Peterson's Four-Year Colleges 2013

PETERSON'S
Publishing

PETERSON'S
Publishing

About Peterson's Publishing
Peterson's Publishing provides the accurate, dependable, high-quality education content and guidance you need to succeed. No matter where you are on your academic or professional path, you can rely on Peterson's print and digital publications for the most up-to-date education exploration data, expert test-prep tools, and top-notch career success resources—everything you need to achieve your goals.

Visit us online at **www.petersonspublishing.com** and let Peterson's help you achieve your goals.

For more information, contact Peterson's Publishing, 2000 Lenox Drive, Lawrenceville, NJ 08648; 800-338-3282 Ext. 54229; or find us on the World Wide Web at www.petersonspublishing.com.

Bernadette Webster, Managing Editor; Jill C. Schwartz, Editor; John Wells, Research Project Manager; Cathleen Fee, Nicole Gallo, Research Associates; Phyllis Johnson, Software Engineer; Ray Golaszewski, Publishing Operations Manager; Linda M. Williams, Composition Manager; Karen Mount, Fulfillment Coordinator; Danielle Vreeland, Shannon White, Client Relations Representatives; Charlotte Thomas, Richard Woodland, Contributing Authors

ISSN 1544-2330
ISBN-13: 978-0-7689-3606-3
ISBN-10: 0-7689-3606-3

Printed in the United States of America

10 9 8 7 6 5 4 3 2 1   14 13 12

Forty-third Edition

Contents

A Note from the Peterson's Editors

For nearly fifty years, Peterson's has given students and parents the most comprehensive, up-to-date information on undergraduate institutions in the United States and Canada. *Peterson's Four-Year Colleges 2013* features advice and tips on the college search and selection process, such as how to consider the factors that truly make a difference during your search, how to understand the application process, and how to get financial aid. Each year, Peterson's researches the data published in *Peterson's Four-Year Colleges*. The information is furnished by the colleges and is accurate at the time of publishing.

Opportunities abound for students, and this guide can help you find what you want in a number of ways:

- For application and admissions advice and guidance, just head to **THE ADVICE CENTER**. Within the **Search, Find, Select** section, the "College Admissions Countdown Calendar" outlines pertinent month-by-month milestones. "Choosing Your Top Ten Colleges" gets you started on putting together the most important top ten list you have ever made. "Surviving Standardized Tests" describes frequently used tests and what you need to know to succeed on them. Of course, part of the college selection process involves visiting the schools themselves, and "The Whys and Whats of College Visits" is just the planner you need to make those trips well worth your while. Next, "Applying 101" provides advice on how best to approach the application phase of the process. If you can't make sense out of the early decision/early action conundrum, "The Early Decision Decision" can help clarify it for you. Finally, "What International Students Need to Know About Admission to U.S. Colleges and Universities" has tips on college admissions for non–U.S. citizens and can also be useful to U.S. citizens. Up next is the **Money, Money, Money** section, which provides all the essential information on how to meet your education expenses, starting with the "Financial Aid Countdown Calendar" and followed by articles covering "Who's Paying for This? Financial Aid Basics" and "Middle Income Families: Making the Financial Aid Process Work." And be sure to check out our **Options, Options, Options** section for some sneak peeks into specific institutions and programs that may be just right for you, including the latest on honors programs, public versus private colleges, women's colleges, and online learning. Finally, you'll want to read through the **How to Use This Guide** section, which explains the information presented for each individual college, how Peterson's collects its data, and how Peterson's determines eligibility for inclusion in this guide.

- Next up is the **PROFILES** section. Here you'll find our unparalleled college profiles, arranged alphabetically by state. They provide need-to-know information about accredited four-year colleges—including entrance difficulty, campus setting, total enrollment, student-faculty ratio, application deadlines, expenses, most frequently chosen baccalaureate fields, and academic programs. All the information you need to apply is placed together at the conclusion of each college profile. Display ads, which appear near some of the institutions' profiles, have been provided and paid for by those colleges or universities that wished to supplement their profile data with additional information about their institution.

- And if you still thirst for even more information, over 350 two-page narrative descriptions appear as **COLLEGE CLOSE-UPS**—descriptions written by admissions or college officials that provide great detail about each school. They are edited to provide a consistent format across entries for your ease of comparison.

- If you already have specifics in mind, such as a particular major or institution, turn to the **INDEXES** section. Here you can search for a school based on major, entrance difficulty, cost ranges, and geography. If you already have colleges in mind that pique your interest, you can use the "Alphabetical Listing of Colleges and Universities" to search for these schools. Page numbers referring to all information presented about a college are conveniently referenced.

Peterson's publishes a full line of books—college and grad guides, education exploration, test preparation, financial aid, and career preparation. Peterson's publications can be found at high school guidance offices, college libraries and career centers, and your local bookstore and library. Peterson's books are now also available as eBooks.

We welcome any comments or suggestions you may have about this publication. Your feedback will help us make educational dreams possible for you—and others like you.

Colleges will be pleased to know that Peterson's helped you in your selection. Admissions staff members are more than happy to answer questions, address specific problems, and help in any way they can. The editors at Peterson's wish you great success in your college search!

The Advice Center

College Admissions Countdown Calendar

T his practical month-by-month calendar is designed to help you stay on top of the process of applying to college. For most students, the process begins in September of the junior year of high school and ends in June of the senior year. You may want to begin considering financial aid options, reviewing your academic schedule, and attending college fairs before your junior year.

JUNIOR YEAR

September
- Check with your counselor to make sure your course credits will meet college requirements.
- Be sure you are involved in one or two extracurricular activities.
- Begin building your personal list of colleges.

October
- Register for and take the PSAT/NMSQT.

November
- Strive to get the best grades you can. A serious effort will provide you with the most options during the application process.

December
- Get involved in a community service activity.
- Begin to read newspapers and a weekly news magazine.
- Buy *Peterson's Master the SAT,* or *The Real ACT* and begin to study for the tests.

January
- With your school counselor, decide when to take the ACT, SAT, and SAT Subject Tests (and which Subject Tests to take). If English is not your primary language and you are planning on attending a college in North America, decide when to take the TOEFL.
- Keep your grades up!

February
- Plan a challenging schedule of classes for your senior year.
- Think about which teachers you will ask to write recommendations.
- Check http://www.nacacnet.org/ and click on "College Fairs" for up-to-date schedules and locations of college fairs.

March
- Register for the tests you will take in the spring (ACT, SAT, SAT Subject Tests, or the TOEFL).
- Meet with your school counselor to discuss college choices.
- Review your transcript and test scores with your counselor to determine how competitive your range of choices should be.
- Develop a preliminary list of fifteen to twenty colleges and universities.
- Start scheduling campus visits. The best time is when school is in session (but never during final exams). Summers are OK but will not show you what the college is really like. If possible, save your top college choices for the fall. Be aware, however, that fall is the busiest visit season, and you will need advance planning. Don't forget to write thank you letters to your interviewers.

April
- Take any standardized tests for which you have registered.
- Create a list of your potential college choices and begin to record personal and academic information that can be transferred later to your college applications.

May
- Plan college visits and make appointments.
- Structure your summer plans to include advanced academic work, travel, volunteer work, or a job.
- Confirm your academic schedule for the fall.

Summer
- Write to any colleges on your list that do not accept the Common Application to request application forms.
- Begin working on your application essays

SENIOR YEAR

September

- ❑ Register for the ACT, SAT, SAT Subject Tests, or TOEFL, as necessary.
- ❑ Check with your school counselor for the fall visiting schedule of college reps.
- ❑ Ask appropriate teachers if they would write recommendations for you. Don't forget to write thank you letters when they accept.
- ❑ Meet with your counselor to compile your final list of colleges.

October

- ❑ Mail or send early applications electronically after carefully checking them to be sure they are completely filled out.
- ❑ Photocopy or print extra copies of your applications to use as a backup.
- ❑ Take the tests for which you have registered.
- ❑ Don't be late! Keep track of all deadlines for transcripts, recommendations, financial aid, etc.

November

- ❑ Be sure that you have requested your ACT and SAT scores be sent to your colleges of choice.
- ❑ Complete and submit all applications. Print or photocopy an extra copy for your records.

December

- ❑ Take any necessary tests: ACT, SAT, SAT Subject Tests, or TOEFL.
- ❑ Meet with your counselor to verify that all is in order and that transcripts are out to colleges.

January

- ❑ Prepare the Free Application for Federal Student Aid (FAFSA), available at www.fafsa.ed.gov or through your school counseling office. An estimated income tax statement (which can be corrected later) can be used. The sooner you apply for financial aid, the better your chances.

February

- ❑ Send in your FAFSA via the Web or U.S. mail.
- ❑ Be sure your midyear report has gone out to the colleges to which you've applied.
- ❑ Let colleges know of any new honors or accomplishments that were not in your original application.

March

- ❑ Register for any Advanced Placement (AP) tests you might take.
- ❑ Be sure you have received a FAFSA acknowledgment.

April

- ❑ Review the acceptances and financial aid offers you receive.
- ❑ Go back to visit one or two of your top-choice colleges.
- ❑ Notify your college of choice that you have accepted its offer (and send in a deposit by May 1).
- ❑ Notify the colleges you have chosen not to attend of your decision.

May

- ❑ Take AP tests.

June

- ❑ Graduate! Congratulations and best of luck.

Choosing Your Top Ten Colleges

By using all the information in the various sections of this guide, you will find colleges worthy of the most important top-ten list on the planet—yours.

The first thing you will need to do is decide what type of institution of higher learning you want to attend. Each of the thousands of four-year colleges and universities in the United States is as unique as the people applying to it. Although listening to the voices and media hype around you can make it sound as though there are only a few elite schools worth attending, this simply is not true. By considering some of the following criteria, you will soon find that the large pool of interesting colleges can be narrowed down to a more reasonable number.

SIZE AND CATEGORY

Schools come in all shapes and sizes, from tiny rural colleges of 400 students to massive state university systems serving 100,000 students or more. If you are coming from a small high school, a college with 3,500 students may seem large to you. If you are currently attending a high school with 3,000 students, selecting a college of a similar size may not feel like a new enough experience. Some students coming from very large impersonal high schools are looking for a place where they will be recognized from the beginning and offered a more personal approach. If you don't have a clue about what size might feel right to you, try visiting a couple of nearby colleges of varying sizes. You do not have to be seriously interested in them; just feel what impact the number of students on campus has on you.

Large Universities

Large universities offer a wide range of educational, athletic, and social experiences. Universities offer a full scope of undergraduate majors and award master's and doctoral degrees as well. Universities are usually composed of several smaller colleges. Depending on your interest in a major field or area of study, you would likely apply to a specific college within the university. Each college has the flexibility to set its own standards for admission, which may differ from the overall average of the university. The colleges within a university system also set their own course requirements for earning a degree.

Universities may be public or private. Some large private universities, such as Harvard, Yale, Princeton, University of Pennsylvania, New York University, Northwestern, and Stanford, are well-known for their high entrance standards, the excellence of their education, and the success rates of their graduates. These institutions place a great deal of emphasis on research and compete aggressively for grants from the federal government to fund these projects. Large public universities,

such as the State University of New York (SUNY) System, University of Michigan, University of Texas, University of Illinois, University of Washington, and University of North Carolina, also support excellent educational programs, compete for and win research funding, and have successful graduates. Public universities usually offer substantially lower tuition rates to in-state students, although their tuition rates for out-of-state residents are often comparable to those of private institutions.

At many large universities, sports play a major role on campus. Athletics can dominate the calendar and set the tone year-round at some schools. Alumni travel from far and wide to attend their alma mater's football or basketball games, and the campus, and frequently the entire town, grinds to a halt when there is a home game. Athletes are heroes and dominate campus social life.

What are some other features of life on a university campus? Every kind of club imaginable, from literature to bioengineering and chorus to politics, can be found on most college campuses. You will be able to play the intramural version of almost every sport in which the university fields interscholastic teams and join fraternities, sororities, and groups dedicated to social action. You can become a member of a band, an orchestra, or perhaps a chamber music group or work on the newspaper, the literary magazine, or the Web site. The list can go on and on. You may want to try out a new interest or two or pursue what you have always been interested in and make like-minded friends along the way.

Take a look at the size of the classrooms in the larger universities and envision yourself sitting in that atmosphere. Would this offer a learning environment that would benefit you?

Liberal Arts Colleges

If you have considered large universities and come to the conclusion that all that action could be a distraction, a small liberal arts college might be right for you. Ideally tucked away on a picture-perfect campus, a liberal arts college generally has fewer than 5,000 students. The mission of most liberal arts schools is learning for the sake of learning, with a strong emphasis on creating lifelong learners who will be able to apply their education to any number of careers. This contrasts with objectives of the profession-based preparation of specialized colleges.

Liberal arts colleges cannot offer the breadth of courses provided by the large universities. As a result, liberal arts colleges try to create a niche for themselves. For instance, a college may place its emphasis on its humanities departments, whose professors are all well-known published authors and international presenters in their areas of expertise. A college may

highlight its science departments by providing state-of-the-art-facilities where undergraduates conduct research side by side with top-notch professors and copublish their findings in the most prestigious scientific journals in the country. The personal approach is very important at liberal arts colleges. Whether in advisement, course selection, athletic programs tailored to students' interests, or dinner with the department head at her home, liberal arts colleges emphasize that they get to know their students.

If they are so perfect, why doesn't everyone choose a liberal arts college? Well, the small size limits options. Fewer people may mean less diversity. The fact that many of these colleges encourage a study-abroad option (a student elects to spend a semester or a year studying in another country) reduces the number of students on campus even further. Some liberal arts colleges have a certain reputation that does not appeal to some students. You should ask yourself questions about the campus life that most appeals to you. Will you fit in with the campus culture? Will the small size mean that you go through your social options quickly? Check out the activities listed on the Student Center bulletin board. Does the student body look diverse enough for you? Will what is happening keep you busy and interested? Do the students have input into decision making? Do they create the social climate of the school?

Small Universities

Smaller universities often combine stringent admissions policies, handpicked faculty members, and attractive scholarship packages. These institutions generally have undergraduate enrollments of about 4,000 students. Some are more famous for their graduate and professional schools but have also established strong undergraduate colleges. Smaller universities balance the great majors options of large universities with a smaller campus community. They offer choices but not to the same extent as large universities. On the other hand, by limiting admissions and enrollment, they manage to cultivate some of the characteristics of a liberal arts college. Like a liberal arts college, a small university may emphasize a particular program and go out of its way to draw strong candidates in a specific area, such as premed, to its campus. Universities such as The Johns Hopkins University, University of Notre Dame, Vanderbilt University, Washington University in St. Louis, and Wesleyan University in Connecticut are a few examples of this category.

Technical or Specialized Colleges

Another alternative to the liberal arts college or large university is the technical or otherwise specialized college. Their goal is to offer a specialized and saturated experience in a particular field of study. Such an institution might limit its course offerings to engineering and science, the performing or fine arts, or business. Schools such as California Institute of Technology, Carnegie Mellon University, Massachusetts Institute of Technology, and Rensselaer Polytechnic Institute concentrate on attracting the finest math and science students in the country. At other schools, like Bentley College in Massachusetts or Bryant College in Rhode Island, students eat, sleep, and breathe business. These institutions are purists at heart and strong believers in the necessity of focused, specialized

study to produce excellence in their graduates' achievements. If you are certain about your chosen path in life and want to immerse yourself in subjects such as math, music, or business, you will fit right in.

Religious Colleges

Many private colleges have religious origins, and many of these have become secular institutions with virtually no trace of their religious roots. Others remain dedicated to a religious way of education. What sets religious colleges apart is the way they combine faith, learning, and student life. Faculty members and administrators are hired with faith as a criterion as much as their academic credentials.

Single-Gender Colleges

There are strong arguments that being able to pursue one's education without the distraction, competition, and stress caused by the presence of the opposite sex helps a student evolve a stronger sense of her or his self-worth; achieve more academically; have a more fulfilling, less pressured social schedule; and achieve more later in life. For various historic, social, and psychological reasons, there are many more all-women than all-men colleges. A strict single-sex environment is rare. Even though the undergraduate day college adheres to an all-female or all-male admissions policy, coeducational evening classes or graduate programs and coordinate facilities and classes shared with nearby coed or opposite-sex institutions can result in a good number of students of the opposite sex being found on campus. If you want to concentrate on your studies and hone your leadership qualities, a single-gender school is an option.

LOCATION

Location and distance from home are two other important considerations. If you have always lived in the suburbs, choosing an urban campus can be an adventure, but after a week of the urban experience, will you long for a grassy campus and open space? On the other hand, if you choose a college in a rural area, will you run screaming into the Student Center some night looking for noise, lights, and people? The location—urban, rural, or suburban—can directly affect how easy or how difficult adjusting to college life will be for you.

Don't forget to factor in distance from home. Everyone going off to college wants to think he or she won't be homesick, but sometimes it's nice to get a home-cooked meal or to do the laundry in a place that does not require quarters. Even your kid sister may seem like less of a nuisance after a couple of months away.

Here are some questions you might ask yourself as you go through the selection process: In what part of the country do I want to be? How far away from home do I want to be? What is the cost of returning home? Do I need to be close to a city? How close? How large of a city? Would city life distract me? Would I concentrate better in a setting that is more rural or more suburban?

ENTRANCE DIFFICULTY

Many students will look at a college's entrance difficulty as an indicator of whether or not they will be admitted. For instance,

if you have an excellent academic record, you might wish to primarily consider those colleges that are highly competitive. Although entrance difficulty does not translate directly to quality of education, it indicates which colleges are attracting large numbers of high-achieving students. A high-achieving student body usually translates into prestige for the college and its graduates. Prestige has some advantages but should definitely be viewed as a secondary factor that might tip the scales when all the other important factors are equal. Never base your decision on prestige alone!

The other principle to keep in mind when considering this factor is to not sell yourself short. If everything else tells you that a college might be right for you, but your numbers just miss that college's average range, apply there anyway. Your numbers—grades and test scores—are undeniably important in the admissions decision, but there are other considerations. First, lower grades in honors or AP courses will impress colleges more than top grades in regular-track courses because they demonstrate that you are the kind of student willing to accept challenges. Second, admissions directors are looking for different qualities in students that can be combined to create a multifaceted class. For example, if you did poorly in your freshman and sophomore years but made a great

improvement in your grades in later years, this usually will impress a college. If you are likely to contribute to your class because of your special personal qualities, a strong sense of commitment and purpose, unusual and valuable experiences, or special interests and talents, these factors can outweigh numbers that are weaker than average. Nevertheless, be practical. Overreach yourself in a few applications, but put the bulk of your effort into gaining admission to colleges where you have a realistic chance for admission.

THE PRICE OF AN EDUCATION

The price tag for higher education continues to rise, and it has become an increasingly important factor for people. While it is necessary to consider your family's resources when choosing a list of colleges to which you might apply, never eliminate a college solely because of cost. There are many ways to pay for college, including loans, and a college education will never depreciate in value, unlike other purchases. It is an investment in yourself and will pay back the expense many times over in your lifetime.

Surviving Standardized Tests

WHAT ARE STANDARDIZED TESTS?

Colleges and universities in the United States use tests to help evaluate applicants' readiness for admission or to place them in appropriate courses. The tests that are most frequently used by colleges are the ACT of American College Testing, Inc., and the College Board's SAT. In addition, the Educational Testing Service (ETS) offers the TOEFL test, which evaluates the English-language proficiency of nonnative speakers. The tests are offered at designated testing centers located at high schools and colleges throughout the United States and U.S. territories and at testing centers in various countries throughout the world.

Upon request, special accommodations for students with documented visual, hearing, physical, or learning disabilities are available. Examples of special accommodations include tests in Braille or large print and such aids as a reader, recorder, magnifying glass, or sign language interpreter. Additional testing time may be allowed in some instances. Contact the appropriate testing program or your guidance counselor for details on how to request special accommodations.

THE ACT

The ACT is a standardized college entrance examination that measures knowledge and skills in English, mathematics, reading, and science reasoning and the application of these skills to future academic tasks. The ACT consists of four multiple-choice tests.

Test 1: English
- 75 questions, 45 minutes
- Usage and mechanics
- Rhetorical skills

Test 2: Mathematics
- 60 questions, 60 minutes
- Pre-algebra
- Elementary algebra
- Intermediate algebra
- Coordinate geometry
- Plane geometry
- Trigonometry

Test 3: Reading
- 40 questions, 35 minutes
- Prose fiction
- Humanities
- Social studies
- Natural sciences

Test 4: Science
- 40 questions, 35 minutes
- Data representation
- Research summary
- Conflicting viewpoints

Each section is scored from 1 to 36 and is scaled for slight variations in difficulty. Students are not penalized for incorrect responses. The composite score is the average of the four scaled scores. The ACT Plus Writing includes the four multiple-choice tests and a writing test, which measures writing skills emphasized in high school English classes and in entry-level college composition courses.

To prepare for the ACT, ask your guidance counselor for a free guidebook called "Preparing for the ACT." Besides providing general test-preparation information and additional test-taking strategies, this guidebook describes the content and format of the four ACT subject area tests, summarizes test administration procedures followed at ACT test centers, and includes a practice test. Peterson's publishes *The Real ACT* that includes five official ACT tests.

THE SAT

The SAT measures developed critical reading and mathematical reasoning abilities as they relate to successful performance in college. It is intended to supplement the secondary school record and other information about the student in assessing readiness for college. There is one unscored, experimental section on the exam, which is used for equating and/or pretesting purposes and can cover either the mathematics or critical reading area.

Critical Reading
- 67 questions, 70 minutes
- Sentence completion
- Passage-based reading

DON'T FORGET TO . . .

- ❑ Take the SAT or ACT before application deadlines.
- ❑ Note that test registration deadlines precede test dates by about six weeks.
- ❑ Register to take the TOEFL test if English is not your native language and you are planning on studying at a North American college.
- ❑ Practice your test-taking skills with *Peterson's Master the SAT,* and *The Real ACT*
- ❑ Contact the College Board or American College Testing, Inc., in advance if you need special accommodations when taking tests.

Mathematics
- 54 questions, 70 minutes
- Multiple-choice
- Student-produced response (grid-ins)

Writing

- 49 questions plus essay, 60 minutes
- Identifying sentence errors
- Improving paragraphs
- Improving sentences
- Essay

Students receive one point for each correct response and lose a fraction of a point for each incorrect response (except for student-produced responses). These points are totaled to produce the raw scores, which are then scaled to equalize the scores for slight variations in difficulty for various editions of the test. The critical reading, writing, and mathematics scaled scores range from 200–800 per section. The total scaled score range is from 600–2400.

Top 10 Ways Not to Take the Test

10. Cramming the night before the test.

9. Not becoming familiar with the directions before you take the test.

8. Not becoming familiar with the format of the test before you take it.

7. Not knowing how the test is graded.

6. Spending too much time on any one question.

5. Second-guessing yourself.

4. Not checking spelling, grammar, and sentence structure in essays.

3. Writing a one-paragraph essay.

2. Forgetting to take a deep breath to keep from—

1. Losing It!

SAT SUBJECT TESTS

Subject Tests are required by some institutions for admission and/or placement in freshman-level courses. Each Subject Test measures one's knowledge of a specific subject and the ability to apply that knowledge. Students should check with each institution for its specific requirements. In general, students are required to take three Subject Tests (one English, one mathematics, and one of their choice).

Subject Tests are given in the following areas: biology, chemistry, Chinese, French, German, Italian, Japanese, Korean, Latin, literature, mathematics, modern Hebrew, physics, Spanish, U.S. history, and world history. These tests are 1 hour long and are primarily multiple-choice tests. Three Subject Tests may be taken on one test date.

Scored like the SAT, students gain a point for each correct answer and lose a fraction of a point for each incorrect answer. The raw scores are then converted to scaled scores that range from 200 to 800.

THE TOEFL INTERNET-BASED TEST (IBT)

The Test of English as a Foreign Language Internet-Based Test (TOEFL iBT) is designed to help assess a student's grasp of English if it is not the student's first language. Performance on the TOEFL test may help interpret scores on the critical reading sections of the SAT. The test consists of four integrated sections: speaking, listening, reading, and writing. The TOEFL iBT emphasizes integrated skills. The paper-based versions of the TOEFL will continue to be administered in certain countries where the Internet-based version has not yet been introduced. For further information, visit www.toefl.org.

WHAT OTHER TESTS SHOULD I KNOW ABOUT?

The AP Program

This program allows high school students to try college-level work and build valuable skills and study habits in the process. Subject matter is explored in more depth in AP courses than in other high school classes. A qualifying score on an AP test—which varies from school to school—can earn you college credit or advanced placement. Getting qualifying grades on enough exams can even earn you a full year's credit and sophomore standing at more than 1,500 higher-education institutions. There are more than thirty AP courses across multiple subject areas, including art history, biology, and computer science. Speak to your guidance counselor for information about your school's offerings.

College-Level Examination Program (CLEP)

The CLEP enables students to earn college credit for what they already know, whether it was learned in school, through independent study, or through other experiences outside of the classroom. More than 2,900 colleges and universities now award credit for qualifying scores on one or more of the 33 CLEP exams. The exams, which are 90 minutes in length and are primarily multiple choice, are administered at participating colleges and universities. For more information, check out the Web site at www.collegeboard.com/clep.

WHAT CAN I DO TO PREPARE FOR THESE TESTS?

Know what to expect. Get familiar with how the tests are structured, how much time is allowed, and the directions for each type of question. Get plenty of rest the night before the test and eat breakfast that morning.

There are a variety of products, from books to software to videos, available to help you prepare for most standardized tests. Find the learning style that suits you best. As for which products to buy, there are two major categories— those created by the test makers and those created by private companies. The best approach is to talk to someone who has been through the process and find out which product or products he or she recommends.

Some students report significant increases in scores after participating in coaching programs. Longer-term programs (40 hours) seem to raise scores more than short-term programs (20

hours), but beyond 40 hours, score gains are minor. Math scores appear to benefit more from coaching than critical reading scores.

Resources

There is a variety of ways to prepare for standardized tests—find a method that fits your schedule and your budget. But you should definitely prepare. Far too many students walk into these tests cold, either because they find standardized tests frightening or annoying or they just haven't found the time to study. The key is that these exams are standardized. That means these tests are largely the same from administration to administration; they always test the same concepts. They have to, or else you couldn't compare the scores of people who took the tests on different dates. The numbers or words may change, but the underlying content doesn't.

So how do you prepare? At the very least, you should review relevant material, such as math formulas and commonly used vocabulary words, and know the directions for each question type or test section. You should take at least one practice test and review your mistakes so you don't make them again on the test day. Beyond that, you know best how much preparation you need. You'll also find lots of material in libraries or bookstores to help you: books and software from the test makers and from other publishers (including Peterson's) or live courses that range from national test-preparation companies to teachers at your high school who offer classes.

The Whys and Whats of College Visits

Dawn B. Sova, Ph.D.

The campus visit should not be a passive activity for you and your parents. Take the initiative and gather information beyond that provided in the official tour. You will see many important indicators during your visit that will tell you more about the true character of a college and its students than the tour guide will reveal. Know what to look for and how to assess the importance of such indicators.

WHAT SHOULD YOU ASK AND WHAT SHOULD YOU LOOK FOR?

Your first stop on a campus visit is the visitor center or admissions office, where you will probably have to wait to meet with a counselor. Colleges usually plan to greet visitors later than the appointed time in order to give them the opportunity to review some of the campus information that is liberally scattered throughout the visitor waiting room. Take advantage of the time to become even more familiar with the college by arriving 15 to 30 minutes before your appointment to observe the behavior of staff members and to browse through the yearbooks and student newspapers that will be available.

If you prepare in advance, you will have already reviewed the college catalog and map of the campus. These materials familiarize you with the academic offerings and the physical layout of the campus, but the true character of the college and its students emerges in other ways.

Begin your investigation with the visitor center staff members. As a student's first official contact with the college, they should make every effort to welcome prospective students and project a friendly image.

- How do they treat you and other prospective students who are waiting? Are they friendly and willing to speak with you, or do they try their hardest to avoid eye contact and conversation?

- Are they friendly with each other and with students who enter the office, or are they curt and unwilling to help?

- Does the waiting room have a friendly feeling or is it cold and sterile?

If the visitor center staff members seem indifferent to prospective students, there is little reason to believe that they will be warm and welcoming to current students. View such behavior as a warning to watch very carefully the interaction of others with you during the tour. An indifferent or unfriendly reception in the admissions office may be simply the first of many signs that attending this college will not be a pleasant experience.

Look through several yearbooks and see the types of activities that are actually photographed, as opposed to the activities that colleges promise in their promotional literature. Some questions are impossible to answer if the college is very large, but for small and moderately sized colleges the yearbook is a good indicator of campus activity.

- Has the number of clubs and organizations increased or decreased in the past five years?

- Do the same students appear repeatedly in activities?

- Do sororities and fraternities dominate campus activities?

- Are participants limited to one sex or one ethnic group, or is there diversity?

- Are all activities limited to the campus, or are students involved in activities in the community?

Use what you observe in the yearbooks as a means of forming a more complete understanding of the college, but don't base your entire impression on just one facet. If time permits, look through several copies of the school newspaper, which should reflect the major concerns and interests of the students. The paper is also a good way to learn about the campus social life.

- Does the paper contain a mix of national and local news?

- What products or services are advertised?

- How assertive are the editorials?

- With what topics are the columnists concerned?

- Are movies and concerts that meet your tastes advertised or reviewed?

- What types of ads appear in the classified section?

The newspaper should be a public forum for students, and, as such, should reflect the character of the campus and of the student body. A paper that deals only with seemingly safe and well-edited topics on the editorial page and in regular feature columns might indicate administrative censorship. A lack of ads for restaurants might indicate either a lack of good places to eat or that area restaurants do not welcome student business. A limited mention of movies, concerts, or other entertainment might reveal a severely limited campus social life. Even if ads and reviews are included, you should still balance how such activities reflect your tastes.

You will have only a limited amount of time to ask questions during your initial meeting with the admissions counselor, for very few schools include a formal interview in the initial campus visit or tour. Instead, this brief meeting is often just a nicety that allows the admissions office to begin a file for the student and to record some initial impressions. Save your questions for the tour guide and for students on campus you meet along the way.

HOW CAN YOU ASSESS THE TRUE CHARACTER OF A COLLEGE AND ITS STUDENTS?

Colleges do not train their tour guides to deceive prospective students, but they do caution guides to avoid unflattering topics and campus sites. Does this mean that you will see only a sugarcoated version of life on a particular college campus? Not at all, especially not if you are observant.

Most organized campus visits include such campus facilities as dormitories, dining halls, libraries, student activity and recreation centers, and the health and student services centers. Some may only be pointed out, while you will walk through others. Either way, you will find that many signs of the true character of the college emerge if you keep your eyes open.

Bulletin boards in dormitories and student centers contain a wealth of information about campus activities, student concerns, and campus groups. Read the posters, notices, and messages to learn what *really* interests students. Unlike ads in the school newspaper, posters put up by students advertise both on-and off-campus events, so they will give you an idea of what is also available in the surrounding community.

Review the notices, which may cover either campuswide events or events that concern only small groups of students. The catalog may not mention a performance group, but an individual dormitory with its own small theater may offer regular productions. Poetry readings, jam sessions, writers' groups, and other activities may be announced and show diversity of student interests.

Even the brief bulletin board messages offering objects for sale and noting objects that people want to purchase reveal a lot about a campus. Are most of the items computer related? Or do the messages specify audio equipment or musical instruments? Are offers to trade goods or services posted? Don't ignore the "ride wanted" messages. Students who want to share rides home during a break may specify widely diverse geographical locations. If so, then you know that the student body is not limited to only the immediate area or one locale. Other messages can also enhance your knowledge of the true character of the campus and its students.

As you walk through various buildings, examine their condition carefully.

- Is the paint peeling, and do the exteriors look worn?
- Are the exteriors and interiors of the building clean?
- Is the equipment in the classrooms up-to-date or outdated?

Pay particular attention to the dormitories, especially to factors that might affect your safety. Observe the appearance of the structure, and ask about the security measures in and around the dormitories.

- Are the dormitories noisy or quiet?
- Do they seem crowded?
- How good is the lighting around each dormitory?
- Are the dormitories spread throughout the campus or are they clustered in one main area?
- Who has access to the dormitories in addition to students?
- How secure are the means by which students enter and leave the dormitory?

While you are on the subject of dormitory safety, you should also ask about campus safety. Don't expect that the guide will rattle off a list of crimes that have been committed in the past year. To obtain that information, access the recent year of issues of *The Chronicle of Higher Education* and locate its yearly report on campus crime. Also ask the guide about safety measures that the campus police take and those that students have initiated.

- Can students request escorts to their residences late at night?
- Do campus shuttle buses run at frequent intervals all night?
- Are "blue-light" telephones liberally placed throughout the campus for students to use to call for help?
- Do the campus police patrol the campus regularly?

If the guide does not answer your questions satisfactorily, wait until after the tour to contact the campus police or traffic office for answers.

Campus tours usually just point out the health services center without taking the time to walk through. Even if you don't see the inside of the building, you should take a close look at the location of the health services center and ask the guide questions about services.

- How far is the health center from the dormitories?
- Is a doctor always on call?
- Does the campus transport sick students from their dormitories or must they walk?
- What are the operating hours of the health center?
- Does the health center refer students to a nearby hospital?

If the guide can't answer your questions, visit the health center later and ask someone there.

Most campus tours take pride in showing students their activities centers, which may contain snack bars, game rooms, workout facilities, and other means of entertainment. Should you scrutinize this building as carefully as the rest? Of course. Outdated and poorly maintained activity equipment contributes to your total impression of the college. You should also ask about the hours, availability, and cost (no, the activities are usually not free) of using the bowling alleys, pool tables, air hockey tables, and other amenities.

As you walk through campus with the tour, also look carefully at the appearance of the students who pass. The way in which both men and women groom themselves, the way they dress, and even their physical bearing communicate a lot more than any guidebook can. If everyone seems to conform to the same look, you might feel that you would be uncomfortable at the college, however nonconformist that look might be. On the other hand, you might not feel comfortable on a campus that stresses diversity of dress and behavior, and your observations now can save you discomfort later.

- Does every student seem to wear a sorority or fraternity t-shirt or jacket?

- Is everyone of your sex sporting the latest fad haircut?

- Do all of the men or the women seem to be wearing expensive name-brand clothes?

- Do most of the students seem to be working hard to look outrageous with regards to clothing, hair color, and body art?

- Would you feel uncomfortable in a room full of these students?

Is appearance important to you? If it is, then you should consider very seriously if you answer yes to any of the above questions. You don't have to be the same as everyone else on campus, but standing out too much may make you unhappy.

As you observe the physical appearance of the students, also listen to their conversations as you pass them. What are they talking about? How are they speaking? Are their voices and accents all the same, or do you hear diversity in their speech? Are you offended by their language? Think how you will feel if surrounded by the same speech habits and patterns for four years.

WHERE SHOULD YOU VISIT ON YOUR OWN?

Your campus visit is not over when the tour ends because you will probably have many questions yet to be answered and many places to still be seen. Where you go depends upon the extent to which the organized tour covers the campus. Your tour should take you to view residential halls, health and student services centers, the gymnasium or field house, dining halls, the library, and recreational centers. If any of the facilities on this list have been omitted, visit them on your own and ask questions of the students and staff members you meet. In addition, you should step off campus and gain an impression of the surrounding community. You will probably become bored with life on campus and spend at least some time off campus. Make certain that you know what the surrounding area is like.

The campus tour leaves little time to ask impromptu questions of current students, but you can do so after the tour. Eat lunch in one of the dining halls. Most will allow visitors to pay cash to experience a typical student meal. Food may not be important to you now while you are living at home and can simply take anything you want from the refrigerator at any time, but it will be when you are away at college with only a meal ticket to feed you.

- How clean is the dining hall? Consider serving tables, floors, and seating.

- What is the quality of the food?

- How big are the portions?

- How much variety do students have at each meal?

- How healthy are the food choices?

While you are eating, try to strike up a conversation with students and tell them that you are considering attending their college. Their reactions and advice can be eye-opening. Ask them questions about the academic atmosphere and the professors.

- Are the classes large or small?

- Do the majority of the professors only lecture or are tutorials and seminars common?

- Is the emphasis of the faculty career-oriented or abstract?

- Are the teaching methods innovative and stimulating or boring and dull?

- Is the academic atmosphere pressured, lax, or somewhere in between?

- Which are the strong majors? The weak majors?

- Is the emphasis on grades or social life or a mix of both at the college?

- How hard do students have to work to receive high grades?

Current students can also give you the inside line on the true nature of the college social life. You may gain some idea through looking in the yearbook, in the newspaper, and on the bulletin boards, but students will reveal the true highs and lows of campus life. Ask them about drug use, partying, dating, drinking, and anything else that may affect your life as a student.

- Which are the most popular club activities?

- What do students do on weekends? Do most go home?

- How frequently do concerts occur on campus? Who has recently performed?

- How can you become involved in specific activities (name them)?

- How strictly are campus rules enforced and how severe are penalties?

- What counseling services are available?

- Are academic tutoring services available?

- Do they feel that the faculty really cares about students, especially freshmen?

You will receive the most valuable information from current students, but you will only be able to speak with them after the tour is over. And you might have to risk rejection as you try to initiate conversations with students who might not want to

reveal how they feel about the campus. Still, the value of this information is worth the chance.

If you have the time, you should also visit the library to see just how accessible research materials are and to observe the physical layout. The catalog usually specifies the days and hours of operation, as well as the number of volumes contained in the library and the number of periodicals to which it subscribes. A library also requires accessibility, good lighting, an adequate number of study carrels, and lounge areas for students. Many colleges have created 24-hour study lounges for students who find the residence halls too noisy for studying, although most colleges claim that they designate areas of the residences as "quiet study" areas. You may not be interested in any of this information, but when you are a student you will have to make frequent use of the campus library so you should know what is available. You should at least ask how extensive their holdings are in your proposed major area. If they have virtually nothing, you will have to spend a lot of time ordering items via interlibrary loan or making copies, which can become expensive. The ready answer of students that they will obtain their information from the Internet is unpleasantly countered by professors who demand journal articles with documentation.

Make a point of at least driving through the community surrounding the college because you will be spending time there shopping, dining, working in a part-time job, or attending events. Even the largest and best-stocked campus will not meet all of your social and personal needs. If you can spare the time, stop in several stores to see if they welcome college students.

- Is the surrounding community suburban, urban, or rural?

- Does the community offer stores of interest, such as bookstores, craft shops, and boutiques?

- Do the businesses employ college students?

- Does the community have a movie or stage theater?

- Are there several types of interesting restaurants?

- Do there seem to be any clubs that court a college clientele?

- Is the center of activity easy to walk to, or do you need other transportation?

You might feel that a day is not enough to answer all of your questions, but even answering some questions will provide you with a stronger basis for choosing a college. Many students visit a college campus several times before making their decision. Keep in mind that for the rest of your life you will be associated with the college that you attend. You will spend four years of your life at this college. The effort of spending several days to obtain the information to make your decision is worthwhile.

Dawn B. Sova, Ph.D., is a former newspaper reporter and columnist, as well as the author of more than eight books and numerous magazine articles. She teaches creative and research writing, as well as scientific and technical writing, newswriting, and journalism.

Applying 101

The words "applying yourself" have several important meanings in the college application process. One meaning refers to the fact that you need to keep focused during this important time in your life, keep your priorities straight, and know the dates that your applications are due so you can apply on time. The phrase might also refer to the person who is really responsible for your application—you.

You are the only person who should compile your college application. You need to take ownership of this process. The guidance counselor is not responsible for completing your applications, and neither are your parents. College applications must be completed in addition to your normal workload at school, college visits, and SAT, ACT, or TOEFL testing.

THE APPLICATION

The application is your way of introducing yourself to a college admissions office. As with any introduction, you want to make a good first impression. The first thing you should do in presenting your application is to find out what the college or university needs from you. Read the application carefully to find out the application fee and deadline, required standardized tests, number of essays, interview requirements, and anything else you can do or submit to help improve your chances for acceptance.

Completing college applications yourself helps you learn more about the schools to which you are applying. The information a college asks for in its application can tell you much about the school. State university applications often tell you how they are going to view their applicants. Usually, they select students based on GPAs and test scores. Colleges that request an interview, ask you to respond to a few open-ended questions, or require an essay are interested in a more personal approach to the application process and may be looking for different types of students than those sought by a state school.

In addition to submitting the actual application, there are several other items that are commonly required. You will be responsible for ensuring that your standardized test scores and your high school transcript arrive at the colleges to which you apply. Most colleges will ask that you submit teacher recommendations as well. Select teachers who know you and your abilities well and allow them plenty of time to complete the recommendations. When all portions of the application have been completed and sent in, whether electronically or by mail, make sure you follow up with the college to ensure their receipt.

FOLLOW THESE TIPS WHEN FILLING OUT YOUR APPLICATIONS

- **Follow the directions to the letter.** You don't want to be in a position to ask an admissions officer for exceptions due to your inattentiveness.
- **Proofread all parts of your application,** including your essay. Again, the final product indicates to the admissions staff how meticulous and careful you are in your work.
- **Submit your application as early as possible,** provided all of the pieces are available. If there is a problem with your application, this will allow you to work through it with the admissions staff in plenty of time. If you wait until the last minute, it not only takes away that cushion but also reflects poorly on your sense of priorities.
- **Keep a copy of the completed application,** whether it is a photocopy or a copy saved on your computer.

THE APPLICATION ESSAY

Whereas the other portions of your application—your transcript, test scores, and involvement in extracurricular activities—are a reflection of what you've accomplished up to this point, your application essay is an opportunity to present yourself in the here and now. The essay shows your originality and verbal skills and how you approach a topic or problem and express your opinion.

Some colleges may request one essay or a combination of essays and short-answer topics to learn more about who you are and how well you can communicate your thoughts. Common essay topics cover such simple themes as writing about yourself and your experiences or why you want to attend that particular school. Other colleges will ask that you show your imaginative or creative side by writing about a favorite author, for instance, or commenting on a hypothetical situation. In such cases, they will be looking at your thought processes and level of creativity.

Admissions officers, particularly those at small or mid-size colleges, use the essay to determine how you, as a student, will fit into life at that college. The essay, therefore, is a critical component of the application process. Here are some tips for writing a winning essay:

- Colleges are looking for an honest representation of who you are and what you think. Make sure that the tone of the essay reflects enthusiasm, maturity, creativity, the ability to communicate, talent, and your leadership skills.

- Be sure you set aside enough time to write the essay, revise it, and revise it *again.* Running "spell check" will only detect a fraction of the errors you probably made on your first pass at writing it. Take a break and then come back to it and reread it. You will probably notice other style, content, and grammar problems—and ways that you can improve the essay overall.

- Always answer the question that is being asked, making sure that you are specific, clear, and true to your personality.

- Enlist the help of reviewers who know you well— friends, parents, teachers—since they are likely to be the most honest and will keep you on track in the presentation of your true self.

THE PERSONAL INTERVIEW

Although it is relatively rare that a personal interview is required, many colleges recommend that you take this opportunity for a face-to-face discussion with a member of the admissions staff. Read through the application materials to determine whether or not a college places great emphasis on the interview. If they strongly recommend that you have one, it may work against you to forego it.

In contrast to a group interview and some alumni interviews, which are intended to provide information about a college, the personal interview is viewed both as an information session and as further evaluation of your skills and strengths. You will meet with a member of the admissions staff who will be assessing your personal qualities, high school preparation, and your capacity to contribute to undergraduate life at the institution. On average, these meetings last about 45 minutes—a relatively short amount of time in which to gather information and leave the desired impression—so here are some suggestions on how to make the most of it.

Scheduling Your Visit

Generally, students choose to visit campuses in the summer or fall of their senior year. Both times have their advantages. A summer visit, when the campus is not in session, generally allows for a less hectic visit and interview. Visiting in the fall, on the other hand, provides the opportunity to see what campus life is like in full swing. If you choose the fall, consider arranging an overnight trip so that you can stay in one of the college dormitories. At the very least, you should make your way around campus to take part in classes, athletic events, and social activities. Always make an appointment and avoid scheduling more than two college interviews on any given day. Multiple interviews in a single day hinder your chances of making a good impression, and your impressions of the colleges will blur into each other as you hurriedly make your way from place to place.

Preparation

Know the basics about the college before going for your interview. Read the college catalog and Web site in addition to this guide. You will be better prepared to ask questions that are not answered in the literature and that will give you a better understanding of what the college has to offer. You should also spend some time thinking about your strengths and weaknesses and, in particular, what you are looking for in a college education. You will find that as you get a few interviews under your belt, they will get easier. You might consider starting with a college that is not a top contender on your list, so that the stakes are not as high.

Asking Questions

Inevitably, your interviewer will ask you, "Do you have any questions?" Not having one may suggest that you're unprepared or, even worse, not interested. When you do ask questions, make sure that they are ones that matter to you and that have a bearing on your decision about whether or not to attend that college. The questions that you ask will give the interviewer some insight into your personality and priorities. Avoid asking questions that are answered in the college literature—again, a sign of unpreparedness. Although the interviewer will undoubtedly pose questions to you, the interview should not be viewed merely as a question-andanswer session. If a conversation evolves out of a particular question, so much the better. Your interviewer can learn a great deal about you from how you sustain a conversation. Similarly, you will be able to learn a great deal about the college in a conversational format.

Separate the Interview from the Interviewer

Many students base their feelings about a college solely on their impressions of the interviewer. Try not to characterize a college based only on your personal reaction, however, since your impressions can be skewed by whether you and your interviewer hit it off. Pay lots of attention to everything else that you see, hear, and learn about a college. Once on campus, you may never see your interviewer again.

In the end, remember to relax and be yourself. Your interviewer will expect you to be somewhat nervous, which will relieve some of the pressure. Don't drink jitters-producing caffeinated beverages prior to the interview, and suppress nervous fidgets like leg-wagging, finger-drumming, or bracelet jangling. Consider your interview an opportunity to put forth your best effort and to enhance everything that the college knows about you up to this point.

THE FINAL DECISION

Once you have received your acceptance letters, it is time to go back and look at the whole picture. Provided you received more than one acceptance, you are now in a position to compare your options. The best way to do this is to compare your original list of important college-ranking criteria with what you've discovered about each college along the way. In addition, you and your family will need to factor in the financial aid component. You will need to look beyond these cost issues and the quantifiable pros and cons of each college, however, and know that you have a good feeling about your final choice. Before sending off your acceptance letter, you need to feel confident that the college will feel like home for the next four years. Once the choice is made, the only hard part will be waiting for an entire summer before heading off to college!

The Early Decision

Maybe a senior you knew last year didn't get into the college he wanted. He said it was because he didn't apply early decision. Maybe your friend's mom told your mom that unless students apply early decision, their chances of getting into top schools are slim to none, even though they have great grades and spectacular essays. Maybe you figure you'd better get in on the early decision action.

All of the above are true—well, sort of—because many students applying to college get the term "early decision" backwards. High school guidance and college counselors run into this kind of thinking all the time and suggest putting "decision" before "early"—as in making a wise decision about committing to a college before applying early. For some students, early decision is a great option. For others, early decision is loaded with pitfalls and dangers.

"When students come back in the fall of their senior year, I often hear 'I know I want to apply early. Can you help me choose the school?'" says Kathy Cleaver, Co-Director of College Counseling at Durham Academy in Durham, North Carolina. She compares that to saying, "I know I want to get married, please help me pick the man." Continues Cleaver, "First you have to fall in love with the school and know it's your first choice and then join the circus for early decision." She's referring to the media hype flying around high school halls about early decision—it's easy to fall prey to the early decision madness. Hot competition to get into "top" schools creates early decision anxiety. Michael "Mickey" Gilbert, Guidance Counselor at Passaic High School in Passaic, New Jersey, throws out some scary numbers that confirm that, yes, the competition for admittance to top schools is white-hot. There are about 30,000 high schools in the United States, and although the majority of high school seniors apply to institutions in their own states, there are still limited spaces in the "top" schools and the eight Ivy League schools. "No wonder kids think that early decision is the way to go," speculates Gilbert. Early decision panic sets in because students are convinced that if they get their applications in early, they have an edge. Sometimes early decision might make the difference, but there are many issues to consider before taking the early decision leap.

EARLY THIS, EARLY THAT

With all the buzz about early decision, do you really know what it means along with all the other early options, such as early action and early notification? And what about the variations of early decision? Each institution can have its own version of early decision, meaning that deadlines and criteria are different. There's the early decision that notifies students by December, there's the early decision round two, and then there is the early action/single choice.

Seeing the confusion, the National Association for College Admission Counseling (NACAC) developed a standard set of definitions. NACAC is an education association of secondary school counselors, college and university admissions and financial aid officers, counselors, and other individuals who work with students as they transition from high school to college. While each institution has its own variations of each early option, an understanding of the basic differences can help. The list that follows was adapted from the definitions found on the NACAC Web site (www.nacacnet.org).

Early Decision

- Early decision is the application process in which students make a commitment to a first-choice institution where, if admitted, they definitely will enroll. Should a student who applies for financial aid not be offered an award that makes attendance possible, the student may decline the offer of admission and be released from the early decision commitment.

- While pursuing admission under an early decision plan, students may apply to other institutions, but may have only one early decision application pending at any time.

- The institution must notify the applicant of the decision within a reasonable and clearly stated period of time after the early decision deadline. Usually, a nonrefundable deposit must be made well in advance of May 1.

- A student applying for financial aid must adhere to institutional early decision aid application deadlines.

- The institution will respond to an application for financial aid at or near the time of an offer of admission.

- The early decision application supercedes all other applications. Immediately upon acceptance of an offer of admission, a student must withdraw all other applications and make no subsequent applications.

- The application form will include a request for a parent and a counselor signature, in addition to the student's signature, indicating an understanding of the early decision commitment and agreement to abide by its terms.

Early Action

- Early action is the application process in which students make application to an institution of preference and receive a decision well in advance of the institution's regular response date. Students who are admitted under early action are not obligated to accept the institution's offer of admission or to submit a deposit until the regular reply date (not prior to May 1).

- A student may apply to other colleges without restriction.

- The institution must notify the applicant of the decision within a reasonable and clearly stated period of time after the early action deadline.

- A student applying for financial aid must adhere to institutional aid application deadlines.

- A student admitted under an early action plan may not be required to make a commitment prior to May 1, but may be encouraged to do so as soon as a final college choice is made. Colleges that solicit commitments to offers of early action admission and/or financial assistance prior to May 1 may do so provided those offers include a clear statement that written requests for extensions until May 1 will be granted, and that such requests will not jeopardize a student's status for admission or financial aid.

Regular Decision

- Regular decision is the application process in which a student submits an application to an institution by a specified date and receives a decision within a reasonable and clearly stated period of time, but not later than April 15.

- A student may apply to other colleges without restriction.

- The institution will state a deadline for completion of applications and will respond to completed applications by a specified date.

- A student applying for financial aid must adhere to institutional aid application deadlines.

- A student admitted under a regular decision plan may not be required to make a commitment prior to May 1, but may be encouraged to do so as soon as a final college choice is made. Colleges that solicit commitments to offers of admission and/or financial assistance prior to May 1 may do so provided those offers include a clear statement that written requests for extensions until May 1 will be granted, and that such requests will not jeopardize a student's status for admission or financial aid.

Rolling Admission

- Rolling admission is the application process in which an institution reviews applications as they are completed and renders admission decisions to students throughout the admission cycle.

- A student may apply to other colleges without restriction.

- The institution will respond to completed applications in a timely manner.

- A student applying for financial aid must adhere to institutional aid application deadlines.

- A student admitted under a rolling admission plan may not be required to make a commitment prior to May 1, but may be encouraged to do so as soon as a final college choice is made. Colleges that solicit commitments to offers of admission and/or financial assistance prior to May 1 may do so provided those offers include a clear statement that written requests for extensions until May 1 will be granted, and that such requests will not jeopardize a student's status for admission or financial aid.

Wait List

- Wait list is an admission decision option utilized by institutions to protect against shortfalls in enrollment. Wait lists are sometimes made necessary because of the uncertainty of the admission process, as students submit applications for admission to multiple institutions and may receive several offers of admission. By placing a student on the wait list, an institution does not initially offer or deny admission, but extends to a candidate the possibility of admission in the future before the institution's admission cycle is concluded.

- The institution will ensure that a wait list, if necessary, is of reasonable length and is maintained for a reasonable period of time, but never later than August 1.

- In the letter offering a wait list position, the institution should provide a past wait list history, which describes the number of students placed on the wait list(s), the number offered admission from the wait list, and the availability of financial aid. Students should be given an indication of when they can expect to be notified of a final admission decision.

- An institution must resolve final status and notify wait list candidates as soon after May 1 as possible.

- The institution will not require students to submit deposits to remain on a wait list or pressure students for a commitment to enroll prior to sending an official offer of admission in writing.

There is one more option, called early action/single choice (EASC), that some highly selective schools such as Harvard, Yale, and Stanford have begun using. Early action/single choice is a nonbinding early admission option for freshman applicants that replaces early decision. With this change, students learn about their admission decision in December without being required to reply until May 1. This option allows students to apply to as many colleges as they want under a regular admission time frame. The difference is that the early action/single choice option does not allow a candidate to apply to other schools under any type of early action, early decision, or early notification program. Students are asked to sign a statement in their application agreeing to file only one early application.

Each of these options has variations, depending on the institution using them. Some schools have a November 1 deadline for early decision round one. Smaller schools have a deadline of November 15, while others have a December 1 deadline. Then there's an early decision round two. To make matters even more complicated, some schools with early decision say that students can't apply to other institutions if they've sent in an early decision application to their admissions office. Others say it's okay to apply to other schools at the same time you're applying early decision to them, but if they send you an acceptance, you must withdraw the other applications.

Just because two institutions have an application process called early decision or early action doesn't mean that their policies are identical. "There is no common terminology, even among the colleges that have early decision," says Christoph Guttentag, Dean of Undergraduate Admissions at Duke University in Durham, North Carolina. He also points out that just when you think you've got the definitions figured out, institu-

PARENTS, SOME ADVICE FOR YOU

Though guidance counselors stress that high school students should make the final decision about which college to attend, they also say that parents are a very important part of the decision equation. Parents can help as organizers of all the information and provide the support needed to make a good choice. "Little things like setting up file folders and keeping track of deadlines can keep a student on track," advises David Gibson, College Advisor at St. Mary's Parish in Annapolis, Maryland.

Along with their children, parents also need to understand the basics of early option terminology as it applies to each institution being considered. Five different colleges might have five different early decision criteria. Read the fine print, and make note of deadlines.

What really will help—you, your child, and your wallet—is to understand the basics about financial aid. Says Shawn Leftwich, Director of Undergraduate Admissions at Wheaton College in Illinois, "Have an in-depth discussion with the financial aid officer so that you are aware of the ramifications, restrictions, and implications of the financial aid offer."

If possible, make an appointment to visit with a financial aid officer at the college while your child is visiting the campus. Bring your tax forms and discuss the prospects of financial aid. "Financial aid people are straight shooters. It's not in their best interest to tell you one thing to get your foot in the door and then turn around and pull the rug out from under you," says Bill McClintick, Director of College Counseling at Mercerburg Academy. "Parents might not like the answer they get from the financial aid officer, but they will get a candid assessment of their eligibility for financial aid."

Leftwich suggests having an honest discussion with your child early in the college selection process. Talk about what you can realistically afford, what colleges will appropriately challenge him or her, if location is a factor, and what kind of environment best suits your child. Whichever option your child uses to apply, you both will know the decision is an informed one.

tions change them. "Colleges are always balancing the needs of their institution and the needs of students," he comments.

EARLY DECISION: A MATCHMAKING TOOL OR A CLEVER STRATEGY?

Despite the differences in what actually constitutes early decision, it has become more of a strategy than a matchmaking tool, according to Bill McClintick, Director of College Counseling at Mercersburg Academy in Mercersburg, Pennsylvania. He also chairs the national steering committee on admissions standards for NACAC. The focus of early decision used to be on matching the student with the college and letting the admissions office know that that institution is where the student wants to be above all others. Today, early decision is

misunderstood and misused. High school seniors think that they must use the early decision tactic to get an edge. The result, says McClintick is "at many of the top places, early decision applications have gone through the roof."

Though high school students may have exaggerated ideas of how much early decision can really help them, it is true that it does give a small segment of students applying at highly selective schools an advantage. Generally, the more selective the institution, the more small differences matter. "Even if it's a small increase, you need everything you can get," states John Latting, Dean of Undergraduate Admissions at Emory University in Atlanta, Georgia.

"Remember," cautions McClintick, "we're only talking about a small slice of kids in the grand scheme of things." He mentions 5 percent of high school seniors nationally who aspire to the "top" institutions. State colleges and universities fill a much lower percentage of their freshman class with early decision applications. "I don't believe that more kids are chasing the same number of spots," says Jon Reider, Director of College Counseling at San Francisco University High School in San Francisco, California. "Students are applying to more and more schools, even with the early decision option on the side. This is inflating the selectivity of some colleges beyond what it used to be." In reality, 90 percent of students apply regular admission. Interest in early decision comes from a relatively small segment of the college applicant pool.

THE BENEFITS OF EARLY DECISION

There are clear benefits for students who apply for early decision. Aside from the fact that early decision does play a role in acceptance rates for a relatively small percentage of students at a small number of schools, early decision is a good option. The caveat is that students must know, without a shred of doubt, that one institution, above all others, is the best match for their goals and their likes and dislikes, and that based on grades and test scores, they solidly match the institution's criteria for admission. The option to go early decision should be taken after extensive research, multiple visits to the campus, and talking to a lot of people. "Early decision is for those who can put their hearts and souls into one application," advises Cleaver.

There are other advantages. You have to make only one choice, and you will know by December if you've been accepted. You have to fill out only one application. You are not chewing your nails over your list of possibilities during the Christmas holiday. Instead, you know where you're going and can sit back and enjoy the rest of your senior year, while others in your class are madly filling out applications, writing essays, and agonizing over the thin envelopes that arrive in the mail. Says Guttentag, "The advantage of having that challenging process over with is not insignificant."

Early decision is helpful for admissions officers at selective colleges because it allows them to make decisions between well-qualified students and select those who really want to be at their institution. As Shawn Leftwich, Director of Undergraduate Admissions at Wheaton College in Illinois, points out, early decision is for the students who are strongly com-

mitted. "We like you. You like us. We know you're coming, and we can fill our freshman class." However, on the flip side, she adds that some students aren't so sure about which college they want to attend, and early decision only makes the process more stressful.

Before you decide to go with early decision, consider early action. Many high school counselors lean toward early action, which is another good option. With early action you're able to apply later in the process. This means you will be able to take the SATs again. Your first-semester grades and AP classes taken in the first semester of your senior year can be used to evaluate your eligibility. You have September and October to visit several campuses while they are in session and plenty of time to do the research to put more than one school on your list.

THE PITFALLS OF EARLY DECISION

Though early decision has benefits, before you jump into it, look at the ramifications of that option. Advises Gilbert, "Early decision might give you an edge, but the tradeoff is not so great."

Perhaps the most compelling reason why students should seriously examine early decision before jumping at it is because they are bound by an agreement to attend that school if accepted. Students sign a pledge to attend that institution and are required to withdraw applications from all other schools. They also are obligated to accept the financial aid award that the institution gives them. An early decision is a binding decision. "Regardless," advises David Gibson, College Advisor at St. Mary's Parish in Annapolis, Maryland, "students don't learn about their financial aid awards until March or April, and if the award funding is not at all acceptable because the family's financial need was not met, they need to decline the offer and begin searching for a new college. March or April is not a good time to start applying to new colleges."

How binding is binding? Though no school can force a student to attend if they've signed an early decision agreement, students who decide not to attend that school hurt others with that decision. High school counselors have to sign the binding agreement, along with parents, and must state that they will not send out transcripts to other institutions. Many institutions will not accept the application of a student who applied early decision elsewhere and backed out of the agreement. Admissions officers may find out in May that an early decision student is not coming, so they'll call the counselor and ask if the student applied to another school. If so, often a phone call to the other institution is made and acceptance denied. Sometimes the counselor loses a good reputation with that institution, putting applicants who follow in subsequent years at a disadvantage.

After the consequences of signing a binding agreement, the financial aspect of early decision is the next biggest pitfall. "You can't compare financial aid offers," says Latting. "You have only one offer." Students won't know if they're eligible for Pell grants or merit scholarships. Government FAFSA forms are not submitted until January, and students might not find out how much aid they can get until March or April, long

What if you don't get accepted early decision—then what? Speaking from the experience of seeing students deal with early decision rejection letters, Reider says, "Some of your friends are getting acceptance letters, and you get one thin envelope and the pain of rejection. You've given the early decision institution your best shot and you lost." Cleaver has seen kids in her high school end up thinking they won't get in anywhere. "This is the first time they've faced a big rejection and news they don't want to hear," she says, noting that because of the timetable of early decision, letters often come right around exam time in December.

When students apply regular decision, meaning they wait until well into their senior year and apply to several different institutions, it's "all or some," quips Latting. "With early decision, it's all or nothing." Many application deadlines for regular decision are in January. If you get that rejection letter from the school you were counting on, that doesn't give you much time to apply to other schools, much less visit them.

Are you ready to make such a drastic decision so early in your senior year? A lot can change in how you think about your future between the beginning of your senior year and graduation. With six or seven months behind you as a senior, you might be in a better position to compare colleges in April than you were back in September. Think about it—you're making the decision about where you want to spend the next four years of your life in early October of your senior year!

Have you given yourself enough time to pick one college above all others? If you want to apply early decision, you should start making plans to do so in your junior year. In order to apply early decision, you must have your ACTs or SATs taken, campus visits done, a final choice made, a dynamite essay written, a stellar application filled out, and teacher recommendation letters collected. That's a lot to cram into the end of your junior year and a few months into your senior year.

Have you given an admissions office enough information to make a decision about you? The more information the admissions office has about grades and classes you took and activities and leadership positions you held, the better they can decide if you're a good match for them. Do you really want decisions being made about you based on sophomore and junior grades and activities? What happens to that AP English class you finally felt ready to take the beginning of your senior year? What about that calculus class you aced in the first semester of your senior year? Admissions won't be able to assess that on an early decision application.

after the early decision agreement was signed and sealed. "This means that if they are accepted, they are then obligated to a college that might not fund them to the level of their financial need," says Gibson. Students who apply early action or regular decision are in a better position to negotiate financial aid packages.

EARLY DECISION REJECTION

In case you haven't heard, fat is good, thin is bad. Thin envelopes from college admissions offices usually mean a single-page letter saying good luck, we wish you the best, but you're not going to be attending our school next fall. However stated, it's hard to be rejected, especially when you've applied early decision, which states to the college and to yourself that this is the college you've decided is the only one you really, really want to attend above all others.

But thin envelopes don't mean the end of the world. Cleaver advises to not let early decision get control of you. "There are too many choices of colleges for you not to get into college. You might not get into Princeton, but there are many other wonderful schools if you do the research to look for a good match. Early decision is a tool to use to apply, but it is not always the best tool."

Objecting to the term "perfect match," Reider asks, "Does it really matter what kind of car you drive? There are twenty different colleges that can get you where you want to go. You'll be successful in most places."

HOW TO DO EARLY DECISION THE RIGHT WAY

Taking the early decision option requires more than gathering information, filling out an application, writing an essay, and waiting for an envelope to come in the mail or an e-mail to hit your In Box. If you're going to be serious about early decision, the time to start is in your junior year.

Research the institutions at the top of your list. Think through what you want out of college—not just in terms of a future career, but also factors such as location, size, distance from home, sports, and other activities. Think about who you want to be. "It has to be a love connection," says Cleaver. Tune out all the early decision talk and do your homework about each college. Then ask yourself if one stands out above all the others you've researched. Is this the one to which you can commit to a binding agreement? Are you in the competition to be admitted? Will you have the funds to attend this college?

"Admissions can tell if your application is from the heart," Cleaver cautions. Students ask her how to make their applications "look like they want to go there." She replies that what they put on an application and in an essay has to pour out of their hearts. Students who visit the campus and sit in on a class or a campus organization have the edge if something really clicked with them. They will write a convincing application. Perhaps they'll tell about how exciting the professor they heard was or how wonderful it is that the college has a chess club. Cleaver observes that kids usually write about an institution's sports team or about the ivy-covered walls of the campus on their application essay instead of writing about some interesting aspect of the university that spoke to them, which takes research, time, and reflection. "Don't make the mistake of chasing a name and not being a good consumer," cautions McClintick. Part of being a good consumer is to make sure you are a reasonably competitive applicant. This means looking at the school's admission criteria and statistics. What percentage of the freshman class is filled with early decision and early action students? If it's a high percentage, then you might want to reconsider where that school falls on your wish list. How many students return for their sophomore year? If more than 10 percent leave after their freshman year, that should tell you something about student satisfaction—and ultimately yours.

One of the most important ways to choose the right school is to visit the campus, perhaps multiple times and preferably with students on campus. "Campus visits are a critical time to talk with undergraduates and to find out what the academic, social, and physical climate is like," advises Guttentag. If you're staying in a dorm on Tuesday night during a visit, you can tell how serious kids are about their work. What kinds of conversations are they having? "Are these the kind of kids you want to spend four years of your life with?" asks McClintick.

After you've thoroughly investigated all the aspects of a college and decided it's at the absolute top of your list, after you are familiar with the early decision requirements at that institution, and after you've determined that you have a good chance of getting into that institution, then you can say early decision is for you. For those who are not so sure, fortunately, colleges and universities have plenty of other options for admission.

What International Students Need to Know About Admission to U.S. Colleges and Universities

Kitty M. Villa

There are two principles to remember about admission to a university in the United States. First, applying is almost never a one-time request for admission but an ongoing process that may involve several exchanges of information between applicant and institution. "Admission process" or "application process" means that a "yes" or "no" is usually not immediate, and requests for additional information are to be expected. To successfully manage this process, you must be prepared to send additional information when requested and then wait for replies. You need a thoughtful balance of persistence to communicate regularly and effectively with your selected universities and patience to endure what can be a very long process.

The second principle involves a marketplace analogy. The most successful applicants are alert to opportunities to create a positive impression that sets them apart from other applicants. They are able to market themselves to their target institution. Institutions are also trying to attract the highest-quality student that they can. The admissions process presents you with the opportunity to analyze your strengths and weaknesses as a student and to look for ways to present yourself in the most marketable manner.

FIRST STEP—SELECTING INSTITUTIONS

With thousands of institutions of higher education in the United States, how do you begin to narrow your choices down to the institutions that are best for you? There are many factors to consider, and you must ultimately decide which factors are most important to you.

Location

You may spend several years studying in the United States. Do you prefer an urban or rural campus? Large or small metropolitan area? If you need to live on campus, will you be unhappy at a university where most students commute from off-campus housing? How do you feel about extremely hot summers or cold winters? Eliminating institutions that do not match your preferences in terms of location will narrow your choices.

Recommendations from Friends, Professors, or Others

There are valid academic reasons to consider the recommendations of people who know you well and have firsthand knowledge about particular institutions. Friends and contacts may be able to provide you with "inside information" about the campus or its academic programs to which published sources have no access. You should carefully balance anecdotal information with your own research and your own impressions. However, current and former students, professors, and others may provide excellent information during the application process.

Your Own Academic and Career Goals

Consideration of your academic goals is more complex than it may seem at first glance. All institutions do not offer the same academic programs. The application form usually provides a definitive listing of the academic programs offered by an institution. A course catalog describes the degree program and all the courses offered. In addition to printed sources, there is a tremendous amount of institutional information available on the Web. Program descriptions, even course descriptions and course syllabi, are often available to peruse online.

You may be interested in the rankings of either the university or of a program of study. Keep in mind, however, that rankings usually assume that quality is quantifiable. Rankings are usually based on presumptions about how data relate to quality and are likely to be unproven. It is important to carefully consider the source and the criteria of any ranking information before believing and acting upon it.

Your Own Educational Background

You may be concerned about the interpretation of your educational credentials, since your country's degree nomenclature and the grading scale may differ from those in the United States. Universities use reference books about the educational systems of other countries to help them understand specific educational credentials. Generally, these credentials are interpreted by each institution; there is not a single interpretation that applies to every institution. The lack of uniformity is good

news for most students, since it means that students from a wide variety of educational backgrounds can find a U.S. university that is appropriate to their needs.

To choose an appropriate institution, you can and should do an informal self-evaluation of your educational background. This self-analysis involves three important questions:

1. How Many Years of Study Have You Completed?

Completion of secondary school with at least twelve total years of education usually qualifies students to apply for undergraduate (bachelor's) degree programs. Completion of a university degree program that involves at least sixteen years of total education qualifies one to apply for admission to graduate (master's) degree programs in the United States.

2. Does the Education That You Have Completed in Your Country Provide Access to Further Study in the United States?

Consider the kind of institution where you completed your previous studies. If educational opportunities in your country are limited, it may be necessary to investigate many U.S. institutions and programs in order to find a match.

3. Are Your Previous Marks or Grades Excellent, Average, or Poor?

Your educational record influences your choice of U.S. institutions. If your grades are average or poor, it may be advisable to apply to several institutions with minimally difficult or non-competitive entrance levels.

YOU are one of the best sources of information about the level and quality of your previous studies. Awareness of your educational assets and liabilities will serve you well throughout the application process.

SECOND STEP—PLANNING AND ASSEMBLING THE APPLICATION

Planning and assembling a university application can be compared to the construction of a building. First, you must start with a solid foundation, which is the application form itself. The application, often available online as well as in paper form, usually contains a wealth of useful information, such as deadlines, fees, and degree programs available at that institution. To build a solid application, it is best to begin well in advance of the application deadline.

How to Obtain the Application Form

Application forms and links to institutional Web sites may also be available at a U.S. educational advising center associated with the American Embassy or Consulate in your country. These centers are excellent resources for international students and provide information about standardized test administration, scholarships, and other matters to students who are interested in studying in the United States. Your local U.S. Embassy or Consulate can guide you to the nearest educational advising center.

What Are the Key Components of a Complete Application?

Institutional requirements vary, but the standard components of a complete application include the following:

- Transcript
- Required standardized examination scores
- Evidence of financial support
- Letters of recommendation
- Application fee

Transcript

A complete academic record or transcript includes all courses completed, grades earned, and degrees awarded. Most universities require an official transcript to be sent directly from the school or university. In many other countries, however, the practice is to issue official transcripts and degree certificates directly to the student. If you have only one official copy of your transcript, it may be a challenge to get additional certified copies that are acceptable to U.S. universities. Some institutions will issue additional official copies for application purposes.

If your institution does not provide this service, you may have to seek an alternate source of certification. As a last resort, you may send a photocopy of your official transcript, explain that you have only one original, and ask the university for advice on how to deal with this situation.

Required Standardized Examination Scores

Arranging to take standardized examinations and earning the required scores seem to cause the most anxiety for international students.

The university application form usually indicates which examinations are required. The standardized examination required most often for undergraduate admission is the Test of English as a Foreign Language (TOEFL). Institutions may also require the SAT of undergraduate applicants. These standardized examinations are administered by the Educational Testing Service (ETS).

These examinations are offered in almost every country of the world. It is advisable to begin planning for standardized examinations at least six months prior to the application deadline of your desired institutions. Test centers fill up quickly, so it is important to register as soon as possible. Information about the examinations is available at U.S. educational advising centers associated with embassies or consulates.

Most universities require that the original test scores, not a student copy, be sent directly by the testing service. When you register for the test, be sure to indicate that the testing service should send the test scores directly to the universities.

You should begin your application process before you receive your test scores. Delaying submission of your application until the test scores arrive may cause you to miss deadlines and negatively affect the outcome of your application. If you want to know your scores in order to assess your chances of admission to an institution with rigorous admission standards, you should take the tests early.

Many universities in the United States set minimum required scores on the TOEFL or other standardized examinations. Test scores are an important factor, but most institutions also look at a number of other factors in their consideration of a candidate for admission.

For More Information

Questions about test formats, locations, dates, and registration may be addressed to:

ETS Corporate Headquarters
Rosedale Road
Princeton, New Jersey 08541
Web sites: http://www.ets.org
http://www.ets.org/toefl/
Phone: 609-921-9000
Fax: 609-734-5410

Evidence of Financial Support

Evidence of financial support is required to issue immigration documents to admitted students. This is part of a complete application package but usually plays no role in determining admission. Most institutions make admissions decisions without regard to the source and amount of financial support.

Letters of Recommendation

Most institutions require one or more letters of recommendation. The best letters are written by former professors, employers, or others who can comment on your academic achievements or professional potential.

Some universities provide a special form for the letters of recommendation. If possible, use the forms provided. If you are applying to a large number of universities, however, or if your recommenders are not available to complete several forms, it may be necessary for you to duplicate a general recommendation letter.

Application Fee

Most universities also require an application fee, ranging from $25 to $100, which must be paid to initiate consideration of the application.

Completing the Application Form

Whether sent by mail or electronically, the application form must be neat and thoroughly filled out. Although parts of the application may not seem to apply to you or your situation, do your best to answer all the questions.

Remember that this is a process. You provide information, and your proposed university then may request clarification and further information. If you have questions, it is better to initiate the entire process by submitting the application form rather than asking questions before you apply. The university will be better able to respond to you after it has your application. Always complete as much as you can. Do not permit uncertainty about the completion of the application form to cause unnecessary delays.

THIRD STEP—DISTINGUISH YOUR APPLICATION

To distinguish your application—to market yourself successfully—is ultimately the most important part of the application process. As you select your prospective universities, begin to analyze your strengths and weaknesses as a prospective student. As you complete your application, you should strive to create a positive impression and set yourself apart from other applicants, to highlight your assets and bring these qualities to the attention of the appropriate university administrators and professors. Applying early is a very easy way to distinguish your application.

Deadline or Guideline?

The application deadline is the last date that an application for a given semester will be accepted. Often, the application will specify that all required documents and information be submitted before the deadline date. To meet the deadlines, start the application process early. This also gives you more time to take—and perhaps retake and improve—the required standardized tests.

Admissions deliberations may take several weeks or months. In the meantime, most institutions accept additional information, including improved test scores, after the posted deadline.

Even if your application is initially rejected, you may be able to provide additional information to change the decision. You can request reconsideration based on additional information, such as improved test scores, strong letters of recommendation, or information about your class rank. Applying early allows more time to improve your application. Also, some students may decide not to accept their offers of admission, leaving room for offers to students on a waiting list. Reconsideration of the admission decisions can occur well beyond the application deadline.

Think of the deadline as a guideline rather than an impermeable barrier. Many factors—the strength of the application, your research interests, the number of spaces available at the proposed institution—can override the enforcement of an application deadline. So, if you lack a test score or transcript by the official deadline, you may still be able to apply and be accepted.

Statement of Purpose

The statement of purpose is your first and perhaps best opportunity to present yourself as an excellent candidate for admission. Whether or not a personal history essay or statement of purpose is required, always include a carefully written statement of purpose with your applications. A compelling statement of purpose does not have to be lengthy, but it should include some basic components:

- Part One—Introduce yourself and describe your educational background. This is your opportunity to describe any facet of your educational experience that you wish to emphasize. Perhaps you attended a highly ranked secondary school or university in your home country. Mention the name and any noteworthy characteristics of the secondary school or university from which you graduated. Explain the grading scale used at your university. Do not forget to mention your rank in your graduating class and any honors you may have received. This is not the time to be modest.

- Part Two—Describe your current academic and career interests and goals. Think about how these will fit into those

of the institution to which you are applying, and mention the reasons why you have selected that institution.

- Part Three—Describe your long-term goals. When you finish your program of study, what do you plan to do next? If you already have a job offer or a career plan, describe it. Give some thought to how you'll demonstrate that studying in the United States. will ultimately benefit others.

Use Personal Contacts When Possible

Appropriate and judicious use of your own network of contacts can be very helpful. Friends, former professors, former students of your selected institutions, and others may be willing to advise you during the application process and provide you with introductions to key administrators or professors. If suggested, you may wish to contact certain professors or administrators by mail, phone, or e-mail. A personal visit to discuss your interest in the institution may be appropriate. Whatever your choice of communication, try to make the encounter pleasant and personal. Your goal is to make a positive impression, not to rush the admission decision.

There is no single right way to be admitted to U.S. universities. The same characteristics that make the educational choice in the United States so difficult—the number of institutions and the variety of programs of study—are the same attributes that allow so many international students to find the institution that's right for them.

Kitty M. Villa is the former Assistant Director, International Office, at the University of Texas at Austin.

Financial Aid Countdown Calendar

JUNIOR YEAR

Fall

Now is the time to get serious about the colleges in which you are interested. Meet with your guidance counselor to help you narrow down your choices. Hopefully by the spring, your list will have five to ten solid choices. College visits are always a great idea—remember this will be the place you will call home for four years, so start your campus visits soon!

❑ Register for the PSAT/NMSQT.

❑ Check out local financial aid nights in the area. Be sure to attend these valuable sessions, especially if this is the first time your family is sending someone off to college. Try to become familiar with common financial aid terms. Start reviewing the literature available and begin to familiarize yourself with the various programs. A good booklet is published by the U.S. Department of Education, "Funding Education Beyond High School: The Guide to Federal Student Aid" and is available at any financial aid office or on the Web at http://studentaid.ed.gov/students/attachments/siteresources/12-13_Guide.pdf

❑ In October, take the PSAT/NMSQT.

❑ Do some Web browsing! There are many free scholarship search engines, such as Petersons.com. Also, head to the bookstore or library and pick up a copy of *Peterson's Scholarships, Grants & Prizes,* which features details on billions of dollars of aid from private sources, or *Best Scholarships for the Best Students,* which offers great info on scholarships, fellowships, and experiential learning programs for top students.

❑ Ask your parents to contact their employers, unions, and any religious and fraternal organizations with which they have a connection to learn about possible scholarship opportunities.

❑ Check with your high school guidance counselor for the qualifications and deadlines of local scholarship awards. Many guidance counselors report that there are few applicants for these awards.

Winter

❑ Keep checking for scholarships! Remember that this is the one area over which you have control. The harder you work, the better your chances for success!

❑ Register and study for the ACT or SAT and SAT Subject Tests.

Spring

❑ Spring Break—a great time to visit colleges. Remember your top ten list? Time to start narrowing it down.

❑ Review the requirements for local scholarships. What can you do now and over the summer to improve your chances?

❑ Take the ACT or SAT. Good luck!

❑ Look for a summer job, especially one that ties in with your college plans. For example, if you want to major in premed, why not try to get a job at a hospital or with a laboratory?

Summer

❑ College visit time! Ask: Is this where I see myself getting my undergraduate degree? Can I adjust to the seasons, the town surrounding the campus, the distance from home, the college size? Does this school feel right for me?

❑ Why not get a jump on college (and maybe save some money!) and enroll for a college course at the local community college? Or, better yet, do some extra prep work for the ACT or SAT!

MONEY, MONEY, MONEY

SENIOR YEAR

Fall

How's the college list coming? Can you get your list down to five or six choices? Your guidance counselor can help with this process. Once you have your top choices, make a list of what each college requires for admission and financial aid. Be sure your list includes all deadlines. Attend a financial aid night presentation with your parents. Some of these sessions offer help in completing forms; others offer a broader view of the process. Contact the presenter (usually a local college financial aid professional) to be sure you are getting the information you need.

❏ Do any of these colleges require the CSS/Financial Aid PROFILE® financial aid application? Many private colleges use this form for institutional aid. You need to file this comprehensive form in late September or early October. For more information or to find out which colleges use this supplemental form, go to http://profileonline.collegeboard.com/index.jsp. (Web site registration is free; however, PROFILE is a fee-based application).

❏ Don't falter now in your scholarship search. Get the applications filed by the published deadlines.

❏ Register now if you are planning to retake the SAT.

❏ Most important, start completing your college applications—the earlier, the better! If you are interested in early decision or early action, now is the time! Remember, accuracy and completeness are a must!

Winter

❏ Ensure all college applications are completed.

❏ Get the Free Application for Federal Student Aid (FAFSA). This is the key form for financial aid for every school across the country. Remember, watch your deadlines, but do not file until after January 1. Be sure to keep a copy of the form, whether you file electronically or with the paper application. Do you have some questions? Call the local financial aid office. Many states have special toll-free call-in programs in

January and February, Financial Aid Awareness Month. Be sure that you have completed each school's required forms.

❏ As the letters of admission start to arrive, the financial aid award letters should be right behind them. Important question for parents: What is the bottom line? Remember, aid at a lower-cost state school will be less than a higher-cost private college. But what will you be required to pay? This can be confusing, so consider gift aid (scholarships and grants), student loans, and parent loans. The school with the lowest sticker price (tuition, fees, and room and board) might not be the best bargain when you look at the overall financial aid package.

Spring

❏ Still not sure where to go? The financial aid package at your top choice just not enough? Call the financial aid office and the admissions office. Talk it over. While schools don't like to bargain, they are usually willing to take a second look. Is there something unusual about your family's financial situation that might impact your parents' ability to pay?

❏ By May 1, you must make your final decision. Notify your chosen college and find out what you need to do next. Tell the other colleges you are not accepting their offers of admission and financial aid.

Summer

❏ Time to crunch the numbers. Parents, get information from the college on the total charges for the coming fall term. Deduct the aid package and then plan for how the balance will be paid. Contact the college financial aid office for the best parental loan program. If you want to arrange for a payment plan, contact the business office for further information. Most schools have deferred payment plans available for a nominal fee.

Congratulations! Remember that you need to reapply for aid every year!

Who's Paying for This? Financial Aid Basics

A college education can be expensive—costing more than $150,000 for four years at some of the higher priced private colleges and universities. Even at the lower cost state colleges and universities, the cost of a four-year education can approach $60,000. Determining how you and your family will come up with the necessary funds to pay for your education requires planning, perseverance, and learning as much as you can about the options that are available to you. But before you get discouraged, College Board statistics show that 53 percent of full-time students attend four-year public and private colleges with tuition and fees less than $9000, while 20 percent attend colleges that have tuition and fees more than $36,000. College costs tend to be less in the western states and higher in New England.

Paying for college should not be looked at as a four-year financial commitment. For many families, paying the total cost of a student's college education out of current income and savings is usually not realistic. For families that have planned ahead and have financial savings established for higher education, the burden is a lot easier. But for most, meeting the cost of college requires the pooling of current income and assets and investing in longer-term loan options. These family resources, together with financial assistance from state, federal, and institutional sources, enable millions of students each year to attend the institution of their choice.

FINANCIAL AID PROGRAMS

There are three types of financial aid:

1. Gift-aid—Scholarships and grants are funds that do not have to be repaid.

2. Loans—Loans must be repaid, usually after graduation; the amount you have to pay back is the total you've borrowed plus any accrued interest. This is considered a source of self-help aid.

3. Student employment—Student employment is a job arranged for you by the financial aid office. This is another source of self-help aid.

The federal government has four major grant programs—the Federal Pell Grant, the Federal Supplemental Educational Opportunity Grant, Academic Competitiveness Grants (ACG), and SMART grants. ACG and SMART grants are limited to students who qualify for a Pell grant and are awarded to a select group of students. Overall, these grants are targeted to low-to-moderate income families with significant financial need. The federal government also sponsors a student employment program called the Federal Work-Study Program, which offers jobs both on and off campus, and several loan programs, including those for students and for parents of undergraduate students.

There are two types of student loan programs: subsidized and unsubsidized. The subsidized Federal Direct Loan and the Federal Perkins Loan are need-based, government-subsidized loans. Students who borrow through these programs do not have to pay interest on the loan until after they graduate or leave school. The unsubsidized Federal Direct Loan and the Federal Direct PLUS Loan Program are not based on need, and borrowers are responsible for the interest while the student is in school. These loans are administered by different methods. Once you choose your college, the financial aid office will guide you through this process.

After you've submitted your financial aid application and you've been accepted for admission, each college will send you a letter describing your financial aid award. Most award letters show estimated college costs, how much you and your family are expected to contribute, and the amount and types of aid you have been awarded. Most students are awarded aid from a combination of sources and programs. Hence, your award is often called a financial aid "package."

SOURCES OF FINANCIAL AID

Millions of students and families apply for financial aid each year. Financial aid from all sources exceeds $143 billion per year. The largest single source of aid is the federal government, which will award more than $100 billion this year.

The next largest source of financial aid is found in the college and university community. Most of this aid is awarded to students who have a demonstrated need based on the Federal Methodology. Some institutions use a different formula, the Institutional Methodology (IM), to award their own funds in conjunction with other forms of aid. Institutional aid may be either need-based or non-need based. Aid that is not based on need is usually awarded for a student's academic performance (merit awards), specific talents or abilities, or to attract the type of students a college seeks to enroll.

Another source of financial aid is from state government. All states offer grant and/or scholarship aid, most of which is need-based. However, more and more states are offering substantial merit-based aid programs. Most state programs award aid only to students attending college in their home state.

Other sources of financial aid include:

- Private agencies
- Foundations
- Corporations
- Clubs
- Fraternal and service organizations

- Civic associations
- Unions
- Religious groups that award grants, scholarships, and low-interest loans
- Employers that provide tuition reimbursement benefits for employees and their children

More information about these different sources of aid is available from high school guidance offices, public libraries, college financial aid offices, directly from the sponsoring organizations, and on the Web at www.petersons.com and www.finaid.org.

HOW NEED-BASED FINANCIAL AID IS AWARDED

When you apply for aid, your family's financial situation is analyzed using a government-approved formula called the Federal Methodology. This formula looks at five items:

1. Demographic information of the family
2. Income of the parents
3. Assets of the parents
4. Income of the student
5. Assets of the student

This analysis determines the amount you and your family are expected to contribute toward your college expenses, called your Expected Family Contribution or EFC. If the EFC is equal to or more than the cost of attendance at a particular college, then you do not demonstrate financial need. However, even if you don't have financial need, you may still qualify for aid, as there are grants, scholarships, and loan programs that are not need-based.

If the cost of your education is greater than your EFC, then you do demonstrate financial need and qualify for assistance. The amount of your financial need that can be met varies from school to school. Some are able to meet your full need, while others can only cover a certain percentage of need. Here's the formula:

$$
\begin{array}{l}
\text{Cost of Attendance} \\
\underline{- \text{ Expected Family Contribution}} \\
= \text{Financial Need}
\end{array}
$$

The EFC remains constant, but your need will vary according to the costs of attendance at a particular college. In general, the higher the tuition and fees at a particular college, the higher the cost of attendance will be. Expenses for books and supplies, room and board, transportation, and other miscellaneous items are included in the overall cost of attendance. It is important to remember that you do not have to be "needy" to qualify for financial aid. Many middle and upper-middle income families qualify for need-based financial aid.

APPLYING FOR FINANCIAL AID

Every student must complete the Free Application for Federal Student Aid (FAFSA) to be considered for financial aid. The FAFSA is available from your high school guidance office, many public libraries, colleges in your area, or directly from the U.S. Department of Education.

Students are encouraged to apply for federal student aid on the Web. The electronic version of the FAFSA can be accessed at http://www.fafsa.ed.gov. Both the student and at least one parent must apply for a federal PIN at http:// www.pin.ed.gov. The PIN serves as your electronic signature when applying for aid on the Web.

To award their own funds, some colleges require an additional application, the CSS/Financial Aid PROFILE® form. The PROFILE asks supplemental questions that some colleges and awarding agencies feel provide a more accurate assessment of the family's ability to pay for college. It is up to the college to decide whether it will use only the FAFSA or both the FAFSA and the PROFILE. PROFILE applications are available from the high school guidance office and on the Web. Both the paper application and the Web site list those colleges and programs that require the PROFILE application.

If Every College You're Applying to for Fall 2013 Requires the FAFSA

. . . then it's pretty simple: Complete the FAFSA after January 1, 2013, being certain to send it in before any college-imposed deadlines. (You are not permitted to send in the 2013–14 FAFSA before January 1, 2013.) Most college FAFSA application deadlines are in February or early March. It is easier if you have all your financial records for the previous year available, but if that is not possible, you are strongly encouraged to use estimated figures.

After you send in your FAFSA, either with the paper application or electronically, you'll receive a Student Aid Report (SAR) that includes all of the information you reported and shows your EFC. If you provided an e-mail address, the SAR is sent to you electronically; otherwise, you will receive a paper copy in the mail. Be sure to review the SAR, checking to see if the information you reported is accurately represented. If you used estimated numbers to complete the FAFSA, you may have to resubmit the SAR with any corrections to the data. The college(s) you have designated on the FAFSA will receive the information you reported and will use that data to make their decision. In many instances, the colleges to which you've applied will ask you to send copies of your and your parents' federal income tax returns for 2011, plus any other documents needed to verify the information you reported.

If a College Requires the PROFILE

Step 1: Register for the CSS/Financial Aid PROFILE in the fall of your senior year in high school. You can apply for the PROFILE online at http://profileonline.collegeboard.com/ prf/ index.jsp. Registration information with a list of the colleges that require the PROFILE is available in most high school guidance offices. There is a fee for using the Financial Aid PROFILE application ($25 for the first college, which includes the $9 application fee, and $16 for each additional college). You must pay for the service by credit card when you register. If you do not have a credit card, you will be billed. A limited number of fee waivers are automatically granted to first-time applicants based on the financial information provided on the PROFILE.

Step 2: Fill out your customized CSS/Financial Aid PROFILE. Once you register, your application will be immediately available online and will have questions that all students must complete, questions which must be completed by the student's parents (unless the student is independent and the colleges or programs selected do not require parental information), and *may* have supplemental questions needed by one or more of your schools or programs. If required, those will be found in Section Q of the application.

In addition to the PROFILE application you complete online, you may also be required to complete a Business/ Farm Supplement via traditional paper format. Completion of this form is not a part of the online process. If this form is required, instructions on how to download and print the supplemental form are provided. If your biological or adoptive parents are separated or divorced and your colleges and programs require it, your noncustodial parent may be asked to complete the Non-custodial PROFILE.

Once you complete and submit your PROFILE application, it will be processed and sent directly to your requested colleges and programs.

IF YOU DON'T QUALIFY FOR NEED-BASED AID

If you are not eligible for need-based aid, you can still find ways to lessen your burden.

Here are some suggestions:

- Search for merit scholarships. You can start at the initial stages of your application process. College merit awards are increasingly important as more and more colleges award these to students they especially want to attract. As a result, applying to a college at which your qualifications put you at the top of the entering class may give you a larger merit award. Another source of aid to look for is private scholarships that are given for special skills and talents. Additional information can be found at and at www.finaid.org.

- Seek employment during the summer and the academic year. The student employment office at your college can help you locate a school-year job. Many colleges and local businesses have vacancies remaining after they have hired students who are receiving Federal Work-Study Program financial aid.

- Borrow through the unsubsidized Federal Direct Loan program. This is generally available to all students. The terms and conditions are similar to the subsidized loans. The biggest difference is that the borrower is responsible for the interest while still in college, although the government permits students to delay paying the interest right away and add the accrued interest to the total amount owed. You must file the FAFSA to be considered.

- After you've secured what you can through scholarships, working, and borrowing, you and your parents will be expected to meet your share of the college bill (the Expected Family Contribution). Many colleges offer monthly payment plans that spread the cost over the academic year. If the monthly payments are too high, parents can borrow through the Federal Direct PLUS Loan Program, through one of the many private education loan programs available, or through home equity loans and lines of credit. Families seeking assistance in financing college expenses should inquire at the financial aid office about what programs are available at the college. Some families seek the advice of professional financial advisers and tax consultants.

Middle-Income Families: Making the Financial Aid Process Work

Richard Woodland

A report from the U.S. Department of Education's National Center for Education Statistics took a close look at how middle-income families finance a college education. The report, *Middle Income Undergraduates: Where They Enroll and How They Pay for Their Education,* was one of the first detailed studies of these families. Even though 31 percent of middle-income families have the entire cost of attendance covered by financial aid, there is widespread angst among middle-income families that, while they earn too much to qualify for grant assistance, they are financially unable to pay the spiraling costs of higher education.

First, we have to agree on what constitutes a "middle-income" family. For the purposes of the federal study, middle income is defined as those families with incomes between $35,000 and $70,000. The good news is that 52 percent of these families received grants, while the balance received loans. Other sources of aid, including work-study, also helped close the gap.

So how do these families do it? Is there a magic key that will open the door to significant amounts of grants and scholarships?

The report found some interesting trends. One way families can make college more affordable is by choosing a less expensive college. In fact, in this income group, 29 percent choose to enroll in low-to moderate-cost schools. These include schools where the total cost is less than $8,500 per year. In this sector, we find the community colleges and lower-priced state colleges and universities. But almost half of these middle-income families choose schools in the upper-level tier, with costs ranging from $8,500 to $16,000. The remaining 23 percent enrolled at the highest-tier schools, with costs above $16,000. Clearly, while cost is a factor, middle-income families are not limiting their choices based on costs alone.

The report shows that families pay these higher costs with a combination of family assets, current income, and long-term borrowing. This is often referred to as the "past-present-future" model of financing. In fact, just by looking at the Expected Family Contributions, it is clear that there is a significant gap in what families need and what the financial aid process can provide. Families are closing this gap by making the financial sacrifices necessary to pay the price at higher-cost schools, especially if they think their child is academically strong. The report concludes that parents are more likely to pay for a higher-priced education if their child scores high on the SAT.

The best place for middle-income families to start is with the high school guidance office. This office has information on financial aid and valuable leads on local scholarships. Most guidance officers report that there are far fewer applicants for these locally based scholarships than one would expect. So read the information they send home and check on the application process. A few of those $500–$1000 scholarships can add up!

Plan to attend a financial aid awareness program. If your school does not offer one, contact your local college financial aid office and see when and where they will be speaking. You can get a lot of "inside" information on how the financial aid process works.

Next, be sure to file the correct applications for aid. Remember, each school can have a different set of requirements. For example, many higher-cost private colleges will require the CSS/Financial Aid PROFILE® application, filed in September or October of the senior year. Other schools may have their own institutional aid application. All schools will require the Free Application for Federal Student Aid (FAFSA). Watch the deadlines! It is imperative that you meet the school's published application deadline. Generally, schools are not flexible about this, so be sure to double-check the due date of all applications.

Finally, become a smart educational consumer. Peterson's has a wide range of resources available to help you understand the process. Be sure to also check your local library, bookstore, and of course, the Internet. A great Web site to check is www.finaid.org.

Once admitted to the various colleges and universities, you will receive an award notice outlining the aid you are eligible to receive. If you feel the offer is not sufficient, or if you have some unique financial circumstances, call the school's financial aid office to see if you can have your application reviewed again. The financial aid office is your best source for putting the pieces together and finding financial solutions.

The financial aid office will help you determine the "net price." This is the actual out-of-pocket cost that you will need to cover. Through a combination of student and parent loans, most families are able to meet these expenses with other forms of financial aid and family resources.

Many students help meet their educational expenses by working while in school. While this works for many students, research shows that too many hours spent away from your studies will negatively impact your academic success. Most experts feel that working 10 to 15 hours a week is optimal.

An overlooked source of aid is the tax credits given to middle-income families. Rather than extending eligibility for traditional sources of grant assistance to middle-income families, the federal tax system has built in a number of significant tax benefits, known as the Hope Scholarship and Lifetime Learning tax credit, for middle-income families. While it may be seven or eight months before you see the tax credit, most families in this income group can count on this benefit, usually between $1500 to $2000 per student. This is real money in your pocket. You do not need to itemize your deductions to qualify for this tax credit.

A tool to help families get a handle on the ever-rising costs of college is to assume that you can pay one third of the "net charges" from savings, another third from available (non-retirement) assets, and the rest from parent borrowing. If any one of these "thirds" is not available, shift that amount to one of the other resources. However, if it looks like you will be financing most or all of the costs from future income (borrowing), it may be wise to consider a lower-cost college.

Millions of middle-income families send their children to colleges and universities every year. Only 8 percent attend the lowest-priced schools. By using the concept of past-present-future financing, institutional assistance, federal and state aid, meaningful targeted tax relief, and student earnings, you can afford even the highest-cost schools.

Richard Woodland is the former Director of Financial Aid at Rutgers University–Camden.

Honors Programs and Colleges: Smart Choices for an Undergraduate Education

Dr. Joan Digby

In general, students and their parents are guided toward a narrow selection of colleges and universities based on reputation, conversations with friends, or promotional material. Few people think to approach the college search focused on honors opportunities. As a result, students with extraordinary talents and interests miss out on a rich variety of untapped financial resources and exciting college experiences.

The smarter approach is to seek out a distinctive education that caters to students' great diversity of intellectual and creative strengths. If you are a strong student filled with ideas, longing for creative expression and ready to take on career-shaping challenges, then an honors education is just for you. Honors programs and colleges offer some of the finest undergraduate degrees available at U.S. colleges and do it with students in mind. The essence of honors is personal attention, top faculty, enlightening seminars, illuminating study-travel experiences, research options, and career-building internships—all designed to enhance a classic education and prepare you for life achievements. And here is an eye-opening bonus: Honors program and colleges may reward your past academic performance by giving you scholarships that will help you pay for your higher education!

Take your choice of institutions: community college, state or private, two-or four-year, college or large research university. There are honors opportunities in each. What they share is an unqualified commitment to academic excellence. Honors education teaches students to think and write clearly, be excited by ideas, and become independent, creative, self-confident learners. It prepares exceptional students for professional choices in every imaginable sphere of life: arts and sciences, engineering, business, health, education, medicine, theater, music, film, journalism, media, law, politics—invent your own professional goal and honors will guide you to it! Whichever honors program or college you choose, you can be sure to enjoy an extraordinarily fulfilling undergraduate education.

WHO ARE HONORS STUDENTS?

Who are you? Perhaps a high school junior filling out your first college application, a community college student seeking to transfer to a four-year college, or possibly a four-year college student doing better than you had expected. You might be an international student, a varsity athlete, captain of the debate team, or second violin in the orchestra. Whether you are the first person in your family to attend college or an adult with a grown family seeking a new career, honors might well be right for you. Honors programs admit students with every imaginable background and educational goal.

How does honors satisfy students and give them something special? Read what students in some honors programs and colleges say. Although they refer to particular honors colleges or programs, their experiences are typical of what students find exciting about honors education on hundreds of campuses around the country.

"Being an honors program student has been a life-changing experience for me. I have gained tremendously in knowledge, experience, and self-esteem. I have learned so much more in the program than any textbook could teach about the value of encouraging support and positive thinking."

—*Cheri Becker, Mount Wachusett Community College*

"I've been in a healing ceremony in Ecuador and have performed music on stage. I've guided my peers and Navajo children, hiked the Grand Canyon, and so much more. Sometimes, experience speaks for itself; always, it creates paths, opens eyes, and helps us find our places. Thanks to my honors program, I've experienced these wonders and accomplishments. Now I know that there are no greater lessons than how to learn and love discovery."

—*April Fisher, University of North Florida*

"The Honors College has been my home away from home. In the midst of a diverse, fairly large university, it has provided me with the intimacy that I needed...My freshman-year living situation on the honors floor... allowed me to find like-minded students early in my college career."

—*Brian Leech, Davidson Honors College, University of Montana*

"I was able to transition from an honors program at a two-year institution into an honors program at a four-year institution without any reservations or tribulations."

—*Rachel Jones Williams, Harrisburg Area Community College*

"Every single professor is in love with what they do and it shows in their research, their amazing teaching, and their interaction with students outside of the classroom. The undergraduate journey can be very difficult at times, but as an Honors College student, you're sure to have plenty of support every step of the way."

—*Walteria Tucker, Wilkes Honors College, Florida Atlantic University*

"The class size is perfect and I've been able to make some of my closest relationships with students and teachers through the program. The majority of honors faculty I have encountered have been overwhelmingly helpful...and my favorite courses have been honors classes."

—*Ellen Daschler, Eastern Illinois University*

"Our professor met us at a local restaurant the last evening of class and we shared a wonderful dinner. It had such a familiar feel to it because these are students I have known throughout my four years in the program."

—*Betsy Porter, University of La Verne*

"For the last two years, I have investigated new synthetic methods under the direction of a professor emeritus. Through the University Honors College, I am able to pursue this interest in chemistry and other academic endeavors . . . that have allowed me to develop my academic potential and contribute to the scientific body of knowledge."

—*Justin Chalker, University of Pittsburgh*

"The most rewarding part of being a member of the honors program is the joy of doing creative, meaningful projects with faculty I love."

—*Meleia Egger, Hartwick College*

"I would... like to add a word of praise for the way the curriculum is structured. It has deepened and enriched my thinking and helped me develop tools to negotiate the complex world we live in."

—*Monideepa Talukdar, Southeastern Louisiana University*

"We have a better time...our discussions get rather heated. In a lot of classes, only one or two students will speak up, but in the honors classes, it's a free-for-all."

—*Jonathan Post, Reinhardt College*

"My internship at a major international bank gave me an in-depth look into the world of investment and accounting. Funded by the Honors College, I was able to study business and culture in Shanghai, China, for a month. These valuable experiences are helping me to develop professionally, academically, and personally."

—*Jenny Lam, Honors College, The College of Staten Island, CUNY*

"The honors thesis was the key factor during the selection process at my future employer....It helped me to get the job and have an advantage over others. It is a lot of work but, in the end, it is worth it."

—*Olgierd Hinz, Lee Honors College, Western Michigan University*

These portraits don't tell the whole story, but they should give you a sense of what it means to be part of an honors program or college. One of the great strengths of honors programs and colleges is that they are nurturing environments that encourage students to be well-rounded and help students make life choices.

WHAT IS AN HONORS PROGRAM?

An honors program is a sequence of courses designed specifically to encourage independent and creative learning. For more than half a century, honors education—given definition by the National Collegiate Honors Council—has been an institution on U.S. campuses. Although honors programs have many different designs, there are typical components. At two-year colleges, the programs often concentrate on special versions of general education courses and may have individual capstone projects that come out of students' special interests. At four-year colleges and universities, honors programs are generally designed for students of almost every major in every college on campus. In growing numbers, they are given additional prominence as honors colleges. Whether a program or a college, honors often includes a general education or "core" component followed by advanced courses (often called colloquia or seminars). Some programs have honors contracts that shape existing courses into honors components to suit the needs of individual students. Many have interdisciplinary or collaborative seminars that bring students of different majors together to discuss a complex topic with faculty members from different disciplines. A good number have final thesis, capstone, or creative projects, which may or may not be in the departmental major. Almost always, honors curriculum is incorporated within whatever number of credits is required of every student for graduation. Honors very rarely requires students to take additional credits. Students who complete an honors program or honors college curriculum frequently receive transcript and diploma notations as well as certificates, medallions, or other citations at graduation ceremonies.

In every case, catering to the student as an individual plays a central role in honors course design. Most honors classes are small (fewer than 20 students); most are discussion-oriented, giving students a chance to present their own interpretations of ideas and even teach a part of the course. Many classes are interdisciplinary, which means they are taught by faculty members from two or more departments, providing different perspectives on a subject. All honors classes help students develop and articulate their own perspectives by cultivating both verbal and written style. They help students mature intel-

OPTIONS, OPTIONS, OPTIONS

lectually, preparing them to engage in their own explorations and research. Some programs even extend the options for self-growth to study abroad and internships in science, government, the arts, or business related to the major. Other programs encourage or require community service as part of the honors experience. In every case, honors is an experiential education that deepens classroom learning and extends far beyond.

Despite their individual differences, all honors programs and honors colleges rely on faculty members who enjoy working with bright, independent students. The ideal honors faculty members are open-minded, encouraging master teachers. They want to see their students achieve at their highest capacity and are glad to spend time with students in discussions and laboratories, on field trips and at conferences, or online in e-mail. They often influence career decisions, are inspiring role models, and remain friends long after they have served as thesis advisers.

WHERE ARE HONORS PROGRAMS AND HONORS COLLEGES LOCATED?

Because honors programs and honors colleges include students from many different departments or colleges, they usually have their own offices and space on campus. Some have their own buildings. Most programs have honors centers or lounges, where students gather together for informal conversations, luncheons, discussions, lectures, and special projects.

Many honors students have cultivated strong personal interests that have nothing to do with classes. They may be multilingual; they may be fine artists or poets, musicians or racing car enthusiasts, mothers or fathers. Some volunteer in hospitals or do landscape gardening to pay for college. Many work in retail stores and catering. Some are avid sports enthusiasts, while others collect antiques. When they get together in honors lounges, there is always an interesting mixture of ideas!

In the honors center, you will also find the honors director or dean. The honors director often serves as a personal adviser to all of the students in the program. Many programs also have peer counselors and mentors who are upperclass honors students and know the ropes from a student's perspective and experience. Some have specially assigned honors advisers who guide honors students through their degrees, assist in registration, and answer every imaginable question. The honors office area usually is a good place to meet people, ask questions, and solve problems.

In general, honors provides an environment in which students feel free to talk about their passionate interests and ideas knowing that they will find good listeners and, sometimes, even arguers. There is no end to conversations among honors students. Like many students in honors, you may feel a great relief in finding a sympathetic group that respects your intelligence and creativity. In honors, you can be eccentric; you can be yourself! Some lifelong friendships, even marriages, are the result of social relationships developed in honors programs.

ARE YOU READY FOR HONORS?

Admission to honors programs and honors colleges is generally based on a combination of several factors: high school or previous college grades, experience taking AP or IB courses, SAT or ACT scores, personal essay, and extracurricular achievements. To stay in honors, students need to maintain a certain grade point average (GPA) and show progress toward the completion of the specific honors program or college requirements. Since you have probably exceeded admissions standards all along, maintaining your GPA will not be as big a problem as it sounds. Your professors and your honors director are there to help you succeed in the program. Most honors programs have very low attrition rates because students enjoy classes and do well.

Of course, you must be careful about how you budget your time for studying. Honors encourages well-rounded, diversified students, so you should play a sport, work at the radio station, join clubs of interest, or pledge a sorority or fraternity. You might find a job in the student center or library that will help you pay for your car expenses and that also is reasonable. But remember, each activity takes time, and you must strike the balance that leaves you enough time to do your homework, write papers, prepare for seminar discussions, do your research, and do well on exams. Choose the jobs and activities that attract you, but never let them overshadow your primary purpose—which is to be a student.

Sometimes even the very best students who apply for admission into an honors program or college are frightened by the thought of speaking in front of a group, giving seminar papers, or writing a thesis. But if you understand how the programs work, you will see that there is nothing to fear. The basis of honors is confidence in the student and building the student's self-confidence. Admittance to an honors program means you have already demonstrated your academic achievement in high school or college classes. Once in the honors environment, you learn how to formulate and structure ideas so that you can apply critical judgment to sets of facts and opinions. In small seminar classes, you practice discussion and arguments, so by the time you come to the senior thesis or project, the method is second nature. For most honors students, the senior thesis, performance, or portfolio presentation is the project that gives them the greatest fulfillment and pride. In many honors programs and colleges, students present their work either to other students or to faculty members in their major departments. Students often present their work at regional and national honors conferences. Some students even publish their work jointly with their faculty mentors. These are great achievements, and they come naturally with the training. There is nothing to fear. Honors will prepare you for life.

Dr. Joan Digby is Director of the Honors Program and Merit Fellowship at Long Island University, C.W. Post Campus. She was also President of the National Collegiate Honors Council from 1999 to 2000.

Public and Private Colleges and Universities— How to Choose

Debra Humphreys

As you survey the thousands of four-year colleges in the country and weigh the options before you, it is important to be aware of how colleges differ and what kind of educational experience each college offers you. In every state in the country, you will find both public and private colleges and universities. What are the differences between public and private colleges, and how should you approach the decision to attend one or the other? What are some common misconceptions regarding both public and private colleges that you should know about before you eliminate an entire category of institution from your list of prospective schools?

WHAT ARE THE BASIC CHARACTERISTICS OF PUBLIC AND PRIVATE INSTITUTIONS?

Over the course of the nation's history, what began as a small group of mostly church-affiliated colleges has grown in both size and complexity. Over the years, education in the United States became increasingly democratized, and more and more state-sponsored institutions and state systems of higher education emerged. These included small colleges, sometimes called "normal schools," designed to train school teachers for the expanding public school system; land-grant colleges and universities brought into existence with federal support in the mid-nineteenth century in order to prepare workers to expand the nation's agricultural and technological capacity; and large state systems that evolved in the twentieth century and now include two-year colleges, basic four-year institutions, and large research universities, all supported at least in part by state revenues.

While there are some clear distinctions to be made, even some of the core characteristics of public and private colleges vary from state to state. In general, a public institution receives at least part of its operating budget from state tax revenues, operates with a mandate and mission from the state where it is located, and is accountable to the elected officials of that state. Most private colleges and universities are independent, not-for-profit institutions. They operate with revenues from tuition, income from endowments, private gifts and bequests, and federal, private, or corporate foundation grants. These institutions are primarily accountable to a board of trustees,

usually made up of local or national business and community leaders and esteemed alumni.

There are also a small but growing number of for-profit colleges whose operating revenues include tuition dollars but also might include investor financing. Some of these colleges are owned and operated by publicly traded corporations. Most of the following generalizations about private institutions however refer to the more familiar not-for-profit independent college previously described.

While the distinction between public and private institutions might seem clear at first, these two kinds of colleges and universities actually share many characteristics. All accredited colleges and universities in the country—whether public or private, for profit or not—are entitled to receive public funds from the federal government in the form of direct grants and loans for eligible students, support for student work-study programs, and competitive grants to support research or campus programs. In exchange for this federal support, all schools undergo a peer-reviewed accreditation process by a regional accreditor authorized by the federal government's Department of Education.

Whether a college is public or private, you should know if it is accredited and therefore an institution whose students are eligible for all available federal financial aid. Accreditation status also provides you with assurance that the school operates in a fiscally responsible manner and that its academic programs have been deemed sound by an outside group of educators from its peer institutions.

HOW ARE PUBLIC AND PRIVATE COLLEGES AND UNIVERSITIES RUN?

In many ways, your experience as a student will not differ significantly based on what type of governance system a college or university uses. However, some knowledge of this might be useful in making choices among the various options. Private colleges and universities tend to have more independence and autonomy in how they are run, with boards of trustees that oversee financial and other program and life on campus at these schools. Public colleges and universities often have more complex governing structures with boards of regents or other types of oversight committees made up of politically

appointed or elected officials exercising more or less oversight and intrusion into their day-to-day operations. New York, for instance, has a board of regents that oversees the system's campuses and is more actively involved in reviewing and revising curricular requirements that apply to institutions throughout the system. Other states have multiple public colleges, each with its own board overseeing each campus' operations with more or less intrusion into day-to-day operations.

Whether an institution is public or private, you will want to ask lots of questions about campus climate and academic programs in order to help you determine if a school is right for you. Being aware of some facts about public and private institutions will help you frame these questions to get truly useful answers.

ARE ALL PUBLIC COLLEGES AND UNIVERSITIES BIG AND IMPERSONAL?

Like private institutions, public colleges come in all shapes and sizes. Some are large institutions offering multiple degrees and majors to both undergraduate and graduate students alike. These institutions offer students many curricular options as well as access to leading scholars and an environment where cutting-edge academic research is conducted. While an institution of this size and scope might seem intimidating at first, remember that there are large institutions that do take very seriously their undergraduate programs. While you may receive less customized attention at a larger institution, many large public and private research universities offer options such as smaller honors programs, academic learning communities with smaller cohorts of students, or theme residence halls that can minimize the potential that you will get lost in the crowd.

If you are considering a large research institution— whether it is public or private—you should ask questions about the undergraduate program. What is the student-faculty ratio for undergraduates? What is the average class size, especially for introductory first-year courses? How many courses are taught by graduate students, and what sort of teacher training do those students receive? Are there opportunities for undergraduate students to participate in research projects with university faculty members?

In addition to the large, public research universities, there are many other smaller, state-funded regional institutions that still offer a wide range of both liberal arts and sciences fields as well as professional fields of study. Many states also offer small, public liberal arts colleges that share many of the defining characteristics of traditional, private liberal arts colleges. In 1987, some of these institutions formed the Council of Public Liberal Arts Colleges (COPLAC). COPLAC schools pride themselves on providing students of high ability and from all backgrounds access to a quality liberal education. These colleges and universities have been nationally recognized as outstanding in many ways. They offer small classes, innovations in teaching, personal interactions with faculty members, opportunities for faculty-supervised research, and supportive atmospheres. Most of them are located on campuses in rural or small-town settings. In addition to offering rigorous and well-integrated undergraduate programs, these

institutions often charge far less tuition than many private colleges do. More information can be found at http://www.coplac.org.

These public liberal arts colleges, along with more traditional private liberal arts institutions, do offer unique learning environments that research suggests often lead to higher levels of student achievement. Liberal arts colleges tend to offer a high degree of student-faculty interaction, high levels of student engagement with both in-class and out-of-class experiences, and lots of opportunities for collaborative and innovative learning practices. Businesses are also increasingly asking for exactly the set of skills and capacities that a liberal education provides, whether offered in a traditional liberal arts college setting or within a larger university that grants degrees in both liberal arts and other fields. Many public liberal arts and more comprehensive colleges and universities also now offer students a rigorous liberal education while integrating liberal learning into professional degree programs, for instance in health sciences, engineering, or education.

ARE PUBLIC COLLEGES CHEAPER THAN PRIVATE COLLEGES?

The cost of college is not easy to calculate and is not limited simply to the advertised price of tuition. It is absolutely not the case that attending a public college will always cost a student less money than attending a private institution. It is true that the basic tuition for in-state or out-of-state students attending public colleges is on average less expensive than the advertised tuition rate at private institutions. It is very important, however, to note that many private colleges and universities offer significant amounts of financial aid—often beyond the basic federal loans and grants available to all students. Many, but not all, private colleges have large endowments that allow them to effectively discount the standard, published tuition rates for a great number of their students. The National Association of College and University Business Officers sampled a small group of private colleges and discovered that only 10 percent of entering students were paying the full, advertised tuition. Ninety percent of their students received price discounts in the form of scholarships or financial aid. In other words, don't write off a college simply because its tuition looks extremely high relative to other institutions.

Both private and public institutions, however, have been fiscally stressed in recent years because of declining values of stock portfolios in endowments or because of declining state revenues resulting from the deteriorating economy. It is safe to say that for many students in the coming years, it will become increasingly difficult to get large amounts of financial aid. Many institutions, however, remain committed to widening access to more students from less economically privileged backgrounds. In addition, students demonstrating high levels of academic achievement are being rewarded at both private and public institutions—both in terms of admission and financial aid.

It is important to look carefully at the tuition and the financial aid requirements and availability at each school you are considering, private or public. In-state and out-of-state tuitions and the difference between them varies substantially from

state to state. Out-of-state tuition also varies from state to state but still tends to be lower than average private tuition levels.

Policies vary as well for determining state residency status. In many states, the policy for dependent students requires that their parents must have lived in the state for at least twelve months prior to attendance in order to qualify for in-state tuition. For independent students, the requirement of twelve months residence prior to enrollment applies to the student. Independent status must be verified and generally entails proof that a student receives no support from parents or other relatives living in or out of the state in question. As budgets have increasingly tightened, states have over the past several years made it increasingly difficult to establish in-state residence after matriculating at a school. Exceptions are sometimes made, however, for students from migrant, refugee, or military families.

IS IT EASIER TO GAIN ADMISSION TO A PUBLIC INSTITUTION ESPECIALLY AS A STATE RESIDENT?

Few public colleges and universities automatically admit students who graduate from a public high school in their state. Many, however, give preference in admissions and financial assistance to in-state residents. Moreover, some states have implemented policies that guarantee admission to at least one of the state's public institutions for all students graduating in a top percentage of their high school classes.

There are, indeed, more highly selective private than public institutions. Many public colleges and universities, however, do admit very few applicants. These highly selective institutions might draw their students from a national pool of applicants and can be among the most selective in the country. However, the national universities and liberal arts colleges with the lowest acceptance rates in the country are mostly all private institutions.

While some public institutions offer virtually open admissions to state residents, it is important for all prospective students to realize that even an open-admission institution will require incoming students to meet certain academic standards before being admitted to credit-bearing courses. In most cases, public and private institutions give incoming students a series of placement exams that determines at what level the student can begin his or her course work. Depending on the results of these exams, a student may be required to take and pass one or more remedial courses before being admitted to courses that will actually count towards a degree.

Since each state's requirements are different and shift often, you should not assume that, regardless of your academic background, admission is automatic to your local state college. In the current climate—with costs rising and competition across systems tightening—admission rates are dropping at many public institutions.

IS THE CLIMATE ON A PUBLIC COLLEGE CAMPUS SIGNIFICANTLY DIFFERENT THAN THAT ON A PRIVATE COLLEGE CAMPUS?

The social and academic climate at colleges and universities varies substantially, and public institutions do not necessarily offer a distinctively different climate than private institutions do. You can find, at some public institutions, the small, residential environment traditionally associated with private liberal arts colleges. You will also find the presence of fraternities and sororities at both public and private institutions. You should look carefully at whether a school in which you are interested has fraternities and sororities and how much influence the Greek system has on college life. At some institutions, fraternities and sororities dominate the entire social life of the campus.

One campus environment that can only be found at a private institution is a highly religious environment. Many early colleges and universities were founded by churches or religious orders. Some of these institutions no longer retain a strong affiliation with one church or denomination. Others do retain a strong affiliation, and church traditions can heavily influence the climate of these institutions. Usually, these campuses will admit a student from any religious background, but they may require students to attend chapel services and/or take religion or theology courses to graduate. In addition, some college missions and curricula are influenced by their religious affiliations. For instance, many Catholic institutions have a strong commitment to community service and social justice. Students may find, at these institutions, curricula related to social justice issues and requirements that they complete a community-service learning activity or course to graduate. Institutions with a strong mission are also often able to develop more coherent, cohesive, and innovative curricula for their students.

Finally, other important climate factors to consider include whether a college or university is in an urban or rural setting; what the diversity of the student body is in terms of geographic, religious, or racial/ethnic background; if most students live on campus or commute from home; and finally if the college dominates the life of the community in which it is located. Each of these options has advantages and disadvantages you will want to weigh in making your decisions.

ARE PRIVATE COLLEGES MORE ACADEMICALLY RIGOROUS THAN PUBLIC COLLEGES?

Private colleges and universities are not necessarily more academically rigorous than public institutions. You will find rigorous, intellectually challenging, and innovative academic programs at both private and public institutions. There is also a common misconception that schools that are more highly selective have the most effective or engaging academic programs. Research suggests that there is no connection between the selectivity of an institution and the presence of effective or innovative teaching and learning practices. There is, however, preliminary research that suggests that the academic quality of

Questions to Ask as You Evaluate Prospective Colleges and Universities

- Does the college offer a distinctive first-year experience?
- Does the college offer a small-size freshman seminar for all students?
- Are all students required to complete a senior project or assignment that allows them to integrate all that they have learned and demonstrate acquired skills and knowledge?
- Are students encouraged or required to completeinternships and/or service learning courses?
- Are students encouraged to study abroad? Is support for study abroad provided to all students and are study abroad experiences integrated into a student's overall curricula?
- Does the college offer learning communities, especially in the student's early years?
- Are students required to complete rigorous writing courses not only in the freshman year but also across the curriculum in whatever major he or she chooses to pursue?
- Are there opportunities for students to pursue independent research or creative projects under the supervision of a senior faculty member?

one's peers does seem to have an impact on the grade point averages of fellow students.

Nothing could be more important in your decision-making process than evaluating the nature of academic programs at prospective colleges or universities. Across both public and private institutions, there have been exciting and important changes in how colleges and universities are organizing undergraduate curricula. Many promising programs have been proven to result in higher levels of student retention, graduation, satisfaction, and academic achievement.

Many colleges and universities also now participate in the National Survey of Student Engagement. This survey asks students in both their first and last years about a series of effective educational practices and the degree to which they are engaged in the academic life of their school. Issues that are examined in the survey include the level of academic challenge, active and collaborative learning opportunities, the nature of student-faculty interactions, the number of enriching educational experiences available, and the supportive nature of the campus environment. Ask if the school you are considering participates in this survey and if you can see the results from recent classes of students.

THE PRIVATE/PUBLIC CHOICE

While there are distinct differences between public and private colleges and universities you should not limit your choice—whatever your background—to only one type of institution. There are wonderful opportunities at many different kinds of schools. The availability of many kinds of financial aid may bring private institutions with high-tuition levels within reach for you, whatever your financial background. Whether a school is highly selective or has open admissions, you should also be able to find a college or university that will challenge you academically and provide you with a supportive environment in which to live, learn, and pursue a college degree of lasting value.

Debra Humphreys is Vice President for Communications and Public Affairs for the Association of American Colleges and Universities.

Distance Education— It's Closer Than You Think

You may not realize it, but as an incoming college student, you are joining a revolution that is radically changing education. It's called distance learning. From kindergarten up to postgraduate degrees, distance learning is fast becoming an essential teaching tool. Most of the colleges and universities you are considering for a bachelor's degree offer distance learning in one form or another. Most likely you will be a distance learner at some point, whether during college or graduate school or throughout your career.

In case you're not familiar with distance learning—or asynchronous learning, online learning, or distance education—it means you don't sit in a classroom facing a teacher. You can be hundreds of miles or minutes from the teacher and other students. Most often you connect through the Internet to the teacher, fellow students, and study materials. However, increasingly sophisticated technologies, such as virtual laboratories, simulations, and interactive multimedia, are also used. You may run across the term "blended learning." Many institutions incorporate online learning into their face-to-face classes. In fact, a number of colleges require that a part of all classes is online.

FROM SNAIL-MAIL COURSES TO LEADING-EDGE TECHNOLOGY

Talk about change. Distance education began in the late 1800s, when schools mailed correspondence courses to farmers who wanted to learn how to grow better crops. Since technology came along, distance learning has become accessible and widespread. At first educators were skeptical, but as name-plate universities began to incorporate it into their teaching methodology, distance education became accepted.

When brick-and-mortar colleges and universities first considered distance education, the goal was to make it as good as face-to-face education. Now, says Ray Schroeder, Professor Emeritus of Communication and Director of the Center for Online Learning, Research, and Service (COLRS), at the University of Illinois at Springfield, "Field research shows that online learning technologies are better than face-to-face learning in a number of ways." Having taught online, he has seen firsthand how students participate more in discussions and learn from one another. Peg Miller, Ph.D., former Coordinator of Academic Support for Distributed Learning, University of Central Florida, cites a survey she conducted every other semester that compares face-to-face and distance learners at her institution. She has found that students from face-to-face and online classes were almost identical in the grades they earned and in their satisfaction with the classes.

ON THE UPSWING

Many reasons have caused the phenomenal growth of distance education. It's convenient and user-friendly, plus the scope of classes is stunning. Not that you'll likely begin your college years with classes in forensics or grading diamonds, but they are offered and indicate the enormous variety of courses. Along with many others in education, Michael P. Lambert, Secretary and Executive Director of the Distance Education Training Council, feels that online learning has transformed how people learn. "You no longer sit in a box with 35 other people where you might never raise your hand," he says. Adds Gerald Heeger, former President of the University of Maryland University College (UMUC), "Online learning gets rid of the limitations of geography and time. And as bandwidth increases, we will do more and more."

PROCEED WITH CAUTION

Now that you're convinced that distance education sounds great, sign me up, it's only fair to warn you that perhaps you shouldn't start your bachelor's degree totally online. Distance learning changes how you study, respond to your teachers, participate in class discussions, and take exams. If you're not prepared for the differences, you can easily fall behind and even fail. Though the age of online students continues to drop, most are older, have had some life experience since graduating from high school, and have the self-discipline, maturity, and self-motivation, that distance education demands. The average age of distance students is in the mid-30s, and 95 percent of them work full-time. They know what they want from college and are willing to meet the rigors of online learning, which are considerable.

Of course, some students straight from high school do successfully start college as distance learners because they've already had some online learning experience. Some take online classes in high school or advanced-placement and college courses. At Stevens Institute of Technology's Web Campus, incoming freshmen brush up on math and precalculus online before their first fall semester. At first, Nathan Kahl, former instructor for the Euclid Program at Stevens Institute of Technology Web Campus, was skeptical that high school graduates could succeed in the online courses he taught, but he saw that "everyone quickly got into the swing of things." He admits that he underestimated the students' ability to learn online. Heeger agrees "There's no reason why a bright junior in high school who is ready to take college freshmen courses can't do it."

The University of Phoenix Online (parent company: Apollo Group, Inc.) has developed a bachelor's degree program specifically for incoming freshmen of any age—including those

just out of high school. In today's job market, a college education is a necessity, yet many students have life situations that prevent them from attending. Notes former president of Apollo Group, Inc., Brian Mueller about the accommodations their program makes for students who are new to higher education, "It is our experience that if you create an online classroom, it must have all the features that incoming students need, which are small, highly interactive, and collaborative classes." Their freshman classes average 15 and require that the instructor has consistent contact with the students. New freshmen also get a tremendous amount of support in writing, math, and online research skills and have the help of an academic counselor who closely tracks them for ten weeks into their first semester. "We think there are more students coming out of high school who must have jobs, so we took the model for working adults and created an environment for traditional students that combines education and work," says Mueller.

However, not all educators have the same experience with incoming freshmen. Jimmy Reeves, Ph.D., Professor and Chair, Department of Chemistry and Biochemistry at the University of North Carolina at Wilmington, teaches both online and face-to-face classes and knows how students can react. Freshmen who fail his face-to-face class sometimes ask to take his class online. He says no because the discipline required is rare among 19-year-old students. "Junior and senior college students do well, but it has more to do with their level of maturity and the reasons why they're in college," he says, referring to the fact that many incoming college students want to experiment or come because their parents demand it. "Without any real desire to learn or sense of why they're in college, it's easy to get distracted in online classes," he notes. You can't hide in the back of a lecture hall half asleep on Monday morning and hope for the best on multiple-choice questions. In online classes, your active participation is noticed and taken into account for final grades.

Attending college isn't just about acquiring knowledge in a particular field in order to get a job. It's also about learning social skills and meeting people with different ideas from diverse backgrounds. "If you want to live in a dorm and have bull sessions on the meaning of life with the kids down the hall, then being a fully online freshman student isn't for you," advises Cynthia Davis, Associate Dean of Academic Affairs in the School of Undergraduate Studies at the University of Maryland University College (UMUC). She adds that sometimes students mistakenly think getting a bachelor's degree online will take less time than physically attending classes or won't require as much work. But as she points out, online classes demand the same amount of effort, if not more than face-to-face classes.

WHAT'S IT GOING TO BE LIKE?

Blended learning or mixed-mode classes, combining face-to-face and online instruction, are becoming a permanent fixture in higher education. Students might sit in a classroom on Monday but take the remaining two classes for that week online. Professors routinely post the syllabus, class calendar, or PowerPoint lectures. Reeves says that it's rare to see college classes without some Web-based materials. Davis comments that UMUC routinely Web-enhances all of its face-to-face classes with companion Web classrooms. Students can have optional online discussions or print copies of class materials.

"We find more students use online technology to enhance their studies and get better grades," comments Schroeder. Educators see a trend of students enrolling in one university and taking courses from other institutions. For instance, say you're in an art class but want to study German cathedral architecture, which your university doesn't have but another one offers online. It's only a matter of time before this will be a standard option for college students.

LOTS TO LOOK FOR, LOTS TO AVOID, LOTS TO ASK

Though much of distance education depends on the Internet, you can't just type in "distance education" and see what comes up in a search for a college. You must seriously research and do background checks to make sure a diploma mill doesn't hand you a bachelor's degree that isn't credible. There are plenty of places to get information. Petersons.com offers a database of colleges and universities that have online courses, as well as totally online distance education providers. "You have to be a good consumer," recommends Heeger. "It's no different from getting a loan. You don't borrow money from people you never heard of. You shouldn't get degrees from people you never heard of." Schroeder suggests checking the course completion of online programs, their enrollment, and growth of programs. "Just as one checks with friends and colleagues about the quality of consumer services, such as computers and cars, one should check with students who are enrolled in online programs," he advises.

Is the Institution Accredited by a Valid Accrediting Body?
There are several kinds of accrediting organizations:

- The six regional accrediting agencies recognized by the U.S. Department of Education
- The Council for Higher Education Accreditation (www.chea.org)
- Other institutional accrediting agencies, such as the Accrediting Council for Independent Colleges and Schools and the Distance Education and Training Council
- Specialized accrediting agencies that cover schools offering everything from acupuncture to veterinary medicine
- Other discipline-based accrediting organizations, such as those for law and business schools

Can You Transfer Credits Received Online from One Institution to Another?
Policies vary greatly among universities and colleges. Though distance education is widely accepted, there are so many places where students can take bogus online courses that institutions are justifiably cautious. If students do decide they want to get a bachelor's degree completely online, they need to be sure the campus-based program and distance education program offer the same degree. At most institutions both on-campus and online degrees are the same, but others do differ-

Test-Drive an Online Class

Just like face-to-face instruction, online classes are different, depending on the course material and how each teacher chooses to structure the course, but here's a typical scenario of what it's like to be a distance learner.

Getting started. First you'll want to get to the general information page for the class, which you'll visit often. The professor's contact information, the class calendar, the syllabus, and announcements on quizzes and tests or links to other pages on which you'll find posted discussion questions may be found here. Some teachers will ask you to tell something about yourself to the other students in the class. Be sure to read the syllabus, which will outline the course and tell you when assignments are due and how grades are determined.

Responding to discussion questions. Those students who never raised their hands will get a shock in online courses. Responding with thoughtful answers to online discussion groups is mandatory. Usually the teacher will assign reading material and then post a discussion question. The material might be from your textbook or Web sites. You must respond to the question and possibly to the postings of other students in the class. Teachers will gauge your participation in the class and how well you learn the material.

Interacting with fellow students and your teacher. Ray Schroeder, Professor Emeritus of Communication and Director of the Center for Online Learning, Research, and Service (COLRS) at the University of Illinois at Springfield, gives talks about distance education. Often he'll ask his audience to recall their favorite class from elementary school up to college and what made it so memorable. Was it the textbook? The actual classroom? The view out the window? When he asks if it was the interaction among students and with the teacher, the audience realizes that's what made the class good. "Both in person and online, learning takes place in the interaction," says Schroeder. "Otherwise, we would do just as well to read a book or watch a video to learn." In online classes, interaction between you and the professor and other students is an enormous part of your success.

Nathan Kahl, former instructor for the Euclid Program at Stevens Institute of Technology Web Campus, explains, "Distance students expect that their teachers will be online at least as much as they are." The level of interaction expected from you will vary by school and course, but you should know that in online courses, you must be an active participant. On the flip side, teachers carefully monitor discussions to make sure the more talkative students don't dominate. Keith W. Miller, Professor of Computer Science at the University of Illinois at Springfield, interacts with his students in a variety of ways. "I make announcements to the whole class on the homepage. I send e-mails to the whole class. I enter into the electronic discussions on the bulletin board forums, and post daily reminders and assignments to the course calendar. The students interact with me using e-mail, notes in their assignments, and via the bulletin boards. Now and then someone calls me at my office on the phone, but that's rare." He likes to answer his e-mails at least once a day, which means that his students get much more feedback than they would if he were physically in a classroom with them.

As do most online teachers, Cynthia Davis, Associate Dean of Academic Affairs in the School of Undergraduate Studies at the University of Maryland University College, gets students to participate with a weekly discussion topic. "If we're reading a novel," she says, "I ask them to discuss the role of the narrator or analyze a passage. The students respond individually and then respond to other students' comments."

Attending virtual lectures. Some online courses allow you to hear and see the professor or other guest speakers who are also online. If you want to ask a question, there's a button to indicate you want to speak. Everyone else can hear you as if you all were in the same room. Other professors add voice to PowerPoint lectures, which you can view when you want to, not at some prearranged time.

Taking quizzes and tests. No more waiting weeks to get your tests back. Online technology in some courses instantly zaps back the corrected test and notes that you missed question six and need to study page 54 of the textbook. Just like in face-to-face classes, you have an allotted amount of time to take the quiz. Some online courses may have automated components, such as instant quizzes and animated and interactive practice sessions. Others have mandatory proctored exams at a nearby community college or learning center for students who are off campus.

entiate in the degrees conferred, and it will show up on your diploma.

What Kind of Refund Policy Does the University Have for Distance Learners?

It might become painfully apparent for students that online learning is not for them, and they want to drop out. Find out ahead of time about the refund policy for online classes. What happens if you're ill during an online class? How can you make up the work? Even before taking any classes, you should find out if you're suited for online learning. Many institutions offer self-assessment tests on their Web sites.

What Online Services Does the College Provide?

Is the dorm wired? Can you get an e-mail address from the university? What about browsers and computer compatibility? Ask how the Internet is part of face-to-face classes. To what extent is the library online, and is it available 24/7 for research? Ask about writing and math labs and help-desk

support. Look for online tutorials that show students how to use the school's specific software. Is there a tech fee?

IF YOU'RE LEARNING ONLINE, YOU BETTER HAVE THESE

Since online learning is part of college, it's helpful to know what to expect ahead of time, rather than three weeks into the class, when you feel like throwing your laptop out the window and would happily settle for sitting in the back row of the nearest classroom. Here are the five skills and abilities that successful online students must have:

1. You must have the self-discipline to do things you don't want to do when you don't want to do them.

If you're a procrastinator, you'll find the catch-up tactics that served you well in face-to-face classes won't work online. "Students get the idea they can whiz by without studying, or they came from high schools where they weren't pushed," cautions Heeger. "Maybe they never got Fs in high school, but they do here." That's because they don't realize they're responsible for learning the material on their own. The burden is on you to keep up with the homework. It doesn't take long to fall far behind in online classes.

Typically, students in face-to-face and online classes need 2 hours for work outside of class for every hour in class. But online students often forget to add that hour. For every hour they would have to sit in a traditional classroom, they should be listening, studying, thinking, writing, responding to discussions, and getting ready for tests, plus the 2 hours outside of class. Three classes a week—that's 9 to 10 hours for one class. Online teachers keep students on track with weekly quizzes and homework assignments. If students start lagging, they're likely to get an e-mail from the professor asking what's going on. Claudine SchWeber, Ph.D., Chair of the Doctor of Management Program at the University of Maryland University College, has taught online for years and states, "My classes are structured by weekly readings, activities, and discussions. Students can't decide to get around to doing the work when they feel like it. It must be done at the instructor's pace. The first shot of online can be a shock to their system."

2. You must have the ability to manage your time without anyone telling you do your homework NOW.

In high school, students usually can put off studying until the weekend. "That doesn't work in college. You can't write complex papers the night before," says Karen L. Kirkendall, Ph.D., Associate Professor of Liberal and Integrative Studies and Director of the Capitol Scholars Honors Program at the University of Illinois at Springfield. She teaches both online and face-to-face classes and has seen first-time online students who have never failed before start to slip and suddenly realize they are in big trouble. "My online classes are extraordinarily structured so I pretty much know when students aren't engaged, which I monitor by seeing how much they participate in online discussions," she notes.

Distance Learning Myths

As distance education becomes more accepted, people will readily discard some of the myths on this list. But for now, they persist.

Distance learning is for people on ranches 200 miles from the nearest freeway. Geography is not a factor. Many distance learners who are located across the campus or a few miles away just don't want to deal with the commute or have a work schedule that conflicts with being in a class at a certain time. They appreciate the flexibility that distance education gives them.

Distance learning is easier than face-to-face classes. Once you start an online class, you'll knock that myth off the list. Still, some students think it will be easier. When they realize they must not only respond to discussion questions but also comment on the responses from other students, they wonder why they ever thought distance education was going to be easy. Online teachers normally keep track of how their students progress with frequent monitoring and quizzes.

I'll get a better education in face-to-face classes. Much research has been conducted comparing the two and consistently, online learning is equivalent or better. Teachers of online courses now have plenty of precedents to follow, training and research to help them teach better, and technology to prepare for classes and keep up with their students' progress.

I'll talk to a computer all day. Yes, you are in front of a computer as a distance learner, but you also interact with professors and other students much more than you ever would in a core freshman class of 200. Teachers have sophisticated software to facilitate interaction. Even though you don't physically see your teachers, they put a great deal of effort into class preparation and reading e-mails. Some get as many as 3,000 e-mails in a ten-week class. Distance learners often get to know fellow students much more easily online than they would walking in and out of a class.

I need to be a computer geek. If you can handle the simplest maneuvers around a computer, such as attaching documents to e-mails or going to a specified Web address, you can be a distance learner. And you'll have tech support to help out if you run into problems.

Distance education is cheaper than face-to-face. Too bad this is a myth. It costs the same as a traditional college if you attend a recognized institution. Most students pay for distance education through student loans.

3. You must have the skills to communicate your thoughts in writing.

"Online participation in class discussions isn't instant messaging. You are what you write in online classes," advises SchWeber. Most of the work in online classes is written, whether it's participation in discussions, homework, quizzes, papers, or tests.

Since you'll communicate by e-mail and post your thoughts, netiquette is essential. You need to think differently online than when speaking on the phone or face-to-face. "You can't write a report that sounds like you are hanging out with friends," advises SchWeber. "When you are totally online, the only image people (including your professor) have of you is how you write." Kirkendall has reprimanded students who sent e-mails showing disrespect to the teacher because they were upset about something. Probably they would never respond that way if face-to-face. "Never hit the submit button when you're angry," Kirkendall cautions.

4. You must have the ability to research worthwhile information on the Web.

You need to know what's junk and what's reliable. In addition, professors take plagiarism very seriously, especially because it's so easy to do.

5. You must have some computer skills and know some computer-speak.

Those who design the software and set up how a distance learning class is taught are careful to make sure the technology doesn't get in the way of learning; however, you should know the basics. "In some classes, certain downloads are required, such as Adobe Acrobat, but in general, the skills are not beyond the abilities used daily by most elementary school children," says Schroeder, pointing out that if distance programs use expensive or exotic technology, they defeat the purpose. He reports that most computers that are five years old have the speed, memory, and capability to support online learning. Some classes might require a microphone. You should be familiar with some of the computer jargon so that if you're asked to post something or use a drop box, add an attachment, or take part in a threaded discussion, you'll know what you need to do. Just about every distance learning provider has online tutorials to familiarize you with their particular online software. If you run into technical problems, help-desk support is available.

Why Not Women's Colleges?

Before we start talking about the many advantages that women's colleges offer, let's get some myths out of the way. It is almost certain that the minute you hear "women's colleges" in the same sentence with "choosing colleges" you immediately think: no boys, no fun, no way!

Maybe that is why some girls who visit Joan Jaffe's office at Mills College in San Francisco, California, rush in to tell her that they just saw some guys on the campus of this women's college. Jaffe, Associate Dean of Admission, frequently gets this reaction from the young women who visit the campus. That's because many think that if they go to a women's college they are never going to see a guy within 2 miles of the campus gates, which, by the way, will clang shut behind them, leaving them secluded inside a heavily guarded male-free zone.

KISS MYTH NUMBER ONE GOOD-BYE

Forget iron gates. The first myth to get rid of is the one that assumes attending a women's college means kissing your social life good-bye. In fact, as Patricia Gibbs, Vice President for Student Affairs, Dean of Students at Wesleyan College in Macon, Georgia, points out, "If you were a guy looking for a date, where would you go?" Not only that, the majority of women's colleges are near, if not next to, coed campuses. Most share activities with other colleges and universities, and many have reciprocal agreements so that guys can take classes at the women's college and vice versa.

When it comes to dating, women's colleges offer the best of both worlds. You can hang out with guys when you want to and then retreat to your own lovely environment (women's dorms usually are beautiful) and hang out with the girls. Julie Binder, who transferred from the University of Wisconsin to all-women's Barnard College in New York City, notes that there is open registration with Columbia University, which just happens to be right next door. "Campus life is shared. Sports are shared," she says.

As you dig deeper into this myth, you will find that attending a women's college is not about isolation, it's about options. You get to choose if you want to be in classes, clubs, and organizations only with women or mingle with the men.

SCRATCH MYTH NUMBER TWO

Myth Number Two: Women's colleges are just a bunch of catty, competitive females waiting for the right moment to scratch each other's eyes out. Scratch that myth, too. Instead, women's colleges cultivate an environment of sisterhood—women who look out for one another. Most women's colleges encourage women in the upper-level classes to help their younger classmates. Talking to their "big sisters," newcomers can find out what classes to take and which professors are best, and they find a sympathetic ear for the problems that most first-year college students face.

The Rich Traditions in Women's Colleges

Tradition plays an important part of the experience women have in women's colleges. They run the gamut from solemn ceremonies of passing along the bond of sisterhood to the fun of secret surprises. "Women's colleges have a strong sense of tradition," says Amy Shaver, former Academic Dean at Stephens College in Columbia, Missouri. It's also a wonderful way to help women from all social, economic, religious, and ethnic backgrounds to share a common experience and pass it on to the next generation of students. "Traditions bond women over the generations," says Jennifer Rickard, Dean of Admissions and Financial Aid at Bryn Mawr College, who notes that it's not unusual at all to have students today singing songs and participating in ceremonies that the class of 1945 did and which will be the same when today's students have their twenty-year reunion.

Here's a sampling of the many traditions you'll find on women's college campuses:

Lantern Night At Bryn Mawr's Lantern Night, women gather around a fountain on campus. Each woman is given a lantern as a symbol of knowledge and learning. Each class has a color, and as the lanterns are passed from the sophomores to the first-year students, songs are sung in Greek that are the same as the ones sung 100 years ago around the same fountain.

Senior Paint Night Mills College seniors get the okay to paint the campus in their class color. Along with brushes and cans of paint, they are given a few guidelines as to what can and cannot be painted, but the rest is up to them.

The Crossing of the Bridge As women students come to Stephens to begin their college education, they cross over a bridge on campus in a ceremony symbolizing their entrance into the world of academia. At graduation, they cross over another bridge on campus and are welcomed into the alumnae society.

Candlelight Induction Ceremony Spelman students dressed in white dresses and black shoes light candles and hear the charge to be the best they can be. While the candles are still lit, they sing the Spelman hymn.

Midnight Breakfast At Barnard, the night before finals, the president of the college, deans, and professors make breakfast for the students.

"The sense of community is very strong at women's colleges," observes Fran Samuels, former Director of College Counseling at The Master's School in Dobbs Ferry, New York. "The myth is that a women's college will be cliquish. In truth, the women are supportive of each other." The strong bonds of

sisterhood that naturally develop connect students to their college, its history, and its students, past, present, and future. Many women's colleges designate a rotating color for each incoming class. For example, if the freshman class you enter is dubbed the golden hearts, by the time you graduate, you are connected to all the golden hearts who graduated ahead of you and all the golden hearts who will graduate after you.

TOSS MYTH NUMBER THREE

Another myth that should be tossed out is that women's colleges don't prepare you for the "real world." Well, try saying that to the 12 women members of Congress who graduated from women's colleges. Or to the 15 women on *Business Week*'s list of the rising stars in corporate America. Although you are not in a totally coed situation, on the other hand you are in an environment in which you can gain skills to think critically and learn to meet challenges. Becky Marsh, Director of Advancement at Whitfield School, in St. Louis, Missouri, points out that when you first ride a bike, training wheels allow you to learn how to balance. Once you are ready to race down the street, you take them off. Same with women's colleges. The focus is on your education and your strengths, and who you are. You graduate ready to take on the obstacles of the real world. "In high school, I had the feeling that boys were given more opportunities to share their knowledge. It was harder and more intimidating for me to share my opinions in a coed class," says Brittany Johnson, from Spelman College in Atlanta, Georgia. "Now I feel like I can do anything."

Graduates of women's colleges feel empowered and willing to confront any limits to their abilities. While in college, they have many opportunities to assume leadership roles and see women in leadership positions as professors and deans. "They don't doubt whether they can do anything. Instead, they ask, 'Why can't I do it now?'" reports Amy Shaver, former Academic Dean at Stephens College in Columbia, Missouri. Women can find their own voices and establish their own ways of approaching things that will ultimately make them successful in a male-dominated world. They learn from seeing other women students and professors engaged in the intellectual process.

THE ADVANTAGES

As more young women find out about the advantages that women's colleges offer them, they like what they see. Maybe that is why attendance at women's colleges is growing. Learning leadership skills tops the list of advantages. Says Shaver, "Women in a same-sex environment are more likely to take risks and speak up in class. They are more willing to stand up and voice an opinion." If you think about it, students get plenty of practice at a women's college because all the leadership roles go to women. From day one on a women's campus, you will see women leading the entire college or involved in interesting and significant research. You get more exposure to what leadership is and what to expect as a leader. "Leadership becomes ingrained," notes Jennifer Fondiller, Dean of Admissions and Financial Aid at Barnard College in New York City.

You might not realize it, but women react differently in classrooms with all women. They tend to speak up with confidence and to test their ideas more readily when they are not competing with men. Researchers find that even as early as the fifth grade, girls are taught differently than boys. Teachers call on boys more frequently and don't ask girls the more thought-provoking questions or to critically analyze problems. In coed situations, the more aggressive and competitive guys take over, whereas in all-female classes, research indicates there is much more give-and-take and exchange of ideas.

Coming from a coed public school, Johnson realized that more attention was given to the guys in her classes, but at Spelman, she says, "Everyone is on the same path." Arlene Cash, Vice President for Enrollment Management at Spelman, notes that women don't have to vie for attention or retreat into the intellectual background in all-women classes. In a coed class, the environment becomes more adversarial. "Women feel they have to perform. In women's colleges they become more academically involved and interact with faculty members more frequently," says Debbie Greenberg, former College Counselor at Whitfield School. Speaking of the rich interaction that occurs in her classes at Barnard, Binder says, "The diversity of experience around the discussion table is unparalleled."

YOU CAN SUCCEED

Shaver characterizes the environment in women's colleges as one in which there is no fear of failing when the social pressures and dynamics of men and women are removed from the classroom. Women's colleges give women the opportunity to explore different avenues without the fear of failing. "We challenge them to become what they want to become," says Gibbs from Wesleyan. "No one says, 'You can't do that because you are a woman.'" At the same time, you are interacting with other women who have the same goals as you, which reinforces who you are. Or, as Jennifer Rickard, Dean of Admissions and Financial Aid at Bryn Mawr College, in Bryn Mawr, Pennsylvania, points out, women are not just sitting in classes to do well on exams and get good grades. They also are figuring out what they want to do with their education. "There's less expectation to conform to an external measure," she says.

Many women's colleges foster self-government and give their students responsibilities they might not find in a coed institution. At Bryn Mawr, for instance, students pay a self-government association fee as part of their tuition. This is put into a fund that is controlled by a student government that takes ownership of how the students want to govern themselves. "This isn't student government making only recommendations to the administration as to how to allocate the budget to the different student groups vying for funds," notes Rickard. "You have students dealing with real-world management issues, such as resource allocation."

Since women's colleges are smaller than big coed universities, women receive all the benefits that students get from a small liberal arts college in addition to the advantages that only a women's college offers. A big plus is interaction with professors and staff, which is hard to achieve when you are one of 200 students in a lecture hall taught by a graduate student.

What Made You Choose a Women's College?

When she got to the point of choosing which college to attend, Wisambi Loundu had plenty of options. Coming from San Diego, the California universities were a logical choice. Women's colleges were not on her list. In fact, she hardly knew they existed. Her first thought when someone suggested a women's college to her was, "I'm not going to a school full of girls minus boys." Her second thought was just as negative. "If it's all girls, they will always be fighting." The third and fourth thoughts assumed that a women's college wouldn't prepare her for the real world, plus she would be isolated.

But then her math teacher's daughter told her about Bryn Mawr, and as Wisambi started exploring the possibility, the advantages of a women's college started lining up. However, it wasn't until she visited Bryn Mawr that she really began to see herself there. "I fell in love with the campus," says Wisambi. "It was like nothing I'd ever seen before." Her stay in the dorm added to her steadily growing thoughts that Bryn Mawr might be it. "The girls I stayed with in the dorm were so friendly. At first I was suspicious, but I saw it was not a front. Plus, there were girls from all over the world."

But Wisambi didn't make her final decision just yet. She decided to look at other schools, like Wellesley and the University of California schools, as well as Stanford. Meanwhile, her friend told her more about Bryn Mawr. "She said I'd make lasting friends and she talked about how the academics would train me for the outside world even if there were no men on campus. Bryn Mawr would build my identity as a woman."

She still wasn't convinced and made a second visit, along with visits to Wellesley and Stanford, which she says were nice, but too big. It would be too hard to make friends there, she thought. When the time came to make her final selection, she chose Bryn Mawr.

Now at Bryn Mawr, how does Wisambi feel about her choice? The academics are more challenging than she anticipated but doable, and she is excited about the internships she will be able to access. She also finds that the staff and teachers at Bryn Mawr go out of their way to make her feel at home. "They match us up with a mentor and professor," she says.

How about dating? Since Bryn Mawr is part of a tri-college community, guys are around, though Wisambi says you have to make an effort to meet people on other campuses.

Talking to seniors who are getting ready to head out to the "real world," Wisambi can see that they are full of confidence and don't think for a minute that they won't do well. "And that's a positive," she says.

Women's colleges tend to foster seminar-style classes taught by full professors, many of them women. "You have an expert teaching you," says Gibbs. Faculty members get to know their students and can challenge them intellectually on an individual basis. "Within two days, all my teachers knew my name," recalls Johnson, who says she was given each professor's e-mail address, home phone number, and all the contact information she needed and was encouraged to reach out to them.

Women are encouraged to achieve their intellectual goals. Professors often will point out specific programs that they know suit the student's interests. Add to this the opportunities to conduct research with a professor, and in many cases actually present research findings to a professional society, and you can see why women graduate with a terrific resume before they even start their careers. Rickard mentions the opportunity that Bryn Mawr students have to work on funded projects with professors during the summer and then present the results along with them at conferences. "It's a window into the academic world and the world of the intellectual," she notes. It's no surprise that women in women's colleges major in math and science at a higher national average than women in coed institutions.

Paid and unpaid internships, too, are more available for women at women's colleges, mainly because of the network of women graduates in business and industry who want to help their "sisters" at their alma maters. "I'm getting my professional edge now," says Binder, who is interested in TV production and had a paid internship as a production assistant while a sophomore at Barnard. "You will have an amazing resume by the time you graduate," she says.

Peggy Hock, Ph.D., former College Counselor at Notre Dame High School in San Jose, California, points out that colleges naturally rely on their alumni to come forward with networking opportunities for students; however, the alumnae of women's colleges tend to be more loyal and willing to give of their time. This translates into many more opportunities for internships, mentoring, and job possibilities. At Barnard, for example, the career office has an alumna mentor network. Students can call, ask questions, and get advice about career choices. At alumnae events, current students mix with the graduates. Binder takes full advantage of the Web log of women who are working all over the world and willing to spend time online with Barnard students. She applied for a job at a public relations firm in New York after contacting a fellow Barnard graduate working there. She met with her and subsequently got a letter of recommendation.

HOW TO CHOOSE

Choosing a women's college isn't any different from choosing a coed college. You should definitely visit the campus and don't be afraid to ask lots of questions—even the ones that might make you uncomfortable. Because women's colleges are similar to small coed liberal arts colleges, make sure that you don't compare a women's campus to a big university.

Janet Ashley, former Interim Director for Admissions at Spelman College, advises high school women to ask what a

women's college can give them academically. "Their choice depends on what their goals are," she says.

If you're worried about the dating scene, ask about the levels of interaction with guys and how close the relationships are with neighboring institutions.

"Look at the individuality of each women's college," suggests Rickard, "because each has its own personality."

Look at the school before looking at the fact that it's a women's college, and on the flip side, don't rule out a school just because it is a women's college. "So many students make quick decisions about where to apply," warns Fondiller, noting that sometimes the decision hinges on what schools a friend is applying to rather than if that institution really fits the student. Many women's colleges specialize in certain fields like science, math, or theater.

Famous Firsts From Women's Colleges

Quick, from which college did the first woman to be named Secretary of State graduate? Or the woman scientist who identified the Hong Kong flu? Or the first woman executive vice president of the American Stock Exchange? Here's a big clue. They were all graduates of women's colleges.

SENATOR
- Barbara Mikulski (MD)—Mount Saint Agnes College

REPRESENTATIVES
- Tammy Baldwin (WI)—Smith College
- Donna Christian-Christensen (VI)—St. Mary's College
- Rosa DeLauro (CT)—Marymount College
- Jane Harman (CA)—Smith College
- Gabrielle Giffords (AZ)—Scripps College
- Eddie Bernice Johnson (TX)—Saint Mary's College
- Barbara Lee (CA)—Mills College
- Nita Lowey (NY)—Mount Holyoke College
- Betty McCollum (MN)—College of Saint Catherine
- Nancy Pelosi (CA), first woman elected as Speaker of the House of Representatives—Trinity College
- Allyson Schwartz (PA)—Simmons College

SECRETARY OF STATE
- Hillary Rodham Clinton (NY)—Wellesley College

OTHER FAMOUS WOMEN FIRSTS
- Madeleine Albright, first woman to be named Secretary of State in the United States, appointed in 1997—Wellesley
- Jane Amsterdam, first woman editor, the New York Post—Cedar Crest College
- Emily Green Balch, first woman to receive the Nobel Peace Prize in 1946—Bryn Mawr College
- Catherine Brewer Benson, first woman to receive a college bachelor's degree—Wesleyan College
- Earla Biekert, first scientist to identify the Hong Kong flu virus—Wesleyan College
- Cathleen Black, first woman leader of the American Newspaper Publishers Association—Trinity Washington University
- Sarah Porter Boehmler, first woman executive vice president of American Stock Exchange—Sweet Briar College
- Jane Matilda Bolin, first African American woman judge in the United States—Wellesley College
- Dorothy L. Brown, first African American woman general surgeon in the South—Bennett College for Women
- Pearl S. Buck, first American woman to win the Nobel Prize in Literature—Randolph-Macon Woman's College
- Ila Burdett, Georgia's first female Rhodes Scholar—Agnes Scott College
- Dorothy Vredenburgh Bush, first woman secretary of the Democratic National Party—Mississippi University for Women
- Hon. Audrey J. S. Carrion, first Hispanic woman judge Circuit Court for Baltimore City—College of Notre Dame of Maryland
- Rachel Carson, first environmentalist who awakened public consciousness through her book, *Silent Spring*—Chatham University
- Barbara Cassani, first woman CEO of a commercial airline—Mount Holyoke College
- Elaine L. Chao, U.S. Secretary of Labor, 2001; First Asian American woman appointed to a President's cabinet—Mount Holyoke College

Adapted from the Web site of the Women's College Coalition at http://www.womenscolleges.org.

How to Use This Guide

PROFILES

The **PROFILES** section contains basic data in capsule form for quick review and comparison. The following outline of the format shows the section headings and the items that each section covers. Any item that does not apply to a particular college or for which no information was supplied is omitted from that college's listing. Display ads, which appear near some of the institutions' profiles, have been provided and paid for by those colleges and universities that chose to supplement their profile with additional information.

Category Overviews

Type of Institution

Private institutions are designated as independent (nonprofit), proprietary (profit-making), or independent with a specific religious denomination or affiliation. Nondenominational or interdenominational religious orientation is possible and would be indicated. Public institutions are designated by the source of funding. Designations include federal, state, province, commonwealth (Puerto Rico), territory (U.S. territories), county, district (an educational administrative unit often having boundaries different from units of local government), city, state and local (local may refer to county, district, or city), or state-related (funded primarily by the state but administratively autonomous). *Religious affiliation* may follow, along with year founded. Each institution is classified as one of the following:

- Primarily two-year: Awards baccalaureate degrees but majority of students are enrolled in two-year programs.

- Four-year: Awards baccalaureate degrees; may also award associate degrees; does not award graduate (postbaccalaureate) degrees.

- Five-year: Awards a five-year baccalaureate in a professional field such as architecture or pharmacy; does not award graduate degrees.

- Upper-level: Awards baccalaureate degrees, but entering students must have at least two years of previous college-level credit; may also offer graduate degrees.

- Comprehensive: Awards baccalaureate degrees; may also award associate degrees; offers graduate degree programs, primarily at the master's, specialist's, or professional level, although one or two doctoral programs may be offered.

- University: Offers four years of undergraduate work, plus graduate degrees through the doctorate in more than two academic or professional fields.

Setting

Designated as *urban* (located within a major city), *suburban* (a residential area within commuting distance of a major city), *small town* (a small but compactly settled area not within commuting distance of a major city), or *rural* (a remote and sparsely populated area).

Endowment

The total dollar value of funds and/or property donated to the institution or the multicampus educational system of which the institution is a part.

Student body

An institution is *coed* (coeducational—admits men and women), *primarily* (80 percent or more) *women, primarily men, women only,* or *men only.* A few schools are designated as *undergraduate: women only; graduate: coed* or *undergraduate: men only; graduate: coed.*

Entrance

The five levels of entrance difficulty *(most difficult, very difficult, moderately difficult, minimally difficult,* and *noncompetitive)* are based on the percentage of applicants who were accepted for fall 2011 freshman admission (or, in the case of upper-level schools, for entering-class admission) and on the high school class rank and standardized test scores of the accepted freshmen who actually enrolled in fall 2011. The colleges were asked to select the level that most closely corresponds to their entrance difficulty, according to these guidelines.

Undergraduates

Percentages of undergraduates who are part-time or full-time students; transfers in; live on campus; out-of-state; Black or African American, non-Hispanic/Latino; Hispanic/Latino; Asian, non-Hispanic/Latino; Native Hawaiian or other Pacific Islander, non-Hispanic/Latino; American Indian or Alaska Native, non-Hispanic/Latino are given. *Retention:* The percentage of freshmen (or, for upper-level institutions, entering students) who returned the following year for the fall term.

Freshmen

Admission: Figures are given for the number of students who applied for fall 2011 admission, the number of those who were admitted, and the number who enrolled. *Average high school GPA:* Freshman statistics include the average high school GPA. *Test scores:* Percentage of freshmen who took the SAT and received critical reading, math, and writing scores above 500, above 600, and above 700; as well as percentage of freshmen taking the ACT who received a composite score of 18 or higher, 24 or higher, and 30 or higher.

Faculty

Total: The total number of faculty members; percentage of full-time faculty members as of fall 2011; and percentage of total faculty members who hold terminal degrees. *Student/faculty ratio:* School's estimate of the ratio of matriculated undergraduate students to faculty members teaching undergraduate courses.

Academics

Calendar: Most colleges indicate one of the following: 4-1-4, 4-4-1, or a similar arrangement (two terms of equal length plus an abbreviated winter or spring term, with the numbers referring to months); semesters; trimesters; quarters; 3-3

(three courses for each of three terms); modular (the academic year is divided into small blocks of time; courses of varying lengths are assembled according to individual programs); or standard year (for most Canadian institutions). *Degrees:* This names the full range of levels of certificates, diplomas, and degrees, including prebaccalaureate, baccalaureate, graduate, and professional, that are offered by this institution: *Special study options:* Details on study options available at each college, such as accelerated degree program, academic remediation for entering students, Advanced Placement credit, cooperative education programs, distance learning, double majors, English as a second language (ESL), and external degree programs. *ROTC:* Army, Naval, or Air Force Reserve Officers' Training Corps programs offered either on campus, at a branch campus [designated by a (b)], or at a cooperating host institution [designated by (c)].

Computers on Campus

Information is provided on the numbers of computers/terminals available on campus for general student use, what computer technology is accessible to students, and availability of a campuswide network and wireless campus network.

Student Life

Housing options: Institution's policy about whether students are permitted to live off-campus or are required to live on campus for a specified period; whether freshmen only, coed, single-sex, cooperative, and disabled student housing options are available; whether campus housing is leased by the school and/or provided by a third party; whether freshman applicants are given priority for college housing. "College housing not available" indicates that no college-owned or -operated housing facilities are provided for undergraduates and that noncommuting students must arrange for their own accommodations. *Activities and organizations:* Information on clubs and organizations, including sororities and fraternities. *Campus security:* Campus safety measures including 24-hour emergency response devices (phones and alarms) and patrols by trained security personnel, student patrols, late-night transport-escort service, and controlled dormitory access (key, security card, etc.). *Student services:* Information indicates services offered to students by the college, such as legal services, health clinics, personal-psychological counseling, and women's centers.

Athletics

Membership in one or more of the following athletic associations is indicated by initials: NCAA: National Collegiate Athletic Association; NAIA: National Association of Intercollegiate Athletics; NCCAA: National Christian College Athletic Association; USCAA: United States Collegiate Athletic Association; and CIS: Canadian Interuniversity Sport. The overall NCAA division in which all or most intercollegiate teams compete is designated by I, II, or III. All teams that do not compete in this division are listed as exceptions.

Sports offered by the college are divided into two groups: *Intercollegiate* ("M" or "W" following the name of each sport indicates that it is offered for men or women) and *Intramural*. An "s" in parentheses following an "M" or "W" for an intercollegiate sport indicates that athletic scholarships (or grants-in-aid) are offered for men or women in that sport, and a "c" indicates a club team as opposed to a varsity team.

Standardized Tests

The most commonly required standardized tests are the ACT, SAT, and SAT Subject Tests. These and other standardized tests may be used for selective admission, as a basis for counseling or course placement, or for both purposes. This section notes if a test is used for admission or placement and whether it is required, required for some, or recommended. In addition to the ACT and SAT, the following standardized entrance and placement examinations are referred to by their initials: ABLE (Adult Basic Learning Examination); ACT ASSET (ACT Assessment of Skills for Successful Entry and Transfer); ACT PEP (ACT Proficiency Examination Program); CAT (California Achievement Tests); CELT (Comprehensive English Language Test); CPAt (Career Programs Assessment); CPT (Computerized Placement Test); DAT (Differential Aptitude Test); LSAT (Law School Admission Test); MAPS (Multiple Assessment Program Service); MCAT (Medical College Admission Test); MMPI (Minnesota Multiphasic Personality Inventory); OAT (Optometry Admission Test); PAA (Prueba de Aptitud Académica—Spanish-language version of SAT); PCAT (Pharmacy College Admission Test); PSAT/NMSQT (Preliminary SAT/National Merit Scholarship Qualifying Test); SCAT (Scholastic College Aptitude Test); TABE (Test of Adult Basic Education); TASP (Texas Academic Skills Program); TOEFL (Test of English as a Foreign Language); WPCT (Washington Pre-College Test).

Costs

Costs are given for the 2012–13 academic year or for the 2011–12 academic year if 2012–13 figures were not yet available. Annual expenses may be expressed as a comprehensive fee (including full-time tuition, mandatory fees, and college room and board) or as separate figures for full-time tuition, fees, room and board, or room only. For public institutions where tuition differs according to residence, separate figures are given for area or state residents and for nonresidents. Part-time tuition is expressed in terms of a per-unit rate (per credit, per semester hour, etc.).

The tuition structure at some institutions is complex in that freshmen and sophomores may be charged a different rate from that for juniors and seniors, a professional or vocational division may have a different fee structure from the liberal arts division of the same institution, or part-time tuition may be prorated on a sliding scale according to the number of credit hours taken. Tuition and fees may vary according to academic program, campus/location, class time (day, evening, weekend), course/credit load, course level, degree level, reciprocity agreements, and student level. *Room and board* charges are reported as an average for one academic year and may vary according to the board plan selected, campus/location, type of housing facility, or student level. *Payment plans* may include tuition prepayment, installment payments, and deferred payment. A tuition prepayment plan gives a student the option of locking in the current tuition rate for the entire term of enrollment by paying the full amount in advance rather than year by year. *Waivers:* availability of full or partial undergraduate tuition waivers to minority students, children of alumni, employees or their children, adult students, and senior citizens may be listed.

Financial Aid

This information represents aid awarded to undergraduates for the available academic year. Figures are given for the number of undergraduates who applied for aid, the number who were judged to have need, and the number who had their need met. The number of Federal Work-Study Programs and/or part-time jobs and average earnings are listed, as well as the number of non-need-based awards. The *Average percent of need met* for those determined to have need, *Average financial aid package* awarded to undergraduates (the amount of scholarships, grants, work-study payments, or loans in the institutionally administered financial aid package divided by the number of students who received any financial aid-amounts used to pay the officially designated Expected Family Contribution (EFC), *Average need-based loan, Average need-based gift aid,* and *Average non-need-based aid* are given. *Average indebtedness upon graduation,* which is the average per-borrower indebtedness of the last graduating undergraduate class from amounts borrowed at this institution through any loan programs, excluding parent loans, is listed last.

Applying

Application and admission *Options* include the following: Early admission—(highly qualified students may matriculate before graduating from high school); Early action—admission plan that allows students to apply and be notified of an admission decision well in advance of the regular notification dates (If accepted, the candidate is not committed to enroll; students may reply to the offer under the college's regular reply policy); Deferred entrance—practice of permitting accepted students to postpone enrollment, usually for a period of one academic term or year; Early decision deadline—plan that permits students to apply and be notified of an admission decision (and financial aid offer, if applicable) well in advance of the regular notification date, and. applicants agree to accept an offer of admission and to withdraw their applications from other colleges. *Application fee:* The fee required with an application is noted. *Required, Required for some,* and *Recommended:* Other application requirements are grouped into three categories and may include an essay, standardized test scores, a high school transcript, a minimum high school grade point average (expressed as a number on a scale of 0 to 4.0, where 4.0 equals A, 3.0 equals B, etc.), letters of recommendation, an interview on campus or with local alumni, and, for certain types of schools or programs, special requirements such as a musical audition or an art portfolio. *Application deadlines and Notification:* Admission application deadlines and dates for notification of acceptance or rejection are given either as specific dates or as rolling and continuous. Rolling means that applications are processed as they are received, and qualified students are accepted as long as there are openings. Continuous means that applicants are notified of acceptance or rejection as applications are processed up until the date indicated or the actual beginning of classes. The application deadline and the notification date for transfers are given if they differ from the dates for freshmen. Early decision and early action application deadlines and notification dates are also indicated when relevant.

Freshman Application Contact

The name, title, mailing address, and phone number of the person to contact for further information are given at the end of the profile. The fax number, e-mail address, and Web site may also be provided.

Additional Information

Each school that has a College Close-Up in this guide will have a cross-reference with the page number of the Close-Up.

COLLEGE CLOSE-UPS

The over 350 two-page descriptions provide an inside look at colleges and universities. The descriptions provide a wealth of information that is crucial in the college decision-making process—components such as tuition, financial aid, and major fields of study. Prepared exclusively by college officials, the descriptions are designed to help give students a better sense of the individuality of each institution, in terms that include campus environment, student activities, and lifestyle. The absence of any college or university does not constitute an editorial decision on the part of Peterson's. In essence, these descriptions are an open forum for colleges and universities, on a voluntary basis, to communicate their particular message to prospective college students. The colleges included have paid a fee to Peterson's to provide this information. The **College Close-Ups** are edited to provide a consistent format across entries for your ease of comparison.

INDEXES

Here you'll find easy-to-use breakdowns of schools' majors, entrance difficulty, and cost ranges. We've also provided an "Advertisers Index," a "Geographical Listing of College Close-Ups," and an "Alphabetical Listing of Colleges and Universities."

Majors

This listing presents hundreds of undergraduate fields of study that are currently offered, according to the colleges' responses on *Peterson's Annual Survey of Undergraduate Institutions*. The majors appear in alphabetical order, each followed by an alphabetical list of the schools that offer a bachelor's-level program in that particular field. Liberal Arts and Studies indicates a general program with no specified major.

The terms used are those of the U.S. Department of Education Classification of Instructional Programs (CIP). Many institutions, however, use different terms. Although the term major is used in this guide, some colleges may use other terms, such as concentration, program of study, or field.

Entrance Difficulty

This listing groups colleges by their own assessment of their entrance difficulty level. The colleges were asked to select the level that most closely corresponds to their entrance difficulty. Institutions for which high school class rank and/or standardized test scores do not apply as admission criteria were asked to select the level that best indicates their entrance difficulty as compared to other institutions.

Cost Ranges

Colleges are grouped into thirteen price ranges, from under $2000 to $30,000 and over.

Institutional Changes Since Peterson's Four-Year Colleges 2012

The following is an alphabetical listing of institutions that have closed, merged with other institutions, or changed their names or status since *Peterson's Four-Year Colleges 2012*.

Andrew Jackson University (Birmingham, AL): *name changed to New Charter University.*

The Art Center Design College (Tucson, AZ): *name changed to Southwest University of Visual Arts.*

The Art Institute of California–Hollywood (North Hollywood, CA): *name changed to The Art Institute of California, a college of Argosy University, Hollywood.*

The Art Institute of California–Inland Empire (San Bernardino, CA): *name changed to The Art Institute of California, a college of Argosy University, Inland Empire.*

The Art Institute of California–Los Angeles (Santa Monica, CA): *name changed to The Art Institute of California, a college of Argosy University, Los Angeles.*

The Art Institute of California–Orange County (Santa Ana, CA): *name changed to The Art Institute of California, a college of Argosy University, Orange County.*

The Art Institute of California–Sacramento (Sacramento, CA): *name changed to The Art Institute of California, a college of Argosy University, Sacramento.*

The Art Institute of California–San Diego (San Diego, CA): *name changed to The Art Institute of California, a college of Argosy University, San Diego.*

The Art Institute of California–San Francisco (San Francisco, CA): *name changed to The Art Institute of California, a college of Argosy University, San Francisco.*

The Art Institute of California–Sunnyvale (Sunnyvale, CA): *name changed to The Art Institute of California, a college of Argosy University, Sunnyvale.*

The Art Institute of Washington–Northern Virginia (Sterling, VA): *name changed to The Art Institute of Washington–Dulles.*

Atlanta Christian College (East Point, GA): *name changed to Point University.*

Atlantic Union College (South Lancaster, MA): *not accredited by an agency recognized by USDE or CHEA at the time of publication.*

Baltimore International College (Baltimore, MD): *name changed to Stratford University.*

Bethany Bible College (Sussex, NB, Canada): *name changed to Kingswood University.*

Bethany University (Scotts Valley, CA): *closed.*

Bethesda Christian University (Anaheim, CA): *name changed to Bethesda University of California.*

Central Pennsylvania College (Summerdale, PA): *name changed to Central Penn College.*

Cleveland Chiropractic College–Los Angeles Campus (Los Angeles, CA): *closed.*

Colegio Pentecostal Mizpa (Río Piedras, PR): *name changed to Universidad Pentecostal Mizpa.*

College of Notre Dame of Maryland (Baltimore, MD): *name changed to Notre Dame of Maryland University.*

The College of Saint Thomas More (Fort Worth, TX): *name changed to The College of Saints John Fisher & Thomas More.*

Colorado Technical University Denver (Greenwood Village, CO): *name changed to Colorado Technical University Denver South.*

Columbia College (Caguas, PR): *name changed to Columbia Centro Universitario.*

Daniel Webster College–Portsmouth Campus (Portsmouth, NH): *closed.*

Emmanuel Bible College (Pasadena, CA): *closed.*

Global College of Long Island University (Brooklyn, NY): *name changed to LIU Global.*

Globe University (Woodbury, MN): *name changed to Globe University–Woodbury.*

Globe University (Sioux Falls, SD): *name changed to Globe University–Sioux Falls.*

Johnson Bible College (Knoxville, TN): *name changed to Johnson University.*

The King's College and Seminary (Van Nuys, CA): *name changed to King's University.*

Lambuth University (Jackson, TN): *merged into a single entry for University of Memphis (Memphis, TN) by request from the institution.*

Lancaster Bible College & Graduate School (Lancaster, PA): *name changed to Lancaster Bible College.*

Long Island University, Brentwood Campus (Brentwood, NY): *name changed to Long Island University–Brentwood Campus.*

Long Island University, Brooklyn Campus (Brooklyn, NY): *name changed to Long Island University–Brooklyn Campus.*

Long Island University, C.W. Post Campus (Brookville, NY): *name changed to Long Island University–C. W. Post Campus.*

Lourdes College (Sylvania, OH): *name changed to Lourdes University.*

Magdalen College (Warner, NH): *name changed to College of Saint Mary Magdalen.*

Mercy College of Northwest Ohio (Toledo, OH): *name changed to Mercy College of Ohio.*

Mesa State College (Grand Junction, CO): *name changed to Colorado Mesa University.*

Midland Lutheran College (Fremont, NE): *name changed to Midland University.*

Midwest University (Wentzville, MO): *not accredited by an agency recognized by USDE or CHEA at the time of publication.*

Northwest College of Art (Poulsbo, WA): *name changed to Northwest College of Art & Design.*

Northwood University (Midland, MI): *name changed to Northwood University, Michigan Campus.*

Peace College (Raleigh, NC): *name changed to William Peace University.*

Piedmont Baptist College and Graduate School (Winston-Salem, NC): *name changed to Piedmont International University.*

Pikeville College (Pikeville, KY): *name changed to University of Pikeville.*

Potomac College (Herndon, VA): *merged into a single entry for Potomac College (Washington, DC) by request from the institution.*

St. Andrews Presbyterian College (Laurinburg, NC): *name changed to St. Andrews University.*

St. Charles Borromeo Seminary, Overbrook (Wynnewood, PA): *name changed to Saint Charles Borromeo Seminary, Overbrook.*

Saint Joseph College (West Hartford, CT): *name changed to University of Saint Joseph.*

St. Louis Christian College (Florissant, MO): *name changed to Saint Louis Christian College.*

Schiller International University (London, United Kingdom): *closed.*

State University of New York College of Agriculture and Technology at Morrisville (Morrisville, NY): *name changed to Morrisville State College.*

Trinity (Washington) University (Washington, DC): *name changed to Trinity Washington University.*

TUI University (Cypress, CA): *name changed to Trident University International.*

University of New Mexico–Gallup (Gallup, NM): *no longer offers bachelor's degrees.*

University of Phoenix–Phoenix Campus (Phoenix, AZ): *name changed to University of Phoenix–Phoenix Hohokam Campus.*

The University of Texas Southwestern Medical Center at Dallas (Dallas, TX): *no longer offers undergraduate degrees.*

Worcester State College (Worcester, MA): *name changed to Worcester State University.*

DATA COLLECTION PROCEDURES

The data contained in the **PROFILES** and **INDEXES** sections were researched between winter 2011 and spring 2012 through *Peterson's Annual Survey of Undergraduate Institutions*. Questionnaires were sent to the more than 2,700 colleges and universities that met the outlined inclusion criteria. All data included in this edition have been submitted by officials (usually admissions and financial aid officers, registrars, or institutional research personnel) at the colleges. Some of the institutions that submitted data were contacted directly by the Peterson's research staff to verify unusual figures, resolve discrepancies, or obtain additional data. All usable information received in time for publication has been included. The omission of any particular item from the **PROFILES** and **INDEXES** sections signifies that the information is either not applicable to that institution or not available. Because of Peterson's comprehensive editorial review and because all material comes directly from college officials, we believe that the information presented is accurate. You should check with a specific college or university at the time of application to verify such figures as tuition and fees, which may have changed since this guide's publication.

CRITERIA FOR INCLUSION IN THIS BOOK

The term "four-year college" is the commonly used designation for institutions that grant the baccalaureate degree. Four years is the expected amount of time required to earn this degree, although some bachelor's degree programs may be completed in three years, others require five years, and part-time programs may take considerably longer. Upper-level institutions offer only the junior and senior years and accept only students with two years of college-level credit. Therefore, "four-year college" is a conventional term that accurately describes most of the institutions included in this guide, but should not be taken literally in all cases.

To be included in this guide, an institution must have full accreditation or be a candidate for accreditation (preaccreditation) status by an institutional or specialized accrediting body recognized by the U.S. Department of Education or the Council for Higher Education Accreditation (CHEA). Institutional accrediting bodies, which review each institution as a whole, include the six regional associations of schools and colleges (Middle States, New England, North Central, Northwest, Southern, and Western), each of which is responsible for a specified portion of the United States and its territories. Other institutional accrediting bodies are national in scope and accredit specific kinds of institutions (e.g., Bible colleges, independent colleges, and rabbinical and Talmudic schools). Program registration by the New York State Board of Regents is considered to be the equivalent of institutional accreditation, since the board requires that all programs offered by an institution meet its standards before recognition is granted. A Canadian institution must be chartered and authorized to grant degrees by the provincial government, affiliated with a chartered institution, or accredited by a recognized U.S. accrediting body. This guide also includes institutions outside the United States that are accredited by these U.S. accrediting bodies. There are recognized specialized or professional accrediting bodies in more than forty different fields, each of which is authorized to accredit institutions or specific programs in its particular field. For specialized institutions that offer programs in one field only, we designate this to be the equivalent of institutional accreditation. A full explanation of the accrediting process and complete information on recognized, institutional (regional and national) and specialized accrediting bodies can be found online at www.chea.org or at www2.ed.gov/admins/finaid/accred/index.html.

Profiles

UNITED STATES AND U.S. TERRITORIES

ALABAMA

Alabama Agricultural and Mechanical University

Huntsville, Alabama

- **State-supported** university, founded 1875
- **Suburban** 2001-acre campus
- **Endowment** $29.3 million
- **Coed**
- **Minimally difficult** entrance level

Faculty *Student/faculty ratio:* 20:1.

Academics *Calendar:* semesters. *Degrees:* bachelor's, master's, doctoral, post-master's, and first professional certificates.

Student Life *Campus security:* 24-hour patrols, late-night transport/escort service, controlled dormitory access.

Athletics Member NCAA. All Division I except football (Division I-AA).

Standardized Tests *Required:* ACT (for admission).

Costs (2011–12) *Tuition:* state resident $6660 full-time, $222 per credit part-time; nonresident $13,320 full-time, $444 per credit part-time. Full-time tuition and fees vary according to course load. Part-time tuition and fees vary according to course load. *Required fees:* $1500 full-time, $587 per term part-time. *Room and board:* $6980; room only: $4200. Room and board charges vary according to board plan, housing facility, and location.

Financial Aid *Of all full-time matriculated undergraduates who enrolled in 2011,* 4,264 applied for aid, 4,037 were judged to have need, 307 had their need fully met. 81 Federal Work-Study jobs (averaging $2820). *In 2011,* 163 non-need-based awards were made. *Average percent of need met:* 8. *Average financial aid package:* $10,377. *Average need-based loan:* $3963. *Average need-based gift aid:* $7559. *Average non-need-based aid:* $10,206. *Average indebtedness upon graduation:* $33,038.

Applying *Options:* electronic application, deferred entrance. *Application fee:* $10. *Required:* high school transcript, minimum 2.0 GPA. *Recommended:* 1 letter of recommendation.

Freshman Application Contact Dr. Evelyn Ellis, Interim Director of Admissions, Alabama Agricultural and Mechanical University, 4900 Meridian Street, Huntsville, AL 35811. *Phone:* 256-372-5245. *Toll-free phone:* 800-553-0816. *Fax:* 256-851-9747. *Web site:* http://www.aamu.edu/.

Alabama State University

Montgomery, Alabama

- **State-supported** comprehensive, founded 1867, part of Alabama Commission on Higher Education
- **Urban** 172-acre campus
- **Coed** 4,747 undergraduate students, 92% full-time, 59% women, 41% men
- **Minimally difficult** entrance level, 46% of applicants were admitted

Undergraduates 4,362 full-time, 385 part-time. 30% are from out of state; 96% Black or African American, non-Hispanic/Latino; 0.7% Hispanic/Latino; 0.1% Asian, non-Hispanic/Latino; 0.1% Two or more races, non-Hispanic/Latino; 2% Race/ethnicity unknown; 0.3% international; 4% transferred in; 35% live on campus. *Retention:* 55% of full-time freshmen returned.

Freshmen *Admission:* 7,592 applied, 3,495 admitted, 1,104 enrolled. *Average high school GPA:* 2.76. *Test scores:* SAT critical reading scores over 500: 17%; SAT math scores over 500: 21%; ACT scores over 18: 39%; SAT critical reading scores over 600: 4%; SAT math scores over 600: 4%; ACT scores over 24: 5%.

Faculty *Total:* 407, 62% full-time, 50% with terminal degrees. *Student/faculty ratio:* 17:1.

Academics *Calendar:* semesters. *Degrees:* bachelor's, master's, doctoral, post-master's, postbachelor's, and first professional certificates. *Special study options:* academic remediation for entering students, advanced placement credit, cooperative education, distance learning, double majors, freshman honors college, honors programs, independent study, internships, part-time degree program, student-designed majors, summer session for credit. *ROTC:* Army (c), Air Force (b).

Computers on Campus Students can access the following: computer help desk, free student e-mail accounts, online (class) grades, online (class) registration, online (class) schedules. Campuswide network is available. Wireless service is available via entire campus.

Student Life *Housing options:* men-only, women-only, disabled students. Campus housing is university owned. *Activities and organizations:* drama/theater group, student-run newspaper, radio station, choral group, marching band,

Kappa Alpha Psi Fraternity Inc., Tribe of Judah, Alpha Kappa Psi Professional Business Fraternity, Inc., Delta Sigma Theta Sorority, Inc., Phi Beta Lambda Professional Business Fraternity, Inc., national fraternities, national sororities. *Campus security:* 24-hour emergency response devices and patrols, late-night transport/escort service, self-defense education, well-lit campus. *Student services:* health clinic, personal/psychological counseling.

Athletics Member NCAA. All Division I. *Intercollegiate sports:* baseball M(s), basketball M(s)/W(s), bowling W(s), cheerleading M/W, cross-country running M(s)/W(s), football M(s), golf M(s)/W(s), soccer W(s), softball W(s), tennis M(s)/W(s), track and field M(s)/W(s), volleyball W(s). *Intramural sports:* baseball M, basketball M/W, softball M/W, swimming and diving M/W, tennis M/W, track and field M/W, volleyball M/W, weight lifting M/W.

Standardized Tests *Required:* SAT or ACT (for admission).

Costs (2012–13) *One-time required fee:* $150. *Tuition:* state resident $7932 full-time, $263 per credit hour part-time; nonresident $14,244 full-time, $526 per credit hour part-time. *Required fees:* $213 per term part-time. *Room and board:* $5366. Room and board charges vary according to board plan and housing facility. *Payment plan:* deferred payment. *Waivers:* employees or children of employees.

Financial Aid Of all full-time matriculated undergraduates who enrolled in 2011, 4,245 applied for aid, 4,156 were judged to have need, 1,730 had their need fully met. 888 Federal Work-Study jobs (averaging $1695). 461 state and other part-time jobs (averaging $1993). In 2011, 106 non-need-based awards were made. *Average percent of need met:* 88%. *Average financial aid package:* $18,455. *Average need-based loan:* $3970. *Average need-based gift aid:* $5315. *Average non-need-based aid:* $9194. *Average indebtedness upon graduation:* $29,795.

Applying *Options:* electronic application, early admission, deferred entrance. *Application fee:* $25. *Required:* high school transcript, minimum 2.0 GPA. *Recommended:* essay or personal statement, interview. *Application deadlines:* 7/31 (freshmen), 7/31 (transfers). *Notification:* continuous (freshmen), continuous (transfers).

Freshman Application Contact Mr. Freddie Williams, Director of Admissions and Recruitment, Alabama State University, 915 South Jackson Street, Montgomery, AL 36101-0271. *Phone:* 334-229-4291. *Toll-free phone:* 800-253-5037. *Fax:* 334-229-4984. *E-mail:* admissions@alasu.edu. *Web site:* http://www.alasu.edu/.

Amridge University

Montgomery, Alabama

- **Independent** university, founded 1967, affiliated with Church of Christ
- **Urban** 9-acre campus
- **Endowment** $750,000
- **Coed** 361 undergraduate students, 61% full-time, 56% women, 44% men
- **Minimally difficult** entrance level

Undergraduates 221 full-time, 140 part-time. Students come from 48 states and territories; 75% are from out of state; 18% Black or African American, non-Hispanic/Latino; 2% Hispanic/Latino; 0.6% Asian, non-Hispanic/Latino; 61% Race/ethnicity unknown; 97% transferred in. *Retention:* 75% of full-time freshmen returned.

Freshmen *Admission:* 10 enrolled.

Faculty *Total:* 74, 64% full-time, 66% with terminal degrees. *Student/faculty ratio:* 11:1.

Academics *Calendar:* semesters. *Degrees:* associate, bachelor's, master's, and doctoral. *Special study options:* accelerated degree program, adult/continuing education programs, advanced placement credit, distance learning, double majors, external degree program, internships, part-time degree program, services for LD students, summer session for credit.

Computers on Campus 5 computers/terminals are available on campus for general student use. Students can access the following: online (class) registration, access to over 20 million monographs and journals online. Campuswide network is available.

Student Life *Housing:* college housing not available.

Costs (2011–12) *Tuition:* $7620 full-time, $330 per semester hour part-time. Full-time tuition and fees vary according to course load. Part-time tuition and fees vary according to course load. *Required fees:* $800 full-time, $400 per term part-time. *Waivers:* employees or children of employees.

Financial Aid Of all full-time matriculated undergraduates who enrolled in 2010, 340 applied for aid, 333 were judged to have need, 333 had their need fully met. In 2010, 12 non-need-based awards were made. *Average percent of need met:* 85%. *Average financial aid package:* $8500. *Average need-based loan:* $6634. *Average need-based gift aid:* $5886. *Average non-need-based aid:* $4000.

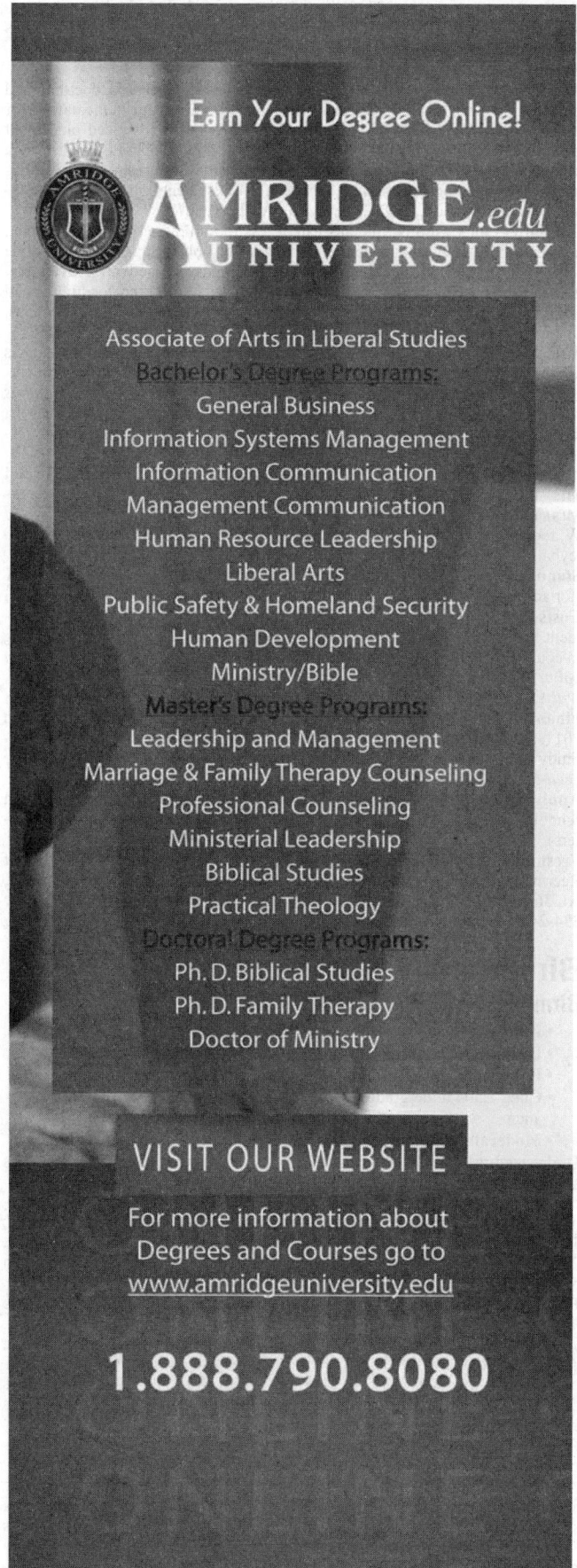
Applying *Options:* electronic application. *Application fee:* $75. *Required:* high school transcript, minimum 2.0 GPA. *Application deadlines:* rolling (freshmen), rolling (out-of-state freshmen), rolling (transfers). **Freshman Application Contact** Mrs. Ora Davis, Admissions Officer, Amridge University, 1200 Taylor Road, Montgomery, AL 36117. *Phone:* 334-387-3877 Ext. 7524. *Toll-free phone:* 888-790-8080. *Fax:* 334-387-3878. *E-mail:* oradavis@amridgeuniversity.edu. *Web site:* http://www.amridgeuniversity.edu/.

See page 1054 for the College Close-Up.

Athens State University

Athens, Alabama

- **State-supported** upper-level, founded 1822, part of Alabama College System
- **Small-town** 45-acre campus
- **Coed** 3,389 undergraduate students, 45% full-time, 65% women, 35% men
- **Noncompetitive** entrance level

Undergraduates 1,518 full-time, 1,871 part-time. Students come from 7 states and territories; 4% are from out of state; 12% Black or African American, non-Hispanic/Latino; 1% Hispanic/Latino; 0.6% Asian, non-Hispanic/Latino; 2% American Indian or Alaska Native, non-Hispanic/Latino; 1% Two or more races, non-Hispanic/Latino; 3% Race/ethnicity unknown; 0.7% international; 26% transferred in.

Faculty *Total:* 219, 39% full-time, 31% with terminal degrees. *Student/faculty ratio:* 17:1.

Academics *Calendar:* semesters. *Degree:* certificates and bachelor's. *Special study options:* adult/continuing education programs, advanced placement credit, cooperative education, distance learning, double majors, independent study, internships, off-campus study, part-time degree program, study abroad, summer session for credit.

Computers on Campus 210 computers/terminals are available on campus for general student use. Students can access the following: online (class) registration, grades, transcripts, schedules, e-mail. Campuswide network is available.

Student Life *Housing:* college housing not available. *Activities and organizations:* drama/theater group, student-run newspaper, national sororities. *Student services:* personal/psychological counseling.

Athletics *Intramural sports:* table tennis M/W, volleyball M/W.

Costs (2011–12) *Tuition:* state resident $4590 full-time, $153 per credit hour part-time; nonresident $9180 full-time, $306 per credit hour part-time. *Required fees:* $750 full-time, $25 per credit hour part-time. *Waivers:* senior citizens and employees or children of employees.

Financial Aid Of all full-time matriculated undergraduates who enrolled in 2010, 1,043 applied for aid. *Average financial aid package:* $10,270. *Average need-based gift aid:* $2791.

Applying *Options:* electronic application, deferred entrance. *Application fee:* $30. *Application deadline:* rolling (transfers). *Notification:* continuous (transfers).

Application Contact Athens State University, 300 North Beaty Street, Athens, AL 35611. *Phone:* 256-233-8151. *Toll-free phone:* 800-522-0272. *Web site:* http://www.athens.edu/.

Auburn University

Auburn University, Alabama

- **State-supported** university, founded 1856
- **Small-town** 1875-acre campus with easy access to Atlanta, Birmingham
- **Endowment** $484.3 million
- **Coed** 20,446 undergraduate students, 91% full-time, 49% women, 51% men
- **Moderately difficult** entrance level, 70% of applicants were admitted

Undergraduates 18,627 full-time, 1,819 part-time. Students come from 53 states and territories; 41 other countries; 38% are from out of state; 7% Black or African American, non-Hispanic/Latino; 3% Hispanic/Latino; 2% Asian, non-Hispanic/Latino; 0.7% American Indian or Alaska Native, non-Hispanic/Latino; 1% Race/ethnicity unknown; 0.7% international; 6% transferred in; 20% live on campus. *Retention:* 89% of full-time freshmen returned.

Freshmen *Admission:* 18,323 applied, 12,827 admitted, 4,202 enrolled. *Average high school GPA:* 3.78. *Test scores:* SAT critical reading scores over 500: 92%; SAT math scores over 500: 95%; SAT writing scores over 500: 89%; ACT scores over 18: 100%; SAT critical reading scores over 600: 52%; SAT math scores over 600: 64%; SAT writing scores over 600: 48%; ACT scores over 24: 84%; SAT critical reading scores over 700: 18%; SAT math scores over 700: 18%; SAT writing scores over 700: 12%; ACT scores over 30: 32%.

Faculty *Total:* 1,358, 87% full-time, 90% with terminal degrees. *Student/faculty ratio:* 18:1.

Academics *Calendar:* semesters. *Degrees:* bachelor's, master's, doctoral, post-master's, postbachelor's, and first professional certificates. *Special study options:* accelerated degree program, adult/continuing education programs, advanced placement credit, cooperative education, distance learning, double majors, English as a second language, freshman honors college, honors programs, independent study, internships, off-campus study, part-time degree program, services for LD students, study abroad, summer session for credit. *ROTC:* Army (b), Navy (b), Air Force (b). *Unusual degree programs:* 3-2 engineering.

Computers on Campus 1,722 computers/terminals are available on campus for general student use. Students can access the following: computer help desk, free student e-mail accounts, online (class) grades, online (class) registration, pay Bursar online, course materials available online. Campuswide network is available. 100% of college-owned or -operated housing units are wired for high-speed Internet access. Wireless service is available via entire campus.

Student Life *Housing options:* coed, men-only, women-only, disabled students. Campus housing is university owned. *Activities and organizations:* drama/theater group, student-run newspaper, radio and television station, choral group, marching band, Student Government Association, University Program Council, IMPACT (volunteer opportunities), International Student Organization, student media (AU Plainsman newspaper, WEGL radio, Glomerata yearbook, Eagle Eye television, AU Circle literary journal), national fraternities, national sororities. *Campus security:* 24-hour emergency response devices and patrols, late-night transport/escort service, controlled dormitory access. *Student services:* health clinic, personal/psychological counseling.

Athletics Member NCAA. All Division I except football (Division I-A). *Intercollegiate sports:* baseball M(s), basketball M(s)/W(s), cross-country running M(s)/W(s), equestrian sports W(s), golf M(s)/W(s), gymnastics W(s), soccer W(s), softball W(s), swimming and diving M(s)/W(s), tennis M(s)/W(s), track and field M(s)/W(s), volleyball W(s). *Intramural sports:* badminton M/W, basketball M/W, bowling M/W, crew M(c)/W(c), football M/W, golf M/W, ice hockey M(c), lacrosse M(c)/W(c), racquetball M/W, rugby M(c)/W(c), sailing M(c)/W(c), soccer M/W, softball M/W, swimming and diving M/W, table tennis M/W, tennis M/W, track and field M/W, ultimate Frisbee M/W, volleyball M/W, water polo M(c)/W(c), wrestling M(c)/W(c).

Standardized Tests *Required:* SAT or ACT (for admission).

Costs (2011–12) *Tuition:* state resident $7296 full-time, $304 per semester hour part-time; nonresident $21,888 full-time, $912 per semester hour part-time. Full-time tuition and fees vary according to program and reciprocity agreements. Part-time tuition and fees vary according to course load, program, and reciprocity agreements. *Required fees:* $1402 full-time, $701 per term part-time. *Room and board:* $9992; room only: $5030. Room and board charges vary according to board plan and housing facility. *Payment plan:* installment. *Waivers:* employees or children of employees.

Financial Aid Of all full-time matriculated undergraduates who enrolled in 2010, 11,380 applied for aid, 6,788 were judged to have need, 1,148 had their need fully met. 240 Federal Work-Study jobs (averaging $4040). In 2010, 2763 non-need-based awards were made. *Average percent of need met:* 52%. *Average financial aid package:* $10,589. *Average need-based loan:* $4455. *Average need-based gift aid:* $6733. *Average non-need-based aid:* $5596. *Average indebtedness upon graduation:* $24,778.

Applying *Options:* electronic application, early admission, early action, deferred entrance. *Application fee:* $50. *Required:* essay or personal statement, high school transcript, minimum 2.0 GPA. *Required for some:* minimum 3.0 GPA. *Recommended:* minimum 3.0 GPA. *Application deadlines:* 2/1 (freshmen), 2/4 (out-of-state freshmen), rolling (transfers), 10/1 (early action). *Notification:* 2/15 (freshmen), continuous (transfers), 10/15 (early action).

Freshman Application Contact Ms. Cindy Singley, Director, University Recruitment, Auburn University, Auburn University, AL 36849. *Phone:* 334-844-4080. *Toll-free phone:* 800-AUBURN9. *E-mail:* admissions@auburn.edu. *Web site:* http://www.auburn.edu/.

Auburn University Montgomery

Montgomery, Alabama

- **State-supported** comprehensive, founded 1967, part of Auburn University
- **Suburban** 500-acre campus
- **Endowment** $38.9 million
- **Coed** 4,404 undergraduate students, 68% full-time, 62% women, 38% men
- **Moderately difficult** entrance level, 74% of applicants were admitted

Undergraduates 2,994 full-time, 1,410 part-time. 5% are from out of state; 30% Black or African American, non-Hispanic/Latino; 2% Hispanic/Latino; 3% Asian, non-Hispanic/Latino; 0.4% American Indian or Alaska Native, non-Hispanic/Latino; 6% Race/ethnicity unknown; 4% international; 8% transferred in; 13% live on campus. *Retention:* 50% of full-time freshmen returned.

Freshmen *Admission:* 1,739 applied, 1,286 admitted, 828 enrolled. *Average high school GPA:* 3.14. *Test scores:* ACT scores over 18: 80%; ACT scores over 24: 15%; ACT scores over 30: 1%.

Faculty *Total:* 321, 61% full-time. *Student/faculty ratio:* 16:1.

Academics *Calendar:* semesters. *Degrees:* bachelor's, master's, doctoral, and post-master's certificates. *Special study options:* academic remediation for entering students, adult/continuing education programs, advanced placement credit, cooperative education, distance learning, double majors, English as a second language, honors programs, independent study, internships, off-campus study, part-time degree program, services for LD students, study abroad, summer session for credit. *ROTC:* Army (b), Air Force (c).

Computers on Campus Students can access the following: campus intranet, computer help desk, free student e-mail accounts, online (class) grades, online (class) registration, online (class) schedules. Campuswide network is available. 100% of college-owned or -operated housing units are wired for high-speed Internet access. Wireless service is available via classrooms, computer labs, libraries, student centers.

Student Life *Housing options:* coed, disabled students. Campus housing is university owned. *Activities and organizations:* drama/theater group, student-run newspaper, choral group, national fraternities, national sororities. *Campus security:* 24-hour emergency response devices and patrols, student patrols, late-night transport/escort service, controlled dormitory access. *Student services:* health clinic, personal/psychological counseling.

Athletics Member NAIA. *Intercollegiate sports:* baseball M(s), basketball M(s)/W(s), cheerleading M(s)/W(s), soccer M(s)/W(s), softball W(s), tennis M(s)/W(s). *Intramural sports:* badminton M/W, basketball M/W, bowling M/W, football M/W, soccer M/W, softball W, table tennis M/W, tennis M/W, volleyball M/W, wrestling M.

Standardized Tests *Required:* ACT (for admission). *Recommended:* SAT (for admission).

Costs (2012–13) *Tuition:* state resident $231 per credit hour part-time; nonresident $693 per credit hour part-time. Full-time tuition and fees vary according to course load. Part-time tuition and fees vary according to course load. *Room only:* $3970. Room and board charges vary according to housing facility. *Waivers:* employees or children of employees.

Financial Aid Of all full-time matriculated undergraduates who enrolled in 2011, 2,182 applied for aid, 472 had their need fully met. 36 Federal Work-Study jobs (averaging $3688). *Average need-based loan:* $4133. *Average need-based gift aid:* $4678.

Applying *Options:* electronic application, deferred entrance. *Required:* high school transcript. *Application deadlines:* rolling (freshmen), rolling (transfers). *Notification:* continuous (freshmen), continuous (transfers).

Freshman Application Contact Mr. Ronnie McKinney, Director of Recruitment, Auburn University Montgomery, PO Box 244023, Montgomery, AL 36124-4023. *Phone:* 334-244-3615. *Toll-free phone:* 800-227-2649. *Fax:* 334-244-3795. *E-mail:* rmckinne@aum.edu. *Web site:* http://www.aum.edu/.

Birmingham-Southern College

Birmingham, Alabama

- **Independent Methodist** 4-year, founded 1856
- **Urban** 196-acre campus with easy access to Birmingham
- **Endowment** $56.6 million
- **Coed** 1,305 undergraduate students, 99% full-time, 49% women, 51% men
- **Moderately difficult** entrance level, 64% of applicants were admitted

Undergraduates 1,295 full-time, 10 part-time. Students come from 33 states and territories; 13 other countries; 38% are from out of state; 8% Black or African American, non-Hispanic/Latino; 3% Hispanic/Latino; 5% Asian, non-Hispanic/Latino; 0.8% American Indian or Alaska Native, non-Hispanic/Latino; 1% Two or more races, non-Hispanic/Latino; 0.8% Race/ethnicity unknown; 2% transferred in; 84% live on campus. *Retention:* 80% of full-time freshmen returned.

Freshmen *Admission:* 1,798 applied, 1,155 admitted, 278 enrolled. *Average high school GPA:* 3.43. *Test scores:* SAT critical reading scores over 500: 78%; SAT math scores over 500: 76%; SAT writing scores over 500: 72%; ACT scores over 18: 100%; SAT critical reading scores over 600: 35%; SAT math scores over 600: 39%; SAT writing scores over 600: 33%; ACT scores over 24: 75%; SAT critical reading scores over 700: 10%; SAT math scores over 700: 9%; SAT writing scores over 700: 8%; ACT scores over 30: 20%.

Faculty *Total:* 107, 76% full-time, 86% with terminal degrees. *Student/faculty ratio:* 13:1.

Academics *Calendar:* 4-1-4. *Degree:* bachelor's. *Special study options:* advanced placement credit, cooperative education, double majors, English as a second language, honors programs, independent study, internships, off-campus study, part-time degree program, student-designed majors, study abroad, summer session for credit. *ROTC:* Army (c), Air Force (c). *Unusual degree programs:* 3-2 engineering with Auburn University, Columbia University,

Washington University in St. Louis, University of Alabama at Birmingham; nursing with Vanderbilt University; environmental studies with Duke University.

Computers on Campus 306 computers/terminals and 306 ports are available on campus for general student use. Students can access the following: campus intranet, computer help desk, free student e-mail accounts, online (class) grades, online (class) registration, online (class) schedules. Campuswide network is available. 100% of college-owned or -operated housing units are wired for high-speed Internet access. Wireless service is available via entire campus.

Student Life *Housing:* on-campus residence required through sophomore year. *Options:* coed, men-only, women-only, disabled students. Campus housing is university owned. Freshman campus housing is guaranteed. *Activities and organizations:* drama/theater group, student-run newspaper, choral group, marching band, Black Student Union, Southern Bouldering Club, Student Government Association, Multi- Cultural Awareness Organization, BSC Chapter of Habitat for Humanity, national fraternities, national sororities. *Campus security:* 24-hour emergency response devices and patrols, late-night transport/escort service, controlled dormitory access, vehicle safety inspections for students, emergency phone stations throughout campus. *Student services:* health clinic, personal/psychological counseling.

Athletics Member NCAA. All Division III. *Intercollegiate sports:* baseball M, basketball M/W, cheerleading M/W, cross-country running M/W, football M, golf M/W, lacrosse M/W, soccer M/W, softball W, swimming and diving M/W, tennis M/W, track and field M/W, volleyball W. *Intramural sports:* basketball M/W, football M/W, racquetball M/W, soccer M/W, softball M, table tennis M/W, tennis M/W, ultimate Frisbee M/W, volleyball M/W, water polo M/W.

Standardized Tests *Required:* SAT or ACT (for admission).

Costs (2011–12) *One-time required fee:* $200. *Comprehensive fee:* $39,240 includes full-time tuition ($28,250), mandatory fees ($1040), and room and board ($9950). Full-time tuition and fees vary according to program and reciprocity agreements. Part-time tuition: $4708 per course. Part-time tuition and fees vary according to course load, program, and reciprocity agreements. *Required fees:* $520 per term part-time. *College room only:* $5450. Room and board charges vary according to board plan, housing facility, and location. *Payment plan:* installment. *Waivers:* employees or children of employees.

Financial Aid Of all full-time matriculated undergraduates who enrolled in 2010, 994 applied for aid, 841 were judged to have need, 227 had their need fully met. 178 Federal Work-Study jobs (averaging $1351). 281 state and other part-time jobs (averaging $1213). In 2010, 598 non-need-based awards were made. *Average percent of need met:* 82%. *Average financial aid package:* $27,468. *Average need-based loan:* $3935. *Average need-based gift aid:* $5341. *Average non-need-based aid:* $9987. *Average indebtedness upon graduation:* $28,157.

Applying *Options:* electronic application, deferred entrance. *Application fee:* $40. *Required:* essay or personal statement, high school transcript, minimum 2.0 GPA, 1 letter of recommendation. *Required for some:* interview. *Recommended:* interview. *Application deadlines:* rolling (freshmen), rolling (transfers). *Notification:* continuous (freshmen), continuous (transfers).

Freshman Application Contact Ms. Jennifer Waters, Director of Admission, Birmingham-Southern College, Box 549008, Birmingham, AL 35254. *Phone:* 205-226-4696. *Toll-free phone:* 800-523-5793. *Fax:* 205-226-3074. *E-mail:* jwaters@bsc.edu. *Web site:* http://www.bsc.edu/.

Brown Mackie College–Birmingham

Birmingham, Alabama

- **Proprietary** 4-year, part of Education Management Corporation
- **Coed**

Academics *Degrees:* diplomas, associate, and bachelor's.

Costs (2011–12) *Tuition:* Tuition varies by program. Students should contact Brown Mackie College for tuition information.

Freshman Application Contact Brown Mackie College–Birmingham, 105 Vulcan Road, Suite 400, Birmingham, AL 35209. *Phone:* 205-909-1500. *Toll-free phone:* 888-299-4699. *Web site:* http://www.brownmackie.edu/birmingham.

See page 1190 for the College Close-Up.

Columbia Southern University

Orange Beach, Alabama

- **Proprietary** comprehensive, founded 1993
- **Small-town** campus
- **Coed** 19,192 undergraduate students, 34% full-time, 37% women, 63% men
- **Noncompetitive** entrance level, 100% of applicants were admitted

Undergraduates 6,594 full-time, 12,598 part-time. Students come from 55 states and territories; 62 other countries; 95% are from out of state; 21% Black

or African American, non-Hispanic/Latino; 6% Hispanic/Latino; 2% Asian, non-Hispanic/Latino; 0.2% Native Hawaiian or other Pacific Islander, non-Hispanic/Latino; 1% American Indian or Alaska Native, non-Hispanic/Latino; 2% Two or more races, non-Hispanic/Latino; 11% Race/ethnicity unknown; 11% transferred in. *Retention:* 84% of full-time freshmen returned.

Freshmen *Admission:* 7,656 applied, 7,656 admitted, 348 enrolled.

Faculty *Total:* 285, 14% full-time. *Student/faculty ratio:* 67:1.

Academics *Calendar:* modular. *Degrees:* certificates, associate, bachelor's, master's, doctoral, postbachelor's, and first professional certificates (offers only distance learning degree programs). *Special study options:* academic remediation for entering students, adult/continuing education programs, distance learning, internships, off-campus study, part-time degree program, services for LD students.

Computers on Campus Students can access the following: computer help desk, online (class) grades, online (class) registration, online (class) schedules.

Costs (2012–13) *Tuition:* $4800 full-time, $200 per credit hour part-time. Full-time tuition and fees vary according to course load and degree level. Part-time tuition and fees vary according to course load and degree level. *Required fees:* $95 full-time. *Waivers:* employees or children of employees.

Applying *Options:* electronic application. *Application fee:* $25. *Required for some:* high school transcript. *Application deadlines:* rolling (freshmen), rolling (transfers).

Freshman Application Contact Director of Admissions, Columbia Southern University, 21982 University Lane, Orange Beach, AL 36561. *Phone:* 251-981-3771. *Toll-free phone:* 800-977-8449. *Fax:* 251-224-0540. *E-mail:* admissions@columbiasouthern.edu. *Web site:* http://www.columbiasouthern.edu/.

Concordia College

Selma, Alabama

Freshman Application Contact Ms. Phyllis Richardson, Director, STARS, Concordia College, 1804 Green Street, Selma, AL 36701. *Phone:* 334-874-5700 Ext. 102. *Fax:* 334-874-5755. *E-mail:* prichrdson@concordiaselma.edu. *Web site:* http://www.concordiaselma.edu/.

Faulkner University

Montgomery, Alabama

- **Independent** comprehensive, founded 1942, affiliated with Church of Christ
- **Urban** 75-acre campus
- **Endowment** $19.7 million
- **Coed** 3,005 undergraduate students, 68% full-time, 64% women, 36% men
- **Minimally difficult** entrance level, 58% of applicants were admitted

Undergraduates 2,051 full-time, 954 part-time. Students come from 34 states and territories; 26 other countries; 12% are from out of state; 48% Black or African American, non-Hispanic/Latino; 1% Hispanic/Latino; 0.8% Asian, non-Hispanic/Latino; 0.2% Native Hawaiian or other Pacific Islander, non-Hispanic/Latino; 0.4% American Indian or Alaska Native, non-Hispanic/Latino; 0.8% Two or more races, non-Hispanic/Latino; 8% Race/ethnicity unknown; 2% international; 4% transferred in; 40% live on campus. *Retention:* 71% of full-time freshmen returned.

Freshmen *Admission:* 1,215 applied, 705 admitted, 327 enrolled. *Average high school GPA:* 3.17. *Test scores:* SAT critical reading scores over 500: 28%; SAT math scores over 500: 46%; SAT writing scores over 500: 27%; ACT scores over 18: 83%; SAT critical reading scores over 600: 5%; SAT math scores over 600: 12%; SAT writing scores over 600: 4%; ACT scores over 24: 19%; SAT critical reading scores over 700: 1%; ACT scores over 30: 2%.

Faculty *Total:* 287, 33% full-time, 38% with terminal degrees. *Student/faculty ratio:* 15:1.

Academics *Calendar:* semesters. *Degrees:* associate, bachelor's, master's, and doctoral. *Special study options:* academic remediation for entering students, accelerated degree program, adult/continuing education programs, advanced placement credit, distance learning, double majors, English as a second language, freshman honors college, honors programs, independent study, internships, off-campus study, part-time degree program, services for LD students, study abroad, summer session for credit. *ROTC:* Army (c), Air Force (c).

Computers on Campus 228 computers/terminals and 150 ports are available on campus for general student use. Students can access the following: campus intranet, computer help desk, free student e-mail accounts, online (class) grades, online (class) registration, online (class) schedules, student account access. Campuswide network is available. 100% of college-owned or -operated housing units are wired for high-speed Internet access. Wireless service is available via entire campus.

Student Life *Housing:* on-campus residence required through junior year. *Options:* men-only, women-only, disabled students. Campus housing is university owned. Freshman campus housing is guaranteed. *Activities and organizations:* drama/theater group, student-run newspaper, choral group, marching band, Student Government, Marching Band, Dinner Theatre, Acappella Chorus, Phi Lambda/Kappa Social Clubs. *Campus security:* 24-hour emergency response devices and patrols, late-night transport/escort service. *Student services:* health clinic, personal/psychological counseling.

Athletics Member NAIA. *Intercollegiate sports:* baseball M(s), basketball M(s)/W(s), cheerleading M(s)(c)/W(s)(c), football M(s), golf M(s)/W(s), soccer M(s)/W(s), softball W(s), volleyball W(s). *Intramural sports:* basketball M/W, bowling M/W, golf M/W, racquetball M/W, soccer M/W, softball M/W, table tennis M/W, ultimate Frisbee M/W, volleyball M/W.

Standardized Tests *Required:* SAT or ACT (for admission).

Costs (2012–13) *One-time required fee:* $1650. *Comprehensive fee:* $23,230 includes full-time tuition ($15,230), mandatory fees ($1350), and room and board ($6650). Full-time tuition and fees vary according to location and program. Part-time tuition: $515 per semester hour. Part-time tuition and fees vary according to location. *Required fees:* $415 per semester part-time. *College room only:* $3250. Room and board charges vary according to board plan and housing facility. *Payment plan:* installment. *Waivers:* adult students, senior citizens, and employees or children of employees.

Financial Aid Of all full-time matriculated undergraduates who enrolled in 2011, 2,734 applied for aid, 2,159 were judged to have need, 191 had their need fully met. 170 Federal Work-Study jobs (averaging $1206). 5 state and other part-time jobs (averaging $340). In 2011, 57 non-need-based awards were made. *Average percent of need met:* 63%. *Average financial aid package:* $6800. *Average need-based loan:* $5200. *Average need-based gift aid:* $3700. *Average non-need-based aid:* $3700. *Average indebtedness upon graduation:* $19,600.

Applying *Options:* electronic application, early admission, deferred entrance. *Application fee:* $25. *Required:* high school transcript, minimum 2.0 GPA. *Recommended:* essay or personal statement, 2 letters of recommendation, interview. *Application deadlines:* rolling (freshmen), rolling (out-of-state freshmen), rolling (transfers). *Notification:* continuous (freshmen), continuous (out-of-state freshmen), continuous (transfers).

Freshman Application Contact Mr. Neil Scott, Director of Admissions, Faulkner University, 5345 Atlanta Highway, Montgomery, AL 36109-3398. *Phone:* 334-386-7200. *Toll-free phone:* 800-879-9816. *Fax:* 334-386-7137. *E-mail:* nscott@faulkner.edu. *Web site:* http://www.faulkner.edu/.

Heritage Christian University

Florence, Alabama

- **Independent** comprehensive, founded 1971, affiliated with Church of Christ
- **Small-town** 43-acre campus
- **Endowment** $6.0 million
- **Coed, primarily men** 63 undergraduate students, 43% full-time, 16% women, 84% men
- **Noncompetitive** entrance level, 100% of applicants were admitted

Undergraduates 27 full-time, 36 part-time. Students come from 14 states and territories; 1 other country; 48% are from out of state; 8% Black or African American, non-Hispanic/Latino; 3% Hispanic/Latino; 11% Race/ethnicity unknown; 3% international; 19% transferred in; 60% live on campus. *Retention:* 33% of full-time freshmen returned.

Freshmen *Admission:* 8 applied, 8 admitted, 8 enrolled.

Faculty *Total:* 20, 25% full-time, 40% with terminal degrees. *Student/faculty ratio:* 5:1.

Academics *Calendar:* semesters. *Degrees:* associate, bachelor's, and master's. *Special study options:* academic remediation for entering students, accelerated degree program, adult/continuing education programs, cooperative education, distance learning, external degree program, independent study, internships, part-time degree program, summer session for credit.

Computers on Campus 12 computers/terminals are available on campus for general student use. Students can access the following: free student e-mail accounts, online (class) grades, online (class) registration, online (class) schedules. Campuswide network is available. 100% of college-owned or -operated housing units are wired for high-speed Internet access. Wireless service is available via entire campus.

Student Life *Housing options:* men-only, women-only, disabled students. Campus housing is university owned. *Activities and organizations:* Missions Club, Preachers Club, Student Government Association, Christian Ladies Organization, HCU Skit Team. *Student services:* personal/psychological counseling.

Standardized Tests *Required for some:* TOEFL (Test of English as a Foreign Language) for international students.

Costs (2012–13) *One-time required fee:* $300. *Comprehensive fee:* $18,202 includes full-time tuition ($11,936), mandatory fees ($840), and room and board ($5426). Part-time tuition: $373 per credit hour. *Required fees:* $35 per credit hour part-time. *College room only:* $3000. Room and board charges vary according to housing facility. *Payment plan:* installment. *Waivers:* employees or children of employees.

Financial Aid Of all full-time matriculated undergraduates who enrolled in 2010, 50 applied for aid, 50 were judged to have need, 49 had their need fully met. *Average percent of need met:* 95%. *Average financial aid package:* $15,000. *Average need-based loan:* $3500. *Average need-based gift aid:* $5500.

Applying *Options:* electronic application, early admission, deferred entrance. *Application fee:* $25. *Required:* high school transcript, minimum 2.0 GPA, 3 letters of recommendation. *Recommended:* interview. *Application deadlines:* rolling (freshmen), rolling (transfers). *Notification:* 7/1 (freshmen), continuous (transfers).

Freshman Application Contact Mr. Brad McKinnon, Dean of Students, Heritage Christian University, PO Box HCU, Florence, AL 35630. *Phone:* 256-766-6610 Ext. 305. *Toll-free phone:* 800-367-3565. *Fax:* 256-766-9289. *E-mail:* bmckinnon@hcu.edu. *Web site:* http://www.hcu.edu/.

Herzing University

Birmingham, Alabama

Director of Admissions Ms. Tess Anderson, Admissions Coordinator, Herzing University, 280 West Valley Avenue, Birmingham, AL 35209. *Phone:* 205-916-2800. *Toll-free phone:* 800-596-0724. *E-mail:* admiss@bhm.herzing.edu. *Web site:* http://www.herzing.edu/birmingham/.

Huntingdon College

Montgomery, Alabama

- **Independent United Methodist** 4-year, founded 1854
- **Suburban** 71-acre campus with easy access to Birmingham
- **Endowment** $41.6 million
- **Coed** 1,123 undergraduate students, 79% full-time, 50% women, 50% men
- **Moderately difficult** entrance level, 62% of applicants were admitted

Undergraduates 885 full-time, 238 part-time. Students come from 26 states and territories; 6 other countries; 15% are from out of state; 17% Black or African American, non-Hispanic/Latino; 2% Hispanic/Latino; 0.5% Asian, non-Hispanic/Latino; 0.3% Native Hawaiian or other Pacific Islander, non-Hispanic/Latino; 0.4% American Indian or Alaska Native, non-Hispanic/Latino; 2% Two or more races, non-Hispanic/Latino; 20% Race/ethnicity unknown; 0.7% international; 11% transferred in; 45% live on campus. *Retention:* 60% of full-time freshmen returned.

Freshmen *Admission:* 1,407 applied, 868 admitted, 256 enrolled. *Average high school GPA:* 3.29. *Test scores:* SAT critical reading scores over 500: 55%; SAT math scores over 500: 63%; SAT writing scores over 500: 42%; ACT scores over 18: 94%; SAT critical reading scores over 600: 26%; SAT math scores over 600: 16%; SAT writing scores over 600: 13%; ACT scores over 24: 25%; ACT scores over 30: 3%.

Faculty *Total:* 115, 42% full-time, 58% with terminal degrees. *Student/faculty ratio:* 14:1.

Academics *Calendar:* semesters. *Degree:* bachelor's. *Special study options:* accelerated degree program, adult/continuing education programs, advanced placement credit, distance learning, double majors, freshman honors college, honors programs, independent study, internships, off-campus study, part-time degree program, services for LD students, student-designed majors, study abroad, summer session for credit. *ROTC:* Army (c), Air Force (c). *Unusual degree programs:* 3-2 engineering with Auburn University.

Computers on Campus 13 computers/terminals are available on campus for general student use. Students can access the following: campus intranet, free student e-mail accounts, online (class) grades, online (class) schedules, online library, student web hosting. Campuswide network is available. 100% of college-owned or -operated housing units are wired for high-speed Internet access. Wireless service is available via classrooms, dorm rooms, learning centers, libraries.

Student Life *Housing:* on-campus residence required through junior year. *Options:* coed, disabled students. Campus housing is university owned. Freshman campus housing is guaranteed. *Activities and organizations:* student-run newspaper, choral group, marching band, Freshman Forum, Commuter Student Organization, Campus Ministries, Student Government Association, Campus Activities Board, national fraternities, national sororities. *Campus security:* 24-hour emergency response devices and patrols, student patrols, late-night transport/escort service, controlled dormitory access, electronic video surveillance. *Student services:* health clinic, personal/psychological counseling.

Athletics Member NCAA. All Division III. *Intercollegiate sports:* baseball M, basketball M/W, cross-country running M/W, football M, golf M/W, lacrosse M, soccer M/W, softball W, tennis M/W, track and field W, volleyball W. *Intramural sports:* basketball M/W, cheerleading M(c)/W(c), soccer M/W, softball M/W, table tennis M/W, volleyball M/W.

Standardized Tests *Required:* SAT or ACT (for admission).

Costs (2011–12) *Comprehensive fee:* $29,990 includes full-time tuition ($20,990), mandatory fees ($1000), and room and board ($8000). Full-time tuition and fees vary according to course load, program, and student level. Part-time tuition: $880 per credit hour. Part-time tuition and fees vary according to course load and program. No tuition increase for student's term of enrollment. *Room and board:* Room and board charges vary according to housing facility. *Payment plan:* deferred payment. *Waivers:* children of alumni and employees or children of employees.

Financial Aid Of all full-time matriculated undergraduates who enrolled in 2011, 734 applied for aid, 651 were judged to have need, 144 had their need fully met. 188 Federal Work-Study jobs (averaging $944). In 2011, 81 non-need-based awards were made. *Average percent of need met:* 69%. *Average financial aid package:* $18,292. *Average need-based loan:* $4409. *Average need-based gift aid:* $7191. *Average non-need-based aid:* $10,418. *Average indebtedness upon graduation:* $17,003.

Applying *Options:* electronic application, deferred entrance. *Required:* high school transcript, minimum 2.3 GPA. *Required for some:* essay or personal statement, 3 letters of recommendation, interview, auditions for music students; portfolios for art. *Application deadlines:* 8/17 (freshmen), 8/17 (transfers). *Notification:* continuous until 9/6 (freshmen), continuous until 9/6 (transfers).

Freshman Application Contact Office of Admission, Huntingdon College, 1500 East Fairview Avenue, Montgomery, AL 36106-2148. *Phone:* 334-833-4497. *Toll-free phone:* 800-763-0313. *Fax:* 334-833-4347. *E-mail:* admiss@huntingdon.edu. *Web site:* http://www.huntingdon.edu/.

ITT Technical Institute

Bessemer, Alabama

- **Proprietary** primarily 2-year, founded 1994, part of ITT Educational Services, Inc.
- **Suburban** campus
- **Coed**
- **Minimally difficult** entrance level

Academics *Calendar:* quarters. *Degrees:* associate and bachelor's.

Student Life *Housing:* college housing not available. *Campus security:* 24-hour emergency response devices.

Freshman Application Contact Director of Recruitment, ITT Technical Institute, 6270 Park South Drive, Bessemer, AL 35022. *Phone:* 205-497-5700. *Toll-free phone:* 800-488-7033. *Web site:* http://www.itt-tech.edu/.

ITT Technical Institute

Madison, Alabama

- **Proprietary** primarily 2-year, part of ITT Educational Services, Inc.
- **Coed**
- **Minimally difficult** entrance level

Academics *Degrees:* associate and bachelor's.

Student Life *Housing:* college housing not available.

Freshman Application Contact Director of Recruitment, ITT Technical Institute, 9238 Madison Boulevard, Suite 500, Madison, AL 35758. *Phone:* 256-542-2900. *Toll-free phone:* 877-628-5960. *Web site:* http://www.itt-tech.edu/.

ITT Technical Institute

Mobile, Alabama

- **Proprietary** primarily 2-year, part of ITT Educational Services, Inc.
- **Coed**
- **Minimally difficult** entrance level

Academics *Degrees:* associate and bachelor's.

Student Life *Housing:* college housing not available.

Freshman Application Contact Director of Recruitment, ITT Technical Institute, Office Mall South, 3100 Cottage Hill Road, Building 3, Mobile, AL 36606. *Phone:* 251-472-4760. *Toll-free phone:* 877-327-1013. *Web site:* http://www.itt-tech.edu/.

Jacksonville State University

Jacksonville, Alabama

- **State-supported** comprehensive, founded 1883
- **Small-town** 459-acre campus with easy access to Birmingham
- **Coed** 8,199 undergraduate students, 75% full-time, 58% women, 42% men
- **Minimally difficult** entrance level, 84% of applicants were admitted

Undergraduates 6,176 full-time, 2,023 part-time. 17% are from out of state; 29% Black or African American, non-Hispanic/Latino; 1% Hispanic/Latino; 0.4% Asian, non-Hispanic/Latino; 0.1% Native Hawaiian or other Pacific Islander, non-Hispanic/Latino; 0.5% American Indian or Alaska Native, non-Hispanic/Latino; 3% Race/ethnicity unknown; 2% international; 9% transferred in; 22% live on campus. *Retention:* 68% of full-time freshmen returned.

Freshmen *Admission:* 3,400 applied, 2,844 admitted, 1,414 enrolled. *Average high school GPA:* 3.11. *Test scores:* SAT critical reading scores over 500: 34%; SAT math scores over 500: 31%; ACT scores over 18: 86%; SAT critical reading scores over 600: 8%; SAT math scores over 600: 8%; ACT scores over 24: 34%; SAT critical reading scores over 700: 1%; ACT scores over 30: 3%.

Faculty *Total:* 484, 66% full-time. *Student/faculty ratio:* 20:1.

Academics *Calendar:* semesters. *Degrees:* bachelor's, master's, doctoral, post-master's, postbachelor's, and first professional certificates. *Special study options:* academic remediation for entering students, accelerated degree program, adult/continuing education programs, advanced placement credit, cooperative education, distance learning, double majors, honors programs, independent study, internships, part-time degree program, services for LD students, summer session for credit. *ROTC:* Army (b).

Computers on Campus 350 computers/terminals are available on campus for general student use. Students can access the following: computer help desk, free student e-mail accounts, online (class) grades, online (class) registration, online (class) schedules. Campuswide network is available.

Student Life *Housing options:* coed, men-only, women-only, disabled students. Campus housing is university owned. *Activities and organizations:* drama/theater group, student-run newspaper, radio and television station, choral group, marching band, Student Government Association, Archaeology Club, Campus Fellowship Clubs, Computer Science Club, Biology Club, national fraternities, national sororities. *Campus security:* 24-hour emergency response devices and patrols, student patrols, late-night transport/escort service, controlled dormitory access, night security officer in female residence halls. *Student services:* health clinic, personal/psychological counseling.

Athletics Member NCAA. All Division I except football (Division I-AA). *Intercollegiate sports:* baseball M(s), basketball M(s)/W(s), cross-country running M(s)/W(s), golf M(s)/W(s), riflery M(s)/W(s), soccer W(s), softball W(s), tennis M(s)/W(s), volleyball W(s). *Intramural sports:* badminton M(c)/W(c), basketball M(c)/W(c), bowling M(c)/W(c), football M(c), golf M(c)/W(c), racquetball M(c)/W(c), soccer M(c)/W(c), softball M(c)/W(c), table tennis M(c)/W(c), tennis M(c)/W(c), volleyball M(c)/W(c).

Standardized Tests *Required:* SAT or ACT (for admission).

Costs (2011–12) *Tuition:* state resident $7650 full-time, $255 per credit hour part-time; nonresident $15,300 full-time, $510 per credit hour part-time. *Room and board:* $5778. Room and board charges vary according to board plan and housing facility. *Payment plan:* installment. *Waivers:* employees or children of employees.

Financial Aid Of all full-time matriculated undergraduates who enrolled in 2008, 4,765 applied for aid. 224 Federal Work-Study jobs (averaging $1302). *Average financial aid package:* $6563. *Average need-based loan:* $3889. *Average need-based gift aid:* $3878.

Applying *Options:* electronic application, early admission, deferred entrance. *Application fee:* $30. *Required:* high school transcript. *Application deadlines:* rolling (freshmen), rolling (out-of-state freshmen), rolling (transfers). *Notification:* continuous (freshmen), continuous (out-of-state freshmen), continuous (transfers).

Freshman Application Contact Mr. Andrew Green, Director of Admission, Jacksonville State University, 700 Pelham Road North, Jacksonville, AL 36265. *Phone:* 256-782-5363. *Toll-free phone:* 800-231-5291. *Fax:* 256-782-5291. *E-mail:* info@jsu.edu. *Web site:* http://www.jsu.edu/.

Judson College

Marion, Alabama

- **Independent Baptist** 4-year, founded 1838
- **Rural** 118-acre campus with easy access to Birmingham
- **Endowment** $14.8 million
- **Coed, primarily women** 353 undergraduate students, 78% full-time, 97% women, 3% men
- **Moderately difficult** entrance level, 74% of applicants were admitted

Undergraduates 276 full-time, 77 part-time. Students come from 21 states and territories; 1 other country; 13% are from out of state; 15% Black or Afri-

can American, non-Hispanic/Latino; 2% Hispanic/Latino; 1% Asian, non-Hispanic/Latino; 0.6% American Indian or Alaska Native, non-Hispanic/Latino; 1% Two or more races, non-Hispanic/Latino; 3% Race/ethnicity unknown; 0.3% international; 13% transferred in; 63% live on campus. *Retention:* 65% of full-time freshmen returned.

Freshmen *Admission:* 269 applied, 200 admitted, 75 enrolled. *Average high school GPA:* 3.39. *Test scores:* SAT critical reading scores over 500: 55%; SAT math scores over 500: 36%; SAT writing scores over 500: 64%; ACT scores over 18: 95%; SAT critical reading scores over 600: 18%; SAT math scores over 600: 18%; ACT scores over 24: 35%; ACT scores over 30: 8%.

Faculty *Total:* 44, 61% full-time, 64% with terminal degrees. *Student/faculty ratio:* 9:1.

Academics *Calendar:* semesters plus 2-month term. *Degrees:* associate and bachelor's. *Special study options:* academic remediation for entering students, accelerated degree program, adult/continuing education programs, advanced placement credit, distance learning, double majors, external degree program, honors programs, independent study, internships, off-campus study, part-time degree program, services for LD students, student-designed majors, study abroad, summer session for credit. *ROTC:* Army (c).

Computers on Campus 54 computers/terminals and 54 ports are available on campus for general student use. Students can access the following: campus intranet, computer help desk, free student e-mail accounts, online (class) grades, online (class) schedules. Campuswide network is available. 100% of college-owned or -operated housing units are wired for high-speed Internet access. Wireless service is available via classrooms, computer labs, dorm rooms, libraries, student centers.

Student Life *Housing:* on-campus residence required through senior year. *Options:* women-only. Campus housing is university owned. Freshman campus housing is guaranteed. *Activities and organizations:* drama/theater group, student-run newspaper, choral group, marching band, Student Government Association, Campus Ministries, Faith-Based Service Learning Activities, Ambassadors, Science Club. *Campus security:* 24-hour emergency response devices and patrols, late-night transport/escort service, controlled dormitory access. *Student services:* personal/psychological counseling.

Athletics Member USCAA. *Intercollegiate sports:* basketball W(s), equestrian sports W, soccer W(s), softball W(s), tennis W(s)(c), volleyball W(s). *Intramural sports:* basketball W, field hockey W, softball W, swimming and diving W, tennis W, volleyball W.

Standardized Tests *Required:* SAT or ACT (for admission).

Costs (2012–13) *One-time required fee:* $240. *Comprehensive fee:* $23,790 includes full-time tuition ($14,200), mandatory fees ($890), and room and board ($8700). Full-time tuition and fees vary according to degree level. Part-time tuition: $480 per hour. Part-time tuition and fees vary according to degree level. *College room only:* $4900. *Payment plans:* installment, deferred payment. *Waivers:* employees or children of employees.

Financial Aid Of all full-time matriculated undergraduates who enrolled in 2009, 209 applied for aid, 196 were judged to have need, 25 had their need fully met. In 2009, 18 non-need-based awards were made. *Average percent of need met:* 76%. *Average financial aid package:* $13,259. *Average need-based loan:* $3926. *Average need-based gift aid:* $9855. *Average non-need-based aid:* $8859. *Average indebtedness upon graduation:* $17,563.

Applying *Options:* electronic application, early admission, deferred entrance. *Application fee:* $35. *Required:* high school transcript, minimum 2.0 GPA. *Application deadlines:* rolling (freshmen), rolling (out-of-state freshmen), rolling (transfers). *Notification:* continuous (freshmen), continuous (out-of-state freshmen), continuous (transfers).

Freshman Application Contact Mrs. Charlotte S. Clements, Vice President for Admissions and Financial Aid, Judson College, 302 Bibb Street, Marion, AL 36756. *Phone:* 334-683-5110. *Toll-free phone:* 800-447-9472. *Fax:* 334-683-5282. *E-mail:* admissions@judson.edu. *Web site:* http://www.judson.edu/

Miles College

Fairfield, Alabama

Freshman Application Contact Mr. Christopher Robertson, Director of Admissions and Recruitment, Miles College, 5500 Myron Massey Boulevard, Bell Building, Fairfield, AL 35064. *Phone:* 205-929-1657. *Toll-free phone:* 800-445-0708. *Fax:* 205-929-1627. *E-mail:* admissions@miles.edu. *Web site:* http://www.miles.edu/.

New Charter University

Birmingham, Alabama

- **Private** comprehensive, founded 1994
- **Suburban** campus with easy access to Birmingham
- **Coed**
- **Noncompetitive** entrance level

Faculty *Student/faculty ratio:* 11:1.

Academics *Degrees:* certificates, associate, bachelor's, master's, and doctoral (offers primarily external degree programs).

Costs (2011–12) *Tuition:* $1592 full-time. No tuition increase for student's term of enrollment. *Required fees:* $796 per term part-time. *Payment plans:* installment, deferred payment.

Applying *Options:* electronic application. *Application fee:* $75. *Required:* interview. *Required for some:* essay or personal statement, high school transcript.

Freshman Application Contact Ms. Tammy J. Kassner, Director of Admissions, New Charter University, 2919 John Hawkins Parkway, Birmingham, AL 35244. *Phone:* 205-871-9288 Ext. 107. *Toll-free phone:* 800-679-1871. *Fax:* 800-871-9294. *E-mail:* admissions@aju.edu. *Web site:* http://new.edu/.

Oakwood University

Huntsville, Alabama

Freshman Application Contact Mr. Jason McCracken, Director of Enrollment Management, Oakwood University, 7000 Adventist Boulevard, NW, Huntsville, AL 35896. *Phone:* 256-726-7354. *Toll-free phone:* 800-824-5312. *Fax:* 256-726-7154. *E-mail:* admission@oakwood.edu. *Web site:* http://www.oakwood.edu/.

Remington College–Mobile Campus

Mobile, Alabama

Freshman Application Contact Remington College–Mobile Campus, 828 Downtowner Loop West, Mobile, AL 36609-5404. *Phone:* 251-343-8200. *Toll-free phone:* 800-560-6192. *Web site:* http://www.remingtoncollege.edu/.

Samford University

Birmingham, Alabama

- **Independent Baptist** university, founded 1841
- **Suburban** 209-acre campus
- **Endowment** $246.5 million
- **Coed** 2,950 undergraduate students, 93% full-time, 64% women, 36% men
- **Moderately difficult** entrance level, 83% of applicants were admitted

Undergraduates 2,754 full-time, 196 part-time. Students come from 40 states and territories; 13 other countries; 61% are from out of state; 7% Black or African American, non-Hispanic/Latino; 2% Hispanic/Latino; 0.7% Asian, non-Hispanic/Latino; 0.1% Native Hawaiian or other Pacific Islander, non-Hispanic/Latino; 0.3% American Indian or Alaska Native, non-Hispanic/Latino; 0.9% Two or more races, non-Hispanic/Latino; 1% Race/ethnicity unknown; 1% international; 4% transferred in; 68% live on campus. *Retention:* 84% of full-time freshmen returned.

Freshmen *Admission:* 2,623 applied, 2,166 admitted, 686 enrolled. *Average high school GPA:* 3.68. *Test scores:* SAT critical reading scores over 500: 83%; SAT math scores over 500: 85%; ACT scores over 18: 99%; SAT critical reading scores over 600: 49%; SAT math scores over 600: 40%; ACT scores over 24: 70%; SAT critical reading scores over 700: 15%; SAT math scores over 700: 6%; ACT scores over 30: 21%.

Faculty *Total:* 478, 64% full-time, 68% with terminal degrees. *Student/faculty ratio:* 12:1.

Academics *Calendar:* 4-1-4. *Degrees:* certificates, associate, bachelor's, master's, doctoral, post-master's, and first professional certificates. *Special study options:* accelerated degree program, adult/continuing education programs, advanced placement credit, cooperative education, distance learning, double majors, English as a second language, honors programs, independent study, internships, off-campus study, part-time degree program, services for LD students, study abroad, summer session for credit. *ROTC:* Army (c), Air Force (b). *Unusual degree programs:* 3-2 engineering with The University of Alabama at Birmingham, Auburn University, and Mercer University (Georgia).

Computers on Campus 330 computers/terminals and 400 ports are available on campus for general student use. Students can access the following: campus intranet, computer help desk, free student e-mail accounts, online (class) grades, online (class) registration, online (class) schedules, free online storage and tech support. Campuswide network is available. 100% of college-owned

or -operated housing units are wired for high-speed Internet access. Wireless service is available via entire campus.

Student Life *Housing:* on-campus residence required through sophomore year. *Options:* men-only, women-only, disabled students. Campus housing is university owned. Freshman campus housing is guaranteed. *Activities and organizations:* drama/theater group, student-run newspaper, radio and television station, choral group, marching band, Alpha Delta Pi sorority, Chi Omega sorority, Phi Mu Sorority, Zeta Tau Alpha sorority, Alpha Omicron Pi sorority, national fraternities, national sororities. *Campus security:* 24-hour emergency response devices and patrols, late-night transport/escort service, self defense education, security escort services, and lighted pathways/sidewalks. *Student services:* health clinic, personal/psychological counseling.

Athletics Member NCAA. All Division I except football (Division I-AA). *Intercollegiate sports:* baseball M(s), basketball M(s)/W(s), cross-country running M(s)/W(s), golf M(s)/W(s), soccer M(c)/W(s), softball W(s), tennis M(s)/W(s), track and field M(s)/W(s), volleyball W(s). *Intramural sports:* basketball M/W, football M/W, soccer M/W, softball M/W, ultimate Frisbee M(c)/W(c), volleyball M/W.

Standardized Tests *Required:* SAT or ACT (for admission).

Costs (2011–12) *Comprehensive fee:* $31,448 includes full-time tuition ($23,423), mandatory fees ($250), and room and board ($7775). Full-time tuition and fees vary according to course load, location, and program. Part-time tuition: $783 per credit hour. Part-time tuition and fees vary according to course load and program. *Required fees:* $220 per year part-time. *College room only:* $3970. Room and board charges vary according to board plan, housing facility, and location. *Waivers:* employees or children of employees.

Financial Aid Of all full-time matriculated undergraduates who enrolled in 2010, 1,663 applied for aid, 1,272 were judged to have need, 231 had their need fully met. 280 Federal Work-Study jobs (averaging $1936). 648 state and other part-time jobs (averaging $1535). In 2010, 862 non-need-based awards were made. *Average percent of need met:* 65%. *Average financial aid package:* $15,777. *Average need-based loan:* $3772. *Average need-based gift aid:* $12,933. *Average non-need-based aid:* $8075. *Average indebtedness upon graduation:* $24,405.

Applying *Options:* electronic application, early admission, deferred entrance. *Application fee:* $35. *Required:* essay or personal statement, high school transcript, 1 letter of recommendation. *Required for some:* interview. *Application deadlines:* rolling (freshmen), rolling (out-of-state freshmen), 7/1 (transfers). *Notification:* continuous (freshmen), continuous (out-of-state freshmen).

Freshman Application Contact Mr. Jason E. Black, Director of Orientation and Visits, Samford University, 800 Lakeshore Drive, Samford Hall, Birmingham, AL 35229-0002. *Phone:* 205-726-3673. *Toll-free phone:* 800-888-7218. *Fax:* 205-726-2171. *E-mail:* jjblack@samford.edu. *Web site:* http://www.samford.edu/.

Selma University

Selma, Alabama

Director of Admissions Mrs. Estella Davis-Baynes, Director of Admissions and Records, Selma University, 1501 Lapsley Street, Selma, AL 36701-5299. *Phone:* 334-872-2533.

Southeastern Bible College

Birmingham, Alabama

- **Independent nondenominational** 4-year, founded 1935
- **Suburban** 10-acre campus
- **Coed** 175 undergraduate students, 78% full-time, 40% women, 60% men
- **Noncompetitive** entrance level, 100% of applicants were admitted

Undergraduates 136 full-time, 39 part-time. Students come from 13 states and territories; 1 other country; 9% are from out of state; 32% Black or African American, non-Hispanic/Latino; 0.6% Hispanic/Latino; 0.6% American Indian or Alaska Native, non-Hispanic/Latino; 9% Race/ethnicity unknown; 0.6% international; 24% transferred in; 33% live on campus. *Retention:* 70% of full-time freshmen returned.

Freshmen *Admission:* 24 applied, 24 admitted, 14 enrolled. *Average high school GPA:* 3.05. *Test scores:* ACT scores over 18: 86%; ACT scores over 24: 43%; ACT scores over 30: 14%.

Faculty *Total:* 20, 30% full-time, 55% with terminal degrees. *Student/faculty ratio:* 14:1.

Academics *Calendar:* semesters. *Degrees:* diplomas, associate, and bachelor's. *Special study options:* academic remediation for entering students, adult/continuing education programs, advanced placement credit, distance learning, double majors, independent study, internships, part-time degree program, services for LD students, summer session for credit.

Computers on Campus 30 computers/terminals are available on campus for general student use. Students can access the following: free student e-mail accounts. Wireless service is available via entire campus.

Student Life *Housing options:* men-only, women-only. Campus housing is university owned. *Activities and organizations:* choral group, Student Council, Student Missions Fellowship, chorale. *Campus security:* controlled dormitory access.

Standardized Tests *Required:* SAT or ACT (for admission).

Costs (2011–12) *Tuition:* $11,250 full-time, $375 per semester hour part-time. Full-time tuition and fees vary according to course load and program. Part-time tuition and fees vary according to course load and program. *Required fees:* $350 full-time, $175 per term part-time. *Room only:* $2550. *Payment plan:* installment. *Waivers:* employees or children of employees.

Applying *Options:* electronic application, deferred entrance. *Application fee:* $30. *Required:* essay or personal statement, high school transcript, minimum 1.5 GPA, 2 letters of recommendation.

Freshman Application Contact Ms. Deidra Whitfield, Admissions Counselor, Southeastern Bible College, 2545 Valleydale Road, Birmingham, AL 35244. *Phone:* 205-970-9210. *Toll-free phone:* 800-749-8878. *Fax:* 205-970-9207. *E-mail:* deidra.whitfield@sebc.edu. *Web site:* http://www.sebc.edu/.

South University

Montgomery, Alabama

- **Proprietary** comprehensive, founded 1887, part of Education Management Corporation
- **Coed**

Academics *Calendar:* quarters. *Degrees:* associate, bachelor's, and master's.

Costs (2011–12) *Tuition:* Information about tuition and fees can be obtained by contacting the South University Admissions Office.

Freshman Application Contact South University, 5355 Vaughn Road, Montgomery, AL 36116-1120. *Phone:* 334-395-8800. *Toll-free phone:* 866-629-2962. *Web site:* http://www.southuniversity.edu/montgomery/.

See page 1596 for the College Close-Up.

Spring Hill College

Mobile, Alabama

- **Independent Roman Catholic (Jesuit)** comprehensive, founded 1830
- **Suburban** 450-acre campus
- **Coed** 1,282 undergraduate students, 92% full-time, 63% women, 37% men
- **Moderately difficult** entrance level, 49% of applicants were admitted

Undergraduates 1,178 full-time, 104 part-time. Students come from 34 states and territories; 8 other countries; 56% are from out of state; 19% Black or African American, non-Hispanic/Latino; 8% Hispanic/Latino; 1% Asian, non-Hispanic/Latino; 0.1% Native Hawaiian or other Pacific Islander, non-Hispanic/Latino; 0.9% American Indian or Alaska Native, non-Hispanic/Latino; 1% Two or more races, non-Hispanic/Latino; 4% Race/ethnicity unknown; 0.5% international; 2% transferred in; 77% live on campus. *Retention:* 76% of full-time freshmen returned.

Freshmen *Admission:* 6,048 applied, 2,935 admitted, 336 enrolled. *Average high school GPA:* 3.45. *Test scores:* SAT critical reading scores over 500: 78%; SAT math scores over 500: 61%; SAT writing scores over 500: 69%; ACT scores over 18: 99%; SAT critical reading scores over 600: 32%; SAT math scores over 600: 21%; SAT writing scores over 600: 19%; ACT scores over 24: 49%; SAT critical reading scores over 700: 6%; SAT math scores over 700: 4%; SAT writing scores over 700: 3%; ACT scores over 30: 4%.

Faculty *Total:* 135, 62% full-time, 70% with terminal degrees. *Student/faculty ratio:* 13:1.

Academics *Calendar:* semesters. *Degrees:* certificates, bachelor's, master's, post-master's, and postbachelor's certificates. *Special study options:* academic remediation for entering students, accelerated degree program, adult/continuing education programs, advanced placement credit, distance learning, double majors, honors programs, independent study, internships, off-campus study, part-time degree program, services for LD students, student-designed majors, study abroad, summer session for credit. *ROTC:* Army (c), Air Force (c). *Unusual degree programs:* 3-2 engineering with Marquette University, University of Alabama at Birmingham, University of Florida, Auburn University, Texas A&M University.

Computers on Campus 194 computers/terminals and 250 ports are available on campus for general student use. Students can access the following: campus intranet, computer help desk, free student e-mail accounts, online (class) grades, online (class) registration, online (class) schedules. Campuswide network is available. 100% of college-owned or -operated housing units are wired for high-speed Internet access. Wireless service is available via computer centers, computer labs, libraries, student centers.

Student Life *Housing:* on-campus residence required through senior year. *Options:* coed. Campus housing is university owned. Freshman campus housing is guaranteed. *Activities and organizations:* drama/theater group, student-

run newspaper, choral group, national fraternities, national sororities. *Campus security:* 24-hour emergency response devices and patrols, late-night transport/ escort service, controlled dormitory access. *Student services:* health clinic, personal/psychological counseling.

Athletics Member NAIA. *Intercollegiate sports:* baseball M(s), basketball M(s)/W(s), cross-country running M(s)/W(s), golf M(s)/W(s), soccer M(s)/ W(s), softball W(s), tennis M(s)/W(s), volleyball W(s). *Intramural sports:* basketball M/W, cheerleading W(c), football M/W, racquetball M/W, rugby M(c), soccer M/W, softball M/W, ultimate Frisbee M/W, volleyball M/W, weight lifting M/W.

Standardized Tests *Required:* SAT or ACT (for admission).

Costs (2011–12) *Comprehensive fee:* $38,820 includes full-time tuition ($26,360), mandatory fees ($1700), and room and board ($10,760). Part-time tuition: $930 per credit hour. *Required fees:* $50 per credit hour part-time. *College room only:* $5620. Room and board charges vary according to board plan and housing facility. *Payment plan:* installment. *Waivers:* employees or children of employees.

Financial Aid Of all full-time matriculated undergraduates who enrolled in 2011, 946 applied for aid, 946 were judged to have need, 161 had their need fully met. In 2011, 305 non-need-based awards were made. *Average percent of need met:* 86%. *Average financial aid package:* $28,012. *Average need-based loan:* $4608. *Average need-based gift aid:* $9512. *Average non-need-based aid:* $14,559. *Average indebtedness upon graduation:* $27,220.

Applying *Options:* electronic application, early admission, deferred entrance. *Application fee:* $25. *Required:* essay or personal statement, high school transcript, 1 letter of recommendation. *Recommended:* minimum 2.5 GPA, interview. *Application deadlines:* 7/15 (freshmen), 7/15 (out-of-state freshmen), rolling (transfers). *Notification:* continuous (freshmen), continuous (out-of-state freshmen), continuous (transfers).

Freshman Application Contact Ms. Ellen G. Richardson, Admissions Office, Spring Hill College, 4000 Dauphin Street, Mobile, AL 36608-1791. *Phone:* 251-380-3030. *Toll-free phone:* 800-SHC-6704. *Fax:* 251-460-2186. *E-mail:* admit@shc.edu. *Web site:* http://www.shc.edu/.

Stillman College
Tuscaloosa, Alabama

- **Independent** 4-year, founded 1876, affiliated with Presbyterian Church (U.S.A.)
- **Urban** 100-acre campus with easy access to Birmingham
- **Endowment** $18.2 million
- **Coed** 1,072 undergraduate students, 96% full-time, 53% women, 47% men
- **Minimally difficult** entrance level, 44% of applicants were admitted

Undergraduates 1,032 full-time, 40 part-time. Students come from 25 states and territories; 10 other countries; 35% are from out of state; 93% Black or African American, non-Hispanic/Latino; 0.8% Hispanic/Latino; 0.1% American Indian or Alaska Native, non-Hispanic/Latino; 2% Race/ethnicity unknown; 13% transferred in; 63% live on campus. *Retention:* 61% of full-time freshmen returned.

Freshmen *Admission:* 3,491 applied, 1,526 admitted, 305 enrolled. *Average high school GPA:* 2.9. *Test scores:* SAT critical reading scores over 500: 23%; SAT math scores over 500: 10%; ACT scores over 18: 50%; SAT critical reading scores over 600: 5%; SAT math scores over 600: 5%; ACT scores over 24: 7%; SAT critical reading scores over 700: 5%.

Faculty *Total:* 61, 89% full-time, 75% with terminal degrees. *Student/faculty ratio:* 18:1.

Academics *Calendar:* semesters. *Degree:* bachelor's. *Special study options:* academic remediation for entering students, advanced placement credit, cooperative education, distance learning, double majors, honors programs, independent study, internships, summer session for credit. *ROTC:* Army (c).

Computers on Campus 150 computers/terminals are available on campus for general student use. Students can access the following: campus intranet, computer help desk, free student e-mail accounts, online (class) grades, online (class) registration, online (class) schedules. Campuswide network is available. 100% of college-owned or -operated housing units are wired for high-speed Internet access. Wireless service is available via entire campus.

Student Life *Housing:* on-campus residence required for freshman year. *Options:* men-only, women-only. Campus housing is university owned. Freshman campus housing is guaranteed. *Activities and organizations:* drama/theater group, student-run newspaper, choral group, marching band, Stillman Blue Pride Marching Band, Sophisticated Unlimited Modeling Troupe, Christian Student Association, Student Government Association, Students in Free Enterprise (SIFE), national fraternities, national sororities. *Campus security:* 24-hour patrols, 24-hour patrols by trained campus police. *Student services:* health clinic, personal/psychological counseling.

Athletics Member NCAA. All Division II. *Intercollegiate sports:* baseball M, basketball M/W, cross-country running M/W, football M, softball W, tennis M/

W, track and field M/W, volleyball W. *Intramural sports:* badminton M(c)/ W(c), baseball M(c), basketball M(c)/W(c), football M(c)/W(c), softball M(c)/ W(c), table tennis M(c)/W(c).

Standardized Tests *Required:* SAT or ACT (for admission), SAT and SAT Subject Tests or ACT (for admission). *Recommended:* SAT (for admission), ACT (for admission), SAT Subject Tests (for admission).

Costs (2012–13) *Comprehensive fee:* $22,721 includes full-time tuition ($13,548), mandatory fees ($2117), and room and board ($7056). Part-time tuition: $534 per credit. No tuition increase for student's term of enrollment. *Required fees:* $2117 per term part-time. *College room only:* $3404. Room and board charges vary according to housing facility. *Payment plan:* deferred payment. *Waivers:* employees or children of employees.

Financial Aid Of all full-time matriculated undergraduates who enrolled in 2011, 980 applied for aid, 973 were judged to have need, 568 had their need fully met. 169 Federal Work-Study jobs (averaging $1056). In 2011, 16 non-need-based awards were made. *Average percent of need met:* 80%. *Average financial aid package:* $24,300. *Average need-based loan:* $5500. *Average need-based gift aid:* $7250. *Average non-need-based aid:* $12,250. *Average indebtedness upon graduation:* $30,429. *Financial aid deadline:* 6/1.

Applying *Options:* electronic application, early admission, early decision, deferred entrance. *Application fee:* $15. *Required:* high school transcript, minimum 2.5 GPA. *Recommended:* essay or personal statement, interview. *Application deadlines:* rolling (freshmen), rolling (transfers). *Early decision deadline:* 7/1. *Notification:* 7/15 (early decision).

Freshman Application Contact Stillman College, PO Drawer 1430, 3600 Stillman Boulevard, Tuscaloosa, AL 35403-9990. *Phone:* 205-366-8837. *Toll-free phone:* 800-841-5722. *Web site:* http://www.stillman.edu/.

Strayer University - Birmingham Campus
Birmingham, Alabama

- **Proprietary** comprehensive
- **Coed**

Academics *Degrees:* certificates, diplomas, associate, bachelor's, master's, and postbachelor's certificates.

Freshman Application Contact Strayer University - Birmingham Campus, 3570 Grandview Parkway, Suite 200, Birmingham, AL 35243. *Web site:* http://www.strayer.edu/birmingham/.

Strayer University - Huntsville Campus
Huntsville, Alabama

- **Proprietary** comprehensive
- **Coed**

Academics *Degrees:* certificates, diplomas, associate, bachelor's, master's, and postbachelor's certificates.

Freshman Application Contact Strayer University - Huntsville Campus, 4955 Corporate Drive, NW, Suite 200, Huntsville, AL 35805. *Web site:* http://www.strayer.edu/huntsville/.

Talladega College
Talladega, Alabama

- **Independent** 4-year, founded 1867
- **Small-town** 130-acre campus with easy access to Birmingham
- **Coed**
- **Moderately difficult** entrance level

Faculty *Student/faculty ratio:* 18:1.

Academics *Calendar:* semesters. *Degree:* bachelor's.

Student Life *Campus security:* 24-hour patrols, late-night transport/escort service, campus police.

Athletics Member USCAA.

Standardized Tests *Recommended:* SAT or ACT (for admission).

Costs (2011–12) *Comprehensive fee:* $17,996 includes full-time tuition ($10,175), mandatory fees ($1317), and room and board ($6504). Full-time tuition and fees vary according to course load. Part-time tuition: $424 per credit hour. *Required fees:* $659 per term part-time. *College room only:* $3020. *Payment plans:* tuition prepayment, installment.

Financial Aid *Of all full-time matriculated undergraduates who enrolled in 2003,* 407 applied for aid, 375 were judged to have need, 100 had their need fully met. 141 Federal Work-Study jobs (averaging $691). *Average percent of need met:* 90. *Average financial aid package:* $5000. *Average need-based loan:* $5335. *Average need-based gift aid:* $3025. *Average non-need-based*

aid: $5774. *Average indebtedness upon graduation:* $12,790. *Financial aid deadline:* 6/30.

Applying *Options:* electronic application, early admission. *Application fee:* $25. *Required:* essay or personal statement, high school transcript, minimum 2.0 GPA, 1 letter of recommendation.

Freshman Application Contact Talladega College, 627 West Battle Street, Talladega, AL 35160-2354. *Phone:* 256-761-6415. *Toll-free phone:* 866-540-3956. *Web site:* http://www.talladega.edu/.

Troy University
Troy, Alabama

- **State-supported** comprehensive, founded 1887, part of Troy University System
- **Small-town** 906-acre campus
- **Endowment** $30.6 million
- **Coed** 22,245 undergraduate students, 50% full-time, 61% women, 39% men
- **Moderately difficult** entrance level, 62% of applicants were admitted

Undergraduates 11,085 full-time, 11,160 part-time. Students come from 52 states and territories; 52 other countries; 42% are from out of state; 41% Black or African American, non-Hispanic/Latino; 3% Hispanic/Latino; 0.9% Asian, non-Hispanic/Latino; 0.1% Native Hawaiian or other Pacific Islander, non-Hispanic/Latino; 1% American Indian or Alaska Native, non-Hispanic/Latino; 0.2% Two or more races, non-Hispanic/Latino; 7% Race/ethnicity unknown; 2% international; 10% transferred in; 31% live on campus. *Retention:* 71% of full-time freshmen returned.

Freshmen *Admission:* 6,269 applied, 3,905 admitted, 2,989 enrolled. *Test scores:* SAT math scores over 500: 38%; ACT scores over 18: 80%; SAT math scores over 600: 11%; ACT scores over 24: 27%; SAT math scores over 700: 3%; ACT scores over 30: 4%.

Faculty *Total:* 1,477, 39% full-time, 48% with terminal degrees. *Student/faculty ratio:* 20:1.

Academics *Calendar:* semesters. *Degrees:* associate, bachelor's, master's, doctoral, and post-master's certificates. *Special study options:* academic remediation for entering students, accelerated degree program, advanced placement credit, distance learning, double majors, English as a second language, honors programs, independent study, internships, part-time degree program, services for LD students, summer session for credit. *ROTC:* Army (b), Air Force (b).

Computers on Campus 1,950 computers/terminals and 5,167 ports are available on campus for general student use. Students can access the following: campus intranet, computer help desk, free student e-mail accounts, online (class) grades, online (class) registration, online (class) schedules. Campuswide network is available. Wireless service is available via classrooms, dorm rooms, libraries.

Student Life *Housing:* on-campus residence required for freshman year. *Options:* coed, men-only, women-only. Campus housing is university owned. Freshman campus housing is guaranteed. *Activities and organizations:* drama/theater group, student-run newspaper, television station, choral group, marching band, T-Day/Athletic Events (Homecoming), Activities Council, Pep Rallies, national fraternities, national sororities. *Campus security:* 24-hour emergency response devices and patrols, student patrols, late-night transport/escort service, controlled dormitory access. *Student services:* health clinic, personal/psychological counseling.

Athletics Member NCAA. All Division I except football (Division I-A). *Intercollegiate sports:* baseball M(s), basketball M(s)/W(s), cross-country running M(s)/W(s), golf M(s)/W(s), soccer W(s), softball W(s), tennis M(s)/W(s), track and field M(s)/W(s), volleyball W(s). *Intramural sports:* basketball M/W, bowling M/W, cross-country running M/W, football M, golf M/W, soccer W, softball W, tennis M/W, track and field M/W, volleyball W.

Standardized Tests *Required:* SAT or ACT (for admission).

Costs (2011–12) *Tuition:* state resident $7050 full-time, $235 per credit hour part-time; nonresident $14,100 full-time, $470 per credit hour part-time. Full-time tuition and fees vary according to location and program. Part-time tuition and fees vary according to location and program. *Required fees:* $940 full-time, $28 per credit hour part-time, $50 per term part-time. *Room and board:* $6534. Room and board charges vary according to board plan and housing facility. *Payment plan:* installment.

Financial Aid Of all full-time matriculated undergraduates who enrolled in 2011, 7,771 applied for aid, 7,748 were judged to have need. In 2011, 2143 non-need-based awards were made. *Average financial aid package:* $4583. *Average need-based loan:* $4587. *Average need-based gift aid:* $4679. *Average non-need-based aid:* $4724.

Applying *Options:* electronic application, deferred entrance. *Application fee:* $30. *Required:* high school transcript. *Recommended:* interview. *Application deadlines:* rolling (freshmen), rolling (transfers).

Freshman Application Contact Mr. Buddy Starling, Dean of Enrollment Management, Troy University, University Avenue, Troy, AL 36082. *Phone:* 334-670-3243. *Toll-free phone:* 800-551-9716. *Fax:* 334-670-3733. *E-mail:* bstar@troy.edu. *Web site:* http://www.troy.edu/.

Tuskegee University
Tuskegee, Alabama

- **Independent** comprehensive, founded 1881
- **Small-town** 5000-acre campus
- **Coed** 2,684 undergraduate students, 97% full-time, 57% women, 43% men
- **Moderately difficult** entrance level, 65% of applicants were admitted

Undergraduates 2,614 full-time, 70 part-time. Students come from 44 states and territories; 19 other countries; 72% are from out of state; 87% Black or African American, non-Hispanic/Latino; 0.1% Hispanic/Latino; 0.1% American Indian or Alaska Native, non-Hispanic/Latino; 12% Race/ethnicity unknown; 1% international; 6% transferred in; 63% live on campus. *Retention:* 71% of full-time freshmen returned.

Freshmen *Admission:* 2,815 applied, 1,816 admitted, 819 enrolled. *Average high school GPA:* 3.2. *Test scores:* SAT critical reading scores over 500: 25%; SAT math scores over 500: 29%; SAT critical reading scores over 600: 6%; SAT math scores over 600: 6%; SAT math scores over 700: 2%.

Faculty *Total:* 297, 91% full-time, 74% with terminal degrees. *Student/faculty ratio:* 12:1.

Academics *Calendar:* semesters. *Degrees:* bachelor's, master's, and doctoral. *Special study options:* academic remediation for entering students, cooperative education, English as a second language, honors programs, internships, off-campus study, part-time degree program, summer session for credit. *ROTC:* Army (b), Air Force (b). *Unusual degree programs:* 3-2 forestry with Auburn University, Iowa State University of Science and Technology, University of Michigan, Idaho State University.

Computers on Campus 1,000 computers/terminals are available on campus for general student use. Students can access the following: online (class) registration. Campuswide network is available.

Student Life *Housing:* on-campus residence required through sophomore year. *Options:* coed, men-only, women-only. Freshman applicants given priority for college housing. *Activities and organizations:* drama/theater group, student-run newspaper, choral group, marching band, national fraternities, national sororities. *Campus security:* 24-hour emergency response devices and patrols, late-night transport/escort service. *Student services:* health clinic, personal/psychological counseling.

Athletics Member NCAA. All Division II. *Intercollegiate sports:* baseball M(s), basketball M(s)/W(s), cross-country running M/W, football M(s), golf M(s), riflery M/W, soccer M, tennis M(s)/W(s), track and field M(s)/W(s), volleyball W(s). *Intramural sports:* badminton M/W, basketball M/W, football M, golf M, gymnastics M/W, riflery M/W, soccer M, swimming and diving M/W, tennis M/W, track and field M/W, volleyball M/W.

Standardized Tests *Required:* SAT or ACT (for admission).

Costs (2011–12) *Comprehensive fee:* $25,670 includes full-time tuition ($17,070), mandatory fees ($650), and room and board ($7950). Full-time tuition and fees vary according to course load and program. Part-time tuition: $705 per credit hour. Part-time tuition and fees vary according to course load and program. *Room and board:* Room and board charges vary according to housing facility. *Payment plan:* installment. *Waivers:* employees or children of employees.

Financial Aid Of all full-time matriculated undergraduates who enrolled in 2010, 2,519 applied for aid, 2,147 were judged to have need, 1,379 had their need fully met. 525 Federal Work-Study jobs (averaging $1879). 424 state and other part-time jobs (averaging $4628). In 2010, 597 non-need-based awards were made. *Average percent of need met:* 85%. *Average financial aid package:* $19,250. *Average need-based loan:* $6006. *Average need-based gift aid:* $8000. *Average non-need-based aid:* $6000. *Average indebtedness upon graduation:* $28,575.

Applying *Options:* electronic application, early admission. *Application fee:* $25. *Required:* high school transcript, minimum 2.0 GPA. *Application deadlines:* 4/15 (freshmen), 4/15 (transfers).

Freshman Application Contact Tuskegee University, Tuskegee, AL 36088. *Phone:* 334-727-8500. *Toll-free phone:* 800-622-6531. *Web site:* http://www.tuskegee.edu/.

United States Sports Academy
Daphne, Alabama

Application Contact United States Sports Academy, One Academy Drive, Daphne, AL 36526-7055. *Toll-free phone:* 800-223-2668. *Web site:* http://www.ussa.edu/.

The University of Alabama

Tuscaloosa, Alabama

- **State-supported** university, founded 1831, part of University of Alabama System
- **Suburban** 1000-acre campus with easy access to Birmingham
- **Endowment** $616.9 million
- **Coed** 26,234 undergraduate students, 91% full-time, 53% women, 47% men
- **Moderately difficult** entrance level, 44% of applicants were admitted

Undergraduates 23,945 full-time, 2,289 part-time. Students come from 51 states and territories; 50 other countries; 35% are from out of state; 12% Black or African American, non-Hispanic/Latino; 2% Hispanic/Latino; 1% Asian, non-Hispanic/Latino; 0.1% Native Hawaiian or other Pacific Islander, non-Hispanic/Latino; 0.5% American Indian or Alaska Native, non-Hispanic/Latino; 1% Two or more races, non-Hispanic/Latino; 0.3% Race/ethnicity unknown; 3% international; 6% transferred in; 28% live on campus. *Retention:* 87% of full-time freshmen returned.

Freshmen *Admission:* 22,136 applied, 9,636 admitted, 5,728 enrolled. *Average high school GPA:* 3.54. *Test scores:* SAT critical reading scores over 500: 76%; SAT math scores over 500: 76%; SAT writing scores over 500: 73%; ACT scores over 18: 100%; SAT critical reading scores over 600: 33%; SAT math scores over 600: 37%; SAT writing scores over 600: 30%; ACT scores over 24: 60%; SAT critical reading scores over 700: 14%; SAT math scores over 700: 13%; SAT writing scores over 700: 10%; ACT scores over 30: 25%.

Faculty *Total:* 1,590, 74% full-time, 77% with terminal degrees. *Student/faculty ratio:* 19:1.

Academics *Calendar:* semesters. *Degrees:* bachelor's, master's, doctoral, post-master's, and first professional certificates. *Special study options:* academic remediation for entering students, accelerated degree program, adult/continuing education programs, advanced placement credit, cooperative education, distance learning, double majors, English as a second language, external degree program, freshman honors college, honors programs, independent study, internships, off-campus study, part-time degree program, services for LD students, student-designed majors, study abroad, summer session for credit. *ROTC:* Army (b), Air Force (b).

Computers on Campus 2,500 computers/terminals are available on campus for general student use. Students can access the following: campus intranet, computer help desk, free student e-mail accounts, online (class) grades, online (class) registration, online (class) schedules. Campuswide network is available. 100% of college-owned or -operated housing units are wired for high-speed Internet access. Wireless service is available via entire campus.

Student Life *Housing:* on-campus residence required for freshman year. *Options:* coed, men-only, women-only, disabled students. Campus housing is university owned and leased by the school. Freshman campus housing is guaranteed. *Activities and organizations:* drama/theater group, student-run newspaper, radio station, choral group, marching band, SOURCE Board of Governors, Residence Hall Association, International Student Association, Student Government Association, Black Student Union, national fraternities, national sororities. *Campus security:* 24-hour emergency response devices and patrols, late-night transport/escort service, controlled dormitory access, 24-hour patrols by University of Alabama Police (UAPD), certified law enforcement personnel. *Student services:* health clinic, personal/psychological counseling, women's center, legal services.

Athletics Member NCAA. All Division I except football (Division I-A). *Intercollegiate sports:* baseball M(s), basketball M(s)/W(s), bowling M(c), cheerleading M(s)/W(s), crew M(c)/W(s), cross-country running M(s)/W(s), equestrian sports W(c), golf M(s)/W, gymnastics W(s), ice hockey M(c), lacrosse M(c)/W(c), racquetball M(c)/W(c), rock climbing M(c)/W(c), rugby M(c)/W(c), soccer M(c)/W(s), softball W(s), swimming and diving M(s)/W(s), table tennis M(c)/W(c), tennis M(s)/W(s), track and field M(s)/W(s), ultimate Frisbee M(c)/W(c), volleyball M(c)/W(s), water polo M(c), wrestling M(c). *Intramural sports:* badminton M/W, basketball M/W, bowling M/W, golf M/W, racquetball M/W, soccer M/W, swimming and diving M/W, table tennis M/W, tennis M/W, ultimate Frisbee M/W, volleyball M/W.

Standardized Tests *Required:* SAT or ACT (for admission).

Costs (2011–12) *Tuition:* state resident $8600 full-time; nonresident $21,900 full-time. Full-time tuition and fees vary according to course load. Part-time tuition and fees vary according to course load. *Room and board:* $8564; room only: $5050. Room and board charges vary according to board plan and housing facility. *Payment plans:* installment, deferred payment. *Waivers:* employees or children of employees.

Financial Aid Of all full-time matriculated undergraduates who enrolled in 2010, 12,045 applied for aid, 9,340 were judged to have need, 1,406 had their need fully met. 384 Federal Work-Study jobs (averaging $3008). In 2010, 4675 non-need-based awards were made. *Average percent of need met:* 55%. *Average financial aid package:* $10,467. *Average need-based loan:* $4182.

Average need-based gift aid: $7445. *Average non-need-based aid:* $7798. *Average indebtedness upon graduation:* $26,714.

Applying *Options:* electronic application, early admission. *Application fee:* $40. *Required:* high school transcript, minimum 3.0 GPA. *Required for some:* essay or personal statement. *Application deadlines:* 6/1 (freshmen), 6/1 (out-of-state freshmen), 8/1 (transfers). *Notification:* continuous (freshmen), continuous (out-of-state freshmen), continuous (transfers).

Freshman Application Contact Ms. Mary K. Spiegel, Executive Director of Undergraduate Admissions, The University of Alabama, Box 870132, Tuscaloosa, AL 35487. *Phone:* 205-348-5666. *Toll-free phone:* 800-933-BAMA. *Fax:* 205-348-9046. *E-mail:* admissions@ua.edu. *Web site:* http://www.ua.edu/.

The University of Alabama at Birmingham

Birmingham, Alabama

- **State-supported** university, founded 1969, part of University of Alabama System
- **Urban** 323-acre campus with easy access to Birmingham
- **Coed** 11,128 undergraduate students, 73% full-time, 58% women, 42% men
- **Moderately difficult** entrance level, 72% of applicants were admitted

Undergraduates 8,137 full-time, 2,991 part-time. Students come from 47 states and territories; 52 other countries; 7% are from out of state; 27% Black or African American, non-Hispanic/Latino; 2% Hispanic/Latino; 4% Asian, non-Hispanic/Latino; 0.1% Native Hawaiian or other Pacific Islander, non-Hispanic/Latino; 0.3% American Indian or Alaska Native, non-Hispanic/Latino; 2% Two or more races, non-Hispanic/Latino; 3% Race/ethnicity unknown; 2% international; 11% transferred in; 21% live on campus. *Retention:* 80% of full-time freshmen returned.

Freshmen *Admission:* 5,575 applied, 4,027 admitted, 1,605 enrolled. *Average high school GPA:* 3.5. *Test scores:* ACT scores over 18: 100%; ACT scores over 24: 53%; ACT scores over 30: 10%.

Faculty *Total:* 943, 91% full-time, 85% with terminal degrees. *Student/faculty ratio:* 18:1.

Academics *Calendar:* semesters. *Degrees:* certificates, bachelor's, master's, doctoral, post-master's, postbachelor's, and first professional certificates. *Special study options:* academic remediation for entering students, accelerated degree program, adult/continuing education programs, advanced placement credit, cooperative education, distance learning, double majors, English as a second language, freshman honors college, honors programs, independent study, internships, off-campus study, part-time degree program, services for LD students, student-designed majors, study abroad, summer session for credit. *ROTC:* Army (b), Air Force (c). *Unusual degree programs:* 3-2 engineering with Biomedical Engineering 5th Year Master's Program; Fast-Track Program - Civil Engineering, Electrical Engineering, Materials Engineering, and Mechanical Engineering; BS/MS in Biology; BS/MS in Computer Science; Public Health Fifth Year Master's Program, and Fast-Track Programs in Mathematics and Accounting.

Computers on Campus Students can access the following: campus intranet, computer help desk, free student e-mail accounts, online (class) grades, online (class) registration, online (class) schedules, transcript requests. Campuswide network is available. 100% of college-owned or -operated housing units are wired for high-speed Internet access. Wireless service is available via classrooms, computer labs, dorm rooms, learning centers, libraries, student centers.

Student Life *Housing options:* coed, disabled students. Campus housing is university owned and is provided by a third party. Freshman applicants given priority for college housing. *Activities and organizations:* drama/theater group, student-run newspaper, radio station, choral group, marching band, campus ministries, service-oriented groups, sports-affiliated groups, national fraternities, national sororities. *Campus security:* 24-hour emergency response devices and patrols, late-night transport/escort service, controlled dormitory access. *Student services:* health clinic, personal/psychological counseling, women's center.

Athletics Member NCAA. All Division I except football (Division I-A). *Intercollegiate sports:* baseball M(s), basketball M(s)/W(s), bowling W, cross-country running W(s), golf M(s)/W(s), riflery W, soccer M(s)/W(s), softball W(s), tennis M(s)/W(s), track and field W(s), volleyball W(s). *Intramural sports:* badminton M/W, basketball M/W, bowling M/W, football M/W, racquetball M/W, skiing (downhill) M/W, soccer M/W, softball M/W, swimming and diving M/W, table tennis M/W, tennis M/W, track and field M/W, ultimate Frisbee M/W, volleyball M/W, water polo M/W, wrestling M.

Standardized Tests *Required:* SAT or ACT (for admission).

Costs (2011–12) *Tuition:* state resident $7740 full-time, $246 per credit hour part-time; nonresident $17,730 full-time, $579 per credit hour part-time. Full-time tuition and fees vary according to program. Part-time tuition and fees vary

according to program. *Room and board:* $9094; room only: $5200. Room and board charges vary according to board plan and housing facility.

Financial Aid Of all full-time matriculated undergraduates who enrolled in 2011, 5,805 applied for aid, 4,899 were judged to have need, 512 had their need fully met. In 2011, 1256 non-need-based awards were made. *Average percent of need met:* 44%. *Average financial aid package:* $9420. *Average need-based loan:* $4511. *Average need-based gift aid:* $4709. *Average non-need-based aid:* $6094. *Average indebtedness upon graduation:* $21,503.

Applying *Options:* electronic application, early admission, deferred entrance. *Application fee:* $30. *Required:* high school transcript, minimum 2.3 GPA. *Application deadlines:* rolling (freshmen), 5/1 (transfers). *Notification:* continuous (freshmen), continuous (transfers).

Freshman Application Contact Mr. Kirk Kluver, Director of Undergraduate Admissions, The University of Alabama at Birmingham, 1530 3rd Avenue South, HUC 260, Birmingham, AL 35294-1150. *Phone:* 205-934-8221. *Toll-free phone:* 800-421-8743. *Fax:* 205-975-7114. *E-mail:* undergradadmit@uab.edu. *Web site:* http://www.uab.edu/.

The University of Alabama in Huntsville
Huntsville, Alabama

- **State-supported** university, founded 1950, part of University of Alabama System
- **Suburban** 400-acre campus
- **Endowment** $56.4 million
- **Coed** 5,935 undergraduate students, 75% full-time, 46% women, 54% men
- **Moderately difficult** entrance level, 64% of applicants were admitted

Undergraduates 4,461 full-time, 1,474 part-time. Students come from 40 states and territories; 68 other countries; 10% are from out of state; 14% Black or African American, non-Hispanic/Latino; 3% Hispanic/Latino; 4% Asian, non-Hispanic/Latino; 2% American Indian or Alaska Native, non-Hispanic/Latino; 1% Two or more races, non-Hispanic/Latino; 3% Race/ethnicity unknown; 3% international; 13% transferred in; 20% live on campus. *Retention:* 79% of full-time freshmen returned.

Freshmen *Admission:* 1,952 applied, 1,243 admitted, 677 enrolled. *Average high school GPA:* 3.62. *Test scores:* SAT critical reading scores over 500: 77%; SAT math scores over 500: 80%; ACT scores over 18: 100%; SAT critical reading scores over 600: 32%; SAT math scores over 600: 51%; ACT scores over 24: 66%; SAT critical reading scores over 700: 7%; SAT math scores over 700: 13%; ACT scores over 30: 22%.

Faculty *Total:* 486, 63% full-time, 69% with terminal degrees. *Student/faculty ratio:* 15:1.

Academics *Calendar:* semesters. *Degrees:* bachelor's, master's, doctoral, post-master's, postbachelor's, and first professional certificates. *Special study options:* academic remediation for entering students, advanced placement credit, cooperative education, distance learning, double majors, English as a second language, honors programs, independent study, internships, off-campus study, part-time degree program, services for LD students, student-designed majors, study abroad, summer session for credit. *ROTC:* Army (c). *Unusual degree programs:* 3-2 engineering with Oakwood College, Morehouse College, Clark Atlanta University, Spelman College.

Computers on Campus 1,227 computers/terminals and 5,330 ports are available on campus for general student use. Students can access the following: campus intranet, computer help desk, free student e-mail accounts, online (class) grades, online (class) registration, online (class) schedules. Campuswide network is available. 100% of college-owned or -operated housing units are wired for high-speed Internet access. Wireless service is available via classrooms, computer centers, computer labs, dorm rooms, learning centers, libraries, student centers.

Student Life *Housing:* on-campus residence required through sophomore year. *Options:* coed, cooperative, disabled students. Campus housing is university owned. Freshman campus housing is guaranteed. *Activities and organizations:* drama/theater group, student-run newspaper, choral group, Black Student Association, Chinese Students and Scholars Association, Baptist Campus Ministry, Indian Student Organization, American Society of Civil Engineers, national fraternities, national sororities. *Campus security:* 24-hour emergency response devices and patrols, late-night transport/escort service, controlled dormitory access, Sworn Police Department with state certified police officers; 24/7 dispatch center; community policing efforts. *Student services:* health clinic, personal/psychological counseling.

Athletics Member NCAA. All Division II except ice hockey (Division I). *Intercollegiate sports:* baseball M(s), basketball M(s)/W(s), cheerleading M(s)/W(s), crew M(c)/W(c), cross-country running M(s)/W(s), ice hockey M(s), lacrosse M(c)/W(c), soccer M(s)/W(s), softball W(s), tennis M(s)/W(s), track and field M(s)/W(s), volleyball W(s). *Intramural sports:* basketball M/W, football M/W, racquetball M/W, soccer M/W, softball M/W, tennis M/W, ultimate Frisbee M/W, volleyball M/W.

Standardized Tests *Required:* SAT or ACT (for admission).

Costs (2011–12) *Tuition:* state resident $8094 full-time, $276 per credit hour part-time; nonresident $19,424 full-time, $666 per credit hour part-time. Full-time tuition and fees vary according to course load. Part-time tuition and fees vary according to course load. *Required fees:* $47 per credit hour part-time. *Room and board:* $7930; room only: $5480. Room and board charges vary according to board plan and housing facility. *Payment plan:* installment. *Waivers:* employees or children of employees.

Financial Aid Of all full-time matriculated undergraduates who enrolled in 2011, 3,577 applied for aid, 2,429 were judged to have need, 257 had their need fully met. 73 Federal Work-Study jobs (averaging $4844). In 2011, 692 non-need-based awards were made. *Average percent of need met:* 56%. *Average financial aid package:* $9319. *Average need-based loan:* $7705. *Average need-based gift aid:* $6195. *Average non-need-based aid:* $6380. *Average indebtedness upon graduation:* $22,854. *Financial aid deadline:* 7/31.

Applying *Options:* electronic application, deferred entrance. *Application fee:* $30. *Required:* high school transcript. *Application deadlines:* 8/22 (freshmen), 8/22 (out-of-state freshmen), 8/22 (transfers). *Notification:* continuous (freshmen), continuous (transfers).

Freshman Application Contact Ms. Sandra Ranae Barinowski, Director of Admissions, The University of Alabama in Huntsville, Enrollment Services, 301 Sparkman Drive, Huntsville, AL 35899. *Phone:* 256-824-2773. *Toll-free phone:* 800-UAH-CALL. *Fax:* 256-824-4539. *E-mail:* admitme@email.uah.edu. *Web site:* http://www.uah.edu/.

University of Mobile
Mobile, Alabama

- **Independent Southern Baptist** comprehensive, founded 1961
- **Suburban** 830-acre campus
- **Endowment** $14.5 million
- **Coed** 1,544 undergraduate students, 87% full-time, 67% women, 33% men
- **Moderately difficult** entrance level, 81% of applicants were admitted

Undergraduates 1,346 full-time, 198 part-time. Students come from 33 states and territories; 30 other countries; 16% are from out of state; 24% Black or African American, non-Hispanic/Latino; 1% Hispanic/Latino; 0.7% Asian, non-Hispanic/Latino; 2% American Indian or Alaska Native, non-Hispanic/Latino; 1% Two or more races, non-Hispanic/Latino; 6% Race/ethnicity unknown; 3% international; 12% transferred in; 39% live on campus. *Retention:* 72% of full-time freshmen returned.

Freshmen *Admission:* 620 applied, 500 admitted, 251 enrolled. *Average high school GPA:* 3.34. *Test scores:* SAT critical reading scores over 500: 49%; SAT math scores over 500: 54%; ACT scores over 18: 91%; SAT critical reading scores over 600: 19%; SAT math scores over 600: 16%; ACT scores over 24: 37%; SAT critical reading scores over 700: 5%; SAT math scores over 700: 3%; ACT scores over 30: 2%.

Faculty *Total:* 178, 47% full-time, 39% with terminal degrees. *Student/faculty ratio:* 13:1.

Academics *Calendar:* semesters. *Degrees:* associate, bachelor's, and master's. *Special study options:* academic remediation for entering students, accelerated degree program, adult/continuing education programs, advanced placement credit, double majors, honors programs, independent study, internships, part-time degree program, services for LD students, summer session for credit. *ROTC:* Army (c), Air Force (c). *Unusual degree programs:* 3-2 engineering with Auburn University and University of South Alabama.

Computers on Campus 120 computers/terminals are available on campus for general student use. Students can access the following: campus intranet, computer help desk, free student e-mail accounts, online (class) grades, online (class) registration, online (class) schedules. Campuswide network is available. 100% of college-owned or -operated housing units are wired for high-speed Internet access. Wireless service is available via classrooms, computer centers, computer labs, dorm rooms, learning centers, libraries, student centers.

Student Life *Housing:* on-campus residence required for freshman year. *Options:* men-only, women-only. Campus housing is university owned. Freshman campus housing is guaranteed. *Activities and organizations:* drama/theater group, choral group, Campus Activity Board, Baptist Campus Ministry, Student Government Association, Fellowship of Christian Athletes. *Campus security:* 24-hour emergency response devices and patrols, controlled dormitory access, text alerts. *Student services:* health clinic, personal/psychological counseling.

Athletics Member NAIA. *Intercollegiate sports:* baseball M(s), basketball M(s)/W(s), cheerleading W(s), cross-country running M(s)/W(s), golf M(s)/W(s), soccer M(s)/W(s), softball W(s), tennis M(s)/W(s), track and field M(s)/W(s), volleyball W(s). *Intramural sports:* basketball M/W, golf M/W, soccer M/W, softball M/W, tennis M/W, track and field M/W, volleyball M/W.

Standardized Tests *Required:* SAT or ACT (for admission). *Recommended:* SAT and SAT Subject Tests or ACT (for admission), SAT Subject Tests (for admission).

Costs (2011–12) *Comprehensive fee:* $25,206 includes full-time tuition ($16,450), mandatory fees ($680), and room and board ($8076). Full-time tuition and fees vary according to course load. Part-time tuition: $585 per credit hour. Part-time tuition and fees vary according to course load. *Required fees:* $346 per degree program part-time. *College room only:* $4766. Room and board charges vary according to housing facility. *Payment plan:* installment. *Waivers:* employees or children of employees.

Financial Aid Of all full-time matriculated undergraduates who enrolled in 2011, 923 applied for aid, 847 were judged to have need, 150 had their need fully met. 54 Federal Work-Study jobs (averaging $2175). In 2011, 79 non-need-based awards were made. *Average percent of need met:* 59%. *Average financial aid package:* $15,545. *Average need-based loan:* $4701. *Average need-based gift aid:* $5415. *Average non-need-based aid:* $5600. *Average indebtedness upon graduation:* $19,900.

Applying *Options:* electronic application, deferred entrance. *Application fee:* $50. *Required:* high school transcript, minimum 2.8 GPA. *Required for some:* interview. *Application deadlines:* rolling (freshmen), rolling (transfers). *Notification:* continuous (freshmen), continuous (transfers).

Freshman Application Contact Mrs. Charity Wittner, Director of Enrollment, University of Mobile, 5735 College Parkway, Mobile, AL 36613-2842. *Phone:* 251-442-2507. *Toll-free phone:* 800-946-7267. *Fax:* 251-442-2498. *E-mail:* cwittner@umobile.edu. *Web site:* http://www.umobile.edu/.

University of Montevallo

Montevallo, Alabama

- **State-supported** comprehensive, founded 1896
- **Small-town** 160-acre campus with easy access to Birmingham
- **Endowment** $2.1 million
- **Coed**
- **Moderately difficult** entrance level

Faculty *Student/faculty ratio:* 17:1.

Academics *Calendar:* semesters. *Degrees:* bachelor's, master's, and post-master's certificates.

Student Life *Campus security:* 24-hour emergency response devices and patrols, late-night transport/escort service, controlled dormitory access.

Athletics Member NCAA. All Division II.

Standardized Tests *Required:* SAT or ACT (for admission). *Recommended:* ACT (for admission).

Costs (2011–12) *Tuition:* state resident $8040 full-time, $268 per credit hour part-time; nonresident $16,080 full-time, $536 per credit hour part-time. *Required fees:* $480 full-time. *Room and board:* $5192. Room and board charges vary according to housing facility.

Financial Aid *Of all full-time matriculated undergraduates who enrolled in 2011,* 1,610 applied for aid, 1,355 were judged to have need, 192 had their need fully met. *In 2011,* 510 non-need-based awards were made. *Average percent of need met:* 58. *Average financial aid package:* $9316. *Average need-based loan:* $4124. *Average need-based gift aid:* $6435. *Average non-need-based aid:* $8290. *Average indebtedness upon graduation:* $10,567.

Applying *Options:* electronic application, early admission, deferred entrance. *Application fee:* $30. *Required:* high school transcript, minimum 2.0 GPA. *Recommended:* interview.

Freshman Application Contact Mr. Ira Lynn Gurganus, Director of Admissions, University of Montevallo, University of Montevallo, Office of Admissions, Station 6030, Montevallo, AL 35115-6030. *Phone:* 205-665-6030. *Toll-free phone:* 800-292-4349. *Fax:* 205-665-6032. *E-mail:* admissions@montevallo.edu. *Web site:* http://www.montevallo.edu/.

University of North Alabama

Florence, Alabama

- **State-supported** comprehensive, founded 1830
- **Urban** 200-acre campus with easy access to Huntsville, AL
- **Endowment** $20.6 million
- **Coed** 6,119 undergraduate students, 80% full-time, 57% women, 43% men
- **Minimally difficult** entrance level, 79% of applicants were admitted

Undergraduates 4,924 full-time, 1,195 part-time. Students come from 39 states and territories; 46 other countries; 16% are from out of state; 12% Black

or African American, non-Hispanic/Latino; 2% Hispanic/Latino; 0.6% Asian, non-Hispanic/Latino; 0.1% Native Hawaiian or other Pacific Islander, non-Hispanic/Latino; 1% American Indian or Alaska Native, non-Hispanic/Latino; 2% Two or more races, non-Hispanic/Latino; 3% Race/ethnicity unknown; 4% international; 10% transferred in; 20% live on campus. *Retention:* 71% of full-time freshmen returned.

Freshmen *Admission:* 2,381 applied, 1,872 admitted, 891 enrolled. *Average high school GPA:* 3.07. *Test scores:* SAT critical reading scores over 500: 28%; SAT math scores over 500: 40%; ACT scores over 18: 84%; SAT critical reading scores over 600: 6%; SAT math scores over 600: 12%; ACT scores over 24: 31%; SAT math scores over 700: 6%; ACT scores over 30: 2%.

Faculty *Total:* 332, 70% full-time, 63% with terminal degrees. *Student/faculty ratio:* 22:1.

Academics *Calendar:* semesters. *Degrees:* bachelor's, master's, and post-master's certificates. *Special study options:* academic remediation for entering students, accelerated degree program, advanced placement credit, cooperative education, distance learning, double majors, English as a second language, freshman honors college, honors programs, independent study, internships, off-campus study, part-time degree program, services for LD students, student-designed majors, study abroad, summer session for credit. *ROTC:* Army (b).

Computers on Campus 1,000 computers/terminals are available on campus for general student use. Students can access the following: computer help desk, free student e-mail accounts, online (class) grades, online (class) registration, online (class) schedules. Campuswide network is available. Wireless service is available via computer labs, learning centers.

Student Life *Housing options:* coed, men-only, women-only. Campus housing is university owned. *Activities and organizations:* drama/theater group, student-run newspaper, radio station, choral group, marching band, Student Government Association, University Program Council, Baptist campus ministries, Physical Education Majors Club, Residence Hall Association, national fraternities, national sororities. *Campus security:* 24-hour emergency response devices and patrols, student patrols, late-night transport/escort service, controlled dormitory access. *Student services:* health clinic, personal/psychological counseling, women's center.

Athletics Member NCAA. All Division II. *Intercollegiate sports:* baseball M(s), basketball M(s)/W(s), cross-country running M(s)/W(s), football M(s), golf M(s), soccer W(s), softball W(s), tennis M(s)/W(s), volleyball W(s). *Intramural sports:* badminton M/W, baseball M, basketball M/W, bowling M/W, cross-country running M/W, football M/W, golf M, racquetball M/W, softball W, swimming and diving M/W, table tennis M/W, tennis M/W, volleyball M/W, weight lifting M/W.

Standardized Tests *Required:* SAT or ACT (for admission).

Costs (2011–12) *Tuition:* state resident $6120 full-time, $204 per credit hour part-time; nonresident $12,240 full-time, $408 per credit hour part-time. Full-time tuition and fees vary according to course load and program. Part-time tuition and fees vary according to course load and program. *Required fees:* $1398 full-time. *Room and board:* $5490. Room and board charges vary according to board plan and housing facility. *Payment plan:* installment. *Waivers:* senior citizens and employees or children of employees.

Financial Aid Of all full-time matriculated undergraduates who enrolled in 2011, 3,623 applied for aid, 3,323 were judged to have need, 1,636 had their need fully met. 163 Federal Work-Study jobs (averaging $1604). 382 state and other part-time jobs (averaging $1413). In 2011, 101 non-need-based awards were made. *Average percent of need met:* 62%. *Average financial aid package:* $7457. *Average need-based loan:* $3825. *Average need-based gift aid:* $4715. *Average non-need-based aid:* $2061. *Average indebtedness upon graduation:* $34,100.

Applying *Options:* electronic application, early admission, deferred entrance. *Application fee:* $25. *Required:* high school transcript. *Application deadlines:* rolling (freshmen), rolling (transfers).

Freshman Application Contact Mrs. Kim O. Mauldin, Director of Admissions, University of North Alabama, One Harrison Plaza, Florence, AL 35632-0001. *Phone:* 256-765-4680. *Toll-free phone:* 800-TALK-UNA. *Fax:* 256-765-4329. *E-mail:* admissions@una.edu. *Web site:* http://www.una.edu/.

University of Phoenix–Birmingham Campus

Birmingham, Alabama

Admissions Office Contact University of Phoenix–Birmingham Campus, One Corporate Center, Suite 400, Birmingham, AL 35244. *Toll-free phone:* 866-766-0766. *Web site:* http://www.phoenix.edu/.

University of South Alabama

Mobile, Alabama

- **State-supported** university, founded 1963
- **Suburban** 1225-acre campus
- **Endowment** $123.1 million
- **Coed** 11,578 undergraduate students, 75% full-time, 56% women, 44% men
- **Moderately difficult** entrance level, 87% of applicants were admitted

Undergraduates 8,678 full-time, 2,900 part-time. Students come from 51 states and territories; 100 other countries; 25% are from out of state; 21% Black or African American, non-Hispanic/Latino; 2% Hispanic/Latino; 3% Asian, non-Hispanic/Latino; 0.3% Native Hawaiian or other Pacific Islander, non-Hispanic/Latino; 0.8% American Indian or Alaska Native, non-Hispanic/Latino; 1% Two or more races, non-Hispanic/Latino; 4% Race/ethnicity unknown; 4% international; 10% transferred in; 21% live on campus. *Retention:* 65% of full-time freshmen returned.

Freshmen *Admission:* 4,473 applied, 3,903 admitted, 1,944 enrolled. *Test scores:* ACT scores over 18: 89%; ACT scores over 24: 35%; ACT scores over 30: 4%.

Faculty *Total:* 834, 63% full-time. *Student/faculty ratio:* 22:1.

Academics *Calendar:* semesters. *Degrees:* certificates, bachelor's, master's, doctoral, post-master's, postbachelor's, and first professional certificates. *Special study options:* academic remediation for entering students, accelerated degree program, adult/continuing education programs, advanced placement credit, cooperative education, distance learning, double majors, English as a second language, external degree program, freshman honors college, honors programs, part-time degree program, services for LD students, study abroad, summer session for credit. *ROTC:* Army (b), Air Force (b).

Computers on Campus 500 computers/terminals are available on campus for general student use. Students can access the following: campus intranet, computer help desk, free student e-mail accounts, online (class) grades, online (class) registration, online (class) schedules. Campuswide network is available. 100% of college-owned or -operated housing units are wired for high-speed Internet access. Wireless service is available via entire campus.

Student Life *Housing options:* coed, disabled students. Campus housing is university owned and is provided by a third party. *Activities and organizations:* drama/theater group, student-run newspaper, television station, choral group, marching band, Student Government Association, African American Student Association, Council of International Student Organizations, Alpha Epsilon Delta Pre-Health Professions, Panhellenic Council, national fraternities, national sororities. *Campus security:* 24-hour emergency response devices and patrols, late-night transport/escort service. *Student services:* health clinic, personal/psychological counseling, legal services.

Athletics Member NCAA. All Division I. *Intercollegiate sports:* baseball M(s), basketball M(s)/W(s), cross-country running M(s)/W(s), fencing M(c)/W(c), football M(c), golf M/W, soccer W(s), tennis M(s)/W(s), track and field M(s)/W(s), volleyball W(s). *Intramural sports:* badminton M/W, basketball M/W, bowling M/W, cheerleading M(c)/W(c), golf M/W, racquetball M/W, sailing M(c)/W(c), soccer M/W, softball M/W, table tennis M/W, tennis M/W, volleyball M/W, water polo M/W.

Standardized Tests *Required for some:* SAT or ACT (for admission).

Costs (2012–13) *Tuition:* state resident $7380 full-time, $246 per hour part-time; nonresident $14,760 full-time, $492 per hour part-time. Full-time tuition and fees vary according to course level, course load, degree level, and program. Part-time tuition and fees vary according to course level, course load, degree level, and program. *Room and board:* $6270; room only: $3220. Room and board charges vary according to board plan and housing facility. *Payment plan:* installment. *Waivers:* employees or children of employees.

Financial Aid Of all full-time matriculated undergraduates who enrolled in 2010, 5,978 applied for aid, 4,939 were judged to have need, 336 had their need fully met. In 2010, 832 non-need-based awards were made. *Average percent of need met:* 49%. *Average financial aid package:* $8902. *Average need-based loan:* $4288. *Average need-based gift aid:* $6018. *Average non-need-based aid:* $4262.

Applying *Options:* electronic application, early admission. *Application fee:* $35. *Required:* high school transcript. *Recommended:* minimum 2.0 GPA. *Application deadlines:* 7/15 (freshmen), 8/10 (transfers). *Notification:* continuous until 8/18 (freshmen), continuous until 8/18 (transfers).

Freshman Application Contact Mr. Christopher A. Lynch, Director, New Student Recruitment, University of South Alabama, Mobile, AL 36688-0002. *Phone:* 251-460-6141. *Toll-free phone:* 800-872-5247. *E-mail:* admiss@usouthal.edu. *Web site:* http://www.southalabama.edu/.

The University of West Alabama

Livingston, Alabama

- **State-supported** comprehensive, founded 1835
- **Small-town** 514-acre campus
- **Endowment** $4.3 million
- **Coed** 2,076 undergraduate students, 86% full-time, 60% women, 40% men
- **Minimally difficult** entrance level, 49% of applicants were admitted

Undergraduates 1,790 full-time, 286 part-time. Students come from 47 states and territories; 13 other countries; 18% are from out of state; 46% Black or African American, non-Hispanic/Latino; 1% Hispanic/Latino; 0.2% Asian, non-Hispanic/Latino; 0.2% Native Hawaiian or other Pacific Islander, non-Hispanic/Latino; 0.4% American Indian or Alaska Native, non-Hispanic/Latino; 0.3% Two or more races, non-Hispanic/Latino; 4% Race/ethnicity unknown; 3% international; 13% transferred in; 30% live on campus. *Retention:* 56% of full-time freshmen returned.

Freshmen *Admission:* 937 applied, 455 admitted, 360 enrolled. *Test scores:* ACT scores over 18: 80%; ACT scores over 24: 23%.

Faculty *Total:* 273, 45% full-time. *Student/faculty ratio:* 28:1.

Academics *Calendar:* semesters. *Degrees:* associate, bachelor's, master's, and post-master's certificates. *Special study options:* academic remediation for entering students, accelerated degree program, advanced placement credit, cooperative education, distance learning, double majors, honors programs, independent study, internships, off-campus study, part-time degree program, services for LD students, summer session for credit. *ROTC:* Army (c), Air Force (c). *Unusual degree programs:* 3-2 engineering with Auburn University, The University of Alabama at Birmingham, Mississippi State University, The University of Alabama; forestry with Auburn University; nursing with University of Alabama.

Computers on Campus 400 computers/terminals are available on campus for general student use. Students can access the following: computer help desk, free student e-mail accounts, online (class) grades, online (class) registration, online (class) schedules, Wireless intranet is available campus wide for all students to use. Campuswide network is available. 100% of college-owned or -operated housing units are wired for high-speed Internet access. Wireless service is available via entire campus.

Student Life *Housing:* on-campus residence required through sophomore year. *Options:* coed. Campus housing is university owned. *Activities and organizations:* drama/theater group, student-run newspaper, television station, choral group, marching band, The Student Government Association, The UWA Band, The UWA Choir, Fellowship of Christian Athletes (FCA), Livingston's Early Alumni Development (LEAD), national fraternities, national sororities. *Campus security:* 24-hour patrols, late-night transport/escort service. *Student services:* health clinic, personal/psychological counseling.

Athletics Member NCAA. All Division II. *Intercollegiate sports:* baseball M(s), basketball M(s)/W(s), cross-country running M(s)/W(s), football M(s), soccer M(s)/W(s), softball W(s), tennis M(s)/W(s), volleyball W(s). *Intramural sports:* archery M/W, basketball M/W, football M/W, golf M/W, soccer M/W, softball M/W, table tennis M/W, tennis M/W, ultimate Frisbee M/W, volleyball M/W, weight lifting M/W.

Standardized Tests *Required:* SAT or ACT (for admission).

Costs (2012–13) *Tuition:* state resident $5848 full-time; nonresident $11,696 full-time. Full-time tuition and fees vary according to course load, degree level, and program. Part-time tuition and fees vary according to course load, degree level, and program. *Required fees:* $1070 full-time. *Room and board:* $5840; room only: $2280. Room and board charges vary according to board plan and housing facility. *Payment plan:* installment. *Waivers:* employees or children of employees.

Financial Aid Of all full-time matriculated undergraduates who enrolled in 2010, 1,682 applied for aid, 1,572 were judged to have need, 39 had their need fully met. 108 Federal Work-Study jobs (averaging $3338). 108 state and other part-time jobs (averaging $3338). In 2010, 55 non-need-based awards were made. *Average percent of need met:* 33%. *Average financial aid package:* $13,712. *Average need-based gift aid:* $5519. *Average non-need-based aid:* $3391. *Average indebtedness upon graduation:* $2137.

Applying *Options:* electronic application, early admission, deferred entrance. *Application fee:* $50. *Required:* high school transcript, minimum 2.0 GPA. *Application deadlines:* rolling (freshmen), rolling (transfers). *Notification:* continuous (freshmen), continuous (transfers).

Freshman Application Contact Mr. Danny Buckalew, Vice President of Student Affairs, The University of West Alabama, Station 4, Livingston, AL 35470. *Phone:* 205-652-3581. *Toll-free phone:* 800-621-8044. *Fax:* 205-652-3881. *E-mail:* dbuckalew@uwa.edu. *Web site:* http://www.uwa.edu/.

Virginia College at Birmingham

Birmingham, Alabama

Director of Admissions Director of Admissions, Virginia College at Birmingham, 488 Palisades Boulevard, Birmingham, AL 35209. *Phone:* 205-802-1200. *Web site:* http://www.vc.edu/.

Virginia College at Huntsville

Huntsville, Alabama

Freshman Application Contact Director of Admission, Virginia College at Huntsville, 2800-A Bob Wallace Avenue, Huntsville, AL 35805. *Phone:* 256-533-7387. *Fax:* 256-533-7785. *Web site:* http://www.vc.edu/.

ALASKA

Alaska Bible College

Glennallen, Alaska

- **Independent nondenominational** 4-year, founded 1966
- **Rural** 80-acre campus
- **Endowment** $48,433
- **Coed** 30 undergraduate students, 80% full-time, 37% women, 63% men
- **Minimally difficult** entrance level

Undergraduates 24 full-time, 6 part-time. Students come from 8 states and territories; 43% are from out of state; 3% Black or African American, non-Hispanic/Latino; 13% American Indian or Alaska Native, non-Hispanic/Latino. *Retention:* 70% of full-time freshmen returned.
Freshmen *Admission:* 9 enrolled.
Academics *Calendar:* semesters. *Degrees:* certificates, associate, and bachelor's. *Special study options:* academic remediation for entering students, advanced placement credit, double majors, independent study, internships, part-time degree program.
Computers on Campus 8 computers/terminals are available on campus for general student use. Students can access the following: campus intranet, computer help desk, free student e-mail accounts, online (class) grades, online (class) registration, online (class) schedules. Campuswide network is available. 100% of college-owned or -operated housing units are wired for high-speed Internet access. Wireless service is available via entire campus.
Student Life *Housing:* on-campus residence required through sophomore year. *Options:* men-only, women-only. Campus housing is university owned. Freshman campus housing is guaranteed. *Campus security:* 24-hour emergency response devices.
Standardized Tests *Required:* SAT or ACT (for admission).
Costs (2012–13) *Comprehensive fee:* $12,630 includes full-time tuition ($6840), mandatory fees ($390), and room and board ($5400). Part-time tuition: $300 per credit hour. *Payment plan:* installment. *Waivers:* employees or children of employees.
Financial Aid Of all full-time matriculated undergraduates who enrolled in 2009, 8 applied for aid, 8 were judged to have need. 20 state and other part-time jobs (averaging $842). *Average need-based gift aid:* $850. *Average indebtedness upon graduation:* $8075. *Financial aid deadline:* 7/1.
Applying *Options:* deferred entrance. *Application fee:* $35. *Required:* essay or personal statement, high school transcript, minimum 2.0 GPA, 2 letters of recommendation, interview. *Application deadlines:* 7/1 (freshmen), 7/1 (transfers). *Notification:* continuous until 7/15 (freshmen), continuous until 7/15 (transfers).
Freshman Application Contact Nikki Palmer, Director of Admissions, Alaska Bible College, PO Box 289, Glennallen, AK 99588. *Phone:* 907-822-3201 Ext. 224. *Toll-free phone:* 800-478-7884. *Fax:* 907-822-5027. *E-mail:* npalmer@akbible.edu. *Web site:* http://www.akbible.edu/.

Alaska Pacific University

Anchorage, Alaska

- **Independent** comprehensive, founded 1959
- **Urban** 170-acre campus
- **Endowment** $51.8 million
- **Coed** 481 undergraduate students, 57% full-time, 67% women, 33% men
- **Moderately difficult** entrance level, 5% of applicants were admitted

Undergraduates 275 full-time, 206 part-time. Students come from 34 states and territories; 29% are from out of state; 5% Black or African American, non-Hispanic/Latino; 4% Hispanic/Latino; 1% Asian, non-Hispanic/Latino; 0.5% Native Hawaiian or other Pacific Islander, non-Hispanic/Latino; 15% American Indian or Alaska Native, non-Hispanic/Latino; 3% Two or more races, non-Hispanic/Latino; 16% Race/ethnicity unknown; 26% live on campus. *Retention:* 75% of full-time freshmen returned.

Freshmen *Admission:* 468 applied, 24 admitted, 24 enrolled. *Average high school GPA:* 3.22. *Test scores:* SAT critical reading scores over 500: 71%; SAT math scores over 500: 64%; SAT writing scores over 500: 64%; ACT scores over 18: 91%; SAT critical reading scores over 600: 21%; SAT math scores over 600: 21%; SAT writing scores over 600: 14%; ACT scores over 24: 27%.

Faculty *Total:* 115, 43% full-time. *Student/faculty ratio:* 15:1.

Academics *Calendar:* semesters. *Degrees:* certificates, associate, bachelor's, master's, doctoral, and postbachelor's certificates. *Special study options:* academic remediation for entering students, adult/continuing education programs, advanced placement credit, distance learning, double majors, independent study, internships, part-time degree program, services for LD students, student-designed majors, study abroad, summer session for credit. *ROTC:* Air Force (c). *Unusual degree programs:* 3-2 business administration.

Computers on Campus 105 computers/terminals and 480 ports are available on campus for general student use. Students can access the following: campus intranet, computer help desk, free student e-mail accounts, online (class) grades, online (class) registration, online (class) schedules. Campuswide network is available. 100% of college-owned or -operated housing units are wired for high-speed Internet access. Wireless service is available via entire campus.

Student Life *Housing:* on-campus residence required for freshman year. *Options:* coed. Campus housing is university owned. Freshman campus housing is guaranteed. *Activities and organizations:* drama/theater group, student-run newspaper, choral group, ASAPU (Associated Students of Alaska Pacific University), Photography Club, Dive Club, basketball club, Spectrum Club. *Campus security:* 24-hour emergency response devices, student patrols, late-night transport/escort service, controlled dormitory access. *Student services:* personal/psychological counseling.

Athletics *Intramural sports:* basketball M/W, skiing (cross-country) M/W, soccer M/W, volleyball M/W.

Standardized Tests *Required:* SAT or ACT (for admission).

Costs (2012–13) *Comprehensive fee:* $39,180 includes full-time tuition ($29,700), mandatory fees ($180), and room and board ($9300). Full-time tuition and fees vary according to course load, degree level, program, and reciprocity agreements. Part-time tuition: $1240 per semester hour. Part-time tuition and fees vary according to course load, degree level, and program. *Required fees:* $55 per term part-time. *College room only:* $4400. Room and board charges vary according to board plan and housing facility. *Payment plans:* installment, deferred payment. *Waivers:* employees or children of employees.

Financial Aid Of all full-time matriculated undergraduates who enrolled in 2011, 185 applied for aid, 118 were judged to have need, 57 had their need fully met. 41 Federal Work-Study jobs (averaging $1010). In 2011, 57 non-need-based awards were made. *Average percent of need met:* 40%. *Average financial aid package:* $17,524. *Average need-based loan:* $3175. *Average need-based gift aid:* $6414. *Average non-need-based aid:* $16,500. *Average indebtedness upon graduation:* $28,000.

Applying *Options:* electronic application, deferred entrance. *Application fee:* $25. *Required:* essay or personal statement, high school transcript, minimum 2.5 GPA, 2 letters of recommendation. *Required for some:* interview. *Application deadlines:* 8/15 (freshmen), 8/15 (transfers).

Freshman Application Contact Mr. Barclay Roeder, Interim Director of Admissions, Alaska Pacific University, 4101 University Drive, Anchorage, AK 99508. *Phone:* 907-564-8248. *Toll-free phone:* 800-252-7528. *Fax:* 907-564-8317. *E-mail:* admissions@alaskapacific.edu. *Web site:* http://www.alaskapacific.edu/.

Charter College

Anchorage, Alaska

Director of Admissions Ms. Lily Sirianni, Vice President, Charter College, 2221 East Northern Lights Boulevard, Suite 120, Anchorage, AK 99508. *Phone:* 907-277-1000. *Toll-free phone:* 888-200-9942. *Web site:* http://www.chartercollege.edu/.

University of Alaska Anchorage

Anchorage, Alaska

- **State-supported** comprehensive, founded 1954, part of University of Alaska System
- **Urban** 428-acre campus
- **Coed** 17,890 undergraduate students, 46% full-time, 58% women, 42% men
- **Noncompetitive** entrance level, 80% of applicants were admitted

Undergraduates 8,156 full-time, 9,734 part-time. 10% are from out of state; 4% Black or African American, non-Hispanic/Latino; 7% Hispanic/Latino; 6% Asian, non-Hispanic/Latino; 0.9% Native Hawaiian or other Pacific Islander, non-Hispanic/Latino; 12% American Indian or Alaska Native, non-Hispanic/Latino; 2% Two or more races, non-Hispanic/Latino; 7% Race/ethnicity unknown; 0.7% international; 6% transferred in. *Retention:* 73% of full-time freshmen returned.

Freshmen *Admission:* 4,267 applied, 3,396 admitted, 2,198 enrolled.

Faculty *Total:* 1,374, 49% full-time, 25% with terminal degrees. *Student/faculty ratio:* 19:1.

Academics *Calendar:* semesters. *Degrees:* certificates, associate, bachelor's, master's, post-master's, and postbachelor's certificates. *Special study options:* academic remediation for entering students, adult/continuing education programs, advanced placement credit, cooperative education, distance learning, double majors, English as a second language, honors programs, independent study, internships, off-campus study, part-time degree program, services for LD students, student-designed majors, study abroad, summer session for credit. *ROTC:* Army (b), Air Force (b).

Computers on Campus Students can access the following: campus intranet, online (class) registration. Campuswide network is available. Wireless service is available via dorm rooms.

Student Life *Housing options:* coed, disabled students. *Activities and organizations:* drama/theater group, student-run newspaper, radio station, choral group, Accounting Club, African-American Students Association, Association of Latin-American Spanish Students, Inter-Varsity Christian Fellowship, Student Nurses Association, national fraternities, national sororities. *Campus security:* 24-hour emergency response devices and patrols, student patrols, late-night transport/escort service, controlled dormitory access. *Student services:* health clinic, personal/psychological counseling, women's center.

Athletics Member NCAA. All Division II. *Intercollegiate sports:* basketball M(s)/W(s), cross-country running M(s)/W, gymnastics W(s), ice hockey M(s), skiing (cross-country) M(s)/W(s), skiing (downhill) M(s)/W(s), track and field M/W, volleyball W(s). *Intramural sports:* basketball M/W, ice hockey M/W, soccer M/W, volleyball M/W.

Standardized Tests *Required:* SAT or ACT (for admission).

Costs (2011–12) *Tuition:* state resident $4620 full-time, $154 per credit part-time; nonresident $16,260 full-time, $542 per credit part-time. Full-time tuition and fees vary according to course level and location. Part-time tuition and fees vary according to course level and location. *Required fees:* $686 full-time, $26 per credit part-time, $31 per term part-time. *Room and board:* $9427. Room and board charges vary according to board plan and housing facility.

Financial Aid Of all full-time matriculated undergraduates who enrolled in 2011, 3,802 applied for aid, 3,174 were judged to have need, 381 had their need fully met. In 2011, 390 non-need-based awards were made. *Average percent of need met:* 62%. *Average financial aid package:* $8189. *Average need-based loan:* $4103. *Average need-based gift aid:* $2440. *Average non-need-based aid:* $2376. *Average indebtedness upon graduation:* $28,001.

Applying *Options:* deferred entrance. *Application fee:* $50. *Required:* minimum 2.0 GPA. *Required for some:* high school transcript. *Application deadlines:* 7/1 (freshmen), rolling (transfers). *Notification:* continuous (freshmen), continuous (transfers).

Freshman Application Contact Enrollment Services, University of Alaska Anchorage, PO Box 141629, 3901 Old Seward Highway, Anchorage, AK 99508-8046. *Phone:* 907-786-1480. *Fax:* 907-786-4888. *E-mail:* enroll@uaa.alaska.edu. *Web site:* http://www.uaa.alaska.edu/.

University of Alaska Anchorage, Kenai Peninsula College

Soldotna, Alaska

- **State-supported** primarily 2-year, founded 1964, part of University of Alaska System
- **Rural** 360-acre campus
- **Coed**
- **Noncompetitive** entrance level

Academics *Calendar:* semesters. *Degrees:* certificates, associate, and bachelor's.

Student Life *Campus security:* 24-hour emergency response devices.

Standardized Tests *Required:* ACT, SAT or ACCUPLACER scores (for admission).

Costs (2011–12) *Tuition:* state resident $4905 full-time, $154 per credit hour part-time; nonresident $4905 full-time, $154 per credit hour part-time. *Required fees:* $405 full-time.

Financial Aid *Of all full-time matriculated undergraduates who enrolled in 2010,* 50 Federal Work-Study jobs (averaging $3000). 50 state and other part-time jobs (averaging $3000).

Applying *Options:* electronic application. *Application fee:* $40. *Required:* high school transcript.

Freshman Application Contact Ms. Shelly Love Blatchford, Admission and Registration Coordinator, University of Alaska Anchorage, Kenai Peninsula College, 156 College Road, Soldotna, AK 99669-9798. *Phone:* 907-262-0311. *Toll-free phone:* 877-262-0330. *Web site:* http://www.kpc.alaska.edu/.

University of Alaska Fairbanks

Fairbanks, Alaska

- **State-supported** university, founded 1917, part of University of Alaska System
- **Small-town** 2250-acre campus
- **Endowment** $715.6 million
- **Coed** 8,622 undergraduate students, 44% full-time, 59% women, 41% men
- **Minimally difficult** entrance level, 79% of applicants were admitted

Undergraduates 3,825 full-time, 4,797 part-time. Students come from 50 states and territories; 51 other countries; 12% are from out of state; 2% Black or African American, non-Hispanic/Latino; 5% Hispanic/Latino; 1% Asian, non-Hispanic/Latino; 0.3% Native Hawaiian or other Pacific Islander, non-Hispanic/Latino; 15% American Indian or Alaska Native, non-Hispanic/Latino; 5% Two or more races, non-Hispanic/Latino; 19% Race/ethnicity unknown; 1% international; 6% transferred in; 24% live on campus. *Retention:* 76% of full-time freshmen returned.

Freshmen *Admission:* 2,034 applied, 1,610 admitted, 1,072 enrolled. *Average high school GPA:* 3.2. *Test scores:* SAT critical reading scores over 500: 61%; SAT math scores over 500: 58%; SAT writing scores over 500: 50%; ACT scores over 18: 81%; SAT critical reading scores over 600: 24%; SAT math scores over 600: 24%; SAT writing scores over 600: 14%; ACT scores over 24: 35%; SAT critical reading scores over 700: 3%; SAT math scores over 700: 2%; SAT writing scores over 700: 1%; ACT scores over 30: 4%.

Faculty *Total:* 1,042, 33% full-time, 47% with terminal degrees. *Student/faculty ratio:* 12:1.

Academics *Calendar:* semesters. *Degrees:* certificates, associate, bachelor's, master's, doctoral, postbachelor's, and first professional certificates. *Special study options:* academic remediation for entering students, accelerated degree program, advanced placement credit, cooperative education, distance learning, double majors, English as a second language, external degree program, honors programs, independent study, internships, off-campus study, part-time degree program, services for LD students, student-designed majors, study abroad, summer session for credit. *ROTC:* Army (b). *Unusual degree programs:* 3-2 engineering; computer science.

Computers on Campus 125 computers/terminals and 22 ports are available on campus for general student use. Students can access the following: campus intranet, computer help desk, free student e-mail accounts, online (class) grades, online (class) registration, online (class) schedules, university portal, campus wireless access. Campuswide network is available. 100% of college-owned or -operated housing units are wired for high-speed Internet access. Wireless service is available via entire campus.

Student Life *Housing options:* coed, disabled students. Campus housing is university owned. Freshman applicants given priority for college housing. *Activities and organizations:* drama/theater group, student-run newspaper, radio and television station, choral group, UAF Chinese Student Association, Alpha Phi Omega, Student Veterans of UAF, Broomball Club, Caribbean Music and Culture Club, national fraternities, national sororities. *Campus security:* 24-hour emergency response devices and patrols, student patrols, late-night transport/escort service, controlled dormitory access, ID check at door of residence halls, crime prevention and safety workshops. *Student services:* health clinic, personal/psychological counseling, women's center, legal services.

Athletics Member NCAA. All Division II except ice hockey (Division I). *Intercollegiate sports:* basketball M(s)/W(s), cross-country running M(s)/W(s), ice hockey M(s), riflery M(s)/W(s), skiing (cross-country) M(s)/W(s), swimming and diving W(s), volleyball W(s). *Intramural sports:* archery M(c)/W(c), basketball M/W, bowling M/W, cross-country running M/W, fencing M(c)/W(c), ice hockey W(c), racquetball M(c)/W(c), rugby W(c), soccer M/W, swimming and diving M(c)/W(c), ultimate Frisbee M/W, volleyball M/W.

Standardized Tests *Required:* SAT or ACT (for admission).

Costs (2012–13) *Tuition:* state resident $5475 full-time, $165 per credit part-time; nonresident $17,925 full-time, $580 per credit part-time. Full-time tuition and fees vary according to course level, course load, location, and reciprocity agreements. Part-time tuition and fees vary according to course level, course load, location, and reciprocity agreements. *Required fees:* $968 full-time. *Room and board:* $6960; room only: $3610. Room and board charges vary according to board plan and housing facility. *Payment plan:* installment. *Waivers:* children of alumni, senior citizens, and employees or children of employees.

Financial Aid Of all full-time matriculated undergraduates who enrolled in 2010, 2,620 applied for aid, 1,849 were judged to have need, 161 had their need fully met. 51 Federal Work-Study jobs (averaging $3938). In 2010, 593 non-need-based awards were made. *Average percent of need met:* 51%. *Average financial aid package:* $7224. *Average need-based loan:* $4850. *Average need-based gift aid:* $6294. *Average non-need-based aid:* $3097. *Average indebtedness upon graduation:* $34,885. *Financial aid deadline:* 7/1.

Applying *Options:* electronic application, deferred entrance. *Application fee:* $50. *Required:* high school transcript, minimum 2.5 GPA. *Application deadlines:* 7/1 (freshmen), 7/1 (out-of-state freshmen), 7/1 (transfers). *Notification:* continuous (freshmen), continuous (out-of-state freshmen), continuous (transfers).

Freshman Application Contact Mike Earnest, Director of Admissions, University of Alaska Fairbanks, PO Box 757480, Fairbanks, AK 99775-7480. *Phone:* 907-474-7500. *Toll-free phone:* 800-478-1823. *Fax:* 907-474-5379. *E-mail:* admissions@uaf.edu. *Web site:* http://www.uaf.edu/.

See below for display ad and page 1658 for the College Close-Up.

University of Alaska Southeast
Juneau, Alaska

- **State-supported** comprehensive, founded 1972, part of University of Alaska System
- **Small-town** 198-acre campus
- **Coed**
- **Noncompetitive** entrance level

Faculty *Student/faculty ratio:* 9:1.
Academics *Calendar:* semesters. *Degrees:* certificates, associate, bachelor's, master's, and post-master's certificates.

Student Life *Campus security:* 24-hour emergency response devices and patrols, late-night transport/escort service, controlled dormitory access.

Standardized Tests *Recommended:* SAT or ACT (for admission).

Costs (2011–12) *Tuition:* state resident $4620 full-time, $154 per semester hour part-time; nonresident $16,260 full-time, $542 per semester hour part-time. Full-time tuition and fees vary according to course level, course load, and location. Part-time tuition and fees vary according to course level, course load, and location. *Required fees:* $857 full-time, $13 per semester hour part-time, $5 per term part-time. *Room and board:* $7100; room only: $4200. Room and board charges vary according to housing facility and location. *Payment plans:* tuition prepayment, installment.

Financial Aid *Of all full-time matriculated undergraduates who enrolled in 2009,* 856 applied for aid, 461 were judged to have need, 62 had their need fully met. *In 2009,* 63 non-need-based awards were made. *Average percent of need met:* 58. *Average financial aid package:* $8261. *Average need-based loan:* $1527. *Average need-based gift aid:* $1185. *Average non-need-based aid:* $1213. *Average indebtedness upon graduation:* $2611.

Applying *Options:* electronic application, deferred entrance. *Application fee:* $50. *Required:* high school transcript, minimum 2.0 GPA. *Required for some:* essay or personal statement.

Freshman Application Contact Ms. Deema Ferguson, Admissions Clerk, University of Alaska Southeast, 11120 Glacier Highway, Juneau, AK 99801-8625. *Phone:* 907-796-6294 Ext. 6100. *Toll-free phone:* 877-465-4827. *Fax:* 907-796-6365. *E-mail:* admissions@uas.alaska.edu. *Web site:* http://www.uas.alaska.edu/.

ARIZONA

American Indian College of the Assemblies of God, Inc.
Phoenix, Arizona

Director of Admissions Sandra Gonzales, Director of Enrollment Management, American Indian College of the Assemblies of God, Inc., 10020 North Fifteenth Avenue, Phoenix, AZ 85021-2199. *Phone:* 602-944-3335 Ext. 226. *E-mail:* sgonzales@aicag.edu. *Web site:* http://www.aicag.edu/.

ALASKA

UNIVERSITY OF ALASKA FAIRBANKS

Is {it} for you?

www.uaf.edu/admissions/

UAF

UNIVERSITY *of* ALASKA FAIRBANKS

The University of Alaska Fairbanks is accredited by the Northwest Commission on Colleges and Universities. UAF is an affirmative action/equal opportunity employer and educational institution.

Anthem College–Phoenix

Phoenix, Arizona

Freshman Application Contact Mr. Glen Husband, Vice President of Admissions, Anthem College–Phoenix, 1515 East Indian School Road, Phoenix, AZ 85014-4901. *Phone:* 602-279-9700. *Toll-free phone:* 855-331-7767. *Web site:* http://anthem.edu/phoenix-arizona/.

Argosy University, Phoenix

Phoenix, Arizona

Freshman Application Contact Argosy University, Phoenix, 2233 West Dunlap Avenue, Phoenix, AZ 85021. *Phone:* 602-216-2600. *Toll-free phone:* 866-216-2777. *Web site:* http://www.argosy.edu/phoenix/.

See page 1062 for the College Close-Up.

Arizona Christian University

Phoenix, Arizona

Freshman Application Contact Rebekah Dubina, Admissions Advisor, Arizona Christian University, 2625 East Cactus Road, Phoenix, AZ 85032. *Phone:* 602-386-4106. *Toll-free phone:* 800-247-2697. *Fax:* 602-404-2159. *E-mail:* rebekah@swcaz.edu. *Web site:* http://arizonachristian.edu/.

Arizona State University

Tempe, Arizona

- **State-supported** university, founded 1885, part of Arizona State University System
- **Urban** 1966-acre campus with easy access to Phoenix
- **Coed** 58,404 undergraduate students, 86% full-time, 50% women, 50% men
- **Moderately difficult** entrance level, 89% of applicants were admitted

Undergraduates 50,484 full-time, 7,920 part-time. Students come from 54 states and territories; 91 other countries; 23% are from out of state; 5% Black or African American, non-Hispanic/Latino; 19% Hispanic/Latino; 6% Asian, non-Hispanic/Latino; 0.2% Native Hawaiian or other Pacific Islander, non-Hispanic/Latino; 2% American Indian or Alaska Native, non-Hispanic/Latino; 2% Two or more races, non-Hispanic/Latino; 2% Race/ethnicity unknown; 3% international; 12% transferred in; 19% live on campus. *Retention:* 84% of full-time freshmen returned.

Freshmen *Admission:* 29,722 applied, 26,425 admitted, 9,254 enrolled. *Average high school GPA:* 3.41. *Test scores:* SAT critical reading scores over 500: 70%; SAT math scores over 500: 75%; ACT scores over 18: 93%; SAT critical reading scores over 600: 29%; SAT math scores over 600: 38%; ACT scores over 24: 54%; SAT critical reading scores over 700: 6%; SAT math scores over 700: 8%; ACT scores over 30: 10%.

Faculty *Total:* 2,698, 93% full-time, 85% with terminal degrees. *Student/faculty ratio:* 24:1.

Academics *Calendar:* semesters. *Degrees:* certificates, bachelor's, master's, doctoral, post-master's, postbachelor's, and first professional certificates (profile includes data for the West, Polytechnic and Downtown Phoenix campuses). *Special study options:* accelerated degree program, adult/continuing education programs, advanced placement credit, cooperative education, distance learning, double majors, English as a second language, freshman honors college, honors programs, independent study, internships, off-campus study, part-time degree program, services for LD students, student-designed majors, study abroad, summer session for credit. *ROTC:* Army (b), Navy (b), Air Force (b). *Unusual degree programs:* 3-2 BA/MA Global Health; BA/MA Political Science; BS/MS Biological Science; Biochemistry (B.S./M.S.) - Emphasis in Medicinal Chemistry; Urban Planning (B.S.P.)/Urban and Environmental Planning (M.U.E.P.).

Computers on Campus 4,250 computers/terminals and 1,000 ports are available on campus for general student use. Students can access the following: campus intranet, computer help desk, free student e-mail accounts, online (class) grades, online (class) registration, online (class) schedules, My Apps offers enrolled students, faculty and staff access to software applications for use online, in the classroom, by download, or for purchase. My Apps is free of charge and is accessible from any computer using your ASURITE UserID and password. Campuswide network is available. 100% of college-owned or -operated housing units are wired for high-speed Internet access. Wireless service is available via classrooms, computer centers, computer labs, dorm rooms, learning centers, libraries, student centers.

Student Life *Housing:* on-campus residence required for freshman year. *Options:* coed. Campus housing is university owned and leased by the school.

Freshman applicants given priority for college housing. *Activities and organizations:* drama/theater group, student-run newspaper, radio and television station, choral group, marching band, Interfraternity Council, Panhellenic Council, Undergraduate Student Government, Business School Council, Residence Hall Association, national fraternities, national sororities. *Campus security:* 24-hour emergency response devices and patrols, late-night transport/escort service. *Student services:* health clinic, personal/psychological counseling, legal services.

Athletics Member NCAA. All Division I except football (Division I-A). *Intercollegiate sports:* baseball M(s), basketball M(s)/W(s), cross-country running M(s)/W(s), golf M(s)/W(s), gymnastics W(s), soccer W(s), softball W(s), swimming and diving M(s)/W(s), tennis W(s), track and field M(s)/W(s), volleyball W(s), water polo W(s), wrestling M(s). *Intramural sports:* badminton M/W, baseball M(c), basketball M/W, cheerleading M(c)/W(c), crew M(c)/W(c), equestrian sports M(c)/W(c), fencing M(c)/W(c), field hockey M(c)/W(c), gymnastics M(c), ice hockey M(c), lacrosse M(c)/W(c), racquetball M(c)/W(c), rugby M(c)/W(c), sailing M(c)/W(c), soccer M(c)/W(c), softball M/W, table tennis M/W, tennis M(c)/W(c), track and field M/W, ultimate Frisbee M(c)/W(c), volleyball M(c)/W, water polo M(c).

Standardized Tests *Required for some:* SAT or ACT (for admission), SAT and SAT Subject Tests or ACT (for admission). *Recommended:* SAT or ACT (for admission).

Costs (2011–12) *Tuition:* state resident $9208 full-time, $658 per credit hour part-time; nonresident $21,807 full-time, $909 per credit hour part-time. Full-time tuition and fees vary according to program. Part-time tuition and fees vary according to program. *Required fees:* $512 full-time, $153 per term part-time. *Room and board:* $11,436; room only: $7164. Room and board charges vary according to board plan, housing facility, and location. *Payment plan:* installment. *Waivers:* employees or children of employees.

Financial Aid Of all full-time matriculated undergraduates who enrolled in 2010, 32,735 applied for aid, 29,261 were judged to have need, 4,775 had their need fully met. 1,220 Federal Work-Study jobs (averaging $1550). 6,765 state and other part-time jobs (averaging $3342). In 2010, 5414 non-need-based awards were made. *Average percent of need met:* 59%. *Average financial aid package:* $11,680. *Average need-based loan:* $4156. *Average need-based gift aid:* $7951. *Average non-need-based aid:* $7848. *Average indebtedness upon graduation:* $19,227.

Applying *Options:* electronic application. *Application fee:* $50. *Required:* high school transcript, minimum 3.0 GPA. *Required for some:* application fee is $65 for nonresidents. *Application deadlines:* rolling (freshmen), rolling (transfers). *Notification:* continuous (freshmen), continuous (transfers).

Freshman Application Contact Arizona State University, PO Box 870112, Tempe, AZ 85287-0112. *Phone:* 480-965-7788. *Fax:* 480-965-3610. *E-mail:* admissions@asu.edu. *Web site:* http://www.asu.edu/.

The Art Institute of Phoenix

Phoenix, Arizona

- **Proprietary** 4-year, founded 1995, part of Education Management Corporation
- **Suburban** campus
- **Coed**

Academics *Calendar:* quarters. *Degrees:* diplomas, associate, and bachelor's.

Costs (2011–12) *Tuition:* Tuition cost varies by program. Prospective students should contact the school for current tuition costs. Other charges include a starting kit for all first-quarter students. Kits vary in price, depending on the program of study.

Freshman Application Contact The Art Institute of Phoenix, 2233 West Dunlap Avenue, Phoenix, AZ 85021-2859. *Phone:* 602-331-7500. *Toll-free phone:* 800-474-2479. *Web site:* http://www.artinstitutes.edu/phoenix/.

See page 1118 for the College Close-Up.

The Art Institute of Tucson

Tucson, Arizona

- **Proprietary** 4-year, founded 2007
- **Coed**

Academics *Degrees:* diplomas, associate, and bachelor's.

Costs (2011–12) *Tuition:* Tuition cost varies by program. Prospective students should contact the school for current tuition costs. Other charges include a starting kit for all first-quarter students. Kits vary in price, depending on the program of study.

Freshman Application Contact The Art Institute of Tucson, 5099 East Grant Road, Suite 100, Tucson, AZ 85712. *Phone:* 520-318-2700. *Toll-free phone:* 866-690-8850. *Web site:* http://www.artinstitutes.edu/tucson/.

See page 1136 for the College Close-Up.

Brookline College
Phoenix, Arizona

- **Proprietary** 4-year, founded 1979
- **Urban** campus with easy access to Phoenix
- **Coed**
- **Noncompetitive** entrance level

Faculty *Student/faculty ratio:* 25:1.
Academics *Calendar:* continuous. *Degrees:* certificates, diplomas, associate, and bachelor's.
Student Life *Campus security:* 24-hour emergency response devices.
Costs (2011–12) *Tuition:* $13,750 full-time. Full-time tuition and fees vary according to degree level and program. No tuition increase for student's term of enrollment.
Applying *Options:* electronic application. *Required:* interview.
Freshman Application Contact Ms. Theresa Dean, Director of Admissions, Brookline College, 2445 West Dunlap Avenue, Suite 100, Phoenix, AZ 85021. *Phone:* 602-242-6265. *Toll-free phone:* 800-793-2428. *Fax:* 602-973-2572. *E-mail:* tdean@brooklinecollege.edu. *Web site:* http://brooklinecollege.edu/.

Brookline College
Tempe, Arizona

- **Proprietary** 4-year, founded 1982
- **Urban** campus with easy access to Phoenix
- **Coed**
- **Noncompetitive** entrance level

Faculty *Student/faculty ratio:* 11:1.
Academics *Calendar:* continuous. *Degrees:* diplomas, associate, and bachelor's.
Student Life *Campus security:* 24-hour emergency response devices.
Costs (2011–12) *Tuition:* $13,750 full-time. Full-time tuition and fees vary according to degree level and program. No tuition increase for student's term of enrollment.
Applying *Options:* electronic application. *Required:* interview.
Freshman Application Contact Ms. Cheryl Kindred, Campus Director, Brookline College, 1140-1150 South Priest Drive, Tempe, AZ 85281. *Phone:* 480-545-8755. *Toll-free phone:* 888-886-2428. *Fax:* 480-926-1371. *E-mail:* ckindred@brooklinecollege.edu. *Web site:* http://brooklinecollege.edu/.

Brookline College
Tucson, Arizona

- **Proprietary** 4-year, founded 1979
- **Urban** campus with easy access to Tucson
- **Coed**
- **Noncompetitive** entrance level

Faculty *Student/faculty ratio:* 16:1.
Academics *Calendar:* continuous. *Degrees:* diplomas, associate, and bachelor's.
Student Life *Campus security:* 24-hour emergency response devices.
Costs (2011–12) *Tuition:* $13,750 full-time. Full-time tuition and fees vary according to degree level and program. No tuition increase for student's term of enrollment.
Applying *Options:* electronic application. *Required:* interview.
Freshman Application Contact Ms. Leigh Anne Pechota, Campus Director, Brookline College, 5441 East 22nd Street, Suite 125, Tucson, AZ 85711. *Phone:* 520-748-9799. *Toll-free phone:* 888-292-2428. *Fax:* 520-748-9355. *E-mail:* lpechota@brooklinecollege.edu. *Web site:* http://brooklinecollege.edu/.

Brown Mackie College–Phoenix
Phoenix, Arizona

- **Proprietary** primarily 2-year, part of Education Management Corporation
- **Coed**

Academics *Degrees:* diplomas, associate, and bachelor's.
Costs (2011–12) *Tuition:* Tuition varies by program. Students should contact Brown Mackie College for tuition information.
Freshman Application Contact Brown Mackie College–Phoenix, 13430 North Black Canyon Highway, Suite 190, Phoenix, AZ 85029. *Phone:* 602-337-3044. *Toll-free phone:* 866-824-4793. *Web site:* http://www.brownmackie.edu/phoenix/.

See page 1218 for the College Close-Up.

Brown Mackie College–Tucson
Tucson, Arizona

- **Proprietary** primarily 2-year, founded 1972, part of Education Management Corporation
- **Suburban** campus
- **Coed**

Academics *Degrees:* diplomas, associate, and bachelor's.
Costs (2011–12) *Tuition:* Tuition varies by program. Students should contact Brown Mackie College for tuition information.
Freshman Application Contact Brown Mackie College–Tucson, 4585 East Speedway, Suite 204, Tucson, AZ 85712. *Phone:* 520-319-3300. *Web site:* http://www.brownmackie.edu/tucson/.

See page 1226 for the College Close-Up.

Chamberlain College of Nursing
Phoenix, Arizona

- **Proprietary** 4-year
- **Coed** 406 undergraduate students, 66% full-time, 84% women, 16% men

Undergraduates 266 full-time, 140 part-time. 8% are from out of state; 5% Black or African American, non-Hispanic/Latino; 11% Hispanic/Latino; 6% Asian, non-Hispanic/Latino; 2% Native Hawaiian or other Pacific Islander, non-Hispanic/Latino; 0.7% American Indian or Alaska Native, non-Hispanic/Latino; 1% Two or more races, non-Hispanic/Latino; 1% Race/ethnicity unknown; 0.2% international; 47% transferred in.
Freshmen *Admission:* 3 enrolled.
Faculty *Total:* 67, 22% full-time. *Student/faculty ratio:* 10:1.
Academics *Calendar:* semesters.
Standardized Tests *Required:* SAT or ACT (for admission).
Freshman Application Contact Admissions, Chamberlain College of Nursing, 2149 West Dunlap Avenue, Phoenix, AZ 85021. *Phone:* 602-331-2720. *Toll-free phone:* 888-556-8CCN. *Web site:* http://www.chamberlain.edu/.

CollegeAmerica–Flagstaff
Flagstaff, Arizona

- **Proprietary** primarily 2-year
- **Coed**
- **Noncompetitive** entrance level

Faculty *Student/faculty ratio:* 33:1.
Academics *Degrees:* associate and bachelor's.
Costs (2011–12) *Tuition:* Tuition cost varies by program. Prospective students should contact the school for current tuition costs.
Freshman Application Contact CollegeAmerica–Flagstaff, 3012 East Route 66, Flagstaff, AZ 86004. *Phone:* 928-213-6060. *Toll-free phone:* 800-622-2894. *Web site:* http://www.collegeamerica.edu/.

College of the Humanities and Sciences, Harrison Middleton University
Tempe, Arizona

- **Independent** comprehensive, founded 1998
- **Suburban** campus with easy access to Phoenix
- **Coed** 79 undergraduate students, 100% full-time, 47% women, 53% men

Undergraduates 79 full-time.
Faculty *Total:* 23, 74% full-time, 43% with terminal degrees.
Academics *Calendar:* continuous. *Degrees:* diplomas, associate, bachelor's, master's, and doctoral. *Special study options:* advanced placement credit, distance learning, double majors, independent study, student-designed majors, summer session for credit.
Costs (2012–13) *One-time required fee:* $400. *Tuition:* $3000 full-time, $250 per credit part-time. *Payment plan:* installment.
Applying *Options:* electronic application. *Application fee:* $50. *Required:* high school transcript, interview. *Required for some:* essay or personal statement, 2 letters of recommendation. *Application deadlines:* rolling (freshmen), rolling (out-of-state freshmen), rolling (transfers). *Notification:* continuous (freshmen), continuous (out-of-state freshmen), continuous (transfers).
Freshman Application Contact College of the Humanities and Sciences, Harrison Middleton University, 1105 East Broadway, Tempe, AZ 85282. *Toll-free phone:* 877-248-6724. *Web site:* http://www.hmu.edu/.

Collins College

Tempe, Arizona

- **Proprietary** 4-year, founded 1978, part of Career Education Corporation
- **Urban** 3-acre campus with easy access to Phoenix
- **Coed**

Academics *Calendar:* trimesters. *Degrees:* associate and bachelor's.

Standardized Tests *Recommended:* SAT and SAT Subject Tests or ACT (for admission).

Financial Aid *Of all full-time matriculated undergraduates who enrolled in 2007,* 935 applied for aid, 935 were judged to have need, 27 had their need fully met. 65 Federal Work-Study jobs (averaging $3000). *In 2007,* 4 non-need-based awards were made. *Average percent of need met:* 65. *Average financial aid package:* $5287. *Average need-based loan:* $3513. *Average need-based gift aid:* $3014. *Average non-need-based aid:* $750.

Applying *Options:* early admission, deferred entrance. *Application fee:* $50. *Required:* high school transcript, interview.

Freshman Application Contact Admissions Department, Collins College, 4750 South 44th Place, Phoenix, AZ 85040. *Phone:* 480-966-3000. *Toll-free phone:* 800-876-7070. *Fax:* 480-966-2599. *E-mail:* contact@collinscollege.edu. *Web site:* http://www.collinscollege.edu/.

DeVry University

Mesa, Arizona

Admissions Office Contact DeVry University, 1201 South Alma School Road, Mesa, AZ 85210-2011. *Toll-free phone:* 866-338-7941. *Web site:* http://www.devry.edu/.

DeVry University

Phoenix, Arizona

- **Proprietary** comprehensive, founded 1967, part of DeVry University
- **Urban** campus
- **Coed** 1,362 undergraduate students, 51% full-time, 30% women, 70% men
- **Minimally difficult** entrance level

Undergraduates 690 full-time, 672 part-time. 5% are from out of state; 6% Black or African American, non-Hispanic/Latino; 26% Hispanic/Latino; 2% Asian, non-Hispanic/Latino; 0.5% Native Hawaiian or other Pacific Islander, non-Hispanic/Latino; 3% American Indian or Alaska Native, non-Hispanic/Latino; 2% Two or more races, non-Hispanic/Latino; 12% Race/ethnicity unknown; 0.7% international; 23% transferred in.

Freshmen *Admission:* 220 enrolled.

Faculty *Total:* 133, 26% full-time. *Student/faculty ratio:* 15:1.

Academics *Calendar:* semesters. *Degrees:* associate, bachelor's, master's, and postbachelor's certificates. *Special study options:* adult/continuing education programs, part-time degree program.

Computers on Campus Students can access the following: online (class) registration.

Student Life *Housing:* college housing not available.

Costs (2011–12) *Tuition:* $15,294 full-time, $597 per credit hour part-time. Full-time tuition and fees vary according to course load. Part-time tuition and fees vary according to course load. *Required fees:* $80 full-time, $40 per term part-time. *Payment plans:* installment, deferred payment. *Waivers:* employees or children of employees.

Financial Aid Of all full-time matriculated undergraduates who enrolled in 2007, 435 applied for aid, 414 were judged to have need, 32 had their need fully met. In 2007, 34 non-need-based awards were made. *Average percent of need met:* 43%. *Average financial aid package:* $13,557. *Average need-based loan:* $8565. *Average need-based gift aid:* $6253. *Average non-need-based aid:* $15,538. *Average indebtedness upon graduation:* $20,667.

Applying *Application fee:* $50. *Required:* high school transcript, interview. *Application deadlines:* rolling (freshmen), rolling (transfers). *Notification:* continuous (freshmen), continuous (transfers).

Freshman Application Contact DeVry University, 2149 West Dunlap Avenue, Phoenix, AZ 85021-2995. *Phone:* 602-870-9222. *Toll-free phone:* 866-338-7941. *Web site:* http://www.devry.edu/.

Dunlap-Stone University

Phoenix, Arizona

Freshman Application Contact Dunlap-Stone University, 11225 North 28th Drive, Suite B-201, Phoenix, AZ 85029. *Phone:* 602-648-5750. *Toll-free phone:* 800-474-8013. *Web site:* http://www.dunlap-stone.edu/.

Embry-Riddle Aeronautical University–Prescott

Prescott, Arizona

- **Independent** comprehensive, founded 1978
- **Small-town** 547-acre campus with easy access to Phoenix
- **Endowment** $62.4 million
- **Coed** 1,672 undergraduate students, 94% full-time, 18% women, 82% men
- **Moderately difficult** entrance level, 82% of applicants were admitted

Undergraduates 1,564 full-time, 108 part-time. Students come from 49 states and territories; 23 other countries; 75% are from out of state; 2% Black or African American, non-Hispanic/Latino; 11% Hispanic/Latino; 5% Asian, non-Hispanic/Latino; 0.4% Native Hawaiian or other Pacific Islander, non-Hispanic/Latino; 1% American Indian or Alaska Native, non-Hispanic/Latino; 4% Two or more races, non-Hispanic/Latino; 7% Race/ethnicity unknown; 4% international; 6% transferred in; 47% live on campus. *Retention:* 78% of full-time freshmen returned.

Freshmen *Admission:* 1,319 applied, 1,086 admitted, 349 enrolled. *Average high school GPA:* 3.55. *Test scores:* SAT critical reading scores over 500: 75%; SAT math scores over 500: 81%; ACT scores over 18: 95%; SAT critical reading scores over 600: 28%; SAT math scores over 600: 43%; ACT scores over 24: 78%; SAT critical reading scores over 700: 4%; SAT math scores over 700: 6%; ACT scores over 30: 19%.

Faculty *Total:* 127, 67% full-time, 57% with terminal degrees. *Student/faculty ratio:* 16:1.

Academics *Calendar:* semesters. *Degrees:* bachelor's and master's. *Special study options:* academic remediation for entering students, accelerated degree program, adult/continuing education programs, advanced placement credit, cooperative education, distance learning, double majors, honors programs, independent study, internships, part-time degree program, services for LD students, student-designed majors, study abroad, summer session for credit. *ROTC:* Army (b), Air Force (b).

Computers on Campus 470 computers/terminals are available on campus for general student use. Students can access the following: campus intranet, computer help desk, free student e-mail accounts, online (class) grades, online (class) registration, online (class) schedules. Campuswide network is available. 100% of college-owned or -operated housing units are wired for high-speed Internet access. Wireless service is available via entire campus.

Student Life *Housing:* on-campus residence required for freshman year. *Options:* coed. Campus housing is university owned. Freshman campus housing is guaranteed. *Activities and organizations:* student-run newspaper, radio station, Hawaii Club, Strike Eagles, Theta XI, American Institute of Aeronautics and Astronautics (AIAA), Arnold Air Society, national fraternities, national sororities. *Campus security:* 24-hour emergency response devices and patrols, student patrols, late-night transport/escort service. *Student services:* health clinic, personal/psychological counseling.

Athletics Member NAIA. *Intercollegiate sports:* golf M(s)/W(s), soccer M(s)/W(s), volleyball W(s), wrestling M(s). *Intramural sports:* basketball M/W, bowling M(c)/W(c), football M/W, racquetball M/W, rock climbing M/W, soccer M/W, softball M/W, table tennis M/W, tennis M/W, ultimate Frisbee M(c)/W(c), volleyball M/W.

Standardized Tests *Required:* SAT or ACT (for admission).

Costs (2012–13) *Comprehensive fee:* $39,760 includes full-time tuition ($29,520), mandatory fees ($900), and room and board ($9340). Part-time tuition: $1230 per credit hour. *College room only:* $5500. Room and board charges vary according to board plan and housing facility. *Payment plans:* installment, deferred payment. *Waivers:* employees or children of employees.

Financial Aid Of all full-time matriculated undergraduates who enrolled in 2011, 1,205 applied for aid, 1,102 were judged to have need. 28 Federal Work-Study jobs (averaging $1527). 454 state and other part-time jobs (averaging $1419). *Average financial aid package:* $16,521. *Average need-based loan:* $5189. *Average need-based gift aid:* $10,661.

Applying *Options:* electronic application, deferred entrance. *Application fee:* $50. *Required:* high school transcript, minimum 2.0 GPA, 2 letters of recommendation, medical examination for flight students. *Required for some:* minimum 3.0 GPA. *Recommended:* essay or personal statement, interview. *Application deadlines:* rolling (freshmen), rolling (transfers). *Notification:* continuous (freshmen), continuous (transfers).

Freshman Application Contact Bryan Dougherty, Director of Admissions, Embry-Riddle Aeronautical University–Prescott, 3700 Willow Creek Road, Prescott, AZ 863013720. *Phone:* 928-777-6600. *Toll-free phone:* 800-888-3728. *Fax:* 928-777-6606. *E-mail:* pradmit@erau.edu. *Web site:* http://www.embryriddle.edu/.

Everest College

Phoenix, Arizona

Freshman Application Contact Mr. Jim Askins, Director of Admissions, Everest College, 10400 North 25th Avenue, Suite 190, Phoenix, AZ 85021. *Phone:* 602-942-4141. *Toll-free phone:* 888-741-4270. *Fax:* 602-943-0960. *E-mail:* jaskins@cci.edu. *Web site:* http://www.everest.edu/.

Everest Online

Tempe, Arizona

Admissions Office Contact Everest Online, 8150 South Hardy Drive #102, Tempe, AZ 85284-1117. *Web site:* http://www.everestonline.edu/.

Grand Canyon University

Phoenix, Arizona

- **Independent Southern Baptist** comprehensive, founded 1949
- **Urban** 100-acre campus with easy access to Phoenix
- **Coed**
- **Moderately difficult** entrance level

Undergraduates 22% Black or African American, non-Hispanic/Latino; 6% Hispanic/Latino; 2% Asian, non-Hispanic/Latino; 0.2% Native Hawaiian or other Pacific Islander, non-Hispanic/Latino; 0.7% American Indian or Alaska Native, non-Hispanic/Latino; 2% Two or more races, non-Hispanic/Latino; 40% Race/ethnicity unknown; 0.1% international; 40% live on campus.

Freshmen *Admission:* 841 admitted.

Academics *Calendar:* semesters. *Degrees:* bachelor's, master's, doctoral, post-master's, and first professional certificates. *Special study options:* academic remediation for entering students, accelerated degree program, adult/continuing education programs, advanced placement credit, cooperative education, distance learning, double majors, English as a second language, freshman honors college, honors programs, independent study, internships, off-campus study, part-time degree program, study abroad, summer session for credit. *ROTC:* Army (b), Air Force (c).

Computers on Campus 65 computers/terminals are available on campus for general student use. Students can access the following: campus intranet, computer help desk, free student e-mail accounts, online (class) grades, online (class) registration, online (class) schedules. Campuswide network is available. 100% of college-owned or -operated housing units are wired for high-speed Internet access. Wireless service is available via classrooms, computer centers, computer labs, dorm rooms, learning centers, libraries, student centers.

Student Life *Housing:* on-campus residence required through sophomore year. *Options:* men-only, women-only, disabled students. Campus housing is university owned and leased by the school. *Activities and organizations:* drama/theater group, choral group, International Student Association, Fellowship of Christian Athletes, Student Nurses Association, Canyon Crazies, AZ Hosa. *Campus security:* 24-hour emergency response devices and patrols, late-night transport/escort service, controlled dormitory access, staffed gates to enter campus after non-business hours. *Student services:* health clinic, personal/psychological counseling.

Athletics Member NCAA. All Division II. *Intercollegiate sports:* baseball M(s), basketball M(s)/W(s), cross-country running M(s)/W(s), golf M(s)/W(s), lacrosse M(c), soccer M(s)/W(s), softball W(s), swimming and diving M(s)/W(s), tennis M(s)/W(s), track and field M(s)/W(s), volleyball M(s)/W(s), wrestling M(s). *Intramural sports:* basketball M/W, football M/W, softball M/W, volleyball M/W.

Standardized Tests *Recommended:* SAT or ACT (for admission).

Costs (2012–13) *Comprehensive fee:* $27,100 includes full-time tuition ($16,500), mandatory fees ($2500), and room and board ($8100). Full-time tuition and fees vary according to course load. Part-time tuition: $688 per credit. Part-time tuition and fees vary according to course load. *College room only:* $4000. Room and board charges vary according to board plan and housing facility. *Payment plan:* installment. *Waivers:* employees or children of employees.

Financial Aid Of all full-time matriculated undergraduates who enrolled in 2007, 1,102 applied for aid, 942 were judged to have need, 155 had their need fully met. *Average financial aid package:* $3371. *Average need-based loan:* $3701. *Average need-based gift aid:* $3360.

Applying *Options:* electronic application, early admission, deferred entrance. *Required:* high school transcript, minimum 2.8 GPA. *Application deadlines:* rolling (freshmen), rolling (transfers). *Notification:* continuous (freshmen), continuous until 9/1 (transfers).

Freshman Application Contact Enrollment, Grand Canyon University, 3300 West Camelback Road, PO Box 11097, Phoenix, AZ 86017-3030. *Phone:* 800-486-7085. *Toll-free phone:* 800-800-9776. *E-mail:* admissionsonline@gcu.edu. *Web site:* http://www.gcu.edu/.

International Baptist College

Chandler, Arizona

Freshman Application Contact Director of Admissions, International Baptist College, 2211 West Germann Road, Chandler, AZ 85286. *Phone:* 480-245-7970. *Toll-free phone:* 800-422-4858. *E-mail:* admissions@ibconline.edu. *Web site:* http://www.ibconline.edu/ibc/.

ITT Technical Institute

Phoenix, Arizona

- **Proprietary** primarily 2-year, founded 1972, part of ITT Educational Services, Inc.
- **Urban** campus
- **Coed**
- **Minimally difficult** entrance level

Academics *Calendar:* quarters. *Degrees:* associate and bachelor's.

Student Life *Housing:* college housing not available.

Financial Aid Of all full-time matriculated undergraduates who enrolled in 2010, 10 Federal Work-Study jobs (averaging $4000).

Freshman Application Contact Director of Recruitment, ITT Technical Institute, 10220 North 25th Avenue, Suite 100, Phoenix, AZ 85021. *Phone:* 602-749-7900. *Toll-free phone:* 877-221-1132. *Web site:* http://www.itt-tech.edu/.

ITT Technical Institute

Phoenix, Arizona

- **Proprietary** primarily 2-year, part of ITT Educational Services, Inc.
- **Coed**

Academics *Calendar:* quarters. *Degrees:* associate and bachelor's.

Freshman Application Contact Director of Recruitment, ITT Technical Institute, 1840 N. 95th Avenue, Suite 132, Phoenix, AZ 85037. *Phone:* 623-474-7900. *Toll-free phone:* 800-210-1178. *Web site:* http://www.itt-tech.edu/.

ITT Technical Institute

Tempe, Arizona

- **Proprietary** 4-year, founded 1963, part of ITT Educational Services, Inc.
- **Coed**
- **Minimally difficult** entrance level

Academics *Degrees:* associate and bachelor's.

Student Life *Housing:* college housing not available.

Freshman Application Contact Director of Recruitment, ITT Technical Institute, 5005 S. Wendler Drive, Tempe, AZ 85282. *Phone:* 602-437-7500. *Toll-free phone:* 800-879-4881. *Web site:* http://www.itt-tech.edu/.

ITT Technical Institute

Tucson, Arizona

- **Proprietary** primarily 2-year, founded 1984, part of ITT Educational Services, Inc.
- **Urban** campus
- **Coed**
- **Minimally difficult** entrance level

Academics *Calendar:* quarters. *Degrees:* associate and bachelor's.

Student Life *Housing:* college housing not available.

Freshman Application Contact Director of Recruitment, ITT Technical Institute, 1455 West River Road, Tucson, AZ 85704. *Phone:* 520-408-7488. *Toll-free phone:* 800-870-9730. *Web site:* http://www.itt-tech.edu/.

Le Cordon Bleu College of Culinary Arts in Scottsdale

Scottsdale, Arizona

Director of Admissions Le Cordon Bleu College of Culinary Arts in Scottsdale, 8100 East Camelback Road, Suite 1001, Scottsdale, AZ 85251-3940. *Toll-free phone:* 888-557-4222. *Web site:* http://www.chefs.edu/SCOTTSDALE.

National Paralegal College

Phoenix, Arizona

Freshman Application Contact Admissions Office, National Paralegal College, 6516 N 7th Street, Suite 103, Phoenix, AZ 85014. *Phone:* 845-371-

9101. *Toll-free phone:* 800-371-6105. *Fax:* 866-347-2744. *E-mail:* info@nationalparalegal.edu. *Web site:* http://nationalparalegal.edu/.

Northcentral University
Prescott Valley, Arizona

- **Proprietary** comprehensive
- **Coed** 480 undergraduate students, 33% full-time, 58% women, 43% men
- **Minimally difficult** entrance level

Undergraduates 156 full-time, 324 part-time. Students come from 45 states and territories; 8 other countries; 3% Black or African American, non-Hispanic/Latino; 0.8% Hispanic/Latino; 0.2% Asian, non-Hispanic/Latino; 0.2% American Indian or Alaska Native, non-Hispanic/Latino; 88% Race/ethnicity unknown.
Freshmen *Admission:* 22 enrolled.
Faculty *Total:* 633, 2% full-time.
Academics *Calendar:* continuous. *Degrees:* certificates, bachelor's, master's, doctoral, post-master's, and first professional certificates (offers only distance learning programs). *Special study options:* accelerated degree program, distance learning, external degree program, services for LD students.
Computers on Campus Students can access the following: campus intranet, computer help desk, online (class) grades, online (class) registration, online (class) schedules. Campuswide network is available.
Costs (2012–13) *Tuition:* $9520 full-time. *Payment plans:* tuition prepayment, installment. *Waivers:* employees or children of employees.
Applying *Options:* electronic application. *Required:* essay or personal statement, high school transcript. *Application deadlines:* rolling (freshmen), rolling (transfers). *Notification:* continuous (freshmen), continuous (transfers).
Freshman Application Contact Northcentral University, 10000 East University Drive, Prescott Valley, AZ 86314. *Phone:* 888-327-2877. *Toll-free phone:* 866-776-0331. *Web site:* http://www.ncu.edu/.

Northern Arizona University
Flagstaff, Arizona

- **State-supported** university, founded 1899, part of Arizona University System, under the Arizona Board of Regents
- **Small-town** 740-acre campus
- **Endowment** $108.9 million
- **Coed** 20,750 undergraduate students, 85% full-time, 58% women, 42% men
- **Moderately difficult** entrance level, 65% of applicants were admitted

Undergraduates 17,610 full-time, 3,140 part-time. Students come from 51 states and territories; 51 other countries; 24% are from out of state; 3% Black or African American, non-Hispanic/Latino; 17% Hispanic/Latino; 2% Asian, non-Hispanic/Latino; 0.4% Native Hawaiian or other Pacific Islander, non-Hispanic/Latino; 4% American Indian or Alaska Native, non-Hispanic/Latino; 3% Two or more races, non-Hispanic/Latino; 0.9% Race/ethnicity unknown; 4% international; 11% transferred in; 32% live on campus. *Retention:* 72% of full-time freshmen returned.
Freshmen *Admission:* 31,995 applied, 20,727 admitted, 3,872 enrolled. *Average high school GPA:* 3.4. *Test scores:* SAT critical reading scores over 500: 67%; SAT math scores over 500: 67%; SAT writing scores over 500: 60%; ACT scores over 18: 89%; SAT critical reading scores over 600: 23%; SAT math scores over 600: 24%; SAT writing scores over 600: 17%; ACT scores over 24: 43%; SAT critical reading scores over 700: 3%; SAT math scores over 700: 2%; SAT writing scores over 700: 1%; ACT scores over 30: 4%.
Faculty *Total:* 1,496, 58% full-time. *Student/faculty ratio:* 20:1.
Academics *Calendar:* semesters. *Degrees:* certificates, bachelor's, master's, doctoral, postbachelor's, and first professional certificates. *Special study options:* accelerated degree program, advanced placement credit, cooperative education, distance learning, double majors, English as a second language, freshman honors college, honors programs, independent study, internships, off-campus study, part-time degree program, services for LD students, study abroad, summer session for credit. *ROTC:* Army (b), Air Force (b).
Computers on Campus 400 computers/terminals are available on campus for general student use. Students can access the following: campus intranet, computer help desk, free student e-mail accounts, online (class) grades, online (class) registration, online (class) schedules. Campuswide network is available. 100% of college-owned or -operated housing units are wired for high-speed Internet access. Wireless service is available via entire campus.
Student Life *Housing options:* coed, men-only, women-only, disabled students. Campus housing is university owned. Freshman campus housing is guaranteed. *Activities and organizations:* drama/theater group, student-run newspaper, radio and television station, choral group, marching band, NAU Jack Pack, Northern Arizona Snow Association, MELT (Minds Expressing Live Thoughts), NAU Hiking Club, Badjacks Dance Club, national fraternities, national sororities. *Campus security:* 24-hour emergency response

devices and patrols, late-night transport/escort service, controlled dormitory access. *Student services:* health clinic, personal/psychological counseling.
Athletics Member NCAA. All Division I. *Intercollegiate sports:* basketball M(s)/W(s), cheerleading M/W, cross-country running M(s)/W(s), football M(s), golf W(s), soccer W(s), swimming and diving W(s), tennis M(s)/W(s), track and field M(s)/W(s), volleyball W(s). *Intramural sports:* archery M(c)/W(c), badminton M(c)/W(c), baseball M(c)/W(c), basketball M/W, bowling M(c)/W(c), football M/W, gymnastics M(c)/W(c), ice hockey M(c)/W(c), lacrosse M(c)/W(c), racquetball M/W, rugby M(c)/W(c), skiing (downhill) M(c)/W(c), soccer M/W, softball M(c)/W(c), tennis M(c)/W(c), ultimate Frisbee M/W, volleyball M/W, water polo M(c)/W(c), weight lifting M/W, wrestling M(c)/W(c).
Standardized Tests *Required for some:* SAT (for admission), ACT (for admission), SAT or ACT (for admission), SAT and SAT Subject Tests or ACT (for admission), SAT Subject Tests (for admission), ACT/SAT test scores required for home-schooled students.
Costs (2011–12) *Tuition:* state resident $8010 full-time, $572 per credit hour part-time; nonresident $20,364 full-time, $849 per credit hour part-time. Full-time tuition and fees vary according to degree level, location, and program. Part-time tuition and fees vary according to course load, degree level, location, and program. No tuition increase for student's term of enrollment. *Required fees:* $820 full-time, $6 per credit hour part-time, $338 per term part-time. *Room and board:* $8474; room only: $4702. Room and board charges vary according to board plan and housing facility. *Payment plan:* installment. *Waivers:* employees or children of employees.
Financial Aid Of all full-time matriculated undergraduates who enrolled in 2010, 12,896 applied for aid, 10,660 were judged to have need, 954 had their need fully met. In 2010, 1998 non-need-based awards were made. *Average percent of need met:* 60%. *Average financial aid package:* $10,057. *Average need-based loan:* $4145. *Average need-based gift aid:* $6771. *Average non-need-based aid:* $4178. *Average indebtedness upon graduation:* $20,602.
Applying *Options:* electronic application, deferred entrance. *Application fee:* $25. *Required:* high school transcript, minimum 3.0 GPA, Completion of 16 required college preparatory courses with minimum 2.0 in each subject area. *Application deadlines:* rolling (freshmen), rolling (out-of-state freshmen), rolling (transfers). *Notification:* continuous (freshmen), continuous (out-of-state freshmen), continuous (transfers).
Freshman Application Contact Undergraduate Admissions, Northern Arizona University, Box 4084, Flagstaff, AZ 86011. *Phone:* 928-523-5511. *Toll-free phone:* 888-MORE-NAU. *Fax:* 928-523-0226. *E-mail:* Admissions@nau.edu. *Web site:* http://www.nau.edu/.

Northern Arizona University–Yuma
Yuma, Arizona

Director of Admissions Eileen Knight, Associate Director of Admissions, Northern Arizona University–Yuma, 2020 South Avenue 8E, PO Box 6236, Yuma, AZ 85365. *Phone:* 928-317-6431. *Toll-free phone:* 888-NAU-Yuma. *E-mail:* eileen.knight@nau.edu. *Web site:* http://www.yuma.nau.edu/.

Penn Foster College
Scottsdale, Arizona

- **Proprietary** 4-year
- **Coed**

Academics *Degrees:* certificates, associate, and bachelor's.
Costs (2011–12) *One-time required fee:* $200. *Tuition:* $90 per credit part-time. Part-time tuition and fees vary according to course load and student level.
Applying *Options:* electronic application. *Application fee:* $75. *Required:* high school transcript.
Freshman Application Contact Admissions, Penn Foster College, 14300 North Northsight Boulevard, Suite 120, Scottsdale, AZ 85260. *Phone:* 480-315-4950. *Toll-free phone:* 800-471-3232. *Web site:* http://www.pennfostercollege.edu/.

Pima Medical Institute
Mesa, Arizona

- **Proprietary** primarily 2-year, founded 1985, part of Vocational Training Institutes, Inc.
- **Urban** campus
- **Coed**
- **Minimally difficult** entrance level

Academics *Calendar:* modular. *Degrees:* certificates, associate, and bachelor's.
Standardized Tests *Required:* Wonderlic aptitude test (for admission).
Applying *Required:* interview. *Required for some:* high school transcript.

Freshman Application Contact Admissions Office, Pima Medical Institute, 957 South Dobson Road, Mesa, AZ 85202. *Phone:* 480-644-0267 Ext. 225. *Toll-free phone:* 800-477-PIMA (in-state); 888-477-PIMA (out-of-state). *Web site:* http://www.pmi.edu/.

Pima Medical Institute
Tucson, Arizona

- **Proprietary** primarily 2-year, founded 1972, part of Vocational Training Institutes, Inc.
- **Urban** campus
- **Coed**
- **Minimally difficult** entrance level

Academics *Calendar:* modular. *Degrees:* certificates, associate, and bachelor's.

Standardized Tests *Required:* Wonderlic Scholastic Level Exam (for admission).

Applying *Options:* early admission. *Required:* interview. *Required for some:* high school transcript.

Freshman Application Contact Admissions Office, Pima Medical Institute, 3350 East Grant Road, Tucson, AZ 85716. *Phone:* 520-326-1600 Ext. 5112. *Toll-free phone:* 800-477-PIMA (in-state); 888-477-PIMA (out-of-state). *Web site:* http://www.pmi.edu/.

Prescott College
Prescott, Arizona

- **Independent** comprehensive, founded 1966
- **Small-town** 14-acre campus
- **Endowment** $844,290
- **Coed** 741 undergraduate students, 80% full-time, 60% women, 40% men
- **Moderately difficult** entrance level, 83% of applicants were admitted

Undergraduates 595 full-time, 146 part-time. Students come from 49 states and territories; 10 other countries; 74% are from out of state; 2% Black or African American, non-Hispanic/Latino; 7% Hispanic/Latino; 0.7% Asian, non-Hispanic/Latino; 0.1% Native Hawaiian or other Pacific Islander, non-Hispanic/Latino; 1% American Indian or Alaska Native, non-Hispanic/Latino; 5% Two or more races, non-Hispanic/Latino; 6% Race/ethnicity unknown; 2% international; 21% transferred in; 4% live on campus. *Retention:* 62% of full-time freshmen returned.

Freshmen *Admission:* 424 applied, 350 admitted, 62 enrolled. *Average high school GPA:* 3.03. *Test scores:* SAT critical reading scores over 500: 83%; SAT writing scores over 500: 83%; ACT scores over 18: 96%; SAT critical reading scores over 600: 52%; SAT writing scores over 600: 28%; ACT scores over 24: 61%; SAT critical reading scores over 700: 10%; SAT writing scores over 700: 3%; ACT scores over 30: 4%.

Faculty *Total:* 90, 83% full-time, 59% with terminal degrees. *Student/faculty ratio:* 9:1.

Academics *Calendar:* quarters (4-week blocks followed by 10-week terms for each quarter). *Degrees:* bachelor's, master's, doctoral, post-master's, post-bachelor's, and first professional certificates. *Special study options:* adult/continuing education programs, advanced placement credit, double majors, external degree program, independent study, internships, off-campus study, services for LD students, student-designed majors, study abroad, summer session for credit.

Computers on Campus 100 computers/terminals and 20 ports are available on campus for general student use. Students can access the following: computer help desk, free student e-mail accounts, Learning Management System (Moodle), free E-portfolios. Campuswide network is available. Wireless service is available via classrooms, computer centers, computer labs, dorm rooms, learning centers, libraries, student centers.

Student Life *Housing:* on-campus residence required for freshman year. *Options:* coed. Campus housing is university owned. Freshman applicants given priority for college housing. *Activities and organizations:* drama/theater group, student-run newspaper, choral group, Student Union, Catalyst, WEB (Women's Empowerment Breakthrough), HUB (Helping Understand Bikes), Aztlan Center. *Campus security:* 24-hour emergency response devices, late-night transport/escort service, controlled dormitory access. *Student services:* personal/psychological counseling.

Standardized Tests *Required:* SAT or ACT (for admission).

Costs (2012–13) *Tuition:* $27,408 full-time, $1142 per credit part-time. Full-time tuition and fees vary according to course load, degree level, and reciprocity agreements. Part-time tuition and fees vary according to course load, degree level, and reciprocity agreements. *Required fees:* $611 full-time, $300 per term part-time. *Room only:* $3400. Room and board charges vary according to board plan and housing facility. *Payment plans:* installment, deferred payment. *Waivers:* employees or children of employees.

Financial Aid Of all full-time matriculated undergraduates who enrolled in 2011, 451 applied for aid, 416 were judged to have need, 19 had their need fully met. In 2011, 115 non-need-based awards were made. *Average percent of need met:* 59%. *Average financial aid package:* $16,909. *Average need-based loan:* $5032. *Average need-based gift aid:* $11,919. *Average non-need-based aid:* $7197. *Average indebtedness upon graduation:* $13,737.

Applying *Options:* electronic application, early decision, deferred entrance. *Application fee:* $25. *Required:* essay or personal statement, high school transcript, 1 letter of recommendation. *Required for some:* interview. *Application deadlines:* 8/15 (freshmen), 8/15 (out-of-state freshmen), 8/15 (transfers). *Early decision deadline:* 12/1. *Notification:* continuous (freshmen), continuous (out-of-state freshmen), continuous (transfers), 12/15 (early decision).

Freshman Application Contact Nancy Simmons, Receptionist, Prescott College, 220 Grove Avenue, Prescott, AZ 86301. *Phone:* 928-350-2100. *Toll-free phone:* 877-350-2100. *Fax:* 928-776-5242. *E-mail:* admissions@prescott.edu. *Web site:* http://www.prescott.edu/.

Southwest University of Visual Arts
Tucson, Arizona

Freshman Application Contact Sarah LaVetter, Director of Admissions, Southwest University of Visual Arts, 2525 North Country Club Road, Tucson, AZ 85716-2505. *Phone:* 520-325-0123. *Toll-free phone:* 800-825-8753. *Fax:* 520-325-5535. *Web site:* http://www.suva.edu/.

University of Advancing Technology
Tempe, Arizona

- **Proprietary** comprehensive, founded 1983
- **Urban** campus
- **Coed, primarily men**

Faculty *Student/faculty ratio:* 14:1.

Academics *Calendar:* semesters. *Degrees:* associate, bachelor's, and master's.

Student Life *Campus security:* 24-hour patrols.

Standardized Tests *Required for some:* SAT or ACT (for admission).

Costs (2011–12) *Comprehensive fee:* $30,560 includes full-time tuition ($19,400), mandatory fees ($100), and room and board ($11,060). *College room only:* $7346. Room and board charges vary according to board plan.

Financial Aid *Of all full-time matriculated undergraduates who enrolled in 2010,* 799 applied for aid, 747 were judged to have need. *Average financial aid package:* $10,343. *Average need-based loan:* $5512. *Average need-based gift aid:* $6767.

Applying *Options:* electronic application. *Required:* essay or personal statement, high school transcript. *Required for some:* minimum 2.5 GPA.

Freshman Application Contact Admissions Office, University of Advancing Technology, 2625 West Baseline Road, Tempe, AZ 85283-1042. *Phone:* 602-383-8228. *Toll-free phone:* 800-658-5744. *Fax:* 602-383-8222. *E-mail:* admissions@uat.edu. *Web site:* http://www.uat.edu/.

The University of Arizona
Tucson, Arizona

- **State-supported** university, founded 1885, part of Arizona Board of Regents
- **Urban** 391-acre campus
- **Endowment** $552.4 million
- **Coed** 30,665 undergraduate students, 89% full-time, 52% women, 48% men
- **Moderately difficult** entrance level, 69% of applicants were admitted

Undergraduates 27,356 full-time, 3,309 part-time. Students come from 111 other countries; 29% are from out of state; 3% Black or African American, non-Hispanic/Latino; 22% Hispanic/Latino; 5% Asian, non-Hispanic/Latino; 0.7% Native Hawaiian or other Pacific Islander, non-Hispanic/Latino; 1% American Indian or Alaska Native, non-Hispanic/Latino; 4% Two or more races, non-Hispanic/Latino; 2% Race/ethnicity unknown; 4% international; 6% transferred in. *Retention:* 77% of full-time freshmen returned.

Freshmen *Admission:* 32,227 applied, 22,116 admitted, 7,300 enrolled. *Average high school GPA:* 3.39. *Test scores:* SAT critical reading scores over 500: 70%; SAT math scores over 500: 74%; SAT writing scores over 500: 68%; ACT scores over 18: 92%; SAT critical reading scores over 600: 29%; SAT math scores over 600: 34%; SAT writing scores over 600: 26%; ACT scores over 24: 51%; SAT critical reading scores over 700: 5%; SAT math scores over 700: 5%; SAT writing scores over 700: 4%; ACT scores over 30: 10%.

Faculty *Total:* 2,021, 76% full-time. *Student/faculty ratio:* 21:1.

Academics *Calendar:* semesters. *Degrees:* bachelor's, master's, doctoral, post-master's, postbachelor's, and first professional certificates. *Special study*

options: accelerated degree program, adult/continuing education programs, advanced placement credit, cooperative education, distance learning, double majors, English as a second language, external degree program, freshman honors college, honors programs, independent study, internships, off-campus study, part-time degree program, services for LD students, student-designed majors, study abroad, summer session for credit. *ROTC:* Army (b), Navy (b), Air Force (b). *Unusual degree programs:* 3-2 business administration with American Graduate School of International Management; engineering; sciences.

Computers on Campus Students can access the following: campus intranet, computer help desk, free student e-mail accounts, online (class) grades, online (class) registration, online (class) schedules. Campuswide network is available. Wireless service is available via classrooms, computer centers, computer labs, dorm rooms, learning centers, libraries, student centers.

Student Life *Housing options:* coed, women-only, disabled students. Campus housing is university owned and leased by the school. Freshman applicants given priority for college housing. *Activities and organizations:* drama/theater group, student-run newspaper, radio and television station, choral group, marching band, national fraternities, national sororities. *Campus security:* 24-hour patrols, student patrols, late-night transport/escort service, emergency telephones. *Student services:* health clinic, personal/psychological counseling, women's center, legal services.

Athletics Member NCAA. All Division I except football (Division I-A). *Intercollegiate sports:* baseball M(s), basketball M(s)/W(s), cross-country running M(s)/W(s), golf M(s)/W(s), gymnastics W(s), ice hockey M(c), lacrosse M(c)/W(c), rugby M(c), soccer M(c)/W(s), softball W(s), swimming and diving M(s)/W(s), tennis M(s)/W(s), track and field M(s)/W(s), volleyball M(c)/W(s). *Intramural sports:* badminton M/W, baseball M, basketball M/W, bowling M/W, cheerleading M/W, cross-country running M/W, equestrian sports M/W, fencing M/W, football M/W, golf M/W, racquetball M/W, rugby M/W, soccer M/W, softball M/W, swimming and diving M/W, table tennis M/W, tennis M/W, track and field M/W, ultimate Frisbee M/W, volleyball M/W, water polo M/W.

Standardized Tests *Recommended:* SAT or ACT (for admission).

Costs (2011–12) *Tuition:* state resident $9286 full-time, $597 per credit hour part-time; nonresident $25,496 full-time, $1024 per credit hour part-time. Full-time tuition and fees vary according to course load, location, program, and student level. Part-time tuition and fees vary according to course load, location, program, and student level. *Required fees:* $922 full-time, $80 per credit hour part-time. *Room and board:* $8540; room only: $5740. Room and board charges vary according to board plan and housing facility. *Waivers:* employees or children of employees.

Financial Aid Of all full-time matriculated undergraduates who enrolled in 2010, 16,572 applied for aid, 13,458 were judged to have need, 1,508 had their need fully met. In 2010, 5620 non-need-based awards were made. *Average percent of need met:* 63%. *Average financial aid package:* $11,903. *Average need-based loan:* $4196. *Average need-based gift aid:* $9767. *Average non-need-based aid:* $6203. *Average indebtedness upon graduation:* $21,247.

Applying *Options:* electronic application, early admission. *Application fee:* $50. *Required:* essay or personal statement, high school transcript. *Required for some:* minimum 3.0 GPA, interview. *Application deadlines:* 5/1 (freshmen), rolling (transfers). *Notification:* continuous (freshmen).

Freshman Application Contact The University of Arizona, Tucson, AZ 85721. *Phone:* 520-621-3087. *Web site:* http://www.arizona.edu/.

University of Phoenix

Phoenix, Arizona

Freshman Application Contact Marc Booker, Sr. Director, Office of Admissions and Evaluation, University of Phoenix, 4035 South Riverpoint Parkway, Mail Stop CF-L101, Phoenix, AZ 85040. *Phone:* 602-557-4609. *Toll-free phone:* 866-766-0766. *Fax:* 480-643-1156. *Web site:* http://www.uopxonline.com/.

University of Phoenix–Phoenix Hohokam Campus

Phoenix, Arizona

Freshman Application Contact Marc Booker, Sr. Director, Office of Admissions and Evaluation, University of Phoenix–Phoenix Hohokam Campus, 4035 South Riverpoint Parkway, Mail Stop CF-L101, Phoenix, AZ

85040. *Phone:* 602-557-4609. *Toll-free phone:* 866-766-0766. *Fax:* 480-643-1156. *Web site:* http://www.phoenix.edu/.

University of Phoenix–Southern Arizona Campus

Tucson, Arizona

Freshman Application Contact Marc Booker, Sr. Director, Office of Admissions and Evaluation, University of Phoenix–Southern Arizona Campus, 4035 South Riverpoint Parkway, Mail Stop CF-L101, Phoenix, AZ 85040-1958. *Phone:* 602-557-4609. *Toll-free phone:* 866-766-0766. *Fax:* 480-643-1156. *Web site:* http://www.phoenix.edu/.

Western International University

Phoenix, Arizona

- **Proprietary** comprehensive, founded 1978, part of Apollo Global and Apollo Group
- **Urban** 4-acre campus with easy access to Phoenix
- **Coed** 2,322 undergraduate students, 100% full-time, 64% women, 36% men
- **Moderately difficult** entrance level

Undergraduates 2,322 full-time. Students come from 59 states and territories; 10 other countries; 17% Black or African American, non-Hispanic/Latino; 12% Hispanic/Latino; 1% Asian, non-Hispanic/Latino; 0.1% Native Hawaiian or other Pacific Islander, non-Hispanic/Latino; 2% American Indian or Alaska Native, non-Hispanic/Latino; 5% Two or more races, non-Hispanic/Latino; 13% Race/ethnicity unknown; 1% international; 0.3% transferred in.

Freshmen *Admission:* 20 enrolled.

Faculty *Total:* 369, 0.5% full-time, 4% with terminal degrees. *Student/faculty ratio:* 24:1.

Academics *Calendar:* continuous. *Degrees:* associate, bachelor's, master's, and postbachelor's certificates. *Special study options:* academic remediation for entering students, accelerated degree program, adult/continuing education programs, advanced placement credit, distance learning, double majors, independent study, part-time degree program, summer session for credit.

Computers on Campus Students can access the following: campus intranet, computer help desk, free student e-mail accounts, online (class) grades, online (class) registration, online (class) schedules. Campuswide network is available. Wireless service is available via entire campus.

Student Life *Housing:* college housing not available. *Campus security:* 24-hour emergency response devices and patrols, late-night transport/escort service.

Costs (2011–12) *One-time required fee:* $25. *Tuition:* $12,900 full-time, $430 per credit hour part-time. Full-time tuition and fees vary according to course level and degree level. Part-time tuition and fees vary according to course level and degree level. *Payment plan:* deferred payment. *Waivers:* employees or children of employees.

Financial Aid *Average financial aid package:* $3321. *Average indebtedness upon graduation:* $5285.

Applying *Options:* electronic application, deferred entrance. *Application fee:* $25. *Required:* high school transcript, minimum 2.5 GPA. *Application deadlines:* rolling (freshmen), rolling (transfers).

Freshman Application Contact Ms. Melissa Machuca, Director of Enrollment, Western International University, 9215 North Black Canyon Highway, Phoenix, AZ 85021-2718. *Phone:* 602-943-2311. *E-mail:* Melissa.Machuca@west.edu. *Web site:* http://www.west.edu.

ARKANSAS

Arkansas Baptist College

Little Rock, Arkansas

Freshman Application Contact Arkansas Baptist College, 1621 Dr. Martin Luther King, Jr. Drive, Little Rock, AR 72202-6067. *Phone:* 501-244-5104 Ext. 5124. *Web site:* http://www.arkansasbaptist.edu/.

Arkansas State University
Jonesboro, Arkansas

- **State-supported** comprehensive, founded 1909, part of Arkansas State University System
- **Small-town** 1376-acre campus with easy access to Memphis
- **Endowment** $39.5 million
- **Coed** 10,113 undergraduate students, 76% full-time, 58% women, 42% men
- **Moderately difficult** entrance level, 63% of applicants were admitted

Undergraduates 7,703 full-time, 2,410 part-time. Students come from 38 states and territories; 47 other countries; 10% are from out of state; 16% Black or African American, non-Hispanic/Latino; 2% Hispanic/Latino; 0.6% Asian, non-Hispanic/Latino; 0.1% Native Hawaiian or other Pacific Islander, non-Hispanic/Latino; 0.4% American Indian or Alaska Native, non-Hispanic/Latino; 1% Two or more races, non-Hispanic/Latino; 3% Race/ethnicity unknown; 5% international; 9% transferred in; 28% live on campus. *Retention:* 71% of full-time freshmen returned.

Freshmen *Admission:* 4,806 applied, 3,040 admitted, 1,562 enrolled. *Average high school GPA:* 3.34. *Test scores:* SAT critical reading scores over 500: 19%; SAT math scores over 500: 48%; SAT writing scores over 500: 32%; ACT scores over 18: 93%; SAT critical reading scores over 600: 3%; SAT math scores over 600: 19%; ACT scores over 24: 42%; SAT math scores over 700: 3%; ACT scores over 30: 5%.

Faculty *Total:* 654, 74% full-time, 55% with terminal degrees. *Student/faculty ratio:* 19:1.

Academics *Calendar:* semesters. *Degrees:* certificates, associate, bachelor's, master's, doctoral, post-master's, postbachelor's, and first professional certificates. *Special study options:* academic remediation for entering students, accelerated degree program, advanced placement credit, distance learning, double majors, English as a second language, honors programs, independent study, internships, off-campus study, part-time degree program, services for LD students, study abroad, summer session for credit. *ROTC:* Army (b).

Computers on Campus 600 computers/terminals and 5,304 ports are available on campus for general student use. Students can access the following: campus intranet, computer help desk, free student e-mail accounts, online (class) grades, online (class) registration, online (class) schedules. Campuswide network is available. 99% of college-owned or -operated housing units are wired for high-speed Internet access. Wireless service is available via entire campus.

Student Life *Housing:* on-campus residence required for freshman year. *Options:* coed, men-only, women-only. Campus housing is university owned. *Activities and organizations:* drama/theater group, student-run newspaper, radio and television station, choral group, marching band, ASU Rugby, Gay Straight Alliance, Student Activities Board, Honors College Association, Student Government Association, national fraternities, national sororities. *Campus security:* 24-hour emergency response devices and patrols, student patrols, late-night transport/escort service, controlled dormitory access, check-in desk; video surveillance cameras. *Student services:* health clinic, personal/psychological counseling.

Athletics Member NCAA. All Division I except football (Division I-A). *Intercollegiate sports:* baseball M(s), basketball M(s)/W(s), bowling W(s), cross-country running M(s)/W(s), golf M(s)/W(s), soccer W(s), tennis W(s), track and field M(s)/W(s), volleyball W(s). *Intramural sports:* badminton M/W, basketball M/W, bowling M/W, football M/W, rugby M(c), soccer M/W, softball M/W, table tennis M/W, tennis M/W, track and field M/W, ultimate Frisbee M/W, volleyball M/W.

Standardized Tests *Required:* SAT or ACT (for admission). *Required for some:* ACT ASSET; ACT COMPASS; TOEFL, IELTS, PTE or Proof of English Proficiency for international students. *Recommended:* ACT (for admission).

Costs (2011–12) *Tuition:* state resident $5304 full-time, $177 per credit hour part-time; nonresident $13,854 full-time, $462 per credit hour part-time. Full-time tuition and fees vary according to course load, location, and program. Part-time tuition and fees vary according to course load, location, and program. *Required fees:* $1630 full-time, $52 per credit hour part-time, $25 per term part-time. *Room and board:* $6920. Room and board charges vary according to board plan, housing facility, and student level. *Payment plan:* installment. *Waivers:* senior citizens and employees or children of employees.

Financial Aid Of all full-time matriculated undergraduates who enrolled in 2011, 7,250 applied for aid, 5,945 were judged to have need, 1,510 had their need fully met. 109 Federal Work-Study jobs (averaging $3320). 300 state and other part-time jobs (averaging $3500). In 2011, 665 non-need-based awards were made. *Average percent of need met:* 50%. *Average financial aid package:* $12,400. *Average need-based loan:* $8700. *Average need-based gift aid:* $6000. *Average non-need-based aid:* $6600. *Average indebtedness upon graduation:* $20,000. *Financial aid deadline:* 7/1.

Applying *Options:* electronic application, early admission. *Application fee:* $15. *Required:* high school transcript, minimum 2.5 GPA, For Fall 2012, ACT composite score of 21 plus a 2.5 high school GPA, immunization, selective service. *Application deadlines:* rolling (freshmen), rolling (transfers). *Notification:* continuous (freshmen), continuous (transfers).

Freshman Application Contact Ms. Tammy Fowler, Director of Admissions, Arkansas State University, PO Box 1630, State University, AR 72467. *Phone:* 870-972-3024. *Toll-free phone:* 800-382-3030. *Fax:* 870-972-3406. *E-mail:* admissions@astate.edu. *Web site:* http://www.astate.edu/.

Arkansas Tech University
Russellville, Arkansas

- **State-supported** comprehensive, founded 1909
- **Small-town** 559-acre campus
- **Endowment** $17.3 million
- **Coed** 9,710 undergraduate students, 72% full-time, 55% women, 45% men
- **Moderately difficult** entrance level, 90% of applicants were admitted

Undergraduates 7,015 full-time, 2,695 part-time. Students come from 44 states and territories; 35 other countries; 5% are from out of state; 6% Black or African American, non-Hispanic/Latino; 4% Hispanic/Latino; 2% Asian, non-Hispanic/Latino; 0.1% Native Hawaiian or other Pacific Islander, non-Hispanic/Latino; 2% American Indian or Alaska Native, non-Hispanic/Latino; 1% Two or more races, non-Hispanic/Latino; 2% international; 6% transferred in; 31% live on campus. *Retention:* 74% of full-time freshmen returned.

Freshmen *Admission:* 3,741 applied, 3,380 admitted, 1,860 enrolled. *Average high school GPA:* 3.15. *Test scores:* SAT critical reading scores over 500: 8%; SAT math scores over 500: 46%; ACT scores over 18: 84%; SAT critical reading scores over 600: 8%; SAT math scores over 600: 15%; ACT scores over 24: 38%; SAT math scores over 700: 8%; ACT scores over 30: 3%.

Faculty *Total:* 496, 62% full-time, 43% with terminal degrees. *Student/faculty ratio:* 17:1.

Academics *Calendar:* semesters. *Degrees:* certificates, associate, bachelor's, master's, and post-master's certificates. *Special study options:* academic remediation for entering students, accelerated degree program, adult/continuing education programs, advanced placement credit, distance learning, double majors, English as a second language, honors programs, independent study, internships, off-campus study, part-time degree program, services for LD students, study abroad, summer session for credit. *ROTC:* Army (c).

Computers on Campus 1,124 computers/terminals are available on campus for general student use. Students can access the following: campus intranet, computer help desk, free student e-mail accounts, online (class) grades, online (class) registration, online (class) schedules. Campuswide network is available. 100% of college-owned or -operated housing units are wired for high-speed Internet access. Wireless service is available via classrooms, computer centers, computer labs, dorm rooms, learning centers, libraries, student centers.

Student Life *Housing:* on-campus residence required through sophomore year. *Options:* coed, men-only, women-only, cooperative, disabled students. Campus housing is university owned. Freshman campus housing is guaranteed. *Activities and organizations:* drama/theater group, student-run newspaper, radio and television station, choral group, marching band, national fraternities, national sororities. *Campus security:* 24-hour emergency response devices and patrols, student patrols, late-night transport/escort service, controlled dormitory access. *Student services:* health clinic, personal/psychological counseling.

Athletics Member NCAA. All Division II. *Intercollegiate sports:* baseball M(s), basketball M(s)/W(s), cheerleading M(s)/W(s), cross-country running W(s), football M(s), golf M(s)/W(s), softball W(s), tennis W(s), volleyball W(s). *Intramural sports:* basketball M/W, bowling M/W, football M/W, racquetball M/W, soccer M/W, softball M/W, table tennis M/W, tennis M/W, ultimate Frisbee M/W, volleyball M/W.

Standardized Tests *Required:* SAT or ACT (for admission).

Costs (2011–12) *Tuition:* state resident $5400 full-time, $180 per credit hour part-time; nonresident $10,800 full-time, $360 per credit hour part-time. Full-time tuition and fees vary according to course load and location. Part-time tuition and fees vary according to course load and location. *Required fees:* $858 full-time, $18 per credit hour part-time, $87 per term part-time. *Room and board:* $5456; room only: $3266. Room and board charges vary according to board plan, housing facility, and location. *Payment plans:* installment, deferred payment. *Waivers:* senior citizens and employees or children of employees.

Financial Aid Of all full-time matriculated undergraduates who enrolled in 2010, 6,195 applied for aid, 4,744 were judged to have need, 1,040 had their need fully met. In 2010, 828 non-need-based awards were made. *Average percent of need met:* 73%. *Average financial aid package:* $9526. *Average need-based loan:* $3649. *Average need-based gift aid:* $5306. *Average non-need-based aid:* $6623. *Average indebtedness upon graduation:* $20,264.

Applying *Options:* electronic application, early action, deferred entrance. *Required:* high school transcript, minimum 2.0 GPA. *Notification:* continuous (freshmen), continuous (transfers).

Freshman Application Contact Ms. Shauna Donnell, Director of Enrollment Management, Arkansas Tech University, Doc Bryan Student Services Building, Suite 141, Russellville, AR 72801. *Phone:* 479-968-0343. *Toll-free phone:* 800-582-6953. *Fax:* 479-964-0522. *E-mail:* tech.enroll@atu.edu. *Web site:* http://www.atu.edu/.

Central Baptist College
Conway, Arkansas

Freshman Application Contact Ms. Rachel Waymire, Admissions Counselor, Central Baptist College, 1501 College Avenue, Conway, AR 72034. *Phone:* 501-329-6872 Ext. 197. *Toll-free phone:* 800-205-6872. *Fax:* 501-329-2941. *E-mail:* rwaymire@cbc.edu. *Web site:* http://www.cbc.edu/.

Ecclesia College
Springdale, Arkansas

Freshman Application Contact Ecclesia College, 9653 Nations Drive, Springdale, AR 72762. *Phone:* 479-248-7236 Ext. 223. *Web site:* http://www.ecollege.edu/.

Harding University
Searcy, Arkansas

- **Independent** university, founded 1924, affiliated with Church of Christ
- **Small-town** 350-acre campus with easy access to Little Rock
- **Endowment** $101.9 million
- **Coed** 4,304 undergraduate students, 94% full-time, 53% women, 47% men
- **Moderately difficult** entrance level, 72% of applicants were admitted

Undergraduates 4,041 full-time, 263 part-time. Students come from 50 states and territories; 51 other countries; 71% are from out of state; 4% Black or African American, non-Hispanic/Latino; 3% Hispanic/Latino; 0.6% Asian, non-Hispanic/Latino; 0.1% Native Hawaiian or other Pacific Islander, non-Hispanic/Latino; 0.5% American Indian or Alaska Native, non-Hispanic/Latino; 2% Two or more races, non-Hispanic/Latino; 0.4% Race/ethnicity unknown; 7% international; 6% transferred in; 77% live on campus. *Retention:* 81% of full-time freshmen returned.

Freshmen *Admission:* 2,121 applied, 1,531 admitted, 1,013 enrolled. *Average high school GPA:* 3.51. *Test scores:* SAT critical reading scores over 500: 79%; SAT math scores over 500: 77%; ACT scores over 18: 95%; SAT critical reading scores over 600: 35%; SAT math scores over 600: 40%; ACT scores over 24: 58%; SAT critical reading scores over 700: 10%; SAT math scores over 700: 10%; ACT scores over 30: 16%.

Faculty *Total:* 485, 54% full-time, 52% with terminal degrees. *Student/faculty ratio:* 17:1.

Academics *Calendar:* semesters. *Degrees:* bachelor's, master's, doctoral, post-master's, and first professional certificates. *Special study options:* academic remediation for entering students, accelerated degree program, adult/continuing education programs, advanced placement credit, cooperative education, distance learning, double majors, English as a second language, freshman honors college, honors programs, independent study, internships, part-time degree program, services for LD students, student-designed majors, study abroad, summer session for credit.

Computers on Campus 482 computers/terminals and 2,400 ports are available on campus for general student use. Students can access the following: campus intranet, computer help desk, free student e-mail accounts, online (class) grades, online (class) registration, online (class) schedules. Campus-wide network is available. 100% of college-owned or -operated housing units are wired for high-speed Internet access. Wireless service is available via entire campus.

Student Life *Housing:* on-campus residence required through senior year. *Options:* men-only, women-only, disabled students. Campus housing is university owned. Freshman campus housing is guaranteed. *Activities and organizations:* drama/theater group, student-run newspaper, radio and television station, choral group, marching band, Bisons for Christ, Harding in Action, Spring Break Campaigns, HUmanity. *Campus security:* 24-hour emergency response devices and patrols, student patrols, late-night transport/escort service, controlled dormitory access. *Student services:* health clinic, personal/psychological counseling.

Athletics Member NCAA. All Division II. *Intercollegiate sports:* baseball M(s), basketball M(s)/W(s), cheerleading W, cross-country running M(s)/W(s), football M(s), golf M(s)/W(s), lacrosse M(c), rugby M(c), soccer M(s)/W(s), tennis M(s)/W(s), track and field M(s)/W(s), ultimate Frisbee M(c)/W(c), volleyball W(s). *Intramural sports:* basketball M/W, cross-country running M/W, football M/W, golf M/W, racquetball M/W, soccer M/W, softball M/W, swimming and diving M/W, table tennis M/W, tennis M/W, track and field M/W, ultimate Frisbee M/W, volleyball M/W, weight lifting M/W.

Standardized Tests *Required:* SAT or ACT (for admission).

Costs (2011–12) *Comprehensive fee:* $20,640 includes full-time tuition ($14,160), mandatory fees ($450), and room and board ($6030). Full-time tuition and fees vary according to course load. Part-time tuition: $472 per credit hour. Part-time tuition and fees vary according to course load. *Required fees:* $23 per credit hour part-time. *College room only:* $2988. Room and board charges vary according to board plan and housing facility. *Payment plans:* tuition prepayment, installment. *Waivers:* senior citizens and employees or children of employees.

Financial Aid Of all full-time matriculated undergraduates who enrolled in 2010, 3,017 applied for aid, 2,405 were judged to have need, 625 had their need fully met. 388 Federal Work-Study jobs (averaging $1112). 1,388 state and other part-time jobs (averaging $1540). In 2010, 497 non-need-based awards were made. *Average percent of need met:* 70%. *Average financial aid package:* $13,059. *Average need-based loan:* $4819. *Average need-based gift aid:* $8493. *Average non-need-based aid:* $5592. *Average indebtedness upon graduation:* $31,706.

Applying *Options:* electronic application, early admission, early action, deferred entrance. *Application fee:* $40. *Required:* essay or personal statement, high school transcript, 2 letters of recommendation. *Application deadlines:* rolling (freshmen), rolling (out-of-state freshmen), rolling (transfers). *Notification:* continuous (freshmen), continuous (out-of-state freshmen), continuous (transfers).

Freshman Application Contact Mr. Glenn Dillard, Assistant Vice President for Enrollment Management, Harding University, Box 12255, Searcy, AR 72149-2255. *Phone:* 501-279-4407. *Toll-free phone:* 800-477-4407. *Fax:* 501-279-4129. *E-mail:* admissions@harding.edu. *Web site:* http://www.harding.edu/.

See next page for display ad and page 1356 for the College Close-Up.

Henderson State University
Arkadelphia, Arkansas

- **State-supported** comprehensive, founded 1890
- **Small-town** 151-acre campus with easy access to Little Rock
- **Endowment** $12.3 million
- **Coed**
- **Moderately difficult** entrance level

Faculty *Student/faculty ratio:* 17:1.

Academics *Calendar:* semesters. *Degrees:* certificates, associate, bachelor's, master's, and postbachelor's certificates.

Student Life *Campus security:* 24-hour emergency response devices and patrols, controlled dormitory access.

Athletics Member NCAA. All Division II.

Standardized Tests *Required:* SAT or ACT (for admission). *Recommended:* ACT (for admission).

Costs (2011–12) *Tuition:* state resident $5610 full-time, $187 per credit hour part-time; nonresident $11,220 full-time, $374 per credit hour part-time. Full-time tuition and fees vary according to course level, course load, degree level, and student level. Part-time tuition and fees vary according to course level, course load, degree level, and student level. *Required fees:* $1104 full-time. *Room and board:* $5084. Room and board charges vary according to board plan and housing facility.

Financial Aid Of all full-time matriculated undergraduates who enrolled in 2009, 3,026 applied for aid, 2,535 were judged to have need, 24 had their need fully met. In 2009, 95 non-need-based awards were made. *Average percent of need met:* 83. *Average financial aid package:* $10,648. *Average need-based loan:* $3984. *Average need-based gift aid:* $11,908. *Average non-need-based aid:* $9096. *Average indebtedness upon graduation:* $16,529.

Applying *Options:* electronic application, deferred entrance. *Required:* high school transcript. *Required for some:* essay or personal statement, 3 letters of recommendation. *Recommended:* minimum 2.5 GPA.

Freshman Application Contact Ms. Vikita Hardwrick, Director of University Relations/Admissions, Henderson State University, 1100 Henderson Street, PO Box 7560, Arkadelphia, AR 71999-0001. *Phone:* 870-230-5028. *Toll-free phone:* 800-228-7333. *Fax:* 870-230-5066. *E-mail:* hardwrv@hsu.edu. *Web site:* http://www.hsu.edu/.

Hendrix College

Conway, Arkansas

- **Independent United Methodist** comprehensive, founded 1876
- **Suburban** 180-acre campus with easy access to Little Rock
- **Endowment** $170.6 million
- **Coed** 1,415 undergraduate students, 99% full-time, 58% women, 42% men
- **Very difficult** entrance level, 83% of applicants were admitted

Undergraduates 1,402 full-time, 13 part-time. Students come from 43 states and territories; 14 other countries; 53% are from out of state; 3% Black or African American, non-Hispanic/Latino; 5% Hispanic/Latino; 3% Asian, non-Hispanic/Latino; 0.5% American Indian or Alaska Native, non-Hispanic/Latino; 2% Two or more races, non-Hispanic/Latino; 7% Race/ethnicity unknown; 4% international; 1% transferred in; 86% live on campus. *Retention:* 80% of full-time freshmen returned.

Freshmen *Admission:* 1,528 applied, 1,261 admitted, 375 enrolled. *Average high school GPA:* 3.94. *Test scores:* SAT critical reading scores over 500: 94%; SAT math scores over 500: 92%; ACT scores over 18: 100%; SAT critical reading scores over 600: 64%; SAT math scores over 600: 58%; ACT scores over 24: 92%; SAT critical reading scores over 700: 21%; SAT math scores over 700: 17%; ACT scores over 30: 48%.

Faculty *Total:* 139, 78% full-time, 82% with terminal degrees. *Student/faculty ratio:* 12:1.

Academics *Calendar:* semesters. *Degrees:* bachelor's and master's. *Special study options:* advanced placement credit, cooperative education, double majors, English as a second language, independent study, internships, off-campus study, services for LD students, student-designed majors, study abroad. *ROTC:* Army (c). *Unusual degree programs:* 3-2 engineering with Columbia University, Vanderbilt University, Washington University in St. Louis; public health BA/MPH with University of Arkansas Medical School.

Computers on Campus 75 computers/terminals are available on campus for general student use. Students can access the following: campus intranet, computer help desk, free student e-mail accounts, online (class) grades, online (class) registration, online (class) schedules. Campuswide network is available. 100% of college-owned or -operated housing units are wired for high-speed Internet access. Wireless service is available via entire campus.

Student Life *Housing:* on-campus residence required through senior year. *Options:* coed, men-only, women-only. Campus housing is university owned. Freshman campus housing is guaranteed. *Activities and organizations:* drama/theater group, student-run newspaper, radio station, choral group, Volunteer Action Center, student government, Music ensembles, Multicultural Development Committee, Social Committee. *Campus security:* 24-hour emergency response devices and patrols, late-night transport/escort service, controlled dormitory access. *Student services:* health clinic, personal/psychological counseling.

Athletics Member NCAA. All Division III. *Intercollegiate sports:* baseball M, basketball M/W, cross-country running M/W, field hockey W, golf M/W, lacrosse M, soccer M/W, softball W, swimming and diving M/W, tennis M/W, track and field M/W, volleyball W. *Intramural sports:* basketball M/W, cheerleading M/W, football M/W, racquetball M/W, soccer M/W, softball M/W, table tennis M/W, tennis M/W, ultimate Frisbee M/W.

Standardized Tests *Required:* SAT or ACT (for admission).

Costs (2011–12) *Comprehensive fee:* $43,944 includes full-time tuition ($33,930), mandatory fees ($300), and room and board ($9714). Full-time tuition and fees vary according to course load. Part-time tuition: $4279 per course. Part-time tuition and fees vary according to course load. *College room only:* $4968. Room and board charges vary according to board plan and housing facility. *Payment plan:* installment. *Waivers:* employees or children of employees.

Financial Aid Of all full-time matriculated undergraduates who enrolled in 2011, 1,151 applied for aid, 875 were judged to have need, 354 had their need fully met. 522 Federal Work-Study jobs (averaging $1429). 269 state and other part-time jobs (averaging $1487). In 2011, 531 non-need-based awards were made. *Average percent of need met:* 83%. *Average financial aid package:* $26,323. *Average need-based loan:* $4440. *Average need-based gift aid:* $22,545. *Average non-need-based aid:* $18,631. *Average indebtedness upon graduation:* $24,388.

Applying *Options:* electronic application, early action. *Application fee:* $40. *Required:* essay or personal statement, high school transcript. *Required for some:* interview. *Recommended:* 1 letter of recommendation. *Application deadlines:* 6/1 (freshmen), 7/1 (transfers). *Notification:* continuous (freshmen), 4/30 (out-of-state freshmen), continuous (transfers).

Freshman Application Contact Mr. Fred Baker, Interim Director of Admission, Hendrix College, 1600 Washington Avenue, Conway, AR 72032. *Phone:* 501-450-1362. *Toll-free phone:* 800-277-9017. *Fax:* 501-450-3843. *E-mail:* baker@hendrix.edu. *Web site:* http://www.hendrix.edu/.

ITT Technical Institute

Little Rock, Arkansas

- **Proprietary** primarily 2-year, founded 1993, part of ITT Educational Services, Inc.
- **Urban** campus
- **Coed**
- **Minimally difficult** entrance level

Academics *Calendar:* quarters. *Degrees:* associate and bachelor's.
Student Life *Housing:* college housing not available.
Freshman Application Contact Director of Recruitment, ITT Technical Institute, 12200 Westhaven Drive, Little Rock, AR 72211. *Phone:* 501-565-5550. *Toll-free phone:* 800-359-4429. *Web site:* http://www.itt-tech.edu/.

John Brown University

Siloam Springs, Arkansas

- **Independent interdenominational** comprehensive, founded 1919
- **Small-town** 200-acre campus
- **Coed** 1,551 undergraduate students, 80% full-time, 54% women, 46% men
- **Moderately difficult** entrance level, 70% of applicants were admitted

Undergraduates 1,236 full-time, 315 part-time. Students come from 41 states and territories; 44 other countries; 71% are from out of state; 2% Black or African American, non-Hispanic/Latino; 4% Hispanic/Latino; 0.9% Asian, non-Hispanic/Latino; 1% American Indian or Alaska Native, non-Hispanic/Latino; 3% Two or more races, non-Hispanic/Latino; 4% Race/ethnicity unknown; 7% international; 4% transferred in; 68% live on campus. *Retention:* 78% of full-time freshmen returned.
Freshmen *Admission:* 1,093 applied, 765 admitted, 360 enrolled. *Average high school GPA:* 3.62. *Test scores:* SAT critical reading scores over 500: 82%; SAT math scores over 500: 79%; SAT writing scores over 500: 74%; ACT scores over 18: 97%; SAT critical reading scores over 600: 46%; SAT math scores over 600: 41%; SAT writing scores over 600: 41%; ACT scores over 24: 64%; SAT critical reading scores over 700: 21%; SAT math scores over 700: 5%; SAT writing scores over 700: 12%; ACT scores over 30: 18%.
Faculty *Total:* 123, 55% full-time, 47% with terminal degrees. *Student/faculty ratio:* 14:1.
Academics *Calendar:* semesters. *Degrees:* associate, bachelor's, and master's. *Special study options:* accelerated degree program, adult/continuing education programs, distance learning, double majors, English as a second language, external degree program, honors programs, independent study, internships, services for LD students, study abroad. *ROTC:* Army (c), Air Force (c).
Computers on Campus 100 computers/terminals are available on campus for general student use. Students can access the following: campus intranet, computer help desk, free student e-mail accounts, online (class) grades, online (class) registration, online (class) schedules. Campuswide network is available. 100% of college-owned or -operated housing units are wired for high-speed Internet access. Wireless service is available via classrooms, dorm rooms, learning centers, libraries, student centers.
Student Life *Housing:* on-campus residence required through junior year. *Options:* coed, men-only, women-only, disabled students. Campus housing is university owned. Freshman campus housing is guaranteed. *Activities and organizations:* drama/theater group, student-run newspaper, radio station, choral group, Student Government Association, Student Ministries Organization, Student Activities Club, Student Missionary Fellowship. *Campus security:* 24-hour emergency response devices and patrols, late-night transport/escort service, controlled dormitory access. *Student services:* health clinic, personal/psychological counseling.
Athletics Member NAIA. *Intercollegiate sports:* basketball M(s)/W(s), cheerleading M(s)/W(s), cross-country running M(s)/W(s), golf M(s), soccer M(s)/W(s), tennis M(s)/W(s), volleyball W(s). *Intramural sports:* baseball M, basketball M/W, football M/W, golf M, racquetball M/W, rugby M, soccer M/W, softball M/W, table tennis M/W, tennis M/W, ultimate Frisbee M/W, volleyball M/W.
Standardized Tests *Required:* SAT or ACT (for admission).
Costs (2011–12) *Comprehensive fee:* $28,328 includes full-time tuition ($19,834), mandatory fees ($932), and room and board ($7562). Full-time tuition and fees vary according to course load. Part-time tuition: $628 per credit. Part-time tuition and fees vary according to course load. *Room and board:* Room and board charges vary according to board plan and housing facility. *Payment plan:* installment. *Waivers:* employees or children of employees.
Financial Aid Of all full-time matriculated undergraduates who enrolled in 2011, 1,002 applied for aid, 891 were judged to have need, 159 had their need fully met. In 2011, 311 non-need-based awards were made. *Average percent of need met:* 82%. *Average financial aid package:* $18,335. *Average need-*

based loan: $2758. *Average need-based gift aid:* $14,234. *Average non-need-based aid:* $13,524. *Average indebtedness upon graduation:* $29,899.
Applying *Options:* electronic application, deferred entrance. *Application fee:* $25. *Required:* essay or personal statement, high school transcript, minimum 2.5 GPA, 2 letters of recommendation. *Recommended:* interview. *Application deadlines:* rolling (freshmen), rolling (transfers). *Notification:* continuous (freshmen), continuous (transfers).
Freshman Application Contact Mr. Jared Burgess, Director of Visitation Program, John Brown University, 2000 West University, Siloam Springs, AR 72761. *Phone:* 479-524-7190. *Toll-free phone:* 877-JBU-INFO. *Fax:* 479-524-4196. *E-mail:* JBurgess@jbu.edu. *Web site:* http://www.jbu.edu/.

Lyon College

Batesville, Arkansas

- **Independent Presbyterian** 4-year, founded 1872
- **Small-town** 136-acre campus
- **Endowment** $39.5 million
- **Coed** 600 undergraduate students, 95% full-time, 54% women, 47% men
- **Moderately difficult** entrance level, 62% of applicants were admitted

Undergraduates 571 full-time, 29 part-time. Students come from 25 states and territories; 7 other countries; 24% are from out of state; 4% Black or African American, non-Hispanic/Latino; 5% Hispanic/Latino; 2% Asian, non-Hispanic/Latino; 8% American Indian or Alaska Native, non-Hispanic/Latino; 6% Race/ethnicity unknown; 3% international; 11% transferred in; 78% live on campus. *Retention:* 61% of full-time freshmen returned.
Freshmen *Admission:* 971 applied, 605 admitted, 158 enrolled. *Average high school GPA:* 3.6. *Test scores:* SAT critical reading scores over 500: 72%; SAT math scores over 500: 78%; SAT writing scores over 500: 84%; ACT scores over 18: 99%; SAT critical reading scores over 600: 50%; SAT math scores over 600: 34%; SAT writing scores over 600: 17%; ACT scores over 24: 67%; SAT critical reading scores over 700: 6%; SAT math scores over 700: 6%; ACT scores over 30: 19%.
Faculty *Total:* 70, 60% full-time. *Student/faculty ratio:* 11:1.
Academics *Calendar:* semesters. *Degree:* bachelor's. *Special study options:* accelerated degree program, advanced placement credit, double majors, independent study, internships, off-campus study, part-time degree program, student-designed majors, study abroad, summer session for credit. *Unusual degree programs:* 3-2 engineering with University of Missouri-Rolla, University of Arkansas, University of Minnesota.
Computers on Campus 101 computers/terminals are available on campus for general student use. Students can access the following: campus intranet, computer help desk, free student e-mail accounts, online (class) grades, online (class) registration, online (class) schedules. Campuswide network is available. 100% of college-owned or -operated housing units are wired for high-speed Internet access. Wireless service is available via entire campus.
Student Life *Housing:* on-campus residence required through junior year. *Options:* coed, men-only, women-only. Campus housing is university owned. *Activities and organizations:* drama/theater group, student-run newspaper, choral group, Wesley Fellowship, Gay-Straight Alliance, Alpha Xi Delta Sorority, Fellowship of Christian Athletes, Young Democrats/Japanese Culture Club, national fraternities, national sororities. *Campus security:* 24-hour patrols, late-night transport/escort service, controlled dormitory access. *Student services:* health clinic, personal/psychological counseling.
Athletics Member NAIA. *Intercollegiate sports:* baseball M(s), basketball M(s)/W(s), cross-country running M(s)/W(s), golf M(s)/W(s), soccer M(s)/W(s), softball W(s), volleyball W(s). *Intramural sports:* badminton M/W, basketball M/W, football M/W, softball M/W, table tennis M/W, tennis M/W, ultimate Frisbee M/W, volleyball M/W.
Standardized Tests *Required:* SAT or ACT (for admission).
Costs (2011–12) *Comprehensive fee:* $30,246 includes full-time tuition ($22,682), mandatory fees ($224), and room and board ($7340). Part-time tuition: $760 per credit hour. *Room and board:* Room and board charges vary according to board plan and housing facility. *Payment plan:* installment. *Waivers:* employees or children of employees.
Financial Aid Of all full-time matriculated undergraduates who enrolled in 2011, 500 applied for aid, 445 were judged to have need, 88 had their need fully met. 190 Federal Work-Study jobs (averaging $957). 6 state and other part-time jobs (averaging $1034). In 2011, 82 non-need-based awards were made. *Average percent of need met:* 79%. *Average financial aid package:* $21,065. *Average need-based loan:* $4064. *Average need-based gift aid:* $17,532. *Average non-need-based aid:* $11,613. *Average indebtedness upon graduation:* $17,092.
Applying *Options:* electronic application, early admission, early action, deferred entrance. *Application fee:* $25. *Required:* high school transcript, minimum 2.5 GPA. *Required for some:* essay or personal statement, 2 letters of recommendation. *Application deadlines:* rolling (freshmen), rolling (transfers). *Notification:* continuous (freshmen), continuous (transfers).

Freshman Application Contact Office of Enrollment Services, Lyon College, 2300 Highland Road, Batesville, AR 72501. *Phone:* 870-307-7250. *Toll-free phone:* 800-423-2542. *Fax:* 870-307-7542. *E-mail:* admissions@lyon.edu. *Web site:* http://www.lyon.edu/.

Ouachita Baptist University
Arkadelphia, Arkansas
- **Independent Baptist** 4-year, founded 1886
- **Small-town** 200-acre campus with easy access to Little Rock
- **Endowment** $81.3 million
- **Coed** 1,594 undergraduate students, 98% full-time, 53% women, 47% men
- **Moderately difficult** entrance level, 64% of applicants were admitted

Undergraduates 1,559 full-time, 35 part-time. Students come from 35 states and territories; 46 other countries; 44% are from out of state; 6% Black or African American, non-Hispanic/Latino; 3% Hispanic/Latino; 0.6% Asian, non-Hispanic/Latino; 0.1% Native Hawaiian or other Pacific Islander, non-Hispanic/Latino; 1% American Indian or Alaska Native, non-Hispanic/Latino; 0.1% Two or more races, non-Hispanic/Latino; 3% international; 3% transferred in; 94% live on campus. *Retention:* 82% of full-time freshmen returned.
Freshmen *Admission:* 1,953 applied, 1,245 admitted, 459 enrolled. *Average high school GPA:* 3.54. *Test scores:* SAT critical reading scores over 500: 65%; SAT math scores over 500: 78%; ACT scores over 18: 96%; SAT critical reading scores over 600: 26%; SAT math scores over 600: 28%; ACT scores over 24: 55%; SAT critical reading scores over 700: 4%; SAT math scores over 700: 2%; ACT scores over 30: 10%.
Faculty *Total:* 158, 68% full-time, 63% with terminal degrees. *Student/faculty ratio:* 13:1.
Academics *Calendar:* semesters. *Degree:* bachelor's. *Special study options:* academic remediation for entering students, accelerated degree program, advanced placement credit, cooperative education, distance learning, double majors, English as a second language, honors programs, independent study, internships, off-campus study, part-time degree program, study abroad, summer session for credit. *ROTC:* Army (b). *Unusual degree programs:* 3-2 engineering with University of Arkansas at Fayetteville.
Computers on Campus 275 computers/terminals and 1,350 ports are available on campus for general student use. Students can access the following: campus intranet, computer help desk, free student e-mail accounts, online (class) grades, online (class) schedules, student Web portal. Campuswide network is available. 100% of college-owned or -operated housing units are wired for high-speed Internet access. Wireless service is available via entire campus.
Student Life *Housing:* on-campus residence required through senior year. *Options:* men-only, women-only, disabled students. Campus housing is university owned and leased by the school. Freshman campus housing is guaranteed. *Activities and organizations:* drama/theater group, student-run newspaper, television station, choral group, marching band, Phi Beta Lambda, Campus Activities Board, Student Education Association, Student Foundation, International Club. *Campus security:* 24-hour emergency response devices and patrols, controlled dormitory access. *Student services:* health clinic, personal/psychological counseling.
Athletics Member NCAA. All Division II. *Intercollegiate sports:* baseball M(s), basketball M(s)/W(s), cheerleading M/W, cross-country running W(s), football M(s), golf M(s)/W(s), soccer M(s)/W(s), softball W(s), swimming and diving M(s)/W(s), tennis M(s)/W(s), volleyball W(s), wrestling M(s). *Intramural sports:* basketball M/W, football M/W, soccer M, softball M/W, table tennis M/W.
Standardized Tests *Required:* SAT or ACT (for admission).
Costs (2011–12) *Comprehensive fee:* $26,670 includes full-time tuition ($20,160), mandatory fees ($470), and room and board ($6040). Part-time tuition: $580 per semester hour. *Room and board:* Room and board charges vary according to housing facility. *Payment plans:* installment, deferred payment. *Waivers:* employees or children of employees.
Financial Aid Of all full-time matriculated undergraduates who enrolled in 2011, 1,209 applied for aid, 954 were judged to have need, 396 had their need fully met. 307 Federal Work-Study jobs (averaging $1800). 26 state and other part-time jobs (averaging $46,845). In 2011, 609 non-need-based awards were made. *Average percent of need met:* 87%. *Average financial aid package:* $19,741. *Average need-based loan:* $5403. *Average need-based gift aid:* $12,743. *Average non-need-based aid:* $8432. *Average indebtedness upon graduation:* $18,510. *Financial aid deadline:* 6/1.
Applying *Options:* deferred entrance. *Required:* high school transcript, minimum 2.8 GPA. *Recommended:* interview. *Application deadlines:* 8/15 (freshmen), 8/15 (transfers). *Notification:* continuous (freshmen), continuous (transfers).
Freshman Application Contact Mrs. Lori Motl, Director of Admissions Counseling, Ouachita Baptist University, OBU Box 3776, Arkadelphia, AR

71998-0001. *Phone:* 870-245-5110. *Toll-free phone:* 800-342-5628. *Fax:* 870-245-5500. *E-mail:* motll@obu.edu. *Web site:* http://www.obu.edu/.

Philander Smith College
Little Rock, Arkansas
- **Independent United Methodist** 4-year, founded 1877
- **Urban** 25-acre campus
- **Coed** 732 undergraduate students, 93% full-time, 65% women, 35% men
- **Minimally difficult** entrance level, 68% of applicants were admitted

Undergraduates 680 full-time, 52 part-time. 42% are from out of state; 92% Black or African American, non-Hispanic/Latino; 0.8% Hispanic/Latino; 0.1% Asian, non-Hispanic/Latino; 0.1% Native Hawaiian or other Pacific Islander, non-Hispanic/Latino; 1% Two or more races, non-Hispanic/Latino; 5% international; 8% transferred in; 40% live on campus. *Retention:* 60% of full-time freshmen returned.
Freshmen *Admission:* 2,906 applied, 1,976 admitted, 197 enrolled. *Average high school GPA:* 2.91. *Test scores:* SAT critical reading scores over 500: 33%; SAT math scores over 500: 24%; SAT writing scores over 500: 24%; ACT scores over 18: 57%; SAT critical reading scores over 600: 4%; ACT scores over 24: 10%.
Faculty *Total:* 84, 56% full-time, 37% with terminal degrees. *Student/faculty ratio:* 13:1.
Academics *Calendar:* semesters. *Degree:* bachelor's. *Special study options:* adult/continuing education programs.
Computers on Campus Campuswide network is available.
Student Life *Housing:* on-campus residence required for freshman year. *Options:* coed. Campus housing is university owned. *Campus security:* 24-hour emergency response devices and patrols, student patrols, controlled dormitory access.
Athletics *Intercollegiate sports:* basketball M/W, volleyball W.
Standardized Tests *Required:* SAT or ACT (for admission).
Costs (2012–13) *Comprehensive fee:* $19,510 includes full-time tuition ($11,350), mandatory fees ($560), and room and board ($7600). Full-time tuition and fees vary according to course load, program, and student level. Part-time tuition: $400 per credit hour. Part-time tuition and fees vary according to course load, program, and student level. *Room and board:* Room and board charges vary according to housing facility. *Payment plans:* installment, deferred payment. *Waivers:* employees or children of employees.
Financial Aid Of all full-time matriculated undergraduates who enrolled in 2011, 690 applied for aid, 668 were judged to have need, 36 had their need fully met. 76 Federal Work-Study jobs (averaging $2600). In 2011, 37 non-need-based awards were made. *Average percent of need met:* 54%. *Average financial aid package:* $11,336. *Average need-based loan:* $3618. *Average need-based gift aid:* $8165. *Average non-need-based aid:* $11,012. *Average indebtedness upon graduation:* $35,000.
Applying *Options:* deferred entrance. *Application fee:* $25. *Required:* high school transcript, minimum 2.0 GPA. *Required for some:* essay or personal statement, interview. *Application deadlines:* 7/1 (freshmen), rolling (transfers). *Notification:* continuous (freshmen), continuous (transfers).
Freshman Application Contact Mr. George Gray, Director of Recruitment and Admissions, Philander Smith College, 812 West 13th Street, Little Rock, AR 72202-3799. *Phone:* 501-370-5310. *Toll-free phone:* 800-446-6772. *Fax:* 501-370-5225. *E-mail:* ggray@philander.edu. *Web site:* http://www.philander.edu/.

Southern Arkansas University–Magnolia
Magnolia, Arkansas
- **State-supported** comprehensive, founded 1909, part of Southern Arkansas University System
- **Small-town** 781-acre campus
- **Endowment** $22.1 million
- **Coed** 2,922 undergraduate students, 87% full-time, 58% women, 42% men
- **Moderately difficult** entrance level, 67% of applicants were admitted

Undergraduates 2,536 full-time, 386 part-time. Students come from 30 states and territories; 23 other countries; 24% are from out of state; 31% Black or African American, non-Hispanic/Latino; 2% Hispanic/Latino; 0.8% Asian, non-Hispanic/Latino; 0.7% Native Hawaiian or other Pacific Islander, non-Hispanic/Latino; 0.4% American Indian or Alaska Native, non-Hispanic/Latino; 0.2% Two or more races, non-Hispanic/Latino; 3% international; 8% transferred in; 48% live on campus. *Retention:* 60% of full-time freshmen returned.
Freshmen *Admission:* 2,499 applied, 1,671 admitted, 646 enrolled. *Average high school GPA:* 3.15. *Test scores:* SAT critical reading scores over 500:

58%; SAT math scores over 500: 44%; ACT scores over 18: 82%; SAT critical reading scores over 600: 25%; SAT math scores over 600: 13%; ACT scores over 24: 36%; SAT critical reading scores over 700: 6%; ACT scores over 30: 4%.

Faculty *Total:* 218, 74% full-time, 49% with terminal degrees. *Student/faculty ratio:* 15:1.

Academics *Calendar:* semesters. *Degrees:* certificates, associate, bachelor's, and master's. *Special study options:* academic remediation for entering students, accelerated degree program, adult/continuing education programs, advanced placement credit, distance learning, double majors, English as a second language, freshman honors college, honors programs, independent study, internships, part-time degree program, services for LD students, study abroad, summer session for credit.

Computers on Campus 199 computers/terminals and 199 ports are available on campus for general student use. Students can access the following: campus intranet, computer help desk, free student e-mail accounts, online (class) grades, online (class) registration, online (class) schedules. Campuswide network is available. 100% of college-owned or -operated housing units are wired for high-speed Internet access. Wireless service is available via computer centers, computer labs, dorm rooms, libraries, student centers.

Student Life *Housing:* on-campus residence required through sophomore year. *Options:* coed, men-only, women-only. Campus housing is university owned and is provided by a third party. Freshman campus housing is guaranteed. *Activities and organizations:* drama/theater group, student-run newspaper, radio station, choral group, marching band, Student Government Association, Student Activities Board, Resident Hall Association, Residential College, International Student Association, national fraternities, national sororities. *Campus security:* 24-hour emergency response devices, student patrols, late-night transport/escort service, controlled dormitory access. *Student services:* health clinic, personal/psychological counseling.

Athletics Member NCAA. All Division II. *Intercollegiate sports:* baseball M(s), basketball M(s)/W(s), cross-country running M(s)/W(s), football M(s), golf M/W, softball W(s), tennis W(s), track and field M(s)/W(s), volleyball W(s). *Intramural sports:* badminton M/W, basketball M/W, football M, golf M/W, softball M/W, swimming and diving M/W, table tennis M/W, tennis M/W, volleyball M/W.

Standardized Tests *Required:* SAT or ACT (for admission). *Recommended:* ACT (for admission).

Costs (2011–12) *Tuition:* state resident $5580 full-time, $186 per hour part-time; nonresident $8460 full-time, $282 per hour part-time. Full-time tuition and fees vary according to course load. Part-time tuition and fees vary according to course load. *Required fees:* $1206 full-time, $39 per hour part-time, $18 per term part-time. *Room and board:* $4700; room only: $2340. Room and board charges vary according to board plan and housing facility. *Payment plan:* installment. *Waivers:* children of alumni, senior citizens, and employees or children of employees.

Financial Aid Of all full-time matriculated undergraduates who enrolled in 2009, 1,959 applied for aid, 1,766 were judged to have need, 1,187 had their need fully met. 1,250 Federal Work-Study jobs (averaging $3097). 303 state and other part-time jobs (averaging $4268). In 2009, 284 non-need-based awards were made. *Average percent of need met:* 100%. *Average financial aid package:* $7679. *Average need-based loan:* $3692. *Average need-based gift aid:* $4106. *Average non-need-based aid:* $5891. *Average indebtedness upon graduation:* $15,672.

Applying *Options:* electronic application, early admission, deferred entrance. *Required:* high school transcript. *Required for some:* interview. *Application deadlines:* 8/27 (freshmen), 8/27 (transfers).

Freshman Application Contact Southern Arkansas University–Magnolia, 100 East University, Magnolia, AR 71753. *Phone:* 870-235-4040. *Toll-free phone:* 800-332-7286. *Web site:* http://www.saumag.edu/.

Strayer University - Little Rock Campus

Little Rock, Arkansas

- **Proprietary** comprehensive
- **Coed**

Academics *Degrees:* bachelor's and master's.

Freshman Application Contact Strayer University - Little Rock Campus, 10825 Financial Centre Parkway, Suite 131, Little Rock, AR 72211. *Web site:* http://www.strayer.edu/little_rock.

University of Arkansas

Fayetteville, Arkansas

- **State-supported** university, founded 1871, part of University of Arkansas System
- **Suburban** 410-acre campus
- **Endowment** $673.1 million
- **Coed** 19,027 undergraduate students, 87% full-time, 49% women, 51% men
- **Moderately difficult** entrance level, 61% of applicants were admitted

Undergraduates 16,617 full-time, 2,410 part-time. Students come from 50 states and territories; 120 other countries; 33% are from out of state; 5% Black or African American, non-Hispanic/Latino; 5% Hispanic/Latino; 3% Asian, non-Hispanic/Latino; 0.1% Native Hawaiian or other Pacific Islander, non-Hispanic/Latino; 1% American Indian or Alaska Native, non-Hispanic/Latino; 3% Two or more races, non-Hispanic/Latino; 0.3% Race/ethnicity unknown; 3% international; 8% transferred in; 33% live on campus. *Retention:* 83% of full-time freshmen returned.

Freshmen *Admission:* 16,633 applied, 10,129 admitted, 4,447 enrolled. *Average high school GPA:* 3.56. *Test scores:* SAT critical reading scores over 500: 79%; SAT math scores over 500: 84%; ACT scores over 18: 100%; SAT critical reading scores over 600: 33%; SAT math scores over 600: 43%; ACT scores over 24: 70%; SAT critical reading scores over 700: 7%; SAT math scores over 700: 7%; ACT scores over 30: 19%.

Faculty *Total:* 1,087, 91% full-time, 82% with terminal degrees. *Student/faculty ratio:* 18:1.

Academics *Calendar:* semesters. *Degrees:* bachelor's, master's, doctoral, post-master's, postbachelor's, and first professional certificates. *Special study options:* accelerated degree program, advanced placement credit, cooperative education, distance learning, double majors, English as a second language, freshman honors college, honors programs, independent study, internships, part-time degree program, services for LD students, study abroad, summer session for credit. *ROTC:* Army (b), Air Force (b). *Unusual degree programs:* 3-2 law.

Computers on Campus 3,335 computers/terminals are available on campus for general student use. Students can access the following: computer help desk, free student e-mail accounts, online (class) grades, online (class) registration, online (class) schedules. Campuswide network is available. 100% of college-owned or -operated housing units are wired for high-speed Internet access. Wireless service is available via entire campus.

Student Life *Housing:* on-campus residence required for freshman year. *Options:* coed, men-only, women-only, disabled students. Campus housing is university owned. Freshman campus housing is guaranteed. *Activities and organizations:* drama/theater group, student-run newspaper, radio and television station, choral group, marching band, Gamma Beta Phi, University Baptist Collegiate Ministry, Associated Student Government, Black Students Association, Hot Pink Ribbon Club, national fraternities, national sororities. *Campus security:* 24-hour emergency response devices and patrols, student patrols, late-night transport/escort service, controlled dormitory access, RAD (Rape Aggression Defense program). *Student services:* health clinic, personal/psychological counseling, women's center, legal services.

Athletics Member NCAA. All Division I except football (Division I-A). *Intercollegiate sports:* baseball M(s), basketball M(s)/W(s), cross-country running M(s)/W(s), golf M(s)/W(s), gymnastics W(s), soccer W(s), softball W(s), swimming and diving W(s), tennis M(s)/W(s), track and field M(s)/W(s), volleyball W(s). *Intramural sports:* badminton M/W, basketball M/W, bowling M/W, cheerleading M(c)/W(c), crew M(c)/W(c), football M, golf M/W, racquetball M/W, rugby M(c)/W(c), soccer M/W, softball M/W, tennis M/W, ultimate Frisbee M/W, volleyball M(c)/W(c), water polo M/W.

Standardized Tests *Required:* SAT or ACT (for admission).

Costs (2011–12) *One-time required fee:* $162. *Tuition:* state resident $5888 full-time, $196 per credit hour part-time; nonresident $16,321 full-time, $544 per credit hour part-time. Full-time tuition and fees vary according to course load and program. Part-time tuition and fees vary according to course load and program. *Required fees:* $946 full-time, $32 per credit hour part-time. *Room and board:* $8204. Room and board charges vary according to board plan and housing facility.

Financial Aid Of all full-time matriculated undergraduates who enrolled in 2010, 10,435 applied for aid, 7,075 were judged to have need, 1,528 had their need fully met. In 2010, 2202 non-need-based awards were made. *Average percent of need met:* 64%. *Average financial aid package:* $9836. *Average need-based loan:* $4335. *Average need-based gift aid:* $7166. *Average non-need-based aid:* $5249. *Average indebtedness upon graduation:* $21,562.

Applying *Options:* electronic application, early admission, early action. *Application fee:* $40. *Required:* high school transcript. *Recommended:* minimum 3.0 GPA. *Application deadlines:* 8/1 (freshmen), 8/1 (transfers), 11/15 (early action). *Notification:* continuous until 9/1 (freshmen), continuous (transfers), 12/15 (early action).

Freshman Application Contact University of Arkansas, 232 Silas H. Hunt Hall, Office of Admissions, Fayetteville, AR 72701-1201. *Phone:* 479-575-5346. *Toll-free phone:* 800-377-8632. *Fax:* 479-575-7515. *E-mail:* uofa@uark.edu. *Web site:* http://www.uark.edu/.

University of Arkansas at Little Rock
Little Rock, Arkansas

- **State-supported** university, founded 1927, part of University of Arkansas System
- **Urban** 150-acre campus
- **Coed** 10,374 undergraduate students, 56% full-time, 60% women, 40% men
- **Minimally difficult** entrance level, 57% of applicants were admitted

Undergraduates 5,783 full-time, 4,591 part-time. 26% Black or African American, non-Hispanic/Latino; 2% Hispanic/Latino; 2% Asian, non-Hispanic/Latino; 0.4% American Indian or Alaska Native, non-Hispanic/Latino; 5% Two or more races, non-Hispanic/Latino; 3% Race/ethnicity unknown; 2% international; 12% transferred in. *Retention:* 62% of full-time freshmen returned.

Freshmen *Admission:* 2,192 applied, 1,252 admitted, 923 enrolled. *Test scores:* ACT scores over 18: 86%; ACT scores over 24: 34%; ACT scores over 30: 5%.

Faculty *Total:* 820, 59% full-time, 45% with terminal degrees. *Student/faculty ratio:* 15:1.

Academics *Calendar:* semesters. *Degrees:* certificates, associate, bachelor's, master's, doctoral, post-master's, postbachelor's, and first professional certificates. *Special study options:* adult/continuing education programs, part-time degree program.

Computers on Campus Campuswide network is available.

Student Life *Housing options:* coed. *Campus security:* 24-hour emergency response devices, student patrols, late-night transport/escort service.

Athletics Member NCAA. All Division I. *Intercollegiate sports:* baseball M(s), basketball M(s), cross-country running M(s)/W(s), golf M(s)/W(s), soccer W(s), swimming and diving W, tennis M(s)/W(s), track and field M/W(s), volleyball W(s). *Intramural sports:* archery M/W, badminton M/W, basketball M, bowling M/W, football M/W, golf M/W, swimming and diving M/W, table tennis M/W, tennis M/W, volleyball M/W.

Standardized Tests *Required:* ACT (for admission).

Costs (2011–12) *Tuition:* state resident $5490 full-time, $183 per credit hour part-time; nonresident $15,000 full-time, $500 per credit hour part-time. Full-time tuition and fees vary according to program. Part-time tuition and fees vary according to program. *Required fees:* $1268 full-time, $42 per credit hour part-time. *Room and board:* $6056. Room and board charges vary according to housing facility. *Waivers:* employees or children of employees.

Applying *Options:* early admission, deferred entrance. *Application fee:* $40. *Required:* high school transcript, minimum 2.5 GPA, proof of immunization. *Application deadlines:* rolling (freshmen), rolling (transfers). *Notification:* continuous (freshmen), continuous (transfers).

Freshman Application Contact Ms. Tammy Harrison, Director of Admissions, University of Arkansas at Little Rock, 2801 South University Avenue, Little Rock, AR 72204-1099. *Phone:* 501-569-3127. *Toll-free phone:* 800-482-8892. *Fax:* 501-569-8956. *E-mail:* twharrison@ualn.edu. *Web site:* http://www.ualr.edu/.

University of Arkansas at Monticello
Monticello, Arkansas

- **State-supported** comprehensive, founded 1909, part of University of Arkansas System
- **Small-town** 1600-acre campus
- **Endowment** $2.5 million
- **Coed** 3,802 undergraduate students, 70% full-time, 60% women, 40% men
- **Noncompetitive** entrance level, 46% of applicants were admitted

Undergraduates 2,676 full-time, 1,126 part-time. 12% are from out of state; 33% Black or African American, non-Hispanic/Latino; 2% Hispanic/Latino; 0.3% Asian, non-Hispanic/Latino; 0.4% American Indian or Alaska Native, non-Hispanic/Latino; 1% Two or more races, non-Hispanic/Latino; 0.4% Race/ethnicity unknown; 0.4% international; 25% live on campus. *Retention:* 40% of full-time freshmen returned.

Freshmen *Admission:* 2,761 applied, 1,277 admitted, 822 enrolled. *Average high school GPA:* 2.71. *Test scores:* ACT scores over 18: 58%; ACT scores over 24: 16%; ACT scores over 30: 1%.

Faculty *Total:* 240, 72% full-time, 29% with terminal degrees. *Student/faculty ratio:* 16:1.

Academics *Calendar:* semesters. *Degrees:* certificates, associate, bachelor's, master's, and postbachelor's certificates. *Special study options:* academic remediation for entering students, accelerated degree program, advanced placement credit, distance learning, double majors, independent study, off-campus study, part-time degree program, services for LD students, summer session for credit. *ROTC:* Army (b).

Computers on Campus 400 computers/terminals are available on campus for general student use. Students can access the following: campus intranet, computer help desk, free student e-mail accounts, online (class) grades, online (class) registration, online (class) schedules. Campuswide network is available. Wireless service is available via libraries.

Student Life *Housing options:* coed, men-only, women-only. Campus housing is university owned. *Activities and organizations:* drama/theater group, student-run newspaper, choral group, marching band, national fraternities, national sororities. *Campus security:* 24-hour emergency response devices and patrols. *Student services:* health clinic, personal/psychological counseling.

Athletics Member NCAA. All Division II. *Intercollegiate sports:* baseball M(s), basketball M(s)/W(s), cross-country running W, football M(s), golf M(s), softball W(s), tennis W. *Intramural sports:* baseball M, basketball M/W, cross-country running M/W, football M/W, golf M/W, racquetball M/W, soccer M/W, softball M/W, table tennis M/W, tennis M/W, track and field M/W, volleyball M/W.

Standardized Tests *Recommended:* used for placement.

Costs (2011–12) *Tuition:* state resident $3780 full-time, $126 per semester hour part-time; nonresident $9000 full-time, $300 per semester hour part-time. Full-time tuition and fees vary according to location and program. Part-time tuition and fees vary according to location and program. *Required fees:* $1650 full-time, $55 per semester hour part-time. *Room and board:* $4610. Room and board charges vary according to board plan and housing facility. *Payment plan:* installment. *Waivers:* senior citizens and employees or children of employees.

Financial Aid Of all full-time matriculated undergraduates who enrolled in 2006, 166 Federal Work-Study jobs (averaging $1159). 292 state and other part-time jobs (averaging $1388).

Applying *Options:* early admission, deferred entrance. *Required:* high school transcript, proof of immunization. *Application deadlines:* 8/1 (freshmen), 8/1 (transfers).

Freshman Application Contact Ms. Mary Whiting, Director of Admissions, University of Arkansas at Monticello, Monticello, AR 71656. *Phone:* 870-460-1026. *Toll-free phone:* 800-844-1826. *E-mail:* admissions@uamont.edu. *Web site:* http://www.uamont.edu/.

University of Arkansas at Pine Bluff
Pine Bluff, Arkansas

- **State-supported** comprehensive, founded 1873, part of University of Arkansas System
- **Urban** 327-acre campus
- **Coed**
- **30%** of applicants were admitted

Faculty *Student/faculty ratio:* 17:1.

Academics *Calendar:* semesters. *Degrees:* certificates, associate, bachelor's, and master's.

Student Life *Campus security:* 24-hour emergency response devices and patrols.

Athletics Member NCAA, NAIA. All NCAA Division I except football (Division I-AA).

Standardized Tests *Required:* SAT or ACT (for admission).

Costs (2011–12) *Tuition:* state resident $3975 full-time, $133 per credit hour part-time; nonresident $9240 full-time, $308 per credit hour part-time. Full-time tuition and fees vary according to course level, degree level, and location. Part-time tuition and fees vary according to course level, degree level, and location. *Required fees:* $8 per credit hour part-time, $24 per term part-time. *Room and board:* $6148; room only: $3118. Room and board charges vary according to board plan and housing facility.

Financial Aid *Of all full-time matriculated undergraduates who enrolled in 2005,* 2,825 applied for aid, 2,825 were judged to have need, 1,200 had their need fully met. 328 Federal Work-Study jobs (averaging $1000). *Average percent of need met:* 70. *Average financial aid package:* $8121. *Average need-based loan:* $4500. *Average need-based gift aid:* $1000.

Applying *Options:* electronic application, early admission, deferred entrance. *Required:* high school transcript, minimum 2.0 GPA.

Freshman Application Contact University of Arkansas at Pine Bluff, 1200 North University Drive, Pine Bluff, AR 71601-2799. *Phone:* 870-575-8461. *Toll-free phone:* 800-621-7440. *Web site:* http://www.uapb.edu/.

University of Arkansas for Medical Sciences
Little Rock, Arkansas

- **State-supported** university, founded 1879, part of University of Arkansas System
- **Urban** 5-acre campus with easy access to Little Rock
- **Endowment** $31.0 million
- **Coed**

Academics *Calendar:* semesters. *Degrees:* certificates, associate, bachelor's, master's, doctoral, postbachelor's, and first professional certificates (bachelor's degree is upper-level).

Student Life *Campus security:* 24-hour emergency response devices and patrols, late-night transport/escort service, controlled dormitory access.

Costs (2011–12) *Tuition:* state resident $6600 full-time; nonresident $15,576 full-time. Full-time tuition and fees vary according to course load, degree level, location, program, and reciprocity agreements. Part-time tuition and fees vary according to course load, degree level, location, program, and reciprocity agreements. *Required fees:* $256 full-time. *Room only:* $5900.

Financial Aid *Of all full-time matriculated undergraduates who enrolled in 2005,* 734 applied for aid, 686 were judged to have need. 9 Federal Work-Study jobs (averaging $1201). *Average percent of need met:* 62. *Average financial aid package:* $3000. *Average need-based loan:* $4000. *Average need-based gift aid:* $500. *Average indebtedness upon graduation:* $7000.

Freshman Application Contact University of Arkansas for Medical Sciences, 4301 West Markham, Little Rock, AR 72205-7199. *Phone:* 501-686-5730. *Web site:* http://www.uams.edu/.

University of Arkansas–Fort Smith
Fort Smith, Arkansas

- **State and locally supported** 4-year, founded 1928, part of University of Arkansas System
- **Suburban** 120-acre campus
- **Endowment** $62.9 million
- **Coed** 7,606 undergraduate students, 69% full-time, 58% women, 42% men
- **Minimally difficult** entrance level, 56% of applicants were admitted

Undergraduates 5,243 full-time, 2,363 part-time. Students come from 34 states and territories; 18 other countries; 10% are from out of state; 4% Black or African American, non-Hispanic/Latino; 8% Hispanic/Latino; 4% Asian, non-Hispanic/Latino; 0.1% Native Hawaiian or other Pacific Islander, non-Hispanic/Latino; 3% American Indian or Alaska Native, non-Hispanic/Latino; 5% Two or more races, non-Hispanic/Latino; 0.8% Race/ethnicity unknown; 0.7% international; 5% transferred in; 10% live on campus. *Retention:* 62% of full-time freshmen returned.

Freshmen *Admission:* 3,989 applied, 2,237 admitted, 1,357 enrolled. *Average high school GPA:* 3.11. *Test scores:* ACT scores over 18: 87%; ACT scores over 24: 31%; ACT scores over 30: 2%.

Faculty *Total:* 448, 54% full-time, 38% with terminal degrees. *Student/faculty ratio:* 19:1.

Academics *Calendar:* semesters. *Degrees:* certificates, associate, and bachelor's. *Special study options:* academic remediation for entering students, accelerated degree program, adult/continuing education programs, advanced placement credit, cooperative education, distance learning, double majors, English as a second language, external degree program, honors programs, internships, off-campus study, part-time degree program, services for LD students, study abroad, summer session for credit. *ROTC:* Army (b), Air Force (c).

Computers on Campus 914 computers/terminals and 2,000 ports are available on campus for general student use. Students can access the following: campus intranet, computer help desk, free student e-mail accounts, online (class) grades, online (class) registration, online (class) schedules, online subscription databases, information portal, online course management system and online courses. Campuswide network is available. 100% of college-owned or -operated housing units are wired for high-speed Internet access. Wireless service is available via classrooms, computer centers, computer labs, dorm rooms, learning centers, libraries, student centers.

Student Life *Housing options:* coed, disabled students. Campus housing is university owned. *Activities and organizations:* drama/theater group, student-run newspaper, choral group, Campus Activities Board, Phi Beta Lambda, Student Alumni Association, Non-Traditional Students, Baptist Collegiate Ministry, national fraternities, national sororities. *Campus security:* 24-hour emergency response devices and patrols, student patrols, late-night transport/escort service, controlled dormitory access, student patrols; new dormitory facilities have electronic card readers entrances. *Student services:* health clinic, personal/psychological counseling.

Athletics Member NCAA. All Division II. *Intercollegiate sports:* baseball M(s), basketball M(s)/W(s), cross-country running M(s)/W(s), golf M(s)/W(s), tennis M(s)/W(s), volleyball W(s). *Intramural sports:* badminton M/W, basketball M/W, bowling M/W, cheerleading M/W, football M/W, riflery M(c)/W(c), soccer M/W, softball M/W, table tennis M/W, ultimate Frisbee M/W, volleyball M/W.

Standardized Tests *Required:* SAT or ACT (for admission), COMPASS (in lieu of SAT or ACT) (for admission).

Costs (2012–13) *Tuition:* state resident $3780 full-time, $126 per credit hour part-time; nonresident $10,230 full-time, $341 per credit hour part-time. Full-time tuition and fees vary according to course load and program. Part-time tuition and fees vary according to course load and program. *Required fees:* $1487 full-time, $44 per credit hour part-time, $91 per credit hour part-time. *Room and board:* $7642; room only: $4707. Room and board charges vary according to board plan and housing facility. *Payment plan:* installment. *Waivers:* senior citizens and employees or children of employees.

Financial Aid *Of all full-time matriculated undergraduates who enrolled in 2004,* 2,564 applied for aid, 2,232 were judged to have need, 215 had their need fully met. 110 Federal Work-Study jobs (averaging $3000). 94 state and other part-time jobs (averaging $3000). In 2004, 350 non-need-based awards were made. *Average percent of need met:* 62%. *Average financial aid package:* $5568. *Average need-based loan:* $3183. *Average need-based gift aid:* $3504. *Average non-need-based aid:* $2643. *Average indebtedness upon graduation:* $7339.

Applying *Options:* electronic application, early admission, deferred entrance. *Required:* high school transcript. *Application deadlines:* rolling (freshmen), rolling (transfers).

Freshman Application Contact Mr. Mark Lloyd, Office of Admissions and School Relations, University of Arkansas–Fort Smith, 5210 Grand Avenue, PO Box 3649, Fort Smith, AR 72913-3649. *Phone:* 479-788-7120. *Toll-free phone:* 888-512-5466. *Fax:* 479-424-6120. *E-mail:* information@uafortsmith.edu. *Web site:* http://www.uafortsmith.edu/.

University of Central Arkansas
Conway, Arkansas

- **State-supported** university, founded 1907
- **Small-town** 365-acre campus
- **Coed** 9,629 undergraduate students, 84% full-time, 57% women, 43% men
- **Moderately difficult** entrance level, 93% of applicants were admitted

Undergraduates 8,077 full-time, 1,552 part-time. Students come from 43 states and territories; 61 other countries; 6% are from out of state; 17% Black or African American, non-Hispanic/Latino; 3% Hispanic/Latino; 0.5% Asian, non-Hispanic/Latino; 0.1% Native Hawaiian or other Pacific Islander, non-Hispanic/Latino; 0.7% American Indian or Alaska Native, non-Hispanic/Latino; 1% Two or more races, non-Hispanic/Latino; 4% Race/ethnicity unknown; 4% international; 6% transferred in. *Retention:* 69% of full-time freshmen returned.

Freshmen *Admission:* 3,370 applied, 3,131 admitted, 1,960 enrolled. *Average high school GPA:* 3.3. *Test scores:* ACT scores over 18: 89%; ACT scores over 24: 43%; ACT scores over 30: 8%.

Faculty *Total:* 715, 74% full-time, 56% with terminal degrees. *Student/faculty ratio:* 16:1.

Academics *Calendar:* semesters. *Degrees:* certificates, associate, bachelor's, master's, doctoral, post-master's, postbachelor's, and first professional certificates. *Special study options:* academic remediation for entering students, accelerated degree program, advanced placement credit, cooperative education, distance learning, double majors, English as a second language, freshman honors college, honors programs, independent study, internships, part-time degree program, summer session for credit. *ROTC:* Army (b). *Unusual degree programs:* 3-2 engineering with University of Arkansas at Fayetteville.

Computers on Campus 608 computers/terminals are available on campus for general student use. Students can access the following: campus intranet, computer help desk, free student e-mail accounts, online (class) grades, online (class) registration, online (class) schedules. Campuswide network is available. Wireless service is available via entire campus.

Student Life *Housing:* on-campus residence required for freshman year. *Options:* coed, men-only, women-only, disabled students. Campus housing is university owned and leased by the school. Freshman campus housing is guaranteed. *Activities and organizations:* drama/theater group, student-run newspaper, radio and television station, choral group, marching band, Student Government Association, national fraternities, national sororities. *Campus security:* 24-hour emergency response devices and patrols, student patrols, late-night transport/escort service, controlled dormitory access, security personnel at entrances during evening hours. *Student services:* health clinic, personal/psychological counseling, women's center.

Athletics Member NCAA. All Division I. *Intercollegiate sports:* baseball M(s), basketball M(s)/W(s), cheerleading M(s)(c)/W(s)(c), cross-country running M(s)/W(s), football M(s), golf M(s)/W(s), soccer M(s)/W(s), softball W(s), tennis W(s), track and field M(s)/W(s), volleyball W(s). *Intramural sports:* basketball M/W, bowling M/W, soccer M/W, softball M/W, table tennis M, tennis W, track and field M/W, volleyball M/W.

Standardized Tests *Required:* SAT or ACT (for admission).

Costs (2011–12) *Tuition:* state resident $5387 full-time, $180 per credit hour part-time; nonresident $10,773 full-time, $359 per credit hour part-time. Full-time tuition and fees vary according to course load. Part-time tuition and fees vary according to course load. *Required fees:* $1796 full-time, $51 per credit hour part-time. *Room and board:* $5260; room only: $2940. Room and board charges vary according to board plan and housing facility. *Payment plan:* installment. *Waivers:* senior citizens and employees or children of employees.

Financial Aid *Financial aid deadline:* 7/1.

Applying *Options:* electronic application, early admission, deferred entrance. *Application fee:* $25. *Required:* high school transcript. *Application deadlines:* rolling (freshmen), rolling (transfers). *Notification:* continuous (freshmen), continuous (transfers).

Freshman Application Contact Penny Hatfield, Interim Director of Admissions, University of Central Arkansas, 201 Donaghey Avenue, Bernard 100, Conway, AR 72035. *Phone:* 501-450-346. *Toll-free phone:* 800-243-8245. *Fax:* 501-450-5228. *E-mail:* phatfield@uca.edu. *Web site:* http://www.uca.edu/.

University of Phoenix–Little Rock Campus

Little Rock, Arkansas

Freshman Application Contact Marc Booker, Sr. Director, Office of Admissions and Evaluation, University of Phoenix–Little Rock Campus, 4035 South Riverpoint Parkway, Mail Stop CF-L101, Phoenix, AZ 85040. *Phone:* 602-557-4609. *Toll-free phone:* 866-766-0766. *Fax:* 480-643-1156. *Web site:* http://www.phoenix.edu/.

University of Phoenix–Northwest Arkansas Campus

Rogers, Arkansas

Admissions Office Contact University of Phoenix–Northwest Arkansas Campus, 903 North 47th Street - Barrington Centre 2, Rogers, AR 72756-9615. *Toll-free phone:* 866-766-0766. *Web site:* http://www.phoenix.edu/.

University of the Ozarks

Clarksville, Arkansas

- **Independent Presbyterian** 4-year, founded 1834
- **Small-town** campus
- **Coed** 630 undergraduate students, 94% full-time, 52% women, 48% men
- **Moderately difficult** entrance level, 85% of applicants were admitted

Undergraduates 595 full-time, 35 part-time. 32% are from out of state; 5% Black or African American, non-Hispanic/Latino; 8% Hispanic/Latino; 0.3% Asian, non-Hispanic/Latino; 1% American Indian or Alaska Native, non-Hispanic/Latino; 3% Two or more races, non-Hispanic/Latino; 0.7% Race/ethnicity unknown; 11% international; 3% transferred in; 70% live on campus. *Retention:* 59% of full-time freshmen returned.

Freshmen *Admission:* 929 applied, 791 admitted, 186 enrolled. *Average high school GPA:* 3.39. *Test scores:* SAT critical reading scores over 500: 46%; SAT math scores over 500: 66%; ACT scores over 18: 94%; SAT critical reading scores over 600: 9%; SAT math scores over 600: 20%; ACT scores over 24: 42%; SAT critical reading scores over 700: 3%; SAT math scores over 700: 3%; ACT scores over 30: 9%.

Faculty *Total:* 79, 61% full-time, 42% with terminal degrees. *Student/faculty ratio:* 11:1.

Academics *Calendar:* semesters. *Degree:* bachelor's. *Special study options:* part-time degree program.

Computers on Campus Students can access the following: campus intranet, computer help desk, free student e-mail accounts. Campuswide network is available. 100% of college-owned or -operated housing units are wired for high-speed Internet access. Wireless service is available via libraries.

Student Life *Housing:* on-campus residence required through sophomore year. *Options:* coed, women-only. Campus housing is university owned. Freshman campus housing is guaranteed. *Campus security:* 24-hour emergency response devices and patrols, late-night transport/escort service.

Athletics Member NCAA. All Division III. *Intercollegiate sports:* baseball M, basketball M/W, cheerleading M/W, cross-country running M/W, soccer M/W, softball W, tennis M/W. *Intramural sports:* badminton M/W, basketball M/W, bowling M/W, football M/W, racquetball M/W, soccer M, softball M/W, table tennis M/W, tennis M/W, ultimate Frisbee M/W, volleyball M/W, weight lifting M/W.

Standardized Tests *Required:* SAT or ACT (for admission).

Costs (2012–13) *Comprehensive fee:* $29,950 includes full-time tuition ($22,650), mandatory fees ($600), and room and board ($6700). Part-time tuition: $950 per credit hour. *College room only:* $3100. Room and board charges vary according to board plan and housing facility. *Payment plan:* installment. *Waivers:* children of alumni and employees or children of employees.

Financial Aid Of all full-time matriculated undergraduates who enrolled in 2010, 445 applied for aid, 418 were judged to have need, 98 had their need fully met. In 2010, 158 non-need-based awards were made. *Average percent of need met:* 81%. *Average financial aid package:* $21,842. *Average need-based loan:* $9752. *Average need-based gift aid:* $16,562. *Average non-need-based aid:* $20,299. *Average indebtedness upon graduation:* $21,520.

Applying *Options:* deferred entrance. *Application fee:* $30. *Required:* minimum 2.0 GPA. *Required for some:* essay or personal statement, high school transcript, interview. *Application deadlines:* rolling (freshmen), rolling (transfers). *Notification:* continuous (freshmen), continuous (transfers).

Freshman Application Contact Ms. Kim Myrick, Vice President for Enrollment Management, University of the Ozarks, 415 North College Avenue, Clarksville, AR 72830-2880. *Phone:* 479-979-1227. *Toll-free phone:* 800-264-8636. *Fax:* 479-979-1417. *E-mail:* admiss@ozarks.edu. *Web site:* http://www.ozarks.edu/.

Williams Baptist College

Walnut Ridge, Arkansas

- **Independent Southern Baptist** 4-year, founded 1941
- **Rural** 180-acre campus
- **Coed** 619 undergraduate students
- **Minimally difficult** entrance level

Undergraduates 17% are from out of state. *Retention:* 60% of full-time freshmen returned.

Freshmen *Average high school GPA:* 3.36.

Faculty *Student/faculty ratio:* 13:1.

Academics *Calendar:* semesters. *Degrees:* associate and bachelor's. *Special study options:* adult/continuing education programs, advanced placement credit, double majors, independent study, internships, off-campus study, part-time degree program, student-designed majors, study abroad, summer session for credit. *ROTC:* Army (c).

Computers on Campus Campuswide network is available.

Student Life *Housing:* on-campus residence required through senior year. *Options:* men-only, women-only. Campus housing is university owned. *Activities and organizations:* drama/theater group, choral group. *Campus security:* 24-hour emergency response devices, student patrols. *Student services:* personal/psychological counseling.

Athletics Member NAIA, NCCAA. *Intercollegiate sports:* baseball M(s), basketball M(s)/W(s), golf M(s), soccer M(s)/W(s), softball W(s), volleyball W(s). *Intramural sports:* basketball M/W, football M, golf M/W, racquetball M/W, softball M/W, table tennis M/W, tennis M/W, volleyball M/W.

Standardized Tests *Required:* SAT or ACT (for admission).

Costs (2011–12) *Comprehensive fee:* $18,520 includes full-time tuition ($11,800), mandatory fees ($820), and room and board ($5900). *Payment plan:* installment. *Waivers:* senior citizens and employees or children of employees.

Financial Aid Of all full-time matriculated undergraduates who enrolled in 2010, 465 applied for aid, 408 were judged to have need. 188 Federal Work-Study jobs (averaging $1192). 36 state and other part-time jobs (averaging $1383). *Average financial aid package:* $13,853. *Average need-based loan:* $3556. *Average need-based gift aid:* $4654. *Average indebtedness upon graduation:* $20,302.

Applying *Options:* electronic application. *Application fee:* $20. *Required:* high school transcript, minimum 2.5 GPA. *Required for some:* essay or personal statement. *Recommended:* interview. *Application deadlines:* rolling (freshmen), rolling (transfers).

Freshman Application Contact Mrs. Angela Flippo, Vice President for Enrollment, Williams Baptist College, 60 West Fulbright Avenue, Walnut Ridge, AR 72476. *Phone:* 870-759-4120. *Toll-free phone:* 800-722-4434. *Fax:* 870-759-4163. *E-mail:* admissions@wbcoll.edu. *Web site:* http://www.wbcoll.edu/.

CALIFORNIA

Academy of Art University

San Francisco, California

- **Proprietary** comprehensive, founded 1929
- **Urban** 3-acre campus
- **Coed** 12,345 undergraduate students, 57% full-time, 57% women, 43% men
- **Noncompetitive** entrance level, 100% of applicants were admitted

Undergraduates 7,019 full-time, 5,326 part-time. Students come from 55 states and territories; 115 other countries; 41% are from out of state; 6% Black or African American, non-Hispanic/Latino; 9% Hispanic/Latino; 9% Asian, non-Hispanic/Latino; 0.1% Native Hawaiian or other Pacific Islander, non-Hispanic/Latino; 0.7% American Indian or Alaska Native, non-Hispanic/Latino; 0.3% Two or more races, non-Hispanic/Latino; 32% Race/ethnicity unknown; 17% international; 6% transferred in; 13% live on campus. *Retention:* 65% of full-time freshmen returned.

Freshmen *Admission:* 4,452 applied, 4,452 admitted, 1,880 enrolled.

Faculty *Total:* 1,347, 17% full-time. *Student/faculty ratio:* 22:1.

Academics *Calendar:* semesters. *Degrees:* certificates, diplomas, associate, bachelor's, and master's. *Special study options:* academic remediation for entering students, adult/continuing education programs, distance learning, English as a second language, independent study, internships, part-time degree program, services for LD students, summer session for credit.

Computers on Campus 800 computers/terminals are available on campus for general student use. Students can access the following: campus intranet, computer help desk, free student e-mail accounts, online (class) registration, online (class) schedules. Campuswide network is available. 15% of college-owned or -operated housing units are wired for high-speed Internet access. Wireless service is available via classrooms, dorm rooms, libraries.

Student Life *Housing options:* coed, men-only, women-only, disabled students. Campus housing is university owned and leased by the school. Freshman campus housing is guaranteed. *Activities and organizations:* drama/theater group, student-run radio and television station, choral group, Korean Student Association, Front Row (Fashion Club), Drama Club, Taiwanese Student Association, national fraternities. *Campus security:* 24-hour emergency response devices and patrols, late-night transport/escort service, controlled dormitory access, ID check at all buildings.

Athletics Member NCAA. All Division II. *Intercollegiate sports:* baseball M(s), basketball M(s)/W(s), cross-country running M(s)/W(s), golf M(s)/W(s), soccer M(s)/W(s), softball W(s), tennis W(s), track and field M(s)/W(s), volleyball W(s).

Costs (2012–13) *Tuition:* $22,950 full-time, $765 per credit part-time. Full-time tuition and fees vary according to course load. Part-time tuition and fees vary according to course load. *Room only:* Room and board charges vary according to housing facility. *Payment plan:* installment.

Financial Aid Of all full-time matriculated undergraduates who enrolled in 2010, 4,230 applied for aid, 3,871 were judged to have need, 12 had their need fully met. 113 Federal Work-Study jobs (averaging $3130). In 2010, 7 non-need-based awards were made. *Average percent of need met:* 27%. *Average financial aid package:* $8643. *Average need-based loan:* $3496. *Average need-based gift aid:* $5524. *Average non-need-based aid:* $3726. *Average indebtedness upon graduation:* $49,265.

Applying *Options:* electronic application, early admission, deferred entrance. *Application fee:* $100. *Required:* high school transcript. *Recommended:* minimum 2.0 GPA, interview, portfolio. *Application deadlines:* rolling (freshmen), rolling (transfers).

Freshman Application Contact Admissions, Academy of Art University, 79 New Montgomery Street, San Francisco, CA 94105. *Phone:* 800-544-2787. *Toll-free phone:* 800-544-ARTS. *Fax:* 415-618-6287. *E-mail:* info@academyart.edu. *Web site:* http://www.academyart.edu/.

See page 1044 for the College Close-Up.

Academy of Couture Art

West Hollywood, California

Admissions Office Contact Academy of Couture Art, Pacific Design Center, 8687 Melrose Avenue, Suite G520, West Hollywood, CA 90069. *Web site:* http://www.academyofcoutureart.com/.

Alliant International University

San Diego, California

- **Independent** university, founded 1952, part of Alliant International University
- **Suburban** 60-acre campus with easy access to San Diego
- **Coed** 140 undergraduate students, 75% full-time, 61% women, 39% men

Undergraduates 105 full-time, 35 part-time. Students come from 8 states and territories; 17 other countries; 5% are from out of state; 40% live on campus. **Faculty** *Total:* 670, 35% full-time, 93% with terminal degrees. *Student/faculty ratio:* 9:1.

Academics *Calendar:* semesters. *Degrees:* certificates, bachelor's, master's, doctoral, postbachelor's, and first professional certificates. *Special study options:* academic remediation for entering students, advanced placement credit, distance learning, English as a second language, honors programs, independent study, internships, part-time degree program, services for LD students, summer session for credit.

Computers on Campus 100 computers/terminals are available on campus for general student use. Students can access the following: campus intranet, computer help desk, free student e-mail accounts, online (class) grades, online (class) registration, online (class) schedules. Campuswide network is available. Wireless service is available via entire campus.

Student Life *Housing options:* coed. Campus housing is university owned. *Activities and organizations:* student-run newspaper, Residence Hall Association, Latino Students Association, Finance Club, student government, Sigma Iota Epsilon. *Campus security:* 24-hour emergency response devices and patrols, student patrols, late-night transport/escort service. *Student services:* health clinic, personal/psychological counseling.

Athletics *Intramural sports:* basketball M/W, cross-country running M/W, football M/W, soccer M/W, softball M/W, table tennis M/W, tennis M/W, volleyball M/W.

Costs (2011–12) *Comprehensive fee:* $24,140 includes full-time tuition ($16,680), mandatory fees ($190), and room and board ($7270). Full-time tuition and fees vary according to course load. Part-time tuition: $610 per semester hour. Part-time tuition and fees vary according to course load. *Room and board:* Room and board charges vary according to board plan. *Payment plan:* installment. *Waivers:* employees or children of employees.

Financial Aid Of all full-time matriculated undergraduates who enrolled in 2010, 161 applied for aid, 161 were judged to have need. 5 Federal Work-Study jobs (averaging $9579). 3 state and other part-time jobs (averaging $3000). In 2010, 34 non-need-based awards were made. *Average percent of need met:* 67%. *Average financial aid package:* $13,550. *Average need-based loan:* $5500. *Average need-based gift aid:* $6750. *Average non-need-based aid:* $1000. *Average indebtedness upon graduation:* $20,000.

Applying *Options:* electronic application, deferred entrance. *Application fee:* $45. *Required:* high school transcript, minimum 2.0 GPA. *Application deadline:* rolling (transfers). *Notification:* continuous (transfers).

Freshman Application Contact Alliant International University, 10455 Pomerado Road, San Diego, CA 92131-1799. *Phone:* 858-635-4772. *Toll-free phone:* 866-825-5426. *Web site:* http://www.alliant.edu/.

Allied American University

Laguna Hills, California

Director of Admissions Lindsay Oglesby, Admissions Director, Allied American University, 22952 Alcade Drive, Laguna Hills, CA 92653. *Phone:* 888-384-0849. *Toll-free phone:* 888-384-0849. *Fax:* 949-707-2978. *E-mail:* info@allied.edu. *Web site:* http://allied.edu/.

American Jewish University

Bel Air, California

- **Independent Jewish** comprehensive, founded 1947
- **Suburban** 28-acre campus with easy access to Los Angeles
- **Endowment** $22.1 million
- **Coed** 132 undergraduate students, 97% full-time, 50% women, 50% men
- **Moderately difficult** entrance level, 95% of applicants were admitted

Undergraduates 128 full-time, 4 part-time. Students come from 17 states and territories; 5 other countries; 24% are from out of state; 2% Black or African American, non-Hispanic/Latino; 4% Hispanic/Latino; 2% Asian, non-Hispanic/Latino; 2% American Indian or Alaska Native, non-Hispanic/Latino; 31% Race/ethnicity unknown; 5% international; 19% transferred in; 47% live on campus. *Retention:* 91% of full-time freshmen returned. **Freshmen** *Admission:* 39 applied, 37 admitted, 11 enrolled. *Average high school GPA:* 3.27. *Test scores:* SAT critical reading scores over 500: 50%; SAT math scores over 500: 63%; SAT writing scores over 500: 63%; ACT scores over 18: 100%; SAT critical reading scores over 600: 25%; SAT math scores over 600: 25%; SAT writing scores over 600: 25%; ACT scores over 24:

25%; SAT critical reading scores over 700: 25%; SAT math scores over 700: 13%; SAT writing scores over 700: 25%. **Faculty** *Total:* 70, 17% full-time, 54% with terminal degrees. *Student/faculty ratio:* 8:1.

Academics *Calendar:* semesters. *Degrees:* bachelor's and master's. *Special study options:* academic remediation for entering students, adult/continuing education programs, advanced placement credit, cooperative education, double majors, independent study, internships, part-time degree program, services for LD students, student-designed majors, study abroad, summer session for credit. *Unusual degree programs:* 3-2 business administration; education.

Computers on Campus 38 computers/terminals and 10 ports are available on campus for general student use. Students can access the following: campus intranet, free student e-mail accounts, online (class) grades, online (class) schedules. Campuswide network is available. 100% of college-owned or -operated housing units are wired for high-speed Internet access. Wireless service is available via computer centers, computer labs, dorm rooms, libraries, student centers.

Student Life *Housing options:* coed. Campus housing is university owned. Freshman campus housing is guaranteed. *Activities and organizations:* drama/theater group, student-run newspaper, choral group, The Giving Tree, Sports Club, Hillel, Israel Action Committee, American Medical Association. *Campus security:* 24-hour emergency response devices and patrols, controlled dormitory access. *Student services:* health clinic, personal/psychological counseling.

Standardized Tests *Required:* SAT or ACT (for admission).

Costs (2012–13) *Comprehensive fee:* $39,104 includes full-time tuition ($24,744), mandatory fees ($1088), and room and board ($13,272). Full-time tuition and fees vary according to course load and degree level. Part-time tuition: $1031 per unit. Part-time tuition and fees vary according to course load and degree level. *Room and board:* Room and board charges vary according to board plan and housing facility. *Payment plan:* installment. *Waivers:* employees or children of employees.

Financial Aid Of all full-time matriculated undergraduates who enrolled in 2010, 136 applied for aid, 136 were judged to have need, 120 had their need fully met. 35 Federal Work-Study jobs (averaging $929). In 2010, 56 non-need-based awards were made. *Average percent of need met:* 96%. *Average financial aid package:* $24,500. *Average need-based loan:* $6500. *Average need-based gift aid:* $9238. *Average non-need-based aid:* $2000. *Average indebtedness upon graduation:* $28,000.

Applying *Options:* electronic application, deferred entrance. *Application fee:* $35. *Required:* essay or personal statement, high school transcript, 2 letters of recommendation. *Recommended:* interview. *Application deadlines:* 5/31 (freshmen), 5/31 (out-of-state freshmen), 5/31 (transfers). *Notification:* continuous (freshmen), continuous (out-of-state freshmen), continuous (transfers).

Freshman Application Contact Mr. Matt Spooner, Director of Undergraduate Admissions, American Jewish University, Familian Campus, 15600 Mulholland Drive, Los Angeles, CA 90077-1599. *Phone:* 310-440-1250. *Toll-free phone:* 888-853-6763. *Fax:* 310-471-3657. *E-mail:* admissions@ajula.edu. *Web site:* http://www.ajula.edu/.

American Musical and Dramatic Academy, Los Angeles

Los Angeles, California

Freshman Application Contact Karen Jackson, Director of Admission, American Musical and Dramatic Academy, Los Angeles, 6305 Yucca Street, Los Angeles, CA 90028. *Phone:* 323-469-3300. *Toll-free phone:* 888-474-9444. *Fax:* 323-469-5246. *E-mail:* kjackson@amda.edu. *Web site:* http://www.amda.edu/.

Antioch University Los Angeles

Culver City, California

Application Contact Admissions, Antioch University Los Angeles, 400 Corporate Pointe, Culver City, CA 90230. *Phone:* 310-578-1080 Ext. 100. *Toll-free phone:* 800-726-8462. *Fax:* 310-822-4824. *E-mail:* admissions@antiochla.edu. *Web site:* http://www.antiochla.edu/.

Antioch University Santa Barbara

Santa Barbara, California

- **Independent** upper-level, founded 1977, part of Antioch University
- **Small-town** campus with easy access to Los Angeles
- **Coed** 148 undergraduate students, 47% full-time, 70% women, 30% men
- **Moderately difficult** entrance level

Undergraduates 69 full-time, 79 part-time. Students come from 3 other countries; 4% Black or African American, non-Hispanic/Latino; 26% Hispanic/

Latino; 3% Asian, non-Hispanic/Latino; 1% American Indian or Alaska Native, non-Hispanic/Latino; 2% Two or more races, non-Hispanic/Latino; 5% Race/ethnicity unknown; 6% international.

Faculty *Total:* 64, 19% full-time. *Student/faculty ratio:* 12:1.

Academics *Calendar:* quarters. *Degrees:* bachelor's, master's, doctoral, and first professional. *Special study options:* academic remediation for entering students, accelerated degree program, distance learning, double majors, external degree program, independent study, internships, off-campus study, part-time degree program, student-designed majors, summer session for credit.

Computers on Campus 14 computers/terminals are available on campus for general student use. Students can access the following: computer help desk, free student e-mail accounts, online (class) grades, online (class) registration, online (class) schedules. Campuswide network is available. Wireless service is available via entire campus.

Student Life *Housing:* college housing not available. *Campus security:* late-night transport/escort service.

Standardized Tests *Required for some:* TOFFL.

Costs (2012–13) *Tuition:* $453 per unit part-time. Full-time tuition and fees vary according to degree level. Part-time tuition and fees vary according to degree level.

Financial Aid Of all full-time matriculated undergraduates who enrolled in 2003, 23 Federal Work-Study jobs (averaging $2120).

Applying *Options:* electronic application, deferred entrance. *Application fee:* $60. *Application deadline:* rolling (transfers). *Notification:* continuous (transfers).

Application Contact Mr. Scott Weatherman, Admissions Advisor, Antioch University Santa Barbara, 602 Anacapa Street, Santa Barbara, CA 93101. *Phone:* 805-962-8179 Ext. 5330. *Toll-free phone:* 866-526-8462. *Fax:* 805-962-4786. *E-mail:* sweatherman@antioch.edu. *Web site:* http://www.antiochsb.edu/.

Argosy University, Inland Empire

San Bernardino, California

Freshman Application Contact Argosy University, Inland Empire, 636 East Brier Drive, Suite 120, San Bernardino, CA 92408. *Phone:* 909-915-3800. *Toll-free phone:* 866-217-9075. *Web site:* http://www.argosy.edu/inland-empire/.

See page 1062 for the College Close-Up.

Argosy University, Los Angeles

Santa Monica, California

Freshman Application Contact Argosy University, Los Angeles, 5230 Pacific Concourse, Suite 200, Santa Monica, CA 90045. *Phone:* 310-866-4000. *Toll-free phone:* 866-505-0332. *Web site:* http://www.argosy.edu/los-angeles/.

See page 1062 for the College Close-Up.

Argosy University, Orange County

Orange, California

Freshman Application Contact Argosy University, Orange County, 601 South Lewis Street, Orange, CA 92868. *Phone:* 714-620-3700. *Toll-free phone:* 800-716-9598. *Web site:* http://www.argosy.edu/locations/los-angeles-orange-county/.

See page 1062 for the College Close-Up.

Argosy University, San Diego

San Diego, California

Freshman Application Contact Argosy University, San Diego, 1615 Murray Canyon Road, Suite 100, San Diego, CA 92108. *Phone:* 619-321-3000. *Toll-free phone:* 866-505-0333. *Web site:* http://www.argosy.edu/sandiego/.

See page 1062 for the College Close-Up.

Argosy University, San Francisco Bay Area

Alameda, California

Freshman Application Contact Argosy University, San Francisco Bay Area, 1005 Atlantic Avenue, Alameda, CA 94501. *Phone:* 510-217-4700. *Toll-free phone:* 866-215-2777. *Web site:* http://www.argosy.edu/sanfrancisco/.

See page 1062 for the College Close-Up.

Art Center College of Design

Pasadena, California

- **Independent** comprehensive, founded 1930
- **Suburban** 175-acre campus with easy access to Los Angeles
- **Coed** 1,650 undergraduate students, 83% full-time, 47% women, 53% men
- **Very difficult** entrance level

Undergraduates 1,370 full-time, 280 part-time. 2% Black or African American, non-Hispanic/Latino; 11% Hispanic/Latino; 37% Asian, non-Hispanic/Latino; 0.8% Native Hawaiian or other Pacific Islander, non-Hispanic/Latino; 0.1% American Indian or Alaska Native, non-Hispanic/Latino; 2% Two or more races, non-Hispanic/Latino; 2% Race/ethnicity unknown; 20% international.

Freshmen *Admission:* 139 enrolled.

Faculty *Total:* 372, 25% full-time. *Student/faculty ratio:* 9:1.

Academics *Calendar:* trimesters. *Degrees:* bachelor's and master's.

Computers on Campus Students can access the following: campus intranet, computer help desk, free student e-mail accounts, online (class) grades, online (class) registration, online (class) schedules. Campuswide network is available. Wireless service is available via entire campus.

Student Life *Housing:* college housing not available. *Campus security:* 24-hour emergency response devices and patrols.

Standardized Tests *Required for some:* SAT or ACT (for admission).

Costs (2012–13) *Tuition:* $33,444 full-time, $1198 per credit hour part-time. *Required fees:* $500 full-time. *Payment plan:* installment. *Waivers:* employees or children of employees.

Financial Aid *Average financial aid package:* $17,803. *Average need-based loan:* $10,169. *Average need-based gift aid:* $14,627.

Applying *Options:* electronic application, deferred entrance. *Application fee:* $50. *Required:* essay or personal statement, high school transcript, portfolio. *Recommended:* interview. *Application deadlines:* rolling (freshmen), rolling (transfers). *Notification:* continuous (freshmen), continuous (transfers).

Freshman Application Contact Ms. Kit Baron, Vice President, Admissions and Enrollment Management, Art Center College of Design, 1700 Lida Street, Pasadena, CA 91103. *Phone:* 626-396-2322. *Fax:* 626-795-0578. *E-mail:* kit.baron@artcenter.edu. *Web site:* http://www.artcenter.edu/.

The Art Institute of California, a college of Argosy University, Hollywood

North Hollywood, California

- **Proprietary** 4-year, founded 1992, part of Education Management Corporation
- **Urban** campus
- **Coed**

Academics *Calendar:* quarters. *Degrees:* associate and bachelor's.

Costs (2011–12) *Tuition:* Tuition cost varies by program. Prospective students should contact the school for current tuition costs. Other charges include a starting kit for all first-quarter students. Kits vary in price, depending on the program of study.

Freshman Application Contact The Art Institute of California, a college of Argosy University, Hollywood, 5250 Lankershim Boulevard, North Hollywood, CA 91601. *Phone:* 818-299-5100. *Toll-free phone:* 877-468-6232. *Web site:* http://www.artinstitutes.edu/hollywood/.

See page 1072 for the College Close-Up.

The Art Institute of California, a college of Argosy University, Inland Empire

San Bernardino, California

- **Proprietary** 4-year, part of Education Management Corporation
- **Suburban** campus
- **Coed**

Academics *Degrees:* associate and bachelor's.

Costs (2011–12) *Tuition:* Tuition cost varies by program. Prospective students should contact the school for current tuition costs. Other charges include a starting kit for all first-quarter students. Kits vary in price, depending on the program of study.

Freshman Application Contact The Art Institute of California, a college of Argosy University, Inland Empire, 674 East Brier Drive, San Bernardino, CA

92408. *Phone:* 909-915-2100. *Toll-free phone:* 800-353-0812. *Web site:* http://www.artinstitutes.edu/inlandempire/.

See page 1074 for the College Close-Up.

The Art Institute of California, a college of Argosy University, Los Angeles

Santa Monica, California

- **Proprietary** 4-year, part of Education Management Corporation
- **Urban** campus
- **Coed**

Academics *Calendar:* quarters. *Degrees:* diplomas, associate, and bachelor's.

Costs (2011–12) *Tuition:* Tuition cost varies by program. Prospective students should contact the school for current tuition costs. Other charges include a starting kit for all first-quarter students. Kits vary in price, depending on the program of study.

Freshman Application Contact The Art Institute of California, a college of Argosy University, Los Angeles, 2900 31st Street, Santa Monica, CA 90405-3035. *Phone:* 310-752-4700. *Toll-free phone:* 888-646-4610. *Web site:* http://www.artinstitutes.edu/losangeles/.

See page 1076 for the College Close-Up.

The Art Institute of California, a college of Argosy University, Orange County

Santa Ana, California

- **Proprietary** 4-year, founded 2000, part of Education Management Corporation
- **Urban** campus with easy access to Orange County
- **Coed**

Academics *Calendar:* quarters. *Degrees:* diplomas, associate, and bachelor's.

Costs (2011–12) *Tuition:* Tuition cost varies by program. Prospective students should contact the school for current tuition costs. Other charges include a starting kit for all first-quarter students. Kits vary in price, depending on the program of study.

Freshman Application Contact The Art Institute of California, a college of Argosy University, Orange County, 3601 West Sunflower Avenue, Santa Ana, CA 92704. *Phone:* 714-830-0200. *Toll-free phone:* 888-549-3055. *Web site:* http://www.artinstitutes.edu/orangecounty/.

See page 1078 for the College Close-Up.

The Art Institute of California, a college of Argosy University, Sacramento

Sacramento, California

- **Proprietary** 4-year
- **Coed**

Academics *Degrees:* diplomas, associate, and bachelor's.

Costs (2011–12) *Tuition:* Tuition cost varies by program. Prospective students should contact the school for current tuition costs. Other charges include a starting kit for all first-quarter students. Kits vary in price, depending on the program of study.

Freshman Application Contact The Art Institute of California, a college of Argosy University, Sacramento, 2850 Gateway Oaks Drive, Suite 100, Sacramento, CA 95833. *Phone:* 916-830-6320. *Toll-free phone:* 800-477-1957. *Web site:* http://www.artinstitutes.edu/sacramento/.

See page 1080 for the College Close-Up.

The Art Institute of California, a college of Argosy University, San Diego

San Diego, California

- **Proprietary** 4-year, founded 1981, part of Education Management Corporation
- **Urban** campus
- **Coed**

Academics *Calendar:* quarters. *Degrees:* associate and bachelor's.

Costs (2011–12) *Tuition:* Tuition cost varies by program. Prospective students should contact the school for current tuition costs. Other charges include a starting kit for all first-quarter students. Kits vary in price, depending on the program of study.

Freshman Application Contact The Art Institute of California, a college of Argosy University, San Diego, 7650 Mission Valley Road, San Diego, CA 92108. *Phone:* 858-598-1200. *Toll-free phone:* 866-275-2422. *Web site:* http://www.artinstitutes.edu/sandiego/.

See page 1082 for the College Close-Up.

The Art Institute of California, a college of Argosy University, San Francisco

San Francisco, California

- **Proprietary** comprehensive, founded 1939, part of Education Management Corporation
- **Urban** campus
- **Coed**

Academics *Calendar:* quarters. *Degrees:* diplomas, associate, bachelor's, and master's.

Costs (2011–12) *Tuition:* Tuition cost varies by program. Prospective students should contact the school for current tuition costs. Other charges include a starting kit for all first-quarter students. Kits vary in price, depending on the program of study.

Freshman Application Contact The Art Institute of California, a college of Argosy University, San Francisco, 1170 Market Street, San Francisco, CA 94102. *Phone:* 415-865-0198. *Toll-free phone:* 888-493-3261. *Web site:* http://www.artinstitutes.edu/sanfrancisco/.

See page 1084 for the College Close-Up.

The Art Institute of California, a college of Argosy University, Sunnyvale

Sunnyvale, California

- **Proprietary** 4-year
- **Coed**

Academics *Degrees:* associate and bachelor's.

Costs (2011–12) *Tuition:* Tuition cost varies by program. Prospective students should contact the school for current tuition costs. Other charges include a starting kit for all first-quarter students. Kits vary in price, depending on the program of study.

Freshman Application Contact The Art Institute of California, a college of Argosy University, Sunnyvale, 1120 Kifer Road, Sunnyvale, CA 94086. *Phone:* 408-962-6400. *Toll-free phone:* 866-583-7961. *Web site:* http://www.artinstitutes.edu/sunnyvale/.

See page 1086 for the College Close-Up.

Azusa Pacific University

Azusa, California

- **Independent nondenominational** university, founded 1899
- **Small-town** 60-acre campus with easy access to Los Angeles
- **Endowment** $52.1 million
- **Coed** 5,998 undergraduate students, 86% full-time, 64% women, 36% men
- **Moderately difficult** entrance level, 49% of applicants were admitted

Undergraduates 5,129 full-time, 869 part-time. Students come from 51 states and territories; 23 other countries; 19% are from out of state; 5% Black or African American, non-Hispanic/Latino; 17% Hispanic/Latino; 8% Asian, non-

Hispanic/Latino; 0.6% Native Hawaiian or other Pacific Islander, non-Hispanic/Latino; 0.3% American Indian or Alaska Native, non-Hispanic/Latino; 2% Two or more races, non-Hispanic/Latino; 11% Race/ethnicity unknown; 2% international; 10% transferred in; 57% live on campus. *Retention:* 88% of full-time freshmen returned.

Freshmen *Admission:* 8,187 applied, 4,028 admitted, 1,180 enrolled. *Average high school GPA:* 3.64. *Test scores:* SAT critical reading scores over 500: 72%; SAT math scores over 500: 74%; ACT scores over 18: 98%; SAT critical reading scores over 600: 26%; SAT math scores over 600: 31%; ACT scores over 24: 50%; SAT critical reading scores over 700: 4%; SAT math scores over 700: 4%; ACT scores over 30: 9%.

Faculty *Total:* 1,102, 35% full-time, 27% with terminal degrees. *Student/faculty ratio:* 13:1.

Academics *Calendar:* semesters. *Degrees:* bachelor's, master's, doctoral, post-master's, postbachelor's, and first professional certificates. *Special study options:* academic remediation for entering students, accelerated degree program, adult/continuing education programs, advanced placement credit, cooperative education, distance learning, double majors, English as a second language, freshman honors college, honors programs, independent study, internships, off-campus study, part-time degree program, services for LD students, study abroad, summer session for credit. *ROTC:* Army (b), Air Force (c).

Computers on Campus Students can access the following: campus intranet, computer help desk, free student e-mail accounts, online (class) grades, online (class) registration. Campuswide network is available. Wireless service is available via entire campus.

Student Life *Housing:* on-campus residence required through sophomore year. *Options:* coed, men-only, women-only. Campus housing is university owned and leased by the school. Freshman applicants given priority for college housing. *Activities and organizations:* drama/theater group, student-run newspaper, radio and television station, choral group, marching band, community service groups, choir, outreach ministries groups, Habitat for Humanity, Multi-Ethnic Student Alliance (MESA). *Campus security:* 24-hour emergency response devices and patrols, student patrols, late-night transport/escort service, controlled dormitory access. *Student services:* health clinic, personal/psychological counseling.

Athletics Member NAIA. *Intercollegiate sports:* baseball M(s), basketball M(s)/W(s), cross-country running M(s)/W(s), football M(s), golf M(s), soccer M(s)/W(s), softball W(s), tennis M(s), track and field M(s)/W(s), volleyball M/W(s). *Intramural sports:* basketball M/W, football M/W, golf M/W, skiing (downhill) M/W, soccer W, volleyball M/W.

Standardized Tests *Required:* SAT or ACT (for admission).

Costs (2011–12) *Comprehensive fee:* $37,161 includes full-time tuition ($29,100), mandatory fees ($840), and room and board ($7221). Part-time tuition: $1213 per credit hour. *College room only:* $4158. Room and board charges vary according to board plan and housing facility. *Payment plan:* installment.

Financial Aid Of all full-time matriculated undergraduates who enrolled in 2010, 4,440 applied for aid, 4,067 were judged to have need, 387 had their need fully met. 1,097 Federal Work-Study jobs (averaging $908). In 2010, 302 non-need-based awards were made. *Average percent of need met:* 67%. *Average financial aid package:* $17,963. *Average need-based loan:* $4330. *Average need-based gift aid:* $9485. *Average non-need-based aid:* $7240. *Average indebtedness upon graduation:* $26,795. *Financial aid deadline:* 7/1.

Applying *Options:* electronic application, early admission, early action, deferred entrance. *Application fee:* $45. *Required:* essay or personal statement, high school transcript, minimum 3.0 GPA, 2 letters of recommendation. *Required for some:* interview. *Application deadlines:* 6/1 (freshmen), 6/1 (transfers), 11/15 (early action). *Notification:* continuous (freshmen), continuous (transfers), 1/15 (early action).

Freshman Application Contact Ms. Lynnette Barnes, Processing Coordinator, Azusa Pacific University, 901 East Alosta Avenue, PO Box 7000, Undergraduate Admissions, 7221, Azusa, CA 91702-7000. *Phone:* 626-815-6000 Ext. 3419. *Toll-free phone:* 800-TALK-APU. *E-mail:* admissions@apu.edu. *Web site:* http://www.apu.edu/.

Bethesda University of California

Anaheim, California

Director of Admissions Jacquie Ha, Director of Admission, Bethesda University of California, 730 North Euclid Street, Anaheim, CA 92801. *Phone:* 714-517-1945. *Fax:* 714-517-1948. *E-mail:* admission@bcu.edu. *Web site:* http://www.buc.edu/.

Biola University

La Mirada, California

- **Independent interdenominational** university, founded 1908
- **Suburban** 95-acre campus with easy access to Los Angeles
- **Endowment** $74.6 million
- **Coed** 4,271 undergraduate students, 94% full-time, 61% women, 39% men
- **Moderately difficult** entrance level, 76% of applicants were admitted

Undergraduates 4,036 full-time, 235 part-time. Students come from 43 states and territories; 20 other countries; 24% are from out of state; 2% Black or African American, non-Hispanic/Latino; 16% Hispanic/Latino; 13% Asian, non-Hispanic/Latino; 0.5% Native Hawaiian or other Pacific Islander, non-Hispanic/Latino; 0.4% American Indian or Alaska Native, non-Hispanic/Latino; 6% Two or more races, non-Hispanic/Latino; 1% Race/ethnicity unknown; 2% international; 8% transferred in; 64% live on campus. *Retention:* 86% of full-time freshmen returned.

Freshmen *Admission:* 3,337 applied, 2,548 admitted, 935 enrolled. *Average high school GPA:* 3.5. *Test scores:* SAT critical reading scores over 500: 76%; SAT math scores over 500: 75%; SAT writing scores over 500: 76%; ACT scores over 18: 95%; SAT critical reading scores over 600: 36%; SAT math scores over 600: 35%; SAT writing scores over 600: 33%; ACT scores over 24: 53%; SAT critical reading scores over 700: 7%; SAT math scores over 700: 6%; SAT writing scores over 700: 6%; ACT scores over 30: 10%.

Faculty *Total:* 497, 49% full-time, 36% with terminal degrees. *Student/faculty ratio:* 14:1.

Academics *Calendar:* 4-1-4. *Degrees:* certificates, bachelor's, master's, doctoral, post-master's, postbachelor's, and first professional certificates. *Special study options:* double majors, English as a second language, honors programs, internships, off-campus study, part-time degree program, services for LD students, study abroad, summer session for credit. *ROTC:* Army (c), Air Force (c). *Unusual degree programs:* 3-2 engineering.

Computers on Campus 200 computers/terminals are available on campus for general student use. Students can access the following: campus intranet, computer help desk, free student e-mail accounts, online (class) grades, online (class) registration, online (class) schedules. Campuswide network is available. 100% of college-owned or -operated housing units are wired for high-speed Internet access. Wireless service is available via entire campus.

Student Life *Housing:* on-campus residence required for freshman year. *Options:* coed, men-only, women-only, disabled students. Campus housing is university owned. Freshman campus housing is guaranteed. *Activities and organizations:* drama/theater group, student-run newspaper, radio and television station, choral group, Social Justice Ministry, Guerilla Film Society, Community Bike Riders, Xopoc Dance Team, Biola Cheese Society. *Campus security:* 24-hour emergency response devices and patrols, late-night transport/escort service, controlled dormitory access. *Student services:* health clinic, personal/psychological counseling.

Athletics Member NAIA. *Intercollegiate sports:* baseball M(s), basketball M(s)/W(s), cross-country running M(s)/W(s), golf M(s)/W(s), soccer M(s)/W(s), softball W(s), swimming and diving M(s)/W(s), tennis M(s)/W(s), track and field M(s)/W(s), volleyball W(s). *Intramural sports:* basketball M/W, cheerleading W(c), football M/W, lacrosse M(c), rugby M, soccer M/W, softball M/W, ultimate Frisbee M/W, volleyball M/W.

Standardized Tests *Required:* SAT or ACT (for admission).

Costs (2011–12) *Comprehensive fee:* $37,478 includes full-time tuition ($29,908) and room and board ($7570). Full-time tuition and fees vary according to course load. Part-time tuition: $1246 per unit. Part-time tuition and fees vary according to course load. *College room only:* $4480. Room and board charges vary according to board plan and housing facility. *Payment plan:* installment. *Waivers:* employees or children of employees.

Financial Aid Of all full-time matriculated undergraduates who enrolled in 2010, 3,036 applied for aid, 2,674 were judged to have need, 165 had their need fully met. 556 Federal Work-Study jobs (averaging $1167). In 2010, 682 non-need-based awards were made. *Average percent of need met:* 53%. *Average financial aid package:* $17,751. *Average need-based loan:* $3449. *Average need-based gift aid:* $13,062. *Average non-need-based aid:* $5792. *Average indebtedness upon graduation:* $32,091.

Applying *Options:* electronic application, early action, deferred entrance. *Application fee:* $45. *Required:* essay or personal statement, high school transcript, minimum 3.0 GPA, 1 letter of recommendation, evangelical believer in the Christian faith. *Required for some:* interview. *Application deadlines:* 3/1 (freshmen), 11/15 (transfers), 11/15 (early action). *Notification:* 4/1 (freshmen), 1/15 (transfers), 1/15 (early action).

Freshman Application Contact Andrea Helmuth, Associate Director of Undergraduate Admissions, Biola University, 13800 Biola Avenue, La Mirada, CA 90639. *Phone:* 562-903-4752. *Toll-free phone:* 800-652-4652. *E-mail:* admissions@biola.edu. *Web site:* http://www.biola.edu/.

Brandman University

Irvine, California

Admissions Office Contact Brandman University, 16355 Laguna Canyon Road, Irvine, CA 92618. *Toll-free phone:* 800-746-0082. *Web site:* http://www.brandman.edu/irvine/.

Brooks Institute

Santa Barbara, California

Freshman Application Contact Admissions Office, Brooks Institute, 27 East Cota Street, Santa Barbara, CA 93101. *Phone:* 805-966-3888. *Toll-free phone:* 888-276-4999. *Fax:* 805-565-1386. *E-mail:* admissions@brooks.edu. *Web site:* http://www.brooks.edu/.

California Baptist University

Riverside, California

- **Independent Southern Baptist** comprehensive, founded 1950
- **Suburban** 128-acre campus with easy access to Los Angeles
- **Endowment** $13.5 million
- **Coed** 4,403 undergraduate students, 88% full-time, 63% women, 37% men
- **Minimally difficult** entrance level, 74% of applicants were admitted

Undergraduates 3,877 full-time, 526 part-time. Students come from 45 states and territories; 25 other countries; 10% are from out of state; 9% Black or African American, non-Hispanic/Latino; 24% Hispanic/Latino; 5% Asian, non-Hispanic/Latino; 0.1% Native Hawaiian or other Pacific Islander, non-Hispanic/Latino; 0.9% American Indian or Alaska Native, non-Hispanic/Latino; 0.7% Two or more races, non-Hispanic/Latino; 7% Race/ethnicity unknown; 3% international; 11% transferred in; 52% live on campus. *Retention:* 77% of full-time freshmen returned.
Freshmen *Admission:* 2,398 applied, 1,776 admitted, 790 enrolled. *Average high school GPA:* 3.4. *Test scores:* SAT critical reading scores over 500: 48%; SAT math scores over 500: 51%; SAT writing scores over 500: 48%; ACT scores over 18: 85%; SAT critical reading scores over 600: 15%; SAT math scores over 600: 17%; SAT writing scores over 600: 12%; ACT scores over 24: 29%; SAT critical reading scores over 700: 1%; SAT math scores over 700: 2%; SAT writing scores over 700: 1%; ACT scores over 30: 1%.
Faculty *Total:* 460, 43% full-time, 45% with terminal degrees. *Student/faculty ratio:* 19:1.
Academics *Calendar:* 2-4-4-2. *Degrees:* bachelor's and master's. *Special study options:* accelerated degree program, adult/continuing education programs, advanced placement credit, distance learning, double majors, English as a second language, honors programs, independent study, internships, off-campus study, part-time degree program, study abroad, summer session for credit. *ROTC:* Army (b), Air Force (c).
Computers on Campus 279 computers/terminals are available on campus for general student use. Students can access the following: campus intranet, computer help desk, free student e-mail accounts, online (class) grades, online (class) registration, online (class) schedules. Campuswide network is available. Wireless service is available via entire campus.
Student Life *Housing:* on-campus residence required for freshman year. *Options:* men-only, women-only. Campus housing is university owned. Freshman applicants given priority for college housing. *Activities and organizations:* drama/theater group, student-run newspaper, choral group, CBU CRAZIES, University Place-Men, University Place-Women, Student Leadership Groups, Commuter Students. *Campus security:* 24-hour emergency response devices and patrols, student patrols, late-night transport/escort service, controlled dormitory access. *Student services:* personal/psychological counseling.
Athletics Member NAIA. *Intercollegiate sports:* baseball M(s), basketball M(s)/W(s), cheerleading M(s)/W(s), cross-country running M(s)/W(s), golf M(s)/W(s), soccer M(s)/W(s), softball W(s), swimming and diving M(s)/W(s), track and field M(s)/W(s), volleyball M(s)/W(s), water polo M(s)/W(s), wrestling M(s). *Intramural sports:* basketball M/W, bowling M/W, football M/W, softball M/W, table tennis M/W, ultimate Frisbee M/W, volleyball M/W.
Standardized Tests *Required:* SAT or ACT (for admission).
Costs (2011–12) *Comprehensive fee:* $34,468 includes full-time tuition ($23,998), mandatory fees ($1770), and room and board ($8700). Full-time tuition and fees vary according to class time and program. Part-time tuition: $923 per semester hour. Part-time tuition and fees vary according to class time and program. *Required fees:* $175 per term part-time. *College room only:* $4360. Room and board charges vary according to board plan and housing facility. *Payment plan:* installment. *Waivers:* employees or children of employees.
Financial Aid Of all full-time matriculated undergraduates who enrolled in 2009, 2,576 applied for aid, 1,894 were judged to have need, 1,605 had their need fully met. 178 Federal Work-Study jobs (averaging $888). In 2009, 449 non-need-based awards were made. *Average percent of need met:* 58%. *Average financial aid package:* $8651. *Average need-based loan:* $2298. *Average need-based gift aid:* $4677. *Average non-need-based:* $3656. *Average indebtedness upon graduation:* $34,650.
Applying *Options:* electronic application, early admission, early action, deferred entrance. *Application fee:* $45. *Required:* essay or personal statement, high school transcript, minimum 2.0 GPA, 2 letters of recommendation. *Recommended:* interview. *Application deadlines:* rolling (freshmen), rolling (out-of-state freshmen), rolling (transfers), 12/1 (early action). *Notification:* continuous until 9/6 (freshmen), continuous until 6/9 (out-of-state freshmen), continuous (transfers), 12/20 (early action).
Freshman Application Contact Mr. Allen Johnson, Director, Undergraduate Admissions, California Baptist University, 8432 Magnolia Avenue, Riverside, CA 92504-3297. *Phone:* 951-343-4212. *Toll-free phone:* 877-228-8866. *Fax:* 951-343-4525. *E-mail:* admissions@calbaptist.edu. *Web site:* http://www.calbaptist.edu/.

California Christian College

Fresno, California

- **Independent Free Will Baptist** 4-year
- **Urban** 5-acre campus
- **Endowment** $122,093
- **Coed** 20 undergraduate students, 85% full-time, 45% women, 55% men
- **Noncompetitive** entrance level, 100% of applicants were admitted

Undergraduates 17 full-time, 3 part-time. Students come from 1 other state; 1 other country; 20% Black or African American, non-Hispanic/Latino; 40% Hispanic/Latino; 10% Asian, non-Hispanic/Latino; 5% international; 10% transferred in; 25% live on campus.
Freshmen *Admission:* 3 applied, 3 admitted, 5 enrolled. *Average high school GPA:* 3.04.
Faculty *Total:* 5, 20% with terminal degrees. *Student/faculty ratio:* 4:1.
Academics *Calendar:* semesters. *Degrees:* associate and bachelor's. *Special study options:* academic remediation for entering students, cooperative education, distance learning, independent study, part-time degree program.
Computers on Campus 5 computers/terminals are available on campus for general student use. Students can access the following: wireless Internet access. Campuswide network is available. 100% of college-owned or -operated housing units are wired for high-speed Internet access. Wireless service is available via entire campus.
Student Life *Housing:* on-campus residence required through sophomore year. *Options:* men-only, women-only. Campus housing is university owned. *Student services:* personal/psychological counseling.
Standardized Tests *Required:* standardized Bible content tests (for admission). *Recommended:* SAT or ACT (for admission).
Costs (2011–12) *Comprehensive fee:* $11,760 includes full-time tuition ($7080), mandatory fees ($530), and room and board ($4150). *Payment plan:* installment.
Financial Aid Of all full-time matriculated undergraduates who enrolled in 2009, 25 applied for aid, 23 were judged to have need, 1 had their need fully met. 4 Federal Work-Study jobs (averaging $1829). *Average percent of need met:* 67%. *Average financial aid package:* $11,676. *Average need-based loan:* $4138. *Average need-based gift aid:* $2625. *Average indebtedness upon graduation:* $26,237.
Applying *Options:* electronic application. *Application fee:* $40. *Required:* essay or personal statement, high school transcript, minimum 2.0 GPA, 2 letters of recommendation, statement of faith, moral/ethical statement. *Recommended:* interview. *Application deadlines:* rolling (freshmen), rolling (transfers). *Notification:* continuous (freshmen), continuous (transfers).
Freshman Application Contact California Christian College, 4881 East University Avenue, Fresno, CA 93703-3533. *Phone:* 559-251-4215. *Web site:* http://www.calchristiancollege.org/.

California Coast University

Santa Ana, California

- **Proprietary** comprehensive, founded 1973
- **Coed**

Academics *Degrees:* associate, bachelor's, master's, and doctoral (distance learning only).
Costs (2011–12) *Tuition:* $150 per unit part-time.
Applying *Application fee:* $75. *Required:* resume, high school transcript or GED equivalent.
Freshman Application Contact California Coast University, 925 North Spurgeon Street, Santa Ana, CA 92701. *Phone:* 714-547-9625. *Toll-free phone:* 888-CCU-UNIV. *Web site:* http://www.calcoast.edu/.

California College

San Diego, California

Director of Admissions Tana Sanderson, Director of Admission, California College, 2820 Camino del Rio South, Suite 300, San Diego, CA 92108. *Phone:* 619-295-5785. *Toll-free phone:* 800-622-3188. *E-mail:* tana.sanderson@cc-sd.edu. *Web site:* http://www.cc-sd.edu/.

California College of the Arts

San Francisco, California

- **Independent** comprehensive, founded 1907
- **Urban** 4-acre campus with easy access to San Francisco, Oakland
- **Endowment** $31.1 million
- **Coed** 1,502 undergraduate students, 93% full-time, 61% women, 39% men
- **Moderately difficult** entrance level, 76% of applicants were admitted

Undergraduates 1,396 full-time, 106 part-time. Students come from 44 states and territories; 51 other countries; 35% are from out of state; 5% Black or African American, non-Hispanic/Latino; 13% Hispanic/Latino; 16% Asian, non-Hispanic/Latino; 0.8% American Indian or Alaska Native, non-Hispanic/Latino; 11% Race/ethnicity unknown; 15% international; 13% transferred in; 15% live on campus. *Retention:* 79% of full-time freshmen returned.

Freshmen *Admission:* 1,352 applied, 1,031 admitted, 234 enrolled. *Average high school GPA:* 3.18. *Test scores:* SAT critical reading scores over 500: 63%; SAT math scores over 500: 68%; SAT writing scores over 500: 68%; ACT scores over 18: 96%; SAT critical reading scores over 600: 33%; SAT math scores over 600: 28%; SAT writing scores over 600: 31%; ACT scores over 24: 41%; SAT critical reading scores over 700: 7%; SAT math scores over 700: 6%; SAT writing scores over 700: 7%; ACT scores over 30: 5%.

Faculty *Total:* 571, 15% full-time, 63% with terminal degrees. *Student/faculty ratio:* 10:1.

Academics *Calendar:* semesters. *Degrees:* bachelor's and master's. *Special study options:* academic remediation for entering students, advanced placement credit, cooperative education, double majors, English as a second language, honors programs, independent study, internships, off-campus study, services for LD students, student-designed majors, study abroad, summer session for credit.

Computers on Campus 346 computers/terminals and 33 ports are available on campus for general student use. Students can access the following: computer help desk, free student e-mail accounts, online (class) grades, online (class) registration, online (class) schedules. Campuswide network is available. 100% of college-owned or -operated housing units are wired for high-speed Internet access. Wireless service is available via classrooms, computer centers, computer labs, dorm rooms, learning centers, libraries.

Student Life *Housing options:* coed. Campus housing is university owned. Freshman applicants given priority for college housing. *Activities and organizations:* Social Projects and Communal Environments (SPACE), Queer/Straight Alliance (QSA), Future Action Reclamation Mob (FARM), Alliance for Multiculturalism in Architecture (NOMAS), Improv Club. *Campus security:* 24-hour emergency response devices and patrols, late-night transport/escort service. *Student services:* personal/psychological counseling.

Standardized Tests *Recommended:* SAT or ACT (for admission).

Costs (2012–13) *Tuition:* $36,960 full-time, $1540 per unit part-time. Full-time tuition and fees vary according to degree level. Part-time tuition and fees vary according to course load and degree level. *Required fees:* $350 full-time. *Room only:* $7400. Room and board charges vary according to housing facility. *Payment plan:* installment. *Waivers:* employees or children of employees.

Financial Aid Of all full-time matriculated undergraduates who enrolled in 2011, 988 applied for aid, 923 were judged to have need, 44 had their need fully met. 862 Federal Work-Study jobs (averaging $2944). 113 state and other part-time jobs (averaging $3252). In 2011, 192 non-need-based awards were made. *Average percent of need met:* 57%. *Average financial aid package:* $24,079. *Average need-based loan:* $4923. *Average need-based gift aid:* $19,901. *Average non-need-based aid:* $8403. *Average indebtedness upon graduation:* $36,690.

Applying *Options:* electronic application, deferred entrance. *Application fee:* $60. *Required:* essay or personal statement, high school transcript, 2 letters of recommendation, portfolio of creative work and statement of artistic and professional goals required. *Required for some:* interview. *Application deadlines:* rolling (freshmen), rolling (transfers). *Notification:* continuous (freshmen), continuous (transfers).

Freshman Application Contact Ms. Robynne Royster, Director of Admissions, California College of the Arts, 1111 Eighth Street, San Francisco, CA 94107. *Phone:* 415-703-9523 Ext. 9532. *Toll-free phone:* 800-447-1ART. *Fax:* 415-703-9539. *E-mail:* enroll@cca.edu. *Web site:* http://www.cca.edu/.

See page 1236 for the College Close-Up.

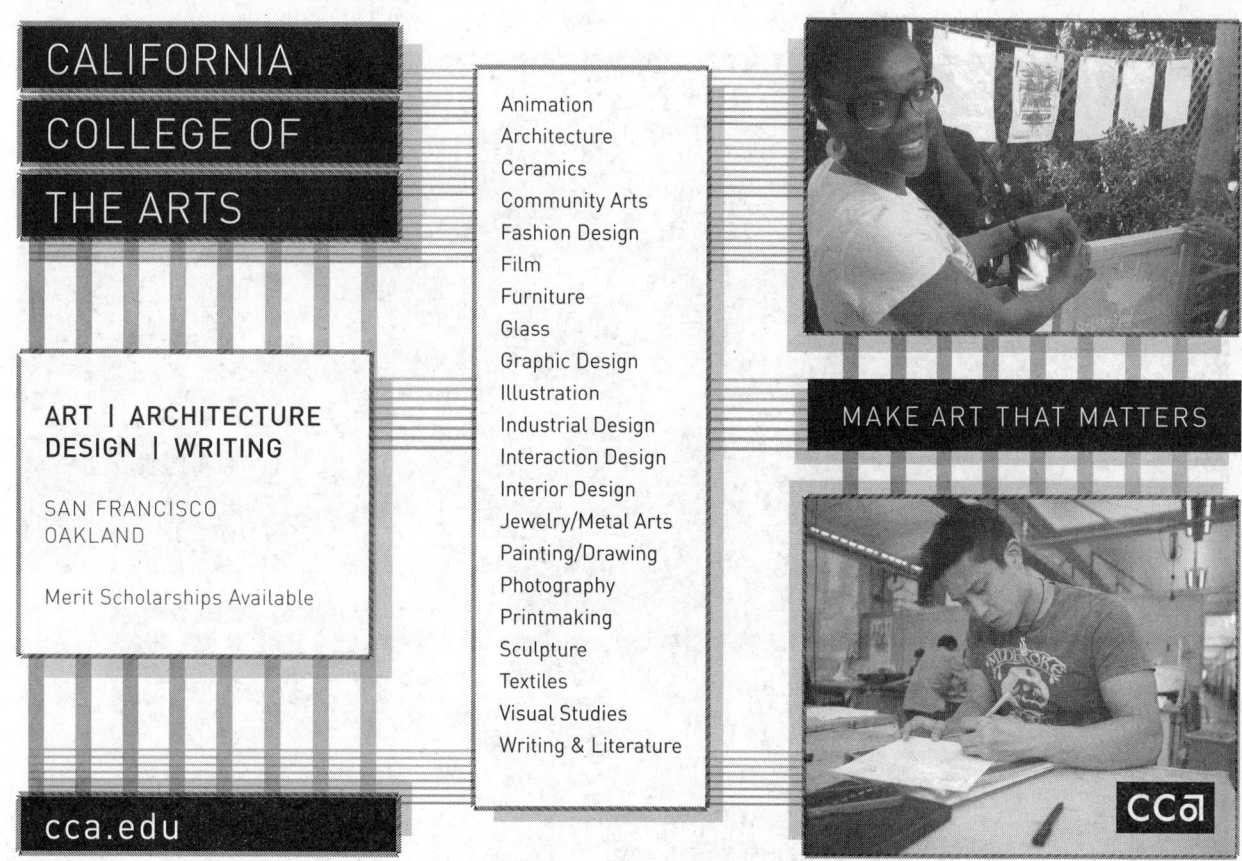

CALIFORNIA COLLEGE OF THE ARTS

ART | ARCHITECTURE
DESIGN | WRITING

SAN FRANCISCO
OAKLAND

Merit Scholarships Available

Animation
Architecture
Ceramics
Community Arts
Fashion Design
Film
Furniture
Glass
Graphic Design
Illustration
Industrial Design
Interaction Design
Interior Design
Jewelry/Metal Arts
Painting/Drawing
Photography
Printmaking
Sculpture
Textiles
Visual Studies
Writing & Literature

MAKE ART THAT MATTERS

CCA

cca.edu

California Institute of Integral Studies

San Francisco, California

Application Contact Admissions Department, California Institute of Integral Studies, 1453 Mission Street, San Francisco, CA 94103. *Phone:* 415-575-6156. *Fax:* 415-575-1268. *E-mail:* admissions@ciis.edu. *Web site:* http://www.ciis.edu/.

California Institute of Technology

Pasadena, California

- **Independent** university, founded 1891
- **Suburban** 124-acre campus with easy access to Los Angeles
- **Endowment** $1.5 billion
- **Coed** 978 undergraduate students, 100% full-time, 39% women, 61% men
- **Most difficult** entrance level, 13% of applicants were admitted

Undergraduates 978 full-time. 65% are from out of state; 1% Black or African American, non-Hispanic/Latino; 8% Hispanic/Latino; 39% Asian, non-Hispanic/Latino; 0.6% Native Hawaiian or other Pacific Islander, non-Hispanic/Latino; 0.3% American Indian or Alaska Native, non-Hispanic/Latino; 3% Two or more races, non-Hispanic/Latino; 0.5% Race/ethnicity unknown; 12% international; 0.6% transferred in; 95% live on campus. *Retention:* 98% of full-time freshmen returned.

Freshmen *Admission:* 5,225 applied, 667 admitted, 244 enrolled. *Test scores:* SAT critical reading scores over 500: 100%; SAT math scores over 500: 100%; SAT writing scores over 500: 100%; ACT scores over 18: 100%; SAT critical reading scores over 600: 98%; SAT math scores over 600: 100%; SAT writing scores over 600: 100%; ACT scores over 24: 100%; SAT critical reading scores over 700: 77%; SAT math scores over 700: 98%; SAT writing scores over 700: 77%; ACT scores over 30: 100%.

Faculty *Total:* 338, 95% full-time, 96% with terminal degrees. *Student/faculty ratio:* 3:1.

Academics *Calendar:* 3 ten-week terms. *Degrees:* bachelor's, master's, doctoral, post-master's, and first professional certificates. *Special study options:* cooperative education, double majors, English as a second language, independent study, off-campus study, services for LD students, student-designed majors, study abroad. *ROTC:* Army (c), Air Force (c). *Unusual degree programs:* 3-2 engineering with Bowdoin College, Bryn Mawr College, Grinnell College, Haverford College, Mt. Holyoke College, Oberlin College, Occidental College, Ohio Wesleyan University, Pomona College, Reed College, Spelman College, Wesleyan University, Whitman College.

Computers on Campus Students can access the following: computer help desk, free student e-mail accounts, online (class) registration. Campuswide network is available. 100% of college-owned or -operated housing units are wired for high-speed Internet access. Wireless service is available via entire campus.

Student Life *Housing:* on-campus residence required for freshman year. *Options:* coed, disabled students. Campus housing is university owned. Freshman campus housing is guaranteed. *Activities and organizations:* drama/theater group, student-run newspaper, choral group, Instrumental music groups, Entrepreneur's Club, Glee Club, theater arts, Ultimate Disc Club. *Campus security:* 24-hour emergency response devices and patrols, late-night transport/escort service, controlled dormitory access. *Student services:* health clinic, personal/psychological counseling, women's center.

Athletics Member NCAA. All Division III. *Intercollegiate sports:* baseball M, basketball M/W, cross-country running M/W, fencing M/W, ice hockey M(c), rugby M(c), soccer M/W(c), swimming and diving M/W, tennis M/W, track and field M/W, volleyball M(c)/W, water polo M/W. *Intramural sports:* badminton M/W, baseball M, basketball M/W, cross-country running M/W, fencing M/W, football M/W, ice hockey M, racquetball M, soccer M/W, softball M/W, squash M/W, swimming and diving M/W, table tennis M/W, tennis M/W, track and field M/W, ultimate Frisbee M/W, volleyball M/W, water polo M/W.

Standardized Tests *Required:* SAT or ACT (for admission), SAT Subject Tests (for admission).

Costs (2011–12) *One-time required fee:* $500. *Comprehensive fee:* $49,380 includes full-time tuition ($36,387), mandatory fees ($1317), and room and board ($11,676). Full-time tuition and fees vary according to course load. Part-time tuition: $337 per unit. Part-time tuition and fees vary according to course load. *College room only:* $6570. *Payment plans:* installment, deferred payment. *Waivers:* employees or children of employees.

Financial Aid Of all full-time matriculated undergraduates who enrolled in 2011, 618 applied for aid, 526 were judged to have need, 526 had their need fully met. 308 Federal Work-Study jobs (averaging $3081). 64 state and other part-time jobs (averaging $2534). In 2011, 9 non-need-based awards were made. *Average percent of need met:* 100%. *Average financial aid package:* $36,483. *Average need-based loan:* $3627. *Average need-based gift aid:* $32,358. *Average non-need-based aid:* $36,626. *Average indebtedness upon graduation:* $13,442.

Applying *Options:* electronic application, early admission, early action, deferred entrance. *Application fee:* $65. *Required:* essay or personal statement, high school transcript, 2 letters of recommendation. *Application deadlines:* 1/3 (freshmen), 2/15 (transfers), 11/1 (early action). *Notification:* 4/1 (freshmen), 5/1 (transfers), 12/15 (early action).

Freshman Application Contact Mr. Jarrid James Whitney, Director of Admissions, California Institute of Technology, 383 South Hill Avenue, Mail Code 10-90, Pasadena, CA 91125. *Phone:* 626-395-6341. *Fax:* 626-683-3026. *Web site:* http://www.caltech.edu/.

California Institute of the Arts
Valencia, California

- **Independent** comprehensive, founded 1961
- **Suburban** 60-acre campus with easy access to Los Angeles
- **Endowment** $101.6 million
- **Coed**
- **Very difficult** entrance level

Faculty *Student/faculty ratio:* 7:1.

Academics *Calendar:* semesters. *Degrees:* bachelor's, master's, doctoral, and postbachelor's certificates.

Student Life *Campus security:* 24-hour emergency response devices and patrols, late-night transport/escort service, controlled dormitory access.

Costs (2011–12) *Comprehensive fee:* $47,886 includes full-time tuition ($37,684), mandatory fees ($576), and room and board ($9626). Part-time tuition and fees vary according to course load. *College room only:* $5450. Room and board charges vary according to board plan, housing facility, and location.

Financial Aid *Of all full-time matriculated undergraduates who enrolled in 2010,* 734 applied for aid, 655 were judged to have need, 36 had their need fully met. 236 Federal Work-Study jobs (averaging $2515). 4 state and other part-time jobs (averaging $1500). *In 2010,* 59 non-need-based awards were made. *Average percent of need met:* 74. *Average financial aid package:* $30,448. *Average need-based loan:* $9445. *Average need-based gift aid:* $16,573. *Average non-need-based aid:* $7043. *Average indebtedness upon graduation:* $49,928.

Applying *Options:* electronic application. *Application fee:* $70. *Required:* essay or personal statement, high school transcript, 2 letters of recommendation, portfolio or audition. *Required for some:* interview.

Freshman Application Contact Molly Ryan, Director of Admissions, California Institute of the Arts, 24700 McBean Parkway, Valencia, CA 91355-2340. *Phone:* 661-255-1050. *Toll-free phone:* 800-545-2787. *Fax:* 661-253-7710. *E-mail:* admiss@calarts.edu. *Web site:* http://www.calarts.edu/.

See page 94 for display ad and page 1238 for the College Close-Up.

California Intercontinental University
Diamond Bar, California

Director of Admissions John Ramsay, Director of Admission, California Intercontinental University, 1470 Valley Vista Drive, Suite 150, Diamond Bar, CA 91765. *Phone:* 909-396-6090. *Toll-free phone:* 866-687-2258. *Fax:* 909-804-5151. *E-mail:* admissions@caluniversity.com. *Web site:* http://caluniversity.edu/.

California Lutheran University
Thousand Oaks, California

- **Independent Lutheran** comprehensive, founded 1959
- **Suburban** 290-acre campus with easy access to Los Angeles
- **Endowment** $55.5 million
- **Coed** 2,713 undergraduate students, 91% full-time, 56% women, 44% men
- **Moderately difficult** entrance level, 44% of applicants were admitted

Undergraduates 2,480 full-time, 233 part-time. Students come from 38 states and territories; 50 other countries; 15% are from out of state; 4% Black or African American, non-Hispanic/Latino; 20% Hispanic/Latino; 6% Asian, non-Hispanic/Latino; 0.6% Native Hawaiian or other Pacific Islander, non-Hispanic/Latino; 1% American Indian or Alaska Native, non-Hispanic/Latino; 4% Two or more races, non-Hispanic/Latino; 6% Race/ethnicity unknown; 4% international; 9% transferred in; 56% live on campus. *Retention:* 85% of full-time freshmen returned.

Freshmen *Admission:* 7,245 applied, 3,187 admitted, 502 enrolled. *Average high school GPA:* 3.7. *Test scores:* SAT critical reading scores over 500: 79%; SAT math scores over 500: 82%; SAT writing scores over 500: 74%; ACT scores over 18: 99%; SAT critical reading scores over 600: 27%; SAT math scores over 600: 31%; SAT writing scores over 600: 25%; ACT scores over 24: 55%; SAT critical reading scores over 700: 3%; SAT math scores over 700: 4%; SAT writing scores over 700: 2%; ACT scores over 30: 8%.

Faculty *Total:* 373, 44% full-time, 57% with terminal degrees. *Student/faculty ratio:* 15:1.

Academics *Calendar:* semesters. *Degrees:* certificates, bachelor's, master's, doctoral, post-master's, and postbachelor's certificates. *Special study options:* accelerated degree program, adult/continuing education programs, advanced placement credit, cooperative education, double majors, honors programs, independent study, internships, off-campus study, part-time degree program,

services for LD students, student-designed majors, study abroad, summer session for credit. *ROTC:* Army (c), Air Force (c). *Unusual degree programs:* 3-2 computer science, political public policy and administration.

Computers on Campus 452 computers/terminals are available on campus for general student use. Students can access the following: campus intranet, computer help desk, free student e-mail accounts, online (class) grades, online (class) registration, online (class) schedules, Wireless campus wide. Campuswide network is available. 100% of college-owned or -operated housing units are wired for high-speed Internet access. Wireless service is available via entire campus.

Student Life *Housing:* on-campus residence required through junior year. *Options:* coed, disabled students. Campus housing is university owned. Freshman campus housing is guaranteed. *Activities and organizations:* drama/theater group, student-run newspaper, radio and television station, choral group, student government, recreation, sports fan, or club sports related, service organizations, campus ministry or other religiously affiliated organization, multicultural organizations. *Campus security:* 24-hour emergency response devices and patrols, late-night transport/escort service, controlled dormitory access, escort service; shuttle service. *Student services:* health clinic, personal/psychological counseling, women's center.

Athletics Member NCAA. All Division III. *Intercollegiate sports:* baseball M, basketball M/W, cheerleading M/W, cross-country running M/W, football M, golf M/W, soccer M/W, softball W, swimming and diving M/W, tennis M/W, track and field M/W, volleyball W, water polo M/W. *Intramural sports:* badminton M(c)/W(c), basketball M(c)/W(c), football M(c)/W(c), lacrosse M(c)/W(c), rugby M(c), soccer M(c)/W(c), softball M(c)/W(c), tennis M(c)/W(c), volleyball M(c)/W(c), water polo M(c)/W(c).

Standardized Tests *Required:* SAT or ACT (for admission).

Costs (2012–13) *Comprehensive fee:* $45,870 includes full-time tuition ($33,910), mandatory fees ($450), and room and board ($11,510). Part-time tuition: $1090 per credit hour. *Required fees:* $225 per term part-time. *College room only:* $6220. Room and board charges vary according to board plan.

Financial Aid Of all full-time matriculated undergraduates who enrolled in 2010, 1,809 applied for aid, 1,590 were judged to have need, 266 had their need fully met. 189 Federal Work-Study jobs (averaging $2500). 440 state and other part-time jobs (averaging $2500). In 2010, 734 non-need-based awards were made. *Average percent of need met:* 70%. *Average financial aid package:* $22,580. *Average need-based loan:* $4430. *Average need-based gift aid:* $18,150. *Average non-need-based aid:* $11,400. *Average indebtedness upon graduation:* $23,900.

Applying *Options:* electronic application, early action, deferred entrance. *Application fee:* $45. *Required:* essay or personal statement, high school transcript, minimum 2.8 GPA, 1 letter of recommendation. *Recommended:* minimum 3.0 GPA, interview. *Application deadline:* 3/15 (freshmen). *Notification:* 12/1 (freshmen), 5/1 (transfers).

Freshman Application Contact Dr. Michael Elgarico, Dean of Undergraduate Enrollment, California Lutheran University, Office of Admission, #1350, Thousand Oaks, CA 91360. *Phone:* 805-493-3135. *Toll-free phone:* 877-258-3678. *Fax:* 805-493-3114. *E-mail:* cluadm@clunet.edu. *Web site:* http://www.callutheran.edu/.

See pagg 95 for display ad and page 1240 for the College Close-Up.

California Maritime Academy
Vallejo, California

- **State-supported** 4-year, founded 1929, part of California State University System
- **Suburban** 64-acre campus with easy access to San Francisco
- **Coed** 863 undergraduate students, 97% full-time, 14% women, 86% men
- **Moderately difficult** entrance level

Undergraduates 838 full-time, 25 part-time. 15% are from out of state; 13% transferred in; 77% live on campus. *Retention:* 86% of full-time freshmen returned.

Freshmen *Admission:* 145 enrolled. *Average high school GPA:* 3.1.

Academics *Calendar:* semesters. *Degree:* bachelor's. *Special study options:* academic remediation for entering students, advanced placement credit, internships, study abroad, summer session for credit. *ROTC:* Navy (c).

Computers on Campus 75 computers/terminals are available on campus for general student use. Students can access the following: campus intranet, computer help desk, free student e-mail accounts, online (class) grades, online (class) registration, online (class) schedules. Campuswide network is available. 100% of college-owned or -operated housing units are wired for high-speed Internet access. Wireless service is available via entire campus.

Student Life *Housing:* on-campus residence required through senior year. *Options:* coed. Campus housing is university owned. Freshman campus housing is guaranteed. *Activities and organizations:* student-run newspaper, choral group, Sailing Club, Dive Club, drill team. *Campus security:* 24-hour patrols,

student patrols. *Student services:* health clinic, personal/psychological counseling.

Athletics Member NAIA. *Intercollegiate sports:* basketball M(s)/W(s), crew M/W, golf M(s)/W, rugby M, sailing M/W, soccer M(s), volleyball W(s), water polo M/W. *Intramural sports:* baseball M, basketball M/W, football M/W, golf M/W, racquetball M/W, rugby M, sailing M/W, softball M/W, tennis M/W, volleyball M/W.

Standardized Tests *Required:* SAT or ACT (for admission).

Applying *Options:* electronic application. *Application fee:* $55. *Required:* high school transcript, minimum 2.0 GPA, health form. *Notification:* continuous (freshmen), continuous (transfers).

Freshman Application Contact California Maritime Academy, 200 Maritime Academy Drive, Vallejo, CA 94590. *Phone:* 707-654-1330. *Toll-free phone:* 800-561-1945. *Web site:* http://www.csum.edu/.

California Miramar University
San Diego, California

Director of Admissions Jean Van Slyke, Director of Admissions, California Miramar University, 9750 Miramar Road, Suite 180, San Diego, CA 92126. *Phone:* 858-653-3000. *Toll-free phone:* 877-570-5678. *Fax:* 858-653-6786. *E-mail:* admissions@calmu.edu. *Web site:* http://www.calmu.edu/.

California National University for Advanced Studies
Northridge, California

Freshman Application Contact Ms. Stephanie Smith, Registrar, California National University for Advanced Studies, Admissions, 8550 Balboa Boulevard, Suite 210, Northridge, CA 91325. *Phone:* 818-830-2411. *Toll-free phone:* 800-782-2422. *Fax:* 818-830-2418. *E-mail:* cnuadms@mail.cnuas.edu. *Web site:* http://www.cnuas.edu/.

California Polytechnic State University, San Luis Obispo
San Luis Obispo, California

- **State-supported** comprehensive, founded 1901, part of California State University System
- **Suburban** 6000-acre campus
- **Coed** 17,725 undergraduate students, 96% full-time, 45% women, 55% men
- **Moderately difficult** entrance level, 37% of applicants were admitted

Undergraduates 17,066 full-time, 659 part-time. 8% are from out of state; 0.8% Black or African American, non-Hispanic/Latino; 13% Hispanic/Latino; 11% Asian, non-Hispanic/Latino; 0.2% Native Hawaiian or other Pacific Islander, non-Hispanic/Latino; 0.4% American Indian or Alaska Native, non-Hispanic/Latino; 5% Two or more races, non-Hispanic/Latino; 6% Race/ethnicity unknown; 1% international; 5% transferred in; 38% live on campus. *Retention:* 93% of full-time freshmen returned.

Freshmen *Admission:* 33,001 applied, 12,341 admitted, 4,316 enrolled. *Average high school GPA:* 3.84. *Test scores:* SAT critical reading scores over 500: 90%; SAT math scores over 500: 95%; ACT scores over 18: 100%; SAT critical reading scores over 600: 50%; SAT math scores over 600: 71%; ACT scores over 24: 85%; SAT critical reading scores over 700: 8%; SAT math scores over 700: 21%; ACT scores over 30: 24%.

Faculty *Total:* 1,244, 64% full-time, 63% with terminal degrees. *Student/faculty ratio:* 19:1.

Academics *Calendar:* quarters. *Degrees:* bachelor's and master's. *Special study options:* academic remediation for entering students, advanced placement credit, cooperative education, distance learning, double majors, English as a second language, honors programs, internships, off-campus study, part-time degree program, services for LD students, study abroad, summer session for credit. *ROTC:* Army (b).

Computers on Campus Students can access the following: campus intranet, free student e-mail accounts, online (class) grades, online (class) registration, online (class) schedules. Campuswide network is available. Wireless service is available via classrooms, computer centers, computer labs, learning centers, libraries, student centers.

Student Life *Housing options:* coed, disabled students. Campus housing is university owned. *Activities and organizations:* drama/theater group, student-run newspaper, radio and television station, choral group, marching band, national fraternities, national sororities. *Campus security:* 24-hour emergency response devices and patrols, student patrols, late-night transport/escort service, controlled dormitory access. *Student services:* health clinic, personal/psychological counseling, women's center, legal services.

Athletics Member NCAA. All Division I except football (Division I-AA). *Intercollegiate sports:* baseball M(s), basketball M(s)/W(s), cross-country running M(s)/W(s), golf M(s)/W(s), soccer M(s)/W(s), softball W(s), swimming and diving M(s)/W(s), tennis M(s)/W(s), track and field M(s)/W(s), volleyball W(s), wrestling M(s). *Intramural sports:* basketball M/W, football M/W, racquetball M/W, soccer M/W, softball M/W, table tennis M/W, tennis M/W, volleyball M/W.

Standardized Tests *Required:* SAT or ACT (for admission).

Costs (2011–12) *Tuition:* state resident $5602 full-time, $3304 per year part-time; nonresident $16,762 full-time, $7768 per year part-time. Full-time tuition and fees vary according to course load, degree level, and program. Part-time tuition and fees vary according to course load, degree level, and program. *Required fees:* $2319 full-time, $633 per term part-time. *Room and board:* $10,444; room only: $5888. Room and board charges vary according to housing facility. *Payment plan:* installment. *Waivers:* employees or children of employees.

Financial Aid Of all full-time matriculated undergraduates who enrolled in 2010, 9,419 applied for aid, 6,674 were judged to have need, 265 had their need fully met. In 2010, 661 non-need-based awards were made. *Average percent of need met:* 61%. *Average financial aid package:* $9642. *Average need-based loan:* $3864. *Average need-based gift aid:* $2969. *Average non-need-based aid:* $1985.

Applying *Options:* electronic application, early admission, early decision. *Application fee:* $55. *Required:* high school transcript. *Application deadlines:* 11/30 (freshmen), 11/30 (transfers). *Early decision deadline:* 10/31. *Notification:* 4/1 (freshmen), 4/1 (transfers), 12/15 (early decision).

Freshman Application Contact Mr. James Maraviglia, Associate Vice Provost for Marketing and Enrollment Development, California Polytechnic State University, San Luis Obispo, Admissions Office, 1 Grand Avenue, San Luis Obispo, CA 93407-0031. *Phone:* 805-756-2311. *Fax:* 805-756-5911. *E-mail:* admissions@calpoly.edu. *Web site:* http://www.calpoly.edu/.

California State Polytechnic University, Pomona

Pomona, California

- **State-supported** comprehensive, founded 1938, part of California State University System
- **Urban** 1400-acre campus with easy access to Los Angeles
- **Endowment** $50.0 million
- **Coed** 19,399 undergraduate students, 87% full-time, 43% women, 57% men
- **Moderately difficult** entrance level, 55% of applicants were admitted

Undergraduates 16,820 full-time, 2,579 part-time. Students come from 43 states and territories; 25 other countries; 1% are from out of state; 3% Black or African American, non-Hispanic/Latino; 34% Hispanic/Latino; 26% Asian, non-Hispanic/Latino; 0.2% Native Hawaiian or other Pacific Islander, non-Hispanic/Latino; 0.3% American Indian or Alaska Native, non-Hispanic/Latino; 3% Two or more races, non-Hispanic/Latino; 6% Race/ethnicity unknown; 4% international; 7% transferred in; 12% live on campus. *Retention:* 90% of full-time freshmen returned.

Freshmen *Admission:* 23,946 applied, 13,191 admitted, 3,249 enrolled. *Average high school GPA:* 3.32. *Test scores:* SAT critical reading scores over 500: 56%; SAT math scores over 500: 70%; ACT scores over 18: 88%; SAT critical reading scores over 600: 16%; SAT math scores over 600: 33%; ACT scores over 24: 41%; SAT critical reading scores over 700: 1%; SAT math scores over 700: 6%; ACT scores over 30: 5%.

Faculty *Total:* 1,023, 50% full-time, 55% with terminal degrees. *Student/faculty ratio:* 25:1.

Academics *Calendar:* quarters. *Degrees:* bachelor's and master's. *Special study options:* academic remediation for entering students, adult/continuing education programs, advanced placement credit, cooperative education, distance learning, double majors, English as a second language, honors programs, internships, off-campus study, part-time degree program, services for LD students, study abroad, summer session for credit. *ROTC:* Army (b).

Computers on Campus 1,875 computers/terminals are available on campus for general student use. Students can access the following: campus intranet, computer help desk, free student e-mail accounts, online (class) grades, online (class) registration, online (class) schedules. Campuswide network is available. 100% of college-owned or -operated housing units are wired for high-speed Internet access. Wireless service is available via entire campus.

Student Life *Housing:* on-campus residence required for freshman year. *Options:* coed, disabled students. Campus housing is university owned and is provided by a third party. Freshman applicants given priority for college housing. *Activities and organizations:* drama/theater group, student-run newspaper, choral group, Rose Float Club, Ridge Runners Ski Club, Barkada (Asian club), American Marketing Association, Cal Poly Society of Accountants, national

fraternities, national sororities. *Campus security:* 24-hour emergency response devices and patrols, student patrols, late-night transport/escort service, controlled dormitory access, video camera surveillance. *Student services:* health clinic, personal/psychological counseling, women's center.

Athletics Member NCAA. All Division II. *Intercollegiate sports:* baseball M(s), basketball M(s)/W(s), cross-country running M(s)/W(s), soccer M(s)/W(s), tennis M(s)/W(s), track and field M(s)/W(s), volleyball W(s). *Intramural sports:* basketball M/W, bowling M/W, football M/W, softball M/W, tennis M/W, volleyball M/W.

Standardized Tests *Required:* SAT or ACT (for admission).

Costs (2012–13) *Tuition:* state resident $5472 full-time; nonresident $11,160 full-time. Full-time tuition and fees vary according to course load, degree level, and program. Part-time tuition and fees vary according to course load, degree level, and program. *Required fees:* $634 full-time. *Room and board:* $10,752; room only: $6708. Room and board charges vary according to board plan and housing facility. *Payment plans:* installment, deferred payment. *Waivers:* employees or children of employees.

Financial Aid Of all full-time matriculated undergraduates who enrolled in 2011, 12,386 applied for aid, 10,843 were judged to have need, 602 had their need fully met. 247 Federal Work-Study jobs (averaging $2626). In 2011, 12 non-need-based awards were made. *Average percent of need met:* 59%. *Average financial aid package:* $10,814. *Average need-based loan:* $4511. *Average need-based gift aid:* $9646. *Average non-need-based aid:* $3042. *Average indebtedness upon graduation:* $16,815.

Applying *Options:* electronic application. *Application fee:* $55. *Required:* high school transcript, minimum 2.0 GPA. *Application deadlines:* 11/30 (freshmen), 11/30 (transfers). *Notification:* continuous until 10/2 (freshmen), 5/1 (transfers).

Freshman Application Contact Ms. Deborah L. Brandon, Executive Director, Admissions and Outreach, California State Polytechnic University, Pomona, 3801 West Temple Avenue, Pomona, CA 91768-2557. *Phone:* 909-869-3427. *Fax:* 909-869-5315. *E-mail:* admissions@csupomona.edu. *Web site:* http://www.csupomona.edu/.

California State University, Bakersfield

Bakersfield, California

- **State-supported** comprehensive, founded 1970, part of California State University System
- **Urban** 575-acre campus
- **Coed** 6,737 undergraduate students, 89% full-time, 61% women, 39% men
- **Moderately difficult** entrance level

Undergraduates 6,022 full-time, 715 part-time. 1% are from out of state; 7% Black or African American, non-Hispanic/Latino; 45% Hispanic/Latino; 7% Asian, non-Hispanic/Latino; 0.5% Native Hawaiian or other Pacific Islander, non-Hispanic/Latino; 1% American Indian or Alaska Native, non-Hispanic/Latino; 2% Two or more races, non-Hispanic/Latino; 7% Race/ethnicity unknown; 2% international; 13% transferred in.

Freshmen *Admission:* 1,060 enrolled. *Test scores:* SAT critical reading scores over 500: 28%; SAT math scores over 500: 34%; ACT scores over 18: 58%; SAT critical reading scores over 600: 5%; SAT math scores over 600: 7%; ACT scores over 24: 11%; ACT scores over 30: 1%.

Faculty *Student/faculty ratio:* 27:1.

Academics *Calendar:* quarters. *Degrees:* bachelor's and master's. *Special study options:* adult/continuing education programs, external degree program, part-time degree program.

Computers on Campus Students can access the following: online (class) registration. Campuswide network is available.

Student Life *Housing options:* coed, disabled students. *Campus security:* 24-hour emergency response devices and patrols, late-night transport/escort service.

Athletics Member NCAA. All Division II except wrestling (Division I). *Intercollegiate sports:* basketball M(s), golf M(s), soccer M(s), softball W(s), swimming and diving M(s)/W(s), tennis W(s), track and field M(s)/W(s), volleyball W(s), water polo W(s), wrestling M(s). *Intramural sports:* archery M/W, badminton M/W, baseball M/W, basketball M/W, fencing M/W, football M/W, golf M/W, gymnastics M/W, racquetball M/W, riflery M/W, soccer M, softball M/W, swimming and diving M/W, tennis W, volleyball M/W, weight lifting M/W, wrestling M/W.

Standardized Tests *Required for some:* SAT or ACT (for admission).

Costs (2011–12) *Tuition:* state resident $5472 full-time; nonresident $16,632 full-time. Full-time tuition and fees vary according to course load, degree level, and reciprocity agreements. Part-time tuition and fees vary according to course load, degree level, and reciprocity agreements. *Required fees:* $1210 full-time. *Room and board:* $7808. Room and board charges vary according to board plan.

Financial Aid Of all full-time matriculated undergraduates who enrolled in 2010, 4,366 applied for aid, 3,453 were judged to have need, 105 had their need fully met. *Average percent of need met:* 3%. *Average financial aid package:* $3890. *Average need-based loan:* $1480. *Average need-based gift aid:* $3099. *Average indebtedness upon graduation:* $6730.
Applying *Options:* electronic application, deferred entrance. *Required:* high school transcript. *Application deadlines:* 3/1 (freshmen), rolling (transfers). *Notification:* continuous (freshmen).
Freshman Application Contact Debra Blowers, Assistant Director, Admissions and Evaluations, California State University, Bakersfield, 9001 Stockdale Highway, Balersfield, CA 93311-1099. *Phone:* 661-664-3036. *Toll-free phone:* 800-788-2782. *E-mail:* admissions@csub.edu. *Web site:* http://www.csub.edu/.

California State University Channel Islands
Camarillo, California

Freshman Application Contact Ms. Ginger Reyes, California State University Channel Islands, One University Drive, Camarillo, CA 93012. *Phone:* 805-437-8520. *Fax:* 805-437-8519. *E-mail:* prospective.student@csuci.edu. *Web site:* http://www.csuci.edu/.

California State University, Chico
Chico, California

- **State-supported** comprehensive, founded 1887, part of California State University System
- **Small-town** 119-acre campus
- **Endowment** $43.0 million
- **Coed** 14,766 undergraduate students, 92% full-time, 51% women, 49% men
- **Moderately difficult** entrance level, 78% of applicants were admitted

Undergraduates 13,634 full-time, 1,132 part-time. Students come from 36 states and territories; 39 other countries; 2% are from out of state; 2% Black or African American, non-Hispanic/Latino; 18% Hispanic/Latino; 5% Asian, non-Hispanic/Latino; 0.2% Native Hawaiian or other Pacific Islander, non-Hispanic/Latino; 0.8% American Indian or Alaska Native, non-Hispanic/Latino; 4% Two or more races, non-Hispanic/Latino; 9% Race/ethnicity unknown; 3% international; 9% transferred in; 1% live on campus. *Retention:* 87% of full-time freshmen returned.
Freshmen *Admission:* 14,509 applied, 11,285 admitted, 2,429 enrolled. *Average high school GPA:* 3.22. *Test scores:* SAT critical reading scores over 500: 54%; SAT math scores over 500: 58%; ACT scores over 18: 84%; SAT critical reading scores over 600: 14%; SAT math scores over 600: 16%; ACT scores over 24: 33%; SAT critical reading scores over 700: 1%; SAT math scores over 700: 1%; ACT scores over 30: 2%.
Faculty *Total:* 872, 53% full-time, 58% with terminal degrees. *Student/faculty ratio:* 23:1.
Academics *Calendar:* semesters. *Degrees:* certificates, bachelor's, master's, post-master's, and postbachelor's certificates. *Special study options:* academic remediation for entering students, adult/continuing education programs, advanced placement credit, cooperative education, distance learning, double majors, English as a second language, external degree program, honors programs, independent study, internships, off-campus study, part-time degree program, services for LD students, student-designed majors, study abroad, summer session for credit.
Computers on Campus 1,212 computers/terminals and 1,205 ports are available on campus for general student use. Students can access the following: campus intranet, computer help desk, free student e-mail accounts, online (class) grades, online (class) registration, online (class) schedules, student account information, calendar, transcripts. Campuswide network is available. 100% of college-owned or -operated housing units are wired for high-speed Internet access. Wireless service is available via entire campus.
Student Life *Housing options:* coed, women-only, disabled students. Campus housing is university owned. Freshman applicants given priority for college housing. *Activities and organizations:* drama/theater group, student-run newspaper, radio station, choral group, Scour and Devour, Panhellenic Council, The Edge Campus Christian Fellowship, Golden Key International Honor Society, Music and Entertainment Industry, national fraternities, national sororities. *Campus security:* 24-hour emergency response devices and patrols, student patrols, late-night transport/escort service, controlled dormitory access, crime prevention workshops, RAD self-defense program, Chico Safe Rides, blue light emergency phones, freshmen safety orientation. *Student services:* health clinic, personal/psychological counseling, women's center, legal services.
Athletics Member NCAA. All Division II. *Intercollegiate sports:* baseball M(s), basketball M(s)/W(s), cross-country running M(s)/W(s), field hockey

W(c), golf M(s)/W(s), racquetball M(c)/W(c), rugby M(c)/W(c), soccer M(s)/W(s), softball W(s), swimming and diving M(c)/W(c), table tennis M(c)/W(c), tennis M(c)/W(c), track and field M(s)/W(s), ultimate Frisbee M(c)/W(c), volleyball W(s), water polo M(c)/W(c), wrestling M(c). *Intramural sports:* badminton M/W, basketball M/W, bowling M/W, football M/W, soccer M/W, softball M/W, volleyball M/W.
Standardized Tests *Required:* SAT or ACT (for admission).
Costs (2012–13) *Tuition:* state resident $6890 full-time; nonresident $18,050 full-time. Full-time tuition and fees vary according to degree level. Part-time tuition and fees vary according to course load and degree level. *Room and board:* $11,138; room only: $7104. Room and board charges vary according to board plan and housing facility. *Payment plans:* installment, deferred payment. *Waivers:* senior citizens and employees or children of employees.
Financial Aid Of all full-time matriculated undergraduates who enrolled in 2010, 8,981 applied for aid, 7,692 were judged to have need, 924 had their need fully met. In 2010, 473 non-need-based awards were made. *Average percent of need met:* 88%. *Average financial aid package:* $12,697. *Average need-based loan:* $4593. *Average need-based gift aid:* $8542. *Average non-need-based aid:* $1530.
Applying *Options:* electronic application, deferred entrance. *Application fee:* $55. *Required:* high school transcript, GPA of 10th /11th grade college preparatory courses only. *Required for some:* minimum 2.0 GPA. *Application deadlines:* 11/30 (freshmen), 11/30 (transfers). *Notification:* 3/1 (freshmen), 3/1 (transfers).
Freshman Application Contact California State University, Chico, Chico, CA 95929-0722. *Phone:* 530-898-4428. *Toll-free phone:* 800-542-4426. *Fax:* 530-898-6456. *Web site:* http://www.csuchico.edu/.

California State University, Dominguez Hills
Carson, California

- **State-supported** comprehensive, founded 1960, part of California State University System
- **Urban** 350-acre campus with easy access to Los Angeles
- **Endowment** $9.1 million
- **Coed** 11,534 undergraduate students, 68% full-time, 64% women, 36% men
- **Moderately difficult** entrance level, 84% of applicants were admitted

Undergraduates 7,798 full-time, 3,736 part-time. Students come from 16 states and territories; 32 other countries; 21% Black or African American, non-Hispanic/Latino; 48% Hispanic/Latino; 9% Asian, non-Hispanic/Latino; 0.4% Native Hawaiian or other Pacific Islander, non-Hispanic/Latino; 0.3% American Indian or Alaska Native, non-Hispanic/Latino; 3% Two or more races, non-Hispanic/Latino; 5% Race/ethnicity unknown; 2% international; 17% transferred in; 6% live on campus. *Retention:* 80% of full-time freshmen returned.
Freshmen *Admission:* 8,759 applied, 7,337 admitted, 1,173 enrolled. *Average high school GPA:* 3.05. *Test scores:* SAT critical reading scores over 500: 14%; SAT math scores over 500: 16%; SAT writing scores over 500: 14%; ACT scores over 18: 42%; SAT critical reading scores over 600: 1%; SAT math scores over 600: 2%; SAT writing scores over 600: 2%; ACT scores over 24: 4%; ACT scores over 30: 1%.
Faculty *Total:* 743, 33% full-time, 54% with terminal degrees. *Student/faculty ratio:* 26:1.
Academics *Calendar:* semesters. *Degrees:* bachelor's, master's, post-master's, and postbachelor's certificates. *Special study options:* academic remediation for entering students, accelerated degree program, advanced placement credit, cooperative education, distance learning, double majors, external degree program, honors programs, independent study, internships, off-campus study, part-time degree program, services for LD students, student-designed majors, study abroad, summer session for credit. *ROTC:* Army (b), Air Force (c).
Computers on Campus 350 computers/terminals and 350 ports are available on campus for general student use. Students can access the following: free student e-mail accounts, online (class) grades, online (class) registration, online (class) schedules. Campuswide network is available. 100% of college-owned or -operated housing units are wired for high-speed Internet access. Wireless service is available via entire campus.
Student Life *Housing options:* coed, disabled students. Campus housing is university owned. *Activities and organizations:* drama/theater group, student-run newspaper, radio station, choral group, Latino Business Students Association, Espirito de Nuestro Futuro, Organization of African Studies, national fraternities, national sororities. *Campus security:* 24-hour emergency response devices, student patrols, late-night transport/escort service, Campus Police Patrol Division is staffed 24 hours a day, 7 days a week. Officers are vested

with full police powers. *Student services:* health clinic, personal/psychological counseling, women's center.

Athletics Member NCAA. All Division II. *Intercollegiate sports:* baseball M(s), basketball M(s)/W(s), cross-country running W(s), golf M, soccer M(s)/W(s), softball W(s), track and field W(s), volleyball W(s). *Intramural sports:* basketball M/W, cross-country running M/W, football M/W, golf M/W, soccer M/W, softball M/W, swimming and diving M/W, tennis M/W, track and field M(c)/W(c), volleyball M/W, water polo M/W, weight lifting M/W.

Standardized Tests *Required for some:* SAT or ACT (for admission).

Costs (2012–13) *Tuition:* state resident $5970 full-time; nonresident $17,130 full-time. *Required fees:* $623 full-time. *Room and board:* $10,320; room only: $5124. Room and board charges vary according to housing facility. *Payment plan:* installment. *Waivers:* senior citizens and employees or children of employees.

Financial Aid Of all full-time matriculated undergraduates who enrolled in 2011, 5,917 applied for aid, 5,701 were judged to have need, 108 had their need fully met. 176 Federal Work-Study jobs (averaging $1901). In 2011, 157 non-need-based awards were made. *Average percent of need met:* 36%. *Average financial aid package:* $6588. *Average need-based loan:* $2398. *Average need-based gift aid:* $4793. *Average non-need-based aid:* $4108. *Average indebtedness upon graduation:* $11,783. *Financial aid deadline:* 5/17.

Applying *Options:* electronic application. *Application fee:* $55. *Required:* high school transcript. *Application deadlines:* rolling (freshmen), rolling (transfers). *Notification:* continuous (freshmen), continuous (transfers).

Freshman Application Contact Information Center, California State University, Dominguez Hills, 1000 East Victoria Street, Carson, CA 90747-0001. *Phone:* 310-243-3696. *Web site:* http://www.csudh.edu/.

California State University, East Bay

Hayward, California

- **State-supported** comprehensive, founded 1957, part of California State University System
- **Suburban** 343-acre campus with easy access to San Francisco Bay Area
- **Endowment** $9.2 million
- **Coed** 10,582 undergraduate students, 87% full-time, 60% women, 40% men
- **Moderately difficult** entrance level, 61% of applicants were admitted

Undergraduates 9,200 full-time, 1,382 part-time. Students come from 36 states and territories; 69 other countries; 1% are from out of state; 10% Black or African American, non-Hispanic/Latino; 19% Hispanic/Latino; 20% Asian, non-Hispanic/Latino; 3% Native Hawaiian or other Pacific Islander, non-Hispanic/Latino; 0.3% American Indian or Alaska Native, non-Hispanic/Latino; 3% Two or more races, non-Hispanic/Latino; 15% Race/ethnicity unknown; 8% international; 19% transferred in. *Retention:* 76% of full-time freshmen returned.

Freshmen *Admission:* 6,655 applied, 4,075 admitted, 1,225 enrolled. *Average high school GPA:* 3. *Test scores:* SAT critical reading scores over 500: 28%; SAT math scores over 500: 31%; SAT writing scores over 500: 26%; ACT scores over 18: 57%; SAT critical reading scores over 600: 7%; SAT math scores over 600: 7%; SAT writing scores over 600: 4%; ACT scores over 24: 11%.

Faculty *Total:* 683, 47% full-time. *Student/faculty ratio:* 30:1.

Academics *Calendar:* quarters. *Degrees:* certificates, bachelor's, master's, doctoral, and postbachelor's certificates. *Special study options:* academic remediation for entering students, accelerated degree program, adult/continuing education programs, advanced placement credit, cooperative education, distance learning, double majors, English as a second language, honors programs, independent study, internships, off-campus study, part-time degree program, services for LD students, student-designed majors, study abroad, summer session for credit.

Computers on Campus 700 computers/terminals are available on campus for general student use. Students can access the following: campus intranet, computer help desk, free student e-mail accounts, online (class) grades, online (class) registration, online (class) schedules. Campuswide network is available. 100% of college-owned or -operated housing units are wired for high-speed Internet access. Wireless service is available via entire campus.

Student Life *Housing options:* coed, disabled students. Campus housing is university owned. *Activities and organizations:* drama/theater group, student-run newspaper, radio and television station, choral group, Vietnamese Student Association, Accounting Association, Filipino-American Students Association, Movimiento Estudiantil Chicano, Hayward Orientation Team, national fraternities, national sororities. *Campus security:* 24-hour emergency response devices and patrols, late-night transport/escort service. *Student services:* health clinic, personal/psychological counseling, legal services.

Athletics Member NCAA, NAIA. All NCAA Division III. *Intercollegiate sports:* baseball M, basketball M/W, cross-country running M/W, soccer M/W, softball W, swimming and diving W, volleyball W, water polo W. *Intramural*

sports: badminton M/W, basketball M/W, golf M/W, gymnastics M, racquetball M/W, soccer M/W, softball M/W, swimming and diving M/W, tennis M/W, volleyball M/W, weight lifting M/W.

Standardized Tests *Required for some:* SAT or ACT (for admission).

Costs (2011–12) *Tuition:* state resident $5472 full-time; nonresident $16,632 full-time. *Required fees:* $861 full-time. *Room and board:* $11,352.

Financial Aid Of all full-time matriculated undergraduates who enrolled in 2011, 5,574 applied for aid, 5,422 were judged to have need, 109 had their need fully met. *Average percent of need met:* 56%. *Average financial aid package:* $11,469. *Average need-based loan:* $6901. *Average need-based gift aid:* $9901. *Average indebtedness upon graduation:* $18,062.

Applying *Options:* electronic application. *Application fee:* $55. *Required:* high school transcript, minimum 2.0 GPA, California State University eligibility index. *Application deadlines:* 11/30 (freshmen), 11/11 (transfers). *Notification:* continuous (freshmen), continuous (transfers).

Freshman Application Contact Greg Smith, Enrollment Development and Management, California State University, East Bay, 25800 Carlos Bee Boulevard, Hayward, CA 94542-3000. *Phone:* 510-885-3249. *E-mail:* admissions@csueastbay.edu. *Web site:* http://www.csueastbay.edu/.

California State University, Fresno

Fresno, California

- **State-supported** comprehensive, founded 1911, part of California State University System
- **Urban** 1399-acre campus
- **Coed** 19,132 undergraduate students, 86% full-time, 57% women, 43% men
- **Minimally difficult** entrance level, 60% of applicants were admitted

Undergraduates 16,541 full-time, 2,591 part-time. 1% are from out of state; 5% Black or African American, non-Hispanic/Latino; 38% Hispanic/Latino; 15% Asian, non-Hispanic/Latino; 0.2% Native Hawaiian or other Pacific Islander, non-Hispanic/Latino; 0.5% American Indian or Alaska Native, non-Hispanic/Latino; 3% Two or more races, non-Hispanic/Latino; 7% Race/ethnicity unknown; 3% international; 10% transferred in; 5% live on campus. *Retention:* 86% of full-time freshmen returned.

Freshmen *Admission:* 15,482 applied, 9,292 admitted, 2,858 enrolled. *Average high school GPA:* 3.33. *Test scores:* SAT critical reading scores over 500: 32%; SAT math scores over 500: 38%; SAT writing scores over 500: 29%; ACT scores over 18: 66%; SAT critical reading scores over 600: 8%; SAT math scores over 600: 10%; SAT writing scores over 600: 7%; ACT scores over 24: 18%; SAT critical reading scores over 700: 1%; SAT math scores over 700: 1%; SAT writing scores over 700: 1%; ACT scores over 30: 2%.

Faculty *Total:* 1,089, 57% full-time, 65% with terminal degrees. *Student/faculty ratio:* 22:1.

Academics *Calendar:* semesters. *Degrees:* certificates, bachelor's, master's, and doctoral. *Special study options:* academic remediation for entering students, accelerated degree program, adult/continuing education programs, advanced placement credit, cooperative education, distance learning, double majors, English as a second language, freshman honors college, honors programs, independent study, internships, off-campus study, part-time degree program, services for LD students, student-designed majors, study abroad, summer session for credit. *ROTC:* Army (b), Air Force (b).

Computers on Campus Students can access the following: campus intranet, computer help desk, free student e-mail accounts, online (class) grades, online (class) registration, online (class) schedules. Campuswide network is available. 100% of college-owned or -operated housing units are wired for high-speed Internet access. Wireless service is available via classrooms, computer centers, computer labs, learning centers, libraries, student centers.

Student Life *Housing options:* coed, men-only, women-only. Campus housing is university owned. *Activities and organizations:* drama/theater group, student-run newspaper, radio station, choral group, marching band, national fraternities, national sororities. *Campus security:* 24-hour emergency response devices and patrols, late-night transport/escort service, controlled dormitory access. *Student services:* health clinic, personal/psychological counseling, women's center.

Athletics Member NCAA. All Division I except football (Division I-A). *Intercollegiate sports:* baseball M(s), basketball M(s)/W(s), cross-country running M(s)/W(s), equestrian sports W(s), golf M(s)/W(s), lacrosse W(s), soccer W(s), softball W(s), swimming and diving W(s), tennis M(s)/W(s), track and field M(s)/W(s), volleyball W(s). *Intramural sports:* archery M/W, badminton M/W, baseball M, basketball M/W, bowling M/W, cross-country running M/W, equestrian sports W, fencing M/W, golf M/W, gymnastics M/W, racquetball M/W, tennis M/W, volleyball M/W.

Standardized Tests *Required:* SAT or ACT (for admission).

Costs (2012–13) *Tuition:* state resident $5472 full-time; nonresident $11,160 full-time, $372 per credit hour part-time. *Required fees:* $790 full-time. *Room*

and board: $10,550; room only: $6679. Room and board charges vary according to board plan. *Payment plan:* installment.

Financial Aid Of all full-time matriculated undergraduates who enrolled in 2011, 13,038 applied for aid, 12,040 were judged to have need, 283 had their need fully met. 199 Federal Work-Study jobs (averaging $3233). In 2011, 142 non-need-based awards were made. *Average percent of need met:* 71%. *Average financial aid package:* $11,437. *Average need-based loan:* $4022. *Average need-based gift aid:* $10,023. *Average non-need-based aid:* $3186. *Average indebtedness upon graduation:* $11,349.

Applying *Options:* electronic application. *Application fee:* $55. *Required:* high school transcript, minimum 2.0 GPA. *Application deadlines:* 11/30 (freshmen), 11/30 (transfers). *Notification:* continuous (freshmen).

Freshman Application Contact Mr. Andy Hernandez, Admissions Officer, California State University, Fresno, 5150 North Maple Avenue, M/S JA 57, Fresno, CA 93740-8026. *Phone:* 559-278-6115. *Fax:* 559-278-4812. *E-mail:* andyhe@csufresno.edu. *Web site:* http://www.csufresno.edu/.

California State University, Fullerton
Fullerton, California

- **State-supported** comprehensive, founded 1957, part of California State University System
- **Suburban** 236-acre campus with easy access to Los Angeles
- **Endowment** $23.7 million
- **Coed** 30,782 undergraduate students, 79% full-time, 56% women, 44% men
- **Moderately difficult** entrance level, 47% of applicants were admitted

Undergraduates 24,354 full-time, 6,428 part-time. Students come from 35 states and territories; 59 other countries; 1% are from out of state; 3% Black or African American, non-Hispanic/Latino; 34% Hispanic/Latino; 22% Asian, non-Hispanic/Latino; 0.3% American Indian or Alaska Native, non-Hispanic/Latino; 3% Two or more races, non-Hispanic/Latino; 5% Race/ethnicity unknown; 4% international; 11% transferred in; 6% live on campus. *Retention:* 85% of full-time freshmen returned.

Freshmen *Admission:* 35,235 applied, 16,452 admitted, 4,195 enrolled. *Average high school GPA:* 3.37. *Test scores:* SAT critical reading scores over 500: 52%; SAT math scores over 500: 61%; ACT scores over 18: 85%; SAT critical reading scores over 600: 12%; SAT math scores over 600: 18%; ACT scores over 24: 29%; SAT critical reading scores over 700: 1%; SAT math scores over 700: 2%; ACT scores over 30: 2%.

Faculty *Total:* 1,680, 50% full-time, 77% with terminal degrees. *Student/faculty ratio:* 26:1.

Academics *Calendar:* semesters. *Degrees:* bachelor's, master's, doctoral, post-master's, and postbachelor's certificates. *Special study options:* academic remediation for entering students, adult/continuing education programs, advanced placement credit, cooperative education, distance learning, double majors, English as a second language, freshman honors college, honors programs, independent study, internships, off-campus study, part-time degree program, services for LD students, student-designed majors, study abroad, summer session for credit. *ROTC:* Army (b).

Computers on Campus 2,000 computers/terminals are available on campus for general student use. Students can access the following: campus intranet, computer help desk, free student e-mail accounts, online (class) grades, online (class) registration, online (class) schedules. Campuswide network is available. Wireless service is available via entire campus.

Student Life *Housing options:* coed. Campus housing is university owned. Freshman applicants given priority for college housing. *Activities and organizations:* drama/theater group, student-run newspaper, radio station, choral group, Pan-Hellenic Council, American Marketing Association, Lacrosse Club, Samaritans (volunteer service club), Human Services Student Association, national fraternities, national sororities. *Campus security:* 24-hour emergency response devices and patrols, student patrols, late-night transport/escort service, controlled dormitory access. *Student services:* health clinic, personal/psychological counseling, women's center, legal services.

Athletics Member NCAA. All Division I. *Intercollegiate sports:* baseball M(s), basketball M(s)/W(s), cross-country running M(s)/W(s), golf M(s)/W(s), gymnastics W(s), soccer M(s)/W(s), softball W(s), tennis W(s), track and field M(s)/W(s), volleyball W(s), wrestling M(s). *Intramural sports:* archery M(c)/W(c), badminton M/W, basketball M/W, bowling M/W, equestrian sports M(c)/W(c), football M/W, gymnastics W, ice hockey M(c)/W(c), lacrosse M/W(c), racquetball M/W, rugby M/W(c), sailing M(c)/W(c), skiing (downhill) M/W, soccer M/W, softball M/W, swimming and diving M/W, table tennis M/W, tennis W, ultimate Frisbee M(c)/W(c), volleyball M/W, water polo M(c)/W(c), wrestling M.

Standardized Tests *Required:* SAT (for admission), SAT or ACT (for admission).

Costs (2012–13) *Tuition:* state resident $0 full-time; nonresident $11,160 full-time, $372 per unit part-time. Full-time tuition and fees vary according to

course load. Part-time tuition and fees vary according to course load. *Required fees:* $6128 full-time, $1915 part-time. *Room and board:* $10,587. Room and board charges vary according to board plan and housing facility. *Payment plans:* installment, deferred payment. *Waivers:* senior citizens and employees or children of employees.

Financial Aid Of all full-time matriculated undergraduates who enrolled in 2010, 12,402 applied for aid, 12,294 were judged to have need, 10,851 had their need fully met. 412 Federal Work-Study jobs (averaging $3356). In 2010, 1230 non-need-based awards were made. *Average percent of need met:* 65%. *Average financial aid package:* $10,298. *Average need-based loan:* $6515. *Average need-based gift aid:* $8427. *Average non-need-based aid:* $6958. *Average indebtedness upon graduation:* $14,904.

Applying *Options:* electronic application. *Application fee:* $55. *Required:* high school transcript, minimum 2.0 GPA. *Application deadlines:* 11/30 (freshmen), 11/30 (transfers). *Notification:* continuous (freshmen), continuous (transfers).

Freshman Application Contact Ms. Nancy J. Dority, Assistant Vice President of Enrollment Services, California State University, Fullerton, Office of Admissions and Records, PO Box 34080, Fullerton, CA 92834-9480. *Phone:* 657-278-2370. *Fax:* 657-278-2356. *E-mail:* admissions@fullerton.edu. *Web site:* http://www.fullerton.edu/.

California State University, Long Beach
Long Beach, California

- **State-supported** comprehensive, founded 1949, part of California State University System
- **Suburban** 320-acre campus with easy access to Los Angeles
- **Endowment** $46.3 million
- **Coed** 29,287 undergraduate students, 84% full-time, 58% women, 42% men
- **Moderately difficult** entrance level, 30% of applicants were admitted

Undergraduates 24,622 full-time, 4,665 part-time. Students come from 43 states and territories; 73 other countries; 1% are from out of state; 4% Black or African American, non-Hispanic/Latino; 33% Hispanic/Latino; 21% Asian, non-Hispanic/Latino; 3% Native Hawaiian or other Pacific Islander, non-Hispanic/Latino; 0.6% American Indian or Alaska Native, non-Hispanic/Latino; 3% Two or more races, non-Hispanic/Latino; 6% Race/ethnicity unknown; 5% international; 9% transferred in; 30% live on campus. *Retention:* 89% of full-time freshmen returned.

Freshmen *Admission:* 49,767 applied, 15,122 admitted, 3,987 enrolled. *Average high school GPA:* 3.43. *Test scores:* SAT critical reading scores over 500: 53%; SAT math scores over 500: 61%; ACT scores over 18: 81%; SAT critical reading scores over 600: 15%; SAT math scores over 600: 24%; ACT scores over 24: 33%; SAT critical reading scores over 700: 1%; SAT math scores over 700: 4%; ACT scores over 30: 3%.

Faculty *Total:* 1,996, 47% full-time, 57% with terminal degrees. *Student/faculty ratio:* 21:1.

Academics *Calendar:* semesters. *Degrees:* bachelor's, master's, doctoral, postbachelor's, and first professional certificates. *Special study options:* academic remediation for entering students, accelerated degree program, adult/continuing education programs, advanced placement credit, distance learning, double majors, English as a second language, honors programs, independent study, internships, off-campus study, part-time degree program, services for LD students, student-designed majors, study abroad, summer session for credit. *ROTC:* Army (b).

Computers on Campus 2,000 computers/terminals are available on campus for general student use. Campuswide network is available.

Student Life *Housing options:* coed. *Activities and organizations:* drama/theater group, student-run newspaper, radio and television station, choral group, national fraternities, national sororities. *Campus security:* 24-hour emergency response devices and patrols, student patrols, late-night transport/escort service. *Student services:* health clinic, personal/psychological counseling, women's center, legal services.

Athletics Member NCAA. All Division I. *Intercollegiate sports:* archery M(c)/W(c), badminton M(c)/W(c), basketball M(s)/W(s), bowling M(c)/W(c), crew M(c)/W(c), cross-country running M(s)/W(s), fencing M(c)/W(c), golf M/W, rugby M(c), sailing M(c)/W(c), skiing (downhill) M(c)/W(c), soccer M(c)/W(s), softball W(s), table tennis M(c), tennis W(s), track and field M(s)/W(s), volleyball M(s)/W(s), water polo M(s)/W(s). *Intramural sports:* basketball M/W, gymnastics M/W, racquetball M/W, softball W, swimming and diving M/W, table tennis W(c), tennis W, track and field M(c)/W(c), volleyball M/W.

Standardized Tests *Required:* SAT or ACT (for admission).

Costs (2012–13) *Tuition:* state resident $0 full-time; nonresident $11,160 full-time, $372 per unit part-time. Full-time tuition and fees vary according to pro-

gram. Part-time tuition and fees vary according to course load and program. *Required fees:* $6738 full-time. *Room and board:* $11,300. Room and board charges vary according to board plan. *Payment plan:* installment. *Waivers:* senior citizens and employees or children of employees.

Financial Aid Of all full-time matriculated undergraduates who enrolled in 2011, 19,149 applied for aid, 18,239 were judged to have need, 9,126 had their need fully met. In 2011, 1018 non-need-based awards were made. *Average percent of need met:* 83%. *Average financial aid package:* $13,491. *Average need-based loan:* $3593. *Average need-based gift aid:* $6001. *Average non-need-based aid:* $2837.

Applying *Options:* electronic application. *Application fee:* $55. *Required:* high school transcript. *Required for some:* minimum 2.0 GPA, minimum GPA of 2.4 for nonresidents. *Application deadlines:* 11/30 (freshmen), 11/30 (transfers). *Notification:* continuous (freshmen), continuous (transfers).

Freshman Application Contact Mr. Thomas Enders, Director of Enrollment Services, California State University, Long Beach, Brotman Hall, 1250 Bellflower Boulevard, Long Beach, CA 90840. *Phone:* 562-985-4641. *Web site:* http://www.csulb.edu/.

California State University, Los Angeles

Los Angeles, California

- **State-supported** comprehensive, founded 1947, part of California State University System
- **Urban** 173-acre campus
- **Endowment** $14.8 million
- **Coed** 17,313 undergraduate students, 83% full-time, 59% women, 41% men
- **Moderately difficult** entrance level, 69% of applicants were admitted

Undergraduates 14,404 full-time, 2,909 part-time. Students come from 50 states and territories; 44 other countries; 0.4% are from out of state; 6% Black or African American, non-Hispanic/Latino; 59% Hispanic/Latino; 17% Asian, non-Hispanic/Latino; 0.1% Native Hawaiian or other Pacific Islander, non-Hispanic/Latino; 0.2% American Indian or Alaska Native, non-Hispanic/Latino; 1% Two or more races, non-Hispanic/Latino; 3% Race/ethnicity unknown; 4% international; 14% transferred in; 5% live on campus. *Retention:* 82% of full-time freshmen returned.

Freshmen *Admission:* 24,218 applied, 16,812 admitted, 2,473 enrolled. *Average high school GPA:* 3.11. *Test scores:* SAT critical reading scores over 500: 21%; SAT math scores over 500: 28%; SAT writing scores over 500: 22%; ACT scores over 18: 47%; SAT critical reading scores over 600: 3%; SAT math scores over 600: 6%; SAT writing scores over 600: 3%; ACT scores over 24: 9%; SAT math scores over 700: 1%; ACT scores over 30: 1%.

Faculty *Total:* 1,233, 59% full-time, 44% with terminal degrees. *Student/faculty ratio:* 20:1.

Academics *Calendar:* quarters. *Degrees:* bachelor's, master's, doctoral, and first professional. *Special study options:* academic remediation for entering students, accelerated degree program, adult/continuing education programs, advanced placement credit, cooperative education, distance learning, double majors, English as a second language, honors programs, independent study, internships, off-campus study, part-time degree program, services for LD students, student-designed majors, study abroad, summer session for credit. *ROTC:* Army (c), Air Force (c). *Unusual degree programs:* 3-2 nursing.

Computers on Campus 1,500 computers/terminals are available on campus for general student use. Students can access the following: campus intranet, computer help desk, free student e-mail accounts, online (class) grades, online (class) registration, online (class) schedules. Campuswide network is available. 100% of college-owned or -operated housing units are wired for high-speed Internet access. Wireless service is available via classrooms, computer centers, computer labs, dorm rooms, learning centers, libraries, student centers.

Student Life *Housing options:* coed. Campus housing is university owned. *Activities and organizations:* drama/theater group, student-run newspaper, choral group, Society of Hispanic Engineering and Science Students, Institute of Electrical and Electronics Engineer, Sigma Delta PI, Asian Unified, Society of Automotive Engineers, national fraternities, national sororities. *Campus security:* 24-hour emergency response devices, student patrols, late-night transport/escort service. *Student services:* health clinic, personal/psychological counseling, women's center, legal services.

Athletics Member NCAA. All Division II. *Intercollegiate sports:* baseball M(s), basketball M(s)/W(s), cross-country running W(s), soccer M(s)/W(s), tennis W(s), track and field M(s)/W(s), volleyball W(s). *Intramural sports:* basketball M/W, bowling M/W, gymnastics M/W, racquetball M/W, skiing (cross-country) M/W, soccer M/W, softball M/W, swimming and diving M/W, tennis M/W, track and field M/W, volleyball M/W, water polo M/W, wrestling M.

Standardized Tests *Required for some:* SAT or ACT (for admission).

Costs (2012–13) *Tuition:* state resident $0 full-time; nonresident $14,434 full-time, $248 per unit part-time. Full-time tuition and fees vary according to course level and course load. Part-time tuition and fees vary according to course level and course load. *Required fees:* $6094 full-time. *Room and board:* $9264. Room and board charges vary according to housing facility. *Payment plan:* installment. *Waivers:* employees or children of employees.

Financial Aid Of all full-time matriculated undergraduates who enrolled in 2008, 9,412 applied for aid, 8,916 were judged to have need, 1,449 had their need fully met. In 2008, 95 non-need-based awards were made. *Average percent of need met:* 66%. *Average financial aid package:* $9484. *Average need-based loan:* $5002. *Average need-based gift aid:* $7561. *Average non-need-based aid:* $4048.

Applying *Options:* electronic application, early admission. *Application fee:* $55. *Required:* high school transcript. *Application deadlines:* 11/30 (freshmen), 11/30 (transfers). *Notification:* 8/30 (freshmen), 8/30 (transfers).

Freshman Application Contact Mr. Vince Lopez, Director of Outreach and Recruitment, California State University, Los Angeles, 5151 State University Drive, Los Angeles, CA 90032-8530. *Phone:* 323-343-3839. *E-mail:* admission@calstatela.edu. *Web site:* http://www.calstatela.edu/.

California State University, Monterey Bay

Seaside, California

- **State-supported** comprehensive, founded 1994, part of California State University System
- **Small-town** 1387-acre campus with easy access to San Jose
- **Endowment** $13.0 million
- **Coed** 4,814 undergraduate students, 93% full-time, 61% women, 39% men
- **Moderately difficult** entrance level, 47% of applicants were admitted

Undergraduates 4,472 full-time, 342 part-time. Students come from 37 states and territories; 14 other countries; 2% are from out of state; 5% Black or African American, non-Hispanic/Latino; 32% Hispanic/Latino; 5% Asian, non-Hispanic/Latino; 0.7% Native Hawaiian or other Pacific Islander, non-Hispanic/Latino; 0.7% American Indian or Alaska Native, non-Hispanic/Latino; 6% Two or more races, non-Hispanic/Latino; 6% Race/ethnicity unknown; 1% international; 12% transferred in; 61% live on campus. *Retention:* 79% of full-time freshmen returned.

Freshmen *Admission:* 11,607 applied, 5,455 admitted, 873 enrolled. *Average high school GPA:* 3.19. *Test scores:* SAT critical reading scores over 500: 46%; SAT math scores over 500: 46%; SAT writing scores over 500: 43%; ACT scores over 18: 81%; SAT critical reading scores over 600: 9%; SAT math scores over 600: 11%; SAT writing scores over 600: 7%; ACT scores over 24: 22%; ACT scores over 30: 1%.

Faculty *Total:* 336, 37% full-time, 46% with terminal degrees. *Student/faculty ratio:* 26:1.

Academics *Calendar:* semesters. *Degrees:* bachelor's and master's. *Special study options:* academic remediation for entering students, advanced placement credit, cooperative education, distance learning, double majors, independent study, internships, off-campus study, part-time degree program, services for LD students, student-designed majors, study abroad, summer session for credit.

Computers on Campus 980 computers/terminals are available on campus for general student use. Students can access the following: campus intranet, computer help desk, free student e-mail accounts, online (class) grades, online (class) registration, online (class) schedules. Campuswide network is available. 100% of college-owned or -operated housing units are wired for high-speed Internet access. Wireless service is available via entire campus.

Student Life *Housing:* on-campus residence required through sophomore year. *Options:* coed, disabled students. Campus housing is university owned. Freshman applicants given priority for college housing. *Activities and organizations:* student-run newspaper, radio station, choral group, Anime Club, Otter Christian Fellowship, Men's Rugby, M.E.Ch.A, National Society of Leadership and Success, national fraternities, national sororities. *Campus security:* 24-hour emergency response devices and patrols, student patrols, late-night transport/escort service, controlled dormitory access. *Student services:* health clinic, personal/psychological counseling.

Athletics Member NCAA. All Division II. *Intercollegiate sports:* baseball M(s), basketball M(s)/W(s), cross-country running M(s)/W(s), golf M(s)/W(s), sailing M/W, soccer M(s)/W(s), softball W(s), volleyball W(s), water polo W(s). *Intramural sports:* basketball M/W, bowling M/W, soccer M/W, volleyball M/W.

Standardized Tests *Required for some:* SAT or ACT (for admission), ELM/EPT.

Costs (2011–12) *Tuition:* state resident $0 full-time; nonresident $11,160 full-time, $372 per unit part-time. Full-time tuition and fees vary according to

degree level. Part-time tuition and fees vary according to degree level. *Required fees:* $5963 full-time, $1833 per term part-time. *Room and board:* $9152. Room and board charges vary according to board plan and housing facility. *Payment plan:* installment. *Waivers:* senior citizens and employees or children of employees.

Financial Aid Of all full-time matriculated undergraduates who enrolled in 2010, 3,014 applied for aid, 2,520 were judged to have need, 834 had their need fully met. *Average percent of need met:* 74%. *Average financial aid package:* $9744. *Average need-based loan:* $4211. *Average need-based gift aid:* $8234. *Average indebtedness upon graduation:* $14,365.

Applying *Options:* electronic application, deferred entrance. *Application fee:* $55. *Required:* high school transcript, minimum 2.0 GPA. *Application deadlines:* 11/30 (freshmen), 11/30 (out-of-state freshmen), 11/30 (transfers). *Notification:* continuous (freshmen), continuous (out-of-state freshmen), continuous (transfers).

Freshman Application Contact Mr. John Larsen, Assistant Director of Recruitment, California State University, Monterey Bay, 100 Campus Center, Seaside, CA 93955. *Phone:* 831-582-3738. *Fax:* 831-582-3783. *E-mail:* admissions@csumb.edu. *Web site:* http://www.csumb.edu/.

California State University, Northridge
Northridge, California

- **State-supported** comprehensive, founded 1958, part of California State University System
- **Urban** 356-acre campus with easy access to Los Angeles
- **Coed**
- **Moderately difficult** entrance level

Faculty *Student/faculty ratio:* 25:1.

Academics *Calendar:* semesters. *Degrees:* bachelor's and master's.

Student Life *Campus security:* 24-hour emergency response devices, late-night transport/escort service.

Athletics Member NCAA. All Division I except football (Division II).

Standardized Tests *Required:* SAT or ACT (for admission).

Costs (2011–12) *Tuition:* state resident $0 full-time; nonresident $11,160 full-time. *Required fees:* $6488 full-time. *Room and board:* $12,276. Room and board charges vary according to board plan and housing facility.

Financial Aid *Of all full-time matriculated undergraduates who enrolled in 2009,* 15,251 applied for aid, 14,019 were judged to have need. *In 2009,* 908 non-need-based awards were made. *Average financial aid package:* $15,296. *Average need-based loan:* $6020. *Average need-based gift aid:* $12,948. *Average non-need-based aid:* $1479. *Average indebtedness upon graduation:* $15,582.

Applying *Options:* electronic application. *Application fee:* $55. *Required:* high school transcript.

Freshman Application Contact Ms. Mary Baxton, Associate Director of Admissions and Records, California State University, Northridge, 18111 Nordhoff Street, Northridge, CA 91330-8207. *Phone:* 818-677-3777. *Fax:* 818-677-3766. *E-mail:* admissions.records@csun.edu. *Web site:* http://www.csun.edu/.

California State University, Sacramento
Sacramento, California

- **State-supported** comprehensive, founded 1947, part of California State University System
- **Urban** 300-acre campus
- **Coed** 24,701 undergraduate students, 83% full-time, 57% women, 43% men
- **Moderately difficult** entrance level, 67% of applicants were admitted

Undergraduates 20,410 full-time, 4,291 part-time. 6% Black or African American, non-Hispanic/Latino; 18% Hispanic/Latino; 20% Asian, non-Hispanic/Latino; 1% Native Hawaiian or other Pacific Islander, non-Hispanic/Latino; 0.8% American Indian or Alaska Native, non-Hispanic/Latino; 4% Two or more races, non-Hispanic/Latino; 8% Race/ethnicity unknown; 1% international; 14% transferred in; 5% live on campus. *Retention:* 83% of full-time freshmen returned.

Freshmen *Admission:* 18,617 applied, 12,496 admitted, 2,912 enrolled. *Average high school GPA:* 3.23. *Test scores:* SAT critical reading scores over 500: 36%; SAT math scores over 500: 44%; ACT scores over 18: 59%; SAT critical reading scores over 600: 7%; SAT math scores over 600: 11%; ACT scores over 24: 19%; SAT critical reading scores over 700: 1%; SAT math scores over 700: 1%; ACT scores over 30: 3%.

Faculty *Total:* 1,400, 50% full-time, 54% with terminal degrees. *Student/faculty ratio:* 26:1.

Academics *Calendar:* semesters. *Degrees:* bachelor's, master's, doctoral, and first professional. *Special study options:* off-campus study, part-time degree program. *ROTC:* Army (b), Air Force (b).

Computers on Campus Students can access the following: computer help desk, free student e-mail accounts, online (class) grades, online (class) registration, online (class) schedules, online transcripts. Campuswide network is available. Wireless service is available via entire campus.

Student Life *Housing options:* coed, disabled students. Campus housing is university owned. *Campus security:* 24-hour emergency response devices and patrols, student patrols, late-night transport/escort service, controlled dormitory access.

Athletics Member NCAA. All Division I except football (Division I-AA). *Intercollegiate sports:* baseball M(s), basketball M(s)/W(s), bowling M(c)/W(c), cheerleading M/W, crew M(s)/W(s), cross-country running M(s)/W(s), golf M(s)/W, gymnastics W(s), ice hockey M(c), lacrosse M(c)/W(c), racquetball M(c)/W(c), rugby M(c), skiing (downhill) M(c)/W(c), soccer M(s)/W(s), softball W(s), tennis M(s)/W(s), track and field M(s)/W(s), volleyball M(c)/W(s). *Intramural sports:* basketball M/W, crew M/W, football M/W, golf M/W, ice hockey M, skiing (downhill) M/W, soccer M/W, softball M/W, table tennis M/W, tennis M/W, volleyball M/W, water polo M/W, weight lifting M/W.

Standardized Tests *Required:* SAT or ACT (for admission).

Costs (2011–12) *Tuition:* state resident $5472 full-time; nonresident $16,632 full-time. *Required fees:* $1100 full-time. *Room and board:* $9628. Room and board charges vary according to board plan and housing facility.

Financial Aid Of all full-time matriculated undergraduates who enrolled in 2010, 14,236 applied for aid, 12,932 were judged to have need, 576 had their need fully met. In 2010, 14 non-need-based awards were made. *Average percent of need met:* 59%. *Average financial aid package:* $10,435. *Average need-based loan:* $4522. *Average need-based gift aid:* $8901. *Average non-need-based aid:* $1670. *Average indebtedness upon graduation:* $3541.

Applying *Options:* electronic application, early action, deferred entrance. *Application fee:* $55. *Required:* minimum 2.0 GPA. *Required for some:* high school transcript.

Freshman Application Contact Mr. Emiliano Diaz, Director of University Outreach Services, California State University, Sacramento, 6000 J Street, Lassen Hall, Sacramento, CA 95819-6048. *Phone:* 916-278-3901. *Fax:* 916-278-5603. *E-mail:* admissions@csus.edu. *Web site:* http://www.csus.edu/.

California State University, San Bernardino
San Bernardino, California

- **State-supported** comprehensive, founded 1965, part of California State University System
- **Suburban** 430-acre campus with easy access to Los Angeles
- **Coed** 14,732 undergraduate students, 88% full-time, 63% women, 37% men
- **Moderately difficult** entrance level, 58% of applicants were admitted

Undergraduates 12,980 full-time, 1,752 part-time. 9% Black or African American, non-Hispanic/Latino; 49% Hispanic/Latino; 7% Asian, non-Hispanic/Latino; 0.3% Native Hawaiian or other Pacific Islander, non-Hispanic/Latino; 0.4% American Indian or Alaska Native, non-Hispanic/Latino; 3% Two or more races, non-Hispanic/Latino; 6% Race/ethnicity unknown; 4% international; 10% transferred in. *Retention:* 89% of full-time freshmen returned.

Freshmen *Admission:* 10,908 applied, 6,353 admitted, 2,131 enrolled. *Average high school GPA:* 3.22. *Test scores:* SAT critical reading scores over 500: 25%; SAT math scores over 500: 32%; SAT writing scores over 500: 25%; ACT scores over 18: 24%; SAT critical reading scores over 600: 4%; SAT math scores over 600: 5%; SAT writing scores over 600: 3%; ACT scores over 24: 3%; SAT math scores over 700: 1%.

Faculty *Total:* 912, 48% full-time, 49% with terminal degrees. *Student/faculty ratio:* 26:1.

Academics *Calendar:* quarters. *Degrees:* bachelor's, master's, doctoral, and first professional. *Special study options:* accelerated degree program, cooperative education, distance learning, double majors, honors programs, independent study, internships, off-campus study, part-time degree program, services for LD students, student-designed majors, study abroad, summer session for credit. *ROTC:* Army (b), Air Force (b).

Computers on Campus 1,300 computers/terminals are available on campus for general student use. Students can access the following: computer help desk, free student e-mail accounts, online (class) grades, online (class) registration, online (class) schedules. Campuswide network is available. Wireless service is available via entire campus.

Student Life *Housing options:* coed, women-only. Campus housing is university owned and is provided by a third party. *Activities and organizations:* drama/theater group, student-run newspaper, radio and television station, cho-

ral group, national fraternities, national sororities. *Campus security:* 24-hour emergency response devices and patrols, student patrols, late-night transport/escort service, residence staff on call 24 hours. *Student services:* health clinic, personal/psychological counseling, women's center, legal services.

Athletics Member NCAA. All Division II. *Intercollegiate sports:* baseball M(s), basketball M(s)/W(s), cross-country running W, golf M(s), soccer M(s)/W(s), softball W(s), swimming and diving M(s)/W(s), tennis W, volleyball W(s), water polo M/W. *Intramural sports:* basketball M/W, field hockey M/W, football M/W, soccer M/W, softball M, volleyball M/W.

Standardized Tests *Recommended:* SAT or ACT (for admission).

Costs (2012–13) *Tuition:* state resident $0 full-time; nonresident $11,160 full-time, $248 per unit part-time. Part-time tuition and fees vary according to course load. *Required fees:* $6453 full-time. *Room and board:* $9796. Room and board charges vary according to board plan and housing facility. *Payment plan:* installment. *Waivers:* senior citizens and employees or children of employees.

Financial Aid Of all full-time matriculated undergraduates who enrolled in 2011, 11,326 applied for aid, 10,128 were judged to have need, 243 had their need fully met. 3,819 Federal Work-Study jobs. In 2011, 31 non-need-based awards were made. *Average percent of need met:* 64%. *Average financial aid package:* $11,235. *Average need-based loan:* $3857. *Average need-based gift aid:* $8472. *Average non-need-based aid:* $2736. *Average indebtedness upon graduation:* $23,656.

Applying *Options:* electronic application, early admission, early action. *Application fee:* $55. *Required:* high school transcript, minimum 2.0 GPA. *Application deadlines:* rolling (freshmen), rolling (transfers). *Notification:* continuous (freshmen), continuous (transfers).

Freshman Application Contact Ms. Julie Mellen, Assistant Director of Admissions and Evaluations, California State University, San Bernardino, 5500 University Parkway, University Hall, Room 107, San Bernardino, CA 92407-2397. *Phone:* 909-537-5211. *Fax:* 909-537-7034. *E-mail:* moreinfo@mail.csusb.edu. *Web site:* http://www.csusb.edu/.

California State University, San Marcos

San Marcos, California

- **State-supported** comprehensive, founded 1990, part of California State University System
- **Suburban** 304-acre campus with easy access to San Diego
- **Coed** 9,482 undergraduate students, 77% full-time, 60% women, 40% men
- **Moderately difficult** entrance level, 59% of applicants were admitted

Undergraduates 7,312 full-time, 2,170 part-time. 2% are from out of state; 3% Black or African American, non-Hispanic/Latino; 30% Hispanic/Latino; 10% Asian, non-Hispanic/Latino; 0.5% American Indian or Alaska Native, non-Hispanic/Latino; 4% Two or more races, non-Hispanic/Latino; 9% Race/ethnicity unknown; 2% international; 11% transferred in; 6% live on campus. *Retention:* 82% of full-time freshmen returned.

Freshmen *Admission:* 9,978 applied, 5,841 admitted, 1,450 enrolled. *Average high school GPA:* 3.17. *Test scores:* SAT critical reading scores over 500: 40%; SAT math scores over 500: 47%; SAT critical reading scores over 600: 9%; SAT math scores over 600: 10%; SAT critical reading scores over 700: 1%; SAT math scores over 700: 1%.

Faculty *Total:* 569, 44% full-time. *Student/faculty ratio:* 24:1.

Academics *Calendar:* semesters. *Degrees:* bachelor's and master's. *Special study options:* academic remediation for entering students, adult/continuing education programs, advanced placement credit, distance learning, double majors, English as a second language, independent study, internships, off-campus study, part-time degree program, services for LD students, student-designed majors, study abroad, summer session for credit. *ROTC:* Army (c), Navy (c), Air Force (c).

Computers on Campus 1,400 computers/terminals are available on campus for general student use. Students can access the following: computer help desk, free student e-mail accounts, online (class) registration, online (class) schedules. Campuswide network is available.

Student Life *Housing options:* disabled students. Campus housing is provided by a third party. *Activities and organizations:* drama/theater group, student-run newspaper, choral group, Accounting Club, Liberal Studies Club, MECHA, Sigma IOTA Epsilon, national fraternities, national sororities. *Campus security:* 24-hour emergency response devices and patrols, student patrols, late-night transport/escort service. *Student services:* health clinic, personal/psychological counseling, women's center.

Athletics Member NAIA. *Intercollegiate sports:* baseball M, basketball M/W, cross-country running M/W, golf M/W, soccer M/W, track and field M/W. *Intramural sports:* softball W.

Standardized Tests *Recommended:* SAT or ACT (for admission).

Costs (2012–13) *Tuition:* nonresident $372 per unit part-time. Part-time tuition and fees vary according to course load. *Room and board:* Room and board charges vary according to housing facility. *Waivers:* senior citizens and employees or children of employees.

Financial Aid Of all full-time matriculated undergraduates who enrolled in 2007, 2,799 applied for aid, 2,208 were judged to have need. 156 Federal Work-Study jobs (averaging $1962). *Average financial aid package:* $6924. *Average need-based loan:* $4001. *Average need-based gift aid:* $4013. *Average indebtedness upon graduation:* $14,584.

Applying *Options:* electronic application. *Application fee:* $55. *Required:* high school transcript, minimum 3.0 GPA. *Application deadlines:* 11/30 (freshmen), 11/30 (transfers). *Notification:* continuous (freshmen), continuous (transfers).

Freshman Application Contact Darren Bush, Director of Admissions, California State University, San Marcos, 333 South Twin Oaks Valley Road, San Marcos, CA 92096-0001. *Phone:* 760-750-4848. *Fax:* 760-750-3248. *E-mail:* apply@csusm.edu. *Web site:* http://www.csusm.edu/.

California State University, Stanislaus

Turlock, California

- **State-supported** comprehensive, founded 1957, part of California State University System
- **Small-town** 228-acre campus
- **Endowment** $10.5 million
- **Coed** 7,921 undergraduate students, 81% full-time, 64% women, 36% men
- **Moderately difficult** entrance level, 77% of applicants were admitted

Undergraduates 6,405 full-time, 1,516 part-time. Students come from 23 states and territories; 22 other countries; 0.5% are from out of state; 3% Black or African American, non-Hispanic/Latino; 39% Hispanic/Latino; 11% Asian, non-Hispanic/Latino; 0.5% Native Hawaiian or other Pacific Islander, non-Hispanic/Latino; 0.5% American Indian or Alaska Native, non-Hispanic/Latino; 4% Two or more races, non-Hispanic/Latino; 8% Race/ethnicity unknown; 1% international; 15% transferred in; 8% live on campus. *Retention:* 87% of full-time freshmen returned.

Freshmen *Admission:* 5,387 applied, 4,128 admitted, 1,251 enrolled. *Average high school GPA:* 3.25. *Test scores:* SAT critical reading scores over 500: 31%; SAT math scores over 500: 36%; SAT writing scores over 500: 30%; ACT scores over 18: 62%; SAT critical reading scores over 600: 5%; SAT math scores over 600: 7%; SAT writing scores over 600: 5%; ACT scores over 24: 14%; SAT critical reading scores over 700: 1%; SAT math scores over 700: 1%; ACT scores over 30: 1%.

Faculty *Total:* 444, 60% full-time, 61% with terminal degrees. *Student/faculty ratio:* 24:1.

Academics *Calendar:* semesters. *Degrees:* bachelor's, master's, doctoral, post-master's, and postbachelor's certificates. *Special study options:* academic remediation for entering students, adult/continuing education programs, advanced placement credit, cooperative education, distance learning, double majors, English as a second language, honors programs, independent study, internships, off-campus study, part-time degree program, services for LD students, student-designed majors, study abroad, summer session for credit.

Computers on Campus 200 computers/terminals are available on campus for general student use. Students can access the following: computer help desk, free student e-mail accounts, online (class) grades, online (class) registration, online (class) schedules. Campuswide network is available. 100% of college-owned or -operated housing units are wired for high-speed Internet access. Wireless service is available via entire campus.

Student Life *Housing options:* coed. Campus housing is university owned and leased by the school. *Activities and organizations:* drama/theater group, student-run newspaper, radio station, choral group, Alpha Xi Delta, Phi Sigma Sigma, Kappa Sigma, Delta Phi Gamma, Nu Alpha Kappa Inc., national fraternities, national sororities. *Campus security:* 24-hour emergency response devices and patrols, student patrols, late-night transport/escort service, controlled dormitory access. *Student services:* health clinic, personal/psychological counseling, women's center.

Athletics Member NCAA. All Division II. *Intercollegiate sports:* baseball M, basketball M/W, cheerleading M(c)/W(c), cross-country running M/W, golf M, soccer M/W, softball W, tennis W, track and field M/W, volleyball W. *Intramural sports:* basketball M/W, football M/W, soccer M/W, ultimate Frisbee M/W, volleyball M/W.

Standardized Tests *Required for some:* SAT or ACT (for admission).

Costs (2011–12) *Tuition:* state resident $5472 full-time; nonresident $16,632 full-time. Full-time tuition and fees vary according to course load and reciprocity agreements. Part-time tuition and fees vary according to course load and reciprocity agreements. *Required fees:* $1110 full-time. *Room and board:* $8553. Room and board charges vary according to board plan and housing facility.

Financial Aid Of all full-time matriculated undergraduates who enrolled in 2011, 5,603 applied for aid, 5,055 were judged to have need, 286 had their need fully met. 131 Federal Work-Study jobs (averaging $3399). In 2011, 47 non-need-based awards were made. *Average percent of need met:* 63%. *Average financial aid package:* $11,142. *Average need-based loan:* $7494. *Average need-based gift aid:* $7769. *Average non-need-based aid:* $1659. *Average indebtedness upon graduation:* $15,894.

Applying *Options:* electronic application. *Application fee:* $55. *Required:* high school transcript. *Required for some:* interview. *Recommended:* minimum 3.0 GPA. *Application deadlines:* 11/30 (freshmen), 11/30 (transfers). *Notification:* continuous (freshmen), continuous (transfers).

Freshman Application Contact Student Outreach, California State University, Stanislaus, One University Circle, Turlock, CA 95382. *Phone:* 209-667-3122. *Toll-free phone:* 800-300-7420. *Fax:* 209-667-3788. *E-mail:* outreach_help_desk@csustan.edu. *Web site:* http://www.csustan.edu/.

Chapman University

Orange, California

- **Independent** comprehensive, founded 1861, affiliated with Christian Church (Disciples of Christ)
- **Suburban** 78-acre campus with easy access to Los Angeles
- **Endowment** $190.6 million
- **Coed** 5,300 undergraduate students, 96% full-time, 57% women, 43% men
- **Very difficult** entrance level, 45% of applicants were admitted

Undergraduates 5,077 full-time, 223 part-time. Students come from 50 states and territories; 62 other countries; 27% are from out of state; 2% Black or African American, non-Hispanic/Latino; 13% Hispanic/Latino; 9% Asian, non-Hispanic/Latino; 0.2% Native Hawaiian or other Pacific Islander, non-Hispanic/Latino; 0.4% American Indian or Alaska Native, non-Hispanic/Latino; 4% Two or more races, non-Hispanic/Latino; 7% Race/ethnicity unknown; 3% international; 7% transferred in; 37% live on campus. *Retention:* 91% of full-time freshmen returned.

Freshmen *Admission:* 9,616 applied, 4,313 admitted, 1,272 enrolled. *Average high school GPA:* 3.7. *Test scores:* SAT critical reading scores over 500: 95%; SAT math scores over 500: 94%; SAT writing scores over 500: 95%; ACT scores over 18: 100%; SAT critical reading scores over 600: 53%; SAT math scores over 600: 60%; SAT writing scores over 600: 61%; ACT scores over 24: 82%; SAT critical reading scores over 700: 9%; SAT math scores over 700: 11%; SAT writing scores over 700: 14%; ACT scores over 30: 18%.

Faculty *Total:* 748, 51% full-time. *Student/faculty ratio:* 14:1.

Academics *Calendar:* 4-1-4. *Degrees:* bachelor's, master's, doctoral, post-bachelor's, and first professional certificates. *Special study options:* academic remediation for entering students, adult/continuing education programs, advanced placement credit, distance learning, double majors, honors programs, independent study, internships, off-campus study, part-time degree program, services for LD students, student-designed majors, study abroad, summer session for credit. *ROTC:* Army (c), Air Force (c). *Unusual degree programs:* 3-2 business administration; engineering with University of California, Irvine.

Computers on Campus Students can access the following: campus intranet, computer help desk, free student e-mail accounts, online (class) grades, online (class) registration, online (class) schedules. Campuswide network is available. 100% of college-owned or -operated housing units are wired for high-speed Internet access. Wireless service is available via entire campus.

Student Life *Housing options:* coed, disabled students. Campus housing is university owned. Freshman campus housing is guaranteed. *Activities and organizations:* drama/theater group, student-run newspaper, radio station, choral group, Gamma Beta Phi, Alpha Kappa Psi Professional Business Fraternity, Public Relations Student Society of America, Black Student Union, Disciples on Campus, national fraternities, national sororities. *Campus security:* 24-hour emergency response devices and patrols, late-night transport/escort service, controlled dormitory access, full safety education program. *Student services:* health clinic, personal/psychological counseling.

Athletics Member NCAA. All Division III. *Intercollegiate sports:* baseball M, basketball M/W, cheerleading W(c), crew M(c)/W, cross-country running M/W, football M, golf M, ice hockey M(c), lacrosse M(c)/W(c), sailing M(c)/W(c), soccer M/W, softball W, swimming and diving M(c)/W, tennis M/W, track and field W, volleyball W, water polo M/W. *Intramural sports:* basketball M/W, soccer M/W, ultimate Frisbee M/W, volleyball M/W.

Standardized Tests *Required:* SAT or ACT (for admission). *Recommended:* SAT Subject Tests (for admission).

Costs (2012–13) *Comprehensive fee:* $54,288 includes full-time tuition ($41,040), mandatory fees ($1044), and room and board ($12,204). Part-time tuition: $1275 per credit. *College room only:* $8238. Room and board charges vary according to board plan and housing facility. *Payment plans:* tuition prepayment, installment, deferred payment. *Waivers:* employees or children of employees.

Financial Aid Of all full-time matriculated undergraduates who enrolled in 2010, 3,270 applied for aid, 2,899 were judged to have need, 401 had their

need fully met. 2,499 Federal Work-Study jobs (averaging $2886). In 2010, 918 non-need-based awards were made. *Average percent of need met:* 53%. *Average financial aid package:* $29,730. *Average need-based loan:* $4586. *Average need-based gift aid:* $15,755. *Average non-need-based aid:* $15,404. *Average indebtedness upon graduation:* $28,761.

Applying *Options:* electronic application, early action. *Application fee:* $60. *Required:* essay or personal statement, high school transcript, 1 letter of recommendation. *Recommended:* interview. *Application deadlines:* 1/15 (freshmen), 3/15 (transfers), 11/15 (early action). *Notification:* 3/15 (freshmen), 4/15 (transfers), 1/10 (early action).

Freshman Application Contact Ms. Marcela Mejia-Martinez, Assistant Vice Chancellor and Chief Admission Officer, Chapman University, One University Drive, Orange, CA 92866. *Phone:* 714-997-6711. *Toll-free phone:* 888-CUAPPLY. *Fax:* 714-997-6713. *E-mail:* admit@chapman.edu. *Web site:* http://www.chapman.edu/.

See page 104 for display ad and page 1256 for the College Close-Up.

Charles Drew University of Medicine and Science

Los Angeles, California

Freshman Application Contact Ms. Yvette Lane, Associate Director, Student Service, Charles Drew University of Medicine and Science, 1731 East 120th Street, Los Angeles, CA 90059. *Phone:* 323-563-4922. *Fax:* 323-563-4923. *E-mail:* yvettelane@cdrewu.edu. *Web site:* http://www.cdrewu.edu/.

Claremont McKenna College

Claremont, California

- **Independent** comprehensive, founded 1946, part of The Claremont Colleges Consortium
- **Small-town** 50-acre campus with easy access to Los Angeles
- **Endowment** $543.2 million
- **Coed** 1,301 undergraduate students, 99% full-time, 47% women, 53% men
- **Most difficult** entrance level, 14% of applicants were admitted

Undergraduates 1,293 full-time, 8 part-time. Students come from 46 states and territories; 30 other countries; 56% are from out of state; 3% Black or African American, non-Hispanic/Latino; 8% Hispanic/Latino; 11% Asian, non-Hispanic/Latino; 0.1% Native Hawaiian or other Pacific Islander, non-Hispanic/Latino; 0.1% American Indian or Alaska Native, non-Hispanic/Latino; 5% Two or more races, non-Hispanic/Latino; 18% Race/ethnicity unknown; 9% international; 3% transferred in; 94% live on campus. *Retention:* 97% of full-time freshmen returned.

Freshmen *Admission:* 4,412 applied, 623 admitted, 305 enrolled. *Test scores:* SAT critical reading scores over 500: 100%; SAT math scores over 500: 100%; SAT writing scores over 500: 100%; ACT scores over 18: 100%; SAT critical reading scores over 600: 90%; SAT math scores over 600: 96%; SAT writing scores over 600: 89%; ACT scores over 24: 100%; SAT critical reading scores over 700: 44%; SAT math scores over 700: 62%; SAT writing scores over 700: 48%; ACT scores over 30: 76%.

Faculty *Total:* 152, 84% full-time, 96% with terminal degrees. *Student/faculty ratio:* 9:1.

Academics *Calendar:* semesters. *Degrees:* bachelor's and master's. *Special study options:* advanced placement credit, double majors, English as a second language, independent study, internships, off-campus study, services for LD students, student-designed majors, study abroad, summer session for credit. *ROTC:* Army (b), Air Force (c). *Unusual degree programs:* 3-2 engineering with Stanford University, Harvey Mudd College, Columbia University, University of California System schools, University of Southern California.

Computers on Campus 220 computers/terminals are available on campus for general student use. Students can access the following: campus intranet, computer help desk, free student e-mail accounts, online (class) grades, online (class) registration, online (class) schedules. Campuswide network is available. 100% of college-owned or -operated housing units are wired for high-speed Internet access. Wireless service is available via entire campus.

Student Life *Housing:* on-campus residence required for freshman year. *Options:* coed, disabled students. Campus housing is university owned. Freshman campus housing is guaranteed. *Activities and organizations:* drama/theater group, student-run newspaper, radio station, choral group, The Forum - student newspaper, ASCMC - student government, Debate/Forensics Club, Amnesty International, Civitas (community service club). *Campus security:* 24-hour emergency response devices and patrols, student patrols, late-night transport/escort service, controlled dormitory access. *Student services:* health clinic, personal/psychological counseling, women's center.

Athletics Member NCAA. All Division III. *Intercollegiate sports:* archery M(c)/W(c), baseball M, basketball M/W, cheerleading M(c)/W(c), cross-country running M/W, equestrian sports M(c)/W(c), fencing M(c)/W(c), field hockey M(c)/W(c), football M, golf M/W, lacrosse M(c)/W, rugby M(c)/W(c), sailing M(c)/W(c), skiing (downhill) M(c)/W(c), soccer M/W, softball W, swimming and diving M/W, tennis M/W, track and field M/W, volleyball M(c)/W, water polo M/W. *Intramural sports:* basketball M/W, bowling M/W, crew M/W, football M, soccer M/W, squash M/W, table tennis M/W, tennis M/W, ultimate Frisbee M/W, volleyball M/W, water polo M/W, weight lifting M/W.

Standardized Tests *Required:* SAT or ACT (for admission).

Costs (2011–12) *Comprehensive fee:* $55,940 includes full-time tuition ($41,995), mandatory fees ($245), and room and board ($13,700). Full-time tuition and fees vary according to reciprocity agreements. Part-time tuition: $6666 per course. Part-time tuition and fees vary according to course load and reciprocity agreements. *College room only:* $7597. Room and board charges vary according to board plan and housing facility. *Payment plan:* installment. *Waivers:* employees or children of employees.

Financial Aid Of all full-time matriculated undergraduates who enrolled in 2011, 564 applied for aid, 538 were judged to have need, 538 had their need fully met. 280 Federal Work-Study jobs (averaging $1850). In 2011, 81 non-need-based awards were made. *Average percent of need met:* 100%. *Average financial aid package:* $38,394. *Average need-based gift aid:* $36,889. *Average non-need-based aid:* $13,752. *Average indebtedness upon graduation:* $9915. *Financial aid deadline:* 2/1.

Applying *Options:* electronic application, early decision, deferred entrance. *Application fee:* $60. *Required:* essay or personal statement, high school transcript, 3 letters of recommendation. *Recommended:* interview. *Application deadlines:* 1/2 (freshmen), 4/1 (transfers). *Early decision deadline:* 11/15 (for plan 1), 1/2 (for plan 2). *Notification:* 4/1 (freshmen), 5/15 (transfers), 12/15 (early decision plan 1), 2/15 (early decision plan 2).

Freshman Application Contact Georgette R. DeVeres, Associate Vice President of Admission and Director of Financial Aid, Claremont McKenna College, Office of Admission and Financial Aid, 888 Columbia Avenue, Claremont, CA 91711. *Phone:* 909-621-8356. *Fax:* 909-607-0661. *E-mail:* gdeveres@cmc.edu. *Web site:* http://www.claremontmckenna.edu/.

Cogswell Polytechnical College

Sunnyvale, California

- **Independent** comprehensive, founded 1887
- **Suburban** 2-acre campus with easy access to San Francisco, San Jose
- **Coed, primarily men** 288 undergraduate students, 65% full-time, 17% women, 83% men
- **Moderately difficult** entrance level, 54% of applicants were admitted

Undergraduates 187 full-time, 101 part-time. Students come from 13 states and territories; 3 other countries; 13% are from out of state; 3% Black or African American, non-Hispanic/Latino; 15% Hispanic/Latino; 8% Asian, non-Hispanic/Latino; 1% Native Hawaiian or other Pacific Islander, non-Hispanic/Latino; 0.7% American Indian or Alaska Native, non-Hispanic/Latino; 5% Two or more races, non-Hispanic/Latino; 14% Race/ethnicity unknown; 4% international; 24% transferred in; 22% live on campus. *Retention:* 67% of full-time freshmen returned.

Freshmen *Admission:* 145 applied, 78 admitted, 45 enrolled. *Average high school GPA:* 2.89. *Test scores:* SAT critical reading scores over 500: 69%; SAT math scores over 500: 70%; SAT writing scores over 500: 41%; ACT scores over 18: 80%; SAT critical reading scores over 600: 6%; SAT math scores over 600: 29%; SAT writing scores over 600: 12%; ACT scores over 24: 40%.

Faculty *Total:* 52, 21% full-time, 17% with terminal degrees. *Student/faculty ratio:* 9:1.

Academics *Calendar:* semesters. *Degrees:* associate, bachelor's, and master's. *Special study options:* advanced placement credit, distance learning, double majors, internships, part-time degree program, student-designed majors, study abroad, summer session for credit.

Computers on Campus 224 computers/terminals are available on campus for general student use. Students can access the following: computer help desk, free student e-mail accounts, online (class) grades, online (class) registration, online (class) schedules. Campuswide network is available. Wireless service is available via entire campus.

Student Life *Housing options:* coed. Campus housing is provided by a third party. Freshman campus housing is guaranteed. *Activities and organizations:* drama/theater group, choral group, ASB, Game Development club, Audio Production and Engineering club, Comic Club, Women's club. *Campus security:* 24-hour emergency response devices.

Standardized Tests *Recommended:* SAT or ACT (for admission).

Costs (2012–13) *Comprehensive fee:* $30,630 includes full-time tuition ($19,488), mandatory fees ($180), and room and board ($10,962). Full-time tuition and fees vary according to course load. Part-time tuition: $812 per credit hour. Part-time tuition and fees vary according to course load. *College room only:* $6000. Room and board charges vary according to housing facility.

Payment plan: deferred payment. *Waivers:* employees or children of employees.

Applying *Options:* electronic application, deferred entrance. *Required:* essay or personal statement, high school transcript, minimum 2.7 GPA. *Required for some:* portfolio for "Digital Art and Animation" and "Digital Audio Technology" majors. *Recommended:* interview. *Application deadlines:* rolling (freshmen), rolling (transfers). *Notification:* continuous (freshmen), continuous (transfers).

Freshman Application Contact Abraham Chacko, Executive Director of Admissions, Cogswell Polytechnical College, 1175 Bordeaux Drive, Sunnyvale, CA 94089-1299. *Phone:* 408-4985123. *Toll-free phone:* 800-264-7955. *Fax:* 408-747-0764. *E-mail:* achacko@cogswell.edu. *Web site:* http://www.cogswell.edu/.

The Colburn School Conservatory of Music
Los Angeles, California

- **Independent** 4-year, founded 1980
- **Urban** campus with easy access to Los Angeles
- **Coed**
- **Most difficult** entrance level

Faculty *Student/faculty ratio:* 4:1.

Academics *Calendar:* semesters. *Degrees:* certificates, diplomas, bachelor's, and postbachelor's certificates.

Student Life *Campus security:* 24-hour emergency response devices and patrols, controlled dormitory access.

Standardized Tests *Recommended:* SAT or ACT (for admission).

Costs (2011–12) *One-time required fee:* $500. *Comprehensive fee:* The Colburn School does not charge its Conservatory students for tuition, room or board.

Applying *Options:* electronic application, deferred entrance. *Application fee:* $110. *Required:* essay or personal statement, high school transcript, 2 letters of recommendation, interview, pre-screening DVD, in-person audition by invitation.

Freshman Application Contact Ms. Kathleen Tesar, Associate Dean, The Colburn School Conservatory of Music, 200 South Grand Avenue, Los Angeles, CA 90012. *Phone:* 213-621-4534. *Fax:* 213-625-0371. *E-mail:* admissions@colburnschool.edu. *Web site:* http://www.colburnschool.edu/.

Coleman University
San Diego, California

Freshman Application Contact Admissions Department, Coleman University, 7380 Parkway Drive, La Mesa, CA 91942-1532. *Phone:* 619-465-3990. *Toll-free phone:* 800-430-2030. *E-mail:* jschafer@cts.com. *Web site:* http://www.coleman.edu/.

Coleman University
San Marcos, California

Director of Admissions Senior Admissions Officer, Coleman University, 1284 West San Marcos Boulevard, San Marcos, CA 92078. *Phone:* 760-747-3990. *Fax:* 760-752-9808. *Web site:* http://www.coleman.edu/.

Columbia College Hollywood
Tarzana, California

Freshman Application Contact Carmen Munoz, Admissions Director, Columbia College Hollywood, 18618 Oxnard Street, Tarzana, CA 91356. *Phone:* 818-345-8414. *Toll-free phone:* 800-785-0585. *Fax:* 818-345-9053. *E-mail:* admissions@columbiacollege.edu. *Web site:* http://www.columbiacollege.edu/.

Concordia University
Irvine, California

- **Independent** comprehensive, founded 1972, affiliated with Lutheran Church–Missouri Synod, part of The Concordia University System
- **Suburban** 70-acre campus with easy access to Los Angeles
- **Endowment** $12.0 million
- **Coed** 1,629 undergraduate students, 95% full-time, 59% women, 41% men
- **Moderately difficult** entrance level, 76% of applicants were admitted

Undergraduates 1,542 full-time, 87 part-time. Students come from 33 states and territories; 12 other countries; 13% are from out of state; 3% Black or African American, non-Hispanic/Latino; 18% Hispanic/Latino; 5% Asian, non-Hispanic/Latino; 0.2% Native Hawaiian or other Pacific Islander, non-Hispanic/Latino; 0.4% American Indian or Alaska Native, non-Hispanic/Latino; 4% Two or more races, non-Hispanic/Latino; 7% Race/ethnicity unknown; 4% international; 13% transferred in; 60% live on campus. *Retention:* 72% of full-time freshmen returned.

Freshmen *Admission:* 1,469 applied, 1,116 admitted, 294 enrolled. *Average high school GPA:* 3.43. *Test scores:* SAT critical reading scores over 500: 56%; SAT math scores over 500: 61%; SAT writing scores over 500: 53%; ACT scores over 18: 92%; SAT critical reading scores over 600: 18%; SAT math scores over 600: 19%; SAT writing scores over 600: 14%; ACT scores over 24: 33%; SAT critical reading scores over 700: 3%; SAT math scores over 700: 2%; SAT writing scores over 700: 1%; ACT scores over 30: 9%.

Faculty *Total:* 320, 22% full-time, 40% with terminal degrees. *Student/faculty ratio:* 18:1.

Academics *Calendar:* semesters. *Degrees:* associate, bachelor's, and master's (associate's degree for international students only). *Special study options:* academic remediation for entering students, accelerated degree program, adult/continuing education programs, advanced placement credit, distance learning, double majors, honors programs, independent study, internships, off-campus study, part-time degree program, services for LD students, study abroad, summer session for credit. *ROTC:* Army (c).

Computers on Campus 89 computers/terminals are available on campus for general student use. Students can access the following: computer help desk, free student e-mail accounts, online (class) grades, online (class) registration, online (class) schedules. Campuswide network is available. 100% of college-owned or -operated housing units are wired for high-speed Internet access. Wireless service is available via entire campus.

Student Life *Housing:* on-campus residence required for freshman year. *Options:* coed, disabled students. Campus housing is university owned. Freshman campus housing is guaranteed. *Activities and organizations:* drama/theater group, student-run newspaper, choral group, intramurals, Screaming Eagles, Lacrosse, abbey west, student activities. *Campus security:* 24-hour emergency response devices and patrols, student patrols, late-night transport/escort service, lighted walkways, 24-hour dispatch. *Student services:* health clinic, personal/psychological counseling.

Athletics *Member* NAIA. *Intercollegiate sports:* baseball M(s), basketball M(s)/W(s), cross-country running M(s)/W(s), lacrosse M(c), soccer M(s)/W(s), softball W(s), swimming and diving M(s)/W(s), tennis M(s)/W(s), track and field M(s)/W(s), volleyball M(s)/W(s), water polo M(s)/W(s). *Intramural sports:* basketball M/W, bowling M/W, cheerleading W(c), football M/W, soccer M/W, softball M/W, track and field M/W, ultimate Frisbee M/W, volleyball M/W.

Standardized Tests *Required:* SAT or ACT (for admission).

Costs (2012–13) *Comprehensive fee:* $37,260 includes full-time tuition ($27,900), mandatory fees ($600), and room and board ($8760). Full-time tuition and fees vary according to course load. Part-time tuition: $870 per unit. Part-time tuition and fees vary according to course load. *Required fees:* $300 per term part-time. *College room only:* $5000. Room and board charges vary according to board plan and housing facility. *Payment plan:* installment. *Waivers:* employees or children of employees.

Financial Aid Of all full-time matriculated undergraduates who enrolled in 2011, 1,255 applied for aid, 1,090 were judged to have need, 135 had their need fully met. 46 Federal Work-Study jobs (averaging $104,750). In 2011, 227 non-need-based awards were made. *Average percent of need met:* 61%. *Average financial aid package:* $17,299. *Average need-based loan:* $4472. *Average need-based gift aid:* $14,131. *Average non-need-based aid:* $8045. *Average indebtedness upon graduation:* $23,807. *Financial aid deadline:* 3/2.

Applying *Options:* electronic application, early action, deferred entrance. *Application fee:* $50. *Required:* essay or personal statement, high school transcript, 1 letter of recommendation. *Recommended:* minimum 2.8 GPA, interview. *Application deadlines:* rolling (freshmen), rolling (transfers), 12/1 (early action). *Notification:* continuous (freshmen), continuous (transfers), 12/15 (early action).

Freshman Application Contact Mr. Rick Hardy, Associate Vice President for Enrollment Management, Concordia University, 1530 Concordia West, Irvine, CA 92612-3299. *Phone:* 949-214-3147. *Toll-free phone:* 800-229-1200. *Fax:* 949-854-6894. *E-mail:* admission@cui.edu. *Web site:* http://www.cui.edu/.

Design Institute of San Diego
San Diego, California

Director of Admissions Ms. Paula Parrish, Director of Admissions, Design Institute of San Diego, 8555 Commerce Avenue, San Diego, CA 92121-2685. *Phone:* 858-566-1200. *Toll-free phone:* 800-619-4337. *Fax:* 858-566-2711. *E-mail:* admissions@disd.edu. *Web site:* http://www.disd.edu/.

DeVry University
Alhambra, California

Admissions Office Contact DeVry University, Unit 100, Building A-11, First Floor, 1000 South Fremont Avenue, Alhambra, CA 91803. *Toll-free phone:* 866-338-7941. *Web site:* http://www.devry.edu/.

DeVry University
Anaheim, California

Admissions Office Contact DeVry University, 1900 South State College Boulevard, Suite 150, Anaheim, CA 92806-6136. *Toll-free phone:* 866-338-7941. *Web site:* http://www.devry.edu/.

DeVry University
Bakersfield, California

Admissions Office Contact DeVry University, 3000 Ming Avenue, Bakersfield, CA 93304-4136. *Toll-free phone:* 866-338-7941. *Web site:* http://www.devry.edu/.

DeVry University
Daly City, California

Admissions Office Contact DeVry University, 2001 Junipero Serra Boulevard, Suite 161, Daly City, CA 94014-3899. *Toll-free phone:* 866-338-7941. *Web site:* http://www.devry.edu/.

DeVry University
Elk Grove, California

Admissions Office Contact DeVry University, Sacramento Center, 2216 Kausen Drive, Elk Grove, CA 95758. *Toll-free phone:* 866-338-7941. *Web site:* http://www.devry.edu/.

DeVry University
Fremont, California

Freshman Application Contact DeVry University, 6600 Dumbarton Circle, Fremont, CA 94555. *Toll-free phone:* 866-338-7941. *Web site:* http://www.devry.edu/.

DeVry University
Irvine, California

Admissions Office Contact DeVry University, 430 Exchange, Suite 250, Irvine, CA 92602-1303. *Toll-free phone:* 866-338-7941. *Web site:* http://www.devry.edu/.

DeVry University
Long Beach, California

Freshman Application Contact DeVry University, 3880 Kilroy Airport Way, Long Beach, CA 90806. *Toll-free phone:* 866-338-7941. *Web site:* http://www.devry.edu/.

DeVry University
Oakland, California

Admissions Office Contact DeVry University, 505 14th Street, Oakland, CA 94612. *Toll-free phone:* 866-338-7941. *Web site:* http://www.devry.edu/.

DeVry University
Palmdale, California

Director of Admissions Admissions Office, DeVry University, One 39115 Trade Center Drive, Suite 100, Palmdale, CA 93551. *Toll-free phone:* 866-338-7941. *Web site:* http://www.devry.edu/.

DeVry University
Pomona, California

- **Proprietary** comprehensive, founded 1983, part of DeVry University
- **Urban** campus
- **Coed** 2,566 undergraduate students, 37% full-time, 39% women, 61% men
- **Minimally difficult** entrance level

Undergraduates 962 full-time, 1,604 part-time. 2% are from out of state; 11% Black or African American, non-Hispanic/Latino; 39% Hispanic/Latino; 10% Asian, non-Hispanic/Latino; 1% Native Hawaiian or other Pacific Islander, non-Hispanic/Latino; 0.6% American Indian or Alaska Native, non-Hispanic/Latino; 1% Two or more races, non-Hispanic/Latino; 7% Race/ethnicity unknown; 0.9% international; 23% transferred in.
Freshmen *Admission:* 330 enrolled.
Faculty *Total:* 107, 20% full-time. *Student/faculty ratio:* 34:1.
Academics *Calendar:* semesters. *Degrees:* associate, bachelor's, master's, and postbachelor's certificates. *Special study options:* adult/continuing education programs, part-time degree program.
Computers on Campus Students can access the following: online (class) registration.
Student Life *Housing:* college housing not available.
Costs (2011–12) *Tuition:* $15,294 full-time, $597 per credit hour part-time. Full-time tuition and fees vary according to course load. Part-time tuition and fees vary according to course load. *Required fees:* $80 full-time, $40 per term part-time. *Payment plans:* installment, deferred payment. *Waivers:* employees or children of employees.
Financial Aid Of all full-time matriculated undergraduates who enrolled in 2007, 414 applied for aid, 394 were judged to have need, 6 had their need fully met. In 2007, 50 non-need-based awards were made. *Average percent of need met:* 36%. *Average financial aid package:* $12,689. *Average need-based loan:* $7876. *Average need-based gift aid:* $8289. *Average non-need-based aid:* $16,971. *Average indebtedness upon graduation:* $33,385.
Applying *Application fee:* $50. *Required:* high school transcript, interview. *Application deadlines:* rolling (freshmen), rolling (transfers). *Notification:* continuous (freshmen), continuous (transfers).
Freshman Application Contact DeVry University, 901 Corporate Center Drive, Pomona, CA 91768-2642. *Phone:* 909-622-8866. *Toll-free phone:* 866-338-7941. *Web site:* http://www.devry.edu/.

DeVry University
San Diego, California

Admissions Office Contact DeVry University, 2655 Camino Del Rio North, Suite 201, San Diego, CA 92108-1633. *Toll-free phone:* 866-338-7941. *Web site:* http://www.devry.edu/.

DeVry University
Sherman Oaks, California

Freshman Application Contact DeVry University, 15301 Ventura Boulevard, D-100, Sherman Oaks, CA 91403. *Toll-free phone:* 866-338-7941. *Web site:* http://www.devry.edu/.

Dominican University of California
San Rafael, California

- **Independent** comprehensive, founded 1890, affiliated with Roman Catholic Church
- **Suburban** 85-acre campus with easy access to San Francisco
- **Endowment** $26.1 million
- **Coed** 1,662 undergraduate students, 82% full-time, 73% women, 27% men
- **Moderately difficult** entrance level, 54% of applicants were admitted

Undergraduates 1,364 full-time, 298 part-time. Students come from 31 states and territories; 17 other countries; 7% are from out of state; 4% Black or African American, non-Hispanic/Latino; 19% Hispanic/Latino; 19% Asian, non-Hispanic/Latino; 2% Native Hawaiian or other Pacific Islander, non-Hispanic/Latino; 0.7% American Indian or Alaska Native, non-Hispanic/Latino; 4% Two or more races, non-Hispanic/Latino; 15% Race/ethnicity unknown; 2% international; 8% transferred in; 31% live on campus. *Retention:* 84% of full-time freshmen returned.
Freshmen *Admission:* 3,093 applied, 1,662 admitted, 279 enrolled. *Average high school GPA:* 3.47. *Test scores:* SAT critical reading scores over 500: 65%; SAT math scores over 500: 70%; ACT scores over 18: 95%; SAT critical reading scores over 600: 16%; SAT math scores over 600: 24%; ACT scores

over 24: 44%; SAT critical reading scores over 700: 2%; SAT math scores over 700: 1%; ACT scores over 30: 3%.

Faculty *Total:* 371, 27% full-time, 51% with terminal degrees. *Student/faculty ratio:* 11:1.

Academics *Calendar:* semesters. *Degrees:* bachelor's, master's, and post-bachelor's certificates. *Special study options:* academic remediation for entering students, adult/continuing education programs, advanced placement credit, double majors, English as a second language, external degree program, honors programs, independent study, internships, off-campus study, part-time degree program, services for LD students, student-designed majors, study abroad, summer session for credit. *Unusual degree programs:* 3-2 occupational therapy.

Computers on Campus 200 computers/terminals and 700 ports are available on campus for general student use. Students can access the following: computer help desk, free student e-mail accounts, online (class) grades, online (class) registration, online (class) schedules, Microsoft Office Applications (Word, Excel, PowerPoint). Campuswide network is available. 100% of college-owned or -operated housing units are wired for high-speed Internet access. Wireless service is available via classrooms, computer centers, computer labs, dorm rooms, learning centers, libraries, student centers.

Student Life *Housing options:* coed. Campus housing is university owned. Freshman applicants given priority for college housing. *Activities and organizations:* drama/theater group, student-run newspaper, radio station, choral group, Students Promoting Dominican Islands, Perceptions, Science Club, Filipino Club, Scripture Union. *Campus security:* 24-hour emergency response devices and patrols, late-night transport/escort service, controlled dormitory access. *Student services:* health clinic, personal/psychological counseling.

Athletics Member NCAA. All Division II. *Intercollegiate sports:* basketball M(s)/W(s), golf M(s)/W(s), lacrosse M(s), soccer M(s)/W(s), softball W(s), tennis W(s), volleyball W(s). *Intramural sports:* cheerleading W.

Standardized Tests *Required:* SAT or ACT (for admission).

Costs (2011–12) *Comprehensive fee:* $51,250 includes full-time tuition ($36,900), mandatory fees ($450), and room and board ($13,900). Full-time tuition and fees vary according to course load, degree level, location, and program. Part-time tuition: $1560 per unit. Part-time tuition and fees vary according to degree level, location, and program. *Room and board:* Room and board charges vary according to board plan. *Payment plan:* installment. *Waivers:* employees or children of employees.

Financial Aid Of all full-time matriculated undergraduates who enrolled in 2009, 934 applied for aid, 862 were judged to have need, 72 had their need fully met. 200 Federal Work-Study jobs (averaging $1778). 46 state and other part-time jobs (averaging $5412). In 2009, 72 non-need-based awards were made. *Average percent of need met:* 55%. *Average financial aid package:* $22,418. *Average need-based loan:* $4458. *Average need-based gift aid:* $18,314. *Average non-need-based aid:* $10,528. *Average indebtedness upon graduation:* $32,314.

Applying *Options:* electronic application, deferred entrance. *Application fee:* $40. *Required:* essay or personal statement, high school transcript, 1 letter of recommendation. *Recommended:* interview. *Application deadlines:* 2/1 (freshmen), 2/1 (transfers). *Notification:* continuous (freshmen), continuous (transfers).

Freshman Application Contact Ms. Rebecca Finn Kenney, Director of Undergraduate Admissions, Dominican University of California, 50 Acacia Avenue, San Rafael, CA 94901-2298. *Phone:* 415-485-3204. *Toll-free phone:* 888-323-6763. *Fax:* 415-485-3214. *E-mail:* enroll@dominican.edu. *Web site:* http://www.dominican.edu/.

See below for display ad and page 1302 for the College Close-Up.

Epic Bible College
Sacramento, California

Director of Admissions Ms. Sheila Knoll, Assistant Director of Records, Epic Bible College, 5225 Hillsdale Boulevard, Sacramento, CA 95842. *Phone:* 916-348-4689. *E-mail:* kclarke@tlbc.edu. *Web site:* http://epic.edu/.

Everest College
Ontario, California

Freshman Application Contact Admissions Office, Everest College, 1819 South Excise Avenue, Ontario, CA 91761. *Phone:* 909-484-4311. *Toll-free phone:* 888-741-4270. *Fax:* 909-484-1162. *Web site:* http://www.everest.edu/campus/ontario/.

Ex'pression College for Digital Arts
Emeryville, California

Admissions Office Contact Ex'pression College for Digital Arts, 6601 Shellmound Street, Emeryville, CA 94608. *Toll-free phone:* 877-833-8800. *Web site:* http://www.expression.edu/.

FIDM/The Fashion Institute of Design & Merchandising, Los Angeles Campus

Los Angeles, California

- **Proprietary** primarily 2-year, founded 1969, part of The Fashion Institute of Design and Merchandising/FIDM
- **Urban** campus
- **Coed**
- **Moderately difficult** entrance level

Faculty *Student/faculty ratio:* 16:1.

Academics *Calendar:* quarters. *Degrees:* associate and bachelor's (also includes Orange County Campus).

Student Life *Campus security:* 24-hour emergency response devices and patrols, late-night transport/escort service.

Standardized Tests *Recommended:* SAT or ACT (for admission).

Financial Aid *Of all full-time matriculated undergraduates who enrolled in 2010,* 88 Federal Work-Study jobs (averaging $2935).

Applying *Options:* electronic application, deferred entrance. *Application fee:* $225. *Required:* essay or personal statement, high school transcript, minimum 2.0 GPA, 3 letters of recommendation, interview, major-determined project.

Freshman Application Contact Ms. Susan Aronson, Director of Admissions, FIDM/The Fashion Institute of Design & Merchandising, Los Angeles Campus, Los Angeles, CA 90015. *Phone:* 213-624-1201. *Toll-free phone:* 800-624-1200. *Fax:* 213-624-4799. *E-mail:* saronson@fidm.com. *Web site:* http://www.fidm.edu/.

See page 1326 for the College Close-Up.

Fresno Pacific University

Fresno, California

Freshman Application Contact Fresno Pacific University, 1717 South Chestnut Avenue, #2005, Fresno, CA 93727. *Phone:* 800-660-6089. *Toll-free phone:* 800-660-6089. *Fax:* 559-453-2007. *E-mail:* ugadmis@fresno.edu. *Web site:* http://www.fresno.edu/.

Golden Gate University

San Francisco, California

Freshman Application Contact Mr. Louis D. Riccardi Jr., Director of Enrollment Services, Golden Gate University, 536 Mission Street, San Francisco, CA 94105-2968. *Phone:* 415-442-7800. *Toll-free phone:* 800-448-3381. *Fax:* 415-442-7807. *E-mail:* info@ggu.edu. *Web site:* http://www.ggu.edu/.

Harvey Mudd College

Claremont, California

- **Independent** 4-year, founded 1955, part of The Claremont Colleges Consortium
- **Suburban** 33-acre campus with easy access to Los Angeles
- **Endowment** $243.1 million
- **Coed** 777 undergraduate students, 100% full-time, 42% women, 58% men
- **Most difficult** entrance level, 22% of applicants were admitted

Undergraduates 776 full-time, 1 part-time. Students come from 45 states and territories; 27 other countries; 62% are from out of state; 1% Black or African American, non-Hispanic/Latino; 6% Hispanic/Latino; 21% Asian, non-Hispanic/Latino; 0.6% American Indian or Alaska Native, non-Hispanic/Latino; 1% Two or more races, non-Hispanic/Latino; 4% Race/ethnicity unknown; 7% international; 99% live on campus. *Retention:* 98% of full-time freshmen returned.

Freshmen *Admission:* 2,957 applied, 660 admitted, 194 enrolled. *Test scores:* SAT critical reading scores over 500: 100%; SAT math scores over 500: 100%; SAT writing scores over 500: 100%; ACT scores over 18: 100%; SAT critical reading scores over 600: 97%; SAT math scores over 600: 100%; SAT writing scores over 600: 98%; ACT scores over 24: 100%; SAT critical reading scores over 700: 71%; SAT math scores over 700: 97%; SAT writing scores over 700: 73%; ACT scores over 30: 94%.

Faculty *Total:* 107, 81% full-time, 100% with terminal degrees. *Student/faculty ratio:* 8:1.

Academics *Calendar:* semesters. *Degree:* bachelor's. *Special study options:* double majors, internships, off-campus study, services for LD students, student-designed majors, study abroad. *ROTC:* Army (c), Air Force (b). *Unusual degree programs:* 3-2 economics/engineering with Claremont McKenna College and /engineering with Scripps College.

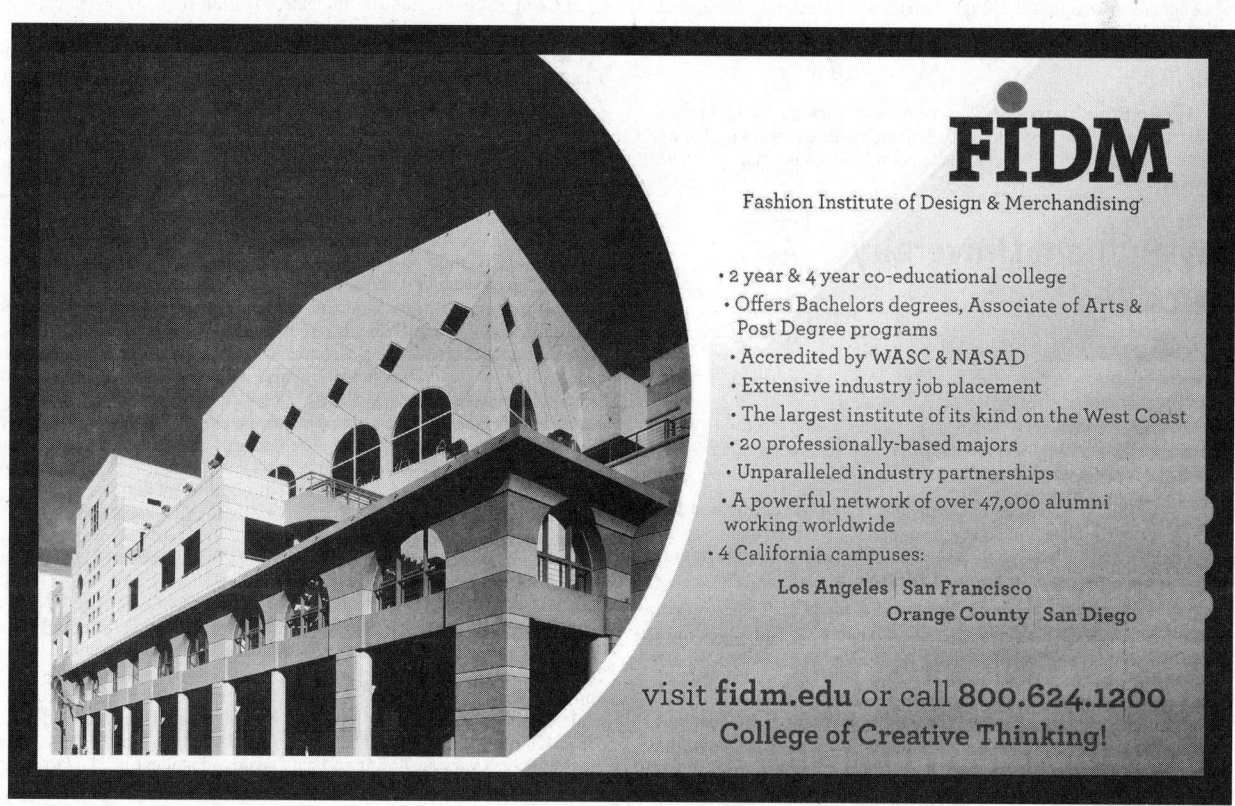

Computers on Campus 120 computers/terminals and 860 ports are available on campus for general student use. Students can access the following: campus intranet, computer help desk, free student e-mail accounts, online (class) grades, online (class) registration, online (class) schedules. Campuswide network is available. 100% of college-owned or -operated housing units are wired for high-speed Internet access. Wireless service is available via entire campus.

Student Life *Housing:* on-campus residence required for freshman year. *Options:* coed. Campus housing is university owned. Freshman campus housing is guaranteed. *Activities and organizations:* drama/theater group, student-run newspaper, radio station, choral group, Ballroom Dancing, Delta-H (outdoors club), Intervarsity Christian Fellowship, Science Bus, SWE (Society of Women Engineers). *Campus security:* 24-hour emergency response devices and patrols, late-night transport/escort service. *Student services:* health clinic, personal/psychological counseling, women's center.

Athletics Member NCAA. All Division III. *Intercollegiate sports:* baseball M, basketball M/W, cross-country running M/W, football M, golf M/W, lacrosse W, soccer M/W, softball W, swimming and diving M/W, tennis M/W, track and field M/W, volleyball W, water polo M/W. *Intramural sports:* badminton M(c)/W(c), equestrian sports M(c)/W(c), fencing M(c)/W(c), football M/W, ice hockey M(c), lacrosse M(c), rock climbing M(c)/W(c), rugby M(c)/W(c), sailing M(c)/W(c), soccer M/W, swimming and diving M/W, table tennis M(c)/W(c), tennis M/W, ultimate Frisbee M(c)/W(c), volleyball M/W.

Standardized Tests *Required:* SAT or ACT (for admission), SAT Subject Tests (for admission), SAT or ACT and the SAT Subject Test in Math 2C and a second SAT II subject exam (for admission).

Costs (2011–12) *Comprehensive fee:* $56,368 includes full-time tuition ($42,140), mandatory fees ($370), and room and board ($13,858). *College room only:* $7282. Room and board charges vary according to board plan. *Payment plan:* installment. *Waivers:* employees or children of employees.

Financial Aid Of all full-time matriculated undergraduates who enrolled in 2011, 462 applied for aid, 398 were judged to have need, 398 had their need fully met. 230 Federal Work-Study jobs (averaging $2245). 23 state and other part-time jobs (averaging $6004). In 2011, 171 non-need-based awards were made. *Average percent of need met:* 100%. *Average financial aid package:* $35,122. *Average need-based loan:* $5411. *Average need-based gift aid:* $30,475. *Average non-need-based aid:* $11,087. *Average indebtedness upon graduation:* $25,265. *Financial aid deadline:* 2/1.

Applying *Options:* electronic application, early admission, early decision, deferred entrance. *Application fee:* $60. *Required:* essay or personal statement, high school transcript, 3 letters of recommendation. *Recommended:* interview. *Application deadlines:* 1/2 (freshmen), 4/1 (transfers). *Early decision deadline:* 11/15 (for plan 1), 1/2 (for plan 2). *Notification:* 4/1 (freshmen), 5/15 (transfers), 12/15 (early decision plan 1), 2/15 (early decision plan 2).

Freshman Application Contact Mr. Peter Osgood, Director of Admission, Harvey Mudd College, 301 Platt Boulevard, Claremont, CA 91711. *Phone:* 909-621-8011. *Fax:* 909-607-7046. *E-mail:* admission@hmc.edu. *Web site:* http://www.hmc.edu/.

Henley-Putnam University

San Jose, California

- **Proprietary** comprehensive, founded 1991

- **Coed**

Academics *Degrees:* certificates, bachelor's, master's, and doctoral (offers only online degree programs). *Special study options:* adult/continuing education programs, part-time degree program.

Costs (2012–13) *Tuition:* $264 per unit part-time. Full-time tuition and fees vary according to course level and course load. Part-time tuition and fees vary according to course level and course load. No tuition increase for student's term of enrollment. *Payment plan:* installment.

Applying *Options:* electronic application. *Required for some:* high school transcript, interview, official transcripts from all colleges and universities attended. *Application deadlines:* rolling (freshmen), rolling (out-of-state freshmen), rolling (transfers).

Freshman Application Contact Henley-Putnam University, 25 Metro Drive, Suite 500, San Jose, CA 95110. *Phone:* 408-453-9900. *Toll-free phone:* 88-852-8746 (in-state); 888-852-8746 (out-of-state). *Web site:* http://www.henley-putnam.edu/.

Holy Names University

Oakland, California

- **Independent Roman Catholic** comprehensive, founded 1868
- **Urban** 60-acre campus with easy access to San Francisco
- **Endowment** $9.8 million
- **Coed, primarily women**
- **Moderately difficult** entrance level

Faculty *Student/faculty ratio:* 14:1.

Academics *Calendar:* semesters. *Degrees:* certificates, bachelor's, master's, post-master's, and postbachelor's certificates.

Student Life *Campus security:* 24-hour emergency response devices, late-night transport/escort service, controlled dormitory access, 24-hour security main gate.

Athletics Member NAIA.

Standardized Tests *Required:* SAT or ACT (for admission).

Costs (2011–12) *Comprehensive fee:* $40,650 includes full-time tuition ($30,050), mandatory fees ($340), and room and board ($10,260). Full-time tuition and fees vary according to course load and reciprocity agreements. Part-time tuition: $995 per credit hour. Part-time tuition and fees vary according to course load and reciprocity agreements. *Room and board:* Room and board charges vary according to board plan and housing facility.

Financial Aid *Of all full-time matriculated undergraduates who enrolled in 2006,* 373 applied for aid, 247 were judged to have need, 58 had their need fully met. 50 Federal Work-Study jobs (averaging $1699). 53 state and other part-time jobs (averaging $1750). *In 2006,* 77 non-need-based awards were made. *Average percent of need met:* 43. *Average financial aid package:* $15,554. *Average need-based loan:* $4154. *Average need-based gift aid:* $13,258. *Average non-need-based aid:* $10,557. *Average indebtedness upon graduation:* $10,500. *Financial aid deadline:* 6/30.

Applying *Options:* electronic application, deferred entrance. *Required:* essay or personal statement, high school transcript. *Required for some:* interview.

Freshman Application Contact Holy Names University, 3500 Mountain Boulevard, Oakland, CA 94619-1699. *Phone:* 510-436-1195. *Toll-free phone:* 800-430-1321. *Web site:* http://www.hnu.edu/.

Hope International University

Fullerton, California

- **Independent** comprehensive, founded 1928, affiliated with Christian Churches and Churches of Christ
- **Suburban** 16-acre campus with easy access to Los Angeles
- **Coed** 964 undergraduate students, 77% full-time, 57% women, 43% men
- **Moderately difficult** entrance level

Undergraduates 738 full-time, 226 part-time. 34% are from out of state; 7% Black or African American, non-Hispanic/Latino; 15% Hispanic/Latino; 3% Asian, non-Hispanic/Latino; 2% Native Hawaiian or other Pacific Islander, non-Hispanic/Latino; 0.5% American Indian or Alaska Native, non-Hispanic/Latino; 9% Two or more races, non-Hispanic/Latino; 20% Race/ethnicity unknown; 0.3% international. *Retention:* 67% of full-time freshmen returned.

Freshmen *Admission:* 143 enrolled.

Faculty *Total:* 188, 19% full-time, 47% with terminal degrees. *Student/faculty ratio:* 12:1.

Academics *Calendar:* 4-1-4. *Degrees:* certificates, associate, bachelor's, master's, and postbachelor's certificates.

Computers on Campus Students can access the following: computer help desk, free student e-mail accounts, online (class) grades, online (class) registration, online (class) schedules. Campuswide network is available. 100% of college-owned or -operated housing units are wired for high-speed Internet access. Wireless service is available via entire campus.

Student Life *Housing:* on-campus residence required through sophomore year. *Options:* men-only, women-only, disabled students. Campus housing is university owned. Freshman campus housing is guaranteed. *Campus security:* 24-hour emergency response devices and patrols, student patrols.

Athletics Member NAIA, NCCAA. *Intercollegiate sports:* basketball M(s)/W(s), cheerleading M(s)/W(s), soccer M(s)/W(s), softball W(s), tennis M(s)/W(s), ultimate Frisbee M/W, volleyball M/W(s). *Intramural sports:* ultimate Frisbee M/W, volleyball M/W.

Costs (2011–12) *One-time required fee:* $160. *Comprehensive fee:* $33,489 includes full-time tuition ($23,600), mandatory fees ($1789), and room and board ($8100). Full-time tuition and fees vary according to course level, course load, degree level, location, program, and reciprocity agreements. Part-time tuition: $995 per unit. Part-time tuition and fees vary according to course level, course load, degree level, location, program, and reciprocity agreements. *Required fees:* $364 per year part-time. *College room only:* $4300. Room and board charges vary according to board plan and student level. *Payment plan:* installment. *Waivers:* employees or children of employees.

Financial Aid Of all full-time matriculated undergraduates who enrolled in 2011, 717 applied for aid, 700 were judged to have need, 126 had their need fully met. 28 Federal Work-Study jobs (averaging $2000). In 2011, 28 non-need-based awards were made. *Average percent of need met:* 60%. *Average financial aid package:* $15,250. *Average need-based loan:* $4750. *Average need-based gift aid:* $7530. *Average non-need-based aid:* $11,250. *Average indebtedness upon graduation:* $31,000.

Applying *Options:* electronic application. *Required:* essay or personal statement, high school transcript, minimum 2.5 GPA, 2 letters of recommendation, rank in upper 50% of high school class. *Required for some:* interview. *Application deadline:* 2/1 (freshmen).

Freshman Application Contact Ms. Midge Madden, Office Manager, Hope International University, 2500 East Nutwood Avenue, Fullerton, CA 92831-3138. *Phone:* 714-879-3901. *Toll-free phone:* 866-722-HOPE. *Fax:* 714-681-7423. *E-mail:* mfmadden@hiu.edu. *Web site:* http://www.hiu.edu/.

Humboldt State University
Arcata, California

- **State-supported** comprehensive, founded 1913, part of California State University System
- **Rural** 161-acre campus
- **Endowment** $18.5 million
- **Coed** 7,385 undergraduate students, 92% full-time, 53% women, 47% men
- **Moderately difficult** entrance level, 93% of applicants were admitted

Undergraduates 6,818 full-time, 567 part-time. Students come from 50 states and territories; 46 other countries; 14% are from out of state; 4% Black or African American, non-Hispanic/Latino; 21% Hispanic/Latino; 3% Asian, non-Hispanic/Latino; 0.3% Native Hawaiian or other Pacific Islander, non-Hispanic/Latino; 1% American Indian or Alaska Native, non-Hispanic/Latino; 6% Two or more races, non-Hispanic/Latino; 0.9% Race/ethnicity unknown; 0.9% international; 13% transferred in; 27% live on campus. *Retention:* 74% of full-time freshmen returned.

Freshmen *Admission:* 9,466 applied, 8,770 admitted, 1,282 enrolled. *Average high school GPA:* 3.13. *Test scores:* SAT critical reading scores over 500: 59%; SAT math scores over 500: 55%; SAT writing scores over 500: 52%; ACT scores over 18: 79%; SAT critical reading scores over 600: 20%; SAT math scores over 600: 17%; SAT writing scores over 600: 13%; ACT scores over 24: 33%; SAT critical reading scores over 700: 2%; SAT math scores over 700: 1%; SAT writing scores over 700: 1%; ACT scores over 30: 3%.

Faculty *Total:* 517, 45% full-time, 54% with terminal degrees. *Student/faculty ratio:* 23:1.

Academics *Calendar:* semesters. *Degrees:* bachelor's, master's, post-master's, and postbachelor's certificates. *Special study options:* academic remediation for entering students, adult/continuing education programs, advanced placement credit, cooperative education, distance learning, double majors, English as a second language, honors programs, independent study, internships, off-campus study, part-time degree program, services for LD students, student-designed majors, study abroad, summer session for credit.

Computers on Campus 1,098 computers/terminals are available on campus for general student use. Students can access the following: computer help desk, free student e-mail accounts, online (class) grades, online (class) registration, online (class) schedules. Campuswide network is available. 100% of college-owned or -operated housing units are wired for high-speed Internet access. Wireless service is available via entire campus.

Student Life *Housing options:* coed. Campus housing is university owned. Freshman applicants given priority for college housing. *Activities and organizations:* drama/theater group, student-run newspaper, radio station, choral group, marching band, student radio station, Student Environmental Action Coalition, Youth Educational Services, Ballet Folklorico, International Student Union, national fraternities, national sororities. *Campus security:* 24-hour emergency response devices and patrols, late-night transport/escort service, controlled dormitory access. *Student services:* health clinic, personal/psychological counseling, women's center.

Athletics Member NCAA. All Division II. *Intercollegiate sports:* basketball M(s)/W(s), cheerleading W(c), crew M(c)/W, cross-country running M(s)/W(s), football M(s), lacrosse M(c), soccer M(s)/W(s), softball W(s), track and field M(s)/W(s), volleyball W(s). *Intramural sports:* baseball M(c), basketball M/W, fencing M(c)/W(c), rugby M(c)/W(c), soccer M/W, ultimate Frisbee M(c)/W(c), volleyball M(c), water polo M(c).

Standardized Tests *Required for some:* SAT or ACT (for admission).

Costs (2012–13) *Tuition:* state resident $0 full-time; nonresident $11,160 full-time, $372 per credit part-time. Full-time tuition and fees vary according to degree level. Part-time tuition and fees vary according to course load and degree level. *Required fees:* $7622 full-time, $2348 per term part-time. *Room and board:* $10,948. Room and board charges vary according to board plan

and housing facility. *Payment plan:* installment. *Waivers:* employees or children of employees.

Financial Aid Of all full-time matriculated undergraduates who enrolled in 2010, 4,957 applied for aid, 4,293 were judged to have need, 26 had their need fully met. 308 Federal Work-Study jobs (averaging $2793). In 2010, 21 non-need-based awards were made. *Average percent of need met:* 67%. *Average financial aid package:* $11,339. *Average need-based loan:* $4498. *Average need-based gift aid:* $9356. *Average non-need-based aid:* $1649. *Average indebtedness upon graduation:* $17,889.

Applying *Options:* electronic application. *Application fee:* $55. *Required:* high school transcript, minimum 2.0 GPA. *Application deadlines:* 11/30 (freshmen), 11/30 (out-of-state freshmen), 11/30 (transfers). *Notification:* continuous (freshmen), continuous (out-of-state freshmen), continuous (transfers).

Freshman Application Contact Ms. Rhonda Geldin, Assistant Director of Admissions, Humboldt State University, 1 Harpst Street, Arcata, CA 95521. *Phone:* 707-826-4402. *Toll-free phone:* 866-850-9556. *Fax:* 707-826-6190. *E-mail:* hsuinfo@humboldt.edu. *Web site:* http://www.humboldt.edu/.

Humphreys College
Stockton, California

Director of Admissions Director of Admission, Humphreys College, 6650 Inglewood Avenue, Stockton, CA 95207-3896. *Phone:* 209-235-2901. *E-mail:* ugadmission@humphreys.edu. *Web site:* http://www.humphreys.edu/.

Interior Designers Institute
Newport Beach, California

Freshman Application Contact Interior Designers Institute, 1061 Camelback Road, Newport Beach, CA 92660. *Web site:* http://www.idi.edu/.

International Technological University
Santa Clara, California

Director of Admissions Manisha Pai, Director of Admissions and Registrar, International Technological University, 1650 Warburton Avenue, Santa Clara, CA 95050. *Phone:* 408-331-1014. *Toll-free phone:* 888-488-8969 (in-state); 888-488-4968 (out-of-state). *Fax:* 408-331-1026. *E-mail:* mpai@itu.edu. *Web site:* http://www.itu.edu/.

ITT Technical Institute
Clovis, California

- **Proprietary** 4-year, founded 2005, part of ITT Educational Services, Inc.
- **Coed**
- **Minimally difficult** entrance level

Academics *Calendar:* quarters. *Degrees:* associate and bachelor's.

Student Life *Housing:* college housing not available.

Freshman Application Contact Director of Recruitment, ITT Technical Institute, 362 North Clovis Avenue, Clovis, CA 93612. *Phone:* 559-325-5400. *Toll-free phone:* 800-564-9771. *Web site:* http://www.itt-tech.edu/.

ITT Technical Institute
Concord, California

- **Proprietary** 4-year, part of ITT Educational Services, Inc.
- **Coed**
- **Minimally difficult** entrance level

Academics *Calendar:* quarters. *Degrees:* associate and bachelor's.

Freshman Application Contact Director of Recruitment, ITT Technical Institute, 1140 Galaxy Way, Suite 400, Concord, CA 94520. *Phone:* 925-674-8200. *Toll-free phone:* 800-211-7062. *Web site:* http://www.itt-tech.edu/.

ITT Technical Institute
Corona, California

- **Proprietary** 4-year
- **Coed**
- **Minimally difficult** entrance level

Academics *Degrees:* associate and bachelor's.

Freshman Application Contact Director of Recruitment, ITT Technical Institute, 4160 Temescal Canyon Road, Suite 100, Corona, CA 92883. *Phone:* 951-277-5400. *Toll-free phone:* 877-764-9661. *Web site:* http://www.itt-tech.edu/.

ITT Technical Institute
Culver City, California

- **Proprietary** primarily 2-year, part of ITT Educational Services, Inc.
- **Coed**

Academics *Calendar:* quarters. *Degrees:* associate and bachelor's.
Freshman Application Contact Director of Recruitment, ITT Technical Institute, 6101 W. Centinela Avenue, Suite 180, Culver City, CA 90230. *Phone:* 310-417-5800. *Toll-free phone:* 800-215-6151. *Web site:* http://www.itt-tech.edu/.

ITT Technical Institute
Lathrop, California

- **Proprietary** primarily 2-year, founded 1997, part of ITT Educational Services, Inc.
- **Coed**
- **Minimally difficult** entrance level

Academics *Calendar:* quarters. *Degrees:* associate and bachelor's.
Student Life *Housing:* college housing not available.
Freshman Application Contact Director of Recruitment, ITT Technical Institute, 16916 South Harlan Road, Lathrop, CA 95330. *Phone:* 209-858-0077. *Toll-free phone:* 800-346-1786. *Web site:* http://www.itt-tech.edu/.

ITT Technical Institute
Oakland, California

- **Proprietary** primarily 2-year, part of ITT Educational Services, Inc.
- **Coed**

Academics *Calendar:* quarters. *Degrees:* associate and bachelor's.
Freshman Application Contact Director of Recruitment, ITT Technical Institute, 7901 Oakport Street, Suite 3000, Oakland, CA 94621. *Phone:* 510-553-2800. *Toll-free phone:* 877-442-5833. *Web site:* http://www.itt-tech.edu/.

ITT Technical Institute
Orange, California

- **Proprietary** primarily 2-year, founded 1982, part of ITT Educational Services, Inc.
- **Suburban** campus
- **Coed**
- **Minimally difficult** entrance level

Academics *Calendar:* quarters. *Degrees:* associate and bachelor's.
Student Life *Housing:* college housing not available.
Financial Aid Of all full-time matriculated undergraduates who enrolled in 2010, 20 Federal Work-Study jobs (averaging $5000).
Freshman Application Contact Director of Recruitment, ITT Technical Institute, 4000 West Metropolitan Drive, Suite 100, Orange, CA 92868. *Phone:* 714-941-2400. *Web site:* http://www.itt-tech.edu/.

ITT Technical Institute
Oxnard, California

- **Proprietary** primarily 2-year, founded 1993, part of ITT Educational Services, Inc.
- **Urban** campus
- **Coed**
- **Minimally difficult** entrance level

Academics *Calendar:* quarters. *Degrees:* associate and bachelor's.
Student Life *Housing:* college housing not available.
Freshman Application Contact Director of Recruitment, ITT Technical Institute, 2051 Solar Drive, Suite 150, Oxnard, CA 93036. *Phone:* 805-988-0143. *Toll-free phone:* 800-530-1582. *Web site:* http://www.itt-tech.edu/.

ITT Technical Institute
Rancho Cordova, California

- **Proprietary** primarily 2-year, founded 1954, part of ITT Educational Services, Inc.
- **Urban** campus
- **Coed**
- **Minimally difficult** entrance level

Academics *Calendar:* quarters. *Degrees:* associate and bachelor's.
Student Life *Housing:* college housing not available.

Freshman Application Contact Director of Recruitment, ITT Technical Institute, 10863 Gold Center Drive, Rancho Cordova, CA 95670-6034. *Phone:* 916-851-3900. *Toll-free phone:* 800-488-8466. *Web site:* http://www.itt-tech.edu/.

ITT Technical Institute
San Bernardino, California

- **Proprietary** primarily 2-year, founded 1987, part of ITT Educational Services, Inc.
- **Urban** campus
- **Coed**
- **Minimally difficult** entrance level

Academics *Calendar:* quarters. *Degrees:* associate and bachelor's.
Student Life *Housing:* college housing not available.
Freshman Application Contact Director of Recruitment, ITT Technical Institute, 670 East Carnegie Drive, San Bernardino, CA 92408. *Phone:* 909-806-4600. *Toll-free phone:* 800-888-3801. *Web site:* http://www.itt-tech.edu/.

ITT Technical Institute
San Diego, California

- **Proprietary** primarily 2-year, founded 1981, part of ITT Educational Services, Inc.
- **Suburban** campus
- **Coed**
- **Minimally difficult** entrance level

Academics *Calendar:* quarters. *Degrees:* associate and bachelor's.
Student Life *Housing:* college housing not available.
Freshman Application Contact Director of Recruitment, ITT Technical Institute, 9680 Granite Ridge Drive, San Diego, CA 92123. *Phone:* 858-571-8500. *Toll-free phone:* 800-883-0380. *Web site:* http://www.itt-tech.edu/.

ITT Technical Institute
San Dimas, California

- **Proprietary** primarily 2-year, founded 1982, part of ITT Educational Services, Inc.
- **Suburban** campus
- **Coed**
- **Minimally difficult** entrance level

Academics *Calendar:* quarters. *Degrees:* associate and bachelor's.
Student Life *Housing:* college housing not available.
Financial Aid Of all full-time matriculated undergraduates who enrolled in 2010, 20 Federal Work-Study jobs (averaging $4500).
Freshman Application Contact Director of Recruitment, ITT Technical Institute, 650 West Cienega Avenue, San Dimas, CA 91773. *Phone:* 909-971-2300. *Toll-free phone:* 800-414-6522. *Web site:* http://www.itt-tech.edu/.

ITT Technical Institute
Sylmar, California

- **Proprietary** primarily 2-year, founded 1982, part of ITT Educational Services, Inc.
- **Urban** campus
- **Coed**
- **Minimally difficult** entrance level

Academics *Calendar:* quarters. *Degrees:* associate and bachelor's.
Student Life *Housing:* college housing not available.
Freshman Application Contact Director of Recruitment, ITT Technical Institute, 12669 Encinitas Avenue, Sylmar, CA 91342-3664. *Phone:* 818-364-5151. *Toll-free phone:* 800-363-2086 (in-state); 800-636-2086 (out-of-state). *Web site:* http://www.itt-tech.edu/.

ITT Technical Institute
Torrance, California

- **Proprietary** primarily 2-year, founded 1987, part of ITT Educational Services, Inc.
- **Urban** campus
- **Coed**
- **Minimally difficult** entrance level

Academics *Calendar:* quarters. *Degrees:* associate and bachelor's.
Student Life *Housing:* college housing not available.
Financial Aid Of all full-time matriculated undergraduates who enrolled in 2010, 6 Federal Work-Study jobs (averaging $4000).

Freshman Application Contact Director of Recruitment, ITT Technical Institute, 2555 West 190th Street, Suite 125, Torrance, CA 90504. *Phone:* 310-965-5900. *Web site:* http://www.itt-tech.edu/.

ITT Technical Institute
West Covina, California

- **Proprietary** primarily 2-year, part of ITT Educational Services, Inc.
- **Coed**

Academics *Calendar:* quarters. *Degrees:* associate and bachelor's.
Freshman Application Contact Director of Recruitment, ITT Technical Institute, 1530 W. Cameron Avenue, West Covina, CA 91790. *Phone:* 626-813-3681. *Toll-free phone:* 877-480-2766. *Web site:* http://www.itt-tech.edu/.

John F. Kennedy University
Pleasant Hill, California

Director of Admissions Ms. Jen Miller-Hogg, Director of Admissions, John F. Kennedy University, 100 Ellinwood Way, Pleasant Hill, CA 94523-4817. *Phone:* 925-969-3584. *Toll-free phone:* 800-696-JFKU. *E-mail:* jmhogg@jfku.edu. *Web site:* http://www.jfku.edu/.

King's University
Van Nuys, California

Freshman Application Contact Mrs. Marilyn J. Chappell, Director of Admissions, King's University, 14800 Sherman Way, Van Nuys, CA 91405-8040. *Phone:* 818-779-8040. *Toll-free phone:* 888-779-8040. *Fax:* 818-779-8429. *E-mail:* mchappell@kingscollege.edu. *Web site:* http://kingsuniversity.edu/.

LA College International
Los Angeles, California

- **Proprietary** 4-year, founded 1981
- **Urban** with easy access to Los Angeles
- **Coed**
- **Noncompetitive** entrance level

Faculty *Student/faculty ratio:* 14:1.
Academics *Calendar:* quarters. *Degrees:* associate and bachelor's.
Student Life *Campus security:* 24-hour emergency response devices.
Applying *Options:* electronic application. *Required:* high school graduate or hold a General Equivalency (Education) Diploma (GED). Complete the Jump Start Orientation Seminar.
Freshman Application Contact LA College International, 3200 Wilshire Boulevard, # 400, Los Angeles, CA 90010-1308. *Toll-free phone:* 877-4LAC-EDU. *Web site:* http://www.lac.edu/.

Laguna College of Art & Design
Laguna Beach, California

Director of Admissions Mike Rivas, Vice President of Enrollment, Laguna College of Art & Design, 2222 Laguna Canyon Road, Laguna Beach, CA 92651-1136. *Phone:* 949-376-6000 Ext. 232. *Toll-free phone:* 800-255-0762. *Web site:* http://www.lagunacollege.edu/.

La Sierra University
Riverside, California

- **Independent Seventh-day Adventist** comprehensive, founded 1922, part of Seventh-Day Adventist Education System
- **Suburban** 100-acre campus with easy access to Los Angeles
- **Endowment** $15.4 million
- **Coed** 1,897 undergraduate students, 89% full-time, 55% women, 45% men
- **Minimally difficult** entrance level, 53% of applicants were admitted

Undergraduates 1,697 full-time, 200 part-time. Students come from 16 states and territories; 8 other countries; 9% are from out of state; 7% Black or African American, non-Hispanic/Latino; 35% Hispanic/Latino; 16% Asian, non-Hispanic/Latino; 3% Native Hawaiian or other Pacific Islander, non-Hispanic/Latino; 0.2% American Indian or Alaska Native, non-Hispanic/Latino; 4% Two or more races, non-Hispanic/Latino; 0.2% Race/ethnicity unknown; 16% international; 13% transferred in; 40% live on campus. *Retention:* 76% of full-time freshmen returned.

Freshmen *Admission:* 1,979 applied, 1,058 admitted, 437 enrolled. *Average high school GPA:* 3.27. *Test scores:* SAT critical reading scores over 500: 37%; SAT math scores over 500: 45%; ACT scores over 18: 66%; SAT critical reading scores over 600: 6%; SAT math scores over 600: 10%; ACT scores over 24: 17%; SAT critical reading scores over 700: 1%; SAT math scores over 700: 3%; ACT scores over 30: 1%.
Faculty *Total:* 250, 38% full-time, 34% with terminal degrees. *Student/faculty ratio:* 20:1.
Academics *Calendar:* quarters. *Degrees:* certificates, bachelor's, master's, doctoral, post-master's, postbachelor's, and first professional certificates. *Special study options:* academic remediation for entering students, accelerated degree program, adult/continuing education programs, advanced placement credit, distance learning, double majors, English as a second language, honors programs, independent study, internships, off-campus study, part-time degree program, services for LD students, student-designed majors, study abroad, summer session for credit. *Unusual degree programs:* business administration with White memorial branch (CA), Riverside branch (CA), Glendale branch (CA), Chino Branch (CA); criminal justice at Corona Branch.
Computers on Campus 300 computers/terminals are available on campus for general student use. Students can access the following: computer help desk, free student e-mail accounts, online (class) grades, online (class) registration, online (class) schedules. Campuswide network is available. Wireless service is available via classrooms, computer centers, computer labs, libraries, student centers.
Student Life *Housing:* on-campus residence required for freshman year. *Options:* men-only, women-only, cooperative. Campus housing is university owned. Freshman campus housing is guaranteed. *Activities and organizations:* drama/theater group, student-run newspaper, choral group, Student Association of LSU, Korean Student Association, Students In Free Enterprise (SIFE), Ol Club, Black Student Association. *Campus security:* 24-hour emergency response devices and patrols, student patrols, late-night transport/escort service. *Student services:* health clinic, personal/psychological counseling, women's center.
Athletics Member NAIA. *Intercollegiate sports:* basketball M/W, golf M, soccer M, softball W, volleyball W. *Intramural sports:* baseball M, basketball M/W, soccer M, softball W, volleyball W.
Standardized Tests *Required:* SAT or ACT (for admission).
Costs (2011–12) *Comprehensive fee:* $35,685 includes full-time tuition ($27,240), mandatory fees ($1095), and room and board ($7350). Full-time tuition and fees vary according to course load, degree level, and location. Part-time tuition: $726 per quarter hour. Part-time tuition and fees vary according to course load, degree level, and location. *Room and board:* Room and board charges vary according to board plan and housing facility. *Payment plan:* installment. *Waivers:* employees or children of employees.
Financial Aid Of all full-time matriculated undergraduates who enrolled in 2006, 1,114 applied for aid, 1,019 were judged to have need, 117 had their need fully met. 269 Federal Work-Study jobs (averaging $2314). In 2006, 373 non-need-based awards were made. *Average percent of need met:* 64%. *Average financial aid package:* $15,006. *Average need-based loan:* $4856. *Average need-based gift aid:* $11,281. *Average non-need-based aid:* $5847. *Average indebtedness upon graduation:* $28,876.
Applying *Options:* electronic application, deferred entrance. *Application fee:* $30. *Required:* essay or personal statement, high school transcript, minimum 2.0 GPA, 2 letters of recommendation, Eligibility Index Table (combination of GPA and test scores). *Required for some:* interview. *Application deadlines* 2/1 (freshmen), 2/1 (out-of-state freshmen), 7/1 (transfers). *Notification:* continuous (freshmen), continuous (out-of-state freshmen), continuous (transfers).
Freshman Application Contact Ms. Ivy Teheda, Ass. Director of Admissions, La Sierra University, 4500 Riverwalk Parkway, Riverside, CA 92515. *Phone:* 951-7852957. *Toll-free phone:* 800-874-5587. *Fax:* 951-7852447. *E-mail:* iteheda@lasierra.edu. *Web site:* http://www.lasierra.edu/.

Life Pacific College
San Dimas, California

Freshman Application Contact Ms. Dorienne Elston, Director of Admissions, Life Pacific College, 1100 Covina Boulevard, San Dimas, CA 91773-3298. *Phone:* 909-599-5433 Ext. 314. *Toll-free phone:* 877-886-5433 Ext. 314. *Fax:* 909-706-3070. *E-mail:* adm@lifepacific.edu. *Web site:* http://www.lifepacific.edu/.

Lincoln University
Oakland, California

Freshman Application Contact Ms. Reenu Shrestha, Admissions Officer, Lincoln University, 401 15th Street, Oakland, CA 94612. *Phone:* 510-628-8010 Ext. 8030. *Toll-free phone:* 888-810-9998. *Fax:* 510-628-8012. *E-mail:* admissions@lincolnuca.edu. *Web site:* http://www.lincolnuca.edu/.

COLLEGES AT-A-GLANCE

Loma Linda University

Loma Linda, California

Freshman Application Contact Admissions Office, Loma Linda University, Loma Linda, CA 92350. *Phone:* 909-558-1000. *Toll-free phone:* 800-422-4558. *Web site:* http://www.llu.edu/.

Loyola Marymount University

Los Angeles, California

- **Independent Roman Catholic** comprehensive, founded 1911
- **Suburban** 142-acre campus with easy access to Los Angeles
- **Endowment** $386.7 million
- **Coed** 6,069 undergraduate students, 96% full-time, 57% women, 43% men
- **Very difficult** entrance level, 53% of applicants were admitted

Undergraduates 5,818 full-time, 251 part-time. Students come from 48 states and territories; 48 other countries; 24% are from out of state; 6% Black or African American, non-Hispanic/Latino; 21% Hispanic/Latino; 10% Asian, non-Hispanic/Latino; 0.2% Native Hawaiian or other Pacific Islander, non-Hispanic/Latino; 0.2% American Indian or Alaska Native, non-Hispanic/Latino; 8% Two or more races, non-Hispanic/Latino; 4% international; 5% transferred in; 53% live on campus. *Retention:* 92% of full-time freshmen returned.

Freshmen *Admission:* 11,309 applied, 6,043 admitted, 1,288 enrolled. *Average high school GPA:* 3.71. *Test scores:* SAT critical reading scores over 500: 90%; SAT math scores over 500: 92%; SAT writing scores over 500: 93%; ACT scores over 18: 99%; SAT critical reading scores over 600: 47%; SAT math scores over 600: 56%; SAT writing scores over 600: 54%; ACT scores over 24: 80%; SAT critical reading scores over 700: 7%; SAT math scores over 700: 10%; SAT writing scores over 700: 9%; ACT scores over 30: 17%.

Faculty *Total:* 1,095, 49% full-time. *Student/faculty ratio:* 11:1.

Academics *Calendar:* semesters. *Degrees:* certificates, bachelor's, master's, doctoral, post-master's, postbachelor's, and first professional certificates. *Special study options:* academic remediation for entering students, accelerated degree program, advanced placement credit, cooperative education, double majors, English as a second language, honors programs, independent study, internships, part-time degree program, services for LD students, student-designed majors, study abroad, summer session for credit. *ROTC:* Army (c), Navy (c), Air Force (b). *Unusual degree programs:* 3-2 engineering.

Computers on Campus 780 computers/terminals and 2,000 ports are available on campus for general student use. Students can access the following: campus intranet, computer help desk, free student e-mail accounts, online (class) grades, online (class) registration, online (class) schedules. Campuswide network is available. 100% of college-owned or -operated housing units are wired for high-speed Internet access. Wireless service is available via entire campus.

Student Life *Housing options:* coed, men-only, women-only, disabled students. Campus housing is university owned. Freshman applicants given priority for college housing. *Activities and organizations:* drama/theater group, student-run newspaper, radio and television station, choral group, Greeks, Intramurals, Christian Life Communities, Black Student Union, Serve LA, national fraternities, national sororities. *Campus security:* 24-hour emergency response devices and patrols, late-night transport/escort service, controlled dormitory access. *Student services:* health clinic, personal/psychological counseling.

Athletics Member NCAA. All Division I. *Intercollegiate sports:* baseball M(s), basketball M(s)/W(s), cheerleading M/W, crew M/W(s), cross-country running M(s)/W(s), golf M(s), soccer M(s)/W(s), softball W(s), swimming and diving W(s), tennis M(s)/W(s), track and field M/W, volleyball W(s), water polo M(s)/W(s). *Intramural sports:* baseball M(c), basketball M/W(c), football M/W, ice hockey M(c), lacrosse M(c)/W(c), rugby M(c), skiing (downhill) M(c)/W(c), soccer M(c)/W(c), tennis M(c)/W(c), volleyball M(c)/W(c), water polo W(c).

Standardized Tests *Required:* SAT or ACT (for admission).

Costs (2011–12) *One-time required fee:* $220. *Comprehensive fee:* $51,805 includes full-time tuition ($36,912), mandatory fees ($693), and room and board ($14,200). Full-time tuition and fees vary according to reciprocity agreements. Part-time tuition: $1540 per credit hour. Part-time tuition and fees vary according to course load. *Required fees:* $5 per credit hour part-time, $60 per term part-time. *College room only:* $9800. Room and board charges vary according to board plan and housing facility. *Payment plans:* installment, deferred payment. *Waivers:* employees or children of employees.

Financial Aid Of all full-time matriculated undergraduates who enrolled in 2010, 4,181 applied for aid, 3,282 were judged to have need, 527 had their need fully met. 1,746 Federal Work-Study jobs (averaging $1997), 2,060 state and other part-time jobs (averaging $2539). In 2010, 948 non-need-based awards were made. *Average percent of need met:* 66%. *Average financial aid package:* $26,322. *Average need-based loan:* $5436. *Average need-based gift

aid:* $19,117. *Average non-need-based aid:* $10,415. *Average indebtedness upon graduation:* $31,246. *Financial aid deadline:* 7/30.

Applying *Options:* electronic application, early admission, early action, deferred entrance. *Application fee:* $60. *Required:* essay or personal statement, high school transcript, 1 letter of recommendation. *Required for some:* portfolios or auditions for animation, dance, music, or theatre arts majors. *Recommended:* interview. *Application deadlines:* 1/15 (freshmen), 3/15 (transfers), 11/1 (early action). *Notification:* continuous (freshmen), continuous (transfers), 12/20 (early action).

Freshman Application Contact Loyola Marymount University, One LMU Drive, Los Angeles, CA 90045-2659. *Phone:* 310-338-2750. *Toll-free phone:* 800-LMU-INFO. *Web site:* http://www.lmu.edu/.

See page 115 for display ad and page 1418 for the College Close-Up.

Marymount College, Palos Verdes, California

Rancho Palos Verdes, California

- **Independent Roman Catholic** 4-year, founded 1932
- **Suburban** 26-acre campus with easy access to Los Angeles
- **Endowment** $9.5 million
- **Coed** 946 undergraduate students, 96% full-time, 51% women, 49% men
- **Minimally difficult** entrance level, 45% of applicants were admitted

Undergraduates 909 full-time, 37 part-time. Students come from 21 states and territories; 27 other countries; 12% are from out of state; 9% Black or African American, non-Hispanic/Latino; 19% Hispanic/Latino; 5% Asian, non-Hispanic/Latino; 1% Native Hawaiian or other Pacific Islander, non-Hispanic/Latino; 0.5% American Indian or Alaska Native, non-Hispanic/Latino; 5% Two or more races, non-Hispanic/Latino; 18% Race/ethnicity unknown; 6% international; 7% transferred in; 58% live on campus. *Retention:* 66% of full-time freshmen returned.

Freshmen *Admission:* 3,169 applied, 1,417 admitted, 426 enrolled. *Average high school GPA:* 2.86. *Test scores:* SAT math scores over 500: 38%; SAT writing scores over 500: 37%; ACT scores over 18: 68%; SAT math scores over 600: 8%; SAT writing scores over 600: 8%; ACT scores over 24: 24%; SAT math scores over 700: 1%; SAT writing scores over 700: 1%; ACT scores over 30: 1%.

Faculty *Total:* 121, 27% full-time, 28% with terminal degrees. *Student/faculty ratio:* 15:1.

Academics *Calendar:* semesters. *Degrees:* certificates, associate, and bachelor's. *Special study options:* academic remediation for entering students, adult/continuing education programs, advanced placement credit, English as a second language, honors programs, independent study, internships, off-campus study, part-time degree program, services for LD students, study abroad, summer session for credit.

Computers on Campus 180 computers/terminals are available on campus for general student use. Students can access the following: campus intranet, computer help desk, free student e-mail accounts, online (class) grades, online (class) registration, online (class) schedules. Campuswide network is available. 100% of college-owned or -operated housing units are wired for high-speed Internet access. Wireless service is available via entire campus.

Student Life *Housing:* on-campus residence required for freshman year. *Options:* coed. Campus housing is university owned. Freshman campus housing is guaranteed. *Activities and organizations:* drama/theater group, student-run newspaper, radio station, choral group. *Campus security:* 24-hour emergency response devices and patrols, late-night transport/escort service, controlled dormitory access. *Student services:* health clinic, personal/psychological counseling.

Athletics Member NAIA. *Intercollegiate sports:* golf M/W, lacrosse M/W, soccer M(s). *Intramural sports:* basketball M/W, golf M/W, lacrosse M/W, soccer M/W, softball M/W, swimming and diving M/W, volleyball M/W.

Standardized Tests *Recommended:* SAT or ACT (for admission).

Costs (2012–13) *Comprehensive fee:* $40,942 includes full-time tuition ($28,217), mandatory fees ($650), and room and board ($12,075). Part-time tuition: $1066 per credit hour. *Room and board:* Room and board charges vary according to board plan and housing facility. *Payment plan:* installment. *Waivers:* senior citizens and employees or children of employees.

Financial Aid Of all full-time matriculated undergraduates who enrolled in 2010, 40 Federal Work-Study jobs (averaging $2000).

Applying *Options:* electronic application, early admission. *Application fee:* $40. *Required:* high school transcript. *Required for some:* essay or personal statement, interview. *Application deadlines:* 7/1 (freshmen), 8/15 (transfers). *Notification:* continuous until 9/1 (freshmen), continuous until 9/1 (transfers).

Freshman Application Contact Ms. Paula Avery, Director of Admissions, Marymount College, Palos Verdes, California, 30800 Palos Verdes Drive East, Rancho Palos Verdes, CA 90275-6299. *Phone:* 310-377-5501 Ext. 211. *Fax:* 310-265-0962.*E-mail:* admissions@marymountpv.edu. *Web site:* http://www.marymountpv.edu/.

The Master's College and Seminary
Santa Clarita, California

- **Independent nondenominational** comprehensive, founded 1927
- **Suburban** 110-acre campus with easy access to Los Angeles
- **Endowment** $14.6 million
- **Coed** 1,156 undergraduate students, 90% full-time, 47% women, 53% men
- **Moderately difficult** entrance level, 66% of applicants were admitted

Undergraduates 1,040 full-time, 116 part-time. Students come from 42 states and territories; 25 other countries; 29% are from out of state; 3% Black or African American, non-Hispanic/Latino; 8% Hispanic/Latino; 6% Asian, non-Hispanic/Latino; 0.5% Native Hawaiian or other Pacific Islander, non-Hispanic/Latino; 0.9% American Indian or Alaska Native, non-Hispanic/Latino; 4% Two or more races, non-Hispanic/Latino; 3% Race/ethnicity unknown; 5% international; 10% transferred in; 75% live on campus. *Retention:* 84% of full-time freshmen returned.

Freshmen *Admission:* 822 applied, 541 admitted, 230 enrolled. *Average high school GPA:* 3.62. *Test scores:* SAT critical reading scores over 500: 70%; SAT math scores over 500: 59%; SAT critical reading scores over 600: 30%; SAT math scores over 600: 19%; SAT critical reading scores over 700: 7%; SAT math scores over 700: 2%.

Faculty *Total:* 195, 28% full-time, 35% with terminal degrees. *Student/faculty ratio:* 19:1.

Academics *Calendar:* semesters. *Degrees:* certificates, bachelor's, master's, and doctoral. *Special study options:* academic remediation for entering students, accelerated degree program, adult/continuing education programs, advanced placement credit, cooperative education, distance learning, double majors, external degree program, independent study, internships, part-time degree program, services for LD students, study abroad, summer session for credit.

Computers on Campus 57 computers/terminals are available on campus for general student use. Students can access the following: free student e-mail accounts, online (class) grades, online (class) registration, online (class) schedules. Campuswide network is available. Wireless service is available via entire campus.

Student Life *Housing:* on-campus residence required through junior year. *Options:* men-only, women-only. Campus housing is university owned. Freshman campus housing is guaranteed. *Activities and organizations:* drama/theater group, choral group, College Chorale, Summer Missions, intramurals, Church Ministries, Drama Club. *Campus security:* 24-hour patrols. *Student services:* health clinic, personal/psychological counseling.

Athletics Member NAIA, NCCAA. *Intercollegiate sports:* baseball M(s), basketball M(s)/W(s), cross-country running M(s)/W(s), golf M(s), soccer M(s)/W(s), tennis W(s), track and field M(s)/W(s), volleyball W(s). *Intramural sports:* basketball M/W, football M/W, soccer M/W, volleyball M/W.

Standardized Tests *Required:* SAT or ACT (for admission).

Costs (2012–13) *Comprehensive fee:* $37,090 includes full-time tuition ($27,300), mandatory fees ($780), and room and board ($9010). Full-time tuition and fees vary according to course load, degree level, and program. Part-time tuition: $1145 per credit hour. Part-time tuition and fees vary according to course load, degree level, and program. *Required fees:* $1145 per credit hour part-time. *College room only:* $5030. Room and board charges vary according to board plan. *Payment plan:* installment. *Waivers:* employees or children of employees.

Financial Aid Of all full-time matriculated undergraduates who enrolled in 2011, 847 applied for aid, 761 were judged to have need, 102 had their need fully met. 49 Federal Work-Study jobs (averaging $1740). 183 state and other part-time jobs (averaging $2842). In 2011, 147 non-need-based awards were made. *Average percent of need met:* 69%. *Average financial aid package:* $20,666. *Average need-based loan:* $4935. *Average need-based gift aid:* $15,957. *Average non-need-based aid:* $9193. *Average indebtedness upon graduation:* $20,265.

Applying *Options:* electronic application, early admission, early action, deferred entrance. *Application fee:* $40. *Required:* essay or personal statement, high school transcript, minimum 2.8 GPA, 2 letters of recommendation. *Recommended:* interview. *Application deadlines:* 9/1 (freshmen), 9/1 (out-of-state freshmen), 9/1 (transfers), 11/15 (early action). *Notification:* 3/15 (freshmen), 3/15 (transfers), 12/22 (early action).

Freshman Application Contact Ms. Hollie Gorsh, Director of Admissions, The Master's College and Seminary, 21726 Placerita Canyon Road, Santa Clarita, CA 91321. *Phone:* 661-259-3540 Ext. 3369. *Toll-free phone:* 800-568-6248. *Fax:* 661-288-1037. *E-mail:* admissions@masters.edu. *Web site:* http://www.masters.edu/.

located in **Silicon Valley**
one of the world's most entrepreneurial areas

Menlo
Means
Business

"Through
collaboration,
strategic
partnership and
understanding
diverse global
perspectives,
Menlo College
students will
become effective
leaders and
innovators who
will define the
future of
business."

~James J. Kelly
President, Menlo College

Office of Admissions
TEL: 650-543-3753
admissions@menlo.edu
www.menlo.edu

MENLO
C O L L E G E
Silicon Valley's Business School

Menlo College
Atherton, California

- **Independent** 4-year, founded 1927
- **Small-town** 45-acre campus with easy access to San Francisco
- **Endowment** $8.0 million
- **Coed** 642 undergraduate students, 98% full-time, 36% women, 64% men
- **Moderately difficult** entrance level, 90% of applicants were admitted

Undergraduates 631 full-time, 11 part-time. Students come from 21 states and territories; 26 other countries; 21% are from out of state; 6% Black or African American, non-Hispanic/Latino; 19% Hispanic/Latino; 7% Asian, non-Hispanic/Latino; 4% Native Hawaiian or other Pacific Islander, non-Hispanic/Latino; 0.2% American Indian or Alaska Native, non-Hispanic/Latino; 8% Two or more races, non-Hispanic/Latino; 10% Race/ethnicity unknown; 12% international; 15% transferred in; 69% live on campus. *Retention:* 74% of full-time freshmen returned.

Freshmen *Admission:* 1,725 applied, 1,556 admitted, 148 enrolled. *Average high school GPA:* 3.26. *Test scores:* SAT critical reading scores over 500: 30%; SAT math scores over 500: 50%; SAT writing scores over 500: 36%; ACT scores over 18: 80%; SAT critical reading scores over 600: 5%; SAT math scores over 600: 9%; SAT writing scores over 600: 3%; ACT scores over 24: 24%; SAT critical reading scores over 700: 1%.

Faculty *Total:* 73, 38% full-time, 55% with terminal degrees. *Student/faculty ratio:* 14:1.

Academics *Calendar:* semesters. *Degree:* bachelor's. *Special study options:* accelerated degree program, adult/continuing education programs, advanced placement credit, cooperative education, double majors, English as a second language, independent study, internships, part-time degree program, services for LD students, student-designed majors, study abroad, summer session for credit. *ROTC:* Army (c), Air Force (c).

Computers on Campus 185 computers/terminals are available on campus for general student use. Students can access the following: campus intranet, computer help desk, free student e-mail accounts, online (class) grades, online (class) registration, online (class) schedules. Campuswide network is available. 100% of college-owned or -operated housing units are wired for high-speed Internet access. Wireless service is available via classrooms, computer centers, computer labs, dorm rooms, learning centers, libraries, student centers.

Student Life *Housing:* on-campus residence required through sophomore year. *Options:* coed, men-only, women-only. Campus housing is university owned. *Activities and organizations:* student-run newspaper, radio station, International Club, Residence Hall Association, SERV, Women Club, Hawaiian Club. *Campus security:* 24-hour emergency response devices and patrols, controlled dormitory access. *Student services:* personal/psychological counseling, women's center.

Athletics Member NAIA. *Intercollegiate sports:* baseball M, basketball M/W, cheerleading M/W, cross-country running M/W, football M, golf M, soccer M/W, softball W, volleyball M/W, wrestling M/W. *Intramural sports:* basketball M(c)/W(c), skiing (downhill) M(c)/W(c).

Standardized Tests *Required:* SAT or ACT (for admission).

Costs (2012–13) *Comprehensive fee:* $47,554 includes full-time tuition ($35,510), mandatory fees ($600), and room and board ($11,444). Part-time tuition: $1480 per credit. *Room and board:* Room and board charges vary according to housing facility. *Payment plan:* installment. *Waivers:* employees or children of employees.

Financial Aid Of all full-time matriculated undergraduates who enrolled in 2011, 458 applied for aid, 436 were judged to have need, 44 had their need fully met. 330 Federal Work-Study jobs (averaging $1068). In 2011, 154 non-need-based awards were made. *Average percent of need met:* 71%. *Average financial aid package:* $28,794. *Average need-based loan:* $3896. *Average need-based gift aid:* $24,865. *Average non-need-based aid:* $11,970. *Average indebtedness upon graduation:* $30,243.

Applying *Options:* electronic application, early admission, early action, deferred entrance. *Application fee:* $40. *Required:* essay or personal statement, high school transcript, 1 letter of recommendation. *Recommended:* minimum 2.5 GPA, interview. *Application deadlines:* rolling (freshmen), rolling (out-of-state freshmen), rolling (transfers), 12/1 (early action). *Notification:* continuous (freshmen), continuous (out-of-state freshmen), continuous (transfers), 12/15 (early action).

Freshman Application Contact Jadelin Felipe, Director, Enrollment Management Operations, Menlo College, 1000 El Camino Real, Atherton, CA 94027. *Phone:* 650-543-3918. *Toll-free phone:* 800-556-3656. *Fax:* 650-543-4496. *E-mail:* admissions@menlo.edu. *Web site:* http://www.menlo.edu/.

See page 1440 for the College Close-Up.

Mills College
Oakland, California

- **Independent** comprehensive, founded 1852
- **Urban** 135-acre campus with easy access to San Francisco
- **Endowment** $183.4 million
- **Undergraduate: women only; graduate: coed** 936 undergraduate students, 94% full-time, 100% women
- **Moderately difficult** entrance level, 57% of applicants were admitted

Undergraduates 881 full-time, 55 part-time. Students come from 34 states and territories; 7 other countries; 20% are from out of state; 8% Black or African American, non-Hispanic/Latino; 17% Hispanic/Latino; 10% Asian, non-Hispanic/Latino; 0.7% Native Hawaiian or other Pacific Islander, non-Hispanic/Latino; 0.6% American Indian or Alaska Native, non-Hispanic/Latino; 7% Two or more races, non-Hispanic/Latino; 13% Race/ethnicity unknown; 2% international; 12% transferred in; 55% live on campus. *Retention:* 78% of full-time freshmen returned.

Freshmen *Admission:* 2,251 applied, 1,284 admitted, 168 enrolled. *Average high school GPA:* 3.72. *Test scores:* SAT critical reading scores over 500: 86%; SAT math scores over 500: 80%; SAT writing scores over 500: 87%; ACT scores over 18: 100%; SAT critical reading scores over 600: 47%; SAT math scores over 600: 36%; SAT writing scores over 600: 38%; ACT scores over 24: 78%; SAT critical reading scores over 700: 13%; SAT math scores over 700: 1%; SAT writing scores over 700: 10%; ACT scores over 30: 20%.

Faculty *Total:* 203, 49% full-time, 76% with terminal degrees. *Student/faculty ratio:* 11:1.

Academics *Calendar:* semesters. *Degrees:* certificates, bachelor's, master's, doctoral, postbachelor's, and first professional certificates. *Special study options:* accelerated degree program, adult/continuing education programs, advanced placement credit, double majors, English as a second language, honors programs, independent study, internships, off-campus study, part-time degree program, services for LD students, student-designed majors, study abroad. *ROTC:* Army (c). *Unusual degree programs:* 3-2 business administration; engineering with University of Southern California; education; public policy.

Computers on Campus 345 computers/terminals and 8 ports are available on campus for general student use. Students can access the following: campus intranet, computer help desk, free student e-mail accounts, online (class) grades, online (class) registration, online (class) schedules, online degree audit. Campuswide network is available. 100% of college-owned or -operated housing units are wired for high-speed Internet access. Wireless service is available via entire campus.

Student Life *Housing options:* coed, women-only, cooperative, disabled students. Campus housing is university owned. Freshman campus housing is guaranteed. *Activities and organizations:* drama/theater group, student-run newspaper, radio station, choral group, Mujeres Unidas, Black Women's Collective, Student Athlete Advisory Committee, Women's Health Resource Center, Phi Alpha Delta Pre-Law Fraternity. *Campus security:* 24-hour emergency response devices and patrols, late-night transport/escort service, controlled dormitory access. *Student services:* health clinic, personal/psychological counseling, women's center.

Athletics Member NCAA, NAIA. All NCAA Division III. *Intercollegiate sports:* crew W, cross-country running W, soccer W, swimming and diving W, tennis W, volleyball W. *Intramural sports:* badminton W, basketball W, soccer W, softball W, tennis W, volleyball W.

Standardized Tests *Required:* SAT or ACT (for admission). *Recommended:* SAT Subject Tests (for admission).

Costs (2012–13) *Comprehensive fee:* $51,660 includes full-time tuition ($38,850), mandatory fees ($1230), and room and board ($11,580). Full-time tuition and fees vary according to course load. Part-time tuition and fees vary according to course load. *College room only:* $5610. Room and board charges vary according to board plan and housing facility. *Payment plan:* installment. *Waivers:* employees or children of employees.

Financial Aid Of all full-time matriculated undergraduates who enrolled in 2011, 792 applied for aid, 748 were judged to have need, 123 had their need fully met. In 2011, 105 non-need-based awards were made. *Average percent of need met:* 78%. *Average financial aid package:* $34,160. *Average need-based loan:* $7568. *Average need-based gift aid:* $19,420. *Average non-need-based aid:* $15,464. *Average indebtedness upon graduation:* $27,342.

Applying *Options:* electronic application, early action, deferred entrance. *Application fee:* $50. *Required:* high school transcript, 2 letters of recommendation, essay or graded paper. *Recommended:* interview. *Application deadlines:* 2/1 (freshmen), 3/1 (transfers), 11/15 (early action). *Notification:* 3/30 (freshmen), 4/1 (transfers), 12/1 (early action).

Freshman Application Contact Ms. Giulietta Aquino, Vice President of Enrollment Management, Mills College, 5000 MacArthur Boulevard, Oakland, CA 94613-1301. *Phone:* 510-430-2135. *Toll-free phone:* 800-87-MILLS. *Fax:* 510-430-3314. *E-mail:* admission@mills.edu. *Web site:* http://www.mills.edu/.

See page 1456 for the College Close-Up.

Mount St. Mary's College
Los Angeles, California

- **Independent Roman Catholic** comprehensive, founded 1925
- **Urban** 49-acre campus with easy access to Los Angeles
- **Endowment** $99.8 million
- **Coed, primarily women** 2,273 undergraduate students, 78% full-time, 93% women, 7% men
- **Moderately difficult** entrance level, 68% of applicants were admitted

Undergraduates 1,770 full-time, 503 part-time. Students come from 18 states and territories; 4 other countries; 2% are from out of state; 10% Black or African American, non-Hispanic/Latino; 50% Hispanic/Latino; 18% Asian, non-Hispanic/Latino; 1% Native Hawaiian or other Pacific Islander, non-Hispanic/Latino; 0.5% American Indian or Alaska Native, non-Hispanic/Latino; 2% Two or more races, non-Hispanic/Latino; 7% Race/ethnicity unknown; 0.5% international; 10% transferred in; 28% live on campus. *Retention:* 84% of full-time freshmen returned.

Freshmen *Admission:* 1,822 applied, 1,237 admitted, 394 enrolled. *Average high school GPA:* 3.34. *Test scores:* SAT critical reading scores over 500: 35%; SAT math scores over 500: 33%; SAT writing scores over 500: 42%; ACT scores over 18: 69%; SAT critical reading scores over 600: 6%; SAT math scores over 600: 7%; SAT writing scores over 600: 10%; ACT scores over 24: 16%; SAT math scores over 700: 1%; SAT writing scores over 700: 1%; ACT scores over 30: 1%.

Faculty *Total:* 359, 28% full-time, 38% with terminal degrees. *Student/faculty ratio:* 13:1.

Academics *Calendar:* semesters. *Degrees:* associate, bachelor's, master's, doctoral, and post-master's certificates. *Special study options:* academic remediation for entering students, accelerated degree program, advanced placement credit, distance learning, double majors, English as a second language, freshman honors college, honors programs, independent study, internships, off-campus study, part-time degree program, services for LD students, student-designed majors, study abroad, summer session for credit. *Unusual degree programs:* 3-2 nursing.

Computers on Campus 300 computers/terminals are available on campus for general student use. Students can access the following: campus intranet, computer help desk, free student e-mail accounts, online (class) grades, online (class) registration, online (class) schedules. Campuswide network is available. 100% of college-owned or -operated housing units are wired for high-speed Internet access. Wireless service is available via entire campus.

Student Life *Housing options:* men-only, women-only. Campus housing is university owned. Freshman applicants given priority for college housing. *Activities and organizations:* drama/theater group, student-run newspaper, choral group, Na Pua O Ka Aina, Pangkat Pilipino, Alpha Tau Delta, California Nursing Student Association, Mount Movement. *Campus security:* 24-hour emergency response devices and patrols, late-night transport/escort service, controlled dormitory access. *Student services:* health clinic, personal/psychological counseling, women's center.

Athletics *Intramural sports:* basketball M/W, soccer M/W, softball M/W, swimming and diving M/W, tennis M/W, volleyball M/W.

Standardized Tests *Required:* SAT or ACT (for admission).

Costs (2012–13) *Comprehensive fee:* $43,424 includes full-time tuition ($31,924), mandatory fees ($970), and room and board ($10,530). Full-time tuition and fees vary according to course load, degree level, and program. Part-time tuition: $1330 per unit. Part-time tuition and fees vary according to course load, degree level, and program. *College room only:* $6423. Room and board charges vary according to board plan and housing facility. *Payment plan:* installment. *Waivers:* employees or children of employees.

Financial Aid Of all full-time matriculated undergraduates who enrolled in 2011, 1,687 applied for aid, 1,635 were judged to have need, 75 had their need fully met. In 2011, 108 non-need-based awards were made. *Average percent of need met:* 70%. *Average financial aid package:* $28,793. *Average need-based loan:* $3950. *Average need-based gift aid:* $18,177. *Average non-need-based aid:* $11,616.

Applying *Options:* electronic application, early action. *Application fee:* $50. *Required:* essay or personal statement, high school transcript, minimum 2.5 GPA, 1 letter of recommendation. *Recommended:* 2 letters of recommendation, interview. *Application deadlines:* 2/15 (freshmen), 3/15 (transfers), 12/1 (early action). *Notification:* continuous (freshmen), continuous (transfers), 1/1 (early action).

Freshman Application Contact Yvonne Berumen, Director of Admissions, Mount St. Mary's College, 12001 Chalon Road, Los Angeles, CA 90049-1599. *Phone:* 310-954-4250. *Toll-free phone:* 800-999-9893. *Fax:* 310-954-4259. *E-mail:* admissions@msmc.la.edu. *Web site:* http://www.msmc.la.edu/.

Mt. Sierra College
Monrovia, California

Freshman Application Contact Mt. Sierra College, 101 East Huntington Drive, Monrovia, CA 91016. *Phone:* 888-486-9818. *Toll-free phone:* 888-828-8000. *Web site:* http://www.mtsierra.edu/.

Musicians Institute
Hollywood, California

- **Proprietary** 4-year, founded 1976
- **Urban** campus
- **Coed** 1,337 undergraduate students
- **Minimally difficult** entrance level, 98% of applicants were admitted

Undergraduates Students come from 54 other countries; 7% Black or African American, non-Hispanic/Latino; 13% Hispanic/Latino; 4% Asian, non-Hispanic/Latino; 0.5% Native Hawaiian or other Pacific Islander, non-Hispanic/Latino; 1% American Indian or Alaska Native, non-Hispanic/Latino; 5% Two or more races, non-Hispanic/Latino; 5% Race/ethnicity unknown; 25% international.

Freshmen *Admission:* 1,201 applied, 1,181 admitted.

Faculty *Total:* 204, 53% full-time. *Student/faculty ratio:* 10:1.

Academics *Calendar:* quarters. *Degrees:* certificates, diplomas, associate, and bachelor's. *Special study options:* internships, part-time degree program, services for LD students, summer session for credit.

Computers on Campus Students can access the following: campus intranet, computer help desk, free student e-mail accounts, online (class) grades, online (class) registration, online (class) schedules. Wireless service is available via entire campus.

Student Life *Housing:* college housing not available. *Campus security:* 24-hour emergency response devices and patrols. *Student services:* personal/psychological counseling.

Standardized Tests *Required for some:* SAT or ACT (for admission).

Costs (2012–13) *Tuition:* $24,720 full-time. Full-time tuition and fees vary according to course load, degree level, and program. Part-time tuition and fees vary according to course load and degree level. *Required fees:* $5700 full-time. *Payment plan:* installment. *Waivers:* employees or children of employees.

Financial Aid Of all full-time matriculated undergraduates who enrolled in 2002, 520 applied for aid, 465 were judged to have need. *Average percent of need met:* 40%. *Average financial aid package:* $6100. *Average need-based loan:* $3100. *Average indebtedness upon graduation:* $14,000.

Applying *Options:* electronic application, deferred entrance. *Application fee:* $100. *Required:* high school transcript, 1 letter of recommendation. *Required for some:* essay or personal statement, 2 letters of recommendation. *Application deadline:* rolling (freshmen). *Notification:* continuous (freshmen).

Freshman Application Contact Musicians Institute, 1655 North McCadden Place, Hollywood, CA 90028. *Phone:* 323-860-4345. *Toll-free phone:* 800-255-PLAY. *Web site:* http://www.mi.edu/.

The National Hispanic University
San Jose, California

Director of Admissions Ms. Pamela Bustillo, Director of Office of Admissions/Registrar, The National Hispanic University, 14271 Story Road, San Jose, CA 95127-3823. *Phone:* 408-273-2772. *E-mail:* chernandez@nhu.edu. *Web site:* http://www.nhu.edu/.

National University
La Jolla, California

- **Independent** comprehensive, founded 1971, part of National University System
- **Urban** campus
- **Endowment** $406.2 million
- **Coed** 10,671 undergraduate students, 47% full-time, 65% women, 35% men
- **Minimally difficult** entrance level, 100% of applicants were admitted

Undergraduates 5,065 full-time, 5,606 part-time. Students come from 48 states and territories; 129 other countries; 10% are from out of state; 12% Black or African American, non-Hispanic/Latino; 22% Hispanic/Latino; 10% Asian, non-Hispanic/Latino; 2% Native Hawaiian or other Pacific Islander, non-Hispanic/Latino; 0.8% American Indian or Alaska Native, non-Hispanic/Latino; 3% Two or more races, non-Hispanic/Latino; 8% Race/ethnicity unknown; 0.8% international; 37% transferred in. *Retention:* 76% of full-time freshmen returned.

Freshmen *Admission:* 3,439 applied, 3,439 admitted, 1,262 enrolled.

Faculty *Total:* 2,914, 10% full-time, 28% with terminal degrees. *Student/faculty ratio:* 19:1.

Academics *Calendar:* continuous. *Degrees:* certificates, associate, bachelor's, master's, and postbachelor's certificates. *Special study options:* accelerated degree program, adult/continuing education programs, advanced placement credit, distance learning, double majors, English as a second language, independent study, internships, off-campus study, part-time degree program, services for LD students, summer session for credit. *ROTC:* Army (c), Air Force (c).

Computers on Campus 3,100 computers/terminals are available on campus for general student use. Students can access the following: computer help desk, online (class) grades, online (class) registration, online (class) schedules. Campuswide network is available. Wireless service is available via libraries.

Student Life *Housing:* college housing not available. *Activities and organizations:* student-run television station. *Campus security:* 24-hour emergency response devices and patrols, late-night transport/escort service.

Costs (2011–12) *Tuition:* $11,376 full-time, $316 per unit part-time. Full-time tuition and fees vary according to course load and location. Part-time tuition and fees vary according to course load and location. *Required fees:* $60 full-time. *Waivers:* employees or children of employees.

Financial Aid Of all full-time matriculated undergraduates who enrolled in 2010, 5,852 applied for aid, 5,765 were judged to have need, 23 had their need fully met. *Average percent of need met:* 86%. *Average financial aid package:* $7867. *Average need-based loan:* $7912. *Average need-based gift aid:* $4462.

Applying *Options:* electronic application, deferred entrance. *Application fee:* $60. *Required:* high school transcript, minimum 2.0 GPA, interview. *Required for some:* essay or personal statement. *Application deadlines:* rolling (freshmen), rolling (transfers). *Notification:* continuous (freshmen), continuous (transfers).

Freshman Application Contact National University, 11255 North Torrey Pines Road, La Jolla, CA 92037-1011. *Phone:* 858-628-8648 Ext. 7701. *Toll-free phone:* 800-NAT-UNIV. *Web site:* http://www.nu.edu/.

NewSchool of Architecture & Design
San Diego, California

Freshman Application Contact Ms. Lexi Rogers, Director of Admissions, Newschool of Architecture & Design, 1249 F Street, San Diego, CA 92101-6634. *Phone:* 619-235-4100 Ext. 106. *Toll-free phone:* 800-490-7081. *Web site:* http://www.newschoolarch.edu/.

New York Film Academy
Los Angeles, California

Freshman Application Contact Admissions Office, New York Film Academy, 3801 Barham Boulevard, Los Angeles, CA 90068. *Phone:* 818-733-2600. *Fax:* 818-733-4074. *E-mail:* studios@nyfa.edu. *Web site:* http://www.nyfa.com/.

Northwestern Polytechnic University
Fremont, California

Freshman Application Contact Mr. Michael Tang, Admission Officer, Northwestern Polytechnic University, 47671 Westinghouse Drive, Fremont, CA 94539. *Phone:* 510-592-9688 Ext. 15. *Fax:* 510-657-8975. *E-mail:* admission@npu.edu. *Web site:* http://www.npu.edu/.

Notre Dame de Namur University
Belmont, California

- **Independent Roman Catholic** comprehensive, founded 1851
- **Suburban** 50-acre campus with easy access to San Francisco
- **Endowment** $11.9 million
- **Coed** 1,147 undergraduate students, 65% full-time, 66% women, 34% men
- **Moderately difficult** entrance level, 71% of applicants were admitted

Undergraduates 745 full-time, 402 part-time. Students come from 28 states and territories; 23 other countries; 6% are from out of state; 7% Black or African American, non-Hispanic/Latino; 26% Hispanic/Latino; 11% Asian, non-Hispanic/Latino; 3% Native Hawaiian or other Pacific Islander, non-Hispanic/Latino; 0.6% American Indian or Alaska Native, non-Hispanic/Latino; 4% Two or more races, non-Hispanic/Latino; 16% Race/ethnicity unknown; 3% international; 58% transferred in; 35% live on campus. *Retention:* 77% of full-time freshmen returned.

Freshmen *Admission:* 1,789 applied, 1,270 admitted, 177 enrolled. *Average high school GPA:* 3.09. *Test scores:* SAT critical reading scores over 500: 38%; SAT math scores over 500: 36%; SAT writing scores over 500: 41%;

ACT scores over 18: 75%; SAT critical reading scores over 600: 7%; SAT math scores over 600: 8%; SAT writing scores over 600: 4%; ACT scores over 24: 17%; SAT critical reading scores over 700: 1%; SAT math scores over 700: 1%; ACT scores over 30: 2%.

Faculty *Total:* 202, 28% full-time. *Student/faculty ratio:* 13:1.

Academics *Calendar:* semesters. *Degrees:* bachelor's, master's, and postbachelor's certificates. *Special study options:* academic remediation for entering students, accelerated degree program, adult/continuing education programs, advanced placement credit, cooperative education, double majors, English as a second language, independent study, internships, off-campus study, part-time degree program, services for LD students, student-designed majors, study abroad, summer session for credit. *ROTC:* Air Force (c).

Computers on Campus 80 computers/terminals and 100 ports are available on campus for general student use. Students can access the following: campus intranet, computer help desk, free student e-mail accounts, online (class) grades, online (class) registration, online (class) schedules. Campuswide network is available. Wireless service is available via classrooms, computer centers, computer labs, dorm rooms, learning centers, libraries, student centers.

Student Life *Housing:* on-campus residence required through sophomore year. *Options:* coed. Campus housing is university owned. Freshman campus housing is guaranteed. *Activities and organizations:* drama/theater group, student-run newspaper, choral group, Associated Students of Notre Dame de Namur University, BizCom, Rotaract, Students for Sustainability, International Club. *Campus security:* 24-hour emergency response devices and patrols, late-night transport/escort service, controlled dormitory access. *Student services:* health clinic, personal/psychological counseling.

Athletics Member NCAA. All Division II. *Intercollegiate sports:* basketball M(s)/W(s), cross-country running M(s)/W(s), golf M(s), lacrosse M(s), soccer M(s)/W(s), softball W(s), tennis W(s), volleyball W(s).

Standardized Tests *Required:* SAT or ACT (for admission).

Costs (2012–13) *Comprehensive fee:* $42,492 includes full-time tuition ($30,202), mandatory fees ($320), and room and board ($11,970). Full-time tuition and fees vary according to degree level and program. Part-time tuition: $974 per unit. Part-time tuition and fees vary according to degree level and program. *Required fees:* $35 per term part-time. *College room only:* $7800. Room and board charges vary according to board plan and housing facility. *Payment plan:* installment. *Waivers:* senior citizens and employees or children of employees.

Financial Aid Of all full-time matriculated undergraduates who enrolled in 2011, 685 applied for aid, 646 were judged to have need, 27 had their need fully met. 96 Federal Work-Study jobs (averaging $1984). In 2011, 31 non-need-based awards were made. *Average percent of need met:* 54%. *Average financial aid package:* $21,243. *Average need-based gift aid:* $17,498. *Average non-need-based aid:* $5994. *Average indebtedness upon graduation:* $27,280.

Applying *Options:* electronic application, early admission, early action, deferred entrance. *Application fee:* $50. *Required:* essay or personal statement, high school transcript, audition is required for music programs. *Required for some:* interview. *Application deadlines:* rolling (freshmen), rolling (transfers). *Notification:* continuous (freshmen), continuous (transfers).

Freshman Application Contact Notre Dame de Namur University, 1500 Ralston Avenue, Belmont, CA 94002-1908. *Phone:* 650-508-3600. *Toll-free phone:* 800-263-0545. *Web site:* http://www.ndnu.edu/.

Occidental College
Los Angeles, California

- **Independent** comprehensive, founded 1887
- **Urban** 120-acre campus
- **Endowment** $342.4 million
- **Coed** 2,123 undergraduate students, 99% full-time, 57% women, 43% men
- **Very difficult** entrance level, 39% of applicants were admitted

Undergraduates 2,111 full-time, 12 part-time. Students come from 43 states and territories; 28 other countries; 54% are from out of state; 4% Black or African American, non-Hispanic/Latino; 10% Hispanic/Latino; 16% Asian, non-Hispanic/Latino; 0.6% American Indian or Alaska Native, non-Hispanic/Latino; 5% Two or more races, non-Hispanic/Latino; 2% Race/ethnicity unknown; 3% international; 2% transferred in; 80% live on campus. *Retention:* 90% of full-time freshmen returned.

Freshmen *Admission:* 6,120 applied, 2,369 admitted, 537 enrolled. *Average high school GPA:* 3.57. *Test scores:* SAT critical reading scores over 500: 98%; SAT math scores over 500: 98%; SAT writing scores over 500: 98%; SAT critical reading scores over 600: 75%; SAT math scores over 600: 76%; SAT writing scores over 600: 79%; SAT critical reading scores over 700: 23%; SAT math scores over 700: 22%; SAT writing scores over 700: 28%.

Faculty *Total:* 265, 69% full-time. *Student/faculty ratio:* 10:1.

Academics *Calendar:* semesters. *Degrees:* diplomas, bachelor's, and master's. *Special study options:* advanced placement credit, cooperative education, double majors, honors programs, independent study, internships, off-campus study, services for LD students, student-designed majors, study abroad. *ROTC:* Army (c), Air Force (c). *Unusual degree programs:* 3-2 engineering with California Institute of Technology, Columbia University; law with Columbia University; bioscience with Keck Graduate Institute.

Computers on Campus 323 computers/terminals and 1,400 ports are available on campus for general student use. Students can access the following: campus intranet, computer help desk, free student e-mail accounts, online (class) grades, online (class) registration, online (class) schedules, moodle class sites. Campuswide network is available. Wireless service is available via classrooms, computer centers, computer labs, dorm rooms, learning centers, libraries, student centers.

Student Life *Housing:* on-campus residence required through junior year. *Options:* coed, women-only. Campus housing is university owned. Freshman campus housing is guaranteed. *Activities and organizations:* drama/theater group, student-run newspaper, radio station, choral group, Dance Production, Vagina Monologues, Glee Clubs, Colleges Against Cancer, Asian/Pacific Islander Graduation, national fraternities, national sororities. *Campus security:* 24-hour emergency response devices and patrols, late-night transport/escort service, controlled dormitory access. *Student services:* health clinic, personal/psychological counseling, women's center.

Athletics Member NCAA. All Division III. *Intercollegiate sports:* baseball M, basketball M/W, cross-country running M/W, football M, golf M/W, lacrosse W, soccer M/W, softball W, swimming and diving M/W, tennis M/W, track and field M/W, volleyball W, water polo M/W. *Intramural sports:* basketball M/W, tennis M/W, volleyball M/W.

Standardized Tests *Required:* SAT or ACT (for admission). *Recommended:* SAT Subject Tests (for admission).

Costs (2012–13) *Comprehensive fee:* $56,990 includes full-time tuition ($43,490), mandatory fees ($1050), and room and board ($12,450). Part-time tuition: $1810 per credit. Part-time tuition and fees vary according to course load. *College room only:* $7080. Room and board charges vary according to board plan and housing facility. *Payment plan:* installment. *Waivers:* employees or children of employees.

Financial Aid Of all full-time matriculated undergraduates who enrolled in 2011, 1,245 applied for aid, 1,078 were judged to have need, 1,072 had their need fully met. In 2011, 388 non-need-based awards were made. *Average percent of need met:* 100%. *Average financial aid package:* $36,048. *Average need-based loan:* $6346. *Average need-based gift aid:* $28,994. *Average non-need-based aid:* $9316. *Average indebtedness upon graduation:* $27,119. *Financial aid deadline:* 2/1.

Applying *Options:* electronic application, early admission, early decision, deferred entrance. *Application fee:* $60. *Required:* essay or personal statement, high school transcript, 2 letters of recommendation, a statement describing structure and mission for home schoolers. *Recommended:* interview. *Application deadlines:* 1/10 (freshmen), 3/15 (transfers). *Early decision deadline:* 11/15 (for plan 1), 1/2 (for plan 2). *Notification:* 4/1 (freshmen), 5/1 (transfers), 12/15 (early decision plan 1), 2/1 (early decision plan 2).

Freshman Application Contact Ms. Sally Stone Richmond, Director of Admission, Occidental College, 1600 Campus Road, Los Angeles, CA 90041. *Phone:* 323-259-2700. *Toll-free phone:* 800-825-5262. *Fax:* 323-341-4875. *E-mail:* admission@oxy.edu. *Web site:* http://www.oxy.edu/.

Otis College of Art and Design

Los Angeles, California

- **Independent** comprehensive, founded 1918
- **Urban** 5-acre campus
- **Coed** 1,141 undergraduate students, 98% full-time, 68% women, 32% men
- **Moderately difficult** entrance level, 51% of applicants were admitted

Undergraduates 1,123 full-time, 18 part-time. Students come from 24 states and territories; 8 other countries; 13% are from out of state; 4% Black or African American, non-Hispanic/Latino; 14% Hispanic/Latino; 34% Asian, non-Hispanic/Latino; 0.4% Native Hawaiian or other Pacific Islander, non-Hispanic/Latino; 0.5% American Indian or Alaska Native, non-Hispanic/Latino; 0.9% Two or more races, non-Hispanic/Latino; 8% Race/ethnicity unknown; 16% international; 12% transferred in; 9% live on campus. *Retention:* 78% of full-time freshmen returned.

Freshmen *Admission:* 1,458 applied, 745 admitted, 185 enrolled. *Average high school GPA:* 3.2. *Test scores:* SAT critical reading scores over 500: 49%; SAT math scores over 500: 66%; ACT scores over 18: 93%; SAT critical reading scores over 600: 19%; SAT math scores over 600: 27%; ACT scores over 24: 45%; SAT critical reading scores over 700: 4%; SAT math scores over 700: 5%; ACT scores over 30: 17%.

Faculty *Total:* 420, 13% full-time, 21% with terminal degrees. *Student/faculty ratio:* 7:1.

Academics *Calendar:* semesters. *Degrees:* bachelor's and master's. *Special study options:* academic remediation for entering students, adult/continuing education programs, advanced placement credit, cooperative education, double majors, freshman honors college, honors programs, independent study, internships, off-campus study, services for LD students, student-designed majors, study abroad, summer session for credit.

Computers on Campus 400 computers/terminals are available on campus for general student use. Students can access the following: campus intranet, computer help desk, free student e-mail accounts, online (class) grades, online (class) registration, online (class) schedules. Campuswide network is available. Wireless service is available via entire campus.

Student Life *Housing options:* Campus housing is provided by a third party. Freshman applicants given priority for college housing. *Activities and organizations:* Student Government Association, international students organization, Otis Students in Service (OASIS), Literary Magazine Club, Campus Crusade. *Campus security:* 24-hour patrols. *Student services:* personal/psychological counseling.

Athletics *Intramural sports:* skiing (downhill) W, soccer M.

Standardized Tests *Required:* SAT or ACT (for admission).

Costs (2011–12) *Tuition:* $34,454 full-time, $1149 per unit part-time. *Required fees:* $900 full-time. *Payment plan:* installment. *Waivers:* employees or children of employees.

Financial Aid Of all full-time matriculated undergraduates who enrolled in 2011, 802 applied for aid, 758 were judged to have need, 20 had their need fully met. 136 Federal Work-Study jobs (averaging $740). 11 state and other part-time jobs (averaging $427). In 2011, 154 non-need-based awards were made. *Average percent of need met:* 52%. *Average financial aid package:* $21,840. *Average need-based loan:* $4716. *Average need-based gift aid:* $18,546. *Average non-need-based aid:* $9896. *Average indebtedness upon graduation:* $9756.

Applying *Options:* electronic application, early admission. *Application fee:* $50. *Required:* essay or personal statement, high school transcript, minimum 2.5 GPA, portfolio. *Recommended:* interview. *Application deadlines:* rolling (freshmen), rolling (transfers). *Notification:* continuous (freshmen), continuous (transfers).

Freshman Application Contact Otis College of Art and Design, 9045 Lincoln Boulevard, Los Angeles, CA 90045-9785. *Phone:* 310-665-6820. *Toll-free phone:* 800-527-OTIS. *Web site:* http://www.otis.edu/.

Pacific Oaks College

Pasadena, California

- **Independent** upper-level, founded 1945, part of The Chicago School Education System
- **Small-town** 2-acre campus with easy access to Los Angeles, San Gabriel Valley
- **Endowment** $7.3 million
- **Coed, primarily women**
- 77% of applicants were admitted

Faculty *Student/faculty ratio:* 22:1.

Academics *Calendar:* semesters summer sessions and 2 intensive sessions. *Degrees:* certificates, bachelor's, master's, and post-master's certificates.

Financial Aid Of all full-time matriculated undergraduates who enrolled in 2006, 11 Federal Work-Study jobs (averaging $5000).

Applying *Options:* electronic application, deferred entrance. *Application fee:* $55.

Application Contact Ms. Augusta Pickens, Office of Admissions, Pacific Oaks College, 5 Westmoreland Place, Pasadena, CA 91103. *Phone:* 626-397-1349. *Toll-free phone:* 877-314-2380. *Fax:* 626-666-1220. *E-mail:* admissions@pacificoaks.edu. *Web site:* http://www.pacificoaks.edu/.

Pacific States University

Los Angeles, California

- **Independent** comprehensive, founded 1928
- **Urban** 1-acre campus
- **Coed** 14 undergraduate students, 100% full-time, 29% women, 71% men
- **Noncompetitive** entrance level

Undergraduates 14 full-time. Students come from 1 other state; 7 other countries; 7% Black or African American, non-Hispanic/Latino; 14% Asian, non-Hispanic/Latino; 14% Race/ethnicity unknown; 57% international; 29% transferred in. *Retention:* 100% of full-time freshmen returned.

Faculty *Total:* 27, 22% full-time, 48% with terminal degrees. *Student/faculty ratio:* 13:1.

Academics *Calendar:* quarters. *Degrees:* bachelor's, master's, doctoral, post-bachelor's, and first professional certificates. *Special study options:* academic

remediation for entering students, accelerated degree program, adult/continuing education programs, distance learning, double majors, English as a second language, independent study.

Computers on Campus 50 computers/terminals are available on campus for general student use. Students can access the following: online (class) schedules. Campuswide network is available. 90% of college-owned or -operated housing units are wired for high-speed Internet access. Wireless service is available via classrooms, computer labs, dorm rooms, libraries, student centers.

Student Life *Housing options:* coed. Campus housing is university owned. *Campus security:* patrols by trained security personnel during campus hours.

Standardized Tests *Required for some:* TOEFL or IELTS. *Recommended:* SAT or ACT (for admission).

Costs (2011–12) *Tuition:* $14,055 full-time, $315 per unit part-time. Full-time tuition and fees vary according to course load, degree level, and program. Part-time tuition and fees vary according to course load, degree level, and program. No tuition increase for student's term of enrollment. *Required fees:* $600 full-time. *Room only:* $7200. Room and board charges vary according to housing facility. *Payment plan:* installment. *Waivers:* employees or children of employees.

Applying *Options:* electronic application, deferred entrance. *Application fee:* $100. *Required:* high school transcript, minimum 2.5 GPA, proof of English proficiency (i.e. TOEFL, IBT, IELTS...). *Recommended:* essay or personal statement. *Application deadlines:* rolling (freshmen), rolling (out-of-state freshmen), rolling (transfers). *Notification:* continuous (freshmen), continuous (out-of-state freshmen), continuous (transfers).

Freshman Application Contact Miss Seohee Yang, Admission officer, Pacific States University, 3450 Wilshire Bjoulevard, #500, Los Angeles, CA 90010. *Phone:* 323-731-2383 Ext. 203. *Toll-free phone:* 888-200-0383. *Fax:* 323-731-7276. *E-mail:* admissions@psuca.edu. *Web site:* http://www.psuca.edu/.

Pacific Union College
Angwin, California

- **Independent Seventh-day Adventist** comprehensive, founded 1882
- **Rural** 200-acre campus with easy access to San Francisco Bay Area
- **Endowment** $22.6 million
- **Coed** 1,529 undergraduate students, 89% full-time, 54% women, 46% men
- **Moderately difficult** entrance level, 47% of applicants were admitted

Undergraduates 1,359 full-time, 170 part-time. Students come from 30 states and territories; 21 other countries; 14% are from out of state; 6% Black or African American, non-Hispanic/Latino; 22% Hispanic/Latino; 20% Asian, non-Hispanic/Latino; 1% Native Hawaiian or other Pacific Islander, non-Hispanic/Latino; 1% American Indian or Alaska Native, non-Hispanic/Latino; 4% Two or more races, non-Hispanic/Latino; 8% Race/ethnicity unknown; 5% international; 8% transferred in; 74% live on campus. *Retention:* 71% of full-time freshmen returned.

Freshmen *Admission:* 2,524 applied, 1,182 admitted, 363 enrolled. *Average high school GPA:* 3.35. *Test scores:* SAT critical reading scores over 500: 56%; SAT math scores over 500: 55%; SAT writing scores over 500: 48%; ACT scores over 18: 79%; SAT critical reading scores over 600: 18%; SAT math scores over 600: 23%; SAT writing scores over 600: 17%; ACT scores over 24: 36%; SAT critical reading scores over 700: 3%; SAT math scores over 700: 6%; ACT scores over 30: 5%.

Faculty *Total:* 130, 68% full-time, 43% with terminal degrees. *Student/faculty ratio:* 14:1.

Academics *Calendar:* quarters. *Degrees:* certificates, associate, bachelor's, and master's. *Special study options:* academic remediation for entering students, adult/continuing education programs, advanced placement credit, cooperative education, double majors, honors programs, independent study, internships, off-campus study, part-time degree program, services for LD students, study abroad, summer session for credit.

Computers on Campus 150 computers/terminals and 1,200 ports are available on campus for general student use. Students can access the following: campus intranet, computer help desk, free student e-mail accounts, online (class) grades, online (class) registration, online (class) schedules, student financial information. Campuswide network is available. 100% of college-owned or -operated housing units are wired for high-speed Internet access. Wireless service is available via computer centers, computer labs, learning centers, libraries, student centers.

Student Life *Housing:* on-campus residence required through senior year. *Options:* men-only, women-only. Campus housing is university owned. *Activities and organizations:* drama/theater group, student-run newspaper, choral group, Student Association, Business Club, Asian Student Association, Korean Adventist Student Association, Student Organization of Latinos. *Campus security:* 24-hour emergency response devices and patrols, late-night transport/

escort service. *Student services:* health clinic, personal/psychological counseling, women's center.

Athletics Member NAIA. *Intercollegiate sports:* basketball M/W, cross-country running M/W, soccer M, volleyball W. *Intramural sports:* badminton M/W, baseball M/W, basketball M/W, cross-country running M/W, football M/W, golf M/W, soccer M/W, softball M/W, tennis M/W, volleyball M/W.

Standardized Tests *Required:* SAT or ACT (for admission).

Costs (2012–13) *Comprehensive fee:* $33,390 includes full-time tuition ($25,740), mandatory fees ($300), and room and board ($7350). Full-time tuition and fees vary according to course load. Part-time tuition: $750 per quarter hour. Part-time tuition and fees vary according to course load. No tuition increase for student's term of enrollment. *College room only:* $4260. *Payment plan:* installment. *Waivers:* senior citizens and employees or children of employees.

Financial Aid Of all full-time matriculated undergraduates who enrolled in 2011, 1,352 applied for aid, 1,050 were judged to have need, 13 had their need fully met. 188 Federal Work-Study jobs (averaging $2662). In 2011, 315 non-need-based awards were made. *Average percent of need met:* 44%. *Average financial aid package:* $20,376. *Average need-based loan:* $4294. *Average need-based gift aid:* $18,457. *Average non-need-based aid:* $2603. *Average indebtedness upon graduation:* $27,000.

Applying *Options:* electronic application, deferred entrance. *Application fee:* $30. *Required:* high school transcript, minimum 2.3 GPA, 3 letters of recommendation. *Application deadlines:* rolling (freshmen), rolling (transfers).

Freshman Application Contact Mr. Craig Philpott, Associate Director, Admissions, Pacific Union College, Enrollment Services, One Angwin Avenue, Angwin, CA 94508. *Phone:* 800-862-7080. *Toll-free phone:* 800-862-7080. *Fax:* 707-965-6671. *E-mail:* enroll@puc.edu. *Web site:* http://www.puc.edu/.

Patten University
Oakland, California

Freshman Application Contact Ms. Kim Guerra, Director of Admissions, Patten University, 2433 Coolidge Avenue, Oakland, CA 94601-2699. *Phone:* 510-261-8500 Ext. 7763. *Toll-free phone:* 877-4PATTEN. *Fax:* 510-534-4344. *Web site:* http://www.patten.edu/.

Pepperdine University
Malibu, California

- **Independent** university, founded 1937, affiliated with Church of Christ
- **Suburban** 830-acre campus with easy access to Los Angeles
- **Endowment** $629.6 million
- **Coed** 3,474 undergraduate students, 88% full-time, 56% women, 44% men
- **Very difficult** entrance level, 32% of applicants were admitted

Undergraduates 3,050 full-time, 424 part-time. Students come from 50 states and territories; 50 other countries; 44% are from out of state; 7% Black or African American, non-Hispanic/Latino; 14% Hispanic/Latino; 11% Asian, non-Hispanic/Latino; 0.8% Native Hawaiian or other Pacific Islander, non-Hispanic/Latino; 0.8% American Indian or Alaska Native, non-Hispanic/Latino; 4% Two or more races, non-Hispanic/Latino; 7% Race/ethnicity unknown; 7% international; 1% transferred in; 58% live on campus. *Retention:* 93% of full-time freshmen returned.

Freshmen *Admission:* 9,384 applied, 2,962 admitted, 676 enrolled. *Average high school GPA:* 3.65. *Test scores:* SAT critical reading scores over 500: 92%; SAT math scores over 500: 94%; SAT writing scores over 500: 93%; ACT scores over 18: 100%; SAT critical reading scores over 600: 48%; SAT math scores over 600: 62%; SAT writing scores over 600: 59%; ACT scores over 24: 88%; SAT critical reading scores over 700: 14%; SAT math scores over 700: 20%; SAT writing scores over 700: 13%; ACT scores over 30: 32%.

Faculty *Total:* 695, 56% full-time, 74% with terminal degrees. *Student/faculty ratio:* 13:1.

Academics *Calendar:* semesters. *Degrees:* certificates, bachelor's, master's, doctoral, and first professional. *Special study options:* advanced placement credit, double majors, honors programs, independent study, internships, student-designed majors, study abroad, summer session for credit. *ROTC:* Army (c), Air Force (c). *Unusual degree programs:* 3-2 business administration; engineering with University of Southern California, Washington University in St. Louis.

Computers on Campus 292 computers/terminals are available on campus for general student use. Students can access the following: campus intranet, computer help desk, free student e-mail accounts, online (class) grades, online (class) registration, online (class) schedules. Campuswide network is available. 100% of college-owned or -operated housing units are wired for high-speed Internet access. Wireless service is available via entire campus.

Student Life *Housing:* on-campus residence required through sophomore year. *Options:* men-only, women-only, disabled students. Campus housing is university owned. Freshman campus housing is guaranteed. *Activities and organizations:* drama/theater group, student-run newspaper, radio and television station, choral group, Latino Student Association, Black Student Union, Panhellenic Council, Interfraternity Council, International Justice Mission, national fraternities, national sororities. *Campus security:* 24-hour emergency response devices and patrols, student patrols, late-night transport/escort service, front gate security, 24-hour security in residence halls, controlled access, crime prevention programs. *Student services:* health clinic, personal/psychological counseling.

Athletics Member NCAA. All Division I. *Intercollegiate sports:* baseball M(s), basketball M(s)/W(s), cheerleading M/W, crew M(c)/W(c), cross-country running M(s)/W(s), field hockey W(c), golf M(s)/W(s), lacrosse M(c), rugby M(c), sailing M(c)/W(c), soccer M(c)/W(s), swimming and diving W(s), tennis M(s)/W(s), volleyball M(s)/W(s), water polo M(s)/W(c). *Intramural sports:* badminton M/W, basketball M/W, cross-country running M/W, football M/W, golf M/W, lacrosse M, soccer M/W, softball M/W, swimming and diving M/W, tennis M/W, volleyball M/W.

Standardized Tests *Required:* SAT or ACT (for admission).

Costs (2011–12) *Comprehensive fee:* $52,596 includes full-time tuition ($40,500), mandatory fees ($252), and room and board ($11,844). Part-time tuition: $1266 per credit hour. *College room only:* $9110. Room and board charges vary according to board plan and housing facility. *Payment plan:* installment. *Waivers:* employees or children of employees.

Financial Aid Of all full-time matriculated undergraduates who enrolled in 2011, 2,343 applied for aid, 1,692 were judged to have need, 470 had their need fully met. In 2011, 457 non-need-based awards were made. *Average percent of need met:* 80%. *Average financial aid package:* $36,983. *Average need-based loan:* $4781. *Average need-based gift aid:* $38,389. *Average non-need-based aid:* $18,672. *Average indebtedness upon graduation:* $30,175. *Financial aid deadline:* 2/15.

Applying *Options:* electronic application. *Application fee:* $65. *Required:* essay or personal statement, high school transcript, 2 letters of recommendation. *Application deadlines:* 1/5 (freshmen), 1/5 (out-of-state freshmen), 1/5 (transfers). *Notification:* 4/1 (freshmen), 4/1 (out-of-state freshmen), 4/1 (transfers).

Freshman Application Contact Mrs. Laura Kalinkewicz, Associate Director of Admission, Enrollment Management, Seaver College, Pepperdine University, 24255 Pacific Coast Highway, Malibu, CA 90263. *Phone:* 310-506-4392. *E-mail:* sarah.e.carter@pepperdine.edu. *Web site:* http://www.pepperdine.edu/.

See below for display ad and page 1500 for the College Close-Up.

Perelandra College
La Mesa, California

- **Independent Christian** comprehensive
- **Suburban** campus with easy access to San Diego
- **Coed** 6 undergraduate students, 67% women, 33% men
- **Minimally difficult** entrance level

Undergraduates 6 part-time. Students come from 10 states and territories; 3 other countries; 90% are from out of state; 100% Race/ethnicity unknown; 83% transferred in. *Retention:* 100% of full-time freshmen returned.

Freshmen *Average high school GPA:* 2.8.

Faculty *Total:* 11, 73% with terminal degrees. *Student/faculty ratio:* 3:1.

Academics *Degrees:* diplomas, bachelor's, and master's. *Special study options:* accelerated degree program, adult/continuing education programs, advanced placement credit, distance learning, external degree program, independent study, off-campus study, part-time degree program, services for LD students, summer session for credit.

Computers on Campus Students can access the following: computer help desk, free student e-mail accounts, online (class) grades, online (class) registration.

Student Life *Housing:* college housing not available. *Student services:* personal/psychological counseling.

Costs (2011–12) *Tuition:* $200 per credit part-time. *Payment plans:* tuition prepayment, installment. *Waivers:* employees or children of employees.

Applying *Options:* electronic application. *Application fee:* $50. *Required:* essay or personal statement, minimum 2.5 GPA, 2 letters of recommendation, letter of intent. *Required for some:* high school transcript. *Notification:* continuous (freshmen), continuous (out-of-state freshmen), continuous (transfers).

Freshman Application Contact Perelandra College, 8697-C La Mesa Boulevard, PMB 21, La Mesa, CA 91941. *Phone:* 619-335-0441. *Web site:* http://www.perelandra.edu/.

Pima Medical Institute

Chula Vista, California

- **Proprietary** primarily 2-year, founded 1998
- **Urban** campus
- **Coed**
- **Minimally difficult** entrance level

Academics *Calendar:* modular. *Degrees:* certificates, associate, and bachelor's.

Standardized Tests *Required:* Wonderlic Scholastic Level Exam (for admission).

Applying *Required:* high school transcript, interview.

Freshman Application Contact Admissions Office, Pima Medical Institute, 780 Bay Boulevard, Suite 101, Chula Vista, CA 91910. *Phone:* 619-425-3200. *Toll-free phone:* 800-477-PIMA (in-state); 888-477-PIMA (out-of-state). *Web site:* http://www.pmi.edu/.

Pitzer College

Claremont, California

- **Independent** 4-year, founded 1963, part of The Claremont Colleges Consortium
- **Suburban** 35-acre campus with easy access to Los Angeles
- **Endowment** $113.7 million
- **Coed** 1,099 undergraduate students, 96% full-time, 62% women, 38% men
- **Moderately difficult** entrance level, 24% of applicants were admitted

Undergraduates 1,058 full-time, 41 part-time. Students come from 40 states and territories; 17 other countries; 52% are from out of state; 6% Black or African American, non-Hispanic/Latino; 16% Hispanic/Latino; 8% Asian, non-Hispanic/Latino; 0.5% American Indian or Alaska Native, non-Hispanic/Latino; 20% Race/ethnicity unknown; 3% international; 1% transferred in; 74% live on campus. *Retention:* 93% of full-time freshmen returned.

Freshmen *Admission:* 3,743 applied, 903 admitted, 278 enrolled. *Average high school GPA:* 3.88. *Test scores:* SAT critical reading scores over 500: 100%; SAT math scores over 500: 100%; SAT critical reading scores over 600: 85%; SAT math scores over 600: 76%; SAT critical reading scores over 700: 25%; SAT math scores over 700: 16%.

Faculty *Total:* 116, 64% full-time, 93% with terminal degrees. *Student/faculty ratio:* 12:1.

Academics *Calendar:* semesters. *Degree:* bachelor's. *Special study options:* adult/continuing education programs, advanced placement credit, cooperative education, double majors, English as a second language, honors programs, independent study, internships, off-campus study, part-time degree program, services for LD students, student-designed majors, study abroad, summer session for credit. *ROTC:* Army (c), Air Force (c). *Unusual degree programs:* 3-2 business administration; public administration, mathematics, psychology with Claremont Graduate University.

Computers on Campus 100 computers/terminals are available on campus for general student use. Students can access the following: campus intranet, computer help desk, free student e-mail accounts, online (class) grades, online (class) registration, online (class) schedules. Campuswide network is available. 100% of college-owned or -operated housing units are wired for high-speed Internet access. Wireless service is available via entire campus.

Student Life *Housing:* on-campus residence required for freshman year. *Options:* coed, women-only, cooperative, disabled students. Campus housing is university owned. Freshman campus housing is guaranteed. *Activities and organizations:* drama/theater group, student-run newspaper, radio station, choral group, Student Senate, The Other Side, Without A Box, Residence Hall Association. *Campus security:* 24-hour emergency response devices and patrols, late-night transport/escort service, controlled dormitory access. *Student services:* health clinic, personal/psychological counseling, women's center.

Athletics Member NCAA. All Division III. *Intercollegiate sports:* baseball M, basketball M/W, cross-country running M/W, football M, golf M, lacrosse W, soccer M/W, softball W, swimming and diving M/W, tennis M/W, track and field M/W, volleyball W, water polo M/W. *Intramural sports:* badminton M/W, baseball M, basketball M/W, fencing M(c)/W(c), football M, lacrosse M(c)/W(c), rugby M(c), sailing M(c)/W(c), skiing (downhill) M(c)/W(c), soccer M/W, softball W, tennis M/W, track and field M/W, ultimate Frisbee M/W, volleyball M(c)/W, water polo M(c)/W(c).

Standardized Tests *Required for some:* SAT or ACT (for admission).

Costs (2011–12) *Comprehensive fee:* $53,080 includes full-time tuition ($37,520), mandatory fees ($3610), and room and board ($11,950). Full-time tuition and fees vary according to course load. Part-time tuition: $5108 per course. Part-time tuition and fees vary according to course load. *College room only:* $7540. Room and board charges vary according to board plan. *Payment*

PITZER COLLEGE
Use Your Education to Transform the World

At Pitzer, five core values distinguish our approach to education:

SOCIAL RESPONSIBILITY

INTERCULTURAL UNDERSTANDING

INTERDISCPLINARY LEARNING

STUDENT ENGAGEMENT

ENVIRONMENTAL SUSTAINABILITY

PITZER COLLEGE
A MEMBER OF THE CLAREMONT COLLEGES
www.pitzer.edu/admission

plans: installment, deferred payment. *Waivers:* employees or children of employees.

Financial Aid Of all full-time matriculated undergraduates who enrolled in 2011, 491 applied for aid, 422 were judged to have need, 414 had their need fully met. 377 Federal Work-Study jobs (averaging $2486). In 2011, 28 non-need-based awards were made. *Average percent of need met:* 100%. *Average financial aid package:* $38,798. *Average need-based loan:* $4336. *Average need-based gift aid:* $33,775. *Average non-need-based aid:* $4821. *Average indebtedness upon graduation:* $22,568. *Financial aid deadline:* 2/1.

Applying *Options:* electronic application, early decision, deferred entrance. *Application fee:* $60. *Required:* essay or personal statement, high school transcript, minimum 2.0 GPA, 3 letters of recommendation. *Recommended:* interview. *Application deadlines:* 1/1 (freshmen), 4/15 (transfers). *Early decision deadline:* 11/15. *Notification:* 4/1 (freshmen), 5/15 (transfers), 1/1 (early decision).

Freshman Application Contact Mr. Angel Perez, Vice President for Admission and Financial Aid, Pitzer College, 1050 North Mills Avenue, Claremont, CA 91711-6101. *Phone:* 909-621-8129. *Toll-free phone:* 800-748-9371. *Fax:* 909-621-8770. *E-mail:* admission@pitzer.edu. *Web site:* http://www.pitzer.edu/.

See page 123 for display ad and page 1504 for the College Close-Up.

Platt College
Huntington Beach, California

Director of Admissions Ms. Lisa Rhodes, President, Platt College, 7755 Center Avenue, Suite 600, Huntington Beach, CA 92647. *Phone:* 949-833-2300 Ext. 222. *Toll-free phone:* 888-80-PLATT. *Web site:* http://www.plattcollege.edu/.

Platt College
Ontario, California

Director of Admissions Ms. Jennifer Abandonato, Director of Admissions, Platt College, 3700 Inland Empire Boulevard, Suite 400, Ontario, CA 91764. *Phone:* 909-941-9410. *Toll-free phone:* 888-80-PLATT. *Web site:* http://www.plattcollege.edu/.

Platt College–Los Angeles
Alhambra, California

Director of Admissions Mr. Detroit Whiteside, Director of Admissions, Platt College–Los Angeles, 1000 South Fremont A9W, Alhambra, CA 91803. *Phone:* 323-258-8050. *Toll-free phone:* 888-866-6697 (in-state); 888-80-PLATT (out-of-state). *Web site:* http://www.plattcollege.edu/.

Platt College San Diego
San Diego, California

Freshman Application Contact Mr. Steve Gallup, Admissions Representative, Platt College San Diego, 6250 El Cajon Boulevard, San Diego, CA 92115-3919. *Phone:* 619-265-0107. *Toll-free phone:* 866-752-8826. *Fax:* 619-265-8655. *E-mail:* sgallup@platt.edu. *Web site:* http://www.platt.edu/.

Point Loma Nazarene University
San Diego, California

- **Independent** *Nazarene* comprehensive, founded 1902
- **Suburban** 93-acre campus with easy access to San Diego
- **Endowment** $34.9 million
- **Coed** 2,376 undergraduate students, 97% full-time, 61% women, 39% men
- **Moderately difficult** entrance level, 52% of applicants were admitted

Undergraduates 2,308 full-time, 68 part-time. Students come from 41 states and territories; 20 other countries; 18% are from out of state; 3% Black or African American, non-Hispanic/Latino; 16% Hispanic/Latino; 7% Asian, non-Hispanic/Latino; 0.5% Native Hawaiian or other Pacific Islander, non-Hispanic/Latino; 2% American Indian or Alaska Native, non-Hispanic/Latino; 1% Two or more races, non-Hispanic/Latino; 0.7% Race/ethnicity unknown; 0.5% international; 6% transferred in; 67% live on campus. *Retention:* 81% of full-time freshmen returned.

Freshmen *Admission:* 3,671 applied, 1,924 admitted, 532 enrolled. *Average high school GPA:* 3.71. *Test scores:* SAT critical reading scores over 500: 84%; SAT math scores over 500: 83%; SAT critical reading scores over 600: 35%; SAT math scores over 600: 39%; SAT critical reading scores over 700: 5%; SAT math scores over 700: 5%.

Faculty *Total:* 143.

Academics *Calendar:* semesters. *Degrees:* bachelor's, master's, and post-master's certificates. *Special study options:* academic remediation for entering students, advanced placement credit, double majors, honors programs, independent study, internships, off-campus study, part-time degree program, services for LD students, study abroad, summer session for credit. *ROTC:* Army (c), Navy (c), Air Force (c).

Computers on Campus Students can access the following: computer help desk, free student e-mail accounts, online (class) grades, online (class) registration, online (class) schedules. Campuswide network is available. 100% of college-owned or -operated housing units are wired for high-speed Internet access. Wireless service is available via entire campus.

Student Life *Housing:* on-campus residence required through junior year. *Options:* men-only, women-only. Campus housing is university owned. Freshman campus housing is guaranteed. *Activities and organizations:* drama/theater group, student-run newspaper, radio and television station, choral group. *Campus security:* 24-hour patrols, student patrols, late-night transport/escort service. *Student services:* health clinic, personal/psychological counseling, women's center.

Athletics Member NAIA. *Intercollegiate sports:* baseball M(s), basketball M(s)/W(s), cross-country running M(s)/W(s), golf M(s)/W, soccer M(s)/W(s), tennis M(s)/W(s), track and field M(s)/W(s), volleyball W(s). *Intramural sports:* basketball M/W, football M, soccer M/W, volleyball M/W.

Standardized Tests *Required:* SAT or ACT (for admission). *Recommended:* SAT (for admission).

Costs (2012–13) *Comprehensive fee:* $39,060 includes full-time tuition ($28,900), mandatory fees ($610), and room and board ($9550). Full-time tuition and fees vary according to course load. Part-time tuition: $1205 per credit hour. Part-time tuition and fees vary according to course load. *College room only:* $5440. Room and board charges vary according to board plan. *Payment plan:* installment. *Waivers:* senior citizens and employees or children of employees.

Financial Aid Of all full-time matriculated undergraduates who enrolled in 2011, 1,863 applied for aid, 1,579 were judged to have need, 239 had their need fully met. In 2011, 332 non-need-based awards were made. *Average percent of need met:* 65%. *Average financial aid package:* $19,951. *Average need-based loan:* $5638. *Average need-based gift aid:* $14,864. *Average non-need-based aid:* $7289. *Average indebtedness upon graduation:* $32,487.

Applying *Options:* electronic application, early action. *Application fee:* $50. *Required:* essay or personal statement, high school transcript, minimum 2.8 GPA, 2 letters of recommendation, interview. *Application deadlines:* 2/15 (freshmen), 11/15 (early action). *Notification:* 4/1 (freshmen), 12/21 (early action).

Freshman Application Contact Eric Groves, Director of Admissions, Point Loma Nazarene University, 3900 Lomaland Drive, San Diego, CA 92106. *Phone:* 619-849-2273. *Toll-free phone:* 800-733-7770. *Fax:* 619-849-2601. *E-mail:* admissions@pointloma.edu. *Web site:* http://www.pointloma.edu/.

Pomona College
Claremont, California

- **Independent** 4-year, founded 1887
- **Suburban** 140-acre campus with easy access to Los Angeles
- **Endowment** $1.7 billion
- **Coed** 1,586 undergraduate students, 99% full-time, 51% women, 49% men
- **Most difficult** entrance level, 14% of applicants were admitted

Undergraduates 1,572 full-time, 14 part-time. Students come from 49 states and territories; 23 other countries; 68% are from out of state; 6% Black or African American, non-Hispanic/Latino; 13% Hispanic/Latino; 10% Asian, non-Hispanic/Latino; 0.1% American Indian or Alaska Native, non-Hispanic/Latino; 6% Two or more races, non-Hispanic/Latino; 13% Race/ethnicity unknown; 5% international; 0.9% transferred in; 98% live on campus. *Retention:* 99% of full-time freshmen returned.

Freshmen *Admission:* 7,207 applied, 1,011 admitted, 394 enrolled. *Test scores:* SAT critical reading scores over 500: 100%; SAT math scores over 500: 100%; SAT writing scores over 500: 100%; ACT scores over 18: 100%; SAT critical reading scores over 600: 96%; SAT math scores over 600: 94%; SAT writing scores over 600: 97%; ACT scores over 24: 99%; SAT critical reading scores over 700: 69%; SAT math scores over 700: 70%; SAT writing scores over 700: 72%; ACT scores over 30: 84%.

Faculty *Total:* 226, 84% full-time, 94% with terminal degrees. *Student/faculty ratio:* 8:1.

Academics *Calendar:* semesters. *Degree:* bachelor's. *Special study options:* advanced placement credit, double majors, independent study, internships, off-campus study, services for LD students, student-designed majors, study abroad. *ROTC:* Army (c), Air Force (c). *Unusual degree programs:* 3-2 engineering with California Institute of Technology, Washington University in St. Louis.

Computers on Campus 180 computers/terminals are available on campus for general student use. Students can access the following: computer help desk, free student e-mail accounts, online (class) grades, online (class) schedules. Campuswide network is available. 100% of college-owned or -operated housing units are wired for high-speed Internet access. Wireless service is available via entire campus.

Student Life *Housing:* on-campus residence required for freshman year. *Options:* coed. Campus housing is university owned. Freshman campus housing is guaranteed. *Activities and organizations:* drama/theater group, student-run newspaper, radio and television station, choral group, student government, music/choral organizations, service organizations, intramural sports, outdoor activities club. *Campus security:* 24-hour emergency response devices and patrols, late-night transport/escort service, controlled dormitory access. *Student services:* health clinic, personal/psychological counseling, women's center.

Athletics Member NCAA. All Division III. *Intercollegiate sports:* baseball M, basketball M/W, cross-country running M/W, football M, golf M/W, lacrosse W, soccer M/W, softball W, swimming and diving M/W, tennis M/W, track and field M/W, ultimate Frisbee M(c)/W(c), volleyball M(c)/W, water polo M/W. *Intramural sports:* badminton M(c)/W(c), basketball M/W, crew W(c), cross-country running M/W, equestrian sports M(c)/W(c), fencing M/W, field hockey M(c)/W(c), football M, golf M/W, lacrosse M(c), racquetball M/W, rock climbing M/W, skiing (cross-country) M(c)/W(c), skiing (downhill) M(c)/W(c), soccer M/W, softball M/W, squash M/W, swimming and diving M/W, tennis M/W, track and field M/W, ultimate Frisbee M, volleyball M/W, water polo M/W.

Standardized Tests *Required:* SAT and SAT Subject Tests or ACT (for admission).

Costs (2011–12) *Comprehensive fee:* $53,110 includes full-time tuition ($39,572), mandatory fees ($311), and room and board ($13,227). *Room and board:* Room and board charges vary according to board plan. *Payment plan:* installment. *Waivers:* employees or children of employees.

Financial Aid Of all full-time matriculated undergraduates who enrolled in 2011, 1,058 applied for aid, 825 were judged to have need, 825 had their need fully met. 270 Federal Work-Study jobs (averaging $925). 790 state and other part-time jobs (averaging $1308). *Average percent of need met:* 100%. *Average financial aid package:* $39,273. *Average need-based gift aid:* $37,607. *Average indebtedness upon graduation:* $7540. *Financial aid deadline:* 2/1.

Applying *Options:* electronic application, early admission, early decision, deferred entrance. *Application fee:* $65. *Required:* essay or personal statement, high school transcript, 2 letters of recommendation. *Recommended:* interview, Supplemental forms for visual and performing arts, athletics, and science research are available. *Application deadlines:* 1/2 (freshmen), 3/15 (transfers). *Early decision deadline:* 11/1 (for plan 1), 12/28 (for plan 2). *Notification:* 4/1 (freshmen), 5/15 (transfers), 12/15 (early decision plan 1), 2/15 (early decision plan 2).

Freshman Application Contact Mr. Seth Allen, Vice President for Enrollment and Dean of Admissions and Financial Aid, Pomona College, 333 North College Way, Claremont, CA 91711. *Phone:* 909-621-8134. *Fax:* 909-621-8952. *E-mail:* admissions@pomona.edu. *Web site:* http://www.pomona.edu/.

Saint Mary's College of California
Moraga, California

- **Independent Roman Catholic** comprehensive, founded 1863
- **Suburban** 420-acre campus with easy access to San Francisco
- **Endowment** $129.4 million
- **Coed** 2,996 undergraduate students, 92% full-time, 62% women, 38% men
- **Moderately difficult** entrance level, 69% of applicants were admitted

Undergraduates 2,764 full-time, 232 part-time. Students come from 40 states and territories; 19 other countries; 12% are from out of state; 5% Black or African American, non-Hispanic/Latino; 23% Hispanic/Latino; 10% Asian, non-Hispanic/Latino; 0.4% Native Hawaiian or other Pacific Islander, non-Hispanic/Latino; 0.7% American Indian or Alaska Native, non-Hispanic/Latino; 4% Two or more races, non-Hispanic/Latino; 9% Race/ethnicity unknown; 2% international; 7% transferred in; 55% live on campus. *Retention:* 87% of full-time freshmen returned.

Freshmen *Admission:* 4,874 applied, 3,355 admitted, 644 enrolled. *Average high school GPA:* 3.56. *Test scores:* SAT critical reading scores over 500: 76%; SAT math scores over 500: 78%; ACT scores over 18: 98%; SAT critical reading scores over 600: 26%; SAT math scores over 600: 31%; ACT scores over 24: 52%; SAT critical reading scores over 700: 3%; SAT math scores over 700: 5%; ACT scores over 30: 8%.

Faculty *Total:* 495, 40% full-time, 92% with terminal degrees. *Student/faculty ratio:* 12:1.

Academics *Calendar:* 4-1-4. *Degrees:* associate, bachelor's, master's, doctoral, and first professional. *Special study options:* adult/continuing education programs, advanced placement credit, double majors, honors programs, independent study, internships, off-campus study, part-time degree program, services for LD students, student-designed majors, study abroad, summer session for credit. *ROTC:* Army (c), Air Force (c). *Unusual degree programs:* 3-2 engineering with Washington University in St. Louis, University of Southern California in Los Angeles.

Computers on Campus 244 computers/terminals and 1,800 ports are available on campus for general student use. Students can access the following: campus intranet, computer help desk, free student e-mail accounts, online (class) grades, online (class) registration, online (class) schedules, student accounts. Campuswide network is available. 100% of college-owned or -operated housing units are wired for high-speed Internet access. Wireless service is available via classrooms, computer centers, computer labs, learning centers, libraries, student centers.

Student Life *Housing:* on-campus residence required for freshman year. *Options:* coed, men-only, women-only, disabled students. Campus housing is university owned. Freshman campus housing is guaranteed. *Activities and organizations:* drama/theater group, student-run newspaper, radio and television station, choral group, Gael Force, Student Alumni Association, LASA-Latin American Student Association-Black Student Union, Inter-Varsity Christian Fellowship, Asian Pacific America Student Association. *Campus security:* 24-hour emergency response devices and patrols, late-night transport/escort service. *Student services:* health clinic, personal/psychological counseling, women's center.

Athletics Member NCAA. All Division I. *Intercollegiate sports:* baseball M(s), basketball M(s)/W(s), cheerleading W, crew M(c)/W(s), cross-country running M(s)/W(s), golf M(s), lacrosse M(c)/W(s), rugby M(c), soccer M(s)/W(s), softball W(s), tennis M(s)/W(s), volleyball M(c)/W(s), water polo M(c)/W(c). *Intramural sports:* badminton M/W, basketball M/W, football M/W, skiing (cross-country) M/W, soccer M(c)/W, softball W, tennis M(c)/W(c), volleyball M/W(c).

Standardized Tests *Required:* SAT or ACT (for admission).

Costs (2012–13) *Comprehensive fee:* $51,290 includes full-time tuition ($38,300), mandatory fees ($150), and room and board ($12,840). Part-time tuition: $4790 per course. Part-time tuition and fees vary according to course load and program. *College room only:* $7040. Room and board charges vary according to board plan and housing facility. *Payment plan:* installment. *Waivers:* employees or children of employees.

Financial Aid Of all full-time matriculated undergraduates who enrolled in 2011, 2,176 applied for aid, 2,050 were judged to have need, 187 had their need fully met. 467 Federal Work-Study jobs (averaging $1822). In 2011, 169 non-need-based awards were made. *Average percent of need met:* 68%. *Average financial aid package:* $27,255. *Average need-based loan:* $4560. *Average need-based gift aid:* $22,878. *Average non-need-based aid:* $12,430. *Average indebtedness upon graduation:* $34,375.

Applying *Options:* electronic application, deferred entrance. *Application fee:* $55. *Required:* essay or personal statement, high school transcript, minimum 2.0 GPA, 1 letter of recommendation. *Required for some:* minimum 3.0 GPA, interview. *Recommended:* minimum 3.0 GPA. *Application deadlines:* 2/1 (freshmen), 7/1 (transfers). *Notification:* 3/15 (freshmen), continuous (transfers).

Freshman Application Contact Mr. Michael McKeon, Dean of Admissions, Saint Mary's College of California, PO Box 4800, Moraga, CA 94575-4800. *Phone:* 925-631-4224. *Toll-free phone:* 800-800-4SMC. *Fax:* 925-376-7193. *E-mail:* smcadmit@stmarys-ca.edu. *Web site:* http://www.stmarys-ca.edu/.

Samuel Merritt University
Oakland, California

- **Independent** upper-level, founded 1909
- **Urban** 1-acre campus with easy access to San Francisco
- **Endowment** $41.6 million
- **Coed, primarily women** 593 undergraduate students, 87% full-time, 84% women, 16% men
- **Moderately difficult** entrance level, 57% of applicants were admitted

Undergraduates 515 full-time, 78 part-time. Students come from 6 states and territories; 2% are from out of state; 5% Black or African American, non-Hispanic/Latino; 10% Hispanic/Latino; 27% Asian, non-Hispanic/Latino; 1% Native Hawaiian or other Pacific Islander, non-Hispanic/Latino; 0.4% American Indian or Alaska Native, non-Hispanic/Latino; 5% Two or more races, non-Hispanic/Latino; 13% Race/ethnicity unknown; 42% transferred in.

Freshmen *Admission:* 261 applied, 148 admitted.

Faculty *Total:* 266, 50% full-time, 36% with terminal degrees. *Student/faculty ratio:* 8:1.

Academics *Calendar:* trimesters. *Degrees:* bachelor's, master's, and doctoral (bachelor's degree offered jointly with Saint Mary's College of California).

Special study options: academic remediation for entering students, accelerated degree program, advanced placement credit, cooperative education, distance learning, independent study, internships, off-campus study, part-time degree program, services for LD students, summer session for credit. *ROTC:* Army (c), Air Force (c).

Computers on Campus 102 computers/terminals are available on campus for general student use. Students can access the following: campus intranet, computer help desk, free student e-mail accounts, online (class) grades, online (class) registration, online (class) schedules. Campuswide network is available. Wireless service is available via entire campus.

Student Life *Housing:* college housing not available. *Activities and organizations:* student-run newspaper, Student Body Association, Green Team, International Health Club, Multicultural Group. *Campus security:* 24-hour emergency response devices and patrols, late-night transport/escort service, controlled dormitory access, 24-hour controlled access. *Student services:* health clinic, personal/psychological counseling.

Costs (2012–13) *One-time required fee:* $1352. *Tuition:* $39,719 full-time, $1674 per unit part-time. Full-time tuition and fees vary according to degree level and program. Part-time tuition and fees vary according to degree level and program. *Payment plan:* installment.

Financial Aid Of all full-time matriculated undergraduates who enrolled in 2009, 495 applied for aid, 448 were judged to have need, 20 had their need fully met. 120 Federal Work-Study jobs (averaging $1583). *Average percent of need met:* 69%. *Average financial aid package:* $32,000. *Average need-based loan:* $10,457. *Average need-based gift aid:* $20,000.

Applying *Options:* deferred entrance. *Application fee:* $50. *Application deadline:* 3/1 (transfers). *Notification:* continuous (transfers).

Application Contact Samuel Merritt University, 3100 Telegraph Avenue, Oakland, CA 94609-3108. *Phone:* 510-869-6610. *Toll-free phone:* 800-607-MERRITT. *Web site:* http://www.samuelmerritt.edu/.

San Diego Christian College
El Cajon, California

- **Independent nondenominational** 4-year, founded 1970
- **Suburban** 55-acre campus with easy access to San Diego
- **Coed** 617 undergraduate students, 89% full-time, 52% women, 48% men
- **Moderately difficult** entrance level, 39% of applicants were admitted

Undergraduates 551 full-time, 66 part-time. Students come from 48 states and territories; 7 other countries; 8% are from out of state; 12% Black or African American, non-Hispanic/Latino; 17% Hispanic/Latino; 1% Asian, non-Hispanic/Latino; 0.5% Native Hawaiian or other Pacific Islander, non-Hispanic/Latino; 1% American Indian or Alaska Native, non-Hispanic/Latino; 3% Two or more races, non-Hispanic/Latino; 20% Race/ethnicity unknown; 1% international; 15% transferred in; 42% live on campus. *Retention:* 64% of full-time freshmen returned.

Freshmen *Admission:* 585 applied, 226 admitted, 92 enrolled. *Average high school GPA:* 3.31. *Test scores:* SAT critical reading scores over 500: 52%; SAT math scores over 500: 40%; ACT scores over 18: 89%; SAT critical reading scores over 600: 15%; SAT math scores over 600: 10%; ACT scores over 24: 21%; SAT critical reading scores over 700: 1%.

Faculty *Total:* 78, 21% full-time, 18% with terminal degrees. *Student/faculty ratio:* 17:1.

Academics *Calendar:* semesters. *Degrees:* certificates, bachelor's, and post-bachelor's certificates. *Special study options:* academic remediation for entering students, accelerated degree program, adult/continuing education programs, advanced placement credit, distance learning, double majors, English as a second language, honors programs, independent study, internships, off-campus study, part-time degree program, student-designed majors, summer session for credit. *ROTC:* Army (c), Air Force (c).

Computers on Campus 187 computers/terminals and 69 ports are available on campus for general student use. Students can access the following: computer help desk, free student e-mail accounts, online (class) grades, online (class) registration, online (class) schedules. Campuswide network is available. 100% of college-owned or -operated housing units are wired for high-speed Internet access. Wireless service is available via classrooms, computer centers, computer labs, learning centers, libraries, student centers.

Student Life *Housing:* on-campus residence required through sophomore year. *Options:* men-only, women-only. Campus housing is leased by the school. *Activities and organizations:* drama/theater group, student-run newspaper, choral group, Senate, Missions Club, Aviators Club, Women of Influence, Hope Ministries. *Campus security:* 24-hour emergency response devices and patrols. *Student services:* health clinic, personal/psychological counseling.

Athletics Member NAIA. *Intercollegiate sports:* baseball M(s), basketball M(s)/W(s), cross-country running M(s)/W(s), soccer M(s)/W(s), volleyball W(s). *Intramural sports:* basketball M/W, football M, golf M/W(c), soccer M/W, softball M/W, swimming and diving M/W, tennis M/W, ultimate Frisbee M/W, volleyball M/W, weight lifting M/W.

Standardized Tests *Required:* SAT or ACT (for admission).

Costs (2012–13) *One-time required fee:* $100. *Comprehensive fee:* $33,948 includes full-time tuition ($23,824), mandatory fees ($1284), and room and board ($8840). Full-time tuition and fees vary according to class time, course load, and program. Part-time tuition: $964 per credit. Part-time tuition and fees vary according to class time, course load, and program. *Required fees:* $239 per term part-time. *Payment plan:* installment. *Waivers:* employees or children of employees.

Financial Aid Of all full-time matriculated undergraduates who enrolled in 2011, 529 applied for aid, 472 were judged to have need, 59 had their need fully met. 22 Federal Work-Study jobs (averaging $2290). 10 state and other part-time jobs (averaging $2140). In 2011, 11 non-need-based awards were made. *Average percent of need met:* 83%. *Average financial aid package:* $14,072. *Average need-based loan:* $4129. *Average need-based gift aid:* $6840. *Average non-need-based aid:* $3273. *Average indebtedness upon graduation:* $27,366. *Financial aid deadline:* 7/15.

Applying *Options:* electronic application, deferred entrance. *Application fee:* $25. *Required:* essay or personal statement, high school transcript, 2 letters of recommendation. *Recommended:* minimum 2.8 GPA, interview. *Application deadlines:* 7/1 (freshmen), 7/1 (transfers). *Notification:* continuous (freshmen), continuous (transfers).

Freshman Application Contact Candice Del Giudice, Director of Admissions, San Diego Christian College, 2100 Greenfield Drive, El Cajon, CA 92019-1157. *Phone:* 619-201-8741. *Toll-free phone:* 800-676-2242. *Fax:* 619-201-8749. *E-mail:* cdelgiudice@sdcc.edu. *Web site:* http://www.sdcc.edu/.

San Diego State University
San Diego, California

- **State-supported** university, founded 1897, part of California State University System
- **Urban** 300-acre campus
- **Endowment** $142.2 million
- **Coed** 26,371 undergraduate students, 87% full-time, 56% women, 44% men
- **Moderately difficult** entrance level, 33% of applicants were admitted

Undergraduates 22,888 full-time, 3,483 part-time. Students come from 54 states and territories; 70 other countries; 6% are from out of state; 4% Black or African American, non-Hispanic/Latino; 29% Hispanic/Latino; 7% Asian, non-Hispanic/Latino; 8% Native Hawaiian or other Pacific Islander, non-Hispanic/Latino; 0.4% American Indian or Alaska Native, non-Hispanic/Latino; 4% Two or more races, non-Hispanic/Latino; 7% Race/ethnicity unknown; 4% international; 8% transferred in; 15% live on campus. *Retention:* 89% of full-time freshmen returned.

Freshmen *Admission:* 45,027 applied, 14,805 admitted, 4,019 enrolled. *Average high school GPA:* 3.62. *Test scores:* SAT critical reading scores over 500: 67%; SAT math scores over 500: 76%; ACT scores over 18: 94%; SAT critical reading scores over 600: 19%; SAT math scores over 600: 32%; ACT scores over 24: 55%; SAT critical reading scores over 700: 1%; SAT math scores over 700: 3%; ACT scores over 30: 4%.

Faculty *Total:* 1,453, 54% full-time, 51% with terminal degrees. *Student/faculty ratio:* 22:1.

Academics *Calendar:* semesters. *Degrees:* bachelor's, master's, doctoral, postbachelor's, and first professional certificates. *Special study options:* academic remediation for entering students, advanced placement credit, distance learning, double majors, English as a second language, external degree program, honors programs, independent study, internships, off-campus study, part-time degree program, services for LD students, study abroad, summer session for credit. *ROTC:* Army (b), Navy (b), Air Force (b). *Unusual degree programs:* 3-2 business administration; engineering with BS/MS 4+1 Degree Program B.S. and M.S. in Mechanical Engineering; BS/MS 4+1 Degree Program B.S. in Mechanical Engineering and M.S. in Bioengineering.

Computers on Campus 2,055 computers/terminals and 400 ports are available on campus for general student use. Students can access the following: computer help desk, free student e-mail accounts, online (class) grades, online (class) registration, online (class) schedules. Campuswide network is available. 100% of college-owned or -operated housing units are wired for high-speed Internet access. Wireless service is available via entire campus.

Student Life *Housing:* on-campus residence required for freshman year. *Options:* coed. Campus housing is university owned. Freshman applicants given priority for college housing. *Activities and organizations:* drama/theater group, student-run newspaper, radio and television station, choral group, marching band, AB Samahan, Asian Pacific Student Alliance, Enviro-Business Society, M.E.Ch.A de SDSU, Social fraternities and Sororities, including both general and culturally based organizations, national fraternities, national sororities. *Campus security:* 24-hour emergency response devices and patrols, stu-

dent patrols, late-night transport/escort service. *Student services:* health clinic, personal/psychological counseling, women's center.

Athletics Member NCAA. All Division I. *Intercollegiate sports:* baseball M(s), basketball M(s)/W(s), crew W(s), cross-country running W(s), football M(s), golf M(s)/W(s), soccer M(s)/W(s), softball W(s), swimming and diving W(s), tennis M(s)/W(s), track and field W(s), volleyball W(s), water polo W(s). *Intramural sports:* basketball M/W, bowling M/W, cheerleading W(c), crew M(c), football M/W, golf M/W, ice hockey M(c), lacrosse M(c)/W(c), racquetball M/W, rugby M(c), skiing (downhill) M(c)/W(c), soccer M(c)/W(c), softball M/W, swimming and diving M/W, tennis M/W, ultimate Frisbee M(c)/W(c), volleyball M(c)/W(c), water polo M(c)/W(c).

Standardized Tests *Required:* SAT or ACT (for admission).

Costs (2012–13) *Tuition:* state resident $0 full-time; nonresident $11,160 full-time, $372 per unit part-time. Full-time tuition and fees vary according to degree level, location, and program. Part-time tuition and fees vary according to course load, degree level, location, and program. *Required fees:* $7076 full-time. *Room and board:* $13,052. Room and board charges vary according to board plan and housing facility. *Payment plan:* installment. *Waivers:* employees or children of employees.

Financial Aid Of all full-time matriculated undergraduates who enrolled in 2011, 18,000 applied for aid, 14,300 were judged to have need, 1,300 had their need fully met. 589 Federal Work-Study jobs (averaging $2300). In 2011, 1200 non-need-based awards were made. *Average percent of need met:* 72%. *Average financial aid package:* $10,100. *Average need-based loan:* $4100. *Average need-based gift aid:* $9200. *Average non-need-based aid:* $1600. *Average indebtedness upon graduation:* $16,400. *Financial aid deadline:* 3/2.

Applying *Options:* electronic application. *Application fee:* $55. *Required:* high school transcript, minimum 2.0 GPA, 2.5 GPA for non-California residents. *Application deadlines:* 11/30 (freshmen), 11/30 (transfers). *Notification:* 3/1 (freshmen), 3/1 (transfers).

Freshman Application Contact Ms. Beverly Arata, Director of Admissions, San Diego State University, 5500 Campanile Drive, San Diego, CA 92182-0771. *Phone:* 619-594-6336. *E-mail:* admissions@sdsu.edu. *Web site:* http://www.sdsu.edu/.

San Diego State University–Imperial Valley Campus

Calexico, California

Freshman Application Contact Aracely Bororquez, Admissions Department, San Diego State University–Imperial Valley Campus, 720 Heber Avenue, Calexico, CA 92231. *Phone:* 760-768-5506. *Fax:* 760-768-5589. *E-mail:* transfer@mail.sdsu.edu. *Web site:* http://www.ivcampus.sdsu.edu/.

San Francisco Art Institute

San Francisco, California

Freshman Application Contact Office of Admissions, San Francisco Art Institute, 800 Chestnut Street, San Francisco, CA 94133. *Phone:* 415-749-4500. *Toll-free phone:* 800-345-SFAI. *E-mail:* admissions@sfai.edu. *Web site:* http://www.sfai.edu/.

San Francisco Conservatory of Music

San Francisco, California

- **Independent** comprehensive, founded 1917
- **Urban** 2-acre campus
- **Endowment** $33.6 million
- **Coed** 188 undergraduate students, 97% full-time, 47% women, 53% men
- **Moderately difficult** entrance level, 38% of applicants were admitted

Undergraduates 183 full-time, 5 part-time. Students come from 26 states and territories; 18 other countries; 33% are from out of state; 3% Black or African American, non-Hispanic/Latino; 6% Hispanic/Latino; 10% Asian, non-Hispanic/Latino; 1% Native Hawaiian or other Pacific Islander, non-Hispanic/Latino; 7% Two or more races, non-Hispanic/Latino; 7% Race/ethnicity unknown; 22% international; 7% transferred in; 42% live on campus. *Retention:* 80% of full-time freshmen returned.

Freshmen *Admission:* 273 applied, 105 admitted, 39 enrolled.

Faculty *Total:* 113, 28% full-time, 20% with terminal degrees. *Student/faculty ratio:* 7:1.

Academics *Calendar:* semesters. *Degrees:* diplomas, bachelor's, master's, and post-master's certificates. *Special study options:* academic remediation for entering students, advanced placement credit, independent study, internships, part-time degree program.

Computers on Campus 15 computers/terminals and 50 ports are available on campus for general student use. Students can access the following: campus intranet, computer help desk, free student e-mail accounts. Campuswide net-

work is available. Wireless service is available via computer labs, libraries, student centers.

Student Life *Housing options:* coed. Campus housing is leased by the school and is provided by a third party. *Activities and organizations:* drama/theater group, choral group, Yoga Group, Meditation Group, Conservatory Ball Planning Committee. *Campus security:* 24-hour emergency response devices and patrols, controlled dormitory access, resident assistant on-call for residential hall residents. *Student services:* personal/psychological counseling.

Standardized Tests *Recommended:* SAT or ACT (for admission).

Costs (2012–13) *Tuition:* $36,500 full-time, $1610 per credit part-time. Part-time tuition and fees vary according to course load and program. *Required fees:* $540 full-time, $270 per term part-time. *Payment plan:* installment. *Waivers:* employees or children of employees.

Financial Aid Of all full-time matriculated undergraduates who enrolled in 2009, 127 applied for aid, 112 were judged to have need, 16 had their need fully met. In 2009, 69 non-need-based awards were made. *Average percent of need met:* 66%. *Average financial aid package:* $22,952. *Average need-based loan:* $6127. *Average need-based gift aid:* $17,133. *Average non-need-based aid:* $12,389. *Average indebtedness upon graduation:* $15,454.

Applying *Options:* electronic application, deferred entrance. *Application fee:* $100. *Required:* essay or personal statement, high school transcript, minimum 2.5 GPA, 2 letters of recommendation, audition, pre-screen recording in select areas. *Application deadlines:* 12/1 (freshmen), 12/1 (out-of-state freshmen), 12/1 (transfers). *Notification:* 4/1 (freshmen), 4/1 (out-of-state freshmen), 4/1 (transfers).

Freshman Application Contact Ms. Melissa Cocco-Mitten, San Francisco Conservatory of Music, 50 Oak Street, San Francisco, CA 94102. *Phone:* 800-899-7326. *Fax:* 415-503-6299. *E-mail:* admit@sfcm.edu. *Web site:* http://www.sfcm.edu/.

San Francisco State University

San Francisco, California

- **State-supported** university, founded 1899, part of California State University System
- **Urban** 142-acre campus
- **Endowment** $49.0 million
- **Coed** 25,383 undergraduate students, 84% full-time, 57% women, 43% men
- **Moderately difficult** entrance level, 65% of applicants were admitted

Undergraduates 21,315 full-time, 4,068 part-time. Students come from 41 states and territories; 90 other countries; 1% are from out of state; 5% Black or African American, non-Hispanic/Latino; 20% Hispanic/Latino; 27% Asian, non-Hispanic/Latino; 0.7% Native Hawaiian or other Pacific Islander, non-Hispanic/Latino; 0.3% American Indian or Alaska Native, non-Hispanic/Latino; 5% Two or more races, non-Hispanic/Latino; 8% Race/ethnicity unknown; 7% international; 12% transferred in; 12% live on campus. *Retention:* 81% of full-time freshmen returned.

Freshmen *Admission:* 30,096 applied, 19,569 admitted, 3,537 enrolled. *Average high school GPA:* 3.15. *Test scores:* SAT critical reading scores over 500: 52%; ACT scores over 18: 86%; SAT critical reading scores over 600: 13%; ACT scores over 24: 32%; SAT critical reading scores over 700: 1%; ACT scores over 30: 2%.

Faculty *Total:* 1,593, 54% full-time, 48% with terminal degrees. *Student/faculty ratio:* 22:1.

Academics *Calendar:* semesters. *Degrees:* certificates, bachelor's, master's, doctoral, postbachelor's, and first professional certificates. *Special study options:* academic remediation for entering students, adult/continuing education programs, advanced placement credit, cooperative education, distance learning, double majors, English as a second language, honors programs, independent study, internships, off-campus study, part-time degree program, services for LD students, student-designed majors, study abroad, summer session for credit. *ROTC:* Army (c), Air Force (c).

Computers on Campus 2,800 computers/terminals and 800 ports are available on campus for general student use. Students can access the following: campus intranet, computer help desk, free student e-mail accounts, online (class) grades, online (class) registration, online (class) schedules. Campuswide network is available. 100% of college-owned or -operated housing units are wired for high-speed Internet access. Wireless service is available via entire campus.

Student Life *Housing options:* coed, disabled students. Campus housing is university owned. Freshman applicants given priority for college housing. *Activities and organizations:* drama/theater group, student-run newspaper, radio and television station, choral group, International Education Exchange Council, Graduate Students Association, Accounting Students Organization, Improv Nation @ San Francisco State University, Asian Student Union, national fraternities, national sororities. *Campus security:* 24-hour emergency response devices and patrols, student patrols, late-night transport/escort ser-

vice, controlled dormitory access. *Student services:* health clinic, personal/psychological counseling, women's center, legal services.
Athletics Member NCAA. All Division II. *Intercollegiate sports:* baseball M(s), basketball M(s)/W(s), cross-country running M(s)/W(s), soccer M(s)/W(s), softball W(s), track and field W(s), volleyball W(s), wrestling M(s). *Intramural sports:* basketball M/W, cheerleading M(c)/W(c), rugby M(c)/W(c), soccer M/W, tennis M/W, volleyball M/W, water polo M(c)/W(c).
Standardized Tests *Required:* SAT or ACT (for admission).
Costs (2011–12) *Tuition:* state resident $5472 full-time; nonresident $16,632 full-time. Full-time tuition and fees vary according to course load. Part-time tuition and fees vary according to course load. *Required fees:* $804 full-time. *Room and board:* $11,408. Room and board charges vary according to board plan and housing facility.
Financial Aid Of all full-time matriculated undergraduates who enrolled in 2011, 14,569 applied for aid, 13,083 were judged to have need, 489 had their need fully met. In 2011, 63 non-need-based awards were made. *Average percent of need met:* 59%. *Average financial aid package:* $11,133. *Average need-based loan:* $3165. *Average need-based gift aid:* $9760. *Average non-need-based aid:* $3132. *Average indebtedness upon graduation:* $18,850.
Applying *Options:* electronic application. *Application fee:* $55. *Required:* high school transcript. *Application deadlines:* 11/30 (freshmen), 8/31 (transfers). *Notification:* 10/1 (freshmen).
Freshman Application Contact Admissions Officer, San Francisco State University, 1600 Holloway Avenue, San Francisco, CA 94132-1722. *Phone:* 415-338-1113. *Fax:* 415-338-7196. *E-mail:* ugadmit@sfsu.edu. *Web site:* http://www.sfsu.edu/.

San Jose State University
San Jose, California

- **State-supported** comprehensive, founded 1857, part of California State University System
- **Urban** 104-acre campus
- **Coed**
- **Very difficult** entrance level

Faculty *Student/faculty ratio:* 25:1.
Academics *Calendar:* semesters. *Degrees:* bachelor's and master's.
Student Life *Campus security:* 24-hour emergency response devices and patrols, student patrols, late-night transport/escort service.
Athletics Member NCAA. All Division I except football (Division I-A).
Standardized Tests *Required for some:* SAT or ACT (for admission).
Costs (2011–12) *Tuition:* state resident $5472 full-time; nonresident $16,632 full-time. *Required fees:* $1368 full-time. *Room and board:* $10,733.
Financial Aid Of all full-time matriculated undergraduates who enrolled in 2010, 12,780 applied for aid, 11,523 were judged to have need, 2,857 had their need fully met. In 2010, 88 non-need-based awards were made. *Average percent of need met:* 80. *Average financial aid package:* $13,986. *Average need-based loan:* $4211. *Average need-based gift aid:* $8387. *Average non-need-based aid:* $3389. *Average indebtedness upon graduation:* $14,549. *Financial aid deadline:* 6/15.
Applying *Options:* electronic application. *Application fee:* $55. *Required:* high school transcript.
Freshman Application Contact Admissions Office, San Jose State University, One Washington Square, San Jose, CA 95192-0001. *Phone:* 408-283-7500. *Fax:* 408-924-2050. *E-mail:* admissions@sjsu.edu. *Web site:* http://www.sjsu.edu/.

Santa Clara University
Santa Clara, California

- **Independent Roman Catholic (Jesuit)** university, founded 1851
- **Suburban** 106-acre campus with easy access to San Francisco, San Jose
- **Endowment** $716.8 million
- **Coed** 5,229 undergraduate students, 98% full-time, 51% women, 49% men
- **Moderately difficult** entrance level, 54% of applicants were admitted

Undergraduates 5,128 full-time, 101 part-time. Students come from 46 states and territories; 40 other countries; 36% are from out of state; 3% Black or African American, non-Hispanic/Latino; 18% Hispanic/Latino; 14% Asian, non-Hispanic/Latino; 0.4% Native Hawaiian or other Pacific Islander, non-Hispanic/Latino; 0.1% American Indian or Alaska Native, non-Hispanic/Latino; 6% Two or more races, non-Hispanic/Latino; 12% Race/ethnicity unknown; 3% international; 4% transferred in; 50% live on campus. *Retention:* 94% of full-time freshmen returned.
Freshmen *Admission:* 13,342 applied, 7,263 admitted, 1,283 enrolled. *Average high school GPA:* 3.61. *Test scores:* SAT critical reading scores over 500: 96%; SAT math scores over 500: 98%; ACT scores over 18: 100%; SAT critical reading scores over 600: 67%; SAT math scores over 600: 76%; ACT

scores over 24: 93%; SAT critical reading scores over 700: 17%; SAT math scores over 700: 21%; ACT scores over 30: 40%.
Faculty *Total:* 832, 58% full-time, 81% with terminal degrees. *Student/faculty ratio:* 13:1.
Academics *Calendar:* quarters. *Degrees:* bachelor's, master's, doctoral, post-master's, postbachelor's, and first professional certificates. *Special study options:* advanced placement credit, cooperative education, double majors, honors programs, independent study, internships, services for LD students, student-designed majors, study abroad, summer session for credit. *ROTC:* Army (b), Air Force (c).
Computers on Campus 826 computers/terminals are available on campus for general student use. Students can access the following: campus intranet, computer help desk, free student e-mail accounts, online (class) grades, online (class) registration, online (class) schedules. Campuswide network is available. 100% of college-owned or -operated housing units are wired for high-speed Internet access. Wireless service is available via entire campus.
Student Life *Housing options:* coed, disabled students. Campus housing is university owned. Freshman applicants given priority for college housing. *Activities and organizations:* drama/theater group, student-run newspaper, radio station, choral group, Ruff Riders, Associated Student Government (ASG), The Multicultural Center (MCC), The SCU Radio Station (KSCU), Santa Clara Community Action Program (SCCAP). *Campus security:* 24-hour emergency response devices and patrols, late-night transport/escort service, controlled dormitory access. *Student services:* health clinic, personal/psychological counseling.
Athletics Member NCAA. All Division I. *Intercollegiate sports:* baseball M(s), basketball M(s)/W(s), crew M/W, cross-country running M(s)/W(s), golf M(s)/W(s), soccer M(s)/W(s), softball W(s), tennis M(s)/W(s), track and field M(s)/W(s), volleyball W(s), water polo M(s)/W(s). *Intramural sports:* badminton M/W, basketball M/W, cheerleading W(c), equestrian sports M(c)/W(c), field hockey W(c), football M/W, ice hockey M(c), lacrosse M(c)/W(c), rugby M(c)/W(c), sailing M(c)/W(c), soccer M/W, softball M/W, swimming and diving M(c)/W(c), table tennis M/W, tennis M/W, volleyball M/W.
Standardized Tests *Required:* SAT or ACT (for admission).
Costs (2011–12) *Comprehensive fee:* $51,045 includes full-time tuition ($39,048) and room and board ($11,997). Part-time tuition: $1085 per unit. Part-time tuition and fees vary according to course load. *Room and board:* Room and board charges vary according to board plan, housing facility, location, and student level. *Payment plan:* installment. *Waivers:* employees or children of employees.
Financial Aid Of all full-time matriculated undergraduates who enrolled in 2011, 3,377 applied for aid, 2,655 were judged to have need, 865 had their need fully met. 310 Federal Work-Study jobs (averaging $3410). In 2011, 1336 non-need-based awards were made. *Average percent of need met:* 67%. *Average financial aid package:* $25,903. *Average need-based loan:* $4755. *Average need-based gift aid:* $19,975. *Average non-need-based aid:* $11,732. *Average indebtedness upon graduation:* $27,121.
Applying *Options:* electronic application, early decision, early action, deferred entrance. *Application fee:* $55. *Required:* essay or personal statement, high school transcript, 1 letter of recommendation. *Application deadlines:* 1/7 (freshmen), 4/1 (transfers), 11/1 (early action). *Early decision deadline:* 11/1. *Notification:* continuous until 4/1 (freshmen), continuous (transfers), 12/15 (early decision), 12/23 (early action).
Freshman Application Contact Ms. Sandra Hayes, Dean of Undergraduate Admissions, Santa Clara University, 500 El Camino Real, Santa Clara, CA 95053. *Phone:* 408-554-4700. *Fax:* 408-554-5255. *E-mail:* ugadmissions@scu.edu. *Web site:* http://www.scu.edu/.

School of Urban Missions
Oakland, California

Freshman Application Contact Admissions, School of Urban Missions, 735 105th Avenue, Oakland, CA 94603. *Phone:* 510-567-6174. *Toll-free phone:* 888-567-6174. *Fax:* 510-568-1024. *Web site:* http://www.sum.edu/.

Scripps College
Claremont, California

- **Independent** 4-year, founded 1926
- **Suburban** 37-acre campus with easy access to Los Angeles
- **Endowment** $266.9 million
- **Women only** 966 undergraduate students, 99% full-time
- **Very difficult** entrance level, 36% of applicants were admitted

Undergraduates 961 full-time, 5 part-time. Students come from 47 states and territories; 20 other countries; 52% are from out of state; 5% Black or African American, non-Hispanic/Latino; 8% Hispanic/Latino; 17% Asian, non-Hispanic/Latino; 0.1% Native Hawaiian or other Pacific Islander, non-Hispanic/Latino; 0.9% American Indian or Alaska Native, non-Hispanic/Latino; 17%

Race/ethnicity unknown; 4% international; 97% live on campus. *Retention:* 91% of full-time freshmen returned.

Freshmen *Admission:* 2,163 applied, 785 admitted, 257 enrolled. *Average high school GPA:* 4.1. *Test scores:* SAT critical reading scores over 500: 100%; SAT math scores over 500: 100%; SAT writing scores over 500: 100%; ACT scores over 18: 100%; SAT critical reading scores over 600: 90%; SAT math scores over 600: 94%; SAT writing scores over 600: 93%; ACT scores over 24: 99%; SAT critical reading scores over 700: 47%; SAT math scores over 700: 38%; SAT writing scores over 700: 51%; ACT scores over 30: 61%.

Faculty *Total:* 115, 74% full-time, 97% with terminal degrees. *Student/faculty ratio:* 11:1.

Academics *Calendar:* semesters. *Degrees:* certificates, bachelor's, and post-bachelor's certificates. *Special study options:* accelerated degree program, advanced placement credit, double majors, independent study, internships, off-campus study, part-time degree program, student-designed majors, study abroad. *ROTC:* Army (c), Air Force (c). *Unusual degree programs:* 3-2 business administration with Claremont Graduate University; engineering with Stanford University, University of Southern California, Harvey Mudd College, University of California, Berkeley, Washington University in St. Louis, Columbia University, Rensselaer and Boston University; American politics, economics, philosophy, public policy, international studies, or religion with Claremont Graduate University.

Computers on Campus 87 computers/terminals are available on campus for general student use. Students can access the following: campus intranet, computer help desk, free student e-mail accounts, online (class) grades, online (class) registration, online (class) schedules, 2 ports per dorm room. Campuswide network is available. 100% of college-owned or -operated housing units are wired for high-speed Internet access. Wireless service is available via entire campus.

Student Life *Housing:* on-campus residence required for freshman year. *Options:* women-only, disabled students. Campus housing is university owned. Freshman campus housing is guaranteed. *Activities and organizations:* drama/theater group, student-run newspaper, radio station, choral group, Scripps Associated Students, Asian/Black/Latina clubs, National Organization for Women, Sexual Assault Task Force. *Campus security:* 24-hour emergency response devices and patrols, late-night transport/escort service, controlled dormitory access. *Student services:* health clinic, personal/psychological counseling, women's center.

Athletics Member NCAA. All Division III. *Intercollegiate sports:* basketball W, cross-country running W, fencing W(c), golf W, lacrosse W, rock climbing W(c), rugby W(c), skiing (downhill) W(c), soccer W, softball W, swimming and diving W, tennis W, track and field W, ultimate Frisbee W(c), volleyball W, water polo W. *Intramural sports:* basketball W, cheerleading W, football W, soccer W, softball W, volleyball W, water polo W.

Standardized Tests *Required:* SAT or ACT (for admission).

Costs (2011–12) *Comprehensive fee:* $54,900 includes full-time tuition ($41,736), mandatory fees ($214), and room and board ($12,950). Full-time tuition and fees vary according to course load. Part-time tuition: $5217 per course. Part-time tuition and fees vary according to course load. *College room only:* $7000. Room and board charges vary according to board plan. *Payment plans:* tuition prepayment, installment. *Waivers:* employees or children of employees.

Financial Aid Of all full-time matriculated undergraduates who enrolled in 2011, 509 applied for aid, 397 were judged to have need, 397 had their need fully met. 307 Federal Work-Study jobs (averaging $1899). 28 state and other part-time jobs (averaging $1899). In 2011, 98 non-need-based awards were made. *Average percent of need met:* 100%. *Average financial aid package:* $36,673. *Average need-based loan:* $3506. *Average need-based gift aid:* $33,988. *Average non-need-based aid:* $22,621. *Average indebtedness upon graduation:* $13,121. *Financial aid deadline:* 5/1.

Applying *Options:* early admission, early decision, deferred entrance. *Application fee:* $60. *Required:* essay or personal statement, high school transcript, 2 letters of recommendation, graded writing sample. *Recommended:* minimum 3.0 GPA, interview. *Application deadlines:* 1/2 (freshmen), 4/1 (transfers). *Early decision deadline:* 11/15 (for plan 1), 1/2 (for plan 2). *Notification:* 4/1 (freshmen), 5/15 (transfers), 12/15 (early decision plan 1), 2/15 (early decision plan 2).

Freshman Application Contact Ms. Laura Stratton, Director of Admission, Scripps College, 1030 Columbia Avenue, Claremont, CA 91711. *Phone:* 909-621-8149. *Toll-free phone:* 800-770-1333. *Fax:* 909-607-7508. *E-mail:* admission@scrippscollege.edu. *Web site:* http://www.scrippscollege.edu/.

Shasta Bible College
Redding, California

Freshman Application Contact Connie Barton, Registrar, Shasta Bible College, 2951 Goodwater Avenue, Redding, CA 96002. *Phone:* 530-221-4275 Ext. 26. *Toll-free phone:* 800-800-4SBC. *Fax:* 530-221-6929. *E-mail:* registrar@shasta.edu. *Web site:* http://www.shasta.edu/.

Silicon Valley University
San Jose, California

- **Proprietary** comprehensive
- **Suburban** 1-acre campus with easy access to San Jose
- **Coed**

Faculty *Student/faculty ratio:* 24:1.

Academics *Calendar:* trimesters. *Degrees:* certificates, diplomas, bachelor's, and master's.

Student Life *Campus security:* 24-hour emergency response devices and patrols.

Standardized Tests *Required:* TOEFL for students whose first language is not English (for admission). *Recommended:* SAT (for admission), ACT (for admission), SAT or ACT (for admission).

Applying *Options:* electronic application, deferred entrance. *Application fee:* $50. *Required:* high school transcript, copy of diploma. *Required for some:* interview. *Recommended:* essay or personal statement.

Freshman Application Contact Admissions Office, Silicon Valley University, 2160 Lundy Avenue, Suite 110, San Jose, CA 95131. *Phone:* 408-435-8989 Ext. 109. *E-mail:* admission-office@svuca.edu. *Web site:* http://www.svuca.edu/.

Simpson University
Redding, California

- **Independent** comprehensive, founded 1921, affiliated with The Christian and Missionary Alliance
- **Suburban** 100-acre campus
- **Endowment** $4.2 million
- **Coed** 1,019 undergraduate students, 97% full-time, 67% women, 33% men
- **Moderately difficult** entrance level, 81% of applicants were admitted

Undergraduates 987 full-time, 32 part-time. Students come from 29 states and territories; 9 other countries; 13% are from out of state; 3% Black or African American, non-Hispanic/Latino; 8% Hispanic/Latino; 5% Asian, non-Hispanic/Latino; 0.5% Native Hawaiian or other Pacific Islander, non-Hispanic/Latino; 3% American Indian or Alaska Native, non-Hispanic/Latino; 1% Two or more races, non-Hispanic/Latino; 15% Race/ethnicity unknown; 0.3% international; 12% transferred in; 45% live on campus. *Retention:* 63% of full-time freshmen returned.

Freshmen *Admission:* 378 applied, 308 admitted, 141 enrolled. *Average high school GPA:* 3.48. *Test scores:* SAT critical reading scores over 500: 65%; SAT math scores over 500: 64%; SAT writing scores over 500: 58%; ACT scores over 18: 95%; SAT critical reading scores over 600: 24%; SAT math scores over 600: 14%; SAT writing scores over 600: 15%; ACT scores over 24: 50%; SAT critical reading scores over 700: 2%.

Faculty *Total:* 128, 37% full-time, 40% with terminal degrees. *Student/faculty ratio:* 14:1.

Academics *Calendar:* semesters. *Degrees:* certificates, associate, bachelor's, and master's. *Special study options:* academic remediation for entering students, accelerated degree program, adult/continuing education programs, advanced placement credit, distance learning, double majors, honors programs, independent study, internships, off-campus study, part-time degree program, services for LD students, student-designed majors, study abroad, summer session for credit. *ROTC:* Army (b).

Computers on Campus 50 computers/terminals are available on campus for general student use. Students can access the following: campus intranet, computer help desk, free student e-mail accounts, online (class) grades, online (class) registration, online (class) schedules. Campuswide network is available. 100% of college-owned or -operated housing units are wired for high-speed Internet access. Wireless service is available via entire campus.

Student Life *Housing:* on-campus residence required through junior year. *Options:* men-only, women-only, disabled students. Campus housing is university owned. Freshman campus housing is guaranteed. *Activities and organizations:* drama/theater group, student-run newspaper, choral group, Summer Missions Trips, Social Action Committee, Asian Fellowship, Vida, Psychology Club. *Campus security:* 24-hour emergency response devices and patrols, student patrols, late-night transport/escort service, controlled dormitory access, emergency whistle program and monthly campus safety meetings. *Student services:* health clinic, personal/psychological counseling.

Athletics Member NAIA, NCCAA. *Intercollegiate sports:* baseball M(s), basketball M(s)/W(s), cross-country running M(s)/W(s), golf M(s)/W(s), soccer M(s)/W(s), softball W(s), volleyball W(s), wrestling M(s). *Intramural sports:* basketball M/W, volleyball M(c).

Standardized Tests *Required:* SAT or ACT (for admission). *Recommended:* SAT Subject Tests (for admission).

Costs (2012–13) *Comprehensive fee:* $29,800 includes full-time tuition ($22,400) and room and board ($7400). Full-time tuition and fees vary accord-

ing to course load. Part-time tuition: $933 per unit. Part-time tuition and fees vary according to course load. *College room only:* $6400. Room and board charges vary according to board plan. *Payment plan:* deferred payment. *Waivers:* employees or children of employees.

Financial Aid Of all full-time matriculated undergraduates who enrolled in 2011, 695 applied for aid, 644 were judged to have need, 62 had their need fully met. 170 Federal Work-Study jobs (averaging $489). In 2011, 50 non-need-based awards were made. *Average percent of need met:* 70%. *Average financial aid package:* $19,313. *Average need-based loan:* $4481. *Average need-based gift aid:* $12,322. *Average non-need-based aid:* $6395. *Average indebtedness upon graduation:* $25,281.

Applying *Options:* electronic application, deferred entrance. *Application fee:* $25. *Required:* essay or personal statement, high school transcript, 2 letters of recommendation, Christian commitment. *Required for some:* interview. *Application deadlines:* rolling (freshmen), rolling (transfers). *Notification:* continuous (freshmen), continuous (transfers).

Freshman Application Contact Mrs. Kendell Kluttz, Director of Undergraduate Admissions, Simpson University, 2211 College View Drive, Redding, CA 96003-8606. *Phone:* 530-226-5600. *Toll-free phone:* 888-9-SIMPSON. *Fax:* 530-226-4861. *E-mail:* admissions@simpsonu.edu. *Web site:* http://www.simpsonu.edu/.

Soka University of America
Aliso Viejo, California

- **Independent** comprehensive, founded 2001
- **Suburban** 103-acre campus
- **Endowment** $774.0 million
- **Coed** 438 undergraduate students, 100% full-time, 65% women, 35% men
- **Very difficult** entrance level, 49% of applicants were admitted

Undergraduates 437 full-time, 1 part-time. Students come from 32 states and territories; 27 other countries; 33% are from out of state; 4% Black or African American, non-Hispanic/Latino; 10% Hispanic/Latino; 22% Asian, non-Hispanic/Latino; 0.2% Native Hawaiian or other Pacific Islander, non-Hispanic/Latino; 0.2% American Indian or Alaska Native, non-Hispanic/Latino; 3% Two or more races, non-Hispanic/Latino; 5% Race/ethnicity unknown; 42% international; 99% live on campus. *Retention:* 94% of full-time freshmen returned.

Freshmen *Admission:* 364 applied, 179 admitted, 110 enrolled. *Average high school GPA:* 3.68. *Test scores:* SAT critical reading scores over 500: 70%; SAT math scores over 500: 90%; SAT writing scores over 500: 89%; ACT scores over 18: 100%; SAT critical reading scores over 600: 34%; SAT math scores over 600: 52%; SAT writing scores over 600: 38%; ACT scores over 24: 56%; SAT critical reading scores over 700: 7%; SAT math scores over 700: 17%; SAT writing scores over 700: 5%; ACT scores over 30: 9%.

Faculty *Total:* 61, 69% full-time, 82% with terminal degrees. *Student/faculty ratio:* 9:1.

Academics *Calendar:* semesters. *Degrees:* bachelor's and master's. *Special study options:* academic remediation for entering students, cooperative education, double majors, English as a second language, independent study, internships, off-campus study, services for LD students, study abroad.

Computers on Campus 100 computers/terminals are available on campus for general student use. Students can access the following: campus intranet, computer help desk, free student e-mail accounts, online (class) grades, online (class) registration, online (class) schedules, Angel courseware/PeopleSoft Portal. Campuswide network is available. 100% of college-owned or -operated housing units are wired for high-speed Internet access. Wireless service is available via entire campus.

Student Life *Housing:* on-campus residence required through senior year. *Options:* coed, disabled students. Campus housing is university owned. Freshman campus housing is guaranteed. *Activities and organizations:* student-run newspaper, choral group, Josho Daiko (Japanese Drum Club), Rhythmission (Hip Hop Dance Club), Sualseros (Salsa Dance Club), Ka Pilina Ho'olokahi (Hawaiian Dance Club), Soul Wings (Choir). *Campus security:* 24-hour emergency response devices and patrols, late-night transport/escort service, controlled dormitory access. *Student services:* health clinic, personal/psychological counseling.

Athletics Member NAIA. *Intercollegiate sports:* cross-country running M(s)/W(s), soccer M(s)/W(s), swimming and diving M(s)/W(s), track and field M(s)/W(s), water polo M/W. *Intramural sports:* badminton M/W, baseball M, basketball M/W, cheerleading M(c)/W(c), football M/W, golf M, racquetball M(c)/W(c), soccer M(c)/W(c), softball M/W, table tennis M(c)/W(c), tennis M/W, volleyball M(c)/W(c), weight lifting M/W.

Standardized Tests *Required:* SAT or ACT (for admission). *Recommended:* SAT Subject Tests (for admission).

Costs (2012–13) *Comprehensive fee:* $38,700 includes full-time tuition ($27,214), mandatory fees ($858), and room and board ($10,628). Full-time

tuition and fees vary according to course load. Part-time tuition: $1134 per credit. Part-time tuition and fees vary according to course load. *Payment plan:* installment. *Waivers:* employees or children of employees.

Financial Aid Of all full-time matriculated undergraduates who enrolled in 2011, 388 applied for aid, 356 were judged to have need, 69 had their need fully met. 58 Federal Work-Study jobs (averaging $498). *Average percent of need met:* 77%. *Average financial aid package:* $25,521. *Average need-based loan:* $4365. *Average need-based gift aid:* $21,357. *Average indebtedness upon graduation:* $26,256. *Financial aid deadline:* 5/1.

Applying *Options:* electronic application, early admission, early action, deferred entrance. *Application fee:* $45. *Required:* essay or personal statement, high school transcript, 2 letters of recommendation. *Recommended:* interview. *Application deadlines:* 1/15 (freshmen), 1/15 (out-of-state freshmen), 10/15 (early action). *Notification:* 3/1 (freshmen), 3/1 (out-of-state freshmen), 12/1 (early action).

Freshman Application Contact Ms. Kelleigh Messer, Admissions Operations Coordinator, Soka University of America, Enrollment Services, 1 University Drive, Aliso Viejo, CA 92656. *Phone:* 949-480-4152 Ext. 4152. *Toll-free phone:* 888-600-SOKA. *Fax:* 949-480-4151. *E-mail:* kmesser@soka.edu. *Web site:* http://www.soka.edu/.

Sonoma State University
Rohnert Park, California

- **State-supported** comprehensive, founded 1960, part of California State University System
- **Small-town** 280-acre campus with easy access to San Francisco
- **Endowment** $28.0 million
- **Coed** 7,761 undergraduate students, 91% full-time, 60% women, 40% men
- **Moderately difficult** entrance level, 85% of applicants were admitted

Undergraduates 7,034 full-time, 727 part-time. Students come from 24 states and territories; 19 other countries; 1% are from out of state; 2% Black or African American, non-Hispanic/Latino; 15% Hispanic/Latino; 4% Asian, non-Hispanic/Latino; 0.6% Native Hawaiian or other Pacific Islander, non-Hispanic/Latino; 0.8% American Indian or Alaska Native, non-Hispanic/Latino; 7% Two or more races, non-Hispanic/Latino; 4% Race/ethnicity unknown; 1% international; 9% transferred in; 36% live on campus. *Retention:* 80% of full-time freshmen returned.

Freshmen *Admission:* 12,151 applied, 10,317 admitted, 1,810 enrolled. *Average high school GPA:* 3.17. *Test scores:* SAT critical reading scores over 500: 56%; SAT math scores over 500: 55%; ACT scores over 18: 85%; SAT critical reading scores over 600: 14%; SAT math scores over 600: 14%; ACT scores over 24: 30%; SAT critical reading scores over 700: 1%; SAT math scores over 700: 1%; ACT scores over 30: 1%.

Faculty *Total:* 539, 48% full-time, 60% with terminal degrees. *Student/faculty ratio:* 25:1.

Academics *Calendar:* semesters. *Degrees:* bachelor's and master's. *Special study options:* academic remediation for entering students, accelerated degree program, adult/continuing education programs, advanced placement credit, cooperative education, distance learning, double majors, English as a second language, honors programs, independent study, internships, off-campus study, part-time degree program, services for LD students, student-designed majors, study abroad, summer session for credit. *ROTC:* Army (c), Air Force (c).

Computers on Campus 400 computers/terminals are available on campus for general student use. Students can access the following: computer help desk, free student e-mail accounts, online (class) grades, online (class) registration, online (class) schedules. Campuswide network is available. 100% of college-owned or -operated housing units are wired for high-speed Internet access. Wireless service is available via entire campus.

Student Life *Housing options:* coed, women-only, disabled students. Campus housing is university owned. Freshman applicants given priority for college housing. *Activities and organizations:* drama/theater group, student-run newspaper, radio station, choral group, Accounting Forum, Sonoma Earth Action, Re-Entry Student Association, Lacrosse Club, Inter-Varsity Christian Fellowship, national fraternities, national sororities. *Campus security:* 24-hour emergency response devices and patrols, student patrols, late-night transport/escort service, controlled dormitory access. *Student services:* health clinic, personal/psychological counseling, women's center, legal services.

Athletics Member NCAA. All Division II. *Intercollegiate sports:* baseball M(s), basketball M(s)/W(s), cross-country running M(s), golf M/W, soccer M(s)/W(s), softball W(s), tennis M(s)/W(s), volleyball W(s), water polo W. *Intramural sports:* baseball M, basketball M/W, cheerleading M/W, crew M/W, cross-country running M, fencing M/W, lacrosse M/W, rock climbing M/W, soccer M/W, softball M/W, swimming and diving M/W, volleyball M/W.

Standardized Tests *Required:* SAT or ACT (for admission).

Costs (2011–12) *Tuition:* state resident $5472 full-time; nonresident $16,632 full-time. Full-time tuition and fees vary according to course load and degree

level. Part-time tuition and fees vary according to course load and degree level. *Required fees:* $1390 full-time. *Room and board:* $10,961. Room and board charges vary according to housing facility.

Financial Aid Of all full-time matriculated undergraduates who enrolled in 2011, 4,617 applied for aid, 3,670 were judged to have need, 264 had their need fully met. 102 Federal Work-Study jobs (averaging $2939). 620 state and other part-time jobs (averaging $2580). In 2011, 211 non-need-based awards were made. *Average percent of need met:* 63%. *Average financial aid package:* $10,617. *Average need-based loan:* $4308. *Average need-based gift aid:* $9971. *Average non-need-based aid:* $1621. *Average indebtedness upon graduation:* $18,659.

Applying *Options:* electronic application, early admission. *Application fee:* $55. *Required:* high school transcript. *Application deadlines:* rolling (freshmen), rolling (transfers). *Notification:* continuous (freshmen), continuous (transfers).

Freshman Application Contact Mr. Gustavo Flores, Director of Admissions, Sonoma State University, 1801 East Cotati Avenue, Rohnert Park, CA 94928-3609. *Phone:* 707-664-2778. *E-mail:* gustavo.flores@sonoma.edu. *Web site:* http://www.sonoma.edu/.

Southern California Institute of Architecture

Los Angeles, California

- **Independent** comprehensive, founded 1972
- **Urban** campus with easy access to Los Angeles
- **Coed**
- **Moderately difficult** entrance level

Faculty *Student/faculty ratio:* 15:1.

Academics *Calendar:* semesters. *Degrees:* certificates, bachelor's, master's, and doctoral.

Student Life *Campus security:* 24-hour emergency response devices and patrols.

Standardized Tests *Required:* SAT or ACT (for admission).

Costs (2011–12) *Tuition:* $30,250 full-time. Full-time tuition and fees vary according to course load. *Required fees:* $400 full-time.

Financial Aid *Of all full-time matriculated undergraduates who enrolled in 2005,* 173 applied for aid, 147 were judged to have need. *In 2005,* 12 non-need-based awards were made. *Average percent of need met:* 19. *Average financial aid package:* $11,946. *Average need-based loan:* $4589. *Average need-based gift aid:* $4271. *Average non-need-based aid:* $2239. *Average indebtedness upon graduation:* $33,000.

Applying *Options:* electronic application, deferred entrance. *Application fee:* $75. *Required:* essay or personal statement, high school transcript, 3 letters of recommendation, portfolio of creative visual work. *Required for some:* interview. *Recommended:* minimum 3.0 GPA.

Freshman Application Contact Mr. J.J. Jackman, Admissions Director, Southern California Institute of Architecture, 960 East Third Street, Los Angeles, CA 90013. *Phone:* 213-613-2200 Ext. 321. *Fax:* 213-613-2260. *E-mail:* jj@sciarc.edu. *Web site:* http://www.sciarc.edu/.

Southern California Institute of Technology

Anaheim, California

- **Proprietary** 4-year, founded 1987
- **Urban** campus with easy access to Anaheim, Los Angeles
- **Coed**

Academics *Degrees:* diplomas, associate, and bachelor's.

Standardized Tests *Required:* entrance exam (for admission).

Financial Aid *Of all full-time matriculated undergraduates who enrolled in 2010,* 8 Federal Work-Study jobs (averaging $2800).

Applying *Application fee:* $100. *Required:* interview. *Required for some:* high school transcript.

Freshman Application Contact Director of Admissions, Southern California Institute of Technology, 222 South Harbor Boulevard, Suite 200, Anaheim, CA 92805. *Phone:* 714-300-0300. *Fax:* 714-300-0311. *E-mail:* admissions@scitech.edu. *Web site:* http://www.scitech.edu.

Southern California Seminary

El Cajon, California

Freshman Application Contact Thomas Pittman, Director of Admissions, Southern California Seminary, 2075 East Madison Avenue, El Cajon, CA 92019. *Phone:* 888-389-7244. *E-mail:* thpittman@socalsem.edu. *Web site:* http://www.socalsem.edu/.

Stanford University

Stanford, California

- **Independent** university, founded 1891
- **Suburban** 8180-acre campus with easy access to San Francisco, San Jose
- **Endowment** $16.5 billion
- **Coed** 6,988 undergraduate students, 98% full-time, 48% women, 52% men
- **Most difficult** entrance level, 7% of applicants were admitted

Undergraduates 6,856 full-time, 132 part-time. Students come from 52 states and territories; 89 other countries; 53% are from out of state; 7% Black or African American, non-Hispanic/Latino; 17% Hispanic/Latino; 18% Asian, non-Hispanic/Latino; 0.5% Native Hawaiian or other Pacific Islander, non-Hispanic/Latino; 0.9% American Indian or Alaska Native, non-Hispanic/Latino; 12% Two or more races, non-Hispanic/Latino; 0.9% Race/ethnicity unknown; 8% international; 0.7% transferred in; 91% live on campus. *Retention:* 98% of full-time freshmen returned.

Freshmen *Admission:* 34,348 applied, 2,437 admitted, 1,704 enrolled. *Test scores:* SAT critical reading scores over 500: 100%; SAT math scores over 500: 100%; SAT writing scores over 500: 99%; ACT scores over 18: 100%; SAT critical reading scores over 600: 94%; SAT math scores over 600: 96%; SAT writing scores over 600: 95%; ACT scores over 24: 98%; SAT critical reading scores over 700: 62%; SAT math scores over 700: 72%; SAT writing scores over 700: 70%; ACT scores over 30: 83%.

Faculty *Total:* 1,452, 99% full-time, 99% with terminal degrees. *Student/faculty ratio:* 5:1.

Academics *Calendar:* quarters. *Degrees:* bachelor's, master's, doctoral, and first professional. *Special study options:* advanced placement credit, distance learning, double majors, English as a second language, honors programs, independent study, internships, off-campus study, services for LD students, student-designed majors, study abroad, summer session for credit. *ROTC:* Army (c), Navy (c), Air Force (c).

Computers on Campus 1,000 computers/terminals and 22,000 ports are available on campus for general student use. Students can access the following: campus intranet, computer help desk, free student e-mail accounts, online (class) grades, online (class) registration, online (class) schedules. Campus-wide network is available. 100% of college-owned or -operated housing units are wired for high-speed Internet access. Wireless service is available via entire campus.

Student Life *Housing:* on-campus residence required for freshman year. *Options:* coed, women-only, cooperative, disabled students. Campus housing is university owned. Freshman campus housing is guaranteed. *Activities and organizations:* drama/theater group, student-run newspaper, radio and television station, choral group, marching band, Ram's Head (theatre club), Axe Committee (athletic support), Business Association of Engineering Students, Asian-American Student Association, Stanford Daily, national fraternities, national sororities. *Campus security:* 24-hour emergency response devices and patrols, late-night transport/escort service, controlled dormitory access. *Student services:* health clinic, personal/psychological counseling, women's center, legal services.

Athletics Member NCAA, NAIA. All NCAA Division I. *Intercollegiate sports:* archery M(c)/W(c), baseball M(s), basketball M(s)/W(s), cheerleading M(c)/W(c), crew M(s)/W(s), cross-country running M(s)/W(s), equestrian sports M(c)/W(c), fencing M(s)/W(s), field hockey W(s), football M(s), golf M(s)/W(s), gymnastics M(s)/W(s), ice hockey M(c), lacrosse M(c)/W(c), racquetball M(c)/W(c), rugby M(c)/W(c), sailing M/W, skiing (downhill) M(c)/W(c), soccer M(s)/W(s), softball W(s), squash M(c)/W, swimming and diving M(s)/W(s), tennis M(s)/W(s), track and field M(s)/W(s), ultimate Frisbee M(c)/W(c), volleyball M(s)/W(s), water polo M(s)/W(s), wrestling M(s). *Intramural sports:* badminton M/W, baseball M, basketball M/W, bowling M/W, cross-country running M/W, field hockey W, football M/W, golf M/W, lacrosse W(c), soccer M(c)/W(c), softball M/W, table tennis M(c)/W(c), tennis M(c)/W(c), track and field M/W, volleyball M/W, water polo M/W.

Standardized Tests *Required:* SAT or ACT (for admission). *Recommended:* SAT Subject Tests (for admission).

Costs (2011–12) *Comprehensive fee:* $53,297 includes full-time tuition ($40,500), mandatory fees ($506), and room and board ($12,291). *Room and board:* Room and board charges vary according to board plan. *Waivers:* employees or children of employees.

Financial Aid Of all full-time matriculated undergraduates who enrolled in 2010, 3,916 applied for aid, 3,583 were judged to have need, 3,024 had their need fully met. 719 Federal Work-Study jobs (averaging $2242). 1,748 state and other part-time jobs (averaging $2058). In 2010, 507 non-need-based awards were made. *Average percent of need met:* 100%. *Average financial aid package:* $41,919. *Average need-based loan:* $2823. *Average need-based gift aid:* $39,105. *Average non-need-based aid:* $5701. *Average indebtedness upon graduation:* $16,458.

Applying *Options:* electronic application, early action, deferred entrance. *Application fee:* $90. *Required:* essay or personal statement, high school transcript, 2 letters of recommendation. *Application deadlines:* 1/1 (freshmen), 3/15 (transfers), 11/1 (early action). *Notification:* 4/1 (freshmen), 5/15 (transfers), 12/15 (early action).

Freshman Application Contact Rick Shaw, Dean of Undergraduate Admission and Financial Aid, Stanford University, Montag Hall, 355 Galvez Street, Stanford, CA 94305-3020. *Phone:* 650-723-2091. *Fax:* 650-725-2846. *E-mail:* admission@stanford.edu. *Web site:* http://www.stanford.edu/.

Thomas Aquinas College

Santa Paula, California

- **Independent Roman Catholic** 4-year, founded 1971
- **Rural** 131-acre campus with easy access to Los Angeles
- **Endowment** $13.4 million
- **Coed** 358 undergraduate students, 100% full-time, 51% women, 49% men
- **Very difficult** entrance level, 79% of applicants were admitted

Undergraduates 358 full-time. Students come from 39 states and territories; 6 other countries; 64% are from out of state; 13% Hispanic/Latino; 0.8% Asian, non-Hispanic/Latino; 0.3% American Indian or Alaska Native, non-Hispanic/Latino; 2% Two or more races, non-Hispanic/Latino; 6% Race/ethnicity unknown; 6% international; 100% live on campus. *Retention:* 90% of full-time freshmen returned.

Freshmen *Admission:* 171 applied, 135 admitted, 92 enrolled. *Average high school GPA:* 3.71. *Test scores:* SAT critical reading scores over 500: 98%; SAT math scores over 500: 96%; SAT writing scores over 500: 100%; ACT scores over 18: 100%; SAT critical reading scores over 600: 86%; SAT math scores over 600: 52%; SAT writing scores over 600: 70%; ACT scores over 24: 91%; SAT critical reading scores over 700: 35%; SAT math scores over 700: 11%; SAT writing scores over 700: 23%; ACT scores over 30: 23%.

Faculty *Total:* 37, 81% full-time, 70% with terminal degrees. *Student/faculty ratio:* 11:1.

Academics *Calendar:* semesters. *Degree:* bachelor's. *Special study options:* cooperative education.

Computers on Campus 20 computers/terminals and 24 ports are available on campus for general student use. Students can access the following: free student e-mail accounts. Campuswide network is available.

Student Life *Housing:* on-campus residence required through senior year. *Options:* men-only, women-only. Campus housing is university owned. Freshman campus housing is guaranteed. *Activities and organizations:* drama/theater group, choral group, Musical Groups (Choir, Chamber Orchestra), Theatre Groups, Language Clubs, Pro-Life Ministry, religious groups. *Campus security:* daily security patrol. *Student services:* personal/psychological counseling.

Athletics *Intramural sports:* basketball M/W, football M, soccer M/W, softball M/W, table tennis M/W, tennis M/W, ultimate Frisbee M/W, volleyball M/W.

Standardized Tests *Required:* SAT or ACT (for admission).

Costs (2012–13) *Comprehensive fee:* $31,400 includes full-time tuition ($23,600) and room and board ($7800). *Payment plan:* installment.

Financial Aid Of all full-time matriculated undergraduates who enrolled in 2011, 280 applied for aid, 277 were judged to have need, 277 had their need fully met. 248 state and other part-time jobs (averaging $3848). *Average percent of need met:* 100%. *Average financial aid package:* $20,081. *Average need-based loan:* $3852. *Average need-based gift aid:* $14,407. *Average indebtedness upon graduation:* $16,582. *Financial aid deadline:* 3/2.

Applying *Options:* electronic application, deferred entrance. *Required:* essay or personal statement, high school transcript, 3 letters of recommendation. *Required for some:* interview. *Recommended:* minimum 3.0 GPA. *Application deadlines:* rolling (freshmen), rolling (out-of-state freshmen). *Notification:* continuous (freshmen), continuous (out-of-state freshmen).

Freshman Application Contact Mr. Jonathan P. Daly, Director of Admissions, Thomas Aquinas College, 10000 Ojai Road, Santa Paula, CA 93060-9621. *Phone:* 805-525-4417 Ext. 5901. *Toll-free phone:* 800-634-9797. *Fax:* 805-421-5905. *E-mail:* admissions@thomasaquinas.edu. *Web site:* http://www.thomasaquinas.edu/.

Trident University International

Cypress, California

- **Independent** university
- **Urban** campus
- **Coed** 2,857 undergraduate students, 56% full-time, 33% women, 67% men
- **Minimally difficult** entrance level

Undergraduates 1,590 full-time, 1,267 part-time. Students come from 50 states and territories; 15 other countries; 88% are from out of state; 13% Black or African American, non-Hispanic/Latino; 5% Hispanic/Latino; 3% Asian, non-Hispanic/Latino; 0.7% Native Hawaiian or other Pacific Islander, non-Hispanic/Latino; 0.5% American Indian or Alaska Native, non-Hispanic/Latino; 59% Race/ethnicity unknown; 0.1% international; 85% transferred in. **Freshmen** *Admission:* 302 enrolled.

Faculty *Total:* 479, 14% full-time. *Student/faculty ratio:* 17:1.

Academics *Calendar:* four 12 week sessions per year. *Degrees:* certificates, diplomas, bachelor's, master's, doctoral, post-master's, postbachelor's, and first professional certificates (offers only online degree programs). *Special study options:* adult/continuing education programs, distance learning, double majors, honors programs, part-time degree program, summer session for credit.

Computers on Campus Students can access the following: computer help desk, free student e-mail accounts, online (class) grades, online (class) registration, online (class) schedules. Campuswide network is available.

Student Life *Housing:* college housing not available.

Costs (2011–12) *Tuition:* $9440 full-time, $295 per semester hour part-time. Full-time tuition and fees vary according to course load, degree level, and program. Part-time tuition and fees vary according to course load, degree level, and program. *Payment plans:* installment, deferred payment. *Waivers:* employees or children of employees.

Financial Aid Of all full-time matriculated undergraduates who enrolled in 2009, 650 applied for aid, 650 were judged to have need, 552 had their need fully met. In 2009, 55 non-need-based awards were made. *Average percent of need met:* 98%. *Average financial aid package:* $4415. *Average need-based gift aid:* $3293. *Average non-need-based aid:* $5898. *Average indebtedness upon graduation:* $38,298.

Applying *Options:* electronic application. *Required:* high school transcript, minimum 3.0 GPA. *Required for some:* essay or personal statement. *Application deadlines:* rolling (freshmen), rolling (out-of-state freshmen), rolling (transfers). *Notification:* continuous (freshmen), continuous (out-of-state freshmen), continuous (transfers).

Freshman Application Contact Trident University International, 5757 Plaza Drive, Suite 100, Cypress, CA 90630. *Phone:* 714-816-0366 Ext. 2015. *Web site:* http://www.trident.edu/.

United States University

Chula Vista, California

Freshman Application Contact Admissions, United States University, 830 Bay Boulevard, Chula Vista, CA 91911. *Phone:* 619-477-6310. *Toll-free phone:* 888-422-3381. *Fax:* 619-477-7340. *Web site:* http://www.usuniversity.edu/sd/.

United States University

Cypress, California

Freshman Application Contact Admissions, United States University, 6251 Katella Avenue, Cypress, CA 90630. *Phone:* 714-252-8592. *Toll-free phone:* 888-422-3381. *Web site:* http://www.usuniversity.edu/oc/.

University of California, Berkeley

Berkeley, California

- **State-supported** university, founded 1868, part of University of California
- **Urban** 1232-acre campus with easy access to San Francisco
- **Endowment** $3.1 billion
- **Coed** 25,885 undergraduate students
- 22% of applicants were admitted

Undergraduates 10% are from out of state; 3% Black or African American, non-Hispanic/Latino; 12% Hispanic/Latino; 39% Asian, non-Hispanic/Latino; 0.2% Native Hawaiian or other Pacific Islander, non-Hispanic/Latino; 0.7% American Indian or Alaska Native, non-Hispanic/Latino; 6% Race/ethnicity unknown; 9% international; 26% live on campus. *Retention:* 97% of full-time freshmen returned.

Freshmen *Admission:* 52,786 applied, 11,440 admitted. *Average high school GPA:* 3.83. *Test scores:* SAT critical reading scores over 500: 95%; SAT math scores over 500: 97%; SAT writing scores over 500: 96%; ACT scores over 18: 100%; SAT critical reading scores over 600: 78%; SAT math scores over 600: 87%; SAT writing scores over 600: 83%; ACT scores over 24: 92%; SAT critical reading scores over 700: 36%; SAT math scores over 700: 58%; SAT writing scores over 700: 46%; ACT scores over 30: 62%.

Academics *Calendar:* semesters. *Degrees:* bachelor's, master's, doctoral, and first professional. *Special study options:* accelerated degree program, adult/continuing education programs, advanced placement credit, double majors, English as a second language, honors programs, independent study, internships, off-campus study, services for LD students, student-designed majors, study abroad, summer session for credit. *ROTC:* Army (b), Navy (b), Air Force (b).

Computers on Campus Students can access the following: computer help desk, free student e-mail accounts, online (class) grades, online (class) registration, online (class) schedules. Campuswide network is available. Wireless service is available via classrooms, computer centers, computer labs, dorm rooms, learning centers, libraries, student centers.

Student Life *Housing options:* coed, men-only, women-only, cooperative, disabled students. Campus housing is university owned and is provided by a third party. Freshman campus housing is guaranteed. *Activities and organizations:* drama/theater group, student-run newspaper, radio and television station, choral group, marching band, national fraternities, national sororities. *Campus security:* 24-hour emergency response devices and patrols, late-night transport/escort service, controlled dormitory access, Office of Emergency Preparedness. *Student services:* health clinic, personal/psychological counseling, women's center, legal services.

Athletics Member NCAA. All Division I. *Intercollegiate sports:* baseball M, basketball M/W, crew M/W, cross-country running M/W, field hockey W, football M, golf M/W, gymnastics M/W, lacrosse M/W, rugby M, soccer M/W, softball W, swimming and diving M/W, tennis M/W, track and field M/W, volleyball W, water polo M/W. *Intramural sports:* basketball M/W, soccer M/W, softball M/W, tennis M/W, ultimate Frisbee M/W, volleyball M/W.

Standardized Tests *Required:* SAT or ACT (for admission). *Recommended:* SAT Subject Tests (for admission).

Costs (2011–12) *Tuition:* state resident $11,220 full-time; nonresident $34,098 full-time. *Required fees:* $1615 full-time. *Room and board:* $14,990. Room and board charges vary according to board plan and housing facility. *Payment plan:* installment.

Financial Aid Of all full-time matriculated undergraduates who enrolled in 2011, 17,065 applied for aid, 14,421 were judged to have need, 2,762 had their need fully met. In 2011, 1225 non-need-based awards were made. *Average percent of need met:* 83%. *Average financial aid package:* $20,471. *Average need-based loan:* $4329. *Average need-based gift aid:* $16,214. *Average non-need-based aid:* $8371. *Average indebtedness upon graduation:* $17,116. *Financial aid deadline:* 3/2.

Applying *Options:* electronic application. *Application fee:* $70. *Required:* essay or personal statement. *Application deadlines:* 11/30 (freshmen), 11/30 (transfers). *Notification:* 3/31 (freshmen), 4/30 (transfers).

Freshman Application Contact University of California, Berkeley, Berkeley, CA 94720-1500. *Web site:* http://www.berkeley.edu/.

University of California, Davis
Davis, California

- **State-supported** university, founded 1905, part of University of California System
- **Suburban** 5993-acre campus with easy access to San Francisco
- **Coed** 25,096 undergraduate students, 99% full-time, 55% women, 45% men
- **Very difficult** entrance level, 46% of applicants were admitted

Undergraduates 24,787 full-time, 309 part-time. Students come from 49 states and territories; 105 other countries; 2% are from out of state; 2% Black or African American, non-Hispanic/Latino; 16% Hispanic/Latino; 37% Asian, non-Hispanic/Latino; 0.5% Native Hawaiian or other Pacific Islander, non-Hispanic/Latino; 0.4% American Indian or Alaska Native, non-Hispanic/Latino; 3% Two or more races, non-Hispanic/Latino; 4% Race/ethnicity unknown; 3% international; 11% transferred in; 25% live on campus. *Retention:* 93% of full-time freshmen returned.

Freshmen *Admission:* 45,806 applied, 21,085 admitted, 4,705 enrolled. *Average high school GPA:* 3.9. *Test scores:* SAT critical reading scores over 500: 83%; SAT math scores over 500: 92%; SAT writing scores over 500: 86%; ACT scores over 18: 92%; SAT critical reading scores over 600: 49%; SAT math scores over 600: 69%; SAT writing scores over 600: 54%; ACT scores over 24: 79%; SAT critical reading scores over 700: 12%; SAT math scores over 700: 25%; SAT writing scores over 700: 16%; ACT scores over 30: 31%.

Faculty *Total:* 1,620, 91% full-time, 98% with terminal degrees. *Student/faculty ratio:* 15:1.

Academics *Calendar:* quarters. *Degrees:* bachelor's, master's, doctoral, postmaster's, postbachelor's, and first professional certificates. *Special study options:* academic remediation for entering students, adult/continuing education programs, advanced placement credit, double majors, English as a second language, freshman honors college, honors programs, independent study, internships, part-time degree program, services for LD students, student-designed majors, study abroad, summer session for credit. *ROTC:* Army (b), Navy (c), Air Force (c).

Computers on Campus 1,500 computers/terminals and 550 ports are available on campus for general student use. Students can access the following: campus intranet, computer help desk, free student e-mail accounts, online (class) grades, online (class) registration, online (class) schedules, software packages. Campuswide network is available. 100% of college-owned or -operated housing units are wired for high-speed Internet access. Wireless service is available via classrooms, libraries.

Student Life *Housing options:* coed, women-only, cooperative, disabled students. Campus housing is university owned, leased by the school and is provided by a third party. Freshman campus housing is guaranteed. *Activities and organizations:* drama/theater group, student-run newspaper, radio and television station, choral group, marching band, Filipino Student Organization, Vietnamese Student Association, Jewish Student Union, Alpha Phi Omega, national fraternities, national sororities. *Campus security:* 24-hour emergency response devices and patrols, student patrols, late-night transport/escort service, controlled dormitory access, Campus Violence Prevention Program (CVPP). *Student services:* health clinic, personal/psychological counseling, women's center, legal services.

Athletics Member NCAA. All Division I except football (Division I-AA). *Intercollegiate sports:* baseball M(s), basketball M(s)/W(s), cross-country running M(s)/W(s), field hockey W(s), golf M(s)/W(s), gymnastics W(s), lacrosse W(s), soccer M(s)/W(s), softball W(s), swimming and diving W(s), tennis M(s)/W(s), track and field M(s)/W(s), volleyball W(s), water polo M(s)/W(s). *Intramural sports:* archery M(c)/W(c), badminton M(c)/W(c), basketball M/W, crew M(c)/W(c), equestrian sports M(c)/W(c), fencing M(c)/W(c), football M/W, golf M/W, gymnastics M(c), ice hockey M(c)/W, lacrosse M(c)/W(c), racquetball M(c)/W(c), riflery M(c)/W(c), rugby M(c), sailing M(c)/W(c), skiing (cross-country) M(c)/W(c), skiing (downhill) M(c)/W(c), soccer M/W, softball M/W, swimming and diving W(c), table tennis M/W, tennis M/W, volleyball M(c)/W, water polo W(c).

Standardized Tests *Required:* SAT or ACT (for admission), SAT Subject Tests (for admission).

Costs (2011–12) *Tuition:* state resident $11,220 full-time; nonresident $34,098 full-time. Fees do not include Health Insurance Fee of $1,263 which can be waived with proof of insurance. *Required fees:* $2640 full-time. *Room and board:* $12,697. Room and board charges vary according to board plan. *Payment plan:* deferred payment.

Financial Aid Of all full-time matriculated undergraduates who enrolled in 2011, 18,170 applied for aid, 15,893 were judged to have need, 2,667 had their need fully met. In 2011, 905 non-need-based awards were made. *Average percent of need met:* 82%. *Average financial aid package:* $19,538. *Average need-based loan:* $5480. *Average need-based gift aid:* $16,072. *Average non-need-based aid:* $5855. *Average indebtedness upon graduation:* $18,386.

Applying *Options:* electronic application. *Application fee:* $70. *Required:* essay or personal statement, high school transcript, minimum 2.8 GPA, high school subject requirements. *Application deadlines:* 11/30 (freshmen), 11/30 (transfers). *Notification:* 3/15 (freshmen), continuous until 3/15 (transfers).

Freshman Application Contact University of California, Davis, CA. *E-mail:* undergraduateadmissions@ucdavis.edu. *Web site:* http://www.ucdavis.edu/.

University of California, Irvine
Irvine, California

- **State-supported** university, founded 1965, part of University of California System
- **Suburban** 1477-acre campus with easy access to Los Angeles
- **Coed** 22,004 undergraduate students, 98% full-time, 54% women, 46% men
- **Very difficult** entrance level, 47% of applicants were admitted

Undergraduates 21,603 full-time, 401 part-time. Students come from 39 states and territories; 69 other countries; 1% are from out of state; 2% Black or African American, non-Hispanic/Latino; 18% Hispanic/Latino; 49% Asian, non-Hispanic/Latino; 0.1% Native Hawaiian or other Pacific Islander, non-Hispanic/Latino; 0.2% American Indian or Alaska Native, non-Hispanic/Latino; 3% Two or more races, non-Hispanic/Latino; 4% Race/ethnicity unknown; 4% international; 8% transferred in; 45% live on campus. *Retention:* 94% of full-time freshmen returned.

Freshmen *Admission:* 49,287 applied, 23,391 admitted, 5,115 enrolled. *Average high school GPA:* 3.87. *Test scores:* SAT critical reading scores over 500: 77%; SAT math scores over 500: 89%; SAT writing scores over 500: 80%; SAT critical reading scores over 600: 38%; SAT math scores over 600: 62%; SAT writing scores over 600: 42%; SAT critical reading scores over 700: 9%; SAT math scores over 700: 21%; SAT writing scores over 700: 9%.
Faculty *Total:* 1,923, 76% full-time, 98% with terminal degrees. *Student/faculty ratio:* 19:1.
Academics *Calendar:* quarters. *Degrees:* bachelor's, master's, doctoral, post-bachelor's, and first professional certificates. *Special study options:* accelerated degree program, advanced placement credit, distance learning, double majors, English as a second language, honors programs, independent study, internships, off-campus study, services for LD students, study abroad, summer session for credit. *ROTC:* Army (b), Air Force (c).
Computers on Campus 1,500 computers/terminals are available on campus for general student use. Students can access the following: campus intranet, computer help desk, free student e-mail accounts, online (class) grades, online (class) registration, online (class) schedules. Campuswide network is available. Wireless service is available via entire campus.
Student Life *Housing options:* coed, men-only, women-only, disabled students. Campus housing is university owned and is provided by a third party. Freshman campus housing is guaranteed. *Activities and organizations:* drama/theater group, student-run newspaper, radio station, choral group, national fraternities, national sororities. *Campus security:* 24-hour emergency response devices and patrols, student patrols, late-night transport/escort service, controlled dormitory access. *Student services:* health clinic, personal/psychological counseling.
Athletics Member NCAA. All Division I. *Intercollegiate sports:* baseball M(s), basketball M(s)/W(s), cross-country running M(s)/W(s), golf M(s)/W(s), soccer M(s)/W(s), tennis M(s)/W(s), track and field M(s)/W(s), volleyball M(s)/W(s), water polo M(s)/W(s). *Intramural sports:* archery M(c)/W(c), badminton M/W, basketball M/W, crew M(c)/W(c), equestrian sports M(c)/W(c), fencing M(c)/W(c), golf M(c)/W(c), ice hockey M(c), lacrosse M(c)/W(c), racquetball M/W, rugby M(c)/W(c), sailing M(c)/W(c), skiing (downhill) M(c)/W(c), soccer M/W, softball M/W, swimming and diving M/W, table tennis M/W, tennis M/W, track and field M/W, ultimate Frisbee M/W, volleyball M/W, water polo M/W, wrestling M/W.
Standardized Tests *Required:* SAT or ACT (for admission). *Recommended:* SAT Subject Tests (for admission).
Costs (2012–13) *Tuition:* state resident $11,220 full-time; nonresident $34,098 full-time. *Required fees:* $2870 full-time. *Room and board:* $11,611. Room and board charges vary according to board plan and housing facility. *Payment plan:* installment. *Waivers:* employees or children of employees.
Financial Aid Of all full-time matriculated undergraduates who enrolled in 2011, 16,562 applied for aid, 14,256 were judged to have need, 4,740 had their need fully met. 2,439 Federal Work-Study jobs (averaging $1486). 1,842 state and other part-time jobs (averaging $1716). In 2011, 479 non-need-based awards were made. *Average percent of need met:* 85%. *Average financial aid package:* $19,671. *Average need-based loan:* $6463. *Average need-based gift aid:* $15,869. *Average non-need-based aid:* $9656. *Average indebtedness upon graduation:* $18,719. *Financial aid deadline:* 5/2.
Applying *Options:* electronic application. *Application fee:* $70. *Required:* essay or personal statement, high school transcript. *Application deadlines:* 11/30 (freshmen), 11/30 (transfers). *Notification:* 3/31 (freshmen), 4/30 (transfers).
Freshman Application Contact University of California, Irvine, Irvine, CA 92697. *Phone:* 949-824-6703. *E-mail:* admissions@uci.edu. *Web site:* http://www.uci.edu/.

University of California, Los Angeles
Los Angeles, California

- **State-supported** university, founded 1919, part of University of California System
- **Urban** 419-acre campus with easy access to Los Angeles
- **Coed** 27,199 undergraduate students, 97% full-time, 55% women, 45% men
- **Very difficult** entrance level, 25% of applicants were admitted

Undergraduates 26,476 full-time, 723 part-time. Students come from 50 states and territories; 116 other countries; 5% are from out of state; 3% Black or African American, non-Hispanic/Latino; 17% Hispanic/Latino; 34% Asian, non-Hispanic/Latino; 0.3% Native Hawaiian or other Pacific Islander, non-Hispanic/Latino; 0.2% American Indian or Alaska Native, non-Hispanic/Latino; 3% Two or more races, non-Hispanic/Latino; 3% Race/ethnicity unknown; 7% international; 11% transferred in; 45% live on campus. *Retention:* 97% of full-time freshmen returned.
Freshmen *Admission:* 61,564 applied, 15,689 admitted, 5,825 enrolled. *Average high school GPA:* 4.22. *Test scores:* SAT critical reading scores over 500:

91%; SAT math scores over 500: 95%; SAT writing scores over 500: 94%; ACT scores over 18: 99%; SAT critical reading scores over 600: 64%; SAT math scores over 600: 79%; SAT writing scores over 600: 74%; ACT scores over 24: 82%; SAT critical reading scores over 700: 22%; SAT math scores over 700: 44%; SAT writing scores over 700: 30%; ACT scores over 30: 41%.
Faculty *Total:* 2,577, 78% full-time, 98% with terminal degrees. *Student/faculty ratio:* 16:1.
Academics *Calendar:* quarters. *Degrees:* bachelor's, master's, doctoral, and first professional. *Special study options:* accelerated degree program, advanced placement credit, distance learning, double majors, freshman honors college, honors programs, independent study, internships, off-campus study, services for LD students, student-designed majors, study abroad, summer session for credit. *ROTC:* Army (b), Navy (b), Air Force (b).
Computers on Campus 3,930 computers/terminals are available on campus for general student use. Students can access the following: campus intranet, computer help desk, free student e-mail accounts, online (class) grades, online (class) registration, online (class) schedules. Campuswide network is available. 100% of college-owned or -operated housing units are wired for high-speed Internet access. Wireless service is available via entire campus.
Student Life *Housing options:* coed, disabled students. Campus housing is university owned. Freshman campus housing is guaranteed. *Activities and organizations:* drama/theater group, student-run newspaper, radio and television station, choral group, marching band, national fraternities, national sororities. *Campus security:* 24-hour emergency response devices and patrols, student patrols, late-night transport/escort service, controlled dormitory access. *Student services:* health clinic, personal/psychological counseling, women's center, legal services.
Athletics Member NCAA. All Division I except football (Division I-A). *Intercollegiate sports:* baseball M(s), basketball M(s)/W(s), crew W(s), cross-country running M(s)/W(s), golf M(s)/W(s), gymnastics W(s), soccer M(s)/W(s), softball W(s), swimming and diving W(s), tennis M(s)/W(s), track and field M(s)/W(s), volleyball M(s)/W(s), water polo M(s)/W(s). *Intramural sports:* archery M/W, badminton M/W, basketball M/W, bowling M/W, crew M/W, cross-country running M/W, fencing M/W, field hockey W, football M/W, golf M/W, gymnastics M/W, ice hockey M/W, lacrosse M/W, racquetball M/W, riflery M/W, rugby M/W, sailing M/W, skiing (cross-country) M/W, skiing (downhill) M/W, soccer M/W, softball M/W, squash M/W, swimming and diving M/W, table tennis M/W, tennis M/W, track and field M/W, ultimate Frisbee M/W, volleyball M/W, water polo M/W.
Standardized Tests *Required:* SAT or ACT (for admission).
Costs (2011–12) *Tuition:* state resident $11,220 full-time; nonresident $34,098 full-time. *Required fees:* $2690 full-time. *Room and board:* $13,979. Room and board charges vary according to board plan and housing facility.
Financial Aid Of all full-time matriculated undergraduates who enrolled in 2011, 16,196 applied for aid, 14,846 were judged to have need, 3,955 had their need fully met. 2,388 Federal Work-Study jobs (averaging $1969). 1,022 state and other part-time jobs (averaging $1203). In 2011, 924 non-need-based awards were made. *Average percent of need met:* 84%. *Average financial aid package:* $20,362. *Average need-based loan:* $6606. *Average need-based gift aid:* $16,659. *Average non-need-based aid:* $5736. *Average indebtedness upon graduation:* $18,814.
Applying *Options:* electronic application. *Application fee:* $70. *Required:* essay or personal statement, high school transcript. *Application deadlines:* 11/30 (freshmen), 11/30 (out-of-state freshmen), 11/30 (transfers). *Notification:* 3/31 (freshmen), 3/31 (out-of-state freshmen), 4/30 (transfers).
Freshman Application Contact Sue Wilbur, Director of Undergraduate Admissions, University of California, Los Angeles, 405 Hilgard Avenue, Box 951436, Los Angeles, CA 90095-1436. *Phone:* 310-825-3101. *E-mail:* ugadm@saonet.ucla.edu. *Web site:* http://www.ucla.edu/.

University of California, Merced
Merced, California

- **State-supported** university, part of University of California System
- **Small-town** 815-acre campus with easy access to Fresno
- **Endowment** $27.6 million
- **Coed** 4,938 undergraduate students, 99% full-time, 50% women, 50% men
- **Moderately difficult** entrance level, 80% of applicants were admitted

Undergraduates 4,901 full-time, 37 part-time. Students come from 20 states and territories; 14 other countries; 1% are from out of state; 7% Black or African American, non-Hispanic/Latino; 37% Hispanic/Latino; 29% Asian, non-Hispanic/Latino; 0.7% Native Hawaiian or other Pacific Islander, non-Hispanic/Latino; 0.3% American Indian or Alaska Native, non-Hispanic/Latino; 3% Two or more races, non-Hispanic/Latino; 3% Race/ethnicity unknown; 1% international; 4% transferred in; 32% live on campus. *Retention:* 85% of full-time freshmen returned.

Freshmen *Admission:* 15,135 applied, 12,108 admitted, 1,444 enrolled. *Average high school GPA:* 3.44. *Test scores:* SAT critical reading scores over 500: 47%; SAT math scores over 500: 60%; SAT writing scores over 500: 48%; SAT critical reading scores over 600: 13%; SAT math scores over 600: 22%; SAT writing scores over 600: 12%; SAT critical reading scores over 700: 2%; SAT math scores over 700: 4%; SAT writing scores over 700: 2%.
Faculty *Total:* 264, 83% full-time, 72% with terminal degrees. *Student/faculty ratio:* 21:1.
Academics *Degrees:* bachelor's, master's, doctoral, and first professional. *Special study options:* academic remediation for entering students, advanced placement credit, double majors, internships, off-campus study, part-time degree program, services for LD students, study abroad, summer session for credit.
Computers on Campus 220 computers/terminals are available on campus for general student use. Students can access the following: campus intranet, computer help desk, free student e-mail accounts, online (class) grades, online (class) registration, online (class) schedules. Campuswide network is available. 100% of college-owned or -operated housing units are wired for high-speed Internet access. Wireless service is available via entire campus.
Student Life *Housing options:* coed, disabled students. Campus housing is university owned. Freshman campus housing is guaranteed. *Activities and organizations:* student-run newspaper, radio station, choral group, marching band, Philipino American Alliance, Vietnamese Student Association, Intervarsity Christian Fellowship, Latino Associated Students, Hip Hop Movement, national fraternities, national sororities. *Campus security:* 24-hour emergency response devices and patrols, student patrols, late-night transport/escort service, controlled dormitory access. *Student services:* health clinic, personal/psychological counseling, women's center, legal services.
Athletics Member NAIA. *Intercollegiate sports:* basketball M(s)/W(s), cross-country running M(s)/W(s), soccer W(s), volleyball W(s). *Intramural sports:* archery M/W, badminton M/W, basketball M/W, cheerleading M/W, lacrosse M, soccer M/W, softball M/W, ultimate Frisbee M/W, volleyball M/W.
Standardized Tests *Required:* SAT or ACT (for admission).
Costs (2011–12) *Tuition:* state resident $9402 full-time, $4701 per year part-time; nonresident $32,280 full-time, $16,140 per year part-time. *Required fees:* $728 full-time. *Room and board:* $12,801.
Financial Aid Of all full-time matriculated undergraduates who enrolled in 2011, 4,390 applied for aid, 4,040 were judged to have need, 1,544 had their need fully met. In 2011, 82 non-need-based awards were made. *Average percent of need met:* 88%. *Average financial aid package:* $20,921. *Average need-based loan:* $5268. *Average need-based gift aid:* $16,550. *Average non-need-based aid:* $11,190. *Average indebtedness upon graduation:* $16,982.
Applying *Options:* electronic application. *Application fee:* $70. *Required:* essay or personal statement, high school transcript, minimum 3.0 high school GPA for California residents. *Application deadlines:* 10/30 (freshmen), 11/30 (transfers). *Notification:* 3/1 (freshmen), 4/30 (transfers).
Freshman Application Contact Ms. Susan Fauroat, Associate Director of Admissions and Outreach, University of California, Merced, 5200 North Lake Road, Merced, CA 95343. *Phone:* 209-228-4241. *E-mail:* admissions@ucmerced.edu. *Web site:* http://www.ucmerced.edu/.

University of California, Riverside
Riverside, California

- **State-supported** university, founded 1954, part of University of California System
- **Urban** 1200-acre campus with easy access to Los Angeles
- **Endowment** $140.5 million
- **Coed** 18,523 undergraduate students, 97% full-time, 52% women, 48% men
- **Very difficult** entrance level, 69% of applicants were admitted

Undergraduates 18,028 full-time, 495 part-time. Students come from 29 states and territories; 61 other countries; 0.5% are from out of state; 6% Black or African American, non-Hispanic/Latino; 34% Hispanic/Latino; 37% Asian, non-Hispanic/Latino; 0.4% Native Hawaiian or other Pacific Islander, non-Hispanic/Latino; 0.3% American Indian or Alaska Native, non-Hispanic/Latino; 1% Two or more races, non-Hispanic/Latino; 3% Race/ethnicity unknown; 2% international; 8% transferred in; 31% live on campus. *Retention:* 87% of full-time freshmen returned.
Freshmen *Admission:* 28,101 applied, 19,389 admitted, 3,664 enrolled. *Average high school GPA:* 3.56. *Test scores:* SAT critical reading scores over 500: 60%; SAT math scores over 500: 72%; SAT writing scores over 500: 63%; ACT scores over 18: 88%; SAT critical reading scores over 600: 19%; SAT math scores over 600: 36%; SAT writing scores over 600: 21%; ACT scores over 24: 36%; SAT critical reading scores over 700: 2%; SAT math scores over 700: 7%; SAT writing scores over 700: 2%; ACT scores over 30: 4%.
Faculty *Total:* 882, 85% full-time, 98% with terminal degrees. *Student/faculty ratio:* 21:1.

Academics *Calendar:* quarters. *Degrees:* bachelor's, master's, doctoral, post-bachelor's, and first professional certificates. *Special study options:* accelerated degree program, adult/continuing education programs, advanced placement credit, distance learning, double majors, honors programs, independent study, internships, off-campus study, services for LD students, study abroad, summer session for credit. *ROTC:* Army (c), Air Force (c). *Unusual degree programs:* 3-2 engineering with five-year joint BS/MS programs in chemical and environmental engineering, computer science and engineering, electrical engineering, mechanical engineering.
Computers on Campus 556 computers/terminals are available on campus for general student use. Students can access the following: campus intranet, computer help desk, free student e-mail accounts, online (class) grades, online (class) registration, online (class) schedules, online viewing of financial information. Campuswide network is available. 100% of college-owned or -operated housing units are wired for high-speed Internet access. Wireless service is available via entire campus.
Student Life *Housing options:* coed. Campus housing is university owned and is provided by a third party. Freshman campus housing is guaranteed. *Activities and organizations:* drama/theater group, student-run newspaper, radio station, choral group, Associated Students, Student Alumni Association, Health Careers Organization, national fraternities, national sororities. *Campus security:* 24-hour emergency response devices and patrols, student patrols, late-night transport/escort service, controlled dormitory access. *Student services:* health clinic, personal/psychological counseling, women's center, legal services.
Athletics Member NCAA. All Division I. *Intercollegiate sports:* baseball M(s), basketball M(s)/W(s), cross-country running M(s)/W(s), golf M(s)/W(s), soccer M(s)/W(s), softball W(s), tennis M(s)/W(s), track and field M(s)/W(s), volleyball W(s). *Intramural sports:* badminton M/W, baseball M, basketball M/W, football M/W, golf M/W, soccer M/W, softball W, table tennis M(c)/W(c), tennis M/W, volleyball W.
Standardized Tests *Required:* SAT or ACT (for admission). *Recommended:* SAT Subject Tests (for admission).
Costs (2012–13) *Tuition:* state resident $13,607 full-time; nonresident $36,485 full-time. Full-time tuition and fees vary according to course load. Part-time tuition and fees vary according to course load. *Required fees:* $1703 full-time. *Room and board:* $12,100. Room and board charges vary according to board plan and housing facility. *Payment plan:* deferred payment.
Financial Aid Of all full-time matriculated undergraduates who enrolled in 2010, 14,753 applied for aid, 13,381 were judged to have need, 4,575 had their need fully met. 3,839 Federal Work-Study jobs (averaging $2063). In 2010, 105 non-need-based awards were made. *Average percent of need met:* 85%. *Average financial aid package:* $19,431. *Average need-based loan:* $6182. *Average need-based gift aid:* $15,329. *Average non-need-based aid:* $6901. *Average indebtedness upon graduation:* $18,094. *Financial aid deadline:* 3/2.
Applying *Options:* electronic application. *Application fee:* $70. *Required:* essay or personal statement, high school transcript, minimum 3.0 GPA. *Application deadlines:* 11/30 (freshmen), 11/30 (transfers). *Notification:* continuous until 3/1 (freshmen), continuous until 5/1 (transfers).
Freshman Application Contact Emily Engelschall, Director, Undergraduate Recruitment, University of California, Riverside, 3221 Student Services, 900 University Avenue, Riverside, CA 92521. *Phone:* 951-827-5307. *Fax:* 951-827-6346. *E-mail:* discover@ucr.edu. *Web site:* http://www.ucr.edu/.

University of California, San Diego
La Jolla, California

Freshman Application Contact Ms. Mae Brown, Assistant Vice Chancellor, Admissions and Relations with Schools, University of California, San Diego, 9500 Gilman Drive, 0021, La Jolla, CA 92093-0021. *Phone:* 858-534-4831. *E-mail:* admissionsreply@ucsd.edu. *Web site:* http://www.ucsd.edu/.

University of California, Santa Barbara
Santa Barbara, California

- **State-supported** university, founded 1909, part of University of California System
- **Suburban** 989-acre campus
- **Endowment** $116.0 million
- **Coed** 18,620 undergraduate students, 98% full-time, 52% women, 48% men
- **Very difficult** entrance level, 46% of applicants were admitted

Undergraduates 18,318 full-time, 302 part-time. Students come from 50 states and territories; 95 other countries; 4% are from out of state; 0.4% Black or African American, non-Hispanic/Latino; 24% Hispanic/Latino; 20% Asian, non-Hispanic/Latino; 0.2% Native Hawaiian or other Pacific Islander, non-

Hispanic/Latino; 0.1% American Indian or Alaska Native, non-Hispanic/Latino; 5% Race/ethnicity unknown; 2% international; 8% transferred in; 33% live on campus. *Retention:* 92% of full-time freshmen returned.

Freshmen *Admission:* 49,008 applied, 22,379 admitted, 4,093 enrolled. *Average high school GPA:* 3.91. *Test scores:* SAT critical reading scores over 500: 89%; SAT math scores over 500: 93%; SAT writing scores over 500: 92%; ACT scores over 18: 98%; SAT critical reading scores over 600: 57%; SAT math scores over 600: 67%; SAT writing scores over 600: 61%; ACT scores over 24: 77%; SAT critical reading scores over 700: 15%; SAT math scores over 700: 22%; SAT writing scores over 700: 17%; ACT scores over 30: 26%.

Faculty *Total:* 1,052, 84% full-time, 100% with terminal degrees. *Student/faculty ratio:* 17:1.

Academics *Calendar:* quarters plus 6-week summer term. *Degrees:* bachelor's, master's, doctoral, post-master's, postbachelor's, and first professional certificates. *Special study options:* accelerated degree program, advanced placement credit, cooperative education, double majors, English as a second language, honors programs, independent study, internships, off-campus study, services for LD students, student-designed majors, study abroad, summer session for credit. *ROTC:* Army (b).

Computers on Campus 700 computers/terminals are available on campus for general student use. Students can access the following: computer help desk, free student e-mail accounts, online (class) grades, online (class) registration, online (class) schedules. Campuswide network is available. 100% of college-owned or -operated housing units are wired for high-speed Internet access. Wireless service is available via classrooms, computer labs, dorm rooms, libraries, student centers.

Student Life *Housing:* on-campus residence required for freshman year. *Options:* coed, cooperative. Campus housing is university owned and is provided by a third party. Freshman applicants given priority for college housing. *Activities and organizations:* drama/theater group, student-run newspaper, radio and television station, choral group, national fraternities, national sororities. *Campus security:* 24-hour emergency response devices, late-night transport/escort service. *Student services:* health clinic, personal/psychological counseling, women's center, legal services.

Athletics Member NCAA. All Division I. *Intercollegiate sports:* baseball M(s), basketball M(s)/W(s), bowling M(c)/W(c), crew M(c)/W(c), cross-country running M(s)/W(s), equestrian sports M(c)/W(c), fencing M(c)/W(c), field hockey W(c), golf M(s), gymnastics M(s)/W(s), lacrosse M(c)/W(c), rugby M(c), sailing M(c)/W(c), skiing (downhill) M(c)/W(c), soccer M(s)/W(s), softball W(s), swimming and diving M(s)/W(s), tennis M(s)/W(s), track and field M(s)/W(s), ultimate Frisbee M(c)/W(c), volleyball M(s)/W(s), water polo M(s)/W(s). *Intramural sports:* badminton M/W, basketball M/W, bowling M/W, cross-country running M/W, football M/W, golf M/W, gymnastics M/W, racquetball M/W, soccer M/W, softball M/W, squash M/W, tennis M/W, ultimate Frisbee M/W, volleyball M/W, water polo M/W.

Standardized Tests *Required:* SAT or ACT (for admission), SAT Subject Tests (for admission).

Costs (2011–12) *Tuition:* state resident $11,220 full-time; nonresident $33,030 full-time. *Required fees:* $2356 full-time. *Room and board:* $13,110. Room and board charges vary according to board plan and housing facility. *Payment plan:* installment.

Financial Aid Of all full-time matriculated undergraduates who enrolled in 2011, 13,071 applied for aid, 11,138 were judged to have need, 3,927 had their need fully met. In 2011, 343 non-need-based awards were made. *Average percent of need met:* 86%. *Average financial aid package:* $21,398. *Average need-based loan:* $6408. *Average need-based gift aid:* $17,223. *Average non-need-based aid:* $8653. *Average indebtedness upon graduation:* $18,627.

Applying *Options:* electronic application. *Application fee:* $60. *Required:* essay or personal statement, high school transcript. *Required for some:* interview. *Application deadlines:* 11/30 (freshmen), 11/30 (transfers). *Notification:* 3/15 (freshmen), 5/1 (transfers).

Freshman Application Contact Office of Admissions, University of California, Santa Barbara, 1210 Cheadle Hall, Santa Barbara, CA 93106-2014. *Phone:* 805-893-2881. *Fax:* 805-893-2676. *E-mail:* admissions@sa.ucsb.edu. *Web site:* http://www.ucsb.edu/.

University of California, Santa Cruz
Santa Cruz, California

- **State-supported** university, founded 1965, part of University of California System
- **Small-town** 2000-acre campus with easy access to San Francisco, San Jose
- **Endowment** $121.9 million
- **Coed** 16,545 undergraduate students, 98% full-time, 51% women, 49% men
- **Very difficult** entrance level, 70% of applicants were admitted

Undergraduates 16,277 full-time, 268 part-time. Students come from 41 states and territories; 14 other countries; 2% are from out of state; 2% Black or African American, non-Hispanic/Latino; 23% Hispanic/Latino; 20% Asian, non-Hispanic/Latino; 0.2% Native Hawaiian or other Pacific Islander, non-Hispanic/Latino; 0.5% American Indian or Alaska Native, non-Hispanic/Latino; 5% Two or more races, non-Hispanic/Latino; 5% Race/ethnicity unknown; 0.4% international; 7% transferred in; 45% live on campus. *Retention:* 89% of full-time freshmen returned.

Freshmen *Admission:* 27,658 applied, 19,228 admitted, 3,610 enrolled. *Average high school GPA:* 3.62. *Test scores:* SAT critical reading scores over 500: 78%; SAT math scores over 500: 82%; SAT writing scores over 500: 79%; ACT scores over 18: 94%; SAT critical reading scores over 600: 39%; SAT math scores over 600: 45%; SAT writing scores over 600: 40%; ACT scores over 24: 63%; SAT critical reading scores over 700: 7%; SAT math scores over 700: 8%; SAT writing scores over 700: 6%; ACT scores over 30: 11%.

Faculty *Total:* 803, 70% full-time, 95% with terminal degrees. *Student/faculty ratio:* 18:1.

Academics *Calendar:* quarters. *Degrees:* bachelor's, master's, doctoral, post-bachelor's, and first professional certificates. *Special study options:* accelerated degree program, advanced placement credit, cooperative education, double majors, freshman honors college, honors programs, independent study, internships, off-campus study, services for LD students, student-designed majors, study abroad, summer session for credit. *ROTC:* Army (c), Navy (c), Air Force (c).

Computers on Campus Students can access the following: campus intranet, computer help desk, free student e-mail accounts, online (class) grades, online (class) registration, online (class) schedules. Campuswide network is available. 100% of college-owned or -operated housing units are wired for high-speed Internet access. Wireless service is available via entire campus.

Student Life *Housing options:* coed, men-only, women-only, cooperative. Campus housing is university owned. Freshman campus housing is guaranteed. *Activities and organizations:* drama/theater group, student-run newspaper, radio and television station, choral group, Filipino Student Association, Movimiento Estudiantil Chicano de Aztlan, CSA (Chinese Student Association), A/BSA (African/Black Student Alliance), SEC (Student Environmental Center), national fraternities, national sororities. *Campus security:* 24-hour emergency response devices and patrols, late-night transport/escort service, controlled dormitory access, evening main gate security, campus police force and fire station. *Student services:* health clinic, personal/psychological counseling, women's center.

Athletics Member NCAA. All Division III. *Intercollegiate sports:* badminton M(c)/W(c), baseball M(c)/W(c), basketball M/W, cheerleading M(c)/W(c), cross-country running M(c)/W, equestrian sports M(c)/W(c), fencing M(c)/W(c), golf W, lacrosse M(c), racquetball M(c)/W(c), rugby M(c)/W(c), soccer M/W, swimming and diving M/W, table tennis M(c)/W(c), tennis M/W, track and field M(c)/W(c), ultimate Frisbee M(c)/W(c), volleyball M/W, water polo M(c)/W(c). *Intramural sports:* basketball M/W, soccer M/W, softball M/W, ultimate Frisbee M/W, volleyball M/W, water polo M/W.

Standardized Tests *Required:* SAT or ACT (for admission), (for admission).

Costs (2012–13) *Tuition:* state resident $13,538 full-time; nonresident $36,416 full-time. Part-time tuition and fees vary according to course load. *Room and board:* $14,871. Room and board charges vary according to board plan and housing facility.

Financial Aid Of all full-time matriculated undergraduates who enrolled in 2011, 12,027 applied for aid, 10,222 were judged to have need, 3,739 had their need fully met. 7,625 Federal Work-Study jobs (averaging $1936). In 2011, 290 non-need-based awards were made. *Average percent of need met:* 88%. *Average financial aid package:* $21,922. *Average need-based loan:* $6248. *Average need-based gift aid:* $16,591. *Average non-need-based aid:* $10,016. *Average indebtedness upon graduation:* $19,851. *Financial aid deadline:* 6/1.

Applying *Options:* electronic application. *Application fee:* $70. *Required:* essay or personal statement, high school transcript, minimum high school GPA of 3.0 for California residents, 3.4 for non-residents. *Application deadlines:* 11/30 (freshmen), 11/30 (transfers). *Notification:* 3/31 (freshmen), 4/30 (transfers).

Freshman Application Contact Michael McCawley, Director, Admissions, University of California, Santa Cruz, 1156 High Street, Santa Cruz, CA 95064.

Phone: 831-459-2374. *Fax:* 831-459-4163. *E-mail:* admissions@ucsc.edu. *Web site:* http://www.ucsc.edu/.

University of La Verne
La Verne, California

- **Independent** university, founded 1891
- **Suburban** 38-acre campus with easy access to Los Angeles
- **Endowment** $37.4 million
- **Coed** 2,172 undergraduate students, 97% full-time, 59% women, 41% men
- **Moderately difficult** entrance level, 40% of applicants were admitted

Undergraduates 2,098 full-time, 74 part-time. Students come from 17 states and territories; 6 other countries; 3% are from out of state; 5% Black or African American, non-Hispanic/Latino; 50% Hispanic/Latino; 5% Asian, non-Hispanic/Latino; 0.4% Native Hawaiian or other Pacific Islander, non-Hispanic/Latino; 0.2% American Indian or Alaska Native, non-Hispanic/Latino; 4% Two or more races, non-Hispanic/Latino; 3% Race/ethnicity unknown; 3% international; 9% transferred in; 45% live on campus. *Retention:* 85% of full-time freshmen returned.

Freshmen *Admission:* 5,734 applied, 2,286 admitted, 506 enrolled. *Average high school GPA:* 3.46. *Test scores:* SAT critical reading scores over 500: 53%; SAT math scores over 500: 61%; SAT writing scores over 500: 54%; ACT scores over 18: 83%; SAT critical reading scores over 600: 11%; SAT math scores over 600: 15%; SAT writing scores over 600: 11%; ACT scores over 24: 22%; SAT critical reading scores over 700: 1%; SAT math scores over 700: 2%; SAT writing scores over 700: 1%; ACT scores over 30: 2%.

Faculty *Total:* 455, 46% full-time. *Student/faculty ratio:* 12:1.

Academics *Calendar:* 4-1-4. *Degrees:* certificates, associate, bachelor's, master's, doctoral, postbachelor's, and first professional certificates (also offers continuing education program with significant enrollment not reflected in profile). *Special study options:* academic remediation for entering students, accelerated degree program, adult/continuing education programs, advanced placement credit, distance learning, double majors, English as a second language, freshman honors college, honors programs, independent study, internships, off-campus study, part-time degree program, services for LD students, student-designed majors, study abroad, summer session for credit. *ROTC:* Army (c).

Computers on Campus 250 computers/terminals and 250 ports are available on campus for general student use. Students can access the following: computer help desk, free student e-mail accounts, online (class) grades, online (class) registration, online (class) schedules, MyLaVerne (online). Campus-wide network is available. 100% of college-owned or -operated housing units are wired for high-speed Internet access. Wireless service is available via entire campus.

Student Life *Housing options:* coed, women-only, disabled students. Campus housing is university owned. Freshman campus housing is guaranteed. *Activities and organizations:* drama/theater group, student-run newspaper, radio and television station, choral group, Latino Student Forum, Black Student Union, Associated Students Federation, Alpha Kappa Psi, national fraternities, national sororities. *Campus security:* 24-hour emergency response devices and patrols, late-night transport/escort service, controlled dormitory access. *Student services:* health clinic, personal/psychological counseling.

Athletics Member NCAA. All Division III. *Intercollegiate sports:* baseball M, basketball M/W, cross-country running M/W, football M, golf M, soccer M/W, softball W, swimming and diving M/W, tennis M/W, track and field M/W, volleyball W, water polo M/W.

Standardized Tests *Required:* SAT or ACT (for admission).

Costs (2012–13) *Comprehensive fee:* $45,010 includes full-time tuition ($32,096), mandatory fees ($1254), and room and board ($11,660). Full-time tuition and fees vary according to degree level and location. Part-time tuition: $890 per unit. Part-time tuition and fees vary according to degree level and location. *College room only:* $6020. Room and board charges vary according to board plan and housing facility. *Payment plans:* installment, deferred payment. *Waivers:* employees or children of employees.

Financial Aid Of all full-time matriculated undergraduates who enrolled in 2011, 1,877 applied for aid, 1,774 were judged to have need, 184 had their need fully met. In 2011, 233 non-need-based awards were made. *Average percent of need met:* 48%. *Average financial aid package:* $26,918. *Average need-based loan:* $4562. *Average need-based gift aid:* $11,957. *Average non-need-based aid:* $16,627. *Average indebtedness upon graduation:* $29,567.

Applying *Options:* electronic application, deferred entrance. *Application fee:* $50. *Required:* essay or personal statement, high school transcript, 2 letters of recommendation. *Recommended:* interview. *Application deadlines:* 2/1 (freshmen), 4/1 (transfers). *Notification:* continuous (freshmen), continuous (transfers).

Freshman Application Contact Ms. Ana Liza V. Zell, Associate Dean of Undergraduate Admissions, University of La Verne, 1950 Third Street, La Verne, CA 91750. *Phone:* 909-593-3511 Ext. 4035. *Toll-free phone:* 800-876-4858. *Fax:* 909-392-2714. *E-mail:* admissions@ulv.edu. *Web site:* http://www.laverne.edu/.

University of Phoenix–Bay Area Campus
San Jose, California

Freshman Application Contact Marc Booker, Sr. Director, Office of Admissions and Evaluation, University of Phoenix–Bay Area Campus, 4035 South Riverpoint Parkway, Mail Stop CF-L101, Phoenix, AZ 85040-1958. *Phone:* 602-557-4609. *Toll-free phone:* 866-766-0766. *Fax:* 480-643-1156. *Web site:* http://www.phoenix.edu/.

University of Phoenix–Central Valley Campus
Fresno, California

Freshman Application Contact Marc Booker, Sr. Director, Office of Admissions and Evaluation, University of Phoenix–Central Valley Campus, 4035 South Riverpoint Parkway, Mail Stop CF-L101, Phoenix, AZ 85040. *Phone:* 602-557-4609. *Toll-free phone:* 866-766-0766. *Fax:* 480-643-1156. *Web site:* http://phoenix.edu/.

University of Phoenix–Sacramento Valley Campus
Sacramento, California

Freshman Application Contact Marc Booker, Sr. Director, Office of Admissions and Evaluation, University of Phoenix–Sacramento Valley Campus, 4035 South Riverpoint Parkway, Mail Stop CF-L101, Phoenix, AZ 85040. *Phone:* 602-557-4609. *Toll-free phone:* 866-766-0766. *Fax:* 480-643-1156. *Web site:* http://www.phoenix.edu/.

University of Phoenix–San Diego Campus
San Diego, California

Freshman Application Contact Marc Booker, Sr. Director, Office of Admissions and Evaluation, University of Phoenix–San Diego Campus, 4035 South Riverpoint Parkway, Mail Stop CF-L101, Phoenix, AZ 85040. *Phone:* 602-557-4609. *Toll-free phone:* 866-766-0766. *Fax:* 480-643-1156. *Web site:* http://www.phoenix.edu/.

University of Phoenix–Southern California Campus
Costa Mesa, California

Freshman Application Contact Marc Booker, Sr. Director, Office of Admissions and Evaluation, University of Phoenix–Southern California Campus, 4035 South Riverpoint Parkway, Mail Stop CF-L101, Phoenix, AZ 85040. *Phone:* 602-557-4609. *Toll-free phone:* 866-766-0766. *Fax:* 480-643-1156. *Web site:* http://www.phoenix.edu/.

University of Redlands
Redlands, California

- **Independent** comprehensive, founded 1907
- **Small-town** 140-acre campus with easy access to Los Angeles
- **Endowment** $109.9 million
- **Coed** 3,302 undergraduate students, 73% full-time, 56% women, 44% men
- **Moderately difficult** entrance level, 65% of applicants were admitted

Undergraduates 2,421 full-time, 881 part-time. Students come from 42 states and territories; 6 other countries; 26% are from out of state; 4% Black or African American, non-Hispanic/Latino; 18% Hispanic/Latino; 4% Asian, non-Hispanic/Latino; 0.8% Native Hawaiian or other Pacific Islander, non-Hispanic/Latino; 0.8% American Indian or Alaska Native, non-Hispanic/Latino; 2% Two or more races, non-Hispanic/Latino; 21% Race/ethnicity unknown; 0.5% international; 53% live on campus. *Retention:* 87% of full-time freshmen returned.

Freshmen *Admission:* 4,125 applied, 2,674 admitted, 644 enrolled. *Average high school GPA:* 3.54. *Test scores:* SAT critical reading scores over 500:

UR UNIQUE
UR CONNECTED
UR BOLD

UR HOME.

UNIVERSITY OF REDLANDS

78%; SAT math scores over 500: 81%; SAT writing scores over 500: 80%; ACT scores over 18: 99%; SAT critical reading scores over 600: 30%; SAT math scores over 600: 27%; SAT writing scores over 600: 32%; ACT scores over 24: 61%; SAT critical reading scores over 700: 4%; SAT math scores over 700: 3%; SAT writing scores over 700: 3%; ACT scores over 30: 7%.

Faculty *Total:* 482, 42% full-time. *Student/faculty ratio:* 15:1.

Academics *Calendar:* 4-4-1. *Degrees:* bachelor's, master's, doctoral, post-master's, and postbachelor's certificates. *Special study options:* academic remediation for entering students, adult/continuing education programs, advanced placement credit, double majors, freshman honors college, honors programs, independent study, internships, off-campus study, part-time degree program, services for LD students, student-designed majors, study abroad. *ROTC:* Army (c), Air Force (c).

Computers on Campus 804 computers/terminals and 1,500 ports are available on campus for general student use. Students can access the following: campus intranet, computer help desk, free student e-mail accounts, online (class) grades, online (class) registration, online (class) schedules. Campus-wide network is available. 100% of college-owned or -operated housing units are wired for high-speed Internet access. Wireless service is available via entire campus.

Student Life *Housing:* on-campus residence required through senior year. *Options:* coed, men-only, women-only, cooperative, disabled students. Campus housing is university owned. Freshman campus housing is guaranteed. *Activities and organizations:* drama/theater group, student-run newspaper, radio station, choral group, Associated Students, service organizations, cultural organizations, social awareness groups. *Campus security:* 24-hour emergency response devices and patrols, student patrols, late-night transport/escort service, controlled dormitory access. *Student services:* health clinic, personal/psychological counseling, women's center.

Athletics Member NCAA. All Division III. *Intercollegiate sports:* baseball M, basketball M/W, cross-country running M/W, football M, golf M/W, lacrosse W, soccer M/W, softball W, swimming and diving M/W, tennis M/W, track and field M/W, volleyball W, water polo M/W. *Intramural sports:* basketball M/W, cheerleading W, football M, racquetball M/W, soccer M/W, softball M/W, table tennis M/W, volleyball W, water polo M/W.

Standardized Tests *Required:* SAT or ACT (for admission).

Costs (2012–13) *Comprehensive fee:* $51,262 includes full-time tuition ($39,038), mandatory fees ($300), and room and board ($11,924). Full-time tuition and fees vary according to program. Part-time tuition and fees vary according to course load and program. *Required fees:* $150 per term part-time. *Room and board:* Room and board charges vary according to board plan and housing facility. *Payment plan:* installment. *Waivers:* employees or children of employees.

Financial Aid Of all full-time matriculated undergraduates who enrolled in 2011, 2,229 applied for aid, 1,836 were judged to have need, 617 had their need fully met. In 2011, 368 non-need-based awards were made. *Average percent of need met:* 88%. *Average financial aid package:* $32,861. *Average need-based loan:* $5208. *Average need-based gift aid:* $26,596. *Average non-need-based aid:* $13,829. *Average indebtedness upon graduation:* $27,779.

Applying *Options:* electronic application, deferred entrance. *Application fee:* $30. *Required:* essay or personal statement, high school transcript, 2 letters of recommendation. *Recommended:* interview. *Application deadlines:* 3/1 (freshmen), 3/1 (transfers). *Notification:* continuous (freshmen), continuous (transfers).

Freshman Application Contact University of Redlands, 1200 East Colton Avenue, PO Box 3080, Redlands, CA 92373-0999. *Phone:* 909-748-8159. *Toll-free phone:* 800-455-5064. *Web site:* http://www.redlands.edu/.

See page 1704 for the College Close-Up.

University of San Diego
San Diego, California

- **Independent Roman Catholic** university, founded 1949
- **Urban** 180-acre campus with easy access to San Diego
- **Endowment** $327.0 million
- **Coed** 5,493 undergraduate students, 97% full-time, 55% women, 45% men
- **Very difficult** entrance level, 48% of applicants were admitted

Undergraduates 5,304 full-time, 189 part-time. Students come from 52 states and territories; 57 other countries; 40% are from out of state; 2% Black or African American, non-Hispanic/Latino; 17% Hispanic/Latino; 6% Asian, non-Hispanic/Latino; 0.2% Native Hawaiian or other Pacific Islander, non-Hispanic/Latino; 0.3% American Indian or Alaska Native, non-Hispanic/Latino; 5% Two or more races, non-Hispanic/Latino; 6% Race/ethnicity unknown; 6% international; 5% transferred in; 46% live on campus. *Retention:* 87% of full-time freshmen returned.

Freshmen *Admission:* 13,867 applied, 6,590 admitted, 1,143 enrolled. *Average high school GPA:* 3.89. *Test scores:* SAT critical reading scores over 500:

95%; SAT math scores over 500: 96%; SAT writing scores over 500: 95%; ACT scores over 18: 100%; SAT critical reading scores over 600: 53%; SAT math scores over 600: 68%; SAT writing scores over 600: 59%; ACT scores over 24: 93%; SAT critical reading scores over 700: 10%; SAT math scores over 700: 11%; SAT writing scores over 700: 10%; ACT scores over 30: 26%. **Faculty** *Total:* 845, 48% full-time, 76% with terminal degrees. *Student/faculty ratio:* 16:1.

Academics *Calendar:* 4-1-4. *Degrees:* bachelor's, master's, doctoral, post-master's, postbachelor's, and first professional certificates. *Special study options:* advanced placement credit, double majors, English as a second language, honors programs, independent study, internships, part-time degree program, services for LD students, study abroad, summer session for credit. *ROTC:* Army (c), Navy (b), Air Force (c).

Computers on Campus 1,300 computers/terminals and 4,250 ports are available on campus for general student use. Students can access the following: campus intranet, computer help desk, free student e-mail accounts, online (class) grades, online (class) registration, online (class) schedules. Campus-wide network is available. 100% of college-owned or -operated housing units are wired for high-speed Internet access. Wireless service is available via entire campus.

Student Life *Housing:* on-campus residence required for freshman year. *Options:* coed, men-only, women-only, disabled students. Campus housing is university owned. Freshman campus housing is guaranteed. *Activities and organizations:* drama/theater group, student-run newspaper, radio and television station, choral group, Panhellenic Council, Interfraternity Council, Residence Hall Association, Adventure Club, Kappa Kappa Gamma Sorority, national fraternities, national sororities. *Campus security:* 24-hour emergency response devices and patrols, late-night transport/escort service, controlled dormitory access. *Student services:* health clinic, personal/psychological counseling, women's center, legal services.

Athletics Member NCAA. All Division I except football (Division I-AA). *Intercollegiate sports:* baseball M(s), basketball M(s)/W(s), crew M/W(s), cross-country running M(s)/W(s), equestrian sports W(c), golf M(s), lacrosse M(c)/W(c), rock climbing M(c), rugby M(c)/W(c), soccer M(s)/W(s), softball W(s), swimming and diving W(s), tennis M(s)/W(s), track and field W(s), ultimate Frisbee M(c)/W(c), volleyball M(c)/W(s). *Intramural sports:* baseball M(c), basketball M/W, football M/W, golf M/W, skiing (downhill) M(c)/W(c), soccer M(c)/W(c), softball M/W, swimming and diving M(c)/W(c), tennis M/W, ultimate Frisbee M/W, volleyball M/W(c), water polo M(c).

Standardized Tests *Required:* SAT or ACT (for admission).

Costs (2011–12) *Comprehensive fee:* $50,330 includes full-time tuition ($38,150), mandatory fees ($428), and room and board ($11,752). Part-time tuition: $1315 per unit. Part-time tuition and fees vary according to course load. *Room and board:* Room and board charges vary according to board plan and housing facility. *Payment plan:* installment. *Waivers:* employees or children of employees.

Financial Aid Of all full-time matriculated undergraduates who enrolled in 2010, 3,081 applied for aid, 2,705 were judged to have need, 368 had their need fully met. 564 Federal Work-Study jobs (averaging $2133). In 2010, 738 non-need-based awards were made. *Average percent of need met:* 69%. *Average financial aid package:* $28,783. *Average need-based loan:* $7969. *Average need-based gift aid:* $22,096. *Average non-need-based aid:* $13,322. *Average indebtedness upon graduation:* $31,937.

Applying *Options:* electronic application, early action, deferred entrance. *Application fee:* $55. *Required:* essay or personal statement, high school transcript, 1 letter of recommendation. *Application deadlines:* 1/15 (freshmen), 3/1 (transfers), 11/15 (early action). *Notification:* 4/1 (freshmen), continuous until 6/30 (transfers), 1/31 (early action).

Freshman Application Contact Mr. Stephen Pultz, Director of Admission, University of San Diego, 5998 Alcala Park, San Diego, CA 92110. *Phone:* 619-260-4506. *Toll-free phone:* 800-248-4873. *Fax:* 619-260-6836. *E-mail:* admissions@sandiego.edu. *Web site:* http://www.sandiego.edu/.

University of San Francisco

San Francisco, California

- **Independent Roman Catholic (Jesuit)** university, founded 1855
- **Urban** 55-acre campus
- **Coed**
- **Moderately difficult** entrance level

Faculty *Student/faculty ratio:* 12:1.

Academics *Calendar:* 4-1-4. *Degrees:* certificates, bachelor's, master's, doctoral, and post-master's certificates.

Student Life *Campus security:* 24-hour emergency response devices and patrols, late-night transport/escort service, controlled dormitory access.

Athletics Member NCAA. All Division I.

Standardized Tests *Required:* SAT or ACT (for admission), Sat Writing and Reading are used for Core Curriculum placement in the Foundation of Communication Core requirements (for admission).

Costs (2011–12) *Comprehensive fee:* $49,674 includes full-time tuition ($37,040), mandatory fees ($384), and room and board ($12,250). Full-time tuition and fees vary according to course load, degree level, program, and reciprocity agreements. Part-time tuition: $1315 per credit hour. Part-time tuition and fees vary according to course load, degree level, program, and reciprocity agreements. *Required fees:* $384 per year part-time. *College room only:* $8240. Room and board charges vary according to housing facility.

Financial Aid Of all full-time matriculated undergraduates who enrolled in 2008, 3,188 applied for aid, 2,896 were judged to have need, 182 had their need fully met. 856 Federal Work-Study jobs (averaging $3737). 535 state and other part-time jobs (averaging $3512). In 2008, 88 non-need-based awards were made. *Average percent of need met:* 65. *Average financial aid package:* $26,830. *Average need-based loan:* $4795. *Average need-based gift aid:* $21,762. *Average non-need-based aid:* $18,254. *Average indebtedness upon graduation:* $26,886.

Applying *Options:* electronic application, early action, deferred entrance. *Application fee:* $55. *Required:* essay or personal statement, high school transcript, 1 letter of recommendation. *Required for some:* interview. *Recommended:* minimum 3.0 GPA.

Freshman Application Contact Mr. Michael Hughes, Director, University of San Francisco, 2130 Fulton Street, San Francisco, CA 94117-1080. *Phone:* 415-422-6563. *Toll-free phone:* 800-CALL-USF. *Fax:* 415-422-2217. *E-mail:* admissions@usfca.edu. *Web site:* http://www.usfca.edu/.

See page 1710 for the College Close-Up.

University of Southern California

Los Angeles, California

- **Independent** university, founded 1880
- **Urban** 229-acre campus with easy access to Los Angeles
- **Endowment** $3.5 billion
- **Coed** 17,414 undergraduate students, 96% full-time, 51% women, 49% men
- **Most difficult** entrance level, 23% of applicants were admitted

Undergraduates 16,753 full-time, 661 part-time. Students come from 55 states and territories; 91 other countries; 35% are from out of state; 5% Black or African American, non-Hispanic/Latino; 14% Hispanic/Latino; 23% Asian, non-Hispanic/Latino; 0.2% Native Hawaiian or other Pacific Islander, non-Hispanic/Latino; 0.2% American Indian or Alaska Native, non-Hispanic/Latino; 5% Two or more races, non-Hispanic/Latino; 0.7% Race/ethnicity unknown; 12% international; 8% transferred in; 38% live on campus. *Retention:* 97% of full-time freshmen returned.

Freshmen *Admission:* 37,210 applied, 8,566 admitted, 2,931 enrolled. *Average high school GPA:* 3.72. *Test scores:* SAT critical reading scores over 500: 99%; SAT math scores over 500: 100%; SAT writing scores over 500: 100%; ACT scores over 18: 100%; SAT critical reading scores over 600: 81%; SAT math scores over 600: 92%; SAT writing scores over 600: 91%; ACT scores over 24: 98%; SAT critical reading scores over 700: 36%; SAT math scores over 700: 60%; SAT writing scores over 700: 49%; ACT scores over 30: 70%.

Faculty *Total:* 3,123, 55% full-time, 79% with terminal degrees. *Student/faculty ratio:* 9:1.

Academics *Calendar:* semesters. *Degrees:* bachelor's, master's, doctoral, post-master's, postbachelor's, and first professional certificates. *Special study options:* accelerated degree program, advanced placement credit, cooperative education, distance learning, double majors, English as a second language, freshman honors college, honors programs, independent study, internships, off-campus study, part-time degree program, services for LD students, student-designed majors, study abroad, summer session for credit. *ROTC:* Army (b), Navy (b), Air Force (b). *Unusual degree programs:* 3-2 engineering.

Computers on Campus 2,500 computers/terminals and 6,000 ports are available on campus for general student use. Students can access the following: campus intranet, computer help desk, free student e-mail accounts, online (class) grades, online (class) registration, online (class) schedules, online degree progress, financial aid applications, document sharing, calendars, personal Web space, customizable Web portal, course management systems (including data and video). Campuswide network is available. 100% of college-owned or -operated housing units are wired for high-speed Internet access. Wireless service is available via entire campus.

Student Life *Housing options:* coed, disabled students. Campus housing is university owned and is provided by a third party. Freshman campus housing is guaranteed. *Activities and organizations:* drama/theater group, student-run newspaper, radio and television station, choral group, marching band, Troy Camp, USC Helenes, Alpha Phi Omega, Student Bar Association, USC Accounting Society, national fraternities, national sororities. *Campus security:* 24-hour emergency response devices and patrols, student patrols, late-night

transport/escort service, controlled dormitory access. *Student services:* health clinic, personal/psychological counseling, women's center, legal services.
Athletics Member NCAA. All Division I except football (Division I-A). *Intercollegiate sports:* archery M(c)/W(c), badminton M(c)/W(c), baseball M(s), basketball M(s)/W(s), cheerleading M(c)/W(c), crew M(c)/W(s), cross-country running M(c)/W(s), equestrian sports W(c), fencing W(c), field hockey W(c), golf M(s)/W(s), ice hockey M(c)/W(c), lacrosse M(c)/W(c), racquetball M(c)/W(c), rock climbing M(c)/W(c), rugby M(c)/W(c), skiing (downhill) M(c)/W(c), soccer M(c)/W(s), softball W(c), squash M(c)/W(c), swimming and diving M(s)/W(s), tennis M(s)/W(s), track and field M(s)/W(s), ultimate Frisbee M(c)/W(c), volleyball M(s)/W(s), water polo M(s)/W(s). *Intramural sports:* badminton M/W, basketball M/W, cross-country running M/W, football M/W, golf M/W, racquetball M/W, soccer M/W, softball M/W, tennis M/W, ultimate Frisbee M/W, volleyball M/W.
Standardized Tests *Required:* SAT or ACT (for admission).
Costs (2011–12) *One-time required fee:* $150. *Comprehensive fee:* $54,896 includes full-time tuition ($42,162), mandatory fees ($656), and room and board ($12,078). Full-time tuition and fees vary according to program. Part-time tuition: $1420 per unit. Part-time tuition and fees vary according to course load and program. *College room only:* $7078. Room and board charges vary according to board plan and housing facility. *Payment plans:* tuition prepayment, installment. *Waivers:* employees or children of employees.
Financial Aid Of all full-time matriculated undergraduates who enrolled in 2009, 8,671 applied for aid, 6,400 were judged to have need, 5,931 had their need fully met. 4,945 Federal Work-Study jobs (averaging $2681). In 2009, 2769 non-need-based awards were made. *Average percent of need met:* 100%. *Average financial aid package:* $35,906. *Average need-based loan:* $5873. *Average need-based gift aid:* $24,777. *Average non-need-based aid:* $15,639. *Average indebtedness upon graduation:* $30,090.
Applying *Options:* electronic application, deferred entrance. *Application fee:* $70. *Required:* essay or personal statement, high school transcript. *Application deadlines:* 1/10 (freshmen), 1/10 (out-of-state freshmen), 2/1 (transfers). *Notification:* 4/1 (freshmen), 6/1 (transfers).
Freshman Application Contact Timothy Brunold, Dean of Admission, University of Southern California, University Park Campus, Los Angeles, CA 90089. *Phone:* 213-740-1111. *Fax:* 213-821-0200. *E-mail:* admitusc@usc.edu. *Web site:* http://www.usc.edu/.

University of the Pacific
Stockton, California

- **Independent** university, founded 1851
- **Suburban** 175-acre campus with easy access to Sacramento
- **Coed** 3,883 undergraduate students, 98% full-time, 55% women, 45% men
- **Moderately difficult** entrance level, 36% of applicants were admitted

Undergraduates 3,799 full-time, 84 part-time. 10% are from out of state; 4% Black or African American, non-Hispanic/Latino; 14% Hispanic/Latino; 31% Asian, non-Hispanic/Latino; 2% Native Hawaiian or other Pacific Islander, non-Hispanic/Latino; 2% American Indian or Alaska Native, non-Hispanic/Latino; 4% Two or more races, non-Hispanic/Latino; 4% Race/ethnicity unknown; 4% international; 6% transferred in; 51% live on campus. *Retention:* 85% of full-time freshmen returned.
Freshmen *Admission:* 21,230 applied, 7,608 admitted, 927 enrolled. *Average high school GPA:* 3.47. *Test scores:* SAT critical reading scores over 500: 79%; SAT math scores over 500: 86%; SAT writing scores over 500: 78%; ACT scores over 18: 98%; SAT critical reading scores over 600: 39%; SAT math scores over 600: 54%; SAT writing scores over 600: 40%; ACT scores over 24: 69%; SAT critical reading scores over 700: 8%; SAT math scores over 700: 21%; SAT writing scores over 700: 11%; ACT scores over 30: 23%.
Faculty *Total:* 812, 56% full-time, 69% with terminal degrees. *Student/faculty ratio:* 13:1.
Academics *Calendar:* semesters. *Degrees:* bachelor's, master's, doctoral, and first professional. *Special study options:* academic remediation for entering students, accelerated degree program, advanced placement credit, cooperative education, double majors, English as a second language, honors programs, independent study, internships, part-time degree program, services for LD students, student-designed majors, summer session for credit. *ROTC:* Air Force (c).
Computers on Campus Students can access the following: online (class) registration. Campuswide network is available. 100% of college-owned or -operated housing units are wired for high-speed Internet access. Wireless service is available via entire campus.
Student Life *Housing:* on-campus residence required through sophomore year. *Options:* coed. Campus housing is university owned. Freshman campus housing is guaranteed. *Activities and organizations:* drama/theater group, student-run newspaper, radio station, choral group, national fraternities, national sororities. *Campus security:* 24-hour emergency response devices and patrols, late-

night transport/escort service, controlled dormitory access. *Student services:* health clinic, personal/psychological counseling, legal services.
Athletics Member NCAA. All Division I. *Intercollegiate sports:* baseball M(s), basketball M(s)/W(s), cross-country running W(s), field hockey W(s), golf M(s), soccer W(s), softball W(s), swimming and diving M(s)/W(s), tennis M(s)/W(s), volleyball M(s)/W(s), water polo M(s)/W(s). *Intramural sports:* badminton M(c)/W(c), basketball M/W, bowling M/W, football M/W, golf M, lacrosse M(c)/W(c), rugby M(c), soccer M(c)/W(c), tennis M/W, volleyball M/W.
Standardized Tests *Required:* SAT or ACT (for admission). *Recommended:* SAT Subject Tests (for admission).
Costs (2011–12) *Comprehensive fee:* $47,978 includes full-time tuition ($35,770), mandatory fees ($520), and room and board ($11,688). Part-time tuition and fees vary according to course load. *Room and board:* Room and board charges vary according to board plan and housing facility. *Payment plan:* deferred payment. *Waivers:* employees or children of employees.
Financial Aid Of all full-time matriculated undergraduates who enrolled in 2011, 3,096 applied for aid, 2,822 were judged to have need, 267 had their need fully met. In 2011, 392 non-need-based awards were made. *Average financial aid package:* $30,355. *Average need-based loan:* $8219. *Average need-based gift aid:* $22,125. *Average non-need-based aid:* $9713.
Applying *Options:* electronic application, early action. *Application fee:* $60. *Required:* essay or personal statement, high school transcript, minimum 2.5 GPA, 1 letter of recommendation. *Required for some:* audition for music program. *Recommended:* minimum 3.0 GPA. *Application deadlines:* 1/15 (freshmen), 6/1 (transfers), 11/15 (early action). *Notification:* continuous (freshmen), continuous (transfers), 1/15 (early action).
Freshman Application Contact Mr. Rich Toledo, Director of Admissions, University of the Pacific, 3601 Pacific Avenue, Stockton, CA 95211-0197. *Phone:* 209-946-2211. *Fax:* 209-946-2413. *E-mail:* admissions@pacific.edu. *Web site:* http://www.pacific.edu/.

University of the West
Rosemead, California

- **Independent** comprehensive, founded 1991
- **Suburban** 10-acre campus
- **Coed**
- **Moderately difficult** entrance level

Faculty *Student/faculty ratio:* 9:1.
Academics *Calendar:* semesters. *Degrees:* certificates, diplomas, bachelor's, master's, doctoral, post-master's, postbachelor's, and first professional certificates.
Student Life *Campus security:* 24-hour patrols.
Costs (2011–12) *One-time required fee:* $75. *Comprehensive fee:* $13,726 includes full-time tuition ($8040), mandatory fees ($250), and room and board ($5436). Full-time tuition and fees vary according to course level, course load, degree level, and program. Part-time tuition: $335 per unit. Part-time tuition and fees vary according to course level, course load, degree level, and program. *Required fees:* $250 per term part-time. *Room and board:* Room and board charges vary according to board plan and housing facility.
Financial Aid *Of all full-time matriculated undergraduates who enrolled in 2003, 30 applied for aid, 18 were judged to have need. 20 state and other part-time jobs.*
Applying *Options:* electronic application, deferred entrance. *Application fee:* $50. *Required:* essay or personal statement, high school transcript, minimum 2.0 GPA, 3 letters of recommendation.
Freshman Application Contact University of the West, 1409 North Walnut Grove Avenue, Rosemead, CA 91770. *Phone:* 626-571-8811 Ext. 120. *Web site:* http://www.uwest.edu/.

See page 141 for display ad and page 1720 for the College Close-Up.

Vanguard University of Southern California
Costa Mesa, California

- **Independent** comprehensive, founded 1920, affiliated with Assemblies of God
- **Suburban** 38-acre campus with easy access to Los Angeles
- **Endowment** $5.0 million
- **Coed** 1,954 undergraduate students, 75% full-time, 64% women, 36% men
- **Moderately difficult** entrance level, 79% of applicants were admitted

Undergraduates 1,461 full-time, 493 part-time. Students come from 37 states and territories; 13 other countries; 14% are from out of state; 5% Black or African American, non-Hispanic/Latino; 26% Hispanic/Latino; 5% Asian, non-Hispanic/Latino; 0.4% Native Hawaiian or other Pacific Islander, non-His-

panic/Latino; 0.7% American Indian or Alaska Native, non-Hispanic/Latino; 4% Two or more races, non-Hispanic/Latino; 4% Race/ethnicity unknown; 1% international; 11% transferred in; 68% live on campus. *Retention:* 73% of full-time freshmen returned.

Freshmen *Admission:* 787 applied, 625 admitted, 402 enrolled. *Average high school GPA:* 3.37.

Faculty *Total:* 203, 31% full-time. *Student/faculty ratio:* 17:1.

Academics *Calendar:* semesters. *Degrees:* bachelor's and master's. *Special study options:* accelerated degree program, adult/continuing education programs, advanced placement credit, double majors, independent study, internships, off-campus study, part-time degree program, services for LD students, study abroad, summer session for credit. *ROTC:* Air Force (c).

Computers on Campus 100 computers/terminals and 50 ports are available on campus for general student use. Students can access the following: free student e-mail accounts, online (class) grades, online (class) registration, online (class) schedules. Campuswide network is available. 100% of college-owned or -operated housing units are wired for high-speed Internet access. Wireless service is available via entire campus.

Student Life *Housing:* on-campus residence required through sophomore year. *Options:* coed, men-only, women-only, disabled students. Campus housing is university owned. Freshman campus housing is guaranteed. *Activities and organizations:* drama/theater group, student-run newspaper, radio and television station, choral group, local outreach, Global Missions, student organizations/clubs, choral groups. *Campus security:* 24-hour emergency response devices and patrols, student patrols, late-night transport/escort service. *Student services:* personal/psychological counseling, women's center.

Athletics Member NAIA. *Intercollegiate sports:* baseball M(s), basketball M(s)/W(s), cross-country running M(s)/W(s), soccer M(s)/W(s), softball W(s), swimming and diving M(s)/W(s), tennis M(s)/W(s), track and field M(s)/W(s), volleyball W(s). *Intramural sports:* basketball M/W, football M/W, soccer M/W, softball M/W, volleyball M/W.

Standardized Tests *Required:* SAT or ACT (for admission).

Costs (2011–12) *Comprehensive fee:* $35,830 includes full-time tuition ($27,400) and room and board ($8430). Full-time tuition and fees vary according to course load. Part-time tuition: $1142 per unit. Part-time tuition and fees vary according to course load. *College room only:* $4150. Room and board charges vary according to board plan and housing facility. *Payment plan:* installment. *Waivers:* employees or children of employees.

Financial Aid Of all full-time matriculated undergraduates who enrolled in 2010, 1,183 applied for aid, 1,110 were judged to have need, 135 had their need fully met. 94 Federal Work-Study jobs (averaging $2386). In 2010, 196 non-need-based awards were made. *Average percent of need met:* 67%. *Average financial aid package:* $19,230. *Average need-based loan:* $4683. *Average need-based gift aid:* $8695. *Average non-need-based aid:* $12,957. *Average indebtedness upon graduation:* $28,256.

Applying *Options:* electronic application, early admission, early action, deferred entrance. *Application fee:* $45. *Required:* essay or personal statement, high school transcript, minimum 2.8 GPA, 2 letters of recommendation. *Required for some:* interview. *Application deadlines:* 1/15 (freshmen), 12/1 (transfers), 12/1 (early action). *Notification:* continuous until 3/1 (freshmen), continuous until 8/31 (transfers), 1/15 (early action).

Freshman Application Contact Kristi Pruett, Undergraduate Inquiry Data Coordinator, Vanguard University of Southern California, 55 Fair Drive, Costa Mesa, CA 92626. *Phone:* 800-722-6279 Ext. 4107. *Toll-free phone:* 800-722-6279. *Fax:* 714-966-5471. *E-mail:* admissions@vanguard.edu. *Web site:* http://www.vanguard.edu/.

West Coast University
North Hollywood, California

Director of Admissions Mr. Roger A. Miller, Dean of Admissions and Registrar, West Coast University, 12215 Victory Boulevard, North Hollywood, CA 91606. *Phone:* 213-427-4400. *Toll-free phone:* 866-508-2684. *E-mail:* info@katz.wcula.edu. *Web site:* http://www.westcoastuniversity.edu/.

Westmont College
Santa Barbara, California

- **Independent nondenominational** 4-year, founded 1937
- **Suburban** 113-acre campus with easy access to Los Angeles
- **Endowment** $60.0 million
- **Coed**
- **Moderately difficult** entrance level

Faculty *Student/faculty ratio:* 12:1.

Academics *Calendar:* semesters. *Degrees:* bachelor's and postbachelor's certificates.

Student Life *Campus security:* 24-hour emergency response devices and patrols, late-night transport/escort service, controlled dormitory access.

Athletics Member NAIA.

Standardized Tests *Required:* SAT or ACT (for admission).

Grow deeper.

1-800-777-9011

www.westmont.edu

Costs (2011–12) *Comprehensive fee:* $46,990 includes full-time tuition ($34,570), mandatory fees ($1080), and room and board ($11,340). *College room only:* $7050. Room and board charges vary according to board plan.
Financial Aid *Of all full-time matriculated undergraduates who enrolled in 2011,* 1,017 applied for aid, 895 were judged to have need, 167 had their need fully met. *In 2011,* 378 non-need-based awards were made. *Average percent of need met:* 79. *Average financial aid package:* $27,953. *Average need-based loan:* $5578. *Average need-based gift aid:* $22,046. *Average non-need-based aid:* $11,086. *Average indebtedness upon graduation:* $30,940.
Applying *Options:* electronic application, early action. *Application fee:* $25. *Required:* essay or personal statement, high school transcript, 1 letter of recommendation. *Required for some:* interview. *Recommended:* interview.
Freshman Application Contact Mrs. Joyce Luy, Dean of Admission, Westmont College, 955 La Paz Road, Santa Barbara, CA 93108. *Phone:* 805-565-6200. *Toll-free phone:* 800-777-9011. *Fax:* 805-565-6234. *E-mail:* admissions@westmont.edu. *Web site:* http://www.westmont.edu/.

See page 1756 for the College Close-Up.

Westwood College–Anaheim
Anaheim, California
Freshman Application Contact Westwood College–Anaheim, 1551 South Douglass Road, Anaheim, CA 92806. *Phone:* 714-704-2721. *Toll-free phone:* 877-840-8999. *Web site:* http://www.westwood.edu/.

Westwood College–Inland Empire
Upland, California
Freshman Application Contact Westwood College–Inland Empire, 20 West 7th Street, Upland, CA 91786. *Phone:* 909-931-7599. *Toll-free phone:* 866-221-5632. *Web site:* http://www.westwood.edu/.

Westwood College–Los Angeles
Los Angeles, California
Freshman Application Contact Westwood College–Los Angeles, 3250 Wilshire Boulevard, 4th Floor, Los Angeles, CA 90010. *Phone:* 213-382-2328. *Toll-free phone:* 866-930-9256. *Web site:* http://www.westwood.edu/.

Westwood College–South Bay Campus
Torrance, California
Freshman Application Contact Westwood College–South Bay Campus, 19700 South Vermont Avenue, Suite 100, Torrance, CA 90502. *Phone:* 310-965-0877. *Toll-free phone:* 888-403-3308. *Web site:* http://www.westwood.edu/.

Whittier College
Whittier, California
- **Independent** comprehensive, founded 1887
- **Suburban** 95-acre campus with easy access to Los Angeles
- **Coed** 1,643 undergraduate students, 98% full-time, 54% women, 46% men
- **Moderately difficult** entrance level, 71% of applicants were admitted

Undergraduates 1,611 full-time, 32 part-time. Students come from 27 states and territories; 20 other countries; 24% are from out of state; 5% Black or African American, non-Hispanic/Latino; 33% Hispanic/Latino; 10% Asian, non-Hispanic/Latino; 0.5% American Indian or Alaska Native, non-Hispanic/Latino; 12% Race/ethnicity unknown; 3% international; 5% transferred in; 59% live on campus. *Retention:* 81% of full-time freshmen returned.
Freshmen *Admission:* 2,989 applied, 2,137 admitted, 430 enrolled. *Average high school GPA:* 3.45. *Test scores:* SAT critical reading scores over 500: 61%; SAT math scores over 500: 64%; SAT writing scores over 500: 61%; ACT scores over 18: 90%; SAT critical reading scores over 600: 17%; SAT math scores over 600: 19%; SAT writing scores over 600: 15%; ACT scores over 24: 38%; SAT critical reading scores over 700: 3%; SAT math scores over 700: 1%; SAT writing scores over 700: 2%; ACT scores over 30: 4%.
Faculty *Total:* 153, 69% full-time, 94% with terminal degrees. *Student/faculty ratio:* 13:1.
Academics *Calendar:* 4-1-4. *Degrees:* bachelor's, master's, and doctoral. *Special study options:* academic remediation for entering students, accelerated degree program, adult/continuing education programs, advanced placement credit, double majors, independent study, internships, off-campus study, services for LD students, student-designed majors, study abroad, summer session

for credit. *ROTC:* Army (c), Air Force (c). *Unusual degree programs:* 3-2 engineering with University of Southern California, University of Minnesota.

Computers on Campus 150 computers/terminals are available on campus for general student use. Students can access the following: computer help desk, free student e-mail accounts, online (class) grades, online (class) registration, online (class) schedules. Campuswide network is available. Wireless service is available via entire campus.

Student Life *Housing:* on-campus residence required through junior year. *Options:* coed, disabled students. Campus housing is university owned. Freshman campus housing is guaranteed. *Activities and organizations:* drama/theater group, student-run newspaper, radio station, choral group, Hispanic Students Association, Hawaiian Islander Club, Choir, Asian Students Association, Students Organized for Multicultural Awareness. *Campus security:* 24-hour emergency response devices and patrols, late-night transport/escort service, controlled dormitory access. *Student services:* health clinic, personal/psychological counseling.

Athletics Member NCAA. All Division III. *Intercollegiate sports:* baseball M, basketball M/W, cross-country running M/W, football M, golf M, lacrosse M/W, soccer M/W, softball W, swimming and diving M/W, tennis M/W, track and field M/W, volleyball W, water polo M/W. *Intramural sports:* basketball M/W, bowling M/W, football M/W, racquetball M/W, skiing (downhill) M/W, softball M/W, table tennis M/W, tennis M/W, volleyball M/W, water polo M/W.

Standardized Tests *Required:* SAT or ACT (for admission). *Recommended:* SAT Subject Tests (for admission).

Costs (2012–13) *One-time required fee:* $200. *Comprehensive fee:* $50,058 includes full-time tuition ($38,280), mandatory fees ($390), and room and board ($11,388). Part-time tuition: $1610 per unit. *College room only:* $6108. Room and board charges vary according to board plan. *Waivers:* children of alumni and employees or children of employees.

Financial Aid Of all full-time matriculated undergraduates who enrolled in 2011, 1,361 applied for aid, 1,243 were judged to have need, 144 had their need fully met. In 2011, 275 non-need-based awards were made. *Average percent of need met:* 73%. *Average financial aid package:* $31,261. *Average need-based loan:* $6905. *Average need-based gift aid:* $26,632. *Average non-need-based aid:* $17,658. *Average indebtedness upon graduation:* $26,541. *Financial aid deadline:* 6/30.

Applying *Options:* electronic application, early action, deferred entrance. *Application fee:* $50. *Required:* essay or personal statement, high school transcript, minimum 2.0 GPA, 2 letters of recommendation. *Required for some:* minimum 3.5 GPA. *Recommended:* minimum 2.5 GPA, interview. *Application deadlines:* rolling (freshmen), rolling (transfers), 12/1 (early action). *Notification:* continuous (freshmen), 3/1 (transfers), 12/31 (early action).

Freshman Application Contact Mr. Kieron Miller, Director of Admission, Whittier College, Office of Admission, 13406 East Philadelphia Street, Whittier, CA 90608-0634. *Phone:* 562-907-4238. *Fax:* 562-907-4870. *E-mail:* admission@whittier.edu. *Web site:* http://www.whittier.edu/.

William Jessup University
Rocklin, California

- **Independent nondenominational** 4-year, founded 1939
- **Suburban** 126-acre campus with easy access to Sacramento
- **Coed** 869 undergraduate students, 81% full-time, 59% women, 41% men
- **Moderately difficult** entrance level, 65% of applicants were admitted

Undergraduates 700 full-time, 169 part-time. Students come from 13 states and territories; 15 other countries; 9% are from out of state; 6% Black or African American, non-Hispanic/Latino; 9% Hispanic/Latino; 3% Asian, non-Hispanic/Latino; 1% Native Hawaiian or other Pacific Islander, non-Hispanic/Latino; 2% American Indian or Alaska Native, non-Hispanic/Latino; 4% Two or more races, non-Hispanic/Latino; 2% Race/ethnicity unknown; 0.3% international; 17% transferred in; 60% live on campus. *Retention:* 78% of full-time freshmen returned.

Freshmen *Admission:* 389 applied, 251 admitted, 121 enrolled. *Average high school GPA:* 3.31. *Test scores:* SAT critical reading scores over 500: 62%; SAT math scores over 500: 53%; SAT writing scores over 500: 58%; ACT scores over 18: 95%; SAT critical reading scores over 600: 18%; SAT math scores over 600: 16%; SAT writing scores over 600: 13%; ACT scores over 24: 39%; SAT critical reading scores over 700: 1%; ACT scores over 30: 5%.

Faculty *Total:* 114, 24% full-time, 35% with terminal degrees. *Student/faculty ratio:* 13:1.

Academics *Calendar:* semesters. *Degrees:* certificates, associate, bachelor's, and postbachelor's certificates. *Special study options:* adult/continuing education programs, advanced placement credit, double majors, independent study, internships, off-campus study, part-time degree program, services for LD students, study abroad, summer session for credit.

Computers on Campus 44 computers/terminals are available on campus for general student use. Students can access the following: campus intranet, com-

puter help desk, free student e-mail accounts, online (class) grades, online (class) registration, online (class) schedules. Campuswide network is available. 100% of college-owned or -operated housing units are wired for high-speed Internet access. Wireless service is available via entire campus.

Student Life *Housing:* on-campus residence required through junior year. *Options:* men-only, women-only. Campus housing is university owned. Freshman campus housing is guaranteed. *Activities and organizations:* drama/theater group, student-run newspaper, choral group. *Campus security:* student patrols, late-night transport/escort service, controlled dormitory access, day and evening patrols by trained security personnel. *Student services:* personal/psychological counseling.

Athletics Member NAIA. *Intercollegiate sports:* basketball M(s)/W(s), cross-country running M(s)/W(s), golf M(s), soccer M(s)/W(s), softball W(s), track and field M(s)/W(s), volleyball W(s). *Intramural sports:* basketball M/W, softball M/W, table tennis M/W, volleyball M/W.

Standardized Tests *Required:* SAT or ACT (for admission).

Costs (2012–13) *Comprehensive fee:* $31,970 includes full-time tuition ($22,900) and room and board ($9070). Full-time tuition and fees vary according to course load. Part-time tuition: $970 per credit hour. Part-time tuition and fees vary according to course load. *Room and board:* Room and board charges vary according to board plan and housing facility. *Payment plan:* deferred payment. *Waivers:* employees or children of employees.

Financial Aid Of all full-time matriculated undergraduates who enrolled in 2011, 630 applied for aid, 585 were judged to have need, 64 had their need fully met. 14 Federal Work-Study jobs (averaging $2857). 39 state and other part-time jobs (averaging $2496). In 2011, 96 non-need-based awards were made. *Average percent of need met:* 67%. *Average financial aid package:* $18,974. *Average need-based loan:* $4421. *Average need-based gift aid:* $15,355. *Average non-need-based aid:* $6160. *Average indebtedness upon graduation:* $20,088.

Applying *Options:* electronic application. *Application fee:* $45. *Required:* essay or personal statement, high school transcript, minimum 2.5 GPA. *Required for some:* 1 letter of recommendation, interview. *Recommended:* 1 letter of recommendation, interview. *Application deadlines:* 8/15 (freshmen), 8/15 (transfers). *Notification:* continuous (freshmen), continuous (transfers).

Freshman Application Contact Mr. Vance Pascua, Director of Admission, William Jessup University, 333 Sunset Boulevard, Rocklin, CA 95765. *Phone:* 916-577-2222. *Toll-free phone:* 800-355-7522. *Fax:* 916-577-2220. *E-mail:* admissions@jessup.edu. *Web site:* http://www.jessup.edu/.

Woodbury University
Burbank, California

- **Independent** comprehensive, founded 1884
- **Suburban** 22-acre campus with easy access to Los Angeles
- **Endowment** $16.7 million
- **Coed** 1,333 undergraduate students, 81% full-time, 52% women, 48% men
- **Moderately difficult** entrance level, 72% of applicants were admitted

Undergraduates 1,086 full-time, 247 part-time. Students come from 8 states and territories; 23 other countries; 4% Black or African American, non-Hispanic/Latino; 33% Hispanic/Latino; 9% Asian, non-Hispanic/Latino; 1% Native Hawaiian or other Pacific Islander, non-Hispanic/Latino; 0.4% American Indian or Alaska Native, non-Hispanic/Latino; 2% Two or more races, non-Hispanic/Latino; 0.1% Race/ethnicity unknown; 13% international; 16% transferred in; 16% live on campus. *Retention:* 80% of full-time freshmen returned.

Freshmen *Admission:* 416 applied, 299 admitted, 120 enrolled. *Average high school GPA:* 3.2. *Test scores:* SAT math scores over 500: 46%; ACT scores over 18: 69%; SAT math scores over 600: 10%; ACT scores over 24: 19%; SAT math scores over 700: 2%.

Faculty *Total:* 291, 24% full-time, 69% with terminal degrees. *Student/faculty ratio:* 10:1.

Academics *Calendar:* semesters. *Degrees:* bachelor's and master's. *Special study options:* academic remediation for entering students, accelerated degree program, adult/continuing education programs, advanced placement credit, double majors, English as a second language, independent study, internships, part-time degree program, services for LD students, student-designed majors, study abroad, summer session for credit.

Computers on Campus 169 computers/terminals are available on campus for general student use. Students can access the following: campus intranet, computer help desk, free student e-mail accounts, online (class) grades, online (class) registration, online (class) schedules. Campuswide network is available. 100% of college-owned or -operated housing units are wired for high-speed Internet access. Wireless service is available via classrooms, computer centers, computer labs, learning centers, libraries, student centers.

Student Life *Housing options:* coed. Campus housing is university owned and is provided by a third party. Freshman applicants given priority for college

housing. *Activities and organizations:* Associated Student Government, American Institute of Architecture Students, Armenian Student Association, La Voz Unida, Collegiate Entrepreneurs' Organization (CEO), national fraternities, national sororities. *Campus security:* 24-hour patrols, late-night transport/escort service, controlled dormitory access. *Student services:* health clinic, personal/psychological counseling.

Athletics *Intramural sports:* basketball M/W, soccer M/W.

Standardized Tests *Required:* SAT or ACT (for admission).

Costs (2011–12) *Comprehensive fee:* $39,914 includes full-time tuition ($29,604), mandatory fees ($390), and room and board ($9920). Full-time tuition and fees vary according to course load, degree level, and program. Part-time tuition: $965 per credit hour. Part-time tuition and fees vary according to course load, degree level, and program. *College room only:* $5990. Room and board charges vary according to board plan, housing facility, and location. *Payment plan:* deferred payment. *Waivers:* employees or children of employees.

Financial Aid Of all full-time matriculated undergraduates who enrolled in 2011, 949 applied for aid, 909 were judged to have need, 19 had their need fully met. 120 Federal Work-Study jobs (averaging $132,695). In 2011, 78 non-need-based awards were made. *Average percent of need met:* 53%. *Average financial aid package:* $20,336. *Average need-based loan:* $4541. *Average need-based gift aid:* $16,137. *Average non-need-based aid:* $8839. *Average indebtedness upon graduation:* $39,359.

Applying *Options:* electronic application, deferred entrance. *Application fee:* $50. *Required:* minimum 2.0 GPA. *Required for some:* high school transcript. *Recommended:* essay or personal statement, minimum 3.0 GPA, 2 letters of recommendation. *Application deadlines:* rolling (freshmen), rolling (transfers). *Notification:* continuous (freshmen), continuous (transfers).

Freshman Application Contact Ms. Sabrina Taylor, Woodbury University, 7500 Glenoaks Boulevard, Burbank, CA 91510-7846. *Phone:* 800-784-9663. *Toll-free phone:* 800-784-WOOD. *Fax:* 818-767-0032. *E-mail:* admissions@woodbury.edu. *Web site:* http://www.woodbury.edu/.

Yeshiva Ohr Elchonon Chabad/West Coast Talmudical Seminary

Los Angeles, California

Director of Admissions Rabbi Ezra Binyomin Schochet, Dean, Yeshiva Ohr Elchonon Chabad/West Coast Talmudical Seminary, 7215 Waring Avenue, Los Angeles, CA 90046-7660. *Phone:* 323-937-3763. *E-mail:* roshyeshiva@yoec.edu. *Web site:* http://www.yoec.edu/.

COLORADO

Adams State College

Alamosa, Colorado

- **State-supported** comprehensive, founded 1921
- **Small-town** 90-acre campus with easy access to Pueblo
- **Coed** 2,430 undergraduate students, 82% full-time, 55% women, 45% men
- **Moderately difficult** entrance level, 64% of applicants were admitted

Undergraduates 2,001 full-time, 429 part-time. Students come from 52 states and territories; 12 other countries; 19% are from out of state; 6% Black or African American, non-Hispanic/Latino; 32% Hispanic/Latino; 1% Asian, non-Hispanic/Latino; 0.2% Native Hawaiian or other Pacific Islander, non-Hispanic/Latino; 1% American Indian or Alaska Native, non-Hispanic/Latino; 2% Two or more races, non-Hispanic/Latino; 6% Race/ethnicity unknown; 9% transferred in; 36% live on campus. *Retention:* 55% of full-time freshmen returned.

Freshmen *Admission:* 2,534 applied, 1,613 admitted, 585 enrolled. *Average high school GPA:* 2.99. *Test scores:* SAT critical reading scores over 500: 47%; SAT math scores over 500: 51%; SAT writing scores over 500: 36%; ACT scores over 18: 72%; SAT critical reading scores over 600: 10%; SAT math scores over 600: 9%; SAT writing scores over 600: 6%; ACT scores over 24: 19%; ACT scores over 30: 2%.

Faculty *Total:* 174, 64% full-time, 45% with terminal degrees. *Student/faculty ratio:* 17:1.

Academics *Calendar:* semesters. *Degrees:* associate, bachelor's, and master's. *Special study options:* academic remediation for entering students, accelerated degree program, adult/continuing education programs, advanced placement credit, distance learning, double majors, independent study, internships, off-campus study, part-time degree program, services for LD students, student-designed majors, study abroad, summer session for credit.

Computers on Campus Students can access the following: campus intranet, computer help desk, free student e-mail accounts, online (class) grades, online (class) registration, online (class) schedules. Campuswide network is available. 100% of college-owned or -operated housing units are wired for high-speed Internet access. Wireless service is available via classrooms, computer centers, computer labs, dorm rooms, learning centers, libraries, student centers.

Student Life *Housing:* on-campus residence required through sophomore year. *Options:* coed, men-only, women-only. Campus housing is university owned. Freshman campus housing is guaranteed. *Activities and organizations:* drama/theater group, student-run newspaper, radio station, choral group, marching band, Student Programming Board, student government, Semillas de la Tierra, Newman Club (Psychology), Fellowship of Christian Athletes. *Campus security:* 24-hour emergency response devices and patrols, student patrols, late-night transport/escort service, controlled dormitory access. *Student services:* personal/psychological counseling.

Athletics Member NCAA. All Division II. *Intercollegiate sports:* basketball M(s)/W(s), cross-country running M(s)/W(s), football M(s), golf M(s)/W(s), lacrosse M(s)/W(s), soccer M(s)/W(s), softball W(s), swimming and diving M(s)/W(s), track and field M(s)/W(s), volleyball W(s), wrestling M(s). *Intramural sports:* basketball M/W, bowling M/W, cheerleading M(c)/W(c), football M/W, golf M(c)/W(c), racquetball M/W, rock climbing M/W, rugby M(c)/W(c), skiing (cross-country) M/W, skiing (downhill) M/W, soccer M/W, softball M/W, swimming and diving M/W, volleyball M/W, water polo M/W.

Standardized Tests *Required:* SAT or ACT (for admission).

Costs (2011–12) *Tuition:* state resident $3312 full-time, $138 per credit hour part-time; nonresident $13,560 full-time, $565 per credit hour part-time. Full-time tuition and fees vary according to course load. Part-time tuition and fees vary according to course load. *Required fees:* $2315 full-time, $96 per credit hour part-time. *Room and board:* $7120; room only: $3300. Room and board charges vary according to board plan and housing facility. *Payment plans:* installment, deferred payment. *Waivers:* senior citizens and employees or children of employees.

Financial Aid Of all full-time matriculated undergraduates who enrolled in 2010, 1,913 applied for aid, 1,682 were judged to have need, 18 had their need fully met. 218 Federal Work-Study jobs (averaging $264,004). 313 state and other part-time jobs (averaging $1144). *Average percent of need met:* 61%. *Average financial aid package:* $12,299. *Average need-based loan:* $3638. *Average need-based gift aid:* $5196. *Average indebtedness upon graduation:* $23,860.

Applying *Options:* electronic application, early admission, deferred entrance. *Application fee:* $30. *Required:* high school transcript, minimum 2.0 GPA. *Required for some:* essay or personal statement, interview, audition for music majors, portfolio for art majors. *Application deadlines:* 8/1 (freshmen), 8/10 (out-of-state freshmen), 8/1 (transfers). *Notification:* continuous (freshmen), continuous (out-of-state freshmen), continuous (transfers).

Freshman Application Contact Mr. Eric Carpio, Director of Admissions, Adams State College, 208 Edgemont Boulevard, Alamosa, CO 81102. *Phone:* 719-587-7712. *Toll-free phone:* 800-824-6494. *Fax:* 719-587-7522. *E-mail:* ascadmit@adams.edu. *Web site:* http://www.adams.edu/.

American Sentinel University

Aurora, Colorado

Director of Admissions Natalie Nixon, Vice President of Admission, American Sentinel University, 2260 South Xanadu Way, Suite 310, Aurora, CO 80014. *Phone:* 800-729-2427. *Toll-free phone:* 800-729-2427. *Fax:* 866-505-2450. *E-mail:* natalie.nixon@AmericanSentinel.edu. *Web site:* http://www.americansentinel.edu/.

Argosy University, Denver

Denver, Colorado

Freshman Application Contact Argosy University, Denver, 7600 East Eastman Avenue, Denver, CO 80231. *Phone:* 303-248-2700. *Toll-free phone:* 866-431-5981. *Web site:* http://www.argosy.edu/denver/.

See page 1062 for the College Close-Up.

The Art Institute of Colorado

Denver, Colorado

- **Proprietary** 4-year, founded 1952, part of Education Management Corporation
- **Urban** campus
- **Coed**

Academics *Calendar:* quarters. *Degrees:* diplomas, associate, and bachelor's.

Costs (2011–12) *Tuition:* Tuition cost varies by program. Prospective students should contact the school for current tuition costs. Other charges include a

starting kit for all first-quarter students. Kits vary in price, depending on the program of study.

Freshman Application Contact The Art Institute of Colorado, 1200 Lincoln Street, Denver, CO 80203. *Phone:* 303-837-0825. *Toll-free phone:* 800-275-2420. *Web site:* http://www.artinstitutes.edu/denver/.

See page 1092 for the College Close-Up.

Aspen University
Denver, Colorado

Director of Admissions Admissions, Aspen University, 501 South Cherry Street, Suite 350, Denver, CO 80246. *Phone:* 303-333-4224. *Toll-free phone:* 800-441-4746. *Fax:* 303-336-1144. *E-mail:* admissions@aspen.edu. *Web site:* http://www.aspen.edu/.

CollegeAmerica–Colorado Springs
Colorado Springs, Colorado

Freshman Application Contact CollegeAmerica–Colorado Springs, 3645 Citadel Drive South, Colorado Springs, CO 80909. *Phone:* 719-637-0600. *Toll-free phone:* 800-622-2894. *Web site:* http://www.collegeamerica.edu/.

CollegeAmerica–Denver
Denver, Colorado

Freshman Application Contact Admissions Office, CollegeAmerica–Denver, 1385 South Colorado Boulevard, Denver, CO 80222. *Phone:* 303-300-8740. *Toll-free phone:* 800-622-2894. *Web site:* http://www.collegeamerica.edu/.

CollegeAmerica–Fort Collins
Fort Collins, Colorado

Director of Admissions Ms. Anna DiTorrice-Mull, Director of Admissions, CollegeAmerica–Fort Collins, 4601 South Mason Street, Fort Collins, CO 80525-3740. *Phone:* 970-223-6060 Ext. 8002. *Toll-free phone:* 800-622-2894. *Web site:* http://www.collegeamerica.edu/.

Colorado Christian University
Lakewood, Colorado

Freshman Application Contact Jo Leda Martin, Associate Director of Admissions, Colorado Christian University, 8787 W Alameda Avenue. *Phone:* 303-963-3000. *Toll-free phone:* 800-44-FAITH. *Fax:* 303-963-3201. *E-mail:* jomartin@ccu.edu. *Web site:* http://www.ccu.edu/.

The Colorado College
Colorado Springs, Colorado

- **Independent** comprehensive, founded 1874
- **Urban** 90-acre campus with easy access to Denver
- **Endowment** $509.4 million
- **Coed** 2,026 undergraduate students, 99% full-time, 54% women, 46% men
- **Very difficult** entrance level, 26% of applicants were admitted

Undergraduates 2,008 full-time, 18 part-time. Students come from 50 states and territories; 58 other countries; 78% are from out of state; 1% Black or African American, non-Hispanic/Latino; 8% Hispanic/Latino; 4% Asian, non-Hispanic/Latino; 0.0% Native Hawaiian or other Pacific Islander, non-Hispanic/Latino; 0.4% American Indian or Alaska Native, non-Hispanic/Latino; 5% Two or more races, non-Hispanic/Latino; 2% Race/ethnicity unknown; 6% international; 1% transferred in; 74% live on campus. *Retention:* 96% of full-time freshmen returned.

Freshmen *Admission:* 4,916 applied, 1,267 admitted, 484 enrolled. *Test scores:* SAT critical reading scores over 500: 99%; SAT math scores over 500: 99%; SAT writing scores over 500: 98%; ACT scores over 18: 100%; SAT critical reading scores over 600: 86%; SAT math scores over 600: 88%; SAT writing scores over 600: 83%; ACT scores over 24: 97%; SAT critical reading scores over 700: 38%; SAT math scores over 700: 29%; SAT writing scores over 700: 31%; ACT scores over 30: 66%.

Faculty *Total:* 202, 85% full-time. *Student/faculty ratio:* 10:1.

Academics *Calendar:* modular. *Degrees:* bachelor's and master's (master's degree in education only). *Special study options:* advanced placement credit, double majors, English as a second language, independent study, off-campus study, services for LD students, student-designed majors, study abroad, summer session for credit. *ROTC:* Army (c). *Unusual degree programs:* 3-2 engi-

neering with Rensselaer Polytechnic Institute, Washington University in St. Louis, University of Southern California, Columbia University.

Computers on Campus 396 computers/terminals are available on campus for general student use. Students can access the following: campus intranet, computer help desk, free student e-mail accounts, online (class) grades, online (class) registration, online (class) schedules. Campuswide network is available. 100% of college-owned or -operated housing units are wired for high-speed Internet access. Wireless service is available via entire campus.

Student Life *Housing:* on-campus residence required through junior year. *Options:* coed, men-only, women-only. Campus housing is university owned. Freshman campus housing is guaranteed. *Activities and organizations:* drama/theater group, student-run newspaper, choral group, national fraternities, national sororities. *Campus security:* 24-hour emergency response devices and patrols, late-night transport/escort service, controlled dormitory access, whistle program, student escort service, good campus lighting. *Student services:* health clinic, personal/psychological counseling, women's center.

Athletics Member NCAA. All Division III except ice hockey (Division I), soccer (Division I). *Intercollegiate sports:* baseball M(c), basketball M/W, cross-country running M/W, equestrian sports M(c)/W(c), field hockey M(c)/W(c), ice hockey M(s)/W(c), lacrosse M/W, rugby M(c)/W(c), skiing (downhill) M(c)/W(c), soccer M/W(s), softball W(c), swimming and diving M/W, tennis M/W, track and field M/W, ultimate Frisbee M(c)/W(c), volleyball W, water polo W(c). *Intramural sports:* basketball M/W, football M/W, ice hockey M, racquetball M/W, soccer M/W, softball M/W, ultimate Frisbee M/W, volleyball M/W, water polo M/W.

Standardized Tests *Required for some:* SAT and SAT Subject Tests or ACT (for admission).

Costs (2011–12) *One-time required fee:* $150. *Comprehensive fee:* $49,516 includes full-time tuition ($39,900), mandatory fees ($200), and room and board ($9416). Part-time tuition: $6650 per course. Part-time tuition and fees vary according to course load. *College room only:* $5184. Room and board charges vary according to board plan and housing facility. *Payment plan:* installment. *Waivers:* employees or children of employees.

Financial Aid Of all full-time matriculated undergraduates who enrolled in 2010, 888 applied for aid, 750 were judged to have need, 469 had their need fully met. 225 Federal Work-Study jobs (averaging $1750). 128 state and other part-time jobs (averaging $1664). In 2010, 158 non-need-based awards were made. *Average percent of need met:* 92%. *Average financial aid package:* $33,298. *Average need-based loan:* $4355. *Average need-based gift aid:* $30,672. *Average non-need-based aid:* $13,573. *Average indebtedness upon graduation:* $18,349. *Financial aid deadline:* 2/15.

Applying *Options:* electronic application, early decision, early action, deferred entrance. *Application fee:* $50. *Required:* essay or personal statement, high school transcript, 2 letters of recommendation. *Recommended:* interview. *Application deadlines:* 1/15 (freshmen), 3/1 (transfers), 11/15 (early action). *Early decision deadline:* 11/15 (for plan 1), 1/1 (for plan 2). *Notification:* 4/1 (freshmen), 5/1 (transfers), 12/15 (early decision plan 1), 2/10 (early decision plan 2), 12/20 (early action).

Freshman Application Contact Mr. Matthew Bonser, Associate Director of Admission, The Colorado College, 14 East Cache La Poudre, Colorado Springs, CO 80903-3294. *Phone:* 719-389-6344. *Toll-free phone:* 800-542-7214. *Fax:* 719-389-6816. *E-mail:* admission@coloradocollege.edu. *Web site:* http://www.coloradocollege.edu/.

Colorado Heights University
Denver, Colorado

Director of Admissions Ashley Henderson, Admissions Coordinator, Colorado Heights University, 3001 South Federal Boulevard, Denver, CO 80236-2711. *Phone:* 303-937-4221. *E-mail:* admissions@tlhu.edu. *Web site:* http://www.chu.edu/.

Colorado Mesa University
Grand Junction, Colorado

- **State-supported** comprehensive, founded 1925
- **Small-town** 78-acre campus
- **Coed** 8,930 undergraduate students, 75% full-time, 55% women, 45% men
- **Minimally difficult** entrance level, 80% of applicants were admitted

Undergraduates 6,723 full-time, 2,207 part-time. Students come from 43 states and territories; 14 other countries; 12% are from out of state; 2% Black or African American, non-Hispanic/Latino; 13% Hispanic/Latino; 1% Asian, non-Hispanic/Latino; 0.8% Native Hawaiian or other Pacific Islander, non-Hispanic/Latino; 1% American Indian or Alaska Native, non-Hispanic/Latino; 2% Two or more races, non-Hispanic/Latino; 5% Race/ethnicity unknown; 0.4% international; 7% transferred in; 21% live on campus. *Retention:* 64% of full-time freshmen returned.

Freshmen *Admission:* 5,840 applied, 4,671 admitted, 2,179 enrolled. *Average high school GPA:* 3. *Test scores:* SAT critical reading scores over 500: 40%; SAT math scores over 500: 48%; ACT scores over 18: 75%; SAT critical reading scores over 600: 8%; SAT math scores over 600: 11%; ACT scores over 24: 22%; SAT critical reading scores over 700: 1%; ACT scores over 30: 1%.
Faculty *Total:* 531, 46% full-time. *Student/faculty ratio:* 22:1.
Academics *Calendar:* semesters. *Degrees:* certificates, associate, bachelor's, master's, and doctoral. *Special study options:* academic remediation for entering students, accelerated degree program, adult/continuing education programs, advanced placement credit, distance learning, double majors, honors programs, independent study, internships, off-campus study, part-time degree program, services for LD students, study abroad, summer session for credit.
Computers on Campus 525 computers/terminals are available on campus for general student use. Students can access the following: campus intranet, computer help desk, free student e-mail accounts, online (class) grades, online (class) registration, online (class) schedules. Campuswide network is available. 100% of college-owned or -operated housing units are wired for high-speed Internet access. Wireless service is available via classrooms, computer centers, libraries, student centers.
Student Life *Housing:* on-campus residence required through sophomore year. *Options:* coed, women-only, disabled students. Campus housing is university owned. Freshman applicants given priority for college housing. *Activities and organizations:* drama/theater group, student-run newspaper, radio and television station, choral group, marching band, Environmental Club, Student Body Association, KMSA radio station, Rodeo Club, Campus Residents Association. *Campus security:* 24-hour emergency response devices and patrols, late-night transport/escort service, controlled dormitory access. *Student services:* health clinic, personal/psychological counseling, legal services.
Athletics Member NCAA. All Division II. *Intercollegiate sports:* baseball M(s), basketball M(s)/W(s), cross-country running M(s)/W(s), football M(s), golf M(s)/W(s), lacrosse M(s)/W(s), rugby M(c)/W(c), soccer M(s)/W(s), softball W(s), swimming and diving M(s)/W(s), tennis M(s)/W(s), track and field M(s)/W(s), volleyball W(s), wrestling M(s). *Intramural sports:* badminton M/W, basketball M/W, equestrian sports M/W, football M/W, racquetball M/W, soccer M/W, softball M/W, tennis M/W, ultimate Frisbee M/W, volleyball M/W, water polo M/W.
Standardized Tests *Required:* SAT or ACT (for admission).
Costs (2011–12) *Tuition:* state resident $5780 full-time, $193 per credit hour part-time; nonresident $15,968 full-time, $532 per credit hour part-time. Full-time tuition and fees vary according to course load. Part-time tuition and fees vary according to course load. *Required fees:* $768 full-time, $26 per credit hour part-time. *Room and board:* $8657. Room and board charges vary according to board plan and housing facility. *Payment plan:* installment. *Waivers:* employees or children of employees.
Financial Aid Of all full-time matriculated undergraduates who enrolled in 2010, 4,875 applied for aid, 4,162 were judged to have need, 460 had their need fully met. In 2010, 422 non-need-based awards were made. *Average percent of need met:* 56%. *Average financial aid package:* $7784. *Average need-based loan:* $3720. *Average need-based gift aid:* $5242. *Average non-need-based aid:* $2252. *Average indebtedness upon graduation:* $25,924.
Applying *Options:* electronic application, deferred entrance. *Application fee:* $30. *Required:* high school transcript. *Recommended:* essay or personal statement, 2 letters of recommendation. *Application deadlines:* rolling (freshmen), rolling (out-of-state freshmen), rolling (transfers). *Notification:* continuous (freshmen), continuous (out-of-state freshmen), continuous (transfers).
Freshman Application Contact Admissions, Colorado Mesa University, 1100 North Avenue, Grand Junction, CO 81501. *Phone:* 970-248-1875. *Toll-free phone:* 800-982-MESA. *Fax:* 970-248-1973. *E-mail:* admissions@coloradomesa.edu. *Web site:* http://www.coloradomesa.edu/.

Colorado Mountain College

Glenwood Springs, Colorado

- **District-supported** primarily 2-year, founded 1965, part of Colorado Mountain College District System
- **Rural** 680-acre campus
- **Coed** 2,465 undergraduate students
- **Noncompetitive** entrance level

Undergraduates 44% live on campus.
Freshmen *Average high school GPA:* 2.4.
Faculty *Total:* 28. *Student/faculty ratio:* 12:1.
Academics *Calendar:* semesters. *Degrees:* certificates, associate, and bachelor's. *Special study options:* academic remediation for entering students, adult/continuing education programs, advanced placement credit, cooperative education, distance learning, double majors, English as a second language, honors programs, independent study, internships, part-time degree program, services for LD students, study abroad, summer session for credit.

Computers on Campus 65 computers/terminals are available on campus for general student use. Students can access the following: campus intranet, computer help desk, free student e-mail accounts, online (class) grades, online (class) registration, online (class) schedules. Campuswide network is available. Wireless service is available via entire campus.
Student Life *Housing:* on-campus residence required for freshman year. *Options:* coed, disabled students. Campus housing is university owned. Freshman applicants given priority for college housing. *Activities and organizations:* drama/theater group, student-run newspaper, student government, Outdoor activities, World Awareness Society, Peer Mentors, Student Activities Board. *Campus security:* 24-hour emergency response devices, student patrols, controlled dormitory access. *Student services:* health clinic, personal/psychological counseling.
Athletics Member NCAA, NJCAA. All NCAA Division I. *Intramural sports:* basketball M/W, rock climbing M/W, skiing (cross-country) M/W, skiing (downhill) M/W, ultimate Frisbee M/W, volleyball M/W.
Standardized Tests *Recommended:* SAT or ACT (for admission).
Costs (2012–13) *Tuition:* area resident $1590 full-time; state resident $2670 full-time; nonresident $8370 full-time. *Required fees:* $180 full-time. *Room and board:* $7928.
Applying *Options:* electronic application, early admission, deferred entrance. *Required:* high school transcript. *Application deadlines:* rolling (freshmen), rolling (out-of-state freshmen), rolling (transfers).
Freshman Application Contact Vicky Butler, Admissions Assistant, Colorado Mountain College, 3000 CR 114, Glenwood Springs, CO 81601. *Phone:* 970-947-8276. *Toll-free phone:* 800-621-8559. *E-mail:* Vvalentine@coloradomtn.edu. *Web site:* http://www.coloradomtn.edu/.

Colorado Mountain College, Alpine Campus

Steamboat Springs, Colorado

- **District-supported** primarily 2-year, founded 1965, part of Colorado Mountain College District System
- **Small-town** 10-acre campus
- **Coed** 1,550 undergraduate students
- **Noncompetitive** entrance level

Undergraduates 44% live on campus.
Freshmen *Average high school GPA:* 2.4.
Faculty *Total:* 25. *Student/faculty ratio:* 12:1.
Academics *Calendar:* semesters. *Degrees:* certificates, associate, and bachelor's. *Special study options:* academic remediation for entering students, adult/continuing education programs, advanced placement credit, cooperative education, distance learning, double majors, English as a second language, honors programs, independent study, internships, off-campus study, part-time degree program, services for LD students, study abroad, summer session for credit.
Computers on Campus 60 computers/terminals are available on campus for general student use. Students can access the following: campus intranet, computer help desk, free student e-mail accounts, online (class) grades, online (class) registration, online (class) schedules. Campuswide network is available. 100% of college-owned or -operated housing units are wired for high-speed Internet access. Wireless service is available via entire campus.
Student Life *Housing:* on-campus residence required for freshman year. *Options:* coed, disabled students. Campus housing is university owned. *Activities and organizations:* student-run newspaper, student government, Forensics Team, Ski Club, International Club, Phi Theta Kappa. *Campus security:* 24-hour emergency response devices, student patrols, controlled dormitory access. *Student services:* health clinic, personal/psychological counseling.
Athletics Member NCAA, NJCAA. All NCAA Division I. *Intercollegiate sports:* skiing (downhill) M/W. *Intramural sports:* basketball M/W, skiing (cross-country) M/W, skiing (downhill) M/W, soccer M/W, ultimate Frisbee M/W, volleyball M/W.
Standardized Tests *Recommended:* SAT or ACT (for admission).
Costs (2012–13) *Tuition:* area resident $1590 full-time; state resident $2670 full-time; nonresident $8370 full-time. *Required fees:* $180 full-time. *Room and board:* $7928; room only: $4160. Room and board charges vary according to board plan. *Payment plan:* installment. *Waivers:* senior citizens.
Financial Aid Of all full-time matriculated undergraduates who enrolled in 2010, 40 Federal Work-Study jobs (averaging $1173). 62 state and other part-time jobs (averaging $1060).
Applying *Options:* electronic application, early admission, deferred entrance. *Required:* high school transcript. *Application deadlines:* rolling (freshmen), rolling (out-of-state freshmen), rolling (transfers).
Freshman Application Contact Ms. Stephanie Fletcher, Admissions Assistant, Colorado Mountain College, Alpine Campus, 1330 Bob Adams Drive, Steamboat Springs, CO 80487. *Phone:* 970-870-4417 Ext. 4417. *Toll-free phone:* 800-621-8559. *E-mail:* stephaniefletcher@coloradomtn.edu. *Web site:* http://www.coloradomtn.edu/.

Colorado Mountain College, Timberline Campus

Leadville, Colorado

- **District-supported** primarily 2-year, founded 1965, part of Colorado Mountain College District System
- **Rural** 200-acre campus
- **Coed** 1,209 undergraduate students
- **Noncompetitive** entrance level

Undergraduates 30% live on campus.

Freshmen *Average high school GPA:* 2.4.

Faculty *Total:* 16. *Student/faculty ratio:* 12:1.

Academics *Calendar:* semesters. *Degrees:* certificates, associate, and bachelor's. *Special study options:* academic remediation for entering students, adult/continuing education programs, advanced placement credit, cooperative education, distance learning, double majors, English as a second language, honors programs, independent study, internships, off-campus study, part-time degree program, services for LD students, student-designed majors, study abroad, summer session for credit.

Computers on Campus 30 computers/terminals are available on campus for general student use. Students can access the following: free student e-mail accounts, online (class) grades, online (class) registration, online (class) schedules. Campuswide network is available. 100% of college-owned or -operated housing units are wired for high-speed Internet access. Wireless service is available via entire campus.

Student Life *Housing:* on-campus residence required for freshman year. *Options:* coed, disabled students. Campus housing is university owned. Freshman applicants given priority for college housing. *Activities and organizations:* Environmental Club, Outdoor Club, Student Activities Board. *Campus security:* 24-hour emergency response devices, student patrols, controlled dormitory access. *Student services:* health clinic, personal/psychological counseling.

Athletics Member NCAA, NJCAA. All NCAA Division I. *Intramural sports:* basketball M, rock climbing M/W, skiing (cross-country) M/W, skiing (downhill) M/W, soccer M/W, volleyball M/W.

Standardized Tests *Recommended:* SAT or ACT (for admission).

Costs (2012–13) *Tuition:* area resident $1590 full-time; state resident $2670 full-time; nonresident $8370 full-time. *Required fees:* $180 full-time. *Room and board:* $7928. Room and board charges vary according to board plan. *Payment plan:* installment. *Waivers:* senior citizens.

Applying *Options:* electronic application, early admission, deferred entrance. *Required:* high school transcript. *Application deadlines:* rolling (freshmen), rolling (out-of-state freshmen), rolling (transfers).

Freshman Application Contact Ms. Kate Kenoyer, Admissions Assistant, Colorado Mountain College, Timberline Campus, 901South Highway 24, Leadville, CO 80461. *Phone:* 719-486-4292. *Toll-free phone:* 800-621-8559. *E-mail:* joinus@coloradomtn.edu. *Web site:* http://www.coloradomtn.edu/.

Colorado School of Mines

Golden, Colorado

- **State-supported** university, founded 1874
- **Small-town** 470-acre campus with easy access to Denver, Boulder
- **Endowment** $196.0 million
- **Coed** 3,946 undergraduate students, 95% full-time, 26% women, 74% men
- **Very difficult** entrance level, 45% of applicants were admitted

Undergraduates 3,729 full-time, 217 part-time. Students come from 53 states and territories; 39 other countries; 28% are from out of state; 1% Black or African American, non-Hispanic/Latino; 8% Hispanic/Latino; 5% Asian, non-Hispanic/Latino; 0.4% American Indian or Alaska Native, non-Hispanic/Latino; 2% Two or more races, non-Hispanic/Latino; 5% Race/ethnicity unknown; 5% international; 2% transferred in; 39% live on campus. *Retention:* 89% of full-time freshmen returned.

Freshmen *Admission:* 10,145 applied, 4,520 admitted, 879 enrolled. *Average high school GPA:* 3.8. *Test scores:* SAT critical reading scores over 500: 96%; SAT math scores over 500: 99%; SAT writing scores over 500: 90%; ACT scores over 18: 100%; SAT critical reading scores over 600: 60%; SAT math scores over 600: 90%; SAT writing scores over 600: 47%; ACT scores over 24: 96%; SAT critical reading scores over 700: 19%; SAT math scores over 700: 37%; SAT writing scores over 700: 7%; ACT scores over 30: 43%.

Faculty *Total:* 337, 71% full-time, 77% with terminal degrees. *Student/faculty ratio:* 17:1.

Academics *Calendar:* semesters. *Degrees:* bachelor's, master's, doctoral, post-master's, and first professional certificates. *Special study options:* accelerated degree program, advanced placement credit, cooperative education, double majors, honors programs, independent study, internships, off-campus study, services for LD students, study abroad, summer session for credit. *ROTC:* Army (b), Air Force (b).

Computers on Campus 400 computers/terminals are available on campus for general student use. Students can access the following: campus intranet, computer help desk, free student e-mail accounts, online (class) grades, online (class) registration, online (class) schedules. Campuswide network is available. 100% of college-owned or -operated housing units are wired for high-speed Internet access. Wireless service is available via entire campus.

Student Life *Housing:* on-campus residence required for freshman year. *Options:* coed. Campus housing is university owned and is provided by a third party. Freshman campus housing is guaranteed. *Activities and organizations:* drama/theater group, student-run newspaper, radio station, choral group, marching band, Society of Women Engineers, Residence Hall Association, Associated Students of Colorado School of Mines, Student Professional Societies, Campus Crusade for Christ/Fellowship for Christian Athletes, national fraternities, national sororities. *Campus security:* 24-hour emergency response devices and patrols, late-night transport/escort service, controlled dormitory access, full service, community oriented law enforcement agency employing fully trained police officers. *Student services:* health clinic, personal/psychological counseling, women's center.

Athletics Member NCAA. All Division II. *Intercollegiate sports:* baseball M(s), basketball M(s)/W(s), bowling M(c)/W(c), cross-country running M(s)/W(s), football M(s), golf M, ice hockey M(c)/W(c), lacrosse M(c), rugby M(c)/W(c), skiing (downhill) M(c)/W(c), soccer M(s)/W(s), softball W(s), swimming and diving M/W, track and field M(s)/W(s), ultimate Frisbee M(c)/W(c), volleyball M(c)/W(s), wrestling M(s). *Intramural sports:* badminton M/W, basketball M/W, bowling M/W, cross-country running M/W, field hockey M/W, football M/W, golf M/W, lacrosse M, racquetball M/W, soccer M/W, softball M/W, swimming and diving M/W, table tennis M/W, tennis M/W, track and field M/W, ultimate Frisbee M/W, volleyball M/W, wrestling M/W.

Standardized Tests *Required:* SAT or ACT (for admission).

Costs (2011–12) *Tuition:* state resident $12,585 full-time, $419 per credit hour part-time; nonresident $27,270 full-time, $909 per credit hour part-time. Part-time tuition and fees vary according to course load. *Required fees:* $1869 full-time. *Room and board:* $8838. Room and board charges vary according to board plan and housing facility. *Payment plan:* installment. *Waivers:* senior citizens and employees or children of employees.

Financial Aid Of all full-time matriculated undergraduates who enrolled in 2010, 2,443 applied for aid, 1,766 were judged to have need, 338 had their need fully met. 293 Federal Work-Study jobs (averaging $1438). 1,110 state and other part-time jobs (averaging $1906). In 2010, 877 non-need-based awards were made. *Average percent of need met:* 67%. *Average financial aid package:* $13,086. *Average need-based loan:* $4664. *Average need-based gift aid:* $6863. *Average non-need-based aid:* $5168. *Average indebtedness upon graduation:* $29,662.

Applying *Options:* electronic application, deferred entrance. *Application fee:* $45. *Required:* high school transcript. *Required for some:* essay or personal statement, interview. *Recommended:* minimum 3.8 GPA, rank in upper one-third of high school class. *Application deadlines:* 5/1 (freshmen), 5/1 (transfers). *Notification:* continuous until 10/1 (freshmen), continuous until 10/1 (transfers).

Freshman Application Contact Mrs. Joanne Lambert, Assistant Director of Enrollment Management, Colorado School of Mines, Student Center, 1600 Maple Street, Golden, CO 80401. *Phone:* 303-273-3220. *Toll-free phone:* 800-446-9488 Ext. 3220. *Fax:* 303-273-3509. *E-mail:* admit@mines.edu. *Web site:* http://www.mines.edu/.

Colorado State University

Fort Collins, Colorado

- **State-supported** university, founded 1870, part of Colorado State University System
- **Urban** 582-acre campus with easy access to Denver
- **Endowment** $221.2 million
- **Coed** 23,261 undergraduate students, 91% full-time, 51% women, 49% men
- **Moderately difficult** entrance level, 76% of applicants were admitted

Undergraduates 21,059 full-time, 2,202 part-time. Students come from 57 states and territories; 51 other countries; 17% are from out of state; 2% Black or African American, non-Hispanic/Latino; 8% Hispanic/Latino; 2% Asian, non-Hispanic/Latino; 0.2% Native Hawaiian or other Pacific Islander, non-Hispanic/Latino; 0.4% American Indian or Alaska Native, non-Hispanic/Latino; 3% Two or more races, non-Hispanic/Latino; 5% Race/ethnicity unknown; 2% international; 7% transferred in; 24% live on campus. *Retention:* 84% of full-time freshmen returned.

Freshmen *Admission:* 16,559 applied, 12,564 admitted, 4,504 enrolled. *Average high school GPA:* 3.59. *Test scores:* SAT critical reading scores over 500: 80%; SAT math scores over 500: 84%; ACT scores over 18: 98%; SAT critical

reading scores over 600: 37%; SAT math scores over 600: 42%; ACT scores over 24: 61%; SAT critical reading scores over 700: 6%; SAT math scores over 700: 7%; ACT scores over 30: 11%.

Faculty *Total:* 961, 96% full-time, 99% with terminal degrees. *Student/faculty ratio:* 18:1.

Academics *Calendar:* semesters. *Degrees:* bachelor's, master's, doctoral, and first professional. *Special study options:* accelerated degree program, advanced placement credit, cooperative education, distance learning, double majors, English as a second language, external degree program, honors programs, independent study, internships, off-campus study, part-time degree program, services for LD students, study abroad, summer session for credit. *ROTC:* Army (b), Air Force (b). *Unusual degree programs:* 3-2 engineering.

Computers on Campus 2,500 computers/terminals and 3,200 ports are available on campus for general student use. Students can access the following: campus intranet, computer help desk, free student e-mail accounts, online (class) grades, online (class) registration, online (class) schedules, personalized portal services including transcripts and financials (billing, financial aid). Campuswide network is available. 100% of college-owned or -operated housing units are wired for high-speed Internet access. Wireless service is available via classrooms, computer centers, computer labs, dorm rooms, libraries, student centers.

Student Life *Housing:* on-campus residence required for freshman year. *Options:* coed, disabled students. Campus housing is university owned. Freshman campus housing is guaranteed. *Activities and organizations:* drama/theater group, student-run newspaper, radio and television station, choral group, marching band, Golden Key International Honor Society, Council of International Student Affairs, Campus Crusade for Christ, Associated Students of CSU (ASCSU Student Government), Snowriders, national fraternities, national sororities. *Campus security:* 24-hour emergency response devices and patrols, student patrols, late-night transport/escort service, controlled dormitory access. *Student services:* health clinic, personal/psychological counseling, women's center, legal services.

Athletics Member NCAA. All Division I except football (Division I-A). *Intercollegiate sports:* baseball M(c), basketball M(s)/W(s), crew M(c)/W(c), cross-country running M(s)/W(s), field hockey M(c)/W(c), golf M(s)/W(s), ice hockey M(c)/W(c), lacrosse M(c)/W(c), rugby M(c)/W(c), skiing (downhill) M(c)/W(c), soccer M(c)/W(c), softball W(s), swimming and diving W(s), tennis M(c)/W(s), track and field M(s)/W(s), ultimate Frisbee M(c)/W(c), volleyball W(s), water polo M(c)/W(c), wrestling M(c)/W(c). *Intramural sports:* basketball M/W, bowling M/W, golf M/W, racquetball M/W, soccer M/W, softball M/W, ultimate Frisbee M/W, volleyball M/W.

Standardized Tests *Required:* SAT or ACT (for admission).

Costs (2011–12) *Tuition:* state resident $6307 full-time, $286 per credit hour part-time; nonresident $22,007 full-time, $1100 per credit hour part-time. Full-time tuition and fees vary according to course load and program. Part-time tuition and fees vary according to course load and program. *Required fees:* $1735 full-time, $30 per credit hour part-time, $148 per term part-time. *Room and board:* $9172; room only: $4538. Room and board charges vary according to board plan and housing facility. *Waivers:* employees or children of employees.

Financial Aid Of all full-time matriculated undergraduates who enrolled in 2009, 13,383 applied for aid, 9,036 were judged to have need, 3,937 had their need fully met. 419 Federal Work-Study jobs (averaging $2063). 997 state and other part-time jobs (averaging $1823). In 2009, 1905 non-need-based awards were made. *Average percent of need met:* 77%. *Average financial aid package:* $11,085. *Average need-based loan:* $6906. *Average need-based gift aid:* $6626. *Average non-need-based aid:* $3539. *Average indebtedness upon graduation:* $21,224.

Applying *Options:* electronic application, early action, deferred entrance. *Application fee:* $50. *Required:* essay or personal statement, high school transcript, 1 letter of recommendation. *Application deadlines:* 2/1 (freshmen), 7/1 (transfers). *Notification:* continuous (freshmen), continuous (transfers).

Freshman Application Contact Mr. Jim Rawlins, Executive Director of Admissions, Colorado State University, Ammons Hall, Fort Collins, CO 80523-1062. *Phone:* 970-491-6909. *Fax:* 970-491-7799. *E-mail:* admissions@colostate.edu. *Web site:* http://www.colostate.edu/.

Colorado State University–Pueblo

Pueblo, Colorado

Freshman Application Contact Mrs. Dana Trujillo, Director of Admissions, Colorado State University–Pueblo, 2200 Bonforte Boulevard, Pueblo, CO 81001-4901. *Phone:* 719-549-2391. *Fax:* 719-549-2419. *E-mail:* dana.trujillo@colostate-pueblo.edu. *Web site:* http://www.colostate-pueblo.edu/.

Colorado Technical University Colorado Springs

Colorado Springs, Colorado

Director of Admissions Beth Braaten, Vice President of Admissions, Colorado Technical University Colorado Springs, 4435 North Chestnut Street, Colorado Springs, CO 80907-3896. *Phone:* 888-404-7555. *Toll-free phone:* 866-942-6555. *E-mail:* bbraaten@coloradotech.edu. *Web site:* http://www.coloradotech.edu/.

Colorado Technical University Denver South

Aurora, Colorado

Director of Admissions Rosaland Giboney, Associate Director of Admissions, Colorado Technical University Denver South, 3151 South Vaughn Way, Aurora, CO 80014. *Phone:* 888-404-7555. *Toll-free phone:* 888-309-6555. *E-mail:* rgiboney@coloradotech.edu. *Web site:* http://www.coloradotech.edu/.

Colorado Technical University Online

Colorado Springs, Colorado

Director of Admissions William Beckley, Chief Admission Officer, Colorado Technical University Online, 4435 North Chestnut Street, Suite E, Colorado Springs, CO 80907. *Phone:* 888-404-7555. *Web site:* http://www.coloradotech.edu/.

Denver School of Nursing

Denver, Colorado

Admissions Office Contact Denver School of Nursing, 1401 19th Street, Denver, CO 80202. *Toll-free phone:* 888-479-5550. *Web site:* http://www.denverschoolofnursing.edu/.

DeVry University

Colorado Springs, Colorado

Director of Admissions Admissions Office, DeVry University, 1175 Kelly Johnson Boulevard, Colorado Springs, CO 80920. *Toll-free phone:* 866-338-7941. *Web site:* http://www.devry.edu/.

DeVry University

Westminster, Colorado

- **Proprietary** comprehensive, founded 1945
- **Urban** campus
- **Coed** 812 undergraduate students, 33% full-time, 37% women, 63% men
- **Noncompetitive** entrance level

Undergraduates 270 full-time, 542 part-time. 6% are from out of state; 6% Black or African American, non-Hispanic/Latino; 16% Hispanic/Latino; 4% Asian, non-Hispanic/Latino; 0.5% Native Hawaiian or other Pacific Islander, non-Hispanic/Latino; 0.6% American Indian or Alaska Native, non-Hispanic/Latino; 2% Two or more races, non-Hispanic/Latino; 9% Race/ethnicity unknown; 0.1% international; 23% transferred in.

Freshmen *Admission:* 83 enrolled.

Faculty *Total:* 87, 15% full-time. *Student/faculty ratio:* 13:1.

Academics *Calendar:* semesters. *Degrees:* associate, bachelor's, master's, and postbachelor's certificates. *Special study options:* adult/continuing education programs.

Student Life *Housing:* college housing not available.

Costs (2011–12) *Tuition:* $15,294 full-time, $597 per credit hour part-time. Full-time tuition and fees vary according to course load. Part-time tuition and fees vary according to course load. *Required fees:* $80 full-time, $40 per term part-time. *Payment plans:* installment, deferred payment. *Waivers:* employees or children of employees.

Financial Aid Of all full-time matriculated undergraduates who enrolled in 2007, 148 applied for aid, 136 were judged to have need, 6 had their need fully met. In 2007, 17 non-need-based awards were made. *Average percent of need met:* 37%. *Average financial aid package:* $11,971. *Average need-based loan:* $8024. *Average need-based gift aid:* $6094. *Average non-need-based aid:* $13,350. *Average indebtedness upon graduation:* $11,071.

Applying *Application fee:* $50. *Required:* high school transcript. *Required for some:* essay or personal statement, interview. *Application deadlines:* rolling (freshmen), rolling (transfers). *Notification:* continuous (freshmen), continuous (transfers).

Freshman Application Contact Admissions Office, DeVry University, 1870 West 122nd Avenue, Westminster, CO 80234-2010. *Phone:* 303-280-7400. *Toll-free phone:* 866-338-7941. *Web site:* http://www.devry.edu/.

Fort Lewis College
Durango, Colorado

- **State-supported** 4-year, founded 1911
- **Small-town** 350-acre campus
- **Endowment** $4.7 million
- **Coed** 3,856 undergraduate students, 91% full-time, 48% women, 52% men
- **Moderately difficult** entrance level, 71% of applicants were admitted

Undergraduates 3,507 full-time, 349 part-time. Students come from 47 states and territories; 19 other countries; 38% are from out of state; 1% Black or African American, non-Hispanic/Latino; 8% Hispanic/Latino; 0.3% Asian, non-Hispanic/Latino; 0.2% Native Hawaiian or other Pacific Islander, non-Hispanic/Latino; 21% American Indian or Alaska Native, non-Hispanic/Latino; 4% Two or more races, non-Hispanic/Latino; 2% Race/ethnicity unknown; 0.7% international; 10% transferred in; 34% live on campus.
Freshmen *Admission:* 2,792 applied, 1,974 admitted, 777 enrolled. *Average high school GPA:* 3.13. *Test scores:* SAT critical reading scores over 500: 54%; SAT math scores over 500: 56%; SAT writing scores over 500: 41%; ACT scores over 18: 91%; SAT critical reading scores over 600: 17%; SAT math scores over 600: 15%; SAT writing scores over 600: 15%; ACT scores over 24: 31%; SAT critical reading scores over 700: 3%; SAT math scores over 700: 1%; SAT writing scores over 700: 2%; ACT scores over 30: 3%.
Faculty *Total:* 229, 72% full-time, 78% with terminal degrees. *Student/faculty ratio:* 19:1.
Academics *Calendar:* modified trimesters. *Degree:* bachelor's. *Special study options:* academic remediation for entering students, advanced placement credit, double majors, honors programs, independent study, internships, services for LD students, student-designed majors, study abroad, summer session for credit. *Unusual degree programs:* 3-2 social work with Psychology or Sociology majors may be able to complete both their Bachelor's degree and their Master of Social Work degrees in a total of five years through the Fort Lewis College and U. of Denver Graduate Degree Program.
Computers on Campus 786 computers/terminals are available on campus for general student use. Students can access the following: campus intranet, computer help desk, free student e-mail accounts, online (class) grades, online (class) registration, online (class) schedules. Campuswide network is available. 100% of college-owned or -operated housing units are wired for high-speed Internet access. Wireless service is available via entire campus.
Student Life *Housing:* on-campus residence required for freshman year. *Options:* coed. Campus housing is university owned. Freshman applicants given priority for college housing. *Activities and organizations:* drama/theater group, student-run newspaper, radio station. *Campus security:* 24-hour emergency response devices and patrols, late-night transport/escort service, controlled dormitory access. *Student services:* health clinic, personal/psychological counseling.
Athletics Member NCAA. All Division II. *Intercollegiate sports:* baseball M(c), basketball M(s)/W(s), cheerleading M(c)/W(c), cross-country running M(s)/W(s), fencing M(c)/W(c), football M(s), golf M(s), ice hockey M(c)/W(c), lacrosse M(c)/W(s), rock climbing M(c)/W(c), rugby M(c)/W(c), skiing (cross-country) M(c)/W(c), skiing (downhill) M(c)/W(c), soccer M(s)/W(s), softball W(s), ultimate Frisbee M(c)/W(c), volleyball W(s), wrestling M(c)/W(c). *Intramural sports:* badminton M/W, basketball M/W, football M/W, golf M/W, racquetball M/W, soccer M/W, softball M/W, ultimate Frisbee M/W, volleyball M/W.
Standardized Tests *Required:* SAT or ACT (for admission).
Costs (2011–12) *One-time required fee:* $135. *Tuition:* state resident $4048 full-time, $169 per credit hour part-time; nonresident $16,072 full-time, $803 per credit hour part-time. Full-time tuition and fees vary according to course load and reciprocity agreements. Part-time tuition and fees vary according to course load and reciprocity agreements. *Required fees:* $1544 full-time. *Room and board:* $8010; room only: $4020. Room and board charges vary according to board plan and housing facility. *Payment plan:* installment. *Waivers:* minority students and employees or children of employees.
Financial Aid Of all full-time matriculated undergraduates who enrolled in 2010, 3,410 applied for aid, 3,003 were judged to have need, 935 had their need fully met. In 2010, 689 non-need-based awards were made. *Average percent of need met:* 73%. *Average financial aid package:* $9554. *Average need-based loan:* $4022. *Average need-based gift aid:* $3764. *Average non-need-based aid:* $2614. *Average indebtedness upon graduation:* $18,780.
Applying *Options:* deferred entrance. *Application fee:* $40. *Required:* high school transcript. *Required for some:* interview. *Recommended:* essay or personal statement, 2 letters of recommendation. *Application deadline:* 8/1 (freshmen).

Freshman Application Contact Fort Lewis College, 1000 Rim Drive, Durango, CO 81301-3999. *Phone:* 970-247-7184. *Toll-free phone:* 877-FLC-COLO. *Web site:* http://www.fortlewis.edu/.

ITT Technical Institute
Aurora, Colorado

- **Proprietary** primarily 2-year
- **Coed**
- **Minimally difficult** entrance level

Academics *Degrees:* associate and bachelor's.
Freshman Application Contact Director of Recruitment, ITT Technical Institute, 12500 East Iliff Avenue, Suite 100, Aurora, CO 80014. *Phone:* 303-695-6317. *Toll-free phone:* 877-832-8460. *Web site:* http://www.itt-tech.edu/.

ITT Technical Institute
Thornton, Colorado

- **Proprietary** primarily 2-year, founded 1984, part of ITT Educational Services, Inc.
- **Suburban** campus
- **Coed**
- **Minimally difficult** entrance level

Academics *Calendar:* quarters. *Degrees:* associate and bachelor's.
Student Life *Housing:* college housing not available.
Freshman Application Contact Director of Recruitment, ITT Technical Institute, 500 East 84th Avenue, Suite B12, Thornton, CO 80229. *Phone:* 303-288-4488. *Toll-free phone:* 800-395-4488. *Web site:* http://www.itt-tech.edu/.

Johnson & Wales University
Denver, Colorado

- **Independent** 4-year, founded 1993
- **Small-town** campus
- **Coed**
- **Moderately difficult** entrance level

Faculty *Student/faculty ratio:* 24:1.
Academics *Calendar:* quarters. *Degrees:* associate and bachelor's.
Student Life *Campus security:* 24-hour emergency response devices and patrols, student patrols, late-night transport/escort service.
Athletics Member NAIA.
Standardized Tests *Required for some:* SAT or ACT (for admission).
Costs (2011–12) *One-time required fee:* $300. *Comprehensive fee:* $35,421 includes full-time tuition ($23,955), mandatory fees ($1152), and room and board ($10,314). Part-time tuition: $164 per credit hour. *Room and board:* Room and board charges vary according to board plan, housing facility, and location.
Financial Aid Of all full-time matriculated undergraduates who enrolled in 2010, 1,279 applied for aid, 1,106 were judged to have need, 153 had their need fully met. In 2010, 265 non-need-based awards were made. *Average percent of need met:* 67. *Average financial aid package:* $16,423. *Average need-based loan:* $5006. *Average need-based gift aid:* $6325. *Average non-need-based aid:* $6332.
Applying *Options:* electronic application, early admission, deferred entrance. *Required:* high school transcript. *Required for some:* essay or personal statement, minimum 2.8 GPA, interview. *Recommended:* minimum 2.0 GPA.
Freshman Application Contact Kim Ostrowski, Director of Admissions, Johnson & Wales University, 7150 Montview Boulevard, Denver, CO 80220. *Phone:* 303-256-9300. *Toll-free phone:* 877-598-3368. *Fax:* 303-598-3368. *E-mail:* den@admissions.jwu.edu. *Web site:* http://www.jwu.edu/.

Jones International University
Centennial, Colorado

- **Proprietary** university, founded 1995
- **Suburban** campus
- **Coed**
- **Noncompetitive** entrance level

Undergraduates Students come from 54 states and territories; 20 other countries; 95% are from out of state.
Faculty *Total:* 131, 8% full-time, 82% with terminal degrees.
Academics *Calendar:* continuous. *Degrees:* certificates, associate, bachelor's, master's, doctoral, and postbachelor's certificates (offers only online degree programs). *Special study options:* advanced placement credit, distance learning, independent study, internships, part-time degree program, services for LD students. *Unusual degree programs:* business administration.

Computers on Campus Students can access the following: computer help desk, free student e-mail accounts, online (class) grades, online (class) registration, online (class) schedules, we are entirely online.

Costs (2012–13) *Tuition:* $12,720 full-time, $530 per credit hour part-time. Full-time tuition and fees vary according to course level, course load, degree level, and program. Part-time tuition and fees vary according to course level, course load, degree level, and program. *Payment plan:* installment. *Waivers:* employees or children of employees.

Financial Aid Of all full-time matriculated undergraduates who enrolled in 2009, 469 applied for aid, 368 were judged to have need. *Average percent of need met:* 80%. *Average financial aid package:* $7020. *Average need-based loan:* $3450. *Average need-based gift aid:* $3570.

Applying *Options:* electronic application, early admission, deferred entrance. *Required:* high school transcript, minimum 2.0 GPA. *Required for some:* minimum 2.0 GPA for transfer applicants. *Application deadlines:* rolling (freshmen), rolling (out-of-state freshmen), rolling (transfers). *Notification:* continuous (freshmen), continuous (out-of-state freshmen), continuous (transfers).

Freshman Application Contact Admissions Center, Jones International University, 9697 East Mineral Avenue, Centennial, CO 80112. *Phone:* 800-811-5663 Ext. 2. *Toll-free phone:* 800-811-5663. *Fax:* 303-799-0966. *Web site:* http://www.jiu.edu/.

Metropolitan State College of Denver
Denver, Colorado

- **State-supported** comprehensive, founded 1963
- **Urban** 175-acre campus with easy access to Denver
- **Coed** 23,538 undergraduate students, 60% full-time, 54% women, 46% men
- **Minimally difficult** entrance level, 63% of applicants were admitted

Undergraduates 14,105 full-time, 9,433 part-time. 4% are from out of state; 6% Black or African American, non-Hispanic/Latino; 18% Hispanic/Latino; 3% Asian, non-Hispanic/Latino; 0.3% Native Hawaiian or other Pacific Islander, non-Hispanic/Latino; 0.8% American Indian or Alaska Native, non-Hispanic/Latino; 3% Two or more races, non-Hispanic/Latino; 5% Race/ethnicity unknown; 0.5% international; 9% transferred in. *Retention:* 66% of full-time freshmen returned.

Freshmen *Admission:* 5,942 applied, 3,744 admitted, 2,405 enrolled. *Average high school GPA:* 2.96. *Test scores:* SAT critical reading scores over 500: 54%; SAT math scores over 500: 47%; ACT scores over 18: 85%; SAT critical reading scores over 600: 17%; SAT math scores over 600: 13%; ACT scores over 24: 22%; SAT critical reading scores over 700: 2%; ACT scores over 30: 1%.

Faculty *Total:* 1,414, 37% full-time. *Student/faculty ratio:* 21:1.

Academics *Calendar:* semesters. *Degrees:* bachelor's, master's, and post-master's certificates. *Special study options:* accelerated degree program, adult/continuing education programs, advanced placement credit, cooperative education, distance learning, double majors, external degree program, honors programs, independent study, internships, off-campus study, part-time degree program, services for LD students, student-designed majors, study abroad, summer session for credit. *ROTC:* Army (c), Air Force (c).

Computers on Campus 808 computers/terminals are available on campus for general student use. Students can access the following: computer help desk, free student e-mail accounts, online (class) grades, online (class) registration, online (class) schedules. Campuswide network is available. Wireless service is available via entire campus.

Student Life *Housing:* college housing not available. *Activities and organizations:* drama/theater group, student-run newspaper, radio and television station, choral group, national fraternities, national sororities. *Campus security:* 24-hour emergency response devices and patrols, late-night transport/escort service. *Student services:* health clinic, personal/psychological counseling, women's center, legal services.

Athletics Member NCAA. All Division II. *Intercollegiate sports:* baseball M(s), basketball M(s)/W(s), cross-country running M/W, soccer M(s)/W(s), softball W(s), tennis M(s)/W(s), track and field M/W, volleyball W(s). *Intramural sports:* baseball M(c)/W(c), cheerleading M(c)/W(c), fencing M(c)/W(c), football M(c), ice hockey M(c), lacrosse M(c), rugby M(c), soccer M(c), squash M(c)/W, swimming and diving M(c)/W(c), ultimate Frisbee M(c)/W(c), volleyball M(c)/W(c).

Standardized Tests *Required:* SAT or ACT (for admission). *Required for some:* SAT (for admission), ACT (for admission).

Costs (2011–12) *Tuition:* state resident $3809 full-time, $159 per credit hour part-time; nonresident $14,665 full-time, $611 per credit hour part-time. Full-time tuition and fees vary according to course load and location. Part-time tuition and fees vary according to course load and location. *Required fees:* $1025 full-time, $233 per credit hour part-time. *Payment plans:* installment, deferred payment. *Waivers:* senior citizens.

Financial Aid Of all full-time matriculated undergraduates who enrolled in 2010, 9,892 applied for aid, 7,856 were judged to have need, 471 had their need fully met. 252 Federal Work-Study jobs (averaging $2733). 569 state and other part-time jobs (averaging $3503). In 2010, 1354 non-need-based awards were made. *Average percent of need met:* 63%. *Average financial aid package:* $7724. *Average need-based loan:* $4059. *Average need-based gift aid:* $5551. *Average non-need-based aid:* $1919. *Average indebtedness upon graduation:* $25,774.

Applying *Options:* electronic application, deferred entrance. *Application fee:* $25. *Required:* high school transcript. *Recommended:* minimum 2.0 GPA. *Application deadline:* rolling (transfers). *Notification:* continuous (freshmen), continuous (transfers).

Freshman Application Contact Ms. Michelle Brown, Associate Director of Admissions, Metropolitan State College of Denver, PO Box 173362, Denver, CO 80217-3362. *Phone:* 303-556-2615. *Web site:* http://www.mscd.edu/.

Naropa University
Boulder, Colorado

- **Independent** comprehensive, founded 1974
- **Urban** 12-acre campus with easy access to Denver
- **Endowment** $4.8 million
- **Coed** 425 undergraduate students, 93% full-time, 60% women, 40% men
- **Moderately difficult** entrance level, 91% of applicants were admitted

Undergraduates 395 full-time, 30 part-time. Students come from 41 states and territories; 9 other countries; 69% are from out of state; 1% Black or African American, non-Hispanic/Latino; 7% Hispanic/Latino; 1% Asian, non-Hispanic/Latino; 0.2% American Indian or Alaska Native, non-Hispanic/Latino; 5% Two or more races, non-Hispanic/Latino; 22% Race/ethnicity unknown; 2% international; 20% transferred in; 18% live on campus.

Freshmen *Admission:* 137 applied, 125 admitted, 54 enrolled.

Faculty *Total:* 175, 27% full-time, 37% with terminal degrees. *Student/faculty ratio:* 9:1.

Academics *Calendar:* semesters. *Degrees:* certificates, bachelor's, and master's. *Special study options:* advanced placement credit, double majors, independent study, internships, part-time degree program, services for LD students, student-designed majors, summer session for credit.

Computers on Campus 51 computers/terminals are available on campus for general student use. Students can access the following: computer help desk, free student e-mail accounts, online (class) grades, online (class) registration, online (class) schedules. Campuswide network is available. 100% of college-owned or -operated housing units are wired for high-speed Internet access. Wireless service is available via entire campus.

Student Life *Housing:* on-campus residence required for freshman year. *Options:* coed. Campus housing is university owned. Freshman campus housing is guaranteed. *Activities and organizations:* drama/theater group, student-run newspaper, choral group, ROOT: Reconnecting on Outdoor Terrain, Restorative Justice Training Group, Team Asana, Naropa Way of Tea, SUN: Students for a United Naropa. *Campus security:* late-night transport/escort service, controlled dormitory access, foot and vehicle patrol 4:30 pm to midnight, 24 hour on-call Safety and Security Manager. *Student services:* personal/psychological counseling.

Costs (2012–13) *Comprehensive fee:* $34,832 includes full-time tuition ($26,230), mandatory fees ($160), and room and board ($8442). Full-time tuition and fees vary according to course load. Part-time tuition: $850 per credit. Part-time tuition and fees vary according to course load. *Room and board:* Room and board charges vary according to board plan. *Payment plan:* installment. *Waivers:* employees or children of employees.

Financial Aid Of all full-time matriculated undergraduates who enrolled in 2011, 286 applied for aid, 271 were judged to have need, 3 had their need fully met. In 2011, 7 non-need-based awards were made. *Average percent of need met:* 83%. *Average financial aid package:* $29,811. *Average need-based loan:* $9912. *Average need-based gift aid:* $18,208. *Average non-need-based aid:* $4597. *Average indebtedness upon graduation:* $26,617.

Applying *Options:* electronic application, deferred entrance. *Application fee:* $50. *Required:* essay or personal statement, high school transcript, 2 letters of recommendation, interview. *Required for some:* supplemental application and/or art samples required for applicants to performance, environmental studies, INTD studies, music, visual arts and writing and literature programs. *Application deadlines:* rolling (freshmen), rolling (transfers). *Notification:* continuous (freshmen), continuous (out-of-state freshmen), continuous (transfers).

Freshman Application Contact Mr. Jason Makowsky, Associate Director of Undergraduate Admissions, Naropa University, 2130 Arapahoe Avenue, Boulder, CO 80302. *Phone:* 303-245-4693. *Toll-free phone:* 800-772-6951. *Fax:* 303-546-3583. *E-mail:* jmakowsky@naropa.edu. *Web site:* http://www.naropa.edu/.

National American University
Colorado Springs, Colorado

Director of Admissions Director of Admissions, National American University, 5125 North Academy Boulevard, Colorado Springs, CO 80918. *Phone:* 719-590-8300. *E-mail:* csadmissions@national.edu. *Web site:* http://www.national.edu/.

National American University
Denver, Colorado

Freshman Application Contact National American University, 1325 South Colorado Blvd, Suite 100, Denver, CO 80222. *Phone:* 303-876-7112. *Web site:* http://www.national.edu/.

Nazarene Bible College
Colorado Springs, Colorado

Freshman Application Contact Dr. Laurel Matson, Director of Admissions/Public Relations, Nazarene Bible College, 1111 Academy Park Loop, Colorado Springs, CO 80910-3704. *Phone:* 719-884-5061. *Toll-free phone:* 800-873-3873. *Fax:* 719-884-5199. *Web site:* http://www.nbc.edu/.

Pima Medical Institute
Denver, Colorado

- **Proprietary** primarily 2-year, founded 1988, part of Vocational Training Institutes, Inc.
- **Urban** campus
- **Coed**
- **Minimally difficult** entrance level

Academics *Calendar:* modular. *Degrees:* certificates, associate, and bachelor's.

Standardized Tests *Required:* Wonderlic Scholastic Level Exam (for admission).

Applying *Required:* interview. *Required for some:* high school transcript.

Freshman Application Contact Admissions Office, Pima Medical Institute, 1701 West 72nd Avenue, Suite 130, Denver, CO 80221. *Phone:* 303-426-1800. *Toll-free phone:* 800-477-PIMA (in-state); 888-477-PIMA (out-of-state). *Web site:* http://www.pmi.edu/.

Platt College
Aurora, Colorado

Freshman Application Contact Admissions Office, Platt College, 3100 South Parker Road, Suite 200, Aurora, CO 80014-3141. *Phone:* 303-369-5151. *Web site:* http://www.plattcolorado.edu/.

Regis University
Denver, Colorado

- **Independent Roman Catholic (Jesuit)** comprehensive, founded 1877
- **Suburban** 90-acre campus with easy access to Denver
- **Coed** 5,643 undergraduate students, 45% full-time, 65% women, 35% men
- **Moderately difficult** entrance level, 87% of applicants were admitted

Undergraduates 2,537 full-time, 3,106 part-time. 6% Black or African American, non-Hispanic/Latino; 14% Hispanic/Latino; 4% Asian, non-Hispanic/Latino; 0.1% Native Hawaiian or other Pacific Islander, non-Hispanic/Latino; 0.7% American Indian or Alaska Native, non-Hispanic/Latino; 1% Two or more races, non-Hispanic/Latino; 9% Race/ethnicity unknown; 0.7% international; 16% transferred in; 50% live on campus. *Retention:* 82% of full-time freshmen returned.

Freshmen *Admission:* 3,701 applied, 3,214 admitted, 514 enrolled. *Test scores:* SAT critical reading scores over 500: 64%; SAT math scores over 500: 61%; SAT writing scores over 500: 68%; ACT scores over 18: 96%; SAT critical reading scores over 600: 21%; SAT math scores over 600: 20%; SAT writing scores over 600: 22%; ACT scores over 24: 52%; SAT critical reading scores over 700: 4%; SAT math scores over 700: 2%; SAT writing scores over 700: 1%; ACT scores over 30: 4%.

Faculty *Total:* 1,093, 25% full-time. *Student/faculty ratio:* 14:1.

Academics *Calendar:* semesters. *Degrees:* certificates, bachelor's, master's, doctoral, post-master's, and postbachelor's certificates. *Special study options:* academic remediation for entering students, accelerated degree program, adult/continuing education programs, advanced placement credit, cooperative education, distance learning, double majors, external degree program, freshman honors college, honors programs, independent study, internships, off-campus study, part-time degree program, services for LD students, student-designed majors, study abroad, summer session for credit. *ROTC:* Army (c), Navy (c), Air Force (c). *Unusual degree programs:* 3-2 engineering with Washington University in St. Louis.

Computers on Campus 450 computers/terminals and 1,000 ports are available on campus for general student use. Students can access the following: campus intranet, computer help desk, free student e-mail accounts, online (class) grades, online (class) registration, online (class) schedules. Campus-wide network is available. 100% of college-owned or -operated housing units are wired for high-speed Internet access. Wireless service is available via entire campus.

Student Life *Housing:* on-campus residence required through sophomore year. *Options:* coed, disabled students. Campus housing is university owned. Freshman applicants given priority for college housing. *Activities and organizations:* drama/theater group, student-run newspaper, radio station, choral group, Musical Theater Club, Student government, Club Sports, Outdoor Adventure, Black Student Association. *Campus security:* 24-hour emergency response devices and patrols, student patrols, late-night transport/escort service, controlled dormitory access. *Student services:* health clinic, personal/psychological counseling.

Athletics Member NCAA. All Division II. *Intercollegiate sports:* baseball M(s), basketball M(s)/W(s), cross-country running M(s)/W(s), golf M(s)/W(s), lacrosse W(s), soccer M(s)/W(s), softball W(s), volleyball W(s). *Intramural sports:* basketball M/W, bowling M/W, cheerleading M/W, football M/W, ice hockey M, lacrosse M, rugby M, soccer M/W, softball W, tennis M/W, ultimate Frisbee M/W, volleyball M/W.

Standardized Tests *Required:* SAT or ACT (for admission).

Costs (2012–13) *Comprehensive fee:* $40,718 includes full-time tuition ($30,588), mandatory fees ($600), and room and board ($9530). Full-time tuition and fees vary according to course load, location, program, and reciprocity agreements. Part-time tuition: $956 per credit hour. Part-time tuition and fees vary according to location, program, and reciprocity agreements. *Required fees:* $956 per credit hour part-time. *Room and board:* Room and board charges vary according to board plan and housing facility. *Payment plans:* installment, deferred payment. *Waivers:* employees or children of employees.

Financial Aid Of all full-time matriculated undergraduates who enrolled in 2009, 2,075 applied for aid, 1,577 were judged to have need, 569 had their need fully met. 280 Federal Work-Study jobs (averaging $1993). 456 state and other part-time jobs (averaging $1734). In 2009, 422 non-need-based awards were made. *Average percent of need met:* 57%. *Average financial aid package:* $15,006. *Average need-based loan:* $3003. *Average need-based gift aid:* $10,312. *Average non-need-based aid:* $12,199. *Average indebtedness upon graduation:* $29,590.

Applying *Options:* electronic application, deferred entrance. *Application fee:* $40. *Required:* essay or personal statement, high school transcript, minimum 2.5 GPA. *Required for some:* 1 letter of recommendation, interview. *Application deadlines:* rolling (freshmen), rolling (out-of-state freshmen), rolling (transfers). *Notification:* continuous (freshmen), continuous (transfers).

Freshman Application Contact Mr. Vic Davolt, Director of Admission, Regis University, 3333 Regis Boulevard, Denver, CO 80221-1099. *Phone:* 303-458-4905. *Toll-free phone:* 800-388-2366 Ext. 4900. *Fax:* 303-964-5534. *E-mail:* regisadm@regis.edu. *Web site:* http://www.regis.edu/.

Remington College–Colorado Springs Campus
Colorado Springs, Colorado

Freshman Application Contact Remington College–Colorado Springs Campus, 6050 Erin Park Drive, #250, Colorado Springs, CO 80918. *Phone:* 719-532-1234 Ext. 202. *Web site:* http://www.remingtoncollege.edu/.

Rocky Mountain College of Art + Design
Lakewood, Colorado

- **Proprietary** 4-year, founded 1963
- **Suburban** 23-acre campus
- **Coed** 635 undergraduate students, 86% full-time, 62% women, 38% men
- **Moderately difficult** entrance level, 100% of applicants were admitted

Undergraduates 547 full-time, 88 part-time. Students come from 47 states and territories; 6 other countries; 32% are from out of state; 3% Black or African American, non-Hispanic/Latino; 9% Hispanic/Latino; 3% Asian, non-Hispanic/Latino; 2% American Indian or Alaska Native, non-Hispanic/Latino; 0.8% Two or more races, non-Hispanic/Latino; 8% Race/ethnicity unknown;

2% international; 11% transferred in. *Retention:* 59% of full-time freshmen returned.

Freshmen *Admission:* 375 applied, 375 admitted, 94 enrolled.

Faculty *Total:* 114, 43% full-time, 11% with terminal degrees. *Student/faculty ratio:* 12:1.

Academics *Calendar:* trimesters. *Degree:* bachelor's. *Special study options:* academic remediation for entering students, accelerated degree program, advanced placement credit, cooperative education, distance learning, double majors, honors programs, independent study, internships, off-campus study, part-time degree program, services for LD students, study abroad, summer session for credit.

Computers on Campus 300 computers/terminals are available on campus for general student use. Students can access the following: campus intranet, computer help desk, free student e-mail accounts, online (class) grades, online (class) registration, online (class) schedules, computer assistance, online library, wireless network, discounted software/hardware. Campuswide network is available. Wireless service is available via entire campus.

Student Life *Housing:* college housing not available. *Activities and organizations:* student-run newspaper, The Sanatorium (student newspaper), The American Society of Interior Designers, The American Institute of Graphic Arts, Belly Dancing Club, writing club. *Campus security:* 24-hour emergency response devices, late-night transport/escort service. *Student services:* personal/psychological counseling.

Costs (2011–12) *Tuition:* $27,648 full-time, $1152 per credit hour part-time. Full-time tuition and fees vary according to location. Part-time tuition and fees vary according to course load and location. No tuition increase for student's term of enrollment. *Payment plan:* installment. *Waivers:* employees or children of employees.

Financial Aid Of all full-time matriculated undergraduates who enrolled in 2011, 349 applied for aid, 320 were judged to have need, 22 had their need fully met. In 2011, 46 non-need-based awards were made. *Average percent of need met:* 72%. *Average financial aid package:* $19,774. *Average need-based loan:* $4648. *Average need-based gift aid:* $4616. *Average non-need-based aid:* $5613. *Average indebtedness upon graduation:* $34,191.

Applying *Options:* electronic application. *Application fee:* $50. *Required:* essay or personal statement, minimum 2.0 GPA, interview, portfolio. *Required for some:* high school transcript. *Application deadlines:* rolling (freshmen), rolling (transfers). *Notification:* continuous (freshmen), continuous (transfers).

Freshman Application Contact Mr. Joe Leonhardt, Vice President of Admissions, Rocky Mountain College of Art + Design, 1600 Pierce Street, Lakewood, CO 80214. *Phone:* 303-225-8567. *Toll-free phone:* 800-888-ARTS. *Fax:* 303-759-4970. *E-mail:* admit@rmcad.edu. *Web site:* http://www.rmcad.edu/.

United States Air Force Academy

Colorado Springs, Colorado

- **Federally supported** 4-year, founded 1954
- **Suburban** 18,000-acre campus with easy access to Colorado Springs, Denver
- **Coed, primarily men** 4,413 undergraduate students, 100% full-time, 22% women, 78% men
- **Most difficult** entrance level, 9% of applicants were admitted

Undergraduates 4,413 full-time. Students come from 54 states and territories; 31 other countries; 93% are from out of state; 7% Black or African American, non-Hispanic/Latino; 9% Hispanic/Latino; 7% Asian, non-Hispanic/Latino; 0.9% Native Hawaiian or other Pacific Islander, non-Hispanic/Latino; 0.8% American Indian or Alaska Native, non-Hispanic/Latino; 2% Race/ethnicity unknown; 1% international; 100% live on campus. *Retention:* 89% of full-time freshmen returned.

Freshmen *Admission:* 12,732 applied, 1,127 admitted, 1,071 enrolled. *Average high school GPA:* 3.88. *Test scores:* SAT critical reading scores over 500: 98%; SAT math scores over 500: 100%; ACT scores over 18: 100%; SAT critical reading scores over 600: 72%; SAT math scores over 600: 89%; ACT scores over 24: 99%; SAT critical reading scores over 700: 16%; SAT math scores over 700: 33%; ACT scores over 30: 56%.

Faculty *Total:* 529, 99% full-time, 54% with terminal degrees. *Student/faculty ratio:* 8:1.

Academics *Calendar:* semesters. *Degree:* bachelor's. *Special study options:* academic remediation for entering students, advanced placement credit, double majors, English as a second language, honors programs, independent study, internships, off-campus study, student-designed majors, study abroad, summer session for credit.

Computers on Campus 4 computers/terminals and 40 ports are available on campus for general student use. Students can access the following: campus intranet, computer help desk, free student e-mail accounts, online (class) grades, online (class) registration, online (class) schedules. Campuswide network is available. 100% of college-owned or -operated housing units are wired

for high-speed Internet access. Wireless service is available via classrooms, computer centers, computer labs, learning centers, libraries, student centers.

Student Life *Housing:* on-campus residence required through senior year. *Options:* coed. Campus housing is university owned. Freshman campus housing is guaranteed. *Activities and organizations:* drama/theater group, student-run radio station, choral group, marching band, Cadet Ski Club, Men's and Women's Rugby Club, Cadet Cycling Club, Aviation Club, Drum and Bugle Corps. *Campus security:* 24-hour emergency response devices and patrols, late-night transport/escort service, controlled dormitory access, self-defense education, well-lit campus. *Student services:* health clinic, personal/psychological counseling, legal services.

Athletics Member NCAA. All Division I. *Intercollegiate sports:* archery M(c)/W(c), baseball M, basketball M/W, cheerleading M/W, cross-country running M/W, equestrian sports M(c)/W(c), fencing M/W, football M, golf M(c), gymnastics M/W, ice hockey M, lacrosse M/W(c), racquetball M(c)/W(c), riflery M/W, rock climbing M(c)/W(c), rugby M(c)/W(c), skiing (cross-country) M(c)/W(c), skiing (downhill) M(c)/W(c), soccer M/W, softball M/W, swimming and diving M/W, tennis M/W, track and field M/W, ultimate Frisbee M(c)/W(c), volleyball M(c)/W, water polo M/W(c), weight lifting M(c)/W(c), wrestling M. *Intramural sports:* basketball M/W, cross-country running M/W, racquetball M/W, rugby M/W, soccer M/W, softball M/W, ultimate Frisbee M/W, volleyball M/W, wrestling M.

Standardized Tests *Required:* SAT or ACT (for admission).

Applying *Options:* electronic application. *Required:* essay or personal statement, high school transcript, minimum 2.0 GPA, interview, authorized nomination. *Recommended:* 3 letters of recommendation. *Application deadlines:* 12/31 (freshmen), 12/31 (transfers). *Notification:* 10/15 (freshmen), 10/15 (transfers).

Freshman Application Contact Selections Division Admission Counselor, United States Air Force Academy, HQ USAFA/RR, 2304 Cadet Drive, Suite 2400, USAF Academy, CO 80840-5025. *Phone:* 800-443-9266. *Toll-free phone:* 800-443-9266. *Fax:* 719-333-3012. *Web site:* http://www.usafa.edu/.

See inside front cover for full-page display ad and page 1652 for the College Close-Up.

University of Colorado at Colorado Springs

Colorado Springs, Colorado

- **State-supported** university, founded 1965, part of University of Colorado System
- **Urban** 532-acre campus with easy access to Colorado Springs
- **Endowment** $31.6 million
- **Coed** 7,909 undergraduate students, 77% full-time, 53% women, 47% men
- **Moderately difficult** entrance level, 68% of applicants were admitted

Undergraduates 6,099 full-time, 1,810 part-time. Students come from 46 states and territories; 16 other countries; 9% are from out of state; 4% Black or African American, non-Hispanic/Latino; 12% Hispanic/Latino; 4% Asian, non-Hispanic/Latino; 0.1% Native Hawaiian or other Pacific Islander, non-Hispanic/Latino; 0.7% American Indian or Alaska Native, non-Hispanic/Latino; 2% Two or more races, non-Hispanic/Latino; 4% Race/ethnicity unknown; 0.5% international; 12% transferred in; 10% live on campus. *Retention:* 71% of full-time freshmen returned.

Freshmen *Admission:* 5,203 applied, 3,549 admitted, 1,352 enrolled. *Average high school GPA:* 3.26. *Test scores:* SAT critical reading scores over 500: 70%; SAT math scores over 500: 70%; ACT scores over 18: 95%; SAT critical reading scores over 600: 20%; SAT math scores over 600: 30%; ACT scores over 24: 43%; SAT critical reading scores over 700: 2%; SAT math scores over 700: 4%; ACT scores over 30: 7%.

Faculty *Total:* 676, 51% full-time, 44% with terminal degrees. *Student/faculty ratio:* 18:1.

Academics *Calendar:* semesters. *Degrees:* bachelor's, master's, doctoral, and first professional. *Special study options:* academic remediation for entering students, accelerated degree program, adult/continuing education programs, advanced placement credit, cooperative education, distance learning, double majors, English as a second language, honors programs, independent study, internships, off-campus study, part-time degree program, services for LD students, student-designed majors, study abroad, summer session for credit. *ROTC:* Army (b). *Unusual degree programs:* 3-2 business administration; engineering; nursing; chemistry.

Computers on Campus Students can access the following: campus intranet, computer help desk, free student e-mail accounts, online (class) grades, online (class) registration, online (class) schedules, wireless network, student portal, learning management system. Campuswide network is available. 100% of college-owned or -operated housing units are wired for high-speed Internet access. Wireless service is available via entire campus.

Student Life *Housing options:* coed, men-only, women-only, disabled students. Campus housing is university owned. Freshman applicants given priority for college housing. *Activities and organizations:* drama/theater group, student-run newspaper, radio station, Fans Initiating Growth Honor and Tradition (spirit club), Pi Beta Phi, Sustainability Club, Gamers (computing), El Circulo, national fraternities, national sororities. *Campus security:* 24-hour emergency response devices and patrols, student patrols, late-night transport/escort service, controlled dormitory access, emergency text messaging. *Student services:* health clinic, personal/psychological counseling.

Athletics Member NCAA. All Division II. *Intercollegiate sports:* baseball M(c), basketball M(s)/W(s), cross-country running M(s)/W(s), golf M(s), ice hockey M(c), lacrosse M(c), rock climbing M(c)/W(c), soccer M(s)/W(s), softball W(s), tennis M(c)/W(c), track and field M(s)/W(s), volleyball M(c)/W(s). *Intramural sports:* badminton M/W, basketball M/W, bowling M/W, soccer M/W, softball M/W, table tennis M/W, ultimate Frisbee M/W, volleyball M/W, water polo M/W.

Standardized Tests *Required:* SAT or ACT (for admission).

Costs (2011–12) *One-time required fee:* $100. *Tuition:* state resident $6720 full-time, $224 per credit hour part-time; nonresident $16,240 full-time, $812 per credit hour part-time. Full-time tuition and fees vary according to course load, degree level, location, program, reciprocity agreements, and student level. Part-time tuition and fees vary according to course load, degree level, location, program, reciprocity agreements, and student level. *Required fees:* $1174 full-time, $242 per term part-time. *Room only:* $7990. Room and board charges vary according to board plan and housing facility. *Payment plan:* installment. *Waivers:* employees or children of employees.

Financial Aid Of all full-time matriculated undergraduates who enrolled in 2010, 4,762 applied for aid, 3,285 were judged to have need, 265 had their need fully met. 104 Federal Work-Study jobs (averaging $3673). 299 state and other part-time jobs (averaging $3795). In 2010, 214 non-need-based awards were made. *Average percent of need met:* 55%. *Average financial aid package:* $8648. *Average need-based loan:* $4285. *Average need-based gift aid:* $6470. *Average non-need-based aid:* $1551. *Average indebtedness upon graduation:* $21,551.

Applying *Options:* electronic application, deferred entrance. *Application fee:* $50. *Required:* high school transcript. *Required for some:* GED certificate in lieu of high school transcript. *Application deadlines:* rolling (freshmen), rolling (out-of-state freshmen), rolling (transfers). *Notification:* continuous (freshmen), continuous (out-of-state freshmen), continuous (transfers).

Freshman Application Contact Mr. Chris Beiswanger, Director of Student Recruitment and Admissions Counseling, University of Colorado at Colorado Springs, 1420 Austin Bluffs Parkway, Colorado Springs, CO 80918. *Phone:* 719-255-3088. *Toll-free phone:* 800-990-8227 Ext. 3383. *E-mail:* cbeiswan@uccs.edu. *Web site:* http://www.uccs.edu/.

University of Colorado Boulder

Boulder, Colorado

- **State-supported** university, founded 1876, part of University of Colorado System
- **Suburban** 600-acre campus with easy access to Denver
- **Endowment** $389.5 million
- **Coed** 26,325 undergraduate students, 92% full-time, 47% women, 53% men
- **Moderately difficult** entrance level, 87% of applicants were admitted

Undergraduates 24,166 full-time, 2,159 part-time. Students come from 52 states and territories; 79 other countries; 35% are from out of state; 2% Black or African American, non-Hispanic/Latino; 8% Hispanic/Latino; 6% Asian, non-Hispanic/Latino; 0.5% American Indian or Alaska Native, non-Hispanic/Latino; 2% Two or more races, non-Hispanic/Latino; 3% Race/ethnicity unknown; 2% international; 5% transferred in; 28% live on campus. *Retention:* 84% of full-time freshmen returned.

Freshmen *Admission:* 20,506 applied, 17,828 admitted, 5,700 enrolled. *Average high school GPA:* 3.55. *Test scores:* SAT critical reading scores over 500: 86%; SAT math scores over 500: 90%; ACT scores over 18: 99%; SAT critical reading scores over 600: 42%; SAT math scores over 600: 52%; ACT scores over 24: 75%; SAT critical reading scores over 700: 8%; SAT math scores over 700: 12%; ACT scores over 30: 17%.

Faculty *Total:* 2,011, 62% full-time, 70% with terminal degrees. *Student/faculty ratio:* 20:1.

Academics *Calendar:* semesters. *Degrees:* bachelor's, master's, doctoral, post-master's, and first professional certificates. *Special study options:* accelerated degree program, adult/continuing education programs, advanced placement credit, cooperative education, distance learning, double majors, English as a second language, freshman honors college, honors programs, independent study, internships, off-campus study, part-time degree program, services for LD students, student-designed majors, study abroad, summer session for credit. *ROTC:* Army (b), Navy (b), Air Force (b).

Computers on Campus 1,800 computers/terminals are available on campus for general student use. Students can access the following: campus intranet, computer help desk, free student e-mail accounts, online (class) grades, online (class) registration, online (class) schedules, training, tutorials, workshops, and seminars; standard and academic software; student government voting. Campuswide network is available. 100% of college-owned or -operated housing units are wired for high-speed Internet access. Wireless service is available via entire campus.

Student Life *Housing:* on-campus residence required for freshman year. *Options:* coed, disabled students. Campus housing is university owned and is provided by a third party. Freshman campus housing is guaranteed. *Activities and organizations:* drama/theater group, student-run newspaper, radio station, choral group, marching band, student government, Environmental Center, Ski and Snowboard Club, AIESEC (international leadership organization), Program Council, national fraternities, national sororities. *Campus security:* 24-hour emergency response devices and patrols, student patrols, late-night transport/escort service, controlled dormitory access, University police department. *Student services:* health clinic, personal/psychological counseling, women's center, legal services.

Athletics Member NCAA. All Division I except football (Division I-A). *Intercollegiate sports:* baseball M(c), basketball M(s)/W(s), crew M(c)/W(c), cross-country running M(s)/W(s), equestrian sports M(c)/W(c), fencing M(c)/W(c), field hockey M(c)/W(c), golf M(s)/W(s), ice hockey M(c)/W(c), lacrosse M(c)/W(c), racquetball M(c)/W(c), rugby M(c)/W(c), skiing (cross-country) M(s)/W(s), skiing (downhill) M(s)/W(s), soccer M(c)/W(s), softball W(c), swimming and diving M(c)/W(c), tennis M(c)/W(s), track and field M(s)/W(s), ultimate Frisbee M(c)/W(c), volleyball M(c)/W(s), water polo M(c)/W(c), wrestling M(c). *Intramural sports:* badminton M/W, basketball M/W, ice hockey M/W, soccer M/W, table tennis M/W, tennis M/W, ultimate Frisbee M/W, volleyball M/W, water polo M/W.

Standardized Tests *Required:* SAT or ACT (for admission).

Costs (2011–12) *One-time required fee:* $182. *Tuition:* state resident $7018 full-time; nonresident $28,000 full-time. Full-time tuition and fees vary according to program. Part-time tuition and fees vary according to course load and program. *Required fees:* $1493 full-time. *Room and board:* $10,792. Room and board charges vary according to board plan, housing facility, and location. *Payment plan:* deferred payment. *Waivers:* senior citizens and employees or children of employees.

Financial Aid Of all full-time matriculated undergraduates who enrolled in 2011, 12,890 applied for aid, 9,735 were judged to have need, 5,473 had their need fully met. 1,126 Federal Work-Study jobs (averaging $1813). 810 state and other part-time jobs (averaging $2387). In 2011, 5055 non-need-based awards were made. *Average percent of need met:* 88%. *Average financial aid package:* $13,693. *Average need-based loan:* $6510. *Average need-based gift aid:* $7589. *Average non-need-based aid:* $7544. *Average indebtedness upon graduation:* $22,683.

Applying *Options:* electronic application, early action, deferred entrance. *Application fee:* $50. *Required:* essay or personal statement, high school transcript. *Required for some:* audition for music program. *Application deadlines:* 1/15 (freshmen), 4/1 (transfers), 12/1 (early action). *Notification:* 4/1 (freshmen), continuous (transfers), 1/15 (early action).

Freshman Application Contact Admissions Office, University of Colorado Boulder, Regent Administrative Center 125, 552 UCB, Boulder, CO 80309. *Phone:* 303-492-6301. *Fax:* 303-492-7115. *E-mail:* apply@colorado.edu. *Web site:* http://www.colorado.edu/.

University of Colorado Denver

Denver, Colorado

- **State-supported** university, founded 1912, part of University of Colorado System
- **Urban** 171-acre campus
- **Endowment** $286.9 million
- **Coed** 13,337 undergraduate students, 57% full-time, 55% women, 45% men
- **Moderately difficult** entrance level, 60% of applicants were admitted

Undergraduates 7,594 full-time, 5,743 part-time. Students come from 50 states and territories; 72 other countries; 6% are from out of state; 6% Black or African American, non-Hispanic/Latino; 13% Hispanic/Latino; 11% Asian, non-Hispanic/Latino; 1% American Indian or Alaska Native, non-Hispanic/Latino; 0.3% Two or more races, non-Hispanic/Latino; 6% Race/ethnicity unknown; 6% international; 11% transferred in; 6% live on campus. *Retention:* 73% of full-time freshmen returned.

Freshmen *Admission:* 5,413 applied, 3,235 admitted, 1,111 enrolled. *Average high school GPA:* 3.35. *Test scores:* SAT critical reading scores over 500: 71%; SAT math scores over 500: 68%; ACT scores over 18: 93%; SAT critical reading scores over 600: 30%; SAT math scores over 600: 33%; ACT scores

over 24: 43%; SAT critical reading scores over 700: 5%; SAT math scores over 700: 6%; ACT scores over 30: 5%.

Faculty *Total:* 3,158, 82% full-time, 72% with terminal degrees. *Student/faculty ratio:* 19:1.

Academics *Calendar:* semesters. *Degrees:* bachelor's, master's, doctoral, post-master's, and first professional certificates. *Special study options:* accelerated degree program, adult/continuing education programs, advanced placement credit, cooperative education, distance learning, double majors, English as a second language, honors programs, independent study, internships, off-campus study, part-time degree program, services for LD students, student-designed majors, study abroad, summer session for credit. *ROTC:* Army (c), Air Force (c). *Unusual degree programs:* 3-2 School of Public Affairs: Criminal Justice Dual BACJ/MCJ.

Computers on Campus 750 computers/terminals are available on campus for general student use. Students can access the following: campus intranet, computer help desk, free student e-mail accounts, online (class) grades, online (class) registration, online (class) schedules. Campuswide network is available. 100% of college-owned or -operated housing units are wired for high-speed Internet access. Wireless service is available via entire campus.

Student Life *Housing:* on-campus residence required for freshman year. *Options:* coed. Campus housing is provided by a third party. Freshman applicants given priority for college housing. *Activities and organizations:* drama/theater group, student-run newspaper, choral group, Veterans Student Organization (Service), Golden Key Honor Society (Academic), Minority Association for Pre-Health Students (Health), Future Doctors of Denver, Intercultural Club Beijing (Cultural and Social). *Campus security:* 24-hour emergency response devices and patrols, student patrols, late-night transport/escort service. *Student services:* health clinic, personal/psychological counseling.

Athletics *Intramural sports:* basketball M/W, cheerleading M(c)/W(c), football M(c)/W(c), ice hockey M(c)/W(c), lacrosse M(c)/W(c), skiing (downhill) M(c)/W(c), soccer M(c)/W(c), squash M(c)/W(c), swimming and diving M(c)/W(c), ultimate Frisbee M(c)/W(c), volleyball M/W.

Standardized Tests *Required:* SAT or ACT (for admission).

Costs (2012–13) *Tuition:* state resident $6336 full-time, $264 per credit hour part-time; nonresident $19,512 full-time, $813 per credit hour part-time. Full-time tuition and fees vary according to course level, course load, degree level, location, program, reciprocity agreements, and student level. Part-time tuition and fees vary according to course level, course load, degree level, location, program, reciprocity agreements, and student level. *Required fees:* $1058 full-time. *Room and board:* $10,090; room only: $6890. Room and board charges vary according to board plan. *Payment plans:* installment, deferred payment. *Waivers:* employees or children of employees.

Financial Aid Of all full-time matriculated undergraduates who enrolled in 2010, 5,266 applied for aid, 4,489 were judged to have need, 185 had their need fully met. 218 Federal Work-Study jobs (averaging $3183). 209 state and other part-time jobs (averaging $3798). In 2010, 171 non-need-based awards were made. *Average percent of need met:* 48%. *Average financial aid package:* $8183. *Average need-based loan:* $4331. *Average need-based gift aid:* $6485. *Average non-need-based aid:* $2851. *Average indebtedness upon graduation:* $18,960.

Applying *Options:* electronic application, deferred entrance. *Application fee:* $50. *Required:* high school transcript, minimum 2.5 GPA. *Required for some:* essay or personal statement, minimum 3.0 GPA, audition, portfolio, entrance exam. *Application deadlines:* 7/22 (freshmen), 7/22 (transfers). *Notification:* continuous (freshmen), continuous (transfers).

Freshman Application Contact Office of Admissions, University of Colorado Denver, PO Box 173354, Campus Box 167, Denver, CO 80217. *Phone:* 303-556-2704. *E-mail:* admissions@ucdenver.edu. *Web site:* http://www.ucdenver.edu/.

University of Denver

Denver, Colorado

- **Independent** university, founded 1864
- **Urban** 125-acre campus with easy access to Denver
- **Endowment** $345.2 million
- **Coed** 5,453 undergraduate students, 92% full-time, 56% women, 44% men
- **Moderately difficult** entrance level, 68% of applicants were admitted

Undergraduates 4,997 full-time, 456 part-time. Students come from 49 states and territories; 61 other countries; 50% are from out of state; 3% Black or African American, non-Hispanic/Latino; 8% Hispanic/Latino; 4% Asian, non-Hispanic/Latino; 0.1% Native Hawaiian or other Pacific Islander, non-Hispanic/Latino; 0.6% American Indian or Alaska Native, non-Hispanic/Latino; 3% Two or more races, non-Hispanic/Latino; 4% Race/ethnicity unknown; 9% international; 4% transferred in; 44% live on campus. *Retention:* 89% of full-time freshmen returned.

Freshmen *Admission:* 10,504 applied, 7,160 admitted, 1,240 enrolled. *Average high school GPA:* 3.7. *Test scores:* SAT critical reading scores over 500: 88%; SAT math scores over 500: 95%; SAT writing scores over 500: 87%;

ACT scores over 18: 100%; SAT critical reading scores over 600: 58%; SAT math scores over 600: 63%; SAT writing scores over 600: 46%; ACT scores over 24: 86%; SAT critical reading scores over 700: 14%; SAT math scores over 700: 14%; SAT writing scores over 700: 8%; ACT scores over 30: 33%.

Faculty *Total:* 1,299, 48% full-time, 46% with terminal degrees. *Student/faculty ratio:* 8:1.

Academics *Calendar:* quarters; semesters for law school. *Degrees:* certificates, bachelor's, master's, doctoral, post-master's, postbachelor's, and first professional certificates. *Special study options:* accelerated degree program, adult/continuing education programs, advanced placement credit, cooperative education, distance learning, double majors, English as a second language, freshman honors college, honors programs, independent study, internships, off-campus study, part-time degree program, services for LD students, student-designed majors, study abroad, summer session for credit. *ROTC:* Army (c), Air Force (c). *Unusual degree programs:* 3-2 business administration; engineering; social work; art history; public policy; accounting; international studies; education; environmental science; and geography.

Computers on Campus 150 computers/terminals and 35,000 ports are available on campus for general student use. Students can access the following: campus intranet, computer help desk, free student e-mail accounts, online (class) grades, online (class) registration, online (class) schedules. Campuswide network is available. 95% of college-owned or -operated housing units are wired for high-speed Internet access. Wireless service is available via entire campus.

Student Life *Housing:* on-campus residence required through sophomore year. *Options:* coed, men-only, women-only, cooperative. Campus housing is university owned. Freshman campus housing is guaranteed. *Activities and organizations:* drama/theater group, student-run newspaper, radio station, choral group, Club Sports Council, Alpine Club, DU Programs Board, Greek Life Council, Residence Hall Association, national fraternities, national sororities. *Campus security:* 24-hour emergency response devices and patrols, late-night transport/escort service, controlled dormitory access, 24-hour locked residence hall entrances. *Student services:* health clinic, personal/psychological counseling, women's center.

Athletics Member NCAA. All Division I. *Intercollegiate sports:* baseball M(c), basketball M(s)/W(s), cross-country running M(c)/W(c), equestrian sports M(c)/W(c), golf M(s)/W(s), gymnastics W(s), ice hockey M(s)/W(c), lacrosse M(s)/W(s), racquetball M(c)/W(c), skiing (cross-country) M(s)/W(s), skiing (downhill) M(s)/W(s), soccer M(s)/W(s), softball W(c), swimming and diving M(s)/W(s), tennis M(s)/W(s), volleyball W(s), water polo M(c)/W(c). *Intramural sports:* basketball M/W, field hockey M(c)/W(c), football M/W, golf M(c)/W(c), ice hockey M(c), lacrosse M(c)/W(c), racquetball M(c)/W(c), rock climbing M(c)/W(c), rugby M(c), skiing (downhill) M(c)/W(c), soccer M(c)/W(c), softball M/W, tennis M(c)/W(c), ultimate Frisbee M(c)/W(c), volleyball M(c)/W(c).

Standardized Tests *Required:* SAT or ACT (for admission).

Costs (2012–13) *Comprehensive fee:* $49,995 includes full-time tuition ($38,232), mandatory fees ($945), and room and board ($10,818). Full-time tuition and fees vary according to class time, course load, and program. Part-time tuition: $1062 per quarter hour. Part-time tuition and fees vary according to class time, course load, and program. *College room only:* $6618. Room and board charges vary according to board plan and housing facility. *Payment plans:* installment, deferred payment. *Waivers:* senior citizens and employees or children of employees.

Financial Aid Of all full-time matriculated undergraduates who enrolled in 2011, 2,622 applied for aid, 2,149 were judged to have need, 638 had their need fully met. 387 Federal Work-Study jobs (averaging $2810). 258 state and other part-time jobs (averaging $3059). In 2011, 1800 non-need-based awards were made. *Average percent of need met:* 82%. *Average financial aid package:* $30,392. *Average need-based loan:* $4326. *Average need-based gift aid:* $24,182. *Average non-need-based aid:* $13,437. *Average indebtedness upon graduation:* $26,628. *Financial aid deadline:* 5/1.

Applying *Options:* electronic application, early admission, early action, deferred entrance. *Application fee:* $50. *Required:* essay or personal statement, high school transcript, 2 letters of recommendation. *Required for some:* minimum 2.0 GPA. *Recommended:* interview. *Application deadlines:* 1/15 (freshmen), rolling (transfers), 11/1 (early action). *Notification:* 3/15 (freshmen), continuous (transfers), 1/15 (early action).

Freshman Application Contact Mr. Todd R. Rinehart, Assistant Vice Chancellor for Enrollment, University of Denver, 2197 South University Boulevard, Denver, CO 80208. *Phone:* 303-871-3125. *Toll-free phone:* 800-525-9495. *Fax:* 303-871-3301. *E-mail:* admission@du.edu. *Web site:* http://www.du.edu/.

See page 154 for display ad and page 1664 for the College Close-Up.

University of Northern Colorado
Greeley, Colorado

- **State-supported** university, founded 1890
- **Suburban** 240-acre campus with easy access to Denver
- **Endowment** $76.5 million
- **Coed** 10,231 undergraduate students, 91% full-time, 62% women, 38% men
- **Moderately difficult** entrance level, 73% of applicants were admitted

Undergraduates 9,299 full-time, 932 part-time. Students come from 50 states and territories; 23 other countries; 12% are from out of state; 5% Black or African American, non-Hispanic/Latino; 13% Hispanic/Latino; 2% Asian, non-Hispanic/Latino; 0.6% Native Hawaiian or other Pacific Islander, non-Hispanic/Latino; 1% American Indian or Alaska Native, non-Hispanic/Latino; 2% Two or more races, non-Hispanic/Latino; 14% Race/ethnicity unknown; 1% international; 8% transferred in; 31% live on campus. *Retention:* 70% of full-time freshmen returned.

Freshmen *Admission:* 8,169 applied, 5,949 admitted, 2,280 enrolled. *Average high school GPA:* 3.22. *Test scores:* SAT critical reading scores over 500: 67%; SAT math scores over 500: 60%; ACT scores over 18: 91%; SAT critical reading scores over 600: 20%; SAT math scores over 600: 22%; ACT scores over 24: 35%; SAT critical reading scores over 700: 2%; SAT math scores over 700: 3%; ACT scores over 30: 4%.

Faculty *Total:* 683, 72% full-time. *Student/faculty ratio:* 20:1.

Academics *Calendar:* semesters. *Degrees:* bachelor's, master's, doctoral, and first professional. *Special study options:* academic remediation for entering students, accelerated degree program, adult/continuing education programs, advanced placement credit, cooperative education, distance learning, double majors, English as a second language, external degree program, honors programs, independent study, internships, off-campus study, part-time degree program, services for LD students, student-designed majors, study abroad, summer session for credit. *ROTC:* Army (b), Air Force (b).

Computers on Campus 1,671 computers/terminals and 800 ports are available on campus for general student use. Students can access the following: computer help desk, free student e-mail accounts, online (class) grades, online (class) registration, online (class) schedules. Campuswide network is available. 100% of college-owned or -operated housing units are wired for high-speed Internet access. Wireless service is available via entire campus.

Student Life *Housing:* on-campus residence required for freshman year. *Options:* coed, women-only, disabled students. Campus housing is university owned. Freshman campus housing is guaranteed. *Activities and organizations:* drama/theater group, student-run newspaper, radio and television station, choral group, marching band, national fraternities, national sororities. *Campus security:* 24-hour emergency response devices and patrols, student patrols, late-night transport/escort service, controlled dormitory access. *Student services:* health clinic, personal/psychological counseling, women's center, legal services.

Athletics Member NCAA. All Division I. *Intercollegiate sports:* baseball M(s), basketball M(s)/W(s), cross-country running W(s), football M(s), golf M(s)/W(s), ice hockey M(c), lacrosse M(c), rugby M(c)/W(c), soccer M(c)/W(s), softball W(s), swimming and diving W(s), tennis M(s)/W(s), track and field M(s)/W(s), volleyball W(s), wrestling M(s). *Intramural sports:* basketball M/W, football M/W, soccer M/W, softball M/W, volleyball M/W, water polo M/W.

Standardized Tests *Required:* SAT or ACT (for admission).

Costs (2011–12) *Tuition:* state resident $5300 full-time, $213 per credit hour part-time; nonresident $16,822 full-time, $684 per credit hour part-time. Full-time tuition and fees vary according to program. Part-time tuition and fees vary according to program. *Required fees:* $1323 full-time, $44 per credit hour part-time. *Room and board:* $9750; room only: $4770. Room and board charges vary according to board plan, housing facility, and student level. *Payment plan:* deferred payment. *Waivers:* employees or children of employees.

Financial Aid Of all full-time matriculated undergraduates who enrolled in 2009, 6,381 applied for aid, 4,156 were judged to have need, 2,049 had their need fully met. In 2009, 934 non-need-based awards were made. *Average percent of need met:* 99%. *Average financial aid package:* $14,255. *Average need-based loan:* $4245. *Average need-based gift aid:* $7007. *Average non-need-based aid:* $3993.

Applying *Options:* electronic application, deferred entrance. *Application fee:* $45. *Required:* high school transcript, minimum 2.9 GPA. *Application deadlines:* 8/1 (freshmen), 8/1 (out-of-state freshmen), rolling (transfers). *Notification:* continuous (freshmen), continuous (transfers).

Freshman Application Contact Sean Broghammer, Director of Admissions, University of Northern Colorado, Campus Box 10, Carter Hall 3006, Greeley, CO 80639. *Phone:* 970-351-2881. *Toll-free phone:* 888-700-4UNC. *Fax:* 970-351-2984. *E-mail:* admissions@unco.edu. *Web site:* http://www.unco.edu/.

University of Phoenix–Denver Campus

Lone Tree, Colorado

Freshman Application Contact Marc Booker, Sr. Director, Office of Admissions and Evaluation, University of Phoenix–Denver Campus, 4035 South Riverpoint Parkway, Mail Stop CF-L101, Phoenix, AZ 85040. *Phone:* 602-557-4609. *Toll-free phone:* 866-766-0766. *Fax:* 480-643-1156. *Web site:* http://www.phoenix.edu/.

University of Phoenix–Southern Colorado Campus

Colorado Springs, Colorado

Freshman Application Contact Marc Booker, Sr. Director, Office of Admissions and Evaluation, University of Phoenix–Southern Colorado Campus, 4035 South Riverpoint Parkway, Mail Stop CF-L101, Phoenix, AZ 85040. *Phone:* 602-557-4609. *Toll-free phone:* 866-766-0766. *Fax:* 480-643-1156. *Web site:* http://www.phoenix.edu/.

Western State College of Colorado

Gunnison, Colorado

- **State-supported** comprehensive, founded 1901
- **Rural** 381-acre campus
- **Coed** 2,039 undergraduate students, 91% full-time, 39% women, 61% men
- **Moderately difficult** entrance level, 93% of applicants were admitted

Undergraduates 1,863 full-time, 176 part-time. Students come from 50 states and territories; 8 other countries; 24% are from out of state; 2% Black or African American, non-Hispanic/Latino; 5% Hispanic/Latino; 0.7% Native Hawaiian or other Pacific Islander, non-Hispanic/Latino; 0.4% American Indian or Alaska Native, non-Hispanic/Latino; 1% Two or more races, non-Hispanic/Latino; 15% Race/ethnicity unknown; 0.4% international; 7% transferred in; 32% live on campus. *Retention:* 64% of full-time freshmen returned.
Freshmen *Admission:* 1,495 applied, 1,383 admitted, 436 enrolled. *Average high school GPA:* 3.04. *Test scores:* SAT critical reading scores over 500: 56%; SAT math scores over 500: 62%; ACT scores over 18: 87%; SAT critical reading scores over 600: 20%; SAT math scores over 600: 15%; ACT scores over 24: 29%; SAT critical reading scores over 700: 3%; SAT math scores over 700: 1%; ACT scores over 30: 3%.
Faculty *Total:* 174, 64% full-time, 63% with terminal degrees. *Student/faculty ratio:* 16:1.
Academics *Calendar:* semesters. *Degrees:* bachelor's, master's, and post-bachelor's certificates. *Special study options:* academic remediation for entering students, adult/continuing education programs, advanced placement credit, double majors, honors programs, independent study, internships, off-campus study, part-time degree program, services for LD students, study abroad, summer session for credit.
Computers on Campus 181 computers/terminals and 600 ports are available on campus for general student use. Students can access the following: computer help desk, free student e-mail accounts, online (class) grades, online (class) registration, online (class) schedules. Campuswide network is available. 100% of college-owned or -operated housing units are wired for high-speed Internet access. Wireless service is available via classrooms, computer centers, computer labs, dorm rooms, learning centers, libraries, student centers.
Student Life *Housing:* on-campus residence required for freshman year. *Options:* coed, men-only, women-only. Campus housing is university owned. Freshman campus housing is guaranteed. *Activities and organizations:* drama/theater group, student-run newspaper, radio and television station, choral group, Mountain Search and Rescue Team, Student Government Association, Rodeo Club, wilderness pursuits, Peak Productions, national fraternities, national sororities. *Campus security:* 24-hour emergency response devices and patrols, student patrols, late-night transport/escort service, controlled dormitory access. *Student services:* health clinic, personal/psychological counseling.
Athletics Member NCAA. All Division II. *Intercollegiate sports:* baseball M(c), basketball M(s)/W(s), cheerleading M(c)/W(c), cross-country running M(s)/W(s), football M(s), ice hockey M(c), lacrosse M(c)/W(c), rock climbing M(c)/W(c), rugby M(c)/W(c), skiing (cross-country) M(c)/W(c), skiing (downhill) M(c)/W(c), soccer M(c)/W(s), swimming and diving W(s), track and field M(s)/W(s), volleyball M(s)/W(s), wrestling M(s)/W(c). *Intramural sports:* basketball M/W, football M/W, golf M/W, soccer M/W, softball M/W, table tennis M/W, tennis M/W, ultimate Frisbee M/W, volleyball M/W.
Standardized Tests *Required:* SAT or ACT (for admission).
Costs (2012–13) *Tuition:* state resident $3922 full-time, $163 per credit hour part-time; nonresident $13,532 full-time, $564 per credit hour part-time. Full-time tuition and fees vary according to course load and reciprocity agreements. Part-time tuition and fees vary according to course load and reciprocity agreements. *Required fees:* $1551 full-time. *Room and board:* $8472; room only: $4618. Room and board charges vary according to board plan and housing facility. *Payment plans:* installment, deferred payment. *Waivers:* senior citizens.
Financial Aid Of all full-time matriculated undergraduates who enrolled in 2011, 1,299 applied for aid, 780 were judged to have need, 78 had their need fully met. 209 Federal Work-Study jobs (averaging $1359). 326 state and other part-time jobs (averaging $1394). In 2011, 453 non-need-based awards were made. *Average percent of need met:* 40%. *Average financial aid package:* $9849. *Average need-based loan:* $4300. *Average need-based gift aid:* $4535. *Average non-need-based aid:* $3500. *Average indebtedness upon graduation:* $18,600.
Applying *Options:* electronic application, deferred entrance. *Application fee:* $30. *Required:* high school transcript. *Required for some:* essay or personal statement, interview. *Recommended:* minimum 2.5 GPA. *Notification:* continuous until 11/15 (freshmen), continuous until 11/15 (out-of-state freshmen), continuous (transfers).
Freshman Application Contact Mr. Timothy Albers, Director of Admissions, Western State College of Colorado, 600 North Adams Street, Gunnison, CO 81231. *Phone:* 970-943-2119. *Toll-free phone:* 800-876-5309. *Fax:* 970-943-2212. *E-mail:* admissions@western.edu. *Web site:* http://www.western.edu/.

Westwood College–Denver North

Denver, Colorado

Freshman Application Contact Westwood College–Denver North, 7350 North Broadway, Denver, CO 80221-3653. *Phone:* 303-426-7000. *Toll-free phone:* 800-281-2978. *Web site:* http://www.westwood.edu/.

Westwood College–Denver South

Denver, Colorado

Freshman Application Contact Westwood College–Denver South, 3150 South Sheridan Boulevard, Denver, CO 80227. *Phone:* 303-934-1122. *Toll-free phone:* 800-281-2978. *Web site:* http://www.westwood.edu/.

Westwood College–Online Campus

Broomfield, Colorado

Freshman Application Contact Westwood College–Online Campus, 10249 Church Ranch Way, Broomfield, CO 80021. *Phone:* 720-887-8888. *Web site:* http://www.westwood.edu/.

Yeshiva Toras Chaim Talmudical Seminary

Denver, Colorado

Director of Admissions Rabbi Israel Kagan, Dean, Yeshiva Toras Chaim Talmudical Seminary, 1555 Stuart Street, Denver, CO 80204-1415. *Phone:* 303-629-8200. *Fax:* 303-623-5949.

Yorktown University

Denver, Colorado

Admissions Office Contact Yorktown University, 4340 East Kentucky Avenue, Suite 457, Denver, CO 80246. *Web site:* http://yorktownuniversity.edu/.

CONNECTICUT

Albertus Magnus College

New Haven, Connecticut

- **Independent Roman Catholic** comprehensive, founded 1925
- **Suburban** 55-acre campus
- **Endowment** $6.1 million
- **Coed** 1,604 undergraduate students, 86% full-time, 66% women, 34% men
- **Moderately difficult** entrance level, 67% of applicants were admitted

Undergraduates 1,376 full-time, 228 part-time. Students come from 7 states and territories; 2 other countries; 17% are from out of state; 22% Black or Afri-

can American, non-Hispanic/Latino; 11% Hispanic/Latino; 1% Asian, non-Hispanic/Latino; 0.1% Native Hawaiian or other Pacific Islander, non-Hispanic/Latino; 1% American Indian or Alaska Native, non-Hispanic/Latino; 21% Race/ethnicity unknown; 0.1% international; 9% transferred in; 46% live on campus. *Retention:* 76% of full-time freshmen returned.

Freshmen *Admission:* 722 applied, 485 admitted, 151 enrolled. *Average high school GPA:* 2.8. *Test scores:* SAT critical reading scores over 500: 37%; SAT writing scores over 500: 40%; SAT critical reading scores over 600: 8%; SAT writing scores over 600: 5%.

Faculty *Total:* 76, 55% full-time, 54% with terminal degrees. *Student/faculty ratio:* 15:1.

Academics *Calendar:* semesters. *Degrees:* associate, bachelor's, and master's. *Special study options:* academic remediation for entering students, accelerated degree program, advanced placement credit, distance learning, double majors, English as a second language, freshman honors college, honors programs, independent study, internships, part-time degree program, services for LD students, student-designed majors, summer session for credit. *Unusual degree programs:* 3-2 business administration.

Computers on Campus 146 computers/terminals are available on campus for general student use. Students can access the following: campus intranet, computer help desk, free student e-mail accounts, online (class) grades, online (class) registration, online (class) schedules, online class sessions - Moodle. Campuswide network is available. 100% of college-owned or -operated housing units are wired for high-speed Internet access. Wireless service is available via entire campus.

Student Life *Housing options:* coed, women-only. Campus housing is university owned. Freshman applicants given priority for college housing. *Activities and organizations:* drama/theater group, choral group, Student Government Association, College Drama, Campus ministry. *Campus security:* 24-hour emergency response devices and patrols, late-night transport/escort service, controlled dormitory access. *Student services:* health clinic, personal/psychological counseling.

Athletics Member NCAA. All Division III. *Intercollegiate sports:* baseball M, basketball M/W, cross-country running M/W, lacrosse M/W, soccer M/W, softball W, tennis M/W, volleyball M/W. *Intramural sports:* basketball M/W, racquetball M/W, soccer M/W, squash M/W, table tennis M/W.

Standardized Tests *Required:* SAT or ACT (for admission). *Recommended:* SAT Subject Tests (for admission).

Costs (2011–12) *Comprehensive fee:* $37,382 includes full-time tuition ($25,824), mandatory fees ($470), and room and board ($11,088). Full-time tuition and fees vary according to program. Part-time tuition: $2586 per course. Part-time tuition and fees vary according to program. *Payment plan:* installment. *Waivers:* senior citizens and employees or children of employees.

Financial Aid Of all full-time matriculated undergraduates who enrolled in 2008, 1,442 applied for aid, 1,307 were judged to have need, 90 had their need fully met. 78 Federal Work-Study jobs (averaging $1583). 34 state and other part-time jobs (averaging $3400). In 2008, 32 non-need-based awards were made. *Average percent of need met:* 53%. *Average financial aid package:* $9074. *Average need-based loan:* $4398. *Average need-based gift aid:* $5739. *Average non-need-based aid:* $3537. *Average indebtedness upon graduation:* $26,404.

Applying *Options:* electronic application, deferred entrance. *Application fee:* $35. *Required:* high school transcript, 1 letter of recommendation. *Required for some:* minimum 2.5 GPA. *Recommended:* essay or personal statement, minimum 2.5 GPA, interview. *Application deadlines:* 8/30 (freshmen), rolling (transfers). *Notification:* continuous (freshmen), continuous (transfers).

Freshman Application Contact Mr. Nilvio Perez, Director of Admission, Albertus Magnus College, 700 Prospect Street, New Haven, CT 06511-1189. *Phone:* 203-773-8501. *Toll-free phone:* 800-578-9160. *Fax:* 203-773-5248. *E-mail:* admissions@albertus.edu. *Web site:* http://www.albertus.edu/.

Bais Binyomin Academy

Stamford, Connecticut

Director of Admissions Director of Admissions, Bais Binyomin Academy, 132 Prospect Street, Stamford, CT 06901-1202. *Phone:* 203-325-4351.

Central Connecticut State University
New Britain, Connecticut

- **State-supported** comprehensive, founded 1849, part of Connecticut State University System
- **Suburban** 294-acre campus
- **Endowment** $38.2 million
- **Coed** 10,092 undergraduate students, 78% full-time, 48% women, 52% men
- **Moderately difficult** entrance level, 63% of applicants were admitted

Undergraduates 7,823 full-time, 2,269 part-time. Students come from 29 states and territories; 41 other countries; 3% are from out of state; 10% Black or African American, non-Hispanic/Latino; 9% Hispanic/Latino; 3% Asian, non-Hispanic/Latino; 0.1% Native Hawaiian or other Pacific Islander, non-Hispanic/Latino; 0.2% American Indian or Alaska Native, non-Hispanic/Latino; 2% Two or more races, non-Hispanic/Latino; 3% Race/ethnicity unknown; 1% international; 11% transferred in; 23% live on campus. *Retention:* 76% of full-time freshmen returned.

Freshmen *Admission:* 6,473 applied, 4,087 admitted, 1,387 enrolled. *Average high school GPA:* 2.97. *Test scores:* SAT critical reading scores over 500: 53%; SAT math scores over 500: 57%; SAT writing scores over 500: 54%; SAT critical reading scores over 600: 9%; SAT math scores over 600: 11%; SAT writing scores over 600: 10%; SAT critical reading scores over 700: 1%; SAT writing scores over 700: 1%.

Faculty *Total:* 968, 45% full-time, 45% with terminal degrees. *Student/faculty ratio:* 16:1.

Academics *Calendar:* semesters. *Degrees:* bachelor's, master's, doctoral, post-master's, and postbachelor's certificates. *Special study options:* academic remediation for entering students, adult/continuing education programs, advanced placement credit, cooperative education, distance learning, English as a second language, honors programs, independent study, internships, off-campus study, part-time degree program, services for LD students, student-designed majors, study abroad, summer session for credit. *ROTC:* Army (c), Air Force (c).

Computers on Campus 750 computers/terminals are available on campus for general student use. Students can access the following: campus intranet, computer help desk, free student e-mail accounts, online (class) grades, online (class) registration, online (class) schedules. Campuswide network is available. 97% of college-owned or -operated housing units are wired for high-speed Internet access. Wireless service is available via entire campus.

Student Life *Housing options:* coed, women-only. Campus housing is university owned. *Activities and organizations:* drama/theater group, student-run newspaper, radio and television station, choral group, Inter-Residence Council, student radio station, Program Council, Outing Club, NAACP, national fraternities, national sororities. *Campus security:* 24-hour emergency response devices and patrols, student patrols, late-night transport/escort service, controlled dormitory access. *Student services:* health clinic, personal/psychological counseling, women's center.

Athletics Member NCAA. All Division I except football (Division I-AA). *Intercollegiate sports:* baseball M(s), basketball M(s)/W(s), cross-country running M(s)/W(s), fencing M(c)/W(c), golf M(s)/W(s), lacrosse M(c)/W(s), soccer M(s)/W(s), softball W(s), swimming and diving W(s), track and field M(s)/W(s), volleyball W(s). *Intramural sports:* basketball M/W, field hockey W(c), football M, rugby M(c)/W(c), soccer M/W, softball M/W, volleyball M/W.

Standardized Tests *Required:* SAT (for admission).

Costs (2011–12) *Tuition:* state resident $4124 full-time, $172 per credit part-time; nonresident $13,346 full-time, $175 per credit part-time. Full-time tuition and fees vary according to course level, course load, program, and reciprocity agreements. Part-time tuition and fees vary according to course level, course load, and program. *Required fees:* $3931 full-time, $212 per credit part-time, $55 per term part-time. *Room and board:* $9814; room only: $5710. Room and board charges vary according to board plan. *Payment plan:* installment. *Waivers:* senior citizens and employees or children of employees.

Financial Aid Of all full-time matriculated undergraduates who enrolled in 2010, 6,898 applied for aid, 5,295 were judged to have need, 478 had their need fully met. In 2010, 147 non-need-based awards were made. *Average percent of need met:* 62%. *Average financial aid package:* $7759. *Average need-based loan:* $4181. *Average need-based gift aid:* $4007. *Average non-need-based aid:* $3615. *Average indebtedness upon graduation:* $19,086.

Applying *Options:* electronic application. *Application fee:* $50. *Required:* essay or personal statement, high school transcript, minimum 2.0 GPA. *Required for some:* interview. *Recommended:* minimum 3.0 GPA, 1 letter of recommendation. *Application deadlines:* 5/1 (freshmen), 6/1 (transfers). *Notification:* continuous until 10/15 (freshmen), continuous until 10/15 (transfers).

Freshman Application Contact Central Connecticut State University, 1615 Stanley Street, New Britain, CT 06050. *Phone:* 860-832-2285. *Fax:* 860-832-2522. *E-mail:* admissions@ccsu.edu. *Web site:* http://www.ccsu.edu/.

Charter Oak State College
New Britain, Connecticut

- **State-supported** 4-year, founded 1973
- **Small-town** campus
- **Endowment** $1.2 million
- **Coed** 2,241 undergraduate students, 11% full-time, 65% women, 35% men
- **Noncompetitive** entrance level

Undergraduates 254 full-time, 1,987 part-time. Students come from 48 states and territories; 3 other countries; 29% are from out of state; 14% Black or African American, non-Hispanic/Latino; 8% Hispanic/Latino; 2% Asian, non-Hispanic/Latino; 0.3% Native Hawaiian or other Pacific Islander, non-Hispanic/Latino; 0.3% American Indian or Alaska Native, non-Hispanic/Latino; 1% Two or more races, non-Hispanic/Latino; 13% Race/ethnicity unknown; 91% transferred in.
Faculty *Total:* 153.
Academics *Calendar:* continuous. *Degrees:* associate and bachelor's (offers only external degree programs). *Special study options:* accelerated degree program, adult/continuing education programs, advanced placement credit, distance learning, external degree program, independent study, part-time degree program, services for LD students, student-designed majors, summer session for credit.
Student Life *Housing:* college housing not available.
Costs (2012–13) *Tuition:* state resident $236 per credit hour part-time; nonresident $310 per credit hour part-time. *Required fees:* $165 per term part-time.
Financial Aid Of all full-time matriculated undergraduates who enrolled in 2003, 355 applied for aid, 226 were judged to have need, 25 had their need fully met. *Average percent of need met:* 75%. *Average financial aid package:* $4464. *Average need-based loan:* $1800.
Applying *Options:* electronic application, deferred entrance. *Application fee:* $75. *Application deadline:* rolling (transfers). *Notification:* continuous (transfers).
Freshman Application Contact Ms. Lori Pendleton, Director of Admissions, Charter Oak State College, 55 Paul J. Manafort Drive, New Britain, CT 06053-2150. *Phone:* 860-515-3701. *Fax:* 860-760-6047. *E-mail:* info@charteroak.edu. *Web site:* http://www.charteroak.edu/.

Connecticut College
New London, Connecticut

- **Independent** comprehensive, founded 1911
- **Small-town** 702-acre campus
- **Endowment** $212.6 million
- **Coed** 1,896 undergraduate students, 98% full-time, 61% women, 39% men
- **Very difficult** entrance level, 34% of applicants were admitted

Undergraduates 1,855 full-time, 41 part-time. Students come from 46 states and territories; 74 other countries; 81% are from out of state; 4% Black or African American, non-Hispanic/Latino; 7% Hispanic/Latino; 3% Asian, non-Hispanic/Latino; 0.1% Native Hawaiian or other Pacific Islander, non-Hispanic/Latino; 0.1% American Indian or Alaska Native, non-Hispanic/Latino; 3% Two or more races, non-Hispanic/Latino; 5% Race/ethnicity unknown; 4% international; 0.7% transferred in; 99% live on campus. *Retention:* 90% of full-time freshmen returned.
Freshmen *Admission:* 5,241 applied, 1,804 admitted, 508 enrolled. *Test scores:* SAT critical reading scores over 500: 99%; SAT math scores over 500: 100%; SAT writing scores over 500: 99%; ACT scores over 18: 100%; SAT critical reading scores over 600: 91%; SAT math scores over 600: 90%; SAT writing scores over 600: 89%; ACT scores over 24: 95%; SAT critical reading scores over 700: 28%; SAT math scores over 700: 26%; SAT writing scores over 700: 39%; ACT scores over 30: 47%.
Faculty *Total:* 243, 73% full-time, 73% with terminal degrees. *Student/faculty ratio:* 9:1.
Academics *Calendar:* semesters. *Degrees:* bachelor's and master's. *Special study options:* accelerated degree program, adult/continuing education programs, advanced placement credit, double majors, independent study, internships, off-campus study, part-time degree program, services for LD students, student-designed majors, study abroad, summer session for credit. *Unusual degree programs:* 3-2 engineering with Washington University in St. Louis.
Computers on Campus Students can access the following: campus intranet, computer help desk, free student e-mail accounts, online (class) grades, online (class) registration, online (class) schedules, Moodle course web pages. Campuswide network is available. 100% of college-owned or -operated housing units are wired for high-speed Internet access. Wireless service is available via classrooms, computer centers, computer labs, dorm rooms, learning centers, libraries, student centers.

Student Life *Housing:* on-campus residence required through sophomore year. *Options:* coed. Campus housing is university owned. Freshman campus housing is guaranteed. *Activities and organizations:* drama/theater group, student-run newspaper, radio station, choral group, Student Government Association, Student Activity Council, Unity House organizations, sports clubs, student radio station. *Campus security:* 24-hour emergency response devices and patrols, late-night transport/escort service, controlled dormitory access. *Student services:* health clinic, personal/psychological counseling, women's center.
Athletics Member NCAA. All Division III. *Intercollegiate sports:* baseball M(c), basketball M/W, crew M/W, cross-country running M/W, equestrian sports M(c)/W(c), field hockey W, ice hockey M/W, lacrosse M/W, rugby W(c), sailing M/W, skiing (cross-country) M(c)/W(c), skiing (downhill) M(c)/W(c), soccer M/W, squash M/W, swimming and diving M/W, tennis M/W, track and field M/W, ultimate Frisbee M(c)/W(c), volleyball M/W, water polo M/W. *Intramural sports:* basketball M/W, football M, golf M/W, ice hockey M/W, lacrosse M, soccer M/W, softball M/W, tennis M/W, volleyball M/W.
Costs (2011–12) *Comprehensive fee:* $54,970 includes full-time tuition ($43,695), mandatory fees ($295), and room and board ($10,980). Part-time tuition: $1275 per credit hour. *College room only:* $5940. *Payment plan:* installment. *Waivers:* senior citizens and employees or children of employees.
Financial Aid Of all full-time matriculated undergraduates who enrolled in 2009, 997 applied for aid, 859 were judged to have need, 859 had their need fully met. 719 Federal Work-Study jobs (averaging $1386). 18 state and other part-time jobs (averaging $992). *Average percent of need met:* 100%. *Average financial aid package:* $31,101. *Average need-based loan:* $4389. *Average need-based gift aid:* $29,616. *Average indebtedness upon graduation:* $22,038. *Financial aid deadline:* 2/1.
Applying *Options:* electronic application, early decision, deferred entrance. *Application fee:* $60. *Required:* essay or personal statement, high school transcript, minimum 2.0 GPA, letters of recommendation, Supplement to Common Application. *Recommended:* interview. *Application deadlines:* 1/1 (freshmen), 4/1 (transfers). *Early decision deadline:* 11/15 (for plan 1), 1/1 (for plan 2). *Notification:* 3/31 (freshmen), 5/15 (transfers), 12/15 (early decision plan 1), 2/15 (early decision plan 2).
Freshman Application Contact Ms. Martha C. Merrill, Dean of Admissions and Financial Aid, Connecticut College, 270 Mohegan Avenue, New London, CT 06320-4196. *Phone:* 860-439-2200. *Fax:* 860-439-4301. *E-mail:* admission@conncoll.edu. *Web site:* http://www.connecticutcollege.edu/.

Eastern Connecticut State University
Willimantic, Connecticut

- **State-supported** comprehensive, founded 1889, part of Connecticut State Colleges and Universities
- **Small-town** 182-acre campus with easy access to Hartford
- **Coed** 5,346 undergraduate students, 83% full-time, 53% women, 47% men
- **Moderately difficult** entrance level, 62% of applicants were admitted

Undergraduates 4,446 full-time, 900 part-time. Students come from 27 states and territories; 42 other countries; 5% are from out of state; 7% Black or African American, non-Hispanic/Latino; 8% Hispanic/Latino; 1% Asian, non-Hispanic/Latino; 0.2% Native Hawaiian or other Pacific Islander, non-Hispanic/Latino; 0.4% American Indian or Alaska Native, non-Hispanic/Latino; 2% Two or more races, non-Hispanic/Latino; 1% Race/ethnicity unknown; 0.8% international; 9% transferred in; 53% live on campus. *Retention:* 76% of full-time freshmen returned.
Freshmen *Admission:* 3,785 applied, 2,355 admitted, 951 enrolled. *Average high school GPA:* 2.99. *Test scores:* SAT critical reading scores over 500: 54%; SAT math scores over 500: 55%; SAT critical reading scores over 600: 10%; SAT math scores over 600: 10%; SAT critical reading scores over 700: 1%; SAT math scores over 700: 1%.
Faculty *Total:* 446, 45% full-time, 54% with terminal degrees. *Student/faculty ratio:* 16:1.
Academics *Calendar:* semesters. *Degrees:* associate, bachelor's, and master's. *Special study options:* academic remediation for entering students, adult/continuing education programs, advanced placement credit, cooperative education, distance learning, double majors, freshman honors college, honors programs, independent study, internships, off-campus study, part-time degree program, services for LD students, student-designed majors, study abroad, summer session for credit. *ROTC:* Army (c), Air Force (c).
Computers on Campus 637 computers/terminals are available on campus for general student use. Students can access the following: computer help desk, free student e-mail accounts, online (class) grades, online (class) registration, online (class) schedules. Campuswide network is available. 100% of college-owned or -operated housing units are wired for high-speed Internet access. Wireless service is available via libraries, student centers.

Student Life *Housing options:* coed. Campus housing is university owned. Freshman campus housing is guaranteed. *Activities and organizations:* drama/theater group, student-run newspaper, radio and television station, choral group, Bowling Club, People Helping People, M.A.L.E.S, Education Club, West Indian Society. *Campus security:* 24-hour emergency response devices and patrols, student patrols, late-night transport/escort service, controlled dormitory access. *Student services:* health clinic, personal/psychological counseling, women's center.

Athletics Member NCAA. All Division III. *Intercollegiate sports:* baseball M, basketball M/W, cheerleading W(c), cross-country running M/W, field hockey W, lacrosse M/W, soccer M/W, softball W, swimming and diving W, track and field M/W, volleyball W. *Intramural sports:* badminton M/W, basketball M/W, bowling M(c)/W(c), cross-country running M/W, football M, gymnastics W, racquetball M/W, rugby M/W(c), skiing (cross-country) M/W, skiing (downhill) M/W, soccer M/W, softball M/W, squash M/W, swimming and diving M/W, tennis M/W, track and field M/W, ultimate Frisbee M/W, volleyball M/W, water polo M/W.

Standardized Tests *Required:* SAT or ACT (for admission).

Costs (2011–12) *Tuition:* state resident $4124 full-time, $386 per credit hour part-time; nonresident $14,748 full-time, $389 per credit hour part-time. Full-time tuition and fees vary according to reciprocity agreements. *Required fees:* $4431 full-time, $40 per term part-time. *Room and board:* $10,256; room only: $5806. Room and board charges vary according to board plan.

Financial Aid Of all full-time matriculated undergraduates who enrolled in 2010, 3,506 applied for aid, 2,869 were judged to have need, 239 had their need fully met. In 2010, 91 non-need-based awards were made. *Average percent of need met:* 52%. *Average financial aid package:* $8677. *Average need-based loan:* $4634. *Average need-based gift aid:* $6657. *Average non-need-based aid:* $2694. *Average indebtedness upon graduation:* $26,192.

Applying *Options:* electronic application, early admission, deferred entrance. *Application fee:* $50. *Required:* high school transcript. *Required for some:* interview. *Recommended:* essay or personal statement, rank in upper 50% of high school class. *Application deadlines:* rolling (freshmen), rolling (transfers). *Notification:* continuous (freshmen), continuous (transfers).

Freshman Application Contact Christopher Dorsey, Interim Director of Admissions and Enrollment Management, Eastern Connecticut State University, 83 Windham Street, Willimantic, CT 06226. *Phone:* 860-465-5286. *Fax:* 860-465-5544. *E-mail:* admissions@easternct.edu. *Web site:* http://www.easternct.edu/.

Fairfield University
Fairfield, Connecticut

- **Independent Roman Catholic (Jesuit)** comprehensive, founded 1942
- **Suburban** 200-acre campus with easy access to New York City
- **Endowment** $254.0 million
- **Coed** 3,835 undergraduate students, 88% full-time, 58% women, 42% men
- **Moderately difficult** entrance level, 69% of applicants were admitted

Undergraduates 3,385 full-time, 450 part-time. Students come from 35 states and territories; 43 other countries; 66% are from out of state; 3% Black or African American, non-Hispanic/Latino; 3% Hispanic/Latino; 1% Asian, non-Hispanic/Latino; 0.1% Native Hawaiian or other Pacific Islander, non-Hispanic/Latino; 0.1% American Indian or Alaska Native, non-Hispanic/Latino; 0.9% Two or more races, non-Hispanic/Latino; 47% Race/ethnicity unknown; 1% international; 0.7% transferred in; 74% live on campus. *Retention:* 88% of full-time freshmen returned.

Freshmen *Admission:* 8,486 applied, 5,892 admitted, 909 enrolled. *Average high school GPA:* 3.37. *Test scores:* SAT critical reading scores over 500: 95%; SAT math scores over 500: 93%; SAT writing scores over 500: 94%; ACT scores over 18: 96%; SAT critical reading scores over 600: 38%; SAT math scores over 600: 47%; SAT writing scores over 600: 46%; ACT scores over 24: 77%; SAT critical reading scores over 700: 3%; SAT math scores over 700: 4%; SAT writing scores over 700: 4%; ACT scores over 30: 17%.

Faculty *Total:* 541, 48% full-time, 45% with terminal degrees. *Student/faculty ratio:* 13:1.

Academics *Calendar:* semesters. *Degrees:* associate, bachelor's, doctoral, and post-master's certificates. *Special study options:* adult/continuing education programs, advanced placement credit, distance learning, double majors, English as a second language, honors programs, independent study, internships, part-time degree program, services for LD students, student-designed majors, study abroad, summer session for credit. *ROTC:* Army (c), Air Force (c). *Unusual degree programs:* 3-2 engineering with University of Connecticut, Rensselaer Polytechnic Institute, Columbia University, Stevens Institute of Technology, Fairfield University.

Computers on Campus 220 computers/terminals and 150 ports are available on campus for general student use. Students can access the following: campus intranet, computer help desk, free student e-mail accounts, online (class)

grades, online (class) registration, online (class) schedules. Campuswide network is available. 100% of college-owned or -operated housing units are wired for high-speed Internet access. Wireless service is available via classrooms, dorm rooms, libraries, student centers.

Student Life *Housing:* on-campus residence required through senior year. *Options:* coed, disabled students. Campus housing is university owned. Freshman campus housing is guaranteed. *Activities and organizations:* drama/theater group, student-run newspaper, radio and television station, choral group, Student government, Glee Club, Residence Hall Council, Stags in the Stands, Campus Ministry. *Campus security:* 24-hour emergency response devices and patrols, late-night transport/escort service, controlled dormitory access, bicycle patrols. *Student services:* health clinic, personal/psychological counseling, women's center.

Athletics Member NCAA. All Division I. *Intercollegiate sports:* baseball M(s), basketball M(s)/W(s), crew M(s)/W(s), cross-country running M(s)/W(s), equestrian sports W(c), field hockey W(s), golf M(s)/W(s), ice hockey M(c)/W(c), lacrosse M(s)/W(s), rugby M(c)/W(c), sailing M(c)/W(c), skiing (downhill) M(c)/W(c), soccer M(s)/W(s), softball W(s), swimming and diving M(s)/W(s), tennis M(s)/W(s), volleyball M(c)/W(s). *Intramural sports:* basketball M/W, field hockey W, golf M/W, lacrosse M/W, soccer M/W, softball W, tennis M/W, volleyball M/W.

Costs (2011–12) *One-time required fee:* $60. *Comprehensive fee:* $52,700 includes full-time tuition ($39,900), mandatory fees ($590), and room and board ($12,210). Part-time tuition: $595 per credit hour. Part-time tuition and fees vary according to course load. *Required fees:* $25 per term part-time. *College room only:* $7480. Room and board charges vary according to board plan and housing facility. *Payment plan:* installment. *Waivers:* employees or children of employees.

Financial Aid Of all full-time matriculated undergraduates who enrolled in 2011, 2,373 applied for aid, 1,987 were judged to have need, 342 had their need fully met. 473 Federal Work-Study jobs (averaging $530). In 2011, 413 non-need-based awards were made. *Average percent of need met:* 82%. *Average financial aid package:* $28,140. *Average need-based loan:* $4723. *Average need-based gift aid:* $21,077. *Average non-need-based aid:* $18,301. *Average indebtedness upon graduation:* $31,099. *Financial aid deadline:* 2/15.

Applying *Options:* electronic application, early admission, early decision, early action, deferred entrance. *Application fee:* $60. *Required:* essay or personal statement, high school transcript, 1 letter of recommendation. *Recommended:* interview. *Application deadlines:* 1/15 (freshmen), 5/1 (transfers), 11/1 (early action). *Early decision deadline:* 1/1. *Notification:* 4/1 (freshmen), continuous (transfers), 2/1 (early decision), 1/1 (early action).

Freshman Application Contact Ms. Karen Pellegrino, Director of Admission, Fairfield University, 1073 North Benson Road, Fairfield, CT 06824-5195. *Phone:* 203-254-4100. *Fax:* 203-254-4199. *E-mail:* admis@fairfield.edu. *Web site:* http://www.fairfield.edu/.

Goodwin College
East Hartford, Connecticut

- **Proprietary** primarily 2-year, founded 1999
- **Suburban** 660-acre campus with easy access to Hartford
- **Endowment** $3.4 million
- **Coed** 3,116 undergraduate students, 16% full-time, 83% women, 17% men
- **Minimally difficult** entrance level, 100% of applicants were admitted

Undergraduates 496 full-time, 2,620 part-time. 1% are from out of state; 24% Black or African American, non-Hispanic/Latino; 19% Hispanic/Latino; 2% Asian, non-Hispanic/Latino; 0.1% Native Hawaiian or other Pacific Islander, non-Hispanic/Latino; 0.3% American Indian or Alaska Native, non-Hispanic/Latino; 2% Two or more races, non-Hispanic/Latino; 0.4% Race/ethnicity unknown; 23% transferred in. *Retention:* 44% of full-time freshmen returned.

Freshmen *Admission:* 537 applied, 537 admitted, 381 enrolled.

Faculty *Total:* 261, 22% full-time. *Student/faculty ratio:* 11:1.

Academics *Calendar:* semesters. *Degrees:* certificates, associate, and bachelor's. *Special study options:* academic remediation for entering students, adult/continuing education programs, advanced placement credit, distance learning, double majors, English as a second language, internships, off-campus study, part-time degree program, services for LD students, summer session for credit.

Computers on Campus 204 computers/terminals are available on campus for general student use. Students can access the following: campus intranet, computer help desk, free student e-mail accounts, online (class) grades, online (class) registration, online (class) schedules. Campuswide network is available. Wireless service is available via entire campus.

Student Life *Housing:* college housing not available. *Activities and organizations:* student-run newspaper, choral group. *Campus security:* 24-hour emergency response devices, evening security patrolman. *Student services:* personal/psychological counseling.

Athletics *Intramural sports:* basketball M, football M/W, soccer M/W, softball M/W.

Costs (2012–13) *Tuition:* $18,900 full-time, $590 per credit hour part-time. Full-time tuition and fees vary according to course load and program. Part-time tuition and fees vary according to course load and program. *Required fees:* $500 full-time. *Payment plan:* installment. *Waivers:* employees or children of employees.

Financial Aid Of all full-time matriculated undergraduates who enrolled in 2010, 662 applied for aid, 644 were judged to have need. 74 Federal Work-Study jobs (averaging $2745). In 2010, 11 non-need-based awards were made. *Average percent of need met:* 25%. *Average financial aid package:* $8029. *Average need-based loan:* $3231. *Average need-based gift aid:* $5404. *Average non-need-based aid:* $3333.

Applying *Options:* electronic application, early admission, early decision, early action, deferred entrance. *Application fee:* $50. *Required:* essay or personal statement, high school transcript, minimum 2.0 GPA, medical exam. *Recommended:* 2 letters of recommendation, interview. *Application deadlines:* rolling (freshmen), rolling (transfers), 6/1 (early action). *Early decision deadline:* 3/1. *Notification:* continuous (freshmen), continuous (transfers), 3/15 (early decision), 6/15 (early action).

Freshman Application Contact Mr. Nicholas Lentino, Director of Admissions, Goodwin College, One Riverside Drive, East Hartford, CT 06118. *Phone:* 860-727-6765. *Toll-free phone:* 800-889-3282. *Fax:* 860-291-9550. *E-mail:* nlantino@goodwin.edu. *Web site:* http://www.goodwin.edu/.

Holy Apostles College and Seminary
Cromwell, Connecticut

- **Independent Roman Catholic** comprehensive, founded 1956
- **Suburban** 17-acre campus with easy access to Hartford, New Haven
- **Endowment** $657,367
- **Coed**
- **Noncompetitive** entrance level

Faculty *Student/faculty ratio:* 2:1.

Academics *Calendar:* semesters. *Degrees:* certificates, associate, bachelor's, master's, post-master's, and postbachelor's certificates.

Standardized Tests *Recommended:* SAT (for admission).

Costs (2011–12) *Tuition:* $9840 full-time, $410 per credit part-time. Part-time tuition and fees vary according to course load.

Applying *Options:* deferred entrance. *Application fee:* $50. *Required:* high school transcript. *Required for some:* interview.

Freshman Application Contact Holy Apostles College and Seminary, 33 Prospect Hill Road, Cromwell, CT 06416-2005. *Phone:* 860-632-3010. *Web site:* http://www.holyapostles.edu/.

Lincoln College of New England
Southington, Connecticut

Freshman Application Contact Anthony Reich, Vice President of Admissions, Lincoln College of New England, 2279 Mount Vernon Road, Southington, CT 06489. *Phone:* 860-628-4751 Ext. 40904. *Toll-free phone:* 800-825-0087. *Fax:* 860-628-6444. *E-mail:* areich@lincolncollegene.edu. *Web site:* http://www.lincolncollegene.edu/.

Lyme Academy College of Fine Arts
Old Lyme, Connecticut

- **Independent** 4-year, founded 1976
- **Rural** 47-acre campus with easy access to New Haven, Hartford
- **Endowment** $4.0 million
- **Coed** 83 undergraduate students, 80% full-time, 60% women, 40% men
- **Moderately difficult** entrance level, 41% of applicants were admitted

Undergraduates 66 full-time, 17 part-time. Students come from 21 states and territories; 2 other countries; 47% are from out of state; 7% transferred in. *Retention:* 89% of full-time freshmen returned.

Freshmen *Admission:* 111 applied, 46 admitted, 19 enrolled. *Average high school GPA:* 3.22.

Faculty *Total:* 21, 43% full-time, 52% with terminal degrees. *Student/faculty ratio:* 4:1.

Academics *Calendar:* semesters. *Degrees:* bachelor's and postbachelor's certificates. *Special study options:* adult/continuing education programs, advanced placement credit, independent study, internships, part-time degree program, services for LD students, study abroad.

Computers on Campus 24 computers/terminals are available on campus for general student use. Students can access the following: campus intranet. Campuswide network is available. Wireless service is available via entire campus.

Student Life *Housing:* college housing not available. *Options:* coed. Campus housing is university owned, leased by the school and is provided by a third party. Freshman campus housing is guaranteed. *Activities and organizations:* Student Organization. *Campus security:* student patrols. *Student services:* personal/psychological counseling.

Athletics *Intramural sports:* volleyball M/W.

Standardized Tests *Required:* SAT or ACT (for admission).

Costs (2012–13) *Comprehensive fee:* $39,336 includes full-time tuition ($26,904), mandatory fees ($1632), and room and board ($10,800). Part-time tuition: $1121 per credit. Part-time tuition and fees vary according to course load. *Required fees:* $68 per credit part-time. *College room only:* $7200. *Payment plan:* installment. *Waivers:* employees or children of employees.

Financial Aid Of all full-time matriculated undergraduates who enrolled in 2010, 52 applied for aid, 48 were judged to have need. In 2010, 9 non-need-based awards were made. *Average financial aid package:* $16,870. *Average non-need-based aid:* $4055. *Average indebtedness upon graduation:* $24,578.

Applying *Options:* electronic application, early admission, early decision, deferred entrance. *Application fee:* $55. *Required:* high school transcript, art portfolio of at least 5 pieces but recommend 10-12 pieces. *Recommended:* essay or personal statement, 2 letters of recommendation, interview. *Application deadlines:* rolling (freshmen), rolling (out-of-state freshmen), rolling (transfers). *Early decision deadline:* 2/15. *Notification:* continuous (freshmen), continuous (out-of-state freshmen), continuous (transfers).

Freshman Application Contact Mr. Karl Holzenthal, Admissions Representative, Lyme Academy College of Fine Arts, 84 Lyme Street, Old Lyme, CT 06371. *Phone:* 860-434-3571 Ext. 127. *Fax:* 860-434-8725. *E-mail:* kholzenthal@lymeacademy.edu. *Web site:* http://www.lymeacademy.edu/.

Mitchell College
New London, Connecticut

- **Independent** 4-year, founded 1938
- **Suburban** 67-acre campus with easy access to Hartford, Providence
- **Coed** 952 undergraduate students, 85% full-time, 47% women, 53% men
- **Moderately difficult** entrance level, 53% of applicants were admitted

Undergraduates 808 full-time, 144 part-time. 45% are from out of state; 11% Black or African American, non-Hispanic/Latino; 11% Hispanic/Latino; 1% Asian, non-Hispanic/Latino; 0.1% Native Hawaiian or other Pacific Islander, non-Hispanic/Latino; 2% American Indian or Alaska Native, non-Hispanic/Latino; 3% Two or more races, non-Hispanic/Latino; 6% Race/ethnicity unknown; 1% international; 5% transferred in; 62% live on campus. *Retention:* 59% of full-time freshmen returned.

Freshmen *Admission:* 1,320 applied, 694 admitted, 194 enrolled. *Average high school GPA:* 2.75.

Faculty *Total:* 110, 33% full-time, 42% with terminal degrees. *Student/faculty ratio:* 14:1.

Academics *Calendar:* semesters. *Degrees:* associate and bachelor's. *Special study options:* advanced placement credit, cooperative education, double majors, independent study, internships, part-time degree program, services for LD students, student-designed majors, summer session for credit.

Computers on Campus 176 computers/terminals are available on campus for general student use. Students can access the following: campus intranet, computer help desk, free student e-mail accounts, online (class) grades, online (class) schedules. Campuswide network is available. 100% of college-owned or -operated housing units are wired for high-speed Internet access. Wireless service is available via classrooms, computer centers, computer labs, dorm rooms, learning centers, libraries, student centers.

Student Life *Housing:* on-campus residence required through senior year. *Options:* coed, men-only, women-only. Campus housing is university owned. Freshman applicants given priority for college housing. *Activities and organizations:* drama/theater group, student-run newspaper, radio station, choral group, Mitchell College Drama Society, Sigma Alpha Pi Leadership Society, Behavioral Science, Early Childhood, Gaming Club. *Campus security:* 24-hour emergency response devices and patrols, student patrols, late-night transport/escort service, controlled dormitory access. *Student services:* health clinic, personal/psychological counseling.

Athletics Member NCAA. All Division III. *Intercollegiate sports:* baseball M, basketball M/W, cross-country running M/W, golf M, lacrosse M, sailing M/W, soccer M/W, softball W, tennis M/W, volleyball W. *Intramural sports:* basketball M/W, cheerleading M/W, rugby M/W, sailing M/W, soccer M/W, softball M/W, tennis M/W, volleyball M/W.

Costs (2012–13) *Comprehensive fee:* $40,206 includes full-time tuition ($25,994), mandatory fees ($1720), and room and board ($12,492). *College room only:* $6496. *Payment plan:* installment. *Waivers:* employees or children of employees.

Financial Aid Of all full-time matriculated undergraduates who enrolled in 2004, 491 applied for aid, 414 were judged to have need. 44 Federal Work-

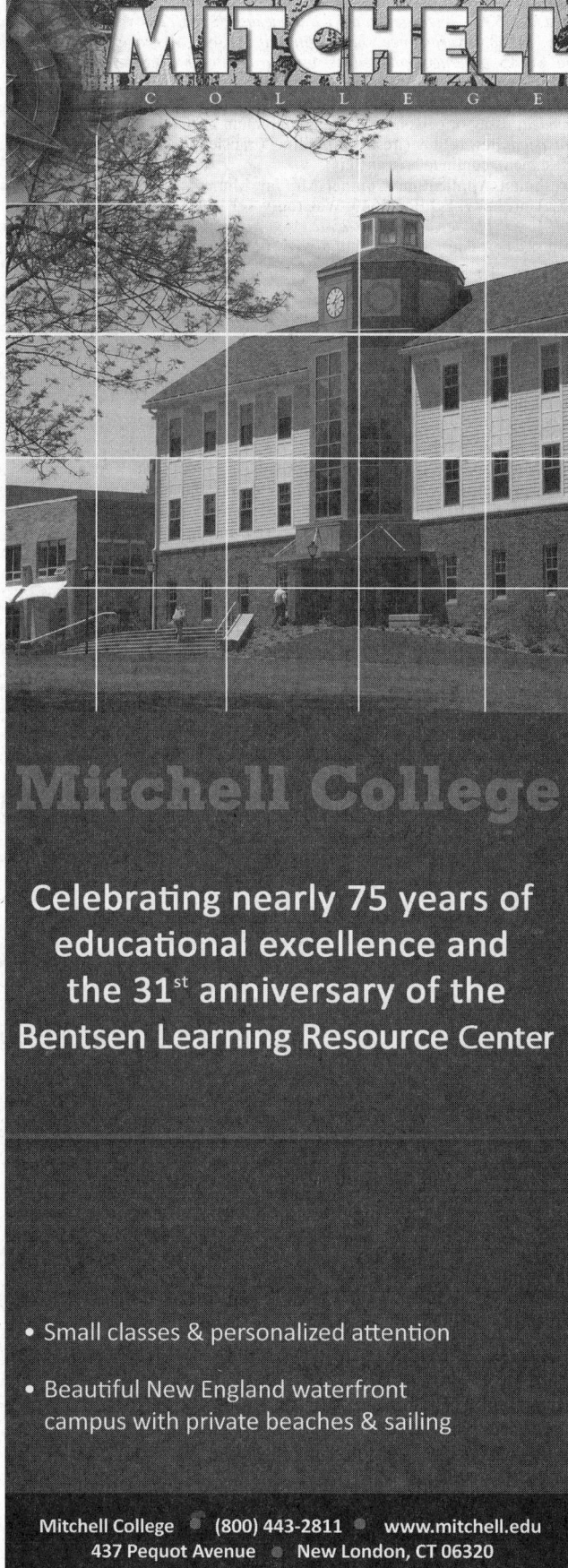

Celebrating nearly 75 years of educational excellence and the 31ˢᵗ anniversary of the Bentsen Learning Resource Center

• Small classes & personalized attention

• Beautiful New England waterfront campus with private beaches & sailing

Mitchell College (800) 443-2811 www.mitchell.edu
437 Pequot Avenue New London, CT 06320

Study jobs (averaging $1000). In 2004, 70 non-need-based awards were made. *Average percent of need met:* 89%. *Average financial aid package:* $16,357. *Average need-based loan:* $2904. *Average need-based gift aid:* $8058. *Average non-need-based aid:* $2890.

Applying *Options:* electronic application, early admission, early decision, deferred entrance. *Application fee:* $30. *Required:* essay or personal statement, high school transcript, minimum 2.0 GPA, 1 letter of recommendation, interview. *Application deadlines:* rolling (freshmen), rolling (transfers). *Early decision deadline:* 11/15. *Notification:* continuous until 12/15 (freshmen), continuous (transfers), 12/1 (early decision).

Freshman Application Contact Ms. Susan Bibeau, Vice President of Enrollment Management, Mitchell College, 437 Pequot Avenue, New London, CT 06320. *Phone:* 860-701-5039. *Toll-free phone:* 800-443-2811. *Fax:* 860-444-1209. *E-mail:* admissions@mitchell.edu. *Web site:* http://www.mitchell.edu/.

See page 1460 for the College Close-Up.

Paier College of Art, Inc.
Hamden, Connecticut

- **Proprietary** 4-year, founded 1946
- **Suburban** 3-acre campus with easy access to New York City
- **Coed** 196 undergraduate students, 74% full-time, 68% women, 32% men
- **Minimally difficult** entrance level, 67% of applicants were admitted

Undergraduates 145 full-time, 51 part-time. Students come from 5 states and territories; 5% Black or African American, non-Hispanic/Latino; 7% Hispanic/Latino; 2% Asian, non-Hispanic/Latino; 8% transferred in. *Retention:* 83% of full-time freshmen returned.

Freshmen *Admission:* 42 applied, 28 admitted, 20 enrolled. *Average high school GPA:* 2.8. *Test scores:* SAT critical reading scores over 500: 31%; SAT math scores over 500: 25%.

Faculty *Total:* 38, 26% full-time, 47% with terminal degrees. *Student/faculty ratio:* 5:1.

Academics *Calendar:* semesters plus 1 summer session. *Degrees:* certificates, diplomas, associate, and bachelor's. *Special study options:* academic remediation for entering students, advanced placement credit, independent study, part-time degree program, services for LD students, study abroad.

Computers on Campus 45 computers/terminals are available on campus for general student use. Wireless service is available via entire campus.

Student Life *Housing:* college housing not available. *Activities and organizations:* student-run newspaper, Student Council, School Newspaper. *Campus security:* evening patrols by security.

Standardized Tests *Required:* SAT or ACT (for admission).

Costs (2012–13) *Tuition:* $12,600 full-time, $400 per credit part-time. Full-time tuition and fees vary according to degree level. Part-time tuition and fees vary according to course load. *Required fees:* $360 full-time, $235 per semester part-time. *Payment plan:* installment.

Financial Aid Of all full-time matriculated undergraduates who enrolled in 1999, 102 applied for aid, 92 were judged to have need, 1 had their need fully met. *Average percent of need met:* 62%. *Average financial aid package:* $6717. *Average need-based loan:* $3446. *Average need-based gift aid:* $3460. *Average indebtedness upon graduation:* $13,536.

Applying *Options:* deferred entrance. *Application fee:* $25. *Required:* high school transcript, minimum 2.0 GPA, 2 letters of recommendation, interview, Portfolio Interview. *Recommended:* essay or personal statement. *Application deadlines:* rolling (freshmen), rolling (transfers). *Notification:* continuous (freshmen), continuous (transfers).

Freshman Application Contact Ms. Lynn Pascale, Admissions Secretary, Paier College of Art, Inc., 20 Gorham Avenue, Hamden, CT 06514 . *Phone:* 203-287-3031. *Fax:* 203-287-3021. *E-mail:* paier.admission@snet.net. *Web site:* http://www.paiercollegeofart.edu/.

Post University
Waterbury, Connecticut

- **Independent** comprehensive, founded 1890
- **Suburban** 70-acre campus with easy access to Hartford
- **Coed** 822 undergraduate students, 97% full-time, 51% women, 49% men
- **Moderately difficult** entrance level, 13% of applicants were admitted

Undergraduates 801 full-time, 21 part-time. Students come from 9 other countries; 46% are from out of state; 18% Black or African American, non-Hispanic/Latino; 7% Hispanic/Latino; 0.6% Asian, non-Hispanic/Latino; 0.5% Two or more races, non-Hispanic/Latino; 51% Race/ethnicity unknown; 2% international; 10% transferred in; 53% live on campus. *Retention:* 52% of full-time freshmen returned.

Freshmen *Admission:* 1,861 applied, 239 admitted, 296 enrolled. *Average high school GPA:* 2.48. *Test scores:* SAT critical reading scores over 500: 15%; SAT math scores over 500: 56%; SAT writing scores over 500: 12%;

ACT scores over 18: 3%; SAT critical reading scores over 600: 1%; SAT math scores over 600: 14%; ACT scores over 24: 1%; SAT math scores over 700: 2%.

Faculty *Total:* 128, 15% full-time, 27% with terminal degrees. *Student/faculty ratio:* 15:1.

Academics *Calendar:* semesters (modular courses offered in the evening). *Degrees:* certificates, associate, bachelor's, and master's. *Special study options:* academic remediation for entering students, accelerated degree program, adult/continuing education programs, advanced placement credit, cooperative education, distance learning, double majors, English as a second language, independent study, internships, part-time degree program, services for LD students, study abroad, summer session for credit.

Computers on Campus 150 computers/terminals and 150 ports are available on campus for general student use. Students can access the following: campus intranet, computer help desk, free student e-mail accounts, online (class) grades, online (class) registration, online (class) schedules, software applications. Campuswide network is available. 100% of college-owned or -operated housing units are wired for high-speed Internet access. Wireless service is available via entire campus.

Student Life *Housing options:* coed. Campus housing is university owned. Freshman campus housing is guaranteed. *Activities and organizations:* drama/theater group, choral group, Art Club, Equine Club, Accounting Society, Post Pride, CIS Club. *Campus security:* 24-hour emergency response devices and patrols, late-night transport/escort service, controlled dormitory access. *Student services:* health clinic, personal/psychological counseling.

Athletics Member NCAA. All Division II. *Intercollegiate sports:* baseball M(s), basketball M(s)/W(s), cross-country running M(s)/W(s), equestrian sports M(s)/W(s), football M, golf M(s), lacrosse M(s)/W(s), soccer M(s)/W(s), softball W(s), swimming and diving M(s)/W(s), tennis M(s)/W(s), volleyball W(s). *Intramural sports:* basketball M/W, lacrosse M/W, soccer M/W, swimming and diving M/W, tennis M/W.

Standardized Tests *Recommended:* SAT or ACT (for admission).

Costs (2011–12) *Comprehensive fee:* $35,850 includes full-time tuition ($24,800), mandatory fees ($1200), and room and board ($9850). Full-time tuition and fees vary according to degree level and program. Part-time tuition: $825 per credit. Part-time tuition and fees vary according to class time, course load, degree level, and program. *College room only:* $5400. Room and board charges vary according to housing facility. *Payment plan:* installment. *Waivers:* senior citizens and employees or children of employees.

Financial Aid Of all full-time matriculated undergraduates who enrolled in 2010, 726 applied for aid, 707 were judged to have need, 27 had their need fully met. In 2010, 58 non-need-based awards were made. *Average percent of need met:* 53%. *Average financial aid package:* $18,672. *Average need-based loan:* $4258. *Average need-based gift aid:* $14,491. *Average non-need-based aid:* $8815. *Average indebtedness upon graduation:* $33,584.

Applying *Options:* electronic application, deferred entrance. *Application fee:* $40. *Required:* high school transcript, 1 letter of recommendation. *Recommended:* essay or personal statement, minimum 2.0 GPA, interview. *Application deadlines:* rolling (freshmen), rolling (transfers). *Notification:* continuous (freshmen), continuous (transfers).

Freshman Application Contact Mr. Jay Murray, Director of Admissions, Post University, PO Box 2540, Waterbury, CT 06723. *Phone:* 203-596-4500. *Toll-free phone:* 800-345-2562. *Fax:* 203-756-5810. *E-mail:* admiss@post.edu. *Web site:* http://www.post.edu/.

Quinnipiac University
Hamden, Connecticut

- **Independent** comprehensive, founded 1929
- **Suburban** 600-acre campus with easy access to New Haven, Hartford
- **Endowment** $275.5 million
- **Coed** 6,262 undergraduate students, 96% full-time, 62% women, 38% men
- **Moderately difficult** entrance level, 63% of applicants were admitted

Undergraduates 5,988 full-time, 274 part-time. Students come from 28 states and territories; 20 other countries; 73% are from out of state; 4% Black or African American, non-Hispanic/Latino; 7% Hispanic/Latino; 3% Asian, non-Hispanic/Latino; 0.4% American Indian or Alaska Native, non-Hispanic/Latino; 0.7% Two or more races, non-Hispanic/Latino; 5% Race/ethnicity unknown; 1% international; 3% transferred in; 78% live on campus. *Retention:* 87% of full-time freshmen returned.

Freshmen *Admission:* 18,642 applied, 11,768 admitted, 1,513 enrolled. *Average high school GPA:* 3.4. *Test scores:* SAT critical reading scores over 500: 82%; SAT math scores over 500: 87%; ACT scores over 18: 100%; SAT critical reading scores over 600: 23%; SAT math scores over 600: 31%; ACT scores over 24: 71%; SAT critical reading scores over 700: 2%; SAT math scores over 700: 3%; ACT scores over 30: 10%.

Faculty *Total:* 925, 38% full-time, 64% with terminal degrees. *Student/faculty ratio:* 12:1.

Academics *Calendar:* semesters. *Degrees:* bachelor's, master's, doctoral, post-master's, and postbachelor's certificates. *Special study options:* acceler-

ated degree program, advanced placement credit, distance learning, double majors, honors programs, independent study, internships, part-time degree program, services for LD students, student-designed majors, study abroad, summer session for credit. *ROTC:* Army (c), Navy (c), Air Force (c).

Computers on Campus 600 computers/terminals and 2,500 ports are available on campus for general student use. Students can access the following: campus intranet, computer help desk, free student e-mail accounts, online (class) grades, online (class) registration, online (class) schedules, e-commerce 'Q' card for local merchants, food service, dorm card access. Campuswide network is available. 100% of college-owned or -operated housing units are wired for high-speed Internet access. Wireless service is available via entire campus.

Student Life *Housing options:* coed. Campus housing is university owned. Freshman campus housing is guaranteed. *Activities and organizations:* drama/theater group, student-run newspaper, radio and television station, choral group, student government, Social Programming Board, Drama Club, Chronicle (student newspaper), dance company, national fraternities, national sororities. *Campus security:* 24-hour emergency response devices and patrols, late-night transport/escort service, controlled dormitory access, text message emergency notification system. *Student services:* health clinic, personal/psychological counseling.

Athletics Member NCAA. All Division I. *Intercollegiate sports:* baseball M(s), basketball M(s)/W(s), cross-country running M(s)/W(s), field hockey W(s), golf W(s), gymnastics W(s), ice hockey M(s)/W(s), lacrosse M(s)/W(s), rugby W(s), soccer M(s)/W(s), softball W(s), tennis M(s)/W(s), track and field W(s), volleyball W(s). *Intramural sports:* baseball M, basketball M/W, bowling M/W, field hockey W, soccer M/W, softball W, tennis M/W, volleyball M/W.

Standardized Tests *Required:* SAT or ACT (for admission).

Costs (2012–13) *Comprehensive fee:* $51,800 includes full-time tuition ($36,510), mandatory fees ($1490), and room and board ($13,800). Part-time tuition: $875 per credit. Part-time tuition and fees vary according to class time and course load. *Required fees:* $35 per credit hour part-time. *Room and board:* Room and board charges vary according to housing facility. *Payment plan:* installment. *Waivers:* employees or children of employees.

Financial Aid Of all full-time matriculated undergraduates who enrolled in 2011, 4,463 applied for aid, 3,826 were judged to have need, 489 had their need fully met. 2,105 Federal Work-Study jobs (averaging $2017). 36 state and other part-time jobs (averaging $1530). In 2011, 856 non-need-based awards were made. *Average percent of need met:* 63%. *Average financial aid package:* $20,999. *Average need-based loan:* $4482. *Average need-based gift aid:* $15,502. *Average non-need-based aid:* $10,942. *Average indebtedness upon graduation:* $39,500.

Applying *Options:* electronic application, early decision, deferred entrance. *Application fee:* $45. *Required:* essay or personal statement, high school transcript, 1 letter of recommendation. *Required for some:* minimum 3.0 GPA. *Recommended:* minimum 3.0 GPA, interview. *Application deadlines:* 2/1 (freshmen), 2/1 (out-of-state freshmen), 4/1 (transfers). *Early decision deadline:* 11/1. *Notification:* continuous (freshmen), continuous (out-of-state freshmen), continuous (transfers), rolling (early decision).

Freshman Application Contact Ms. Joan Isaac Mohr, Vice President and Dean of Admissions, Quinnipiac University, 275 Mount Carmel Avenue, Hamden, CT 06518. *Phone:* 203-582-8600. *Toll-free phone:* 800-462-1944. *Fax:* 203-582-8906. *E-mail:* admissions@quinnipiac.edu. *Web site:* http://www.quinnipiac.edu/.

See page 162 for display ad and page 1512 for the College Close-Up.

Sacred Heart University

Fairfield, Connecticut

- **Independent Roman Catholic** comprehensive, founded 1963
- **Suburban** 71-acre campus with easy access to New York City
- **Endowment** $82.8 million
- **Coed** 4,143 undergraduate students, 83% full-time, 63% women, 37% men
- **Moderately difficult** entrance level, 54% of applicants were admitted

Undergraduates 3,458 full-time, 685 part-time. Students come from 21 states and territories; 2 other countries; 70% are from out of state; 5% Black or African American, non-Hispanic/Latino; 6% Hispanic/Latino; 2% Asian, non-Hispanic/Latino; 0.1% Native Hawaiian or other Pacific Islander, non-Hispanic/Latino; 0.3% American Indian or Alaska Native, non-Hispanic/Latino; 0.9% Two or more races, non-Hispanic/Latino; 18% Race/ethnicity unknown; 1% international; 61% live on campus. *Retention:* 74% of full-time freshmen returned.

Freshmen *Admission:* 8,321 applied, 4,470 admitted, 950 enrolled. *Average high school GPA:* 3.3. *Test scores:* SAT critical reading scores over 500: 77%; SAT math scores over 500: 83%; SAT writing scores over 500: 81%; ACT scores over 18: 98%; SAT critical reading scores over 600: 19%; SAT math scores over 600: 27%; SAT writing scores over 600: 23%; ACT scores over 24:

49%; SAT critical reading scores over 700: 1%; SAT math scores over 700: 2%; SAT writing scores over 700: 2%; ACT scores over 30: 4%.

Faculty *Total:* 570, 41% full-time. *Student/faculty ratio:* 14:1.

Academics *Calendar:* semesters. *Degrees:* certificates, associate, bachelor's, master's, doctoral, post-master's, and postbachelor's certificates (also offers part-time program with significant enrollment not reflected in profile). *Special study options:* academic remediation for entering students, accelerated degree program, adult/continuing education programs, advanced placement credit, cooperative education, distance learning, double majors, English as a second language, honors programs, independent study, internships, off-campus study, part-time degree program, services for LD students, student-designed majors, study abroad, summer session for credit. *ROTC:* Army (c).

Computers on Campus 111 computers/terminals and 3,100 ports are available on campus for general student use. Students can access the following: campus intranet, computer help desk, free student e-mail accounts, online (class) grades, online (class) registration, online (class) schedules. Campuswide network is available. 100% of college-owned or -operated housing units are wired for high-speed Internet access. Wireless service is available via entire campus.

Student Life *Housing:* on-campus residence required through sophomore year. *Options:* coed, men-only, women-only, disabled students. Campus housing is university owned and leased by the school. Freshman campus housing is guaranteed. *Activities and organizations:* drama/theater group, student-run newspaper, radio and television station, choral group, marching band, Habitat for Humanity, Student Events Team, Student Athletic Training Organizations, SHU FORCE (Dance Ensemble), American Chemical Society, national fraternities, national sororities. *Campus security:* 24-hour emergency response devices and patrols, late-night transport/escort service, controlled dormitory access, Campus Emergency Plan, Personal Safety Escort Program, Security Alarm Systems, Crime Prevention Announcements, Security Surveys. *Student services:* health clinic, personal/psychological counseling.

Athletics Member NCAA. All Division I except football (Division I-AA). *Intercollegiate sports:* baseball M(s), basketball M(s)/W(s), bowling W(s), cheerleading W(c), crew W, cross-country running M(s)/W(s), equestrian sports W, fencing M(s)/W(s), field hockey W(s), golf M(s)/W(s), ice hockey M(s)/W(s), lacrosse M(s)/W(s), soccer M(s)/W(s), softball W(s), swimming and diving W(s), tennis M(s)/W(s), track and field M(s)/W(s), volleyball M(s)/W(s), wrestling M(s). *Intramural sports:* baseball M(c), basketball M(c)/W(c), bowling M(c), cross-country running M(c)/W(c), field hockey W(c), golf M(c)/W(c), gymnastics W(c), ice hockey M(c), lacrosse M(c)/W(c), rugby M(c)/W(c), sailing M(c)/W(c), soccer M(c)/W(c), softball W(c), tennis M(c)/W(c), ultimate Frisbee M(c)/W(c), volleyball M(c)/W(c), weight lifting M(c)/W(c).

Standardized Tests *Recommended:* Test-Optional Admissions Policy, SAT/ACT scores will be considered if submitted.

Costs (2012–13) *Comprehensive fee:* $45,500 includes full-time tuition ($32,474), mandatory fees ($250), and room and board ($12,776). Full-time tuition and fees vary according to course load, degree level, and program. Part-time tuition: $500 per credit. Part-time tuition and fees vary according to degree level and program. *Required fees:* $90 per term part-time. *Room and board:* Room and board charges vary according to board plan and housing facility. *Payment plan:* installment. *Waivers:* employees or children of employees.

Financial Aid Of all full-time matriculated undergraduates who enrolled in 2010, 3,076 applied for aid, 2,570 were judged to have need, 309 had their need fully met. 978 Federal Work-Study jobs (averaging $996). 787 state and other part-time jobs (averaging $958). In 2010, 491 non-need-based awards were made. *Average percent of need met:* 58%. *Average financial aid package:* $18,253. *Average need-based loan:* $5150. *Average need-based gift aid:* $13,718. *Average non-need-based aid:* $5712. *Average indebtedness upon graduation:* $46,812.

Applying *Options:* electronic application, early admission, early decision. *Application fee:* $50. *Required:* essay or personal statement, high school transcript, 1 letter of recommendation. *Required for some:* interview, interview required for Early Decision candidates. *Recommended:* minimum 3.2 GPA, interview. *Early decision deadline:* 12/1. *Notification:* continuous (freshmen), continuous (transfers), 12/15 (early decision).

Freshman Application Contact Mr. Kenneth Higgins, Director of Undergraduate Admissions, Sacred Heart University, 5151 Park Avenue, Fairfield, CT 06825-1000. *Phone:* 203-610-9388. *Fax:* 203-365-7607. *E-mail:* higginsk2288@sacredheart.edu. *Web site:* http://www.sacredheart.edu/.

See page 164 for display ad and page 1536 for the College Close-Up.

Southern Connecticut State University
New Haven, Connecticut

- **State-supported** comprehensive, founded 1893, part of Connecticut State Colleges and Universities (ConnSCU)
- **Suburban** 168-acre campus with easy access to New York City
- **Endowment** $1.4 million
- **Coed** 8,696 undergraduate students, 87% full-time, 61% women, 39% men
- **Moderately difficult** entrance level, 72% of applicants were admitted

Undergraduates 7,524 full-time, 1,172 part-time. Students come from 24 states and territories; 7 other countries; 6% are from out of state; 14% Black or African American, non-Hispanic/Latino; 10% Hispanic/Latino; 2% Asian, non-Hispanic/Latino; 0.1% Native Hawaiian or other Pacific Islander, non-Hispanic/Latino; 0.3% American Indian or Alaska Native, non-Hispanic/Latino; 2% Two or more races, non-Hispanic/Latino; 4% Race/ethnicity unknown; 0.4% international; 11% transferred in; 32% live on campus. *Retention:* 76% of full-time freshmen returned.

Freshmen *Admission:* 5,332 applied, 3,831 admitted, 1,334 enrolled. *Average high school GPA:* 2.73. *Test scores:* SAT critical reading scores over 500: 35%; SAT math scores over 500: 34%; SAT writing scores over 500: 40%; ACT scores over 18: 71%; SAT critical reading scores over 600: 6%; SAT math scores over 600: 6%; SAT writing scores over 600: 7%; ACT scores over 24: 19%; ACT scores over 30: 2%.

Faculty *Total:* 1,046, 41% full-time, 33% with terminal degrees. *Student/faculty ratio:* 15:1.

Academics *Calendar:* semesters. *Degrees:* bachelor's, master's, doctoral, post-master's, and postbachelor's certificates. *Special study options:* academic remediation for entering students, accelerated degree program, advanced placement credit, cooperative education, distance learning, double majors, freshman honors college, honors programs, independent study, internships, off-campus study, part-time degree program, services for LD students, student-designed majors, study abroad, summer session for credit. *ROTC:* Army (c), Air Force (c).

Computers on Campus 800 computers/terminals are available on campus for general student use. Students can access the following: computer help desk, free student e-mail accounts, online (class) grades, online (class) registration, online (class) schedules. Campuswide network is available. 100% of college-owned or -operated housing units are wired for high-speed Internet access. Wireless service is available via classrooms, computer centers, computer labs, learning centers, libraries, student centers.

Student Life *Housing options:* coed, disabled students. Campus housing is university owned. Freshman campus housing is guaranteed. *Activities and organizations:* drama/theater group, student-run newspaper, radio and television station, choral group, marching band, Student Government Association, Psychology Club, Habitat for Humanity, Crescent Players, Black Student Union, national fraternities, national sororities. *Campus security:* 24-hour emergency response devices and patrols, late-night transport/escort service, controlled dormitory access. *Student services:* health clinic, personal/psychological counseling, women's center.

Athletics Member NCAA. All Division II. *Intercollegiate sports:* baseball M(s), basketball M(s)/W(s), cheerleading M(c)/W(c), cross-country running M(s)/W(s), field hockey W(s), football M(s), gymnastics W(s), lacrosse W(s), rugby M(c)/W(c), soccer M(s)/W(s), softball W(s), swimming and diving M(s)/W(s), track and field M(s)/W(s), ultimate Frisbee M(c)/W(c), volleyball W(s). *Intramural sports:* badminton M/W, basketball M/W, football M/W, ice hockey M(c)/W(c), soccer M/W, softball M/W, tennis M/W, volleyball M/W.

Standardized Tests *Required:* SAT or ACT (for admission).

Costs (2011–12) *Tuition:* state resident $4124 full-time, $413 per credit part-time; nonresident $13,346 full-time, $426 per credit part-time. Full-time tuition and fees vary according to course load and reciprocity agreements. Part-time tuition and fees vary according to course load. *Required fees:* $4124 full-time, $55 per term part-time. *Room and board:* $10,087; room only: $5633. Room and board charges vary according to board plan and housing facility. *Payment plans:* installment, deferred payment. *Waivers:* senior citizens and employees or children of employees.

Financial Aid Of all full-time matriculated undergraduates who enrolled in 2011, 7,321 applied for aid, 5,012 were judged to have need, 1,986 had their need fully met. 107 Federal Work-Study jobs (averaging $3190). In 2011, 311 non-need-based awards were made. *Average percent of need met:* 84%. *Average financial aid package:* $13,244. *Average need-based loan:* $4370. *Average need-based gift aid:* $5581. *Average non-need-based aid:* $5300. *Average indebtedness upon graduation:* $23,753. *Financial aid deadline:* 3/9.

Applying *Options:* electronic application, deferred entrance. *Application fee:* $50. *Required:* essay or personal statement, high school transcript. *Application deadlines:* 4/1 (freshmen), 8/1 (transfers). *Notification:* continuous (freshmen), continuous (transfers).

Freshman Application Contact Ms. Paula Kennedy, Associate Director of Admissions, Southern Connecticut State University, Admissions House, 131 Farnham Avenue, New Haven, CT 06515-1202. *Phone:* 203-392-5651. *Fax:* 203-392-5727. *Web site:* http://www.southernct.edu/.

See page 1592 for the College Close-Up.

Trinity College
Hartford, Connecticut

- **Independent** comprehensive, founded 1823
- **Urban** 100-acre campus
- **Endowment** $436,652
- **Coed** 2,344 undergraduate students, 95% full-time, 49% women, 51% men
- **Most difficult** entrance level, 30% of applicants were admitted

Undergraduates 2,236 full-time, 108 part-time. Students come from 48 states and territories; 51 other countries; 83% are from out of state; 6% Black or African American, non-Hispanic/Latino; 8% Hispanic/Latino; 5% Asian, non-Hispanic/Latino; 0.1% American Indian or Alaska Native, non-Hispanic/Latino; 4% Two or more races, non-Hispanic/Latino; 5% Race/ethnicity unknown; 7% international; 0.8% transferred in; 90% live on campus. *Retention:* 92% of full-time freshmen returned.

Freshmen *Admission:* 6,967 applied, 2,118 admitted, 590 enrolled. *Test scores:* SAT critical reading scores over 500: 97%; SAT math scores over 500: 97%; SAT writing scores over 500: 97%; ACT scores over 18: 99%; SAT critical reading scores over 600: 69%; SAT math scores over 600: 76%; SAT writing scores over 600: 78%; ACT scores over 24: 89%; SAT critical reading scores over 700: 18%; SAT math scores over 700: 20%; SAT writing scores over 700: 25%; ACT scores over 30: 21%.

Faculty *Total:* 243, 71% full-time, 87% with terminal degrees. *Student/faculty ratio:* 10:1.

Academics *Calendar:* semesters. *Degrees:* bachelor's and master's. *Special study options:* accelerated degree program, adult/continuing education programs, advanced placement credit, double majors, honors programs, independent study, internships, off-campus study, student-designed majors, study abroad, summer session for credit. *ROTC:* Army (c). *Unusual degree programs:* 3-2 engineering with Rensselaer Polytechnic Institute.

Computers on Campus 249 computers/terminals and 3,000 ports are available on campus for general student use. Students can access the following: campus intranet, computer help desk, free student e-mail accounts, online (class) grades, online (class) registration, online (class) schedules, Web pages. Campuswide network is available. 100% of college-owned or -operated housing units are wired for high-speed Internet access. Wireless service is available via classrooms, computer centers, computer labs, learning centers, libraries, student centers.

Student Life *Housing:* on-campus residence required for freshman year. *Options:* coed, disabled students. Campus housing is university owned. Freshman campus housing is guaranteed. *Activities and organizations:* drama/theater group, student-run newspaper, radio station, choral group, Friends Active in Community Engagement and Service (FACES), The Mill, Student Government Association, Relay for Life, Multi-Cultural Affairs Council, national fraternities, national sororities. *Campus security:* 24-hour emergency response devices and patrols, late-night transport/escort service, controlled dormitory access. *Student services:* health clinic, personal/psychological counseling, women's center.

Athletics Member NCAA. All Division III. *Intercollegiate sports:* baseball M, basketball M/W, crew M/W, cross-country running M/W, equestrian sports M(c)/W(c), fencing M(c)/W(c), football M, golf M, ice hockey M/W, lacrosse M/W, rugby M(c)/W(c), sailing M(c)/W(c), skiing (downhill) M(c)/W(c), soccer M/W, softball W, squash M/W, swimming and diving M/W, tennis M/W, track and field M/W, ultimate Frisbee M(c)/W(c), volleyball W, water polo M(c)/W(c), wrestling M. *Intramural sports:* badminton M/W, basketball M/W, soccer M/W, softball M/W, squash M/W, tennis M/W.

Standardized Tests *Required for some:* SAT or ACT (for admission), SAT Subject Tests (for admission).

Costs (2012–13) *One-time required fee:* $25. *Comprehensive fee:* $57,530 includes full-time tuition ($43,570), mandatory fees ($2160), and room and board ($11,800). Full-time tuition and fees vary according to course load and program. Part-time tuition: $4841 per course. Part-time tuition and fees vary according to course load and program. *College room only:* $7660. Room and board charges vary according to board plan. *Payment plan:* installment. *Waivers:* adult students and employees or children of employees.

Financial Aid Of all full-time matriculated undergraduates who enrolled in 2011, 1,018 applied for aid, 964 were judged to have need, 964 had their need fully met. 733 Federal Work-Study jobs (averaging $1758). In 2011, 25 non-need-based awards were made. *Average percent of need met:* 100%. *Average financial aid package:* $40,226. *Average need-based loan:* $4491. *Average need-based gift aid:* $37,923. *Average non-need-based aid:* $36,743. *Average indebtedness upon graduation:* $20,367. *Financial aid deadline:* 3/1.

Applying *Options:* electronic application, early admission, early decision, deferred entrance. *Application fee:* $60. *Required:* essay or personal state-

ment, high school transcript, 3 letters of recommendation. *Recommended:* interview. *Application deadlines:* 1/1 (freshmen), 4/1 (transfers). *Early decision deadline:* 11/15 (for plan 1), 1/1 (for plan 2). *Notification:* 4/1 (freshmen), 6/10 (transfers), 12/15 (early decision plan 1), 2/15 (early decision plan 2).

Freshman Application Contact Trinity College, 300 Summit Street, Hartford, CT 06106-3100. *Phone:* 860-297-2180. *Web site:* http://www.trincoll.edu/.

See page 165 for display ad and page 1644 for the College Close-Up.

United States Coast Guard Academy
New London, Connecticut

- **Federally supported** 4-year, founded 1876
- **Suburban** 110-acre campus with easy access to Providence, Hartford
- **Endowment** $1.3 million
- **Coed** 1,055 undergraduate students, 100% full-time, 30% women, 70% men
- **Very difficult** entrance level, 16% of applicants were admitted

Undergraduates 1,055 full-time. Students come from 53 states and territories; 19 other countries; 94% are from out of state; 3% Black or African American, non-Hispanic/Latino; 10% Hispanic/Latino; 4% Asian, non-Hispanic/Latino; 0.9% Native Hawaiian or other Pacific Islander, non-Hispanic/Latino; 0.7% American Indian or Alaska Native, non-Hispanic/Latino; 3% Two or more races, non-Hispanic/Latino; 1% Race/ethnicity unknown; 2% international; 100% live on campus. *Retention:* 95% of full-time freshmen returned.
Freshmen *Admission:* 2,374 applied, 383 admitted, 288 enrolled. *Average high school GPA:* 3.78. *Test scores:* SAT critical reading scores over 500: 93%; SAT math scores over 500: 97%; SAT writing scores over 500: 92%; ACT scores over 18: 99%; SAT critical reading scores over 600: 49%; SAT math scores over 600: 71%; SAT writing scores over 600: 46%; ACT scores over 24: 87%; SAT critical reading scores over 700: 10%; SAT math scores over 700: 12%; SAT writing scores over 700: 6%; ACT scores over 30: 23%.
Faculty *Total:* 143, 93% full-time, 50% with terminal degrees. *Student/faculty ratio:* 8:1.
Academics *Calendar:* semesters. *Degree:* bachelor's. *Special study options:* academic remediation for entering students, double majors, English as a second language, honors programs, independent study, internships, off-campus study, summer session for credit.
Computers on Campus 325 computers/terminals are available on campus for general student use. Students can access the following: campus intranet, computer help desk, free student e-mail accounts, online (class) grades, online (class) registration, online (class) schedules. Campuswide network is available. 100% of college-owned or -operated housing units are wired for high-speed Internet access. Wireless service is available via classrooms, dorm rooms, libraries, student centers.
Student Life *Housing:* on-campus residence required through senior year. *Options:* coed. Campus housing is university owned. Freshman campus housing is guaranteed. *Activities and organizations:* drama/theater group, choral group, marching band, Companneros Club - Latino culture and traditions, Genesis Club - Multicultural awareness, Men's and Women's Lacrosse Club, Men's and Women's Rugby Club, Officers' Christian Fellowship. *Campus security:* 24-hour patrols, student patrols, late-night transport/escort service. *Student services:* health clinic, personal/psychological counseling, legal services.
Athletics Member NCAA. All Division III. *Intercollegiate sports:* baseball M, basketball M/W, bowling M(c)/W(c), cheerleading W, crew M/W, cross-country running M/W, fencing M(c)/W(c), football M, golf M(c)/W(c), ice hockey M(c), lacrosse M(c)/W(c), riflery M/W, rugby M(c)/W(c), sailing M/W, skiing (downhill) M(c)/W(c), soccer M/W, softball W, swimming and diving M/W, tennis M, track and field M/W, volleyball M(c)/W, water polo M(c), weight lifting M(c), wrestling M. *Intramural sports:* basketball M/W, football M/W, golf M/W, racquetball M/W, soccer M/W, softball M/W, swimming and diving M/W, tennis M/W.
Standardized Tests *Required:* SAT or ACT (for admission).
Costs (2012–13) *Comprehensive fee:* Tuition, room and board, and medical and dental care are provided by the US government. Each cadet receives a salary from which to pay for uniforms, supplies, and personal expenses.
Applying *Options:* electronic application, early action. *Required:* essay or personal statement, high school transcript, 3 letters of recommendation, medical examination, physical fitness examination. *Recommended:* interview. *Application deadlines:* 2/1 (freshmen), 2/1 (out-of-state freshmen), 2/1 (transfers), 11/1 (early action). *Notification:* continuous until 4/15 (freshmen), continuous until 4/15 (out-of-state freshmen), continuous until 4/15 (transfers), 1/15 (early action).
Freshman Application Contact Capt. Stephan P. Finton, Director of Admissions, United States Coast Guard Academy, 31 Mohegan Avenue, New London, CT 06320-4195. *Phone:* 860-444-8500. *Toll-free phone:* 800-883-

8724. *Fax:* 860-701-6700. *E-mail:* admissions@uscga.edu. *Web site:* http://www.uscga.edu/.

University of Bridgeport
Bridgeport, Connecticut

- **Independent** comprehensive, founded 1927
- **Urban** 86-acre campus with easy access to New York City
- **Endowment** $18.3 million
- **Coed** 2,503 undergraduate students, 67% full-time, 68% women, 32% men
- **Moderately difficult** entrance level, 57% of applicants were admitted

Undergraduates 1,684 full-time, 819 part-time. Students come from 39 states and territories; 56 other countries; 39% are from out of state; 37% Black or African American, non-Hispanic/Latino; 19% Hispanic/Latino; 3% Asian, non-Hispanic/Latino; 0.1% Native Hawaiian or other Pacific Islander, non-Hispanic/Latino; 0.4% American Indian or Alaska Native, non-Hispanic/Latino; 4% Two or more races, non-Hispanic/Latino; 9% international; 7% transferred in; 44% live on campus. *Retention:* 53% of full-time freshmen returned.
Freshmen *Admission:* 5,595 applied, 3,171 admitted, 403 enrolled. *Average high school GPA:* 2.88. *Test scores:* SAT critical reading scores over 500: 33%; SAT math scores over 500: 30%; SAT writing scores over 500: 26%; ACT scores over 18: 73%; SAT critical reading scores over 600: 6%; SAT math scores over 600: 7%; SAT writing scores over 600: 3%; ACT scores over 24: 8%; SAT math scores over 700: 1%.
Faculty *Total:* 473, 26% full-time. *Student/faculty ratio:* 15:1.
Academics *Calendar:* semesters. *Degrees:* certificates, associate, bachelor's, master's, doctoral, post-master's, postbachelor's, and first professional certificates. *Special study options:* academic remediation for entering students, accelerated degree program, adult/continuing education programs, advanced placement credit, cooperative education, distance learning, double majors, English as a second language, honors programs, independent study, internships, off-campus study, part-time degree program, services for LD students, student-designed majors, study abroad, summer session for credit. *ROTC:* Army (b).
Computers on Campus 100 computers/terminals and 100 ports are available on campus for general student use. Students can access the following: computer help desk, free student e-mail accounts, online (class) grades, online (class) registration, online (class) schedules. Campuswide network is available. 100% of college-owned or -operated housing units are wired for high-speed Internet access. Wireless service is available via classrooms, computer centers, computer labs, dorm rooms, learning centers, libraries, student centers.
Student Life *Housing:* on-campus residence required through sophomore year. *Options:* coed. Campus housing is university owned. Freshman campus housing is guaranteed. *Activities and organizations:* student-run newspaper, choral group, Student Congress, International Relations Club, Black Students Alliance, Latin America Club, Martial Arts Club, national fraternities, national sororities. *Campus security:* 24-hour emergency response devices and patrols, student patrols, late-night transport/escort service, controlled dormitory access. *Student services:* health clinic, personal/psychological counseling, women's center.
Athletics Member NCAA. All Division II. *Intercollegiate sports:* baseball M(s), basketball M(s)/W(s), cross-country running M(s)/W(s), gymnastics W(s), lacrosse W(s), soccer M(s)/W(s), softball W(s), swimming and diving M(s)/W(s), volleyball W(s). *Intramural sports:* basketball M/W, football M/W, golf M/W, racquetball M/W, soccer M/W, softball M/W, tennis M/W.
Standardized Tests *Required:* SAT or ACT (for admission).
Costs (2011–12) *Comprehensive fee:* $39,030 includes full-time tuition ($25,200), mandatory fees ($2130), and room and board ($11,700). Full-time tuition and fees vary according to course load and program. Part-time tuition: $840 per credit hour. Part-time tuition and fees vary according to course load and program. *Required fees:* $95 per term part-time. *Room and board:* Room and board charges vary according to board plan and student level. *Payment plans:* installment, deferred payment. *Waivers:* senior citizens and employees or children of employees.
Financial Aid Of all full-time matriculated undergraduates who enrolled in 2010, 1,400 applied for aid, 1,380 were judged to have need. *Average percent of need met:* 61%. *Average financial aid package:* $23,400. *Average need-based loan:* $4380. *Average need-based gift aid:* $15,178.
Applying *Options:* electronic application, early admission, deferred entrance. *Application fee:* $25. *Required:* essay or personal statement, high school transcript, minimum 2.0 GPA. *Required for some:* 2 letters of recommendation, interview, portfolio, audition. *Recommended:* 1 letter of recommendation, interview. *Application deadlines:* rolling (freshmen), rolling (out-of-state freshmen), rolling (transfers). *Notification:* continuous (freshmen), continuous (out-of-state freshmen), continuous (transfers).

Freshman Application Contact Ms. Jessica Crowley, Director Undergraduate Admissions, University of Bridgeport, 126 Park Avenue, Bridgeport, CT 06604. *Phone:* 203-576-4812. *Toll-free phone:* 800-EXCEL-UB. *Fax:* 203-576-4941. *E-mail:* admit@bridgeport.edu. *Web site:* http://www.bridgeport.edu/.

University of Connecticut

Storrs, Connecticut

- **State-supported** university, founded 1881
- **Rural** 4108-acre campus
- **Endowment** $329.0 million
- **Coed** 17,815 undergraduate students, 96% full-time, 49% women, 51% men
- **Moderately difficult** entrance level, 47% of applicants were admitted

Undergraduates 17,063 full-time, 752 part-time. Students come from 44 states and territories; 58 other countries; 23% are from out of state; 6% Black or African American, non-Hispanic/Latino; 7% Hispanic/Latino; 8% Asian, non-Hispanic/Latino; 0.1% Native Hawaiian or other Pacific Islander, non-Hispanic/Latino; 0.2% American Indian or Alaska Native, non-Hispanic/Latino; 1% Two or more races, non-Hispanic/Latino; 11% Race/ethnicity unknown; 2% international; 5% transferred in; 73% live on campus. *Retention:* 92% of full-time freshmen returned.

Freshmen *Admission:* 27,247 applied, 12,894 admitted, 3,327 enrolled. *Test scores:* SAT critical reading scores over 500: 90%; SAT math scores over 500: 95%; SAT writing scores over 500: 92%; ACT scores over 18: 99%; SAT critical reading scores over 600: 49%; SAT math scores over 600: 68%; SAT writing scores over 600: 53%; ACT scores over 24: 87%; SAT critical reading scores over 700: 9%; SAT math scores over 700: 15%; SAT writing scores over 700: 11%; ACT scores over 30: 21%.

Faculty *Total:* 1,363, 76% full-time, 78% with terminal degrees. *Student/faculty ratio:* 18:1.

Academics *Calendar:* semesters. *Degrees:* associate, bachelor's, master's, doctoral, post-master's, postbachelor's, and first professional certificates. *Special study options:* accelerated degree program, adult/continuing education programs, advanced placement credit, cooperative education, distance learning, double majors, English as a second language, honors programs, independent study, internships, off-campus study, part-time degree program, services for LD students, student-designed majors, study abroad, summer session for credit. *ROTC:* Army (b), Air Force (b). *Unusual degree programs:* 3-2 education, pharmacy.

Computers on Campus 1,318 computers/terminals are available on campus for general student use. Students can access the following: computer help desk, free student e-mail accounts, online (class) grades, online (class) registration, online (class) schedules. Campuswide network is available. 100% of college-owned or -operated housing units are wired for high-speed Internet access. Wireless service is available via classrooms, computer centers, computer labs, dorm rooms, learning centers, libraries, student centers.

Student Life *Housing options:* coed, men-only, women-only, disabled students. Campus housing is university owned and is provided by a third party. Freshman campus housing is guaranteed. *Activities and organizations:* drama/theater group, student-run newspaper, radio and television station, choral group, marching band, national fraternities, national sororities. *Campus security:* 24-hour emergency response devices, late-night transport/escort service. *Student services:* health clinic, personal/psychological counseling, women's center.

Athletics Member NCAA. All Division I except football (Division I-A). *Intercollegiate sports:* baseball M(s), basketball M(s)/W(s), crew W, cross-country running M(s)/W(s), field hockey W(s), golf M(s), ice hockey M(s)/W(s), lacrosse W, soccer M(s)/W(s), softball W(s), swimming and diving M(s)/W(s), tennis M(s)/W(s), track and field M(s)/W(s), volleyball W(s). *Intramural sports:* badminton M/W, baseball M, basketball M/W, bowling M(c)/W(c), crew M(c), cross-country running M/W, equestrian sports M(c)/W(c), fencing M(c)/W(c), football M, gymnastics M(c)/W(c), ice hockey M(c)/W(c), lacrosse M(c)/W(c), racquetball M/W, rugby M(c)/W(c), sailing M(c)/W(c), skiing (downhill) M(c)/W(c), soccer M/W, softball M/W, squash M/W, swimming and diving M/W, table tennis M/W, tennis M/W, track and field M/W, volleyball M/W, water polo W, weight lifting M(c), wrestling M(c).

Standardized Tests *Required:* SAT or ACT (for admission).

Costs (2012–13) *Tuition:* state resident $8712 full-time, $363 per credit part-time; nonresident $26,544 full-time, $1106 per credit part-time. Part-time tuition and fees vary according to course load. *Required fees:* $2530 full-time. *Room and board:* $11,380; room only: $6096. Room and board charges vary according to board plan and housing facility. *Payment plans:* installment, deferred payment. *Waivers:* senior citizens and employees or children of employees.

Financial Aid Of all full-time matriculated undergraduates who enrolled in 2011, 12,476 applied for aid, 9,683 were judged to have need, 1,388 had their need fully met. 1,958 Federal Work-Study jobs (averaging $1703). 5,263 state and other part-time jobs (averaging $3125). In 2011, 1491 non-need-based awards were made. *Average percent of need met:* 65%. *Average financial aid package:* $12,739. *Average need-based loan:* $4173. *Average need-based gift aid:* $7868. *Average non-need-based aid:* $6661. *Average indebtedness upon graduation:* $23,822.

Applying *Options:* electronic application, early action, deferred entrance. *Application fee:* $70. *Required:* essay or personal statement, high school transcript. *Recommended:* 1 letter of recommendation. *Application deadlines:* 2/1 (freshmen), 4/1 (transfers), 12/1 (early action). *Notification:* 1/1 (freshmen), continuous (transfers), 2/1 (early action).

Freshman Application Contact Nathan Fuerst, Director of Undergraduate Admissions, University of Connecticut, 2131 Hillside Road, U-88, Storrs, CT 06269. *Phone:* 860-486-3137. *Fax:* 860-486-1476. *E-mail:* beahusky@uconnvm.uconn.edu. *Web site:* http://www.uconn.edu/.

University of Hartford

West Hartford, Connecticut

- **Independent** comprehensive, founded 1877
- **Suburban** 320-acre campus with easy access to Hartford
- **Endowment** $115.8 million
- **Coed** 5,350 undergraduate students, 86% full-time, 52% women, 48% men
- **Moderately difficult** entrance level, 71% of applicants were admitted

Undergraduates 4,596 full-time, 754 part-time. Students come from 49 states and territories; 35 other countries; 57% are from out of state; 14% Black or African American, non-Hispanic/Latino; 7% Hispanic/Latino; 3% Asian, non-Hispanic/Latino; 0.1% Native Hawaiian or other Pacific Islander, non-Hispanic/Latino; 0.4% American Indian or Alaska Native, non-Hispanic/Latino; 1% Two or more races, non-Hispanic/Latino; 10% Race/ethnicity unknown; 4% international; 4% transferred in; 60% live on campus. *Retention:* 72% of full-time freshmen returned.

Freshmen *Admission:* 11,997 applied, 8,534 admitted, 1,331 enrolled. *Test scores:* SAT critical reading scores over 500: 54%; SAT math scores over 500: 57%; ACT scores over 18: 84%; SAT critical reading scores over 600: 15%; SAT math scores over 600: 19%; ACT scores over 24: 33%; SAT critical reading scores over 700: 1%; SAT math scores over 700: 2%; ACT scores over 30: 5%.

Faculty *Total:* 848, 41% full-time. *Student/faculty ratio:* 10:1.

Academics *Calendar:* semesters. *Degrees:* certificates, diplomas, associate, bachelor's, master's, doctoral, post-master's, postbachelor's, and first professional certificates. *Special study options:* academic remediation for entering students, adult/continuing education programs, advanced placement credit, cooperative education, distance learning, double majors, English as a second language, honors programs, independent study, internships, off-campus study, part-time degree program, services for LD students, student-designed majors, study abroad, summer session for credit. *ROTC:* Army (c), Air Force (c).

Computers on Campus 400 computers/terminals are available on campus for general student use. Students can access the following: campus intranet, computer help desk, free student e-mail accounts, online (class) grades, online (class) registration, online (class) schedules, student Web pages. Campuswide network is available. 100% of college-owned or -operated housing units are wired for high-speed Internet access. Wireless service is available via classrooms, computer centers, computer labs, libraries, student centers.

Student Life *Housing options:* coed, women-only, disabled students. Campus housing is university owned and leased by the school. Freshman campus housing is guaranteed. *Activities and organizations:* drama/theater group, student-run newspaper, radio and television station, choral group, Program Council, Brothers and Sisters United, Hillel, Student Government Association, Residence Hall Association, national fraternities, national sororities. *Campus security:* 24-hour emergency response devices and patrols, late-night transport/escort service, controlled dormitory access, bicycle patrols. *Student services:* health clinic, personal/psychological counseling, women's center, legal services.

Athletics Member NCAA. All Division I. *Intercollegiate sports:* badminton M(c)/W(c), baseball M(s), basketball M(s)/W(s), cross-country running M(s)/W(s), golf M(s)/W(s), lacrosse M(s), racquetball M(c)/W(c), rugby M(c)/W(c), soccer M(s)/W(s), softball W(s), squash M(c)/W(c), tennis M(s)/W(s), track and field M/W, volleyball M(c)/W(c). *Intramural sports:* basketball M/W, football M/W, racquetball M/W, soccer M/W, softball M/W, tennis M/W, ultimate Frisbee M/W, volleyball M/W, water polo M/W.

Standardized Tests *Required:* SAT or ACT (for admission).

Costs (2012–13) *Comprehensive fee:* $44,276 includes full-time tuition ($30,618), mandatory fees ($1554), and room and board ($12,104). Full-time tuition and fees vary according to program. Part-time tuition: $440 per credit hour. Part-time tuition and fees vary according to course load and program. *College room only:* $7328. Room and board charges vary according to board

plan and housing facility. *Payment plans:* tuition prepayment, installment. *Waivers:* senior citizens and employees or children of employees.

Financial Aid Of all full-time matriculated undergraduates who enrolled in 2010, 4,376 applied for aid, 3,698 were judged to have need, 925 had their need fully met. 723 Federal Work-Study jobs (averaging $6719). In 2010, 919 non-need-based awards were made. *Average percent of need met:* 80%. *Average financial aid package:* $5464. *Average need-based loan:* $9814. *Average need-based gift aid:* $4153. *Average non-need-based aid:* $3578. *Average indebtedness upon graduation:* $14,855.

Applying *Options:* electronic application, early admission, deferred entrance. *Application fee:* $40. *Required:* high school transcript. *Recommended:* essay or personal statement, 2 letters of recommendation, interview. *Application deadlines:* rolling (freshmen), rolling (transfers). *Notification:* continuous (freshmen), continuous (transfers).

Freshman Application Contact Mr. Richard Zeiser, Dean of Admissions, University of Hartford, 200 Bloomfield Avenue, West Hartford, CT 06117. *Phone:* 860-768-4296. *Toll-free phone:* 800-947-4303. *Fax:* 860-768-4961. *E-mail:* admissions@hartford.edu. *Web site:* http://www.hartford.edu/.

See page 170 for display ad and page 1672 for the College Close-Up.

University of New Haven

West Haven, Connecticut

- **Independent** comprehensive, founded 1920
- **Suburban** 82-acre campus with easy access to Hartford, New Haven
- **Coed** 4,607 undergraduate students, 89% full-time, 51% women, 49% men
- **Moderately difficult** entrance level, 64% of applicants were admitted

Undergraduates 4,119 full-time, 488 part-time. Students come from 43 states and territories; 28 other countries; 54% are from out of state; 8% Black or African American, non-Hispanic/Latino; 5% Hispanic/Latino; 2% Asian, non-Hispanic/Latino; 0.4% American Indian or Alaska Native, non-Hispanic/Latino; 1% Two or more races, non-Hispanic/Latino; 29% Race/ethnicity unknown; 5% international; 5% transferred in; 56% live on campus. *Retention:* 75% of full-time freshmen returned.

Freshmen *Admission:* 11,181 applied, 7,129 admitted, 1,296 enrolled. *Average high school GPA:* 3.34. *Test scores:* SAT critical reading scores over 500: 63%; SAT math scores over 500: 70%; SAT writing scores over 500: 63%; ACT scores over 18: 94%; SAT critical reading scores over 600: 18%; SAT math scores over 600: 21%; SAT writing scores over 600: 17%; ACT scores over 24: 45%; SAT critical reading scores over 700: 2%; SAT math scores over 700: 2%; SAT writing scores over 700: 2%; ACT scores over 30: 4%.

Faculty *Total:* 572, 37% full-time, 52% with terminal degrees. *Student/faculty ratio:* 17:1.

Academics *Calendar:* 4-1-4. *Degrees:* certificates, associate, bachelor's, master's, doctoral, post-master's, postbachelor's, and first professional certificates. *Special study options:* academic remediation for entering students, accelerated degree program, adult/continuing education programs, advanced placement credit, cooperative education, distance learning, double majors, English as a second language, honors programs, independent study, internships, off-campus study, part-time degree program, services for LD students, study abroad, summer session for credit. *ROTC:* Army (b), Air Force (c).

Computers on Campus 300 computers/terminals and 250 ports are available on campus for general student use. Students can access the following: campus intranet, computer help desk, free student e-mail accounts, online (class) grades, online (class) registration, online (class) schedules, computer repair services. Campuswide network is available. 100% of college-owned or -operated housing units are wired for high-speed Internet access. Wireless service is available via entire campus.

Student Life *Housing options:* coed, disabled students. Campus housing is university owned and leased by the school. Freshman applicants given priority for college housing. *Activities and organizations:* drama/theater group, student-run newspaper, radio station, choral group, marching band, student government, Criminal Justice Club, Music Entertainment and Industry Association, Black Student Union, Fire Science Club, national fraternities, national sororities. *Campus security:* 24-hour emergency response devices and patrols, late-night transport/escort service, escort service, vehicle, bicycle and foot patrols, crime prevention programs. *Student services:* health clinic, personal/psychological counseling.

Athletics Member NCAA. All Division II. *Intercollegiate sports:* baseball M(s), basketball M(s)/W(s), cheerleading M/W, cross-country running M(s)/W(s), field hockey W(c), football M(s), ice hockey M(c), lacrosse M(c)/W(s), soccer M(s)/W(s), softball W(s), tennis W(s), track and field M(s)/W(s), ultimate Frisbee M(c)/W(c), volleyball W(s), wrestling M(c). *Intramural sports:* basketball M/W, bowling M/W, cross-country running M/W, football M, racquetball M/W, soccer M/W, softball M/W, table tennis M/W, ultimate Frisbee M/W, volleyball M/W, weight lifting M/W.

Standardized Tests *Required:* SAT or ACT (for admission).

Costs (2011–12) *Comprehensive fee:* $44,980 includes full-time tuition ($30,500), mandatory fees ($1250), and room and board ($13,230). Full-time tuition and fees vary according to course load and program. Part-time tuition:

$510 per credit hour. Part-time tuition and fees vary according to class time, course load, and program. *Required fees:* $75 per term part-time. *College room only:* $8340. Room and board charges vary according to board plan and housing facility. *Payment plan:* installment. *Waivers:* senior citizens and employees or children of employees.

Financial Aid Of all full-time matriculated undergraduates who enrolled in 2011, 3,652 applied for aid, 3,368 were judged to have need, 511 had their need fully met. In 2011, 433 non-need-based awards were made. *Average percent of need met:* 61%. *Average financial aid package:* $19,433. *Average need-based loan:* $4214. *Average need-based gift aid:* $15,843. *Average non-need-based aid:* $11,270. *Average indebtedness upon graduation:* $42,600.

Applying *Options:* electronic application, early action. *Application fee:* $75. *Required:* essay or personal statement, high school transcript, 1 letter of recommendation. *Recommended:* interview. *Application deadlines:* rolling (freshmen), rolling (transfers), 11/15 (early action). *Notification:* continuous (freshmen), continuous (transfers), 12/15 (early action).

Freshman Application Contact Mr. Kevin Phillips, Associate Vice President for Enrollment Management, University of New Haven, Bayer Hall, 300 Boston Post Road, West Haven, CT 06516. *Phone:* 203-932-7318. *Toll-free phone:* 800-DIAL-UNH. *Fax:* 203-931-6093. *E-mail:* adminfo@newhaven.edu. *Web site:* http://www.newhaven.edu/.

See page 168 for display ad and page 1694 for the College Close-Up.

University of Phoenix–Fairfield County Campus

Norwalk, Connecticut

Admissions Office Contact University of Phoenix–Fairfield County Campus, 535 Connecticut Avenue Suite 400, Norwalk, CT 06854-1799. *Toll-free phone:* 866-766-0766. *Web site:* http://www.phoenix.edu/.

University of Saint Joseph

West Hartford, Connecticut

- **Independent Roman Catholic** comprehensive, founded 1932
- **Suburban** 84-acre campus with easy access to Hartford
- **Endowment** $21.4 million
- **Undergraduate: women only; graduate: coed** 1,039 undergraduate students, 78% full-time, 99% women, 1% men
- **Moderately difficult** entrance level, 78% of applicants were admitted

Undergraduates 809 full-time, 230 part-time. 6% are from out of state; 10% Black or African American, non-Hispanic/Latino; 11% Hispanic/Latino; 2% Asian, non-Hispanic/Latino; 0.3% American Indian or Alaska Native, non-Hispanic/Latino; 1% Two or more races, non-Hispanic/Latino; 22% Race/ethnicity unknown; 11% transferred in; 40% live on campus. *Retention:* 75% of full-time freshmen returned.

Freshmen *Admission:* 1,335 applied, 1,047 admitted, 158 enrolled. *Average high school GPA:* 3.3. *Test scores:* SAT critical reading scores over 500: 55%; SAT math scores over 500: 52%; ACT scores over 18: 100%; SAT critical reading scores over 600: 10%; SAT math scores over 600: 12%.

Faculty *Total:* 290, 37% full-time. *Student/faculty ratio:* 12:1.

Academics *Calendar:* semesters. *Degrees:* certificates, bachelor's, master's, doctoral, post-master's, and postbachelor's certificates. *Special study options:* accelerated degree program, adult/continuing education programs, advanced placement credit, distance learning, double majors, honors programs, independent study, internships, off-campus study, part-time degree program, services for LD students, student-designed majors, study abroad, summer session for credit.

Computers on Campus Students can access the following: campus intranet, computer help desk, free student e-mail accounts, online (class) grades, online (class) registration, online (class) schedules. Campuswide network is available. 100% of college-owned or -operated housing units are wired for high-speed Internet access. Wireless service is available via computer centers, computer labs, dorm rooms, libraries, student centers.

Student Life *Housing options:* women-only, disabled students. Campus housing is university owned. *Activities and organizations:* drama/theater group, choral group. *Campus security:* 24-hour emergency response devices and patrols, late-night transport/escort service, controlled dormitory access. *Student services:* health clinic, personal/psychological counseling.

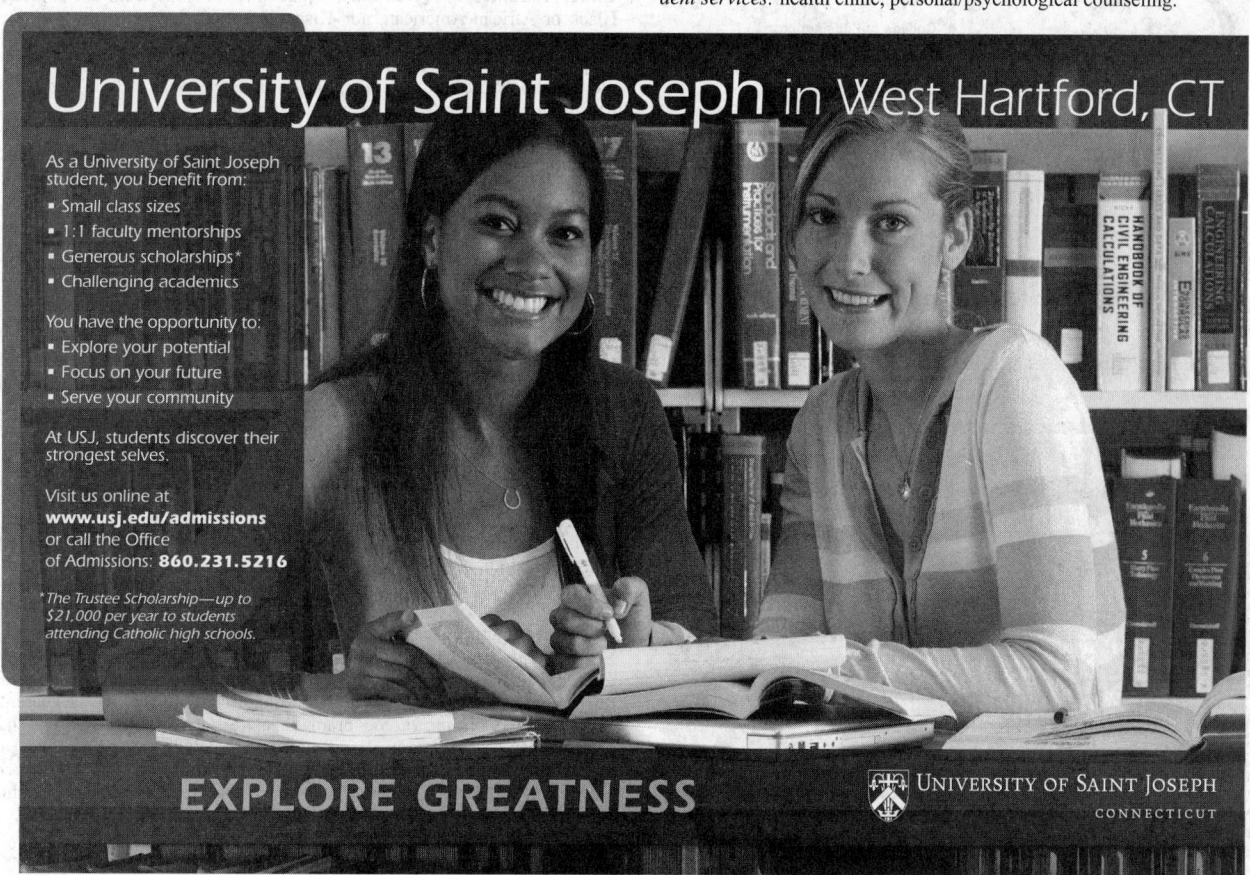

Athletics Member NCAA. All Division III. *Intercollegiate sports:* basketball W, cross-country running W, lacrosse W, soccer W, softball W, swimming and diving W, tennis W, volleyball W.

Standardized Tests *Required:* SAT or ACT (for admission). *Recommended:* SAT (for admission).

Costs (2012–13) *Comprehensive fee:* $45,424 includes full-time tuition ($30,408), mandatory fees ($1418), and room and board ($13,598). Full-time tuition and fees vary according to course load, degree level, location, program, and student level. Part-time tuition: $688 per credit. Part-time tuition and fees vary according to course load, degree level, location, program, and student level. *Required fees:* $45 per credit part-time. *College room only:* $6274. Room and board charges vary according to board plan and housing facility. *Payment plan:* installment. *Waivers:* employees or children of employees.

Financial Aid Of all full-time matriculated undergraduates who enrolled in 2011, 756 applied for aid, 717 were judged to have need, 76 had their need fully met. In 2011, 78 non-need-based awards were made. *Average percent of need met:* 68%. *Average financial aid package:* $21,631. *Average need-based loan:* $5307. *Average need-based gift aid:* $16,859. *Average non-need-based aid:* $9711.

Applying *Options:* electronic application, deferred entrance. *Application fee:* $50. *Required:* high school transcript. *Recommended:* essay or personal statement, interview. *Application deadlines:* rolling (freshmen), rolling (out-of-state freshmen), rolling (transfers). *Notification:* continuous (freshmen), continuous (out-of-state freshmen), continuous (transfers).

Freshman Application Contact Office of Admissions, University of Saint Joseph, 1678 Asylum Avenue, West Hartford, CT 06117. *Phone:* 860-231-5216. *Toll-free phone:* 866-442-8752. *Fax:* 860-231-5744. *E-mail:* admissions@sjc.edu. *Web site:* http://www.sjc.edu/.

See page 169 for display ad and page 1708 for the College Close-Up.

Wesleyan University
Middletown, Connecticut

- **Independent** university, founded 1831
- **Small-town** 240-acre campus
- **Endowment** $601.5 million
- **Coed** 2,882 undergraduate students, 100% full-time, 51% women, 49% men
- **Most difficult** entrance level, 24% of applicants were admitted

Undergraduates 2,879 full-time, 3 part-time. 91% are from out of state; 7% Black or African American, non-Hispanic/Latino; 10% Hispanic/Latino; 8% Asian, non-Hispanic/Latino; 0.1% American Indian or Alaska Native, non-Hispanic/Latino; 5% Two or more races, non-Hispanic/Latino; 10% Race/ethnicity unknown; 8% international; 0.9% transferred in; 99% live on campus. *Retention:* 94% of full-time freshmen returned.

Freshmen *Admission:* 9,658 applied, 2,340 admitted, 808 enrolled. *Average high school GPA:* 3.77. *Test scores:* SAT critical reading scores over 500: 99%; SAT math scores over 500: 99%; SAT writing scores over 500: 99%; ACT scores over 18: 100%; SAT critical reading scores over 600: 87%; SAT math scores over 600: 92%; SAT writing scores over 600: 90%; ACT scores over 24: 97%; SAT critical reading scores over 700: 53%; SAT math scores over 700: 55%; SAT writing scores over 700: 58%; ACT scores over 30: 67%.

Faculty *Total:* 375, 90% full-time, 91% with terminal degrees. *Student/faculty ratio:* 9:1.

Academics *Calendar:* semesters. *Degrees:* bachelor's, master's, doctoral, post-master's, and first professional certificates. *Special study options:* adult/continuing education programs, advanced placement credit, double majors, honors programs, independent study, off-campus study, services for LD students, student-designed majors, study abroad, summer session for credit. *ROTC:* Army (c), Air Force (c). *Unusual degree programs:* 3-2 engineering with Columbia University, California Institute of Technology.

Computers on Campus 1,600 computers/terminals are available on campus for general student use. Students can access the following: campus intranet, computer help desk, free student e-mail accounts, online (class) grades, online (class) registration, online (class) schedules, electronic portfolio, online course drop/add, Blackboard course management system. Campuswide network is available. 100% of college-owned or -operated housing units are wired for high-speed Internet access. Wireless service is available via entire campus.

Student Life *Housing:* on-campus residence required through senior year. *Options:* coed, men-only, women-only, cooperative, disabled students. Campus housing is university owned. Freshman campus housing is guaranteed. *Activities and organizations:* drama/theater group, student-run newspaper, radio station, choral group, Environmental Organizers Network, WesDems, Ajuacampos (Latino affinity group), national fraternities, national sororities. *Campus security:* 24-hour emergency response devices and patrols, student patrols, late-night transport/escort service, controlled dormitory access. *Student services:* health clinic, personal/psychological counseling, women's center.

Athletics Member NCAA. All Division III. *Intercollegiate sports:* baseball M, basketball M/W, crew M/W, cross-country running M/W, equestrian sports M(c)/W(c), field hockey W, football M, golf M, ice hockey M/W, lacrosse M/W, rugby M(c)/W(c), sailing M(c)/W(c), skiing (cross-country) M(c)/W(c), skiing (downhill) M(c)/W(c), soccer M/W, softball M/W, squash M/W, swimming and diving M/W, tennis M/W, track and field M/W, volleyball M(c)/W, water polo M(c), wrestling M. *Intramural sports:* basketball M/W, ice hockey M/W, soccer M/W, softball M/W, squash M/W, ultimate Frisbee M/W, water polo M/W.

Standardized Tests *Required:* SAT and SAT Subject Tests or ACT (for admission).

Costs (2011–12) *One-time required fee:* $300. *Comprehensive fee:* $55,706 includes full-time tuition ($43,404), mandatory fees ($270), and room and board ($12,032). *Room and board:* Room and board charges vary according to board plan and housing facility. *Payment plan:* installment.

Financial Aid Of all full-time matriculated undergraduates who enrolled in 2011, 1,509 applied for aid, 1,413 were judged to have need, 1,311 had their need fully met. 1,183 Federal Work-Study jobs (averaging $2369). 100 state and other part-time jobs (averaging $2325). In 2011, 32 non-need-based awards were made. *Average percent of need met:* 100%. *Average financial aid package:* $40,364. *Average need-based loan:* $4283. *Average need-based gift aid:* $36,316. *Average non-need-based aid:* $42,362. *Average indebtedness upon graduation:* $25,864. *Financial aid deadline:* 2/15.

Applying *Options:* electronic application, early admission, early decision, deferred entrance. *Application fee:* $55. *Required:* essay or personal statement, high school transcript, 2 letters of recommendation. *Required for some:* interview. *Recommended:* interview. *Application deadlines:* 1/1 (freshmen), 3/15 (transfers). *Early decision deadline:* 11/15 (for plan 1), 1/1 (for plan 2). *Notification:* 4/1 (freshmen), 5/15 (transfers), 12/15 (early decision plan 1), 2/15 (early decision plan 2).

Freshman Application Contact Ms. Nancy Meislahn, Dean of Admission and Financial Aid, Wesleyan University, Stewart M. Reid House, 70 Wyllys Avenue, Middletown, CT 06459-0265. *Phone:* 860-685-3000. *Fax:* 860-685-3001. *E-mail:* admissions@wesleyan.edu. *Web site:* http://www.wesleyan.edu/.

Western Connecticut State University
Danbury, Connecticut

- **State-supported** comprehensive, founded 1903, part of Connecticut State University System
- **Urban** 340-acre campus with easy access to New York City
- **Coed** 5,815 undergraduate students, 82% full-time, 54% women, 46% men
- **Moderately difficult** entrance level, 62% of applicants were admitted

Undergraduates 4,763 full-time, 1,052 part-time. 8% are from out of state; 8% Black or African American, non-Hispanic/Latino; 12% Hispanic/Latino; 3% Asian, non-Hispanic/Latino; 0.1% Native Hawaiian or other Pacific Islander, non-Hispanic/Latino; 0.4% American Indian or Alaska Native, non-Hispanic/Latino; 2% Two or more races, non-Hispanic/Latino; 2% Race/ethnicity unknown; 0.1% international; 9% transferred in; 29% live on campus. *Retention:* 72% of full-time freshmen returned.

Freshmen *Admission:* 4,157 applied, 2,593 admitted, 887 enrolled. *Average high school GPA:* 2.79. *Test scores:* SAT critical reading scores over 500: 51%; SAT math scores over 500: 48%; SAT critical reading scores over 600: 9%; SAT math scores over 600: 8%; SAT critical reading scores over 700: 1%.

Faculty *Total:* 528, 43% full-time. *Student/faculty ratio:* 16:1.

Academics *Calendar:* semesters. *Degrees:* associate, bachelor's, master's, and doctoral. *Special study options:* part-time degree program. *ROTC:* Army (c), Air Force (c).

Computers on Campus Students can access the following: computer help desk, free student e-mail accounts, online (class) grades, online (class) registration, online (class) schedules. Campuswide network is available. Wireless service is available via classrooms, computer labs, libraries.

Student Life *Housing options:* coed, women-only. Campus housing is university owned. Freshman campus housing is guaranteed. *Activities and organizations:* drama/theater group, student-run newspaper, radio station, choral group, national fraternities, national sororities. *Campus security:* 24-hour emergency response devices and patrols, student patrols, late-night transport/escort service, controlled dormitory access. *Student services:* health clinic, personal/psychological counseling.

Athletics Member NCAA. All Division III. *Intercollegiate sports:* baseball M, basketball M/W, cheerleading W(c), field hockey W, football M, lacrosse M/W, soccer M/W, softball W, swimming and diving W, tennis M/W, volleyball W. *Intramural sports:* basketball M/W, football M, ice hockey M(c), rock climbing M(c)/W(c), softball M/W.

Standardized Tests *Required:* SAT or ACT (for admission).

Costs (2011–12) *Tuition:* state resident $4124 full-time, $172 per credit hour part-time; nonresident $13,346 full-time, $175 per credit hour part-time. Full-time tuition and fees vary according to program and reciprocity agreements. *Required fees:* $3980 full-time, $201 per credit hour part-time. *Room and board:* $10,223; room only: $5844. Room and board charges vary according to board plan and housing facility. *Payment plan:* installment. *Waivers:* senior citizens and employees or children of employees.

Financial Aid Of all full-time matriculated undergraduates who enrolled in 2009, 3,814 applied for aid, 2,923 were judged to have need, 83 had their need fully met. 116 Federal Work-Study jobs (averaging $1501). 29 state and other part-time jobs (averaging $2138). In 2009, 35 non-need-based awards were made. *Average percent of need met:* 65%. *Average financial aid package:* $7368. *Average need-based loan:* $3973. *Average need-based gift aid:* $4468. *Average non-need-based aid:* $6883. *Average indebtedness upon graduation:* $23,487. *Financial aid deadline:* 4/15.

Applying *Options:* electronic application, early admission, deferred entrance. *Application fee:* $50. *Required:* high school transcript, 2 letters of recommendation. *Required for some:* essay or personal statement, interview. *Application deadlines:* rolling (freshmen), rolling (transfers). *Notification:* continuous (freshmen), continuous (transfers).

Freshman Application Contact Office of University Admissions, Western Connecticut State University, 181 White Street, Danbury, CT 06810. *Phone:* 203-837-9000. *Toll-free phone:* 877-837-WCSU. *E-mail:* admissions@wcsu.edu. *Web site:* http://www.wcsu.edu/.

See page 1754 for the College Close-Up.

Yale University
New Haven, Connecticut

- **Independent** university, founded 1701
- **Urban** 200-acre campus with easy access to New York City
- **Coed** 5,349 undergraduate students, 100% full-time, 50% women, 50% men
- **Most difficult** entrance level, 8% of applicants were admitted

Undergraduates 5,341 full-time, 8 part-time. 93% are from out of state; 6% Black or African American, non-Hispanic/Latino; 10% Hispanic/Latino; 15% Asian, non-Hispanic/Latino; 0.1% Native Hawaiian or other Pacific Islander, non-Hispanic/Latino; 0.5% American Indian or Alaska Native, non-Hispanic/Latino; 6% Two or more races, non-Hispanic/Latino; 5% Race/ethnicity unknown; 10% international; 0.4% transferred in; 88% live on campus. *Retention:* 99% of full-time freshmen returned.

Freshmen *Admission:* 27,283 applied, 2,109 admitted, 1,349 enrolled. *Test scores:* SAT critical reading scores over 500: 100%; SAT math scores over 500: 100%; SAT writing scores over 500: 99%; SAT critical reading scores over 600: 98%; SAT math scores over 600: 99%; SAT writing scores over 600: 97%; SAT critical reading scores over 700: 78%; SAT math scores over 700: 79%; SAT writing scores over 700: 81%.

Faculty *Total:* 816, 99% full-time, 93% with terminal degrees. *Student/faculty ratio:* 5:1.

Academics *Calendar:* semesters. *Degrees:* bachelor's, master's, doctoral, post-master's, and first professional certificates. *Special study options:* part-time degree program. *ROTC:* Army (c), Air Force (c).

Computers on Campus Students can access the following: campus intranet, computer help desk, free student e-mail accounts, online (class) grades, online (class) registration, online (class) schedules. Campuswide network is available. 100% of college-owned or -operated housing units are wired for high-speed Internet access. Wireless service is available via classrooms, computer centers, computer labs, learning centers, libraries, student centers.

Student Life *Housing:* on-campus residence required through sophomore year. *Options:* coed, disabled students. Campus housing is university owned. Freshman campus housing is guaranteed. *Campus security:* 24-hour emergency response devices and patrols, late-night transport/escort service, controlled dormitory access.

Athletics Member NCAA. All Division I except football (Division I-AA). *Intercollegiate sports:* archery M(c)/W(c), baseball M, basketball M/W, crew M/W, cross-country running M/W, equestrian sports M(c)/W(c), fencing M/W, field hockey W, golf M/W, gymnastics W, ice hockey M/W, lacrosse M/W, riflery M(c)/W(c), rock climbing M(c)/W(c), rugby M(c)/W(c), sailing M/W, skiing (cross-country) M(c)/W(c), skiing (downhill) M(c)/W(c), soccer M/W, softball W, squash M/W, swimming and diving M/W, table tennis M(c)/W(c), tennis M/W, track and field M/W, ultimate Frisbee M(c)/W(c), volleyball M(c)/W, water polo M(c)/W(c), wrestling M(c). *Intramural sports:* badminton M(c)/W(c), baseball M, basketball M/W, bowling M/W, cheerleading M(c)/W(c), cross-country running M/W, field hockey M/W, football M/W, golf M/W, ice hockey M/W, soccer M/W, softball M/W, squash M/W, swimming and diving M/W, table tennis M/W, tennis M/W, ultimate Frisbee M/W, volleyball M/W, water polo M/W.

Standardized Tests *Required:* SAT and SAT Subject Tests or ACT (for admission).

Costs (2011–12) *Comprehensive fee:* $52,700 includes full-time tuition ($40,500) and room and board ($12,200). *College room only:* $6700. Room and board charges vary according to board plan.

Financial Aid Of all full-time matriculated undergraduates who enrolled in 2010, 3,145 applied for aid, 3,004 were judged to have need, 3,004 had their need fully met. 649 Federal Work-Study jobs (averaging $2335). 1,660 state and other part-time jobs (averaging $2486). *Average percent of need met:* 100%. *Average financial aid package:* $40,990. *Average need-based loan:* $2434. *Average need-based gift aid:* $38,914. *Average indebtedness upon graduation:* $9254. *Financial aid deadline:* 3/1.

Applying *Options:* electronic application, early admission, early action, deferred entrance. *Application fee:* $75. *Required:* essay or personal statement, high school transcript, 3 letters of recommendation. *Recommended:* interview. *Application deadlines:* 12/31 (freshmen), 3/1 (transfers), 11/1 (early action). *Notification:* 4/1 (freshmen), 5/15 (transfers), 12/15 (early action).

Freshman Application Contact Admissions Director, Yale University, PO Box 208234, New Haven, CT 06520. *Phone:* 203-432-9300. *E-mail:* student.questions@yale.edu. *Web site:* http://www.yale.edu/.

DELAWARE

Delaware State University
Dover, Delaware

- **State-supported** university, founded 1891, part of Delaware Higher Education Commission
- **Small-town** 400-acre campus
- **Coed** 3,744 undergraduate students, 93% full-time, 62% women, 38% men
- **Moderately difficult** entrance level, 43% of applicants were admitted

Undergraduates 3,467 full-time, 277 part-time. Students come from 31 states and territories; 22 other countries; 49% are from out of state; 73% Black or African American, non-Hispanic/Latino; 5% Hispanic/Latino; 3% Asian, non-Hispanic/Latino; 0.2% Native Hawaiian or other Pacific Islander, non-Hispanic/Latino; 0.2% American Indian or Alaska Native, non-Hispanic/Latino; 4% Two or more races, non-Hispanic/Latino; 2% Race/ethnicity unknown; 2% international; 6% transferred in; 64% live on campus. *Retention:* 71% of full-time freshmen returned.

Freshmen *Admission:* 9,221 applied, 3,933 admitted, 1,086 enrolled. *Average high school GPA:* 2.94. *Test scores:* SAT critical reading scores over 500: 15%; SAT math scores over 500: 16%; ACT scores over 18: 43%; SAT critical reading scores over 600: 1%; SAT math scores over 600: 2%; ACT scores over 24: 3%.

Faculty *Total:* 357, 59% full-time. *Student/faculty ratio:* 15:1.

Academics *Calendar:* semesters. *Degrees:* bachelor's, master's, doctoral, and first professional. *Special study options:* academic remediation for entering students, accelerated degree program, adult/continuing education programs, advanced placement credit, cooperative education, distance learning, double majors, English as a second language, honors programs, internships, off-campus study, part-time degree program, services for LD students, study abroad, summer session for credit. *ROTC:* Army (b), Air Force (c).

Computers on Campus 641 computers/terminals are available on campus for general student use. Students can access the following: campus intranet, computer help desk, free student e-mail accounts, online (class) grades, online (class) registration, online (class) schedules. Campuswide network is available. 100% of college-owned or -operated housing units are wired for high-speed Internet access. Wireless service is available via classrooms, computer centers, computer labs, learning centers, libraries, student centers.

Student Life *Housing options:* coed, men-only, women-only, disabled students. Campus housing is university owned. Freshman applicants given priority for college housing. *Activities and organizations:* drama/theater group, student-run newspaper, radio and television station, choral group, marching band, SGA, NPHC, Women's Senate, RHA, Men's Council, national fraternities, national sororities. *Campus security:* 24-hour emergency response devices and patrols, student patrols, late-night transport/escort service, controlled dormitory access. *Student services:* health clinic, personal/psychological counseling, women's center.

Athletics Member NCAA. All Division I except football (Division I-AA). *Intercollegiate sports:* baseball M(s), basketball M(s)/W(s), bowling W(s), cheerleading M(s)/W(s), cross-country running M(s)/W(s), equestrian sports W(s), soccer W(s), softball W(s), tennis W(s), track and field M(s)/W(s), volleyball W(s). *Intramural sports:* basketball M/W, football M(c)/W(c), soccer M/W, softball M/W, swimming and diving M/W, table tennis M/W, tennis M/W, track and field M/W, volleyball W.

Standardized Tests *Required:* SAT or ACT (for admission).

Costs (2011–12) *Tuition:* state resident $7056 full-time, $260 per credit hour part-time; nonresident $15,052 full-time, $593 per credit hour part-time. Full-time tuition and fees vary according to course load. Part-time tuition and fees vary according to course load. *Required fees:* $830 full-time, $105 per term part-time, $56 per credit part-time. *Room and board:* $10,244; room only: $6676. Room and board charges vary according to board plan and housing facility. *Payment plan:* deferred payment. *Waivers:* minority students, senior citizens, and employees or children of employees.

Financial Aid Of all full-time matriculated undergraduates who enrolled in 2010, 2,817 applied for aid, 2,595 were judged to have need, 876 had their need fully met. In 2010, 401 non-need-based awards were made. *Average percent of need met:* 48%. *Average financial aid package:* $11,274. *Average need-based loan:* $3481. *Average need-based gift aid:* $11,274. *Average non-need-based aid:* $7131. *Average indebtedness upon graduation:* $36,410.

Applying *Options:* electronic application, early admission. *Application fee:* $35. *Required:* high school transcript, minimum 2.0 GPA.

Freshman Application Contact Mrs. Erin Hill, Executive Director for Admissions, Delaware State University, 1200 North DuPont Highway, Dover, DE 19901-2277. *Phone:* 302-857-6351. *Toll-free phone:* 800-845-2544. *Fax:* 302-857-6352. *E-mail:* ehill@desu.edu. *Web site:* http://www.desu.edu/.

Goldey-Beacom College
Wilmington, Delaware

- **Independent** comprehensive, founded 1886
- **Suburban** 24-acre campus with easy access to Philadelphia
- **Endowment** $47.4 million
- **Coed** 707 undergraduate students, 71% full-time, 53% women, 47% men
- **Moderately difficult** entrance level

Undergraduates 505 full-time, 202 part-time. 23% Black or African American, non-Hispanic/Latino; 8% Hispanic/Latino; 5% Asian, non-Hispanic/Latino; 0.1% Native Hawaiian or other Pacific Islander, non-Hispanic/Latino; 0.3% American Indian or Alaska Native, non-Hispanic/Latino; 2% Two or more races, non-Hispanic/Latino; 3% Race/ethnicity unknown; 7% international; 4% transferred in; 27% live on campus. *Retention:* 85% of full-time freshmen returned.

Freshmen *Admission:* 104 admitted, 104 enrolled. *Average high school GPA:* 2.9.

Faculty *Total:* 54, 35% full-time, 52% with terminal degrees. *Student/faculty ratio:* 24:1.

Academics *Calendar:* semesters. *Degrees:* associate, bachelor's, master's, and postbachelor's certificates. *Special study options:* academic remediation for entering students, accelerated degree program, advanced placement credit, cooperative education, double majors, honors programs, internships, part-time degree program, summer session for credit. *ROTC:* Air Force (c).

Computers on Campus 159 computers/terminals are available on campus for general student use. Students can access the following: campus intranet, computer help desk, free student e-mail accounts, online (class) grades, online (class) schedules, campus Web. Campuswide network is available. 100% of college-owned or -operated housing units are wired for high-speed Internet access. Wireless service is available via entire campus.

Student Life *Housing options:* coed. Campus housing is university owned. *Activities and organizations:* student-run newspaper, Student Athletic Advisory Committee, Alpha Chi, Resident Student Association, Student Ambassadors, International Student Association. *Campus security:* 24-hour emergency response devices and patrols, student patrols, late-night transport/escort service.

Athletics Member NCAA. All Division II. *Intercollegiate sports:* basketball M(s)/W(s), cross-country running M(s)/W(s), golf M(s)/W, soccer M(s)/W(s), softball W(s), tennis W(s), volleyball W(s).

Standardized Tests *Required:* SAT or ACT (for admission).

Costs (2012–13) *Tuition:* $20,820 full-time, $694 per credit hour part-time. Full-time tuition and fees vary according to course load. Part-time tuition and fees vary according to course load. *Required fees:* $300 full-time, $10 per credit hour part-time. *Room only:* $5248. Room and board charges vary according to housing facility. *Payment plans:* installment, deferred payment. *Waivers:* employees or children of employees.

Applying *Options:* electronic application, early admission, deferred entrance. *Required:* high school transcript, minimum 2.0 GPA. *Required for some:* 1 letter of recommendation, interview. *Application deadlines:* rolling (freshmen), rolling (transfers). *Notification:* continuous until 8/15 (freshmen), continuous until 8/15 (transfers).

Freshman Application Contact Mr. Larry Eby, Director of Admissions, Goldey-Beacom College, 4701 Limestone Road, Wilmington, DE 19808. *Phone:* 302-225-6289. *Toll-free phone:* 800-833-4877. *Fax:* 302-996-5408. *E-mail:* admissions@gbc.edu. *Web site:* http://www.gbc.edu/.

Strayer University - Christiana Campus
Newark, Delaware

- **Proprietary** comprehensive
- **Coed**

Academics *Degrees:* certificates, diplomas, associate, bachelor's, master's, and postbachelor's certificates.

Freshman Application Contact Strayer University - Christiana Campus, 240 Continental Drive, Suite 108, Newark, DE 19713. *Web site:* http://www.strayer.edu/christiana.

University of Delaware
Newark, Delaware

- **State-related** university, founded 1743
- **Small-town** 1000-acre campus with easy access to Philadelphia, Baltimore
- **Coed** 17,120 undergraduate students, 91% full-time, 57% women, 43% men
- **Moderately difficult** entrance level, 58% of applicants were admitted

Undergraduates 15,558 full-time, 1,562 part-time. 59% are from out of state; 4% Black or African American, non-Hispanic/Latino; 6% Hispanic/Latino; 4% Asian, non-Hispanic/Latino; 0.2% Native Hawaiian or other Pacific Islander, non-Hispanic/Latino; 0.1% American Indian or Alaska Native, non-Hispanic/Latino; 2% Two or more races, non-Hispanic/Latino; 2% Race/ethnicity unknown; 4% international; 3% transferred in; 44% live on campus. *Retention:* 93% of full-time freshmen returned.

Freshmen *Admission:* 23,647 applied, 13,768 admitted, 3,914 enrolled. *Average high school GPA:* 3.62. *Test scores:* SAT critical reading scores over 500: 93%; SAT math scores over 500: 94%; SAT writing scores over 500: 93%; ACT scores over 18: 100%; SAT critical reading scores over 600: 48%; SAT math scores over 600: 60%; SAT writing scores over 600: 52%; ACT scores over 24: 85%; SAT critical reading scores over 700: 7%; SAT math scores over 700: 13%; SAT writing scores over 700: 9%; ACT scores over 30: 17%.

Faculty *Total:* 1,485, 80% full-time, 77% with terminal degrees. *Student/faculty ratio:* 13:1.

Academics *Calendar:* 4-1-4. *Degrees:* associate, bachelor's, master's, doctoral, and first professional. *Special study options:* academic remediation for entering students, accelerated degree program, adult/continuing education programs, advanced placement credit, distance learning, double majors, English as a second language, honors programs, independent study, internships, off-campus study, part-time degree program, services for LD students, student-designed majors, study abroad, summer session for credit. *ROTC:* Army (b), Air Force (b).

Computers on Campus Students can access the following: campus intranet, computer help desk, free student e-mail accounts, online (class) grades, online (class) registration, online (class) schedules, personal Web page, google apps. Campuswide network is available. 100% of college-owned or -operated housing units are wired for high-speed Internet access. Wireless service is available via entire campus.

Student Life *Housing:* on-campus residence required for freshman year. *Options:* coed, women-only, disabled students. Campus housing is university owned. Freshman campus housing is guaranteed. *Activities and organizations:* drama/theater group, student-run newspaper, radio station, choral group, marching band, national fraternities, national sororities. *Campus security:* 24-hour emergency response devices and patrols, student patrols, late-night transport/escort service, controlled dormitory access. *Student services:* health clinic, personal/psychological counseling, women's center.

Athletics Member NCAA. All Division I except football (Division I-AA). *Intercollegiate sports:* baseball M(s), basketball M(s)/W(s), bowling M(c)/W(c), cheerleading M(s)/W(s), crew M(c)/W(s), cross-country running M(c)/W, equestrian sports M(c)/W(c), field hockey W(s), golf M/W, ice hockey M(c)/W(c), lacrosse M(s)/W(s), rugby M(c)/W(c), sailing M(c)/W(c), soccer M(s)/W(s), softball W(s), swimming and diving M/W(s), tennis M/W, track and field M(c)/W(s), volleyball W(s), wrestling M(c). *Intramural sports:* badminton M/W, basketball M/W, field hockey W(c), football M/W, golf M/W, lacrosse M(c)/W(c), racquetball M/W, soccer M(c)/W(c), softball M/W, squash M/W, swimming and diving M/W, table tennis M/W, tennis M/W, track and field M/W, ultimate Frisbee M/W, volleyball M(c)/W(c), water polo M/W.

Standardized Tests *Required:* SAT or ACT (for admission). *Required for some:* SAT Subject Tests (for admission). *Recommended:* SAT Subject Tests (for admission).

Costs (2011–12) *Tuition:* state resident $9670 full-time, $403 per credit hour part-time; nonresident $25,940 full-time, $1081 per credit hour part-time. *Required fees:* $1522 full-time. *Room and board:* $10,470; room only: $6450. Room and board charges vary according to board plan, housing facility, and

student level. *Payment plan:* installment. *Waivers:* senior citizens and employees or children of employees.

Financial Aid Of all full-time matriculated undergraduates who enrolled in 2011, 10,991 applied for aid, 7,464 were judged to have need, 3,457 had their need fully met. In 2011, 2663 non-need-based awards were made. *Average percent of need met:* 73%. *Average financial aid package:* $14,083. *Average need-based loan:* $7889. *Average need-based gift aid:* $7385. *Average non-need-based aid:* $6461. *Average indebtedness upon graduation:* $31,002. *Financial aid deadline:* 3/15.

Applying *Options:* electronic application, early admission, deferred entrance. *Application fee:* $75. *Required:* essay or personal statement, high school transcript, 1 letter of recommendation. *Application deadlines:* 1/15 (freshmen), 5/1 (transfers). *Notification:* 3/15 (freshmen), continuous (transfers).

Freshman Application Contact Mr. Lou Hirsh, Director of Admissions, University of Delaware, 116 Hullihen Hall, Newark, DE 19716. *Phone:* 302-831-8123. *Fax:* 302-831-6905. *E-mail:* admissions@udel.edu. *Web site:* http://www.udel.edu/.

Wesley College
Dover, Delaware

Freshman Application Contact Mr. Arthur Jacobs, Director of Undergraduate Admissions, Wesley College, 120 North State Street, Dover, DE 19901-3875. *Phone:* 302-736-2400. *Toll-free phone:* 800-937-5398. *Fax:* 302-736-2382. *E-mail:* admissions@wesley.edu. *Web site:* http://www.wesley.edu/.

Wilmington University
New Castle, Delaware

- **Independent** comprehensive, founded 1967
- **Suburban** 17-acre campus with easy access to Philadelphia
- **Endowment** $15.5 million
- **Coed** 6,628 undergraduate students, 51% full-time, 62% women, 38% men
- **Noncompetitive** entrance level, 96% of applicants were admitted

Undergraduates 3,386 full-time, 3,242 part-time. Students come from 29 states and territories; 22 other countries; 23% are from out of state; 19% transferred in. *Retention:* 58% of full-time freshmen returned.

Freshmen *Admission:* 1,396 applied, 1,340 admitted, 577 enrolled.

Faculty *Total:* 1,116, 8% full-time, 23% with terminal degrees. *Student/faculty ratio:* 14:1.

Academics *Calendar:* semesters. *Degrees:* certificates, associate, bachelor's, master's, doctoral, post-master's, postbachelor's, and first professional certificates. *Special study options:* academic remediation for entering students, accelerated degree program, adult/continuing education programs, cooperative education, distance learning, double majors, external degree program, independent study, internships, part-time degree program, summer session for credit. *ROTC:* Army (c), Air Force (c).

Computers on Campus 600 computers/terminals are available on campus for general student use. Students can access the following: free student e-mail accounts, online (class) grades, online (class) registration, online (class) schedules. Campuswide network is available. Wireless service is available via entire campus.

Student Life *Housing:* college housing not available. *Activities and organizations:* Student Government Association, Green Team, Photography Club, WU Student United Way, Wildcat Cheerleaders. *Campus security:* 24-hour emergency response devices and patrols, late-night transport/escort service.

Athletics Member NCAA. All Division II. *Intercollegiate sports:* baseball M(s), basketball M(s)/W(s), cross-country running M(s)/W(s), softball W(s), volleyball W(s).

Costs (2011–12) *Tuition:* $7536 full-time, $314 per credit hour part-time. Full-time tuition and fees vary according to degree level and location. Part-time tuition and fees vary according to degree level and location. *Required fees:* $50 full-time. *Payment plan:* installment. *Waivers:* employees or children of employees.

Financial Aid Of all full-time matriculated undergraduates who enrolled in 2004, 1,217 applied for aid, 900 were judged to have need. 25 Federal Work-Study jobs (averaging $2000). In 2004, 74 non-need-based awards were made. *Average percent of need met:* 48%. *Average financial aid package:* $5770. *Average need-based loan:* $3889. *Average need-based gift aid:* $2464. *Average non-need-based aid:* $1100. *Average indebtedness upon graduation:* $17,486.

Applying *Options:* early admission, deferred entrance. *Application fee:* $25. *Required:* high school transcript. *Recommended:* interview. *Application deadlines:* rolling (freshmen), rolling (transfers). *Notification:* continuous (freshmen), continuous (transfers).

Freshman Application Contact Ms. Laura Morris, Director of Admissions, Wilmington University, 320 North DuPont Highway, New Castle, DE 19720-6491. *Phone:* 302-295-1179. *Toll-free phone:* 877-967-5464. *E-mail:* undergradadmissions@wilmu.edu. *Web site:* http://www.wilmu.edu/.

DISTRICT OF COLUMBIA

American University
Washington, District of Columbia

- **Independent Methodist** university, founded 1893
- **Suburban** 84-acre campus with easy access to Washington, D.C.
- **Endowment** $455.0 million
- **Coed** 7,212 undergraduate students, 96% full-time, 59% women, 41% men
- **Very difficult** entrance level, 42% of applicants were admitted

Undergraduates 6,941 full-time, 271 part-time. Students come from 55 states and territories; 89 other countries; 87% are from out of state; 5% Black or African American, non-Hispanic/Latino; 8% Hispanic/Latino; 6% Asian, non-Hispanic/Latino; 0.2% Native Hawaiian or other Pacific Islander, non-Hispanic/Latino; 0.5% American Indian or Alaska Native, non-Hispanic/Latino; 3% Two or more races, non-Hispanic/Latino; 14% Race/ethnicity unknown; 7% international; 4% transferred in. *Retention:* 90% of full-time freshmen returned.
Freshmen *Admission:* 18,706 applied, 7,788 admitted, 1,541 enrolled. *Average high school GPA:* 3.82. *Test scores:* SAT critical reading scores over 500: 96%; SAT math scores over 500: 95%; SAT writing scores over 500: 97%; ACT scores over 18: 100%; SAT critical reading scores over 600: 75%; SAT math scores over 600: 64%; SAT writing scores over 600: 69%; ACT scores over 24: 90%; SAT critical reading scores over 700: 27%; SAT math scores over 700: 16%; SAT writing scores over 700: 20%; ACT scores over 30: 35%.
Faculty *Total:* 1,277, 56% full-time. *Student/faculty ratio:* 12:1.
Academics *Calendar:* semesters. *Degrees:* certificates, associate, bachelor's, master's, doctoral, postbachelor's, and first professional certificates. *Special study options:* accelerated degree program, advanced placement credit, cooperative education, distance learning, double majors, honors programs, independent study, internships, off-campus study, part-time degree program, services for LD students, student-designed majors, study abroad, summer session for credit. *ROTC:* Army (c), Air Force (c). *Unusual degree programs:* 3-2 engineering with University of Maryland College Park.
Computers on Campus 650 computers/terminals are available on campus for general student use. Students can access the following: campus intranet, computer help desk, free student e-mail accounts, online (class) grades, online (class) registration, online (class) schedules. Campuswide network is available. 100% of college-owned or -operated housing units are wired for high-speed Internet access. Wireless service is available via entire campus.
Student Life *Housing options:* coed, disabled students. Campus housing is university owned and leased by the school. Freshman campus housing is guaranteed. *Activities and organizations:* drama/theater group, student-run newspaper, radio and television station, choral group, Kennedy Political Union, Habitat for Humanity, Student Government, Amnesty International, Ethnic and religious organizations, national fraternities, national sororities. *Campus security:* 24-hour emergency response devices and patrols, late-night transport/escort service, controlled dormitory access, E-mail and text emergency notification system. *Student services:* health clinic, personal/psychological counseling, women's center.
Athletics Member NCAA. All Division I. *Intercollegiate sports:* basketball M(s)/W(s), cross-country running M(s)/W(s), field hockey W(s), lacrosse W(s), soccer M(s)/W(s), swimming and diving M/W, track and field M(s)/W(s), volleyball W(s), wrestling M(s). *Intramural sports:* basketball M(c)/W, crew M(c)/W(c), equestrian sports M(c)/W(c), field hockey M(c)/W(c), football M/W, gymnastics M(c)/W(c), ice hockey M(c)/W(c), lacrosse M(c), rugby M(c)/W(c), sailing M(c)/W(c), soccer M(c)/W(c), softball M/W, tennis M(c)/W(c), ultimate Frisbee M(c)/W(c), volleyball M/W(c), weight lifting M.
Standardized Tests *Required:* SAT or ACT (for admission).
Costs (2012–13) *Comprehensive fee:* $53,419 includes full-time tuition ($38,982), mandatory fees ($517), and room and board ($13,920). Full-time tuition and fees vary according to degree level. Part-time tuition: $1299 per credit hour. Part-time tuition and fees vary according to course load. *Required fees:* $170 per term part-time. *College room only:* $9290. Room and board charges vary according to board plan, housing facility, and location. *Payment plans:* tuition prepayment, installment.
Financial Aid Of all full-time matriculated undergraduates who enrolled in 2011, 4,060 applied for aid, 3,298 were judged to have need, 669 had their need fully met. In 2011, 1166 non-need-based awards were made. *Average percent of need met:* 61%. *Average financial aid package:* $25,990. *Average*

need-based loan: $5053. *Average need-based gift aid:* $17,893. *Average non-need-based aid:* $17,486. *Financial aid deadline:* 2/15.
Applying *Options:* electronic application, early decision, deferred entrance. *Application fee:* $65. *Required:* essay or personal statement, high school transcript. *Required for some:* If home schooled: statement describing home school structure and mission. *Recommended:* 2 letters of recommendation. *Application deadlines:* 1/15 (freshmen), 3/1 (transfers). *Early decision deadline:* 11/15. *Notification:* 4/1 (freshmen), continuous (transfers), 12/31 (early decision).
Freshman Application Contact Greg Grauman, Director of Admissions, American University, 4400 Massachusetts Avenue, NW, Washington, DC 20016-8001. *Phone:* 202-885-6000. *E-mail:* admissions@american.edu. *Web site:* http://www.american.edu/.

The Catholic University of America
Washington, District of Columbia

- **Independent** university, founded 1887, affiliated with Roman Catholic Church
- **Urban** 184-acre campus
- **Coed** 3,633 undergraduate students, 94% full-time, 55% women, 45% men
- **Moderately difficult** entrance level, 75% of applicants were admitted

Undergraduates 3,397 full-time, 236 part-time. Students come from 47 states and territories; 43 other countries; 96% are from out of state; 5% Black or African American, non-Hispanic/Latino; 8% Hispanic/Latino; 3% Asian, non-Hispanic/Latino; 0.2% Native Hawaiian or other Pacific Islander, non-Hispanic/Latino; 0.2% American Indian or Alaska Native, non-Hispanic/Latino; 1% Two or more races, non-Hispanic/Latino; 17% Race/ethnicity unknown; 4% international; 3% transferred in; 61% live on campus. *Retention:* 80% of full-time freshmen returned.
Freshmen *Admission:* 6,617 applied, 4,971 admitted, 904 enrolled. *Average high school GPA:* 3.35. *Test scores:* SAT critical reading scores over 500: 81%; SAT math scores over 500: 79%; ACT scores over 18: 98%; SAT critical reading scores over 600: 35%; SAT math scores over 600: 29%; ACT scores over 24: 61%; SAT critical reading scores over 700: 7%; SAT math scores over 700: 3%; ACT scores over 30: 11%.
Faculty *Total:* 797, 49% full-time. *Student/faculty ratio:* 9:1.
Academics *Calendar:* semesters. *Degrees:* associate, bachelor's, master's, doctoral, post-master's, postbachelor's, and first professional certificates. *Special study options:* accelerated degree program, adult/continuing education programs, advanced placement credit, cooperative education, distance learning, double majors, English as a second language, honors programs, independent study, internships, off-campus study, part-time degree program, services for LD students, study abroad, summer session for credit. *ROTC:* Army (c), Navy (c), Air Force (c). *Unusual degree programs:* 3-2 engineering; nursing; architecture, accounting, education, psychology.
Computers on Campus 500 computers/terminals and 50 ports are available on campus for general student use. Students can access the following: campus intranet, computer help desk, free student e-mail accounts, online (class) grades, online (class) registration, online (class) schedules, Internet 2, video streaming, online voting, pedagogical software. Campuswide network is available. 100% of college-owned or -operated housing units are wired for high-speed Internet access. Wireless service is available via computer centers, computer labs, dorm rooms, libraries, student centers.
Student Life *Housing:* on-campus residence required through sophomore year. *Options:* coed, men-only, women-only, disabled students. Campus housing is university owned. Freshman campus housing is guaranteed. *Activities and organizations:* drama/theater group, student-run newspaper, radio station, choral group, Habitat for Humanity, College Democrats, College Republicans, Students for Life, Centerstage Theatre Company, national fraternities, national sororities. *Campus security:* 24-hour emergency response devices and patrols, late-night transport/escort service, controlled dormitory access, controlled access of academic buildings. *Student services:* health clinic, personal/psychological counseling, legal services.
Athletics Member NCAA. All Division III. *Intercollegiate sports:* baseball M, basketball M/W, cross-country running M/W, field hockey W, football M, lacrosse M/W, soccer M/W, softball W, swimming and diving M/W, tennis M/W, track and field M/W, volleyball W. *Intramural sports:* badminton M/W, basketball M/W, cheerleading M(c)/W(c), crew M(c)/W(c), fencing M(c)/W(c), football M/W, ice hockey M(c), rugby M(c)/W(c), soccer M/W, softball M/W, tennis M/W, ultimate Frisbee M(c)/W(c), volleyball M/W.
Standardized Tests *Required:* SAT or ACT (for admission). *Recommended:* SAT Subject Tests (for admission).
Costs (2011–12) *One-time required fee:* $425. *Comprehensive fee:* $49,284 includes full-time tuition ($35,260), mandatory fees ($200), and room and board ($13,824). Full-time tuition and fees vary according to program. Part-time tuition: $1380 per credit hour. Part-time tuition and fees vary according to

course load. *Required fees:* $100 per year part-time. *College room only:* $8618. Room and board charges vary according to board plan and housing facility. *Payment plan:* installment. *Waivers:* employees or children of employees.

Financial Aid Of all full-time matriculated undergraduates who enrolled in 2011, 2,381 applied for aid, 2,087 were judged to have need, 907 had their need fully met. 840 Federal Work-Study jobs (averaging $1988). In 2011, 914 non-need-based awards were made. *Average percent of need met:* 79%. *Average financial aid package:* $22,163. *Average need-based loan:* $4724. *Average need-based gift aid:* $17,747. *Average non-need-based aid:* $12,881. *Financial aid deadline:* 4/10.

Applying *Options:* electronic application, early action, deferred entrance. *Application fee:* $55. *Required:* essay or personal statement, high school transcript, 1 letter of recommendation. *Required for some:* interview. *Recommended:* minimum 3.0 GPA. *Application deadlines:* 2/15 (freshmen), 7/15 (transfers), 11/15 (early action). *Notification:* 3/15 (freshmen), 12/15 (early action).

Freshman Application Contact Ms. Christine Mica, Dean, University Admissions, The Catholic University of America, 102 McMahon Hall, 620 Michigan Avenue, NE, Washington, DC 20064. *Phone:* 202-319-5305. *Toll-free phone:* 800-673-2772. *Fax:* 202-319-6533. *E-mail:* cua-admissions@cua.edu. *Web site:* http://www.cua.edu/.

Corcoran College of Art and Design
Washington, District of Columbia

- **Independent** comprehensive, founded 1890
- **Urban** 7-acre campus with easy access to Washington, D.C.
- **Endowment** $19.5 million
- **Coed** 406 undergraduate students, 79% full-time, 66% women, 34% men
- **Moderately difficult** entrance level, 28% of applicants were admitted

Undergraduates 319 full-time, 87 part-time. Students come from 30 states and territories; 26 other countries; 73% are from out of state; 9% Black or African American, non-Hispanic/Latino; 9% Hispanic/Latino; 8% Asian, non-Hispanic/Latino; 0.7% Native Hawaiian or other Pacific Islander, non-Hispanic/Latino; 0.5% American Indian or Alaska Native, non-Hispanic/Latino; 1% Two or more races, non-Hispanic/Latino; 7% Race/ethnicity unknown; 5% international; 12% transferred in; 21% live on campus. *Retention:* 79% of full-time freshmen returned.

Freshmen *Admission:* 575 applied, 160 admitted, 58 enrolled. *Average high school GPA:* 3.15. *Test scores:* SAT critical reading scores over 500: 60%; SAT math scores over 500: 42%; SAT writing scores over 500: 49%; ACT scores over 18: 92%; SAT critical reading scores over 600: 18%; SAT math scores over 600: 6%; SAT writing scores over 600: 9%; ACT scores over 24: 30%.

Faculty *Total:* 258, 11% full-time. *Student/faculty ratio:* 10:1.

Academics *Calendar:* semesters. *Degrees:* certificates, associate, bachelor's, and master's. *Special study options:* academic remediation for entering students, adult/continuing education programs, advanced placement credit, independent study, internships, off-campus study, part-time degree program, services for LD students, study abroad, summer session for credit. *Unusual degree programs:* 3-2 BFA/MAT Art Education.

Computers on Campus 154 computers/terminals are available on campus for general student use. Students can access the following: campus intranet, computer help desk, free student e-mail accounts, online (class) grades, online (class) schedules. 100% of college-owned or -operated housing units are wired for high-speed Internet access. Wireless service is available via classrooms, computer centers, computer labs, dorm rooms, libraries.

Student Life *Housing options:* coed. Campus housing is leased by the school. Freshman applicants given priority for college housing. *Activities and organizations:* Student Activities Programming Board, American Society of Interior Designers, National Art Education Association, Corcoran Student Council, Society of Environmental Designers. *Campus security:* 24-hour emergency response devices and patrols, controlled dormitory access, ID check at all entrances. *Student services:* personal/psychological counseling.

Standardized Tests *Required:* SAT or ACT (for admission).

Costs (2011–12) *Comprehensive fee:* $42,610 includes full-time tuition ($29,940), mandatory fees ($200), and room and board ($12,470). Part-time tuition: $998 per credit hour. Part-time tuition and fees vary according to course load and degree level. *Required fees:* $998 per credit hour part-time, $200 per year part-time. *College room only:* $9970. *Payment plan:* installment. *Waivers:* employees or children of employees.

Financial Aid Of all full-time matriculated undergraduates who enrolled in 2010, 248 applied for aid, 248 were judged to have need. 48 Federal Work-Study jobs (averaging $1857). In 2010, 73 non-need-based awards were made. *Average percent of need met:* 28%. *Average financial aid package:* $19,972. *Average need-based loan:* $4090. *Average need-based gift aid:* $9234. *Aver-*

age non-need-based aid: $6507. *Average indebtedness upon graduation:* $35,562.

Applying *Options:* electronic application, early admission, early action, deferred entrance. *Application fee:* $45. *Required:* high school transcript, minimum 2.5 GPA, portfolio. *Required for some:* essay or personal statement, 1 letter of recommendation, interview. *Recommended:* essay or personal statement, minimum 3.0 GPA, 1 letter of recommendation, interview. *Application deadlines:* rolling (freshmen), rolling (transfers), 11/15 (early action). *Notification:* continuous until 3/15 (freshmen), continuous until 3/15 (transfers), 12/15 (early action).

Freshman Application Contact Corcoran College of Art and Design, 500 17th Street NW, Washington, DC 20006-4804. *Phone:* 202-639-1864. *Toll-free phone:* 888-CORCORAN. *Web site:* http://www.corcoran.edu/.

Gallaudet University
Washington, District of Columbia

- **Independent** university, founded 1864
- **Urban** 99-acre campus
- **Coed** 1,118 undergraduate students, 92% full-time, 54% women, 46% men
- **Moderately difficult** entrance level, 69% of applicants were admitted

Undergraduates 1,029 full-time, 89 part-time. Students come from 47 states and territories; 21 other countries; 96% are from out of state; 11% Black or African American, non-Hispanic/Latino; 8% Hispanic/Latino; 4% Asian, non-Hispanic/Latino; 0.1% Native Hawaiian or other Pacific Islander, non-Hispanic/Latino; 0.3% American Indian or Alaska Native, non-Hispanic/Latino; 6% Two or more races, non-Hispanic/Latino; 0.9% Race/ethnicity unknown; 5% international; 9% transferred in. *Retention:* 70% of full-time freshmen returned.

Freshmen *Admission:* 413 applied, 284 admitted, 201 enrolled. *Test scores:* ACT scores over 18: 42%; ACT scores over 24: 15%; ACT scores over 30: 2%.

Faculty *Total:* 185, 100% full-time, 89% with terminal degrees. *Student/faculty ratio:* 8:1.

Academics *Calendar:* semesters. *Degrees:* bachelor's, master's, doctoral, postbachelor's, and first professional certificates (undergraduate programs are open primarily to the students with hearing-impairments). *Special study options:* academic remediation for entering students, accelerated degree program, adult/continuing education programs, advanced placement credit, distance learning, double majors, English as a second language, honors programs, independent study, internships, off-campus study, part-time degree program, services for LD students, student-designed majors, study abroad, summer session for credit.

Computers on Campus Students can access the following: campus intranet, computer help desk, free student e-mail accounts, online (class) grades, online (class) registration, online (class) schedules. Campuswide network is available.

Student Life *Housing options:* coed, disabled students. Campus housing is university owned. *Activities and organizations:* drama/theater group, student-run newspaper, Student Body Government, Delta Epsilon, Rainbow Society, Black Deaf Student Union, national fraternities, national sororities. *Campus security:* 24-hour emergency response devices and patrols, late-night transport/escort service, controlled dormitory access. *Student services:* health clinic, personal/psychological counseling.

Athletics Member NCAA. All Division III. *Intercollegiate sports:* baseball M, basketball M/W, cross-country running M/W, football M, soccer M/W, softball W, swimming and diving M/W, track and field M/W, volleyball M(c)/W. *Intramural sports:* basketball M/W, football M/W, soccer M, softball W.

Standardized Tests *Required:* SAT or ACT (for admission). *Recommended:* ACT (for admission).

Costs (2012–13) *Comprehensive fee:* $23,596 includes full-time tuition ($12,430), mandatory fees ($376), and room and board ($10,790). Full-time tuition and fees vary according to degree level. Part-time tuition: $622 per credit hour. Part-time tuition and fees vary according to degree level. *College room only:* $5960. Room and board charges vary according to board plan. *Payment plans:* installment, deferred payment. *Waivers:* employees or children of employees.

Financial Aid Of all full-time matriculated undergraduates who enrolled in 2011, 939 applied for aid, 877 were judged to have need, 156 had their need fully met. 76 Federal Work-Study jobs (averaging $942). In 2011, 56 non-need-based awards were made. *Average percent of need met:* 83%. *Average financial aid package:* $18,392. *Average need-based loan:* $3642. *Average need-based gift aid:* $17,206. *Average non-need-based aid:* $13,382. *Average indebtedness upon graduation:* $15,299.

Applying *Options:* electronic application, deferred entrance. *Application fee:* $50. *Required:* essay or personal statement, high school transcript, 2 letters of recommendation, audiogram. *Required for some:* interview. *Application*

deadline: rolling (freshmen). *Notification:* continuous (freshmen), continuous (transfers).

Freshman Application Contact Gallaudet University, 800 Florida Avenue, NE, Washington, DC 20002-3625. *Phone:* 202-651-5750. *Toll-free phone:* 800-995-0550. *Web site:* http://www.gallaudet.edu/.

Georgetown University
Washington, District of Columbia

- **Independent Roman Catholic (Jesuit)** university, founded 1789
- **Urban** 110-acre campus
- **Coed**
- **Most difficult** entrance level

Academics *Calendar:* semesters. *Degrees:* certificates, bachelor's, master's, doctoral, and first professional.

Student Life *Campus security:* 24-hour emergency response devices and patrols, late-night transport/escort service, controlled dormitory access, student guards at residence halls and academic facilities.

Athletics Member NCAA. All Division I except football (Division I-AA).

Standardized Tests *Required:* SAT or ACT (for admission). *Recommended:* SAT Subject Tests (for admission).

Costs (2011-12) *Comprehensive fee:* $53,910 includes full-time tuition ($40,920), mandatory fees ($473), and room and board ($12,517). Full-time tuition and fees vary according to course load and program. Part-time tuition: $1705 per credit hour. Part-time tuition and fees vary according to course load and program. *Required fees:* $473 per year part-time. *College room only:* $8945. Room and board charges vary according to board plan and housing facility.

Financial Aid *Of all full-time matriculated undergraduates who enrolled in 2011,* 4,150 applied for aid, 2,931 were judged to have need, 2,931 had their need fully met. 1,900 Federal Work-Study jobs (averaging $2630). *Average percent of need met:* 100. *Average financial aid package:* $33,566. *Average need-based loan:* $4394. *Average need-based gift aid:* $31,830. *Average indebtedness upon graduation:* $28,035. *Financial aid deadline:* 2/1.

Applying *Options:* electronic application, early action, deferred entrance. *Application fee:* $65. *Required:* essay or personal statement, high school transcript, 2 letters of recommendation, interview.

Freshman Application Contact Mr. Charles A. Deacon, Dean of Undergraduate Admissions, Georgetown University, 37th and O Street, NW, Washington, DC 20057. *Phone:* 202-687-3600. *Fax:* 202-687-5084. *Web site:* http://www.georgetown.edu/.

The George Washington University
Washington, District of Columbia

- **Independent** university, founded 1821
- **Urban** 36-acre campus
- **Endowment** $1.6 billion
- **Coed** 10,406 undergraduate students, 94% full-time, 56% women, 44% men
- **Very difficult** entrance level, 33% of applicants were admitted

Undergraduates 9,747 full-time, 659 part-time. Students come from 54 states and territories; 87 other countries; 98% are from out of state; 7% Black or African American, non-Hispanic/Latino; 7% Hispanic/Latino; 10% Asian, non-Hispanic/Latino; 0.1% Native Hawaiian or other Pacific Islander, non-Hispanic/Latino; 0.3% American Indian or Alaska Native, non-Hispanic/Latino; 2% Two or more races, non-Hispanic/Latino; 10% Race/ethnicity unknown; 8% international; 4% transferred in; 68% live on campus. *Retention:* 94% of full-time freshmen returned.

Freshmen *Admission:* 21,591 applied, 7,124 admitted, 2,241 enrolled. *Test scores:* SAT critical reading scores over 500: 98%; SAT math scores over 500: 99%; SAT writing scores over 500: 99%; ACT scores over 18: 100%; SAT critical reading scores over 600: 76%; SAT math scores over 600: 79%; SAT writing scores over 600: 84%; ACT scores over 24: 96%; SAT critical reading scores over 700: 24%; SAT math scores over 700: 24%; SAT writing scores over 700: 31%; ACT scores over 30: 42%.

Faculty *Total:* 2,220, 43% full-time. *Student/faculty ratio:* 14:1.

Academics *Calendar:* semesters. *Degrees:* certificates, associate, bachelor's, master's, doctoral, post-master's, postbachelor's, and first professional certificates. *Special study options:* accelerated degree program, adult/continuing education programs, advanced placement credit, cooperative education, distance learning, double majors, honors programs, independent study, internships, off-campus study, part-time degree program, services for LD students, student-designed majors, study abroad, summer session for credit. *ROTC:* Army (c), Navy (b), Air Force (c). *Unusual degree programs:* 3-2 business administration; engineering; chemical toxicology, art therapy, economics, engineering economics, operations research.

Computers on Campus Campuswide network is available.

Student Life *Housing:* on-campus residence required through sophomore year. *Options:* coed. Campus housing is university owned. Freshman campus housing is guaranteed. *Activities and organizations:* drama/theater group, student-run newspaper, radio and television station, choral group, marching band, Program Board, Student Association, Residence Hall Association, College Democrats, College Republicans, national fraternities, national sororities. *Campus security:* 24-hour emergency response devices and patrols, late-night transport/escort service, controlled dormitory access. *Student services:* health clinic, personal/psychological counseling, legal services.

Athletics Member NCAA. All Division I. *Intercollegiate sports:* baseball M(s), basketball M(s)/W(s), crew M(s)/W(s), cross-country running M(s)/W(s), golf M(s), gymnastics W(s), soccer M(s)/W(s), swimming and diving M(s)/W(s), tennis M(s)/W(s), volleyball W(s), water polo M(s). *Intramural sports:* badminton M(c)/W(c), basketball M/W, bowling M(c)/W(c), equestrian sports M(c)/W(c), fencing M(c)/W(c), football M/W, lacrosse M(c), racquetball M/W, rugby M(c), sailing M(c)/W(c), soccer M/W, softball M/W, squash M(c)/W, swimming and diving M/W, tennis M/W, volleyball M(c)/W, water polo M/W.

Standardized Tests *Required:* SAT or ACT (for admission).

Costs (2012-13) *Comprehensive fee:* $56,310 includes full-time tuition ($45,735), mandatory fees ($45), and room and board ($10,530). Full-time tuition and fees vary according to student level. Part-time tuition and fees vary according to course load. No tuition increase for student's term of enrollment. *College room only:* $7130. Room and board charges vary according to housing facility. *Payment plan:* installment. *Waivers:* employees or children of employees.

Financial Aid Of all full-time matriculated undergraduates who enrolled in 2011, 5,313 applied for aid, 4,509 were judged to have need, 3,119 had their need fully met. In 2011, 1310 non-need-based awards were made. *Average percent of need met:* 90%. *Average financial aid package:* $39,558. *Average need-based loan:* $5725. *Average need-based gift aid:* $27,270. *Average non-need-based aid:* $15,510. *Average indebtedness upon graduation:* $32,714. *Financial aid deadline:* 2/1.

Applying *Options:* electronic application, early admission, early decision, deferred entrance. *Application fee:* $75. *Required:* essay or personal statement, high school transcript, 2 letters of recommendation. *Recommended:* interview. *Application deadlines:* 1/10 (freshmen), rolling (transfers). *Early decision deadline:* 11/10 (for plan 1), 1/10 (for plan 2). *Notification:* 4/1 (freshmen), continuous (transfers), 12/15 (early decision plan 1), 2/1 (early decision plan 2).

Freshman Application Contact The George Washington University, 2121 Eye Street, NW, Washington, DC 20052. *Phone:* 202-994-6040. *Web site:* http://www.gwu.edu/.

See page 1344 for the College Close-Up.

Howard University
Washington, District of Columbia

Director of Admissions Ms. Linda Sanders-Hawkins, Interim Director of Admissions, Howard University, 2400 Sixth Street, NW, Washington, DC 20059-0002. *Phone:* 202-806-2700. *Toll-free phone:* 800-822-6363. *Fax:* 202-806-4467. *E-mail:* lsanders-hawkins@howard.edu. *Web site:* http://www.howard.edu/.

Potomac College
Washington, District of Columbia

- **Proprietary** 4-year, founded 1991
- **Urban** campus with easy access to Washington, D.C.
- **Coed** 298 undergraduate students, 85% full-time, 57% women, 43% men
- **Noncompetitive** entrance level

Undergraduates 253 full-time, 45 part-time. Students come from 29 states and territories; 60% Black or African American, non-Hispanic/Latino; 6% Hispanic/Latino; 1% Asian, non-Hispanic/Latino; 0.3% American Indian or Alaska Native, non-Hispanic/Latino; 21% Race/ethnicity unknown; 0.3% international.

Freshmen *Admission:* 62 enrolled.

Faculty *Total:* 38, 13% full-time, 11% with terminal degrees. *Student/faculty ratio:* 10:1.

Academics *Calendar:* 6-week modules. *Degrees:* associate and bachelor's. *Special study options:* adult/continuing education programs, distance learning, external degree program, honors programs, independent study, part-time degree program, services for LD students.

Computers on Campus 28 computers/terminals are available on campus for general student use. Students can access the following: campus intranet, free student e-mail accounts, online (class) grades, online (class) schedules, Student Portal and access to Course Management System. Wireless service is available via entire campus.

Student Life *Housing:* college housing not available. *Campus security:* late-night transport/escort service.

Costs (2012–13) *Tuition:* $10,680 full-time, $445 per credit part-time. No tuition increase for student's term of enrollment. *Required fees:* $1000 full-time, $50 per term part-time.

Applying *Options:* electronic application. *Required:* interview. *Application deadlines:* rolling (freshmen), rolling (transfers). *Notification:* continuous (freshmen), continuous (transfers).

Freshman Application Contact Angeliqua Wesley, Director of Admissions, Potomac, Potomac College, 4000 Chesapeake Street, NW, Washington, DC 20016. *Phone:* 202-274-2322. *Toll-free phone:* 888-686-0876. *E-mail:* admissions@potomac.edu. *Web site:* http://www.potomac.edu/.

Strayer University - Takoma Park Campus
Washington, District of Columbia

- **Proprietary** comprehensive
- **Coed**

Academics *Degrees:* certificates, diplomas, associate, bachelor's, master's, and postbachelor's certificates.

Freshman Application Contact Strayer University - Takoma Park Campus, 6830 Laurel Street, NW, Washington, DC 20012. *Web site:* http://www.strayer.edu/takoma_park.

Strayer University - Washington Campus
Washington, District of Columbia

- **Proprietary** comprehensive
- **Coed**

Academics *Degrees:* certificates, diplomas, associate, bachelor's, master's, and postbachelor's certificates.

Freshman Application Contact Strayer University - Washington Campus, 1133 15th Street, NW, Washington, DC 200025. *Web site:* http://www.strayer.edu/washington_dc.

Trinity Washington University
Washington, District of Columbia

Director of Admissions Director of Admissions, Trinity Washington University, 125 Michigan Avenue, NE, Washington, DC 20017-1094. *Phone:* 800-492-6882. *Toll-free phone:* 800-IWANTTC. *E-mail:* admissions@trinitydc.edu. *Web site:* http://www.trinitydc.edu/.

University of Phoenix–Washington D.C. Campus
Washington, District of Columbia

Freshman Application Contact Marc Booker, Sr. Director, Office of Admissions and Evaluation, University of Phoenix–Washington D.C. Campus, 4035 South Riverpoint Parkway, Mail Stop CF-L101, Phoenix, AZ 85040. *Phone:* 602-557-4609. *Toll-free phone:* 866-766-0766. *Fax:* 480-643-1156. *Web site:* http://www.phoenix.edu/.

University of the District of Columbia
Washington, District of Columbia

- **District-supported** comprehensive, founded 1976
- **Urban** 28-acre campus
- **Coed** 4,658 undergraduate students, 47% full-time, 52% women, 48% men
- **Noncompetitive** entrance level, 33% of applicants were admitted

Undergraduates 2,178 full-time, 2,480 part-time. Students come from 39 states and territories; 95 other countries; 20% are from out of state; 46% Black or African American, non-Hispanic/Latino; 4% Hispanic/Latino; 0.4% Asian, non-Hispanic/Latino; 0.1% American Indian or Alaska Native, non-Hispanic/Latino; 37% Race/ethnicity unknown; 10% international; 9% transferred in. *Retention:* 43% of full-time freshmen returned.

Freshmen *Admission:* 6,269 applied, 2,054 admitted, 1,115 enrolled. *Average high school GPA:* 2.

Faculty *Total:* 312, 71% full-time, 36% with terminal degrees. *Student/faculty ratio:* 13:1.

Academics *Calendar:* semesters. *Degrees:* associate, bachelor's, and master's. *Special study options:* academic remediation for entering students, accelerated degree program, adult/continuing education programs, cooperative education, English as a second language, external degree program, honors programs, internships, off-campus study, part-time degree program, services for LD students, summer session for credit. *ROTC:* Army (c), Air Force (c).

Computers on Campus 1,586 computers/terminals are available on campus for general student use. Students can access the following: campus intranet, computer help desk, free student e-mail accounts, online (class) grades, online (class) registration, online (class) schedules. Campuswide network is available. Wireless service is available via classrooms, computer labs, learning centers, libraries.

Student Life *Activities and organizations:* drama/theater group, student-run newspaper, choral group, marching band, Caribbean Student Association, Theater Arts Ensemble, National Association for the Advancement of Colored People, national fraternities, national sororities. *Campus security:* 24-hour emergency response devices and patrols. *Student services:* health clinic, personal/psychological counseling.

Athletics Member NCAA. All Division II. *Intercollegiate sports:* golf M(s), soccer M(s), tennis M(s)/W(s), track and field M(s)/W(s), volleyball W(s).

Standardized Tests *Recommended:* SAT (for admission).

Costs (2012–13) *Tuition:* district resident $6380 full-time, $266 per credit hour part-time; nonresident $13,380 full-time, $558 per credit hour part-time. Full-time tuition and fees vary according to course load. Part-time tuition and fees vary according to course load. *Required fees:* $620 full-time, $30 per credit hour part-time. *Room and board:* $6600. *Payment plans:* installment, deferred payment. *Waivers:* senior citizens and employees or children of employees.

Financial Aid Of all full-time matriculated undergraduates who enrolled in 2011, 2,160 applied for aid, 1,965 were judged to have need, 789 had their need fully met. 87 Federal Work-Study jobs (averaging $2500). 92 state and other part-time jobs (averaging $2500). In 2011, 141 non-need-based awards were made. *Average percent of need met:* 98%. *Average financial aid package:* $5600. *Average need-based loan:* $2750. *Average need-based gift aid:* $3275. *Average non-need-based aid:* $2750.

Applying *Options:* deferred entrance. *Application fee:* $35. *Required:* high school transcript. *Required for some:* GED. *Application deadlines:* 8/1 (freshmen), 8/1 (transfers). *Notification:* continuous until 8/15 (freshmen), continuous until 8/15 (transfers).

Freshman Application Contact Mr. Pete Nacy, Acting Director, University of the District of Columbia, 4200 Connecticut Ave. NW, Washington, DC 20008. *Phone:* 202-274-6110. *Web site:* http://www.udc.edu/.

FLORIDA

American InterContinental University South Florida
Weston, Florida

Freshman Application Contact American InterContinental University South Florida, 2250 North Commerce Parkway, Suite 100, Weston, FL 33326. *Phone:* 877-564-6248. *Toll-free phone:* 888-603-4888. *Fax:* 877-564-6248. *Web site:* http://www.aiuniv.edu/.

Argosy University, Sarasota
Sarasota, Florida

Freshman Application Contact Argosy University, Sarasota, 5250 17th Street, Sarasota, FL 34235. *Phone:* 941-379-0404. *Toll-free phone:* 800-331-5995. *Web site:* http://www.argosy.edu/sarasota/.

See page 1062 for the College Close-Up.

Argosy University, Tampa
Tampa, Florida

Freshman Application Contact Argosy University, Tampa, 1403 North Howard Avenue, Tampa, FL 33607. *Phone:* 813-393-5290. *Toll-free phone:* 800-850-6488. *Web site:* http://www.argosy.edu/tampa/.

See page 1062 for the College Close-Up.

The Art Institute of Fort Lauderdale

Fort Lauderdale, Florida

- **Proprietary** 4-year, founded 1968, part of Education Management Corporation
- **Urban** campus
- **Coed**

Academics *Calendar:* quarters. *Degrees:* diplomas, associate, and bachelor's.

Costs (2011–12) *Tuition:* Tuition cost varies by program. Prospective students should contact the school for current tuition costs. Other charges include a starting kit for all first-quarter students. Kits vary in price, depending on the program of study.

Freshman Application Contact The Art Institute of Fort Lauderdale, 1799 Southeast 17th Street, Fort Lauderdale, FL 33316. *Phone:* 954-463-3000. *Toll-free phone:* 800-275-7603. *Web site:* http://www.artinstitutes.edu/fortlauderdale/.

See page 1096 for the College Close-Up.

The Art Institute of Jacksonville

Jacksonville, Florida

- **Proprietary** 4-year, founded 2006, part of Education Management Corporation
- **Suburban** campus
- **Coed**

Academics *Degrees:* diplomas, associate, and bachelor's.

Costs (2011–12) *Tuition:* Tuition cost varies by program. Prospective students should contact the school for current tuition costs. Other charges include a starting kit for all first-quarter students. Kits vary in price, depending on the program of study.

Freshman Application Contact The Art Institute of Jacksonville, 8775 Baypine Road, Jacksonville, FL 32256. *Phone:* 904-486-3000. *Toll-free phone:* 800-924-1589. *Web site:* http://www.artinstitutes.edu/jacksonville/.

See page 1106 for the College Close-Up.

The Art Institute of Tampa

Tampa, Florida

- **Proprietary** 4-year, part of Education Management Corporation
- **Suburban** campus
- **Coed**

Academics *Calendar:* quarters. *Degrees:* diplomas, associate, and bachelor's.

Costs (2011–12) *Tuition:* Tuition cost varies by program. Prospective students should contact the school for current tuition costs. Other charges include a starting kit for all first-quarter students. Kits vary in price, depending on the program of study.

Freshman Application Contact The Art Institute of Tampa, Parkside at Tampa Bay Park, 4401 North Himes Avenue, Suite 150, Tampa, FL 33614. *Phone:* 813-873-2112. *Toll-free phone:* 866-703-3277. *Web site:* http://www.artinstitutes.edu/tampa/.

See page 1132 for the College Close-Up.

Ave Maria University

Ave Maria, Florida

Freshman Application Contact Ave Maria University, 5050 Ave Maria Boulevard, Ave Maria, FL 34142. *Phone:* 239-280-2487. *Toll-free phone:* 877-283-8648. *Fax:* 239-280-2559. *Web site:* http://www.avemaria.edu/.

See page 1154 for the College Close-Up.

The Baptist College of Florida

Graceville, Florida

- **Independent Southern Baptist** comprehensive, founded 1943
- **Small-town** 165-acre campus
- **Endowment** $5.8 million
- **Coed** 596 undergraduate students, 73% full-time, 39% women, 61% men
- **Noncompetitive** entrance level, 40% of applicants were admitted

Undergraduates 438 full-time, 158 part-time. Students come from 20 states and territories; 37% are from out of state; 6% Black or African American, non-Hispanic/Latino; 3% Hispanic/Latino; 0.2% Asian, non-Hispanic/Latino; 0.2% American Indian or Alaska Native, non-Hispanic/Latino; 1% Two or more races, non-Hispanic/Latino; 9% Race/ethnicity unknown; 12% transferred in; 44% live on campus. *Retention:* 82% of full-time freshmen returned.

Freshmen *Admission:* 162 applied, 65 admitted, 63 enrolled.

Faculty *Total:* 63, 41% full-time, 57% with terminal degrees. *Student/faculty ratio:* 13:1.

Academics *Calendar:* semesters. *Degrees:* certificates, associate, bachelor's, and master's. *Special study options:* academic remediation for entering students, advanced placement credit, distance learning, double majors, independent study, internships, part-time degree program, services for LD students, summer session for credit.

Computers on Campus 25 computers/terminals are available on campus for general student use. Students can access the following: free student e-mail accounts, online (class) grades, online (class) registration. Campuswide network is available. Wireless service is available via entire campus.

Student Life *Housing:* on-campus residence required through sophomore year. *Options:* men-only, women-only. Campus housing is university owned. Freshman campus housing is guaranteed. *Activities and organizations:* drama/theater group, student-run radio station, choral group, Baptist Collegiate Ministry, College Choir, AACC. *Campus security:* student patrols, patrols by police officers 11 pm to 7 am. *Student services:* personal/psychological counseling.

Athletics Member NCCAA. *Intercollegiate sports:* golf M, volleyball W. *Intramural sports:* basketball M/W, football M/W, soccer M/W, softball M/W, table tennis M/W, tennis M/W, ultimate Frisbee M/W, volleyball M/W.

Standardized Tests *Required:* SAT or ACT (for admission).

Financial Aid Of all full-time matriculated undergraduates who enrolled in 2011, 710 applied for aid, 638 were judged to have need, 22 had their need fully met. 20 Federal Work-Study jobs (averaging $2645). In 2011, 6 non-need-based awards were made. *Average percent of need met:* 35%. *Average financial aid package:* $7399. *Average need-based loan:* $3422. *Average need-based gift aid:* $5165. *Average non-need-based aid:* $1833. *Average indebtedness upon graduation:* $12,535. *Financial aid deadline:* 4/15.

Applying *Options:* electronic application, deferred entrance. *Application fee:* $25. *Required:* essay or personal statement, high school transcript, 2 letters of recommendation, Christian/Church Member for 1 year minimum. *Recommended:* interview. *Application deadlines:* 8/11 (freshmen), 8/11 (transfers). *Notification:* continuous (freshmen), continuous (transfers).

Freshman Application Contact The Baptist College of Florida, 5400 College Drive, Graceville, FL 32440-1898. *Phone:* 850-263-3261 Ext. 460. *Toll-free phone:* 800-328-2660 Ext. 460. *Web site:* http://www.baptistcollege.edu/.

Barry University
Miami Shores, Florida

- **Independent Roman Catholic** university, founded 1940
- **Suburban** 122-acre campus with easy access to Miami
- **Endowment** $25.1 million
- **Coed** 4,698 undergraduate students, 84% full-time, 66% women, 34% men
- **Moderately difficult** entrance level, 59% of applicants were admitted

Undergraduates 3,941 full-time, 757 part-time. Students come from 44 states and territories; 67 other countries; 19% are from out of state; 15% Black or African American, non-Hispanic/Latino; 13% Hispanic/Latino; 0.6% Asian, non-Hispanic/Latino; 0.2% American Indian or Alaska Native, non-Hispanic/Latino; 57% Race/ethnicity unknown; 7% international; 16% transferred in; 28% live on campus. *Retention:* 56% of full-time freshmen returned.

Freshmen *Admission:* 6,918 applied, 4,060 admitted, 662 enrolled. *Average high school GPA:* 2.9. *Test scores:* SAT critical reading scores over 500: 30%; SAT math scores over 500: 28%; SAT critical reading scores over 600: 5%; SAT math scores over 600: 4%.

Faculty *Total:* 838, 44% full-time. *Student/faculty ratio:* 20:1.

Academics *Calendar:* semesters. *Degrees:* certificates, bachelor's, master's, doctoral, post-master's, postbachelor's, and first professional certificates. *Special study options:* academic remediation for entering students, accelerated degree program, adult/continuing education programs, advanced placement credit, distance learning, double majors, English as a second language, honors programs, independent study, internships, off-campus study, part-time degree program, services for LD students, study abroad, summer session for credit. *ROTC:* Army (c), Air Force (c). *Unusual degree programs:* 3-2 engineering with University of Miami.

Computers on Campus 368 computers/terminals are available on campus for general student use. Students can access the following: campus intranet, computer help desk, free student e-mail accounts, online (class) grades, online (class) registration, online (class) schedules, Blackboard. Campuswide network is available. Wireless service is available via computer centers, computer labs, learning centers, student centers.

Student Life *Housing:* on-campus residence required for freshman year. *Options:* coed, men-only, women-only, disabled students. Campus housing is university owned. *Activities and organizations:* drama/theater group, student-run newspaper, radio and television station, choral group, Student Government Association, Campus Activities Board, SCUBA Society, Caribbean Students

Association, Jamaican Association, national fraternities, national sororities. *Campus security:* 24-hour emergency response devices and patrols, late-night transport/escort service. *Student services:* health clinic, personal/psychological counseling.

Athletics Member NCAA. All Division II. *Intercollegiate sports:* baseball M(s), basketball M(s)/W(s), crew W(s), golf M(s)/W(s), soccer M(s)/W(s), softball W(s), tennis M(s)/W(s), volleyball W(s). *Intramural sports:* basketball M/W, football M/W, golf M/W, soccer M/W, softball M/W, volleyball M/W.

Standardized Tests *Required:* SAT or ACT (for admission).

Costs (2011–12) *Comprehensive fee:* $37,190 includes full-time tuition ($28,160) and room and board ($9030). Part-time tuition: $845 per credit. Part-time tuition and fees vary according to course load. *Room and board:* Room and board charges vary according to board plan.

Financial Aid Of all full-time matriculated undergraduates who enrolled in 2009, 3,482 applied for aid, 3,370 were judged to have need, 128 had their need fully met. In 2009, 395 non-need-based awards were made. *Average percent of need met:* 53%. *Average financial aid package:* $20,365. *Average need-based loan:* $5212. *Average need-based gift aid:* $8596. *Average non-need-based aid:* $6786. *Average indebtedness upon graduation:* $35,880.

Applying *Options:* electronic application, early admission, deferred entrance. *Application fee:* $30. *Required:* high school transcript, minimum 2.0 GPA. *Required for some:* essay or personal statement. *Recommended:* interview. *Application deadlines:* rolling (freshmen), rolling (transfers). *Notification:* continuous (freshmen), continuous (transfers).

Freshman Application Contact Barry University, 11300 Northeast Second Avenue, Miami Shores, FL 33161-6695. *Phone:* 305-899-3100. *Toll-free phone:* 800-695-2279. *Web site:* http://www.barry.edu/.

See page 179 for display ad and page 1164 for the College Close-Up.

Beacon College

Leesburg, Florida

- **Independent** 4-year, founded 1989
- **Small-town** 5-acre campus with easy access to Orlando
- **Coed** 153 undergraduate students, 99% full-time, 38% women, 62% men
- **Moderately difficult** entrance level, 30% of applicants were admitted

Undergraduates 151 full-time, 2 part-time. Students come from 30 states and territories; 4 other countries; 75% are from out of state; 9% Black or African American, non-Hispanic/Latino; 8% Hispanic/Latino; 1% Asian, non-Hispanic/Latino; 0.7% Native Hawaiian or other Pacific Islander, non-Hispanic/Latino; 0.7% American Indian or Alaska Native, non-Hispanic/Latino; 5% international; 10% transferred in; 94% live on campus. *Retention:* 65% of full-time freshmen returned.

Freshmen *Admission:* 117 applied, 35 admitted, 35 enrolled. *Average high school GPA:* 2.8.

Faculty *Total:* 20, 65% full-time, 35% with terminal degrees. *Student/faculty ratio:* 8:1.

Academics *Calendar:* semesters. *Degrees:* associate and bachelor's. *Special study options:* academic remediation for entering students, adult/continuing education programs, advanced placement credit, cooperative education, double majors, independent study, internships, services for LD students, summer session for credit.

Computers on Campus 54 computers/terminals and 216 ports are available on campus for general student use. Students can access the following: campus intranet, computer help desk, free student e-mail accounts, online (class) grades, online (class) schedules. Campuswide network is available. 100% of college-owned or -operated housing units are wired for high-speed Internet access. Wireless service is available via classrooms, computer centers, computer labs, dorm rooms, learning centers, libraries, student centers.

Student Life *Housing options:* coed. Campus housing is university owned and leased by the school. Freshman campus housing is guaranteed. *Activities and organizations:* drama/theater group, student-run newspaper, choral group, Lambda Epsilon Omega fraternity, Activities Club, Performance Club, Theater Goers Club, World Dance Club, national fraternities, national sororities. *Campus security:* 24-hour emergency response devices, student patrols, late-night transport/escort service. *Student services:* health clinic, personal/psychological counseling.

Standardized Tests *Recommended:* SAT or ACT (for admission).

Costs (2012–13) *One-time required fee:* $412. *Comprehensive fee:* $39,030 includes full-time tuition ($29,500), mandatory fees ($930), and room and board ($8600). Part-time tuition: $833 per course. *College room only:* $5305. Room and board charges vary according to board plan and housing facility. *Payment plan:* installment.

Applying *Options:* early admission, deferred entrance. *Application fee:* $50. *Required:* essay or personal statement, high school transcript, 3 letters of recommendation, psycho-educational evaluation. *Recommended:* minimum 2.5

GPA. *Application deadlines:* rolling (freshmen), rolling (transfers). *Notification:* 8/1 (freshmen), 8/1 (transfers).

Freshman Application Contact Ms. Brenda Meli, Director of Admissions, Beacon College, 105 East Main Street, Leesburg, FL 34748. *Phone:* 352-638-9732. *Fax:* 352-787-0796. *E-mail:* bmeli@beaconcollege.edu. *Web site:* http://www.beaconcollege.edu/.

Belhaven University

Orlando, Florida

Director of Admissions Jeremy Couch, Director of Admission, Belhaven University, 5200 Vineland Road, Suite 100, Orlando, FL 32811. *Phone:* 407-804-1424. *Toll-free phone:* 877-804-1424. *Fax:* 407-661-1732. *E-mail:* orlando@belhaven.edu. *Web site:* http://orlando.belhaven.edu/.

Bethune-Cookman University

Daytona Beach, Florida

- **Independent Methodist** comprehensive, founded 1904
- **Urban** 60-acre campus with easy access to Orlando
- **Endowment** $34.0 million
- **Coed** 3,545 undergraduate students, 96% full-time, 61% women, 39% men
- **Minimally difficult** entrance level, 70% of applicants were admitted

Undergraduates 3,405 full-time, 140 part-time. Students come from 39 states and territories; 18 other countries; 31% are from out of state; 92% Black or African American, non-Hispanic/Latino; 2% Hispanic/Latino; 0.2% Asian, non-Hispanic/Latino; 1% Native Hawaiian or other Pacific Islander, non-Hispanic/Latino; 0.8% Two or more races, non-Hispanic/Latino; 0.2% Race/ethnicity unknown; 2% international; 3% transferred in; 55% live on campus. *Retention:* 68% of full-time freshmen returned.

Freshmen *Admission:* 4,763 applied, 3,312 admitted, 928 enrolled. *Average high school GPA:* 2.9. *Test scores:* SAT critical reading scores over 500: 14%; SAT math scores over 500: 12%; SAT writing scores over 500: 14%; ACT scores over 18: 34%; SAT critical reading scores over 600: 1%; SAT math scores over 600: 2%; SAT writing scores over 600: 1%; ACT scores over 24: 3%; SAT math scores over 700: 1%; ACT scores over 30: 1%.

Faculty *Total:* 230, 88% full-time, 47% with terminal degrees. *Student/faculty ratio:* 17:1.

Academics *Calendar:* semesters. *Degrees:* bachelor's and master's. *Special study options:* academic remediation for entering students, accelerated degree program, adult/continuing education programs, advanced placement credit, cooperative education, distance learning, double majors, honors programs, independent study, internships, part-time degree program, study abroad, summer session for credit. *ROTC:* Army (c), Air Force (c). *Unusual degree programs:* 3-2 engineering with Tuskegee University, University of Florida, Florida Atlantic University, Florida Agricultural and Mechanical University, University of Central Florida.

Computers on Campus 451 computers/terminals are available on campus for general student use. Students can access the following: campus intranet, computer help desk, free student e-mail accounts, online (class) grades, online (class) registration, online (class) schedules. Campuswide network is available. 100% of college-owned or -operated housing units are wired for high-speed Internet access. Wireless service is available via entire campus.

Student Life *Housing:* on-campus residence required for freshman year. *Options:* men-only, women-only. Campus housing is university owned. Freshman campus housing is guaranteed. *Activities and organizations:* drama/theater group, student-run newspaper, radio station, choral group, marching band, Concert Chorale, marching band, Inspirational Gospel Choir, Student Government Association, national fraternities, national sororities. *Campus security:* 24-hour emergency response devices and patrols, student patrols, late-night transport/escort service. *Student services:* health clinic, personal/psychological counseling.

Athletics Member NCAA. All Division I except football (Division I-AA). *Intercollegiate sports:* baseball M(s), basketball M(s)/W(s), bowling W(s), cheerleading W, cross-country running M(s)/W(s), golf M(s)/W(s), softball W(s), tennis M(s)/W(s), track and field M(s)/W(s), volleyball W(s). *Intramural sports:* basketball M/W, bowling M/W, football M, racquetball W, soccer M/W, table tennis W.

Standardized Tests *Required:* SAT or ACT (for admission).

Costs (2011–12) *Comprehensive fee:* $22,290 includes full-time tuition ($13,990) and room and board ($8300). Full-time tuition and fees vary according to course load. Part-time tuition: $583 per credit hour. Part-time tuition and fees vary according to course load. *Payment plan:* installment. *Waivers:* employees or children of employees.

Financial Aid Of all full-time matriculated undergraduates who enrolled in 2011, 3,268 applied for aid, 3,176 were judged to have need, 141 had their need fully met. 265 Federal Work-Study jobs (averaging $1900). 135 state and

other part-time jobs (averaging $2200). In 2011, 27 non-need-based awards were made. *Average percent of need met:* 48%. *Average financial aid package:* $13,131. *Average need-based loan:* $4378. *Average need-based gift aid:* $9271. *Average non-need-based aid:* $7655. *Average indebtedness upon graduation:* $21,528.

Applying *Options:* electronic application, early admission, deferred entrance. *Application fee:* $25. *Required:* high school transcript, minimum 2.3 GPA, 1 letter of recommendation, medical history. *Required for some:* interview. *Recommended:* essay or personal statement. *Application deadlines:* 6/30 (freshmen), 6/30 (transfers). *Notification:* continuous (freshmen), continuous (transfers).

Freshman Application Contact Mrs. Aixa Melendez, Director of Admissions, Bethune-Cookman University, 640 Dr. Mary McLeod Bethune Boulevard, Daytona Beach, FL 32114-3099. *Phone:* 386-481-2600. *Toll-free phone:* 800-448-0228. *Fax:* 386-481-2601. *E-mail:* admissions@cookman.edu. *Web site:* http://www.cookman.edu/.

Broward College
Fort Lauderdale, Florida

Freshman Application Contact Willie J. Alexander, Associate Vice President for Student Affairs/College Registrar, Broward College, 225 East Las Olas Boulevard, Fort Lauderdale, FL 33301. *Phone:* 954-201-7471. *Fax:* 954-201-7466. *E-mail:* walexand@broward.edu. *Web site:* http://www.broward.edu/.

Brown Mackie College–Miami
Miami, Florida

- **Proprietary** primarily 2-year, part of Education Management Corporation
- **Coed**

Academics *Degrees:* diplomas, associate, and bachelor's.
Costs (2011–12) *Tuition:* Tuition varies by program. Students should contact Brown Mackie College for tuition information.
Freshman Application Contact Brown Mackie College–Miami, One Herald Plaza, Miami, FL 33132. *Phone:* 305-341-6600. *Toll-free phone:* 866-505-0335. *Web site:* http://www.brownmackie.edu/miami/.

See page 1210 for the College Close-Up.

Carlos Albizu University, Miami Campus
Miami, Florida

- **Independent** comprehensive, founded 1980, part of Carlos Albizu University
- **Urban** 18-acre campus
- **Coed, primarily women** 307 undergraduate students, 60% full-time, 76% women, 24% men
- 36% of applicants were admitted

Undergraduates 183 full-time, 124 part-time. 4% Black or African American, non-Hispanic/Latino; 73% Hispanic/Latino; 0.3% Asian, non-Hispanic/Latino; 0.3% American Indian or Alaska Native, non-Hispanic/Latino; 18% Race/ethnicity unknown; 3% international; 25% transferred in. *Retention:* 68% of full-time freshmen returned.
Freshmen *Admission:* 36 applied, 13 admitted, 9 enrolled. *Average high school GPA:* 2.5.
Faculty *Total:* 66, 8% full-time, 38% with terminal degrees. *Student/faculty ratio:* 13:1.
Academics *Calendar:* trimesters. *Degrees:* certificates, diplomas, bachelor's, master's, doctoral, and first professional. *Special study options:* academic remediation for entering students, accelerated degree program, adult/continuing education programs, advanced placement credit, cooperative education, distance learning, double majors, English as a second language, independent study, internships, part-time degree program, services for LD students, summer session for credit.
Computers on Campus 142 computers/terminals are available on campus for general student use. Students can access the following: computer help desk, free student e-mail accounts, online (class) grades, online (class) schedules, Campus Portal. Wireless service is available via entire campus.
Student Life *Housing:* college housing not available. *Activities and organizations:* student-run newspaper, Student Council, Psi Chi, Kappa Delta Pi, Nu Sigma Si, Future Educators of America. *Campus security:* 24-hour emergency response devices and patrols, late-night transport/escort service.
Costs (2012–13) *Tuition:* $11,304 full-time, $314 per credit part-time. Full-time tuition and fees vary according to course load, degree level, and program. Part-time tuition and fees vary according to course load, degree level, and pro-

gram. *Required fees:* $744 full-time, $248 per term part-time. *Payment plan:* installment. *Waivers:* employees or children of employees.
Financial Aid Of all full-time matriculated undergraduates who enrolled in 2003, 121 applied for aid, 118 were judged to have need. 27 Federal Work-Study jobs (averaging $3059). *Average percent of need met:* 50%. *Average financial aid package:* $7925. *Average need-based loan:* $3549. *Average need-based gift aid:* $5300. *Average indebtedness upon graduation:* $23,000.
Applying *Options:* electronic application. *Application fee:* $25. *Required:* high school transcript, minimum 2.0 GPA. *Recommended:* interview. *Application deadlines:* rolling (freshmen), rolling (transfers). *Notification:* continuous (freshmen).
Freshman Application Contact Ms. Dayanes Rodriguez, Admissions Officer, Carlos Albizu University, Miami Campus, 2173 NW 99 Avenue, Miami, FL 33172. *Phone:* 305-593-1223 Ext. 218. *Toll-free phone:* 888-GO-TO-CAU (in-state); 800-GO-TO-CAU (out-of-state). *Fax:* 305-593-1854. *E-mail:* mtriana@albizu.edu. *Web site:* http://www.mia.albizu.edu/.

Chamberlain College of Nursing
Jacksonville, Florida

- **Proprietary** 4-year
- **Coed** 270 undergraduate students, 60% full-time, 87% women, 13% men

Undergraduates 163 full-time, 107 part-time. 5% are from out of state; 24% Black or African American, non-Hispanic/Latino; 7% Hispanic/Latino; 8% Asian, non-Hispanic/Latino; 0.7% Native Hawaiian or other Pacific Islander, non-Hispanic/Latino; 3% Two or more races, non-Hispanic/Latino; 7% Race/ethnicity unknown; 0.7% international; 53% transferred in.
Faculty *Total:* 18, 56% full-time. *Student/faculty ratio:* 16:1.
Academics *Calendar:* semesters.
Standardized Tests *Required:* SAT or ACT (for admission).
Freshman Application Contact Admissions, Chamberlain College of Nursing, 5200 Belfort Road, Jacksonville, FL 32256-6040. *Phone:* 904-251-8100. *Toll-free phone:* 888-556-8CCN. *Web site:* http://www.chamberlain.edu/.

Chamberlain College of Nursing
Miramar, Florida

- **Proprietary** 4-year
- **Coed** 69 undergraduate students, 70% full-time, 90% women, 10% men
- **Moderately difficult** entrance level

Undergraduates 48 full-time, 21 part-time. 3% are from out of state; 16% Black or African American, non-Hispanic/Latino; 42% Hispanic/Latino; 1% Asian, non-Hispanic/Latino; 35% Race/ethnicity unknown; 96% transferred in.
Freshmen *Admission:* 2 enrolled.
Faculty *Total:* 3, 100% full-time. *Student/faculty ratio:* 18:1.
Academics *Degree:* bachelor's.
Student Life *Housing:* college housing not available.
Standardized Tests *Required:* SAT or ACT (for admission).
Applying *Application fee:* $95. *Application deadlines:* rolling (freshmen), rolling (transfers). *Notification:* continuous (freshmen), continuous (transfers).
Freshman Application Contact Director of Recruitment, Chamberlain College of Nursing, 2300 SW 145th Avenue, Miramar, FL 33027. *Phone:* 954-885-3510. *Web site:* http://www.chamberlain.edu/.

Chipola College
Marianna, Florida

- **State-supported** primarily 2-year, founded 1947
- **Rural** 105-acre campus
- **Coed** 2,341 undergraduate students, 43% full-time, 61% women, 39% men
- **Noncompetitive** entrance level

Undergraduates 1,016 full-time, 1,325 part-time. Students come from 7 states and territories; 6 other countries; 8% are from out of state; 16% Black or African American, non-Hispanic/Latino; 2% Hispanic/Latino; 0.9% Asian, non-Hispanic/Latino; 0.8% American Indian or Alaska Native, non-Hispanic/Latino; 2% Two or more races, non-Hispanic/Latino; 0.2% Race/ethnicity unknown; 6% transferred in.
Freshmen *Admission:* 249 enrolled. *Average high school GPA:* 2.5. *Test scores:* SAT critical reading scores over 500: 16%; SAT math scores over 500: 36%; ACT scores over 18: 81%; SAT critical reading scores over 600: 4%; SAT math scores over 600: 12%; ACT scores over 24: 25%; ACT scores over 30: 3%.
Faculty *Total:* 133, 30% full-time, 14% with terminal degrees. *Student/faculty ratio:* 24:1.

Academics *Calendar:* semesters. *Degrees:* certificates, associate, and bachelor's. *Special study options:* academic remediation for entering students, adult/continuing education programs, advanced placement credit, distance learning, honors programs, independent study, part-time degree program, services for LD students, summer session for credit.

Computers on Campus 80 computers/terminals are available on campus for general student use. Campuswide network is available.

Student Life *Housing:* college housing not available. *Activities and organizations:* drama/theater group, student-run newspaper, choral group, Drama/Theater Group. *Campus security:* night security personnel.

Athletics Member NJCAA. *Intercollegiate sports:* baseball M(s), basketball M(s)/W(s), softball W(s).

Costs (2011–12) *Tuition:* state resident $3000 full-time, $100 per semester hour part-time; nonresident $8557 full-time, $285 per semester hour part-time. Full-time tuition and fees vary according to degree level. Part-time tuition and fees vary according to degree level. *Required fees:* $40 full-time.

Applying *Options:* early admission. *Required:* high school transcript. *Application deadlines:* rolling (freshmen), rolling (transfers). *Notification:* continuous (freshmen), continuous (transfers).

Freshman Application Contact Mrs. Kathy L. Rehberg, Registrar, Chipola College, 3094 Indian Circle, Marianna, FL 32446-3065. *Phone:* 850-718-2233. *Fax:* 850-718-2287. *E-mail:* rehbergk@chipola.edu. *Web site:* http://www.chipola.edu/.

City College
Casselberry, Florida

Director of Admissions Ms. Kimberly Bowden, Director of Admissions, City College, 853 Semoran Boulevard, Suite 200, Casselberry, FL 32707-5342. *Phone:* 352-335-4000. *Fax:* 352-335-4303. *E-mail:* kbowden@citycollege.edu. *Web site:* http://www.citycollegeorlando.edu/.

City College
Fort Lauderdale, Florida

Freshman Application Contact City College, 2000 West Commercial Boulevard, Suite 200, Fort Lauderdale, FL 33309. *Phone:* 954-492-5353. *Toll-free phone:* 866-314-5681. *Web site:* http://www.citycollege.edu/.

City College
Gainesville, Florida

Freshman Application Contact Admissions Office, City College, 7001 Northwest 4th Boulevard, Gainesville, FL 32607. *Phone:* 352-335-4000. *Web site:* http://www.citycollege.edu/.

City College
Miami, Florida

Freshman Application Contact Admissions Office, City College, 9300 South Dadeland Boulevard, Suite PH, Miami, FL 33156. *Phone:* 305-666-9242. *Fax:* 305-666-9243. *Web site:* http://www.citycollege.edu/.

Clearwater Christian College
Clearwater, Florida

- **Independent nondenominational** comprehensive, founded 1966
- **Suburban** 138-acre campus with easy access to Tampa-St. Petersburg
- **Endowment** $594,825
- **Coed** 510 undergraduate students, 97% full-time, 48% women, 52% men
- **Minimally difficult** entrance level, 72% of applicants were admitted

Undergraduates 494 full-time, 16 part-time. Students come from 43 states and territories; 4 other countries; 49% are from out of state; 5% Black or African American, non-Hispanic/Latino; 3% Hispanic/Latino; 0.2% Asian, non-Hispanic/Latino; 0.4% Native Hawaiian or other Pacific Islander, non-Hispanic/Latino; 1% American Indian or Alaska Native, non-Hispanic/Latino; 7% Race/ethnicity unknown; 1% international; 75% live on campus.

Freshmen *Admission:* 340 applied, 245 admitted, 120 enrolled. *Average high school GPA:* 3.4. *Test scores:* SAT critical reading scores over 500: 66%; SAT math scores over 500: 54%; ACT scores over 18: 86%; SAT critical reading scores over 600: 21%; SAT math scores over 600: 21%; ACT scores over 24: 28%; SAT critical reading scores over 700: 5%; ACT scores over 30: 4%.

Faculty *Total:* 43, 67% full-time, 72% with terminal degrees. *Student/faculty ratio:* 15:1.

Academics *Calendar:* semesters. *Degrees:* certificates, associate, bachelor's, and master's. *Special study options:* academic remediation for entering stu-

dents, advanced placement credit, distance learning, double majors, independent study, internships, off-campus study, part-time degree program, services for LD students, study abroad, summer session for credit. *ROTC:* Army (c), Navy (c), Air Force (c).

Computers on Campus 45 computers/terminals are available on campus for general student use. Students can access the following: campus intranet, computer help desk, free student e-mail accounts, online (class) grades, online (class) registration, online (class) schedules. Campuswide network is available. 100% of college-owned or -operated housing units are wired for high-speed Internet access. Wireless service is available via entire campus.

Student Life *Housing:* on-campus residence required through senior year. *Options:* men-only, women-only. Campus housing is university owned. Freshman campus housing is guaranteed. *Activities and organizations:* drama/theater group, student-run newspaper, choral group, Drama Club, Alpha Chi, College Republicans, Science Club, Student Missionary Fellowship. *Campus security:* 24-hour emergency response devices and patrols. *Student services:* personal/psychological counseling.

Athletics Member NCCAA. *Intercollegiate sports:* baseball M, basketball M/W, golf M/W, soccer M/W, softball W, volleyball W. *Intramural sports:* basketball M/W, football M, table tennis M/W, tennis M/W, volleyball M/W.

Standardized Tests *Required:* SAT or ACT (for admission).

Costs (2011–12) *Comprehensive fee:* $23,720 includes full-time tuition ($16,250) and room and board ($7470). Full-time tuition and fees vary according to student level. Part-time tuition: $635 per credit. No tuition increase for student's term of enrollment. *College room only:* $4600. Room and board charges vary according to board plan. *Payment plan:* installment. *Waivers:* employees or children of employees.

Financial Aid Of all full-time matriculated undergraduates who enrolled in 2009, 543 applied for aid, 433 were judged to have need, 65 had their need fully met. 50 Federal Work-Study jobs (averaging $670). 20 state and other part-time jobs (averaging $612). In 2009, 132 non-need-based awards were made. *Average percent of need met:* 60%. *Average financial aid package:* $10,353. *Average need-based loan:* $4324. *Average need-based gift aid:* $7918. *Average non-need-based aid:* $2848. *Average indebtedness upon graduation:* $18,000.

Applying *Options:* electronic application, early admission, deferred entrance. *Application fee:* $35. *Required:* essay or personal statement, high school transcript, minimum 2.0 GPA, 2 letters of recommendation, Christian testimony. *Recommended:* interview. *Application deadlines:* rolling (freshmen), rolling (transfers). *Notification:* continuous (freshmen), continuous (transfers).

Freshman Application Contact Miss Colleen Gumbert, Admissions Administrative Assistant, Clearwater Christian College, 3400 Gulf-to-Bay Boulevard, Clearwater, FL 33759-4595. *Phone:* 727-726-1153 Ext. 228. *Toll-free phone:* 800-348-4463. *Fax:* 813-726-8597. *E-mail:* admissions@clearwater.edu. *Web site:* http://www.clearwater.edu/.

College of Business and Technology
Miami, Florida

- **Proprietary** primarily 2-year, founded 1988
- **Coed** 1,098 undergraduate students, 100% full-time, 37% women, 63% men
- **Minimally difficult** entrance level, 75% of applicants were admitted

Undergraduates 1,098 full-time. Students come from 4 states and territories; 11% Black or African American, non-Hispanic/Latino; 85% Hispanic/Latino; 0.1% Asian, non-Hispanic/Latino; 0.1% Native Hawaiian or other Pacific Islander, non-Hispanic/Latino; 0.7% American Indian or Alaska Native, non-Hispanic/Latino; 0.2% Two or more races, non-Hispanic/Latino; 0.8% Race/ethnicity unknown; 3% transferred in.

Freshmen *Admission:* 1,463 applied, 1,098 admitted, 1,098 enrolled. *Average high school GPA:* 2.8.

Faculty *Total:* 28, 43% full-time, 100% with terminal degrees. *Student/faculty ratio:* 15:1.

Academics *Calendar:* semesters. *Degrees:* certificates, diplomas, associate, and bachelor's. *Special study options:* academic remediation for entering students, accelerated degree program, adult/continuing education programs, advanced placement credit, cooperative education, distance learning, double majors, English as a second language, honors programs, independent study, internships, off-campus study, part-time degree program, services for LD students, summer session for credit.

Computers on Campus 150 computers/terminals are available on campus for general student use. Students can access the following: online (class) registration. Campuswide network is available.

Student Life *Housing options:* Campus housing is provided by a third party. *Activities and organizations:* student-run newspaper.

Costs (2012–13) *Tuition:* $10,920 full-time. *Required fees:* $1400 full-time. *Payment plan:* installment.

Applying *Options:* electronic application. *Application fee:* $25. *Required:* essay or personal statement, high school transcript, minimum 2.6 GPA, 2 letters of recommendation, interview.
Freshman Application Contact Ms. Ivis Delgado, Admissions Representative, College of Business and Technology, 8230 West Flagler Street, Miami, FL 33144. *Phone:* 305-273-4499 Ext. 2204. *Toll-free phone:* 866-626-8842. *Fax:* 305-485-4411. *E-mail:* admissions@cbt.edu. *Web site:* http://www.cbt.edu/.

College of Central Florida
Ocala, Florida

- **State and locally supported** primarily 2-year, founded 1957, part of Florida Community College System
- **Small-town** 139-acre campus
- **Endowment** $40.1 million
- **Coed** 8,766 undergraduate students, 42% full-time, 62% women, 38% men
- **Noncompetitive** entrance level

Undergraduates 3,666 full-time, 5,100 part-time.
Freshmen *Admission:* 1,345 enrolled. *Test scores:* SAT critical reading scores over 500: 42%; SAT math scores over 500: 39%; SAT writing scores over 500: 42%; ACT scores over 18: 77%; SAT math scores over 600: 8%; ACT scores over 24: 29%; ACT scores over 30: 5%.
Faculty *Total:* 611, 21% full-time, 10% with terminal degrees. *Student/faculty ratio:* 18:1.
Academics *Calendar:* semesters. *Degrees:* certificates, diplomas, associate, and bachelor's. *Special study options:* academic remediation for entering students, adult/continuing education programs, advanced placement credit, cooperative education, distance learning, English as a second language, freshman honors college, honors programs, independent study, internships, part-time degree program, services for LD students, summer session for credit.
Computers on Campus 737 computers/terminals are available on campus for general student use. Students can access the following: online (class) registration. Campuswide network is available.
Student Life *Housing:* college housing not available. *Activities and organizations:* drama/theater group, student-run newspaper, choral group, Student Activities Board, African-American Student Union, ROC (Realizing Our Cause), Gay Straight Alliance, Musagettas. *Campus security:* 24-hour emergency response devices and patrols, student patrols, late-night transport/escort service. *Student services:* personal/psychological counseling.
Athletics Member NJCAA. *Intercollegiate sports:* baseball M(s), basketball M(s)/W(s), softball W(s), tennis W(s), volleyball W(s).
Standardized Tests *Recommended:* SAT (for admission), ACT (for admission), SAT or ACT (for admission), SAT and SAT Subject Tests or ACT (for admission), SAT Subject Tests (for admission).
Costs (2011–12) *Tuition:* state resident $2274 full-time, $99 per credit hour part-time; nonresident $9096 full-time, $371 per credit hour part-time. Full-time tuition and fees vary according to course level, degree level, and program. Part-time tuition and fees vary according to course level, degree level, and program. *Required fees:* $682 full-time, $23 per credit hour part-time. *Waivers:* employees or children of employees.
Financial Aid Of all full-time matriculated undergraduates who enrolled in 2010, 85 Federal Work-Study jobs (averaging $1505).
Applying *Options:* early admission. *Application fee:* $30. *Required:* high school transcript. *Application deadlines:* rolling (freshmen), rolling (transfers). *Notification:* continuous (freshmen), continuous (transfers).
Freshman Application Contact Ms. Devona Sewell, Registrar, Admission and Records, College of Central Florida, 3001 SW College Road, Ocala, FL 34474. *Phone:* 352-237-2111 Ext. 1398. *Fax:* 352-873-5882. *E-mail:* sewelld@cf.edu. *Web site:* http://www.cf.edu/.

Daytona State College
Daytona Beach, Florida

- **State-supported** primarily 2-year, founded 1958, part of Florida Community College System
- **Suburban** 100-acre campus with easy access to Orlando
- **Coed**
- **Noncompetitive** entrance level

Faculty *Student/faculty ratio:* 22:1.
Academics *Calendar:* semesters. *Degrees:* certificates, diplomas, associate, bachelor's, and postbachelor's certificates.
Student Life *Campus security:* 24-hour emergency response devices and patrols, late-night transport/escort service.
Athletics Member NJCAA.
Costs (2011–12) *Tuition:* state resident $2847 full-time, $95 per credit hour part-time; nonresident $10,737 full-time, $358 per credit hour part-time. Full-

time tuition and fees vary according to course level, course load, degree level, and program. Part-time tuition and fees vary according to course level, course load, degree level, and program. *Required fees:* $60 full-time, $30 per term part-time.
Financial Aid *Of all full-time matriculated undergraduates who enrolled in 2010,* 193 Federal Work-Study jobs (averaging $1542).
Applying *Options:* electronic application, early admission, deferred entrance. *Required:* high school transcript.
Freshman Application Contact Mrs. Karen Sanders, Director of Admissions and Recruitment, Daytona State College, 1200 International Speedway Boulevard, Daytona Beach, FL 32114. *Phone:* 386-506-3050. *E-mail:* sanderk@daytonastate.edu. *Web site:* http://www.daytonastate.edu/.

DeVry University
Jacksonville, Florida

Admissions Office Contact DeVry University, 5200 Belfort Road, Jacksonville, FL 32256-6040. *Web site:* http://www.devry.edu/locations/campuses/loc_jacksonville.jsp.

DeVry University
Miami, Florida

Admissions Office Contact DeVry University, 8700 West Flagler Street, Suite 100, Miami, FL 33174-2535. *Toll-free phone:* 866-338-7941. *Web site:* http://www.devry.edu/.

DeVry University
Miramar, Florida

- **Proprietary** comprehensive, founded 2002, part of DeVry University
- **Coed** 977 undergraduate students, 39% full-time, 41% women, 59% men
- **Minimally difficult** entrance level

Undergraduates 383 full-time, 594 part-time. 5% are from out of state; 24% Black or African American, non-Hispanic/Latino; 41% Hispanic/Latino; 0.9% Asian, non-Hispanic/Latino; 0.1% American Indian or Alaska Native, non-Hispanic/Latino; 0.6% Two or more races, non-Hispanic/Latino; 10% Race/ethnicity unknown; 9% international; 22% transferred in.
Freshmen *Admission:* 71 enrolled.
Faculty *Total:* 77, 23% full-time. *Student/faculty ratio:* 19:1.
Academics *Calendar:* semesters. *Degrees:* associate, bachelor's, master's, and postbachelor's certificates. *Special study options:* part-time degree program.
Student Life *Housing:* college housing not available.
Costs (2011–12) *Tuition:* $15,294 full-time, $597 per credit hour part-time. Full-time tuition and fees vary according to course load. Part-time tuition and fees vary according to course load. *Required fees:* $80 full-time, $40 per term part-time. *Payment plans:* installment, deferred payment. *Waivers:* employees or children of employees.
Financial Aid Of all full-time matriculated undergraduates who enrolled in 2007, 204 applied for aid, 197 were judged to have need, 2 had their need fully met. In 2007, 35 non-need-based awards were made. *Average percent of need met:* 38%. *Average financial aid package:* $12,172. *Average need-based loan:* $7414. *Average need-based gift aid:* $7044. *Average non-need-based aid:* $12,256. *Average indebtedness upon graduation:* $51,131.
Applying *Application fee:* $50. *Required:* high school transcript, interview. *Application deadlines:* rolling (freshmen), rolling (transfers). *Notification:* continuous (freshmen), continuous (transfers).
Freshman Application Contact DeVry University, 2300 Southwest 145th Avenue, Miramar, FL 33027-4150. *Phone:* 954-499-9775. *Toll-free phone:* 866-338-7941. *Web site:* http://www.devry.edu/.

DeVry University
Orlando, Florida

- **Proprietary** comprehensive, founded 2000, part of DeVry University
- **Urban** campus
- **Coed** 1,656 undergraduate students, 41% full-time, 38% women, 63% men
- **Minimally difficult** entrance level

Undergraduates 678 full-time, 978 part-time. 7% are from out of state; 21% Black or African American, non-Hispanic/Latino; 23% Hispanic/Latino; 2% Asian, non-Hispanic/Latino; 0.2% Native Hawaiian or other Pacific Islander, non-Hispanic/Latino; 0.3% American Indian or Alaska Native, non-Hispanic/Latino; 1% Two or more races, non-Hispanic/Latino; 9% Race/ethnicity unknown; 2% international; 24% transferred in.
Freshmen *Admission:* 182 enrolled.

Faculty *Total:* 144, 15% full-time. *Student/faculty ratio:* 18:1.
Academics *Calendar:* semesters. *Degrees:* associate, bachelor's, master's, and postbachelor's certificates. *Special study options:* adult/continuing education programs, part-time degree program.
Computers on Campus Students can access the following: online (class) registration.
Student Life *Housing:* college housing not available.
Costs (2011–12) *Tuition:* $15,294 full-time, $597 per credit hour part-time. Full-time tuition and fees vary according to course load. Part-time tuition and fees vary according to course load. *Required fees:* $80 full-time, $40 per term part-time. *Payment plans:* installment, deferred payment. *Waivers:* employees or children of employees.
Financial Aid Of all full-time matriculated undergraduates who enrolled in 2007, 314 applied for aid, 294 were judged to have need, 2 had their need fully met. In 2007, 35 non-need-based awards were made. *Average percent of need met:* 33%. *Average financial aid package:* $10,774. *Average need-based loan:* $7062. *Average need-based gift aid:* $5608. *Average non-need-based aid:* $18,240. *Average indebtedness upon graduation:* $23,511.
Applying *Application fee:* $50. *Required:* high school transcript, interview. *Application deadlines:* rolling (freshmen), rolling (transfers). *Notification:* continuous (freshmen), continuous (transfers).
Freshman Application Contact DeVry University, 4000 Millenia Boulevard, Orlando, FL 32839. *Phone:* 407-345-2800. *Toll-free phone:* 866-338-7941. *Web site:* http://www.devry.edu/.

DeVry University
Tampa, Florida

Admissions Office Contact DeVry University, 3030 North Rocky Point Drive West, Suite 100, Tampa, FL 33607-5901. *Toll-free phone:* 866-338-7941. *Web site:* http://www.devry.edu/.

Eckerd College
St. Petersburg, Florida

- **Independent Presbyterian** 4-year, founded 1958
- **Suburban** 188-acre campus with easy access to Tampa
- **Endowment** $47.5 million
- **Coed** 1,843 undergraduate students, 98% full-time, 59% women, 41% men
- **Moderately difficult** entrance level, 53% of applicants were admitted

Undergraduates 1,815 full-time, 28 part-time. Students come from 48 states and territories; 30 other countries; 76% are from out of state; 3% Black or African American, non-Hispanic/Latino; 7% Hispanic/Latino; 1% Asian, non-Hispanic/Latino; 0.2% Native Hawaiian or other Pacific Islander, non-Hispanic/Latino; 0.3% American Indian or Alaska Native, non-Hispanic/Latino; 3% Two or more races, non-Hispanic/Latino; 2% Race/ethnicity unknown; 4% international; 4% transferred in; 80% live on campus. *Retention:* 81% of full-time freshmen returned.
Freshmen *Admission:* 3,713 applied, 1,977 admitted, 502 enrolled. *Average high school GPA:* 3.3. *Test scores:* SAT critical reading scores over 500: 81%; SAT math scores over 500: 76%; SAT writing scores over 500: 76%; ACT scores over 18: 97%; SAT critical reading scores over 600: 35%; SAT math scores over 600: 31%; SAT writing scores over 600: 30%; ACT scores over 24: 63%; SAT critical reading scores over 700: 6%; SAT math scores over 700: 3%; SAT writing scores over 700: 3%; ACT scores over 30: 11%.
Faculty *Total:* 163, 67% full-time, 82% with terminal degrees. *Student/faculty ratio:* 13:1.
Academics *Calendar:* 4-1-4. *Degree:* bachelor's. *Special study options:* accelerated degree program, adult/continuing education programs, advanced placement credit, double majors, external degree program, honors programs, independent study, internships, off-campus study, part-time degree program, services for LD students, student-designed majors, study abroad, summer session for credit. *ROTC:* Army (c), Air Force (c). *Unusual degree programs:* 3-2 engineering with Columbia University, Washington University in St. Louis.
Computers on Campus 300 computers/terminals and 2,000 ports are available on campus for general student use. Students can access the following: campus intranet, computer help desk, free student e-mail accounts, online (class) grades, online (class) registration, online (class) schedules, free computer repair shop. Campuswide network is available. 100% of college-owned or -operated housing units are wired for high-speed Internet access. Wireless service is available via entire campus.
Student Life *Housing:* on-campus residence required for freshman year. *Options:* coed, women-only. Campus housing is university owned. Freshman campus housing is guaranteed. *Activities and organizations:* drama/theater group, student-run newspaper, radio and television station, choral group, Earth Society, Water Search and Rescue Team, The Current (student newspaper), College Choir, Organization of Students. *Campus security:* 24-hour emer-

gency response devices and patrols, student patrols, late-night transport/escort service, controlled dormitory access. *Student services:* health clinic, personal/psychological counseling, women's center.
Athletics Member NCAA. All Division II. *Intercollegiate sports:* baseball M(s), basketball M(s)/W(s), golf M(s)/W(s), sailing M/W, soccer M(s)/W(s), softball W(s), tennis M(s)/W(s), volleyball W(s). *Intramural sports:* baseball M, basketball M/W, bowling M/W, cheerleading M(c)/W(c), equestrian sports M(c)/W(c), field hockey M(c)/W(c), football M(c)/W(c), golf M(c)/W(c), lacrosse M(c)/W(c), rugby M(c)/W(c), sailing M/W, soccer M(c)/W(c), softball M/W, swimming and diving M(c)/W(c), table tennis M/W, tennis M(c)/W(c), ultimate Frisbee M(c)/W(c), volleyball M/W.
Standardized Tests *Required:* SAT or ACT (for admission). *Recommended:* SAT Subject Tests (for admission).
Costs (2012–13) *Comprehensive fee:* $45,772 includes full-time tuition ($35,620), mandatory fees ($306), and room and board ($9846). Part-time tuition: $4192 per course. *College room only:* $4956. Room and board charges vary according to board plan and housing facility. *Payment plan:* installment. *Waivers:* employees or children of employees.
Financial Aid Of all full-time matriculated undergraduates who enrolled in 2011, 1,314 applied for aid, 1,074 were judged to have need, 210 had their need fully met. In 2011, 606 non-need-based awards were made. *Average percent of need met:* 87%. *Average financial aid package:* $28,312. *Average need-based loan:* $4540. *Average need-based gift aid:* $18,696. *Average non-need-based aid:* $11,730. *Average indebtedness upon graduation:* $32,245.
Applying *Options:* electronic application, early action, deferred entrance. *Application fee:* $40. *Required:* essay or personal statement, high school transcript, 1 letter of recommendation. *Recommended:* minimum 3.0 GPA, interview. *Application deadlines:* rolling (freshmen), rolling (transfers), 11/15 (early action). *Notification:* continuous (freshmen), continuous (transfers), 12/15 (early action).
Freshman Application Contact Ms. Donna Grosso, Eckerd College, 4200 54th Avenue South, St. Petersburg, FL 33711. *Phone:* 727-864-8331. *Toll-free phone:* 800-456-9009. *Fax:* 727-866-2304. *E-mail:* admissions@eckerd.edu. *Web site:* http://www.eckerd.edu/.

Edison State College
Fort Myers, Florida

Freshman Application Contact Lauren Willison, Admissions Specialist, Edison State College, 8099 College Parkway, Fort Myers, FL 33919. *Phone:* 239-489-9257. *Toll-free phone:* 800-749-2ECC. *E-mail:* Lauren.Willison@edison.edu. *Web site:* http://www.edison.edu/.

Edward Waters College
Jacksonville, Florida

- **Independent African Methodist Episcopal** 4-year, founded 1866
- **Urban** 50-acre campus
- **Coed** 751 undergraduate students, 98% full-time, 45% women, 55% men
- **Noncompetitive** entrance level, 23% of applicants were admitted

Undergraduates 739 full-time, 12 part-time. Students come from 21 states and territories; 4 other countries; 19% are from out of state; 94% Black or African American, non-Hispanic/Latino; 1% Hispanic/Latino; 0.1% Native Hawaiian or other Pacific Islander, non-Hispanic/Latino; 0.3% American Indian or Alaska Native, non-Hispanic/Latino; 1% Two or more races, non-Hispanic/Latino; 1% Race/ethnicity unknown. *Retention:* 53% of full-time freshmen returned.
Freshmen *Admission:* 1,611 applied, 365 admitted. *Average high school GPA:* 2.64.
Faculty *Total:* 81, 44% full-time. *Student/faculty ratio:* 9:1.
Academics *Calendar:* semesters. *Degree:* bachelor's. *Special study options:* academic remediation for entering students, adult/continuing education programs, cooperative education, honors programs, internships, off-campus study, part-time degree program, services for LD students, student-designed majors, summer session for credit. *ROTC:* Army (c). *Unusual degree programs:* 3-2 engineering with University of Miami.
Computers on Campus 200 computers/terminals and 200 ports are available on campus for general student use. Students can access the following: campus intranet, computer help desk, free student e-mail accounts, online (class) grades, online (class) registration, online (class) schedules. Campuswide network is available. Wireless service is available via entire campus.
Student Life *Housing options:* coed. Campus housing is university owned. *Activities and organizations:* drama/theater group, choral group, marching band, national fraternities, national sororities. *Campus security:* 24-hour emergency response devices and patrols, student patrols, late-night transport/escort service, controlled dormitory access. *Student services:* health clinic, personal/psychological counseling.

Athletics Member NAIA. *Intercollegiate sports:* basketball M(s)/W(s), tennis M(s)/W(s), track and field M(s)/W(s). *Intramural sports:* basketball M/W, football M, golf M, tennis M/W, volleyball M/W.

Standardized Tests *Required:* SAT or ACT (for admission).

Costs (2011–12) *Comprehensive fee:* $17,586 includes full-time tuition ($10,994) and room and board ($6592). Part-time tuition: $458 per credit hour. *College room only:* $3124. *Payment plan:* installment. *Waivers:* employees or children of employees.

Financial Aid Of all full-time matriculated undergraduates who enrolled in 2001, 1,242 applied for aid, 1,242 were judged to have need, 11 had their need fully met. 318 Federal Work-Study jobs (averaging $851). In 2001, 262 non-need-based awards were made. *Average percent of need met:* 61%. *Average financial aid package:* $4835. *Average need-based loan:* $2625. *Average need-based gift aid:* $4835. *Average non-need-based aid:* $1488. *Average indebtedness upon graduation:* $9000.

Applying *Options:* electronic application. *Application fee:* $25. *Required:* high school transcript, 2 letters of recommendation, medical forms. *Application deadlines:* rolling (freshmen), rolling (transfers). *Notification:* continuous (freshmen), continuous (transfers).

Freshman Application Contact Edward Waters College, 1658 Kings Road, Jacksonville, FL 32209-6199. *Phone:* 904-470-8202. *Toll-free phone:* 888-898-3191. *Web site:* http://www.ewc.edu/.

Embry-Riddle Aeronautical University–Daytona

Daytona Beach, Florida

- **Independent** comprehensive, founded 1926
- **Suburban** 178-acre campus with easy access to Orlando
- **Endowment** $62.4 million
- **Coed** 4,597 undergraduate students, 92% full-time, 15% women, 85% men
- **Moderately difficult** entrance level, 79% of applicants were admitted

Undergraduates 4,237 full-time, 360 part-time. Students come from 54 states and territories; 84 other countries; 64% are from out of state; 7% Black or African American, non-Hispanic/Latino; 10% Hispanic/Latino; 5% Asian, non-Hispanic/Latino; 0.2% Native Hawaiian or other Pacific Islander, non-Hispanic/Latino; 0.6% American Indian or Alaska Native, non-Hispanic/Latino; 1% Two or more races, non-Hispanic/Latino; 7% Race/ethnicity unknown; 14% international; 5% transferred in; 41% live on campus. *Retention:* 72% of full-time freshmen returned.

Freshmen *Admission:* 4,176 applied, 3,280 admitted, 1,046 enrolled. *Average high school GPA:* 3.29. *Test scores:* SAT math scores over 500: 78%; ACT scores over 18: 91%; SAT math scores over 600: 39%; ACT scores over 24: 61%; SAT math scores over 700: 9%; ACT scores over 30: 14%.

Faculty *Total:* 365, 72% full-time, 54% with terminal degrees. *Student/faculty ratio:* 15:1.

Academics *Calendar:* semesters. *Degrees:* associate, bachelor's, master's, and doctoral. *Special study options:* academic remediation for entering students, accelerated degree program, adult/continuing education programs, advanced placement credit, cooperative education, distance learning, double majors, English as a second language, honors programs, independent study, internships, part-time degree program, services for LD students, study abroad, summer session for credit. *ROTC:* Army (b), Navy (b), Air Force (b).

Computers on Campus 1,049 computers/terminals are available on campus for general student use. Students can access the following: campus intranet, computer help desk, free student e-mail accounts, online (class) grades, online (class) registration, online (class) schedules. Campuswide network is available. 100% of college-owned or -operated housing units are wired for high-speed Internet access. Wireless service is available via entire campus.

Student Life *Housing:* on-campus residence required for freshman year. *Options:* coed. Campus housing is university owned. Freshman campus housing is guaranteed. *Activities and organizations:* drama/theater group, student-run newspaper, radio station, choral group, Eagle Wing, Future Professional Pilots Association, African Student Association, Caribbean Student Association, Sigma Gamma Tau, national fraternities, national sororities. *Campus security:* 24-hour emergency response devices and patrols, student patrols, late-night transport/escort service, controlled dormitory access. *Student services:* health clinic, personal/psychological counseling, women's center.

Athletics Member NAIA. *Intercollegiate sports:* baseball M(s), basketball M(s), cheerleading M/W, cross-country running M(s)/W(s), golf M(s)/W(s), soccer M(s)/W(s), softball W(s), tennis M(s)/W(s), track and field M(s)/W(s), volleyball W(s). *Intramural sports:* basketball M/W, bowling M/W, crew M(c)/W(c), football M/W, golf M/W, ice hockey M(c), lacrosse M(c), racquetball M/W, rugby M(c), soccer M/W, softball M/W, swimming and diving M(c)/W(c), table tennis M/W, tennis M/W, ultimate Frisbee M(c)/W(c), volleyball M/W.

Standardized Tests *Required:* SAT or ACT (for admission).

Costs (2012–13) *Comprehensive fee:* $40,060 includes full-time tuition ($29,520), mandatory fees ($1200), and room and board ($9340). Part-time tuition: $1230 per credit hour. *College room only:* $5500. Room and board charges vary according to board plan and housing facility. *Payment plan:* deferred payment. *Waivers:* employees or children of employees.

Financial Aid Of all full-time matriculated undergraduates who enrolled in 2011, 3,111 applied for aid, 2,775 were judged to have need. 123 Federal Work-Study jobs (averaging $1008). 1,171 state and other part-time jobs (averaging $1700). *Average financial aid package:* $14,942. *Average need-based loan:* $4822. *Average need-based gift aid:* $9321.

Applying *Options:* electronic application, deferred entrance. *Application fee:* $50. *Required:* high school transcript, minimum 2.0 GPA, 2 letters of recommendation. *Required for some:* minimum 3.0 GPA, medical examination for flight students. *Recommended:* essay or personal statement, interview. *Application deadlines:* rolling (freshmen), 6/1 (transfers). *Notification:* continuous (freshmen), continuous (transfers).

Freshman Application Contact Embry-Riddle Aeronautical University–Daytona, 600 South Clyde Morris Boulevard, Daytona Beach, FL 32114-3900. *Phone:* 386-226-6100. *Toll-free phone:* 800-862-2416. *Fax:* 386-226-7070. *E-mail:* dbadmit@erau.edu. *Web site:* http://www.embryriddle.edu/.

See page 186 for display ad and page 1318 for the College Close-Up.

Embry-Riddle Aeronautical University–Worldwide

Daytona Beach, Florida

- **Independent** comprehensive, founded 1970
- **Endowment** $62.4 million
- **Coed** 10,907 undergraduate students, 25% full-time, 12% women, 88% men
- **Minimally difficult** entrance level

Undergraduates 2,719 full-time, 8,188 part-time. 6% Black or African American, non-Hispanic/Latino; 11% Hispanic/Latino; 2% Asian, non-Hispanic/Latino; 0.2% Native Hawaiian or other Pacific Islander, non-Hispanic/Latino; 0.3% American Indian or Alaska Native, non-Hispanic/Latino; 0.3% Two or more races, non-Hispanic/Latino; 44% Race/ethnicity unknown; 0.7% international.

Freshmen *Admission:* 515 enrolled.

Faculty *Total:* 2,650, 5% full-time, 21% with terminal degrees.

Academics *Calendar:* 5 9-week terms. *Degrees:* associate, bachelor's, master's, and doctoral (programs offered at 100 military bases worldwide). *Special study options:* adult/continuing education programs, advanced placement credit, cooperative education, distance learning, external degree program, independent study, off-campus study, part-time degree program, services for LD students.

Student Life *Housing:* college housing not available.

Standardized Tests *Required for some:* SAT or ACT (for admission).

Costs (2012–13) *Tuition:* $7320 full-time, $305 per credit part-time. *Waivers:* employees or children of employees.

Financial Aid Of all full-time matriculated undergraduates who enrolled in 2011, 899 applied for aid, 769 were judged to have need. *Average financial aid package:* $6690. *Average need-based loan:* $4438. *Average need-based gift aid:* $4249.

Applying *Options:* electronic application, deferred entrance. *Application fee:* $50. *Required for some:* essay or personal statement, high school transcript, 2 letters of recommendation, college transcript, statement of good standing from prior institution. *Application deadlines:* rolling (freshmen), rolling (transfers). *Notification:* continuous (freshmen), continuous (transfers).

Freshman Application Contact Embry-Riddle Aeronautical University–Worldwide, 600 South Clyde Morris Boulevard, Daytona Beach, FL 32114-3900. *Phone:* 866-509-0743. *Toll-free phone:* 800-522-6787. *Fax:* 386-226-6984. *E-mail:* ecinfo@erau.edu. *Web site:* http://www.embryriddle.edu/.

Everest University

Clearwater, Florida

Freshman Application Contact Mr. Kevin Buskirk, Director of Admissions, Everest University, 2471 McMullen Road, Clearwater, FL 33759. *Phone:* 727-725-2688. *Toll-free phone:* 888-741-4270. *Fax:* 727-796-3406. *E-mail:* kbuskirk@cci.edu. *Web site:* http://www.everest.edu/.

Everest University

Jacksonville, Florida

Director of Admissions Mr. Robin Manning, Admissions Director, Everest University, 8226 Phillips Highway, Jacksonville, FL 32256. *Phone:* 904-731-

4949. *Toll-free phone:* 888-741-4270. *E-mail:* rmanning@cci.edu. *Web site:* http://www.everest.edu/.

Everest University
Lakeland, Florida

- **Proprietary** 4-year, founded 1890, part of Corinthian Colleges, Inc.
- **Urban** 3-acre campus with easy access to Orlando, Tampa-St. Petersburg
- **Coed** 683 undergraduate students, 50% full-time, 79% women, 21% men
- **Minimally difficult** entrance level

Undergraduates 343 full-time, 340 part-time. Students come from 5 states and territories; 0.5% are from out of state; 28% Black or African American, non-Hispanic/Latino; 13% Hispanic/Latino; 0.5% Asian, non-Hispanic/Latino; 1% American Indian or Alaska Native, non-Hispanic/Latino; 2% Two or more races, non-Hispanic/Latino; 2% Race/ethnicity unknown; 1% transferred in. *Retention:* 3% of full-time freshmen returned.

Freshmen *Admission:* 302 enrolled.

Faculty *Total:* 36, 28% full-time, 100% with terminal degrees. *Student/faculty ratio:* 18:1.

Academics *Calendar:* quarters. *Degrees:* certificates, diplomas, associate, and bachelor's (bachelor's degree in business administration only). *Special study options:* academic remediation for entering students, accelerated degree program, adult/continuing education programs, distance learning, external degree program, independent study, internships, part-time degree program, services for LD students, summer session for credit.

Computers on Campus 50 computers/terminals are available on campus for general student use.

Student Life *Housing:* college housing not available. *Activities and organizations:* C. J. Association, Paralegal Society, Club Med, Phi Beta Lambda. *Campus security:* 24-hour patrols.

Standardized Tests *Required:* CPAt (for admission). *Recommended:* SAT or ACT (for admission).

Costs (2012–13) *Tuition:* $452 per credit part-time. Full-time tuition and fees vary according to course load, degree level, and program. Part-time tuition and fees vary according to course load, degree level, and program. *Payment plan:* installment.

Financial Aid Of all full-time matriculated undergraduates who enrolled in 2002, 679 applied for aid, 646 were judged to have need, 10 had their need fully met. 6 Federal Work-Study jobs (averaging $4863). *Average percent of need met:* 76%. *Average financial aid package:* $3510. *Average need-based loan:* $3875. *Average need-based gift aid:* $1000. *Average indebtedness upon graduation:* $29,852.

Applying *Options:* early admission. *Required:* high school transcript, interview. *Recommended:* essay or personal statement, high school transcript.

Freshman Application Contact Ms. Patricia Sabol, Director of Student Services, Everest University, 995 East Memorial Boulevard, Suite 110, Lakeland, FL 33801. *Phone:* 863-686-1444 Ext. 144. *Toll-free phone:* 888-741-4270. *E-mail:* psabol@cci.edu. *Web site:* http://www.everest.edu/.

Everest University
Melbourne, Florida

Director of Admissions Mr. Timothy Alexander, Director of Admissions, Everest University, 2401 North Harbor City Boulevard, Melbourne, FL 32935-6657. *Phone:* 321-253-2929 Ext. 121. *Web site:* http://www.everest.edu/.

Everest University
Orange Park, Florida

Freshman Application Contact Admissions Office, Everest University, 805 Wells Road, Orange Park, FL 32073. *Phone:* 904-264-9122. *Web site:* http://www.everest.edu/.

Everest University
Orlando, Florida

Freshman Application Contact Joann Derosa-Weber, Director of Admissions, Everest University, 5421 Diplomat Circle, Orlando, FL 32810-5674. *Phone:* 407-628-5870. *Toll-free phone:* 800-628-5870. *Fax:* 407-628-1344. *Web site:* http://www.everest.edu/.

Everest University
Orlando, Florida

Director of Admissions Ms. Annette Cloin, Director of Admissions, Everest University, 9200 South Park Center Loop, Orlando, FL 32819. *Phone:* 407-

851-2525 Ext. 111. *Toll-free phone:* 888-741-4270 (in-state); 888-471-4270 (out-of-state). *Fax:* 407-354-7946. *Web site:* http://www.everest.edu/.

Everest University
Pompano Beach, Florida

Freshman Application Contact Martin Levert, Director of Admissions, Everest University, 225 North Federal Highway, Pompano Beach, FL 33062. *Phone:* 954-783-7339. *Fax:* 954-943-2571. *Web site:* http://www.everest.edu/.

Everest University
Tampa, Florida

- **Proprietary** comprehensive, founded 1890, part of Corinthian Colleges, Inc.
- **Urban** 4-acre campus
- **Coed**
- **Minimally difficult** entrance level

Faculty *Student/faculty ratio:* 20:1.
Academics *Calendar:* quarters. *Degrees:* diplomas, associate, bachelor's, and master's.
Student Life *Campus security:* 24-hour emergency response devices, evening and Saturday afternoon patrols by trained security personnel.
Standardized Tests *Required:* CPAt (for admission). *Required for some:* SAT (for admission), ACT (for admission).
Costs (2011–12) *Tuition:* $15,336 full-time. *Payment plans:* installment, deferred payment.
Financial Aid *Of all full-time matriculated undergraduates who enrolled in 2006,* 1,054 applied for aid, 1,054 were judged to have need, 850 had their need fully met. 25 Federal Work-Study jobs (averaging $4000). *Average percent of need met:* 83. *Average financial aid package:* $6625. *Average need-based loan:* $2625. *Average need-based gift aid:* $1350. *Average indebtedness upon graduation:* $12,000.
Applying *Options:* deferred entrance. *Application fee:* $25. *Required:* high school transcript.
Freshman Application Contact Everest University, 3319 West Hillsborough Avenue, Tampa, FL 33614-5899. *Phone:* 813-879-6000 Ext. 129. *Web site:* http://www.everest.edu/.

Everest University
Tampa, Florida

- **Proprietary** comprehensive, founded 1890, part of Corinthian Colleges, Inc.
- **Urban** 5-acre campus with easy access to Tampa
- **Coed**
- **Minimally difficult** entrance level

Faculty *Student/faculty ratio:* 17:1.
Academics *Calendar:* quarters. *Degrees:* diplomas, associate, bachelor's, and master's.
Student Life *Campus security:* 24-hour emergency response devices, on-campus security guard on duty during business hours.
Costs (2011–12) *Tuition:* $16,272 full-time, $452 per credit hour part-time. Full-time tuition and fees vary according to degree level and program. Part-time tuition and fees vary according to degree level and program. *Required fees:* $180 full-time, $60 per term part-time. *Payment plans:* installment, deferred payment.
Financial Aid *Of all full-time matriculated undergraduates who enrolled in 2001,* 1,000 applied for aid, 900 were judged to have need. 41 Federal Work-Study jobs (averaging $2500). *In 2001,* 200 non-need-based awards were made. *Average percent of need met:* 15. *Average need-based loan:* $3500. *Average need-based gift aid:* $4000. *Average indebtedness upon graduation:* $15,000.
Applying *Options:* early admission, deferred entrance. *Application fee:* $25. *Required:* high school transcript, interview.
Freshman Application Contact Everest University, 3924 Coconut Palm Drive, Tampa, FL 33619. *Phone:* 813-621-0041 Ext. 106. *Toll-free phone:* 888-741-4270. *Web site:* http://www.everest.edu/.

Everglades University
Altamonte Springs, Florida

Freshman Application Contact Everglades University, 887 East Altamonte Drive, Altamonte Springs, FL 32701. *Phone:* 407-277-0311. *Toll-free phone:* 866-289-1078. *Web site:* http://www.evergladesuniversity.edu/.

Everglades University
Boca Raton, Florida

Freshman Application Contact Everglades University, 5002 T-Rex Avenue, Suite 100, Boca Raton, FL 33431. *Phone:* 561-912-1211. *Toll-free phone:* 888-772-6077. *Web site:* http://www.evergladesuniversity.edu/.

Everglades University
Sarasota, Florida

Director of Admissions Director of Admissions, Everglades University, 6001 Lake Osprey Drive #110, Sarasota, FL 34240. *Phone:* 941-907-2262. *Toll-free phone:* 866-907-2262. *Fax:* 941-907-6634. *E-mail:* admissions-sar@evergladesuniversity.edu. *Web site:* http://www.evergladesuniversity.edu/.

Flagler College
St. Augustine, Florida

- **Independent** 4-year, founded 1968
- **Small-town** 32-acre campus with easy access to Jacksonville
- **Endowment** $53.6 million
- **Coed** 2,878 undergraduate students, 97% full-time, 58% women, 42% men
- **Moderately difficult** entrance level, 40% of applicants were admitted

Undergraduates 2,787 full-time, 91 part-time. Students come from 44 states and territories; 35 other countries; 37% are from out of state; 3% Black or African American, non-Hispanic/Latino; 7% Hispanic/Latino; 0.6% Asian, non-Hispanic/Latino; 0.1% Native Hawaiian or other Pacific Islander, non-Hispanic/Latino; 0.6% American Indian or Alaska Native, non-Hispanic/Latino; 2% Two or more races, non-Hispanic/Latino; 5% Race/ethnicity unknown; 2% international; 6% transferred in; 40% live on campus. *Retention:* 84% of full-time freshmen returned.
Freshmen *Admission:* 3,933 applied, 1,588 admitted, 665 enrolled. *Average high school GPA:* 3.41. *Test scores:* SAT critical reading scores over 500: 90%; SAT math scores over 500: 87%; SAT writing scores over 500: 87%; ACT critical reading scores over 18: 99%; SAT critical reading scores over 600: 27%; SAT math scores over 600: 17%; SAT writing scores over 600: 14%; ACT scores over 24: 57%; SAT critical reading scores over 700: 3%; SAT math scores over 700: 1%; SAT writing scores over 700: 2%; ACT scores over 30: 3%.
Faculty *Total:* 223, 46% full-time, 40% with terminal degrees. *Student/faculty ratio:* 19:1.
Academics *Calendar:* semesters. *Degree:* bachelor's. *Special study options:* academic remediation for entering students, advanced placement credit, double majors, independent study, internships, services for LD students, study abroad, summer session for credit.
Computers on Campus 265 computers/terminals are available on campus for general student use. Students can access the following: campus intranet, computer help desk, free student e-mail accounts, online (class) grades, online (class) registration, online (class) schedules. Campuswide network is available. 100% of college-owned or -operated housing units are wired for high-speed Internet access. Wireless service is available via entire campus.
Student Life *Housing:* on-campus residence required for freshman year. *Options:* men-only, women-only. Campus housing is university owned. Freshman campus housing is guaranteed. *Activities and organizations:* drama/theater group, student-run newspaper, radio station, choral group, Student Government Association, Inter-Varsity, Campus Crusade, Mu Epsilon Nu (men's service club), Phi Alpha Omega (women's service club). *Campus security:* 24-hour emergency response devices and patrols, late-night transport/escort service, controlled dormitory access. *Student services:* health clinic, personal/psychological counseling.
Athletics Member NCAA. All Division II. *Intercollegiate sports:* baseball M(s), basketball M(s)/W(s), cross-country running M(s)/W(s), golf M(s)/W(s), lacrosse M(c), soccer M(s)/W(s), softball W(s), tennis M(s)/W(s), volleyball M(c)/W(s). *Intramural sports:* badminton M/W, basketball M/W, bowling M/W, football M/W, soccer M/W, softball M/W, swimming and diving M/W, table tennis M/W, tennis M/W, volleyball M/W, weight lifting M/W.
Standardized Tests *Required:* SAT or ACT (for admission).
Costs (2011–12) *Comprehensive fee:* $22,500 includes full-time tuition ($14,510) and room and board ($7990). Part-time tuition: $485 per credit hour. *Room and board:* Room and board charges vary according to board plan and housing facility. *Waivers:* employees or children of employees.
Financial Aid Of all full-time matriculated undergraduates who enrolled in 2011, 2,432 applied for aid, 1,797 were judged to have need, 292 had their need fully met. 243 Federal Work-Study jobs (averaging $1172). 70 state and other part-time jobs (averaging $1197). In 2011, 99 non-need-based awards were made. *Average percent of need met:* 80. *Average financial aid package:* $11,139. *Average need-based loan:* $4272. *Average need-based gift aid:*

$5122. *Average non-need-based aid:* $2850. *Average indebtedness upon graduation:* $23,424.

Applying *Options:* electronic application, early admission, early decision, deferred entrance. *Application fee:* $40. *Required:* essay or personal statement, high school transcript. *Recommended:* minimum 2.0 GPA, 1 letter of recommendation, interview, rank in upper 50% of high school class. *Application deadlines:* 3/1 (freshmen), 3/1 (transfers). *Early decision deadline:* 12/1. *Notification:* 3/30 (freshmen), 3/30 (transfers), 12/15 (early decision).

Freshman Application Contact Mr. Marc Williar, Director of Admissions, Flagler College, 74 King Street, St. Augustine, FL 32085. *Phone:* 904-819-6220. *Toll-free phone:* 800-304-4208. *Fax:* 904-819-6466. *E-mail:* admiss@flagler.edu. *Web site:* http://www.flagler.edu/.

Florida Agricultural and Mechanical University

Tallahassee, Florida

- **State-supported** university, founded 1887, part of State University System of Florida
- **Urban** 419-acre campus with easy access to Jacksonville
- **Endowment** $79.7 million
- **Coed** 11,180 undergraduate students, 91% full-time, 60% women, 40% men
- **Moderately difficult** entrance level, 48% of applicants were admitted

Undergraduates 10,165 full-time, 1,015 part-time. Students come from 42 states and territories; 71 other countries; 17% are from out of state; 94% Black or African American, non-Hispanic/Latino; 1% Hispanic/Latino; 0.7% Asian, non-Hispanic/Latino; 0.2% American Indian or Alaska Native, non-Hispanic/Latino; 0.1% Two or more races, non-Hispanic/Latino; 0.7% international; 5% transferred in; 25% live on campus. *Retention:* 79% of full-time freshmen returned.

Freshmen *Admission:* 7,322 applied, 3,540 admitted, 1,970 enrolled. *Average high school GPA:* 3.1. *Test scores:* SAT critical reading scores over 500: 33%; SAT math scores over 500: 35%; SAT writing scores over 500: 29%; ACT scores over 18: 87%; SAT critical reading scores over 600: 7%; SAT math scores over 600: 7%; SAT writing scores over 600: 6%; ACT scores over 24: 17%; SAT critical reading scores over 700: 1%; SAT math scores over 700: 1%; ACT scores over 30: 1%.

Faculty *Total:* 720, 75% full-time, 57% with terminal degrees. *Student/faculty ratio:* 21:1.

Academics *Calendar:* semesters. *Degrees:* associate, bachelor's, master's, doctoral, post-master's, and first professional certificates. *Special study options:* academic remediation for entering students, accelerated degree program, adult/continuing education programs, advanced placement credit, cooperative education, distance learning, double majors, honors programs, independent study, internships, off-campus study, part-time degree program, services for LD students, study abroad, summer session for credit. *ROTC:* Army (b), Navy (b), Air Force (c). *Unusual degree programs:* 3-2 business administration; occupational therapy, architecture.

Computers on Campus 3,500 computers/terminals and 5,900 ports are available on campus for general student use. Students can access the following: campus intranet, computer help desk, free student e-mail accounts, online (class) grades, online (class) registration, online (class) schedules. Campuswide network is available. 100% of college-owned or -operated housing units are wired for high-speed Internet access. Wireless service is available via classrooms, computer centers, computer labs, dorm rooms, learning centers, libraries, student centers.

Student Life *Housing:* on-campus residence required for freshman year. *Options:* coed, men-only, women-only, disabled students. Campus housing is university owned. Freshman applicants given priority for college housing. *Activities and organizations:* drama/theater group, student-run newspaper, radio and television station, choral group, marching band, National Council of Negro Women, FAMU Chapter, American Society of Mechanical Engineers, Psi Chi International Honor Society, Caribbean Student Association, Academy of Student Pharmacists/Student National Pharmaceutical Association, national fraternities, national sororities. *Campus security:* 24-hour emergency response devices and patrols, late-night transport/escort service, controlled dormitory access. *Student services:* health clinic, personal/psychological counseling.

Athletics Member NCAA. All Division I except football (Division I-AA). *Intercollegiate sports:* baseball M(s), basketball M(s)/W(s), bowling W(s), cheerleading M/W, cross-country running M(s)/W(s), golf M(s)/W(s), softball W(s), swimming and diving M(s)/W(s), tennis M(s)/W(s), track and field M(s)/W(s), volleyball W(s). *Intramural sports:* badminton M/W, basketball M/W, bowling M/W, cheerleading W, football M, golf M/W, gymnastics M/W, racquetball M/W, skiing (downhill) M/W, soccer M/W, softball M/W, swimming and diving M/W, table tennis M/W, tennis M/W, track and field M/W, ultimate Frisbee M/W, volleyball M/W, weight lifting M/W, wrestling M/W.

Standardized Tests *Required:* SAT or ACT (for admission).

Costs (2012–13) *Tuition:* state resident $4929 full-time, $164 per credit part-time; nonresident $16,869 full-time, $562 per credit part-time. *Required fees:* $258 full-time, $129 per term part-time. *Room and board:* $8754; room only: $4928. Room and board charges vary according to board plan and housing facility. *Payment plan:* tuition prepayment. *Waivers:* senior citizens and employees or children of employees.

Financial Aid Of all full-time matriculated undergraduates who enrolled in 2010, 8,426 applied for aid, 8,245 were judged to have need, 2,003 had their need fully met. 394 Federal Work-Study jobs (averaging $1763). In 2010, 85 non-need-based awards were made. *Average percent of need met:* 77%. *Average financial aid package:* $12,829. *Average need-based loan:* $4072. *Average need-based gift aid:* $6328. *Average non-need-based aid:* $2629. *Average indebtedness upon graduation:* $29,554.

Applying *Options:* electronic application, early admission. *Application fee:* $30. *Required:* essay or personal statement, high school transcript, minimum 2.5 GPA, 3 letters of recommendation. *Required for some:* interview, audition required of music major applicants. *Recommended:* minimum 3.0 GPA. *Application deadlines:* 5/15 (freshmen), 5/15 (out-of-state freshmen), 5/15 (transfers). *Notification:* continuous (freshmen), continuous (out-of-state freshmen), continuous (transfers).

Freshman Application Contact Ms. Barbara R. Cox, Director, Admissions, Florida Agricultural and Mechanical University, Office of Admissions, Florida A & M University, Tallahassee, FL 32307. *Phone:* 850-599-3796. *Toll-free phone:* 866-642-1198. *Fax:* 850-599-3069. *E-mail:* ugrdadmissions@famu.edu. *Web site:* http://www.famu.edu/.

Florida Atlantic University

Boca Raton, Florida

- **State-supported** university, founded 1961, part of State University System of Florida
- **Suburban** 850-acre campus with easy access to Miami, Fort Lauderdale, Palm Beach
- **Coed** 24,281 undergraduate students, 62% full-time, 57% women, 43% men
- **Moderately difficult** entrance level, 35% of applicants were admitted

Undergraduates 15,164 full-time, 9,117 part-time. Students come from 50 states and territories; 138 other countries; 4% are from out of state; 18% Black or African American, non-Hispanic/Latino; 23% Hispanic/Latino; 4% Asian, non-Hispanic/Latino; 0.1% Native Hawaiian or other Pacific Islander, non-Hispanic/Latino; 0.2% American Indian or Alaska Native, non-Hispanic/Latino; 2% Two or more races, non-Hispanic/Latino; 0.7% Race/ethnicity unknown; 1% international; 14% transferred in; 6% live on campus. *Retention:* 79% of full-time freshmen returned.

Freshmen *Admission:* 28,197 applied, 9,805 admitted, 3,347 enrolled. *Average high school GPA:* 3.3. *Test scores:* SAT critical reading scores over 500: 70%; SAT math scores over 500: 73%; SAT writing scores over 500: 65%; ACT scores over 18: 100%; SAT critical reading scores over 600: 16%; SAT math scores over 600: 20%; SAT writing scores over 600: 13%; ACT scores over 24: 39%; SAT critical reading scores over 700: 2%; SAT math scores over 700: 2%; SAT writing scores over 700: 2%; ACT scores over 30: 4%.

Faculty *Total:* 1,332, 60% full-time, 52% with terminal degrees. *Student/faculty ratio:* 20:1.

Academics *Calendar:* semesters. *Degrees:* certificates, associate, bachelor's, master's, doctoral, post-master's, and first professional certificates. *Special study options:* accelerated degree program, adult/continuing education programs, advanced placement credit, cooperative education, distance learning, double majors, English as a second language, freshman honors college, honors programs, independent study, internships, off-campus study, part-time degree program, services for LD students, study abroad, summer session for credit. *ROTC:* Army (b), Air Force (c).

Computers on Campus 1,000 computers/terminals are available on campus for general student use. Students can access the following: campus intranet, computer help desk, free student e-mail accounts, online (class) grades, online (class) registration, online (class) schedules. Campuswide network is available. Wireless service is available via entire campus.

Student Life *Housing:* on-campus residence required for freshman year. *Options:* coed, women-only. Campus housing is university owned. Freshman campus housing is guaranteed. *Activities and organizations:* drama/theater group, student-run newspaper, radio and television station, choral group, marching band, American Society of Civil Engineers, Dive Club, Pre-Law Society, Submarine Club, American Criminal Justice Society, national fraternities, national sororities. *Campus security:* 24-hour emergency response devices and patrols, student patrols, late-night transport/escort service, controlled dormitory access. *Student services:* health clinic, personal/psychological counseling, women's center.

Athletics Member NCAA. All Division I. *Intercollegiate sports:* baseball M(s), basketball M(s)/W(s), cheerleading M/W, cross-country running M/W, football M(s), golf M(s)/W(s), soccer M/W, softball W(s), swimming and diving M/W, tennis M/W, track and field W, volleyball W(s). *Intramural sports:* baseball M/W, bowling M/W, football M, ice hockey M(c)/W(c), lacrosse M(c), rock climbing M(c)/W(c), rugby M(c)/W(c), sailing M(c)/W(c), soccer M/W, softball W, table tennis M/W, ultimate Frisbee M/W, volleyball M/W, weight lifting M(c), wrestling M(c).

Standardized Tests *Required:* SAT or ACT (for admission).

Costs (2011–12) *Tuition:* state resident $5330 full-time, $178 per credit hour part-time; nonresident $19,715 full-time, $657 per credit hour part-time. Full-time tuition and fees vary according to course load. Part-time tuition and fees vary according to course load. *Room and board:* $10,940. Room and board charges vary according to board plan and housing facility. *Payment plans:* tuition prepayment, installment, deferred payment. *Waivers:* senior citizens and employees or children of employees.

Financial Aid Of all full-time matriculated undergraduates who enrolled in 2011, 12,489 applied for aid, 9,973 were judged to have need, 1,409 had their need fully met. 156 Federal Work-Study jobs (averaging $3444). 5 state and other part-time jobs (averaging $2000). In 2011, 182 non-need-based awards were made. *Average percent of need met:* 67%. *Average financial aid package:* $10,278. *Average need-based loan:* $6457. *Average need-based gift aid:* $5742. *Average non-need-based aid:* $3151. *Average indebtedness upon graduation:* $19,100.

Applying *Options:* electronic application, early admission, deferred entrance. *Application fee:* $30. *Required:* high school transcript. *Application deadline:* 5/1 (freshmen).

Freshman Application Contact Assistant Director, Florida Atlantic University, 777 Glades Road, PO Box 3091, Boca Raton, FL 33431-0991. *Phone:* 561-297-3040. *Fax:* 561-297-2758. *Web site:* http://www.fau.edu/.

See page 1332 for the College Close-Up.

Florida Christian College

Kissimmee, Florida

Director of Admissions Admissions Office, Florida Christian College, 1011 Bill Beck Boulevard, Kissimmee, FL 34744-5301. *Phone:* 407-569-1172. *Toll-free phone:* 888-GO-TO-FCC. *E-mail:* admissionsforms@fcc.edu. *Web site:* http://www.fcc.edu/.

Florida College

Temple Terrace, Florida

- **Independent** 4-year, founded 1944
- **Small-town** 95-acre campus with easy access to Tampa
- **Endowment** $10.4 million
- **Coed** 502 undergraduate students, 94% full-time, 53% women, 47% men
- **Moderately difficult** entrance level, 94% of applicants were admitted

Undergraduates 474 full-time, 28 part-time. Students come from 4 other countries; 66% are from out of state; 5% Black or African American, non-Hispanic/Latino; 6% Hispanic/Latino; 0.4% Asian, non-Hispanic/Latino; 0.6% Native Hawaiian or other Pacific Islander, non-Hispanic/Latino; 0.4% American Indian or Alaska Native, non-Hispanic/Latino; 3% Two or more races, non-Hispanic/Latino; 0.8% international; 3% transferred in; 81% live on campus.

Freshmen *Admission:* 378 applied, 356 admitted, 181 enrolled. *Test scores:* SAT critical reading scores over 500: 66%; SAT math scores over 500: 55%; SAT writing scores over 500: 51%; ACT scores over 18: 84%; SAT critical reading scores over 600: 23%; SAT math scores over 600: 20%; SAT writing scores over 600: 17%; ACT scores over 24: 38%; SAT critical reading scores over 700: 4%; SAT math scores over 700: 1%; SAT writing scores over 700: 3%; ACT scores over 30: 7%.

Faculty *Total:* 56, 66% full-time, 30% with terminal degrees. *Student/faculty ratio:* 11:1.

Academics *Calendar:* semesters. *Degrees:* associate and bachelor's. *Special study options:* academic remediation for entering students, advanced placement credit, independent study, summer session for credit. *ROTC:* Army (c), Air Force (c).

Computers on Campus 36 computers/terminals are available on campus for general student use. Students can access the following: campus intranet, computer help desk, free student e-mail accounts, online (class) grades, online (class) schedules. Campuswide network is available. 100% of college-owned or -operated housing units are wired for high-speed Internet access. Wireless service is available via classrooms, computer centers, computer labs, dorm rooms, libraries, student centers.

Student Life *Housing:* on-campus residence required through sophomore year. *Options:* men-only, women-only. Campus housing is university owned. Freshman campus housing is guaranteed. *Activities and organizations:* drama/theater group, choral group, Co-ed Societies, Circle K, NAFME, SBGA, Footlighters. *Campus security:* controlled dormitory access, evening patrols

by trained security personnel. *Student services:* health clinic, personal/psychological counseling.

Athletics Member USCAA. *Intercollegiate sports:* basketball M(s)/W(c), cheerleading W, cross-country running M/W, soccer M(s)/W(s), volleyball W(s). *Intramural sports:* basketball M/W, football M/W, soccer M/W, softball M/W, ultimate Frisbee M/W, volleyball M/W.

Standardized Tests *Required:* SAT or ACT (for admission).

Costs (2012–13) *One-time required fee:* $150. *Comprehensive fee:* $20,730 includes full-time tuition ($12,400), mandatory fees ($780), and room and board ($7550). Part-time tuition: $500 per credit hour. Part-time tuition and fees vary according to course load. *Room and board:* Room and board charges vary according to board plan and housing facility. *Payment plan:* installment. *Waivers:* employees or children of employees.

Financial Aid Of all full-time matriculated undergraduates who enrolled in 2010, 389 applied for aid, 321 were judged to have need, 29 had their need fully met. 25 Federal Work-Study jobs (averaging $831). In 2010, 65 non-need-based awards were made. *Average percent of need met:* 56%. *Average financial aid package:* $12,257. *Average need-based loan:* $3980. *Average need-based gift aid:* $6069. *Average non-need-based aid:* $2524.

Applying *Options:* electronic application. *Application fee:* $30. *Required:* high school transcript, minimum 2.0 GPA, 2 letters of recommendation. *Required for some:* essay required for international students. *Application deadlines:* 8/1 (freshmen), 8/1 (transfers). *Notification:* continuous (freshmen), continuous (transfers).

Freshman Application Contact Mrs. Colleen Engel, Assistant Director of Admissions, Florida College, 119 North Glen Arven Avenue, Temple Terrace, FL 33617. *Phone:* 813-988-5131 Ext. 152. *Fax:* 813-899-6772. *E-mail:* admissions@floridacollege.edu. *Web site:* http://www.floridacollege.edu/.

Florida Gateway College

Lake City, Florida

Freshman Application Contact Florida Gateway College, Lake City, FL 32025-8703. *Fax:* 386-755-1521. *E-mail:* admissions@mail.lakecity.cc.fl.us. *Web site:* http://www.fgc.edu/.

Florida Gulf Coast University

Fort Myers, Florida

- **State-supported** comprehensive, founded 1991, part of State University System of Florida
- **Suburban** 760-acre campus
- **Endowment** $56.7 million
- **Coed** 11,291 undergraduate students, 81% full-time, 55% women, 45% men
- **Moderately difficult** entrance level, 66% of applicants were admitted

Undergraduates 9,110 full-time, 2,181 part-time. Students come from 47 states and territories; 87 other countries; 7% are from out of state; 6% Black or African American, non-Hispanic/Latino; 16% Hispanic/Latino; 2% Asian, non-Hispanic/Latino; 0.2% Native Hawaiian or other Pacific Islander, non-Hispanic/Latino; 0.3% American Indian or Alaska Native, non-Hispanic/Latino; 2% Two or more races, non-Hispanic/Latino; 1% Race/ethnicity unknown; 1% international; 10% transferred in; 30% live on campus. *Retention:* 65% of full-time freshmen returned.

Freshmen *Admission:* 2,709 applied, 1,789 admitted, 2,581 enrolled. *Average high school GPA:* 3.32. *Test scores:* SAT critical reading scores over 500: 57%; SAT math scores over 500: 60%; SAT writing scores over 500: 49%; ACT scores over 18: 93%; SAT critical reading scores over 600: 12%; SAT math scores over 600: 12%; SAT writing scores over 600: 8%; ACT scores over 24: 23%; SAT critical reading scores over 700: 2%; SAT math scores over 700: 1%; ACT scores over 30: 1%.

Faculty *Total:* 630, 63% full-time, 47% with terminal degrees. *Student/faculty ratio:* 22:1.

Academics *Calendar:* semesters. *Degrees:* certificates, associate, bachelor's, master's, and doctoral. *Special study options:* academic remediation for entering students, accelerated degree program, advanced placement credit, cooperative education, distance learning, double majors, honors programs, independent study, internships, off-campus study, part-time degree program, services for LD students, study abroad, summer session for credit.

Computers on Campus 871 computers/terminals are available on campus for general student use. Students can access the following: online (class) registration, online admissions and advising. Campuswide network is available. 100% of college-owned or -operated housing units are wired for high-speed Internet access.

Student Life *Housing options:* coed. Campus housing is university owned. *Activities and organizations:* drama/theater group, student-run newspaper, student government, Ignite (Religious Organization), International Club, Martial Arts Club, Physical Therapy Association, national fraternities, national sorori-

ties. *Campus security:* 24-hour emergency response devices and patrols, late-night transport/escort service. *Student services:* health clinic, personal/psychological counseling.

Athletics Member NCAA. All Division I. *Intercollegiate sports:* baseball M(s), basketball M(s)/W(s), cheerleading W, cross-country running M(s)/W(s), golf M(s)/W(s), soccer M(s)/W(s), softball W(s), swimming and diving W(s), tennis M(s)/W(s), volleyball W(s). *Intramural sports:* basketball M/W, cross-country running M(c)/W(c), fencing M(c)/W(c), football M/W, ice hockey M(c), lacrosse M(c)/W(c), sailing M(c)/W(c), skiing (downhill) M(c)/W(c), soccer M/W, softball M/W, swimming and diving M(c)/W(c), table tennis M/W, tennis M(c)/W(c), ultimate Frisbee M/W, volleyball M/W, water polo M/W, weight lifting M(c)/W(c), wrestling M(c)/W(c).

Standardized Tests *Required:* SAT or ACT (for admission), SAT and SAT Subject Tests or ACT (for admission).

Costs (2011–12) *Tuition:* state resident $5352 full-time, $184 per credit hour part-time; nonresident $22,822 full-time, $772 per credit hour part-time. Full-time tuition and fees vary according to course load. Part-time tuition and fees vary according to course load. *Room and board:* $8771. Room and board charges vary according to board plan.

Financial Aid Of all full-time matriculated undergraduates who enrolled in 2010, 6,702 applied for aid, 3,730 were judged to have need, 346 had their need fully met. In 2010, 285 non-need-based awards were made. *Average percent of need met:* 68%. *Average financial aid package:* $9780. *Average need-based loan:* $7235. *Average need-based gift aid:* $5391. *Average non-need-based aid:* $3576. *Average indebtedness upon graduation:* $22,171. *Financial aid deadline:* 6/30.

Applying *Options:* electronic application, deferred entrance. *Application fee:* $30. *Required:* high school transcript, minimum 2.0 GPA. *Application deadlines:* 7/1 (freshmen), 7/1 (transfers). *Notification:* continuous (freshmen), continuous (transfers).

Freshman Application Contact Florida Gulf Coast University, 10501 FGCU Boulevard South, Fort Myers, FL 33965-6565. *Phone:* 239-590-7878. *Toll-free phone:* 888-889-1095. *Web site:* http://www.fgcu.edu/.

Florida Hospital College of Health Sciences

Orlando, Florida

Freshman Application Contact Florida Hospital College of Health Sciences, 671 Winyah Drive, Orlando, FL 32803. *Phone:* 407-303-7742. *Toll-free phone:* 800-500-7747. *Web site:* http://www.fhchs.edu/.

Florida Institute of Technology

Melbourne, Florida

- **Independent** university, founded 1958
- **Small-town** 130-acre campus with easy access to Orlando
- **Endowment** $49.6 million
- **Coed** 5,387 undergraduate students, 77% full-time, 48% women, 52% men
- **Moderately difficult** entrance level, 57% of applicants were admitted

Undergraduates 4,155 full-time, 1,232 part-time. Students come from 51 states and territories; 88 other countries; 62% are from out of state; 15% Black or African American, non-Hispanic/Latino; 6% Hispanic/Latino; 2% Asian, non-Hispanic/Latino; 0.2% Native Hawaiian or other Pacific Islander, non-Hispanic/Latino; 0.7% American Indian or Alaska Native, non-Hispanic/Latino; 1% Two or more races, non-Hispanic/Latino; 9% Race/ethnicity unknown; 15% international; 4% transferred in; 51% live on campus. *Retention:* 80% of full-time freshmen returned.

Freshmen *Admission:* 6,841 applied, 3,925 admitted, 669 enrolled. *Average high school GPA:* 3.5. *Test scores:* SAT critical reading scores over 500: 76%; SAT math scores over 500: 90%; ACT scores over 18: 98%; SAT critical reading scores over 600: 30%; SAT math scores over 600: 53%; ACT scores over 24: 63%; SAT critical reading scores over 700: 5%; SAT math scores over 700: 10%; ACT scores over 30: 15%.

Faculty *Total:* 616, 38% full-time, 68% with terminal degrees. *Student/faculty ratio:* 19:1.

Academics *Calendar:* semesters. *Degrees:* associate, bachelor's, master's, doctoral, post-master's, and first professional certificates. *Special study options:* academic remediation for entering students, accelerated degree program, adult/continuing education programs, advanced placement credit, cooperative education, distance learning, double majors, English as a second language, independent study, internships, part-time degree program, services for LD students, student-designed majors, study abroad, summer session for credit. *ROTC:* Army (b).

Computers on Campus 415 computers/terminals and 75 ports are available on campus for general student use. Students can access the following: com-

puter help desk, free student e-mail accounts, online (class) grades, online (class) registration, online (class) schedules. Campuswide network is available. 100% of college-owned or -operated housing units are wired for high-speed Internet access. Wireless service is available via classrooms, computer centers, computer labs, dorm rooms, learning centers, libraries, student centers.

Student Life *Housing:* on-campus residence required through sophomore year. *Options:* coed. Campus housing is university owned. Freshman campus housing is guaranteed. *Activities and organizations:* drama/theater group, student-run newspaper, radio and television station, choral group, FITSSFF, College Players, Saudi Student House, Squamish, Phi Eta Sigma National Honor Society, national fraternities, national sororities. *Campus security:* 24-hour emergency response devices and patrols, late-night transport/escort service, controlled dormitory access. *Student services:* health clinic, personal/psychological counseling.

Athletics Member NCAA. All Division II. *Intercollegiate sports:* baseball M(s), basketball M(s)/W(s), crew W(s), cross-country running M(s)/W(s), football M(c)/W(c), golf M(s)/W(s), soccer M(s)/W(s), softball W(s), tennis M(s)/W(s), ultimate Frisbee M(c)/W(c), volleyball W(s), water polo M(c)/W(c). *Intramural sports:* badminton M/W, baseball M(c)/W(c), basketball M/W, bowling M/W, cheerleading M(c)/W(c), crew M(c)/W(c), fencing M(c)/W(c), football M/W, golf M/W, ice hockey M/W, sailing M(c)/W(c), soccer M/W, softball M/W, swimming and diving M(c)/W(c), table tennis M(c)/W(c), tennis M/W, ultimate Frisbee M/W, volleyball M/W, water polo M/W, weight lifting M/W, wrestling M(c)/W(c).

Standardized Tests *Required:* SAT or ACT (for admission).

Costs (2011–12) *Comprehensive fee:* $46,810 includes full-time tuition ($34,430), mandatory fees ($560), and room and board ($11,820). Full-time tuition and fees vary according to course load, program, and student level. Part-time tuition: $995 per credit hour. *College room only:* $6940. Room and board charges vary according to board plan and housing facility. *Payment plan:* installment. *Waivers:* senior citizens and employees or children of employees.

Financial Aid Of all full-time matriculated undergraduates who enrolled in 2011, 1,690 applied for aid, 1,503 were judged to have need, 357 had their need fully met. 677 Federal Work-Study jobs (averaging $1262). 3 state and other part-time jobs (averaging $1975). In 2011, 592 non-need-based awards were made. *Average percent of need met:* 81%. *Average financial aid package:* $30,585. *Average need-based loan:* $4767. *Average need-based gift aid:* $20,597. *Average non-need-based aid:* $11,214. *Average indebtedness upon graduation:* $39,007.

Applying *Options:* electronic application, deferred entrance. *Application fee:* $50. *Required:* essay or personal statement, high school transcript, minimum 2.6 GPA, 2 letters of recommendation, SAT or ACT. *Recommended:* minimum 3.3 GPA, interview. *Application deadlines:* rolling (freshmen), rolling (transfers). *Notification:* continuous (freshmen), continuous (transfers).

Freshman Application Contact Bob Rowe, Director of Undergraduate Admission, Florida Institute of Technology, 150 West University Boulevard, Melbourne, FL 32901-6975. *Phone:* 321-674-7554. *Toll-free phone:* 800-888-4348. *Fax:* 321-723-9468. *E-mail:* admission@fit.edu. *Web site:* http://www.fit.edu/.

Florida International University

Miami, Florida

- **State-supported** university, founded 1965, part of State University System of Florida
- **Urban** 573-acre campus with easy access to Miami
- **Endowment** $136.2 million
- **Coed** 35,875 undergraduate students, 65% full-time, 55% women, 45% men
- **Moderately difficult** entrance level, 39% of applicants were admitted

Undergraduates 23,152 full-time, 12,723 part-time. Students come from 51 states and territories; 147 other countries; 3% are from out of state; 12% Black or African American, non-Hispanic/Latino; 66% Hispanic/Latino; 3% Asian, non-Hispanic/Latino; 0.1% Native Hawaiian or other Pacific Islander, non-Hispanic/Latino; 0.4% American Indian or Alaska Native, non-Hispanic/Latino; 1% Two or more races, non-Hispanic/Latino; 1% Race/ethnicity unknown; 5% international; 13% transferred in; 7% live on campus. *Retention:* 82% of full-time freshmen returned.

Freshmen *Admission:* 16,626 applied, 6,545 admitted, 4,473 enrolled. *Average high school GPA:* 3.7. *Test scores:* SAT critical reading scores over 500: 93%; SAT math scores over 500: 91%; SAT writing scores over 500: 92%; ACT scores over 18: 100%; SAT critical reading scores over 600: 35%; SAT

math scores over 600: 31%; SAT writing scores over 600: 28%; ACT scores over 24: 76%; SAT critical reading scores over 700: 4%; SAT math scores over 700: 2%; SAT writing scores over 700: 2%; ACT scores over 30: 5%.

Faculty *Total:* 1,941, 52% full-time, 68% with terminal degrees. *Student/faculty ratio:* 27:1.

Academics *Calendar:* semesters. *Degrees:* bachelor's, master's, doctoral, postbachelor's, and first professional certificates. *Special study options:* accelerated degree program, adult/continuing education programs, advanced placement credit, cooperative education, distance learning, double majors, freshman honors college, honors programs, independent study, internships, off-campus study, part-time degree program, services for LD students, study abroad, summer session for credit. *ROTC:* Army (b), Air Force (b).

Computers on Campus Students can access the following: computer help desk, free student e-mail accounts, online (class) grades, online (class) registration, online (class) schedules, online financial and cashier's information; class schedule, financial, campus maps information available on cell phones. Campuswide network is available. 100% of college-owned or -operated housing units are wired for high-speed Internet access. Wireless service is available via entire campus.

Student Life *Housing options:* coed. Campus housing is university owned. *Activities and organizations:* drama/theater group, student-run newspaper, radio station, choral group, marching band, Students for Community Service, Black Student Leadership Council, Hospitality Management Student Club, Hispanic Students Association, Haitian Students Organization, national fraternities, national sororities. *Campus security:* 24-hour emergency response devices and patrols, late-night transport/escort service, controlled dormitory access. *Student services:* health clinic, personal/psychological counseling, women's center.

Athletics Member NCAA. All Division I. *Intercollegiate sports:* baseball M(s), basketball M(s)/W(s), cross-country running M(s)/W(s), football M(s), golf W(s), soccer M(s)/W(s), softball W(s), swimming and diving W(s), tennis W(s), track and field M(s)/W(s), volleyball W(s). *Intramural sports:* badminton M(c)/W(c), baseball M(c), basketball M/W, cheerleading M(c)/W(c), crew M(c)/W(c), cross-country running M(c)/W(c), equestrian sports M(c)/W(c), golf W, lacrosse M(c)/W(c), racquetball M/W, rugby M(c)/W(c), sailing M/W, soccer M/W, softball M/W, swimming and diving M(c)/W(c), table tennis M/W, tennis M(c)/W(c), ultimate Frisbee M/W, volleyball M/W, water polo M(c), weight lifting M/W, wrestling M(c)/W(c).

Standardized Tests *Required:* SAT or ACT (for admission), TOEFL is required of all applicants whose native language is not English (for admission). *Recommended:* SAT Subject Tests (for admission).

Costs (2011–12) *Tuition:* state resident $5327 full-time, $178 per credit hour part-time; nonresident $17,726 full-time, $591 per credit hour part-time. Full-time tuition and fees vary according to course load. Part-time tuition and fees vary according to course load. *Required fees:* $351 full-time. *Room and board:* $11,330. Room and board charges vary according to board plan and housing facility. *Payment plan:* installment. *Waivers:* senior citizens and employees or children of employees.

Financial Aid Of all full-time matriculated undergraduates who enrolled in 2011, 14,484 applied for aid, 14,259 were judged to have need, 1,662 had their need fully met. 478 Federal Work-Study jobs (averaging $3511). 14 state and other part-time jobs (averaging $5651). In 2011, 985 non-need-based awards were made. *Average percent of need met:* 21%. *Average financial aid package:* $9060. *Average need-based loan:* $9565. *Average need-based gift aid:* $6488. *Average non-need-based aid:* $661. *Average indebtedness upon graduation:* $17,231. *Financial aid deadline:* 5/15.

Applying *Options:* electronic application. *Application fee:* $30. *Required:* high school transcript, minimum 3.0 GPA. *Required for some:* portfolio, audition. *Application deadlines:* rolling (freshmen), rolling (out-of-state freshmen), rolling (transfers). *Notification:* continuous (freshmen), continuous (out-of-state freshmen), continuous (transfers).

Freshman Application Contact Mr. Barry Taylor, Director of Admissions, Florida International University, 11200 SW Eighth Street, PC 140, Miami, FL 33199. *Phone:* 305-348-2363. *Fax:* 305-348-3648. *E-mail:* admiss@fiu.edu. *Web site:* http://www.fiu.edu/.

Florida Memorial University

Miami-Dade, Florida

Director of Admissions Mrs. Peggy Murray Martin, Director of Admissions and International Student Advisor, Florida Memorial University, 15800 NW 42nd Avenue, Miami-Dade, FL 33054. *Phone:* 305-626-3147. *Toll-free phone:* 800-822-1362. *Web site:* http://www.fmuniv.edu/.

Florida National College
Hialeah, Florida

- **Proprietary** comprehensive, founded 1982
- **Urban** 4-acre campus with easy access to Miami
- **Coed** 2,744 undergraduate students, 72% full-time, 70% women, 30% men
- **Moderately difficult** entrance level, 93% of applicants were admitted

Undergraduates 1,973 full-time, 771 part-time. Students come from 13 states and territories; 16 other countries; 1% are from out of state; 6% Black or African American, non-Hispanic/Latino; 88% Hispanic/Latino; 0.5% Asian, non-Hispanic/Latino; 0.1% American Indian or Alaska Native, non-Hispanic/Latino; 0.4% Two or more races, non-Hispanic/Latino; 4% international; 4% transferred in. *Retention:* 69% of full-time freshmen returned.

Freshmen *Admission:* 1,947 applied, 1,819 admitted, 564 enrolled.

Faculty *Total:* 147, 57% full-time, 13% with terminal degrees. *Student/faculty ratio:* 21:1.

Academics *Calendar:* semesters. *Degrees:* certificates, diplomas, associate, bachelor's, and master's. *Special study options:* academic remediation for entering students, accelerated degree program, adult/continuing education programs, advanced placement credit, cooperative education, distance learning, English as a second language, independent study, internships, part-time degree program, services for LD students, summer session for credit.

Computers on Campus 230 computers/terminals are available on campus for general student use. Students can access the following: computer help desk, online (class) grades, online (class) registration, online (class) schedules. Campuswide network is available. Wireless service is available via entire campus.

Student Life *Housing:* college housing not available. *Activities and organizations:* student-run newspaper, Student Government Association, Bible Club, Salsa Club, W.I.C.S (Women Community Service), Criminal Justice Society, national fraternities. *Campus security:* 24-hour emergency response devices.

Standardized Tests *Required:* SAT or ACT (for admission).

Costs (2012–13) *Tuition:* $12,600 full-time, $525 per credit part-time. No tuition increase for student's term of enrollment. *Required fees:* $570 full-time. *Payment plans:* tuition prepayment, installment. *Waivers:* employees or children of employees.

Financial Aid Of all full-time matriculated undergraduates who enrolled in 2009, 1,344 applied for aid, 1,330 were judged to have need. 14 Federal Work-Study jobs (averaging $7253). *Average need-based gift aid:* $4650. *Average indebtedness upon graduation:* $8750.

Applying *Options:* electronic application, deferred entrance. *Required:* high school transcript, interview. *Application deadlines:* rolling (freshmen), rolling (transfers). *Notification:* continuous (freshmen), continuous (transfers).

Freshman Application Contact Mr. Guillermo Araya, Director of Admissions, Florida National College, 4425 West Dr. Jose Regueiro Avenue (20th), Hialeah, FL 33012. *Phone:* 305-821-3333 Ext. 1015. *Fax:* 305-362-0595. *E-mail:* garaya@mm.fnc.edu. *Web site:* http://www.fnc.edu/.

Florida Southern College
Lakeland, Florida

- **Independent** comprehensive, founded 1885, affiliated with United Methodist Church
- **Suburban** 100-acre campus with easy access to Tampa, Orlando
- **Endowment** $80.8 million
- **Coed** 2,040 undergraduate students, 98% full-time, 58% women, 42% men
- **Moderately difficult** entrance level, 65% of applicants were admitted

Undergraduates 2,001 full-time, 39 part-time. Students come from 43 states and territories; 39 other countries; 34% are from out of state; 6% Black or African American, non-Hispanic/Latino; 8% Hispanic/Latino; 2% Asian, non-Hispanic/Latino; 0.0% Native Hawaiian or other Pacific Islander, non-Hispanic/Latino; 0.5% American Indian or Alaska Native, non-Hispanic/Latino; 2% Two or more races, non-Hispanic/Latino; 0.1% Race/ethnicity unknown; 4% international; 6% transferred in; 74% live on campus. *Retention:* 77% of full-time freshmen returned.

Freshmen *Admission:* 3,159 applied, 2,056 admitted, 525 enrolled. *Average high school GPA:* 3.51. *Test scores:* SAT critical reading scores over 500: 74%; SAT math scores over 500: 74%; SAT writing scores over 500: 64%; ACT scores over 18: 100%; SAT critical reading scores over 600: 23%; SAT math scores over 600: 20%; SAT writing scores over 600: 16%; ACT scores over 24: 46%; SAT critical reading scores over 700: 2%; SAT math scores over 700: 2%; SAT writing scores over 700: 1%; ACT scores over 30: 6%.

Faculty *Total:* 223, 52% full-time, 53% with terminal degrees. *Student/faculty ratio:* 13:1.

Academics *Calendar:* semesters. *Degrees:* bachelor's and master's. *Special study options:* adult/continuing education programs, advanced placement credit, double majors, honors programs, independent study, internships, off-campus study, part-time degree program, student-designed majors, study abroad, summer session for credit. *ROTC:* Army (b), Air Force (c). *Unusual*

degree programs: 3-2 business administration with Students can now follow a focused enrollment track that includes summer enrollment to complete the BA in Business Administration in three years and proceed directly into the MBA. Students still must meet all MBA admission requirements.

Computers on Campus 483 computers/terminals and 50 ports are available on campus for general student use. Students can access the following: campus intranet, computer help desk, free student e-mail accounts, online (class) grades, online (class) registration, online (class) schedules, campus portal. Campuswide network is available. 100% of college-owned or -operated housing units are wired for high-speed Internet access. Wireless service is available via classrooms, computer labs, dorm rooms, libraries, student centers.

Student Life *Housing:* on-campus residence required through senior year. *Options:* coed, men-only, women-only, disabled students. Campus housing is university owned. Freshman campus housing is guaranteed. *Activities and organizations:* drama/theater group, student-run newspaper, television station, choral group, Student Government Association, Toastmasters, Association of Campus Entertainment, Beyond (Campus Ministry), Fellowship of Christian Athletes, national fraternities, national sororities. *Campus security:* 24-hour emergency response devices and patrols, student patrols, late-night transport/escort service, controlled dormitory access. *Student services:* health clinic, personal/psychological counseling.

Athletics Member NCAA. All Division II. *Intercollegiate sports:* baseball M(s), basketball M(s)/W(s), cheerleading W(c), cross-country running M(s)/W(s), golf M(s)/W(s), lacrosse M(s)/W(s), soccer M(s)/W(s), softball W(s), swimming and diving M(s)/W(s), tennis M(s)/W(s), track and field M(s)/W(s), volleyball M(c)/W(s). *Intramural sports:* basketball M/W, bowling M/W, cross-country running M/W, football M/W, golf M/W, soccer M/W, softball M/W, swimming and diving M/W, table tennis M/W, tennis M/W, ultimate Frisbee M/W, volleyball M/W.

Standardized Tests *Required:* SAT or ACT (for admission).

Costs (2012–13) *Comprehensive fee:* $36,300 includes full-time tuition ($26,600), mandatory fees ($600), and room and board ($9100). Full-time tuition and fees vary according to student level. Part-time tuition: $780 per semester hour. Part-time tuition and fees vary according to class time. *College room only:* $5000. Room and board charges vary according to board plan and housing facility. *Payment plan:* installment. *Waivers:* children of alumni and employees or children of employees.

Financial Aid Of all full-time matriculated undergraduates who enrolled in 2011, 1,744 applied for aid, 1,466 were judged to have need, 403 had their need fully met. 168 Federal Work-Study jobs (averaging $1500). 370 state and other part-time jobs (averaging $1200). In 2011, 331 non-need-based awards were made. *Average percent of need met:* 72%. *Average financial aid package:* $21,405. *Average need-based loan:* $4345. *Average need-based gift aid:* $8562. *Average non-need-based aid:* $9861. *Average indebtedness upon graduation:* $20,580. *Financial aid deadline:* 7/1.

Applying *Options:* electronic application, early admission, early decision, deferred entrance. *Application fee:* $30. *Required:* essay or personal statement, high school transcript, 1 letter of recommendation. *Recommended:* minimum 2.0 GPA, interview. *Application deadlines:* 3/1 (freshmen), rolling (transfers). *Early decision deadline:* 12/1. *Notification:* continuous (freshmen), continuous (transfers), 12/15 (early decision).

Freshman Application Contact Florida Southern College, 111 Lake Hollingsworth Drive, Lakeland, FL 33801-5698. *Phone:* 863-680-4131. *Toll-free phone:* 800-274-4131. *Web site:* http://www.flsouthern.edu/.

See page 1334 for the College Close-Up.

Florida State College at Jacksonville

Jacksonville, Florida

- **State-supported** primarily 2-year, founded 1963, part of Florida College System
- **Urban** 825-acre campus
- **Endowment** $28.8 million
- **Coed** 30,863 undergraduate students, 35% full-time, 60% women, 40% men
- **Noncompetitive** entrance level, 48% of applicants were admitted

Undergraduates 10,778 full-time, 20,085 part-time. 28% Black or African American, non-Hispanic/Latino; 4% Hispanic/Latino; 3% Asian, non-Hispanic/Latino; 0.6% Native Hawaiian or other Pacific Islander, non-Hispanic/Latino; 0.5% American Indian or Alaska Native, non-Hispanic/Latino; 1% Two or more races, non-Hispanic/Latino; 15% Race/ethnicity unknown; 0.8% international; 7% transferred in. *Retention:* 36% of full-time freshmen returned.

Freshmen *Admission:* 8,562 applied, 4,148 admitted, 4,864 enrolled.

Faculty *Total:* 1,205, 34% full-time, 18% with terminal degrees. *Student/faculty ratio:* 29:1.

Academics *Calendar:* semesters. *Degrees:* certificates, diplomas, associate, and bachelor's. *Special study options:* academic remediation for entering stu-

dents, accelerated degree program, adult/continuing education programs, advanced placement credit, cooperative education, distance learning, double majors, English as a second language, honors programs, independent study, internships, off-campus study, part-time degree program, services for LD students, study abroad, summer session for credit. *ROTC:* Navy (c).

Computers on Campus 2,500 computers/terminals are available on campus for general student use. Students can access the following: campus intranet, computer help desk, free student e-mail accounts, online (class) grades, online (class) registration, online (class) schedules. Campuswide network is available. Wireless service is available via entire campus.

Student Life *Activities and organizations:* drama/theater group, student-run newspaper, radio and television station, choral group, Phi Theta Kappa, Forensic Team, Brain Bowl Team, International Student Association, DramaWorks. *Campus security:* 24-hour emergency response devices and patrols, late-night transport/escort service. *Student services:* personal/psychological counseling, women's center.

Athletics Member NJCAA. *Intercollegiate sports:* baseball M(s), basketball M(s)/W(s), softball W(s), tennis W(s), volleyball W(s). *Intramural sports:* badminton M/W, basketball M/W, bowling M/W, football M/W, golf M/W, soccer M/W, softball M/W, table tennis M/W, tennis M/W, volleyball M/W.

Costs (2011–12) *Tuition:* state resident $2387 full-time, $99 per credit hour part-time; nonresident $9171 full-time, $382 per credit hour part-time. Full-time tuition and fees vary according to degree level and program. Part-time tuition and fees vary according to degree level and program. *Payment plan:* installment. *Waivers:* employees or children of employees.

Applying *Options:* electronic application, early admission, deferred entrance. *Application fee:* $25. *Required:* high school transcript. *Application deadlines:* rolling (freshmen), rolling (out-of-state freshmen), rolling (transfers).

Freshman Application Contact Dr. Peter Biegel, AVP, Enrollment Management, Florida State College at Jacksonville, 501 West State Street, Jacksonville, FL 32202. *Phone:* 904-632-3131. *Toll-free phone:* 888-873-1145. *Fax:* 904-632-5105. *E-mail:* pbiegel@fscj.edu. *Web site:* http://www.fscj.edu/.

Florida State University

Tallahassee, Florida

- **State-supported** university, founded 1851, part of State University System of Florida
- **Suburban** 451-acre campus
- **Endowment** $525.3 million
- **Coed** 32,201 undergraduate students, 90% full-time, 55% women, 45% men
- **Very difficult** entrance level, 58% of applicants were admitted

Undergraduates 28,864 full-time, 3,337 part-time. Students come from 52 states and territories; 101 other countries; 9% are from out of state; 10% Black or African American, non-Hispanic/Latino; 14% Hispanic/Latino; 4% Asian, non-Hispanic/Latino; 1% American Indian or Alaska Native, non-Hispanic/Latino; 1% Race/ethnicity unknown; 0.8% international; 7% transferred in; 15% live on campus. *Retention:* 93% of full-time freshmen returned.

Freshmen *Admission:* 28,313 applied, 16,561 admitted, 6,121 enrolled. *Average high school GPA:* 3.79. *Test scores:* SAT critical reading scores over 500: 97%; SAT math scores over 500: 97%; SAT writing scores over 500: 96%; ACT scores over 18: 100%; SAT critical reading scores over 600: 52%; SAT math scores over 600: 53%; SAT writing scores over 600: 50%; ACT scores over 24: 90%; SAT critical reading scores over 700: 10%; SAT math scores over 700: 7%; SAT writing scores over 700: 8%; ACT scores over 30: 14%.

Faculty *Total:* 1,624, 77% full-time, 92% with terminal degrees. *Student/faculty ratio:* 26:1.

Academics *Calendar:* semesters. *Degrees:* certificates, associate, bachelor's, master's, doctoral, post-master's, postbachelor's, and first professional certificates. *Special study options:* accelerated degree program, advanced placement credit, cooperative education, distance learning, double majors, English as a second language, honors programs, independent study, internships, off-campus study, part-time degree program, services for LD students, study abroad, summer session for credit. *ROTC:* Army (b), Navy (c), Air Force (b).

Computers on Campus 3,821 computers/terminals are available on campus for general student use. Students can access the following: computer help desk, free student e-mail accounts, online (class) grades, online (class) registration, online (class) schedules, course home pages, course search, online fee payment. Campuswide network is available. 90% of college-owned or -operated housing units are wired for high-speed Internet access. Wireless service is available via entire campus.

Student Life *Housing options:* coed, women-only, cooperative, disabled students. Campus housing is university owned. Freshman applicants given priority for college housing. *Activities and organizations:* drama/theater group, student-run newspaper, radio and television station, choral group, marching band, student government, honors program, Golden Key Honor Society,

Marching Chiefs, intramural sports, national fraternities, national sororities. *Campus security:* 24-hour emergency response devices and patrols, late-night transport/escort service, controlled dormitory access. *Student services:* health clinic, personal/psychological counseling, women's center, legal services.

Athletics Member NCAA. All Division I except football (Division I-A). *Intercollegiate sports:* baseball M(s), basketball M(s)/W(s), bowling M(c)/W(c), cheerleading M/W, cross-country running M(s)/W(s), golf M(s)/W(s), rugby M(c)/W(c), soccer M(c)/W(s), softball W(s), swimming and diving M(s)/W(s), table tennis M(c)/W(c), tennis M(s)/W(s), track and field M(s)/W(s), volleyball M(c)/W(s), wrestling M(c)/W(c). *Intramural sports:* badminton M(c)/W(c), baseball M(c), basketball M/W, bowling M/W, crew M(c)/W(c), equestrian sports M(c)/W(c), fencing M(c)/W(c), field hockey W(c), football M/W, golf M/W, gymnastics W(c), ice hockey M(c)/W(c), lacrosse M(c)/W(c), racquetball M/W, sailing M(c)/W(c), soccer M/W, softball M/W, squash M(c)/W(c), swimming and diving M/W, table tennis M/W, tennis M/W, track and field M/W, ultimate Frisbee M(c)/W(c), volleyball M/W, water polo M(c)/W(c), weight lifting M/W, wrestling M/W.

Standardized Tests *Required:* SAT or ACT (for admission).

Costs (2011–12) *Tuition:* state resident $3397 full-time, $135 per credit hour part-time; nonresident $18,564 full-time, $617 per credit hour part-time. Full-time tuition and fees vary according to course load, degree level, and location. Part-time tuition and fees vary according to course load, degree level, and location. *Required fees:* $2428 full-time, $20 per credit hour part-time. *Room and board:* $9412; room only: $5668. Room and board charges vary according to board plan and housing facility. *Payment plans:* tuition prepayment, installment. *Waivers:* senior citizens and employees or children of employees.

Financial Aid Of all full-time matriculated undergraduates who enrolled in 2011, 25,375 applied for aid, 11,812 were judged to have need, 7,660 had their need fully met. 834 Federal Work-Study jobs (averaging $1200). 28 state and other part-time jobs (averaging $1200). In 2011, 2040 non-need-based awards were made. *Average percent of need met:* 64%. *Average financial aid package:* $9464. *Average need-based loan:* $3862. *Average need-based gift aid:* $3779. *Average non-need-based aid:* $2298. *Average indebtedness upon graduation:* $22,139.

Applying *Options:* electronic application, early admission. *Application fee:* $30. *Required:* high school transcript. *Recommended:* essay or personal statement. *Application deadlines:* 1/14 (freshmen), 1/14 (out-of-state freshmen), 7/1 (transfers). *Notification:* 3/20 (freshmen), 3/20 (out-of-state freshmen), continuous (transfers).

Freshman Application Contact Florida State University, Tallahassee, FL 32306. *Phone:* 850-644-6200. *Web site:* http://www.fsu.edu/.

Full Sail University
Winter Park, Florida

Freshman Application Contact Ms. Mary Beth Plank, Director of Admissions, Full Sail University, 3300 University Boulevard, Winter Park, FL 32792-7437. *Phone:* 407-679-6333. *Toll-free phone:* 800-226-7625. *E-mail:* admissions@fullsail.com. *Web site:* http://www.fullsail.edu/.

Gulf Coast State College
Panama City, Florida

- **State-supported** primarily 2-year, founded 1957
- **Suburban** 80-acre campus
- **Endowment** $25.9 million
- **Coed** 6,436 undergraduate students, 38% full-time, 63% women, 37% men
- **Noncompetitive** entrance level

Undergraduates 2,414 full-time, 4,022 part-time. Students come from 21 states and territories; 6% are from out of state; 11% Black or African American, non-Hispanic/Latino; 8% Hispanic/Latino; 2% Asian, non-Hispanic/Latino; 0.2% Native Hawaiian or other Pacific Islander, non-Hispanic/Latino; 0.5% American Indian or Alaska Native, non-Hispanic/Latino; 3% Two or more races, non-Hispanic/Latino; 2% Race/ethnicity unknown; 0.6% international; 4% transferred in.

Freshmen *Admission:* 653 enrolled.

Faculty *Total:* 304, 38% full-time. *Student/faculty ratio:* 21:1.

Academics *Calendar:* semesters. *Degrees:* certificates, associate, and bachelor's. *Special study options:* academic remediation for entering students, accelerated degree program, adult/continuing education programs, advanced placement credit, cooperative education, distance learning, double majors, English as a second language, external degree program, honors programs, independent study, off-campus study, part-time degree program, services for LD students, summer session for credit.

Computers on Campus 1,000 computers/terminals are available on campus for general student use. Students can access the following: computer help desk, free student e-mail accounts, online (class) grades, online (class) registration,

online (class) schedules. Campuswide network is available. Wireless service is available via entire campus.

Student Life *Housing:* college housing not available. *Activities and organizations:* drama/theater group, student-run newspaper, television station, choral group. *Campus security:* late-night transport/escort service, patrols by trained security personnel during campus hours. *Student services:* personal/psychological counseling.

Athletics Member NJCAA. *Intercollegiate sports:* baseball M(s), basketball M(s)/W(s), softball W(s), volleyball W(s).

Costs (2012–13) *One-time required fee:* $20. *Tuition:* state resident $2370 full-time, $99 per credit hour part-time; nonresident $8635 full-time, $360 per credit hour part-time. Full-time tuition and fees vary according to degree level. Part-time tuition and fees vary according to degree level.

Financial Aid Of all full-time matriculated undergraduates who enrolled in 2010, 145 Federal Work-Study jobs (averaging $3200). 60 state and other part-time jobs (averaging $2600).

Applying *Options:* electronic application, early admission, deferred entrance. *Application fee:* $20. *Required:* high school transcript. *Application deadlines:* rolling (freshmen), rolling (transfers). *Notification:* continuous (freshmen).

Freshman Application Contact Mrs. Jackie Kuczenski, Administrative Secretary of Admissions, Gulf Coast State College, 5230 West U.S. Highway 98, Panama City, FL 32401. *Phone:* 850-769-1551 Ext. 4892. *Fax:* 850-913-3308. *E-mail:* jkuczenski@gulfcoast.edu. *Web site:* http://www.gulfcoast.edu/.

Herzing University
Winter Park, Florida

Director of Admissions Tessie Uranga, Director of Admissions, Herzing University, 1595 South Semoran Boulevard, Winter Park, FL 32792. *Phone:* 407-478-0500. *Toll-free phone:* 800-596-0724. *Fax:* 407-380-0269. *Web site:* http://www.herzing.edu/.

Hobe Sound Bible College
Hobe Sound, Florida

Freshman Application Contact Director of Admissions, Hobe Sound Bible College, PO Box 1065, Hobe Sound, FL 33475-1065. *Phone:* 772-545-1400. *E-mail:* info@hsbc.edu. *Web site:* http://www.hsbc.edu/.

Hodges University
Naples, Florida

- **Independent** comprehensive, founded 1990
- **Suburban** campus with easy access to Miami
- **Endowment** $4.7 million
- **Coed** 2,172 undergraduate students, 72% full-time, 67% women, 33% men
- **Minimally difficult** entrance level, 78% of applicants were admitted

Undergraduates 1,559 full-time, 613 part-time. Students come from 36 states and territories; 1 other country; 6% are from out of state; 16% Black or African American, non-Hispanic/Latino; 33% Hispanic/Latino; 0.9% Asian, non-Hispanic/Latino; 0.1% Native Hawaiian or other Pacific Islander, non-Hispanic/Latino; 0.5% American Indian or Alaska Native, non-Hispanic/Latino; 0.4% Two or more races, non-Hispanic/Latino; 2% Race/ethnicity unknown; 18% transferred in.

Freshmen *Admission:* 217 applied, 170 admitted, 162 enrolled.

Faculty *Total:* 168, 55% full-time, 44% with terminal degrees. *Student/faculty ratio:* 15:1.

Academics *Calendar:* trimesters. *Degrees:* certificates, associate, bachelor's, and master's. *Special study options:* academic remediation for entering students, accelerated degree program, adult/continuing education programs, advanced placement credit, cooperative education, distance learning, double majors, English as a second language, external degree program, independent study, internships, part-time degree program, services for LD students, summer session for credit.

Computers on Campus 1,020 computers/terminals are available on campus for general student use. Students can access the following: computer help desk, free student e-mail accounts, online (class) grades, online (class) registration, online (class) schedules. Campuswide network is available. Wireless service is available via entire campus.

Student Life *Housing:* college housing not available. *Activities and organizations:* Ambassadors, Paralegal Club, Institute of Managerial Accountants, running club, Entrepreneurial Club. *Campus security:* late-night transport/escort service, building security. *Student services:* personal/psychological counseling.

Standardized Tests *Required for some:* CPAt.

Costs (2011–12) *Tuition:* $11,280 full-time, $470 per credit hour part-time. *Required fees:* $500 full-time, $250 per term part-time. *Payment plan:* installment. *Waivers:* employees or children of employees.

Financial Aid Of all full-time matriculated undergraduates who enrolled in 2010, 1,558 applied for aid, 1,402 were judged to have need, 285 had their need fully met. 50 Federal Work-Study jobs (averaging $3931). In 2010, 71 non-need-based awards were made. *Average percent of need met:* 76%. *Average financial aid package:* $9275. *Average need-based loan:* $4310. *Average need-based gift aid:* $4625. *Average non-need-based aid:* $220. *Average indebtedness upon graduation:* $18,900.

Applying *Options:* electronic application, deferred entrance. *Application fee:* $20. *Required:* essay or personal statement, high school transcript, interview. *Required for some:* 2 letters of recommendation. *Application deadlines:* rolling (freshmen), rolling (transfers). *Notification:* continuous (freshmen), continuous (transfers).

Freshman Application Contact Hodges University, 2655 Northbrooke Drive, Naples, FL 34119. *Phone:* 239-513-1122 Ext. 104. *Toll-free phone:* 800-466-8017. *Web site:* http://www.hodges.edu/.

Indian River State College

Fort Pierce, Florida

- **State-supported** primarily 2-year, founded 1960, part of Florida Community College System
- **Small-town** 310-acre campus
- **Coed** 17,528 undergraduate students, 35% full-time, 60% women, 40% men
- **Noncompetitive** entrance level, 100% of applicants were admitted

Undergraduates 6,177 full-time, 11,351 part-time. Students come from 28 states and territories; 130 other countries; 13% are from out of state; 17% Black or African American, non-Hispanic/Latino; 14% Hispanic/Latino; 2% Asian, non-Hispanic/Latino; 0.2% Native Hawaiian or other Pacific Islander, non-Hispanic/Latino; 0.2% American Indian or Alaska Native, non-Hispanic/Latino; 0.8% Two or more races, non-Hispanic/Latino; 3% Race/ethnicity unknown; 1% international; 14% transferred in.

Freshmen *Admission:* 1,855 applied, 1,855 admitted, 2,123 enrolled. *Average high school GPA:* 2.83.

Faculty *Total:* 967, 22% full-time, 16% with terminal degrees. *Student/faculty ratio:* 22:1.

Academics *Calendar:* semesters. *Degrees:* certificates, diplomas, associate, and bachelor's. *Special study options:* academic remediation for entering students, adult/continuing education programs, advanced placement credit, distance learning, English as a second language, independent study, part-time degree program, services for LD students, summer session for credit.

Computers on Campus 2,000 computers/terminals are available on campus for general student use. Students can access the following: computer help desk, free student e-mail accounts, online (class) grades, online (class) registration, online (class) schedules. Campuswide network is available. Wireless service is available via classrooms, computer centers, computer labs, learning centers, libraries, student centers.

Student Life *Housing:* college housing not available. *Activities and organizations:* drama/theater group, choral group. *Campus security:* 24-hour emergency response devices and patrols. *Student services:* health clinic, personal/psychological counseling, women's center.

Athletics Member NJCAA. *Intercollegiate sports:* baseball M(s), basketball M(s)/W(s), softball W(s), swimming and diving M(s)/W(s), volleyball W(s). *Intramural sports:* basketball M/W, racquetball M/W, soccer M, volleyball M/W.

Applying *Options:* early admission, deferred entrance. *Required:* high school transcript. *Application deadlines:* rolling (freshmen), rolling (transfers). *Notification:* continuous (freshmen), continuous (transfers).

Freshman Application Contact Mr. Steven Payne, Dean of Educational Services, Indian River State College, 3209 Virginia Avenue, Fort Pierce, FL 34981-5596. *Phone:* 772-462-7805. *Toll-free phone:* 866-792-4772. *E-mail:* spayne@ircc.edu. *Web site:* http://www.irsc.edu/.

International Academy of Design & Technology

Tampa, Florida

- **Proprietary** 4-year, founded 1984, part of Career Education Corporation
- **Urban** 1-acre campus
- **Coed**
- **Noncompetitive** entrance level

Faculty *Total:* 95. *Student/faculty ratio:* 21:1.

Academics *Calendar:* quarters. *Degrees:* associate and bachelor's. *Special study options:* academic remediation for entering students, accelerated degree program, cooperative education, distance learning, independent study, internships, part-time degree program, services for LD students, study abroad, summer session for credit.

Computers on Campus 485 computers/terminals are available on campus for general student use. Campuswide network is available.

Student Life *Housing:* college housing not available. *Options:* Campus housing is provided by a third party. *Activities and organizations:* Student Chapter ASID, IIDA, Emerging Professionals, United States Greenbuilding Council (USGBC), American Advertising Federation. *Campus security:* 24-hour emergency response devices, late night patrols by trained security personnel.

Standardized Tests *Required:* Wonderlic Assessment (for admission).

Costs (2011–12) *Comprehensive fee:* $20,756 includes full-time tuition ($13,860), mandatory fees ($600), and room and board ($6296). Part-time tuition: $385 per credit hour. *College room only:* $3392. *Payment plans:* installment, deferred payment. *Waivers:* employees or children of employees.

Financial Aid *Average percent of need met:* 48%.

Applying *Options:* electronic application, early admission, deferred entrance. *Application fee:* $50. *Required:* interview, Wonderlic Assessment. *Application deadlines:* rolling (freshmen), rolling (out-of-state freshmen), rolling (transfers). *Notification:* continuous (freshmen), continuous (out-of-state freshmen), continuous (transfers).

Freshman Application Contact International Academy of Design & Technology, 5104 Eisenhower Boulevard, Tampa, FL 33634-7350. *Phone:* 813-881-0007. *Toll-free phone:* 888-315-6111. *Web site:* http://www.academy.edu/.

ITT Technical Institute

Bradenton, Florida

- **Proprietary** primarily 2-year, part of ITT Educational Services, Inc.
- **Coed**

Academics *Calendar:* quarters. *Degrees:* associate and bachelor's.

Freshman Application Contact Director of Recruitment, ITT Technical Institute, 8039 Cooper Creek Boulevard, Bradenton, FL 34201. *Phone:* 941-309-9200. *Toll-free phone:* 800-342-8684. *Web site:* http://www.itt-tech.edu/.

ITT Technical Institute

Deerfield Beach, Florida

- **Proprietary** 4-year
- **Coed**
- **Minimally difficult** entrance level

Academics *Degrees:* associate and bachelor's.

Freshman Application Contact Director of Recruitment, ITT Technical Institute, 700 W. Hillsboro Boulevard, Suite 100, Building 1, Deerfield Beach, FL 33441. *Phone:* 954-360-4701. *Toll-free phone:* 877-243-8548. *Web site:* http://www.itt-tech.edu/.

ITT Technical Institute

Fort Lauderdale, Florida

- **Proprietary** primarily 2-year, founded 1991, part of ITT Educational Services, Inc.
- **Suburban** campus
- **Coed**
- **Minimally difficult** entrance level

Academics *Calendar:* quarters. *Degrees:* associate and bachelor's.

Student Life *Housing:* college housing not available.

Freshman Application Contact Director of Recruitment, ITT Technical Institute, 3401 South University Drive, Fort Lauderdale, FL 33328-2021. *Phone:* 954-476-9300. *Toll-free phone:* 800-488-7797. *Web site:* http://www.itt-tech.edu/.

ITT Technical Institute

Fort Myers, Florida

- **Proprietary** primarily 2-year
- **Coed**
- **Minimally difficult** entrance level

Academics *Degrees:* associate and bachelor's.

Freshman Application Contact Director of Recruitment, ITT Technical Institute, 13500 Powers Court, Suite 100, Fort Myers, FL 33912. *Phone:* 239-603-8700. *Toll-free phone:* 877-485-5313. *Web site:* http://www.itt-tech.edu/.

ITT Technical Institute

Jacksonville, Florida

- **Proprietary** primarily 2-year, founded 1991, part of ITT Educational Services, Inc.
- **Urban** campus
- **Coed**
- **Minimally difficult** entrance level

Academics *Calendar:* quarters. *Degrees:* associate and bachelor's.

Student Life *Housing:* college housing not available.

Financial Aid Of all full-time matriculated undergraduates who enrolled in 2010, 5 Federal Work-Study jobs.

Freshman Application Contact Director of Recruitment, ITT Technical Institute, 7011 A.C. Skinner Parkway, Suite 140, Jacksonville, FL 32256. *Phone:* 904-573-9100. *Toll-free phone:* 800-318-1264. *Web site:* http://www.itt-tech.edu/.

ITT Technical Institute

Lake Mary, Florida

- **Proprietary** primarily 2-year, founded 1989, part of ITT Educational Services, Inc.
- **Suburban** campus
- **Coed**
- **Minimally difficult** entrance level

Academics *Calendar:* quarters. *Degrees:* associate and bachelor's.

Freshman Application Contact Director of Recruitment, ITT Technical Institute, 1400 South International Parkway, Lake Mary, FL 32746. *Phone:* 407-660-2900. *Toll-free phone:* 866-489-8441. *Fax:* 407-660-2566. *Web site:* http://www.itt-tech.edu/.

ITT Technical Institute

Miami, Florida

- **Proprietary** primarily 2-year, founded 1996, part of ITT Educational Services, Inc.
- **Coed**
- **Minimally difficult** entrance level

Academics *Calendar:* quarters. *Degrees:* associate and bachelor's.

Student Life *Housing:* college housing not available.

Freshman Application Contact Director of Recruitment, ITT Technical Institute, 7955 NW 12th Street, Suite 119, Miami, FL 33126. *Phone:* 305-477-3080. *Web site:* http://www.itt-tech.edu/.

ITT Technical Institute

Orlando, Florida

- **Proprietary** primarily 2-year, part of ITT Educational Services, Inc.
- **Coed**

Academics *Calendar:* quarters. *Degrees:* associate and bachelor's.

Freshman Application Contact Director of Recruitment, ITT Technical Institute, 8301 Southpark Circle, Suite 100, Orlando, FL 32819. *Phone:* 407-371-6000. *Toll-free phone:* 877-201-4367. *Web site:* http://www.itt-tech.edu/.

ITT Technical Institute

Pinellas Park, Florida

- **Proprietary** primarily 2-year, part of ITT Educational Services, Inc.
- **Coed**
- **Minimally difficult** entrance level

Academics *Degrees:* associate and bachelor's.

Student Life *Housing:* college housing not available.

Freshman Application Contact Director of Recruitment, ITT Technical Institute, 877 Executive Center Drive W, Suite 100, Pinellas Park, FL 33702. *Phone:* 727-209-4700. *Toll-free phone:* 866-488-5084. *Web site:* http://www.itt-tech.edu/.

ITT Technical Institute

Tallahassee, Florida

- **Proprietary** primarily 2-year
- **Coed**
- **Minimally difficult** entrance level

Academics *Degrees:* associate and bachelor's.

Freshman Application Contact Director of Recruitment, ITT Technical Institute, 2639 North Monroe Street, Building A, Suite 100, Tallahassee, FL 32303. *Phone:* 850-422-6300. *Toll-free phone:* 877-230-3559. *Web site:* http://www.itt-tech.edu/.

ITT Technical Institute

Tampa, Florida

- **Proprietary** primarily 2-year, founded 1981, part of ITT Educational Services, Inc.
- **Suburban** campus
- **Coed**
- **Minimally difficult** entrance level

Academics *Calendar:* quarters. *Degrees:* associate and bachelor's.

Student Life *Housing:* college housing not available.

Freshman Application Contact Director of Recruitment, ITT Technical Institute, 4809 Memorial Highway, Tampa, FL 33634-7151. *Phone:* 813-885-2244. *Toll-free phone:* 800-825-2831. *Web site:* http://www.itt-tech.edu/.

ITT Technical Institute

West Palm Beach, Florida

- **Proprietary** 4-year
- **Coed**
- **Minimally difficult** entrance level

Academics *Degrees:* associate and bachelor's.

Freshman Application Contact Director of Recruitment, ITT Technical Institute, 1756 N. Congress Avenue, West Palm Beach, FL 33409. *Phone:* 561-233-4900. *Toll-free phone:* 877-236-8164. *Web site:* http://www.itt-tech.edu/.

Jacksonville University

Jacksonville, Florida

- **Independent** comprehensive, founded 1934
- **Suburban** 198-acre campus
- **Coed** 3,194 undergraduate students, 69% full-time, 59% women, 41% men
- **Moderately difficult** entrance level, 42% of applicants were admitted

Undergraduates 2,201 full-time, 993 part-time. 29% are from out of state; 19% Black or African American, non-Hispanic/Latino; 7% Hispanic/Latino; 4% Asian, non-Hispanic/Latino; 0.4% Native Hawaiian or other Pacific Islander, non-Hispanic/Latino; 1% American Indian or Alaska Native, non-Hispanic/Latino; 8% Two or more races, non-Hispanic/Latino; 0.4% international; 8% transferred in; 34% live on campus. *Retention:* 60% of full-time freshmen returned.

Freshmen *Admission:* 8,096 applied, 3,369 admitted, 529 enrolled. *Average high school GPA:* 3.47. *Test scores:* SAT critical reading scores over 500: 60%; SAT math scores over 500: 67%; ACT scores over 18: 96%; SAT critical reading scores over 600: 14%; SAT math scores over 600: 16%; ACT scores over 24: 39%; SAT critical reading scores over 700: 2%; SAT math scores over 700: 1%; ACT scores over 30: 5%.

Faculty *Total:* 318, 57% full-time, 60% with terminal degrees. *Student/faculty ratio:* 13:1.

Academics *Calendar:* semesters. *Degrees:* bachelor's, master's, and post-master's certificates. *Special study options:* adult/continuing education programs, part-time degree program. *ROTC:* Army (c), Navy (b).

Computers on Campus Students can access the following: online (class) registration. Campuswide network is available.

Student Life *Housing options:* coed, men-only, women-only, disabled students. Campus housing is university owned. Freshman campus housing is guaranteed. *Campus security:* 24-hour emergency response devices and patrols, student patrols, late-night transport/escort service, controlled dormitory access, code lock doors in residence halls, trained security patrols during evening hours.

Athletics Member NCAA. All Division I except football (Division I-AA). *Intercollegiate sports:* baseball M(s), basketball M(s)/W(s), crew M(s)/W(s), cross-country running M/W(s), golf M(s)/W(s), soccer M(s)/W(s), softball W(s), tennis M(s)/W(s), track and field W(s), volleyball W(s). *Intramural sports:* basketball M/W, bowling M/W, cross-country running M/W, football M/W, golf M/W, racquetball M/W, soccer M, softball M/W, swimming and diving M/W, table tennis M/W, tennis M/W, track and field M, volleyball M/W.

Standardized Tests *Required:* SAT or ACT (for admission).

Costs (2011–12) *Comprehensive fee:* $37,068 includes full-time tuition ($27,900) and room and board ($9168). Part-time tuition: $926 per credit hour. *College room only:* $5408. Room and board charges vary according to board plan and housing facility.

Financial Aid Of all full-time matriculated undergraduates who enrolled in 2010, 2,260 applied for aid, 1,730 were judged to have need, 257 had their

need fully met. In 2010, 492 non-need-based awards were made. *Average percent of need met: 57%. Average financial aid package: $19,750. Average need-based loan: $4284. Average need-based gift aid: $16,333. Average non-need-based aid: $12,269.*
Applying *Options:* electronic application, early admission, deferred entrance. *Application fee:* $30. *Required:* high school transcript, minimum 2.0 GPA. *Required for some:* essay or personal statement. *Recommended:* interview. *Application deadlines:* rolling (freshmen), rolling (transfers). *Notification:* continuous (freshmen).
Freshman Application Contact Ms. Lisa Hannasch, Director of First Year Student Admission and Enrollment, Jacksonville University, 2800 University Boulevard North, Office of Admissions, Jacksonville, FL 32211. *Phone:* 904-256-7000. *Toll-free phone:* 800-225-2027. *Fax:* 904-256-7012. *E-mail:* admissions@ju.edu. *Web site:* http://www.ju.edu/.

Johnson & Wales University
North Miami, Florida
- **Independent** 4-year, founded 1992
- **Suburban** 8-acre campus with easy access to Miami
- **Coed**
- **Moderately difficult** entrance level

Faculty *Student/faculty ratio:* 28:1.
Academics *Calendar:* quarters. *Degrees:* associate and bachelor's.
Student Life *Campus security:* 24-hour emergency response devices and patrols, video camera surveillance throughout campus.
Athletics Member NAIA.
Standardized Tests *Required for some:* SAT or ACT (for admission).
Costs (2011–12) *One-time required fee:* $300. *Comprehensive fee:* $34,368 includes full-time tuition ($23,955), mandatory fees ($1152), and room and board ($9261). *Room and board:* Room and board charges vary according to board plan and housing facility.
Financial Aid *Of all full-time matriculated undergraduates who enrolled in 2010,* 1,776 applied for aid, 1,635 were judged to have need, 172 had their need fully met. *In 2010,* 247 non-need-based awards were made. *Average percent of need met:* 68. *Average financial aid package:* $18,719. *Average need-based loan:* $5150. *Average need-based gift aid:* $8710. *Average non-need-based aid:* $5454.
Applying *Options:* early admission, deferred entrance. *Required:* high school transcript. *Required for some:* essay or personal statement, interview. *Recommended:* minimum 2.0 GPA.
Freshman Application Contact Jeff Greenip, Director of Admissions, Johnson & Wales University, 1701 Northeast 127th Street, North Miami, FL 33181. *Phone:* 305-892-7600. *Toll-free phone:* 866-598-3567. *Fax:* 305-892-7020. *E-mail:* mia@admissions.jwu.edu. *Web site:* http://www.jwu.edu/northmiami/.

Jones College
Jacksonville, Florida
- **Independent** 4-year, founded 1918
- **Urban** 5-acre campus
- **Coed** 748 undergraduate students, 33% full-time, 79% women, 21% men
- **Noncompetitive** entrance level

Undergraduates 249 full-time, 499 part-time. Students come from 25 states and territories; 2 other countries; 14% are from out of state; 70% Black or African American, non-Hispanic/Latino; 5% Hispanic/Latino; 0.4% Asian, non-Hispanic/Latino; 0.4% Native Hawaiian or other Pacific Islander, non-Hispanic/Latino; 0.4% American Indian or Alaska Native, non-Hispanic/Latino; 2% Two or more races, non-Hispanic/Latino; 0.5% Race/ethnicity unknown; 0.4% international; 9% transferred in. *Retention:* 55% of full-time freshmen returned.
Freshmen *Admission:* 27 admitted, 27 enrolled.
Faculty *Total:* 75, 4% full-time, 24% with terminal degrees. *Student/faculty ratio:* 15:1.
Academics *Calendar:* trimesters. *Degrees:* associate and bachelor's. *Special study options:* academic remediation for entering students, accelerated degree program, adult/continuing education programs, advanced placement credit, cooperative education, distance learning, double majors, independent study, internships, part-time degree program, student-designed majors, summer session for credit.
Computers on Campus 80 computers/terminals are available on campus for general student use. Students can access the following: campus intranet, computer help desk, free student e-mail accounts, online (class) registration, online (class) schedules. Campuswide network is available. Wireless service is available via classrooms, computer centers, computer labs.
Student Life *Housing:* college housing not available. *Campus security:* late-night transport/escort service.

Standardized Tests *Required for some:* CPAt.
Costs (2011–12) *Tuition:* $7320 full-time, $305 per credit part-time. *Required fees:* $90 full-time, $45 per term part-time. *Payment plans:* installment, deferred payment. *Waivers:* children of alumni and employees or children of employees.
Applying *Options:* electronic application. *Required:* interview. *Required for some:* high school transcript. *Application deadline:* rolling (freshmen). *Notification:* continuous (transfers).
Freshman Application Contact Jones College, 555 Arlington Expressway, Jacksonville, FL 32211-5588. *Phone:* 904-743-1122 Ext. 141. *Toll-free phone:* 800-631-4056. *Web site:* http://www.jones.edu/.

Keiser University
Fort Lauderdale, Florida
Freshman Application Contact Keiser University, 1500 NW 49th Street, Fort Lauderdale, FL 33309. *Toll-free phone:* 888-534-7379. *Web site:* http://www.keiseruniversity.edu/.

Lincoln College of Technology
West Palm Beach, Florida
Director of Admissions Mr. Kevin Cassidy, Director of Admissions, Lincoln College of Technology, 2410 Metro Centre Boulevard, West Palm Beach, FL 33407. *Phone:* 561-842-8324 Ext. 117. *Fax:* 561-842-9503. *Web site:* http://www.lincolnedu.com/.

Lincoln Culinary Institute
West Palm Beach, Florida
- **Proprietary** 4-year
- **Urban** 14-acre campus with easy access to West Palm Beach, Fort Lauderdale, Miami
- **Coed** 600 undergraduate students, 100% full-time, 35% women, 65% men

Undergraduates 600 full-time.
Faculty *Total:* 19.
Academics *Degrees:* diplomas, associate, and bachelor's (degree in science only (18 or 24 month program)).
Financial Aid Of all full-time matriculated undergraduates who enrolled in 2010, 28 Federal Work-Study jobs (averaging $4160).
Freshman Application Contact Lincoln Culinary Institute, 2410 Metrocentre Boulevard, West Palm Beach, FL 33407. *Phone:* 561-842-8324 Ext. 202. *Web site:* http://www.lincolnedu.com/campus/west-palm-beach-culinary-fl.

Lynn University
Boca Raton, Florida
- **Independent** comprehensive, founded 1962
- **Suburban** 123-acre campus with easy access to Fort Lauderdale
- **Coed** 1,619 undergraduate students, 90% full-time, 48% women, 52% men
- **Moderately difficult** entrance level, 63% of applicants were admitted

Undergraduates 1,453 full-time, 166 part-time. Students come from 48 states and territories; 80 other countries; 47% are from out of state; 7% Black or African American, non-Hispanic/Latino; 11% Hispanic/Latino; 0.8% Asian, non-Hispanic/Latino; 0.1% Native Hawaiian or other Pacific Islander, non-Hispanic/Latino; 0.4% American Indian or Alaska Native, non-Hispanic/Latino; 0.8% Two or more races, non-Hispanic/Latino; 13% Race/ethnicity unknown; 18% international; 8% transferred in; 45% live on campus. *Retention:* 60% of full-time freshmen returned.
Freshmen *Admission:* 2,953 applied, 1,862 admitted, 411 enrolled. *Average high school GPA:* 2.75. *Test scores:* SAT critical reading scores over 500: 23%; SAT math scores over 500: 29%; ACT scores over 18: 68%; SAT critical reading scores over 600: 4%; SAT math scores over 600: 4%; ACT scores over 24: 15%; SAT critical reading scores over 700: 1%; SAT math scores over 700: 1%; ACT scores over 30: 1%.
Faculty *Total:* 170, 52% full-time, 48% with terminal degrees. *Student/faculty ratio:* 16:1.
Academics *Calendar:* semesters plus 3 summer sessions. *Degrees:* certificates, bachelor's, master's, doctoral, post-master's, postbachelor's, and first professional certificates. *Special study options:* academic remediation for entering students, accelerated degree program, adult/continuing education programs, advanced placement credit, cooperative education, distance learning, double majors, English as a second language, freshman honors college, honors programs, independent study, internships, part-time degree program, services

for LD students, study abroad, summer session for credit. *ROTC:* Air Force (c).

Computers on Campus Students can access the following: campus intranet, computer help desk, free student e-mail accounts, online (class) grades, online (class) registration, online (class) schedules. Campuswide network is available. Wireless service is available via entire campus.

Student Life *Housing:* on-campus residence required for freshman year. *Options:* coed, women-only, disabled students. Campus housing is university owned. Freshman campus housing is guaranteed. *Activities and organizations:* drama/theater group, student-run newspaper, radio and television station, choral group, Knights of the Round Table, intramural groups, student newspaper, Residence Hall Council, Activities Board, national fraternities, national sororities. *Campus security:* 24-hour emergency response devices and patrols, late-night transport/escort service, video monitor at residence entrances. *Student services:* health clinic, personal/psychological counseling.

Athletics Member NCAA. All Division II. *Intercollegiate sports:* baseball M(s), basketball M(s)/W(s), golf M(s)/W(s), soccer M(s)/W(s), softball W(s), tennis M(s)/W(s), volleyball W(s).

Standardized Tests *Required:* SAT or ACT (for admission).

Costs (2012–13) *Comprehensive fee:* $43,500 includes full-time tuition ($31,100), mandatory fees ($1500), and room and board ($10,900). Full-time tuition and fees vary according to reciprocity agreements. Part-time tuition: $900 per credit. Part-time tuition and fees vary according to class time and course load. *Required fees:* $30 per term part-time. *Room and board:* Room and board charges vary according to board plan and housing facility. *Payment plans:* installment, deferred payment. *Waivers:* employees or children of employees.

Financial Aid Of all full-time matriculated undergraduates who enrolled in 2011, 1,095 applied for aid, 676 were judged to have need, 667 had their need fully met. 115 Federal Work-Study jobs (averaging $1947). 35 state and other part-time jobs (averaging $7670). In 2011, 265 non-need-based awards were made. *Average percent of need met:* 54%. *Average financial aid package:* $19,434. *Average need-based loan:* $5019. *Average need-based gift aid:* $11,130. *Average non-need-based aid:* $8907. *Average indebtedness upon graduation:* $40,101.

Applying *Options:* electronic application, early admission, deferred entrance. *Application fee:* $45. *Required:* essay or personal statement, high school transcript, minimum 2.0 GPA. *Recommended:* minimum 3.0 GPA, interview. *Application deadlines:* rolling (freshmen), rolling (transfers). *Notification:* continuous (freshmen), continuous (transfers).

Freshman Application Contact Stefano Papaleo, Director of Undergraduate Admission, Lynn University, Admission, 3601 North Military Trail, Boca Raton, FL 33431. *Phone:* 561-237-7831. *Toll-free phone:* 800-888-5966. *Fax:* 561-237-7100. *E-mail:* spapaleo@lynn.edu. *Web site:* http://www.lynn.edu/.

Miami Dade College

Miami, Florida

- **State and locally supported** primarily 2-year, founded 1960, part of Florida College System
- **Urban** campus
- **Endowment** $176.1 million
- **Coed** 63,766 undergraduate students, 42% full-time, 59% women, 41% men
- **Noncompetitive** entrance level, 100% of applicants were admitted

Undergraduates 26,634 full-time, 37,132 part-time. Students come from 45 states and territories; 186 other countries; 1% are from out of state; 16% Black or African American, non-Hispanic/Latino; 70% Hispanic/Latino; 1% Asian, non-Hispanic/Latino; 0.1% Native Hawaiian or other Pacific Islander, non-Hispanic/Latino; 0.1% American Indian or Alaska Native, non-Hispanic/Latino; 0.2% Two or more races, non-Hispanic/Latino; 2% Race/ethnicity unknown; 2% international; 2% transferred in.

Freshmen *Admission:* 11,764 applied, 11,764 admitted, 13,498 enrolled. **Faculty** *Total:* 2,462, 29% full-time, 19% with terminal degrees. *Student/faculty ratio:* 30:1.

Academics *Calendar:* 16-16-6-6. *Degrees:* certificates, associate, bachelor's, and postbachelor's certificates. *Special study options:* academic remediation for entering students, accelerated degree program, adult/continuing education programs, advanced placement credit, cooperative education, distance learning, English as a second language, freshman honors college, honors programs, independent study, internships, off-campus study, part-time degree program, services for LD students, study abroad, summer session for credit. *ROTC:* Army (b), Air Force (b).

Computers on Campus 9,655 computers/terminals and 1,500 ports are available on campus for general student use. Students can access the following: campus intranet, computer help desk, free student e-mail accounts, online (class) grades, online (class) registration, online (class) schedules, admissions;

student feedback of faculty; financial aid; IRS Form 1098. Wireless service is available via classrooms, computer centers, computer labs, learning centers, libraries, student centers.

Student Life *Housing:* college housing not available. *Activities and organizations:* drama/theater group, student-run newspaper, radio and television station, choral group, Student Government Association, Phi Theta Kappa, Phi Beta Lambda (Business), Future Educators of America Professional, Kappa Delta Pi Honor Society (Education), national fraternities. *Campus security:* 24-hour emergency response devices and patrols, mass communication emergency notification systems. *Student services:* personal/psychological counseling, legal services.

Athletics Member NCAA, NJCAA. All NCAA Division I. *Intercollegiate sports:* baseball M(s), basketball M(s)/W(s), softball W(s), volleyball W(s).

Costs (2011–12) *One-time required fee:* $30. *Tuition:* state resident $2365 full-time, $79 per credit hour part-time; nonresident $9466 full-time, $316 per credit hour part-time. Full-time tuition and fees vary according to course load, degree level, and program. Part-time tuition and fees vary according to course load, degree level, and program. *Required fees:* $780 full-time, $27 per credit hour part-time. *Waivers:* employees or children of employees.

Financial Aid Of all full-time matriculated undergraduates who enrolled in 2010, 800 Federal Work-Study jobs (averaging $5000). 125 state and other part-time jobs (averaging $5000).

Applying *Options:* electronic application, early admission. *Application fee:* $30. *Required:* high school transcript. *Required for some:* some programs such as Honors College have additional admissions requirements. *Application deadlines:* rolling (freshmen), rolling (out-of-state freshmen), rolling (transfers). *Notification:* continuous (freshmen), continuous (out-of-state freshmen), continuous (transfers).

Freshman Application Contact Mrs. Dulce Beltran, College Registrar, Miami Dade College, 11011 SW 104th Street, Miami, FL 33176. *Phone:* 305-237-2206. *Fax:* 305-237-2532. *E-mail:* dbeltran@mdc.edu. *Web site:* http://www.mdc.edu/.

Miami International University of Art & Design

Miami, Florida

- **Proprietary** comprehensive, founded 1965, part of Education Management Corporation
- **Urban** campus
- **Coed**

Academics *Calendar:* quarters. *Degrees:* diplomas, associate, bachelor's, and master's.

Freshman Application Contact Miami International University of Art & Design, 1501 Biscayne Boulevard, Suite 100, Miami, FL 33132-1418. *Phone:* 305-428-5700. *Toll-free phone:* 800-225-9023. *Web site:* http://www.artinstitutes.edu/miami/.

See page 1446 for the College Close-Up.

New College of Florida

Sarasota, Florida

- **State-supported** 4-year, founded 1960, part of State University System of Florida
- **Suburban** 119-acre campus with easy access to Tampa-St. Petersburg
- **Endowment** $29.7 million
- **Coed** 845 undergraduate students, 100% full-time, 61% women, 39% men
- **Very difficult** entrance level, 56% of applicants were admitted

Undergraduates 845 full-time. Students come from 40 states and territories; 16 other countries; 21% are from out of state; 1% Black or African American, non-Hispanic/Latino; 13% Hispanic/Latino; 3% Asian, non-Hispanic/Latino; 0.1% Native Hawaiian or other Pacific Islander, non-Hispanic/Latino; 0.5% American Indian or Alaska Native, non-Hispanic/Latino; 4% Two or more races, non-Hispanic/Latino; 2% Race/ethnicity unknown; 0.1% international; 4% transferred in; 78% live on campus. *Retention:* 86% of full-time freshmen returned.

Freshmen *Admission:* 1,272 applied, 715 admitted, 237 enrolled. *Average high school GPA:* 3.98. *Test scores:* SAT critical reading scores over 500: 100%; SAT math scores over 500: 99%; SAT writing scores over 500: 97%; ACT scores over 18: 100%; SAT critical reading scores over 600: 89%; SAT math scores over 600: 63%; SAT writing scores over 600: 76%; ACT scores over 24: 95%; SAT critical reading scores over 700: 43%; SAT math scores over 700: 16%; SAT writing scores over 700: 23%; ACT scores over 30: 39%. **Faculty** *Total:* 106, 65% full-time, 92% with terminal degrees. *Student/faculty ratio:* 10:1.

Academics *Calendar:* 4-1-4. *Degree:* bachelor's. *Special study options:* cooperative education, double majors, honors programs, independent study, internships, off-campus study, services for LD students, student-designed majors, study abroad.

Computers on Campus 41 computers/terminals and 1,000 ports are available on campus for general student use. Students can access the following: campus intranet, computer help desk, free student e-mail accounts, online (class) grades, online (class) registration, online (class) schedules. Campuswide network is available. 100% of college-owned or -operated housing units are wired for high-speed Internet access. Wireless service is available via classrooms, dorm rooms, learning centers, libraries, student centers.

Student Life *Housing:* on-campus residence required through senior year. *Options:* coed, disabled students. Campus housing is university owned. Freshman campus housing is guaranteed. *Activities and organizations:* drama/theater group, student-run newspaper, radio station, choral group, PRIDE, Interfaith groups, New College Student Alliance, Feminist Majority Leadership Alliance, Sailing Club. *Campus security:* 24-hour emergency response devices and patrols, student patrols, late-night transport/escort service, controlled dormitory access, campus police are state certified police officers and available 24/7. *Student services:* health clinic, personal/psychological counseling, women's center.

Athletics *Intercollegiate sports:* sailing M/W. *Intramural sports:* archery M(c)/W(c), basketball M/W, fencing M/W, football M, racquetball M/W, sailing M(c)/W(c), soccer M(c)/W(c), softball M(c)/W(c), swimming and diving M(c)/W(c), table tennis M(c)/W(c), tennis M(c)/W(c), ultimate Frisbee M(c)/W(c), volleyball M/W, weight lifting M(c)/W(c), wrestling M/W.

Standardized Tests *Required:* SAT or ACT (for admission).

Costs (2011–12) *Tuition:* state resident $6060 full-time; nonresident $29,088 full-time. Full-time tuition and fees vary according to course load. *Room and board:* $8598; room only: $5901. Room and board charges vary according to board plan and housing facility. *Payment plan:* installment.

Financial Aid Of all full-time matriculated undergraduates who enrolled in 2011, 764 applied for aid, 491 were judged to have need, 487 had their need fully met. 8 Federal Work-Study jobs (averaging $3325). In 2011, 237 non-need-based awards were made. *Average percent of need met:* 100%. *Average financial aid package:* $12,720. *Average need-based loan:* $4472. *Average need-based gift aid:* $8659. *Average non-need-based aid:* $2182. *Average indebtedness upon graduation:* $14,172.

Applying *Options:* electronic application, early admission, deferred entrance. *Application fee:* $30. *Required:* essay or personal statement, high school transcript, 1 letter of recommendation. *Required for some:* interview. *Recommended:* minimum 3.0 GPA. *Application deadlines:* 4/15 (freshmen), 4/15 (out-of-state freshmen), 4/15 (transfers). *Notification:* 4/25 (freshmen), 4/25 (out-of-state freshmen), 4/25 (transfers).

Freshman Application Contact Office of Admissions, New College of Florida, 5800 Bay Shore Road, Sarasota, FL 34243-2109. *Phone:* 941-487-5000. *Fax:* 941-487-5010. *E-mail:* admissions@ncf.edu. *Web site:* http://www.ncf.edu/.

New World School of the Arts
Miami, Florida

- **State-supported** 4-year, founded 1984, part of New World School of the Arts is a partnership of Miami Dade County Public Schools, Miami Dade College and the University of Florida
- **Urban** 5-acre campus with easy access to Broward, Palm Beach Counties
- **Endowment** $8.3 million
- **Coed** 335 undergraduate students, 100% full-time, 57% women, 43% men
- **Noncompetitive** entrance level, 52% of applicants were admitted

Undergraduates 335 full-time. Students come from 12 states and territories; 9 other countries; 4% are from out of state; 13% Black or African American, non-Hispanic/Latino; 62% Hispanic/Latino; 4% Asian, non-Hispanic/Latino; 6% Two or more races, non-Hispanic/Latino; 6% transferred in. *Retention:* 70% of full-time freshmen returned.

Freshmen *Admission:* 384 applied, 200 admitted, 123 enrolled. *Average high school GPA:* 3.

Faculty *Total:* 77, 29% full-time. *Student/faculty ratio:* 5:1.

Academics *Calendar:* semesters. *Degrees:* associate and bachelor's. *Special study options:* academic remediation for entering students, advanced placement credit, cooperative education, distance learning, double majors, English as a second language, freshman honors college, independent study, internships, services for LD students, study abroad, summer session for credit.

Computers on Campus 100 computers/terminals are available on campus for general student use. Students can access the following: campus intranet, computer help desk, free student e-mail accounts, online (class) grades, online (class) registration. Campuswide network is available.

Student Life *Housing:* college housing not available. *Activities and organizations:* student government. *Campus security:* 24-hour patrols. *Student services:* personal/psychological counseling.

Standardized Tests *Recommended:* SAT or ACT (for admission).

Applying *Options:* early decision. *Required:* essay or personal statement, high school transcript, 2 letters of recommendation, interview, audition. *Application deadline:* rolling (freshmen). *Notification:* continuous (freshmen), continuous (out-of-state freshmen), continuous (transfers), rolling (early decision).

Freshman Application Contact Recruitment and Admissions Coordinator, New World School of the Arts, 300 NE Second Avenue, Miami, FL 33132. *Phone:* 305-237-7408. *Fax:* 305-237-3794. *E-mail:* nwsaadm@mdc.edu. *Web site:* http://www.mdc.edu/nwsa/.

Northwest Florida State College
Niceville, Florida

- **State and locally supported** primarily 2-year, founded 1963, part of Florida College System
- **Small-town** 264-acre campus
- **Endowment** $28.6 million
- **Coed** 10,317 undergraduate students
- **Noncompetitive** entrance level

Undergraduates Students come from 18 states and territories.

Faculty *Total:* 310, 31% full-time. *Student/faculty ratio:* 15:1.

Academics *Calendar:* semesters plus summer sessions. *Degrees:* certificates, associate, and bachelor's. *Special study options:* academic remediation for entering students, accelerated degree program, adult/continuing education programs, advanced placement credit, distance learning, English as a second language, independent study, part-time degree program, services for LD students, summer session for credit. *ROTC:* Army (b).

Computers on Campus 643 computers/terminals are available on campus for general student use. Students can access the following: online (class) registration. Campuswide network is available.

Student Life *Housing:* college housing not available. *Activities and organizations:* drama/theater group, choral group. *Student services:* women's center.

Athletics Member NJCAA. *Intercollegiate sports:* baseball M(s), basketball M(s)/W(s), softball W(s). *Intramural sports:* basketball M/W.

Standardized Tests *Required for some:* ACT, SAT I, ACT ASSET, MAPS, or Florida College Entry Placement Test are used for placement not admission.

Financial Aid Of all full-time matriculated undergraduates who enrolled in 2010, 81 Federal Work-Study jobs (averaging $1500). 11 state and other part-time jobs (averaging $1460).

Applying *Options:* electronic application. *Required:* high school transcript. *Application deadlines:* rolling (freshmen), rolling (transfers). *Notification:* continuous (freshmen), continuous (transfers).

Freshman Application Contact Ms. Christine Bishop, Dean Enrollment Services, Northwest Florida State College, 100 College Boulevard, Niceville, FL 32578. *Phone:* 850-729-5373. *Fax:* 850-729-5323. *E-mail:* registrar@nwfsc.edu. *Web site:* http://www.nwfsc.edu/.

Northwood University, Florida Campus
West Palm Beach, Florida

- **Private** comprehensive, founded 1982
- **Suburban** 90-acre campus
- **Endowment** $31.1 million
- **Coed** 523 undergraduate students, 96% full-time, 40% women, 60% men
- **Moderately difficult** entrance level, 50% of applicants were admitted

Undergraduates 500 full-time, 23 part-time. 38% are from out of state; 12% Black or African American, non-Hispanic/Latino; 14% Hispanic/Latino; 0.6% Asian, non-Hispanic/Latino; 0.8% American Indian or Alaska Native, non-Hispanic/Latino; 4% Race/ethnicity unknown; 36% international; 23% transferred in; 50% live on campus. *Retention:* 56% of full-time freshmen returned.

Freshmen *Admission:* 844 applied, 418 admitted, 95 enrolled. *Average high school GPA:* 3.09. *Test scores:* SAT critical reading scores over 500: 18%; SAT math scores over 500: 33%; SAT writing scores over 500: 23%; ACT scores over 18: 75%; SAT critical reading scores over 600: 4%; SAT math scores over 600: 5%; SAT writing scores over 600: 3%; ACT scores over 24: 12%.

Faculty *Total:* 43, 37% full-time, 26% with terminal degrees. *Student/faculty ratio:* 20:1.

Academics *Calendar:* quarters. *Degrees:* bachelor's and master's. *Special study options:* academic remediation for entering students, accelerated degree program, adult/continuing education programs, advanced placement credit, distance learning, double majors, external degree program, honors programs,

THE BUSINESS UNIVERSITY *for* BUSINESS-MINDED STUDENTS.

■ Start courses in your major on day one

■ Engage in hands-on, industry-specific learning opportunities in your first year

■ High employment rate

■ Generous academic and business club scholarships

■ NAIA, Member of The Sun Conference

OUR GRADUATES EMERGE AS LEADERS, MANAGERS, EXECUTIVES, AND ENTREPRENEURS.

■ Four Year BBA/MBA (available to those who qualify)

■ Accounting

■ Advertising & Marketing

■ Aftermarket Management

■ Automotive Marketing & Management

■ Economics

■ Entertainment, Sport & Promotion Management

■ Entrepreneurship

■ Finance

■ Hotel, Restaurant & Resort Management

■ International Business

■ Management

■ Marketing

www.northwood.edu

---

independent study, internships, off-campus study, part-time degree program, study abroad, summer session for credit.

Computers on Campus 89 computers/terminals are available on campus for general student use. Students can access the following: campus intranet, computer help desk, free student e-mail accounts, online (class) grades, online (class) registration, online (class) schedules. Campuswide network is available. 100% of college-owned or -operated housing units are wired for high-speed Internet access. Wireless service is available via entire campus.

Student Life *Housing:* on-campus residence required for freshman year. *Options:* coed, men-only. Campus housing is university owned. Freshman campus housing is guaranteed. *Activities and organizations:* drama/theater group, student-run newspaper, Student Government Association, International Club, Auto Show. *Campus security:* 24-hour emergency response devices and patrols, student patrols, late-night transport/escort service. *Student services:* health clinic, personal/psychological counseling.

Athletics Member NAIA. *Intercollegiate sports:* baseball M(s), basketball M/W, cheerleading M/W, golf M(s)/W(s), soccer M(s)/W(s), softball W(s), tennis M(s)/W(s), volleyball W(s). *Intramural sports:* basketball M/W, bowling M/W, football M, racquetball M/W, tennis M/W.

Standardized Tests *Required:* SAT or ACT (for admission).

Costs (2012–13) *Comprehensive fee:* $30,746 includes full-time tuition ($20,040), mandatory fees ($956), and room and board ($9750). Part-time tuition: $776 per credit hour. *College room only:* $5030.

Financial Aid Of all full-time matriculated undergraduates who enrolled in 2011, 266 applied for aid, 244 were judged to have need, 53 had their need fully met. In 2011, 54 non-need-based awards were made. *Average percent of need met:* 59%. *Average financial aid package:* $18,449. *Average need-based loan:* $4117. *Average need-based gift aid:* $6462. *Average non-need-based aid:* $6750. *Average indebtedness upon graduation:* $28,457.

Applying *Options:* electronic application, early admission, deferred entrance. *Application fee:* $25. *Required:* essay or personal statement, high school transcript. *Recommended:* minimum 2.0 GPA, 1 letter of recommendation, interview. *Application deadlines:* rolling (freshmen), rolling (transfers). *Notification:* continuous (freshmen), continuous (transfers).

Freshman Application Contact Ms. Emily Mass, Associate Director of Admissions, Northwood University, Florida Campus, 2600 North Military Trail, West Palm Beach, FL 33409-2911. *Phone:* 800-622-9000. *Toll-free phone:* 800-622-9000. *Fax:* 561-681-7901. *E-mail:* fladmit@northwood.edu. *Web site:* http://www.northwood.edu/.

See page 1486 for the College Close-Up.

Nova Southeastern University
Fort Lauderdale, Florida

- **Independent** university, founded 1964
- **Suburban** 300-acre campus
- **Endowment** $64.5 million
- **Coed** 6,397 undergraduate students, 65% full-time, 71% women, 29% men
- **Moderately difficult** entrance level, 58% of applicants were admitted

Undergraduates 4,165 full-time, 2,232 part-time. Students come from 44 states and territories; 69 other countries; 16% are from out of state; 23% Black or African American, non-Hispanic/Latino; 33% Hispanic/Latino; 6% Asian, non-Hispanic/Latino; 0.2% Native Hawaiian or other Pacific Islander, non-Hispanic/Latino; 0.4% American Indian or Alaska Native, non-Hispanic/Latino; 1% Two or more races, non-Hispanic/Latino; 4% Race/ethnicity unknown; 4% international; 18% transferred in; 15% live on campus. *Retention:* 70% of full-time freshmen returned.

Freshmen *Admission:* 3,780 applied, 2,180 admitted, 791 enrolled. *Average high school GPA:* 3.65. *Test scores:* SAT critical reading scores over 500: 59%; SAT math scores over 500: 63%; ACT scores over 18: 95%; SAT critical reading scores over 600: 18%; SAT math scores over 600: 23%; ACT scores over 24: 40%; SAT critical reading scores over 700: 2%; SAT math scores over 700: 4%; ACT scores over 30: 6%.

Faculty *Total:* 1,737, 47% full-time, 80% with terminal degrees. *Student/faculty ratio:* 20:1.

Academics *Calendar:* trimesters. *Degrees:* associate, bachelor's, master's, doctoral, post-master's, and first professional certificates. *Special study options:* academic remediation for entering students, adult/continuing education programs, advanced placement credit, distance learning, double majors, honors programs, independent study, internships, off-campus study, part-time degree program, services for LD students, study abroad, summer session for credit. *Unusual degree programs:* 3-2 business administration; marine biology, occupational therapy, criminal justice, psychology, mental health counseling, speech language pathology, computer science, education, physical therapy.

Computers on Campus 3,000 computers/terminals and 6,000 ports are available on campus for general student use. Students can access the following: campus intranet, computer help desk, free student e-mail accounts, online

(class) grades, online (class) registration, online (class) schedules. Campus-wide network is available. 100% of college-owned or -operated housing units are wired for high-speed Internet access. Wireless service is available via entire campus.

Student Life *Housing:* on-campus residence required through sophomore year. *Options:* coed, disabled students. Campus housing is university owned. Freshman campus housing is guaranteed. *Activities and organizations:* drama/theater group, student-run newspaper, radio station, choral group, Delta Epsilon Iota, Students for Stress Resilience, International Muslim Association at NSU (IMAN), Preventative Medicine Initiative (PMI), Pre-Med Society, national fraternities, national sororities. *Campus security:* 24-hour emergency response devices and patrols, late-night transport/escort service, controlled dormitory access, shuttle bus service. *Student services:* health clinic, personal/psychological counseling, women's center.

Athletics Member NCAA. All Division II. *Intercollegiate sports:* baseball M(s), basketball M(s)/W(s), cheerleading W, crew W(s), cross-country running M(s)/W(s), golf M(s)/W(s), soccer M(s)/W(s), softball W(s), swimming and diving M(s)/W(s), tennis W(s), track and field M(s)/W(s), volleyball W(s). *Intramural sports:* basketball M/W, golf M/W, racquetball M/W, soccer M/W, softball M/W, ultimate Frisbee M/W, volleyball M/W.

Standardized Tests *Required:* SAT or ACT (for admission).

Costs (2012–13) *Comprehensive fee:* $34,016 includes full-time tuition ($23,850), mandatory fees ($650), and room and board ($9516). Full-time tuition and fees vary according to class time and program. Part-time tuition: $795 per credit hour. Part-time tuition and fees vary according to class time, course load, and program. *College room only:* $6916. Room and board charges vary according to board plan and housing facility. *Payment plans:* installment, deferred payment. *Waivers:* employees or children of employees.

Financial Aid Of all full-time matriculated undergraduates who enrolled in 2009, 3,301 applied for aid, 2,943 were judged to have need, 204 had their need fully met. 278 Federal Work-Study jobs (averaging $2850). 1,511 state and other part-time jobs (averaging $3614). In 2009, 247 non-need-based awards were made. *Average percent of need met:* 67%. *Average financial aid package:* $16,863. *Average need-based loan:* $5568. *Average need-based gift aid:* $6287. *Average non-need-based aid:* $5631. *Average indebtedness upon graduation:* $36,908.

Applying *Options:* electronic application, deferred entrance. *Application fee:* $50. *Recommended:* minimum 2.6 GPA, essay and transcript of high school record recommended of some. *Application deadlines:* rolling (freshmen), rolling (out-of-state freshmen), rolling (transfers). *Notification:* continuous (freshmen), continuous (out-of-state freshmen), continuous (transfers).

Freshman Application Contact Ms. Maria Dillard, Director of Enrollment Management, Nova Southeastern University, Enrollment Processing Services, 3301 College Avenue, Ft. Lauderdale, FL 33329-9905. *Phone:* 954-262-8000. *Toll-free phone:* 800-541-NOVA. *Fax:* 954-262-3811. *E-mail:* nsuinfo@nova.edu. *Web site:* http://www.nova.edu/.

Palm Beach Atlantic University
West Palm Beach, Florida

- **Independent nondenominational** comprehensive, founded 1968
- **Urban** 27-acre campus with easy access to Orlando, the Caribbean
- **Endowment** $62.5 million
- **Coed** 2,836 undergraduate students, 78% full-time, 62% women, 38% men
- **Moderately difficult** entrance level, 83% of applicants were admitted

Undergraduates 2,225 full-time, 611 part-time. Students come from 46 states and territories; 40 other countries; 29% are from out of state; 16% Black or African American, non-Hispanic/Latino; 12% Hispanic/Latino; 2% Asian, non-Hispanic/Latino; 0.2% Native Hawaiian or other Pacific Islander, non-Hispanic/Latino; 0.3% American Indian or Alaska Native, non-Hispanic/Latino; 0.4% Two or more races, non-Hispanic/Latino; 5% Race/ethnicity unknown; 4% international; 12% transferred in; 44% live on campus. *Retention:* 72% of full-time freshmen returned.

Freshmen *Admission:* 1,373 applied, 1,139 admitted, 477 enrolled. *Test scores:* SAT critical reading scores over 500: 60%; SAT math scores over 500: 53%; SAT writing scores over 500: 60%; ACT scores over 18: 97%; SAT critical reading scores over 600: 22%; SAT math scores over 600: 19%; SAT writing scores over 600: 17%; ACT scores over 24: 43%; SAT critical reading scores over 700: 3%; SAT math scores over 700: 1%; SAT writing scores over 700: 2%; ACT scores over 30: 7%.

Faculty *Total:* 343, 45% full-time, 56% with terminal degrees. *Student/faculty ratio:* 12:1.

Academics *Calendar:* semesters. *Degrees:* associate, bachelor's, master's, and doctoral. *Special study options:* academic remediation for entering students, accelerated degree program, adult/continuing education programs, advanced placement credit, distance learning, double majors, honors programs, independent study, internships, part-time degree program, services for LD stu-

dents, student-designed majors, study abroad, summer session for credit. *ROTC:* Army (c).

Computers on Campus 585 computers/terminals are available on campus for general student use. Students can access the following: campus intranet, computer help desk, free student e-mail accounts, online (class) grades, online (class) registration, online (class) schedules. Campuswide network is available. 100% of college-owned or -operated housing units are wired for high-speed Internet access. Wireless service is available via entire campus.

Student Life *Housing:* on-campus residence required through sophomore year. *Options:* men-only, women-only. Campus housing is university owned and leased by the school. Freshman campus housing is guaranteed. *Activities and organizations:* drama/theater group, student-run newspaper, radio station, choral group, Christian Pharmacist Fellowship International, American Latino Intercultural Coalition, N.O.W. (Night of Worship), Student Government, Club S.A.I.L.. *Campus security:* 24-hour emergency response devices and patrols, late-night transport/escort service, controlled dormitory access. *Student services:* health clinic, personal/psychological counseling.

Athletics Member NCAA, NCCAA. All NCAA Division II. *Intercollegiate sports:* baseball M(s), basketball M(s)/W(s), cheerleading M(c)/W(c), cross-country running W(s), fencing M(c)/W(c), lacrosse M(c)/W(c), soccer M(s)/W(s), softball W(s), tennis M(s)/W(s), volleyball W(s). *Intramural sports:* badminton M/W, basketball M/W, bowling M/W, golf M/W, racquetball M/W, soccer M/W, softball M/W, table tennis M/W, ultimate Frisbee M/W, volleyball M/W, water polo M/W.

Standardized Tests *Required:* SAT or ACT (for admission).

Costs (2011–12) *Comprehensive fee:* $32,312 includes full-time tuition ($23,800), mandatory fees ($300), and room and board ($8212). Full-time tuition and fees vary according to course load, degree level, location, program, and reciprocity agreements. Part-time tuition and fees vary according to course load, degree level, location, program, and reciprocity agreements. *College room only:* $4570. Room and board charges vary according to board plan and housing facility. *Payment plan:* installment. *Waivers:* employees or children of employees.

Financial Aid Of all full-time matriculated undergraduates who enrolled in 2011, 1,968 applied for aid, 1,692 were judged to have need, 162 had their need fully met. 244 Federal Work-Study jobs (averaging $2288). 7 state and other part-time jobs (averaging $1607). In 2011, 431 non-need-based awards were made. *Average percent of need met:* 53%. *Average financial aid package:* $14,924. *Average need-based loan:* $4185. *Average need-based gift aid:* $11,479. *Average non-need-based aid:* $7536. *Average indebtedness upon graduation:* $27,222. *Financial aid deadline:* 8/1.

Applying *Options:* electronic application, early admission, early action, deferred entrance. *Application fee:* $50. *Required:* essay or personal statement, high school transcript. *Required for some:* interview. *Application deadlines:* rolling (freshmen), rolling (transfers). *Notification:* continuous (freshmen), continuous (transfers).

Freshman Application Contact Mr. James Zugelder, Director of Admission, Palm Beach Atlantic University, 901 South Flagler Drive, PO Box 24708, West Palm Beach, FL 33416-4708. *Phone:* 561-803-2101. *Toll-free phone:* 888-GO-TO-PBA. *E-mail:* admissions_admissions@pba.edu. *Web site:* http://www.pba.edu/.

Palm Beach State College
Lake Worth, Florida

- **State-supported** primarily 2-year, founded 1933, part of Florida College System
- **Urban** 150-acre campus with easy access to West Palm Beach
- **Endowment** $23.0 million
- **Coed** 29,534 undergraduate students, 37% full-time, 58% women, 42% men
- **Noncompetitive** entrance level, 100% of applicants were admitted

Undergraduates 10,913 full-time, 18,621 part-time. Students come from 49 states and territories; 146 other countries; 5% are from out of state; 5% transferred in.

Freshmen *Admission:* 5,127 applied, 5,127 admitted, 5,127 enrolled.

Faculty *Total:* 1,473, 19% full-time, 16% with terminal degrees. *Student/faculty ratio:* 43:1.

Academics *Calendar:* semesters. *Degrees:* certificates, diplomas, associate, and bachelor's. *Special study options:* academic remediation for entering students, adult/continuing education programs, advanced placement credit, cooperative education, distance learning, double majors, English as a second language, freshman honors college, honors programs, independent study, internships, off-campus study, part-time degree program, services for LD students, student-designed majors, study abroad, summer session for credit.

Computers on Campus 2,300 computers/terminals are available on campus for general student use. Students can access the following: computer help desk,

free student e-mail accounts, online (class) registration. Campuswide network is available. Wireless service is available via entire campus.
Student Life *Housing:* college housing not available. *Activities and organizations:* drama/theater group, student-run newspaper, choral group, student government, Phi Theta Kappa, Students for International Understanding, Black Student Union, Drama Club, national fraternities. *Campus security:* 24-hour emergency response devices and patrols. *Student services:* health clinic, women's center.
Athletics Member NJCAA. *Intercollegiate sports:* baseball M(s), basketball M(s)/W(s), softball W(s), volleyball W(s).
Standardized Tests *Recommended:* SAT and SAT Subject Tests or ACT (for admission).
Costs (2011–12) *One-time required fee:* $20. *Tuition:* state resident $2304 full-time, $96 per credit hour part-time; nonresident $8376 full-time, $349 per credit hour part-time. *Required fees:* $10 full-time, $10 per term part-time. *Waivers:* employees or children of employees.
Applying *Options:* electronic application, early admission, deferred entrance. *Application fee:* $20. *Application deadlines:* 8/20 (freshmen), 8/20 (transfers). *Notification:* continuous until 8/20 (freshmen), continuous until 8/20 (transfers).
Freshman Application Contact Ms. Anne Guiler, Coordinator of Distance Learning, Palm Beach State College, Lake Worth, FL 33461. *Phone:* 561-868-3032. *Fax:* 561-868-3584. *E-mail:* enrollmt@palmbeachstate.edu. *Web site:* http://www.palmbeachstate.edu/.

Pensacola State College

Pensacola, Florida

- **State-supported** primarily 2-year, founded 1948, part of Florida College System
- **Urban** 130-acre campus
- **Coed** 11,531 undergraduate students, 42% full-time, 62% women, 38% men
- **Noncompetitive** entrance level

Undergraduates 4,799 full-time, 6,732 part-time. Students come from 15 states and territories; 1% are from out of state; 16% Black or African American, non-Hispanic/Latino; 5% Hispanic/Latino; 3% Asian, non-Hispanic/Latino; 0.3% Native Hawaiian or other Pacific Islander, non-Hispanic/Latino; 1% American Indian or Alaska Native, non-Hispanic/Latino; 4% Two or more races, non-Hispanic/Latino; 1% Race/ethnicity unknown; 0.4% international; 6% transferred in.
Freshmen *Admission:* 1,359 enrolled.
Faculty *Total:* 203, 100% full-time, 20% with terminal degrees. *Student/faculty ratio:* 25:1.
Academics *Calendar:* semesters. *Degrees:* certificates, diplomas, associate, and bachelor's. *Special study options:* academic remediation for entering students, adult/continuing education programs, advanced placement credit, cooperative education, distance learning, double majors, external degree program, honors programs, independent study, part-time degree program, services for LD students, summer session for credit. *ROTC:* Army (b).
Computers on Campus 500 computers/terminals are available on campus for general student use. Students can access the following: campus intranet, computer help desk, free student e-mail accounts, online (class) grades, online (class) registration, online (class) schedules. Campuswide network is available. Wireless service is available via entire campus.
Student Life *Housing:* college housing not available. *Activities and organizations:* drama/theater group, student-run newspaper, choral group. *Campus security:* 24-hour emergency response devices and patrols, student patrols, late-night transport/escort service. *Student services:* health clinic, personal/psychological counseling.
Athletics Member NJCAA. *Intercollegiate sports:* baseball M(s), basketball M(s)/W(s), softball W(s), volleyball W. *Intramural sports:* archery M/W, badminton M/W, basketball M/W, bowling M/W, cross-country running M/W, gymnastics M/W, racquetball M/W, sailing M/W, swimming and diving M/W, tennis M/W, track and field M/W, volleyball M/W, weight lifting M/W, wrestling M.
Costs (2011–12) *One-time required fee:* $30. *Tuition:* state resident $2352 full-time, $98 per credit hour part-time; nonresident $8870 full-time, $370 per credit hour part-time. Full-time tuition and fees vary according to degree level. Part-time tuition and fees vary according to degree level. *Waivers:* senior citizens and employees or children of employees.
Financial Aid Of all full-time matriculated undergraduates who enrolled in 2010, 120 Federal Work-Study jobs (averaging $3000).
Applying *Options:* early admission. *Application fee:* $30. *Required:* high school transcript. *Application deadlines:* 8/30 (freshmen), 8/30 (transfers). *Notification:* continuous until 8/30 (freshmen), continuous until 8/30 (transfers).

Freshman Application Contact Ms. Martha Caughey, Registrar, Pensacola State College, 1000 College Boulevard, Pensacola, FL 32504-8998. *Phone:* 850-484-1600. *Fax:* 850-484-1829. *Web site:* http://www.pensacolastate.edu/.

Polk State College

Winter Haven, Florida

- **State-supported** primarily 2-year, founded 1964, part of Florida College System
- **Suburban** 98-acre campus with easy access to Orlando, Tampa
- **Endowment** $14.7 million
- **Coed** 11,529 undergraduate students, 34% full-time, 63% women, 37% men
- **Noncompetitive** entrance level

Undergraduates 3,914 full-time, 7,615 part-time. Students come from 9 states and territories; 60 other countries; 1% are from out of state; 19% Black or African American, non-Hispanic/Latino; 15% Hispanic/Latino; 2% Asian, non-Hispanic/Latino; 0.1% Native Hawaiian or other Pacific Islander, non-Hispanic/Latino; 0.3% American Indian or Alaska Native, non-Hispanic/Latino; 2% Two or more races, non-Hispanic/Latino; 3% Race/ethnicity unknown; 0.8% international; 2% transferred in. *Retention:* 62% of full-time freshmen returned.
Freshmen *Admission:* 2,055 enrolled. *Test scores:* SAT math scores over 500: 56%; SAT writing scores over 500: 45%; ACT scores over 18: 100%; SAT math scores over 600: 2%; SAT writing scores over 600: 5%; ACT scores over 24: 20%; SAT math scores over 700: 1%; ACT scores over 30: 2%.
Faculty *Total:* 707, 26% full-time, 13% with terminal degrees. *Student/faculty ratio:* 19:1.
Academics *Calendar:* semesters 16-16-6-6. *Degrees:* certificates, associate, and bachelor's. *Special study options:* academic remediation for entering students, accelerated degree program, adult/continuing education programs, advanced placement credit, cooperative education, distance learning, double majors, English as a second language, honors programs, independent study, off-campus study, part-time degree program, services for LD students, study abroad, summer session for credit. *ROTC:* Army (c).
Computers on Campus 250 computers/terminals are available on campus for general student use. Students can access the following: computer help desk, free student e-mail accounts, online (class) grades, online (class) registration, online (class) schedules. Campuswide network is available. Wireless service is available via entire campus.
Student Life *Housing:* college housing not available. *Activities and organizations:* drama/theater group, choral group, Florida Student Nursing Association, SLAM (Student's Living a Message), Eagleteers, Student Government Association, SALO (Student Activities and Leadership Office). *Campus security:* 24-hour emergency response devices and patrols. *Student services:* personal/psychological counseling.
Athletics Member NJCAA. *Intercollegiate sports:* baseball M(s), basketball M(s), soccer W(s), softball W(s), volleyball W(s). *Intramural sports:* basketball M/W, bowling M/W, football M/W, volleyball M/W.
Costs (2011–12) *Tuition:* state resident $3114 full-time, $104 per credit hour part-time; nonresident $11,677 full-time, $389 per credit hour part-time. Full-time tuition and fees vary according to course level, course load, and degree level. Part-time tuition and fees vary according to course level, course load, and degree level. *Waivers:* employees or children of employees.
Applying *Options:* electronic application, early admission, deferred entrance. *Required:* high school transcript. *Application deadlines:* rolling (freshmen), rolling (transfers). *Notification:* continuous (freshmen), continuous (transfers).
Freshman Application Contact Polk State College, 999 Avenue H, NE, Winter Haven, FL 33881-4299. *Phone:* 863-297-1010 Ext. 5016. *Web site:* http://www.polk.edu/.

Polytechnic University of Puerto Rico, Miami Campus

Miami, Florida

Director of Admissions Admissions Department, Polytechnic University of Puerto Rico, Miami Campus, 8180 Northwest 36th Street, Suite 401, Miami, FL 33166. *Phone:* 305-418-4220. *Toll-free phone:* 888-729-7659. *Fax:* 305-418-4325. *Web site:* http://www.pupr.edu/miami/.

Polytechnic University of Puerto Rico, Orlando Campus

Winter Park, Florida

Director of Admissions Teresa Cardona, Director of Recruitment and Admission, Polytechnic University of Puerto Rico, Orlando Campus, 4800

Howell Branch Road, Winter Park, FL 32792. *Phone:* 407-677-7000. *Toll-free phone:* 888-577-POLY. *Fax:* 407-677-5082. *Web site:* http://www.pupr.edu/orlando/.

Rasmussen College Fort Myers

Fort Myers, Florida

- **Proprietary** primarily 2-year, part of Rasmussen College System
- **Suburban** campus
- **Coed** 723 undergraduate students
- **Minimally difficult** entrance level

Faculty *Student/faculty ratio:* 22:1.

Academics *Degrees:* certificates, diplomas, associate, and bachelor's. *Special study options:* academic remediation for entering students, accelerated degree program, adult/continuing education programs, distance learning, double majors, internships, part-time degree program, summer session for credit.

Computers on Campus 129 computers/terminals are available on campus for general student use. Students can access the following: computer help desk, free student e-mail accounts, online (class) grades, online (class) schedules. Campuswide network is available. Wireless service is available via entire campus.

Student Life *Housing:* college housing not available.

Standardized Tests *Required:* Internal Exam (for admission).

Costs (2012–13) *Tuition:* $12,600 full-time. Full-time tuition and fees vary according to course level, course load, degree level, location, and program. Part-time tuition and fees vary according to course level, course load, degree level, location, and program. *Required fees:* $40 full-time. *Payment plans:* installment, deferred payment. *Waivers:* employees or children of employees.

Applying *Options:* electronic application, early admission, deferred entrance. *Application fee:* $20. *Required:* high school transcript, minimum 2.0 GPA, interview. *Application deadlines:* rolling (freshmen), rolling (transfers).

Freshman Application Contact Susan Hammerstrom, Director of Admissions, Rasmussen College Fort Myers, 9160 Forum Corporate Parkway, Suite 100, Fort Myers, FL 33905. *Phone:* 239-477-2100. *Toll-free phone:* 888-549-6755. *E-mail:* susan.hammerstrom@rasmussen.edu. *Web site:* http://www.rasmussen.edu/.

Rasmussen College Land O' Lakes

Land O' Lakes, Florida

- **Proprietary** 4-year, part of Rasmussen College System
- **Suburban** campus
- **Coed** 41 undergraduate students
- **Minimally difficult** entrance level

Faculty *Student/faculty ratio:* 22:1.

Academics *Degrees:* certificates, diplomas, associate, and bachelor's. *Special study options:* academic remediation for entering students, accelerated degree program, adult/continuing education programs, distance learning, double majors, internships, part-time degree program, summer session for credit.

Computers on Campus 61 computers/terminals are available on campus for general student use. Students can access the following: computer help desk, free student e-mail accounts, online (class) grades, online (class) schedules. Campuswide network is available. Wireless service is available via entire campus.

Student Life *Housing:* college housing not available.

Standardized Tests *Required:* Internal Exam (for admission).

Costs (2012–13) *Tuition:* $12,600 full-time. Full-time tuition and fees vary according to course level, course load, degree level, location, and program. Part-time tuition and fees vary according to course level, course load, degree level, location, and program. *Required fees:* $40 full-time. *Payment plans:* installment, deferred payment. *Waivers:* employees or children of employees.

Applying *Options:* electronic application, early admission, deferred entrance. *Application fee:* $20. *Required:* high school transcript, minimum 2.0 GPA, interview. *Application deadlines:* rolling (freshmen), rolling (transfers).

Freshman Application Contact Susan Hammerstrom, Director of Admissions, Rasmussen College Land O' Lakes, 18600 Fernview Street, Land O' Lakes, FL 34638. *Phone:* 813-435-3601. *Toll-free phone:* 888-549-6755. *E-mail:* susan.hammerstrom@rasmussen.edu. *Web site:* http://www.rasmussen.edu/.

Rasmussen College New Port Richey

New Port Richey, Florida

- **Proprietary** primarily 2-year, part of Rasmussen College System
- **Suburban** campus
- **Coed** 896 undergraduate students
- **Minimally difficult** entrance level

Faculty *Student/faculty ratio:* 22:1.

Academics *Degrees:* certificates, diplomas, associate, and bachelor's. *Special study options:* academic remediation for entering students, accelerated degree program, adult/continuing education programs, distance learning, double majors, internships, part-time degree program, summer session for credit.

Computers on Campus 118 computers/terminals are available on campus for general student use. Students can access the following: computer help desk, free student e-mail accounts, online (class) grades, online (class) schedules. Campuswide network is available. Wireless service is available via entire campus.

Student Life *Housing:* college housing not available.

Standardized Tests *Required:* Internal Exam (for admission).

Costs (2012–13) *Tuition:* $12,600 full-time. Full-time tuition and fees vary according to course level, course load, degree level, location, and program. Part-time tuition and fees vary according to course level, course load, degree level, location, and program. *Required fees:* $40 full-time. *Payment plans:* installment, deferred payment. *Waivers:* employees or children of employees.

Financial Aid Of all full-time matriculated undergraduates who enrolled in 2010, 6 Federal Work-Study jobs.

Applying *Options:* electronic application, early admission, deferred entrance. *Application fee:* $20. *Required:* high school transcript, minimum 2.0 GPA, interview. *Application deadlines:* rolling (freshmen), rolling (transfers).

Freshman Application Contact Susan Hammerstrom, Director of Admissions, Rasmussen College New Port Richey, 8661 Citizens Drive, New Port Richey, FL 34654. *Phone:* 727-942-0069. *Toll-free phone:* 888-549-6755. *E-mail:* susan.hammerstrom@rasmussen.edu. *Web site:* http://www.rasmussen.edu/.

Rasmussen College Ocala

Ocala, Florida

- **Proprietary** primarily 2-year, founded 1984, part of Rasmussen College System
- **Suburban** campus with easy access to Orlando
- **Coed, primarily women** 1,256 undergraduate students
- **Minimally difficult** entrance level

Faculty *Student/faculty ratio:* 22:1.

Academics *Calendar:* quarters. *Degrees:* certificates, diplomas, associate, and bachelor's. *Special study options:* academic remediation for entering students, accelerated degree program, adult/continuing education programs, distance learning, double majors, internships, part-time degree program, summer session for credit.

Computers on Campus 124 computers/terminals are available on campus for general student use. Students can access the following: computer help desk, free student e-mail accounts, online (class) grades, online (class) schedules. Campuswide network is available. Wireless service is available via entire campus.

Student Life *Housing:* college housing not available.

Standardized Tests *Required:* Internal Exam (for admission).

Costs (2012–13) *Tuition:* $12,600 full-time. Full-time tuition and fees vary according to course level, course load, degree level, location, and program. Part-time tuition and fees vary according to course level, course load, degree level, location, and program. *Required fees:* $40 full-time. *Payment plans:* installment, deferred payment. *Waivers:* employees or children of employees.

Applying *Options:* electronic application, early admission, deferred entrance. *Application fee:* $20. *Required:* high school transcript, minimum 2.0 GPA, interview. *Application deadlines:* rolling (freshmen), rolling (transfers).

Freshman Application Contact Susan Hammerstrom, Director of Admissions, Rasmussen College Ocala, 2221 Southwest 19th Avenue Road, Ocala, FL 34471. *Phone:* 352-629-1941. *Toll-free phone:* 888-549-6755. *E-mail:* susan.hammerstrom@rasmussen.edu. *Web site:* http://www.rasmussen.edu/.

Rasmussen College Ocala School of Nursing

Ocala, Florida

- **Proprietary** 4-year, part of Rasmussen College System
- **Suburban** campus
- **Coed**
- **Minimally difficult** entrance level

Faculty *Student/faculty ratio:* 22:1.

Academics *Degrees:* associate and bachelor's. *Special study options:* academic remediation for entering students, accelerated degree program, adult/continuing education programs, distance learning, double majors, internships, part-time degree program, summer session for credit.

Computers on Campus Students can access the following: computer help desk, free student e-mail accounts, online (class) grades, online (class) schedules. Campuswide network is available. Wireless service is available via entire campus.

Student Life *Housing:* college housing not available.

Standardized Tests *Required:* Internal Exam (for admission).

Costs (2012–13) *Tuition:* $12,600 full-time. Full-time tuition and fees vary according to course level, course load, degree level, location, and program. Part-time tuition and fees vary according to course level, course load, degree level, location, and program. *Required fees:* $40 full-time. *Payment plans:* installment, deferred payment. *Waivers:* employees or children of employees.

Applying *Options:* electronic application, early admission, deferred entrance. *Application fee:* $20. *Required:* high school transcript, minimum 2.0 GPA, interview. *Application deadlines:* rolling (freshmen), rolling (transfers).

Freshman Application Contact Susan Hammerstrom, Director of Admissions, Rasmussen College Ocala School of Nursing, 2100 SW 22nd Place, Ocala, FL 34471. *Phone:* 352-291-8560. *Toll-free phone:* 888-549-6755. *E-mail:* susan.hammerstrom@rasmussen.edu. *Web site:* http://www.rasmussen.edu/.

Rasmussen College Tampa/Brandon

Tampa, Florida

- **Proprietary** 4-year, part of Rasmussen College System
- **Suburban** campus
- **Coed** 129 undergraduate students
- **Minimally difficult** entrance level

Faculty *Student/faculty ratio:* 22:1.

Academics *Degrees:* certificates, diplomas, associate, and bachelor's. *Special study options:* academic remediation for entering students, accelerated degree program, adult/continuing education programs, distance learning, double majors, internships, part-time degree program, summer session for credit.

Computers on Campus 47 computers/terminals are available on campus for general student use. Students can access the following: computer help desk, free student e-mail accounts, online (class) grades, online (class) schedules. Campuswide network is available. Wireless service is available via entire campus.

Student Life *Housing:* college housing not available.

Standardized Tests *Required:* Internal Exam (for admission).

Costs (2012–13) *Tuition:* $12,600 full-time. Full-time tuition and fees vary according to course level, course load, degree level, location, and program. Part-time tuition and fees vary according to course level, course load, degree level, location, and program. *Required fees:* $40 full-time. *Payment plans:* installment, deferred payment. *Waivers:* employees or children of employees.

Applying *Options:* electronic application, early admission, deferred entrance. *Application fee:* $20. *Required:* high school transcript, minimum 2.0 GPA, interview. *Application deadlines:* rolling (freshmen), rolling (transfers).

Freshman Application Contact Susan Hammerstrom, Director of Admissions, Rasmussen College Tampa/Brandon, 4042 Park Oaks Boulevard, Tampa, FL 33610. *Phone:* 813-246-7600. *Toll-free phone:* 888-549-6755. *E-mail:* susan.hammerstrom@rasmussen.edu. *Web site:* http://www.rasmussen.edu/.

Remington College–Largo Campus

Largo, Florida

Director of Admissions Kathy McCabe, Director of Recruitment, Remington College–Largo Campus, 8550 Ulmerton Road, Largo, FL 33771. *Phone:* 727-532-1999. *Toll-free phone:* 800-560-6192. *Fax:* 727-530-7710.

E-mail: kathy.mccabe@remingtoncollege.edu. *Web site:* http://www.remingtoncollege.edu/.

Remington College–Tampa Campus

Tampa, Florida

Freshman Application Contact Remington College–Tampa Campus, 2410 East Busch Boulevard, Tampa, FL 33612-8410. *Phone:* 813-932-0701. *Toll-free phone:* 800-560-6192. *Web site:* http://www.remingtoncollege.edu/.

Ringling College of Art and Design

Sarasota, Florida

- **Independent** 4-year, founded 1931
- **Small-town** 49-acre campus with easy access to Tampa-St. Petersburg
- **Endowment** $27.4 million
- **Coed** 1,376 undergraduate students, 96% full-time, 60% women, 40% men
- **Moderately difficult** entrance level, 73% of applicants were admitted

Undergraduates 1,326 full-time, 50 part-time. Students come from 42 states and territories; 38 other countries; 44% are from out of state; 3% Black or African American, non-Hispanic/Latino; 13% Hispanic/Latino; 6% Asian, non-Hispanic/Latino; 0.2% Native Hawaiian or other Pacific Islander, non-Hispanic/Latino; 0.4% American Indian or Alaska Native, non-Hispanic/Latino; 3% Two or more races, non-Hispanic/Latino; 9% international; 7% transferred in; 59% live on campus. *Retention:* 83% of full-time freshmen returned.

Freshmen *Admission:* 1,313 applied, 963 admitted, 286 enrolled. *Average high school GPA:* 3.15.

Faculty *Total:* 155, 59% full-time, 50% with terminal degrees. *Student/faculty ratio:* 12:1.

Academics *Calendar:* semesters. *Degree:* certificates and bachelor's. *Special study options:* academic remediation for entering students, advanced placement credit, independent study, internships, off-campus study, part-time degree program, services for LD students, study abroad.

Computers on Campus 850 computers/terminals are available on campus for general student use. Students can access the following: campus intranet, computer help desk, free student e-mail accounts, online (class) grades, online (class) registration, online (class) schedules, central file storage, high performance computing labs. Campuswide network is available. 100% of college-owned or -operated housing units are wired for high-speed Internet access. Wireless service is available via entire campus.

Student Life *Housing options:* coed, men-only, women-only. Campus housing is university owned. Freshman applicants given priority for college housing. *Activities and organizations:* drama/theater group, Student Government Association, Digital Painting Sketch Club, Resident Student Association, MOSAIC, Quidditch Team. *Campus security:* 24-hour emergency response devices and patrols, late-night transport/escort service, controlled dormitory access, lighted campus. *Student services:* personal/psychological counseling.

Athletics *Intramural sports:* basketball M(c)/W(c), football M(c)/W(c), soccer M(c)/W(c), table tennis M(c)/W(c), ultimate Frisbee M(c)/W(c), volleyball M(c)/W(c), weight lifting M(c)/W(c).

Costs (2011–12) *Comprehensive fee:* $44,520 includes full-time tuition ($32,280), mandatory fees ($950), and room and board ($11,290). Full-time tuition and fees vary according to course load, program, and student level. Part-time tuition: $1505 per semester hour. Part-time tuition and fees vary according to course load, program, and student level. *College room only:* $5950. Room and board charges vary according to board plan and housing facility. *Payment plan:* installment. *Waivers:* employees or children of employees.

Financial Aid Of all full-time matriculated undergraduates who enrolled in 2011, 1,043 applied for aid, 944 were judged to have need, 33 had their need fully met. 103 Federal Work-Study jobs (averaging $1175). In 2011, 95 non-need-based awards were made. *Average percent of need met:* 41%. *Average financial aid package:* $17,098. *Average need-based loan:* $7609. *Average need-based gift aid:* $10,368. *Average non-need-based aid:* $16,601.

Applying *Options:* electronic application, deferred entrance. *Application fee:* $70. *Required:* essay or personal statement, high school transcript, minimum 2.0 GPA, 2 letters of recommendation, portfolio, resume. *Recommended:* interview. *Application deadlines:* rolling (freshmen), rolling (transfers). *Notification:* continuous (freshmen), continuous (transfers).

Freshman Application Contact Ms. Tracy Stephanski, Director of Admissions, Ringling College of Art and Design, 2700 North Tamiami Trail, Sarasota, FL 34234-5895. *Phone:* 941-359-7526. *Toll-free phone:* 800-255-7695. *Fax:* 941-359-7517. *E-mail:* admissions@ringling.edu. *Web site:* http://www.ringling.edu/.

Rollins College
Winter Park, Florida

- **Independent** comprehensive, founded 1885
- **Suburban** 70-acre campus with easy access to Orlando
- **Endowment** $353.4 million
- **Coed** 1,818 undergraduate students, 100% full-time, 59% women, 41% men
- **Very difficult** entrance level, 54% of applicants were admitted

Undergraduates 1,818 full-time. 43% are from out of state; 4% Black or African American, non-Hispanic/Latino; 10% Hispanic/Latino; 2% Asian, non-Hispanic/Latino; 0.1% Native Hawaiian or other Pacific Islander, non-Hispanic/Latino; 0.1% American Indian or Alaska Native, non-Hispanic/Latino; 3% Two or more races, non-Hispanic/Latino; 8% Race/ethnicity unknown; 6% international; 4% transferred in; 66% live on campus. *Retention:* 81% of full-time freshmen returned.

Freshmen *Admission:* 4,416 applied, 2,378 admitted, 555 enrolled. *Average high school GPA:* 3.27. *Test scores:* SAT critical reading scores over 500: 94%; SAT math scores over 500: 93%; ACT scores over 18: 100%; SAT critical reading scores over 600: 47%; SAT math scores over 600: 46%; ACT scores over 24: 85%; SAT critical reading scores over 700: 9%; SAT math scores over 700: 6%; ACT scores over 30: 14%.

Faculty *Total:* 174, 100% full-time, 90% with terminal degrees. *Student/faculty ratio:* 10:1.

Academics *Calendar:* semesters. *Degrees:* bachelor's and master's. *Special study options:* academic remediation for entering students, accelerated degree program, adult/continuing education programs, advanced placement credit, double majors, honors programs, independent study, internships, off-campus study, part-time degree program, services for LD students, student-designed majors, study abroad, summer session for credit. *Unusual degree programs:* 3-2 business administration with Crummer Graduate School of Business, Rollins College; engineering with Columbia University, Washington University in St. Louis, or Auburn University; forestry with Duke University School of the Environment; environmental management with Duke University School of the Environment.

Computers on Campus 240 computers/terminals and 155 ports are available on campus for general student use. Students can access the following: campus intranet, computer help desk, free student e-mail accounts, online (class) grades, online (class) registration, online (class) schedules. Campuswide network is available. 100% of college-owned or -operated housing units are wired for high-speed Internet access. Wireless service is available via entire campus.

Student Life *Housing:* on-campus residence required through sophomore year. *Options:* coed, men-only, women-only, disabled students. Campus housing is university owned. Freshman campus housing is guaranteed. *Activities and organizations:* drama/theater group, student-run newspaper, radio and television station, choral group, Interfraternity Council, Panhellenic Association, Student Government Association, Rollins Entertainment Programs, National Society of Collegiate Scholars, national fraternities, national sororities. *Campus security:* 24-hour emergency response devices and patrols, late-night transport/escort service, controlled dormitory access. *Student services:* health clinic, personal/psychological counseling, women's center.

Athletics Member NCAA. All Division II. *Intercollegiate sports:* baseball M(s), basketball M(s)/W(s), crew M/W, cross-country running M/W, golf M(s)/W(s), lacrosse M/W, sailing M/W, skiing (downhill) M/W, soccer M(s)/W(s), softball W(s), swimming and diving M/W, tennis M(s)/W(s), volleyball W(s). *Intramural sports:* baseball M(c), basketball M/W, bowling M(c)/W(c), cheerleading W(c), equestrian sports W(c), football M/W, ice hockey M(c), rock climbing M(c)/W(c), soccer M(c)/W(c), softball M/W, table tennis M/W, tennis M/W, ultimate Frisbee M(c)/W(c), volleyball W(c).

Standardized Tests *Required for some:* SAT or ACT (for admission), Selection of Test Score Waived Option (TSWO) or official SAT/ACT scores (TSWO is not appropriate for applicants seeking academic merit scholarship, Honors Program, or 3/2 Accelerated Management Program consideration).

Costs (2011–12) *Comprehensive fee:* $50,400 includes full-time tuition ($38,400) and room and board ($12,000). *College room only:* $7060. Room and board charges vary according to housing facility. *Payment plan:* installment. *Waivers:* employees or children of employees.

Financial Aid Of all full-time matriculated undergraduates who enrolled in 2011, 1,212 applied for aid, 992 were judged to have need, 198 had their need fully met. 353 Federal Work-Study jobs (averaging $1955). In 2011, 322 non-need-based awards were made. *Average percent of need met:* 80%. *Average financial aid package:* $32,947. *Average need-based loan:* $4808. *Average need-based gift aid:* $29,097. *Average non-need-based aid:* $17,031. *Average indebtedness upon graduation:* $22,719.

Applying *Options:* electronic application, early admission, early decision, deferred entrance. *Application fee:* $40. *Required:* essay or personal statement, high school transcript, 1 letter of recommendation. *Recommended:* minimum 2.0 GPA, interview. *Application deadlines:* 2/15 (freshmen), 4/15 (transfers). *Early decision deadline:* 11/15 (for plan 1), 1/15 (for plan 2). *Notification:* 4/1 (freshmen), continuous (transfers), 12/15 (early decision plan 1), 2/1 (early decision plan 2).

Freshman Application Contact Mr. David Erdmann, Dean of Admission and Enrollment, Rollins College, 1000 Holt Avenue, Campus Box 2720, Winter Park, FL 32789. *Phone:* 407-646-2161. *Fax:* 407-646-1502. *E-mail:* admission@rollins.edu. *Web site:* http://www.rollins.edu/.

St. John Vianney College Seminary
Miami, Florida

Freshman Application Contact Br. Edward Van Merrienboer, Academic Dean, St. John Vianney College Seminary, 2900 Southwest 87th Avenue, Miami, FL 33165-3244. *Phone:* 305-223-4561 Ext. 13. *Web site:* http://www.sjvcs.edu/.

Saint Leo University
Saint Leo, Florida

- **Independent Roman Catholic** comprehensive, founded 1889
- **Rural** 186-acre campus with easy access to Tampa, Orlando
- **Endowment** $34.6 million
- **Coed** 1,926 undergraduate students, 97% full-time, 51% women, 49% men
- **Minimally difficult** entrance level, 93% of applicants were admitted

Undergraduates 1,861 full-time, 65 part-time. Students come from 39 states and territories; 58 other countries; 28% are from out of state; 10% Black or African American, non-Hispanic/Latino; 13% Hispanic/Latino; 1% Asian, non-Hispanic/Latino; 0.2% Native Hawaiian or other Pacific Islander, non-Hispanic/Latino; 0.4% American Indian or Alaska Native, non-Hispanic/Latino; 0.5% Two or more races, non-Hispanic/Latino; 11% Race/ethnicity unknown; 9% international; 5% transferred in; 62% live on campus. *Retention:* 67% of full-time freshmen returned.

Freshmen *Admission:* 1,981 applied, 1,841 admitted, 544 enrolled. *Average high school GPA:* 3.3. *Test scores:* SAT critical reading scores over 500: 41%; SAT math scores over 500: 40%; SAT writing scores over 500: 28%; ACT scores over 18: 88%; SAT critical reading scores over 600: 8%; SAT math scores over 600: 6%; SAT writing scores over 600: 3%; ACT scores over 24: 21%; ACT scores over 30: 1%.

Faculty *Total:* 153, 66% full-time, 61% with terminal degrees. *Student/faculty ratio:* 16:1.

Academics *Calendar:* semesters. *Degrees:* associate, bachelor's, master's, and postbachelor's certificates. *Special study options:* academic remediation for entering students, adult/continuing education programs, advanced placement credit, distance learning, double majors, honors programs, independent study, internships, part-time degree program, services for LD students, study abroad, summer session for credit. *ROTC:* Army (b), Air Force (c).

Computers on Campus 141 computers/terminals are available on campus for general student use. Students can access the following: campus intranet, computer help desk, free student e-mail accounts, online (class) grades, online (class) registration, online (class) schedules, campus residents are issued a laptop for their personal use. Campuswide network is available. 100% of college-owned or -operated housing units are wired for high-speed Internet access. Wireless service is available via classrooms, computer centers, computer labs, dorm rooms, learning centers, libraries, student centers.

Student Life *Housing:* on-campus residence required through junior year. *Options:* coed, men-only, women-only, disabled students. Campus housing is university owned. Freshman applicants given priority for college housing. *Activities and organizations:* drama/theater group, student-run newspaper, radio station, choral group, Student Government Union, Campus Activities Board, Caribbean Student Association, Samaritans, Intercultural Student Association, national fraternities, national sororities. *Campus security:* 24-hour emergency response devices and patrols, late-night transport/escort service, controlled dormitory access, surveillance cameras in parking lots. *Student services:* health clinic, personal/psychological counseling.

Athletics Member NCAA. All Division II. *Intercollegiate sports:* baseball M(s), basketball M(s)/W(s), cross-country running M(s)/W(s), golf M(s)/W(s), lacrosse M(s)/W(s), soccer M(s)/W(s), softball W(s), swimming and diving M(s)/W(s), tennis M(s)/W(s), volleyball W(s). *Intramural sports:* basketball M/W, field hockey M/W, football M/W, soccer M/W, softball M/W, tennis M/W, ultimate Frisbee M/W, volleyball M/W.

Standardized Tests *Recommended:* SAT or ACT (for admission).

Costs (2011–12) *Comprehensive fee:* $27,990 includes full-time tuition ($18,200), mandatory fees ($670), and room and board ($9120). *College room only:* $4720. Room and board charges vary according to board plan and housing facility. *Payment plans:* installment, deferred payment. *Waivers:* employees or children of employees.

Financial Aid Of all full-time matriculated undergraduates who enrolled in 2011, 1,566 applied for aid, 1,375 were judged to have need, 284 had their need fully met. 711 Federal Work-Study jobs (averaging $3220). In 2011, 92 non-need-based awards were made. *Average percent of need met:* 73%. *Average financial aid package:* $18,859. *Average need-based loan:* $4148. *Average need-based gift aid:* $13,057. *Average non-need-based aid:* $1816. *Average indebtedness upon graduation:* $30,015.

Applying *Options:* electronic application, early admission, deferred entrance. *Application fee:* $40. *Required:* high school transcript, minimum 2.5 GPA, 1 letter of recommendation. *Recommended:* minimum 3.0 GPA, interview. *Application deadlines:* 8/15 (freshmen), 8/1 (transfers). *Notification:* continuous (freshmen), continuous (transfers).

Freshman Application Contact Mr. Scott Rhodes, Associate Vice President of Enrollment, Saint Leo University, MC 2008, PO Box 6665, Saint Leo, FL 33574-6665. *Phone:* 352-588-8283. *Toll-free phone:* 800-334-5532. *Fax:* 352-588-8257. *E-mail:* admissions@saintleo.edu. *Web site:* http://www.saintleo.edu/.

See below for display ad and page 1558 for the College Close-Up.

St. Petersburg College
St. Petersburg, Florida

- **State and locally supported** 4-year, founded 1927
- **Suburban** 410-acre campus with easy access to Tampa
- **Endowment** $25.8 million
- **Coed**
- **Noncompetitive** entrance level

Academics *Calendar:* semesters. *Degrees:* certificates, diplomas, associate, and bachelor's.

Student Life *Campus security:* late-night transport/escort service.

Athletics Member NJCAA.

Costs (2011–12) *Tuition:* state resident $2424 full-time, $78 per credit hour part-time; nonresident $9300 full-time, $310 per credit hour part-time. Full-time tuition and fees vary according to course level, degree level, and program. Part-time tuition and fees vary according to course level, degree level, and program. *Required fees:* $664 full-time, $22 per credit hour part-time.

Financial Aid *Of all full-time matriculated undergraduates who enrolled in 2010,* 350 Federal Work-Study jobs (averaging $2500).

Applying *Options:* electronic application, early admission. *Application fee:* $40. *Required:* high school transcript.

Freshman Application Contact Ms. Susan Fell, Director of Admissions and Records, St. Petersburg College, PO Box 13489, St. Petersburg, FL 33733-3489. *Phone:* 727-341-3166. *E-mail:* information@spcollege.edu. *Web site:* http://www.spcollege.edu.

St. Thomas University
Miami Gardens, Florida

- **Independent Roman Catholic** comprehensive, founded 1961
- **Suburban** 140-acre campus
- **Coed** 1,085 undergraduate students, 93% full-time, 56% women, 44% men
- **Minimally difficult** entrance level, 39% of applicants were admitted

Undergraduates 1,013 full-time, 72 part-time. 20% are from out of state; 26% Black or African American, non-Hispanic/Latino; 41% Hispanic/Latino; 0.4% Asian, non-Hispanic/Latino; 0.2% American Indian or Alaska Native, non-Hispanic/Latino; 0.9% Two or more races, non-Hispanic/Latino; 7% Race/ethnicity unknown; 13% international; 16% transferred in; 25% live on campus. *Retention:* 67% of full-time freshmen returned.

Freshmen *Admission:* 681 applied, 268 admitted, 209 enrolled. *Average high school GPA:* 2.94. *Test scores:* SAT critical reading scores over 500: 21%; SAT math scores over 500: 29%; SAT writing scores over 500: 13%; ACT scores over 18: 69%; SAT critical reading scores over 600: 2%; SAT math scores over 600: 6%; SAT writing scores over 600: 2%; ACT scores over 24: 6%.

Faculty *Total:* 238, 43% full-time, 52% with terminal degrees. *Student/faculty ratio:* 14:1.

Academics *Calendar:* semesters. *Degrees:* certificates, bachelor's, master's, doctoral, post-master's, postbachelor's, and first professional certificates. *Special study options:* academic remediation for entering students, adult/continuing education programs, advanced placement credit, distance learning, double majors, freshman honors college, honors programs, independent study, internships, part-time degree program, services for LD students, summer session for credit.

Computers on Campus Students can access the following: campus intranet, free student e-mail accounts, online (class) grades, online (class) registration, online (class) schedules. Campuswide network is available. Wireless service is available via entire campus.

Student Life *Housing options:* men-only, women-only. Campus housing is university owned. *Activities and organizations:* student-run television station,

choral group. *Campus security:* 24-hour emergency response devices and patrols, late-night transport/escort service, controlled dormitory access. *Student services:* health clinic, personal/psychological counseling.

Athletics Member NAIA. *Intercollegiate sports:* baseball M(s), cross-country running M(s)/W(s), golf M(s)/W(s), soccer M(s)/W(s), softball W(s), tennis M(s)/W(s), volleyball W(s). *Intramural sports:* baseball M, basketball M/W, cross-country running M/W, football M, golf M, soccer M/W, softball M/W, table tennis M/W, tennis M/W, volleyball M/W, water polo M/W, weight lifting M/W.

Standardized Tests *Required:* SAT or ACT (for admission).

Costs (2011–12) *Comprehensive fee:* $31,050 includes full-time tuition ($23,910) and room and board ($7140). Full-time tuition and fees vary according to program. Part-time tuition and fees vary according to program. *Room and board:* Room and board charges vary according to board plan and housing facility. *Payment plan:* installment. *Waivers:* minority students, children of alumni, and employees or children of employees.

Financial Aid Of all full-time matriculated undergraduates who enrolled in 2011, 862 applied for aid, 775 were judged to have need, 153 had their need fully met. In 2011, 174 non-need-based awards were made. *Average need-based loan:* $4220. *Average need-based gift aid:* $3093. *Average non-need-based aid:* $9121.

Applying *Options:* electronic application, deferred entrance. *Application fee:* $40. *Required:* high school transcript, minimum 2.0 GPA. *Recommended:* essay or personal statement, 1 letter of recommendation, interview. *Application deadlines:* rolling (freshmen), rolling (transfers). *Notification:* continuous (freshmen), continuous (transfers).

Freshman Application Contact Mr. Andre Lightbourne, Director of Admissions, St. Thomas University, 16401 Northwest 37th Avenue, Miami Gardens, FL 33054-6459. *Phone:* 305-628-6712. *Toll-free phone:* 800-367-9010. *Fax:* 305-628-6591. *E-mail:* signup@stu.edu. *Web site:* http://www.stu.edu/.

Santa Fe College

Gainesville, Florida

- **State and locally supported** 4-year, founded 1966, part of Florida College System
- **Suburban** 187-acre campus with easy access to Jacksonville
- **Coed**
- **Noncompetitive** entrance level

Faculty *Student/faculty ratio:* 25:1.

Academics *Calendar:* semesters. *Degrees:* certificates, associate, and bachelor's (offers bachelor's degrees in conjunction with Saint Leo College).

Student Life *Campus security:* 24-hour emergency response devices and patrols.

Athletics Member NJCAA.

Costs (2011–12) *Tuition:* state resident $2456 full-time, $102 per credit hour part-time; nonresident $9057 full-time, $377 per credit hour part-time. Full-time tuition and fees vary according to degree level. Part-time tuition and fees vary according to degree level.

Financial Aid *Of all full-time matriculated undergraduates who enrolled in 2010,* 190 Federal Work-Study jobs.

Applying *Options:* electronic application, early admission. *Required:* high school transcript. *Required for some:* essay or personal statement, high school transcript, interview.

Freshman Application Contact Santa Fe College, 3000 Northwest 83rd Street, Gainesville, FL 32606. *Phone:* 352-395-4177. *Web site:* http://www.sfcollege.edu/.

Schiller International University

Largo, Florida

Freshman Application Contact Donald Trippe, Admissions Officer, Schiller International University, 300 East Bay Drive, Largo, FL 33770. *Phone:* 727-738-6365. *Toll-free phone:* 800-261-9571 (in-state); 800-261-9751 (out-of-state). *Fax:* 727-738-6376. *E-mail:* admissions@schiller.edu. *Web site:* http://www.schiller.edu/.

Seminole State College of Florida

Sanford, Florida

- **State and locally supported** primarily 2-year, founded 1966
- **Small-town** 200-acre campus with easy access to Orlando
- **Endowment** $8.3 million
- **Coed** 18,514 undergraduate students, 42% full-time, 59% women, 41% men
- **Noncompetitive** entrance level, 100% of applicants were admitted

Undergraduates 7,692 full-time, 10,822 part-time. Students come from 88 other countries; 0.5% are from out of state; 18% Black or African American, non-Hispanic/Latino; 21% Hispanic/Latino; 2% Asian, non-Hispanic/Latino; 0.3% Native Hawaiian or other Pacific Islander, non-Hispanic/Latino; 0.3% American Indian or Alaska Native, non-Hispanic/Latino; 2% Two or more races, non-Hispanic/Latino; 2% Race/ethnicity unknown; 2% international; 4% transferred in.

Freshmen *Admission:* 8,978 applied, 8,978 admitted, 2,844 enrolled.

Faculty *Total:* 795, 30% full-time, 14% with terminal degrees. *Student/faculty ratio:* 27:1.

Academics *Calendar:* semesters. *Degrees:* certificates, diplomas, associate, and bachelor's. *Special study options:* academic remediation for entering students, accelerated degree program, adult/continuing education programs, advanced placement credit, cooperative education, distance learning, double majors, English as a second language, external degree program, honors programs, independent study, internships, part-time degree program, services for LD students, study abroad, summer session for credit. *ROTC:* Army (b).

Computers on Campus 250 computers/terminals are available on campus for general student use. Students can access the following: online (class) registration, online (class) schedules. Campuswide network is available. Wireless service is available via entire campus.

Student Life *Housing:* college housing not available. *Activities and organizations:* drama/theater group, student-run newspaper, choral group, Phi Beta Lambda, Phi Theta Kappa, Student Government Association, Sigma Phi Gamma, Hispanic Student Association. *Campus security:* 24-hour emergency response devices and patrols. *Student services:* personal/psychological counseling.

Athletics Member NJCAA. *Intercollegiate sports:* baseball M(s), golf W(s), softball W(s).

Standardized Tests *Required:* CPT (for admission). *Recommended:* ACT (for admission).

Costs (2012–13) *Tuition:* state resident $3131 full-time, $104 per credit hour part-time; nonresident $11,456 full-time, $382 per credit hour part-time. Full-time tuition and fees vary according to degree level and program. Part-time tuition and fees vary according to degree level and program. *Payment plan:* deferred payment. *Waivers:* senior citizens and employees or children of employees.

Applying *Options:* electronic application, early admission, deferred entrance. *Required:* high school transcript, minimum 2.0 GPA. *Application deadlines:* rolling (freshmen), rolling (transfers). *Notification:* continuous (freshmen), continuous (transfers).

Freshman Application Contact Ms. Pamela Mennechey, Associate Vice President - Student Recruitment and Enrollment, Seminole State College of Florida, Sanford, FL 32773-6199. *Phone:* 407-708-2050. *Fax:* 407-708-2395. *E-mail:* admissions@scc-fl.edu. *Web site:* http://www.seminolestate.edu/.

Southeastern University

Lakeland, Florida

- **Independent** comprehensive, founded 1935, affiliated with Assemblies of God
- **Suburban** 87-acre campus with easy access to Tampa, Orlando
- **Coed** 2,320 undergraduate students, 87% full-time, 56% women, 44% men
- **Minimally difficult** entrance level, 70% of applicants were admitted

Undergraduates 2,029 full-time, 291 part-time. 33% are from out of state; 11% Black or African American, non-Hispanic/Latino; 15% Hispanic/Latino; 0.9% Asian, non-Hispanic/Latino; 0.4% American Indian or Alaska Native, non-Hispanic/Latino; 0.8% Two or more races, non-Hispanic/Latino; 4% Race/ethnicity unknown; 1% international; 7% transferred in; 54% live on campus. *Retention:* 66% of full-time freshmen returned.

Freshmen *Admission:* 1,234 applied, 859 admitted, 472 enrolled. *Test scores:* SAT critical reading scores over 500: 54%; SAT math scores over 500: 45%; SAT writing scores over 500: 50%; ACT scores over 18: 81%; SAT critical reading scores over 600: 15%; SAT math scores over 600: 11%; SAT writing scores over 600: 10%; ACT scores over 24: 24%; SAT critical reading scores over 700: 2%; SAT math scores over 700: 1%; SAT writing scores over 700: 2%; ACT scores over 30: 3%.

Faculty *Total:* 169, 57% full-time, 46% with terminal degrees. *Student/faculty ratio:* 19:1.

Academics *Calendar:* semesters. *Degrees:* bachelor's and master's. *Special study options:* adult/continuing education programs, part-time degree program. *ROTC:* Army (c).

Computers on Campus Students can access the following: campus intranet, computer help desk, free student e-mail accounts, online (class) grades, online (class) registration, online (class) schedules, network programs. Campuswide network is available. 100% of college-owned or -operated housing units are wired for high-speed Internet access. Wireless service is available via entire campus.

Student Life *Housing:* on-campus residence required through senior year. *Options:* men-only, women-only. Campus housing is university owned. Freshman campus housing is guaranteed. *Campus security:* 24-hour emergency response devices and patrols, late-night transport/escort service.

Athletics Member NAIA, NCCAA. *Intercollegiate sports:* baseball M, basketball M/W, cheerleading M/W, golf M, soccer M/W, tennis W, volleyball W. *Intramural sports:* basketball M/W, football M/W, soccer M/W, softball M/W, ultimate Frisbee M/W, volleyball M/W.

Standardized Tests *Required:* SAT or ACT (for admission).

Costs (2011–12) *Comprehensive fee:* $25,938 includes full-time tuition ($17,118), mandatory fees ($600), and room and board ($8220). Full-time tuition and fees vary according to class time, degree level, and reciprocity agreements. Part-time tuition: $713 per credit hour. Part-time tuition and fees vary according to class time, course load, degree level, and reciprocity agreements. *Required fees:* $150 per term part-time. *Room and board:* Room and board charges vary according to board plan and housing facility. *Payment plan:* installment. *Waivers:* employees or children of employees.

Financial Aid Of all full-time matriculated undergraduates who enrolled in 2011, 2,057 applied for aid, 1,814 were judged to have need, 172 had their need fully met. In 2011, 245 non-need-based awards were made. *Average percent of need met:* 2%. *Average financial aid package:* $11,535. *Average need-based loan:* $3861. *Average need-based gift aid:* $8187. *Average non-need-based aid:* $3846. *Average indebtedness upon graduation:* $24,398.

Applying *Options:* early admission, deferred entrance. *Application fee:* $40. *Required:* essay or personal statement, high school transcript, 2 letters of recommendation. *Required for some:* interview. *Application deadlines:* 5/1 (freshmen), 7/1 (transfers). *Notification:* 6/1 (freshmen), continuous (transfers).

Freshman Application Contact Southeastern University, 1000 Longfellow Boulevard, Lakeland, FL 33801-6099. *Phone:* 800-500-8760. *Toll-free phone:* 800-500-8760. *Web site:* http://www.seu.edu/.

South University

Royal Palm Beach, Florida

- **Proprietary** comprehensive, founded 1899, part of Education Management Corporation
- **Coed**

Academics *Calendar:* quarters. *Degrees:* associate, bachelor's, and master's.

Costs (2011–12) *Tuition:* Information about tuition and fees can be obtained by contacting the South University Admissions Office.

Freshman Application Contact South University, University Centre, 9801 Belvedere Road, Royal Palm Beach, FL 33411. *Phone:* 561-273-6500. *Toll-free phone:* 866-629-2902. *Web site:* http://www.southuniversity.edu/westpalm-beach/.

See page 1596 for the College Close-Up.

South University

Tampa, Florida

- **Proprietary** comprehensive, part of Education Management Corporation
- **Coed**

Academics *Degrees:* associate, bachelor's, and master's.

Costs (2011–12) *Tuition:* Information about tuition and fees can be obtained by contacting the South University Admissions Office.

Freshman Application Contact South University, 4401 North Himes Avenue, Suite 175, Tampa, FL 33614. *Phone:* 813-393-3800. *Toll-free phone:* 800-846-1472. *Web site:* http://www.southuniversity.edu/tampa/.

See page 1596 for the College Close-Up.

Southwest Florida College

Fort Myers, Florida

Freshman Application Contact Mr. Ken Reynolds, Director of Admissions, Southwest Florida College, 1685 Medical Lane, Fort Myers, FL 33907. *Phone:* 239-939-4766. *Toll-free phone:* 877-493-5147 (in-state); 877-793-5147 (out-of-state). *Fax:* 239-936-4040. *E-mail:* kreynolds@swfc.edu. *Web site:* http://www.swfc.edu/.

Southwest Florida College

Tampa, Florida

Director of Admissions Admissions, Southwest Florida College, 3910 Riga Boulevard, Tampa, FL 33619. *Phone:* 813-630-4401. *Toll-free phone:* 877-493-5147. *Web site:* http://www.swfc.edu/.

State College of Florida Manatee-Sarasota

Bradenton, Florida

- **State-supported** primarily 2-year, founded 1957, part of Florida Community College System
- **Suburban** 100-acre campus with easy access to Tampa-St. Petersburg
- **Coed** 11,303 undergraduate students, 43% full-time, 60% women, 40% men
- **Noncompetitive** entrance level, 100% of applicants were admitted

Undergraduates 4,881 full-time, 6,422 part-time. Students come from 29 states and territories; 47 other countries; 2% are from out of state; 10% Black or African American, non-Hispanic/Latino; 12% Hispanic/Latino; 2% Asian, non-Hispanic/Latino; 0.5% American Indian or Alaska Native, non-Hispanic/Latino; 0.7% Two or more races, non-Hispanic/Latino; 4% Race/ethnicity unknown; 1% international; 5% transferred in. *Retention:* 59% of full-time freshmen returned.

Freshmen *Admission:* 2,736 applied, 2,736 admitted, 1,541 enrolled. *Test scores:* SAT critical reading scores over 500: 32%; SAT math scores over 500: 31%; SAT writing scores over 500: 33%; ACT scores over 18: 56%; SAT critical reading scores over 600: 6%; SAT math scores over 600: 6%; SAT writing scores over 600: 6%; ACT scores over 24: 16%; ACT scores over 30: 3%.

Faculty *Total:* 407, 37% full-time.

Academics *Calendar:* semesters. *Degrees:* certificates, associate, and bachelor's. *Special study options:* academic remediation for entering students, advanced placement credit, cooperative education, distance learning, English as a second language, honors programs, independent study, part-time degree program, services for LD students, summer session for credit.

Computers on Campus 1,000 computers/terminals are available on campus for general student use. Students can access the following: computer help desk, free student e-mail accounts, online (class) registration, online (class) schedules. Campuswide network is available. Wireless service is available via libraries, student centers.

Student Life *Housing:* college housing not available. *Activities and organizations:* drama/theater group, student-run newspaper, choral group, Student Government Association, Phi Theta Kappa, American Chemical Society Student Affiliate, Campus Ministry, Medical Community Club. *Campus security:* 24-hour emergency response devices and patrols, late-night transport/escort service.

Athletics Member NJCAA. *Intercollegiate sports:* baseball M(s), basketball M(s), softball W(s), volleyball W(s). *Intramural sports:* basketball M/W, softball M/W, volleyball M/W, weight lifting M/W.

Costs (2012–13) *Tuition:* state resident $2460 full-time, $102 per credit part-time; nonresident $9276 full-time, $387 per credit part-time.

Financial Aid Of all full-time matriculated undergraduates who enrolled in 2010, 82 Federal Work-Study jobs (averaging $2800). *Financial aid deadline:* 8/15.

Applying *Options:* early admission. *Required:* high school transcript. *Application deadlines:* 8/20 (freshmen), 8/20 (transfers). *Notification:* continuous (freshmen), continuous (transfers).

Freshman Application Contact Ms. MariLynn Lewy, AVP, Student Services, State College of Florida Manatee-Sarasota, Bradenton, FL 34206. *Phone:* 941-752-5384. *Fax:* 941-727-6380. *E-mail:* lewym@scf.edu. *Web site:* http://www.scf.edu/.

Stetson University

DeLand, Florida

- **Independent** comprehensive, founded 1883
- **Small-town** 140-acre campus with easy access to Orlando
- **Endowment** $143.9 million
- **Coed** 2,291 undergraduate students, 97% full-time, 58% women, 42% men
- **Moderately difficult** entrance level, 66% of applicants were admitted

Undergraduates 2,233 full-time, 58 part-time. Students come from 45 states and territories; 41 other countries; 19% are from out of state; 7% Black or Afri-

can American, non-Hispanic/Latino; 14% Hispanic/Latino; 2% Asian, non-Hispanic/Latino; 0.1% Native Hawaiian or other Pacific Islander, non-Hispanic/Latino; 0.2% American Indian or Alaska Native, non-Hispanic/Latino; 4% Two or more races, non-Hispanic/Latino; 1% Race/ethnicity unknown; 4% international; 6% transferred in; 63% live on campus. *Retention:* 77% of full-time freshmen returned.

Freshmen *Admission:* 3,454 applied, 2,295 admitted, 715 enrolled. *Average high school GPA:* 3.74. *Test scores:* SAT critical reading scores over 500: 85%; SAT math scores over 500: 82%; SAT writing scores over 500: 77%; ACT scores over 18: 99%; SAT critical reading scores over 600: 40%; SAT math scores over 600: 32%; SAT writing scores over 600: 29%; ACT scores over 24: 60%; SAT critical reading scores over 700: 6%; SAT math scores over 700: 4%; SAT writing scores over 700: 3%; ACT scores over 30: 8%.

Faculty *Total:* 375, 62% full-time, 84% with terminal degrees. *Student/faculty ratio:* 12:1.

Academics *Calendar:* semesters. *Degrees:* bachelor's, master's, doctoral, and post-master's certificates. *Special study options:* accelerated degree program, adult/continuing education programs, advanced placement credit, distance learning, double majors, honors programs, independent study, internships, off-campus study, part-time degree program, services for LD students, student-designed majors, study abroad, summer session for credit. *ROTC:* Army (c). *Unusual degree programs:* 3-2 engineering; forestry with Duke University; Master of Public Administration with American University, JD with Stetson University College of Law.

Computers on Campus 487 computers/terminals are available on campus for general student use. Students can access the following: campus intranet, computer help desk, free student e-mail accounts, online (class) grades, online (class) registration, online (class) schedules. Campuswide network is available. 100% of college-owned or -operated housing units are wired for high-speed Internet access. Wireless service is available via entire campus.

Student Life *Housing:* on-campus residence required through junior year. *Options:* coed, men-only, women-only. Campus housing is university owned and leased by the school. Freshman campus housing is guaranteed. *Activities and organizations:* drama/theater group, student-run newspaper, radio station, choral group, Into the Streets, Multicultural Student Council, Student Government Association, Kaleidoscope, Hatter Harvest, national fraternities, national sororities. *Campus security:* 24-hour emergency response devices and patrols, late-night transport/escort service, controlled dormitory access. *Student services:* health clinic, personal/psychological counseling, women's center.

Athletics Member NCAA. All Division I. *Intercollegiate sports:* baseball M(s), basketball M(s)/W(s), crew M/W(s), cross-country running M(s)/W(s), golf M(s)/W(s), soccer M(s)/W(s), softball W(s), tennis M(s)/W(s), volleyball W(s). *Intramural sports:* baseball M, basketball M/W, bowling M/W, equestrian sports M(c)/W(c), golf M/W, lacrosse M(c)/W(c), riflery M(c)/W(c), soccer M(c)/W, softball M/W, swimming and diving M(c)/W(c), table tennis M(c)/W(c), tennis M(c)/W(c), ultimate Frisbee M(c)/W(c), volleyball M/W.

Standardized Tests *Required for some:* SAT or ACT (for admission).

Costs (2012–13) *Comprehensive fee:* $47,332 includes full-time tuition ($36,344), mandatory fees ($300), and room and board ($10,688). Part-time tuition: $3785 per course. Part-time tuition and fees vary according to course load, location, and program. *College room only:* $6088. Room and board charges vary according to board plan and housing facility. *Payment plan:* installment. *Waivers:* employees or children of employees.

Financial Aid Of all full-time matriculated undergraduates who enrolled in 2011, 1,926 applied for aid, 1,641 were judged to have need, 349 had their need fully met. 731 Federal Work-Study jobs (averaging $1964). 159 state and other part-time jobs (averaging $3623). In 2011, 448 non-need-based awards were made. *Average percent of need met:* 78%. *Average financial aid package:* $30,449. *Average need-based loan:* $4981. *Average need-based gift aid:* $23,528. *Average non-need-based aid:* $16,011. *Average indebtedness upon graduation:* $31,206.

Applying *Options:* electronic application, early admission, early decision, deferred entrance. *Application fee:* $25. *Required:* essay or personal statement, high school transcript, 1 letter of recommendation. *Recommended:* interview. *Application deadlines:* 3/15 (freshmen), rolling (transfers). *Early decision deadline:* 11/1. *Notification:* 12/1 (freshmen), continuous (transfers), 11/15 (early decision).

Freshman Application Contact Mr. Robert Stewart, Director of Admissions, Stetson University, Unit 8378, Griffith Hall, DeLand, FL 32723. *Phone:* 386-822-7100. *Toll-free phone:* 800-688-0101. *Fax:* 386-822-7112. *E-mail:* admissions@stetson.edu. *Web site:* http://www.stetson.edu/.

Strayer University - Baymeadows Campus

Jacksonville, Florida

- **Proprietary** comprehensive
- **Coed**

Academics *Degrees:* certificates, diplomas, associate, bachelor's, master's, and postbachelor's certificates.

Freshman Application Contact Strayer University - Baymeadows Campus, 8375 Dix Ellis Trail, Suite 200, Jacksonville, FL 32256. *Web site:* http://www.strayer.edu/baymeadows/.

Strayer University - Brickell Campus

Miami, Florida

- **Proprietary** comprehensive
- **Coed**

Academics *Degrees:* certificates, diplomas, associate, bachelor's, master's, and postbachelor's certificates.

Freshman Application Contact Strayer University - Brickell Campus, 1201 Brickell Avenue, Suite 700, Miami, FL 33131. *Web site:* http://www.strayer.edu/brickell.

Strayer University - Coral Springs Campus

Coral Springs, Florida

- **Proprietary** comprehensive
- **Coed**

Academics *Degrees:* certificates, diplomas, associate, bachelor's, master's, and postbachelor's certificates.

Freshman Application Contact Strayer University - Coral Springs Campus, 5830 Coral Ridge Drive, Suite 300, Coral Springs, FL 33076. *Web site:* http://www.strayer.edu/coral_springs/.

Strayer University - Doral Campus

Miami, Florida

- **Proprietary** comprehensive
- **Coed**

Academics *Degrees:* certificates, diplomas, associate, bachelor's, master's, and postbachelor's certificates.

Freshman Application Contact Strayer University - Doral Campus, 11430 Northwest 20th Street, Suite 150, Miami, FL 33172. *Web site:* http://www.strayer.edu/doral.

Strayer University - Fort Lauderdale Campus

Fort Lauderdale, Florida

- **Proprietary** comprehensive
- **Coed**

Academics *Degrees:* certificates, diplomas, associate, bachelor's, master's, and postbachelor's certificates.

Freshman Application Contact Strayer University - Fort Lauderdale Campus, 2307 West Broward Boulevard, Suite 100, Fort Lauderdale, FL 33312. *Web site:* http://www.strayer.edu/fort_lauderdale/.

Strayer University - Maitland Campus

Maitland, Florida

- **Proprietary** comprehensive
- **Coed**

Academics *Degrees:* certificates, diplomas, associate, bachelor's, master's, and postbachelor's certificates.

Freshman Application Contact Strayer University - Maitland Campus, 850 Trafalgar Court, Suite 360, Maitland, FL 32751. *Web site:* http://www.strayer.edu/maitland/.

Strayer University - Miramar Campus

Miramar, Florida

- **Proprietary** comprehensive
- **Coed**

Academics *Degrees:* certificates, diplomas, associate, bachelor's, master's, and postbachelor's certificates.

Freshman Application Contact Strayer University - Miramar Campus, 15620 Southwest 29th Street, Miramar, FL 33027. *Web site:* http://www.strayer.edu/miramar.

Strayer University - Orlando East Campus

Orlando, Florida

- **Proprietary** comprehensive
- **Coed**

Academics *Degrees:* certificates, diplomas, associate, bachelor's, master's, and postbachelor's certificates.

Freshman Application Contact Strayer University - Orlando East Campus, 2200 North Alafaya Trail, Suite 500, Orlando, FL 32826. *Web site:* http://www.strayer.edu/orlando_east/.

Strayer University - Palm Beach Gardens Campus

Palm Beach Gardens, Florida

- **Proprietary** comprehensive
- **Coed**

Academics *Degrees:* certificates, diplomas, associate, bachelor's, master's, and postbachelor's certificates.

Freshman Application Contact Strayer University - Palm Beach Gardens Campus, 11025 RCA Center Drive, Suite 200, Palm Beach Gardens, FL 33410. *Web site:* http://www.strayer.edu/palm_beach_gardens.

Strayer University - Sand Lake Campus

Orlando, Florida

- **Proprietary** comprehensive
- **Coed**

Academics *Degrees:* certificates, diplomas, associate, bachelor's, master's, and postbachelor's certificates.

Freshman Application Contact Strayer University - Sand Lake Campus, 8541 South Park Circle, Building 900, Orlando, FL 32819. *Web site:* http://www.strayer.edu/sand_lake/.

Strayer University - Tampa East Campus

Tampa, Florida

- **Proprietary** comprehensive
- **Coed**

Academics *Degrees:* certificates, diplomas, associate, bachelor's, master's, and postbachelor's certificates.

Freshman Application Contact Strayer University - Tampa East Campus, 6302 East Martin Luther King Boulevard, Suite 450, Tampa, FL 33619. *Web site:* http://www.strayer.edu/tampa_east.

Strayer University - Tampa Westshore Campus

Tampa, Florida

- **Proprietary** comprehensive
- **Coed**

Academics *Degrees:* certificates, diplomas, associate, bachelor's, master's, and postbachelor's certificates.

Freshman Application Contact Strayer University - Tampa Westshore Campus, 4902 Eisenhower Boulevard, Suite 100, Tampa, FL 33634. *Web site:* http://www.strayer.edu/tampa_westshore.

Talmudic College of Florida

Miami Beach, Florida

Freshman Application Contact Rabbi Yeshaya Greenberg, Dean of Students, Talmudic College of Florida, 1910 Alton Road, Miami Beach, FL 33139. *Phone:* 305-534-7050. *Fax:* 305-534-8444. *E-mail:* yandtg@gmail.com. *Web site:* http://www.talmudicu.edu/.

Trinity Baptist College

Jacksonville, Florida

- **Independent Baptist** comprehensive, founded 1974
- **Urban** 148-acre campus with easy access to Jacksonville
- **Coed** 268 undergraduate students
- **Moderately difficult** entrance level

Freshmen *Admission:* 130 applied.

Faculty *Total:* 50. *Student/faculty ratio:* 9:1.

Academics *Calendar:* semesters. *Degrees:* associate, bachelor's, and master's. *Special study options:* academic remediation for entering students, accelerated degree program, adult/continuing education programs, advanced placement credit, distance learning, double majors, independent study, internships, part-time degree program, services for LD students, summer session for credit.

Computers on Campus 30 computers/terminals are available on campus for general student use. Students can access the following: campus intranet, free student e-mail accounts, online (class) grades, online (class) registration. Campuswide network is available. 100% of college-owned or -operated housing units are wired for high-speed Internet access. Wireless service is available via entire campus.

Student Life *Housing:* on-campus residence required through junior year. *Options:* men-only, women-only. Campus housing is university owned. Freshman campus housing is guaranteed. *Activities and organizations:* drama/theater group, student-run newspaper, choral group. *Campus security:* 24-hour emergency response devices and patrols, controlled dormitory access. *Student services:* health clinic, personal/psychological counseling.

Athletics Member NCCAA. *Intercollegiate sports:* basketball M/W, cheerleading W, soccer M, volleyball W. *Intramural sports:* baseball M, basketball M/W, football M, soccer M, softball M/W, table tennis M/W, volleyball M/W.

Standardized Tests *Required:* SAT or ACT (for admission).

Costs (2012–13) *Comprehensive fee:* $14,550 includes full-time tuition ($7990), mandatory fees ($1050), and room and board ($5510). Part-time tuition: $335 per credit hour. *College room only:* $2510. Room and board charges vary according to board plan. *Payment plan:* installment. *Waivers:* employees or children of employees.

Financial Aid Of all full-time matriculated undergraduates who enrolled in 2001, 264 applied for aid, 168 were judged to have need, 37 had their need fully met. In 2001, 10 non-need-based awards were made. *Average percent of need met:* 55%. *Average financial aid package:* $4458. *Average need-based loan:* $2912. *Average need-based gift aid:* $2791. *Average non-need-based aid:* $1279. *Average indebtedness upon graduation:* $6425. *Financial aid deadline:* 4/15.

Applying *Options:* electronic application. *Application fee:* $30. *Required:* essay or personal statement, high school transcript, minimum 2.0 GPA, 2 letters of recommendation. *Application deadlines:* rolling (freshmen), rolling (transfers). *Notification:* continuous until 8/15 (freshmen), continuous until 8/15 (transfers).

Freshman Application Contact Trinity Baptist College, FL. *Phone:* 904-596-2538. *Toll-free phone:* 800-786-2206. *E-mail:* trinity@tbc.edu. *Web site:* http://www.tbc.edu/.

Trinity College of Florida

New Port Richey, Florida

- **Independent nondenominational** 4-year, founded 1932
- **Small-town** 40-acre campus with easy access to Tampa
- **Endowment** $2.1 million
- **Coed** 192 undergraduate students, 88% full-time, 43% women, 57% men
- **Minimally difficult** entrance level, 35% of applicants were admitted

Undergraduates 168 full-time, 24 part-time. Students come from 8 states and territories; 2 other countries; 4% are from out of state; 10% Black or African American, non-Hispanic/Latino; 14% Hispanic/Latino; 0.5% Asian, non-Hispanic/Latino; 3% Two or more races, non-Hispanic/Latino; 1% Race/ethnicity unknown; 2% international; 16% transferred in; 36% live on campus. *Retention:* 52% of full-time freshmen returned.

Freshmen *Admission:* 243 applied, 85 admitted, 30 enrolled. *Average high school GPA:* 2.56. *Test scores:* SAT critical reading scores over 500: 45%; SAT math scores over 500: 45%; SAT writing scores over 500: 22%; ACT scores over 18: 69%; SAT critical reading scores over 600: 18%; SAT math

scores over 600: 18%; SAT writing scores over 600: 11%; ACT scores over 24: 31%.
Faculty *Total:* 28, 29% full-time, 36% with terminal degrees. *Student/faculty ratio:* 11:1.
Academics *Calendar:* semesters. *Degrees:* certificates, associate, and bachelor's. *Special study options:* academic remediation for entering students, accelerated degree program, adult/continuing education programs, advanced placement credit, cooperative education, distance learning, double majors, independent study, internships, off-campus study, part-time degree program, services for LD students, student-designed majors, summer session for credit.
Computers on Campus 17 computers/terminals and 144 ports are available on campus for general student use. Students can access the following: campus intranet, computer help desk, free student e-mail accounts, online (class) grades, online (class) registration, online (class) schedules. Campuswide network is available. 100% of college-owned or -operated housing units are wired for high-speed Internet access. Wireless service is available via entire campus.
Student Life *Housing:* on-campus residence required through senior year. *Options:* men-only, women-only, disabled students. Campus housing is university owned and leased by the school. Freshman campus housing is guaranteed. *Activities and organizations:* drama/theater group, choral group, Great Commission Missionary Fellowship, Ad Honorem, Student Government, Dead to Sin Poets Society. *Campus security:* student patrols. *Student services:* personal/psychological counseling.
Athletics Member NCAA, NCCAA. All NCAA Division II. *Intercollegiate sports:* basketball M, volleyball W. *Intramural sports:* softball M.
Standardized Tests *Required:* SAT or ACT (for admission).
Costs (2012–13) *Comprehensive fee:* $19,674 includes full-time tuition ($11,808), mandatory fees ($800), and room and board ($7066). Part-time tuition: $492 per credit hour. Part-time tuition and fees vary according to course load. *Required fees:* $400 per term part-time. *Payment plan:* installment. *Waivers:* senior citizens and employees or children of employees.
Financial Aid Of all full-time matriculated undergraduates who enrolled in 2011, 155 applied for aid, 152 were judged to have need, 4 had their need fully met. 21 Federal Work-Study jobs (averaging $3451). In 2011, 1 non-need-based awards were made. *Average percent of need met:* 50%. *Average financial aid package:* $9960. *Average need-based loan:* $4073. *Average need-based gift aid:* $6771. *Average non-need-based aid:* $500. *Average indebtedness upon graduation:* $25,344.
Applying *Options:* electronic application, early admission, deferred entrance. *Application fee:* $25. *Required:* essay or personal statement, high school transcript, 2 letters of recommendation, interview. *Recommended:* minimum 2.8 GPA. *Application deadlines:* 8/20 (freshmen), 8/20 (out-of-state freshmen), 8/20 (transfers). *Notification:* continuous until 8/20 (freshmen), continuous (out-of-state freshmen).
Freshman Application Contact Mr. Kevin D. O'Farrell, Admissions Committee Chairman, Trinity College of Florida, 2430 Welbilt Boulevard, Trinity, FL 34655. *Phone:* 727-376-6911 Ext. 309. *Toll-free phone:* 800-388-0869. *Fax:* 727-569-1410. *E-mail:* kofarrell@trinitycollege.edu. *Web site:* http://www.trinitycollege.edu/.

Universidad FLET
Miami, Florida
Director of Admissions Dalia Sosa, Admissions Director, Universidad FLET, 14540 Southwest 136th Street, Suite 108, Miami, FL 33186. *Phone:* 305-378-8700. *Toll-free phone:* 888-376-3538. *Fax:* 305-232-5832. *E-mail:* admissiones@flet.edu. *Web site:* http://www.flet.edu/.

University of Central Florida
Orlando, Florida
- **State-supported** university, founded 1963, part of State University System of Florida
- **Suburban** 1415-acre campus with easy access to Orlando
- **Endowment** $125.7 million
- **Coed** 49,900 undergraduate students, 75% full-time, 54% women, 46% men
- **Moderately difficult** entrance level, 45% of applicants were admitted

Undergraduates 37,271 full-time, 12,629 part-time. Students come from 50 states and territories; 131 other countries; 5% are from out of state; 10% Black or African American, non-Hispanic/Latino; 19% Hispanic/Latino; 6% Asian, non-Hispanic/Latino; 0.2% Native Hawaiian or other Pacific Islander, non-Hispanic/Latino; 0.3% American Indian or Alaska Native, non-Hispanic/Latino; 2% Two or more races, non-Hispanic/Latino; 1% Race/ethnicity unknown; 1% international; 13% transferred in; 15% live on campus. *Retention:* 87% of full-time freshmen returned.
Freshmen *Admission:* 33,968 applied, 15,303 admitted, 6,301 enrolled. *Average high school GPA:* 3.78. *Test scores:* SAT critical reading scores over 500:

91%; SAT math scores over 500: 95%; SAT writing scores over 500: 82%; ACT scores over 18: 100%; SAT critical reading scores over 600: 42%; SAT math scores over 600: 54%; SAT writing scores over 600: 30%; ACT scores over 24: 78%; SAT critical reading scores over 700: 7%; SAT math scores over 700: 9%; SAT writing scores over 700: 4%; ACT scores over 30: 10%.

Faculty *Total:* 1,834, 71% full-time, 65% with terminal degrees. *Student/faculty ratio:* 32:1.

Academics *Calendar:* semesters. *Degrees:* certificates, associate, bachelor's, master's, doctoral, postbachelor's, and first professional certificates. *Special study options:* accelerated degree program, adult/continuing education programs, advanced placement credit, cooperative education, distance learning, double majors, English as a second language, freshman honors college, honors programs, independent study, internships, off-campus study, part-time degree program, services for LD students, study abroad, summer session for credit. *ROTC:* Army (b), Air Force (b). *Unusual degree programs:* 3-2 engineering; nursing; history; communicative sciences and disorders; economics; computer science.

Computers on Campus 3,200 computers/terminals and 200 ports are available on campus for general student use. Students can access the following: campus intranet, computer help desk, free student e-mail accounts, online (class) grades, online (class) registration, online (class) schedules. Campuswide network is available. 100% of college-owned or -operated housing units are wired for high-speed Internet access. Wireless service is available via entire campus.

Student Life *Housing options:* coed, men-only, women-only, disabled students. Campus housing is university owned and is provided by a third party. Freshman applicants given priority for college housing. *Activities and organizations:* drama/theater group, student-run newspaper, radio station, choral group, marching band, Volunteer UCF, Intramural Sports, Recreation and Wellness Center Group Exercise Programs, Multicultural Student Center and Organizations, Campus Religious Organizations, national fraternities, national sororities. *Campus security:* 24-hour emergency response devices and patrols, late-night transport/escort service, controlled dormitory access. *Student services:* health clinic, personal/psychological counseling, women's center, legal services.

Athletics Member NCAA. All Division I except football (Division I-A). *Intercollegiate sports:* baseball M(s), basketball M(s)/W(s), cheerleading M(s)/W(s), crew W, cross-country running W(s), golf M(s)/W(s), soccer M(s)/W(s), tennis M(s)/W(s), track and field W(s), volleyball W(s). *Intramural sports:* badminton M(c)/W(c), baseball M(c), basketball M/W, bowling M(c)/W(c), crew M(c)/W(c), equestrian sports M(c)/W(c), fencing M(c)/W(c), ice hockey M(c)/W(c), lacrosse M(c)/W(c), racquetball M/W, rock climbing M(c)/W(c), rugby M(c)/W(c), soccer M(c)/W(c), softball M/W, swimming and diving M(c)/W(c), table tennis M(c)/W(c), tennis M(c)/W(c), ultimate Frisbee M(c)/W(c), volleyball M(c)/W(c), water polo M(c)/W(c), wrestling M.

Standardized Tests *Required:* SAT or ACT (for admission).

Costs (2011–12) *Tuition:* state resident $5584 full-time, $186 per credit hour part-time; nonresident $21,063 full-time, $702 per credit hour part-time. Full-time tuition and fees vary according to course load. Part-time tuition and fees vary according to course load. *Room and board:* $9063; room only: $5300. Room and board charges vary according to board plan and housing facility. *Payment plans:* tuition prepayment, deferred payment. *Waivers:* senior citizens and employees or children of employees.

Financial Aid Of all full-time matriculated undergraduates who enrolled in 2010, 25,512 applied for aid, 23,075 were judged to have need, 2,184 had their need fully met. 427 Federal Work-Study jobs (averaging $3521). In 2010, 643 non-need-based awards were made. *Average percent of need met:* 60%. *Average financial aid package:* $8396. *Average need-based loan:* $4789. *Average need-based gift aid:* $5847. *Average non-need-based aid:* $2527. *Average indebtedness upon graduation:* $20,624. *Financial aid deadline:* 6/15.

Applying *Options:* electronic application, early admission. *Application fee:* $30. *Required:* high school transcript, minimum 2.0 GPA. *Recommended:* essay or personal statement. *Application deadlines:* 3/1 (freshmen), 5/1 (transfers). *Notification:* continuous (freshmen), continuous (transfers).

Freshman Application Contact Dr. Gordon Chavis Jr., Associate Vice President, Undergraduate Admissions, Student Financial Assistance and Outreach Programs, University of Central Florida, PO Box 160111, Orlando, FL 32816-0111. *Phone:* 407-823-3000. *Fax:* 407-823-5625. *E-mail:* admission@ucf.edu. *Web site:* http://www.ucf.edu/.

See page 212 for display ad and page 1660 for the College Close-Up.

UCF
UNIVERSITY OF CENTRAL FLORIDA

From thrilling theme parks to forward-thinking research parks, Orlando has made its mark on the world's stage. Home to the nation's second-largest university, this dynamic area has the ability to attract, develop and unleash creative talent.

To learn more about the UCF Knights, visit **ucf.edu**.

1204 ADM243 4/12

University of Florida
Gainesville, Florida

- **State-supported** university, founded 1853, part of Board of Trustees
- **Suburban** 2000-acre campus with easy access to Jacksonville
- **Endowment** $1.3 billion
- **Coed** 32,598 undergraduate students, 93% full-time, 55% women, 45% men
- **Very difficult** entrance level, 43% of applicants were admitted

Undergraduates 30,342 full-time, 2,256 part-time. Students come from 49 states and territories; 128 other countries; 3% are from out of state; 9% Black or African American, non-Hispanic/Latino; 17% Hispanic/Latino; 8% Asian, non-Hispanic/Latino; 0.4% Native Hawaiian or other Pacific Islander, non-Hispanic/Latino; 0.3% American Indian or Alaska Native, non-Hispanic/Latino; 2% Two or more races, non-Hispanic/Latino; 3% Race/ethnicity unknown; 1% international; 5% transferred in; 22% live on campus. *Retention:* 95% of full-time freshmen returned.

Freshmen *Admission:* 27,295 applied, 11,786 admitted, 6,429 enrolled. *Test scores:* SAT critical reading scores over 500: 94%; SAT math scores over 500: 96%; ACT scores over 18: 98%; SAT critical reading scores over 600: 64%; SAT math scores over 600: 73%; ACT scores over 24: 76%; SAT critical reading scores over 700: 17%; SAT math scores over 700: 22%; ACT scores over 30: 27%.

Academics *Calendar:* semesters. *Degrees:* bachelor's, master's, doctoral, and first professional. *Special study options:* accelerated degree program, adult/continuing education programs, cooperative education, distance learning, double majors, English as a second language, external degree program, honors programs, independent study, internships, off-campus study, part-time degree program, student-designed majors, study abroad. *ROTC:* Army (b), Navy (b), Air Force (b). *Unusual degree programs:* 3-2 business administration.

Computers on Campus 2,200 computers/terminals and 1,000 ports are available on campus for general student use. Students can access the following: campus intranet, computer help desk, free student e-mail accounts, online (class) grades, online (class) registration, online (class) schedules, course management system. Campuswide network is available. 100% of college-owned or -operated housing units are wired for high-speed Internet access. Wireless service is available via classrooms, computer centers, computer labs, dorm rooms, learning centers, libraries, student centers.

Student Life *Housing options:* coed, disabled students. Campus housing is university owned. Freshman applicants given priority for college housing. *Activities and organizations:* drama/theater group, student-run newspaper, radio and television station, choral group, marching band, VISA - Volunteers for International Student Affairs, Fellowship of Christian Athletes, Black Student Union, Hispanic Student Association, Asian American Student Union, national fraternities, national sororities. *Campus security:* 24-hour emergency response devices and patrols, student patrols, late-night transport/escort service, controlled dormitory access, crime and rape prevention programs. *Student services:* health clinic, personal/psychological counseling, legal services.

Athletics Member NCAA. All Division I. *Intercollegiate sports:* baseball M(s), basketball M(s)/W(s), bowling M/W, cheerleading M(s)/W(s), crew M/W, cross-country running M(s)/W(s), equestrian sports M/W; fencing M/W, football M(s), golf M(s)/W(s), gymnastics W(s), ice hockey M, lacrosse M/W(s), racquetball M/W, rock climbing M/W, rugby M/W, sailing M/W, soccer M/W(s), softball W(s), swimming and diving M(s)/W(s), table tennis M/W, tennis M(s)/W(s), track and field M(s)/W(s), ultimate Frisbee M/W, volleyball M/W(s), water polo M/W, wrestling M/W. *Intramural sports:* basketball M/W, bowling M/W, football M/W, golf M/W, racquetball M/W, soccer M/W, softball M/W, swimming and diving M/W, table tennis M/W, tennis M/W, track and field M/W, ultimate Frisbee M/W, volleyball M/W, weight lifting M/W, wrestling M/W.

Standardized Tests *Required:* SAT or ACT with writing section (for admission).

Costs (2011–12) *Tuition:* state resident $5657 full-time, $135 per credit hour part-time; nonresident $27,934 full-time, $843 per credit hour part-time. *Room and board:* $8800; room only: $5250. Room and board charges vary according to board plan and housing facility. *Waivers:* senior citizens.

Financial Aid Of all full-time matriculated undergraduates who enrolled in 2010, 19,400 applied for aid, 15,998 were judged to have need, 4,045 had their need fully met. 865 Federal Work-Study jobs (averaging $1994). 4,255 state and other part-time jobs (averaging $2449). In 2010, 1901 non-need-based awards were made. *Average percent of need met:* 80%. *Average financial aid package:* $13,746. *Average need-based loan:* $4300. *Average need-based gift aid:* $7853. *Average non-need-based aid:* $1867. *Average indebtedness upon graduation:* $16,841.

Applying *Options:* electronic application, early admission. *Application fee:* $30. *Required:* essay or personal statement, high school transcript. *Application deadlines:* 11/1 (freshmen), rolling (transfers). *Notification:* 2/10 (freshmen), continuous (transfers).

Freshman Application Contact Office of Admissions, University of Florida, PO Box 114000, Gainesville, FL 32611-4000. *Phone:* 352-392-1365. *Web site:* http://www.ufl.edu/.

University of Miami
Coral Gables, Florida

- **Independent** university, founded 1925
- **Suburban** 230-acre campus with easy access to Miami
- **Coed** 10,509 undergraduate students, 94% full-time, 51% women, 49% men
- **Very difficult** entrance level, 38% of applicants were admitted

Undergraduates 9,833 full-time, 676 part-time. 51% are from out of state; 7% Black or African American, non-Hispanic/Latino; 24% Hispanic/Latino; 6% Asian, non-Hispanic/Latino; 0.1% Native Hawaiian or other Pacific Islander, non-Hispanic/Latino; 0.2% American Indian or Alaska Native, non-Hispanic/Latino; 2% Two or more races, non-Hispanic/Latino; 6% Race/ethnicity unknown; 11% international; 6% transferred in; 41% live on campus. *Retention:* 91% of full-time freshmen returned.

Freshmen *Admission:* 27,747 applied, 10,635 admitted, 2,172 enrolled. *Average high school GPA:* 4.2. *Test scores:* SAT critical reading scores over 500: 97%; SAT math scores over 500: 98%; SAT writing scores over 500: 97%; ACT scores over 18: 99%; SAT critical reading scores over 600: 79%; SAT math scores over 600: 88%; SAT writing scores over 600: 77%; ACT scores over 24: 95%; SAT critical reading scores over 700: 24%; SAT math scores over 700: 35%; SAT writing scores over 700: 23%; ACT scores over 30: 54%.

Faculty *Total:* 1,402, 74% full-time, 81% with terminal degrees. *Student/faculty ratio:* 11:1.

Academics *Calendar:* semesters. *Degrees:* certificates, bachelor's, master's, doctoral, post-master's, postbachelor's, and first professional certificates. *Special study options:* adult/continuing education programs, part-time degree program. *ROTC:* Army (b), Air Force (b).

Computers on Campus Students can access the following: campus intranet, computer help desk, free student e-mail accounts, online (class) grades, online (class) registration, online (class) schedules, online student account information. Campuswide network is available. 100% of college-owned or -operated housing units are wired for high-speed Internet access. Wireless service is available via entire campus.

Student Life *Housing:* on-campus residence required for freshman year. *Options:* coed, disabled students. Campus housing is university owned. Freshman campus housing is guaranteed. *Campus security:* 24-hour emergency response devices and patrols, student patrols, late-night transport/escort service, controlled dormitory access, crime prevention and safety workshops, residential college crime watch.

Athletics Member NCAA. All Division I except football (Division I-A). *Intercollegiate sports:* baseball M(s), basketball M(s)/W(s), cheerleading M/W, crew M(s), cross-country running M(s)/W(s), golf W(s), soccer W(s), swimming and diving W(s), tennis M(s)/W(s), track and field M(s)/W(s), volleyball W(s). *Intramural sports:* badminton M(c)/W(c), basketball M/W, bowling M(c)/W(c), equestrian sports M(c)/W(c), fencing M(c)/W(c), field hockey M(c)/W(c), golf M(c)/W(c), lacrosse M(c)/W(c), racquetball M(c)/W(c), rugby M(c)/W(c), sailing M(c)/W(c), soccer M(c)/W(c), softball M/W(c), swimming and diving M(c)/W(c), table tennis M(c)/W(c), tennis M(c)/W(c), ultimate Frisbee M(c)/W(c), volleyball M(c)/W(c), water polo M(c)/W(c), weight lifting M(c)/W(c).

Standardized Tests *Required:* SAT or ACT (for admission). *Required for some:* SAT Subject Tests (for admission).

Costs (2011–12) *Comprehensive fee:* $51,182 includes full-time tuition ($38,440), mandatory fees ($1214), and room and board ($11,528). Part-time tuition: $1600 per credit hour. Part-time tuition and fees vary according to course load. *College room only:* $6706. Room and board charges vary according to board plan and housing facility. *Payment plans:* tuition prepayment, installment, deferred payment. *Waivers:* employees or children of employees.

Financial Aid Of all full-time matriculated undergraduates who enrolled in 2011, 5,976 applied for aid, 4,575 were judged to have need, 1,599 had their need fully met. In 2011, 1739 non-need-based awards were made. *Average percent of need met:* 79%. *Average financial aid package:* $31,709. *Average need-based loan:* $5550. *Average need-based gift aid:* $23,200. *Average non-need-based aid:* $21,445. *Average indebtedness upon graduation:* $26,297.

Applying *Options:* electronic application, early admission, early decision, early action, deferred entrance. *Application fee:* $70. *Required:* essay or personal statement, high school transcript, counselor evaluation. *Application deadlines:* 1/1 (freshmen), 3/1 (transfers), 11/1 (early action). *Early decision deadline:* 11/1. *Notification:* 4/15 (freshmen), 5/1 (transfers), 12/15 (early decision), 2/1 (early action).

Freshman Application Contact University of Miami, University of Miami Branch, Coral Gables, FL 33124. *Phone:* 305-284-4323. *E-mail:* admission@miami.edu. *Web site:* http://www.miami.edu/.

University of North Florida
Jacksonville, Florida

- **State-supported** comprehensive, founded 1965, part of State University System of Florida
- **Urban** 1300-acre campus
- **Endowment** $77.4 million
- **Coed** 14,363 undergraduate students, 73% full-time, 56% women, 44% men
- **Very difficult** entrance level, 49% of applicants were admitted

Undergraduates 10,460 full-time, 3,903 part-time. Students come from 46 states and territories; 63 other countries; 3% are from out of state; 10% Black or African American, non-Hispanic/Latino; 8% Hispanic/Latino; 5% Asian, non-Hispanic/Latino; 0.1% Native Hawaiian or other Pacific Islander, non-Hispanic/Latino; 0.2% American Indian or Alaska Native, non-Hispanic/Latino; 3% Two or more races, non-Hispanic/Latino; 0.7% Race/ethnicity unknown; 2% international; 11% transferred in; 18% live on campus. *Retention:* 82% of full-time freshmen returned.

Freshmen *Admission:* 11,053 applied, 5,471 admitted, 1,777 enrolled. *Average high school GPA:* 3.7. *Test scores:* SAT critical reading scores over 500: 90%; SAT math scores over 500: 92%; SAT writing scores over 500: 100%; ACT scores over 18: 100%; SAT critical reading scores over 600: 35%; SAT math scores over 600: 37%; SAT writing scores over 600: 62%; ACT scores over 24: 62%; SAT critical reading scores over 700: 6%; SAT math scores over 700: 4%; SAT writing scores over 700: 4%; ACT scores over 30: 4%.

Faculty *Total:* 816, 66% full-time, 61% with terminal degrees. *Student/faculty ratio:* 20:1.

Academics *Calendar:* semesters. *Degrees:* associate, bachelor's, master's, doctoral, post-master's, postbachelor's, and first professional certificates (doctoral degree in education only). *Special study options:* accelerated degree program, adult/continuing education programs, advanced placement credit, cooperative education, distance learning, double majors, English as a second language, honors programs, independent study, internships, off-campus study, part-time degree program, services for LD students, student-designed majors, study abroad, summer session for credit. *ROTC:* Army (b), Navy (c).

Computers on Campus 750 computers/terminals are available on campus for general student use. Students can access the following: campus intranet, computer help desk, free student e-mail accounts, online (class) grades, online (class) registration, online (class) schedules, applications software. Campuswide network is available. 100% of college-owned or -operated housing units are wired for high-speed Internet access. Wireless service is available via entire campus.

Student Life *Housing options:* coed, disabled students. Campus housing is university owned. Freshman applicants given priority for college housing. *Activities and organizations:* drama/theater group, student-run newspaper, radio and television station, choral group, Student Government Association, African Student Association, International Student Association, Filipino Student Association, National Education Association, national fraternities, national sororities. *Campus security:* 24-hour emergency response devices and patrols, late-night transport/escort service, controlled dormitory access, electronic parking lot security. *Student services:* health clinic, personal/psychological counseling, women's center.

Athletics Member NCAA. All Division I. *Intercollegiate sports:* baseball M(s), basketball M(s)/W(s), cross-country running M(s)/W(s), golf M(s)/W, soccer M(s)/W(s), softball W(s), swimming and diving W(s), tennis M(s)/W(s), track and field M(s)/W(s), volleyball W(s). *Intramural sports:* badminton M/W, basketball M/W, bowling M/W, fencing M(c)/W(c), football M/W, golf M/W, lacrosse M(c)/W(c), racquetball M(c)/W(c), rugby M(c), sailing M(c)/W(c), soccer M/W, swimming and diving M/W, table tennis M/W, track and field M/W, ultimate Frisbee M(c)/W(c), volleyball M(c)/W(c).

Standardized Tests *Required:* SAT or ACT (for admission).

Costs (2011–12) *Tuition:* state resident $3742 full-time, $182 per credit hour part-time; nonresident $18,002 full-time, $681 per credit hour part-time. Full-time tuition and fees vary according to course load. Part-time tuition and fees vary according to course load. *Required fees:* $1707 full-time. *Room and board:* $8452. Room and board charges vary according to board plan and housing facility. *Payment plan:* installment. *Waivers:* senior citizens and employees or children of employees.

Financial Aid Of all full-time matriculated undergraduates who enrolled in 2011, 8,800 applied for aid, 6,316 were judged to have need, 815 had their need fully met. 166 Federal Work-Study jobs (averaging $2586). In 2011, 1391 non-need-based awards were made. *Average percent of need met:* 89%. *Average financial aid package:* $8114. *Average need-based loan:* $2700. *Average need-based gift aid:* $5837. *Average non-need-based aid:* $2594. *Average indebtedness upon graduation:* $16,572.

Applying *Options:* electronic application, deferred entrance. *Application fee:* $30. *Required:* high school transcript, minimum 2.5 GPA, meet minimum test score requirements (460 SAT Critical Reading, 460 SAT Math, 440 SAT Writ-

ing; or 19 ACT Reading, 19 ACT Math, 18 ACT English/Writing). *Required for some:* essay or personal statement. *Recommended:* minimum 3.0 GPA. *Application deadlines:* rolling (freshmen), 5/11 (transfers). *Notification:* continuous until 1/11 (freshmen), continuous (transfers).

Freshman Application Contact Mr. John Yancey, Director of Admissions, University of North Florida, 1 UNF Drive, Jacksonville, FL 32224. *Phone:* 904-620-2624. *Fax:* 904-620-2014. *E-mail:* admissions@unf.edu. *Web site:* http://www.unf.edu/.

University of Phoenix–Central Florida Campus

Maitland, Florida

Freshman Application Contact Marc Booker, Sr. Director, Office of Admissions and Evaluation, University of Phoenix–Central Florida Campus, 4035 South Riverpoint Parkway, Mail Stop CF-L101, Phoenix, AZ 85040. *Phone:* 602-557-4609. *Toll-free phone:* 866-766-0766. *Fax:* 480-643-1156. *Web site:* http://www.phoenix.edu/.

University of Phoenix–North Florida Campus

Jacksonville, Florida

Freshman Application Contact Marc Booker, Sr. Director, Office of Admissions and Evaluation, University of Phoenix–North Florida Campus, 4035 South Riverpoint Parkway, Mail Stop CF-L101, Phoenix, AZ 85040. *Phone:* 602-557-4609. *Toll-free phone:* 866-766-0766. *Fax:* 480-643-1156. *Web site:* http://www.phoenix.edu/.

University of Phoenix–South Florida Campus

Fort Lauderdale, Florida

Freshman Application Contact Marc Booker, Sr. Director, Office of Admissions and Evaluation, University of Phoenix–South Florida Campus, 4035 South Riverpoint Parkway, Mail Stop CF-L101, Phoenix, AZ 85040.

Phone: 602-557-4609. *Toll-free phone:* 866-766-0766. *Fax:* 480-643-1156. *Web site:* http://www.phoenix.edu/.

University of Phoenix–West Florida Campus

Temple Terrace, Florida

Freshman Application Contact Marc Booker, Sr. Director, Office of Admissions and Evaluation, University of Phoenix–West Florida Campus, 4615 East Elwood Street, Mail Stop AA-K101, Phoenix, AZ 85040-1958. *Phone:* 602-557-4609. *Toll-free phone:* 866-766-0766. *Fax:* 480-643-1156. *Web site:* http://www.phoenix.edu/.

University of South Florida

Tampa, Florida

- **State-supported** university, founded 1956, part of State University System of Florida
- **Urban** 1561-acre campus
- **Coed** 29,975 undergraduate students, 77% full-time, 56% women, 44% men
- **Moderately difficult** entrance level, 37% of applicants were admitted

Undergraduates 23,014 full-time, 6,961 part-time. Students come from 51 states and territories; 141 other countries; 4% are from out of state; 12% Black or African American, non-Hispanic/Latino; 18% Hispanic/Latino; 6% Asian, non-Hispanic/Latino; 0.2% Native Hawaiian or other Pacific Islander, non-Hispanic/Latino; 0.4% American Indian or Alaska Native, non-Hispanic/Latino; 2% Two or more races, non-Hispanic/Latino; 2% Race/ethnicity unknown; 2% international; 12% transferred in; 16% live on campus. *Retention:* 89% of full-time freshmen returned.

Freshmen *Admission:* 30,194 applied, 11,107 admitted, 3,378 enrolled. *Average high school GPA:* 3.78. *Test scores:* SAT critical reading scores over 500: 86%; SAT math scores over 500: 90%; SAT writing scores over 500: 78%; ACT scores over 18: 100%; SAT critical reading scores over 600: 38%; SAT math scores over 600: 45%; SAT writing scores over 600: 27%; ACT scores over 24: 74%; SAT critical reading scores over 700: 6%; SAT math scores over 700: 6%; SAT writing scores over 700: 3%; ACT scores over 30: 11%.

Faculty *Total:* 1,190, 92% full-time, 79% with terminal degrees. *Student/faculty ratio:* 27:1.

COLLEGES AT-A-GLANCE

Academics *Calendar:* semesters. *Degrees:* associate, bachelor's, master's, doctoral, and first professional. *Special study options:* academic remediation for entering students, accelerated degree program, adult/continuing education programs, advanced placement credit, cooperative education, distance learning, double majors, English as a second language, freshman honors college, honors programs, independent study, internships, off-campus study, part-time degree program, services for LD students, student-designed majors, study abroad, summer session for credit. *ROTC:* Army (b), Navy (b), Air Force (b).

Computers on Campus 500 computers/terminals are available on campus for general student use. Students can access the following: computer help desk, free student e-mail accounts, online (class) registration, online (class) schedules. Campuswide network is available. 100% of college-owned or -operated housing units are wired for high-speed Internet access. Wireless service is available via classrooms, computer centers, computer labs, dorm rooms, libraries, student centers.

Student Life *Housing:* on-campus residence required for freshman year. *Options:* coed, men-only, women-only, cooperative, disabled students. Campus housing is university owned. Freshman campus housing is guaranteed. *Activities and organizations:* drama/theater group, student-run newspaper, radio and television station, choral group, marching band, student government, Campus Activities Board, USF Ambassadors, Student Admissions Representatives, national fraternities, national sororities. *Campus security:* 24-hour emergency response devices and patrols, student patrols, late-night transport/escort service, controlled dormitory access, residence hall lobby personnel 8 pm to 6 am. *Student services:* health clinic, personal/psychological counseling, women's center, legal services.

Athletics Member NCAA. All Division I. *Intercollegiate sports:* baseball M(s), basketball M(s)/W(s), cross-country running M(s)/W(s), football M(s), golf M(s)/W(s), soccer M(s)/W(s), softball W(s), tennis M(s)/W(s), track and field M(s)/W(s), volleyball W(s). *Intramural sports:* badminton M/W, basketball M/W, bowling M/W, cross-country running M/W, football M, golf M/W, racquetball M/W, soccer M/W, softball M/W, swimming and diving M/W, table tennis M/W, tennis M/W, track and field M/W, volleyball M/W, wrestling M/W.

Standardized Tests *Required:* SAT or ACT (for admission).

Costs (2011–12) *Tuition:* state resident $5732 full-time, $191 per credit hour part-time; nonresident $14,920 full-time, $497 per credit hour part-time. Full-time tuition and fees vary according to course level, course load, and location. Part-time tuition and fees vary according to course level, course load, and location. *Required fees:* $74 full-time, $37 per term part-time. *Room only:* $5232. Room and board charges vary according to board plan, housing facility, and location. *Payment plan:* installment. *Waivers:* senior citizens.

Financial Aid Of all full-time matriculated undergraduates who enrolled in 2009, 19,172 applied for aid, 16,347 were judged to have need, 16 had their need fully met. In 2009, 3950 non-need-based awards were made. *Average percent of need met:* 49%. *Average financial aid package:* $9374. *Average need-based loan:* $4645. *Average need-based gift aid:* $5966. *Average non-need-based aid:* $1940. *Average indebtedness upon graduation:* $21,679.

Applying *Options:* electronic application, early admission. *Application fee:* $30. *Required:* minimum 2.0 GPA. *Required for some:* high school transcript, 1 letter of recommendation. *Application deadlines:* 4/15 (freshmen), 4/15 (transfers). *Notification:* continuous (freshmen), continuous (transfers).

Freshman Application Contact Ms. Lisa Rycroft, Freshman Recruiter and Advisor, University of South Florida, Office of Undergraduate Admissions, 4202 East Fowler Avenue, Tampa, FL 33620-9951. *Phone:* 813-974-6431. *Fax:* 813-974-9689. *E-mail:* bullseye@admin.usf.edu. *Web site:* http://www.usf.edu/.

See page 1712 for the College Close-Up.

University of South Florida– Polytechnic

Lakeland, Florida

- **State-supported** upper-level, founded 1988, part of University of South Florida System

- **Coed**

Academics *Calendar:* semesters. *Degrees:* bachelor's, master's, and post-master's certificates.

Admissions Office Contact University of South Florida–Polytechnic, 3433 Winter Lake Road, Lakeland, FL 33803. *Web site:* http://www.poly.usf.edu/.

University of South Florida– St. Petersburg Campus

St. Petersburg, Florida

- **State-supported** comprehensive, founded 1965, part of University of South Florida System
- **Urban** 50-acre campus with easy access to Tampa
- **Coed** 3,926 undergraduate students, 65% full-time, 60% women, 40% men

Undergraduates 2,542 full-time, 1,383 part-time. Students come from 28 states and territories; 2% are from out of state; 7% Black or African American, non-Hispanic/Latino; 12% Hispanic/Latino; 4% Asian, non-Hispanic/Latino; 0.3% Native Hawaiian or other Pacific Islander, non-Hispanic/Latino; 0.3% American Indian or Alaska Native, non-Hispanic/Latino; 2% Two or more races, non-Hispanic/Latino; 1% Race/ethnicity unknown; 0.5% international; 16% transferred in. *Retention:* 68% of full-time freshmen returned.

Freshmen *Admission:* 421 enrolled. *Average high school GPA:* 3.6. *Test scores:* SAT critical reading scores over 500: 77%; SAT math scores over 500: 82%; SAT writing scores over 500: 65%; SAT critical reading scores over 600: 22%; SAT math scores over 600: 26%; SAT writing scores over 600: 15%; SAT critical reading scores over 700: 3%; SAT math scores over 700: 1%; SAT writing scores over 700: 2%.

Faculty *Total:* 255, 56% full-time. *Student/faculty ratio:* 13:1.

Academics *Calendar:* semesters. *Degrees:* bachelor's and master's. *Special study options:* distance learning, double majors, freshman honors college, honors programs, independent study, internships, services for LD students, study abroad, summer session for credit. *ROTC:* Army (b).

Computers on Campus 125 computers/terminals and 350 ports are available on campus for general student use. Students can access the following: computer help desk, free student e-mail accounts, online (class) grades, online (class) registration, online (class) schedules. Campuswide network is available. 100% of college-owned or -operated housing units are wired for high-speed Internet access. Wireless service is available via entire campus.

Student Life *Housing:* on-campus residence required for freshman year. *Options:* coed. Campus housing is university owned and is provided by a third party. Freshman applicants given priority for college housing. *Activities and organizations:* student-run newspaper. *Campus security:* 24-hour emergency response devices and patrols, late-night transport/escort service, controlled dormitory access. *Student services:* personal/psychological counseling.

Athletics *Intramural sports:* basketball M/W, football M/W, sailing M/W, soccer M/W, volleyball M/W.

Standardized Tests *Required:* SAT or ACT (for admission).

Costs (2012–13) *Tuition:* state resident $5189 full-time, $173 per credit hour part-time; nonresident $14,377 full-time, $392 per credit hour part-time. *Required fees:* $10 full-time. *Room only:* $7570.

Applying *Required:* high school transcript, minimum 2.5 GPA.

Freshman Application Contact Ms. Holly Kickliter, Director, Enrollment Services, University of South Florida–St. Petersburg Campus, 140 Seventh Avenue South, St. Petersburg, FL 33701. *Phone:* 727-873-4142. *Fax:* 727-873-4525. *E-mail:* admissions@usfsp.edu. *Web site:* http://www.stpt.usf.edu/.

University of South Florida Sarasota-Manatee

Sarasota, Florida

- **State-supported** upper-level, founded 1956, part of University of South Florida System
- **Coed**

Academics *Calendar:* semesters. *Degrees:* bachelor's, master's, and post-master's certificates.

Admissions Office Contact University of South Florida Sarasota-Manatee, 8350 N Tamiami Trail, Sarasota, FL 34243. *Web site:* http://www.sarasota.usf.edu/.

The University of Tampa

Tampa, Florida

- **Independent** comprehensive, founded 1931
- **Urban** 100-acre campus with easy access to Tampa-St. Petersburg, Clearwater
- **Coed** 6,050 undergraduate students, 94% full-time, 57% women, 43% men
- **Moderately difficult** entrance level, 53% of applicants were admitted

Undergraduates 5,703 full-time, 347 part-time. Students come from 50 states and territories; 117 other countries; 59% are from out of state; 6% Black or African American, non-Hispanic/Latino; 12% Hispanic/Latino; 1% Asian,

non-Hispanic/Latino; 0.1% Native Hawaiian or other Pacific Islander, non-Hispanic/Latino; 0.2% American Indian or Alaska Native, non-Hispanic/Latino; 3% Two or more races, non-Hispanic/Latino; 9% Race/ethnicity unknown; 9% international; 6% transferred in; 60% live on campus. *Retention:* 74% of full-time freshmen returned.

Freshmen *Admission:* 13,690 applied, 7,245 admitted, 1,631 enrolled. *Average high school GPA:* 3.3. *Test scores:* SAT critical reading scores over 500: 67%; SAT math scores over 500: 72%; SAT writing scores over 500: 65%; ACT scores over 18: 98%; SAT critical reading scores over 600: 16%; SAT math scores over 600: 20%; SAT writing scores over 600: 15%; ACT scores over 24: 46%; SAT critical reading scores over 700: 1%; SAT math scores over 700: 2%; SAT writing scores over 700: 1%; ACT scores over 30: 3%.

Faculty *Total:* 564, 47% full-time, 59% with terminal degrees. *Student/faculty ratio:* 16:1.

Academics *Calendar:* semesters. *Degrees:* certificates, associate, bachelor's, master's, and post-master's certificates. *Special study options:* academic remediation for entering students, adult/continuing education programs, advanced placement credit, cooperative education, double majors, English as a second language, honors programs, independent study, internships, part-time degree program, services for LD students, study abroad, summer session for credit. *ROTC:* Army (b), Navy (c), Air Force (c). *Unusual degree programs:* 3-2 chemistry/MBA joint program.

Computers on Campus 800 computers/terminals and 8,000 ports are available on campus for general student use. Students can access the following: campus intranet, computer help desk, free student e-mail accounts, online (class) grades, online (class) registration, online (class) schedules. Campus-wide network is available. 100% of college-owned or -operated housing units are wired for high-speed Internet access. Wireless service is available via entire campus.

Student Life *Housing options:* coed, disabled students. Campus housing is university owned. *Activities and organizations:* drama/theater group, student-run newspaper, radio and television station, choral group, Greek Life, student government, PEACE (volunteer organization), Student Productions, Minaret, national fraternities, national sororities. *Campus security:* 24-hour emergency response devices and patrols, student patrols, late-night transport/escort service, controlled dormitory access. *Student services:* health clinic, personal/psychological counseling, women's center.

Athletics Member NCAA. All Division II. *Intercollegiate sports:* baseball M(s), basketball M(s)/W(s), crew W(s), cross-country running M(s)/W(s), golf M(s)/W(s), lacrosse M(s), soccer M(s)/W(s), softball W(s), swimming and diving M(s)/W(s), tennis W(s), volleyball W(s). *Intramural sports:* basketball M/W, cheerleading W(c), crew M(c), field hockey W, football M/W, golf M/W, soccer M/W, softball M/W, swimming and diving M/W, table tennis W, tennis M/W, track and field M/W, ultimate Frisbee M/W, volleyball M/W.

Standardized Tests *Required:* SAT or ACT (for admission).

Costs (2012–13) *Comprehensive fee:* $32,806 includes full-time tuition ($22,834), mandatory fees ($1142), and room and board ($8830). Full-time tuition and fees vary according to class time. Part-time tuition: $486 per credit hour. Part-time tuition and fees vary according to class time. *College room only:* $4700. Room and board charges vary according to board plan and housing facility. *Payment plan:* installment. *Waivers:* employees or children of employees.

Financial Aid Of all full-time matriculated undergraduates who enrolled in 2011, 4,346 applied for aid, 3,438 were judged to have need, 636 had their need fully met. 299 Federal Work-Study jobs (averaging $2000). 3 state and other part-time jobs (averaging $2000). In 2011, 1737 non-need-based awards were made. *Average percent of need met:* 62%. *Average financial aid package:* $16,253. *Average need-based loan:* $4219. *Average need-based gift aid:* $12,463. *Average non-need-based aid:* $6076. *Average indebtedness upon graduation:* $31,437.

Applying *Options:* electronic application, early admission, early action, deferred entrance. *Application fee:* $40. *Required:* essay or personal statement, high school transcript, minimum 2.0 GPA. *Required for some:* 1 letter of recommendation. *Recommended:* interview. *Application deadlines:* rolling (freshmen), rolling (out-of-state freshmen), rolling (transfers), 5/1 (early action). *Notification:* continuous (freshmen), continuous (out-of-state freshmen), continuous (transfers), 12/15 (early action).

Freshman Application Contact Dennis Nostrand, Vice President for Enrollment, The University of Tampa, 401 West Kennedy Boulevard, Tampa, FL 33606-1480. *Phone:* 813-257-1808. *Toll-free phone:* 888-646-2738 (in-state); 888-MINARET (out-of-state). *Fax:* 813-258-7398. *E-mail:* admissions@ut.edu. *Web site:* http://www.ut.edu/.

University of West Florida
Pensacola, Florida

- **State-supported** comprehensive, founded 1963, part of State University System of Florida
- **Suburban** 1600-acre campus
- **Endowment** $52.9 million
- **Coed** 9,826 undergraduate students, 72% full-time, 58% women, 42% men
- **Moderately difficult** entrance level, 63% of applicants were admitted

Undergraduates 7,051 full-time, 2,775 part-time. Students come from 43 states and territories; 90 other countries; 10% are from out of state; 11% Black or African American, non-Hispanic/Latino; 7% Hispanic/Latino; 4% Asian, non-Hispanic/Latino; 0.3% Native Hawaiian or other Pacific Islander, non-Hispanic/Latino; 0.8% American Indian or Alaska Native, non-Hispanic/Latino; 3% Two or more races, non-Hispanic/Latino; 0.1% Race/ethnicity unknown; 2% international; 13% transferred in; 19% live on campus. *Retention:* 72% of full-time freshmen returned.

Freshmen *Admission:* 5,744 applied, 3,616 admitted, 1,324 enrolled. *Average high school GPA:* 3.23. *Test scores:* SAT critical reading scores over 500: 51%; SAT math scores over 500: 46%; SAT writing scores over 500: 40%; ACT scores over 18: 94%; SAT critical reading scores over 600: 12%; SAT math scores over 600: 11%; SAT writing scores over 600: 7%; ACT scores over 24: 32%; SAT critical reading scores over 700: 1%; ACT scores over 30: 2%.

Faculty *Total:* 543, 55% full-time, 54% with terminal degrees. *Student/faculty ratio:* 24:1.

Academics *Calendar:* semesters. *Degrees:* associate, bachelor's, master's, doctoral, and post-master's certificates. *Special study options:* advanced placement credit, cooperative education, distance learning, English as a second language, honors programs, independent study, internships, off-campus study, part-time degree program, services for LD students, study abroad, summer session for credit. *ROTC:* Army (b), Air Force (b). *Unusual degree programs:* 3-2 business administration.

Computers on Campus 1,111 computers/terminals and 100 ports are available on campus for general student use. Students can access the following: campus intranet, computer help desk, free student e-mail accounts, online (class) grades, online (class) registration, online (class) schedules. Campus-wide network is available. 100% of college-owned or -operated housing units are wired for high-speed Internet access. Wireless service is available via entire campus.

Student Life *Housing options:* coed. Campus housing is university owned. *Activities and organizations:* drama/theater group, student-run newspaper, choral group, Marketing Association, Student Council for Exceptional Children, Inter-Varsity Christian Fellowship, Baptist Student Ministry, Golden Key Honor Society, national fraternities, national sororities. *Campus security:* 24-hour emergency response devices and patrols, student patrols, late-night transport/escort service, controlled dormitory access. *Student services:* health clinic, personal/psychological counseling.

Athletics Member NCAA. All Division II. *Intercollegiate sports:* baseball M(s), basketball M(s)/W(s), cross-country running M(s)/W(s), golf M(s)/W(s), soccer M(s)/W(s), softball W(s), tennis M(s)/W(s), volleyball W. *Intramural sports:* basketball M/W, bowling M/W, cheerleading W, fencing M/W, football M/W, sailing M/W, soccer M/W, softball W, swimming and diving M/W, tennis M/W, volleyball M/W.

Standardized Tests *Required:* SAT or ACT (for admission), SAT and SAT Subject Tests or ACT (for admission).

Costs (2011–12) *Tuition:* state resident $3742 full-time, $181 per semester hour part-time; nonresident $16,010 full-time, $610 per semester hour part-time. Full-time tuition and fees vary according to location and reciprocity agreements. Part-time tuition and fees vary according to location and reciprocity agreements. *Required fees:* $1683 full-time, $181 per semester hour part-time. *Room and board:* $8684. Room and board charges vary according to housing facility. *Payment plans:* tuition prepayment, deferred payment. *Waivers:* senior citizens and employees or children of employees.

Financial Aid Of all full-time matriculated undergraduates who enrolled in 2011, 169 Federal Work-Study jobs (averaging $1595).

Applying *Options:* electronic application, early admission, deferred entrance. *Application fee:* $30. *Required:* high school transcript, minimum 2.0 GPA. *Application deadlines:* 6/30 (freshmen), 6/30 (transfers). *Notification:* continuous (freshmen), continuous (transfers).

Freshman Application Contact Stephen McKellips, Director of Admissions, University of West Florida, Admissions, 11000 University Parkway, Pensacola, FL 32514. *Phone:* 850-474-2230. *Toll-free phone:* 800-263-1074. *Fax:* 850-474-3460. *E-mail:* admissions@uwf.edu. *Web site:* http://www.uwf.edu/.

Warner University

Lake Wales, Florida

Freshman Application Contact Mr. Jason Roe, Director of Admissions, Warner University, Warner Southern Center, 13895 Highway 27, Lake Wales, FL 33859. *Phone:* 863-638-7212 Ext. 7213. *Toll-free phone:* 800-309-9563. *Fax:* 863-638-1472. *E-mail:* admissions@warner.edu. *Web site:* http://www.warner.edu/.

Webber International University

Babson Park, Florida

- **Independent** comprehensive, founded 1927
- **Small-town** 110-acre campus with easy access to Orlando
- **Endowment** $4.4 million
- **Coed** 680 undergraduate students, 92% full-time, 36% women, 64% men
- **Moderately difficult** entrance level, 57% of applicants were admitted

Undergraduates 626 full-time, 54 part-time. Students come from 26 states and territories; 35 other countries; 8% are from out of state; 23% Black or African American, non-Hispanic/Latino; 8% Hispanic/Latino; 0.9% Asian, non-Hispanic/Latino; 0.4% American Indian or Alaska Native, non-Hispanic/Latino; 0.9% Two or more races, non-Hispanic/Latino; 23% international; 13% transferred in; 52% live on campus. *Retention:* 50% of full-time freshmen returned.

Freshmen *Admission:* 579 applied, 331 admitted, 179 enrolled. *Average high school GPA:* 3.19. *Test scores:* SAT critical reading scores over 500: 24%; SAT math scores over 500: 39%; ACT scores over 18: 72%; SAT math scores over 600: 3%; ACT scores over 24: 5%.

Faculty *Total:* 43, 44% full-time, 49% with terminal degrees. *Student/faculty ratio:* 24:1.

Academics *Calendar:* semesters. *Degrees:* associate, bachelor's, and master's. *Special study options:* academic remediation for entering students, accelerated degree program, adult/continuing education programs, advanced placement credit, cooperative education, distance learning, double majors, English as a second language, internships, part-time degree program, services for LD students, study abroad, summer session for credit.

Computers on Campus 89 computers/terminals are available on campus for general student use. Students can access the following: campus intranet, free student e-mail accounts, online (class) grades, online (class) schedules. Campuswide network is available. 100% of college-owned or -operated housing units are wired for high-speed Internet access. Wireless service is available via computer labs, libraries, student centers.

Student Life *Housing:* on-campus residence required for freshman year. *Options:* men-only, women-only. Campus housing is university owned and leased by the school. Freshman campus housing is guaranteed. *Activities and organizations:* student-run newspaper, marching band, Student Leadership Association, Phi Beta Lambda, Society of International Students, Fellowship of Christian Athletes, Marketing Club. *Campus security:* 24-hour emergency response devices and patrols, late-night transport/escort service, controlled dormitory access. *Student services:* health clinic, personal/psychological counseling.

Athletics Member NAIA. *Intercollegiate sports:* baseball M(s), basketball M(s)/W(s), bowling M(s)/W(s), cheerleading M(s)/W(s), cross-country running M(s)/W(s), football M(s), golf M(s)/W(s), soccer M(s)/W(s), softball W(s), tennis M(s)/W(s), track and field M(s)/W(s), volleyball W(s). *Intramural sports:* basketball M/W, football M/W, soccer M/W, softball W, table tennis M/W, tennis M/W, volleyball M(c)/W(c).

Standardized Tests *Required:* SAT or ACT (for admission).

Costs (2011–12) *Comprehensive fee:* $27,280 includes full-time tuition ($19,670) and room and board ($7610). Full-time tuition and fees vary according to class time and course load. Part-time tuition: $272 per credit hour. Part-time tuition and fees vary according to course load. *College room only:* $4886. Room and board charges vary according to board plan, gender, and housing facility. *Payment plan:* installment. *Waivers:* children of alumni, adult students, senior citizens, and employees or children of employees.

Financial Aid Of all full-time matriculated undergraduates who enrolled in 2011, 628 applied for aid, 382 were judged to have need, 38 had their need fully met. 19 Federal Work-Study jobs (averaging $1417). 33 state and other part-time jobs (averaging $2504). In 2011, 208 non-need-based awards were made. *Average percent of need met:* 58%. *Average financial aid package:* $13,062. *Average need-based loan:* $4396. *Average need-based gift aid:* $3185. *Average non-need-based aid:* $8021. *Average indebtedness upon graduation:* $27,171. *Financial aid deadline:* 8/1.

Applying *Options:* electronic application, early action. *Application fee:* $35. *Required:* high school transcript, minimum 2.0 GPA. *Required for some:* interview. *Recommended:* essay or personal statement. *Application deadlines:* 8/1 (freshmen), 8/1 (transfers), 4/1 (early action).

Freshman Application Contact Mr. Mike Mattison, Director of Admissions, Webber International University, P. O. Box 96, Babson Park, FL 33827.

Phone: 863-638-2910. *Toll-free phone:* 800-741-1844. *Fax:* 863-638-1591. *E-mail:* admissions@webber.edu. *Web site:* http://www.webber.edu/.

See page 217 for display ad and page 1744 for the College Close-Up.

Yeshiva Gedolah Rabbinical College
Miami Beach, Florida

Admissions Office Contact Yeshiva Gedolah Rabbinical College, 1140 Alton Road, Miami Beach, FL 33139.

GEORGIA

Abraham Baldwin Agricultural College
Tifton, Georgia

Freshman Application Contact Mrs. Donna Webb, Director of Enrollment Services, Abraham Baldwin Agricultural College, Box 4, 2802 Moore Highway, Tifton, GA 31793-2601. *Phone:* 229-391-5004. *Toll-free phone:* 800-733-3653. *Fax:* 229-391-5002. *E-mail:* dwebb@abac.edu. *Web site:* http://www.abac.edu/.

Agnes Scott College
Decatur, Georgia

- **Independent** 4-year, founded 1889, affiliated with Presbyterian Church (U.S.A.)
- **Urban** 100-acre campus with easy access to Atlanta
- **Undergraduate: women only; graduate: coed** 871 undergraduate students, 98% full-time, 99% women, 1% men
- **Very difficult** entrance level, 46% of applicants were admitted

Undergraduates 855 full-time, 16 part-time. Students come from 41 states and territories; 29 other countries; 37% are from out of state; 30% Black or African American, non-Hispanic/Latino; 7% Hispanic/Latino; 3% Asian, non-Hispanic/Latino; 4% Two or more races, non-Hispanic/Latino; 5% Race/ethnicity unknown; 11% international; 2% transferred in; 86% live on campus. *Retention:* 84% of full-time freshmen returned.
Freshmen *Admission:* 2,284 applied, 1,048 admitted, 227 enrolled. *Average high school GPA:* 3.67. *Test scores:* SAT critical reading scores over 500: 83%; SAT math scores over 500: 77%; SAT writing scores over 500: 91%; ACT scores over 18: 99%; SAT critical reading scores over 600: 46%; SAT math scores over 600: 38%; SAT writing scores over 600: 43%; ACT scores over 24: 70%; SAT critical reading scores over 700: 14%; SAT math scores over 700: 12%; SAT writing scores over 700: 9%; ACT scores over 30: 12%.
Faculty *Total:* 95, 76% full-time, 91% with terminal degrees. *Student/faculty ratio:* 11:1.
Academics *Calendar:* semesters. *Degree:* bachelor's. *Special study options:* accelerated degree program, adult/continuing education programs, advanced placement credit, double majors, independent study, internships, off-campus study, part-time degree program, services for LD students, student-designed majors, study abroad, summer session for credit. *ROTC:* Army (c), Air Force (c). *Unusual degree programs:* 3-2 engineering with Georgia Institute of Technology; nursing with Emory University; computer science with Emory University.
Computers on Campus 458 computers/terminals and 3,819 ports are available on campus for general student use. Students can access the following: campus intranet, computer help desk, free student e-mail accounts, online (class) grades, online (class) registration, online (class) schedules. Campuswide network is available. 100% of college-owned or -operated housing units are wired for high-speed Internet access. Wireless service is available via entire campus.
Student Life *Housing:* on-campus residence required through senior year. *Options:* women-only. Campus housing is university owned. Freshman campus housing is guaranteed. *Activities and organizations:* drama/theater group, student-run newspaper, television station, choral group, marching band, Programming Board, Witkaze (African-American Student organization), Student Senate, ASC-TV, International Students Association. *Campus security:* 24-hour emergency response devices and patrols, late-night transport/escort service, controlled dormitory access, security systems in apartments, public safety facility, surveillance equipment, key required for residence hall entry. *Student services:* health clinic, personal/psychological counseling.
Athletics Member NCAA. All Division III. *Intercollegiate sports:* basketball W, lacrosse W, soccer W, softball W, tennis W, volleyball W. *Intramural sports:* cross-country running W(c), swimming and diving W(c), tennis W.

Standardized Tests *Required:* SAT or ACT scores or graded writing sample, home-schooled students must submit SAT or ACT (for admission). *Required for some:* SAT and SAT Subject Tests or ACT (for admission).
Costs (2011–12) *Comprehensive fee:* $42,345 includes full-time tuition ($31,980), mandatory fees ($215), and room and board ($10,150). Full-time tuition and fees vary according to course load. Part-time tuition: $1332 per credit hour. Part-time tuition and fees vary according to course load. *College room only:* $4830. Room and board charges vary according to board plan and housing facility. *Payment plan:* installment. *Waivers:* employees or children of employees.
Financial Aid Of all full-time matriculated undergraduates who enrolled in 2010, 660 applied for aid, 599 were judged to have need, 209 had their need fully met. 498 Federal Work-Study jobs (averaging $2300). 116 state and other part-time jobs (averaging $2300). In 2010, 218 non-need-based awards were made. *Average percent of need met:* 92%. *Average financial aid package:* $31,243. *Average need-based loan:* $3763. *Average need-based gift aid:* $24,148. *Average non-need-based aid:* $17,628. *Average indebtedness upon graduation:* $26,493. *Financial aid deadline:* 5/1.
Applying *Options:* electronic application, early admission, early action, deferred entrance. *Application fee:* $35. *Required:* essay or personal statement, high school transcript, 2 letters of recommendation. *Recommended:* interview. *Application deadlines:* 3/1 (freshmen), 3/1 (transfers), 11/15 (early action). *Notification:* continuous (transfers), 12/15 (early action).
Freshman Application Contact Agnes Scott College, 141 East College Avenue, Decatur, GA 30030-3797. *Phone:* 404-471-6285. *Toll-free phone:* 800-868-8602. *Web site:* http://www.agnesscott.edu/.

Albany State University
Albany, Georgia

- **State-supported** comprehensive, founded 1903, part of University System of Georgia
- **Urban** 232-acre campus
- **Endowment** $1.5 million
- **Coed** 4,187 undergraduate students, 87% full-time, 66% women, 34% men
- **Minimally difficult** entrance level, 29% of applicants were admitted

Undergraduates 3,662 full-time, 525 part-time. Students come from 32 states and territories; 18 other countries; 4% are from out of state; ####% Black or African American, non-Hispanic/Latino; ####% Hispanic/Latino; 125% Asian, non-Hispanic/Latino; 25% Native Hawaiian or other Pacific Islander, non-Hispanic/Latino; 125% American Indian or Alaska Native, non-Hispanic/Latino; 75% Two or more races, non-Hispanic/Latino; ####% Race/ethnicity unknown; 350% international; 6% transferred in; 43% live on campus. *Retention:* 65% of full-time freshmen returned.
Freshmen *Admission:* 6,554 applied, 1,878 admitted, 1,062 enrolled. *Average high school GPA:* 2.94. *Test scores:* SAT critical reading scores over 500: 9%; SAT math scores over 500: 11%; ACT scores over 18: 47%; ACT scores over 24: 1%.
Faculty *Total:* 270, 61% full-time, 56% with terminal degrees. *Student/faculty ratio:* 21:1.
Academics *Calendar:* semesters. *Degrees:* bachelor's, master's, and post-master's certificates. *Special study options:* academic remediation for entering students, advanced placement credit, cooperative education, distance learning, double majors, honors programs, independent study, internships, off-campus study, part-time degree program, services for LD students, study abroad, summer session for credit. *ROTC:* Army (b). *Unusual degree programs:* engineering with Engineering with Georgia Institute of Technology.
Computers on Campus Students can access the following: campus intranet, computer help desk, free student e-mail accounts, online (class) grades, online (class) registration, online (class) schedules, academic advising tools, online payment, and campus one stop portal. Campuswide network is available. 100% of college-owned or -operated housing units are wired for high-speed Internet access. Wireless service is available via entire campus.
Student Life *Housing:* on-campus residence required for freshman year. *Options:* coed, men-only, women-only. Campus housing is university owned. Freshman applicants given priority for college housing. *Activities and organizations:* drama/theater group, student-run newspaper, radio and television station, choral group, marching band, ASU Anointed Gospel Choir, ASU Pan-Hellenic Council (Greeks), Peer Educators, SIFE (Students In Free Enterprise), Student Government Association, national fraternities, national sororities. *Campus security:* 24-hour emergency response devices and patrols, late-night transport/escort service, controlled dormitory access, Connect Ed.- Emergency E-mail, Emergency sirens, Active Shooter Team, Certified Police Officers. *Student services:* health clinic, personal/psychological counseling.
Athletics Member NCAA. All Division II. *Intercollegiate sports:* baseball M(s), basketball M(s)/W(s), cheerleading M/W, cross-country running M(s)/

W(s), football M(s), softball W(s), tennis W(s), track and field M(s)/W(s), volleyball W(s). *Intramural sports:* basketball M/W, football M.

Standardized Tests *Required:* SAT or ACT (for admission).

Costs (2011–12) *Tuition:* state resident $4402 full-time, $147 per credit hour part-time; nonresident $16,016 full-time, $534 per credit hour part-time. Full-time tuition and fees vary according to course load and degree level. Part-time tuition and fees vary according to course load and degree level. *Required fees:* $1400 full-time, $379 per semester part-time. *Room and board:* $6124. Room and board charges vary according to board plan and housing facility. *Waivers:* senior citizens and employees or children of employees.

Financial Aid Of all full-time matriculated undergraduates who enrolled in 2003, 2,524 applied for aid, 2,182 were judged to have need, 615 had their need fully met. 440 Federal Work-Study jobs (averaging $1050). 178 state and other part-time jobs (averaging $1655). In 2003, 164 non-need-based awards were made. *Average percent of need met:* 68%. *Average financial aid package:* $7057.

Applying *Options:* electronic application, early admission, deferred entrance. *Application fee:* $20. *Required:* high school transcript, minimum 2.2 GPA. *Required for some:* COMPASS Test. *Application deadlines:* 6/1 (freshmen), 6/1 (out-of-state freshmen), 6/1 (transfers). *Notification:* continuous (freshmen), continuous (out-of-state freshmen), continuous (transfers).

Freshman Application Contact Mr. James Burrell, Interim Director, Enrollment Services, Albany State University, 504 College Drive, Albany, GA 31705-2717. *Phone:* 229-430-4646. *Toll-free phone:* 866-579-3498. *Fax:* 229-430-4105. *E-mail:* enrollmentservices@asurams.edu. *Web site:* http://www.asurams.edu/.

American InterContinental University Atlanta

Atlanta, Georgia

Freshman Application Contact American InterContinental University Atlanta, 6600 Peachtree-Dunwoody Road, 500 Embassy Row, Atlanta, GA 30328. *Phone:* 877-564-6248. *Toll-free phone:* 800-353-1744. *Fax:* 877-564-6248. *Web site:* http://www.aiuniv.edu/.

Argosy University, Atlanta

Atlanta, Georgia

Freshman Application Contact Argosy University, Atlanta, 980 Hammond Drive, Suite 100, Atlanta, GA 30328. *Phone:* 770-671-1200. *Toll-free phone:* 888-671-4777. *Web site:* http://www.argosy.edu/atlanta/.

See page 1062 for the College Close-Up.

Armstrong Atlantic State University

Savannah, Georgia

- **State-supported** comprehensive, founded 1935, part of University System of Georgia
- **Suburban** 250-acre campus
- **Endowment** $7.7 million
- **Coed** 6,813 undergraduate students, 71% full-time, 64% women, 36% men
- **Minimally difficult** entrance level, 76% of applicants were admitted

Undergraduates 4,834 full-time, 1,979 part-time. Students come from 45 states and territories; 69 other countries; 12% are from out of state; 24% Black or African American, non-Hispanic/Latino; 6% Hispanic/Latino; 3% Asian, non-Hispanic/Latino; 0.2% Native Hawaiian or other Pacific Islander, non-Hispanic/Latino; 0.4% American Indian or Alaska Native, non-Hispanic/Latino; 4% Two or more races, non-Hispanic/Latino; 0.2% Race/ethnicity unknown; 2% international; 10% transferred in; 20% live on campus. *Retention:* 65% of full-time freshmen returned.

Freshmen *Admission:* 2,856 applied, 2,158 admitted, 1,176 enrolled. *Average high school GPA:* 3.17. *Test scores:* SAT critical reading scores over 500: 56%; SAT math scores over 500: 52%; ACT scores over 18: 92%; SAT critical reading scores over 600: 13%; SAT math scores over 600: 16%; ACT scores over 24: 26%; SAT critical reading scores over 700: 1%; SAT math scores over 700: 2%; ACT scores over 30: 2%.

Faculty *Total:* 424, 61% full-time. *Student/faculty ratio:* 19:1.

Academics *Calendar:* semesters. *Degrees:* certificates, associate, bachelor's, master's, doctoral, post-master's, postbachelor's, and first professional certificates. *Special study options:* academic remediation for entering students, adult/continuing education programs, advanced placement credit, cooperative education, distance learning, double majors, honors programs, independent study, internships, off-campus study, part-time degree program, services for

LD students, study abroad, summer session for credit. *ROTC:* Army (b), Navy (c).

Computers on Campus 300 computers/terminals are available on campus for general student use. Students can access the following: campus intranet, computer help desk, free student e-mail accounts, online (class) grades, online (class) registration, online (class) schedules. Campuswide network is available. 100% of college-owned or -operated housing units are wired for high-speed Internet access. Wireless service is available via entire campus.

Student Life *Housing:* on-campus residence required for freshman year. *Options:* coed. Campus housing is university owned. *Activities and organizations:* drama/theater group, student-run newspaper, choral group, Wesley Fellowship, Hispanic Outreach and Leadership at Armstrong (HOLA), Ebony Coalition, American Chemical Society, Phi Alpha Theta, national fraternities, national sororities. *Campus security:* 24-hour emergency response devices and patrols, student patrols, late-night transport/escort service. *Student services:* health clinic, personal/psychological counseling.

Athletics Member NCAA. All Division II. *Intercollegiate sports:* baseball M(s), basketball M(s)/W(s), cheerleading M/W, golf M(s)/W(s), softball W(s), tennis M(s)/W(s), volleyball W(s). *Intramural sports:* badminton M/W, basketball M/W, bowling M/W, football M/W, golf M/W, rugby M, soccer M/W, softball M/W, table tennis M/W, tennis M/W, ultimate Frisbee M/W, volleyball M/W.

Standardized Tests *Required:* SAT or ACT (for admission). *Required for some:* SAT Subject Tests (for admission).

Costs (2012–13) *Tuition:* state resident $4402 full-time, $147 per credit hour part-time; nonresident $16,016 full-time, $534 per credit hour part-time. Full-time tuition and fees vary according to location and program. Part-time tuition and fees vary according to location and program. *Required fees:* $1332 full-time, $666 per term part-time. *Room and board:* $9342; room only: $5897. Room and board charges vary according to board plan and housing facility. *Waivers:* employees or children of employees.

Financial Aid Of all full-time matriculated undergraduates who enrolled in 2009, 4,275 applied for aid, 2,835 were judged to have need, 1,743 had their need fully met. In 2009, 882 non-need-based awards were made. *Average percent of need met:* 82%. *Average financial aid package:* $7750. *Average need-based loan:* $4500. *Average need-based gift aid:* $4000. *Average non-need-based aid:* $3000. *Average indebtedness upon graduation:* $19,000.

Applying *Options:* electronic application, early admission, deferred entrance. *Application fee:* $25. *Required:* high school transcript, minimum 2.0 GPA, proof of immunization. *Application deadlines:* 7/15 (freshmen), 7/15 (transfers). *Notification:* continuous (freshmen), continuous (transfers).

Freshman Application Contact Armstrong Atlantic State University, 11935 Abercorn Street, Savannah, GA 31419-1997. *Phone:* 912-344-2503. *Toll-free phone:* 800-633-2349. *Web site:* http://www.armstrong.edu/.

The Art Institute of Atlanta

Atlanta, Georgia

- **Proprietary** 4-year, founded 1949, part of Education Management Corporation
- **Suburban** 7-acre campus
- **Coed**

Academics *Calendar:* quarters. *Degrees:* diplomas, associate, and bachelor's.

Costs (2011–12) *Tuition:* Tuition cost varies by program. Prospective students should contact the school for current tuition costs. Other charges include a starting kit for all first-quarter students. Kits vary in price, depending on the program of study.

Freshman Application Contact The Art Institute of Atlanta, 6600 Peachtree Dunwoody Road, NE, 100 Embassy Row, Atlanta, GA 30328. *Phone:* 770-394-8300. *Toll-free phone:* 800-275-4242. *Web site:* http://www.artinstitutes.edu/atlanta/.

See page 1066 for the College Close-Up.

The Art Institute of Atlanta–Decatur

Decatur, Georgia

- **Proprietary** 4-year, founded 2007, part of Education Management Corporation
- **Coed**

Academics *Calendar:* quarters. *Degrees:* diplomas, associate, and bachelor's.

Costs (2011–12) *Tuition:* Tuition cost varies by program. Prospective students should contact the school for current tuition costs. Other charges include a starting kit for all first-quarter students. Kits vary in price, depending on the program of study.

Freshman Application Contact The Art Institute of Atlanta–Decatur, One West Court Square, Suite 110, Decatur, GA 30030. *Phone:* 404-942-1800.

Toll-free phone: 866-856-6203. *Web site:* http://www.artinstitutes.edu/decatur/
.

See page 1068 for the College Close-Up.

Ashworth College

Norcross, Georgia

- **Proprietary** comprehensive
- **Suburban** campus with easy access to Atlanta
- **Coed**
- **Noncompetitive** entrance level

Academics *Calendar:* semesters. *Degrees:* certificates, diplomas, associate, bachelor's, master's, post-master's, and postbachelor's certificates.
Costs (2011–12) *Tuition:* $1846 full-time, $83 per credit hour part-time. Full-time tuition and fees vary according to degree level.
Applying *Options:* electronic application. *Required:* high school transcript.
Freshman Application Contact Eric Ryall, Registrar, Ashworth College, 6625 The Corners Parkway, Suite 500, Norcross, GA 30092. *Phone:* 770-729-8400 Ext. 5297. *Toll-free phone:* 800-957-5412. *Web site:* http://www.ashworthcollege.edu/.

Augusta State University

Augusta, Georgia

Freshman Application Contact Ms. Jody Wilson, Coordinator of Publications and Marketing, Augusta State University, 2500 Walton Way, Augusta, GA 30904-2200. *Phone:* 706-737-1632. *Toll-free phone:* 800-341-4373. *Fax:* 706-667-4355. *E-mail:* admissions@aug.edu. *Web site:* http://www.aug.edu/.

Bauder College

Atlanta, Georgia

- **Proprietary** 4-year, founded 1964
- **Urban** campus
- **Coed**

Academics *Calendar:* quarters. *Degrees:* certificates, associate, and bachelor's.
Freshman Application Contact Bauder College, 384 Northyards Boulevard NW, Suites 190 and 400, Atlanta, GA 30313. *Phone:* 404-237-7573. *Toll-free phone:* 800-935-1857. *Web site:* http://atlanta.bauder.edu/.

Berry College

Mount Berry, Georgia

- **Independent interdenominational** comprehensive, founded 1902
- **Suburban** 26,000-acre campus with easy access to Atlanta
- **Endowment** $761.5 million
- **Coed** 1,944 undergraduate students, 98% full-time, 67% women, 33% men
- **Moderately difficult** entrance level, 62% of applicants were admitted

Undergraduates 1,912 full-time, 32 part-time. Students come from 36 states and territories; 16 other countries; 26% are from out of state; 5% Black or African American, non-Hispanic/Latino; 5% Hispanic/Latino; 2% Asian, non-Hispanic/Latino; 0.1% Native Hawaiian or other Pacific Islander, non-Hispanic/Latino; 0.2% American Indian or Alaska Native, non-Hispanic/Latino; 1% Two or more races, non-Hispanic/Latino; 3% Race/ethnicity unknown; 1% international; 2% transferred in; 87% live on campus. *Retention:* 79% of full-time freshmen returned.
Freshmen *Admission:* 3,231 applied, 2,014 admitted, 557 enrolled. *Average high school GPA:* 3.7. *Test scores:* SAT critical reading scores over 500: 90%; SAT math scores over 500: 86%; SAT writing scores over 500: 83%; ACT scores over 18: 100%; SAT critical reading scores over 600: 49%; SAT math scores over 600: 38%; SAT writing scores over 600: 34%; ACT scores over 24: 74%; SAT critical reading scores over 700: 9%; SAT math scores over 700: 6%; SAT writing scores over 700: 4%; ACT scores over 30: 18%.
Faculty *Total:* 211, 69% full-time, 75% with terminal degrees. *Student/faculty ratio:* 13:1.
Academics *Calendar:* semesters. *Degrees:* bachelor's and master's. *Special study options:* adult/continuing education programs, advanced placement credit, cooperative education, double majors, honors programs, independent study, internships, part-time degree program, student-designed majors, study abroad, summer session for credit. *Unusual degree programs:* 3-2 engineering with Georgia Institute of Technology; nursing with Emory University.
Computers on Campus 200 computers/terminals and 80 ports are available on campus for general student use. Students can access the following: campus intranet, computer help desk, free student e-mail accounts, online (class)

grades, online (class) registration, online (class) schedules. Campuswide network is available. 100% of college-owned or -operated housing units are wired for high-speed Internet access. Wireless service is available via classrooms, computer centers, computer labs, dorm rooms, learning centers, libraries, student centers.
Student Life *Housing:* on-campus residence required through senior year. *Options:* coed, men-only, women-only. Campus housing is university owned. Freshman campus housing is guaranteed. *Activities and organizations:* drama/theater group, student-run newspaper, choral group, Student Government Association, Campus Outreach, Block-n-Bridle, Allied Health, Athletes Bettering the Community. *Campus security:* 24-hour emergency response devices and patrols, controlled dormitory access, lighted pathways, gated campus, mobile police patrols, identification of valuables, limited access to campus, on campus police officers. *Student services:* health clinic, personal/psychological counseling.
Athletics Member NCAA. All Division III. *Intercollegiate sports:* baseball M, basketball M/W, cross-country running M/W, equestrian sports W, golf M/W, lacrosse M/W, soccer M/W, softball W, swimming and diving M/W, tennis M/W, track and field M/W, volleyball W. *Intramural sports:* badminton M/W, basketball M/W, bowling M/W, cheerleading M(c)/W(c), crew M(c)/W(c), cross-country running M/W, football M/W, golf M/W, racquetball M/W, rock climbing M/W, soccer M/W, softball M/W, swimming and diving M/W, table tennis M/W, tennis M/W, ultimate Frisbee M/W, volleyball M/W, water polo M/W, weight lifting M/W.
Standardized Tests *Required:* SAT or ACT (for admission).
Costs (2011–12) *Comprehensive fee:* $35,248 includes full-time tuition ($25,890), mandatory fees ($200), and room and board ($9158). Part-time tuition: $863 per credit hour. *College room only:* $5138. Room and board charges vary according to board plan and housing facility. *Payment plan:* installment. *Waivers:* senior citizens and employees or children of employees.
Financial Aid Of all full-time matriculated undergraduates who enrolled in 2011, 1,632 applied for aid, 1,334 were judged to have need, 351 had their need fully met. 246 Federal Work-Study jobs (averaging $2874). 2,056 state and other part-time jobs (averaging $3680). In 2011, 549 non-need-based awards were made. *Average percent of need met:* 81%. *Average financial aid package:* $21,740. *Average need-based loan:* $4411. *Average need-based gift aid:* $17,315. *Average non-need-based aid:* $11,126. *Average indebtedness upon graduation:* $19,049.
Applying *Options:* electronic application, early admission. *Application fee:* $50. *Required:* essay or personal statement, high school transcript. *Recommended:* interview. *Application deadlines:* 7/27 (freshmen), 7/27 (transfers). *Notification:* continuous (freshmen), continuous (transfers).
Freshman Application Contact Mr. Timothy Tarpley, Director of Operations, Enrollment Management, Berry College, PO Box 490159, 2277 Martha Berry Highway, NW, Mount Berry, GA 30149-0159. *Phone:* 706-236-2215. *Toll-free phone:* 800-237-7942. *Fax:* 706-290-2178. *E-mail:* admissions@berry.edu. *Web site:* http://www.berry.edu/.

Beulah Heights University

Atlanta, Georgia

- **Independent Pentecostal** comprehensive, founded 1918
- **Urban** 10-acre campus with easy access to Atlanta
- **Coed** 641 undergraduate students, 51% full-time, 56% women, 44% men
- **Noncompetitive** entrance level, 100% of applicants were admitted

Undergraduates 329 full-time, 312 part-time. Students come from 22 states and territories; 12 other countries; 30% are from out of state; 8% transferred in; 10% live on campus. *Retention:* 57% of full-time freshmen returned.
Freshmen *Admission:* 78 applied, 78 admitted, 78 enrolled. *Average high school GPA:* 3.
Faculty *Total:* 64, 41% full-time, 75% with terminal degrees. *Student/faculty ratio:* 13:1.
Academics *Calendar:* semesters. *Degrees:* associate, bachelor's, and master's. *Special study options:* academic remediation for entering students, accelerated degree program, adult/continuing education programs, advanced placement credit, cooperative education, distance learning, double majors, independent study, internships, off-campus study, part-time degree program, services for LD students, summer session for credit. *Unusual degree programs:* Bachelor of Arts in Religious Studies, B.A. in Leadership Studies, Master of Divinity, M.A. in Leadership and M.A. in Religious Studies can be complete at the Griffin campus extension.
Computers on Campus 28 computers/terminals are available on campus for general student use. Students can access the following: campus intranet, computer help desk, free student e-mail accounts, online (class) registration, online (class) schedules. Campuswide network is available. 100% of college-owned or -operated housing units are wired for high-speed Internet access. Wireless service is available via entire campus.

Student Life *Housing options:* men-only, women-only. Campus housing is university owned. *Activities and organizations:* student-run newspaper, choral group, Chapel Choir, Student Government, Club Give. *Campus security:* 24-hour emergency response devices and patrols. *Student services:* personal/psychological counseling.

Athletics *Intercollegiate sports:* ultimate Frisbee M(s)/W(s), volleyball M(s)/W(s). *Intramural sports:* ultimate Frisbee M/W, volleyball M/W.

Standardized Tests *Required:* TOFEL required for international students (for admission). *Recommended:* SAT or ACT (for admission).

Costs (2012–13) *Tuition:* $5760 full-time, $240 per credit part-time. Full-time tuition and fees vary according to course load. *Room only:* $2500. Room and board charges vary according to housing facility. *Payment plans:* installment, deferred payment. *Waivers:* employees or children of employees.

Financial Aid Of all full-time matriculated undergraduates who enrolled in 2009, 113 applied for aid, 113 were judged to have need. 13 Federal Work-Study jobs (averaging $4335). *Average percent of need met:* 75%. *Average financial aid package:* $5619. *Average need-based loan:* $2250. *Average need-based gift aid:* $3500. *Average indebtedness upon graduation:* $40,000.

Applying *Options:* electronic application, early admission. *Application fee:* $30. *Required:* essay or personal statement, high school transcript, minimum 2.0 GPA, 2 letters of recommendation, Statement of Faith. *Recommended:* interview. *Application deadlines:* rolling (freshmen), rolling (transfers). *Notification:* continuous (freshmen), continuous (transfers).

Freshman Application Contact John Dreher, Director of Admissions, Beulah Heights University, 892 Berne Street, SE, Atlanta, GA 30316. *Phone:* 404-627-2681 Ext. 117. *Toll-free phone:* 888-777-BHBC. *E-mail:* john.dreher@beulah.org. *Web site:* http://www.beulah.org/.

Brenau University

Gainesville, Georgia

- **Independent** comprehensive, founded 1878
- **Small-town** 57-acre campus with easy access to Atlanta
- **Endowment** $31.7 million
- **Women only** 802 undergraduate students, 89% full-time
- **Moderately difficult** entrance level, 47% of applicants were admitted

Undergraduates 715 full-time, 87 part-time. Students come from 13 states and territories; 12 other countries; 8% are from out of state; 21% Black or African American, non-Hispanic/Latino; 9% Hispanic/Latino; 2% Asian, non-Hispanic/Latino; 0.4% American Indian or Alaska Native, non-Hispanic/Latino; 3% Two or more races, non-Hispanic/Latino; 6% Race/ethnicity unknown; 5% international; 17% transferred in; 58% live on campus. *Retention:* 69% of full-time freshmen returned.

Freshmen *Admission:* 2,696 applied, 1,263 admitted, 175 enrolled. *Test scores:* SAT critical reading scores over 500: 51%; SAT math scores over 500: 45%; SAT writing scores over 500: 48%; ACT scores over 18: 90%; SAT critical reading scores over 600: 15%; SAT math scores over 600: 9%; SAT writing scores over 600: 14%; SAT critical reading scores over 700: 1%; SAT math scores over 700: 1%; SAT writing scores over 700: 1%.

Faculty *Total:* 115, 62% full-time, 62% with terminal degrees. *Student/faculty ratio:* 9:1.

Academics *Calendar:* semesters. *Degrees:* associate, bachelor's, and master's (also offers coed evening and weekend programs with significant enrollment not reflected in profile). *Special study options:* academic remediation for entering students, advanced placement credit, distance learning, double majors, English as a second language, honors programs, independent study, internships, part-time degree program, services for LD students, student-designed majors, study abroad, summer session for credit.

Computers on Campus 130 computers/terminals and 200 ports are available on campus for general student use. Students can access the following: campus intranet, computer help desk, free student e-mail accounts, online (class) grades, online (class) registration, online (class) schedules, students can create own Web sites, videos and other things made possible by Google apps. Campuswide network is available. 100% of college-owned or -operated housing units are wired for high-speed Internet access. Wireless service is available via classrooms, computer centers, computer labs, dorm rooms, learning centers, libraries, student centers.

Student Life *Housing:* on-campus residence required through junior year. *Options:* women-only, disabled students. Campus housing is university owned. Freshman campus housing is guaranteed. *Activities and organizations:* drama/theater group, student-run newspaper, radio station, choral group, Sigma Alpha Pi Leadership Society, Student Government Association/Student Activities Board, Circle K, Silhouettes, International Club, national sororities. *Campus security:* 24-hour emergency response devices and patrols, late-night transport/escort service. *Student services:* health clinic, personal/psychological counseling.

Athletics Member NAIA. *Intercollegiate sports:* basketball W(s), cheerleading W(c), crew W(c), cross-country running W(s), soccer W(s), softball W(s), swimming and diving W(s), tennis W(s), volleyball W(s).

Standardized Tests *Required:* SAT or ACT (for admission).

Costs (2011–12) *Comprehensive fee:* $31,490 includes full-time tuition ($20,864), mandatory fees ($260), and room and board ($10,366). Full-time tuition and fees vary according to location and program. Part-time tuition: $695 per credit hour. Part-time tuition and fees vary according to course load, location, and program. *Required fees:* $130 per term part-time. *Payment plan:* installment. *Waivers:* employees or children of employees.

Financial Aid Of all full-time matriculated undergraduates who enrolled in 2010, 634 applied for aid, 592 were judged to have need, 113 had their need fully met. 108 Federal Work-Study jobs (averaging $1944). In 2010, 141 non-need-based awards were made. *Average percent of need met:* 70%. *Average financial aid package:* $18,714. *Average need-based loan:* $4206. *Average need-based gift aid:* $14,609. *Average non-need-based aid:* $12,542. *Average indebtedness upon graduation:* $20,634.

Applying *Options:* electronic application, deferred entrance. *Application fee:* $35. *Required:* high school transcript, minimum 2.5 GPA. *Required for some:* interview. *Application deadlines:* rolling (freshmen), rolling (out-of-state freshmen), rolling (transfers). *Notification:* continuous (freshmen), continuous (out-of-state freshmen), continuous (transfers).

Freshman Application Contact Mr. Scott Briell, Senior Vice President, Enrollment Management and Student Services, Brenau University, Admissions, 500 Washington Street, SE, Gainesville, GA 30501. *Phone:* 770-538-4704. *Toll-free phone:* 800-252-5119. *Fax:* 770-538-4701. *E-mail:* admissions@brenau.edu. *Web site:* http://www.brenau.edu/.

Brewton-Parker College

Mt. Vernon, Georgia

- **Independent Southern Baptist** 4-year, founded 1904
- **Rural** 280-acre campus
- **Coed** 629 undergraduate students, 74% full-time, 50% women, 50% men
- **Minimally difficult** entrance level

Undergraduates 468 full-time, 161 part-time. Students come from 11 states and territories; 12 other countries; 12% are from out of state; 24% Black or African American, non-Hispanic/Latino; 5% Hispanic/Latino; 0.5% Asian, non-Hispanic/Latino; 0.5% Native Hawaiian or other Pacific Islander, non-Hispanic/Latino; 0.3% American Indian or Alaska Native, non-Hispanic/Latino; 0.6% Two or more races, non-Hispanic/Latino; 12% Race/ethnicity unknown; 4% international; 55% live on campus. *Retention:* 41% of full-time freshmen returned.

Freshmen *Admission:* 293 applied, 123 enrolled. *Average high school GPA:* 3.04. *Test scores:* SAT critical reading scores over 500: 35%; SAT math scores over 500: 35%; SAT writing scores over 500: 38%; ACT scores over 18: 54%; SAT critical reading scores over 600: 6%; SAT math scores over 600: 6%; SAT writing scores over 600: 7%; ACT scores over 24: 7%; SAT critical reading scores over 700: 1%; ACT scores over 30: 4%.

Faculty *Total:* 85, 36% full-time, 40% with terminal degrees. *Student/faculty ratio:* 11:1.

Academics *Calendar:* semesters. *Degrees:* associate and bachelor's. *Special study options:* academic remediation for entering students, accelerated degree program, advanced placement credit, cooperative education, honors programs, independent study, internships, part-time degree program, services for LD students, summer session for credit.

Computers on Campus 104 computers/terminals are available on campus for general student use. Students can access the following: computer help desk, free student e-mail accounts, online (class) grades, online (class) registration, online (class) schedules. Campuswide network is available. 100% of college-owned or -operated housing units are wired for high-speed Internet access. Wireless service is available via classrooms, computer centers, computer labs, dorm rooms, libraries, student centers.

Student Life *Housing:* on-campus residence required through junior year. *Options:* men-only, women-only. Campus housing is university owned. Freshman campus housing is guaranteed. *Activities and organizations:* drama/theater group, student-run newspaper, Council of Intramural Activities, Student Activities Council, Student Government Association, Circle K, Baptist Student Union. *Campus security:* 24-hour emergency response devices, controlled dormitory access, Campus security is provided from 6 pm to 6 am. *Student services:* personal/psychological counseling.

Athletics Member NAIA. *Intercollegiate sports:* baseball M(s), basketball M(s)/W(s), cheerleading M(s)/W(s), cross-country running M(s)/W(s), soccer M(s)/W(s), softball W(s), volleyball M(s), wrestling M(s). *Intramural sports:* basketball M/W, football M/W, softball M/W, table tennis M/W, tennis M/W, ultimate Frisbee M/W, volleyball M/W.

Standardized Tests *Required:* SAT or ACT (for admission).

Costs (2011–12) *One-time required fee:* $200. *Comprehensive fee:* $19,388 includes full-time tuition ($11,600), mandatory fees ($690), and room and board ($7098). Full-time tuition and fees vary according to course load, location, and program. Part-time tuition: $325 per credit hour. Part-time tuition and fees vary according to course load, location, and program. *College room only:* $3150. Room and board charges vary according to board plan and housing facility. *Payment plan:* installment. *Waivers:* senior citizens and employees or children of employees.

Financial Aid Of all full-time matriculated undergraduates who enrolled in 2009, 819 applied for aid, 736 were judged to have need, 118 had their need fully met. 170 Federal Work-Study jobs (averaging $676). 114 state and other part-time jobs (averaging $466). In 2009, 96 non-need-based awards were made. *Average percent of need met:* 71%. *Average financial aid package:* $11,736. *Average need-based loan:* $3436. *Average need-based gift aid:* $9011. *Average non-need-based aid:* $3915. *Average indebtedness upon graduation:* $28,231. *Financial aid deadline:* 5/1.

Applying *Options:* electronic application. *Application fee:* $35. *Required:* high school transcript, minimum 2.0 GPA. *Application deadlines:* 8/1 (freshmen), rolling (out-of-state freshmen), rolling (transfers). *Notification:* continuous (freshmen), continuous (out-of-state freshmen), continuous (transfers).

Freshman Application Contact Director of Admissions, Brewton-Parker College, PO Box 197, Mount Vernon, GA 30445. *Phone:* 912-583-3247. *Toll-free phone:* 800-342-1087. *Fax:* 912-583-3598. *E-mail:* admissions@bpc.edu. *Web site:* http://www.bpc.edu/.

Carver Bible College

Atlanta, Georgia

- **Independent nondenominational** 4-year, founded 1943
- **Urban** 16-acre campus
- **Coed** 104 undergraduate students, 60% full-time, 33% women, 67% men
- **Noncompetitive** entrance level, 100% of applicants were admitted

Undergraduates 62 full-time, 42 part-time. Students come from 4 states and territories; 4 other countries; 1% are from out of state; 65% Black or African American, non-Hispanic/Latino; 1% Asian, non-Hispanic/Latino; 34% international; 35% live on campus. *Retention:* 56% of full-time freshmen returned.

Freshmen *Admission:* 49 applied, 49 admitted. *Average high school GPA:* 2.

Faculty *Total:* 19, 11% full-time. *Student/faculty ratio:* 6:1.

Academics *Calendar:* semesters. *Degrees:* certificates, associate, and bachelor's. *Special study options:* part-time degree program.

Computers on Campus 7 computers/terminals are available on campus for general student use. Students can access the following: campus intranet, computer help desk, free student e-mail accounts, online (class) grades, online (class) schedules.

Student Life *Housing options:* coed, men-only, women-only. Campus housing is university owned. *Activities and organizations:* Student Government Association, Student Missions Organization, Carver Praise Team.

Athletics Member NCCAA. *Intercollegiate sports:* basketball M.

Costs (2012–13) *Comprehensive fee:* $11,840 includes full-time tuition ($6960) and room and board ($4880). Part-time tuition: $290 per credit hour.

Applying *Application fee:* $35. *Required:* essay or personal statement, high school transcript, minimum 2.0 GPA, 2 letters of recommendation. *Required for some:* interview. *Recommended:* interview. *Application deadline:* 8/1 (freshmen).

Freshman Application Contact Bertha Mack, Admissions Officer, Carver Bible College, 3870 Cascade Road SW, Atlanta, GA 30331. *Phone:* 404-527-4520. *Fax:* 404-527-4524. *E-mail:* info@carver.edu. *Web site:* http://www.carver.edu/.

Clark Atlanta University

Atlanta, Georgia

- **Independent United Methodist** university, founded 1865
- **Urban** 126-acre campus
- **Endowment** $52.5 million
- **Coed** 3,127 undergraduate students, 94% full-time, 75% women, 25% men
- **Moderately difficult** entrance level, 72% of applicants were admitted

Undergraduates 2,955 full-time, 172 part-time. Students come from 45 states and territories; 10 other countries; 62% are from out of state; 91% Black or African American, non-Hispanic/Latino; 0.3% Hispanic/Latino; 0.2% Asian, non-Hispanic/Latino; 0.4% American Indian or Alaska Native, non-Hispanic/Latino; 7% Race/ethnicity unknown; 0.6% international; 5% transferred in; 32% live on campus. *Retention:* 65% of full-time freshmen returned.

Freshmen *Admission:* 5,261 applied, 3,772 admitted, 833 enrolled. *Average high school GPA:* 3. *Test scores:* SAT critical reading scores over 500: 21%; SAT math scores over 500: 20%; ACT scores over 18: 74%; SAT critical reading scores over 600: 2%; SAT math scores over 600: 3%; ACT scores over 24: 8%.

Faculty *Total:* 306, 56% full-time, 60% with terminal degrees. *Student/faculty ratio:* 18:1.

Academics *Calendar:* semesters. *Degrees:* bachelor's, master's, doctoral, post-master's, postbachelor's, and first professional certificates. *Special study options:* academic remediation for entering students, accelerated degree program, adult/continuing education programs, advanced placement credit, cooperative education, double majors, honors programs, independent study, internships, off-campus study, part-time degree program, services for LD students, study abroad, summer session for credit. *ROTC:* Army (c), Navy (c). *Unusual degree programs:* 3-2 engineering with Georgia Institute of Technology, Boston University, North Carolina Agricultural and Technical State University.

Computers on Campus 741 computers/terminals and 2,000 ports are available on campus for general student use. Students can access the following: computer help desk, free student e-mail accounts, online (class) grades, online (class) registration, online (class) schedules. Campuswide network is available. 100% of college-owned or -operated housing units are wired for high-speed Internet access. Wireless service is available via entire campus.

Student Life *Housing:* on-campus residence required through sophomore year. *Options:* coed, men-only, women-only. Campus housing is university owned and is provided by a third party. Freshman applicants given priority for college housing. *Activities and organizations:* drama/theater group, student-run newspaper, radio and television station, choral group, marching band, Spirit Boosters, Pre-Alumni Council, Campus Activities Board, Orientation Guides, National Association for the Advancement of Colored People, national fraternities, national sororities. *Campus security:* 24-hour emergency response devices and patrols, late-night transport/escort service, controlled dormitory access. *Student services:* health clinic, personal/psychological counseling.

Athletics Member NCAA. All Division II. *Intercollegiate sports:* baseball M(s), basketball M(s)/W(s), cross-country running M(s)/W(s), football M(s), softball W(s), tennis W(s), track and field M(s)/W(s), volleyball W(s). *Intramural sports:* basketball M/W, football M, softball W, tennis W, track and field M/W, volleyball M/W.

Standardized Tests *Required:* SAT or ACT (for admission).

Costs (2012–13) *Comprehensive fee:* $28,197 includes full-time tuition ($18,106), mandatory fees ($806), and room and board ($9285). Part-time tuition: $754 per credit hour. *Required fees:* $403 part-time. *Room and board:* Room and board charges vary according to board plan and housing facility.

Financial Aid Of all full-time matriculated undergraduates who enrolled in 2005, 3,883 applied for aid, 3,712 were judged to have need, 1,567 had their need fully met. 229 Federal Work-Study jobs (averaging $1335). *Average percent of need met:* 8%. *Average financial aid package:* $10,935. *Average need-based loan:* $4526. *Average need-based gift aid:* $3818. *Average indebtedness upon graduation:* $17,751.

Applying *Options:* electronic application, early admission, deferred entrance. *Application fee:* $35. *Required:* essay or personal statement, high school transcript, minimum 2.5 GPA, 2 letters of recommendation. *Required for some:* interview. *Application deadlines:* 6/1 (freshmen), 6/1 (out-of-state freshmen), 6/1 (transfers). *Notification:* continuous (freshmen), continuous (out-of-state freshmen), continuous (transfers).

Freshman Application Contact Ms. Michelle Davis, Interim Director, Office of Admissions, Clark Atlanta University, 223 James P. Brawley Drive, SW, Atlanta, GA 30314. *Phone:* 404-880-8918. *Toll-free phone:* 800-688-3228. *Fax:* 404-880-6174. *E-mail:* cauadmissions@cau.edu. *Web site:* http://www.cau.edu/.

Clayton State University

Morrow, Georgia

- **State-supported** comprehensive, founded 1969, part of University System of Georgia
- **Suburban** 163-acre campus with easy access to Atlanta
- **Coed** 6,564 undergraduate students, 59% full-time, 71% women, 29% men
- **Minimally difficult** entrance level, 37% of applicants were admitted

Undergraduates 3,843 full-time, 2,721 part-time. Students come from 29 states and territories; 35 other countries; 2% are from out of state; 63% Black or African American, non-Hispanic/Latino; 2% Hispanic/Latino; 4% Asian, non-Hispanic/Latino; 0.2% American Indian or Alaska Native, non-Hispanic/Latino; 0.5% Two or more races, non-Hispanic/Latino; 6% Race/ethnicity unknown; 1% international; 13% transferred in; 7% live on campus. *Retention:* 66% of full-time freshmen returned.

Freshmen *Admission:* 2,574 applied, 964 admitted, 499 enrolled. *Average high school GPA:* 3.14. *Test scores:* SAT critical reading scores over 500: 35%; SAT math scores over 500: 31%; SAT critical reading scores over 600:

8%; SAT math scores over 600: 6%; SAT critical reading scores over 700: 1%; SAT math scores over 700: 1%.

Faculty *Total:* 380, 59% full-time. *Student/faculty ratio:* 18:1.

Academics *Calendar:* semesters. *Degrees:* certificates, associate, bachelor's, and master's. *Special study options:* academic remediation for entering students, adult/continuing education programs, advanced placement credit, cooperative education, distance learning, double majors, English as a second language, freshman honors college, honors programs, independent study, internships, off-campus study, part-time degree program, services for LD students, student-designed majors, study abroad, summer session for credit. *ROTC:* Army (b), Navy (c), Air Force (c).

Computers on Campus 3,500 computers/terminals are available on campus for general student use. Students can access the following: online (class) grades, online (class) registration, online (class) schedules. Campuswide network is available. 100% of college-owned or -operated housing units are wired for high-speed Internet access. Wireless service is available via entire campus.

Student Life *Housing:* on-campus residence required for freshman year. *Options:* coed. Campus housing is university owned. Freshman applicants given priority for college housing. *Activities and organizations:* drama/theater group, student-run newspaper, choral group, Accounting Club, International Awareness Club, Black Cultural Awareness Association, Student Government Association, music club, national fraternities, national sororities. *Campus security:* 24-hour emergency response devices and patrols, late-night transport/escort service, controlled dormitory access, lighted pathways. *Student services:* health clinic, personal/psychological counseling.

Athletics Member NCAA. All Division II. *Intercollegiate sports:* basketball M(s)/W(s), cheerleading W(s)(c), cross-country running M(s)/W(s), golf M(s), soccer M(s)/W(s), tennis W(s), track and field M(s)/W(s). *Intramural sports:* bowling M/W, softball M/W, table tennis M/W, volleyball M/W.

Standardized Tests *Required:* SAT or ACT (for admission). *Required for some:* SAT Subject Tests (for admission).

Costs (2011–12) *Tuition:* state resident $3522 full-time, $147 per credit hour part-time; nonresident $12,813 full-time, $534 per credit hour part-time. Full-time tuition and fees vary according to course load. Part-time tuition and fees vary according to course load. *Required fees:* $1404 full-time, $702 per term part-time. *Room and board:* $8634; room only: $5412. Room and board charges vary according to board plan and housing facility. *Waivers:* senior citizens and employees or children of employees.

Financial Aid Of all full-time matriculated undergraduates who enrolled in 2007, 2,633 applied for aid, 2,402 were judged to have need, 138 had their need fully met. In 2007, 144 non-need-based awards were made. *Average percent of need met:* 33%. *Average financial aid package:* $3855. *Average need-based loan:* $2133. *Average need-based gift aid:* $2126. *Average non-need-based aid:* $699.

Applying *Options:* electronic application, early admission, deferred entrance. *Application fee:* $40. *Required:* high school transcript, proof of immunization. *Application deadline:* 7/17 (freshmen). *Notification:* continuous (freshmen), continuous (transfers).

Freshman Application Contact Ms. Carol S. Montgomery, Admissions, Clayton State University, 2000 Clayton State Boulevard, Morrow, GA 30260-0285. *Phone:* 678-466-4115. *Fax:* 678-466-4149. *E-mail:* csc-info@clayton.edu. *Web site:* http://www.clayton.edu/.

College of Coastal Georgia
Brunswick, Georgia

- **State-supported** 4-year, founded 1961, part of University System of Georgia
- **Small-town** 193-acre campus with easy access to Jacksonville
- **Endowment** $5.6 million
- **Coed** 3,474 undergraduate students, 57% full-time, 68% women, 32% men
- **Minimally difficult** entrance level, 68% of applicants were admitted

Undergraduates 1,982 full-time, 1,492 part-time. Students come from 43 states and territories; 33 other countries; 9% are from out of state; 15% Black or African American, non-Hispanic/Latino; 4% Hispanic/Latino; 0.8% Asian, non-Hispanic/Latino; 0.2% Native Hawaiian or other Pacific Islander, non-Hispanic/Latino; 0.3% American Indian or Alaska Native, non-Hispanic/Latino; 1% Two or more races, non-Hispanic/Latino; 28% Race/ethnicity unknown; 0.6% international; 5% transferred in; 8% live on campus. *Retention:* 53% of full-time freshmen returned.

Freshmen *Admission:* 1,958 applied, 1,329 admitted, 770 enrolled. *Average high school GPA:* 2.87. *Test scores:* SAT critical reading scores over 500: 30%; SAT math scores over 500: 28%; ACT scores over 18: 53%; SAT critical reading scores over 600: 7%; SAT math scores over 600: 4%; ACT scores over 24: 14%; ACT scores over 30: 1%.

Faculty *Total:* 176, 49% full-time, 40% with terminal degrees. *Student/faculty ratio:* 21:1.

Academics *Calendar:* semesters. *Degrees:* associate and bachelor's. *Special study options:* academic remediation for entering students, advanced placement credit, distance learning, double majors, internships, part-time degree program, services for LD students, study abroad, summer session for credit.

Computers on Campus 395 computers/terminals and 300 ports are available on campus for general student use. Students can access the following: computer help desk, free student e-mail accounts, online (class) grades, online (class) registration, online (class) schedules. Campuswide network is available. 100% of college-owned or -operated housing units are wired for high-speed Internet access. Wireless service is available via entire campus.

Student Life *Housing options:* coed. Campus housing is university owned. Freshman campus housing is guaranteed. *Activities and organizations:* student-run newspaper, Brunswick Association of Nursing Students, Minority Advisement and Social Development Association, Student Government Association, Programming Board, Phi Theta Kappa. *Campus security:* 24-hour emergency response devices and patrols, late-night transport/escort service, controlled dormitory access. *Student services:* health clinic, personal/psychological counseling.

Athletics Member NAIA. *Intercollegiate sports:* basketball M(s)/W(s), cross-country running M(s)/W(s), golf M(s)/W(s), softball W(s), tennis M(s)/W(s), volleyball W(s). *Intramural sports:* basketball M/W, bowling M/W, golf M/W, soccer M, tennis M/W, volleyball M/W.

Standardized Tests *Required for some:* SAT or ACT (for admission).

Costs (2012–13) *Tuition:* state resident $2221 full-time, $93 per credit hour part-time; nonresident $8207 full-time, $342 per credit hour part-time. Full-time tuition and fees vary according to course load. Part-time tuition and fees vary according to course load. *Required fees:* $1260 full-time, $630 per term part-time. *Room and board:* $7475; room only: $5075. Room and board charges vary according to board plan and housing facility. *Waivers:* senior citizens and employees or children of employees.

Financial Aid Of all full-time matriculated undergraduates who enrolled in 2010, 80 Federal Work-Study jobs (averaging $1500).

Applying *Options:* electronic application, early admission, deferred entrance. *Application fee:* $25. *Required:* high school transcript, minimum 2.0 GPA, Immunization records, proof of residency and SAT or ACT scores(for applicants graduating from high school within the last five years). *Application deadlines:* 7/15 (freshmen), 7/15 (transfers). *Notification:* continuous (freshmen), continuous (transfers).

Freshman Application Contact Mr. Clayton Daniels, Assistant Vice President for Enrollment Management, College of Coastal Georgia, One College Drive, Brunswick, GA 31520. *Phone:* 912-279-5730. *Toll-free phone:* 800-675-7235. *Fax:* 912-262-3072. *E-mail:* admiss@ccga.edu. *Web site:* http://www.ccga.edu/.

Columbus State University
Columbus, Georgia

- **State-supported** comprehensive, founded 1958, part of University System of Georgia
- **Suburban** 132-acre campus with easy access to Atlanta
- **Endowment** $1.8 million
- **Coed** 7,037 undergraduate students, 71% full-time, 60% women, 40% men
- **Minimally difficult** entrance level, 56% of applicants were admitted

Undergraduates 5,020 full-time, 2,017 part-time. Students come from 42 states and territories; 43 other countries; 15% are from out of state; 36% Black or African American, non-Hispanic/Latino; 5% Hispanic/Latino; 2% Asian, non-Hispanic/Latino; 0.3% Native Hawaiian or other Pacific Islander, non-Hispanic/Latino; 0.6% American Indian or Alaska Native, non-Hispanic/Latino; 2% Two or more races, non-Hispanic/Latino; 0.9% international; 8% transferred in; 20% live on campus. *Retention:* 69% of full-time freshmen returned.

Freshmen *Admission:* 3,843 applied, 2,144 admitted, 1,189 enrolled. *Average high school GPA:* 3.03. *Test scores:* SAT critical reading scores over 500: 45%; SAT math scores over 500: 38%; SAT writing scores over 500: 37%; ACT scores over 18: 73%; SAT critical reading scores over 600: 10%; SAT math scores over 600: 8%; SAT writing scores over 600: 5%; ACT scores over 24: 9%; SAT critical reading scores over 700: 1%; SAT math scores over 700: 1%; SAT writing scores over 700: 1%; ACT scores over 30: 1%.

Faculty *Total:* 469, 58% full-time, 54% with terminal degrees. *Student/faculty ratio:* 18:1.

Academics *Calendar:* semesters. *Degrees:* certificates, associate, bachelor's, master's, post-master's, and postbachelor's certificates. *Special study options:* academic remediation for entering students, adult/continuing education programs, advanced placement credit, cooperative education, distance learning, double majors, English as a second language, freshman honors college, honors programs, independent study, internships, off-campus study, part-time degree program, services for LD students, study abroad, summer session for credit.

ROTC: Army (b). *Unusual degree programs:* 3-2 engineering with Georgia Institute of Technology.

Computers on Campus 1,135 computers/terminals are available on campus for general student use. Students can access the following: campus intranet, computer help desk, free student e-mail accounts, online (class) grades, online (class) registration, online (class) schedules. Campuswide network is available. 100% of college-owned or -operated housing units are wired for high-speed Internet access. Wireless service is available via entire campus.

Student Life *Housing:* on-campus residence required for freshman year. *Options:* coed, men-only, women-only, disabled students. Campus housing is university owned. Freshman applicants given priority for college housing. *Activities and organizations:* drama/theater group, student-run newspaper, choral group, Student Government Association, Student Activities Council, Campus Ministry Association, African Students Association, SABER Student Newspaper, national fraternities, national sororities. *Campus security:* 24-hour emergency response devices and patrols, late-night transport/escort service, controlled dormitory access. *Student services:* health clinic, personal/psychological counseling.

Athletics Member NCAA. All Division II except men's and women's riflery (Division I). *Intercollegiate sports:* baseball M(s), basketball M(s)/W(s), cross-country running M(s)/W(s), golf M(s)/W, riflery M/W, soccer W(s), softball W(s), tennis M(s)/W(s). *Intramural sports:* badminton M/W, basketball M/W, bowling M/W, cross-country running M/W, football M/W, golf M/W, racquetball M/W, skiing (downhill) M/W, soccer M/W, softball M/W, table tennis M/W, tennis M/W, track and field M/W, volleyball M/W.

Standardized Tests *Required:* SAT or ACT (for admission).

Costs (2011–12) *Tuition:* state resident $4734 full-time, $158 per semester hour part-time; nonresident $16,710 full-time, $557 per semester hour part-time. *Required fees:* $1670 full-time, $835 per term part-time. *Room and board:* $7560. Room and board charges vary according to board plan.

Financial Aid Of all full-time matriculated undergraduates who enrolled in 2010, 4,019 applied for aid, 3,231 were judged to have need, 953 had their need fully met. 73 Federal Work-Study jobs (averaging $1953). In 2010, 129 non-need-based awards were made. *Average percent of need met:* 78%. *Average financial aid package:* $8501. *Average need-based loan:* $3912. *Average need-based gift aid:* $4862. *Average non-need-based aid:* $1681. *Average indebtedness upon graduation:* $21,486.

Applying *Options:* electronic application, early admission, deferred entrance. *Application fee:* $30. *Required:* high school transcript, minimum 2.3 GPA, proof of immunization. *Application deadlines:* 6/30 (freshmen), 6/30 (transfers). *Notification:* continuous (freshmen), continuous (transfers).

Freshman Application Contact Columbus State University, 4225 University Avenue, Columbus, GA 31907-5645. *Phone:* 706-507-8806. *Toll-free phone:* 866-264-2035. *Web site:* http://www.columbusstate.edu/.

Covenant College
Lookout Mountain, Georgia

- **Independent** comprehensive, founded 1955, affiliated with Presbyterian Church in America
- **Suburban** 350-acre campus
- **Endowment** $25.1 million
- **Coed** 1,030 undergraduate students, 97% full-time, 55% women, 45% men
- **Moderately difficult** entrance level, 57% of applicants were admitted

Undergraduates 1,002 full-time, 28 part-time. Students come from 43 states and territories; 20 other countries; 76% are from out of state; 3% Black or African American, non-Hispanic/Latino; 2% Hispanic/Latino; 2% Asian, non-Hispanic/Latino; 0.5% American Indian or Alaska Native, non-Hispanic/Latino; 2% Two or more races, non-Hispanic/Latino; 2% international; 3% transferred in; 83% live on campus. *Retention:* 81% of full-time freshmen returned.

Freshmen *Admission:* 1,057 applied, 607 admitted, 286 enrolled. *Average high school GPA:* 3.6. *Test scores:* SAT critical reading scores over 500: 91%; SAT math scores over 500: 87%; SAT writing scores over 500: 86%; ACT scores over 18: 98%; SAT critical reading scores over 600: 52%; SAT math scores over 600: 40%; SAT writing scores over 600: 44%; ACT scores over 24: 71%; SAT critical reading scores over 700: 14%; SAT math scores over 700: 7%; SAT writing scores over 700: 5%; ACT scores over 30: 21%.

Faculty *Total:* 93, 69% full-time, 70% with terminal degrees. *Student/faculty ratio:* 14:1.

Academics *Calendar:* semesters. *Degrees:* associate, bachelor's, and master's (master's degree in education only). *Special study options:* academic remediation for entering students, adult/continuing education programs, advanced placement credit, double majors, independent study, internships, off-campus study, part-time degree program, services for LD students, student-designed majors, study abroad, summer session for credit. *ROTC:* Army (c).

Computers on Campus Students can access the following: computer help desk, free student e-mail accounts, online (class) registration, online student information system. Campuswide network is available. 100% of college-owned or -operated housing units are wired for high-speed Internet access. Wireless service is available via classrooms, computer labs, dorm rooms, libraries.

Student Life *Housing:* on-campus residence required through junior year. *Options:* men-only, women-only. Campus housing is university owned. Freshman campus housing is guaranteed. *Activities and organizations:* drama/theater group, student-run newspaper, radio station, choral group. *Campus security:* controlled dormitory access, night security guards. *Student services:* health clinic, personal/psychological counseling, women's center.

Athletics Member NCAA, NAIA, NCCAA. All NCAA Division III. *Intercollegiate sports:* baseball M, basketball M/W, cross-country running M/W, golf M/W, soccer M/W, softball W, tennis M/W, volleyball W. *Intramural sports:* badminton M/W, basketball M/W, football M, soccer M/W, volleyball M/W.

Standardized Tests *Required:* SAT or ACT (for admission).

Costs (2011–12) *Comprehensive fee:* $33,676 includes full-time tuition ($25,476), mandatory fees ($750), and room and board ($7450). Full-time tuition and fees vary according to course load. Part-time tuition and fees vary according to course load. *Payment plan:* installment. *Waivers:* senior citizens and employees or children of employees.

Financial Aid Of all full-time matriculated undergraduates who enrolled in 2009, 689 applied for aid, 587 were judged to have need, 168 had their need fully met. In 2009, 212 non-need-based awards were made. *Average percent of need met:* 77%. *Average financial aid package:* $18,953. *Average need-based loan:* $4331. *Average need-based gift aid:* $14,127. *Average non-need-based aid:* $8392. *Average indebtedness upon graduation:* $20,519.

Applying *Options:* electronic application, early admission, deferred entrance. *Application fee:* $35. *Required:* essay or personal statement, high school transcript, minimum 2.5 GPA, 2 letters of recommendation, interview. *Application deadlines:* rolling (freshmen), rolling (transfers). *Notification:* continuous (freshmen).

Freshman Application Contact Mr. Philip Howlett, Assistant Director of Admissions, Covenant College, 14049 Scenic Highway, Lookout Mountain, GA 30750. *Phone:* 706-419-1145. *Toll-free phone:* 888-451-2683. *Fax:* 706-820-0893. *E-mail:* admissions@covenant.edu. *Web site:* http://www.covenant.edu/.

Dalton State College
Dalton, Georgia

- **State-supported** 4-year, founded 1963, part of University System of Georgia
- **Small-town** 144-acre campus
- **Endowment** $20.3 million
- **Coed** 5,485 undergraduate students, 59% full-time, 62% women, 38% men
- **Noncompetitive** entrance level, 47% of applicants were admitted

Undergraduates 3,226 full-time, 2,259 part-time. 1% are from out of state; 4% Black or African American, non-Hispanic/Latino; 16% Hispanic/Latino; 0.9% Asian, non-Hispanic/Latino; 0.1% Native Hawaiian or other Pacific Islander, non-Hispanic/Latino; 0.5% American Indian or Alaska Native, non-Hispanic/Latino; 0.9% Two or more races, non-Hispanic/Latino; 7% Race/ethnicity unknown; 1% international; 29% transferred in; 4% live on campus. *Retention:* 63% of full-time freshmen returned.

Freshmen *Admission:* 3,592 applied, 1,676 admitted, 1,224 enrolled. *Average high school GPA:* 3.1. *Test scores:* SAT critical reading scores over 500: 42%; SAT math scores over 500: 37%; ACT scores over 18: 71%; SAT critical reading scores over 600: 7%; SAT math scores over 600: 6%; ACT scores over 24: 17%; ACT scores over 30: 1%.

Faculty *Total:* 237, 66% full-time, 42% with terminal degrees. *Student/faculty ratio:* 20:1.

Academics *Calendar:* semesters. *Degrees:* certificates, associate, and bachelor's. *Special study options:* academic remediation for entering students, adult/continuing education programs, advanced placement credit, cooperative education, double majors, English as a second language, internships, off-campus study, part-time degree program, services for LD students, study abroad, summer session for credit.

Computers on Campus 730 computers/terminals are available on campus for general student use. Students can access the following: free student e-mail accounts, online (class) grades, online (class) registration, online (class) schedules. Campuswide network is available. Wireless service is available via computer centers, computer labs, learning centers, libraries, student centers.

Student Life *Housing options:* coed, disabled students. Campus housing is university owned. *Activities and organizations:* student-run newspaper, Kappa Delta Pi, Phi Theta Kappa, Phi Beta Lambda, Environmental Club, Radiological Technology Club. *Campus security:* 24-hour emergency response devices and patrols.

Athletics *Intercollegiate sports:* basketball M(c)/W(c), golf W(c), softball M(c)/W(c), table tennis M(c)/W(c), tennis M(c)/W(c), volleyball M(c)/W(c). *Intramural sports:* badminton M/W, basketball M/W, football M/W, softball M/W, table tennis M/W, tennis M/W, volleyball M/W.

Standardized Tests *Required:* SAT or ACT (for admission).

Costs (2012–13) *One-time required fee:* $300. *Tuition:* state resident $2160 full-time, $93 per credit hour part-time; nonresident $8160 full-time, $342 per credit hour part-time. Full-time tuition and fees vary according to course load. Part-time tuition and fees vary according to course load. *Required fees:* $846 full-time. *Room only:* $4750. Room and board charges vary according to housing facility. *Waivers:* senior citizens and employees or children of employees.

Financial Aid Of all full-time matriculated undergraduates who enrolled in 2009, 2,749 applied for aid, 2,034 were judged to have need, 947 had their need fully met. In 2009, 25 non-need-based awards were made. *Average percent of need met:* 77%. *Average financial aid package:* $8985. *Average need-based loan:* $3476. *Average need-based gift aid:* $3636. *Average non-need-based aid:* $1295. *Average indebtedness upon graduation:* $11,953. *Financial aid deadline:* 7/1.

Applying *Options:* electronic application, deferred entrance. *Application fee:* $30. *Required:* high school transcript. *Application deadlines:* 7/1 (freshmen), 7/1 (transfers). *Notification:* continuous (freshmen).

Freshman Application Contact Dr. Angela Harris, Assistant Vice President of Enrollment Services, Dalton State College, 650 College Drive, Dalton, GA 30720-3797. *Phone:* 706-272-4476. *Toll-free phone:* 800-829-4436. *Fax:* 706-272-2530. *Web site:* http://www.daltonstate.edu/.

DeVry University

Alpharetta, Georgia

Freshman Application Contact DeVry University, 2555 Northwinds Parkway, Alpharetta, GA 30009. *Toll-free phone:* 866-338-7941. *Web site:* http://www.devry.edu/.

DeVry University

Decatur, Georgia

- **Proprietary** comprehensive, founded 1969, part of DeVry University
- **Suburban** campus
- **Coed** 2,720 undergraduate students, 38% full-time, 52% women, 48% men
- **Minimally difficult** entrance level

Undergraduates 1,022 full-time, 1,698 part-time. 6% are from out of state; 61% Black or African American, non-Hispanic/Latino; 4% Hispanic/Latino; 2% Asian, non-Hispanic/Latino; 0.2% Native Hawaiian or other Pacific Islander, non-Hispanic/Latino; 0.1% American Indian or Alaska Native, non-Hispanic/Latino; 1% Two or more races, non-Hispanic/Latino; 10% Race/ethnicity unknown; 0.3% international; 23% transferred in.

Freshmen *Admission:* 344 enrolled.

Faculty *Total:* 143, 26% full-time. *Student/faculty ratio:* 24:1.

Academics *Calendar:* semesters. *Degrees:* associate, bachelor's, master's, and postbachelor's certificates. *Special study options:* adult/continuing education programs, part-time degree program.

Student Life *Housing:* college housing not available.

Athletics *Intramural sports:* basketball M/W, football M/W, softball M/W, volleyball M/W.

Costs (2011–12) *Tuition:* $15,294 full-time, $597 per term part-time. Full-time tuition and fees vary according to course load. Part-time tuition and fees vary according to course load. *Required fees:* $80 full-time, $40 per term part-time. *Payment plans:* installment, deferred payment. *Waivers:* employees or children of employees.

Financial Aid Of all full-time matriculated undergraduates who enrolled in 2007, 488 applied for aid, 477 were judged to have need, 14 had their need fully met. In 2007, 17 non-need-based awards were made. *Average percent of need met:* 43%. *Average financial aid package:* $14,044. *Average need-based loan:* $8002. *Average need-based gift aid:* $6480. *Average non-need-based aid:* $15,251. *Average indebtedness upon graduation:* $47,994.

Applying *Application fee:* $50. *Required:* high school transcript, interview. *Application deadlines:* rolling (freshmen), rolling (transfers). *Notification:* continuous (freshmen), continuous (transfers).

Freshman Application Contact DeVry University, 1 West Court Square, Suite 100, Decatur, GA 30030-2556. *Phone:* 404-270-2700. *Toll-free phone:* 866-338-7941. *Web site:* http://www.devry.edu/.

DeVry University

Duluth, Georgia

Admissions Office Contact DeVry University, 3505 Koger Boulevard, Suite 170, Duluth, GA 30096-7671. *Toll-free phone:* 866-338-7941. *Web site:* http://www.devry.edu/.

Emmanuel College

Franklin Springs, Georgia

- **Independent** 4-year, founded 1919, affiliated with Pentecostal Holiness Church
- **Rural** 90-acre campus with easy access to Atlanta
- **Endowment** $3.3 million
- **Coed** 788 undergraduate students, 88% full-time, 54% women, 46% men
- **Moderately difficult** entrance level, 56% of applicants were admitted

Undergraduates 695 full-time, 93 part-time. Students come from 20 states and territories; 19 other countries; 21% are from out of state; 19% Black or African American, non-Hispanic/Latino; 5% Hispanic/Latino; 0.9% Asian, non-Hispanic/Latino; 0.1% American Indian or Alaska Native, non-Hispanic/Latino; 0.4% Two or more races, non-Hispanic/Latino; 4% international; 8% transferred in; 50% live on campus. *Retention:* 52% of full-time freshmen returned.

Freshmen *Admission:* 1,108 applied, 615 admitted, 188 enrolled. *Average high school GPA:* 3.28.

Faculty *Total:* 87, 54% full-time, 37% with terminal degrees. *Student/faculty ratio:* 12:1.

Academics *Calendar:* semesters. *Degrees:* associate and bachelor's. *Special study options:* academic remediation for entering students, accelerated degree program, advanced placement credit, distance learning, honors programs, independent study, internships, part-time degree program, services for LD students, study abroad, summer session for credit.

Computers on Campus 50 computers/terminals are available on campus for general student use. Students can access the following: campus intranet, computer help desk, free student e-mail accounts, online (class) grades, online (class) registration, online (class) schedules. Campuswide network is available. 100% of college-owned or -operated housing units are wired for high-speed Internet access. Wireless service is available via entire campus.

Student Life *Housing:* on-campus residence required through sophomore year. *Options:* men-only, women-only. Campus housing is university owned. Freshman campus housing is guaranteed. *Activities and organizations:* drama/theater group, choral group, Students in Free Enterprise (SIFE), FCA, SOS, BSU, International Students Club. *Campus security:* 24-hour patrols. *Student services:* personal/psychological counseling.

Athletics Member NAIA, NCCAA. *Intercollegiate sports:* baseball M(s), basketball M(s)/W(s), cross-country running M(s)/W(s), golf M(s)/W(s), soccer M(s)/W(s), softball W(s), tennis M(s)/W(s), track and field M(s)/W(s), volleyball W(s). *Intramural sports:* basketball M/W, football M/W, golf M/W, soccer M/W, tennis M/W, track and field M/W, volleyball M/W, weight lifting M/W.

Standardized Tests *Required:* SAT or ACT (for admission).

Costs (2011–12) *Comprehensive fee:* $20,650 includes full-time tuition ($14,550) and room and board ($6100). Part-time tuition: $600 per credit hour. *Room and board:* Room and board charges vary according to housing facility. *Payment plan:* installment. *Waivers:* senior citizens and employees or children of employees.

Financial Aid Of all full-time matriculated undergraduates who enrolled in 2010, 634 applied for aid, 589 were judged to have need, 55 had their need fully met. 286 Federal Work-Study jobs (averaging $1871). In 2010, 68 non-need-based awards were made. *Average percent of need met:* 66%. *Average financial aid package:* $12,455. *Average need-based loan:* $3512. *Average need-based gift aid:* $8768. *Average non-need-based aid:* $4658. *Average indebtedness upon graduation:* $28,298. *Financial aid deadline:* 6/15.

Applying *Options:* electronic application, early admission, deferred entrance. *Application fee:* $25. *Required:* high school transcript. *Application deadlines:* 8/1 (freshmen), 8/1 (transfers). *Notification:* 8/1 (freshmen), continuous until 8/1 (transfers).

Freshman Application Contact Ms. Amanda Strickland, Admissions Counselor, Emmanuel College, PO Box 129, 181 Spring Street, Franklin Springs, GA 30639-0129. *Phone:* 706-245-7226 Ext. 2907. *Toll-free phone:* 800-860-8800. *E-mail:* admissions@ec.edu. *Web site:* http://www.ec.edu/.

Emory University
Atlanta, Georgia

- **Independent Methodist** university, founded 1836
- **Suburban** 634-acre campus with easy access to Atlanta
- **Endowment** $5.4 billion
- **Coed** 7,441 undergraduate students, 99% full-time, 55% women, 45% men
- **Most difficult** entrance level, 27% of applicants were admitted

Undergraduates 7,368 full-time, 73 part-time. Students come from 53 states and territories; 66 other countries; 72% are from out of state; 10% Black or African American, non-Hispanic/Latino; 5% Hispanic/Latino; 23% Asian, non-Hispanic/Latino; 0.3% American Indian or Alaska Native, non-Hispanic/Latino; 1% Two or more races, non-Hispanic/Latino; 7% Race/ethnicity unknown; 11% international; 2% transferred in; 70% live on campus. *Retention:* 96% of full-time freshmen returned.

Freshmen *Admission:* 17,027 applied, 4,548 admitted, 1,780 enrolled. *Average high school GPA:* 3.86. *Test scores:* SAT critical reading scores over 500: 100%; SAT math scores over 500: 100%; SAT writing scores over 500: 100%; ACT scores over 18: 100%; SAT critical reading scores over 600: 92%; SAT math scores over 600: 96%; SAT writing scores over 600: 94%; ACT scores over 24: 100%; SAT critical reading scores over 700: 49%; SAT math scores over 700: 64%; SAT writing scores over 700: 59%; ACT scores over 30: 81%.

Faculty *Total:* 1,534, 84% full-time, 99% with terminal degrees. *Student/faculty ratio:* 7:1.

Academics *Calendar:* semesters. *Degrees:* associate, bachelor's, master's, doctoral, post-master's, postbachelor's, and first professional certificates (enrollment figures include Emory University, Oxford College; application data for main campus only). *Special study options:* advanced placement credit, double majors, English as a second language, honors programs, independent study, internships, off-campus study, services for LD students, student-designed majors, study abroad, summer session for credit. *ROTC:* Army (c), Navy (c), Air Force (c). *Unusual degree programs:* 3-2 engineering with Georgia Institute of Technology.

Computers on Campus 1,000 computers/terminals and 300 ports are available on campus for general student use. Students can access the following: campus intranet, computer help desk, free student e-mail accounts, online (class) grades, online (class) registration, online (class) schedules, Computer Repair System, Online Library, iTunes University. Campuswide network is available. 100% of college-owned or -operated housing units are wired for high-speed Internet access. Wireless service is available via entire campus.

Student Life *Housing:* on-campus residence required through sophomore year. *Options:* coed, disabled students. Campus housing is university owned. Freshman campus housing is guaranteed. *Activities and organizations:* drama/theater group, student-run newspaper, radio and television station, choral group, Volunteer Emory, music/theater, student government, Outdoor Emory, Hillel, national fraternities, national sororities. *Campus security:* 24-hour emergency response devices and patrols, student patrols, late-night transport/escort service, controlled dormitory access. *Student services:* health clinic, personal/psychological counseling, women's center, legal services.

Athletics Member NCAA. All Division III. *Intercollegiate sports:* badminton M(c)/W(c), baseball M, basketball M/W, cheerleading M(c)/W(c), crew M(c)/W(c), cross-country running M/W, equestrian sports W(c), fencing M(c)/W(c), field hockey W(c), golf M, gymnastics M(c)/W(c), ice hockey M(c), lacrosse M(c)/W(c), racquetball M(c)/W(c), rock climbing M(c)/W(c), rugby M(c)/W(c), sailing M(c)/W(c), soccer M/W, softball W, swimming and diving M/W, tennis M/W, track and field M/W, ultimate Frisbee M(c)/W(c), volleyball M(c)/W, water polo M(c)/W(c), weight lifting M(c)/W(c), wrestling M(c). *Intramural sports:* basketball M/W, cross-country running M/W, football M/W, ice hockey M, racquetball M/W, soccer M/W, softball M/W, swimming and diving M/W, table tennis M/W, tennis M/W, track and field M/W, volleyball M/W.

Standardized Tests *Required:* SAT or ACT (for admission). *Recommended:* SAT Subject Tests (for admission).

Costs (2011–12) *Comprehensive fee:* $52,792 includes full-time tuition ($40,600), mandatory fees ($564), and room and board ($11,628). Full-time tuition and fees vary according to degree level and location. Part-time tuition: $1692 per credit hour. *College room only:* $6988. Room and board charges vary according to board plan, housing facility, location, and student level. *Payment plan:* installment. *Waivers:* employees or children of employees.

Financial Aid Of all full-time matriculated undergraduates who enrolled in 2011, 3,940 applied for aid, 3,591 were judged to have need, 3,591 had their need fully met. In 2011, 457 non-need-based awards were made. *Average percent of need met:* 100%. *Average financial aid package:* $36,807. *Average need-based loan:* $4179. *Average need-based gift aid:* $33,323. *Average non-need-based aid:* $21,821. *Average indebtedness upon graduation:* $28,076. *Financial aid deadline:* 3/1.

Applying *Options:* electronic application, early admission, early decision, deferred entrance. *Application fee:* $50. *Required:* essay or personal statement, high school transcript, 1 letter of recommendation. *Recommended:* minimum 3.0 GPA. *Application deadlines:* 1/15 (freshmen), 6/1 (transfers). *Early decision deadline:* 11/1 (for plan 1), 1/1 (for plan 2). *Notification:* 4/1 (freshmen), continuous (transfers), 12/15 (early decision plan 1), 2/15 (early decision plan 2).

Freshman Application Contact Mr. John Latting, Dean of Admission, Emory University, 1390 Oxford Road NE, 3rd Floor, Atlanta, GA 30322-1100. *Phone:* 404-727-6036. *Toll-free phone:* 800-727-6036. *Fax:* 404-727-4303. *E-mail:* admiss@emory.edu. *Web site:* http://www.emory.edu/.

Emory University, Oxford College
Oxford, Georgia

- **Independent Methodist** primarily 2-year, founded 1836
- **Small-town** 150-acre campus with easy access to Atlanta
- **Endowment** $39.0 million
- **Coed** 936 undergraduate students, 100% full-time, 53% women, 47% men
- **Very difficult** entrance level, 55% of applicants were admitted

Undergraduates 936 full-time. Students come from 45 states and territories; 29 other countries; 61% are from out of state; 14% Black or African American, non-Hispanic/Latino; 6% Hispanic/Latino; 29% Asian, non-Hispanic/Latino; 0.1% Native Hawaiian or other Pacific Islander, non-Hispanic/Latino; 0.3% American Indian or Alaska Native, non-Hispanic/Latino; 3% Two or more races, non-Hispanic/Latino; 4% Race/ethnicity unknown; 15% international; 99% live on campus. *Retention:* 90% of full-time freshmen returned.

Freshmen *Admission:* 3,683 applied, 2,013 admitted, 440 enrolled. *Average high school GPA:* 3.54. *Test scores:* SAT critical reading scores over 500: 95%; SAT math scores over 500: 97%; SAT writing scores over 500: 95%; ACT scores over 18: 100%; SAT critical reading scores over 600: 60%; SAT math scores over 600: 71%; SAT writing scores over 600: 65%; ACT scores over 24: 88%; SAT critical reading scores over 700: 19%; SAT math scores over 700: 26%; SAT writing scores over 700: 21%; ACT scores over 30: 29%.

Faculty *Total:* 85, 67% full-time, 74% with terminal degrees. *Student/faculty ratio:* 14:1.

Academics *Calendar:* semesters. *Degrees:* associate and bachelor's. *Special study options:* advanced placement credit, double majors, independent study, internships, off-campus study, services for LD students, study abroad, summer session for credit. *ROTC:* Army (c), Navy (c), Air Force (c). *Unusual degree programs:* 3-2 engineering with Georgia Institute of Technology.

Computers on Campus 110 computers/terminals are available on campus for general student use. Students can access the following: campus intranet, computer help desk, free student e-mail accounts, online (class) grades, online (class) registration, online (class) schedules. Campuswide network is available. Wireless service is available via entire campus.

Student Life *Housing:* on-campus residence required through sophomore year. *Options:* coed, women-only, disabled students. Campus housing is university owned. Freshman campus housing is guaranteed. *Activities and organizations:* drama/theater group, student-run newspaper, choral group, Residence Hall Association, intramurals/junior varsity sports, Student Government Association, Student Admissions Association, Volunteer Oxford. *Campus security:* 24-hour emergency response devices and patrols, student patrols, late-night transport/escort service, controlled dormitory access. *Student services:* health clinic, personal/psychological counseling.

Athletics Member NJCAA. *Intercollegiate sports:* basketball M, soccer W, tennis M/W. *Intramural sports:* badminton M/W, baseball M(c), basketball M/W, football M, soccer M/W, swimming and diving M/W, tennis M/W, ultimate Frisbee M/W, volleyball M/W.

Standardized Tests *Required:* SAT or ACT (for admission). *Required for some:* SAT Subject Tests (for admission).

Costs (2012–13) *Comprehensive fee:* $47,054 includes full-time tuition ($36,100), mandatory fees ($478), and room and board ($10,476). Part-time tuition: $1504 per contact hour. *College room only:* $7196. *Payment plan:* installment. *Waivers:* employees or children of employees.

Financial Aid Of all full-time matriculated undergraduates who enrolled in 2010, 225 Federal Work-Study jobs (averaging $1600).

Applying *Options:* electronic application, early admission, early action, deferred entrance. *Application fee:* $50. *Required:* essay or personal statement, high school transcript, 1 letter of recommendation. *Required for some:* interview. *Recommended:* minimum 3.0 GPA, 2 letters of recommendation. *Application deadlines:* 1/15 (freshmen), 11/1 (early action). *Notification:* continuous until 4/1 (freshmen), 12/15 (early action).

Freshman Application Contact Emory University, Oxford College, 100 Hamill Street, PO Box 1328, Oxford, GA 30054. *Phone:* 770-784-8328. *Toll-free phone:* 800-723-8328. *Web site:* http://oxford.emory.edu/.

Fort Valley State University

Fort Valley, Georgia

Freshman Application Contact Mr. Donald Moore, Director of Admissions and Recruitment, Fort Valley State University, 1005 State University Drive, Fort Valley, GA 31030. *Phone:* 478-825-6307. *Toll-free phone:* 877-462-3878. *Fax:* 478-825-6169. *E-mail:* admissap@fvsu.edu. *Web site:* http://www.fvsu.edu/.

Gainesville State College

Oakwood, Georgia

Freshman Application Contact Mr. Mack Palmour, Director of Admissions, Gainesville State College, PO Box 1358, Gainesville, GA 30503. *Phone:* 678-717-3641. *Fax:* 678-717-3751. *E-mail:* admissions@gsc.edu. *Web site:* http://www.gsc.edu/.

Georgia College & State University

Milledgeville, Georgia

- **State-supported** comprehensive, founded 1889, part of University System of Georgia
- **Small-town** 590-acre campus
- **Endowment** $25.3 million
- **Coed** 5,635 undergraduate students, 91% full-time, 60% women, 40% men
- **Moderately difficult** entrance level, 70% of applicants were admitted

Undergraduates 5,139 full-time, 496 part-time. 1% are from out of state; 6% Black or African American, non-Hispanic/Latino; 4% Hispanic/Latino; 1% Asian, non-Hispanic/Latino; 0.1% Native Hawaiian or other Pacific Islander, non-Hispanic/Latino; 0.3% American Indian or Alaska Native, non-Hispanic/Latino; 2% Two or more races, non-Hispanic/Latino; 0.5% Race/ethnicity unknown; 1% international; 6% transferred in; 36% live on campus. *Retention:* 83% of full-time freshmen returned.

Freshmen *Admission:* 3,779 applied, 2,651 admitted, 1,209 enrolled. *Average high school GPA:* 3.4. *Test scores:* SAT critical reading scores over 500: 87%; SAT math scores over 500: 86%; SAT writing scores over 500: 81%; ACT scores over 18: 100%; SAT critical reading scores over 600: 33%; SAT math scores over 600: 34%; SAT writing scores over 600: 25%; ACT scores over 24: 57%; SAT critical reading scores over 700: 3%; SAT math scores over 700: 2%; SAT writing scores over 700: 2%; ACT scores over 30: 3%.

Faculty *Total:* 436, 70% full-time. *Student/faculty ratio:* 17:1.

Academics *Calendar:* semesters. *Degrees:* bachelor's, master's, and post-master's certificates. *Special study options:* accelerated degree program, advanced placement credit, distance learning, double majors, English as a second language, freshman honors college, honors programs, independent study, internships, part-time degree program, services for LD students, student-designed majors, study abroad, summer session for credit. *ROTC:* Army (c). *Unusual degree programs:* 3-2 engineering with Georgia Institute of Technology.

Computers on Campus 766 computers/terminals and 6,295 ports are available on campus for general student use. Students can access the following: campus intranet, computer help desk, free student e-mail accounts, online (class) grades, online (class) registration, online (class) schedules. Campuswide network is available. 100% of college-owned or -operated housing units are wired for high-speed Internet access. Wireless service is available via entire campus.

Student Life *Housing:* on-campus residence required for freshman year. *Options:* coed, disabled students. Campus housing is university owned and leased by the school. Freshman applicants given priority for college housing. *Activities and organizations:* drama/theater group, student-run newspaper, radio station, choral group, Alpha Lambda Delta, Delta Zeta, Alpha Delta Pi, Phi Mu, Honors Program, national fraternities, national sororities. *Campus security:* 24-hour emergency response devices and patrols, student patrols, late-night transport/escort service, controlled dormitory access. *Student services:* health clinic, personal/psychological counseling, women's center.

Athletics Member NCAA. All Division II. *Intercollegiate sports:* baseball M(s), basketball M(s)/W(s), cheerleading M/W, cross-country running M(s)/W(s), golf M(s), soccer W(s), softball W(s), tennis M(s)/W(s). *Intramural sports:* basketball M/W, football M/W, ice hockey M(c), lacrosse M(c)/W(c), rugby M(c), soccer M(c)/W(c), softball M/W, swimming and diving M(c)/W(c), ultimate Frisbee M/W, volleyball M(c)/W(c), water polo M/W.

Standardized Tests *Required:* SAT or ACT (for admission). *Required for some:* SAT Subject Tests (for admission).

Costs (2011–12) *Tuition:* state resident $6472 full-time; nonresident $23,510 full-time. Full-time tuition and fees vary according to course load and location. Part-time tuition and fees vary according to course load and location. *Required fees:* $1872 full-time, $936 per term part-time. *Room and board:* $8998; room only: $5114. Room and board charges vary according to board plan and housing facility. *Payment plan:* installment. *Waivers:* senior citizens and employees or children of employees.

Financial Aid Of all full-time matriculated undergraduates who enrolled in 2011, 4,800 applied for aid, 2,702 were judged to have need. In 2011, 52 non-need-based awards were made. *Average financial aid package:* $7418. *Average need-based loan:* $3299. *Average need-based gift aid:* $4424. *Average non-need-based aid:* $1325. *Average indebtedness upon graduation:* $18,985.

Applying *Options:* electronic application, early admission, early action, deferred entrance. *Application fee:* $40. *Required:* essay or personal statement, proof of immunization. *Required for some:* interview. *Application deadlines:* 4/1 (freshmen), 7/1 (transfers), 11/1 (early action). *Notification:* continuous (freshmen), continuous (transfers), 12/1 (early action).

Freshman Application Contact Ms. Suzanne Pittman, Assistant Vice President for Enrollment Management, Georgia College & State University, CPO Box 023, Milledgeville, GA 31061. *Phone:* 478-445-6283. *Toll-free phone:* 800-342-0471. *Fax:* 478-445-1336. *E-mail:* admissions@gcsu.edu. *Web site:* http://www.gcsu.edu/.

Georgia Gwinnett College

Lawrenceville, Georgia

- **State-supported** 4-year, part of University System of Georgia
- **Suburban** 260-acre campus with easy access to Atlanta
- **Coed** 7,742 undergraduate students, 72% full-time, 54% women, 46% men
- **92%** of applicants were admitted

Undergraduates 5,602 full-time, 2,140 part-time. Students come from 10 states and territories; 1% are from out of state; 31% Black or African American, non-Hispanic/Latino; 10% Hispanic/Latino; 8% Asian, non-Hispanic/Latino; 0.3% Native Hawaiian or other Pacific Islander, non-Hispanic/Latino; 0.2% American Indian or Alaska Native, non-Hispanic/Latino; 3% Two or more races, non-Hispanic/Latino; 2% Race/ethnicity unknown; 0.7% international; 11% transferred in; 10% live on campus. *Retention:* 68% of full-time freshmen returned.

Freshmen *Admission:* 4,588 applied, 4,216 admitted, 2,364 enrolled. *Average high school GPA:* 2.7. *Test scores:* SAT critical reading scores over 500: 33%; SAT math scores over 500: 38%; ACT scores over 18: 64%; SAT critical reading scores over 600: 6%; SAT math scores over 600: 7%; ACT scores over 24: 12%; ACT scores over 30: 1%.

Faculty *Total:* 489, 61% full-time. *Student/faculty ratio:* 17:1.

Academics *Degree:* bachelor's. *Special study options:* advanced placement credit, English as a second language, internships, services for LD students, summer session for credit. *ROTC:* Army (c).

Computers on Campus 207 computers/terminals are available on campus for general student use. Students can access the following: campus intranet, computer help desk, free student e-mail accounts, online (class) grades, online (class) registration, online (class) schedules. Campuswide network is available. 100% of college-owned or -operated housing units are wired for high-speed Internet access. Wireless service is available via entire campus.

Student Life *Housing options:* coed. Campus housing is university owned. *Campus security:* 24-hour emergency response devices and patrols. *Student services:* personal/psychological counseling.

Athletics *Intramural sports:* basketball M/W, golf M/W, racquetball M/W, soccer M/W, tennis M/W, volleyball M/W.

Standardized Tests *Recommended:* SAT or ACT (for admission).

Costs (2012–13) *Tuition:* state resident $3296 full-time; nonresident $12,296 full-time. No tuition increase for student's term of enrollment. *Required fees:* $1994 full-time. *Room and board:* $9000. Room and board charges vary according to board plan. *Payment plans:* installment, deferred payment. *Waivers:* senior citizens and employees or children of employees.

Applying *Options:* electronic application. *Application fee:* $20. *Required:* high school transcript, minimum 2.0 GPA. *Application deadlines:* 6/1 (freshmen), 6/1 (out-of-state freshmen), rolling (transfers).

Freshman Application Contact Admissions Office, Georgia Gwinnett College, 1000 University Center Lane, Lawrenceville, GA 60043. *Phone:* 678-407-5313. *Toll-free phone:* 877-704-4422. *E-mail:* ggcadmissions@ggc.edu. *Web site:* http://www.ggc.usg.edu/.

Georgia Health Sciences University
Augusta, Georgia

- **State-supported** upper-level, founded 1828, part of University System of Georgia
- **Urban** 100-acre campus
- **Endowment** $6.6 million
- **Coed**
- 33% of applicants were admitted

Academics *Calendar:* semesters. *Degrees:* bachelor's, master's, doctoral, post-master's, and postbachelor's certificates.
Student Life *Campus security:* 24-hour emergency response devices and patrols, late-night transport/escort service.
Costs (2011–12) *Tuition:* state resident $7282 full-time, $243 per credit hour part-time; nonresident $25,492 full-time, $850 per credit hour part-time. Full-time tuition and fees vary according to course load, location, program, and reciprocity agreements. Part-time tuition and fees vary according to course load, location, program, and reciprocity agreements. *Required fees:* $1626 full-time. *Room only:* $2372. Room and board charges vary according to housing facility and location.
Financial Aid *Of all full-time matriculated undergraduates who enrolled in 2010,* 403 applied for aid, 403 were judged to have need. 22 Federal Work-Study jobs (averaging $1561). *Average financial aid package:* $8594. *Average need-based loan:* $3747. *Average need-based gift aid:* $1897.
Applying *Options:* electronic application. *Application fee:* $30.
Application Contact Georgia Health Sciences University, 1120 15th Street, Augusta, GA 30912. *Phone:* 706-721-2725. *Toll-free phone:* 800-519-3388. *Web site:* http://www.georgiahealth.edu.

Georgia Institute of Technology
Atlanta, Georgia

- **State-supported** university, founded 1885, part of University System of Georgia
- **Urban** 400-acre campus
- **Endowment** $1.6 billion
- **Coed** 13,948 undergraduate students, 91% full-time, 32% women, 68% men
- **Very difficult** entrance level, 51% of applicants were admitted

Undergraduates 12,701 full-time, 1,247 part-time. Students come from 53 states and territories; 122 other countries; 26% are from out of state; 7% Black or African American, non-Hispanic/Latino; 6% Hispanic/Latino; 17% Asian, non-Hispanic/Latino; 0.1% Native Hawaiian or other Pacific Islander, non-Hispanic/Latino; 0.2% American Indian or Alaska Native, non-Hispanic/Latino; 3% Two or more races, non-Hispanic/Latino; 0.6% Race/ethnicity unknown; 8% international; 5% transferred in; 56% live on campus. *Retention:* 95% of full-time freshmen returned.
Freshmen *Admission:* 14,088 applied, 7,210 admitted, 2,695 enrolled. *Average high school GPA:* 3.89. *Test scores:* SAT critical reading scores over 500: 99%; SAT math scores over 500: 99%; SAT writing scores over 500: 98%; ACT scores over 18: 100%; SAT critical reading scores over 600: 76%; SAT math scores over 600: 93%; SAT writing scores over 600: 78%; ACT scores over 24: 98%; SAT critical reading scores over 700: 24%; SAT math scores over 700: 55%; SAT writing scores over 700: 26%; ACT scores over 30: 54%.
Faculty *Total:* 1,225, 85% full-time, 83% with terminal degrees. *Student/faculty ratio:* 17:1.
Academics *Calendar:* semesters. *Degrees:* bachelor's, master's, doctoral, and first professional. *Special study options:* academic remediation for entering students, accelerated degree program, advanced placement credit, cooperative education, distance learning, double majors, English as a second language, honors programs, independent study, internships, off-campus study, part-time degree program, services for LD students, student-designed majors, study abroad, summer session for credit. *ROTC:* Army (b), Navy (b), Air Force (b).
Unusual degree programs: 3-2 engineering with Many of the schools in the University System of Georgia, Morehouse College, Spelman College, Clark Atlanta University, and other liberal arts colleges, historically black colleges, and women's colleges in the Southeast.
Computers on Campus 1,000 computers/terminals and 16,776 ports are available on campus for general student use. Students can access the following: campus intranet, computer help desk, free student e-mail accounts, online (class) grades, online (class) registration, online (class) schedules. Campus-wide network is available. 100% of college-owned or -operated housing units are wired for high-speed Internet access. Wireless service is available via entire campus.
Student Life *Housing options:* coed, men-only, women-only, disabled students. Campus housing is university owned. Freshman campus housing is guaranteed. *Activities and organizations:* drama/theater group, student-run newspaper, radio and television station, choral group, marching band, India

Club, Christian Campus Fellowship, Muslim Student Association, National Society of Black Engineers, national fraternities, national sororities. *Campus security:* 24-hour emergency response devices and patrols, late-night transport/escort service, controlled dormitory access, self defense education, lighted pathways and walks, video cameras, email and phone alerts of emergency situations. *Student services:* health clinic, personal/psychological counseling, women's center, legal services.
Athletics Member NCAA. All Division I except football (Division I-A). *Intercollegiate sports:* baseball M(s), basketball M(s)/W(s), cheerleading M(s)/W(s), cross-country running M(s)/W(s), golf M(s), softball W(s), swimming and diving M(s)/W(s), tennis M(s)/W(s), track and field M(s)/W(s), volleyball W(s). *Intramural sports:* archery M(c)/W(c), badminton M(c)/W(c), baseball M(c), basketball M/W, bowling M/W, crew M(c)/W(c), equestrian sports M(c)/W(c), fencing M(c)/W(c), field hockey M(c)/W(c), football M/W, golf M(c)/W(c), gymnastics M(c)/W(c), ice hockey M(c), lacrosse M(c)/W(c), racquetball M/W, rugby M(c)/W(c), sailing M(c)/W(c), soccer M(c)/W(c), softball M/W, swimming and diving M(c)/W(c), table tennis M(c)/W(c), tennis M(c)/W(c), ultimate Frisbee M(c)/W(c), volleyball M(c)/W(c), water polo M(c)/W(c), wrestling M(c).
Standardized Tests *Required:* SAT or ACT (for admission).
Costs (2011–12) *Tuition:* state resident $7282 full-time, $361 per credit hour part-time; nonresident $25,492 full-time, $1261 per credit hour part-time. Part-time tuition and fees vary according to course load. *Required fees:* $2370 full-time, $727 per course part-time, $1185 per term part-time. *Room and board:* $8826; room only: $5312. Room and board charges vary according to board plan and housing facility. *Waivers:* employees or children of employees.
Financial Aid Of all full-time matriculated undergraduates who enrolled in 2010, 8,131 applied for aid, 5,553 were judged to have need, 1,757 had their need fully met. 369 Federal Work-Study jobs (averaging $1739). In 2010, 674 non-need-based awards were made. *Average percent of need met:* 58%. *Average financial aid package:* $11,529. *Average need-based loan:* $5066. *Average need-based gift aid:* $10,049. *Average non-need-based aid:* $4221. *Average indebtedness upon graduation:* $23,427. *Financial aid deadline:* 3/1.
Applying *Options:* electronic application, early admission, early action. *Application fee:* $65. *Required:* essay or personal statement, high school transcript. *Application deadlines:* 1/10 (freshmen), 2/1 (transfers), 10/15 (early action). *Notification:* 3/15 (freshmen), continuous (transfers), 12/15 (early action).
Freshman Application Contact Mr. Rick A. Clark Jr., Director of Undergraduate Admissions, Georgia Institute of Technology, Office of Undergraduate Admission, Atlanta, GA 30332-0320. *Phone:* 404-894-4154. *Fax:* 404-894-9511. *E-mail:* admission@gatech.edu. *Web site:* http://www.gatech.edu/.

Georgia Southern University
Statesboro, Georgia

- **State-supported** university, founded 1906, part of University System of Georgia
- **Small-town** 700-acre campus with easy access to None
- **Endowment** $37.6 million
- **Coed** 17,525 undergraduate students, 89% full-time, 50% women, 50% men
- **Moderately difficult** entrance level, 49% of applicants were admitted

Undergraduates 15,634 full-time, 1,891 part-time. Students come from 47 states and territories; 78 other countries; 3% are from out of state; 24% Black or African American, non-Hispanic/Latino; 4% Hispanic/Latino; 1% Asian, non-Hispanic/Latino; 0.2% Native Hawaiian or other Pacific Islander, non-Hispanic/Latino; 0.5% American Indian or Alaska Native, non-Hispanic/Latino; 2% Two or more races, non-Hispanic/Latino; 1% Race/ethnicity unknown; 1% international; 7% transferred in; 25% live on campus. *Retention:* 80% of full-time freshmen returned.
Freshmen *Admission:* 11,032 applied, 5,456 admitted, 3,543 enrolled. *Average high school GPA:* 3.2. *Test scores:* SAT critical reading scores over 500: 86%; SAT math scores over 500: 87%; SAT writing scores over 500: 68%; ACT scores over 18: 99%; SAT critical reading scores over 600: 23%; SAT math scores over 600: 25%; SAT writing scores over 600: 14%; ACT scores over 24: 34%; SAT critical reading scores over 700: 2%; SAT math scores over 700: 2%; SAT writing scores over 700: 1%; ACT scores over 30: 3%.
Faculty *Total:* 870, 87% full-time, 76% with terminal degrees. *Student/faculty ratio:* 22:1.
Academics *Calendar:* semesters. *Degrees:* bachelor's, master's, doctoral, post-master's, and first professional certificates. *Special study options:* academic remediation for entering students, accelerated degree program, adult/continuing education programs, advanced placement credit, cooperative education, distance learning, double majors, English as a second language, honors programs, independent study, internships, off-campus study, part-time degree program, services for LD students, student-designed majors, study abroad,

summer session for credit. *ROTC:* Army (b). *Unusual degree programs:* 3-2 engineering with Georgia Institute of Technology.

Computers on Campus 3,320 computers/terminals and 5,200 ports are available on campus for general student use. Students can access the following: campus intranet, computer help desk, free student e-mail accounts, online (class) grades, online (class) registration, online (class) schedules. Campuswide network is available. 100% of college-owned or -operated housing units are wired for high-speed Internet access. Wireless service is available via entire campus.

Student Life *Housing:* on-campus residence required for freshman year. *Options:* coed, disabled students. Campus housing is university owned. Freshman applicants given priority for college housing. *Activities and organizations:* drama/theater group, student-run newspaper, radio and television station, choral group, marching band, Residence Hall Association, Campus Religious Ministries, Student Government Association, Club Sports and Recreation, Greek Life, national fraternities, national sororities. *Campus security:* 24-hour emergency response devices and patrols, student patrols, late-night transport/escort service, bike police and environmental safety services. *Student services:* health clinic, personal/psychological counseling, women's center, legal services.

Athletics Member NCAA. All Division I except football (Division I-AA). *Intercollegiate sports:* baseball M(s), basketball M(s)/W(s), cheerleading M/W, cross-country running W(s), golf M(s), soccer M(s)/W(s), softball W(s), swimming and diving W(s), tennis M(s)/W(s), track and field W(s), volleyball W(s). *Intramural sports:* baseball M(c), basketball M/W, bowling M/W, football M/W, golf M/W, soccer M/W, softball M/W, tennis M/W, track and field M(c)/W(c), volleyball M/W.

Standardized Tests *Required:* SAT or ACT (for admission).

Costs (2011–12) *Tuition:* state resident $4734 full-time, $158 per credit hour part-time; nonresident $16,710 full-time, $557 per credit hour part-time. Full-time tuition and fees vary according to degree level, location, and program. Part-time tuition and fees vary according to degree level, location, and program. *Required fees:* $1872 full-time, $936 per term part-time. *Room and board:* $9020; room only: $5420. Room and board charges vary according to board plan and housing facility. *Waivers:* senior citizens and employees or children of employees.

Financial Aid Of all full-time matriculated undergraduates who enrolled in 2010, 13,603 applied for aid, 10,012 were judged to have need, 945 had their need fully met. 224 Federal Work-Study jobs (averaging $1734). In 2010, 331 non-need-based awards were made. *Average percent of need met:* 55%. *Average financial aid package:* $9595. *Average need-based loan:* $4211. *Average need-based gift aid:* $7479. *Average non-need-based aid:* $1920. *Average indebtedness upon graduation:* $20,595.

Applying *Options:* electronic application, early admission, deferred entrance. *Application fee:* $30. *Required:* minimum 2.0 GPA, proof of immunization prior to enrollment. *Required for some:* high school transcript. *Application deadlines:* 5/1 (freshmen), 5/1 (out-of-state freshmen), 8/1 (transfers). *Notification:* continuous (freshmen), continuous (out-of-state freshmen), continuous (transfers).

Freshman Application Contact Mrs. Sarah Smith, Director, Georgia Southern University, PO Box 8024, Statesboro, GA 30460. *Phone:* 912-478-5391. *Fax:* 912-478-7240. *E-mail:* admissions@georgiasouthern.edu. *Web site:* http://www.georgiasouthern.edu/.

Georgia Southwestern State University
Americus, Georgia

- **State-supported** comprehensive, founded 1906, part of University System of Georgia
- **Small-town** 255-acre campus
- **Coed** 2,811 undergraduate students, 72% full-time, 62% women, 38% men
- **Moderately difficult** entrance level, 68% of applicants were admitted

Undergraduates 2,031 full-time, 780 part-time. Students come from 37 states and territories; 22 other countries; 3% are from out of state; 29% Black or African American, non-Hispanic/Latino; 2% Hispanic/Latino; 1% Asian, non-Hispanic/Latino; 0.1% Native Hawaiian or other Pacific Islander, non-Hispanic/Latino; 1% Two or more races, non-Hispanic/Latino; 0.9% Race/ethnicity unknown; 3% international; 12% transferred in; 28% live on campus. *Retention:* 65% of full-time freshmen returned.

Freshmen *Admission:* 1,267 applied, 866 admitted, 413 enrolled. *Average high school GPA:* 3.2. *Test scores:* SAT critical reading scores over 500: 43%; SAT math scores over 500: 42%; SAT writing scores over 500: 39%; ACT scores over 18: 70%; SAT critical reading scores over 600: 10%; SAT math scores over 600: 7%; SAT writing scores over 600: 5%; ACT scores over 24: 9%; SAT critical reading scores over 700: 1%.

Faculty *Total:* 160, 67% full-time, 58% with terminal degrees. *Student/faculty ratio:* 20:1.

Academics *Calendar:* semesters. *Degrees:* bachelor's, master's, post-master's, and postbachelor's certificates. *Special study options:* academic remediation for entering students, advanced placement credit, distance learning, double majors, English as a second language, honors programs, internships, off-campus study, part-time degree program, services for LD students, study abroad, summer session for credit. *Unusual degree programs:* 3-2 engineering with Georgia Institute of Technology.

Computers on Campus 550 computers/terminals are available on campus for general student use. Students can access the following: free student e-mail accounts, online (class) grades, online (class) registration, online (class) schedules. Campuswide network is available. Wireless service is available via dorm rooms.

Student Life *Housing:* on-campus residence required through sophomore year. *Options:* coed. Campus housing is university owned. Freshman campus housing is guaranteed. *Activities and organizations:* drama/theater group, student-run newspaper, television station, choral group, SUAVE - Strong United Assertive Virtuous Educated, BOLD - Beautiful Outstanding Ladies of Distinction, Residence Hall Association, Baptist Collegiate Ministries, national fraternities, national sororities. *Campus security:* 24-hour emergency response devices and patrols, late-night transport/escort service, controlled dormitory access. *Student services:* health clinic, personal/psychological counseling.

Athletics Member NCAA. All Division II. *Intercollegiate sports:* baseball M(s), basketball M(s)/W(s), cross-country running W(s), golf M(s), soccer M(s)/W(s), softball W(s), tennis M(s)/W(s). *Intramural sports:* badminton M/W, basketball M/W, football M/W, golf M/W, racquetball M/W, softball M/W, table tennis M/W, tennis M/W, ultimate Frisbee M/W, volleyball M/W, weight lifting M/W.

Standardized Tests *Required:* SAT or ACT (for admission).

Costs (2011–12) *Tuition:* state resident $4402 full-time, $147 per credit hour part-time; nonresident $16,016 full-time, $534 per credit hour part-time. Full-time tuition and fees vary according to course load. Part-time tuition and fees vary according to course load. *Required fees:* $1258 full-time, $292 per term part-time. *Room and board:* $6344. Room and board charges vary according to board plan and housing facility.

Financial Aid Of all full-time matriculated undergraduates who enrolled in 2009, 1,563 applied for aid, 1,300 were judged to have need, 270 had their need fully met. 58 Federal Work-Study jobs (averaging $1493). In 2009, 114 non-need-based awards were made. *Average percent of need met:* 56%. *Average financial aid package:* $7655. *Average need-based loan:* $3914. *Average need-based gift aid:* $4475. *Average non-need-based aid:* $1886. *Average indebtedness upon graduation:* $20,505.

Applying *Options:* electronic application, early admission, early decision. *Application fee:* $25. *Required:* high school transcript, minimum 2.0 GPA, proof of immunization; SAT or ACT scores. *Recommended:* interview. *Application deadlines:* 7/21 (freshmen), 7/21 (transfers). *Early decision deadline:* 12/15. *Notification:* continuous (freshmen), continuous (transfers), 1/15 (early decision).

Freshman Application Contact Mr. David Jenkins, Assistant Director of Admissions, Georgia Southwestern State University, Americus, GA 31709. *Phone:* 229-928-1273. *Toll-free phone:* 800-338-0082. *Fax:* 229-931-2983. *E-mail:* gswapps@canes.gsw.edu. *Web site:* http://www.gsw.edu/.

Georgia State University
Atlanta, Georgia

- **State-supported** university, founded 1913, part of University System of Georgia
- **Urban** 60-acre campus with easy access to Atlanta
- **Endowment** $113.2 million
- **Coed** 24,101 undergraduate students, 73% full-time, 59% women, 41% men
- **Moderately difficult** entrance level, 51% of applicants were admitted

Undergraduates 17,565 full-time, 6,536 part-time. Students come from 58 states and territories; 154 other countries; 5% are from out of state; 38% Black or African American, non-Hispanic/Latino; 8% Hispanic/Latino; 11% Asian, non-Hispanic/Latino; 0.2% Native Hawaiian or other Pacific Islander, non-Hispanic/Latino; 0.3% American Indian or Alaska Native, non-Hispanic/Latino; 4% Two or more races, non-Hispanic/Latino; 2% Race/ethnicity unknown; 2% international; 11% transferred in; 14% live on campus. *Retention:* 83% of full-time freshmen returned.

Freshmen *Admission:* 12,869 applied, 6,567 admitted, 2,755 enrolled. *Average high school GPA:* 3.38. *Test scores:* SAT critical reading scores over 500: 75%; SAT math scores over 500: 77%; ACT scores over 18: 98%; SAT critical reading scores over 600: 23%; SAT math scores over 600: 26%; ACT scores over 24: 39%; SAT critical reading scores over 700: 3%; SAT math scores over 700: 3%; ACT scores over 30: 2%.

Faculty *Total:* 1,633, 70% full-time, 76% with terminal degrees. *Student/faculty ratio:* 21:1.

Academics *Calendar:* semesters. *Degrees:* certificates, bachelor's, master's, doctoral, post-master's, postbachelor's, and first professional certificates. *Special study options:* accelerated degree program, advanced placement credit, cooperative education, distance learning, double majors, English as a second language, honors programs, independent study, internships, part-time degree program, services for LD students, study abroad, summer session for credit. *ROTC:* Army (b), Navy (c), Air Force (c). *Unusual degree programs:* 3-2 business administration.

Computers on Campus 574 computers/terminals and 13,685 ports are available on campus for general student use. Students can access the following: computer help desk, free student e-mail accounts, online (class) grades, online (class) registration, online (class) schedules. Campuswide network is available. 100% of college-owned or -operated housing units are wired for high-speed Internet access. Wireless service is available via entire campus.

Student Life *Housing options:* coed, disabled students. Campus housing is university owned and leased by the school. Freshman applicants given priority for college housing. *Activities and organizations:* drama/theater group, student-run newspaper, radio and television station, choral group, marching band, Spotlight Programs Board, Greek Organizations, International Student Associations Council, Academic Clubs, Sports Clubs, national fraternities, national sororities. *Campus security:* 24-hour emergency response devices and patrols, late-night transport/escort service, controlled dormitory access, Emergency Notification Center. *Student services:* health clinic, personal/psychological counseling.

Athletics Member NCAA. All Division I. *Intercollegiate sports:* baseball M(s), basketball M(s)/W(s), crew M(c)/W(c), cross-country running M(s)/W(s), equestrian sports M(c)/W(c), football M(s), golf M(s)/W(s), ice hockey M(c), lacrosse M(c), rugby M(c), soccer M(s)/W(s), softball W(s), squash M(c)/W(c), swimming and diving M(c)/W(c), table tennis M(c)/W(c), tennis M(s)/W(s), track and field M(s)/W(s), ultimate Frisbee M(c)/W(c), volleyball W(s). *Intramural sports:* badminton M(c)/W(c), basketball M/W, bowling M/W, football M/W, golf M/W, racquetball M/W, soccer M/W, softball M/W, ultimate Frisbee M/W, volleyball M/W, water polo M/W, weight lifting M/W.

Standardized Tests *Required:* SAT or ACT (for admission).

Costs (2011–12) *Tuition:* state resident $7282 full-time, $243 per credit hour part-time; nonresident $25,492 full-time, $850 per credit hour part-time. Part-time tuition and fees vary according to course load. *Required fees:* $2128 full-time, $1064 per hour part-time. *Room and board:* $11,390; room only: $7800. Room and board charges vary according to housing facility. *Waivers:* senior citizens and employees or children of employees.

Financial Aid Of all full-time matriculated undergraduates who enrolled in 2011, 14,922 applied for aid, 12,979 were judged to have need, 1,679 had their need fully met. In 2011, 1898 non-need-based awards were made. *Average percent of need met:* 30%. *Average financial aid package:* $12,812. *Average need-based loan:* $4448. *Average need-based gift aid:* $4485. *Average non-need-based aid:* $4205. *Average indebtedness upon graduation:* $20,439. *Financial aid deadline:* 11/1.

Applying *Options:* electronic application, early action, deferred entrance. *Application fee:* $60. *Required:* high school transcript, minimum 2.8 GPA, college preparatory curriculum as specified by the University System of Georgia Board of Regents. Combined SAT of 900 or ACT composite of 19. *Application deadlines:* 3/1 (freshmen), 6/1 (transfers), 11/1 (early action). *Notification:* 5/1 (freshmen), continuous (transfers), 1/8 (early action).

Freshman Application Contact Scott Burke, Director of Admissions, Georgia State University, PO Box 4009, Atlanta, GA 30302-4009. *Phone:* 404-413-2500. *Fax:* 404-413-2002. *E-mail:* onestopshop@gsu.edu. *Web site:* http://www.gsu.edu/.

Gordon College
Barnesville, Georgia

Freshman Application Contact Gordon College, 419 College Drive, Barnesville, GA 30204-1762. *Phone:* 678-359-5021. *Toll-free phone:* 800-282-6504. *Web site:* http://www.gdn.edu/.

Herzing University
Atlanta, Georgia

- **Proprietary** 4-year, founded 1949, part of Herzing, Inc.
- **Urban** campus with easy access to Atlanta
- **Coed**
- **Moderately difficult** entrance level

Faculty *Student/faculty ratio:* 8:1.

Academics *Calendar:* semesters. *Degrees:* diplomas, associate, and bachelor's.

Student Life *Campus security:* 24-hour patrols.

Standardized Tests *Required:* Wonderlic aptitude test (for admission).

Costs (2011–12) *One-time required fee:* $100. *Tuition:* $10,200 full-time, $440 per credit part-time. Full-time tuition and fees vary according to class time and course load. Part-time tuition and fees vary according to class time and course load.

Applying *Application fee:* $25. *Required:* high school transcript, interview.

Freshman Application Contact Miss Anissa Elder, Director of Admissions, Herzing University, 3393 Peachtree Road, NE, Suite 1003, Atlanta, GA 30326. *Phone:* 404-816-4533. *Toll-free phone:* 800-596-0724. *Fax:* 404-816-5576. *E-mail:* aelder@atl.herzing.edu. *Web site:* http://www.herzing.edu/atlanta/.

ITT Technical Institute
Atlanta, Georgia

- **Proprietary** primarily 2-year, part of ITT Educational Services, Inc.
- **Coed**
- **Minimally difficult** entrance level

Academics *Degrees:* associate and bachelor's.

Student Life *Housing:* college housing not available.

Freshman Application Contact Director of Recruitment, ITT Technical Institute, 485 Oak Place, Suite 800, Atlanta, GA 30349. *Phone:* 404-765-4600. *Toll-free phone:* 877-488-6102 (in-state); 877-788-6102 (out-of-state). *Web site:* http://www.itt-tech.edu/.

ITT Technical Institute
Duluth, Georgia

- **Proprietary** primarily 2-year, founded 2003, part of ITT Educational Services, Inc.
- **Coed**
- **Minimally difficult** entrance level

Academics *Calendar:* quarters. *Degrees:* associate and bachelor's.

Student Life *Housing:* college housing not available.

Freshman Application Contact Director of Recruitment, ITT Technical Institute, 10700 Abbotts Bridge Road, Duluth, GA 30097. *Phone:* 678-957-8510. *Toll-free phone:* 866-489-8818. *Web site:* http://www.itt-tech.edu/.

ITT Technical Institute
Kennesaw, Georgia

- **Proprietary** primarily 2-year, founded 2004, part of ITT Educational Services, Inc.
- **Coed**
- **Minimally difficult** entrance level

Academics *Calendar:* quarters. *Degrees:* associate and bachelor's.

Freshman Application Contact Director of Recruitment, ITT Technical Institute, 2065 ITT Tech Way NW, Kennesaw, GA 30144. *Phone:* 770-426-2300. *Toll-free phone:* 877-231-6415 (in-state); 800-231-6415 (out-of-state). *Web site:* http://www.itt-tech.edu/.

Kennesaw State University
Kennesaw, Georgia

- **State-supported** comprehensive, founded 1963, part of University System of Georgia
- **Suburban** 384-acre campus with easy access to Atlanta
- **Endowment** $24.5 million
- **Coed** 22,333 undergraduate students, 75% full-time, 58% women, 42% men
- **Moderately difficult** entrance level, 62% of applicants were admitted

Undergraduates 16,713 full-time, 5,620 part-time. Students come from 54 states and territories; 125 other countries; 6% are from out of state; 15% Black or African American, non-Hispanic/Latino; 6% Hispanic/Latino; 3% Asian, non-Hispanic/Latino; 0.2% Native Hawaiian or other Pacific Islander, non-Hispanic/Latino; 0.3% American Indian or Alaska Native, non-Hispanic/Latino; 3% Two or more races, non-Hispanic/Latino; 4% Race/ethnicity unknown; 2% international; 10% transferred in; 13% live on campus. *Retention:* 77% of full-time freshmen returned.

Freshmen *Admission:* 8,773 applied, 5,483 admitted, 2,880 enrolled. *Average high school GPA:* 3.21. *Test scores:* SAT critical reading scores over 500: 77%; SAT math scores over 500: 74%; SAT writing scores over 500: 62%; ACT scores over 18: 99%; SAT critical reading scores over 600: 19%; SAT math scores over 600: 19%; SAT writing scores over 600: 13%; ACT scores over 24: 31%; SAT critical reading scores over 700: 2%; SAT math scores over 700: 1%; SAT writing scores over 700: 1%; ACT scores over 30: 1%.

Faculty *Total:* 1,295, 57% full-time, 56% with terminal degrees. *Student/faculty ratio:* 21:1.

Academics *Calendar:* semesters. *Degrees:* bachelor's, master's, doctoral, post-master's, postbachelor's, and first professional certificates. *Special study options:* adult/continuing education programs, advanced placement credit, cooperative education, distance learning, double majors, English as a second language, honors programs, internships, off-campus study, part-time degree program, services for LD students, study abroad, summer session for credit. *ROTC:* Army (c), Air Force (c).

Computers on Campus 1,700 computers/terminals and 12,000 ports are available on campus for general student use. Students can access the following: campus intranet, computer help desk, free student e-mail accounts, online (class) grades, online (class) registration, online (class) schedules. Campuswide network is available. 100% of college-owned or -operated housing units are wired for high-speed Internet access. Wireless service is available via classrooms, computer centers, computer labs, dorm rooms, learning centers, libraries, student centers.

Student Life *Housing options:* coed, disabled students. Campus housing is provided by a third party. Freshman applicants given priority for college housing. *Activities and organizations:* drama/theater group, student-run newspaper, radio station, choral group, Golden Key National Honor Society, Student Government Association, Kennesaw Activities Board, African-American Student Alliance, International Student Association, national fraternities, national sororities. *Campus security:* 24-hour emergency response devices and patrols, student patrols, late-night transport/escort service, controlled dormitory access. *Student services:* health clinic, personal/psychological counseling.

Athletics Member NCAA. All Division I. *Intercollegiate sports:* baseball M(s), basketball M(s)/W(s), cheerleading W(c), cross-country running M(s)/W(s), golf M(s)/W(s), soccer W(s), softball W(s), tennis M(s)/W(s), track and field M(s)/W(s), ultimate Frisbee M(c), volleyball W(s). *Intramural sports:* baseball M, basketball M, cross-country running M(c)/W(c), equestrian sports M(c)/W(c), fencing M(c)/W(c), football M/W, golf M/W, ice hockey M(c), lacrosse M(c)/W(c), rugby M(c)/W(c), soccer M(c)/W(c), softball M/W, swimming and diving M(c)/W(c), tennis M/W, ultimate Frisbee M/W, volleyball M/W, weight lifting M(c)/W(c), wrestling M(c).

Standardized Tests *Required:* SAT or ACT (for admission).

Costs (2011–12) *Tuition:* state resident $4734 full-time, $158 per credit hour part-time; nonresident $16,710 full-time, $557 per credit hour part-time. Part-time tuition and fees vary according to course load. *Required fees:* $1548 full-time, $774 per term part-time. *Room and board:* $9557. Room and board charges vary according to board plan and housing facility.

Financial Aid Of all full-time matriculated undergraduates who enrolled in 2011, 13,355 applied for aid, 11,390 were judged to have need, 2,118 had their need fully met. 140 Federal Work-Study jobs (averaging $2257). In 2011, 42 non-need-based awards were made. *Average percent of need met:* 80%. *Average financial aid package:* $7214. *Average need-based loan:* $3046. *Average need-based gift aid:* $6103. *Average non-need-based aid:* $1048. *Average indebtedness upon graduation:* $20,423.

Applying *Options:* electronic application, early admission, deferred entrance. *Application fee:* $40. *Required:* high school transcript, minimum 2.5 GPA, proof of immunization. *Application deadlines:* 5/11 (freshmen), 6/22 (transfers). *Notification:* continuous (freshmen), continuous (transfers).

Freshman Application Contact Admissions Office, Kennesaw State University, 1000 Chastain Road, Campus Box #0115, Kennesaw, GA 30144-5591. *Phone:* 770-423-6300. *Fax:* 770-420-4435. *E-mail:* ksuadmit@kennesaw.edu. *Web site:* http://www.kennesaw.edu/.

LaGrange College
LaGrange, Georgia

- **Independent United Methodist** comprehensive, founded 1831
- **Small-town** 120-acre campus with easy access to Atlanta
- **Endowment** $57.8 million
- **Coed** 857 undergraduate students, 93% full-time, 56% women, 44% men
- **Moderately difficult** entrance level, 59% of applicants were admitted

Undergraduates 797 full-time, 60 part-time. Students come from 19 states and territories; 10 other countries; 10% are from out of state; 23% Black or African American, non-Hispanic/Latino; 3% Hispanic/Latino; 1% Asian, non-Hispanic/Latino; 0.4% American Indian or Alaska Native, non-Hispanic/Latino; 2% Race/ethnicity unknown; 2% international; 8% transferred in; 69% live on campus. *Retention:* 64% of full-time freshmen returned.

Freshmen *Admission:* 1,232 applied, 722 admitted, 228 enrolled. *Average high school GPA:* 3.36. *Test scores:* SAT critical reading scores over 500: 46%; SAT math scores over 500: 58%; ACT scores over 18: 98%; SAT critical reading scores over 600: 12%; SAT math scores over 600: 13%; ACT scores over 24: 23%; SAT critical reading scores over 700: 2%; ACT scores over 30: 1%.

Faculty *Total:* 130, 56% full-time, 52% with terminal degrees. *Student/faculty ratio:* 10:1.

Academics *Calendar:* 4-1-4. *Degrees:* bachelor's and master's. *Special study options:* accelerated degree program, adult/continuing education programs, advanced placement credit, double majors, independent study, internships, part-time degree program, services for LD students, student-designed majors, study abroad, summer session for credit. *Unusual degree programs:* 3-2 engineering with Georgia Institute of Technology, Auburn University.

Computers on Campus 175 computers/terminals and 960 ports are available on campus for general student use. Students can access the following: campus intranet, free student e-mail accounts, online (class) grades, online (class) registration, online (class) schedules. Campuswide network is available. 100% of college-owned or -operated housing units are wired for high-speed Internet access. Wireless service is available via entire campus.

Student Life *Housing:* on-campus residence required through senior year. *Options:* coed, men-only, women-only. Campus housing is university owned. Freshman campus housing is guaranteed. *Activities and organizations:* drama/theater group, student-run newspaper, choral group, Greek Life, Student Government Association, Baptist Collegiate Ministries, Wesley Fellowship, Fellowship of Christian Athletes, national fraternities, national sororities. *Campus security:* 24-hour patrols, controlled dormitory access. *Student services:* health clinic, personal/psychological counseling.

Athletics Member NCAA. All Division III. *Intercollegiate sports:* baseball M, basketball M/W, cheerleading W, cross-country running M/W, football M, golf M, lacrosse W, soccer M/W, softball W, swimming and diving M/W, tennis M/W, volleyball W. *Intramural sports:* basketball M/W, softball M/W, table tennis M/W, water polo M/W.

Standardized Tests *Required:* SAT or ACT (for admission).

Costs (2011–12) *Comprehensive fee:* $32,727 includes full-time tuition ($23,212), mandatory fees ($60), and room and board ($9455). Full-time tuition and fees vary according to class time, course load, degree level, and program. Part-time tuition: $956 per semester hour. Part-time tuition and fees vary according to class time, course load, degree level, and program. *College room only:* $5538. Room and board charges vary according to board plan and housing facility. *Payment plan:* installment. *Waivers:* senior citizens and employees or children of employees.

Applying *Options:* electronic application, early admission, early action, deferred entrance. *Application fee:* $30. *Required:* essay or personal statement, high school transcript, SAT or ACT. *Required for some:* minimum 2.8 GPA, 1 letter of recommendation, interview. *Application deadlines:* rolling (freshmen), rolling (transfers), 12/31 (early action). *Notification:* continuous (freshmen), continuous (transfers).

Freshman Application Contact Mr. Michael Thomas, Director of Admission, LaGrange College, 601 Broad Street, LaGrange, GA 30240-2999. *Phone:* 706-880-8217. *Toll-free phone:* 800-593-2885. *Fax:* 706-880-8010. *E-mail:* dpaul@lagrange.edu. *Web site:* http://www.lagrange.edu/.

Life University
Marietta, Georgia

- **Independent** comprehensive, founded 1974
- **Suburban** 96-acre campus
- **Coed** 862 undergraduate students, 72% full-time, 53% women, 47% men
- **Minimally difficult** entrance level, 70% of applicants were admitted

Undergraduates 619 full-time, 243 part-time. Students come from 52 states and territories; 14 other countries; 54% are from out of state; 34% Black or African American, non-Hispanic/Latino; 8% Hispanic/Latino; 3% Asian, non-Hispanic/Latino; 0.7% American Indian or Alaska Native, non-Hispanic/Latino; 7% Race/ethnicity unknown; 4% international; 15% transferred in. *Retention:* 71% of full-time freshmen returned.

Freshmen *Admission:* 775 applied, 544 admitted, 50 enrolled.

Faculty *Total:* 172, 69% full-time, 77% with terminal degrees. *Student/faculty ratio:* 18:1.

Academics *Calendar:* quarters. *Degrees:* associate, bachelor's, master's, and doctoral. *Special study options:* academic remediation for entering students, accelerated degree program, advanced placement credit, double majors, English as a second language, independent study, internships, off-campus study, services for LD students, summer session for credit.

Computers on Campus Students can access the following: campus intranet, free student e-mail accounts, online (class) grades, online (class) registration. Campuswide network is available. 100% of college-owned or -operated housing units are wired for high-speed Internet access. Wireless service is available via classrooms, computer centers, computer labs, learning centers, libraries.

Student Life *Housing options:* Campus housing is university owned. *Activities and organizations:* student-run newspaper. *Campus security:* 24-hour emergency response devices and patrols, controlled dormitory access. *Student services:* health clinic.

Athletics Member NAIA. *Intramural sports:* basketball M/W, football M, rugby M, softball M/W, volleyball M/W.

Standardized Tests *Required:* SAT or ACT (for admission).

Costs (2011–12) *Comprehensive fee:* $24,505 includes full-time tuition ($10,904), mandatory fees ($747), and room and board ($12,854). Full-time tuition and fees vary according to course load. Part-time tuition: $182 per credit hour. Part-time tuition and fees vary according to course load. *Required fees:* $249 per term part-time. *Payment plan:* installment. *Waivers:* employees or children of employees.

Financial Aid Of all full-time matriculated undergraduates who enrolled in 2011, 492 applied for aid, 463 were judged to have need, 2 had their need fully met. 54 Federal Work-Study jobs (averaging $1800). In 2011, 2 non-need-based awards were made. *Average percent of need met:* 89%. *Average financial aid package:* $10,850. *Average need-based loan:* $4650. *Average need-based gift aid:* $5200. *Average non-need-based aid:* $3000. *Average indebtedness upon graduation:* $21,000.

Applying *Options:* electronic application. *Application fee:* $50. *Required:* high school transcript, minimum 2.0 GPA. *Application deadline:* 9/1 (freshmen). *Notification:* continuous (freshmen), continuous (transfers).

Freshman Application Contact Mr. Brian Gipson, Office of New Student Development, Life University, 1269 Barclay Circle, Marietta, GA 30060. *Phone:* 800-543-3202. *Toll-free phone:* 800-543-3202. *Fax:* 770-426-2895. *E-mail:* admissions@life.edu. *Web site:* http://www.life.edu/.

Luther Rice University

Lithonia, Georgia

Freshman Application Contact Mr. Steve Pray, Admissions Counselor, Luther Rice University, 3038 Evans Mill Road, Lithonia, GA 30038-2454. *Phone:* 770-484-1204. *Toll-free phone:* 800-442-1577. *E-mail:* admissions@lru.edu. *Web site:* http://www.lru.edu/.

Macon State College

Macon, Georgia

- **State-supported** 4-year, founded 1968, part of University System of Georgia
- **Urban** 419-acre campus
- **Coed** 5,702 undergraduate students, 57% full-time, 65% women, 35% men
- **Minimally difficult** entrance level, 66% of applicants were admitted

Undergraduates 3,234 full-time, 2,468 part-time. Students come from 41 states and territories; 21 other countries; 8% are from out of state; 31% Black or African American, non-Hispanic/Latino; 3% Hispanic/Latino; 2% Asian, non-Hispanic/Latino; 0.1% Native Hawaiian or other Pacific Islander, non-Hispanic/Latino; 0.2% American Indian or Alaska Native, non-Hispanic/Latino; 3% Two or more races, non-Hispanic/Latino; 0.8% Race/ethnicity unknown; 0.6% international; 7% transferred in; 5% live on campus. *Retention:* 74% of full-time freshmen returned.

Freshmen *Admission:* 1,770 applied, 1,161 admitted, 593 enrolled. *Average high school GPA:* 2.99. *Test scores:* SAT critical reading scores over 500: 36%; SAT math scores over 500: 31%; ACT scores over 18: 64%; SAT critical reading scores over 600: 7%; SAT math scores over 600: 5%; ACT scores over 24: 12%; SAT critical reading scores over 700: 1%; ACT scores over 30: 1%.

Faculty *Total:* 289, 62% full-time, 37% with terminal degrees. *Student/faculty ratio:* 19:1.

Academics *Calendar:* semesters. *Degrees:* certificates, associate, and bachelor's. *Special study options:* academic remediation for entering students, advanced placement credit, cooperative education, distance learning, double majors, honors programs, independent study, internships, part-time degree program, services for LD students, study abroad, summer session for credit. *ROTC:* Army (c).

Computers on Campus Students can access the following: campus intranet, free student e-mail accounts, online (class) grades, online (class) registration, online (class) schedules. Campuswide network is available. 100% of college-owned or -operated housing units are wired for high-speed Internet access. Wireless service is available via entire campus.

Student Life *Housing:* on-campus residence required for freshman year. *Options:* coed. Campus housing is university owned. *Activities and organizations:* drama/theater group, student-run newspaper, television station, choral group, MSCANS, ISSA, NSN, PBL. *Campus security:* 24-hour emergency response devices and patrols, late-night transport/escort service. *Student services:* health clinic, personal/psychological counseling.

Athletics *Intramural sports:* baseball M(c), basketball M(c)/W(c), cheerleading W(c), rugby M(c), soccer M(c), softball W(c), tennis M(c)/W(c).

Standardized Tests *Required:* SAT or ACT (for admission).

Costs (2011–12) *Tuition:* state resident $2776 full-time, $93 per credit hour part-time; nonresident $10,258 full-time, $342 per credit hour part-time. Full-time tuition and fees vary according to course load and program. Part-time tuition and fees vary according to course load and program. *Required fees:*

$868 full-time, $434 per term part-time. *Room and board:* $6750; room only: $4750.

Financial Aid Of all full-time matriculated undergraduates who enrolled in 2005, 1,352 were judged to have need, 39 had their need fully met. 106 Federal Work-Study jobs. In 2005, 507 non-need-based awards were made. *Average percent of need met:* 46%. *Average financial aid package:* $5984. *Average need-based loan:* $2749. *Average need-based gift aid:* $3031. *Average non-need-based aid:* $1826.

Applying *Options:* electronic application, early admission, early decision. *Application fee:* $20. *Required:* high school transcript, minimum 2.0 GPA. *Application deadlines:* rolling (freshmen), rolling (transfers). *Notification:* continuous (freshmen), continuous (transfers).

Freshman Application Contact Mr. Ryan Tucker, Admissions Representative, Macon State College, 100 College Station Drive, Macon, GA 31206. *Toll-free phone:* 800-272-7619. *E-mail:* mscinfo@mail.maconstate.edu. *Web site:* http://www.maconstate.edu/.

Mercer University

Macon, Georgia

- **Independent Baptist** university, founded 1833
- **Suburban** 150-acre campus with easy access to Atlanta
- **Endowment** $197.0 million
- **Coed** 2,304 undergraduate students, 96% full-time, 53% women, 47% men
- **Moderately difficult** entrance level, 83% of applicants were admitted

Undergraduates 2,212 full-time, 92 part-time. Students come from 41 states and territories; 35 other countries; 16% are from out of state; 19% Black or African American, non-Hispanic/Latino; 4% Hispanic/Latino; 7% Asian, non-Hispanic/Latino; 0.4% American Indian or Alaska Native, non-Hispanic/Latino; 2% Two or more races, non-Hispanic/Latino; 6% Race/ethnicity unknown; 4% international; 3% transferred in; 67% live on campus. *Retention:* 84% of full-time freshmen returned.

Freshmen *Admission:* 2,582 applied, 2,137 admitted, 565 enrolled. *Average high school GPA:* 3.66. *Test scores:* SAT critical reading scores over 500: 88%; SAT math scores over 500: 92%; SAT writing scores over 500: 79%; ACT scores over 18: 100%; SAT critical reading scores over 600: 40%; SAT math scores over 600: 41%; SAT writing scores over 600: 33%; ACT scores over 24: 79%; SAT critical reading scores over 700: 8%; SAT math scores over 700: 7%; SAT writing scores over 700: 4%; ACT scores over 30: 23%.

Faculty *Total:* 677, 55% full-time, 72% with terminal degrees. *Student/faculty ratio:* 12:1.

Academics *Calendar:* semesters. *Degrees:* bachelor's, master's, doctoral, post-master's, and first professional certificates. *Special study options:* accelerated degree program, adult/continuing education programs, advanced placement credit, cooperative education, distance learning, double majors, English as a second language, honors programs, independent study, internships, off-campus study, part-time degree program, services for LD students, student-designed majors, study abroad, summer session for credit. *ROTC:* Army (b). *Unusual degree programs:* pharmacy, physical therapy, physicians assistant.

Computers on Campus Students can access the following: campus intranet, computer help desk, free student e-mail accounts, online (class) grades, online (class) registration, online (class) schedules. Campuswide network is available. 100% of college-owned or -operated housing units are wired for high-speed Internet access. Wireless service is available via entire campus.

Student Life *Housing:* on-campus residence required through sophomore year. *Options:* coed, men-only, women-only, disabled students. Campus housing is university owned. Freshman campus housing is guaranteed. *Activities and organizations:* drama/theater group, student-run newspaper, radio and television station, choral group, national fraternities, national sororities. *Campus security:* 24-hour emergency response devices and patrols, student patrols, late-night transport/escort service, controlled dormitory access, patrols by police officers. *Student services:* health clinic, personal/psychological counseling.

Athletics Member NCAA. All Division I. *Intercollegiate sports:* baseball M(s), basketball M(s)/W(s), cross-country running M(s)/W(s), football M, golf M(s)/W(s), lacrosse M(s)/W(c), soccer M(s)/W(s), softball W(s), tennis M(s)/W(s), volleyball W(s). *Intramural sports:* basketball M/W, bowling M/W, equestrian sports W(c), football M/W, golf M/W, soccer M/W, softball M/W, tennis M/W, ultimate Frisbee M/W, volleyball M/W, water polo M/W, wrestling M(c).

Standardized Tests *Required:* SAT or ACT (for admission).

Costs (2011–12) *Comprehensive fee:* $41,956 includes full-time tuition ($31,248), mandatory fees ($300), and room and board ($10,408). Full-time tuition and fees vary according to class time and location. Part-time tuition: $1042 per credit hour. Part-time tuition and fees vary according to class time, course load, and location. *Required fees:* $10 per credit hour part-time. *Room and board:* Room and board charges vary according to board plan, housing

facility, and location. *Payment plan:* installment. *Waivers:* employees or children of employees.

Financial Aid Of all full-time matriculated undergraduates who enrolled in 2011, 2,228 applied for aid, 1,539 were judged to have need, 397 had their need fully met. In 2011, 628 non-need-based awards were made. *Average percent of need met:* 77%. *Average financial aid package:* $28,019. *Average need-based loan:* $5569. *Average need-based gift aid:* $28,166. *Average non-need-based aid:* $18,061. *Average indebtedness upon graduation:* $30,851.

Applying *Options:* electronic application, early admission, early action, deferred entrance. *Application fee:* $50. *Required:* high school transcript, minimum 3.0 GPA. *Required for some:* 2 letters of recommendation, interview. *Recommended:* interview, counselor's evaluation. *Application deadlines:* 7/1 (freshmen), rolling (transfers), 11/1 (early action). *Notification:* continuous (freshmen), continuous (transfers), 11/15 (early action).

Freshman Application Contact Mr. Emory Dunn, Director of Freshman Admissions, Mercer University, 1400 Coleman Avenue, Macon, GA 31207-0003. *Phone:* 478-301-2312. *Toll-free phone:* 800-MERCER-U. *E-mail:* dunn_e@mercer.edu. *Web site:* http://www.mercer.edu/.

Middle Georgia College
Cochran, Georgia

Freshman Application Contact Ms. Jennifer Brannon, Director of Admissions, Middle Georgia College, 1100 2nd Street, Southeast, Cochran, GA 31014. *Phone:* 478-934-3103. *Fax:* 478-934-3403. *E-mail:* admissions@mgc.edu. *Web site:* http://www.mgc.edu/.

Morehouse College
Atlanta, Georgia

- **Independent** 4-year, founded 1867
- **Urban** 61-acre campus
- **Endowment** $139.8 million
- **Men only** 2,438 undergraduate students, 94% full-time
- **Moderately difficult** entrance level, 62% of applicants were admitted

Undergraduates 2,290 full-time, 148 part-time. Students come from 43 states and territories; 17 other countries; 70% are from out of state; 96% Black or African American, non-Hispanic/Latino; 0.3% Hispanic/Latino; 0.1% American Indian or Alaska Native, non-Hispanic/Latino; 1% Race/ethnicity unknown; 2% international; 3% transferred in; 95% live on campus. *Retention:* 86% of full-time freshmen returned.

Freshmen *Admission:* 2,186 applied, 1,366 admitted, 500 enrolled. *Average high school GPA:* 3.24. *Test scores:* SAT critical reading scores over 500: 64%; SAT math scores over 500: 59%; SAT writing scores over 500: 52%; ACT scores over 18: 91%; SAT critical reading scores over 600: 24%; SAT math scores over 600: 21%; SAT writing scores over 600: 19%; ACT scores over 24: 36%; SAT critical reading scores over 700: 4%; SAT math scores over 700: 3%; SAT writing scores over 700: 2%; ACT scores over 30: 3%.

Faculty *Total:* 214, 77% full-time, 75% with terminal degrees. *Student/faculty ratio:* 13:1.

Academics *Calendar:* semesters. *Degree:* bachelor's. *Special study options:* academic remediation for entering students, advanced placement credit, cooperative education, double majors, honors programs, internships, off-campus study, part-time degree program, services for LD students, study abroad, summer session for credit. *ROTC:* Army (b), Navy (b), Air Force (b). *Unusual degree programs:* 3-2 engineering with Georgia Tech, Boston Univ., Auburn Univ., Rensselaer Polytechnic Univ., Rochester Institute of Technology, Columbia Univ., Dartmouth College, North Carolina A&T State Univ., Univ. of Florida, Univ. of Missouri-Rolla. Univ. of Michigan.

Computers on Campus 500 computers/terminals are available on campus for general student use. Students can access the following: campus intranet, computer help desk, free student e-mail accounts, online (class) grades, online (class) registration, online (class) schedules. Campuswide network is available. 100% of college-owned or -operated housing units are wired for high-speed Internet access. Wireless service is available via entire campus.

Student Life *Housing:* on-campus residence required for freshman year. *Options:* men-only. Campus housing is university owned. Freshman campus housing is guaranteed. *Activities and organizations:* drama/theater group, student-run newspaper, choral group, marching band, Morehouse College Glee Club, Morehouse Business Association, NAACP, Morehouse Public Health Association, Pre-Law Society, national fraternities. *Campus security:* 24-hour emergency response devices and patrols, late-night transport/escort service, controlled dormitory access. *Student services:* health clinic, personal/psychological counseling.

Athletics Member NCAA. All Division II. *Intercollegiate sports:* basketball M(s), cross-country running M(s), football M(s), tennis M(s), track and field M(s). *Intramural sports:* baseball M, basketball M, football M, golf M, soccer M, softball M, swimming and diving M, table tennis M, tennis M, weight lifting M.

Standardized Tests *Required:* SAT or ACT (for admission).

Costs (2011–12) *Comprehensive fee:* $35,976 includes full-time tuition ($21,618), mandatory fees ($2174), and room and board ($12,184). Full-time tuition and fees vary according to course load and student level. Part-time tuition: $901 per credit hour. Part-time tuition and fees vary according to course load. *Required fees:* $1087 per term part-time. *College room only:* $6942. Room and board charges vary according to board plan. *Waivers:* employees or children of employees.

Financial Aid Of all full-time matriculated undergraduates who enrolled in 2011, 2,240 applied for aid, 2,240 were judged to have need, 196 had their need fully met. *Average percent of need met:* 60%. *Average financial aid package:* $15,450. *Average need-based loan:* $5500. *Average need-based gift aid:* $10,000. *Financial aid deadline:* 4/1.

Applying *Options:* electronic application, early admission, early decision, early action, deferred entrance. *Application fee:* $50. *Required:* essay or personal statement, high school transcript. *Recommended:* minimum 3.0 GPA, interview. *Application deadlines:* 2/15 (freshmen), 2/15 (transfers), 11/1 (early action). *Early decision deadline:* 11/1. *Notification:* 4/1 (freshmen), 4/1 (transfers), 12/15 (early decision), 12/15 (early action).

Freshman Application Contact Morehouse College, 830 Westview Drive, SW, Atlanta, GA 30314. *Phone:* 404-215-2632. *Toll-free phone:* 800-851-1254. *Web site:* http://www.morehouse.edu/.

North Georgia College & State University
Dahlonega, Georgia

- **State-supported** comprehensive, founded 1873, part of University System of Georgia
- **Small-town** 140-acre campus with easy access to Atlanta
- **Endowment** $26.4 million
- **Coed** 5,541 undergraduate students, 83% full-time, 57% women, 43% men
- **Moderately difficult** entrance level, 53% of applicants were admitted

Undergraduates 4,605 full-time, 936 part-time. Students come from 38 states and territories; 47 other countries; 5% are from out of state; 3% Black or African American, non-Hispanic/Latino; 3% Hispanic/Latino; 1% Asian, non-Hispanic/Latino; 0.1% Native Hawaiian or other Pacific Islander, non-Hispanic/Latino; 0.3% American Indian or Alaska Native, non-Hispanic/Latino; 2% Two or more races, non-Hispanic/Latino; 2% Race/ethnicity unknown; 1% international; 8% transferred in; 36% live on campus. *Retention:* 77% of full-time freshmen returned.

Freshmen *Admission:* 4,077 applied, 2,160 admitted, 986 enrolled. *Average high school GPA:* 3.5. *Test scores:* SAT critical reading scores over 500: 85%; SAT math scores over 500: 78%; ACT scores over 18: 98%; SAT critical reading scores over 600: 27%; SAT math scores over 600: 26%; ACT scores over 24: 50%; SAT critical reading scores over 700: 4%; SAT math scores over 700: 2%; ACT scores over 30: 4%.

Faculty *Total:* 372, 67% full-time. *Student/faculty ratio:* 18:1.

Academics *Calendar:* semesters. *Degrees:* certificates, associate, bachelor's, master's, doctoral, and post-master's certificates. *Special study options:* academic remediation for entering students, accelerated degree program, advanced placement credit, cooperative education, distance learning, double majors, English as a second language, external degree program, freshman honors college, honors programs, independent study, internships, part-time degree program, services for LD students, study abroad, summer session for credit. *ROTC:* Army (b). *Unusual degree programs:* 3-2 engineering with Georgia Institute of Technology, Clemson University; industrial management, computer science with Georgia Institute of Technology.

Computers on Campus 707 computers/terminals are available on campus for general student use. Students can access the following: computer help desk, free student e-mail accounts, online (class) grades, online (class) registration, online (class) schedules. Campuswide network is available. 100% of college-owned or -operated housing units are wired for high-speed Internet access. Wireless service is available via classrooms, computer centers, computer labs, dorm rooms, learning centers, libraries, student centers.

Student Life *Housing:* on-campus residence required through sophomore year. *Options:* coed, men-only, women-only. Campus housing is university owned. Freshman campus housing is guaranteed. *Activities and organizations:* drama/theater group, student-run newspaper, choral group, Student Government Association, Commuter Council, Graduate Student Senate, Baptist Student Union, Greek organizations, national fraternities, national sororities. *Campus security:* 24-hour emergency response devices and patrols, late-night transport/escort service, controlled dormitory access. *Student services:* health clinic, personal/psychological counseling.

Athletics Member NCAA. All Division II. *Intercollegiate sports:* baseball M(s), basketball M(s)/W(s), cheerleading M/W, cross-country running M(c)/W(s), equestrian sports W(c), golf M(s)/W(s), lacrosse M(c)/W(c), riflery M(s)/W(s), rugby M(c)/W(c), soccer M(s)/W(s), softball W(s), tennis M(s)/W(s), wrestling M(c). *Intramural sports:* basketball M/W, football M/W, golf M(c)/W(c), soccer M/W, softball M/W, table tennis M/W, ultimate Frisbee M/W, volleyball M/W, water polo M/W.

Standardized Tests *Required:* SAT or ACT (for admission).

Costs (2011–12) *Tuition:* state resident $4734 full-time, $158 per credit hour part-time; nonresident $16,710 full-time, $557 per credit hour part-time. Part-time tuition and fees vary according to course load. *Required fees:* $1718 full-time. *Room and board:* $6550; room only: $3022. Room and board charges vary according to board plan and housing facility. *Waivers:* senior citizens and employees or children of employees.

Financial Aid Of all full-time matriculated undergraduates who enrolled in 2011, 3,524 applied for aid, 2,643 were judged to have need, 539 had their need fully met. 78 Federal Work-Study jobs (averaging $2000). 92 state and other part-time jobs (averaging $1500). In 2011, 37 non-need-based awards were made. *Average percent of need met:* 62%. *Average financial aid package:* $11,187. *Average need-based loan:* $4823. *Average need-based gift aid:* $4732. *Average non-need-based aid:* $1201. *Average indebtedness upon graduation:* $10,128.

Applying *Options:* electronic application, early admission. *Application fee:* $30. *Required:* high school transcript, minimum 2.0 GPA, proof of immunization. *Application deadlines:* 7/1 (freshmen), rolling (transfers). *Notification:* continuous (freshmen), continuous (transfers).

Freshman Application Contact Jennifer Chadwick, Director of Admissions, North Georgia College & State University, 110 South Chestatee Street, Dahlonega, GA 30597. *Phone:* 706-864-1800. *Toll-free phone:* 800-498-9581. *Fax:* 706-864-1478. *E-mail:* admissions@northgeorgia.edu. *Web site:* http://www.northgeorgia.edu/.

Oglethorpe University
Atlanta, Georgia

- **Independent** comprehensive, founded 1835
- **Suburban** 102-acre campus
- **Coed** 1,094 undergraduate students, 91% full-time, 59% women, 41% men
- **Very difficult** entrance level, 85% of applicants were admitted

Undergraduates 997 full-time, 97 part-time. Students come from 28 states and territories; 25 other countries; 28% are from out of state; 23% Black or African American, non-Hispanic/Latino; 8% Hispanic/Latino; 4% Asian, non-Hispanic/Latino; 0.2% Native Hawaiian or other Pacific Islander, non-Hispanic/Latino; 0.4% American Indian or Alaska Native, non-Hispanic/Latino; 1% Two or more races, non-Hispanic/Latino; 18% Race/ethnicity unknown; 4% international; 4% transferred in; 62% live on campus. *Retention:* 73% of full-time freshmen returned.

Freshmen *Admission:* 2,376 applied, 2,027 admitted, 262 enrolled. *Average high school GPA:* 3.51. *Test scores:* SAT critical reading scores over 500: 93%; SAT math scores over 500: 87%; SAT writing scores over 500: 81%; ACT scores over 18: 99%; SAT critical reading scores over 600: 44%; SAT math scores over 600: 31%; SAT writing scores over 600: 37%; ACT scores over 24: 57%; SAT critical reading scores over 700: 8%; SAT math scores over 700: 6%; SAT writing scores over 700: 5%; ACT scores over 30: 6%.

Faculty *Total:* 102, 48% full-time, 65% with terminal degrees. *Student/faculty ratio:* 16:1.

Academics *Calendar:* semesters. *Degrees:* bachelor's and master's. *Special study options:* accelerated degree program, adult/continuing education programs, advanced placement credit, cooperative education, double majors, honors programs, independent study, internships, off-campus study, part-time degree program, services for LD students, student-designed majors, study abroad, summer session for credit. *ROTC:* Air Force (c). *Unusual degree programs:* 3-2 engineering with Auburn University, Georgia Institute of Technology, University of Florida, University of Southern California.

Computers on Campus Students can access the following: campus intranet, computer help desk, free student e-mail accounts, online (class) grades, online (class) registration, online (class) schedules. Campuswide network is available. 100% of college-owned or -operated housing units are wired for high-speed Internet access. Wireless service is available via classrooms, computer centers, computer labs, learning centers, libraries, student centers.

Student Life *Housing:* on-campus residence required through sophomore year. *Options:* coed. Campus housing is university owned. Freshman campus housing is guaranteed. *Activities and organizations:* drama/theater group, student-run newspaper, radio station, choral group, national fraternities, national sororities. *Campus security:* 24-hour emergency response devices and patrols, late-night transport/escort service, controlled dormitory access. *Student services:* health clinic, personal/psychological counseling.

Athletics Member NCAA. All Division III. *Intercollegiate sports:* baseball M, basketball M/W, cross-country running M/W, golf M/W, lacrosse M/W, soccer M/W, tennis M/W, track and field M/W, volleyball W. *Intramural sports:* badminton M/W, basketball M/W, football M/W, softball M/W, table tennis M/W, ultimate Frisbee M/W, volleyball M/W.

Standardized Tests *Required:* SAT or ACT (for admission).

Costs (2011–12) *Comprehensive fee:* $39,590 includes full-time tuition ($28,900), mandatory fees ($250), and room and board ($10,440). Full-time tuition and fees vary according to degree level and program. Part-time tuition: $1170 per credit hour. Part-time tuition and fees vary according to course load, degree level, and program. *Room and board:* Room and board charges vary according to housing facility and location. *Payment plans:* tuition prepayment, installment. *Waivers:* employees or children of employees.

Financial Aid Of all full-time matriculated undergraduates who enrolled in 2011, 797 applied for aid, 733 were judged to have need, 115 had their need fully met. In 2011, 201 non-need-based awards were made. *Average percent of need met:* 74%. *Average financial aid package:* $25,967. *Average need-based loan:* $4036. *Average need-based gift aid:* $20,846. *Average non-need-based aid:* $14,405. *Average indebtedness upon graduation:* $20,867.

Applying *Options:* electronic application, early admission, early action, deferred entrance. *Application fee:* $40. *Required:* essay or personal statement, high school transcript, 1 letter of recommendation. *Required for some:* interview. *Recommended:* minimum 2.5 GPA, interview. *Application deadlines:* rolling (freshmen), rolling (transfers), 12/5 (early action). *Notification:* continuous (freshmen), continuous (transfers), 12/20 (early action).

Freshman Application Contact Ms. Lucy Leusch, Vice President for Enrollment and Financial Aid, Oglethorpe University, 4484 Peachtree Road, NE, Atlanta, GA 30319. *Phone:* 404-364-8307. *Toll-free phone:* 800-428-4484. *Fax:* 404-364-8491. *E-mail:* admission@oglethorpe.edu. *Web site:* http://www.oglethorpe.edu/.

Paine College
Augusta, Georgia

- **Independent Methodist** 4-year, founded 1882
- **Urban** 65-acre campus with easy access to Atlanta
- **Endowment** $8.1 million
- **Coed** 891 undergraduate students, 91% full-time, 63% women, 37% men
- **Minimally difficult** entrance level, 69% of applicants were admitted

Undergraduates 815 full-time, 76 part-time. Students come from 32 states and territories; 1 other country; 23% are from out of state; 94% Black or African American, non-Hispanic/Latino; 1% Hispanic/Latino; 0.1% Asian, non-Hispanic/Latino; 0.2% Native Hawaiian or other Pacific Islander, non-Hispanic/Latino; 0.1% American Indian or Alaska Native, non-Hispanic/Latino; 1% Two or more races, non-Hispanic/Latino; 1% Race/ethnicity unknown; 0.2% international; 6% transferred in; 52% live on campus. *Retention:* 62% of full-time freshmen returned.

Freshmen *Admission:* 1,923 applied, 1,335 admitted, 192 enrolled. *Average high school GPA:* 2.8. *Test scores:* SAT critical reading scores over 500: 13%; SAT math scores over 500: 11%; SAT writing scores over 500: 10%; ACT scores over 18: 29%; SAT critical reading scores over 600: 3%; SAT math scores over 600: 2%; SAT writing scores over 600: 2%; ACT scores over 24: 2%; SAT critical reading scores over 700: 1%.

Faculty *Total:* 84, 71% full-time, 58% with terminal degrees. *Student/faculty ratio:* 12:1.

Academics *Calendar:* semesters. *Degree:* bachelor's. *Special study options:* academic remediation for entering students, accelerated degree program, advanced placement credit, cooperative education, distance learning, double majors, honors programs, independent study, internships, off-campus study, part-time degree program, services for LD students, study abroad, summer session for credit. *ROTC:* Army (c). *Unusual degree programs:* 3-2 engineering with Tuskegee University.

Computers on Campus 130 computers/terminals and 696 ports are available on campus for general student use. Students can access the following: campus intranet, computer help desk, free student e-mail accounts, online (class) grades, online (class) registration, online (class) schedules. Campuswide network is available. 100% of college-owned or -operated housing units are wired for high-speed Internet access. Wireless service is available via entire campus.

Student Life *Housing options:* men-only, women-only. Campus housing is university owned. Freshman applicants given priority for college housing. *Activities and organizations:* drama/theater group, student-run newspaper, choral group, Wesley Fellowship, Alpha Kappa Mu National Honor Society, Pre-Alumni Council, Honda All-Stars, Creme de la Creme Models, national fraternities, national sororities. *Campus security:* 24-hour emergency response devices and patrols, late-night transport/escort service. *Student services:* health clinic, personal/psychological counseling.

Athletics Member NCAA. All Division II. *Intercollegiate sports:* baseball M(s), basketball M(s)/W(s), cross-country running M(s)/W(s), golf M(s), soft-

ball W(s), track and field M(s)/W(s), volleyball W(s). *Intramural sports:* baseball M, basketball M/W, cheerleading M/W, football M, soccer M/W, softball M/W, table tennis M/W, tennis M/W, track and field M/W, volleyball M/W, weight lifting M/W.

Standardized Tests *Required:* SAT or ACT (for admission).

Costs (2011–12) *Comprehensive fee:* $18,596 includes full-time tuition ($11,550), mandatory fees ($952), and room and board ($6094). Full-time tuition and fees vary according to course load, location, and reciprocity agreements. Part-time tuition: $481 per semester hour. Part-time tuition and fees vary according to course load, location, and reciprocity agreements. *Room and board:* Room and board charges vary according to housing facility. *Payment plans:* installment, deferred payment. *Waivers:* children of alumni and employees or children of employees.

Financial Aid *Average indebtedness upon graduation:* $2304.

Applying *Options:* electronic application, early admission, deferred entrance. *Application fee:* $35. *Required:* essay or personal statement, high school transcript, minimum 2.0 GPA, 3 letters of recommendation. *Required for some:* score of 500 on each Georgia high school exit exam. *Application deadlines:* 7/1 (freshmen), 7/1 (out-of-state freshmen), 7/1 (transfers). *Notification:* continuous (freshmen), continuous (out-of-state freshmen), continuous (transfers).

Freshman Application Contact Mr. Joseph D. Tinsley, Director of Admissions, Paine College, 1235 15th Street, Augusta, GA 30901-3182. *Phone:* 706-821-8320. *Toll-free phone:* 800-476-7703. *Fax:* 706-821-8691. *E-mail:* jtinsley@paine.edu. *Web site:* http://www.paine.edu/.

Piedmont College
Demorest, Georgia

- **Independent** comprehensive, founded 1897, affiliated with United Church of Christ
- **Rural** 186-acre campus with easy access to Atlanta
- **Endowment** $49.5 million
- **Coed** 1,303 undergraduate students, 85% full-time, 67% women, 33% men
- **Moderately difficult** entrance level, 64% of applicants were admitted

Undergraduates 1,110 full-time, 193 part-time. Students come from 24 states and territories; 10 other countries; 5% are from out of state; 11% Black or African American, non-Hispanic/Latino; 2% Hispanic/Latino; 1% Asian, non-Hispanic/Latino; 0.5% American Indian or Alaska Native, non-Hispanic/Latino; 2% Race/ethnicity unknown; 0.4% international; 9% transferred in; 42% live on campus. *Retention:* 78% of full-time freshmen returned.

Freshmen *Admission:* 876 applied, 563 admitted, 388 enrolled. *Average high school GPA:* 3.45. *Test scores:* SAT critical reading scores over 500: 57%; SAT math scores over 500: 58%; ACT scores over 18: 93%; SAT critical reading scores over 600: 15%; SAT math scores over 600: 12%; ACT scores over 24: 37%; SAT critical reading scores over 700: 2%; SAT math scores over 700: 1%; ACT scores over 30: 2%.

Faculty *Total:* 274, 46% full-time, 75% with terminal degrees. *Student/faculty ratio:* 16:1.

Academics *Calendar:* semesters. *Degrees:* bachelor's, master's, doctoral, and post-master's certificates. *Special study options:* accelerated degree program, adult/continuing education programs, advanced placement credit, cooperative education, distance learning, double majors, honors programs, independent study, internships, off-campus study, part-time degree program, services for LD students, student-designed majors, study abroad, summer session for credit. *Unusual degree programs:* 3-2 engineering with Georgia Institute of Technology; Engineering Physics (Primarily for Mechanical Engineering).

Computers on Campus 150 computers/terminals are available on campus for general student use. Students can access the following: free student e-mail accounts, online (class) grades, online (class) schedules. Campuswide network is available. Wireless service is available via classrooms, computer centers, computer labs, dorm rooms, learning centers, libraries, student centers.

Student Life *Housing:* on-campus residence required through sophomore year. *Options:* coed, men-only, women-only, disabled students. Campus housing is university owned. Freshman campus housing is guaranteed. *Activities and organizations:* drama/theater group, student-run newspaper, radio and television station, choral group, Campus Activity Board, Residence Hall Council, Outdoor Club, Team Piedmont, Alpha PSI Omega. *Campus security:* 24-hour emergency response devices and patrols, late-night transport/escort service. *Student services:* personal/psychological counseling.

Athletics Member NCAA. All Division III. *Intercollegiate sports:* baseball M, basketball M/W, cross-country running M/W, golf M/W, lacrosse M/W, soccer M/W, softball W, tennis M/W, volleyball W.

Standardized Tests *Required:* SAT or ACT (for admission).

Costs (2011–12) *Comprehensive fee:* $26,500 includes full-time tuition ($19,000) and room and board ($7500). Full-time tuition and fees vary according to course load, degree level, location, and program. Part-time tuition: $792 per semester hour. Part-time tuition and fees vary according to course load,

degree level, location, and program. *Payment plan:* installment. *Waivers:* employees or children of employees.

Financial Aid Of all full-time matriculated undergraduates who enrolled in 2011, 981 applied for aid, 909 were judged to have need, 178 had their need fully met. 82 Federal Work-Study jobs (averaging $2210). 224 state and other part-time jobs (averaging $2331). In 2011, 132 non-need-based awards were made. *Average percent of need met:* 73%. *Average financial aid package:* $16,330. *Average need-based loan:* $4351. *Average need-based gift aid:* $12,943. *Average non-need-based aid:* $10,867. *Average indebtedness upon graduation:* $20,407.

Applying *Options:* electronic application, early admission, deferred entrance. *Required:* high school transcript, minimum 2.0 GPA. *Required for some:* interview. *Recommended:* essay or personal statement. *Application deadlines:* 7/1 (freshmen), 7/1 (transfers).

Freshman Application Contact Ms. Cynthia L. Peterson, Director of Undergraduate Admissions, Piedmont College, PO Box 10, 165 Central Avenue, Demorest, GA 30535. *Phone:* 706-776-0103 Ext. 1188. *Toll-free phone:* 800-277-7020. *Fax:* 706-776-6635. *E-mail:* cpeterson@piedmont.edu. *Web site:* http://www.piedmont.edu/.

Point University
East Point, Georgia

- **Independent Christian** 4-year, founded 1937
- **Suburban** 52-acre campus with easy access to Atlanta
- **Coed** 1,288 undergraduate students, 92% full-time, 60% women, 40% men
- **Moderately difficult** entrance level, 47% of applicants were admitted

Undergraduates 1,179 full-time, 109 part-time. 10% are from out of state; 67% Black or African American, non-Hispanic/Latino; 3% Hispanic/Latino; 0.2% Asian, non-Hispanic/Latino; 3% Race/ethnicity unknown; 12% transferred in; 62% live on campus. *Retention:* 63% of full-time freshmen returned.

Freshmen *Admission:* 443 applied, 210 admitted, 151 enrolled. *Average high school GPA:* 3.13. *Test scores:* SAT critical reading scores over 500: 26%; SAT math scores over 500: 33%; ACT scores over 18: 69%; SAT critical reading scores over 600: 9%; SAT math scores over 600: 7%; ACT scores over 24: 19%; SAT critical reading scores over 700: 1%.

Faculty *Total:* 114, 23% full-time, 31% with terminal degrees. *Student/faculty ratio:* 22:1.

Academics *Calendar:* semesters. *Degrees:* associate and bachelor's. *Special study options:* academic remediation for entering students, accelerated degree program, adult/continuing education programs, advanced placement credit, cooperative education, distance learning, double majors, independent study, internships, part-time degree program, services for LD students, summer session for credit.

Computers on Campus Students can access the following: campus intranet, computer help desk, free student e-mail accounts, online (class) grades, online (class) registration, online (class) schedules. Campuswide network is available. 100% of college-owned or -operated housing units are wired for high-speed Internet access. Wireless service is available via entire campus.

Student Life *Housing:* on-campus residence required for freshman year. *Options:* men-only, women-only. Campus housing is university owned. Freshman campus housing is guaranteed. *Activities and organizations:* drama/theater group, student-run newspaper, choral group, Student Government Association, Global Mission Conference, Campus Life Ministers, Student Transition Team. *Campus security:* 24-hour patrols, student patrols, controlled dormitory access. *Student services:* health clinic, personal/psychological counseling.

Athletics Member NAIA, NCCAA. *Intercollegiate sports:* baseball M(s), basketball M(s)/W(s), cheerleading W(s), cross-country running M(s)/W(s), football M(s)(c), soccer M(s)/W(s), softball W(s), volleyball W(s). *Intramural sports:* basketball W, table tennis M/W, ultimate Frisbee M/W, volleyball M/W, weight lifting M/W.

Standardized Tests *Required:* SAT or ACT (for admission).

Costs (2011–12) *Comprehensive fee:* $22,206 includes full-time tuition ($15,476), mandatory fees ($750), and room and board ($5980). Part-time tuition: $620 per credit hour. Part-time tuition and fees vary according to course load. *Required fees:* $375 per term part-time. *Room and board:* Room and board charges vary according to board plan and housing facility. *Payment plan:* installment. *Waivers:* employees or children of employees.

Applying *Options:* electronic application, early admission, deferred entrance. *Application fee:* $25. *Required:* high school transcript, minimum 2.0 GPA, 1 letter of recommendation. *Required for some:* essay or personal statement, interview. *Application deadlines:* 8/1 (freshmen), rolling (transfers).

Freshman Application Contact Ms. Tiffany Wood, Director of Admission, Point University, 2605 Ben Hill Road, East Point, GA 30344-1999. *Phone:* 404-669-3202. *Toll-free phone:* 855-37-POINT. *Fax:* 404-460-2451. *E-mail:* admissions@acc.edu. *Web site:* http://point.edu/.

Reinhardt University
Waleska, Georgia

- **Independent** comprehensive, founded 1883, affiliated with United Methodist Church
- **Rural** 600-acre campus with easy access to Atlanta
- **Endowment** $41.5 million
- **Coed** 1,035 undergraduate students, 91% full-time, 56% women, 44% men
- **Moderately difficult** entrance level, 59% of applicants were admitted

Undergraduates 938 full-time, 97 part-time. Students come from 4 states and territories; 40 other countries; 27% are from out of state; 12% Black or African American, non-Hispanic/Latino; 4% Hispanic/Latino; 1% Asian, non-Hispanic/Latino; 0.5% American Indian or Alaska Native, non-Hispanic/Latino; 6% Race/ethnicity unknown; 9% transferred in; 43% live on campus. *Retention:* 58% of full-time freshmen returned.

Freshmen *Admission:* 1,310 applied, 769 admitted, 237 enrolled. *Average high school GPA:* 3.04. *Test scores:* SAT critical reading scores over 500: 40%; SAT math scores over 500: 40%; SAT critical reading scores over 600: 10%; SAT math scores over 600: 8%.

Faculty *Total:* 157, 39% full-time, 57% with terminal degrees. *Student/faculty ratio:* 12:1.

Academics *Calendar:* semesters. *Degrees:* associate, bachelor's, and master's. *Special study options:* academic remediation for entering students, adult/continuing education programs, advanced placement credit, cooperative education, distance learning, double majors, freshman honors college, honors programs, independent study, internships, off-campus study, part-time degree program, services for LD students, student-designed majors, study abroad, summer session for credit.

Computers on Campus 164 computers/terminals and 164 ports are available on campus for general student use. Students can access the following: campus intranet, computer help desk, free student e-mail accounts, online (class) grades, online (class) registration, online (class) schedules. Campuswide network is available. 100% of college-owned or -operated housing units are wired for high-speed Internet access. Wireless service is available via classrooms, computer centers, computer labs, dorm rooms, learning centers, libraries, student centers.

Student Life *Housing:* on-campus residence required for freshman year. *Options:* coed, men-only, women-only, disabled students. Campus housing is university owned. Freshman campus housing is guaranteed. *Activities and organizations:* drama/theater group, student-run newspaper, television station, choral group, Real Deal, International and Historical Film Society, Student Government Association, SOAR (Student Orientation Leaders), Communication Club. *Campus security:* 24-hour emergency response devices and patrols, late-night transport/escort service, controlled dormitory access. *Student services:* health clinic, personal/psychological counseling.

Athletics Member NAIA. *Intercollegiate sports:* baseball M(s), basketball M(s)/W(s), cross-country running M(s)/W(s), football M(s), golf M(s), lacrosse M(s)/W(s), soccer M(s)/W(s), softball W(s), tennis M(s)/W(s), volleyball W(s). *Intramural sports:* basketball M/W, cheerleading M/W, football M/W, soccer M/W, softball M/W, volleyball M/W.

Standardized Tests *Required:* SAT or ACT (for admission).

Costs (2011–12) *Comprehensive fee:* $24,420 includes full-time tuition ($17,500), mandatory fees ($340), and room and board ($6580). Full-time tuition and fees vary according to location and program. Part-time tuition: $592 per credit hour. Part-time tuition and fees vary according to course load, location, and program. *Required fees:* $85 per term part-time. *Room and board:* Room and board charges vary according to board plan and housing facility. *Payment plan:* installment. *Waivers:* senior citizens and employees or children of employees.

Financial Aid Of all full-time matriculated undergraduates who enrolled in 2009, 1,601 applied for aid, 1,382 were judged to have need, 56 had their need fully met. In 2009, 235 non-need-based awards were made. *Average percent of need met:* 27%. *Average financial aid package:* $9523. *Average need-based loan:* $3631. *Average need-based gift aid:* $7417. *Average non-need-based aid:* $4221. *Average indebtedness upon graduation:* $21,096.

Applying *Options:* electronic application, early admission, deferred entrance. *Application fee:* $25. *Required:* high school transcript, minimum 2.0 GPA. *Application deadlines:* rolling (freshmen), rolling (transfers). *Notification:* continuous (freshmen), continuous (transfers).

Freshman Application Contact Ms. Julie Fleming, Director of Admissions, Reinhardt University, 7300 Reinhardt College Circle, Waleska, GA 30183-0128. *Phone:* 770-720-5526. *Fax:* 770-720-5602. *E-mail:* admissions@mail.reinhardt.edu. *Web site:* http://www.reinhardt.edu/.

Savannah College of Art and Design
Savannah, Georgia

- **Independent** comprehensive, founded 1978
- **Urban** campus
- **Coed** 8,948 undergraduate students, 86% full-time, 63% women, 37% men
- **Moderately difficult** entrance level, 63% of applicants were admitted

Undergraduates 7,701 full-time, 1,247 part-time. Students come from 55 states and territories; 104 other countries; 78% are from out of state; 8% Black or African American, non-Hispanic/Latino; 5% Hispanic/Latino; 4% Asian, non-Hispanic/Latino; 0.2% Native Hawaiian or other Pacific Islander, non-Hispanic/Latino; 0.5% American Indian or Alaska Native, non-Hispanic/Latino; 0.3% Two or more races, non-Hispanic/Latino; 30% Race/ethnicity unknown; 10% international; 9% transferred in; 42% live on campus. *Retention:* 81% of full-time freshmen returned.

Freshmen *Admission:* 8,533 applied, 5,377 admitted, 1,790 enrolled. *Average high school GPA:* 3.42. *Test scores:* SAT critical reading scores over 500: 70%; SAT math scores over 500: 62%; SAT writing scores over 500: 66%; ACT scores over 18: 94%; SAT critical reading scores over 600: 27%; SAT math scores over 600: 21%; SAT writing scores over 600: 22%; ACT scores over 24: 48%; SAT critical reading scores over 700: 4%; SAT math scores over 700: 3%; SAT writing scores over 700: 2%; ACT scores over 30: 7%.

Faculty *Total:* 724, 72% full-time, 72% with terminal degrees. *Student/faculty ratio:* 17:1.

Academics *Calendar:* quarters. *Degrees:* certificates, bachelor's, master's, and postbachelor's certificates. *Special study options:* advanced placement credit, cooperative education, distance learning, double majors, English as a second language, independent study, internships, off-campus study, part-time degree program, services for LD students, study abroad, summer session for credit. *ROTC:* Army (c).

Computers on Campus 3,400 computers/terminals are available on campus for general student use. Students can access the following: campus intranet, computer help desk, free student e-mail accounts, online (class) grades, online (class) registration, online (class) schedules. Campuswide network is available. 100% of college-owned or -operated housing units are wired for high-speed Internet access. Wireless service is available via entire campus.

Student Life *Housing options:* coed, women-only, disabled students. Campus housing is university owned and leased by the school. Freshman applicants given priority for college housing. *Activities and organizations:* drama/theater group, student-run newspaper, radio station, choral group, Gamers' Guild, Contemporary Animation Society, Circus Club, Expressions Dance Club, Queers and Allies. *Campus security:* 24-hour emergency response devices and patrols, student patrols, late-night transport/escort service, controlled dormitory access, Video camera surveillance. *Student services:* health clinic, personal/psychological counseling.

Athletics Member NAIA. *Intercollegiate sports:* baseball M(s), cheerleading M(c)/W(c), cross-country running M(s)/W(s), equestrian sports M(s)/W(s), fencing M(c)/W(c), golf M(s)/W(s), lacrosse W(s), soccer M(s)/W(s), softball W(s), swimming and diving M(s)/W(s), tennis M(s)/W(s), volleyball W(s). *Intramural sports:* basketball M/W, equestrian sports M(c)/W(c), lacrosse M(c), softball M/W, tennis M/W, ultimate Frisbee M/W, volleyball M/W.

Standardized Tests *Required:* SAT or ACT (for admission).

Costs (2012–13) *Comprehensive fee:* $44,850 includes full-time tuition ($31,905) and room and board ($12,945). Full-time tuition and fees vary according to course load and degree level. Part-time tuition: $709 per quarter hour. Part-time tuition and fees vary according to course load and degree level. *College room only:* $8220. Room and board charges vary according to board plan, housing facility, and location. *Payment plan:* installment. *Waivers:* employees or children of employees.

Financial Aid Of all full-time matriculated undergraduates who enrolled in 2011, 5,109 applied for aid, 4,531 were judged to have need, 335 had their need fully met. In 2011, 2249 non-need-based awards were made. *Average percent of need met:* 21%. *Average financial aid package:* $22,755. *Average need-based loan:* $3814. *Average need-based gift aid:* $5692. *Average non-need-based aid:* $8977. *Average indebtedness upon graduation:* $35,549.

Applying *Options:* electronic application, early admission, deferred entrance. *Application fee:* $35. *Required:* high school transcript. *Required for some:* essay or personal statement, high school transcript, College transcripts required for transfer students; Portfolio/audition recommended for all performing arts, riding, writing, or visual arts applicants. *Recommended:* essay or personal statement, minimum 3.0 GPA, 3 letters of recommendation, interview. *Application deadlines:* rolling (freshmen), rolling (transfers). *Notification:* continuous (freshmen), continuous (transfers).

Freshman Application Contact Ms. Ginger Hansen, Executive Director of Recruitment, Savannah College of Art and Design, 342 Bull Street, PO Box 3146, Savannah, GA 31402-3146. *Phone:* 912-525-5100. *Toll-free phone:* 800-869-7223. *Fax:* 912-525-5983. *E-mail:* admission@scad.edu. *Web site:* http://www.scad.edu/.

Savannah State University

Savannah, Georgia

- **State-supported** comprehensive, founded 1890, part of University System of Georgia
- **Suburban** 173-acre campus
- **Endowment** $3.7 million
- **Coed**
- **Minimally difficult** entrance level

Faculty *Student/faculty ratio:* 23:1.

Academics *Calendar:* semesters. *Degrees:* bachelor's and master's.

Student Life *Campus security:* 24-hour emergency response devices and patrols, late-night transport/escort service, controlled dormitory access.

Athletics Member NCAA. All Division I.

Standardized Tests *Required:* SAT or ACT (for admission). *Required for some:* SAT Subject Tests (for admission). *Recommended:* SAT (for admission).

Costs (2011–12) *Tuition:* state resident $4401 full-time, $147 per credit hour part-time; nonresident $16,016 full-time, $534 per credit hour part-time. Full-time tuition and fees vary according to course load and program. Part-time tuition and fees vary according to course load and program. *Required fees:* $1630 full-time, $815 per term part-time. *Room and board:* $6604; room only: $3012. Room and board charges vary according to board plan and housing facility.

Applying *Options:* electronic application, early admission, deferred entrance. *Application fee:* $20. *Required:* high school transcript, minimum 2.3 GPA. *Required for some:* essay or personal statement, interview.

Freshman Application Contact Mrs. Carol Dolan, Assistant Director of Admissions for Operations, Savannah State University, PO Box 20209, Savannah, GA 31404. *Phone:* 912-358-4014. *Toll-free phone:* 800-788-0478. *Fax:* 912-358-4517. *E-mail:* dolanc@savannahstate.edu. *Web site:* http://www.savannahstate.edu/.

Shorter University

Rome, Georgia

- **Independent Baptist** comprehensive, founded 1873
- **Small-town** 155-acre campus with easy access to Atlanta
- **Endowment** $20.1 million
- **Coed** 1,642 undergraduate students, 92% full-time, 54% women, 46% men
- **Moderately difficult** entrance level, 65% of applicants were admitted

Undergraduates 1,510 full-time, 132 part-time. Students come from 35 states and territories; 23 other countries; 14% are from out of state; 17% Black or African American, non-Hispanic/Latino; 4% Hispanic/Latino; 0.7% Asian, non-Hispanic/Latino; 0.1% Native Hawaiian or other Pacific Islander, non-Hispanic/Latino; 0.2% American Indian or Alaska Native, non-Hispanic/Latino; 1% Two or more races, non-Hispanic/Latino; 5% Race/ethnicity unknown; 3% international; 10% transferred in; 54% live on campus. *Retention:* 68% of full-time freshmen returned.

Freshmen *Admission:* 1,944 applied, 1,263 admitted, 405 enrolled. *Average high school GPA:* 3.32. *Test scores:* SAT critical reading scores over 500: 44%; SAT math scores over 500: 48%; SAT writing scores over 500: 35%; ACT scores over 18: 77%; SAT critical reading scores over 600: 12%; SAT math scores over 600: 14%; SAT writing scores over 600: 9%; ACT scores over 24: 27%; SAT critical reading scores over 700: 1%; SAT math scores over 700: 1%; ACT scores over 30: 3%.

Faculty *Total:* 186, 49% full-time, 38% with terminal degrees. *Student/faculty ratio:* 13:1.

Academics *Calendar:* semesters. *Degrees:* associate, bachelor's, and master's. *Special study options:* academic remediation for entering students, adult/continuing education programs, advanced placement credit, double majors, honors programs, independent study, internships, off-campus study, part-time degree program, services for LD students, student-designed majors, study abroad, summer session for credit.

Computers on Campus 100 computers/terminals are available on campus for general student use. Students can access the following: campus intranet, computer help desk, free student e-mail accounts, online (class) grades, online (class) registration, online (class) schedules. Campuswide network is available. 100% of college-owned or -operated housing units are wired for high-speed Internet access. Wireless service is available via classrooms, computer centers, computer labs, dorm rooms, learning centers, libraries, student centers.

Student Life *Housing options:* men-only, women-only. Campus housing is university owned. Freshman applicants given priority for college housing. *Activities and organizations:* drama/theater group, student-run newspaper, radio and television station, choral group, marching band, Baptist Collegiate Ministries, Student Government Association, Fellowship of Christian Athletes, Habitat for Humanity, SAVE (Students Advocating Volunteer Efforts), national fraternities, national sororities. *Campus security:* 24-hour emergency response devices and patrols. *Student services:* health clinic, personal/psychological counseling.

Athletics Member NAIA. *Intercollegiate sports:* baseball M(s), basketball M(s)/W(s), cheerleading M(s)/W(s), cross-country running M(s)/W(s), football M(s), golf M(s)/W(s), soccer M(s)/W(s), softball W(s), tennis M(s)/W(s), track and field M(s)/W(s), volleyball W(s). *Intramural sports:* basketball M/W, bowling M/W, soccer M/W, table tennis M/W, tennis M/W, ultimate Frisbee M/W, volleyball W.

Standardized Tests *Required:* SAT or ACT (for admission).

Costs (2011–12) *One-time required fee:* $99. *Comprehensive fee:* $26,470 includes full-time tuition ($17,500), mandatory fees ($370), and room and board ($8600). Full-time tuition and fees vary according to course load. Part-time tuition: $480 per credit hour. *College room only:* $4600. Room and board charges vary according to board plan and housing facility. *Payment plan:* installment. *Waivers:* senior citizens and employees or children of employees.

Financial Aid Of all full-time matriculated undergraduates who enrolled in 2011, 1,312 applied for aid, 1,176 were judged to have need, 235 had their need fully met. 133 Federal Work-Study jobs (averaging $2417). 82 state and other part-time jobs (averaging $2335). In 2011, 159 non-need-based awards were made. *Average percent of need met:* 65%. *Average financial aid package:* $16,072. *Average need-based loan:* $4054. *Average need-based gift aid:* $12,875. *Average non-need-based aid:* $5738. *Average indebtedness upon graduation:* $25,441.

Applying *Options:* electronic application, early admission, deferred entrance. *Application fee:* $25. *Required:* essay or personal statement, high school transcript. *Required for some:* interview, audition for music and theater programs. *Recommended:* minimum 2.0 GPA, 1 letter of recommendation, interview. *Application deadlines:* 8/25 (freshmen), 8/25 (transfers). *Notification:* continuous (freshmen), continuous (transfers).

Freshman Application Contact Shorter University, 315 Shorter Avenue, Rome, GA 30165. *Phone:* 706-233-7342. *Toll-free phone:* 800-868-6980. *Web site:* http://www.shorter.edu/.

See page 238 for display ad and page 1580 for the College Close-Up.

Southern Polytechnic State University

Marietta, Georgia

- **State-supported** comprehensive, founded 1948, part of University System of Georgia
- **Suburban** 198-acre campus with easy access to Atlanta
- **Endowment** $3.2 million
- **Coed** 5,024 undergraduate students, 72% full-time, 18% women, 82% men
- **Moderately difficult** entrance level, 74% of applicants were admitted

Undergraduates 3,631 full-time, 1,393 part-time. Students come from 23 states and territories; 57 other countries; 2% are from out of state; 22% Black or African American, non-Hispanic/Latino; 7% Hispanic/Latino; 6% Asian, non-Hispanic/Latino; 0.3% American Indian or Alaska Native, non-Hispanic/Latino; 3% Two or more races, non-Hispanic/Latino; 2% Race/ethnicity unknown; 5% international; 13% transferred in; 30% live on campus. *Retention:* 76% of full-time freshmen returned.

Freshmen *Admission:* 1,320 applied, 978 admitted, 604 enrolled. *Average high school GPA:* 3.27. *Test scores:* SAT critical reading scores over 500: 77%; SAT math scores over 500: 91%; SAT writing scores over 500: 60%; ACT scores over 18: 97%; SAT critical reading scores over 600: 24%; SAT math scores over 600: 39%; SAT writing scores over 600: 10%; ACT scores over 24: 43%; SAT critical reading scores over 700: 4%; SAT math scores over 700: 5%; SAT writing scores over 700: 1%; ACT scores over 30: 7%.

Faculty *Total:* 305, 64% full-time, 53% with terminal degrees. *Student/faculty ratio:* 19:1.

Academics *Calendar:* semesters. *Degrees:* certificates, associate, bachelor's, master's, and postbachelor's certificates. *Special study options:* advanced placement credit, cooperative education, distance learning, double majors, honors programs, independent study, internships, off-campus study, part-time degree program, services for LD students, student-designed majors, study abroad, summer session for credit. *ROTC:* Army (c), Navy (c), Air Force (c).

Computers on Campus 1,400 computers/terminals and 250 ports are available on campus for general student use. Students can access the following: campus intranet, computer help desk, free student e-mail accounts, online (class) grades, online (class) registration, online (class) schedules. Campuswide network is available. 100% of college-owned or -operated housing units are wired for high-speed Internet access. Wireless service is available via classrooms, computer centers, computer labs, dorm rooms, learning centers, libraries, student centers.

Excellence. Since 1873.

From our founding in 1873, Shorter University has offered a top quality education within a caring Christian environment. To us, the true value of an education is the person a student becomes because of it. At Shorter University, our students receive individualized attention to help them succeed in our academically challenging environment. We pair that with opportunities for personal and spiritual growth. The result is a unique environment where students can become everything God intended them to be.

SHORTER UNIVERSITY™

At the Crossroads of Faith & Learning

www.shorter.edu

315 Shorter Avenue, Rome, Georgia 30165
800-868-6980 • admissions@shorter.edu

Perennially ranked as one of the South's best colleges by U.S. News & World Report and The Princeton Review.

Student Life *Housing:* on-campus residence required for freshman year. *Options:* coed, men-only, women-only, cooperative, disabled students. Campus housing is university owned and is provided by a third party. Freshman applicants given priority for college housing. *Activities and organizations:* drama/theater group, student-run newspaper, radio station, choral group, International Student Association, Campus Activities Board, National Society of Black Engineers, Baptist Collegiate Ministries, American Society of Civil Engineers, national fraternities, national sororities. *Campus security:* 24-hour emergency response devices and patrols, late-night transport/escort service, controlled dormitory access. *Student services:* health clinic, personal/psychological counseling.

Athletics Member NAIA. *Intercollegiate sports:* baseball M(s), basketball M(s)/W(s), cheerleading M/W, soccer M(s). *Intramural sports:* badminton M/W, basketball M/W, football M/W, golf M/W, racquetball M/W, soccer M/W, softball M/W, ultimate Frisbee M/W, volleyball M/W.

Standardized Tests *Required:* SAT or ACT (for admission).

Costs (2011–12) *Tuition:* state resident $5128 full-time, $171 per semester hour part-time; nonresident $18,248 full-time, $608 per semester hour part-time. Full-time tuition and fees vary according to course load. Part-time tuition and fees vary according to course load. *Required fees:* $1396 full-time, $698 per term part-time. *Room and board:* $6892; room only: $3900. Room and board charges vary according to housing facility. *Waivers:* senior citizens and employees or children of employees.

Financial Aid Of all full-time matriculated undergraduates who enrolled in 2010, 3,675 applied for aid, 3,161 were judged to have need, 399 had their need fully met. 107 Federal Work-Study jobs (averaging $4000). In 2010, 4 non-need-based awards were made. *Average percent of need met:* 65%. *Average financial aid package:* $3943. *Average need-based loan:* $4562. *Average need-based gift aid:* $4215. *Average non-need-based aid:* $7219. *Average indebtedness upon graduation:* $24,957.

Applying *Options:* electronic application, deferred entrance. *Application fee:* $40. *Required:* high school transcript, minimum 2.5 GPA, proof of immunization, international students have additional requirements, 18 academic CPC units. *Application deadlines:* 7/1 (freshmen), 7/1 (out-of-state freshmen), 7/1 (transfers). *Notification:* continuous (freshmen), continuous (out-of-state freshmen), continuous (transfers).

Freshman Application Contact Mr. Gary Bush, Director of Admissions, Southern Polytechnic State University, 1100 South Marietta Parkway, Marietta, GA 30060. *Phone:* 678-915-7468. *Toll-free phone:* 800-635-3204. *Fax:* 678-915-7292. *E-mail:* gbush@spsu.edu. *Web site:* http://www.spsu.edu/.

South University

Savannah, Georgia

- **Proprietary** comprehensive, founded 1899, part of Education Management Corporation
- **Coed**

Academics *Calendar:* quarters. *Degrees:* associate, bachelor's, master's, doctoral, and first professional.

Costs (2011–12) *Tuition:* Information about tuition and fees can be obtained by contacting the South University Admissions Office.

Freshman Application Contact South University, 709 Mall Boulevard, Savannah, GA 31406. *Phone:* 912-201-8000. *Toll-free phone:* 866-629-2901. *Web site:* http://www.southuniversity.edu/savannah/.

See page 1596 for the College Close-Up.

Spelman College

Atlanta, Georgia

- **Independent** 4-year, founded 1881
- **Urban** 32-acre campus with easy access to Atlanta
- **Women only** 2,170 undergraduate students, 96% full-time
- **Very difficult** entrance level, 38% of applicants were admitted

Undergraduates 2,082 full-time, 88 part-time. 87% are from out of state; 81% Black or African American, non-Hispanic/Latino; 0.2% Hispanic/Latino; 0.1% American Indian or Alaska Native, non-Hispanic/Latino; 2% Two or more races, non-Hispanic/Latino; 16% Race/ethnicity unknown; 0.7% international; 2% transferred in; 39% live on campus. *Retention:* 89% of full-time freshmen returned.

Freshmen *Admission:* 5,864 applied, 2,204 admitted, 531 enrolled. *Average high school GPA:* 3.63. *Test scores:* SAT critical reading scores over 500: 69%; SAT math scores over 500: 60%; ACT scores over 18: 92%; SAT critical reading scores over 600: 15%; SAT math scores over 600: 12%; ACT scores over 24: 36%; SAT critical reading scores over 700: 1%; SAT math scores over 700: 1%; ACT scores over 30: 3%.

Faculty *Total:* 250, 69% full-time, 73% with terminal degrees. *Student/faculty ratio:* 11:1.

Academics *Calendar:* semesters. *Degree:* bachelor's. *Special study options:* adult/continuing education programs, part-time degree program. *ROTC:* Army (c), Navy (b), Air Force (c).

Computers on Campus Students can access the following: online (class) registration. Campuswide network is available.

Student Life *Housing:* on-campus residence required for freshman year. *Options:* women-only. Campus housing is university owned and leased by the school. Freshman applicants given priority for college housing. *Campus security:* 24-hour emergency response devices and patrols, late-night transport/escort service, controlled dormitory access.

Athletics Member NCAA. *Intercollegiate sports:* basketball W, cross-country running W, golf W, soccer W, tennis W, track and field W, volleyball W. *Intramural sports:* softball W, swimming and diving W.

Standardized Tests *Required:* SAT or ACT (for admission).

Costs (2011–12) *One-time required fee:* $250. *Comprehensive fee:* $34,240 includes full-time tuition ($19,684), mandatory fees ($3570), and room and board ($10,986). *Part-time tuition:* $820 per credit hour. *Payment plan:* deferred payment. *Waivers:* employees or children of employees.

Financial Aid Of all full-time matriculated undergraduates who enrolled in 2009, 1,997 applied for aid, 1,669 were judged to have need, 563 had their need fully met. *Average percent of need met:* 47%. *Average financial aid package:* $15,439. *Average need-based loan:* $4307. *Average need-based gift aid:* $12,829. *Average indebtedness upon graduation:* $14,070.

Applying *Options:* electronic application, early decision, early action. *Application fee:* $35. *Required:* essay or personal statement, high school transcript, minimum 2.0 GPA, 2 letters of recommendation. *Required for some:* interview. *Application deadlines:* 2/1 (freshmen), 4/1 (transfers), 11/15 (early action). *Early decision deadline:* 11/1. *Notification:* 4/1 (freshmen), 5/1 (transfers), 12/15 (early decision), 12/31 (early action).

Freshman Application Contact Ms. Arlene Cash, Vice President for Admissions and Orientation, Spelman College, 350 Spelman Lane, SW, Atlanta, GA 30314-4399. *Phone:* 404-681-3643. *Toll-free phone:* 800-982-2411. *Fax:* 404-270-5201. *E-mail:* admiss@spelman.edu. *Web site:* http://www.spelman.edu/.

Strayer University - Augusta Campus
Augusta, Georgia
- **Proprietary** comprehensive
- **Coed**

Academics *Degrees:* certificates, diplomas, associate, bachelor's, master's, and postbachelor's certificates.

Freshman Application Contact Strayer University - Augusta Campus, 1330 Augusta West Parkway, Augusta, GA 30909. *Web site:* http://www.strayer.edu/augusta/.

Strayer University - Chamblee Campus
Atlanta, Georgia
- **Proprietary** comprehensive
- **Coed**

Academics *Degrees:* certificates, diplomas, associate, bachelor's, master's, and postbachelor's certificates.

Freshman Application Contact Strayer University - Chamblee Campus, 3355 Northeast Expressway, Suite 100, Atlanta, GA 30341. *Web site:* http://www.strayer.edu/chamblee/.

Strayer University - Cobb County Campus
Atlanta, Georgia
- **Proprietary** comprehensive
- **Coed**

Academics *Degrees:* certificates, diplomas, associate, bachelor's, master's, and postbachelor's certificates.

Freshman Application Contact Strayer University - Cobb County Campus, 3101 Towercreek Parkway, SE, Suite 700, Atlanta, GA 30339-3256. *Web site:* http://www.strayer.edu/cobb_county/.

Strayer University - Columbus Campus
Columbus, Georgia
- **Proprietary** comprehensive
- **Coed**

Academics *Degrees:* certificates, diplomas, associate, bachelor's, master's, and postbachelor's certificates.

Freshman Application Contact Strayer University - Columbus Campus, 6003 Veterans Parkway, Suite 100, Columbus, GA 31909. *Web site:* http://www.strayer.edu/columbus_ga.

Strayer University - Douglasville Campus
Douglasville, Georgia
- **Proprietary** comprehensive
- **Coed**

Academics *Degrees:* certificates, diplomas, associate, bachelor's, master's, and postbachelor's certificates.

Freshman Application Contact Strayer University - Douglasville Campus, 4655 Timber Ridge Drive, Douglasville, GA 30135. *Web site:* http://www.strayer.edu/douglasville/.

Strayer University - Lithonia Campus
Lithonia, Georgia
- **Proprietary** comprehensive
- **Coed**

Academics *Degrees:* certificates, diplomas, associate, bachelor's, master's, and postbachelor's certificates.

Freshman Application Contact Strayer University - Lithonia Campus, 3120 Stonecrest Boulevard, Suite 200, Lithonia, GA 30038. *Web site:* http://www.strayer.edu/lithonia/.

Strayer University - Morrow Campus
Morrow, Georgia
- **Proprietary** comprehensive
- **Coed**

Academics *Degrees:* certificates, diplomas, associate, bachelor's, master's, and postbachelor's certificates.

Freshman Application Contact Strayer University - Morrow Campus, 3000 Corporate Center Drive, Suite 100, Morrow, GA 30260. *Web site:* http://www.strayer.edu/morrow.

Strayer University - Roswell Campus
Roswell, Georgia
- **Proprietary** comprehensive
- **Coed**

Academics *Degrees:* certificates, diplomas, associate, bachelor's, master's, and postbachelor's certificates.

Freshman Application Contact Strayer University - Roswell Campus, 100 Mansell Court East, Suite 100, Roswell, GA 30076. *Web site:* http://www.strayer.edu/roswell.

Strayer University - Savannah Campus
Savannah, Georgia
- **Proprietary** comprehensive
- **Coed**

Academics *Degrees:* certificates, diplomas, associate, bachelor's, master's, and postbachelor's certificates.

Freshman Application Contact Strayer University - Savannah Campus, 20 Martin Court, Savannah, GA 31419. *Web site:* http://www.strayer.edu/savannah/.

Thomas University
Thomasville, Georgia

- **Independent** comprehensive, founded 1950
- **Small-town** 24-acre campus
- **Endowment** $3.3 million
- **Coed** 863 undergraduate students, 53% full-time, 56% women, 44% men
- **Noncompetitive** entrance level

Undergraduates 454 full-time, 409 part-time. Students come from 8 states and territories; 13 other countries; 5% are from out of state; 31% Black or African American, non-Hispanic/Latino; 3% Hispanic/Latino; 0.8% Asian, non-Hispanic/Latino; 2% American Indian or Alaska Native, non-Hispanic/Latino; 9% Race/ethnicity unknown; 2% international; 11% transferred in; 9% live on campus. *Retention:* 63% of full-time freshmen returned.
Freshmen *Admission:* 71 applied, 97 enrolled.
Faculty *Total:* 53, 96% full-time, 70% with terminal degrees. *Student/faculty ratio:* 6:1.
Academics *Calendar:* semesters. *Degrees:* associate, bachelor's, master's, and postbachelor's certificates. *Special study options:* academic remediation for entering students, accelerated degree program, adult/continuing education programs, advanced placement credit, cooperative education, distance learning, double majors, independent study, internships, part-time degree program, services for LD students, study abroad, summer session for credit.
Computers on Campus 50 computers/terminals are available on campus for general student use. Students can access the following: free student e-mail accounts, online (class) schedules. Campuswide network is available.
Student Life *Housing options:* coed. Campus housing is university owned. Freshman applicants given priority for college housing. *Activities and organizations:* drama/theater group, student-run newspaper, choral group, Student Government Association, Professional Management Association, National Society for Leadership and Success. *Campus security:* late-night transport/escort service, controlled dormitory access, evening security guards. *Student services:* personal/psychological counseling.
Athletics Member NAIA. *Intercollegiate sports:* baseball M(s), golf M(s)/W, soccer M(s)/W(s), softball W(s). *Intramural sports:* football M/W, table tennis M/W, tennis M/W, volleyball M/W.
Standardized Tests *Recommended:* SAT (for admission), SAT and SAT Subject Tests or ACT (for admission).
Costs (2011–12) *One-time required fee:* $150. *Tuition:* $12,600 full-time, $500 per credit hour part-time. Full-time tuition and fees vary according to course level, course load, program, and student level. Part-time tuition and fees vary according to course level, course load, program, and student level. *Required fees:* $720 full-time, $150 per term part-time. *Room only:* $3550. *Payment plan:* installment. *Waivers:* employees or children of employees.
Applying *Options:* electronic application, early admission, deferred entrance. *Application fee:* $25. *Required:* high school transcript. *Application deadlines:* rolling (freshmen), rolling (transfers). *Notification:* continuous (freshmen), continuous (transfers).
Freshman Application Contact Mrs. Kerri Knight, Thomas University Office of Admission, Thomas University, 1501 Millpond Road, Thomasville, GA 31792. *Phone:* 229-227-6942 Ext. 1074. *Toll-free phone:* 800-538-9784. *Fax:* 229-227-6919. *E-mail:* kknight@thomasu.edu. *Web site:* http://www.thomasu.edu/.

Toccoa Falls College
Toccoa Falls, Georgia

Freshman Application Contact Toccoa Falls College, 107 North Chapel Drive, Toccoa Falls, GA 30598. *Phone:* 888-785-5624. *Web site:* http://www.tfc.edu/.

Truett-McConnell College
Cleveland, Georgia

- **Independent Baptist** 4-year, founded 1946
- **Rural** 310-acre campus with easy access to Atlanta
- **Coed** 921 undergraduate students, 64% full-time, 48% women, 52% men
- **Minimally difficult** entrance level, 83% of applicants were admitted

Undergraduates 586 full-time, 335 part-time. Students come from 17 states and territories; 7 other countries; 6% are from out of state; 8% Black or African American, non-Hispanic/Latino; 4% Hispanic/Latino; 0.7% American Indian or Alaska Native, non-Hispanic/Latino; 4% Race/ethnicity unknown; 3% international; 6% transferred in; 49% live on campus. *Retention:* 74% of full-time freshmen returned.
Freshmen *Admission:* 400 applied, 332 admitted, 179 enrolled. *Average high school GPA:* 3.06.
Faculty *Total:* 89, 38% full-time. *Student/faculty ratio:* 13:1.

Academics *Calendar:* semesters. *Degrees:* associate and bachelor's. *Special study options:* academic remediation for entering students, accelerated degree program, advanced placement credit, distance learning, double majors, services for LD students, summer session for credit.
Computers on Campus Students can access the following: computer help desk, free student e-mail accounts, online (class) grades, online (class) registration, online (class) schedules. Campuswide network is available. 100% of college-owned or -operated housing units are wired for high-speed Internet access. Wireless service is available via classrooms, computer labs, dorm rooms, libraries, student centers.
Student Life *Housing:* on-campus residence required through senior year. *Options:* men-only, women-only. Campus housing is university owned. *Activities and organizations:* choral group. *Campus security:* 24-hour weekday patrols, 10-hour weekend patrols by trained security personnel. *Student services:* health clinic.
Athletics Member NAIA, NCCAA. *Intercollegiate sports:* baseball M(s), basketball M(s)/W(s), cross-country running M(s)/W(s), golf M(s)/W(s), soccer M(s)/W(s), softball W(s), volleyball W(s), wrestling M(s). *Intramural sports:* basketball M/W, football M/W, ultimate Frisbee M/W, volleyball M/W.
Standardized Tests *Required:* SAT or ACT (for admission).
Costs (2011–12) *Comprehensive fee:* $21,190 includes full-time tuition ($14,460), mandatory fees ($550), and room and board ($6180). Full-time tuition and fees vary according to course load. Part-time tuition: $482 per semester hour. Part-time tuition and fees vary according to course load. *Required fees:* $275 per term part-time. *Room and board:* Room and board charges vary according to housing facility. *Payment plan:* installment. *Waivers:* employees or children of employees.
Financial Aid Of all full-time matriculated undergraduates who enrolled in 2011, 509 applied for aid, 330 were judged to have need, 37 had their need fully met. 24 Federal Work-Study jobs (averaging $1205). In 2011, 40 non-need-based awards were made. *Average percent of need met:* 67%. *Average financial aid package:* $13,759. *Average need-based loan:* $3581. *Average need-based gift aid:* $11,135. *Average non-need-based aid:* $6872. *Average indebtedness upon graduation:* $19,921.
Applying *Options:* electronic application, early admission, deferred entrance. *Application fee:* $25. *Required:* essay or personal statement, high school transcript, minimum 2.0 GPA. *Required for some:* 1 letter of recommendation, interview. *Application deadlines:* 8/1 (freshmen), 8/1 (transfers). *Notification:* continuous (freshmen), continuous (transfers).
Freshman Application Contact Truett-McConnell College, 100 Alumni Drive, Cleveland, GA 30528. *Phone:* 706-865-2134 Ext. 210. *Toll-free phone:* 800-226-8621. *Web site:* http://www.truett.edu/.

University of Atlanta
Atlanta, Georgia

Freshman Application Contact Bill Kay, Vice President for Enrollment Management, University of Atlanta, 6685 Peachtree Industrial Boulevard, Atlanta, GA 30360. *Phone:* 404-424-8410 Ext. 5555. *Toll-free phone:* 800-533-3378. *Fax:* 678-736-8042. *E-mail:* bkay@uofa.edu. *Web site:* http://www.uofa.edu/.

University of Georgia
Athens, Georgia

- **State-supported** comprehensive, founded 1785, part of University System of Georgia
- **Suburban** 759-acre campus with easy access to Atlanta
- **Endowment** $745.8 million
- **Coed** 26,373 undergraduate students, 94% full-time, 58% women, 42% men
- **Moderately difficult** entrance level, 63% of applicants were admitted

Undergraduates 24,705 full-time, 1,668 part-time. Students come from 53 states and territories; 121 other countries; 9% are from out of state; 7% Black or African American, non-Hispanic/Latino; 4% Hispanic/Latino; 8% Asian, non-Hispanic/Latino; 0.1% Native Hawaiian or other Pacific Islander, non-Hispanic/Latino; 0.2% American Indian or Alaska Native, non-Hispanic/Latino; 2% Two or more races, non-Hispanic/Latino; 2% Race/ethnicity unknown; 0.8% international; 5% transferred in; 30% live on campus. *Retention:* 94% of full-time freshmen returned.
Freshmen *Admission:* 17,569 applied, 11,062 admitted, 5,482 enrolled. *Average high school GPA:* 3.63. *Test scores:* SAT critical reading scores over 500: 93%; SAT math scores over 500: 95%; SAT writing scores over 500: 93%; ACT scores over 18: 100%; SAT critical reading scores over 600: 54%; SAT math scores over 600: 61%; SAT writing scores over 600: 54%; ACT scores over 24: 87%; SAT critical reading scores over 700: 11%; SAT math scores over 700: 12%; SAT writing scores over 700: 11%; ACT scores over 30: 26%.

Faculty *Total:* 2,187, 82% full-time, 89% with terminal degrees. *Student/faculty ratio:* 18:1.

Academics *Calendar:* semesters. *Degrees:* certificates, bachelor's, master's, doctoral, post-master's, postbachelor's, and first professional certificates. *Special study options:* academic remediation for entering students, accelerated degree program, adult/continuing education programs, advanced placement credit, cooperative education, distance learning, double majors, honors programs, independent study, internships, off-campus study, part-time degree program, services for LD students, student-designed majors, study abroad, summer session for credit. *ROTC:* Army (b), Air Force (b).

Computers on Campus 3,096 computers/terminals are available on campus for general student use. Students can access the following: campus intranet, computer help desk, free student e-mail accounts, online (class) grades, online (class) registration, online (class) schedules. Campuswide network is available. 100% of college-owned or -operated housing units are wired for high-speed Internet access. Wireless service is available via classrooms, computer centers, computer labs, dorm rooms, learning centers, libraries, student centers.

Student Life *Housing:* on-campus residence required for freshman year. *Options:* coed, women-only, disabled students. Campus housing is university owned. Freshman campus housing is guaranteed. *Activities and organizations:* drama/theater group, student-run newspaper, radio and television station, choral group, marching band, intramurals, Recreational sports program, Communiversity, University Union, Red Coat Band, national fraternities, national sororities. *Campus security:* 24-hour emergency response devices and patrols, late-night transport/escort service, controlled dormitory access. *Student services:* health clinic, personal/psychological counseling, women's center, legal services.

Athletics Member NCAA. All Division I except football (Division I-A). *Intercollegiate sports:* baseball M(s), basketball M(s)/W(s), cross-country running M(s)/W(s), equestrian sports W(s), golf M(s)/W(s), gymnastics W(s), soccer W(s), softball W(s), swimming and diving M(s)/W(s), tennis M(s)/W(s), track and field M(s)/W(s), volleyball W(s). *Intramural sports:* badminton M(c)/W(c), baseball M(c), basketball M/W, cheerleading M(c)/W(c), crew M(c)/W(c), cross-country running M(c)/W(c), equestrian sports W(c)/W(c), fencing M(c)/W(c), football M/W, golf M/W, gymnastics M(c)/W(c), ice hockey M(c), lacrosse M(c)/W(c), racquetball M/W, rugby M(c)/W(c), sailing M(c)/W(c), soccer M/W, softball M/W, squash M/W, swimming and diving M(c)/W(c), tennis M/W, track and field M/W, volleyball M/W, water polo M(c)/W(c), wrestling M(c).

Standardized Tests *Required:* SAT or ACT (for admission). *Recommended:* SAT Subject Tests (for admission).

Costs (2011–12) *Tuition:* state resident $7282 full-time; nonresident $25,492 full-time. Full-time tuition and fees vary according to course load, location, and program. Part-time tuition and fees vary according to course load, location, and program. *Required fees:* $2190 full-time, $1095 per term part-time. *Room and board:* $8708. Room and board charges vary according to board plan and housing facility. *Waivers:* senior citizens.

Financial Aid Of all full-time matriculated undergraduates who enrolled in 2011, 15,966 applied for aid, 9,793 were judged to have need, 1,838 had their need fully met. 398 Federal Work-Study jobs (averaging $2830). In 2011, 1447 non-need-based awards were made. *Average percent of need met:* 67%. *Average financial aid package:* $10,479. *Average need-based loan:* $4154. *Average need-based gift aid:* $8149. *Average non-need-based aid:* $1798. *Average indebtedness upon graduation:* $18,569.

Applying *Options:* electronic application, early admission, early action, deferred entrance. *Application fee:* $60. *Required:* high school transcript, counselor evaluation. *Recommended:* essay or personal statement, minimum 2.0 GPA. *Application deadlines:* 1/15 (freshmen), 4/1 (transfers), 10/15 (early action). *Notification:* 4/1 (freshmen), continuous (transfers), 12/1 (early action).

Freshman Application Contact Mr. Charles Carabello, Associate Director for Enrollment Management, University of Georgia, Terrell Hall, Athens, GA 30602. *Phone:* 706-542-8776. *Fax:* 706-542-1466. *E-mail:* admproc@uga.edu. *Web site:* http://www.uga.edu/.

University of Phoenix–Atlanta Campus

Sandy Springs, Georgia

Freshman Application Contact Marc Booker, Sr. Director, Office of Admissions and Evaluation, University of Phoenix–Atlanta Campus, 4035 South Riverpoint Parkway, Mail Stop CF-L101, Phoenix, AZ 85040. *Phone:* 602-557-4609. *Toll-free phone:* 866-766-0766. *Fax:* 480-643-1156. *Web site:* http://www.phoenix.edu/.

University of Phoenix–Augusta Campus

Augusta, Georgia

Admissions Office Contact University of Phoenix–Augusta Campus, 3150 Perimeter Parkway, Augusta, GA 30909-4583. *Toll-free phone:* 866-766-0766. *Web site:* http://www.phoenix.edu/.

University of Phoenix–Columbus Georgia Campus

Columbus, Georgia

Freshman Application Contact Marc Booker, Sr. Director, Office of Admissions and Evaluation, University of Phoenix–Columbus Georgia Campus, 4035 South Riverpoint Parkway, Mail Stop CF-L101, Phoenix, AZ 85040. *Phone:* 602-557-4609. *Toll-free phone:* 866-766-0766. *Fax:* 480-643-1156. *Web site:* http://www.phoenix.edu/.

University of Phoenix–Savannah Campus

Savannah, Georgia

Admissions Office Contact University of Phoenix–Savannah Campus, 8001 Chatham Center Drive, Suite 200, Savannah, GA 31405-7400. *Toll-free phone:* 866-766-0766. *Web site:* http://www.phoenix.edu/.

University of West Georgia

Carrollton, Georgia

- **State-supported** comprehensive, founded 1933, part of University System of Georgia
- **Small-town** 645-acre campus with easy access to Atlanta
- **Endowment** $16.7 million
- **Coed** 10,029 undergraduate students, 82% full-time, 61% women, 39% men
- **Minimally difficult** entrance level, 55% of applicants were admitted

Undergraduates 8,265 full-time, 1,764 part-time. Students come from 36 states and territories; 62 other countries; 3% are from out of state; 29% Black or African American, non-Hispanic/Latino; 4% Hispanic/Latino; 1% Asian, non-Hispanic/Latino; 0.1% Native Hawaiian or other Pacific Islander, non-Hispanic/Latino; 0.2% American Indian or Alaska Native, non-Hispanic/Latino; 3% Two or more races, non-Hispanic/Latino; 5% Race/ethnicity unknown; 1% international; 6% transferred in; 28% live on campus. *Retention:* 73% of full-time freshmen returned.

Freshmen *Admission:* 6,634 applied, 3,637 admitted, 1,991 enrolled. *Average high school GPA:* 3.06. *Test scores:* SAT critical reading scores over 500: 45%; SAT math scores over 500: 42%; SAT writing scores over 500: 35%; ACT scores over 18: 89%; SAT critical reading scores over 600: 9%; SAT math scores over 600: 7%; SAT writing scores over 600: 4%; ACT scores over 24: 15%.

Faculty *Total:* 602, 72% full-time, 59% with terminal degrees. *Student/faculty ratio:* 19:1.

Academics *Calendar:* semesters. *Degrees:* certificates, bachelor's, master's, doctoral, post-master's, and postbachelor's certificates. *Special study options:* academic remediation for entering students, accelerated degree program, adult/continuing education programs, advanced placement credit, cooperative education, distance learning, double majors, external degree program, honors programs, independent study, internships, off-campus study, part-time degree program, services for LD students, study abroad, summer session for credit. *ROTC:* Air Force (b). *Unusual degree programs:* 3-2 engineering with Georgia Institute of Technology, Auburn University, Mercer University, University of Georgia.

Computers on Campus 1,200 computers/terminals are available on campus for general student use. Students can access the following: campus intranet, computer help desk, free student e-mail accounts, online (class) grades, online (class) registration, online (class) schedules. Campuswide network is available. 100% of college-owned or -operated housing units are wired for high-speed Internet access. Wireless service is available via classrooms, computer centers, computer labs, dorm rooms, learning centers, libraries, student centers.

Student Life *Housing:* on-campus residence required for freshman year. *Options:* coed, women-only, disabled students. Campus housing is university owned and leased by the school. Freshman campus housing is guaranteed. *Activities and organizations:* drama/theater group, student-run newspaper, radio and television station, choral group, marching band, Black Student Alliance, Student Activities Council, Baptist Student Union, Campus Outreach,

United Voices Gospel Choir, national fraternities, national sororities. *Campus security:* 24-hour emergency response devices and patrols, late-night transport/ escort service, controlled dormitory access. *Student services:* health clinic, personal/psychological counseling.

Athletics Member NCAA. All Division II. *Intercollegiate sports:* baseball M(s), basketball M(s)/W(s), cheerleading M(s)/W(s), cross-country running M(s)/W(s), football M(s), golf M(s)/W(s), soccer W(s), softball W(s), tennis W(s), volleyball W(s). *Intramural sports:* basketball M/W, football M/W, soccer M/W, softball M/W, tennis M/W, ultimate Frisbee M/W, volleyball M/W.

Standardized Tests *Required:* SAT or ACT (for admission).

Costs (2011–12) *Tuition:* state resident $4734 full-time, $158 per semester hour part-time; nonresident $16,710 full-time, $557 per semester hour part-time. Full-time tuition and fees vary according to course load, degree level, and location. Part-time tuition and fees vary according to course load, degree level, and location. *Required fees:* $1858 full-time, $46 per semester hour part-time, $512 per term part-time. *Room and board:* $7168; room only: $3900. Room and board charges vary according to board plan and housing facility. *Waivers:* senior citizens and employees or children of employees.

Financial Aid Of all full-time matriculated undergraduates who enrolled in 2011, 7,042 applied for aid, 6,064 were judged to have need, 683 had their need fully met. In 2011, 348 non-need-based awards were made. *Average percent of need met:* 52%. *Average financial aid package:* $5900. *Average need-based loan:* $4136. *Average need-based gift aid:* $5597. *Average non-need-based aid:* $1551. *Average indebtedness upon graduation:* $20,712. *Financial aid deadline:* 7/1.

Applying *Options:* electronic application, early admission, deferred entrance. *Application fee:* $30. *Required:* high school transcript, minimum 2.4 GPA, proof of immunization. *Application deadlines:* 6/1 (freshmen), 6/10 (out-of-state freshmen), 6/1 (transfers). *Notification:* continuous (freshmen), continuous (out-of-state freshmen), continuous (transfers).

Freshman Application Contact Ms. Ketty Ballard, Associate Director of Admissions, University of West Georgia, 1601 Maple Street, Carrollton, GA 30118. *Phone:* 678-839-4000. *Fax:* 678-839-4747. *E-mail:* admiss@westga.edu. *Web site:* http://www.westga.edu/.

Valdosta State University
Valdosta, Georgia

- **State-supported** university, founded 1906, part of University System of Georgia
- **Small-town** 180-acre campus
- **Coed** 10,728 undergraduate students, 86% full-time, 60% women, 40% men
- **Moderately difficult** entrance level, 58% of applicants were admitted

Undergraduates 9,273 full-time, 1,455 part-time. Students come from 45 states and territories; 66 other countries; 4% are from out of state; 34% Black or African American, non-Hispanic/Latino; 4% Hispanic/Latino; 1% Asian, non-Hispanic/Latino; 0.2% Native Hawaiian or other Pacific Islander, non-Hispanic/Latino; 0.3% American Indian or Alaska Native, non-Hispanic/Latino; 3% Two or more races, non-Hispanic/Latino; 2% Race/ethnicity unknown; 1% international; 7% transferred in; 27% live on campus. *Retention:* 67% of full-time freshmen returned.

Freshmen *Admission:* 7,950 applied, 4,648 admitted, 2,204 enrolled. *Average high school GPA:* 3.07. *Test scores:* SAT critical reading scores over 500: 49%; SAT math scores over 500: 41%; SAT writing scores over 500: 38%; ACT scores over 18: 91%; SAT critical reading scores over 600: 9%; SAT math scores over 600: 7%; SAT writing scores over 600: 5%; ACT scores over 24: 15%; SAT critical reading scores over 700: 1%; ACT scores over 30: 1%.

Faculty *Total:* 616, 79% full-time, 66% with terminal degrees. *Student/faculty ratio:* 23:1.

Academics *Calendar:* semesters. *Degrees:* certificates, associate, bachelor's, master's, doctoral, postbachelor's, and first professional certificates. *Special study options:* accelerated degree program, adult/continuing education programs, advanced placement credit, cooperative education, distance learning, double majors, English as a second language, external degree program, honors programs, independent study, internships, off-campus study, part-time degree program, services for LD students, study abroad, summer session for credit. *ROTC:* Air Force (b). *Unusual degree programs:* 3-2 engineering with Georgia Institute of Technology, Atlanta, GA.

Computers on Campus 1,225 computers/terminals are available on campus for general student use. Students can access the following: campus intranet, computer help desk, free student e-mail accounts, online (class) grades, online (class) registration, online (class) schedules. Campuswide network is available. 100% of college-owned or -operated housing units are wired for high-speed Internet access. Wireless service is available via classrooms, computer centers, computer labs, dorm rooms, learning centers, libraries, student centers.

Student Life *Housing:* on-campus residence required for freshman year. *Options:* coed, disabled students. Campus housing is university owned. Freshman applicants given priority for college housing. *Activities and organizations:* drama/theater group, student-run newspaper, radio station, choral group, marching band, Interfraternity Council, College Panhellenic Council, Black Student League, Residence Hall Association, Alpha Lambda Delta Freshmen Honor Society, national fraternities, national sororities. *Campus security:* 24-hour emergency response devices and patrols, late-night transport/escort service, controlled dormitory access, bicycle patrols, security cameras. *Student services:* health clinic, personal/psychological counseling.

Athletics Member NCAA. All Division II. *Intercollegiate sports:* baseball M(s), basketball M(s)/W(s), cross-country running M(s)/W(s), football M(s), golf M(s), soccer W, softball W(s), tennis M(s)/W(s), volleyball W(s). *Intramural sports:* badminton M/W, basketball M/W, bowling M/W, field hockey M/W, football M/W, golf M/W, racquetball M/W, soccer M/W, softball M/W, table tennis W, tennis M/W, ultimate Frisbee M/W, volleyball M/W.

Standardized Tests *Required:* SAT or ACT (for admission).

Costs (2011–12) *Tuition:* state resident $3787 full-time, $158 per credit hour part-time; nonresident $13,368 full-time, $557 per credit hour part-time. Full-time tuition and fees vary according to course load, location, program, and reciprocity agreements. Part-time tuition and fees vary according to course load, location, program, and reciprocity agreements. *Required fees:* $1910 full-time, $955 per term part-time. *Room and board:* $6850; room only: $3460. Room and board charges vary according to board plan and housing facility. *Waivers:* senior citizens and employees or children of employees.

Financial Aid Of all full-time matriculated undergraduates who enrolled in 2010, 8,259 applied for aid, 6,980 were judged to have need, 2,185 had their need fully met. 174 Federal Work-Study jobs (averaging $2828). In 2010, 108 non-need-based awards were made. *Average percent of need met:* 73%. *Average financial aid package:* $12,731. *Average need-based loan:* $4042. *Average need-based gift aid:* $6450. *Average non-need-based aid:* $1648. *Average indebtedness upon graduation:* $21,166.

Applying *Options:* electronic application, deferred entrance. *Application fee:* $40. *Required:* high school transcript. *Application deadlines:* 6/1 (freshmen), 6/1 (out-of-state freshmen), 6/1 (transfers). *Notification:* continuous (freshmen), continuous (transfers).

Freshman Application Contact Mr. Ryan M. Hogan, Associate Director of Admissions, Valdosta State University, Office of Admissions, 1500 North Patterson Street, Valdosta, GA 31698. *Phone:* 229-333-5791. *Toll-free phone:* 800-618-1878. *Fax:* 229-333-5482. *E-mail:* rmhogan@valdosta.edu. *Web site:* http://www.valdosta.edu/.

Wesleyan College
Macon, Georgia

- **Independent United Methodist** comprehensive, founded 1836
- **Suburban** 200-acre campus with easy access to Atlanta
- **Endowment** $44.0 million
- **Undergraduate: women only; graduate: coed** 762 undergraduate students, 52% full-time, 100% women
- **Moderately difficult** entrance level, 54% of applicants were admitted

Undergraduates 394 full-time, 368 part-time. Students come from 34 states and territories; 24 other countries; 4% are from out of state; 35% Black or African American, non-Hispanic/Latino; 6% Hispanic/Latino; 2% Asian, non-Hispanic/Latino; 0.2% Native Hawaiian or other Pacific Islander, non-Hispanic/Latino; 2% Two or more races, non-Hispanic/Latino; 2% Race/ethnicity unknown; 20% international; 3% transferred in; 82% live on campus. *Retention:* 78% of full-time freshmen returned.

Freshmen *Admission:* 519 applied, 280 admitted, 158 enrolled. *Average high school GPA:* 3.25. *Test scores:* SAT critical reading scores over 500: 68%; SAT math scores over 500: 61%; SAT writing scores over 500: 57%; ACT scores over 18: 85%; SAT critical reading scores over 600: 26%; SAT math scores over 600: 28%; SAT writing scores over 600: 21%; ACT scores over 24: 35%; SAT critical reading scores over 700: 3%; SAT math scores over 700: 4%; SAT writing scores over 700: 9%.

Faculty *Total:* 88, 55% full-time, 61% with terminal degrees. *Student/faculty ratio:* 9:1.

Academics *Calendar:* semesters. *Degrees:* bachelor's and master's. *Special study options:* adult/continuing education programs, advanced placement credit, cooperative education, double majors, honors programs, independent study, internships, off-campus study, part-time degree program, services for LD students, student-designed majors, study abroad, summer session for credit. *ROTC:* Army (c). *Unusual degree programs:* 3-2 engineering with Georgia Tech, Auburn University and Mercer University.

Computers on Campus 40 computers/terminals are available on campus for general student use. Students can access the following: campus intranet, computer help desk, free student e-mail accounts, online (class) grades, online (class) registration, online (class) schedules, online payment. Campuswide net-

work is available. 85% of college-owned or -operated housing units are wired for high-speed Internet access. Wireless service is available via classrooms, computer centers, computer labs, learning centers, libraries, student centers.

Student Life *Housing:* on-campus residence required through senior year. *Options:* women-only, disabled students. Campus housing is university owned. Freshman campus housing is guaranteed. *Activities and organizations:* drama/ theater group, student-run newspaper, choral group, Student Recreation Council, Campus Activities Board, Student Government Association, Council on Religious Concerns, Christian Fellowship. *Campus security:* 24-hour emergency response devices and patrols, late-night transport/escort service, controlled dormitory access. *Student services:* health clinic, women's center.

Athletics Member NCAA. All Division III. *Intercollegiate sports:* basketball W, cross-country running W, equestrian sports W, soccer W, softball W, tennis W, volleyball W. *Intramural sports:* basketball W, cross-country running W, equestrian sports W, soccer W, softball W, tennis W, volleyball W.

Standardized Tests *Required:* SAT or ACT (for admission).

Costs (2011–12) *Comprehensive fee:* $27,450 includes full-time tuition ($18,500), mandatory fees ($750), and room and board ($8200). Full-time tuition and fees vary according to degree level, program, and reciprocity agreements. Part-time tuition: $435 per credit hour. Part-time tuition and fees vary according to degree level, program, and reciprocity agreements. *Room and board:* Room and board charges vary according to board plan and housing facility. *Payment plans:* installment, deferred payment. *Waivers:* senior citizens and employees or children of employees.

Financial Aid Of all full-time matriculated undergraduates who enrolled in 2010, 276 applied for aid, 230 were judged to have need, 73 had their need fully met. 65 Federal Work-Study jobs (averaging $941). 79 state and other part-time jobs (averaging $1244). In 2010, 131 non-need-based awards were made. *Average percent of need met:* 81%. *Average financial aid package:* $16,418. *Average need-based loan:* $4925. *Average need-based gift aid:* $12,632. *Average non-need-based aid:* $18,887. *Average indebtedness upon graduation:* $20,896.

Applying *Options:* electronic application, early admission, early decision, early action, deferred entrance. *Application fee:* $30. *Required:* high school transcript, minimum 2.0 GPA, 1 letter of recommendation. *Required for some:* interview. *Recommended:* essay or personal statement, 2 letters of recommendation. *Application deadlines:* 2/15 (freshmen), rolling (transfers), 1/15 (early action). *Early decision deadline:* 11/15. *Notification:* continuous (freshmen), continuous (transfers), 12/15 (early decision).

Freshman Application Contact Mr. Stephen Farr, Vice President for Enrollment Services, Wesleyan College, 4760 Forsyth Road, Macon, GA 31210-4462. *Phone:* 478-757-3700. *Toll-free phone:* 800-447-6610. *Fax:* 478-757-4030. *E-mail:* admissions@wesleyancollege.edu. *Web site:* http://www.wesleyancollege.edu/.

Westwood College–Atlanta Midtown
Atlanta, Georgia

Freshman Application Contact Westwood College–Atlanta Midtown, 1100 Spring Street, Suite 102, Atlanta, GA 30309. *Phone:* 404-745-9862. *Toll-free phone:* 800-613-4595. *Web site:* http://www.westwood.edu/.

Westwood College–Atlanta Northlake
Atlanta, Georgia

Freshman Application Contact Westwood College–Atlanta Northlake, 2309 Parklake Drive, NE, Building 10, Atlanta, GA 30345. *Phone:* 404-962-2998. *Toll-free phone:* 866-821-6145. *Web site:* http://www.westwood.edu/.

Young Harris College
Young Harris, Georgia

- **Independent United Methodist** 4-year, founded 1886
- **Small-town** 800-acre campus
- **Endowment** $91.4 million
- **Coed**
- **Moderately difficult** entrance level

Faculty *Student/faculty ratio:* 10:1.

Academics *Calendar:* semesters. *Degrees:* associate and bachelor's.

Student Life *Campus security:* 24-hour emergency response devices and patrols.

Standardized Tests *Required:* SAT or ACT (for admission).

Costs (2011–12) *Comprehensive fee:* $29,635 includes full-time tuition ($21,500), mandatory fees ($655), and room and board ($7480). Full-time tuition and fees vary according to course load. Part-time tuition: $675 per credit hour. Part-time tuition and fees vary according to course load. *Room and board:* Room and board charges vary according to housing facility.

Financial Aid Of all full-time matriculated undergraduates who enrolled in 2009, 592 applied for aid, 492 were judged to have need, 111 had their need fully met. In 2009, 209 non-need-based awards were made. *Average percent of need met:* 79. *Average financial aid package:* $15,202. *Average need-based loan:* $3003. *Average need-based gift aid:* $13,075. *Average non-need-based aid:* $10,554.

Applying *Options:* electronic application. *Required:* high school transcript.

Freshman Application Contact Mr. Clinton G. Hobbs, Vice President for Enrollment Management, Young Harris College, PO Box 116, Young Harris, GA 30582-0098. *Phone:* 706-379-3111. *Toll-free phone:* 800-241-3754. *Fax:* 706-379-3108. *E-mail:* admissions@yhc.edu. *Web site:* http://www.yhc.edu/.

HAWAII

Argosy University, Hawai`i
Honolulu, Hawaii

Freshman Application Contact Argosy University, Hawai`i, 400 ASB Tower, 1001 Bishop Street, Honolulu, HI 96813. *Phone:* 808-536-5555. *Toll-free phone:* 888-323-2777. *Web site:* http://www.argosy.edu/hawaii/.

See page 1062 for the College Close-Up.

Brigham Young University–Hawaii
Laie, Hawaii

Freshman Application Contact Mr. Arapata P. Meha, Brigham Young University–Hawaii, 55-220 Kulanui Street, Laie, HI 96762-1294. *Phone:* 808-675-3731. *Fax:* 808-675-3741. *E-mail:* admissions@byuh.edu. *Web site:* http://www.byuh.edu/.

Chaminade University of Honolulu
Honolulu, Hawaii

- **Independent Roman Catholic** comprehensive, founded 1955
- **Urban** 62-acre campus with easy access to Honolulu
- **Endowment** $9.3 million
- **Coed** 1,294 undergraduate students, 98% full-time, 68% women, 32% men
- **Moderately difficult** entrance level, 90% of applicants were admitted

Undergraduates 1,262 full-time, 32 part-time. Students come from 38 states and territories; 12 other countries; 35% are from out of state; 3% Black or African American, non-Hispanic/Latino; 6% Hispanic/Latino; 27% Asian, non-Hispanic/Latino; 15% Native Hawaiian or other Pacific Islander, non-Hispanic/Latino; 0.7% American Indian or Alaska Native, non-Hispanic/Latino; 24% Two or more races, non-Hispanic/Latino; 6% Race/ethnicity unknown; 2% international; 11% transferred in; 32% live on campus. *Retention:* 72% of full-time freshmen returned.

Freshmen *Admission:* 1,008 applied, 908 admitted, 306 enrolled. *Average high school GPA:* 3.31. *Test scores:* SAT critical reading scores over 500: 36%; SAT math scores over 500: 35%; SAT writing scores over 500: 32%; ACT scores over 18: 77%; SAT critical reading scores over 600: 4%; SAT math scores over 600: 7%; SAT writing scores over 600: 4%; ACT scores over 24: 10%; ACT scores over 30: 2%.

Faculty *Student/faculty ratio:* 13:1.

Academics *Calendar:* semesters. *Degrees:* associate, bachelor's, master's, and postbachelor's certificates. *Special study options:* academic remediation for entering students, accelerated degree program, adult/continuing education programs, advanced placement credit, distance learning, double majors, independent study, internships, off-campus study, part-time degree program, student-designed majors, study abroad, summer session for credit. *ROTC:* Army (c), Air Force (c). *Unusual degree programs:* 3-2 engineering with University of Dayton, St. Mary's University of San Antonio; mathematics with St. Mary's University of San Antonio.

Computers on Campus 100 computers/terminals are available on campus for general student use. Students can access the following: computer help desk, free student e-mail accounts, online (class) grades, online (class) registration, online (class) schedules. Campuswide network is available. Wireless service is available via entire campus.

Student Life *Housing options:* coed, women-only. Campus housing is university owned and leased by the school. *Activities and organizations:* drama/theater group, student-run newspaper, choral group, Lumana O Samoa (Samoan Club), Kaimi Lalakea (Hawaiian Club), Rotaract, Residence Hall Association, Chaminade Student Government Association. *Campus security:* 24-hour emergency response devices and patrols, late-night transport/escort service,

controlled dormitory access. *Student services:* personal/psychological counseling.

Athletics Member NCAA. All Division II. *Intercollegiate sports:* basketball M(s), cross-country running M(s)/W(s), golf M/W, softball W(s), tennis M(s)/W(s), volleyball W(s), water polo M(s).

Standardized Tests *Required:* SAT or ACT (for admission), TOEFL for international students (for admission).

Costs (2011–12) *Comprehensive fee:* $29,540 includes full-time tuition ($18,300), mandatory fees ($140), and room and board ($11,100). Full-time tuition and fees vary according to course load. Part-time tuition: $610 per credit hour. Part-time tuition and fees vary according to course load. *Room and board:* Room and board charges vary according to board plan and housing facility.

Applying *Options:* electronic application, deferred entrance. *Application fee:* $50. *Required:* essay or personal statement, high school transcript, minimum 2.5 GPA. *Required for some:* minimum 2.8 GPA, 2 letters of recommendation, interview. *Recommended:* minimum 3.0 GPA, 2 letters of recommendation. *Application deadlines:* rolling (freshmen), rolling (transfers). *Notification:* continuous (freshmen), continuous (transfers).

Freshman Application Contact Ms. Shauna Pimentel, Associate Director of Admissions, Chaminade University of Honolulu, 3140 Waialae Avenue, Honolulu, HI 96816-1578. *Phone:* 808-739-8364. *Toll-free phone:* 800-735-3733. *Fax:* 808-739-4647. *E-mail:* admissions@chaminade.edu. *Web site:* http://www.chaminade.edu/.

Hawai`i Pacific University

Honolulu, Hawaii

- **Independent** comprehensive, founded 1965
- **Urban** 140-acre campus
- **Endowment** $81.8 million
- **Coed** 6,740 undergraduate students, 63% full-time, 55% women, 45% men
- **Moderately difficult** entrance level, 70% of applicants were admitted

Undergraduates 4,228 full-time, 2,512 part-time. Students come from 51 states and territories; 60 other countries; 29% are from out of state; 6% Black or African American, non-Hispanic/Latino; 13% Hispanic/Latino; 20% Asian, non-Hispanic/Latino; 3% Native Hawaiian or other Pacific Islander, non-Hispanic/Latino; 0.5% American Indian or Alaska Native, non-Hispanic/Latino; 11% Two or more races, non-Hispanic/Latino; 7% Race/ethnicity unknown; 10% international; 13% transferred in; 10% live on campus. *Retention:* 66% of full-time freshmen returned.

Freshmen *Admission:* 4,367 applied, 3,038 admitted, 555 enrolled. *Average high school GPA:* 3.33. *Test scores:* SAT critical reading scores over 500: 44%; SAT writing scores over 500: 42%; ACT scores over 18: 78%; SAT critical reading scores over 600: 13%; SAT writing scores over 600: 8%; ACT scores over 24: 33%; SAT critical reading scores over 700: 2%; SAT writing scores over 700: 1%; ACT scores over 30: 2%.

Faculty *Total:* 642, 41% full-time, 48% with terminal degrees. *Student/faculty ratio:* 15:1.

Academics *Calendar:* semesters. *Degrees:* certificates, associate, bachelor's, master's, post-master's, and postbachelor's certificates. *Special study options:* academic remediation for entering students, accelerated degree program, adult/continuing education programs, advanced placement credit, cooperative education, distance learning, double majors, English as a second language, freshman honors college, honors programs, independent study, internships, off-campus study, part-time degree program, services for LD students, student-designed majors, study abroad, summer session for credit. *ROTC:* Army (c), Air Force (c). *Unusual degree programs:* 3-2 engineering with Washington University in St. Louis, University of Southern California.

Computers on Campus 590 computers/terminals are available on campus for general student use. Students can access the following: campus intranet, computer help desk, free student e-mail accounts, online (class) grades, online (class) registration, online (class) schedules. Campuswide network is available. Wireless service is available via entire campus.

Student Life *Housing options:* coed. Campus housing is university owned and is provided by a third party. Freshman applicants given priority for college housing. *Activities and organizations:* drama/theater group, student-run newspaper, choral group, Student Government Association, Circle K International, Psychology Club, Student Nurses Association, Outspoken LGBT Cooperative. *Campus security:* 24-hour emergency response devices and patrols, student patrols, late-night transport/escort service, controlled dormitory access, Rave Alert System. *Student services:* personal/psychological counseling.

Athletics Member NCAA. All Division II. *Intercollegiate sports:* baseball M(s), basketball M(s)/W(s), cheerleading M(s)/W(s), cross-country running M(s)/W(s), golf M(s), soccer M(s)/W(s), softball W(s), tennis M(s)/W(s), volleyball W(s). *Intramural sports:* basketball M/W, football M/W, soccer M/W, softball M/W, table tennis M/W, tennis M/W, ultimate Frisbee M/W, volleyball M/W.

Standardized Tests *Required:* SAT or ACT (for admission).

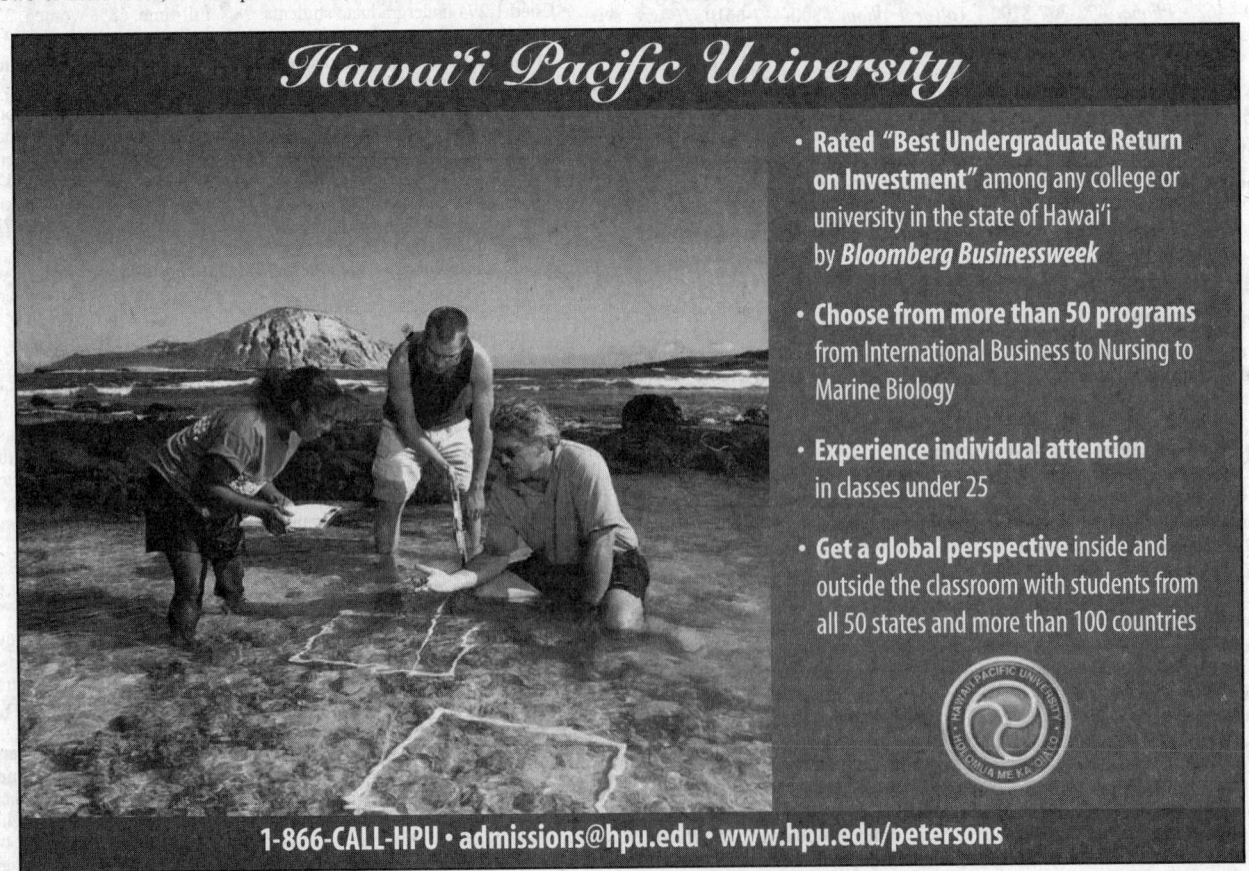

Costs (2012–13) *Comprehensive fee:* $30,830 includes full-time tuition ($18,500), mandatory fees ($100), and room and board ($12,230). Full-time tuition and fees vary according to course level, course load, degree level, location, program, and student level. Part-time tuition: $617 per credit hour. Part-time tuition and fees vary according to course level, course load, degree level, location, program, and student level. *Room and board:* Room and board charges vary according to housing facility. *Payment plan:* installment. *Waivers:* employees or children of employees.

Financial Aid Of all full-time matriculated undergraduates who enrolled in 2010, 3,031 applied for aid, 1,933 were judged to have need, 470 had their need fully met. 157 Federal Work-Study jobs (averaging $3000). In 2010, 182 non-need-based awards were made. *Average percent of need met:* 78%. *Average financial aid package:* $17,448. *Average need-based loan:* $6159. *Average need-based gift aid:* $2031. *Average non-need-based aid:* $2153. *Average indebtedness upon graduation:* $32,172.

Applying *Options:* electronic application, early admission, deferred entrance. *Application fee:* $50. *Required:* high school transcript, minimum 2.5 GPA. *Required for some:* interview. *Recommended:* essay or personal statement, 2 letters of recommendation. *Application deadlines:* rolling (freshmen), rolling (transfers). *Notification:* continuous (transfers).

Freshman Application Contact Mr. Scott Stensrud, Vice President, Enrollment Management, Hawai'i Pacific University, 1164 Bishop Street, Honolulu, HI 96813-2785. *Phone:* 808-544-0238. *Toll-free phone:* 866-225-5478. *Fax:* 808-544-1136. *E-mail:* admissions@hpu.edu. *Web site:* http://www.hpu.edu/.

See page 1360 for the College Close-Up.

Remington College–Honolulu Campus

Honolulu, Hawaii

Director of Admissions Louis LaMair, Director of Recruitment, Remington College–Honolulu Campus, 1111 Bishop Street, Suite 400, Honolulu, HI 96813. *Phone:* 808-942-1000. *Fax:* 808-533-3064. *E-mail:* louis.lamair@remingtoncollege.edu. *Web site:* http://www.remingtoncollege.edu/.

University of Hawaii at Hilo

Hilo, Hawaii

- **State-supported** comprehensive, founded 1970, part of University of Hawaii System
- **Small-town** 115-acre campus
- **Endowment** $2.8 million
- **Coed** 3,529 undergraduate students, 80% full-time, 59% women, 41% men
- **Moderately difficult** entrance level, 72% of applicants were admitted

Undergraduates 2,822 full-time, 707 part-time. Students come from 50 states and territories; 26 other countries; 26% are from out of state; 1% Black or African American, non-Hispanic/Latino; 10% Hispanic/Latino; 19% Asian, non-Hispanic/Latino; 13% Native Hawaiian or other Pacific Islander, non-Hispanic/Latino; 0.6% American Indian or Alaska Native, non-Hispanic/Latino; 27% Two or more races, non-Hispanic/Latino; 0.2% Race/ethnicity unknown; 5% international; 44% transferred in; 22% live on campus. *Retention:* 69% of full-time freshmen returned.

Freshmen *Admission:* 1,500 applied, 1,084 admitted, 471 enrolled. *Average high school GPA:* 3.5. *Test scores:* SAT critical reading scores over 500: 40%; SAT math scores over 500: 43%; SAT writing scores over 500: 30%; ACT scores over 18: 81%; SAT critical reading scores over 600: 9%; SAT math scores over 600: 12%; SAT writing scores over 600: 7%; ACT scores over 24: 27%; SAT critical reading scores over 700: 1%; SAT math scores over 700: 1%; ACT scores over 30: 1%.

Faculty *Total:* 300, 76% full-time. *Student/faculty ratio:* 14:1.

Academics *Calendar:* semesters. *Degrees:* certificates, bachelor's, master's, doctoral, postbachelor's, and first professional certificates. *Special study options:* advanced placement credit, distance learning, double majors, English as a second language, honors programs, independent study, internships, off-campus study, part-time degree program, services for LD students, student-designed majors, study abroad, summer session for credit.

Computers on Campus 600 computers/terminals are available on campus for general student use. Students can access the following: online (class) registration. Campuswide network is available.

Student Life *Housing options:* coed. Campus housing is university owned. *Activities and organizations:* drama/theater group, student-run newspaper, choral group, International Student Association, Hawaiian Leadership and Development, Delta Sigma Pi Business Fraternity, University Canoe Club, Samoan Club. *Campus security:* 24-hour emergency response devices and patrols, con-

trolled dormitory access. *Student services:* health clinic, personal/psychological counseling, women's center.

Athletics Member NCAA. All Division II except baseball (Division I). *Intercollegiate sports:* baseball M(s), basketball M(s), cross-country running M(s)/W(s), golf M(s), softball W(s), tennis M(s)/W(s), volleyball W(s). *Intramural sports:* archery M/W, badminton M/W, basketball M/W, bowling M/W, golf M/W, soccer M/W, softball M/W, table tennis M/W, tennis M/W, volleyball M/W, weight lifting M/W.

Standardized Tests *Required:* SAT or ACT (for admission).

Costs (2011–12) *Tuition:* state resident $5640 full-time, $235 per credit hour part-time; nonresident $17,112 full-time, $713 per credit hour part-time. Full-time tuition and fees vary according to reciprocity agreements. Part-time tuition and fees vary according to course load. *Required fees:* $304 full-time, $119 per term part-time. *Room and board:* $7134. Room and board charges vary according to board plan and housing facility.

Financial Aid Of all full-time matriculated undergraduates who enrolled in 2010, 2,191 applied for aid, 1,697 were judged to have need, 377 had their need fully met. 158 Federal Work-Study jobs (averaging $2065). 531 state and other part-time jobs (averaging $3993). In 2010, 12 non-need-based awards were made. *Average percent of need met:* 72%. *Average financial aid package:* $10,683. *Average need-based loan:* $4423. *Average need-based gift aid:* $4970. *Average non-need-based aid:* $1615. *Average indebtedness upon graduation:* $11,944.

Applying *Options:* electronic application, deferred entrance. *Application fee:* $50. *Required:* high school transcript. *Recommended:* minimum 3.0 GPA. *Application deadlines:* 7/1 (freshmen), 7/1 (transfers). *Notification:* 7/31 (freshmen), 7/31 (transfers).

Freshman Application Contact Mr. James Cromwell, Student Services Specialist/Director of Admissions, University of Hawaii at Hilo, 200 West Kawili Street, Hilo, HI 96720-4091. *Phone:* 808-974-7414. *Toll-free phone:* 800-897-4456. *Fax:* 808-933-0861. *E-mail:* uhhao@hawaii.edu. *Web site:* http://www.uhh.hawaii.edu/.

University of Hawaii at Manoa

Honolulu, Hawaii

- **State-supported** university, founded 1907, part of University of Hawaii System
- **Urban** 320,300-acre campus with easy access to Honolulu
- **Endowment** $145.1 million
- **Coed** 14,402 undergraduate students, 81% full-time, 54% women, 46% men
- **Moderately difficult** entrance level, 78% of applicants were admitted

Undergraduates 11,634 full-time, 2,768 part-time. Students come from 56 states and territories; 54 other countries; 23% are from out of state; 1% Black or African American, non-Hispanic/Latino; 2% Hispanic/Latino; 41% Asian, non-Hispanic/Latino; 17% Native Hawaiian or other Pacific Islander, non-Hispanic/Latino; 0.4% American Indian or Alaska Native, non-Hispanic/Latino; 14% Two or more races, non-Hispanic/Latino; 0.1% Race/ethnicity unknown; 3% international; 13% transferred in; 23% live on campus.

Freshmen *Admission:* 6,541 applied, 5,130 admitted, 2,010 enrolled. *Average high school GPA:* 3.43. *Test scores:* SAT critical reading scores over 500: 66%; SAT math scores over 500: 76%; SAT writing scores over 500: 65%; ACT scores over 18: 97%; SAT critical reading scores over 600: 20%; SAT math scores over 600: 30%; SAT writing scores over 600: 14%; ACT scores over 24: 42%; SAT critical reading scores over 700: 2%; SAT math scores over 700: 4%; SAT writing scores over 700: 2%; ACT scores over 30: 5%.

Faculty *Total:* 1,229, 95% full-time, 85% with terminal degrees. *Student/faculty ratio:* 14:1.

Academics *Calendar:* semesters. *Degrees:* certificates, bachelor's, master's, doctoral, postbachelor's, and first professional certificates. *Special study options:* accelerated degree program, advanced placement credit, cooperative education, distance learning, double majors, English as a second language, honors programs, independent study, internships, off-campus study, part-time degree program, services for LD students, student-designed majors, study abroad, summer session for credit. *ROTC:* Army (b), Air Force (b).

Computers on Campus 400 computers/terminals are available on campus for general student use. Students can access the following: campus intranet, computer help desk, free student e-mail accounts, online (class) grades, online (class) registration, online (class) schedules. Campuswide network is available. 99% of college-owned or -operated housing units are wired for high-speed Internet access. Wireless service is available via entire campus.

Student Life *Housing options:* coed, disabled students. Campus housing is university owned. Freshman applicants given priority for college housing. *Activities and organizations:* drama/theater group, student-run newspaper, radio station, choral group, marching band, Associated Students of University of Hawaii, Campus Center Board, Broadcast Communication Authority, Board of Publications, Student Activities and Program Fee Board, national fraterni-

ties, national sororities. *Campus security:* 24-hour emergency response devices and patrols, student patrols, late-night transport/escort service, controlled dormitory access. *Student services:* health clinic, personal/psychological counseling, women's center.

Athletics Member NCAA. All Division I except football (Division I-A). *Intercollegiate sports:* archery M, baseball M(s), basketball M(s)/W(s), cheerleading M(s)/W(s), cross-country running W(s), golf M(s)/W(s), sailing M/W, soccer W(s), softball W(s), swimming and diving M(s)/W(s), tennis M(s)/W(s), track and field W(s), volleyball M(s)/W(s), water polo W(s). *Intramural sports:* badminton M/W, basketball M/W, crew M/W, cross-country running M/W, golf M/W, rugby M, sailing M/W, soccer M, softball M, swimming and diving M/W, table tennis M/W, tennis M/W, track and field M/W, ultimate Frisbee M/W, volleyball M/W, weight lifting M/W, wrestling M/W.

Standardized Tests *Required:* SAT or ACT (for admission).

Costs (2012–13) *Tuition:* state resident $8664 full-time, $361 per credit hour part-time; nonresident $24,912 full-time, $1038 per credit hour part-time. Full-time tuition and fees vary according to class time, course level, course load, degree level, program, reciprocity agreements, and student level. Part-time tuition and fees vary according to class time, course level, course load, degree level, program, reciprocity agreements, and student level. *Required fees:* $740 full-time. *Room and board:* $10,279; room only: $6304. Room and board charges vary according to board plan and housing facility. *Payment plan:* installment. *Waivers:* minority students, adult students, senior citizens, and employees or children of employees.

Financial Aid Of all full-time matriculated undergraduates who enrolled in 2010, 8,850 applied for aid, 5,929 were judged to have need, 1,873 had their need fully met. 438 Federal Work-Study jobs (averaging $2265). In 2010, 1367 non-need-based awards were made. *Average percent of need met:* 73%. *Average financial aid package:* $11,938. *Average need-based loan:* $4518. *Average need-based gift aid:* $8524. *Average non-need-based aid:* $8697. *Average indebtedness upon graduation:* $17,447.

Applying *Options:* electronic application. *Application fee:* $70. *Required:* high school transcript, minimum 2.8 GPA. *Application deadlines:* 5/1 (freshmen), 5/1 (transfers). *Notification:* continuous (freshmen), continuous (transfers).

Freshman Application Contact Ms. Lisa Buto, Student Services Specialist, University of Hawaii at Manoa, 2600 Campus Road, Room 001, Honolulu, HI 96822. *Phone:* 808-956-8975. *Toll-free phone:* 800-823-9771. *Fax:* 808-956-4148. *E-mail:* ar-info@hawaii.edu. *Web site:* http://manoa.hawaii.edu/.

University of Hawaii Maui College

Kahului, Hawaii

Freshman Application Contact Mr. Stephen Kameda, Director of Admissions and Records, University of Hawaii Maui College, 310 Kaahumanu Avenue, Kahului, HI 96732. *Phone:* 808-984-3267. *Toll-free phone:* 800-479-6692. *Fax:* 808-242-9618. *E-mail:* kameda@hawaii.edu. *Web site:* http://maui.hawaii.edu/.

University of Hawaii–West Oahu

Pearl City, Hawaii

- **State-supported** 4-year, founded 1976, part of University of Hawaii System
- **Small-town** campus with easy access to Honolulu
- **Coed** 1,662 undergraduate students, 30% full-time, 68% women, 32% men
- **Moderately difficult** entrance level, 72% of applicants were admitted

Undergraduates 500 full-time, 1,162 part-time. 10% are from out of state; 1% Black or African American, non-Hispanic/Latino; 2% Hispanic/Latino; 40% Asian, non-Hispanic/Latino; 28% Native Hawaiian or other Pacific Islander, non-Hispanic/Latino; 0.4% American Indian or Alaska Native, non-Hispanic/Latino; 13% Two or more races, non-Hispanic/Latino; 0.3% Race/ethnicity unknown; 0.5% international; 30% transferred in. *Retention:* 37% of full-time freshmen returned.

Freshmen *Admission:* 448 applied, 324 admitted, 122 enrolled. *Average high school GPA:* 3.22.

Faculty *Total:* 74, 66% full-time, 70% with terminal degrees. *Student/faculty ratio:* 16:1.

Academics *Calendar:* semesters. *Degree:* certificates and bachelor's. *Special study options:* part-time degree program. *ROTC:* Army (c), Air Force (c).

Computers on Campus Students can access the following: computer help desk, free student e-mail accounts, online (class) grades, online (class) registration, online (class) schedules. Campuswide network is available. Wireless service is available via classrooms.

Student Life *Housing:* college housing not available. *Campus security:* 24-hour emergency response devices and patrols, late-night transport/escort service. *Student services:* personal/psychological counseling.

Standardized Tests *Recommended:* SAT or ACT (for admission).

Costs (2011–12) *Tuition:* state resident $5136 full-time, $214 per credit part-time; nonresident $15,744 full-time, $656 per credit part-time. *Required fees:* $10 full-time. *Payment plan:* installment. *Waivers:* employees or children of employees.

Financial Aid Of all full-time matriculated undergraduates who enrolled in 2010, 282 applied for aid, 282 were judged to have need. In 2010, 2 non-need-based awards were made. *Average percent of need met:* 50%. *Average financial aid package:* $6192. *Average need-based loan:* $4118. *Average need-based gift aid:* $3652. *Average non-need-based aid:* $1000.

Applying *Options:* deferred entrance. *Application fee:* $50. *Required:* minimum 2.7 GPA. *Required for some:* high school transcript, 2 letters of recommendation, college transcripts. *Application deadlines:* 3/1 (freshmen), 3/1 (transfers). *Notification:* continuous (freshmen), continuous (transfers).

Freshman Application Contact Robyn Oshiro, University of Hawaii–West Oahu, 96-129 Ala Ike Street, Pearl City, HI 96782. *Phone:* 808-454-4700. *Toll-free phone:* 866-299-8656. *Fax:* 808-453-6075. *E-mail:* admissions@hawaii.edu. *Web site:* http://www.uhwo.hawaii.edu/.

University of Phoenix–Hawaii Campus

Honolulu, Hawaii

Freshman Application Contact Marc Booker, Sr. Director, Office of Admissions and Evaluation, University of Phoenix–Hawaii Campus, 4035 South Riverpoint Parkway, Mail Stop CF-L101, Phoenix, AZ 85040. *Phone:* 602-557-4609. *Toll-free phone:* 866-766-0766. *Fax:* 480-643-1156. *Web site:* http://www.phoenix.edu/.

IDAHO

Boise Bible College

Boise, Idaho

Freshman Application Contact Russell Grove, Director of Admissions, Boise Bible College, 8695 West Marigold Street, Boise, ID 83714-1220. *Phone:* 208-376-7731. *Toll-free phone:* 800-893-7755. *Fax:* 208-376-7743. *E-mail:* rgrove@boisebible.edu. *Web site:* http://www.boisebible.edu/.

Boise State University

Boise, Idaho

- **State-supported** university, founded 1932, part of Idaho System of Higher Education
- **Urban** 175-acre campus
- **Endowment** $75.6 million
- **Coed** 17,369 undergraduate students, 73% full-time, 53% women, 47% men
- **Moderately difficult** entrance level, 81% of applicants were admitted

Undergraduates 12,711 full-time, 4,658 part-time. Students come from 47 states and territories; 64 other countries; 12% are from out of state; 2% Black or African American, non-Hispanic/Latino; 7% Hispanic/Latino; 3% Asian, non-Hispanic/Latino; 0.6% Native Hawaiian or other Pacific Islander, non-Hispanic/Latino; 1% American Indian or Alaska Native, non-Hispanic/Latino; 1% Two or more races, non-Hispanic/Latino; 5% Race/ethnicity unknown; 2% international; 6% transferred in; 12% live on campus. *Retention:* 69% of full-time freshmen returned.

Freshmen *Admission:* 5,298 applied, 4,291 admitted, 2,330 enrolled. *Average high school GPA:* 3.31. *Test scores:* SAT critical reading scores over 500: 60%; SAT math scores over 500: 66%; SAT writing scores over 500: 49%; ACT scores over 18: 93%; SAT critical reading scores over 600: 17%; SAT math scores over 600: 19%; SAT writing scores over 600: 10%; ACT scores over 24: 39%; SAT critical reading scores over 700: 2%; SAT math scores over 700: 2%; SAT writing scores over 700: 1%; ACT scores over 30: 3%.

Faculty *Total:* 1,251, 46% full-time, 44% with terminal degrees. *Student/faculty ratio:* 19:1.

Academics *Calendar:* semesters. *Degrees:* associate, bachelor's, master's, doctoral, postbachelor's, and first professional certificates. *Special study options:* academic remediation for entering students, adult/continuing education programs, advanced placement credit, cooperative education, distance learning, double majors, English as a second language, freshman honors college, honors programs, independent study, internships, off-campus study, part-time degree program, services for LD students, student-designed majors, study abroad, summer session for credit. *ROTC:* Army (b).

Computers on Campus 900 computers/terminals are available on campus for general student use. Students can access the following: online (class) registration. Campuswide network is available. 100% of college-owned or -operated housing units are wired for high-speed Internet access. Wireless service is available via classrooms, libraries, student centers.

Student Life *Housing options:* coed, men-only, women-only. Campus housing is university owned. Freshman applicants given priority for college housing. *Activities and organizations:* drama/theater group, student-run newspaper, choral group, marching band, Latter-Day Saints Student Association, Residence Hall Association, Organization of Student Social Workers, Marching Band Association, Teacher Education Association, national fraternities, national sororities. *Campus security:* 24-hour emergency response devices and patrols. *Student services:* health clinic, personal/psychological counseling, women's center, legal services.

Athletics Member NCAA. All Division I except football (Division I-A). *Intercollegiate sports:* basketball M(s)/W(s), cross-country running M(s)/W(s), golf M(s)/W(s), gymnastics W(s), soccer W(s), softball W(s), swimming and diving W(s)(c), tennis M(s)/W(s), track and field M(s)/W(s), volleyball W(s), wrestling M(s). *Intramural sports:* baseball M, basketball M/W, bowling M/W, lacrosse W(c), racquetball M/W, rock climbing M/W, skiing (downhill) M(c)/W(c), soccer M/W, softball M/W, tennis M/W, volleyball M/W, weight lifting M/W.

Standardized Tests *Required for some:* SAT or ACT (for admission).

Costs (2011–12) *One-time required fee:* $75. *Tuition:* state resident $3724 full-time, $151 per credit hour part-time; nonresident $14,124 full-time, $243 per credit hour part-time. Full-time tuition and fees vary according to reciprocity agreements. *Required fees:* $1842 full-time, $88 per credit hour part-time. *Room and board:* $6020; room only: $2840. Room and board charges vary according to board plan and housing facility. *Payment plan:* installment. *Waivers:* senior citizens and employees or children of employees.

Financial Aid Of all full-time matriculated undergraduates who enrolled in 2011, 9,175 applied for aid, 8,877 were judged to have need, 2,536 had their need fully met. 819 Federal Work-Study jobs (averaging $3815). 880 state and other part-time jobs (averaging $3796). In 2011, 1124 non-need-based awards were made. *Average percent of need met:* 22%. *Average financial aid package:* $9464. *Average need-based loan:* $7321. *Average need-based gift aid:* $4641. *Average non-need-based aid:* $1392. *Average indebtedness upon graduation:* $24,905. *Financial aid deadline:* 6/30.

Applying *Options:* electronic application. *Application fee:* $55. *Required for some:* high school transcript, minimum 2.0 GPA. *Recommended:* high school transcript. *Application deadlines:* 5/15 (freshmen), 5/15 (transfers). *Notification:* continuous (freshmen), continuous (transfers).

Freshman Application Contact Ms. Jenny Cerda, Dean of Admissions, Boise State University, Enrollment Services, 1910 University Drive, Boise, ID 83725. *Phone:* 208-426-1177. *Toll-free phone:* 800-824-7017. *E-mail:* bsuinfo@boisestate.edu. *Web site:* http://www.boisestate.edu/.

Brigham Young University–Idaho
Rexburg, Idaho

Freshman Application Contact Brigham Young University–Idaho, Rexburg, ID 83460. *Phone:* 208-496-1310. *Web site:* http://www.byui.edu/.

Broadview University-Boise
Meridian, Idaho

- **Proprietary** 4-year, part of Globe Education Network (GEN) which is composed of Globe University, Minnesota School of Business, Broadview University, The Institute of Production and Recording and Minnesota School of Cosmetology
- **Small-town** 4-acre campus
- **Coed**

Faculty *Total:* 16, 25% full-time, 31% with terminal degrees. *Student/faculty ratio:* 5:1.

Academics *Degrees:* diplomas, associate, and bachelor's. *Special study options:* academic remediation for entering students, accelerated degree program, adult/continuing education programs, advanced placement credit, internships, part-time degree program, services for LD students, summer session for credit.

Computers on Campus 45 computers/terminals and 128 ports are available on campus for general student use. Students can access the following: computer help desk, free student e-mail accounts, online (class) grades, online (class) registration, online (class) schedules. Campuswide network is available. Wireless service is available via entire campus.

Student Life *Housing:* college housing not available. *Campus security:* 24-hour emergency response devices, late-night transport/escort service.

Standardized Tests *Required:* AccuPlacer is required of all applicants unless documentation of a minimum ACT composite score of 21 or documentation of a minimum composite score of 1485 on the SAT is presented (for admission).

Applying *Options:* electronic application. *Application fee:* $50. *Required:* high school transcript, interview. *Required for some:* essay or personal statement, 2 letters of recommendation, GED certificate in lieu of high school transcript. *Application deadlines:* rolling (freshmen), rolling (out-of-state freshmen), rolling (transfers). *Notification:* continuous (freshmen), continuous (out-of-state freshmen), continuous (transfers).

Freshman Application Contact Broadview University-Boise, 2750 East Gala Court, Meridian, ID 83642. *Phone:* 208-577-2900. *Toll-free phone:* 877-572-5757. *Web site:* http://www.broadviewuniversity.edu/.

Brown Mackie College–Boise
Boise, Idaho

- **Proprietary** primarily 2-year, part of Education Management Corporation
- **Coed**

Academics *Degrees:* diplomas, associate, and bachelor's.

Costs (2011–12) *Tuition:* Tuition varies by program. Students should contact Brown Mackie College for tuition information.

Freshman Application Contact Brown Mackie College–Boise, 9050 West Overland Road, Suite 100, Boise, ID 83709. *Phone:* 208-321-8800. *Web site:* http://www.brownmackie.edu/boise/.

See page 1192 for the College Close-Up.

The College of Idaho
Caldwell, Idaho

- **Independent** comprehensive, founded 1891
- **Suburban** 50-acre campus
- **Coed** 1,018 undergraduate students, 95% full-time, 58% women, 42% men
- **Moderately difficult** entrance level, 66% of applicants were admitted

Undergraduates 970 full-time, 48 part-time. 19% are from out of state; 1% Black or African American, non-Hispanic/Latino; 13% Hispanic/Latino; 2% Asian, non-Hispanic/Latino; 0.7% Native Hawaiian or other Pacific Islander, non-Hispanic/Latino; 0.9% American Indian or Alaska Native, non-Hispanic/Latino; 0.5% Two or more races, non-Hispanic/Latino; 19% Race/ethnicity unknown; 10% international; 4% transferred in; 52% live on campus. *Retention:* 80% of full-time freshmen returned.

Freshmen *Admission:* 1,185 applied, 777 admitted, 240 enrolled. *Average high school GPA:* 3.7. *Test scores:* SAT critical reading scores over 500: 68%; SAT math scores over 500: 71%; SAT writing scores over 500: 64%; ACT scores over 18: 99%; SAT critical reading scores over 600: 42%; SAT math scores over 600: 38%; SAT writing scores over 600: 25%; ACT scores over 24: 66%; SAT critical reading scores over 700: 8%; SAT math scores over 700: 9%; SAT writing scores over 700: 7%; ACT scores over 30: 10%.

Faculty *Total:* 101, 73% full-time, 67% with terminal degrees. *Student/faculty ratio:* 12:1.

Academics *Calendar:* 12-6-12 week calendar. *Degrees:* bachelor's and master's. *Special study options:* part-time degree program. *ROTC:* Army (c). *Unusual degree programs:* 3-2 business administration with Boise State University, Gonzaga University; engineering with University of Idaho, Columbia University, Washington University in St. Louis, Boise State University; nursing with Idaho State University; law, natural resources with University of Idaho; speech language pathology, occupational therapy, physical therapy, physician assistant, pharmacy with Idaho State University.

Computers on Campus Students can access the following: campus intranet, computer help desk, free student e-mail accounts, online (class) grades, online (class) schedules, online course syllabi, course assignments, course discussion, College of Idaho catalog. Campuswide network is available. 100% of college-owned or -operated housing units are wired for high-speed Internet access. Wireless service is available via entire campus.

Student Life *Housing:* on-campus residence required through sophomore year. *Options:* coed, disabled students. Campus housing is university owned. Freshman campus housing is guaranteed. *Campus security:* 24-hour emergency response devices and patrols, student patrols, late-night transport/escort service, controlled dormitory access.

Athletics Member NAIA. *Intercollegiate sports:* baseball M(s), basketball M(s)/W(s), cross-country running M(s)/W(s), golf M(s)/W(s), skiing (downhill) M(s)/W(s), soccer M(s)/W(s), softball W(s), swimming and diving M(s)/W(s), tennis M(s)/W(s), track and field M(s)/W(s), volleyball W(s). *Intramural sports:* badminton M/W, basketball M/W, football M/W, soccer M/W, softball M/W, ultimate Frisbee M/W, volleyball M/W.

Standardized Tests *Required:* SAT or ACT (for admission).

Costs (2012–13) *Comprehensive fee:* $31,088 includes full-time tuition ($22,600), mandatory fees ($375), and room and board ($8113). Part-time tuition: $940 per credit hour. Part-time tuition and fees vary according to course load. *Room and board:* Room and board charges vary according to board plan and housing facility.

Financial Aid Of all full-time matriculated undergraduates who enrolled in 2011, 755 applied for aid, 742 were judged to have need, 85 had their need fully met. In 2011, 276 non-need-based awards were made. *Average percent of need met:* 77%. *Average financial aid package:* $18,958. *Average need-based loan:* $4464. *Average need-based gift aid:* $6837. *Average non-need-based aid:* $11,656. *Average indebtedness upon graduation:* $24,939.

Applying *Options:* electronic application, early admission, early action, deferred entrance. *Required:* essay or personal statement, high school transcript, minimum 2.0 GPA, 1 letter of recommendation. *Recommended:* interview, class rank, extracurricular resume. *Application deadlines:* 8/1 (freshmen), 8/1 (transfers), 11/15 (early action). *Notification:* continuous (freshmen), continuous (transfers), 11/15 (early action).

Freshman Application Contact Brian Bava, Interim Dean of Enrollment Management, The College of Idaho, 2112 Cleveland Boulevard, Caldwell, ID 83605-4432. *Phone:* 208-459-5319. *Toll-free phone:* 800-244-3246. *Fax:* 208-459-5757. *E-mail:* admission@collegeofidaho.edu. *Web site:* http://www.collegeofidaho.edu/.

Idaho State University

Pocatello, Idaho

- **State-supported** university, founded 1901
- **Urban** 1100-acre campus
- **Coed** 10,536 undergraduate students
- **Minimally difficult** entrance level, 93% of applicants were admitted

Undergraduates 6% are from out of state; 1% Black or African American, non-Hispanic/Latino; 8% Hispanic/Latino; 1% Asian, non-Hispanic/Latino; 0.2% Native Hawaiian or other Pacific Islander, non-Hispanic/Latino; 2% American Indian or Alaska Native, non-Hispanic/Latino; 1% Two or more races, non-Hispanic/Latino; 6% Race/ethnicity unknown; 3% international; 7% live on campus.

Freshmen *Admission:* 3,253 applied, 3,035 admitted. *Average high school GPA:* 3.16. *Test scores:* SAT critical reading scores over 500: 54%; SAT math scores over 500: 71%; SAT writing scores over 500: 49%; ACT scores over 18: 80%; SAT critical reading scores over 600: 20%; SAT math scores over 600: 35%; SAT writing scores over 600: 13%; ACT scores over 24: 29%; SAT critical reading scores over 700: 7%; SAT math scores over 700: 5%; ACT scores over 30: 4%.

Faculty *Total:* 846, 71% full-time. *Student/faculty ratio:* 15:1.

Academics *Calendar:* semesters. *Degrees:* certificates, associate, bachelor's, master's, doctoral, post-master's, postbachelor's, and first professional certificates. *Special study options:* adult/continuing education programs, part-time degree program. *ROTC:* Army (b).

Computers on Campus 697 computers/terminals are available on campus for general student use. Students can access the following: computer help desk, free student e-mail accounts, online (class) grades, online (class) registration, online (class) schedules. Campuswide network is available. 100% of college-owned or -operated housing units are wired for high-speed Internet access. Wireless service is available via classrooms, computer centers, computer labs, dorm rooms, learning centers, libraries, student centers.

Student Life *Housing options:* coed, men-only, women-only, disabled students. Campus housing is university owned. *Campus security:* 24-hour emergency response devices and patrols, late-night transport/escort service, controlled dormitory access.

Athletics Member NCAA. All Division I except football (Division I-AA). *Intercollegiate sports:* basketball M(s)/W(s), cross-country running M(s)/W(s), golf W(s), soccer W(s), softball W(s), tennis M(s)/W(s), track and field M(s)/W(s), volleyball W(s). *Intramural sports:* badminton M/W, basketball M/W, bowling M/W, cross-country running M/W, fencing M(c)/W(c), football M, golf M/W, racquetball M/W, skiing (cross-country) M/W, soccer M/W, softball M/W, table tennis M/W, tennis M/W, track and field M/W, ultimate Frisbee M/W, volleyball M/W, water polo M/W, wrestling M.

Standardized Tests *Required:* SAT or ACT (for admission). *Recommended:* ACT (for admission).

Costs (2011–12) *One-time required fee:* $40. *Tuition:* state resident $4180 full-time, $290 per credit part-time; nonresident $15,416 full-time, $451 per credit part-time. Full-time tuition and fees vary according to course load, program, and reciprocity agreements. Part-time tuition and fees vary according to course load and reciprocity agreements. *Required fees:* $1616 full-time. *Room and board:* $5322; room only: $2422. Room and board charges vary according to board plan and housing facility. *Payment plan:* deferred payment. *Waivers:* senior citizens and employees or children of employees.

Financial Aid Of all full-time matriculated undergraduates who enrolled in 2010, 6,664 applied for aid, 6,040 were judged to have need, 157 had their need fully met. In 2010, 353 non-need-based awards were made. *Average percent of need met:* 53%. *Average financial aid package:* $9376. *Average need-based loan:* $3869. *Average need-based gift aid:* $4792. *Average non-need-based aid:* $1810. *Average indebtedness upon graduation:* $21,939. *Financial aid deadline:* 3/1.

Applying *Options:* electronic application, early admission, deferred entrance. *Application fee:* $40. *Required:* high school transcript, minimum 2.0 GPA. *Application deadlines:* rolling (freshmen), rolling (transfers). *Notification:* continuous (freshmen), continuous (transfers).

Freshman Application Contact Admissions and Registration Office, Idaho State University, 921 South 7th, Stop 8270, Pocatello, ID 83209-8270. *Phone:* 208-282-2475. *Fax:* 208-282-4511. *E-mail:* info@isu.edu. *Web site:* http://www.isu.edu/.

ITT Technical Institute

Boise, Idaho

- **Proprietary** primarily 2-year, founded 1906, part of ITT Educational Services, Inc.
- **Urban** campus
- **Coed**
- **Minimally difficult** entrance level

Academics *Calendar:* quarters. *Degrees:* associate and bachelor's.

Student Life *Housing:* college housing not available.

Financial Aid Of all full-time matriculated undergraduates who enrolled in 2010, 9 Federal Work-Study jobs (averaging $5500).

Freshman Application Contact Director of Recruitment, ITT Technical Institute, 12302 West Explorer Drive, Boise, ID 83713. *Phone:* 208-322-8844. *Toll-free phone:* 800-666-4888. *Fax:* 208-322-0173. *Web site:* http://www.itt-tech.edu/.

Lewis-Clark State College

Lewiston, Idaho

- **State-supported** 4-year, founded 1893
- **Small-town** 44-acre campus
- **Coed** 4,693 undergraduate students, 60% full-time, 59% women, 41% men
- **Minimally difficult** entrance level, 63% of applicants were admitted

Undergraduates 2,794 full-time, 1,899 part-time. 19% are from out of state; 0.7% Black or African American, non-Hispanic/Latino; 5% Hispanic/Latino; 0.7% Asian, non-Hispanic/Latino; 0.2% Native Hawaiian or other Pacific Islander, non-Hispanic/Latino; 3% American Indian or Alaska Native, non-Hispanic/Latino; 4% Two or more races, non-Hispanic/Latino; 1% Race/ethnicity unknown; 3% international; 9% transferred in.

Freshmen *Admission:* 1,365 applied, 866 admitted, 625 enrolled. *Average high school GPA:* 2.98. *Test scores:* SAT critical reading scores over 500: 47%; SAT math scores over 500: 40%; ACT scores over 18: 74%; SAT critical reading scores over 600: 9%; SAT math scores over 600: 9%; ACT scores over 24: 15%; SAT critical reading scores over 700: 2%; ACT scores over 30: 1%.

Faculty *Total:* 249, 64% full-time, 43% with terminal degrees. *Student/faculty ratio:* 18:1.

Academics *Calendar:* semesters. *Degrees:* certificates, associate, and bachelor's. *Special study options:* adult/continuing education programs, part-time degree program, study abroad. *ROTC:* Army (c), Navy (c), Air Force (c).

Computers on Campus Students can access the following: online (class) registration. Campuswide network is available.

Student Life *Housing options:* coed. Campus housing is university owned, leased by the school and is provided by a third party. *Campus security:* 24-hour emergency response devices and patrols, student patrols, late-night transport/escort service.

Athletics Member NAIA. *Intercollegiate sports:* baseball M(s), basketball M(s)/W(s), cross-country running M(s)/W(s), golf M(s)/W(s), tennis M(s)/W(s), volleyball W(s). *Intramural sports:* badminton M/W, baseball M/W, basketball M/W, bowling M/W, field hockey M/W, football M/W, golf M/W, lacrosse M/W, rock climbing M/W, rugby M/W, skiing (cross-country) M/W, skiing (downhill) M/W, soccer M/W, softball M/W, table tennis M/W, tennis M/W, track and field M/W, volleyball M/W, weight lifting M/W.

Standardized Tests *Required for some:* SAT or ACT (for admission).

Costs (2011–12) *Tuition:* state resident $5348 full-time, $273 per credit part-time; nonresident $14,880 full-time. Full-time tuition and fees vary according to course load and reciprocity agreements. *Room and board:* Room and board charges vary according to board plan and housing facility. *Payment plan:* deferred payment. *Waivers:* senior citizens and employees or children of employees.

Financial Aid Of all full-time matriculated undergraduates who enrolled in 2010, 2,266 applied for aid, 2,037 were judged to have need, 298 had their need fully met. 75 Federal Work-Study jobs (averaging $1304). 80 state and other part-time jobs (averaging $1387). In 2010, 170 non-need-based awards were made. *Average percent of need met:* 15%. *Average financial aid package:* $8244. *Average need-based loan:* $3884. *Average need-based gift aid:* $4583. *Average non-need-based aid:* $2392.

Applying *Options:* electronic application, deferred entrance. *Application fee:* $35. *Required:* high school transcript, minimum 2.0 GPA. *Required for some:* interview. *Application deadlines:* rolling (freshmen), rolling (transfers). *Notification:* continuous (freshmen), continuous (transfers).

Freshman Application Contact Soo Lee Bruce-Smith, Coordinator of New Student Recruitment, Lewis-Clark State College, 500 Eighth Avenue, Lewiston, ID 83501-2698. *Phone:* 208-792-2210. *Toll-free phone:* 800-933-5272. *Fax:* 208-792-2876. *E-mail:* admissions@lcsc.edu. *Web site:* http://www.lcsc.edu/.

New Saint Andrews College
Moscow, Idaho

- **Independent Christian** comprehensive, founded 1993
- **Small-town** campus
- **Coed** 151 undergraduate students, 88% full-time, 51% women, 49% men
- **Moderately difficult** entrance level, 77% of applicants were admitted

Undergraduates 133 full-time, 18 part-time. Students come from 26 states and territories, 7 other countries; 83% are from out of state; 3% Hispanic/Latino; 17% Race/ethnicity unknown; 3% international; 5% transferred in. *Retention:* 86% of full-time freshmen returned.

Freshmen *Admission:* 87 applied, 67 admitted, 44 enrolled. *Test scores:* SAT critical reading scores over 500: 100%; SAT math scores over 500: 82%; SAT writing scores over 500: 85%; ACT scores over 18: 100%; SAT critical reading scores over 600: 85%; SAT math scores over 600: 35%; SAT writing scores over 600: 50%; ACT scores over 24: 79%; SAT critical reading scores over 700: 29%; SAT math scores over 700: 6%; SAT writing scores over 700: 6%.

Faculty *Total:* 17, 35% full-time, 53% with terminal degrees. *Student/faculty ratio:* 15:1.

Academics *Calendar:* 4 8-week terms. *Degrees:* associate, bachelor's, master's, and postbachelor's certificates. *Special study options:* advanced placement credit, independent study, part-time degree program, summer session for credit.

Computers on Campus 6 computers/terminals and 6 ports are available on campus for general student use. Students can access the following: campus intranet, free student e-mail accounts, online (class) grades, online (class) registration, online (class) schedules. Campuswide network is available. Wireless service is available via entire campus.

Student Life *Housing:* college housing not available. *Activities and organizations:* choral group, Students for the Relief of the Oppressed, Nursing Home Visits and Elderly Assistance (snow and leaf removal), Blood Drives, Fall Carnival, St. Andrews Day Food Bank Drive. *Campus security:* 24-hour emergency response devices. *Student services:* personal/psychological counseling.

Standardized Tests *Required:* SAT or ACT (for admission).

Costs (2012–13) *Tuition:* $10,750 full-time, $850 per course part-time. Full-time tuition and fees vary according to program. Part-time tuition and fees vary according to program. No tuition increase for student's term of enrollment. *Payment plan:* installment. *Waivers:* employees or children of employees.

Applying *Options:* electronic application, deferred entrance. *Application fee:* $40. *Required:* essay or personal statement, high school transcript, 2 letters of recommendation. *Required for some:* interview. *Application deadlines:* 2/15 (freshmen), 2/15 (transfers). *Notification:* 3/15 (freshmen), 3/15 (transfers).

Freshman Application Contact Mr. John Sawyer, Director of Student Recruitment, New Saint Andrews College, PO Box 9025, Moscow, ID 83843. *Phone:* 208-882-1566 Ext. 100. *Fax:* 208-882-4293. *E-mail:* info@nsa.edu. *Web site:* http://www.nsa.edu/.

Northwest Nazarene University
Nampa, Idaho

- **Independent** comprehensive, founded 1913, affiliated with Church of the Nazarene
- **Small-town** 85-acre campus with easy access to Boise
- **Endowment** $27.0 million
- **Coed** 1,347 undergraduate students, 88% full-time, 59% women, 41% men
- **Moderately difficult** entrance level, 69% of applicants were admitted

Undergraduates 1,183 full-time, 164 part-time. 50% are from out of state; 1% Black or African American, non-Hispanic/Latino; 6% Hispanic/Latino; 2% Asian, non-Hispanic/Latino; 0.3% Native Hawaiian or other Pacific Islander, non-Hispanic/Latino; 0.7% American Indian or Alaska Native, non-Hispanic/Latino; 0.7% Two or more races, non-Hispanic/Latino; 13% Race/ethnicity unknown; 2% international; 60% live on campus. *Retention:* 72% of full-time freshmen returned.

Freshmen *Admission:* 984 applied, 679 admitted, 284 enrolled. *Average high school GPA:* 3.53. *Test scores:* SAT critical reading scores over 500: 65%; SAT math scores over 500: 69%; SAT writing scores over 500: 61%; ACT scores over 18: 88%; SAT critical reading scores over 600: 26%; SAT math scores over 600: 32%; SAT writing scores over 600: 22%; ACT scores over 24: 47%; SAT critical reading scores over 700: 6%; SAT math scores over 700: 4%; SAT writing scores over 700: 2%; ACT scores over 30: 5%.

Faculty *Total:* 110, 97% full-time, 74% with terminal degrees. *Student/faculty ratio:* 12:1.

Academics *Calendar:* semesters. *Degrees:* bachelor's, master's, and post-master's certificates. *Special study options:* academic remediation for entering students, accelerated degree program, adult/continuing education programs, advanced placement credit, cooperative education, distance learning, double majors, English as a second language, freshman honors college, honors programs, independent study, internships, off-campus study, part-time degree program, services for LD students, student-designed majors, study abroad, summer session for credit. *ROTC:* Army (b).

Computers on Campus 174 computers/terminals and 1,200 ports are available on campus for general student use. Students can access the following: campus intranet, computer help desk, free student e-mail accounts, online (class) grades, online (class) registration, online (class) schedules, various software packages. Campuswide network is available. 99% of college-owned or -operated housing units are wired for high-speed Internet access. Wireless service is available via entire campus.

Student Life *Housing:* on-campus residence required through sophomore year. *Options:* men-only, women-only, disabled students. Campus housing is university owned. Freshman campus housing is guaranteed. *Activities and organizations:* drama/theater group, student-run newspaper, choral group, Students in Free Enterprise (SIFE), Student Government Association, Fellowship of Christian Athletes, The Crusader newspaper, The Oasis yearbook. *Campus security:* 24-hour emergency response devices and patrols, student patrols, late-night transport/escort service, controlled dormitory access, residence hall check-in system, on-campus police hub. *Student services:* health clinic, personal/psychological counseling.

Athletics Member NCAA. All Division II. *Intercollegiate sports:* baseball M(s), basketball M(s)/W(s), cheerleading W(c), cross-country running M(s)/W(s), golf M(s)/W(s), soccer M/W(s), softball W(s), track and field M(s)/W(s), volleyball W(s). *Intramural sports:* basketball M/W, cross-country running M/W, football M/W, softball M/W, table tennis M/W, tennis M/W, ultimate Frisbee M/W, volleyball M/W.

Standardized Tests *Required:* SAT or ACT (for admission).

Costs (2012–13) *Comprehensive fee:* $31,490 includes full-time tuition ($24,790), mandatory fees ($300), and room and board ($6400). Full-time tuition and fees vary according to course load, degree level, program, and reciprocity agreements. Part-time tuition: $1074 per semester hour. *Room and board:* Room and board charges vary according to board plan. *Payment plans:* tuition prepayment, installment. *Waivers:* minority students, children of alumni, and employees or children of employees.

Financial Aid Of all full-time matriculated undergraduates who enrolled in 2009, 993 applied for aid, 881 were judged to have need, 166 had their need fully met. 145 Federal Work-Study jobs (averaging $996). In 2009, 273 non-need-based awards were made. *Average percent of need met:* 66%. *Average financial aid package:* $14,946. *Average need-based loan:* $8292. *Average need-based gift aid:* $16,314. *Average non-need-based aid:* $6577. *Average indebtedness upon graduation:* $26,752.

Applying *Options:* electronic application, early action, deferred entrance. *Application fee:* $25. *Required:* essay or personal statement, high school transcript, minimum 2.5 GPA, 2 letters of recommendation. *Required for some:* interview. *Application deadlines:* 8/15 (freshmen), 8/15 (transfers), 12/15 (early action). *Notification:* continuous (freshmen), continuous (transfers), 1/15 (early action).

Freshman Application Contact Northwest Nazarene University, 623 Holly Street, Nampa, ID 83686-5897. *Phone:* 208-467-8950. *Toll-free phone:* 877-668-4968. *Web site:* http://www.nnu.edu/.

Stevens-Henager College
Boise, Idaho

Director of Admissions David Breck, Director of Admission, Stevens-Henager College, 730 Americana Boulevard, Boise, ID 83702. *Phone:* 208-383-4540. *Toll-free phone:* 800-622-2670 (in-state); 800-622-2640 (out-of-state). *Fax:* 208-345-6999. *Web site:* http://www.stevenshenager.edu/.

University of Idaho
Moscow, Idaho

- **State-supported** university, founded 1889
- **Small-town** 1450-acre campus
- **Endowment** $190.7 million
- **Coed** 9,586 undergraduate students, 91% full-time, 47% women, 53% men
- **Moderately difficult** entrance level, 61% of applicants were admitted

Undergraduates 8,705 full-time, 881 part-time. Students come from 45 states and territories; 39 other countries; 29% are from out of state; 1% Black or African American, non-Hispanic/Latino; 7% Hispanic/Latino; 1% Asian, non-Hispanic/Latino; 0.3% Native Hawaiian or other Pacific Islander, non-Hispanic/Latino; 1% American Indian or Alaska Native, non-Hispanic/Latino; 3% Two or more races, non-Hispanic/Latino; 2% Race/ethnicity unknown; 2% international; 8% transferred in; 34% live on campus. *Retention:* 80% of full-time freshmen returned.

Freshmen *Admission:* 8,248 applied, 5,020 admitted, 1,631 enrolled. *Average high school GPA:* 3.33. *Test scores:* SAT critical reading scores over 500: 67%; SAT math scores over 500: 71%; SAT writing scores over 500: 57%; ACT scores over 18: 92%; SAT critical reading scores over 600: 30%; SAT math scores over 600: 29%; SAT writing scores over 600: 19%; ACT scores over 24: 43%; SAT critical reading scores over 700: 6%; SAT math scores over 700: 6%; SAT writing scores over 700: 3%; ACT scores over 30: 6%.

Faculty *Total:* 677, 80% full-time, 67% with terminal degrees. *Student/faculty ratio:* 18:1.

Academics *Calendar:* semesters. *Degrees:* certificates, bachelor's, master's, doctoral, post-master's, postbachelor's, and first professional certificates. *Special study options:* academic remediation for entering students, accelerated degree program, adult/continuing education programs, advanced placement credit, cooperative education, distance learning, double majors, English as a second language, honors programs, independent study, internships, off-campus study, part-time degree program, services for LD students, student-designed majors, study abroad, summer session for credit. *ROTC:* Army (b), Navy (b), Air Force (c).

Computers on Campus 575 computers/terminals are available on campus for general student use. Students can access the following: campus intranet, computer help desk, free student e-mail accounts, online (class) grades, online (class) registration, online (class) schedules. Campuswide network is available. 100% of college-owned or -operated housing units are wired for high-speed Internet access. Wireless service is available via entire campus.

Student Life *Housing:* on-campus residence required for freshman year. *Options:* coed, men-only, women-only, cooperative, disabled students. Campus housing is university owned. Freshman campus housing is guaranteed. *Activities and organizations:* drama/theater group, student-run newspaper, radio and television station, choral group, marching band, ASUI - Associated Student of the University of Idaho, Student Alumni Relations Board, Multicultural Greek Council, Gay Straight Alliance, Campus Crusade for Christ, national fraternities, national sororities. *Campus security:* 24-hour emergency response devices and patrols, late-night transport/escort service, controlled dormitory access, contracted services with the city of Moscow police department. *Student services:* health clinic, personal/psychological counseling, women's center, legal services.

Athletics Member NCAA. All Division I except football (Division I-A). *Intercollegiate sports:* basketball M(s)/W(s), cross-country running M(s)/W(s), golf M(s)/W(s), soccer W(s), swimming and diving W(s), tennis M(s)/W(s), track and field M(s)/W(s), volleyball W(s). *Intramural sports:* badminton M/W, basketball M/W, bowling M/W, football M, golf M/W, racquetball M/W, rugby M/W, skiing (cross-country) M/W, skiing (downhill) M/W, soccer M/W, softball M/W, squash M/W, swimming and diving M/W, table tennis M/W, tennis M/W, track and field M/W, ultimate Frisbee M/W, volleyball M/W, water polo M, weight lifting M/W, wrestling M.

Standardized Tests *Required:* SAT or ACT (for admission).

Costs (2011–12) *Tuition:* state resident $3874 full-time, $235 per credit hour part-time; nonresident $16,394 full-time, $861 per credit hour part-time. Full-time tuition and fees vary according to course load, degree level, program, and reciprocity agreements. Part-time tuition and fees vary according to course load, degree level, and program. *Required fees:* $1982 full-time, $59 per credit hour part-time. *Room and board:* $7304. Room and board charges vary according to board plan and housing facility. *Payment plans:* installment, deferred payment. *Waivers:* senior citizens and employees or children of employees.

Financial Aid Of all full-time matriculated undergraduates who enrolled in 2010, 7,046 applied for aid, 5,900 were judged to have need, 1,611 had their need fully met. 416 Federal Work-Study jobs (averaging $1870). 161 state and other part-time jobs (averaging $1848). In 2010, 1722 non-need-based awards were made. *Average percent of need met:* 75%. *Average financial aid package:* $12,961. *Average need-based loan:* $7462. *Average need-based gift aid:*

$4678. *Average non-need-based aid:* $4899. *Average indebtedness upon graduation:* $24,396.

Applying *Options:* electronic application, deferred entrance. *Application fee:* $50. *Required:* high school transcript, minimum 2.2 GPA. *Required for some:* essay or personal statement. *Application deadlines:* 8/1 (freshmen), rolling (transfers). *Notification:* continuous (freshmen), continuous (transfers).

Freshman Application Contact Ms. Melissa Goodwin, Associate Director, Admissions, University of Idaho, PO Box 444264, Moscow, ID 83844-4264. *Phone:* 208-885-6326. *Toll-free phone:* 888-884-3246. *Fax:* 208-885-9119. *E-mail:* admissions@uidaho.edu. *Web site:* http://www.uidaho.edu/.

University of Phoenix–Idaho Campus
Meridian, Idaho

Freshman Application Contact Marc Booker, Sr. Director, Office of Admissions and Evaluation, University of Phoenix–Idaho Campus, 4305 South Riverpoint Parkway, Mail Stop CF-L101, Phoenix, AZ 85040. *Phone:* 602-557-4609. *Toll-free phone:* 866-766-0766. *Fax:* 480-643-1156. *Web site:* http://www.phoenix.edu/.

ILLINOIS

American Academy of Art
Chicago, Illinois

Freshman Application Contact Mr. Stuart Rosenbloom, Director of Admissions, American Academy of Art, 332 South Michigan Avenue, Suite 300, Chicago, IL 60604-4302. *Phone:* 312-461-0600 Ext. 159. *Toll-free phone:* 888-461-0600. *E-mail:* srosenbloom@aaart.edu. *Web site:* http://www.aaart.edu/.

American InterContinental University Online
Hoffman Estates, Illinois

Director of Admissions Jennifer Ziegenmier, Senior Vice President of Admissions and Marketing, American InterContinental University Online, 5550 Prairie Stone Parkway, Suite 400, Hoffman Estates, IL 60192. *Phone:* 877-564-6248. *Toll-free phone:* 877-701-3800. *E-mail:* jziegenmier@aiuonline.edu. *Web site:* http://www.aiuniv.edu/.

Argosy University, Chicago
Chicago, Illinois

Freshman Application Contact Argosy University, Chicago, 225 North Michigan Avenue, Suite 1300, Chicago, IL 60601. *Phone:* 312-777-7600. *Toll-free phone:* 800-626-4123. *Web site:* http://www.argosy.edu/chicago/.

See page 1062 for the College Close-Up.

Argosy University, Schaumburg
Schaumburg, Illinois

Freshman Application Contact Argosy University, Schaumburg, 999 North Plaza Drive, Suite 111, Schaumburg, IL 60173-5403. *Phone:* 847-969-4900. *Toll-free phone:* 866-290-2777. *Web site:* http://www.argosy.edu/schaumburg/

See page 1062 for the College Close-Up.

Augustana College
Rock Island, Illinois

- **Independent** 4-year, founded 1860, affiliated with Evangelical Lutheran Church in America
- **Suburban** 115-acre campus
- **Endowment** $99.3 million
- **Coed** 2,518 undergraduate students, 99% full-time, 57% women, 43% men
- **Moderately difficult** entrance level, 62% of applicants were admitted

Undergraduates 2,505 full-time, 13 part-time. Students come from 29 states and territories; 23 other countries; 13% are from out of state; 3% Black or African American, non-Hispanic/Latino; 6% Hispanic/Latino; 2% Asian, non-Hispanic/Latino; 0.2% Native Hawaiian or other Pacific Islander, non-Hispanic/

Latino; 0.3% American Indian or Alaska Native, non-Hispanic/Latino; 2% Two or more races, non-Hispanic/Latino; 7% Race/ethnicity unknown; 2% transferred in; 73% live on campus. *Retention:* 87% of full-time freshmen returned.

Freshmen *Admission:* 4,609 applied, 2,838 admitted, 708 enrolled. *Average high school GPA:* 3.26. *Test scores:* ACT scores over 18: 98%; ACT scores over 24: 68%; ACT scores over 30: 12%.

Faculty *Total:* 307, 61% full-time, 67% with terminal degrees. *Student/faculty ratio:* 11:1.

Academics *Calendar:* quarters. *Degree:* bachelor's. *Special study options:* advanced placement credit, double majors, honors programs, independent study, internships, part-time degree program, services for LD students, student-designed majors, study abroad, summer session for credit. *Unusual degree programs:* 3-2 engineering with Washington University in St. Louis, University of Illinois, Iowa State University of Science and Technology, Purdue University; forestry with Duke University; occupational therapy with Washington University in St. Louis, landscape architecture with University of Illinois, environmental studies with Duke University.

Computers on Campus 600 computers/terminals and 1,800 ports are available on campus for general student use. Students can access the following: campus intranet, computer help desk, free student e-mail accounts, online (class) grades, online (class) registration, online (class) schedules. Campuswide network is available. 100% of college-owned or -operated housing units are wired for high-speed Internet access. Wireless service is available via classrooms, computer centers, computer labs, libraries, student centers.

Student Life *Housing:* on-campus residence required through junior year. *Options:* coed, men-only, women-only. Campus housing is university owned. Freshman campus housing is guaranteed. *Activities and organizations:* drama/theater group, student-run newspaper, radio station, choral group, College Union Board of Managers, Student Government Association, student newspaper, student radio station, service organizations (APO, Dance Marathon committee). *Campus security:* 24-hour emergency response devices and patrols, late-night transport/escort service, controlled dormitory access. *Student services:* health clinic, personal/psychological counseling, women's center.

Athletics Member NCAA. All Division III. *Intercollegiate sports:* baseball M, basketball M/W, cheerleading M(c)/W(c), crew M(c)/W(c), cross-country running M/W, equestrian sports M(c)/W(c), fencing M(c)/W(c), football M, golf M/W, ice hockey M(c), lacrosse M/W, soccer M/W, softball W, swimming and diving M/W, tennis M/W, track and field M/W, ultimate Frisbee M(c)/W(c), volleyball M(c)/W, wrestling M. *Intramural sports:* badminton M/W, basketball M/W, bowling M/W, cross-country running M/W, football M/W, golf M/W, racquetball M/W, rugby M, skiing (cross-country) M/W, skiing (downhill) M/W, soccer M/W, softball M/W, swimming and diving M/W, table tennis M/W, tennis M/W, track and field M/W, ultimate Frisbee M/W, volleyball M/W, wrestling M.

Standardized Tests *Required for some:* SAT or ACT (for admission). *Recommended:* SAT or ACT (for admission).

Costs (2012–13) *Comprehensive fee:* $121,466 includes full-time tuition ($33,582) and room and board ($87,884). Full-time tuition and fees vary according to student level. Part-time tuition and fees vary according to course load. *Room and board:* Room and board charges vary according to board plan and housing facility. *Payment plans:* tuition prepayment, installment. *Waivers:* employees or children of employees.

Financial Aid Of all full-time matriculated undergraduates who enrolled in 2010, 2,121 applied for aid, 1,843 were judged to have need, 439 had their need fully met. 1,216 Federal Work-Study jobs (averaging $2320). In 2010, 593 non-need-based awards were made. *Average percent of need met:* 85%. *Average financial aid package:* $23,118. *Average need-based loan:* $4616. *Average need-based gift aid:* $17,349. *Average non-need-based aid:* $13,324. *Average indebtedness upon graduation:* $31,205.

Applying *Options:* electronic application, deferred entrance. *Application fee:* $35. *Required:* high school transcript. *Required for some:* essay or personal statement, interview. *Recommended:* essay or personal statement, 1 letter of recommendation, interview. *Application deadlines:* rolling (freshmen), rolling (transfers). *Notification:* continuous (freshmen), continuous (transfers).

Freshman Application Contact Kent Barnds, Director of Admissions, Augustana College, 639 38th Street, Rock Island, IL 61201-2296. *Phone:* 309-794-7341. *Toll-free phone:* 800-798-8100. *Fax:* 309-794-8797. *E-mail:* admissions@augustana.edu. *Web site:* http://www.augustana.edu/.

Aurora University
Aurora, Illinois

Freshman Application Contact Mr. James Lancaster, Director, Freshman Admission, Aurora University, 347 South Gladstone Avenue, Aurora, IL 60506-4892. *Phone:* 630-844-5533. *Toll-free phone:* 800-742-5281. *Fax:* 630-844-5535. *E-mail:* admission@aurora.edu. *Web site:* http://www.aurora.edu/.

Benedictine University
Lisle, Illinois

- **Independent Roman Catholic** comprehensive, founded 1887
- **Suburban** 108-acre campus with easy access to Chicago
- **Endowment** $31.4 million
- **Coed** 3,825 undergraduate students, 78% full-time, 61% women, 39% men
- **Moderately difficult** entrance level, 76% of applicants were admitted

Undergraduates 2,971 full-time, 854 part-time. Students come from 50 states and territories; 15 other countries; 15% are from out of state; 10% Black or African American, non-Hispanic/Latino; 7% Hispanic/Latino; 13% Asian, non-Hispanic/Latino; 0.5% Native Hawaiian or other Pacific Islander, non-Hispanic/Latino; 0.3% American Indian or Alaska Native, non-Hispanic/Latino; 0.1% Two or more races, non-Hispanic/Latino; 29% Race/ethnicity unknown; 1% international; 12% transferred in; 32% live on campus. *Retention:* 81% of full-time freshmen returned.

Freshmen *Admission:* 1,531 applied, 1,159 admitted, 537 enrolled. *Average high school GPA:* 3.29. *Test scores:* ACT scores over 18: 89%; ACT scores over 24: 40%; ACT scores over 30: 6%.

Faculty *Total:* 709, 20% full-time, 28% with terminal degrees. *Student/faculty ratio:* 18:1.

Academics *Calendar:* semesters. *Degrees:* certificates, associate, bachelor's, master's, doctoral, postbachelor's, and first professional certificates. *Special study options:* academic remediation for entering students, accelerated degree program, adult/continuing education programs, advanced placement credit, distance learning, double majors, English as a second language, honors programs, independent study, internships, off-campus study, part-time degree program, services for LD students, study abroad, summer session for credit. *ROTC:* Army (c). *Unusual degree programs:* 3-2 engineering with University of Illinois at Urbana–Champaign, Illinois Institute of Technology, Purdue University.

Computers on Campus 200 computers/terminals are available on campus for general student use. Students can access the following: computer help desk, free student e-mail accounts, online (class) grades, online (class) registration, online (class) schedules. Campuswide network is available. 100% of college-owned or -operated housing units are wired for high-speed Internet access. Wireless service is available via computer centers, dorm rooms, libraries, student centers.

Student Life *Housing options:* coed, men-only, women-only. Campus housing is university owned and is provided by a third party. Freshman campus housing is guaranteed. *Activities and organizations:* drama/theater group, student-run newspaper, television station, choral group, Student Senate, MSA-Muslim Student Association, AMSA-American Medical Student Association, The Candor-Student Newspaper, SEWATE. *Campus security:* 24-hour emergency response devices and patrols, late-night transport/escort service, controlled dormitory access. *Student services:* health clinic, personal/psychological counseling.

Athletics Member NCAA. All Division III. *Intercollegiate sports:* baseball M, basketball M/W, cross-country running M/W, football M, golf M/W, soccer M/W, softball W, tennis W, track and field M/W, volleyball W. *Intramural sports:* basketball M/W, bowling M/W, cheerleading W(c), football M/W, lacrosse M(c), softball M/W, table tennis M/W, volleyball M/W.

Standardized Tests *Required:* SAT or ACT (for admission).

Costs (2011–12) *Comprehensive fee:* $32,710 includes full-time tuition ($23,650), mandatory fees ($1000), and room and board ($8060). Full-time tuition and fees vary according to class time, degree level, and location. Part-time tuition: $790 per credit hour. Part-time tuition and fees vary according to class time and degree level. *Required fees:* $15 per credit hour part-time. *College room only:* $2820. Room and board charges vary according to board plan, housing facility, and location. *Payment plans:* installment, deferred payment. *Waivers:* employees or children of employees.

Financial Aid Of all full-time matriculated undergraduates who enrolled in 2011, 2,409 applied for aid, 2,218 were judged to have need. 1,269 Federal Work-Study jobs (averaging $2630). 1,264 state and other part-time jobs (averaging $3957). In 2011, 307 non-need-based awards were made. *Average financial aid package:* $16,945. *Average need-based loan:* $4382. *Average need-based gift aid:* $7364. *Average non-need-based aid:* $9044. *Average indebtedness upon graduation:* $30,946.

Applying *Options:* electronic application, deferred entrance. *Application fee:* $40. *Required:* essay or personal statement, high school transcript. *Required for some:* interview. *Recommended:* rank in upper 50% of high school class. *Application deadlines:* rolling (freshmen), rolling (transfers). *Notification:* continuous (freshmen), continuous (transfers).

Freshman Application Contact Ms. Kari Gibbons, Dean of Enrollment, Benedictine University, 5700 College Road, Lisle, IL 60532-0900. *Phone:* 630-829-6300. *Toll-free phone:* 888-829-6363. *Fax:* 630-829-6301. *E-mail:* admissions@ben.edu. *Web site:* http://www.ben.edu/.

Blackburn College

Carlinville, Illinois

- **Independent Presbyterian** 4-year, founded 1837
- **Small-town** 80-acre campus with easy access to St. Louis
- **Endowment** $10.9 million
- **Coed** 549 undergraduate students, 96% full-time, 57% women, 43% men
- **Moderately difficult** entrance level, 68% of applicants were admitted

Undergraduates 527 full-time, 22 part-time. Students come from 17 states and territories; 1 other country; 9% are from out of state; 8% Black or African American, non-Hispanic/Latino; 1% Hispanic/Latino; 0.2% Asian, non-Hispanic/Latino; 0.2% Native Hawaiian or other Pacific Islander, non-Hispanic/Latino; 3% Two or more races, non-Hispanic/Latino; 0.4% Race/ethnicity unknown; 0.2% international; 7% transferred in; 67% live on campus. *Retention:* 61% of full-time freshmen returned.

Freshmen *Admission:* 660 applied, 452 admitted, 142 enrolled. *Average high school GPA:* 3.21. *Test scores:* ACT scores over 18: 77%; ACT scores over 24: 21%; ACT scores over 30: 1%.

Faculty *Total:* 76, 50% full-time, 57% with terminal degrees. *Student/faculty ratio:* 10:1.

Academics *Calendar:* semesters. *Degree:* bachelor's. *Special study options:* advanced placement credit, cooperative education, double majors, honors programs, independent study, internships, off-campus study, services for LD students, student-designed majors, study abroad, summer session for credit. *Unusual degree programs:* 3-2 engineering with Washington University in St. Louis or University of Missouri, Kansas City.

Computers on Campus 202 computers/terminals are available on campus for general student use. Students can access the following: computer help desk, free student e-mail accounts, online (class) grades, online (class) registration, online (class) schedules. Campuswide network is available. 100% of college-owned or -operated housing units are wired for high-speed Internet access. Wireless service is available via libraries, student centers.

Student Life *Housing:* on-campus residence required through junior year. *Options:* coed, men-only, women-only. Campus housing is university owned. Freshman campus housing is guaranteed. *Activities and organizations:* drama/theater group, student-run newspaper, radio station, choral group, Habitat for Humanity, Residence Hall Association, Newman Club, Blackburn Common Ground. *Campus security:* student patrols, late-night transport/escort service. *Student services:* personal/psychological counseling.

Athletics Member NCAA. All Division III. *Intercollegiate sports:* baseball M, basketball M/W, cross-country running M/W, golf M, soccer M/W, softball W, tennis W, volleyball W. *Intramural sports:* badminton M/W, basketball M/W, football M/W, golf M/W, racquetball M/W, soccer M/W, softball M/W, table tennis M/W, tennis M/W, ultimate Frisbee M/W, volleyball M/W.

Standardized Tests *Required:* SAT or ACT (for admission).

Costs (2012–13) *Comprehensive fee:* $22,934 includes full-time tuition ($17,282), mandatory fees ($220), and room and board ($5432). Full-time tuition and fees vary according to student level. Part-time tuition: $576 per credit. *College room only:* $2848. Room and board charges vary according to board plan and housing facility. *Payment plan:* installment. *Waivers:* employees or children of employees.

Financial Aid Of all full-time matriculated undergraduates who enrolled in 2009, 581 applied for aid, 502 were judged to have need, 194 had their need fully met. 388 Federal Work-Study jobs (averaging $2653). 113 state and other part-time jobs (averaging $2337). In 2009, 62 non-need-based awards were made. *Average percent of need met:* 80%. *Average financial aid package:* $13,873. *Average need-based loan:* $4107. *Average need-based gift aid:* $11,209. *Average non-need-based aid:* $5163. *Average indebtedness upon graduation:* $20,077.

Applying *Options:* electronic application, deferred entrance. *Application fee:* $20. *Required:* high school transcript, minimum 2.0 GPA. *Required for some:* essay or personal statement, 3 letters of recommendation, interview. *Recommended:* minimum 2.5 GPA. *Application deadlines:* rolling (freshmen), rolling (out-of-state freshmen), rolling (transfers). *Notification:* continuous (freshmen), continuous (out-of-state freshmen), continuous (transfers).

Freshman Application Contact Mrs. Alisha Kapp, Director of Admission, Blackburn College, 700 College Avenue, Carlinville, IL 62626. *Phone:* 217-854-3231 Ext. 4252. *Toll-free phone:* 800-233-3550. *E-mail:* admit@mail.blackburn.edu. *Web site:* http://www.blackburn.edu/.

Blessing-Rieman College of Nursing

Quincy, Illinois

- **Independent** comprehensive, founded 1985
- **Small-town** 1-acre campus
- **Endowment** $6.7 million
- **Coed, primarily women** 266 undergraduate students, 83% full-time, 91% women, 9% men
- **Moderately difficult** entrance level, 77% of applicants were admitted

Undergraduates 221 full-time, 45 part-time. Students come from 10 states and territories; 32% are from out of state; 10% transferred in; 82% live on campus.

Freshmen *Admission:* 39 applied, 30 admitted. *Test scores:* ACT scores over 18: 100%; ACT scores over 24: 67%.

Faculty *Total:* 18, 100% full-time, 28% with terminal degrees. *Student/faculty ratio:* 12:1.

Academics *Calendar:* semesters. *Degrees:* bachelor's and master's. *Special study options:* academic remediation for entering students, adult/continuing education programs, advanced placement credit, distance learning, double majors, honors programs, internships, part-time degree program, summer session for credit.

Computers on Campus 28 computers/terminals are available on campus for general student use. Students can access the following: campus intranet, computer help desk, free student e-mail accounts. Campuswide network is available. 100% of college-owned or -operated housing units are wired for high-speed Internet access.

Student Life *Housing:* on-campus residence required through sophomore year. *Options:* coed. Campus housing is university owned. Freshman campus housing is guaranteed. *Activities and organizations:* drama/theater group, student-run newspaper, radio station, choral group, Student Nurses Organization, national fraternities, national sororities. *Campus security:* 24-hour patrols, late-night transport/escort service, controlled dormitory access. *Student services:* health clinic, personal/psychological counseling.

Athletics *Intercollegiate sports:* baseball M(s)/W(s), basketball M(s)/W(s), football M(s), soccer M(s)/W(s), volleyball M(s)/W(s). *Intramural sports:* baseball M/W, basketball M/W, football M, soccer M/W, volleyball M/W.

Standardized Tests *Required:* SAT or ACT (for admission).

Financial Aid Of all full-time matriculated undergraduates who enrolled in 2009, 186 applied for aid, 186 were judged to have need, 186 had their need fully met. *Average percent of need met:* 100%. *Average need-based loan:* $2394. *Average need-based gift aid:* $7902. *Average indebtedness upon graduation:* $20,000.

Applying *Options:* electronic application, deferred entrance. *Required:* high school transcript, minimum 3.0 GPA. *Recommended:* essay or personal statement, interview. *Application deadlines:* rolling (freshmen), rolling (transfers).

Freshman Application Contact Ms. Heather Mutter, Admissions Counselor, Blessing-Rieman College of Nursing, Broadway at 11th Street, POB 7005, Quincy, IL 62305-7005. *Phone:* 217-228-5520 Ext. 6979. *Toll-free phone:* 800-877-9140 Ext. 6964. *Fax:* 217-223-4661. *E-mail:* admissions@brcn.edu. *Web site:* http://www.brcn.edu/.

Bradley University

Peoria, Illinois

- **Independent** comprehensive, founded 1897
- **Suburban** 85-acre campus
- **Endowment** $249.5 million
- **Coed** 4,955 undergraduate students, 94% full-time, 54% women, 46% men
- **Moderately difficult** entrance level, 70% of applicants were admitted

Undergraduates 4,680 full-time, 275 part-time. Students come from 39 states and territories; 28 other countries; 11% are from out of state; 8% Black or African American, non-Hispanic/Latino; 6% Hispanic/Latino; 3% Asian, non-Hispanic/Latino; 0.1% Native Hawaiian or other Pacific Islander, non-Hispanic/Latino; 0.2% American Indian or Alaska Native, non-Hispanic/Latino; 2% Two or more races, non-Hispanic/Latino; 0.5% Race/ethnicity unknown; 0.7% international; 6% transferred in; 66% live on campus. *Retention:* 86% of full-time freshmen returned.

Freshmen *Admission:* 6,454 applied, 4,529 admitted, 1,018 enrolled. *Average high school GPA:* 3.58. *Test scores:* SAT critical reading scores over 500: 78%; SAT math scores over 500: 90%; ACT scores over 18: 99%; SAT critical reading scores over 600: 40%; SAT math scores over 600: 52%; ACT scores over 24: 65%; SAT critical reading scores over 700: 9%; SAT math scores over 700: 9%; ACT scores over 30: 13%.

Faculty *Total:* 536, 65% full-time, 55% with terminal degrees. *Student/faculty ratio:* 12:1.

Academics *Calendar:* semesters. *Degrees:* certificates, bachelor's, master's, and doctoral. *Special study options:* advanced placement credit, cooperative

education, distance learning, double majors, honors programs, independent study, internships, off-campus study, part-time degree program, services for LD students, student-designed majors, study abroad, summer session for credit. *ROTC:* Army (b). *Unusual degree programs:* 3-2 business administration.

Computers on Campus 2,500 computers/terminals are available on campus for general student use. Students can access the following: computer help desk, free student e-mail accounts, online (class) grades, online (class) registration, online (class) schedules. Campuswide network is available. 100% of college-owned or -operated housing units are wired for high-speed Internet access. Wireless service is available via classrooms, computer centers, computer labs, dorm rooms, learning centers, libraries, student centers.

Student Life *Housing:* on-campus residence required through sophomore year. *Options:* coed. Campus housing is university owned, leased by the school and is provided by a third party. Freshman campus housing is guaranteed. *Activities and organizations:* drama/theater group, student-run newspaper, radio station, choral group, Habitat for Humanity, Alpha Phi Omega Co-Ed Service Fraternity, Activities Council of Bradley University, CRU (Campus Christian group), Dance Marathon, national fraternities, national sororities. *Campus security:* 24-hour emergency response devices and patrols, late-night transport/escort service, controlled dormitory access, emergency text messaging, mass notification/emergency communication system in 20 academic buildings. *Student services:* health clinic, personal/psychological counseling.

Athletics Member NCAA. All Division I. *Intercollegiate sports:* baseball M(s), basketball M(s)/W(s), cheerleading M/W, cross-country running M(s)/W(s), golf M(s)/W(s), ice hockey M(c), soccer M(s), softball W(s), tennis M(s)/W(s), track and field M(s)/W(s), volleyball M(c)/W(s). *Intramural sports:* badminton M/W, basketball M/W, bowling M/W, football M, racquetball M/W, rock climbing M/W, soccer M/W, swimming and diving M/W, table tennis M/W, tennis M/W, ultimate Frisbee M/W, volleyball M/W, water polo M/W, wrestling M.

Standardized Tests *Required:* SAT or ACT (for admission).

Costs (2012–13) *One-time required fee:* $200. *Comprehensive fee:* $36,964 includes full-time tuition ($27,920), mandatory fees ($344), and room and board ($8700). Full-time tuition and fees vary according to course load and program. Part-time tuition: $710 per credit. Part-time tuition and fees vary according to course load and program. *College room only:* $5146. Room and board charges vary according to board plan. *Payment plans:* installment, deferred payment. *Waivers:* senior citizens and employees or children of employees.

Financial Aid Of all full-time matriculated undergraduates who enrolled in 2010, 4,171 applied for aid, 3,692 were judged to have need, 508 had their need fully met. In 2010, 984 non-need-based awards were made. *Average percent of need met:* 62%. *Average financial aid package:* $16,725. *Average need-based loan:* $5376. *Average need-based gift aid:* $12,988. *Average non-need-based aid:* $6718.

Applying *Options:* electronic application, early admission, deferred entrance. *Application fee:* $35. *Required:* essay or personal statement, high school transcript, 1 letter of recommendation. *Recommended:* interview. *Application deadlines:* rolling (freshmen), rolling (out-of-state freshmen), rolling (transfers).

Freshman Application Contact Rodney San Jose, Director of Admissions, Bradley University, 1501 West Bradley Avenue, Peoria, IL 61625-0002. *Phone:* 309-677-1000. *Toll-free phone:* 800-447-6460. *Fax:* 309-677-2797. *E-mail:* admissions@bradley.edu. *Web site:* http://www.bradley.edu/.

Chamberlain College of Nursing

Addison, Illinois

- **Proprietary** 4-year
- **Coed** 906 undergraduate students, 68% full-time, 89% women, 11% men

Undergraduates 620 full-time, 286 part-time. 1% are from out of state; 6% Black or African American, non-Hispanic/Latino; 12% Hispanic/Latino; 20% Asian, non-Hispanic/Latino; 2% Native Hawaiian or other Pacific Islander, non-Hispanic/Latino; 0.1% American Indian or Alaska Native, non-Hispanic/Latino; 1% Two or more races, non-Hispanic/Latino; 3% Race/ethnicity unknown; 0.1% international; 40% transferred in.

Freshmen *Admission:* 13 enrolled.

Faculty *Total:* 100, 31% full-time. *Student/faculty ratio:* 23:1.

Academics *Calendar:* semesters.

Standardized Tests *Required:* SAT or ACT (for admission).

Freshman Application Contact Admissions, Chamberlain College of Nursing, 1221 N. Swift Road, Addison, IL 60101-6106. *Phone:* 630-953-3680. *Toll-free phone:* 888-556-8CCN. *Web site:* http://www.chamberlain.edu/.

Chamberlain College of Nursing

Chicago, Illinois

- **Proprietary** 4-year
- **Coed** 450 undergraduate students, 67% full-time, 87% women, 13% men

Undergraduates 302 full-time, 148 part-time. 1% are from out of state; 20% Black or African American, non-Hispanic/Latino; 23% Hispanic/Latino; 18% Asian, non-Hispanic/Latino; 1% Native Hawaiian or other Pacific Islander, non-Hispanic/Latino; 0.2% American Indian or Alaska Native, non-Hispanic/Latino; 3% Two or more races, non-Hispanic/Latino; 2% Race/ethnicity unknown; 0.4% international; 63% transferred in.

Freshmen *Admission:* 8 enrolled.

Faculty *Total:* 29, 52% full-time. *Student/faculty ratio:* 18:1.

Academics *Calendar:* semesters.

Standardized Tests *Required:* SAT or ACT (for admission).

Freshman Application Contact Admissions, Chamberlain College of Nursing, 3300 N. Campbell Avenue, Chicago, IL 60618. *Phone:* 773-961-3000. *Toll-free phone:* 888-556-8CCN. *Web site:* http://www.chamberlain.edu/.

Chicago State University

Chicago, Illinois

- **State-supported** comprehensive, founded 1867
- **Urban** 161-acre campus
- **Endowment** $2.0 million
- **Coed** 5,280 undergraduate students, 68% full-time, 72% women, 28% men
- **Minimally difficult** entrance level, 43% of applicants were admitted

Undergraduates 3,585 full-time, 1,695 part-time. Students come from 22 states and territories; 13 other countries; 2% are from out of state; 84% Black or African American, non-Hispanic/Latino; 7% Hispanic/Latino; 0.8% Asian, non-Hispanic/Latino; 0.2% American Indian or Alaska Native, non-Hispanic/Latino; 5% Two or more races, non-Hispanic/Latino; 0.1% international; 11% transferred in. *Retention:* 54% of full-time freshmen returned.

Freshmen *Admission:* 3,876 applied, 1,673 admitted, 486 enrolled.

Faculty *Total:* 499, 65% full-time. *Student/faculty ratio:* 11:1.

Academics *Calendar:* semesters. *Degrees:* bachelor's, master's, doctoral, postbachelor's, and first professional certificates. *Special study options:* academic remediation for entering students, accelerated degree program, adult/continuing education programs, advanced placement credit, cooperative education, distance learning, double majors, external degree program, freshman honors college, honors programs, independent study, internships, off-campus study, part-time degree program, services for LD students, student-designed majors, study abroad, summer session for credit. *ROTC:* Army (b), Navy (c), Air Force (c).

Computers on Campus 75 computers/terminals and 250 ports are available on campus for general student use. Students can access the following: free student e-mail accounts, online (class) grades, online (class) registration, online (class) schedules. Campuswide network is available. 100% of college-owned or -operated housing units are wired for high-speed Internet access. Wireless service is available via libraries.

Student Life *Housing options:* coed. Campus housing is university owned. *Activities and organizations:* drama/theater group, student-run newspaper, radio station, choral group, Math/Computer Science Club, Geographic Society Club, Gospel Choir, Movie Club, national fraternities, national sororities. *Campus security:* 24-hour emergency response devices and patrols, student patrols, late-night transport/escort service, controlled dormitory access. *Student services:* health clinic, personal/psychological counseling, women's center.

Athletics Member NCAA. All Division I. *Intercollegiate sports:* baseball M(s), basketball M(s)/W(s), cross-country running M(s)/W(s), golf M(s)/W(s), tennis M(s)/W(s), track and field M(s)/W(s), volleyball W(s).

Standardized Tests *Required:* SAT or ACT (for admission).

Costs (2011–12) *Tuition:* state resident $6648 full-time, $277 per credit hour part-time; nonresident $13,248 full-time, $552 per credit hour part-time. No tuition increase for student's term of enrollment. *Required fees:* $2414 full-time, $423 per term part-time. *Room and board:* $8221. *Payment plan:* tuition prepayment.

Financial Aid Of all full-time matriculated undergraduates who enrolled in 2010, 3,699 applied for aid, 3,685 were judged to have need. 252 Federal Work-Study jobs (averaging $1682). 234 state and other part-time jobs (averaging $1567). *Average percent of need met:* 48%. *Average financial aid package:* $4850. *Average need-based loan:* $980. *Average need-based gift aid:* $3850. *Average indebtedness upon graduation:* $27,322. *Financial aid deadline:* 6/30.

Applying *Options:* electronic application. *Application fee:* $25. *Required:* high school transcript, minimum 2.5 GPA. *Required for some:* essay or per-

sonal statement, interview. *Notification:* continuous (freshmen), continuous (transfers).

Freshman Application Contact Mr. John Martinez, Associate Director of Admissions, Chicago State University, 95th Street at King Drive, ADM 200, Chicago, IL 60628. *Phone:* 773-995-3578. *Fax:* 773-995-3820. *E-mail:* jmarti21@csu.edu. *Web site:* http://www.csu.edu/.

Christian Life College
Mount Prospect, Illinois

- **Independent Christian** 4-year, founded 1950
- **Suburban** 5-acre campus with easy access to Chicago
- **Coed**
- **Noncompetitive** entrance level

Faculty *Student/faculty ratio:* 4:1.
Academics *Degrees:* diplomas, associate, and bachelor's.
Student Life *Campus security:* controlled dormitory access.
Standardized Tests *Required:* SAT or ACT (for admission).
Costs (2011–12) *Tuition:* $9440 full-time. *Required fees:* $1190 full-time. *Room only:* $3700.
Financial Aid *Of all full-time matriculated undergraduates who enrolled in 2002,* 33 applied for aid, 28 were judged to have need. 4 Federal Work-Study jobs (averaging $1646). *In 2002,* 6 non-need-based awards were made. *Average percent of need met:* 75. *Average financial aid package:* $4464. *Average need-based loan:* $2393. *Average need-based gift aid:* $3160. *Average non-need-based aid:* $871.
Applying *Options:* early admission, deferred entrance. *Application fee:* $40. *Required:* high school transcript, minimum 2.0 GPA. *Required for some:* essay or personal statement, minimum 2.5 GPA, interview. *Recommended:* minimum 2.5 GPA.
Freshman Application Contact Christian Life College, 400 East Gregory Street, Mount Prospect, IL 60056. *Phone:* 847-259-1840 Ext. 100. *Web site:* http://www.christianlifecollege.edu/.

Columbia College Chicago
Chicago, Illinois

- **Independent** comprehensive, founded 1890
- **Urban** campus with easy access to Chicago
- **Endowment** $1.1 billion
- **Coed** 11,138 undergraduate students, 89% full-time, 53% women, 47% men
- **Moderately difficult** entrance level, 84% of applicants were admitted

Undergraduates 9,941 full-time, 1,197 part-time. Students come from 39 other countries; 36% are from out of state; 17% Black or African American, non-Hispanic/Latino; 12% Hispanic/Latino; 2% Asian, non-Hispanic/Latino; 0.3% Native Hawaiian or other Pacific Islander, non-Hispanic/Latino; 0.4% American Indian or Alaska Native, non-Hispanic/Latino; 4% Two or more races, non-Hispanic/Latino; 1% Race/ethnicity unknown; 1% international; 10% transferred in; 22% live on campus. *Retention:* 68% of full-time freshmen returned.
Freshmen *Admission:* 7,132 applied, 5,973 admitted, 2,148 enrolled. *Average high school GPA:* 2.98. *Test scores:* SAT critical reading scores over 500: 60%; SAT math scores over 500: 46%; SAT writing scores over 500: 60%; ACT scores over 18: 82%; SAT critical reading scores over 600: 25%; SAT math scores over 600: 16%; SAT writing scores over 600: 16%; ACT scores over 24: 32%; SAT critical reading scores over 700: 3%; SAT math scores over 700: 1%; SAT writing scores over 700: 3%; ACT scores over 30: 4%.
Faculty *Total:* 2,037, 19% full-time. *Student/faculty ratio:* 11:1.
Academics *Calendar:* semesters. *Degrees:* certificates, diplomas, bachelor's, master's, and postbachelor's certificates. *Special study options:* academic remediation for entering students, adult/continuing education programs, advanced placement credit, cooperative education, distance learning, English as a second language, honors programs, independent study, internships, off-campus study, part-time degree program, services for LD students, student-designed majors, study abroad, summer session for credit.
Computers on Campus 851 computers/terminals are available on campus for general student use. Students can access the following: campus intranet, computer help desk, free student e-mail accounts, online (class) grades, online (class) registration, online (class) schedules. Campuswide network is available. 100% of college-owned or -operated housing units are wired for high-speed Internet access. Wireless service is available via entire campus.
Student Life *Housing options:* coed. Campus housing is university owned and leased by the school. Freshman applicants given priority for college housing. *Activities and organizations:* drama/theater group, student-run newspaper, radio and television station, choral group, Columbia Urban Music Association, International Student Organization, Acianza Latina, Marketing Club. *Campus security:* 24-hour emergency response devices and patrols, late-night transport/

escort service, controlled dormitory access, escort upon request. *Student services:* health clinic, personal/psychological counseling.
Athletics *Intercollegiate sports:* baseball M(c), basketball M(c), lacrosse M(c). *Intramural sports:* cheerleading M/W, cross-country running M/W, fencing M/W, football M/W, rugby M/W, soccer M/W, softball W, swimming and diving M/W, tennis M/W, ultimate Frisbee M/W, volleyball M/W.
Standardized Tests *Recommended:* SAT or ACT (for admission).
Costs (2012–13) *Comprehensive fee:* $33,670 includes full-time tuition ($21,200), mandatory fees ($550), and room and board ($11,920). Full-time tuition and fees vary according to course load. Part-time tuition: $732 per credit hour. Part-time tuition and fees vary according to course load. *Room and board:* Room and board charges vary according to housing facility.
Financial Aid Of all full-time matriculated undergraduates who enrolled in 2009, 7,243 applied for aid, 6,428 were judged to have need, 5,780 had their need fully met. *Average percent of need met:* 29%. *Average financial aid package:* $8922. *Average need-based loan:* $4337. *Average need-based gift aid:* $2347.
Applying *Options:* electronic application, deferred entrance. *Application fee:* $35. *Required:* essay or personal statement, high school transcript, 1 letter of recommendation. *Recommended:* minimum 2.0 GPA, interview. *Application deadlines:* rolling (freshmen), rolling (out-of-state freshmen), rolling (transfers). *Notification:* continuous (freshmen), continuous (out-of-state freshmen), continuous (transfers).
Freshman Application Contact Mr. Murphy Monroe, Executive Director of Admissions, Columbia College Chicago, 600 South Michigan Avenue, Chicago, IL 60605-1996. *Phone:* 312-369-7133. *Fax:* 312-344-8024. *E-mail:* admissions@colum.edu. *Web site:* http://www.colum.edu/.

See page 255 for display ad and page 1280 for the College Close-Up.

Concordia University Chicago
River Forest, Illinois

- **Independent** comprehensive, founded 1864, affiliated with Lutheran Church–Missouri Synod, part of Concordia University System
- **Suburban** 40-acre campus with easy access to Chicago
- **Coed** 1,452 undergraduate students, 94% full-time, 59% women, 41% men
- **Moderately difficult** entrance level, 57% of applicants were admitted

Undergraduates 1,361 full-time, 91 part-time. 28% are from out of state; 13% Black or African American, non-Hispanic/Latino; 19% Hispanic/Latino; 2% Asian, non-Hispanic/Latino; 0.1% Native Hawaiian or other Pacific Islander, non-Hispanic/Latino; 0.2% American Indian or Alaska Native, non-Hispanic/Latino; 2% Two or more races, non-Hispanic/Latino; 2% Race/ethnicity unknown; 0.1% international; 8% transferred in; 55% live on campus. *Retention:* 63% of full-time freshmen returned.
Freshmen *Admission:* 3,309 applied, 1,873 admitted, 343 enrolled. *Average high school GPA:* 2.98. *Test scores:* SAT critical reading scores over 500: 62%; SAT math scores over 500: 40%; ACT scores over 18: 90%; SAT critical reading scores over 600: 14%; SAT math scores over 600: 14%; ACT scores over 24: 33%; SAT critical reading scores over 700: 2%; SAT math scores over 700: 2%; ACT scores over 30: 3%.
Faculty *Total:* 426, 36% full-time.
Academics *Calendar:* semesters. *Degrees:* certificates, bachelor's, master's, doctoral, post-master's, and first professional certificates. *Special study options:* adult/continuing education programs, part-time degree program.
Computers on Campus Students can access the following: campus intranet, computer help desk, free student e-mail accounts, online (class) grades, online (class) registration, online (class) schedules. Campuswide network is available. 100% of college-owned or -operated housing units are wired for high-speed Internet access. Wireless service is available via libraries, student centers.
Student Life *Housing options:* coed, disabled students. Campus housing is university owned. *Campus security:* 24-hour emergency response devices and patrols, student patrols, late-night transport/escort service, controlled dormitory access, emergency call boxes.
Athletics Member NCAA. All Division III. *Intercollegiate sports:* baseball M, basketball M/W, cheerleading M/W, cross-country running M/W, football M, golf M, soccer M/W, softball W, tennis M/W, track and field M/W, volleyball M/W. *Intramural sports:* badminton M/W, basketball M/W, bowling M/W, football W, swimming and diving M/W, table tennis M/W, tennis M/W, volleyball M/W.
Standardized Tests *Required:* SAT or ACT (for admission).
Costs (2012–13) *Comprehensive fee:* $35,236 includes full-time tuition ($25,942), mandatory fees ($714), and room and board ($8580). Full-time tuition and fees vary according to program. Part-time tuition: $810 per semester hour. Part-time tuition and fees vary according to program. *Payment plan:* installment. *Waivers:* minority students, children of alumni, senior citizens, and employees or children of employees.

Financial Aid Of all full-time matriculated undergraduates who enrolled in 2010, 1,217 applied for aid, 1,105 were judged to have need, 215 had their need fully met. In 2010, 159 non-need-based awards were made. *Average percent of need met:* 77%. *Average financial aid package:* $18,748. *Average need-based loan:* $4141. *Average need-based gift aid:* $13,938. *Average non-need-based aid:* $9594. *Average indebtedness upon graduation:* $31,856. *Financial aid deadline:* 8/15.

Applying *Options:* electronic application, deferred entrance. *Required:* high school transcript, minimum 2.0 GPA, 1 letter of recommendation. *Required for some:* essay or personal statement, interview. *Application deadlines:* rolling (freshmen), rolling (transfers).

Freshman Application Contact Ms. Gwen Kanelos, Director of Admission, Concordia University Chicago, 7400 Augusta Street, River Forest, IL 60305. *Phone:* 708-209-3101. *Toll-free phone:* 800-285-2668. *Fax:* 708-209-3473. *E-mail:* gwen.kanelos@cuchicago.edu. *Web site:* http://www.cuchicago.edu/.

DePaul University
Chicago, Illinois

- **Independent Roman Catholic** university, founded 1898
- **Urban** 36-acre campus with easy access to Chicago
- **Coed** 16,384 undergraduate students, 82% full-time, 54% women, 46% men
- **Moderately difficult** entrance level, 64% of applicants were admitted

Undergraduates 13,457 full-time, 2,927 part-time. 18% are from out of state; 9% Black or African American, non-Hispanic/Latino; 16% Hispanic/Latino; 7% Asian, non-Hispanic/Latino; 0.4% Native Hawaiian or other Pacific Islander, non-Hispanic/Latino; 0.1% American Indian or Alaska Native, non-Hispanic/Latino; 3% Two or more races, non-Hispanic/Latino; 7% Race/ethnicity unknown; 2% international; 11% transferred in; 16% live on campus. *Retention:* 86% of full-time freshmen returned.

Freshmen *Admission:* 16,711 applied, 10,714 admitted, 2,458 enrolled. *Average high school GPA:* 3.55. *Test scores:* SAT critical reading scores over 500: 87%; SAT math scores over 500: 82%; ACT scores over 18: 99%; SAT critical reading scores over 600: 45%; SAT math scores over 600: 37%; ACT scores over 24: 70%; SAT critical reading scores over 700: 10%; SAT math scores over 700: 6%; ACT scores over 30: 13%.

Faculty *Total:* 1,908, 50% full-time, 52% with terminal degrees. *Student/faculty ratio:* 17:1.

Academics *Calendar:* quarters; semesters for law school. *Degrees:* certificates, bachelor's, master's, doctoral, post-master's, postbachelor's, and first professional certificates. *Special study options:* adult/continuing education programs, part-time degree program. *ROTC:* Army (b).

Computers on Campus Students can access the following: campus intranet, computer help desk, free student e-mail accounts, online (class) grades, online (class) registration, online (class) schedules, tuition payments, degree progress, financial aid, transcript requests, housing services, student employment information. Campuswide network is available. 100% of college-owned or -operated housing units are wired for high-speed Internet access. Wireless service is available via entire campus.

Student Life *Housing options:* coed, disabled students. Campus housing is university owned, leased by the school and is provided by a third party. Freshman applicants given priority for college housing. *Campus security:* 24-hour emergency response devices and patrols, late-night transport/escort service, controlled dormitory access, security lighting, prevention/awareness programs, on-campus police officers, video cameras, smoke detectors in residence halls, etc.

Athletics Member NCAA. All Division I. *Intercollegiate sports:* basketball M(s)/W(s), cross-country running M(s)/W(s), golf M(s), soccer M(s)/W(s), softball W(s), tennis M(s)/W(s), track and field M(s)/W(s), volleyball W(s). *Intramural sports:* badminton M/W, basketball M/W, football M/W, golf M(c)/W(c), ice hockey M(c)/W(c), lacrosse M(c)/W(c), racquetball M/W, rugby M(c)/W(c), skiing (downhill) M(c)/W(c), soccer M/W, softball M/W, table tennis M/W, tennis M/W, ultimate Frisbee M(c)/W(c), volleyball M/W, water polo M/W.

Standardized Tests *Recommended:* SAT and SAT Subject Tests or ACT (for admission).

Costs (2011–12) *Comprehensive fee:* $41,953 includes full-time tuition ($30,000), mandatory fees ($618), and room and board ($11,335). Full-time tuition and fees vary according to program. Part-time tuition: $510 per quarter hour. Part-time tuition and fees vary according to program. *College room only:* $8245. Room and board charges vary according to board plan, housing facility, and location. *Payment plans:* installment, deferred payment. *Waivers:* employees or children of employees.

Financial Aid Of all full-time matriculated undergraduates who enrolled in 2011, 10,211 applied for aid, 9,991 were judged to have need, 653 had their need fully met. In 2011, 697 non-need-based awards were made. *Average percent of need met:* 61%. *Average financial aid package:* $19,411. *Average*

need-based loan: $4621. *Average need-based gift aid:* $14,031. *Average non-need-based aid:* $8882. *Average indebtedness upon graduation:* $27,486.

Applying *Options:* electronic application, early action, deferred entrance. *Application fee:* $40. *Required:* essay or personal statement, high school transcript, minimum 2.0 GPA. *Required for some:* minimum 3.0 GPA, audition/interviews required for the School of Music and Theatre School applicants. *Recommended:* minimum 2.5 GPA. *Application deadlines:* 2/1 (freshmen), rolling (transfers), 11/15 (early action). *Notification:* 3/15 (freshmen), continuous (transfers), 1/15 (early action).

Freshman Application Contact Carlene Klaas-Kennelly, Dean of Undergraduate Admissions, DePaul University, 1 East Jackson Boulevard, Suite 9000, Chicago, IL 60604. *Phone:* 312-362-8300. *Toll-free phone:* 800-4DE-PAUL. *E-mail:* admission@depaul.edu. *Web site:* http://www.depaul.edu/.

DeVry University
Addison, Illinois

Freshman Application Contact DeVry University, 1221 North Swift Road, Addison, IL 60101-6106. *Toll-free phone:* 866-338-7941. *Web site:* http://www.devry.edu/.

DeVry University
Chicago, Illinois

- **Proprietary** comprehensive, founded 1931, part of DeVry University
- **Urban** campus
- **Coed** 2,006 undergraduate students, 60% full-time, 42% women, 58% men
- **Minimally difficult** entrance level

Undergraduates 1,204 full-time, 802 part-time. 2% are from out of state; 38% Black or African American, non-Hispanic/Latino; 34% Hispanic/Latino; 5% Asian, non-Hispanic/Latino; 0.4% Native Hawaiian or other Pacific Islander, non-Hispanic/Latino; 0.2% American Indian or Alaska Native, non-Hispanic/Latino; 1% Two or more races, non-Hispanic/Latino; 5% Race/ethnicity unknown; 2% international; 13% transferred in.

Freshmen *Admission:* 227 enrolled.

Faculty *Total:* 196, 20% full-time. *Student/faculty ratio:* 17:1.

Academics *Calendar:* semesters. *Degrees:* associate, bachelor's, master's, and postbachelor's certificates. *Special study options:* adult/continuing education programs, part-time degree program.

Student Life *Housing:* college housing not available.

Costs (2011–12) *Tuition:* $15,294 full-time, $597 per credit hour part-time. Full-time tuition and fees vary according to course load. Part-time tuition and fees vary according to course load. *Required fees:* $80 full-time, $40 per term part-time. *Payment plans:* installment, deferred payment. *Waivers:* employees or children of employees.

Financial Aid Of all full-time matriculated undergraduates who enrolled in 2007, 479 applied for aid, 467 were judged to have need, 5 had their need fully met. In 2007, 14 non-need-based awards were made. *Average percent of need met:* 48%. *Average financial aid package:* $16,145. *Average need-based loan:* $8033. *Average need-based gift aid:* $8371. *Average non-need-based aid:* $11,220. *Average indebtedness upon graduation:* $49,157.

Applying *Application fee:* $50. *Required:* high school transcript, interview. *Application deadlines:* rolling (freshmen), rolling (transfers). *Notification:* continuous (freshmen), continuous (transfers).

Freshman Application Contact DeVry University, 3300 North Campbell Avenue, Chicago, IL 60618-5994. *Phone:* 773-929-8500. *Toll-free phone:* 866-338-7941. *Web site:* http://www.devry.edu/.

DeVry University
Downers Grove, Illinois

Admissions Office Contact DeVry University, 3005 Highland Parkway, Downers Grove, IL 60515. *Toll-free phone:* 866-338-7941. *Web site:* http://www.devry.edu/.

DeVry University
Elgin, Illinois

Admissions Office Contact DeVry University, Randall Point, 2250 Point Boulevard, Suite 250, Elgin, IL 60123. *Toll-free phone:* 866-338-7941. *Web site:* http://www.devry.edu/.

DeVry University
Gurnee, Illinois

Admissions Office Contact DeVry University, 1075 Tri-State Parkway, Suite 800, Gurnee, IL 60031-9126. *Toll-free phone:* 866-338-7941. *Web site:* http://www.devry.edu/.

DeVry University
Naperville, Illinois

Director of Admissions Admissions Office, DeVry University, 2056 Westings Avenue, Suite 40, Naperville, IL 60563-2361. *Toll-free phone:* 866-338-7941. *Web site:* http://www.devry.edu/.

DeVry University
Tinley Park, Illinois

Freshman Application Contact DeVry University, 18624 West Creek Drive, Tinley Park, IL 60477. *Toll-free phone:* 866-338-7941. *Web site:* http://www.devry.edu/.

DeVry University Online
Addison, Illinois

- **Proprietary** comprehensive, founded 2000
- **Coed** 21,826 undergraduate students, 23% full-time, 54% women, 46% men
- **Minimally difficult** entrance level

Undergraduates 5,011 full-time, 16,815 part-time. 89% are from out of state; 22% Black or African American, non-Hispanic/Latino; 8% Hispanic/Latino; 2% Asian, non-Hispanic/Latino; 0.4% Native Hawaiian or other Pacific Islander, non-Hispanic/Latino; 0.7% American Indian or Alaska Native, non-Hispanic/Latino; 2% Two or more races, non-Hispanic/Latino; 12% Race/ethnicity unknown; 0.2% international; 30% transferred in.

Freshmen *Admission:* 2,729 enrolled.

Faculty *Total:* 3,215, 0.3% full-time. *Student/faculty ratio:* 12:1.

Academics *Calendar:* semesters. *Degrees:* associate, bachelor's, master's, and postbachelor's certificates.

Costs (2011–12) *Tuition:* $15,294 full-time, $597 per credit hour part-time. Full-time tuition and fees vary according to course load. Part-time tuition and fees vary according to course load. *Required fees:* $80 full-time, $40 per term part-time. *Payment plans:* installment, deferred payment. *Waivers:* employees or children of employees.

Financial Aid Of all full-time matriculated undergraduates who enrolled in 2006, 810 applied for aid, 785 were judged to have need, 9 had their need fully met. In 2006, 146 non-need-based awards were made. *Average percent of need met:* 36%. *Average financial aid package:* $10,560. *Average need-based loan:* $6201. *Average need-based gift aid:* $7114. *Average non-need-based aid:* $10,591. *Average indebtedness upon graduation:* $35,423.

Applying *Application fee:* $50. *Required:* high school transcript, interview. *Application deadlines:* rolling (freshmen), rolling (transfers). *Notification:* continuous (freshmen), continuous (transfers).

Freshman Application Contact DeVry University Online, 1221 North Swift Road, Addison, IL 60101-6106. *Phone:* 877-496-9050. *Toll-free phone:* 866-338-7941. *Web site:* http://www.devry.edu/.

Dominican University
River Forest, Illinois

- **Independent Roman Catholic** comprehensive, founded 1901
- **Suburban** 30-acre campus with easy access to Chicago
- **Endowment** $24.3 million
- **Coed** 1,953 undergraduate students, 91% full-time, 67% women, 33% men
- **Moderately difficult** entrance level, 59% of applicants were admitted

Undergraduates 1,768 full-time, 185 part-time. Students come from 27 states and territories; 18 other countries; 7% are from out of state; 8% Black or African American, non-Hispanic/Latino; 34% Hispanic/Latino; 2% Asian, non-Hispanic/Latino; 0.2% Native Hawaiian or other Pacific Islander, non-Hispanic/Latino; 0.2% American Indian or Alaska Native, non-Hispanic/Latino; 2% Two or more races, non-Hispanic/Latino; 0.8% Race/ethnicity unknown; 2% international; 5% transferred in; 31% live on campus. *Retention:* 82% of full-time freshmen returned.

Freshmen *Admission:* 2,732 applied, 1,611 admitted, 416 enrolled. *Average high school GPA:* 3.47. *Test scores:* SAT critical reading scores over 500: 78%; SAT math scores over 500: 61%; SAT writing scores over 500: 67%; ACT scores over 18: 94%; SAT critical reading scores over 600: 28%; SAT

math scores over 600: 22%; SAT writing scores over 600: 11%; ACT scores over 24: 31%; ACT scores over 30: 2%.

Faculty *Total:* 394, 40% full-time, 62% with terminal degrees. *Student/faculty ratio:* 12:1.

Academics *Calendar:* semesters. *Degrees:* certificates, bachelor's, master's, doctoral, post-master's, postbachelor's, and first professional certificates. *Special study options:* accelerated degree program, adult/continuing education programs, advanced placement credit, distance learning, double majors, English as a second language, honors programs, independent study, internships, off-campus study, part-time degree program, services for LD students, student-designed majors, study abroad, summer session for credit. *Unusual degree programs:* 3-2 business administration; engineering with Illinois Institute of Technology; nursing with Rush University; social work; library science, occupational therapy with Rush University, pharmacy with Midwestern University.

Computers on Campus 552 computers/terminals are available on campus for general student use. Students can access the following: campus intranet, computer help desk, free student e-mail accounts, online (class) grades, online (class) registration, online (class) schedules, online student account information, online financial aid information. Campuswide network is available. 100% of college-owned or -operated housing units are wired for high-speed Internet access. Wireless service is available via computer centers, learning centers, libraries, student centers.

Student Life *Housing options:* coed, men-only, women-only. Campus housing is university owned and leased by the school. Freshman applicants given priority for college housing. *Activities and organizations:* drama/theater group, student-run newspaper, choral group, student government, Student Theater, Commuter Student Association, Resident Student Association, International Club. *Campus security:* 24-hour emergency response devices and patrols, student patrols, late-night transport/escort service, controlled dormitory access, door alarms. *Student services:* health clinic, personal/psychological counseling.

Athletics Member NCAA. All Division III. *Intercollegiate sports:* baseball M, basketball M/W, cross-country running M/W, golf M, soccer M/W, softball W, tennis M/W, volleyball W. *Intramural sports:* basketball M/W, bowling M/W, racquetball M/W, soccer M/W, softball W, tennis M/W, ultimate Frisbee M/W, volleyball W.

Standardized Tests *Required:* SAT or ACT (for admission).

Costs (2012–13) *One-time required fee:* $150. *Comprehensive fee:* $36,250 includes full-time tuition ($27,480), mandatory fees ($250), and room and board ($8520). Full-time tuition and fees vary according to course load. Part-time tuition: $916 per credit. Part-time tuition and fees vary according to course load. *Required fees:* $15 per term part-time. *College room only:* $4760. Room and board charges vary according to board plan and housing facility. *Payment plan:* deferred payment. *Waivers:* employees or children of employees.

Financial Aid Of all full-time matriculated undergraduates who enrolled in 2010, 1,521 applied for aid, 1,401 were judged to have need, 193 had their need fully met. 393 Federal Work-Study jobs (averaging $2270). 125 state and other part-time jobs (averaging $2421). In 2010, 194 non-need-based awards were made. *Average percent of need met:* 73%. *Average financial aid package:* $18,162. *Average need-based loan:* $4125. *Average need-based gift aid:* $14,312. *Average non-need-based aid:* $8039. *Average indebtedness upon graduation:* $22,605.

Applying *Options:* electronic application, deferred entrance. *Application fee:* $25. *Required:* essay or personal statement, high school transcript, minimum 2.8 GPA. *Required for some:* 2 letters of recommendation, interview. *Recommended:* interview. *Application deadlines:* rolling (freshmen), rolling (transfers). *Notification:* continuous (freshmen), continuous (transfers).

Freshman Application Contact Mr. Glenn Hamilton, Assistant Vice President, Enrollment Management, Dominican University, 7900 West Division Street, River Forest, IL 60305. *Phone:* 708-524-6800. *Toll-free phone:* 800-828-8475. *Fax:* 708-524-6864. *E-mail:* domadmis@dom.edu. *Web site:* http://www.dom.edu/.

Eastern Illinois University
Charleston, Illinois

- **State-supported** comprehensive, founded 1895
- **Small-town** 320-acre campus
- **Endowment** $51.6 million
- **Coed** 9,657 undergraduate students, 89% full-time, 59% women, 41% men
- **Moderately difficult** entrance level, 68% of applicants were admitted

Undergraduates 8,602 full-time, 1,055 part-time. Students come from 33 states and territories; 28 other countries; 2% are from out of state; 15% Black or African American, non-Hispanic/Latino; 4% Hispanic/Latino; 0.8% Asian, non-Hispanic/Latino; 0.1% Native Hawaiian or other Pacific Islander, non-Hispanic/Latino; 0.3% American Indian or Alaska Native, non-Hispanic/

Latino; 1% Two or more races, non-Hispanic/Latino; 4% Race/ethnicity unknown; 0.6% international; 12% transferred in; 49% live on campus. *Retention:* 79% of full-time freshmen returned.

Freshmen *Admission:* 7,076 applied, 4,808 admitted, 1,371 enrolled. *Average high school GPA:* 3.1. *Test scores:* ACT scores over 18: 89%; ACT scores over 24: 24%; ACT scores over 30: 2%.

Faculty *Total:* 741, 81% full-time, 60% with terminal degrees. *Student/faculty ratio:* 15:1.

Academics *Calendar:* semesters. *Degrees:* bachelor's, master's, post-master's, and postbachelor's certificates. *Special study options:* academic remediation for entering students, accelerated degree program, adult/continuing education programs, advanced placement credit, cooperative education, distance learning, double majors, freshman honors college, honors programs, independent study, internships, off-campus study, part-time degree program, services for LD students, study abroad, summer session for credit. *ROTC:* Army (b). *Unusual degree programs:* 3-2 engineering with University of Illinois at Urbana-Champaign and Southern Illinois University at Carbondale.

Computers on Campus 766 computers/terminals and 10,000 ports are available on campus for general student use. Students can access the following: computer help desk, free student e-mail accounts, online (class) grades, online (class) registration, online (class) schedules. Campuswide network is available. 100% of college-owned or -operated housing units are wired for high-speed Internet access. Wireless service is available via classrooms, computer centers, computer labs, dorm rooms, learning centers, libraries, student centers.

Student Life *Housing:* on-campus residence required for freshman year. *Options:* coed, men-only, women-only. Campus housing is university owned. Freshman campus housing is guaranteed. *Activities and organizations:* drama/theater group, student-run newspaper, radio and television station, choral group, marching band, Illinois Student Education Association, Math Energy at Eastern Illinois University, Black Student Union, Alpha Gamma, Alpha Phi, national fraternities, national sororities. *Campus security:* 24-hour emergency response devices and patrols, student patrols, late-night transport/escort service, AlertEIU and warning sirens. *Student services:* health clinic, personal/psychological counseling, women's center, legal services.

Athletics Member NCAA. All Division I except football (Division I-AA). *Intercollegiate sports:* badminton M(c)/W(c), baseball M(s), basketball M(s)/W(s), cross-country running M(s)/W(s), equestrian sports M(c)/W(c), golf M(s)/W(s), ice hockey M(c)/W(c), lacrosse M(c)/W(c), racquetball M(c)/W(c), rugby M(c)/W(s), soccer M(s)/W(s), softball W(s), swimming and diving M(s)/W(s), tennis M(s)/W(s), track and field M(s)/W(s), ultimate Frisbee M(c)/W(c), volleyball W(s), water polo M(c)/W(c). *Intramural sports:* badminton M/W, basketball M/W, bowling M/W, racquetball M/W, soccer M/W, softball M/W, table tennis M/W, tennis M/W, volleyball M/W, weight lifting M/W.

Standardized Tests *Required:* SAT or ACT (for admission).

Costs (2011–12) *Tuition:* state resident $8070 full-time, $269 per credit hour part-time; nonresident $24,210 full-time, $807 per credit hour part-time. Full-time tuition and fees vary according to course load and student level. Part-time tuition and fees vary according to course load and student level. No tuition increase for student's term of enrollment. *Required fees:* $2464 full-time, $89 per credit hour part-time. *Room and board:* $8884. Room and board charges vary according to board plan and housing facility. *Payment plan:* installment. *Waivers:* senior citizens and employees or children of employees.

Financial Aid Of all full-time matriculated undergraduates who enrolled in 2011, 7,621 applied for aid, 5,669 were judged to have need, 417 had their need fully met. 150 Federal Work-Study jobs (averaging $790). 2,469 state and other part-time jobs (averaging $1679). In 2011, 245 non-need-based awards were made. *Average percent of need met:* 60%. *Average financial aid package:* $9785. *Average need-based loan:* $3900. *Average need-based gift aid:* $3817. *Average non-need-based aid:* $4117. *Average indebtedness upon graduation:* $26,500.

Applying *Options:* electronic application. *Application fee:* $30. *Required:* high school transcript, minimum 2.3 GPA, standardized test scores, audition for music program. *Required for some:* essay or personal statement, 2 letters of recommendation, standardized test scores, audition for music program. *Application deadlines:* rolling (freshmen), rolling (out-of-state freshmen), rolling (transfers). *Notification:* continuous (freshmen), continuous (out-of-state freshmen), continuous (transfers).

Freshman Application Contact Brenda Major, Director of Admissions, Eastern Illinois University, 600 Lincoln Avenue, Charleston, IL 61920. *Phone:* 217-581-2223. *Toll-free phone:* 877-581-2348 (in-state); 800-252-5711 (out-of-state). *Fax:* 217-581-7060. *E-mail:* admissions@eiu.edu. *Web site:* http://www.eiu.edu/.

East-West University
Chicago, Illinois

Freshman Application Contact Mr. Ho Chung, Director of Admissions, East-West University, 816 South Michigan Avenue, Chicago, IL 60605-2103,

Phone: 312-939-0111 Ext. 1829. *Fax:* 312-939-0083. *E-mail:* ho@eastwest.edu. *Web site:* http://www.eastwest.edu/.

Ellis University
Chicago, Illinois

Freshman Application Contact Office of Admissions, Ellis University, 111 North Canal Street, Suite 380, Chicago, IL 60606-7204. *Phone:* 312-669-5000. *Toll-free phone:* 877-355-4762. *E-mail:* admissions@ellis.edu. *Web site:* http://www.ellis.edu/.

Elmhurst College
Elmhurst, Illinois

- **Independent** comprehensive, founded 1871, affiliated with United Church of Christ
- **Suburban** 38-acre campus with easy access to Chicago
- **Endowment** $92.0 million
- **Coed** 3,190 undergraduate students, 93% full-time, 62% women, 38% men
- **Moderately difficult** entrance level, 72% of applicants were admitted

Undergraduates 2,974 full-time, 216 part-time. Students come from 19 states and territories; 38 other countries; 9% are from out of state; 4% Black or African American, non-Hispanic/Latino; 10% Hispanic/Latino; 4% Asian, non-Hispanic/Latino; 0.3% Native Hawaiian or other Pacific Islander, non-Hispanic/Latino; 0.5% American Indian or Alaska Native, non-Hispanic/Latino; 2% Two or more races, non-Hispanic/Latino; 3% Race/ethnicity unknown; 0.7% international; 10% transferred in; 40% live on campus. *Retention:* 77% of full-time freshmen returned.

Freshmen *Admission:* 2,899 applied, 2,093 admitted, 608 enrolled. *Average high school GPA:* 3.39. *Test scores:* SAT critical reading scores over 500: 59%; SAT math scores over 500: 67%; SAT writing scores over 500: 51%; ACT scores over 18: 97%; SAT critical reading scores over 600: 19%; SAT math scores over 600: 23%; SAT writing scores over 600: 16%; ACT scores over 24: 53%; SAT writing scores over 700: 2%; ACT scores over 30: 8%.

Faculty *Total:* 399, 45% full-time, 28% with terminal degrees. *Student/faculty ratio:* 14:1.

Academics *Calendar:* 4-1-4. *Degrees:* bachelor's and master's. *Special study options:* academic remediation for entering students, accelerated degree program, adult/continuing education programs, advanced placement credit, cooperative education, double majors, honors programs, independent study, internships, off-campus study, part-time degree program, services for LD students, study abroad, summer session for credit. *ROTC:* Army (c), Air Force (c). *Unusual degree programs:* 3-2 engineering with University of Illinois at Urbana-Champaign, University of Southern California.

Computers on Campus 800 computers/terminals are available on campus for general student use. Students can access the following: campus intranet, computer help desk, free student e-mail accounts, online (class) grades, online (class) registration, online (class) schedules. Campuswide network is available. 100% of college-owned or -operated housing units are wired for high-speed Internet access. Wireless service is available via classrooms, computer labs, dorm rooms, libraries, student centers.

Student Life *Housing options:* coed. Campus housing is university owned, leased by the school and is provided by a third party. Freshman applicants given priority for college housing. *Activities and organizations:* drama/theater group, student-run newspaper, radio station, choral group, Programming Board and Student Government, theater and music groups, Black Student Union, residence life groups, Hablamos, national fraternities, national sororities. *Campus security:* 24-hour emergency response devices and patrols, late-night transport/escort service, controlled dormitory access. *Student services:* health clinic, personal/psychological counseling.

Athletics Member NCAA. All Division III. *Intercollegiate sports:* baseball M, basketball M/W, bowling W, cross-country running M/W, football M, golf M/W, lacrosse M/W, soccer M/W, softball W, tennis M/W, track and field M/W, volleyball W, wrestling M. *Intramural sports:* basketball M/W, football M, golf M/W, racquetball M/W, soccer M/W, softball W, volleyball M/W.

Standardized Tests *Required:* SAT or ACT (for admission).

Costs (2011–12) *Comprehensive fee:* $38,578 includes full-time tuition ($29,994), mandatory fees ($60), and room and board ($8524). Part-time tuition: $854 per semester hour. Part-time tuition and fees vary according to course load. *College room only:* $5154. Room and board charges vary according to board plan and housing facility. *Payment plan:* installment. *Waivers:* senior citizens and employees or children of employees.

Financial Aid Of all full-time matriculated undergraduates who enrolled in 2011, 2,439 applied for aid, 2,233 were judged to have need, 672 had their need fully met. 432 Federal Work-Study jobs (averaging $912). 438 state and other part-time jobs (averaging $1584). In 2011, 549 non-need-based awards were made. *Average percent of need met:* 79%. *Average financial aid package:* $22,881. *Average need-based loan:* $4391. *Average need-based gift aid:* $17,773. *Average non-need-based aid:* $12,314. *Average indebtedness upon graduation:* $26,507.

Applying *Options:* electronic application, deferred entrance. *Required:* high school transcript. *Required for some:* essay or personal statement, interview. *Recommended:* essay or personal statement, interview. *Application deadlines:* rolling (freshmen), rolling (transfers). *Notification:* continuous (freshmen), continuous (transfers).

Freshman Application Contact Mrs. Stephanie Levenson, Director of Admission, Elmhurst College, Elmhurst College, Admission Office, 190 South Prospect Avenue, Elmhurst, IL 60126-3296. *Phone:* 630-617-3400. *Toll-free phone:* 800-697-1871. *Fax:* 630-617-5501. *E-mail:* admit@elmhurst.edu. *Web site:* http://www.elmhurst.edu/.

Eureka College
Eureka, Illinois

Freshman Application Contact Dr. Brian Sajko, Dean of Admissions and Financial Aid, Eureka College, 300 East College Avenue, Eureka, IL 61530. *Phone:* 309-467-6350. *Toll-free phone:* 888-4-EUREKA. *Fax:* 309-467-6576. *E-mail:* admissions@eureka.edu. *Web site:* http://www.eureka.edu/.

Governors State University
University Park, Illinois

- **State-supported** upper-level, founded 1969
- **Suburban** 750-acre campus with easy access to Chicago
- **Coed** 2,943 undergraduate students, 39% full-time, 69% women, 31% men

Undergraduates 1,150 full-time, 1,793 part-time. 2% are from out of state; 37% Black or African American, non-Hispanic/Latino; 9% Hispanic/Latino; 2% Asian, non-Hispanic/Latino; 0.3% American Indian or Alaska Native, non-Hispanic/Latino; 0.5% Two or more races, non-Hispanic/Latino; 5% Race/ethnicity unknown; 0.3% international; 28% transferred in.

Academics *Calendar:* trimesters. *Degrees:* certificates, bachelor's, master's, doctoral, post-master's, and postbachelor's certificates. *Special study options:* adult/continuing education programs, advanced placement credit, distance learning, double majors, honors programs, independent study, internships, off-campus study, part-time degree program, services for LD students, student-designed majors, summer session for credit.

Computers on Campus Students can access the following: computer help desk, free student e-mail accounts, online (class) grades, online (class) registration, online (class) schedules, student portal. Campuswide network is available.

Student Life *Housing:* college housing not available. *Activities and organizations:* student-run newspaper, choral group. *Campus security:* 24-hour emergency response devices and patrols, late-night transport/escort service. *Student services:* personal/psychological counseling.

Athletics *Intramural sports:* badminton M/W, basketball M/W, racquetball M/W, skiing (cross-country) M/W, softball M/W, table tennis M/W, volleyball M/W.

Costs (2011–12) *Tuition:* state resident $7290 full-time, $243 per credit hour part-time; nonresident $14,580 full-time, $486 per credit hour part-time. Full-time tuition and fees vary according to reciprocity agreements and student level. Part-time tuition and fees vary according to reciprocity agreements and student level. No tuition increase for student's term of enrollment. *Required fees:* $1646 full-time, $46 per credit hour part-time, $133 per credit hour part-time. *Payment plans:* installment, deferred payment. *Waivers:* senior citizens and employees or children of employees.

Financial Aid Of all full-time matriculated undergraduates who enrolled in 2010, 859 applied for aid, 807 were judged to have need, 120 had their need fully met. In 2010, 40 non-need-based awards were made. *Average percent of need met:* 65%. *Average financial aid package:* $4795. *Average need-based loan:* $2227. *Average need-based gift aid:* $3087. *Average non-need-based aid:* $2055.

Applying *Options:* electronic application, deferred entrance. *Application deadline:* rolling (transfers).

Application Contact Ms. Sharon Evans, Director of Admissions, Governors State University, One University Parkway, University Park, IL 60466. *Phone:* 708-534-4490. *Toll-free phone:* 800-GSU-8GSU. *Fax:* 708-235-7455. *E-mail:* s-evans@govst.edu. *Web site:* http://www.govst.edu/.

Greenville College

Greenville, Illinois

- **Independent Free Methodist** comprehensive, founded 1892
- **Small-town** 12-acre campus with easy access to St. Louis
- **Endowment** $13.3 million
- **Coed** 1,279 undergraduate students, 96% full-time, 49% women, 51% men
- **Moderately difficult** entrance level, 74% of applicants were admitted

Undergraduates 1,230 full-time, 49 part-time. Students come from 40 states and territories; 10 other countries; 32% are from out of state; 10% Black or African American, non-Hispanic/Latino; 3% Hispanic/Latino; 0.7% Asian, non-Hispanic/Latino; 0.1% Native Hawaiian or other Pacific Islander, non-Hispanic/Latino; 0.1% American Indian or Alaska Native, non-Hispanic/Latino; 2% Two or more races, non-Hispanic/Latino; 8% Race/ethnicity unknown; 2% international; 7% transferred in; 80% live on campus. *Retention:* 67% of full-time freshmen returned.

Freshmen *Admission:* 1,107 applied, 823 admitted, 276 enrolled. *Average high school GPA:* 3.24. *Test scores:* SAT critical reading scores over 500: 68%; SAT math scores over 500: 55%; ACT scores over 18: 82%; SAT critical reading scores over 600: 19%; SAT math scores over 600: 29%; ACT scores over 24: 35%; SAT critical reading scores over 700: 8%; SAT math scores over 700: 3%; ACT scores over 30: 6%.

Faculty *Total:* 161, 37% full-time, 33% with terminal degrees. *Student/faculty ratio:* 15:1.

Academics *Calendar:* 4-1-4. *Degrees:* bachelor's and master's. *Special study options:* academic remediation for entering students, accelerated degree program, adult/continuing education programs, advanced placement credit, cooperative education, double majors, external degree program, honors programs, independent study, internships, off-campus study, part-time degree program, student-designed majors, study abroad, summer session for credit. *Unusual degree programs:* 3-2 engineering with University of Illinois at Urbana-Champaign; Washington University in St. Louis; nursing with St. John's College of Nursing; chiropractic at Logan College of Chiropractic.

Computers on Campus 65 computers/terminals are available on campus for general student use. Students can access the following: campus intranet, computer help desk, free student e-mail accounts, online (class) grades, online (class) registration, online (class) schedules. Campuswide network is available. 100% of college-owned or -operated housing units are wired for high-speed Internet access. Wireless service is available via entire campus.

Student Life *Housing:* on-campus residence required through senior year. *Options:* men-only, women-only. Campus housing is university owned. Freshman campus housing is guaranteed. *Activities and organizations:* drama/theater group, student-run newspaper, radio station, choral group, marching band, Campus Activity Board, Greenville Student Outreach, Fellowship of Christian Athletes, Greenville College Student Association, African American Student Union. *Campus security:* 24-hour emergency response devices and patrols, late-night transport/escort service, controlled dormitory access. *Student services:* personal/psychological counseling.

Athletics Member NCAA, NCCAA. All NCAA Division III. *Intercollegiate sports:* baseball M, basketball M/W, cross-country running M/W, football M, soccer M/W, softball W, tennis M/W, track and field M/W, volleyball W. *Intramural sports:* basketball M/W, cheerleading W, football M/W, softball M/W, ultimate Frisbee M/W, volleyball M/W.

Standardized Tests *Required:* SAT or ACT (for admission).

Costs (2011–12) *Comprehensive fee:* $29,536 includes full-time tuition ($22,034), mandatory fees ($164), and room and board ($7338). Part-time tuition: $467 per credit hour. Part-time tuition and fees vary according to course load. *College room only:* $3550. Room and board charges vary according to housing facility. *Waivers:* senior citizens and employees or children of employees.

Financial Aid Of all full-time matriculated undergraduates who enrolled in 2011, 1,136 applied for aid, 1,052 were judged to have need, 89 had their need fully met. In 2011, 149 non-need-based awards were made. *Average percent of need met:* 68%. *Average financial aid package:* $16,597. *Average need-based loan:* $4288. *Average need-based gift aid:* $12,880. *Average non-need-based aid:* $6970. *Average indebtedness upon graduation:* $23,976.

Applying *Options:* electronic application, early admission, deferred entrance. *Application fee:* $30. *Required:* essay or personal statement, high school transcript, minimum 2.5 GPA, 2 letters of recommendation, agreement to code of conduct. *Required for some:* interview. *Application deadlines:* rolling (freshmen), rolling (transfers). *Notification:* continuous (freshmen), continuous (transfers).

Freshman Application Contact Mr. John R. Massena, Director of Undergraduate Admissions, Greenville College, 315 East College Avenue, Greenville, IL 62246. *Phone:* 618-664-7100. *Toll-free phone:* 800-345-4440. *Fax:* 618-664-9841. *E-mail:* admissions@greenville.edu. *Web site:* http://www.greenville.edu/.

Harrington College of Design

Chicago, Illinois

- **Proprietary** comprehensive, founded 1931, part of Career Education Corporation
- **Urban** campus with easy access to Chicago
- **Coed, primarily women** 645 undergraduate students, 38% full-time, 76% women, 24% men
- **Noncompetitive** entrance level, 89% of applicants were admitted

Undergraduates 247 full-time, 398 part-time. Students come from 17 states and territories; 11 other countries; 11% are from out of state; 13% Black or African American, non-Hispanic/Latino; 16% Hispanic/Latino; 3% Asian, non-Hispanic/Latino; 0.9% Native Hawaiian or other Pacific Islander, non-Hispanic/Latino; 0.2% American Indian or Alaska Native, non-Hispanic/Latino; 2% Two or more races, non-Hispanic/Latino; 4% Race/ethnicity unknown; 2% international; 10% transferred in. *Retention:* 69% of full-time freshmen returned.

Freshmen *Admission:* 73 applied, 65 admitted, 33 enrolled. *Average high school GPA:* 2.95.

Faculty *Total:* 77, 22% full-time, 4% with terminal degrees. *Student/faculty ratio:* 14:1.

Academics *Calendar:* semesters. *Degrees:* associate, bachelor's, and master's. *Special study options:* academic remediation for entering students, internships, part-time degree program, study abroad, summer session for credit.

Computers on Campus 249 computers/terminals are available on campus for general student use. Students can access the following: campus intranet, computer help desk, free student e-mail accounts, online (class) grades, online (class) registration, online (class) schedules, we have wireless access for student use and network file storage for students. Campuswide network is available. Wireless service is available via entire campus.

Student Life *Housing:* college housing not available. *Activities and organizations:* student-run newspaper, American Society of Interior Designers, International Interior Design Association, American Industry of Graphic Artists, student government, Digital Photography Focus Group. *Campus security:* 24-hour emergency response devices and patrols. *Student services:* personal/psychological counseling.

Standardized Tests *Recommended:* SAT or ACT (for admission).

Costs (2012–13) *Tuition:* $18,250 full-time, $4750 per term part-time. Full-time tuition and fees vary according to course load and program. Part-time tuition and fees vary according to course load and program. *Required fees:* $1050 full-time, $410 per term part-time. *Payment plan:* installment. *Waivers:* employees or children of employees.

Financial Aid *Average percent of need met:* 30%. *Average financial aid package:* $3500.

Applying *Options:* electronic application. *Application fee:* $50. *Required:* high school transcript, interview. *Recommended:* essay or personal statement, 1 letter of recommendation. *Application deadlines:* rolling (freshmen), rolling (out-of-state freshmen), rolling (transfers). *Notification:* continuous (freshmen), continuous (out-of-state freshmen), continuous (transfers).

Freshman Application Contact Harrington College of Design, 200 West Madison Street, Chicago, IL 60605-1496. *Phone:* 312-697-8051. *Toll-free phone:* 866-590-4423 (in-state); 877-939-4975 (out-of-state). *Web site:* http://www.interiordesign.edu/.

Hebrew Theological College

Skokie, Illinois

Freshman Application Contact Rabbi Berish Cardash, Hebrew Theological College, 7135 North Carpenter Road, Skokie, IL 60077-3263. *Phone:* 847-982-2500. *Web site:* http://www.htc.edu/.

Illinois College

Jacksonville, Illinois

- **Independent interdenominational** comprehensive, founded 1829
- **Small-town** 62-acre campus with easy access to St. Louis
- **Coed** 938 undergraduate students, 97% full-time, 48% women, 52% men
- **Moderately difficult** entrance level, 65% of applicants were admitted

Undergraduates 913 full-time, 25 part-time. 12% are from out of state; 8% Black or African American, non-Hispanic/Latino; 3% Hispanic/Latino; 0.8% Asian, non-Hispanic/Latino; 0.2% American Indian or Alaska Native, non-Hispanic/Latino; 4% Two or more races, non-Hispanic/Latino; 3% Race/ethnicity unknown; 2% international; 5% transferred in; 83% live on campus. *Retention:* 83% of full-time freshmen returned.

Freshmen *Admission:* 1,626 applied, 1,054 admitted, 288 enrolled. *Average high school GPA:* 3.33. *Test scores:* SAT critical reading scores over 500: 45%; SAT math scores over 500: 45%; SAT writing scores over 500: 55%;

ACT scores over 18: 86%; SAT critical reading scores over 600: 14%; SAT math scores over 600: 23%; SAT writing scores over 600: 5%; ACT scores over 24: 39%; SAT math scores over 700: 5%; ACT scores over 30: 6%. **Faculty** *Total:* 93, 82% full-time, 71% with terminal degrees. *Student/faculty ratio:* 11:1.

Academics *Calendar:* semesters. *Degrees:* bachelor's and master's.

Computers on Campus Students can access the following: computer help desk, free student e-mail accounts, online (class) grades, online (class) registration, online (class) schedules. Campuswide network is available. Wireless service is available via entire campus.

Student Life *Housing:* on-campus residence required through sophomore year. *Options:* coed, men-only, women-only. Campus housing is university owned. Freshman campus housing is guaranteed. *Campus security:* 24-hour emergency response devices and patrols, late-night transport/escort service, controlled dormitory access.

Athletics Member NCAA. All Division III. *Intercollegiate sports:* baseball M, cheerleading W, cross-country running M/W, football M, golf M/W, soccer M/W, softball W, swimming and diving M/W, tennis M/W, track and field M/W, volleyball W. *Intramural sports:* badminton M/W, basketball M/W, fencing M/W, football M, racquetball M/W, softball M/W, swimming and diving M/W, volleyball M/W, water polo M/W, weight lifting M/W.

Costs (2011–12) *Comprehensive fee:* $32,730 includes full-time tuition ($24,030), mandatory fees ($500), and room and board ($8200). Part-time tuition: $800 per semester hour. *College room only:* $4300. Room and board charges vary according to board plan and housing facility.

Financial Aid Of all full-time matriculated undergraduates who enrolled in 2010, 778 applied for aid, 711 were judged to have need, 181 had their need fully met. In 2010, 127 non-need-based awards were made. *Average percent of need met:* 89%. *Average financial aid package:* $20,096. *Average need-based loan:* $4580. *Average need-based gift aid:* $15,409. *Average non-need-based aid:* $10,944. *Average indebtedness upon graduation:* $24,401.

Applying *Options:* electronic application, early admission, early action, deferred entrance. *Required:* high school transcript, 1 letter of recommendation. *Required for some:* essay or personal statement. *Recommended:* essay or personal statement, minimum 2.5 GPA, interview. *Application deadlines:* rolling (freshmen), 12/15 (early action). *Notification:* continuous (freshmen).

Freshman Application Contact Mr. Rick Bystry, Associate Director of Admission, Illinois College, 1101 West College, Jacksonville, IL 62650. *Phone:* 217-245-3030. *Toll-free phone:* 866-464-5265. *Fax:* 217-245-3034. *E-mail:* admissions@ic.edu. *Web site:* http://www.ic.edu/.

The Illinois Institute of Art–Chicago
Chicago, Illinois

- **Proprietary** 4-year, founded 1916, part of Education Management Corporation
- **Urban** campus
- **Coed**

Academics *Calendar:* quarters. *Degrees:* diplomas, associate, and bachelor's.
Freshman Application Contact The Illinois Institute of Art–Chicago, 350 North Orleans Street, Chicago, IL 60654. *Phone:* 312-280-3500. *Toll-free phone:* 800-351-3450. *Web site:* http://www.artinstitutes.edu/chicago/.

See page 1376 for the College Close-Up.

The Illinois Institute of Art–Schaumburg
Schaumburg, Illinois

- **Proprietary** 4-year, part of Education Management Corporation
- **Suburban** campus
- **Coed**

Academics *Calendar:* quarters. *Degrees:* diplomas, associate, and bachelor's.
Freshman Application Contact The Illinois Institute of Art–Schaumburg, 1000 North Plaza Drive, Suite 100, Schaumburg, IL 60173. *Phone:* 847-619-3450. *Toll-free phone:* 800-314-3450. *Web site:* http://www.artinstitutes.edu/schaumburg/.

See page 1378 for the College Close-Up.

The Illinois Institute of Art–Tinley Park
Tinley Park, Illinois

- **Proprietary** 4-year, part of Education Management Corporation
- **Coed**

Academics *Degrees:* diplomas, associate, and bachelor's.

Freshman Application Contact The Illinois Institute of Art–Tinley Park, 18670 Graphic Drive, Tinley Park, IL 60477. *Phone:* 708-781-4200. *Toll-free phone:* 877-342-3298. *Web site:* http://www.artinstitutes.edu/tinleypark.

See page 1380 for the College Close-Up.

Illinois Institute of Technology
Chicago, Illinois

- **Independent** comprehensive, founded 1890
- **Urban** 120-acre campus with easy access to Chicago
- **Endowment** $194.2 million
- **Coed** 2,714 undergraduate students, 93% full-time, 31% women, 69% men
- **Moderately difficult** entrance level, 64% of applicants were admitted

Undergraduates 2,513 full-time, 201 part-time. Students come from 51 states and territories; 100 other countries; 26% are from out of state; 7% Black or African American, non-Hispanic/Latino; 11% Hispanic/Latino; 11% Asian, non-Hispanic/Latino; 0.7% Native Hawaiian or other Pacific Islander, non-Hispanic/Latino; 0.5% American Indian or Alaska Native, non-Hispanic/Latino; 0.5% Two or more races, non-Hispanic/Latino; 8% Race/ethnicity unknown; 21% international; 11% transferred in; 60% live on campus. *Retention:* 95% of full-time freshmen returned.

Freshmen *Admission:* 2,466 applied, 1,566 admitted, 448 enrolled. *Average high school GPA:* 3.97. *Test scores:* SAT critical reading scores over 500: 83%; SAT math scores over 500: 98%; SAT writing scores over 500: 83%; ACT scores over 18: 100%; SAT critical reading scores over 600: 43%; SAT math scores over 600: 83%; SAT writing scores over 600: 46%; ACT scores over 24: 79%; SAT critical reading scores over 700: 16%; SAT math scores over 700: 36%; SAT writing scores over 700: 11%; ACT scores over 30: 31%.

Faculty *Total:* 714, 56% full-time. *Student/faculty ratio:* 11:1.

Academics *Calendar:* semesters. *Degrees:* bachelor's, master's, doctoral, and first professional. *Special study options:* advanced placement credit, cooperative education, distance learning, double majors, English as a second language, independent study, internships, off-campus study, part-time degree program, services for LD students, study abroad, summer session for credit. *ROTC:* Army (b), Navy (b), Air Force (b). *Unusual degree programs:* 3-2 engineering; BS in Political Science/Master of Public Administration; BS in Psychology/MS in Personnel and Human Resources Development; BS in Psychology/MS. in Rehabilitation Counseling Dual Degree Program.

Computers on Campus 500 computers/terminals are available on campus for general student use. Students can access the following: campus intranet, computer help desk, free student e-mail accounts, online (class) grades, online (class) registration, online (class) schedules. Campuswide network is available. 100% of college-owned or -operated housing units are wired for high-speed Internet access. Wireless service is available via classrooms, computer centers, computer labs, dorm rooms, learning centers, libraries, student centers.

Student Life *Housing:* on-campus residence required for freshman year. *Options:* coed. Campus housing is university owned and is provided by a third party. Freshman applicants given priority for college housing. *Activities and organizations:* drama/theater group, student-run newspaper, radio station, choral group, Union Board, International Students Association, Student Government Association, Greek Council, Commuter Student Associate, national fraternities, national sororities. *Campus security:* 24-hour emergency response devices and patrols, late-night transport/escort service, controlled dormitory access. *Student services:* health clinic, personal/psychological counseling, women's center, legal services.

Athletics Member NAIA. *Intercollegiate sports:* badminton M(c)/W(c), baseball M(s), bowling M(c)/W(c), cross-country running M(s)/W(s), lacrosse M(c)/W(c), rugby M(c)/W(c), soccer M(s)/W(s), swimming and diving M(s)/W(s), track and field M/W, ultimate Frisbee M(c)/W(c), volleyball M(c)/W(s). *Intramural sports:* badminton M/W, basketball M/W, bowling M/W, field hockey M/W, football M/W, racquetball M/W, soccer M/W, softball M/W, squash M/W, table tennis M/W, tennis M(c)/W(c), track and field M(c)/W(c), ultimate Frisbee M/W, volleyball M/W.

Standardized Tests *Required:* SAT or ACT (for admission).

Costs (2012–13) *One-time required fee:* $165. *Comprehensive fee:* $48,128 includes full-time tuition ($36,504), mandatory fees ($1160), and room and board ($10,464). Full-time tuition and fees vary according to student level. Part-time tuition: $1119 per credit hour. Part-time tuition and fees vary according to course load and student level. *Required fees:* $25 per course part-time, $100 per term part-time. *College room only:* $5384. Room and board charges vary according to board plan and housing facility. *Payment plan:* installment. *Waivers:* employees or children of employees.

Financial Aid Of all full-time matriculated undergraduates who enrolled in 2010, 1,576 applied for aid, 1,487 were judged to have need, 223 had their need fully met. 741 Federal Work-Study jobs (averaging $2415). In 2010, 860 non-need-based awards were made. *Average percent of need met:* 77%. *Aver-*

age financial aid package: $27,639. *Average need-based loan:* $4829. *Average need-based gift aid:* $22,054. *Average non-need-based aid:* $14,481.

Applying *Options:* electronic application, early admission, early action, deferred entrance. *Required:* essay or personal statement, high school transcript, 1 letter of recommendation. *Recommended:* interview. *Application deadlines:* 8/1 (freshmen), 6/1 (transfers), 12/1 (early action). *Notification:* continuous (freshmen), continuous (transfers), 11/15 (early action).

Freshman Application Contact Mr. Alfred Nunez, Acting Director, Undergraduate Admissions Office, Illinois Institute of Technology, Office of Undergraduate Admission, Perlstein 101, 10 West 33rd Street, Chicago, IL 60616. *Phone:* 312-567-3025. *Toll-free phone:* 866-472-3448. *Fax:* 312-567-6939. *E-mail:* admission@iit.edu. *Web site:* http://www.iit.edu/.

Illinois State University
Normal, Illinois

- **State-supported** university, founded 1857
- **Urban** 490-acre campus
- **Endowment** $88.4 million
- **Coed** 18,594 undergraduate students, 94% full-time, 55% women, 45% men
- **Moderately difficult** entrance level, 63% of applicants were admitted

Undergraduates 17,536 full-time, 1,058 part-time. Students come from 41 states and territories; 33 other countries; 2% are from out of state; 6% Black or African American, non-Hispanic/Latino; 6% Hispanic/Latino; 2% Asian, non-Hispanic/Latino; 0.1% Native Hawaiian or other Pacific Islander, non-Hispanic/Latino; 0.2% American Indian or Alaska Native, non-Hispanic/Latino; 1% Two or more races, non-Hispanic/Latino; 2% Race/ethnicity unknown; 0.5% international; 10% transferred in; 30% live on campus. *Retention:* 85% of full-time freshmen returned.

Freshmen *Admission:* 13,156 applied, 8,339 admitted, 3,316 enrolled. *Average high school GPA:* 3.33. *Test scores:* ACT scores over 18: 99%; ACT scores over 24: 52%; ACT scores over 30: 4%.

Faculty *Total:* 1,205, 73% full-time, 68% with terminal degrees. *Student/faculty ratio:* 19:1.

Academics *Calendar:* semesters. *Degrees:* bachelor's, master's, doctoral, post-master's, postbachelor's, and first professional certificates. *Special study options:* academic remediation for entering students, accelerated degree program, adult/continuing education programs, advanced placement credit, cooperative education, distance learning, double majors, English as a second language, honors programs, independent study, internships, off-campus study, part-time degree program, services for LD students, student-designed majors, study abroad, summer session for credit. *ROTC:* Army (b). *Unusual degree programs:* 3-2 engineering with University of Illinois or Bradley University.

Computers on Campus 2,204 computers/terminals and 2,204 ports are available on campus for general student use. Students can access the following: campus intranet, computer help desk, free student e-mail accounts, online (class) grades, online (class) registration, online (class) schedules. Campuswide network is available. 100% of college-owned or -operated housing units are wired for high-speed Internet access. Wireless service is available via classrooms, computer centers, computer labs, libraries, student centers.

Student Life *Housing:* on-campus residence required through sophomore year. *Options:* coed, women-only, disabled students. Campus housing is university owned. Freshman campus housing is guaranteed. *Activities and organizations:* drama/theater group, student-run newspaper, radio and television station, choral group, marching band, national fraternities, national sororities. *Campus security:* 24-hour emergency response devices and patrols, late-night transport/escort service, controlled dormitory access. *Student services:* health clinic, personal/psychological counseling, women's center, legal services.

Athletics Member NCAA. All Division I except football (Division I-AA). *Intercollegiate sports:* baseball M(s), basketball M(s)/W(s), cross-country running M(s)/W(s), golf M(s)/W(s), gymnastics W(s), soccer W(s), softball W(s), swimming and diving W(s), tennis M(s)/W(s), track and field M(s)/W(s), volleyball W(s). *Intramural sports:* badminton M/W, baseball M, basketball M/W, bowling M(c)/W(c), field hockey M/W, football M, golf M/W, gymnastics M(c), ice hockey M(c), lacrosse M(c), racquetball M/W, rugby M(c)/W(c), soccer M/W, softball M/W, tennis M/W, ultimate Frisbee M/W, volleyball M(c)/W.

Standardized Tests *Required:* SAT or ACT (for admission).

Costs (2011–12) *Tuition:* state resident $9630 full-time, $321 per credit hour part-time; nonresident $16,590 full-time, $553 per credit hour part-time. Full-time tuition and fees vary according to course load and degree level. Part-time tuition and fees vary according to course load and degree level. No tuition increase for student's term of enrollment. *Required fees:* $2600 full-time, $73 per credit hour part-time. *Room and board:* $9090. Room and board charges vary according to board plan, housing facility, and location. *Payment plan:* installment. *Waivers:* minority students, senior citizens, and employees or children of employees.

Financial Aid Of all full-time matriculated undergraduates who enrolled in 2011, 13,855 applied for aid, 10,919 were judged to have need, 3,777 had their need fully met. 625 Federal Work-Study jobs (averaging $2410). 47 state and other part-time jobs (averaging $1315). In 2011, 261 non-need-based awards were made. *Average percent of need met:* 77%. *Average financial aid package:* $12,939. *Average need-based loan:* $6837. *Average need-based gift aid:* $9457. *Average non-need-based aid:* $3226. *Average indebtedness upon graduation:* $24,767.

Applying *Options:* electronic application. *Application fee:* $40. *Required:* essay or personal statement, high school transcript. *Application deadlines:* 3/1 (freshmen), 4/1 (transfers). *Notification:* continuous (freshmen), continuous (transfers).

Freshman Application Contact Ms. Doris Groves, Director of Admissions, Illinois State University, Campus Box 2200, Normal, IL 61790-2200. *Phone:* 309-438-2181. *Toll-free phone:* 800-366-2478. *Fax:* 309-438-3932. *E-mail:* admissions@ilstu.edu. *Web site:* http://www.illinoisstate.edu/.

Illinois Wesleyan University
Bloomington, Illinois

- **Independent** 4-year, founded 1850
- **Suburban** 79-acre campus
- **Coed** 2,090 undergraduate students, 100% full-time, 57% women, 43% men
- **Very difficult** entrance level, 61% of applicants were admitted

Undergraduates 2,082 full-time, 8 part-time. 12% are from out of state; 4% Black or African American, non-Hispanic/Latino; 5% Hispanic/Latino; 5% Asian, non-Hispanic/Latino; 0.5% American Indian or Alaska Native, non-Hispanic/Latino; 0.3% Two or more races, non-Hispanic/Latino; 8% Race/ethnicity unknown; 4% international; 2% transferred in; 77% live on campus. *Retention:* 90% of full-time freshmen returned.

Freshmen *Admission:* 3,319 applied, 2,017 admitted, 510 enrolled. *Average high school GPA:* 3.8. *Test scores:* SAT critical reading scores over 500: 88%; SAT math scores over 500: 96%; ACT scores over 18: 100%; SAT critical reading scores over 600: 55%; SAT math scores over 600: 74%; ACT scores over 24: 88%; SAT critical reading scores over 700: 15%; SAT math scores over 700: 34%; ACT scores over 30: 31%.

Faculty *Total:* 226, 71% full-time, 78% with terminal degrees. *Student/faculty ratio:* 11:1.

Academics *Calendar:* 4-4-1. *Degree:* bachelor's. *ROTC:* Army (c). *Unusual degree programs:* 3-2 engineering with Case Western Reserve University, Northwestern University, Washington University in St. Louis, Dartmouth College, University of Illinois; forestry with Duke University; occupational therapy.

Computers on Campus Students can access the following: campus intranet, computer help desk, free student e-mail accounts, online (class) grades, online (class) registration, online (class) schedules. Campuswide network is available. Wireless service is available via entire campus.

Student Life *Housing:* on-campus residence required through sophomore year. *Options:* coed, disabled students. Campus housing is university owned. Freshman campus housing is guaranteed. *Campus security:* 24-hour emergency response devices and patrols, late-night transport/escort service, controlled dormitory access, emergency response team.

Athletics Member NCAA. All Division III. *Intercollegiate sports:* baseball M, basketball M/W, cheerleading M(c)/W(c), cross-country running M/W, football M, golf M/W, lacrosse M(c), soccer M/W, softball W, swimming and diving M/W, tennis M/W, track and field M/W, ultimate Frisbee M(c)/W(c), volleyball M(c)/W, water polo M(c). *Intramural sports:* badminton M/W, basketball M/W, football M/W, golf M/W, racquetball M/W, soccer M/W, softball M/W, tennis M/W, volleyball M/W.

Standardized Tests *Required:* SAT or ACT (for admission).

Costs (2011–12) *Comprehensive fee:* $45,048 includes full-time tuition ($36,392), mandatory fees ($180), and room and board ($8476). *College room only:* $5318. *Payment plan:* installment.

Financial Aid Of all full-time matriculated undergraduates who enrolled in 2011, 1,616 applied for aid, 1,391 were judged to have need, 517 had their need fully met. In 2011, 571 non-need-based awards were made. *Average percent of need met:* 95%. *Average financial aid package:* $25,532. *Average need-based loan:* $5020. *Average need-based gift aid:* $19,297. *Average non-need-based aid:* $12,887. *Average indebtedness upon graduation:* $31,091. *Financial aid deadline:* 3/1.

Applying *Options:* electronic application, early admission, early action, deferred entrance. *Required:* essay or personal statement, high school transcript, minimum 2.0 GPA, 1 letter of recommendation. *Recommended:* minimum 3.0 GPA, 2 letters of recommendation, interview. *Application deadlines:* rolling (freshmen), 8/15 (transfers), 11/15 (early action). *Notification:* continuous (freshmen), continuous (transfers), 1/15 (early action).

Freshman Application Contact Mr. Tony Bankston, Dean of Admissions, Illinois Wesleyan University, PO Box 2900, Bloomington, IL 61702-2900. *Phone:* 309-556-3031. *Toll-free phone:* 800-332-2498. *Fax:* 309-556-3820. *E-mail:* iwuadmit@iwu.edu. *Web site:* http://www.iwu.edu/.

International Academy of Design & Technology

Chicago, Illinois

Freshman Application Contact Ms. Suzanne Reichart, Director of Student Management, International Academy of Design & Technology, One North State Street, Suite 500, Chicago, IL 60602. *Phone:* 312-980-9200. *Toll-free phone:* 877-458-6111. *Fax:* 312-541-3929. *E-mail:* sreichart@iadtchicago.edu. *Web site:* http://www.iadtchicago.edu/.

ITT Technical Institute

Mount Prospect, Illinois

- **Proprietary** primarily 2-year, founded 1986, part of ITT Educational Services, Inc.
- **Suburban** campus
- **Coed**
- **Minimally difficult** entrance level

Academics *Calendar:* quarters. *Degrees:* associate and bachelor's.

Student Life *Housing:* college housing not available.

Freshman Application Contact Director of Recruitment, ITT Technical Institute, 1401 Feehanville Drive, Mount Prospect, IL 60056. *Phone:* 847-375-8800. *Web site:* http://www.itt-tech.edu/.

ITT Technical Institute

Oak Brook, Illinois

- **Proprietary** primarily 2-year, founded 1998, part of ITT Educational Services, Inc.
- **Coed**
- **Minimally difficult** entrance level

Academics *Calendar:* quarters. *Degrees:* associate and bachelor's.

Student Life *Housing:* college housing not available.

Freshman Application Contact Director of Recruitment, ITT Technical Institute, 800 Jorie Boulevard, Suite 100, Oak Brook, IL 60523. *Phone:* 630-472-7000. *Toll-free phone:* 877-488-0001. *Web site:* http://www.itt-tech.edu/.

ITT Technical Institute

Orland Park, Illinois

- **Proprietary** primarily 2-year, founded 1993, part of ITT Educational Services, Inc.
- **Suburban** campus
- **Coed**
- **Minimally difficult** entrance level

Academics *Calendar:* quarters. *Degrees:* associate and bachelor's.

Student Life *Housing:* college housing not available.

Financial Aid Of all full-time matriculated undergraduates who enrolled in 2010, 6 Federal Work-Study jobs (averaging $4000).

Freshman Application Contact Director of Recruitment, ITT Technical Institute, 11551 184th Place, Orland Park, IL 60467. *Phone:* 708-326-3200. *Web site:* http://www.itt-tech.edu/.

ITT Technical Institute

Springfield, Illinois

- **Proprietary** 4-year
- **Coed**
- **Minimally difficult** entrance level

Academics *Degrees:* associate and bachelor's.

Freshman Application Contact Director of Recruitment, ITT Technical Institute, 2501 Wabash Avenue, Springfield, IL 62704. *Phone:* 217-547-5700. *Toll-free phone:* 877-263-2374. *Web site:* http://www.itt-tech.edu/.

Judson University

Elgin, Illinois

- **Independent Baptist** comprehensive, founded 1963
- **Suburban** 90-acre campus with easy access to Chicago
- **Endowment** $10.4 million
- **Coed** 995 undergraduate students, 80% full-time, 53% women, 47% men
- **Moderately difficult** entrance level, 64% of applicants were admitted

Undergraduates 800 full-time, 195 part-time. Students come from 36 states and territories; 25 other countries; 18% are from out of state; 4% Black or African American, non-Hispanic/Latino; 6% Hispanic/Latino; 1% Asian, non-Hispanic/Latino; 0.1% American Indian or Alaska Native, non-Hispanic/Latino; 1% Two or more races, non-Hispanic/Latino; 19% Race/ethnicity unknown; 4% international; 8% transferred in; 65% live on campus. *Retention:* 79% of full-time freshmen returned.

Freshmen *Admission:* 705 applied, 452 admitted, 161 enrolled. *Average high school GPA:* 3.3. *Test scores:* SAT critical reading scores over 500: 63%; SAT math scores over 500: 71%; ACT scores over 18: 100%; SAT critical reading scores over 600: 21%; SAT math scores over 600: 25%; ACT scores over 24: 45%; SAT critical reading scores over 700: 13%; SAT math scores over 700: 13%; ACT scores over 30: 7%.

Faculty *Total:* 200, 31% full-time, 48% with terminal degrees. *Student/faculty ratio:* 9:1.

Academics *Calendar:* semesters. *Degrees:* bachelor's, master's, and post-bachelor's certificates. *Special study options:* academic remediation for entering students, accelerated degree program, adult/continuing education programs, advanced placement credit, distance learning, double majors, honors programs, independent study, internships, off-campus study, part-time degree program, services for LD students, student-designed majors, study abroad, summer session for credit. *ROTC:* Army (c).

Computers on Campus 90 computers/terminals are available on campus for general student use. Students can access the following: campus intranet, computer help desk, free student e-mail accounts, online (class) grades, online (class) registration, online (class) schedules. Campuswide network is available. 100% of college-owned or -operated housing units are wired for high-speed Internet access. Wireless service is available via entire campus.

Student Life *Housing:* on-campus residence required through senior year. *Options:* coed, men-only, women-only, disabled students. Campus housing is university owned. Freshman campus housing is guaranteed. *Activities and organizations:* drama/theater group, choral group, Judson Student Organization, University Ministries, Judson Choir, Fellowship of Christian Athletes, Judson Business Network. *Campus security:* 24-hour emergency response devices and patrols, controlled dormitory access. *Student services:* health clinic, personal/psychological counseling.

Athletics Member NAIA, NCCAA. *Intercollegiate sports:* baseball M(s), basketball M(s)/W(s), cheerleading W(s), cross-country running M(s)/W(s), golf M(s)/W(s), lacrosse M(s), soccer M(s)/W(s), softball W(s), tennis M(s)/W(s), track and field M(s)/W(s), volleyball W(s). *Intramural sports:* basketball M/W, football M, racquetball M/W, soccer M/W, ultimate Frisbee M/W, volleyball M/W.

Standardized Tests *Required:* SAT or ACT (for admission).

Costs (2012–13) *Comprehensive fee:* $35,990 includes full-time tuition ($26,220), mandatory fees ($780), and room and board ($8990). Full-time tuition and fees vary according to course load and program. Part-time tuition: $1075 per credit. Part-time tuition and fees vary according to course load and program. *Room and board:* Room and board charges vary according to board plan. *Payment plan:* installment. *Waivers:* adult students, senior citizens, and employees or children of employees.

Applying *Options:* electronic application. *Application fee:* $50. *Required:* high school transcript, minimum 2.5 GPA, Minimum 21 ACT; lifestyle statement; portfolios for some majors. *Application deadlines:* rolling (freshmen), rolling (out-of-state freshmen), rolling (transfers). *Notification:* continuous (freshmen), continuous (out-of-state freshmen), continuous (transfers).

Freshman Application Contact Mrs. Nancy Binger, Director of Enrollment Services, Judson University, Judson University, 1151 N State St, Elgin, IL 60123. *Phone:* 847-628-1581. *Toll-free phone:* 800-879-5376. *Fax:* 847-628-2526. *E-mail:* nbinger@judsonu.edu. *Web site:* http://www.judsonu.edu/.

Kendall College

Chicago, Illinois

- **Proprietary** 4-year, founded 1934, part of Laureate International Universities
- **Urban** campus with easy access to Chicago
- **Coed**
- **Minimally difficult** entrance level

Faculty *Student/faculty ratio:* 18:1.

Academics *Calendar:* quarters. *Degrees:* certificates, associate, and bachelor's.

Student Life *Campus security:* 24-hour emergency response devices and patrols, controlled dormitory access, late night security in dorms.

Standardized Tests *Required for some:* SAT or ACT (for admission).

Costs (2011–12) *Comprehensive fee:* $32,820 includes full-time tuition ($22,095), mandatory fees ($825), and room and board ($9900). Full-time tuition and fees vary according to program. Part-time tuition: $600 per credit. Part-time tuition and fees vary according to course load and program. *Required fees:* $275 per term part-time. *College room only:* $9450. Room and board charges vary according to housing facility.

Financial Aid *Of all full-time matriculated undergraduates who enrolled in 2008,* 30 Federal Work-Study jobs (averaging $1100). *Average indebtedness upon graduation:* $14,125.

Applying *Options:* electronic application, deferred entrance. *Application fee:* $50. *Required:* essay or personal statement, high school transcript, interview. *Recommended:* minimum 2.0 GPA.

Freshman Application Contact Mr. Thomas Marigliano, Director of Enrollment, Kendall College, 900 North North Branch Street, Chicago, IL 60642. *Toll-free phone:* 888-90-KENDALL.

E-mail: admissions@kendall.edu. *Web site:* http://www.kendall.edu/.

See page 1388 for the College Close-Up.

Knox College
Galesburg, Illinois

- **Independent** 4-year, founded 1837
- **Small-town** 82-acre campus with easy access to Peoria; Quad Cities
- **Endowment** $84.1 million
- **Coed** 1,420 undergraduate students, 99% full-time, 58% women, 42% men
- **Very difficult** entrance level, 72% of applicants were admitted

Undergraduates 1,400 full-time, 20 part-time. Students come from 48 states and territories; 37 other countries; 46% are from out of state; 5% Black or African American, non-Hispanic/Latino; 8% Hispanic/Latino; 5% Asian, non-Hispanic/Latino; 0.1% Native Hawaiian or other Pacific Islander, non-Hispanic/Latino; 0.1% American Indian or Alaska Native, non-Hispanic/Latino; 4% Two or more races, non-Hispanic/Latino; 2% Race/ethnicity unknown; 9% international; 4% transferred in; 85% live on campus. *Retention:* 89% of full-time freshmen returned.

Freshmen *Admission:* 2,385 applied, 1,706 admitted, 343 enrolled. *Average high school GPA:* 3.35. *Test scores:* SAT critical reading scores over 500: 90%; SAT math scores over 500: 91%; SAT writing scores over 500: 92%; ACT scores over 18: 100%; SAT critical reading scores over 600: 77%; SAT math scores over 600: 67%; SAT writing scores over 600: 63%; ACT scores over 24: 87%; SAT critical reading scores over 700: 25%; SAT math scores over 700: 25%; SAT writing scores over 700: 17%; ACT scores over 30: 31%.

Faculty *Total:* 130, 88% full-time, 88% with terminal degrees. *Student/faculty ratio:* 12:1.

Academics *Calendar:* trimesters. *Degree:* bachelor's. *Special study options:* advanced placement credit, double majors, honors programs, independent study, internships, off-campus study, part-time degree program, services for LD students, student-designed majors, study abroad. *Unusual degree programs:* 3-2 engineering with University of Illinois at Urbana, Washington University, Columbia University, Rensselaer Polytechnic Institute; forestry with Duke University; nursing with Rush University's College of Nursing.

Computers on Campus 335 computers/terminals are available on campus for general student use. Students can access the following: campus intranet, computer help desk, free student e-mail accounts, online (class) grades, online (class) registration, online (class) schedules, Transcripts, EDR, Moodle. Campuswide network is available. 100% of college-owned or -operated housing units are wired for high-speed Internet access. Wireless service is available via entire campus.

Student Life *Housing:* on-campus residence required through sophomore year. *Options:* coed, men-only, women-only, disabled students. Campus housing is university owned. Freshman campus housing is guaranteed. *Activities and organizations:* drama/theater group, student-run newspaper, radio station, choral group, Student-Run Radio Station (WVKC), International Club, Student Newspaper (The Knox Student), Common Ground, Terpsichore (Dance Collective), national fraternities, national sororities. *Campus security:* 24-hour emergency response devices and patrols, late-night transport/escort service. *Student services:* health clinic, personal/psychological counseling.

Athletics Member NCAA. All Division III. *Intercollegiate sports:* baseball M, basketball M/W, cross-country running M/W, football M, golf M/W, soccer M/W, softball W, swimming and diving M/W, tennis M/W, track and field M/W, volleyball W, wrestling M. *Intramural sports:* basketball M/W, fencing M(c)/W(c), lacrosse M(c)/W(c), rugby W(c), soccer M/W, softball M/W, ultimate Frisbee M(c)/W(c), volleyball M/W, water polo M(c)/W(c).

Costs (2012–13) *Comprehensive fee:* $44,424 includes full-time tuition ($36,138), mandatory fees ($354), and room and board ($7932). Full-time tuition and fees vary according to course load. Part-time tuition and fees vary according to course load. *College room only:* $3972. Room and board charges vary according to housing facility. *Payment plan:* installment. *Waivers:* employees or children of employees.
Financial Aid Of all full-time matriculated undergraduates who enrolled in 2011, 1,181 applied for aid, 1,082 were judged to have need, 310 had their need fully met. 684 Federal Work-Study jobs (averaging $2313). 95 state and other part-time jobs (averaging $2351). In 2011, 303 non-need-based awards were made. *Average percent of need met:* 88%. *Average financial aid package:* $27,341. *Average need-based loan:* $5276. *Average need-based gift aid:* $21,332. *Average non-need-based aid:* $12,009. *Average indebtedness upon graduation:* $28,169.
Applying *Options:* electronic application, early admission, early action, deferred entrance. *Application fee:* $40. *Required:* essay or personal statement, high school transcript, 2 letters of recommendation. *Recommended:* interview. *Application deadlines:* 2/1 (freshmen), 4/1 (transfers), 12/1 (early action). *Notification:* 3/31 (freshmen), 5/15 (transfers), 12/31 (early action).
Freshman Application Contact Mr. Paul Steenis, Dean of Admission, Knox College, 2 East South Street, Campus Box148, Galesburg, IL 61401. *Phone:* 309-341-7100. *Toll-free phone:* 800-678-KNOX. *Fax:* 309-341-7070. *E-mail:* admission@knox.edu. *Web site:* http://www.knox.edu/.

Lake Forest College

Lake Forest, Illinois

- **Independent** comprehensive, founded 1857
- **Suburban** 107-acre campus with easy access to Chicago
- **Endowment** $70.9 million
- **Coed** 1,497 undergraduate students, 99% full-time, 59% women, 41% men
- **Moderately difficult** entrance level, 54% of applicants were admitted

Undergraduates 1,481 full-time, 16 part-time. Students come from 49 states and territories; 78 other countries; 40% are from out of state; 6% Black or African American, non-Hispanic/Latino; 12% Hispanic/Latino; 4% Asian, non-Hispanic/Latino; 0.1% Native Hawaiian or other Pacific Islander, non-Hispanic/Latino; 0.2% American Indian or Alaska Native, non-Hispanic/Latino; 3% Two or more races, non-Hispanic/Latino; 1% Race/ethnicity unknown; 12% international; 4% transferred in; 80% live on campus. *Retention:* 84% of full-time freshmen returned.
Freshmen *Admission:* 3,198 applied, 1,711 admitted, 406 enrolled. *Average high school GPA:* 3.65.
Faculty *Total:* 161, 58% full-time, 76% with terminal degrees. *Student/faculty ratio:* 13:1.
Academics *Calendar:* semesters. *Degrees:* bachelor's, master's, and post-bachelor's certificates. *Special study options:* accelerated degree program, advanced placement credit, double majors, honors programs, independent study, internships, off-campus study, part-time degree program, services for LD students, student-designed majors, study abroad, summer session for credit. *Unusual degree programs:* 3-2 engineering with Washington University in St. Louis.
Computers on Campus 130 computers/terminals and 1,200 ports are available on campus for general student use. Students can access the following: campus intranet, computer help desk, free student e-mail accounts, online (class) grades, online (class) registration, online (class) schedules, file storage. Campuswide network is available. 100% of college-owned or -operated housing units are wired for high-speed Internet access. Wireless service is available via classrooms, computer centers, computer labs, dorm rooms, learning centers, libraries, student centers.
Student Life *Housing options:* coed, women-only, disabled students. Campus housing is university owned. Freshman applicants given priority for college housing. *Activities and organizations:* drama/theater group, student-run newspaper, radio station, choral group, WMXM, eTeam, Habitat for Humanity, United Black Association, International Student Organization, national fraternities, national sororities. *Campus security:* 24-hour emergency response devices and patrols, student patrols, late-night transport/escort service, controlled dormitory access. *Student services:* health clinic, personal/psychological counseling.
Athletics Member NCAA. All Division III. *Intercollegiate sports:* baseball M(c), basketball M/W, cheerleading M(c)/W(c), equestrian sports M/W, fencing M(c)/W(c), football M, golf M(c)/W(c), ice hockey M/W, rugby M(c)/W(c), sailing M(c)/W(c), soccer M/W, softball W, swimming and diving M/W, tennis M/W, track and field M(c)/W(c), ultimate Frisbee M(c)/W(c), volleyball W, water polo M(c)/W(c). *Intramural sports:* archery M, basketball M/W, racquetball M/W, soccer M/W, table tennis M/W, volleyball M/W.
Standardized Tests *Required for some:* SAT or ACT (for admission).

Costs (2012–13) *Comprehensive fee:* $47,350 includes full-time tuition ($37,660), mandatory fees ($640), and room and board ($9050). *College room only:* $4440. *Payment plan:* installment.
Financial Aid Of all full-time matriculated undergraduates who enrolled in 2010, 1,196 applied for aid, 1,110 were judged to have need, 320 had their need fully met. 611 Federal Work-Study jobs (averaging $2216). In 2010, 240 non-need-based awards were made. *Average percent of need met:* 81%. *Average financial aid package:* $30,013. *Average need-based loan:* $4713. *Average need-based gift aid:* $25,350. *Average non-need-based aid:* $12,558. *Average indebtedness upon graduation:* $31,790. *Financial aid deadline:* 5/1.
Applying *Options:* electronic application, early decision, early action, deferred entrance. *Required:* essay or personal statement, high school transcript, 1 letter of recommendation. *Recommended:* interview. *Application deadlines:* 2/15 (freshmen), rolling (transfers), 12/1 (early action). *Early decision deadline:* 12/1. *Notification:* 3/20 (freshmen), continuous (transfers), rolling (early decision), 1/20 (early action).
Freshman Application Contact Mr. William Motzer Jr., Vice President for Admissions and Career Services, Lake Forest College, 555 North Sheridan Road, Lake Forest, IL 60045-2338. *Phone:* 847-735-5000. *Toll-free phone:* 800-828-4751. *Fax:* 847-735-6271. *E-mail:* admissions@lakeforest.edu. *Web site:* http://www.lakeforest.edu/.

Lakeview College of Nursing

Danville, Illinois

Application Contact Admissions Office, Lakeview College of Nursing, 903 North Logan Avenue, Danville, IL 61832. *Phone:* 217-443-5238. *Fax:* 217-442-2279. *E-mail:* admission@lakeviewcol.edu. *Web site:* http://www.lakeviewcol.edu/.

Lewis University

Romeoville, Illinois

- **Independent** comprehensive, founded 1932, affiliated with Roman Catholic Church
- **Suburban** 376-acre campus with easy access to Chicago
- **Endowment** $39.8 million
- **Coed** 4,474 undergraduate students, 80% full-time, 57% women, 43% men
- **Moderately difficult** entrance level, 62% of applicants were admitted

Undergraduates 3,557 full-time, 917 part-time. Students come from 34 states and territories; 30 other countries; 6% are from out of state; 9% Black or African American, non-Hispanic/Latino; 14% Hispanic/Latino; 3% Asian, non-Hispanic/Latino; 0.2% Native Hawaiian or other Pacific Islander, non-Hispanic/Latino; 0.2% American Indian or Alaska Native, non-Hispanic/Latino; 0.8% Two or more races, non-Hispanic/Latino; 8% Race/ethnicity unknown; 1% international; 9% transferred in; 30% live on campus. *Retention:* 77% of full-time freshmen returned.
Freshmen *Admission:* 4,726 applied, 2,927 admitted, 736 enrolled. *Average high school GPA:* 3.31. *Test scores:* SAT critical reading scores over 500: 50%; SAT math scores over 500: 60%; SAT writing scores over 500: 25%; ACT scores over 18: 97%; SAT critical reading scores over 600: 15%; SAT math scores over 600: 30%; ACT scores over 24: 37%; SAT math scores over 700: 5%; ACT scores over 30: 2%.
Faculty *Total:* 655, 31% full-time, 31% with terminal degrees. *Student/faculty ratio:* 13:1.
Academics *Calendar:* semesters. *Degrees:* certificates, associate, bachelor's, master's, doctoral, post-master's, and first professional certificates. *Special study options:* academic remediation for entering students, accelerated degree program, adult/continuing education programs, advanced placement credit, distance learning, double majors, English as a second language, honors programs, independent study, internships, off-campus study, part-time degree program, services for LD students, student-designed majors, study abroad, summer session for credit. *ROTC:* Army (c), Air Force (c).
Computers on Campus 267 computers/terminals are available on campus for general student use. Students can access the following: campus intranet, computer help desk, free student e-mail accounts, online (class) grades, online (class) registration, online (class) schedules, online help, online billing, online financial aid, online payments, online application for admission, online housing application, online application for graduation, Blackboard course management system. Campuswide network is available. 100% of college-owned or -operated housing units are wired for high-speed Internet access. Wireless service is available via entire campus.
Student Life *Housing options:* coed. Campus housing is university owned. Freshman campus housing is guaranteed. *Activities and organizations:* drama/theater group, student-run newspaper, radio and television station, choral group, Student Governing Board, The PULSE, Black Student Union, Delta Sigma Pi (business fraternity), Student Nursing Association, national fraterni-

ties, national sororities. *Campus security:* 24-hour emergency response devices and patrols, student patrols, late-night transport/escort service, controlled dormitory access. *Student services:* health clinic, personal/psychological counseling.

Athletics Member NCAA. All Division II. *Intercollegiate sports:* baseball M(s), basketball M(s)/W(s), cheerleading M(s)(c)/W(s)(c), cross-country running M(s)/W(s), golf M(s)/W(s), ice hockey M(c), rugby M(c), soccer M(s)/W(s), softball W(s), swimming and diving M(s)/W(s), tennis M(s)/W(s), track and field M(s)/W(s), volleyball M(s)/W(s). *Intramural sports:* basketball M/W, bowling M/W, cross-country running M/W, football M/W, golf M/W, soccer M/W, softball M/W, swimming and diving M/W, table tennis M/W, tennis M/W, track and field M/W, ultimate Frisbee M/W, volleyball M(c)/W.

Standardized Tests *Required:* SAT or ACT (for admission).

Costs (2011–12) *Comprehensive fee:* $33,670 includes full-time tuition ($24,770) and room and board ($8900). Full-time tuition and fees vary according to course load and program. Part-time tuition: $750 per semester hour. Part-time tuition and fees vary according to course load and program. *College room only:* $5780. Room and board charges vary according to board plan and housing facility. *Payment plan:* installment. *Waivers:* children of alumni, adult students, and employees or children of employees.

Financial Aid Of all full-time matriculated undergraduates who enrolled in 2011, 3,060 applied for aid, 2,775 were judged to have need, 623 had their need fully met. 1,728 Federal Work-Study jobs (averaging $3322). 213 state and other part-time jobs (averaging $3088). In 2011, 555 non-need-based awards were made. *Average percent of need met:* 76%. *Average financial aid package:* $18,608. *Average need-based loan:* $4224. *Average need-based gift aid:* $12,977. *Average non-need-based aid:* $7970. *Average indebtedness upon graduation:* $27,156. *Financial aid deadline:* 5/1.

Applying *Options:* electronic application, deferred entrance. *Application fee:* $40. *Required:* high school transcript, minimum 2.0 GPA. *Required for some:* interview. *Application deadlines:* 8/1 (freshmen), rolling (transfers). *Notification:* continuous (freshmen), continuous (transfers).

Freshman Application Contact Mr. Ryan Cockerill, Director of Admission, Lewis University, Box 297, One University Parkway, Romeoville, IL 60446. *Phone:* 815-836-5237. *Toll-free phone:* 800-897-9000. *Fax:* 815-836-5002. *E-mail:* admissions@lewisu.edu. *Web site:* http://www.lewisu.edu/.

Lexington College

Chicago, Illinois

- **Independent** 4-year, founded 1977
- **Urban** campus
- **Endowment** $29,600
- **Women only**
- **Noncompetitive** entrance level

Faculty *Student/faculty ratio:* 6:1.

Academics *Calendar:* semesters. *Degrees:* certificates, associate, and bachelor's.

Student Life *Campus security:* 24-hour emergency response devices and patrols, patrols by municipal security personnel.

Standardized Tests *Required for some:* SAT or ACT (for admission).

Financial Aid *Financial aid deadline:* 10/1.

Applying *Options:* electronic application. *Application fee:* $30. *Required:* essay or personal statement, high school transcript, minimum 2.0 GPA. *Recommended:* interview.

Freshman Application Contact Mrs. Carmen Larios, Admissions Director, Lexington College, 310 South Peoria Street, Suite 512, Chicago, IL 60607-3534. *Phone:* 312-226-6294 Ext. 226. *Fax:* 312-226-6405. *E-mail:* admissions@lexingtoncollege.edu. *Web site:* http://www.lexingtoncollege.edu/.

Lincoln Christian University

Lincoln, Illinois

- **Independent** comprehensive, founded 1944, affiliated with Christian Churches and Churches of Christ
- **Small-town** 227-acre campus
- **Endowment** $7.3 million
- **Coed** 672 undergraduate students, 81% full-time, 53% women, 47% men
- **Moderately difficult** entrance level, 68% of applicants were admitted

Undergraduates 545 full-time, 127 part-time. Students come from 27 states and territories; 5 other countries; 194% are from out of state; 6% Black or African American, non-Hispanic/Latino; 3% Hispanic/Latino; 0.7% Asian, non-Hispanic/Latino; 0.7% American Indian or Alaska Native, non-Hispanic/Latino; 0.9% Two or more races, non-Hispanic/Latino; 2% Race/ethnicity unknown; 1% international; 15% transferred in; 71% live on campus. *Retention:* 68% of full-time freshmen returned.

Freshmen *Admission:* 234 applied, 160 admitted, 75 enrolled. *Average high school GPA:* 3.19. *Test scores:* ACT scores over 18: 81%; ACT scores over 24: 48%; ACT scores over 30: 7%.

Faculty *Total:* 111, 35% full-time, 39% with terminal degrees. *Student/faculty ratio:* 16:1.

Academics *Calendar:* semesters. *Degrees:* certificates, associate, bachelor's, and master's. *Special study options:* academic remediation for entering students, adult/continuing education programs, advanced placement credit, distance learning, double majors, external degree program, honors programs, independent study, internships, off-campus study, part-time degree program, services for LD students, study abroad, summer session for credit. *Unusual degree programs:* 3-2 teacher education.

Computers on Campus 51 computers/terminals are available on campus for general student use. Students can access the following: campus intranet, computer help desk, free student e-mail accounts, online (class) grades, online (class) registration, online (class) schedules. Campuswide network is available. 100% of college-owned or -operated housing units are wired for high-speed Internet access. Wireless service is available via entire campus.

Student Life *Housing:* on-campus residence required through senior year. *Options:* men-only, women-only. Campus housing is university owned. Freshman campus housing is guaranteed. *Activities and organizations:* drama/theater group, student-run newspaper, choral group, Chorale, Student Cabinet, American Association of Christian Counselors (AACC) - Student Chapter, Cheerleading. *Campus security:* 24-hour emergency response devices, student patrols, controlled dormitory access. *Student services:* personal/psychological counseling.

Athletics Member NCCAA. *Intercollegiate sports:* baseball M, basketball M/W, soccer M/W, volleyball W. *Intramural sports:* badminton M/W, basketball M/W, soccer M/W, ultimate Frisbee M/W, volleyball M/W.

Standardized Tests *Required:* SAT or ACT (for admission).

Costs (2011–12) *One-time required fee:* $240. *Comprehensive fee:* $21,019 includes full-time tuition ($14,340) and room and board ($6679). Part-time tuition: $478 per credit hour. *Required fees:* $8 per credit hour part-time. *College room only:* $2805. *Payment plans:* installment, deferred payment. *Waivers:* employees or children of employees.

Financial Aid Of all full-time matriculated undergraduates who enrolled in 2010, 631 applied for aid, 559 were judged to have need, 50 had their need fully met. 97 Federal Work-Study jobs (averaging $1107). 156 state and other part-time jobs (averaging $1345). In 2010, 49 non-need-based awards were made. *Average percent of need met:* 53%. *Average financial aid package:* $10,423. *Average need-based loan:* $3991. *Average need-based gift aid:* $3897. *Average non-need-based aid:* $5210. *Average indebtedness upon graduation:* $16,165.

Applying *Options:* electronic application, deferred entrance. *Application fee:* $25. *Required:* essay or personal statement, high school transcript, 3 letters of recommendation. *Required for some:* interview. *Application deadlines:* rolling (freshmen), rolling (out-of-state freshmen), rolling (transfers). *Notification:* continuous (freshmen), continuous (out-of-state freshmen), continuous (transfers).

Freshman Application Contact Mrs. Mary K. Davis, Admissions Office Manager, Lincoln Christian University, 100 Campus View Drive, Lincoln, IL 62656. *Phone:* 217-732-3168 Ext. 2251. *Toll-free phone:* 888-522-5228. *Fax:* 217-732-4199. *E-mail:* admissions@lincolnchristian.edu. *Web site:* http://www.lincolnchristian.edu/.

Lincoln College–Normal

Normal, Illinois

Freshman Application Contact Mr. Steve Puck, Director of Admissions, Lincoln College–Normal, 715 West Raab Road, Normal, IL 61761. *Phone:* 309-268-4314. *Toll-free phone:* 800-569-0558. *Fax:* 309-862-3352. *E-mail:* spuck@lincolncollege.edu. *Web site:* http://www.lincolncollege.edu/normal/.

Loyola University Chicago

Chicago, Illinois

- **Independent Roman Catholic (Jesuit)** university, founded 1870
- **Urban** 105-acre campus
- **Endowment** $388.7 million
- **Coed** 9,856 undergraduate students, 92% full-time, 63% women, 37% men
- **Moderately difficult** entrance level, 55% of applicants were admitted

Undergraduates 9,084 full-time, 772 part-time. Students come from 50 states and territories; 82 other countries; 35% are from out of state; 4% Black or African American, non-Hispanic/Latino; 11% Hispanic/Latino; 11% Asian, non-Hispanic/Latino; 0.1% Native Hawaiian or other Pacific Islander, non-Hispanic/Latino; 0.2% American Indian or Alaska Native, non-Hispanic/Latino; 4% Two or more races, non-Hispanic/Latino; 4% Race/ethnicity unknown; 1%

international; 6% transferred in; 38% live on campus. *Retention:* 87% of full-time freshmen returned.

Freshmen *Admission:* 17,828 applied, 9,793 admitted, 1,930 enrolled. *Average high school GPA:* 3.7. *Test scores:* SAT critical reading scores over 500: 88%; SAT math scores over 500: 89%; SAT writing scores over 500: 88%; ACT scores over 18: 100%; SAT critical reading scores over 600: 50%; SAT math scores over 600: 50%; SAT writing scores over 600: 46%; ACT scores over 24: 85%; SAT critical reading scores over 700: 12%; SAT math scores over 700: 9%; SAT writing scores over 700: 9%; ACT scores over 30: 20%.

Faculty *Total:* 1,367, 50% full-time. *Student/faculty ratio:* 15:1.

Academics *Calendar:* semesters. *Degrees:* bachelor's, master's, doctoral, post-master's, postbachelor's, and first professional certificates (also offers adult part-time program with significant enrollment not reflected in profile). *Special study options:* academic remediation for entering students, accelerated degree program, adult/continuing education programs, advanced placement credit, cooperative education, distance learning, double majors, English as a second language, freshman honors college, honors programs, independent study, internships, off-campus study, part-time degree program, services for LD students, study abroad, summer session for credit. *ROTC:* Army (c), Navy (c), Air Force (c). *Unusual degree programs:* 3-2 business administration; engineering with BS Physics and Engineering, Columbia University in NYC; BS Physics and Engineering, Washington University, St. Louis; social work; political science, sociology, psychology, computer science, biology, education, accounting, information technology, criminal justice, environmental studies.

Computers on Campus 1,363 computers/terminals are available on campus for general student use. Students can access the following: campus intranet, computer help desk, free student e-mail accounts, online (class) grades, online (class) registration, online (class) schedules. Campuswide network is available. 100% of college-owned or -operated housing units are wired for high-speed Internet access. Wireless service is available via entire campus.

Student Life *Housing:* on-campus residence required through sophomore year. *Options:* coed, disabled students. Campus housing is university owned. Freshman campus housing is guaranteed. *Activities and organizations:* drama/theater group, student-run newspaper, radio station, Department of Programming, Panhellenic Sororities, American Medical Association, Habitat for Humanity, Cooking Club, national fraternities, national sororities. *Campus security:* 24-hour emergency response devices and patrols, late-night transport/escort service, controlled dormitory access, Loyola Alert, a special service to provide personalized, time-sensitive alerts to students, faculty, staff & other personnel at Loyola. *Student services:* health clinic, personal/psychological counseling, women's center.

Athletics Member NCAA. All Division I. *Intercollegiate sports:* basketball M(s)/W(s), cheerleading M/W, cross-country running M(s)/W(s), golf M(s)/W(s), soccer M(s)/W(s), softball W(s), track and field M(s)/W(s), volleyball M(s)/W(s). *Intramural sports:* badminton M/W, baseball M(c), basketball M/W, cross-country running M(c)/W(c), fencing M(c)/W(c), football M/W, ice hockey M(c)/W(c), lacrosse M(c)/W(c), racquetball M/W, rugby M(c)/W(c), soccer M(c)/W(c), softball W(c), swimming and diving M(c)/W(c), table tennis M(c)/W(c), tennis M(c)/W(c), ultimate Frisbee M(c)/W(c), volleyball M(c)/W(c), water polo M(c)/W(c).

Standardized Tests *Required:* SAT or ACT (for admission).

Costs (2012–13) *Comprehensive fee:* $46,588 includes full-time tuition ($33,450), mandatory fees ($1128), and room and board ($12,010). Full-time tuition and fees vary according to location, program, and student level. Part-time tuition: $675 per credit. Part-time tuition and fees vary according to course load. *Required fees:* $149 per term part-time. *College room only:* $7820. Room and board charges vary according to board plan, housing facility, and location. *Payment plans:* installment, deferred payment. *Waivers:* senior citizens and employees or children of employees.

Financial Aid Of all full-time matriculated undergraduates who enrolled in 2011, 7,266 applied for aid, 6,595 were judged to have need, 627 had their need fully met. 5,294 Federal Work-Study jobs (averaging $2179). In 2011, 1565 non-need-based awards were made. *Average percent of need met:* 79%. *Average financial aid package:* $29,009. *Average need-based loan:* $4876. *Average need-based gift aid:* $17,878. *Average non-need-based aid:* $9260.

Applying *Options:* electronic application. *Required:* essay or personal statement, high school transcript, minimum 2.0 GPA. *Recommended:* interview. *Notification:* continuous (freshmen), continuous (out-of-state freshmen), continuous (transfers).

Freshman Application Contact Ms. Lori Greene, Director of Undergraduate Admissions, Loyola University Chicago, 1032 West Sheridan Road, Chicago, IL 60660. *Phone:* 773-508-3075. *Toll-free phone:* 800-262-2373. *E-mail:* admission@luc.edu. *Web site:* http://www.luc.edu/.

MacMurray College
Jacksonville, Illinois

- **Independent United Methodist** 4-year, founded 1846
- **Small-town** 60-acre campus
- **Endowment** $7.1 million
- **Coed**
- **Moderately difficult** entrance level

Faculty *Student/faculty ratio:* 11:1.
Academics *Calendar:* 4-1-4. *Degrees:* associate and bachelor's.
Student Life *Campus security:* 24-hour emergency response devices and patrols, late-night transport/escort service.
Athletics Member NCAA. All Division III.
Standardized Tests *Recommended:* SAT or ACT (for admission).
Costs (2011–12) *Comprehensive fee:* $28,050 includes full-time tuition ($19,900), mandatory fees ($500), and room and board ($7650). Part-time tuition: $660 per credit hour. Part-time tuition and fees vary according to course load. *Required fees:* $30 per credit hour part-time. *Room and board:* Room and board charges vary according to housing facility and student level.
Financial Aid *Of all full-time matriculated undergraduates who enrolled in 2009,* 463 applied for aid, 448 were judged to have need, 210 had their need fully met. 114 Federal Work-Study jobs (averaging $564). *In 2009,* 12 non-need-based awards were made. *Average percent of need met:* 93. *Average financial aid package:* $24,166. *Average need-based loan:* $10,059. *Average need-based gift aid:* $14,107. *Average non-need-based aid:* $9212. *Average indebtedness upon graduation:* $27,524.
Applying *Options:* electronic application, early admission. *Required:* high school transcript. *Required for some:* essay or personal statement, minimum 2.5 GPA, 1 letter of recommendation, interview.
Freshman Application Contact Ms. Alicia Zeone, Assistant Director of Admission, MacMurray College, MacMurray College, 447 East College Avenue, Jacksonville, IL 62650. *Phone:* 217-479-7059. *Toll-free phone:* 800-252-7485. *Fax:* 217-291-0702. *E-mail:* alicia.zeone@mac.edu. *Web site:* http://www.mac.edu/.

McKendree University
Lebanon, Illinois

- **Independent** comprehensive, founded 1828, affiliated with United Methodist Church
- **Suburban** 116-acre campus with easy access to St. Louis, MO; Belleville, IL
- **Endowment** $28.2 million
- **Coed** 2,356 undergraduate students, 71% full-time, 56% women, 44% men
- **Moderately difficult** entrance level, 68% of applicants were admitted

Undergraduates 1,667 full-time, 689 part-time. Students come from 24 states and territories; 9 other countries; 23% are from out of state; 9% Black or African American, non-Hispanic/Latino; 2% Hispanic/Latino; 1% Asian, non-Hispanic/Latino; 0.2% American Indian or Alaska Native, non-Hispanic/Latino; 4% Two or more races, non-Hispanic/Latino; 1% international; 10% transferred in; 60% live on campus. *Retention:* 81% of full-time freshmen returned.
Freshmen *Admission:* 1,359 applied, 925 admitted, 290 enrolled. *Average high school GPA:* 3.4. *Test scores:* SAT critical reading scores over 500: 63%; SAT math scores over 500: 63%; SAT writing scores over 500: 13%; ACT scores over 18: 93%; SAT math scores over 600: 13%; ACT scores over 24: 37%; ACT scores over 30: 4%.
Faculty *Total:* 316, 29% full-time. *Student/faculty ratio:* 14:1.
Academics *Calendar:* semesters. *Degrees:* associate, bachelor's, master's, doctoral, post-master's, and first professional certificates. *Special study options:* academic remediation for entering students, accelerated degree program, adult/continuing education programs, advanced placement credit, double majors, honors programs, independent study, internships, off-campus study, part-time degree program, services for LD students, student-designed majors, study abroad, summer session for credit. *ROTC:* Army (c), Air Force (c). *Unusual degree programs:* 3-2 occupational therapy with Washington University in St. Louis.
Computers on Campus 168 computers/terminals and 1,061 ports are available on campus for general student use. Students can access the following: campus intranet, computer help desk, free student e-mail accounts, online (class) grades, online (class) registration, online (class) schedules. Campuswide network is available. 100% of college-owned or -operated housing units are wired for high-speed Internet access. Wireless service is available via entire campus.
Student Life *Housing:* on-campus residence required through junior year. *Options:* coed, disabled students. Campus housing is university owned and leased by the school. Freshman campus housing is guaranteed. *Activities and organizations:* drama/theater group, student-run newspaper, choral group,

marching band, Wonders of Wellness, Center for Public Service, Campus Ministries, national fraternities, national sororities. *Campus security:* 24-hour emergency response devices and patrols, student patrols, late-night transport/escort service, controlled dormitory access. *Student services:* health clinic, personal/psychological counseling.

Athletics Member NCAA. All Division II. *Intercollegiate sports:* baseball M(s), basketball M(s)/W(s), bowling M(c)/W(s), cheerleading M(s)/W(s), cross-country running M(s)/W(s), football M(s), golf M(s)/W(s), ice hockey M(c), lacrosse W(s), soccer M(s)/W(s), softball M(s), tennis M(s)/W(s), track and field M(s)/W(s), volleyball W(s), wrestling M(s). *Intramural sports:* basketball M/W, football M/W, softball M/W, table tennis M/W, ultimate Frisbee M/W, volleyball M/W.

Standardized Tests *Required:* SAT or ACT (for admission).

Costs (2012–13) *Comprehensive fee:* $32,620 includes full-time tuition ($23,290), mandatory fees ($900), and room and board ($8430). Full-time tuition and fees vary according to course load, degree level, and location. Part-time tuition: $780 per credit hour. Part-time tuition and fees vary according to course load, degree level, and location. *College room only:* $4440. Room and board charges vary according to board plan and housing facility. *Payment plans:* installment, deferred payment. *Waivers:* children of alumni and employees or children of employees.

Financial Aid Of all full-time matriculated undergraduates who enrolled in 2011, 1,470 applied for aid, 1,365 were judged to have need, 261 had their need fully met. 862 Federal Work-Study jobs (averaging $1675). 81 state and other part-time jobs (averaging $1390). In 2011, 179 non-need-based awards were made. *Average percent of need met:* 77%. *Average financial aid package:* $18,277. *Average need-based loan:* $3874. *Average need-based gift aid:* $14,805. *Average non-need-based aid:* $7497. *Average indebtedness upon graduation:* $19,581.

Applying *Options:* electronic application, deferred entrance. *Required:* essay or personal statement, high school transcript, minimum 2.5 GPA, 1 letter of recommendation, rank in upper 50% of high school class, ACT score of 20 or higher. *Required for some:* interview. *Application deadlines:* rolling (freshmen), rolling (transfers). *Notification:* continuous (freshmen), continuous (transfers).

Freshman Application Contact Josie Blasdel, Director of Undergraduate Admission, McKendree University, 701 College Road, Lebanon, IL 62254. *Phone:* 618-537-6836. *Toll-free phone:* 800-232-7228. *Fax:* 618-537-6496. *E-mail:* jlblasdel@mckendree.edu. *Web site:* http://www.mckendree.edu/.

Midstate College
Peoria, Illinois

Freshman Application Contact Ms. Jessica Hancock, Director of Admissions, Midstate College, 411 West Northmoor Road, Peoria, IL 61614. *Phone:* 309-692-4092. *Toll-free phone:* 800-251-4299. *Fax:* 309-692-3893. *E-mail:* jhancock2@midstate.edu. *Web site:* http://www.midstate.edu/.

Millikin University
Decatur, Illinois

- **Independent** comprehensive, founded 1901, affiliated with Presbyterian Church (U.S.A.)
- **Suburban** 75-acre campus
- **Endowment** $106.2 million
- **Coed** 2,258 undergraduate students, 95% full-time, 60% women, 40% men
- **Moderately difficult** entrance level, 56% of applicants were admitted

Undergraduates 2,141 full-time, 117 part-time. Students come from 39 states and territories; 13 other countries; 11% are from out of state; 12% Black or African American, non-Hispanic/Latino; 5% Hispanic/Latino; 0.6% Asian, non-Hispanic/Latino; 0.2% Native Hawaiian or other Pacific Islander, non-Hispanic/Latino; 0.3% American Indian or Alaska Native, non-Hispanic/Latino; 3% Two or more races, non-Hispanic/Latino; 0.3% Race/ethnicity unknown; 2% international; 6% transferred in; 64% live on campus. *Retention:* 77% of full-time freshmen returned.

Freshmen *Admission:* 3,285 applied, 1,856 admitted, 432 enrolled. *Average high school GPA:* 3.34. *Test scores:* SAT critical reading scores over 500: 69%; SAT math scores over 500: 57%; SAT writing scores over 500: 60%; ACT scores over 18: 97%; SAT critical reading scores over 600: 30%; SAT math scores over 600: 13%; SAT writing scores over 600: 10%; ACT scores over 24: 42%; ACT scores over 30: 8%.

Faculty *Total:* 302, 52% full-time, 52% with terminal degrees. *Student/faculty ratio:* 11:1.

Academics *Calendar:* semesters. *Degrees:* bachelor's and master's. *Special study options:* accelerated degree program, adult/continuing education programs, advanced placement credit, double majors, English as a second language, honors programs, independent study, internships, off-campus study,

part-time degree program, services for LD students, student-designed majors, study abroad, summer session for credit. *Unusual degree programs:* 3-2 engineering with Washington University in St. Louis; occupational therapy with Washington University; pharmacy with Midwestern University.

Computers on Campus 280 computers/terminals and 318 ports are available on campus for general student use. Students can access the following: computer help desk, free student e-mail accounts, online (class) grades, online (class) registration, online (class) schedules, online degree audit; online financials (view and pay bills; view financial aid). Campuswide network is available. 100% of college-owned or -operated housing units are wired for high-speed Internet access. Wireless service is available via classrooms, computer centers, computer labs, dorm rooms, learning centers, libraries, student centers.

Student Life *Housing:* on-campus residence required through junior year. *Options:* coed, men-only, women-only, disabled students. Campus housing is university owned, leased by the school and is provided by a third party. Freshman campus housing is guaranteed. *Activities and organizations:* drama/theater group, student-run newspaper, radio station, choral group, University Center Board, Multicultural Student Council, Student Housing Council, Panhellenic Council, Interfraternity Council, national fraternities, national sororities. *Campus security:* 24-hour emergency response devices and patrols, late-night transport/escort service, controlled dormitory access. *Student services:* health clinic, personal/psychological counseling.

Athletics Member NCAA. All Division III. *Intercollegiate sports:* baseball M, basketball M/W, cheerleading M/W, cross-country running M/W, football M, golf M/W, soccer M/W, softball W, swimming and diving M/W, tennis W, track and field M/W, volleyball W. *Intramural sports:* basketball M/W, bowling M/W, football M, soccer M/W, softball M/W, volleyball M/W.

Standardized Tests *Required:* SAT or ACT (for admission).

Costs (2012–13) *Comprehensive fee:* $37,614 includes full-time tuition ($27,852), mandatory fees ($792), and room and board ($8970). Part-time tuition: $931 per credit hour. *Required fees:* $22 per credit hour part-time. *College room only:* $5000. Room and board charges vary according to board plan and housing facility. *Payment plan:* installment. *Waivers:* employees or children of employees.

Financial Aid Of all full-time matriculated undergraduates who enrolled in 2010, 1,937 applied for aid, 1,750 were judged to have need, 862 had their need fully met. 382 Federal Work-Study jobs (averaging $1108). 174 state and other part-time jobs (averaging $798). In 2010, 157 non-need-based awards were made. *Average percent of need met:* 90%. *Average financial aid package:* $21,775. *Average need-based loan:* $4357. *Average need-based gift aid:* $9282. *Average non-need-based aid:* $10,077. *Average indebtedness upon graduation:* $31,174.

Applying *Options:* electronic application, deferred entrance. *Required:* high school transcript, minimum 2.0 GPA, 2 letters of recommendation. *Required for some:* audition for music/theatre, art portfolio review. *Recommended:* interview. *Application deadlines:* rolling (freshmen), rolling (out-of-state freshmen), rolling (transfers). *Notification:* continuous (freshmen), continuous (out-of-state freshmen), continuous (transfers).

Freshman Application Contact Mr. Joe Havis, Director, Office of Admission, Millikin University, 1184 West Main Street, Decatur, IL 62522-2084. *Phone:* 217-424-6210. *Toll-free phone:* 800-373-7733. *Fax:* 217-425-4669. *E-mail:* admis@millikin.edu. *Web site:* http://www.millikin.edu/.

Monmouth College
Monmouth, Illinois

- **Independent** 4-year, founded 1853, affiliated with Presbyterian Church
- **Small-town** 106-acre campus with easy access to Chicago
- **Endowment** $78.6 million
- **Coed** 1,316 undergraduate students, 97% full-time, 52% women, 48% men
- **Moderately difficult** entrance level, 65% of applicants were admitted

Undergraduates 1,274 full-time, 42 part-time. Students come from 27 states and territories; 9 other countries; 7% are from out of state; 9% Black or African American, non-Hispanic/Latino; 7% Hispanic/Latino; 0.5% Asian, non-Hispanic/Latino; 0.2% Native Hawaiian or other Pacific Islander, non-Hispanic/Latino; 0.7% American Indian or Alaska Native, non-Hispanic/Latino; 0.3% Two or more races, non-Hispanic/Latino; 3% Race/ethnicity unknown; 1% international; 5% transferred in; 94% live on campus. *Retention:* 74% of full-time freshmen returned.

Freshmen *Admission:* 2,170 applied, 1,401 admitted, 341 enrolled. *Average high school GPA:* 3.2. *Test scores:* ACT scores over 18: 91%; ACT scores over 24: 32%; ACT scores over 30: 2%.

Faculty *Total:* 121, 69% full-time, 64% with terminal degrees. *Student/faculty ratio:* 14:1.

Academics *Calendar:* semesters. *Degree:* bachelor's. *Special study options:* academic remediation for entering students, advanced placement credit, double majors, English as a second language, honors programs, independent study,

internships, off-campus study, part-time degree program, services for LD students, student-designed majors, study abroad. *ROTC:* Army (c). *Unusual degree programs:* engineering with Case Western Reserve University; University of Southern California (joint five-year and six-year coordinated programs); nursing with Rush University College of Nursing; Joint five-year and six-year occupational therapy and medical technology Masters programs with Rush University; atmospheric science with Creighton University.

Computers on Campus 140 computers/terminals are available on campus for general student use. Students can access the following: campus intranet, computer help desk, free student e-mail accounts, online (class) grades, online (class) registration, online (class) schedules, 11 PC labs and 3 specialized Mac labs. Campuswide network is available. 100% of college-owned or -operated housing units are wired for high-speed Internet access. Wireless service is available via entire campus.

Student Life *Housing:* on-campus residence required through senior year. *Options:* coed, men-only, women-only, disabled students. Campus housing is university owned. Freshman campus housing is guaranteed. *Activities and organizations:* drama/theater group, student-run newspaper, radio and television station, choral group, marching band, Fighting Scots Marching Band and Jazz Band, Associated Students of Monmouth College, Crimson Masque (theatre), Alternative Spring Break, Coalition for Ethnic Awareness, national fraternities, national sororities. *Campus security:* 24-hour emergency response devices, late-night transport/escort service, controlled dormitory access, night security. *Student services:* personal/psychological counseling.

Athletics Member NCAA. All Division III. *Intercollegiate sports:* baseball M, basketball M/W, cross-country running M/W, football M, golf M/W, soccer M/W, softball M/W, swimming and diving M/W, tennis M/W, track and field M/W, volleyball W. *Intramural sports:* archery M/W, badminton M/W, baseball M/W, basketball M/W, cheerleading M/W, cross-country running M/W, golf M/W, soccer M/W, softball M/W, swimming and diving M/W, table tennis M/W, tennis M/W, track and field M/W, ultimate Frisbee M/W, volleyball M/W, water polo M(c)/W(c), wrestling M.

Standardized Tests *Required:* SAT or ACT (for admission).

Costs (2012–13) *Tuition:* $895 per credit hour part-time. Full-time tuition and fees vary according to course load. *Room only:* Room and board charges vary according to board plan and housing facility. *Payment plan:* installment. *Waivers:* employees or children of employees.

Financial Aid Of all full-time matriculated undergraduates who enrolled in 2011, 1,221 applied for aid, 1,138 were judged to have need, 222 had their need fully met. In 2011, 83 non-need-based awards were made. *Average percent of need met:* 86%. *Average financial aid package:* $25,302. *Average need-based loan:* $4292. *Average need-based gift aid:* $19,914. *Average non-need-based aid:* $11,854. *Average indebtedness upon graduation:* $28,934.

Applying *Options:* electronic application, deferred entrance. *Required:* essay or personal statement, high school transcript, letters of recommendation. *Required for some:* interview. *Recommended:* minimum 2.7 GPA, interview. *Application deadlines:* rolling (freshmen), rolling (transfers). *Notification:* continuous (freshmen), continuous (transfers).

Freshman Application Contact Mr. Omar Correa, Vice President for Enrollment Management, Monmouth College, 700 East Broadway, Monmouth, IL 61462-1988. Phone: 309-457-2210. *Toll-free phone:* 800-747-2687. *Fax:* 309-457-2141. *E-mail:* admissions@monmouthcollege.edu. *Web site:* http://www.monm.edu/.

Moody Bible Institute
Chicago, Illinois

- **Independent nondenominational** comprehensive, founded 1886
- **Urban** 25-acre campus with easy access to Chicago
- **Endowment** $27.8 million
- **Coed** 2,928 undergraduate students, 78% full-time, 44% women, 56% men
- **Moderately difficult** entrance level, 89% of applicants were admitted

Undergraduates 2,275 full-time, 653 part-time. Students come from 24 other countries; 4% Black or African American, non-Hispanic/Latino; 4% Hispanic/Latino; 3% Asian, non-Hispanic/Latino; 0.1% Native Hawaiian or other Pacific Islander, non-Hispanic/Latino; 0.2% American Indian or Alaska Native, non-Hispanic/Latino; 0.2% Two or more races, non-Hispanic/Latino; 14% Race/ethnicity unknown; 6% international. *Retention:* 78% of full-time freshmen returned.

Freshmen *Admission:* 816 applied, 723 admitted, 430 enrolled. *Average high school GPA:* 3.37.

Faculty *Total:* 211, 43% full-time. *Student/faculty ratio:* 20:1.

Academics *Calendar:* semesters. *Degrees:* associate, bachelor's, master's, and postbachelor's certificates. *Special study options:* adult/continuing education programs, advanced placement credit, distance learning, double majors, English as a second language, external degree program, independent study,

internships, off-campus study, part-time degree program, study abroad, summer session for credit.

Computers on Campus Students can access the following: campus intranet, computer help desk, free student e-mail accounts, online (class) grades, online (class) registration, online (class) schedules. Campuswide network is available. 100% of college-owned or -operated housing units are wired for high-speed Internet access. Wireless service is available via entire campus.

Student Life *Housing:* on-campus residence required through senior year. *Options:* men-only, women-only. Campus housing is university owned. *Activities and organizations:* drama/theater group, student-run newspaper, radio station, choral group. *Campus security:* 24-hour emergency response devices and patrols, student patrols, late-night transport/escort service, controlled dormitory access. *Student services:* health clinic, personal/psychological counseling.

Athletics Member NCCAA. *Intercollegiate sports:* basketball M/W, soccer M, volleyball M/W. *Intramural sports:* basketball M/W, football M/W, racquetball M/W, soccer M/W, softball M/W, tennis M, ultimate Frisbee M/W, volleyball M/W, water polo M/W.

Standardized Tests *Required:* SAT and SAT Subject Tests or ACT (for admission).

Applying *Options:* electronic application, early admission, early decision. *Required:* essay or personal statement, high school transcript, minimum 2.0 GPA, 4 letters of recommendation, Christian testimony. *Required for some:* interview. *Application deadlines:* 3/1 (freshmen), 3/1 (transfers). *Early decision deadline:* 12/1. *Notification:* continuous until 4/1 (freshmen), continuous until 4/1 (transfers), 1/15 (early decision).

Freshman Application Contact Ms. Jacqueline Holman, Admissions Office, Moody Bible Institute, 820 North LaSalle Boulevard, Chicago, IL 60610. *Phone:* 312-329-4307. *Toll-free phone:* 800-967-4MBI. *Fax:* 312-329-8987. *E-mail:* admissions@moody.edu. *Web site:* http://www.moody.edu/.

National-Louis University
Chicago, Illinois

- **Independent** university, founded 1886
- **Urban** 12-acre campus
- **Endowment** $29.0 million
- **Coed** 1,437 undergraduate students, 59% full-time, 79% women, 21% men
- **Minimally difficult** entrance level, 30% of applicants were admitted

Undergraduates 849 full-time, 588 part-time. Students come from 6 states and territories; 39% Black or African American, non-Hispanic/Latino; 20% Hispanic/Latino; 2% Asian, non-Hispanic/Latino; 0.2% Native Hawaiian or other Pacific Islander, non-Hispanic/Latino; 0.4% American Indian or Alaska Native, non-Hispanic/Latino; 0.7% Two or more races, non-Hispanic/Latino; 7% Race/ethnicity unknown; 0.5% international.

Freshmen *Admission:* 161 applied, 48 admitted, 26 enrolled.

Faculty *Total:* 521, 41% full-time, 31% with terminal degrees. *Student/faculty ratio:* 8:1.

Academics *Calendar:* quarters. *Degrees:* bachelor's, master's, doctoral, postmaster's, postbachelor's, and first professional certificates. *Special study options:* academic remediation for entering students, accelerated degree program, adult/continuing education programs, advanced placement credit, distance learning, English as a second language, honors programs, independent study, internships, services for LD students, summer session for credit.

Computers on Campus 165 computers/terminals are available on campus for general student use. Students can access the following: campus intranet, computer help desk, free student e-mail accounts, online (class) grades, online (class) registration, online (class) schedules. Campuswide network is available. Wireless service is available via classrooms, computer centers, computer labs, learning centers, libraries, student centers.

Student Life *Housing:* college housing not available. *Activities and organizations:* drama/theater group. *Campus security:* 24-hour emergency response devices and patrols. *Student services:* personal/psychological counseling.

Standardized Tests *Required for some:* SAT or ACT (for admission).

Costs (2011–12) *Tuition:* $18,855 full-time, $419 per quarter hour part-time. Full-time tuition and fees vary according to course level, course load, degree level, and program. Part-time tuition and fees vary according to course level, course load, degree level, and program. *Required fees:* $120 full-time, $20 per term part-time.

Financial Aid Of all full-time matriculated undergraduates who enrolled in 2010, 844 applied for aid, 799 were judged to have need, 85 had their need fully met. 69 Federal Work-Study jobs (averaging $3185). In 2010, 40 non-need-based awards were made. *Average percent of need met:* 51%. *Average financial aid package:* $11,138. *Average need-based loan:* $4504. *Average need-based gift aid:* $7358. *Average non-need-based aid:* $5395. *Average indebtedness upon graduation:* $33,732.

Applying *Options:* electronic application, deferred entrance. *Application fee:* $40. *Required:* high school transcript, minimum 2.0 GPA. *Required for some:*

2 letters of recommendation. *Recommended:* interview. *Application deadlines:* rolling (freshmen), rolling (transfers). *Notification:* continuous (freshmen), continuous (transfers).

Freshman Application Contact National-Louis University, 1000 Capitol Drive, Wheeling, IL 60090. *Phone:* 888-NLU-TODAY. *Toll-free phone:* 888-658-8632. *Web site:* http://www.nl.edu/.

North Central College
Naperville, Illinois

- **Independent United Methodist** comprehensive, founded 1861
- **Suburban** 62-acre campus with easy access to Chicago
- **Endowment** $94.1 million
- **Coed** 2,729 undergraduate students, 92% full-time, 56% women, 44% men
- **Moderately difficult** entrance level, 65% of applicants were admitted

Undergraduates 2,516 full-time, 213 part-time. Students come from 32 states and territories; 27 other countries; 7% are from out of state; 4% Black or African American, non-Hispanic/Latino; 7% Hispanic/Latino; 2% Asian, non-Hispanic/Latino; 0.2% American Indian or Alaska Native, non-Hispanic/Latino; 2% Two or more races, non-Hispanic/Latino; 5% Race/ethnicity unknown; 1% international; 10% transferred in; 55% live on campus. *Retention:* 82% of full-time freshmen returned.

Freshmen *Admission:* 3,052 applied, 1,972 admitted, 574 enrolled. *Average high school GPA:* 3.6. *Test scores:* ACT scores over 18: 99%; ACT scores over 24: 61%; ACT scores over 30: 11%.

Faculty *Total:* 247, 52% full-time, 64% with terminal degrees. *Student/faculty ratio:* 16:1.

Academics *Calendar:* quarters. *Degrees:* bachelor's, master's, and postbachelor's certificates. *Special study options:* academic remediation for entering students, accelerated degree program, advanced placement credit, double majors, English as a second language, honors programs, independent study, internships, off-campus study, part-time degree program, services for LD students, student-designed majors, study abroad, summer session for credit. *ROTC:* Army (c), Air Force (c). *Unusual degree programs:* 3-2 engineering with Washington University in St. Louis; University of Illinois at Urbana-Champaign; Marquette University; University of Minnesota, Twin Cities Campus.

Computers on Campus 232 computers/terminals and 31 ports are available on campus for general student use. Students can access the following: campus intranet, computer help desk, free student e-mail accounts, online (class) grades, online (class) registration, online (class) schedules, software packages. Campuswide network is available. 100% of college-owned or -operated housing units are wired for high-speed Internet access. Wireless service is available via computer centers, computer labs, dorm rooms, learning centers, libraries, student centers.

Student Life *Housing options:* coed, men-only, women-only, disabled students. Campus housing is university owned. Freshman applicants given priority for college housing. *Activities and organizations:* drama/theater group, student-run newspaper, radio station, choral group, College Union Activities Board, WONC (student radio station), Cardinals in Action (service group), Students in Free Enterprise (SIFE), Residence Hall Association. *Campus security:* 24-hour emergency response devices and patrols, late-night transport/escort service, controlled dormitory access. *Student services:* health clinic, personal/psychological counseling.

Athletics Member NCAA. All Division III. *Intercollegiate sports:* baseball M, basketball M/W, cheerleading W, cross-country running M/W, football M, golf M/W, lacrosse W, soccer M/W, softball W, swimming and diving M/W, tennis M/W, track and field M/W, volleyball W, wrestling M. *Intramural sports:* badminton M/W, basketball M/W, football M/W, golf M/W, racquetball M/W, soccer M/W, softball M/W, ultimate Frisbee M/W, volleyball M/W.

Standardized Tests *Required:* SAT or ACT (for admission). *Recommended:* ACT (for admission).

Costs (2011–12) *Comprehensive fee:* $38,343 includes full-time tuition ($29,493), mandatory fees ($240), and room and board ($8610). Part-time tuition: $716 per credit hour. Part-time tuition and fees vary according to course load. *Required fees:* $20 per term part-time. *Room and board:* Room and board charges vary according to housing facility. *Payment plan:* installment. *Waivers:* senior citizens and employees or children of employees.

Financial Aid Of all full-time matriculated undergraduates who enrolled in 2011, 2,109 applied for aid, 1,927 were judged to have need, 447 had their need fully met. 1,336 Federal Work-Study jobs (averaging $169). In 2011, 500 non-need-based awards were made. *Average percent of need met:* 76%. *Average financial aid package:* $21,681. *Average need-based loan:* $4673. *Average need-based gift aid:* $16,597. *Average non-need-based aid:* $11,962. *Average indebtedness upon graduation:* $29,162.

Applying *Options:* electronic application, deferred entrance. *Application fee:* $25. *Required:* high school transcript, minimum 2.5 GPA. *Required for some:*

interview. *Recommended:* essay or personal statement, 1 letter of recommendation. *Application deadlines:* rolling (freshmen), rolling (out-of-state freshmen), rolling (transfers). *Notification:* continuous (freshmen), continuous (out-of-state freshmen), continuous (transfers).

Freshman Application Contact Ms. Martha Stolze, Director of Freshman Admission, North Central College, 30 North Brainard Street, PO Box 3063, Naperville, IL 60566-7063. *Phone:* 630-637-5800. *Toll-free phone:* 800-411-1861. *Fax:* 630-637-5819. *E-mail:* admissions@noctrl.edu. *Web site:* http://www.northcentralcollege.edu/.

Northeastern Illinois University
Chicago, Illinois

- **State-supported** comprehensive, founded 1961
- **Urban** 67-acre campus with easy access to Chicago
- **Endowment** $2.9 million
- **Coed** 9,498 undergraduate students, 59% full-time, 58% women, 42% men
- **Minimally difficult** entrance level, 65% of applicants were admitted

Undergraduates 5,623 full-time, 3,875 part-time. Students come from 20 states and territories; 104 other countries; 1% are from out of state; 10% Black or African American, non-Hispanic/Latino; 31% Hispanic/Latino; 10% Asian, non-Hispanic/Latino; 0.2% Native Hawaiian or other Pacific Islander, non-Hispanic/Latino; 0.2% American Indian or Alaska Native, non-Hispanic/Latino; 0.7% Two or more races, non-Hispanic/Latino; 4% Race/ethnicity unknown; 4% international; 15% transferred in. *Retention:* 67% of full-time freshmen returned.

Freshmen *Admission:* 5,104 applied, 3,341 admitted, 1,042 enrolled. *Average high school GPA:* 2.87. *Test scores:* ACT scores over 18: 62%; ACT scores over 24: 11%; ACT scores over 30: 1%.

Faculty *Total:* 718, 58% full-time, 52% with terminal degrees. *Student/faculty ratio:* 15:1.

Academics *Calendar:* semesters. *Degrees:* bachelor's and master's. *Special study options:* academic remediation for entering students, adult/continuing education programs, advanced placement credit, cooperative education, distance learning, double majors, English as a second language, external degree program, honors programs, independent study, internships, off-campus study, part-time degree program, services for LD students, study abroad, summer session for credit. *ROTC:* Army (c), Air Force (c).

Computers on Campus 520 computers/terminals are available on campus for general student use. Students can access the following: computer help desk, free student e-mail accounts, online (class) grades, online (class) registration, online (class) schedules, productivity software. Campuswide network is available. Wireless service is available via classrooms, computer centers, computer labs, learning centers, libraries, student centers.

Student Life *Housing:* college housing not available. *Activities and organizations:* student-run newspaper, radio station, choral group, Student Government Association, WZRD radio club, Anime Club, Future Health Professionals, Green Cycle Club, national fraternities, national sororities. *Campus security:* 24-hour emergency response devices and patrols, late-night transport/escort service. *Student services:* health clinic, personal/psychological counseling, women's center.

Athletics *Intramural sports:* baseball M(c), basketball M(c), rugby M(c), volleyball M(c)/W(c).

Standardized Tests *Required:* ACT (for admission).

Costs (2011–12) *Tuition:* state resident $8250 full-time, $275 per credit hour part-time; nonresident $16,500 full-time, $550 per credit hour part-time. Full-time tuition and fees vary according to student level. Part-time tuition and fees vary according to student level. No tuition increase for student's term of enrollment. *Required fees:* $1599 full-time, $53 per credit hour part-time, $3 per term part-time. *Payment plan:* deferred payment. *Waivers:* senior citizens and employees or children of employees.

Financial Aid Of all full-time matriculated undergraduates who enrolled in 2011, 4,410 applied for aid, 3,912 were judged to have need, 80 had their need fully met. 65 Federal Work-Study jobs (averaging $3073). 221 state and other part-time jobs (averaging $3757). In 2011, 141 non-need-based awards were made. *Average percent of need met:* 31%. *Average financial aid package:* $8196. *Average need-based loan:* $4610. *Average need-based gift aid:* $6735. *Average non-need-based aid:* $3240. *Average indebtedness upon graduation:* $12,100.

Applying *Options:* electronic application, deferred entrance. *Application fee:* $25. *Required:* high school transcript. *Application deadlines:* 7/1 (freshmen), 7/1 (transfers). *Notification:* 9/1 (freshmen), continuous (transfers).

Freshman Application Contact Ms. Zarrin Kerwell, Admissions Counselor, Northeastern Illinois University, 5500 North St. Louis Avenue, Chicago, IL 60625. *Phone:* 773-442-4026. *Fax:* 773-794-6243. *E-mail:* admrec@neiu.edu. *Web site:* http://www.neiu.edu/.

Northern Illinois University

De Kalb, Illinois

- **State-supported** university, founded 1895
- **Small-town** 650-acre campus with easy access to Chicago
- **Endowment** $3.0 million
- **Coed** 17,306 undergraduate students, 88% full-time, 50% women, 50% men
- **Moderately difficult** entrance level, 53% of applicants were admitted

Undergraduates 15,233 full-time, 2,073 part-time. Students come from 28 states and territories; 88 other countries; 4% are from out of state; 15% Black or African American, non-Hispanic/Latino; 11% Hispanic/Latino; 5% Asian, non-Hispanic/Latino; 0.1% Native Hawaiian or other Pacific Islander, non-Hispanic/Latino; 0.2% American Indian or Alaska Native, non-Hispanic/Latino; 2% Two or more races, non-Hispanic/Latino; 3% Race/ethnicity unknown; 1% international; 12% transferred in; 33% live on campus. *Retention:* 71% of full-time freshmen returned.

Freshmen *Admission:* 17,586 applied, 9,239 admitted, 2,590 enrolled. *Test scores:* ACT scores over 18: 87%; ACT scores over 24: 31%; ACT scores over 30: 4%.

Faculty *Total:* 1,145, 77% full-time, 73% with terminal degrees. *Student/faculty ratio:* 14:1.

Academics *Calendar:* semesters. *Degrees:* bachelor's, master's, doctoral, and first professional. *Special study options:* accelerated degree program, adult/continuing education programs, advanced placement credit, cooperative education, double majors, honors programs, independent study, internships, off-campus study, part-time degree program, services for LD students, student-designed majors, study abroad, summer session for credit. *ROTC:* Army (b), Air Force (c). *Unusual degree programs:* 3-2 engineering with University of Illinois.

Computers on Campus 1,500 computers/terminals are available on campus for general student use. Students can access the following: computer help desk, free student e-mail accounts, online (class) registration. Campuswide network is available.

Student Life *Housing:* on-campus residence required for freshman year. *Options:* coed. Campus housing is university owned. Freshman applicants given priority for college housing. *Activities and organizations:* drama/theater group, student-run newspaper, radio station, choral group, marching band, American Marketing Association, Delta Sigma Pi, Pi Sigma Epsilon, Black Choir, Student Volunteer Choir, national fraternities, national sororities. *Campus security:* 24-hour emergency response devices and patrols, student patrols, late-night transport/escort service, controlled dormitory access. *Student services:* health clinic, personal/psychological counseling, women's center, legal services.

Athletics Member NCAA. All Division I except football (Division I-A). *Intercollegiate sports:* baseball M(s), basketball M(s)/W(s), cross-country running W, golf M(s)/W(s), gymnastics W(s), soccer M(s)/W(s), softball W(s), swimming and diving M(s)/W(s), tennis M(s)/W(s), volleyball W(s), wrestling M(s). *Intramural sports:* archery M(c)/W(c), badminton M/W, basketball M/W, bowling M(c)/W(c), cross-country running W, football M/W, golf M/W, ice hockey M(c)/W(c), lacrosse M(c)/W(c), racquetball M/W, rugby M(c)/W(c), skiing (downhill) M(c)/W(c), soccer M/W, softball M/W, table tennis M/W, tennis M/W, track and field M(c)/W(c), volleyball M/W, water polo M(c)/W(c), weight lifting M(c)/W(c).

Standardized Tests *Required:* SAT or ACT (for admission).

Costs (2011–12) *Tuition:* state resident $8491 full-time, $315 per credit hour part-time; nonresident $16,981 full-time, $629 per credit hour part-time. Full-time tuition and fees vary according to course load, location, and student level. Part-time tuition and fees vary according to course load, location, and student level. No tuition increase for student's term of enrollment. *Required fees:* $2534 full-time, $84 per credit hour part-time, $125 per term part-time. *Room and board:* $10,420. Room and board charges vary according to board plan and housing facility.

Financial Aid Of all full-time matriculated undergraduates who enrolled in 2010, 13,489 applied for aid, 11,823 were judged to have need, 1,150 had their need fully met. 6,227 Federal Work-Study jobs (averaging $3188). *Average percent of need met:* 63%. *Average financial aid package:* $11,281. *Average need-based loan:* $4277. *Average need-based gift aid:* $7511. *Average indebtedness upon graduation:* $29,267.

Applying *Options:* electronic application. *Application fee:* $40. *Required:* high school transcript, high school rank. *Application deadlines:* 8/1 (freshmen), 8/1 (transfers). *Notification:* continuous (freshmen), continuous (transfers).

Freshman Application Contact Dr. Kimberley Buster-Williams, Director of Admissions, Northern Illinois University, Office of Admissions, DeKalb, IL 60115-2857. *Phone:* 815-753-0446. *Toll-free phone:* 800-892-3050. *E-mail:* admission-info@niu.edu. *Web site:* http://www.niu.edu/.

North Park University

Chicago, Illinois

Freshman Application Contact Office of Admissions, North Park University, 3225 West Foster Avenue, Chicago, IL 60625-4895. *Phone:* 773-244-5500. *Toll-free phone:* 800-888-NPC8. *Fax:* 773-583-0858. *E-mail:* afao@northpark.edu. *Web site:* http://www.northpark.edu/.

Northwestern University

Evanston, Illinois

Freshman Application Contact Mr. Christopher Watson, Dean of Undergraduate Admission, Northwestern University, PO Box 3060, Evanston, IL 60204-3060. *Phone:* 847-491-7271. *E-mail:* ug-admission@northwestern.edu. *Web site:* http://www.northwestern.edu/.

Olivet Nazarene University

Bourbonnais, Illinois

Freshman Application Contact Olivet Nazarene University, One University Avenue, Bourbonnais, IL 60914. *Phone:* 815-939-5203. *Toll-free phone:* 800-648-1463. *Web site:* http://www.olivet.edu/.

See page 271 for display ad and page 1496 for the College Close-Up.

Principia College

Elsah, Illinois

- **Independent Christian Science** 4-year, founded 1910
- **Rural** 2600-acre campus with easy access to St. Louis
- **Endowment** $493.7 million
- **Coed**
- **Moderately difficult** entrance level

Faculty *Student/faculty ratio:* 8:1.

Academics *Calendar:* quarters. *Degree:* bachelor's.

Student Life *Campus security:* 24-hour patrols.

Athletics Member NCAA. All Division III.

Standardized Tests *Required:* SAT or ACT (for admission). *Recommended:* SAT Subject Tests (for admission).

Costs (2011–12) *Comprehensive fee:* $35,140 includes full-time tuition ($25,200), mandatory fees ($440), and room and board ($9500). Full-time tuition and fees vary according to course load. *College room only:* $4620.

Financial Aid Of all full-time matriculated undergraduates who enrolled in 2010, 361 applied for aid, 350 were judged to have need, 297 had their need fully met. 142 state and other part-time jobs (averaging $1252). *In 2010,* 85 non-need-based awards were made. *Average percent of need met:* 85. *Average financial aid package:* $24,175. *Average need-based loan:* $5342. *Average need-based gift aid:* $20,119. *Average non-need-based aid:* $16,727. *Average indebtedness upon graduation:* $14,963.

Applying *Options:* electronic application, deferred entrance. *Required:* essay or personal statement, high school transcript, minimum 2.3 GPA, 4 letters of recommendation, Christian Science commitment. *Required for some:* interview. *Recommended:* interview.

Freshman Application Contact Mr. Brian McCauley, Dean of Enrollment Management, Principia College, One Maybeck Place, Elsah, IL 62028-9799. *Phone:* 618-374-5180. *Toll-free phone:* 800-277-4648 Ext. 2804. *Web site:* http://www.principiacollege.edu.

Quincy University

Quincy, Illinois

- **Independent Roman Catholic** comprehensive, founded 1860
- **Small-town** 70-acre campus
- **Endowment** $15.5 million
- **Coed** 1,268 undergraduate students, 91% full-time, 56% women, 44% men
- **Moderately difficult** entrance level, 91% of applicants were admitted

Undergraduates 1,149 full-time, 119 part-time. Students come from 24 states and territories; 3 other countries; 27% are from out of state; 11% Black or African American, non-Hispanic/Latino; 2% Hispanic/Latino; 0.6% Asian, non-Hispanic/Latino; 0.2% Native Hawaiian or other Pacific Islander, non-Hispanic/Latino; 0.8% American Indian or Alaska Native, non-Hispanic/Latino; 0.7% Two or more races, non-Hispanic/Latino; 19% Race/ethnicity unknown; 0.6% international; 10% transferred in; 54% live on campus. *Retention:* 72% of full-time freshmen returned.

Freshmen *Admission:* 1,023 applied, 928 admitted, 276 enrolled. *Average high school GPA:* 3.26. *Test scores:* SAT critical reading scores over 500:

38%; SAT math scores over 500: 44%; ACT scores over 18: 92%; SAT critical reading scores over 600: 13%; SAT math scores over 600: 6%; ACT scores over 24: 31%; SAT critical reading scores over 700: 13%; ACT scores over 30: 2%.

Faculty *Total:* 176, 31% full-time, 36% with terminal degrees. *Student/faculty ratio:* 14:1.

Academics *Calendar:* semesters. *Degrees:* associate, bachelor's, and master's. *Special study options:* academic remediation for entering students, accelerated degree program, adult/continuing education programs, advanced placement credit, distance learning, double majors, honors programs, independent study, internships, off-campus study, part-time degree program, student-designed majors, study abroad, summer session for credit. *Unusual degree programs:* 3-2 engineering with Washington University in St. Louis.

Computers on Campus 107 computers/terminals are available on campus for general student use. Students can access the following: campus intranet, computer help desk, free student e-mail accounts, online (class) grades, online (class) registration, online (class) schedules. Campuswide network is available. 100% of college-owned or -operated housing units are wired for high-speed Internet access. Wireless service is available via classrooms, computer centers, computer labs, dorm rooms, learning centers, libraries, student centers.

Student Life *Housing:* on-campus residence required through junior year. *Options:* coed, men-only, women-only, disabled students. Campus housing is university owned. Freshman campus housing is guaranteed. *Activities and organizations:* drama/theater group, student-run newspaper, choral group, marching band, Student Senate, Kappa Kappa Psi, Student Programming Board, Minority Student Association, Students in Free Enterprise (SIFE), national fraternities, national sororities. *Campus security:* 24-hour emergency response devices and patrols, student patrols, late-night transport/escort service, controlled dormitory access, self-defense education, shuttle buses, lighted pathways/sidewalks. *Student services:* health clinic, personal/psychological counseling.

Athletics Member NCAA, NAIA. All NCAA Division II except volleyball (Division I). *Intercollegiate sports:* baseball M(s), basketball M(s)/W(s), cheerleading M(c)/W(c), cross-country running M(s)/W(s), football M(s), golf M(s)/W(s), soccer M(s)/W(s), softball W(s), tennis M(s)/W(s), volleyball M(s)/W(s). *Intramural sports:* basketball M/W, bowling M/W, football M/W, racquetball M/W, soccer M/W, softball M/W, table tennis M/W, volleyball M/W.

Standardized Tests *Required:* SAT or ACT (for admission).

Costs (2011–12) *Comprehensive fee:* $33,560 includes full-time tuition ($23,340), mandatory fees ($800), and room and board ($9420). Part-time

tuition: $565 per semester hour. Part-time tuition and fees vary according to course load. *Required fees:* $15 per semester hour part-time. *College room only:* $5210. Room and board charges vary according to board plan and housing facility. *Payment plan:* installment. *Waivers:* senior citizens and employees or children of employees.

Financial Aid Of all full-time matriculated undergraduates who enrolled in 2011, 1,049 applied for aid, 970 were judged to have need, 179 had their need fully met. 389 Federal Work-Study jobs (averaging $2000). 22 state and other part-time jobs (averaging $2273). In 2011, 43 non-need-based awards were made. *Average percent of need met:* 76%. *Average financial aid package:* $22,177. *Average need-based loan:* $4360. *Average need-based gift aid:* $18,977. *Average non-need-based aid:* $11,423. *Average indebtedness upon graduation:* $25,248.

Applying *Options:* electronic application, deferred entrance. *Application fee:* $25. *Required:* essay or personal statement, high school transcript, minimum 2.5 GPA. *Required for some:* 1 letter of recommendation, audition required of music majors, portfolio recommended for art majors. *Recommended:* interview. *Application deadlines:* rolling (freshmen), rolling (out-of-state freshmen), rolling (transfers). *Notification:* continuous (freshmen), continuous (out-of-state freshmen), continuous (transfers).

Freshman Application Contact Mrs. Syndi Peck, Vice President of Enrollment Management, Quincy University, Admissions Office, 1800 College Avenue, Quincy, IL 62301-2699. *Phone:* 217-228-5210. *Toll-free phone:* 800-688-4295. *E-mail:* admissions@quincy.edu. *Web site:* http://www.quincy.edu/.

Rasmussen College Aurora

Aurora, Illinois

- **Proprietary** primarily 2-year, part of Rasmussen College System
- **Suburban** campus
- **Coed** 443 undergraduate students
- **Minimally difficult** entrance level

Faculty *Student/faculty ratio:* 22:1.

Academics *Degrees:* certificates, diplomas, associate, and bachelor's. *Special study options:* academic remediation for entering students, accelerated degree program, adult/continuing education programs, distance learning, double majors, internships, part-time degree program, summer session for credit.

Computers on Campus 87 computers/terminals are available on campus for general student use. Students can access the following: computer help desk,

Nearly 100 percent of our students receive some type of financial assistance.

Scan this code or go to:
http://undergrad.olivet.edu
to find out your potential award.

OLIVET NAZARENE UNIVERSITY

www.olivet.edu

we believe. you belong here.

For more information or to schedule a campus visit, go to www.olivet.edu or call the Office of Admissions at 800-648-1463.

free student e-mail accounts, online (class) grades, online (class) schedules. Campuswide network is available. Wireless service is available via entire campus.

Student Life *Housing:* college housing not available.

Standardized Tests *Required:* Internal Exam (for admission).

Costs (2012–13) *Tuition:* $12,600 full-time. Full-time tuition and fees vary according to course level, course load, degree level, location, and program. Part-time tuition and fees vary according to course level, course load, degree level, location, and program. *Required fees:* $40 full-time. *Payment plans:* installment, deferred payment. *Waivers:* employees or children of employees.

Applying *Options:* electronic application, early admission, deferred entrance. *Application fee:* $40. *Required:* high school transcript, minimum 2.0 GPA, interview. *Application deadlines:* rolling (freshmen), rolling (transfers).

Freshman Application Contact Susan Hammerstrom, Director of Admissions, Rasmussen College Aurora, 2363 Sequoia Drive, Aurora, IL 60506. *Phone:* 630-888-3500. *Toll-free phone:* 888-549-6755. *E-mail:* susan.hammerstrom@rasmussen.edu. *Web site:* http://www.rasmussen.edu/.

Rasmussen College Mokena/Tinley Park

Mokena, Illinois

- **Proprietary** 4-year, part of Rasmussen College System
- **Suburban** campus
- **Coed** 176 undergraduate students
- **Minimally difficult** entrance level

Faculty *Student/faculty ratio:* 22:1.

Academics *Degrees:* certificates, diplomas, associate, and bachelor's. *Special study options:* academic remediation for entering students, accelerated degree program, adult/continuing education programs, distance learning, double majors, internships, part-time degree program, summer session for credit.

Computers on Campus 73 computers/terminals are available on campus for general student use. Students can access the following: computer help desk, free student e-mail accounts, online (class) grades, online (class) schedules. Campuswide network is available. Wireless service is available via entire campus.

Student Life *Housing:* college housing not available.

Standardized Tests *Required:* Internal Exam (for admission).

Costs (2012–13) *Tuition:* $12,600 full-time. Full-time tuition and fees vary according to course level, course load, degree level, location, and program. Part-time tuition and fees vary according to course level, course load, degree level, location, and program. *Required fees:* $40 full-time. *Payment plans:* installment, deferred payment. *Waivers:* employees or children of employees.

Applying *Options:* electronic application, early admission, deferred entrance. *Application fee:* $40. *Required:* high school transcript, minimum 2.0 GPA, interview. *Application deadlines:* rolling (freshmen), rolling (transfers).

Freshman Application Contact Susan Hammerstrom, Director of Admissions, Rasmussen College Mokena/Tinley Park, 8650 West Spring Lake Road, Mokena, IL 60448. *Phone:* 815-534-3300. *Toll-free phone:* 888-549-6755. *Web site:* http://www.rasmussen.edu/.

Rasmussen College Rockford

Rockford, Illinois

- **Proprietary** primarily 2-year, part of Rasmussen College System
- **Suburban** campus
- **Coed** 881 undergraduate students
- **Minimally difficult** entrance level

Faculty *Student/faculty ratio:* 22:1.

Academics *Degrees:* certificates, diplomas, associate, and bachelor's. *Special study options:* academic remediation for entering students, accelerated degree program, adult/continuing education programs, distance learning, double majors, internships, part-time degree program, summer session for credit.

Computers on Campus 103 computers/terminals are available on campus for general student use. Students can access the following: computer help desk, free student e-mail accounts, online (class) grades, online (class) schedules. Campuswide network is available. Wireless service is available via entire campus.

Student Life *Housing:* college housing not available.

Standardized Tests *Required:* Internal Exam (for admission).

Costs (2012–13) *Tuition:* $12,600 full-time. Full-time tuition and fees vary according to course level, course load, degree level, location, and program. Part-time tuition and fees vary according to course level, course load, degree level, location, and program. *Required fees:* $40 full-time. *Payment plans:* installment, deferred payment. *Waivers:* employees or children of employees.

Applying *Options:* electronic application, early admission, deferred entrance. *Application fee:* $40. *Required:* high school transcript, minimum 2.0 GPA, interview. *Application deadlines:* rolling (freshmen), rolling (transfers).

Freshman Application Contact Susan Hammerstrom, Director of Admissions, Rasmussen College Rockford, 6000 East State Street, Fourth Floor, Rockford, IL 61108-2513. *Phone:* 815-316-4800. *Toll-free phone:* 888-549-6755. *E-mail:* susan.hammerstrom@rasmussen.edu. *Web site:* http://www.rasmussen.edu/.

Rasmussen College Romeoville/Joliet

Romeoville, Illinois

- **Proprietary** 4-year, part of Rasmussen College System
- **Suburban** campus
- **Coed** 437 undergraduate students
- **Minimally difficult** entrance level

Faculty *Student/faculty ratio:* 22:1.

Academics *Degrees:* certificates, diplomas, associate, and bachelor's. *Special study options:* academic remediation for entering students, accelerated degree program, adult/continuing education programs, distance learning, double majors, internships, part-time degree program, summer session for credit.

Computers on Campus 87 computers/terminals are available on campus for general student use. Students can access the following: computer help desk, free student e-mail accounts, online (class) grades, online (class) schedules. Campuswide network is available. Wireless service is available via entire campus.

Student Life *Housing:* college housing not available.

Standardized Tests *Required:* Internal Exam (for admission).

Costs (2012–13) *Tuition:* $12,600 full-time. Full-time tuition and fees vary according to course level, course load, degree level, location, and program. Part-time tuition and fees vary according to course level, course load, degree level, location, and program. *Required fees:* $40 full-time. *Payment plans:* installment, deferred payment. *Waivers:* employees or children of employees.

Applying *Options:* electronic application, early admission, deferred entrance. *Application fee:* $40. *Required:* high school transcript, minimum 2.0 GPA, interview. *Application deadlines:* rolling (freshmen), rolling (transfers).

Freshman Application Contact Susan Hammerstrom, Director of Admissions, Rasmussen College Romeoville/Joliet, 1400 W. Normantown Road, Romeoville, IL 60446. *Phone:* 815-306-2600. *Toll-free phone:* 888-549-6755. *E-mail:* susan.hammerstrom@rasmussen.edu. *Web site:* http://www.rasmussen.edu/.

Resurrection University

Oak Park, Illinois

- **Independent** upper-level, founded 1982
- **Suburban** 10-acre campus with easy access to Chicago
- **Coed, primarily women**
- **Moderately difficult** entrance level

Faculty *Student/faculty ratio:* 8:1.

Academics *Calendar:* semesters. *Degrees:* bachelor's and master's.

Student Life *Campus security:* 24-hour emergency response devices and patrols, late-night transport/escort service.

Costs (2011–12) *Tuition:* $711 per credit hour part-time. Full-time tuition and fees vary according to program. Part-time tuition and fees vary according to course load and program. *Required fees:* $135 per term part-time.

Financial Aid *Of all full-time matriculated undergraduates who enrolled in 2011,* 291 applied for aid, 291 were judged to have need, 152 had their need fully met. 9 Federal Work-Study jobs (averaging $4800). *Average percent of need met:* 85. *Average financial aid package:* $15,550. *Average need-based loan:* $5500. *Average need-based gift aid:* $3000.

Applying *Options:* electronic application, deferred entrance. *Application fee:* $30.

Application Contact Resurrection University, 3 Erie Court, Oak Park, IL 60302. *Phone:* 708-763-6530. *Web site:* http://www.resu.edu/.

Robert Morris University Illinois

Chicago, Illinois

- **Independent** comprehensive, founded 1913
- **Urban** campus with easy access to Chicago
- **Endowment** $53.3 million
- **Coed** 3,688 undergraduate students, 94% full-time, 55% women, 45% men
- **Minimally difficult** entrance level, 33% of applicants were admitted

Undergraduates 3,480 full-time, 208 part-time. Students come from 27 states and territories; 16 other countries; 8% are from out of state; 32% Black or Afri-

can American, non-Hispanic/Latino; 23% Hispanic/Latino; 2% Asian, non-Hispanic/Latino; 0.4% Native Hawaiian or other Pacific Islander, non-Hispanic/Latino; 0.2% American Indian or Alaska Native, non-Hispanic/Latino; 1% Two or more races, non-Hispanic/Latino; 2% Race/ethnicity unknown; 0.8% international; 16% transferred in; 9% live on campus. *Retention:* 49% of full-time freshmen returned.

Freshmen *Admission:* 3,132 applied, 1,037 admitted, 852 enrolled. *Average high school GPA:* 2.67. *Test scores:* ACT scores over 18: 57%; ACT scores over 24: 17%; ACT scores over 30: 2%.

Faculty *Total:* 275, 44% full-time, 18% with terminal degrees. *Student/faculty ratio:* 22:1.

Academics *Calendar:* 5 ten-week academic sessions per year. *Degrees:* associate, bachelor's, and master's. *Special study options:* accelerated degree program, adult/continuing education programs, advanced placement credit, double majors, honors programs, internships, part-time degree program, services for LD students, study abroad, summer session for credit. *ROTC:* Army (c).

Computers on Campus 1,671 computers/terminals are available on campus for general student use. Students can access the following: computer help desk, free student e-mail accounts, online (class) grades, online (class) schedules, online credentials, online payments, online student accounts, online degree audit. Campuswide network is available. Wireless service is available via entire campus.

Student Life *Housing options:* coed. *Activities and organizations:* student-run newspaper, choral group, marching band, Cooks for a Cause, Students in Free Enterprise (SIFE), Sigma Beta Delta, Student Chapter of Society for Human Resource Management, Veteran's Club. *Campus security:* 24-hour emergency response devices, controlled dormitory access, roaming security visits our metropolitan campuses on an intermittent schedule and are sent to other campuses as needed. *Student services:* personal/psychological counseling.

Athletics Member NAIA, USCAA. *Intercollegiate sports:* baseball M(s), basketball M(s)/W(s), bowling M(s)/W(s), cheerleading M(s)(c)/W(s)(c), crew W(s), cross-country running M(s)/W(s), equestrian sports W(s), field hockey W(s)(c), football M(s), golf M(s)/W(s), ice hockey M/W, lacrosse M(s)/W(s), sailing M(s)(c)/W(s)(c), soccer M(s)/W(s), softball W(s), swimming and diving W(s), tennis W(s), track and field W(s), volleyball M(s)/W(s). *Intramural sports:* bowling M/W, cross-country running M/W, golf M/W, softball M/W.

Standardized Tests *Required for some:* SAT or ACT (for admission).

Costs (2012–13) *Comprehensive fee:* $33,540 includes full-time tuition ($22,200) and room and board ($11,340). Full-time tuition and fees vary according to program. Part-time tuition: $617 per credit hour. Part-time tuition and fees vary according to course load and program. *College room only:* $10,500. Room and board charges vary according to housing facility. *Payment plan:* installment. *Waivers:* employees or children of employees.

Financial Aid Of all full-time matriculated undergraduates who enrolled in 2009, 5,485 applied for aid, 5,314 were judged to have need, 158 had their need fully met. 326 Federal Work-Study jobs (averaging $2056). In 2009, 119 non-need-based awards were made. *Average percent of need met:* 48%. *Average financial aid package:* $12,862. *Average need-based loan:* $4767. *Average need-based gift aid:* $10,127. *Average non-need-based aid:* $5320. *Average indebtedness upon graduation:* $28,103.

Applying *Options:* electronic application, deferred entrance. *Application fee:* $20. *Required for some:* high school transcript. *Recommended:* interview. *Application deadlines:* rolling (freshmen), rolling (out-of-state freshmen), rolling (transfers). *Notification:* continuous (freshmen), continuous (out-of-state freshmen), continuous (transfers).

Freshman Application Contact Ms. Connie Esparza, Vice President for Marketing, Robert Morris University Illinois, 401 South State Street, Chicago, IL 60605. *Phone:* 312-935-4141. *Toll-free phone:* 800-RMC-5960. *Fax:* 312-935-4440. *E-mail:* enroll@robertmorris.edu. *Web site:* http://www.robertmorris.edu/.

See page 1526 for the College Close-Up.

Rockford College
Rockford, Illinois

- **Independent** comprehensive, founded 1847
- **Suburban** 130-acre campus with easy access to Chicago
- **Coed** 997 undergraduate students, 85% full-time, 62% women, 38% men
- **Moderately difficult** entrance level, 44% of applicants were admitted

Undergraduates 849 full-time, 148 part-time. Students come from 25 states and territories; 11 other countries; 10% are from out of state; 8% Black or African American, non-Hispanic/Latino; 9% Hispanic/Latino; 2% Asian, non-Hispanic/Latino; 0.4% Native Hawaiian or other Pacific Islander, non-Hispanic/Latino; 1% American Indian or Alaska Native, non-Hispanic/Latino; 8% Race/ethnicity unknown; 16% transferred in; 31% live on campus. *Retention:* 69% of full-time freshmen returned.

Freshmen *Admission:* 1,245 applied, 550 admitted, 164 enrolled. *Average high school GPA:* 3.19. *Test scores:* ACT scores over 18: 90%; ACT scores over 24: 29%; ACT scores over 30: 3%.
Faculty *Total:* 157, 45% full-time, 37% with terminal degrees. *Student/faculty ratio:* 8:1.
Academics *Calendar:* semesters. *Degrees:* bachelor's and master's. *Special study options:* academic remediation for entering students, accelerated degree program, adult/continuing education programs, advanced placement credit, double majors, English as a second language, honors programs, independent study, internships, off-campus study, part-time degree program, services for LD students, study abroad, summer session for credit. *ROTC:* Army (c).
Computers on Campus 75 computers/terminals are available on campus for general student use. Students can access the following: campus intranet, computer help desk, free student e-mail accounts, online (class) grades, online (class) registration, online (class) schedules, online bill payment. Campuswide network is available. 100% of college-owned or -operated housing units are wired for high-speed Internet access. Wireless service is available via entire campus.
Student Life *Housing options:* coed, disabled students. Campus housing is university owned. *Activities and organizations:* drama/theater group, student-run newspaper, radio station, choral group, Student Government Association, Multicultural Club, RAGE (Regent Athletics Getting Excited), Psychology Society, Nursing Student Organization. *Campus security:* 24-hour emergency response devices and patrols, late-night transport/escort service, controlled dormitory access. *Student services:* health clinic, personal/psychological counseling.
Athletics Member NCAA. All Division III. *Intercollegiate sports:* baseball M, basketball M/W, cross-country running M/W, football M, golf M/W, soccer M/W, softball W, tennis M/W, track and field M/W, volleyball M(c)/W. *Intramural sports:* basketball M/W, bowling M/W, cheerleading M(c)/W(c), football M/W, table tennis M/W, tennis M/W, volleyball M/W.
Standardized Tests *Required:* SAT or ACT (for admission).
Costs (2012–13) *Comprehensive fee:* $33,670 includes full-time tuition ($26,250), mandatory fees ($100), and room and board ($7320). Full-time tuition and fees vary according to course load. Part-time tuition: $715 per credit. Part-time tuition and fees vary according to course load. *College room only:* $4070. Room and board charges vary according to board plan and housing facility.
Financial Aid Of all full-time matriculated undergraduates who enrolled in 2010, 846 applied for aid, 799 were judged to have need, 88 had their need fully met. In 2010, 68 non-need-based awards were made. *Average percent of need met:* 68%. *Average financial aid package:* $17,513. *Average need-based loan:* $4755. *Average need-based gift aid:* $12,447. *Average non-need-based aid:* $8810. *Average indebtedness upon graduation:* $28,343.
Applying *Options:* electronic application, early admission, deferred entrance. *Required:* high school transcript. *Required for some:* essay or personal statement, minimum 2.7 GPA, 2 letters of recommendation. *Recommended:* minimum 2.7 GPA, interview, campus visit. *Application deadlines:* rolling (freshmen), rolling (out-of-state freshmen), rolling (transfers). *Notification:* continuous until 9/15 (freshmen), continuous (out-of-state freshmen), continuous (transfers).
Freshman Application Contact Ms. Rebecca Miziniak, Assistant Director of Admission, Rockford College, 5050 East State Street, Rockford, IL 61108-2393. *Phone:* 815-226-4050. *Toll-free phone:* 800-892-2984. *Fax:* 815-226-2822. *E-mail:* rcadmissions@rockford.edu. *Web site:* http://www.rockford.edu/.

Roosevelt University
Chicago, Illinois

- **Independent** comprehensive, founded 1945
- **Urban** campus with easy access to Chicago
- **Endowment** $80.2 million
- **Coed** 3,908 undergraduate students, 71% full-time, 65% women, 35% men
- **Moderately difficult** entrance level, 75% of applicants were admitted

Undergraduates 2,772 full-time, 1,136 part-time. Students come from 46 states and territories; 34 other countries; 15% are from out of state; 21% Black or African American, non-Hispanic/Latino; 15% Hispanic/Latino; 6% Asian, non-Hispanic/Latino; 0.1% Native Hawaiian or other Pacific Islander, non-Hispanic/Latino; 0.2% American Indian or Alaska Native, non-Hispanic/Latino; 4% Two or more races, non-Hispanic/Latino; 2% Race/ethnicity unknown; 2% international; 18% transferred in; 23% live on campus. *Retention:* 65% of full-time freshmen returned.
Freshmen *Admission:* 3,773 applied, 2,833 admitted, 448 enrolled. *Average high school GPA:* 3.1. *Test scores:* SAT critical reading scores over 500: 80%; SAT math scores over 500: 58%; SAT writing scores over 500: 74%; ACT scores over 18: 99%; SAT critical reading scores over 600: 27%; SAT math

scores over 600: 26%; SAT writing scores over 600: 25%; ACT scores over 24: 37%; SAT critical reading scores over 700: 3%; SAT math scores over 700: 2%; SAT writing scores over 700: 2%; ACT scores over 30: 3%.
Faculty *Total:* 722, 34% full-time. *Student/faculty ratio:* 12:1.
Academics *Calendar:* semesters. *Degrees:* bachelor's, master's, doctoral, postbachelor's, and first professional certificates. *Special study options:* academic remediation for entering students, accelerated degree program, adult/continuing education programs, advanced placement credit, distance learning, double majors, English as a second language, honors programs, independent study, internships, off-campus study, part-time degree program, services for LD students, student-designed majors, study abroad, summer session for credit.
Computers on Campus 646 computers/terminals are available on campus for general student use. Students can access the following: campus intranet, computer help desk, free student e-mail accounts, online (class) grades, online (class) registration, online (class) schedules. Campuswide network is available. 100% of college-owned or -operated housing units are wired for high-speed Internet access. Wireless service is available via classrooms, computer centers, computer labs, dorm rooms, libraries, student centers.
Student Life *Housing:* on-campus residence required through sophomore year. *Options:* coed. Campus housing is university owned, leased by the school and is provided by a third party. Freshman campus housing is guaranteed. *Activities and organizations:* student-run newspaper, radio station, International Student Union, RU Proud, Association of Latin Americans (ALAS), student government, Residence Hall Council, national fraternities, national sororities. *Campus security:* 24-hour emergency response devices and patrols, late-night transport/escort service, controlled dormitory access. *Student services:* personal/psychological counseling.
Athletics Member NAIA. *Intercollegiate sports:* baseball M, basketball M/W, cross-country running M/W, golf M, soccer M/W, softball W, tennis M/W, volleyball W.
Standardized Tests *Required:* SAT or ACT (for admission).
Costs (2012–13) *Comprehensive fee:* $38,050 includes full-time tuition ($25,950) and room and board ($12,100). Full-time tuition and fees vary according to course load, program, and reciprocity agreements. Part-time tuition: $699 per credit. Part-time tuition and fees vary according to course load, program, and reciprocity agreements. *Room and board:* Room and board charges vary according to board plan and housing facility. *Payment plan:* installment. *Waivers:* employees or children of employees.
Financial Aid Of all full-time matriculated undergraduates who enrolled in 2010, 2,675 applied for aid, 2,281 were judged to have need, 177 had their need fully met. In 2010, 529 non-need-based awards were made. *Average percent of need met:* 75%. *Average financial aid package:* $20,970. *Average need-based loan:* $8827. *Average need-based gift aid:* $8927. *Average non-need-based aid:* $6718.
Applying *Options:* electronic application, deferred entrance. *Application fee:* $25. *Required:* high school transcript, minimum 2.5 GPA, audition for music and theater programs. *Required for some:* essay or personal statement, interview. *Recommended:* essay or personal statement. *Application deadlines:* 8/15 (freshmen), rolling (transfers). *Notification:* continuous (freshmen), continuous (transfers).
Freshman Application Contact Ms. Asia Mitchell, Director of Admission, Roosevelt University, 430 South Michigan Avenue, Chicago, IL 60605-1394. *Phone:* 312-341-2107. *Toll-free phone:* 877-APPLYRU. *Fax:* 312-341-3253. *E-mail:* amitchell@roosevelt.edu. *Web site:* http://www.roosevelt.edu/.

Rush University
Chicago, Illinois

Application Contact Rush University, 600 South Paulina, Chicago, IL 60612-3832. *Phone:* 312-942-7100. *Web site:* http://www.rushu.rush.edu/.

Saint Anthony College of Nursing
Rockford, Illinois

Application Contact Ms. Nancy Sanders, Assistant Dean for Admissions and Student Affairs, Saint Anthony College of Nursing, 5658 East State Street, Rockford, IL 61108-2468. *Phone:* 815-395-5100. *Fax:* 815-395-2275. *E-mail:* info@sacn.edu. *Web site:* http://www.sacn.edu/.

St. Augustine College
Chicago, Illinois

Freshman Application Contact Ms. Gloria Quiroz, Director of Admissions, St. Augustine College, 1333-1345 West Argyle, Chicago, IL 60640-3501. *Phone:* 773-878-3256. *Fax:* 773-878-0937. *E-mail:* info@staugustine.edu. *Web site:* http://www.staugustine.edu/.

Saint Francis Medical Center College of Nursing
Peoria, Illinois

- **Independent Roman Catholic** upper-level, founded 1986
- **Urban** campus
- **Coed, primarily women** 354 undergraduate students, 81% full-time, 89% women, 11% men
- 56% of applicants were admitted

Undergraduates 286 full-time, 68 part-time. Students come from 2 states and territories; 4 other countries; 1% are from out of state; 7% Black or African American, non-Hispanic/Latino; 2% Hispanic/Latino; 2% Asian, non-Hispanic/Latino; 0.7% Native Hawaiian or other Pacific Islander, non-Hispanic/Latino; 0.5% American Indian or Alaska Native, non-Hispanic/Latino; 24% transferred in; 3% live on campus.
Freshmen *Admission:* 320 applied, 180 admitted.
Faculty *Total:* 49, 69% full-time, 16% with terminal degrees. *Student/faculty ratio:* 7:1.
Academics *Calendar:* semesters. *Degrees:* bachelor's, master's, doctoral, and post-master's certificates. *Special study options:* advanced placement credit, distance learning, independent study, summer session for credit.
Computers on Campus 49 computers/terminals and 53 ports are available on campus for general student use. Students can access the following: campus intranet, computer help desk, free student e-mail accounts, online (class) grades, online (class) registration, online (class) schedules. Campuswide network is available. 100% of college-owned or -operated housing units are wired for high-speed Internet access. Wireless service is available via entire campus.
Student Life *Housing options:* coed. Campus housing is university owned. *Activities and organizations:* Student Senate, SNAI, Minority Student Association. *Campus security:* 24-hour emergency response devices, controlled dormitory access. *Student services:* health clinic, personal/psychological counseling.
Costs (2012–13) *Tuition:* $15,810 full-time, $510 per degree program part-time. Full-time tuition and fees vary according to course load. Part-time tuition and fees vary according to course load. *Required fees:* $556 full-time. *Room only:* $3000.
Financial Aid Of all full-time matriculated undergraduates who enrolled in 2011, 259 applied for aid, 223 were judged to have need, 13 had their need fully met. In 2011, 6 non-need-based awards were made. *Average percent of need met:* 50%. *Average financial aid package:* $10,365. *Average need-based loan:* $4398. *Average need-based gift aid:* $7405. *Average non-need-based aid:* $1717.
Applying *Options:* deferred entrance. *Application fee:* $50.
Application Contact Saint Francis Medical Center College of Nursing, 511 Northeast Greenleaf Street, Peoria, IL 61603-3783. *Phone:* 309-624-8980. *Web site:* http://www.sfmccon.edu/.

St. John's College
Springfield, Illinois

Application Contact St. John's College, 729 East Carpenter Street, Springfield, IL 62702. *Phone:* 217-525-5628. *Web site:* http://www.stjohnscollegespringfield.edu/.

Saint Xavier University
Chicago, Illinois

- **Independent Roman Catholic** comprehensive, founded 1847
- **Urban** 70-acre campus
- **Endowment** $7.1 million
- **Coed** 2,993 undergraduate students, 85% full-time, 68% women, 32% men
- **Moderately difficult** entrance level, 83% of applicants were admitted

Undergraduates 2,537 full-time, 456 part-time. 5% are from out of state; 17% Black or African American, non-Hispanic/Latino; 17% Hispanic/Latino; 2% Asian, non-Hispanic/Latino; 0.5% American Indian or Alaska Native, non-Hispanic/Latino; 2% Two or more races, non-Hispanic/Latino; 7% Race/ethnicity unknown; 0.3% international; 13% transferred in; 29% live on campus. *Retention:* 72% of full-time freshmen returned.
Freshmen *Admission:* 5,520 applied, 4,579 admitted, 583 enrolled. *Average high school GPA:* 3.4. *Test scores:* SAT critical reading scores over 500: 69%; SAT math scores over 500: 58%; SAT writing scores over 500: 74%; ACT scores over 18: 95%; SAT critical reading scores over 600: 32%; SAT math scores over 600: 21%; SAT writing scores over 600: 21%; ACT scores over 24: 37%; ACT scores over 30: 4%.
Faculty *Total:* 431, 40% full-time, 49% with terminal degrees. *Student/faculty ratio:* 14:1.
Academics *Calendar:* semesters. *Degrees:* certificates, bachelor's, master's, post-master's, and postbachelor's certificates. *Special study options:* academic remediation for entering students, accelerated degree program, adult/continuing education programs, advanced placement credit, cooperative education, double majors, English as a second language, honors programs, independent study, internships, part-time degree program, services for LD students, student-designed majors, study abroad, summer session for credit. *ROTC:* Air Force (c).
Computers on Campus 500 computers/terminals are available on campus for general student use. Students can access the following: campus intranet, computer help desk, free student e-mail accounts, online (class) grades, online (class) registration, online (class) schedules. Campuswide network is available. 100% of college-owned or -operated housing units are wired for high-speed Internet access. Wireless service is available via classrooms, computer centers, computer labs, dorm rooms, learning centers, libraries, student centers.
Student Life *Housing options:* coed. Campus housing is university owned. *Activities and organizations:* drama/theater group, student-run newspaper, radio station, choral group, marching band, Student Activities Board, Black Student Union, UNIDOS (Hispanic Organization), Student Nurses Association, Business Students Association. *Campus security:* 24-hour emergency response devices and patrols, late-night transport/escort service. *Student services:* health clinic, personal/psychological counseling, women's center.
Athletics Member NAIA. *Intercollegiate sports:* baseball M(s), basketball M(s)/W(s), cross-country running W(s), football M(s), golf M(s), soccer M(s)/W(s), softball W(s), volleyball W(s). *Intramural sports:* basketball M, bowling M/W, volleyball M/W, weight lifting M.
Standardized Tests *Required:* SAT or ACT (for admission).
Costs (2011–12) *Comprehensive fee:* $36,100 includes full-time tuition ($26,280), mandatory fees ($780), and room and board ($9040). Part-time tuition: $650 per credit hour. *Required fees:* $540 per year part-time. *College room only:* $5350. Room and board charges vary according to board plan and housing facility. *Payment plan:* installment. *Waivers:* senior citizens and employees or children of employees.
Financial Aid Of all full-time matriculated undergraduates who enrolled in 2011, 2,362 applied for aid, 2,233 were judged to have need, 395 had their need fully met. 1,757 Federal Work-Study jobs (averaging $2377). In 2011, 206 non-need-based awards were made. *Average percent of need met:* 79%. *Average financial aid package:* $21,941. *Average need-based loan:* $4584. *Average need-based gift aid:* $15,477. *Average non-need-based aid:* $8470. *Average indebtedness upon graduation:* $32,095.
Applying *Options:* electronic application, deferred entrance. *Application fee:* $25. *Required:* high school transcript. *Recommended:* essay or personal statement, minimum 2.5 GPA, interview. *Application deadlines:* rolling (freshmen), rolling (transfers). *Notification:* continuous (freshmen), continuous (transfers).
Freshman Application Contact Dr. Kathleen Carlson, Vice President, Saint Xavier University, 3700 West 103rd Street, Chicago, IL 60655-3105. *Phone:* 773-298-3305. *Toll-free phone:* 800-462-9288. *E-mail:* carlson@sxu.edu. *Web site:* http://www.sxu.edu/.

School of the Art Institute of Chicago
Chicago, Illinois

Freshman Application Contact Mr. Scott Ramon, Director, Undergraduate Admissions, School of the Art Institute of Chicago, 36 South Wabash, Chicago, IL 60603. *Phone:* 312-629-6100. *Toll-free phone:* 800-232-SAIC. *Fax:* 312-629-6101. *E-mail:* ugadmiss@saic.edu. *Web site:* http://www.saic.edu/.

See page 276 for display ad and page 1572 for the College Close-Up.

Shimer College
Chicago, Illinois

- **Independent** 4-year, founded 1853
- **Urban** 3-acre campus with easy access to Chicago, Milwaukee
- **Coed** 127 undergraduate students, 83% full-time, 48% women, 52% men
- **Moderately difficult** entrance level, 48% of applicants were admitted

Undergraduates 105 full-time, 22 part-time. 56% are from out of state; 2% Black or African American, non-Hispanic/Latino; 4% Hispanic/Latino; 4% Asian, non-Hispanic/Latino; 10% Two or more races, non-Hispanic/Latino; 4% Race/ethnicity unknown; 12% transferred in; 17% live on campus. *Retention:* 85% of full-time freshmen returned.
Freshmen *Admission:* 119 applied, 57 admitted, 16 enrolled. *Average high school GPA:* 3.24. *Test scores:* SAT critical reading scores over 500: 100%; SAT math scores over 500: 75%; SAT writing scores over 500: 100%; ACT scores over 18: 100%; SAT critical reading scores over 600: 100%; SAT writing scores over 600: 75%; ACT scores over 24: 89%; SAT critical reading scores over 700: 50%; ACT scores over 30: 45%.

Faculty *Total:* 16, 63% full-time, 88% with terminal degrees. *Student/faculty ratio:* 9:1.

Academics *Calendar:* semesters. *Degree:* bachelor's. *Special study options:* adult/continuing education programs, cooperative education, double majors, independent study, internships, off-campus study, part-time degree program, student-designed majors, study abroad, summer session for credit. *ROTC:* Army (c), Navy (c), Air Force (c).

Computers on Campus Students can access the following: campus intranet, computer help desk, free student e-mail accounts, online (class) schedules. Campuswide network is available. 100% of college-owned or -operated housing units are wired for high-speed Internet access. Wireless service is available via entire campus.

Student Life *Housing options:* coed, disabled students. Campus housing is university owned and leased by the school. Freshman campus housing is guaranteed. *Activities and organizations:* drama/theater group, student-run newspaper, radio station, choral group. *Campus security:* 24-hour emergency response devices, late-night transport/escort service. *Student services:* personal/psychological counseling.

Athletics *Intramural sports:* baseball M, basketball M/W, cross-country running M/W, soccer M/W, softball W, track and field M/W, volleyball M/W.

Costs (2011–12) *Tuition:* $26,510 full-time, $970 per credit hour part-time. Full-time tuition and fees vary according to class time, course load, and program. Part-time tuition and fees vary according to class time, course load, and program. *Required fees:* $2350 full-time. *Room only:* Room and board charges vary according to housing facility. *Payment plan:* installment. *Waivers:* adult students, senior citizens, and employees or children of employees.

Financial Aid Of all full-time matriculated undergraduates who enrolled in 2010, 95 applied for aid, 84 were judged to have need, 4 had their need fully met. In 2010, 14 non-need-based awards were made. *Average percent of need met:* 59%. *Average financial aid package:* $20,388. *Average need-based loan:* $5630. *Average need-based gift aid:* $13,889. *Average non-need-based aid:* $6525. *Average indebtedness upon graduation:* $33,500.

Applying *Options:* electronic application. *Application fee:* $25. *Required:* essay or personal statement, high school transcript, 1 letter of recommendation, interview. *Application deadlines:* rolling (freshmen), rolling (transfers). *Notification:* continuous (freshmen), continuous (transfers).

Freshman Application Contact Ms. Amy Pritts, Director of Admission, Shimer College, 3424 South State Street, Chicago, IL 60616. *Phone:* 312-235-3504. *Toll-free phone:* 800-215-7173. *Fax:* 888-808-3133. *E-mail:* admission@shimer.edu. *Web site:* http://www.shimer.edu/.

Southern Illinois University Carbondale

Carbondale, Illinois

- **State-supported** university, founded 1869, part of Southern Illinois University
- **Rural** 1136-acre campus with easy access to St. Louis
- **Endowment** $95.9 million
- **Coed** 15,000 undergraduate students, 87% full-time, 44% women, 56% men
- **Moderately difficult** entrance level, 44% of applicants were admitted

Undergraduates 13,066 full-time, 1,934 part-time. Students come from 46 states and territories; 50 other countries; 12% are from out of state; 22% Black or African American, non-Hispanic/Latino; 5% Hispanic/Latino; 2% Asian, non-Hispanic/Latino; 0.2% Native Hawaiian or other Pacific Islander, non-Hispanic/Latino; 0.5% American Indian or Alaska Native, non-Hispanic/Latino; 2% Two or more races, non-Hispanic/Latino; 0.5% Race/ethnicity unknown; 2% international; 14% transferred in; 29% live on campus. *Retention:* 67% of full-time freshmen returned.

Freshmen *Admission:* 14,511 applied, 6,402 admitted, 2,417 enrolled. *Test scores:* SAT math scores over 500: 62%; ACT scores over 18: 83%; SAT math scores over 600: 28%; ACT scores over 24: 29%; SAT math scores over 700: 4%; ACT scores over 30: 5%.

Faculty *Total:* 1,054, 85% full-time, 78% with terminal degrees. *Student/faculty ratio:* 15:1.

Academics *Calendar:* semesters plus 8-week summer session. *Degrees:* associate, bachelor's, master's, doctoral, postbachelor's, and first professional certificates. *Special study options:* academic remediation for entering students, adult/continuing education programs, advanced placement credit, cooperative education, distance learning, double majors, English as a second language, honors programs, independent study, internships, off-campus study, part-time degree program, services for LD students, student-designed majors, study abroad, summer session for credit. *ROTC:* Army (b), Air Force (b).

Computers on Campus 1,820 computers/terminals are available on campus for general student use. Students can access the following: campus intranet, computer help desk, free student e-mail accounts, online (class) grades, online (class) registration, online (class) schedules. Campuswide network is available. 80% of college-owned or -operated housing units are wired for high-speed

Internet access. Wireless service is available via classrooms, computer centers, computer labs, learning centers, libraries, student centers.

Student Life *Housing:* on-campus residence required for freshman year. *Options:* coed, women-only, disabled students. Campus housing is university owned. Freshman campus housing is guaranteed. *Activities and organizations:* drama/theater group, student-run newspaper, radio and television station, choral group, marching band, Inter-Greek Council, Black Affairs Council, International Student Council, Undergraduate Student government, Graduate and Professional Student Council, national fraternities, national sororities. *Campus security:* 24-hour emergency response devices and patrols, student patrols, late-night transport/escort service, controlled dormitory access, well-lit pathways, night safety vans, student transit system. *Student services:* health clinic, personal/psychological counseling, women's center, legal services.

Athletics Member NCAA. All Division I except football (Division I-AA). *Intercollegiate sports:* baseball M(s), basketball M(s)/W(s), cheerleading M/W, cross-country running M(s)/W(s), golf M(s)/W(s), softball W(s), swimming and diving M(s)/W(s), tennis M(s)/W(s), track and field M(s)/W(s), volleyball W(s). *Intramural sports:* archery M(c)/W(c), badminton M(c)/W(c), baseball M(c), basketball M/W, bowling M(c)/W(c), equestrian sports M(c)/W(c), fencing M(c)/W(c), football M/W, gymnastics M(c)/W(c), lacrosse M(c)/W(c), racquetball M/W, rock climbing M(c)/W(c), rugby M(c)/W(c), sailing M(c)/W(c), soccer M(c)/W(c), softball M/W(c), swimming and diving M/W, table tennis M(c)/W(c), tennis M(c)/W(c), track and field M/W, ultimate Frisbee M(c)/W(c), volleyball M(c)/W(c), water polo M(c)/W(c), weight lifting M(c)/W(c).

Standardized Tests *Required:* SAT or ACT (for admission).

Costs (2011–12) *Tuition:* state resident $7794 full-time, $260 per credit hour part-time; nonresident $19,485 full-time, $650 per credit hour part-time. Full-time tuition and fees vary according to course load and student level. Part-time tuition and fees vary according to course load and student level. No tuition increase for student's term of enrollment. *Required fees:* $3244 full-time, $300 per credit hour part-time. *Room and board:* $8648. Room and board charges vary according to board plan and housing facility. *Payment plan:* installment. *Waivers:* children of alumni, senior citizens, and employees or children of employees.

Financial Aid Of all full-time matriculated undergraduates who enrolled in 2010, 10,432 applied for aid, 9,243 were judged to have need, 450 had their need fully met. In 2010, 179 non-need-based awards were made. *Average percent of need met:* 30%. *Average financial aid package:* $10,615. *Average need-based loan:* $4261. *Average need-based gift aid:* $1806. *Average non-need-based aid:* $3555. *Average indebtedness upon graduation:* $40,143.

Applying *Options:* electronic application, deferred entrance. *Application fee:* $30. *Required:* high school transcript, SAT or ACT. *Application deadlines:* rolling (freshmen), rolling (transfers). *Notification:* continuous (freshmen), continuous (transfers).

Freshman Application Contact Katharine Suski, Associate Director, Southern Illinois University Carbondale, Undergraduate Admissions, 425 Clocktower Drive, Carbondale, IL 62901. *Phone:* 618-453-2987. *Fax:* 618-453-4609. *E-mail:* ksuski@siu.edu. *Web site:* http://www.siuc.edu/.

Southern Illinois University Edwardsville
Edwardsville, Illinois

- **State-supported** comprehensive, founded 1957, part of Southern Illinois University
- **Suburban** 2660-acre campus with easy access to St. Louis
- **Endowment** $16.5 million
- **Coed** 11,428 undergraduate students, 85% full-time, 53% women, 47% men
- **Moderately difficult** entrance level, 80% of applicants were admitted

Undergraduates 9,720 full-time, 1,708 part-time. Students come from 43 states and territories; 40 other countries; 8% are from out of state; 14% Black or African American, non-Hispanic/Latino; 3% Hispanic/Latino; 2% Asian, non-Hispanic/Latino; 0.1% Native Hawaiian or other Pacific Islander, non-Hispanic/Latino; 0.3% American Indian or Alaska Native, non-Hispanic/Latino; 2% Two or more races, non-Hispanic/Latino; 2% Race/ethnicity unknown; 0.8% international; 11% transferred in; 30% live on campus. *Retention:* 70% of full-time freshmen returned.

Freshmen *Admission:* 7,542 applied, 6,070 admitted, 2,060 enrolled.

Faculty Total: 874, 68% full-time. *Student/faculty ratio:* 17:1.

Academics *Calendar:* semesters. *Degrees:* bachelor's, master's, doctoral, post-master's, postbachelor's, and first professional certificates. *Special study options:* academic remediation for entering students, accelerated degree program, advanced placement credit, cooperative education, distance learning, double majors, English as a second language, honors programs, independent study, internships, off-campus study, part-time degree program, services for LD students, student-designed majors, study abroad, summer session for

credit. *ROTC:* Army (b), Air Force (c). *Unusual degree programs:* 3-2 engineering.

Computers on Campus 600 computers/terminals are available on campus for general student use. Students can access the following: campus intranet, computer help desk, free student e-mail accounts, online (class) grades, online (class) registration, online (class) schedules, online job finder. Campuswide network is available. 100% of college-owned or -operated housing units are wired for high-speed Internet access. Wireless service is available via entire campus.

Student Life *Housing options:* coed, disabled students. Campus housing is university owned. Freshman applicants given priority for college housing. *Activities and organizations:* drama/theater group, student-run newspaper, radio and television station, choral group, national fraternities, national sororities. *Campus security:* 24-hour emergency response devices and patrols, student patrols, late-night transport/escort service, controlled dormitory access, 24-hour ID check at residence hall entrances, emergency call boxes located throughout campus. *Student services:* health clinic, personal/psychological counseling, legal services.

Athletics Member NCAA. All Division I. *Intercollegiate sports:* baseball M(s), basketball M(s)/W(s), cross-country running M(s)/W(s), golf M(s)/W(s), soccer M(s)/W(s), softball W(s), tennis M(s)/W(s), track and field M(s)/W(s), volleyball W(s), wrestling M(s). *Intramural sports:* badminton M/W, basketball M/W, bowling M/W, cheerleading M/W, fencing M/W, ice hockey M, racquetball M/W, rock climbing M/W, rugby M, soccer M/W, softball M/W, table tennis M/W, tennis M/W, ultimate Frisbee M/W, volleyball M/W, water polo M/W, weight lifting M/W.

Standardized Tests *Required:* SAT or ACT (for admission).

Costs (2011–12) *Tuition:* state resident $6630 full-time, $221 per credit hour part-time; nonresident $16,575 full-time. Full-time tuition and fees vary according to course load. Part-time tuition and fees vary according to course load. No tuition increase for student's term of enrollment. *Required fees:* $2235 full-time, $265 per credit hour part-time. *Room and board:* $8051. Room and board charges vary according to board plan and housing facility. *Payment plan:* installment. *Waivers:* senior citizens and employees or children of employees.

Financial Aid Of all full-time matriculated undergraduates who enrolled in 2011, 7,771 applied for aid, 6,344 were judged to have need, 2,642 had their need fully met. In 2011, 190 non-need-based awards were made. *Average percent of need met:* 66%. *Average financial aid package:* $11,387. *Average need-based loan:* $4529. *Average need-based gift aid:* $8923. *Average non-need-based aid:* $8100. *Average indebtedness upon graduation:* $25,998.

Applying *Options:* electronic application, deferred entrance. *Application fee:* $30. *Required:* high school transcript. *Recommended:* minimum 2.5 GPA. *Application deadline:* 5/1 (freshmen). *Notification:* continuous (freshmen), continuous (transfers).

Freshman Application Contact Mr. Todd Burrell, Director of Admissions, Southern Illinois University Edwardsville, Campus Box 1600, Rendleman Hall, Edwardsville, IL 62026-1600. *Phone:* 618-650-3705. *Toll-free phone:* 800-447-SIUE. *Fax:* 618-650-5013. *E-mail:* admissions@siue.edu. *Web site:* http://www.siue.edu/.

Telshe Yeshiva–Chicago
Chicago, Illinois

Freshman Application Contact Rosh Hayeshiva, Telshe Yeshiva–Chicago, 3535 West Foster Avenue, Chicago, IL 60625-5598. *Phone:* 773-463-7738.

Trinity Christian College
Palos Heights, Illinois

- **Independent Christian Reformed** 4-year, founded 1959
- **Suburban** 53-acre campus with easy access to Chicago
- **Endowment** $8.0 million
- **Coed** 1,470 undergraduate students, 79% full-time, 65% women, 35% men
- **Moderately difficult** entrance level, 29% of applicants were admitted

Undergraduates 1,155 full-time, 315 part-time. Students come from 37 states and territories; 7 other countries; 33% are from out of state; 9% Black or African American, non-Hispanic/Latino; 8% Hispanic/Latino; 1% Asian, non-Hispanic/Latino; 0.2% Native Hawaiian or other Pacific Islander, non-Hispanic/Latino; 0.3% American Indian or Alaska Native, non-Hispanic/Latino; 0.8% Two or more races, non-Hispanic/Latino; 3% Race/ethnicity unknown; 2% international; 6% transferred in; 56% live on campus. *Retention:* 80% of full-time freshmen returned.

Freshmen *Admission:* 799 applied, 235 admitted, 235 enrolled. *Average high school GPA:* 3.38. *Test scores:* SAT critical reading scores over 500: 67%; SAT math scores over 500: 66%; ACT scores over 18: 90%; SAT critical reading scores over 600: 34%; SAT math scores over 600: 16%; ACT scores over

24: 47%; SAT critical reading scores over 700: 17%; ACT scores over 30: 10%.

Faculty *Total:* 161, 55% full-time, 39% with terminal degrees. *Student/faculty ratio:* 11:1.

Academics *Calendar:* semesters plus 2 week interim term. *Degrees:* bachelor's and postbachelor's certificates. *Special study options:* academic remediation for entering students, adult/continuing education programs, advanced placement credit, cooperative education, double majors, honors programs, independent study, internships, off-campus study, part-time degree program, services for LD students, study abroad.

Computers on Campus 170 computers/terminals are available on campus for general student use. Students can access the following: campus intranet, computer help desk, free student e-mail accounts, online (class) grades, online (class) registration, online (class) schedules. Campuswide network is available. 100% of college-owned or -operated housing units are wired for high-speed Internet access. Wireless service is available via entire campus.

Student Life *Housing:* on-campus residence required through junior year. *Options:* coed. Campus housing is university owned. Freshman campus housing is guaranteed. *Activities and organizations:* drama/theater group, student-run newspaper, choral group, Student Association, student ministries, campus newspaper, Pro-Life Task Force, PACE (prison tutoring program). *Campus security:* 24-hour emergency response devices and patrols, student patrols, late-night transport/escort service, security cameras, Code Blue Emergency Phones. *Student services:* health clinic, personal/psychological counseling.

Athletics Member NAIA, NCCAA. *Intercollegiate sports:* baseball M(s), basketball M(s)/W(s), cross-country running M(s)/W(s), golf M(s), soccer M(s)/W(s), softball W(s), track and field M(s)/W(s), volleyball W(s). *Intramural sports:* badminton M/W, basketball M/W, football M/W, soccer M/W, volleyball M/W.

Standardized Tests *Required:* SAT or ACT (for admission). *Recommended:* ACT (for admission).

Costs (2011–12) *Comprehensive fee:* $30,800 includes full-time tuition ($22,232), mandatory fees ($120), and room and board ($8448). Full-time tuition and fees vary according to course load. Part-time tuition and fees vary according to course load. *Room and board:* Room and board charges vary according to board plan. *Payment plans:* installment, deferred payment. *Waivers:* employees or children of employees.

Financial Aid Of all full-time matriculated undergraduates who enrolled in 2011, 1,016 applied for aid, 885 were judged to have need, 61 had their need fully met. 150 Federal Work-Study jobs (averaging $1500). In 2011, 208 non-need-based awards were made. *Average percent of need met:* 48%. *Average financial aid package:* $12,520. *Average need-based loan:* $4501. *Average need-based gift aid:* $4180. *Average non-need-based aid:* $5730. *Average indebtedness upon graduation:* $22,270.

Applying *Options:* electronic application, deferred entrance. *Application fee:* $20. *Required:* essay or personal statement, high school transcript, minimum 2.3 GPA, interview. *Required for some:* 1 letter of recommendation. *Application deadline:* rolling (freshmen). *Notification:* continuous (freshmen), continuous (transfers).

Freshman Application Contact Jeremy Klyn, Director of Admissions, Trinity Christian College, 6601 West College Drive, Palos Heights, IL 60463. *Phone:* 708-239-4708. *Fax:* 708-239-4826. *E-mail:* admissions@trnty.edu. *Web site:* http://www.trnty.edu/.

Trinity College of Nursing and Health Sciences

Rock Island, Illinois

- **Independent** 4-year, founded 1994
- **Urban** 2-acre campus
- **Endowment** $1.2 million
- **Coed** 222 undergraduate students, 49% full-time, 87% women, 13% men
- **Moderately difficult** entrance level, 50% of applicants were admitted

Undergraduates 109 full-time, 113 part-time. 46% are from out of state; 4% Black or African American, non-Hispanic/Latino; 5% Hispanic/Latino; 2% Asian, non-Hispanic/Latino; 1% Two or more races, non-Hispanic/Latino; 4% Race/ethnicity unknown; 18% transferred in. *Retention:* 100% of full-time freshmen returned.

Freshmen *Admission:* 4 applied, 2 admitted, 2 enrolled. *Average high school GPA:* 3.42. *Test scores:* ACT scores over 18: 82%; ACT scores over 24: 24%; ACT scores over 30: 1%.

Faculty *Total:* 20, 70% full-time, 15% with terminal degrees. *Student/faculty ratio:* 14:1.

Academics *Calendar:* semesters. *Degrees:* associate and bachelor's (general education requirements are taken off campus, usually at Black Hawk College, Eastern Iowa Community College District and Western Illinois University). *Special study options:* accelerated degree program, adult/continuing education programs, advanced placement credit, distance learning, honors programs,

independent study, internships, off-campus study, part-time degree program, services for LD students, study abroad, summer session for credit.

Computers on Campus 20 computers/terminals are available on campus for general student use. Students can access the following: computer help desk, free student e-mail accounts, online (class) grades, online (class) schedules. Campuswide network is available. Wireless service is available via entire campus.

Student Life *Housing:* college housing not available. *Activities and organizations:* Student Government Association, Phi Theta Kappa, BSN Honor Society. *Campus security:* 24-hour emergency response devices. *Student services:* personal/psychological counseling.

Standardized Tests *Required for some:* ACT (for admission).

Costs (2012–13) *Tuition:* $15,552 full-time, $648 per credit hour part-time. Full-time tuition and fees vary according to course level, course load, degree level, program, and student level. Part-time tuition and fees vary according to course level, course load, degree level, program, and student level. *Required fees:* $331 full-time. *Payment plan:* installment.

Financial Aid Of all full-time matriculated undergraduates who enrolled in 2011, 98 applied for aid, 98 were judged to have need. *Average indebtedness upon graduation:* $9500.

Applying *Options:* electronic application, early admission, early decision. *Application fee:* $50. *Required:* minimum 2.5 GPA. *Required for some:* essay or personal statement, high school transcript, minimum 3.0 GPA, interview. *Application deadlines:* rolling (freshmen), rolling (out-of-state freshmen), rolling (transfers). *Early decision deadline:* 12/1. *Notification:* continuous until 2/1 (freshmen), continuous until 2/1 (out-of-state freshmen), continuous until 2/1 (transfers), 12/15 (early decision).

Freshman Application Contact Ms. Lori Perez, Admissions Representative, Trinity College of Nursing and Health Sciences, 2122 - 25th Avenue, Rock Island, IL 61201. *Phone:* 309-779-7700. *Fax:* 309-779-7748. *E-mail:* PerezLJ@ihs.org. *Web site:* http://www.trinitycollegeqc.edu/.

Trinity International University
Deerfield, Illinois

Freshman Application Contact Mr. Aaron Mahl, Director of Undergraduate Admissions, Trinity International University, 2065 Half Day Road, Deerfield, IL 60015-1284. *Phone:* 847-317-7000. *Toll-free phone:* 800-822-3225. *Fax:* 847-317-8097. *E-mail:* tcadmissions@tiu.edu. *Web site:* http://www.tiu.edu/.

University of Chicago
Chicago, Illinois

- **Independent** university, founded 1891
- **Urban** 215-acre campus
- **Endowment** $6.6 million
- **Coed** 5,388 undergraduate students, 99% full-time, 48% women, 52% men
- **Most difficult** entrance level, 16% of applicants were admitted

Undergraduates 5,320 full-time, 68 part-time. 79% are from out of state; 5% Black or African American, non-Hispanic/Latino; 6% Hispanic/Latino; 17% Asian, non-Hispanic/Latino; 0.1% Native Hawaiian or other Pacific Islander, non-Hispanic/Latino; 0.2% American Indian or Alaska Native, non-Hispanic/Latino; 6% Two or more races, non-Hispanic/Latino; 13% Race/ethnicity unknown; 9% international; 0.8% transferred in; 60% live on campus. *Retention:* 99% of full-time freshmen returned.

Freshmen *Admission:* 21,762 applied, 3,539 admitted, 1,411 enrolled. *Average high school GPA:* 4.16. *Test scores:* SAT critical reading scores over 500: 100%; SAT math scores over 500: 100%; SAT writing scores over 500: 100%; ACT scores over 18: 100%; SAT critical reading scores over 600: 98%; SAT math scores over 600: 99%; SAT writing scores over 600: 98%; ACT scores over 24: 99%; SAT critical reading scores over 700: 79%; SAT math scores over 700: 78%; SAT writing scores over 700: 75%; ACT scores over 30: 86%.

Faculty *Total:* 1,701, 67% full-time, 88% with terminal degrees. *Student/faculty ratio:* 7:1.

Academics *Calendar:* quarters. *Degrees:* bachelor's, master's, doctoral, and first professional. *Special study options:* accelerated degree program, adult/continuing education programs, advanced placement credit, double majors, honors programs, independent study, internships, off-campus study, student-designed majors, study abroad, summer session for credit. *ROTC:* Army (c), Air Force (c). *Unusual degree programs:* 3-2 business administration; social work; public policy, social sciences (MAPSS), international relations.

Computers on Campus 1,000 computers/terminals are available on campus for general student use. Students can access the following: campus intranet, computer help desk, free student e-mail accounts, online (class) grades, online (class) registration, online (class) schedules. Campuswide network is available. Wireless service is available via entire campus.

Student Life *Housing:* on-campus residence required for freshman year. *Options:* coed, disabled students. Campus housing is university owned. Freshman campus housing is guaranteed. *Activities and organizations:* drama/theater group, student-run newspaper, radio station, choral group, marching band, University Theatre, Model United Nations, Council on University Programming, Documentary Films, South Asian Students Association, national fraternities, national sororities. *Campus security:* 24-hour emergency response devices and patrols, student patrols, late-night transport/escort service, controlled dormitory access. *Student services:* health clinic, personal/psychological counseling, women's center.

Athletics Member NCAA. All Division III. *Intercollegiate sports:* baseball M, basketball M/W, cross-country running M/W, football M, soccer M/W, softball W, swimming and diving M/W, tennis M/W, track and field M/W, volleyball W, wrestling M.

Standardized Tests *Required:* SAT or ACT (for admission).

Costs (2011–12) *One-time required fee:* $997. *Comprehensive fee:* $55,416 includes full-time tuition ($41,853), mandatory fees ($930), and room and board ($12,633). Part-time tuition and fees vary according to course load. *Room and board:* Room and board charges vary according to board plan and housing facility. *Payment plans:* tuition prepayment, installment.

Financial Aid Of all full-time matriculated undergraduates who enrolled in 2011, 2,866 applied for aid, 2,483 were judged to have need, 2,483 had their need fully met. In 2011, 635 non-need-based awards were made. *Average percent of need met:* 100%. *Average financial aid package:* $40,089. *Average need-based loan:* $4697. *Average need-based gift aid:* $36,600. *Average non-need-based aid:* $11,955. *Average indebtedness upon graduation:* $22,663. *Financial aid deadline:* 2/1.

Applying *Options:* electronic application, early admission, early action, deferred entrance. *Application fee:* $75. *Required:* essay or personal statement, high school transcript, 2 letters of recommendation, 2 teacher recommendations required. *Recommended:* interview. *Application deadlines:* 1/3 (freshmen), 3/1 (transfers), 11/1 (early action).

Freshman Application Contact Mr. James G. Nondorf, Vice President, Dean of College Admissions and Financial Aid, University of Chicago, Rosenwald Hall, 1101 East 58th Street, Suite 105, Chicago, IL 60637. *Phone:* 773-702-8650. *Fax:* 773-702-4199. *E-mail:* collegeadmissions@uchicago.edu. *Web site:* http://www.uchicago.edu/.

University of Illinois at Chicago
Chicago, Illinois

- **State-supported** university, founded 1946, part of University of Illinois System
- **Urban** 240-acre campus with easy access to Chicago
- **Endowment** $220.0 million
- **Coed** 16,925 undergraduate students, 92% full-time, 52% women, 48% men
- **Moderately difficult** entrance level, 63% of applicants were admitted

Undergraduates 15,532 full-time, 1,393 part-time. Students come from 42 states and territories; 43 other countries; 2% are from out of state; 8% Black or African American, non-Hispanic/Latino; 22% Hispanic/Latino; 21% Asian, non-Hispanic/Latino; 0.5% Native Hawaiian or other Pacific Islander, non-Hispanic/Latino; 0.1% American Indian or Alaska Native, non-Hispanic/Latino; 2% Two or more races, non-Hispanic/Latino; 2% Race/ethnicity unknown; 1% international; 9% transferred in; 19% live on campus. *Retention:* 79% of full-time freshmen returned.

Freshmen *Admission:* 14,564 applied, 9,151 admitted, 3,115 enrolled. *Average high school GPA:* 3.13. *Test scores:* SAT critical reading scores over 500: 60%; SAT math scores over 500: 77%; SAT writing scores over 500: 69%; ACT scores over 18: 99%; SAT critical reading scores over 600: 27%; SAT math scores over 600: 48%; SAT writing scores over 600: 28%; ACT scores over 24: 49%; SAT critical reading scores over 700: 9%; SAT math scores over 700: 17%; SAT writing scores over 700: 10%; ACT scores over 30: 7%.

Faculty *Total:* 1,590, 73% full-time, 67% with terminal degrees. *Student/faculty ratio:* 19:1.

Academics *Calendar:* semesters. *Degrees:* bachelor's, master's, doctoral, post-master's, postbachelor's, and first professional certificates. *Special study options:* academic remediation for entering students, accelerated degree program, advanced placement credit, cooperative education, distance learning, double majors, honors programs, independent study, internships, off-campus study, part-time degree program, services for LD students, student-designed majors, study abroad, summer session for credit. *ROTC:* Army (b), Navy (c), Air Force (c).

Computers on Campus 910 computers/terminals are available on campus for general student use. Students can access the following: campus intranet, computer help desk, free student e-mail accounts, online (class) grades, online (class) registration, online (class) schedules. Campuswide network is available. 100% of college-owned or -operated housing units are wired for high-speed

Internet access. Wireless service is available via classrooms, computer centers, computer labs, dorm rooms, libraries, student centers.

Student Life *Housing options:* coed. Campus housing is university owned. *Activities and organizations:* drama/theater group, student-run newspaper, radio station, choral group, MBA Association, StudentsMuslim Student Association, Society of Automotive Engineers, Pakistani Student Organization, Society of Future Physicians, national fraternities, national sororities. *Campus security:* 24-hour emergency response devices and patrols, student patrols, late-night transport/escort service, controlled dormitory access, housing ID stickers, guest escort policy, 24-hour closed circuit videos for exits and entrances, security screen for first floor. *Student services:* health clinic, personal/psychological counseling, women's center, legal services.

Athletics Member NCAA. All Division I. *Intercollegiate sports:* baseball M(s), basketball M(s)/W(s), cross-country running M(s)/W(s), gymnastics M(s)/W(s), soccer M(s), softball W(s), swimming and diving M(s)/W(s), tennis M(s)/W(s), track and field M(s)/W(s), volleyball W(s). *Intramural sports:* badminton M/W, basketball M/W, bowling M/W, fencing M(c)/W(c), field hockey W, football M/W, golf M/W, racquetball M/W, rugby M(c)/W(c), soccer M/W, softball M/W, squash M/W, table tennis M/W, tennis M/W, volleyball M(c)/W, water polo M(c)/W(c), wrestling M.

Standardized Tests *Required:* SAT or ACT (for admission).

Costs (2012–13) *Tuition:* state resident $9744 full-time, $1627 part-time; nonresident $22,154 full-time, $3692 part-time. Full-time tuition and fees vary according to degree level and program. Part-time tuition and fees vary according to course load, degree level, and program. No tuition increase for student's term of enrollment. *Required fees:* $2892 full-time, $888 part-time. *Room and board:* $10,194; room only: $7318. Room and board charges vary according to board plan and housing facility. *Payment plan:* installment. *Waivers:* senior citizens and employees or children of employees.

Financial Aid Of all full-time matriculated undergraduates who enrolled in 2010, 12,545 applied for aid, 11,077 were judged to have need, 719 had their need fully met. 918 Federal Work-Study jobs (averaging $1900). 2,619 state and other part-time jobs (averaging $2500). In 2010, 582 non-need-based awards were made. *Average percent of need met:* 70%. *Average financial aid package:* $13,874. *Average need-based loan:* $4441. *Average need-based gift aid:* $12,416. *Average non-need-based aid:* $3172. *Average indebtedness upon graduation:* $20,196.

Applying *Options:* electronic application. *Application fee:* $50. *Required:* essay or personal statement, high school transcript, auditions required of music and theater majors; portfolios required of art majors. *Application deadlines:* 1/15 (freshmen), 3/31 (transfers). *Notification:* continuous until 11/30 (freshmen), continuous (transfers).

Freshman Application Contact Mr. Thomas Glenn, Executive Director of Admissions, University of Illinois at Chicago, 1100 SSB, m/c 018, Chicago, IL 60607-7128. *Phone:* 312-996-5133. *Fax:* 312-996-2953. *E-mail:* uic.admit@uic.edu. *Web site:* http://www.uic.edu/.

University of Illinois at Springfield
Springfield, Illinois

- **State-supported** comprehensive, founded 1969, part of University of Illinois System
- **Suburban** 746-acre campus
- **Endowment** $10.7 million
- **Coed** 3,112 undergraduate students, 66% full-time, 53% women, 47% men
- **Moderately difficult** entrance level, 60% of applicants were admitted

Undergraduates 2,047 full-time, 1,065 part-time. Students come from 50 states and territories; 10 other countries; 10% are from out of state; 11% Black or African American, non-Hispanic/Latino; 4% Hispanic/Latino; 3% Asian, non-Hispanic/Latino; 0.2% Native Hawaiian or other Pacific Islander, non-Hispanic/Latino; 0.4% American Indian or Alaska Native, non-Hispanic/Latino; 2% Two or more races, non-Hispanic/Latino; 4% Race/ethnicity unknown; 2% international; 19% transferred in; 27% live on campus. *Retention:* 75% of full-time freshmen returned.

Freshmen *Admission:* 1,243 applied, 747 admitted, 241 enrolled. *Average high school GPA:* 3.38. *Test scores:* ACT scores over 18: 96%; ACT scores over 24: 41%; ACT scores over 30: 7%.

Faculty *Total:* 358, 58% full-time. *Student/faculty ratio:* 13:1.

Academics *Calendar:* semesters. *Degrees:* bachelor's, master's, doctoral, post-master's, postbachelor's, and first professional certificates. *Special study options:* academic remediation for entering students, advanced placement credit, cooperative education, distance learning, double majors, English as a second language, honors programs, independent study, internships, off-campus study, part-time degree program, services for LD students, study abroad, summer session for credit.

Computers on Campus 357 computers/terminals and 27 ports are available on campus for general student use. Students can access the following: campus

intranet, computer help desk, free student e-mail accounts, online (class) grades, online (class) registration, online (class) schedules. Campuswide network is available. 100% of college-owned or -operated housing units are wired for high-speed Internet access. Wireless service is available via entire campus. **Student Life** *Housing:* on-campus residence required for freshman year. *Options:* coed, disabled students. Campus housing is university owned. Freshman campus housing is guaranteed. *Activities and organizations:* drama/theater group, student-run newspaper, radio station, choral group, Student Activities Committee, Christian Student Fellowship, Indian Student Organization, Black Student Union, DODGE - Dodge Ball Club. *Campus security:* 24-hour emergency response devices and patrols, late-night transport/escort service, controlled dormitory access. *Student services:* health clinic, personal/psychological counseling, women's center.

Athletics Member NCAA. All Division II. *Intercollegiate sports:* baseball M(s), basketball M(s)/W(s), golf M(s)/W(s), soccer M(s)/W(s), softball W(s), tennis M(s)/W(s), volleyball W(s). *Intramural sports:* badminton M/W, baseball M(c), basketball M/W, football M/W, racquetball M/W, soccer M/W, softball M/W, squash M(c)/W, ultimate Frisbee M/W, volleyball M/W.

Standardized Tests *Required:* SAT or ACT (for admission).

Costs (2012–13) *Tuition:* state resident $9090 full-time, $303 per credit hour part-time; nonresident $18,240 full-time, $608 per credit hour part-time. Full-time tuition and fees vary according to course load. Part-time tuition and fees vary according to course load. No tuition increase for student's term of enrollment. *Required fees:* $1775 full-time, $16 per credit hour part-time. *Room and board:* $9870; room only: $6720. Room and board charges vary according to board plan and housing facility. *Payment plan:* installment. *Waivers:* senior citizens and employees or children of employees.

Financial Aid Of all full-time matriculated undergraduates who enrolled in 2010, 1,762 applied for aid, 1,483 were judged to have need, 99 had their need fully met. In 2010, 273 non-need-based awards were made. *Average percent of need met:* 65%. *Average financial aid package:* $10,805. *Average need-based loan:* $4289. *Average need-based gift aid:* $8340. *Average non-need-based aid:* $4732. *Average indebtedness upon graduation:* $20,323. *Financial aid deadline:* 11/15.

Applying *Options:* electronic application, deferred entrance. *Application fee:* $50. *Required:* high school transcript. *Application deadlines:* rolling (freshmen), rolling (transfers). *Notification:* continuous (transfers).

Freshman Application Contact Dr. Lori Giordano, Interim Director of Student Services/ Admissions, University of Illinois at Springfield, Springfield, IL 62703. *Phone:* 217-206-4847. *Toll-free phone:* 888-977-4847. *E-mail:* admissions@uis.edu. *Web site:* http://www.uis.edu/.

University of Illinois at Urbana–Champaign
Champaign, Illinois

- **State-supported** university, founded 1867, part of University of Illinois System
- **Endowment** $24.0 billion
- **Coed** 32,256 undergraduate students, 97% full-time, 45% women, 55% men
- **Very difficult** entrance level, 68% of applicants were admitted

Undergraduates 31,311 full-time, 945 part-time. Students come from 52 states and territories; 119 other countries; 7% are from out of state; 6% Black or African American, non-Hispanic/Latino; 7% Hispanic/Latino; 13% Asian, non-Hispanic/Latino; 0.2% Native Hawaiian or other Pacific Islander, non-Hispanic/Latino; 0.1% American Indian or Alaska Native, non-Hispanic/Latino; 2% Two or more races, non-Hispanic/Latino; 0.7% Race/ethnicity unknown; 13% international; 4% transferred in; 50% live on campus. *Retention:* 94% of full-time freshmen returned.

Freshmen *Admission:* 28,751 applied, 19,434 admitted, 7,252 enrolled. *Test scores:* SAT critical reading scores over 500: 88%; SAT math scores over 500: 98%; SAT writing scores over 500: 96%; ACT scores over 18: 99%; SAT critical reading scores over 600: 50%; SAT math scores over 600: 93%; SAT writing scores over 600: 71%; ACT scores over 24: 90%; SAT critical reading scores over 700: 14%; SAT math scores over 700: 73%; SAT writing scores over 700: 18%; ACT scores over 30: 40%.

Faculty *Total:* 1,872, 100% full-time, 92% with terminal degrees. *Student/faculty ratio:* 18:1.

Academics *Calendar:* semesters. *Degrees:* certificates, bachelor's, master's, doctoral, post-master's, postbachelor's, and first professional certificates. *Special study options:* academic remediation for entering students, accelerated degree program, advanced placement credit, cooperative education, distance learning, double majors, English as a second language, honors programs, independent study, internships, off-campus study, services for LD students, student-designed majors, study abroad, summer session for credit. *ROTC:* Army (b), Navy (b), Air Force (b). *Unusual degree programs:* 3-2 business administration; engineering; accounting.

Computers on Campus Students can access the following: computer help desk, free student e-mail accounts, online (class) grades, online (class) registration, online (class) schedules. Campuswide network is available. 100% of college-owned or -operated housing units are wired for high-speed Internet access. Wireless service is available via entire campus.

Student Life *Housing:* on-campus residence required for freshman year. *Options:* coed, men-only, women-only, cooperative, disabled students. Campus housing is university owned and is provided by a third party. Freshman campus housing is guaranteed. *Activities and organizations:* drama/theater group, student-run newspaper, radio and television station, choral group, marching band, Volunteer Illini Project, October Lovers, Illini Pride Student Board, National Society of Collegiate Scholars, Phi Eta Sigma Freshman Honor Society, national fraternities, national sororities. *Campus security:* 24-hour emergency response devices and patrols, student patrols, late-night transport/escort service, controlled dormitory access, safety training classes, ID cards with safety numbers. *Student services:* health clinic, personal/psychological counseling, women's center, legal services.

Athletics Member NCAA. All Division I except football (Division I-A). *Intercollegiate sports:* baseball M(s), basketball M(s)/W(s), cheerleading M/W, cross-country running M(s)/W(s), golf M(s)/W(s), gymnastics M(s)/W(s), soccer W(s), softball W(s), swimming and diving W(s), tennis M(s)/W(s), track and field M(s)/W(s), volleyball W(s), wrestling M(s). *Intramural sports:* archery M(c)/W(c), badminton M/W, baseball M(c), basketball M/W, bowling M(c)/W(c), cheerleading M(c)/W(c), crew M(c)/W(c), cross-country running M/W, equestrian sports M(c)/W(c), fencing M(c)/W(c), field hockey M(c)/W(c), football M/W(c), golf M/W, gymnastics M(c)/W(c), ice hockey M(c)/W(c), lacrosse M(c)/W(c), racquetball M/W, riflery M(c)/W(c), rock climbing M(c)/W(c), rugby M(c)/W(c), sailing M(c)/W(c), skiing (cross-country) M(c)/W(c), skiing (downhill) M(c)/W(c), soccer M/W, softball M/W, squash M(c)/W(c), swimming and diving W(c), table tennis M(c)/W(c), tennis M/W, ultimate Frisbee M(c)/W(c), volleyball M/W, water polo M(c)/W(c), weight lifting M(c)/W(c), wrestling M.

Standardized Tests *Required:* SAT or ACT (for admission).

Costs (2012–13) *Tuition:* state resident $11,636 full-time; nonresident $25,778 full-time. Full-time tuition and fees vary according to program and student level. No tuition increase for student's term of enrollment. *Required fees:* $3324 full-time. *Room and board:* $10,332. Room and board charges vary according to board plan, housing facility, and location. *Payment plan:* installment. *Waivers:* senior citizens and employees or children of employees.

Financial Aid Of all full-time matriculated undergraduates who enrolled in 2009, 17,991 applied for aid, 13,790 were judged to have need, 3,978 had their need fully met. In 2009, 3667 non-need-based awards were made. *Average percent of need met:* 68%. *Average financial aid package:* $12,933. *Average need-based loan:* $4536. *Average need-based gift aid:* $10,885. *Average non-need-based aid:* $3286. *Average indebtedness upon graduation:* $21,543.

Applying *Options:* electronic application, early admission, deferred entrance. *Application fee:* $50. *Required:* essay or personal statement, high school transcript. *Required for some:* An application essay is required for all potential students. Auditions or portfolios may be required of some applicants depending on their field of study. *Application deadlines:* 1/2 (freshmen), 3/1 (transfers). *Notification:* 2/17 (freshmen), 4/15 (transfers).

Freshman Application Contact Stacey Kostell, Director of Admissions, University of Illinois at Urbana–Champaign, 901 West Illinois, Urbana, IL 61801. *Phone:* 217-333-0302. *Fax:* 217-244-4614. *E-mail:* ugradadmissions@uiuc.edu. *Web site:* http://www.illinois.edu/.

University of Phoenix–Chicago Campus
Schaumburg, Illinois

Freshman Application Contact Marc Booker, Sr. Director, Office of Admissions and Evaluation, University of Phoenix–Chicago Campus, 4035 South Riverpoint Parkway, Mail Stop CF-L101, Phoenix, AZ 85040-1958. *Phone:* 602-557-4609. *Toll-free phone:* 866-766-0766. *Fax:* 480-643-1156. *Web site:* http://www.phoenix.edu/.

University of St. Francis
Joliet, Illinois

- **Independent Roman Catholic** comprehensive, founded 1920
- **Suburban** 24-acre campus with easy access to Chicago
- **Endowment** $28.9 million
- **Coed** 1,402 undergraduate students, 96% full-time, 67% women, 33% men
- **Moderately difficult** entrance level, 45% of applicants were admitted

Undergraduates 1,343 full-time, 59 part-time. Students come from 17 states and territories; 5% are from out of state; 7% Black or African American, non-

Hispanic/Latino; 14% Hispanic/Latino; 2% Asian, non-Hispanic/Latino; 0.3% Native Hawaiian or other Pacific Islander, non-Hispanic/Latino; 0.1% American Indian or Alaska Native, non-Hispanic/Latino; 2% Two or more races, non-Hispanic/Latino; 0.1% Race/ethnicity unknown; 0.8% international; 16% transferred in; 25% live on campus. *Retention:* 79% of full-time freshmen returned.
Freshmen *Admission:* 1,482 applied, 662 admitted, 180 enrolled. *Average high school GPA:* 3.23. *Test scores:* SAT critical reading scores over 500: 17%; SAT math scores over 500: 67%; SAT writing scores over 500: 17%; ACT scores over 18: 99%; ACT scores over 24: 49%; ACT scores over 30: 4%.
Faculty *Total:* 248, 36% full-time, 40% with terminal degrees. *Student/faculty ratio:* 12:1.
Academics *Calendar:* semesters. *Degrees:* bachelor's, master's, doctoral, post-master's, and first professional certificates. *Special study options:* academic remediation for entering students, accelerated degree program, adult/continuing education programs, advanced placement credit, distance learning, double majors, external degree program, honors programs, independent study, internships, off-campus study, part-time degree program, services for LD students, student-designed majors, study abroad, summer session for credit. *ROTC:* Army (c).
Computers on Campus 446 computers/terminals and 1,500 ports are available on campus for general student use. Students can access the following: campus intranet, computer help desk, free student e-mail accounts, online (class) grades, online (class) registration, online (class) schedules, billing/payment. Campuswide network is available. 100% of college-owned or -operated housing units are wired for high-speed Internet access. Wireless service is available via entire campus.
Student Life *Housing options:* coed. Campus housing is university owned. Freshman campus housing is guaranteed. *Activities and organizations:* drama/theater group, student-run newspaper, radio and television station, choral group, Unidos Vamos Alcanzar, Student Nurses Association, Student Business Association, TV Club, Justice League of USF. *Campus security:* 24-hour emergency response devices and patrols, student patrols, late-night transport/escort service, controlled dormitory access, First Response trained security personnel. *Student services:* personal/psychological counseling.
Athletics Member NAIA. *Intercollegiate sports:* baseball M(s), basketball M(s)/W(s), cheerleading W(s), cross-country running M(s)/W(s), football M(s), golf M(s)/W(s), soccer M(s)/W(s), softball W(s), tennis M(s)/W(s), track and field M(s)/W(s), volleyball W(s). *Intramural sports:* basketball M/W, bowling M/W, volleyball M/W.
Standardized Tests *Required:* SAT or ACT (for admission).
Costs (2011–12) *Comprehensive fee:* $34,394 includes full-time tuition ($25,482), mandatory fees ($450), and room and board ($8462). Full-time tuition and fees vary according to degree level and location. Part-time tuition: $795 per credit hour. Part-time tuition and fees vary according to degree level and location. *Room and board:* Room and board charges vary according to board plan and housing facility. *Payment plans:* installment, deferred payment. *Waivers:* children of alumni and employees or children of employees.
Financial Aid Of all full-time matriculated undergraduates who enrolled in 2010, 1,190 applied for aid, 1,084 were judged to have need, 539 had their need fully met. 174 Federal Work-Study jobs (averaging $1107). 241 state and other part-time jobs (averaging $1470). In 2010, 192 non-need-based awards were made. *Average percent of need met:* 67%. *Average financial aid package:* $19,955. *Average need-based loan:* $4457. *Average need-based gift aid:* $8409. *Average non-need-based aid:* $8266. *Average indebtedness upon graduation:* $27,088.
Applying *Options:* electronic application, deferred entrance. *Application fee:* $30. *Required:* high school transcript, minimum 2.5 GPA. *Required for some:* essay or personal statement, 2 letters of recommendation, interview. *Application deadline:* 8/1 (freshmen). *Notification:* continuous (freshmen), continuous (transfers).
Freshman Application Contact Ms. Julie Marlatt, Director of Undergraduate Admissions, University of St. Francis, 500 North Wilcox Street, Joliet, IL 60435-6188. *Phone:* 800-735-7500. *Toll-free phone:* 800-735-7500. *Fax:* 815-740-5032. *E-mail:* jmarlatt@stfrancis.edu. *Web site:* http://www.stfrancis.edu/.

VanderCook College of Music
Chicago, Illinois

- **Independent** comprehensive, founded 1909
- **Urban** 1-acre campus
- **Endowment** $2.1 million
- **Coed** 178 undergraduate students, 71% full-time, 48% women, 52% men
- **Moderately difficult** entrance level, 69% of applicants were admitted

Undergraduates 126 full-time, 52 part-time. Students come from 15 states and territories; 4 other countries; 27% are from out of state; 7% Black or African American, non-Hispanic/Latino; 12% Hispanic/Latino; 1% Asian, non-Hispanic/Latino; 0.7% Two or more races, non-Hispanic/Latino; 1% Race/ethnicity unknown; 4% international; 4% transferred in; 19% live on campus. *Retention:* 82% of full-time freshmen returned.
Freshmen *Admission:* 75 applied, 52 admitted, 21 enrolled. *Average high school GPA:* 3.35. *Test scores:* ACT scores over 18: 100%; ACT scores over 24: 40%; ACT scores over 30: 5%.
Faculty *Total:* 33, 30% full-time, 27% with terminal degrees. *Student/faculty ratio:* 10:1.
Academics *Calendar:* semesters. *Degrees:* bachelor's, master's, and post-bachelor's certificates. *Special study options:* advanced placement credit, distance learning, independent study, internships, part-time degree program.
Computers on Campus 21 computers/terminals are available on campus for general student use. Students can access the following: campus intranet, free student e-mail accounts. Campuswide network is available. Wireless service is available via entire campus.
Student Life *Housing options:* coed, disabled students. Campus housing is provided by a third party. *Activities and organizations:* choral group, NAME (National Association for Music Education), ACDA (American Choral Directors Association), NBA (National Band Association), ASTA (American String Teachers Association), national fraternities, national sororities. *Campus security:* 24-hour emergency response devices and patrols, late-night transport/escort service, controlled dormitory access.
Standardized Tests *Required for some:* SAT or ACT (for admission).
Costs (2011–12) *Comprehensive fee:* $32,844 includes full-time tuition ($21,090), mandatory fees ($1290), and room and board ($10,464). Full-time tuition and fees vary according to course level, course load, degree level, and program. Part-time tuition: $925 per semester hour. Part-time tuition and fees vary according to course level, course load, degree level, and program. *Required fees:* $1010 per year part-time. *College room only:* $5384. Room and board charges vary according to board plan and housing facility. *Payment plan:* installment. *Waivers:* employees or children of employees.
Financial Aid Of all full-time matriculated undergraduates who enrolled in 2006, 7 Federal Work-Study jobs (averaging $500). 37 state and other part-time jobs (averaging $959).
Applying *Options:* deferred entrance. *Application fee:* $35. *Required:* essay or personal statement, high school transcript, 3 letters of recommendation, interview, audition. *Required for some:* minimum 3.0 GPA. *Recommended:* minimum 3.0 GPA. *Application deadlines:* rolling (freshmen), rolling (out-of-state freshmen), rolling (transfers). *Notification:* continuous (freshmen), continuous (out-of-state freshmen), continuous (transfers).
Freshman Application Contact Ms. Amy Lenting, Director of Admissions, VanderCook College of Music, 3140 South Federal Street, Chicago, IL 60616. *Phone:* 312-225-6288 Ext. 230. *Fax:* 312-225-5211. *E-mail:* admissions@vandercook.edu. *Web site:* http://www.vandercook.edu/.

Western Illinois University
Macomb, Illinois

- **State-supported** comprehensive, founded 1899
- **Small-town** 1050-acre campus
- **Endowment** $27.9 million
- **Coed** 10,520 undergraduate students, 90% full-time, 48% women, 52% men
- **Moderately difficult** entrance level, 66% of applicants were admitted

Undergraduates 9,520 full-time, 1,000 part-time. Students come from 38 states and territories; 57 other countries; 14% Black or African American, non-Hispanic/Latino; 6% Hispanic/Latino; 0.8% Asian, non-Hispanic/Latino; 0.1% Native Hawaiian or other Pacific Islander, non-Hispanic/Latino; 0.2% American Indian or Alaska Native, non-Hispanic/Latino; 2% Two or more races, non-Hispanic/Latino; 4% Race/ethnicity unknown; 1% international; 12% transferred in; 44% live on campus. *Retention:* 71% of full-time freshmen returned.
Freshmen *Admission:* 9,731 applied, 6,384 admitted, 1,955 enrolled. *Average high school GPA:* 2.99. *Test scores:* ACT scores over 18: 83%; ACT scores over 24: 20%; ACT scores over 30: 2%.
Faculty *Total:* 731, 91% full-time, 68% with terminal degrees. *Student/faculty ratio:* 16:1.
Academics *Calendar:* semesters. *Degrees:* bachelor's, master's, doctoral, postbachelor's, and first professional certificates. *Special study options:* academic remediation for entering students, adult/continuing education programs, advanced placement credit, distance learning, double majors, English as a second language, external degree program, freshman honors college, honors programs, independent study, internships, off-campus study, part-time degree program, services for LD students, student-designed majors, study abroad, summer session for credit. *ROTC:* Army (b).
Computers on Campus 1,000 computers/terminals are available on campus for general student use. Students can access the following: online (class) regis-

tration. Campuswide network is available. 100% of college-owned or -operated housing units are wired for high-speed Internet access. Wireless service is available via classrooms, computer labs, dorm rooms, libraries, student centers.

Student Life *Housing:* on-campus residence required through sophomore year. *Options:* coed, men-only, women-only. Campus housing is university owned. Freshman campus housing is guaranteed. *Activities and organizations:* drama/theater group, student-run newspaper, radio and television station, choral group, marching band, Student Government Association, Black Student Association, University Union Board, International Friendship Club, Bureau of Cultural Affairs, national fraternities, national sororities. *Campus security:* 24-hour emergency response devices and patrols, student patrols, late-night transport/escort service, controlled dormitory access. *Student services:* health clinic, personal/psychological counseling, women's center, legal services.

Athletics Member NCAA. All Division I except football (Division I-AA). *Intercollegiate sports:* baseball M(s), basketball M(s)/W(s), cross-country running M(s)/W(s), golf M(s)/W, soccer M(s)/W(s), softball W(s), swimming and diving M(s)/W(s), tennis M(s)/W(s), track and field M(s)/W(s), volleyball W(s). *Intramural sports:* badminton M/W, basketball M/W, bowling M/W, cheerleading M/W, cross-country running M/W, football M/W, golf M/W, lacrosse M, racquetball M/W, rugby M/W, soccer M/W, softball M/W, swimming and diving M/W, table tennis M/W, tennis M/W, volleyball M/W, water polo M/W.

Standardized Tests *Required:* SAT or ACT (for admission).

Costs (2011–12) *Tuition:* state resident $7649 full-time, $255 per credit hour part-time; nonresident $11,473 full-time, $382 per credit hour part-time. Full-time tuition and fees vary according to course load and student level. Part-time tuition and fees vary according to course load and student level. No tuition increase for student's term of enrollment. *Required fees:* $2332 full-time, $78 per credit hour part-time. *Room and board:* $8460; room only: $5160. Room and board charges vary according to board plan, housing facility, and student level. *Waivers:* senior citizens and employees or children of employees.

Financial Aid Of all full-time matriculated undergraduates who enrolled in 2011, 7,763 applied for aid, 6,813 were judged to have need, 2,003 had their need fully met. 159 Federal Work-Study jobs (averaging $2712). 1,424 state and other part-time jobs (averaging $968). In 2011, 218 non-need-based awards were made. *Average percent of need met:* 57%. *Average financial aid package:* $9818. *Average need-based loan:* $4303. *Average need-based gift aid:* $7780. *Average non-need-based aid:* $3582. *Average indebtedness upon graduation:* $23,227.

Applying *Options:* electronic application, deferred entrance. *Application fee:* $30. *Required:* high school transcript, minimum 2.5 GPA. *Application deadlines:* 5/15 (freshmen), rolling (transfers). *Notification:* continuous (freshmen), continuous (transfers).

Freshman Application Contact Western Illinois University, 1 University Circle, Macomb, IL 61455-1390. *Phone:* 309-298-3157. *Toll-free phone:* 877-742-5948. *Web site:* http://www.wiu.edu/.

Westwood College–Chicago Du Page

Woodridge, Illinois

Freshman Application Contact Westwood College–Chicago Du Page, 7155 Janes Avenue, Woodridge, IL 60517. *Phone:* 630-434-8250. *Toll-free phone:* 866-721-7647. *Web site:* http://www.westwood.edu/.

Westwood College–Chicago Loop Campus

Chicago, Illinois

Freshman Application Contact Westwood College–Chicago Loop Campus, 17 North State Street, Suite 300, Chicago, IL 60602. *Phone:* 312-739-0890. *Toll-free phone:* 800-693-5411. *Web site:* http://www.westwood.edu/.

Westwood College–Chicago O'Hare Airport

Chicago, Illinois

Freshman Application Contact Westwood College–Chicago O'Hare Airport, 8501 West Higgins Road, Suite 100, Chicago, IL 60631. *Phone:* 773-380-6801. *Toll-free phone:* 866-235-2457. *Web site:* http://www.westwood.edu/.

Westwood College–Chicago River Oaks

Calumet City, Illinois

Freshman Application Contact Westwood College–Chicago River Oaks, 80 River Oaks Drive, Suite 111, Calumet City, IL 60409. *Phone:* 708-832-9760. *Toll-free phone:* 888-549-4960. *Web site:* http://www.westwood.edu/.

Wheaton College

Wheaton, Illinois

- **Independent nondenominational** comprehensive, founded 1860
- **Suburban** 80-acre campus with easy access to Chicago
- **Endowment** $322.6 million
- **Coed** 2,433 undergraduate students, 97% full-time, 50% women, 50% men
- **Very difficult** entrance level, 65% of applicants were admitted

Undergraduates 2,359 full-time, 74 part-time. Students come from 50 states and territories; 40 other countries; 75% are from out of state; 3% Black or African American, non-Hispanic/Latino; 4% Hispanic/Latino; 8% Asian, non-Hispanic/Latino; 0.1% Native Hawaiian or other Pacific Islander, non-Hispanic/Latino; 0.1% American Indian or Alaska Native, non-Hispanic/Latino; 2% Two or more races, non-Hispanic/Latino; 1% Race/ethnicity unknown; 1% international; 3% transferred in; 90% live on campus. *Retention:* 95% of full-time freshmen returned.

Freshmen *Admission:* 2,050 applied, 1,327 admitted, 596 enrolled. *Average high school GPA:* 3.7. *Test scores:* SAT critical reading scores over 500: 99%; SAT math scores over 500: 97%; SAT writing scores over 500: 98%; ACT scores over 18: 100%; SAT critical reading scores over 600: 80%; SAT math scores over 600: 81%; SAT writing scores over 600: 78%; ACT scores over 24: 93%; SAT critical reading scores over 700: 36%; SAT math scores over 700: 23%; SAT writing scores over 700: 29%; ACT scores over 30: 47%.

Faculty *Total:* 272, 72% full-time, 85% with terminal degrees. *Student/faculty ratio:* 12:1.

Academics *Calendar:* semesters. *Degrees:* bachelor's, master's, doctoral, postbachelor's, and first professional certificates. *Special study options:* advanced placement credit, double majors, independent study, internships, off-campus study, services for LD students, student-designed majors, study abroad, summer session for credit. *ROTC:* Army (b), Air Force (c). *Unusual degree programs:* 3-2 engineering with University of Illinois, Washington University in St. Louis, Illinois Institute of Technology, University of Minnesota; nursing with Emory University, Johns Hopkins University, Rush University, Vanderbilt University, Case Western Reserve University.

Computers on Campus 125 computers/terminals and 3,500 ports are available on campus for general student use. Students can access the following: campus intranet, computer help desk, free student e-mail accounts, online (class) grades, online (class) registration, online (class) schedules, financial information, degree requirements evaluation. Campuswide network is available. 100% of college-owned or -operated housing units are wired for high-speed Internet access. Wireless service is available via entire campus.

Student Life *Housing:* on-campus residence required through senior year. *Options:* coed, men-only, women-only, cooperative, disabled students. Campus housing is university owned. Freshman campus housing is guaranteed. *Activities and organizations:* drama/theater group, student-run newspaper, choral group, Discipleship small groups, Christian Service Council, Orientation Committee, Resident Assistant Staff. *Campus security:* 24-hour emergency response devices and patrols, student patrols, late-night transport/escort service, controlled dormitory access. *Student services:* health clinic, personal/psychological counseling.

Athletics Member NCAA. All Division III. *Intercollegiate sports:* baseball M, basketball M/W, cheerleading W(c), crew M(c)/W(c), cross-country running M/W, football M, golf M/W, ice hockey M(c), lacrosse M(c)/W(c), soccer M/W, softball W, swimming and diving M/W, tennis M/W, track and field M/W, volleyball M(c)/W, water polo M(c)/W, wrestling M. *Intramural sports:* basketball M/W, golf M/W, soccer M/W, softball M, ultimate Frisbee M/W, volleyball M/W.

Standardized Tests *Required:* SAT or ACT (for admission).

Costs (2011–12) *Comprehensive fee:* $37,180 includes full-time tuition ($28,960) and room and board ($8220). Part-time tuition: $1207 per credit hour. Part-time tuition and fees vary according to course load. *College room only:* $4850. Room and board charges vary according to board plan and housing facility. *Payment plans:* installment, deferred payment.

Financial Aid Of all full-time matriculated undergraduates who enrolled in 2010, 1,598 applied for aid, 1,286 were judged to have need, 342 had their need fully met. 199 Federal Work-Study jobs (averaging $1273). In 2010, 303 non-need-based awards were made. *Average percent of need met:* 89%. *Average financial aid package:* $23,176. *Average need-based loan:* $4941. *Aver-*

age need-based gift aid: $16,076. *Average non-need-based aid:* $4424. *Average indebtedness upon graduation:* $23,022.

Applying *Options:* electronic application, early action, deferred entrance. *Application fee:* $50. *Required:* essay or personal statement, high school transcript, 2 letters of recommendation. *Recommended:* interview. *Application deadlines:* 1/10 (freshmen), 3/1 (transfers), 11/1 (early action). *Notification:* 4/1 (freshmen), 4/1 (transfers), 12/31 (early action).

Freshman Application Contact Ms. Shawn Leftwich, Director of Admissions, Wheaton College, 501 College Avenue, Wheaton, IL 60187-5593. *Phone:* 630-752-5011. *Toll-free phone:* 800-222-2419. *Fax:* 630-752-5285. *E-mail:* admissions@wheaton.edu. *Web site:* http://www.wheaton.edu/.

See below for display ad and page 1760 for the College Close-Up.

INDIANA

Anderson University
Anderson, Indiana

- **Independent** comprehensive, founded 1917, affiliated with Church of God
- **Suburban** 163-acre campus with easy access to Indianapolis
- **Endowment** $24.6 million
- **Coed** 2,044 undergraduate students, 93% full-time, 58% women, 42% men
- **Moderately difficult** entrance level, 56% of applicants were admitted

Undergraduates 1,901 full-time, 143 part-time. Students come from 41 states and territories; 22 other countries; 26% are from out of state; 6% Black or African American, non-Hispanic/Latino; 2% Hispanic/Latino; 0.5% Asian, non-Hispanic/Latino; 0.1% Native Hawaiian or other Pacific Islander, non-Hispanic/Latino; 0.3% American Indian or Alaska Native, non-Hispanic/Latino; 0.4% Two or more races, non-Hispanic/Latino; 6% Race/ethnicity unknown; 3% international; 5% transferred in; 63% live on campus. *Retention:* 79% of full-time freshmen returned.

Freshmen *Admission:* 3,079 applied, 1,736 admitted, 506 enrolled. *Average high school GPA:* 3.4. *Test scores:* SAT critical reading scores over 500: 61%; SAT math scores over 500: 67%; ACT scores over 18: 93%; SAT critical reading scores over 600: 20%; SAT math scores over 600: 24%; ACT scores over 24: 50%; SAT critical reading scores over 700: 1%; SAT math scores over 700: 2%; ACT scores over 30: 5%.

Faculty *Total:* 253, 53% full-time, 38% with terminal degrees. *Student/faculty ratio:* 12:1.

Academics *Calendar:* semesters. *Degrees:* associate, bachelor's, master's, doctoral, and first professional. *Special study options:* academic remediation for entering students, accelerated degree program, adult/continuing education programs, advanced placement credit, distance learning, double majors, honors programs, independent study, internships, off-campus study, part-time degree program, services for LD students, student-designed majors, study abroad, summer session for credit. *Unusual degree programs:* 3-2 engineering with Purdue University.

Computers on Campus 338 computers/terminals are available on campus for general student use. Students can access the following: campus intranet, computer help desk, free student e-mail accounts, online (class) grades, online (class) registration, online (class) schedules, microcomputer software. Campuswide network is available. 100% of college-owned or -operated housing units are wired for high-speed Internet access. Wireless service is available via entire campus.

Student Life *Housing:* on-campus residence required through junior year. *Options:* men-only, women-only. Campus housing is university owned. Freshman campus housing is guaranteed. *Activities and organizations:* drama/theater group, student-run newspaper, radio station, choral group, Adult and Continuing Education Students Association, Multicultural Student Union, Campus Ministries. *Campus security:* 24-hour emergency response devices and patrols, student patrols, late-night transport/escort service, controlled dormitory access, 24-hour crime line. *Student services:* health clinic, personal/psychological counseling.

Athletics Member NCAA. All Division III. *Intercollegiate sports:* baseball M, basketball M/W, cross-country running M/W, football M, golf M/W, soccer M/W, softball W, tennis M/W, track and field M/W, volleyball W. *Intramural sports:* badminton M/W, basketball M/W, bowling M/W, cheerleading M(c)/W(c), rugby M(c), soccer M/W, softball M/W, tennis M/W, volleyball M/W.

Standardized Tests *Required:* SAT or ACT (for admission).

Costs (2012–13) *Comprehensive fee:* $34,340 includes full-time tuition ($25,400), mandatory fees ($80), and room and board ($8860). Part-time tuition: $1059 per semester hour. Part-time tuition and fees vary according to course load. *College room only:* $5670. Room and board charges vary according to board plan and housing facility. *Payment plan:* installment. *Waivers:* employees or children of employees.

Financial Aid Of all full-time matriculated undergraduates who enrolled in 2008, 1,740 applied for aid, 1,572 were judged to have need, 346 had their need fully met. 1,500 Federal Work-Study jobs (averaging $2200). In 2008, 356 non-need-based awards were made. *Average percent of need met:* 93%. *Average financial aid package:* $20,553. *Average need-based loan:* $1651. *Average need-based gift aid:* $13,414. *Average non-need-based aid:* $9500. *Average indebtedness upon graduation:* $25,401.

Applying *Options:* electronic application, deferred entrance. *Application fee:* $25. *Required:* high school transcript, minimum 2.0 GPA, 2 letters of recommendation, lifestyle statement. *Required for some:* interview. *Recommended:* essay or personal statement. *Application deadlines:* 7/1 (freshmen), rolling (transfers). *Notification:* 9/1 (freshmen), continuous until 9/1 (transfers).

Freshman Application Contact Mr. Joe Davis, Director of Admissions, Anderson University, 1100 East 5th Street, Anderson, IN 46012-3495. *Phone:* 765-641-4076. *Toll-free phone:* 800-428-6414. *Fax:* 765-641-3851. *E-mail:* info@anderson.edu. *Web site:* http://www.anderson.edu/.

The Art Institute of Indianapolis

Indianapolis, Indiana

- **Proprietary** 4-year, part of Education Management Corporation
- **Suburban** campus
- **Coed**

Academics *Degrees:* certificates, associate, and bachelor's.

Costs (2011–12) *Tuition:* Tuition cost varies by program. Prospective students should contact the school for current tuition costs. Other charges include a starting kit for all first-quarter students. Kits vary in price, depending on the program of study.

Freshman Application Contact The Art Institute of Indianapolis, 3500 Depauw Boulevard, Suite 1010, Indianapolis, IN 46268. *Phone:* 317-613-4800. *Toll-free phone:* 866-441-9031. *Web site:* http://www.artinstitutes.edu/indianapolis/.

See page 1104 for the College Close-Up.

Ball State University

Muncie, Indiana

- **State-supported** university, founded 1918
- **Suburban** 1140-acre campus with easy access to Indianapolis
- **Endowment** $140.3 million
- **Coed** 17,627 undergraduate students, 92% full-time, 56% women, 44% men
- **Moderately difficult** entrance level, 68% of applicants were admitted

Undergraduates 16,218 full-time, 1,409 part-time. Students come from 50 states and territories; 56 other countries; 11% are from out of state; 6% Black or African American, non-Hispanic/Latino; 3% Hispanic/Latino; 0.7% Asian, non-Hispanic/Latino; 0.1% Native Hawaiian or other Pacific Islander, non-Hispanic/Latino; 0.2% American Indian or Alaska Native, non-Hispanic/Latino; 2% Two or more races, non-Hispanic/Latino; 2% Race/ethnicity unknown; 2% international; 4% transferred in; 43% live on campus. *Retention:* 79% of full-time freshmen returned.

Freshmen *Admission:* 14,302 applied, 9,659 admitted, 3,844 enrolled. *Average high school GPA:* 3.33. *Test scores:* SAT critical reading scores over 500: 66%; SAT math scores over 500: 67%; SAT writing scores over 500: 59%; ACT scores over 18: 98%; SAT critical reading scores over 600: 19%; SAT math scores over 600: 20%; SAT writing scores over 600: 13%; ACT scores over 24: 29%; SAT critical reading scores over 700: 2%; SAT math scores over 700: 1%; SAT writing scores over 700: 1%; ACT scores over 30: 3%.

Faculty *Total:* 1,145, 82% full-time, 67% with terminal degrees. *Student/faculty ratio:* 18:1.

Academics *Calendar:* semesters. *Degrees:* associate, bachelor's, master's, doctoral, post-master's, postbachelor's, and first professional certificates. *Special study options:* accelerated degree program, adult/continuing education programs, advanced placement credit, cooperative education, distance learning, double majors, English as a second language, external degree program, freshman honors college, honors programs, independent study, internships, part-time degree program, services for LD students, student-designed majors, study abroad, summer session for credit. *ROTC:* Army (b). *Unusual degree programs:* 3-2 engineering with Purdue University, Tri-State University.

Computers on Campus 888 computers/terminals and 21,135 ports are available on campus for general student use. Students can access the following: campus intranet, computer help desk, free student e-mail accounts, online (class) grades, online (class) registration, online (class) schedules, room reservations, testing and test results, manage and pay tuition, order/buy textbooks, request room repairs, order transcripts, manage meal plan, manage and prepay long distance service, undergraduate degree progress report. Campuswide net-

work is available. 100% of college-owned or -operated housing units are wired for high-speed Internet access. Wireless service is available via entire campus.

Student Life *Housing:* on-campus residence required for freshman year. *Options:* coed, men-only, women-only, disabled students. Campus housing is university owned. Freshman campus housing is guaranteed. *Activities and organizations:* drama/theater group, student-run newspaper, radio and television station, choral group, marching band, Epsilon Sigma Alpha International, WCRD- Student Radio Station, Golden Key Honor Society, Excellence in Leadership (EIL), Student Voluntary Services, national fraternities, national sororities. *Campus security:* 24-hour emergency response devices and patrols, late-night transport/escort service, controlled dormitory access. *Student services:* health clinic, personal/psychological counseling, women's center, legal services.

Athletics Member NCAA. All Division I except football (Division I-A). *Intercollegiate sports:* baseball M(s)/W(c), basketball M(s)/W(s), bowling M(c)/W(c), cheerleading M/W, cross-country running W(s), equestrian sports M(c)/W(c), fencing M(c)/W(c), field hockey W(s), golf M(s)/W(s), gymnastics W(s), lacrosse M(c)/W(c), racquetball M(c)/W(c), rock climbing M(c)/W(c), rugby M(c)/W(c), soccer M(c)/W(s), softball W(s), swimming and diving M(s)/W(s), tennis M(s)/W(s), track and field W(s), ultimate Frisbee M(c)/W(c), volleyball M(s)/W(s), water polo M(c)/W(c), wrestling M(c). *Intramural sports:* badminton M/W, basketball M/W, bowling M/W, golf M/W, racquetball M/W, soccer M/W, softball M/W, swimming and diving M/W, table tennis M/W, tennis M/W, track and field M/W, ultimate Frisbee M/W, volleyball M/W.

Standardized Tests *Required for some:* SAT or ACT (for admission).

Costs (2012–13) *Tuition:* state resident $8318 full-time, $270 per credit hour part-time; nonresident $22,988 full-time, $906 per credit hour part-time. Full-time tuition and fees vary according to course load, program, and reciprocity agreements. Part-time tuition and fees vary according to course load and reciprocity agreements. *Required fees:* $662 full-time. *Room and board:* $8714. Room and board charges vary according to board plan and housing facility. *Payment plan:* installment. *Waivers:* senior citizens and employees or children of employees.

Financial Aid Of all full-time matriculated undergraduates who enrolled in 2011, 13,106 applied for aid, 10,449 were judged to have need, 2,153 had their need fully met. 830 Federal Work-Study jobs (averaging $2238). In 2011, 1528 non-need-based awards were made. *Average percent of need met:* 56%. *Average financial aid package:* $10,653. *Average need-based loan:* $4245. *Average need-based gift aid:* $6370. *Average non-need-based aid:* $6933. *Average indebtedness upon graduation:* $25,667.

Applying *Options:* electronic application, deferred entrance. *Application fee:* $55. *Required:* high school transcript. *Required for some:* essay or personal statement. *Application deadlines:* 8/15 (freshmen), rolling (transfers). *Notification:* continuous (freshmen), continuous (transfers).

Freshman Application Contact Ball State University, 2000 West University Avenue, Muncie, IN 47306-1099. *Phone:* 765-285-8300. *Toll-free phone:* 800-482-4BSU. *Web site:* http://www.bsu.edu/.

Bethel College

Mishawaka, Indiana

- **Independent** comprehensive, founded 1947, affiliated with Missionary Church
- **Suburban** 80-acre campus
- **Endowment** $8.2 million
- **Coed** 1,885 undergraduate students, 79% full-time, 66% women, 34% men
- **Minimally difficult** entrance level, 69% of applicants were admitted

Undergraduates 1,483 full-time, 402 part-time. Students come from 31 states and territories; 17 other countries; 25% are from out of state; 12% Black or African American, non-Hispanic/Latino; 4% Hispanic/Latino; 0.7% Asian, non-Hispanic/Latino; 0.5% American Indian or Alaska Native, non-Hispanic/Latino; 2% Two or more races, non-Hispanic/Latino; 2% international; 11% transferred in; 46% live on campus. *Retention:* 84% of full-time freshmen returned.

Freshmen *Admission:* 1,128 applied, 777 admitted, 279 enrolled. *Average high school GPA:* 3.43. *Test scores:* SAT critical reading scores over 500: 54%; SAT math scores over 500: 56%; SAT writing scores over 500: 51%; ACT scores over 18: 88%; SAT critical reading scores over 600: 20%; SAT math scores over 600: 19%; SAT writing scores over 600: 15%; ACT scores over 24: 42%; SAT critical reading scores over 700: 2%; SAT math scores over 700: 4%; SAT writing scores over 700: 2%; ACT scores over 30: 8%.

Faculty *Total:* 217, 39% full-time, 31% with terminal degrees. *Student/faculty ratio:* 13:1.

Academics *Calendar:* semesters. *Degrees:* associate, bachelor's, and master's. *Special study options:* academic remediation for entering students, accelerated degree program, adult/continuing education programs, advanced

placement credit, distance learning, double majors, honors programs, independent study, internships, off-campus study, part-time degree program, services for LD students, student-designed majors, study abroad, summer session for credit. *ROTC:* Army (c), Air Force (c). *Unusual degree programs:* 3-2 engineering with University of Notre Dame, Tri-State University.

Computers on Campus 160 computers/terminals are available on campus for general student use. Students can access the following: computer help desk, free student e-mail accounts, online (class) grades, online (class) registration, online (class) schedules. Campuswide network is available. 100% of college-owned or -operated housing units are wired for high-speed Internet access. Wireless service is available via entire campus.

Student Life *Housing:* on-campus residence required through sophomore year. *Options:* men-only, women-only. Campus housing is university owned. *Activities and organizations:* drama/theater group, student-run newspaper, radio station, choral group, International Student Fellowship, Students for Life, Student Council, Spiritual Life Team. *Campus security:* 24-hour emergency response devices and patrols, late-night transport/escort service, controlled dormitory access. *Student services:* health clinic, personal/psychological counseling.

Athletics Member NAIA, NCCAA. *Intercollegiate sports:* baseball M(s), basketball M(s)/W(s), cheerleading M(s)/W(s), cross-country running M(s)/W(s), golf M(s)/W(s), soccer M(s)/W(s), softball W(s), tennis M(s)/W(s), track and field M(s)/W(s), volleyball W(s). *Intramural sports:* badminton M/W, basketball M/W, football M/W, soccer M/W, softball M/W, table tennis M/W, tennis M/W, ultimate Frisbee M/W, volleyball M/W.

Standardized Tests *Required:* SAT or ACT (for admission).

Costs (2012–13) *Comprehensive fee:* $31,560 includes full-time tuition ($23,930), mandatory fees ($350), and room and board ($7280). Full-time tuition and fees vary according to program. Part-time tuition: $760 per hour. Part-time tuition and fees vary according to course load and program. *College room only:* $3560. Room and board charges vary according to board plan and housing facility. *Payment plan:* installment. *Waivers:* employees or children of employees.

Financial Aid Of all full-time matriculated undergraduates who enrolled in 2011, 1,376 applied for aid, 1,263 were judged to have need, 173 had their need fully met. 357 Federal Work-Study jobs (averaging $1654). In 2011, 144 non-need-based awards were made. *Average percent of need met:* 64%. *Average financial aid package:* $15,802. *Average need-based loan:* $4324. *Average need-based gift aid:* $7789. *Average non-need-based aid:* $7310. *Average indebtedness upon graduation:* $23,474. *Financial aid deadline:* 3/10.

Applying *Options:* electronic application, early admission, deferred entrance. *Application fee:* $25. *Required:* essay or personal statement, high school transcript, minimum 2.0 GPA, 1 letter of recommendation. *Recommended:* minimum 2.5 GPA, interview. *Application deadlines:* 8/15 (freshmen), 8/15 (transfers). *Notification:* continuous (freshmen), continuous (transfers).

Freshman Application Contact Ms. Stephanie Hochstetler, Associate Director of Admission, Bethel College, 1001 Bethel Circle, Mishawaka, IN 46545. *Phone:* 574-807-7600. *Toll-free phone:* 800-422-4101. *Fax:* 574-807-7650. *E-mail:* admissions@bethelcollege.edu. *Web site:* http://www.bethelcollege.edu/.

Brown Mackie College–Fort Wayne

Fort Wayne, Indiana

- **Proprietary** primarily 2-year, part of Education Management Corporation
- **Coed**

Academics *Calendar:* quarters. *Degrees:* certificates, diplomas, associate, and bachelor's.

Costs (2011–12) *Tuition:* Tuition varies by program. Students should contact Brown Mackie College for tuition information.

Freshman Application Contact Brown Mackie College–Fort Wayne, 3000 East Coliseum Boulevard, Fort Wayne, IN 46805. *Phone:* 260-484-4400. *Toll-free phone:* 866-433-2289. *Web site:* http://www.brownmackie.edu/fortwayne/.

See page 1200 for the College Close-Up.

Brown Mackie College–Indianapolis

Indianapolis, Indiana

- **Proprietary** primarily 2-year, part of Education Management Corporation
- **Coed**

Academics *Degrees:* certificates, diplomas, associate, and bachelor's.

Costs (2011–12) *Tuition:* Tuition varies by program. Students should contact Brown Mackie College for tuition information.

Freshman Application Contact Brown Mackie College–Indianapolis, 1200 North Meridian Street, Suite 100, Indianapolis, IN 46204. *Phone:* 317-554-

8301. *Toll-free phone:* 866-255-0279. *Web site:* http://www.brownmackie.edu/indianapolis/.

See page 1204 for the College Close-Up.

Brown Mackie College–Merrillville

Merrillville, Indiana

- **Proprietary** primarily 2-year, founded 1890, part of Education Management Corporation
- **Small-town** campus
- **Coed**

Academics *Calendar:* quarters. *Degrees:* certificates, diplomas, associate, and bachelor's.

Costs (2011–12) *Tuition:* Tuition varies by program. Students should contact Brown Mackie College for tuition information.

Freshman Application Contact Brown Mackie College–Merrillville, 1000 East 80th Place, Suite 205S, Merrillville, IN 46410. *Phone:* 219-769-3321. *Toll-free phone:* 800-258-3321. *Web site:* http://www.brownmackie.edu/merrillville/.

See page 1208 for the College Close-Up.

Brown Mackie College–Michigan City

Michigan City, Indiana

- **Proprietary** primarily 2-year, part of Education Management Corporation
- **Rural** campus
- **Coed**

Academics *Calendar:* quarters. *Degrees:* certificates, diplomas, associate, and bachelor's.

Costs (2011–12) *Tuition:* Tuition varies by program. Students should contact Brown Mackie College for tuition information.

Freshman Application Contact Brown Mackie College–Michigan City, 325 East US Highway 20, Michigan City, IN 46360. *Phone:* 219-877-3100. *Toll-free phone:* 800-519-2416. *Web site:* http://www.brownmackie.edu/michigancity/.

See page 1212 for the College Close-Up.

Brown Mackie College–South Bend

South Bend, Indiana

- **Proprietary** primarily 2-year, founded 1882, part of Education Management Corporation
- **Urban** campus
- **Coed, primarily women**

Academics *Calendar:* quarters. *Degrees:* certificates, associate, and bachelor's.

Costs (2011–12) *Tuition:* Tuition varies by program. Students should contact Brown Mackie College for tuition information.

Freshman Application Contact Brown Mackie College–South Bend, 3454 Douglas Road, South Bend, IN 46635. *Phone:* 574-237-0774. *Toll-free phone:* 800-743-2447. *Web site:* http://www.brownmackie.edu/southbend/.

See page 1224 for the College Close-Up.

Butler University

Indianapolis, Indiana

- **Independent** comprehensive, founded 1855
- **Urban** 290-acre campus with easy access to Indianapolis
- **Endowment** $160.0 million
- **Coed** 3,889 undergraduate students, 98% full-time, 59% women, 41% men
- **Very difficult** entrance level, 61% of applicants were admitted

Undergraduates 3,807 full-time, 82 part-time. Students come from 45 states and territories; 45 other countries; 45% are from out of state; 4% Black or African American, non-Hispanic/Latino; 3% Hispanic/Latino; 3% Asian, non-Hispanic/Latino; 0.3% American Indian or Alaska Native, non-Hispanic/Latino; 0.8% Two or more races, non-Hispanic/Latino; 5% Race/ethnicity unknown; 2% international; 3% transferred in; 68% live on campus. *Retention:* 87% of full-time freshmen returned.

Freshmen *Admission:* 9,518 applied, 5,792 admitted, 927 enrolled. *Average high school GPA:* 3.78. *Test scores:* SAT critical reading scores over 500: 91%; SAT math scores over 500: 92%; SAT writing scores over 500: 85%; ACT scores over 18: 100%; SAT critical reading scores over 600: 39%; SAT math scores over 600: 48%; SAT writing scores over 600: 35%; ACT scores

over 24: 86%; SAT critical reading scores over 700: 6%; SAT math scores over 700: 7%; SAT writing scores over 700: 5%; ACT scores over 30: 32%.

Faculty *Total:* 475, 71% full-time, 60% with terminal degrees. *Student/faculty ratio:* 11:1.

Academics *Calendar:* semesters. *Degrees:* associate, bachelor's, master's, and doctoral. *Special study options:* adult/continuing education programs, advanced placement credit, cooperative education, double majors, honors programs, independent study, internships, off-campus study, part-time degree program, services for LD students, student-designed majors, study abroad, summer session for credit. *ROTC:* Army (b), Air Force (c). *Unusual degree programs:* 3-2 engineering with Indiana University-Purdue University Indianapolis.

Computers on Campus 450 computers/terminals are available on campus for general student use. Students can access the following: campus intranet, computer help desk, free student e-mail accounts, online (class) grades, online (class) registration, online (class) schedules. Campuswide network is available. 100% of college-owned or -operated housing units are wired for high-speed Internet access. Wireless service is available via entire campus.

Student Life *Housing:* on-campus residence required through junior year. *Options:* coed, women-only. Campus housing is university owned. Freshman campus housing is guaranteed. *Activities and organizations:* drama/theater group, student-run newspaper, television station, choral group, marching band, Dawg Pound, Student Government Association, Academic Service Honoraries, Alpha Phi Omega, Mortar Board, national fraternities, national sororities. *Campus security:* 24-hour emergency response devices and patrols, late-night transport/escort service, controlled dormitory access. *Student services:* health clinic, personal/psychological counseling.

Athletics Member NCAA. All Division I except football (Division III). *Intercollegiate sports:* baseball M(s), basketball M(s)/W(s), crew M(c)/W(c), cross-country running M(s)/W(s), football M, golf M(s)/W(s), ice hockey M(c), rugby M(c), soccer M(s)/W(s), softball W(s), swimming and diving W, tennis M(s)/W(s), track and field M/W, volleyball W(s). *Intramural sports:* badminton M/W, baseball M, basketball M/W, bowling M/W, football M, soccer M/W, softball M/W, swimming and diving M/W, table tennis M/W, tennis M/W, track and field M/W, volleyball M/W, weight lifting M/W.

Standardized Tests *Required:* SAT or ACT (for admission).

Costs (2011–12) *Comprehensive fee:* $42,548 includes full-time tuition ($31,110), mandatory fees ($838), and room and board ($10,600). Full-time tuition and fees vary according to course load, degree level, and program. Part-time tuition: $1310 per credit hour. Part-time tuition and fees vary according to course load, degree level, and program. *College room only:* $5190. Room and board charges vary according to housing facility. *Payment plan:* installment. *Waivers:* employees or children of employees.

Financial Aid Of all full-time matriculated undergraduates who enrolled in 2011, 3,650 applied for aid, 2,676 were judged to have need, 438 had their need fully met. 269 Federal Work-Study jobs (averaging $1392). In 2011, 869 non-need-based awards were made. *Average percent of need met:* 73%. *Average financial aid package:* $22,485. *Average need-based loan:* $5272. *Average need-based gift aid:* $17,705. *Average non-need-based aid:* $11,231. *Average indebtedness upon graduation:* $36,925.

Applying *Options:* electronic application, early action, deferred entrance. *Application fee:* $35. *Required:* essay or personal statement, high school transcript, 1 letter of recommendation. *Required for some:* Audition/interview/portfolio required for applicants to JCFA. Four years of math and science STRONGLY recommended for students interested in COPHS majors and natural sciences. *Recommended:* 1 letter of recommendation. *Application deadlines:* rolling (freshmen), rolling (out-of-state freshmen), 8/15 (transfers), 11/1 (early action). *Notification:* continuous (freshmen), continuous (out-of-state freshmen), continuous (transfers), 12/15 (early action).

Freshman Application Contact Mr. Scott Ham, Director of Admissions, Butler University, 4600 Sunset Avenue, Indianapolis, IN 46208-3485. *Phone:* 317-940-8100. *Toll-free phone:* 888-940-8100. *Fax:* 317-940-8150. *E-mail:* admission@butler.edu. *Web site:* http://www.butler.edu/.

Calumet College of Saint Joseph

Whiting, Indiana

- **Independent Roman Catholic** comprehensive, founded 1951
- **Urban** 25-acre campus with easy access to Chicago
- **Endowment** $3.6 million
- **Coed** 980 undergraduate students, 52% full-time, 49% women, 51% men
- **Noncompetitive** entrance level, 40% of applicants were admitted

Undergraduates 508 full-time, 472 part-time. Students come from 2 states and territories; 1% are from out of state; 25% Black or African American, non-Hispanic/Latino; 30% Hispanic/Latino; 0.7% Asian, non-Hispanic/Latino; 0.4% American Indian or Alaska Native, non-Hispanic/Latino; 8% transferred in. *Retention:* 69% of full-time freshmen returned.

Freshmen *Admission:* 576 applied, 228 admitted, 120 enrolled. *Average high school GPA:* 2.45. *Test scores:* SAT critical reading scores over 500: 10%; SAT math scores over 500: 8%; SAT writing scores over 500: 4%; ACT scores over 18: 40%; SAT critical reading scores over 600: 3%; SAT writing scores over 600: 2%; ACT scores over 24: 3%; SAT critical reading scores over 700: 3%.

Faculty *Total:* 50, 68% full-time, 50% with terminal degrees. *Student/faculty ratio:* 11:1.

Academics *Calendar:* semesters. *Degrees:* certificates, associate, bachelor's, and master's. *Special study options:* academic remediation for entering students, accelerated degree program, adult/continuing education programs, advanced placement credit, cooperative education, distance learning, double majors, external degree program, independent study, internships, part-time degree program, services for LD students, summer session for credit.

Computers on Campus 132 computers/terminals are available on campus for general student use. Students can access the following: computer help desk, free student e-mail accounts, online (class) grades, online (class) registration, online (class) schedules. Campuswide network is available. Wireless service is available via classrooms, libraries, student centers.

Student Life *Housing:* college housing not available. *Activities and organizations:* drama/theater group, student-run newspaper, Student Government, Los Amigos Hispanic Club, Criminal Justice Club, Drama Club, Black Student Union, national fraternities, national sororities. *Campus security:* day and night security. *Student services:* personal/psychological counseling.

Athletics Member NAIA. *Intercollegiate sports:* baseball M, basketball M/W, bowling M/W, cross-country running M/W, golf M, soccer M/W, softball W, tennis M/W, track and field M/W, volleyball W, wrestling M.

Standardized Tests *Required for some:* ACT COMPASS. *Recommended:* SAT or ACT (for admission).

Costs (2011–12) *Tuition:* $14,680 full-time, $465 per credit hour part-time. Full-time tuition and fees vary according to course load and program. Part-time tuition and fees vary according to course load and program. *Required fees:* $200 full-time, $100 per term part-time. *Payment plan:* installment. *Waivers:* children of alumni, senior citizens, and employees or children of employees.

Financial Aid Of all full-time matriculated undergraduates who enrolled in 2011, 444 applied for aid, 409 were judged to have need, 17 had their need fully met. 27 Federal Work-Study jobs (averaging $2003). In 2011, 14 non-need-based awards were made. *Average percent of need met:* 66%. *Average financial aid package:* $12,475. *Average need-based loan:* $2033. *Average need-based gift aid:* $7962. *Average non-need-based aid:* $3110. *Average indebtedness upon graduation:* $24,215.

Applying *Options:* electronic application, deferred entrance. *Required:* high school transcript. *Required for some:* essay or personal statement, interview. *Recommended:* minimum 2.0 GPA. *Application deadlines:* rolling (freshmen), rolling (out-of-state freshmen), rolling (transfers). *Notification:* continuous (transfers).

Freshman Application Contact Miss Rebecca Leevey, Assistant Director of Recruitment and Enrollment, Calumet College of Saint Joseph, 2400 New York Avenue, Whiting, IN 46394. *Phone:* 219-473-4218. *Toll-free phone:* 877-700-9100. *Fax:* 219-473-4336. *E-mail:* admissions@ccsj.edu. *Web site:* http://www.ccsj.edu/.

Crossroads Bible College

Indianapolis, Indiana

- **Independent Baptist** 4-year, founded 1980
- **Urban** 6-acre campus with easy access to Indianapolis
- **Coed** 232 undergraduate students, 55% full-time, 56% women, 44% men
- **Noncompetitive** entrance level, 95% of applicants were admitted

Undergraduates 127 full-time, 105 part-time. Students come from 12 states and territories; 7 other countries; 9% are from out of state; 55% Black or African American, non-Hispanic/Latino; 2% Hispanic/Latino; 0.4% Asian, non-Hispanic/Latino; 0.4% Native Hawaiian or other Pacific Islander, non-Hispanic/Latino; 0.4% American Indian or Alaska Native, non-Hispanic/Latino; 0.4% Race/ethnicity unknown; 22% transferred in; 5% live on campus. *Retention:* 45% of full-time freshmen returned.

Freshmen *Admission:* 42 applied, 40 admitted, 27 enrolled. *Average high school GPA:* 2.75.

Faculty *Total:* 35, 17% full-time, 20% with terminal degrees. *Student/faculty ratio:* 7:1.

Academics *Calendar:* semesters. *Degrees:* certificates, associate, and bachelor's. *Special study options:* academic remediation for entering students, accelerated degree program, adult/continuing education programs, cooperative education, distance learning, double majors, external degree program, independent study, internships, part-time degree program, summer session for credit.

Computers on Campus 15 computers/terminals are available on campus for general student use. Students can access the following: campus intranet, free student e-mail accounts, online (class) grades, online (class) registration,

online (class) schedules. Campuswide network is available. Wireless service is available via entire campus.

Student Life *Housing options:* men-only, women-only. Campus housing is leased by the school. *Activities and organizations:* choral group. *Campus security:* 24-hour emergency response devices, student patrols, late-night transport/escort service. *Student services:* personal/psychological counseling.

Costs (2012–13) *Tuition:* $9480 full-time, $395 per credit hour part-time. *Required fees:* $370 full-time. *Room only:* $3400. *Payment plan:* installment. *Waivers:* employees or children of employees.

Financial Aid Of all full-time matriculated undergraduates who enrolled in 2010, 133 applied for aid, 133 were judged to have need, 130 had their need fully met. 14 Federal Work-Study jobs (averaging $1509). *Average percent of need met:* 98%. *Average financial aid package:* $7945. *Average need-based loan:* $5500. *Average need-based gift aid:* $5662. *Average indebtedness upon graduation:* $9618. *Financial aid deadline:* 6/30.

Applying *Options:* electronic application, deferred entrance. *Application fee:* $10. *Required:* essay or personal statement, high school transcript. *Required for some:* interview. *Application deadlines:* 8/8 (freshmen), rolling (out-of-state freshmen), 8/8 (transfers). *Notification:* continuous (freshmen), continuous (out-of-state freshmen), continuous (transfers).

Freshman Application Contact Michael Garrison, Admissions Counselor, Crossroads Bible College, 601 North Shortridge Road, Indianapolis, IN 46219. *Phone:* 317-789-8266. *Toll-free phone:* 800-822-3119. *E-mail:* admissions@crossroads.edu. *Web site:* http://www.crossroads.edu/.

DePauw University
Greencastle, Indiana

- **Independent** 4-year, founded 1837, affiliated with United Methodist Church
- **Small-town** 655-acre campus with easy access to Indianapolis
- **Coed** 2,352 undergraduate students, 99% full-time, 56% women, 44% men
- **Moderately difficult** entrance level, 57% of applicants were admitted

Undergraduates 2,331 full-time, 21 part-time. 59% are from out of state; 7% Black or African American, non-Hispanic/Latino; 4% Hispanic/Latino; 3% Asian, non-Hispanic/Latino; 0.3% American Indian or Alaska Native, non-Hispanic/Latino; 4% Two or more races, non-Hispanic/Latino; 2% Race/ethnicity unknown; 11% international; 0.5% transferred in; 94% live on campus. *Retention:* 92% of full-time freshmen returned.

Freshmen *Admission:* 5,131 applied, 2,950 admitted, 584 enrolled. *Average high school GPA:* 3.55. *Test scores:* SAT critical reading scores over 500: 88%; SAT math scores over 500: 94%; ACT scores over 18: 100%; SAT critical reading scores over 600: 50%; SAT math scores over 600: 68%; ACT scores over 24: 79%; SAT critical reading scores over 700: 14%; SAT math scores over 700: 21%; ACT scores over 30: 25%.

Faculty *Total:* 275, 81% full-time, 83% with terminal degrees. *Student/faculty ratio:* 10:1.

Academics *Calendar:* 4-1-4. *Degree:* bachelor's. *Special study options:* part-time degree program. *ROTC:* Army (c), Air Force (c). *Unusual degree programs:* 3-2 engineering with Columbia University, Washington University in St. Louis.

Computers on Campus Students can access the following: online (class) registration. Campuswide network is available.

Student Life *Housing:* on-campus residence required through senior year. *Options:* coed, disabled students. Campus housing is university owned. Freshman campus housing is guaranteed. *Activities and organizations:* drama/theater group, student-run newspaper, radio and television station, choral group, national fraternities, national sororities. *Campus security:* 24-hour emergency response devices and patrols, student patrols, late-night transport/escort service, controlled dormitory access. *Student services:* health clinic, personal/psychological counseling, women's center.

Athletics Member NCAA. All Division III. *Intercollegiate sports:* baseball M, basketball M/W, cheerleading M(c)/W(c), crew M(c)/W(c), cross-country running M/W, field hockey W, football M, golf M/W, rugby M(c), soccer M/W, softball W, swimming and diving M/W, tennis M/W, track and field M/W, volleyball W. *Intramural sports:* badminton M/W, basketball M/W, bowling M/W, football M/W, golf M, racquetball M/W, soccer M/W, softball M/W, table tennis M/W, tennis M/W, ultimate Frisbee M/W, volleyball M/W.

Standardized Tests *Required:* SAT or ACT (for admission).

Costs (2011–12) *Comprehensive fee:* $46,700 includes full-time tuition ($36,500), mandatory fees ($470), and room and board ($9730). Part-time tuition: $1141 per credit hour. *Room and board:* Room and board charges vary according to board plan. *Payment plan:* installment. *Waivers:* employees or children of employees.

Financial Aid Of all full-time matriculated undergraduates who enrolled in 2011, 1,509 applied for aid, 1,318 were judged to have need, 377 had their need fully met. 518 Federal Work-Study jobs (averaging $1658). 260 state and

other part-time jobs (averaging $2800). In 2011, 948 non-need-based awards were made. *Average percent of need met:* 87%. *Average financial aid package:* $29,804. *Average need-based loan:* $4284. *Average need-based gift aid:* $25,718. *Average non-need-based aid:* $16,638. *Average indebtedness upon graduation:* $19,522. *Financial aid deadline:* 3/1.

Applying *Options:* electronic application, early admission, early decision, early action, deferred entrance. *Application fee:* $40. *Required:* essay or personal statement, high school transcript, 1 letter of recommendation. *Recommended:* interview. *Application deadlines:* 2/1 (freshmen), 3/1 (transfers), 12/1 (early action). *Early decision deadline:* 11/1. *Notification:* 4/1 (transfers), 1/1 (early decision), 1/31 (early action).

Freshman Application Contact Earl Macam, Director of Admission, DePauw University, 313 South Locust Street, Greencastle, IN 46135. *Phone:* 765-658-4006. *Toll-free phone:* 800-447-2495. *Fax:* 765-658-4007. *E-mail:* emacam@depauw.edu. *Web site:* http://www.depauw.edu/.

DeVry University
Indianapolis, Indiana

Freshman Application Contact DeVry University, 9100 Keystone Crossing, Suite 350, Indianapolis, IN 46240-2158. *Toll-free phone:* 866-338-7941. *Web site:* http://www.devry.edu/.

DeVry University
Merrillville, Indiana

Admissions Office Contact DeVry University, Twin Towers, 1000 East 80th Place, Suite 222 Mall, Merrillville, IN 46410-5673. *Toll-free phone:* 866-338-7941. *Web site:* http://www.devry.edu/.

Earlham College
Richmond, Indiana

- **Independent** comprehensive, founded 1847, affiliated with Society of Friends
- **Small-town** 800-acre campus with easy access to Cincinnati, Indianapolis, and Dayton
- **Endowment** $335.5 million
- **Coed** 1,063 undergraduate students, 99% full-time, 57% women, 43% men
- **Very difficult** entrance level, 68% of applicants were admitted

Undergraduates 1,052 full-time, 11 part-time. Students come from 42 states and territories; 75 other countries; 78% are from out of state; 8% Black or African American, non-Hispanic/Latino; 4% Hispanic/Latino; 2% Asian, non-Hispanic/Latino; 0.2% Native Hawaiian or other Pacific Islander, non-Hispanic/Latino; 0.8% American Indian or Alaska Native, non-Hispanic/Latino; 1% Two or more races, non-Hispanic/Latino; 12% Race/ethnicity unknown; 18% international; 2% transferred in; 96% live on campus. *Retention:* 86% of full-time freshmen returned.

Freshmen *Admission:* 1,620 applied, 1,109 admitted, 234 enrolled. *Average high school GPA:* 3.4. *Test scores:* SAT critical reading scores over 500: 73%; SAT math scores over 500: 77%; SAT writing scores over 500: 73%; ACT scores over 18: 98%; SAT critical reading scores over 600: 48%; SAT math scores over 600: 38%; SAT writing scores over 600: 36%; ACT scores over 24: 77%; SAT critical reading scores over 700: 13%; SAT math scores over 700: 5%; SAT writing scores over 700: 11%; ACT scores over 30: 25%.

Faculty *Total:* 107, 87% full-time, 90% with terminal degrees. *Student/faculty ratio:* 11:1.

Academics *Calendar:* semesters. *Degrees:* bachelor's and master's. *Special study options:* accelerated degree program, advanced placement credit, double majors, English as a second language, independent study, internships, off-campus study, services for LD students, student-designed majors, study abroad. *Unusual degree programs:* 3-2 engineering with Columbia University, University of Michigan, Rensselaer Polytechnic Institute; forestry with Duke University; nursing with Case Western Reserve University, Washington University in St. Louis, Emory University, Columbia University.

Computers on Campus 175 computers/terminals and 30 ports are available on campus for general student use. Students can access the following: campus intranet, computer help desk, free student e-mail accounts, online (class) grades, online (class) registration, online (class) schedules. Campuswide network is available. 100% of college-owned or -operated housing units are wired for high-speed Internet access. Wireless service is available via classrooms, computer centers, computer labs, learning centers, libraries, student centers.

Student Life *Housing:* on-campus residence required through senior year. *Options:* coed, men-only, women-only, disabled students. Campus housing is university owned. Freshman campus housing is guaranteed. *Activities and organizations:* drama/theater group, student-run newspaper, radio station, cho-

ral group, Gospel Revelations Chorus, Dance Alloy, club sports, student government, Black Student Union. *Campus security:* 24-hour emergency response devices and patrols, student patrols, late-night transport/escort service, controlled dormitory access. *Student services:* health clinic, personal/psychological counseling, women's center.

Athletics Member NCAA. All Division III. *Intercollegiate sports:* baseball M, basketball M/W, cheerleading W(c), cross-country running M/W, equestrian sports W(c), field hockey W, football M, lacrosse M(c)/W(c), rugby M(c)/W(c), soccer M/W, tennis M/W, track and field M/W, ultimate Frisbee M(c)/W(c), volleyball M(c)/W. *Intramural sports:* basketball M/W, bowling M/W, football M, racquetball M/W, soccer M/W.

Costs (2011–12) *Comprehensive fee:* $45,854 includes full-time tuition ($37,500), mandatory fees ($784), and room and board ($7570). Part-time tuition: $1250 per credit. *College room only:* $3800. Room and board charges vary according to board plan. *Payment plans:* tuition prepayment, installment, deferred payment. *Waivers:* employees or children of employees.

Financial Aid Of all full-time matriculated undergraduates who enrolled in 2011, 713 applied for aid, 659 were judged to have need, 321 had their need fully met. In 2011, 109 non-need-based awards were made. *Average percent of need met:* 96%. *Average financial aid package:* $33,818. *Average need-based loan:* $5217. *Average need-based gift aid:* $21,950. *Average non-need-based aid:* $8811. *Average indebtedness upon graduation:* $24,018. *Financial aid deadline:* 3/1.

Applying *Options:* electronic application, early admission, early decision, early action, deferred entrance. *Required:* essay or personal statement, high school transcript, minimum 2.8 GPA, 2 letters of recommendation. *Recommended:* interview. *Application deadlines:* 2/15 (freshmen), 4/1 (transfers), 1/1 (early action). *Early decision deadline:* 12/1. *Notification:* 3/15 (freshmen), 4/15 (transfers), 12/15 (early decision), 2/1 (early action).

Freshman Application Contact Ms. Nancy Sinex, Director of Admissions, Earlham College, 801 National Road West, Richmond, IN 47374. *Phone:* 765-983-1600. *Toll-free phone:* 800-327-5426. *Fax:* 765-983-1560. *E-mail:* admission@earlham.edu. *Web site:* http://www.earlham.edu/.

See page 1338 for the College Close-Up.

Franklin College
Franklin, Indiana

- **Independent** 4-year, founded 1834, affiliated with American Baptist Churches in the U.S.A.
- **Small-town** 187-acre campus with easy access to Indianapolis
- **Endowment** $80.1 million
- **Coed** 1,051 undergraduate students, 95% full-time, 48% women, 52% men
- **Moderately difficult** entrance level, 60% of applicants were admitted

Undergraduates 996 full-time, 55 part-time. Students come from 20 states and territories; 4 other countries; 3% are from out of state; 5% Black or African American, non-Hispanic/Latino; 0.4% Hispanic/Latino; 0.2% Asian, non-Hispanic/Latino; 0.1% Native Hawaiian or other Pacific Islander, non-Hispanic/Latino; 0.2% American Indian or Alaska Native, non-Hispanic/Latino; 2% Two or more races, non-Hispanic/Latino; 8% Race/ethnicity unknown; 0.4% international; 3% transferred in; 69% live on campus. *Retention:* 77% of full-time freshmen returned.

Freshmen *Admission:* 1,926 applied, 1,147 admitted, 275 enrolled. *Average high school GPA:* 3.4. *Test scores:* SAT critical reading scores over 500: 44%; SAT math scores over 500: 56%; SAT writing scores over 500: 38%; ACT scores over 18: 96%; SAT critical reading scores over 600: 9%; SAT math scores over 600: 14%; SAT writing scores over 600: 7%; ACT scores over 24: 33%; ACT scores over 30: 3%.

Faculty *Total:* 111, 68% full-time, 64% with terminal degrees. *Student/faculty ratio:* 13:1.

Academics *Calendar:* 4-1-4. *Degree:* bachelor's. *Special study options:* academic remediation for entering students, advanced placement credit, cooperative education, double majors, independent study, internships, off-campus study, part-time degree program, services for LD students, study abroad, summer session for credit. *ROTC:* Army (c). *Unusual degree programs:* 3-2 engineering with Indiana University - Purdue University Indianapolis.

Computers on Campus 150 computers/terminals are available on campus for general student use. Students can access the following: online (class) registration. Campuswide network is available. Wireless service is available via classrooms, computer centers, computer labs, learning centers, libraries, student centers.

Student Life *Housing:* on-campus residence required through junior year. *Options:* coed. Campus housing is university owned. Freshman campus housing is guaranteed. *Activities and organizations:* drama/theater group, student-

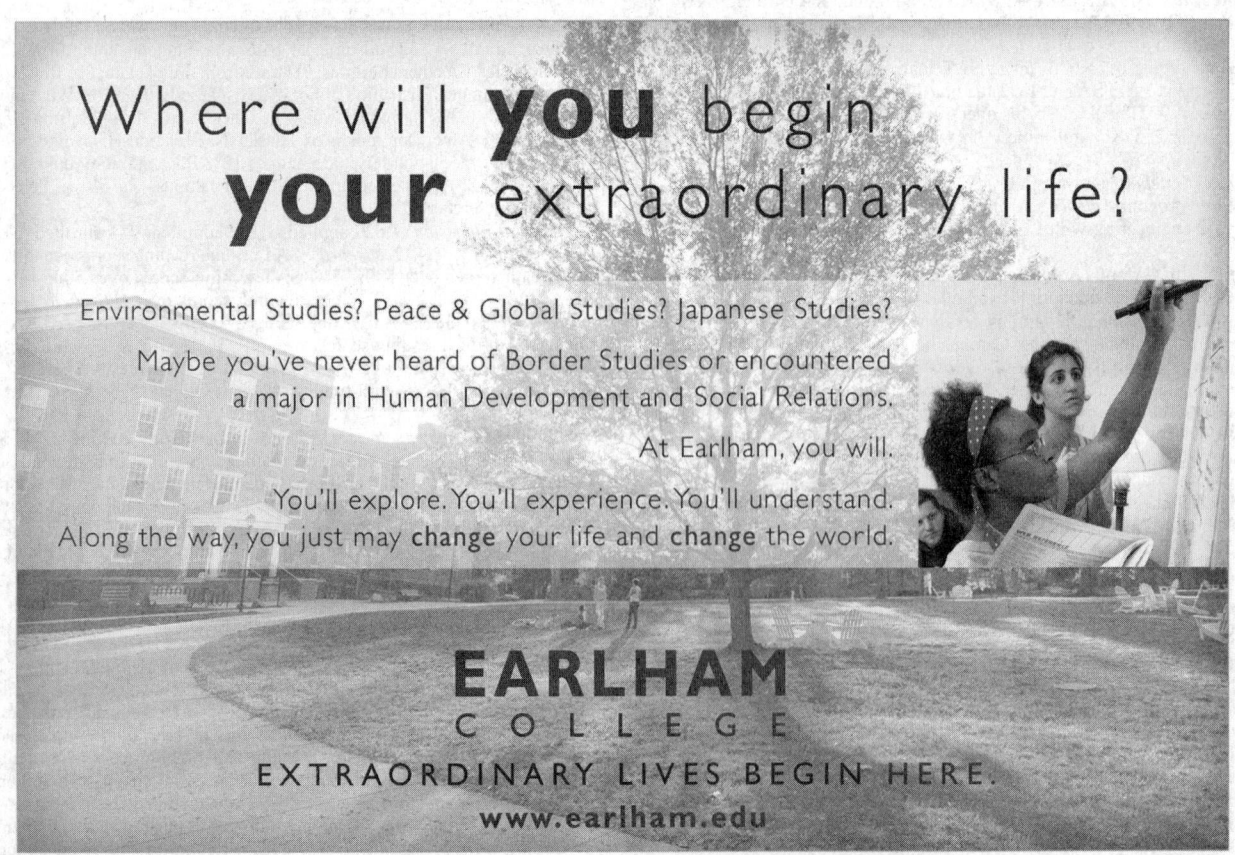

run newspaper, radio and television station, choral group, FLOW, FC Volunteers, Student Entertainment Board, Student Congress, national fraternities, national sororities. *Campus security:* 24-hour emergency response devices and patrols, late-night transport/escort service. *Student services:* health clinic, personal/psychological counseling.

Athletics Member NCAA. All Division III. *Intercollegiate sports:* baseball M, basketball M/W, cross-country running M/W, football M, golf M/W, soccer M/W, softball W, tennis M/W, track and field M/W, volleyball W. *Intramural sports:* basketball M/W, softball W, volleyball W.

Standardized Tests *Required:* SAT or ACT (for admission).

Costs (2011–12) *Comprehensive fee:* $33,515 includes full-time tuition ($25,680), mandatory fees ($185), and room and board ($7650). Part-time tuition and fees vary according to course load. *College room only:* $4540. Room and board charges vary according to board plan and housing facility. *Payment plan:* installment. *Waivers:* senior citizens and employees or children of employees.

Financial Aid Of all full-time matriculated undergraduates who enrolled in 2009, 1,034 applied for aid, 912 were judged to have need, 144 had their need fully met. 328 Federal Work-Study jobs (averaging $863). 31 state and other part-time jobs (averaging $637). In 2009, 158 non-need-based awards were made. *Average percent of need met:* 81%. *Average financial aid package:* $18,496. *Average need-based loan:* $5051. *Average need-based gift aid:* $14,213. *Average non-need-based aid:* $8197. *Average indebtedness upon graduation:* $29,387.

Applying *Options:* electronic application, deferred entrance. *Application fee:* $30. *Required:* essay or personal statement, high school transcript. *Required for some:* interview. *Application deadline:* rolling (freshmen). *Notification:* continuous (freshmen), continuous (transfers).

Freshman Application Contact Ms. Alan Hill, Director of Admissions, Franklin College, 101 Branigin Boulevard, Franklin, IN 46131-2623. *Phone:* 317-738-8062. *Toll-free phone:* 800-852-0232. *Fax:* 317-738-8274. *E-mail:* jacosta@franklincollege.edu. *Web site:* http://www.franklincollege.edu/.

See page 1338 for the College Close-Up.

Goshen College
Goshen, Indiana

- **Independent Mennonite** comprehensive, founded 1894
- **Small-town** 135-acre campus
- **Endowment** $99.3 million
- **Coed** 893 undergraduate students, 91% full-time, 56% women, 44% men
- **Moderately difficult** entrance level, 60% of applicants were admitted

Undergraduates 814 full-time, 79 part-time. Students come from 36 states and territories; 30 other countries; 47% are from out of state; 3% Black or African American, non-Hispanic/Latino; 8% Hispanic/Latino; 1% Asian, non-Hispanic/Latino; 0.1% American Indian or Alaska Native, non-Hispanic/Latino; 1% Two or more races, non-Hispanic/Latino; 1% Race/ethnicity unknown; 8% international; 6% transferred in; 70% live on campus. *Retention:* 79% of full-time freshmen returned.

Freshmen *Admission:* 616 applied, 368 admitted, 168 enrolled. *Average high school GPA:* 3.5. *Test scores:* SAT critical reading scores over 500: 76%; SAT math scores over 500: 75%; SAT writing scores over 500: 67%; ACT scores over 18: 97%; SAT critical reading scores over 600: 36%; SAT math scores over 600: 37%; SAT writing scores over 600: 34%; ACT scores over 24: 66%; SAT critical reading scores over 700: 8%; SAT math scores over 700: 12%; SAT writing scores over 700: 8%; ACT scores over 30: 9%.

Faculty *Total:* 109, 63% full-time, 43% with terminal degrees. *Student/faculty ratio:* 12:1.

Academics *Calendar:* semesters. *Degrees:* certificates, bachelor's, and master's. *Special study options:* academic remediation for entering students, accelerated degree program, adult/continuing education programs, advanced placement credit, distance learning, double majors, independent study, internships, off-campus study, part-time degree program, services for LD students, student-designed majors, study abroad, summer session for credit. *Unusual degree programs:* 3-2 engineering with Case Western Reserve University, University of Illinois at Urbana-Champaign, University of Notre Dame, Washington University in St. Louis.

Computers on Campus 160 computers/terminals and 2,000 ports are available on campus for general student use. Students can access the following: campus intranet, computer help desk, free student e-mail accounts, online (class) grades, online (class) registration, online (class) schedules. Campus-wide network is available. 100% of college-owned or -operated housing units are wired for high-speed Internet access. Wireless service is available via entire campus.

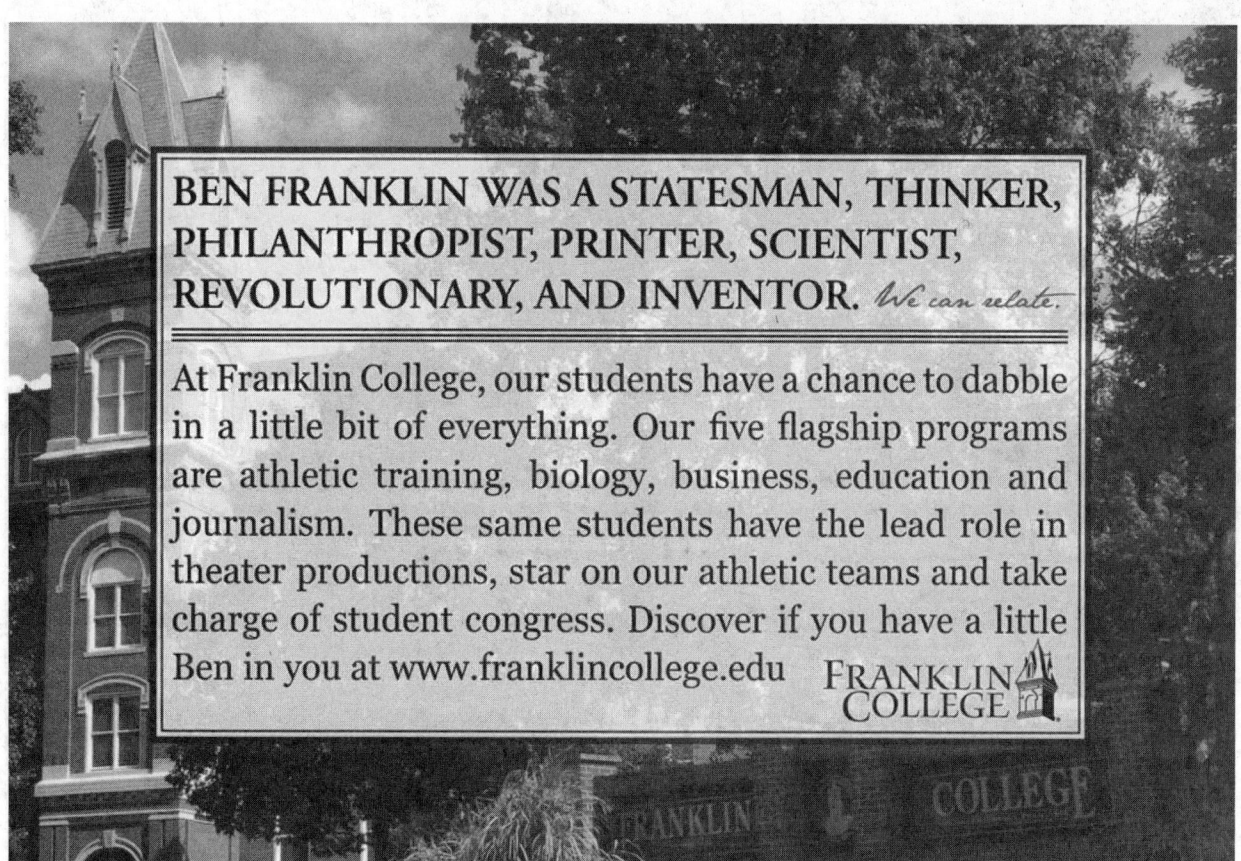

Student Life *Housing:* on-campus residence required through senior year. *Options:* coed, men-only, women-only, disabled students. Campus housing is university owned. Freshman campus housing is guaranteed. *Activities and organizations:* drama/theater group, student-run newspaper, radio and television station, choral group, Business Club, Black Student Union, Non-Traditional Student Network, Goshen Student Women's Organization, International Student Club. *Campus security:* 24-hour emergency response devices and patrols, late-night transport/escort service. *Student services:* health clinic, personal/psychological counseling, women's center.

Athletics Member NAIA. *Intercollegiate sports:* baseball M(s), basketball M(s)/W(s), cross-country running M(s)/W(s), golf M(s)/W(s), soccer M(s)/W(s), softball W(s), tennis M(s)/W(s), track and field M(s)/W(s), volleyball W(s). *Intramural sports:* badminton M/W, baseball M, basketball M/W, cross-country running M/W, racquetball M/W, skiing (cross-country) M/W, soccer M/W, softball W, swimming and diving M/W, table tennis M/W, tennis M/W, volleyball M/W, weight lifting M/W.

Standardized Tests *Required:* SAT or ACT (for admission).

Costs (2012–13) *Comprehensive fee:* $35,900 includes full-time tuition ($26,900) and room and board ($9000). Full-time tuition and fees vary according to degree level. Part-time tuition: $1120 per credit hour. Part-time tuition and fees vary according to course load and degree level. *College room only:* $4750. Room and board charges vary according to board plan and housing facility. *Waivers:* employees or children of employees.

Financial Aid Of all full-time matriculated undergraduates who enrolled in 2010, 749 applied for aid, 686 were judged to have need, 106 had their need fully met. 250 Federal Work-Study jobs (averaging $800). 50 state and other part-time jobs (averaging $995). In 2010, 198 non-need-based awards were made. *Average percent of need met:* 80%. *Average financial aid package:* $18,798. *Average need-based loan:* $4480. *Average need-based gift aid:* $15,544. *Average non-need-based aid:* $9838. *Average indebtedness upon graduation:* $15,416.

Applying *Options:* electronic application, deferred entrance. *Application fee:* $25. *Required:* essay or personal statement, high school transcript, minimum 2.0 GPA, 2 letters of recommendation. *Recommended:* minimum 2.6 GPA, interview, rank in upper 50% of high school class. *Application deadlines:* 8/15 (freshmen), 8/15 (transfers). *Notification:* continuous (freshmen), continuous (transfers).

Freshman Application Contact Dr. Dan Koop Liechty, Director of Admission, Goshen College, 1700 South Main Street, Goshen, IN 46526-4794. *Phone:* 574-535-7535. *Toll-free phone:* 800-348-7422. *Fax:* 574-535-7609. *E-mail:* dankl@goshen.edu. *Web site:* http://www.goshen.edu/.

Grace College
Winona Lake, Indiana

- **Independent** comprehensive, founded 1948, affiliated with Fellowship of Grace Brethren Churches
- **Small-town** 160-acre campus
- **Endowment** $8.3 million
- **Coed** 1,310 undergraduate students, 82% full-time, 57% women, 43% men
- **Moderately difficult** entrance level, 95% of applicants were admitted

Undergraduates 1,078 full-time, 232 part-time. Students come from 34 states and territories; 5 other countries; 42% are from out of state; 4% Black or African American, non-Hispanic/Latino; 3% Hispanic/Latino; 1% Asian, non-Hispanic/Latino; 0.2% Native Hawaiian or other Pacific Islander, non-Hispanic/Latino; 0.3% American Indian or Alaska Native, non-Hispanic/Latino; 2% Two or more races, non-Hispanic/Latino; 3% Race/ethnicity unknown; 1% international; 4% transferred in; 61% live on campus. *Retention:* 79% of full-time freshmen returned.

Freshmen *Admission:* 1,821 applied, 1,731 admitted, 293 enrolled. *Average high school GPA:* 3.47. *Test scores:* SAT critical reading scores over 500: 57%; SAT math scores over 500: 51%; ACT scores over 18: 94%; SAT critical reading scores over 600: 18%; SAT math scores over 600: 17%; ACT scores over 24: 53%; SAT critical reading scores over 700: 1%; SAT math scores over 700: 3%; ACT scores over 30: 14%.

Faculty *Total:* 85, 52% full-time, 41% with terminal degrees. *Student/faculty ratio:* 27:1.

Academics *Calendar:* semesters. *Degrees:* certificates, diplomas, associate, bachelor's, master's, and doctoral. *Special study options:* academic remediation for entering students, accelerated degree program, adult/continuing education programs, advanced placement credit, cooperative education, distance learning, double majors, honors programs, independent study, internships, off-campus study, part-time degree program, services for LD students, study abroad, summer session for credit.

Computers on Campus 150 computers/terminals are available on campus for general student use. Students can access the following: campus intranet, computer help desk, free student e-mail accounts, online (class) grades, online (class) registration, online (class) schedules. Campuswide network is available. 100% of college-owned or -operated housing units are wired for high-speed Internet access. Wireless service is available via entire campus.

Student Life *Housing:* on-campus residence required through senior year. *Options:* men-only, women-only. Campus housing is university owned. Freshman campus housing is guaranteed. *Activities and organizations:* drama/theater group, student-run newspaper, choral group, Grace Ministries in Action, Student Activities Board, Funfest, women's ministries, Breakout. *Campus security:* student patrols, late-night transport/escort service, controlled dormitory access, evening patrols by trained security personnel. *Student services:* health clinic, personal/psychological counseling.

Athletics Member NAIA, NCCAA. *Intercollegiate sports:* baseball M(s), basketball M(s)/W(s), cheerleading M(s)/W(s), cross-country running M(s)/W(s), golf M(s), soccer M(s)/W(s), softball W(s), tennis M(s)/W(s), track and field M(s)/W(s), volleyball W(s). *Intramural sports:* basketball M/W, soccer M/W, volleyball M/W.

Standardized Tests *Required:* SAT or ACT (for admission).

Costs (2011–12) *Comprehensive fee:* $29,760 includes full-time tuition ($22,546) and room and board ($7214). Full-time tuition and fees vary according to course load, degree level, location, and program. Part-time tuition: $750 per credit hour. Part-time tuition and fees vary according to course load, degree level, location, and program. *College room only:* $3774. Room and board charges vary according to board plan and housing facility. *Payment plan:* installment. *Waivers:* senior citizens and employees or children of employees.

Financial Aid Of all full-time matriculated undergraduates who enrolled in 2009, 1,276 applied for aid, 1,273 were judged to have need. *Average financial aid package:* $11,338.

Applying *Options:* electronic application, early admission, early action, deferred entrance. *Application fee:* $30. *Required:* essay or personal statement, high school transcript, minimum 2.3 GPA, 2 letters of recommendation, personal statement of faith. *Required for some:* interview. *Application deadlines:* 8/1 (freshmen), 8/1 (transfers), 12/1 (early action). *Notification:* 8/15 (freshmen), continuous until 8/15 (transfers).

Freshman Application Contact Mrs. Jessica Hauck, Admissions Office, Grace College, 200 Seminary Drive, Winona Lake, IN 46590. *Phone:* 574-372-5100 Ext. 6008. *Toll-free phone:* 800-54-GRACE. *Fax:* 574-372-5120. *E-mail:* enroll@grace.edu. *Web site:* http://www.grace.edu/.

See page 1346 for the College Close-Up.

Hanover College
Hanover, Indiana

- **Independent Presbyterian** 4-year, founded 1827
- **Rural** 630-acre campus with easy access to Louisville
- **Endowment** $137.3 million
- **Coed** 1,068 undergraduate students, 99% full-time, 55% women, 45% men
- **Moderately difficult** entrance level, 68% of applicants were admitted

Undergraduates 1,061 full-time, 7 part-time. Students come from 25 states and territories; 9 other countries; 35% are from out of state; 5% Black or African American, non-Hispanic/Latino; 2% Hispanic/Latino; 0.7% Asian, non-Hispanic/Latino; 0.1% Native Hawaiian or other Pacific Islander, non-Hispanic/Latino; 0.4% American Indian or Alaska Native, non-Hispanic/Latino; 3% Two or more races, non-Hispanic/Latino; 3% Race/ethnicity unknown; 3% international; 0.9% transferred in; 95% live on campus. *Retention:* 80% of full-time freshmen returned.

Freshmen *Admission:* 3,015 applied, 2,058 admitted, 321 enrolled. *Average high school GPA:* 3.61. *Test scores:* SAT critical reading scores over 500: 79%; SAT math scores over 500: 80%; SAT writing scores over 500: 63%; ACT scores over 18: 100%; SAT critical reading scores over 600: 33%; SAT math scores over 600: 30%; SAT writing scores over 600: 20%; ACT scores over 24: 63%; SAT critical reading scores over 700: 5%; SAT math scores over 700: 4%; SAT writing scores over 700: 3%; ACT scores over 30: 17%.

Faculty *Total:* 100, 94% full-time, 98% with terminal degrees. *Student/faculty ratio:* 12:1.

Academics *Calendar:* 4-4-1. *Degree:* bachelor's. *Special study options:* advanced placement credit, cooperative education, double majors, independent study, internships, off-campus study, services for LD students, student-designed majors, study abroad.

Computers on Campus 120 computers/terminals and 1,550 ports are available on campus for general student use. Students can access the following: campus intranet, computer help desk, free student e-mail accounts, online (class) grades, online (class) registration, online (class) schedules. Campuswide network is available. 100% of college-owned or -operated housing units are wired for high-speed Internet access. Wireless service is available via entire campus.

Student Life *Housing:* on-campus residence required through senior year. *Options:* coed, men-only, women-only. Campus housing is university owned and leased by the school. Freshman campus housing is guaranteed. *Activities and organizations:* drama/theater group, student-run newspaper, radio and television station, choral group, marching band, Student Senate, Campus Crusade

for Christ, Campus Activities Board, People for Peace, Love Out Loud, national fraternities, national sororities. *Campus security:* 24-hour emergency response devices and patrols, late-night transport/escort service, controlled dormitory access. *Student services:* health clinic, personal/psychological counseling.

Athletics Member NCAA. All Division III. *Intercollegiate sports:* baseball M, basketball M/W, cross-country running M/W, football M, golf M/W, lacrosse M, soccer M/W, softball W, tennis M/W, track and field M/W, volleyball W. *Intramural sports:* basketball M/W, football M/W, rugby M(c), soccer M/W, softball M/W, ultimate Frisbee M(c), volleyball M/W.

Standardized Tests *Required:* SAT or ACT (for admission).

Costs (2011–12) *One-time required fee:* $250. *Comprehensive fee:* $37,500 includes full-time tuition ($28,250), mandatory fees ($600), and room and board ($8650). Full-time tuition and fees vary according to reciprocity agreements. Part-time tuition: $3140 per unit. Part-time tuition and fees vary according to course load and reciprocity agreements. *College room only:* $4300. Room and board charges vary according to housing facility and location. *Payment plan:* installment. *Waivers:* senior citizens and employees or children of employees.

Financial Aid Of all full-time matriculated undergraduates who enrolled in 2010, 955 applied for aid, 870 were judged to have need, 208 had their need fully met. 360 Federal Work-Study jobs (averaging $1208). In 2010, 190 non-need-based awards were made. *Average percent of need met:* 85%. *Average financial aid package:* $25,101. *Average need-based loan:* $4780. *Average need-based gift aid:* $20,486. *Average non-need-based aid:* $13,942. *Average indebtedness upon graduation:* $27,410.

Applying *Options:* electronic application, early admission, early action, deferred entrance. *Application fee:* $40. *Required:* essay or personal statement, high school transcript, 1 letter of recommendation. *Recommended:* interview. *Application deadlines:* 3/1 (freshmen), rolling (transfers), 12/1 (early action). *Notification:* continuous (freshmen), continuous (transfers), 12/20 (early action).

Freshman Application Contact Mr. Christopher Gage, Dean of Admission, Hanover College, PO Box 108, Hanover, IN 47243-0108. *Phone:* 812-866-7021. *Toll-free phone:* 800-213-2178. *Fax:* 812-866-7098. *E-mail:* admission@hanover.edu. *Web site:* http://www.hanover.edu/.

Harrison College
Elkhart, Indiana

Freshman Application Contact Matt Brady, Director of Admissions, Harrison College, 56075 Parkway Avenue, Elkhart, IN 46516. *Phone:* 574-522-0397. *Toll-free phone:* 888-544-4422. *E-mail:* matt.brady@harrison.edu. *Web site:* http://www.harrison.edu/.

Harrison College
Evansville, Indiana

Freshman Application Contact Mr. Bryan Barber, Harrison College, 4601 Theater Drive, Evansville, IN 47715. *Phone:* 812-476-6000. *Toll-free phone:* 888-544-4422 (in-state); 888-554-4422 (out-of-state). *Fax:* 812-471-8576. *E-mail:* bryan.barber@harrison.edu. *Web site:* http://www.harrison.edu/.

Harrison College
Fort Wayne, Indiana

Freshman Application Contact Mr. Matt Wallace, Associate Director of Admissions, Harrison College, 6413 North Clinton Street, Fort Wayne, IN 46825. *Phone:* 260-471-7667. *Toll-free phone:* 888-544-4422. *Fax:* 260-471-6918. *E-mail:* matt.wallace@harrison.edu. *Web site:* http://www.harrison.edu/.

Harrison College
Indianapolis, Indiana

- **Proprietary** primarily 2-year, founded 1902
- **Urban** 1-acre campus with easy access to Indianapolis
- **Coed**
- **Moderately difficult** entrance level

Faculty *Student/faculty ratio:* 16:1.

Academics *Calendar:* quarters. *Degrees:* certificates, diplomas, associate, and bachelor's.

Student Life *Campus security:* 24-hour patrols.

Standardized Tests *Required:* Wonderlic Scholastic Level Exam (SLE) (for admission).

Costs (2011–12) *Tuition:* Full-time tuition and fees vary according to course load and program. Part-time tuition and fees vary according to course load and

program. No tuition increase for student's term of enrollment. Tuition ranges from $300 to $400 a credit depending upon program of study. *Required fees:* $435 full-time, $145 per term part-time.
Applying *Options:* electronic application. *Application fee:* $50. *Required:* high school transcript, interview.
Freshman Application Contact Mr. Ted Lukomski, Director of Admissions, Harrison College, 550 East Washington Street, Indianapolis, IN 46204. *Phone:* 317-264-5656. *Toll-free phone:* 888-544-4422. *Fax:* 317-264-5650. *E-mail:* ted.lukomski@ibcschools.edu. *Web site:* http://www.harrison.edu/.

Harrison College
Lafayette, Indiana

- **Proprietary** primarily 2-year
- **Small-town** campus
- **Coed**
- **Moderately difficult** entrance level

Faculty *Student/faculty ratio:* 15:1.
Academics *Calendar:* quarters. *Degrees:* certificates, diplomas, associate, and bachelor's.
Standardized Tests *Required:* Wonderlic Scholastic Level Exam (SLE) (for admission).
Costs (2011–12) *Tuition:* Full-time tuition and fees vary according to course load and program. Part-time tuition and fees vary according to course load and program. No tuition increase for student's term of enrollment. Tuition ranges from $300 to $400 a credit depending upon program of study. *Required fees:* $435 full-time, $145 per term part-time.
Applying *Options:* electronic application. *Application fee:* $50. *Required:* high school transcript, interview.
Freshman Application Contact Ms. Stacy Golleher, Associate Director of Admissions, Harrison College, 4705 Meijer Court, Lafayette, IN 47905. *Phone:* 765-447-9550. *Toll-free phone:* 888-544-4422. *Fax:* 765-447-0868. *E-mail:* stacy.golleher@harrison.edu. *Web site:* http://www.harrison.edu/.

Harrison College
Muncie, Indiana

- **Proprietary** primarily 2-year
- **Small-town** campus
- **Coed, primarily women**
- **Moderately difficult** entrance level

Faculty *Student/faculty ratio:* 16:1.
Academics *Calendar:* quarters. *Degrees:* certificates, diplomas, associate, and bachelor's.
Standardized Tests *Required:* Wonderlic Scholastic Level Exam (SLE) (for admission).
Costs (2011–12) *Tuition:* Full-time tuition and fees vary according to course load and program. Part-time tuition and fees vary according to course load and program. No tuition increase for student's term of enrollment. Tuition ranges from $300 to $400 a credit depending upon program of study. *Required fees:* $435 full-time, $145 per term part-time.
Applying *Options:* electronic application. *Application fee:* $50. *Required:* high school transcript, interview.
Freshman Application Contact Mr. Jeremy Linder, Associate Director of Admissions, Harrison College, Muncie, IN 47303. *Phone:* 765-288-8681. *Toll-free phone:* 888-544-4422. *Fax:* 765-288-8797. *E-mail:* Jeremy.linder@harrison.edu. *Web site:* http://www.harrison.edu/.

Harrison College
Terre Haute, Indiana

Freshman Application Contact Sarah Stultz, Associate Director of Admissions, Harrison College, 1378 South State Road 46, Terre Haute, IN 47803. *Phone:* 812-877-2100. *Toll-free phone:* 888-544-4422. *Fax:* 812-877-4440. *E-mail:* sarah.stultz@harrison.edu. *Web site:* http://www.harrison.edu/.

Holy Cross College
Notre Dame, Indiana

- **Independent Roman Catholic** 4-year, founded 1966
- **Suburban** 150-acre campus with easy access to Chicago, Indianapolis
- **Endowment** $1.4 million
- **Coed** 449 undergraduate students, 96% full-time, 35% women, 65% men
- **Moderately difficult** entrance level, 83% of applicants were admitted

Undergraduates 430 full-time, 19 part-time. Students come from 31 states and territories; 11 other countries; 47% are from out of state; 7% Black or African American, non-Hispanic/Latino; 10% Hispanic/Latino; 0.9% Asian, non-Hispanic/Latino; 0.2% Native Hawaiian or other Pacific Islander, non-Hispanic/Latino; 1% Two or more races, non-Hispanic/Latino; 0.2% Race/ethnicity unknown; 6% international; 8% transferred in; 54% live on campus. *Retention:* 57% of full-time freshmen returned.
Freshmen *Admission:* 387 applied, 322 admitted, 137 enrolled. *Average high school GPA:* 2.94. *Test scores:* SAT critical reading scores over 500: 40%; SAT math scores over 500: 42%; SAT writing scores over 500: 37%; ACT scores over 18: 95%; SAT critical reading scores over 600: 15%; SAT math scores over 600: 11%; SAT writing scores over 600: 8%; ACT scores over 24: 36%; SAT critical reading scores over 700: 2%; SAT math scores over 700: 2%; ACT scores over 30: 2%.
Faculty *Total:* 48, 46% full-time, 27% with terminal degrees. *Student/faculty ratio:* 14:1.
Academics *Calendar:* semesters. *Degrees:* associate and bachelor's. *Special study options:* academic remediation for entering students, advanced placement credit, double majors, English as a second language, freshman honors college, honors programs, independent study, internships, off-campus study, student-designed majors, study abroad, summer session for credit. *ROTC:* Army (c), Air Force (c).
Computers on Campus 91 computers/terminals are available on campus for general student use. Students can access the following: campus intranet, free student e-mail accounts, online (class) registration, online (class) schedules. Campuswide network is available. 100% of college-owned or -operated housing units are wired for high-speed Internet access. Wireless service is available via entire campus.
Student Life *Housing options:* men-only, women-only, disabled students. Campus housing is university owned. Freshman applicants given priority for college housing. *Activities and organizations:* drama/theater group, student-run newspaper, choral group, marching band, Student Government Association, Campus Ministry, Intramural athletics, Commuter Student Organization, Circle K. *Campus security:* 24-hour emergency response devices and patrols, late-night transport/escort service, controlled dormitory access, 24-hour patrols by trained personnel on certain days. *Student services:* personal/psychological counseling.
Athletics Member NAIA. *Intercollegiate sports:* baseball M(s), basketball M(s), crew M, ice hockey M, lacrosse M, soccer M(s)/W(s), track and field M(s)/W(s), water polo M/W. *Intramural sports:* basketball M/W, cheerleading M/W, football M/W, golf M/W, lacrosse M, rugby M, skiing (downhill) M(c)/W(c), soccer M, softball M/W, table tennis M/W, tennis M/W, ultimate Frisbee M/W, volleyball M/W, weight lifting M/W.
Standardized Tests *Required:* SAT or ACT (for admission).
Costs (2012–13) *Comprehensive fee:* $32,300 includes full-time tuition ($22,700), mandatory fees ($1200), and room and board ($8400). No tuition increase for student's term of enrollment. *Room and board:* Room and board charges vary according to board plan and housing facility. *Payment plan:* installment. *Waivers:* employees or children of employees.
Applying *Options:* electronic application, deferred entrance. *Required:* high school transcript. *Required for some:* essay or personal statement. *Recommended:* minimum 2.5 GPA, interview. *Application deadlines:* rolling (freshmen), rolling (out-of-state freshmen), rolling (transfers).
Freshman Application Contact Mr. Adam DeBeck, Office of Admissions, Holy Cross College, Notre Dame, IN 46556. *Phone:* 574-239-8400. *Fax:* 574-239-8323. *E-mail:* admissions@hcc-nd.edu. *Web site:* http://www.hcc-nd.edu/.

Huntington University
Huntington, Indiana

- **Independent** comprehensive, founded 1897, affiliated with Church of the United Brethren in Christ
- **Small-town** 170-acre campus with easy access to Fort Wayne
- **Endowment** $20.6 million
- **Coed** 1,163 undergraduate students, 91% full-time, 57% women, 43% men
- **Moderately difficult** entrance level, 88% of applicants were admitted

Undergraduates 1,059 full-time, 104 part-time. Students come from 35 states and territories; 23 other countries; 39% are from out of state; 2% Black or African American, non-Hispanic/Latino; 2% Hispanic/Latino; 0.6% Asian, non-Hispanic/Latino; 0.2% American Indian or Alaska Native, non-Hispanic/Latino; 0.9% Two or more races, non-Hispanic/Latino; 3% international; 5% transferred in; 77% live on campus. *Retention:* 79% of full-time freshmen returned.
Freshmen *Admission:* 968 applied, 856 admitted, 245 enrolled. *Average high school GPA:* 3.39. *Test scores:* SAT critical reading scores over 500: 56%; SAT math scores over 500: 57%; SAT writing scores over 500: 48%; ACT scores over 18: 93%; SAT critical reading scores over 600: 15%; SAT math scores over 600: 19%; SAT writing scores over 600: 10%; ACT scores over 24:

54%; SAT critical reading scores over 700: 1%; SAT math scores over 700: 5%; SAT writing scores over 700: 1%; ACT scores over 30: 9%.

Faculty *Total:* 113, 52% full-time, 50% with terminal degrees. *Student/faculty ratio:* 14:1.

Academics *Calendar:* 4-1-4. *Degrees:* associate, bachelor's, and master's. *Special study options:* academic remediation for entering students, accelerated degree program, adult/continuing education programs, advanced placement credit, distance learning, double majors, English as a second language, independent study, internships, off-campus study, part-time degree program, services for LD students, study abroad, summer session for credit.

Computers on Campus 270 computers/terminals and 3,167 ports are available on campus for general student use. Students can access the following: campus intranet, computer help desk, free student e-mail accounts, online (class) grades, online (class) registration, online (class) schedules. Campuswide network is available. 100% of college-owned or -operated housing units are wired for high-speed Internet access. Wireless service is available via classrooms, computer centers, computer labs, dorm rooms, learning centers, libraries, student centers.

Student Life *Housing:* on-campus residence required through junior year. *Options:* men-only, women-only, disabled students. Campus housing is university owned. Freshman campus housing is guaranteed. *Activities and organizations:* drama/theater group, student-run newspaper, radio and television station, choral group, Film Club, Ultimate Frisbee Club, Mu Kappa, Social Work Student Council, Investment Club. *Campus security:* 24-hour emergency response devices, late-night transport/escort service, campus police on duty from 6 pm to 6 am.

Athletics Member NAIA, NCCAA. *Intercollegiate sports:* baseball M(s), basketball M(s)/W(s), bowling M(s)/W(s), cheerleading M/W, cross-country running M(s)/W(s), golf M(s), soccer M(s)/W(s), softball W(s), tennis M(s)/W(s), track and field M(s)/W(s), ultimate Frisbee M(c), volleyball W(s). *Intramural sports:* basketball M/W, football M/W, racquetball M/W, soccer M/W, table tennis M/W, volleyball M/W.

Standardized Tests *Required:* SAT or ACT (for admission).

Costs (2012–13) *Comprehensive fee:* $31,720 includes full-time tuition ($23,300), mandatory fees ($480), and room and board ($7940). Full-time tuition and fees vary according to course load, degree level, and program. Part-time tuition and fees vary according to course load, degree level, and program. *Room and board:* Room and board charges vary according to board plan. *Payment plan:* installment. *Waivers:* employees or children of employees.

Financial Aid Of all full-time matriculated undergraduates who enrolled in 2011, 917 applied for aid, 847 were judged to have need, 64 had their need fully met. 107 Federal Work-Study jobs (averaging $1854). In 2011, 143 non-need-based awards were made. *Average percent of need met:* 66%. *Average financial aid package:* $15,967. *Average need-based loan:* $4707. *Average need-based gift aid:* $13,295. *Average non-need-based aid:* $9934. *Average indebtedness upon graduation:* $28,860.

Applying *Options:* electronic application, deferred entrance. *Application fee:* $20. *Required:* essay or personal statement, high school transcript, minimum 2.3 GPA. *Recommended:* interview. *Application deadlines:* 8/1 (freshmen), rolling (transfers). *Notification:* 10/1 (freshmen), continuous (transfers).

Freshman Application Contact Huntington University, 2303 College Avenue, Huntington, IN 46750-1299. *Phone:* 260-356-6000 Ext. 4016. *Toll-free phone:* 800-642-6493. *Web site:* http://www.huntington.edu/.

Indiana State University
Terre Haute, Indiana

- **State-supported** university, founded 1865
- **Small-town** 91-acre campus with easy access to Indianapolis
- **Endowment** $47.0 million
- **Coed** 9,449 undergraduate students, 87% full-time, 53% women, 47% men
- **Moderately difficult** entrance level, 51% of applicants were admitted

Undergraduates 8,234 full-time, 1,215 part-time. Students come from 53 states and territories; 66 other countries; 15% are from out of state; 16% Black or African American, non-Hispanic/Latino; 3% Hispanic/Latino; 1% Asian, non-Hispanic/Latino; 0.3% American Indian or Alaska Native, non-Hispanic/Latino; 3% Two or more races, non-Hispanic/Latino; 1% Race/ethnicity unknown; 3% international; 8% transferred in; 36% live on campus. *Retention:* 58% of full-time freshmen returned.

Freshmen *Admission:* 13,030 applied, 6,588 admitted, 2,521 enrolled. *Average high school GPA:* 3.04. *Test scores:* SAT critical reading scores over 500: 31%; SAT math scores over 500: 33%; SAT writing scores over 500: 24%; ACT scores over 18: 65%; SAT critical reading scores over 600: 6%; SAT math scores over 600: 6%; SAT writing scores over 600: 3%; ACT scores over 24: 14%; ACT scores over 30: 1%.

Faculty *Total:* 661, 71% full-time, 61% with terminal degrees. *Student/faculty ratio:* 19:1.

Academics *Calendar:* semesters. *Degrees:* certificates, associate, bachelor's, master's, doctoral, post-master's, postbachelor's, and first professional certificates. *Special study options:* academic remediation for entering students, accelerated degree program, adult/continuing education programs, advanced placement credit, cooperative education, distance learning, double majors, English as a second language, freshman honors college, honors programs, independent study, internships, off-campus study, part-time degree program, services for LD students, study abroad, summer session for credit. *ROTC:* Army (b), Air Force (b).

Computers on Campus 395 computers/terminals are available on campus for general student use. Students can access the following: campus intranet, computer help desk, free student e-mail accounts, online (class) grades, online (class) registration, online (class) schedules. Campuswide network is available. 100% of college-owned or -operated housing units are wired for high-speed Internet access. Wireless service is available via entire campus.

Student Life *Housing:* on-campus residence required for freshman year. *Options:* coed, men-only, women-only, disabled students. Campus housing is university owned. Freshman campus housing is guaranteed. *Activities and organizations:* drama/theater group, student-run newspaper, radio station, choral group, marching band, Union Board, Student Government Association, Panhellenic Council (sororities), Interfraternity Council (fraternities), Pan-Hellenic Council (African American fraternities/sororities), national fraternities, national sororities. *Campus security:* 24-hour emergency response devices and patrols, student patrols, late-night transport/escort service. *Student services:* health clinic, personal/psychological counseling, women's center.

Athletics Member NCAA. All Division I except football (Division I-AA). *Intercollegiate sports:* baseball M(s), basketball M(s)/W(s), cross-country running M(s)/W(s), golf W(s), soccer W(s), softball W(s), track and field M(s)/W(s), volleyball W(s). *Intramural sports:* badminton M/W, basketball M/W, racquetball M/W, soccer M/W, softball M/W, swimming and diving M/W, track and field M/W, ultimate Frisbee M/W, volleyball M/W.

Standardized Tests *Required:* SAT or ACT (for admission).

Costs (2012–13) *Tuition:* state resident $7898 full-time, $286 per credit hour part-time; nonresident $17,444 full-time, $617 per credit hour part-time. Part-time tuition and fees vary according to course load. *Required fees:* $200 full-time, $100 per term part-time. *Room and board:* $8262. Room and board charges vary according to board plan, housing facility, and student level. *Payment plans:* installment, deferred payment. *Waivers:* senior citizens and employees or children of employees.

Financial Aid Of all full-time matriculated undergraduates who enrolled in 2010, 7,133 applied for aid, 6,113 were judged to have need, 702 had their need fully met. 1,262 Federal Work-Study jobs (averaging $2019). In 2010, 708 non-need-based awards were made. *Average percent of need met:* 77%. *Average financial aid package:* $9562. *Average need-based loan:* $3862. *Average need-based gift aid:* $6096. *Average non-need-based aid:* $4428. *Average indebtedness upon graduation:* $18,445.

Applying *Options:* electronic application, deferred entrance. *Application fee:* $25. *Required:* high school transcript. *Required for some:* interview. *Application deadline:* 8/15 (freshmen). *Notification:* continuous (freshmen), continuous (transfers).

Freshman Application Contact Mr. Richard Toomey, Assistant Vice President Enrollment Management, Indiana State University, 218 North Sixth Street, Erickson Hall, Terre Haute, IN 47809-9989. *Phone:* 812-237-2121. *Toll-free phone:* 800-468-6478. *Fax:* 812-237-8023. *E-mail:* admisu@isugw.indstate.edu. *Web site:* http://www.indstate.edu/.

Indiana Tech
Fort Wayne, Indiana

- **Independent** comprehensive, founded 1930
- **Urban** 42-acre campus
- **Endowment** $47.1 million
- **Coed** 4,470 undergraduate students, 66% full-time, 58% women, 42% men
- **Moderately difficult** entrance level, 65% of applicants were admitted

Undergraduates 2,969 full-time, 1,501 part-time. Students come from 41 states and territories; 10 other countries; 16% are from out of state; 25% Black or African American, non-Hispanic/Latino; 3% Hispanic/Latino; 0.4% Asian, non-Hispanic/Latino; 0.2% Native Hawaiian or other Pacific Islander, non-Hispanic/Latino; 0.3% American Indian or Alaska Native, non-Hispanic/Latino; 2% Two or more races, non-Hispanic/Latino; 21% Race/ethnicity unknown; 0.4% international; 2% transferred in; 48% live on campus. *Retention:* 73% of full-time freshmen returned.

Freshmen *Admission:* 3,172 applied, 2,054 admitted, 593 enrolled. *Average high school GPA:* 2.82. *Test scores:* SAT critical reading scores over 500: 33%; SAT math scores over 500: 43%; SAT writing scores over 500: 22%; ACT scores over 18: 74%; SAT critical reading scores over 600: 4%; SAT

math scores over 600: 11%; SAT writing scores over 600: 2%; ACT scores over 24: 17%; SAT math scores over 700: 1%.

Faculty *Total:* 306, 13% full-time. *Student/faculty ratio:* 19:1.

Academics *Calendar:* semesters. *Degrees:* associate, bachelor's, master's, doctoral, and first professional. *Special study options:* academic remediation for entering students, accelerated degree program, adult/continuing education programs, advanced placement credit, cooperative education, distance learning, double majors, external degree program, honors programs, independent study, internships, part-time degree program, services for LD students, student-designed majors, summer session for credit. *ROTC:* Army (c).

Computers on Campus 360 computers/terminals and 20 ports are available on campus for general student use. Students can access the following: computer help desk, free student e-mail accounts, online (class) grades, online (class) registration, online (class) schedules. Campuswide network is available. 100% of college-owned or -operated housing units are wired for high-speed Internet access. Wireless service is available via entire campus.

Student Life *Housing:* on-campus residence required through sophomore year. *Options:* coed. Campus housing is university owned. Freshman campus housing is guaranteed. *Activities and organizations:* student-run newspaper, Student Board, Student Ambassadors, NSBE, SHRM, Sport Recreation and Leisure Society, national fraternities. *Campus security:* 24-hour emergency response devices and patrols, student patrols, controlled dormitory access.

Athletics Member NAIA. *Intercollegiate sports:* baseball M(s), basketball M(s)/W(s), bowling M(s)/W(s), cheerleading M(s)/W(s), cross-country running M(s)/W(s), golf M(s)/W(s), lacrosse M(s)/W(s), soccer M(s)/W(s), softball W(s), tennis M(s)/W(s), track and field M(s)/W(s), volleyball W(s), wrestling M(s). *Intramural sports:* badminton M/W, basketball M/W, bowling M/W, football M/W, golf M/W, soccer M/W, softball M/W, table tennis M/W, tennis M/W, ultimate Frisbee M/W, volleyball M/W.

Standardized Tests *Required:* SAT or ACT (for admission).

Costs (2012–13) *Comprehensive fee:* $33,530 includes full-time tuition ($23,970), mandatory fees ($400), and room and board ($9160). Full-time tuition and fees vary according to class time, course load, and program. Part-time tuition: $470 per credit hour. Part-time tuition and fees vary according to class time, course load, and program. *Room and board:* Room and board charges vary according to housing facility. *Payment plan:* installment. *Waivers:* employees or children of employees.

Financial Aid *Average financial aid package:* $9125. *Average indebtedness upon graduation:* $16,500.

Applying *Options:* electronic application. *Application fee:* $50. *Required:* minimum 2.0 GPA. *Required for some:* high school transcript, minimum 3.0 GPA, 2 letters of recommendation, Interview with the Director of Software Engineering and college-level math courses for the Software Engineering program, Interview with the Director for the Pre-Law program. *Recommended:* Interview with the Director of Software Engineering and college-level math courses for the Software Engineering program, Interview with the Director for the Pre-Law program. *Application deadlines:* 8/15 (freshmen), 8/15 (transfers). *Notification:* continuous until 8/15 (freshmen), continuous until 8/15 (transfers).

Freshman Application Contact Ms. Monica Chamberlain, Associate Vice President of Enrollment Management, Indiana Tech, 1600 East Washington Boulevard, Fort Wayne, IN 46803. *Phone:* 260-422-5561 Ext. 2348. *Toll-free phone:* 800-937-2448. *Fax:* 260-422-7696. *E-mail:* admissions@indianatech.edu. *Web site:* http://www.indianatech.edu/.

Indiana University Bloomington

Bloomington, Indiana

- **State-supported** university, founded 1820, part of Indiana University System
- **Small-town** 1937-acre campus with easy access to Indianapolis
- **Endowment** $723.9 million
- **Coed** 32,543 undergraduate students, 96% full-time, 50% women, 50% men
- **Moderately difficult** entrance level, 72% of applicants were admitted

Undergraduates 31,093 full-time, 1,450 part-time. Students come from 51 states and territories; 139 other countries; 29% are from out of state; 4% Black or African American, non-Hispanic/Latino; 4% Hispanic/Latino; 4% Asian, non-Hispanic/Latino; 0.1% Native Hawaiian or other Pacific Islander, non-Hispanic/Latino; 0.2% American Indian or Alaska Native, non-Hispanic/Latino; 2% Two or more races, non-Hispanic/Latino; 0.7% Race/ethnicity

unknown; 10% international; 3% transferred in. *Retention:* 89% of full-time freshmen returned.

Freshmen *Admission:* 35,218 applied, 25,455 admitted, 7,057 enrolled. *Average high school GPA:* 3.63. *Test scores:* SAT critical reading scores over 500: 83%; SAT math scores over 500: 90%; ACT scores over 18: 99%; SAT critical reading scores over 600: 39%; SAT math scores over 600: 50%; ACT scores over 24: 81%; SAT critical reading scores over 700: 8%; SAT math scores over 700: 13%; ACT scores over 30: 25%.

Faculty *Total:* 2,297, 85% full-time, 71% with terminal degrees. *Student/faculty ratio:* 19:1.

Academics *Calendar:* semesters plus 2 summer sessions. *Degrees:* certificates, bachelor's, master's, doctoral, post-master's, postbachelor's, and first professional certificates. *Special study options:* academic remediation for entering students, accelerated degree program, adult/continuing education programs, advanced placement credit, cooperative education, distance learning, double majors, English as a second language, external degree program, freshman honors college, honors programs, independent study, internships, off-campus study, part-time degree program, services for LD students, student-designed majors, study abroad, summer session for credit. *ROTC:* Army (b), Air Force (b). *Unusual degree programs:* 3-2 accounting.

Computers on Campus Students can access the following: campus intranet, computer help desk, free student e-mail accounts, online (class) grades, online (class) registration, online (class) schedules, various software packages. Campuswide network is available. 100% of college-owned or -operated housing units are wired for high-speed Internet access. Wireless service is available via entire campus.

Student Life *Housing:* on-campus residence required for freshman year. *Options:* coed, men-only, women-only, cooperative, disabled students. Campus housing is university owned. Freshman applicants given priority for college housing. *Activities and organizations:* drama/theater group, student-run newspaper, radio and television station, choral group, marching band, Union Board, Student Association, Student Foundation, Habitat for Humanity, Student Athletic Board, national fraternities, national sororities. *Campus security:* 24-hour emergency response devices and patrols, late-night transport/escort service, safety seminars, lighted pathways, escort service, shuttle bus service, emergency telephones. *Student services:* health clinic, personal/psychological counseling, women's center, legal services.

Athletics Member NCAA. All Division I except football (Division I-A). *Intercollegiate sports:* baseball M(s), basketball M(s)/W(s), crew W(s), cross-country running M(s)/W(s), field hockey W, golf M(s)/W(s), soccer M(s)/W(s), softball W(s), swimming and diving M(s)/W(s), tennis M(s)/W(s), track and field M(s)/W(s), volleyball W(s), water polo W(s), wrestling M(s). *Intramural sports:* archery M/W, badminton M(c)/W(c), baseball M/W, basketball M/W, bowling M(c)/W(c), crew M(c)/W(c), cross-country running M/W, equestrian sports M(c)/W(c), fencing M(c)/W(c), field hockey W(c), golf M/W, gymnastics M/W, ice hockey M/W, lacrosse M(c)/W(c), racquetball M(c)/W(c), riflery M(c)/W(c), rugby M(c)/W(c), sailing M(c)/W(c), skiing (downhill) M(c)/W(c), soccer M/W(c), softball M/W, squash M/W, swimming and diving M/W, table tennis M/W, tennis M(c)/W, track and field M/W, volleyball M/W, water polo M(c)/W, weight lifting M(c)/W(c), wrestling M(c).

Standardized Tests *Required:* SAT or ACT (for admission). *Recommended:* SAT Subject Tests (for admission).

Costs (2012–13) *Tuition:* state resident $8750 full-time, $273 per credit hour part-time; nonresident $30,200 full-time, $944 per credit hour part-time. Full-time tuition and fees vary according to location and program. Part-time tuition and fees vary according to course load, location, and program. *Required fees:* $1283 full-time. *Room and board:* Room and board charges vary according to board plan and housing facility. *Payment plan:* deferred payment. *Waivers:* employees or children of employees.

Financial Aid Of all full-time matriculated undergraduates who enrolled in 2010, 18,807 applied for aid, 14,152 were judged to have need, 1,698 had their need fully met. In 2010, 7655 non-need-based awards were made. *Average percent of need met:* 90%. *Average financial aid package:* $11,254. *Average need-based loan:* $4416. *Average need-based gift aid:* $9215. *Average non-need-based aid:* $5226. *Average indebtedness upon graduation:* $28,434.

Applying *Options:* electronic application, deferred entrance. *Application fee:* $55. *Required:* high school transcript. *Recommended:* interview. *Application deadlines:* rolling (freshmen), rolling (transfers). *Notification:* continuous (freshmen), continuous (transfers).

Freshman Application Contact Ms. Mary Ellen Anderson, Director of Admissions, Indiana University Bloomington, 300 North Jordan Avenue, Bloomington, IN 47405-1106. *Phone:* 812-855-0661. *Fax:* 812-855-5102. *E-mail:* iuadmit@indiana.edu. *Web site:* http://www.iub.edu/.

Indiana University East

Richmond, Indiana

- **State-supported** comprehensive, founded 1971, part of Indiana University System
- **Small-town** 182-acre campus with easy access to Indianapolis
- **Endowment** $4.3 million
- **Coed** 3,623 undergraduate students, 53% full-time, 66% women, 34% men
- **Moderately difficult** entrance level, 64% of applicants were admitted

Undergraduates 1,904 full-time, 1,719 part-time. Students come from 29 states and territories; 22 other countries; 18% are from out of state; 3% Black or African American, non-Hispanic/Latino; 2% Hispanic/Latino; 0.6% Asian, non-Hispanic/Latino; 0.1% Native Hawaiian or other Pacific Islander, non-Hispanic/Latino; 0.2% American Indian or Alaska Native, non-Hispanic/Latino; 1% Two or more races, non-Hispanic/Latino; 2% Race/ethnicity unknown; 0.2% international; 10% transferred in. *Retention:* 66% of full-time freshmen returned.

Freshmen *Admission:* 1,122 applied, 714 admitted, 407 enrolled. *Average high school GPA:* 3.04. *Test scores:* SAT critical reading scores over 500: 29%; SAT math scores over 500: 28%; ACT scores over 18: 80%; SAT critical reading scores over 600: 6%; SAT math scores over 600: 4%; ACT scores over 24: 19%; ACT scores over 30: 1%.

Faculty *Total:* 258, 37% full-time, 32% with terminal degrees. *Student/faculty ratio:* 16:1.

Academics *Calendar:* semesters. *Degrees:* certificates, associate, bachelor's, master's, and postbachelor's certificates. *Special study options:* academic remediation for entering students, adult/continuing education programs, advanced placement credit, cooperative education, distance learning, double majors, external degree program, honors programs, independent study, internships, off-campus study, part-time degree program, services for LD students, study abroad, summer session for credit.

Computers on Campus Students can access the following: campus intranet, computer help desk, free student e-mail accounts, online (class) grades, online (class) registration, online (class) schedules. Campuswide network is available. Wireless service is available via entire campus.

Student Life *Housing:* college housing not available. *Activities and organizations:* drama/theater group, student-run newspaper, television station, Student Government Association, Phi Beta Lambda, Multicultural Awareness Association, Psychology Club, Sociology Club. *Campus security:* 24-hour emergency response devices, late-night transport/escort service, safety awareness, lighted pathways, 14-hour foot and vehicle patrol. *Student services:* personal/psychological counseling.

Athletics Member NAIA. *Intercollegiate sports:* basketball M, cheerleading W, cross-country running M/W, golf M/W, tennis M/W, track and field M/W, volleyball W. *Intramural sports:* basketball M(c)/W(c), softball M/W, volleyball M/W.

Standardized Tests *Required:* SAT or ACT (for admission).

Costs (2012–13) *Tuition:* state resident $5964 full-time, $199 per credit hour part-time; nonresident $16,894 full-time, $563 per credit hour part-time. Full-time tuition and fees vary according to course load, location, program, and reciprocity agreements. Part-time tuition and fees vary according to course load, location, program, and reciprocity agreements. *Required fees:* $532 full-time. *Payment plan:* deferred payment. *Waivers:* employees or children of employees.

Financial Aid Of all full-time matriculated undergraduates who enrolled in 2010, 1,602 applied for aid, 1,433 were judged to have need, 83 had their need fully met. In 2010, 96 non-need-based awards were made. *Average percent of need met:* 96%. *Average financial aid package:* $8166. *Average need-based loan:* $3777. *Average need-based gift aid:* $5964. *Average non-need-based aid:* $1262. *Average indebtedness upon graduation:* $26,897.

Applying *Options:* electronic application, early admission, deferred entrance. *Application fee:* $35. *Required:* high school transcript. *Recommended:* minimum 2.0 GPA. *Application deadlines:* rolling (freshmen), rolling (transfers). *Notification:* continuous (freshmen), continuous (transfers).

Freshman Application Contact Ms. Molly Vanderpool, Director of Admissions, Indiana University East, 2325 Chester Boulevard, Whitewater Hall 151, Richmond, IN 47374-1289. *Phone:* 765-973-8208. *Toll-free phone:* 800-959-EAST. *Fax:* 765-973-8209. *E-mail:* applynow@iue.edu. *Web site:* http://www.iue.edu/.

Indiana University Kokomo

Kokomo, Indiana

- **State-supported** comprehensive, founded 1945, part of Indiana University System
- **Small-town** 51-acre campus with easy access to Indianapolis
- **Endowment** $4.2 million
- **Coed** 3,204 undergraduate students, 55% full-time, 65% women, 35% men
- **Minimally difficult** entrance level, 70% of applicants were admitted

Undergraduates 1,755 full-time, 1,449 part-time. Students come from 10 states and territories; 18 other countries; 1% are from out of state; 4% Black or African American, non-Hispanic/Latino; 3% Hispanic/Latino; 1% Asian, non-Hispanic/Latino; 0.1% Native Hawaiian or other Pacific Islander, non-Hispanic/Latino; 0.2% American Indian or Alaska Native, non-Hispanic/Latino; 1% Two or more races, non-Hispanic/Latino; 7% Race/ethnicity unknown; 8% transferred in. *Retention:* 64% of full-time freshmen returned.

Freshmen *Admission:* 932 applied, 653 admitted, 435 enrolled. *Average high school GPA:* 3. *Test scores:* SAT critical reading scores over 500: 43%; SAT math scores over 500: 40%; ACT scores over 18: 75%; SAT critical reading scores over 600: 7%; SAT math scores over 600: 8%; ACT scores over 24: 17%; SAT critical reading scores over 700: 1%; SAT math scores over 700: 1%.

Faculty *Total:* 187, 53% full-time, 37% with terminal degrees. *Student/faculty ratio:* 17:1.

Academics *Calendar:* semesters. *Degrees:* certificates, associate, bachelor's, master's, and postbachelor's certificates. *Special study options:* academic remediation for entering students, accelerated degree program, adult/continuing education programs, advanced placement credit, distance learning, double majors, external degree program, freshman honors college, honors programs, independent study, internships, part-time degree program, services for LD students, study abroad, summer session for credit. *ROTC:* Army (c).

Computers on Campus Students can access the following: campus intranet, computer help desk, free student e-mail accounts, online (class) grades, online (class) registration, online (class) schedules. Campuswide network is available. Wireless service is available via entire campus.

Student Life *Housing:* college housing not available. *Activities and organizations:* drama/theater group, student-run newspaper, choral group. *Campus security:* 24-hour patrols, late-night transport/escort service, campus police, lighted pathways. *Student services:* personal/psychological counseling.

Athletics *Intramural sports:* basketball M, soccer M/W, softball M/W, volleyball M/W.

Standardized Tests *Required:* SAT or ACT (for admission).

Costs (2012–13) *Tuition:* state resident $5949 full-time, $198 per credit hour part-time; nonresident $16,894 full-time, $563 per credit hour part-time. Full-time tuition and fees vary according to course load, location, and program. Part-time tuition and fees vary according to course load, location, and program. *Required fees:* $592 full-time. *Payment plan:* deferred payment. *Waivers:* employees or children of employees.

Financial Aid Of all full-time matriculated undergraduates who enrolled in 2010, 1,485 applied for aid, 1,263 were judged to have need, 48 had their need fully met. In 2010, 104 non-need-based awards were made. *Average percent of need met:* 93%. *Average financial aid package:* $7933. *Average need-based loan:* $3605. *Average need-based gift aid:* $6189. *Average non-need-based aid:* $1027. *Average indebtedness upon graduation:* $25,839.

Applying *Options:* electronic application, deferred entrance. *Application fee:* $35. *Required:* high school transcript. *Application deadline:* rolling (freshmen). *Notification:* continuous (freshmen), continuous (transfers).

Freshman Application Contact Indiana University Kokomo, Kelley Student Center, Room 230, 2300 South Washington Street, Kokomo, IN 46904-9003. *Phone:* 765-455-9217. *Toll-free phone:* 888-875-4485. *Fax:* 765-455-9537. *E-mail:* iuadmis@iuk.edu. *Web site:* http://www.iuk.edu/.

Indiana University Northwest

Gary, Indiana

- **State-supported** comprehensive, founded 1959, part of Indiana University System
- **Urban** 38-acre campus with easy access to Chicago
- **Endowment** $7.3 million
- **Coed** 5,421 undergraduate students, 61% full-time, 69% women, 31% men
- **Minimally difficult** entrance level, 76% of applicants were admitted

Undergraduates 3,298 full-time, 2,123 part-time. Students come from 10 states and territories; 35 other countries; 1% are from out of state; 21% Black or African American, non-Hispanic/Latino; 15% Hispanic/Latino; 2% Asian, non-Hispanic/Latino; 0.1% Native Hawaiian or other Pacific Islander, non-Hispanic/Latino; 0.2% American Indian or Alaska Native, non-Hispanic/

Latino; 1% Two or more races, non-Hispanic/Latino; 3% Race/ethnicity unknown; 0.1% international; 7% transferred in. *Retention:* 63% of full-time freshmen returned.
Freshmen *Admission:* 1,793 applied, 1,364 admitted, 904 enrolled. *Average high school GPA:* 2.72. *Test scores:* SAT critical reading scores over 500: 25%; SAT math scores over 500: 26%; ACT scores over 18: 65%; SAT critical reading scores over 600: 5%; SAT math scores over 600: 6%; ACT scores over 24: 24%; SAT critical reading scores over 700: 1%.
Faculty *Total:* 401, 46% full-time, 40% with terminal degrees. *Student/faculty ratio:* 16:1.
Academics *Calendar:* semesters. *Degrees:* certificates, associate, bachelor's, master's, and postbachelor's certificates. *Special study options:* academic remediation for entering students, accelerated degree program, adult/continuing education programs, advanced placement credit, cooperative education, distance learning, double majors, external degree program, honors programs, independent study, internships, off-campus study, part-time degree program, services for LD students, student-designed majors, study abroad, summer session for credit. *ROTC:* Army (b).
Computers on Campus Students can access the following: campus intranet, computer help desk, free student e-mail accounts, online (class) grades, online (class) registration, online (class) schedules. Campuswide network is available. Wireless service is available via entire campus.
Student Life *Housing:* college housing not available. *Activities and organizations:* drama/theater group, student-run newspaper, radio station, choral group, Student Government Association, Student Guides Organization, Nursing Association, Dental Association, International Affairs Club, national fraternities, national sororities. *Campus security:* 24-hour emergency response devices and patrols, late-night transport/escort service, lighted pathways. *Student services:* personal/psychological counseling.
Athletics Member NAIA. *Intercollegiate sports:* baseball M, basketball M/W, golf M/W, volleyball W. *Intramural sports:* basketball M(c), bowling M(c)/W(c), cheerleading W(c), fencing M(c)/W(c), golf M(c)/W(c), soccer M(c), softball M(c)/W(c), table tennis M(c)/W(c), tennis M(c)/W(c), volleyball M(c)/W(c).
Standardized Tests *Required:* SAT or ACT (for admission).
Costs (2012–13) *Tuition:* state resident $6043 full-time, $201 per credit hour part-time; nonresident $16,894 full-time, $563 per credit hour part-time. Full-time tuition and fees vary according to course load, location, and program. Part-time tuition and fees vary according to course load, location, and program. *Required fees:* $583 full-time. *Payment plans:* installment, deferred payment. *Waivers:* employees or children of employees.
Financial Aid Of all full-time matriculated undergraduates who enrolled in 2010, 2,871 applied for aid, 2,630 were judged to have need, 45 had their need fully met. In 2010, 216 non-need-based awards were made. *Average percent of need met:* 91%. *Average financial aid package:* $8077. *Average need-based loan:* $3845. *Average need-based gift aid:* $6019. *Average non-need-based aid:* $2385. *Average indebtedness upon graduation:* $31,686.
Applying *Options:* electronic application, deferred entrance. *Application fee:* $35. *Required:* high school transcript, minimum 2.0 GPA. *Application deadlines:* rolling (freshmen), rolling (transfers). *Notification:* continuous (freshmen), continuous (transfers).
Freshman Application Contact Dr. Linda B. Templeton, Director of Admissions, Indiana University Northwest, Hawthorn Hall 101, 3400 Broadway, Gary, IN 46408-1197. *Phone:* 219-980-6991. *Toll-free phone:* 800-968-7486. *Fax:* 219-981-4219. *E-mail:* admit@iun.edu. *Web site:* http://www.iun.edu/.

Indiana University–Purdue University Fort Wayne

Fort Wayne, Indiana

- **State-supported** comprehensive, founded 1917, part of Indiana University System and Purdue University System
- **Urban** 682-acre campus
- **Endowment** $42.4 million
- **Coed** 13,608 undergraduate students, 63% full-time, 55% women, 45% men
- **Minimally difficult** entrance level, 91% of applicants were admitted

Undergraduates 8,585 full-time, 5,023 part-time. Students come from 42 states and territories; 64 other countries; 4% are from out of state; 8% Black or African American, non-Hispanic/Latino; 5% Hispanic/Latino; 2% Asian, non-Hispanic/Latino; 0.4% American Indian or Alaska Native, non-Hispanic/Latino; 2% Two or more races, non-Hispanic/Latino; 1% Race/ethnicity unknown; 2% international; 5% transferred in; 7% live on campus. *Retention:* 58% of full-time freshmen returned.
Freshmen *Admission:* 2,779 applied, 2,530 admitted, 2,044 enrolled. *Average high school GPA:* 3.08. *Test scores:* SAT critical reading scores over 500:

40%; SAT math scores over 500: 46%; SAT writing scores over 500: 33%; ACT scores over 18: 83%; SAT critical reading scores over 600: 10%; SAT math scores over 600: 13%; SAT writing scores over 600: 5%; ACT scores over 24: 30%; SAT critical reading scores over 700: 2%; SAT math scores over 700: 1%; ACT scores over 30: 5%.
Faculty *Total:* 880, 49% full-time, 46% with terminal degrees. *Student/faculty ratio:* 18:1.
Academics *Calendar:* semesters. *Degrees:* certificates, associate, bachelor's, master's, and postbachelor's certificates. *Special study options:* academic remediation for entering students, accelerated degree program, adult/continuing education programs, advanced placement credit, cooperative education, distance learning, double majors, English as a second language, honors programs, independent study, internships, off-campus study, part-time degree program, services for LD students, student-designed majors, study abroad, summer session for credit. *ROTC:* Army (b).
Computers on Campus 642 computers/terminals are available on campus for general student use. Students can access the following: computer help desk, free student e-mail accounts, online (class) grades, online (class) registration, online (class) schedules, student academic records. Campuswide network is available. 100% of college-owned or -operated housing units are wired for high-speed Internet access. Wireless service is available via entire campus.
Student Life *Housing options:* coed. Campus housing is provided by a third party. *Activities and organizations:* drama/theater group, student-run newspaper, television station, choral group, Campus Ministry, Big Heart, Students Today, Alumni Tomorrow, Psychology Club, Sociology Club. *Campus security:* 24-hour emergency response devices and patrols, late-night transport/escort service, controlled dormitory access. *Student services:* health clinic, personal/psychological counseling, women's center.
Athletics Member NCAA. All Division I. *Intercollegiate sports:* baseball M(s), basketball M(s)/W(s), cross-country running M(s)/W(s), golf M(s)/W(s), soccer M(s)/W(s), softball W(s), tennis M(s)/W(s), track and field W(s), volleyball M(s)/W(s). *Intramural sports:* basketball M/W, golf M/W, soccer M/W, softball W, table tennis M/W, tennis M/W, ultimate Frisbee M/W, volleyball M/W.
Standardized Tests *Required:* SAT or ACT (for admission).
Costs (2011–12) *Tuition:* state resident $5855 full-time, $217 per credit hour part-time; nonresident $15,259 full-time, $565 per credit hour part-time. Full-time tuition and fees vary according to course load. Part-time tuition and fees vary according to course load. *Required fees:* $853 full-time, $32 per credit hour part-time. *Room only:* $5900. Room and board charges vary according to housing facility. *Payment plans:* installment, deferred payment. *Waivers:* senior citizens and employees or children of employees.
Financial Aid Of all full-time matriculated undergraduates who enrolled in 2010, 7,730 applied for aid, 6,851 were judged to have need, 3 had their need fully met. 918 Federal Work-Study jobs (averaging $3000). In 2010, 83 non-need-based awards were made. *Average percent of need met:* 46%. *Average financial aid package:* $9490. *Average need-based loan:* $3800. *Average need-based gift aid:* $5989. *Average non-need-based aid:* $2083. *Average indebtedness upon graduation:* $25,190.
Applying *Options:* electronic application, deferred entrance. *Application fee:* $50. *Required:* high school transcript, minimum 2.8 GPA. *Recommended:* rank in upper 50% of high school class. *Application deadlines:* 8/1 (freshmen), 8/1 (out-of-state freshmen), 8/1 (transfers). *Notification:* continuous (freshmen), continuous (out-of-state freshmen), continuous (transfers).
Freshman Application Contact Angela Morren, Undergraduate Applications Coordinator, Indiana University–Purdue University Fort Wayne, 2101 East Coliseum Boulevard, Fort Wayne, IN 46805-1499. *Phone:* 260-481-6142. *Toll-free phone:* 800-324-4739. *Fax:* 260-481-6880. *E-mail:* morrena@ipfw.edu. *Web site:* http://www.ipfw.edu/.

Indiana University–Purdue University Indianapolis

Indianapolis, Indiana

- **State-supported** university, founded 1969, part of Indiana University System
- **Urban** 509-acre campus
- **Endowment** $512.9 million
- **Coed** 22,236 undergraduate students, 72% full-time, 57% women, 43% men
- **Moderately difficult** entrance level, 69% of applicants were admitted

Undergraduates 16,085 full-time, 6,151 part-time. Students come from 51 states and territories; 134 other countries; 2% are from out of state; 11% Black or African American, non-Hispanic/Latino; 4% Hispanic/Latino; 3% Asian, non-Hispanic/Latino; 0.1% Native Hawaiian or other Pacific Islander, non-Hispanic/Latino; 0.2% American Indian or Alaska Native, non-Hispanic/Latino; 2% Two or more races, non-Hispanic/Latino; 2% Race/ethnicity

unknown; 3% international; 8% transferred in; 5% live on campus. *Retention:* 82% of full-time freshmen returned.

Freshmen *Admission:* 10,164 applied, 7,048 admitted, 2,996 enrolled. *Average high school GPA:* 3.26. *Test scores:* SAT critical reading scores over 500: 47%; SAT math scores over 500: 51%; ACT scores over 18: 86%; SAT critical reading scores over 600: 13%; SAT math scores over 600: 14%; ACT scores over 24: 35%; SAT critical reading scores over 700: 2%; SAT math scores over 700: 2%; ACT scores over 30: 6%.

Faculty *Total:* 3,208, 68% full-time, 65% with terminal degrees. *Student/faculty ratio:* 18:1.

Academics *Calendar:* semesters. *Degrees:* certificates, associate, bachelor's, master's, doctoral, postbachelor's, and first professional certificates. *Special study options:* academic remediation for entering students, accelerated degree program, adult/continuing education programs, advanced placement credit, cooperative education, distance learning, double majors, English as a second language, external degree program, honors programs, independent study, internships, off-campus study, part-time degree program, services for LD students, student-designed majors, study abroad, summer session for credit. *ROTC:* Army (b), Air Force (c).

Computers on Campus Students can access the following: campus intranet, computer help desk, free student e-mail accounts, online (class) grades, online (class) registration, online (class) schedules. Campuswide network is available. Wireless service is available via entire campus.

Student Life *Housing options:* coed. Campus housing is university owned. *Activities and organizations:* drama/theater group, student-run newspaper, choral group, Undergraduate Student Assembly, Black Student Union, Student Activities Programming Board, national fraternities, national sororities. *Campus security:* 24-hour emergency response devices and patrols, late-night transport/escort service, controlled dormitory access, lighted pathways, self-defense education. *Student services:* health clinic, personal/psychological counseling, women's center.

Athletics Member NCAA. All Division I. *Intercollegiate sports:* basketball M(s)/W(s), cross-country running M(s)/W(s), golf M(s)/W(s), soccer M(s)/W(s), softball W(s), swimming and diving M(s)/W(s), tennis M(s)/W(s), volleyball W(s). *Intramural sports:* badminton M/W, baseball M, basketball M/W, cross-country running M/W, football M, golf M/W, racquetball M/W, soccer M/W, softball M/W, swimming and diving M/W, table tennis M/W, tennis M/W, track and field M/W, volleyball M/W, water polo M/W.

Standardized Tests *Required:* SAT or ACT (for admission).

Costs (2012–13) *Tuition:* state resident $7623 full-time, $254 per credit hour part-time; nonresident $28,080 full-time, $936 per credit hour part-time. Full-time tuition and fees vary according to course load, location, and program. Part-time tuition and fees vary according to course load, location, and program. *Required fees:* $982 full-time. *Room and board:* Room and board charges vary according to housing facility. *Payment plans:* installment, deferred payment. *Waivers:* employees or children of employees.

Financial Aid Of all full-time matriculated undergraduates who enrolled in 2010, 13,069 applied for aid, 11,354 were judged to have need, 494 had their need fully met. In 2010, 1537 non-need-based awards were made. *Average percent of need met:* 91%. *Average financial aid package:* $9409. *Average need-based loan:* $4163. *Average need-based gift aid:* $7003. *Average non-need-based aid:* $2929. *Average indebtedness upon graduation:* $29,673.

Applying *Options:* electronic application, deferred entrance. *Application fee:* $50. *Required:* high school transcript. *Required for some:* interview. *Recommended:* portfolio for art program. *Application deadlines:* 5/1 (freshmen), rolling (transfers). *Notification:* continuous (freshmen), continuous (transfers).

Freshman Application Contact Mr. Chris J. Foley, Director of Admissions, Indiana University–Purdue University Indianapolis, Cavanaugh Hall 129, 425 University Boulevard, Indianapolis, IN 46202-5143. *Phone:* 317-274-4591. *Fax:* 317-278-1862. *E-mail:* apply@iupui.edu. *Web site:* http://www.iupui.edu/.

Indiana University South Bend

South Bend, Indiana

- **State-supported** comprehensive, founded 1922, part of Indiana University System
- **Suburban** 102-acre campus with easy access to Chicago
- **Endowment** $9.2 million
- **Coed** 7,737 undergraduate students, 56% full-time, 61% women, 39% men
- **Moderately difficult** entrance level, 71% of applicants were admitted

Undergraduates 4,321 full-time, 3,416 part-time. Students come from 26 states and territories; 80 other countries; 4% are from out of state; 7% Black or African American, non-Hispanic/Latino; 6% Hispanic/Latino; 2% Asian, non-Hispanic/Latino; 0.1% Native Hawaiian or other Pacific Islander, non-Hispanic/Latino; 0.2% American Indian or Alaska Native, non-Hispanic/Latino; 2% Two or more races, non-Hispanic/Latino; 3% Race/ethnicity unknown; 2%

international; 6% transferred in. *Retention:* 64% of full-time freshmen returned.

Freshmen *Admission:* 2,441 applied, 1,725 admitted, 975 enrolled. *Average high school GPA:* 2.94. *Test scores:* SAT critical reading scores over 500: 37%; SAT math scores over 500: 44%; ACT scores over 18: 85%; SAT critical reading scores over 600: 10%; SAT math scores over 600: 9%; ACT scores over 24: 23%; SAT critical reading scores over 700: 1%; SAT math scores over 700: 1%; ACT scores over 30: 1%.

Faculty *Total:* 542, 53% full-time, 40% with terminal degrees. *Student/faculty ratio:* 14:1.

Academics *Calendar:* semesters. *Degrees:* certificates, diplomas, associate, bachelor's, master's, and postbachelor's certificates. *Special study options:* accelerated degree program, adult/continuing education programs, distance learning, double majors, English as a second language, external degree program, honors programs, independent study, internships, off-campus study, part-time degree program, study abroad, summer session for credit. *ROTC:* Army (c), Navy (c), Air Force (c).

Computers on Campus Students can access the following: campus intranet, computer help desk, free student e-mail accounts, online (class) grades, online (class) registration, online (class) schedules. Campuswide network is available. Wireless service is available via entire campus.

Student Life *Housing options:* Campus housing is university owned. *Activities and organizations:* drama/theater group, student-run newspaper, choral group, national fraternities. *Campus security:* 24-hour emergency response devices and patrols, late-night transport/escort service, safety seminars, lighted pathways. *Student services:* personal/psychological counseling, women's center.

Athletics Member NAIA. *Intercollegiate sports:* basketball M(s)/W(s), volleyball W. *Intramural sports:* badminton M/W, baseball M, basketball M(c)/W(c), bowling M(c)/W(c), cheerleading W(c), cross-country running M/W, football M/W, golf M/W, racquetball M/W, soccer M(c)/W(c), softball M/W, table tennis M/W, tennis M/W, volleyball M(c)/W(c).

Standardized Tests *Required:* SAT or ACT (for admission).

Costs (2012–13) *Tuition:* state resident $6138 full-time, $205 per credit hour part-time; nonresident $16,894 full-time, $563 per credit hour part-time. Full-time tuition and fees vary according to course load, location, and program. Part-time tuition and fees vary according to course load, location, and program. *Required fees:* $590 full-time. *Payment plan:* deferred payment. *Waivers:* employees or children of employees.

Financial Aid Of all full-time matriculated undergraduates who enrolled in 2010, 3,832 applied for aid, 3,369 were judged to have need, 93 had their need fully met. In 2010, 265 non-need-based awards were made. *Average percent of need met:* 94%. *Average financial aid package:* $8267. *Average need-based loan:* $3793. *Average need-based gift aid:* $6148. *Average non-need-based aid:* $2067. *Average indebtedness upon graduation:* $25,014.

Applying *Options:* electronic application, deferred entrance. *Application fee:* $35. *Required:* high school transcript, minimum 2.0 GPA. *Required for some:* interview. *Application deadlines:* rolling (freshmen), rolling (transfers). *Notification:* continuous (freshmen), continuous (transfers).

Freshman Application Contact Mr. Michael Renfrow, Director of Admissions, Indiana University South Bend, 1700 Mishawaka Avenue, PO Box 7111, South Bend, IN 46634-7111. *Phone:* 574-520-4839. *Toll-free phone:* 877-GO-2-IUSB. *Fax:* 574-520-4834. *E-mail:* admissions@iusb.edu. *Web site:* http://www.iusb.edu/.

Indiana University Southeast

New Albany, Indiana

- **State-supported** comprehensive, founded 1941, part of Indiana University System
- **Suburban** 178-acre campus with easy access to Louisville
- **Endowment** $10.6 million
- **Coed** 6,423 undergraduate students, 64% full-time, 58% women, 42% men
- **Minimally difficult** entrance level, 77% of applicants were admitted

Undergraduates 4,100 full-time, 2,323 part-time. Students come from 13 states and territories; 43 other countries; 28% are from out of state; 6% Black or African American, non-Hispanic/Latino; 2% Hispanic/Latino; 1% Asian, non-Hispanic/Latino; 0.1% Native Hawaiian or other Pacific Islander, non-Hispanic/Latino; 0.3% American Indian or Alaska Native, non-Hispanic/Latino; 2% Two or more races, non-Hispanic/Latino; 2% Race/ethnicity unknown; 0.3% international; 8% transferred in. *Retention:* 64% of full-time freshmen returned.

Freshmen *Admission:* 2,102 applied, 1,617 admitted, 969 enrolled. *Average high school GPA:* 3.05. *Test scores:* SAT critical reading scores over 500: 39%; SAT math scores over 500: 35%; ACT scores over 18: 79%; SAT critical reading scores over 600: 8%; SAT math scores over 600: 7%; ACT scores over 24: 16%; SAT critical reading scores over 700: 1%; ACT scores over 30: 2%.

Faculty *Total:* 487, 43% full-time, 41% with terminal degrees. *Student/faculty ratio:* 17:1.

Academics *Calendar:* semesters. *Degrees:* certificates, associate, bachelor's, master's, and postbachelor's certificates. *Special study options:* academic remediation for entering students, accelerated degree program, adult/continuing education programs, advanced placement credit, distance learning, double majors, external degree program, honors programs, independent study, internships, off-campus study, part-time degree program, services for LD students, student-designed majors, study abroad, summer session for credit. *ROTC:* Army (c), Air Force (c).

Computers on Campus Students can access the following: campus intranet, computer help desk, free student e-mail accounts, online (class) grades, online (class) registration, online (class) schedules. Campuswide network is available. Wireless service is available via entire campus.

Student Life *Housing options:* coed. Campus housing is university owned. *Activities and organizations:* drama/theater group, student-run newspaper, choral group, national fraternities, national sororities. *Campus security:* 24-hour emergency response devices and patrols, self-defense education, lighted pathways, police department on campus. *Student services:* personal/psychological counseling.

Athletics Member NAIA. *Intercollegiate sports:* baseball M, basketball M(s)/W(s), cheerleading W, softball W, tennis M/W, volleyball W(s). *Intramural sports:* basketball M/W, bowling M/W, cross-country running M/W, softball M/W, tennis M/W, volleyball W.

Standardized Tests *Required:* SAT or ACT (for admission).

Costs (2012–13) *Tuition:* state resident $5960 full-time, $199 per credit hour part-time; nonresident $16,894 full-time, $563 per credit hour part-time. Full-time tuition and fees vary according to course load, location, program, and reciprocity agreements. Part-time tuition and fees vary according to course load, location, program, and reciprocity agreements. *Required fees:* $616 full-time. *Room and board:* Room and board charges vary according to board plan and housing facility. *Payment plan:* deferred payment. *Waivers:* employees or children of employees.

Financial Aid Of all full-time matriculated undergraduates who enrolled in 2010, 3,384 applied for aid, 2,854 were judged to have need, 84 had their need fully met. In 2010, 309 non-need-based awards were made. *Average percent of need met:* 93%. *Average financial aid package:* $7724. *Average need-based loan:* $3800. *Average need-based gift aid:* $5762. *Average non-need-based aid:* $1092. *Average indebtedness upon graduation:* $23,532.

Applying *Options:* electronic application, early admission, deferred entrance. *Application fee:* $35. *Required:* high school transcript. *Required for some:* interview. *Application deadlines:* rolling (freshmen), rolling (transfers). *Notification:* continuous (freshmen), continuous (transfers).

Freshman Application Contact Ms. Anne Skuce, Director of Admissions/Assistant Vice Chancellor for Enrollment Management, Indiana University Southeast, University Center South Room 102, 4201 Grant Line Road, New Albany, IN 47150. *Phone:* 812-941-2212. *Toll-free phone:* 800-852-8835. *Fax:* 812-941-2595. *E-mail:* admissions@ius.edu. *Web site:* http://www.ius.edu/.

Indiana Wesleyan University

Marion, Indiana

- **Independent Wesleyan** comprehensive, founded 1920
- **Small-town** 300-acre campus with easy access to Indianapolis
- **Endowment** $88.7 million
- **Coed** 3,188 undergraduate students, 93% full-time, 63% women, 37% men
- **Moderately difficult** entrance level, 67% of applicants were admitted

Undergraduates 2,970 full-time, 218 part-time. Students come from 3 states and territories; 48 other countries; 47% are from out of state; 2% Black or African American, non-Hispanic/Latino; 3% Hispanic/Latino; 0.6% Asian, non-Hispanic/Latino; 0.2% Native Hawaiian or other Pacific Islander, non-Hispanic/Latino; 0.2% American Indian or Alaska Native, non-Hispanic/Latino; 2% Two or more races, non-Hispanic/Latino; 0.3% Race/ethnicity unknown; 0.3% international; 4% transferred in; 81% live on campus. *Retention:* 75% of full-time freshmen returned.

Freshmen *Admission:* 3,512 applied, 2,340 admitted, 753 enrolled. *Average high school GPA:* 3.57. *Test scores:* SAT critical reading scores over 500: 67%; SAT math scores over 500: 62%; SAT writing scores over 500: 59%; SAT critical reading scores over 600: 25%; SAT math scores over 600: 22%; SAT writing scores over 600: 18%; SAT critical reading scores over 700: 2%; SAT math scores over 700: 2%; SAT writing scores over 700: 2%.

Faculty *Total:* 292, 61% full-time, 40% with terminal degrees. *Student/faculty ratio:* 14:1.

Academics *Calendar:* semesters. *Degrees:* certificates, associate, bachelor's, master's, doctoral, post-master's, and postbachelor's certificates (also offers adult program with significant enrollment not reflected in profile). *Special*

study options: academic remediation for entering students, advanced placement credit, distance learning, double majors, freshman honors college, honors programs, independent study, internships, off-campus study, part-time degree program, services for LD students, study abroad, summer session for credit. *ROTC:* Army (b).

Computers on Campus 691 computers/terminals are available on campus for general student use. Students can access the following: campus intranet, computer help desk, free student e-mail accounts, online (class) grades, online (class) registration, online (class) schedules. Campuswide network is available. 100% of college-owned or -operated housing units are wired for high-speed Internet access. Wireless service is available via entire campus.

Student Life *Housing:* on-campus residence required through junior year. *Options:* men-only, women-only. Campus housing is university owned. Freshman campus housing is guaranteed. *Activities and organizations:* drama/theater group, student-run newspaper, radio and television station, choral group, Student Government Organization, Student Activities Council, University Players, World Christian Fellowship, Sixth Man Club. *Campus security:* 24-hour emergency response devices and patrols, late-night transport/escort service, controlled dormitory access. *Student services:* health clinic, personal/psychological counseling.

Athletics Member NAIA, NCCAA. *Intercollegiate sports:* baseball M(s), basketball M(s)/W(s), cheerleading M(s)/W(s), cross-country running M(s)/W(s), golf M(s)/W(s), soccer M(s)/W(s), softball W(s), tennis M(s)/W(s), track and field M(s)/W(s), volleyball W(s). *Intramural sports:* badminton M/W, basketball M/W, bowling M/W, football M/W, golf M/W, racquetball M/W, soccer M/W, softball M/W, swimming and diving M/W, table tennis M/W, tennis M/W, ultimate Frisbee M/W, volleyball M/W, weight lifting M/W.

Standardized Tests *Required:* SAT or ACT (for admission), TOEFL for non-English speaking, and some non-resident alien students (for admission).

Costs (2012–13) *Comprehensive fee:* $30,676 includes full-time tuition ($23,165) and room and board ($7511). Full-time tuition and fees vary according to course load. Part-time tuition and fees vary according to course load. *College room only:* $3649. Room and board charges vary according to board plan. *Payment plan:* installment. *Waivers:* employees or children of employees.

Financial Aid Of all full-time matriculated undergraduates who enrolled in 2010, 2,893 applied for aid, 2,402 were judged to have need, 873 had their need fully met. 730 Federal Work-Study jobs (averaging $809). In 2010, 407 non-need-based awards were made. *Average percent of need met:* 80%. *Average financial aid package:* $20,023. *Average need-based loan:* $7047. *Average need-based gift aid:* $12,953. *Average non-need-based aid:* $4967. *Average indebtedness upon graduation:* $28,793.

Applying *Options:* electronic application, deferred entrance. *Application fee:* $25. *Required:* essay or personal statement, high school transcript, minimum 2.5 GPA, 2 letters of recommendation. *Application deadlines:* rolling (freshmen), rolling (out-of-state freshmen), rolling (transfers). *Notification:* continuous (freshmen), continuous (out-of-state freshmen), continuous (transfers).

Freshman Application Contact Mr. Daniel Solms, Director of Admissions, Indiana Wesleyan University, 4201 South Washington Street, Marion, IN 46953. *Phone:* 866-468-6498 Ext. 2138. *Toll-free phone:* 866-468-6498. *Fax:* 765-677-2333. *E-mail:* admissions@indwes.edu. *Web site:* http://www.indwes.edu/.

International Business College

Fort Wayne, Indiana

- **Private** 4-year, founded 1889
- **Suburban** campus
- **Coed** 580 undergraduate students
- 73% of applicants were admitted

Freshmen *Admission:* 975 applied, 716 admitted.

Academics *Calendar:* semesters. *Degrees:* diplomas, associate, and bachelor's. *Special study options:* accelerated degree program, internships.

Freshman Application Contact Admissions Office, International Business College, 5699 Coventry Lane, Fort Wayne, IN 46804. *Phone:* 260-459-4500. *Toll-free phone:* 800-589-6363. *Web site:* http://www.ibcfortwayne.edu/.

ITT Technical Institute

Fort Wayne, Indiana

- **Proprietary** primarily 2-year, founded 1967, part of ITT Educational Services, Inc.
- **Coed**
- **Minimally difficult** entrance level

Academics *Calendar:* quarters. *Degrees:* associate and bachelor's.

Student Life *Housing:* college housing not available.

Freshman Application Contact Director of Recruitment, ITT Technical Institute, 2810 Dupont Commerce Court, Fort Wayne, IN 46825. *Phone:* 260-

497-6200. *Toll-free phone:* 800-866-4488. *Fax:* 260-497-6299. *Web site:* http://www.itt-tech.edu/.

ITT Technical Institute

Indianapolis, Indiana

- **Proprietary** 4-year
- **Coed**
- **Minimally difficult** entrance level

Academics *Degrees:* associate and bachelor's.

Freshman Application Contact Director of Recruitment, ITT Technical Institute, 2525 N. Shadeland Avenue, Suite 103, Indianapolis, IN 46219. *Phone:* 317-351-3800. *Toll-free phone:* 877-264-1057. *Web site:* http://www.itt-tech.edu/.

ITT Technical Institute

Indianapolis, Indiana

- **Proprietary** comprehensive, founded 1966, part of ITT Educational Services, Inc.
- **Suburban** campus
- **Coed**
- **Minimally difficult** entrance level

Academics *Calendar:* quarters. *Degrees:* associate, bachelor's, and master's.

Freshman Application Contact Director of Recruitment, ITT Technical Institute, 9511 Angola Court, Indianapolis, IN 46268-1119. *Phone:* 317-875-8640. *Toll-free phone:* 800-937-4488. *Web site:* http://www.itt-tech.edu/.

ITT Technical Institute

Merrillville, Indiana

- **Proprietary** primarily 2-year
- **Coed**
- **Minimally difficult** entrance level

Academics *Degrees:* associate and bachelor's.

Freshman Application Contact Director of Recruitment, ITT Technical Institute, 8488 Georgia Street, Merrillville, IN 46410. *Phone:* 219-738-6100. *Toll-free phone:* 877-418-8134. *Web site:* http://www.itt-tech.edu/.

ITT Technical Institute

Newburgh, Indiana

- **Proprietary** primarily 2-year, founded 1966, part of ITT Educational Services, Inc.
- **Coed**
- **Minimally difficult** entrance level

Academics *Calendar:* quarters. *Degrees:* associate and bachelor's.

Student Life *Housing:* college housing not available.

Freshman Application Contact Director of Recruitment, ITT Technical Institute, 10999 Stahl Road, Newburgh, IN 47630-7430. *Phone:* 812-858-1600. *Toll-free phone:* 800-832-4488. *Web site:* http://www.itt-tech.edu/.

ITT Technical Institute

South Bend, Indiana

- **Proprietary** 4-year, part of ITT Educational Services, Inc.
- **Coed**
- **Minimally difficult** entrance level

Academics *Calendar:* quarters. *Degrees:* associate and bachelor's.

Student Life *Housing:* college housing not available.

Freshman Application Contact Director of Recruitment, ITT Technical Institute, 17390 Dugdale Drive, Suite 100, South Bend, IN 46635. *Phone:* 574-247-8300. *Toll-free phone:* 877-474-1926. *Web site:* http://www.itt-tech.edu/.

Manchester College

North Manchester, Indiana

- **Independent** comprehensive, founded 1889, affiliated with Church of the Brethren
- **Small-town** 125-acre campus
- **Endowment** $42.9 million
- **Coed** 1,297 undergraduate students, 98% full-time, 53% women, 47% men
- **Moderately difficult** entrance level, 65% of applicants were admitted

Undergraduates 1,276 full-time, 21 part-time. Students come from 23 states and territories; 23 other countries; 11% are from out of state; 3% Black or African American, non-Hispanic/Latino; 3% Hispanic/Latino; 0.6% Asian, non-Hispanic/Latino; 0.1% Native Hawaiian or other Pacific Islander, non-Hispanic/Latino; 0.4% American Indian or Alaska Native, non-Hispanic/Latino; 2% Two or more races, non-Hispanic/Latino; 0.3% Race/ethnicity unknown; 3% international; 2% transferred in; 74% live on campus. *Retention:* 72% of full-time freshmen returned.

Freshmen *Admission:* 3,622 applied, 2,348 admitted, 373 enrolled. *Average high school GPA:* 3.3. *Test scores:* SAT critical reading scores over 500: 53%; SAT math scores over 500: 61%; SAT writing scores over 500: 41%; ACT scores over 18: 90%; SAT critical reading scores over 600: 13%; SAT math scores over 600: 17%; SAT writing scores over 600: 8%; ACT scores over 24: 45%; SAT critical reading scores over 700: 1%; SAT math scores over 700: 2%; ACT scores over 30: 3%.

Faculty *Total:* 103, 73% full-time, 69% with terminal degrees. *Student/faculty ratio:* 16:1.

Academics *Calendar:* 4-1-4. *Degrees:* certificates, associate, bachelor's, and master's. *Special study options:* accelerated degree program, advanced placement credit, distance learning, double majors, honors programs, independent study, internships, off-campus study, part-time degree program, services for LD students, student-designed majors, study abroad, summer session for credit. *Unusual degree programs:* 3-2 engineering with Washington University in St. Louis.

Computers on Campus 222 computers/terminals are available on campus for general student use. Students can access the following: campus intranet, computer help desk, free student e-mail accounts, online (class) grades, online (class) registration, online (class) schedules. Campuswide network is available. 100% of college-owned or -operated housing units are wired for high-speed Internet access. Wireless service is available via computer centers, computer labs, dorm rooms, learning centers, libraries, student centers.

Student Life *Housing:* on-campus residence required through junior year. *Options:* coed, disabled students. Campus housing is university owned. Freshman campus housing is guaranteed. *Activities and organizations:* drama/theater group, student-run newspaper, radio station, choral group, A Cappella Choir, American Chemical Society, Accounting and Business Club, Circle K, Student Education Association. *Campus security:* 24-hour emergency response devices and patrols, student patrols, late-night transport/escort service, alarm system, locked residence hall entrances. *Student services:* health clinic, personal/psychological counseling.

Athletics Member NCAA. All Division III. *Intercollegiate sports:* baseball M, basketball M/W, cheerleading W, cross-country running M/W, equestrian sports W, football M, golf M/W, soccer M/W, softball W, tennis M/W, track and field M/W, volleyball W, wrestling M. *Intramural sports:* badminton M/W, basketball M/W, football M/W, racquetball M/W, soccer M/W, softball M/W, table tennis M/W, tennis M/W, ultimate Frisbee M/W, volleyball M/W.

Standardized Tests *Required:* SAT or ACT (for admission).

Costs (2011–12) *One-time required fee:* $250. *Comprehensive fee:* $35,070 includes full-time tuition ($25,100), mandatory fees ($870), and room and board ($9100). Part-time tuition: $700 per credit hour. Part-time tuition and fees vary according to course load. *Required fees:* $25 per credit hour part-time. *College room only:* $5500. Room and board charges vary according to board plan and housing facility. *Payment plan:* installment. *Waivers:* employees or children of employees.

Financial Aid Of all full-time matriculated undergraduates who enrolled in 2011, 1,178 applied for aid, 1,106 were judged to have need, 247 had their need fully met. In 2011, 135 non-need-based awards were made. *Average percent of need met:* 85%. *Average financial aid package:* $23,885. *Average need-based loan:* $4240. *Average need-based gift aid:* $19,268. *Average non-need-based aid:* $13,456. *Average indebtedness upon graduation:* $29,958.

Applying *Options:* electronic application. *Application fee:* $25. *Required:* high school transcript, 1 letter of recommendation, rank in upper 50% of high school class. *Required for some:* essay or personal statement, minimum 3.0 GPA. *Recommended:* minimum 2.3 GPA. *Application deadlines:* rolling (freshmen), rolling (transfers). *Notification:* continuous (freshmen), continuous (transfers).

Freshman Application Contact Mr. Adam Hohman, Associate Director of Admissions, Manchester College, 604 East College Avenue, North

Manchester, IN 46962-1225. *Phone:* 260-982-5235. *Toll-free phone:* 800-852-3648. *Fax:* 260-982-5239. *E-mail:* arhohman@manchester.edu. *Web site:* http://www.manchester.edu/.

Marian University

Indianapolis, Indiana

Freshman Application Contact Marian University, 3200 Cold Spring Road, Indianapolis, IN 46222-1997. *Phone:* 317-955-6300. *Toll-free phone:* 800-772-7264. *Fax:* 317-955-6401. *E-mail:* admissions@marian.edu. *Web site:* http://www.marian.edu/.

Martin University

Indianapolis, Indiana

Freshman Application Contact Ms. Brenda Shaheed, Director of Enrollment Management, Martin University, 2171 Avondale Place, PO Box 18567, Indianapolis, IN 46218-3867. *Phone:* 317-543-3237. *Fax:* 317-543-4790. *Web site:* http://www.martin.edu/.

Mid-America College of Funeral Service

Jeffersonville, Indiana

Freshman Application Contact Mr. Richard Nelson, Dean of Students, Mid-America College of Funeral Service, 3111 Hamburg Pike, Jeffersonville, IN 47130-9630. *Phone:* 812-288-8878. *Toll-free phone:* 800-221-6158. *Fax:* 812-288-5942. *E-mail:* macfs@mindspring.com. *Web site:* http://www.mid-america.edu/.

Oakland City University

Oakland City, Indiana

- **Independent General Baptist** comprehensive, founded 1885
- **Rural** 20-acre campus
- **Endowment** $3.8 million
- **Coed** 2,382 undergraduate students, 52% full-time, 55% women, 45% men
- **Minimally difficult** entrance level, 44% of applicants were admitted

Undergraduates 1,228 full-time, 1,154 part-time. Students come from 17 states and territories; 12 other countries; 7% are from out of state; 4% transferred in; 49% live on campus. *Retention:* 69% of full-time freshmen returned.
Freshmen *Admission:* 597 applied, 262 admitted, 230 enrolled. *Average high school GPA:* 3.15. *Test scores:* SAT critical reading scores over 500: 32%; SAT math scores over 500: 38%; SAT writing scores over 500: 34%; ACT scores over 18: 72%; SAT critical reading scores over 600: 7%; SAT math scores over 600: 7%; SAT writing scores over 600: 5%; ACT scores over 24: 19%; SAT math scores over 700: 1%; SAT writing scores over 700: 1%; ACT scores over 30: 2%.
Faculty *Total:* 178, 31% full-time, 16% with terminal degrees. *Student/faculty ratio:* 14:1.
Academics *Calendar:* semesters. *Degrees:* certificates, diplomas, associate, bachelor's, master's, and doctoral. *Special study options:* academic remediation for entering students, accelerated degree program, adult/continuing education programs, advanced placement credit, external degree program, part-time degree program, services for LD students, summer session for credit.
Computers on Campus 92 computers/terminals are available on campus for general student use. Students can access the following: campus intranet, free student e-mail accounts, online (class) grades, online (class) schedules. Campuswide network is available. 100% of college-owned or -operated housing units are wired for high-speed Internet access. Wireless service is available via entire campus.
Student Life *Housing:* on-campus residence required for freshman year. *Options:* men-only, women-only. Campus housing is university owned. Freshman campus housing is guaranteed. *Activities and organizations:* drama/theater group, student-run newspaper, choral group, Student Government Association, Good News Players, Art Guild, FOCUS, intramural sports. *Campus security:* 24-hour patrols, student patrols. *Student services:* personal/psychological counseling.
Athletics Member NCAA, NCCAA. All NCAA Division II. *Intercollegiate sports:* baseball M(s), basketball M(s)/W(s), cheerleading W(s), cross-country running M(s)/W(s), golf M(s)/W(s), soccer M(s)/W(s), softball W(s), tennis M(s)/W(s), volleyball W(s). *Intramural sports:* archery M/W, badminton M/W, basketball M/W, bowling M/W, football M, golf M/W, soccer M/W, softball M/W, table tennis M/W, tennis M/W, volleyball M/W.
Standardized Tests *Required:* SAT or ACT (for admission).

Costs (2011–12) *Comprehensive fee:* $24,340 includes full-time tuition ($16,200), mandatory fees ($440), and room and board ($7700). Full-time tuition and fees vary according to degree level. Part-time tuition: $500 per credit hour. *College room only:* $2600. Room and board charges vary according to board plan and housing facility. *Payment plan:* deferred payment.
Financial Aid Of all full-time matriculated undergraduates who enrolled in 2007, 150 Federal Work-Study jobs (averaging $1600). 4 state and other part-time jobs (averaging $1500). *Average percent of need met:* 90%.
Applying *Options:* electronic application, early admission, deferred entrance. *Application fee:* $35. *Required:* essay or personal statement, high school transcript, minimum 2.0 GPA. *Recommended:* interview. *Application deadlines:* rolling (freshmen), rolling (transfers). *Notification:* continuous (freshmen), continuous (transfers).
Freshman Application Contact Ms. Kim Heldt, Director of Admissions, Oakland City University, 138 North Lucretia Street, Oakland City, IN 47660. *Phone:* 812-749-1222. *Toll-free phone:* 800-737-5125. *Web site:* http://www.oak.edu/.

Purdue University

West Lafayette, Indiana

- **State-supported** university, founded 1869, part of Purdue University System
- **Suburban** 2539-acre campus with easy access to Indianapolis
- **Endowment** $2.0 billion
- **Coed** 30,776 undergraduate students, 95% full-time, 43% women, 57% men
- **Moderately difficult** entrance level, 69% of applicants were admitted

Undergraduates 29,332 full-time, 1,444 part-time. Students come from 52 states and territories; 122 other countries; 30% are from out of state; 4% Black or African American, non-Hispanic/Latino; 3% Hispanic/Latino; 5% Asian, non-Hispanic/Latino; 0.3% American Indian or Alaska Native, non-Hispanic/Latino; 1% Two or more races, non-Hispanic/Latino; 1% Race/ethnicity unknown; 15% international; 3% transferred in; 35% live on campus. *Retention:* 91% of full-time freshmen returned.
Freshmen *Admission:* 29,149 applied, 20,163 admitted, 6,684 enrolled. *Average high school GPA:* 3.6. *Test scores:* SAT critical reading scores over 500: 74%; SAT math scores over 500: 91%; SAT writing scores over 500: 76%; ACT scores over 18: 99%; SAT critical reading scores over 600: 32%; SAT math scores over 600: 60%; SAT writing scores over 600: 31%; ACT scores over 24: 76%; SAT critical reading scores over 700: 5%; SAT math scores over 700: 19%; SAT writing scores over 700: 4%; ACT scores over 30: 26%.
Faculty *Total:* 2,325, 88% full-time, 97% with terminal degrees. *Student/faculty ratio:* 14:1.
Academics *Calendar:* semesters. *Degrees:* certificates, associate, bachelor's, master's, doctoral, post-master's, postbachelor's, and first professional certificates. *Special study options:* accelerated degree program, adult/continuing education programs, advanced placement credit, cooperative education, distance learning, double majors, freshman honors college, honors programs, independent study, internships, part-time degree program, services for LD students, study abroad, summer session for credit. *ROTC:* Army (b), Navy (b), Air Force (b). *Unusual degree programs:* 3-2 business administration; engineering; forestry; nursing; social work; pharmacy.
Computers on Campus 5,330 computers/terminals and 17,822 ports are available on campus for general student use. Students can access the following: campus intranet, computer help desk, free student e-mail accounts, online (class) grades, online (class) registration, online (class) schedules. Campus-wide network is available. 100% of college-owned or -operated housing units are wired for high-speed Internet access. Wireless service is available via classrooms, computer centers, computer labs, learning centers, libraries, student centers.
Student Life *Housing options:* coed, men-only, women-only, cooperative, disabled students. Campus housing is university owned. Freshman applicants given priority for college housing. *Activities and organizations:* drama/theater group, student-run newspaper, radio and television station, choral group, marching band, student government, Golden Key National Honor Society, Society of Women Engineers, Purdue student union board, Krannert Graduate Student Association, national fraternities, national sororities. *Campus security:* 24-hour emergency response devices and patrols, student patrols, late-night transport/escort service, controlled dormitory access. *Student services:* health clinic, personal/psychological counseling, women's center.
Athletics Member NCAA. All Division I except football (Division I-A). *Intercollegiate sports:* baseball M(s), basketball M(s)/W(s), cross-country running M(s)/W(s), golf M(s)/W(s), soccer W(s), softball W(s), swimming and diving M(s)/W(s), tennis M(s)/W(s), track and field M(s)/W(s), volleyball W(s), wrestling M(s). *Intramural sports:* archery M(c)/W(c), badminton M(c)/W(c), baseball M(c), bowling M(c)/W(c), crew M(c)/W(c), cross-country running M(c)/W(c), equestrian sports M(c)/W(c), fencing M(c)/W(c), gym-

nastics M(c)/W(c), ice hockey M(c), lacrosse M(c)/W(c), racquetball M(c)/W(c), riflery M(c)/W(c), rock climbing M(c)/W(c), rugby M(c)/W(c), sailing M(c)/W(c), soccer M(c)/W(c), squash M(c)/W(c), swimming and diving M(c)/W(c), table tennis M(c)/W(c), tennis M(c)/W(c), track and field M(c)/W(c), ultimate Frisbee M(c)/W(c), volleyball M(c)/W(c), water polo M(c)/W(c).
Standardized Tests *Required:* SAT or ACT (for admission).
Costs (2011–12) *Tuition:* state resident $9478 full-time, $336 per credit hour part-time; nonresident $27,646 full-time, $916 per credit hour part-time. Full-time tuition and fees vary according to course load and program. Part-time tuition and fees vary according to course load. *Required fees:* $585 full-time. *Room and board:* $9794; room only: $5104. Room and board charges vary according to board plan and housing facility. *Payment plan:* installment. *Waivers:* senior citizens and employees or children of employees.
Financial Aid Of all full-time matriculated undergraduates who enrolled in 2011, 18,951 applied for aid, 14,829 were judged to have need, 5,894 had their need fully met. 646 Federal Work-Study jobs (averaging $710). In 2011, 2360 non-need-based awards were made. *Average percent of need met: 95%. Average financial aid package:* $11,572. *Average need-based loan:* $4861. *Average need-based gift aid:* $10,216. *Average non-need-based aid:* $6552. *Average indebtedness upon graduation:* $27,286.
Applying *Options:* electronic application, early admission, deferred entrance. *Application fee:* $50. *Required:* high school transcript. *Application deadlines:* 3/1 (freshmen), rolling (transfers). *Notification:* continuous (freshmen).
Freshman Application Contact Ms. Pamela T. Horne, Assistant Vice President for Enrollment Management and Dean of Admissions, Purdue University, 475 Stadium Mall Drive, Schleman Hall, West Lafayette, IN 47907-2050. *Phone:* 765-494-1776. *Fax:* 765-494-0544. *E-mail:* admissions@purdue.edu. *Web site:* http://www.purdue.edu/.

Purdue University Calumet
Hammond, Indiana

- **State-supported** comprehensive, founded 1951, part of Purdue University System
- **Urban** 202-acre campus with easy access to Chicago
- **Endowment** $13.6 million
- **Coed** 8,639 undergraduate students, 64% full-time, 55% women, 45% men
- **Moderately difficult** entrance level, 48% of applicants were admitted

Undergraduates 5,535 full-time, 3,104 part-time. Students come from 32 states and territories; 39 other countries; 14% are from out of state; 17% Black or African American, non-Hispanic/Latino; 17% Hispanic/Latino; 2% Asian, non-Hispanic/Latino; 0.3% American Indian or Alaska Native, non-Hispanic/Latino; 1% Two or more races, non-Hispanic/Latino; 0.8% Race/ethnicity unknown; 6% international; 4% transferred in; 7% live on campus. *Retention:* 69% of full-time freshmen returned.
Freshmen *Admission:* 4,072 applied, 1,943 admitted, 961 enrolled. *Average high school GPA:* 3.23. *Test scores:* SAT critical reading scores over 500: 42%; SAT math scores over 500: 42%; SAT writing scores over 500: 32%; SAT critical reading scores over 600: 7%; SAT math scores over 600: 9%; SAT writing scores over 600: 5%; SAT math scores over 700: 1%.
Faculty *Total:* 604, 51% full-time, 41% with terminal degrees. *Student/faculty ratio:* 18:1.
Academics *Calendar:* semesters. *Degrees:* certificates, associate, bachelor's, master's, post-master's, and postbachelor's certificates. *Special study options:* academic remediation for entering students, accelerated degree program, adult/continuing education programs, advanced placement credit, cooperative education, distance learning, double majors, English as a second language, freshman honors college, honors programs, independent study, internships, part-time degree program, services for LD students, study abroad, summer session for credit. *ROTC:* Army (b).
Computers on Campus 1,500 computers/terminals and 100 ports are available on campus for general student use. Students can access the following: campus intranet, computer help desk, free student e-mail accounts, online (class) grades, online (class) registration, online (class) schedules. Campuswide network is available. 100% of college-owned or -operated housing units are wired for high-speed Internet access. Wireless service is available via learning centers, libraries, student centers.
Student Life *Housing options:* coed. Campus housing is university owned. *Activities and organizations:* drama/theater group, student-run newspaper, choral group, Finance & Accounting Club, Muslim Student Association, College Mentors for Kids, Biology Club, Inter-Varsity Christian Fellowship, national fraternities, national sororities. *Campus security:* 24-hour emergency response devices and patrols, student patrols, late-night transport/escort service. *Student services:* health clinic, personal/psychological counseling.
Athletics Member NAIA. *Intercollegiate sports:* basketball M(s)/W(s), cross-country running M/W, golf M, tennis M/W, volleyball W. *Intramural sports:* badminton M/W, bowling M/W, football M/W, golf M/W, racquetball M/W,

sailing M/W, soccer M/W, softball M/W, table tennis M/W, ultimate Frisbee M/W, volleyball M/W.
Standardized Tests *Required:* SAT or ACT (for admission).
Costs (2011–12) *Tuition:* state resident $6821 full-time, $226 per credit hour part-time; nonresident $14,798 full-time, $511 per credit hour part-time. Full-time tuition and fees vary according to course load and program. Part-time tuition and fees vary according to course load and program. *Room and board:* $7515; room only: $5040. Room and board charges vary according to housing facility. *Payment plan:* deferred payment. *Waivers:* senior citizens and employees or children of employees.
Financial Aid Of all full-time matriculated undergraduates who enrolled in 2010, 5,222 applied for aid, 4,548 were judged to have need, 393 had their need fully met. 92 Federal Work-Study jobs (averaging $2051). In 2010, 247 non-need-based awards were made. *Average percent of need met:* 20%. *Average financial aid package:* $7455. *Average need-based loan:* $3449. *Average need-based gift aid:* $5530. *Average non-need-based aid:* $3656. *Average indebtedness upon graduation:* $24,066.
Applying *Options:* electronic application. *Required:* high school transcript, minimum 2.0 GPA. *Application deadlines:* 8/3 (freshmen), 8/3 (out-of-state freshmen), 8/3 (transfers). *Notification:* continuous (freshmen), continuous (out-of-state freshmen), continuous (transfers).
Freshman Application Contact Purdue University Calumet, 2200 169th Street, Hammond, IN 46323-2094. *Phone:* 219-989-2144. *Toll-free phone:* 800-447-8738. *Web site:* http://www.purduecal.edu/.

Purdue University North Central
Westville, Indiana

- **State-supported** comprehensive, founded 1967, part of Purdue University System
- **Rural** 305-acre campus with easy access to Chicago
- **Endowment** $3.5 million
- **Coed** 5,201 undergraduate students, 50% full-time, 59% women, 41% men
- **Minimally difficult** entrance level, 71% of applicants were admitted

Undergraduates 2,589 full-time, 2,612 part-time. Students come from 15 states and territories; 8 other countries; 2% are from out of state; 7% Black or African American, non-Hispanic/Latino; 8% Hispanic/Latino; 1% Asian, non-Hispanic/Latino; 0.1% Native Hawaiian or other Pacific Islander, non-Hispanic/Latino; 0.5% American Indian or Alaska Native, non-Hispanic/Latino; 1% Two or more races, non-Hispanic/Latino; 0.1% international; 4% transferred in. *Retention:* 51% of full-time freshmen returned.
Freshmen *Admission:* 1,659 applied, 1,177 admitted, 612 enrolled. *Average high school GPA:* 2.94. *Test scores:* SAT critical reading scores over 500: 39%; SAT math scores over 500: 45%; SAT writing scores over 500: 33%; ACT scores over 18: 84%; SAT critical reading scores over 600: 8%; SAT math scores over 600: 11%; SAT writing scores over 600: 4%; ACT scores over 24: 24%; ACT scores over 30: 2%.
Faculty *Total:* 282, 42% full-time, 34% with terminal degrees. *Student/faculty ratio:* 15:1.
Academics *Calendar:* semesters. *Degrees:* certificates, associate, bachelor's, master's, and postbachelor's certificates. *Special study options:* academic remediation for entering students, advanced placement credit, distance learning, double majors, honors programs, independent study, internships, off-campus study, part-time degree program, services for LD students, study abroad, summer session for credit.
Computers on Campus 450 computers/terminals and 65 ports are available on campus for general student use. Students can access the following: campus intranet, computer help desk, free student e-mail accounts, online (class) grades, online (class) registration, online (class) schedules. Campuswide network is available. Wireless service is available via entire campus.
Student Life *Housing:* college housing not available. *Activities and organizations:* drama/theater group, student-run newspaper, choral group, Dean's Leadership Group, Society of Human Resource Management, PLAYCE (Early Childhood Education), Astronomy Club, PNC Veteran's. *Campus security:* 24-hour emergency response devices and patrols, late-night transport/escort service. *Student services:* personal/psychological counseling.
Athletics Member NAIA. *Intercollegiate sports:* cheerleading M/W.
Standardized Tests *Required for some:* SAT or ACT (for admission). *Recommended:* SAT or ACT (for admission).
Costs (2012–13) *Tuition:* state resident $6440 full-time, $215 per credit hour part-time; nonresident $16,164 full-time, $539 per credit hour part-time. Full-time tuition and fees vary according to reciprocity agreements. Part-time tuition and fees vary according to reciprocity agreements. *Required fees:* $605 full-time, $20 per credit hour part-time. *Payment plans:* installment, deferred payment. *Waivers:* senior citizens and employees or children of employees.
Financial Aid Of all full-time matriculated undergraduates who enrolled in 2010, 2,809 applied for aid, 2,150 were judged to have need, 438 had their

need fully met. 62 Federal Work-Study jobs (averaging $1607). In 2010, 25 non-need-based awards were made. *Average percent of need met:* 50%. *Average financial aid package:* $7339. *Average need-based loan:* $3702. *Average need-based gift aid:* $5930. *Average non-need-based aid:* $1473. *Average indebtedness upon graduation:* $20,153. *Financial aid deadline:* 6/30.

Applying *Options:* electronic application, deferred entrance. *Required:* high school transcript. *Required for some:* minimum 2.0 GPA. *Application deadlines:* 8/15 (freshmen), 8/15 (transfers). *Notification:* continuous (freshmen), continuous (transfers).

Freshman Application Contact Ms. Janice Whisler, Director Enrollment/ Outreach Recruitment, Purdue University North Central, 1401 South U.S. Highway 421, Westville, IN 46391. *Phone:* 219-785-5415. *Toll-free phone:* 800-872-1231. *Fax:* 219-785-5538. *E-mail:* jwhisler@pnc.edu. *Web site:* http://www.pnc.edu/.

Rose-Hulman Institute of Technology
Terre Haute, Indiana

- **Independent** comprehensive, founded 1874
- **Suburban** 200-acre campus with easy access to Indianapolis
- **Endowment** $181.9 million
- **Coed, primarily men** 1,895 undergraduate students, 100% full-time, 21% women, 79% men
- **Very difficult** entrance level, 62% of applicants were admitted

Undergraduates 1,888 full-time, 7 part-time. Students come from 48 states and territories; 15 other countries; 58% are from out of state; 2% Black or African American, non-Hispanic/Latino; 3% Hispanic/Latino; 3% Asian, non-Hispanic/Latino; 0.2% Native Hawaiian or other Pacific Islander, non-Hispanic/Latino; 0.2% American Indian or Alaska Native, non-Hispanic/Latino; 3% Two or more races, non-Hispanic/Latino; 0.4% Race/ethnicity unknown; 6% international; 2% transferred in; 57% live on campus. *Retention:* 92% of full-time freshmen returned.

Freshmen *Admission:* 4,298 applied, 2,675 admitted, 506 enrolled. *Average high school GPA:* 3.91. *Test scores:* SAT critical reading scores over 500: 92%; SAT math scores over 500: 99%; SAT writing scores over 500: 89%; ACT scores over 18: 100%; SAT critical reading scores over 600: 54%; SAT math scores over 600: 86%; SAT writing scores over 600: 42%; ACT scores over 24: 94%; SAT critical reading scores over 700: 16%; SAT math scores over 700: 37%; SAT writing scores over 700: 9%; ACT scores over 30: 53%.

Faculty *Total:* 177, 92% full-time, 98% with terminal degrees. *Student/faculty ratio:* 12:1.

Academics *Calendar:* quarters. *Degrees:* bachelor's and master's. *Special study options:* accelerated degree program, adult/continuing education programs, advanced placement credit, cooperative education, double majors, independent study, internships, off-campus study, services for LD students, study abroad, summer session for credit. *ROTC:* Army (b), Air Force (b).

Computers on Campus 45 computers/terminals and 8,000 ports are available on campus for general student use. Students can access the following: campus intranet, computer help desk, free student e-mail accounts, online (class) grades, online (class) registration, online (class) schedules. Campuswide network is available. 100% of college-owned or -operated housing units are wired for high-speed Internet access. Wireless service is available via classrooms, computer centers, computer labs, learning centers, libraries, student centers.

Student Life *Housing:* on-campus residence required for freshman year. *Options:* coed, men-only. Campus housing is university owned. Freshman campus housing is guaranteed. *Activities and organizations:* drama/theater group, student-run newspaper, radio station, choral group, Drama Club, yoga club, Intervarsity Christian Fellowship, Chinese Culture Club, lacrosse club, national fraternities, national sororities. *Campus security:* 24-hour emergency response devices and patrols, late-night transport/escort service, controlled dormitory access. *Student services:* health clinic, personal/psychological counseling.

Athletics Member NCAA. All Division III. *Intercollegiate sports:* baseball M, basketball M/W, cross-country running M/W, football M, golf M/W, riflery M/W, soccer M/W, softball W, swimming and diving M/W, tennis M/W, track and field M/W, volleyball W. *Intramural sports:* basketball M/W, bowling M/ W, cross-country running M/W, fencing M(c)/W(c), football M/W, golf M/W, lacrosse M(c)/W(c), racquetball M/W, soccer M/W, softball M/W, swimming and diving M/W, table tennis M/W, tennis M/W, track and field M/W, ultimate Frisbee M/W, volleyball M/W, water polo M(c)/W(c).

Standardized Tests *Required:* SAT or ACT (for admission).

Costs (2011–12) *One-time required fee:* $2500. *Comprehensive fee:* $48,402 includes full-time tuition ($37,197), mandatory fees ($750), and room and board ($10,455). Full-time tuition and fees vary according to course load. Part-time tuition: $1085 per credit hour. Part-time tuition and fees vary according to course load. *College room only:* $6387. Room and board charges vary according to board plan. *Payment plans:* tuition prepayment, installment. *Waivers:* employees or children of employees.

Financial Aid Of all full-time matriculated undergraduates who enrolled in 2011, 1,482 applied for aid, 1,305 were judged to have need, 252 had their need fully met. 407 Federal Work-Study jobs (averaging $1351). 596 state and other part-time jobs (averaging $1351). In 2011, 542 non-need-based awards were made. *Average percent of need met:* 82%. *Average financial aid package:* $26,129. *Average need-based loan:* $4949. *Average need-based gift aid:* $21,248. *Average non-need-based aid:* $10,882. *Average indebtedness upon graduation:* $42,689.

Applying *Options:* electronic application, deferred entrance. *Application fee:* $40. *Required:* high school transcript, 1 letter of recommendation, curricular. *Recommended:* essay or personal statement, interview. *Application deadline:* 3/1 (freshmen). *Notification:* continuous (freshmen), continuous (transfers).

Freshman Application Contact Mrs. Lisa Norton, Director of Admissions, Rose-Hulman Institute of Technology, 5500 Wabash Avenue, CM 1, Terre Haute, IN 47803-3920. *Phone:* 812-877-8213. *Toll-free phone:* 800-248-7448. *Fax:* 812-877-8941. *E-mail:* admissions@rose-hulman.edu. *Web site:* http://www.rose-hulman.edu/.

Saint Joseph's College
Rensselaer, Indiana

- **Independent Roman Catholic** comprehensive, founded 1889
- **Small-town** 180-acre campus
- **Endowment** $20.2 million
- **Coed** 1,090 undergraduate students, 92% full-time, 59% women, 41% men
- **Moderately difficult** entrance level, 60% of applicants were admitted

Undergraduates 1,001 full-time, 89 part-time. Students come from 22 states and territories; 3 other countries; 22% are from out of state; 10% Black or African American, non-Hispanic/Latino; 5% Hispanic/Latino; 1% Asian, non-Hispanic/Latino; 0.7% American Indian or Alaska Native, non-Hispanic/Latino; 1% Two or more races, non-Hispanic/Latino; 0.2% Race/ethnicity unknown; 0.3% international; 2% transferred in; 67% live on campus. *Retention:* 66% of full-time freshmen returned.

Freshmen *Admission:* 1,799 applied, 1,081 admitted, 285 enrolled. *Average high school GPA:* 3.12. *Test scores:* SAT critical reading scores over 500: 33%; SAT math scores over 500: 39%; ACT scores over 18: 90%; SAT critical reading scores over 600: 10%; SAT math scores over 600: 10%; ACT scores over 24: 31%; SAT math scores over 700: 1%; ACT scores over 30: 4%.

Faculty *Total:* 113, 50% full-time, 42% with terminal degrees. *Student/faculty ratio:* 14:1.

Academics *Calendar:* semesters. *Degrees:* certificates, diplomas, associate, bachelor's, and master's. *Special study options:* academic remediation for entering students, accelerated degree program, advanced placement credit, double majors, honors programs, independent study, internships, part-time degree program, services for LD students, student-designed majors, study abroad, summer session for credit.

Computers on Campus 69 computers/terminals and 200 ports are available on campus for general student use. Students can access the following: campus intranet, computer help desk, free student e-mail accounts, online (class) grades, online (class) registration, online (class) schedules. Campuswide network is available. 100% of college-owned or -operated housing units are wired for high-speed Internet access. Wireless service is available via entire campus.

Student Life *Housing:* on-campus residence required through senior year. *Options:* coed, men-only, women-only, disabled students. Campus housing is university owned. Freshman campus housing is guaranteed. *Activities and organizations:* drama/theater group, student-run newspaper, radio and television station, choral group, marching band, Gallagher Charitable Society, Cup O' Joe, Habitat for Humanity, Science Club, Alpha Lambda Delta. *Campus security:* 24-hour emergency response devices and patrols, student patrols, late-night transport/escort service. *Student services:* health clinic, personal/ psychological counseling.

Athletics Member NCAA. All Division II. *Intercollegiate sports:* baseball M(s), basketball M(s)/W(s), cheerleading M(s)(c)/W(s)(c), cross-country running M(s)/W(s), football M(s), golf M(s)/W(s), soccer M(s)/W(s), softball W(s), tennis M(s)/W(s), track and field M(s)/W(s), volleyball W(s). *Intramural sports:* basketball M/W, lacrosse M(c)/W(c), rugby M(c)/W(c), soccer M/ W, softball M/W, ultimate Frisbee M/W, volleyball M/W.

Standardized Tests *Required:* SAT or ACT (for admission).

Costs (2012–13) *Comprehensive fee:* $35,600 includes full-time tuition ($27,160), mandatory fees ($190), and room and board ($8250). Full-time tuition and fees vary according to reciprocity agreements. Part-time tuition: $910 per credit. Part-time tuition and fees vary according to course load and reciprocity agreements. *College room only:* $4010. Room and board charges vary according to housing facility. *Payment plan:* installment. *Waivers:* minority students, children of alumni, and employees or children of employees.

Financial Aid Of all full-time matriculated undergraduates who enrolled in 2010, 765 applied for aid, 676 were judged to have need, 206 had their need fully met. 77 Federal Work-Study jobs (averaging $1301). In 2010, 83 non-need-based awards were made. *Average percent of need met:* 81%. *Average financial aid package:* $23,475. *Average need-based loan:* $4199. *Average need-based gift aid:* $16,962. *Average non-need-based aid:* $13,496. *Average indebtedness upon graduation:* $34,488.

Applying *Options:* electronic application, deferred entrance. *Application fee:* $25. *Required:* high school transcript, minimum 2.0 GPA. *Required for some:* essay or personal statement. *Recommended:* interview. *Application deadlines:* rolling (freshmen), rolling (transfers). *Notification:* continuous (freshmen), continuous (transfers).

Freshman Application Contact Mr. John Wadell, Assistant Vice President for Enrollment Management, Saint Joseph's College, PO Box 815, Rensselaer, IN 47978-0850. *Phone:* 219-866-6170. *Toll-free phone:* 800-447-8781. *Fax:* 219-866-6122. *E-mail:* admissions@saintjoe.edu. *Web site:* http://www.saintjoe.edu/.

Saint Mary-of-the-Woods College
Saint Mary-of-the-Woods, Indiana

- **Independent Roman Catholic** comprehensive, founded 1840
- **Rural** 67-acre campus with easy access to Indianapolis
- **Endowment** $10.8 million
- **Coed, primarily women** 1,233 undergraduate students, 37% full-time, 94% women, 6% men
- **Moderately difficult** entrance level, 66% of applicants were admitted

Undergraduates 456 full-time, 777 part-time. Students come from 40 states and territories; 7 other countries; 23% are from out of state; 5% Black or African American, non-Hispanic/Latino; 2% Hispanic/Latino; 0.7% Asian, non-Hispanic/Latino; 0.1% Native Hawaiian or other Pacific Islander, non-Hispanic/Latino; 0.5% American Indian or Alaska Native, non-Hispanic/Latino; 12% Race/ethnicity unknown; 2% international; 19% transferred in; 75% live on campus. *Retention:* 74% of full-time freshmen returned.

Freshmen *Admission:* 475 applied, 314 admitted, 102 enrolled. *Average high school GPA:* 3.2. *Test scores:* SAT critical reading scores over 500: 41%; SAT math scores over 500: 28%; SAT writing scores over 500: 37%; ACT scores over 18: 72%; SAT critical reading scores over 600: 12%; SAT math scores over 600: 12%; SAT writing scores over 600: 9%; ACT scores over 24: 28%; SAT critical reading scores over 700: 2%; ACT scores over 30: 7%.

Faculty *Total:* 176, 38% full-time, 23% with terminal degrees. *Student/faculty ratio:* 9:1.

Academics *Calendar:* semesters. *Degrees:* certificates, associate, bachelor's, master's, post-master's, and postbachelor's certificates (also offers external degree program with significant enrollment not reflected in profile). *Special study options:* academic remediation for entering students, accelerated degree program, adult/continuing education programs, advanced placement credit, distance learning, double majors, external degree program, honors programs, independent study, internships, off-campus study, part-time degree program, student-designed majors, study abroad, summer session for credit. *ROTC:* Army (c), Air Force (c).

Computers on Campus 65 computers/terminals and 150 ports are available on campus for general student use. Students can access the following: campus intranet, computer help desk, free student e-mail accounts, online (class) grades, online (class) registration, online (class) schedules. Campuswide network is available. 100% of college-owned or -operated housing units are wired for high-speed Internet access. Wireless service is available via entire campus.

Student Life *Housing:* on-campus residence required through senior year. *Options:* women-only. Campus housing is university owned. Freshman campus housing is guaranteed. *Activities and organizations:* drama/theater group, student-run newspaper, choral group, Student Activities Committee, Chorale, Student Senate, Woods Newspaper, Dance Team. *Campus security:* 24-hour emergency response devices and patrols, late-night transport/escort service. *Student services:* health clinic, personal/psychological counseling.

Athletics Member USCAA. *Intercollegiate sports:* basketball W(s), cross-country running W(s), equestrian sports W(s), golf W(s), soccer W(s), softball W(s).

Standardized Tests *Required:* SAT or ACT (for admission).

Costs (2011–12) *Comprehensive fee:* $36,956 includes full-time tuition ($26,872), mandatory fees ($750), and room and board ($9334). Full-time tuition and fees vary according to program. Part-time tuition: $473 per credit hour. Part-time tuition and fees vary according to program. No tuition increase for student's term of enrollment. *Required fees:* $100 per term part-time. *College room only:* $3644. *Payment plan:* installment. *Waivers:* employees or children of employees.

Financial Aid Of all full-time matriculated undergraduates who enrolled in 2009, 540 applied for aid, 513 were judged to have need, 184 had their need fully met. 104 Federal Work-Study jobs (averaging $883). In 2009, 11 non-need-based awards were made. *Average percent of need met:* 80%. *Average financial aid package:* $21,155. *Average need-based loan:* $2245. *Average need-based gift aid:* $8210. *Average non-need-based aid:* $6000. *Average indebtedness upon graduation:* $35,223.

Applying *Options:* electronic application, early admission, deferred entrance. *Application fee:* $30. *Required:* essay or personal statement, high school transcript, minimum 2.5 GPA, 1 letter of recommendation. *Required for some:* interview. *Application deadlines:* 8/1 (freshmen), 8/1 (transfers). *Notification:* 8/20 (freshmen), 8/20 (out-of-state freshmen), continuous until 8/20 (transfers).

Freshman Application Contact Ms. Beth Terrell, Vice President for Enrollment Management, Saint Mary-of-the-Woods College, Rooney Library, SMWC, Saint Mary-of-the-Woods, IN 47876. *Phone:* 812-535-5106. *Toll-free phone:* 800-926-SMWC. *Fax:* 812-535-5010. *E-mail:* smwcadms@smwc.edu. *Web site:* http://www.smwc.edu/.

Saint Mary's College
Notre Dame, Indiana

- **Independent Roman Catholic** 4-year, founded 1844
- **Suburban** 100-acre campus with easy access to Chicago
- **Endowment** $134.8 million
- **Women only** 1,510 undergraduate students, 99% full-time
- **Moderately difficult** entrance level, 84% of applicants were admitted

Undergraduates 1,499 full-time, 11 part-time. Students come from 46 states and territories; 14 other countries; 72% are from out of state; 2% Black or African American, non-Hispanic/Latino; 9% Hispanic/Latino; 1% Asian, non-Hispanic/Latino; 0.1% American Indian or Alaska Native, non-Hispanic/Latino; 2% Two or more races, non-Hispanic/Latino; 4% Race/ethnicity unknown; 2% international; 1% transferred in; 82% live on campus. *Retention:* 86% of full-time freshmen returned.

Freshmen *Admission:* 1,453 applied, 1,220 admitted, 393 enrolled. *Average high school GPA:* 3.7. *Test scores:* SAT critical reading scores over 500: 80%; SAT math scores over 500: 82%; SAT writing scores over 500: 84%; ACT scores over 18: 99%; SAT critical reading scores over 600: 36%; SAT math scores over 600: 33%; SAT writing scores over 600: 36%; ACT scores over 24: 63%; SAT critical reading scores over 700: 6%; SAT math scores over 700: 5%; SAT writing scores over 700: 5%; ACT scores over 30: 10%.

Faculty *Total:* 219, 54% full-time, 66% with terminal degrees. *Student/faculty ratio:* 10:1.

Academics *Calendar:* semesters. *Degree:* bachelor's. *Special study options:* academic remediation for entering students, accelerated degree program, advanced placement credit, cooperative education, distance learning, double majors, English as a second language, independent study, internships, off-campus study, part-time degree program, services for LD students, student-designed majors, study abroad, summer session for credit. *ROTC:* Army (c), Navy (c), Air Force (c). *Unusual degree programs:* 3-2 engineering with University of Notre Dame.

Computers on Campus 291 computers/terminals and 1,456 ports are available on campus for general student use. Students can access the following: campus intranet, computer help desk, free student e-mail accounts, online (class) grades, online (class) registration, online (class) schedules. Campuswide network is available. 60% of college-owned or -operated housing units are wired for high-speed Internet access. Wireless service is available via classrooms, computer centers, computer labs, dorm rooms, learning centers, libraries, student centers.

Student Life *Housing:* on-campus residence required through junior year. *Options:* women-only. Campus housing is university owned. Freshman campus housing is guaranteed. *Activities and organizations:* drama/theater group, student-run newspaper, radio and television station, choral group, marching band, Student Government Association, Dance Marathon, Class Boards, Residence Hall Association, Student Diversity Board. *Campus security:* 24-hour emergency response devices and patrols, late-night transport/escort service, controlled dormitory access. *Student services:* health clinic, personal/psychological counseling, women's center.

Athletics Member NCAA. All Division III. *Intercollegiate sports:* basketball W, cross-country running W, equestrian sports W(c), field hockey W(c), golf W, gymnastics W(c), skiing (downhill) W(c), soccer W, softball W, swimming and diving W, tennis W, ultimate Frisbee W(c), volleyball W, water polo W(c). *Intramural sports:* baseball W(c), basketball W, cheerleading W(c), lacrosse W(c), soccer W, volleyball W(c).

Standardized Tests *Required:* SAT or ACT (for admission).

Costs (2011–12) *Comprehensive fee:* $41,800 includes full-time tuition ($31,300), mandatory fees ($700), and room and board ($9800). Part-time tuition: $1240 per credit hour. *Required fees:* $350 per term part-time. *College room only:* $6040. Room and board charges vary according to board plan and housing facility. *Payment plan:* installment. *Waivers:* employees or children of employees.

SAINT MARY'S COLLEGE
NOTRE DAME · INDIANA

We Promise You
Discovery

*"Discovery of yourselves,
discovery of the universe,
and your place in it."*

—Sister M. Madeleva Wolff, CSC
President of Saint Mary's College, 1934–1961

*Study Abroad Program
Maynooth, Ireland*

Visit saintmarys.edu/Discover

Saint Mary's College ranks among the top 100
"Best National Liberal Arts Colleges" in the
U.S.News & World Report 2012 College Guide.

Financial Aid Of all full-time matriculated undergraduates who enrolled in 2011, 1,148 applied for aid, 1,075 were judged to have need, 174 had their need fully met. In 2011, 326 non-need-based awards were made. *Average percent of need met:* 71%. *Average financial aid package:* $24,471. *Average need-based loan:* $4631. *Average need-based gift aid:* $19,309. *Average non-need-based aid:* $11,280. *Average indebtedness upon graduation:* $30,072. *Financial aid deadline:* 3/1.

Applying *Options:* electronic application, early admission, early decision, deferred entrance. *Required:* essay or personal statement, high school transcript, 1 letter of recommendation, 16 high school academic units; at least two years of study of the same foreign language. *Recommended:* interview. *Application deadlines:* 2/15 (freshmen), 4/15 (transfers). *Early decision deadline:* 11/15. *Notification:* continuous (freshmen), continuous (transfers), 12/15 (early decision).

Freshman Application Contact Ms. Kristin McAndrew, Director of Admission, Saint Mary's College, Notre Dame, IN 46556. *Phone:* 574-284-4587. *Toll-free phone:* 800-551-7621. *Fax:* 574-284-4841. *E-mail:* admission@saintmarys.edu. *Web site:* http://www.saintmarys.edu/.

See page 1562 for the College Close-Up.

Strayer University - North Indianapolis Campus

Indianapolis, Indiana

- **Proprietary** comprehensive
- **Coed**

Academics *Degrees:* bachelor's and master's.

Freshman Application Contact Strayer University - North Indianapolis Campus, 9025 N. River Road, Suite 400, Indianapolis, IN 46240. *Web site:* http://www.strayer.edu/northindianapolis.

Taylor University

Upland, Indiana

- **Independent interdenominational** comprehensive, founded 1846
- **Rural** 950-acre campus with easy access to Indianapolis
- **Endowment** $72.2 million
- **Coed** 2,288 undergraduate students, 81% full-time, 57% women, 43% men
- **Moderately difficult** entrance level, 84% of applicants were admitted

Undergraduates 1,847 full-time, 441 part-time. Students come from 44 states and territories; 22 other countries; 65% are from out of state; 2% Black or African American, non-Hispanic/Latino; 2% Hispanic/Latino; 2% Asian, non-Hispanic/Latino; 0.1% Native Hawaiian or other Pacific Islander, non-Hispanic/Latino; 0.3% American Indian or Alaska Native, non-Hispanic/Latino; 1% Two or more races, non-Hispanic/Latino; 4% international; 2% transferred in; 86% live on campus. *Retention:* 85% of full-time freshmen returned.

Freshmen *Admission:* 1,839 applied, 1,541 admitted, 462 enrolled. *Average high school GPA:* 3.62. *Test scores:* SAT critical reading scores over 500: 80%; SAT math scores over 500: 78%; SAT writing scores over 500: 77%; ACT scores over 18: 98%; SAT critical reading scores over 600: 44%; SAT math scores over 600: 42%; SAT writing scores over 600: 35%; ACT scores over 24: 79%; SAT critical reading scores over 700: 12%; SAT math scores over 700: 9%; SAT writing scores over 700: 8%; ACT scores over 30: 22%.

Faculty *Total:* 251, 55% full-time, 61% with terminal degrees. *Student/faculty ratio:* 12:1.

Academics *Calendar:* 4-1-4. *Degrees:* certificates, diplomas, associate, bachelor's, and master's. *Special study options:* academic remediation for entering students, advanced placement credit, cooperative education, distance learning, double majors, English as a second language, honors programs, independent study, internships, off-campus study, part-time degree program, services for LD students, student-designed majors, study abroad, summer session for credit.

Computers on Campus 340 computers/terminals are available on campus for general student use. Students can access the following: campus intranet, computer help desk, free student e-mail accounts, online (class) grades, online (class) registration, online (class) schedules. Campuswide network is available. 100% of college-owned or -operated housing units are wired for high-speed Internet access. Wireless service is available via entire campus.

Student Life *Housing:* on-campus residence required through junior year. *Options:* men-only, women-only. Campus housing is university owned and is provided by a third party. Freshman campus housing is guaranteed. *Activities and organizations:* drama/theater group, student-run newspaper, radio and television station, choral group, TWO (Taylor World Outreach), IFC (Integration of Faith and Culture), Spring Break Mission Trips, Community Outreach. *Campus security:* 24-hour patrols, student patrols, late-night transport/escort service. *Student services:* health clinic, personal/psychological counseling.

Athletics Member NAIA. *Intercollegiate sports:* baseball M(s), basketball M(s)/W(s), cross-country running M(s)/W(s), football M(s), golf M(s)/W, soccer M(s)/W(s), softball W(s), tennis M(s)/W(s), track and field M(s)/W(s), volleyball W(s). *Intramural sports:* badminton M/W, basketball M/W, equestrian sports W(c), lacrosse M(c)/W(c), racquetball M/W, soccer M/W, softball M/W, tennis M/W, ultimate Frisbee M/W, volleyball M/W.

Standardized Tests *Required:* SAT or ACT (for admission).

Costs (2011–12) *Comprehensive fee:* $34,970 includes full-time tuition ($27,200), mandatory fees ($238), and room and board ($7532). Full-time tuition and fees vary according to course load. Part-time tuition: $973 per credit hour. Part-time tuition and fees vary according to course load. *Required fees:* $37 per term part-time. *Room and board:* Room and board charges vary according to board plan and housing facility. *Payment plan:* installment. *Waivers:* senior citizens and employees or children of employees.

Financial Aid Of all full-time matriculated undergraduates who enrolled in 2010, 1,358 applied for aid, 1,154 were judged to have need, 243 had their need fully met. 860 Federal Work-Study jobs (averaging $630). In 2010, 421 non-need-based awards were made. *Average percent of need met:* 73%. *Average financial aid package:* $18,328. *Average need-based loan:* $4782. *Average need-based gift aid:* $14,416. *Average non-need-based aid:* $6632. *Average indebtedness upon graduation:* $21,302. *Financial aid deadline:* 3/10.

Applying *Options:* electronic application, early action, deferred entrance. *Application fee:* $25. *Required:* essay or personal statement, high school transcript, 2 letters of recommendation, interview. *Recommended:* minimum 2.8 GPA. *Application deadlines:* rolling (freshmen), rolling (transfers), 12/1 (early action). *Notification:* continuous (freshmen), continuous (transfers), 12/20 (early action).

Freshman Application Contact Ms. Laura Brocker, Manager of On-Campus Recruitment, Taylor University, 236 West Reade Avenue, Upland, IN 46989-1001. *Phone:* 800-882-3456. *Toll-free phone:* 800-882-3456. *Fax:* 765-998-4925. *E-mail:* admissions@taylor.edu. *Web site:* http://www.taylor.edu/.

Trine University
Angola, Indiana

- **Independent** comprehensive, founded 1884
- **Small-town** 400-acre campus
- **Endowment** $23.2 million
- **Coed** 1,773 undergraduate students, 83% full-time, 35% women, 65% men
- **Moderately difficult** entrance level, 72% of applicants were admitted

Undergraduates 1,465 full-time, 308 part-time. Students come from 31 states and territories; 14 other countries; 37% are from out of state; 4% Black or African American, non-Hispanic/Latino; 2% Hispanic/Latino; 0.9% Asian, non-Hispanic/Latino; 0.1% Native Hawaiian or other Pacific Islander, non-Hispanic/Latino; 0.9% American Indian or Alaska Native, non-Hispanic/Latino; 9% Race/ethnicity unknown; 4% international; 2% transferred in; 97% live on campus. *Retention:* 73% of full-time freshmen returned.

Freshmen *Admission:* 2,867 applied, 2,052 admitted, 422 enrolled. *Average high school GPA:* 3.41. *Test scores:* SAT critical reading scores over 500: 55%; SAT math scores over 500: 77%; ACT scores over 18: 98%; SAT critical reading scores over 600: 11%; SAT math scores over 600: 33%; ACT scores over 24: 54%; SAT critical reading scores over 700: 4%; SAT math scores over 700: 5%; ACT scores over 30: 12%.

Faculty *Total:* 137, 58% full-time, 39% with terminal degrees. *Student/faculty ratio:* 15:1.

Academics *Calendar:* semesters. *Degrees:* associate, bachelor's, and master's. *Special study options:* academic remediation for entering students, adult/continuing education programs, advanced placement credit, cooperative education, distance learning, double majors, English as a second language, honors programs, internships, part-time degree program, student-designed majors, study abroad, summer session for credit. *ROTC:* Air Force (c). *Unusual degree programs:* 3-2 engineering.

Computers on Campus 600 computers/terminals are available on campus for general student use. Students can access the following: computer help desk, free student e-mail accounts, online (class) grades, online (class) registration, online (class) schedules, online campus billing accounts. Campuswide network is available. 100% of college-owned or -operated housing units are wired for high-speed Internet access. Wireless service is available via entire campus.

Student Life *Housing:* on-campus residence required through senior year. *Options:* coed, men-only, women-only. Campus housing is university owned and is provided by a third party. Freshman campus housing is guaranteed. *Activities and organizations:* drama/theater group, student-run newspaper, radio station, choral group, marching band, Campus Christian House, Drama Club, Habitat for Humanity, student newspaper, student radio station, national fraternities, national sororities. *Campus security:* 24-hour emergency response

devices and patrols, late-night transport/escort service, controlled dormitory access. *Student services:* health clinic, personal/psychological counseling.

Athletics Member NCAA. All Division III. *Intercollegiate sports:* baseball M, basketball M/W, cross-country running M/W, field hockey W, football M, golf M/W, lacrosse M/W, soccer M/W, softball W, tennis M/W, track and field M/W, volleyball W, wrestling M. *Intramural sports:* badminton M/W, basketball M/W, football M, golf M/W, racquetball M/W, softball M/W, table tennis M/W, volleyball M/W.

Standardized Tests *Required:* SAT or ACT (for admission).

Costs (2011–12) *Comprehensive fee:* $35,530 includes full-time tuition ($26,600), mandatory fees ($130), and room and board ($8800). Full-time tuition and fees vary according to degree level, location, and program. Part-time tuition: $830 per credit hour. Part-time tuition and fees vary according to degree level, location, and program. *Room and board:* Room and board charges vary according to board plan and housing facility. *Payment plan:* installment. *Waivers:* employees or children of employees.

Financial Aid Of all full-time matriculated undergraduates who enrolled in 2011, 1,383 applied for aid, 1,267 were judged to have need, 212 had their need fully met. In 2011, 139 non-need-based awards were made. *Average percent of need met:* 77%. *Average financial aid package:* $22,080. *Average need-based loan:* $5110. *Average need-based gift aid:* $4355. *Average non-need-based aid:* $11,213. *Average indebtedness upon graduation:* $30,400.

Applying *Options:* electronic application, deferred entrance. *Required:* high school transcript, minimum 2.5 GPA. *Recommended:* essay or personal statement, 2 letters of recommendation, interview. *Application deadlines:* 8/1 (freshmen), 8/1 (transfers). *Notification:* 8/15 (freshmen), continuous until 8/15 (transfers).

Freshman Application Contact Mr. Scott Goplin, Dean of Admission, Trine University, 1 University Avenue, Angola, IN 46703. *Phone:* 260-665-4365. *Toll-free phone:* 800-347-4TSU. *Fax:* 260-665-4578. *E-mail:* admit@trine.edu. *Web site:* http://www.trine.edu/.

See page 307 for display ad and page 1642 for the College Close-Up.

University of Evansville
Evansville, Indiana

- **Independent** comprehensive, founded 1854, affiliated with United Methodist Church
- **Urban** 75-acre campus
- **Endowment** $78.7 million
- **Coed** 2,708 undergraduate students, 91% full-time, 60% women, 40% men
- **Moderately difficult** entrance level, 83% of applicants were admitted

Undergraduates 2,471 full-time, 237 part-time. Students come from 41 states and territories; 47 other countries; 42% are from out of state; 3% Black or African American, non-Hispanic/Latino; 2% Hispanic/Latino; 1% Asian, non-Hispanic/Latino; 0.1% Native Hawaiian or other Pacific Islander, non-Hispanic/Latino; 0.1% American Indian or Alaska Native, non-Hispanic/Latino; 2% Two or more races, non-Hispanic/Latino; 7% Race/ethnicity unknown; 5% international; 3% transferred in; 70% live on campus. *Retention:* 83% of full-time freshmen returned.

Freshmen *Admission:* 3,522 applied, 2,915 admitted, 622 enrolled. *Average high school GPA:* 3.76. *Test scores:* SAT critical reading scores over 500: 81%; SAT math scores over 500: 83%; SAT writing scores over 500: 77%; ACT scores over 18: 100%; SAT critical reading scores over 600: 36%; SAT math scores over 600: 39%; SAT writing scores over 600: 29%; ACT scores over 24: 75%; SAT critical reading scores over 700: 6%; SAT math scores over 700: 5%; SAT writing scores over 700: 4%; ACT scores over 30: 15%.

Faculty *Total:* 230, 77% full-time, 73% with terminal degrees. *Student/faculty ratio:* 13:1.

Academics *Calendar:* semesters. *Degrees:* associate, bachelor's, master's, and doctoral. *Special study options:* accelerated degree program, adult/continuing education programs, advanced placement credit, cooperative education, distance learning, double majors, English as a second language, external degree program, honors programs, independent study, internships, part-time degree program, services for LD students, student-designed majors, study abroad, summer session for credit. *ROTC:* Army (b).

Computers on Campus 385 computers/terminals and 3,000 ports are available on campus for general student use. Students can access the following: campus intranet, computer help desk, free student e-mail accounts, online (class) grades, online (class) registration, online (class) schedules. Campuswide network is available. 100% of college-owned or -operated housing units are wired for high-speed Internet access. Wireless service is available via entire campus.

Student Life *Housing:* on-campus residence required for freshman year. *Options:* coed, men-only, women-only. Campus housing is university owned. Freshman campus housing is guaranteed. *Activities and organizations:* drama/theater group, student-run newspaper, radio station, choral group, Phi Eta

Sigma, International Club, PT Club, Student Christian Fellowship, Alpha Omicron Pi, national fraternities, national sororities. *Campus security:* 24-hour emergency response devices and patrols, student patrols, late-night transport/escort service, controlled dormitory access. *Student services:* health clinic, personal/psychological counseling.

Athletics Member NCAA. All Division I. *Intercollegiate sports:* baseball M(s), basketball M(s)/W(s), cross-country running M(s)/W(s), golf M(s)/W(s), soccer M(s)/W(s), softball W(s), swimming and diving M(s)/W(s), tennis W(s), volleyball W(s). *Intramural sports:* badminton M/W, basketball M/W, cross-country running M/W, racquetball M/W, soccer M/W, softball M/W, swimming and diving M/W, table tennis M/W, tennis M/W, ultimate Frisbee M/W, volleyball M/W.

Standardized Tests *Required:* SAT or ACT (for admission).

Costs (2011–12) *Comprehensive fee:* $38,946 includes full-time tuition ($28,620), mandatory fees ($796), and room and board ($9530). Part-time tuition: $800 per credit hour. Part-time tuition and fees vary according to course load. *Required fees:* $50 per term part-time. *College room only:* $4940. Room and board charges vary according to board plan and housing facility. *Payment plan:* installment. *Waivers:* minority students, children of alumni, adult students, senior citizens, and employees or children of employees.

Financial Aid Of all full-time matriculated undergraduates who enrolled in 2011, 2,134 applied for aid, 1,782 were judged to have need, 446 had their need fully met. 401 Federal Work-Study jobs (averaging $1343). 39 state and other part-time jobs (averaging $1400). In 2011, 519 non-need-based awards were made. *Average percent of need met:* 80%. *Average financial aid package:* $24,205. *Average need-based loan:* $4868. *Average need-based gift aid:* $20,804. *Average non-need-based aid:* $15,504. *Average indebtedness upon graduation:* $28,527.

Applying *Options:* electronic application, early action, deferred entrance. *Application fee:* $35. *Required:* essay or personal statement, high school transcript, 1 letter of recommendation. *Required for some:* interview. *Recommended:* minimum 3.0 GPA, interview. *Application deadlines:* 2/1 (freshmen), rolling (transfers), 12/1 (early action). *Notification:* 2/15 (freshmen), continuous (transfers), 12/15 (early action).

Freshman Application Contact Don Vos, Dean of Admission, University of Evansville, 1800 Lincoln Avenue, Evansville, IN 47722. *Phone:* 812-488-2468. *Toll-free phone:* 800-423-8633 Ext. 2468. *Fax:* 812-488-4076. *E-mail:* admission@evansville.edu. *Web site:* http://www.evansville.edu/.

University of Indianapolis
Indianapolis, Indiana

- **Independent** comprehensive, founded 1902, affiliated with United Methodist Church
- **Urban** 65-acre campus with easy access to Indianapolis
- **Endowment** $72.7 million
- **Coed** 4,205 undergraduate students, 72% full-time, 68% women, 32% men
- **Moderately difficult** entrance level, 79% of applicants were admitted

Undergraduates 3,036 full-time, 1,169 part-time. 9% are from out of state; 13% Black or African American, non-Hispanic/Latino; 2% Hispanic/Latino; 0.6% Asian, non-Hispanic/Latino; 0.1% Native Hawaiian or other Pacific Islander, non-Hispanic/Latino; 0.2% American Indian or Alaska Native, non-Hispanic/Latino; 2% Two or more races, non-Hispanic/Latino; 5% Race/ethnicity unknown; 5% international; 36% live on campus. *Retention:* 74% of full-time freshmen returned.

Freshmen *Admission:* 5,396 applied, 4,245 admitted, 794 enrolled. *Average high school GPA:* 3.42. *Test scores:* SAT critical reading scores over 500: 52%; SAT math scores over 500: 58%; ACT scores over 18: 87%; SAT critical reading scores over 600: 15%; SAT math scores over 600: 17%; ACT scores over 24: 36%; SAT critical reading scores over 700: 2%; SAT math scores over 700: 1%; ACT scores over 30: 4%.

Faculty *Total:* 493, 44% full-time. *Student/faculty ratio:* 15:1.

Academics *Calendar:* semesters. *Degrees:* associate, bachelor's, master's, doctoral, and first professional. *Special study options:* academic remediation for entering students, accelerated degree program, adult/continuing education programs, advanced placement credit, cooperative education, distance learning, double majors, English as a second language, freshman honors college, honors programs, independent study, internships, off-campus study, part-time degree program, services for LD students, student-designed majors, study abroad, summer session for credit. *ROTC:* Army (c). *Unusual degree programs:* 3-2 business administration with BS/MBA (Accounting); engineering with Indiana University - Purdue University Indianapolis; physical therapy, occupational therapy.

Computers on Campus 222 computers/terminals are available on campus for general student use. Students can access the following: campus intranet, computer help desk, free student e-mail accounts, online (class) grades, online (class) schedules. Campuswide network is available. 100% of college-owned

or -operated housing units are wired for high-speed Internet access. Wireless service is available via entire campus.

Student Life *Housing options:* coed, women-only. Campus housing is university owned. *Activities and organizations:* drama/theater group, student-run newspaper, radio and television station, choral group, Fellowship of Christian Athletes, Intercultural Association, Circle K, Indianapolis Student Government, Residence Hall Association. *Campus security:* 24-hour emergency response devices and patrols, student patrols, late-night transport/escort service, emergency call boxes. *Student services:* health clinic, personal/psychological counseling.

Athletics Member NCAA. All Division II. *Intercollegiate sports:* baseball M(s), basketball M(s)/W(s), cross-country running M(s)/W(s), football M(s), golf M(s)/W(s), soccer M(s)/W(s), softball W(s), swimming and diving M(s)/W(s), tennis M(s)/W(s), track and field M(s)/W(s), volleyball W(s), wrestling M(s). *Intramural sports:* badminton M/W, basketball M/W, cheerleading M/W, football M/W, racquetball M/W, softball M/W, table tennis M/W, tennis M/W, volleyball M/W.

Standardized Tests *Required:* SAT or ACT (for admission).

Costs (2011–12) *Comprehensive fee:* $31,740 includes full-time tuition ($22,790), mandatory fees ($220), and room and board ($8730). Part-time tuition: $949 per credit hour. Part-time tuition and fees vary according to course load. *College room only:* $4150. Room and board charges vary according to board plan and housing facility. *Waivers:* employees or children of employees.

Financial Aid Of all full-time matriculated undergraduates who enrolled in 2010, 3,445 applied for aid, 3,092 were judged to have need, 272 had their need fully met. In 2010, 524 non-need-based awards were made. *Average percent of need met:* 62%. *Average financial aid package:* $15,132. *Average need-based loan:* $4182. *Average need-based gift aid:* $7973. *Average non-need-based aid:* $7089. *Average indebtedness upon graduation:* $31,004.

Applying *Options:* electronic application, deferred entrance. *Application fee:* $25. *Required:* high school transcript, minimum 2.0 GPA. *Required for some:* interview. *Application deadlines:* rolling (freshmen), rolling (out-of-state freshmen), rolling (transfers). *Notification:* continuous (freshmen), continuous (out-of-state freshmen), continuous (transfers).

Freshman Application Contact Mr. Ronald Wilks, Director of Admissions, University of Indianapolis, 1400 East Hanna Avenue, Indianapolis, IN 46227-3697. *Phone:* 317-788-3216. *Toll-free phone:* 800-232-8634 Ext. 3216. *Fax:* 317-788-3300. *E-mail:* admissions@uindy.edu. *Web site:* http://www.uindy.edu/.

See page 306 for display ad and page 1674 for the College Close-Up.

University of Notre Dame
Notre Dame, Indiana

- **Independent Roman Catholic** university, founded 1842
- **Suburban** 1250-acre campus
- **Endowment** $7.5 billion
- **Coed** 8,452 undergraduate students, 100% full-time, 46% women, 54% men
- **Most difficult** entrance level, 24% of applicants were admitted

Undergraduates 8,428 full-time, 24 part-time. Students come from 51 states and territories; 40 other countries; 92% are from out of state; 3% Black or African American, non-Hispanic/Latino; 9% Hispanic/Latino; 6% Asian, non-Hispanic/Latino; 0.5% Native Hawaiian or other Pacific Islander, non-Hispanic/Latino; 0.4% American Indian or Alaska Native, non-Hispanic/Latino; 3% Two or more races, non-Hispanic/Latino; 0.7% Race/ethnicity unknown; 3% international; 78% live on campus. *Retention:* 97% of full-time freshmen returned.

Freshmen *Admission:* 16,548 applied, 4,019 admitted, 2,020 enrolled.

Faculty *Total:* 1,085, 91% full-time. *Student/faculty ratio:* 12:1.

Academics *Calendar:* semesters. *Degrees:* bachelor's, master's, doctoral, and first professional. *Special study options:* advanced placement credit, double majors, honors programs, independent study, internships, off-campus study, services for LD students, student-designed majors, study abroad, summer session for credit. *ROTC:* Army (b), Navy (b), Air Force (b).

Computers on Campus Students can access the following: computer help desk, free student e-mail accounts, online (class) grades, online (class) registration, online (class) schedules. Campuswide network is available. Wireless service is available via entire campus.

Student Life *Housing:* on-campus residence required for freshman year. *Options:* men-only, women-only. Campus housing is university owned. Freshman campus housing is guaranteed. *Activities and organizations:* drama/theater group, student-run newspaper, radio station, choral group, marching band, marching band, Circle K, Finance Club, Notre Dame/St. Mary's Right to Life. *Campus security:* 24-hour emergency response devices and patrols, student patrols, late-night transport/escort service, controlled dormitory access, crime prevention and personal safety workshops, full-time trained police investiga-

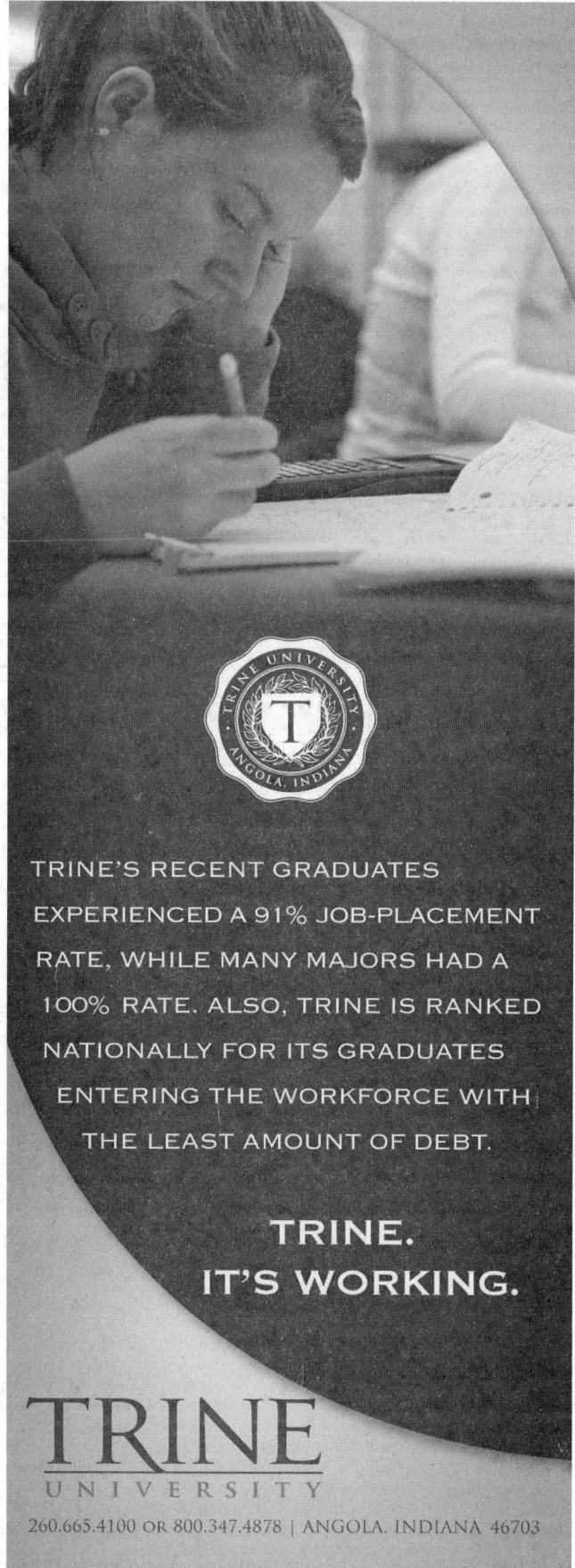

tors, fire sprinklers in all residence halls. *Student services:* health clinic, personal/psychological counseling, women's center.

Athletics Member NCAA. All Division I except football (Division I-A). *Intercollegiate sports:* baseball M(s), basketball M(s)/W(s), crew W(s), cross-country running M(s)/W(s), fencing M(s)/W(s), golf M(s)/W(s), ice hockey M(s), lacrosse M(s)/W(s), soccer M(s)/W(s), softball W(s), swimming and diving M(s)/W(s), tennis M(s)/W(s), track and field M(s)/W(s), volleyball W(s). *Intramural sports:* badminton M/W, baseball M, basketball M/W, bowling M(c)/W(c), crew M(c), cross-country running M/W, equestrian sports M(c)/W(c), field hockey M(c)/W(c), football M/W, golf M/W, gymnastics M(c)/W(c), ice hockey M(c)/W(c), lacrosse M/W, racquetball M/W, rock climbing M(c)/W(c), rugby M(c)/W(c), sailing M(c)/W(c), skiing (cross-country) M(c)/W(c), skiing (downhill) M(c)/W(c), soccer M/W, softball M/W, squash M(c)/W(c), tennis M/W, ultimate Frisbee M/W, volleyball M(c)/W(c), water polo M(c)/W(c).

Standardized Tests *Required:* SAT or ACT (for admission). *Required for some:* SAT Subject Tests (for admission).

Costs (2011–12) *Comprehensive fee:* $52,805 includes full-time tuition ($40,910), mandatory fees ($507), and room and board ($11,388). Part-time tuition: $1705 per credit hour. *Payment plan:* installment. *Waivers:* employees or children of employees.

Financial Aid Of all full-time matriculated undergraduates who enrolled in 2011, 5,194 applied for aid, 4,229 were judged to have need, 4,195 had their need fully met. 1,790 Federal Work-Study jobs (averaging $2358). 3,220 state and other part-time jobs (averaging $2957). In 2011, 349 non-need-based awards were made. *Average percent of need met:* 100%. *Average financial aid package:* $37,234. *Average need-based loan:* $8176. *Average need-based gift aid:* $28,324. *Average non-need-based aid:* $8799. *Average indebtedness upon graduation:* $30,170. *Financial aid deadline:* 2/15.

Applying *Options:* electronic application, early action, deferred entrance. *Application fee:* $75. *Required:* essay or personal statement, high school transcript, 1 letter of recommendation. *Application deadlines:* 12/31 (freshmen), 4/15 (transfers), 11/1 (early action). *Notification:* 4/10 (freshmen), 12/21 (early action).

Freshman Application Contact Office of Undergraduate Admissions, University of Notre Dame, 220 Main Building, Notre Dame, IN 46556-5612. *Phone:* 574-631-7505. *Fax:* 574-631-8865. *E-mail:* admissions@nd.edu. *Web site:* http://www.nd.edu/.

University of Phoenix–Indianapolis Campus

Indianapolis, Indiana

Freshman Application Contact Marc Booker, Sr. Director, Office of Admissions and Evaluation, University of Phoenix–Indianapolis Campus, 4035 South Riverpoint Parkway, Mail Stop CF-L101, Phoenix, AZ 85040. *Phone:* 602-557-4609. *Toll-free phone:* 866-766-0766. *Fax:* 480-643-1156. *Web site:* http://www.phoenix.edu/.

University of Phoenix–Northwest Indiana Campus

Merrillville, Indiana

Admissions Office Contact University of Phoenix–Northwest Indiana Campus, 359 East 81st Avenue, Merrillville, IN 46410. *Toll-free phone:* 866-766-0766. *Web site:* http://www.phoenix.edu/.

University of Saint Francis

Fort Wayne, Indiana

- **Independent Roman Catholic** comprehensive, founded 1890
- **Suburban** 74-acre campus
- **Endowment** $14.8 million
- **Coed** 2,013 undergraduate students, 79% full-time, 68% women, 31% men
- **Moderately difficult** entrance level, 54% of applicants were admitted

Undergraduates 1,584 full-time, 417 part-time. Students come from 17 states and territories; 12 other countries; 10% are from out of state; 7% Black or African American, non-Hispanic/Latino; 5% Hispanic/Latino; 0.7% Asian, non-Hispanic/Latino; 2% Two or more races, non-Hispanic/Latino; 0.7% Race/ethnicity unknown; 0.3% international; 11% transferred in; 26% live on campus. **Freshmen** *Admission:* 1,782 applied, 960 admitted, 379 enrolled. *Average high school GPA:* 3.24. *Test scores:* SAT critical reading scores over 500: 38%; SAT math scores over 500: 50%; SAT writing scores over 500: 35%; ACT scores over 18: 80%; SAT critical reading scores over 600: 9%; SAT

math scores over 600: 8%; SAT writing scores over 600: 6%; ACT scores over 24: 30%; SAT critical reading scores over 700: 1%; ACT scores over 30: 2%.
Faculty *Total:* 249, 51% full-time. *Student/faculty ratio:* 15:1.
Academics *Calendar:* semesters. *Degrees:* certificates, associate, bachelor's, master's, and postbachelor's certificates. *Special study options:* academic remediation for entering students, advanced placement credit, cooperative education, distance learning, double majors, freshman honors college, honors programs, independent study, internships, off-campus study, part-time degree program, services for LD students, study abroad, summer session for credit. *ROTC:* Army (c).
Computers on Campus 139 computers/terminals and 275 ports are available on campus for general student use. Students can access the following: campus intranet, computer help desk, free student e-mail accounts, online (class) grades, online (class) registration, online (class) schedules. Campuswide network is available. 100% of college-owned or -operated housing units are wired for high-speed Internet access. Wireless service is available via entire campus.
Student Life *Housing:* on-campus residence required through sophomore year. *Options:* coed. Campus housing is university owned. Freshman applicants given priority for college housing. *Activities and organizations:* drama/theater group, student-run newspaper, choral group, Student Activities Council, Art Club, Student Government Organization, Student Nursing Association, Residence Hall Council. *Campus security:* 24-hour emergency response devices and patrols, late-night transport/escort service, controlled dormitory access. *Student services:* personal/psychological counseling.
Athletics Member NAIA. *Intercollegiate sports:* baseball M(s), basketball M(s)/W(s), cheerleading M(s)/W(s), cross-country running M(s)/W(s), football M(s), golf M(s)/W(s), soccer M(s)/W(s), softball W(s), tennis M(s)/W(s), track and field M(s)/W(s), volleyball W(s). *Intramural sports:* basketball M/W, bowling M/W, soccer M/W, ultimate Frisbee M/W, volleyball W.
Standardized Tests *Required:* SAT or ACT (for admission).
Costs (2012–13) *Comprehensive fee:* $32,730 includes full-time tuition ($23,560), mandatory fees ($1000), and room and board ($8170). Full-time tuition and fees vary according to course load. Part-time tuition: $730 per credit hour. Part-time tuition and fees vary according to course load. *Required fees:* $20 per credit hour part-time. *Room and board:* Room and board charges vary according to board plan and housing facility. *Payment plan:* installment. *Waivers:* senior citizens and employees or children of employees.
Financial Aid Of all full-time matriculated undergraduates who enrolled in 2009, 1,477 applied for aid, 1,316 were judged to have need, 258 had their need fully met. 629 Federal Work-Study jobs (averaging $1411). In 2009, 146 non-need-based awards were made. *Average percent of need met:* 72%. *Average financial aid package:* $16,158. *Average need-based loan:* $4028. *Average need-based gift aid:* $12,247. *Average non-need-based aid:* $5446. *Average indebtedness upon graduation:* $28,428. *Financial aid deadline:* 6/30.
Applying *Options:* electronic application, deferred entrance. *Application fee:* $20. *Required:* high school transcript, minimum 2.3 GPA. *Required for some:* interview. *Recommended:* essay or personal statement. *Application deadlines:* rolling (freshmen), rolling (transfers). *Notification:* 8/15 (freshmen), continuous until 8/15 (transfers).
Freshman Application Contact Mr. JP Spagnolo, Director of Admissions, University of Saint Francis, 2701 Spring Street, Fort Wayne, IN 46808. *Phone:* 260-399-8000. *Toll-free phone:* 800-729-4732. *E-mail:* admis@sf.edu. *Web site:* http://www.sf.edu/.

University of Southern Indiana

Evansville, Indiana

- **State-supported** comprehensive, founded 1965, part of Indiana Commission for Higher Education
- **Suburban** 330-acre campus
- **Coed** 9,871 undergraduate students, 83% full-time, 59% women, 41% men
- **Moderately difficult** entrance level, 72% of applicants were admitted

Undergraduates 8,149 full-time, 1,722 part-time. Students come from 39 states and territories; 36 other countries; 11% are from out of state; 6% Black or African American, non-Hispanic/Latino; 1% Hispanic/Latino; 0.8% Asian, non-Hispanic/Latino; 0.1% Native Hawaiian or other Pacific Islander, non-Hispanic/Latino; 0.4% American Indian or Alaska Native, non-Hispanic/Latino; 0.3% Two or more races, non-Hispanic/Latino; 3% Race/ethnicity unknown; 3% international; 8% transferred in; 27% live on campus. *Retention:* 65% of full-time freshmen returned.
Freshmen *Admission:* 6,469 applied, 4,632 admitted, 2,025 enrolled. *Average high school GPA:* 3.08. *Test scores:* SAT critical reading scores over 500: 47%; SAT math scores over 500: 49%; SAT writing scores over 500: 34%; ACT scores over 18: 84%; SAT critical reading scores over 600: 10%; SAT math scores over 600: 11%; SAT writing scores over 600: 6%; ACT scores

over 24: 28%; SAT critical reading scores over 700: 1%; SAT math scores over 700: 1%; ACT scores over 30: 2%.

Faculty *Total:* 660, 51% full-time, 47% with terminal degrees. *Student/faculty ratio:* 18:1.

Academics *Calendar:* semesters. *Degrees:* certificates, associate, bachelor's, master's, doctoral, and postbachelor's certificates. *Special study options:* academic remediation for entering students, adult/continuing education programs, advanced placement credit, cooperative education, distance learning, double majors, English as a second language, honors programs, independent study, internships, part-time degree program, services for LD students, study abroad, summer session for credit. *ROTC:* Army (b).

Computers on Campus 306 computers/terminals are available on campus for general student use. Students can access the following: computer help desk, free student e-mail accounts, online (class) grades, online (class) registration, online (class) schedules. Campuswide network is available. 100% of college-owned or -operated housing units are wired for high-speed Internet access. Wireless service is available via entire campus.

Student Life *Housing options:* coed. Campus housing is university owned. *Activities and organizations:* drama/theater group, student-run newspaper, radio station, choral group, student government, national fraternities, national sororities. *Campus security:* 24-hour emergency response devices and patrols, student patrols, late-night transport/escort service, controlled dormitory access. *Student services:* health clinic, personal/psychological counseling.

Athletics Member NCAA. All Division II. *Intercollegiate sports:* baseball M(s), basketball M(s)/W(s), bowling M(c)/W(c), cheerleading M/W, cross-country running M(s)/W(s), golf M(s)/W(s), lacrosse M(c), rugby M(c)/W(c), soccer M(s)/W(s), softball W(s), tennis M(s)/W(s), ultimate Frisbee M(c)/W(c), volleyball W(s), wrestling M(c). *Intramural sports:* badminton M/W, basketball M/W, bowling M/W, football M/W, golf M/W, rock climbing M/W, skiing (downhill) M/W, soccer M/W, softball M/W, swimming and diving M/W, table tennis M/W, tennis M/W, volleyball M/W.

Standardized Tests *Required:* SAT or ACT (for admission).

Costs (2012–13) *Tuition:* state resident $5792 full-time, $193 per credit hour part-time; nonresident $13,787 full-time, $460 per credit hour part-time. Full-time tuition and fees vary according to course load and reciprocity agreements. Part-time tuition and fees vary according to course load and reciprocity agreements. *Required fees:* $240 full-time, $23 per term part-time. *Room and board:* $7200; room only: $3840. Room and board charges vary according to board plan and housing facility. *Payment plan:* installment. *Waivers:* employees or children of employees.

Financial Aid Of all full-time matriculated undergraduates who enrolled in 2011, 7,987 applied for aid, 5,433 were judged to have need, 713 had their need fully met. 74 Federal Work-Study jobs (averaging $2269). In 2011, 707 non-need-based awards were made. *Average percent of need met:* 77%. *Average financial aid package:* $8172. *Average need-based loan:* $3996. *Average need-based gift aid:* $6168. *Average non-need-based aid:* $3109. *Average indebtedness upon graduation:* $18,046. *Financial aid deadline:* 3/1.

Applying *Options:* electronic application. *Application fee:* $35. *Required:* high school transcript. *Required for some:* interview. *Recommended:* essay or personal statement, minimum 2.0 GPA. *Application deadline:* 8/15 (freshmen). *Notification:* 8/27 (freshmen), continuous (transfers).

Freshman Application Contact Mr. Eric Otto, Director of Admission, University of Southern Indiana, 8600 University Boulevard, Evansville, IN 47712-3590. *Phone:* 812-464-1765. *Toll-free phone:* 800-467-1965. *Fax:* 812-465-7154. *E-mail:* enroll@usi.edu. *Web site:* http://www.usi.edu/.

Valparaiso University
Valparaiso, Indiana

- **Independent** university, founded 1859, affiliated with Lutheran Church
- **Small-town** 320-acre campus with easy access to Chicago
- **Endowment** $163.7 million
- **Coed** 2,827 undergraduate students, 95% full-time, 55% women, 45% men
- **Moderately difficult** entrance level, 74% of applicants were admitted

Undergraduates 2,692 full-time, 135 part-time. Students come from 42 states and territories; 49 other countries; 59% are from out of state; 5% Black or African American, non-Hispanic/Latino; 6% Hispanic/Latino; 2% Asian, non-Hispanic/Latino; 0.2% Native Hawaiian or other Pacific Islander, non-Hispanic/Latino; 0.2% American Indian or Alaska Native, non-Hispanic/Latino; 2% Two or more races, non-Hispanic/Latino; 1% Race/ethnicity unknown; 4% international; 6% transferred in; 66% live on campus. *Retention:* 81% of full-time freshmen returned.

Freshmen *Admission:* 5,418 applied, 4,027 admitted, 698 enrolled. *Average high school GPA:* 3.63. *Test scores:* SAT critical reading scores over 500: 70%; SAT math scores over 500: 73%; SAT writing scores over 500: 64%; ACT scores over 18: 99%; SAT critical reading scores over 600: 31%; SAT math scores over 600: 31%; SAT writing scores over 600: 24%; ACT scores

over 24: 72%; SAT critical reading scores over 700: 4%; SAT math scores over 700: 5%; SAT writing scores over 700: 3%; ACT scores over 30: 19%.

Faculty *Total:* 375, 70% full-time, 73% with terminal degrees. *Student/faculty ratio:* 12:1.

Academics *Calendar:* semesters. *Degrees:* certificates, associate, bachelor's, master's, doctoral, post-master's, postbachelor's, and first professional certificates. *Special study options:* accelerated degree program, adult/continuing education programs, advanced placement credit, cooperative education, distance learning, double majors, English as a second language, freshman honors college, honors programs, independent study, internships, off-campus study, part-time degree program, services for LD students, student-designed majors, study abroad, summer session for credit. *ROTC:* Army (c), Air Force (c).

Computers on Campus 515 computers/terminals and 10 ports are available on campus for general student use. Students can access the following: campus intranet, computer help desk, free student e-mail accounts, online (class) grades, online (class) registration, online (class) schedules, Web academic information, degree audit. Campuswide network is available. 100% of college-owned or -operated housing units are wired for high-speed Internet access. Wireless service is available via classrooms, computer centers, computer labs, dorm rooms, learning centers, libraries, student centers.

Student Life *Housing:* on-campus residence required through junior year. *Options:* coed, women-only. Campus housing is university owned and leased by the school. Freshman campus housing is guaranteed. *Activities and organizations:* drama/theater group, student-run newspaper, radio station, choral group, Union Board, student government, student volunteer organization, chapel programs, national fraternities. *Campus security:* 24-hour emergency response devices and patrols, late-night transport/escort service, controlled dormitory access. *Student services:* health clinic, personal/psychological counseling, legal services.

Athletics Member NCAA. All Division I. *Intercollegiate sports:* baseball M(s), basketball M(s)/W(s), bowling W(s), cross-country running M(s)/W(s), football M, golf M(s)/W(s), soccer M(s)/W(s), softball W(s), swimming and diving M(s)/W(s), tennis M(s)/W(s), track and field M(s)/W(s), volleyball W(s). *Intramural sports:* badminton M(c)/W(c), basketball M/W, bowling M/W, fencing M(c)/W(c), football M/W, golf M/W, racquetball M/W, soccer M(c)/W(c), softball M/W, swimming and diving M/W, table tennis M/W, tennis M/W, ultimate Frisbee M(c)/W(c), volleyball M(c)/W.

Standardized Tests *Required:* SAT or ACT (for admission).

Costs (2011–12) *Comprehensive fee:* $39,796 includes full-time tuition ($30,000), mandatory fees ($1040), and room and board ($8756). Full-time tuition and fees vary according to course load. Part-time tuition: $1355 per credit hour. *Required fees:* $95 per semester part-time. *College room only:* $5356. Room and board charges vary according to housing facility and student level. *Payment plans:* tuition prepayment, installment. *Waivers:* employees or children of employees.

Financial Aid Of all full-time matriculated undergraduates who enrolled in 2011, 2,248 applied for aid, 2,061 were judged to have need, 468 had their need fully met. In 2011, 486 non-need-based awards were made. *Average percent of need met:* 78%. *Average financial aid package:* $22,770. *Average need-based loan:* $4924. *Average need-based gift aid:* $19,010. *Average non-need-based aid:* $10,080. *Average indebtedness upon graduation:* $33,104.

Applying *Options:* electronic application, deferred entrance. *Required:* essay or personal statement, high school transcript. *Required for some:* interview. *Recommended:* 2 letters of recommendation, interview. *Application deadlines:* rolling (freshmen), rolling (out-of-state freshmen), rolling (transfers). *Notification:* continuous (freshmen), continuous (out-of-state freshmen), continuous (transfers).

Freshman Application Contact Mr. T. Scott Henne, Director of Freshman Recruitment, Valparaiso University, Kretzmann Hall, 1700 Chapel Drive, Valparaiso, IN 46383-6493. *Phone:* 219-464-5011. *Toll-free phone:* 888-GO-VALPO. *Fax:* 219-464-6898. *E-mail:* Undergrad.Admission@valpo.edu. *Web site:* http://www.valpo.edu/.

Vincennes University
Vincennes, Indiana

- **State-supported** primarily 2-year, founded 1801
- **Small-town** 100-acre campus
- **Coed** 17,140 undergraduate students, 39% full-time, 46% women, 54% men
- **Noncompetitive** entrance level

Undergraduates 6,701 full-time, 10,439 part-time. Students come from 36 states and territories; 32 other countries; 11% Black or African American, non-Hispanic/Latino; 2% Hispanic/Latino; 0.5% Asian, non-Hispanic/Latino; 0.2% Native Hawaiian or other Pacific Islander, non-Hispanic/Latino; 0.3% American Indian or Alaska Native, non-Hispanic/Latino; 1% Two or more races, non-Hispanic/Latino; 12% Race/ethnicity unknown; 0.7% international; 2% transferred in.

Freshmen *Admission:* 3,833 enrolled.

Faculty *Student/faculty ratio:* 17:1.

Academics *Calendar:* semesters. *Degrees:* certificates, associate, and bachelor's. *Special study options:* academic remediation for entering students, adult/continuing education programs, advanced placement credit, distance learning, double majors, external degree program, off-campus study, part-time degree program, summer session for credit. *ROTC:* Army (c), Air Force (c).

Computers on Campus Campuswide network is available.

Student Life *Housing:* on-campus residence required for freshman year. *Options:* coed, men-only, women-only, disabled students. Campus housing is university owned. Freshman campus housing is guaranteed. *Activities and organizations:* drama/theater group, student-run newspaper, radio and television station, choral group, national fraternities, national sororities. *Campus security:* 24-hour emergency response devices and patrols, student patrols, late-night transport/escort service, controlled dormitory access, surveillance cameras. *Student services:* health clinic, personal/psychological counseling.

Athletics Member NJCAA. *Intercollegiate sports:* baseball M, basketball M/W, bowling M, cross-country running M/W, golf M, swimming and diving M/W, tennis M, track and field M/W, volleyball W.

Financial Aid Of all full-time matriculated undergraduates who enrolled in 2010, 220 Federal Work-Study jobs (averaging $1072).

Applying *Options:* electronic application, early admission, deferred entrance. *Application fee:* $20. *Required:* high school transcript. *Required for some:* interview. *Application deadlines:* rolling (freshmen), rolling (transfers). *Notification:* continuous until 8/1 (freshmen), continuous (transfers).

Freshman Application Contact Vincennes University, 1002 North First Street, Vincennes, IN 47591-5202. *Phone:* 800-742-9198. *Toll-free phone:* 800-742-9198. *Web site:* http://www.vinu.edu/.

Vincennes University Jasper Campus

Jasper, Indiana

- **State-supported** primarily 2-year, founded 1970, part of Vincennes University
- **Small-town** 140-acre campus
- **Coed**
- **Noncompetitive** entrance level

Faculty *Student/faculty ratio:* 16:1.

Academics *Calendar:* semesters. *Degrees:* certificates, associate, and bachelor's.

Financial Aid *Of all full-time matriculated undergraduates who enrolled in 2010,* 3 Federal Work-Study jobs (averaging $3200).

Applying *Application fee:* $20. *Required:* high school transcript.

Freshman Application Contact Ms. Louann Gilbert, Admissions Director, Vincennes University Jasper Campus, 850 College Avenue, Jasper, IN 47546-9393. *Phone:* 812-482-3030. *Toll-free phone:* 800-809-VUJC. *Fax:* 812-481-5960. *E-mail:* lagilbert@vinu.edu. *Web site:* http://vujc.vinu.edu/.

Wabash College

Crawfordsville, Indiana

- **Independent** 4-year, founded 1832
- **Small-town** 60-acre campus with easy access to Indianapolis
- **Endowment** $326.0 million
- **Men only** 910 undergraduate students, 100% full-time
- **Moderately difficult** entrance level, 63% of applicants were admitted

Undergraduates 908 full-time, 2 part-time. Students come from 35 states and territories; 12 other countries; 27% are from out of state; 5% Black or African American, non-Hispanic/Latino; 5% Hispanic/Latino; 2% Asian, non-Hispanic/Latino; 0.4% Native Hawaiian or other Pacific Islander, non-Hispanic/Latino; 0.8% American Indian or Alaska Native, non-Hispanic/Latino; 2% Two or more races, non-Hispanic/Latino; 2% Race/ethnicity unknown; 7% international; 86% live on campus. *Retention:* 83% of full-time freshmen returned.

Freshmen *Admission:* 1,456 applied, 916 admitted, 293 enrolled. *Average high school GPA:* 3.64. *Test scores:* SAT critical reading scores over 500: 80%; SAT math scores over 500: 92%; SAT writing scores over 500: 72%; ACT scores over 18: 95%; SAT critical reading scores over 600: 33%; SAT math scores over 600: 47%; SAT writing scores over 600: 24%; ACT scores over 24: 57%; SAT critical reading scores over 700: 5%; SAT math scores over 700: 12%; SAT writing scores over 700: 5%; ACT scores over 30: 14%.

Faculty *Total:* 89, 91% full-time, 99% with terminal degrees. *Student/faculty ratio:* 11:1.

Academics *Calendar:* semesters. *Degree:* bachelor's. *Special study options:* advanced placement credit, double majors, independent study, internships, off-campus study, services for LD students, study abroad. *Unusual degree programs:* 3-2 engineering with Purdue University, Columbia University, Washington University in St. Louis; law with Columbia University; accounting with Indiana University.

Computers on Campus 350 computers/terminals are available on campus for general student use. Students can access the following: campus intranet, computer help desk, free student e-mail accounts, online (class) grades, online (class) schedules, online course management, degree audit, expenses. Campuswide network is available. 100% of college-owned or -operated housing units are wired for high-speed Internet access. Wireless service is available via entire campus.

Student Life *Housing:* on-campus residence required through sophomore year. *Options:* men-only. Campus housing is university owned. Freshman campus housing is guaranteed. *Activities and organizations:* drama/theater group, student-run newspaper, radio station, choral group, Sphinx Club, Alpha Phi Omega, The Bachelor, Malcolm X Institute of Black Studies, Wabash Christian Fellowship, national fraternities. *Campus security:* 24-hour emergency response devices and patrols, late-night transport/escort service. *Student services:* health clinic, personal/psychological counseling.

Athletics Member NCAA. All Division III. *Intercollegiate sports:* baseball M, basketball M, crew M(c), cross-country running M, football M, golf M, lacrosse M(c), rugby M(c), sailing M(c), soccer M, swimming and diving M, tennis M, track and field M, volleyball M(c), water polo M(c), wrestling M. *Intramural sports:* badminton M, basketball M, bowling M, cross-country running M, football M, golf M, racquetball M, soccer M, softball M, swimming and diving M, table tennis M, tennis M, track and field M, volleyball M, weight lifting M, wrestling M.

Standardized Tests *Required:* SAT or ACT (for admission).

Costs (2011–12) *Comprehensive fee:* $40,950 includes full-time tuition ($31,800), mandatory fees ($650), and room and board ($8500). Part-time tuition: $5300 per course. *Required fees:* $650 per year part-time. *College room only:* $3900. Room and board charges vary according to board plan and housing facility. *Payment plans:* tuition prepayment, installment. *Waivers:* employees or children of employees.

Financial Aid Of all full-time matriculated undergraduates who enrolled in 2011, 796 applied for aid, 732 were judged to have need, 620 had their need fully met. 786 state and other part-time jobs (averaging $3055). In 2011, 135 non-need-based awards were made. *Average percent of need met:* 98%. *Average financial aid package:* $28,861. *Average need-based loan:* $6691. *Average need-based gift aid:* $17,950. *Average non-need-based aid:* $17,164. *Average indebtedness upon graduation:* $28,311. *Financial aid deadline:* 3/1.

Applying *Options:* electronic application, early admission, early decision, early action, deferred entrance. *Application fee:* $40. *Required:* high school transcript. *Recommended:* essay or personal statement, 1 letter of recommendation, interview. *Application deadlines:* rolling (freshmen), 3/15 (transfers), 12/1 (early action). *Early decision deadline:* 11/15. *Notification:* continuous (freshmen), continuous until 4/1 (transfers), 12/1 (early decision), 12/22 (early action).

Freshman Application Contact Mr. Steven J. Klein, Dean of Admissions, Wabash College, PO Box 362, Crawfordsville, IN 47933-0352. *Phone:* 765-361-6225. *Toll-free phone:* 800-345-5385. *Fax:* 765-361-6437. *E-mail:* admissions@wabash.edu. *Web site:* http://www.wabash.edu/.

IOWA

AIB College of Business

Des Moines, Iowa

- **Independent** 4-year, founded 1921
- **Urban** 20-acre campus
- **Endowment** $7.2 million
- **Coed** 840 undergraduate students, 68% full-time, 67% women, 33% men
- **Minimally difficult** entrance level, 58% of applicants were admitted

Undergraduates 571 full-time, 269 part-time. Students come from 23 states and territories; 8% are from out of state; 3% Black or African American, non-Hispanic/Latino; 4% Hispanic/Latino; 3% Asian, non-Hispanic/Latino; 0.1% Native Hawaiian or other Pacific Islander, non-Hispanic/Latino; 0.8% American Indian or Alaska Native, non-Hispanic/Latino; 3% Two or more races, non-Hispanic/Latino; 5% Race/ethnicity unknown; 0.1% international; 12% transferred in; 32% live on campus. *Retention:* 65% of full-time freshmen returned.

Freshmen *Admission:* 349 applied, 201 admitted, 119 enrolled. *Average high school GPA:* 3.11. *Test scores:* ACT scores over 18: 79%; ACT scores over 24: 20%; ACT scores over 30: 1%.

Faculty *Total:* 62, 34% full-time, 8% with terminal degrees. *Student/faculty ratio:* 18:1.

Academics *Calendar:* quarters. *Degrees:* associate and bachelor's. *Special study options:* academic remediation for entering students, advanced place-

ment credit, cooperative education, distance learning, double majors, independent study, internships, part-time degree program, services for LD students, study abroad, summer session for credit.

Computers on Campus 372 computers/terminals and 1,256 ports are available on campus for general student use. Students can access the following: campus intranet, computer help desk, free student e-mail accounts, online (class) grades. Campuswide network is available. 100% of college-owned or -operated housing units are wired for high-speed Internet access. Wireless service is available via entire campus.

Student Life *Housing options:* coed, disabled students. Campus housing is university owned. *Activities and organizations:* Phi Theta Kappa, Business Management Association, Student Court Reporters and Captioners Association, Students in Free Enterprise (SIFE), Student Government Association, national sororities. *Campus security:* 24-hour emergency response devices and patrols, late-night transport/escort service, controlled dormitory access, video security. *Student services:* personal/psychological counseling.

Athletics Member NAIA. *Intercollegiate sports:* basketball M(s)/W(s), cheerleading M(s)/W(s), golf M(s)/W(s), soccer M(s)/W(s), volleyball W(s). *Intramural sports:* badminton M/W, basketball M/W, bowling M/W, football M/W, softball M/W, table tennis M/W, ultimate Frisbee M/W, volleyball M(c)/W(c).

Standardized Tests *Required for some:* Nelson-Denny if no ACT score. *Recommended:* ACT (for admission).

Costs (2012–13) *Tuition:* $13,800 full-time, $1150 per course part-time. Full-time tuition and fees vary according to course load. Part-time tuition and fees vary according to course load. No tuition increase for student's term of enrollment. *Required fees:* $240 full-time, $80 per term part-time. *Room only:* $3525. Room and board charges vary according to housing facility. *Payment plans:* installment, deferred payment. *Waivers:* employees or children of employees.

Financial Aid Of all full-time matriculated undergraduates who enrolled in 2010, 104 Federal Work-Study jobs (averaging $1135). 1 state and other part-time job (averaging $457).

Applying *Options:* electronic application. *Required:* high school transcript, minimum 2.0 GPA. *Recommended:* interview. *Application deadlines:* rolling (freshmen), rolling (out-of-state freshmen), rolling (transfers). *Notification:* continuous (freshmen), continuous (out-of-state freshmen), continuous (transfers).

Freshman Application Contact AIB College of Business, 2500 Fleur Drive, Des Moines, IA 50321-1799. *Phone:* 515-246-5336. *Toll-free phone:* 800-444-1921. *Web site:* http://www.aib.edu/.

Allen College
Waterloo, Iowa

- **Independent** comprehensive, founded 1989
- **Suburban** 20-acre campus
- **Endowment** $1.8 million
- **Coed, primarily women** 348 undergraduate students, 74% full-time, 92% women, 8% men
- **Moderately difficult** entrance level, 75% of applicants were admitted

Undergraduates 256 full-time, 92 part-time. Students come from 7 states and territories; 2 other countries; 4% are from out of state; 3% Black or African American, non-Hispanic/Latino; 0.9% Hispanic/Latino; 2% Asian, non-Hispanic/Latino; 0.3% American Indian or Alaska Native, non-Hispanic/Latino; 0.3% Two or more races, non-Hispanic/Latino; 0.6% international; 32% transferred in; 5% live on campus.

Freshmen *Admission:* 4 applied, 3 admitted, 2 enrolled.

Faculty *Total:* 39, 77% full-time, 23% with terminal degrees. *Student/faculty ratio:* 12:1.

Academics *Calendar:* semesters. *Degrees:* certificates, associate, bachelor's, master's, doctoral, and post-master's certificates (liberal arts and general education courses offered at either University of North Iowa or Wartburg College). *Special study options:* accelerated degree program, advanced placement credit, cooperative education, distance learning, honors programs, independent study, internships, off-campus study, part-time degree program. *ROTC:* Army (c). *Unusual degree programs:* 3-2 nursing with Wartburg College, Loras College, Central College, Simpson College.

Computers on Campus 32 computers/terminals are available on campus for general student use. Students can access the following: campus intranet, computer help desk, free student e-mail accounts, online (class) grades, online (class) schedules. Campuswide network is available. 100% of college-owned or -operated housing units are wired for high-speed Internet access. Wireless service is available via entire campus.

Student Life *Housing options:* coed. Campus housing is university owned. *Activities and organizations:* choral group, Allen Student Nurses' Association, Nurses' Christian Fellowship. *Campus security:* 24-hour patrols, controlled dormitory access. *Student services:* health clinic, personal/psychological counseling.

Standardized Tests *Required for some:* SAT or ACT (for admission).

Costs (2011–12) *Comprehensive fee:* $24,897 includes full-time tuition ($15,936), mandatory fees ($1680), and room and board ($7281). Full-time tuition and fees vary according to course load and program. Part-time tuition: $510 per credit hour. Part-time tuition and fees vary according to course load and program. *Required fees:* $69 per credit hour part-time. *College room only:* $3641. Room and board charges vary according to housing facility. *Payment plan:* deferred payment. *Waivers:* employees or children of employees.

Financial Aid Of all full-time matriculated undergraduates who enrolled in 2010, 288 applied for aid, 252 were judged to have need, 6 had their need fully met. 15 Federal Work-Study jobs (averaging $2380). In 2010, 14 non-need-based awards were made. *Average percent of need met:* 33%. *Average financial aid package:* $10,231. *Average need-based loan:* $10,088. *Average need-based gift aid:* $6524. *Average non-need-based aid:* $3928. *Average indebtedness upon graduation:* $20,231.

Applying *Options:* electronic application. *Application fee:* $50. *Required for some:* essay or personal statement, high school transcript, 1 letter of recommendation, interview. *Recommended:* minimum 2.7 GPA, GPA requirements are based on grades in specific general education courses, not on a cumulative GPA. *Application deadlines:* 2/1 (freshmen), 2/1 (transfers). *Notification:* continuous until 3/1 (freshmen), continuous until 3/1 (transfers).

Freshman Application Contact Dina Dowden, Education Secretary, Student Services, Allen College, Barrett Forum, 1825 Logan Avenue, Waterloo, IA 50703. *Phone:* 319-226-2000. *Fax:* 319-226-2010. *E-mail:* allencollegeadmissions@ihs.org. *Web site:* http://www.allencollege.edu/.

Ashford University
Clinton, Iowa

Director of Admissions Ms. Waunita M. Sullivan, Director of Enrollment, Ashford University, 400 North Bluff Boulevard, PO Box 2967, Clinton, IA 52733-2967. *Phone:* 563-242-4023 Ext. 3401. *Toll-free phone:* 866-711-1700. *E-mail:* admissns@tfu.edu. *Web site:* http://www.ashford.edu/.

Briar Cliff University
Sioux City, Iowa

- **Independent Roman Catholic** comprehensive, founded 1930
- **Suburban** 75-acre campus
- **Endowment** $9.5 million
- **Coed** 1,088 undergraduate students, 78% full-time, 57% women, 43% men
- **Moderately difficult** entrance level, 54% of applicants were admitted

Undergraduates 851 full-time, 237 part-time. Students come from 32 states and territories; 11 other countries; 42% are from out of state; 7% Black or African American, non-Hispanic/Latino; 9% Hispanic/Latino; 2% Asian, non-Hispanic/Latino; 0.3% Native Hawaiian or other Pacific Islander, non-Hispanic/Latino; 1% American Indian or Alaska Native, non-Hispanic/Latino; 2% Two or more races, non-Hispanic/Latino; 2% international; 12% transferred in. *Retention:* 69% of full-time freshmen returned.

Freshmen *Admission:* 2,400 applied, 1,299 admitted, 237 enrolled. *Average high school GPA:* 3.2. *Test scores:* ACT scores over 18: 91%; ACT scores over 24: 37%; ACT scores over 30: 4%.

Faculty *Total:* 106, 58% full-time, 48% with terminal degrees. *Student/faculty ratio:* 12:1.

Academics *Calendar:* (3 10-week terms plus 2 5-week summer sessions). *Degrees:* associate, bachelor's, master's, post-master's, and postbachelor's certificates. *Special study options:* academic remediation for entering students, accelerated degree program, adult/continuing education programs, advanced placement credit, distance learning, double majors, honors programs, independent study, internships, off-campus study, part-time degree program, services for LD students, student-designed majors, study abroad, summer session for credit. *ROTC:* Army (c).

Computers on Campus 100 computers/terminals and 1,000 ports are available on campus for general student use. Students can access the following: campus intranet, computer help desk, free student e-mail accounts, online (class) grades, online (class) schedules. Campuswide network is available. 100% of college-owned or -operated housing units are wired for high-speed Internet access. Wireless service is available via classrooms, computer centers, computer labs, libraries, student centers.

Student Life *Housing:* on-campus residence required through junior year. *Options:* coed. Campus housing is university owned. Freshman campus housing is guaranteed. *Activities and organizations:* drama/theater group, student-run newspaper, radio station, choral group, Residence Hall Association, Briar Cliff Student Government, Choices, Blue Crew, Catholic Daughters of America. *Campus security:* 24-hour emergency response devices and patrols, student patrols, late-night transport/escort service, controlled dormitory access. *Student services:* health clinic, personal/psychological counseling.

Athletics Member NAIA. *Intercollegiate sports:* baseball M(s), basketball M(s)/ W(s), cheerleading W(s), cross-country running M(s)/W(s), football M(s), golf M(s)/W(s), soccer M(s)/W(s), softball W(s), tennis M(s)/W(s), track and field M(s)/W(s), volleyball W(s), wrestling M(s). *Intramural sports:* basketball M/W, bowling M/W, football M, golf M/W, softball M/W, table tennis M/W, tennis M/W, volleyball M/W.

Standardized Tests *Required:* SAT or ACT (for admission).

Costs (2012–13) *Comprehensive fee:* $33,184 includes full-time tuition ($24,520), mandatory fees ($1122), and room and board ($7542). Part-time tuition: $810 per hour. *Room and board:* Room and board charges vary according to board plan and housing facility. *Payment plans:* installment, deferred payment. *Waivers:* adult students, senior citizens, and employees or children of employees.

Financial Aid Of all full-time matriculated undergraduates who enrolled in 2011, 803 applied for aid, 618 were judged to have need, 340 had their need fully met. 245 Federal Work-Study jobs (averaging $1500). 125 state and other part-time jobs (averaging $1500). In 2011, 251 non-need-based awards were made. *Average percent of need met:* 46%. *Average financial aid package:* $20,452. *Average need-based loan:* $4990. *Average need-based gift aid:* $4542. *Average non-need-based aid:* $15,750. *Average indebtedness upon graduation:* $32,400. *Financial aid deadline:* 3/15.

Applying *Options:* electronic application, early admission, deferred entrance. *Application fee:* $20. *Required:* high school transcript, minimum 2.0 GPA. *Required for some:* essay or personal statement, 3 letters of recommendation, interview. *Application deadlines:* rolling (freshmen), rolling (out-of-state freshmen), rolling (transfers). *Notification:* continuous (transfers).

Freshman Application Contact Mr. Brian Eben, Assistant Vice President for Enrollment Management, Briar Cliff University, 3303 Rebecca Street, Sioux City, IA 51104. *Phone:* 712-279-5200. *Toll-free phone:* 800-662-3303. *Fax:* 712-279-1632. *E-mail:* admissions@briarcliff.edu. *Web site:* http://www.briarcliff.edu/.

See below for display ad and page 1182 for the College Close-Up.

Buena Vista University
Storm Lake, Iowa

- **Independent** comprehensive, founded 1891, affiliated with Presbyterian Church (U.S.A.)
- **Small-town** 60-acre campus
- **Endowment** $125.0 million
- **Coed** 941 undergraduate students, 98% full-time, 50% women, 50% men
- **Moderately difficult** entrance level, 64% of applicants were admitted

Undergraduates 924 full-time, 17 part-time. Students come from 27 states and territories; 10 other countries; 23% are from out of state; 4% Black or African American, non-Hispanic/Latino; 6% Hispanic/Latino; 1% Asian, non-Hispanic/Latino; 0.4% American Indian or Alaska Native, non-Hispanic/Latino; 1% Two or more races, non-Hispanic/Latino; 3% Race/ethnicity unknown; 6% international; 6% transferred in; 84% live on campus. *Retention:* 73% of full-time freshmen returned.

Freshmen *Admission:* 896 applied, 572 admitted, 203 enrolled. *Average high school GPA:* 3.41. *Test scores:* ACT scores over 18: 92%; ACT scores over 24: 35%; ACT scores over 30: 6%.

Faculty *Total:* 108, 80% full-time, 58% with terminal degrees. *Student/faculty ratio:* 10:1.

Academics *Calendar:* 4-1-4. *Degrees:* bachelor's and master's. *Special study options:* academic remediation for entering students, adult/continuing education programs, advanced placement credit, distance learning, double majors, English as a second language, external degree program, honors programs, independent study, internships, off-campus study, part-time degree program, services for LD students, student-designed majors, study abroad, summer session for credit. *ROTC:* Army (b). *Unusual degree programs:* 3-2 engineering with Washington University in St. Louis.

Computers on Campus 400 computers/terminals are available on campus for general student use. Students can access the following: computer help desk, free student e-mail accounts, online (class) grades, online (class) registration, online (class) schedules. Campuswide network is available. 100% of college-owned or -operated housing units are wired for high-speed Internet access. Wireless service is available via entire campus.

Student Life *Housing:* on-campus residence required through senior year. *Options:* coed, men-only, women-only. Campus housing is university owned. Freshman campus housing is guaranteed. *Activities and organizations:* drama/theater group, student-run newspaper, radio and television station, choral group, Student Activities Board, Student orientation staff, Esprit De Corps, Student Senate, Marketing Association. *Campus security:* 24-hour emergency response devices, late-night transport/escort service, controlled dormitory access, night security patrols. *Student services:* health clinic, personal/psychological counseling.

Athletics Member NCAA. All Division III. *Intercollegiate sports:* baseball M, basketball M/W, cross-country running M/W, football M, golf M/W, soccer M/W, softball M/W, tennis M/W, track and field M/W, volleyball W, wrestling M. *Intramural sports:* basketball M/W, football M, racquetball M/W, softball M/W, ultimate Frisbee M/W, volleyball M/W.

Standardized Tests *Required:* SAT or ACT (for admission).

Costs (2011–12) *Comprehensive fee:* $34,996 includes full-time tuition ($27,226) and room and board ($7770). Full-time tuition and fees vary according to location. Part-time tuition: $915 per credit hour. Part-time tuition and fees vary according to location. No tuition increase for student's term of enrollment. *Room and board:* Room and board charges vary according to board plan. *Payment plan:* installment. *Waivers:* employees or children of employees.

Financial Aid Of all full-time matriculated undergraduates who enrolled in 2011, 831 applied for aid, 777 were judged to have need, 356 had their need fully met. 384 Federal Work-Study jobs (averaging $1130). 242 state and other part-time jobs (averaging $1608). In 2011, 20 non-need-based awards were made. *Average percent of need met:* 82%. *Average financial aid package:* $24,781. *Average need-based loan:* $5080. *Average need-based gift aid:* $18,119. *Average non-need-based aid:* $15,015.

Applying *Options:* electronic application, deferred entrance. *Required:* high school transcript. *Required for some:* essay or personal statement, interview. *Recommended:* minimum 3.0 GPA. *Notification:* continuous (freshmen), continuous (transfers).

Freshman Application Contact Bridget Kurkowski, Director of Admissions, Buena Vista University, 610 West Fourth Street, Storm Lake, IA 50588. *Phone:* 712-749-2078. *Toll-free phone:* 800-383-9600. *E-mail:* admissions@bvu.edu. *Web site:* http://www.bvu.edu/.

Central College

Pella, Iowa

- **Independent** 4-year, founded 1853, affiliated with Reformed Church in America
- **Small-town** 169-acre campus with easy access to Des Moines
- **Endowment** $73.1 million
- **Coed** 1,604 undergraduate students, 98% full-time, 54% women, 46% men
- **Moderately difficult** entrance level, 73% of applicants were admitted

Undergraduates 1,567 full-time, 37 part-time. Students come from 34 states and territories; 10 other countries; 17% are from out of state; 2% Black or African American, non-Hispanic/Latino; 3% Hispanic/Latino; 2% Asian, non-Hispanic/Latino; 0.1% Native Hawaiian or other Pacific Islander, non-Hispanic/Latino; 0.3% American Indian or Alaska Native, non-Hispanic/Latino; 1% Two or more races, non-Hispanic/Latino; 2% Race/ethnicity unknown; 1% international; 2% transferred in; 94% live on campus. *Retention:* 79% of full-time freshmen returned.

Freshmen *Admission:* 2,633 applied, 1,926 admitted, 412 enrolled. *Average high school GPA:* 3.48. *Test scores:* SAT critical reading scores over 500: 50%; SAT math scores over 500: 70%; ACT scores over 18: 98%; SAT critical reading scores over 600: 5%; SAT math scores over 600: 30%; ACT scores over 24: 49%; ACT scores over 30: 8%.

Faculty *Total:* 129, 80% full-time, 73% with terminal degrees. *Student/faculty ratio:* 13:1.

Academics *Calendar:* semesters. *Degree:* bachelor's. *Special study options:* cooperative education, double majors, honors programs, independent study, internships, off-campus study, part-time degree program, services for LD students, student-designed majors, study abroad, summer session for credit. *Unusual degree programs:* 3-2 engineering with Washington University in St. Louis, University of Iowa, and Iowa State University; nursing with Allen College; Palmer College of Chiropractic.

Computers on Campus 391 computers/terminals and 1,500 ports are available on campus for general student use. Students can access the following: campus intranet, computer help desk, free student e-mail accounts, online (class) grades, online (class) registration, online (class) schedules. Campuswide network is available. 100% of college-owned or -operated housing units are wired for high-speed Internet access. Wireless service is available via entire campus.

Student Life *Housing:* on-campus residence required through senior year. *Options:* coed, men-only, women-only, disabled students. Campus housing is university owned. Freshman campus housing is guaranteed. *Activities and organizations:* drama/theater group, student-run newspaper, choral group, Campus Activities Board, Fellowship of Christian Athletes, Central Volunteer Center, Residence Hall Council, Economics, Accounting, Management (EAM) Club. *Campus security:* 24-hour emergency response devices and patrols, late-night transport/escort service, controlled dormitory access. *Student services:* health clinic, personal/psychological counseling.

Athletics Member NCAA. All Division III. *Intercollegiate sports:* baseball M, basketball M/W, cross-country running M/W, football M, golf M/W, soccer M/W, softball M/W, tennis M/W, track and field M/W, volleyball W, wrestling M. *Intramural sports:* basketball M/W, football M, racquetball M/W, rugby M, soccer M/W, softball M/W, volleyball M/W.

Standardized Tests *Required:* SAT or ACT (for admission).

Costs (2011–12) *Comprehensive fee:* $36,980 includes full-time tuition ($27,414), mandatory fees ($430), and room and board ($9136). Part-time tuition: $952 per semester hour. Part-time tuition and fees vary according to course load. *College room only:* $4480. Room and board charges vary according to board plan. *Payment plan:* installment. *Waivers:* employees or children of employees.

Financial Aid Of all full-time matriculated undergraduates who enrolled in 2011, 1,368 applied for aid, 1,257 were judged to have need, 229 had their need fully met. In 2011, 236 non-need-based awards were made. *Average percent of need met:* 77%. *Average financial aid package:* $22,283. *Average need-based loan:* $4535. *Average need-based gift aid:* $17,858. *Average non-need-based aid:* $12,620. *Average indebtedness upon graduation:* $35,047.

Applying *Options:* electronic application, deferred entrance. *Application fee:* $25. *Required:* high school transcript. *Required for some:* essay or personal statement, 3 letters of recommendation, interview. *Recommended:* minimum 2.7 GPA, interview. *Application deadlines:* 8/15 (freshmen), rolling (transfers). *Notification:* continuous (freshmen), continuous (transfers).

Freshman Application Contact Chevy Freiburger, Director of Admissions, Central College, 812 University, Pella, IA 50112. *Phone:* 641-628-7637. *Toll-free phone:* 877-462-3687. *Fax:* 641-628-5983. *E-mail:* freiburgerc@central.edu. *Web site:* http://www.central.edu/.

Clarke University

Dubuque, Iowa

- **Independent Roman Catholic** comprehensive, founded 1843
- **Urban** 55-acre campus
- **Endowment** $24.3 million
- **Coed** 979 undergraduate students, 87% full-time, 68% women, 32% men
- **Moderately difficult** entrance level, 74% of applicants were admitted

Undergraduates 855 full-time, 124 part-time. Students come from 29 states and territories; 12 other countries; 39% are from out of state; 3% Black or African American, non-Hispanic/Latino; 3% Hispanic/Latino; 0.8% Asian, non-Hispanic/Latino; 0.2% Native Hawaiian or other Pacific Islander, non-Hispanic/Latino; 0.3% American Indian or Alaska Native, non-Hispanic/Latino; 11% Race/ethnicity unknown; 2% international; 9% transferred in; 42% live on campus. *Retention:* 80% of full-time freshmen returned.

Freshmen *Admission:* 901 applied, 670 admitted, 163 enrolled. *Average high school GPA:* 3.46. *Test scores:* SAT critical reading scores over 500: 25%; SAT math scores over 500: 63%; ACT scores over 18: 98%; ACT scores over 24: 42%; ACT scores over 30: 5%.

Faculty *Total:* 149, 57% full-time, 38% with terminal degrees. *Student/faculty ratio:* 10:1.

Academics *Calendar:* semesters. *Degrees:* associate, bachelor's, master's, and doctoral. *Special study options:* accelerated degree program, adult/continuing education programs, advanced placement credit, cooperative education, distance learning, double majors, English as a second language, honors programs, independent study, internships, off-campus study, part-time degree program, student-designed majors, study abroad, summer session for credit. *ROTC:* Army (c).

Computers on Campus 237 computers/terminals are available on campus for general student use. Students can access the following: campus intranet, computer help desk, free student e-mail accounts, online (class) grades, online (class) registration, online (class) schedules. Campuswide network is available. Wireless service is available via classrooms, computer centers, computer labs, dorm rooms, learning centers, libraries, student centers.

Student Life *Housing:* on-campus residence required through sophomore year. *Options:* coed, men-only, women-only. Campus housing is university owned. Freshman campus housing is guaranteed. *Activities and organizations:* drama/theater group, student-run newspaper, radio station, choral group, Admissions Student Team, Student Multicultural Organization, concert choir, campus ministry, student government. *Campus security:* 24-hour emergency response

devices and patrols, late-night transport/escort service, controlled dormitory access. *Student services:* health clinic, personal/psychological counseling.

Athletics Member NAIA. *Intercollegiate sports:* baseball M(s), basketball M(s)/W(s), bowling M(s)/W(s), cheerleading W, cross-country running M(s)/W(s), golf M(s)/W(s), soccer M(s)/W(s), softball W(s), tennis W(s), track and field M(s)/W(s), volleyball M(s)/W(s). *Intramural sports:* badminton M/W, basketball M/W, bowling M/W, football M/W, golf M/W, racquetball M/W, skiing (cross-country) M/W, skiing (downhill) M/W, softball M/W, table tennis M/W, tennis M/W, track and field M/W, volleyball M/W, water polo M/W, weight lifting M/W.

Standardized Tests *Required:* SAT or ACT (for admission).

Costs (2011–12) *Comprehensive fee:* $33,500 includes full-time tuition ($24,950), mandatory fees ($810), and room and board ($7740). Part-time tuition: $630 per credit hour. *College room only:* $3800. Room and board charges vary according to housing facility. *Payment plans:* installment, deferred payment. *Waivers:* children of alumni, adult students, senior citizens, and employees or children of employees.

Financial Aid Of all full-time matriculated undergraduates who enrolled in 2011, 773 applied for aid, 721 were judged to have need, 127 had their need fully met. 255 Federal Work-Study jobs (averaging $1386). In 2011, 81 non-need-based awards were made. *Average percent of need met:* 69%. *Average financial aid package:* $20,251. *Average need-based loan:* $4587. *Average need-based gift aid:* $15,857. *Average non-need-based aid:* $15,622. *Average indebtedness upon graduation:* $34,650.

Applying *Options:* electronic application, deferred entrance. *Application fee:* $25. *Required:* high school transcript, minimum 2.0 GPA. *Application deadlines:* rolling (freshmen), rolling (transfers). *Notification:* 7/15 (freshmen), continuous until 8/15 (transfers).

Freshman Application Contact Ms. Emily Kruse, Director of Admissions, Clarke University, 1550 Clarke Drive, Dubuque, IA 52001-3198. *Phone:* 563-588-6436. *Toll-free phone:* 800-383-2345. *E-mail:* admissions@clarke.edu. *Web site:* http://www.clarke.edu/.

Coe College
Cedar Rapids, Iowa

- **Independent** comprehensive, founded 1851, affiliated with Presbyterian Church
- **Urban** 53-acre campus
- **Endowment** $81.3 million
- **Coed** 1,369 undergraduate students, 96% full-time, 54% women, 46% men
- **Moderately difficult** entrance level, 64% of applicants were admitted

Undergraduates 1,312 full-time, 57 part-time. Students come from 36 states and territories; 22 other countries; 40% are from out of state; 3% Black or African American, non-Hispanic/Latino; 2% Hispanic/Latino; 2% Asian, non-Hispanic/Latino; 0.1% Native Hawaiian or other Pacific Islander, non-Hispanic/Latino; 0.1% American Indian or Alaska Native, non-Hispanic/Latino; 4% Two or more races, non-Hispanic/Latino; 6% Race/ethnicity unknown; 3% international; 3% transferred in; 84% live on campus. *Retention:* 80% of full-time freshmen returned.

Freshmen *Admission:* 2,405 applied, 1,547 admitted, 361 enrolled. *Average high school GPA:* 3.64. *Test scores:* SAT critical reading scores over 500: 75%; SAT math scores over 500: 84%; SAT writing scores over 500: 75%; ACT scores over 18: 100%; SAT critical reading scores over 600: 42%; SAT math scores over 600: 49%; SAT writing scores over 600: 35%; ACT scores over 24: 68%; SAT critical reading scores over 700: 11%; SAT math scores over 700: 16%; SAT writing scores over 700: 2%; ACT scores over 30: 16%.

Faculty *Total:* 169, 51% full-time, 61% with terminal degrees. *Student/faculty ratio:* 11:1.

Academics *Calendar:* 4-4-1. *Degrees:* bachelor's and master's. *Special study options:* accelerated degree program, advanced placement credit, double majors, English as a second language, honors programs, independent study, internships, off-campus study, part-time degree program, services for LD students, student-designed majors, study abroad, summer session for credit. *ROTC:* Army (c), Air Force (c).

Computers on Campus Students can access the following: campus intranet, computer help desk, free student e-mail accounts, online (class) grades, online (class) registration, online (class) schedules. Campuswide network is available. 100% of college-owned or -operated housing units are wired for high-speed Internet access. Wireless service is available via entire campus.

Student Life *Housing:* on-campus residence required through senior year. *Options:* coed, men-only, women-only. Campus housing is university owned. Freshman campus housing is guaranteed. *Activities and organizations:* drama/theater group, student-run newspaper, radio station, choral group, Student Activities Committee, Student Senate, Up 'til Dawn, Cedar Rapids Dance Marathon, Alpha Sigma Alpha Sorority, national fraternities, national sororities. *Campus security:* 24-hour emergency response devices and patrols, late-

night transport/escort service, controlled dormitory access. *Student services:* health clinic, personal/psychological counseling.

Athletics Member NCAA. All Division III. *Intercollegiate sports:* baseball M, basketball M/W, cheerleading W, cross-country running M/W, football M, golf M/W, soccer M/W, softball W, swimming and diving M/W, tennis M/W, track and field M/W, volleyball W, wrestling M. *Intramural sports:* badminton M/W, basketball M/W, football M/W, racquetball M/W, rock climbing M/W, rugby M(c)/W(c), soccer M/W, softball M/W, squash M/W, table tennis M/W, tennis M/W, ultimate Frisbee M(c)/W(c), volleyball M/W.

Standardized Tests *Required:* SAT or ACT (for admission).

Costs (2012–13) *Comprehensive fee:* $41,920 includes full-time tuition ($33,900), mandatory fees ($320), and room and board ($7700). Part-time tuition: $3915 per course. Part-time tuition and fees vary according to course load. *College room only:* $3400. Room and board charges vary according to housing facility. *Payment plan:* installment. *Waivers:* adult students, senior citizens, and employees or children of employees.

Financial Aid Of all full-time matriculated undergraduates who enrolled in 2011, 1,135 applied for aid, 1,030 were judged to have need, 237 had their need fully met. 394 Federal Work-Study jobs (averaging $1580). 256 state and other part-time jobs (averaging $1400). In 2011, 254 non-need-based awards were made. *Average percent of need met:* 81%. *Average financial aid package:* $25,221. *Average need-based loan:* $4879. *Average need-based gift aid:* $20,765. *Average non-need-based aid:* $17,669. *Average indebtedness upon graduation:* $32,614.

Applying *Options:* electronic application, early admission, early action, deferred entrance. *Application fee:* $30. *Required:* essay or personal statement, high school transcript, 1 letter of recommendation. *Recommended:* minimum 3.0 GPA, interview. *Application deadlines:* 3/1 (freshmen), rolling (transfers), 12/10 (early action). *Notification:* 3/15 (freshmen), continuous (transfers), 1/20 (early action).

Freshman Application Contact Ms. Julie Staker, Dean of Admission, Coe College, 1220 1st Avenue, NE, Cedar Rapids, IA 52402-5070. *Phone:* 319-399-8500. *Toll-free phone:* 877-225-5263. *Fax:* 319-399-8816. *E-mail:* admission@coe.edu. *Web site:* http://www.coe.edu/.

Cornell College
Mount Vernon, Iowa

- **Independent** Methodist 4-year, founded 1853
- **Small-town** 129-acre campus
- **Endowment** $65.0 million
- **Coed** 1,197 undergraduate students, 99% full-time, 54% women, 46% men
- **Moderately difficult** entrance level, 46% of applicants were admitted

Undergraduates 1,185 full-time, 12 part-time. Students come from 49 states and territories; 20 other countries; 77% are from out of state; 5% Black or African American, non-Hispanic/Latino; 8% Hispanic/Latino; 4% Asian, non-Hispanic/Latino; 1% American Indian or Alaska Native, non-Hispanic/Latino; 0.9% Two or more races, non-Hispanic/Latino; 5% Race/ethnicity unknown; 6% international; 3% transferred in; 91% live on campus. *Retention:* 79% of full-time freshmen returned.

Freshmen *Admission:* 3,202 applied, 1,457 admitted, 338 enrolled. *Average high school GPA:* 3.54. *Test scores:* SAT critical reading scores over 500: 89%; SAT math scores over 500: 90%; SAT writing scores over 500: 83%; ACT scores over 18: 99%; SAT critical reading scores over 600: 61%; SAT math scores over 600: 52%; SAT writing scores over 600: 45%; ACT scores over 24: 70%; SAT critical reading scores over 700: 20%; SAT math scores over 700: 23%; SAT writing scores over 700: 16%; ACT scores over 30: 21%.

Faculty *Total:* 90, 93% full-time, 91% with terminal degrees. *Student/faculty ratio:* 13:1.

Academics *Calendar:* 9 3&S1/&I2-week terms. *Degree:* bachelor's. *Special study options:* advanced placement credit, double majors, English as a second language, honors programs, independent study, internships, off-campus study, services for LD students, student-designed majors, study abroad. *Unusual degree programs:* 3-2 engineering with University of Minnesota; forestry with Duke University; environmental management with Duke University; Architecture with Washington University–St. Louis.

Computers on Campus 270 computers/terminals and 1,200 ports are available on campus for general student use. Students can access the following: campus intranet, computer help desk, free student e-mail accounts, online (class) grades, online (class) registration, online (class) schedules. Campuswide network is available. 100% of college-owned or -operated housing units are wired for high-speed Internet access. Wireless service is available via entire campus.

Student Life *Housing:* on-campus residence required through senior year. *Options:* coed, women-only. Campus housing is university owned. Freshman campus housing is guaranteed. *Activities and organizations:* drama/theater group, student-run newspaper, radio station, choral group, Student-initiated

Living-learning Community, Lunch Buddies/Youth Mentoring, Chess and Games Club, PAAC (Performing Arts and Activities Council), Fellowship of Christian Athletes (FCA). *Campus security:* 24-hour emergency response devices and patrols, late-night transport/escort service, controlled dormitory access. *Student services:* health clinic, personal/psychological counseling, women's center.

Athletics Member NCAA. All Division III. *Intercollegiate sports:* baseball M, basketball M/W, cheerleading M/W, cross-country running M/W, fencing M(c)/W(c), football M, lacrosse M(c)/W(c), soccer M/W, softball W, tennis M/W, track and field M/W, ultimate Frisbee M(c)/W(c), volleyball M(c)/W, wrestling M. *Intramural sports:* badminton M/W, basketball M/W, bowling M/W, cross-country running M/W, football M/W, golf M/W, ice hockey M/W, racquetball M/W, soccer M/W, softball M/W, table tennis M/W, tennis M/W, track and field M/W, ultimate Frisbee M/W, volleyball M/W, weight lifting M/W, wrestling M/W.

Standardized Tests *Required:* SAT or ACT (for admission). *Recommended:* SAT Subject Tests (for admission).

Costs (2012–13) *Comprehensive fee:* $42,605 includes full-time tuition ($34,480), mandatory fees ($225), and room and board ($7900). Part-time tuition: $2586 per course. Part-time tuition and fees vary according to course load and reciprocity agreements. *Required fees:* $113 per year part-time. *College room only:* $3700. Room and board charges vary according to board plan and housing facility. *Payment plan:* installment. *Waivers:* employees or children of employees.

Financial Aid Of all full-time matriculated undergraduates who enrolled in 2011, 991 applied for aid, 904 were judged to have need, 243 had their need fully met. 609 Federal Work-Study jobs (averaging $1195). In 2011, 232 non-need-based awards were made. *Average percent of need met:* 87%. *Average financial aid package:* $29,475. *Average need-based loan:* $4786. *Average need-based gift aid:* $22,760. *Average non-need-based aid:* $14,273. *Average indebtedness upon graduation:* $27,805. *Financial aid deadline:* 3/1.

Applying *Options:* electronic application, early admission, early decision, early action, deferred entrance. *Application fee:* $30. *Required:* essay or personal statement, high school transcript, 1 letter of recommendation. *Recommended:* interview. *Application deadlines:* 2/1 (freshmen), 3/1 (transfers), 12/1 (early action). *Early decision deadline:* 11/1 (for plan 1), 2/1 (for plan 2). *Notification:* 3/20 (freshmen), continuous (transfers), 12/15 (early decision plan 1), 3/15 (early decision plan 2), 2/1 (early action).

Freshman Application Contact Mr. Jonathan Stroud, Vice President for Enrollment and Dean of Admissions, Cornell College, 600 First Street SW, Mount Vernon, IA 52314-1098. *Phone:* 319-895-4477. *Toll-free phone:* 800-747-1112. *Fax:* 319-895-4451. *E-mail:* admissions@cornellcollege.edu. *Web site:* http://www.cornellcollege.edu/.

Divine Word College

Epworth, Iowa

- **Independent Roman Catholic** 4-year, founded 1912
- **Rural** 35-acre campus
- **Coed**

Academics *Calendar:* semesters. *Degrees:* associate and bachelor's.

Student Life *Campus security:* controlled dormitory access.

Standardized Tests *Recommended:* SAT or ACT (for admission).

Costs (2011–12) *Comprehensive fee:* $14,850 includes full-time tuition ($11,600), mandatory fees ($100), and room and board ($3150). Part-time tuition: $387 per credit. *Payment plans:* installment, deferred payment.

Applying *Options:* early admission. *Application fee:* $25. *Required:* essay or personal statement, high school transcript, 3 letters of recommendation, interview, medical history.

Freshman Application Contact Divine Word College, 102 Jacoby Drive SW, Epworth, IA 52045-0380. *Phone:* 563-876-3353. *Toll-free phone:* 800-553-3321. *Web site:* http://www.dwci.edu/.

Dordt College

Sioux Center, Iowa

- **Independent Christian Reformed** comprehensive, founded 1955
- **Small-town** 110-acre campus
- **Endowment** $28.0 million
- **Coed** 1,394 undergraduate students, 98% full-time, 47% women, 53% men
- **Moderately difficult** entrance level, 80% of applicants were admitted

Undergraduates 1,362 full-time, 32 part-time. Students come from 37 states and territories; 17 other countries; 63% are from out of state; 1% Black or African American, non-Hispanic/Latino; 1% Hispanic/Latino; 0.6% Asian, non-Hispanic/Latino; 0.1% American Indian or Alaska Native, non-Hispanic/Latino; 3% Two or more races, non-Hispanic/Latino; 10% international; 3%

transferred in; 90% live on campus. *Retention:* 80% of full-time freshmen returned.

Freshmen *Admission:* 1,196 applied, 952 admitted, 370 enrolled. *Average high school GPA:* 3.5. *Test scores:* SAT critical reading scores over 500: 60%; SAT math scores over 500: 70%; SAT writing scores over 500: 56%; ACT scores over 18: 96%; SAT critical reading scores over 600: 20%; SAT math scores over 600: 21%; SAT writing scores over 600: 17%; ACT scores over 24: 56%; SAT critical reading scores over 700: 4%; SAT math scores over 700: 5%; SAT writing scores over 700: 3%; ACT scores over 30: 10%.

Faculty *Total:* 122, 61% full-time, 61% with terminal degrees. *Student/faculty ratio:* 14:1.

Academics *Calendar:* semesters. *Degrees:* associate, bachelor's, and master's. *Special study options:* academic remediation for entering students, advanced placement credit, distance learning, double majors, English as a second language, freshman honors college, honors programs, independent study, internships, off-campus study, part-time degree program, services for LD students, student-designed majors, study abroad.

Computers on Campus 200 computers/terminals are available on campus for general student use. Students can access the following: campus intranet, computer help desk, free student e-mail accounts, online (class) grades, online (class) registration, online (class) schedules. Campuswide network is available. 100% of college-owned or -operated housing units are wired for high-speed Internet access. Wireless service is available via entire campus.

Student Life *Housing:* on-campus residence required through senior year. *Options:* men-only, women-only, disabled students. Campus housing is university owned. Freshman campus housing is guaranteed. *Activities and organizations:* drama/theater group, student-run newspaper, radio station, choral group, PLIA, Future Teachers, Ag Club, Lacrosse Club, Defenders of Life. *Campus security:* 24-hour emergency response devices, student patrols, late-night transport/escort service, controlled dormitory access. *Student services:* health clinic, personal/psychological counseling.

Athletics Member NAIA. *Intercollegiate sports:* baseball M(s), basketball M(s)/W(s), cross-country running M(s)/W(s), football M(s), golf M(s)/W(s), ice hockey M(s), lacrosse M, soccer M(s)/W(s), softball W(s), track and field M(s)/W(s), volleyball W(s). *Intramural sports:* basketball M/W, bowling M/W, field hockey M/W, gymnastics M/W, ice hockey M, lacrosse M, racquetball M/W, skiing (cross-country) M/W, soccer M/W, softball M/W, swimming and diving M/W, table tennis M/W, tennis M/W, track and field M/W, volleyball M/W, weight lifting M/W.

Standardized Tests *Required:* SAT or ACT (for admission).

Costs (2011–12) *Comprehensive fee:* $31,170 includes full-time tuition ($23,900), mandatory fees ($400), and room and board ($6870). Full-time tuition and fees vary according to course load. Part-time tuition: $950 per semester hour. *College room only:* $3510. Room and board charges vary according to board plan and housing facility. *Payment plan:* installment. *Waivers:* senior citizens and employees or children of employees.

Financial Aid Of all full-time matriculated undergraduates who enrolled in 2011, 1,119 applied for aid, 990 were judged to have need, 161 had their need fully met. 510 Federal Work-Study jobs (averaging $1500). 501 state and other part-time jobs (averaging $1500). In 2011, 261 non-need-based awards were made. *Average percent of need met:* 87%. *Average financial aid package:* $21,918. *Average need-based loan:* $5629. *Average need-based gift aid:* $12,192. *Average non-need-based aid:* $12,181. *Average indebtedness upon graduation:* $21,900.

Applying *Options:* electronic application, deferred entrance. *Application fee:* $25. *Required:* high school transcript, minimum 2.3 GPA. *Required for some:* essay or personal statement, interview. *Application deadlines:* 8/1 (freshmen), 8/1 (transfers). *Notification:* 8/1 (freshmen), continuous until 9/1 (transfers).

Freshman Application Contact Mr. Quentin Van Essen, Executive Director of Admissions, Dordt College, 498 4th Avenue, NE, Sioux Center, IA 51250-1697. *Phone:* 712-722-6080. *Toll-free phone:* 800-343-6738. *Fax:* 712-722-6035. *E-mail:* admissions@dordt.edu. *Web site:* http://www.dordt.edu/.

Drake University

Des Moines, Iowa

- **Independent** university, founded 1881
- **Suburban** 120-acre campus
- **Endowment** $153.1 million
- **Coed** 3,438 undergraduate students, 93% full-time, 56% women, 44% men
- **Moderately difficult** entrance level, 63% of applicants were admitted

Undergraduates 3,203 full-time, 235 part-time. Students come from 46 states and territories; 39 other countries; 62% are from out of state; 3% Black or African American, non-Hispanic/Latino; 3% Hispanic/Latino; 3% Asian, non-Hispanic/Latino; 0.1% Native Hawaiian or other Pacific Islander, non-Hispanic/Latino; 0.2% American Indian or Alaska Native, non-Hispanic/Latino; 1% Two or more races, non-Hispanic/Latino; 2% Race/ethnicity unknown; 7%

international; 4% transferred in; 71% live on campus. *Retention:* 88% of full-time freshmen returned.

Freshmen *Admission:* 6,093 applied, 3,849 admitted, 812 enrolled. *Average high school GPA:* 3.7. *Test scores:* SAT critical reading scores over 500: 85%; SAT math scores over 500: 89%; ACT scores over 18: 100%; SAT critical reading scores over 600: 40%; SAT math scores over 600: 70%; ACT scores over 24: 83%; SAT critical reading scores over 700: 13%; SAT math scores over 700: 18%; ACT scores over 30: 24%.

Faculty *Total:* 461, 61% full-time, 55% with terminal degrees. *Student/faculty ratio:* 12:1.

Academics *Calendar:* semesters. *Degrees:* certificates, bachelor's, master's, doctoral, post-master's, postbachelor's, and first professional certificates. *Special study options:* accelerated degree program, advanced placement credit, cooperative education, distance learning, double majors, English as a second language, honors programs, independent study, internships, off-campus study, part-time degree program, services for LD students, student-designed majors, study abroad, summer session for credit. *ROTC:* Army (b), Air Force (c). *Unusual degree programs:* 3-2 journalism and law, arts and sciences and law, accounting.

Computers on Campus 1,000 computers/terminals are available on campus for general student use. Students can access the following: campus intranet, computer help desk, free student e-mail accounts, online (class) grades, online (class) registration, online (class) schedules. Campuswide network is available. 100% of college-owned or -operated housing units are wired for high-speed Internet access. Wireless service is available via classrooms, computer centers, computer labs, dorm rooms, libraries, student centers.

Student Life *Housing:* on-campus residence required through sophomore year. *Options:* coed, disabled students. Campus housing is university owned and is provided by a third party. Freshman campus housing is guaranteed. *Activities and organizations:* drama/theater group, student-run newspaper, radio and television station, choral group, marching band, Student Activities Board, Drake Magazine, Dog Pound Pep Squad, Alpha Phi Omega, Residence Hall Association, national fraternities, national sororities. *Campus security:* 24-hour emergency response devices and patrols, late-night transport/escort service, 24-hour desk attendants in residence halls. *Student services:* health clinic, personal/psychological counseling, legal services.

Athletics Member NCAA. All Division I except football (Division I-AA). *Intercollegiate sports:* basketball M(s)/W(s), cheerleading M(s)/W(s), crew W, cross-country running M(s)/W(s), golf M(s)/W, soccer M(s)/W(s), softball W(s), tennis M(s)/W(s), track and field M(s)/W(s), volleyball W(s). *Intramural sports:* badminton M/W, basketball M/W, football M/W, golf M/W, racquetball M/W, soccer M(c)/W, softball M/W, swimming and diving M/W, tennis M/W, volleyball M/W(c).

Standardized Tests *Required:* SAT or ACT (for admission).

Costs (2012–13) *Comprehensive fee:* $38,236 includes full-time tuition ($29,410), mandatory fees ($146), and room and board ($8680). Full-time tuition and fees vary according to course load, program, and student level. Part-time tuition and fees vary according to class time and program. *College room only:* $4560. Room and board charges vary according to board plan. *Payment plan:* installment. *Waivers:* children of alumni, senior citizens, and employees or children of employees.

Financial Aid Of all full-time matriculated undergraduates who enrolled in 2011, 2,410 applied for aid, 1,971 were judged to have need, 529 had their need fully met. 1,652 Federal Work-Study jobs (averaging $1921). In 2011, 1007 non-need-based awards were made. *Average percent of need met:* 76%. *Average financial aid package:* $21,372. *Average need-based loan:* $4439. *Average need-based gift aid:* $14,753. *Average non-need-based aid:* $11,568. *Average indebtedness upon graduation:* $32,604.

Applying *Options:* electronic application, early admission, deferred entrance. *Application fee:* $25. *Required:* essay or personal statement, high school transcript. *Recommended:* interview. *Application deadlines:* 3/1 (freshmen), rolling (transfers). *Notification:* continuous (freshmen), continuous (transfers).

Freshman Application Contact Ms. Laura Linn, Director of Admission, Drake University, 2507 University Avenue, Des Moines, IA 50311. *Phone:* 515-271-3181 Ext. 3182. *Toll-free phone:* 800-44-DRAKE Ext. 3181. *Fax:* 515-271-2831. *E-mail:* admission@drake.edu. *Web site:* http://www.drake.edu/.

Emmaus Bible College

Dubuque, Iowa

- **Independent nondenominational** 4-year, founded 1941
- **Small-town** 22-acre campus
- **Coed** 244 undergraduate students
- **Noncompetitive** entrance level, 74% of applicants were admitted

Freshmen *Admission:* 162 applied, 120 admitted. *Test scores:* SAT critical reading scores over 500: 55%; SAT math scores over 500: 31%; ACT scores

over 18: 85%; SAT critical reading scores over 600: 16%; SAT math scores over 600: 16%; ACT scores over 24: 47%; ACT scores over 30: 2%.

Academics *Calendar:* semesters. *Degrees:* certificates, associate, and bachelor's. *Special study options:* advanced placement credit, double majors, independent study, internships, off-campus study, part-time degree program.

Computers on Campus Campuswide network is available.

Student Life *Housing:* on-campus residence required through senior year. *Options:* men-only, women-only. Campus housing is university owned. Freshman campus housing is guaranteed. *Activities and organizations:* choral group. *Campus security:* 24-hour emergency response devices, student patrols, controlled dormitory access. *Student services:* personal/psychological counseling.

Athletics Member NCCAA. *Intercollegiate sports:* basketball M/W, soccer M, volleyball W. *Intramural sports:* badminton M/W, basketball M/W, golf M/W, racquetball M/W, soccer M/W, softball M/W, table tennis M/W, tennis M/W, ultimate Frisbee M/W, volleyball M/W.

Standardized Tests *Required:* SAT or ACT (for admission).

Costs (2012–13) *Comprehensive fee:* $20,700 includes full-time tuition ($13,750), mandatory fees ($750), and room and board ($6200). Full-time tuition and fees vary according to course load and program. Part-time tuition and fees vary according to course load and program. *Payment plan:* installment. *Waivers:* employees or children of employees.

Financial Aid Of all full-time matriculated undergraduates who enrolled in 2005, 212 applied for aid, 145 were judged to have need. *Average percent of need met:* 74%. *Average financial aid package:* $5216. *Average need-based loan:* $3652. *Average need-based gift aid:* $2852.

Applying *Options:* electronic application, deferred entrance. *Application fee:* $25. *Required:* essay or personal statement, high school transcript, 2 letters of recommendation. *Application deadlines:* 6/1 (freshmen), 8/1 (transfers). *Notification:* continuous (freshmen), continuous (transfers).

Freshman Application Contact Emmaus Bible College, 2570 Asbury Road, Dubuque, IA 52001-3097. *Phone:* 563-588-8000 Ext. 1310. *Toll-free phone:* 800-397-2425. *Web site:* http://www.emmaus.edu/.

Faith Baptist Bible College and Theological Seminary

Ankeny, Iowa

- **Independent** comprehensive, founded 1921, affiliated with General Association of Regular Baptist Churches
- **Suburban** 52-acre campus
- **Endowment** $3.6 million
- **Coed** 302 undergraduate students, 90% full-time, 55% women, 45% men
- **Minimally difficult** entrance level, 75% of applicants were admitted

Undergraduates 272 full-time, 30 part-time. Students come from 27 states and territories; 9 other countries; 39% are from out of state; 1% Black or African American, non-Hispanic/Latino; 2% Hispanic/Latino; 2% Asian, non-Hispanic/Latino; 0.3% Native Hawaiian or other Pacific Islander, non-Hispanic/Latino; 1% American Indian or Alaska Native, non-Hispanic/Latino; 0.3% Two or more races, non-Hispanic/Latino; 1% international; 5% transferred in; 75% live on campus. *Retention:* 80% of full-time freshmen returned.

Freshmen *Admission:* 147 applied, 110 admitted, 85 enrolled. *Average high school GPA:* 3.45. *Test scores:* SAT critical reading scores over 500: 60%; SAT math scores over 500: 40%; SAT writing scores over 500: 40%; ACT scores over 18: 82%; SAT critical reading scores over 600: 40%; SAT writing scores over 600: 20%; ACT scores over 24: 41%; SAT critical reading scores over 700: 20%; ACT scores over 30: 7%.

Faculty *Total:* 34, 56% full-time, 50% with terminal degrees. *Student/faculty ratio:* 13:1.

Academics *Calendar:* semesters. *Degrees:* certificates, associate, bachelor's, master's, and doctoral. *Special study options:* academic remediation for entering students, adult/continuing education programs, advanced placement credit, double majors, independent study, internships, part-time degree program, summer session for credit.

Computers on Campus 45 computers/terminals and 250 ports are available on campus for general student use. Students can access the following: free student e-mail accounts, online (class) registration. Campuswide network is available. 100% of college-owned or -operated housing units are wired for high-speed Internet access. Wireless service is available via entire campus.

Student Life *Housing:* on-campus residence required through senior year. *Options:* men-only, women-only, disabled students. Campus housing is university owned. Freshman campus housing is guaranteed. *Activities and organizations:* drama/theater group, choral group, Student Association, Student Missionary Fellowship, Intramural Sports, Photo Club, Chapel Orchestra. *Campus security:* 24-hour emergency response devices and patrols, late-night transport/escort service. *Student services:* personal/psychological counseling.

Athletics Member NCCAA. *Intercollegiate sports:* basketball M/W, cross-country running M/W, soccer M/W, track and field M/W, volleyball W. *Intra-*

mural sports: basketball M/W, football M, ultimate Frisbee M/W, volleyball M/W.

Standardized Tests *Required:* SAT or ACT (for admission).

Costs (2011–12) *One-time required fee:* $200. *Comprehensive fee:* $20,290 includes full-time tuition ($14,058), mandatory fees ($420), and room and board ($5812). Full-time tuition and fees vary according to course load and degree level. Part-time tuition: $514 per credit hour. Part-time tuition and fees vary according to course load and degree level. *Required fees:* $210 per term part-time. *College room only:* $2636. *Payment plan:* installment. *Waivers:* employees or children of employees.

Financial Aid Of all full-time matriculated undergraduates who enrolled in 2004, 311 applied for aid, 290 were judged to have need, 5 had their need fully met. In 2004, 21 non-need-based awards were made. *Average percent of need met:* 48%. *Average financial aid package:* $7124. *Average need-based loan:* $3142. *Average need-based gift aid:* $6299. *Average non-need-based aid:* $2465. *Average indebtedness upon graduation:* $15,006.

Applying *Options:* electronic application, deferred entrance. *Required:* essay or personal statement, high school transcript, 2 letters of recommendation. *Required for some:* interview. *Recommended:* minimum 2.0 GPA. *Application deadlines:* 8/1 (freshmen), 8/1 (transfers). *Notification:* 9/1 (freshmen), continuous until 9/1 (transfers).

Freshman Application Contact Mrs. Krisanna Sternquist, Admissions Secretary, Faith Baptist Bible College and Theological Seminary, 1900 NW 4th Street, Ankeny, IA 50023. *Phone:* 515-964-0601. *Toll-free phone:* 888-FAITH 4U. *Fax:* 515-964-1638. *E-mail:* admissions@faith.edu. *Web site:* http://www.faith.edu/.

Graceland University

Lamoni, Iowa

- **Independent Community of Christ** comprehensive, founded 1895
- **Rural** 170-acre campus with easy access to Des Moines
- **Endowment** $37.6 million
- **Coed** 1,515 undergraduate students, 79% full-time, 57% women, 43% men
- **Moderately difficult** entrance level, 50% of applicants were admitted

Undergraduates 1,203 full-time, 312 part-time. Students come from 44 states and territories; 40 other countries; 69% are from out of state; 9% Black or African American, non-Hispanic/Latino; 2% Hispanic/Latino; 0.3% Asian, non-Hispanic/Latino; 1% Native Hawaiian or other Pacific Islander, non-Hispanic/Latino; 0.5% American Indian or Alaska Native, non-Hispanic/Latino; 3% Two or more races, non-Hispanic/Latino; 8% Race/ethnicity unknown; 8% international; 6% transferred in; 65% live on campus. *Retention:* 68% of full-time freshmen returned.

Freshmen *Admission:* 1,512 applied, 762 admitted, 260 enrolled. *Average high school GPA:* 3.2. *Test scores:* SAT critical reading scores over 500: 25%; SAT math scores over 500: 41%; ACT scores over 18: 76%; SAT critical reading scores over 600: 13%; SAT math scores over 600: 16%; ACT scores over 24: 28%; SAT critical reading scores over 700: 2%; SAT math scores over 700: 2%; ACT scores over 30: 3%.

Faculty *Total:* 172, 47% full-time, 57% with terminal degrees. *Student/faculty ratio:* 15:1.

Academics *Calendar:* 4-1-4. *Degrees:* bachelor's, master's, doctoral, and post-master's certificates. *Special study options:* academic remediation for entering students, accelerated degree program, adult/continuing education programs, advanced placement credit, cooperative education, distance learning, double majors, English as a second language, freshman honors college, honors programs, independent study, internships, off-campus study, part-time degree program, services for LD students, student-designed majors, study abroad, summer session for credit.

Computers on Campus 249 computers/terminals and 1,046 ports are available on campus for general student use. Students can access the following: campus intranet, computer help desk, free student e-mail accounts, online (class) grades, online (class) registration, online (class) schedules. Campuswide network is available. 100% of college-owned or -operated housing units are wired for high-speed Internet access. Wireless service is available via classrooms, computer centers, computer labs, dorm rooms, learning centers, libraries, student centers.

Student Life *Housing:* on-campus residence required through sophomore year. *Options:* men-only, women-only. Campus housing is university owned. Freshman campus housing is guaranteed. *Activities and organizations:* drama/theater group, student-run newspaper, radio station, choral group, International Club, Student Athletic Trainers, Outreach International, Art Student Society, Students in Free Enterprise (SIFE). *Campus security:* 24-hour emergency response devices and patrols, late-night transport/escort service, controlled dormitory access. *Student services:* health clinic, personal/psychological counseling.

Athletics Member NAIA. *Intercollegiate sports:* baseball M(s), basketball M(s)/W(s), cheerleading M(s)/W(s), cross-country running M(s)/W(s), football M(s), golf M(s)/W(s), soccer M(s)/W(s), softball W(s), tennis M(s)/W(s), track and field M(s)/W(s), ultimate Frisbee M(c)/W(c), volleyball M(s)/W(s). *Intramural sports:* basketball M/W, football M/W, golf M/W, racquetball M/W, soccer M/W, softball M/W, swimming and diving M/W, table tennis M/W, ultimate Frisbee M/W, volleyball M/W.

Standardized Tests *Required:* SAT or ACT (for admission), TOEFL for all students whose first language is not English (for admission).

Costs (2012–13) *Comprehensive fee:* $30,260 includes full-time tuition ($22,330), mandatory fees ($350), and room and board ($7580). Full-time tuition and fees vary according to course load. Part-time tuition: $700 per semester hour. Part-time tuition and fees vary according to course load. *Room and board:* Room and board charges vary according to board plan, housing facility, and location. *Payment plan:* installment. *Waivers:* senior citizens and employees or children of employees.

Financial Aid Of all full-time matriculated undergraduates who enrolled in 2011, 1,071 applied for aid, 930 were judged to have need, 133 had their need fully met. 194 Federal Work-Study jobs (averaging $1553). 383 state and other part-time jobs (averaging $1283). In 2011, 274 non-need-based awards were made. *Average percent of need met:* 75%. *Average financial aid package:* $19,065. *Average need-based loan:* $5212. *Average need-based gift aid:* $15,020. *Average non-need-based aid:* $10,426. *Average indebtedness upon graduation:* $37,570.

Applying *Options:* electronic application, deferred entrance. *Required:* high school transcript, minimum 2.5 GPA, Students must meet 2 out of the following 3 requirements to be considered for admission: rank in top half of class; score a minimum of 21 on ACT or 960 on the SAT; have a 2.5 high school GPA (on a 4.0 scale). *Required for some:* essay or personal statement, 2 letters of recommendation, interview. *Application deadlines:* rolling (freshmen), rolling (out-of-state freshmen), rolling (transfers). *Notification:* continuous (freshmen), continuous (out-of-state freshmen), continuous (transfers).

Freshman Application Contact Mr. Kevin Brown, Director of Admissions, Graceland University, 1 University Place, Lamoni, IA 50140. *Phone:* 641-784-5149. *Toll-free phone:* 866-GRACELAND. *Fax:* 641-784-5480. *E-mail:* admissions@graceland.edu. *Web site:* http://www.graceland.edu/.

Grand View University

Des Moines, Iowa

- **Independent** comprehensive, founded 1896, affiliated with Evangelical Lutheran Church in America
- **Urban** 25-acre campus
- **Endowment** $15.5 million
- **Coed** 2,195 undergraduate students, 82% full-time, 60% women, 40% men
- **Minimally difficult** entrance level, 93% of applicants were admitted

Undergraduates 1,801 full-time, 394 part-time. Students come from 30 states and territories; 15 other countries; 12% are from out of state; 7% Black or African American, non-Hispanic/Latino; 3% Hispanic/Latino; 2% Asian, non-Hispanic/Latino; 0.2% Native Hawaiian or other Pacific Islander, non-Hispanic/Latino; 0.4% American Indian or Alaska Native, non-Hispanic/Latino; 2% Two or more races, non-Hispanic/Latino; 8% Race/ethnicity unknown; 2% international; 17% transferred in; 37% live on campus. *Retention:* 66% of full-time freshmen returned.

Freshmen *Admission:* 949 applied, 883 admitted, 358 enrolled. *Average high school GPA:* 3.14. *Test scores:* SAT critical reading scores over 500: 9%; SAT math scores over 500: 23%; SAT writing scores over 500: 7%; ACT scores over 18: 87%; SAT critical reading scores over 600: 2%; SAT math scores over 600: 2%; ACT scores over 24: 20%; ACT scores over 30: 2%.

Faculty *Total:* 238, 39% full-time, 30% with terminal degrees. *Student/faculty ratio:* 14:1.

Academics *Calendar:* semesters. *Degrees:* certificates, associate, bachelor's, master's, and postbachelor's certificates. *Special study options:* academic remediation for entering students, accelerated degree program, adult/continuing education programs, advanced placement credit, cooperative education, distance learning, double majors, freshman honors college, honors programs, independent study, internships, off-campus study, part-time degree program, services for LD students, student-designed majors, study abroad, summer session for credit. *ROTC:* Army (c), Air Force (c). *Unusual degree programs:* 3-2 engineering with Iowa State University; hospital administration with The University of Iowa.

Computers on Campus 275 computers/terminals are available on campus for general student use. Students can access the following: campus intranet, computer help desk, free student e-mail accounts, online (class) grades, online (class) registration, online (class) schedules. Campuswide network is available. 100% of college-owned or -operated housing units are wired for high-speed

Internet access. Wireless service is available via classrooms, computer labs, libraries, student centers.

Student Life *Housing:* on-campus residence required through sophomore year. *Options:* coed. Campus housing is university owned. Freshman applicants given priority for college housing. *Activities and organizations:* drama/theater group, student-run newspaper, radio and television station, choral group, Nursing Student Association, Art Club, Science Club, Education Club, Business Club. *Campus security:* 24-hour emergency response devices and patrols, late-night transport/escort service, controlled dormitory access, night security patrols. *Student services:* health clinic, personal/psychological counseling.

Athletics Member NAIA. *Intercollegiate sports:* baseball M(s), basketball M(s)/W(s), bowling M(s)/W(s), cheerleading W(s), cross-country running M(s)/W(s), football M(s), golf M(s)/W(s), soccer M(s)/W(s), softball W(s), tennis M(s)/W(s), track and field M(s)/W(s), volleyball M(s)/W(s), wrestling M(s). *Intramural sports:* basketball M/W, football M/W, soccer M/W, table tennis M/W, ultimate Frisbee M/W, volleyball M/W.

Standardized Tests *Required:* SAT or ACT (for admission).

Costs (2012–13) *Comprehensive fee:* $29,566 includes full-time tuition ($21,436), mandatory fees ($534), and room and board ($7596). Full-time tuition and fees vary according to class time and course load. Part-time tuition and fees vary according to class time and course load. *Room and board:* Room and board charges vary according to board plan and housing facility. *Payment plan:* installment. *Waivers:* children of alumni, senior citizens, and employees or children of employees.

Financial Aid Of all full-time matriculated undergraduates who enrolled in 2011, 1,650 applied for aid, 1,506 were judged to have need, 312 had their need fully met. 376 Federal Work-Study jobs (averaging $1255). In 2011, 234 non-need-based awards were made. *Average percent of need met:* 73%. *Average financial aid package:* $15,750. *Average need-based loan:* $4254. *Average need-based gift aid:* $12,773. *Average non-need-based aid:* $6229. *Average indebtedness upon graduation:* $30,275.

Applying *Options:* electronic application. *Required:* high school transcript. *Recommended:* minimum 2.0 GPA. *Application deadlines:* 8/15 (freshmen), 8/15 (transfers). *Notification:* 9/15 (freshmen), continuous until 9/15 (transfers).

Freshman Application Contact Ms. Diane Schaefer, Director of Admissions, Grand View University, 1200 Grandview Avenue, Des Moines, IA 50316-1599. *Phone:* 515-263-2810. *Toll-free phone:* 800-444-6083. *Fax:* 515-263-2974. *E-mail:* admissions@grandview.edu. *Web site:* http://www.grandview.edu/.

See below for display ad and page 1348 for the College Close-Up.

Grinnell College
Grinnell, Iowa

- **Independent** 4-year, founded 1846
- **Small-town** 120-acre campus
- **Endowment** $1.5 billion
- **Coed** 1,693 undergraduate students, 97% full-time, 54% women, 46% men
- **Very difficult** entrance level, 51% of applicants were admitted

Undergraduates 1,646 full-time, 47 part-time. Students come from 50 states and territories; 54 other countries; 88% are from out of state; 5% Black or African American, non-Hispanic/Latino; 8% Hispanic/Latino; 6% Asian, non-Hispanic/Latino; 0.3% American Indian or Alaska Native, non-Hispanic/Latino; 4% Two or more races, non-Hispanic/Latino; 6% Race/ethnicity unknown; 11% international; 0.6% transferred in; 88% live on campus. *Retention:* 93% of full-time freshmen returned.

Freshmen *Admission:* 2,613 applied, 1,330 admitted, 448 enrolled. *Test scores:* SAT critical reading scores over 500: 97%; SAT math scores over 500: 96%; ACT scores over 18: 100%; SAT critical reading scores over 600: 76%; SAT math scores over 600: 79%; ACT scores over 24: 95%; SAT critical reading scores over 700: 37%; SAT math scores over 700: 32%; ACT scores over 30: 63%.

Faculty *Total:* 206, 77% full-time, 81% with terminal degrees. *Student/faculty ratio:* 9:1.

Academics *Calendar:* semesters. *Degree:* bachelor's. *Special study options:* accelerated degree program, advanced placement credit, double majors, independent study, internships, off-campus study, services for LD students, student-designed majors, study abroad. *Unusual degree programs:* 3-2 engineering with Columbia University, California Institute of Technology, Rensselaer Polytechnic Institute, Washington University in St. Louis; architecture with Washington University in St. Louis, law at Columbia University.

Computers on Campus Students can access the following: campus intranet, computer help desk, free student e-mail accounts, online (class) grades, online (class) schedules. Campuswide network is available. 100% of college-owned or -operated housing units are wired for high-speed Internet access. Wireless service is available via entire campus.

Student Life *Housing:* on-campus residence required through sophomore year. *Options:* coed, cooperative, disabled students. Campus housing is university owned. Freshman campus housing is guaranteed. *Activities and organizations:* drama/theater group, student-run newspaper, radio station, choral group, Con-

cerned Black Students, International Student Organization, Student Organization of Latinas/Latinos, Campus Democrats, Ultimate Frisbee. *Campus security:* 24-hour emergency response devices and patrols, student patrols, late-night transport/escort service, controlled dormitory access. *Student services:* health clinic, personal/psychological counseling.

Athletics Member NCAA. All Division III. *Intercollegiate sports:* baseball M, basketball M/W, cross-country running M/W, football M, golf M/W, soccer M/W, softball W, swimming and diving M/W, tennis M/W, track and field M/W, volleyball W. *Intramural sports:* archery M(c)/W(c), badminton M/W, baseball M(c), basketball M/W, equestrian sports M(c)/W(c), fencing M(c)/W, rugby M(c)/W(c), soccer M/W, softball M/W, swimming and diving M(c)/W(c), table tennis M(c)/W(c), tennis M/W, ultimate Frisbee M(c)/W, volleyball M/W, water polo M/W.

Standardized Tests *Required:* SAT or ACT (for admission).

Costs (2011–12) *Comprehensive fee:* $49,144 includes full-time tuition ($39,250), mandatory fees ($560), and room and board ($9334). Part-time tuition: $1227 per credit. *College room only:* $4372. Room and board charges vary according to board plan and housing facility. *Payment plan:* installment. *Waivers:* employees or children of employees.

Financial Aid Of all full-time matriculated undergraduates who enrolled in 2011, 1,249 applied for aid, 1,157 were judged to have need, 1,157 had their need fully met. 498 Federal Work-Study jobs (averaging $1192). 331 state and other part-time jobs (averaging $1334). In 2011, 263 non-need-based awards were made. *Average percent of need met:* 100%. *Average financial aid package:* $37,556. *Average need-based loan:* $3400. *Average need-based gift aid:* $32,282. *Average non-need-based aid:* $11,582. *Average indebtedness upon graduation:* $15,720. *Financial aid deadline:* 2/1.

Applying *Options:* electronic application, early admission, early decision, deferred entrance. *Application fee:* $30. *Required:* essay or personal statement, high school transcript, 3 letters of recommendation. *Recommended:* interview. *Application deadlines:* 1/15 (freshmen), 4/1 (transfers). *Early decision deadline:* 11/15 (for plan 1), 1/1 (for plan 2). *Notification:* 4/1 (freshmen), 5/20 (transfers), 12/15 (early decision plan 1), 2/1 (early decision plan 2).

Freshman Application Contact Mr. Joseph Bagnoli, Vice President for Enrollment, Grinnell College, 1103 Park Street, Grinnell, IA 50112. *Phone:* 641-269-3600. *Toll-free phone:* 800-247-0113. *Fax:* 641-269-4800. *E-mail:* askgrin@grinnell.edu. *Web site:* http://www.grinnell.edu/.

Hamilton Technical College

Davenport, Iowa

- **Proprietary** 4-year, founded 1969
- **Urban** campus
- **Coed**
- **Noncompetitive** entrance level

Faculty *Student/faculty ratio:* 20:1.

Academics *Calendar:* continuous. *Degrees:* diplomas, associate, and bachelor's.

Student Life *Campus security:* 24-hour emergency response devices.

Applying *Options:* deferred entrance. *Application fee:* $25. *Required:* high school transcript, interview.

Freshman Application Contact Hamilton Technical College, 1011 East 53rd Street, Davenport, IA 52807-2653. *Phone:* 563-386-3570. *Toll-free phone:* 866-966-4825. *Web site:* http://www.hamiltontechcollege.com/.

INSTE Bible College

Ankeny, Iowa

Director of Admissions Admissions, INSTE Bible College, 2302 SW 3rd Street, Ankeny, IA 50023. *Phone:* 515-289-9200. *Fax:* 515-289-9201. *E-mail:* inste@inste.edu. *Web site:* http://www.inste.edu/.

Iowa State University of Science and Technology

Ames, Iowa

- **State-supported** university, founded 1858
- **Suburban** 1795-acre campus with easy access to Des Moines
- **Endowment** $612.3 million
- **Coed** 24,343 undergraduate students, 95% full-time, 44% women, 56% men
- **Moderately difficult** entrance level, 86% of applicants were admitted

Undergraduates 23,103 full-time, 1,240 part-time. Students come from 54 states and territories; 103 other countries; 26% are from out of state; 3% Black

or African American, non-Hispanic/Latino; 4% Hispanic/Latino; 3% Asian, non-Hispanic/Latino; 0.1% Native Hawaiian or other Pacific Islander, non-Hispanic/Latino; 0.2% American Indian or Alaska Native, non-Hispanic/Latino; 1% Two or more races, non-Hispanic/Latino; 3% Race/ethnicity unknown; 8% international; 7% transferred in; 39% live on campus. *Retention:* 88% of full-time freshmen returned.

Freshmen *Admission:* 14,540 applied, 12,541 admitted, 5,048 enrolled. *Average high school GPA:* 3.53. *Test scores:* SAT critical reading scores over 500: 69%; SAT math scores over 500: 82%; ACT scores over 18: 98%; SAT critical reading scores over 600: 34%; SAT math scores over 600: 51%; ACT scores over 24: 62%; SAT critical reading scores over 700: 7%; SAT math scores over 700: 15%; ACT scores over 30: 13%.

Faculty *Total:* 1,667, 84% full-time, 88% with terminal degrees. *Student/faculty ratio:* 18:1.

Academics *Calendar:* semesters. *Degrees:* bachelor's, master's, doctoral, post-master's, postbachelor's, and first professional certificates. *Special study options:* academic remediation for entering students, accelerated degree program, adult/continuing education programs, advanced placement credit, cooperative education, distance learning, double majors, English as a second language, external degree program, freshman honors college, honors programs, independent study, internships, off-campus study, part-time degree program, services for LD students, student-designed majors, study abroad, summer session for credit. *ROTC:* Army (b), Navy (b), Air Force (b). *Unusual degree programs:* 3-2 engineering with William Penn College.

Computers on Campus 2,430 computers/terminals are available on campus for general student use. Students can access the following: campus intranet, computer help desk, free student e-mail accounts, online (class) grades, online (class) registration, online (class) schedules, network services. Campuswide network is available. 100% of college-owned or -operated housing units are wired for high-speed Internet access. Wireless service is available via entire campus.

Student Life *Housing options:* coed, men-only, women-only, disabled students. Campus housing is university owned. Freshman applicants given priority for college housing. *Activities and organizations:* drama/theater group, student-run newspaper, radio and television station, choral group, marching band, student government, Student Alumni Association, Residence Hall Associations, national fraternities, national sororities. *Campus security:* 24-hour emergency response devices and patrols, student patrols, late-night transport/escort service, controlled dormitory access, crime prevention programs, threat assessment team, motor vehicle help van. *Student services:* health clinic, personal/psychological counseling, women's center, legal services.

Athletics Member NCAA. All Division I except football (Division I-A). *Intercollegiate sports:* basketball M(s)/W(s), cross-country running M(s)/W(s), golf M(s)/W(s), gymnastics W(s), soccer W(s), softball W(s), swimming and diving M(s)/W(s), tennis W(s), track and field M(s)/W(s), volleyball W(s), wrestling M(s). *Intramural sports:* archery M(c)/W(c), badminton M(c)/W(c), basketball M/W, bowling M(c)/W(c), cross-country running M/W, equestrian sports M(c)/W(c), fencing M(c)/W(c), football M/W, golf M/W, ice hockey M(c)/W(c), lacrosse M(c)/W(c), racquetball M(c)/W(c), riflery M(c)/W(c), rugby M(c)/W(c), sailing M(c)/W(c), skiing (cross-country) M(c)/W(c), skiing (downhill) M(c)/W(c), soccer M/W, softball M/W, squash M/W, swimming and diving M/W, table tennis M(c)/W(c), tennis M/W, volleyball M(c)/W(c), water polo M(c)/W(c), weight lifting M(c)/W(c), wrestling M/W.

Standardized Tests *Required:* SAT or ACT (for admission).

Costs (2012–13) *Tuition:* state resident $6648 full-time, $277 per semester hour part-time; nonresident $18,760 full-time, $782 per semester hour part-time. Full-time tuition and fees vary according to class time, degree level, and program. Part-time tuition and fees vary according to class time, course load, degree level, and program. *Required fees:* $1078 full-time. *Room and board:* $7878; room only: $4126. Room and board charges vary according to board plan and housing facility. *Payment plans:* installment, deferred payment.

Financial Aid Of all full-time matriculated undergraduates who enrolled in 2010, 16,487 applied for aid, 12,210 were judged to have need, 4,916 had their need fully met. In 2010, 6060 non-need-based awards were made. *Average percent of need met:* 81%. *Average financial aid package:* $11,954. *Average need-based loan:* $4453. *Average need-based gift aid:* $6720. *Average non-need-based aid:* $2613. *Average indebtedness upon graduation:* $29,455.

Applying *Options:* electronic application, early admission, deferred entrance. *Application fee:* $40. *Required:* high school transcript, Regent Admission Index (RAI) of at least 245 and meet minimum HS course requirements. *Application deadlines:* 7/1 (freshmen), 7/1 (transfers). *Notification:* continuous (freshmen), continuous (transfers).

Freshman Application Contact Mr. Phil Caffrey, Associate Director for Freshman Admissions, Iowa State University of Science and Technology, 100 Enrollment Services Center, Ames, IA 50011-2010. *Phone:* 515-294-5836. *Toll-free phone:* 800-262-3810. *Fax:* 515-294-2592. *E-mail:* admissions@iastate.edu. *Web site:* http://www.iastate.edu/.

Iowa Wesleyan College

Mount Pleasant, Iowa

- **Independent United Methodist** 4-year, founded 1842
- **Small-town** 60-acre campus
- **Endowment** $12.3 million
- **Coed** 741 undergraduate students, 78% full-time, 57% women, 43% men
- **Moderately difficult** entrance level, 63% of applicants were admitted

Undergraduates 576 full-time, 165 part-time. Students come from 34 states and territories; 17 other countries; 43% are from out of state; 8% Black or African American, non-Hispanic/Latino; 6% Hispanic/Latino; 0.1% Asian, non-Hispanic/Latino; 0.8% Native Hawaiian or other Pacific Islander, non-Hispanic/Latino; 0.7% Two or more races, non-Hispanic/Latino; 14% Race/ethnicity unknown; 8% international; 20% transferred in; 68% live on campus. *Retention:* 42% of full-time freshmen returned.

Freshmen *Admission:* 1,109 applied, 696 admitted, 113 enrolled. *Average high school GPA:* 2.99. *Test scores:* SAT critical reading scores over 500: 47%; SAT math scores over 500: 59%; ACT scores over 18: 83%; ACT scores over 24: 11%; ACT scores over 30: 1%.

Faculty *Total:* 107, 45% full-time, 32% with terminal degrees. *Student/faculty ratio:* 12:1.

Academics *Calendar:* semesters. *Degree:* bachelor's. *Special study options:* academic remediation for entering students, adult/continuing education programs, advanced placement credit, cooperative education, distance learning, double majors, independent study, internships, off-campus study, part-time degree program, services for LD students, student-designed majors, study abroad, summer session for credit. *Unusual degree programs:* 3-2 forestry with Iowa State University of Science and Technology, Duke University; pre-physical therapy program with St. Ambrose University; medical technology program with St. Luke's Hospital in Cedar Rapids, IA.

Computers on Campus 97 computers/terminals are available on campus for general student use. Students can access the following: campus intranet, computer help desk, free student e-mail accounts, online (class) grades, online (class) schedules. Campuswide network is available. 100% of college-owned or -operated housing units are wired for high-speed Internet access. Wireless service is available via entire campus.

Student Life *Housing:* on-campus residence required through senior year. *Options:* coed, men-only, women-only. Campus housing is university owned. Freshman campus housing is guaranteed. *Activities and organizations:* student-run radio station, choral group, Student Union Board, Student Senate, Commuter Club, Choir, Student Ambassadors, national sororities. *Campus security:* late-night transport/escort service, controlled dormitory access, evening patrols by trained security personnel. *Student services:* health clinic, personal/psychological counseling.

Athletics Member NCAA. All Division III except track and field (Division II). *Intercollegiate sports:* baseball M, basketball M/W, cross-country running M/W, football M, golf M/W, soccer M/W, softball W, track and field M/W, volleyball W. *Intramural sports:* badminton M/W, basketball M/W, bowling M/W, cheerleading M/W, football M/W, soccer M/W, softball M/W, table tennis M/W, tennis M/W, track and field M/W, volleyball M/W, weight lifting M/W.

Standardized Tests *Required:* SAT or ACT (for admission).

Costs (2011–12) *Comprehensive fee:* $30,630 includes full-time tuition ($23,160) and room and board ($7470). Part-time tuition: $580 per credit hour. Part-time tuition and fees vary according to class time, course load, and location. *College room only:* $2990. Room and board charges vary according to board plan and housing facility. *Payment plans:* installment, deferred payment. *Waivers:* employees or children of employees.

Financial Aid Of all full-time matriculated undergraduates who enrolled in 2010, 514 applied for aid, 496 were judged to have need, 6 had their need fully met. 108 Federal Work-Study jobs (averaging $2000). In 2010, 107 non-need-based awards were made. *Average percent of need met:* 59%. *Average financial aid package:* $18,000. *Average need-based loan:* $4800. *Average need-based gift aid:* $13,200. *Average non-need-based aid:* $11,533. *Average indebtedness upon graduation:* $29,780.

Applying *Options:* electronic application, early admission, deferred entrance. *Application fee:* $20. *Required:* high school transcript, minimum 2.5 GPA, minimum ACT score of 19 or SAT of 890. *Required for some:* essay or personal statement, 1 letter of recommendation, interview. *Application deadlines:* 8/15 (freshmen), 8/15 (transfers).

Freshman Application Contact Dean Mark T. Petty, Associate Vice President and Dean for Admissions, Iowa Wesleyan College, 601 N Main Street, Mount Pleasant, IA 52641. *Phone:* 319-385-6231. *Toll-free phone:* 800-582-2383. *Fax:* 319-385-6240. *E-mail:* mpetty@iwc.edu. *Web site:* http://www.iwc.edu/.

ITT Technical Institute

Cedar Rapids, Iowa

- **Proprietary** primarily 2-year
- **Coed**
- **Minimally difficult** entrance level

Academics *Degrees:* associate and bachelor's.

Freshman Application Contact Director of Recruitment, ITT Technical Institute, 3735 Queen Court SW, Cedar Rapids, IA 52404. *Phone:* 319-297-3400. *Toll-free phone:* 877-320-4625. *Web site:* http://www.itt-tech.edu/.

ITT Technical Institute

Clive, Iowa

- **Proprietary** primarily 2-year, part of ITT Educational Services, Inc.
- **Coed**
- **Minimally difficult** entrance level

Academics *Degrees:* associate and bachelor's.

Student Life *Housing:* college housing not available.

Freshman Application Contact Director of Recruitment, ITT Technical Institute, 1860 Northwest 118th Street, Suite 110, Clive, IA 50325. *Phone:* 515-327-5500. *Toll-free phone:* 877-526-7312. *Web site:* http://www.itt-tech.edu/.

Kaplan University, Cedar Falls

Cedar Falls, Iowa

Freshman Application Contact Kaplan University, Cedar Falls, 7009 Nordic Drive, Cedar Falls, IA 50613. *Phone:* 319-277-0220. *Toll-free phone:* 866-527-5268 (in-state); 800-527-5268 (out-of-state). *Web site:* http://www.cedarfalls.kaplanuniversity.edu/.

Kaplan University, Cedar Rapids

Cedar Rapids, Iowa

Freshman Application Contact Kaplan University, Cedar Rapids, 3165 Edgewood Parkway, SW, Cedar Rapids, IA 52404. *Phone:* 319-363-0481. *Toll-free phone:* 866-527-5268 (in-state); 800-527-5268 (out-of-state). *Web site:* http://www.cedarrapids.kaplanuniversity.edu/.

Kaplan University, Council Bluffs

Council Bluffs, Iowa

Freshman Application Contact Kaplan University, Council Bluffs, 1751 Madison Avenue, Council Bluffs, IA 51503. *Phone:* 712-328-4212. *Toll-free phone:* 866-527-5268 (in-state); 800-527-5268 (out-of-state). *Web site:* http://www.councilbluffs.kaplanuniversity.edu/.

Kaplan University, Davenport Campus

Davenport, Iowa

Freshman Application Contact Kaplan University, Davenport Campus, 1801 East Kimberly Road, Suite 1, Davenport, IA 52807-2095. *Phone:* 563-355-3500. *Toll-free phone:* 866-527-5268 (in-state); 800-527-5268 (out-of-state). *Web site:* http://www.davenport.kaplanuniversity.edu/.

Kaplan University, Des Moines

Urbandale, Iowa

Freshman Application Contact Kaplan University, Des Moines, 4655 121st Street, Urbandale, IA 50323. *Phone:* 515-727-2100. *Toll-free phone:* 866-527-5268 (in-state); 800-527-5268 (out-of-state). *Web site:* http://www.desmoines.kaplanuniversity.edu/.

Kaplan University, Mason City Campus

Mason City, Iowa

Freshman Application Contact Kaplan University, Mason City Campus, 2570 4th Street, SW, Mason City, IA 50401. *Phone:* 641-423-2530. *Toll-free phone:* 866-527-5268 (in-state); 800-527-5268 (out-of-state). *Web site:* http://masoncity.kaplanuniversity.edu/Pages/Homepage.aspx.

Loras College

Dubuque, Iowa

- **Independent Roman Catholic** comprehensive, founded 1839
- **Suburban** 60-acre campus
- **Endowment** $22.0 million
- **Coed** 1,517 undergraduate students, 97% full-time, 49% women, 51% men
- **Moderately difficult** entrance level, 76% of applicants were admitted

Undergraduates 1,467 full-time, 47 part-time. Students come from 23 states and territories; 13 other countries; 55% are from out of state; 2% Black or African American, non-Hispanic/Latino; 3% Hispanic/Latino; 0.9% Asian, non-Hispanic/Latino; 0.2% Native Hawaiian or other Pacific Islander, non-Hispanic/Latino; 0.5% American Indian or Alaska Native, non-Hispanic/Latino; 3% Race/ethnicity unknown; 4% international; 4% transferred in; 67% live on campus. *Retention:* 79% of full-time freshmen returned.

Freshmen *Admission:* 1,540 applied, 1,174 admitted, 361 enrolled. *Average high school GPA:* 3.42. *Test scores:* ACT scores over 18: 99%; ACT scores over 24: 48%; ACT scores over 30: 6%.

Faculty *Total:* 141, 78% full-time, 50% with terminal degrees. *Student/faculty ratio:* 12:1.

Academics *Calendar:* semesters. *Degrees:* associate, bachelor's, and master's. *Special study options:* academic remediation for entering students, advanced placement credit, cooperative education, double majors, honors programs, independent study, internships, off-campus study, part-time degree program, services for LD students, student-designed majors, study abroad, summer session for credit. *ROTC:* Army (c). *Unusual degree programs:* 3-2 nursing.

Computers on Campus 20 computers/terminals are available on campus for general student use. Students can access the following: online (class) registration. Campuswide network is available. Wireless service is available via entire campus.

Student Life *Housing:* on-campus residence required through junior year. *Options:* coed, men-only, women-only. Campus housing is university owned. Freshman campus housing is guaranteed. *Activities and organizations:* drama/theater group, student-run newspaper, radio and television station, choral group, Student Senate, Campus Ministry, College Activities Board, residence hall councils, national sororities. *Campus security:* 24-hour emergency response devices and patrols, late-night transport/escort service, controlled dormitory access. *Student services:* health clinic, personal/psychological counseling.

Athletics Member NCAA. All Division III. *Intercollegiate sports:* baseball M, basketball M/W, cross-country running M/W, football M, golf M/W, ice hockey M(c), rugby M(c), skiing (downhill) M(c), soccer M/W, softball W, swimming and diving M/W, tennis M/W, track and field M/W, volleyball M(c)/W, water polo M, wrestling M. *Intramural sports:* badminton M/W, baseball M, basketball M/W, cross-country running M/W, football M, golf M/W, ice hockey M, racquetball M/W, rugby M, skiing (cross-country) M/W, skiing (downhill) M/W, soccer M/W, softball M/W, swimming and diving M/W, table tennis M/W, tennis M/W, track and field M/W, volleyball M/W, water polo M/W, weight lifting M/W, wrestling M.

Standardized Tests *Required for some:* SAT (for admission). *Recommended:* ACT (for admission).

Costs (2012–13) *Comprehensive fee:* $35,992 includes full-time tuition ($26,942), mandatory fees ($1225), and room and board ($7825). Full-time tuition and fees vary according to course load and degree level. Part-time tuition: $562 per credit hour. *College room only:* $3957. Room and board charges vary according to board plan and housing facility. *Payment plan:* installment. *Waivers:* employees or children of employees.

Financial Aid Of all full-time matriculated undergraduates who enrolled in 2011, 1,222 applied for aid, 1,064 were judged to have need, 585 had their need fully met. In 2011, 378 non-need-based awards were made. *Average percent of need met:* 76%. *Average financial aid package:* $20,663. *Average need-based loan:* $4772. *Average need-based gift aid:* $16,144. *Average non-need-based aid:* $13,567. *Average indebtedness upon graduation:* $32,704.

Applying *Options:* electronic application, deferred entrance. *Application fee:* $25. *Required:* high school transcript, minimum 2.5 GPA. *Required for some:* interview. *Recommended:* essay or personal statement, 1 letter of recommendation. *Application deadlines:* rolling (freshmen), rolling (transfers). *Notification:* continuous (freshmen), continuous (transfers).

Freshman Application Contact Ms. Sharon Lyons, Director of Admissions, Loras College, 1450 Alta Vista, Dubuque, IA 52004-0178. *Phone:* 563-588-7829. *Toll-free phone:* 800-245-6727. *Fax:* 563-588-7119. *E-mail:* adms@loras.edu. *Web site:* http://www.loras.edu/.

Luther College

Decorah, Iowa

- **Independent** 4-year, founded 1861, affiliated with Evangelical Lutheran Church in America
- **Small-town** 200-acre campus
- **Endowment** $116.7 million
- **Coed** 2,471 undergraduate students, 99% full-time, 57% women, 43% men
- **Moderately difficult** entrance level, 71% of applicants were admitted

Undergraduates 2,434 full-time, 37 part-time. Students come from 33 states and territories; 44 other countries; 67% are from out of state; 1% Black or African American, non-Hispanic/Latino; 3% Hispanic/Latino; 2% Asian, non-Hispanic/Latino; 0.1% American Indian or Alaska Native, non-Hispanic/Latino; 2% Two or more races, non-Hispanic/Latino; 0.2% Race/ethnicity unknown; 5% international; 2% transferred in; 86% live on campus. *Retention:* 87% of full-time freshmen returned.

Freshmen *Admission:* 3,683 applied, 2,631 admitted, 627 enrolled. *Average high school GPA:* 3.61. *Test scores:* SAT critical reading scores over 500: 66%; SAT math scores over 500: 81%; SAT writing scores over 500: 64%; ACT scores over 18: 99%; SAT critical reading scores over 600: 33%; SAT math scores over 600: 36%; SAT writing scores over 600: 36%; ACT scores over 24: 75%; SAT critical reading scores over 700: 5%; SAT math scores over 700: 12%; SAT writing scores over 700: 7%; ACT scores over 30: 20%.

Faculty *Total:* 257, 69% full-time, 79% with terminal degrees. *Student/faculty ratio:* 12:1.

Academics *Calendar:* 4-1-4. *Degree:* bachelor's. *Special study options:* academic remediation for entering students, advanced placement credit, double majors, honors programs, independent study, internships, off-campus study, part-time degree program, services for LD students, student-designed majors, study abroad, summer session for credit. *Unusual degree programs:* 3-2 engineering with Washington University in St. Louis; University of Minnesota, Twin Cities Campus; environmental management, resource management with Duke University.

Computers on Campus 560 computers/terminals are available on campus for general student use. Students can access the following: campus intranet, computer help desk, free student e-mail accounts, online (class) grades, online (class) registration, online (class) schedules. Campuswide network is available. 100% of college-owned or -operated housing units are wired for high-speed Internet access. Wireless service is available via entire campus.

Student Life *Housing:* on-campus residence required through senior year. *Options:* coed, disabled students. Campus housing is university owned. Freshman campus housing is guaranteed. *Activities and organizations:* drama/theater group, student-run newspaper, radio station, choral group, Alpha Phi Omega, college ministries, recreational sports, Student Activities Council, Diversity groups. *Campus security:* 24-hour emergency response devices and patrols, late-night transport/escort service, controlled dormitory access. *Student services:* health clinic, personal/psychological counseling.

Athletics Member NCAA. All Division III. *Intercollegiate sports:* baseball M, basketball M/W, cross-country running M/W, football M, golf M/W, soccer M/W, softball W, swimming and diving M/W, tennis M/W, track and field M/W, volleyball W, wrestling M. *Intramural sports:* archery M/W, badminton M/W, basketball M/W, bowling M/W, football M/W, golf M/W, racquetball M/W, rugby M(c)/W(c), soccer M/W, softball M/W, table tennis M/W, tennis M/W, track and field M/W, ultimate Frisbee M(c)/W(c), volleyball M/W.

Standardized Tests *Required:* SAT or ACT (for admission).

Costs (2012–13) *Comprehensive fee:* $42,320 includes full-time tuition ($35,950), mandatory fees ($150), and room and board ($6220). Full-time tuition and fees vary according to course load. Part-time tuition and fees vary according to course load. *College room only:* $2890. Room and board charges vary according to board plan and housing facility. *Payment plan:* installment. *Waivers:* employees or children of employees.

Financial Aid Of all full-time matriculated undergraduates who enrolled in 2011, 1,999 applied for aid, 1,712 were judged to have need, 469 had their need fully met. 1,035 Federal Work-Study jobs (averaging $2062). 1,106 state and other part-time jobs (averaging $1996). In 2011, 270 non-need-based awards were made. *Average percent of need met:* 86%. *Average financial aid package:* $26,706. *Average need-based loan:* $5036. *Average need-based gift aid:* $19,436. *Average non-need-based aid:* $13,716. *Average indebtedness upon graduation:* $32,107.

Applying *Options:* electronic application, deferred entrance. *Application fee:* $25. *Required:* essay or personal statement, high school transcript, 1 letter of recommendation. *Recommended:* interview. *Notification:* continuous (freshmen), continuous (transfers).

Freshman Application Contact Kirk Neubauer, Director of Recruiting Services, Luther College, 700 College Drive, Decorah, IA 52101. *Phone:* 563-

387-1287. *Toll-free phone:* 800-458-8437. *Fax:* 563-387-2159. *E-mail:* admissions@luther.edu. *Web site:* http://www.luther.edu/.

See below for display ad and page 1424 for the College Close-Up.

Maharishi University of Management
Fairfield, Iowa

- **Independent** university, founded 1971
- **Small-town** campus
- **Coed** 350 undergraduate students, 95% full-time, 50% women, 50% men
- **Moderately difficult** entrance level

Undergraduates 332 full-time, 18 part-time. 84% are from out of state; 8% Black or African American, non-Hispanic/Latino; 10% Hispanic/Latino; 3% Asian, non-Hispanic/Latino; 0.3% Native Hawaiian or other Pacific Islander, non-Hispanic/Latino; 6% Two or more races, non-Hispanic/Latino; 3% Race/ethnicity unknown; 15% international; 27% transferred in; 52% live on campus. *Retention:* 76% of full-time freshmen returned.
Freshmen *Admission:* 129 applied, 24 enrolled. *Average high school GPA:* 3.1.
Faculty *Total:* 98, 68% full-time, 42% with terminal degrees. *Student/faculty ratio:* 15:1.
Academics *Calendar:* semesters. *Degrees:* diplomas, associate, bachelor's, master's, doctoral, postbachelor's, and first professional certificates. *Special study options:* adult/continuing education programs.
Computers on Campus Students can access the following: campus intranet, computer help desk, free student e-mail accounts, online (class) grades, online (class) schedules. Campuswide network is available. 100% of college-owned or -operated housing units are wired for high-speed Internet access.
Student Life *Housing:* on-campus residence required through senior year. *Options:* men-only, women-only, disabled students. Campus housing is university owned. Freshman campus housing is guaranteed. *Campus security:* 24-hour emergency response devices and patrols, late-night transport/escort service, controlled dormitory access.
Athletics *Intercollegiate sports:* soccer M(c)/W(c), ultimate Frisbee M(c)/W(c), volleyball M(c)/W(c). *Intramural sports:* archery M/W, badminton M/W, basketball M/W, football M/W, gymnastics M/W, rock climbing M/W, sailing M/W, soccer M/W, table tennis M/W, tennis M/W, ultimate Frisbee M/W, volleyball M/W.
Costs (2012–13) *Comprehensive fee:* $33,830 includes full-time tuition ($26,000), mandatory fees ($430), and room and board ($7400). Part-time

tuition: $350 per credit. Part-time tuition and fees vary according to course load. *Payment plan:* installment.
Financial Aid Of all full-time matriculated undergraduates who enrolled in 2006, 150 applied for aid, 148 were judged to have need, 32 had their need fully met. 120 Federal Work-Study jobs (averaging $1422). 7 state and other part-time jobs (averaging $2729). In 2006, 5 non-need-based awards were made. *Average percent of need met:* 89%. *Average financial aid package:* $23,963. *Average need-based loan:* $8281. *Average need-based gift aid:* $14,082. *Average non-need-based aid:* $9300. *Average indebtedness upon graduation:* $22,691.
Applying *Options:* electronic application, early admission, deferred entrance. *Application fee:* $25. *Required:* essay or personal statement, high school transcript, minimum 2.5 GPA, 2 letters of recommendation. *Recommended:* interview. *Application deadline:* 8/1 (freshmen). *Notification:* continuous until 8/15 (freshmen).
Freshman Application Contact Maharishi University of Management, Office of Admissions, Fairfield, IA 52557. *Phone:* 641-472-1110. *Toll-free phone:* 800-369-6480. *Fax:* 641-472-1179. *E-mail:* admissions@mum.edu. *Web site:* http://www.mum.edu/.

Mercy College of Health Sciences
Des Moines, Iowa

- **Independent** 4-year, founded 1995, affiliated with Roman Catholic Church
- **Urban** 5-acre campus
- **Endowment** $3.0 million
- **Coed, primarily women** 833 undergraduate students, 52% full-time, 87% women, 13% men

Undergraduates 431 full-time, 402 part-time. Students come from 12 states and territories; 2% are from out of state; 4% Black or African American, non-Hispanic/Latino; 3% Hispanic/Latino; 2% Asian, non-Hispanic/Latino; 0.2% American Indian or Alaska Native, non-Hispanic/Latino; 0.1% Two or more races, non-Hispanic/Latino; 7% Race/ethnicity unknown.
Faculty *Total:* 123, 45% full-time, 8% with terminal degrees.
Academics *Calendar:* semesters. *Degrees:* certificates, associate, and bachelor's. *Special study options:* academic remediation for entering students, accelerated degree program, advanced placement credit, cooperative education, distance learning, double majors, English as a second language, off-cam-

pus study, part-time degree program, services for LD students, summer session for credit.

Computers on Campus 46 computers/terminals are available on campus for general student use. Students can access the following: campus intranet, computer help desk, free student e-mail accounts, online (class) grades, online (class) schedules. Campuswide network is available. Wireless service is available via entire campus.

Student Life *Housing:* college housing not available. *Activities and organizations:* Student senate, Campus Ministry. *Campus security:* 24-hour emergency response devices and patrols, late-night transport/escort service. *Student services:* personal/psychological counseling.

Standardized Tests *Required for some:* ACT (for admission).

Costs (2012–13) *Tuition:* $13,900 full-time, $480 per credit part-time. Full-time tuition and fees vary according to course load. Part-time tuition and fees vary according to course load.

Financial Aid Of all full-time matriculated undergraduates who enrolled in 2003, 331 applied for aid, 322 were judged to have need, 3 had their need fully met. 11 Federal Work-Study jobs (averaging $1964). In 2003, 9 non-need-based awards were made. *Average percent of need met:* 29%. *Average financial aid package:* $7670. *Average need-based loan:* $2492. *Average need-based gift aid:* $5132. *Average non-need-based aid:* $6697. *Average indebtedness upon graduation:* $17,567. *Financial aid deadline:* 7/1.

Applying *Options:* electronic application. *Application fee:* $30. *Required:* high school transcript, minimum 2.3 GPA. *Required for some:* interview. *Application deadlines:* rolling (freshmen), rolling (out-of-state freshmen), rolling (transfers). *Notification:* continuous (freshmen), continuous (out-of-state freshmen), continuous (transfers).

Freshman Application Contact Kara Donovan, Admissions Manager, Mercy College of Health Sciences, 928 Sixth Avenue, Des Moines, IA 50309-1239. *Phone:* 515-643-6604. *Toll-free phone:* 800-637-2994. *Fax:* 515-643-6698. *E-mail:* kdonovan@mercydesmoines.org. *Web site:* http://www.mchs.edu/.

Morningside College
Sioux City, Iowa

- **Independent** comprehensive, founded 1894, affiliated with United Methodist Church
- **Suburban** 69-acre campus
- **Endowment** $37.6 million
- **Coed** 1,320 undergraduate students, 96% full-time, 53% women, 47% men
- **Moderately difficult** entrance level, 60% of applicants were admitted

Undergraduates 1,269 full-time, 51 part-time. Students come from 20 states and territories; 10 other countries; 35% are from out of state; 1% Black or African American, non-Hispanic/Latino; 5% Hispanic/Latino; 0.5% Asian, non-Hispanic/Latino; 0.2% Native Hawaiian or other Pacific Islander, non-Hispanic/Latino; 0.5% American Indian or Alaska Native, non-Hispanic/Latino; 1% Two or more races, non-Hispanic/Latino; 4% Race/ethnicity unknown; 1% international; 6% transferred in; 66% live on campus. *Retention:* 75% of full-time freshmen returned.

Freshmen *Admission:* 2,978 applied, 1,792 admitted, 377 enrolled. *Average high school GPA:* 3.4. *Test scores:* ACT scores over 18: 98%; ACT scores over 24: 44%; ACT scores over 30: 4%.

Faculty *Total:* 184, 41% full-time, 30% with terminal degrees. *Student/faculty ratio:* 13:1.

Academics *Calendar:* semesters. *Degrees:* bachelor's and master's. *Special study options:* academic remediation for entering students, adult/continuing education programs, advanced placement credit, distance learning, double majors, English as a second language, honors programs, independent study, internships, off-campus study, part-time degree program, services for LD students, student-designed majors, study abroad, summer session for credit. *ROTC:* Army (c).

Computers on Campus 150 computers/terminals are available on campus for general student use. Students can access the following: campus intranet, computer help desk, free student e-mail accounts, online (class) grades, online (class) registration, online (class) schedules, academic and financial records. Campuswide network is available. 100% of college-owned or -operated housing units are wired for high-speed Internet access. Wireless service is available via entire campus.

Student Life *Housing:* on-campus residence required through junior year. *Options:* coed. Campus housing is university owned. Freshman campus housing is guaranteed. *Activities and organizations:* drama/theater group, student-run newspaper, radio and television station, choral group, Student Government/Activities Council, Student Ambassadors, Homecoming Committee, national fraternities, national sororities. *Campus security:* 24-hour emergency response devices, student patrols, late-night transport/escort service, controlled dormitory access, 20-hour patrols by trained security personnel. *Student services:* health clinic, personal/psychological counseling, women's center.

Athletics Member NCAA, NAIA. All NCAA Division II. *Intercollegiate sports:* baseball M(s), basketball M(s)/W(s), cross-country running M(s)/W(s), football M(s), golf M(s)/W(s), soccer M(s)/W(s), softball W(s), swimming and diving M(s)/W(s), tennis M(s)/W(s), track and field M(s)/W(s), volleyball W(s), wrestling M(s). *Intramural sports:* basketball M/W, bowling M/W, ultimate Frisbee M/W, volleyball M/W.

Standardized Tests *Required:* SAT or ACT (for admission).

Costs (2011–12) *Comprehensive fee:* $31,370 includes full-time tuition ($22,880), mandatory fees ($1170), and room and board ($7320). Part-time tuition and fees vary according to course load. *College room only:* $3750. Room and board charges vary according to housing facility. *Payment plan:* installment. *Waivers:* children of alumni, senior citizens, and employees or children of employees.

Financial Aid Of all full-time matriculated undergraduates who enrolled in 2011, 1,184 applied for aid, 1,084 were judged to have need, 239 had their need fully met. 600 Federal Work-Study jobs (averaging $1127). 492 state and other part-time jobs (averaging $1463). In 2011, 161 non-need-based awards were made. *Average percent of need met:* 81%. *Average financial aid package:* $19,709. *Average need-based loan:* $4500. *Average need-based gift aid:* $6804. *Average non-need-based aid:* $10,252. *Average indebtedness upon graduation:* $36,309.

Applying *Options:* electronic application, deferred entrance. *Required:* high school transcript, 20 ACT/1410 SAT and either rank in top half of class or 2.5 GPA required. *Recommended:* minimum 2.5 GPA, interview. *Application deadlines:* rolling (freshmen), rolling (transfers). *Notification:* continuous (freshmen), continuous (out-of-state freshmen), continuous (transfers).

Freshman Application Contact Mrs. Stephanie Peters, Director of Admissions, Morningside College, 1501 Morningside Avenue, Sioux City, IA 51106. *Phone:* 712-274-5111. *Toll-free phone:* 800-831-0806 Ext. 5111. *Fax:* 712-274-5101. *E-mail:* mscadm@morningside.edu. *Web site:* http://www.morningside.edu/.

See page 324 for display ad and page 1466 for the College Close-Up.

Mount Mercy University
Cedar Rapids, Iowa

- **Independent Roman Catholic** comprehensive, founded 1928
- **Suburban** 40-acre campus
- **Endowment** $23.5 million
- **Coed** 1,538 undergraduate students, 59% full-time, 69% women, 31% men
- **Moderately difficult** entrance level, 70% of applicants were admitted

Undergraduates 914 full-time, 624 part-time. Students come from 16 states and territories; 10 other countries; 10% are from out of state; 3% Black or African American, non-Hispanic/Latino; 3% Hispanic/Latino; 1% Asian, non-Hispanic/Latino; 0.1% American Indian or Alaska Native, non-Hispanic/Latino; 0.4% Two or more races, non-Hispanic/Latino; 6% Race/ethnicity unknown; 3% international; 20% transferred in; 38% live on campus. *Retention:* 76% of full-time freshmen returned.

Freshmen *Admission:* 529 applied, 370 admitted, 151 enrolled. *Average high school GPA:* 3.4. *Test scores:* ACT scores over 18: 95%; ACT scores over 24: 28%; ACT scores over 30: 1%.

Faculty *Total:* 151, 56% full-time, 42% with terminal degrees. *Student/faculty ratio:* 11:1.

Academics *Calendar:* 4-1-4. *Degrees:* bachelor's and master's. *Special study options:* academic remediation for entering students, accelerated degree program, adult/continuing education programs, advanced placement credit, double majors, honors programs, independent study, internships, off-campus study, part-time degree program, services for LD students, study abroad, summer session for credit.

Computers on Campus 120 computers/terminals and 200 ports are available on campus for general student use. Students can access the following: campus intranet, computer help desk, free student e-mail accounts, online (class) grades, online (class) registration, online (class) schedules. Campuswide network is available. 100% of college-owned or -operated housing units are wired for high-speed Internet access. Wireless service is available via entire campus.

Student Life *Housing:* on-campus residence required through sophomore year. *Options:* coed, men-only, women-only. Campus housing is university owned. Freshman campus housing is guaranteed. *Activities and organizations:* drama/theater group, student-run newspaper, choral group, Student Ambassadors, Mount Mercy University Association of Nursing Students, Cheerleaders, Best Buddies, Student Government Association. *Campus security:* 24-hour emergency response devices and patrols, student patrols, late-night transport/escort service, controlled dormitory access, The Mount Mercy University Department of Public Safety is operational 24 hours a day, seven days a week. *Student services:* health clinic, personal/psychological counseling.

Athletics Member NAIA. *Intercollegiate sports:* baseball M(s), basketball M(s)/W(s), bowling M/W, cross-country running M(s)/W(s), golf M(s)/W(s),

MORNINGSIDE COLLEGE

DISCOVER YOURSELF
DEFINE YOUR WORLD
DESIGN YOUR FUTURE

MORNINGSIDE
C O L L E G E

Sioux City, Iowa
www.morningside.edu
(800) 831-0806

*The Morningside College experience cultivates a
passion for life-long learning and a dedication
to ethical leadership and civic responsibility.*

soccer M(s)/W(s), softball W(s), track and field M(s)/W(s), volleyball W(s). *Intramural sports:* baseball M, basketball M/W, bowling M/W, cheerleading W, football M/W, racquetball M/W, tennis M/W, volleyball M/W, weight lifting M/W.

Standardized Tests *Required:* SAT or ACT (for admission).

Costs (2011–12) *Comprehensive fee:* $31,830 includes full-time tuition ($24,360) and room and board ($7470). Full-time tuition and fees vary according to course load. Part-time tuition: $670 per credit hour. Part-time tuition and fees vary according to course load. *Required fees:* $670 per credit hour part-time. *Room and board:* Room and board charges vary according to board plan and housing facility. *Payment plan:* installment. *Waivers:* employees or children of employees.

Financial Aid Of all full-time matriculated undergraduates who enrolled in 2011, 996 applied for aid, 909 were judged to have need, 133 had their need fully met. 311 Federal Work-Study jobs (averaging $1906). 116 state and other part-time jobs (averaging $2000). In 2011, 129 non-need-based awards were made. *Average percent of need met:* 67%. *Average financial aid package:* $16,415. *Average need-based loan:* $4432. *Average need-based gift aid:* $12,050. *Average non-need-based aid:* $9285. *Average indebtedness upon graduation:* $28,900.

Applying *Options:* electronic application, deferred entrance. *Required:* high school transcript, minimum 2.5 GPA. *Required for some:* 1 letter of recommendation. *Application deadlines:* 8/15 (freshmen), 8/15 (transfers). *Notification:* continuous (freshmen), continuous (transfers).

Freshman Application Contact Ms. Liz Metz, Assistant Director of Admissions, Mount Mercy University, 1330 Elmhurst Drive, NE, Cedar Rapids, IA 52402. *Phone:* 319-368-6460. *Toll-free phone:* 800-248-4504. *Fax:* 319-363-5270. *E-mail:* emetz@mtmercy.edu. *Web site:* http://www.mtmercy.edu/.

Northwestern College

Orange City, Iowa

- **Independent** 4-year, founded 1882, affiliated with Reformed Church in America
- **Rural** 100-acre campus
- **Endowment** $42.5 million
- **Coed** 1,211 undergraduate students, 96% full-time, 58% women, 42% men
- **Moderately difficult** entrance level, 75% of applicants were admitted

Undergraduates 1,163 full-time, 48 part-time. Students come from 31 states and territories; 17 other countries; 46% are from out of state; 1% Black or African American, non-Hispanic/Latino; 4% Hispanic/Latino; 0.8% Asian, non-Hispanic/Latino; 0.4% American Indian or Alaska Native, non-Hispanic/Latino; 0.2% Two or more races, non-Hispanic/Latino; 0.2% Race/ethnicity unknown; 3% international; 3% transferred in; 95% live on campus. *Retention:* 76% of full-time freshmen returned.

Freshmen *Admission:* 1,422 applied, 1,060 admitted, 324 enrolled. *Average high school GPA:* 3.52. *Test scores:* SAT critical reading scores over 500: 50%; SAT math scores over 500: 54%; SAT writing scores over 500: 34%; ACT scores over 18: 98%; SAT critical reading scores over 600: 16%; SAT math scores over 600: 16%; SAT writing scores over 600: 6%; ACT scores over 24: 56%; ACT scores over 30: 8%.

Faculty *Total:* 134, 63% full-time, 51% with terminal degrees. *Student/faculty ratio:* 12:1.

Academics *Calendar:* semesters. *Degree:* certificates and bachelor's. *Special study options:* academic remediation for entering students, advanced placement credit, cooperative education, distance learning, double majors, English as a second language, honors programs, independent study, internships, off-campus study, services for LD students, student-designed majors, study abroad, summer session for credit.

Computers on Campus 250 computers/terminals are available on campus for general student use. Students can access the following: campus intranet, computer help desk, free student e-mail accounts, online (class) grades, online (class) registration, online (class) schedules, online degree audits. Campuswide network is available. 100% of college-owned or -operated housing units are wired for high-speed Internet access. Wireless service is available via entire campus.

Student Life *Housing:* on-campus residence required through senior year. *Options:* men-only, women-only, disabled students. Campus housing is university owned. Freshman campus housing is guaranteed. *Activities and organizations:* drama/theater group, student-run newspaper, television station, choral group, Drama Ministries Ensemble, Acappella Choir, Psi Chi, Fellowship of Christian Athletes, International Club. *Campus security:* 24-hour emergency response devices, controlled dormitory access. *Student services:* health clinic, personal/psychological counseling.

Athletics Member NAIA. *Intercollegiate sports:* baseball M(s), basketball M(s)/W(s), cheerleading M/W, cross-country running M(s)/W(s), football

M(s), golf M(s)/W(s), soccer M(s)/W(s), softball W(s), tennis W(s), track and field M(s)/W(s), volleyball W(s), wrestling M(s). *Intramural sports:* badminton M/W, basketball M/W, bowling M/W, cheerleading M/W, football M/W, golf M/W, lacrosse M/W, racquetball M/W, softball M, table tennis M/W, tennis M/W, volleyball M/W.

Standardized Tests *Required:* SAT or ACT (for admission).

Costs (2012–13) *Comprehensive fee:* $33,510 includes full-time tuition ($25,590), mandatory fees ($150), and room and board ($7770). Full-time tuition and fees vary according to program. *Part-time tuition:* $520 per credit hour. Part-time tuition and fees vary according to course load and program. *Required fees:* $50 part-time. *Room and board:* Room and board charges vary according to board plan and housing facility. *Payment plans:* tuition prepayment, installment. *Waivers:* employees or children of employees.

Financial Aid Of all full-time matriculated undergraduates who enrolled in 2007, 997 applied for aid, 997 were judged to have need, 418 had their need fully met. 354 Federal Work-Study jobs (averaging $1120). 412 state and other part-time jobs (averaging $1120). In 2007, 229 non-need-based awards were made. *Average percent of need met:* 87%. *Average financial aid package:* $16,330. *Average need-based loan:* $4453. *Average need-based gift aid:* $6289. *Average non-need-based aid:* $5562. *Average indebtedness upon graduation:* $23,817.

Applying *Options:* electronic application, early admission, deferred entrance. *Application fee:* $25. *Required:* essay or personal statement, high school transcript, minimum 2.0 GPA, 1 letter of recommendation. *Recommended:* minimum 2.5 GPA, interview. *Application deadlines:* rolling (freshmen), rolling (transfers). *Notification:* continuous (freshmen), continuous (transfers).

Freshman Application Contact Mr. Kenton Pauls, Dean of Enrollment Management, Northwestern College, 101 7th Street SW, Orange City, IA 51041-1996. *Phone:* 712-737-7130. *Toll-free phone:* 800-747-4757. *Fax:* 712-707-7164. *E-mail:* admissions@nwciowa.edu. *Web site:* http://www.nwciowa.edu/.

Palmer College of Chiropractic

Davenport, Iowa

- **Independent** comprehensive, founded 1897
- **Urban** 31-acre campus
- **Coed**
- **Noncompetitive** entrance level

Faculty *Student/faculty ratio:* 3:1.

Academics *Calendar:* trimesters. *Degrees:* certificates, associate, incidental bachelor's, master's, and doctoral.

Student Life *Campus security:* 24-hour emergency response devices and patrols, late-night transport/escort service.

Applying *Options:* electronic application, deferred entrance. *Application fee:* $50. *Required:* high school transcript, minimum 2.0 GPA, minimum 2.0 in math, science, and English courses. *Required for some:* essay or personal statement, interview.

Freshman Application Contact Ms. Lisa Gisel, Undergraduate Admissions Representative, Palmer College of Chiropractic, 1000 Brady Street, Davenport, IA 52803-5287. *Phone:* 563-884-5743. *Toll-free phone:* 800-722-3648. *Fax:* 563-884-5226. *E-mail:* lisa.gisel@palmer.edu. *Web site:* http://www.palmer.edu/.

St. Ambrose University

Davenport, Iowa

- **Independent Roman Catholic** comprehensive, founded 1882
- **Urban** 118-acre campus
- **Endowment** $107.3 million
- **Coed** 2,752 undergraduate students, 86% full-time, 59% women, 41% men
- **Moderately difficult** entrance level, 84% of applicants were admitted

Undergraduates 2,373 full-time, 379 part-time. Students come from 25 states and territories; 18 other countries; 58% are from out of state; 3% Black or African American, non-Hispanic/Latino; 6% Hispanic/Latino; 1% Asian, non-Hispanic/Latino; 0.1% Native Hawaiian or other Pacific Islander, non-Hispanic/Latino; 0.1% American Indian or Alaska Native, non-Hispanic/Latino; 1% Two or more races, non-Hispanic/Latino; 5% Race/ethnicity unknown; 0.5% international; 8% transferred in; 57% live on campus. *Retention:* 78% of full-time freshmen returned.

Freshmen *Admission:* 2,257 applied, 1,894 admitted, 551 enrolled. *Average high school GPA:* 3.19. *Test scores:* ACT scores over 18: 95%; ACT scores over 24: 36%; ACT scores over 30: 5%.

Faculty *Total:* 401, 53% full-time, 41% with terminal degrees. *Student/faculty ratio:* 11:1.

Academics *Calendar:* 4-1-4. *Degrees:* certificates, bachelor's, master's, doctoral, post-master's, postbachelor's, and first professional certificates. *Special*

study options: academic remediation for entering students, accelerated degree program, adult/continuing education programs, advanced placement credit, cooperative education, distance learning, double majors, external degree program, independent study, internships, off-campus study, part-time degree program, services for LD students, student-designed majors, study abroad, summer session for credit. *Unusual degree programs:* 3-2 physical therapy, occupational therapy, special education.

Computers on Campus 276 computers/terminals and 517 ports are available on campus for general student use. Students can access the following: campus intranet, computer help desk, free student e-mail accounts, online (class) grades, online (class) registration, online (class) schedules, online course syllabi, online class listings, and online payments. Campuswide network is available. 100% of college-owned or -operated housing units are wired for high-speed Internet access. Wireless service is available via classrooms, libraries, student centers.

Student Life *Housing:* on-campus residence required through sophomore year. *Options:* coed, men-only, women-only, disabled students. Campus housing is university owned. Freshman campus housing is guaranteed. *Activities and organizations:* drama/theater group, student-run newspaper, radio and television station, choral group, Up til Dawn, SOTA, Ambrosinas for Obama, Amnesty International, SPTO. *Campus security:* 24-hour emergency response devices and patrols, late-night transport/escort service, controlled dormitory access, police officer on campus 10 pm to 6 am. *Student services:* health clinic, personal/psychological counseling, women's center.

Athletics Member NAIA. *Intercollegiate sports:* baseball M(s), basketball M(s)/W(s), bowling M(s)/W(s), cheerleading M(s)/W(s), cross-country running M(s)/W(s), football M(s), golf M(s)/W(s), soccer M(s)/W(s), softball W(s), tennis M(s)/W(s), track and field M(s)/W(s), volleyball M(s)/W(s). *Intramural sports:* badminton M/W, baseball M/W, basketball M/W, bowling M/W, football M/W, golf M/W, racquetball M/W, skiing (downhill) M/W, soccer M/W, softball M/W, table tennis M/W, tennis M/W, volleyball M/W.

Standardized Tests *Required:* SAT or ACT (for admission). *Recommended:* ACT (for admission).

Costs (2012–13) *Comprehensive fee:* $35,165 includes full-time tuition ($25,730), mandatory fees ($240), and room and board ($9195). Full-time tuition and fees vary according to course load, location, program, and reciprocity agreements. *Part-time tuition:* $798 per credit hour. Part-time tuition and fees vary according to course load and location. *Room and board:* Room and board charges vary according to board plan and housing facility. *Payment plan:* installment. *Waivers:* senior citizens and employees or children of employees.

Financial Aid Of all full-time matriculated undergraduates who enrolled in 2010, 2,400 applied for aid, 1,874 were judged to have need, 223 had their need fully met. In 2010, 513 non-need-based awards were made. *Average percent of need met:* 14%. *Average financial aid package:* $7207. *Average need-based loan:* $4369. *Average need-based gift aid:* $11,304. *Average non-need-based aid:* $17,174. *Average indebtedness upon graduation:* $32,530.

Applying *Options:* electronic application, deferred entrance. *Application fee:* $25. *Required:* high school transcript, minimum 2.5 GPA, rank in upper 50% of high school class. *Required for some:* interview. *Recommended:* interview. *Application deadlines:* rolling (freshmen), rolling (transfers). *Notification:* 10/1 (freshmen), continuous (transfers).

Freshman Application Contact St. Ambrose University, 518 West Locust Street, Davenport, IA 52803-2898. *Phone:* 563-333-6300 Ext. 6311. *Toll-free phone:* 800-383-2627. *Web site:* http://www.sau.edu/.

Simpson College

Indianola, Iowa

- **Independent United Methodist** comprehensive, founded 1860
- **Suburban** 80-acre campus with easy access to Des Moines
- **Endowment** $73.0 million
- **Coed** 1,817 undergraduate students, 77% full-time, 56% women, 44% men
- **Moderately difficult** entrance level, 85% of applicants were admitted

Undergraduates 1,395 full-time, 422 part-time. Students come from 24 states and territories; 7 other countries; 11% are from out of state; 3% Black or African American, non-Hispanic/Latino; 2% Hispanic/Latino; 0.9% Asian, non-Hispanic/Latino; 0.4% American Indian or Alaska Native, non-Hispanic/Latino; 3% Two or more races, non-Hispanic/Latino; 0.4% Race/ethnicity unknown; 1% international; 3% transferred in; 83% live on campus. *Retention:* 77% of full-time freshmen returned.

Freshmen *Admission:* 1,343 applied, 1,145 admitted, 338 enrolled. *Test scores:* ACT scores over 18: 100%; ACT scores over 24: 47%; ACT scores over 30: 8%.

Faculty *Total:* 190, 48% full-time, 53% with terminal degrees. *Student/faculty ratio:* 12:1.

Academics *Calendar:* 4-4-1. *Degrees:* bachelor's, master's, and postbachelor's certificates. *Special study options:* accelerated degree program, adult/continuing education programs, advanced placement credit, cooperative education, double majors, independent study, internships, off-campus study, part-time degree program, services for LD students, student-designed majors, study abroad, summer session for credit. *Unusual degree programs:* 3-2 engineering with Washington University in St. Louis, MO; Iowa State University in Ames, IA; Institute of Technology (University of Minnesota) in Minneapolis, MN; nursing with Allen College (Waterloo, IA).

Computers on Campus 374 computers/terminals are available on campus for general student use. Students can access the following: campus intranet, computer help desk, free student e-mail accounts, online (class) grades, online (class) registration, online (class) schedules, wireless campus. Campuswide network is available. 100% of college-owned or -operated housing units are wired for high-speed Internet access. Wireless service is available via entire campus.

Student Life *Housing:* on-campus residence required through junior year. *Options:* coed. Campus housing is university owned. Freshman campus housing is guaranteed. *Activities and organizations:* drama/theater group, student-run newspaper, radio station, choral group, Religious Life Community, Campus Activities Board, Student Government Association, Residence Hall Association, intramurals, national fraternities, national sororities. *Campus security:* 24-hour emergency response devices and patrols, student patrols, late-night transport/escort service, controlled dormitory access, Safe (Simpson Alert for Emergencies) Students and staff/faculty will receive phone calls in case of campus emergency, including weather. *Student services:* health clinic, personal/psychological counseling, women's center.

Athletics Member NCAA. All Division III. *Intercollegiate sports:* baseball M, basketball M/W, cheerleading M/W, cross-country running M/W, football M, golf M/W, soccer M/W, softball W, swimming and diving M/W, tennis M/W, track and field M/W, volleyball M/W, wrestling M. *Intramural sports:* badminton M/W, basketball M/W, bowling M/W, football M/W, golf M/W, racquetball M/W, soccer M/W, softball M/W, swimming and diving M/W, table tennis M/W, tennis M/W, ultimate Frisbee M/W, volleyball M/W.

Standardized Tests *Required:* SAT or ACT (for admission).

Costs (2012–13) *One-time required fee:* $200. *Comprehensive fee:* $37,489 includes full-time tuition ($28,974), mandatory fees ($555), and room and board ($7960). Full-time tuition and fees vary according to class time, course load, degree level, and program. Part-time tuition: $333 per credit. Part-time tuition and fees vary according to class time, course load, degree level, and program. *College room only:* $3860. Room and board charges vary according to board plan and housing facility. *Payment plan:* installment. *Waivers:* minority students, children of alumni, senior citizens, and employees or children of employees.

Financial Aid Of all full-time matriculated undergraduates who enrolled in 2011, 1,389 applied for aid, 1,203 were judged to have need, 297 had their need fully met. 394 Federal Work-Study jobs (averaging $994). 397 state and other part-time jobs (averaging $1456). In 2011, 188 non-need-based awards were made. *Average percent of need met:* 87%. *Average financial aid package:* $26,567. *Average need-based loan:* $3920. *Average need-based gift aid:* $17,712. *Average non-need-based aid:* $15,273. *Average indebtedness upon graduation:* $35,045.

Applying *Options:* electronic application, deferred entrance. *Required:* high school transcript, online or paper application, guidance counselor recommendation form. *Recommended:* minimum 3.0 GPA, interview. *Application deadlines:* 8/15 (freshmen), 8/15 (transfers). *Notification:* continuous (freshmen), continuous (transfers).

Freshman Application Contact Deborah Tierney, Vice President for Enrollment, Simpson College, 701 North C Street, Indianola, IA 50125. *Phone:* 515-961-1624. *Toll-free phone:* 800-362-2454. *Fax:* 515-961-1870. *E-mail:* admiss@simpson.edu. *Web site:* http://www.simpson.edu/.

See page 327 for display ad and page 1584 for the College Close-Up.

University of Dubuque
Dubuque, Iowa

- **Independent Presbyterian** comprehensive, founded 1852
- **Suburban** 77-acre campus
- **Endowment** $87.1 million
- **Coed** 1,674 undergraduate students, 91% full-time, 43% women, 57% men
- **Moderately difficult** entrance level, 80% of applicants were admitted

Undergraduates 1,524 full-time, 150 part-time. Students come from 41 states and territories; 8 other countries; 52% are from out of state; 11% Black or African American, non-Hispanic/Latino; 1% Hispanic/Latino; 2% Asian, non-Hispanic/Latino; 0.1% Native Hawaiian or other Pacific Islander, non-Hispanic/Latino; 2% American Indian or Alaska Native, non-Hispanic/Latino; 0.8% Two or more races, non-Hispanic/Latino; 9% Race/ethnicity unknown; 1% international; 10% transferred in; 42% live on campus. *Retention:* 72% of full-time freshmen returned.

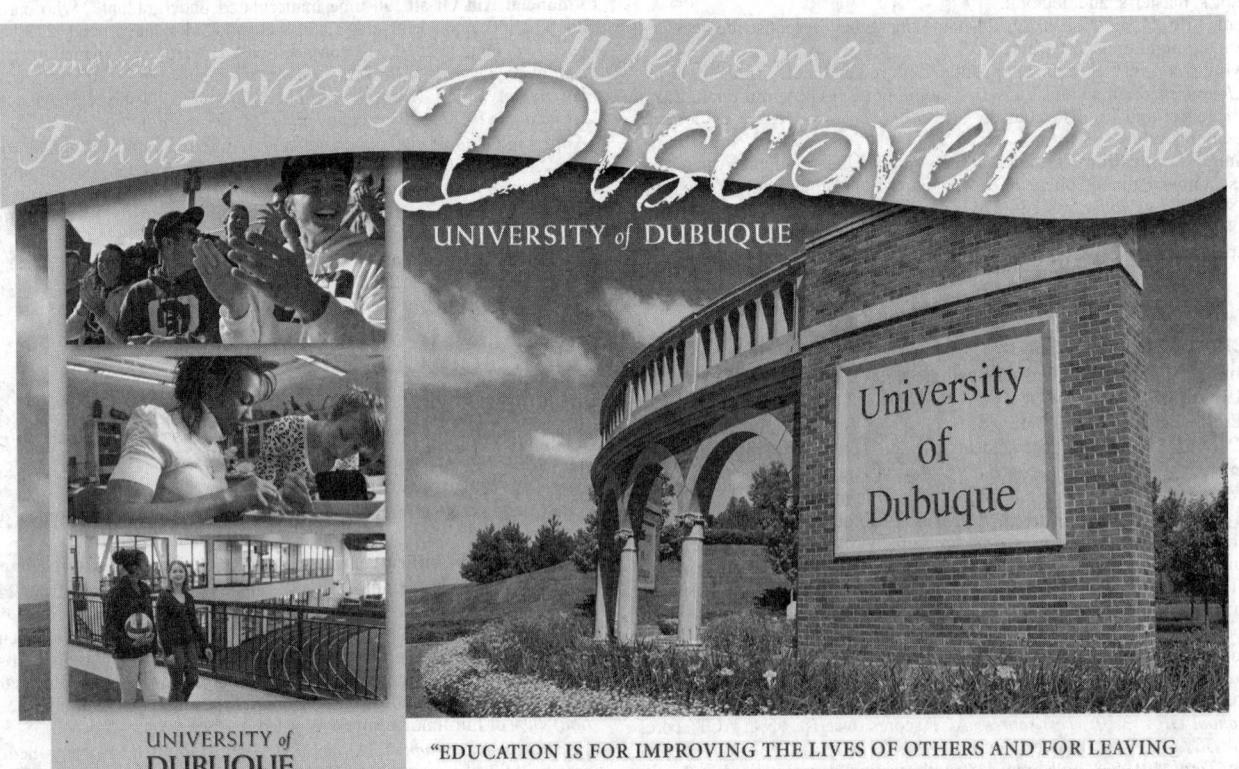

UNIVERSITY of DUBUQUE
www.dbq.edu

"EDUCATION IS FOR IMPROVING THE LIVES OF OTHERS AND FOR LEAVING YOUR COMMUNITY AND WORLD BETTER THAN YOU FOUND IT."
– MARIAN WRIGHT EDELMAN

This is SIMPSON

- Simpson College offers more than 50 majors, minors and pre-professional programs and is recognized for quality and value by national publications.

- Located just miles from Iowa's capital city.

- Combines an energetic academic environment with personal attention; 13:1 student/faculty ratio.

- Guaranteed Internship Program and Study abroad opportunities.

- Student organizations and activities include award-winning fine arts programs and nationally-ranked athletic teams.

- Over 98 percent of Simpson students receive financial assistance.

Indianola, Iowa
800-362-2454 | www.simpson.edu

Freshmen *Admission:* 1,264 applied, 1,009 admitted, 406 enrolled. *Average high school GPA:* 3. *Test scores:* SAT critical reading scores over 500: 24%; SAT math scores over 500: 38%; ACT scores over 18: 80%; SAT critical reading scores over 600: 3%; SAT math scores over 600: 3%; ACT scores over 24: 19%; ACT scores over 30: 1%. **Faculty** *Total:* 166, 52% full-time, 30% with terminal degrees. *Student/faculty ratio:* 15:1.

Academics *Calendar:* semesters. *Degrees:* associate, bachelor's, master's, doctoral, and first professional. *Special study options:* academic remediation for entering students, accelerated degree program, adult/continuing education programs, advanced placement credit, distance learning, double majors, English as a second language, honors programs, independent study, internships, off-campus study, part-time degree program, services for LD students, student-designed majors, study abroad, summer session for credit. *ROTC:* Army (b). *Unusual degree programs:* 3-2 business administration; communications, theology.

Computers on Campus 220 computers/terminals are available on campus for general student use. Students can access the following: campus intranet, computer help desk, free student e-mail accounts, online (class) grades, online (class) registration, online (class) schedules. Campuswide network is available. 100% of college-owned or -operated housing units are wired for high-speed Internet access. Wireless service is available via libraries, student centers.

Student Life *Housing:* on-campus residence required through junior year. *Options:* coed, disabled students. Campus housing is university owned. Freshman campus housing is guaranteed. *Activities and organizations:* drama/theater group, student-run newspaper, choral group, Black Student Union, Flight Team, Fellowship of Christian Athletes, Teacher Education Student Organization, Students in Free Enterprise (SIFE). *Campus security:* 24-hour patrols, late-night transport/escort service, controlled dormitory access. *Student services:* health clinic, personal/psychological counseling.

Athletics Member NCAA. All Division III. *Intercollegiate sports:* baseball M, basketball M/W, cross-country running M/W, football M, golf M/W, soccer M/W, softball W, tennis M/W, track and field M/W, volleyball W, wrestling M. *Intramural sports:* archery M/W, badminton M/W, baseball M, basketball M/W, bowling M/W, cheerleading M/W, football M, golf M/W, racquetball M/W, soccer M/W, softball M/W, table tennis M/W, tennis M/W, track and field M/W, ultimate Frisbee M/W, volleyball M/W, wrestling M.

Standardized Tests *Required:* SAT or ACT (for admission).

Costs (2011–12) *One-time required fee:* $100. *Comprehensive fee:* $29,200 includes full-time tuition ($21,000), mandatory fees ($620), and room and board ($7580). *Part-time tuition:* $515 per credit. *College room only:* $3660. Room and board charges vary according to board plan, housing facility, and location. *Payment plan:* installment. *Waivers:* employees or children of employees.

Financial Aid Of all full-time matriculated undergraduates who enrolled in 2011, 1,487 applied for aid, 1,364 were judged to have need, 230 had their need fully met. 185 Federal Work-Study jobs (averaging $1500). 194 state and other part-time jobs (averaging $1500). In 2011, 164 non-need-based awards were made. *Average percent of need met:* 71%. *Average financial aid package:* $19,029. *Average need-based loan:* $6655. *Average need-based gift aid:* $13,102. *Average non-need-based aid:* $7912. *Average indebtedness upon graduation:* $31,906.

Applying *Options:* electronic application. *Application fee:* $25. *Required:* essay or personal statement, high school transcript, minimum 2.5 GPA, 2 letters of recommendation. *Recommended:* interview. *Application deadlines:* rolling (freshmen), rolling (transfers). *Notification:* continuous (freshmen), continuous (transfers).

Freshman Application Contact Mr. Jesse James, Director of Admissions, University of Dubuque, 2000 University Avenue, Dubuque, IA 52001-5099. *Phone:* 563-589-3214. *Toll-free phone:* 800-722-5583. *Fax:* 563-589-3690. *E-mail:* admissns@dbq.edu. *Web site:* http://www.dbq.edu/.

See page 326 for display ad and page 1666 for the College Close-Up.

The University of Iowa
Iowa City, Iowa

- **State-supported** university, founded 1847
- **Small-town** 1900-acre campus
- **Endowment** $1.0 billion
- **Coed** 21,564 undergraduate students, 90% full-time, 52% women, 48% men
- **Moderately difficult** entrance level, 80% of applicants were admitted

Undergraduates 19,354 full-time, 2,210 part-time. Students come from 53 states and territories; 60 other countries; 38% are from out of state; 3% Black or African American, non-Hispanic/Latino; 5% Hispanic/Latino; 3% Asian, non-Hispanic/Latino; 0.1% Native Hawaiian or other Pacific Islander, non-Hispanic/Latino; 0.3% American Indian or Alaska Native, non-Hispanic/Latino; 1% Two or more races, non-Hispanic/Latino; 4% Race/ethnicity

unknown; 8% international; 6% transferred in; 29% live on campus. *Retention:* 86% of full-time freshmen returned.

Freshmen *Admission:* 18,939 applied, 15,105 admitted, 4,565 enrolled. *Average high school GPA:* 3.61. *Test scores:* SAT critical reading scores over 500: 61%; SAT math scores over 500: 91%; SAT writing scores over 500: 68%; ACT scores over 18: 99%; SAT critical reading scores over 600: 35%; SAT math scores over 600: 62%; SAT writing scores over 600: 31%; ACT scores over 24: 69%; SAT critical reading scores over 700: 11%; SAT math scores over 700: 22%; SAT writing scores over 700: 8%; ACT scores over 30: 15%.

Faculty *Total:* 1,613, 94% full-time, 97% with terminal degrees. *Student/faculty ratio:* 16:1.

Academics *Calendar:* semesters. *Degrees:* bachelor's, master's, doctoral, post-master's, postbachelor's, and first professional certificates. *Special study options:* accelerated degree program, adult/continuing education programs, advanced placement credit, cooperative education, distance learning, double majors, English as a second language, external degree program, honors programs, independent study, internships, off-campus study, part-time degree program, services for LD students, student-designed majors, study abroad, summer session for credit. *ROTC:* Army (b), Air Force (b).

Computers on Campus 1,386 computers/terminals are available on campus for general student use. Students can access the following: computer help desk, free student e-mail accounts, online (class) grades, online (class) registration, online (class) schedules, online degree process, financial aid summary, university bill. Campuswide network is available. 100% of college-owned or -operated housing units are wired for high-speed Internet access. Wireless service is available via classrooms, computer centers, computer labs, dorm rooms, learning centers, libraries, student centers.

Student Life *Housing options:* coed, disabled students. Campus housing is university owned and leased by the school. *Activities and organizations:* drama/theater group, student-run newspaper, radio and television station, choral group, marching band, Association of Residence Halls, Graduate Student Senate, National Society of Collegiate Scholars, Organization for the Active Support of International Students (OASIS), Dance Marathon, national fraternities, national sororities. *Campus security:* 24-hour emergency response devices and patrols, late-night transport/escort service, controlled dormitory access. *Student services:* health clinic, personal/psychological counseling, women's center, legal services.

Athletics Member NCAA. All Division I except football (Division I-A). *Intercollegiate sports:* baseball M(s), basketball M(s)/W(s), crew M(c)/W(s), cross-country running M(s)/W(s), field hockey W(s), golf M(s)/W(s), gymnastics M(s)/W(s), ice hockey M(c), lacrosse M(c)/W(c), rugby M(c)/W(c), sailing M(c)/W(c), soccer M(c)/W(s), softball W(s), swimming and diving M(s)/W(s), table tennis M(c)/W(c), tennis M(s)/W(s), track and field M(s)/W(s), ultimate Frisbee M(c)/W(c), volleyball M(c)/W(s), wrestling M(s). *Intramural sports:* badminton M/W, basketball M/W, bowling M/W, fencing M(c)/W(c), football M/W, golf M/W, racquetball M/W, rugby M(c)/W(c), sailing M(c)/W(c), skiing (cross-country) M(c)/W(c), skiing (downhill) M(c)/W(c), soccer M/W, softball M/W, table tennis M/W, tennis M/W, track and field M/W, ultimate Frisbee M/W, volleyball M/W, water polo M(c)/W(c), wrestling M.

Standardized Tests *Required:* SAT or ACT (for admission).

Costs (2011–12) *Tuition:* state resident $6436 full-time, $268 per semester hour part-time; nonresident $23,770 full-time, $990 per semester hour part-time. Full-time tuition and fees vary according to course load, program, and student level. Part-time tuition and fees vary according to course load, program, and student level. *Required fees:* $1329 full-time, $89 per semester hour part-time. *Room and board:* $8750. Room and board charges vary according to board plan and housing facility. *Payment plan:* installment.

Financial Aid Of all full-time matriculated undergraduates who enrolled in 2009, 12,183 applied for aid, 8,400 were judged to have need, 2,700 had their need fully met. 1,516 Federal Work-Study jobs (averaging $2156). In 2009, 6125 non-need-based awards were made. *Average percent of need met:* 68%. *Average financial aid package:* $11,289. *Average need-based loan:* $5155. *Average need-based gift aid:* $6486. *Average non-need-based aid:* $4147. *Average indebtedness upon graduation:* $27,391.

Applying *Options:* electronic application, early admission, deferred entrance. *Application fee:* $40. *Required:* high school transcript, Must submit ACT or SAT score; must meet Regent Admission Index (RAI) requirement: residents 245 or above; nonresidents 255 or above. *Application deadlines:* 4/1 (freshmen), 4/1 (transfers). *Notification:* continuous (freshmen), continuous (transfers).

Freshman Application Contact Mr. Michael Barron, Assistant Provost for Enrollment Management and Executive Director of Admissions, The University of Iowa, 107 Calvin Hall, Iowa City, IA 52242. *Phone:* 319-335-3847. *Toll-free phone:* 800-553-4692. *Fax:* 319-335-1535. *E-mail:* admissions@uiowa.edu. *Web site:* http://www.uiowa.edu/.

University of Northern Iowa
Cedar Falls, Iowa

- **State-supported** comprehensive, founded 1876, part of Board of Regents, State of Iowa
- **Small-town** 916-acre campus
- **Endowment** $76.8 million
- **Coed** 11,408 undergraduate students, 89% full-time, 56% women, 44% men
- **Moderately difficult** entrance level, 77% of applicants were admitted

Undergraduates 10,209 full-time, 1,199 part-time. Students come from 38 states and territories; 45 other countries; 5% are from out of state; 3% Black or African American, non-Hispanic/Latino; 2% Hispanic/Latino; 1% Asian, non-Hispanic/Latino; 0.1% American Indian or Alaska Native, non-Hispanic/Latino; 1% Two or more races, non-Hispanic/Latino; 1% Race/ethnicity unknown; 3% international; 9% transferred in; 38% live on campus. *Retention:* 82% of full-time freshmen returned.

Freshmen *Admission:* 4,666 applied, 3,607 admitted, 1,937 enrolled. *Average high school GPA:* 3.49. *Test scores:* ACT scores over 18: 97%; ACT scores over 24: 44%; ACT scores over 30: 6%.

Faculty *Total:* 832, 78% full-time, 65% with terminal degrees. *Student/faculty ratio:* 16:1.

Academics *Calendar:* semesters. *Degrees:* bachelor's, master's, and doctoral. *Special study options:* academic remediation for entering students, accelerated degree program, adult/continuing education programs, advanced placement credit, cooperative education, distance learning, double majors, English as a second language, external degree program, honors programs, independent study, internships, off-campus study, part-time degree program, services for LD students, student-designed majors, study abroad, summer session for credit. *ROTC:* Army (b). *Unusual degree programs:* 3-2 nursing with University of Iowa; medical technology with St. Luke's Hospital/University of Iowa Medical School, cytotechnology with Mayo School of Health-Related Sciences, Wisconsin State Laboratory of Hygiene and Mercy School of Cytotechnology, chiropractic with Logan College of Chiropractic.

Computers on Campus 1,900 computers/terminals are available on campus for general student use. Students can access the following: campus intranet, computer help desk, free student e-mail accounts, online (class) grades, online (class) registration, online (class) schedules, course registration, student account, degree audit, program of study. Campuswide network is available. 100% of college-owned or -operated housing units are wired for high-speed Internet access. Wireless service is available via entire campus.

Student Life *Housing options:* coed, women-only, disabled students. Campus housing is university owned. Freshman campus housing is guaranteed. *Activities and organizations:* drama/theater group, student-run newspaper, radio and television station, choral group, marching band, Catholic Student Association, National Society of Collegiate Scholars, Accounting Club, The River, Orchard Hill Church, national fraternities, national sororities. *Campus security:* 24-hour emergency response devices and patrols, student patrols, late-night transport/escort service, controlled dormitory access. *Student services:* health clinic, personal/psychological counseling.

Athletics Member NCAA. All Division I except football (Division I-AA). *Intercollegiate sports:* basketball M(s)/W(s), cross-country running M(s)/W(s), golf M(s)/W(s), soccer W(s), softball W(s), swimming and diving W(s), tennis W(s), track and field M(s)/W(s), volleyball W(s), wrestling M(s). *Intramural sports:* badminton M/W, baseball M(c), basketball M/W, bowling M(c)/W(c), cheerleading M/W, crew M(c)/W(c), cross-country running M(c)/W(c), football M(c), golf M(c)/W(c), ice hockey M(c), racquetball M(c)/W(c), rugby M(c)/W(c), skiing (cross-country) M(c)/W(c), skiing (downhill) M(c)/W(c), soccer M(c)/W(c), softball M(c)/W(c), swimming and diving M(c)/W(c), table tennis M/W, tennis M(c)/W(c), track and field M(c)/W(c), ultimate Frisbee M(c)/W(c), volleyball M/W(c), weight lifting M/W, wrestling M.

Standardized Tests *Required:* SAT or ACT (for admission). *Recommended:* ACT (for admission).

Costs (2012–13) *Tuition:* state resident $6648 full-time, $277 per hour part-time; nonresident $15,734 full-time, $656 per hour part-time. Full-time tuition and fees vary according to course load and program. Part-time tuition and fees vary according to course load and program. *Required fees:* $987 full-time. *Room and board:* Room and board charges vary according to board plan and housing facility. *Payment plan:* installment.

Financial Aid Of all full-time matriculated undergraduates who enrolled in 2010, 8,759 applied for aid, 6,727 were judged to have need, 1,168 had their need fully met. 551 Federal Work-Study jobs (averaging $1829). In 2010, 1446 non-need-based awards were made. *Average percent of need met:* 62%. *Average financial aid package:* $8098. *Average need-based loan:* $4311. *Average need-based gift aid:* $4590. *Average non-need-based aid:* $3376. *Average indebtedness upon graduation:* $25,523.

Applying *Options:* electronic application, deferred entrance. *Application fee:* $40. *Required:* high school transcript, A Regent Admission Index (RAI) score

of 245 guarantees admission. High school requirements include 4 years of English; 3 years each of math, science and social studies, and 2 or more years of electives, which may include foreign language and fine arts. *Required for some:* interview. *Application deadlines:* 8/15 (freshmen), 8/15 (transfers). *Notification:* 9/1 (freshmen), 9/1 (transfers).

Freshman Application Contact Ms. Amy Schipper, Assistant Director, University of Northern Iowa, 002 Gilchrist, Cedar Falls, IA 50614. *Phone:* 319-273-2281. *Toll-free phone:* 800-772-2037. *Fax:* 319-273-2885. *E-mail:* admissions@uni.edu. *Web site:* http://www.uni.edu/.

University of Phoenix–Des Moines Campus

Des Moines, Iowa

Admissions Office Contact University of Phoenix–Des Moines Campus, 6600 Westown Parkway, Des Moines, IA 50266. *Toll-free phone:* 866-766-0766. *Web site:* http://www.phoenix.edu/.

Upper Iowa University

Fayette, Iowa

- **Independent** comprehensive, founded 1857
- **Rural** 80-acre campus with easy access to Minneapolis, Chicago
- **Endowment** $9.0 million
- **Coed** 5,179 undergraduate students, 59% full-time, 60% women, 40% men
- **Moderately difficult** entrance level, 60% of applicants were admitted

Undergraduates 3,077 full-time, 2,102 part-time. Students come from 51 states and territories; 32 other countries; 59% are from out of state; 18% Black or African American, non-Hispanic/Latino; 4% Hispanic/Latino; 1% Asian, non-Hispanic/Latino; 0.1% Native Hawaiian or other Pacific Islander, non-Hispanic/Latino; 0.4% American Indian or Alaska Native, non-Hispanic/Latino; 0.3% Two or more races, non-Hispanic/Latino; 9% Race/ethnicity unknown; 2% international; 2% transferred in; 45% live on campus. *Retention:* 56% of full-time freshmen returned.

Freshmen *Admission:* 1,186 applied, 713 admitted, 204 enrolled. *Average high school GPA:* 3.11. *Test scores:* SAT math scores over 500: 33%; ACT scores over 18: 87%; ACT scores over 24: 30%; ACT scores over 30: 2%.

Faculty *Total:* 508, 15% full-time, 44% with terminal degrees. *Student/faculty ratio:* 21:1.

Academics *Calendar:* 4 8-week terms. *Degrees:* certificates, associate, bachelor's, and master's (enrollment figures include extended learning centers and online and distance education programs). *Special study options:* academic remediation for entering students, accelerated degree program, adult/continuing education programs, advanced placement credit, cooperative education, distance learning, double majors, English as a second language, external degree program, independent study, internships, off-campus study, part-time degree program, services for LD students, student-designed majors, study abroad, summer session for credit.

Computers on Campus 600 computers/terminals and 444 ports are available on campus for general student use. Students can access the following: campus intranet, computer help desk, free student e-mail accounts, online (class) grades, online (class) registration, online (class) schedules. Campuswide network is available. 100% of college-owned or -operated housing units are wired for high-speed Internet access. Wireless service is available via classrooms, computer centers, computer labs, dorm rooms, learning centers, libraries, student centers.

Student Life *Housing:* on-campus residence required through sophomore year. *Options:* coed, men-only, women-only. Campus housing is university owned. Freshman campus housing is guaranteed. *Activities and organizations:* drama/theater group, student-run newspaper, radio station, choral group, Beta Phi Omega, Student Activities Board, Greek Council, Student Government Association, International Student Association. *Campus security:* late-night transport/escort service, controlled dormitory access. *Student services:* health clinic, personal/psychological counseling.

Athletics Member NCAA. All Division II. *Intercollegiate sports:* baseball M(s), basketball M(s)/W(s), football M(s), golf M(s)/W(s), soccer M(s)/W(s), softball W(s), tennis M/W, volleyball W(s), wrestling M. *Intramural sports:* badminton M/W, basketball M/W, bowling M/W, cheerleading M(c)/W(c), football M, golf M/W, soccer M/W, softball M/W, table tennis M/W, ultimate Frisbee M/W, volleyball M/W.

Standardized Tests *Required:* SAT or ACT (for admission).

Costs (2012–13) *Comprehensive fee:* $31,690 includes full-time tuition ($24,400) and room and board ($7290). Full-time tuition and fees vary according to degree level, location, and program. Part-time tuition: $850 per credit hour. *College room only:* $2940. Room and board charges vary according to

board plan, housing facility, and location. *Payment plan:* installment. *Waivers:* employees or children of employees.

Financial Aid Of all full-time matriculated undergraduates who enrolled in 2011, 2,698 applied for aid, 2,152 were judged to have need. 278 Federal Work-Study jobs (averaging $1587). In 2011, 240 non-need-based awards were made. *Average percent of need met:* 75%. *Average financial aid package:* $13,200. *Average need-based loan:* $5000. *Average need-based gift aid:* $8200. *Average non-need-based aid:* $4000. *Average indebtedness upon graduation:* $22,825.

Applying *Options:* electronic application. *Application fee:* $50. *Required:* high school transcript, minimum 2.0 GPA. *Required for some:* essay or personal statement, interview. *Application deadlines:* rolling (freshmen), rolling (out-of-state freshmen), rolling (transfers).

Freshman Application Contact Ms. Jobyna A. Eastman Johnston, Vice President of Admissions and Financial Aid, Upper Iowa University, 605 Washington Street, Parker Fox Hall, Fayette, IA 52142. *Phone:* 563-425-5279. *Toll-free phone:* 800-553-4150. *Fax:* 563-4255323. *E-mail:* admission@uiu.edu. *Web site:* http://www.uiu.edu/.

Vatterott College

Des Moines, Iowa

Freshman Application Contact Mr. Henry Franken, Co-Director, Vatterott College, 7000 Fleur Drive, Suite 290, Des Moines, IA 50321. *Phone:* 515-309-9000. *Toll-free phone:* 888-553-6627. *Fax:* 515-309-0366. *Web site:* http://www.vatterott-college.edu/.

Waldorf College

Forest City, Iowa

- **Independent Lutheran** 4-year, founded 1903
- **Rural** 51-acre campus
- **Coed** 817 undergraduate students, 85% full-time, 39% women, 61% men
- **Moderately difficult** entrance level, 49% of applicants were admitted

Undergraduates 691 full-time, 126 part-time. Students come from 34 states and territories; 65% are from out of state; 18% Black or African American, non-Hispanic/Latino; 8% Hispanic/Latino; 1% Asian, non-Hispanic/Latino; 0.7% American Indian or Alaska Native, non-Hispanic/Latino; 1% Two or more races, non-Hispanic/Latino; 0.1% Race/ethnicity unknown; 8% transferred in; 70% live on campus. *Retention:* 37% of full-time freshmen returned.

Freshmen *Admission:* 1,915 applied, 929 admitted, 159 enrolled. *Average high school GPA:* 3.01. *Test scores:* ACT scores over 18: 81%; ACT scores over 24: 17%; ACT scores over 30: 2%.

Faculty *Total:* 50, 94% full-time, 54% with terminal degrees. *Student/faculty ratio:* 15:1.

Academics *Calendar:* semesters. *Degrees:* associate and bachelor's. *Special study options:* academic remediation for entering students, adult/continuing education programs, advanced placement credit, cooperative education, distance learning, double majors, freshman honors college, honors programs, independent study, internships, part-time degree program, services for LD students, student-designed majors, study abroad, summer session for credit.

Computers on Campus 500 computers/terminals are available on campus for general student use. Students can access the following: campus intranet, computer help desk, free student e-mail accounts, online (class) grades, all students receive laptops. Campuswide network is available. 100% of college-owned or -operated housing units are wired for high-speed Internet access. Wireless service is available via computer centers, computer labs, learning centers, libraries, student centers.

Student Life *Housing:* on-campus residence required through junior year. *Options:* coed, men-only, women-only, cooperative, disabled students. Campus housing is university owned and leased by the school. Freshman campus housing is guaranteed. *Activities and organizations:* drama/theater group, student-run newspaper, radio and television station, choral group, Student Activities Team, Education Club, Campus Ministry groups, Intramurals, Radio/TV/Newspaper. *Campus security:* 24-hour emergency response devices, student patrols, late-night transport/escort service, controlled dormitory access, evening and night patrols by trained security personnel, camera surveillance system. *Student services:* health clinic, personal/psychological counseling.

Athletics Member NAIA. *Intercollegiate sports:* baseball M(s), basketball M(s)/W(s), cheerleading W(s), cross-country running M(s)/W(s), football M(s), golf M(s)/W(s), ice hockey M(s)(c), soccer M(s)/W(s), softball W(s), track and field M(c)/W(c), volleyball W(s), wrestling M(s)/W(s). *Intramural sports:* basketball M/W, bowling M/W, football M/W, racquetball M/W, skiing (cross-country) M/W, skiing (downhill) M/W, soccer M/W, softball M/W, table tennis M/W, tennis M/W, ultimate Frisbee M/W, volleyball M/W.

Standardized Tests *Required:* SAT or ACT (for admission).

Costs (2012–13) *Comprehensive fee:* $26,508 includes full-time tuition ($18,796), mandatory fees ($1024), and room and board ($6688). Full-time

tuition and fees vary according to class time, course load, and program. *Room and board:* Room and board charges vary according to board plan and housing facility. *Payment plans:* installment, deferred payment. *Waivers:* employees or children of employees.

Financial Aid Of all full-time matriculated undergraduates who enrolled in 2011, 958 applied for aid, 745 were judged to have need, 84 had their need fully met. In 2011, 51 non-need-based awards were made. *Average percent of need met:* 64%. *Average financial aid package:* $12,615. *Average need-based loan:* $3966. *Average need-based gift aid:* $9483. *Average non-need-based aid:* $4661. *Average indebtedness upon graduation:* $19,744.

Applying *Options:* electronic application, early admission. *Required:* high school transcript. *Required for some:* interview. *Recommended:* minimum 2.0 GPA. *Application deadlines:* rolling (freshmen), rolling (transfers). *Notification:* continuous (freshmen), continuous (transfers).

Freshman Application Contact Scott Pitcher, Waldorf College, 106 South 6th Street, Forest City, IA 50436-1713. *Phone:* 641-585-8112. *Toll-free phone:* 800-292-1903. *Fax:* 641-85-8125. *E-mail:* admissions@waldorf.edu. *Web site:* http://www.waldorf.edu/.

Wartburg College
Waverly, Iowa

- **Independent Lutheran** 4-year, founded 1852
- **Small-town** 118-acre campus
- **Endowment** $49.2 million
- **Coed** 1,805 undergraduate students, 96% full-time, 53% women, 47% men
- **Moderately difficult** entrance level, 76% of applicants were admitted

Undergraduates 1,735 full-time, 70 part-time. Students come from 26 states and territories; 49 other countries; 31% are from out of state; 7% Black or African American, non-Hispanic/Latino; 2% Hispanic/Latino; 0.8% Asian, non-Hispanic/Latino; 0.3% American Indian or Alaska Native, non-Hispanic/Latino; 2% Two or more races, non-Hispanic/Latino; 0.5% Race/ethnicity unknown; 7% international; 2% transferred in; 86% live on campus. *Retention:* 81% of full-time freshmen returned.

Freshmen *Admission:* 2,346 applied, 1,784 admitted, 510 enrolled. *Average high school GPA:* 3.52. *Test scores:* SAT critical reading scores over 500: 41%; SAT math scores over 500: 57%; SAT writing scores over 500: 45%; ACT scores over 18: 93%; SAT critical reading scores over 600: 15%; SAT math scores over 600: 30%; SAT writing scores over 600: 10%; ACT scores over 24: 54%; SAT critical reading scores over 700: 2%; SAT math scores over 700: 13%; ACT scores over 30: 9%.

Faculty *Total:* 171, 64% full-time, 51% with terminal degrees. *Student/faculty ratio:* 12:1.

Academics *Calendar:* 4-4-1. *Degree:* bachelor's. *Special study options:* academic remediation for entering students, accelerated degree program, advanced placement credit, double majors, honors programs, independent study, internships, off-campus study, part-time degree program, services for LD students, student-designed majors, study abroad, summer session for credit. *Unusual degree programs:* 3-2 nursing with Allen College.

Computers on Campus 250 computers/terminals are available on campus for general student use. Students can access the following: campus intranet, computer help desk, free student e-mail accounts, online (class) grades, online (class) registration, online (class) schedules. Campuswide network is available. 100% of college-owned or -operated housing units are wired for high-speed Internet access. Wireless service is available via classrooms, dorm rooms, libraries, student centers.

Student Life *Housing:* on-campus residence required through senior year. *Options:* coed, men-only, women-only, disabled students. Campus housing is university owned. Freshman campus housing is guaranteed. *Activities and organizations:* drama/theater group, student-run newspaper, radio and television station, choral group, Entertainment To Knight, Student Senate, Campus Ministry, Symphonic Band, Wartburg Choir. *Campus security:* 24-hour emergency response devices and patrols, late-night transport/escort service, controlled dormitory access. *Student services:* health clinic, personal/psychological counseling.

Athletics Member NCAA. All Division III. *Intercollegiate sports:* baseball M, basketball M/W, cheerleading W, cross-country running M/W, football M, golf M/W, soccer M/W, softball W, tennis M/W, track and field M/W, volleyball W, wrestling M. *Intramural sports:* badminton M/W, basketball M/W, bowling M/W, golf M/W, racquetball M/W, rugby W(c), softball M/W, tennis M/W, ultimate Frisbee M/W, volleyball M/W.

Standardized Tests *Required:* SAT or ACT (for admission).

Costs (2012–13) *Comprehensive fee:* $41,055 includes full-time tuition ($31,890), mandatory fees ($850), and room and board ($8315). Part-time tuition: $1540 per course. *Required fees:* $90 per term part-time. *College room only:* $3985. Room and board charges vary according to board plan.

Payment plan: installment. *Waivers:* minority students, children of alumni, and employees or children of employees.

Financial Aid Of all full-time matriculated undergraduates who enrolled in 2010, 1,531 applied for aid, 1,364 were judged to have need, 422 had their need fully met. In 2010, 343 non-need-based awards were made. *Average percent of need met:* 83%. *Average financial aid package:* $22,962. *Average need-based loan:* $4887. *Average need-based gift aid:* $18,038. *Average non-need-based aid:* $14,385. *Average indebtedness upon graduation:* $33,572.

Applying *Options:* electronic application, early action, deferred entrance. *Required:* high school transcript, minimum 2.0 GPA. *Required for some:* interview. *Recommended:* secondary school report. *Application deadlines:* rolling (freshmen), rolling (transfers), 12/1 (early action). *Notification:* continuous (freshmen), continuous (transfers).

Freshman Application Contact Mr. Todd Coleman, Assistant Vice President for Admissions, Wartburg College, 100 Wartburg Boulevard, PO Box 1003, Waverly, IA 50677-0903. *Phone:* 319-352-8264. *Toll-free phone:* 800-772-2085. *Fax:* 319-352-8579. *E-mail:* admissions@wartburg.edu. *Web site:* http://www.wartburg.edu/.

William Penn University
Oskaloosa, Iowa

- **Independent** comprehensive, founded 1873, affiliated with Society of Friends
- **Rural** 60-acre campus with easy access to Des Moines
- **Endowment** $5.7 million
- **Coed** 1,848 undergraduate students, 88% full-time, 49% women, 51% men
- **Moderately difficult** entrance level, 55% of applicants were admitted

Undergraduates 1,633 full-time, 215 part-time. Students come from 43 states and territories; 14 other countries; 29% are from out of state; 13% Black or African American, non-Hispanic/Latino; 7% Hispanic/Latino; 1% Asian, non-Hispanic/Latino; 0.7% Native Hawaiian or other Pacific Islander, non-Hispanic/Latino; 0.6% American Indian or Alaska Native, non-Hispanic/Latino; 1% Two or more races, non-Hispanic/Latino; 6% Race/ethnicity unknown; 1% international; 11% transferred in; 40% live on campus. *Retention:* 61% of full-time freshmen returned.

Freshmen *Admission:* 872 applied, 481 admitted, 278 enrolled. *Average high school GPA:* 2.88. *Test scores:* ACT scores over 18: 69%; ACT scores over 24: 11%; ACT scores over 30: 1%.

Faculty *Total:* 50, 98% full-time, 30% with terminal degrees. *Student/faculty ratio:* 15:1.

Academics *Calendar:* semesters. *Degrees:* associate, bachelor's, and master's. *Special study options:* academic remediation for entering students, adult/continuing education programs, advanced placement credit, cooperative education, distance learning, double majors, honors programs, independent study, internships, part-time degree program, services for LD students, study abroad, summer session for credit. *Unusual degree programs:* 3-2 engineering with Iowa State University College of Engineering.

Computers on Campus 85 computers/terminals are available on campus for general student use. Students can access the following: computer help desk, free student e-mail accounts, online (class) grades, online (class) schedules. Campuswide network is available. 100% of college-owned or -operated housing units are wired for high-speed Internet access. Wireless service is available via classrooms, computer labs, libraries.

Student Life *Housing:* on-campus residence required through sophomore year. *Options:* coed, men-only, women-only. Campus housing is university owned. Freshman campus housing is guaranteed. *Activities and organizations:* drama/theater group, student-run newspaper, radio and television station, choral group, marching band, Student Government Association, Computer Club, InterVarsity/Campus Ministries, College Republicans, Education Club. *Campus security:* 24-hour emergency response devices and patrols, late-night transport/escort service, controlled dormitory access. *Student services:* health clinic, personal/psychological counseling.

Athletics Member NAIA. *Intercollegiate sports:* baseball M(s), basketball M(s)/W(s), bowling M(s)/W(s), cheerleading M(s)/W(s), cross-country running M(s)/W(s), football M(s), golf M(s)/W(s), soccer M(s)/W(s), softball W(s), track and field M(s)/W(s), volleyball W(s), wrestling M(s). *Intramural sports:* basketball M/W, football M, table tennis M/W, volleyball M/W, weight lifting M/W.

Standardized Tests *Required:* SAT or ACT (for admission).

Costs (2012–13) *Comprehensive fee:* $28,682 includes full-time tuition ($22,750), mandatory fees ($460), and room and board ($5472). Part-time tuition: $450 per credit hour. *College room only:* $2002. Room and board charges vary according to board plan and housing facility. *Payment plan:* installment. *Waivers:* senior citizens and employees or children of employees.

Financial Aid Of all full-time matriculated undergraduates who enrolled in 2005, 808 applied for aid, 768 were judged to have need, 238 had their need

fully met. 511 Federal Work-Study jobs (averaging $1287). 1 state and other part-time job (averaging $1103). In 2005, 2 non-need-based awards were made. *Average percent of need met:* 82%. *Average financial aid package:* $17,782. *Average need-based loan:* $4600. *Average need-based gift aid:* $11,300. *Average non-need-based aid:* $4500. *Average indebtedness upon graduation:* $22,169.

Applying *Options:* electronic application, deferred entrance. *Application fee:* $20. *Required:* high school transcript, minimum 2.0 GPA. *Required for some:* essay or personal statement, interview. *Notification:* continuous (freshmen), continuous (out-of-state freshmen), continuous (transfers).

Freshman Application Contact John Ottosson, Vice President for Enrollment Management, William Penn University, 201 Trueblood Avenue, Oskaloosa, IA 52577-1799. *Phone:* 641-673-1012. *Toll-free phone:* 800-779-7366. *Fax:* 641-673-2113. *E-mail:* admissions@wmpenn.edu. *Web site:* http://www.wmpenn.edu/.

KANSAS

The Art Institutes International–Kansas City

Lenexa, Kansas

- **Proprietary** 4-year, founded 2008, part of Education Management Corporation
- **Coed**

Academics *Degrees:* diplomas, associate, and bachelor's.

Costs (2011–12) *Tuition:* Tuition cost varies by program. Prospective students should contact the school for current tuition costs. Other charges include a starting kit for all first-quarter students. Kits vary in price, depending on the program of study.

Freshman Application Contact The Art Institutes International–Kansas City, 8208 Melrose Drive, Lenexa, KS 66214. *Phone:* 913-217-4600. *Toll-free phone:* 866-530-8508. *Web site:* http://www.artinstitutes.edu/kansascity/.

See page 1148 for the College Close-Up.

Baker University

Baldwin City, Kansas

- **Independent United Methodist** comprehensive, founded 1858
- **Small-town** 26-acre campus with easy access to Kansas City
- **Endowment** $35.3 million
- **Coed** 935 undergraduate students, 88% full-time, 50% women, 50% men
- **Moderately difficult** entrance level, 92% of applicants were admitted

Undergraduates 827 full-time, 108 part-time. Students come from 25 states and territories; 9 other countries; 24% are from out of state; 9% Black or African American, non-Hispanic/Latino; 2% Hispanic/Latino; 1% Asian, non-Hispanic/Latino; 2% American Indian or Alaska Native, non-Hispanic/Latino; 4% Race/ethnicity unknown; 1% international; 5% transferred in; 55% live on campus. *Retention:* 77% of full-time freshmen returned.

Freshmen *Admission:* 710 applied, 654 admitted, 200 enrolled. *Average high school GPA:* 3.44. *Test scores:* ACT scores over 18: 95%; ACT scores over 24: 45%; ACT scores over 30: 6%.

Faculty *Total:* 85, 68% full-time, 58% with terminal degrees. *Student/faculty ratio:* 13:1.

Academics *Calendar:* 4-1-4, semesters for nursing program. *Degrees:* bachelor's, master's, doctoral, and first professional (profile includes information primarily for undergraduate residential campus in Baldwin City, KS). *Special study options:* advanced placement credit, double majors, honors programs, independent study, internships, services for LD students, student-designed majors, study abroad, summer session for credit. *ROTC:* Army (c), Air Force (c). *Unusual degree programs:* 3-2 engineering with Washington University in St. Louis, University of Kansas, University of Missouri Kansas City; forestry with Duke University.

Computers on Campus 140 computers/terminals are available on campus for general student use. Students can access the following: computer help desk, free student e-mail accounts, online (class) grades, online (class) registration, online (class) schedules. Campuswide network is available. 100% of college-owned or -operated housing units are wired for high-speed Internet access. Wireless service is available via classrooms, computer labs, libraries, student centers.

Student Life *Housing:* on-campus residence required through senior year. *Options:* coed, men-only, women-only, disabled students. Campus housing is university owned. Freshman campus housing is guaranteed. *Activities and organizations:* drama/theater group, student-run newspaper, radio and televi-

sion station, choral group, Cardinal Key, Earth We Are, Mungano, Fellowship of Christian Athletes, Student Activities Council, national fraternities, national sororities. *Campus security:* 24-hour emergency response devices and patrols, student patrols, controlled dormitory access. *Student services:* health clinic, personal/psychological counseling.

Athletics Member NAIA. *Intercollegiate sports:* baseball M(s), basketball M(s)/W(s), bowling W(s), cheerleading M(s)/W(s), cross-country running M(s)/W(s), football M(s), golf M(s)/W(s), soccer M(s)/W(s), softball W(s), tennis M(s)/W(s), track and field M(s)/W(s), volleyball W(s), wrestling M(s). *Intramural sports:* basketball M/W, football M/W, softball M/W, table tennis M/W, volleyball M/W.

Standardized Tests *Required:* SAT or ACT (for admission).

Costs (2011–12) *One-time required fee:* $80. *Comprehensive fee:* $30,810 includes full-time tuition ($23,310) and room and board ($7500). Full-time tuition and fees vary according to course load, degree level, location, and program. *Part-time tuition:* $705 per credit hour. Part-time tuition and fees vary according to course load, degree level, location, and program. *College room only:* $3580. Room and board charges vary according to board plan and housing facility. *Payment plan:* installment. *Waivers:* senior citizens and employees or children of employees.

Financial Aid Of all full-time matriculated undergraduates who enrolled in 2008, 839 applied for aid, 713 were judged to have need, 268 had their need fully met. In 2008, 180 non-need-based awards were made. *Average percent of need met:* 84%. *Average financial aid package:* $13,600. *Average need-based loan:* $5622. *Average need-based gift aid:* $6787. *Average non-need-based aid:* $9006. *Average indebtedness upon graduation:* $26,869.

Applying *Options:* electronic application, deferred entrance. *Required:* high school transcript, 1 letter of recommendation. *Required for some:* essay or personal statement, interview. *Application deadlines:* rolling (freshmen), rolling (transfers).

Freshman Application Contact Mr. Kevin Kropf, Director of Enrollment Management, Baker University, PO Box 65, Baldwin City, KS 66006-0065. *Phone:* 785-594-8327. *Toll-free phone:* 800-873-4282. *Fax:* 785-594-8353. *E-mail:* admissions@bakeru.edu. *Web site:* http://www.bakeru.edu/.

Barclay College

Haviland, Kansas

- **Independent** comprehensive, founded 1917, affiliated with Society of Friends
- **Rural** 17-acre campus
- **Endowment** $700,000
- **Coed** 232 undergraduate students, 90% full-time, 50% women, 50% men
- **Minimally difficult** entrance level, 37% of applicants were admitted

Undergraduates 209 full-time, 23 part-time. Students come from 31 states and territories; 2 other countries; 69% are from out of state; 3% Black or African American, non-Hispanic/Latino; 5% Hispanic/Latino; 0.9% Native Hawaiian or other Pacific Islander, non-Hispanic/Latino; 0.9% American Indian or Alaska Native, non-Hispanic/Latino; 1% Two or more races, non-Hispanic/Latino; 0.9% Race/ethnicity unknown; 1% international; 16% transferred in; 78% live on campus. *Retention:* 76% of full-time freshmen returned.

Freshmen *Admission:* 102 applied, 38 admitted, 39 enrolled. *Test scores:* SAT critical reading scores over 500: 46%; SAT math scores over 500: 27%; SAT writing scores over 500: 37%; ACT scores over 18: 72%; SAT critical reading scores over 600: 10%; SAT writing scores over 600: 10%; ACT scores over 24: 36%.

Faculty *Total:* 30, 50% full-time, 33% with terminal degrees. *Student/faculty ratio:* 11:1.

Academics *Calendar:* semesters. *Degrees:* certificates, associate, bachelor's, and master's. *Special study options:* academic remediation for entering students, adult/continuing education programs, advanced placement credit, distance learning, double majors, external degree program, independent study, internships, off-campus study, part-time degree program. *Unusual degree programs:* 3-2 nursing with Pratt Community College.

Computers on Campus 28 computers/terminals are available on campus for general student use. Students can access the following: campus intranet, computer help desk, free student e-mail accounts, online (class) grades, online (class) registration, online (class) schedules. Campuswide network is available. 100% of college-owned or -operated housing units are wired for high-speed Internet access. Wireless service is available via entire campus.

Student Life *Housing:* on-campus residence required through senior year. *Options:* men-only, women-only. Campus housing is university owned. Freshman campus housing is guaranteed. *Activities and organizations:* drama/theater group, choral group, Pep Club, Drama Club, Missions Club. *Campus security:* student patrols. *Student services:* personal/psychological counseling.

Athletics *Intercollegiate sports:* basketball M/W, cheerleading M/W, soccer M, tennis M/W, volleyball W. *Intramural sports:* basketball M/W, volleyball M/W.

Standardized Tests *Required:* SAT or ACT (for admission).

Costs (2011–12) *Comprehensive fee:* $20,590 includes full-time tuition ($11,000), mandatory fees ($2790), and room and board ($6800). Part-time tuition: $250 per hour. Part-time tuition and fees vary according to course load. *Room and board:* Room and board charges vary according to board plan and housing facility. *Payment plan:* installment. *Waivers:* employees or children of employees.

Financial Aid Of all full-time matriculated undergraduates who enrolled in 2003, 163 applied for aid, 163 were judged to have need, 145 had their need fully met. 33 Federal Work-Study jobs (averaging $1200). 67 state and other part-time jobs (averaging $600). In 2003, 4 non-need-based awards were made. *Average percent of need met:* 85%. *Average financial aid package:* $6700. *Average need-based loan:* $3750. *Average need-based gift aid:* $1500. *Average non-need-based aid:* $1500. *Average indebtedness upon graduation:* $10,000.

Applying *Options:* electronic application, early admission, deferred entrance. *Application fee:* $15. *Required:* essay or personal statement, high school transcript, minimum 2.3 GPA, 2 letters of recommendation, interview. *Application deadlines:* 9/1 (freshmen), 9/1 (transfers). *Notification:* continuous (freshmen), continuous (transfers).

Freshman Application Contact Mr. Justin Kendall, Admissions Recruiter, Barclay College, 607 North Kingman, Haviland, KS 67059. *Phone:* 620-862-5252 Ext. 21. *Toll-free phone:* 800-862-0226. *Fax:* 620-862-5242. *E-mail:* jkendall@barclaycollege.edu. *Web site:* http://www.barclaycollege.edu/.

Benedictine College

Atchison, Kansas

- **Independent Roman Catholic** comprehensive, founded 1859
- **Small-town** 225-acre campus with easy access to Kansas City
- **Endowment** $16.4 million
- **Coed** 1,992 undergraduate students, 84% full-time, 54% women, 46% men
- **Moderately difficult** entrance level, 59% of applicants were admitted

Undergraduates 1,664 full-time, 328 part-time. Students come from 45 states and territories; 14 other countries; 70% are from out of state; 4% Black or African American, non-Hispanic/Latino; 8% Hispanic/Latino; 1% Asian, non-Hispanic/Latino; 0.3% Native Hawaiian or other Pacific Islander, non-Hispanic/Latino; 0.5% American Indian or Alaska Native, non-Hispanic/Latino; 2% Two or more races, non-Hispanic/Latino; 4% Race/ethnicity unknown; 2% international; 4% transferred in; 78% live on campus. *Retention:* 79% of full-time freshmen returned.

Freshmen *Admission:* 3,538 applied, 2,081 admitted, 470 enrolled. *Average high school GPA:* 3.44. *Test scores:* ACT scores over 18: 96%; ACT scores over 24: 48%; ACT scores over 30: 9%.

Faculty *Total:* 138, 67% full-time, 69% with terminal degrees. *Student/faculty ratio:* 15:1.

Academics *Calendar:* semesters. *Degrees:* associate, bachelor's, and master's. *Special study options:* academic remediation for entering students, advanced placement credit, cooperative education, distance learning, double majors, English as a second language, independent study, internships, off-campus study, part-time degree program, services for LD students, student-designed majors, study abroad, summer session for credit. *ROTC:* Army (c). *Unusual degree programs:* 3-2 engineering with Kansas State University, University of Missouri–Columbia, South Dakota School of Mines and Technology; occupational therapy with Washington University in St. Louis.

Computers on Campus 100 computers/terminals are available on campus for general student use. Students can access the following: computer help desk, free student e-mail accounts, online (class) grades, online (class) registration, online (class) schedules. Campuswide network is available. 100% of college-owned or -operated housing units are wired for high-speed Internet access. Wireless service is available via entire campus.

Student Life *Housing:* on-campus residence required through senior year. *Options:* men-only, women-only. Campus housing is university owned. Freshman campus housing is guaranteed. *Activities and organizations:* drama/theater group, student-run newspaper, choral group, marching band, student government, Students in Free Enterprise (SIFE), Knights of Columbus, Concert Chorale/Chamber Singers, Campus Activities Board. *Campus security:* 24-hour emergency response devices and patrols, late-night transport/escort service, controlled dormitory access. *Student services:* health clinic, personal/psychological counseling.

Athletics Member NAIA. *Intercollegiate sports:* baseball M(s), basketball M(s)/W(s), cheerleading M(s)/W(s), cross-country running M(s)/W(s), football M(s), golf M(s)/W(s), soccer M(s)/W(s), softball W(s), track and field M(s)/W(s), volleyball W(s), wrestling M. *Intramural sports:* basketball M/W, football M/W, racquetball M/W, rugby M/W, soccer M/W, softball M/W, table tennis M/W, volleyball M/W.

Standardized Tests *Required:* SAT or ACT (for admission).

Costs (2011–12) *Comprehensive fee:* $29,180 includes full-time tuition ($21,475) and room and board ($7705). Full-time tuition and fees vary according to course load and degree level. Part-time tuition: $630 per credit hour. Part-time tuition and fees vary according to course load and degree level. *College room only:* $4325. Room and board charges vary according to board plan and housing facility. *Payment plan:* installment. *Waivers:* senior citizens and employees or children of employees.

Financial Aid Of all full-time matriculated undergraduates who enrolled in 2011, 1,372 applied for aid, 1,201 were judged to have need, 217 had their need fully met. 322 Federal Work-Study jobs (averaging $641). 205 state and other part-time jobs (averaging $640). In 2011, 300 non-need-based awards were made. *Average percent of need met:* 71%. *Average financial aid package:* $17,413. *Average need-based loan:* $4758. *Average need-based gift aid:* $4164. *Average non-need-based aid:* $8920. *Average indebtedness upon graduation:* $26,576.

Applying *Options:* electronic application, deferred entrance. *Application fee:* $25. *Required:* high school transcript, minimum 2.0 GPA. *Required for some:* interview. *Notification:* continuous (freshmen), continuous (transfers).

Freshman Application Contact Benedictine College, 1020 North 2nd Street, Atchison, KS 66002-1499. *Phone:* 913-367-5340 Ext. 2476. *Toll-free phone:* 800-467-5340. *Web site:* http://www.benedictine.edu/.

Bethany College

Lindsborg, Kansas

- **Independent Lutheran** 4-year, founded 1881
- **Small-town** 80-acre campus
- **Endowment** $23.0 million
- **Coed** 626 undergraduate students, 93% full-time, 46% women, 54% men
- **Moderately difficult** entrance level, 60% of applicants were admitted

Undergraduates 582 full-time, 44 part-time. Students come from 32 states and territories; 15 other countries; 40% are from out of state; 6% Black or African American, non-Hispanic/Latino; 5% Hispanic/Latino; 0.9% Native Hawaiian or other Pacific Islander, non-Hispanic/Latino; 0.2% American Indian or Alaska Native, non-Hispanic/Latino; 1% Two or more races, non-Hispanic/Latino; 2% Race/ethnicity unknown; 4% international; 13% transferred in; 76% live on campus. *Retention:* 64% of full-time freshmen returned.

Freshmen *Admission:* 831 applied, 496 admitted, 149 enrolled. *Average high school GPA:* 3.26. *Test scores:* SAT critical reading scores over 500: 37%; SAT math scores over 500: 55%; SAT writing scores over 500: 29%; ACT scores over 18: 89%; SAT critical reading scores over 600: 7%; SAT math scores over 600: 7%; SAT writing scores over 600: 7%; ACT scores over 24: 34%; ACT scores over 30: 3%.

Faculty *Total:* 72, 49% full-time, 47% with terminal degrees. *Student/faculty ratio:* 13:1.

Academics *Calendar:* 4-1-4. *Degree:* bachelor's. *Special study options:* academic remediation for entering students, accelerated degree program, advanced placement credit, double majors, honors programs, independent study, internships, off-campus study, services for LD students, student-designed majors, study abroad, summer session for credit. *Unusual degree programs:* 3-2 engineering with Wichita State University.

Computers on Campus 65 computers/terminals are available on campus for general student use. Students can access the following: campus intranet, computer help desk, free student e-mail accounts, online (class) grades, online (class) registration, online (class) schedules. Campuswide network is available. 100% of college-owned or -operated housing units are wired for high-speed Internet access. Wireless service is available via entire campus.

Student Life *Housing:* on-campus residence required through junior year. *Options:* coed, women-only. Campus housing is university owned. Freshman campus housing is guaranteed. *Activities and organizations:* drama/theater group, student-run newspaper, choral group, Student Activities Board (SAB), Alpha Theta Chi, Alpha Sigma Nu, Fellowship of Christian Athletes (FCA), Bethany Youth Ministries Team. *Campus security:* 24-hour emergency response devices, late-night transport/escort service, controlled dormitory access, night patrols by security personnel. *Student services:* health clinic, personal/psychological counseling.

Athletics Member NAIA. *Intercollegiate sports:* baseball M(s), basketball M(s)/W(s), cross-country running M(s)/W(s), football M(s), golf M(s)/W(s), soccer M(s)/W(s), softball W(s), tennis M(s)/W(s), track and field M(s)/W(s), volleyball W(s), wrestling M(s). *Intramural sports:* basketball M/W, softball M/W, volleyball M/W.

Standardized Tests *Required:* SAT or ACT (for admission).

Costs (2011–12) *Comprehensive fee:* $28,193 includes full-time tuition ($21,077), mandatory fees ($600), and room and board ($6516). Part-time tuition: $425 per hour. Part-time tuition and fees vary according to course load. *College room only:* $3426. Room and board charges vary according to board plan and housing facility. *Payment plan:* installment. *Waivers:* employees or children of employees.

Financial Aid Of all full-time matriculated undergraduates who enrolled in 2011, 541 applied for aid, 466 were judged to have need, 188 had their need fully met. 381 Federal Work-Study jobs (averaging $1342). In 2011, 1 non-need-based awards were made. *Average percent of need met:* 91%. *Average financial aid package:* $22,887. *Average need-based loan:* $7529. *Average need-based gift aid:* $6935. *Average non-need-based aid:* $4800. *Average indebtedness upon graduation:* $22,015.

Applying *Options:* electronic application, deferred entrance. *Required:* high school transcript, minimum 2.5 GPA. *Required for some:* essay or personal statement, letters of recommendation, interview. *Application deadlines:* rolling (freshmen), rolling (out-of-state freshmen), rolling (transfers). *Notification:* continuous (freshmen), continuous (out-of-state freshmen), continuous (transfers).

Freshman Application Contact Vicki Cornett, Assistant director of Recruitment, Bethany College, 335 East Swensson Avenue, Lindsborg, KS 67456-1895. *Phone:* 785-227-3311 Ext. 8388. *Toll-free phone:* 800-826-2281. *Fax:* 785-227-8993. *E-mail:* cornettv@bethanylb.edu. *Web site:* http://www.bethanylb.edu/.

Bethel College

North Newton, Kansas

- **Independent** 4-year, founded 1887, affiliated with Mennonite Church USA
- **Small-town** 60-acre campus with easy access to Wichita
- **Coed** 523 undergraduate students, 95% full-time, 51% women, 49% men
- **Moderately difficult** entrance level, 70% of applicants were admitted

Undergraduates 497 full-time, 26 part-time. 29% are from out of state; 9% Black or African American, non-Hispanic/Latino; 7% Hispanic/Latino; 0.8% Asian, non-Hispanic/Latino; 0.4% American Indian or Alaska Native, non-Hispanic/Latino; 2% Two or more races, non-Hispanic/Latino; 2% international; 15% transferred in; 76% live on campus. *Retention:* 77% of full-time freshmen returned.

Freshmen *Admission:* 469 applied, 327 admitted, 126 enrolled. *Average high school GPA:* 3.45. *Test scores:* SAT critical reading scores over 500: 19%; SAT math scores over 500: 43%; SAT writing scores over 500: 11%; ACT scores over 18: 97%; ACT scores over 24: 48%; ACT scores over 30: 7%.

Faculty *Total:* 59, 61% full-time, 46% with terminal degrees. *Student/faculty ratio:* 12:1.

Academics *Calendar:* 4-1-4. *Degree:* certificates and bachelor's. *Special study options:* part-time degree program. *Unusual degree programs:* 3-2 engineering with Kansas State University, University of Kansas, Wichita State University.

Computers on Campus Students can access the following: campus intranet, computer help desk, free student e-mail accounts, online (class) grades, online (class) registration, online (class) schedules. Campuswide network is available. Wireless service is available via entire campus.

Student Life *Housing:* on-campus residence required through senior year. *Options:* coed, disabled students. Campus housing is university owned. Freshman campus housing is guaranteed. *Activities and organizations:* drama/theater group, student-run newspaper, radio and television station, choral group. *Student services:* health clinic, personal/psychological counseling.

Athletics Member NAIA. *Intercollegiate sports:* basketball M(s)/W(s), cross-country running M(s)/W(s), football M(s), golf M(s)/W(s), soccer M(s)/W(s), tennis M(s)/W(s), track and field M(s)/W(s), volleyball W(s). *Intramural sports:* badminton M/W, baseball M, basketball M/W, bowling M/W, cross-country running M/W, golf M/W, soccer M/W, softball M/W, table tennis M/W, tennis M/W, ultimate Frisbee M/W, volleyball M/W.

Standardized Tests *Required:* SAT or ACT (for admission).

Costs (2011–12) *One-time required fee:* $100. *Comprehensive fee:* $29,100 includes full-time tuition ($21,700) and room and board ($7400). Full-time tuition and fees vary according to course load. Part-time tuition: $780 per semester hour. Part-time tuition and fees vary according to course load. *College room only:* $3950. Room and board charges vary according to board plan and housing facility. *Payment plans:* installment, deferred payment. *Waivers:* children of alumni, senior citizens, and employees or children of employees.

Financial Aid Of all full-time matriculated undergraduates who enrolled in 2009, 357 applied for aid, 338 were judged to have need, 160 had their need fully met. 194 Federal Work-Study jobs (averaging $1711). 193 state and other part-time jobs (averaging $1195). In 2009, 78 non-need-based awards were made. *Average percent of need met:* 94%. *Average financial aid package:* $21,698. *Average need-based loan:* $6764. *Average need-based gift aid:* $5359. *Average non-need-based aid:* $8932. *Average indebtedness upon graduation:* $24,860.

Applying *Options:* deferred entrance. *Application fee:* $20. *Required:* high school transcript, minimum 2.5 GPA. *Required for some:* essay or personal statement, 2 letters of recommendation. *Recommended:* interview. *Application deadlines:* rolling (freshmen), rolling (transfers). *Notification:* continuous (freshmen), continuous (transfers).

Freshman Application Contact Mr. Todd H. Moore, Vice President for Admissions, Bethel College, 300 East 27th Street, North Newton, KS 67117-0531. *Phone:* 316-284-5230. *Toll-free phone:* 800-522-1887 Ext. 230. *Fax:* 316-284-5870. *E-mail:* admissions@bethelks.edu. *Web site:* http://www.bethelks.edu/.

Central Christian College of Kansas

McPherson, Kansas

Freshman Application Contact Central Christian College of Kansas, 1200 South Main, PO Box 1403, McPherson, KS 67460-5799. *Phone:* 620-241-0723 Ext. 380. *Toll-free phone:* 800-835-0078. *Web site:* http://www.centralchristian.edu/.

Cleveland Chiropractic College–Kansas City Campus

Overland Park, Kansas

- **Independent** comprehensive, founded 1922
- **Suburban** 34-acre campus with easy access to Kansas City
- **Coed** 99 undergraduate students, 81% full-time, 33% women, 67% men
- **Noncompetitive** entrance level, 100% of applicants were admitted

Undergraduates 80 full-time, 19 part-time. Students come from 18 states and territories; 2 other countries; 78% are from out of state; 3% Black or African American, non-Hispanic/Latino; 7% Hispanic/Latino; 6% Asian, non-Hispanic/Latino; 4% American Indian or Alaska Native, non-Hispanic/Latino; 2% Two or more races, non-Hispanic/Latino; 15% Race/ethnicity unknown; 1% international; 42% transferred in. *Retention:* 20% of full-time freshmen returned.

Freshmen *Admission:* 2 applied, 2 admitted, 3 enrolled. *Test scores:* ACT scores over 18: 100%; ACT scores over 24: 50%.

Faculty *Total:* 53, 81% full-time, 89% with terminal degrees. *Student/faculty ratio:* 11:1.

Academics *Calendar:* trimesters. *Degrees:* associate, bachelor's, and doctoral. *Special study options:* academic remediation for entering students, accelerated degree program, advanced placement credit, cooperative education, internships, services for LD students, summer session for credit.

Computers on Campus 30 computers/terminals are available on campus for general student use. Students can access the following: computer help desk, free student e-mail accounts, online (class) grades, online (class) schedules, educational software. Campuswide network is available. Wireless service is available via entire campus.

Student Life *Housing:* college housing not available. *Campus security:* 24-hour patrols. *Student services:* health clinic, personal/psychological counseling.

Standardized Tests *Required for some:* SAT or ACT (for admission).

Costs (2012–13) *Tuition:* $7000 full-time, $214 per credit part-time. Full-time tuition and fees vary according to course load and program. Part-time tuition and fees vary according to course load and program. *Required fees:* $390 full-time. *Payment plan:* installment.

Applying *Options:* electronic application, deferred entrance. *Application fee:* $50. *Required:* high school transcript, minimum 2.5 GPA. *Required for some:* interview. *Application deadlines:* rolling (freshmen), rolling (out-of-state freshmen), rolling (transfers). *Notification:* continuous (freshmen), continuous (out-of-state freshmen), continuous (transfers).

Freshman Application Contact Ms. Melissa Denton, Director of Admissions, Cleveland Chiropractic College–Kansas City Campus, 10850 Lowell Avenue, Overland Park, KS 66210. *Phone:* 913-234-0750. *Toll-free phone:* 800-467-2252. *Fax:* 913-234-0906. *E-mail:* kc.admissions@cleveland.edu. *Web site:* http://www.cleveland.edu/.

Donnelly College

Kansas City, Kansas

Freshman Application Contact Mr. Edward Marquez, Director of Admissions, Donnelly College, 608 North 18th Street, Kansas City, KS 66102. *Phone:* 913-621-8713. *Fax:* 913-621-8719. *E-mail:* admissions@donnelly.edu. *Web site:* http://www.donnelly.edu/.

Emporia State University

Emporia, Kansas

- **State-supported** comprehensive, founded 1863, part of Kansas State Board of Regents
- **Small-town** 207-acre campus with easy access to Wichita
- **Endowment** $61.9 million
- **Coed** 3,846 undergraduate students, 89% full-time, 60% women, 40% men
- **Noncompetitive** entrance level, 82% of applicants were admitted

Undergraduates 3,435 full-time, 411 part-time. Students come from 28 states and territories; 19 other countries; 9% are from out of state; 6% Black or African American, non-Hispanic/Latino; 5% Hispanic/Latino; 1% Asian, non-Hispanic/Latino; 0.2% Native Hawaiian or other Pacific Islander, non-Hispanic/Latino; 0.5% American Indian or Alaska Native, non-Hispanic/Latino; 3% Two or more races, non-Hispanic/Latino; 3% Race/ethnicity unknown; 7% international; 11% transferred in; 20% live on campus. *Retention:* 69% of full-time freshmen returned.

Freshmen *Admission:* 1,488 applied, 1,224 admitted, 587 enrolled. *Average high school GPA:* 3.24. *Test scores:* ACT scores over 18: 87%; ACT scores over 24: 33%; ACT scores over 30: 2%.

Faculty *Total:* 272, 93% full-time, 73% with terminal degrees. *Student/faculty ratio:* 17:1.

Academics *Calendar:* semesters. *Degrees:* bachelor's, master's, doctoral, post-master's, postbachelor's, and first professional certificates. *Special study options:* academic remediation for entering students, accelerated degree program, adult/continuing education programs, advanced placement credit, cooperative education, distance learning, double majors, English as a second language, honors programs, independent study, internships, off-campus study, part-time degree program, services for LD students, study abroad, summer session for credit. *Unusual degree programs:* 3-2 engineering with Kansas State University, University of Kansas, Wichita State University.

Computers on Campus 410 computers/terminals are available on campus for general student use. Students can access the following: campus intranet, computer help desk, free student e-mail accounts, online (class) grades, online (class) registration, online (class) schedules, various software packages. Campuswide network is available. 100% of college-owned or -operated housing units are wired for high-speed Internet access. Wireless service is available via classrooms, computer centers, computer labs, libraries.

Student Life *Housing:* on-campus residence required for freshman year. *Options:* coed, men-only, women-only, disabled students. Campus housing is university owned. Freshman campus housing is guaranteed. *Activities and organizations:* drama/theater group, student-run newspaper, radio station, choral group, marching band, Union Activities Council, Associated Student Government, Black Student Union, national fraternities, national sororities. *Campus security:* 24-hour emergency response devices and patrols, student patrols, late-night transport/escort service, controlled dormitory access, 24-hour residence hall monitoring, safety and self-awareness programs. *Student services:* health clinic, personal/psychological counseling, women's center, legal services.

Athletics Member NCAA. All Division II. *Intercollegiate sports:* baseball M(s), basketball M(s)/W(s), cheerleading M(s)/W(s), cross-country running M(s)/W(s), football M(s), soccer W(s), softball W(s), tennis M(s)/W(s), track and field M(s)/W(s), volleyball W(s). *Intramural sports:* badminton M/W, basketball M/W, fencing M(c)/W(c), football M/W, rugby M(c), soccer M(c)/W(c), softball M/W, table tennis M/W, tennis M/W, volleyball M/W.

Standardized Tests *Required:* SAT or ACT (for admission).

Costs (2011–12) *Tuition:* state resident $3864 full-time, $129 per credit hour part-time; nonresident $14,244 full-time, $475 per credit hour part-time. Full-time tuition and fees vary according to course load, degree level, and location. Part-time tuition and fees vary according to course load, degree level, and location. *Required fees:* $1088 full-time, $66 per credit hour part-time, $66 per credit hour part-time. *Room and board:* $6380; room only: $3270. Room and board charges vary according to board plan and housing facility. *Payment plans:* installment, deferred payment. *Waivers:* senior citizens and employees or children of employees.

Financial Aid Of all full-time matriculated undergraduates who enrolled in 2011, 2,617 applied for aid, 2,148 were judged to have need, 328 had their need fully met. 21 Federal Work-Study jobs (averaging $1991). 9 state and other part-time jobs (averaging $1638). In 2011, 467 non-need-based awards were made. *Average percent of need met:* 66%. *Average financial aid package:* $5040. *Average need-based loan:* $6308. *Average need-based gift aid:* $4911. *Average non-need-based aid:* $1406. *Average indebtedness upon graduation:* $23,215.

Applying *Options:* electronic application, early admission, deferred entrance. *Application fee:* $30. *Required:* high school transcript. *Recommended:* minimum 2.0 GPA. *Application deadlines:* rolling (freshmen), rolling (transfers). *Notification:* continuous (freshmen), continuous (transfers).

Freshman Application Contact Ms. Laura Eddy, Director of Admissions, Emporia State University, 1200 Commercial Street, Campus Box 4034, Emporia, KS 66801-5087. *Phone:* 620-341-5465. *Toll-free phone:* 877-GOTOESU (in-state); 877-468-6378 (out-of-state). *Fax:* 620-341-5599. *E-mail:* go2esu@emporia.edu. *Web site:* http://www.emporia.edu/.

Fort Hays State University

Hays, Kansas

- **State-supported** comprehensive, founded 1902
- **Small-town** 200-acre campus
- **Coed** 11,158 undergraduate students, 47% full-time, 58% women, 42% men
- **Noncompetitive** entrance level, 68% of applicants were admitted

Undergraduates 5,224 full-time, 5,934 part-time. 3% Black or African American, non-Hispanic/Latino; 4% Hispanic/Latino; 0.7% Asian, non-Hispanic/Latino; 0.1% Native Hawaiian or other Pacific Islander, non-Hispanic/Latino; 0.3% American Indian or Alaska Native, non-Hispanic/Latino; 1% Two or more races, non-Hispanic/Latino; 1% Race/ethnicity unknown; 35% international.

Freshmen *Admission:* 2,536 applied, 1,718 admitted, 1,017 enrolled.

Faculty *Total:* 479, 60% full-time, 47% with terminal degrees. *Student/faculty ratio:* 18:1.

Academics *Calendar:* semesters. *Degrees:* certificates, associate, bachelor's, master's, and post-master's certificates. *Special study options:* academic remediation for entering students, distance learning, double majors, English as a second language, honors programs, independent study, internships, part-time degree program, student-designed majors, study abroad.

Computers on Campus Students can access the following: campus intranet, computer help desk, free student e-mail accounts, online (class) grades, online (class) registration, online (class) schedules. Campuswide network is available. Wireless service is available via entire campus.

Student Life *Housing:* on-campus residence required for freshman year. *Options:* coed, women-only. *Activities and organizations:* marching band. *Campus security:* 24-hour emergency response devices and patrols. *Student services:* health clinic.

Athletics *Intramural sports:* badminton M/W.

Standardized Tests *Required:* SAT or ACT (for admission).

Costs (2011–12) *One-time required fee:* $60. *Tuition:* state resident $105 per credit hour part-time; nonresident $381 per credit hour part-time. Full-time tuition and fees vary according to course load. Part-time tuition and fees vary according to course load. *Required fees:* $30 per credit hour part-time. *Room and board:* $6625; room only: $3335. Room and board charges vary according to board plan and housing facility.

Financial Aid Of all full-time matriculated undergraduates who enrolled in 2007, 3,244 applied for aid, 2,653 were judged to have need, 483 had their need fully met. In 2007, 1162 non-need-based awards were made. *Average percent of need met:* 62%. *Average financial aid package:* $5955. *Average need-based loan:* $3634. *Average need-based gift aid:* $3390. *Average non-need-based aid:* $3358. *Average indebtedness upon graduation:* $15,601.

Applying *Application fee:* $35. *Required:* high school transcript. *Application deadline:* rolling (freshmen).

Freshman Application Contact Tricia Cline, Director, Admissions, Fort Hays State University, 600 Park Street, Hays, KS 67601-4099. *Phone:* 785-628-4091. *Toll-free phone:* 800-628-FHSU. *E-mail:* tcline@fhsu.edu. *Web site:* http://www.fhsu.edu/.

Friends University

Wichita, Kansas

- **Independent** comprehensive, founded 1898, affiliated with Christian non-denominational
- **Urban** 55-acre campus
- **Endowment** $41.7 million
- **Coed** 1,971 undergraduate students, 80% full-time, 56% women, 44% men
- **Moderately difficult** entrance level, 64% of applicants were admitted

Undergraduates 1,581 full-time, 390 part-time. Students come from 34 states and territories; 9 other countries; 12% are from out of state; 10% Black or African American, non-Hispanic/Latino; 4% Hispanic/Latino; 2% Asian, non-Hispanic/Latino; 0.1% Native Hawaiian or other Pacific Islander, non-Hispanic/Latino; 2% American Indian or Alaska Native, non-Hispanic/Latino; 3% Two or more races, non-Hispanic/Latino; 9% Race/ethnicity unknown; 16% transferred in; 39% live on campus. *Retention:* 66% of full-time freshmen returned.

Freshmen *Admission:* 792 applied, 507 admitted, 237 enrolled. *Average high school GPA:* 3.23. *Test scores:* SAT critical reading scores over 500: 42%; SAT math scores over 500: 50%; ACT scores over 18: 88%; SAT critical read-

ing scores over 600: 17%; SAT math scores over 600: 25%; ACT scores over 24: 38%; ACT scores over 30: 4%.

Faculty *Total:* 629, 12% full-time. *Student/faculty ratio:* 11:1.

Academics *Calendar:* semesters. *Degrees:* associate, bachelor's, and master's. *Special study options:* academic remediation for entering students, accelerated degree program, adult/continuing education programs, advanced placement credit, cooperative education, distance learning, double majors, honors programs, independent study, internships, off-campus study, part-time degree program, services for LD students, student-designed majors, study abroad, summer session for credit.

Computers on Campus 360 computers/terminals are available on campus for general student use. Students can access the following: campus intranet, computer help desk, free student e-mail accounts, online (class) grades, online (class) registration, online (class) schedules. Campuswide network is available. 90% of college-owned or -operated housing units are wired for high-speed Internet access. Wireless service is available via entire campus.

Student Life *Housing options:* coed. Campus housing is university owned. *Activities and organizations:* drama/theater group, student-run newspaper, choral group, Concert Choir, Singing Quakers, Zoo Science Club, Psychology Club, Spanish Club. *Campus security:* 24-hour patrols, late-night transport/escort service, controlled dormitory access. *Student services:* health clinic, personal/psychological counseling.

Athletics Member NAIA. *Intercollegiate sports:* baseball M(s), basketball M(s)/W(s), cheerleading M(s)/W(s), cross-country running M(s)/W(s), football M(s), golf M(s), soccer M(s)/W(s), softball W(s), tennis M(s)/W(s), track and field M(s)/W(s), volleyball W(s). *Intramural sports:* basketball M/W, football M/W, racquetball M/W, soccer M/W, table tennis M/W, tennis M/W, ultimate Frisbee M/W, volleyball M/W.

Standardized Tests *Required:* SAT or ACT (for admission). *Required for some:* SAT or ACT (for admission). *Recommended:* ACT (for admission).

Costs (2011–12) *Comprehensive fee:* $26,996 includes full-time tuition ($20,880), mandatory fees ($150), and room and board ($5966). Full-time tuition and fees vary according to course load. Part-time tuition: $696 per credit hour. Part-time tuition and fees vary according to course load. *Required fees:* $5 per credit hour part-time, $75 per term part-time. *College room only:* $2700. Room and board charges vary according to board plan and housing facility. *Payment plan:* installment. *Waivers:* senior citizens and employees or children of employees.

Financial Aid Of all full-time matriculated undergraduates who enrolled in 2006, 1,290 applied for aid, 1,160 were judged to have need, 279 had their need fully met. 239 Federal Work-Study jobs (averaging $1221). 185 state and other part-time jobs (averaging $1608). In 2006, 227 non-need-based awards were made. *Average percent of need met:* 66%. *Average financial aid package:* $11,219. *Average need-based loan:* $4098. *Average need-based gift aid:* $7092. *Average non-need-based aid:* $7792. *Average indebtedness upon graduation:* $17,750.

Applying *Options:* electronic application. *Application fee:* $35. *Required:* High school transcripts are not required for adult students enrolling in degree completion programs. Auditions are required for music, dance and theater programs. Portfolios are required for art program. Admission for traditional undergraduate students is based on student's hs GPA x ACT score. *Required for some:* high school transcript, interview. *Application deadlines:* rolling (freshmen), rolling (out-of-state freshmen), rolling (transfers). *Notification:* continuous (freshmen), continuous (out-of-state freshmen), continuous (transfers).

Freshman Application Contact Ms. Erin Haneberg, Executive Director of Admissions, Friends University, 2100 West University Avenue, Wichita, KS 67213. *Phone:* 316-295-5100. *Toll-free phone:* 800-794-6945. *Fax:* 316-295-5101. *E-mail:* haneberg@friends.edu. *Web site:* http://www.friends.edu/.

Haskell Indian Nations University
Lawrence, Kansas

Freshman Application Contact Ms. Patty Grant, Recruitment Officer, Haskell Indian Nations University, 155 Indian Avenue, #5031, Lawrence, KS 66046-4800. *Phone:* 785-749-8437 Ext. 437. *Web site:* http://www.haskell.edu/.

ITT Technical Institute
Overland Park, Kansas

- **Proprietary** 4-year
- **Coed**
- **Minimally difficult** entrance level

Academics *Degrees:* associate and bachelor's.

Freshman Application Contact Director of Recruitment, ITT Technical Institute, 7600 West 119th Street, Suite 100, Overland Park, KS 66213.

Phone: 913-253-1300. *Toll-free phone:* 877-327-9026. *Web site:* http://www.itt-tech.edu/.

ITT Technical Institute
Wichita, Kansas

- **Proprietary** 4-year, part of ITT Educational Services, Inc.
- **Coed**
- **Minimally difficult** entrance level

Academics *Calendar:* quarters. *Degrees:* associate and bachelor's.

Student Life *Housing:* college housing not available.

Freshman Application Contact Director of Recruitment, ITT Technical Institute, 8111 E. 32nd Street North, Suite 103, Wichita, KS 67226. *Phone:* 316-609-4100. *Toll-free phone:* 877-207-1047. *Web site:* http://www.itt-tech.edu/.

Kansas State University
Manhattan, Kansas

- **State-supported** university, founded 1863, part of Kansas Board of Regents
- **Suburban** 668-acre campus
- **Endowment** $337.5 million
- **Coed** 19,385 undergraduate students, 89% full-time, 48% women, 52% men
- **Noncompetitive** entrance level, 99% of applicants were admitted

Undergraduates 17,245 full-time, 2,140 part-time. Students come from 51 states and territories; 61 other countries; 16% are from out of state; 4% Black or African American, non-Hispanic/Latino; 5% Hispanic/Latino; 1% Asian, non-Hispanic/Latino; 0.2% Native Hawaiian or other Pacific Islander, non-Hispanic/Latino; 0.4% American Indian or Alaska Native, non-Hispanic/Latino; 2% Two or more races, non-Hispanic/Latino; 1% Race/ethnicity unknown; 5% international; 8% transferred in. *Retention:* 82% of full-time freshmen returned.

Freshmen *Admission:* 8,292 applied, 8,204 admitted, 3,644 enrolled. *Average high school GPA:* 3.42. *Test scores:* ACT scores over 18: 95%; ACT scores over 24: 56%; ACT scores over 30: 13%.

Faculty *Total:* 1,154, 84% full-time, 81% with terminal degrees. *Student/faculty ratio:* 20:1.

Academics *Calendar:* semesters. *Degrees:* certificates, associate, bachelor's, master's, doctoral, postbachelor's, and first professional certificates. *Special study options:* academic remediation for entering students, accelerated degree program, adult/continuing education programs, advanced placement credit, cooperative education, distance learning, double majors, English as a second language, freshman honors college, honors programs, independent study, internships, off-campus study, part-time degree program, services for LD students, study abroad, summer session for credit. *ROTC:* Army (b), Air Force (b). *Unusual degree programs:* 3-2 engineering; biology, kinesiology, horticulture, master of public health, biochemistry.

Computers on Campus Students can access the following: computer help desk, free student e-mail accounts, online (class) grades, online (class) registration, online (class) schedules. Campuswide network is available. Wireless service is available via entire campus.

Student Life *Housing options:* coed, men-only, women-only, cooperative. Campus housing is university owned. *Activities and organizations:* drama/theater group, student-run newspaper, radio and television station, choral group, marching band, athletic department groups, marching band, Union Governing Board, theater productions, debate team, national fraternities, national sororities. *Campus security:* 24-hour emergency response devices and patrols, late-night transport/escort service, controlled dormitory access. *Student services:* health clinic, personal/psychological counseling, women's center, legal services.

Athletics Member NCAA. All Division I except football (Division I-A). *Intercollegiate sports:* baseball M(s), basketball M(s)/W(s), crew W(s), cross-country running M(s)/W(s), golf M(s)/W(s), tennis W(s), track and field M(s)/W(s), volleyball W(s). *Intramural sports:* badminton M/W, basketball M/W, bowling M/W, crew M/W, cross-country running M/W, football M/W, golf M/W, ice hockey M, lacrosse M, racquetball M/W, soccer M/W, softball M/W, table tennis M/W, tennis M/W, track and field M/W, volleyball M/W, water polo M/W, weight lifting M/W, wrestling M.

Standardized Tests *Required for some:* SAT or ACT (for admission). *Recommended:* SAT or ACT (for admission).

Costs (2011–12) *Tuition:* state resident $6936 full-time; nonresident $18,402 full-time. Full-time tuition and fees vary according to course load, degree level, location, program, and reciprocity agreements. Part-time tuition and fees vary according to course load, degree level, location, program, and reciprocity agreements. *Required fees:* $721 full-time. *Room and board:* $7198. Room and board charges vary according to board plan, housing facility, and location.

Payment plans: installment, deferred payment. *Waivers:* employees or children of employees.

Financial Aid Of all full-time matriculated undergraduates who enrolled in 2010, 11,628 applied for aid, 8,988 were judged to have need, 1,518 had their need fully met. In 2010, 1069 non-need-based awards were made. *Average percent of need met:* 80%. *Average financial aid package:* $11,207. *Average need-based loan:* $4263. *Average need-based gift aid:* $4290. *Average non-need-based aid:* $3265. *Average indebtedness upon graduation:* $23,857.

Applying *Options:* electronic application, early admission. *Application fee:* $30. *Required:* high school transcript, minimum 2.0 GPA. *Application deadlines:* rolling (freshmen), rolling (out-of-state freshmen), rolling (transfers). *Notification:* continuous (freshmen), continuous (out-of-state freshmen), continuous (transfers).

Freshman Application Contact Ms. Molly McGaughey, Associate Director of Admissions, Kansas State University, 119 Anderson Hall, Manhattan, KS 66506. *Phone:* 785-532-6250. *Toll-free phone:* 800-432-8270. *Fax:* 785-532-6393. *E-mail:* k-state@k-state.edu. *Web site:* http://www.k-state.edu/.

Kansas Wesleyan University

Salina, Kansas

Freshman Application Contact Kansas Wesleyan University, 100 East Claflin Avenue, Salina, KS 67401-6196. *Phone:* 785-827-5541 Ext. 1283. *Toll-free phone:* 800-874-1154 Ext. 1285. *Web site:* http://www.kwu.edu/.

Manhattan Christian College

Manhattan, Kansas

Director of Admissions Eric Ingmire, Director of Admissions, Manhattan Christian College, 1415 Anderson Avenue, Manhattan, KS 66502-4081. *Phone:* 785-539-3571 Ext. 324. *Toll-free phone:* 877-246-4622. *E-mail:* admit@mccks.edu. *Web site:* http://www.mccks.edu/.

McPherson College

McPherson, Kansas

- **Independent** 4-year, founded 1887, affiliated with Church of the Brethren
- **Small-town** 26-acre campus
- **Coed** 620 undergraduate students, 94% full-time, 40% women, 60% men
- **Moderately difficult** entrance level, 86% of applicants were admitted

Undergraduates 585 full-time, 35 part-time. 12% Black or African American, non-Hispanic/Latino; 7% Hispanic/Latino; 0.5% Asian, non-Hispanic/Latino; 0.7% Native Hawaiian or other Pacific Islander, non-Hispanic/Latino; 0.8% American Indian or Alaska Native, non-Hispanic/Latino; 2% Two or more races, non-Hispanic/Latino; 2% international; 12% transferred in; 74% live on campus. *Retention:* 59% of full-time freshmen returned.

Freshmen *Admission:* 487 applied, 420 admitted, 134 enrolled. *Average high school GPA:* 3.15. *Test scores:* SAT critical reading scores over 500: 22%; SAT math scores over 500: 39%; ACT scores over 18: 94%; SAT critical reading scores over 600: 9%; SAT math scores over 600: 4%; ACT scores over 24: 26%; SAT critical reading scores over 700: 4%; ACT scores over 30: 2%.

Faculty *Total:* 65, 60% full-time, 62% with terminal degrees. *Student/faculty ratio:* 13:1.

Academics *Calendar:* 4-1-4. *Degree:* bachelor's. *Special study options:* adult/continuing education programs, part-time degree program.

Computers on Campus Students can access the following: campus intranet, computer help desk, free student e-mail accounts, online (class) grades. Campuswide network is available. Wireless service is available via computer labs, dorm rooms, libraries, student centers.

Student Life *Housing:* on-campus residence required through senior year. *Options:* coed, men-only, women-only, disabled students. Campus housing is university owned. Freshman campus housing is guaranteed. *Campus security:* student patrols, controlled dormitory access.

Athletics Member NAIA. *Intercollegiate sports:* basketball M/W, cheerleading M/W, cross-country running M/W, football M, soccer M/W, softball W, tennis M/W, track and field M/W, volleyball W. *Intramural sports:* basketball M/W, football M/W, racquetball M/W, soccer M/W, softball M/W, table tennis M/W, volleyball M/W.

Standardized Tests *Required:* SAT or ACT (for admission).

Costs (2011–12) *Comprehensive fee:* $28,138 includes full-time tuition ($20,600) and room and board ($7538). Full-time tuition and fees vary according to course load and program. *College room only:* $3113. *Payment plan:* installment. *Waivers:* employees or children of employees.

Financial Aid Of all full-time matriculated undergraduates who enrolled in 2011, 572 applied for aid, 518 were judged to have need, 125 had their need fully met. 239 Federal Work-Study jobs (averaging $875). In 2011, 88 non-need-based awards were made. *Average percent of need met:* 83%. *Average*

financial aid package: $20,849. *Average need-based loan:* $8097. *Average need-based gift aid:* $6191. *Average non-need-based aid:* $7898. *Average indebtedness upon graduation:* $28,949.

Applying *Options:* electronic application, deferred entrance. *Application fee:* $25. *Required:* high school transcript, minimum 2.0 GPA. *Application deadlines:* 8/12 (freshmen), rolling (transfers). *Notification:* continuous (freshmen), continuous (transfers).

Freshman Application Contact Mr. Matt Pfannenstiel, Director of Admissions, McPherson College, 1600 East Euclid, McPherson, KS 67460. *Phone:* 800-365-7402. *Toll-free phone:* 800-365-7402. *E-mail:* admiss@mcpherson.edu. *Web site:* http://www.mcpherson.edu/.

MidAmerica Nazarene University

Olathe, Kansas

- **Independent** comprehensive, founded 1966, affiliated with Church of the Nazarene
- **Suburban** 105-acre campus with easy access to Kansas City
- **Coed** 1,377 undergraduate students, 75% full-time, 56% women, 44% men
- **Moderately difficult** entrance level, 98% of applicants were admitted

Undergraduates 1,031 full-time, 346 part-time. Students come from 31 states and territories; 4 other countries; 30% are from out of state; 12% Black or African American, non-Hispanic/Latino; 4% Hispanic/Latino; 2% Asian, non-Hispanic/Latino; 0.1% Native Hawaiian or other Pacific Islander, non-Hispanic/Latino; 0.7% American Indian or Alaska Native, non-Hispanic/Latino; 1% Two or more races, non-Hispanic/Latino; 6% Race/ethnicity unknown; 0.1% international; 21% transferred in; 44% live on campus. *Retention:* 72% of full-time freshmen returned.

Freshmen *Admission:* 509 applied, 498 admitted, 167 enrolled. *Average high school GPA:* 3.32. *Test scores:* ACT scores over 18: 84%; ACT scores over 24: 39%; ACT scores over 30: 5%.

Faculty *Total:* 264, 30% full-time, 28% with terminal degrees. *Student/faculty ratio:* 10:1.

Academics *Calendar:* semesters. *Degrees:* associate, bachelor's, master's, post-master's, and postbachelor's certificates. *Special study options:* academic remediation for entering students, accelerated degree program, adult/continuing education programs, advanced placement credit, distance learning, double majors, honors programs, independent study, internships, off-campus study, part-time degree program, services for LD students, student-designed majors, study abroad, summer session for credit. *ROTC:* Army (c), Air Force (c).

Computers on Campus Students can access the following: campus intranet, computer help desk, free student e-mail accounts, online (class) grades, online (class) registration, online (class) schedules. Campuswide network is available. Wireless service is available via entire campus.

Student Life *Housing:* on-campus residence required through senior year. *Options:* men-only, women-only, disabled students. Campus housing is university owned. Freshman campus housing is guaranteed. *Activities and organizations:* drama/theater group, student-run newspaper, radio and television station, choral group. *Campus security:* 24-hour emergency response devices and patrols, student patrols, late-night transport/escort service, controlled dormitory access. *Student services:* personal/psychological counseling.

Athletics Member NAIA. *Intercollegiate sports:* baseball M(s), basketball M(s)/W(s), cheerleading M(s)/W(s), football M(s), soccer M(s)/W(s), softball W(s), volleyball W(s). *Intramural sports:* basketball M/W, bowling M/W, football M/W, golf M/W, soccer M/W, softball M/W, table tennis M/W, tennis M/W, ultimate Frisbee M/W, volleyball M/W.

Standardized Tests *Required:* SAT or ACT (for admission).

Costs (2012–13) *Comprehensive fee:* $28,500 includes full-time tuition ($20,500), mandatory fees ($1000), and room and board ($7000). Full-time tuition and fees vary according to course load. Part-time tuition: $700 per credit hour. Part-time tuition and fees vary according to course load. *Required fees:* $250 per term part-time. *Room and board:* Room and board charges vary according to board plan and housing facility. *Payment plan:* installment. *Waivers:* senior citizens and employees or children of employees.

Financial Aid Of all full-time matriculated undergraduates who enrolled in 2008, 796 applied for aid, 692 were judged to have need, 97 had their need fully met. In 2008, 187 non-need-based awards were made. *Average percent of need met:* 65%. *Average financial aid package:* $13,686. *Average need-based loan:* $5638. *Average need-based gift aid:* $8989. *Average non-need-based aid:* $4891. *Average indebtedness upon graduation:* $28,859.

Applying *Options:* electronic application, deferred entrance. *Application fee:* $25. *Required:* high school transcript, minimum 2.0 GPA. *Recommended:* TOEFL recommended. *Application deadlines:* 8/1 (freshmen), 8/1 (transfers). *Notification:* continuous (freshmen), continuous (transfers).

Freshman Application Contact Mr. Dennis Miller, Associate Director of Admissions, MidAmerica Nazarene University, 2030 East College Way, Olathe, KS 66062-1899. *Phone:* 913-971-3380. *Toll-free phone:* 800-800-

8887. *Fax:* 913-971-3481. *E-mail:* admissions@mnu.edu. *Web site:* http://www.mnu.edu/.

See below for display ad and page 1450 for the College Close-Up.

Newman University
Wichita, Kansas

- **Independent Roman Catholic** comprehensive, founded 1933
- **Urban** 61-acre campus
- **Endowment** $15.9 million
- **Coed** 2,193 undergraduate students, 51% full-time, 65% women, 35% men
- **Minimally difficult** entrance level, 44% of applicants were admitted

Undergraduates 1,124 full-time, 1,069 part-time. Students come from 22 states and territories; 25 other countries; 12% are from out of state; 7% Black or African American, non-Hispanic/Latino; 10% Hispanic/Latino; 5% Asian, non-Hispanic/Latino; 0.1% Native Hawaiian or other Pacific Islander, non-Hispanic/Latino; 2% American Indian or Alaska Native, non-Hispanic/Latino; 3% Two or more races, non-Hispanic/Latino; 0.3% Race/ethnicity unknown; 5% international; 12% transferred in; 14% live on campus. *Retention:* 68% of full-time freshmen returned.

Freshmen *Admission:* 2,521 applied, 1,097 admitted, 170 enrolled. *Average high school GPA:* 3.57. *Test scores:* SAT math scores over 500: 83%; SAT writing scores over 500: 58%; ACT scores over 18: 99%; SAT math scores over 600: 42%; SAT writing scores over 600: 25%; ACT scores over 24: 51%; SAT math scores over 700: 8%; SAT writing scores over 700: 8%; ACT scores over 30: 16%.

Faculty *Total:* 264, 31% full-time. *Student/faculty ratio:* 15:1.

Academics *Calendar:* semesters. *Degrees:* associate, bachelor's, and master's. *Special study options:* academic remediation for entering students, accelerated degree program, adult/continuing education programs, advanced placement credit, cooperative education, distance learning, double majors, honors programs, independent study, internships, off-campus study, part-time degree program, services for LD students, student-designed majors, study abroad, summer session for credit. *Unusual degree programs:* 3-2 occupational therapy with Washington University in St. Louis.

Computers on Campus 90 computers/terminals and 300 ports are available on campus for general student use. Students can access the following: computer help desk, free student e-mail accounts, online (class) grades, online (class) registration, online (class) schedules. Campuswide network is available.

100% of college-owned or -operated housing units are wired for high-speed Internet access. Wireless service is available via classrooms, computer centers, dorm rooms, learning centers, libraries, student centers.

Student Life *Housing:* on-campus residence required through sophomore year. *Options:* coed, men-only, women-only, cooperative, disabled students. Campus housing is university owned. Freshman campus housing is guaranteed. *Activities and organizations:* drama/theater group, student-run newspaper, choral group, Koinonia, Multicultural Leadership Organization, Pep Band, Psychology Club (Psi Upsilon Chi), Theatre Troupe (Sloppy Joe's). *Campus security:* 24-hour emergency response devices and patrols, student patrols, late-night transport/escort service, controlled dormitory access. *Student services:* personal/psychological counseling.

Athletics Member NCAA. All Division II. *Intercollegiate sports:* baseball M(s)/W, basketball M(s)/W(s), bowling M(s)(c)/W(s)(c), cross-country running M(s)/W(s), golf M(s)/W(s), soccer M(s)/W(s), softball W(s), tennis M(s)/W(s), volleyball W(s), wrestling M(s). *Intramural sports:* baseball M, basketball M/W, bowling M/W, cheerleading M(c)/W(c), football M/W, golf M/W, soccer M/W, softball M/W, table tennis M/W, volleyball M/W, weight lifting M/W.

Standardized Tests *Required:* SAT or ACT (for admission).

Costs (2012–13) *Comprehensive fee:* $28,688 includes full-time tuition ($21,388), mandatory fees ($910), and room and board ($6390). Full-time tuition and fees vary according to class time, course load, location, and program. Part-time tuition: $713 per credit hour. Part-time tuition and fees vary according to class time, course load, location, and program. *Required fees:* $15 per credit hour part-time. *College room only:* $3200. Room and board charges vary according to board plan and housing facility. *Payment plan:* installment. *Waivers:* employees or children of employees.

Financial Aid Of all full-time matriculated undergraduates who enrolled in 2009, 1,074 applied for aid, 919 were judged to have need, 146 had their need fully met. 66 Federal Work-Study jobs (averaging $1037). 80 state and other part-time jobs (averaging $994). In 2009, 43 non-need-based awards were made. *Average percent of need met:* 62%. *Average financial aid package:* $14,370. *Average need-based loan:* $4065. *Average need-based gift aid:* $4869. *Average non-need-based aid:* $5673. *Average indebtedness upon graduation:* $23,996.

Applying *Options:* electronic application, early admission, deferred entrance. *Application fee:* $20. *Required:* high school transcript, minimum 2.0 GPA. *Recommended:* interview. *Application deadlines:* rolling (freshmen), rolling (out-of-state freshmen), rolling (transfers). *Notification:* continuous (freshmen), continuous (out-of-state freshmen), continuous (transfers).

With purpose.

www.mnu.edu   800.800.8887   MIDAMERICA NAZARENE UNIVERSITY

Freshman Application Contact Jann Reusser, Admissions Coordinator, Newman University, 3100 McCormick Avenue, Wichita, KS 67213. *Phone:* 316-942-4291 Ext. 2144. *Toll-free phone:* 877-NEWMANU. *Fax:* 316-942-4483. *E-mail:* reusserj@newmanu.edu. *Web site:* http://www.newmanu.edu/.

Ottawa University
Ottawa, Kansas

Freshman Application Contact Ottawa University, 1001 South Cedar, Ottawa, KS 66067-3399. *Phone:* 785-229-1051. *Toll-free phone:* 800-755-5200. *Web site:* http://www.ottawa.edu/.

Pittsburg State University
Pittsburg, Kansas

- **State-supported** comprehensive, founded 1903, part of Kansas State Board of Regents
- **Small-town** 630-acre campus
- **Endowment** $59.3 million
- **Coed** 6,076 undergraduate students, 94% full-time, 47% women, 53% men
- **Minimally difficult** entrance level, 77% of applicants were admitted

Undergraduates 5,732 full-time, 344 part-time. Students come from 37 states and territories; 30 other countries; 26% are from out of state; 4% Black or African American, non-Hispanic/Latino; 4% Hispanic/Latino; 0.6% Asian, non-Hispanic/Latino; 0.1% Native Hawaiian or other Pacific Islander, non-Hispanic/Latino; 2% American Indian or Alaska Native, non-Hispanic/Latino; 3% Two or more races, non-Hispanic/Latino; 0.3% Race/ethnicity unknown; 5% international; 9% transferred in; 18% live on campus. *Retention:* 73% of full-time freshmen returned.

Freshmen *Admission:* 2,889 applied, 2,220 admitted, 1,161 enrolled. *Average high school GPA:* 3.3. *Test scores:* ACT scores over 18: 89%; ACT scores over 24: 30%; ACT scores over 30: 3%.

Faculty *Total:* 417, 76% full-time, 64% with terminal degrees. *Student/faculty ratio:* 19:1.

Academics *Calendar:* semesters. *Degrees:* certificates, associate, bachelor's, master's, and post-master's certificates. *Special study options:* academic remediation for entering students, adult/continuing education programs, advanced placement credit, cooperative education, distance learning, double majors, English as a second language, freshman honors college, honors programs, independent study, internships, off-campus study, part-time degree program, services for LD students, student-designed majors, study abroad, summer session for credit. *ROTC:* Army (b).

Computers on Campus 425 computers/terminals are available on campus for general student use. Students can access the following: campus intranet, computer help desk, free student e-mail accounts, online (class) grades, online (class) registration, online (class) schedules. Campuswide network is available. 100% of college-owned or -operated housing units are wired for high-speed Internet access. Wireless service is available via entire campus.

Student Life *Housing:* on-campus residence required for freshman year. *Options:* coed, disabled students. Campus housing is university owned. Freshman applicants given priority for college housing. *Activities and organizations:* drama/theater group, student-run newspaper, radio and television station, choral group, marching band, Student Government Association, student yearbook, student newspaper, Student Activities Council, Students in Free Enterprise (SIFE), national fraternities, national sororities. *Campus security:* 24-hour emergency response devices and patrols, controlled dormitory access. *Student services:* health clinic, personal/psychological counseling, legal services.

Athletics Member NCAA. All Division II. *Intercollegiate sports:* baseball M(s), basketball M(s)/W(s), cheerleading M(s)/W(s), cross-country running M(s)/W(s), football M(s), golf M(s), softball W(s), track and field M(s)/W(s), volleyball W(s). *Intramural sports:* badminton M/W, basketball M/W, football M/W, lacrosse M(c), racquetball M/W, rugby M(c), soccer M(c)/W(c), softball M/W, table tennis M/W, tennis M/W, ultimate Frisbee M/W, volleyball M/W.

Standardized Tests *Required:* ACT (for admission).

Costs (2011–12) *Tuition:* state resident $5162 full-time, $184 per credit hour part-time; nonresident $14,166 full-time, $484 per credit hour part-time. Part-time tuition and fees vary according to course load. *Room and board:* $6288. Room and board charges vary according to board plan and housing facility. *Payment plan:* installment. *Waivers:* employees or children of employees.

Financial Aid Of all full-time matriculated undergraduates who enrolled in 2010, 4,141 applied for aid, 3,260 were judged to have need, 258 had their need fully met. In 2010, 430 non-need-based awards were made. *Average percent of need met:* 75%. *Average financial aid package:* $9900. *Average need-based loan:* $3889. *Average need-based gift aid:* $4525. *Average non-need-based aid:* $2450. *Average indebtedness upon graduation:* $18,516.

Applying *Options:* electronic application. *Application fee:* $30. *Required:* high school transcript. *Required for some:* minimum 2.0 GPA. *Application deadlines:* rolling (freshmen), rolling (transfers).

Freshman Application Contact Director of Admission, Pittsburg State University, 1701 South Broadway, Pittsburg, KS 66762. *Phone:* 620-235-4251. *Toll-free phone:* 800-854-7488. *Fax:* 620-235-6003. *E-mail:* psuadmit@pittstate.edu. *Web site:* http://www.pittstate.edu/.

Southwestern College
Winfield, Kansas

- **Independent United Methodist** comprehensive, founded 1885
- **Small-town** 70-acre campus with easy access to Wichita
- **Endowment** $21.1 million
- **Coed** 1,401 undergraduate students, 41% full-time, 48% women, 52% men
- **Minimally difficult** entrance level, 87% of applicants were admitted

Undergraduates 578 full-time, 823 part-time. Students come from 45 states and territories; 7 other countries; 38% are from out of state; 10% Black or African American, non-Hispanic/Latino; 7% Hispanic/Latino; 1% Asian, non-Hispanic/Latino; 0.1% Native Hawaiian or other Pacific Islander, non-Hispanic/Latino; 1% American Indian or Alaska Native, non-Hispanic/Latino; 3% Two or more races, non-Hispanic/Latino; 11% Race/ethnicity unknown; 2% international; 4% transferred in; 72% live on campus. *Retention:* 63% of full-time freshmen returned.

Freshmen *Admission:* 378 applied, 330 admitted, 160 enrolled. *Average high school GPA:* 3.45. *Test scores:* SAT critical reading scores over 500: 15%; SAT math scores over 500: 30%; SAT writing scores over 500: 15%; ACT scores over 18: 90%; SAT critical reading scores over 600: 4%; ACT scores over 24: 34%; ACT scores over 30: 3%.

Faculty *Total:* 113, 42% full-time, 32% with terminal degrees. *Student/faculty ratio:* 12:1.

Academics *Calendar:* semesters. *Degrees:* certificates, bachelor's, master's, post-master's, and postbachelor's certificates. *Special study options:* accelerated degree program, adult/continuing education programs, advanced placement credit, distance learning, double majors, honors programs, independent study, internships, off-campus study, part-time degree program, student-designed majors, study abroad, summer session for credit.

Computers on Campus 15 computers/terminals and 100 ports are available on campus for general student use. Students can access the following: campus intranet, computer help desk, free student e-mail accounts, online (class) grades, online (class) registration, online (class) schedules. Campuswide network is available. 100% of college-owned or -operated housing units are wired for high-speed Internet access. Wireless service is available via entire campus.

Student Life *Housing:* on-campus residence required through sophomore year. *Options:* coed, men-only, women-only. Campus housing is university owned. Freshman campus housing is guaranteed. *Activities and organizations:* drama/theater group, student-run newspaper, radio and television station, choral group, Discipleship SC, Leadership SC, Acappella Choir, Concert Band, Southwestern Singers, national fraternities, national sororities. *Campus security:* 24-hour emergency response devices and patrols, late-night transport/escort service, controlled dormitory access. *Student services:* health clinic, personal/psychological counseling.

Athletics Member NAIA. *Intercollegiate sports:* basketball M(s)/W(s), cross-country running M(s)/W(s), football M(s), golf M(s)/W(s), soccer M(s)/W(s), softball W(s), tennis M(s)/W(s), track and field M(s)/W(s), volleyball W(s). *Intramural sports:* badminton M(c)/W(c), basketball M/W, softball M/W, tennis M/W, ultimate Frisbee M(c)/W(c), volleyball M/W.

Standardized Tests *Required:* SAT or ACT (for admission).

Costs (2012–13) *Comprehensive fee:* $29,270 includes full-time tuition ($22,606), mandatory fees ($150), and room and board ($6514). Full-time tuition and fees vary according to class time, course load, degree level, location, and program. Part-time tuition: $942 per credit hour. Part-time tuition and fees vary according to class time, course load, degree level, location, and program. *College room only:* $3000. Room and board charges vary according to board plan and housing facility. *Payment plan:* installment. *Waivers:* senior citizens and employees or children of employees.

Financial Aid Of all full-time matriculated undergraduates who enrolled in 2010, 543 applied for aid, 506 were judged to have need, 53 had their need fully met. 188 Federal Work-Study jobs (averaging $1320). 132 state and other part-time jobs (averaging $1063). In 2010, 97 non-need-based awards were made. *Average percent of need met:* 71%. *Average financial aid package:* $18,005. *Average need-based loan:* $5132. *Average need-based gift aid:* $12,775. *Average non-need-based aid:* $7899. *Average indebtedness upon graduation:* $31,280. *Financial aid deadline:* 8/15.

Applying *Options:* electronic application. *Application fee:* $25. *Required:* high school transcript, minimum 2.5 GPA. *Required for some:* 2 letters of recommendation, interview. *Recommended:* essay or personal statement. *Appli-*

cation deadlines: 8/1 (freshmen), 8/1 (out-of-state freshmen), 8/1 (transfers). *Notification:* continuous (freshmen), continuous (out-of-state freshmen), continuous (transfers).

Freshman Application Contact Southwestern College, 100 College Street, Winfield, KS 67156-2499. *Phone:* 620-229-6364. *Toll-free phone:* 800-846-1543. *Web site:* http://www.sckans.edu/.

Sterling College
Sterling, Kansas

- **Independent Presbyterian** 4-year, founded 1887
- **Rural** 46-acre campus
- **Endowment** $13.4 million
- **Coed** 674 undergraduate students, 89% full-time, 46% women, 54% men
- **Minimally difficult** entrance level, 49% of applicants were admitted

Undergraduates 597 full-time, 77 part-time. Students come from 36 states and territories; 2 other countries; 55% are from out of state; 8% Black or African American, non-Hispanic/Latino; 6% Hispanic/Latino; 2% Native Hawaiian or other Pacific Islander, non-Hispanic/Latino; 1% American Indian or Alaska Native, non-Hispanic/Latino; 0.7% Race/ethnicity unknown; 0.4% international; 7% transferred in; 85% live on campus. *Retention:* 62% of full-time freshmen returned.

Freshmen *Admission:* 1,050 applied, 514 admitted, 140 enrolled. *Average high school GPA:* 3.14. *Test scores:* SAT critical reading scores over 500: 26%; SAT math scores over 500: 47%; SAT writing scores over 500: 10%; ACT scores over 18: 88%; SAT math scores over 600: 5%; ACT scores over 24: 38%; ACT scores over 30: 2%.

Faculty *Total:* 80, 51% full-time, 26% with terminal degrees. *Student/faculty ratio:* 14:1.

Academics *Calendar:* 4-1-4. *Degree:* bachelor's. *Special study options:* advanced placement credit, distance learning, double majors, honors programs, independent study, internships, off-campus study, services for LD students, student-designed majors, study abroad, summer session for credit. *Unusual degree programs:* 3-2 biology/medical technology with Wichita State University.

Computers on Campus 50 computers/terminals are available on campus for general student use. Students can access the following: campus intranet, computer help desk, free student e-mail accounts, online (class) grades, online (class) registration, online (class) schedules. Campuswide network is available. 100% of college-owned or -operated housing units are wired for high-speed Internet access. Wireless service is available via entire campus.

Student Life *Housing:* on-campus residence required through senior year. *Options:* men-only, women-only. Campus housing is university owned. Freshman campus housing is guaranteed. *Activities and organizations:* drama/theater group, student-run newspaper, radio and television station, choral group, Fellowship of Christian Athletes, Student Activities Council, Bible study groups, theatre, Mission teams. *Campus security:* controlled dormitory access, late night security patrol. *Student services:* health clinic, personal/psychological counseling.

Athletics Member NAIA. *Intercollegiate sports:* baseball M(s), basketball M(s)/W(s), cross-country running M(s)/W(s), football M(s), golf M(s)/W(s), soccer M(s)/W(s), softball W(s), track and field M(s)/W(s), volleyball W(s). *Intramural sports:* basketball M/W, softball M/W, ultimate Frisbee M/W, volleyball M/W.

Standardized Tests *Required:* SAT or ACT (for admission).

Costs (2012–13) *Comprehensive fee:* $27,902 includes full-time tuition ($20,950), mandatory fees ($200), and room and board ($6752). Part-time tuition: $392 per credit hour. *Room and board:* Room and board charges vary according to board plan and housing facility. *Payment plan:* installment. *Waivers:* senior citizens and employees or children of employees.

Financial Aid Of all full-time matriculated undergraduates who enrolled in 2004, 449 applied for aid, 363 were judged to have need, 176 had their need fully met. 169 Federal Work-Study jobs (averaging $501). 196 state and other part-time jobs (averaging $808). In 2004, 77 non-need-based awards were made. *Average percent of need met:* 100%. *Average financial aid package:* $15,375. *Average need-based loan:* $4214. *Average need-based gift aid:* $7863. *Average non-need-based aid:* $6817. *Average indebtedness upon graduation:* $9647.

Applying *Options:* electronic application, deferred entrance. *Application fee:* $25. *Required:* high school transcript, minimum 2.2 GPA. *Required for some:* 2 letters of recommendation. *Recommended:* essay or personal statement, interview. *Application deadlines:* rolling (freshmen), rolling (transfers). *Notification:* continuous (freshmen), continuous (transfers).

Freshman Application Contact Marge Jones, Admissions Office Manager, Sterling College, 125 West Cooper, Sterling, KS 67579. *Phone:* 620-278-4275. *Toll-free phone:* 800-346-1017. *Fax:* 620-278-4416. *E-mail:* admissions@sterling.edu. *Web site:* http://www.sterling.edu/.

Tabor College
Hillsboro, Kansas

- **Independent Mennonite Brethren** comprehensive, founded 1908
- **Small-town** 87-acre campus with easy access to Wichita
- **Endowment** $5.3 million
- **Coed** 721 undergraduate students, 80% full-time, 49% women, 51% men
- **Moderately difficult** entrance level, 91% of applicants were admitted

Undergraduates 580 full-time, 141 part-time. Students come from 27 states and territories; 6 other countries; 46% are from out of state; 7% Black or African American, non-Hispanic/Latino; 10% Hispanic/Latino; 0.4% Asian, non-Hispanic/Latino; 0.7% Native Hawaiian or other Pacific Islander, non-Hispanic/Latino; 0.7% American Indian or Alaska Native, non-Hispanic/Latino; 2% Two or more races, non-Hispanic/Latino; 1% Race/ethnicity unknown; 2% international; 10% transferred in; 86% live on campus. *Retention:* 70% of full-time freshmen returned.

Freshmen *Admission:* 407 applied, 371 admitted, 151 enrolled. *Average high school GPA:* 3.25. *Test scores:* SAT critical reading scores over 500: 23%; SAT math scores over 500: 56%; ACT scores over 18: 87%; SAT critical reading scores over 600: 4%; SAT math scores over 600: 8%; ACT scores over 24: 37%; SAT critical reading scores over 700: 4%; SAT math scores over 700: 4%; ACT scores over 30: 5%.

Faculty *Total:* 85, 34% full-time, 36% with terminal degrees. *Student/faculty ratio:* 14:1.

Academics *Calendar:* 4-1-4. *Degrees:* associate, bachelor's, and master's. *Special study options:* academic remediation for entering students, accelerated degree program, adult/continuing education programs, advanced placement credit, cooperative education, distance learning, double majors, honors programs, independent study, internships, off-campus study, part-time degree program, services for LD students, student-designed majors, study abroad.

Computers on Campus 40 computers/terminals are available on campus for general student use. Students can access the following: campus intranet, computer help desk, free student e-mail accounts, online (class) grades, online (class) schedules. Campuswide network is available. 100% of college-owned or -operated housing units are wired for high-speed Internet access. Wireless service is available via entire campus.

Student Life *Housing:* on-campus residence required through junior year. *Options:* men-only, women-only, disabled students. Campus housing is university owned. Freshman campus housing is guaranteed. *Activities and organizations:* drama/theater group, student-run newspaper, choral group, Student Activities Board, Campus Ministries Council, Multi-Cultural Student Union, Business Club, Science Club.

Athletics Member NAIA. *Intercollegiate sports:* baseball M(s), basketball M(s)/W(s), bowling M(s)/W(s), cheerleading M(s)/W(s), cross-country running M(s)/W(s), football M(s), soccer M(s)/W(s), softball W(s), tennis M(s)/W(s), track and field M(s)/W(s), volleyball W(s). *Intramural sports:* basketball M/W, football M/W, racquetball M/W, soccer M/W, volleyball M/W.

Standardized Tests *Required:* SAT or ACT (for admission).

Costs (2012–13) *Comprehensive fee:* $29,860 includes full-time tuition ($21,160), mandatory fees ($580), and room and board ($8120). Full-time tuition and fees vary according to course load. Part-time tuition and fees vary according to course load. *Required fees:* $880 per credit part-time. *College room only:* $3220. Room and board charges vary according to board plan, housing facility, and location. *Payment plan:* installment. *Waivers:* employees or children of employees.

Financial Aid Of all full-time matriculated undergraduates who enrolled in 2010, 590 applied for aid, 490 were judged to have need, 87 had their need fully met. 213 Federal Work-Study jobs (averaging $593). In 2010, 86 non-need-based awards were made. *Average percent of need met:* 79%. *Average financial aid package:* $20,301. *Average need-based loan:* $7704. *Average need-based gift aid:* $4702. *Average non-need-based aid:* $7559. *Average indebtedness upon graduation:* $27,380. *Financial aid deadline:* 8/15.

Applying *Options:* electronic application, early admission, deferred entrance. *Application fee:* $30. *Required:* essay or personal statement, high school transcript, minimum 2.0 GPA. *Required for some:* letters of recommendation. *Recommended:* interview. *Application deadlines:* rolling (freshmen), rolling (out-of-state freshmen), rolling (transfers).

Freshman Application Contact Mrs. Natalie Wright, Director of Student Recruitment, Tabor College, Tabor College, 400 South Jefferson, Hillsboro, KS 67063. *Phone:* 620-947-3121 Ext. 1723. *Toll-free phone:* 800-822-6799. *Fax:* 620-947-6276. *E-mail:* nataliew@tabor.edu. *Web site:* http://www.tabor.edu/.

The University of Kansas

Lawrence, Kansas

- **State-supported** university, founded 1866, part of Kansas Board of Regents System
- **Suburban** 1000-acre campus with easy access to Kansas City
- **Endowment** $1.7 billion
- **Coed** 19,700 undergraduate students, 90% full-time, 50% women, 50% men
- **Moderately difficult** entrance level, 93% of applicants were admitted

Undergraduates 17,670 full-time, 2,030 part-time. Students come from 52 states and territories; 70 other countries; 21% are from out of state; 4% Black or African American, non-Hispanic/Latino; 5% Hispanic/Latino; 4% Asian, non-Hispanic/Latino; 0.1% Native Hawaiian or other Pacific Islander, non-Hispanic/Latino; 0.6% American Indian or Alaska Native, non-Hispanic/Latino; 3% Two or more races, non-Hispanic/Latino; 0.7% Race/ethnicity unknown; 5% international; 7% transferred in; 22% live on campus. *Retention:* 80% of full-time freshmen returned.

Freshmen *Admission:* 10,035 applied, 9,306 admitted, 3,580 enrolled. *Average high school GPA:* 3.5. *Test scores:* ACT scores over 18: 97%; ACT scores over 24: 62%; ACT scores over 30: 15%.

Faculty *Total:* 1,703, 77% full-time, 80% with terminal degrees. *Student/faculty ratio:* 20:1.

Academics *Calendar:* semesters. *Degrees:* certificates, bachelor's, master's, doctoral, post-master's, postbachelor's, and first professional certificates (University of Kansas is a single institution with academic programs and facilities at two primary locations: Lawrence and Kansas City). *Special study options:* academic remediation for entering students, accelerated degree program, advanced placement credit, cooperative education, distance learning, double majors, English as a second language, honors programs, independent study, internships, part-time degree program, services for LD students, study abroad, summer session for credit. *ROTC:* Army (b), Navy (b), Air Force (b).

Computers on Campus 1,500 computers/terminals are available on campus for general student use. Students can access the following: campus intranet, computer help desk, free student e-mail accounts, online (class) grades, online (class) registration, online (class) schedules. Campuswide network is available. 100% of college-owned or -operated housing units are wired for high-speed Internet access. Wireless service is available via entire campus.

Student Life *Housing options:* coed, women-only, cooperative. Campus housing is university owned. *Activities and organizations:* drama/theater group, student-run newspaper, radio and television station, choral group, marching band, Association of University Residence Halls, Hillel, Panhellenic Association, International Student Association, McCollum Leadership Involvement Team, national fraternities, national sororities. *Campus security:* 24-hour emergency response devices and patrols, late-night transport/escort service, controlled dormitory access, University police department. *Student services:* health clinic, personal/psychological counseling, women's center, legal services.

Athletics Member NCAA. All Division I except football (Division I-A). *Intercollegiate sports:* baseball M(s), basketball M(s)/W(s), crew W(s), cross-country running M(s)/W(s), golf M(s)/W(s), ice hockey M(c), rugby M(c), soccer W(s), softball W(s), swimming and diving W(s), tennis W(s), track and field M(s)/W(s), ultimate Frisbee M(c)/W(c), volleyball W(s). *Intramural sports:* baseball M(c), basketball M/W, bowling M/W, crew M(c)/W(c), equestrian sports M(c)/W(c), fencing M(c)/W(c), football M/W, golf M(c)/W(c), lacrosse M(c)/W(c), racquetball M(c)/W(c), rock climbing M(c)/W(c), rugby W(c), sailing M(c)/W(c), soccer M(c)/W(c), softball M/W, swimming and diving M(c)/W(c), table tennis M(c)/W(c), tennis M(c)/W(c), ultimate Frisbee M(c)/W(c), volleyball M(c)/W(c), water polo M(c), wrestling M(c).

Standardized Tests *Required:* SAT or ACT (for admission).

Costs (2011–12) *Tuition:* state resident $8364 full-time, $278 per credit hour part-time; nonresident $21,750 full-time, $725 per credit hour part-time. Full-time tuition and fees vary according to program, reciprocity agreements, and student level. Part-time tuition and fees vary according to program, reciprocity agreements, and student level. No tuition increase for student's term of enrollment. *Required fees:* $858 full-time, $71 per credit hour part-time. *Room and board:* $7080; room only: $3700. Room and board charges vary according to board plan and housing facility. *Payment plan:* installment. *Waivers:* employees or children of employees.

Financial Aid Of all full-time matriculated undergraduates who enrolled in 2010, 11,196 applied for aid, 8,259 were judged to have need, 1,179 had their need fully met. 399 Federal Work-Study jobs (averaging $2925). 51 state and other part-time jobs (averaging $3984). In 2010, 1826 non-need-based awards were made. *Average percent of need met:* 61%. *Average financial aid package:* $9449. *Average need-based loan:* $4274. *Average need-based gift aid:* $5813. *Average non-need-based aid:* $3633. *Average indebtedness upon graduation:* $22,114.

Applying *Options:* electronic application. *Application fee:* $30. *Required:* high school transcript, minimum 2.0 GPA, Kansas Board of Regents admissions criteria. *Required for some:* minimum 2.5 GPA. *Application deadlines:* 4/1 (freshmen), 4/1 (out-of-state freshmen), 5/1 (transfers). *Notification:* continuous (freshmen), continuous (out-of-state freshmen), continuous (transfers).
Freshman Application Contact Ms. Lisa Pinamonti Kress, Director of Admissions, The University of Kansas, KU Visitor Center, 1502 Iowa Street, Lawrence, KS 66045-7576. *Phone:* 785-864-3911. *Toll-free phone:* 888-686-7323. *Fax:* 785-864-5006. *E-mail:* adm@ku.edu. *Web site:* http://www.ku.edu/.

University of Phoenix–Wichita Campus

Wichita, Kansas

Freshman Application Contact Marc Booker, Sr. Director, Office of Admissions and Evaluation, University of Phoenix–Wichita Campus, 4035 South Riverpoint Parkway, Mail Stop CF-L101, Phoenix, AZ 85040. *Phone:* 602-557-4609. *Toll-free phone:* 866-766-0766. *Fax:* 480-643-1156. *Web site:* http://www.phoenix.edu/.

University of Saint Mary

Leavenworth, Kansas

- **Independent Roman Catholic** comprehensive, founded 1923
- **Small-town** 240-acre campus with easy access to Kansas City
- **Coed** 816 undergraduate students, 67% full-time, 64% women, 36% men
- **Moderately difficult** entrance level, 55% of applicants were admitted

Undergraduates 544 full-time, 272 part-time. Students come from 41 states and territories; 5 other countries; 40% are from out of state; 14% Black or African American, non-Hispanic/Latino; 6% Hispanic/Latino; 2% Asian, non-Hispanic/Latino; 0.3% Native Hawaiian or other Pacific Islander, non-Hispanic/Latino; 0.7% American Indian or Alaska Native, non-Hispanic/Latino; 11% Race/ethnicity unknown; 0.7% international; 13% transferred in; 30% live on campus. *Retention:* 74% of full-time freshmen returned.

Freshmen *Admission:* 751 applied, 416 admitted, 103 enrolled. *Test scores:* SAT critical reading scores over 500: 26%; SAT math scores over 500: 29%; ACT scores over 18: 89%; SAT critical reading scores over 600: 1%; SAT math scores over 600: 7%; ACT scores over 24: 30%; ACT scores over 30: 5%.

Faculty *Total:* 118, 37% full-time, 33% with terminal degrees. *Student/faculty ratio:* 11:1.

Academics *Calendar:* semesters. *Degrees:* certificates, associate, bachelor's, and master's. *Special study options:* adult/continuing education programs, advanced placement credit, cooperative education, distance learning, double majors, honors programs, independent study, internships, off-campus study, part-time degree program, services for LD students, student-designed majors, study abroad, summer session for credit. *ROTC:* Army (c), Air Force (c).

Computers on Campus 45 computers/terminals are available on campus for general student use. Students can access the following: campus intranet, computer help desk, free student e-mail accounts, online (class) grades, online (class) registration, online (class) schedules. Campuswide network is available. 100% of college-owned or -operated housing units are wired for high-speed Internet access. Wireless service is available via entire campus.

Student Life *Housing:* on-campus residence required through sophomore year. *Options:* coed. Campus housing is university owned. Freshman campus housing is guaranteed. *Activities and organizations:* drama/theater group, choral group, Student Government Association, BACCHUS, Theatrical Union, campus ministry, Amnesty International. *Campus security:* late-night transport/escort service, controlled dormitory access. *Student services:* health clinic, personal/psychological counseling.

Athletics Member NAIA. *Intercollegiate sports:* baseball M(s), basketball M(s)/W(s), cheerleading M(s)/W(s), cross-country running M(s)/W(s), football M(s), soccer M(s)/W(s), softball W(s), track and field M(s)/W(s), volleyball W(s). *Intramural sports:* badminton M/W, basketball M/W, bowling M/W, football M, racquetball M/W, soccer M/W, softball W, table tennis M/W, ultimate Frisbee M/W, volleyball M/W, weight lifting M/W.

Standardized Tests *Required:* SAT or ACT (for admission).

Costs (2012–13) *Comprehensive fee:* $29,230 includes full-time tuition ($21,500), mandatory fees ($480), and room and board ($7250). Full-time tuition and fees vary according to class time, course load, location, and program. Part-time tuition: $410 per credit. Part-time tuition and fees vary according to class time, course load, location, and program. *Required fees:* $115 per term part-time. *Room and board:* Room and board charges vary according to board plan and housing facility. *Waivers:* senior citizens and employees or children of employees.

Financial Aid *Average percent of need met:* 82%.

Applying *Options:* electronic application. *Application fee:* $25. *Required:* high school transcript, minimum 2.5 GPA. *Recommended:* 1 letter of recommendation, interview. *Application deadlines:* rolling (freshmen), rolling (transfers). *Notification:* continuous (freshmen), continuous (transfers).

Freshman Application Contact Mr. Ken Wuertzberger, Director of Admissions, University of Saint Mary, 4100 South Fourth Street, Leavenworth, KS 66048. *Phone:* 913-758-6118. *Toll-free phone:* 800-752-7043. *Fax:* 913-758-6140. *E-mail:* admiss@stmary.edu. *Web site:* http://www.stmary.edu/.

Washburn University
Topeka, Kansas

- **City-supported** comprehensive, founded 1865
- **Urban** 160-acre campus with easy access to Kansas City
- **Endowment** $110.0 million
- **Coed** 6,446 undergraduate students, 65% full-time, 59% women, 41% men
- **Noncompetitive** entrance level, 100% of applicants were admitted

Undergraduates 4,192 full-time, 2,254 part-time. Students come from 44 states and territories; 36 other countries; 7% are from out of state; 9% transferred in; 12% live on campus. *Retention:* 62% of full-time freshmen returned. **Freshmen** *Admission:* 1,817 applied, 1,817 admitted, 935 enrolled. *Average high school GPA:* 3.3. *Test scores:* ACT scores over 18: 87%; ACT scores over 24: 37%; ACT scores over 30: 4%.

Faculty *Total:* 558, 47% full-time, 60% with terminal degrees. *Student/faculty ratio:* 15:1.

Academics *Calendar:* semesters. *Degrees:* certificates, associate, bachelor's, master's, doctoral, and postbachelor's certificates. *Special study options:* academic remediation for entering students, adult/continuing education programs, advanced placement credit, cooperative education, distance learning, double majors, English as a second language, honors programs, independent study, internships, off-campus study, part-time degree program, services for LD students, student-designed majors, study abroad, summer session for credit. *ROTC:* Army (b), Navy (c), Air Force (c). *Unusual degree programs:* 3-2 engineering with University of Kansas, Kansas State University.

Computers on Campus 577 computers/terminals are available on campus for general student use. Students can access the following: campus intranet, computer help desk, free student e-mail accounts, online (class) grades, online (class) registration, online (class) schedules. Campuswide network is available. 100% of college-owned or -operated housing units are wired for high-speed Internet access. Wireless service is available via entire campus.

Student Life *Housing options:* coed. Campus housing is university owned. *Activities and organizations:* drama/theater group, student-run newspaper, television station, choral group, marching band, national fraternities, national sororities. *Campus security:* 24-hour emergency response devices and patrols, student patrols, late-night transport/escort service. *Student services:* health clinic, personal/psychological counseling, legal services.

Athletics Member NCAA. All Division II. *Intercollegiate sports:* baseball M(s), basketball M(s)/W(s), cheerleading M(s)/W(s), football M(s), golf M(s), soccer W(s), softball W(s), tennis M(s)/W(s), volleyball W(s). *Intramural sports:* badminton M/W, basketball M/W, crew M(c)/W(c), football M/W, golf M/W, rugby M(c), soccer M/W, softball M/W, table tennis M/W, tennis M/W, volleyball M/W.

Standardized Tests *Required:* ACT (for admission).

Costs (2011–12) *Tuition:* state resident $6480 full-time, $216 per credit hour part-time; nonresident $14,670 full-time, $489 per credit hour part-time. Full-time tuition and fees vary according to program. Part-time tuition and fees vary according to program. *Required fees:* $86 full-time, $21 per term part-time. *Room and board:* $6059; room only: $3399. Room and board charges vary according to board plan and housing facility. *Payment plan:* installment. *Waivers:* senior citizens and employees or children of employees.

Financial Aid Of all full-time matriculated undergraduates who enrolled in 2010, 3,612 applied for aid, 2,624 were judged to have need, 305 had their need fully met. 241 Federal Work-Study jobs (averaging $2698). 5 state and other part-time jobs (averaging $7877). In 2010, 582 non-need-based awards were made. *Average percent of need met:* 45%. *Average financial aid package:* $9078. *Average need-based loan:* $4298. *Average need-based gift aid:* $4938. *Average non-need-based aid:* $1861. *Average indebtedness upon graduation:* $17,017.

Applying *Options:* electronic application. *Application fee:* $20. *Required:* high school transcript. *Application deadlines:* 8/1 (freshmen), 8/1 (transfers). *Notification:* continuous (freshmen), continuous (transfers).

Freshman Application Contact Susan E. Smith, Interim Director of Admissions, Washburn University, 1700 SW College, MO 114, Topeka, KS 66621. *Phone:* 785-670-1030. *Toll-free phone:* 800-332-0291. *Fax:* 785-670-1113. *E-mail:* admissions@washburn.edu. *Web site:* http://www.washburn.edu/.

Wichita State University
Wichita, Kansas

- **State-supported** university, founded 1895, part of Kansas State Board of Education
- **Urban** 335-acre campus
- **Endowment** $224.4 million
- **Coed** 12,243 undergraduate students, 70% full-time, 54% women, 46% men
- **Noncompetitive** entrance level, 94% of applicants were admitted

Undergraduates 8,529 full-time, 3,714 part-time. Students come from 46 states and territories; 111 other countries; 4% are from out of state; 7% Black or African American, non-Hispanic/Latino; 7% Hispanic/Latino; 6% Asian, non-Hispanic/Latino; 0.1% Native Hawaiian or other Pacific Islander, non-Hispanic/Latino; 1% American Indian or Alaska Native, non-Hispanic/Latino; 2% Two or more races, non-Hispanic/Latino; 6% Race/ethnicity unknown; 6% international; 12% transferred in; 8% live on campus. *Retention:* 73% of full-time freshmen returned.

Freshmen *Admission:* 3,304 applied, 3,102 admitted, 1,366 enrolled. *Average high school GPA:* 3.39. *Test scores:* SAT critical reading scores over 500: 56%; SAT math scores over 500: 70%; ACT scores over 18: 93%; SAT critical reading scores over 600: 28%; SAT math scores over 600: 36%; ACT scores over 24: 46%; SAT critical reading scores over 700: 7%; SAT math scores over 700: 13%; ACT scores over 30: 6%.

Faculty *Total:* 507, 88% full-time, 76% with terminal degrees. *Student/faculty ratio:* 20:1.

Academics *Calendar:* semesters. *Degrees:* certificates, associate, bachelor's, master's, doctoral, post-master's, postbachelor's, and first professional certificates. *Special study options:* academic remediation for entering students, accelerated degree program, advanced placement credit, cooperative education, distance learning, double majors, English as a second language, freshman honors college, honors programs, independent study, internships, off-campus study, part-time degree program, services for LD students, study abroad, summer session for credit. *Unusual degree programs:* 3-2 nursing; accounting.

Computers on Campus 1,500 computers/terminals are available on campus for general student use. Students can access the following: computer help desk, free student e-mail accounts, online (class) grades, online (class) registration, online (class) schedules, online Blackboard. Campuswide network is available. 100% of college-owned or -operated housing units are wired for high-speed Internet access. Wireless service is available via entire campus.

Student Life *Housing:* on-campus residence required for freshman year. *Options:* coed, disabled students. Campus housing is university owned. *Activities and organizations:* drama/theater group, student-run newspaper, radio and television station, choral group, Golden Key Honor Society, WSU Green Group, Criminal Justice Society, Future Health Care Professionals, Students in Free Enterprise (SIFE), national fraternities, national sororities. *Campus security:* 24-hour emergency response devices and patrols, student patrols, late-night transport/escort service, controlled dormitory access, bicycle patrols by campus security. *Student services:* health clinic, personal/psychological counseling, women's center, legal services.

Athletics Member NCAA. All Division I. *Intercollegiate sports:* baseball M(s), basketball M(s)/W(s), bowling M(s)/W(s), cheerleading M/W, cross-country running M(s)/W(s), golf M(s)/W(s), ice hockey M(c), rock climbing M(c)/W(c), soccer M(c), softball W(s), table tennis M(c)/W(c), tennis M(s)/W(s), track and field M(s)/W(s), volleyball M(c)/W(s), wrestling M(c)/W(c). *Intramural sports:* badminton M/W, basketball M/W, bowling M/W, crew M/W, football M/W, golf M/W, racquetball M/W, soccer M/W, softball M/W, swimming and diving M/W, table tennis M/W, tennis M/W, track and field M/W, volleyball M/W.

Standardized Tests *Required for some:* SAT or ACT (for admission). *Recommended:* SAT or ACT (for admission).

Costs (2011–12) *Tuition:* state resident $5005 full-time, $167 per credit hour part-time; nonresident $13,040 full-time, $435 per credit hour part-time. Full-time tuition and fees vary according to course load, degree level, and student level. Part-time tuition and fees vary according to course load, degree level, and student level. *Required fees:* $1184 full-time. *Room and board:* $6350. Room and board charges vary according to board plan and housing facility. *Payment plan:* installment. *Waivers:* senior citizens and employees or children of employees.

Financial Aid Of all full-time matriculated undergraduates who enrolled in 2010, 6,527 applied for aid, 3,703 were judged to have need, 2,538 had their need fully met. 129 Federal Work-Study jobs (averaging $3310). In 2010, 1456 non-need-based awards were made. *Average percent of need met:* 51%. *Average financial aid package:* $11,057. *Average need-based loan:* $4755. *Average need-based gift aid:* $4540. *Average non-need-based aid:* $2012. *Average indebtedness upon graduation:* $21,738.

Applying *Options:* electronic application, deferred entrance. *Application fee:* $30. *Required for some:* minimum 2.5 GPA, rank in upper one-third of high

school class or complete the pre-college curriculum with a minimum 2.0 GPA (2.5 GPA for nonresidents). *Recommended:* high school transcript. *Application deadlines:* rolling (freshmen), rolling (transfers). *Notification:* continuous (freshmen), continuous (transfers).

Freshman Application Contact Wichita State University, 1845 North Fairmount, Wichita, KS 67260. *Phone:* 316-978-3085. *Toll-free phone:* 800-362-2594. *Web site:* http://www.wichita.edu/.

KENTUCKY

Alice Lloyd College
Pippa Passes, Kentucky

Freshman Application Contact Mr. Ronnie Collins, Director of Admissions, Alice Lloyd College, 100 Purpose Road, Pippa Passes, KY 41844. *Phone:* 606-368-6036. *Toll-free phone:* 888-280-4252. *Fax:* 606-368-6215. *E-mail:* ronniecollins@alc.edu. *Web site:* http://www.alc.edu/.

Asbury University
Wilmore, Kentucky

- **Independent nondenominational** comprehensive, founded 1890
- **Small-town** 400-acre campus with easy access to Lexington
- **Endowment** $33.8 million
- **Coed** 1,452 undergraduate students, 91% full-time, 62% women, 38% men
- **Moderately difficult** entrance level, 63% of applicants were admitted

Undergraduates 1,320 full-time, 132 part-time. Students come from 44 states and territories; 15 other countries; 50% are from out of state; 3% Black or African American, non-Hispanic/Latino; 3% Hispanic/Latino; 0.7% Asian, non-Hispanic/Latino; 0.1% Native Hawaiian or other Pacific Islander, non-Hispanic/Latino; 0.4% American Indian or Alaska Native, non-Hispanic/Latino; 2% Two or more races, non-Hispanic/Latino; 2% Race/ethnicity unknown; 1% international; 4% transferred in; 80% live on campus. *Retention:* 80% of full-time freshmen returned.

Freshmen *Admission:* 1,427 applied, 899 admitted, 308 enrolled. *Average high school GPA:* 3.63. *Test scores:* SAT critical reading scores over 500: 79%; SAT math scores over 500: 69%; ACT scores over 18: 97%; SAT critical reading scores over 600: 43%; SAT math scores over 600: 26%; ACT scores over 24: 50%; SAT critical reading scores over 700: 5%; SAT math scores over 700: 5%; ACT scores over 30: 9%.

Faculty *Total:* 154, 56% full-time, 56% with terminal degrees. *Student/faculty ratio:* 14:1.

Academics *Calendar:* semesters. *Degrees:* associate, bachelor's, and master's. *Special study options:* adult/continuing education programs, advanced placement credit, distance learning, double majors, off-campus study, study abroad, summer session for credit. *ROTC:* Army (c), Air Force (c). *Unusual degree programs:* 3-2 engineering with University of Kentucky.

Computers on Campus 200 computers/terminals are available on campus for general student use. Students can access the following: campus intranet, computer help desk, free student e-mail accounts, online (class) grades, online (class) registration, online (class) schedules. Campuswide network is available. 100% of college-owned or -operated housing units are wired for high-speed Internet access. Wireless service is available via classrooms, computer centers, computer labs, dorm rooms, learning centers, libraries, student centers.

Student Life *Housing:* on-campus residence required through senior year. *Options:* men-only, women-only. Campus housing is university owned. Freshman campus housing is guaranteed. *Activities and organizations:* drama/theater group, student-run newspaper, radio and television station, choral group, Fellowship of Christian Athletes, Impact (community service), Christian Service Association, ministry teams, Student-Faculty Council. *Campus security:* 24-hour emergency response devices, late-night transport/escort service, controlled dormitory access, late night security personnel. *Student services:* health clinic, personal/psychological counseling.

Athletics Member NAIA, NCCAA. *Intercollegiate sports:* baseball M(s), basketball M(s)/W(s), cross-country running M(s)/W(s), golf M(s)/W(s), soccer M(s)/W(s), softball W(s), swimming and diving M(s)/W(s), tennis M(s)/W(s), volleyball W(s). *Intramural sports:* basketball M/W, football M/W, golf M/W, racquetball M/W, soccer M/W, softball M/W, ultimate Frisbee M/W, volleyball M/W.

Standardized Tests *Required:* SAT or ACT (for admission). *Required for some:* ACT (for admission).

Costs (2012–13) *Comprehensive fee:* $31,103 includes full-time tuition ($25,140), mandatory fees ($171), and room and board ($5792). Full-time tuition and fees vary according to course load, location, and program. Part-time

tuition: $966 per credit. Part-time tuition and fees vary according to course load, location, and program. *College room only:* $3352. Room and board charges vary according to board plan, housing facility, and location. *Payment plan:* installment. *Waivers:* senior citizens and employees or children of employees.

Financial Aid Of all full-time matriculated undergraduates who enrolled in 2011, 1,027 applied for aid, 900 were judged to have need, 206 had their need fully met. 623 Federal Work-Study jobs (averaging $1636). In 2011, 123 non-need-based awards were made. *Average percent of need met:* 81%. *Average financial aid package:* $19,493. *Average need-based loan:* $3997. *Average need-based gift aid:* $12,605. *Average non-need-based aid:* $11,277. *Average indebtedness upon graduation:* $27,023.

Applying *Options:* electronic application, early admission, deferred entrance. *Required:* essay or personal statement, high school transcript, minimum 2.5 GPA, 1 letter of recommendation. *Required for some:* interview. *Application deadlines:* rolling (freshmen), rolling (transfers). *Notification:* continuous (freshmen), continuous (transfers).

Freshman Application Contact Mrs. Lisa D. Harper, Director of Admissions, Asbury University, One Macklem Drive, Wilmore, KY 40390. *Phone:* 800-888-1818. *Toll-free phone:* 800-888-1818. *E-mail:* admissions@asbury.edu. *Web site:* http://www.asbury.edu/.

Beckfield College
Florence, Kentucky

Freshman Application Contact Mrs. Leah Boerger, Director of Admissions, Beckfield College, 16 Spiral Drive, Florence, KY 41042. *Phone:* 859-371-9393. *E-mail:* lboerger@beckfield.edu. *Web site:* http://www.beckfield.edu/.

Bellarmine University
Louisville, Kentucky

- **Independent Roman Catholic** comprehensive, founded 1950
- **Suburban** 144-acre campus with easy access to Louisville
- **Coed** 2,640 undergraduate students, 87% full-time, 66% women, 34% men
- **Moderately difficult** entrance level, 52% of applicants were admitted

Undergraduates 2,289 full-time, 351 part-time. Students come from 35 states and territories; 29 other countries; 33% are from out of state; 0.2% Black or African American, non-Hispanic/Latino; 4% Hispanic/Latino; 4% Asian, non-Hispanic/Latino; 2% Native Hawaiian or other Pacific Islander, non-Hispanic/Latino; 0.2% American Indian or Alaska Native, non-Hispanic/Latino; 82% Two or more races, non-Hispanic/Latino; 4% Race/ethnicity unknown; 2% international; 3% transferred in; 44% live on campus. *Retention:* 78% of full-time freshmen returned.

Freshmen *Admission:* 6,955 applied, 3,604 admitted, 601 enrolled. *Average high school GPA:* 3.5. *Test scores:* SAT critical reading scores over 500: 71%; SAT math scores over 500: 73%; ACT scores over 18: 100%; SAT critical reading scores over 600: 23%; SAT math scores over 600: 26%; ACT scores over 24: 58%; SAT critical reading scores over 700: 5%; SAT math scores over 700: 1%; ACT scores over 30: 7%.

Faculty *Total:* 363, 41% full-time, 51% with terminal degrees. *Student/faculty ratio:* 12:1.

Academics *Calendar:* semesters. *Degrees:* bachelor's, master's, doctoral, and postbachelor's certificates. *Special study options:* adult/continuing education programs, part-time degree program. *ROTC:* Army (c), Air Force (c).

Computers on Campus 434 computers/terminals and 434 ports are available on campus for general student use. Students can access the following: campus intranet, computer help desk, free student e-mail accounts, online (class) grades, online (class) registration, online (class) schedules. Campuswide network is available. 100% of college-owned or -operated housing units are wired for high-speed Internet access. Wireless service is available via classrooms, computer centers, computer labs, dorm rooms, learning centers, libraries, student centers.

Student Life *Housing:* on-campus residence required through junior year. *Options:* coed, men-only, women-only, disabled students. Campus housing is university owned. Freshman campus housing is guaranteed. *Activities and organizations:* student government, Bellarmine Activities Council, Knights Nation, Fellowship of Christian Athletes, Delta Sigma Pi. *Campus security:* 24-hour emergency response devices and patrols, student patrols, late-night transport/escort service, controlled dormitory access, 24-hour locked residence hall entrances, security cameras.

Athletics Member NCAA. All Division II except lacrosse (Division I). *Intercollegiate sports:* baseball M(s), basketball M(s)/W(s), bowling M/W(s), cross-country running M(s)/W(s), field hockey W(s), golf M(s)/W(s), lacrosse M(s), soccer M(s)/W(s), softball W(s), swimming and diving M(c)/W(c), tennis M(s)/W(s), track and field M(s)/W(s), volleyball W(s). *Intramural sports:* basketball M/W, bowling M/W, football M/W, golf M/W, soccer M/W, softball

M/W, table tennis M/W, tennis M/W, ultimate Frisbee M/W, volleyball M/W, weight lifting M/W.

Standardized Tests *Required:* SAT or ACT (for admission).

Costs (2011–12) *One-time required fee:* $400. *Comprehensive fee:* $41,700 includes full-time tuition ($30,900), mandatory fees ($1240), and room and board ($9560). Part-time tuition: $730 per credit hour. *Required fees:* $45 per course part-time. *College room only:* $5760. Room and board charges vary according to board plan and housing facility. *Payment plan:* installment. *Waivers:* senior citizens and employees or children of employees.

Financial Aid Of all full-time matriculated undergraduates who enrolled in 2011, 1,879 applied for aid, 1,728 were judged to have need, 195 had their need fully met. 273 Federal Work-Study jobs (averaging $1697). In 2011, 484 non-need-based awards were made. *Average percent of need met:* 54%. *Average financial aid package:* $20,705. *Average need-based loan:* $3247. *Average need-based gift aid:* $17,758. *Average non-need-based aid:* $17,677. *Average indebtedness upon graduation:* $26,212.

Applying *Options:* electronic application, early action. *Application fee:* $25. *Required:* high school transcript, minimum 2.5 GPA, 1 letter of recommendation. *Required for some:* essay or personal statement. *Recommended:* interview. *Application deadlines:* 8/15 (freshmen), rolling (transfers), 11/1 (early action). *Notification:* continuous (freshmen), continuous (transfers), 11/15 (early action).

Freshman Application Contact Mr. Timothy A. Sturgeon, Dean of Admission, Bellarmine University, 2001 Newburg Road, Louisville, KY 40205-0671. *Phone:* 502-272-8131. *Toll-free phone:* 800-274-4723 Ext. 8131. *E-mail:* admissions@bellarmine.edu. *Web site:* http://www.bellarmine.edu/.

Berea College

Berea, Kentucky

- **Independent** 4-year, founded 1855
- **Small-town** 140-acre campus
- **Endowment** $978.7 million
- **Coed** 1,661 undergraduate students, 97% full-time, 57% women, 43% men
- **Moderately difficult** entrance level, 12% of applicants were admitted

Undergraduates 1,619 full-time, 42 part-time. Students come from 46 states and territories; 58 other countries; 56% are from out of state; 15% Black or African American, non-Hispanic/Latino; 3% Hispanic/Latino; 1% Asian, non-Hispanic/Latino; 0.1% Native Hawaiian or other Pacific Islander, non-Hispanic/Latino; 0.4% American Indian or Alaska Native, non-Hispanic/Latino; 5% Two or more races, non-Hispanic/Latino; 3% Race/ethnicity unknown; 7% international; 6% transferred in; 86% live on campus. *Retention:* 79% of full-time freshmen returned.

Freshmen *Admission:* 4,707 applied, 586 admitted, 418 enrolled. *Average high school GPA:* 3.4. *Test scores:* SAT critical reading scores over 500: 74%; SAT math scores over 500: 70%; SAT writing scores over 500: 80%; ACT scores over 18: 98%; SAT critical reading scores over 600: 42%; SAT math scores over 600: 23%; SAT writing scores over 600: 38%; ACT scores over 24: 63%; SAT critical reading scores over 700: 10%; SAT math scores over 700: 5%; SAT writing scores over 700: 4%; ACT scores over 30: 9%.

Faculty *Total:* 158, 75% full-time, 73% with terminal degrees. *Student/faculty ratio:* 11:1.

Academics *Calendar:* 4-1-4. *Degree:* bachelor's. *Special study options:* academic remediation for entering students, advanced placement credit, double majors, English as a second language, honors programs, independent study, internships, off-campus study, services for LD students, student-designed majors, study abroad, summer session for credit. *Unusual degree programs:* 3-2 engineering with Washington University in St. Louis, University of Kentucky.

Computers on Campus 7,000 ports are available on campus for general student use. Students can access the following: campus intranet, computer help desk, free student e-mail accounts, online (class) grades, online (class) registration, online (class) schedules. Campuswide network is available. 100% of college-owned or -operated housing units are wired for high-speed Internet access. Wireless service is available via classrooms, learning centers, libraries, student centers.

Student Life *Housing:* on-campus residence required through senior year. *Options:* men-only, women-only. Campus housing is university owned. Freshman campus housing is guaranteed. *Activities and organizations:* drama/theater group, student-run newspaper, choral group, Campus Activities Board, Cosmopolitan Club, CELTS (Center for Excellence in Learning through Service), Black Cultural Center, African Student Association. *Campus security:* 24-hour emergency response devices and patrols, late-night transport/escort service, controlled dormitory access, crime prevention programs. *Student services:* health clinic, personal/psychological counseling, women's center.

Athletics Member NAIA. *Intercollegiate sports:* baseball M, basketball M/W, cross-country running M/W, golf M, soccer M/W, softball W, swimming and diving M/W, tennis M/W, track and field M/W, volleyball W. *Intramural sports:* basketball M/W, football M/W, racquetball M/W, soccer M/W, softball M/W, ultimate Frisbee M/W, volleyball M/W.

Standardized Tests *Required:* SAT or ACT (for admission).

Costs (2011–12) *Comprehensive fee:* includes mandatory fees ($910) and room and board ($5792). Financial aid is provided to all students for tuition costs.

Financial Aid Of all full-time matriculated undergraduates who enrolled in 2011, 1,612 applied for aid, 1,612 were judged to have need. *Average percent of need met:* 92%. *Average financial aid package:* $28,192. *Average need-based loan:* $1562. *Average need-based gift aid:* $25,905. *Average indebtedness upon graduation:* $7661. *Financial aid deadline:* 5/1.

Applying *Options:* electronic application. *Required:* essay or personal statement, high school transcript, interview, financial aid application. *Recommended:* 2 letters of recommendation. *Application deadlines:* 4/30 (freshmen), rolling (transfers). *Notification:* continuous (freshmen), continuous (transfers).

Freshman Application Contact Mr. Luke Hodson, Director of Admissions/Operations, Berea College, CPO 2220, Berea, KY 40404. *Phone:* 859-985-3500. *Toll-free phone:* 800-326-5948. *Fax:* 859-985-3512. *E-mail:* admissions@berea.edu. *Web site:* http://www.berea.edu/.

Brescia University

Owensboro, Kentucky

- **Independent Roman Catholic** comprehensive, founded 1950
- **Urban** 9-acre campus
- **Endowment** $10.3 million
- **Coed** 733 undergraduate students, 74% full-time, 64% women, 36% men
- **Moderately difficult** entrance level, 48% of applicants were admitted

Undergraduates 546 full-time, 187 part-time. Students come from 41 states and territories; 6 other countries; 37% are from out of state; 11% Black or African American, non-Hispanic/Latino; 3% Hispanic/Latino; 0.1% Asian, non-Hispanic/Latino; 0.3% American Indian or Alaska Native, non-Hispanic/Latino; 11% Race/ethnicity unknown; 2% international; 15% transferred in; 41% live on campus. *Retention:* 57% of full-time freshmen returned.

Freshmen *Admission:* 2,437 applied, 1,167 admitted, 150 enrolled. *Average high school GPA:* 3.02. *Test scores:* SAT math scores over 500: 20%; ACT scores over 18: 87%; ACT scores over 24: 29%; ACT scores over 30: 2%.

Faculty *Total:* 65, 57% full-time, 43% with terminal degrees. *Student/faculty ratio:* 13:1.

Academics *Calendar:* semesters. *Degrees:* certificates, associate, bachelor's, master's, and postbachelor's certificates. *Special study options:* academic remediation for entering students, adult/continuing education programs, advanced placement credit, distance learning, double majors, honors programs, independent study, internships, off-campus study, part-time degree program, services for LD students, student-designed majors, study abroad, summer session for credit.

Computers on Campus 90 computers/terminals and 90 ports are available on campus for general student use. Students can access the following: computer help desk, free student e-mail accounts, online (class) grades, online (class) schedules. Campuswide network is available. 100% of college-owned or -operated housing units are wired for high-speed Internet access. Wireless service is available via entire campus.

Student Life *Housing:* on-campus residence required for freshman year. *Options:* coed, men-only, women-only. Campus housing is university owned. *Activities and organizations:* drama/theater group, student-run newspaper, choral group, Fellowship of Christian Athletes, Social Work Club, Ichabod Society, Habitat for Humanity, Spanish Club. *Campus security:* 24-hour emergency response devices, late-night transport/escort service, controlled dormitory access. *Student services:* personal/psychological counseling, women's center.

Athletics Member NAIA. *Intercollegiate sports:* baseball M(s), basketball M(s)/W(s), cross-country running M(s)/W(s), golf M(s)/W(s), soccer M(s)/W(s), softball W(s), track and field M/W(s), volleyball W(s). *Intramural sports:* basketball M/W, soccer M/W, table tennis M/W, volleyball M/W.

Standardized Tests *Required:* SAT or ACT (for admission).

Costs (2011–12) *One-time required fee:* $120. *Comprehensive fee:* $26,140 includes full-time tuition ($17,700), mandatory fees ($440), and room and board ($8000). Full-time tuition and fees vary according to class time, course load, and degree level. Part-time tuition: $525 per credit hour. Part-time tuition and fees vary according to class time, course load, and degree level. *Room and board:* Room and board charges vary according to board plan and housing facility. *Payment plan:* installment. *Waivers:* employees or children of employees.

Financial Aid Of all full-time matriculated undergraduates who enrolled in 2009, 609 applied for aid, 581 were judged to have need. 64 Federal Work-

Study jobs (averaging $1200). 15 state and other part-time jobs (averaging $2500). *Average indebtedness upon graduation:* $18,638.

Applying *Options:* electronic application, deferred entrance. *Application fee:* $25. *Required:* high school transcript, GPA coincides with test scores. *Required for some:* essay or personal statement, 1 letter of recommendation, interview. *Application deadlines:* rolling (freshmen), rolling (out-of-state freshmen), rolling (transfers). *Notification:* continuous (freshmen), continuous (out-of-state freshmen), continuous (transfers).

Freshman Application Contact Brescia University, 717 Frederica Street, Owensboro, KY 42301-3023. *Phone:* 270-686-4241 Ext. 241. *Toll-free phone:* 877-273-7242. *Web site:* http://www.brescia.edu/.

Brown Mackie College–Louisville
Louisville, Kentucky

- **Proprietary** primarily 2-year, founded 1972, part of Education Management Corporation
- **Suburban** campus
- **Coed**

Academics *Calendar:* quarters. *Degrees:* certificates, diplomas, associate, and bachelor's.

Costs (2011–12) *Tuition:* Tuition varies by program. Students should contact Brown Mackie College for tuition information.

Freshman Application Contact Brown Mackie College–Louisville, 3605 Fern Valley Road, Louisville, KY 40219. *Phone:* 502-968-7191. *Toll-free phone:* 800-999-7387. *Web site:* http://www.brownmackie.edu/louisville/.

See page 1206 for the College Close-Up.

Brown Mackie College–Northern Kentucky
Fort Mitchell, Kentucky

- **Proprietary** primarily 2-year, founded 1927, part of Education Management Corporation
- **Suburban** campus
- **Coed**

Academics *Calendar:* quarters. *Degrees:* certificates, diplomas, associate, and bachelor's.

Costs (2011–12) *Tuition:* Tuition varies by program. Students should contact Brown Mackie College for tuition information.

Freshman Application Contact Brown Mackie College–Northern Kentucky, 309 Buttermilk Pike, Fort Mitchell, KY 41017-2191. *Phone:* 859-341-5627. *Toll-free phone:* 800-888-1445. *Web site:* http://www.brownmackie.edu/northernkentucky/.

See page 1216 for the College Close-Up.

Campbellsville University
Campbellsville, Kentucky

- **Independent** comprehensive, founded 1906, affiliated with Kentucky Baptist Convention
- **Small-town** 90-acre campus
- **Endowment** $9.9 million
- **Coed** 3,074 undergraduate students, 61% full-time, 58% women, 42% men
- **Moderately difficult** entrance level, 63% of applicants were admitted

Undergraduates 1,882 full-time, 1,192 part-time. Students come from 34 states and territories; 36 other countries; 12% are from out of state; 10% Black or African American, non-Hispanic/Latino; 1% Hispanic/Latino; 0.4% Asian, non-Hispanic/Latino; 0.1% Native Hawaiian or other Pacific Islander, non-Hispanic/Latino; 0.2% American Indian or Alaska Native, non-Hispanic/Latino; 0.5% Two or more races, non-Hispanic/Latino; 4% Race/ethnicity unknown; 5% international; 8% transferred in; 58% live on campus. *Retention:* 65% of full-time freshmen returned.

Freshmen *Admission:* 2,279 applied, 1,442 admitted, 521 enrolled. *Average high school GPA:* 3.19. *Test scores:* SAT critical reading scores over 500: 47%; SAT math scores over 500: 47%; SAT writing scores over 500: 29%; ACT scores over 18: 78%; SAT critical reading scores over 600: 8%; SAT math scores over 600: 22%; SAT writing scores over 600: 8%; ACT scores over 24: 24%; SAT math scores over 700: 4%; SAT writing scores over 700: 4%; ACT scores over 30: 3%.

Faculty *Total:* 309, 46% full-time, 29% with terminal degrees. *Student/faculty ratio:* 13:1.

Academics *Calendar:* semesters. *Degrees:* certificates, associate, bachelor's, master's, and postbachelor's certificates. *Special study options:* academic remediation for entering students, accelerated degree program, adult/continu-

ing education programs, advanced placement credit, distance learning, double majors, English as a second language, honors programs, independent study, internships, off-campus study, part-time degree program, study abroad, summer session for credit. *ROTC:* Army (c). *Unusual degree programs:* 3-2 engineering with University of Kentucky.

Computers on Campus 190 computers/terminals are available on campus for general student use. Students can access the following: campus intranet, computer help desk, free student e-mail accounts, online (class) grades, online (class) registration, online (class) schedules. Campuswide network is available.

Student Life *Housing:* on-campus residence required through sophomore year. *Options:* men-only, women-only. Campus housing is university owned. Freshman campus housing is guaranteed. *Activities and organizations:* drama/theater group, student-run newspaper, radio and television station, choral group, marching band, Student Government Association, Baptist Student Union, Phi Beta Lambda, African-American Leadership League, Fellowship of Christian Athletes. *Campus security:* 24-hour emergency response devices and patrols, student patrols, late-night transport/escort service, controlled dormitory access. *Student services:* health clinic, personal/psychological counseling.

Athletics Member NAIA. *Intercollegiate sports:* baseball M(s), basketball M(s)/W(s), bowling M(s)/W(s), cheerleading M(s)/W(s), cross-country running M(s)/W(s), football M(s), golf M(s)/W(s), soccer M(s)/W(s), softball W(s), swimming and diving M(s)/W(s), tennis M(s)/W(s), track and field M(s)/W(s), volleyball W(s), wrestling M(s)/W(s). *Intramural sports:* basketball M/W, bowling M/W, football M/W, racquetball M/W, soccer M/W, swimming and diving M/W, table tennis M/W, tennis M/W, volleyball M/W, weight lifting M/W.

Standardized Tests *Required:* SAT or ACT (for admission).

Costs (2012–13) *Comprehensive fee:* $28,720 includes full-time tuition ($21,100), mandatory fees ($500), and room and board ($7120). Part-time tuition: $880 per credit. *Room and board:* Room and board charges vary according to housing facility. *Payment plan:* installment. *Waivers:* adult students, senior citizens, and employees or children of employees.

Financial Aid Of all full-time matriculated undergraduates who enrolled in 2011, 1,655 applied for aid, 1,575 were judged to have need, 178 had their need fully met. 375 Federal Work-Study jobs (averaging $1675). 32 state and other part-time jobs (averaging $1650). In 2011, 101 non-need-based awards were made. *Average percent of need met:* 72%. *Average financial aid package:* $16,981. *Average need-based loan:* $3726. *Average need-based gift aid:* $13,923. *Average non-need-based aid:* $7358. *Average indebtedness upon graduation:* $16,432.

Applying *Options:* electronic application, deferred entrance. *Application fee:* $20. *Required:* high school transcript, minimum 2.0 GPA. *Recommended:* essay or personal statement, minimum 3.0 GPA, interview. *Application deadlines:* rolling (freshmen), rolling (transfers). *Notification:* continuous (freshmen), continuous (transfers).

Freshman Application Contact Mr. David Walters, Vice President for Admissions and Student Services, Campbellsville University, 1 University Drive, Campbellsville, KY 42718-2799. *Phone:* 270-789-5220 Ext. 5007. *Toll-free phone:* 800-264-6014. *Fax:* 270-789-5071. *E-mail:* admissions@campbellsville.edu. *Web site:* http://www.campbellsville.edu/.

Centre College
Danville, Kentucky

- **Independent** 4-year, founded 1819, affiliated with Presbyterian Church (U.S.A.)
- **Small-town** 152-acre campus
- **Endowment** $181.4 million
- **Coed** 1,309 undergraduate students, 100% full-time, 53% women, 47% men
- **Very difficult** entrance level, 70% of applicants were admitted

Undergraduates 1,309 full-time. Students come from 44 states and territories; 10 other countries; 40% are from out of state; 4% Black or African American, non-Hispanic/Latino; 3% Hispanic/Latino; 2% Asian, non-Hispanic/Latino; 2% Two or more races, non-Hispanic/Latino; 0.1% Race/ethnicity unknown; 3% international; 1% transferred in; 97% live on campus. *Retention:* 91% of full-time freshmen returned.

Freshmen *Admission:* 2,413 applied, 1,700 admitted, 374 enrolled. *Average high school GPA:* 3.7. *Test scores:* SAT critical reading scores over 500: 92%; SAT math scores over 500: 90%; SAT writing scores over 500: 91%; ACT scores over 18: 100%; SAT critical reading scores over 600: 61%; SAT math scores over 600: 62%; SAT writing scores over 600: 65%; ACT scores over 24: 91%; SAT critical reading scores over 700: 22%; SAT math scores over 700: 17%; SAT writing scores over 700: 17%; ACT scores over 30: 34%.

Faculty *Total:* 141, 77% full-time, 86% with terminal degrees. *Student/faculty ratio:* 11:1.

Academics *Calendar:* 4-1-4. *Degree:* bachelor's. *Special study options:* advanced placement credit, cooperative education, double majors, honors pro-

grams, independent study, internships, off-campus study, services for LD students, student-designed majors, study abroad. *ROTC:* Army (c), Air Force (c). *Unusual degree programs:* 3-2 engineering with Washington University in St. Louis, Columbia University, Vanderbilt University, University of Kentucky.

Computers on Campus 450 computers/terminals and 2,000 ports are available on campus for general student use. Students can access the following: campus intranet, computer help desk, free student e-mail accounts, online (class) grades, online (class) registration, online (class) schedules. Campus-wide network is available. 100% of college-owned or -operated housing units are wired for high-speed Internet access. Wireless service is available via classrooms, computer centers, computer labs, dorm rooms, learning centers, libraries, student centers.

Student Life *Housing:* on-campus residence required through senior year. *Options:* coed, men-only, disabled students. Campus housing is university owned. Freshman campus housing is guaranteed. *Activities and organizations:* drama/theater group, student-run newspaper, radio and television station, choral group, Student Government Association, campus newspaper, admission tour guides and hosts, Christian fellowship group, Diversity Student Union, national fraternities, national sororities. *Campus security:* 24-hour emergency response devices and patrols, late-night transport/escort service, controlled dormitory access. *Student services:* health clinic, personal/psychological counseling.

Athletics Member NCAA. All Division III. *Intercollegiate sports:* baseball M, basketball M/W, cheerleading W, cross-country running M/W, field hockey W, football M, golf M/W, lacrosse M/W, soccer M/W, softball W, swimming and diving M/W, tennis M/W, track and field M/W, volleyball W. *Intramural sports:* badminton M/W, basketball M/W, bowling M/W, equestrian sports M/W, football M/W, golf M/W, racquetball M/W, soccer M/W, softball M/W, swimming and diving M/W, table tennis M/W, tennis M/W, track and field M/W, ultimate Frisbee M/W, volleyball M/W, weight lifting M/W, wrestling M.

Standardized Tests *Required:* SAT or ACT (for admission).

Costs (2011–12) *Comprehensive fee:* $42,500. *Payment plan:* installment. *Waivers:* employees or children of employees.

Financial Aid Of all full-time matriculated undergraduates who enrolled in 2011, 974 applied for aid, 834 were judged to have need, 261 had their need fully met. 374 Federal Work-Study jobs (averaging $1560). 5 state and other part-time jobs (averaging $2250). In 2011, 440 non-need-based awards were made. *Average percent of need met:* 85%. *Average financial aid package:* $26,306. *Average need-based loan:* $4329. *Average need-based gift aid:* $23,011. *Average non-need-based aid:* $16,280. *Average indebtedness upon graduation:* $26,700. *Financial aid deadline:* 3/1.

Applying *Options:* electronic application, early admission, early action, deferred entrance. *Application fee:* $40. *Required:* essay or personal statement, high school transcript, 1 letter of recommendation. *Recommended:* interview. *Application deadlines:* 2/1 (freshmen), rolling (transfers), 12/1 (early action). *Notification:* 3/15 (freshmen), 1/15 (early action).

Freshman Application Contact Mr. Bob Nesmith, Director of Admissions, Centre College, 600 West Walnut Street, Danville, KY 40422-1394. *Phone:* 859-238-5350. *Toll-free phone:* 800-423-6236. *Fax:* 859-238-5373. *E-mail:* admission@centre.edu. *Web site:* http://www.centre.edu/.

Clear Creek Baptist Bible College
Pineville, Kentucky

- **Independent Southern Baptist** 4-year, founded 1926
- **Rural** 700-acre campus
- **Coed, primarily men** 172 undergraduate students, 62% full-time, 25% women, 75% men
- **Noncompetitive** entrance level, 88% of applicants were admitted

Undergraduates 106 full-time, 66 part-time. *Retention:* 88% of full-time freshmen returned.

Freshmen *Admission:* 52 applied, 46 admitted.

Faculty *Total:* 16, 50% full-time. *Student/faculty ratio:* 13:1.

Academics *Calendar:* semesters. *Degrees:* certificates, diplomas, associate, and bachelor's. *Special study options:* part-time degree program, summer session for credit.

Computers on Campus 15 computers/terminals are available on campus for general student use. Campuswide network is available.

Student Life *Housing options:* coed, men-only, women-only. Campus housing is university owned. *Activities and organizations:* choral group. *Campus security:* 24-hour emergency response devices, student patrols. *Student services:* health clinic, personal/psychological counseling.

Athletics *Intramural sports:* basketball M/W, table tennis M/W, tennis M/W, volleyball M/W.

Costs (2012–13) *Comprehensive fee:* $8840 includes full-time tuition ($5220), mandatory fees ($150), and room and board ($3470). *College room only:* $1870.

Financial Aid Of all full-time matriculated undergraduates who enrolled in 2011, 118 applied for aid, 106 were judged to have need, 8 had their need fully met. 39 Federal Work-Study jobs (averaging $976). In 2011, 13 non-need-based awards were made. *Average percent of need met:* 71%. *Average financial aid package:* $7263. *Average need-based gift aid:* $7263. *Average non-need-based aid:* $1175.

Applying *Options:* electronic application, deferred entrance. *Application fee:* $50. *Required:* essay or personal statement, 4 letters of recommendation. *Recommended:* high school transcript, interview. *Application deadlines:* 7/15 (freshmen), 7/15 (transfers). *Notification:* continuous (freshmen), continuous (transfers).

Freshman Application Contact Mr. Billy Howell, Director of Admissions, Clear Creek Baptist Bible College, 300 Clear Creek Road, Pineville, KY 40977. *Phone:* 606-337-3196 Ext. 103. *Fax:* 606-337-1631. *E-mail:* bhowell@ccbbc.edu. *Web site:* http://www.ccbbc.edu/.

Daymar College
Paducah, Kentucky

Freshman Application Contact Daymar College, 509 South 30th Street, Paducah, KY 42001. *Phone:* 270-444-9950. *Toll-free phone:* 877-258-7796. *Web site:* http://www.daymarcollege.edu/.

DeVry University
Louisville, Kentucky

Freshman Application Contact DeVry University, 10172 Linn Station Road, Suite 300, Louisville, KY 40223. *Toll-free phone:* 866-338-7941. *Web site:* http://www.devry.edu/.

Eastern Kentucky University
Richmond, Kentucky

- **State-supported** comprehensive, founded 1906
- **Small-town** 500-acre campus with easy access to Lexington
- **Endowment** $55.6 million
- **Coed** 13,902 undergraduate students, 81% full-time, 56% women, 44% men
- **Noncompetitive** entrance level, 66% of applicants were admitted

Undergraduates 11,288 full-time, 2,614 part-time. Students come from 46 states and territories; 38 other countries; 13% are from out of state; 6% Black or African American, non-Hispanic/Latino; 2% Hispanic/Latino; 1% Asian, non-Hispanic/Latino; 0.2% Native Hawaiian or other Pacific Islander, non-Hispanic/Latino; 0.4% American Indian or Alaska Native, non-Hispanic/Latino; 2% Two or more races, non-Hispanic/Latino; 1% international; 9% transferred in. *Retention:* 62% of full-time freshmen returned.

Freshmen *Admission:* 9,461 applied, 6,272 admitted, 2,421 enrolled.

Faculty *Total:* 1,114, 61% full-time, 42% with terminal degrees. *Student/faculty ratio:* 15:1.

Academics *Calendar:* semesters. *Degrees:* associate, bachelor's, master's, doctoral, post-master's, and postbachelor's certificates. *Special study options:* academic remediation for entering students, accelerated degree program, adult/continuing education programs, advanced placement credit, cooperative education, distance learning, double majors, English as a second language, external degree program, honors programs, independent study, internships, part-time degree program, services for LD students, student-designed majors, study abroad, summer session for credit. *ROTC:* Army (b), Air Force (c). *Unusual degree programs:* 3-2 engineering with University of Kentucky, Auburn University.

Computers on Campus 1,200 computers/terminals are available on campus for general student use. Students can access the following: online (class) registration. Campuswide network is available.

Student Life *Housing options:* coed, men-only, women-only. Campus housing is university owned. Freshman campus housing is guaranteed. *Activities and organizations:* drama/theater group, student-run newspaper, radio station, choral group, marching band, Honor Society, Regular Society, national fraternities, national sororities. *Campus security:* 24-hour emergency response devices and patrols, student patrols, late-night transport/escort service, controlled dormitory access. *Student services:* health clinic, personal/psychological counseling.

Athletics Member NCAA. All Division I. *Intercollegiate sports:* baseball M(s), basketball M(s)/W(s), cheerleading M/W, cross-country running M(s)/W(s), football M(s), golf M(s)/W(s), softball W(s), tennis M(s)/W(s), track and field M(s)/W(s), volleyball W(s). *Intramural sports:* badminton M/W, basketball M/W, fencing M(c)/W(c), football M/W, golf M/W, ice hockey M(c), racquetball M/W, rock climbing M(c)/W(c), soccer M(c)/W(c), softball M/W, tennis M/W, track and field M/W, ultimate Frisbee M/W, volleyball M/W, weight lifting M/W.

Standardized Tests *Required:* SAT or ACT (for admission).

Costs (2011–12) *Tuition:* state resident $6960 full-time, $290 per credit hour part-time; nonresident $19,056 full-time, $794 per credit hour part-time. Part-time tuition and fees vary according to course load. *Room and board:* $7012. Room and board charges vary according to board plan and housing facility.

Financial Aid Of all full-time matriculated undergraduates who enrolled in 2011, 9,334 applied for aid, 7,852 were judged to have need, 2,886 had their need fully met. 1,000 Federal Work-Study jobs (averaging $1800). 1,000 state and other part-time jobs (averaging $1800). In 2011, 1193 non-need-based awards were made. *Average percent of need met:* 82%. *Average financial aid package:* $9537. *Average need-based loan:* $3725. *Average need-based gift aid:* $5398. *Average non-need-based aid:* $6000. *Average indebtedness upon graduation:* $24,224.

Applying *Options:* electronic application, deferred entrance. *Application fee:* $30. *Required:* high school transcript, minimum 2.0 GPA. *Application deadlines:* 8/1 (freshmen), rolling (transfers). *Notification:* continuous (freshmen), continuous (transfers).

Freshman Application Contact Mr. Stephen Byrn, Director of Admissions, Eastern Kentucky University, SSB CPO 54, 521 Lancaster Avenue, Richmond, KY 40475-3102. *Phone:* 859-622-2106. *Toll-free phone:* 800-465-9191. *Fax:* 859-622-8024. *E-mail:* admissions@eku.edu. *Web site:* http://www.eku.edu/.

Georgetown College

Georgetown, Kentucky

- **Independent** comprehensive, founded 1829, affiliated with Baptist Church
- **Suburban** 110-acre campus with easy access to Cincinnati
- **Endowment** $43.1 million
- **Coed** 1,273 undergraduate students, 96% full-time, 55% women, 45% men
- **Moderately difficult** entrance level, 89% of applicants were admitted

Undergraduates 1,225 full-time, 48 part-time. Students come from 34 states and territories; 8 other countries; 18% are from out of state; 9% Black or African American, non-Hispanic/Latino; 2% Hispanic/Latino; 0.5% Asian, non-Hispanic/Latino; 0.2% American Indian or Alaska Native, non-Hispanic/Latino; 0.5% Two or more races, non-Hispanic/Latino; 0.6% Race/ethnicity unknown; 2% international; 4% transferred in; 91% live on campus. *Retention:* 71% of full-time freshmen returned.

Freshmen *Admission:* 2,125 applied, 1,895 admitted, 352 enrolled. *Average high school GPA:* 3.45. *Test scores:* SAT critical reading scores over 500: 48%; SAT math scores over 500: 61%; ACT scores over 18: 96%; SAT critical reading scores over 600: 17%; SAT math scores over 600: 20%; ACT scores over 24: 51%; SAT critical reading scores over 700: 2%; SAT math scores over 700: 2%; ACT scores over 30: 5%.

Faculty *Total:* 161, 72% full-time, 73% with terminal degrees. *Student/faculty ratio:* 11:1.

Academics *Calendar:* semesters. *Degrees:* bachelor's and master's. *Special study options:* advanced placement credit, cooperative education, distance learning, double majors, English as a second language, honors programs, independent study, internships, off-campus study, part-time degree program, student-designed majors, study abroad, summer session for credit. *ROTC:* Army (c), Air Force (c). *Unusual degree programs:* 3-2 engineering with University of Kentucky; nursing with University of Kentucky; University of Kentucky, Patterson School of Diplomacy.

Computers on Campus 175 computers/terminals are available on campus for general student use. Students can access the following: campus intranet, computer help desk, free student e-mail accounts, online (class) grades, online (class) registration, online (class) schedules. Campuswide network is available. 100% of college-owned or -operated housing units are wired for high-speed Internet access. Wireless service is available via classrooms, computer centers, computer labs, dorm rooms, learning centers, libraries, student centers.

Student Life *Housing:* on-campus residence required through senior year. *Options:* men-only, women-only. Campus housing is university owned. Freshman campus housing is guaranteed. *Activities and organizations:* drama/theater group, student-run newspaper, radio station, choral group, Campus Ministries, Association of Georgetown Students, Harper-Gatton Leadership Center, President's Ambassadors, Phi Beta Lambda, national fraternities, national sororities. *Campus security:* 24-hour patrols, late-night transport/escort service. *Student services:* health clinic, personal/psychological counseling.

Athletics Member NAIA. *Intercollegiate sports:* baseball M(s), basketball M(s)/W(s), cheerleading W(s), cross-country running M(s)/W(s), football M(s), golf M(s)/W(s), soccer M(s)/W(s), softball W(s), tennis M(s)/W(s), track and field M(s)/W(s), volleyball W(s). *Intramural sports:* basketball M/W, football M/W, golf M/W, racquetball M/W, soccer M/W, softball M/W, table tennis M/W, tennis M/W, ultimate Frisbee M/W, volleyball M/W.

Standardized Tests *Required:* SAT or ACT (for admission). *Recommended:* ACT (for admission).

Costs (2011–12) *Comprehensive fee:* $36,910 includes full-time tuition ($29,300) and room and board ($7610). Full-time tuition and fees vary according to course load and degree level. Part-time tuition: $1210 per credit hour. Part-time tuition and fees vary according to degree level. *College room only:* $3670. Room and board charges vary according to board plan and housing facility. *Payment plan:* installment. *Waivers:* senior citizens and employees or children of employees.

Financial Aid Of all full-time matriculated undergraduates who enrolled in 2011, 1,054 applied for aid, 988 were judged to have need, 425 had their need fully met. In 2011, 242 non-need-based awards were made. *Average percent of need met:* 87%. *Average financial aid package:* $26,945. *Average need-based loan:* $4690. *Average need-based gift aid:* $23,361. *Average non-need-based aid:* $16,434. *Average indebtedness upon graduation:* $21,475. *Financial aid deadline:* 3/15.

Applying *Options:* electronic application, early decision, early action, deferred entrance. *Application fee:* $30. *Required:* high school transcript, minimum 2.5 GPA. *Required for some:* essay or personal statement, interview. *Application deadlines:* 8/1 (freshmen), rolling (transfers). *Notification:* 10/1 (freshmen), continuous (out-of-state freshmen), continuous (transfers).

Freshman Application Contact Ms. Julie Sams, Assistant Director of Admissions, Georgetown College, 400 East College Street, Georgetown, KY 40324. *Phone:* 502-863-8013. *Toll-free phone:* 800-788-9985. *Fax:* 502-868-7733. *E-mail:* admissions@georgetowncollege.edu. *Web site:* http://www.georgetowncollege.edu/.

ITT Technical Institute

Lexington, Kentucky

- **Proprietary** 4-year, founded 2006, part of ITT Educational Services, Inc.
- **Coed**
- **Minimally difficult** entrance level

Academics *Degrees:* associate and bachelor's.

Student Life *Housing:* college housing not available.

Freshman Application Contact Director of Recruitment, ITT Technical Institute, 2473 Fortune Drive, Suite 180, Lexington, KY 40509. *Phone:* 859-246-3300. *Toll-free phone:* 800-519-8151. *Web site:* http://www.itt-tech.edu/.

ITT Technical Institute

Louisville, Kentucky

- **Proprietary** primarily 2-year, founded 1993, part of ITT Educational Services, Inc.
- **Suburban** campus
- **Coed**
- **Minimally difficult** entrance level

Academics *Calendar:* quarters. *Degrees:* associate and bachelor's.

Student Life *Housing:* college housing not available.

Freshman Application Contact Director of Recruitment, ITT Technical Institute, 9500 Ormsby Station Road, Suite 100, Louisville, KY 40223. *Phone:* 502-327-7424. *Toll-free phone:* 888-790-7427. *Web site:* http://www.itt-tech.edu/.

Kentucky Christian University

Grayson, Kentucky

- **Independent** comprehensive, founded 1919, affiliated with Christian Churches and Churches of Christ
- **Small-town** 121-acre campus
- **Endowment** $5.9 million
- **Coed** 607 undergraduate students, 84% full-time, 48% women, 52% men
- **Moderately difficult** entrance level, 76% of applicants were admitted

Undergraduates 510 full-time, 97 part-time. Students come from 26 states and territories; 6 other countries; 55% are from out of state; 10% Black or African American, non-Hispanic/Latino; 0.7% Hispanic/Latino; 0.3% Asian, non-Hispanic/Latino; 0.2% American Indian or Alaska Native, non-Hispanic/Latino; 4% Race/ethnicity unknown; 3% international; 6% transferred in; 82% live on campus. *Retention:* 44% of full-time freshmen returned.

Freshmen *Admission:* 357 applied, 271 admitted, 187 enrolled. *Average high school GPA:* 3.46. *Test scores:* SAT critical reading scores over 500: 100%; SAT math scores over 500: 40%; SAT writing scores over 500: 20%; ACT scores over 18: 80%; SAT critical reading scores over 600: 20%; ACT scores over 24: 21%; ACT scores over 30: 4%.

Faculty *Total:* 52, 69% full-time, 40% with terminal degrees. *Student/faculty ratio:* 15:1.

Academics *Calendar:* semesters. *Degrees:* bachelor's and master's. *Special study options:* academic remediation for entering students, accelerated degree program, advanced placement credit, cooperative education, double majors, independent study, internships, off-campus study, summer session for credit.

Computers on Campus 55 computers/terminals and 48 ports are available on campus for general student use. Students can access the following: computer help desk, free student e-mail accounts, online (class) grades, online (class) registration, online (class) schedules. Campuswide network is available. 100% of college-owned or -operated housing units are wired for high-speed Internet access. Wireless service is available via classrooms, dorm rooms, learning centers, libraries, student centers.

Student Life *Housing:* on-campus residence required through sophomore year. *Options:* men-only, women-only, disabled students. Campus housing is university owned. Freshman campus housing is guaranteed. *Activities and organizations:* drama/theater group, choral group, marching band. *Campus security:* 24-hour emergency response devices, late-night transport/escort service, controlled dormitory access. *Student services:* health clinic, personal/psychological counseling.

Athletics Member NCAA, NAIA, NCCAA. All NCAA Division II. *Intercollegiate sports:* basketball M/W, cross-country running M/W, football M, soccer M/W, volleyball W.

Standardized Tests *Required:* SAT or ACT (for admission).

Costs (2012–13) *Comprehensive fee:* $22,500 includes full-time tuition ($15,420), mandatory fees ($330), and room and board ($6750). Part-time tuition: $514 per credit hour. Part-time tuition and fees vary according to class time, program, and reciprocity agreements. *Room and board:* Room and board charges vary according to housing facility. *Payment plan:* installment. *Waivers:* employees or children of employees.

Financial Aid Of all full-time matriculated undergraduates who enrolled in 2007, 507 applied for aid, 458 were judged to have need, 57 had their need fully met. 241 Federal Work-Study jobs (averaging $1219). 56 state and other part-time jobs (averaging $1403). In 2007, 55 non-need-based awards were made. *Average percent of need met:* 67%. *Average financial aid package:* $9798. *Average need-based loan:* $3792. *Average need-based gift aid:* $4474. *Average non-need-based aid:* $4320. *Average indebtedness upon graduation:* $24,703.

Applying *Options:* electronic application. *Application fee:* $35. *Required:* essay or personal statement, high school transcript, 2 letters of recommendation. *Required for some:* 3 letters of recommendation, interview. *Application deadlines:* rolling (freshmen), rolling (transfers). *Notification:* continuous (freshmen), continuous (transfers).

Freshman Application Contact Ms. Sheree Greer, Director of Admissions, Kentucky Christian University, 100 Academic Parkway, Grayson, KY 41143. *Phone:* 606-474-3186. *Toll-free phone:* 800-522-3181. *Fax:* 606-474-3155. *E-mail:* sgreer@kcu.edu. *Web site:* http://www.kcu.edu/.

Kentucky Mountain Bible College

Vancleve, Kentucky

- **Independent interdenominational** 4-year, founded 1931
- **Rural** 400-acre campus with easy access to Lexington
- **Coed** 73 undergraduate students, 89% full-time, 52% women, 48% men
- **Minimally difficult** entrance level, 54% of applicants were admitted

Undergraduates 65 full-time, 8 part-time. Students come from 19 states and territories; 2 other countries; 58% are from out of state; 1% Black or African American, non-Hispanic/Latino; 1% Hispanic/Latino; 1% American Indian or Alaska Native, non-Hispanic/Latino; 4% international; 10% transferred in; 95% live on campus. *Retention:* 53% of full-time freshmen returned.

Freshmen *Admission:* 56 applied, 30 admitted, 14 enrolled. *Average high school GPA:* 3.19.

Faculty *Total:* 16, 6% with terminal degrees. *Student/faculty ratio:* 5:1.

Academics *Calendar:* semesters. *Degrees:* associate and bachelor's. *Special study options:* academic remediation for entering students, cooperative education, distance learning, independent study, internships, part-time degree program.

Computers on Campus 10 computers/terminals are available on campus for general student use. Students can access the following: campus intranet, free student e-mail accounts, online (class) schedules. Campuswide network is available. 100% of college-owned or -operated housing units are wired for high-speed Internet access. Wireless service is available via entire campus.

Student Life *Housing:* on-campus residence required through senior year. *Options:* men-only, women-only. Campus housing is university owned. Freshman campus housing is guaranteed. *Activities and organizations:* drama/theater group, student-run newspaper, choral group, Student Involvement. *Campus security:* student patrols. *Student services:* personal/psychological counseling, women's center.

Athletics *Intramural sports:* basketball M, volleyball W.

Standardized Tests *Required:* ACT (for admission).

Costs (2012–13) *Comprehensive fee:* $10,790 includes full-time tuition ($6000), mandatory fees ($690), and room and board ($4100). Full-time tuition and fees vary according to program. Part-time tuition: $200 per credit. Part-time tuition and fees vary according to program. *Required fees:* $585 per year part-time. *College room only:* $1400. Room and board charges vary according to board plan and housing facility. *Payment plan:* installment. *Waivers:* employees or children of employees.

Applying *Application fee:* $25. *Required:* essay or personal statement, high school transcript, minimum 2.0 GPA, testimony of religious life. *Recommended:* interview. *Application deadlines:* rolling (freshmen), rolling (transfers). *Notification:* continuous (freshmen), continuous (transfers).

Freshman Application Contact Mr. David Lorimer, Director of Recruiting, Kentucky Mountain Bible College, PO Box 10, Vancleve, KY 41385. *Phone:* 606-693-5000 Ext. 138. *Toll-free phone:* 800-879-KMBC. *Fax:* 606-693-4884. *E-mail:* kmbc@kmbc.edu. *Web site:* http://www.kmbc.edu/.

Kentucky State University

Frankfort, Kentucky

- **State-related** comprehensive, founded 1886
- **Small-town** 915-acre campus with easy access to Louisville
- **Endowment** $10.6 million
- **Coed** 2,490 undergraduate students, 79% full-time, 61% women, 39% men
- **Minimally difficult** entrance level, 30% of applicants were admitted

Undergraduates 1,979 full-time, 511 part-time. Students come from 32 states and territories; 9 other countries; 48% are from out of state; 54% Black or African American, non-Hispanic/Latino; 1% Hispanic/Latino; 0.2% Asian, non-Hispanic/Latino; 0.1% Native Hawaiian or other Pacific Islander, non-Hispanic/Latino; 0.2% American Indian or Alaska Native, non-Hispanic/Latino; 1% Two or more races, non-Hispanic/Latino; 22% Race/ethnicity unknown; 2% international; 5% transferred in; 38% live on campus. *Retention:* 50% of full-time freshmen returned.

Freshmen *Admission:* 10,322 applied, 3,126 admitted, 558 enrolled. *Average high school GPA:* 2.63. *Test scores:* SAT critical reading scores over 500: 20%; SAT math scores over 500: 19%; SAT writing scores over 500: 13%; ACT scores over 18: 45%; SAT critical reading scores over 600: 4%; SAT writing scores over 600: 3%; ACT scores over 24: 9%; ACT scores over 30: 1%.

Faculty *Total:* 176, 75% full-time, 61% with terminal degrees. *Student/faculty ratio:* 16:1.

Academics *Calendar:* semesters. *Degrees:* associate, bachelor's, and master's. *Special study options:* academic remediation for entering students, adult/continuing education programs, advanced placement credit, cooperative education, distance learning, double majors, English as a second language, honors programs, independent study, internships, off-campus study, part-time degree program, services for LD students, student-designed majors, study abroad, summer session for credit. *ROTC:* Army (c), Air Force (c). *Unusual degree programs:* 3-2 engineering with University of Kentucky, University of Maryland at College Park, Vanderbilt University, Florida A&M University.

Computers on Campus 450 computers/terminals and 200 ports are available on campus for general student use. Students can access the following: campus intranet, computer help desk, free student e-mail accounts, online (class) grades, online (class) registration, online (class) schedules, accept financial aid awards. Campuswide network is available. 100% of college-owned or -operated housing units are wired for high-speed Internet access. Wireless service is available via entire campus.

Student Life *Housing:* on-campus residence required through sophomore year. *Options:* coed, men-only, women-only. Campus housing is university owned. Freshman applicants given priority for college housing. *Activities and organizations:* drama/theater group, student-run newspaper, choral group, marching band, Student Government Association, Pan-Hellenic Council, Fellowship of Christian Athletes, Kappa Kappa Psi, NAACP, national fraternities, national sororities. *Campus security:* 24-hour emergency response devices and patrols, controlled dormitory access. *Student services:* health clinic, personal/psychological counseling.

Athletics Member NCAA. All Division II. *Intercollegiate sports:* baseball M(s), basketball M(s)/W(s), cross-country running M(s)/W(s), football M(s), golf M(s), softball W(s), track and field M(s)/W(s), volleyball W(s).

Standardized Tests *Required:* SAT or ACT (for admission).

Costs (2011–12) *Tuition:* state resident $6532 full-time, $242 per credit hour part-time; nonresident $15,674 full-time, $581 per credit hour part-time. Full-time tuition and fees vary according to course load. Part-time tuition and fees vary according to course load. *Room and board:* $6480; room only: $3240. Room and board charges vary according to board plan and housing facility. *Payment plan:* deferred payment. *Waivers:* senior citizens and employees or children of employees.

Financial Aid Of all full-time matriculated undergraduates who enrolled in 2011, 1,770 applied for aid, 1,758 were judged to have need, 85 had their need fully met. 270 Federal Work-Study jobs (averaging $1705). In 2011, 25 non-need-based awards were made. *Average percent of need met:* 47%. *Average financial aid package:* $10,261. *Average need-based loan:* $4065. *Average need-based gift aid:* $6591. *Average non-need-based aid:* $6530. *Average indebtedness upon graduation:* $36,293.

Applying *Options:* electronic application, early admission. *Application fee:* $30. *Required:* high school transcript. *Required for some:* essay or personal statement, 2 letters of recommendation, interview. *Recommended:* minimum 2.0 GPA. *Application deadlines:* rolling (freshmen), rolling (transfers).

Freshman Application Contact Director of Admission, Kentucky State University, 400 East Main Street, Academic Suite Building 312, Frankfort, KY 40601. *Phone:* 502-597-6813. *Fax:* 502-597-5814. *Web site:* http://www.kysu.edu/.

Kentucky Wesleyan College

Owensboro, Kentucky

- **Independent Methodist** 4-year, founded 1858
- **Suburban** 52-acre campus
- **Endowment** $29.3 million
- **Coed** 741 undergraduate students, 95% full-time, 47% women, 53% men
- **Moderately difficult** entrance level, 52% of applicants were admitted

Undergraduates 702 full-time, 39 part-time. Students come from 22 states and territories; 8 other countries; 29% are from out of state; 10% Black or African American, non-Hispanic/Latino; 1% Hispanic/Latino; 0.3% Asian, non-Hispanic/Latino; 0.5% American Indian or Alaska Native, non-Hispanic/Latino; 13% Race/ethnicity unknown; 1% international; 11% transferred in; 50% live on campus. *Retention:* 54% of full-time freshmen returned.

Freshmen *Admission:* 2,000 applied, 1,043 admitted, 188 enrolled. *Average high school GPA:* 3.14. *Test scores:* SAT critical reading scores over 500: 37%; SAT math scores over 500: 54%; SAT writing scores over 500: 19%; ACT scores over 18: 87%; SAT critical reading scores over 600: 5%; SAT math scores over 600: 8%; SAT writing scores over 600: 5%; ACT scores over 24: 32%; ACT scores over 30: 3%.

Faculty *Total:* 81, 54% full-time, 44% with terminal degrees. *Student/faculty ratio:* 13:1.

Academics *Calendar:* semesters. *Degree:* bachelor's. *Special study options:* academic remediation for entering students, accelerated degree program, adult/continuing education programs, advanced placement credit, cooperative education, distance learning, double majors, honors programs, independent study, internships, off-campus study, part-time degree program, services for LD students, student-designed majors, study abroad, summer session for credit. *ROTC:* Army (c). *Unusual degree programs:* 3-2 engineering with Auburn University, University of Kentucky; nursing with University of Louisville.

Computers on Campus 125 computers/terminals are available on campus for general student use. Students can access the following: campus intranet, computer help desk, free student e-mail accounts, online (class) grades, online (class) registration, online (class) schedules. Campuswide network is available. 100% of college-owned or -operated housing units are wired for high-speed Internet access. Wireless service is available via entire campus.

Student Life *Housing:* on-campus residence required through senior year. *Options:* coed, men-only, women-only, disabled students. Campus housing is university owned. Freshman campus housing is guaranteed. *Activities and organizations:* drama/theater group, student-run newspaper, radio station, choral group, Student Government Association, Student Activities Programming Board, Campus Ministries, Pre-Professional Society, St Jude Up 'Til Dawn Executive Board, national fraternities, national sororities. *Campus security:* 24-hour emergency response devices, late-night transport/escort service, controlled dormitory access, 12-hour patrols by trained security personnel. *Student services:* health clinic, personal/psychological counseling, women's center.

Athletics Member NCAA. All Division II. *Intercollegiate sports:* baseball M(s), basketball M(s)/W(s), cheerleading M/W, cross-country running M(s)/W(s), football M(s), golf M(s)/W(s), soccer M(s)/W(s), softball W(s), tennis W(s), volleyball W(s). *Intramural sports:* basketball M/W, soccer M/W, softball M, volleyball M/W.

Standardized Tests *Required:* SAT or ACT (for admission).

Costs (2012–13) *Comprehensive fee:* $27,440 includes full-time tuition ($19,640), mandatory fees ($600), and room and board ($7200). Full-time tuition and fees vary according to course load. Part-time tuition and fees vary according to course load. *Room and board:* Room and board charges vary according to board plan and housing facility. *Payment plans:* installment, deferred payment. *Waivers:* children of alumni, senior citizens, and employees or children of employees.

Financial Aid Of all full-time matriculated undergraduates who enrolled in 2011, 621 applied for aid, 579 were judged to have need, 121 had their need fully met. 141 Federal Work-Study jobs (averaging $1174). In 2011, 84 non-need-based awards were made. *Average percent of need met:* 73%. *Average financial aid package:* $17,386. *Average need-based loan:* $4339. *Average need-based gift aid:* $13,900. *Average non-need-based aid:* $10,295. *Average indebtedness upon graduation:* $30,212. *Financial aid deadline:* 3/15.

Applying *Options:* electronic application, early admission, deferred entrance. *Required:* high school transcript. *Notification:* continuous (freshmen), continuous (transfers).

Freshman Application Contact Kentucky Wesleyan College, 3000 Frederica Street, Owensboro, KY 42301. *Phone:* 270-852-3120. *Toll-free phone:* 800-999-0592 (in-state); 800-990-0592 (out-of-state). *Web site:* http://www.kwc.edu/.

Lindsey Wilson College

Columbia, Kentucky

- **Independent United Methodist** comprehensive, founded 1903
- **Rural** 225-acre campus
- **Endowment** $11.7 million
- **Coed** 2,187 undergraduate students, 95% full-time, 59% women, 41% men
- **Minimally difficult** entrance level, 66% of applicants were admitted

Undergraduates 2,072 full-time, 115 part-time. Students come from 28 states and territories; 30 other countries; 17% are from out of state; 9% Black or African American, non-Hispanic/Latino; 0.4% Hispanic/Latino; 0.5% Asian, non-Hispanic/Latino; 0.6% American Indian or Alaska Native, non-Hispanic/Latino; 2% Two or more races, non-Hispanic/Latino; 6% Race/ethnicity unknown; 0.5% international; 16% transferred in; 47% live on campus. *Retention:* 54% of full-time freshmen returned.

Freshmen *Admission:* 3,255 applied, 2,164 admitted, 551 enrolled. *Average high school GPA:* 3.16. *Test scores:* ACT scores over 18: 78%; ACT scores over 24: 22%; ACT scores over 30: 1%.

Faculty *Total:* 233, 47% full-time. *Student/faculty ratio:* 14:1.

Academics *Calendar:* semesters. *Degrees:* associate, bachelor's, and master's. *Special study options:* academic remediation for entering students, accelerated degree program, adult/continuing education programs, advanced placement credit, cooperative education, double majors, English as a second language, independent study, internships, off-campus study, part-time degree program, services for LD students, student-designed majors, study abroad, summer session for credit.

Computers on Campus 120 computers/terminals are available on campus for general student use. Students can access the following: campus intranet, computer help desk, free student e-mail accounts, online (class) grades, online (class) registration, online (class) schedules. Campuswide network is available. 100% of college-owned or -operated housing units are wired for high-speed Internet access. Wireless service is available via entire campus.

Student Life *Housing:* on-campus residence required through senior year. *Options:* men-only, women-only. Campus housing is university owned. Freshman campus housing is guaranteed. *Activities and organizations:* drama/theater group, student-run newspaper, choral group, marching band. *Campus security:* 24-hour emergency response devices and patrols. *Student services:* health clinic, personal/psychological counseling, women's center.

Athletics Member NAIA. *Intercollegiate sports:* baseball M(s), basketball M(s)/W(s), bowling M(s)/W(s), cheerleading M(s)/W(s), cross-country running M(s)/W(s), football M(s)/W(s), golf M(s)/W(s), soccer M(s)/W(s), softball W(s), swimming and diving M(s)/W(s), tennis M(s)/W(s), track and field M(s)/W(s), volleyball W(s), wrestling M(s). *Intramural sports:* basketball M/W, football M/W, softball M/W, table tennis M/W, tennis M/W, volleyball M/W, weight lifting M/W.

Standardized Tests *Required for some:* SAT or ACT (for admission).

Costs (2012–13) *Comprehensive fee:* $29,460 includes full-time tuition ($21,000), mandatory fees ($230), and room and board ($8230). Full-time tuition and fees vary according to location. Part-time tuition: $875 per credit hour. Part-time tuition and fees vary according to location. *College room only:* $3038. *Payment plan:* installment. *Waivers:* senior citizens and employees or children of employees.

Financial Aid Of all full-time matriculated undergraduates who enrolled in 2011, 2,053 applied for aid, 1,951 were judged to have need, 449 had their need fully met. 291 Federal Work-Study jobs (averaging $2036). 21 state and other part-time jobs (averaging $2258). *Average indebtedness upon graduation:* $26,117.

Applying *Options:* electronic application. *Required:* high school transcript. *Recommended:* interview. *Application deadlines:* rolling (freshmen), rolling (transfers). *Notification:* continuous (freshmen), continuous (transfers).

Freshman Application Contact Mrs. Charity Ferguson, Assistant Director of Admissions, Lindsey Wilson College, 210 Lindsey Wilson Street, Columbia, KY 42728-1298. *Phone:* 270-384-8100. *Toll-free phone:* 800-264-0138. *Fax:* 270-384-8591. *Web site:* http://www.lindsey.edu/.

Mid-Continent University
Mayfield, Kentucky

- **Independent Southern Baptist** comprehensive, founded 1949
- **Small-town** 60-acre campus
- **Endowment** $3.4 million
- **Coed** 2,369 undergraduate students, 83% full-time, 62% women, 38% men
- **Minimally difficult** entrance level, 95% of applicants were admitted

Undergraduates 1,967 full-time, 402 part-time. Students come from 21 states and territories; 10 other countries; 19% are from out of state; 15% Black or African American, non-Hispanic/Latino; 2% Hispanic/Latino; 0.3% Asian, non-Hispanic/Latino; 0.3% American Indian or Alaska Native, non-Hispanic/Latino; 0.8% Two or more races, non-Hispanic/Latino; 2% Race/ethnicity unknown; 0.9% international; 23% transferred in; 5% live on campus. *Retention:* 65% of full-time freshmen returned.
Freshmen *Admission:* 401 applied, 382 admitted, 299 enrolled. *Average high school GPA:* 2.87.
Faculty *Total:* 199, 23% full-time, 18% with terminal degrees. *Student/faculty ratio:* 23:1.
Academics *Calendar:* semesters. *Degrees:* certificates, associate, bachelor's, and master's. *Special study options:* academic remediation for entering students, accelerated degree program, adult/continuing education programs, advanced placement credit, distance learning, double majors, English as a second language, independent study, off-campus study, part-time degree program, student-designed majors, summer session for credit.
Computers on Campus 43 computers/terminals are available on campus for general student use. Students can access the following: free student e-mail accounts. Campuswide network is available. 100% of college-owned or -operated housing units are wired for high-speed Internet access. Wireless service is available via libraries, student centers.
Student Life *Housing:* on-campus residence required through sophomore year. *Options:* men-only, women-only. Campus housing is university owned. *Activities and organizations:* Student Government Association, Baptist Student Union, Psychology Club, International Club, Ministry Association. *Campus security:* 24-hour emergency response devices, late-night transport/escort service, controlled dormitory access, night patrols by trained security personnel. *Student services:* personal/psychological counseling.
Athletics Member NAIA, NCCAA. *Intercollegiate sports:* baseball M(s), basketball M(s)/W(s), soccer M(s), softball W(s), volleyball W(s). *Intramural sports:* cheerleading M/W.
Standardized Tests *Required for some:* SAT or ACT (for admission).
Costs (2011–12) *Comprehensive fee:* $20,150 includes full-time tuition ($12,100), mandatory fees ($1250), and room and board ($6800). Full-time tuition and fees vary according to course load and program. Part-time tuition: $425 per credit hour. Part-time tuition and fees vary according to course load and program. *Required fees:* $610 per term part-time. *Room and board:* Room and board charges vary according to housing facility. *Payment plans:* installment, deferred payment. *Waivers:* employees or children of employees.
Financial Aid Of all full-time matriculated undergraduates who enrolled in 2009, 2,161 applied for aid, 2,117 were judged to have need, 58 had their need fully met. 72 Federal Work-Study jobs (averaging $2126). In 2009, 52 non-need-based awards were made. *Average percent of need met:* 35%. *Average financial aid package:* $8454. *Average need-based loan:* $3523. *Average need-based gift aid:* $6356. *Average non-need-based aid:* $8564. *Average indebtedness upon graduation:* $11,005.
Applying *Options:* electronic application, early admission. *Application fee:* $50. *Required for some:* essay or personal statement, high school transcript, minimum 2.0 GPA, 1 letter of recommendation, interview. *Application deadlines:* rolling (freshmen), rolling (out-of-state freshmen), rolling (transfers). *Notification:* continuous (freshmen), continuous (out-of-state freshmen), continuous (transfers).
Freshman Application Contact Mr. Chris Austin, Director of Admission, Advantage Program, Mid-Continent University, 99 Powell Road East, Mayfield, KY 42066. *Phone:* 270-247-8521 Ext. 277. *Toll-free phone:* 866-894-8878. *Fax:* 270-247-9475. *E-mail:* advantage@midcontinent.edu. *Web site:* http://www.midcontinent.edu/.

Midway College
Midway, Kentucky

- **Independent** comprehensive, founded 1847, affiliated with Christian Church (Disciples of Christ)
- **Small-town** 110-acre campus with easy access to Louisville, Lexington
- **Coed, primarily women**
- **Minimally difficult** entrance level

Faculty *Student/faculty ratio:* 16:1.

Academics *Calendar:* semesters. *Degrees:* associate, bachelor's, master's, and doctoral.
Student Life *Campus security:* 24-hour emergency response devices and patrols, late-night transport/escort service.
Athletics Member NAIA.
Standardized Tests *Required:* SAT or ACT (for admission).
Costs (2011–12) *Comprehensive fee:* $27,440 includes full-time tuition ($19,800) and room and board ($7640). Full-time tuition and fees vary according to class time, location, and program. Part-time tuition: $660 per credit hour. Part-time tuition and fees vary according to class time, location, and program. *Room and board:* Room and board charges vary according to housing facility.
Financial Aid *Of all full-time matriculated undergraduates who enrolled in 2007,* 771 applied for aid, 705 were judged to have need, 180 had their need fully met. 113 Federal Work-Study jobs (averaging $1372). *In 2007,* 8 non-need-based awards were made. *Average percent of need met:* 59. *Average financial aid package:* $12,196. *Average need-based loan:* $3658. *Average need-based gift aid:* $5792. *Average non-need-based aid:* $3756. *Average indebtedness upon graduation:* $15,407.
Applying *Options:* electronic application, early admission, deferred entrance. *Application fee:* $25. *Required:* high school transcript. *Required for some:* essay or personal statement, interview. *Recommended:* minimum 2.2 GPA.
Freshman Application Contact Midway College, 512 East Stephens Street, Midway, KY 40347-1120. *Phone:* 859-846-5799. *Toll-free phone:* 800-755-0031. *Web site:* http://www.midway.edu/.

Morehead State University
Morehead, Kentucky

- **State-supported** comprehensive, founded 1922
- **Small-town** 1016-acre campus
- **Coed** 9,417 undergraduate students, 59% full-time, 61% women, 39% men
- **Minimally difficult** entrance level, 86% of applicants were admitted

Undergraduates 5,553 full-time, 3,864 part-time. Students come from 49 states and territories; 32 other countries; 11% are from out of state; 4% Black or African American, non-Hispanic/Latino; 0.9% Hispanic/Latino; 0.4% Asian, non-Hispanic/Latino; 0.2% American Indian or Alaska Native, non-Hispanic/Latino; 0.6% Two or more races, non-Hispanic/Latino; 2% Race/ethnicity unknown; 0.7% international; 6% transferred in; 27% live on campus. *Retention:* 73% of full-time freshmen returned.
Freshmen *Admission:* 3,461 applied, 2,968 admitted, 1,372 enrolled. *Average high school GPA:* 3.3. *Test scores:* SAT critical reading scores over 500: 38%; SAT math scores over 500: 55%; ACT scores over 18: 86%; SAT critical reading scores over 600: 13%; SAT math scores over 600: 19%; ACT scores over 24: 32%; SAT critical reading scores over 700: 1%; SAT math scores over 700: 3%; ACT scores over 30: 3%.
Faculty *Total:* 462, 81% full-time. *Student/faculty ratio:* 17:1.
Academics *Calendar:* semesters. *Degrees:* associate, bachelor's, master's, post-master's, and postbachelor's certificates. *Special study options:* academic remediation for entering students, accelerated degree program, adult/continuing education programs, advanced placement credit, cooperative education, distance learning, double majors, honors programs, independent study, internships, off-campus study, part-time degree program, services for LD students, student-designed majors, study abroad, summer session for credit. *ROTC:* Army (b). *Unusual degree programs:* 3-2 engineering with Chemical Engineering : 3 years (96 hours) at Morehead State University, transfer to University of Kentucky to an approved engineering program.
Computers on Campus 1,000 computers/terminals and 1,820 ports are available on campus for general student use. Students can access the following: campus intranet, computer help desk, free student e-mail accounts, online (class) grades, online (class) registration, online (class) schedules. Campuswide network is available. 100% of college-owned or -operated housing units are wired for high-speed Internet access. Wireless service is available via entire campus.
Student Life *Housing:* on-campus residence required through sophomore year. *Options:* coed, disabled students. Campus housing is university owned. Freshman applicants given priority for college housing. *Activities and organizations:* drama/theater group, student-run newspaper, radio and television station, choral group, marching band, national fraternities, national sororities. *Campus security:* 24-hour emergency response devices and patrols, student patrols, late-night transport/escort service, controlled dormitory access. *Student services:* health clinic, personal/psychological counseling.
Athletics Member NCAA. All Division I except football (Division I-AA). *Intercollegiate sports:* baseball M(s), basketball M(s)/W(s), bowling M(c)/W(c), cheerleading M/W, cross-country running M(s)/W(s), equestrian sports M(c)/W(c), golf M(s), riflery M(s)/W(s), soccer W(s), softball W(s), tennis M(s)/W(s), track and field M(s)/W(s), volleyball W(s). *Intramural sports:* archery M/W, badminton M/W, basketball M/W, bowling M/W, football M/W,

golf M/W, racquetball M/W, soccer M(c)/W(c), softball M/W, swimming and diving M/W, table tennis M/W, tennis M/W, track and field M/W, volleyball M/W.

Standardized Tests *Required:* SAT or ACT (for admission).

Costs (2011–12) *Tuition:* state resident $6942 full-time, $263 per credit hour part-time; nonresident $17,370 full-time, $658 per credit hour part-time. Full-time tuition and fees vary according to course load, degree level, location, reciprocity agreements, and student level. Part-time tuition and fees vary according to course load, degree level, location, reciprocity agreements, and student level. *Room and board:* $7014. Room and board charges vary according to board plan and housing facility. *Payment plan:* installment. *Waivers:* children of alumni, senior citizens, and employees or children of employees.

Financial Aid Of all full-time matriculated undergraduates who enrolled in 2011, 4,767 applied for aid, 4,201 were judged to have need, 1,353 had their need fully met. 436 Federal Work-Study jobs (averaging $2082). 746 state and other part-time jobs (averaging $2221). In 2011, 686 non-need-based awards were made. *Average percent of need met:* 67%. *Average financial aid package:* $10,046. *Average need-based loan:* $3915. *Average need-based gift aid:* $4816. *Average non-need-based aid:* $6493. *Average indebtedness upon graduation:* $29,462.

Applying *Options:* electronic application, early admission, deferred entrance. *Application fee:* $30. *Required:* high school transcript. *Required for some:* essay or personal statement, 1 letter of recommendation, interview. *Application deadlines:* rolling (freshmen), rolling (transfers). *Notification:* continuous (freshmen), continuous (transfers).

Freshman Application Contact Mr. Jeffrey Liles, Assistant Vice President for Enrollment Services, Morehead State University, 100 Admissions Center, Morehead, KY 40351. *Phone:* 606-783-2000. *Toll-free phone:* 800-585-6781. *Fax:* 606-783-5038. *E-mail:* admissions@moreheadstate.edu. *Web site:* http://www.moreheadstate.edu/.

Murray State University
Murray, Kentucky

- **State-supported** comprehensive, founded 1922, part of Kentucky Council on Post Secondary Education
- **Small-town** 238-acre campus
- **Endowment** $47.5 million
- **Coed**
- **Moderately difficult** entrance level

Faculty *Student/faculty ratio:* 15:1.

Academics *Calendar:* semesters. *Degrees:* certificates, associate, bachelor's, master's, and post-master's certificates.

Student Life *Campus security:* 24-hour emergency response devices and patrols, student patrols, late-night transport/escort service, controlled dormitory access.

Athletics Member NCAA. All Division I except football (Division I-AA).

Standardized Tests *Required:* ACT (for admission).

Costs (2011–12) *Tuition:* state resident $5802 full-time, $242 per hour part-time; nonresident $17,118 full-time, $713 per hour part-time. Full-time tuition and fees vary according to reciprocity agreements. Part-time tuition and fees vary according to reciprocity agreements. *Required fees:* $774 full-time, $32 per hour part-time. *Room and board:* $7076. Room and board charges vary according to board plan and housing facility.

Financial Aid Of all full-time matriculated undergraduates who enrolled in 2011, 4,296 applied for aid, 4,090 were judged to have need, 511 had their need fully met. 288 Federal Work-Study jobs (averaging $2088). 1,513 state and other part-time jobs (averaging $2000). In 2011, 700 non-need-based awards were made. *Average percent of need met:* 69. *Average financial aid package:* $9986. *Average need-based loan:* $3800. *Average need-based gift aid:* $5014. *Average non-need-based aid:* $3221. *Average indebtedness upon graduation:* $19,881.

Applying *Options:* electronic application. *Application fee:* $30. *Required:* high school transcript, minimum 3.0 GPA.

Freshman Application Contact Ms. Stacy Bell, Undergraduate Admissions Specialist, Murray State University, 113 Sparks Hall, Murray, KY 42701-0009. *Phone:* 270-809-3035. *Toll-free phone:* 800-272-4678. *Fax:* 270-809-3050. *E-mail:* admissions@murraystate.edu. *Web site:* http://www.murraystate.edu/.

National College
Lexington, Kentucky

Director of Admissions Kim Thomasson, Campus Director, National College, 2376 Sir Barton Way, Lexington, KY 40509. *Phone:* 859-253-0621. *Toll-free phone:* 888-9-JOBREADY. *Web site:* http://www.national-college.edu/.

National College
Louisville, Kentucky

Director of Admissions Vincent C. Tinebra, Campus Director, National College, 3950 Dixie Highway, Louisville, KY 40216. *Phone:* 502-447-7634. *Toll-free phone:* 888-9-JOBREADY. *Web site:* http://www.national-college.edu/.

Northern Kentucky University
Highland Heights, Kentucky

- **State-supported** comprehensive, founded 1968
- **Suburban** 398-acre campus with easy access to Cincinnati
- **Endowment** $68.9 million
- **Coed** 13,308 undergraduate students, 75% full-time, 55% women, 45% men
- **Moderately difficult** entrance level, 64% of applicants were admitted

Undergraduates 10,009 full-time, 3,299 part-time. Students come from 43 states and territories; 51 other countries; 33% are from out of state; 7% Black or African American, non-Hispanic/Latino; 2% Hispanic/Latino; 0.9% Asian, non-Hispanic/Latino; 0.1% Native Hawaiian or other Pacific Islander, non-Hispanic/Latino; 0.3% American Indian or Alaska Native, non-Hispanic/Latino; 1% Two or more races, non-Hispanic/Latino; 4% Race/ethnicity unknown; 2% international; 5% transferred in; 13% live on campus. *Retention:* 66% of full-time freshmen returned.

Freshmen *Admission:* 7,330 applied, 4,704 admitted, 2,271 enrolled. *Average high school GPA:* 3.18. *Test scores:* SAT critical reading scores over 500: 48%; SAT math scores over 500: 46%; ACT scores over 18: 93%; SAT critical reading scores over 600: 13%; SAT math scores over 600: 13%; ACT scores over 24: 30%; SAT critical reading scores over 700: 2%; SAT math scores over 700: 1%; ACT scores over 30: 2%.

Faculty *Total:* 1,018, 54% full-time. *Student/faculty ratio:* 17:1.

Academics *Calendar:* semesters. *Degrees:* certificates, associate, bachelor's, master's, doctoral, post-master's, postbachelor's, and first professional certificates. *Special study options:* academic remediation for entering students, accelerated degree program, adult/continuing education programs, advanced placement credit, cooperative education, distance learning, double majors, English as a second language, honors programs, independent study, internships, off-campus study, part-time degree program, services for LD students, student-designed majors, study abroad, summer session for credit. *ROTC:* Army (c), Air Force (c).

Computers on Campus 250 computers/terminals and 500 ports are available on campus for general student use. Students can access the following: campus intranet, computer help desk, free student e-mail accounts, online (class) grades, online (class) registration, online (class) schedules. Campuswide network is available. 100% of college-owned or -operated housing units are wired for high-speed Internet access. Wireless service is available via entire campus.

Student Life *Housing options:* coed, cooperative, disabled students. Campus housing is university owned. *Activities and organizations:* drama/theater group, student-run newspaper, radio and television station, choral group, Sororities, Fraternities, Freshmen Service Leadership Committee, Student Alumni Association, Activities Programming Board, national fraternities, national sororities. *Campus security:* 24-hour emergency response devices and patrols, late-night transport/escort service, controlled dormitory access. *Student services:* health clinic, personal/psychological counseling, women's center.

Athletics Member NCAA. All Division II. *Intercollegiate sports:* baseball M(s), basketball M(s)/W(s), cheerleading M/W, cross-country running M(s)/W(s), golf M(s)/W(s), soccer M(s)/W(s), softball W(s), tennis M(s)/W(s), volleyball W(s). *Intramural sports:* badminton M(c)/W(c), baseball M(c), basketball M/W, bowling M/W, equestrian sports M(c)/W(c), football M/W, ice hockey M(c), lacrosse M(c), racquetball M/W, soccer M(c)/W(c), softball M(c)/W(c), tennis M/W, ultimate Frisbee M(c)/W(c), volleyball M(c)/W(c), water polo M/W, weight lifting M/W.

Standardized Tests *Required:* SAT or ACT (for admission).

Costs (2011–12) *Tuition:* state resident $7488 full-time, $312 per credit hour part-time; nonresident $14,976 full-time, $624 per credit hour part-time. Full-time tuition and fees vary according to course load and reciprocity agreements. Part-time tuition and fees vary according to course load and reciprocity agreements. *Required fees:* $96 full-time. *Room and board:* $7152. Room and board charges vary according to board plan and housing facility. *Payment plan:* installment. *Waivers:* senior citizens and employees or children of employees.

Financial Aid Of all full-time matriculated undergraduates who enrolled in 2009, 7,451 applied for aid, 5,965 were judged to have need, 920 had their need fully met. In 2009, 765 non-need-based awards were made. *Average percent of need met:* 53%. *Average financial aid package:* $8482. *Average need-*

based loan: $3874. *Average need-based gift aid:* $5801. *Average non-need-based aid:* $4438. *Average indebtedness upon graduation:* $21,535.

Applying *Options:* electronic application, early admission, deferred entrance. *Application fee:* $40. *Required:* high school transcript. *Required for some:* some programs require separate applications. *Application deadlines:* 7/15 (freshmen), 7/15 (out-of-state freshmen), 8/1 (transfers). *Notification:* continuous (freshmen), continuous (out-of-state freshmen), continuous (transfers).

Freshman Application Contact Office of Admissions, Northern Kentucky University, Lucas Administrative Center, 400 Nunn Drive, Highland Heights, KY 41099. *Phone:* 859-572-5220. *Toll-free phone:* 800-637-9948. *Fax:* 859-572-6665. *E-mail:* admitnku@nku.edu. *Web site:* http://www.nku.edu/.

See below for display ad and page 1484 for the College Close-Up.

St. Catharine College

St. Catharine, Kentucky

Director of Admissions Ms. Amy C. Carrico, Director of Admissions, St. Catharine College, 2735 Bardstown Road, St. Catharine, KY 40061-9499. *Phone:* 859-336-5082. *Toll-free phone:* 800-599-2000. *Web site:* http://www.sccky.edu/.

Southern Baptist Theological Seminary

Louisville, Kentucky

Freshman Application Contact Dr. Daniel DeWitt, Southern Baptist Theological Seminary, 2825 Lexington Road, Louisville, KY 40280-0004. *Phone:* 502-897-4011 Ext. 4617. *Web site:* http://www.sbts.edu/.

Spalding University

Louisville, Kentucky

- **Independent** comprehensive, founded 1814, affiliated with Roman Catholic Church
- **Urban** 5-acre campus with easy access to Louisville
- **Endowment** $11.5 million
- **Coed** 1,371 undergraduate students, 72% full-time, 74% women, 26% men
- **Moderately difficult** entrance level, 43% of applicants were admitted

Undergraduates 983 full-time, 388 part-time. Students come from 13 states and territories; 7 other countries; 10% are from out of state; 29% Black or African American, non-Hispanic/Latino; 3% Hispanic/Latino; 1% Asian, non-Hispanic/Latino; 0.1% Native Hawaiian or other Pacific Islander, non-Hispanic/Latino; 0.4% American Indian or Alaska Native, non-Hispanic/Latino; 3% Two or more races, non-Hispanic/Latino; 4% Race/ethnicity unknown; 0.4% international; 14% transferred in; 8% live on campus. *Retention:* 73% of full-time freshmen returned.

Freshmen *Admission:* 790 applied, 338 admitted, 171 enrolled. *Average high school GPA:* 3.04. *Test scores:* SAT critical reading scores over 500: 22%; SAT math scores over 500: 17%; ACT scores over 18: 66%; ACT scores over 24: 8%.

Faculty *Total:* 169, 53% full-time, 51% with terminal degrees. *Student/faculty ratio:* 11:1.

Academics *Calendar:* other. *Degrees:* certificates, associate, bachelor's, master's, doctoral, post-master's, postbachelor's, and first professional certificates. *Special study options:* academic remediation for entering students, accelerated degree program, adult/continuing education programs, advanced placement credit, cooperative education, distance learning, double majors, independent study, internships, off-campus study, part-time degree program, services for LD students, study abroad, summer session for credit. *ROTC:* Army (c), Air Force (c). *Unusual degree programs:* 3-2 occupational therapy.

Computers on Campus 250 computers/terminals are available on campus for general student use. Students can access the following: computer help desk, free student e-mail accounts, online (class) grades, online (class) registration, online (class) schedules. Campuswide network is available. 100% of college-owned or -operated housing units are wired for high-speed Internet access. Wireless service is available via entire campus.

Student Life *Housing options:* coed, disabled students. Campus housing is university owned. *Activities and organizations:* Egan Service Learning Pro-

gram, Student Government Association, Student Occupational Therapy Association, Residence Hall Advisory Council, Best Buddies. *Campus security:* 24-hour emergency response devices and patrols, late-night transport/escort service, controlled dormitory access, outdoor emergency call stations located in various locations around campus. *Student services:* personal/psychological counseling.

Athletics Member NCAA, USCAA. All Division III. *Intercollegiate sports:* baseball M, basketball M/W, bowling W, cross-country running M/W, golf M/W, soccer M/W, softball W, track and field M/W, volleyball W.

Standardized Tests *Required:* SAT or ACT (for admission).

Costs (2011–12) *Comprehensive fee:* $28,150 includes full-time tuition ($19,350) and room and board ($8800). Full-time tuition and fees vary according to course load and program. Part-time tuition: $645 per credit hour. Part-time tuition and fees vary according to course load and program. *College room only:* $5400. Room and board charges vary according to board plan. *Payment plans:* installment, deferred payment. *Waivers:* employees or children of employees.

Financial Aid *Average percent of need met:* 75%. *Average financial aid package:* $11,500.

Applying *Options:* electronic application, early admission, deferred entrance. *Application fee:* $20. *Required:* high school transcript, minimum 2.5 GPA. *Required for some:* essay or personal statement. *Recommended:* interview. *Application deadlines:* rolling (freshmen), rolling (out-of-state freshmen), rolling (transfers). *Notification:* continuous (freshmen), continuous (out-of-state freshmen), continuous (transfers).

Freshman Application Contact Mr. Matt Elder, Associate Director of Admissions, Spalding University, 845 South Third Street, Louisville, KY 40203. *Phone:* 502-873-4177. *Toll-free phone:* 800-896-8941. *E-mail:* admissions@spalding.edu. *Web site:* http://www.spalding.edu/.

Strayer University - Florence Campus

Florence, Kentucky

- **Proprietary** comprehensive
- **Coed**

Academics *Degrees:* certificates, diplomas, associate, bachelor's, master's, and postbachelor's certificates.

Freshman Application Contact Strayer University - Florence Campus, 7300 Turfway Road, Suite 250, Florence, KY 41042. *Web site:* http://strayer.edu/florence.

Strayer University - Lexington Campus

Lexington, Kentucky

- **Proprietary** comprehensive
- **Coed**

Academics *Degrees:* certificates, diplomas, associate, bachelor's, master's, and postbachelor's certificates.

Freshman Application Contact Strayer University - Lexington Campus, 220 Lexington Green Circle, Suite 550, Lexington, KY 40503. *Web site:* http://www.strayer.edu/lexington/.

Strayer University - Louisville Campus

Louisville, Kentucky

- **Proprietary** comprehensive
- **Coed**

Academics *Degrees:* certificates, diplomas, associate, bachelor's, master's, and postbachelor's certificates.

Freshman Application Contact Strayer University - Louisville Campus, 2650 Eastpoint Parkway, Suite 100, Louisville, KY 40223. *Web site:* http://www.strayer.edu/louisville/.

Sullivan College of Technology and Design

Louisville, Kentucky

- **Proprietary** primarily 2-year, founded 1961, part of The Sullivan University System, Inc.
- **Suburban** 10-acre campus with easy access to Louisville
- **Coed** 582 undergraduate students, 62% full-time, 34% women, 66% men
- **Moderately difficult** entrance level, 47% of applicants were admitted

Undergraduates 360 full-time, 222 part-time. Students come from 16 states and territories; 5 other countries; 15% are from out of state; 20% Black or African American, non-Hispanic/Latino; 4% Hispanic/Latino; 0.7% Asian, non-Hispanic/Latino; 0.2% Native Hawaiian or other Pacific Islander, non-Hispanic/Latino; 7% Two or more races, non-Hispanic/Latino; 4% transferred in; 6% live on campus. *Retention:* 72% of full-time freshmen returned.

Freshmen *Admission:* 323 applied, 151 admitted, 121 enrolled.

Faculty *Total:* 81, 42% full-time. *Student/faculty ratio:* 12:1.

Academics *Calendar:* quarters. *Degrees:* certificates, diplomas, associate, and bachelor's. *Special study options:* academic remediation for entering students, accelerated degree program, adult/continuing education programs, advanced placement credit, double majors, independent study, internships, part-time degree program, services for LD students, summer session for credit.

Computers on Campus 232 computers/terminals and 16 ports are available on campus for general student use. Students can access the following: campus intranet, computer help desk, free student e-mail accounts, online (class) grades, online (class) schedules, wireless Internet. Campuswide network is available. 50% of college-owned or -operated housing units are wired for high-speed Internet access. Wireless service is available via classrooms, computer centers, computer labs, dorm rooms, learning centers, libraries, student centers.

Student Life *Housing options:* coed. Campus housing is university owned and leased by the school. Freshman campus housing is guaranteed. *Activities and organizations:* ASID, IIDA, ADDA, ADFED, Skills USA. *Campus security:* late-night transport/escort service, controlled dormitory access, telephone alarm device during hours school is open; patrols by trained security personnel while classes are in session.

Standardized Tests *Required:* Career Performance Assessment Test (CPAt) or ACT or SAT scores in place of CPAt results (for admission). *Recommended:* SAT or ACT (for admission).

Costs (2012–13) *Tuition:* $16,890 full-time. Full-time tuition and fees vary according to course load, degree level, and program. Part-time tuition and fees vary according to course load, degree level, and program. No tuition increase for student's term of enrollment. *Room only:* Room and board charges vary according to board plan. *Payment plan:* installment. *Waivers:* employees or children of employees.

Applying *Options:* electronic application, deferred entrance. *Application fee:* $100. *Required:* high school transcript, interview. *Application deadlines:* rolling (freshmen), rolling (out-of-state freshmen), rolling (transfers). *Notification:* continuous (freshmen), continuous (out-of-state freshmen), continuous (transfers).

Freshman Application Contact Mr. Aamer Z. Chauhdri, Director of Admissions, Sullivan College of Technology and Design, 3901 Atkinson Square Drive, Louisville, KY 40218. *Phone:* 502-456-6509 Ext. 8220. *Toll-free phone:* 800-884-6528. *Fax:* 502-456-2341. *E-mail:* achauhdri@sctd.edu. *Web site:* http://www.sctd.edu/.

Sullivan University

Louisville, Kentucky

- **Proprietary** comprehensive, founded 1864
- **Urban** 15-acre campus
- **Coed** 4,600 undergraduate students, 60% full-time, 59% women, 41% men
- **Minimally difficult** entrance level, 73% of applicants were admitted

Undergraduates 2,776 full-time, 1,824 part-time. Students come from 44 states and territories; 42 other countries; 18% are from out of state; 21% Black or African American, non-Hispanic/Latino; 0.3% Hispanic/Latino; 8% Asian, non-Hispanic/Latino; 0.1% Native Hawaiian or other Pacific Islander, non-Hispanic/Latino; 0.5% American Indian or Alaska Native, non-Hispanic/Latino; 8% Two or more races, non-Hispanic/Latino; 6% Race/ethnicity unknown; 0.9% international; 10% live on campus.

Freshmen *Admission:* 771 applied, 565 admitted, 386 enrolled.

Faculty *Total:* 340, 45% full-time, 35% with terminal degrees. *Student/faculty ratio:* 28:1.

Academics *Calendar:* quarters. *Degrees:* certificates, diplomas, associate, bachelor's, master's, doctoral, post-master's, postbachelor's, and first professional certificates. *Special study options:* academic remediation for entering students, accelerated degree program, adult/continuing education programs,

cooperative education, distance learning, double majors, independent study, internships, part-time degree program, services for LD students, summer session for credit.

Computers on Campus 92 computers/terminals are available on campus for general student use. Students can access the following: campus intranet, computer help desk, free student e-mail accounts, online (class) grades, online (class) schedules. Campuswide network is available. Wireless service is available via entire campus.

Student Life *Housing options:* men-only, women-only. Campus housing is university owned. Freshman campus housing is guaranteed. *Activities and organizations:* choral group, Student Activities Committee, Student Veterans Association. *Campus security:* 24-hour patrols, late-night transport/escort service, controlled dormitory access. *Student services:* personal/psychological counseling.

Athletics *Intramural sports:* basketball M/W, bowling M/W, soccer M/W, softball M/W, volleyball M/W.

Standardized Tests *Required:* Acceptable SAT, ACT, APT or CPAt Scores Required (for admission).

Financial Aid Of all full-time matriculated undergraduates who enrolled in 2002, 6,028 applied for aid, 5,247 were judged to have need. 31 Federal Work-Study jobs (averaging $2065). In 2002, 374 non-need-based awards were made. *Average non-need-based aid:* $2000. *Average indebtedness upon graduation:* $15,000.

Applying *Application fee:* $100. *Required:* high school transcript, interview. *Required for some:* essay or personal statement, 2 letters of recommendation, Certain programs require criminal background checks and no felony convictions. Some drug and abuse related misdemeanors will exclude applicants from being accepted into several programs. *Application deadlines:* rolling (freshmen), rolling (transfers). *Notification:* continuous (freshmen), continuous (transfers).

Freshman Application Contact Ms. Terri Thomas, Director of Admissions, Sullivan University, 3101 Bardstown Road, Louisville, KY 40205. *Phone:* 502-456-6505. *Toll-free phone:* 800-844-1354. *Fax:* 502-456-0040. *E-mail:* admissions@sullivan.edu. *Web site:* http://www.sullivan.edu/.

Thomas More College
Crestview Hills, Kentucky

- **Independent Roman Catholic** comprehensive, founded 1921
- **Suburban** 100-acre campus with easy access to Cincinnati
- **Endowment** $14.9 million
- **Coed** 1,692 undergraduate students, 77% full-time, 54% women, 46% men
- **Moderately difficult** entrance level, 75% of applicants were admitted

Undergraduates 1,296 full-time, 396 part-time. Students come from 16 states and territories; 3 other countries; 48% are from out of state; 7% Black or African American, non-Hispanic/Latino; 0.4% Hispanic/Latino; 0.7% Asian, non-Hispanic/Latino; 0.1% Native Hawaiian or other Pacific Islander, non-Hispanic/Latino; 0.4% American Indian or Alaska Native, non-Hispanic/Latino; 0.9% Two or more races, non-Hispanic/Latino; 15% Race/ethnicity unknown; 0.5% international; 5% transferred in; 34% live on campus. *Retention:* 68% of full-time freshmen returned.

Freshmen *Admission:* 891 applied, 670 admitted, 259 enrolled. *Average high school GPA:* 3.29. *Test scores:* SAT critical reading scores over 500: 52%; SAT math scores over 500: 50%; ACT scores over 18: 98%; SAT critical reading scores over 600: 21%; SAT math scores over 600: 29%; ACT scores over 24: 39%; SAT critical reading scores over 700: 8%; SAT math scores over 700: 4%; ACT scores over 30: 5%.

Faculty *Total:* 149, 50% full-time, 48% with terminal degrees. *Student/faculty ratio:* 14:1.

Academics *Calendar:* semesters. *Degrees:* certificates, associate, bachelor's, and master's. *Special study options:* academic remediation for entering students, accelerated degree program, adult/continuing education programs, advanced placement credit, cooperative education, double majors, honors programs, independent study, internships, off-campus study, part-time degree program, services for LD students, student-designed majors, study abroad, summer session for credit. *ROTC:* Army (c), Air Force (c). *Unusual degree programs:* 3-2 engineering.

Computers on Campus 95 computers/terminals are available on campus for general student use. Students can access the following: campus intranet, computer help desk, free student e-mail accounts, online (class) grades, online (class) registration, online (class) schedules. Campuswide network is available. 100% of college-owned or -operated housing units are wired for high-speed Internet access. Wireless service is available via entire campus.

Student Life *Housing options:* coed, men-only, women-only, disabled students. Campus housing is university owned. *Activities and organizations:* drama/theater group, choral group, Student Government Association, Student Activities Board, More Ministry, Outdoors Adventure Club, International Student Society, national fraternities, national sororities. *Campus security:* 24-hour emergency response devices and patrols, late-night transport/escort service, controlled dormitory access. *Student services:* health clinic, personal/psychological counseling.

Athletics Member NCAA. All Division III. *Intercollegiate sports:* baseball M, basketball M/W, cross-country running M/W, football M, golf M/W, soccer M/W, softball W, tennis M/W, volleyball W. *Intramural sports:* basketball M/W, football M, soccer M/W, softball M/W, volleyball M/W.

Standardized Tests *Required:* SAT or ACT (for admission).

Costs (2011–12) *Comprehensive fee:* $32,750 includes full-time tuition ($25,000), mandatory fees ($720), and room and board ($7030). Full-time tuition and fees vary according to program and student level. Part-time tuition: $560 per credit hour. Part-time tuition and fees vary according to course load and program. *Required fees:* $30 per credit hour part-time, $15 per term part-time. *College room only:* $3300. Room and board charges vary according to board plan and housing facility. *Payment plans:* installment, deferred payment. *Waivers:* senior citizens and employees or children of employees.

Financial Aid Of all full-time matriculated undergraduates who enrolled in 2011, 1,069 applied for aid, 898 were judged to have need, 172 had their need fully met. 109 Federal Work-Study jobs (averaging $1610). In 2011, 181 non-need-based awards were made. *Average percent of need met:* 65%. *Average financial aid package:* $16,148. *Average need-based loan:* $4268. *Average need-based gift aid:* $13,076. *Average non-need-based aid:* $13,667. *Average indebtedness upon graduation:* $29,947.

Applying *Options:* electronic application, deferred entrance. *Application fee:* $25. *Required:* high school transcript, minimum 2.5 GPA. *Required for some:* 2 letters of recommendation. *Application deadlines:* 8/1 (freshmen), 8/1 (transfers). *Notification:* continuous (freshmen), continuous (transfers).

Freshman Application Contact Mr. Billy Sarge, Associate Director of Admissions, Thomas More College, 333 Thomas More Parkway, Crestview Hills, KY 41017-3495. *Phone:* 859-344-3332. *Toll-free phone:* 800-825-4557. *Fax:* 859-344-3444. *E-mail:* admissions@thomasmore.edu. *Web site:* http://www.thomasmore.edu/.

See page 353 for display ad and page 1640 for the College Close-Up.

Transylvania University
Lexington, Kentucky

- **Independent** 4-year, founded 1780, affiliated with Christian Church (Disciples of Christ)
- **Urban** 40-acre campus with easy access to Cincinnati, Louisville
- **Endowment** $124.8 million
- **Coed** 1,029 undergraduate students, 98% full-time, 60% women, 40% men
- **Very difficult** entrance level, 85% of applicants were admitted

Undergraduates 1,011 full-time, 18 part-time. Students come from 29 states and territories; 7 other countries; 15% are from out of state; 4% Black or African American, non-Hispanic/Latino; 1% Hispanic/Latino; 1% Asian, non-Hispanic/Latino; 0.2% American Indian or Alaska Native, non-Hispanic/Latino; 2% Two or more races, non-Hispanic/Latino; 4% Race/ethnicity unknown; 0.9% international; 1% transferred in; 76% live on campus. *Retention:* 87% of full-time freshmen returned.

Freshmen *Admission:* 1,267 applied, 1,075 admitted, 245 enrolled. *Average high school GPA:* 3.76. *Test scores:* SAT critical reading scores over 500: 90%; SAT math scores over 500: 86%; ACT scores over 18: 100%; SAT critical reading scores over 600: 54%; SAT math scores over 600: 51%; ACT scores over 24: 80%; SAT critical reading scores over 700: 18%; SAT math scores over 700: 9%; ACT scores over 30: 26%.

Faculty *Total:* 104, 85% full-time, 81% with terminal degrees. *Student/faculty ratio:* 11:1.

Academics *Calendar:* 4-4-1. *Degree:* bachelor's. *Special study options:* advanced placement credit, double majors, independent study, internships, off-campus study, part-time degree program, student-designed majors, study abroad, summer session for credit. *ROTC:* Army (c), Air Force (c). *Unusual degree programs:* 3-2 engineering with University of Kentucky, Vanderbilt University.

Computers on Campus 200 computers/terminals and 200 ports are available on campus for general student use. Students can access the following: campus intranet, computer help desk, free student e-mail accounts, online (class) grades, online (class) registration, online (class) schedules. Campuswide network is available. 100% of college-owned or -operated housing units are wired for high-speed Internet access. Wireless service is available via classrooms, computer centers, computer labs, dorm rooms, learning centers, libraries, student centers.

Student Life *Housing:* on-campus residence required through junior year. *Options:* coed, men-only, women-only, disabled students. Campus housing is university owned. Freshman campus housing is guaranteed. *Activities and organizations:* drama/theater group, student-run newspaper, radio station, choral group, Student Alumni Association, Student Government Association, Student Activities Board, Crimson Crew, Transylvania Environmental Rights and Responsibility Alliance (TERRA), national fraternities, national sororities. *Campus security:* 24-hour emergency response devices and patrols, late-night transport/escort service, controlled dormitory access. *Student services:* health clinic, personal/psychological counseling.

Athletics Member NCAA. All Division III. *Intercollegiate sports:* baseball M, basketball M/W, cheerleading M/W, cross-country running M/W, equestrian sports M/W, field hockey W, golf M/W, lacrosse M/W, soccer M/W, softball W, swimming and diving M/W, tennis M/W, track and field M/W, volleyball W. *Intramural sports:* badminton M/W, basketball M/W, cross-country running M/W, equestrian sports M/W, football M/W, golf M/W, lacrosse M/W, racquetball M/W, soccer M/W, softball M/W, swimming and diving M/W, table tennis M/W, tennis M/W, track and field M/W, ultimate Frisbee M/W, volleyball M/W, weight lifting M/W.

Standardized Tests *Required:* SAT or ACT (for admission).

Costs (2012–13) *Comprehensive fee:* $38,615 includes full-time tuition ($28,645), mandatory fees ($1220), and room and board ($8750). Part-time tuition: $3175 per course. Part-time tuition and fees vary according to course load. *Room and board:* Room and board charges vary according to board plan, housing facility, and location. *Payment plan:* installment. *Waivers:* employees or children of employees.

Financial Aid Of all full-time matriculated undergraduates who enrolled in 2010, 841 applied for aid, 752 were judged to have need, 161 had their need fully met. 450 Federal Work-Study jobs (averaging $1727). 57 state and other part-time jobs (averaging $6178). In 2010, 325 non-need-based awards were made. *Average percent of need met:* 81%. *Average financial aid package:* $21,914. *Average need-based loan:* $4230. *Average need-based gift aid:* $17,573. *Average non-need-based aid:* $10,995. *Average indebtedness upon graduation:* $22,432.

Applying *Options:* electronic application, early admission, early action, deferred entrance. *Application fee:* $30. *Required:* essay or personal statement, high school transcript, minimum 2.8 GPA, 2 letters of recommendation. *Required for some:* interview. *Recommended:* interview. *Application deadlines:* 2/1 (freshmen), rolling (transfers), 12/1 (early action). *Notification:* 3/1 (freshmen), 1/15 (early action).

Freshman Application Contact Mr. Bradley Goan, Vice President for Enrollment and Dean of Admissions, Transylvania University, 300 North Broadway, Lexington, KY 40508-1797. *Phone:* 859-233-4242. *Toll-free phone:* 800-872-6798. *Fax:* 859-281-3649. *E-mail:* admissions@transy.edu. *Web site:* http://www.transy.edu/.

Union College
Barbourville, Kentucky

- **Independent United Methodist** comprehensive, founded 1879
- **Small-town** 100-acre campus
- **Endowment** $19.3 million
- **Coed** 830 undergraduate students, 92% full-time, 49% women, 51% men
- **Moderately difficult** entrance level, 87% of applicants were admitted

Undergraduates 767 full-time, 63 part-time. Students come from 30 states and territories; 11 other countries; 28% are from out of state; 10% Black or African American, non-Hispanic/Latino; 2% Hispanic/Latino; 0.2% Asian, non-Hispanic/Latino; 0.5% American Indian or Alaska Native, non-Hispanic/Latino; 0.7% Two or more races, non-Hispanic/Latino; 1% Race/ethnicity unknown; 4% international; 11% transferred in; 39% live on campus. *Retention:* 56% of full-time freshmen returned.

Freshmen *Admission:* 1,039 applied, 900 admitted, 194 enrolled. *Average high school GPA:* 3. *Test scores:* ACT scores over 18: 90%; ACT scores over 24: 21%; ACT scores over 30: 3%.

Faculty *Total:* 107, 58% full-time, 51% with terminal degrees. *Student/faculty ratio:* 14:1.

Academics *Calendar:* semesters. *Degrees:* bachelor's, master's, post-master's, and postbachelor's certificates. *Special study options:* academic remediation for entering students, accelerated degree program, advanced placement credit, double majors, honors programs, independent study, off-campus study, part-time degree program, services for LD students, student-designed majors, study abroad, summer session for credit. *ROTC:* Army (b). *Unusual degree programs:* 3-2 engineering with University of Kentucky.

Computers on Campus 230 computers/terminals and 450 ports are available on campus for general student use. Students can access the following: campus intranet, computer help desk, free student e-mail accounts, online (class) grades, online (class) registration, online (class) schedules. Campuswide network is available. 100% of college-owned or -operated housing units are wired

for high-speed Internet access. Wireless service is available via classrooms, computer centers, computer labs, dorm rooms, learning centers, libraries, student centers.

Student Life *Housing:* on-campus residence required through sophomore year. *Options:* men-only, women-only. Campus housing is university owned. Freshman campus housing is guaranteed. *Activities and organizations:* drama/theater group, choral group, Special Performers, Off-campus Trips, Open Mic Night, Bingo Night, Movie Fest. *Campus security:* 24-hour emergency response devices and patrols, late-night transport/escort service, controlled dormitory access. *Student services:* health clinic, personal/psychological counseling.

Athletics Member NAIA. *Intercollegiate sports:* baseball M(s), basketball M(s)/W(s), bowling M(s)/W(s), cheerleading M(s)/W(s), cross-country running M(s)/W(s), football M(s), golf M(s)/W(s), soccer M(s)/W(s), softball W(s), swimming and diving M(s)/W(s), volleyball W(s). *Intramural sports:* basketball M/W, football M, soccer M/W, table tennis M/W, ultimate Frisbee M/W, volleyball M/W.

Standardized Tests *Required:* SAT or ACT (for admission).

Costs (2012–13) *Comprehensive fee:* $27,450 includes full-time tuition ($19,900), mandatory fees ($900), and room and board ($6650). Full-time tuition and fees vary according to course load. Part-time tuition: $325 per credit hour. Part-time tuition and fees vary according to course load. *College room only:* $3000. Room and board charges vary according to board plan and housing facility. *Payment plan:* installment. *Waivers:* senior citizens and employees or children of employees.

Financial Aid Of all full-time matriculated undergraduates who enrolled in 2011, 727 applied for aid, 688 were judged to have need, 102 had their need fully met. 111 Federal Work-Study jobs (averaging $1337). 82 state and other part-time jobs (averaging $1337). In 2011, 70 non-need-based awards were made. *Average percent of need met:* 69%. *Average financial aid package:* $17,853. *Average need-based loan:* $4476. *Average need-based gift aid:* $13,602. *Average non-need-based aid:* $12,189. *Average indebtedness upon graduation:* $26,833.

Applying *Options:* electronic application, deferred entrance. *Application fee:* $10. *Required:* high school transcript, minimum 2.0 GPA. *Required for some:* interview. *Application deadlines:* rolling (freshmen), rolling (out-of-state freshmen), rolling (transfers). *Notification:* continuous (freshmen), continuous (out-of-state freshmen), continuous (transfers).

Freshman Application Contact Dr. Jerry Jackson EdD, Vice President for Enrollment Management, Union College, 310 College Street, Barbourville, KY 40906. *Phone:* 606-546-1222. *Toll-free phone:* 800-489-8646. *Fax:* 606-546-1667. *E-mail:* jjackson@unionky.edu. *Web site:* http://www.unionky.edu/

University of Kentucky

Lexington, Kentucky

Freshman Application Contact Ms. Michelle Nordin, Associate Director of Admissions, University of Kentucky, 100 W.D. Funkhouser Building, Lexington, KY 40506-0054. *Phone:* 859-257-2000. *Toll-free phone:* 866-900-GO-UK. *E-mail:* admissio@uky.edu. *Web site:* http://www.uky.edu/.

University of Louisville

Louisville, Kentucky

- **State-supported** university, founded 1798
- **Urban** 345-acre campus with easy access to Louisville
- **Endowment** $772.2 million
- **Coed** 15,597 undergraduate students, 78% full-time, 51% women, 49% men
- **Moderately difficult** entrance level, 73% of applicants were admitted

Undergraduates 12,177 full-time, 3,420 part-time. Students come from 53 states and territories; 65 other countries; 15% are from out of state; 12% Black or African American, non-Hispanic/Latino; 3% Hispanic/Latino; 3% Asian, non-Hispanic/Latino; 0.1% Native Hawaiian or other Pacific Islander, non-Hispanic/Latino; 0.1% American Indian or Alaska Native, non-Hispanic/Latino; 3% Two or more races, non-Hispanic/Latino; 0.2% Race/ethnicity unknown; 1% international; 7% transferred in; 29% live on campus. *Retention:* 78% of full-time freshmen returned.

Freshmen *Admission:* 7,892 applied, 5,738 admitted, 2,569 enrolled. *Average high school GPA:* 3.46. *Test scores:* SAT critical reading scores over 500: 72%; SAT math scores over 500: 76%; ACT scores over 18: 99%; SAT critical reading scores over 600: 32%; SAT math scores over 600: 39%; ACT scores over 24: 57%; SAT critical reading scores over 700: 8%; SAT math scores over 700: 9%; ACT scores over 30: 15%.

Faculty *Total:* 1,280, 66% full-time, 67% with terminal degrees. *Student/faculty ratio:* 16:1.

Academics *Calendar:* semesters. *Degrees:* certificates, associate, bachelor's, master's, doctoral, post-master's, postbachelor's, and first professional certificates. *Special study options:* academic remediation for entering students, accelerated degree program, adult/continuing education programs, advanced placement credit, cooperative education, distance learning, double majors, English as a second language, honors programs, independent study, internships, off-campus study, part-time degree program, services for LD students, student-designed majors, study abroad, summer session for credit. *ROTC:* Army (b), Air Force (b). *Unusual degree programs:* 3-2 engineering; Bachelor of Music and Bachelor of Music Education, Bachelor of Arts/Science and Master of Public Health.

Computers on Campus 1,226 computers/terminals and 57 ports are available on campus for general student use. Students can access the following: campus intranet, computer help desk, free student e-mail accounts, online (class) grades, online (class) registration, online (class) schedules. Campuswide network is available. 100% of college-owned or -operated housing units are wired for high-speed Internet access. Wireless service is available via classrooms, computer centers, libraries, student centers.

Student Life *Housing options:* coed, cooperative, disabled students. Campus housing is university owned and is provided by a third party. Freshman applicants given priority for college housing. *Activities and organizations:* drama/theater group, student-run newspaper, radio station, choral group, marching band, Baptist Campus Ministry, Society of Porter Scholars, Association of Black Students, commonGround, Phi Eta Sigma, national fraternities, national sororities. *Campus security:* 24-hour emergency response devices and patrols, late-night transport/escort service, controlled dormitory access, The University of Louisville Alert notification system. *Student services:* health clinic, personal/psychological counseling, women's center.

Athletics Member NCAA. All Division I except football (Division I-A). *Intercollegiate sports:* baseball M(s), basketball M(s)/W(s), crew W(s), cross-country running M(s)/W(s), field hockey W(s), golf M(s)/W(s), lacrosse W(s), soccer M(s)/W(s), softball W(s), swimming and diving M(s)/W(s), tennis M(s)/W(s), track and field M(s)/W(s), volleyball W(s). *Intramural sports:* badminton M/W, basketball M/W, bowling M/W, cross-country running M/W, equestrian sports W(c), fencing M/W, football M/W, golf M/W, gymnastics W(c), ice hockey M, lacrosse M(c)/W(c), racquetball M/W, rugby M(c), soccer M/W, softball W, swimming and diving M/W, table tennis M/W, tennis M/W, track and field M/W, ultimate Frisbee M/W, volleyball M/W.

Standardized Tests *Required:* SAT or ACT (for admission). *Required for some:* TOEFL for students whose primary language is not English.

Costs (2012–13) *Tuition:* state resident $8930 full-time, $373 per credit hour part-time; nonresident $21,650 full-time, $903 per credit hour part-time. Full-time tuition and fees vary according to reciprocity agreements. Part-time tuition and fees vary according to course load and reciprocity agreements. *Room and board:* $7440; room only: $4520. Room and board charges vary according to board plan and housing facility. *Payment plan:* installment. *Waivers:* senior citizens and employees or children of employees.

Financial Aid Of all full-time matriculated undergraduates who enrolled in 2010, 10,402 applied for aid, 8,833 were judged to have need, 1,571 had their need fully met. 395 Federal Work-Study jobs (averaging $3280). In 2010, 1573 non-need-based awards were made. *Average percent of need met:* 59%. *Average financial aid package:* $9987. *Average need-based loan:* $4070. *Average need-based gift aid:* $7561. *Average non-need-based aid:* $7368. *Average indebtedness upon graduation:* $19,812.

Applying *Options:* electronic application, deferred entrance. *Application fee:* $40. *Required:* high school transcript, minimum 2.5 GPA. *Application deadlines:* 2/15 (freshmen), 7/1 (transfers). *Notification:* continuous (freshmen), continuous (transfers).

Freshman Application Contact Ms. Jenny L. Sawyer, Executive Director of Admissions, University of Louisville, 2301 South Third Street, Houchens Room 150, Louisville, KY 40292-0001. *Phone:* 502-852-6531. *Toll-free phone:* 800-334-8635. *Fax:* 502-852-4776. *E-mail:* admitme@louisville.edu. *Web site:* http://www.louisville.edu/.

University of Phoenix–Louisville Campus

Louisville, Kentucky

Admissions Office Contact University of Phoenix–Louisville Campus, 10400 Linn Station Road, Louisville, KY 40223-3839. *Toll-free phone:* 866-766-0766. *Web site:* http://www.phoenix.edu/.

University of Pikeville

Pikeville, Kentucky

- **Independent** comprehensive, founded 1889, affiliated with Presbyterian Church (U.S.A.)
- **Small-town** 25-acre campus
- **Endowment** $10.6 million
- **Coed** 1,507 undergraduate students, 77% full-time, 50% women, 50% men
- **Noncompetitive** entrance level, 100% of applicants were admitted

Undergraduates 1,164 full-time, 343 part-time. Students come from 30 states and territories; 14 other countries; 20% are from out of state; 9% Black or African American, non-Hispanic/Latino; 1% Hispanic/Latino; 0.5% Asian, non-Hispanic/Latino; 0.2% American Indian or Alaska Native, non-Hispanic/Latino; 0.3% Race/ethnicity unknown; 1% international; 8% transferred in; 60% live on campus. *Retention:* 50% of full-time freshmen returned.

Freshmen *Admission:* 1,665 applied, 1,665 admitted, 484 enrolled. *Average high school GPA:* 3.14. *Test scores:* ACT scores over 18: 68%; ACT scores over 24: 17%; ACT scores over 30: 2%.

Faculty *Total:* 105, 59% full-time, 37% with terminal degrees. *Student/faculty ratio:* 17:1.

Academics *Calendar:* semesters. *Degrees:* associate, bachelor's, master's, and doctoral. *Special study options:* academic remediation for entering students, advanced placement credit, double majors, independent study, internships, part-time degree program, services for LD students, student-designed majors, study abroad, summer session for credit. *ROTC:* Army (b).

Computers on Campus 166 computers/terminals are available on campus for general student use. Students can access the following: free student e-mail accounts, online (class) grades, online (class) schedules. Campuswide network is available. 90% of college-owned or -operated housing units are wired for high-speed Internet access. Wireless service is available via entire campus.

Student Life *Housing options:* coed, men-only, women-only. Campus housing is university owned. *Activities and organizations:* drama/theater group, student-run newspaper, choral group, student government, Phi Beta Lambda, Lambda Sigma, Concert Choir, Student Nurses at PC. *Campus security:* 24-hour emergency response devices and patrols, controlled dormitory access. *Student services:* personal/psychological counseling.

Athletics Member NAIA. *Intercollegiate sports:* baseball M(s), basketball M(s)/W(s), bowling M(s)/W(s), cheerleading M(s)/W(s), cross-country running M(s)/W(s), football M(s), golf M(s)/W(s), soccer M(s)/W(s), softball W(s), tennis M(s)/W(s), volleyball W(s).

Costs (2012–13) *Comprehensive fee:* $23,750 includes full-time tuition ($17,050) and room and board ($6700). Full-time tuition and fees vary according to course load. Part-time tuition: $710 per credit hour. Part-time tuition and fees vary according to course load. *Room and board:* Room and board charges vary according to housing facility. *Payment plan:* installment. *Waivers:* senior citizens and employees or children of employees.

Financial Aid Of all full-time matriculated undergraduates who enrolled in 2011, 1,141 applied for aid, 1,141 were judged to have need, 478 had their need fully met. 168 Federal Work-Study jobs (averaging $1695). *Average percent of need met:* 84%. *Average financial aid package:* $17,716. *Average need-based loan:* $3903. *Average need-based gift aid:* $14,279. *Average indebtedness upon graduation:* $22,440.

Applying *Options:* electronic application, deferred entrance. *Required:* high school transcript. *Application deadlines:* 8/15 (freshmen), 8/15 (out-of-state freshmen), 8/15 (transfers). *Notification:* continuous (freshmen), continuous (out-of-state freshmen), continuous (transfers).

Freshman Application Contact Mr. Gary Justice, Director of Admissions and Student Financial Aid, University of Pikeville, 147 Sycamore Street, Pikeville, KY 41501. *Phone:* 606-218-5251. *Toll-free phone:* 866-232-7700. *Fax:* 606-218-5255. *E-mail:* wewantyou@pc.edu. *Web site:* http://www.upike.edu/.

University of the Cumberlands

Williamsburg, Kentucky

- **Independent Kentucky Baptist** comprehensive, founded 1889
- **Rural** 60-acre campus with easy access to Knoxville
- **Endowment** $61.6 million
- **Coed** 1,726 undergraduate students, 80% full-time, 51% women, 49% men
- **Moderately difficult** entrance level, 70% of applicants were admitted

Undergraduates 1,384 full-time, 342 part-time. Students come from 34 states and territories; 27 other countries; 31% are from out of state; 6% Black or African American, non-Hispanic/Latino; 3% Hispanic/Latino; 0.7% Asian, non-Hispanic/Latino; 0.1% Native Hawaiian or other Pacific Islander, non-Hispanic/Latino; 0.2% American Indian or Alaska Native, non-Hispanic/Latino; 0.1% Two or more races, non-Hispanic/Latino; 1% Race/ethnicity unknown; 4% international; 5% transferred in; 77% live on campus. *Retention:* 62% of full-time freshmen returned.

Experience UNCOMMON

UNIVERSITY of the CUMBERLANDS

Williamsburg, KY

www.ucumberlands.edu • 1.800.343.1609

Freshmen *Admission:* 2,290 applied, 1,598 admitted, 402 enrolled. *Average high school GPA:* 3.3. *Test scores:* SAT critical reading scores over 500: 30%; SAT math scores over 500: 34%; ACT scores over 18: 92%; SAT critical reading scores over 600: 2%; SAT math scores over 600: 9%; ACT scores over 24: 30%; ACT scores over 30: 3%.

Faculty *Total:* 182, 59% full-time, 71% with terminal degrees. *Student/faculty ratio:* 13:1.

Academics *Calendar:* semesters. *Degrees:* associate, bachelor's, master's, doctoral, post-master's, and postbachelor's certificates. *Special study options:* academic remediation for entering students, accelerated degree program, adult/continuing education programs, advanced placement credit, cooperative education, distance learning, double majors, English as a second language, honors programs, independent study, internships, part-time degree program, student-designed majors, study abroad, summer session for credit. *ROTC:* Army (b).

Computers on Campus 240 computers/terminals are available on campus for general student use. Students can access the following: computer help desk, free student e-mail accounts, online (class) grades, online (class) registration, online (class) schedules. Campuswide network is available. 100% of college-owned or -operated housing units are wired for high-speed Internet access. Wireless service is available via entire campus.

Student Life *Housing:* on-campus residence required through senior year. *Options:* men-only, women-only. Campus housing is university owned. Freshman campus housing is guaranteed. *Activities and organizations:* drama/theater group, student-run newspaper, radio and television station, choral group, marching band, Baptist Student Union, Student Government Association, Campus Activity Board, Mountain Outreach, Fellowship of Christian Athletes. *Campus security:* 24-hour emergency response devices and patrols, student patrols, late-night transport/escort service, patrols by trained security personnel 11pm to 7am.

Athletics Member NAIA. *Intercollegiate sports:* baseball M(s), basketball M(s)/W(s), cheerleading M(s)/W(s), cross-country running M(s)/W(s), football M(s), golf M(s)/W(s), soccer M(s)/W(s), softball M/W(s), swimming and diving M(s)/W(s), tennis M(s)/W(s), track and field M(s)/W(s), volleyball W(s), wrestling M(s)/W(s). *Intramural sports:* basketball M/W, football M/W, golf M/W, soccer M/W, softball M/W, table tennis M/W, tennis M/W, volleyball M/W.

Standardized Tests *Required:* SAT or ACT (for admission).

Costs (2012–13) *Comprehensive fee:* $26,000 includes full-time tuition ($18,640), mandatory fees ($360), and room and board ($7000). Part-time tuition: $590 per credit. Part-time tuition and fees vary according to course load. *Required fees:* $360 per term part-time. *Payment plan:* installment. *Waivers:* employees or children of employees.

Financial Aid Of all full-time matriculated undergraduates who enrolled in 2011, 1,271 applied for aid, 1,191 were judged to have need, 205 had their need fully met. 658 Federal Work-Study jobs (averaging $2235). 10 state and other part-time jobs (averaging $2434). In 2011, 168 non-need-based awards were made. *Average percent of need met:* 77%. *Average financial aid package:* $18,203. *Average need-based loan:* $4012. *Average need-based gift aid:* $14,008. *Average non-need-based aid:* $8507. *Average indebtedness upon graduation:* $13,373.

Applying *Options:* electronic application. *Application fee:* $30. *Required:* high school transcript, minimum 2.0 GPA. *Required for some:* essay or personal statement, interview. *Application deadline:* rolling (freshmen). *Notification:* continuous (freshmen), continuous (transfers).

Freshman Application Contact Mrs. Erica Harris, Director of Admissions, University of the Cumberlands, 6178 College Station Drive, Williamsburg, KY 40769. *Phone:* 606-539-4241. *Toll-free phone:* 800-343-1609. *Fax:* 606-539-4303. *E-mail:* admiss@ucumberlands.edu. *Web site:* http://www.ucumberlands.edu/.

See page 1716 for the College Close-Up.

Western Kentucky University

Bowling Green, Kentucky

- **State-supported** comprehensive, founded 1906
- **Suburban** 235-acre campus with easy access to Nashville
- **Endowment** $108.5 million
- **Coed** 17,970 undergraduate students, 78% full-time, 58% women, 42% men
- **Minimally difficult** entrance level, 92% of applicants were admitted

Undergraduates 13,952 full-time, 4,018 part-time. Students come from 49 states and territories; 51 other countries; 15% are from out of state; 11% Black or African American, non-Hispanic/Latino; 2% Hispanic/Latino; 0.9% Asian, non-Hispanic/Latino; 0.1% Native Hawaiian or other Pacific Islander, non-Hispanic/Latino; 0.3% American Indian or Alaska Native, non-Hispanic/Latino; 1% Two or more races, non-Hispanic/Latino; 0.9% Race/ethnicity unknown; 2% international; 6% transferred in; 29% live on campus. *Retention:* 73% of full-time freshmen returned.

Freshmen *Admission:* 8,017 applied, 7,355 admitted, 3,385 enrolled. *Average high school GPA:* 3.15. *Test scores:* SAT critical reading scores over 500: 55%; SAT math scores over 500: 53%; ACT scores over 18: 81%; SAT critical reading scores over 600: 21%; SAT math scores over 600: 23%; ACT scores over 24: 31%; SAT critical reading scores over 700: 5%; SAT math scores over 700: 3%; ACT scores over 30: 5%.

Faculty *Total:* 1,200, 64% full-time, 52% with terminal degrees. *Student/faculty ratio:* 19:1.

Academics *Calendar:* semesters. *Degrees:* certificates, associate, bachelor's, master's, doctoral, post-master's, postbachelor's, and first professional certificates. *Special study options:* academic remediation for entering students, accelerated degree program, adult/continuing education programs, advanced placement credit, cooperative education, distance learning, double majors, English as a second language, external degree program, freshman honors college, honors programs, independent study, internships, off-campus study, part-time degree program, services for LD students, student-designed majors, study abroad, summer session for credit. *ROTC:* Army (b), Air Force (c). *Unusual degree programs:* 3-2 engineering with Western Kentucky University has cooperative agreements with a number of engineering schools.

Computers on Campus 2,081 computers/terminals are available on campus for general student use. Students can access the following: campus intranet, computer help desk, free student e-mail accounts, online (class) grades, online (class) registration, online (class) schedules. Campuswide network is available. 100% of college-owned or -operated housing units are wired for high-speed Internet access. Wireless service is available via entire campus.

Student Life *Housing:* on-campus residence required through sophomore year. *Options:* coed, men-only, women-only. Campus housing is university owned. Freshman applicants given priority for college housing. *Activities and organizations:* drama/theater group, student-run newspaper, radio and television station, choral group, marching band, Student Government Association, Campus Activities Board, Campus Crusade for Christ, Campus Ministries, Residence Hall Association, national fraternities, national sororities. *Campus security:* 24-hour emergency response devices and patrols, student patrols, late-night transport/escort service, controlled dormitory access. *Student services:* health clinic, personal/psychological counseling, women's center.

Athletics Member NCAA. All Division I except football (Division I-A). *Intercollegiate sports:* baseball M(s), basketball M(s)/W(s), cross-country running M(s)/W(s), golf M(s)/W(s), soccer W, softball W(s), swimming and diving M(s)/W(s), tennis M(s)/W(s), track and field M(s)/W(s), volleyball W(s). *Intramural sports:* badminton M/W, basketball M/W, bowling M(c)/W(c), fencing M(c)/W(c), field hockey M(c)/W(c), football M/W, golf M/W, lacrosse M(c)/W(c), racquetball M/W, rugby M(c)/W(c), soccer M/W, softball M/W, table tennis M/W, tennis M(c)/W(c), ultimate Frisbee M(c)/W(c), volleyball M/W.

Standardized Tests *Required:* SAT or ACT (for admission).

Costs (2011–12) *Tuition:* state resident $8084 full-time, $337 per credit hour part-time; nonresident $20,016 full-time, $834 per credit hour part-time. Full-time tuition and fees vary according to course load, location, program, and reciprocity agreements. Part-time tuition and fees vary according to course load, location, program, and reciprocity agreements. *Room and board:* $7320; room only: $4170. Room and board charges vary according to board plan and housing facility. *Payment plan:* installment. *Waivers:* children of alumni, senior citizens, and employees or children of employees.

Financial Aid Of all full-time matriculated undergraduates who enrolled in 2010, 11,356 applied for aid, 9,304 were judged to have need, 2,432 had their need fully met. 906 Federal Work-Study jobs (averaging $2274). 1,622 state and other part-time jobs (averaging $2683). In 2010, 1111 non-need-based awards were made. *Average percent of need met:* 26%. *Average financial aid package:* $12,877. *Average need-based loan:* $3825. *Average need-based gift aid:* $5199. *Average non-need-based aid:* $5182. *Average indebtedness upon graduation:* $22,560.

Applying *Options:* electronic application. *Application fee:* $40. *Required:* high school transcript, minimum 2.5 GPA. *Required for some:* minimum 2.0 GPA. *Recommended:* minimum 2.5 GPA. *Application deadlines:* 8/1 (freshmen), 8/1 (transfers). *Notification:* continuous (freshmen), continuous (transfers).

Freshman Application Contact Western Kentucky University, 1906 College Heights Boulevard, Bowling Green, KY 42101. *Phone:* 270-745-2551. *Toll-free phone:* 800-495-8463. *Web site:* http://www.wku.edu/.

LOUISIANA

Centenary College of Louisiana
Shreveport, Louisiana

- **Independent United Methodist** comprehensive, founded 1825
- **Suburban** 65-acre campus
- **Coed** 805 undergraduate students, 98% full-time, 56% women, 44% men
- **Moderately difficult** entrance level, 63% of applicants were admitted

Undergraduates 790 full-time, 15 part-time. Students come from 32 states and territories; 13 other countries; 35% are from out of state; 13% Black or African American, non-Hispanic/Latino; 5% Hispanic/Latino; 2% Asian, non-Hispanic/Latino; 0.2% Native Hawaiian or other Pacific Islander, non-Hispanic/Latino; 0.5% American Indian or Alaska Native, non-Hispanic/Latino; 3% Two or more races, non-Hispanic/Latino; 0.2% Race/ethnicity unknown; 3% international; 4% transferred in; 55% live on campus. *Retention:* 68% of full-time freshmen returned.
Freshmen *Admission:* 1,094 applied, 690 admitted, 238 enrolled. *Average high school GPA:* 3.42. *Test scores:* SAT critical reading scores over 500: 67%; SAT math scores over 500: 67%; ACT scores over 18: 100%; SAT critical reading scores over 600: 29%; SAT math scores over 600: 27%; ACT scores over 24: 57%; SAT critical reading scores over 700: 4%; SAT math scores over 700: 4%; ACT scores over 30: 13%.
Faculty *Total:* 102, 61% full-time, 72% with terminal degrees. *Student/faculty ratio:* 11:1.
Academics *Calendar:* 4-4-1. *Degrees:* bachelor's and master's. *Special study options:* adult/continuing education programs, advanced placement credit, double majors, honors programs, independent study, internships, off-campus study, part-time degree program, services for LD students, student-designed majors, study abroad, summer session for credit. *Unusual degree programs:* 3-2 engineering with Columbia University, University of Southern California, Case Western Reserve University, Texas A&M University, Louisiana, Washington University in St. Louis; communication disorders with Louisiana State University Medical Center School of Medicine in Shreveport.
Computers on Campus Students can access the following: free student e-mail accounts, online (class) grades, online (class) registration, online (class) schedules. Campuswide network is available. Wireless service is available via classrooms, dorm rooms, libraries, student centers.
Student Life *Housing:* on-campus residence required through senior year. *Options:* coed, women-only. Campus housing is university owned. Freshman campus housing is guaranteed. *Activities and organizations:* drama/theater group, student-run newspaper, radio station, choral group, intramural sports, Residence Life, FCA, Church Career/Campus Ministries, student media, national fraternities, national sororities. *Campus security:* 24-hour emergency response devices and patrols, late-night transport/escort service, controlled dormitory access. *Student services:* health clinic, personal/psychological counseling.
Athletics Member NCAA. All Division III. *Intercollegiate sports:* baseball M, basketball M/W, cheerleading M(c)/W(c), cross-country running M/W, golf M/W, gymnastics W, lacrosse M(c), soccer M/W, softball W, swimming and diving M/W, tennis M/W, volleyball W. *Intramural sports:* basketball M/W, cheerleading W, football M/W, golf M, lacrosse M, soccer M/W, softball M/W, table tennis M/W, tennis M/W, volleyball M/W.
Standardized Tests *Required:* SAT or ACT (for admission).
Costs (2011–12) *Comprehensive fee:* $34,020 includes full-time tuition ($24,030), mandatory fees ($1260), and room and board ($8730). Part-time tuition: $800 per credit hour. Part-time tuition and fees vary according to course load and program. *Required fees:* $70 per credit hour part-time. *College room only:* $4430. Room and board charges vary according to board plan and housing facility. *Payment plans:* installment, deferred payment. *Waivers:* employees or children of employees.
Financial Aid Of all full-time matriculated undergraduates who enrolled in 2011, 705 applied for aid, 603 were judged to have need, 142 had their need fully met. 187 Federal Work-Study jobs (averaging $1974). 39 state and other part-time jobs (averaging $1218). In 2011, 176 non-need-based awards were made. *Average percent of need met:* 81%. *Average financial aid package:* $21,689. *Average need-based loan:* $3967. *Average need-based gift aid:* $18,692. *Average non-need-based aid:* $11,565. *Average indebtedness upon graduation:* $21,900.
Applying *Options:* electronic application, early admission, early action, deferred entrance. *Application fee:* $30. *Required:* essay or personal statement, high school transcript, minimum 2.0 GPA, 1 letter of recommendation. *Recommended:* interview, class rank. *Application deadlines:* 8/1 (freshmen), 8/1 (out-of-state freshmen), 8/15 (transfers), 1/15 (early action). *Notification:* continuous (freshmen), continuous (out-of-state freshmen), continuous (transfers), 2/1 (early action).
Freshman Application Contact Mrs. Gail Roberson, Director of Admission, Centenary College of Louisiana, Office of Admission, 2911 Centenary Boulevard, Shreveport, LA 71134-1188. *Phone:* 318-869-5701. *Toll-free phone:* 800-234-4448. *Fax:* 318-869-5005. *Web site:* http://www.centenary.edu/.

Dillard University
New Orleans, Louisiana

- **Independent interdenominational** 4-year, founded 1869
- **Urban** 55-acre campus
- **Endowment** $32.5 million
- **Coed** 1,249 undergraduate students, 94% full-time, 72% women, 28% men
- **Moderately difficult** entrance level, 93% of applicants were admitted

Undergraduates 1,180 full-time, 69 part-time. Students come from 32 states and territories; 10 other countries; 31% are from out of state; 96% Black or African American, non-Hispanic/Latino; 0.6% Hispanic/Latino; 0.2% Asian, non-Hispanic/Latino; 0.5% Two or more races, non-Hispanic/Latino; 0.6% Race/ethnicity unknown; 2% international; 5% transferred in; 42% live on campus. *Retention:* 64% of full-time freshmen returned.
Freshmen *Admission:* 2,643 applied, 2,456 admitted, 354 enrolled. *Average high school GPA:* 3. *Test scores:* SAT critical reading scores over 500: 18%; SAT math scores over 500: 16%; SAT writing scores over 500: 18%; ACT scores over 18: 52%; SAT critical reading scores over 600: 2%; SAT math scores over 600: 1%; SAT writing scores over 600: 2%; ACT scores over 24: 4%; SAT critical reading scores over 700: 1%; SAT writing scores over 700: 1%.
Faculty *Student/faculty ratio:* 12:1.
Academics *Calendar:* semesters. *Degree:* bachelor's. *Special study options:* academic remediation for entering students, advanced placement credit, cooperative education, double majors, English as a second language, external degree program, honors programs, independent study, internships, part-time degree program, services for LD students, study abroad, summer session for credit. *ROTC:* Army (c), Air Force (c). *Unusual degree programs:* 3-2 engineering with Columbia University, Tulane University, University of New Orleans, Georgia Institute of Technology; biology with Boston University School of Medicine, Meharry Medical College School of Medicine, New York College of Podiatric Medicine and Ohio College of Medicine; public health with LSU Health Sciences Center School of Public Health and Tulane School of Public Health and Tropical Medicine.
Computers on Campus 97 computers/terminals and 300 ports are available on campus for general student use. Students can access the following: free student e-mail accounts, online (class) grades, online (class) registration, online (class) schedules. Campuswide network is available. 100% of college-owned or -operated housing units are wired for high-speed Internet access. Wireless service is available via classrooms, computer centers, libraries.
Student Life *Housing:* on-campus residence required for freshman year. *Options:* coed, men-only, women-only, disabled students. Campus housing is university owned and leased by the school. Freshman campus housing is guaranteed. *Activities and organizations:* drama/theater group, student-run newspaper, radio and television station, choral group, Student Government Association, Student Activities Board, National Pan-Hellenic Council, Collegiate 100, Class Councils, national fraternities, national sororities. *Campus security:* 24-hour emergency response devices and patrols, late-night transport/escort service, controlled dormitory access. *Student services:* health clinic, personal/psychological counseling, legal services.
Athletics Member NAIA. *Intercollegiate sports:* basketball M(s)/W(s), cross-country running M(s)/W(s), track and field M(s)/W(s), volleyball W(s). *Intramural sports:* basketball M/W, football M/W, tennis M/W, volleyball M/W, weight lifting M/W.
Standardized Tests *Required:* SAT or ACT (for admission), minimum SAT score of 870 (math and verbal) or minimum ACT composite score of 18 (for admission).
Costs (2012–13) *Comprehensive fee:* $23,536 includes full-time tuition ($13,650), mandatory fees ($1200), and room and board ($8686). Part-time tuition: $569 per credit hour. Part-time tuition and fees vary according to course load. *College room only:* $5690. Room and board charges vary according to housing facility. *Payment plan:* installment. *Waivers:* employees or children of employees.
Financial Aid Of all full-time matriculated undergraduates who enrolled in 2010, 1,177 applied for aid, 1,135 were judged to have need, 276 had their need fully met. 291 Federal Work-Study jobs (averaging $1565). *Average percent of need met:* 69%. *Average financial aid package:* $18,745. *Average need-based loan:* $3563. *Average need-based gift aid:* $9469. *Average indebtedness upon graduation:* $26,250.
Applying *Options:* electronic application, early admission. *Application fee:* $30. *Required:* high school transcript, minimum 2.5 GPA, 2 letters of recommendation. *Required for some:* essay or personal statement, interview. *Application deadlines:* rolling (freshmen), rolling (out-of-state freshmen), rolling

(transfers). *Notification:* continuous (freshmen), continuous (out-of-state freshmen), continuous (transfers).
Freshman Application Contact Mr. Anthony Austin, Director of Recruitment, Admissions and Programming, Dillard University, 2601 Gentilly Boulevard, New Orleans, LA 70122-3097. *Phone:* 504-816-4362. *Toll-free phone:* 800-216-8094. *Fax:* 504-816-4895. *E-mail:* aaustin@dillard.edu. *Web site:* http://www.dillard.edu/.

Grambling State University
Grambling, Louisiana

- **State-supported** university, founded 1901, part of University of Louisiana System
- **Small-town** 383-acre campus with easy access to Shreveport
- **Endowment** $9.9 million
- **Coed** 4,461 undergraduate students, 93% full-time, 60% women, 40% men
- **Noncompetitive** entrance level, 21% of applicants were admitted

Undergraduates 4,151 full-time, 310 part-time. Students come from 40 states and territories; 28 other countries; 39% are from out of state; 87% Black or African American, non-Hispanic/Latino; 1% Hispanic/Latino; 0.2% Asian, non-Hispanic/Latino; 0.1% Native Hawaiian or other Pacific Islander, non-Hispanic/Latino; 0.2% American Indian or Alaska Native, non-Hispanic/Latino; 0.6% Two or more races, non-Hispanic/Latino; 2% Race/ethnicity unknown; 8% international; 5% transferred in; 50% live on campus. *Retention:* 68% of full-time freshmen returned.
Freshmen *Admission:* 3,656 applied, 760 admitted, 760 enrolled. *Average high school GPA:* 2.9. *Test scores:* SAT critical reading scores over 500: 16%; SAT math scores over 500: 19%; ACT scores over 18: 49%; SAT critical reading scores over 600: 1%; SAT math scores over 600: 4%; ACT scores over 24: 7%; SAT math scores over 700: 1%.
Faculty *Total:* 260, 88% full-time, 55% with terminal degrees. *Student/faculty ratio:* 19:1.
Academics *Calendar:* semesters. *Degrees:* associate, bachelor's, master's, doctoral, and post-master's certificates. *Special study options:* academic remediation for entering students, adult/continuing education programs, advanced placement credit, cooperative education, distance learning, double majors, honors programs, internships, off-campus study, part-time degree program, services for LD students, study abroad, summer session for credit. *ROTC:* Army (b), Air Force (c).
Computers on Campus 400 computers/terminals and 400 ports are available on campus for general student use. Students can access the following: campus intranet, computer help desk, free student e-mail accounts, online (class) grades, online (class) registration, online (class) schedules. Campuswide network is available. 81% of college-owned or -operated housing units are wired for high-speed Internet access. Wireless service is available via classrooms, computer centers, computer labs, dorm rooms, learning centers, libraries, student centers.
Student Life *Housing:* on-campus residence required for freshman year. *Options:* coed, men-only, women-only, disabled students. Campus housing is university owned. Freshman applicants given priority for college housing. *Activities and organizations:* drama/theater group, student-run newspaper, radio and television station, choral group, marching band, Tiger Marching Band, Black Dynasty Modeling Troupe, CALYPSO, sororities, fraternities, national fraternities, national sororities. *Campus security:* 24-hour patrols, student patrols, controlled dormitory access. *Student services:* health clinic, personal/psychological counseling.
Athletics Member NCAA. All Division I except football (Division I-AA). *Intercollegiate sports:* baseball M(s), basketball M(s)/W(s), bowling W(s), cross-country running M/W, tennis M/W(s), track and field M(s)/W(s), volleyball W(s). *Intramural sports:* bowling W, gymnastics M/W, softball M/W, swimming and diving M/W, table tennis M/W, track and field M/W, volleyball M/W, weight lifting M/W.
Standardized Tests *Required:* SAT or ACT (for admission).
Costs (2012–13) *Tuition:* state resident $3456 full-time, $144 per credit hour part-time; nonresident $10,673 full-time, $144 per credit hour part-time. Full-time tuition and fees vary according to course load. Part-time tuition and fees vary according to course load. *Required fees:* $1426 full-time, $144 per credit hour part-time, $440 per term part-time. *Room and board:* $8498; room only: $5606. Room and board charges vary according to housing facility.
Financial Aid Of all full-time matriculated undergraduates who enrolled in 2007, 4,191 applied for aid, 3,931 were judged to have need, 309 had their need fully met. 1,141 Federal Work-Study jobs (averaging $1310). 431 state and other part-time jobs (averaging $1487). In 2007, 200 non-need-based awards were made. *Average percent of need met:* 80%. *Average financial aid package:* $6800. *Average need-based loan:* $3813. *Average need-based gift aid:* $2928. *Average non-need-based aid:* $2328. *Average indebtedness upon graduation:* $29,416. *Financial aid deadline:* 4/1.

Applying *Options:* electronic application, early admission. *Application fee:* $20. *Required:* high school transcript, minimum 2.0 GPA. *Application deadlines:* 6/30 (freshmen), 6/30 (transfers). *Notification:* 8/1 (freshmen), continuous until 8/1 (transfers).
Freshman Application Contact Ms. Annie L. Moss, Director of Admissions and Recruitment, Grambling State University, GSU Box 4200, Grambling, LA 71270. *Phone:* 318-274-6183. *Toll-free phone:* 800-569-4714. *Fax:* 318-274-3292. *E-mail:* mossa@gram.edu. *Web site:* http://www.gram.edu/.

Herzing University
Kenner, Louisiana

Director of Admissions Genny Bordelon, Director of Admissions, Herzing University, 2500 Williams Boulevard, Kenner, LA 70062. *Phone:* 504-733-0074. *Toll-free phone:* 800-596-0724. *Fax:* 504-733-0020. *Web site:* http://www.herzing.edu/.

ITT Technical Institute
Baton Rouge, Louisiana

- **Proprietary** primarily 2-year
- **Coed**

Academics *Degrees:* associate and bachelor's.
Student Life *Housing:* college housing not available.
Freshman Application Contact Director of Recruitment, ITT Technical Institute, 14111 Airline Highway, Suite 101, Baton Rouge, LA 70817. *Phone:* 225-754-5800. *Toll-free phone:* 800-295-8485. *Web site:* http://www.itt-tech.edu/.

ITT Technical Institute
St. Rose, Louisiana

- **Proprietary** primarily 2-year, founded 1998, part of ITT Educational Services, Inc.
- **Coed**
- **Minimally difficult** entrance level

Academics *Calendar:* quarters. *Degrees:* associate and bachelor's.
Student Life *Housing:* college housing not available.
Freshman Application Contact Director of Recruitment, ITT Technical Institute, 140 James Drive East, St. Rose, LA 70087. *Phone:* 504-463-0338. *Toll-free phone:* 866-463-0338. *Web site:* http://www.itt-tech.edu/.

Louisiana College
Pineville, Louisiana

- **Independent Southern Baptist** comprehensive, founded 1906
- **Small-town** 81-acre campus
- **Endowment** $29.3 million
- **Coed** 1,153 undergraduate students, 93% full-time, 50% women, 50% men
- **Moderately difficult** entrance level, 74% of applicants were admitted

Undergraduates 1,068 full-time, 85 part-time. 18% Black or African American, non-Hispanic/Latino; 3% Hispanic/Latino; 1% Asian, non-Hispanic/Latino; 0.1% Native Hawaiian or other Pacific Islander, non-Hispanic/Latino; 1% American Indian or Alaska Native, non-Hispanic/Latino; 0.9% Two or more races, non-Hispanic/Latino; 2% Race/ethnicity unknown; 1% international; 60% live on campus. *Retention:* 56% of full-time freshmen returned.
Freshmen *Admission:* 820 applied, 606 admitted, 461 enrolled. *Average high school GPA:* 3.17. *Test scores:* ACT scores over 18: 86%; ACT scores over 24: 31%; ACT scores over 30: 5%.
Faculty *Total:* 115, 70% full-time, 48% with terminal degrees. *Student/faculty ratio:* 14:1.
Academics *Calendar:* semesters. *Degrees:* associate, bachelor's, and master's. *Special study options:* academic remediation for entering students, accelerated degree program, adult/continuing education programs, advanced placement credit, distance learning, double majors, honors programs, independent study, internships, part-time degree program, services for LD students, student-designed majors, study abroad, summer session for credit. *ROTC:* Army (b).
Computers on Campus 247 computers/terminals are available on campus for general student use. Students can access the following: campus intranet, free student e-mail accounts, online (class) grades. Campuswide network is available. 100% of college-owned or -operated housing units are wired for high-speed Internet access.
Student Life *Housing:* on-campus residence required through senior year. *Options:* men-only, women-only. Campus housing is university owned. Freshman campus housing is guaranteed. *Activities and organizations:* drama/the-

ater group, student-run newspaper, radio station, choral group, marching band, Baptist Student Union, Delta Xi Omega, Student Government Association, Union Board, Lambda Chi Beta. *Campus security:* 24-hour patrols, student patrols, late-night transport/escort service, controlled dormitory access. *Student services:* health clinic, personal/psychological counseling.

Athletics Member NCAA, NCCAA. All NCAA Division III. *Intercollegiate sports:* baseball M, basketball M/W, cheerleading M/W, cross-country running W, football M, golf M, soccer M/W, softball W, tennis W. *Intramural sports:* badminton M/W, basketball M/W, football M/W, racquetball M/W, soccer M/W, softball M/W, table tennis M/W, tennis M/W, ultimate Frisbee M/W, volleyball M/W, water polo M/W.

Standardized Tests *Required:* SAT or ACT (for admission).

Costs (2011–12) *Comprehensive fee:* $17,728 includes full-time tuition ($11,850), mandatory fees ($1430), and room and board ($4448). Full-time tuition and fees vary according to program. Part-time tuition: $395 per hour. Part-time tuition and fees vary according to program. *Room and board:* Room and board charges vary according to board plan and housing facility. *Payment plan:* installment. *Waivers:* employees or children of employees.

Financial Aid Of all full-time matriculated undergraduates who enrolled in 2010, 1,123 applied for aid, 895 were judged to have need, 286 had their need fully met. *Average percent of need met:* 39%. *Average financial aid package:* $7640. *Average need-based loan:* $4068. *Average need-based gift aid:* $2900.

Applying *Options:* electronic application, early admission. *Application fee:* $25. *Required:* high school transcript, minimum 2.0 GPA, class rank. *Required for some:* 3 letters of recommendation. *Recommended:* interview. *Application deadline:* 8/15 (freshmen). *Notification:* continuous (freshmen), continuous (transfers).

Freshman Application Contact Mr. Byron McGee, Director of Enrollment Management, Louisiana College, LC Box 566, Pineville, LA 71359. *Phone:* 318-487-7439. *Toll-free phone:* 800-487-1906. *Fax:* 318-487-7550. *E-mail:* admissions@lacollege.edu. *Web site:* http://www.lacollege.edu/.

Louisiana State University and Agricultural and Mechanical College

Baton Rouge, Louisiana

- **State-supported** university, founded 1860, part of Louisiana State University System
- **Urban** 2000-acre campus with easy access to New Orleans
- **Endowment** $364.1 million
- **Coed** 23,977 undergraduate students, 93% full-time, 51% women, 49% men
- **Moderately difficult** entrance level, 80% of applicants were admitted

Undergraduates 22,277 full-time, 1,700 part-time. Students come from 50 states and territories; 81 other countries; 20% are from out of state; 10% Black or African American, non-Hispanic/Latino; 4% Hispanic/Latino; 3% Asian, non-Hispanic/Latino; 0.1% Native Hawaiian or other Pacific Islander, non-Hispanic/Latino; 0.4% American Indian or Alaska Native, non-Hispanic/Latino; 2% Two or more races, non-Hispanic/Latino; 1% Race/ethnicity unknown; 2% international; 3% transferred in; 24% live on campus. *Retention:* 84% of full-time freshmen returned.

Freshmen *Admission:* 14,818 applied, 11,789 admitted, 5,290 enrolled. *Average high school GPA:* 3.45. *Test scores:* SAT critical reading scores over 500: 79%; SAT math scores over 500: 87%; ACT scores over 18: 100%; SAT critical reading scores over 600: 33%; SAT math scores over 600: 42%; ACT scores over 24: 68%; SAT critical reading scores over 700: 9%; SAT math scores over 700: 7%; ACT scores over 30: 13%.

Faculty *Total:* 1,366, 87% full-time, 87% with terminal degrees. *Student/faculty ratio:* 23:1.

Academics *Calendar:* semesters. *Degrees:* bachelor's, master's, doctoral, post-master's, and first professional certificates. *Special study options:* accelerated degree program, adult/continuing education programs, advanced placement credit, cooperative education, distance learning, double majors, English as a second language, freshman honors college, honors programs, independent study, internships, off-campus study, part-time degree program, services for LD students, student-designed majors, study abroad, summer session for credit. *ROTC:* Army (b), Navy (c), Air Force (b).

Computers on Campus 1,400 computers/terminals and 8,500 ports are available on campus for general student use. Students can access the following: computer help desk, free student e-mail accounts, online (class) grades, online (class) registration, online (class) schedules, free software for download, personal Web sites, storage, discounts on hardware, virtual computer lab. Campuswide network is available. 100% of college-owned or -operated housing units are wired for high-speed Internet access. Wireless service is available via entire campus.

Student Life *Housing options:* coed, men-only, women-only, disabled students. Campus housing is university owned. *Activities and organizations:*

drama/theater group, student-run newspaper, radio and television station, choral group, marching band, intramural athletics, student political organizations, student professional organizations, religious organizations, national fraternities, national sororities. *Campus security:* 24-hour emergency response devices and patrols, late-night transport/escort service, controlled dormitory access, self-defense education, crime prevention programs. *Student services:* health clinic, personal/psychological counseling, women's center, legal services.

Athletics Member NCAA. All Division I except football (Division I-A). *Intercollegiate sports:* baseball M(s), basketball M(s)/W(s), cheerleading M/W, cross-country running M(s)/W(s), golf M(s)/W(s), gymnastics W(s), soccer W(s), softball W(s), swimming and diving M(s)/W(s), tennis M(s)/W(s), track and field M(s)/W(s), volleyball W(s). *Intramural sports:* badminton M/W, basketball M/W, bowling M(c)/W(c), crew M(c)/W(c), equestrian sports W(c), football M/W, lacrosse M(c), racquetball M/W, rugby M(c), soccer M(c)/W(c), softball M/W, table tennis M/W, tennis M(c)/W(c), ultimate Frisbee M(c)/W, volleyball M(c)/W(c), weight lifting M(c)/W(c).

Standardized Tests *Required:* SAT or ACT (for admission).

Costs (2011–12) *Tuition:* state resident $4558 full-time; nonresident $17,566 full-time. Part-time tuition and fees vary according to course load. *Required fees:* $1796 full-time. *Room and board:* $8670; room only: $5180. Room and board charges vary according to board plan and housing facility. *Payment plan:* deferred payment. *Waivers:* employees or children of employees.

Financial Aid Of all full-time matriculated undergraduates who enrolled in 2010, 11,874 applied for aid, 8,488 were judged to have need, 2,447 had their need fully met. 752 Federal Work-Study jobs (averaging $1300). 4,442 state and other part-time jobs (averaging $2500). In 2010, 3697 non-need-based awards were made. *Average percent of need met:* 74%. *Average financial aid package:* $13,746. *Average need-based loan:* $6140. *Average need-based gift aid:* $8974. *Average non-need-based aid:* $5673. *Average indebtedness upon graduation:* $20,337.

Applying *Options:* electronic application, early admission, deferred entrance. *Application fee:* $40. *Required:* high school transcript, minimum 3.0 GPA. *Required for some:* essay or personal statement. *Application deadlines:* 4/15 (freshmen), 4/15 (transfers). *Notification:* continuous (freshmen), continuous (transfers).

Freshman Application Contact Ms. Guadalupe Lamadrid, Associate Director, Undergraduate Admissions, Louisiana State University and Agricultural and Mechanical College, 1146 Pleasant Hall, Baton Rouge, LA 70803. *Phone:* 225-578-1175. *Fax:* 225-578-4433. *E-mail:* glamadrid@lsu.edu. *Web site:* http://www.lsu.edu/.

Louisiana State University at Alexandria

Alexandria, Louisiana

Freshman Application Contact Ms. Shelly Kieffer, Director of Admissions and Recruiting, Louisiana State University at Alexandria, 8100 Highway 71 South, Alexandria, LA 71302-9121. *Phone:* 318-473-6424. *Toll-free phone:* 888-473-6417. *Fax:* 318-473-6418. *E-mail:* admissions@lsua.edu. *Web site:* http://www.lsua.edu/.

Louisiana State University Health Sciences Center

New Orleans, Louisiana

Freshman Application Contact Louisiana State University Health Sciences Center, 433 Bolivar Street, New Orleans, LA 70112-2223. *Phone:* 504-568-4829. *Web site:* http://www.lsuhsc.edu/.

Louisiana State University in Shreveport

Shreveport, Louisiana

- **State-supported** comprehensive, founded 1965, part of Louisiana State University System
- **Urban** 200-acre campus
- **Endowment** $16.3 million
- **Coed** 4,134 undergraduate students, 57% full-time, 60% women, 40% men
- **Moderately difficult** entrance level, 48% of applicants were admitted

Undergraduates 2,348 full-time, 1,786 part-time. Students come from 41 states and territories; 39 other countries; 6% are from out of state; 23% Black or African American, non-Hispanic/Latino; 4% Hispanic/Latino; 2% Asian, non-Hispanic/Latino; 0.1% Native Hawaiian or other Pacific Islander, non-

Hispanic/Latino; 0.9% American Indian or Alaska Native, non-Hispanic/Latino; 7% Race/ethnicity unknown; 2% international; 11% transferred in. *Retention:* 65% of full-time freshmen returned.

Freshmen *Admission:* 888 applied, 430 admitted, 321 enrolled. *Average high school GPA:* 3.26. *Test scores:* ACT scores over 18: 96%; ACT scores over 24: 32%; ACT scores over 30: 3%.

Faculty *Total:* 193, 67% full-time, 52% with terminal degrees. *Student/faculty ratio:* 21:1.

Academics *Calendar:* semesters plus 8-week and two 4-week summer terms. *Degrees:* certificates, bachelor's, master's, and post-master's certificates. *Special study options:* academic remediation for entering students, accelerated degree program, adult/continuing education programs, advanced placement credit, cooperative education, distance learning, double majors, honors programs, independent study, internships, off-campus study, part-time degree program, services for LD students, student-designed majors, summer session for credit. *ROTC:* Army (b).

Computers on Campus Students can access the following: computer help desk, free student e-mail accounts, online (class) grades, online (class) registration, online (class) schedules. Campuswide network is available. Wireless service is available via entire campus.

Student Life *Housing:* college housing not available. *Options:* Campus housing is provided by a third party. *Activities and organizations:* drama/theater group, student-run newspaper, choral group, national fraternities, national sororities. *Campus security:* 24-hour emergency response devices and patrols, student patrols, controlled dormitory access. *Student services:* personal/psychological counseling.

Athletics Member NAIA. *Intercollegiate sports:* baseball M(s), basketball M(s)/W(s), soccer M(s)/W(s), tennis W(s). *Intramural sports:* archery M, basketball M/W, football M/W, lacrosse M, racquetball M/W, softball M/W, table tennis M/W, volleyball M/W.

Standardized Tests *Required:* SAT or ACT (for admission).

Costs (2011–12) *Tuition:* state resident $3583 full-time, $143 per credit hour part-time; nonresident $10,319 full-time, $424 per credit hour part-time. Part-time tuition and fees vary according to course load. *Required fees:* $1091 full-time, $44 per credit hour part-time. *Room only:* $6228. *Waivers:* employees or children of employees.

Applying *Options:* early admission, early decision. *Application fee:* $10. *Required for some:* high school transcript, minimum 2.0 GPA. *Application deadline:* rolling (freshmen).

Freshman Application Contact Louisiana State University in Shreveport, 1 University Place, Shreveport, LA 71115-2399. *Phone:* 318-797-5063. *Toll-free phone:* 800-229-5957. *Web site:* http://www.lsus.edu/.

Louisiana Tech University
Ruston, Louisiana

Freshman Application Contact Mrs. Jan B. Albritton, Director of Admissions, Louisiana Tech University, PO Box 3168, Ruston, LA 71272. *Phone:* 318-257-3036. *Toll-free phone:* 800-528-3241. *Fax:* 318-257-2499. *E-mail:* bulldog@latech.edu. *Web site:* http://www.latech.edu/.

Loyola University New Orleans
New Orleans, Louisiana

- **Independent Roman Catholic (Jesuit)** comprehensive, founded 1912
- **Suburban** 26-acre campus with easy access to New Orleans
- **Endowment** $272.0 million
- **Coed** 3,165 undergraduate students, 94% full-time, 57% women, 43% men
- **Moderately difficult** entrance level, 65% of applicants were admitted

Undergraduates 2,963 full-time, 202 part-time. Students come from 51 states and territories; 52% are from out of state; 15% Black or African American, non-Hispanic/Latino; 12% Hispanic/Latino; 4% Asian, non-Hispanic/Latino; 0.8% American Indian or Alaska Native, non-Hispanic/Latino; 1% Two or more races, non-Hispanic/Latino; 8% Race/ethnicity unknown; 4% international; 5% transferred in; 49% live on campus. *Retention:* 77% of full-time freshmen returned.

Freshmen *Admission:* 6,386 applied, 4,143 admitted, 858 enrolled. *Average high school GPA:* 3.66. *Test scores:* SAT critical reading scores over 500: 96%; SAT math scores over 500: 93%; SAT writing scores over 500: 93%; ACT scores over 18: 100%; SAT critical reading scores over 600: 53%; SAT math scores over 600: 43%; SAT writing scores over 600: 49%; ACT scores over 24: 73%; SAT critical reading scores over 700: 10%; SAT math scores over 700: 4%; SAT writing scores over 700: 7%; ACT scores over 30: 12%.

Faculty *Total:* 481, 64% full-time, 79% with terminal degrees. *Student/faculty ratio:* 11:1.

Academics *Calendar:* semesters. *Degrees:* bachelor's, master's, doctoral, post-master's, and postbachelor's certificates. *Special study options:* accelerated degree program, adult/continuing education programs, advanced place-

ment credit, cooperative education, distance learning, double majors, English as a second language, external degree program, honors programs, independent study, internships, off-campus study, part-time degree program, services for LD students, student-designed majors, study abroad, summer session for credit. *ROTC:* Army (c), Navy (c), Air Force (c). *Unusual degree programs:* 3-2 engineering with Tulane University.

Computers on Campus 525 computers/terminals and 2,500 ports are available on campus for general student use. Students can access the following: campus intranet, computer help desk, free student e-mail accounts, online (class) grades, online (class) registration, online (class) schedules. Campuswide network is available. 100% of college-owned or -operated housing units are wired for high-speed Internet access. Wireless service is available via entire campus.

Student Life *Housing:* on-campus residence required through sophomore year. *Options:* coed, disabled students. Campus housing is university owned. Freshman campus housing is guaranteed. *Activities and organizations:* drama/theater group, student-run newspaper, radio station, choral group, University Programming Board, Student Government Association, Black Student Union, Loyola University Community Action Program (LUCAP), Panhellic Council, national fraternities, national sororities. *Campus security:* 24-hour emergency response devices and patrols, student patrols, late-night transport/escort service, controlled dormitory access, self-defense education, bicycle patrols, closed circuit TV monitors, door alarms, crime prevention programs, card access control. *Student services:* health clinic, personal/psychological counseling, women's center.

Athletics Member NAIA. *Intercollegiate sports:* baseball M, basketball M(s)/W(s), cheerleading M(c)/W(c), cross-country running M/W, golf M(c)/W(c), racquetball M/W, rugby M(c), sailing M(c)/W(c), soccer M(c)/W(c), swimming and diving M/W, tennis M/W, track and field M/W, ultimate Frisbee M(c)/W(c), volleyball W, wrestling M(c). *Intramural sports:* basketball M/W, soccer M/W, softball M/W, swimming and diving M/W, volleyball M/W, weight lifting M/W.

Standardized Tests *Required:* SAT or ACT (for admission).

Costs (2012–13) *Comprehensive fee:* $46,581 includes full-time tuition ($33,846), mandatory fees ($1106), and room and board ($11,629). Part-time tuition: $965 per credit. *College room only:* $6914. Room and board charges vary according to board plan and housing facility. *Payment plan:* installment. *Waivers:* senior citizens and employees or children of employees.

Financial Aid Of all full-time matriculated undergraduates who enrolled in 2011, 2,157 applied for aid, 1,719 were judged to have need, 320 had their need fully met. In 2011, 890 non-need-based awards were made. *Average percent of need met:* 70%. *Average financial aid package:* $24,545. *Average need-based loan:* $4305. *Average need-based gift aid:* $20,506. *Average non-need-based aid:* $15,091. *Average indebtedness upon graduation:* $12,597. *Financial aid deadline:* 6/1.

Applying *Options:* electronic application, early admission. *Application fee:* $20. *Required:* essay or personal statement, high school transcript, 1 letter of recommendation. *Required for some:* interview. *Recommended:* interview. *Application deadlines:* rolling (freshmen), rolling (transfers). *Notification:* continuous (freshmen).

Freshman Application Contact Mr. Keith E. Gramling, Director, Admissions, Loyola University New Orleans, 6363 St. Charles Avenue, Campus Box 18, New Orleans, LA 70118. *Phone:* 504-865-3240. *Toll-free phone:* 800-4-LOYOLA. *Fax:* 504-865-3383. *E-mail:* admit@loyno.edu. *Web site:* http://www.loyno.edu/.

See page 361 for display ad and page 1422 for the College Close-Up.

McNeese State University
Lake Charles, Louisiana

- **State-supported** comprehensive, founded 1939, part of University of Louisiana System
- **Suburban** 766-acre campus
- **Coed** 7,802 undergraduate students, 79% full-time, 61% women, 39% men
- **Moderately difficult** entrance level, 69% of applicants were admitted

Undergraduates 6,144 full-time, 1,658 part-time. Students come from 38 states and territories; 49 other countries; 6% are from out of state; 18% Black or African American, non-Hispanic/Latino; 2% Hispanic/Latino; 1% Asian, non-Hispanic/Latino; 0.1% Native Hawaiian or other Pacific Islander, non-Hispanic/Latino; 0.7% American Indian or Alaska Native, non-Hispanic/Latino; 0.7% Two or more races, non-Hispanic/Latino; 0.4% Race/ethnicity unknown; 4% international; 5% transferred in. *Retention:* 68% of full-time freshmen returned.

Freshmen *Admission:* 2,964 applied, 2,035 admitted, 1,386 enrolled. *Average high school GPA:* 3.31. *Test scores:* ACT scores over 18: 92%; ACT scores over 24: 26%; ACT scores over 30: 2%.

Faculty *Total:* 434, 68% full-time, 51% with terminal degrees. *Student/faculty ratio:* 21:1.

Academics *Calendar:* semesters. *Degrees:* associate, bachelor's, master's, post-master's, and postbachelor's certificates. *Special study options:* academic remediation for entering students, accelerated degree program, advanced placement credit, cooperative education, distance learning, double majors, English as a second language, freshman honors college, honors programs, independent study, internships, off-campus study, part-time degree program, services for LD students, study abroad, summer session for credit. *ROTC:* Army (b).

Computers on Campus 700 computers/terminals are available on campus for general student use. Students can access the following: computer help desk, free student e-mail accounts, online (class) grades, online (class) registration, online (class) schedules. Campuswide network is available. Wireless service is available via entire campus.

Student Life *Housing:* on-campus residence required for freshman year. *Options:* coed. Campus housing is university owned and is provided by a third party. *Activities and organizations:* drama/theater group, student-run newspaper, choral group, marching band, Student Government Association, International Students Association, Resident Student Association, national fraternities, national sororities. *Campus security:* 24-hour emergency response devices and patrols, late-night transport/escort service, controlled dormitory access. *Student services:* health clinic, personal/psychological counseling, women's center.

Athletics Member NCAA. All Division I except football (Division I-AA). *Intercollegiate sports:* baseball M(s), basketball M(s)/W(s), cross-country running M(s)/W(s), golf M(s)/W(s), soccer W(s), softball W(s), tennis W(s), track and field M(s)/W(s), volleyball W(s). *Intramural sports:* badminton M/W, baseball M, basketball M/W, football M/W, golf M/W, racquetball M/W, soccer M/W, softball W, swimming and diving M/W, table tennis M/W, tennis M/W, volleyball M/W, water polo M/W, weight lifting M/W.

Standardized Tests *Required:* SAT or ACT (for admission).

Costs (2011–12) *Tuition:* state resident $4400 full-time; nonresident $8822 full-time. Full-time tuition and fees vary according to course load. Part-time tuition and fees vary according to course load. *Room and board:* $7198. Room and board charges vary according to board plan and housing facility.

Financial Aid Of all full-time matriculated undergraduates who enrolled in 2007, 3,331 were judged to have need, 556 had their need fully met. In 2007, 1527 non-need-based awards were made. *Average percent of need met:* 64%. *Average financial aid package:* $6705. *Average need-based loan:* $3899. *Average need-based gift aid:* $4085. *Average non-need-based aid:* $2847.

Applying *Options:* electronic application, early admission. *Application fee:* $20. *Required:* high school transcript, minimum 2.0 GPA. *Application deadlines:* rolling (freshmen), rolling (transfers). *Notification:* continuous (freshmen), continuous (transfers).

Freshman Application Contact Ms. Kara Smith, Director of Admissions and Recruiting, McNeese State University, Box 91740, Lake Charles, LA 70609. *Phone:* 337-475-5504. *Toll-free phone:* 800-622-3352. *Fax:* 337-475-5978. *E-mail:* ksmith2@mcneese.edu. *Web site:* http://www.mcneese.edu/.

New Orleans Baptist Theological Seminary
New Orleans, Louisiana

Director of Admissions Dr. Paul E. Gregoire Jr., Registrar/Director of Admissions, New Orleans Baptist Theological Seminary, 3939 Gentilly Boulevard, New Orleans, LA 70126-4858. *Phone:* 504-282-4455 Ext. 3337. *Toll-free phone:* 800-662-8701. *Web site:* http://www.nobts.edu/.

Nicholls State University
Thibodaux, Louisiana

- **State-supported** comprehensive, founded 1948, part of University of Louisiana System
- **Small-town** 210-acre campus with easy access to New Orleans
- **Endowment** $15.2 million
- **Coed** 6,141 undergraduate students, 80% full-time, 63% women, 37% men
- **Noncompetitive** entrance level, 84% of applicants were admitted

Undergraduates 4,885 full-time, 1,256 part-time. Students come from 18 states and territories; 42 other countries; 4% are from out of state; 19% Black or African American, non-Hispanic/Latino; 2% Hispanic/Latino; 0.8% Asian, non-Hispanic/Latino; 0.1% Native Hawaiian or other Pacific Islander, non-Hispanic/Latino; 2% American Indian or Alaska Native, non-Hispanic/Latino; 2% Two or more races, non-Hispanic/Latino; 2% Race/ethnicity unknown; 2% international; 5% transferred in; 26% live on campus. *Retention:* 69% of full-time freshmen returned.

Freshmen *Admission:* 2,174 applied, 1,830 admitted, 1,135 enrolled. *Average high school GPA:* 3.22. *Test scores:* ACT scores over 18: 93%; ACT scores over 24: 27%; ACT scores over 30: 2%.

Faculty *Total:* 262, 100% full-time, 53% with terminal degrees. *Student/faculty ratio:* 21:1.

Academics *Calendar:* semesters. *Degrees:* associate, bachelor's, master's, and post-master's certificates. *Special study options:* academic remediation for entering students, accelerated degree program, adult/continuing education programs, advanced placement credit, cooperative education, distance learning, double majors, English as a second language, honors programs, independent study, internships, off-campus study, part-time degree program, services for LD students, study abroad, summer session for credit.

Computers on Campus 1,500 computers/terminals and 1,500 ports are available on campus for general student use. Students can access the following: campus intranet, free student e-mail accounts, online (class) grades, online (class) registration, online (class) schedules, course management system—Moodle. Campuswide network is available. 100% of college-owned or -operated housing units are wired for high-speed Internet access. Wireless service is available via entire campus.

Student Life *Housing:* on-campus residence required for freshman year. *Options:* coed, men-only, women-only, disabled students. Campus housing is university owned. Freshman campus housing is guaranteed. *Activities and organizations:* drama/theater group, student-run newspaper, radio and television station, choral group, marching band, Student Government Association, Student Programming Association, Residence Hall Association, Food Advisory Association, national fraternities, national sororities. *Campus security:* 24-hour emergency response devices and patrols, student patrols, late-night transport/escort service. *Student services:* health clinic, personal/psychological counseling, women's center, legal services.

Athletics Member NCAA. All Division I except football (Division I-AA). *Intercollegiate sports:* baseball M(s), basketball M(s)/W(s), cross-country running M(s)/W(s), golf M(s)/W(s), soccer W(s), softball W(s), tennis M/W(s), track and field M(s)/W(s), volleyball W(s). *Intramural sports:* basketball M/W, football M/W, softball M/W, volleyball M/W.

Standardized Tests *Required:* SAT or ACT (for admission).

Costs (2011–12) *Tuition:* state resident $4737 full-time; nonresident $12,687 full-time. Part-time tuition and fees vary according to course load. *Required fees:* $1287 full-time. *Room and board:* $8580; room only: $5972. Room and board charges vary according to board plan and housing facility. *Payment plans:* installment, deferred payment. *Waivers:* employees or children of employees.

Financial Aid Of all full-time matriculated undergraduates who enrolled in 2010, 4,109 applied for aid, 2,833 were judged to have need, 471 had their need fully met. In 2010, 437 non-need-based awards were made. *Average percent of need met:* 66%. *Average financial aid package:* $8358. *Average need-based loan:* $3153. *Average need-based gift aid:* $6401. *Average non-need-based aid:* $3731. *Average indebtedness upon graduation:* $25,036. *Financial aid deadline:* 6/30.

Applying *Options:* electronic application, early admission, deferred entrance. *Application fee:* $20. *Required:* high school transcript. *Application deadlines:* rolling (freshmen), rolling (transfers). *Notification:* 9/1 (freshmen), continuous until 8/28 (transfers).

Freshman Application Contact Mrs. Becky L. Durocher, Director of Admissions, Nicholls State University, PO Box 2004-NSU, Thibodaux, LA 70310. *Phone:* 985-448-4507. *Toll-free phone:* 877-NICHOLLS. *Fax:* 985-448-4929. *E-mail:* nicholls@nicholls.edu. *Web site:* http://www.nicholls.edu/.

Northwestern State University of Louisiana

Natchitoches, Louisiana

- **State-supported** comprehensive, founded 1884, part of University of Louisiana System
- **Small-town** 916-acre campus
- **Endowment** $11.1 million
- **Coed** 8,080 undergraduate students, 66% full-time, 68% women, 32% men
- **Moderately difficult** entrance level, 82% of applicants were admitted

Undergraduates 5,319 full-time, 2,761 part-time. Students come from 41 states and territories; 26 other countries; 9% are from out of state; 30% Black or African American, non-Hispanic/Latino; 3% Hispanic/Latino; 0.9% Asian, non-Hispanic/Latino; 0.2% Native Hawaiian or other Pacific Islander, non-

Hispanic/Latino; 1% American Indian or Alaska Native, non-Hispanic/Latino; 3% Two or more races, non-Hispanic/Latino; 5% Race/ethnicity unknown; 0.7% international; 8% transferred in; 18% live on campus. *Retention:* 69% of full-time freshmen returned.

Freshmen *Admission:* 2,756 applied, 2,270 admitted, 1,222 enrolled. *Average high school GPA:* 3.19. *Test scores:* SAT critical reading scores over 500: 53%; SAT math scores over 500: 54%; ACT scores over 18: 89%; SAT critical reading scores over 600: 17%; SAT math scores over 600: 16%; ACT scores over 24: 24%; SAT critical reading scores over 700: 1%; SAT math scores over 700: 1%; ACT scores over 30: 2%.

Faculty *Total:* 517, 54% full-time, 44% with terminal degrees. *Student/faculty ratio:* 19:1.

Academics *Calendar:* semesters. *Degrees:* associate, bachelor's, master's, post-master's, and postbachelor's certificates. *Special study options:* academic remediation for entering students, adult/continuing education programs, advanced placement credit, cooperative education, distance learning, double majors, freshman honors college, honors programs, independent study, internships, part-time degree program, services for LD students, study abroad, summer session for credit. *ROTC:* Army (b), Air Force (c).

Computers on Campus Students can access the following: computer help desk, free student e-mail accounts, online (class) grades, online (class) registration, online (class) schedules. Campuswide network is available. Wireless service is available via classrooms, computer centers, computer labs, dorm rooms, learning centers, libraries, student centers.

Student Life *Housing:* on-campus residence required through junior year. *Options:* coed, disabled students. Campus housing is university owned and is provided by a third party. Freshman applicants given priority for college housing. *Activities and organizations:* drama/theater group, student-run newspaper, radio and television station, choral group, marching band, national fraternities, national sororities. *Campus security:* 24-hour emergency response devices and patrols, late-night transport/escort service, controlled dormitory access. *Student services:* health clinic, personal/psychological counseling.

Athletics Member NCAA. All Division I except football (Division I-AA). *Intercollegiate sports:* baseball M(s), basketball M(s)/W(s), cross-country running M(s)/W(s), soccer W(s), softball W(s), tennis W(s), track and field M(s)/W(s), volleyball W(s). *Intramural sports:* badminton M/W, basketball M/W, bowling M/W, cheerleading M(c)/W(c), crew M(c)/W(c), football M/W, golf M/W, racquetball M/W, soccer M/W, softball M/W, swimming and diving M/W, table tennis M/W, tennis M/W, volleyball M/W.

Standardized Tests *Required:* SAT or ACT (for admission).

Costs (2012–13) *Tuition:* state resident $3440 full-time, $240 per credit part-time; nonresident $12,010 full-time, $240 per credit part-time. Full-time tuition and fees vary according to course load and location. Part-time tuition and fees vary according to course load and location. *Required fees:* $1532 full-time. *Room and board:* $7350; room only: $4708. Room and board charges vary according to board plan, housing facility, and location. *Payment plan:* installment. *Waivers:* senior citizens and employees or children of employees.

Financial Aid Of all full-time matriculated undergraduates who enrolled in 2010, 3,016 applied for aid, 2,673 were judged to have need, 983 had their need fully met. 211 Federal Work-Study jobs (averaging $1455). 114 state and other part-time jobs (averaging $2). In 2010, 2596 non-need-based awards were made. *Average percent of need met:* 48%. *Average financial aid package:* $7433. *Average need-based loan:* $7419. *Average need-based gift aid:* $5236. *Average non-need-based aid:* $5057. *Average indebtedness upon graduation:* $15,176.

Applying *Options:* electronic application, deferred entrance. *Application fee:* $20. *Required:* high school transcript, minimum 2.0 GPA, college preparatory curriculum. *Application deadlines:* 7/6 (freshmen), 7/6 (out-of-state freshmen), 7/6 (transfers). *Notification:* continuous (freshmen), continuous (out-of-state freshmen), continuous (transfers).

Freshman Application Contact Ms. Jana Lucky, Director of University Recruiting, Northwestern State University of Louisiana, South Hall, Natchitoches, LA 71497. *Phone:* 318-357-4503. *Toll-free phone:* 800-327-1903. *Fax:* 318-357-5567. *E-mail:* recruiting@nsula.edu. *Web site:* http://www.nsula.edu/.

Our Lady of Holy Cross College

New Orleans, Louisiana

Director of Admissions Donna Kennedy, Director of Admissions and Financial Aid, Our Lady of Holy Cross College, 4123 Woodland Drive, New Orleans, LA 70131-7399. *Phone:* 504-398-2175. *Toll-free phone:* 800-259-7744. *E-mail:* dkennedy@olhcc.edu. *Web site:* http://www.olhcc.edu/.

Our Lady of the Lake College

Baton Rouge, Louisiana

- **Independent Roman Catholic** comprehensive, founded 1990
- **Suburban** 5-acre campus with easy access to New Orleans
- **Endowment** $8.6 million
- **Coed, primarily women** 1,620 undergraduate students, 32% full-time, 86% women, 14% men
- **Minimally difficult** entrance level

Undergraduates 524 full-time, 1,096 part-time. Students come from 10 states and territories; 2% are from out of state; 26% Black or African American, non-Hispanic/Latino; 0.9% Hispanic/Latino; 3% Asian, non-Hispanic/Latino; 0.4% Native Hawaiian or other Pacific Islander, non-Hispanic/Latino; 1% American Indian or Alaska Native, non-Hispanic/Latino; 7% Race/ethnicity unknown; 9% transferred in. *Retention:* 63% of full-time freshmen returned.
Freshmen *Admission:* 100 enrolled. *Test scores:* ACT scores over 18: 91%; ACT scores over 24: 14%.
Faculty *Total:* 183, 53% full-time, 26% with terminal degrees. *Student/faculty ratio:* 18:1.
Academics *Calendar:* semesters. *Degrees:* certificates, diplomas, associate, bachelor's, master's, and postbachelor's certificates. *Special study options:* academic remediation for entering students, accelerated degree program, advanced placement credit, off-campus study, part-time degree program, services for LD students, summer session for credit. *ROTC:* Army (c), Air Force (c).
Computers on Campus 150 computers/terminals are available on campus for general student use. Students can access the following: campus intranet, computer help desk, free student e-mail accounts, online (class) grades, online (class) registration, online (class) schedules. Campuswide network is available. Wireless service is available via entire campus.
Student Life *Housing:* college housing not available. *Activities and organizations:* Student Government Association, Cultural Arts Association, Christian Fellowship Association, Mathematics/Science Association. *Campus security:* 24-hour patrols. *Student services:* health clinic, personal/psychological counseling.
Standardized Tests *Required:* SAT or ACT (for admission), ACT ASSET (for admission).
Financial Aid Of all full-time matriculated undergraduates who enrolled in 2008, 684 applied for aid, 546 were judged to have need, 10 had their need fully met. *Average financial aid package:* $5175. *Average need-based loan:* $3664. *Average need-based gift aid:* $2486. *Average indebtedness upon graduation:* $12,019.
Applying *Options:* electronic application, early admission, deferred entrance. *Application fee:* $35. *Required:* high school transcript, minimum 2.0 GPA. *Application deadlines:* 8/15 (freshmen), rolling (transfers). *Notification:* continuous (freshmen).
Freshman Application Contact Mrs. Rebecca Cannon, Director of Admissions, Our Lady of the Lake College, 7434 Perkins Road, Baton Rouge, LA 70808. *Phone:* 225-768-1718. *E-mail:* admissions@ololcollege.edu. *Web site:* http://www.ololcollege.edu/.

Saint Joseph Seminary College

Saint Benedict, Louisiana

- **Independent Roman Catholic** 4-year, founded 1891
- **Rural** 1300-acre campus with easy access to New Orleans
- **Endowment** $1.1 million
- **Coed, primarily men** 87 undergraduate students, 97% full-time, 100% men
- **Minimally difficult** entrance level

Undergraduates 84 full-time, 3 part-time. Students come from 8 states and territories; 7 other countries; 50% are from out of state; 5% Black or African American, non-Hispanic/Latino; 22% Hispanic/Latino; 6% Asian, non-Hispanic/Latino; 1% American Indian or Alaska Native, non-Hispanic/Latino; 23% transferred in; 100% live on campus. *Retention:* 50% of full-time freshmen returned.
Freshmen *Admission:* 10 admitted, 10 enrolled. *Average high school GPA:* 3.25. *Test scores:* ACT scores over 18: 55%; ACT scores over 24: 22%.
Faculty *Total:* 22, 45% full-time, 32% with terminal degrees. *Student/faculty ratio:* 3:1.
Academics *Calendar:* semesters. *Degrees:* certificates and bachelor's (Religious Studies Institute is coed). *Special study options:* academic remediation for entering students, adult/continuing education programs, advanced placement credit, English as a second language, services for LD students.
Computers on Campus 14 computers/terminals and 90 ports are available on campus for general student use. Students can access the following: campus intranet, computer help desk, free student e-mail accounts. Campuswide net-

work is available. 100% of college-owned or -operated housing units are wired for high-speed Internet access. Wireless service is available via entire campus.
Student Life *Housing:* on-campus residence required through senior year. *Options:* men-only. Campus housing is university owned. Freshman campus housing is guaranteed. *Activities and organizations:* drama/theater group, student-run newspaper, choral group, student government, yearbook. *Campus security:* 24-hour emergency response devices, controlled dormitory access, entrance gate. *Student services:* health clinic, personal/psychological counseling.
Athletics *Intramural sports:* football M, golf M.
Standardized Tests *Required:* ACT (for admission).
Costs (2011–12) *One-time required fee:* $150. *Comprehensive fee:* $26,810 includes full-time tuition ($12,860), mandatory fees ($1510), and room and board ($12,440). Part-time tuition: $175 per credit hour. *College room only:* $6540.
Financial Aid Of all full-time matriculated undergraduates who enrolled in 2009, 33 applied for aid, 33 were judged to have need, 33 had their need fully met. *Average percent of need met:* 100%. *Average financial aid package:* $4105. *Average need-based gift aid:* $4105. *Average indebtedness upon graduation:* $5000.
Applying *Options:* early admission, deferred entrance. *Required:* high school transcript, minimum 2.0 GPA. *Application deadlines:* rolling (freshmen), rolling (transfers). *Notification:* continuous (freshmen), continuous (transfers).
Freshman Application Contact Saint Joseph Seminary College, 75376 River Road, St. Benedict, LA 70457. *Phone:* 985-867-2273. *Fax:* 985-327-1085. *E-mail:* registrar@sjasc.edu. *Web site:* http://www.sjasc.edu/.

Southeastern Louisiana University

Hammond, Louisiana

- **State-supported** comprehensive, founded 1925, part of University of Louisiana System
- **Small-town** 375-acre campus with easy access to New Orleans
- **Endowment** $21.1 million
- **Coed** 14,072 undergraduate students, 76% full-time, 60% women, 40% men
- **Moderately difficult** entrance level, 80% of applicants were admitted

Undergraduates 10,676 full-time, 3,396 part-time. Students come from 46 states and territories; 43 other countries; 3% are from out of state; 15% Black or African American, non-Hispanic/Latino; 3% Hispanic/Latino; 0.8% Asian, non-Hispanic/Latino; 0.1% Native Hawaiian or other Pacific Islander, non-Hispanic/Latino; 0.4% American Indian or Alaska Native, non-Hispanic/Latino; 2% Two or more races, non-Hispanic/Latino; 2% Race/ethnicity unknown; 2% international; 5% transferred in; 18% live on campus. *Retention:* 69% of full-time freshmen returned.
Freshmen *Admission:* 3,811 applied, 3,034 admitted, 2,437 enrolled. *Average high school GPA:* 3.18. *Test scores:* ACT scores over 18: 95%; ACT scores over 24: 31%; ACT scores over 30: 2%.
Faculty *Total:* 630, 83% full-time, 61% with terminal degrees. *Student/faculty ratio:* 22:1.
Academics *Calendar:* semesters. *Degrees:* associate, bachelor's, master's, doctoral, and first professional. *Special study options:* academic remediation for entering students, adult/continuing education programs, advanced placement credit, distance learning, double majors, English as a second language, honors programs, independent study, internships, off-campus study, part-time degree program, services for LD students, study abroad, summer session for credit. *ROTC:* Army (c).
Computers on Campus 1,440 computers/terminals and 568 ports are available on campus for general student use. Students can access the following: campus intranet, computer help desk, free student e-mail accounts, online (class) grades, online (class) registration, online (class) schedules, campus Webmail, student newspaper, transcripts, bookstore. Campuswide network is available. 100% of college-owned or -operated housing units are wired for high-speed Internet access. Wireless service is available via classrooms, computer centers, computer labs, dorm rooms, learning centers, libraries, student centers.
Student Life *Housing:* on-campus residence required through sophomore year. *Options:* coed, women-only, disabled students. Campus housing is university owned. *Activities and organizations:* drama/theater group, student-run newspaper, radio and television station, choral group, marching band, Gamma Beta Phi, Kappa Delta Pi, National Society of Collegiate Scholars, National Student Speech, Language and Hearing Association, national fraternities, national sororities. *Campus security:* 24-hour emergency response devices and patrols, student patrols, late-night transport/escort service, controlled dormitory access, video cameras, motorist assistance. *Student services:* health clinic, personal/psychological counseling.
Athletics Member NCAA. All Division I except football (Division I-AA). *Intercollegiate sports:* baseball M(s), basketball M(s)/W(s), cross-country run-

ning M(s)/W(s), golf M(s), soccer W(s), softball W(s), tennis W(s), track and field M(s)/W(s), volleyball W(s). *Intramural sports:* baseball M/W, basketball M/W, football M/W, racquetball M/W, rugby M(c), soccer M/W, softball M/W, tennis M/W, volleyball M/W, weight lifting M/W.

Standardized Tests *Required:* SAT or ACT (for admission).

Costs (2011–12) *Tuition:* state resident $4634 full-time; nonresident $14,139 full-time. Full-time tuition and fees vary according to course load. Part-time tuition and fees vary according to course load. *Room and board:* $6620. Room and board charges vary according to board plan and housing facility.

Financial Aid Of all full-time matriculated undergraduates who enrolled in 2010, 8,595 applied for aid, 6,266 were judged to have need, 1,066 had their need fully met. 301 Federal Work-Study jobs (averaging $1743). 1,059 state and other part-time jobs (averaging $2082). In 2010, 1647 non-need-based awards were made. *Average financial aid package:* $7971. *Average need-based loan:* $3767. *Average need-based gift aid:* $5082. *Average non-need-based aid:* $7531. *Average indebtedness upon graduation:* $20,044.

Applying *Options:* electronic application, early admission, deferred entrance. *Application fee:* $20. *Required:* proof of immunization required for all, college transcripts and statement of good standing required for some, *Required for some:* high school transcript, minimum 2.5 GPA. *Application deadlines:* 8/1 (freshmen), 8/1 (out-of-state freshmen), 8/1 (transfers). *Notification:* continuous (freshmen), continuous (out-of-state freshmen), continuous (transfers).

Freshman Application Contact Ms. Lori Fairburn, Director, Enrollment Services, Southeastern Louisiana University, SLU 10752, Hammond, LA 70402. *Phone:* 985-549-5637. *Toll-free phone:* 800-222-7358. *Fax:* 985-549-5882. *E-mail:* admissions@selu.edu. *Web site:* http://www.selu.edu/.

Southern University and Agricultural and Mechanical College

Baton Rouge, Louisiana

Freshman Application Contact Ms. Velva Thomas, Director of Admissions, Southern University and Agricultural and Mechanical College, PO Box 9901, Baton Rouge, LA 70813. *Phone:* 225-771-2430. *Fax:* 225-771-2500. *E-mail:* velva_thomas@subr.edu. *Web site:* http://www.subr.edu/.

Southern University at New Orleans

New Orleans, Louisiana

Freshman Application Contact Southern University at New Orleans, 6400 Press Drive, New Orleans, LA 70126-1009. *Phone:* 504-286-5033. *Web site:* http://www.suno.edu/.

Southwest University

Kenner, Louisiana

- **Proprietary** comprehensive
- **Coed**

Academics *Degrees:* certificates, associate, bachelor's, and master's.

Applying *Application fee:* $75. *Required:* high school transcript, resume.

Freshman Application Contact Admissions Office, Southwest University, 2200 Veterans Memorial Blvd., Kenner, LA 70062. *Phone:* 504-468-2900. *Toll-free phone:* 800-433-5923. *Fax:* 504-468-3213. *E-mail:* admissions@southwest.edu. *Web site:* http://www.southwest.edu/.

Strayer University - Metairie Campus

Metairie, Louisiana

- **Proprietary** comprehensive
- **Coed**

Academics *Degrees:* associate, bachelor's, master's, and postbachelor's certificates.

Freshman Application Contact Strayer University - Metairie Campus, 111 Veterans Memorial Boulevard, Suite 420, Metairie, LA 70005. *Web site:* http://www.strayer.edu/metairie.

Tulane University

New Orleans, Louisiana

- **Independent** university, founded 1834
- **Urban** 110-acre campus
- **Endowment** $1.3 billion
- **Coed** 8,338 undergraduate students, 77% full-time, 58% women, 42% men
- **Very difficult** entrance level, 25% of applicants were admitted

Undergraduates 6,403 full-time, 1,935 part-time. Students come from 53 states and territories; 79 other countries; 70% are from out of state; 8% Black or African American, non-Hispanic/Latino; 4% Hispanic/Latino; 4% Asian, non-Hispanic/Latino; 0.4% American Indian or Alaska Native, non-Hispanic/Latino; 2% Two or more races, non-Hispanic/Latino; 11% Race/ethnicity unknown; 3% international; 1% transferred in; 44% live on campus. *Retention:* 90% of full-time freshmen returned.

Freshmen *Admission:* 37,767 applied, 9,422 admitted, 1,642 enrolled. *Average high school GPA:* 3.55. *Test scores:* SAT critical reading scores over 500: 98%; SAT math scores over 500: 98%; SAT writing scores over 500: 98%; ACT scores over 18: 100%; SAT critical reading scores over 600: 84%; SAT math scores over 600: 86%; SAT writing scores over 600: 88%; ACT scores over 24: 97%; SAT critical reading scores over 700: 28%; SAT math scores over 700: 28%; SAT writing scores over 700: 34%; ACT scores over 30: 59%.

Faculty *Total:* 1,070, 59% full-time, 73% with terminal degrees. *Student/faculty ratio:* 11:1.

Academics *Calendar:* semesters plus 3 summer sessions. *Degrees:* certificates, associate, bachelor's, master's, doctoral, postbachelor's, and first professional certificates. *Special study options:* accelerated degree program, adult/continuing education programs, advanced placement credit, cooperative education, distance learning, double majors, English as a second language, freshman honors college, honors programs, independent study, internships, off-campus study, part-time degree program, services for LD students, student-designed majors, study abroad, summer session for credit. *ROTC:* Army (b), Navy (b), Air Force (b). *Unusual degree programs:* 3-2 business administration; engineering; public health, tropical medicine.

Computers on Campus 556 computers/terminals are available on campus for general student use. Students can access the following: campus intranet, computer help desk, free student e-mail accounts, online (class) grades, online (class) registration, online (class) schedules. Campuswide network is available. 100% of college-owned or -operated housing units are wired for high-speed Internet access. Wireless service is available via entire campus.

Student Life *Housing:* on-campus residence required through sophomore year. *Options:* coed, women-only, disabled students. Campus housing is university owned. Freshman campus housing is guaranteed. *Activities and organizations:* drama/theater group, student-run newspaper, radio and television station, choral group, marching band, Community Action Council of Tulane Students (CACTUS), Associated Student Body, Tulane University Campus Programming (TUCP), Association of Club Sports (ACS), National Pan-Hellenic Council, national fraternities, national sororities. *Campus security:* 24-hour emergency response devices and patrols, student patrols, late-night transport/escort service, controlled dormitory access, on and off-campus shuttle service, crime prevention programs, lighted pathways. *Student services:* health clinic, personal/psychological counseling, women's center, legal services.

Athletics Member NCAA. All Division I except football (Division I-A). *Intercollegiate sports:* baseball M(s), basketball M(s)/W(s), crew M(c)/W(c), cross-country running M(s)/W(s), golf W(s), gymnastics M(c)/W(c), ice hockey M(c)/W(c), lacrosse M(c)/W(c), rugby M(c), sailing M(c)/W(c), soccer M(c)/W(s), swimming and diving M(c)/W(s), tennis M(s)/W(s), track and field M(c)/W(s), volleyball M(c)/W(s), water polo M(c)/W(c). *Intramural sports:* baseball M(c), cheerleading M(c)/W(c), crew M(c)/W(c), cross-country running M(c), fencing M(c)/W(c), field hockey M(c)/W(c), gymnastics M(c)/W(c), ice hockey M(c), lacrosse M(c)/W(c), racquetball M(c)/W(c), rock climbing M(c)/W(c), rugby M(c), sailing M(c)/W(c), soccer M(c)/W(c), swimming and diving M(c)/W(c), tennis M(c)/W(c), track and field M(c)/W, ultimate Frisbee M(c)/W(c), volleyball M(c)/W(c), water polo M(c)/W(c).

Standardized Tests *Required:* SAT or ACT (for admission). *Required for some:* SAT Subject Tests (for admission).

Costs (2011–12) *Comprehensive fee:* $54,884 includes full-time tuition ($39,850), mandatory fees ($3584), and room and board ($11,450). *College room only:* $6700. Room and board charges vary according to board plan and housing facility. *Payment plans:* tuition prepayment, installment. *Waivers:* employees or children of employees.

Financial Aid Of all full-time matriculated undergraduates who enrolled in 2010, 3,220 applied for aid, 2,470 were judged to have need, 1,300 had their need fully met. In 2010, 2102 non-need-based awards were made. *Average percent of need met:* 89%. *Average financial aid package:* $37,240. *Average need-based loan:* $5970. *Average need-based gift aid:* $25,824. *Average non-need-based aid:* $21,443. *Average indebtedness upon graduation:* $31,172.

Applying *Options:* electronic application, early action, deferred entrance. *Required:* essay or personal statement, high school transcript, 1 letter of recommendation. *Application deadlines:* 1/15 (freshmen), 6/1 (transfers). *Notification:* 4/1 (freshmen), continuous (transfers).

Freshman Application Contact Earl Retif, Vice President for Enrollment Management and University Registrar, Tulane University, Office of Admissions, 210 Gibson Hall, New Orleans, LA 70118. *Phone:* 504-865-5731. *Toll-free phone:* 800-873-9283. *Fax:* 504-862-8715. *E-mail:* undergrad.admission@tulane.edu. *Web site:* http://www.tulane.edu/.

University of Louisiana at Lafayette

Lafayette, Louisiana

- **State-supported** university, founded 1898, part of University of Louisiana System
- **Urban** 1375-acre campus
- **Endowment** $86.6 million
- **Coed** 15,321 undergraduate students, 85% full-time, 57% women, 43% men
- **Moderately difficult** entrance level, 66% of applicants were admitted

Undergraduates 13,007 full-time, 2,314 part-time. Students come from 42 states and territories; 75 other countries; 4% are from out of state; 21% Black or African American, non-Hispanic/Latino; 3% Hispanic/Latino; 2% Asian, non-Hispanic/Latino; 0.5% American Indian or Alaska Native, non-Hispanic/Latino; 1% Two or more races, non-Hispanic/Latino; 0.7% Race/ethnicity unknown; 2% international; 5% transferred in; 14% live on campus. *Retention:* 74% of full-time freshmen returned.

Freshmen *Admission:* 9,062 applied, 5,975 admitted, 2,966 enrolled. *Average high school GPA:* 3.23. *Test scores:* SAT critical reading scores over 500: 53%; SAT math scores over 500: 61%; ACT scores over 18: 96%; SAT critical reading scores over 600: 14%; SAT math scores over 600: 17%; ACT scores over 24: 31%; SAT critical reading scores over 700: 2%; SAT math scores over 700: 2%; ACT scores over 30: 2%.

Faculty *Total:* 743, 79% full-time, 61% with terminal degrees. *Student/faculty ratio:* 23:1.

Academics *Calendar:* semesters. *Degrees:* bachelor's, master's, doctoral, post-master's, postbachelor's, and first professional certificates. *Special study options:* academic remediation for entering students, accelerated degree program, adult/continuing education programs, advanced placement credit, cooperative education, distance learning, double majors, honors programs, independent study, internships, part-time degree program, services for LD students, student-designed majors, study abroad, summer session for credit. *ROTC:* Army (b).

Computers on Campus 600 computers/terminals and 855 ports are available on campus for general student use. Students can access the following: campus intranet, computer help desk, free student e-mail accounts, online (class) grades, online (class) registration, online (class) schedules. Campuswide network is available. 63% of college-owned or -operated housing units are wired for high-speed Internet access. Wireless service is available via libraries.

Student Life *Housing options:* men-only, women-only. Campus housing is university owned. Freshman campus housing is guaranteed. *Activities and organizations:* drama/theater group, student-run newspaper, radio station, choral group, marching band, Union Program Council, Chi Alpha, Student Government Association, Greek Council, Newman Club, national fraternities, national sororities. *Campus security:* 24-hour emergency response devices and patrols, late-night transport/escort service, controlled dormitory access. *Student services:* health clinic, personal/psychological counseling, women's center, legal services.

Athletics Member NCAA. All Division I except football (Division I-A). *Intercollegiate sports:* baseball M(s), basketball M(s)/W(s), cross-country running M(s)/W(s), golf M(s), soccer W, softball W(s), tennis M(s)/W(s), track and field M(s)/W(s), volleyball W(s). *Intramural sports:* badminton M/W, baseball M, basketball M/W, bowling M/W, cross-country running M/W, football M/W, golf M/W, ice hockey M, lacrosse M, racquetball M/W, rugby M/W, sailing M/W, soccer M/W, softball M/W, swimming and diving M/W, table tennis M/W, tennis M/W, track and field M/W, volleyball M/W, water polo M/W, weight lifting M/W.

Standardized Tests *Required:* SAT or ACT (for admission).

Costs (2011–12) *Tuition:* state resident $4864 full-time; nonresident $13,486 full-time. Full-time tuition and fees vary according to course load. Part-time tuition and fees vary according to course load. *Room and board:* $5558. Room and board charges vary according to housing facility.

Financial Aid Of all full-time matriculated undergraduates who enrolled in 2010, 10,201 applied for aid, 6,804 were judged to have need, 689 had their need fully met. 446 Federal Work-Study jobs (averaging $1739). 257 state and other part-time jobs (averaging $1649). In 2010, 925 non-need-based awards were made. *Average percent of need met:* 56%. *Average financial aid package:* $7311. *Average need-based loan:* $3595. *Average need-based gift aid:* $5657. *Average non-need-based aid:* $1856.

Applying *Options:* electronic application, early admission, deferred entrance. *Application fee:* $25. *Required:* high school transcript, minimum 2.0 GPA, core requirements, no remedial courses. *Application deadlines:* rolling (freshmen), rolling (transfers).

Freshman Application Contact Mr. Andy Benoit Jr., Director of Enrollment Services and Recruitment, University of Louisiana at Lafayette, PO Drawer 41210, Lafayette, LA 70504. *Phone:* 337-482-6473. *Toll-free phone:* 800-752-6553. *Fax:* 337-482-1317. *E-mail:* admissions@louisiana.edu. *Web site:* http://www.louisiana.edu/.

University of Louisiana at Monroe

Monroe, Louisiana

- **State-supported** university, founded 1931, part of University of Louisiana System
- **Urban** 238-acre campus
- **Coed** 7,243 undergraduate students, 73% full-time, 64% women, 36% men
- **Moderately difficult** entrance level, 51% of applicants were admitted

Undergraduates 5,255 full-time, 1,988 part-time. Students come from 40 states and territories; 43 other countries; 7% are from out of state; 26% Black or African American, non-Hispanic/Latino; 2% Hispanic/Latino; 2% Asian, non-Hispanic/Latino; 0.1% Native Hawaiian or other Pacific Islander, non-Hispanic/Latino; 0.3% American Indian or Alaska Native, non-Hispanic/Latino; 1% Two or more races, non-Hispanic/Latino; 2% Race/ethnicity unknown; 2% international; 8% transferred in; 22% live on campus. *Retention:* 72% of full-time freshmen returned.

Freshmen *Admission:* 2,273 applied, 1,149 admitted, 1,151 enrolled. *Average high school GPA:* 3.28. *Test scores:* SAT critical reading scores over 500: 36%; SAT math scores over 500: 46%; ACT scores over 18: 92%; SAT critical reading scores over 600: 11%; SAT math scores over 600: 24%; ACT scores over 24: 29%; SAT critical reading scores over 700: 2%; SAT math scores over 700: 4%; ACT scores over 30: 3%.

Faculty *Total:* 361, 90% full-time. *Student/faculty ratio:* 18:1.

Academics *Calendar:* semesters. *Degrees:* associate, bachelor's, master's, doctoral, post-master's, postbachelor's, and first professional certificates. *Special study options:* academic remediation for entering students, accelerated degree program, advanced placement credit, cooperative education, distance learning, double majors, English as a second language, external degree program, honors programs, independent study, internships, off-campus study, study abroad, summer session for credit. *ROTC:* Army (c), Air Force (c).

Computers on Campus Students can access the following: campus intranet, computer help desk, free student e-mail accounts, online (class) grades, online (class) registration, online (class) schedules. Campuswide network is available. 100% of college-owned or -operated housing units are wired for high-speed Internet access. Wireless service is available via entire campus.

Student Life *Housing:* on-campus residence required through sophomore year. *Options:* coed, men-only, women-only. Campus housing is university owned and leased by the school. Freshman applicants given priority for college housing. *Activities and organizations:* drama/theater group, student-run newspaper, radio station, marching band, Maroon Platoon, Alpha Lambda Delta, Louisiana Pharmacist Alliance, Association for Students in Kinesiology, Pre-Pharmacy Organization/Sound of Today, national fraternities, national sororities. *Campus security:* 24-hour emergency response devices and patrols, student patrols, late-night transport/escort service. *Student services:* health clinic, personal/psychological counseling.

Athletics Member NCAA. All Division I except football (Division I-A). *Intercollegiate sports:* baseball M(s), basketball M(s)/W(s), cheerleading M(s)/W(s), cross-country running M(s)/W(s), golf M(s)/W, racquetball M/W, soccer M/W(s), softball W(s), swimming and diving M(s)/W(s), tennis M/W, track and field M(s)/W(s), volleyball M/W(s), weight lifting M/W. *Intramural sports:* archery M/W, badminton M/W, basketball M/W, bowling M/W, cross-country running M/W, football M/W, golf M/W, soccer M/W, softball M/W, swimming and diving M/W, table tennis M/W, tennis W, track and field M/W, volleyball W.

Standardized Tests *Required:* SAT or ACT (for admission).

Costs (2011–12) *Tuition:* state resident $5101 full-time; nonresident $13,047 full-time. Full-time tuition and fees vary according to course load, degree level, location, and program. Part-time tuition and fees vary according to course load, degree level, location, and program. *Room and board:* $6212; room only: $3682. Room and board charges vary according to board plan and housing facility. *Payment plan:* deferred payment. *Waivers:* children of alumni, senior citizens, and employees or children of employees.

Applying *Options:* electronic application, early admission, deferred entrance. *Application fee:* $20. *Required:* high school transcript. *Application deadlines:* rolling (freshmen), rolling (out-of-state freshmen), rolling (transfers). *Notifi-*

cation: continuous (freshmen), continuous (out-of-state freshmen), continuous (transfers).

Freshman Application Contact Ms. Frances Self, Assistant Director of Admissions, University of Louisiana at Monroe, Office of Recruitment and Admissions, Sandel Hall, 4020 Northeast Drive, Monroe, LA 71209. *Phone:* 318-342-5430. *Toll-free phone:* 800-372-5127. *Fax:* 318-342-1915. *E-mail:* admissions@ulm.edu. *Web site:* http://www.ulm.edu/.

University of New Orleans
New Orleans, Louisiana

- **State-supported** university, founded 1958, part of University of Louisiana System
- **Urban** 345-acre campus
- **Endowment** $17.6 million
- **Coed** 8,263 undergraduate students, 75% full-time, 49% women, 51% men
- **Moderately difficult** entrance level, 56% of applicants were admitted

Undergraduates 6,177 full-time, 2,086 part-time. Students come from 45 states and territories; 68 other countries; 4% are from out of state; 16% Black or African American, non-Hispanic/Latino; 8% Hispanic/Latino; 7% Asian, non-Hispanic/Latino; 0.1% Native Hawaiian or other Pacific Islander, non-Hispanic/Latino; 0.5% American Indian or Alaska Native, non-Hispanic/Latino; 1% Two or more races, non-Hispanic/Latino; 8% Race/ethnicity unknown; 4% international; 11% transferred in; 8% live on campus. *Retention:* 67% of full-time freshmen returned.

Freshmen *Admission:* 3,353 applied, 1,862 admitted, 1,104 enrolled. *Average high school GPA:* 3.03. *Test scores:* SAT critical reading scores over 500: 70%; SAT math scores over 500: 66%; SAT writing scores over 500: 56%; ACT scores over 18: 93%; SAT critical reading scores over 600: 24%; SAT math scores over 600: 22%; SAT writing scores over 600: 12%; ACT scores over 24: 29%; SAT critical reading scores over 700: 4%; SAT math scores over 700: 1%; ACT scores over 30: 2%.

Faculty *Total:* 550, 67% full-time, 57% with terminal degrees. *Student/faculty ratio:* 20:1.

Academics *Calendar:* semesters. *Degrees:* bachelor's, master's, doctoral, and first professional. *Special study options:* academic remediation for entering students, adult/continuing education programs, advanced placement credit, cooperative education, distance learning, double majors, English as a second language, honors programs, independent study, internships, off-campus study, part-time degree program, services for LD students, student-designed majors, study abroad, summer session for credit. *ROTC:* Army (c), Navy (c), Air Force (c). *Unusual degree programs:* 3-2 engineering with Xavier University of Louisiana; Southern University at New Orleans; Loyola University, New Orleans; Dillard University.

Computers on Campus 1,208 computers/terminals and 1,191 ports are available on campus for general student use. Students can access the following: campus intranet, computer help desk, free student e-mail accounts, online (class) grades, online (class) registration, online (class) schedules, classes in Moodle. Campuswide network is available. 100% of college-owned or -operated housing units are wired for high-speed Internet access. Wireless service is available via entire campus.

Student Life *Housing options:* coed, disabled students. Campus housing is university owned, leased by the school and is provided by a third party. *Activities and organizations:* drama/theater group, student-run newspaper, choral group, Student Activities Council, student government, International Student Organization, Golden Key Honor Society, UNO Ambassadors, national fraternities, national sororities. *Campus security:* 24-hour emergency response devices and patrols, late-night transport/escort service, controlled dormitory access. *Student services:* health clinic, personal/psychological counseling, women's center, legal services.

Athletics Member NCAA. All Division I. *Intercollegiate sports:* baseball M(s), basketball M(s)/W(s), cross-country running M(s)/W(s), golf M(s)/W(s), tennis M(s)/W(s), volleyball W(s). *Intramural sports:* basketball M/W, football M/W, racquetball M/W, soccer M/W, softball M/W, table tennis M/W, tennis M/W, volleyball M/W.

Standardized Tests *Required:* SAT or ACT (for admission).

Costs (2011–12) *Tuition:* state resident $4644 full-time, $155 per credit hour part-time; nonresident $16,168 full-time, $539 per credit hour part-time. Full-time tuition and fees vary according to course load, location, and program. Part-time tuition and fees vary according to course load, location, and program. *Required fees:* $613 full-time. *Room and board:* $8310. Room and board charges vary according to board plan and housing facility. *Payment plans:* installment, deferred payment. *Waivers:* senior citizens and employees or children of employees.

Financial Aid Of all full-time matriculated undergraduates who enrolled in 2011, 4,960 applied for aid, 4,317 were judged to have need, 251 had their need fully met. 158 Federal Work-Study jobs (averaging $2139). 446 state and other part-time jobs (averaging $1720). In 2011, 70 non-need-based awards were made. *Average percent of need met:* 50%. *Average financial aid package:* $8300. *Average need-based loan:* $4317. *Average need-based gift aid:* $5924. *Average non-need-based aid:* $1608. *Average indebtedness upon graduation:* $18,106.

Applying *Options:* electronic application, early admission, deferred entrance. *Application fee:* $50. *Required:* high school transcript, Core Requirements (19 units) (effective Fall 2012). *Required for some:* minimum 2.5 GPA. *Application deadlines:* 7/1 (freshmen), 6/1 (out-of-state freshmen), 7/1 (transfers). *Notification:* continuous (freshmen), continuous (out-of-state freshmen), continuous (transfers).

Freshman Application Contact University of New Orleans, 2000 Lakeshore Drive, New Orleans, LA 70148. *Phone:* 504-280-7013. *Toll-free phone:* 800-256-5866. *Web site:* http://www.uno.edu/.

University of Phoenix–Louisiana Campus
Metairie, Louisiana

Freshman Application Contact Marc Booker, Sr. Director, Office of Admissions and Evaluation, University of Phoenix–Louisiana Campus, 4035 South Riverpoint Parkway, Mail Stop CF-L101, Phoenix, AZ 85040. *Phone:* 602-557-4609. *Toll-free phone:* 866-766-0766. *Fax:* 480-643-1156. *Web site:* http://www.phoenix.edu/.

Xavier University of Louisiana
New Orleans, Louisiana

- **Independent Roman Catholic** comprehensive, founded 1925
- **Urban** 23-acre campus
- **Endowment** $117.3 million
- **Coed** 2,750 undergraduate students, 96% full-time, 71% women, 29% men
- **Moderately difficult** entrance level, 64% of applicants were admitted

Undergraduates 2,635 full-time, 115 part-time. Students come from 36 states and territories; 7 other countries; 57% are from out of state; 79% Black or African American, non-Hispanic/Latino; 2% Hispanic/Latino; 9% Asian, non-Hispanic/Latino; 0.1% American Indian or Alaska Native, non-Hispanic/Latino; 0.3% Two or more races, non-Hispanic/Latino; 1% Race/ethnicity unknown; 2% international; 5% transferred in; 36% live on campus. *Retention:* 69% of full-time freshmen returned.

Freshmen *Admission:* 4,463 applied, 2,860 admitted, 786 enrolled. *Average high school GPA:* 3.26. *Test scores:* SAT math scores over 500: 43%; SAT writing scores over 500: 37%; ACT scores over 18: 86%; SAT math scores over 600: 11%; SAT writing scores over 600: 6%; ACT scores over 24: 30%; ACT scores over 30: 1%.

Faculty *Total:* 267, 90% full-time, 80% with terminal degrees. *Student/faculty ratio:* 13:1.

Academics *Calendar:* semesters. *Degrees:* bachelor's, master's, and doctoral. *Special study options:* academic remediation for entering students, accelerated degree program, adult/continuing education programs, advanced placement credit, cooperative education, double majors, freshman honors college, honors programs, independent study, internships, off-campus study, part-time degree program, services for LD students, study abroad, summer session for credit. *ROTC:* Army (c), Navy (c), Air Force (c). *Unusual degree programs:* 3-2 business administration with Tulane University; engineering with Tulane University, University of Maryland, University of New Orleans, Georgia Institute of Technology, University of Wisconsin-Madison, Morgan State University, Southern University and Agricultural and Mechanical College; biostatistics with Louisiana State University Medical Center.

Computers on Campus 155 computers/terminals are available on campus for general student use. Students can access the following: computer help desk, free student e-mail accounts, online (class) grades, online (class) registration, online (class) schedules. Campuswide network is available. 100% of college-owned or -operated housing units are wired for high-speed Internet access. Wireless service is available via entire campus.

Student Life *Housing options:* coed, men-only, women-only, disabled students. Campus housing is university owned. Freshman applicants given priority for college housing. *Activities and organizations:* drama/theater group, student-run newspaper, television station, choral group, Mobilization at Xavier, AWARE, NAACP, California Club, Beta Beta Beta (Biology Club), national fraternities, national sororities. *Campus security:* 24-hour emergency response devices and patrols, student patrols, bicycle patrols. *Student services:* health clinic, personal/psychological counseling.

Athletics Member NAIA. *Intercollegiate sports:* basketball M(s)/W(s), cross-country running M/W, tennis M(s)/W(s). *Intramural sports:* badminton M/W,

basketball M/W, football M/W, golf M/W, softball M/W, swimming and diving M/W, table tennis M/W, tennis M/W, track and field M/W, volleyball M/W.
Standardized Tests *Required:* SAT or ACT (for admission).
Costs (2012–13) *Comprehensive fee:* $26,300 includes full-time tuition ($17,700), mandatory fees ($1000), and room and board ($7600). Part-time tuition and fees vary according to course load. *Room and board:* Room and board charges vary according to housing facility. *Payment plan:* installment. *Waivers:* employees or children of employees.
Financial Aid Of all full-time matriculated undergraduates who enrolled in 2010, 2,455 applied for aid, 2,271 were judged to have need, 17 had their need fully met. 319 Federal Work-Study jobs (averaging $1082). In 2010, 73 non-need-based awards were made. *Average percent of need met:* 13%. *Average financial aid package:* $17,465. *Average need-based loan:* $4729. *Average need-based gift aid:* $6179. *Average non-need-based aid:* $9257. *Average indebtedness upon graduation:* $46,474.
Applying *Options:* electronic application, early action. *Application fee:* $25. *Required:* high school transcript, minimum 2.0 GPA, 1 letter of recommendation. *Required for some:* interview. *Application deadlines:* 7/1 (freshmen), 6/1 (transfers), 1/15 (early action). *Notification:* continuous (freshmen), continuous (transfers), 2/15 (early action).
Freshman Application Contact Mr. Winston Brown, Dean of Admissions, Xavier University of Louisiana, 7325 Palmetto Street, New Orleans, LA 70125. *Phone:* 504-520-7388. *Toll-free phone:* 877-XAVIERU. *Fax:* 504-520-7941. *E-mail:* apply@xula.edu. *Web site:* http://www.xula.edu/.

MAINE

Bates College

Lewiston, Maine

- **Independent** 4-year, founded 1855
- **Small-town** 109-acre campus
- **Endowment** $231.5 million
- **Coed** 1,769 undergraduate students, 100% full-time, 53% women, 47% men
- **Most difficult** entrance level, 27% of applicants were admitted

Undergraduates 1,769 full-time. Students come from 42 states and territories; 68 other countries; 89% are from out of state; 5% Black or African American, non-Hispanic/Latino; 5% Hispanic/Latino; 5% Asian, non-Hispanic/Latino; 0.1% Native Hawaiian or other Pacific Islander, non-Hispanic/Latino; 0.5% American Indian or Alaska Native, non-Hispanic/Latino; 3% Two or more races, non-Hispanic/Latino; 2% Race/ethnicity unknown; 6% international; 0.4% transferred in; 94% live on campus. *Retention:* 93% of full-time freshmen returned.
Freshmen *Admission:* 5,196 applied, 1,405 admitted, 502 enrolled. *Test scores:* SAT critical reading scores over 500: 100%; SAT math scores over 500: 100%; SAT writing scores over 500: 100%; ACT scores over 18: 100%; SAT critical reading scores over 600: 90%; SAT math scores over 600: 90%; SAT writing scores over 600: 88%; ACT scores over 24: 100%; SAT critical reading scores over 700: 32%; SAT math scores over 700: 33%; SAT writing scores over 700: 42%; ACT scores over 30: 65%.
Faculty *Total:* 189, 87% full-time, 84% with terminal degrees. *Student/faculty ratio:* 10:1.
Academics *Calendar:* 4-4-1. *Degree:* bachelor's. *Special study options:* accelerated degree program, advanced placement credit, double majors, honors programs, independent study, internships, off-campus study, services for LD students, student-designed majors, study abroad. *Unusual degree programs:* 3-2 engineering with Columbia University, Rensselaer Polytechnic Institute, Case Western Reserve University, Washington University in St. Louis, Dartmouth College.
Computers on Campus 175 computers/terminals and 2,075 ports are available on campus for general student use. Students can access the following: computer help desk, free student e-mail accounts, online (class) grades, online (class) registration, online (class) schedules, course web pages, course evaluation, financial records. Campuswide network is available. 100% of college-owned or -operated housing units are wired for high-speed Internet access. Wireless service is available via classrooms, computer labs, dorm rooms, learning centers, libraries, student centers.
Student Life *Housing:* on-campus residence required through senior year. *Options:* coed, men-only, women-only. Campus housing is university owned. Freshman campus housing is guaranteed. *Activities and organizations:* drama/theater group, student-run newspaper, radio station, choral group, Outing Club (outdoor recreation), International Club, Chase Hall Committee (student activities planning), Representative Assembly, WRBC (student radio station). *Campus security:* 24-hour emergency response devices and patrols, student patrols, late-night transport/escort service, controlled dormitory access. *Stu-

dent services: health clinic, personal/psychological counseling, women's center.
Athletics Member NCAA. All Division III. *Intercollegiate sports:* baseball M, basketball M/W, crew M/W, cross-country running M/W, equestrian sports M(c)/W(c), fencing M(c)/W(c), field hockey W, football M, golf M/W, ice hockey M(c)/W(c), lacrosse M/W, rugby M(c)/W(c), sailing M(c)/W(c), skiing (cross-country) M/W, skiing (downhill) M/W, soccer M/W, softball W, squash M/W, swimming and diving M/W, tennis M/W, track and field M/W, ultimate Frisbee M(c)/W(c), volleyball M(c)/W, water polo M(c)/W(c). *Intramural sports:* basketball M/W, bowling M/W, ice hockey M/W, racquetball M/W, soccer M/W, softball M/W, squash M/W, tennis M/W, volleyball M/W.
Costs (2011–12) *Comprehensive fee:* $55,300. *Payment plans:* tuition prepayment, installment. *Waivers:* employees or children of employees.
Financial Aid Of all full-time matriculated undergraduates who enrolled in 2010, 870 applied for aid, 800 were judged to have need, 720 had their need fully met. 606 Federal Work-Study jobs (averaging $1678). 101 state and other part-time jobs (averaging $1728). *Average percent of need met:* 100%. *Average financial aid package:* $35,741. *Average need-based loan:* $4347. *Average need-based gift aid:* $32,910. *Average indebtedness upon graduation:* $18,699. *Financial aid deadline:* 2/1.
Applying *Options:* electronic application, early admission, early decision, deferred entrance. *Application fee:* $60. *Required:* essay or personal statement, high school transcript, 3 letters of recommendation. *Recommended:* interview. *Application deadlines:* 1/1 (freshmen), 3/1 (transfers). *Early decision deadline:* 11/15 (for plan 1), 1/1 (for plan 2). *Notification:* 3/31 (freshmen), 6/1 (transfers), 12/20 (early decision plan 1), 2/14 (early decision plan 2).
Freshman Application Contact Leigh Weisenburger, Director of Admissions, Bates College, 23 Campus Ave, Lindholm House, Bates College, Lewiston, ME 04240-6028. *Phone:* 207-786-6000. *Fax:* 207-786-6025. *E-mail:* admission@bates.edu. *Web site:* http://www.bates.edu/.

Bowdoin College

Brunswick, Maine

- **Independent** 4-year, founded 1794
- **Small-town** 205-acre campus with easy access to Portland
- **Endowment** $904.2 million
- **Coed** 1,778 undergraduate students, 100% full-time, 49% women, 51% men
- **Most difficult** entrance level, 16% of applicants were admitted

Undergraduates 1,773 full-time, 5 part-time. Students come from 48 states and territories; 35 other countries; 88% are from out of state; 5% Black or African American, non-Hispanic/Latino; 12% Hispanic/Latino; 7% Asian, non-Hispanic/Latino; 0.1% Native Hawaiian or other Pacific Islander, non-Hispanic/Latino; 0.1% American Indian or Alaska Native, non-Hispanic/Latino; 6% Two or more races, non-Hispanic/Latino; 0.7% Race/ethnicity unknown; 4% international; 0.1% transferred in; 92% live on campus. *Retention:* 97% of full-time freshmen returned.
Freshmen *Admission:* 6,554 applied, 1,056 admitted, 483 enrolled. *Test scores:* SAT critical reading scores over 500: 100%; SAT math scores over 500: 100%; SAT writing scores over 500: 100%; ACT scores over 18: 100%; SAT critical reading scores over 600: 94%; SAT math scores over 600: 96%; SAT writing scores over 600: 93%; ACT scores over 24: 99%; SAT critical reading scores over 700: 56%; SAT math scores over 700: 54%; SAT writing scores over 700: 59%; ACT scores over 30: 75%.
Faculty *Total:* 222, 82% full-time, 98% with terminal degrees. *Student/faculty ratio:* 9:1.
Academics *Calendar:* semesters. *Degrees:* bachelor's (SAT or ACT considered if submitted. Test scores are required for home-schooled applicants). *Special study options:* accelerated degree program, advanced placement credit, double majors, independent study, off-campus study, services for LD students, student-designed majors, study abroad. *Unusual degree programs:* 3-2 engineering with California Institute of Technology, Columbia University, Dartmouth College, University of Maine Orono; law with Columbia University.
Computers on Campus 450 computers/terminals and 5,500 ports are available on campus for general student use. Students can access the following: campus intranet, computer help desk, free student e-mail accounts, online (class) grades, online (class) schedules, training classes on variety of desktop and academic software. Campuswide network is available. 100% of college-owned or -operated housing units are wired for high-speed Internet access. Wireless service is available via entire campus.
Student Life *Housing:* on-campus residence required through sophomore year. *Options:* coed, disabled students. Campus housing is university owned. Freshman campus housing is guaranteed. *Activities and organizations:* drama/theater group, student-run newspaper, radio and television station, choral group, Outing Club, Intramural Sports, Community Service Volunteer Programs, WBOR 91.1 FM, Bowdoin Orient. *Campus security:* 24-hour emergency

response devices and patrols, late-night transport/escort service, controlled dormitory access, self-defense education, whistle program, safe ride service. *Student services:* health clinic, personal/psychological counseling, women's center.

Athletics Member NCAA. All Division III except men's and women's sailing (Division I), men's and women's skiing (cross-country) (Division I), men's and women's squash (Division I). *Intercollegiate sports:* baseball M, basketball M/W, crew M(c)/W(c), cross-country running M/W, equestrian sports M(c)/W(c), fencing M(c)/W(c), field hockey W, football M, golf M/W, ice hockey M/W, lacrosse M/W, rugby M(c)/W(c), sailing M/W, skiing (cross-country) M/W, skiing (downhill) M(c)/W(c), soccer M/W, softball W, squash M/W, swimming and diving M/W, tennis M/W, track and field M/W, ultimate Frisbee M(c)/W(c), volleyball M(c)/W(c), water polo M(c)/W(c). *Intramural sports:* badminton M/W, basketball M/W, cheerleading M(c)/W(c), football M/W, ice hockey M/W, lacrosse M(c)/W(c), rock climbing M(c)/W(c), skiing (cross-country) M(c)/W(c), soccer M/W, softball M/W, table tennis M(c)/W(c), tennis M/W.

Costs (2011–12) *Comprehensive fee:* $54,470 includes full-time tuition ($42,386), mandatory fees ($430), and room and board ($11,654). *College room only:* $5454. Room and board charges vary according to board plan. *Payment plans:* installment, deferred payment. *Waivers:* employees or children of employees.

Financial Aid Of all full-time matriculated undergraduates who enrolled in 2011, 974 applied for aid, 813 were judged to have need, 813 had their need fully met. 412 Federal Work-Study jobs (averaging $1338). 322 state and other part-time jobs (averaging $2236). In 2011, 89 non-need-based awards were made. *Average percent of need met:* 100%. *Average financial aid package:* $40,196. *Average need-based gift aid:* $35,975. *Average non-need-based aid:* $1000. *Average indebtedness upon graduation:* $17,569. *Financial aid deadline:* 2/15.

Applying *Options:* electronic application, early admission, early decision, deferred entrance. *Application fee:* $60. *Required:* essay or personal statement, high school transcript, 3 letters of recommendation. *Recommended:* interview. *Application deadlines:* 1/1 (freshmen), 1/1 (out-of-state freshmen), 3/1 (transfers). *Early decision deadline:* 11/15 (for plan 1), 1/1 (for plan 2). *Notification:* 4/5 (freshmen), 4/5 (out-of-state freshmen), 5/1 (transfers), 12/15 (early decision plan 1), 2/15 (early decision plan 2).

Freshman Application Contact Peter T. Wiley, Associate Dean of Admissions, Bowdoin College, 5000 College Station, Brunswick, ME 04011-8411. *Phone:* 207-725-3190. *Fax:* 207-725-3101. *E-mail:* admissions@bowdoin.edu. *Web site:* http://www.bowdoin.edu/.

Colby College

Waterville, Maine

- **Independent** 4-year, founded 1813
- **Small-town** 714-acre campus
- **Endowment** $611.4 million
- **Coed** 1,815 undergraduate students, 100% full-time, 53% women, 47% men
- **Most difficult** entrance level, 29% of applicants were admitted

Undergraduates 1,815 full-time. Students come from 45 states and territories; 70 other countries; 86% are from out of state; 3% Black or African American, non-Hispanic/Latino; 4% Hispanic/Latino; 5% Asian, non-Hispanic/Latino; 0.1% Native Hawaiian or other Pacific Islander, non-Hispanic/Latino; 0.2% American Indian or Alaska Native, non-Hispanic/Latino; 3% Two or more races, non-Hispanic/Latino; 18% Race/ethnicity unknown; 6% international; 0.5% transferred in; 93% live on campus. *Retention:* 94% of full-time freshmen returned.

Freshmen *Admission:* 5,186 applied, 1,527 admitted, 467 enrolled. *Test scores:* SAT critical reading scores over 500: 97%; SAT math scores over 500: 99%; SAT writing scores over 500: 97%; ACT scores over 18: 100%; SAT critical reading scores over 600: 83%; SAT math scores over 600: 90%; SAT writing scores over 600: 81%; ACT scores over 24: 100%; SAT critical reading scores over 700: 33%; SAT math scores over 700: 35%; SAT writing scores over 700: 36%; ACT scores over 30: 60%.

Faculty *Total:* 200, 81% full-time, 94% with terminal degrees. *Student/faculty ratio:* 10:1.

Academics *Calendar:* 4-1-4. *Degree:* bachelor's. *Special study options:* advanced placement credit, double majors, honors programs, independent study, internships, off-campus study, services for LD students, student-designed majors, study abroad. *ROTC:* Army (c). *Unusual degree programs:* 3-2 engineering with Dartmouth College.

Computers on Campus 350 computers/terminals are available on campus for general student use. Students can access the following: campus intranet, computer help desk, free student e-mail accounts, online (class) grades, online (class) registration, online (class) schedules, portal. Campuswide network is available. 100% of college-owned or -operated housing units are wired for high-speed Internet access. Wireless service is available via classrooms, computer centers, computer labs, dorm rooms, learning centers, libraries, student centers.

Student Life *Housing:* on-campus residence required through senior year. *Options:* coed. Campus housing is university owned. Freshman campus housing is guaranteed. *Activities and organizations:* drama/theater group, student-run newspaper, radio station, choral group, Outing Club, volunteer center, WMHB-FM (College Radio Station), student government, Powder and Wig (theater). *Campus security:* 24-hour emergency response devices and patrols, late-night transport/escort service, controlled dormitory access, campus lighting, student emergency response team, self-defense class, property id program, party monitors. *Student services:* health clinic, personal/psychological counseling, women's center.

Athletics Member NCAA. All Division III except men's and women's skiing (downhill) (Division I). *Intercollegiate sports:* baseball M, basketball M/W, crew M/W, cross-country running M/W, equestrian sports M(c)/W(c), fencing M(c)/W(c), field hockey W, football M, golf M/W, ice hockey M/W, lacrosse M/W, rugby M(c)/W(c), skiing (downhill) M/W, soccer M/W, softball W, squash M/W, swimming and diving M/W, tennis M/W, track and field M/W, ultimate Frisbee M(c)/W(c), volleyball M(c)/W, water polo M(c)/W(c). *Intramural sports:* basketball M/W, field hockey M/W, football M, soccer M/W, softball M/W.

Standardized Tests *Required:* Students must submit either (a) SAT, (b) ACT, or (c) three SAT Subject Tests of their choice (for admission).

Costs (2011–12) *Comprehensive fee:* $53,800. Full-time tuition and fees vary according to course load. Part-time tuition and fees vary according to course load. *Room and board:* Room and board charges vary according to housing facility. *Payment plan:* installment. *Waivers:* employees or children of employees.

Financial Aid Of all full-time matriculated undergraduates who enrolled in 2011, 991 applied for aid, 748 were judged to have need, 746 had their need fully met. 434 Federal Work-Study jobs (averaging $1645). 159 state and other part-time jobs (averaging $1696). In 2011, 41 non-need-based awards were made. *Average percent of need met:* 100%. *Average financial aid package:* $36,666. *Average need-based loan:* $2640. *Average need-based gift aid:* $34,993. *Average non-need-based aid:* $3357. *Average indebtedness upon graduation:* $22,367. *Financial aid deadline:* 2/1.

Applying *Options:* electronic application, early admission, early decision, deferred entrance. *Required:* essay or personal statement, high school transcript, 2 letters of recommendation. *Recommended:* interview. *Application deadlines:* 1/1 (freshmen), 3/1 (transfers). *Early decision deadline:* 11/15 (for plan 1), 1/1 (for plan 2). *Notification:* 4/1 (freshmen), 5/15 (transfers), 12/15 (early decision plan 1), 2/10 (early decision plan 2).

Freshman Application Contact Mr. Steve Thomas, Director of Admissions, Colby College, Mayflower Hill, Waterville, ME 04901-8840. *Phone:* 207-859-4800. *Toll-free phone:* 800-723-3032. *Fax:* 207-859-4828. *E-mail:* admissions@colby.edu. *Web site:* http://www.colby.edu/.

See page 369 for display ad and page 1268 for the College Close-Up.

College of the Atlantic
Bar Harbor, Maine

- **Independent** comprehensive, founded 1969
- **Small-town** 35-acre campus
- **Endowment** $25.4 million
- **Coed** 354 undergraduate students, 95% full-time, 72% women, 28% men
- **Very difficult** entrance level, 58% of applicants were admitted

Undergraduates 335 full-time, 19 part-time. Students come from 37 states and territories; 34 other countries; 79% are from out of state; 1% Black or African American, non-Hispanic/Latino; 2% Hispanic/Latino; 1% Asian, non-Hispanic/Latino; 0.3% American Indian or Alaska Native, non-Hispanic/Latino; 3% Two or more races, non-Hispanic/Latino; 7% Race/ethnicity unknown; 17% international; 5% transferred in; 41% live on campus. *Retention:* 86% of full-time freshmen returned.

Freshmen *Admission:* 400 applied, 233 admitted, 76 enrolled. *Average high school GPA:* 3.65. *Test scores:* SAT critical reading scores over 500: 100%; SAT math scores over 500: 97%; SAT writing scores over 500: 100%; ACT scores over 18: 100%; SAT critical reading scores over 600: 83%; SAT math scores over 600: 64%; SAT writing scores over 600: 67%; ACT scores over 24: 94%; SAT critical reading scores over 700: 30%; SAT math scores over 700: 10%; SAT writing scores over 700: 13%; ACT scores over 30: 44%.

Faculty *Total:* 41, 68% full-time, 73% with terminal degrees. *Student/faculty ratio:* 11:1.

Academics *Calendar:* trimesters. *Degrees:* bachelor's and master's. *Special study options:* academic remediation for entering students, accelerated degree program, advanced placement credit, cooperative education, independent study, internships, off-campus study, part-time degree program, services for LD students, student-designed majors, study abroad.

Computers on Campus 38 computers/terminals and 50 ports are available on campus for general student use. Students can access the following: computer help desk, free student e-mail accounts, online (class) grades, online (class)

registration, online (class) schedules, online billing, grades, transcript, financial aid and course management system. Campuswide network is available. 100% of college-owned or -operated housing units are wired for high-speed Internet access. Wireless service is available via entire campus.

Student Life *Housing:* on-campus residence required for freshman year. *Options:* coed. Campus housing is university owned. Freshman campus housing is guaranteed. *Activities and organizations:* drama/theater group, student-run newspaper, choral group, All College Meeting, Open Mic, Outdoor Program, Campus Committee on Sustainability, Theater Club. *Campus security:* 24-hour emergency response devices and patrols, late-night transport/escort service. *Student services:* health clinic, personal/psychological counseling.

Athletics *Intramural sports:* badminton M/W, basketball M, bowling M/W, ice hockey M/W, rock climbing M/W, sailing M/W, skiing (cross-country) M/W, soccer M/W, softball M/W, table tennis M/W, ultimate Frisbee M/W, volleyball M/W, water polo M/W.

Standardized Tests *Recommended:* SAT or ACT (for admission).

Costs (2012–13) *Comprehensive fee:* $46,959 includes full-time tuition ($37,152), mandatory fees ($549), and room and board ($9258). Part-time tuition: $4128 per credit. *Required fees:* $183 per term part-time. *College room only:* $5952. Room and board charges vary according to board plan. *Payment plan:* installment. *Waivers:* employees or children of employees.

Financial Aid Of all full-time matriculated undergraduates who enrolled in 2011, 291 applied for aid, 285 were judged to have need, 73 had their need fully met. 214 Federal Work-Study jobs (averaging $2511). 60 state and other part-time jobs (averaging $1983). In 2011, 10 non-need-based awards were made. *Average percent of need met:* 96%. *Average financial aid package:* $36,655. *Average need-based loan:* $3074. *Average need-based gift aid:* $28,770. *Average non-need-based aid:* $3846. *Average indebtedness upon graduation:* $20,858.

Applying *Options:* electronic application, early admission, early decision, deferred entrance. *Application fee:* $50. *Required:* essay or personal statement, high school transcript, 3 letters of recommendation. *Required for some:* interview. *Recommended:* minimum 3.0 GPA, interview. *Application deadlines:* 2/15 (freshmen), 4/1 (transfers). *Early decision deadline:* 12/1 (for plan 1), 1/10 (for plan 2). *Notification:* 4/1 (freshmen), 4/25 (transfers), 12/15 (early decision plan 1), 1/25 (early decision plan 2).

Freshman Application Contact Ms. Sarah Baker, Dean of Admission, College of the Atlantic, 105 Eden Street, Bar Harbor, ME 04609-1198. *Phone:* 207-801-5640. *Toll-free phone:* 800-528-0025. *Fax:* 207-288-4126. *E-mail:* inquiry@coa.edu. *Web site:* http://www.coa.edu/.

Husson University
Bangor, Maine

- **Independent** comprehensive, founded 1898
- **Suburban** 200-acre campus
- **Endowment** $8.0 million
- **Coed** 2,501 undergraduate students, 80% full-time, 59% women, 41% men
- **Moderately difficult** entrance level, 75% of applicants were admitted

Undergraduates 1,999 full-time, 502 part-time. Students come from 20 states and territories; 9 other countries; 15% are from out of state; 4% Black or African American, non-Hispanic/Latino; 1% Hispanic/Latino; 1% Asian, non-Hispanic/Latino; 0.2% Native Hawaiian or other Pacific Islander, non-Hispanic/Latino; 0.4% American Indian or Alaska Native, non-Hispanic/Latino; 0.8% Two or more races, non-Hispanic/Latino; 2% Race/ethnicity unknown; 1% international; 6% transferred in; 39% live on campus. *Retention:* 72% of full-time freshmen returned.

Freshmen *Admission:* 1,560 applied, 1,172 admitted, 448 enrolled. *Average high school GPA:* 3.02. *Test scores:* SAT critical reading scores over 500: 36%; SAT math scores over 500: 39%; SAT writing scores over 500: 35%; ACT scores over 18: 76%; SAT critical reading scores over 600: 5%; SAT math scores over 600: 5%; SAT writing scores over 600: 4%; ACT scores over 24: 28%; SAT critical reading scores over 700: 1%.

Faculty *Total:* 309, 35% full-time, 41% with terminal degrees. *Student/faculty ratio:* 16:1.

Academics *Calendar:* semesters. *Degrees:* certificates, associate, bachelor's, master's, doctoral, post-master's, and postbachelor's certificates. *Special study options:* academic remediation for entering students, adult/continuing education programs, advanced placement credit, cooperative education, double majors, independent study, internships, part-time degree program, services for LD students, student-designed majors, summer session for credit. *ROTC:* Army (b), Navy (c). *Unusual degree programs:* 3-2 business administration; occupational therapy.

Computers on Campus 116 computers/terminals and 116 ports are available on campus for general student use. Students can access the following: campus intranet, computer help desk, free student e-mail accounts, online (class) grades, online (class) registration, online (class) schedules. Campuswide net-

work is available. 100% of college-owned or -operated housing units are wired for high-speed Internet access. Wireless service is available via entire campus.

Student Life *Housing:* on-campus residence required through sophomore year. *Options:* coed. Campus housing is university owned and leased by the school. Freshman campus housing is guaranteed. *Activities and organizations:* drama/theater group, student-run newspaper, radio station, student government, Organization of Student Nurses, Organization of Physical Therapy Students, Accounting Society, Criminal Justice Club, national fraternities. *Campus security:* 24-hour emergency response devices and patrols, late-night transport/escort service, controlled dormitory access. *Student services:* health clinic, personal/psychological counseling.

Athletics Member NCAA. All Division III. *Intercollegiate sports:* baseball M, basketball M/W, cross-country running W, field hockey W, football M, golf M, lacrosse M/W, soccer M/W, softball W, swimming and diving W, track and field W, volleyball W. *Intramural sports:* baseball M, basketball M/W, cheerleading M/W, football M, ice hockey M/W, lacrosse M, soccer M/W, softball M/W, swimming and diving M/W, tennis M/W, volleyball M/W, water polo M/W, wrestling M.

Standardized Tests *Required:* SAT or ACT (for admission).

Costs (2011–12) *One-time required fee:* $455. *Comprehensive fee:* $21,500 includes full-time tuition ($13,650), mandatory fees ($330), and room and board ($7520). Full-time tuition and fees vary according to class time. Part-time tuition: $455 per credit. Part-time tuition and fees vary according to class time and course load. *Room and board:* Room and board charges vary according to board plan. *Payment plans:* tuition prepayment, installment. *Waivers:* senior citizens and employees or children of employees.

Financial Aid Of all full-time matriculated undergraduates who enrolled in 2011, 1,941 applied for aid, 1,742 were judged to have need, 95 had their need fully met. 1,000 Federal Work-Study jobs (averaging $1300). In 2011, 118 non-need-based awards were made. *Average percent of need met:* 60%. *Average financial aid package:* $11,645. *Average need-based loan:* $3928. *Average need-based gift aid:* $7789. *Average non-need-based aid:* $2411. *Average indebtedness upon graduation:* $27,089.

Applying *Options:* electronic application, early admission, deferred entrance. *Application fee:* $40. *Required:* essay or personal statement, high school transcript, 1 letter of recommendation. *Recommended:* interview. *Application deadlines:* 8/15 (freshmen), 8/15 (transfers). *Notification:* continuous (freshmen), continuous (transfers).

Freshman Application Contact Ms. Carlena Bean, Director of Admissions, Husson University, 1 College Circle, Bangor, ME 04401-2999. *Phone:* 207-941-7067. *Toll-free phone:* 800-4-HUSSON. *Fax:* 207-941-7935. *E-mail:* beanc@husson.edu. *Web site:* http://www.husson.edu/.

Maine College of Art

Portland, Maine

- **Independent** comprehensive, founded 1882
- **Urban** campus with easy access to Boston
- **Endowment** $3.8 million
- **Coed**
- **Moderately difficult** entrance level

Faculty *Student/faculty ratio:* 10:1.

Academics *Calendar:* semesters. *Degrees:* bachelor's, master's, and post-bachelor's certificates.

Student Life *Campus security:* 24-hour emergency response devices and patrols, controlled dormitory access.

Costs (2011–12) *One-time required fee:* $50. *Comprehensive fee:* $39,085 includes full-time tuition ($28,665), mandatory fees ($680), and room and board ($9740). Full-time tuition and fees vary according to program. Part-time tuition and fees vary according to course load and program. *College room only:* $4870. Room and board charges vary according to board plan and housing facility.

Applying *Options:* electronic application, early admission, early action, deferred entrance. *Application fee:* $40. *Required:* essay or personal statement, high school transcript, 2 letters of recommendation, portfolio. *Recommended:* minimum 2.0 GPA, interview.

Freshman Application Contact Stacy Howe, Admissions Operations Coordinator, Maine College of Art, 522 Congress Street, Portland, ME 04101-3987. *Phone:* 207-699-5026. *Toll-free phone:* 800-699-1509. *Fax:* 207-699-5080. *E-mail:* admissions@meca.edu. *Web site:* http://www.meca.edu/.

Maine Maritime Academy

Castine, Maine

Freshman Application Contact Maine Maritime Academy, Castine, ME 04420. *Phone:* 207-326-2215. *Toll-free phone:* 800-464-6565 (in-state); 800-227-8465 (out-of-state). *Web site:* http://www.mainemaritime.edu/.

New England School of Communications

Bangor, Maine

- **Independent** 4-year, founded 1981
- **Small-town** 200-acre campus
- **Coed, primarily men** 531 undergraduate students, 95% full-time, 26% women, 74% men
- **Minimally difficult** entrance level, 61% of applicants were admitted

Undergraduates 507 full-time, 24 part-time. Students come from 11 states and territories; 1 other country; 29% are from out of state; 2% Black or African American, non-Hispanic/Latino; 1% Hispanic/Latino; 0.8% Asian, non-Hispanic/Latino; 0.8% American Indian or Alaska Native, non-Hispanic/Latino; 0.2% international; 4% transferred in; 50% live on campus. *Retention:* 65% of full-time freshmen returned.

Freshmen *Admission:* 399 applied, 244 admitted, 119 enrolled.

Faculty *Total:* 64, 28% full-time, 13% with terminal degrees. *Student/faculty ratio:* 15:1.

Academics *Calendar:* semesters. *Degrees:* associate and bachelor's. *Special study options:* adult/continuing education programs, advanced placement credit, cooperative education, internships, off-campus study, part-time degree program, services for LD students, summer session for credit. *ROTC:* Army (c).

Computers on Campus 195 computers/terminals are available on campus for general student use. Students can access the following: campus intranet, computer help desk, free student e-mail accounts, online (class) grades, online (class) schedules. Campuswide network is available. 100% of college-owned or -operated housing units are wired for high-speed Internet access. Wireless service is available via classrooms, computer centers, computer labs, dorm rooms, learning centers, libraries, student centers.

Student Life *Housing:* on-campus residence required through sophomore year. *Options:* coed, disabled students. Campus housing is university owned and leased by the school. Freshman applicants given priority for college housing. *Activities and organizations:* drama/theater group, student-run newspaper, radio and television station, choral group, marching band, drama, newspaper, student government, radio station, Audio Engineering Society, national fraternities, national sororities. *Campus security:* 24-hour emergency response devices and patrols, late-night transport/escort service. *Student services:* health clinic, personal/psychological counseling.

Athletics *Intramural sports:* baseball M, basketball M/W, cheerleading M/W, field hockey W, football M, lacrosse M/W, skiing (downhill) M/W, soccer M/W, softball M/W, swimming and diving M/W, table tennis M/W, tennis M/W, ultimate Frisbee M/W, volleyball M/W, water polo M/W.

Standardized Tests *Required:* Wonderlic aptitude test (for admission). *Recommended:* SAT or ACT (for admission).

Costs (2011–12) *One-time required fee:* $100. *Comprehensive fee:* $20,214 includes full-time tuition ($11,814), mandatory fees ($830), and room and board ($7570). Part-time tuition: $394 per credit hour. Part-time tuition and fees vary according to course load. *Payment plan:* installment. *Waivers:* employees or children of employees.

Financial Aid Of all full-time matriculated undergraduates who enrolled in 2010, 499 applied for aid, 436 were judged to have need. 23 Federal Work-Study jobs (averaging $1246). 65 state and other part-time jobs (averaging $911). In 2010, 9 non-need-based awards were made. *Average need-based loan:* $3972. *Average need-based gift aid:* $4578. *Average non-need-based aid:* $1923. *Average indebtedness upon graduation:* $28,077.

Applying *Options:* electronic application, deferred entrance. *Application fee:* $25. *Required:* essay or personal statement, high school transcript, minimum 2.0 GPA, 2 letters of recommendation, interview. *Required for some:* placement test. *Application deadlines:* rolling (freshmen), rolling (out-of-state freshmen), rolling (transfers). *Notification:* continuous (freshmen), continuous (out-of-state freshmen), continuous (transfers).

Freshman Application Contact Ms. Louise Grant, Director of Admissions, New England School of Communications, 1 College Circle, Bangor, ME 04401. *Phone:* 207-941-7176 Ext. 1093. *Toll-free phone:* 888-877-1876. *Fax:* 207-947-3987. *E-mail:* info@nescom.edu. *Web site:* http://www.nescom.edu/.

Saint Joseph's College of Maine
Standish, Maine

- **Independent** comprehensive, founded 1912, affiliated with Roman Catholic Church
- **Small-town** 350-acre campus
- **Endowment** $9.2 million
- **Coed** 2,384 undergraduate students, 72% full-time, 72% women, 28% men
- **Moderately difficult** entrance level, 88% of applicants were admitted

Undergraduates 1,728 full-time, 656 part-time. Students come from 15 states and territories; 1 other country; 45% are from out of state; 3% Black or African American, non-Hispanic/Latino; 2% Hispanic/Latino; 1% Asian, non-Hispanic/Latino; 22% Race/ethnicity unknown; 1% transferred in; 74% live on campus. *Retention:* 76% of full-time freshmen returned.
Freshmen *Admission:* 1,321 applied, 1,164 admitted, 277 enrolled. *Average high school GPA:* 3.
Faculty *Total:* 126, 54% full-time, 53% with terminal degrees. *Student/faculty ratio:* 14:1.
Academics *Calendar:* semesters. *Degrees:* certificates, bachelor's, master's, and post-master's certificates (profile does not include enrollment in distance learning master's program). *Special study options:* adult/continuing education programs, advanced placement credit, cooperative education, distance learning, double majors, honors programs, independent study, internships, off-campus study, part-time degree program, services for LD students, student-designed majors, study abroad, summer session for credit. *ROTC:* Army (c). *Unusual degree programs:* 3-2 engineering with Manhattan College; pharmacy with Massachusetts College of Pharmacy, optometry with Pennsylvania College of Optometry.
Computers on Campus 102 computers/terminals are available on campus for general student use. Students can access the following: campus intranet, computer help desk, free student e-mail accounts, online (class) grades, online (class) registration, online (class) schedules. Campuswide network is available. 100% of college-owned or -operated housing units are wired for high-speed Internet access. Wireless service is available via entire campus.
Student Life *Housing options:* coed, men-only, women-only. Campus housing is university owned. Freshman campus housing is guaranteed. *Activities and organizations:* drama/theater group, student-run newspaper, radio station, choral group, Campus ministry, Superkids, Student Government Association and Senate, Business Club, Inter-Hall Council. *Campus security:* 24-hour emergency response devices and patrols, late-night transport/escort service, controlled dormitory access. *Student services:* health clinic, personal/psychological counseling.
Athletics Member NCAA. All Division III. *Intercollegiate sports:* baseball M, basketball M/W, cheerleading M(c)/W(c), cross-country running M/W, field hockey W, golf M, ice hockey M(c)/W(c), soccer M/W, softball W, volleyball W. *Intramural sports:* basketball M/W, lacrosse M(c)/W(c), rock climbing M(c)/W(c), soccer M/W, softball M/W, swimming and diving M(c)/W(c), volleyball M/W.
Standardized Tests *Required:* SAT or ACT (for admission).
Costs (2012–13) *Comprehensive fee:* $39,700 includes full-time tuition ($28,700) and room and board ($11,000). Part-time tuition and fees vary according to course load. *Room and board:* Room and board charges vary according to board plan.
Financial Aid Of all full-time matriculated undergraduates who enrolled in 2009, 946 applied for aid, 864 were judged to have need, 99 had their need fully met. 408 Federal Work-Study jobs (averaging $1382). In 2009, 172 non-need-based awards were made. *Average percent of need met:* 78%. *Average financial aid package:* $20,192. *Average need-based loan:* $6858. *Average need-based gift aid:* $13,447. *Average non-need-based aid:* $8155. *Average indebtedness upon graduation:* $36,071.
Applying *Options:* electronic application, early action, deferred entrance. *Required:* essay or personal statement, high school transcript, minimum 2.0 GPA, 2 letters of recommendation, SAT or ACT Scores. *Recommended:* interview. *Application deadlines:* rolling (freshmen), rolling (transfers), 11/15 (early action). *Notification:* continuous (freshmen), continuous (transfers), 12/17 (early action).
Freshman Application Contact Mr. Kathleen Davis, Vice President for Enrollment Management, Saint Joseph's College of Maine, 278 Whites Bridge Road, Standish, ME 04084-5263. *Phone:* 207-893-7746. *Toll-free phone:* 800-338-7057. *Fax:* 207-893-7862. *E-mail:* admission@sjcme.edu. *Web site:* http://www.sjcme.edu/.

Thomas College
Waterville, Maine

Freshman Application Contact Mr. James Love, Dean of Admissions, Thomas College, 180 West River Road, Waterville, ME 04901. *Phone:* 207-859-1101. *Toll-free phone:* 800-339-7001. *Fax:* 207-859-1114. *E-mail:* admiss@thomas.edu. *Web site:* http://www.thomas.edu/.

Unity College
Unity, Maine

Freshman Application Contact Mr. Gary Zane, Dean of Students, Unity College, 90 Quaker Hill Road, Unity, ME 04988. *Phone:* 207-948-3131. *Fax:* 207-948-6277. *E-mail:* gzane@unity.edu. *Web site:* http://www.unity.edu/.

University of Maine
Orono, Maine

- **State-supported** university, founded 1865, part of University of Maine System
- **Small-town** 3300-acre campus
- **Endowment** $159.6 million
- **Coed** 8,911 undergraduate students, 85% full-time, 49% women, 51% men
- **Moderately difficult** entrance level, 78% of applicants were admitted

Undergraduates 7,549 full-time, 1,362 part-time. 16% are from out of state; 2% Black or African American, non-Hispanic/Latino; 1% Hispanic/Latino; 1% Asian, non-Hispanic/Latino; 1% American Indian or Alaska Native, non-Hispanic/Latino; 2% Two or more races, non-Hispanic/Latino; 10% Race/ethnicity unknown; 2% international; 5% transferred in; 27% live on campus. *Retention:* 78% of full-time freshmen returned.
Freshmen *Admission:* 8,093 applied, 6,289 admitted, 1,785 enrolled. *Average high school GPA:* 3.31. *Test scores:* SAT critical reading scores over 500: 62%; SAT math scores over 500: 67%; SAT writing scores over 500: 58%; ACT scores over 18: 94%; SAT critical reading scores over 600: 20%; SAT math scores over 600: 23%; SAT writing scores over 600: 16%; ACT scores over 24: 51%; SAT critical reading scores over 700: 3%; SAT math scores over 700: 2%; SAT writing scores over 700: 2%; ACT scores over 30: 6%.
Faculty *Total:* 789, 70% full-time, 63% with terminal degrees. *Student/faculty ratio:* 15:1.
Academics *Calendar:* semesters. *Degrees:* bachelor's, master's, doctoral, post-master's, and first professional certificates. *Special study options:* accelerated degree program, advanced placement credit, cooperative education, distance learning, double majors, English as a second language, freshman honors college, honors programs, independent study, internships, off-campus study, part-time degree program, services for LD students, student-designed majors, study abroad, summer session for credit. *ROTC:* Army (b), Navy (c).
Computers on Campus 500 computers/terminals are available on campus for general student use. Students can access the following: campus intranet, computer help desk, free student e-mail accounts, online (class) grades, online (class) registration, online (class) schedules, online housing and financial aid information. Campuswide network is available. 100% of college-owned or -operated housing units are wired for high-speed Internet access. Wireless service is available via classrooms, computer centers, computer labs, learning centers, libraries, student centers.
Student Life *Housing:* on-campus residence required for freshman year. *Options:* coed, disabled students. Campus housing is university owned. Freshman campus housing is guaranteed. *Activities and organizations:* drama/theater group, student-run newspaper, radio and television station, choral group, marching band, Alternative Spring Break, Circle K, Campus Crusade for Christ, Outing Club, Wilde Stein, national fraternities, national sororities. *Campus security:* 24-hour emergency response devices and patrols, late-night transport/escort service, controlled dormitory access, area emergency text and email message system. *Student services:* health clinic, personal/psychological counseling, women's center, legal services.
Athletics Member NCAA. All Division I except football (Division I-AA). *Intercollegiate sports:* baseball M(s), basketball M(s)/W(s), cheerleading M/W, crew W(c), cross-country running M(s)/W(s), field hockey W(s), ice hockey M(s)/W(s), soccer W(s), softball W(s), swimming and diving M/W(s), tennis M(c)/W(c), track and field M(s)/W(s). *Intramural sports:* badminton M/W, basketball M/W, crew M(c)/W(c), cross-country running M/W, equestrian sports M(c)/W(c), fencing M(c)/W(c), field hockey M(c)/W(c), football M(c), golf M/W, ice hockey M(c)/W(c), lacrosse M(c)/W(c), racquetball M/W, rock climbing M(c)/W(c), rugby M(c)/W(c), skiing (cross-country) M/W, skiing (downhill) M(c)/W(c), soccer M/W, softball M/W, swimming and diving M/W, table tennis M/W, tennis M/W, track and field M/W, ultimate Frisbee M(c)/W(c), volleyball M(c)/W(c), water polo M/W, weight lifting M(c)/W(c), wrestling M(c).
Standardized Tests *Required:* SAT or ACT (for admission).
Costs (2012–13) *Tuition:* state resident $8370 full-time, $279 per credit part-time; nonresident $24,090 full-time, $803 per credit part-time. Full-time tuition and fees vary according to course load and program. Part-time tuition and fees vary according to course load and program. *Required fees:* $2218

full-time. *Room and board:* $8644. Room and board charges vary according to board plan and housing facility. *Payment plan:* installment. *Waivers:* senior citizens and employees or children of employees.

Financial Aid Of all full-time matriculated undergraduates who enrolled in 2010, 7,023 applied for aid, 6,114 were judged to have need, 1,870 had their need fully met. In 2010, 680 non-need-based awards were made. *Average percent of need met:* 76%. *Average financial aid package:* $11,599. *Average need-based loan:* $6944. *Average need-based gift aid:* $7370. *Average non-need-based aid:* $4617. *Average indebtedness upon graduation:* $29,143.

Applying *Options:* electronic application, early admission, early action, deferred entrance. *Application fee:* $40. *Required:* essay or personal statement, high school transcript, 1 letter of recommendation. *Required for some:* audition for music majors. *Application deadlines:* rolling (freshmen), rolling (out-of-state freshmen), rolling (transfers), 12/15 (early action). *Notification:* continuous (freshmen), continuous (out-of-state freshmen), continuous (transfers), 1/31 (early action).

Freshman Application Contact Ms. Sharon Oliver, Director of Admissions, University of Maine, 5713 Chadbourne Hall, Orono, ME 04469-5713. *Phone:* 207-581-1561. *Toll-free phone:* 877-486-2364. *Fax:* 207-581-1213. *E-mail:* um-admit@maine.edu. *Web site:* http://www.umaine.edu/.

See below for display ad and page 1676 for the College Close-Up.

University of Maine at Augusta
Augusta, Maine

- **State-supported** 4-year, founded 1965, part of University of Maine System
- **Small-town** 159-acre campus
- **Endowment** $5.0 million
- **Coed** 4,943 undergraduate students, 36% full-time, 72% women, 28% men
- **Noncompetitive** entrance level, 96% of applicants were admitted

Undergraduates 1,768 full-time, 3,175 part-time. Students come from 37 states and territories; 10 other countries; 3% are from out of state; 0.9% Black or African American, non-Hispanic/Latino; 1% Hispanic/Latino; 0.5% Asian, non-Hispanic/Latino; 2% American Indian or Alaska Native, non-Hispanic/Latino; 1% Two or more races, non-Hispanic/Latino; 13% Race/ethnicity unknown; 0.3% international; 13% transferred in. *Retention:* 54% of full-time freshmen returned.

Freshmen *Admission:* 948 applied, 907 admitted, 583 enrolled.

Faculty *Total:* 290, 36% full-time, 24% with terminal degrees. *Student/faculty ratio:* 17:1.

Academics *Calendar:* semesters. *Degrees:* certificates, associate, bachelor's, and postbachelor's certificates (also offers some graduate courses and continuing education programs with significant enrollment not reflected in profile). *Special study options:* academic remediation for entering students, adult/continuing education programs, advanced placement credit, distance learning, double majors, honors programs, independent study, internships, off-campus study, part-time degree program, services for LD students, student-designed majors, study abroad, summer session for credit. *ROTC:* Army (c), Navy (c), Air Force (c).

Computers on Campus 315 computers/terminals are available on campus for general student use. Students can access the following: computer help desk, free student e-mail accounts, online (class) grades, online (class) registration, online (class) schedules, Wireless internet available everywhere on campus. Campuswide network is available. Wireless service is available via entire campus.

Student Life *Housing:* college housing not available. *Activities and organizations:* drama/theater group, student-run newspaper, Honors Program Student Association, Arts and Architecture Students of UMA, Student Nurse Association, Student American Dental Hygiene Association, International Student Club. *Campus security:* 24-hour emergency response devices, late-night transport/escort service. *Student services:* personal/psychological counseling.

Athletics Member USCAA. *Intercollegiate sports:* basketball M(s)/W(s), golf M/W, soccer M/W(s). *Intramural sports:* racquetball M/W, soccer M, softball M/W, tennis M/W, volleyball M/W.

Standardized Tests *Recommended:* SAT or ACT (for admission).

Costs (2012–13) *Tuition:* state resident $6510 full-time, $217 per credit hour part-time; nonresident $15,750 full-time, $525 per credit hour part-time. Full-time tuition and fees vary according to course load, location, program, and reciprocity agreements. Part-time tuition and fees vary according to course load, location, program, and reciprocity agreements. *Required fees:* $938 full-time, $31 per credit hour part-time. *Payment plan:* installment. *Waivers:* minority students, senior citizens, and employees or children of employees.

Financial Aid Of all full-time matriculated undergraduates who enrolled in 2008, 1,604 applied for aid, 1,435 were judged to have need, 258 had their need fully met. 220 Federal Work-Study jobs (averaging $1500). In 2008, 135 non-need-based awards were made. *Average percent of need met:* 70%. *Average financial aid package:* $8467. *Average need-based loan:* $4063. *Average need-based gift aid:* $4828. *Average non-need-based aid:* $4862. *Average indebtedness upon graduation:* $15,842.

Applying *Options:* electronic application, early admission, deferred entrance. *Application fee:* $40. *Required:* high school transcript. *Required for some:* interview, music audition. *Recommended:* essay or personal statement. *Application deadlines:* rolling (freshmen), rolling (out-of-state freshmen), rolling (transfers). *Notification:* continuous (freshmen), continuous (out-of-state freshmen), continuous (transfers).

Freshman Application Contact Jonathan H. Henry, VP of Enrollment Management and Director of Admissions, University of Maine at Augusta, 46 University Drive, Robinson Hall, Augusta, ME 04330. *Phone:* 207-621-3136. *Toll-free phone:* 877-862-1234 Ext. 3185 (in-state); 877-862-1234 (out-of-state). *Fax:* 207-621-3333. *E-mail:* umaadm@maine.edu. *Web site:* http://www.uma.maine.edu/.

University of Maine at Farmington
Farmington, Maine

- **State-supported** comprehensive, founded 1863, part of University of Maine System
- **Small-town** 50-acre campus
- **Endowment** $10.2 million
- **Coed** 2,213 undergraduate students, 89% full-time, 65% women, 35% men
- **Moderately difficult** entrance level, 82% of applicants were admitted

Undergraduates 1,977 full-time, 236 part-time. Students come from 24 states and territories; 7 other countries; 15% are from out of state; 1% Black or African American, non-Hispanic/Latino; 1% Hispanic/Latino; 0.9% Asian, non-Hispanic/Latino; 0.1% Native Hawaiian or other Pacific Islander, non-Hispanic/Latino; 0.4% American Indian or Alaska Native, non-Hispanic/Latino; 2% Two or more races, non-Hispanic/Latino; 11% Race/ethnicity unknown; 6% transferred in; 50% live on campus. *Retention:* 74% of full-time freshmen returned.

Freshmen *Admission:* 1,580 applied, 1,291 admitted, 482 enrolled. *Test scores:* SAT critical reading scores over 500: 56%; SAT math scores over 500: 46%; SAT critical reading scores over 600: 18%; SAT math scores over 600: 9%; SAT critical reading scores over 700: 2%; SAT math scores over 700: 1%.

Faculty *Total:* 172, 70% full-time, 81% with terminal degrees. *Student/faculty ratio:* 15:1.

Academics *Calendar:* semesters plus May term and 2 5-week summer terms. *Degrees:* certificates, bachelor's, and master's. *Special study options:* academic remediation for entering students, accelerated degree program, advanced placement credit, distance learning, double majors, honors programs, independent study, internships, off-campus study, part-time degree program, services for LD students, student-designed majors, study abroad, summer session for credit.

Computers on Campus 180 computers/terminals are available on campus for general student use. Students can access the following: campus intranet, computer help desk, free student e-mail accounts, online (class) grades, online (class) registration, online (class) schedules, laptop initiative. Campuswide network is available. 100% of college-owned or -operated housing units are wired for high-speed Internet access. Wireless service is available via entire campus.

Student Life *Housing options:* coed, women-only. Campus housing is university owned and is provided by a third party. Freshman campus housing is guaranteed. *Activities and organizations:* drama/theater group, student-run newspaper, radio station, choral group, Program Board, Intramural Board, Campus Residence Council, campus radio station, Commuter Council. *Campus security:* 24-hour emergency response devices and patrols, late-night transport/escort service, controlled dormitory access, safety whistles. *Student services:* health clinic, personal/psychological counseling.

Athletics Member NCAA, NAIA. All NCAA Division III. *Intercollegiate sports:* baseball M, basketball M/W, cross-country running M/W, field hockey W, golf M, ice hockey M(c), lacrosse M(c)/W(c), soccer M/W, softball W, tennis M(c)/W(c), ultimate Frisbee M(c)/W(c), volleyball W. *Intramural sports:* basketball M/W, cheerleading M(c)/W(c), football M/W, ice hockey M(c)/W(c), rugby M(c)/W(c), skiing (cross-country) M(c)/W(c), skiing (downhill) M(c)/W(c), soccer M/W, softball M/W, swimming and diving M/W, tennis M/W, ultimate Frisbee M/W, volleyball M/W.

Standardized Tests *Required for some:* SAT or ACT (for admission).

Costs (2011–12) *Tuition:* state resident $8352 full-time, $261 per credit hour part-time; nonresident $17,440 full-time, $545 per credit hour part-time. Full-time tuition and fees vary according to course load, reciprocity agreements, and student level. Part-time tuition and fees vary according to course load, reciprocity agreements, and student level. *Required fees:* $1015 full-time. *Room and board:* $8168; room only: $4348. Room and board charges vary according to board plan and housing facility. *Payment plan:* installment. *Waivers:* minority students, senior citizens, and employees or children of employees.

Financial Aid Of all full-time matriculated undergraduates who enrolled in 2007, 1,709 applied for aid, 1,418 were judged to have need, 189 had their

need fully met. 519 Federal Work-Study jobs (averaging $1448). 406 state and other part-time jobs (averaging $1719). In 2007, 65 non-need-based awards were made. *Average percent of need met:* 73%. *Average financial aid package:* $8719. *Average need-based loan:* $4300. *Average need-based gift aid:* $4210. *Average non-need-based aid:* $1770. *Average indebtedness upon graduation:* $19,490.

Applying *Options:* electronic application, early admission, early action, deferred entrance. *Application fee:* $40. *Required:* essay or personal statement, high school transcript, minimum 2.0 GPA, 1 letter of recommendation. *Required for some:* minimum 2.5 GPA. *Recommended:* interview. *Application deadlines:* rolling (freshmen), 12/1 (early action). *Notification:* continuous (freshmen), continuous (transfers), 1/8 (early action).

Freshman Application Contact Ms. Lisa Elrich, Associate Director of Admissions, University of Maine at Farmington, 246 Main Street, Farmington, ME 04938-1994. *Phone:* 207-778-7050. *Fax:* 207-778-8182. *E-mail:* umfadmit@maine.edu. *Web site:* http://www.umf.maine.edu/.

University of Maine at Fort Kent
Fort Kent, Maine

- **State-supported** 4-year, founded 1878, part of University of Maine System
- **Rural** 52-acre campus
- **Endowment** $2.0 million
- **Coed** 1,077 undergraduate students, 52% full-time, 65% women, 35% men
- **Minimally difficult** entrance level, 69% of applicants were admitted

Undergraduates 562 full-time, 515 part-time. Students come from 17 states and territories; 10 other countries; 6% are from out of state; 1% Black or African American, non-Hispanic/Latino; 0.6% Hispanic/Latino; 1% American Indian or Alaska Native, non-Hispanic/Latino; 2% Two or more races, non-Hispanic/Latino; 10% Race/ethnicity unknown; 8% international; 9% transferred in; 29% live on campus. *Retention:* 64% of full-time freshmen returned.

Freshmen *Admission:* 534 applied, 370 admitted, 166 enrolled. *Average high school GPA:* 2.98. *Test scores:* SAT critical reading scores over 500: 23%; SAT math scores over 500: 29%; SAT writing scores over 500: 19%; SAT critical reading scores over 600: 3%; SAT math scores over 600: 3%; SAT writing scores over 600: 3%.

Faculty *Total:* 75, 48% full-time. *Student/faculty ratio:* 14:1.

Academics *Calendar:* semesters. *Degrees:* associate and bachelor's. *Special study options:* academic remediation for entering students, accelerated degree program, advanced placement credit, cooperative education, distance learning, double majors, English as a second language, external degree program, honors programs, independent study, internships, part-time degree program, services for LD students, student-designed majors, summer session for credit.

Computers on Campus 100 computers/terminals are available on campus for general student use. Students can access the following: campus intranet, computer help desk, free student e-mail accounts, online (class) grades, online (class) registration, online (class) schedules. Campuswide network is available. Wireless service is available via entire campus.

Student Life *Housing:* on-campus residence required for freshman year. *Options:* Campus housing is university owned. Freshman applicants given priority for college housing. *Activities and organizations:* drama/theater group, choral group, Student Nurses Organization, Student Teachers Educational Professional Society, Student Senate, Performing Arts Club, Dorm Council, national fraternities, national sororities. *Campus security:* controlled dormitory access, 8-hour night patrols by security personnel 11pm-7am. *Student services:* health clinic, personal/psychological counseling.

Athletics Member USCAA. *Intercollegiate sports:* basketball M/W, soccer M/W, volleyball W. *Intramural sports:* basketball M/W, ice hockey M, racquetball M/W, soccer M/W, softball M/W, volleyball M/W.

Standardized Tests *Required for some:* SAT (for admission), SAT and SAT Subject Tests or ACT (for admission). *Recommended:* SAT and SAT Subject Tests or ACT (for admission).

Costs (2012–13) *Tuition:* state resident $6600 full-time, $220 per credit hour part-time; nonresident $16,560 full-time, $552 per credit hour part-time. Full-time tuition and fees vary according to reciprocity agreements. Part-time tuition and fees vary according to reciprocity agreements. *Required fees:* $975 full-time, $33 per credit hour part-time. *Room and board:* $7400; room only: $4000. Room and board charges vary according to board plan and housing facility.

Financial Aid Of all full-time matriculated undergraduates who enrolled in 2010, 444 applied for aid, 402 were judged to have need, 87 had their need fully met. In 2010, 1 non-need-based awards were made. *Average percent of need met:* 70%. *Average financial aid package:* $10,121. *Average need-based loan:* $5696. *Average need-based gift aid:* $5991. *Average non-need-based aid:* $3000. *Average indebtedness upon graduation:* $9506.

Applying *Options:* electronic application, deferred entrance. *Application fee:* $40. *Required:* essay or personal statement, high school transcript. *Required for some:* interview. *Application deadlines:* rolling (freshmen), rolling (out-of-state freshmen), rolling (transfers). *Notification:* continuous (freshmen), continuous (out-of-state freshmen), continuous (transfers).
Freshman Application Contact University of Maine at Fort Kent, 23 University Drive, Fort Kent, ME 04743-1292. *Phone:* 207-834-7600. *Toll-free phone:* 888-TRY-UMFK. *Web site:* http://www.umfk.maine.edu/.

University of Maine at Machias
Machias, Maine

- **State-supported** 4-year, founded 1909, part of University of Maine System
- **Rural** 42-acre campus
- **Coed**
- **Moderately difficult** entrance level

Faculty *Student/faculty ratio:* 13:1.
Academics *Calendar:* semesters. *Degrees:* certificates, associate, and bachelor's.
Athletics Member NAIA.
Standardized Tests *Required:* SAT or ACT (for admission).
Costs (2011–12) *Tuition:* state resident $6660 full-time, $222 per credit hour part-time; nonresident $18,480 full-time, $616 per credit hour part-time. *Required fees:* $820 full-time. *Room and board:* $7648.
Financial Aid *Of all full-time matriculated undergraduates who enrolled in 2002,* 512 applied for aid, 419 were judged to have need, 108 had their need fully met. 140 Federal Work-Study jobs (averaging $1621). 83 state and other part-time jobs (averaging $1660). *In 2002,* 44 non-need-based awards were made. *Average percent of need met:* 83. *Average financial aid package:* $8182. *Average need-based loan:* $3356. *Average need-based gift aid:* $4847. *Average non-need-based aid:* $5051. *Average indebtedness upon graduation:* $14,873.
Applying *Options:* electronic application, early admission, early action, deferred entrance. *Application fee:* $40. *Required:* essay or personal statement, high school transcript, 1 letter of recommendation. *Required for some:* minimum 2.0 GPA, interview. *Recommended:* minimum 2.5 GPA, 2 letters of recommendation, interview.
Freshman Application Contact Director of Admissions, University of Maine at Machias, 9 O'Brien Avenue, Machias, ME 04654. *Phone:* 207-255-1318.

Toll-free phone: 888-GOTOUMM (in-state); 888-468-6866 (out-of-state). *Fax:* 207-255-1363. *E-mail:* ummadmissions@maine.edu. *Web site:* http://umm.maine.edu/.

See page 1678 for the College Close-Up.

University of Maine at Presque Isle
Presque Isle, Maine

- **State-supported** 4-year, founded 1903, part of University of Maine System
- **Small-town** 150-acre campus
- **Endowment** $6.1 million
- **Coed** 1,453 undergraduate students, 59% full-time, 63% women, 37% men
- **Minimally difficult** entrance level, 82% of applicants were admitted

Undergraduates 851 full-time, 602 part-time. 1% Black or African American, non-Hispanic/Latino; 1% Hispanic/Latino; 0.1% Asian, non-Hispanic/Latino; 5% American Indian or Alaska Native, non-Hispanic/Latino; 1% Two or more races, non-Hispanic/Latino; 4% Race/ethnicity unknown; 11% international; 22% live on campus. *Retention:* 63% of full-time freshmen returned.
Freshmen *Admission:* 504 applied, 411 admitted, 197 enrolled.
Faculty *Total:* 103, 44% full-time. *Student/faculty ratio:* 22:1.
Academics *Calendar:* semesters. *Degrees:* certificates, associate, and bachelor's. *Special study options:* academic remediation for entering students, accelerated degree program, adult/continuing education programs, advanced placement credit, cooperative education, distance learning, double majors, honors programs, independent study, internships, off-campus study, part-time degree program, services for LD students, student-designed majors, study abroad, summer session for credit.
Computers on Campus 85 computers/terminals are available on campus for general student use. Students can access the following: campus intranet, computer help desk, free student e-mail accounts, online (class) grades, online (class) registration, online (class) schedules. Campuswide network is available. 98% of college-owned or -operated housing units are wired for high-speed Internet access. Wireless service is available via entire campus.
Student Life *Housing options:* coed, disabled students. Campus housing is university owned and leased by the school. Freshman campus housing is guaranteed. *Activities and organizations:* student-run newspaper, radio station, PE Majors Club, Student Senate, Athletic Training Student Club, Student Organization of Social Workers, Criminal Justice Club, national fraternities, national

Environmental Liberal Arts on the coast of Maine

At UMM, we look at the world through a different lens by applying the traditional liberal arts to issues of environmental and community sustainability. Through our distinct Environmental Liberal Arts core seminars, called "The Maine Coastal Odyssey," our students gain a real sense of place and purpose while pursuing a degree in one of eleven fields of study.

We're an affordable liberal arts college, a community of individuals committed to the environment, and an unspoiled Maine coast location.

THE UNIVERSITY OF MAINE AT MACHIAS *Naturally!*

New England's Only Public Environmental Liberal Arts College

1-888-468-6866 • www.machias.edu

sororities. *Campus security:* student patrols, controlled dormitory access, crime prevention programs, lighted pathways, security cameras. *Student services:* health clinic, personal/psychological counseling.

Athletics Member NCAA, USCAA. All Division III except men's and women's skiing (cross-country) (Division I). *Intercollegiate sports:* baseball M, basketball M/W, cross-country running M/W, golf M, skiing (cross-country) M/W, soccer M/W, softball W, volleyball W. *Intramural sports:* archery M/W, badminton M/W, basketball M/W, bowling M/W, cross-country running M/W, football M/W, ice hockey M(c)/W(c), skiing (cross-country) M/W, skiing (downhill) M/W, soccer M/W, softball M/W, table tennis M/W, tennis M/W, track and field M/W, volleyball M/W, weight lifting M/W.

Standardized Tests *Recommended:* SAT or ACT (for admission).

Costs (2012–13) *Tuition:* state resident $6600 full-time, $220 per credit part-time; nonresident $16,560 full-time, $552 per credit part-time. Full-time tuition and fees vary according to course load, location, and reciprocity agreements. Part-time tuition and fees vary according to course load, location, and reciprocity agreements. *Required fees:* $835 full-time, $18 per credit part-time, $51 per term part-time. *Room and board:* $7422; room only: $4240. Room and board charges vary according to board plan and housing facility. *Payment plans:* installment, deferred payment. *Waivers:* minority students, senior citizens, and employees or children of employees.

Financial Aid Of all full-time matriculated undergraduates who enrolled in 2011, 696 applied for aid, 637 were judged to have need, 165 had their need fully met. 240 Federal Work-Study jobs (averaging $2632). In 2011, 81 non-need-based awards were made. *Average percent of need met:* 80%. *Average financial aid package:* $10,604. *Average need-based loan:* $5264. *Average need-based gift aid:* $5354. *Average non-need-based aid:* $4123. *Average indebtedness upon graduation:* $18,698.

Applying *Options:* electronic application, early admission, early action, deferred entrance. *Application fee:* $40. *Required:* essay or personal statement, high school transcript, minimum 2.0 GPA. *Required for some:* 1 letter of recommendation, interview. *Application deadlines:* rolling (freshmen), rolling (out-of-state freshmen), rolling (transfers), 10/31 (early action). *Notification:* continuous (freshmen), continuous (out-of-state freshmen), continuous (transfers), 4/1 (early action).

Freshman Application Contact University of Maine at Presque Isle, 181 Main Street, Presque Isle, ME 04769-2888. *Phone:* 207-768-9453. *Web site:* http://www.umpi.edu/.

University of New England
Biddeford, Maine

- **Independent** comprehensive, founded 1831
- **Small-town** 540-acre campus
- **Coed** 2,790 undergraduate students, 78% full-time, 67% women, 33% men
- **Moderately difficult** entrance level, 82% of applicants were admitted

Undergraduates 2,166 full-time, 624 part-time. Students come from 49 states and territories; 13 other countries; 63% are from out of state; 1% Black or African American, non-Hispanic/Latino; 0.6% Hispanic/Latino; 2% Asian, non-Hispanic/Latino; 0.2% Native Hawaiian or other Pacific Islander, non-Hispanic/Latino; 0.4% American Indian or Alaska Native, non-Hispanic/Latino; 1% Two or more races, non-Hispanic/Latino; 18% Race/ethnicity unknown; 0.9% international; 3% transferred in; 52% live on campus. *Retention:* 75% of full-time freshmen returned.

Freshmen *Admission:* 3,717 applied, 3,034 admitted, 640 enrolled. *Average high school GPA:* 3.2. *Test scores:* SAT critical reading scores over 500: 64%; SAT math scores over 500: 68%; ACT scores over 18: 93%; SAT critical reading scores over 600: 15%; SAT math scores over 600: 22%; ACT scores over 24: 51%; SAT critical reading scores over 700: 2%; SAT math scores over 700: 1%; ACT scores over 30: 2%.

Faculty *Total:* 439, 56% full-time, 47% with terminal degrees. *Student/faculty ratio:* 13:1.

Academics *Calendar:* semesters. *Degrees:* associate, bachelor's, master's, doctoral, post-master's, and postbachelor's certificates. *Special study options:* academic remediation for entering students, accelerated degree program, advanced placement credit, cooperative education, distance learning, double majors, independent study, internships, off-campus study, part-time degree program, services for LD students, study abroad, summer session for credit. *ROTC:* Army (c).

Computers on Campus 150 computers/terminals are available on campus for general student use. Students can access the following: campus intranet, computer help desk, free student e-mail accounts, online (class) grades, online (class) registration, online (class) schedules. Campuswide network is available. Wireless service is available via classrooms, computer centers, computer labs, learning centers, libraries, student centers.

Student Life *Housing:* on-campus residence required through junior year. *Options:* coed, women-only. Campus housing is university owned. *Activities and organizations:* student government, Outing Club, Campus Programming

Beauty and purpose make for a powerful connection.

At **University of New England,** it's about connecting... with world-renowned scholars, with nature, with unforgettable adventures, with a community.

UNE is a leader in health sciences education, biomedical research, marine sciences, and the liberal arts. Our undergraduate programs provide a challenging liberal arts education with more than 30 majors in a variety of subject areas, and our exceptional graduate and professional programs prepare you for a lifetime of career opportunities.

UNE UNIVERSITY OF NEW ENGLAND

Biddeford and Portland, Maine
Connections. For Life. | www.une.edu

Board, Earth's Eco, Dance Team. *Campus security:* 24-hour emergency response devices and patrols, late-night transport/escort service, controlled dormitory access. *Student services:* health clinic, personal/psychological counseling.

Athletics Member NCAA. All Division III. *Intercollegiate sports:* basketball M/W, cross-country running M/W, field hockey W, golf M, lacrosse M/W, soccer M/W, softball W, swimming and diving W, volleyball W. *Intramural sports:* baseball M(c), basketball M/W, gymnastics M/W, racquetball M/W, soccer M/W, softball M/W, table tennis M/W, ultimate Frisbee M(c)/W(c), volleyball M(c)/W, water polo M/W.

Standardized Tests *Required:* SAT or ACT (for admission).

Costs (2011–12) *Comprehensive fee:* $42,520 includes full-time tuition ($29,430), mandatory fees ($1070), and room and board ($12,020). Part-time tuition: $1040 per credit hour. *Room and board:* Room and board charges vary according to board plan, housing facility, and location. *Payment plan:* installment. *Waivers:* children of alumni and employees or children of employees.

Financial Aid Of all full-time matriculated undergraduates who enrolled in 2008, 1,777 applied for aid, 1,648 were judged to have need, 306 had their need fully met. 850 Federal Work-Study jobs (averaging $1946). In 2008, 332 non-need-based awards were made. *Average percent of need met:* 83%. *Average financial aid package:* $23,956. *Average need-based loan:* $10,836. *Average need-based gift aid:* $12,857. *Average non-need-based aid:* $8424. *Average indebtedness upon graduation:* $44,325.

Applying *Options:* electronic application, deferred entrance. *Application fee:* $40. *Required:* high school transcript. *Recommended:* essay or personal statement, letters of recommendation, interview. *Application deadlines:* 2/15 (freshmen), rolling (transfers). *Notification:* continuous (freshmen), continuous (transfers).

Freshman Application Contact Mr. Robert J. Pecchia, Associate Dean of Admissions, University of New England, Hills Beach Road, Biddeford, ME 04005-9526. *Phone:* 207-283-0170 Ext. 2297. *Toll-free phone:* 800-477-4UNE. *Fax:* 207-602-5900. *E-mail:* admissions@une.edu. *Web site:* http://www.une.edu/.

See page 1690 for the College Close-Up.

University of Southern Maine
Portland, Maine

- **State-supported** comprehensive, founded 1878, part of University of Maine System
- **Urban** 144-acre campus
- **Endowment** $30.4 million
- **Coed** 7,311 undergraduate students, 61% full-time, 55% women, 45% men
- **Moderately difficult** entrance level, 80% of applicants were admitted

Undergraduates 4,473 full-time, 2,838 part-time. Students come from 42 states and territories; 15 other countries; 9% are from out of state; 3% Black or African American, non-Hispanic/Latino; 2% Hispanic/Latino; 2% Asian, non-Hispanic/Latino; 0.1% Native Hawaiian or other Pacific Islander, non-Hispanic/Latino; 1% American Indian or Alaska Native, non-Hispanic/Latino; 2% Two or more races, non-Hispanic/Latino; 8% Race/ethnicity unknown; 0.5% international; 11% transferred in; 14% live on campus. *Retention:* 66% of full-time freshmen returned.

Freshmen *Admission:* 4,108 applied, 3,285 admitted, 710 enrolled. *Average high school GPA:* 2.95. *Test scores:* SAT math scores over 500: 55%; ACT scores over 18: 90%; SAT math scores over 600: 15%; ACT scores over 24: 29%; SAT math scores over 700: 5%; ACT scores over 30: 2%.

Faculty *Total:* 643, 58% full-time, 56% with terminal degrees. *Student/faculty ratio:* 15:1.

Academics *Calendar:* semesters. *Degrees:* certificates, bachelor's, master's, doctoral, post-master's, postbachelor's, and first professional certificates. *Special study options:* academic remediation for entering students, accelerated degree program, adult/continuing education programs, advanced placement credit, cooperative education, distance learning, double majors, English as a second language, honors programs, independent study, internships, off-campus study, part-time degree program, services for LD students, student-designed majors, study abroad, summer session for credit. *ROTC:* Army (c), Air Force (c). *Unusual degree programs:* 3-2 business administration.

Computers on Campus 219 computers/terminals are available on campus for general student use. Students can access the following: campus intranet, computer help desk, free student e-mail accounts, online (class) grades, online (class) registration, online (class) schedules. Campuswide network is available. 100% of college-owned or -operated housing units are wired for high-speed Internet access. Wireless service is available via entire campus.

Student Life *Housing options:* coed. Campus housing is university owned. Freshman applicants given priority for college housing. *Activities and organizations:* drama/theater group, student-run newspaper, radio and television station, choral group, Outing and Ski Clubs, Gorham Events Board, Commuter

Student Group, Circle K, national fraternities, national sororities. *Campus security:* 24-hour emergency response devices and patrols, late-night transport/escort service, controlled dormitory access, security lighting, preventive programs within residence halls. *Student services:* health clinic, personal/psychological counseling, women's center, legal services.

Athletics Member NCAA. All Division III. *Intercollegiate sports:* baseball M, basketball M/W, cross-country running M/W, fencing M/W(c), field hockey W, golf M/W, ice hockey M/W, lacrosse M/W, sailing M/W, soccer M/W, softball W, tennis M/W, track and field M/W, volleyball W, wrestling M. *Intramural sports:* baseball M, basketball M/W, cheerleading M(c)/W(c), football M/W, ice hockey M/W, lacrosse M(c)/W(c), racquetball M/W, rugby M(c)/W(c), skiing (downhill) M(c)/W(c), soccer M/W, softball M/W, squash M/W, table tennis M/W, tennis M/W, ultimate Frisbee M/W, volleyball M/W, weight lifting M/W.

Standardized Tests *Required:* SAT or ACT (for admission).

Costs (2012–13) *Tuition:* state resident $7590 full-time, $253 per credit hour part-time; nonresident $19,950 full-time, $665 per credit hour part-time. Full-time tuition and fees vary according to course load, degree level, and reciprocity agreements. Part-time tuition and fees vary according to course load, degree level, and reciprocity agreements. *Required fees:* $1310 full-time. *Room and board:* $9666; room only: $4978. Room and board charges vary according to board plan, housing facility, and location. *Payment plan:* installment.

Financial Aid Of all full-time matriculated undergraduates who enrolled in 2010, 4,449 applied for aid, 4,021 were judged to have need, 260 had their need fully met. In 2010, 131 non-need-based awards were made. *Average percent of need met:* 56%. *Average financial aid package:* $10,296. *Average need-based loan:* $10,040. *Average need-based gift aid:* $5147. *Average non-need-based aid:* $4246. *Average indebtedness upon graduation:* $26,249.

Applying *Options:* electronic application, early admission, deferred entrance. *Application fee:* $40. *Required:* essay or personal statement, high school transcript. *Required for some:* interview, auditions for music majors. *Recommended:* minimum 2.8 GPA, 1 letter of recommendation, interview. *Application deadlines:* 2/15 (freshmen), 2/15 (transfers). *Notification:* continuous (freshmen), continuous (out-of-state freshmen), continuous (transfers).

Freshman Application Contact Mrs. Susan Campbell, Chief Student Success Officer, University of Southern Maine, Portland, ME 04104-9300. *Phone:* 207-780-4547. *Toll-free phone:* 800-800-4USM Ext. 5670. *E-mail:* usmadm@usm.maine.edu. *Web site:* http://www.usm.maine.edu/.

MARYLAND

Bowie State University
Bowie, Maryland

- **State-supported** comprehensive, founded 1865, part of University System of Maryland
- **Small-town** 295-acre campus with easy access to Baltimore and Washington, D.C.
- **Endowment** $5.4 million
- **Coed** 4,452 undergraduate students, 82% full-time, 61% women, 39% men
- **Minimally difficult** entrance level, 21% of applicants were admitted

Undergraduates 3,669 full-time, 783 part-time. Students come from 31 states and territories; 12% are from out of state; 91% Black or African American, non-Hispanic/Latino; 2% Hispanic/Latino; 1% Asian, non-Hispanic/Latino; 0.3% American Indian or Alaska Native, non-Hispanic/Latino; 0.8% Two or more races, non-Hispanic/Latino; 1% Race/ethnicity unknown; 0.6% international; 9% transferred in; 34% live on campus. *Retention:* 67% of full-time freshmen returned.

Freshmen *Admission:* 3,153 applied, 671 admitted, 634 enrolled. *Average high school GPA:* 2.53. *Test scores:* SAT critical reading scores over 500: 24%; SAT math scores over 500: 17%; SAT critical reading scores over 600: 4%; SAT math scores over 600: 2%.

Faculty *Total:* 410, 55% full-time, 66% with terminal degrees. *Student/faculty ratio:* 16:1.

Academics *Calendar:* semesters. *Degrees:* certificates, bachelor's, master's, doctoral, postbachelor's, and first professional certificates. *Special study options:* academic remediation for entering students, adult/continuing education programs, advanced placement credit, cooperative education, distance learning, double majors, external degree program, honors programs, independent study, internships, off-campus study, part-time degree program, services for LD students, study abroad, summer session for credit. *ROTC:* Army (b). *Unusual degree programs:* 3-2 engineering with George Washington University, University of Maryland College Park, Howard University.

Computers on Campus 3,144 computers/terminals are available on campus for general student use. Students can access the following: online (class) registration. Campuswide network is available. Wireless service is available via entire campus.

Student Life *Housing options:* coed, men-only, women-only. Campus housing is university owned and is provided by a third party. Freshman applicants given priority for college housing. *Activities and organizations:* drama/theater group, student-run newspaper, radio and television station, choral group, marching band, NSAP Student Leadership Institute, Honda Campus All-Star Challenge, national fraternities, national sororities. *Campus security:* 24-hour emergency response devices and patrols, student patrols, late-night transport/escort service, controlled dormitory access. *Student services:* health clinic, personal/psychological counseling.

Athletics Member NCAA. All Division II. *Intercollegiate sports:* basketball M(s)/W(s), bowling W, cross-country running M(s)/W(s), football M(s), softball W(s), tennis W(s), track and field M(s)/W(s), volleyball W(s).

Standardized Tests *Required:* SAT or ACT (for admission).

Costs (2011–12) *Tuition:* state resident $4547 full-time, $201 per credit hour part-time; nonresident $15,088 full-time, $635 per credit hour part-time. Part-time tuition and fees vary according to course load. *Required fees:* $1800 full-time, $80 per credit hour part-time. *Room and board:* $8998. Room and board charges vary according to board plan and housing facility. *Payment plans:* installment, deferred payment. *Waivers:* senior citizens and employees or children of employees.

Financial Aid Of all full-time matriculated undergraduates who enrolled in 2011, 2,664 applied for aid, 2,658 were judged to have need, 1,071 had their need fully met. 68 Federal Work-Study jobs (averaging $2627). In 2011, 40 non-need-based awards were made. *Average percent of need met:* 46%. *Average financial aid package:* $8287. *Average need-based loan:* $4161. *Average need-based gift aid:* $6335. *Average non-need-based aid:* $78. *Average indebtedness upon graduation:* $24,291.

Applying *Options:* electronic application. *Application fee:* $40. *Required:* high school transcript, minimum 2.0 GPA. *Application deadlines:* 4/1 (freshmen), 4/1 (transfers). *Notification:* continuous (freshmen), continuous (transfers).

Freshman Application Contact Don Kiah, Director of Admissions, Bowie State University, Administration Building, 1st Floor. *Phone:* 301-860-3415. *Toll-free phone:* 877-772-6943. *Fax:* 301-860-3438. *E-mail:* sholt@bowiestate.edu. *Web site:* http://www.bowiestate.edu/.

See below for display ad and page 1180 for the College Close-Up.

Capitol College

Laurel, Maryland

Director of Admissions Mr. George Walls, Director of Recruiting and Admissions, Capitol College, 11301 Springfield Road, Laurel, MD 20708-9759. *Phone:* 301-953-3200 Ext. 3033. *Toll-free phone:* 800-950-1992. *E-mail:* ghwalls@capitol-college.edu. *Web site:* http://www.capitol-college.edu/.

Coppin State University

Baltimore, Maryland

- **State-supported** comprehensive, founded 1900, part of University System of Maryland
- **Urban** 33-acre campus
- **Coed**
- **Moderately difficult** entrance level

Faculty *Student/faculty ratio:* 15:1.

Academics *Calendar:* semesters. *Degrees:* bachelor's, master's, and post-bachelor's certificates.

Student Life *Campus security:* 24-hour emergency response devices and patrols, late-night transport/escort service, controlled dormitory access.

Athletics Member NCAA. All Division I.

Standardized Tests *Required:* SAT or ACT (for admission).

Costs (2011–12) *Tuition:* state resident $3742 full-time, $160 per credit hour part-time; nonresident $8233 full-time, $459 per credit hour part-time. Full-time tuition and fees vary according to course load. Part-time tuition and fees vary according to course load. *Required fees:* $1990 full-time, $67 per semester hour part-time, $116 per term part-time. *Room and board:* $8018; room only: $4920. Room and board charges vary according to board plan.

Financial Aid Of all full-time matriculated undergraduates who enrolled in 2010, 2,303 applied for aid, 2,182 were judged to have need, 417 had their need fully met. 165 Federal Work-Study jobs (averaging $3212). In 2010, 9 non-need-based awards were made. *Average percent of need met:* 74. *Average financial aid package:* $8873. *Average need-based loan:* $4036. *Average need-based gift aid:* $5887. *Average non-need-based aid:* $1056. *Average indebtedness upon graduation:* $8559.

Applying *Options:* electronic application, early admission, deferred entrance. *Application fee:* $35. *Required:* high school transcript. *Required for some:* 2 letters of recommendation. *Recommended:* minimum 2.5 GPA, interview.

Freshman Application Contact Ms. Michelle Gross, Director of Admissions, Coppin State University, 2500 West North Avenue, Baltimore, MD 21216-3698. *Phone:* 410-951-3600. *Toll-free phone:* 800-635-3674. *Fax:* 410-523-7351. *E-mail:* mgross@coppin.edu. *Web site:* http://www.coppin.edu/.

DeVry University
Bethesda, Maryland

Freshman Application Contact DeVry University, 4550 Montgomery Avenue, Suite 100 North, Bethesda, MD 20814-3304. *Toll-free phone:* 866-338-7941. *Web site:* http://www.devry.edu/.

Faith Theological Seminary
Baltimore, Maryland

- **Independent** comprehensive, affiliated with Christian non-denominational
- **Urban** campus
- **Coed**

Academics *Degrees:* bachelor's, master's, and doctoral.
Student Life *Housing:* college housing not available.
Costs (2012–13) *Tuition:* $4800 full-time, $200 per hour part-time. *Required fees:* $280 full-time. *Payment plans:* tuition prepayment, installment. *Waivers:* senior citizens.
Applying *Application fee:* $50. *Required:* essay or personal statement, high school transcript, 2 letters of recommendation, photos. *Required for some:* interview. *Recommended:* interview.
Freshman Application Contact Faith Theological Seminary, 529 Walker Avenue, Baltimore, MD 21212. *Phone:* 410-323-6211. *Web site:* http://www.faiththeological.org/.

Frostburg State University
Frostburg, Maryland

Freshman Application Contact Frostburg State University, 101 Braddock Road, Frostburg, MD 21532-1099. *Phone:* 301-687-4201. *Web site:* http://www.frostburg.edu/.

Goucher College
Baltimore, Maryland

- **Independent** comprehensive, founded 1885
- **Suburban** 287-acre campus
- **Endowment** $188.3 million
- **Coed** 1,446 undergraduate students, 97% full-time, 67% women, 33% men
- **Moderately difficult** entrance level, 73% of applicants were admitted

Undergraduates 1,409 full-time, 37 part-time. Students come from 47 states and territories; 27 other countries; 72% are from out of state; 10% Black or African American, non-Hispanic/Latino; 6% Hispanic/Latino; 4% Asian, non-Hispanic/Latino; 1% American Indian or Alaska Native, non-Hispanic/Latino; 0.6% Two or more races, non-Hispanic/Latino; 12% Race/ethnicity unknown; 2% international; 4% transferred in; 86% live on campus. *Retention:* 81% of full-time freshmen returned.
Freshmen *Admission:* 3,763 applied, 2,764 admitted, 367 enrolled. *Average high school GPA:* 3.1. *Test scores:* SAT critical reading scores over 500: 80%; SAT math scores over 500: 75%; SAT writing scores over 500: 78%; ACT scores over 18: 97%; SAT critical reading scores over 600: 49%; SAT math scores over 600: 31%; SAT writing scores over 600: 43%; ACT scores over 24: 62%; SAT critical reading scores over 700: 14%; SAT math scores over 700: 5%; SAT writing scores over 700: 9%; ACT scores over 30: 16%.
Faculty *Total:* 212, 63% full-time, 69% with terminal degrees. *Student/faculty ratio:* 9:1.
Academics *Calendar:* semesters. *Degrees:* bachelor's, master's, and post-bachelor's certificates. *Special study options:* adult/continuing education programs, advanced placement credit, cooperative education, distance learning, double majors, independent study, internships, off-campus study, part-time degree program, services for LD students, student-designed majors, study abroad. *ROTC:* Army (c), Air Force (c). *Unusual degree programs:* 3-2 engineering with Johns Hopkins University.
Computers on Campus 200 computers/terminals are available on campus for general student use. Students can access the following: campus intranet, computer help desk, free student e-mail accounts, online (class) grades, online (class) registration, online (class) schedules, transcripts, financial aid information, billing, ePortfolios, academic progress reports, study abroad plan. Campuswide network is available. 100% of college-owned or -operated housing

units are wired for high-speed Internet access. Wireless service is available via entire campus.
Student Life *Housing:* on-campus residence required through sophomore year. *Options:* coed, men-only, women-only, cooperative, disabled students. Campus housing is university owned. Freshman campus housing is guaranteed. *Activities and organizations:* drama/theater group, student-run newspaper, radio station, choral group, The Quindecim, Red Hot Blue (a co-ed Acappella group), Umoja: The African Alliance, Hillel, Student Government Association. *Campus security:* 24-hour emergency response devices and patrols, late-night transport/escort service, controlled dormitory access. *Student services:* health clinic, personal/psychological counseling, women's center.
Athletics Member NCAA. All Division III. *Intercollegiate sports:* basketball M/W, cross-country running M/W, equestrian sports M/W, field hockey W, lacrosse M/W, soccer M/W, swimming and diving M/W, tennis M/W, track and field M/W, volleyball W. *Intramural sports:* basketball M/W, fencing M(c)/W(c), soccer M/W, tennis M/W, ultimate Frisbee M/W, volleyball M/W, water polo M/W, weight lifting M/W.
Costs (2011–12) *Comprehensive fee:* $47,122 includes full-time tuition ($36,011), mandatory fees ($542), and room and board ($10,569). *College room only:* $6404. Room and board charges vary according to board plan and housing facility. *Payment plans:* tuition prepayment, installment. *Waivers:* adult students, senior citizens, and employees or children of employees.
Financial Aid Of all full-time matriculated undergraduates who enrolled in 2011, 982 applied for aid, 861 were judged to have need, 114 had their need fully met. 433 Federal Work-Study jobs (averaging $1062). In 2011, 264 non-need-based awards were made. *Average percent of need met:* 75%. *Average financial aid package:* $26,895. *Average need-based loan:* $4184. *Average need-based gift aid:* $23,239. *Average non-need-based aid:* $12,335. *Average indebtedness upon graduation:* $28,147.
Applying *Options:* electronic application, early admission, early decision, early action, deferred entrance. *Application fee:* $55. *Required:* essay or personal statement, high school transcript. *Recommended:* 3 letters of recommendation, interview. *Application deadlines:* 2/1 (freshmen), 4/1 (transfers), 12/1 (early action). *Notification:* 4/1 (freshmen), 6/1 (transfers), 2/1 (early action).
Freshman Application Contact Mr. Carlton E. Surbeck, Director of Admissions, Goucher College, 1021 Dulaney Valley Road, Baltimore, MD 21204. *Phone:* 410-337-6100. *Toll-free phone:* 800-468-2437. *Fax:* 410-337-6354. *E-mail:* admissions@goucher.edu. *Web site:* http://www.goucher.edu/.

Griggs University
Silver Spring, Maryland

Freshman Application Contact Ms. Linda Lundberg, Enrollment Officer, Griggs University, PO Box 4437, Silver Spring, MD 20914-4437. *Phone:* 301-680-6590. *Toll-free phone:* 800-782-4769. *Fax:* 301-680-6577. *E-mail:* LLundberg@griggs.edu. *Web site:* http://www.griggs.edu/.

Hood College
Frederick, Maryland

- **Independent** comprehensive, founded 1893
- **Suburban** 50-acre campus with easy access to Baltimore and Washington, D.C.
- **Endowment** $63.4 million
- **Coed** 1,487 undergraduate students, 91% full-time, 66% women, 34% men
- **Moderately difficult** entrance level, 79% of applicants were admitted

Undergraduates 1,348 full-time, 139 part-time. Students come from 33 states and territories; 24 other countries; 20% are from out of state; 12% Black or African American, non-Hispanic/Latino; 7% Hispanic/Latino; 3% Asian, non-Hispanic/Latino; 0.1% Native Hawaiian or other Pacific Islander, non-Hispanic/Latino; 0.2% American Indian or Alaska Native, non-Hispanic/Latino; 4% Two or more races, non-Hispanic/Latino; 2% Race/ethnicity unknown; 2% international; 9% transferred in; 54% live on campus. *Retention:* 76% of full-time freshmen returned.
Freshmen *Admission:* 1,684 applied, 1,334 admitted, 311 enrolled. *Average high school GPA:* 3.51. *Test scores:* SAT critical reading scores over 500: 71%; SAT math scores over 500: 64%; SAT writing scores over 500: 63%; ACT scores over 18: 94%; SAT critical reading scores over 600: 28%; SAT math scores over 600: 25%; SAT writing scores over 600: 24%; ACT scores over 24: 38%; SAT critical reading scores over 700: 5%; SAT math scores over 700: 3%; SAT writing scores over 700: 3%.
Faculty *Total:* 259, 34% full-time, 59% with terminal degrees. *Student/faculty ratio:* 12:1.
Academics *Calendar:* semesters. *Degrees:* certificates, bachelor's, master's, and postbachelor's certificates (also offers adult program with significant enrollment not reflected in profile). *Special study options:* academic remediation for entering students, advanced placement credit, double majors, English

as a second language, honors programs, independent study, internships, off-campus study, part-time degree program, services for LD students, student-designed majors, study abroad, summer session for credit. *ROTC:* Army (b). *Unusual degree programs:* 3-2 engineering with George Washington University.

Computers on Campus 283 computers/terminals are available on campus for general student use. Students can access the following: campus intranet, computer help desk, free student e-mail accounts, online (class) grades, online (class) registration, online (class) schedules. Campuswide network is available. 100% of college-owned or -operated housing units are wired for high-speed Internet access. Wireless service is available via entire campus.

Student Life *Housing:* on-campus residence required through sophomore year. *Options:* coed, women-only. Campus housing is university owned and leased by the school. Freshman campus housing is guaranteed. *Activities and organizations:* drama/theater group, student-run newspaper, radio station, choral group, Education Club, Black Student Union, Campus Activities Board, International Club, Hood Today (newspaper). *Campus security:* 24-hour emergency response devices and patrols, late-night transport/escort service, controlled dormitory access. *Student services:* health clinic, personal/psychological counseling.

Athletics Member NCAA. All Division III. *Intercollegiate sports:* basketball M/W, cross-country running M/W, equestrian sports M(c)/W(c), field hockey W, golf M/W, lacrosse M/W, soccer M/W, softball W, swimming and diving M/W, tennis M/W, track and field M/W, volleyball W.

Standardized Tests *Required:* SAT or ACT (for admission).

Costs (2011–12) *Comprehensive fee:* $41,450 includes full-time tuition ($30,620), mandatory fees ($440), and room and board ($10,390). Part-time tuition: $885 per credit hour. *Required fees:* $145 per term part-time. *College room only:* $5430. Room and board charges vary according to board plan. *Payment plan:* installment. *Waivers:* senior citizens and employees or children of employees.

Financial Aid Of all full-time matriculated undergraduates who enrolled in 2010, 1,272 applied for aid, 1,189 were judged to have need, 225 had their need fully met. In 2010, 134 non-need-based awards were made. *Average percent of need met:* 76%. *Average financial aid package:* $23,553. *Average need-based loan:* $4195. *Average need-based gift aid:* $20,186. *Average non-need-based aid:* $13,967. *Average indebtedness upon graduation:* $17,144.

Applying *Options:* electronic application, early decision, early action, deferred entrance. *Application fee:* $35. *Required:* essay or personal statement, high school transcript, minimum 2.0 GPA, 2 letters of recommendation. *Recommended:* interview. *Application deadlines:* 2/15 (freshmen), 2/15 (out-of-state freshmen), rolling (transfers), 12/1 (early action). *Early decision deadline:* 11/15 (for plan 1), 12/15 (for plan 2). *Notification:* 3/1 (freshmen), 3/1 (out-of-state freshmen), continuous (transfers), 12/1 (early decision plan 1), 1/1 (early decision plan 2), 12/15 (early action).

Freshman Application Contact Mr. David Adams, Director of Admissions, Hood College, 401 Rosemont Avenue, Frederick, MD 21701. *Phone:* 301-696-3400. *Toll-free phone:* 800-922-1599. *Fax:* 301-696-3819. *E-mail:* admissions@hood.edu. *Web site:* http://www.hood.edu/.

See below for display ad and page 1370 for the College Close-Up.

ITT Technical Institute
Hanover, Maryland

- **Proprietary** 4-year
- **Coed**
- **Minimally difficult** entrance level

Academics *Degrees:* associate and bachelor's.

Freshman Application Contact Director of Recruitment, ITT Technical Institute, 7030 Dorsey Road, Suite 100, Hanover, MD 21076. *Phone:* 410-694-4700. *Toll-free phone:* 877-243-6993. *Web site:* http://www.itt-tech.edu/.

ITT Technical Institute
Owings Mills, Maryland

- **Proprietary** primarily 2-year, founded 2005
- **Coed**
- **Minimally difficult** entrance level

Academics *Calendar:* quarters. *Degrees:* associate and bachelor's.

Student Life *Housing:* college housing not available.

Freshman Application Contact Director of Recruitment, ITT Technical Institute, 11301 Red Run Boulevard, Owings Mills, MD 21117. *Phone:* 443-394-7115. *Toll-free phone:* 877-411-6782. *Web site:* http://www.itt-tech.edu/.

The Johns Hopkins University

Baltimore, Maryland

- **Independent** university, founded 1876
- **Urban** 140-acre campus with easy access to Washington, D.C.
- **Coed** 5,066 undergraduate students, 100% full-time, 47% women, 53% men
- **Most difficult** entrance level, 18% of applicants were admitted

Undergraduates 5,051 full-time, 15 part-time. 87% are from out of state; 5% Black or African American, non-Hispanic/Latino; 9% Hispanic/Latino; 20% Asian, non-Hispanic/Latino; 0.1% Native Hawaiian or other Pacific Islander, non-Hispanic/Latino; 0.1% American Indian or Alaska Native, non-Hispanic/Latino; 4% Two or more races, non-Hispanic/Latino; 2% Race/ethnicity unknown; 9% international; 1% transferred in; 53% live on campus. *Retention:* 96% of full-time freshmen returned.

Freshmen *Admission:* 19,391 applied, 3,576 admitted, 1,279 enrolled. *Average high school GPA:* 3.74. *Test scores:* SAT critical reading scores over 500: 99%; SAT math scores over 500: 100%; SAT writing scores over 500: 99%; ACT scores over 18: 100%; SAT critical reading scores over 600: 89%; SAT math scores over 600: 96%; SAT writing scores over 600: 89%; ACT scores over 24: 100%; SAT critical reading scores over 700: 44%; SAT math scores over 700: 64%; SAT writing scores over 700: 53%; ACT scores over 30: 83%.

Faculty *Total:* 609, 83% full-time, 91% with terminal degrees. *Student/faculty ratio:* 13:1.

Academics *Calendar:* 4-1-4. *Degrees:* certificates, diplomas, bachelor's, master's, doctoral, post-master's, postbachelor's, and first professional certificates. *Special study options:* adult/continuing education programs, part-time degree program. *ROTC:* Army (b), Air Force (c). *Unusual degree programs:* 3-2 engineering; international studies with Johns Hopkins University, School of Advanced International Studies (Washington, DC); biology; classics; German; history; neuroscience; public policy; mathematics; education.

Computers on Campus 100% of college-owned or -operated housing units are wired for high-speed Internet access.

Student Life *Housing:* on-campus residence required through sophomore year. *Options:* coed, men-only, women-only. Campus housing is university owned. Freshman campus housing is guaranteed. *Campus security:* 24-hour emergency response devices and patrols, student patrols, late-night transport/escort service, controlled dormitory access, CCTV monitoring of public areas.

Athletics Member NCAA. All Division III except men's and women's lacrosse (Division I). *Intercollegiate sports:* baseball M, basketball M/W, cross-country running M/W, fencing M/W, field hockey W, football M, lacrosse M(s)/W(s), soccer M/W, swimming and diving M/W, tennis M/W, track and field M/W, volleyball W, water polo M, wrestling M. *Intramural sports:* badminton M/W, basketball M/W, cheerleading M/W, field hockey M/W, football M/W, ice hockey M/W, lacrosse M/W, rock climbing M/W, rugby M/W, sailing M/W, skiing (downhill) M/W, soccer M/W, softball M/W, table tennis M/W, tennis M/W, ultimate Frisbee M/W, volleyball M/W.

Standardized Tests *Required:* SAT or ACT (for admission). *Recommended:* SAT Subject Tests (for admission).

Costs (2011–12) *One-time required fee:* $500. *Comprehensive fee:* $55,242 includes full-time tuition ($42,280) and room and board ($12,962). *Room and board:* Room and board charges vary according to board plan and housing facility. *Payment plan:* installment. *Waivers:* employees or children of employees.

Financial Aid Of all full-time matriculated undergraduates who enrolled in 2011, 2,695 applied for aid, 2,306 were judged to have need, 2,295 had their need fully met. 1,741 Federal Work-Study jobs (averaging $2298). In 2011, 57 non-need-based awards were made. *Average percent of need met:* 100%. *Average financial aid package:* $34,619. *Average need-based loan:* $4429. *Average need-based gift aid:* $31,409. *Average non-need-based aid:* $28,643. *Average indebtedness upon graduation:* $25,266. *Financial aid deadline:* 3/1.

Applying *Options:* electronic application, early decision. *Application fee:* $70. *Required:* essay or personal statement, high school transcript, 2 letters of recommendation. *Recommended:* 3 letters of recommendation, interview. *Application deadlines:* 1/1 (freshmen), 3/15 (transfers). *Early decision deadline:* 11/1. *Notification:* 4/1 (freshmen), 5/31 (transfers), 12/15 (early decision).

Freshman Application Contact Mr. John Birney, Senior Associate Director of Undergraduate Admissions, The Johns Hopkins University, Mason Hall, 3400 North Charles Street, Baltimore, MD 21218-2699. *Phone:* 410-516-8341. *Fax:* 410-516-6025. *E-mail:* gotojhu@jhu.edu. *Web site:* http://www.jhu.edu/.

See page 1384 for the College Close-Up.

Undergraduate studies in liberal arts and engineering

JOHNS HOPKINS
UNIVERSITY

apply.jhu.edu

Kaplan University, Hagerstown Campus

Hagerstown, Maryland

Freshman Application Contact Kaplan University, Hagerstown Campus, 18618 Crestwood Drive, Hagerstown, MD 21742-2797. *Phone:* 301-739-2680 Ext. 217. *Toll-free phone:* 866-527-5268 (in-state); 800-527-5268 (out-of-state). *Web site:* http://www.ku-hagerstown.com/.

Loyola University Maryland

Baltimore, Maryland

- **Independent Roman Catholic (Jesuit)** university, founded 1852
- **Urban** 89-acre campus with easy access to Washington, D.C.
- **Endowment** $167.1 million
- **Coed** 3,863 undergraduate students, 99% full-time, 61% women, 39% men
- **Moderately difficult** entrance level, 63% of applicants were admitted

Undergraduates 3,816 full-time, 47 part-time. Students come from 38 states and territories; 33 other countries; 82% are from out of state; 4% Black or African American, non-Hispanic/Latino; 7% Hispanic/Latino; 3% Asian, non-Hispanic/Latino; 0.2% American Indian or Alaska Native, non-Hispanic/Latino; 2% Two or more races, non-Hispanic/Latino; 1% Race/ethnicity unknown; 0.9% international; 2% transferred in; 83% live on campus. *Retention:* 89% of full-time freshmen returned.

Freshmen *Admission:* 12,066 applied, 7,651 admitted, 1,071 enrolled. *Average high school GPA:* 3.44. *Test scores:* SAT critical reading scores over 500: 94%; SAT math scores over 500: 95%; ACT scores over 18: 100%; SAT critical reading scores over 600: 47%; SAT math scores over 600: 58%; ACT scores over 24: 86%; SAT critical reading scores over 700: 9%; SAT math scores over 700: 9%; ACT scores over 30: 13%.

Faculty *Total:* 531, 62% full-time, 56% with terminal degrees. *Student/faculty ratio:* 13:1.

Academics *Calendar:* semesters. *Degrees:* bachelor's, master's, doctoral, post-master's, postbachelor's, and first professional certificates. *Special study options:* accelerated degree program, advanced placement credit, cooperative education, double majors, honors programs, independent study, internships, off-campus study, part-time degree program, services for LD students, study abroad, summer session for credit. *ROTC:* Army (b), Air Force (c). *Unusual degree programs:* nursing with Johns Hopkins University School of Nursing (The Loyola-Hopkins dual-degree program allows students to earn two degrees in five years).

Computers on Campus 775 computers/terminals and 775 ports are available on campus for general student use. Students can access the following: campus intranet, computer help desk, free student e-mail accounts, online (class) grades, online (class) registration, online (class) schedules. Campuswide network is available. 100% of college-owned or -operated housing units are wired for high-speed Internet access. Wireless service is available via entire campus.

Student Life *Housing:* on-campus residence required for freshman year. *Options:* coed, cooperative. Campus housing is university owned. Freshman campus housing is guaranteed. *Activities and organizations:* drama/theater group, student-run newspaper, radio and television station, choral group, Student Government Association, Resident Affairs Council (RAC), Relay for Life, Resident Assistants (RA), The Evergreens. *Campus security:* 24-hour emergency response devices and patrols, late-night transport/escort service, controlled dormitory access. *Student services:* health clinic, personal/psychological counseling, women's center.

Athletics Member NCAA. All Division I. *Intercollegiate sports:* basketball M(s)/W(s), crew M(s)/W(s), cross-country running M(s)/W(s), golf M(s), lacrosse M(s)/W(s), soccer M(s)/W(s), swimming and diving M(s)/W(s), tennis M(s)/W(s), track and field W(s), volleyball W(s). *Intramural sports:* badminton M(c)/W(c), baseball M(c), basketball M(c)/W(c), field hockey W(c), ice hockey M(c), lacrosse M(c), riflery M(c)/W(c), rugby M(c), sailing M(c)/W(c), soccer M(c)/W(c), softball W(c), swimming and diving M(c)/W(c), tennis M(c)/W(c), ultimate Frisbee M(c)/W(c), volleyball M(c)/W(c), water polo M(c)/W(c).

Costs (2012–13) *One-time required fee:* $165. *Comprehensive fee:* $54,550 includes full-time tuition ($41,030), mandatory fees ($1400), and room and board ($12,120). Full-time tuition and fees vary according to course load. Part-time tuition: $665 per credit. Part-time tuition and fees vary according to course load. *Required fees:* $25 per term part-time. *College room only:* $9120. Room and board charges vary according to housing facility and location. *Payment plan:* installment. *Waivers:* employees or children of employees.

Financial Aid Of all full-time matriculated undergraduates who enrolled in 2010, 2,422 applied for aid, 2,096 were judged to have need, 2,080 had their need fully met. In 2010, 343 non-need-based awards were made. *Average percent of need met:* 97%. *Average financial aid package:* $27,360. *Average need-based loan:* $5820. *Average need-based gift aid:* $19,150. *Average non-*

need-based aid: $15,085. *Average indebtedness upon graduation:* $31,655. *Financial aid deadline:* 2/15.

Applying *Options:* electronic application, early admission, early action, deferred entrance. *Application fee:* $50. *Required:* essay or personal statement, high school transcript. *Application deadlines:* 1/15 (freshmen), 1/15 (out-of-state freshmen), 7/15 (transfers), 11/1 (early action). *Notification:* 4/1 (freshmen), 4/1 (out-of-state freshmen), continuous (transfers), 1/15 (early action).

Freshman Application Contact Loyola University Maryland, 4501 North Charles Street, Baltimore, MD 21210-2699. *Phone:* 410-617-2000. *Toll-free phone:* 800-221-9107. *Web site:* http://www.loyola.edu/.

See page 382 for display ad and page 1420 for the College Close-Up.

Maple Springs Baptist Bible College and Seminary
Capitol Heights, Maryland

- **Independent Baptist** comprehensive, founded 1986
- **Suburban** 1-acre campus with easy access to Washington, D.C.
- **Coed** 77 undergraduate students, 3% full-time, 57% women, 43% men
- **Minimally difficult** entrance level, 100% of applicants were admitted

Undergraduates 2 full-time, 75 part-time. Students come from 3 states and territories; 21% are from out of state; 96% Black or African American, non-Hispanic/Latino; 4% Hispanic/Latino; 1% transferred in.
Freshmen *Admission:* 2 applied, 2 admitted, 2 enrolled.
Faculty *Total:* 23, 13% full-time, 100% with terminal degrees.
Academics *Calendar:* semesters. *Degrees:* certificates, diplomas, associate, bachelor's, master's, and doctoral. *Special study options:* academic remediation for entering students, accelerated degree program, adult/continuing education programs, external degree program, independent study, internships, part-time degree program.
Student Life *Housing:* college housing not available. *Activities and organizations:* student-run newspaper. *Campus security:* 24-hour emergency response devices, part-time security personnel.
Standardized Tests *Required:* math and English placement examination for all new students who do not have college English and math grades of C or above (for admission).
Costs (2011–12) *Tuition:* $4470 full-time, $2230 per term part-time. *Required fees:* $120 full-time, $165 per credit part-time, $60 per term part-time. *Payment plan:* installment.
Financial Aid *Financial aid deadline:* 4/30.
Applying *Options:* deferred entrance. *Application fee:* $50. *Required:* essay or personal statement, high school transcript, 2 letters of recommendation, interview. *Application deadlines:* rolling (freshmen), rolling (transfers). *Notification:* continuous (freshmen), continuous (transfers).
Freshman Application Contact Ms. Jeannie Bowman, Assistant Director of Admissions and Records, Maple Springs Baptist Bible College and Seminary, 4130 Belt Road, Capitol Heights, MD 20743. *Phone:* 301-736-3631. *Fax:* 301-735-6507. *Web site:* http://www.msbbcs.edu/.

Maryland Institute College of Art
Baltimore, Maryland

- **Independent** comprehensive, founded 1826
- **Urban** 16-acre campus with easy access to Washington, D.C.
- **Endowment** $66.9 million
- **Coed** 1,834 undergraduate students, 99% full-time, 71% women, 29% men
- **Very difficult** entrance level, 55% of applicants were admitted

Undergraduates 1,807 full-time, 27 part-time. Students come from 46 states and territories; 49 other countries; 79% are from out of state; 5% Black or African American, non-Hispanic/Latino; 5% Hispanic/Latino; 10% Asian, non-Hispanic/Latino; 0.2% American Indian or Alaska Native, non-Hispanic/Latino; 7% Two or more races, non-Hispanic/Latino; 12% Race/ethnicity unknown; 6% international; 5% transferred in; 88% live on campus. *Retention:* 85% of full-time freshmen returned.
Freshmen *Admission:* 3,233 applied, 1,777 admitted, 496 enrolled. *Average high school GPA:* 3.45. *Test scores:* SAT critical reading scores over 500: 87%; SAT math scores over 500: 78%; SAT writing scores over 500: 86%; SAT critical reading scores over 600: 53%; SAT math scores over 600: 35%; SAT writing scores over 600: 44%; SAT critical reading scores over 700: 17%; SAT math scores over 700: 5%; SAT writing scores over 700: 10%.
Faculty *Total:* 369, 40% full-time, 82% with terminal degrees. *Student/faculty ratio:* 10:1.
Academics *Calendar:* semesters. *Degrees:* bachelor's, master's, and post-bachelor's certificates. *Special study options:* accelerated degree program, adult/continuing education programs, advanced placement credit, distance

learning, double majors, English as a second language, independent study, internships, off-campus study, services for LD students, student-designed majors, study abroad, summer session for credit. *ROTC:* Army (c).
Computers on Campus 650 computers/terminals and 750 ports are available on campus for general student use. Students can access the following: campus intranet, computer help desk, free student e-mail accounts, online (class) grades, online (class) registration, online (class) schedules, campus Portal, online gallery space, network storage space, personal Web sites, online software training tutorials (Lynda.com), and Learning management system (Moodle). Campuswide network is available. 100% of college-owned or -operated housing units are wired for high-speed Internet access. Wireless service is available via classrooms, computer centers, computer labs, dorm rooms, learning centers, libraries, student centers.
Student Life *Housing options:* coed, disabled students. Campus housing is university owned. Freshman campus housing is guaranteed. *Activities and organizations:* drama/theater group, student-run radio station, choral group, Soccer Club, Urban Gaming Club, Black Student Union, Students of Sustainability, National Art Educators Association. *Campus security:* 24-hour emergency response devices and patrols, student patrols, late-night transport/escort service, controlled dormitory access, self-defense education, 24-hour building security, safety awareness programs, campus patrols by city police. *Student services:* health clinic, personal/psychological counseling.
Athletics *Intramural sports:* soccer M(c)/W(c), volleyball M(c)/W(c).
Standardized Tests *Required:* SAT or ACT (for admission).
Costs (2012–13) *One-time required fee:* $160. *Comprehensive fee:* $50,220 includes full-time tuition ($37,900), mandatory fees ($1440), and room and board ($10,880). Part-time tuition: $1580 per credit. *Required fees:* $720 per term part-time. *College room only:* $8200. Room and board charges vary according to board plan and housing facility. *Payment plan:* installment. *Waivers:* employees or children of employees.
Financial Aid *Average indebtedness upon graduation:* $17,472.
Applying *Options:* early admission, early decision, deferred entrance. *Application fee:* $60. *Required:* essay or personal statement, high school transcript, 3 letters of recommendation, art portfolio. *Recommended:* interview. *Application deadlines:* 2/15 (freshmen), 3/1 (transfers). *Early decision deadline:* 11/15. *Notification:* 3/12 (freshmen), 4/24 (transfers), 12/15 (early decision).
Freshman Application Contact Ms. Christine Seese, Director of Undergraduate Admission, Maryland Institute College of Art, 1300 Mount Royal Avenue, Baltimore, MD 21217. *Phone:* 410-225-2222. *Fax:* 410-225-2337. *E-mail:* cgyland@mica.edu. *Web site:* http://www.mica.edu/.

McDaniel College
Westminster, Maryland

- **Independent** comprehensive, founded 1867
- **Suburban** 160-acre campus with easy access to Baltimore and Washington, D.C.
- **Endowment** $88.9 million
- **Coed** 1,629 undergraduate students, 97% full-time, 52% women, 48% men
- **Moderately difficult** entrance level, 75% of applicants were admitted

Undergraduates 1,582 full-time, 47 part-time. Students come from 36 states and territories; 16 other countries; 37% are from out of state; 10% Black or African American, non-Hispanic/Latino; 5% Hispanic/Latino; 4% Asian, non-Hispanic/Latino; 1% American Indian or Alaska Native, non-Hispanic/Latino; 2% Race/ethnicity unknown; 4% transferred in; 81% live on campus. *Retention:* 79% of full-time freshmen returned.
Freshmen *Admission:* 2,754 applied, 2,074 admitted, 424 enrolled. *Average high school GPA:* 3.42. *Test scores:* SAT critical reading scores over 500: 71%; SAT math scores over 500: 75%; ACT scores over 18: 98%; SAT critical reading scores over 600: 31%; SAT math scores over 600: 31%; ACT scores over 24: 42%; SAT critical reading scores over 700: 5%; SAT math scores over 700: 6%; ACT scores over 30: 6%.
Faculty *Total:* 356, 28% full-time, 51% with terminal degrees. *Student/faculty ratio:* 11:1.
Academics *Calendar:* 4-1-4. *Degrees:* bachelor's, master's, and postbachelor's certificates. *Special study options:* academic remediation for entering students, adult/continuing education programs, advanced placement credit, distance learning, double majors, honors programs, independent study, internships, off-campus study, part-time degree program, services for LD students, student-designed majors, study abroad, summer session for credit. *ROTC:* Army (b). *Unusual degree programs:* 3-2 engineering with University of Maryland; environmental policy science with Duke University.
Computers on Campus 315 computers/terminals and 1,228 ports are available on campus for general student use. Students can access the following: campus intranet, computer help desk, free student e-mail accounts, online (class) grades, online (class) registration, online (class) schedules, online billing summaries, financial aid letter, tax information. Campuswide network is

available. 100% of college-owned or -operated housing units are wired for high-speed Internet access. Wireless service is available via entire campus.

Student Life *Housing:* on-campus residence required through junior year. *Options:* coed, men-only, women-only, disabled students. Campus housing is university owned. Freshman campus housing is guaranteed. *Activities and organizations:* drama/theater group, student-run newspaper, radio and television station, choral group, Student Government Association, Black Student Union, International Club, Maryland State Legislature, Up Till Dawn, national fraternities, national sororities. *Campus security:* 24-hour emergency response devices and patrols, late-night transport/escort service, About half patrol force sworn as campus police. All are certified to US DOT First Responder standards. *Student services:* health clinic, personal/psychological counseling.

Athletics Member NCAA. All Division III. *Intercollegiate sports:* baseball M, basketball M/W, cross-country running M/W, field hockey W, football M, golf M/W, lacrosse M/W, soccer M/W, softball W, swimming and diving M/W, tennis M/W, track and field M/W, volleyball W, wrestling M. *Intramural sports:* badminton M/W, basketball M/W, cheerleading M(c)/W(c), cross-country running M/W, football M, golf M/W, rugby M(c)/W(c), soccer M/W, softball M/W, tennis M/W, ultimate Frisbee M(c)/W(c), volleyball M/W.

Standardized Tests *Required:* SAT or ACT (for admission), SAT Optional Plan for students who are in the top 10% of their class if their HS ranks; otherwise, a cumulative GPA of a 3.5 or higher. SAT Subject Tests considered if submitted (for admission).

Costs (2012–13) *Comprehensive fee:* $43,540 includes full-time tuition ($35,800) and room and board ($7740). Full-time tuition and fees vary according to course load. Part-time tuition: $1119 per credit hour. Part-time tuition and fees vary according to course load and reciprocity agreements. *College room only:* $4040. Room and board charges vary according to board plan and housing facility. *Payment plans:* tuition prepayment, installment. *Waivers:* employees or children of employees.

Financial Aid Of all full-time matriculated undergraduates who enrolled in 2011, 1,236 applied for aid, 1,120 were judged to have need, 227 had their need fully met. 418 Federal Work-Study jobs (averaging $858). 241 state and other part-time jobs (averaging $625). In 2011, 371 non-need-based awards were made. *Average percent of need met:* 81%. *Average financial aid package:* $28,449. *Average need-based loan:* $4874. *Average need-based gift aid:* $23,935. *Average non-need-based aid:* $17,264. *Average indebtedness upon graduation:* $29,023.

Applying *Options:* electronic application, early admission, early action, deferred entrance. *Application fee:* $50. *Required:* essay or personal statement, high school transcript, minimum 2.5 GPA, 2 letters of recommendation. *Required for some:* interview. *Recommended:* interview. *Application deadlines:* 2/15 (freshmen), 2/5 (out-of-state freshmen), 4/1 (transfers), 12/1 (early action). *Notification:* 3/9 (freshmen), 3/9 (out-of-state freshmen), 4/15 (transfers), 12/21 (early action).

Freshman Application Contact Ms. Florence Hines, Vice President for Enrollment Management and Dean of Admissions, McDaniel College, 2 College Hill, Westminster, MD 21157-4390. *Phone:* 410-857-2230. *Toll-free phone:* 800-638-5005. *Fax:* 410-857-2757. *E-mail:* admissions@mcdaniel.edu. *Web site:* http://www.mcdaniel.edu/.

Morgan State University

Baltimore, Maryland

Director of Admissions Ms. Shonda Gray, Acting Director of Admissions and Recruitment, Morgan State University, 1700 East Cold Spring Lane, Baltimore, MD 21251. *Phone:* 443-885-3000. *Toll-free phone:* 800-332-6674. *E-mail:* shantell.saunders@morgan.edu. *Web site:* http://www.morgan.edu/.

Mount St. Mary's University

Emmitsburg, Maryland

- **Independent Roman Catholic** comprehensive, founded 1808
- **Rural** 1400-acre campus with easy access to Baltimore and Washington, D.C.
- **Endowment** $44.8 million
- **Coed** 1,783 undergraduate students, 94% full-time, 56% women, 44% men
- **Moderately difficult** entrance level, 66% of applicants were admitted

Undergraduates 1,683 full-time, 100 part-time. Students come from 34 states and territories; 15 other countries; 46% are from out of state; 10% Black or African American, non-Hispanic/Latino; 9% Hispanic/Latino; 2% Asian, non-Hispanic/Latino; 0.1% Native Hawaiian or other Pacific Islander, non-Hispanic/Latino; 0.2% American Indian or Alaska Native, non-Hispanic/Latino; 3% Two or more races, non-Hispanic/Latino; 1% Race/ethnicity unknown; 1%

international; 2% transferred in; 86% live on campus. *Retention:* 82% of full-time freshmen returned.

Freshmen *Admission:* 5,166 applied, 3,389 admitted, 572 enrolled. *Average high school GPA:* 3.33. *Test scores:* SAT critical reading scores over 500: 72%; SAT math scores over 500: 69%; SAT writing scores over 500: 66%; ACT scores over 18: 86%; SAT critical reading scores over 600: 24%; SAT math scores over 600: 21%; SAT writing scores over 600: 21%; ACT scores over 24: 22%; SAT critical reading scores over 700: 4%; SAT math scores over 700: 1%; SAT writing scores over 700: 4%; ACT scores over 30: 3%.

Faculty *Total:* 181, 60% full-time, 67% with terminal degrees. *Student/faculty ratio:* 14:1.

Academics *Calendar:* semesters. *Degrees:* bachelor's, master's, post-master's, and postbachelor's certificates. *Special study options:* academic remediation for entering students, accelerated degree program, adult/continuing education programs, advanced placement credit, double majors, honors programs, independent study, internships, off-campus study, part-time degree program, services for LD students, student-designed majors, study abroad, summer session for credit. *ROTC:* Army (c). *Unusual degree programs:* 3-2 nursing with Johns Hopkins University, Shenandoah University.

Computers on Campus 80 computers/terminals are available on campus for general student use. Students can access the following: campus intranet, computer help desk, free student e-mail accounts, online (class) grades, online (class) registration, online (class) schedules, tuition payment, course management system. Campuswide network is available. 100% of college-owned or -operated housing units are wired for high-speed Internet access. Wireless service is available via entire campus.

Student Life *Housing:* on-campus residence required for freshman year. *Options:* coed, disabled students. Campus housing is university owned. Freshman campus housing is guaranteed. *Activities and organizations:* drama/theater group, student-run newspaper, radio and television station, choral group, Mount Students for Life, CRUX - Outdoor Adventures, Campus Ministry Student Organization, Circle K, Mount Chorale. *Campus security:* 24-hour emergency response devices and patrols, late-night transport/escort service, controlled dormitory access. *Student services:* health clinic, personal/psychological counseling.

Athletics Member NCAA. All Division I. *Intercollegiate sports:* baseball M(s), basketball M(s)/W(s), cheerleading W(c), cross-country running M(s)/W(s), equestrian sports M(c)/W(c), golf M(s)/W(s), ice hockey M(c), lacrosse M(s)/W(s), rugby M(c)/W(c), soccer M(s)/W(s), softball W(s), swimming and diving W(s), tennis M(s)/W(s), track and field M(s)/W(s), ultimate Frisbee W(c). *Intramural sports:* basketball M/W, field hockey W, football M, racquetball M/W, skiing (downhill) M/W, soccer M/W, softball M/W, swimming and diving M/W, tennis M/W, ultimate Frisbee M/W, volleyball M/W.

Standardized Tests *Required:* SAT or ACT (for admission).

Costs (2012–13) *Comprehensive fee:* $43,972 includes full-time tuition ($32,224), mandatory fees ($730), and room and board ($11,018). Full-time tuition and fees vary according to program. Part-time tuition: $1076 per credit hour. Part-time tuition and fees vary according to program. *College room only:* $5392.

Financial Aid Of all full-time matriculated undergraduates who enrolled in 2011, 1,357 applied for aid, 1,176 were judged to have need, 281 had their need fully met. 281 Federal Work-Study jobs (averaging $1180). 421 state and other part-time jobs (averaging $1060). In 2011, 451 non-need-based awards were made. *Average percent of need met:* 75%. *Average financial aid package:* $21,971. *Average need-based loan:* $4607. *Average need-based gift aid:* $17,706. *Average non-need-based aid:* $12,120. *Average indebtedness upon graduation:* $32,453. *Financial aid deadline:* 3/1.

Applying *Options:* electronic application, early action, deferred entrance. *Application fee:* $35. *Required:* high school transcript, minimum 2.0 GPA, 1 letter of recommendation. *Recommended:* essay or personal statement, minimum 3.0 GPA, interview. *Application deadlines:* rolling (freshmen), 6/1 (transfers), 12/1 (early action). *Notification:* continuous (freshmen), continuous (transfers), 12/25 (early action).

Freshman Application Contact Mr. Michael Post, Dean of Admissions and Enrollment Management, Mount St. Mary's University, 16300 Old Emmitsburg Road, Emmitsburg, MD 21727. *Phone:* 301-447-5214. *Toll-free phone:* 800-448-4347. *Fax:* 301-447-5860. *E-mail:* admissions@msmary.edu. *Web site:* http://www.msmary.edu/.

National Labor College

Silver Spring, Maryland

Director of Admissions Carol Rodgers, Associate Provost for External Relations and Director of Admissions, National Labor College, 10000 New Hampshire Avenue, Silver Spring, MD 20903. *Phone:* 301-431-5440. *Toll-free phone:* 888-427-8100. *E-mail:* crodgers@nlc.edu. *Web site:* http://www.nlc.edu/.

Ner Israel Rabbinical College

Baltimore, Maryland

Freshman Application Contact Ner Israel Rabbinical College, 400 Mount Wilson Lane, Baltimore, MD 21208. *Phone:* 410-484-7200.

Notre Dame of Maryland University

Baltimore, Maryland

- **Independent Roman Catholic** comprehensive, founded 1873
- **Urban** 58-acre campus with easy access to Baltimore and Washington, D.C.
- **Endowment** $26.3 million
- **Coed, primarily women** 1,296 undergraduate students, 39% full-time, 95% women, 5% men
- **Moderately difficult** entrance level, 55% of applicants were admitted

Undergraduates 510 full-time, 786 part-time. Students come from 18 states and territories; 12 other countries; 16% are from out of state; 35% Black or African American, non-Hispanic/Latino; 6% Hispanic/Latino; 7% Asian, non-Hispanic/Latino; 1% American Indian or Alaska Native, non-Hispanic/Latino; 0.4% Race/ethnicity unknown; 3% international; 4% transferred in; 55% live on campus. *Retention:* 71% of full-time freshmen returned.

Freshmen *Admission:* 756 applied, 418 admitted, 137 enrolled. *Average high school GPA:* 3.56. *Test scores:* SAT critical reading scores over 500: 61%; SAT math scores over 500: 50%; SAT critical reading scores over 600: 22%; SAT math scores over 600: 16%; SAT critical reading scores over 700: 2%; SAT math scores over 700: 1%.

Faculty *Total:* 121, 86% full-time, 83% with terminal degrees. *Student/faculty ratio:* 12:1.

Academics *Calendar:* 4-1-4. *Degrees:* bachelor's, master's, doctoral, postmaster's, postbachelor's, and first professional certificates (offers coed undergraduate program for adult students). *Special study options:* accelerated degree program, adult/continuing education programs, advanced placement credit, double majors, English as a second language, honors programs, independent study, internships, off-campus study, part-time degree program, services for LD students, student-designed majors, study abroad, summer session for credit. *ROTC:* Army (c). *Unusual degree programs:* 3-2 engineering with University of Maryland, College Park; Johns Hopkins University; nursing with Johns Hopkins University; radiological science with Johns Hopkins University.

Computers on Campus 60 computers/terminals are available on campus for general student use. Students can access the following: campus intranet, computer help desk, free student e-mail accounts, online (class) grades, online (class) registration, online (class) schedules, online classroom assignments and information. Campuswide network is available. 100% of college-owned or -operated housing units are wired for high-speed Internet access. Wireless service is available via entire campus.

Student Life *Housing options:* women-only. Campus housing is university owned. Freshman campus housing is guaranteed. *Activities and organizations:* drama/theater group, student-run newspaper, radio and television station, choral group, Omega Phi Alpha Service Sorority, Maryland Student Legislature, Business and Economics Society, Sigma Tau Delta Honor Society, Residence Hall Council. *Campus security:* 24-hour emergency response devices and patrols, late-night transport/escort service, controlled dormitory access, emergency call boxes. *Student services:* health clinic, personal/psychological counseling, women's center.

Athletics Member NCAA. All Division III. *Intercollegiate sports:* basketball W, field hockey W, lacrosse W, soccer W, softball W, swimming and diving W, tennis W, volleyball W.

Standardized Tests *Required:* SAT or ACT (for admission).

Costs (2012–13) *Comprehensive fee:* $41,000 includes full-time tuition ($29,850), mandatory fees ($1000), and room and board ($10,150). *Room and board:* Room and board charges vary according to board plan.

Financial Aid Of all full-time matriculated undergraduates who enrolled in 2010, 456 applied for aid, 419 were judged to have need, 112 had their need fully met. 92 Federal Work-Study jobs (averaging $962). In 2010, 50 non-need-based awards were made. *Average percent of need met:* 68%. *Average financial aid package:* $20,927. *Average need-based loan:* $3569. *Average need-based gift aid:* $17,012. *Average non-need-based aid:* $12,711. *Average indebtedness upon graduation:* $30,801.

Applying *Options:* electronic application, early admission, early action, deferred entrance. *Application fee:* $45. *Required:* essay or personal state-ment, high school transcript, minimum 2.0 GPA, 2 letters of recommendation. *Recommended:* minimum 3.0 GPA, interview, resume. *Application deadlines:* 2/15 (freshmen), 2/15 (transfers), 12/3 (early action). *Notification:* continuous until 6/30 (freshmen), continuous until 6/30 (transfers), 1/1 (early action).

Freshman Application Contact Notre Dame of Maryland University, 4701 North Charles Street, Baltimore, MD 21210-2476. *Phone:* 410-532-5332. *Toll-free phone:* 800-435-0200. *Web site:* http://www.ndm.edu/.

Peabody Conservatory of The Johns Hopkins University

Baltimore, Maryland

- **Independent** comprehensive, founded 1857
- **Urban** 1-acre campus with easy access to Washington, D.C.
- **Endowment** $85.7 million
- **Coed** 329 undergraduate students, 100% full-time, 47% women, 53% men
- **Very difficult** entrance level, 49% of applicants were admitted

Undergraduates 328 full-time, 1 part-time. Students come from 37 states and territories; 15 other countries; 77% are from out of state; 2% Black or African American, non-Hispanic/Latino; 4% Hispanic/Latino; 12% Asian, non-Hispanic/Latino; 0.6% Native Hawaiian or other Pacific Islander, non-Hispanic/Latino; 5% Two or more races, non-Hispanic/Latino; 3% Race/ethnicity unknown; 22% international; 6% transferred in; 40% live on campus. *Retention:* 88% of full-time freshmen returned.

Freshmen *Admission:* 740 applied, 362 admitted, 78 enrolled.

Faculty *Total:* 163, 52% full-time, 23% with terminal degrees. *Student/faculty ratio:* 5:1.

Academics *Calendar:* semesters. *Degrees:* certificates, diplomas, bachelor's, master's, doctoral, post-master's, and postbachelor's certificates. *Special study options:* academic remediation for entering students, accelerated degree program, advanced placement credit, double majors, English as a second language, honors programs, independent study, internships, off-campus study, services for LD students.

Computers on Campus 40 computers/terminals are available on campus for general student use. Students can access the following: campus intranet, computer help desk, free student e-mail accounts, online (class) grades, online (class) registration, online (class) schedules, word processing, music processing. Campuswide network is available. 100% of college-owned or -operated housing units are wired for high-speed Internet access. Wireless service is available via entire campus.

Student Life *Housing:* on-campus residence required through sophomore year. *Options:* coed. Campus housing is university owned. Freshman campus housing is guaranteed. *Activities and organizations:* choral group. *Campus security:* 24-hour emergency response devices and patrols, late-night transport/escort service, controlled dormitory access. *Student services:* health clinic, personal/psychological counseling.

Standardized Tests *Required for some:* SAT or ACT (for admission).

Costs (2011–12) *One-time required fee:* $700. *Comprehensive fee:* $49,625 includes full-time tuition ($37,000), mandatory fees ($425), and room and board ($12,200). Full-time tuition and fees vary according to program. Part-time tuition: $1055 per semester hour. Part-time tuition and fees vary according to course load. *Room and board:* Room and board charges vary according to board plan. *Payment plan:* installment.

Financial Aid Of all full-time matriculated undergraduates who enrolled in 2011, 231 applied for aid, 199 were judged to have need, 41 had their need fully met. 103 Federal Work-Study jobs (averaging $1892). In 2011, 85 non-need-based awards were made. *Average percent of need met:* 75%. *Average financial aid package:* $16,689. *Average need-based loan:* $5406. *Average need-based gift aid:* $13,085. *Average non-need-based aid:* $17,035. *Average indebtedness upon graduation:* $33,888.

Applying *Application fee:* $100. *Required:* essay or personal statement, high school transcript, 3 letters of recommendation, interview, audition. *Recommended:* minimum 3.0 GPA. *Application deadlines:* 12/1 (freshmen), 12/1 (transfers). *Notification:* 4/1 (freshmen), 4/1 (transfers).

Freshman Application Contact Mr. David Lane, Director of Admissions, Peabody Conservatory of The Johns Hopkins University, Peabody Conservatory Admissions Office, One East Mount Vernon Place, Baltimore, MD 21202-2397. *Phone:* 410-234-4848. *Toll-free phone:* 800-368-2521. *Web site:* http://www.peabody.jhu.edu/.

St. John's College

Annapolis, Maryland

- **Independent** comprehensive, founded 1784
- **Small-town** 36-acre campus with easy access to Baltimore and Washington, D.C.
- **Endowment** $77.9 million
- **Coed** 490 undergraduate students, 100% full-time, 43% women, 57% men
- **Moderately difficult** entrance level, 78% of applicants were admitted

Undergraduates 488 full-time, 2 part-time. Students come from 42 states and territories; 15 other countries; 85% are from out of state; 0.8% Black or African American, non-Hispanic/Latino; 4% Hispanic/Latino; 2% Asian, non-Hispanic/Latino; 0.4% American Indian or Alaska Native, non-Hispanic/Latino; 4% Two or more races, non-Hispanic/Latino; 1% Race/ethnicity unknown; 7% international; 69% live on campus. *Retention:* 82% of full-time freshmen returned.

Freshmen *Admission:* 433 applied, 338 admitted, 150 enrolled. *Test scores:* SAT critical reading scores over 500: 98%; SAT math scores over 500: 98%; ACT scores over 18: 100%; SAT critical reading scores over 600: 89%; SAT math scores over 600: 62%; ACT scores over 24: 86%; SAT critical reading scores over 700: 55%; SAT math scores over 700: 14%; ACT scores over 30: 33%.

Faculty *Total:* 75, 93% full-time, 77% with terminal degrees. *Student/faculty ratio:* 8:1.

Academics *Calendar:* semesters. *Degrees:* bachelor's and master's. *Special study options:* internships, off-campus study.

Computers on Campus Students can access the following: computer help desk, free student e-mail accounts. Campuswide network is available. 100% of college-owned or -operated housing units are wired for high-speed Internet access. Wireless service is available via computer labs, dorm rooms, libraries.

Student Life *Housing:* on-campus residence required for freshman year. *Options:* coed, disabled students. Campus housing is university owned. Freshman campus housing is guaranteed. *Activities and organizations:* drama/theater group, student-run newspaper, choral group. *Campus security:* 24-hour emergency response devices and patrols, late-night transport/escort service, controlled dormitory access. *Student services:* health clinic, personal/psychological counseling.

Athletics *Intercollegiate sports:* crew M(c)/W(c), fencing M(c)/W(c). *Intramural sports:* badminton M/W, basketball M/W, fencing M/W, football W, racquetball M/W, sailing M/W, soccer M/W, softball M/W, squash M/W, table tennis M/W, tennis M/W, track and field M/W, volleyball M/W, weight lifting M/W.

Standardized Tests *Required for some:* SAT or ACT (for admission). *Recommended:* SAT or ACT (for admission).

Costs (2012–13) *Comprehensive fee:* $55,648 includes full-time tuition ($44,554), mandatory fees ($450), and room and board ($10,644). *Room and board:* Room and board charges vary according to board plan. *Payment plan:* installment. *Waivers:* employees or children of employees.

Financial Aid Of all full-time matriculated undergraduates who enrolled in 2011, 398 applied for aid, 352 were judged to have need, 26 had their need fully met. 110 Federal Work-Study jobs (averaging $1743). 96 state and other part-time jobs (averaging $2217). In 2011, 13 non-need-based awards were made. *Average percent of need met:* 98%. *Average financial aid package:* $33,643. *Average need-based loan:* $4764. *Average need-based gift aid:* $28,951. *Average non-need-based aid:* $19,217. *Average indebtedness upon graduation:* $27,470.

Applying *Options:* electronic application, early admission, deferred entrance. *Required:* essay or personal statement, high school transcript, 2 letters of recommendation. *Recommended:* interview. *Application deadlines:* rolling (freshmen), rolling (transfers). *Notification:* continuous (freshmen), continuous (transfers).

Freshman Application Contact Ms. Sarah Morse, Director of Admissions, St. John's College, PO Box 2800, 60 College Avenue, Annapolis, MD 21404. *Phone:* 410-626-2522. *Toll-free phone:* 800-727-9238. *Fax:* 410-269-7916. *E-mail:* admissions@sjca.edu. *Web site:* http://www.stjohnscollege.edu/.

See page 1550 for the College Close-Up.

St. Mary's College of Maryland

St. Mary's City, Maryland

- **State-supported** comprehensive, founded 1840
- **Rural** 361-acre campus
- **Endowment** $25.9 million
- **Coed** 1,962 undergraduate students, 97% full-time, 59% women, 41% men
- **Very difficult** entrance level, 61% of applicants were admitted

Undergraduates 1,901 full-time, 61 part-time. Students come from 31 states and territories; 35 other countries; 13% are from out of state; 8% Black or African American, non-Hispanic/Latino; 4% Hispanic/Latino; 3% Asian, non-His-

panic/Latino; 0.1% Native Hawaiian or other Pacific Islander, non-Hispanic/Latino; 3% Two or more races, non-Hispanic/Latino; 3% Race/ethnicity unknown; 2% international; 4% transferred in; 86% live on campus. *Retention:* 87% of full-time freshmen returned.

Freshmen *Admission:* 2,398 applied, 1,472 admitted, 446 enrolled. *Average high school GPA:* 3.29. *Test scores:* SAT critical reading scores over 500: 90%; SAT math scores over 500: 88%; SAT writing scores over 500: 89%; ACT scores over 18: 97%; SAT critical reading scores over 600: 63%; SAT math scores over 600: 50%; SAT writing scores over 600: 56%; ACT scores over 24: 84%; SAT critical reading scores over 700: 18%; SAT math scores over 700: 8%; SAT writing scores over 700: 15%; ACT scores over 30: 21%.

Faculty *Total:* 226, 60% full-time, 75% with terminal degrees. *Student/faculty ratio:* 12:1.

Academics *Calendar:* semesters. *Degrees:* bachelor's and master's. *Special study options:* advanced placement credit, cooperative education, double majors, freshman honors college, honors programs, independent study, internships, off-campus study, part-time degree program, services for LD students, student-designed majors, study abroad, summer session for credit. *Unusual degree programs:* 3-2 engineering with University of Maryland, College Park.

Computers on Campus 390 computers/terminals and 500 ports are available on campus for general student use. Students can access the following: campus intranet, computer help desk, free student e-mail accounts, online (class) grades, online (class) registration, online (class) schedules, Blackboard. Campuswide network is available. 100% of college-owned or -operated housing units are wired for high-speed Internet access. Wireless service is available via classrooms, computer centers, computer labs, learning centers, libraries, student centers.

Student Life *Housing options:* coed, men-only, women-only, cooperative, disabled students. Campus housing is university owned. Freshman campus housing is guaranteed. *Activities and organizations:* drama/theater group, student-run newspaper, radio station, choral group, Crew, Acappella groups, SEAC (Student Environmental Action Coalition), Dance Club, Outdoors Club. *Campus security:* 24-hour emergency response devices and patrols, late-night transport/escort service, controlled dormitory access. *Student services:* health clinic, personal/psychological counseling.

Athletics Member NCAA. All Division III. *Intercollegiate sports:* badminton M/W, baseball M, basketball M/W, cheerleading M/W, crew M(c)/W(c), cross-country running M/W, equestrian sports M(c)/W(c), fencing M(c)/W(c), field hockey W, lacrosse M/W, rock climbing M(c)/W(c), rugby M(c)/W(c), sailing M/W, soccer M/W, swimming and diving M/W, tennis M/W, ultimate Frisbee M(c)/W(c), volleyball W. *Intramural sports:* badminton M/W, basketball M/W, football M/W, lacrosse M/W, soccer M/W, softball M/W, volleyball M/W.

Standardized Tests *Required:* SAT or ACT (for admission).

Costs (2011–12) *Tuition:* state resident $12,005 full-time, $185 per credit hour part-time; nonresident $24,082 full-time, $185 per credit hour part-time. Full-time tuition and fees vary according to course load and degree level. Part-time tuition and fees vary according to course load and degree level. *Required fees:* $2440 full-time. *Room and board:* $10,915; room only: $6140. Room and board charges vary according to board plan and housing facility. *Payment plan:* installment. *Waivers:* senior citizens and employees or children of employees.

Financial Aid Of all full-time matriculated undergraduates who enrolled in 2010, 1,233 applied for aid, 850 were judged to have need, 19 had their need fully met. 111 Federal Work-Study jobs (averaging $780). In 2010, 447 non-need-based awards were made. *Average percent of need met:* 63%. *Average financial aid package:* $11,255. *Average need-based loan:* $4212. *Average need-based gift aid:* $7961. *Average non-need-based aid:* $3799. *Average indebtedness upon graduation:* $17,505. *Financial aid deadline:* 3/1.

Applying *Options:* electronic application, early admission, early decision, deferred entrance. *Application fee:* $50. *Required:* essay or personal statement, high school transcript, minimum 2.0 GPA, resume of co-curricular activities. *Recommended:* 2 letters of recommendation, interview. *Application deadlines:* 1/1 (freshmen), 2/1 (transfers). *Early decision deadline:* 11/1 (for plan 1), 12/1 (for plan 2). *Notification:* 4/1 (freshmen), 5/1 (transfers), 11/20 (early decision plan 1), 12/20 (early decision plan 2).

Freshman Application Contact Mr. Richard J. Edgar, Director of Admissions, St. Mary's College of Maryland, 18952 East Fisher Road, St. Mary's City, MD 20686-3001. *Phone:* 240-895-5000. *Toll-free phone:* 800-492-7181. *Fax:* 240-895-5001. *E-mail:* admissions@smcm.edu. *Web site:* http://www.smcm.edu/.

Salisbury University
Salisbury, Maryland

- **State-supported** comprehensive, founded 1925, part of University System of Maryland
- **Small-town** 160-acre campus
- **Endowment** $52.8 million
- **Coed** 7,892 undergraduate students, 93% full-time, 57% women, 43% men
- **Moderately difficult** entrance level, 53% of applicants were admitted

Undergraduates 7,304 full-time, 588 part-time. Students come from 28 states and territories; 64 other countries; 13% are from out of state; 11% Black or African American, non-Hispanic/Latino; 4% Hispanic/Latino; 2% Asian, non-Hispanic/Latino; 0.1% Native Hawaiian or other Pacific Islander, non-Hispanic/Latino; 0.3% American Indian or Alaska Native, non-Hispanic/Latino; 2% Two or more races, non-Hispanic/Latino; 1% Race/ethnicity unknown; 0.8% international; 12% transferred in; 29% live on campus. *Retention:* 83% of full-time freshmen returned.

Freshmen *Admission:* 8,021 applied, 4,232 admitted, 1,248 enrolled. *Average high school GPA:* 3.66. *Test scores:* SAT critical reading scores over 500: 93%; SAT math scores over 500: 93%; SAT writing scores over 500: 90%; ACT scores over 18: 95%; SAT critical reading scores over 600: 30%; SAT math scores over 600: 41%; SAT writing scores over 600: 29%; ACT scores over 24: 41%; SAT critical reading scores over 700: 2%; SAT math scores over 700: 2%; SAT writing scores over 700: 1%; ACT scores over 30: 4%.

Faculty *Total:* 614, 64% full-time, 58% with terminal degrees. *Student/faculty ratio:* 17:1.

Academics *Calendar:* 4-1-4. *Degrees:* bachelor's, master's, and postbachelor's certificates. *Special study options:* accelerated degree program, adult/continuing education programs, advanced placement credit, cooperative education, distance learning, double majors, English as a second language, honors programs, independent study, internships, off-campus study, part-time degree program, services for LD students, student-designed majors, study abroad, summer session for credit. *ROTC:* Army (b), Air Force (c). *Unusual degree programs:* 3-2 engineering with Pre-Engineering Program with University of Maryland College Park, Old Dominion University, and Widener University; social work with Social Work and Sociology Dual Degree Program with University of Maryland Eastern Shore; biology and environmental marine science dual degree program with University of Maryland Eastern Shore.

Computers on Campus 390 computers/terminals and 3,568 ports are available on campus for general student use. Students can access the following: computer help desk, free student e-mail accounts, online (class) grades, online (class) registration, online (class) schedules, accounts for all students. Campuswide network is available. 100% of college-owned or -operated housing units are wired for high-speed Internet access. Wireless service is available via entire campus.

Student Life *Housing options:* coed, disabled students. Campus housing is university owned. Freshman applicants given priority for college housing. *Activities and organizations:* drama/theater group, student-run newspaper, radio and television station, choral group, Student Government Association, Radio (WXSU), Student Organization for Activity Planning (SOAP), Campus Crusade for Christ, Greek Council, national fraternities, national sororities. *Campus security:* 24-hour emergency response devices and patrols, late-night transport/escort service, controlled dormitory access. *Student services:* health clinic, personal/psychological counseling.

Athletics Member NCAA. All Division III. *Intercollegiate sports:* baseball M, basketball M/W, cross-country running M/W, field hockey W, football M, lacrosse M/W, soccer M/W, softball W, swimming and diving M/W, tennis M/W, track and field M/W, volleyball W. *Intramural sports:* basketball M(c)/W(c), equestrian sports W(c), fencing M(c)/W(c), field hockey W(c), football M/W, golf M(c)/W(c), ice hockey M(c), lacrosse M(c)/W(c), racquetball M/W, rock climbing M/W, rugby M(c)/W(c), sailing M(c)/W(c), soccer W(c), softball M/W, ultimate Frisbee M(c)/W(c), volleyball M/W, water polo M/W.

Standardized Tests *Required for some:* SAT or ACT (for admission).

Costs (2011–12) *Tuition:* state resident $5260 full-time, $218 per credit hour part-time; nonresident $13,606 full-time, $565 per credit hour part-time. Full-time tuition and fees vary according to course load. Part-time tuition and fees vary according to course load. *Required fees:* $2072 full-time, $68 per credit hour part-time. *Room and board:* $8586; room only: $4750. Room and board charges vary according to board plan and housing facility. *Payment plan:* installment. *Waivers:* senior citizens and employees or children of employees.

Financial Aid Of all full-time matriculated undergraduates who enrolled in 2010, 5,031 applied for aid, 3,523 were judged to have need, 435 had their need fully met. 76 Federal Work-Study jobs (averaging $1970). In 2010, 690 non-need-based awards were made. *Average percent of need met:* 53%. *Average financial aid package:* $7488. *Average need-based loan:* $4023. *Average need-based gift aid:* $4933. *Average non-need-based aid:* $2067. *Average indebtedness upon graduation:* $20,693.

Applying *Options:* electronic application, early admission, early action. *Application fee:* $45. *Required:* essay or personal statement, high school transcript, minimum 2.0 GPA. *Application deadlines:* 1/15 (freshmen), rolling (transfers), 12/1 (early action). *Notification:* 3/15 (freshmen), continuous (transfers), 1/15 (early action).

Freshman Application Contact Mr. Aaron Basko, Director of Admissions, Salisbury University, Admissions House, 1101 Camden Avenue, Salisbury, MD 21801. *Phone:* 410-543-6161. *Toll-free phone:* 888-543-0148. *Fax:* 410-546-6016. *E-mail:* admissions@salisbury.edu. *Web site:* http://www.salisbury.edu/.

See below for display ad and page 1570 for the College Close-Up.

Sojourner-Douglass College

Baltimore, Maryland

- **Independent** comprehensive, founded 1980
- **Urban** 15-acre campus with easy access to Baltimore
- **Coed, primarily women** 1,207 undergraduate students, 68% full-time, 88% women, 12% men
- **Noncompetitive** entrance level

Undergraduates 826 full-time, 381 part-time. Students come from 7 states and territories; 14 other countries; 4% are from out of state; 93% Black or African American, non-Hispanic/Latino; 0.2% Hispanic/Latino; 0.1% Asian, non-Hispanic/Latino; 0.1% Native Hawaiian or other Pacific Islander, non-Hispanic/Latino; 0.9% Race/ethnicity unknown; 3% international; 35% transferred in. *Retention:* 43% of full-time freshmen returned.

Freshmen *Admission:* 130 enrolled.

Faculty *Total:* 240, 43% full-time, 31% with terminal degrees. *Student/faculty ratio:* 5:1.

Academics *Calendar:* trimesters. *Degrees:* bachelor's and master's (offers only evening and weekend programs). *Special study options:* academic remediation for entering students, accelerated degree program, adult/continuing education programs, external degree program, honors programs, internships, part-time degree program, services for LD students, student-designed majors, summer session for credit.

Computers on Campus 200 computers/terminals are available on campus for general student use. Students can access the following: campus intranet, computer help desk, free student e-mail accounts, online (class) grades, online (class) registration, online (class) schedules. Campuswide network is available.

100% of college-owned or -operated housing units are wired for high-speed Internet access. Wireless service is available via entire campus.

Student Life *Housing:* college housing not available. *Activities and organizations:* Student Government Association, Criminal Justice Club, Social Work Club, national fraternities, national sororities. *Student services:* personal/psychological counseling.

Costs (2012–13) *Tuition:* $8650 full-time. *Required fees:* $100 full-time.

Financial Aid Of all full-time matriculated undergraduates who enrolled in 2008, 1,412 applied for aid, 1,412 were judged to have need. 16 Federal Work-Study jobs (averaging $7462). *Average percent of need met:* 35%. *Average financial aid package:* $4080. *Average need-based loan:* $6722. *Average need-based gift aid:* $4800. *Average indebtedness upon graduation:* $34,750.

Applying *Options:* deferred entrance. *Application fee:* $25. *Required:* essay or personal statement, high school transcript, 2 letters of recommendation, interview, resume. *Application deadlines:* rolling (freshmen), rolling (transfers).

Freshman Application Contact Sojourner-Douglass College, 500 North Caroline Street, Baltimore, MD 21205-1814. *Phone:* 410-276-0306 Ext. 251. *Web site:* http://sdc.edu/.

Stevenson University

Stevenson, Maryland

- **Independent** comprehensive, founded 1952
- **Suburban** 168-acre campus with easy access to Baltimore
- **Endowment** $44.8 million
- **Coed** 3,872 undergraduate students, 83% full-time, 65% women, 35% men
- **Moderately difficult** entrance level, 58% of applicants were admitted

Undergraduates 3,201 full-time, 671 part-time. 12% are from out of state; 26% Black or African American, non-Hispanic/Latino; 3% Hispanic/Latino; 3% Asian, non-Hispanic/Latino; 0.3% Native Hawaiian or other Pacific Islander, non-Hispanic/Latino; 0.4% American Indian or Alaska Native, non-Hispanic/Latino; 0.3% Two or more races, non-Hispanic/Latino; 4% Race/ethnicity unknown; 0.5% international; 7% transferred in; 46% live on campus. *Retention:* 75% of full-time freshmen returned.

Freshmen *Admission:* 5,794 applied, 3,369 admitted, 868 enrolled. *Average high school GPA:* 3.28. *Test scores:* SAT critical reading scores over 500: 46%; SAT math scores over 500: 50%; SAT writing scores over 500: 43%; ACT scores over 18: 68%; SAT critical reading scores over 600: 10%; SAT

math scores over 600: 14%; SAT writing scores over 600: 10%; ACT scores over 24: 12%; SAT critical reading scores over 700: 2%; SAT math scores over 700: 1%; SAT writing scores over 700: 1%; ACT scores over 30: 1%.

Faculty *Total:* 448, 26% full-time. *Student/faculty ratio:* 16:1.

Academics *Calendar:* semesters. *Degrees:* bachelor's and master's. *Special study options:* academic remediation for entering students, accelerated degree program, adult/continuing education programs, advanced placement credit, cooperative education, distance learning, double majors, honors programs, independent study, internships, off-campus study, part-time degree program, services for LD students, student-designed majors, study abroad, summer session for credit. *ROTC:* Army (c), Air Force (c).

Computers on Campus 300 computers/terminals and 1,000 ports are available on campus for general student use. Students can access the following: campus intranet, computer help desk, free student e-mail accounts, online (class) grades, online (class) registration, online (class) schedules. Campuswide network is available. 100% of college-owned or -operated housing units are wired for high-speed Internet access. Wireless service is available via entire campus.

Student Life *Housing options:* coed, men-only, women-only, cooperative, disabled students. Campus housing is university owned. Freshman applicants given priority for college housing. *Activities and organizations:* drama/theater group, student-run newspaper, radio station, choral group, marching band, Student Government Association, MAP, Black Student Union, National Student Nurses Association, Phi Sigma, national sororities. *Campus security:* 24-hour emergency response devices and patrols, late-night transport/escort service, controlled dormitory access, patrols by trained security personnel during campus hours. *Student services:* health clinic, personal/psychological counseling.

Athletics Member NCAA. All Division III. *Intercollegiate sports:* baseball M, basketball M/W, cheerleading M/W, cross-country running M/W, field hockey W, football M, golf M/W, ice hockey W, lacrosse M/W, soccer M/W, softball W, tennis M/W, track and field M/W, volleyball M/W. *Intramural sports:* badminton M/W, baseball M, basketball M/W, fencing M(c)/W(c), field hockey W, football M/W, sailing M(c)/W(c), skiing (cross-country) M/W(c), skiing (downhill) M/W, softball W, table tennis M/W, tennis M/W, volleyball M.

Standardized Tests *Required:* SAT or ACT (for admission).

Costs (2011–12) *Comprehensive fee:* $35,058 includes full-time tuition ($22,020), mandatory fees ($1616), and room and board ($11,422). Full-time tuition and fees vary according to degree level. Part-time tuition: $557 per credit hour. Part-time tuition and fees vary according to course load and degree level. *Required fees:* $75 per term part-time. *College room only:* $7514.

Room and board charges vary according to board plan and housing facility. *Payment plans:* installment, deferred payment. *Waivers:* employees or children of employees.

Financial Aid Of all full-time matriculated undergraduates who enrolled in 2009, 2,097 applied for aid, 1,806 were judged to have need, 530 had their need fully met. 225 Federal Work-Study jobs (averaging $2000). In 2009, 555 non-need-based awards were made. *Average percent of need met:* 63%. *Average financial aid package:* $14,124. *Average need-based loan:* $4095. *Average need-based gift aid:* $10,967. *Average non-need-based aid:* $6920. *Average indebtedness upon graduation:* $20,779.

Applying *Options:* electronic application, early admission, deferred entrance. *Application fee:* $40. *Required:* essay or personal statement, high school transcript, 2 letters of recommendation. *Recommended:* interview. *Application deadlines:* rolling (freshmen), rolling (transfers). *Notification:* continuous (freshmen), continuous (transfers).

Freshman Application Contact Mr. Mark Hergan, Vice President, Enrollment Management, Stevenson University, 1525 Greenspring Valley Road, Stevenson, MD 21153. *Phone:* 410-486-7001. *Toll-free phone:* 877-468-6852 (in-state); 877-468-3852 (out-of-state). *Fax:* 410-352-4440. *E-mail:* admissions@stevenson.edu. *Web site:* http://www.stevenson.edu/.

See below for display ad and page 1624 for the College Close-Up.

Stratford University
Baltimore, Maryland

Freshman Application Contact Director of Admissions, Stratford University, Commerce Exchange, 17 Commerce Street, Baltimore, MD 21202-3230. *Phone:* 410-752-4710 Ext. 120. *Toll-free phone:* 800-624-9926 (in-state); 800-624-9926 Ext. 120 (out-of-state). *Fax:* 410-752-3730. *E-mail:* admissions@bic.edu. *Web site:* http://www.stratford.edu/.

Strayer University - Anne Arundel Campus
Millersville, Maryland

- **Proprietary** comprehensive
- **Coed**

Academics *Degrees:* certificates, diplomas, associate, bachelor's, master's, and postbachelor's certificates.

Freshman Application Contact Strayer University - Anne Arundel Campus, 1520 Jabez Run, Millersville, MD 21108. *Web site:* http://www.strayer.edu/anne_arundel.

Strayer University - Owings Mills Campus

Owings Mills, Maryland

- **Proprietary** comprehensive
- **Coed**

Academics *Degrees:* certificates, diplomas, associate, bachelor's, master's, and postbachelor's certificates.

Freshman Application Contact Strayer University - Owings Mills Campus, 500 Redland Court, Suite 100, Owings Mills, MD 21117. *Web site:* http://www.strayer.edu/owings_mills.

Strayer University - Prince George's Campus

Suitland, Maryland

- **Proprietary** comprehensive
- **Coed**

Academics *Degrees:* certificates, diplomas, associate, bachelor's, master's, and postbachelor's certificates.

Freshman Application Contact Strayer University - Prince George's Campus, 4710 Auth Place, First Floor, Suitland, MD 20746. *Web site:* http://www.strayer.edu/prince_georges.

Strayer University - Rockville Campus

Rockville, Maryland

- **Proprietary** comprehensive
- **Coed**

Academics *Degrees:* certificates, diplomas, associate, bachelor's, master's, and postbachelor's certificates.

Freshman Application Contact Strayer University - Rockville Campus, 4 Research Place, Suite 100, Rockville, MD 20850. *Web site:* http://www.strayer.edu/rockville.

Strayer University - White Marsh Campus

Baltimore, Maryland

- **Proprietary** comprehensive, founded 1892
- **Coed**

Academics *Degrees:* certificates, diplomas, associate, bachelor's, master's, and postbachelor's certificates.

Freshman Application Contact Strayer University - White Marsh Campus, 9920 Franklin Square Drive, Suite 200, Baltimore, MD 21236. *Web site:* http://www.strayer.edu/white_marsh.

Towson University

Towson, Maryland

- **State-supported** university, founded 1866, part of University System of Maryland
- **Suburban** 321-acre campus with easy access to Baltimore and Washington, D.C.
- **Endowment** $4.4 million
- **Coed** 17,517 undergraduate students, 89% full-time, 60% women, 40% men
- **Moderately difficult** entrance level, 54% of applicants were admitted

Undergraduates 15,590 full-time, 1,927 part-time. Students come from 46 states and territories; 61 other countries; 20% are from out of state; 13% Black or African American, non-Hispanic/Latino; 4% Hispanic/Latino; 4% Asian, non-Hispanic/Latino; 0.1% Native Hawaiian or other Pacific Islander, non-Hispanic/Latino; 0.3% American Indian or Alaska Native, non-Hispanic/Latino; 2% Two or more races, non-Hispanic/Latino; 5% Race/ethnicity unknown; 2% international; 11% transferred in; 27% live on campus. *Retention:* 84% of full-time freshmen returned.

Freshmen *Admission:* 15,880 applied, 8,610 admitted, 2,543 enrolled. *Average high school GPA:* 3.62. *Test scores:* SAT critical reading scores over 500: 74%; SAT math scores over 500: 77%; SAT writing scores over 500: 79%; ACT scores over 18: 99%; SAT critical reading scores over 600: 20%; SAT math scores over 600: 24%; SAT writing scores over 600: 23%; ACT scores over 24: 45%; SAT critical reading scores over 700: 1%; SAT math scores over 700: 2%; SAT writing scores over 700: 2%; ACT scores over 30: 1%.

Faculty *Total:* 1,671, 50% full-time, 50% with terminal degrees. *Student/faculty ratio:* 17:1.

Academics *Calendar:* semesters. *Degrees:* bachelor's, master's, doctoral, post-master's, postbachelor's, and first professional certificates. *Special study options:* academic remediation for entering students, accelerated degree program, adult/continuing education programs, advanced placement credit, cooperative education, distance learning, double majors, English as a second language, freshman honors college, honors programs, independent study, internships, off-campus study, part-time degree program, services for LD students, student-designed majors, study abroad, summer session for credit. *ROTC:* Army (c), Air Force (c). *Unusual degree programs:* 3-2 engineering with University of Maryland College Park; law with University of Baltimore.

Computers on Campus 1,200 computers/terminals are available on campus for general student use. Students can access the following: computer help desk, free student e-mail accounts, online (class) grades, online (class) registration, online (class) schedules. Campuswide network is available. 100% of college-owned or -operated housing units are wired for high-speed Internet access. Wireless service is available via entire campus.

Student Life *Housing options:* coed, disabled students. Campus housing is university owned and is provided by a third party. Freshman campus housing is guaranteed. *Activities and organizations:* drama/theater group, student-run newspaper, radio and television station, choral group, marching band, University Residence Government, Queer Student Union, Black Student Union, Hillel, African Diaspora Club, national fraternities, national sororities. *Campus security:* 24-hour emergency response devices and patrols, late-night transport/escort service, controlled dormitory access. *Student services:* health clinic, personal/psychological counseling, women's center.

Athletics Member NCAA. All Division I except football (Division I-AA). *Intercollegiate sports:* baseball M(s), basketball M(s)/W(s), cheerleading W, cross-country running W(s), field hockey W(s), golf M(s)/W(s), gymnastics W(s), lacrosse M(s)/W(s), soccer M(s)/W(s), softball W(s), swimming and diving M(s)/W(s), tennis W(s), track and field W(s), volleyball W(s). *Intramural sports:* badminton M(c)/W(c), baseball M(c), basketball M(c)/W(c), equestrian sports M(c)/W(c), field hockey W(c), football M/W, golf M(c), ice hockey M, lacrosse M/W(c), rock climbing M(c)/W(c), rugby M(c)/W(c), sailing M(c)/W(c), skiing (downhill) M(c)/W(c), soccer M(c)/W(c), softball M(c)/W(c), swimming and diving M(c)/W(c), tennis M(c)/W(c), track and field M(c)/W(c), ultimate Frisbee M(c)/W(c), volleyball M(c)/W(c), water polo M(c)/W(c), wrestling M(c)/W(c).

Standardized Tests *Required:* SAT or ACT (for admission).

Costs (2011–12) *Tuition:* state resident $5496 full-time, $239 per credit part-time; nonresident $17,008 full-time, $709 per credit part-time. Full-time tuition and fees vary according to course load. No tuition increase for student's term of enrollment. *Required fees:* $2410 full-time, $99 per credit part-time. *Room and board:* $9942; room only: $5684. Room and board charges vary according to board plan and housing facility. *Payment plans:* tuition prepayment, installment. *Waivers:* senior citizens and employees or children of employees.

Financial Aid Of all full-time matriculated undergraduates who enrolled in 2011, 10,937 applied for aid, 8,239 were judged to have need, 1,117 had their need fully met. 537 Federal Work-Study jobs (averaging $1676). 1,344 state and other part-time jobs (averaging $2465). In 2011, 999 non-need-based awards were made. *Average percent of need met:* 63%. *Average financial aid package:* $9180. *Average need-based loan:* $4089. *Average need-based gift aid:* $7750. *Average non-need-based aid:* $4687. *Average indebtedness upon graduation:* $22,072.

Applying *Options:* electronic application, early admission, deferred entrance. *Application fee:* $45. *Required:* high school transcript. *Required for some:* essay or personal statement, interview. *Recommended:* minimum 3.0 GPA, 2 letters of recommendation. *Application deadlines:* 2/15 (freshmen), 2/15 (transfers). *Notification:* continuous (freshmen), continuous (transfers).

Freshman Application Contact Mr. Brian Hazlett, Director of Admissions, Towson University, 8000 York Road, Towson, MD 21252. *Phone:* 410-704-2113. *Fax:* 410-704-3030. *E-mail:* admissions@towson.edu. *Web site:* http://www.towson.edu/.

United States Naval Academy
Annapolis, Maryland

- **Federally supported** 4-year, founded 1845
- **Small-town** 338-acre campus with easy access to Baltimore and Washington, D.C.
- **Coed, primarily men** 4,576 undergraduate students, 100% full-time, 20% women, 80% men
- **Very difficult** entrance level, 6% of applicants were admitted

Undergraduates 4,576 full-time. Students come from 54 states and territories; 26 other countries; 93% are from out of state; 6% Black or African American, non-Hispanic/Latino; 12% Hispanic/Latino; 5% Asian, non-Hispanic/Latino; 0.7% Native Hawaiian or other Pacific Islander, non-Hispanic/Latino; 0.3% American Indian or Alaska Native, non-Hispanic/Latino; 7% Two or more races, non-Hispanic/Latino; 0.9% Race/ethnicity unknown; 1% international; 100% live on campus. *Retention:* 95% of full-time freshmen returned.
Freshmen *Admission:* 19,145 applied, 1,229 admitted, 1,194 enrolled. *Test scores:* SAT critical reading scores over 500: 93%; SAT math scores over 500: 98%; SAT critical reading scores over 600: 61%; SAT math scores over 600: 79%; SAT critical reading scores over 700: 18%; SAT math scores over 700: 28%.
Faculty *Total:* 528, 91% full-time, 68% with terminal degrees. *Student/faculty ratio:* 10:1.
Academics *Calendar:* semesters. *Degree:* bachelor's. *Special study options:* academic remediation for entering students, advanced placement credit, double majors, honors programs, independent study, off-campus study, study abroad, summer session for credit.
Computers on Campus 6,100 computers/terminals and 8,000 ports are available on campus for general student use. Students can access the following: campus intranet, computer help desk, free student e-mail accounts, online (class) grades, online (class) registration, online (class) schedules. Campus-wide network is available. 100% of college-owned or -operated housing units are wired for high-speed Internet access. Wireless service is available via classrooms, computer labs, libraries.
Student Life *Housing:* on-campus residence required through senior year. *Options:* coed. Campus housing is university owned. Freshman campus housing is guaranteed. *Activities and organizations:* drama/theater group, student-run radio station, choral group, marching band, Mountaineering Club, Semper Fi, Black Studies Club, Midshipmen Action Club, Martial Arts Club. *Campus security:* 24-hour emergency response devices and patrols, campus gate security. *Student services:* health clinic, personal/psychological counseling, legal services.
Athletics Member NCAA. All Division I except football (Division I-A). *Intercollegiate sports:* baseball M, basketball M/W, cheerleading M(c)/W(c), crew M/W, cross-country running M/W, fencing M(c)/W(c), field hockey W(c), golf M, gymnastics M/W(c), ice hockey M(c)/W(c), lacrosse M/W, riflery M/W, rugby M(c)/W(c), sailing M/W, skiing (downhill) M(c)/W(c), soccer M/W, softball W(c), squash M, swimming and diving M/W, tennis M/W, track and field M/W, volleyball M(c)/W, water polo M, weight lifting M(c)/W(c), wrestling M. *Intramural sports:* basketball M/W, cross-country running M/W, football M/W, lacrosse M(c)/W(c), racquetball M/W, sailing M/W, soccer M/W, softball M/W, volleyball M/W, weight lifting M/W.
Standardized Tests *Required:* SAT or ACT (for admission).
Costs (2012–13) *Comprehensive fee:* Tuition, room and board, and medical and dental care are provided by the U.S. government. Each midshipman receives a salary from which to pay for uniforms, books, supplies, and personal expenses.
Applying *Options:* electronic application, early action. *Required:* essay or personal statement, high school transcript, 2 letters of recommendation, interview, age 17-22, medical exam, authorized nomination, candidate fitness test. *Application deadline:* 1/31 (freshmen). *Notification:* continuous until 4/15 (freshmen).
Freshman Application Contact Capt. Angela Cyrus, Director of Admissions, United States Naval Academy, 117 Decatur Road, Annapolis, MD 21402. *Phone:* 410-293-4361. *Fax:* 410-293-4348. *E-mail:* webmail@usna.edu. *Web site:* http://www.usna.edu/.

University of Baltimore
Baltimore, Maryland

- **State-supported** comprehensive, founded 1925, part of University System of Maryland
- **Urban** 49-acre campus
- **Coed**
- **Minimally difficult** entrance level

Faculty *Student/faculty ratio:* 19:1.
Academics *Calendar:* semesters. *Degrees:* bachelor's, master's, doctoral, postbachelor's, and first professional certificates.

Student Life *Campus security:* 24-hour emergency response devices and patrols, late-night transport/escort service.
Standardized Tests *Required:* SAT or ACT (for admission).
Financial Aid *Of all full-time matriculated undergraduates who enrolled in 2007,* 1,036 applied for aid, 912 were judged to have need, 113 had their need fully met. 93 Federal Work-Study jobs (averaging $4801). 48 state and other part-time jobs (averaging $6727). *In 2007,* 86 non-need-based awards were made. *Average percent of need met:* 55. *Average financial aid package:* $9919. *Average need-based loan:* $4326. *Average need-based gift aid:* $2206. *Average non-need-based aid:* $4148.
Applying *Options:* electronic application, deferred entrance. *Application fee:* $30. *Required:* essay or personal statement, high school transcript. *Recommended:* minimum 3.0 GPA, 2 letters of recommendation, interview.
Freshman Application Contact Ms. Brigid H. Lawler, Director, Freshman Admission, University of Baltimore, 1420 North Charles Street, Baltimore, MD 21201. *Phone:* 410-837-4777. *Fax:* 410-837-4793. *E-mail:* admissions@ubalt.edu. *Web site:* http://www.ubalt.edu/.

University of Maryland, Baltimore County
Baltimore, Maryland

- **State-supported** university, founded 1963, part of University System of Maryland
- **Suburban** 530-acre campus with easy access to Washington, D.C.
- **Endowment** $48.9 million
- **Coed** 10,573 undergraduate students, 86% full-time, 45% women, 55% men
- **Moderately difficult** entrance level, 61% of applicants were admitted

Undergraduates 9,051 full-time, 1,522 part-time. Students come from 49 states and territories; 84 other countries; 6% are from out of state; 16% Black or African American, non-Hispanic/Latino; 5% Hispanic/Latino; 21% Asian, non-Hispanic/Latino; 0.4% Native Hawaiian or other Pacific Islander, non-Hispanic/Latino; 0.3% American Indian or Alaska Native, non-Hispanic/Latino; 3% Two or more races, non-Hispanic/Latino; 2% Race/ethnicity unknown; 4% international; 12% transferred in; 35% live on campus. *Retention:* 85% of full-time freshmen returned.
Freshmen *Admission:* 8,099 applied, 4,925 admitted, 1,425 enrolled. *Average high school GPA:* 3.58. *Test scores:* SAT critical reading scores over 500: 91%; SAT math scores over 500: 95%; SAT writing scores over 500: 88%; ACT scores over 18: 96%; SAT critical reading scores over 600: 46%; SAT math scores over 600: 63%; SAT writing scores over 600: 42%; ACT scores over 24: 79%; SAT critical reading scores over 700: 9%; SAT math scores over 700: 14%; SAT writing scores over 700: 9%; ACT scores over 30: 21%.
Faculty *Total:* 740, 65% full-time, 65% with terminal degrees. *Student/faculty ratio:* 20:1.
Academics *Calendar:* 4-1-4. *Degrees:* bachelor's, master's, doctoral, post-bachelor's, and first professional certificates. *Special study options:* academic remediation for entering students, adult/continuing education programs, advanced placement credit, cooperative education, distance learning, double majors, English as a second language, external degree program, freshman honors college, honors programs, independent study, internships, off-campus study, part-time degree program, services for LD students, student-designed majors, study abroad, summer session for credit. *ROTC:* Army (c), Air Force (c).
Computers on Campus 875 computers/terminals are available on campus for general student use. Students can access the following: campus intranet, computer help desk, free student e-mail accounts, online (class) grades, online (class) registration, online (class) schedules, student account information. Campuswide network is available. 100% of college-owned or -operated housing units are wired for high-speed Internet access. Wireless service is available via classrooms, computer centers, computer labs, libraries, student centers.
Student Life *Housing options:* coed, disabled students. Campus housing is university owned and is provided by a third party. Freshman campus housing is guaranteed. *Activities and organizations:* drama/theater group, student-run newspaper, radio station, choral group, Student Government Association, Student Events Board, Filipino American Student Association, Resident Student Association, Humans Versus Zombies, national fraternities, national sororities. *Campus security:* 24-hour emergency response devices and patrols, late-night transport/escort service. *Student services:* health clinic, personal/psychological counseling, women's center, legal services.
Athletics Member NCAA. All Division I. *Intercollegiate sports:* badminton M(c)/W(c), baseball M(s), basketball M(s)/W(s), bowling M(c)/W(c), crew M(c)/W(c), cross-country running M(s)/W(s), fencing M(c)/W(c), field hockey W(c), ice hockey M(c), lacrosse M(s)/W(s), rugby M(c)/W(c), sailing M(c)/W(c), skiing (downhill) M(c)/W(c), soccer M(s)/W(s), softball W(s), swimming and diving M(s)/W(s), tennis M(s)/W(s), track and field M(s)/W(s), ulti-

mate Frisbee M(c)/W(c), volleyball M(c)/W(s), wrestling M(c). *Intramural sports:* basketball M/W, football M/W, lacrosse M(c)/W(c), soccer M(c)/W(c), softball M/W, tennis M(c)/W(c), volleyball M/W(c).

Standardized Tests *Required:* SAT or ACT (for admission).

Costs (2011–12) *One-time required fee:* $125. *Tuition:* state resident $6879 full-time, $278 per credit hour part-time; nonresident $17,282 full-time, $691 per credit hour part-time. Full-time tuition and fees vary according to location and program. Part-time tuition and fees vary according to location and program. *Required fees:* $2588 full-time, $111 per credit hour part-time. *Room and board:* $9937; room only: $6065. Room and board charges vary according to board plan and housing facility. *Payment plan:* installment. *Waivers:* senior citizens and employees or children of employees.

Financial Aid Of all full-time matriculated undergraduates who enrolled in 2011, 5,842 applied for aid, 4,679 were judged to have need, 533 had their need fully met. 101 Federal Work-Study jobs (averaging $2133). In 2011, 1023 non-need-based awards were made. *Average percent of need met:* 56%. *Average financial aid package:* $10,282. *Average need-based loan:* $4204. *Average need-based gift aid:* $7226. *Average non-need-based aid:* $8399. *Average indebtedness upon graduation:* $20,921.

Applying *Options:* electronic application, early admission, early action, deferred entrance. *Application fee:* $50. *Required:* essay or personal statement, high school transcript. *Recommended:* minimum 3.0 GPA, 2 letters of recommendation. *Application deadlines:* 2/1 (freshmen), 5/31 (transfers), 11/1 (early action). *Notification:* continuous (freshmen), continuous (transfers), 12/15 (early action).

Freshman Application Contact Mr. Dale Bittinger, Director of Admissions, University of Maryland, Baltimore County, 1000 Hilltop Circle, Baltimore, MD 21250. *Phone:* 410-455-2291. *Toll-free phone:* 800-UMBC-4U2 (instate); 800-862-2402 (out-of-state). *Fax:* 410-455-1094. *E-mail:* admissions@umbc.edu. *Web site:* http://www.umbc.edu/.

University of Maryland, College Park
College Park, Maryland

- **State-supported** university, founded 1856, part of University System of Maryland
- **Suburban** 1500-acre campus with easy access to Baltimore and Washington, D.C.
- **Endowment** $382.8 million
- **Coed** 26,802 undergraduate students, 92% full-time, 47% women, 53% men
- **Moderately difficult** entrance level, 45% of applicants were admitted

Undergraduates 24,667 full-time, 2,135 part-time. Students come from 49 states and territories; 125 other countries; 23% are from out of state; 12% Black or African American, non-Hispanic/Latino; 8% Hispanic/Latino; 15% Asian, non-Hispanic/Latino; 0.1% Native Hawaiian or other Pacific Islander, non-Hispanic/Latino; 0.1% American Indian or Alaska Native, non-Hispanic/Latino; 3% Two or more races, non-Hispanic/Latino; 3% Race/ethnicity unknown; 3% international; 7% transferred in; 44% live on campus. *Retention:* 95% of full-time freshmen returned.

Freshmen *Admission:* 26,310 applied, 11,762 admitted, 3,992 enrolled. *Average high school GPA:* 4.01. *Test scores:* SAT critical reading scores over 500: 93%; SAT math scores over 500: 95%; SAT critical reading scores over 600: 69%; SAT math scores over 600: 79%; SAT critical reading scores over 700: 20%; SAT math scores over 700: 35%.

Faculty *Total:* 2,328, 72% full-time, 81% with terminal degrees. *Student/faculty ratio:* 18:1.

Academics *Calendar:* semesters. *Degrees:* certificates, bachelor's, master's, doctoral, post-master's, postbachelor's, and first professional certificates. *Special study options:* academic remediation for entering students, accelerated degree program, adult/continuing education programs, advanced placement credit, cooperative education, distance learning, double majors, English as a second language, external degree program, honors programs, independent study, internships, off-campus study, part-time degree program, services for LD students, student-designed majors, study abroad, summer session for credit. *ROTC:* Army (b), Navy (c), Air Force (b).

Computers on Campus 3,890 computers/terminals are available on campus for general student use. Students can access the following: campus intranet, computer help desk, free student e-mail accounts, online (class) grades, online (class) registration, online (class) schedules, student account information, financial aid summary. Campuswide network is available. 100% of college-owned or -operated housing units are wired for high-speed Internet access. Wireless service is available via entire campus.

Student Life *Housing options:* coed, women-only, cooperative, disabled students. Campus housing is university owned and is provided by a third party. Freshman campus housing is guaranteed. *Activities and organizations:* drama/theater group, student-run newspaper, radio and television station, choral group, marching band, Student Government Association, Residence Hall

Association, Black Student Union, Asian-American Student Union/Jewish Student Union, Commuter Students Association, national fraternities, national sororities. *Campus security:* 24-hour emergency response devices and patrols, student patrols, late-night transport/escort service, controlled dormitory access, campus police, video camera surveillance. *Student services:* health clinic, personal/psychological counseling, women's center, legal services.

Athletics Member NCAA. All Division I except football (Division I-A). *Intercollegiate sports:* baseball M(s), basketball M(s)/W(s), cheerleading W(s), cross-country running M/W(s), field hockey W(s), golf M(s)/W(s), gymnastics W, lacrosse M(s)/W(s), soccer M(s)/W(s), softball W(s), swimming and diving M/W, tennis M/W, track and field M/W(s), volleyball W(s), water polo W(s), wrestling M(s). *Intramural sports:* badminton M(c)/W(c), baseball M(c), basketball M/W, crew M(c)/W(c), cross-country running M/W, equestrian sports M(c)/W(c), fencing M(c)/W(c), field hockey W(c), football M/W, golf M/W, ice hockey M(c)/W(c), lacrosse M(c)/W(c), racquetball M(c)/W(c), rock climbing M(c)/W(c), rugby M(c)/W(c), sailing M(c)/W(c), soccer M(c)/W(c), softball W, squash M(c)/W(c), swimming and diving M(c)/W(c), table tennis M/W, tennis M/W, track and field M/W, ultimate Frisbee M/W, volleyball M(c)/W(c), water polo M(c)/W(c), weight lifting M/W, wrestling M.

Standardized Tests *Required:* SAT or ACT (for admission).

Costs (2011–12) *Tuition:* state resident $6966 full-time, $290 per credit hour part-time; nonresident $24,337 full-time, $1014 per credit hour part-time. Part-time tuition and fees vary according to course load. *Required fees:* $1689 full-time, $390 per term part-time. *Room and board:* $9677; room only: $5793. Room and board charges vary according to board plan. *Payment plans:* installment, deferred payment. *Waivers:* employees or children of employees.

Financial Aid Of all full-time matriculated undergraduates who enrolled in 2010, 14,695 applied for aid, 10,827 were judged to have need, 1,285 had their need fully met. 653 Federal Work-Study jobs (averaging $1408). In 2010, 2934 non-need-based awards were made. *Average percent of need met:* 58%. *Average financial aid package:* $10,333. *Average need-based loan:* $4559. *Average need-based gift aid:* $7432. *Average non-need-based aid:* $6416. *Average indebtedness upon graduation:* $24,180.

Applying *Options:* electronic application, early admission, early action, deferred entrance. *Application fee:* $65. *Required:* essay or personal statement, high school transcript. *Required for some:* Resume of activities; audition for music applicants; drawing requirement for architecture applicants. *Recommended:* 2 letters of recommendation. *Application deadlines:* 1/20 (freshmen), 6/1 (transfers), 11/1 (early action). *Notification:* 4/1 (freshmen), continuous (transfers), 1/31 (early action).

Freshman Application Contact Ms. Barbara Gill, Director of Undergraduate Admissions, University of Maryland, College Park, College Park, MD 20742. *Phone:* 301-314-8385. *Toll-free phone:* 800-422-5867. *Fax:* 301-314-9693. *Web site:* http://www.maryland.edu/.

University of Maryland Eastern Shore
Princess Anne, Maryland

- **State-supported** university, founded 1886, part of University System of Maryland
- **Rural** 744-acre campus
- **Coed** 3,862 undergraduate students, 92% full-time, 57% women, 43% men
- **Moderately difficult** entrance level, 50% of applicants were admitted

Undergraduates 3,536 full-time, 326 part-time. 21% are from out of state; 77% Black or African American, non-Hispanic/Latino; 2% Hispanic/Latino; 1% Asian, non-Hispanic/Latino; 0.1% Native Hawaiian or other Pacific Islander, non-Hispanic/Latino; 0.1% American Indian or Alaska Native, non-Hispanic/Latino; 4% Two or more races, non-Hispanic/Latino; 2% Race/ethnicity unknown; 3% international; 5% transferred in; 38% live on campus.

Freshmen *Admission:* 4,201 applied, 2,100 admitted, 756 enrolled. *Average high school GPA:* 2.84. *Test scores:* SAT critical reading scores over 500: 19%; SAT math scores over 500: 19%; SAT writing scores over 500: 15%; ACT scores over 18: 45%; SAT critical reading scores over 600: 2%; SAT math scores over 600: 3%; SAT writing scores over 600: 1%; ACT scores over 24: 7%; ACT scores over 30: 1%.

Faculty *Total:* 354, 58% full-time, 51% with terminal degrees. *Student/faculty ratio:* 17:1.

Academics *Calendar:* semesters. *Degrees:* certificates, bachelor's, master's, doctoral, and first professional. *Special study options:* part-time degree program. *ROTC:* Army (c).

Computers on Campus Students can access the following: computer help desk, free student e-mail accounts, online (class) grades, online (class) registration, online (class) schedules. Campuswide network is available. Wireless service is available via classrooms, computer centers, computer labs, learning centers, libraries, student centers.

Student Life *Housing options:* men-only, women-only, disabled students. Campus housing is university owned. *Campus security:* 24-hour emergency

response devices and patrols, student patrols, late-night transport/escort service, controlled dormitory access.

Athletics Member NCAA. All Division I. *Intercollegiate sports:* baseball M(s), basketball M(s)/W(s), cheerleading M/W, cross-country running M/W, softball W, tennis M(s)/W, track and field M/W, volleyball W, wrestling M. *Intramural sports:* basketball M/W, bowling W, cheerleading M/W, cross-country running M/W, soccer M/W, softball W, swimming and diving M/W, table tennis M/W, tennis M/W, track and field M/W, volleyball M/W, wrestling M.

Standardized Tests *Required:* SAT or ACT (for admission).

Costs (2012–13) *Tuition:* state resident $6482 full-time, $181 per credit hour part-time; nonresident $14,263 full-time, $447 per credit hour part-time. Full-time tuition and fees vary according to course load. Part-time tuition and fees vary according to course load. *Required fees:* $2120 full-time, $43 per term part-time. *Room and board:* $7758; room only: $4158. Room and board charges vary according to board plan and housing facility. *Payment plans:* installment, deferred payment. *Waivers:* senior citizens and employees or children of employees.

Financial Aid Of all full-time matriculated undergraduates who enrolled in 2010, 3,496 applied for aid, 2,983 were judged to have need, 1,130 had their need fully met. 84 Federal Work-Study jobs (averaging $3556). In 2010, 453 non-need-based awards were made. *Average percent of need met:* 75%. *Average financial aid package:* $14,069. *Average need-based gift aid:* $7110. *Average non-need-based aid:* $7816. *Average indebtedness upon graduation:* $8500.

Applying *Options:* electronic application, deferred entrance. *Application fee:* $25. *Required:* essay or personal statement, high school transcript, minimum 2.5 GPA, 3 letters of recommendation. *Required for some:* essay or personal statement, interview. *Application deadlines:* 7/15 (freshmen), 5/1 (transfers). **Freshman Application Contact** University of Maryland Eastern Shore, Princess Anne, MD 21853-1299. *Phone:* 410-651-6410. *Web site:* http://www.umes.edu/.

University of Maryland University College

Adelphi, Maryland

- **State-supported** comprehensive, founded 1947, part of University System of Maryland
- **Suburban** campus with easy access to Washington, D.C.
- **Coed** 28,119 undergraduate students, 20% full-time, 53% women, 47% men
- **Noncompetitive** entrance level, 100% of applicants were admitted

Undergraduates 5,653 full-time, 22,466 part-time. Students come from 50 states and territories; 28 other countries; 41% are from out of state; 33% Black or African American, non-Hispanic/Latino; 8% Hispanic/Latino; 4% Asian, non-Hispanic/Latino; 0.3% Native Hawaiian or other Pacific Islander, non-Hispanic/Latino; 0.5% American Indian or Alaska Native, non-Hispanic/Latino; 2% Two or more races, non-Hispanic/Latino; 10% Race/ethnicity unknown; 1% international; 15% transferred in.

Freshmen *Admission:* 2,603 applied, 2,603 admitted, 1,197 enrolled.

Faculty *Total:* 2,402, 9% full-time, 66% with terminal degrees. *Student/faculty ratio:* 19:1.

Academics *Calendar:* semesters. *Degrees:* certificates, associate, bachelor's, master's, doctoral, post-master's, and postbachelor's certificates (offers primarily part-time evening and weekend degree programs at more than 30 off-campus locations in Maryland and the Washington, DC area, and more than 180 military communities in Europe and Asia with military enrollment not reflected in this profile; associate of arts program available to military students only). *Special study options:* accelerated degree program, advanced placement credit, cooperative education, distance learning, double majors, external degree program, independent study, off-campus study, part-time degree program, services for LD students, summer session for credit.

Computers on Campus 280 computers/terminals are available on campus for general student use. Students can access the following: computer help desk, online (class) grades, online (class) registration, online (class) schedules. Campuswide network is available. Wireless service is available via entire campus.

Student Life *Housing:* college housing not available. *Campus security:* 24-hour emergency response devices and patrols, late-night transport/escort service.

Costs (2011–12) *Tuition:* state resident $5856 full-time, $244 per credit hour part-time; nonresident $11,976 full-time, $499 per credit hour part-time. *Required fees:* $312 full-time, $13 per credit hour part-time. *Payment plan:* installment. *Waivers:* senior citizens and employees or children of employees.

Financial Aid Of all full-time matriculated undergraduates who enrolled in 2009, 2,303 applied for aid, 2,180 were judged to have need, 20 had their need fully met. *Average percent of need met:* 28%. *Average financial aid package:* $7206. *Average need-based loan:* $4269. *Average need-based gift aid:* $4578.

Applying *Options:* electronic application, deferred entrance. *Application fee:* $50. *Required:* high school transcript. *Application deadlines:* rolling (freshmen), rolling (transfers). *Notification:* continuous (freshmen), continuous (transfers).

Freshman Application Contact University of Maryland University College, 3501 University Boulevard East, Adelphi, MD 20783. *Phone:* 800-888-UMUC (8682). *Toll-free phone:* 800-888-8682. *E-mail:* enroll@umuc.edu. *Web site:* http://www.umuc.edu/.

University of Phoenix–Maryland Campus

Columbia, Maryland

Freshman Application Contact Marc Booker, Sr. Director, Office of Admissions and Evaluation, University of Phoenix–Maryland Campus, 4035 South Riverpoint Parkway, Mail Stop CF-L101, Phoenix, AZ 85040. *Phone:* 602-557-4609. *Toll-free phone:* 866-766-0766. *Fax:* 480-643-1156. *Web site:* http://www.phoenix.edu/.

Washington Adventist University

Takoma Park, Maryland

- **Independent Seventh-day Adventist** comprehensive, founded 1904
- **Suburban** campus
- **Coed** 1,327 undergraduate students, 80% full-time, 68% women, 32% men
- **Moderately difficult** entrance level

Undergraduates 1,058 full-time, 269 part-time. 34% are from out of state; 60% Black or African American, non-Hispanic/Latino; 10% Hispanic/Latino; 7% Asian, non-Hispanic/Latino; 0.5% American Indian or Alaska Native, non-Hispanic/Latino; 0.6% Two or more races, non-Hispanic/Latino; 13% Race/ethnicity unknown. *Retention:* 69% of full-time freshmen returned.

Freshmen *Admission:* 164 enrolled.

Faculty *Total:* 134, 39% full-time, 19% with terminal degrees. *Student/faculty ratio:* 14:1.

Academics *Calendar:* semesters. *Degrees:* certificates, associate, bachelor's, and master's. *Special study options:* adult/continuing education programs, external degree program, part-time degree program.

Computers on Campus Students can access the following: campus intranet, free student e-mail accounts, online (class) grades. Campuswide network is available. Wireless service is available via entire campus.

Student Life *Housing options:* men-only, women-only. Campus housing is university owned. Freshman campus housing is guaranteed. *Campus security:* 24-hour emergency response devices and patrols, late-night transport/escort service.

Athletics Member NCAA. All Division II. *Intercollegiate sports:* baseball M(s), basketball M(s)/W(s), cross-country running M(s)/W(s), soccer M(s)/W(s), softball W(s), track and field M(s)/W(s). *Intramural sports:* basketball M/W, cross-country running M/W, football M, golf M, gymnastics M/W, racquetball M/W, soccer M/W, track and field M/W.

Standardized Tests *Required:* SAT or ACT (for admission).

Costs (2011–12) *Comprehensive fee:* $27,780 includes full-time tuition ($18,900), mandatory fees ($1280), and room and board ($7600). Part-time tuition: $760 per credit hour. Part-time tuition and fees vary according to class time and course load. *Required fees:* $433 per term part-time. *Room and board:* Room and board charges vary according to housing facility. *Payment plan:* installment. *Waivers:* senior citizens and employees or children of employees.

Financial Aid Of all full-time matriculated undergraduates who enrolled in 2009, 883 applied for aid, 702 were judged to have need.

Applying *Options:* electronic application, early admission, deferred entrance. *Application fee:* $25. *Required:* essay or personal statement, high school transcript, minimum 2.5 GPA, 2 letters of recommendation. *Required for some:* interview. *Application deadlines:* 8/1 (freshmen), 8/1 (transfers). *Notification:* continuous (freshmen), continuous (transfers).

Freshman Application Contact Elaine Oliver, Associate Vice President, Enrollment Services, Washington Adventist University, 7600 Flower Avenue, Takoma Park, MD 20912. *Phone:* 301-891-4502. *Toll-free phone:* 800-835-4212. *Fax:* 301-971-4230. *E-mail:* enroll@cuc.edu. *Web site:* http://www.wau.edu/.

Washington Bible College

Lanham, Maryland

Freshman Application Contact Mr. Mark D. Johnson, Director of Admissions, Washington Bible College, 6511 Princess Garden Parkway, Lanham, MD 20706-3599. *Phone:* 877-793-7227. *Toll-free phone:* 877-793-

7227 Ext. 1212. *Fax:* 301-552-2775. *E-mail:* admissions@bible.edu. *Web site:* http://www.bible.edu/.

Washington College
Chestertown, Maryland

- **Independent** comprehensive, founded 1782
- **Small-town** 140-acre campus with easy access to Baltimore and Washington, D.C.
- **Endowment** $173.0 million
- **Coed** 1,515 undergraduate students, 97% full-time, 58% women, 42% men
- **Moderately difficult** entrance level, 57% of applicants were admitted

Undergraduates 1,473 full-time, 42 part-time. Students come from 37 states and territories; 19 other countries; 49% are from out of state; 4% Black or African American, non-Hispanic/Latino; 3% Hispanic/Latino; 2% Asian, non-Hispanic/Latino; 0.1% Native Hawaiian or other Pacific Islander, non-Hispanic/Latino; 0.2% American Indian or Alaska Native, non-Hispanic/Latino; 0.9% Two or more races, non-Hispanic/Latino; 4% Race/ethnicity unknown; 0.8% international; 3% transferred in; 86% live on campus. *Retention:* 82% of full-time freshmen returned.

Freshmen *Admission:* 4,799 applied, 2,715 admitted, 399 enrolled. *Average high school GPA:* 3.56. *Test scores:* SAT critical reading scores over 500: 93%; SAT math scores over 500: 91%; SAT writing scores over 500: 84%; ACT scores over 18: 100%; SAT critical reading scores over 600: 41%; SAT math scores over 600: 35%; SAT writing scores over 600: 37%; ACT scores over 24: 55%; SAT critical reading scores over 700: 7%; SAT math scores over 700: 4%; SAT writing scores over 700: 7%; ACT scores over 30: 4%.

Faculty *Total:* 166, 60% full-time, 70% with terminal degrees. *Student/faculty ratio:* 12:1.

Academics *Calendar:* semesters. *Degrees:* bachelor's and master's. *Special study options:* advanced placement credit, double majors, English as a second language, honors programs, independent study, internships, off-campus study, part-time degree program, services for LD students, student-designed majors, study abroad. *Unusual degree programs:* 3-2 engineering with University of Maryland, College Park; nursing with Johns Hopkins University.

Computers on Campus 100 computers/terminals and 225 ports are available on campus for general student use. Students can access the following: campus intranet, computer help desk, free student e-mail accounts, online (class) grades, online (class) registration, online (class) schedules, thousands of wireless addresses available for students. Campuswide network is available. 100% of college-owned or -operated housing units are wired for high-speed Internet access. Wireless service is available via entire campus.

Student Life *Housing:* on-campus residence required through sophomore year. *Options:* coed, men-only, women-only, disabled students. Campus housing is university owned. Freshman campus housing is guaranteed. *Activities and organizations:* drama/theater group, student-run newspaper, radio station, choral group, Writers Union, Student Government Association, Hands Out, Omicron Delta Kappa, Dale Adams Society, national fraternities, national sororities. *Campus security:* 24-hour emergency response devices and patrols, student patrols, late-night transport/escort service, controlled dormitory access. *Student services:* health clinic, personal/psychological counseling.

Athletics Member NCAA. All Division III. *Intercollegiate sports:* baseball M, basketball M/W, cheerleading W(c), crew M/W, equestrian sports M(c)/W(c), field hockey W, ice hockey M(c), lacrosse M/W, rugby M(c)/W(c), sailing M/W, soccer M/W, softball W, swimming and diving M/W, tennis M/W, volleyball M/W, water polo M(c)/W(c). *Intramural sports:* basketball M/W, football M/W, lacrosse M(c), racquetball M/W, rugby M/W, sailing M/W, soccer M/W, squash M/W, table tennis M/W, tennis M/W, ultimate Frisbee M/W.

Standardized Tests *Required:* SAT or ACT (for admission).

Costs (2011–12) *Comprehensive fee:* $46,770 includes full-time tuition ($37,882), mandatory fees ($660), and room and board ($8228). Part-time tuition and fees vary according to course load. *College room only:* $4180. Room and board charges vary according to board plan, housing facility, and location. *Payment plan:* installment. *Waivers:* employees or children of employees.

Financial Aid Of all full-time matriculated undergraduates who enrolled in 2011, 1,040 applied for aid, 914 were judged to have need, 265 had their need fully met. In 2011, 358 non-need-based awards were made. *Average percent of need met:* 75%. *Average financial aid package:* $24,814. *Average need-based loan:* $3812. *Average need-based gift aid:* $21,015. *Average non-need-based aid:* $14,063. *Average indebtedness upon graduation:* $37,303.

Applying *Options:* electronic application, early admission, early decision, early action, deferred entrance. *Application fee:* $50. *Required:* essay or personal statement, high school transcript, 1 letter of recommendation. *Required for some:* interview. *Recommended:* interview. *Application deadlines:* rolling (freshmen), 12/1 (early action). *Early decision deadline:* 11/1. *Notification:* continuous (freshmen), 12/1 (early decision), 1/15 (early action).

Freshman Application Contact Mr. Kevin Coveney, Vice President for Admissions and Enrollment Management, Washington College, 300 Washington Avenue, Chesterton, MD 21620. *Phone:* 410-778-7700. *Toll-free phone:* 800-422-1782. *Fax:* 410-778-7287. *E-mail:* admissions_office@washcoll.edu. *Web site:* http://www.washcoll.edu/.

Yeshiva College of the Nation's Capital
Silver Spring, Maryland

Admissions Office Contact Yeshiva College of the Nation's Capital, 1216 Arcola Avenue, Silver Spring, MD 20902. *Web site:* http://www.yeshiva.edu/.

MASSACHUSETTS

American International College
Springfield, Massachusetts

Freshman Application Contact Miss Kim LaBlanc, Director of Freshman Admissions, American International College, 1000 State Street, Springfield, MA 01109-3189. *Phone:* 413-205-3275. *Toll-free phone:* 800-242-3142. *Fax:* 413-205-3051. *E-mail:* kim.lablanc@aic.edu. *Web site:* http://www.aic.edu/.

Amherst College
Amherst, Massachusetts

- **Independent** 4-year, founded 1821
- **Small-town** 1020-acre campus
- **Endowment** $1.6 billion
- **Coed** 1,795 undergraduate students, 100% full-time, 51% women, 49% men
- **Most difficult** entrance level, 13% of applicants were admitted

Undergraduates 1,795 full-time. Students come from 34 states and territories; 23 other countries; 89% are from out of state; 12% Black or African American, non-Hispanic/Latino; 12% Hispanic/Latino; 11% Asian, non-Hispanic/Latino; 7% Two or more races, non-Hispanic/Latino; 7% Race/ethnicity unknown; 9% international; 1% transferred in; 97% live on campus. *Retention:* 94% of full-time freshmen returned.

Freshmen *Admission:* 8,461 applied, 1,127 admitted, 490 enrolled. *Test scores:* SAT critical reading scores over 500: 100%; SAT math scores over 500: 100%; SAT writing scores over 500: 100%; ACT scores over 18: 100%; SAT critical reading scores over 600: 95%; SAT math scores over 600: 94%; SAT writing scores over 600: 93%; ACT scores over 24: 100%; SAT critical reading scores over 700: 64%; SAT math scores over 700: 63%; SAT writing scores over 700: 68%; ACT scores over 30: 77%.

Faculty *Total:* 236, 83% full-time, 98% with terminal degrees. *Student/faculty ratio:* 8:1.

Academics *Calendar:* semesters. *Degree:* bachelor's. *Special study options:* double majors, honors programs, independent study, off-campus study, student-designed majors, study abroad. *ROTC:* Army (c), Air Force (c).

Computers on Campus 182 computers/terminals are available on campus for general student use. Students can access the following: campus intranet, computer help desk, free student e-mail accounts, online (class) grades, online (class) schedules. Campuswide network is available. 100% of college-owned or -operated housing units are wired for high-speed Internet access. Wireless service is available via entire campus.

Student Life *Housing:* on-campus residence required for freshman year. *Options:* coed, cooperative, disabled students. Campus housing is university owned. Freshman campus housing is guaranteed. *Activities and organizations:* drama/theater group, student-run newspaper, radio station, choral group, choral groups, WAMH (campus radio station), OUTREACH (community service), literary magazines, The Amherst Student (school newspaper). *Campus security:* 24-hour emergency response devices and patrols, student patrols, late-night transport/escort service, controlled dormitory access. *Student services:* health clinic, personal/psychological counseling, women's center.

Athletics Member NCAA. All Division III. *Intercollegiate sports:* baseball M, basketball M/W, crew M(c)/W(c), cross-country running M/W, equestrian sports M(c)/W(c), fencing M(c)/W(c), field hockey W, football M, golf M/W, ice hockey M/W, lacrosse M/W, rugby M(c)/W(c), sailing M(c)/W(c), skiing (downhill) M(c)/W(c), soccer M/W, softball W, squash M/W, swimming and diving M/W, tennis M/W, track and field M/W, ultimate Frisbee M(c)/W(c), volleyball M(c)/W, water polo M(c)/W(c), wrestling M(c)/W(c). *Intramural sports:* badminton M/W, basketball M/W, golf M/W, ice hockey M/W, soccer

M/W, softball M/W, squash M/W, table tennis M/W, tennis M/W, track and field M/W, volleyball M/W.

Standardized Tests *Required:* SAT and SAT Subject Tests or ACT (for admission).

Costs (2011–12) *Comprehensive fee:* $54,074 includes full-time tuition ($42,172), mandatory fees ($702), and room and board ($11,200). *College room only:* $6070. *Payment plans:* installment, deferred payment.

Financial Aid Of all full-time matriculated undergraduates who enrolled in 2011, 1,120 applied for aid, 1,105 were judged to have need, 1,105 had their need fully met. 591 Federal Work-Study jobs (averaging $1684). 257 state and other part-time jobs (averaging $1650). *Average percent of need met:* 100%. *Average financial aid package:* $41,012. *Average need-based loan:* $571. *Average need-based gift aid:* $41,991. *Average indebtedness upon graduation:* $12,713.

Applying *Options:* electronic application, early admission, early decision, deferred entrance. *Application fee:* $60. *Required:* essay or personal statement, high school transcript, 3 letters of recommendation. *Application deadlines:* 1/1 (freshmen), 3/1 (transfers). *Early decision deadline:* 11/15. *Notification:* 4/5 (freshmen), 6/1 (transfers), 12/15 (early decision).

Freshman Application Contact Mr. Thomas H. Parker, Dean of Admission and Financial Aid, Amherst College, PO Box 5000, Amherst, MA 01002-5000. *Phone:* 413-542-2328. *Fax:* 413-542-2040. *E-mail:* admission@amherst.edu. *Web site:* http://www.amherst.edu/.

Anna Maria College
Paxton, Massachusetts

- **Independent Roman Catholic** comprehensive, founded 1946
- **Rural** 192-acre campus with easy access to Boston
- **Endowment** $4.7 million
- **Coed** 1,017 undergraduate students, 79% full-time, 51% women, 49% men
- **Minimally difficult** entrance level, 60% of applicants were admitted

Undergraduates 803 full-time, 214 part-time. Students come from 28 states and territories; 22% are from out of state; 8% Black or African American, non-Hispanic/Latino; 8% Hispanic/Latino; 1% Asian, non-Hispanic/Latino; 0.5% American Indian or Alaska Native, non-Hispanic/Latino; 1% Two or more races, non-Hispanic/Latino; 11% Race/ethnicity unknown; 4% transferred in; 46% live on campus.

Freshmen *Admission:* 2,394 applied, 1,445 admitted, 223 enrolled. *Average high school GPA:* 2.81. *Test scores:* SAT critical reading scores over 500: 21%; SAT math scores over 500: 33%; SAT writing scores over 500: 19%; SAT critical reading scores over 600: 2%; SAT math scores over 600: 5%; SAT writing scores over 600: 1%; SAT critical reading scores over 700: 1%; SAT math scores over 700: 1%; ACT scores over 30: 4%.

Faculty *Total:* 200, 24% full-time, 30% with terminal degrees. *Student/faculty ratio:* 12:1.

Academics *Calendar:* semesters. *Degrees:* certificates, associate, bachelor's, master's, post-master's, and postbachelor's certificates. *Special study options:* academic remediation for entering students, accelerated degree program, adult/continuing education programs, advanced placement credit, cooperative education, distance learning, double majors, honors programs, independent study, internships, off-campus study, part-time degree program, services for LD students, student-designed majors, study abroad, summer session for credit. *ROTC:* Air Force (c).

Computers on Campus 85 computers/terminals are available on campus for general student use. Students can access the following: campus intranet, computer help desk, free student e-mail accounts, online (class) grades, online (class) registration, online (class) schedules, student account information. Campuswide network is available. 100% of college-owned or -operated housing units are wired for high-speed Internet access. Wireless service is available via entire campus.

Student Life *Housing options:* coed, disabled students. Campus housing is university owned. Freshman campus housing is guaranteed. *Activities and organizations:* drama/theater group, choral group, marching band, Habitat for Humanity, Social Action Group, Chorus Club, Alana, Programming Board - AMCAB. *Campus security:* 24-hour emergency response devices and patrols, late-night transport/escort service, controlled dormitory access. *Student services:* health clinic, personal/psychological counseling.

Athletics Member NCAA. All Division III. *Intercollegiate sports:* baseball M, basketball M/W, cross-country running M, field hockey W, football M, golf M, lacrosse M/W, soccer M/W, softball W, tennis M/W, volleyball W. *Intramural sports:* basketball M/W, football M, soccer M/W, softball M/W, volleyball M/W.

Standardized Tests *Required:* SAT or ACT (for admission).

Costs (2012–13) *Comprehensive fee:* $41,861 includes full-time tuition ($28,752), mandatory fees ($1704), and room and board ($11,405). Full-time tuition and fees vary according to course load and program. Part-time tuition and fees vary according to class time, course load, and program. *Room and*

board: Room and board charges vary according to board plan and housing facility.

Financial Aid Of all full-time matriculated undergraduates who enrolled in 2009, 1,001 applied for aid, 932 were judged to have need, 106 had their need fully met. 215 Federal Work-Study jobs (averaging $454). In 2009, 59 non-need-based awards were made. *Average percent of need met:* 92%. *Average financial aid package:* $28,535. *Average need-based loan:* $4744. *Average need-based gift aid:* $5862. *Average non-need-based aid:* $7300. *Average indebtedness upon graduation:* $36,200.

Applying *Options:* electronic application, deferred entrance. *Application fee:* $40. *Required:* high school transcript, minimum 2.0 GPA. *Required for some:* essay or personal statement, audition for music programs, portfolio for art programs. *Recommended:* 1 letter of recommendation, interview. *Application deadlines:* rolling (freshmen), rolling (transfers). *Notification:* continuous (freshmen), continuous (transfers).

Freshman Application Contact Ms. Meghan McDonough, Director of Admissions, Anna Maria College, Box O, Sunset Lane, Paxton, MA 01612. *Phone:* 508-849-3586. *Fax:* 508-849-3362. *E-mail:* admissions@annamaria.edu. *Web site:* http://www.annamaria.edu/.

See page 395 for display ad and page 1056 for the College Close-Up.

The Art Institute of Boston at Lesley University
Boston, Massachusetts

- **Independent** comprehensive, founded 1912
- **Urban** 1-acre campus
- **Coed**
- **67%** of applicants were admitted

Faculty *Student/faculty ratio:* 10:1.

Academics *Calendar:* semesters. *Degrees:* associate, bachelor's, master's, doctoral, post-master's, postbachelor's, and first professional certificates.

Student Life *Campus security:* 24-hour emergency response devices and patrols, late-night transport/escort service, controlled dormitory access.

Athletics Member NCAA. All Division III.

Standardized Tests *Required:* SAT or ACT (for admission).

Costs (2011–12) *Comprehensive fee:* $42,000 includes full-time tuition ($28,000), mandatory fees ($750), and room and board ($13,250). Full-time tuition and fees vary according to class time, course level, course load, degree level, location, program, reciprocity agreements, and student level. *College room only:* $8150. Room and board charges vary according to housing facility.

Financial Aid Of all full-time matriculated undergraduates who enrolled in 2008, 1,070 applied for aid, 636 were judged to have need, 55 had their need fully met. 225 Federal Work-Study jobs (averaging $1800). 150 state and other part-time jobs (averaging $1500). In 2008, 234 non-need-based awards were made. *Average percent of need met:* 70. *Average financial aid package:* $15,652. *Average need-based loan:* $3636. *Average need-based gift aid:* $13,218. *Average non-need-based aid:* $8439. *Average indebtedness upon graduation:* $17,000.

Applying *Options:* electronic application, early action, deferred entrance. *Application fee:* $40. *Required:* essay or personal statement, high school transcript. *Recommended:* interview.

Freshman Application Contact The Art Institute of Boston at Lesley University, 700 Beacon Street, Boston, MA 02215-2598. *Phone:* 617-585-6710. *Toll-free phone:* 800-773-0494. *Web site:* http://www.aiboston.edu/.

Assumption College
Worcester, Massachusetts

- **Independent Roman Catholic** comprehensive, founded 1904
- **Suburban** 180-acre campus with easy access to Boston
- **Endowment** $82.7 million
- **Coed** 2,089 undergraduate students, 100% full-time, 60% women, 40% men
- **Moderately difficult** entrance level, 75% of applicants were admitted

Undergraduates 2,080 full-time, 9 part-time. 36% are from out of state; 3% Black or African American, non-Hispanic/Latino; 6% Hispanic/Latino; 2% Asian, non-Hispanic/Latino; 0.1% American Indian or Alaska Native, non-Hispanic/Latino; 1% Two or more races, non-Hispanic/Latino; 13% Race/ethnicity unknown; 0.7% international; 2% transferred in; 88% live on campus. *Retention:* 86% of full-time freshmen returned.

Freshmen *Admission:* 4,380 applied, 3,290 admitted, 607 enrolled. *Average high school GPA:* 3.29. *Test scores:* SAT critical reading scores over 500: 80%; SAT math scores over 500: 85%; ACT scores over 18: 100%; SAT critical reading scores over 600: 22%; SAT math scores over 600: 35%; ACT scores over 24: 65%; SAT critical reading scores over 700: 2%; SAT math scores over 700: 1%; ACT scores over 30: 4%.

Faculty *Total:* 222, 66% full-time, 81% with terminal degrees. *Student/faculty ratio:* 12:1.

Academics *Calendar:* semesters. *Degrees:* bachelor's, master's, post-master's, and postbachelor's certificates. *Special study options:* advanced placement credit, double majors, honors programs, independent study, internships, off-campus study, part-time degree program, services for LD students, student-designed majors, study abroad, summer session for credit. *ROTC:* Army (c), Air Force (c). *Unusual degree programs:* 3-2 business administration; forestry with Duke University; nursing with Massachusetts College of Pharmacy and Health Sciences; special education, social rehabilitation counseling, school counseling; law with Duquesne Uni. School of Law; optometry with New England College of Optometry; osteopathic medicine with DesMoines Univ.; pharmacy and phys therapy with MA College of Pharmacy & Health Science; podiatry with Barry Univ.

Computers on Campus 315 computers/terminals and 1,900 ports are available on campus for general student use. Students can access the following: campus intranet, computer help desk, free student e-mail accounts, online (class) grades, online (class) registration, online (class) schedules. Campus-wide network is available. 100% of college-owned or -operated housing units are wired for high-speed Internet access. Wireless service is available via entire campus.

Student Life *Housing options:* coed, women-only, disabled students. Campus housing is university owned. Freshman campus housing is guaranteed. *Activities and organizations:* drama/theater group, student-run newspaper, television station, choral group. *Campus security:* 24-hour emergency response devices and patrols, student patrols, late-night transport/escort service, controlled dormitory access, front gate security, well-lit pathways. *Student services:* health clinic, personal/psychological counseling.

Athletics Member NCAA. All Division II. *Intercollegiate sports:* baseball M, basketball M(s)/W(s), crew W, cross-country running M/W, field hockey W, football M, golf M, ice hockey M, lacrosse M/W, soccer M/W, softball W, swimming and diving W, tennis M/W, track and field M/W, volleyball W. *Intramural sports:* basketball M/W, cheerleading M(c)/W(c), equestrian sports M(c)/W(c), football M, golf M/W, ice hockey M/W, racquetball M/W, soccer M/W, softball M/W, ultimate Frisbee M/W, volleyball M(c)/W(c).

Costs (2012–13) *Comprehensive fee:* $44,395 includes full-time tuition ($33,390), mandatory fees ($415), and room and board ($10,590). Full-time tuition and fees vary according to course load and reciprocity agreements. Part-time tuition: $1113 per credit hour. Part-time tuition and fees vary according to course load. *College room only:* $6660. Room and board charges vary according to housing facility. *Waivers:* employees or children of employees.

Financial Aid Of all full-time matriculated undergraduates who enrolled in 2011, 1,781 applied for aid, 1,601 were judged to have need, 334 had their need fully met. 374 Federal Work-Study jobs (averaging $1655). In 2011, 348 non-need-based awards were made. *Average percent of need met:* 74%. *Average financial aid package:* $23,169. *Average need-based loan:* $4821. *Average need-based gift aid:* $17,173. *Average non-need-based aid:* $10,676. *Average indebtedness upon graduation:* $37,103. *Financial aid deadline:* 2/15.

Applying *Options:* electronic application, early action, deferred entrance. *Application fee:* $50. *Required:* essay or personal statement, high school transcript, 1 letter of recommendation. *Recommended:* interview. *Application deadlines:* 2/15 (freshmen), 7/1 (transfers), 11/1 (early action). *Notification:* continuous (freshmen), continuous (transfers), 12/15 (early action).

Freshman Application Contact Ms. Kathleen Murphy, Dean of Enrollment, Assumption College, 500 Salisbury Street, Worcester, MA 01609-1296. *Phone:* 508-767-7110. *Toll-free phone:* 866-477-7776. *Fax:* 508-799-4412. *E-mail:* admiss@assumption.edu. *Web site:* http://www.assumption.edu/.

See page 401 for display ad and page 1152 for the College Close-Up.

Babson College
Wellesley, Massachusetts

- **Independent** comprehensive, founded 1919
- **Suburban** 370-acre campus with easy access to Boston
- **Coed** 2,007 undergraduate students, 100% full-time, 44% women, 56% men
- **Very difficult** entrance level, 34% of applicants were admitted

Undergraduates 2,007 full-time. 69% are from out of state; 4% Black or African American, non-Hispanic/Latino; 10% Hispanic/Latino; 12% Asian, non-Hispanic/Latino; 0.3% American Indian or Alaska Native, non-Hispanic/Latino; 0.9% Two or more races, non-Hispanic/Latino; 8% Race/ethnicity unknown; 27% international; 2% transferred in; 85% live on campus. *Retention:* 94% of full-time freshmen returned.

Freshmen *Admission:* 5,079 applied, 1,718 admitted, 487 enrolled. *Average high school GPA:* 3.56. *Test scores:* SAT critical reading scores over 500: 96%; SAT math scores over 500: 100%; SAT writing scores over 500: 97%; ACT scores over 18: 100%; SAT critical reading scores over 600: 49%; SAT

math scores over 600: 84%; SAT writing scores over 600: 64%; ACT scores over 24: 95%; SAT critical reading scores over 700: 9%; SAT math scores over 700: 32%; SAT writing scores over 700: 15%; ACT scores over 30: 16%.

Faculty *Total:* 267, 61% full-time, 68% with terminal degrees. *Student/faculty ratio:* 15:1.

Academics *Calendar:* semesters. *Degrees:* bachelor's, master's, and post-master's certificates. *Special study options:* advanced placement credit, freshman honors college, honors programs, independent study, internships, off-campus study, services for LD students, student-designed majors, study abroad, summer session for credit. *ROTC:* Army (c), Navy (c), Air Force (c).

Computers on Campus Students can access the following: campus intranet, computer help desk, free student e-mail accounts, online (class) grades, online (class) registration, online (class) schedules, network drives and folders; students are also issued an IBM Thinkpad. Campuswide network is available. Wireless service is available via entire campus.

Student Life *Housing:* on-campus residence required for freshman year. *Options:* coed, men-only, disabled students. Campus housing is university owned. Freshman campus housing is guaranteed. *Activities and organizations:* drama/theater group, student-run newspaper, radio station, choral group, Student Government Association, Free Press, Dance Ensemble, Asian Pacific Student Association, College Radio, national fraternities, national sororities. *Campus security:* 24-hour emergency response devices and patrols, late-night transport/escort service, controlled dormitory access. *Student services:* health clinic, personal/psychological counseling, women's center.

Athletics Member NCAA. All Division III. *Intercollegiate sports:* baseball M, basketball M/W, cheerleading W(c), cross-country running M/W, field hockey W, golf M, ice hockey M/W(c), lacrosse M/W, rugby M(c)/W(c), skiing (downhill) M/W, soccer M/W, softball W, swimming and diving M/W, tennis M/W, track and field M/W, volleyball W. *Intramural sports:* basketball M/W, football M, ice hockey M/W, racquetball M/W, soccer M/W, softball M/W, squash M/W, tennis M/W, ultimate Frisbee M/W, volleyball M/W, wrestling M(c).

Standardized Tests *Required:* SAT or ACT (for admission).

Costs (2011–12) *Comprehensive fee:* $53,730 includes full-time tuition ($40,400) and room and board ($13,330). *College room only:* $8600. Room and board charges vary according to board plan and housing facility.

Financial Aid Of all full-time matriculated undergraduates who enrolled in 2010, 946 applied for aid, 884 were judged to have need, 400 had their need fully met. 697 Federal Work-Study jobs (averaging $1982). 8 state and other part-time jobs (averaging $2200). In 2010, 102 non-need-based awards were made. *Average percent of need met:* 94%. *Average financial aid package:*

$32,105. *Average need-based loan:* $3948. *Average need-based gift aid:* $27,950. *Average non-need-based aid:* $20,000. *Average indebtedness upon graduation:* $30,357. *Financial aid deadline:* 2/15.

Applying *Options:* electronic application, early action, deferred entrance. *Application fee:* $65. *Required:* essay or personal statement, high school transcript, 2 letters of recommendation. *Recommended:* interview. *Application deadlines:* 1/15 (freshmen), 4/1 (transfers), 11/1 (early action). *Early decision deadline:* 11/1. *Notification:* 4/1 (freshmen), 5/15 (transfers), 12/15 (early decision), 1/1 (early action).

Freshman Application Contact Ms. Adrienne Ramsey, Senior Assistant Director of Undergraduate Admission, Babson College, Lunder Undergraduate Admission Center, Babson Park, MA 02457-0310. *Phone:* 781-239-5522. *Toll-free phone:* 800-488-3696. *Fax:* 781-239-4135. *E-mail:* ugradadmission@babson.edu. *Web site:* http://www.babson.edu/.

See page 1156 for the College Close-Up.

Bard College at Simon's Rock
Great Barrington, Massachusetts

- **Independent** 4-year, founded 1964
- **Small-town** 210-acre campus with easy access to Boston, New York City
- **Coed** 350 undergraduate students, 98% full-time, 65% women, 35% men
- **Moderately difficult** entrance level, 87% of applicants were admitted

Undergraduates 344 full-time, 6 part-time. Students come from 36 states and territories; 13 other countries; 87% are from out of state; 10% Black or African American, non-Hispanic/Latino; 5% Hispanic/Latino; 7% Asian, non-Hispanic/Latino; 0.3% American Indian or Alaska Native, non-Hispanic/Latino; 9% Two or more races, non-Hispanic/Latino; 10% Race/ethnicity unknown; 5% international; 0.3% transferred in; 88% live on campus. *Retention:* 81% of full-time freshmen returned.

Freshmen *Admission:* 290 applied, 253 admitted, 118 enrolled. *Average high school GPA:* 3.36. *Test scores:* SAT critical reading scores over 500: 100%; SAT math scores over 500: 100%; SAT writing scores over 500: 92%; ACT scores over 18: 100%; SAT critical reading scores over 600: 100%; SAT math scores over 600: 58%; SAT writing scores over 600: 83%; ACT scores over 24: 60%; SAT critical reading scores over 700: 50%; SAT math scores over 700: 25%; SAT writing scores over 700: 58%; ACT scores over 30: 20%.

Faculty *Total:* 71, 63% full-time, 76% with terminal degrees. *Student/faculty ratio:* 7:1.

Academics *Calendar:* semesters. *Degrees:* associate and bachelor's. *Special study options:* cooperative education, double majors, independent study, internships, off-campus study, services for LD students, student-designed majors, study abroad. *Unusual degree programs:* 3-2 engineering with Columbia University, Dartmouth College.

Computers on Campus 80 computers/terminals and 200 ports are available on campus for general student use. Students can access the following: campus intranet, computer help desk, free student e-mail accounts. Campuswide network is available. 100% of college-owned or -operated housing units are wired for high-speed Internet access. Wireless service is available via classrooms, computer centers, computer labs, libraries, student centers.

Student Life *Housing:* on-campus residence required through junior year. *Options:* coed, men-only, women-only. Campus housing is university owned. Freshman campus housing is guaranteed. *Activities and organizations:* drama/theater group, student-run newspaper, choral group, Black Student Union, QueerSA, Student Action Service Learning, U.S.O. (Untitled Student Organization), Boffing. *Campus security:* 24-hour patrols, controlled dormitory access. *Student services:* health clinic, personal/psychological counseling, women's center.

Athletics *Intercollegiate sports:* basketball M/W, soccer M/W, swimming and diving M/W. *Intramural sports:* archery M/W, basketball M/W, cross-country running M/W, racquetball M/W, soccer M/W, squash M/W, swimming and diving M/W, tennis M/W, ultimate Frisbee M/W, water polo M/W, weight lifting M/W.

Costs (2011–12) *One-time required fee:* $575. *Comprehensive fee:* $55,800 includes full-time tuition ($43,000), mandatory fees ($840), and room and board ($11,960). Full-time tuition and fees vary according to course load. Part-time tuition: $1730 per credit. Part-time tuition and fees vary according to course load. *College room only:* $6070. *Payment plan:* installment. *Waivers:* employees or children of employees.

Financial Aid Of all full-time matriculated undergraduates who enrolled in 2011, 271 applied for aid, 245 were judged to have need, 38 had their need fully met. 156 Federal Work-Study jobs (averaging $1000). In 2011, 73 non-need-based awards were made. *Average percent of need met:* 77%. *Average financial aid package:* $34,687. *Average need-based loan:* $4721. *Average need-based gift aid:* $17,845. *Average non-need-based aid:* $16,504. *Average indebtedness upon graduation:* $30,000.

Applying *Application fee:* $50. *Required:* essay or personal statement, high school transcript, 3 letters of recommendation, interview, school report, parent supplement. *Application deadlines:* 5/31 (freshmen), 5/31 (out-of-state freshmen), 5/31 (transfers). *Notification:* continuous (freshmen), continuous (transfers).

Freshman Application Contact Steven Coleman, Director of Admissions, Bard College at Simon's Rock, 84 Alford Road, Great Barrington, MA 01230-9702. *Phone:* 413-528-7228. *Toll-free phone:* 800-235-7186. *Fax:* 413-541-0081. *E-mail:* admit@simons-rock.edu. *Web site:* http://www.simons-rock.edu/.

See below for display ad and page 1160 for the College Close-Up.

Bay Path College
Longmeadow, Massachusetts

- **Independent** comprehensive, founded 1897
- **Suburban** 48-acre campus with easy access to Hartford, CT and Boston, MA
- **Endowment** $31.9 million
- **Undergraduate: women only; graduate: coed** 1,572 undergraduate students, 80% full-time, 100% women
- **Moderately difficult** entrance level, 59% of applicants were admitted

Undergraduates 1,255 full-time, 317 part-time. Students come from 19 states and territories; 11 other countries; 33% are from out of state; 11% Black or African American, non-Hispanic/Latino; 13% Hispanic/Latino; 2% Asian, non-Hispanic/Latino; 0.3% American Indian or Alaska Native, non-Hispanic/Latino; 3% Two or more races, non-Hispanic/Latino; 14% Race/ethnicity unknown; 0.4% international; 19% transferred in; 66% live on campus. *Retention:* 76% of full-time freshmen returned.

Freshmen *Admission:* 993 applied, 583 admitted, 148 enrolled. *Average high school GPA:* 3.19. *Test scores:* SAT critical reading scores over 500: 35%; SAT math scores over 500: 34%; SAT writing scores over 500: 39%; ACT scores over 18: 92%; SAT critical reading scores over 600: 8%; SAT math scores over 600: 7%; SAT writing scores over 600: 7%; ACT scores over 24: 22%; SAT critical reading scores over 700: 1%.

Faculty *Total:* 236, 20% full-time. *Student/faculty ratio:* 12:1.

Academics *Calendar:* semesters. *Degrees:* certificates, associate, bachelor's, master's, post-master's, and postbachelor's certificates. *Special study options:* academic remediation for entering students, accelerated degree program, adult/continuing education programs, advanced placement credit, cooperative education, distance learning, double majors, English as a second language, honors programs, independent study, internships, off-campus study, part-time degree

program, services for LD students, student-designed majors, study abroad, summer session for credit. *ROTC:* Army (c), Air Force (c).

Computers on Campus 340 computers/terminals are available on campus for general student use. Students can access the following: campus intranet, computer help desk, free student e-mail accounts, online (class) grades, online (class) registration, online (class) schedules. Campuswide network is available. 100% of college-owned or -operated housing units are wired for high-speed Internet access. Wireless service is available via entire campus.

Student Life *Housing:* on-campus residence required through sophomore year. *Options:* women-only. Campus housing is university owned. Freshman campus housing is guaranteed. *Activities and organizations:* drama/theater group, choral group, student government, Black Student Association, Golden Z Service Club, Alliance, Women of Culture. *Campus security:* 24-hour emergency response devices and patrols, late-night transport/escort service, controlled dormitory access. *Student services:* health clinic, personal/psychological counseling.

Athletics Member NCAA. All Division III. *Intercollegiate sports:* basketball W, cross-country running W, field hockey W, soccer W, softball W, tennis W, volleyball W. *Intramural sports:* ice hockey W(c), lacrosse W(c).

Standardized Tests *Required:* SAT or ACT (for admission).

Costs (2011–12) *Comprehensive fee:* $37,995 includes full-time tuition ($27,045) and room and board ($10,950). Part-time tuition: $475 per credit. Part-time tuition and fees vary according to course load. *Room and board:* Room and board charges vary according to board plan. *Payment plan:* installment. *Waivers:* employees or children of employees.

Financial Aid Of all full-time matriculated undergraduates who enrolled in 2011, 567 applied for aid, 546 were judged to have need, 49 had their need fully met. 140 Federal Work-Study jobs (averaging $2200). In 2011, 71 non-need-based awards were made. *Average percent of need met:* 68%. *Average financial aid package:* $22,783. *Average need-based loan:* $5238. *Average need-based gift aid:* $17,055. *Average non-need-based aid:* $11,523. *Average indebtedness upon graduation:* $38,398.

Applying *Options:* electronic application, early admission, early action, deferred entrance. *Application fee:* $25. *Required:* high school transcript. *Required for some:* interview. *Recommended:* essay or personal statement, minimum 2.0 GPA, interview. *Application deadlines:* rolling (freshmen), rolling (transfers), 12/15 (early action). *Notification:* continuous (freshmen), continuous (transfers), 1/2 (early action).

Freshman Application Contact Stefanie Sanchez, Bay Path College, 588 Longmeadow Street, Longmeadow, MA 01106-2292. *Phone:* 413-565-1000. *Toll-free phone:* 800-782-7284 Ext. 1331. *Web site:* http://www.baypath.edu/.

Bay State College
Boston, Massachusetts

Freshman Application Contact Kim Olds, Director of Admissions, Bay State College, 122 Commonwealth Avenue, Boston, MA 02116. *Phone:* 617-217-9115. *Toll-free phone:* 800-81-LEARN. *Fax:* 617-536-1735. *E-mail:* admissions@baystate.edu. *Web site:* http://www.baystate.edu/.

See page 1166 for the College Close-Up.

Becker College
Worcester, Massachusetts

- **Independent** 4-year, founded 1784
- **Urban** 100-acre campus with easy access to Boston
- **Coed** 1,814 undergraduate students, 79% full-time, 61% women, 39% men
- **Moderately difficult** entrance level, 72% of applicants were admitted

Undergraduates 1,430 full-time, 384 part-time. Students come from 30 states and territories; 14 other countries; 27% are from out of state; 8% Black or African American, non-Hispanic/Latino; 8% Hispanic/Latino; 1% Asian, non-Hispanic/Latino; 0.1% Native Hawaiian or other Pacific Islander, non-Hispanic/Latino; 0.6% American Indian or Alaska Native, non-Hispanic/Latino; 1% Two or more races, non-Hispanic/Latino; 29% Race/ethnicity unknown; 0.2% international; 6% transferred in; 36% live on campus. *Retention:* 64% of full-time freshmen returned.

Freshmen *Admission:* 2,509 applied, 1,818 admitted, 416 enrolled. *Average high school GPA:* 2.82. *Test scores:* SAT critical reading scores over 500: 34%; SAT math scores over 500: 36%; SAT writing scores over 500: 26%; ACT scores over 18: 51%; SAT critical reading scores over 600: 9%; SAT math scores over 600: 9%; SAT writing scores over 600: 2%; ACT scores over 24: 14%; SAT math scores over 700: 1%; SAT writing scores over 700: 1%.

Faculty *Total:* 177, 25% full-time. *Student/faculty ratio:* 17:1.

Academics *Calendar:* semesters. *Degrees:* associate and bachelor's (also includes Leicester, MA small town campus). *Special study options:* academic remediation for entering students, accelerated degree program, adult/continuing education programs, advanced placement credit, cooperative education, distance learning, honors programs, independent study, internships, off-campus study, part-time degree program, services for LD students, study abroad. *ROTC:* Army (c).

Computers on Campus 155 computers/terminals are available on campus for general student use. Students can access the following: campus intranet, computer help desk, free student e-mail accounts, online (class) grades, online (class) registration, online (class) schedules. Campuswide network is available. 100% of college-owned or -operated housing units are wired for high-speed Internet access. Wireless service is available via entire campus.

Student Life *Housing options:* coed, men-only, women-only. Campus housing is university owned and leased by the school. Freshman campus housing is guaranteed. *Activities and organizations:* drama/theater group, student-run newspaper, television station, choral group, Student government, Student Activities Committee, Black Student Union, Animal Health Club, Drama Club. *Campus security:* 24-hour emergency response devices and patrols, late-night transport/escort service, controlled dormitory access. *Student services:* health clinic, personal/psychological counseling.

Athletics Member NCAA. *Intercollegiate sports:* baseball M, basketball M/W, cheerleading M/W, equestrian sports M/W, field hockey W, football M, golf M, ice hockey M, lacrosse M/W, soccer M/W, softball W, tennis M/W, volleyball W. *Intramural sports:* basketball M/W, bowling M/W, skiing (downhill) M(c)/W(c), soccer M/W, table tennis M/W, volleyball M/W.

Standardized Tests *Required:* SAT or ACT (for admission).

Costs (2011–12) *Comprehensive fee:* $38,910 includes full-time tuition ($27,050), mandatory fees ($1440), and room and board ($10,420). Full-time tuition and fees vary according to class time, course load, and program. Part-time tuition: $1140 per credit hour. Part-time tuition and fees vary according to class time, course load, and program. *College room only:* $4900. Room and board charges vary according to board plan and housing facility. *Payment plan:* installment. *Waivers:* senior citizens and employees or children of employees.

Financial Aid Of all full-time matriculated undergraduates who enrolled in 2009, 1,679 applied for aid, 1,524 were judged to have need, 27 had their need fully met. 338 Federal Work-Study jobs (averaging $1404). In 2009, 504 non-need-based awards were made. *Average percent of need met:* 74%. *Average financial aid package:* $14,056. *Average need-based loan:* $4031. *Average need-based gift aid:* $12,854. *Average non-need-based aid:* $14,032. *Average indebtedness upon graduation:* $31,800.

Applying *Options:* electronic application, early admission, early action, deferred entrance. *Application fee:* $30. *Required:* high school transcript, minimum 1.0 GPA, 1 letter of recommendation. *Required for some:* interview. *Recommended:* essay or personal statement. *Application deadlines:* rolling (freshmen), rolling (transfers), 11/15 (early action). *Notification:* continuous (freshmen), continuous (transfers), 12/15 (early action).

Freshman Application Contact Office of Admissions, Becker College, 61 Sever Street, Worcester, MA 01609. *Phone:* 508-373-9400. *Toll-free phone:* 877-5BECKER. *Fax:* 508-890-1500. *E-mail:* admissions@becker.edu. *Web site:* http://www.becker.edu/.

Benjamin Franklin Institute of Technology
Boston, Massachusetts

Freshman Application Contact Ms. Brittainy Johnson, Associate Director of Admissions, Benjamin Franklin Institute of Technology, Boston, MA 02116. *Phone:* 617-423-4630 Ext. 122. *Toll-free phone:* 877-400-BFIT. *Fax:* 617-482-3706. *E-mail:* bjohnson@bfit.edu. *Web site:* http://www.bfit.edu/.

Bentley University
Waltham, Massachusetts

- **Independent** comprehensive, founded 1917
- **Suburban** 163-acre campus with easy access to Boston
- **Endowment** $207.8 million
- **Coed** 4,228 undergraduate students, 96% full-time, 41% women, 59% men
- **Very difficult** entrance level, 43% of applicants were admitted

Undergraduates 4,066 full-time, 162 part-time. Students come from 40 states and territories; 83 other countries; 52% are from out of state; 3% Black or African American, non-Hispanic/Latino; 7% Hispanic/Latino; 7% Asian, non-Hispanic/Latino; 0.1% American Indian or Alaska Native, non-Hispanic/Latino; 1% Two or more races, non-Hispanic/Latino; 8% Race/ethnicity unknown; 13% international; 3% transferred in; 79% live on campus. *Retention:* 94% of full-time freshmen returned.

Freshmen *Admission:* 6,695 applied, 2,902 admitted, 911 enrolled. *Test scores:* SAT critical reading scores over 500: 92%; SAT math scores over 500: 99%; SAT writing scores over 500: 93%; ACT scores over 18: 100%; SAT critical reading scores over 600: 48%; SAT math scores over 600: 78%; SAT writing scores over 600: 50%; ACT scores over 24: 91%; SAT critical reading scores over 700: 7%; SAT math scores over 700: 19%; SAT writing scores over 700: 10%; ACT scores over 30: 20%.

Faculty *Total:* 448, 63% full-time, 67% with terminal degrees. *Student/faculty ratio:* 14:1.

ASSUMPTION COLLEGE

Find yourself *here.*

:: Choose among **40** majors and **45** minors in the liberal arts, sciences, business and professional studies

:: **2,000+** undergraduates from **26** states and **23** countries

:: **90%** of the undergraduates live on campus for all **4** years

:: Located in the **2nd-largest** city in New England, with the **3rd-largest** job growth in the nation

:: **Ranked as one of the best colleges** in the northeast by *Princeton Review* and one of the nation's **"best values"** by *Barron's*

Visit the 4th-oldest Catholic college in New England

www.assumption.edu

500 Salisbury Street
Worcester, Massachusetts

Academics *Calendar:* semesters. *Degrees:* associate, bachelor's, master's, doctoral, post-master's, postbachelor's, and first professional certificates. *Special study options:* accelerated degree program, adult/continuing education programs, advanced placement credit, double majors, honors programs, independent study, internships, off-campus study, services for LD students, student-designed majors, study abroad, summer session for credit. *ROTC:* Army (c), Air Force (c).

Computers on Campus 4,489 computers/terminals and 10,752 ports are available on campus for general student use. Students can access the following: campus intranet, computer help desk, free student e-mail accounts, online (class) grades, online (class) registration, online (class) schedules, Grade checking, online admission, Blackboard, resume review, student employment, interlibrary loan, free software. Campuswide network is available. 100% of college-owned or -operated housing units are wired for high-speed Internet access. Wireless service is available via entire campus.

Student Life *Housing options:* coed, disabled students. Campus housing is university owned and leased by the school. Freshman campus housing is guaranteed. *Activities and organizations:* drama/theater group, student-run newspaper, radio and television station, choral group, Bentley Entrepreneurship Society, Campus Activities Board, Delta Sigma Pi, Bentley Investment Group, National Association of Black Accountants, national fraternities, national sororities. *Campus security:* 24-hour emergency response devices and patrols, late-night transport/escort service, controlled dormitory access, security cameras, Community Policing Team, self-defense classes, CPR and first-aid training. *Student services:* health clinic, personal/psychological counseling, women's center.

Athletics Member NCAA. All Division II except ice hockey (Division I). *Intercollegiate sports:* baseball M, basketball M(s)/W(s), cross-country running M/W, field hockey W, football M, golf M, ice hockey M(s), lacrosse M/W, soccer M/W, softball W, swimming and diving M/W, tennis M/W, track and field M/W. *Intramural sports:* basketball M/W, cheerleading W(c), football M, golf M(c)/W(c), racquetball M(c)/W(c), rugby M(c)/W(c), sailing M(c)/W(c), skiing (cross-country) M(c)/W(c), skiing (downhill) M(c)/W(c), soccer M/W, softball M/W, volleyball M/W, water polo M(c), wrestling M(c).

Standardized Tests *Required:* SAT or ACT (for admission). *Required for some:* TOEFL (or IELTS) is required form non-native English speakers unless the student receives at least 577 (paper-based) or 90 (Internet-based) on the writing section of the SAT.

Costs (2011–12) *Comprehensive fee:* $50,848 includes full-time tuition ($36,840), mandatory fees ($1488), and room and board ($12,520). Part-time tuition: $1866 per course. Part-time tuition and fees vary according to class time and course load. *Required fees:* $45 per term part-time. *College room only:* $7530. Room and board charges vary according to board plan and housing facility. *Payment plan:* installment. *Waivers:* employees or children of employees.

Financial Aid Of all full-time matriculated undergraduates who enrolled in 2010, 2,561 applied for aid, 2,037 were judged to have need, 884 had their need fully met. 1,109 Federal Work-Study jobs (averaging $1409). 661 state and other part-time jobs (averaging $1617). In 2010, 589 non-need-based awards were made. *Average percent of need met:* 95%. *Average financial aid package:* $30,521. *Average need-based loan:* $5471. *Average need-based gift aid:* $23,188. *Average non-need-based aid:* $15,050. *Average indebtedness upon graduation:* $33,066. *Financial aid deadline:* 2/1.

Applying *Options:* electronic application, early admission, early action, deferred entrance. *Application fee:* $50. *Required:* essay or personal statement, high school transcript, 2 letters of recommendation. *Required for some:* interview. *Application deadlines:* 1/15 (freshmen), 1/15 (out-of-state freshmen), 11/15 (early action). *Notification:* 4/1 (freshmen), 4/1 (out-of-state freshmen), 1/15 (early action).

Freshman Application Contact Office of Undergraduate Admissions, Bentley University, 175 Forest Street, Waltham, MA 02452. *Phone:* 781-891-2244. *Toll-free phone:* 800-523-2354. *Fax:* 781-891-3414. *E-mail:* ugadmission@bentley.edu. *Web site:* http://www.bentley.edu/.

See page 400 for display ad and page 1172 for the College Close-Up.

Berklee College of Music
Boston, Massachusetts

- **Independent** 4-year, founded 1945
- **Urban** campus
- **Coed** 4,307 undergraduate students, 90% full-time, 30% women, 70% men
- **Moderately difficult** entrance level, 28% of applicants were admitted

Undergraduates 3,888 full-time, 419 part-time. 84% are from out of state; 7% Black or African American, non-Hispanic/Latino; 9% Hispanic/Latino; 3% Asian, non-Hispanic/Latino; 0.1% Native Hawaiian or other Pacific Islander, non-Hispanic/Latino; 0.3% American Indian or Alaska Native, non-Hispanic/Latino; 2% Two or more races, non-Hispanic/Latino; 8% Race/ethnicity

unknown; 23% international; 4% transferred in; 18% live on campus. *Retention:* 83% of full-time freshmen returned.

Freshmen *Admission:* 4,956 applied, 1,388 admitted, 669 enrolled.

Faculty *Total:* 577, 42% full-time. *Student/faculty ratio:* 12:1.

Academics *Calendar:* semesters. *Degree:* diplomas and bachelor's.

Computers on Campus Students can access the following: free student e-mail accounts, online (class) grades, online (class) registration, online (class) schedules. Campuswide network is available. Wireless service is available via entire campus.

Student Life *Housing options:* coed. Campus housing is university owned. Freshman applicants given priority for college housing. *Campus security:* 24-hour patrols.

Athletics *Intramural sports:* ice hockey M/W, rock climbing M/W, soccer M/W, table tennis M/W.

Financial Aid Of all full-time matriculated undergraduates who enrolled in 2010, 2,050 applied for aid, 1,852 were judged to have need, 79 had their need fully met. In 2010, 958 non-need-based awards were made. *Average percent of need met:* 37%. *Average financial aid package:* $15,824. *Average need-based loan:* $5070. *Average need-based gift aid:* $8513. *Average non-need-based aid:* $13,020. *Financial aid deadline:* 5/1.

Applying *Options:* electronic application, early action, deferred entrance. *Application fee:* $150. *Required:* essay or personal statement, high school transcript, 2 letters of recommendation, interview, 2 years of formal music study and audition. *Application deadlines:* 1/15 (freshmen), 1/15 (transfers), 11/1 (early action). *Notification:* 3/31 (freshmen), 3/31 (transfers), 1/31 (early action).

Freshman Application Contact Mr. Damien Bracken, Director of Admissions, Berklee College of Music, 1140 Boylston Street, Boston, MA 02215-3693. *Phone:* 617-747-2222. *Toll-free phone:* 800-BERKLEE. *Fax:* 617-747-2047. *E-mail:* admissions@berklee.edu. *Web site:* http://www.berklee.edu/.

See page 1174 for the College Close-Up.

Boston Architectural College

Boston, Massachusetts

- **Independent** comprehensive, founded 1889
- **Urban** 1-acre campus
- **Endowment** $8.7 million
- **Coed** 615 undergraduate students, 98% full-time, 31% women, 69% men
- **Noncompetitive** entrance level, 100% of applicants were admitted

Undergraduates 600 full-time, 15 part-time. Students come from 35 states and territories; 4 other countries; 51% are from out of state; 7% Black or African American, non-Hispanic/Latino; 13% Hispanic/Latino; 6% Asian, non-Hispanic/Latino; 0.3% American Indian or Alaska Native, non-Hispanic/Latino; 2% Two or more races, non-Hispanic/Latino; 7% Race/ethnicity unknown; 31% transferred in. *Retention:* 49% of full-time freshmen returned.

Freshmen *Admission:* 100 applied, 100 admitted, 41 enrolled. *Average high school GPA:* 2.9.

Faculty *Total:* 229, 5% full-time, 26% with terminal degrees. *Student/faculty ratio:* 4:1.

Academics *Calendar:* semesters. *Degrees:* certificates, bachelor's, and master's. *Special study options:* adult/continuing education programs, advanced placement credit, distance learning, independent study, internships, off-campus study, summer session for credit.

Computers on Campus 63 computers/terminals are available on campus for general student use. Students can access the following: campus intranet, computer help desk, free student e-mail accounts, online (class) grades, online (class) registration, online (class) schedules. Campuswide network is available. Wireless service is available via entire campus.

Student Life *Activities and organizations:* Atelier, Student Government, American Institute of Architectural Students, BAC Interior Design Society (IIDA and ASID), National Organization of Minority Architecture Students (NOMAS), Student American Society of Landscape Architects (SASLA). *Campus security:* 24-hour emergency response devices and patrols, late-night transport/escort service, electronically operated building access and CCTV systems. *Student services:* personal/psychological counseling.

Financial Aid Of all full-time matriculated undergraduates who enrolled in 2010, 864 applied for aid, 794 were judged to have need, 17 had their need fully met. 45 Federal Work-Study jobs (averaging $3066). In 2010, 22 non-need-based awards were made. *Average percent of need met:* 26%. *Average financial aid package:* $9124. *Average need-based loan:* $4580. *Average need-based gift aid:* $5201. *Average non-need-based aid:* $3198. *Average indebtedness upon graduation:* $31,385.

Applying *Options:* electronic application. *Application fee:* $50. *Required:* essay or personal statement, high school transcript, resumes, creative exercise. *Recommended:* interview. *Application deadlines:* rolling (freshmen), rolling

(out-of-state freshmen), rolling (transfers). *Notification:* continuous (freshmen), continuous (out-of-state freshmen), continuous (transfers).

Freshman Application Contact Richard Moyer, Director of Admission, Boston Architectural College, 320 Newbury Street, Boston, MA 02115-2795. *Phone:* 617-585-0256. *Toll-free phone:* 877-585-0100. *Fax:* 617-585-0121. *E-mail:* admissions@the-bac.edu. *Web site:* http://www.the-bac.edu/.

Boston Baptist College

Boston, Massachusetts

- **Independent Baptist** 4-year, founded 1976
- **Suburban** 8-acre campus with easy access to Boston, Providence
- **Coed** 103 undergraduate students, 83% full-time, 48% women, 52% men
- **Moderately difficult** entrance level, 58% of applicants were admitted

Undergraduates 85 full-time, 18 part-time. Students come from 18 states and territories; 5 other countries; 63% are from out of state; 7% Black or African American, non-Hispanic/Latino; 4% Hispanic/Latino; 1% Asian, non-Hispanic/Latino; 3% international; 3% transferred in; 65% live on campus. *Retention:* 72% of full-time freshmen returned.

Freshmen *Admission:* 60 applied, 35 admitted, 20 enrolled. *Average high school GPA:* 2.75.

Faculty *Total:* 22, 14% full-time. *Student/faculty ratio:* 9:1.

Academics *Calendar:* semesters. *Degrees:* certificates, diplomas, associate, and bachelor's. *Special study options:* academic remediation for entering students, adult/continuing education programs, advanced placement credit, distance learning, honors programs, off-campus study, part-time degree program, summer session for credit.

Computers on Campus 10 computers/terminals and 10 ports are available on campus for general student use. Students can access the following: campus intranet, computer help desk, free student e-mail accounts, online (class) grades. Campuswide network is available. 100% of college-owned or -operated housing units are wired for high-speed Internet access. Wireless service is available via entire campus.

Student Life *Housing:* on-campus residence required through senior year. *Options:* men-only, women-only, disabled students. Campus housing is university owned. Freshman campus housing is guaranteed. *Activities and organizations:* choral group, Community Service Organization, Recruitment, Campus Life. *Campus security:* 24-hour emergency response devices, student patrols, late-night transport/escort service, controlled dormitory access. *Student services:* personal/psychological counseling.

Athletics *Intercollegiate sports:* basketball M.

Standardized Tests *Required for some:* SAT or ACT (for admission).

Costs (2012–13) *Comprehensive fee:* $22,750 includes full-time tuition ($13,500), mandatory fees ($1500), and room and board ($7750). Part-time tuition: $391 per credit. *College room only:* $4600. Room and board charges vary according to board plan. *Payment plan:* installment.

Applying *Options:* deferred entrance. *Application fee:* $50. *Required:* essay or personal statement, high school transcript, 1 letter of recommendation. *Recommended:* 1 letter of recommendation. *Application deadlines:* rolling (freshmen), rolling (out-of-state freshmen), rolling (transfers).

Freshman Application Contact Mrs. Karen Fox, Director of Admissions, Boston Baptist College, 950 Metropolitan Avenue, Boston, MA 02136. *Phone:* 617-364-3510 Ext. 217. *Toll-free phone:* 888-235-2014. *Fax:* 617-399-8220. *E-mail:* kfox@boston.edu. *Web site:* http://www.boston.edu/.

Boston College

Chestnut Hill, Massachusetts

- **Independent Roman Catholic (Jesuit)** university, founded 1863
- **Suburban** 338-acre campus with easy access to Boston
- **Endowment** $1.6 billion
- **Coed** 9,088 undergraduate students, 100% full-time, 53% women, 47% men
- **Very difficult** entrance level, 28% of applicants were admitted

Undergraduates 9,088 full-time. Students come from 54 states and territories; 58 other countries; 73% are from out of state; 4% Black or African American, non-Hispanic/Latino; 10% Hispanic/Latino; 9% Asian, non-Hispanic/Latino; 0.1% American Indian or Alaska Native, non-Hispanic/Latino; 2% Two or more races, non-Hispanic/Latino; 9% Race/ethnicity unknown; 4% international; 2% transferred in; 85% live on campus. *Retention:* 95% of full-time freshmen returned.

Freshmen *Admission:* 32,974 applied, 9,227 admitted, 2,113 enrolled. *Test scores:* SAT critical reading scores over 500: 97%; SAT math scores over 500:

98%; SAT writing scores over 500: 97%; ACT scores over 18: 100%; SAT critical reading scores over 600: 83%; SAT math scores over 600: 90%; SAT writing scores over 600: 87%; ACT scores over 24: 96%; SAT critical reading scores over 700: 30%; SAT math scores over 700: 43%; SAT writing scores over 700: 44%; ACT scores over 30: 71%.

Faculty *Total:* 1,371, 54% full-time, 96% with terminal degrees. *Student/faculty ratio:* 14:1.

Academics *Calendar:* semesters. *Degrees:* bachelor's, master's, doctoral, post-master's, and first professional certificates (also offers continuing education program with significant enrollment not reflected in profile). *Special study options:* accelerated degree program, advanced placement credit, double majors, honors programs, independent study, internships, off-campus study, part-time degree program, services for LD students, student-designed majors, study abroad, summer session for credit. *ROTC:* Army (c), Navy (c), Air Force (c).

Computers on Campus 1,000 computers/terminals are available on campus for general student use. Students can access the following: campus intranet, computer help desk, free student e-mail accounts, online (class) grades, online (class) registration, online (class) schedules. Campuswide network is available. 100% of college-owned or -operated housing units are wired for high-speed Internet access. Wireless service is available via entire campus.

Student Life *Housing options:* coed, women-only. Campus housing is university owned. Freshman campus housing is guaranteed. *Activities and organizations:* drama/theater group, student-run newspaper, radio and television station, choral group, marching band, UGBC and individual School Senates, Asian Caucus, Appalachia Volunteers, Dance Marathon, 4Boston. *Campus security:* 24-hour emergency response devices and patrols, late-night transport/escort service, controlled dormitory access. *Student services:* health clinic, personal/psychological counseling, women's center.

Athletics Member NCAA. All Division I except football (Division I-A). *Intercollegiate sports:* baseball M(s), basketball M(s)/W(s), cheerleading M(c)/W(c), crew W(s), cross-country running M(s)/W(s), fencing M/W, field hockey W(s), golf M(s)/W(s), ice hockey M(s)/W(s), lacrosse W(s), sailing M/W, skiing (downhill) M/W, soccer M(s)/W(s), softball W(s), swimming and diving M(s)/W(s), tennis M(s)/W(s), track and field M(s)/W(s), volleyball W(s). *Intramural sports:* badminton M/W, basketball M(c)/W(c), crew M(c), cross-country running M(c)/W(c), equestrian sports M(c)/W(c), field hockey W(c), golf M(c)/W(c), ice hockey M/W, lacrosse M(c)/W(c), racquetball M/W, rugby M(c)/W(c), soccer M(c)/W(c), softball M/W, squash M/W, tennis M/W, track and field M(c)/W(c), ultimate Frisbee M(c)/W(c), volleyball M(c)/W, water polo M(c)/W(c).

Standardized Tests *Required:* SAT and SAT Subject Tests or ACT (for admission).

Costs (2011–12) *One-time required fee:* $450. *Comprehensive fee:* $54,528 includes full-time tuition ($41,480), mandatory fees ($724), and room and board ($12,324). *College room only:* $7600. Room and board charges vary according to housing facility. *Payment plan:* installment. *Waivers:* employees or children of employees.

Financial Aid Of all full-time matriculated undergraduates who enrolled in 2010, 4,451 applied for aid, 3,943 were judged to have need, 3,943 had their need fully met. 3,156 Federal Work-Study jobs (averaging $2143). In 2010, 167 non-need-based awards were made. *Average percent of need met:* 100%. *Average financial aid package:* $33,023. *Average need-based loan:* $4858. *Average need-based gift aid:* $27,633. *Average non-need-based aid:* $16,753. *Average indebtedness upon graduation:* $20,598.

Applying *Options:* electronic application, early admission, early action, deferred entrance. *Application fee:* $70. *Required:* essay or personal statement, high school transcript, 2 letters of recommendation. *Application deadlines:* 1/1 (freshmen), 3/15 (transfers), 11/1 (early action). *Notification:* 4/15 (freshmen), 6/1 (transfers), 12/25 (early action).

Freshman Application Contact Office of Undergraduate Admissions, Boston College, 140 Commonwealth Avenue, Devlin 208, Chestnut Hill, MA 02467-3809. *Phone:* 617-552-3100. *Toll-free phone:* 800-360-2522. *Fax:* 617-552-0798. *Web site:* http://www.bc.edu/.

See page 1176 for the College Close-Up.

The Boston Conservatory

Boston, Massachusetts

Freshman Application Contact The Boston Conservatory, 8 The Fenway, Boston, MA 02215. *Phone:* 617-912-9153. *Web site:* http://www.bostonconservatory.edu/.

Boston University

Boston, Massachusetts

- **Independent** university, founded 1839
- **Urban** 132-acre campus
- **Endowment** $1.2 billion
- **Coed** 18,645 undergraduate students, 92% full-time, 59% women, 41% men
- **Very difficult** entrance level, 52% of applicants were admitted

Undergraduates 17,209 full-time, 1,436 part-time. Students come from 52 states and territories; 104 other countries; 76% are from out of state; 3% Black or African American, non-Hispanic/Latino; 9% Hispanic/Latino; 14% Asian, non-Hispanic/Latino; 0.1% Native Hawaiian or other Pacific Islander, non-Hispanic/Latino; 0.2% American Indian or Alaska Native, non-Hispanic/Latino; 0.9% Two or more races, non-Hispanic/Latino; 9% Race/ethnicity unknown; 12% international; 1% transferred in; 66% live on campus. *Retention:* 92% of full-time freshmen returned.

Freshmen *Admission:* 41,802 applied, 21,662 admitted, 4,023 enrolled. *Average high school GPA:* 3.53. *Test scores:* SAT critical reading scores over 500: 94%; SAT math scores over 500: 99%; SAT writing scores over 500: 98%; ACT scores over 18: 100%; SAT critical reading scores over 600: 65%; SAT math scores over 600: 82%; SAT writing scores over 600: 76%; ACT scores over 24: 96%; SAT critical reading scores over 700: 15%; SAT math scores over 700: 29%; SAT writing scores over 700: 21%; ACT scores over 30: 32%.

Faculty *Total:* 2,630, 62% full-time. *Student/faculty ratio:* 13:1.

Academics *Calendar:* semesters. *Degrees:* associate, bachelor's, master's, doctoral, post-master's, postbachelor's, and first professional certificates. *Special study options:* accelerated degree program, adult/continuing education programs, advanced placement credit, cooperative education, distance learning, double majors, English as a second language, honors programs, independent study, internships, off-campus study, part-time degree program, services for LD students, student-designed majors, study abroad, summer session for credit. *ROTC:* Army (b), Navy (b), Air Force (b).

Computers on Campus 250 computers/terminals and 1,650 ports are available on campus for general student use. Students can access the following: campus intranet, computer help desk, free student e-mail accounts, online (class) grades, online (class) registration, online (class) schedules, research and educational networks. Campuswide network is available. 77% of college-owned or -operated housing units are wired for high-speed Internet access. Wireless service is available via classrooms, computer labs, dorm rooms, libraries, student centers.

Student Life *Housing:* on-campus residence required for freshman year. *Options:* coed, women-only, cooperative, disabled students. Campus housing is university owned. Freshman campus housing is guaranteed. *Activities and organizations:* drama/theater group, student-run newspaper, radio and television station, choral group, marching band, performing and acappella groups, cultural organizations, service organizations, student government, residence hall associations, national fraternities, national sororities. *Campus security:* 24-hour emergency response devices and patrols, late-night transport/escort service, controlled dormitory access, security personnel at residence hall entrances, self-defense education, well-lit sidewalks. *Student services:* health clinic, personal/psychological counseling, women's center.

Athletics Member NCAA. All Division I. *Intercollegiate sports:* badminton M(c)/W(c), baseball M(c), basketball M(s)/W(s), cheerleading M(c)/W(c), crew M(s)/W(s), cross-country running M(s)/W(s), equestrian sports M(c)/W(c), fencing M(c)/W(c), field hockey W(s), golf M(c)/W, gymnastics M(c)/W(c), ice hockey M(s)/W(s), lacrosse M(c)/W(s), rugby M(c)/W(c), sailing M(c)/W(c), skiing (downhill) M(c)/W(c), soccer M(s)/W(s), softball W(s), squash M(c)/W(c), swimming and diving M(s)/W(s), table tennis M(c)/W(c), tennis M/W(s), track and field M(s)/W(s), ultimate Frisbee M(c)/W(c), volleyball M(c)/W(c), water polo M(c)/W(c), wrestling M(s). *Intramural sports:* basketball M/W, football M/W, ice hockey M, soccer M/W, softball M/W, swimming and diving M/W, tennis M/W, volleyball M/W.

Standardized Tests *Required:* SAT or ACT (for admission), SAT and SAT Subject Tests or ACT (for admission), SAT Subject Tests (for admission).

Costs (2011–12) *Comprehensive fee:* $54,130 includes full-time tuition ($40,848), mandatory fees ($572), and room and board ($12,710). Full-time tuition and fees vary according to class time and degree level. Part-time tuition: $1276 per credit. Part-time tuition and fees vary according to class time, course load, and degree level. *Required fees:* $40 per term part-time. *College room only:* $8280. Room and board charges vary according to board plan and housing facility. *Payment plans:* tuition prepayment, installment. *Waivers:* employees or children of employees.

Financial Aid Of all full-time matriculated undergraduates who enrolled in 2010, 8,200 applied for aid, 7,498 were judged to have need, 3,613 had their need fully met. 3,483 Federal Work-Study jobs (averaging $2122). 115 state and other part-time jobs (averaging $11,339). In 2010, 1224 non-need-based awards were made. *Average percent of need met:* 89%. *Average financial aid package:* $35,198. *Average need-based loan:* $7185. *Average need-based gift aid:* $23,454. *Average non-need-based aid:* $19,843. *Average indebtedness upon graduation:* $31,809. *Financial aid deadline:* 2/15.

Applying *Options:* electronic application, early admission, early decision, deferred entrance. *Application fee:* $75. *Required:* essay or personal statement, high school transcript, 2 letters of recommendation. *Required for some:* interview, audition, portfolio. *Recommended:* minimum 3.0 GPA. *Application deadlines:* 1/1 (freshmen), 4/1 (transfers). *Early decision deadline:* 11/1. *Notification:* continuous until 4/15 (freshmen), 12/15 (early decision).

Freshman Application Contact Ms. Kelly Walter, Director of Undergraduate Admissions, Boston University, 121 Bay State Road, Boston, MA 02215. *Phone:* 617-353-2300. *Fax:* 617-353-9695. *E-mail:* admissions@bu.edu. *Web site:* http://www.bu.edu/.

See page 405 for display ad and page 1178 for the College Close-Up.

Brandeis University

Waltham, Massachusetts

- **Independent** university, founded 1948
- **Suburban** 235-acre campus with easy access to Boston
- **Endowment** $703.7 million
- **Coed** 3,504 undergraduate students, 100% full-time, 57% women, 43% men
- **Most difficult** entrance level, 40% of applicants were admitted

Undergraduates 3,490 full-time, 14 part-time. Students come from 48 states and territories; 65 other countries; 72% are from out of state; 4% Black or African American, non-Hispanic/Latino; 6% Hispanic/Latino; 13% Asian, non-Hispanic/Latino; 0.3% American Indian or Alaska Native, non-Hispanic/Latino; 2% Two or more races, non-Hispanic/Latino; 14% Race/ethnicity unknown; 12% international; 2% transferred in; 81% live on campus. *Retention:* 93% of full-time freshmen returned.

Freshmen *Admission:* 8,917 applied, 3,566 admitted, 858 enrolled. *Average high school GPA:* 3.8. *Test scores:* SAT critical reading scores over 500: 96%; SAT math scores over 500: 97%; SAT writing scores over 500: 96%; ACT scores over 18: 100%; SAT critical reading scores over 600: 76%; SAT math scores over 600: 86%; SAT writing scores over 600: 85%; ACT scores over 24: 98%; SAT critical reading scores over 700: 32%; SAT math scores over 700: 43%; SAT writing scores over 700: 39%; ACT scores over 30: 59%.

Faculty *Total:* 507, 72% full-time, 87% with terminal degrees. *Student/faculty ratio:* 10:1.

Academics *Calendar:* semesters. *Degrees:* bachelor's, master's, doctoral, postbachelor's, and first professional certificates. *Special study options:* adult/continuing education programs, advanced placement credit, double majors, English as a second language, honors programs, independent study, internships, off-campus study, services for LD students, student-designed majors, study abroad, summer session for credit. *ROTC:* Army (c), Air Force (c). *Unusual degree programs:* engineering with Columbia University.

Computers on Campus 118 computers/terminals are available on campus for general student use. Students can access the following: computer help desk, free student e-mail accounts, online (class) grades, online (class) registration, online (class) schedules, educational software. Campuswide network is available. 100% of college-owned or -operated housing units are wired for high-speed Internet access. Wireless service is available via entire campus.

Student Life *Housing:* on-campus residence required for freshman year. *Options:* coed, men-only, women-only, disabled students. Campus housing is university owned. Freshman campus housing is guaranteed. *Activities and organizations:* drama/theater group, student-run newspaper, radio and television station, choral group, Waltham Group, Student Events, Student Environmental Action, Liquid Latex, Culinary Arts Club. *Campus security:* 24-hour emergency response devices and patrols, late-night transport/escort service, controlled dormitory access. *Student services:* health clinic, personal/psychological counseling.

Athletics Member NCAA. All Division III. *Intercollegiate sports:* baseball M, basketball M/W, crew M(c)/W(c), cross-country running M/W, fencing M/W, field hockey W(c), golf M(c), lacrosse M(c)/W(c), rugby M(c)/W(c), sailing M(c)/W(c), skiing (downhill) M(c)/W(c), soccer M/W, softball W, squash M(c), swimming and diving M(c)/W(c), tennis M/W, track and field M/W, ultimate Frisbee M(c)/W(c), volleyball W. *Intramural sports:* archery M(c)/W(c), badminton M(c)/W(c), basketball M(c)/W(c), bowling M(c)/W(c), cheerleading M(c)/W(c), crew M(c)/W(c), equestrian sports M(c)/W(c), field hockey M(c)/W(c), football M/W, golf M(c)/W(c), ice hockey M(c)/W(c), lacrosse W(c), rugby M(c)/W(c), sailing M(c)/W(c), soccer M/W, softball M/W, squash M/W, swimming and diving M(c)/W(c), table tennis M/W, tennis M/W, ultimate Frisbee M(c)/W(c), volleyball M/W, water polo M(c)/W(c).

Standardized Tests *Required:* SAT or ACT (for admission).

Costs (2011–12) *Comprehensive fee:* $53,954 includes full-time tuition ($40,514), mandatory fees ($1546), and room and board ($11,894). Part-time

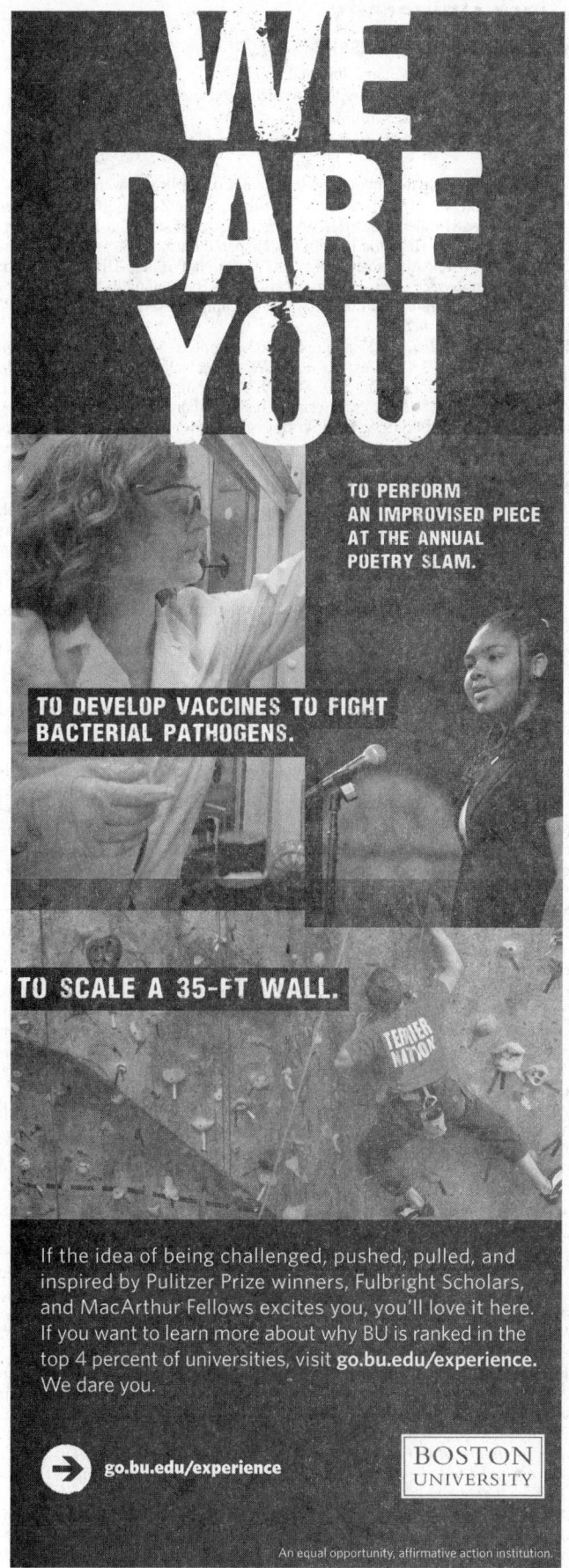

tuition and fees vary according to course load. *College room only:* $6556. Room and board charges vary according to board plan and housing facility. *Payment plans:* tuition prepayment, installment. *Waivers:* employees or children of employees.

Financial Aid Of all full-time matriculated undergraduates who enrolled in 2010, 1,998 applied for aid, 1,785 were judged to have need, 119 had their need fully met. In 2010, 274 non-need-based awards were made. *Average percent of need met:* 82%. *Average financial aid package:* $32,246. *Average need-based loan:* $5060. *Average need-based gift aid:* $27,321. *Average non-need-based aid:* $22,494. *Average indebtedness upon graduation:* $28,531. *Financial aid deadline:* 2/1.

Applying *Options:* electronic application, early decision, deferred entrance. *Application fee:* $55. *Required:* essay or personal statement, high school transcript, 2 letters of recommendation. *Recommended:* interview. *Application deadlines:* 1/15 (freshmen), 4/1 (transfers). *Early decision deadline:* 11/15 (for plan 1), 1/1 (for plan 2). *Notification:* 4/1 (freshmen), 6/1 (transfers), 12/15 (early decision plan 1), 2/1 (early decision plan 2).

Freshman Application Contact Mr. Mark D. Spencer, Dean of Admissions, Brandeis University, 415 South Street, PO Box 549110, Waltham, MA 02454-9110. *Phone:* 781-736-3500. *Toll-free phone:* 800-622-0622. *Fax:* 781-736-3536. *E-mail:* admissions@brandeis.edu. *Web site:* http://www.brandeis.edu/.

Bridgewater State University
Bridgewater, Massachusetts

- **State-supported** comprehensive, founded 1840, part of Massachusetts Public Higher Education System
- **Suburban** 235-acre campus with easy access to Boston
- **Endowment** $10.4 million
- **Coed** 9,552 undergraduate students, 83% full-time, 59% women, 41% men
- **Moderately difficult** entrance level, 65% of applicants were admitted

Undergraduates 7,921 full-time, 1,631 part-time. Students come from 24 states and territories; 24 other countries; 4% are from out of state; 5% Black or African American, non-Hispanic/Latino; 5% Hispanic/Latino; 2% Asian, non-Hispanic/Latino; 0.1% Native Hawaiian or other Pacific Islander, non-Hispanic/Latino; 0.2% American Indian or Alaska Native, non-Hispanic/Latino; 2% Two or more races, non-Hispanic/Latino; 3% Race/ethnicity unknown; 0.6% international; 11% transferred in; 30% live on campus. *Retention:* 81% of full-time freshmen returned.

Freshmen *Admission:* 7,039 applied, 4,549 admitted, 1,494 enrolled. *Average high school GPA:* 3.1. *Test scores:* SAT critical reading scores over 500: 53%; SAT math scores over 500: 59%; ACT scores over 18: 97%; SAT critical reading scores over 600: 11%; SAT math scores over 600: 12%; ACT scores over 24: 36%; SAT critical reading scores over 700: 1%; SAT math scores over 700: 1%; ACT scores over 30: 3%.

Faculty *Total:* 733, 43% full-time. *Student/faculty ratio:* 20:1.

Academics *Calendar:* semesters. *Degrees:* bachelor's, master's, post-master's, and postbachelor's certificates. *Special study options:* academic remediation for entering students, accelerated degree program, adult/continuing education programs, advanced placement credit, distance learning, double majors, English as a second language, honors programs, independent study, internships, off-campus study, part-time degree program, services for LD students, study abroad, summer session for credit. *ROTC:* Army (c), Air Force (c).

Computers on Campus 675 computers/terminals are available on campus for general student use. Students can access the following: campus intranet, computer help desk, free student e-mail accounts, online (class) grades, online (class) registration, online (class) schedules, student account information, application software. Campuswide network is available. Wireless service is available via entire campus.

Student Life *Housing options:* coed, disabled students. Campus housing is university owned. Freshman applicants given priority for college housing. *Activities and organizations:* drama/theater group, student-run newspaper, radio station, choral group, marching band, Dance Company, Afro-Am Society, Program Committee, Panhellenic Association, Inter-Fraternity Council, national fraternities, national sororities. *Campus security:* 24-hour emergency response devices and patrols, late-night transport/escort service, controlled dormitory access. *Student services:* health clinic, personal/psychological counseling, women's center.

Athletics Member NCAA. All Division III. *Intercollegiate sports:* baseball M, basketball M/W, cross-country running M/W, field hockey W, football M, lacrosse W, soccer M/W, softball W, swimming and diving M/W, tennis M/W, track and field M/W, volleyball W, wrestling M. *Intramural sports:* badminton M/W, baseball M(c)/W(c), basketball M/W, cheerleading W(c), equestrian sports M(c)/W(c), field hockey W, football M/W, golf M(c)/W(c), ice hockey M(c), lacrosse M(c), rugby W(c), soccer M/W, softball M/W, ultimate Frisbee M(c)/W(c), volleyball M/W.

Standardized Tests *Required:* SAT or ACT (for admission).

Costs (2012–13) *Tuition:* state resident $910 full-time, $38 per credit hour part-time; nonresident $7050 full-time, $294 per credit hour part-time. *Required fees:* $6642 full-time, $271 per credit hour part-time. *Room and board:* $10,400; room only: $6800. Room and board charges vary according to board plan and housing facility. *Payment plan:* installment. *Waivers:* employees or children of employees.

Financial Aid Of all full-time matriculated undergraduates who enrolled in 2008, 5,109 applied for aid, 3,991 were judged to have need. In 2008, 60 non-need-based awards were made. *Average percent of need met: 75%. Average financial aid package:* $7345. *Average need-based loan:* $3913. *Average need-based gift aid:* $3679. *Average non-need-based aid:* $5710. *Average indebtedness upon graduation:* $22,093.

Applying *Options:* electronic application, early admission, early action, deferred entrance. *Application fee:* $40. *Required:* essay or personal statement, high school transcript, minimum 3.0 GPA. *Application deadlines:* 2/15 (freshmen), 4/1 (transfers), 11/15 (early action). *Notification:* continuous (freshmen), 12/15 (early action).

Freshman Application Contact Mr. Gregg Meyer, Director of Admissions, Bridgewater State University, Gates House, 40 Cedar Street, Bridgewater, MA 02325-0001. *Phone:* 508-531-1237. *Fax:* 508-531-1746. *E-mail:* admission@bridgew.edu. *Web site:* http://www.bridgew.edu/.

Cambridge College

Cambridge, Massachusetts

- **Independent** comprehensive, founded 1971
- **Urban** campus with easy access to Boston
- **Endowment** $11.7 million
- **Coed** 1,271 undergraduate students, 36% full-time, 67% women, 33% men
- **Noncompetitive** entrance level

Undergraduates 459 full-time, 812 part-time. Students come from 9 states and territories; 18% are from out of state; 31% Black or African American, non-Hispanic/Latino; 24% Hispanic/Latino; 3% Asian, non-Hispanic/Latino; 0.3% Native Hawaiian or other Pacific Islander, non-Hispanic/Latino; 0.5% American Indian or Alaska Native, non-Hispanic/Latino; 1% Two or more races, non-Hispanic/Latino; 15% Race/ethnicity unknown; 7% international; 10% transferred in. *Retention:* 21% of full-time freshmen returned.

Freshmen *Admission:* 13 enrolled.

Faculty *Total:* 453, 4% full-time, 59% with terminal degrees. *Student/faculty ratio:* 16:1.

Academics *Calendar:* trimesters. *Degrees:* certificates, bachelor's, master's, doctoral, post-master's, and first professional certificates. *Special study options:* accelerated degree program, adult/continuing education programs, advanced placement credit, distance learning, independent study, internships, part-time degree program, services for LD students, summer session for credit.

Computers on Campus Students can access the following: computer help desk, free student e-mail accounts, online (class) grades, online (class) registration, online (class) schedules. Campuswide network is available. Wireless service is available via entire campus.

Student Life *Housing:* college housing not available.

Costs (2011–12) *Tuition:* $13,140 full-time, $365 per credit hour part-time. *Required fees:* $140 full-time. *Payment plan:* installment. *Waivers:* employees or children of employees.

Financial Aid Of all full-time matriculated undergraduates who enrolled in 2009, 232 applied for aid, 222 were judged to have need. *Average percent of need met: 31%. Average financial aid package:* $8198. *Average need-based loan:* $4313. *Average need-based gift aid:* $5653.

Applying *Options:* electronic application, deferred entrance. *Application fee:* $30. *Required:* essay or personal statement, high school transcript, 1 letter of recommendation, resume, health insurance, immunizations form, application form. *Recommended:* interview. *Application deadlines:* rolling (freshmen), rolling (out-of-state freshmen), rolling (transfers). *Notification:* continuous (freshmen), continuous (out-of-state freshmen), continuous (transfers).

Freshman Application Contact Denise Haile, Director of Admissions, Cambridge College, 1000 Massachusetts Avenue, Cambridge, MA 02138-5304. *Phone:* 800-877-4725. *Toll-free phone:* 800-877-4723. *Fax:* 617-349-3561. *E-mail:* denise.haile@cambridgecollege.edu. *Web site:* http://www.cambridgecollege.edu/.

Clark University

Worcester, Massachusetts

- **Independent** university, founded 1887
- **Urban** 50-acre campus with easy access to Boston
- **Endowment** $320.5 million
- **Coed** 2,311 undergraduate students, 96% full-time, 59% women, 41% men
- **Moderately difficult** entrance level, 68% of applicants were admitted

Undergraduates 2,218 full-time, 93 part-time. Students come from 46 states and territories; 81 other countries; 59% are from out of state; 4% Black or African American, non-Hispanic/Latino; 6% Hispanic/Latino; 5% Asian, non-Hispanic/Latino; 0.1% American Indian or Alaska Native, non-Hispanic/Latino; 3% Two or more races, non-Hispanic/Latino; 6% Race/ethnicity unknown; 9% international; 3% transferred in; 71% live on campus. *Retention:* 87% of full-time freshmen returned.

Freshmen *Admission:* 4,127 applied, 2,803 admitted, 546 enrolled. *Average high school GPA:* 3.48. *Test scores:* SAT critical reading scores over 500: 89%; SAT math scores over 500: 88%; SAT writing scores over 500: 89%; ACT scores over 18: 98%; SAT critical reading scores over 600: 49%; SAT math scores over 600: 49%; SAT writing scores over 600: 51%; ACT scores over 24: 71%; SAT critical reading scores over 700: 13%; SAT math scores over 700: 10%; SAT writing scores over 700: 10%; ACT scores over 30: 16%.

Faculty *Total:* 245, 80% full-time. *Student/faculty ratio:* 10:1.

Academics *Calendar:* semesters. *Degrees:* bachelor's, master's, doctoral, post-master's, and first professional certificates. *Special study options:* academic remediation for entering students, accelerated degree program, adult/continuing education programs, advanced placement credit, double majors, English as a second language, honors programs, independent study, internships, off-campus study, part-time degree program, services for LD students, student-designed majors, study abroad, summer session for credit. *ROTC:* Army (c), Navy (c), Air Force (c). *Unusual degree programs:* 3-2 business administration; engineering with Columbia University, Washington University in St. Louis, Worcester Polytechnic Institute; environmental studies, international development, community planning, biology, biochemistry, chemistry, physics, economics, history, communication, public administration, geographic information systems.

Computers on Campus 108 computers/terminals and 4,000 ports are available on campus for general student use. Students can access the following: campus intranet, computer help desk, free student e-mail accounts, online (class) grades, online (class) registration, online (class) schedules, online course support. Campuswide network is available. 100% of college-owned or -operated housing units are wired for high-speed Internet access. Wireless service is available via entire campus.

Student Life *Housing:* on-campus residence required through sophomore year. *Options:* coed, women-only, disabled students. Campus housing is university owned. Freshman campus housing is guaranteed. *Activities and organizations:* drama/theater group, student-run newspaper, radio and television station, choral group, marching band, International Students Association, Outing Club, Science Fiction People of Clark, Ballroom Dance Team and Club, Hillel. *Campus security:* 24-hour emergency response devices and patrols, student patrols, late-night transport/escort service, controlled dormitory access. *Student services:* health clinic, personal/psychological counseling, women's center.

Athletics Member NCAA. All Division III. *Intercollegiate sports:* baseball M, basketball M/W, crew M/W, cross-country running M/W, field hockey W, lacrosse M, soccer M/W, softball W, swimming and diving M/W, tennis M/W, volleyball W. *Intramural sports:* basketball M/W, equestrian sports M(c)/W(c), football M/W, ice hockey M(c)/W(c), lacrosse W(c), racquetball M/W, soccer M/W, softball M/W, track and field M(c)/W(c), ultimate Frisbee M(c)/W(c), volleyball M(c)/W(c), water polo M/W.

Costs (2012–13) *Comprehensive fee:* $45,770 includes full-time tuition ($38,100), mandatory fees ($350), and room and board ($7320). Part-time tuition: $1191 per course. *Required fees:* $1191 per course part-time. *College room only:* $4120. Room and board charges vary according to board plan and housing facility. *Payment plans:* tuition prepayment, installment. *Waivers:* employees or children of employees.

Financial Aid Of all full-time matriculated undergraduates who enrolled in 2011, 1,701 applied for aid, 1,307 were judged to have need, 942 had their need fully met. 1,000 Federal Work-Study jobs (averaging $2000). In 2011, 706 non-need-based awards were made. *Average percent of need met: 95%. Average financial aid package:* $31,830. *Average need-based loan:* $3605. *Average need-based gift aid:* $24,810. *Average non-need-based aid:* $14,305. *Average indebtedness upon graduation:* $27,600. *Financial aid deadline:* 2/1.

Applying *Options:* electronic application, early admission, early action, deferred entrance. *Application fee:* $55. *Required:* essay or personal statement, high school transcript, 2 letters of recommendation. *Recommended:* interview. *Application deadlines:* 1/15 (freshmen), 4/15 (transfers), 11/15

(early action). *Notification:* 4/1 (freshmen), 6/1 (transfers), 12/23 (early action).

Freshman Application Contact Mr. Donald Honeman, Dean of Admissions, Clark University, Admissions House, 950 Main Street, Worcester, MA 01610. *Phone:* 508-793-7431. *Toll-free phone:* 800-GO-CLARK. *Fax:* 508-793-8821. *E-mail:* admissions@clarku.edu. *Web site:* http://www.clarku.edu/.

College of the Holy Cross
Worcester, Massachusetts

- **Independent Roman Catholic (Jesuit)** 4-year, founded 1843
- **Suburban** 174-acre campus with easy access to Boston
- **Endowment** $607.7 million
- **Coed** 2,905 undergraduate students, 99% full-time, 53% women, 47% men
- **Very difficult** entrance level, 33% of applicants were admitted

Undergraduates 2,872 full-time, 33 part-time. Students come from 47 states and territories; 21 other countries; 63% are from out of state; 5% Black or African American, non-Hispanic/Latino; 10% Hispanic/Latino; 5% Asian, non-Hispanic/Latino; 0.1% Native Hawaiian or other Pacific Islander, non-Hispanic/Latino; 0.2% American Indian or Alaska Native, non-Hispanic/Latino; 1% Two or more races, non-Hispanic/Latino; 11% Race/ethnicity unknown; 1% international; 0.5% transferred in; 90% live on campus. *Retention:* 95% of full-time freshmen returned.

Freshmen *Admission:* 7,353 applied, 2,435 admitted, 751 enrolled. *Average high school GPA:* 3.84. *Test scores:* SAT critical reading scores over 500: 98%; SAT math scores over 500: 99%; SAT writing scores over 500: 98%; ACT scores over 18: 100%; SAT critical reading scores over 600: 75%; SAT math scores over 600: 85%; SAT writing scores over 600: 78%; ACT scores over 24: 95%; SAT critical reading scores over 700: 20%; SAT math scores over 700: 24%; SAT writing scores over 700: 26%; ACT scores over 30: 40%.

Faculty *Total:* 325, 79% full-time, 90% with terminal degrees. *Student/faculty ratio:* 10:1.

Academics *Calendar:* semesters. *Degrees:* bachelor's (standardized tests are optional for admission to the College of Holy Cross). *Special study options:* accelerated degree program, advanced placement credit, double majors, honors programs, independent study, internships, off-campus study, services for LD students, student-designed majors, study abroad. *ROTC:* Army (c), Navy (b), Air Force (c). *Unusual degree programs:* 3-2 engineering with Columbia University.

Computers on Campus 485 computers/terminals are available on campus for general student use. Students can access the following: computer help desk, free student e-mail accounts, online (class) registration. Campuswide network is available. 100% of college-owned or -operated housing units are wired for high-speed Internet access. Wireless service is available via classrooms, computer centers, computer labs, dorm rooms, libraries, student centers.

Student Life *Housing:* on-campus residence required through sophomore year. *Options:* coed, disabled students. Campus housing is university owned. Freshman campus housing is guaranteed. *Activities and organizations:* drama/theater group, student-run newspaper, radio station, choral group, marching band, SPUD (community service organization), choral and music groups, Campus Activities Board, Student Government Association, Purple Key Society. *Campus security:* 24-hour emergency response devices and patrols, late-night transport/escort service, controlled dormitory access. *Student services:* health clinic, personal/psychological counseling.

Athletics Member NCAA. All Division I except football (Division I-AA). *Intercollegiate sports:* baseball M, basketball M(s)/W(s), crew M/W, cross-country running M/W, field hockey W(s), golf M/W, ice hockey M(s)/W, lacrosse M/W, soccer M(s)/W(s), softball W, swimming and diving M/W, tennis M/W, track and field M/W, volleyball W. *Intramural sports:* baseball M(c), basketball M(c)/W, cross-country running M(c)/W(c), equestrian sports M(c)/W(c), field hockey W(c), football M/W, golf M(c)/W(c), ice hockey M(c), lacrosse M(c)/W(c), rugby M(c)/W(c), sailing M(c)/W(c), skiing (downhill) M(c)/W(c), soccer M(c)/W(c), softball M/W, swimming and diving M(c)/W(c), tennis M(c)/W(c), ultimate Frisbee M(c)/W(c), volleyball M(c)/W(c), water polo M(c)/W(c).

Costs (2012–13) *Comprehensive fee:* $55,130 includes full-time tuition ($42,800), mandatory fees ($600), and room and board ($11,730). *College room only:* $6330. Room and board charges vary according to housing facility. *Payment plan:* installment. *Waivers:* employees or children of employees.

Financial Aid Of all full-time matriculated undergraduates who enrolled in 2011, 1,849 applied for aid, 1,635 were judged to have need, 1,633 had their need fully met. 1,062 Federal Work-Study jobs (averaging $1556). In 2011, 26 non-need-based awards were made. *Average percent of need met:* 100%. *Average financial aid package:* $31,430. *Average need-based loan:* $5323. *Average need-based gift aid:* $29,630. *Average non-need-based aid:* $26,927. *Average indebtedness upon graduation:* $26,434. *Financial aid deadline:* 2/1.

Applying *Options:* electronic application, early admission, early decision, deferred entrance. *Application fee:* $60. *Required:* essay or personal statement, high school transcript, 2 letters of recommendation. *Recommended:* interview. *Application deadlines:* 1/15 (freshmen), 4/1 (transfers). *Early decision deadline:* 12/15. *Notification:* 4/1 (freshmen), continuous (transfers), 1/15 (early decision).

Freshman Application Contact College of the Holy Cross, 1 College Street, Worcester, MA 01610-2395. *Phone:* 508-793-2443. *Toll-free phone:* 800-442-2421. *Web site:* http://www.holycross.edu/.

Curry College
Milton, Massachusetts

- **Independent** comprehensive, founded 1879
- **Suburban** 135-acre campus with easy access to Boston
- **Endowment** $62.5 million
- **Coed** 2,693 undergraduate students, 73% full-time, 61% women, 39% men
- **Moderately difficult** entrance level, 72% of applicants were admitted

Undergraduates 1,976 full-time, 717 part-time. Students come from 34 states and territories; 25 other countries; 23% are from out of state; 7% Black or African American, non-Hispanic/Latino; 4% Hispanic/Latino; 1% Asian, non-Hispanic/Latino; 0.3% American Indian or Alaska Native, non-Hispanic/Latino; 0.8% Two or more races, non-Hispanic/Latino; 18% Race/ethnicity unknown; 1% international; 2% transferred in; 62% live on campus. *Retention:* 66% of full-time freshmen returned.

Freshmen *Admission:* 5,063 applied, 3,636 admitted, 621 enrolled. *Average high school GPA:* 2.7. *Test scores:* SAT critical reading scores over 500: 26%; SAT math scores over 500: 29%; SAT writing scores over 500: 29%; ACT scores over 18: 79%; SAT critical reading scores over 600: 3%; SAT math scores over 600: 3%; SAT writing scores over 600: 5%; ACT scores over 24: 14%; SAT writing scores over 700: 1%.

Faculty *Total:* 500, 25% full-time. *Student/faculty ratio:* 10:1.

Academics *Calendar:* semesters. *Degrees:* certificates, bachelor's, and master's. *Special study options:* academic remediation for entering students, accelerated degree program, adult/continuing education programs, advanced placement credit, double majors, external degree program, honors programs, independent study, internships, off-campus study, part-time degree program, services for LD students, student-designed majors, study abroad, summer session for credit. *ROTC:* Army (c).

Computers on Campus 245 computers/terminals and 2,500 ports are available on campus for general student use. Students can access the following: campus intranet, computer help desk, free student e-mail accounts, online (class) grades, online (class) registration, online (class) schedules, library online catalog and research databases. Campuswide network is available. 100% of college-owned or -operated housing units are wired for high-speed Internet access. Wireless service is available via entire campus.

Student Life *Housing options:* coed, men-only, women-only. Campus housing is university owned. *Activities and organizations:* drama/theater group, student-run newspaper, radio and television station, choral group, student radio station, student government, Campus Activities Board, student newspaper, Drama Club. *Campus security:* 24-hour emergency response devices and patrols, late-night transport/escort service, controlled dormitory access. *Student services:* health clinic, personal/psychological counseling.

Athletics Member NCAA. All Division III. *Intercollegiate sports:* baseball M, basketball M/W, cross-country running W, football M, ice hockey M, lacrosse M/W, soccer M/W, softball W, tennis M/W. *Intramural sports:* basketball M/W, cheerleading M/W, equestrian sports W, rugby M/W, skiing (downhill) M/W, softball M/W, tennis M/W, ultimate Frisbee M/W, volleyball M/W.

Standardized Tests *Required for some:* SAT or ACT (for admission), TOEFL for international applicants.

Costs (2011–12) *One-time required fee:* $280. *Comprehensive fee:* $44,495 includes full-time tuition ($30,700), mandatory fees ($1510), and room and board ($12,285). Part-time tuition: $1023 per credit. Part-time tuition and fees vary according to course load. *College room only:* $6895. Room and board charges vary according to board plan and housing facility. *Payment plan:* installment. *Waivers:* children of alumni and employees or children of employees.

Financial Aid Of all full-time matriculated undergraduates who enrolled in 2011, 1,411 applied for aid, 1,407 were judged to have need, 27 had their need fully met. 766 Federal Work-Study jobs (averaging $1859). In 2011, 159 non-need-based awards were made. *Average percent of need met:* 62%. *Average financial aid package:* $18,630. *Average need-based loan:* $4436. *Average need-based gift aid:* $11,607. *Average non-need-based aid:* $5336. *Average indebtedness upon graduation:* $41,281.

Applying *Options:* electronic application, early admission, early action, deferred entrance. *Application fee:* $50. *Required:* essay or personal state-

ment, high school transcript, minimum 2.0 GPA, 1 letter of recommendation, supplemental form for Common Application subscribers and Program for Advancement of Learning. *Required for some:* interview. *Recommended:* interview. *Application deadlines:* 4/1 (freshmen), 7/1 (transfers), 12/1 (early action). *Notification:* continuous (freshmen), continuous (transfers), 12/15 (early action).

Freshman Application Contact Ms. Jane P. Fidler, Dean of Admission, Curry College, 1071 Blue Hill Avenue, Milton, MA 02186. *Phone:* 617-333-2210. *Toll-free phone:* 800-669-0686. *Fax:* 617-333-2114. *E-mail:* curryadm@curry.edu. *Web site:* http://www.curry.edu/.

See below for display ad and page 1288 for the College Close-Up.

Dean College

Franklin, Massachusetts

Freshman Application Contact Mr. James Fowler, Dean College, 99 Main Street, Franklin, MA 02038. *Phone:* 508-541-1547. *Toll-free phone:* 877-TRY-DEAN. *Fax:* 508-541-8726. *E-mail:* jfowler@dean.edu. *Web site:* http://www.dean.edu/.

See page 1292 for the College Close-Up.

Eastern Nazarene College

Quincy, Massachusetts

Freshman Application Contact Mr. Andrew R. Wright, Director of Admissions, Eastern Nazarene College, 23 East Elm Avenue, Quincy, MA 02170. *Phone:* 617-745-3864. *Toll-free phone:* 800-88-ENC88. *Fax:* 617-745-3992. *E-mail:* andrew.wright@enc.edu. *Web site:* http://www.enc.edu/.

Elms College

Chicopee, Massachusetts

Freshman Application Contact Mr. Joseph Wagner, Director of Admissions, Elms College, Chicopee, MA 01013-2839. *Phone:* 413-592-3189 Ext. 350. *Toll-free phone:* 800-255-ELMS. *Fax:* 413-594-2781. *E-mail:* admissions@elms.edu. *Web site:* http://www.elms.edu/.

Emerson College

Boston, Massachusetts

Freshman Application Contact Emerson College, 120 Boylston Street, Boston, MA 02116-4624. *Phone:* 617-824-8600. *Web site:* http://www.emerson.edu/.

See page 409 for display ad and page 1320 for the College Close-Up.

Emmanuel College

Boston, Massachusetts

- **Independent Roman Catholic** comprehensive, founded 1919
- **Urban** 17-acre campus
- **Endowment** $64.5 million
- **Coed** 2,224 undergraduate students, 80% full-time, 72% women, 28% men
- **Moderately difficult** entrance level, 56% of applicants were admitted

Undergraduates 1,783 full-time, 441 part-time. Students come from 33 states and territories; 36 other countries; 39% are from out of state; 6% Black or African American, non-Hispanic/Latino; 6% Hispanic/Latino; 3% Asian, non-Hispanic/Latino; 0.2% American Indian or Alaska Native, non-Hispanic/Latino; 2% Two or more races, non-Hispanic/Latino; 12% Race/ethnicity unknown; 1% international; 2% transferred in; 72% live on campus. *Retention:* 82% of full-time freshmen returned.

Freshmen *Admission:* 6,640 applied, 3,701 admitted, 550 enrolled. *Average high school GPA:* 3.5. *Test scores:* SAT critical reading scores over 500: 74%; SAT math scores over 500: 71%; SAT writing scores over 500: 76%; ACT scores over 18: 100%; SAT critical reading scores over 600: 23%; SAT math scores over 600: 21%; SAT writing scores over 600: 25%; ACT scores over 24: 49%; SAT critical reading scores over 700: 3%; SAT math scores over 700: 1%; SAT writing scores over 700: 2%; ACT scores over 30: 4%.

Faculty *Total:* 231, 42% full-time, 54% with terminal degrees. *Student/faculty ratio:* 15:1.

Academics *Calendar:* semesters. *Degrees:* certificates, bachelor's, master's, post-master's, and postbachelor's certificates. *Special study options:* academic remediation for entering students, accelerated degree program, adult/continuing education programs, advanced placement credit, distance learning, double majors, honors programs, independent study, internships, off-campus study, part-time degree program, services for LD students, student-designed majors, study abroad, summer session for credit. *ROTC:* Army (c).

20 MAJORS TO CHOOSE FROM:

Biology	Elementary Education	Philosophy
Business Management	English	Politics & History
Child, Youth, and Community Education	Environmental Science	Psychology
Communication	Graphic Design	Sociology
Community Health and Wellness	Information Technology	Special Education
Criminal Justice	Integrated Liberal Studies	Visual Arts
Early Childhood Education	Nursing	

In the shadow of New England's Blue Hills sits the picturesque main campus of Curry College, a private, liberal arts-based institution where students are empowered to achieve their dreams.

Curry's dynamic academic curriculum inspires students to challenge themselves, develop new skills and discover an educational path that supports their individual learning style. Small class sizes help ensure that each student at Curry is recognized and encouraged by professors and peers alike. Internship opportunities and study abroad programs support learning outside the classroom, and help to broaden each student's academic perspective.

Visit our website to learn how you can make Curry College the first stop on your path to success!

 www.curry.edu

 CurryCollegeVideo

 @CurryAdmission

 Curry College Admissions

CURRY COLLEGE
1071 Blue Hill Avenue, Milton, MA
(800) 669-0686

Computers on Campus 216 computers/terminals are available on campus for general student use. Students can access the following: campus intranet, computer help desk, free student e-mail accounts, online (class) grades, online (class) registration, online (class) schedules, software applications. Campuswide network is available. 100% of college-owned or -operated housing units are wired for high-speed Internet access. Wireless service is available via entire campus.

Student Life *Housing options:* coed, disabled students. Campus housing is university owned and leased by the school. Freshman campus housing is guaranteed. *Activities and organizations:* drama/theater group, student-run newspaper, radio station, choral group, EC Superfans, Black Student Union, LEADERS Program, Bang (Literary Magazine), Rainbow Connection (LGBTQ Club). *Campus security:* 24-hour emergency response devices and patrols, late-night transport/escort service, controlled dormitory access, 24-hour staffed residence hall desks and security office, closed-circuit surveillance in public areas, off-campus escorts, bike patrol. *Student services:* health clinic, personal/psychological counseling.

Athletics Member NCAA. All Division III. *Intercollegiate sports:* basketball M/W, cross-country running M/W, golf M, lacrosse M/W, soccer M/W, softball W, tennis W, track and field M/W, volleyball M/W. *Intramural sports:* badminton M/W, baseball M(c)/W(c), basketball M/W, bowling M/W, cheerleading W(c), field hockey W(c), racquetball M/W, sailing M(c)/W(c), soccer M/W, softball M/W, tennis M/W, ultimate Frisbee M(c)/W(c), volleyball M/W.

Standardized Tests *Required:* SAT or ACT (for admission).

Costs (2011–12) *One-time required fee:* $175. *Comprehensive fee:* $45,225 includes full-time tuition ($32,100), mandatory fees ($375), and room and board ($12,750). Full-time tuition and fees vary according to course load, degree level, and program. Part-time tuition and fees vary according to program. *Room and board:* Room and board charges vary according to housing facility. *Payment plan:* installment. *Waivers:* employees or children of employees.

Financial Aid Of all full-time matriculated undergraduates who enrolled in 2011, 1,567 applied for aid, 1,451 were judged to have need, 822 had their need fully met. In 2011, 249 non-need-based awards were made. *Average percent of need met:* 77%. *Average financial aid package:* $25,426. *Average need-based loan:* $4571. *Average need-based gift aid:* $10,150. *Average non-need-based aid:* $10,457.

Applying *Options:* electronic application, early admission, early decision, early action, deferred entrance. *Application fee:* $60. *Required:* essay or personal statement, high school transcript, 2 letters of recommendation, Official SAT or ACT report. *Recommended:* interview. *Application deadlines:* 2/15 (freshmen), 4/1 (transfers), 11/15 (early action). *Early decision deadline:* 11/1. *Notification:* 12/1 (freshmen), 12/1 (transfers), 12/1 (early decision), 12/15 (early action).

Freshman Application Contact Ms. Sandra Robbins, Dean for Enrollment, Emmanuel College, Admissions Office, 400 The Fenway, Boston, MA 02115. *Phone:* 617-735-9715. *Fax:* 617-735-9801. *E-mail:* enroll@emmanuel.edu. *Web site:* http://www.emmanuel.edu/.

Endicott College
Beverly, Massachusetts

- **Independent** comprehensive, founded 1939
- **Suburban** 235-acre campus with easy access to Boston
- **Endowment** $38.7 million
- **Coed** 2,655 undergraduate students, 91% full-time, 58% women, 42% men
- **Moderately difficult** entrance level, 67% of applicants were admitted

Undergraduates 2,418 full-time, 237 part-time. Students come from 28 states and territories; 30 other countries; 52% are from out of state; 2% Black or African American, non-Hispanic/Latino; 3% Hispanic/Latino; 0.8% Asian, non-Hispanic/Latino; 0.1% Native Hawaiian or other Pacific Islander, non-Hispanic/Latino; 0.4% American Indian or Alaska Native, non-Hispanic/Latino; 1% Two or more races, non-Hispanic/Latino; 11% Race/ethnicity unknown; 2% international; 2% transferred in; 85% live on campus. *Retention:* 88% of full-time freshmen returned.

Freshmen *Admission:* 3,477 applied, 2,328 admitted, 642 enrolled. *Average high school GPA:* 3.1. *Test scores:* SAT critical reading scores over 500: 64%; SAT math scores over 500: 75%; SAT writing scores over 500: 69%; ACT scores over 18: 98%; SAT critical reading scores over 600: 14%; SAT math scores over 600: 19%; SAT writing scores over 600: 14%; ACT scores over 24: 33%; SAT critical reading scores over 700: 1%; SAT math scores over 700: 1%; SAT writing scores over 700: 1%; ACT scores over 30: 1%.

Faculty *Total:* 335, 28% full-time, 40% with terminal degrees. *Student/faculty ratio:* 15:1.

Academics *Calendar:* semesters. *Degrees:* associate, bachelor's, master's, and postbachelor's certificates. *Special study options:* accelerated degree program, adult/continuing education programs, advanced placement credit, cooperative education, distance learning, honors programs, independent study, internships, off-campus study, part-time degree program, services for LD stu-

dents, student-designed majors, study abroad, summer session for credit. *ROTC:* Army (c).

Computers on Campus 158 computers/terminals are available on campus for general student use. Students can access the following: campus intranet, computer help desk, free student e-mail accounts, online (class) grades, online (class) registration, online (class) schedules. Campuswide network is available. 100% of college-owned or -operated housing units are wired for high-speed Internet access. Wireless service is available via entire campus.

Student Life *Housing options:* coed, women-only, disabled students. Campus housing is university owned. Freshman campus housing is guaranteed. *Activities and organizations:* drama/theater group, student-run newspaper, radio and television station, choral group, Campus Activities Board, Student Senate, Intramurals, Sailing Club, Shipmates. *Campus security:* 24-hour emergency response devices and patrols, student patrols, late-night transport/escort service, controlled dormitory access, license plate recognition, crime prevention programs, rape awareness defense, property identification, security cameras, front gate. *Student services:* health clinic, personal/psychological counseling.

Athletics Member NCAA. All Division III. *Intercollegiate sports:* baseball M, basketball M/W, cheerleading W(c), crew M(c)/W(c), cross-country running M/W, equestrian sports M/W, field hockey W, football M, golf M/W(c), ice hockey M(c)/W(c), lacrosse M/W, sailing M(c)/W(c), soccer M/W, softball W, tennis M/W, volleyball M/W. *Intramural sports:* basketball M/W, football M/W, racquetball M/W, soccer M/W, softball M/W, tennis M/W, volleyball M/W.

Standardized Tests *Required:* SAT or ACT (for admission).

Costs (2011–12) *Comprehensive fee:* $39,890 includes full-time tuition ($26,730), mandatory fees ($400), and room and board ($12,760). Part-time tuition: $820 per credit hour. *Required fees:* $250 per term part-time. *College room only:* $8836. Room and board charges vary according to board plan and housing facility. *Payment plans:* tuition prepayment, installment. *Waivers:* employees or children of employees.

Financial Aid Of all full-time matriculated undergraduates who enrolled in 2010, 1,852 applied for aid, 1,356 were judged to have need, 157 had their need fully met. 461 Federal Work-Study jobs (averaging $2000). In 2010, 379 non-need-based awards were made. *Average percent of need met:* 62%. *Average financial aid package:* $17,981. *Average need-based loan:* $4541. *Average need-based gift aid:* $9901. *Average non-need-based aid:* $7512. *Average indebtedness upon graduation:* $39,168.

Applying *Options:* electronic application. *Application fee:* $50. *Required:* essay or personal statement, high school transcript, minimum 2.5 GPA, 1 letter of recommendation. *Required for some:* interview. *Recommended:* interview. *Application deadlines:* 2/15 (freshmen), 3/15 (transfers). *Notification:* continuous (freshmen), continuous (transfers).

Freshman Application Contact Mr. Thomas J. Redman, Vice President of Admission and Financial Aid, Endicott College, 376 Hale Street, Beverly, MA 01915. *Phone:* 978-921-1000. *Toll-free phone:* 800-325-1114. *Fax:* 978-232-2520. *E-mail:* admissio@endicott.edu. *Web site:* http://www.endicott.edu/.

Fisher College

Boston, Massachusetts

- **Independent** 4-year, founded 1903
- **Urban** campus with easy access to Boston
- **Coed**
- **Minimally difficult** entrance level

Faculty *Student/faculty ratio:* 18:1.

Academics *Calendar:* semesters. *Degrees:* certificates, associate, and bachelor's.

Student Life *Campus security:* 24-hour emergency response devices and patrols, controlled dormitory access.

Athletics Member NAIA.

Standardized Tests *Required for some:* SAT or ACT (for admission).

Costs (2011–12) *Comprehensive fee:* $39,564 includes full-time tuition ($24,783), mandatory fees ($995), and room and board ($13,786). Full-time tuition and fees vary according to course load. Part-time tuition: $285 per credit. Part-time tuition and fees vary according to course load and program. *Room and board:* Room and board charges vary according to housing facility.

Financial Aid *Of all full-time matriculated undergraduates who enrolled in 2011,* 955 applied for aid, 922 were judged to have need.

Applying *Options:* electronic application, deferred entrance. *Application fee:* $50. *Required:* high school transcript. *Required for some:* essay or personal statement, interview. *Recommended:* minimum 2.0 GPA.

Freshman Application Contact Mr. Robert Melaragni, Dean of Admissions, Fisher College, Boston, MA 02116. *Phone:* 617-236-8818. *Fax:* 617-236-5473. *E-mail:* admissions@fisher.edu. *Web site:* http://www.fisher.edu/.

Fitchburg State University

Fitchburg, Massachusetts

- **State-supported** comprehensive, founded 1894, part of Massachusetts Public Higher Education System
- **Suburban** 78-acre campus with easy access to Boston
- **Endowment** $15.0 million
- **Coed** 4,172 undergraduate students, 82% full-time, 54% women, 46% men
- **Moderately difficult** entrance level, 70% of applicants were admitted

Undergraduates 3,430 full-time, 742 part-time. Students come from 23 states and territories; 6 other countries; 8% are from out of state; 4% Black or African American, non-Hispanic/Latino; 6% Hispanic/Latino; 2% Asian, non-Hispanic/Latino; 0.1% Native Hawaiian or other Pacific Islander, non-Hispanic/Latino; 0.3% American Indian or Alaska Native, non-Hispanic/Latino; 2% Two or more races, non-Hispanic/Latino; 5% Race/ethnicity unknown; 0.4% international; 9% transferred in; 41% live on campus. *Retention:* 73% of full-time freshmen returned.

Freshmen *Admission:* 3,104 applied, 2,163 admitted, 698 enrolled. *Average high school GPA:* 3.1. *Test scores:* SAT critical reading scores over 500: 52%; SAT math scores over 500: 60%; SAT writing scores over 500: 49%; ACT scores over 18: 89%; SAT critical reading scores over 600: 12%; SAT math scores over 600: 14%; SAT writing scores over 600: 10%; ACT scores over 24: 22%; SAT critical reading scores over 700: 1%; SAT math scores over 700: 1%; SAT writing scores over 700: 1%; ACT scores over 30: 1%.

Faculty *Total:* 274, 67% full-time, 71% with terminal degrees. *Student/faculty ratio:* 16:1.

Academics *Calendar:* semesters. *Degrees:* certificates, bachelor's, master's, post-master's, and postbachelor's certificates. *Special study options:* academic remediation for entering students, accelerated degree program, adult/continuing education programs, advanced placement credit, distance learning, double majors, honors programs, independent study, internships, off-campus study, part-time degree program, services for LD students, student-designed majors, study abroad, summer session for credit. *ROTC:* Army (b).

Computers on Campus 500 computers/terminals are available on campus for general student use. Students can access the following: computer help desk, free student e-mail accounts, online (class) grades, online (class) registration, online (class) schedules. Campuswide network is available. 100% of college-owned or -operated housing units are wired for high-speed Internet access. Wireless service is available via entire campus.

Student Life *Housing options:* coed, disabled students. Campus housing is university owned. Freshman applicants given priority for college housing. *Activities and organizations:* drama/theater group, student-run newspaper, radio station, choral group, Student Government Association, Dance Club, Activities Board, Greek Council, MASSPIRG, national fraternities, national sororities. *Campus security:* 24-hour emergency response devices and patrols, student patrols, late-night transport/escort service, controlled dormitory access. *Student services:* health clinic, personal/psychological counseling.

Athletics Member NCAA. All Division III. *Intercollegiate sports:* baseball M, basketball M/W, cross-country running M/W, field hockey W, football M, ice hockey M, lacrosse W, soccer M/W, softball W, track and field M/W. *Intramural sports:* basketball M/W, football M/W, racquetball M/W, soccer M/W, softball M/W, swimming and diving M/W, table tennis M/W, ultimate Frisbee M/W, volleyball M/W, water polo M/W.

Standardized Tests *Required:* SAT or ACT (for admission).

Costs (2011–12) *Tuition:* state resident $970 full-time, $40 per credit part-time; nonresident $7050 full-time, $294 per credit part-time. Full-time tuition and fees vary according to class time and reciprocity agreements. Part-time tuition and fees vary according to class time and reciprocity agreements. *Required fees:* $7330 full-time, $305 per credit part-time. *Room and board:* $8256. Room and board charges vary according to board plan and housing facility. *Payment plan:* installment. *Waivers:* senior citizens and employees or children of employees.

Financial Aid Of all full-time matriculated undergraduates who enrolled in 2009, 3,132 applied for aid, 1,934 were judged to have need, 1,742 had their need fully met. 248 Federal Work-Study jobs (averaging $1076). In 2009, 76 non-need-based awards were made. *Average percent of need met:* 93%. *Average financial aid package:* $8645. *Average need-based loan:* $3679. *Average need-based gift aid:* $4336. *Average non-need-based aid:* $1292. *Average indebtedness upon graduation:* $19,902.

Applying *Options:* electronic application, deferred entrance. *Application fee:* $25. *Required:* essay or personal statement, high school transcript, minimum 2.0 GPA, 16 core courses. *Application deadlines:* rolling (freshmen), rolling (out-of-state freshmen), rolling (transfers). *Notification:* continuous (freshmen), continuous (out-of-state freshmen), continuous (transfers).

Freshman Application Contact Kay Reynolds, Director of Admissions, Fitchburg State University, 160 Pearl Street, Fitchburg, MA 01420-2697. *Phone:* 978-665-3144. *Toll-free phone:* 800-705-9692. *Fax:* 978-665-4540.

E-mail: admissions@fitchburgstate.edu. *Web site:* http://www.fitchburgstate.edu/.

See below for display ad and page 1328 for the College Close-Up.

Framingham State University
Framingham, Massachusetts

- **State-supported** comprehensive, founded 1839, part of Massachusetts Public Higher Education System
- **Suburban** 50-acre campus with easy access to Boston
- **Endowment** $21.3 million
- **Coed** 4,321 undergraduate students, 84% full-time, 63% women, 37% men
- **Moderately difficult** entrance level, 30% of applicants were admitted

Undergraduates 3,621 full-time, 700 part-time. 6% are from out of state; 6% Black or African American, non-Hispanic/Latino; 7% Hispanic/Latino; 2% Asian, non-Hispanic/Latino; 0.1% Native Hawaiian or other Pacific Islander, non-Hispanic/Latino; 0.3% American Indian or Alaska Native, non-Hispanic/Latino; 12% Race/ethnicity unknown; 0.8% international; 10% transferred in; 50% live on campus. *Retention:* 74% of full-time freshmen returned.

Freshmen *Admission:* 4,909 applied, 1,493 admitted, 924 enrolled. *Average high school GPA:* 3.13. *Test scores:* SAT critical reading scores over 500: 58%; SAT math scores over 500: 60%; SAT writing scores over 500: 55%; ACT scores over 18: 96%; SAT critical reading scores over 600: 13%; SAT math scores over 600: 14%; SAT writing scores over 600: 13%; ACT scores over 24: 44%; SAT critical reading scores over 700: 2%; SAT math scores over 700: 1%; SAT writing scores over 700: 1%; ACT scores over 30: 2%.

Faculty *Total:* 298, 59% full-time, 61% with terminal degrees. *Student/faculty ratio:* 16:1.

Academics *Calendar:* semesters. *Degrees:* bachelor's, master's, and post-bachelor's certificates. *Special study options:* advanced placement credit, distance learning, double majors, English as a second language, honors programs, independent study, internships, off-campus study, part-time degree program, services for LD students, study abroad, summer session for credit.

Computers on Campus 232 computers/terminals and 3,500 ports are available on campus for general student use. Students can access the following: computer help desk, free student e-mail accounts, online (class) grades, online (class) registration, online (class) schedules. Campuswide network is available. 100% of college-owned or -operated housing units are wired for high-speed Internet access. Wireless service is available via entire campus.

Student Life *Housing options:* coed, women-only. Campus housing is university owned. Freshman applicants given priority for college housing. *Activities and organizations:* drama/theater group, student-run newspaper, radio station, choral group, Dance Club, Student Union Activities Board, Gatepost (student newspaper), Student Government Association, Hilltop Players (theater group). *Campus security:* 24-hour emergency response devices and patrols, student patrols, late-night transport/escort service, controlled dormitory access. *Student services:* health clinic, personal/psychological counseling.

Athletics Member NCAA. All Division III. *Intercollegiate sports:* baseball M, basketball M/W, cross-country running M/W, field hockey W, football M, ice hockey M, lacrosse W, soccer M/W, softball W, volleyball W. *Intramural sports:* badminton M(c)/W(c), basketball M/W, cheerleading M(c)/W(c), football M/W, golf M/W, rugby M(c)/W(c), skiing (downhill) M(c)/W(c), soccer M/W, tennis M/W, ultimate Frisbee M/W, volleyball M/W, weight lifting M/W.

Standardized Tests *Required:* SAT or ACT (for admission).

Costs (2011–12) *Tuition:* state resident $970 full-time, $162 per course part-time; nonresident $7050 full-time, $1175 per course part-time. Full-time tuition and fees vary according to class time. Part-time tuition and fees vary according to class time and course load. *Required fees:* $6610 full-time, $1167 per course part-time. *Room and board:* $9170; room only: $6090. Room and board charges vary according to board plan and housing facility. *Payment plans:* tuition prepayment, installment. *Waivers:* senior citizens and employees or children of employees.

Financial Aid Of all full-time matriculated undergraduates who enrolled in 2009, 2,362 applied for aid, 1,624 were judged to have need, 895 had their need fully met. In 2009, 74 non-need-based awards were made. *Average percent of need met:* 76%. *Average financial aid package:* $6880. *Average need-based loan:* $4950. *Average need-based gift aid:* $4090. *Average non-need-based aid:* $2208. *Average indebtedness upon graduation:* $19,300.

Applying *Options:* electronic application, early action, deferred entrance. *Application fee:* $45. *Required:* high school transcript, minimum 2.0 GPA, minimum of 16 college preparatory courses in specified areas. *Recommended:* minimum 3.0 GPA. *Application deadlines:* 2/15 (freshmen), 2/15 (transfers), 11/15 (early action). *Notification:* continuous (freshmen), continuous (transfers), 12/15 (early action).

Freshman Application Contact Ms. Shayna Eddy, Assistant Dean of Admissions, Framingham State University, 100 State Street, PO Box 9101, Framingham, MA 01701-9101. *Phone:* 508-626-4500. *Fax:* 508-626-4017. *E-mail:* admissions@framingham.edu. *Web site:* http://www.framingham.edu/.

Franklin W. Olin College of Engineering

Needham, Massachusetts

- **Independent** 4-year, founded 2002
- **Suburban** 75-acre campus with easy access to Boston
- **Endowment** $369.1 million
- **Coed** 344 undergraduate students, 100% full-time, 46% women, 54% men
- **Most difficult** entrance level, 16% of applicants were admitted

Undergraduates 344 full-time. Students come from 38 states and territories; 17 other countries; 87% are from out of state; 1% Black or African American, non-Hispanic/Latino; 1% Hispanic/Latino; 15% Asian, non-Hispanic/Latino; 4% Two or more races, non-Hispanic/Latino; 10% Race/ethnicity unknown; 10% international; 100% live on campus. *Retention:* 91% of full-time freshmen returned.

Freshmen *Admission:* 768 applied, 126 admitted, 81 enrolled. *Average high school GPA:* 4. *Test scores:* SAT critical reading scores over 500: 100%; SAT math scores over 500: 100%; SAT writing scores over 500: 100%; ACT scores over 18: 100%; SAT critical reading scores over 600: 98%; SAT math scores over 600: 100%; SAT writing scores over 600: 95%; ACT scores over 24: 100%; SAT critical reading scores over 700: 74%; SAT math scores over 700: 87%; SAT writing scores over 700: 46%; ACT scores over 30: 100%.

Faculty *Total:* 44, 80% full-time, 95% with terminal degrees. *Student/faculty ratio:* 9:1.

Academics *Degree:* bachelor's. *Special study options:* independent study, internships, off-campus study, services for LD students, student-designed majors, study abroad.

Computers on Campus 15 computers/terminals and 5,500 ports are available on campus for general student use. Students can access the following: campus intranet, computer help desk, free student e-mail accounts, online (class) grades, online (class) registration, online (class) schedules. Campuswide network is available. 100% of college-owned or -operated housing units are wired for high-speed Internet access. Wireless service is available via entire campus.

Student Life *Housing:* on-campus residence required through senior year. *Options:* coed, disabled students. Campus housing is university owned. Freshman campus housing is guaranteed. *Activities and organizations:* drama/theater group, student-run newspaper, choral group, Greening Olin, Olin Fire Arts Club, Support, Encourage and Recognize Volunteerism (SERV), Olin Entrepreneurial Group, Open. *Campus security:* 24-hour emergency response devices and patrols, controlled dormitory access. *Student services:* health clinic, personal/psychological counseling.

Athletics *Intercollegiate sports:* soccer M(c)/W(c), ultimate Frisbee M(c)/W(c). *Intramural sports:* basketball M/W, softball M/W, volleyball M/W.

Standardized Tests *Required:* SAT or ACT (for admission), SAT Subject Tests (for admission).

Costs (2012–13) *One-time required fee:* $2500. *Comprehensive fee:* $54,675 includes full-time tuition ($40,000), mandatory fees ($475), and room and board ($14,200). Part-time tuition: $1333 per credit. *College room only:* $9000. *Payment plan:* installment.

Financial Aid Of all full-time matriculated undergraduates who enrolled in 2011, 155 applied for aid, 123 were judged to have need, 123 had their need fully met. In 2011, 203 non-need-based awards were made. *Average percent of need met:* 100%. *Average financial aid package:* $32,290. *Average need-based loan:* $3156. *Average need-based gift aid:* $18,228. *Average non-need-based aid:* $36,022. *Average indebtedness upon graduation:* $11,900. *Financial aid deadline:* 2/15.

Applying *Options:* electronic application, deferred entrance. *Application fee:* $80. *Required:* essay or personal statement, high school transcript, 3 letters of recommendation, interview. *Application deadline:* 1/1 (freshmen). *Notification:* 3/21 (freshmen).

Freshman Application Contact Franklin W. Olin College of Engineering, Olin Way, Needham, MA 02492-1200. *Phone:* 781-292-2250. *Fax:* 781-292-2310. *E-mail:* info@olin.edu. *Web site:* http://www.olin.edu/.

Gordon College

Wenham, Massachusetts

- **Independent nondenominational** comprehensive, founded 1889
- **Suburban** 450-acre campus with easy access to Boston
- **Endowment** $26.8 million
- **Coed** 1,573 undergraduate students, 98% full-time, 61% women, 39% men
- **Moderately difficult** entrance level, 40% of applicants were admitted

Undergraduates 1,534 full-time, 39 part-time. Students come from 44 states and territories; 56 other countries; 69% are from out of state; 2% Black or Afri-

can American, non-Hispanic/Latino; 7% Hispanic/Latino; 2% Asian, non-Hispanic/Latino; 0.5% Native Hawaiian or other Pacific Islander, non-Hispanic/Latino; 0.2% American Indian or Alaska Native, non-Hispanic/Latino; 3% Two or more races, non-Hispanic/Latino; 4% international; 4% transferred in; 89% live on campus. *Retention:* 82% of full-time freshmen returned.

Freshmen *Admission:* 4,315 applied, 1,713 admitted, 464 enrolled. *Average high school GPA:* 3.53. *Test scores:* SAT critical reading scores over 500: 87%; SAT math scores over 500: 84%; SAT writing scores over 500: 87%; ACT scores over 18: 99%; SAT critical reading scores over 600: 50%; SAT math scores over 600: 46%; SAT writing scores over 600: 46%; ACT scores over 24: 71%; SAT critical reading scores over 700: 12%; SAT math scores over 700: 8%; SAT writing scores over 700: 12%; ACT scores over 30: 13%.

Faculty *Total:* 173, 57% full-time, 49% with terminal degrees. *Student/faculty ratio:* 13:1.

Academics *Calendar:* semesters. *Degrees:* bachelor's and master's. *Special study options:* academic remediation for entering students, advanced placement credit, cooperative education, double majors, honors programs, independent study, internships, off-campus study, part-time degree program, services for LD students, student-designed majors, study abroad, summer session for credit. *ROTC:* Army (c). *Unusual degree programs:* 3-2 engineering with University of Southern California.

Computers on Campus 100 computers/terminals are available on campus for general student use. Students can access the following: campus intranet, computer help desk, free student e-mail accounts, online (class) grades, online (class) registration, online (class) schedules. Campuswide network is available. 100% of college-owned or -operated housing units are wired for high-speed Internet access. Wireless service is available via entire campus.

Student Life *Housing:* on-campus residence required through senior year. *Options:* coed, men-only, women-only, disabled students. Campus housing is university owned. Freshman campus housing is guaranteed. *Activities and organizations:* drama/theater group, student-run newspaper, radio station, choral group, Student government association, Student ministries and volunteer programs, Diverse music ensembles, Intramural sports, Short-term missions. *Campus security:* 24-hour emergency response devices and patrols, late-night transport/escort service, controlled dormitory access, video cameras. *Student services:* health clinic, personal/psychological counseling.

Athletics Member NCAA. All Division III. *Intercollegiate sports:* baseball M, basketball M/W, cross-country running M/W, field hockey W, golf M(c)/W(c), lacrosse M/W, soccer M/W, softball W, swimming and diving M/W, tennis M/W, track and field M/W, volleyball W. *Intramural sports:* basketball M/W, cheerleading W(c), football M/W, ice hockey M(c)/W(c), racquetball M/W, rock climbing M/W, skiing (downhill) M(c)/W(c), soccer M/W, softball W, table tennis M/W, tennis M/W, track and field M/W, ultimate Frisbee M/W, volleyball M.

Standardized Tests *Required:* SAT or ACT (for admission). *Recommended:* SAT Subject Tests (for admission).

Costs (2012–13) *Comprehensive fee:* $40,940 includes full-time tuition ($30,740), mandatory fees ($1360), and room and board ($8840). Full-time tuition and fees vary according to course load and program. Part-time tuition: $1085 per credit. Part-time tuition and fees vary according to course load and program. *College room only:* $5900. Room and board charges vary according to board plan and housing facility. *Payment plan:* installment. *Waivers:* employees or children of employees.

Financial Aid Of all full-time matriculated undergraduates who enrolled in 2011, 1,289 applied for aid, 1,153 were judged to have need, 165 had their need fully met. 808 Federal Work-Study jobs (averaging $1529). In 2011, 313 non-need-based awards were made. *Average percent of need met:* 68%. *Average financial aid package:* $19,051. *Average need-based loan:* $4461. *Average need-based gift aid:* $14,487. *Average non-need-based aid:* $11,641. *Average indebtedness upon graduation:* $34,919.

Applying *Options:* electronic application, early admission, early decision, early action, deferred entrance. *Application fee:* $50. *Required:* high school transcript, 2 letters of recommendation, interview, Pastoral recommendation and statement of Christian faith. *Recommended:* essay or personal statement, minimum 3.0 GPA. *Application deadlines:* rolling (freshmen), rolling (transfers), 11/15 (early action). *Early decision deadline:* 11/1. *Notification:* continuous until 9/15 (freshmen), continuous (transfers), 12/1 (early decision), 12/15 (early action).

Freshman Application Contact Ms. June Bodoni, Executive Director of Admissions and Advancement Operations, Gordon College, 255 Grapevine Road, Wenham, MA 01984. *Phone:* 978-867-4218. *Toll-free phone:* 866-464-6736. *Fax:* 978-867-4682. *E-mail:* admissions@gordon.edu. *Web site:* http://www.gordon.edu/.

Hampshire College

Amherst, Massachusetts

- **Independent** 4-year, founded 1965
- **Small-town** 800-acre campus
- **Endowment** $28.9 million
- **Coed** 1,500 undergraduate students, 100% full-time, 59% women, 41% men
- **Moderately difficult** entrance level, 71% of applicants were admitted

Undergraduates 1,500 full-time. Students come from 47 states and territories; 19 other countries; 82% are from out of state; 3% Black or African American, non-Hispanic/Latino; 9% Hispanic/Latino; 2% Asian, non-Hispanic/Latino; 0.1% Native Hawaiian or other Pacific Islander, non-Hispanic/Latino; 0.3% American Indian or Alaska Native, non-Hispanic/Latino; 4% Two or more races, non-Hispanic/Latino; 11% Race/ethnicity unknown; 6% international; 3% transferred in; 80% live on campus. *Retention:* 78% of full-time freshmen returned.

Freshmen *Admission:* 2,517 applied, 1,797 admitted, 356 enrolled. *Average high school GPA:* 3.31. *Test scores:* SAT critical reading scores over 500: 91%; SAT math scores over 500: 88%; SAT writing scores over 500: 93%; ACT scores over 18: 99%; SAT critical reading scores over 600: 71%; SAT math scores over 600: 49%; SAT writing scores over 600: 67%; ACT scores over 24: 84%; SAT critical reading scores over 700: 27%; SAT math scores over 700: 10%; SAT writing scores over 700: 20%; ACT scores over 30: 24%.

Faculty *Total:* 160, 61% full-time, 78% with terminal degrees. *Student/faculty ratio:* 12:1.

Academics *Calendar:* 4-1-4. *Degree:* bachelor's. *Special study options:* independent study, internships, off-campus study, services for LD students, student-designed majors, study abroad. *ROTC:* Army (c).

Computers on Campus 215 computers/terminals are available on campus for general student use. Students can access the following: campus intranet, computer help desk, free student e-mail accounts, online (class) grades, online (class) registration, online (class) schedules. Campuswide network is available. 100% of college-owned or -operated housing units are wired for high-speed Internet access. Wireless service is available via entire campus.

Student Life *Housing:* on-campus residence required through senior year. *Options:* coed, men-only, women-only, cooperative, disabled students. Campus housing is university owned. Freshman campus housing is guaranteed. *Activities and organizations:* drama/theater group, student-run newspaper, radio station, choral group, Red Scare Frisbee, Queer Community Alliance, Excalibur (fantasy/role playing), Sports Coop, Circus Folks Unite. *Campus security:* 24-hour emergency response devices and patrols. *Student services:* health clinic, personal/psychological counseling, women's center.

Athletics Member USCAA. *Intercollegiate sports:* basketball M(c)/W(c), cross-country running M/W, equestrian sports M(c)/W(c), fencing M/W, soccer M/W, ultimate Frisbee M/W. *Intramural sports:* basketball M/W, equestrian sports M(c)/W(c), rock climbing M(c)/W(c), soccer M/W, table tennis M(c)/W(c), ultimate Frisbee M/W.

Standardized Tests *Recommended:* SAT and SAT Subject Tests or ACT (for admission).

Costs (2011–12) *One-time required fee:* $110. *Comprehensive fee:* $54,080 includes full-time tuition ($41,900), mandatory fees ($1000), and room and board ($11,180). *College room only:* $7130. Room and board charges vary according to board plan. *Payment plan:* installment. *Waivers:* employees or children of employees.

Financial Aid Of all full-time matriculated undergraduates who enrolled in 2010, 1,047 applied for aid, 920 were judged to have need, 666 had their need fully met. In 2010, 275 non-need-based awards were made. *Average percent of need met:* 95%. *Average financial aid package:* $37,165. *Average need-based loan:* $4750. *Average need-based gift aid:* $29,940. *Average non-need-based aid:* $6880. *Average indebtedness upon graduation:* $21,673.

Applying *Options:* electronic application, early admission, early decision, early action, deferred entrance. *Application fee:* $60. *Required:* essay or personal statement, high school transcript, 1 letter of recommendation. *Recommended:* interview. *Application deadlines:* 1/1 (freshmen), 3/1 (transfers), 12/1 (early action). *Early decision deadline:* 11/15 (for plan 1), 1/1 (for plan 2). *Notification:* 4/1 (freshmen), 4/15 (transfers), 12/15 (early decision plan 1), 2/1 (early decision plan 2), 2/1 (early action).

Freshman Application Contact Ms. Julie Richardson, Director of Admissions, Hampshire College, Hampshire College, 893 West Street, Amherst, MA 01002. *Phone:* 413-559-5471. *Toll-free phone:* 877-937-4267. *Fax:* 413-559-5631. *E-mail:* admissions@hampshire.edu. *Web site:* http://www.hampshire.edu/.

Harvard University

Cambridge, Massachusetts

- **Independent** university, founded 1636
- **Urban** 380-acre campus with easy access to Boston
- **Endowment** $32.0 billion
- **Coed** 6,676 undergraduate students, 100% full-time, 50% women, 50% men
- **Most difficult** entrance level, 6% of applicants were admitted

Undergraduates 6,671 full-time, 5 part-time. Students come from 55 states and territories; 111 other countries; 85% are from out of state; 7% Black or African American, non-Hispanic/Latino; 9% Hispanic/Latino; 18% Asian, non-Hispanic/Latino; 0.3% American Indian or Alaska Native, non-Hispanic/Latino; 5% Two or more races, non-Hispanic/Latino; 6% Race/ethnicity unknown; 10% international; 0.2% transferred in; 96% live on campus. *Retention:* 97% of full-time freshmen returned.

Freshmen *Admission:* 34,950 applied, 2,188 admitted, 1,657 enrolled. *Average high school GPA:* 4. *Test scores:* SAT critical reading scores over 500: 100%; SAT math scores over 500: 100%; SAT writing scores over 500: 100%; ACT scores over 18: 100%; SAT critical reading scores over 600: 96%; SAT math scores over 600: 98%; SAT writing scores over 600: 97%; ACT scores over 24: 100%; SAT critical reading scores over 700: 73%; SAT math scores over 700: 77%; SAT writing scores over 700: 75%; ACT scores over 30: 87%.

Faculty *Total:* 1,113, 83% full-time, 83% with terminal degrees. *Student/faculty ratio:* 7:1.

Academics *Calendar:* semesters. *Degrees:* bachelor's, master's, doctoral, and first professional. *Special study options:* accelerated degree program, advanced placement credit, double majors, honors programs, independent study, internships, off-campus study, services for LD students, student-designed majors, study abroad, summer session for credit. *ROTC:* Army (c), Navy (b), Air Force (c).

Computers on Campus 605 computers/terminals are available on campus for general student use. Students can access the following: computer help desk, free student e-mail accounts, online (class) grades, online (class) registration, online (class) schedules. Campuswide network is available. 100% of college-owned or -operated housing units are wired for high-speed Internet access. Wireless service is available via entire campus.

Student Life *Housing:* on-campus residence required for freshman year. *Options:* coed, cooperative, disabled students. Campus housing is university owned. Freshman campus housing is guaranteed. *Activities and organizations:* drama/theater group, student-run newspaper, radio and television station, choral group, marching band, Phillips Brooks House Association, Asian-American Association, International Relations Council, Harvard Crimson (newspaper), Harvard/Radcliffe Chorus. *Campus security:* 24-hour emergency response devices and patrols, late-night transport/escort service, controlled dormitory access, required and optional safety courses. *Student services:* health clinic, personal/psychological counseling, women's center.

Athletics Member NCAA. All Division I except football (Division I-AA). *Intercollegiate sports:* baseball M, basketball M/W, crew M/W, cross-country running M/W, fencing M/W, field hockey W, golf M/W, ice hockey M/W, lacrosse M/W, sailing M/W, skiing (cross-country) M/W, skiing (downhill) M/W, soccer M/W, softball W, squash M/W, swimming and diving M/W, tennis M/W, track and field M/W, volleyball M/W, water polo M/W, wrestling M. *Intramural sports:* archery M(c)/W(c), badminton M(c)/W(c), baseball M(c), basketball M/W, cheerleading M(c)/W(c), crew M/W, cross-country running M/W, fencing M/W, field hockey W(c), football M/W, ice hockey M/W, lacrosse M(c)/W(c), riflery M(c)/W(c), rugby M(c)/W(c), skiing (cross-country) M(c)/W(c), skiing (downhill) M(c)/W(c), soccer M/W, softball M/W, squash M/W, swimming and diving M/W, table tennis M/W, tennis M/W, ultimate Frisbee M/W, volleyball M/W, water polo M(c)/W(c), weight lifting M(c)/W(c), wrestling M(c)/W(c).

Standardized Tests *Required:* SAT or ACT (for admission), SAT Subject Tests (for admission).

Costs (2011–12) *Comprehensive fee:* $52,652 includes full-time tuition ($36,305), mandatory fees ($3546), and room and board ($12,801). *College room only:* $7811.

Financial Aid Of all full-time matriculated undergraduates who enrolled in 2011, 4,516 applied for aid, 4,054 were judged to have need, 4,054 had their need fully met. 1,014 Federal Work-Study jobs (averaging $2733). 2,158 state and other part-time jobs (averaging $2744). *Average percent of need met:* 100%. *Average financial aid package:* $44,228. *Average need-based loan:* $4425. *Average need-based gift aid:* $41,507. *Average indebtedness upon graduation:* $11,780.

Applying *Options:* electronic application, early action, deferred entrance. *Application fee:* $75. *Required:* essay or personal statement, high school transcript. *Recommended:* 2 letters of recommendation, interview. *Application deadlines:* 1/1 (freshmen), 3/1 (transfers). *Notification:* 4/1 (freshmen), 6/15 (transfers).

Freshman Application Contact Harvard University, Cambridge, MA 02138. *Phone:* 617-495-1551. *Web site:* http://www.harvard.edu/.

Hebrew College
Newton Centre, Massachusetts

- **Independent Jewish** comprehensive, founded 1921
- **Suburban** 3-acre campus with easy access to Boston
- **Coed** 8 undergraduate students, 38% women, 63% men
- **Minimally difficult** entrance level

Undergraduates 8 part-time. Students come from 3 states and territories; 1 other country; 1% are from out of state.

Faculty *Total:* 41, 49% full-time, 73% with terminal degrees.

Academics *Calendar:* semesters. *Degrees:* bachelor's, master's, post-master's, and postbachelor's certificates. *Special study options:* adult/continuing education programs, distance learning, double majors, independent study, off-campus study, part-time degree program, summer session for credit. *Unusual degree programs:* 3-2 BA/MA (Jewish Studies, Jewish Education).

Computers on Campus 10 computers/terminals are available on campus for general student use.

Student Life *Housing:* college housing not available.

Standardized Tests *Required for some:* GRE. *Recommended:* SAT or ACT (for admission).

Costs (2012–13) *Tuition:* $18,000 full-time. Full-time tuition and fees vary according to course load, degree level, and program. Part-time tuition and fees vary according to course load, degree level, and program. *Required fees:* $200 full-time. *Payment plan:* installment. *Waivers:* employees or children of employees.

Financial Aid Of all full-time matriculated undergraduates who enrolled in 2011, 1 applied for aid, 1 were judged to have need. *Average percent of need met:* 30%. *Average financial aid package:* $1500. *Average need-based gift aid:* $1500. *Average indebtedness upon graduation:* $9000.

Applying *Options:* early admission, deferred entrance. *Application fee:* $50. *Required:* essay or personal statement, high school transcript, 3 letters of recommendation, interview. *Required for some:* 60 credits of undergraduate transfer work for BA students. *Application deadlines:* rolling (freshmen), 4/15 (transfers). *Notification:* continuous (freshmen), continuous until 8/1 (transfers).

Freshman Application Contact Director of Enrollment Management, Hebrew College, 160 Herreck Road, Newton Centre, MA 02459. *Phone:* 617-559-8610. *Toll-free phone:* 800-866-4814. *Fax:* 617-559-8601. *E-mail:* admissions@lhebrewcollege.edu. *Web site:* http://www.hebrewcollege.edu/.

Hellenic College
Brookline, Massachusetts

- **Independent Greek Orthodox** comprehensive, founded 1937
- **Suburban** 52-acre campus with easy access to Boston
- **Endowment** $25.9 million
- **Coed** 99 undergraduate students, 100% full-time, 38% women, 62% men
- **Minimally difficult** entrance level, 59% of applicants were admitted

Undergraduates 99 full-time. Students come from 30 states and territories; 5 other countries; 80% are from out of state; 2% Hispanic/Latino; 8% international; 11% transferred in; 95% live on campus. *Retention:* 94% of full-time freshmen returned.

Freshmen *Admission:* 64 applied, 38 admitted, 27 enrolled. *Average high school GPA:* 3.1.

Faculty *Total:* 50, 36% full-time. *Student/faculty ratio:* 9:1.

Academics *Calendar:* semesters. *Degrees:* bachelor's and master's (also offers graduate degree programs through Holy Cross Greek Orthodox School of Theology). *Special study options:* academic remediation for entering students, advanced placement credit, double majors, independent study, internships, off-campus study, part-time degree program, summer session for credit.

Computers on Campus 35 computers/terminals and 100 ports are available on campus for general student use. Students can access the following: campus intranet, computer help desk, free student e-mail accounts, online (class) grades, online (class) registration, online (class) schedules. Campuswide network is available. 75% of college-owned or -operated housing units are wired for high-speed Internet access. Wireless service is available via dorm rooms, learning centers.

Student Life *Housing:* on-campus residence required through senior year. *Options:* coed. Campus housing is university owned. Freshman campus housing is guaranteed. *Activities and organizations:* student-run newspaper, choral group. *Campus security:* controlled dormitory access. *Student services:* health clinic, personal/psychological counseling.

Athletics *Intramural sports:* baseball M, basketball M/W, football M, golf M, soccer M, table tennis M/W, volleyball M/W.

Standardized Tests *Required:* SAT or ACT (for admission). *Required for some:* SAT Subject Tests (for admission).

Costs (2011–12) *Comprehensive fee:* $33,090 includes full-time tuition ($19,900), mandatory fees ($450), and room and board ($12,740). Part-time tuition: $829 per credit hour. *Room and board:* Room and board charges vary according to housing facility. *Payment plans:* installment, deferred payment. *Waivers:* children of alumni and employees or children of employees.

Financial Aid Of all full-time matriculated undergraduates who enrolled in 2008, 59 applied for aid, 57 were judged to have need. In 2008, 1 non-need-based awards were made. *Average percent of need met:* 80%. *Average financial aid package:* $9500. *Average need-based loan:* $5500. *Average non-need-based aid:* $5000. *Average indebtedness upon graduation:* $15,000.

Applying *Options:* electronic application, early action, deferred entrance. *Application fee:* $50. *Required:* essay or personal statement, high school transcript, minimum 2.0 GPA, interview, health certificate, SAT or ACT Scores. *Application deadlines:* rolling (freshmen), rolling (transfers), 12/1 (early action). *Notification:* continuous (freshmen), continuous (transfers).

Freshman Application Contact Mr. Gregory Floor, Director of Admissions, Hellenic College, 50 Goddard Avenue, Brookline, MA 02445-7496. *Phone:* 617-850-1285. *Toll-free phone:* 866-424-2338. *Fax:* 617-850-1460. *E-mail:* admissions@hchc.edu. *Web site:* http://www.hchc.edu/.

ITT Technical Institute
Norwood, Massachusetts

- **Proprietary** primarily 2-year, founded 1990, part of ITT Educational Services, Inc.
- **Suburban** campus
- **Coed**
- **Minimally difficult** entrance level

Academics *Calendar:* quarters. *Degrees:* associate and bachelor's.

Student Life *Housing:* college housing not available.

Freshman Application Contact Director of Recruitment, ITT Technical Institute, 333 Providence Highway, Norwood, MA 02062. *Phone:* 781-278-7200. *Toll-free phone:* 800-879-8324. *Web site:* http://www.itt-tech.edu/.

ITT Technical Institute
Wilmington, Massachusetts

- **Proprietary** primarily 2-year, founded 2000, part of ITT Educational Services, Inc.
- **Coed**
- **Minimally difficult** entrance level

Academics *Calendar:* quarters. *Degrees:* associate and bachelor's.

Student Life *Housing:* college housing not available.

Freshman Application Contact Director of Recruitment, ITT Technical Institute, 200 Ballardvale Street, Suite 200, Wilmington, MA 01887. *Phone:* 978-658-2636. *Toll-free phone:* 800-430-5097. *Web site:* http://www.itt-tech.edu/.

Lasell College
Newton, Massachusetts

- **Independent** comprehensive, founded 1851
- **Suburban** 50-acre campus with easy access to Boston
- **Endowment** $28.3 million
- **Coed** 1,537 undergraduate students, 98% full-time, 64% women, 36% men
- **Moderately difficult** entrance level, 74% of applicants were admitted

Undergraduates 1,508 full-time, 29 part-time. Students come from 28 states and territories; 20 other countries; 48% are from out of state; 7% Black or African American, non-Hispanic/Latino; 8% Hispanic/Latino; 3% Asian, non-Hispanic/Latino; 0.3% Native Hawaiian or other Pacific Islander, non-Hispanic/Latino; 0.3% American Indian or Alaska Native, non-Hispanic/Latino; 3% Two or more races, non-Hispanic/Latino; 0.8% Race/ethnicity unknown; 2% international; 5% transferred in; 78% live on campus. *Retention:* 64% of full-time freshmen returned.

Freshmen *Admission:* 2,867 applied, 2,125 admitted, 374 enrolled. *Average high school GPA:* 2.8. *Test scores:* SAT critical reading scores over 500: 43%; SAT math scores over 500: 45%; SAT writing scores over 500: 39%; ACT scores over 18: 90%; SAT critical reading scores over 600: 5%; SAT math scores over 600: 10%; SAT writing scores over 600: 5%; ACT scores over 24: 21%; SAT math scores over 700: 1%.

Faculty *Total:* 202, 37% full-time, 50% with terminal degrees. *Student/faculty ratio:* 13:1.

Academics *Calendar:* semesters. *Degrees:* bachelor's and master's. *Special study options:* advanced placement credit, cooperative education, double

majors, English as a second language, honors programs, independent study, internships, part-time degree program, student-designed majors, study abroad.

Computers on Campus 150 computers/terminals are available on campus for general student use. Students can access the following: campus intranet, computer help desk, free student e-mail accounts, online (class) grades, online (class) registration, online (class) schedules. Campuswide network is available. 100% of college-owned or -operated housing units are wired for high-speed Internet access. Wireless service is available via computer centers, computer labs, dorm rooms, learning centers, libraries, student centers.

Student Life *Housing options:* coed, women-only, cooperative. Campus housing is university owned. Freshman campus housing is guaranteed. *Activities and organizations:* drama/theater group, student-run newspaper, radio station, choral group, Campus Activities Board, Tennis Club, Lasell College Radio Station, Students Advocating for Equality, Lasell Environmental Action Force. *Campus security:* 24-hour emergency response devices and patrols, late-night transport/escort service, controlled dormitory access. *Student services:* health clinic, personal/psychological counseling.

Athletics Member NCAA. All Division III. *Intercollegiate sports:* baseball M, basketball M/W, cross-country running M/W, field hockey W, lacrosse M/W, soccer M/W, softball W, track and field M/W, volleyball M/W. *Intramural sports:* basketball M/W, cheerleading M(c)/W(c), crew M(c)/W(c), rugby M(c), skiing (downhill) M(c)/W(c), tennis M(c)/W(c).

Standardized Tests *Required:* SAT or ACT (for admission).

Costs (2011–12) *Comprehensive fee:* $39,800 includes full-time tuition ($26,500), mandatory fees ($1000), and room and board ($12,300). Full-time tuition and fees vary according to program. Part-time tuition: $900 per credit hour. Part-time tuition and fees vary according to program. *Required fees:* $270 per term part-time. *Room and board:* Room and board charges vary according to board plan. *Payment plan:* installment. *Waivers:* children of alumni and employees or children of employees.

Financial Aid Of all full-time matriculated undergraduates who enrolled in 2011, 1,343 applied for aid, 1,220 were judged to have need, 180 had their need fully met. 654 Federal Work-Study jobs (averaging $1600). In 2011, 251 non-need-based awards were made. *Average percent of need met:* 68%. *Average financial aid package:* $20,529. *Average need-based loan:* $4243. *Average need-based gift aid:* $16,088. *Average non-need-based aid:* $8500. *Average indebtedness upon graduation:* $38,645.

Applying *Options:* electronic application, deferred entrance. *Application fee:* $40. *Required:* essay or personal statement, high school transcript, 2 letters of recommendation, college preparatory program. *Recommended:* interview. *Application deadlines:* rolling (freshmen), rolling (transfers). *Notification:* continuous (freshmen), continuous (transfers).

Freshman Application Contact Lasell College, 1844 Commonwealth Avenue, Newton, MA 02466-2709. *Phone:* 617-243-2225. *Toll-free phone:* 888-LASELL-4. *Web site:* http://www.lasell.edu/.

Lesley University

Cambridge, Massachusetts

- **Independent** comprehensive, founded 1909
- **Urban** campus with easy access to Boston
- **Coed, primarily women**
- 67% of applicants were admitted

Faculty *Student/faculty ratio:* 10:1.

Academics *Calendar:* semesters. *Degrees:* associate, bachelor's, master's, doctoral, post-master's, postbachelor's, and first professional certificates.

Student Life *Campus security:* 24-hour emergency response devices and patrols, late-night transport/escort service, controlled dormitory access.

Athletics Member NCAA. All Division III except baseball (Division II).

Standardized Tests *Required:* SAT or ACT (for admission).

Costs (2011–12) *Comprehensive fee:* $43,670 includes full-time tuition ($30,170), mandatory fees ($250), and room and board ($13,250). Full-time tuition and fees vary according to class time, course level, course load, degree level, location, program, reciprocity agreements, and student level. *College room only:* $8150. Room and board charges vary according to housing facility.

Financial Aid *Of all full-time matriculated undergraduates who enrolled in 2010,* 1,337 applied for aid, 1,034 were judged to have need, 155 had their need fully met. *In 2010,* 224 non-need-based awards were made. *Average percent of need met:* 70. *Average financial aid package:* $16,579. *Average need-based loan:* $4534. *Average need-based gift aid:* $14,563. *Average non-need-based aid:* $10,358. *Average indebtedness upon graduation:* $18,000.

Applying *Options:* electronic application, early action, deferred entrance. *Application fee:* $50. *Required:* essay or personal statement, high school transcript. *Recommended:* interview.

Freshman Application Contact Lesley University, 29 Everett Street, Cambridge, MA 02138-2790. *Phone:* 617-349-8800. *Toll-free phone:* 800-999-1959 Ext. 8800. *Web site:* http://www.lesley.edu/.

Massachusetts College of Art and Design

Boston, Massachusetts

- **State-supported** comprehensive, founded 1873, part of Massachusetts Public Higher Education System
- **Urban** 5-acre campus
- **Endowment** $13.0 million
- **Coed** 2,250 undergraduate students, 73% full-time, 69% women, 31% men
- **Very difficult** entrance level, 64% of applicants were admitted

Undergraduates 1,638 full-time, 612 part-time. Students come from 26 states and territories; 49 other countries; 29% are from out of state; 3% Black or African American, non-Hispanic/Latino; 5% Hispanic/Latino; 6% Asian, non-Hispanic/Latino; 0.1% Native Hawaiian or other Pacific Islander, non-Hispanic/Latino; 0.4% American Indian or Alaska Native, non-Hispanic/Latino; 2% Two or more races, non-Hispanic/Latino; 11% Race/ethnicity unknown; 2% international; 7% transferred in; 23% live on campus. *Retention:* 90% of full-time freshmen returned.

Freshmen *Admission:* 1,418 applied, 913 admitted, 311 enrolled. *Average high school GPA:* 3.42. *Test scores:* SAT critical reading scores over 500: 73%; SAT math scores over 500: 70%; SAT writing scores over 500: 75%; SAT critical reading scores over 600: 30%; SAT math scores over 600: 24%; SAT writing scores over 600: 24%; SAT critical reading scores over 700: 3%; SAT math scores over 700: 1%; SAT writing scores over 700: 2%.

Faculty *Total:* 281, 36% full-time. *Student/faculty ratio:* 10:1.

Academics *Calendar:* semesters. *Degrees:* certificates, bachelor's, master's, and postbachelor's certificates. *Special study options:* double majors, independent study, internships, off-campus study, part-time degree program, student-designed majors, study abroad, summer session for credit.

Computers on Campus 370 computers/terminals are available on campus for general student use. Students can access the following: campus intranet, computer help desk, free student e-mail accounts, online (class) grades, online (class) registration, online (class) schedules. Campuswide network is available. 100% of college-owned or -operated housing units are wired for high-speed Internet access. Wireless service is available via entire campus.

Student Life *Housing options:* coed. Campus housing is university owned. Freshman campus housing is guaranteed. *Activities and organizations:* drama/theater group, student-run newspaper, radio station, International Students' Club, Design Research Unit, Spectrum, film society, Event Works. *Campus security:* 24-hour emergency response devices and patrols, late-night transport/escort service, security lighting, self-defense workshops. *Student services:* health clinic, personal/psychological counseling, women's center.

Athletics *Intramural sports:* basketball M/W, ice hockey M, sailing M/W, softball M/W, table tennis M/W, volleyball M/W.

Standardized Tests *Required:* SAT or ACT (for admission).

Costs (2011–12) *Tuition:* state resident $9700 full-time; nonresident $26,400 full-time. Part-time tuition and fees vary according to course load. *Room and board:* $12,150. Room and board charges vary according to board plan and housing facility. *Payment plan:* installment. *Waivers:* senior citizens and employees or children of employees.

Financial Aid Of all full-time matriculated undergraduates who enrolled in 2011, 1,326 applied for aid, 1,112 were judged to have need. 171 Federal Work-Study jobs (averaging $1217). In 2011, 43 non-need-based awards were made. *Average financial aid package:* $9074. *Average need-based loan:* $4251. *Average need-based gift aid:* $6670. *Average non-need-based aid:* $4551.

Applying *Options:* electronic application, early admission, early action, deferred entrance. *Application fee:* $50. *Required:* essay or personal statement, high school transcript, 2 letters of recommendation, portfolio required; for GPA between 2.0 and 2.9, SAT/ACT scores considered with GPA on sliding scale. *Recommended:* minimum 3.0 GPA. *Application deadlines:* 2/1 (freshmen), 2/1 (transfers), 12/1 (early action). *Notification:* 1/5 (early action).

Freshman Application Contact Massachusetts College of Art and Design, 621 Huntington Avenue, Boston, MA 02115. *Phone:* 617-879-7230. *Fax:* 617-879-7250. *E-mail:* admissions@massart.edu. *Web site:* http://www.massart.edu/.

Massachusetts College of Liberal Arts

North Adams, Massachusetts

- **State-supported** comprehensive, founded 1894, part of Massachusetts State University System
- **Small-town** 105-acre campus
- **Coed** 1,673 undergraduate students, 87% full-time, 58% women, 42% men
- **Moderately difficult** entrance level, 67% of applicants were admitted

Undergraduates 1,452 full-time, 221 part-time. Students come from 15 states and territories; 1 other country; 23% are from out of state; 8% Black or African American, non-Hispanic/Latino; 6% Hispanic/Latino; 1% Asian, non-Hispanic/Latino; 0.2% Native Hawaiian or other Pacific Islander, non-Hispanic/Latino; 0.3% American Indian or Alaska Native, non-Hispanic/Latino; 0.6% Two or more races, non-Hispanic/Latino; 4% Race/ethnicity unknown; 11% transferred in; 67% live on campus. *Retention:* 72% of full-time freshmen returned.

Freshmen *Admission:* 1,698 applied, 1,136 admitted, 308 enrolled. *Average high school GPA:* 3.04. *Test scores:* SAT critical reading scores over 500: 56%; SAT critical reading scores over 600: 19%; SAT critical reading scores over 700: 2%.

Faculty *Total:* 171, 49% full-time. *Student/faculty ratio:* 14:1.

Academics *Calendar:* semesters. *Degrees:* certificates, bachelor's, master's, and post-master's certificates. *Special study options:* academic remediation for entering students, accelerated degree program, advanced placement credit, cooperative education, distance learning, double majors, honors programs, independent study, internships, off-campus study, part-time degree program, services for LD students, student-designed majors, study abroad, summer session for credit. *Unusual degree programs:* 3-2 engineering with University of Massachusetts at Amherst; podiatric medicine with the New York School of Podiatric Medicine.

Computers on Campus 140 computers/terminals are available on campus for general student use. Students can access the following: campus intranet, computer help desk, free student e-mail accounts, online (class) grades, online (class) registration, online (class) schedules. Campuswide network is available. 100% of college-owned or -operated housing units are wired for high-speed Internet access. Wireless service is available via entire campus.

Student Life *Housing:* on-campus residence required through junior year. *Options:* coed, disabled students. Campus housing is university owned. Freshman applicants given priority for college housing. *Activities and organizations:* drama/theater group, student-run newspaper, radio and television station, choral group, Student Activities Council, Student Government Association, The Beacon (Student Newspaper), Harlequin-Musical Theatre Company, Dance Company, national fraternities, national sororities. *Campus security:* 24-hour emergency response devices and patrols, late-night transport/escort service, controlled dormitory access, escort service. *Student services:* health clinic, personal/psychological counseling, women's center.

Athletics Member NCAA. All Division III. *Intercollegiate sports:* baseball M, basketball M/W, cross-country running M/W, golf M, soccer M/W, softball W, tennis M/W. *Intramural sports:* basketball M/W, cross-country running M/W, equestrian sports M(c)/W(c), football M, golf M/W, lacrosse M(c)/W(c), racquetball M/W, rugby M(c)/W(c), skiing (cross-country) M(c)/W(c), skiing (downhill) M(c)/W(c), soccer M/W, softball M/W, squash M/W, swimming and diving M/W, tennis M/W, volleyball M/W, weight lifting M(c)/W(c), wrestling M(c)/W(c).

Standardized Tests *Required:* SAT or ACT (for admission).

Costs (2011–12) *Tuition:* state resident $1030 full-time, $43 per credit part-time; nonresident $9975 full-time, $416 per credit part-time. Part-time tuition and fees vary according to course load. *Required fees:* $7045 full-time, $238 per credit part-time. *Room and board:* $8658. Room and board charges vary according to board plan and housing facility. *Payment plan:* installment. *Waivers:* senior citizens and employees or children of employees.

Financial Aid Of all full-time matriculated undergraduates who enrolled in 2011, 1,286 applied for aid, 1,033 were judged to have need, 730 had their need fully met. 300 Federal Work-Study jobs (averaging $1797). In 2011, 77 non-need-based awards were made. *Average percent of need met:* 85%. *Average financial aid package:* $13,891. *Average need-based loan:* $4003. *Average need-based gift aid:* $6191. *Average non-need-based aid:* $2859. *Average indebtedness upon graduation:* $29,738.

Applying *Options:* electronic application, early admission, early action, deferred entrance. *Application fee:* $35. *Required:* essay or personal statement, high school transcript, minimum 3.0 GPA. *Required for some:* 3 letters of recommendation, interview, sliding scale applies (GPA and SAT) if below 3.0. *Application deadlines:* rolling (freshmen), rolling (transfers), 12/1 (early action). *Notification:* continuous (freshmen), continuous (transfers), 12/15 (early action).

Freshman Application Contact Ms. Gina Puc, Assistant Director of Freshman Admission, Massachusetts College of Liberal Arts, 375 Church Street, North Adams, MA 01247. *Phone:* 413-662-5428. *Toll-free phone:* 800-989-MCLA. *E-mail:* g.puc@mcla.edu. *Web site:* http://www.mcla.edu/.

Massachusetts College of Pharmacy and Health Sciences

Boston, Massachusetts

- **Independent** university, founded 1823
- **Urban** 3-acre campus
- **Endowment** $126.0 million
- **Coed** 3,246 undergraduate students, 95% full-time, 69% women, 31% men
- **88%** of applicants were admitted

Undergraduates 3,077 full-time, 169 part-time. Students come from 42 states and territories; 32 other countries; 38% are from out of state; 5% Black or African American, non-Hispanic/Latino; 3% Hispanic/Latino; 2% Asian, non-Hispanic/Latino; 0.2% American Indian or Alaska Native, non-Hispanic/Latino; 0.8% Two or more races, non-Hispanic/Latino; 15% Race/ethnicity unknown; 5% international; 15% transferred in; 20% live on campus. *Retention:* 88% of full-time freshmen returned.

Freshmen *Admission:* 4,728 applied, 4,154 admitted, 822 enrolled. *Average high school GPA:* 3.47. *Test scores:* SAT critical reading scores over 500: 66%; SAT math scores over 500: 87%; SAT writing scores over 500: 74%; ACT scores over 18: 98%; SAT critical reading scores over 600: 18%; SAT math scores over 600: 41%; SAT writing scores over 600: 23%; ACT scores over 24: 55%; SAT critical reading scores over 700: 1%; SAT math scores over 700: 8%; SAT writing scores over 700: 2%; ACT scores over 30: 5%.

Faculty *Total:* 212, 99% full-time, 84% with terminal degrees. *Student/faculty ratio:* 24:1.

Academics *Calendar:* semesters. *Degrees:* certificates, bachelor's, master's, doctoral, postbachelor's, and first professional certificates. *Special study options:* accelerated degree program, adult/continuing education programs, advanced placement credit, distance learning, double majors, independent study, internships, off-campus study, part-time degree program, services for LD students, study abroad, summer session for credit.

Computers on Campus 507 computers/terminals are available on campus for general student use. Students can access the following: computer help desk, free student e-mail accounts, online (class) grades, online (class) registration, online (class) schedules. Campuswide network is available. 100% of college-owned or -operated housing units are wired for high-speed Internet access. Wireless service is available via entire campus.

Student Life *Housing options:* coed. Campus housing is university owned, leased by the school and is provided by a third party. Freshman campus housing is guaranteed. *Activities and organizations:* drama/theater group, student-run newspaper, choral group, Residence Hall Council, Vietnamese Student Association, Student Government Association, Campus Activities Board, Student Indian Organization, national fraternities. *Campus security:* 24-hour emergency response devices and patrols, late-night transport/escort service, controlled dormitory access, electronically operated academic area entrances, security guards at entrance. *Student services:* health clinic, personal/psychological counseling.

Athletics *Intramural sports:* basketball M/W, bowling M/W, cross-country running M/W, field hockey M/W, football M/W, racquetball M/W, soccer M/W, softball M/W, tennis M/W, ultimate Frisbee M/W, volleyball M/W.

Standardized Tests *Required:* SAT or ACT (for admission).

Costs (2011–12) *Comprehensive fee:* $39,280 includes full-time tuition ($25,650), mandatory fees ($805), and room and board ($12,825). Full-time tuition and fees vary according to course load, degree level, location, program, and student level. Part-time tuition: $945 per credit. *Required fees:* $210 per term part-time. *College room only:* $10,300. Room and board charges vary according to board plan, housing facility, and location. *Payment plan:* installment. *Waivers:* employees or children of employees.

Financial Aid Of all full-time matriculated undergraduates who enrolled in 2009, 2,146 applied for aid, 1,953 were judged to have need, 953 had their need fully met. In 2009, 371 non-need-based awards were made. *Average percent of need met:* 41%. *Average financial aid package:* $12,035. *Average need-based loan:* $5305. *Average need-based gift aid:* $8612. *Average non-need-based gift:* $11,269.

Applying *Options:* electronic application, early action, deferred entrance. *Application fee:* $70. *Required:* essay or personal statement, 2 letters of recommendation. *Required for some:* high school transcript, interview. *Application deadlines:* rolling (freshmen), 2/1 (transfers), 11/15 (early action). *Notification:* continuous until 2/15 (freshmen), continuous (transfers), 12/19 (early action).

Freshman Application Contact Sandra Hernandez, Visit Concierge, Massachusetts College of Pharmacy and Health Sciences, 179 Longwood

Avenue, Boston, MA 02115. *Phone:* 617-732-2850. *Fax:* 617-732-2118. *E-mail:* admissions@mcphs.edu. *Web site:* http://www.mcphs.edu/.

Massachusetts Institute of Technology
Cambridge, Massachusetts

- **Independent** university, founded 1861
- **Urban** 168-acre campus with easy access to Boston
- **Endowment** $9.7 billion
- **Coed** 4,384 undergraduate students, 99% full-time, 45% women, 55% men
- **Most difficult** entrance level, 10% of applicants were admitted

Undergraduates 4,354 full-time, 30 part-time. Students come from 54 states and territories; 94 other countries; 91% are from out of state; 7% Black or African American, non-Hispanic/Latino; 15% Hispanic/Latino; 24% Asian, non-Hispanic/Latino; 0.6% American Indian or Alaska Native, non-Hispanic/Latino; 3% Two or more races, non-Hispanic/Latino; 4% Race/ethnicity unknown; 10% international; 0.9% transferred in; 90% live on campus. *Retention:* 98% of full-time freshmen returned.
Freshmen *Admission:* 17,909 applied, 1,742 admitted, 1,126 enrolled. *Test scores:* SAT critical reading scores over 500: 99%; SAT math scores over 500: 100%; SAT writing scores over 500: 100%; ACT scores over 18: 100%; SAT critical reading scores over 600: 93%; SAT math scores over 600: 100%; SAT writing scores over 600: 95%; ACT scores over 24: 100%; SAT critical reading scores over 700: 62%; SAT math scores over 700: 92%; SAT writing scores over 700: 68%; ACT scores over 30: 94%.
Faculty *Total:* 1,432, 82% full-time, 88% with terminal degrees. *Student/faculty ratio:* 8:1.
Academics *Calendar:* 4-1-4. *Degrees:* bachelor's, master's, doctoral, and first professional. *Special study options:* advanced placement credit, cooperative education, double majors, English as a second language, independent study, internships, off-campus study, services for LD students, study abroad. *ROTC:* Army (b), Navy (b), Air Force (b).
Computers on Campus 1,100 computers/terminals and 50,000 ports are available on campus for general student use. Students can access the following: campus intranet, computer help desk, free student e-mail accounts, online (class) grades, online (class) registration, online (class) schedules. Campuswide network is available. 100% of college-owned or -operated housing units are wired for high-speed Internet access. Wireless service is available via entire campus.
Student Life *Housing:* on-campus residence required for freshman year. *Options:* coed, women-only, cooperative, disabled students. Campus housing is university owned. Freshman campus housing is guaranteed. *Activities and organizations:* drama/theater group, student-run newspaper, radio and television station, choral group, marching band, Tech Catholic Community, Outing Club, Society of Women Engineers, Hillel, South Asian-American Students, national fraternities, national sororities. *Campus security:* 24-hour emergency response devices and patrols, late-night transport/escort service, controlled dormitory access. *Student services:* health clinic, personal/psychological counseling.
Athletics Member NCAA. All Division III except men's and women's crew (Division I). *Intercollegiate sports:* baseball M, basketball M/W, crew M/W, cross-country running M/W, fencing M/W, field hockey W, football M, lacrosse M/W, riflery M/W, sailing M/W, soccer M/W, softball W, squash M, swimming and diving M/W, tennis M/W, track and field M/W, volleyball M/W, water polo M. *Intramural sports:* archery M(c)/W(c), badminton M/W, basketball M/W, bowling M/W, cheerleading M(c)/W(c), crew M(c)/W(c), golf M(c)/W(c), gymnastics M(c)/W(c), ice hockey M/W, rugby M(c)/W(c), soccer M/W, softball M/W, table tennis M/W, tennis M/W, ultimate Frisbee M/W, volleyball M/W, water polo M/W, wrestling M(c).
Standardized Tests *Required:* SAT or ACT (for admission), SAT Subject Tests (for admission).
Costs (2011–12) *Comprehensive fee:* $52,507 includes full-time tuition ($40,460), mandatory fees ($272), and room and board ($11,775). Part-time tuition: $630 per unit. Part-time tuition and fees vary according to course load. *College room only:* $7275. Room and board charges vary according to board plan and housing facility. *Payment plan:* installment. *Waivers:* employees or children of employees.
Financial Aid Of all full-time matriculated undergraduates who enrolled in 2010, 3,154 applied for aid, 2,745 were judged to have need, 2,745 had their need fully met. 848 Federal Work-Study jobs (averaging $3017). 1,301 state and other part-time jobs (averaging $2693). *Average percent of need met:* 100%. *Average financial aid package:* $37,919. *Average need-based loan:* $3514. *Average need-based gift aid:* $35,289. *Average indebtedness upon graduation:* $18,127. *Financial aid deadline:* 2/15.
Applying *Options:* electronic application, early action, deferred entrance. *Application fee:* $75. *Required:* essay or personal statement, high school tran-

script, 2 letters of recommendation, SAT, ACT or TOEFL. Two SAT II Subject tests: one in math and one in science. *Recommended:* interview. *Application deadlines:* 1/1 (freshmen), 2/15 (transfers), 11/1 (early action). *Notification:* 3/20 (freshmen), 5/1 (transfers), 12/20 (early action).
Freshman Application Contact Admissions Counselors, Massachusetts Institute of Technology, 77 Massachusetts Avenue, Building 3-108, Cambridge, MA 02139-4307. *Phone:* 617-253-3400. *Fax:* 617-258-8304. *E-mail:* admissions@mit.edu. *Web site:* http://web.mit.edu/.

Massachusetts Maritime Academy
Buzzards Bay, Massachusetts

- **State-supported** comprehensive, founded 1891, part of Massachusetts Public Higher Education University System
- **Small-town** 55-acre campus with easy access to Boston, Providence
- **Endowment** $7.4 million
- **Coed, primarily men** 1,278 undergraduate students, 96% full-time, 9% women, 91% men
- **Moderately difficult** entrance level, 63% of applicants were admitted

Undergraduates 1,231 full-time, 47 part-time. 2% Black or African American, non-Hispanic/Latino; 2% Hispanic/Latino; 2% Asian, non-Hispanic/Latino; 0.2% American Indian or Alaska Native, non-Hispanic/Latino; 0.7% Two or more races, non-Hispanic/Latino; 0.8% Race/ethnicity unknown; 0.5% international; 5% transferred in; 96% live on campus. *Retention:* 90% of full-time freshmen returned.
Freshmen *Admission:* 761 applied, 478 admitted, 277 enrolled.
Faculty *Total:* 137, 52% full-time, 31% with terminal degrees. *Student/faculty ratio:* 14:1.
Academics *Calendar:* semesters plus sea term. *Degrees:* bachelor's and master's. *Special study options:* academic remediation for entering students, advanced placement credit, cooperative education, distance learning, double majors, internships, off-campus study, part-time degree program, services for LD students, study abroad, summer session for credit. *ROTC:* Army (c), Navy (b).
Computers on Campus 150 computers/terminals and 1,000 ports are available on campus for general student use. Students can access the following: campus intranet, computer help desk, free student e-mail accounts, online (class) grades, online (class) registration, online (class) schedules, course-supported e-learning, wireless available campus wide. Campuswide network is available. 100% of college-owned or -operated housing units are wired for high-speed Internet access. Wireless service is available via entire campus.
Student Life *Housing:* on-campus residence required for freshman year. *Options:* coed, disabled students. Campus housing is university owned. Freshman campus housing is guaranteed. *Activities and organizations:* drama/theater group, student-run newspaper, choral group, marching band, club hockey, water sports, sailing/crew, rugby club, scuba club. *Campus security:* 24-hour emergency response devices and patrols, student patrols, late-night transport/escort service, controlled dormitory access. *Student services:* health clinic, personal/psychological counseling, women's center.
Athletics Member NCAA. All Division III. *Intercollegiate sports:* baseball M, crew M/W, cross-country running M/W, football M, lacrosse M/W, riflery M/W, sailing M/W, soccer M/W, softball W, track and field M/W, volleyball W. *Intramural sports:* basketball M/W, golf M(c)/W(c), ice hockey M(c), racquetball M/W, rugby M(c), skiing (cross-country) M(c)/W(c), skiing (downhill) M(c)/W(c), soccer M, softball M/W, squash M/W, swimming and diving M/W, table tennis M/W, tennis M/W, ultimate Frisbee M/W, volleyball M/W, water polo M/W, weight lifting M(c)/W(c).
Standardized Tests *Required:* SAT and SAT Subject Tests or ACT (for admission).
Costs (2011–12) *One-time required fee:* $2210. *Tuition:* state resident $1395 full-time; nonresident $15,592 full-time. Full-time tuition and fees vary according to course load, program, reciprocity agreements, and student level. Part-time tuition and fees vary according to class time, course load, reciprocity agreements, and student level. No tuition increase for student's term of enrollment. *Required fees:* $5472 full-time. *Room and board:* $9700; room only: $5300. *Payment plans:* installment, deferred payment. *Waivers:* minority students, senior citizens, and employees or children of employees.
Financial Aid Of all full-time matriculated undergraduates who enrolled in 2009, 874 applied for aid, 527 were judged to have need. 118 Federal Work-Study jobs (averaging $1000). *Average percent of need met:* 54%. *Average financial aid package:* $7065. *Average need-based loan:* $3570. *Average need-based gift aid:* $3200. *Average indebtedness upon graduation:* $32,553.
Applying *Options:* electronic application, early action. *Application fee:* $50. *Required:* essay or personal statement, high school transcript, minimum 2.0 GPA, 2 letters of recommendation, for students transferring between 12 and 23 credits minimum college GPA 2.5; for less than 23 transferable credits minimum college GPA 2.0 and meet admission standards for freshman applicants; for more than 24 transferable credits minimum college GPA 2.0. *Recom-*

mended: interview. *Application deadlines:* rolling (freshmen), rolling (out-of-state freshmen), rolling (transfers), 11/1 (early action). *Notification:* continuous (freshmen), continuous (out-of-state freshmen), continuous (transfers). **Freshman Application Contact** John McLaughlin, Director of Admissions, Massachusetts Maritime Academy, 101 Academy Drive, Blinn Hall, Buzzards Bay, MA 02532. *Phone:* 508-830-5031. *Toll-free phone:* 800-544-3411. *Fax:* 508-830-5077. *E-mail:* jmclaughlin@maritime.edu. *Web site:* http://www.maritime.edu/.

Merrimack College
North Andover, Massachusetts

- **Independent Roman Catholic** comprehensive, founded 1947
- **Suburban** 220-acre campus with easy access to Boston
- **Endowment** $37.2 million
- **Coed** 2,319 undergraduate students, 94% full-time, 48% women, 52% men
- **Moderately difficult** entrance level, 88% of applicants were admitted

Undergraduates 2,170 full-time, 149 part-time. Students come from 20 states and territories; 22 other countries; 26% are from out of state; 3% Black or African American, non-Hispanic/Latino; 7% Hispanic/Latino; 2% Asian, non-Hispanic/Latino; 0.1% American Indian or Alaska Native, non-Hispanic/Latino; 1% Two or more races, non-Hispanic/Latino; 10% Race/ethnicity unknown; 2% international; 4% transferred in; 81% live on campus. *Retention:* 87% of full-time freshmen returned.
Freshmen *Admission:* 3,869 applied, 3,400 admitted, 610 enrolled.
Faculty *Total:* 271, 49% full-time. *Student/faculty ratio:* 12:1.
Academics *Calendar:* semesters. *Degrees:* certificates, associate, bachelor's, and master's. *Special study options:* academic remediation for entering students, adult/continuing education programs, advanced placement credit, cooperative education, double majors, English as a second language, honors programs, independent study, internships, off-campus study, part-time degree program, services for LD students, student-designed majors, study abroad, summer session for credit. *ROTC:* Air Force (c).
Computers on Campus Students can access the following: campus intranet, computer help desk, free student e-mail accounts, online (class) grades, online (class) registration, online (class) schedules. Campuswide network is available. 100% of college-owned or -operated housing units are wired for high-speed Internet access. Wireless service is available via entire campus.
Student Life *Housing options:* coed, disabled students. Campus housing is university owned. Freshman campus housing is guaranteed. *Activities and organizations:* drama/theater group, student-run newspaper, television station, choral group, Programming Board, Student Government; Class Councils, Greek Life, A.L.A.N.A, national fraternities, national sororities. *Campus security:* 24-hour emergency response devices and patrols, student patrols, late-night transport/escort service, controlled dormitory access, staffed dorm entrances. *Student services:* health clinic, personal/psychological counseling.
Athletics Member NCAA. All Division II except ice hockey (Division I). *Intercollegiate sports:* baseball M(s), basketball M(s)/W(s), crew W(s), cross-country running M(s)/W(s), field hockey W(s), football M(s), golf W(s), ice hockey M(s), lacrosse M(s)/W(s), soccer M(s)/W(s), softball W(s), swimming and diving M(s)/W(s), tennis M(s)/W(s), track and field M(s)/W(s), volleyball W(s). *Intramural sports:* baseball M(c), basketball M/W, cheerleading W(c), field hockey W, football M, ice hockey M(c)/W, lacrosse M(c)/W(c), rugby M(c)/W(c), soccer M/W, ultimate Frisbee M(c)/W(c).
Costs (2011–12) *Comprehensive fee:* $44,215 includes full-time tuition ($31,765), mandatory fees ($1100), and room and board ($11,350). Part-time tuition and fees vary according to class time, course level, course load, and degree level. *Room and board:* Room and board charges vary according to board plan and housing facility. *Payment plan:* installment. *Waivers:* senior citizens and employees or children of employees.
Financial Aid Of all full-time matriculated undergraduates who enrolled in 2010, 1,612 applied for aid, 1,545 were judged to have need, 417 had their need fully met. 204 Federal Work-Study jobs (averaging $1329). 359 state and other part-time jobs (averaging $1779). In 2010, 283 non-need-based awards were made. *Average percent of need met:* 60%. *Average financial aid package:* $18,124. *Average need-based loan:* $5144. *Average need-based gift aid:* $12,510. *Average non-need-based aid:* $10,019. *Average indebtedness upon graduation:* $27,000. *Financial aid deadline:* 2/1.
Applying *Options:* electronic application, early admission, early decision, early action, deferred entrance. *Required:* essay or personal statement, high school transcript, 1 letter of recommendation, first quarter senior grades. *Required for some:* interview. *Recommended:* interview. *Application deadlines:* 2/15 (freshmen), 8/19 (transfers), 11/30 (early action). *Early decision deadline:* 11/15. *Notification:* continuous until 3/15 (freshmen), continuous (transfers), 1/1 (early decision), 1/1 (early action).
Freshman Application Contact Admissions Office, Merrimack College, Austin Hall, A22, North Andover, MA 01845. *Phone:* 978-837-5100. *Fax:*

978-837-5133. *E-mail:* admission@merrimack.edu. *Web site:* http://www.merrimack.edu/.

Montserrat College of Art
Beverly, Massachusetts

- **Independent** 4-year, founded 1970
- **Suburban** 10-acre campus with easy access to Boston
- **Endowment** $670,985
- **Coed** 397 undergraduate students, 98% full-time, 73% women, 27% men
- **Moderately difficult** entrance level, 79% of applicants were admitted

Undergraduates 389 full-time, 8 part-time. Students come from 23 states and territories; 1 other country; 52% are from out of state; 2% Black or African American, non-Hispanic/Latino; 4% Hispanic/Latino; 2% Native Hawaiian or other Pacific Islander, non-Hispanic/Latino; 0.3% American Indian or Alaska Native, non-Hispanic/Latino; 3% Two or more races, non-Hispanic/Latino; 5% Race/ethnicity unknown; 0.5% international; 5% transferred in; 63% live on campus. *Retention:* 79% of full-time freshmen returned.
Freshmen *Admission:* 404 applied, 320 admitted, 129 enrolled. *Average high school GPA:* 2.93. *Test scores:* SAT critical reading scores over 500: 71%; SAT math scores over 500: 48%; SAT critical reading scores over 600: 23%; SAT math scores over 600: 10%; SAT critical reading scores over 700: 2%.
Faculty *Total:* 77, 25% full-time, 8% with terminal degrees. *Student/faculty ratio:* 12:1.
Academics *Calendar:* semesters. *Degrees:* diplomas, bachelor's, and post-bachelor's certificates. *Special study options:* academic remediation for entering students, adult/continuing education programs, advanced placement credit, cooperative education, double majors, independent study, internships, off-campus study, part-time degree program, services for LD students, student-designed majors, study abroad.
Computers on Campus 98 computers/terminals and 100 ports are available on campus for general student use. Students can access the following: computer help desk, free student e-mail accounts. Campuswide network is available. 100% of college-owned or -operated housing units are wired for high-speed Internet access. Wireless service is available via entire campus.
Student Life *Housing options:* men-only, women-only. Campus housing is university owned and leased by the school. *Activities and organizations:* drama/theater group, student-run newspaper, Student Voice, Theatre Club, Bear Gallery, Dance Club, InterVarsity. *Campus security:* 24-hour emergency response devices and patrols, student patrols, late-night transport/escort service, controlled dormitory access. *Student services:* health clinic, personal/psychological counseling.
Athletics *Intramural sports:* badminton M/W, basketball M/W, bowling M/W, football M/W, skiing (downhill) M/W, volleyball M/W.
Standardized Tests *Required for some:* SAT or ACT (for admission).
Costs (2012–13) *Tuition:* $25,500 full-time, $1065 per credit part-time. *Required fees:* $1100 full-time, $50 per credit part-time. *Room only:* $7300. *Payment plan:* installment. *Waivers:* employees or children of employees.
Financial Aid Of all full-time matriculated undergraduates who enrolled in 2005, 281 applied for aid, 227 were judged to have need. 65 Federal Work-Study jobs (averaging $847). *Average financial aid package:* $9947. *Average need-based loan:* $4196. *Average need-based gift aid:* $4548.
Applying *Options:* electronic application, early action, deferred entrance. *Application fee:* $50. *Required:* essay or personal statement, high school transcript, minimum 2.0 GPA, 2 letters of recommendation, portfolio. *Recommended:* minimum 2.0 GPA, interview. *Application deadlines:* 8/15 (freshmen), 8/15 (out-of-state freshmen), 8/15 (transfers), 12/1 (early action). *Notification:* continuous until 12/15 (freshmen), continuous until 12/15 (out-of-state freshmen), continuous until 12/15 (transfers), 12/15 (early action).
Freshman Application Contact Mr. Jeffrey Newell, Director of Admissions, Montserrat College of Art, 23 Essex Street, Beverly, MA 01915. *Phone:* 978-921-4242 Ext. 1152. *Toll-free phone:* 800-836-0487. *Fax:* 978-921-4241. *E-mail:* jeffrey.newell@montserrat.edu. *Web site:* http://www.montserrat.edu/.

Mount Holyoke College
South Hadley, Massachusetts

- **Independent** comprehensive, founded 1837
- **Small-town** 800-acre campus with easy access to Springfield
- **Endowment** $617.3 million
- **Women only** 2,352 undergraduate students, 98% full-time
- **Very difficult** entrance level, 51% of applicants were admitted

Undergraduates 2,316 full-time, 36 part-time. Students come from 46 states and territories; 79 other countries; 76% are from out of state; 6% Black or African American, non-Hispanic/Latino; 9% Hispanic/Latino; 7% Asian, non-Hispanic/Latino; 0.1% Native Hawaiian or other Pacific Islander, non-Hispanic/Latino; 4% Two or more races, non-Hispanic/Latino; 5% Race/ethnicity

unknown; 23% international; 3% transferred in; 94% live on campus. *Retention:* 92% of full-time freshmen returned.

Freshmen *Admission:* 3,416 applied, 1,759 admitted, 592 enrolled. *Average high school GPA:* 3.71. *Test scores:* SAT critical reading scores over 500: 99%; SAT math scores over 500: 97%; ACT scores over 18: 100%; SAT critical reading scores over 600: 82%; SAT math scores over 600: 74%; ACT scores over 24: 94%; SAT critical reading scores over 700: 37%; SAT math scores over 700: 27%; ACT scores over 30: 47%.

Faculty *Total:* 283, 82% full-time, 89% with terminal degrees. *Student/faculty ratio:* 9:1.

Academics *Calendar:* semesters. *Degrees:* bachelor's, master's, and post-bachelor's certificates. *Special study options:* adult/continuing education programs, advanced placement credit, cooperative education, double majors, English as a second language, independent study, internships, off-campus study, part-time degree program, services for LD students, student-designed majors, study abroad. *ROTC:* Army (c), Air Force (c). *Unusual degree programs:* 3-2 engineering with Dartmouth College, University of Massachusetts, California Institute of Technology.

Computers on Campus 447 computers/terminals and 800 ports are available on campus for general student use. Students can access the following: campus intranet, computer help desk, free student e-mail accounts, online (class) grades, online (class) registration, online (class) schedules, personal Web pages. Campuswide network is available. 100% of college-owned or -operated housing units are wired for high-speed Internet access. Wireless service is available via classrooms, computer centers, computer labs, dorm rooms, learning centers, libraries, student centers.

Student Life *Housing:* on-campus residence required through senior year. *Options:* women-only, disabled students. Campus housing is university owned. Freshman campus housing is guaranteed. *Activities and organizations:* drama/theater group, student-run newspaper, radio station, choral group, Student Government Association, Model UN, Mount Holyoke African and Caribbean Student Association (MHCASA), Ice Hockey, Rugby. *Campus security:* 24-hour emergency response devices and patrols, student patrols, late-night transport/escort service, controlled dormitory access, police officers on-campus. *Student services:* health clinic, personal/psychological counseling.

Athletics Member NCAA. All Division III. *Intercollegiate sports:* basketball W, crew W, cross-country running W, equestrian sports W, field hockey W, golf W, lacrosse W, soccer W, squash W, swimming and diving W, tennis W, track and field W, volleyball W. *Intramural sports:* cheerleading W(c), equestrian sports W(c), fencing W(c), ice hockey W(c), rugby W(c), sailing W(c), ultimate Frisbee W(c).

Standardized Tests *Required for some:* SAT Subject Tests (for admission).

Costs (2011–12) *Comprehensive fee:* $53,596 includes full-time tuition ($41,270), mandatory fees ($186), and room and board ($12,140). Part-time tuition: $1290 per credit hour. *College room only:* $5940. *Payment plans:* tuition prepayment, installment. *Waivers:* employees or children of employees.

Financial Aid Of all full-time matriculated undergraduates who enrolled in 2011, 1,769 applied for aid, 1,695 were judged to have need, 1,695 had their need fully met. 922 Federal Work-Study jobs (averaging $1990). 457 state and other part-time jobs (averaging $2023). In 2011, 254 non-need-based awards were made. *Average percent of need met:* 100%. *Average financial aid package:* $36,888. *Average need-based loan:* $4755. *Average need-based gift aid:* $31,661. *Average non-need-based aid:* $15,718. *Average indebtedness upon graduation:* $23,254. *Financial aid deadline:* 3/1.

Applying *Options:* electronic application, early admission, early decision, deferred entrance. *Application fee:* $60. *Required:* essay or personal statement, high school transcript, 2 letters of recommendation. *Recommended:* interview. *Application deadlines:* 1/15 (freshmen), 5/15 (transfers). *Early decision deadline:* 11/15 (for plan 1), 1/1 (for plan 2). *Notification:* 4/1 (freshmen), continuous (transfers), 1/1 (early decision plan 1), 2/1 (early decision plan 2).

Freshman Application Contact Ms. Diane Anci, Interim Vice President for Enrollment and College Relations/Dean of Admission, Mount Holyoke College, Office of Admission, Mount Holyoke College, South Hadley, MA 01075. *Phone:* 413-538-2023. *Fax:* 413-538-2409. *E-mail:* admission@mtholyoke.edu. *Web site:* http://www.mtholyoke.edu/.

Mount Ida College
Newton, Massachusetts

- **Independent** comprehensive, founded 1899
- **Suburban** 72-acre campus with easy access to Boston
- **Coed** 1,461 undergraduate students, 93% full-time, 66% women, 34% men
- **Moderately difficult** entrance level, 75% of applicants were admitted

Undergraduates 1,365 full-time, 96 part-time. Students come from 32 states and territories; 22 other countries; 41% are from out of state; 15% Black or

African American, non-Hispanic/Latino; 8% Hispanic/Latino; 2% Asian, non-Hispanic/Latino; 0.4% American Indian or Alaska Native, non-Hispanic/Latino; 0.3% Two or more races, non-Hispanic/Latino; 13% Race/ethnicity unknown; 4% international; 7% transferred in; 63% live on campus. *Retention:* 64% of full-time freshmen returned.

Freshmen *Admission:* 1,730 applied, 1,297 admitted, 394 enrolled. *Average high school GPA:* 2.6. *Test scores:* SAT critical reading scores over 500: 19%; SAT math scores over 500: 22%; SAT writing scores over 500: 17%; ACT scores over 18: 54%; SAT critical reading scores over 600: 4%; SAT math scores over 600: 3%; SAT writing scores over 600: 2%; ACT scores over 24: 11%.

Faculty *Total:* 189, 35% full-time, 39% with terminal degrees. *Student/faculty ratio:* 14:1.

Academics *Calendar:* semesters. *Degrees:* certificates, associate, bachelor's, and master's. *Special study options:* academic remediation for entering students, advanced placement credit, cooperative education, distance learning, double majors, English as a second language, honors programs, independent study, internships, part-time degree program, services for LD students, study abroad, summer session for credit.

Computers on Campus 82 computers/terminals are available on campus for general student use. Students can access the following: computer help desk, free student e-mail accounts, online (class) grades, online (class) schedules. Campuswide network is available. 100% of college-owned or -operated housing units are wired for high-speed Internet access. Wireless service is available via computer labs, dorm rooms, student centers.

Student Life *Housing options:* coed, women-only, disabled students. Campus housing is university owned and is provided by a third party. Freshman campus housing is guaranteed. *Activities and organizations:* drama/theater group, student-run newspaper, radio station, choral group, Student Government Association, Campus Activities Team, Balfour Peer Leaders, Black Student Achievement Coalition, Alpha Chi. *Campus security:* 24-hour emergency response devices and patrols, student patrols, late-night transport/escort service, controlled dormitory access, secured campus entrance. *Student services:* health clinic, personal/psychological counseling.

Athletics Member NCAA. All Division III. *Intercollegiate sports:* baseball M(c), basketball M/W, cheerleading M/W, cross-country running M/W, equestrian sports W, football M, lacrosse M/W, soccer M/W, softball W, tennis W, volleyball M/W. *Intramural sports:* basketball M/W, soccer M/W, ultimate Frisbee M/W, volleyball M/W.

Standardized Tests *Required:* SAT or ACT (for admission).

Costs (2012–13) *Comprehensive fee:* $39,429 includes full-time tuition ($26,664), mandatory fees ($265), and room and board ($12,500). Part-time tuition: $705 per credit. Part-time tuition and fees vary according to course load. *Payment plan:* installment. *Waivers:* employees or children of employees.

Financial Aid Of all full-time matriculated undergraduates who enrolled in 2009, 1,231 applied for aid, 1,111 were judged to have need, 77 had their need fully met. In 2009, 234 non-need-based awards were made. *Average percent of need met:* 58%. *Average financial aid package:* $15,105. *Average need-based loan:* $4063. *Average need-based gift aid:* $11,328. *Average indebtedness upon graduation:* $34,911.

Applying *Options:* electronic application, deferred entrance. *Application fee:* $45. *Required:* high school transcript, 1 letter of recommendation, SAT or ACT scores. *Required for some:* interview. *Recommended:* essay or personal statement, minimum 2.0 GPA. *Application deadlines:* rolling (freshmen), rolling (transfers). *Notification:* continuous (freshmen), continuous (transfers).

Freshman Application Contact Calvin Conyers, Assistant Dean of Admissions, Mount Ida College, 777 Dedham Street, Newton, MA 02459-3310. *Phone:* 617-928-4553. *Fax:* 617-928-4507. *E-mail:* admissions@mountida.edu. *Web site:* http://www.mountida.edu/.

Newbury College
Brookline, Massachusetts

- **Independent** 4-year, founded 1962
- **Suburban** 9-acre campus with easy access to Boston
- **Endowment** $1.6 million
- **Coed** 1,024 undergraduate students, 86% full-time, 58% women, 42% men
- **Minimally difficult** entrance level, 61% of applicants were admitted

Undergraduates 879 full-time, 145 part-time. Students come from 20 states and territories; 11 other countries; 27% are from out of state; 31% Black or African American, non-Hispanic/Latino; 14% Hispanic/Latino; 7% Asian, non-Hispanic/Latino; 4% international; 3% transferred in; 33% live on campus. *Retention:* 60% of full-time freshmen returned.

Freshmen *Admission:* 4,726 applied, 2,873 admitted, 312 enrolled. *Average high school GPA:* 2.53. *Test scores:* SAT critical reading scores over 500: 15%; SAT math scores over 500: 18%; SAT writing scores over 500: 15%;

ACT scores over 18: 54%; SAT critical reading scores over 600: 1%; SAT math scores over 600: 1%; SAT writing scores over 600: 1%; ACT scores over 24: 8%.

Faculty *Total:* 111, 31% full-time, 19% with terminal degrees. *Student/faculty ratio:* 15:1.

Academics *Calendar:* semesters. *Degrees:* certificates, associate, and bachelor's. *Special study options:* academic remediation for entering students, adult/continuing education programs, advanced placement credit, cooperative education, distance learning, double majors, honors programs, independent study, internships, off-campus study, part-time degree program, services for LD students, student-designed majors, study abroad, summer session for credit.

Computers on Campus 115 computers/terminals are available on campus for general student use. Students can access the following: campus intranet, computer help desk, free student e-mail accounts, online (class) grades, online (class) registration, online (class) schedules. Campuswide network is available. 100% of college-owned or -operated housing units are wired for high-speed Internet access. Wireless service is available via entire campus.

Student Life *Housing options:* coed. Campus housing is university owned and leased by the school. Freshman applicants given priority for college housing. *Activities and organizations:* drama/theater group, student-run radio and television station, choral group, Class Council, Campus Activities Board, Step Team, Fashion Forward Club, Commuter Council. *Campus security:* 24-hour emergency response devices and patrols, late-night transport/escort service. *Student services:* personal/psychological counseling.

Athletics Member NCAA. All Division III. *Intercollegiate sports:* baseball M, basketball M/W, cross-country running M/W, golf M, soccer M/W, softball W, tennis M/W, volleyball M/W.

Costs (2011–12) *One-time required fee:* $150. *Comprehensive fee:* $38,750 includes full-time tuition ($25,500), mandatory fees ($1100), and room and board ($12,150). Full-time tuition and fees vary according to program and reciprocity agreements. Part-time tuition: $310 per credit hour. Part-time tuition and fees vary according to class time, course load, program, and reciprocity agreements. *Room and board:* Room and board charges vary according to housing facility. *Payment plan:* installment. *Waivers:* employees or children of employees.

Financial Aid Of all full-time matriculated undergraduates who enrolled in 2007, 618 applied for aid, 618 were judged to have need. 147 Federal Work-Study jobs (averaging $2000). *Average percent of need met:* 84%. *Average financial aid package:* $4250. *Average need-based loan:* $4500. *Average non-need-based aid:* $7695. *Average indebtedness upon graduation:* $8400.

Applying *Options:* electronic application. *Application fee:* $25. *Required:* essay or personal statement, high school transcript, 2 letters of recommendation. *Required for some:* interview. *Recommended:* minimum 2.0 GPA. *Application deadlines:* 9/1 (freshmen), 9/1 (transfers). *Notification:* continuous (freshmen), continuous (transfers).

Freshman Application Contact Nora Harrington, Assistant Director of Admissions Operations, Newbury College, 129 Fisher Avenue, Brookline, MA 02445-5796. *Phone:* 617-730-7038. *Toll-free phone:* 800-NEWBURY. *Fax:* 617-731-9618. *E-mail:* admissions@newbury.edu. *Web site:* http://www.newbury.edu/.

New England College of Business and Finance

Boston, Massachusetts

Freshman Application Contact New England College of Business and Finance, 10 High Street, Suite 204, Boston, MA 02111-2645. *Phone:* 617-951-2350 Ext. 6912. *Toll-free phone:* 800-997-1673. *Web site:* http://necb.edu/.

New England Conservatory of Music

Boston, Massachusetts

- **Independent** comprehensive, founded 1867
- **Urban** 2-acre campus
- **Endowment** $112.1 million
- **Coed** 416 undergraduate students, 93% full-time, 44% women, 56% men
- **Very difficult** entrance level, 27% of applicants were admitted

Undergraduates 385 full-time, 31 part-time. Students come from 39 states and territories; 23 other countries; 86% are from out of state; 4% Black or African American, non-Hispanic/Latino; 6% Hispanic/Latino; 9% Asian, non-Hispanic/Latino; 4% Two or more races, non-Hispanic/Latino; 4% Race/ethnicity unknown; 29% international; 4% transferred in; 30% live on campus. *Retention:* 95% of full-time freshmen returned.

Freshmen *Admission:* 1,259 applied, 340 admitted, 95 enrolled.

Faculty *Total:* 235, 40% full-time, 10% with terminal degrees. *Student/faculty ratio:* 5:1.

Academics *Calendar:* semesters. *Degrees:* certificates, diplomas, bachelor's, master's, doctoral, post-master's, postbachelor's, and first professional certificates. *Special study options:* advanced placement credit, double majors, English as a second language, independent study, internships, off-campus study, services for LD students, study abroad, summer session for credit.

Computers on Campus 70 computers/terminals and 200 ports are available on campus for general student use. Students can access the following: campus intranet, computer help desk, free student e-mail accounts, online (class) grades, online (class) registration, online (class) schedules, online activity effective Fall 2010. Campuswide network is available. 100% of college-owned or -operated housing units are wired for high-speed Internet access. Wireless service is available via entire campus.

Student Life *Housing:* on-campus residence required for freshman year. *Options:* coed. Campus housing is university owned. Freshman campus housing is guaranteed. *Activities and organizations:* drama/theater group, student-run newspaper, choral group, Fellowship with Christ, Hillel, The Penguin (newspaper), Rockin' Rangers Theatre Improv. *Campus security:* 24-hour patrols, late-night transport/escort service. *Student services:* health clinic, personal/psychological counseling.

Costs (2012–13) *Comprehensive fee:* $50,805 includes full-time tuition ($38,000), mandatory fees ($455), and room and board ($12,350). Part-time tuition: $1210 per credit. *Room and board:* Room and board charges vary according to board plan. *Waivers:* employees or children of employees.

Financial Aid Of all full-time matriculated undergraduates who enrolled in 2011, 263 applied for aid, 214 were judged to have need, 36 had their need fully met. 121 Federal Work-Study jobs (averaging $1573). In 2011, 158 non-need-based awards were made. *Average percent of need met:* 62%. *Average financial aid package:* $22,644. *Average need-based loan:* $5679. *Average need-based gift aid:* $16,966. *Average non-need-based aid:* $15,071. *Average indebtedness upon graduation:* $45,418.

Applying *Options:* electronic application, deferred entrance. *Application fee:* $115. *Required:* essay or personal statement, high school transcript, minimum 2.8 GPA, 2 letters of recommendation, audition recording, repertoire list. *Application deadlines:* 12/1 (freshmen), 12/1 (transfers). *Notification:* 4/1 (freshmen), 4/1 (transfers).

Freshman Application Contact New England Conservatory of Music, 290 Huntington Avenue, Boston, MA 02115-5000. *Phone:* 617-585-1103. *Web site:* http://necmusic.edu/.

The New England Institute of Art

Brookline, Massachusetts

- **Proprietary** 4-year, part of Education Management Corporation
- **Urban** campus
- **Coed**

Academics *Calendar:* semesters. *Degrees:* certificates, associate, and bachelor's.

Freshman Application Contact The New England Institute of Art, 10 Brookline Place West, Brookline, MA 02445. *Phone:* 617-739-1700. *Toll-free phone:* 800-903-4425. *Web site:* http://www.artinstitutes.edu/boston/.

See page 1474 for the College Close-Up.

Nichols College

Dudley, Massachusetts

- **Independent** comprehensive, founded 1815
- **Suburban** 210-acre campus with easy access to Boston
- **Endowment** $11.9 million
- **Coed** 1,337 undergraduate students, 87% full-time, 41% women, 59% men
- **Moderately difficult** entrance level, 74% of applicants were admitted

Undergraduates 1,159 full-time, 178 part-time. Students come from 25 states and territories; 4 other countries; 39% are from out of state; 3% transferred in; 80% live on campus. *Retention:* 66% of full-time freshmen returned.

Freshmen *Admission:* 1,983 applied, 1,463 admitted, 250 enrolled. *Average high school GPA:* 2.58. *Test scores:* SAT critical reading scores over 500: 27%; SAT math scores over 500: 36%; SAT writing scores over 500: 28%; ACT scores over 18: 72%; SAT critical reading scores over 600: 3%; SAT math scores over 600: 9%; SAT writing scores over 600: 2%; ACT scores over 24: 16%.

Faculty *Total:* 80, 45% full-time, 39% with terminal degrees. *Student/faculty ratio:* 18:1.

Academics *Calendar:* semesters. *Degrees:* certificates, associate, bachelor's, and master's. *Special study options:* academic remediation for entering students, accelerated degree program, adult/continuing education programs, advanced placement credit, cooperative education, distance learning, double majors, honors programs, independent study, internships, off-campus study,

part-time degree program, services for LD students, study abroad, summer session for credit. *ROTC:* Army (c).

Computers on Campus 69 computers/terminals are available on campus for general student use. Students can access the following: computer help desk, free student e-mail accounts, online (class) grades, online (class) registration, online (class) schedules. Campuswide network is available. 100% of college-owned or -operated housing units are wired for high-speed Internet access. Wireless service is available via classrooms, computer centers, computer labs, learning centers, libraries, student centers.

Student Life *Housing options:* coed, men-only, women-only, disabled students. Campus housing is university owned. *Activities and organizations:* drama/theater group, student-run newspaper, radio station, Rugby Club, Accounting Club, Racquetball Club, student publications, Theater Club. *Campus security:* 24-hour emergency response devices and patrols, student patrols, late-night transport/escort service. *Student services:* health clinic, personal/ psychological counseling.

Athletics Member NCAA. All Division III. *Intercollegiate sports:* baseball M, basketball M/W, field hockey W, football M, golf M, ice hockey M/W, lacrosse M/W, racquetball M(c)/W(c), rugby M(c)/W(c), soccer M/W, softball W, tennis M/W, track and field M(c)/W(c), volleyball M(c)/W(c). *Intramural sports:* basketball M/W, cheerleading M/W, ice hockey M(c)/W(c), soccer M/ W.

Standardized Tests *Required:* SAT or ACT (for admission).

Costs (2012–13) *Comprehensive fee:* $42,440 includes full-time tuition ($31,440), mandatory fees ($300), and room and board ($10,700). *College room only:* $5800. Room and board charges vary according to housing facility. *Payment plan:* installment. *Waivers:* employees or children of employees.

Financial Aid Of all full-time matriculated undergraduates who enrolled in 2009, 1,098 applied for aid, 1,078 were judged to have need, 61 had their need fully met. 327 Federal Work-Study jobs (averaging $1435). In 2009, 61 non-need-based awards were made. *Average percent of need met:* 78%. *Average financial aid package:* $27,426. *Average need-based loan:* $3654. *Average need-based gift aid:* $7542. *Average non-need-based aid:* $9983. *Average indebtedness upon graduation:* $27,715.

Applying *Options:* electronic application, deferred entrance. *Application fee:* $25. *Required:* essay or personal statement, high school transcript, 1 letter of recommendation. *Required for some:* interview. *Application deadlines:* rolling (freshmen), rolling (transfers). *Notification:* continuous (freshmen), continuous (transfers).

Freshman Application Contact Ms. Marie Keegan, Admissions Assistant, Nichols College, 124 Center Road, Dudley, MA 01571. *Phone:* 508-213-2203. *Toll-free phone:* 800-470-3379. *Fax:* 508-943-9885. *E-mail:* admissions@nichols.edu. *Web site:* http://www.nichols.edu/.

Northeastern University

Boston, Massachusetts

- **Independent** university, founded 1898
- **Urban** 73-acre campus
- **Endowment** $601.0 million
- **Coed** 16,385 undergraduate students, 100% full-time, 50% women, 50% men
- **Very difficult** entrance level, 35% of applicants were admitted

Undergraduates 16,385 full-time. Students come from 52 states and territories; 122 other countries; 64% are from out of state; 3% Black or African American, non-Hispanic/Latino; 5% Hispanic/Latino; 9% Asian, non-Hispanic/Latino; 0.1% American Indian or Alaska Native, non-Hispanic/Latino; 3% Two or more races, non-Hispanic/Latino; 15% Race/ethnicity unknown; 13% international; 3% transferred in; 53% live on campus. *Retention:* 95% of full-time freshmen returned.

Freshmen *Admission:* 43,255 applied, 14,938 admitted, 3,082 enrolled. *Test scores:* SAT critical reading scores over 500: 97%; SAT math scores over 500: 99%; SAT writing scores over 500: 97%; ACT scores over 18: 100%; SAT critical reading scores over 600: 83%; SAT math scores over 600: 92%; SAT writing scores over 600: 78%; ACT scores over 24: 98%; SAT critical reading scores over 700: 27%; SAT math scores over 700: 43%; SAT writing scores over 700: 27%; ACT scores over 30: 60%.

Faculty *Total:* 1,530, 72% full-time. *Student/faculty ratio:* 13:1.

Academics *Calendar:* semesters. *Degrees:* bachelor's, master's, doctoral, post-master's, and first professional certificates. *Special study options:* academic remediation for entering students, accelerated degree program, adult/ continuing education programs, advanced placement credit, cooperative education, distance learning, double majors, English as a second language, honors programs, independent study, internships, off-campus study, part-time degree program, services for LD students, student-designed majors, study abroad, summer session for credit. *ROTC:* Army (b), Navy (c), Air Force (c). *Unusual degree programs:* 3-2 engineering; nursing; biochemistry/biotechnology, biology/biotechnology, chemistry, communication studies/communication, media & cultural studies, computer science, criminal justice, economics, English, health sciences/public health, history, math, physics, poli. science, sociology, speech-language pathology/audiology.

Don't just take classes, take classes further.

At Northeastern University in Boston, we have perfected the integration of classroom study with opportunities for professional work, research, and civic engagement in the US and more than 85 countries around the globe. Here you'll find the flexibility to pursue the education that best matches up with your goals and gain experience that will inspire you to ask new questions and pursue new challenges, enabling you to discover your passion and find your path. It's the world's most powerful learning experience. Find out more at www.northeastern.edu

Northeastern University

Computers on Campus 1,993 computers/terminals and 1,382 ports are available on campus for general student use. Students can access the following: campus intranet, computer help desk, free student e-mail accounts, online (class) grades, online (class) registration, online (class) schedules. Campuswide network is available. 100% of college-owned or -operated housing units are wired for high-speed Internet access. Wireless service is available via entire campus.

Student Life *Housing:* on-campus residence required for freshman year. *Options:* coed. Campus housing is university owned and leased by the school. Freshman campus housing is guaranteed. *Activities and organizations:* drama/theater group, student-run newspaper, radio and television station, choral group, Student Government Association, Council for University Programs, Resident Student Association, Society of Collegiate Scholars, No Limits Dance Crew, national fraternities, national sororities. *Campus security:* 24-hour emergency response devices and patrols, student patrols, late-night transport/escort service, controlled dormitory access, Public Safety website. *Student services:* health clinic, personal/psychological counseling.

Athletics Member NCAA. All Division I. *Intercollegiate sports:* baseball M(s), basketball M(s)/W(s), cheerleading M(c)/W(c), crew M(s)/W(s), cross-country running M(s)/W(s), field hockey W(s), golf M(c)/W(c), ice hockey M(s)/W(s), lacrosse M(c)/W(c), racquetball M(c)/W(c), rugby M(c)/W(c), sailing M(c)/W(c), soccer M(s)/W(s), softball M(c)/W, swimming and diving W(s), table tennis M(c)/W(c), tennis M(c)/W, track and field M(s)/W(s), ultimate Frisbee M(c)/W, volleyball W(s), water polo M(c)/W(c), wrestling M(c). *Intramural sports:* basketball M/W, cheerleading M(c)/W(c), field hockey W(c), golf M(c)/W(c), racquetball M/W, skiing (cross-country) M(c)/W(c), skiing (downhill) M(c)/W(c), soccer M/W, squash M(c)/W(c), swimming and diving M(c)/W(c), volleyball M(c)/W(c), weight lifting M(c).

Standardized Tests *Required:* SAT or ACT (for admission). *Required for some:* SAT and SAT Subject Tests or ACT (for admission).

Costs (2011–12) *Comprehensive fee:* $51,472 includes full-time tuition ($37,840), mandatory fees ($412), and room and board ($13,220). *College room only:* $7030. Room and board charges vary according to board plan and housing facility. *Payment plan:* installment. *Waivers:* employees or children of employees.

Financial Aid Of all full-time matriculated undergraduates who enrolled in 2011, 9,482 applied for aid, 7,573 were judged to have need, 1,970 had their need fully met. In 2011, 4222 non-need-based awards were made. *Average percent of need met:* 69%. *Average financial aid package:* $21,237. *Average need-based loan:* $4714. *Average need-based gift aid:* $16,760. *Average non-need-based aid:* $10,483.

Applying *Options:* electronic application, early admission, early action, deferred entrance. *Application fee:* $75. *Required:* essay or personal statement, high school transcript, 2 letters of recommendation. *Application deadlines:* 1/15 (freshmen), 5/1 (transfers), 11/1 (early action). *Notification:* continuous until 4/1 (freshmen), continuous (transfers), 12/31 (early action).

Freshman Application Contact Ronne Turner, Associate Vice President of Enrollment, Northeastern University, 360 Huntington Avenue, 510 International Village, Boston, MA 02115. *Phone:* 617-373-2200. *Fax:* 617-373-8780. *E-mail:* admissions@neu.edu. *Web site:* http://www.northeastern.edu/.

See page 421 for display ad and page 1482 for the College Close-Up.

Pine Manor College
Chestnut Hill, Massachusetts

- **Independent** comprehensive, founded 1911
- **Suburban** 60-acre campus
- **Endowment** $8.8 million
- **Women only** 309 undergraduate students, 97% full-time
- **Moderately difficult** entrance level, 21% of applicants were admitted

Undergraduates 300 full-time, 9 part-time. Students come from 17 states and territories; 12 other countries; 20% are from out of state; 29% Black or African American, non-Hispanic/Latino; 15% Hispanic/Latino; 6% Asian, non-Hispanic/Latino; 1% American Indian or Alaska Native, non-Hispanic/Latino; 19% Two or more races, non-Hispanic/Latino; 13% Race/ethnicity unknown; 5% international; 6% transferred in. *Retention:* 55% of full-time freshmen returned.

Freshmen *Admission:* 330 applied, 69 admitted, 79 enrolled.
Faculty *Total:* 49. *Student/faculty ratio:* 12:1.
Academics *Calendar:* semesters. *Degrees:* certificates, associate, bachelor's, and master's. *Special study options:* academic remediation for entering students, adult/continuing education programs, advanced placement credit, double majors, English as a second language, external degree program, honors programs, independent study, internships, off-campus study, part-time degree program, services for LD students, student-designed majors, study abroad, summer session for credit.

Computers on Campus 85 computers/terminals are available on campus for general student use. Students can access the following: computer help desk, free student e-mail accounts, online (class) grades, online (class) schedules. Campuswide network is available.

Student Life *Housing options:* women-only. Campus housing is university owned. *Activities and organizations:* drama/theater group, student-run newspaper, radio station, choral group, African American, Latina, Asian, Native American and All (ALANA), Community Service Committee, International Student Club, The Model UN, Student Government Association (SGA). *Campus security:* 24-hour emergency response devices and patrols, student patrols, late-night transport/escort service, controlled dormitory access. *Student services:* health clinic, personal/psychological counseling, women's center.

Athletics Member NCAA. All Division III. *Intercollegiate sports:* basketball W, cross-country running W, field hockey W, lacrosse W, soccer W, softball W, tennis W, volleyball W.

Standardized Tests *Required:* SAT or ACT (for admission).

Costs (2011–12) *Comprehensive fee:* $34,542 includes full-time tuition ($22,042) and room and board ($12,500). Full-time tuition and fees vary according to course load. Part-time tuition: $650 per credit. Part-time tuition and fees vary according to course load. *Room and board:* Room and board charges vary according to housing facility. *Payment plan:* installment. *Waivers:* children of alumni and employees or children of employees.

Financial Aid Of all full-time matriculated undergraduates who enrolled in 2006, 449 applied for aid, 436 were judged to have need, 21 had their need fully met. In 2006, 33 non-need-based awards were made. *Average percent of need met:* 67%. *Average financial aid package:* $15,545. *Average need-based loan:* $3556. *Average need-based gift aid:* $12,008. *Average non-need-based aid:* $8326. *Average indebtedness upon graduation:* $32,875.

Applying *Options:* electronic application, deferred entrance. *Required:* essay or personal statement, high school transcript. *Recommended:* interview. *Application deadlines:* rolling (freshmen), rolling (transfers). *Notification:* continuous (freshmen), continuous (transfers).

Freshman Application Contact Pine Manor College, 400 Heath Street, Chestnut Hill, MA 02467. *Phone:* 617-731-7154. *Toll-free phone:* 800-762-1357. *Web site:* http://www.pmc.edu/.

Regis College
Weston, Massachusetts

- **Independent Roman Catholic** comprehensive, founded 1927
- **Small-town** 131-acre campus with easy access to Boston
- **Endowment** $14.8 million
- **Coed** 1,151 undergraduate students, 78% full-time, 77% women, 23% men
- **Moderately difficult** entrance level, 76% of applicants were admitted

Undergraduates 898 full-time, 253 part-time. Students come from 20 states and territories; 11 other countries; 11% are from out of state; 20% Black or African American, non-Hispanic/Latino; 11% Hispanic/Latino; 5% Asian, non-Hispanic/Latino; 0.1% Native Hawaiian or other Pacific Islander, non-Hispanic/Latino; 0.1% American Indian or Alaska Native, non-Hispanic/Latino; 1% Two or more races, non-Hispanic/Latino; 14% Race/ethnicity unknown; 1% international; 5% transferred in; 65% live on campus. *Retention:* 82% of full-time freshmen returned.

Freshmen *Admission:* 2,015 applied, 1,532 admitted, 262 enrolled. *Average high school GPA:* 2.87. *Test scores:* SAT critical reading scores over 500: 31%; SAT math scores over 500: 37%; SAT writing scores over 500: 32%; ACT scores over 18: 48%; SAT critical reading scores over 600: 5%; SAT math scores over 600: 6%; SAT writing scores over 600: 6%; ACT scores over 24: 8%; SAT math scores over 700: 1%.

Faculty *Total:* 156, 46% full-time, 54% with terminal degrees. *Student/faculty ratio:* 14:1.

Academics *Calendar:* semesters. *Degrees:* associate, bachelor's, master's, doctoral, and post-master's certificates. *Special study options:* academic remediation for entering students, accelerated degree program, adult/continuing education programs, advanced placement credit, double majors, English as a second language, honors programs, independent study, internships, off-campus study, part-time degree program, services for LD students, student-designed majors, study abroad, summer session for credit. *ROTC:* Army (c). *Unusual degree programs:* 3-2 business administration; communication.

Computers on Campus 196 computers/terminals are available on campus for general student use. Students can access the following: campus intranet, computer help desk, free student e-mail accounts, online (class) grades, online (class) registration, online (class) schedules, online bills, financial aid award letters and check-in requirements. Campuswide network is available. 100% of college-owned or -operated housing units are wired for high-speed Internet access. Wireless service is available via computer labs, dorm rooms, learning centers, libraries, student centers.

Student Life *Housing options:* coed, women-only. Campus housing is university owned. Freshman campus housing is guaranteed. *Activities and organizations:* drama/theater group, student-run newspaper, radio station, choral group, Campus Ministry, SGA-Student Government Association, Asian American Student Organization, Latin American Student Organization, Black Student Organization. *Campus security:* 24-hour emergency response devices and patrols, late-night transport/escort service, controlled dormitory access. *Student services:* health clinic, personal/psychological counseling.

Athletics Member NCAA. All Division III. *Intercollegiate sports:* basketball M/W, cheerleading M(c)/W(c), field hockey W, lacrosse M/W, soccer M/W, softball W, swimming and diving M/W, tennis M/W, track and field M/W, volleyball M/W.

Standardized Tests *Required:* SAT or ACT (for admission).

Costs (2011–12) *One-time required fee:* $200. *Comprehensive fee:* $44,585 includes full-time tuition ($31,785) and room and board ($12,800). Full-time tuition and fees vary according to course load. Part-time tuition and fees vary according to class time. *College room only:* $6570. *Payment plan:* installment. *Waivers:* employees or children of employees.

Financial Aid Of all full-time matriculated undergraduates who enrolled in 2008, 695 applied for aid, 644 were judged to have need, 93 had their need fully met. 436 Federal Work-Study jobs (averaging $2000). 40 state and other part-time jobs (averaging $1500). In 2008, 66 non-need-based awards were made. *Average percent of need met:* 59%. *Average financial aid package:* $22,111. *Average need-based loan:* $4849. *Average need-based gift aid:* $12,529. *Average non-need-based aid:* $8231. *Average indebtedness upon graduation:* $24,178.

Applying *Options:* electronic application, early admission, early action, deferred entrance. *Application fee:* $50. *Required:* essay or personal statement, high school transcript, minimum 2.0 GPA, 2 letters of recommendation. *Required for some:* interview. *Recommended:* minimum 3.0 GPA, interview, rank in upper 50% of high school class. *Application deadlines:* rolling (freshmen), rolling (transfers), 12/1 (early action). *Notification:* 12/23 (early action).

Freshman Application Contact Ms. Wanda Suriel, Director of Admission, Regis College, 235 Wellesley Street, Weston, MA 02493. *Phone:* 781-768-7100. *Toll-free phone:* 866-438-7344. *Fax:* 781-768-7071. *E-mail:* admission@regiscollege.edu. *Web site:* http://www.regiscollege.edu/.

Salem State University

Salem, Massachusetts

- **State-supported** comprehensive, founded 1854, part of Massachusetts Public Higher Education System
- **Urban** 62-acre campus with easy access to Boston
- **Coed** 7,704 undergraduate students, 77% full-time, 61% women, 39% men
- **Minimally difficult** entrance level, 67% of applicants were admitted

Undergraduates 5,913 full-time, 1,791 part-time. 8% Black or African American, non-Hispanic/Latino; 9% Hispanic/Latino; 3% Asian, non-Hispanic/Latino; 0.1% Native Hawaiian or other Pacific Islander, non-Hispanic/Latino; 0.2% American Indian or Alaska Native, non-Hispanic/Latino; 2% Two or more races, non-Hispanic/Latino; 3% Race/ethnicity unknown; 4% international; 11% transferred in; 27% live on campus. *Retention:* 73% of full-time freshmen returned.

Freshmen *Admission:* 4,760 applied, 3,193 admitted, 1,005 enrolled. *Average high school GPA:* 3.08. *Test scores:* SAT critical reading scores over 500: 47%; SAT math scores over 500: 50%; SAT critical reading scores over 600: 10%; SAT math scores over 600: 7%; SAT critical reading scores over 700: 1%.

Faculty *Total:* 761, 44% full-time. *Student/faculty ratio:* 15:1.

Academics *Calendar:* semesters. *Degrees:* certificates, bachelor's, master's, and post-master's certificates. *Special study options:* academic remediation for entering students, accelerated degree program, adult/continuing education programs, advanced placement credit, distance learning, double majors, English as a second language, honors programs, independent study, internships, off-campus study, part-time degree program, services for LD students, student-designed majors, study abroad, summer session for credit. *ROTC:* Army (c), Air Force (c).

Computers on Campus 160 computers/terminals are available on campus for general student use. Students can access the following: campus intranet, computer help desk, free student e-mail accounts, online (class) grades, online (class) registration, online (class) schedules. Campuswide network is available. 100% of college-owned or -operated housing units are wired for high-speed Internet access. Wireless service is available via entire campus.

Student Life *Housing options:* coed. Campus housing is university owned. Freshman applicants given priority for college housing. *Activities and organizations:* drama/theater group, student-run newspaper, radio and television station, choral group, Student Government Association, Program Council, Residence Hall Association, Multicultural Student Association, Hispanic-

American Society. *Campus security:* 24-hour emergency response devices and patrols, late-night transport/escort service, controlled dormitory access. *Student services:* health clinic, personal/psychological counseling, women's center, legal services.

Athletics Member NCAA. All Division III. *Intercollegiate sports:* baseball M, basketball M/W, cross-country running M/W, field hockey W, golf M, ice hockey M, lacrosse M, soccer M/W, softball W, tennis M/W, track and field M/W, volleyball W. *Intramural sports:* basketball M/W, cheerleading M/W, football M/W, ice hockey M/W, lacrosse W, soccer M/W, softball M/W, ultimate Frisbee M/W, volleyball M/W.

Standardized Tests *Required:* SAT or ACT (for admission).

Costs (2011–12) *Tuition:* state resident $910 full-time, $38 per credit part-time; nonresident $7050 full-time, $294 per credit part-time. Full-time tuition and fees vary according to class time and course load. Part-time tuition and fees vary according to class time and course load. *Required fees:* $6760 full-time, $282 per credit part-time. *Room only:* $8130. Room and board charges vary according to board plan and housing facility. *Payment plan:* installment. *Waivers:* senior citizens and employees or children of employees.

Financial Aid Of all full-time matriculated undergraduates who enrolled in 2009, 286 Federal Work-Study jobs (averaging $3000).

Applying *Options:* electronic application, early action, deferred entrance. *Application fee:* $75. *Required:* high school transcript, minimum 2.0 GPA. *Required for some:* interview. *Application deadlines:* 5/1 (freshmen), rolling (transfers). *Notification:* continuous (freshmen), continuous (transfers).

Freshman Application Contact Dr. Mary Dunn, Assistant Dean for Undergraduate Admissions, Salem State University, 352 Lafayette Street, Salem, MA 01970. *Phone:* 978-542-6202. *Fax:* 978-542-6893. *E-mail:* admissions@salemstate.edu. *Web site:* http://www.salemstate.edu/.

School of the Museum of Fine Arts, Boston

Boston, Massachusetts

- **Independent** comprehensive, founded 1876
- **Urban** 14-acre campus with easy access to Boston
- **Endowment** $22.4 million
- **Coed** 593 undergraduate students, 77% full-time, 67% women, 33% men
- **Moderately difficult** entrance level, 71% of applicants were admitted

Undergraduates 455 full-time, 138 part-time. Students come from 35 states and territories; 36 other countries; 72% are from out of state; 3% Black or African American, non-Hispanic/Latino; 9% Hispanic/Latino; 5% Asian, non-Hispanic/Latino; 0.5% American Indian or Alaska Native, non-Hispanic/Latino; 5% Two or more races, non-Hispanic/Latino; 18% Race/ethnicity unknown; 7% international; 11% transferred in; 12% live on campus. *Retention:* 75% of full-time freshmen returned.

Freshman *Admission:* 681 applied, 485 admitted, 91 enrolled.

Faculty *Total:* 151, 30% full-time, 69% with terminal degrees. *Student/faculty ratio:* 9:1.

Academics *Calendar:* semesters. *Degrees:* certificates, diplomas, bachelor's, master's, and postbachelor's certificates. *Special study options:* adult/continuing education programs, double majors, independent study, internships, off-campus study, part-time degree program, services for LD students, student-designed majors, study abroad, summer session for credit. *Unusual degree programs:* 3-2 fine arts with Tufts University (BFA/BA).

Computers on Campus 170 computers/terminals are available on campus for general student use. Students can access the following: campus intranet, free student e-mail accounts, online (class) grades, online (class) registration, online (class) schedules. Campuswide network is available. 100% of college-owned or -operated housing units are wired for high-speed Internet access. Wireless service is available via entire campus.

Student Life *Housing options:* coed. Campus housing is leased by the school. Freshman applicants given priority for college housing. *Activities and organizations:* Gay/Lesbian/Bisexual Alliance (Open Forum), Student Body, Inc, Metals Club, Kreep Attack Komics Kult, Bikes Are Really Fun (B.A.R.F.). *Campus security:* 24-hour emergency response devices and patrols, late night taxis service between buildings. *Student services:* health clinic, personal/psychological counseling.

Standardized Tests *Recommended:* Test scores are considered if submitted.

Costs (2012–13) *Comprehensive fee:* $50,018 includes full-time tuition ($36,828), mandatory fees ($1200), and room and board ($11,990). Full-time tuition and fees vary according to course load, degree level, program, and student level. Part-time tuition: $1370 per unit. Part-time tuition and fees vary according to class time, course load, program, and student level. *Room and board:* Room and board charges vary according to housing facility. *Payment plan:* installment. *Waivers:* employees or children of employees.

Financial Aid Of all full-time matriculated undergraduates who enrolled in 2011, 322 applied for aid, 287 were judged to have need, 52 had their need fully met. In 2011, 30 non-need-based awards were made. *Average percent of*

need met: 52%. *Average financial aid package:* $21,284. *Average need-based loan:* $4462. *Average need-based gift aid:* $13,373. *Average non-need-based aid:* $8782.

Applying *Options:* electronic application, deferred entrance. *Application fee:* $65. *Required:* essay or personal statement, high school transcript, 2 letters of recommendation, portfolio. *Recommended:* interview. *Application deadlines:* rolling (freshmen), rolling (out-of-state freshmen), rolling (transfers). *Notification:* continuous (freshmen), continuous (out-of-state freshmen), continuous (transfers).

Freshman Application Contact Ms. Robyn Reed, Associate Dean of Admissions, School of the Museum of Fine Arts, Boston, 230 The Fenway, Boston, MA 02115. *Phone:* 617-369-3626. *Toll-free phone:* 800-643-6078. *Fax:* 617-369-4264. *E-mail:* admissions@smfa.edu. *Web site:* http://www.smfa.edu/.

Simmons College

Boston, Massachusetts

- **Independent** university, founded 1899
- **Urban** 12-acre campus with easy access to Boston
- **Undergraduate: women only; graduate: coed** 1,785 undergraduate students, 90% full-time, 100% women
- **Moderately difficult** entrance level, 47% of applicants were admitted

Undergraduates 1,614 full-time, 171 part-time. 38% are from out of state; 7% Black or African American, non-Hispanic/Latino; 6% Hispanic/Latino; 8% Asian, non-Hispanic/Latino; 0.2% Native Hawaiian or other Pacific Islander, non-Hispanic/Latino; 0.9% American Indian or Alaska Native, non-Hispanic/Latino; 6% Race/ethnicity unknown; 3% international; 3% transferred in; 51% live on campus. *Retention:* 85% of full-time freshmen returned.

Freshmen *Admission:* 4,528 applied, 2,109 admitted, 343 enrolled. *Average high school GPA:* 3.29. *Test scores:* SAT critical reading scores over 500: 81%; SAT math scores over 500: 83%; SAT writing scores over 500: 89%; ACT scores over 18: 99%; SAT critical reading scores over 600: 33%; SAT math scores over 600: 30%; SAT writing scores over 600: 35%; ACT scores over 24: 59%; SAT critical reading scores over 700: 4%; SAT math scores over 700: 3%; SAT writing scores over 700: 5%; ACT scores over 30: 6%.

Faculty *Student/faculty ratio:* 13:1.

Academics *Calendar:* semesters. *Degrees:* bachelor's, master's, doctoral, post-master's, postbachelor's, and first professional certificates. *Special study options:* academic remediation for entering students, accelerated degree pro-

gram, adult/continuing education programs, advanced placement credit, cooperative education, double majors, English as a second language, external degree program, honors programs, independent study, internships, off-campus study, part-time degree program, services for LD students, student-designed majors, study abroad, summer session for credit. *Unusual degree programs:* 3-2 business administration; nursing; social work; teaching, physician assistant, pharmacy with Massachusetts College of Pharmacy & Health Sciences.

Computers on Campus 350 computers/terminals and 1,000 ports are available on campus for general student use. Students can access the following: campus intranet, computer help desk, free student e-mail accounts, online (class) grades, online (class) registration, online (class) schedules. Campuswide network is available. 100% of college-owned or -operated housing units are wired for high-speed Internet access. Wireless service is available via entire campus.

Student Life *Housing options:* coed, women-only, disabled students. Campus housing is university owned. Freshman applicants given priority for college housing. *Activities and organizations:* drama/theater group, student-run newspaper, radio station, choral group, Student Government Association, Black Students Organization, Campus Activities Board, Asian Students Association, Simmons Voice. *Campus security:* 24-hour emergency response devices and patrols, late-night transport/escort service, controlled dormitory access. *Student services:* health clinic, personal/psychological counseling, women's center.

Athletics Member NCAA. All Division III. *Intercollegiate sports:* basketball W, crew W, cross-country running W, field hockey W, lacrosse W, soccer W, softball W, swimming and diving W, tennis W, volleyball W. *Intramural sports:* basketball M/W, rugby W(c), soccer M/W, volleyball M/W.

Standardized Tests *Required:* SAT or ACT (for admission).

Costs (2011–12) *Comprehensive fee:* $46,262 includes full-time tuition ($32,376), mandatory fees ($980), and room and board ($12,906). Full-time tuition and fees vary according to course load and program. Part-time tuition: $1012 per credit. Part-time tuition and fees vary according to course load and program. *Required fees:* $490 per term part-time. *Room and board:* Room and board charges vary according to board plan. *Payment plan:* installment. *Waivers:* employees or children of employees.

Financial Aid Of all full-time matriculated undergraduates who enrolled in 2010, 1,363 applied for aid, 1,252 were judged to have need, 100 had their need fully met. 1,040 Federal Work-Study jobs (averaging $2333). In 2010, 289 non-need-based awards were made. *Average percent of need met:* 64%. *Average financial aid package:* $22,495. *Average need-based loan:* $4800. *Average need-based gift aid:* $16,075. *Average non-need-based aid:* $8815.

Applying *Options:* electronic application, early admission, early action, deferred entrance. *Application fee:* $55. *Required:* essay or personal statement, high school transcript, 2 letters of recommendation, Test scores.*Recommended:* minimum 3.0 GPA, interview. *Application deadlines:* 2/1 (freshmen), 2/1 (out-of-state freshmen), 4/1 (transfers), 12/1 (early action). *Notification:* 4/15 (freshmen), 4/15 (out-of-state freshmen), continuous (transfers), 1/20 (early action).

Freshman Application Contact Simmons College, 300 The Fenway, Boston, MA 02115. *Phone:* 617-521-2057. *Toll-free phone:* 800-345-8468. *Web site:* http://www.simmons.edu/.

See page 1582 for the College Close-Up.

Smith College
Northampton, Massachusetts

- **Independent** comprehensive, founded 1871
- **Small-town** 147-acre campus with easy access to Hartford
- **Undergraduate: women only; graduate: coed** 2,627 undergraduate students, 99% full-time, 100% women, 0% men
- **Very difficult** entrance level, 45% of applicants were admitted

Undergraduates 2,610 full-time, 17 part-time. 79% are from out of state; 5% Black or African American, non-Hispanic/Latino; 8% Hispanic/Latino; 12% Asian, non-Hispanic/Latino; 0.2% Native Hawaiian or other Pacific Islander, non-Hispanic/Latino; 0.3% American Indian or Alaska Native, non-Hispanic/Latino; 4% Two or more races, non-Hispanic/Latino; 16% Race/ethnicity unknown; 11% international; 2% transferred in; 95% live on campus. *Retention:* 94% of full-time freshmen returned.

Freshmen *Admission:* 4,128 applied, 1,877 admitted, 694 enrolled. *Average high school GPA:* 3.88. *Test scores:* SAT critical reading scores over 500: 99%; SAT math scores over 500: 97%; SAT writing scores over 500: 99%; ACT scores over 18: 100%; SAT critical reading scores over 600: 77%; SAT math scores over 600: 76%; SAT writing scores over 600: 85%; ACT scores over 24: 96%; SAT critical reading scores over 700: 35%; SAT math scores over 700: 30%; SAT writing scores over 700: 38%; ACT scores over 30: 50%.

Faculty *Total:* 300, 91% full-time, 98% with terminal degrees. *Student/faculty ratio:* 9:1.

Academics *Calendar:* semesters. *Degrees:* bachelor's, master's, doctoral, post-master's, postbachelor's, and first professional certificates. *Special study options:* adult/continuing education programs, part-time degree program. *ROTC:* Army (c), Air Force (c).

Computers on Campus Students can access the following: campus intranet, computer help desk, free student e-mail accounts, online (class) grades, online (class) registration, online (class) schedules. Campuswide network is available. 100% of college-owned or -operated housing units are wired for high-speed Internet access. Wireless service is available via classrooms, computer centers, computer labs, dorm rooms, learning centers, libraries, student centers.

Student Life *Housing:* on-campus residence required through senior year. *Options:* women-only, cooperative. Campus housing is university owned. Freshman campus housing is guaranteed. *Campus security:* 24-hour emergency response devices and patrols, late-night transport/escort service, self-defense workshops, emergency telephones, programs in crime and sexual assault prevention.

Athletics Member NCAA. All Division III. *Intercollegiate sports:* basketball W, crew W, cross-country running W, equestrian sports W, field hockey W, lacrosse W, skiing (downhill) W, soccer W, softball W, squash W, swimming and diving W, tennis W, track and field W, volleyball W. *Intramural sports:* badminton W(c), cheerleading W(c), crew W, equestrian sports W(c), fencing W(c), golf W(c), ice hockey W(c), rock climbing W, rugby W(c), soccer W, squash W, ultimate Frisbee W(c).

Costs (2011–12) *Comprehensive fee:* $53,460 includes full-time tuition ($39,800), mandatory fees ($270), and room and board ($13,390). Part-time tuition: $1245 per credit hour. *College room only:* $6700. *Payment plans:* tuition prepayment, installment. *Waivers:* employees or children of employees.

Financial Aid Of all full-time matriculated undergraduates who enrolled in 2011, 1,883 applied for aid, 1,646 were judged to have need, 1,646 had their need fully met. In 2011, 112 non-need-based awards were made. *Average percent of need met:* 100%. *Average financial aid package:* $37,618. *Average need-based loan:* $4478. *Average need-based gift aid:* $33,487. *Average non-need-based aid:* $15,702. *Average indebtedness upon graduation:* $22,531. *Financial aid deadline:* 2/15.

Applying *Options:* electronic application, early admission, early decision, deferred entrance. *Application fee:* $60. *Required:* essay or personal statement, high school transcript, 3 letters of recommendation. *Recommended:* interview. *Application deadlines:* 1/15 (freshmen), 5/15 (transfers). *Early decision deadline:* 11/15 (for plan 1), 1/2 (for plan 2). *Notification:* 4/1 (freshmen), 6/1 (transfers), 12/15 (early decision plan 1), 2/2 (early decision plan 2).

Freshman Application Contact Ms. Debra Shaver, Director of Admissions, Smith College, 7 College Lane, Northampton, MA 01063. *Phone:* 413-585-

2500. *Toll-free phone:* 800-383-3232. *Fax:* 413-585-2527. *E-mail:* admission@smith.edu. *Web site:* http://www.smith.edu/.

See page 427 for display ad and page 1588 for the College Close-Up.

Springfield College

Springfield, Massachusetts

- **Independent** comprehensive, founded 1885
- **Suburban** 150-acre campus
- **Coed**
- **Moderately difficult** entrance level

Faculty *Student/faculty ratio:* 13:1.

Academics *Calendar:* semesters. *Degrees:* bachelor's, master's, doctoral, and postbachelor's certificates.

Athletics Member NCAA. All Division III.

Standardized Tests *Required:* SAT or ACT (for admission).

Costs (2011–12) *Comprehensive fee:* $40,940 includes full-time tuition ($30,660) and room and board ($10,280). Part-time tuition: $910 per credit hour. *College room only:* $5590. Room and board charges vary according to board plan and housing facility.

Financial Aid *Of all full-time matriculated undergraduates who enrolled in 2010,* 2,102 applied for aid, 1,919 were judged to have need, 160 had their need fully met. *In 2010,* 231 non-need-based awards were made. *Average percent of need met:* 73. *Average financial aid package:* $20,042. *Average need-based loan:* $4483. *Average need-based gift aid:* $14,766. *Average non-need-based aid:* $6404. *Average indebtedness upon graduation:* $33,697.

Applying *Options:* electronic application, early admission, early decision, deferred entrance. *Application fee:* $50. *Required:* high school transcript, 1 letter of recommendation. *Required for some:* portfolio. *Recommended:* interview.

Freshman Application Contact Richard K. Veres, Director of Undergraduate Admissions, Springfield College, 263 Alden Street, Springfield, MA 01109. *Phone:* 413-748-3136. *Toll-free phone:* 800-343-1257. *Fax:* 413-748-3694. *E-mail:* admissions@spfldcol.edu. *Web site:* http://www.spfldcol.edu/.

See page 425 for display ad and page 1616 for the College Close-Up.

Stonehill College

Easton, Massachusetts

- **Independent Roman Catholic** 4-year, founded 1948
- **Suburban** 384-acre campus with easy access to Boston
- **Endowment** $151.2 million
- **Coed** 2,471 undergraduate students, 99% full-time, 61% women, 39% men
- **Very difficult** entrance level, 65% of applicants were admitted

Undergraduates 2,449 full-time, 22 part-time. Students come from 31 states and territories; 9 other countries; 45% are from out of state; 3% Black or African American, non-Hispanic/Latino; 3% Hispanic/Latino; 1% Asian, non-Hispanic/Latino; 1% Two or more races, non-Hispanic/Latino; 2% Race/ethnicity unknown; 0.6% international; 2% transferred in; 91% live on campus. *Retention:* 88% of full-time freshmen returned.

Freshmen *Admission:* 7,200 applied, 4,693 admitted, 568 enrolled. *Average high school GPA:* 3.35. *Test scores:* SAT critical reading scores over 500: 93%; SAT math scores over 500: 94%; ACT scores over 18: 98%; SAT critical reading scores over 600: 49%; SAT math scores over 600: 57%; ACT scores over 24: 81%; SAT critical reading scores over 700: 7%; SAT math scores over 700: 5%; ACT scores over 30: 14%.

Faculty *Total:* 267, 60% full-time, 69% with terminal degrees. *Student/faculty ratio:* 13:1.

Academics *Calendar:* semesters. *Degree:* bachelor's. *Special study options:* advanced placement credit, double majors, honors programs, independent study, internships, off-campus study, part-time degree program, services for LD students, student-designed majors, study abroad, summer session for credit. *ROTC:* Army (b). *Unusual degree programs:* 3-2 engineering with University of Notre Dame.

Computers on Campus 403 computers/terminals and 300 ports are available on campus for general student use. Students can access the following: campus intranet, computer help desk, free student e-mail accounts, online (class) grades, online (class) registration, online (class) schedules, Learning Management System; online degree evaluation and planning; add funds to ID online and use at off campus locations; online housing contracts and room lottery; online financial aid awards; online time sheets and payments for campus jobs. Campuswide network is available. 100% of college-owned or -operated housing units are wired for high-speed Internet access. Wireless service is available via entire campus.

Student Life *Housing options:* coed, women-only, disabled students. Campus housing is university owned. *Activities and organizations:* drama/theater group, student-run newspaper, radio station, choral group, Into the Streets, student radio station, student government, Summit (student newspaper), sports clubs. *Campus security:* 24-hour emergency response devices and patrols, late-night transport/escort service, controlled dormitory access. *Student services:* health clinic, personal/psychological counseling, women's center.

Athletics Member NCAA. All Division II. *Intercollegiate sports:* baseball M(s), basketball M(s)/W(s), bowling M(c)/W(c), cheerleading M(c)/W(c), cross-country running M(s)/W(s), equestrian sports W, field hockey W(s), football M(s), golf M(c)/W(c), ice hockey M, lacrosse M(c)/W(s), rugby M(c)/W(c), soccer M(s)/W(s), softball W(s), tennis M(s)/W(s), track and field M(s)/W(s), ultimate Frisbee M(c)/W(c), volleyball M(c)/W(s). *Intramural sports:* basketball M/W, field hockey M/W, soccer M/W, softball M/W, tennis M/W, volleyball M/W.

Costs (2012–13) *Comprehensive fee:* $48,420 includes full-time tuition ($35,110) and room and board ($13,310). Part-time tuition: $1170 per credit hour. Part-time tuition and fees vary according to course load. *Room and board:* Room and board charges vary according to board plan. *Payment plans:* tuition prepayment, installment. *Waivers:* employees or children of employees.

Financial Aid Of all full-time matriculated undergraduates who enrolled in 2011, 1,996 applied for aid, 1,412 were judged to have need, 723 had their need fully met. 745 Federal Work-Study jobs (averaging $2245). 371 state and other part-time jobs (averaging $1585). In 2011, 689 non-need-based awards were made. *Average percent of need met:* 91%. *Average financial aid package:* $24,511. *Average need-based loan:* $5039. *Average need-based gift aid:* $18,871. *Average non-need-based aid:* $9848. *Average indebtedness upon graduation:* $29,440.

Applying *Options:* electronic application, early decision, early action, deferred entrance. *Application fee:* $60. *Required:* essay or personal statement, high school transcript, 2 letters of recommendation. *Required for some:* interview. *Recommended:* campus visit. *Application deadlines:* 1/15 (freshmen), 4/1 (transfers), 11/1 (early action). *Early decision deadline:* 11/1. *Notification:* 3/15 (freshmen), continuous until 5/31 (transfers), 12/25 (early decision), 1/15 (early action).

Freshman Application Contact Stonehill College, 320 Washington Street, Easton, MA 02357-5610. *Phone:* 508-565-1373. *Fax:* 508-565-1545. *E-mail:* admissions@stonehill.edu. *Web site:* http://www.stonehill.edu/.

See page 1626 for the College Close-Up.

Suffolk University

Boston, Massachusetts

- **Independent** comprehensive, founded 1906
- **Urban** 2-acre campus
- **Endowment** $121.9 million
- **Coed** 5,811 undergraduate students, 93% full-time, 57% women, 43% men
- **Moderately difficult** entrance level, 79% of applicants were admitted

Undergraduates 5,382 full-time, 429 part-time. Students come from 42 states and territories; 107 other countries; 34% are from out of state; 5% Black or African American, non-Hispanic/Latino; 9% Hispanic/Latino; 6% Asian, non-Hispanic/Latino; 0.2% American Indian or Alaska Native, non-Hispanic/Latino; 0.9% Two or more races, non-Hispanic/Latino; 17% Race/ethnicity unknown; 15% international; 8% transferred in; 23% live on campus. *Retention:* 75% of full-time freshmen returned.

Freshmen *Admission:* 9,137 applied, 7,217 admitted, 1,239 enrolled. *Average high school GPA:* 3.01. *Test scores:* SAT critical reading scores over 500: 57%; SAT math scores over 500: 60%; SAT writing scores over 500: 62%; ACT scores over 18: 95%; SAT critical reading scores over 600: 17%; SAT math scores over 600: 17%; SAT writing scores over 600: 16%; ACT scores over 24: 36%; SAT critical reading scores over 700: 2%; SAT math scores over 700: 1%; SAT writing scores over 700: 1%; ACT scores over 30: 4%.

Faculty *Total:* 963, 44% full-time, 48% with terminal degrees. *Student/faculty ratio:* 11:1.

Academics *Calendar:* semesters. *Degrees:* certificates, diplomas, associate, bachelor's, master's, doctoral, post-master's, postbachelor's, and first professional certificates (doctoral degree in law). *Special study options:* academic remediation for entering students, accelerated degree program, adult/continuing education programs, advanced placement credit, cooperative education, distance learning, double majors, English as a second language, freshman honors college, honors programs, independent study, internships, off-campus study, part-time degree program, services for LD students, study abroad, summer session for credit. *ROTC:* Army (c).

Computers on Campus 539 computers/terminals are available on campus for general student use. Students can access the following: campus intranet, computer help desk, free student e-mail accounts, online (class) grades, online

(class) registration, online (class) schedules. Campuswide network is available. 100% of college-owned or -operated housing units are wired for high-speed Internet access. Wireless service is available via entire campus.

Student Life *Housing options:* coed. Campus housing is university owned. Freshman applicants given priority for college housing. *Activities and organizations:* drama/theater group, student-run newspaper, radio and television station, choral group, Student Government Association, Program Committee, Suffolk Free Radio, Black Student Union, Journey Leadership Program, national fraternities. *Campus security:* 24-hour emergency response devices, late-night transport/escort service, controlled dormitory access. *Student services:* health clinic, personal/psychological counseling, women's center.

Athletics Member NCAA. All Division III. *Intercollegiate sports:* baseball M, basketball M/W, cross-country running M/W, golf M, ice hockey M, soccer M, softball W, tennis M/W, volleyball W. *Intramural sports:* basketball M/W, soccer M/W, softball M/W, volleyball M/W.

Standardized Tests *Required:* SAT or ACT (for admission).

Costs (2011–12) *One-time required fee:* $200. *Comprehensive fee:* $44,519 includes full-time tuition ($29,779), mandatory fees ($116), and room and board ($14,624). Part-time tuition: $730 per credit hour. Part-time tuition and fees vary according to course load. *Required fees:* $10 per term part-time. *College room only:* $12,094. Room and board charges vary according to board plan and housing facility. *Payment plans:* installment, deferred payment. *Waivers:* senior citizens and employees or children of employees.

Financial Aid Of all full-time matriculated undergraduates who enrolled in 2011, 3,770 applied for aid, 3,414 were judged to have need, 367 had their need fully met. 1,667 Federal Work-Study jobs (averaging $2335). 458 state and other part-time jobs (averaging $3053). In 2011, 380 non-need-based awards were made. *Average percent of need met:* 67%. *Average financial aid package:* $21,287. *Average need-based loan:* $4570. *Average need-based gift aid:* $13,405. *Average non-need-based aid:* $8906. *Average indebtedness upon graduation:* $31,364. *Financial aid deadline:* 2/15.

Applying *Options:* electronic application, early action, deferred entrance. *Application fee:* $50. *Required:* essay or personal statement, high school transcript, 2 letters of recommendation. *Required for some:* interview. *Recommended:* minimum 2.5 GPA. *Application deadlines:* 2/15 (freshmen), 6/30 (transfers), 11/15 (early action). *Notification:* 3/20 (freshmen), continuous (transfers), 12/20 (early action).

Freshman Application Contact Mr. John Hamel, Associate VP/Director Undergraduate Admissions, Suffolk University, 8 Ashburton Place, Boston, MA 02108. *Phone:* 617-573-8460. *Toll-free phone:* 800-6-SUFFOLK. *Fax:* 617-742-4291. *E-mail:* admission@suffolk.edu. *Web site:* http://www.suffolk.edu/.

Tufts University
Medford, Massachusetts

- **Independent** university, founded 1852
- **Suburban** 150-acre campus with easy access to Boston
- **Coed** 5,194 undergraduate students, 98% full-time, 51% women, 49% men
- **Most difficult** entrance level, 22% of applicants were admitted

Undergraduates 5,106 full-time, 88 part-time. Students come from 54 states and territories; 105 other countries; 77% are from out of state; 4% Black or African American, non-Hispanic/Latino; 7% Hispanic/Latino; 10% Asian, non-Hispanic/Latino; 0.1% American Indian or Alaska Native, non-Hispanic/Latino; 3% Two or more races, non-Hispanic/Latino; 11% Race/ethnicity unknown; 7% international; 2% transferred in; 64% live on campus. *Retention:* 96% of full-time freshmen returned.

Freshmen *Admission:* 17,104 applied, 3,743 admitted, 1,315 enrolled. *Test scores:* SAT critical reading scores over 500: 99%; SAT math scores over 500: 100%; SAT writing scores over 500: 100%; ACT scores over 18: 100%; SAT critical reading scores over 600: 95%; SAT math scores over 600: 97%; SAT writing scores over 600: 96%; ACT scores over 24: 99%; SAT critical reading scores over 700: 63%; SAT math scores over 700: 67%; SAT writing scores over 700: 67%; ACT scores over 30: 82%.

Faculty *Total:* 1,025, 67% full-time, 83% with terminal degrees. *Student/faculty ratio:* 9:1.

Academics *Calendar:* semesters. *Degrees:* bachelor's, master's, doctoral, post-master's, postbachelor's, and first professional certificates. *Special study options:* adult/continuing education programs, advanced placement credit, double majors, honors programs, independent study, internships, off-campus study, services for LD students, student-designed majors, study abroad, summer session for credit. *ROTC:* Army (c), Navy (c), Air Force (c). *Unusual degree programs:* 3-2 New England Conservatory of Music, School of the Museum of Fine Arts.

Computers on Campus 300 computers/terminals are available on campus for general student use. Students can access the following: computer help desk, free student e-mail accounts, online (class) grades, online (class) registration,

---

online (class) schedules. Campuswide network is available. 100% of college-owned or -operated housing units are wired for high-speed Internet access. Wireless service is available via classrooms, computer centers, computer labs, learning centers, libraries, student centers.

Student Life *Housing:* on-campus residence required through sophomore year. *Options:* coed, women-only, cooperative. Campus housing is university owned. Freshman campus housing is guaranteed. *Activities and organizations:* drama/theater group, student-run newspaper, radio and television station, choral group, marching band, Leonard Carmichael Society, Mountain Club, intramural sports, Tufts Daily (newspaper), Admissions Student Outreach, national fraternities, national sororities. *Campus security:* 24-hour emergency response devices and patrols, late-night transport/escort service, controlled dormitory access, security lighting, call boxes to campus police. *Student services:* health clinic, legal services.

Athletics Member NCAA. All Division III. *Intercollegiate sports:* baseball M, basketball M/W, crew M/W, cross-country running M/W, fencing W, field hockey W, football M, golf M, ice hockey M, lacrosse M/W, sailing M/W, soccer M/W, softball W, squash M/W, swimming and diving M/W, tennis M/W, track and field M/W, volleyball W. *Intramural sports:* basketball M/W, cheerleading M/W, cross-country running M/W, equestrian sports M/W, fencing M, football M, racquetball M/W, rugby M/W, skiing (downhill) M/W, soccer M/W, softball M/W, squash M/W, tennis M/W, track and field M/W, ultimate Frisbee M/W, volleyball M, water polo M.

Standardized Tests *Required:* SAT and SAT Subject Tests or ACT (for admission).

Costs (2011–12) *Comprehensive fee:* $54,474 includes full-time tuition ($41,998), mandatory fees ($964), and room and board ($11,512). *College room only:* $6162. Room and board charges vary according to board plan. *Payment plans:* tuition prepayment, installment. *Waivers:* employees or children of employees.

Financial Aid Of all full-time matriculated undergraduates who enrolled in 2010, 2,555 applied for aid, 2,228 were judged to have need, 2,187 had their need fully met. 1,721 Federal Work-Study jobs (averaging $1912). 85 state and other part-time jobs (averaging $1955). In 2010, 84 non-need-based awards were made. *Average percent of need met:* 100%. *Average financial aid package:* $32,696. *Average need-based loan:* $3554. *Average need-based gift aid:* $29,916. *Average non-need-based aid:* $500. *Average indebtedness upon graduation:* $27,443. *Financial aid deadline:* 2/15.

Applying *Options:* electronic application, early admission, early decision, deferred entrance. *Application fee:* $70. *Required:* essay or personal statement, high school transcript, 1 letter of recommendation. *Recommended:* interview. *Application deadlines:* 1/1 (freshmen), 3/1 (transfers). *Early decision deadline:* 11/1 (for plan 1), 1/1 (for plan 2). *Notification:* 4/1 (freshmen), 5/1 (transfers), 12/15 (early decision plan 1), 2/1 (early decision plan 2).

Freshman Application Contact Mr. Lee Coffin, Office of Undergraduate Admissions, Tufts University, Bendetson Hall, Medford, MA 02155. *Phone:* 617-627-3170. *Fax:* 617-627-3860. *E-mail:* admissions.inquiry@ase.tufts.edu. *Web site:* http://www.tufts.edu/.

University of Massachusetts Amherst
Amherst, Massachusetts

- **State-supported** university, founded 1863, part of University of Massachusetts
- **Small-town** 1463-acre campus with easy access to Hartford
- **Endowment** $181.5 million
- **Coed** 21,812 undergraduate students, 93% full-time, 50% women, 50% men
- **Moderately difficult** entrance level, 66% of applicants were admitted

Undergraduates 20,253 full-time, 1,559 part-time. Students come from 48 states and territories; 53 other countries; 17% are from out of state; 4% Black or African American, non-Hispanic/Latino; 5% Hispanic/Latino; 7% Asian, non-Hispanic/Latino; 0.1% Native Hawaiian or other Pacific Islander, non-Hispanic/Latino; 0.2% American Indian or Alaska Native, non-Hispanic/Latino; 2% Two or more races, non-Hispanic/Latino; 12% Race/ethnicity unknown; 2% international; 5% transferred in; 61% live on campus. *Retention:* 89% of full-time freshmen returned.

Freshmen *Admission:* 32,564 applied, 21,373 admitted, 4,777 enrolled. *Average high school GPA:* 3.64. *Test scores:* SAT critical reading scores over 500: 89%; SAT math scores over 500: 95%; ACT scores over 18: 99%; SAT critical reading scores over 600: 42%; SAT math scores over 600: 57%; ACT scores over 24: 71%; SAT critical reading scores over 700: 8%; SAT math scores over 700: 10%; ACT scores over 30: 11%.

Faculty *Total:* 1,345, 89% full-time, 90% with terminal degrees. *Student/faculty ratio:* 19:1.

Academics *Calendar:* semesters. *Degrees:* certificates, associate, bachelor's, master's, doctoral, post-master's, postbachelor's, and first professional certificates. *Special study options:* academic remediation for entering students,

---

adult/continuing education programs, advanced placement credit, cooperative education, distance learning, double majors, English as a second language, freshman honors college, honors programs, independent study, internships, off-campus study, part-time degree program, services for LD students, student-designed majors, study abroad, summer session for credit. *ROTC:* Army (b), Air Force (b).

Computers on Campus 419 computers/terminals are available on campus for general student use. Students can access the following: computer help desk, free student e-mail accounts, online (class) grades, online (class) registration, online (class) schedules, online housing assignments, bill payment, Learning Management System, file storage, web hosting, blogs. Campuswide network is available. 100% of college-owned or -operated housing units are wired for high-speed Internet access. Wireless service is available via classrooms, computer centers, computer labs, learning centers, libraries, student centers.

Student Life *Housing:* on-campus residence required for freshman year. *Options:* coed, men-only, women-only, disabled students. Campus housing is university owned. Freshman campus housing is guaranteed. *Activities and organizations:* drama/theater group, student-run newspaper, radio and television station, choral group, marching band, Minutemen Marching Band, Theater Guild, Ski Club, Outing Club, student newspaper, national fraternities, national sororities. *Campus security:* 24-hour emergency response devices and patrols, student patrols, late-night transport/escort service, controlled dormitory access. *Student services:* health clinic, personal/psychological counseling, women's center, legal services.

Athletics Member NCAA. All Division I except football (Division I-AA). *Intercollegiate sports:* baseball M(s), basketball M(s)/W(s), crew W(s), cross-country running M(s)/W(s), field hockey W(s), ice hockey M(s), lacrosse M(s)/W(s), soccer M(s)/W(s), softball W(s), swimming and diving M(s)/W(s), tennis W(s), track and field M(s)/W(s). *Intramural sports:* archery M(c)/W(c), baseball M(c), basketball M/W, cheerleading M/W, equestrian sports M(c)/W(c), fencing M(c)/W(c), field hockey W, football M/W, golf M(c)/W(c), ice hockey M, lacrosse M/W, rugby M(c)/W(c), sailing M(c)/W(c), skiing (downhill) M(c)/W(c), soccer M/W, softball M/W, swimming and diving M(c)/W(c), tennis M/W, ultimate Frisbee M(c)/W(c), volleyball M/W, water polo M(c), wrestling M(c)/W(c).

Standardized Tests *Required:* SAT or ACT (for admission).

Costs (2011–12) *One-time required fee:* $185. *Tuition:* state resident $1714 full-time, $72 per credit part-time; nonresident $9937 full-time, $414 per credit part-time. Full-time tuition and fees vary according to class time, course load, degree level, location, program, reciprocity agreements, and student level. Part-time tuition and fees vary according to class time, course load, degree

level, location, program, reciprocity agreements, and student level. *Required fees:* $10,898 full-time. *Room and board:* $10,310; room only: $5306. Room and board charges vary according to board plan and housing facility. *Payment plan:* installment. *Waivers:* senior citizens and employees or children of employees.

Financial Aid Of all full-time matriculated undergraduates who enrolled in 2010, 16,008 applied for aid, 11,922 were judged to have need, 2,540 had their need fully met. 3,469 Federal Work-Study jobs (averaging $1709). In 2010, 1111 non-need-based awards were made. *Average percent of need met:* 84%. *Average financial aid package:* $14,771. *Average need-based loan:* $4400. *Average need-based gift aid:* $9503. *Average non-need-based aid:* $2830. *Average indebtedness upon graduation:* $26,893.

Applying *Options:* electronic application, early action, deferred entrance. *Application fee:* $70. *Required:* essay or personal statement, high school transcript, SAT or ACT. *Recommended:* minimum 3.0 GPA. *Application deadlines:* 1/15 (freshmen), 1/15 (out-of-state freshmen), 4/15 (transfers), 11/1 (early action). *Notification:* continuous (freshmen), continuous (out-of-state freshmen), continuous (transfers), 12/15 (early action).

Freshman Application Contact Mr. Kevin Kelly, Director, Undergraduate Admissions, University of Massachusetts Amherst, 37 Mather Drive, Amherst, MA 01003. *Phone:* 413-545-0222. *Fax:* 413-545-4312. *E-mail:* mail@admissions.umass.edu. *Web site:* http://www.umass.edu/.

University of Massachusetts Boston
Boston, Massachusetts

- **State-supported** university, founded 1964, part of University of Massachusetts
- **Urban** 177-acre campus
- **Endowment** $47.4 million
- **Coed** 11,866 undergraduate students, 70% full-time, 56% women, 44% men
- **Moderately difficult** entrance level, 68% of applicants were admitted

Undergraduates 8,252 full-time, 3,614 part-time. Students come from 34 states and territories; 140 other countries; 5% are from out of state; 15% Black or African American, non-Hispanic/Latino; 11% Hispanic/Latino; 11% Asian, non-Hispanic/Latino; 0.1% Native Hawaiian or other Pacific Islander, non-Hispanic/Latino; 0.3% American Indian or Alaska Native, non-Hispanic/Latino; 2% Two or more races, non-Hispanic/Latino; 9% Race/ethnicity

unknown; 6% international; 15% transferred in. *Retention:* 75% of full-time freshmen returned.

Freshmen *Admission:* 6,454 applied, 4,417 admitted, 1,297 enrolled. *Average high school GPA:* 3.1. *Test scores:* SAT critical reading scores over 500: 54%; SAT math scores over 500: 66%; SAT critical reading scores over 600: 17%; SAT math scores over 600: 19%; SAT critical reading scores over 700: 2%; SAT math scores over 700: 2%.

Faculty *Total:* 1,088, 50% full-time, 63% with terminal degrees. *Student/faculty ratio:* 16:1.

Academics *Calendar:* semesters. *Degrees:* certificates, bachelor's, master's, doctoral, post-master's, postbachelor's, and first professional certificates. *Special study options:* academic remediation for entering students, accelerated degree program, adult/continuing education programs, advanced placement credit, cooperative education, distance learning, double majors, English as a second language, freshman honors college, honors programs, independent study, internships, off-campus study, part-time degree program, services for LD students, student-designed majors, study abroad, summer session for credit. *ROTC:* Army (c), Navy (c), Air Force (c). *Unusual degree programs:* 3-2 engineering with University of Massachusetts Lowell, University of Massachusetts Amherst, Northeastern University.

Computers on Campus 350 computers/terminals are available on campus for general student use. Students can access the following: computer help desk, free student e-mail accounts, online (class) grades, online (class) registration, online (class) schedules. Campuswide network is available. Wireless service is available via entire campus.

Student Life *Housing:* college housing not available. *Activities and organizations:* drama/theater group, student-run newspaper, radio station, choral group, Student Arts & Events Council, Haitian Student Association, Golden Key Honor Society, Campus Kitchens, Mass Media. *Campus security:* 24-hour emergency response devices and patrols, late-night transport/escort service, crime prevention program, bicycle patrols. *Student services:* health clinic, personal/psychological counseling, women's center, legal services.

Athletics Member NCAA. All Division III. *Intercollegiate sports:* baseball M, basketball M/W, cross-country running M/W, ice hockey M, lacrosse M, soccer M/W, softball W, tennis M/W, track and field M/W, volleyball W. *Intramural sports:* badminton M/W, basketball M/W, golf M/W, ice hockey M/W, racquetball M/W, sailing M/W, soccer M/W, softball M/W, squash M/W, swimming and diving M/W, tennis M/W, volleyball M/W, weight lifting M/W.

Standardized Tests *Required:* SAT (for admission), ACT (for admission), SAT or ACT (for admission). *Recommended:* SAT and SAT Subject Tests or ACT (for admission), SAT Subject Tests (for admission).

Costs (2011–12) *Tuition:* state resident $10,761 full-time; nonresident $24,281 full-time. Full-time tuition and fees vary according to program. Part-time tuition and fees vary according to program. *Required fees:* $646 full-time.

Financial Aid Of all full-time matriculated undergraduates who enrolled in 2010, 5,988 applied for aid, 5,228 were judged to have need, 2,921 had their need fully met. 522 Federal Work-Study jobs (averaging $3696). In 2010, 225 non-need-based awards were made. *Average percent of need met:* 93%. *Average financial aid package:* $13,990. *Average need-based loan:* $6774. *Average need-based gift aid:* $7709. *Average non-need-based aid:* $4437. *Average indebtedness upon graduation:* $24,203.

Applying *Options:* electronic application, deferred entrance. *Application fee:* $40. *Required:* high school transcript, minimum 2.5 GPA. *Required for some:* essay or personal statement, minimum 2.8 GPA, interview. *Recommended:* essay or personal statement. *Application deadlines:* 4/1 (freshmen), 7/1 (transfers). *Notification:* continuous (freshmen), continuous (transfers).

Freshman Application Contact Mr. John Drew, Director of Undergraduate Admissions, University of Massachusetts Boston, 100 Morrissey Boulevard, Boston, MA 02125-3393. *Phone:* 617-287-6000. *Fax:* 617-287-5999. *E-mail:* enrollment.info@umb.edu. *Web site:* http://www.umb.edu/.

See page 429 for display ad and page 1680 for the College Close-Up.

University of Massachusetts Dartmouth

North Dartmouth, Massachusetts

- **State-supported** university, founded 1895, part of University of Massachusetts
- **Suburban** 710-acre campus with easy access to Boston, Providence
- **Endowment** $37.3 million
- **Coed** 7,580 undergraduate students, 87% full-time, 48% women, 52% men
- **Moderately difficult** entrance level, 70% of applicants were admitted

Undergraduates 6,560 full-time, 1,020 part-time. Students come from 29 states and territories; 26 other countries; 4% are from out of state; 10% Black or African American, non-Hispanic/Latino; 6% Hispanic/Latino; 3% Asian, non-Hispanic/Latino; 0.3% American Indian or Alaska Native, non-Hispanic/Latino; 3% Two or more races, non-Hispanic/Latino; 3% Race/ethnicity unknown; 0.4% international; 6% transferred in; 55% live on campus. *Retention:* 73% of full-time freshmen returned.

Freshmen *Admission:* 8,164 applied, 5,681 admitted, 1,570 enrolled. *Average high school GPA:* 3.16. *Test scores:* SAT critical reading scores over 500: 60%; SAT math scores over 500: 70%; SAT writing scores over 500: 53%; ACT scores over 18: 94%; SAT critical reading scores over 600: 15%; SAT math scores over 600: 21%; SAT writing scores over 600: 11%; ACT scores over 24: 45%; SAT critical reading scores over 700: 2%; SAT math scores over 700: 2%; SAT writing scores over 700: 1%; ACT scores over 30: 4%.

Faculty *Total:* 636, 60% full-time, 58% with terminal degrees. *Student/faculty ratio:* 19:1.

Academics *Calendar:* semesters. *Degrees:* certificates, bachelor's, master's, doctoral, post-master's, postbachelor's, and first professional certificates. *Special study options:* academic remediation for entering students, advanced placement credit, cooperative education, distance learning, double majors, honors programs, independent study, internships, off-campus study, part-time degree program, services for LD students, student-designed majors, study abroad, summer session for credit. *ROTC:* Army (c).

Computers on Campus 368 computers/terminals are available on campus for general student use. Students can access the following: campus intranet, computer help desk, free student e-mail accounts, online (class) grades, online (class) registration, online (class) schedules. Campuswide network is available. 100% of college-owned or -operated housing units are wired for high-speed Internet access. Wireless service is available via entire campus.

Student Life *Housing options:* coed, disabled students. Campus housing is university owned. *Activities and organizations:* drama/theater group, student-run newspaper, radio station, choral group, Student Activities Board, Outing Club, Phi Sigma Sigma, Portuguese Language Club, United Brothers and Sisters, national fraternities, national sororities. *Campus security:* 24-hour emergency response devices and patrols, student patrols, late-night transport/escort service, controlled dormitory access. *Student services:* health clinic, personal/psychological counseling, women's center, legal services.

Athletics Member NCAA. All Division III. *Intercollegiate sports:* baseball M, basketball M/W, cheerleading W, cross-country running M/W, equestrian sports W(c), field hockey W, football M, golf M, ice hockey M, lacrosse M/W, rugby M(c)/W(c), soccer M/W, softball W, swimming and diving M/W, tennis M/W, track and field M/W, volleyball W. *Intramural sports:* badminton M/W, basketball M/W, field hockey W, rock climbing M(c)/W(c), sailing M/W, skiing (downhill) M(c)/W(c), soccer M/W, softball M/W, table tennis M/W, tennis M/W, ultimate Frisbee M/W, volleyball M/W.

Standardized Tests *Required:* SAT or ACT (for admission).

Costs (2011–12) *One-time required fee:* $75. *Tuition:* state resident $1417 full-time, $59 per credit hour part-time; nonresident $8099 full-time, $337 per credit hour part-time. Full-time tuition and fees vary according to class time, program, and reciprocity agreements. Part-time tuition and fees vary according to class time, course load, program, and reciprocity agreements. *Required fees:* $9718 full-time, $405 per credit hour part-time. *Room and board:* $9408; room only: $6506. Room and board charges vary according to board plan and housing facility. *Payment plan:* installment. *Waivers:* senior citizens and employees or children of employees.

Financial Aid Of all full-time matriculated undergraduates who enrolled in 2010, 5,497 applied for aid, 4,545 were judged to have need, 1,973 had their need fully met. In 2010, 357 non-need-based awards were made. *Average percent of need met:* 88%. *Average financial aid package:* $14,195. *Average need-based loan:* $7337. *Average need-based gift aid:* $7987. *Average non-need-based aid:* $3741. *Average indebtedness upon graduation:* $23,200.

Applying *Options:* electronic application, early admission, early action, deferred entrance. *Application fee:* $40. *Required:* essay or personal statement, high school transcript, minimum 3.0 GPA. *Recommended:* essay or personal statement, 1 letter of recommendation. *Application deadlines:* rolling (freshmen), rolling (transfers), 11/15 (early action). *Notification:* continuous (freshmen), continuous (transfers), 12/15 (early action).

Freshman Application Contact University of Massachusetts Dartmouth, 285 Old Westport Road, North Dartmouth, MA 02747-2300. *Phone:* 508-999-8605. *Fax:* 508-999-8755. *E-mail:* admissions@umassd.edu. *Web site:* http://www.umassd.edu/.

See page 430 for display ad and page 1682 for the College Close-Up.

University of Massachusetts Lowell
Lowell, Massachusetts

- **State-supported** university, founded 1894, part of University of Massachusetts
- **Urban** 100-acre campus with easy access to Boston
- **Endowment** $49.5 million
- **Coed** 11,729 undergraduate students, 72% full-time, 40% women, 60% men
- **Moderately difficult** entrance level, 65% of applicants were admitted

Undergraduates 8,424 full-time, 3,305 part-time. Students come from 32 other countries; 14% are from out of state; 7% Black or African American, non-Hispanic/Latino; 9% Hispanic/Latino; 9% Asian, non-Hispanic/Latino; 0.1% American Indian or Alaska Native, non-Hispanic/Latino; 2% Two or more races, non-Hispanic/Latino; 5% Race/ethnicity unknown; 0.7% interna-

UMass Lowell
Work Ready Life Ready World Ready

"I chose UMass Lowell because it had the academic quality I was looking for, it had an Honors Program and I could spend a semester in New Zealand."
— *Commonwealth Scholar Ianna Hondros-McCarthy '12, psychology, English and pre-med*

- Ranked as a top tier national research university and in the top 100 public campuses in the country (U.S. News and World Report)
- Leading New England public research institutions in increased student success (Chronicle of Higher Education)
- Highest mid-career salaries among New England public grads, two of the last three years (Payscale.com)
- The best value in Massachusetts for student-to-faculty ratio — 14:1 (Mass Inc.)

www.uml.edu

UMASS LOWELL
Learning with Purpose

tional; 9% transferred in; 39% live on campus. *Retention:* 79% of full-time freshmen returned.

Freshmen *Admission:* 7,720 applied, 5,020 admitted, 1,433 enrolled. *Average high school GPA:* 3.27. *Test scores:* SAT critical reading scores over 500: 70%; SAT math scores over 500: 84%; SAT critical reading scores over 600: 22%; SAT math scores over 600: 39%; SAT critical reading scores over 700: 3%; SAT math scores over 700: 6%.

Faculty *Student/faculty ratio:* 14:1.

Academics *Calendar:* semesters. *Degrees:* associate, bachelor's, master's, doctoral, post-master's, postbachelor's, and first professional certificates. *Special study options:* accelerated degree program, adult/continuing education programs, advanced placement credit, cooperative education, distance learning, double majors, honors programs, independent study, internships, off-campus study, part-time degree program, services for LD students, study abroad, summer session for credit. *ROTC:* Army (c), Air Force (b).

Computers on Campus 3,125 computers/terminals and 13,078 ports are available on campus for general student use. Students can access the following: campus intranet, computer help desk, free student e-mail accounts, online (class) grades, online (class) registration, online (class) schedules. Campuswide network is available. 100% of college-owned or -operated housing units are wired for high-speed Internet access. Wireless service is available via classrooms, computer centers, computer labs, dorm rooms, learning centers, libraries, student centers.

Student Life *Housing options:* coed, men-only, women-only. Campus housing is university owned and leased by the school. *Activities and organizations:* drama/theater group, student-run newspaper, radio station, choral group, marching band, Student Government Association, Recreational Sports Club, Association of Students of African Origin, WUML (radio station), Campus Activities Programming Association, national fraternities, national sororities. *Campus security:* 24-hour emergency response devices and patrols, late-night transport/escort service, controlled dormitory access. *Student services:* health clinic, personal/psychological counseling.

Athletics Member NCAA. All Division II except ice hockey (Division I). *Intercollegiate sports:* baseball M(s), basketball M(s)/W(s), crew W, cross-country running M(s)/W(s), field hockey W(s), golf M, ice hockey M(s), soccer M(s)/W(s), softball W(s), track and field M(s)/W(s), volleyball W(s). *Intramural sports:* badminton M/W, basketball M/W, cheerleading M(c)/W(c), crew M(c), fencing M(c)/W(c), football M/W, ice hockey M(c)/W(c), lacrosse M(c)/W(c), racquetball M/W, rock climbing M/W, rugby M(c)/W(c), skiing (cross-country) M/W, skiing (downhill) M/W, soccer M/W, softball M/W, squash M/W, swimming and diving M(c)/W(c), table tennis M/W, tennis M/W, ultimate Frisbee M(c)/W(c), volleyball M(c)/W(c), weight lifting M/W.

Standardized Tests *Required:* SAT or ACT (for admission).

Costs (2012–13) *Tuition:* state resident $1454 full-time, $61 per credit part-time; nonresident $8567 full-time, $357 per credit part-time. Part-time tuition and fees vary according to course load. *Required fees:* $9668 full-time. *Room and board:* $9520; room only: $6346. Room and board charges vary according to board plan and housing facility. *Payment plan:* installment. *Waivers:* senior citizens and employees or children of employees.

Financial Aid Of all full-time matriculated undergraduates who enrolled in 2010, 6,393 applied for aid, 4,998 were judged to have need, 3,260 had their need fully met. 154 Federal Work-Study jobs (averaging $2226). 748 state and other part-time jobs (averaging $2874). In 2010, 578 non-need-based awards were made. *Average percent of need met:* 95%. *Average financial aid package:* $12,868. *Average need-based loan:* $6520. *Average need-based gift aid:* $6902. *Average non-need-based aid:* $3203. *Average indebtedness upon graduation:* $27,620.

Applying *Options:* electronic application, early action, deferred entrance. *Application fee:* $60. *Required:* essay or personal statement, high school transcript, minimum 3.0 GPA, 1 letter of recommendation, Audition for music students. *Application deadlines:* 2/15 (freshmen), 2/15 (out-of-state freshmen), rolling (transfers), 12/1 (early action). *Notification:* continuous (freshmen), continuous (out-of-state freshmen), continuous (transfers), 1/20 (early action).

Freshman Application Contact Admissions Office, University of Massachusetts Lowell, 883 Broadway Street, Room 110, Lowell, MA 01854-5104. *Phone:* 978-934-3931. *Fax:* 978-934-3086. *E-mail:* admissions@uml.edu. *Web site:* http://www.uml.edu/.

See page 431 for display ad and page 1684 for the College Close-Up.

University of Phoenix–Boston Campus

Braintree, Massachusetts

Freshman Application Contact Marc Booker, Sr. Director, Office of Admissions and Evaluation, University of Phoenix–Boston Campus, 4035 South Riverpoint Parkway, Mail Stop CF-L101, Phoenix, AZ 85040. *Phone:* 602-557-4609. *Toll-free phone:* 866-766-0766. *Fax:* 480-643-1156. *Web site:* http://www.phoenix.edu/.

University of Phoenix–Central Massachusetts Campus

Westborough, Massachusetts

Freshman Application Contact Marc Booker, Sr. Director, Office of Admissions and Evaluation, University of Phoenix–Central Massachusetts Campus, 4035 South Riverpoint Parkway, Mail Stop CF-L101, Phoenix, AZ 85040. *Phone:* 602-557-4609. *Toll-free phone:* 866-766-0766. *Fax:* 480-643-1156. *Web site:* http://www.phoenix.edu/.

Wellesley College

Wellesley, Massachusetts

- **Independent** 4-year, founded 1870
- **Suburban** 500-acre campus with easy access to Boston
- **Endowment** $1.3 billion
- **Women only** 2,502 undergraduate students, 94% full-time
- **Most difficult** entrance level, 31% of applicants were admitted

Undergraduates 2,364 full-time, 138 part-time. Students come from 52 states and territories; 83 other countries; 86% are from out of state; 6% Black or African American, non-Hispanic/Latino; 7% Hispanic/Latino; 21% Asian, non-Hispanic/Latino; 0.2% American Indian or Alaska Native, non-Hispanic/Latino; 6% Two or more races, non-Hispanic/Latino; 8% Race/ethnicity unknown; 11% international; 0.8% transferred in; 93% live on campus. *Retention:* 95% of full-time freshmen returned.

Freshmen *Admission:* 4,400 applied, 1,362 admitted, 573 enrolled. *Test scores:* SAT critical reading scores over 500: 100%; SAT math scores over 500: 100%; SAT writing scores over 500: 100%; ACT scores over 18: 100%; SAT critical reading scores over 600: 92%; SAT math scores over 600: 90%; SAT writing scores over 600: 94%; ACT scores over 24: 98%; SAT critical reading scores over 700: 50%; SAT math scores over 700: 49%; SAT writing scores over 700: 57%; ACT scores over 30: 64%.

Faculty *Total:* 351, 82% full-time, 89% with terminal degrees. *Student/faculty ratio:* 8:1.

Academics *Calendar:* semesters. *Degrees:* bachelor's (double bachelor's degree with Massachusetts Institute of Technology). *Special study options:* adult/continuing education programs, advanced placement credit, double majors, honors programs, independent study, internships, off-campus study, part-time degree program, services for LD students, student-designed majors, study abroad, summer session for credit. *ROTC:* Army (c), Air Force (c). *Unusual degree programs:* 3-2 engineering with Massachusetts Institute of Technology, Dartmouth College, Columbia University; architecture; aeronautics and astronautics; urban studies and planning with Massachusetts Institute of Technology; international economics and finance with Brandeis University.

Computers on Campus 200 computers/terminals and 200 ports are available on campus for general student use. Students can access the following: campus intranet, computer help desk, free student e-mail accounts, online (class) grades, online (class) registration, online (class) schedules. Campuswide network is available. 100% of college-owned or -operated housing units are wired for high-speed Internet access. Wireless service is available via entire campus.

Student Life *Housing options:* women-only, cooperative. Campus housing is university owned. Freshman campus housing is guaranteed. *Activities and organizations:* drama/theater group, student-run newspaper, radio and television station, choral group, student government, radio station, cultural clubs, rugby club, theater groups. *Campus security:* 24-hour emergency response devices and patrols, late-night transport/escort service, controlled dormitory access. *Student services:* health clinic, personal/psychological counseling, women's center.

Athletics Member NCAA. All Division III. *Intercollegiate sports:* basketball W, crew W, cross-country running W, fencing W, field hockey W, golf W, lacrosse W, rugby W(c), sailing W(c), skiing (downhill) W(c), soccer W, softball W, squash W, swimming and diving W, tennis W, track and field W, ultimate Frisbee W(c), volleyball W. *Intramural sports:* archery W, badminton W(c), basketball W, cheerleading W(c), crew W, equestrian sports W(c), ice hockey W(c), racquetball W(c), sailing W(c), skiing (cross-country) W, skiing (downhill) W, soccer W, softball W, squash W(c), swimming and diving W, table tennis W(c), tennis W, volleyball W, water polo W, weight lifting W.

Standardized Tests *Required:* SAT and SAT Subject Tests or ACT (for admission).

Costs (2011–12) *Comprehensive fee:* $53,250 includes full-time tuition ($40,410), mandatory fees ($250), and room and board ($12,590). Part-time tuition: $1263 per credit hour. Part-time tuition and fees vary according to course load. *Required fees:* $31 per credit part-time. *College room only:* $6390. *Payment plans:* tuition prepayment, installment. *Waivers:* employees or children of employees.

Financial Aid Of all full-time matriculated undergraduates who enrolled in 2011, 1,596 applied for aid, 1,395 were judged to have need, 1,395 had their

need fully met. *Average percent of need met:* 100%. *Average financial aid package:* $38,903. *Average need-based loan:* $3145. *Average need-based gift aid:* $36,971. *Average indebtedness upon graduation:* $13,579.

Applying *Options:* electronic application, early admission, early decision, deferred entrance. *Application fee:* $50. *Required:* essay or personal statement, high school transcript, 3 letters of recommendation, first senior marking period grades and mid-year report. *Required for some:* interview. *Recommended:* interview. *Application deadlines:* 1/15 (freshmen), 1/15 (out-of-state freshmen), 3/1 (transfers). *Early decision deadline:* 11/1. *Notification:* 4/1 (freshmen), 4/1 (out-of-state freshmen), 5/1 (transfers), 12/15 (early decision).

Freshman Application Contact Director of Admission, Wellesley College, 106 Central Street, Wellesley, MA 02481. *Phone:* 781-283-2270. *Fax:* 781-283-3678. *E-mail:* admission@wellesley.edu. *Web site:* http://www.wellesley.edu/.

Wentworth Institute of Technology
Boston, Massachusetts

- **Independent** comprehensive, founded 1904
- **Urban** 31-acre campus
- **Endowment** $77.5 million
- **Coed** 3,855 undergraduate students, 90% full-time, 19% women, 81% men
- **Moderately difficult** entrance level, 61% of applicants were admitted

Undergraduates 3,454 full-time, 401 part-time. Students come from 38 states and territories; 49 other countries; 40% are from out of state; 5% Black or African American, non-Hispanic/Latino; 4% Hispanic/Latino; 6% Asian, non-Hispanic/Latino; 0.2% American Indian or Alaska Native, non-Hispanic/Latino; 2% Two or more races, non-Hispanic/Latino; 12% Race/ethnicity unknown; 4% international; 4% transferred in; 49% live on campus. *Retention:* 79% of full-time freshmen returned.

Freshmen *Admission:* 4,967 applied, 3,043 admitted, 1,007 enrolled. *Average high school GPA:* 2.98. *Test scores:* SAT critical reading scores over 500: 59%; SAT math scores over 500: 83%; SAT writing scores over 500: 53%; ACT scores over 18: 95%; SAT critical reading scores over 600: 18%; SAT math scores over 600: 36%; SAT writing scores over 600: 15%; ACT scores over 24: 46%; SAT critical reading scores over 700: 1%; SAT math scores over 700: 5%; SAT writing scores over 700: 1%; ACT scores over 30: 4%.

Faculty *Total:* 290, 52% full-time, 34% with terminal degrees. *Student/faculty ratio:* 16:1.

Academics *Calendar:* semesters for freshmen and sophomores, trimesters for juniors and seniors. *Degrees:* associate, bachelor's, and master's. *Special study options:* academic remediation for entering students, advanced placement credit, cooperative education, internships, off-campus study, part-time degree program, services for LD students, study abroad, summer session for credit. *ROTC:* Army (c), Air Force (c).

Computers on Campus 150 computers/terminals and 200 ports are available on campus for general student use. Students can access the following: campus intranet, computer help desk, free student e-mail accounts, online (class) grades, online (class) registration, online (class) schedules. Campuswide network is available. 100% of college-owned or -operated housing units are wired for high-speed Internet access. Wireless service is available via entire campus.

Student Life *Housing:* on-campus residence required through sophomore year. *Options:* coed. Campus housing is university owned. Freshman campus housing is guaranteed. *Activities and organizations:* student-run radio station, intramural sports, Wentworth Events Board, Multicultural Student Association, Phi Sigma Pi, Major Particular Professional Student Associations. *Campus security:* 24-hour emergency response devices and patrols, student patrols, late-night transport/escort service, controlled dormitory access. *Student services:* health clinic, personal/psychological counseling, women's center.

Athletics Member NCAA. All Division III. *Intercollegiate sports:* baseball M, basketball M/W, crew M(c)/W(c), golf M, ice hockey M, lacrosse M/W(c), riflery M/W, rugby M(c)/W(c), soccer M/W, softball W, tennis M/W, ultimate Frisbee M(c)/W(c), volleyball M/W.

Standardized Tests *Required:* SAT or ACT (for admission).

Costs (2011–12) *Comprehensive fee:* $35,300 includes full-time tuition ($24,000) and room and board ($11,300). Part-time tuition: $750 per credit hour. Part-time tuition and fees vary according to course load and degree level. *Required fees:* $420 per credit hour part-time. *Room and board:* Room and board charges vary according to board plan and housing facility. *Payment plan:* installment. *Waivers:* employees or children of employees.

Financial Aid Of all full-time matriculated undergraduates who enrolled in 2010, 2,571 applied for aid, 2,338 were judged to have need, 60 had their need fully met. 2,026 Federal Work-Study jobs (averaging $1354). In 2010, 157 non-need-based awards were made. *Average financial aid package:* $14,453. *Average need-based loan:* $4674. *Average need-based gift aid:* $5568. *Average non-need-based aid:* $6766. *Average indebtedness upon graduation:* $20,208.

Applying *Options:* electronic application, deferred entrance. *Application fee:* $50. *Required:* essay or personal statement, high school transcript, 1 letter of recommendation. *Recommended:* minimum 2.0 GPA, interview. *Application deadlines:* 5/1 (freshmen), 5/1 (out-of-state freshmen), 5/1 (transfers). *Notification:* continuous (freshmen), continuous (transfers).

Freshman Application Contact Ms. Amy Dufour, Associate Director of Admissions, Wentworth Institute of Technology, 550 Huntington Avenue, Boston, MA 02115. *Phone:* 617-989-4116. *Toll-free phone:* 800-556-0610. *Fax:* 617-989-4010. *E-mail:* dufoura@wit.edu. *Web site:* http://www.wit.edu/.

See page 434 for display ad and page 1750 for the College Close-Up.

Western New England University
Springfield, Massachusetts

- **Independent** comprehensive, founded 1919
- **Suburban** 215-acre campus
- **Endowment** $34.1 million
- **Coed** 2,673 undergraduate students, 92% full-time, 39% women, 61% men
- **Moderately difficult** entrance level, 80% of applicants were admitted

Undergraduates 2,472 full-time, 201 part-time. 54% are from out of state; 5% Black or African American, non-Hispanic/Latino; 6% Hispanic/Latino; 3% Asian, non-Hispanic/Latino; 0.2% American Indian or Alaska Native, non-Hispanic/Latino; 2% Two or more races, non-Hispanic/Latino; 4% Race/ethnicity unknown; 0.6% international; 4% transferred in; 72% live on campus. *Retention:* 73% of full-time freshmen returned.

Freshmen *Admission:* 5,752 applied, 4,625 admitted, 786 enrolled. *Average high school GPA:* 3.25. *Test scores:* SAT critical reading scores over 500: 61%; SAT math scores over 500: 76%; ACT scores over 18: 99%; SAT critical reading scores over 600: 14%; SAT math scores over 600: 29%; ACT scores over 24: 47%; SAT critical reading scores over 700: 1%; SAT math scores over 700: 3%; ACT scores over 30: 4%.

Faculty *Total:* 337, 61% full-time. *Student/faculty ratio:* 14:1.

Academics *Calendar:* semesters. *Degrees:* associate, bachelor's, master's, doctoral, and first professional. *Special study options:* accelerated degree program, adult/continuing education credit, advanced placement credit, distance learning, double majors, honors programs, independent study, internships, off-campus study, part-time degree program, services for LD students, student-designed majors, study abroad, summer session for credit. *ROTC:* Army (b), Air Force (c). *Unusual degree programs:* 3-2 business administration; engineering.

Computers on Campus 400 computers/terminals are available on campus for general student use. Students can access the following: computer help desk, free student e-mail accounts, online (class) grades, online (class) registration, online (class) schedules. Campuswide network is available. 100% of college-owned or -operated housing units are wired for high-speed Internet access.

Student Life *Housing options:* coed. Campus housing is university owned. Freshman campus housing is guaranteed. *Activities and organizations:* drama/theater group, student-run newspaper, radio station, choral group, Student Senate, Residence Hall Association, Campus Activities Board, student radio station, The Westerner (student newspaper). *Campus security:* 24-hour emergency response devices and patrols, student patrols, late-night transport/escort service, controlled dormitory access, security cameras. *Student services:* health clinic, personal/psychological counseling.

Athletics Member NCAA. All Division III. *Intercollegiate sports:* baseball M, basketball M/W, bowling M/W, cross-country running M/W, field hockey W, football M, golf M, ice hockey M, lacrosse M/W, soccer M/W, softball W, swimming and diving W, tennis M/W, volleyball W, wrestling M. *Intramural sports:* badminton M/W, basketball M/W, football M/W, rugby M/W, soccer M/W, softball M/W, table tennis M/W, ultimate Frisbee M/W, volleyball M/W, water polo M/W.

Standardized Tests *Required:* SAT or ACT (for admission).

Costs (2011–12) *Comprehensive fee:* $42,576 includes full-time tuition ($28,734), mandatory fees ($2110), and room and board ($11,732). Full-time tuition and fees vary according to program. Part-time tuition: $541 per credit hour. Part-time tuition and fees vary according to location and program. *Room and board:* Room and board charges vary according to board plan and housing facility. *Payment plans:* tuition prepayment, installment. *Waivers:* senior citizens and employees or children of employees.

Financial Aid Of all full-time matriculated undergraduates who enrolled in 2011, 2,166 applied for aid, 1,966 were judged to have need, 258 had their need fully met. In 2011, 318 non-need-based awards were made. *Average percent of need met:* 69%. *Average financial aid package:* $20,654. *Average need-based loan:* $4749. *Average need-based gift aid:* $15,378. *Average non-need-based aid:* $10,616. *Financial aid deadline:* 4/15.

Applying *Options:* electronic application. *Application fee:* $40. *Required:* high school transcript, 1 letter of recommendation. *Recommended:* essay or

WENTWORTH
Institute of Technology

personal statement, interview. *Application deadlines:* rolling (freshmen), rolling (transfers). *Notification:* continuous (freshmen), continuous (transfers).
Freshman Application Contact Dr. Charles R. Pollock, Vice President of Enrollment Management, Western New England University, Springfield, MA 01119. *Phone:* 413-782-1321. *Toll-free phone:* 800-325-1122 Ext. 1321. *Fax:* 413-782-1777. *E-mail:* learn@wne.edu. *Web site:* http://www.wne.edu/.

Westfield State University
Westfield, Massachusetts

- **State-supported** comprehensive, founded 1838, part of Massachusetts Public Higher Education System
- **Suburban** 227-acre campus
- **Coed** 5,397 undergraduate students, 89% full-time, 53% women, 47% men
- **Moderately difficult** entrance level, 61% of applicants were admitted

Undergraduates 4,801 full-time, 596 part-time. Students come from 23 states and territories; 15 other countries; 7% are from out of state; 4% Black or African American, non-Hispanic/Latino; 5% Hispanic/Latino; 0.8% Asian, non-Hispanic/Latino; 0.1% Native Hawaiian or other Pacific Islander, non-Hispanic/Latino; 0.2% American Indian or Alaska Native, non-Hispanic/Latino; 2% Two or more races, non-Hispanic/Latino; 4% Race/ethnicity unknown; 0.5% international; 7% transferred in; 55% live on campus. *Retention:* 80% of full-time freshmen returned.
Freshmen *Admission:* 5,192 applied, 3,178 admitted, 1,133 enrolled. *Average high school GPA:* 3.09. *Test scores:* SAT critical reading scores over 500: 54%; SAT math scores over 500: 63%; ACT scores over 18: 90%; SAT critical reading scores over 600: 12%; SAT math scores over 600: 14%; ACT scores over 24: 41%; SAT critical reading scores over 700: 1%; SAT math scores over 700: 1%; ACT scores over 30: 3%.
Faculty *Total:* 465, 48% full-time, 56% with terminal degrees. *Student/faculty ratio:* 18:1.
Academics *Calendar:* semesters. *Degrees:* bachelor's, master's, post-master's, and postbachelor's certificates. *Special study options:* adult/continuing education programs, advanced placement credit, cooperative education, distance learning, double majors, honors programs, independent study, internships, off-campus study, part-time degree program, services for LD students, student-designed majors, study abroad, summer session for credit. *ROTC:* Army (c), Air Force (c).
Computers on Campus 369 computers/terminals are available on campus for general student use. Students can access the following: computer help desk, free student e-mail accounts, online (class) grades, online (class) registration, online (class) schedules, online transcripts and billing information. Campus-wide network is available. 100% of college-owned or -operated housing units are wired for high-speed Internet access. Wireless service is available via entire campus.
Student Life *Housing options:* coed, disabled students. Campus housing is university owned. Freshman applicants given priority for college housing. *Activities and organizations:* drama/theater group, student-run newspaper, radio and television station, choral group, Student National Education Association, Student Government Association, Campus Activities Board, The Dance Company, Multicultural Student Association. *Campus security:* 24-hour emergency response devices and patrols, student patrols, late-night transport/escort service, controlled dormitory access. *Student services:* health clinic, personal/psychological counseling, legal services.
Athletics Member NCAA. All Division III. *Intercollegiate sports:* baseball M, basketball M/W, cheerleading W, cross-country running M/W, equestrian sports M(c)/W(c), field hockey W, football M, golf M/W, ice hockey M, lacrosse M(c)/W, soccer M/W, softball W, swimming and diving W, track and field M/W, volleyball W. *Intramural sports:* badminton M/W, basketball M/W, ice hockey M(c)/W(c), rock climbing M/W, rugby M(c), ultimate Frisbee M/W.
Standardized Tests *Required:* SAT or ACT (for admission).
Costs (2011–12) *Tuition:* state resident $970 full-time; nonresident $7050 full-time. Full-time tuition and fees vary according to reciprocity agreements. *Required fees:* $6916 full-time. *Room and board:* $8665. Room and board charges vary according to board plan and housing facility. *Payment plan:* installment. *Waivers:* senior citizens and employees or children of employees.
Financial Aid Of all full-time matriculated undergraduates who enrolled in 2010, 4,035 applied for aid, 2,853 were judged to have need, 392 had their need fully met. 302 Federal Work-Study jobs (averaging $1526). In 2010, 55 non-need-based awards were made. *Average percent of need met:* 69%. *Average financial aid package:* $7682. *Average need-based loan:* $4087. *Average need-based gift aid:* $5113. *Average non-need-based aid:* $4258. *Average indebtedness upon graduation:* $23,095.
Applying *Options:* electronic application, deferred entrance. *Application fee:* $50. *Required:* high school transcript, minimum 2.0 GPA. *Required for some:* interview, audition for music major, portfolio for art major. *Application dead-

lines: 3/1 (freshmen), 3/1 (out-of-state freshmen), 3/1 (transfers). *Notification:* continuous until 3/15 (freshmen), continuous until 3/15 (out-of-state freshmen), continuous until 3/15 (transfers).

Freshman Application Contact Dr. Kelly Hart, Director of Admissions, Westfield State University, 333 Western Avenue, Westfield, MA 01002. *Phone:* 413-572-5218. *Fax:* 413-572-0520. *E-mail:* admission@westfield.ma.edu. *Web site:* http://www.wsc.ma.edu/.

Wheaton College
Norton, Massachusetts

- **Independent** 4-year, founded 1834
- **Suburban** 400-acre campus with easy access to Boston
- **Endowment** $164.9 million
- **Coed** 1,622 undergraduate students, 100% full-time, 64% women, 36% men
- **Very difficult** entrance level, 60% of applicants were admitted

Undergraduates 1,621 full-time, 1 part-time. Students come from 39 states and territories; 41 other countries; 65% are from out of state; 5% Black or African American, non-Hispanic/Latino; 7% Hispanic/Latino; 2% Asian, non-Hispanic/Latino; 0.2% American Indian or Alaska Native, non-Hispanic/Latino; 3% Two or more races, non-Hispanic/Latino; 0.8% Race/ethnicity unknown; 8% international; 0.9% transferred in; 95% live on campus. *Retention:* 86% of full-time freshmen returned.

Freshmen *Admission:* 3,448 applied, 2,075 admitted, 437 enrolled. *Average high school GPA:* 3.5.

Faculty *Total:* 166, 84% full-time, 80% with terminal degrees. *Student/faculty ratio:* 11:1.

Academics *Calendar:* semesters. *Degree:* bachelor's. *Special study options:* accelerated degree program, advanced placement credit, double majors, honors programs, independent study, internships, off-campus study, part-time degree program, student-designed majors, study abroad. *ROTC:* Army (c). *Unusual degree programs:* 3-2 business administration with University of Rochester; engineering with Dartmouth College, George Washington University; theology with Andover Newton Theological School, optometry with New England College of Optometry, integrated marketing communications studies with Emerson College, studio art with School of the Museum of Fine Arts.

Computers on Campus 289 computers/terminals and 2,175 ports are available on campus for general student use. Students can access the following: campus intranet, computer help desk, free student e-mail accounts, online (class) grades, online (class) registration, online (class) schedules. Campus-wide network is available. 100% of college-owned or -operated housing units are wired for high-speed Internet access. Wireless service is available via entire campus.

Student Life *Housing:* on-campus residence required through senior year. *Options:* coed, men-only, women-only, disabled students. Campus housing is university owned. Freshman campus housing is guaranteed. *Activities and organizations:* drama/theater group, student-run newspaper, radio station, choral group, Student Government Association, Community Service Network, Amnesty International, a cappella singing groups, Programming Council. *Campus security:* 24-hour emergency response devices and patrols, student patrols, late-night transport/escort service, controlled dormitory access. *Student services:* health clinic, personal/psychological counseling, women's center.

Athletics Member NCAA. All Division III. *Intercollegiate sports:* baseball M, basketball M/W, cross-country running M/W, field hockey W, lacrosse M/W, soccer M/W, softball W, swimming and diving M/W, tennis M/W, track and field M/W, volleyball W. *Intramural sports:* archery M(c)/W, badminton M/W, basketball M/W, equestrian sports M(c)/W(c), field hockey W(c), golf M(c)/W(c), ice hockey M(c)/W(c), rugby M(c)/W(c), sailing M(c)/W(c), soccer M/W, softball M/W, tennis M/W, ultimate Frisbee M(c)/W(c), volleyball M/W, wrestling M(c)/W(c).

Costs (2011–12) *One-time required fee:* $50. *Comprehensive fee:* $52,564 includes full-time tuition ($41,600), mandatory fees ($294), and room and board ($10,670). *College room only:* $5700. *Payment plans:* tuition prepayment, installment. *Waivers:* employees or children of employees.

Financial Aid Of all full-time matriculated undergraduates who enrolled in 2011, 1,132 applied for aid, 1,007 were judged to have need, 501 had their need fully met. 807 Federal Work-Study jobs (averaging $1672). 295 state and other part-time jobs (averaging $1590). In 2011, 231 non-need-based awards were made. *Average percent of need met:* 96%. *Average financial aid package:* $33,908. *Average need-based loan:* $4431. *Average need-based gift aid:* $27,876. *Average non-need-based aid:* $12,374. *Average indebtedness upon graduation:* $25,778. *Financial aid deadline:* 2/1.

Applying *Options:* electronic application, early admission, early decision, early action, deferred entrance. *Application fee:* $55. *Required:* essay or personal statement, high school transcript, 2 letters of recommendation. *Recommended:* interview. *Application deadlines:* 1/15 (freshmen), 3/1 (transfers),

11/15 (early action). *Early decision deadline:* 11/15. *Notification:* 4/1 (freshmen), continuous (transfers), 12/15 (early decision), 1/15 (early action).

Freshman Application Contact Gail Berson, Vice President for Enrollment and Dean of Admission and Student Aid, Wheaton College, 26 East Main Street, Norton, MA 02766. *Phone:* 508-286-8251. *Toll-free phone:* 800-394-6003. *Fax:* 508-286-8271. *E-mail:* admission@wheatoncollege.edu. *Web site:* http://www.wheatoncollege.edu/.

Wheelock College
Boston, Massachusetts

- **Independent** comprehensive, founded 1888
- **Urban** 6-acre campus
- **Endowment** $43.7 million
- **Coed, primarily women** 916 undergraduate students, 91% full-time, 89% women, 11% men
- **Minimally difficult** entrance level, 71% of applicants were admitted

Undergraduates 837 full-time, 79 part-time. Students come from 15 states and territories; 8 other countries; 35% are from out of state; 12% Black or African American, non-Hispanic/Latino; 11% Hispanic/Latino; 2% Asian, non-Hispanic/Latino; 0.7% Two or more races, non-Hispanic/Latino; 13% Race/ethnicity unknown; 0.5% international; 15% transferred in; 70% live on campus. *Retention:* 80% of full-time freshmen returned.

Freshmen *Admission:* 1,537 applied, 1,086 admitted, 230 enrolled. *Average high school GPA:* 3. *Test scores:* SAT critical reading scores over 500: 47%; SAT math scores over 500: 40%; SAT writing scores over 500: 51%; ACT scores over 18: 74%; SAT critical reading scores over 600: 11%; SAT math scores over 600: 9%; SAT writing scores over 600: 10%; ACT scores over 24: 16%; SAT critical reading scores over 700: 1%; SAT writing scores over 700: 1%; ACT scores over 30: 2%.

Faculty *Total:* 167, 39% full-time, 41% with terminal degrees. *Student/faculty ratio:* 9:1.

Academics *Calendar:* semesters. *Degrees:* bachelor's, master's, post-master's, and postbachelor's certificates. *Special study options:* advanced placement credit, double majors, freshman honors college, honors programs, independent study, internships, off-campus study, part-time degree program, services for LD students, study abroad, summer session for credit.

Computers on Campus 100 computers/terminals and 1,100 ports are available on campus for general student use. Students can access the following: campus intranet, computer help desk, free student e-mail accounts, online (class) grades, online (class) registration, online (class) schedules. Campus-wide network is available. Wireless service is available via classrooms, computer labs, dorm rooms, learning centers, libraries, student centers.

Student Life *Housing options:* coed, women-only, cooperative, disabled students. Campus housing is university owned. Freshman campus housing is guaranteed. *Activities and organizations:* drama/theater group, choral group. *Campus security:* 24-hour patrols, late-night transport/escort service, controlled dormitory access. *Student services:* health clinic, personal/psychological counseling, women's center.

Athletics Member NCAA. All Division III. *Intercollegiate sports:* basketball M/W, cross-country running M/W, field hockey W, lacrosse M/W, soccer M/W, softball W, tennis M. *Intramural sports:* basketball M/W, racquetball M/W, soccer M, softball M/W, squash M/W, table tennis M/W, ultimate Frisbee M/W, volleyball M/W, water polo M/W.

Standardized Tests *Required:* SAT or ACT (for admission).

Costs (2012–13) *Comprehensive fee:* $43,755 includes full-time tuition ($29,860), mandatory fees ($1095), and room and board ($12,800). Part-time tuition: $933 per credit hour. *Payment plan:* installment. *Waivers:* employees or children of employees.

Financial Aid Of all full-time matriculated undergraduates who enrolled in 2011, 753 applied for aid, 683 were judged to have need, 94 had their need fully met. 186 Federal Work-Study jobs (averaging $1800). In 2011, 130 non-need-based awards were made. *Average percent of need met:* 64%. *Average financial aid package:* $21,063. *Average need-based loan:* $4688. *Average need-based gift aid:* $16,546. *Average non-need-based aid:* $11,645. *Average indebtedness upon graduation:* $45,391.

Applying *Options:* electronic application, early admission, early action, deferred entrance. *Application fee:* $15. *Required:* essay or personal statement, high school transcript, minimum 2.0 GPA, 1 letter of recommendation. *Recommended:* interview. *Application deadlines:* 3/1 (freshmen), 6/1 (transfers), 12/1 (early action). *Notification:* continuous (freshmen), continuous (transfers).

Freshman Application Contact Ms. Kristen Harrington, Director of Undergraduate Admissions, Wheelock College, 200 The Riverway, Boston, MA 02215. *Phone:* 617-879-2206. *Toll-free phone:* 800-734-5212. *Fax:* 617-879-2449. *E-mail:* kharrington@wheelock.edu. *Web site:* http://www.wheelock.edu/.

Williams College

Williamstown, Massachusetts

- **Independent** comprehensive, founded 1793
- **Small-town** 450-acre campus with easy access to Albany, NY
- **Endowment** $1.8 million
- **Coed** 2,053 undergraduate students, 98% full-time, 51% women, 49% men
- **Most difficult** entrance level, 17% of applicants were admitted

Undergraduates 2,012 full-time, 41 part-time. Students come from 50 states and territories; 56 other countries; 86% are from out of state; 8% Black or African American, non-Hispanic/Latino; 11% Hispanic/Latino; 11% Asian, non-Hispanic/Latino; 0.1% American Indian or Alaska Native, non-Hispanic/Latino; 5% Two or more races, non-Hispanic/Latino; 7% international; 0.3% transferred in; 94% live on campus. *Retention:* 97% of full-time freshmen returned.

Freshmen *Admission:* 7,030 applied, 1,215 admitted, 546 enrolled. *Test scores:* SAT critical reading scores over 500: 100%; SAT math scores over 500: 100%; ACT scores over 18: 100%; SAT critical reading scores over 600: 90%; SAT math scores over 600: 91%; ACT scores over 24: 99%; SAT critical reading scores over 700: 63%; SAT math scores over 700: 60%; ACT scores over 30: 78%.

Faculty *Total:* 320, 82% full-time, 92% with terminal degrees. *Student/faculty ratio:* 7:1.

Academics *Calendar:* 4-1-4. *Degrees:* bachelor's and master's. *Special study options:* double majors, independent study, internships, off-campus study, study abroad. *ROTC:* Air Force (c). *Unusual degree programs:* 3-2 engineering with Columbia University, Washington University in St. Louis, Oxford-Style tutorials, Dartmouth College.

Computers on Campus 252 computers/terminals are available on campus for general student use. Students can access the following: computer help desk, free student e-mail accounts, online (class) grades, online (class) registration. Campuswide network is available. 100% of college-owned or -operated housing units are wired for high-speed Internet access. Wireless service is available via entire campus.

Student Life *Housing:* on-campus residence required for freshman year. *Options:* coed, cooperative. Campus housing is university owned. *Activities and organizations:* drama/theater group, student-run newspaper, radio station, choral group. *Student services:* health clinic, personal/psychological counseling.

Athletics Member NCAA. All Division III except men's and women's skiing (cross-country) (Division I), men's and women's skiing (downhill) (Division I). *Intercollegiate sports:* baseball M, basketball M/W, crew M/W, cross-country running M/W, equestrian sports M(c)/W(c), field hockey W, football M, golf M/W(c), ice hockey M/W, lacrosse M/W, rugby M(c)/W(c), sailing M(c)/W(c), skiing (cross-country) M/W, skiing (downhill) M/W, soccer M/W, softball W, squash M/W, swimming and diving M/W, tennis M/W, track and field M/W, volleyball M(c)/W, water polo M(c)/W(c), wrestling M. *Intramural sports:* badminton M/W, baseball M(c), basketball M/W, fencing M(c)/W(c), gymnastics M(c)/W(c), ice hockey M/W, skiing (cross-country) M/W, skiing (downhill) M/W, soccer M/W, softball M/W, ultimate Frisbee M(c)/W(c), volleyball M/W, water polo M/W.

Standardized Tests *Required:* SAT and SAT Subject Tests or ACT (for admission).

Costs (2011–12) *Comprehensive fee:* $54,560 includes full-time tuition ($42,938), mandatory fees ($252), and room and board ($11,370). *College room only:* $5780. Room and board charges vary according to board plan. *Payment plan:* installment.

Financial Aid Of all full-time matriculated undergraduates who enrolled in 2010, 1,275 applied for aid, 1,163 were judged to have need, 1,163 had their need fully met. 468 Federal Work-Study jobs (averaging $1846). 463 state and other part-time jobs (averaging $1886). *Average percent of need met:* 100%. *Average financial aid package:* $40,485. *Average need-based gift aid:* $38,035. *Average indebtedness upon graduation:* $8065. *Financial aid deadline:* 2/1.

Applying *Options:* electronic application, early admission, early decision, deferred entrance. *Application fee:* $65. *Required:* essay or personal statement, high school transcript, 2 letters of recommendation.

Freshman Application Contact Mr. Richard L. Nesbitt, Director of Admission, Williams College, 33 Stetson Court, Williamstown, MA 01267. *Phone:* 413-597-2211. *Fax:* 413-597-4052. *E-mail:* admission@williams.edu. *Web site:* http://www.williams.edu/.

Worcester Polytechnic Institute

Worcester, Massachusetts

- **Independent** university, founded 1865
- **Suburban** 80-acre campus with easy access to Boston
- **Endowment** $374.4 million
- **Coed** 3,849 undergraduate students, 96% full-time, 31% women, 69% men
- **Very difficult** entrance level, 57% of applicants were admitted

Undergraduates 3,681 full-time, 168 part-time. Students come from 46 states and territories; 63 other countries; 53% are from out of state; 3% Black or African American, non-Hispanic/Latino; 8% Hispanic/Latino; 5% Asian, non-Hispanic/Latino; 0.2% American Indian or Alaska Native, non-Hispanic/Latino; 2% Two or more races, non-Hispanic/Latino; 2% Race/ethnicity unknown; 11% international; 1% transferred in; 50% live on campus. *Retention:* 95% of full-time freshmen returned.

Freshmen *Admission:* 7,049 applied, 3,998 admitted, 1,005 enrolled. *Average high school GPA:* 3.8. *Test scores:* SAT critical reading scores over 500: 90%; SAT math scores over 500: 100%; SAT writing scores over 500: 93%; ACT scores over 18: 99%; SAT critical reading scores over 600: 60%; SAT math scores over 600: 92%; SAT writing scores over 600: 57%; ACT scores over 24: 94%; SAT critical reading scores over 700: 15%; SAT math scores over 700: 43%; SAT writing scores over 700: 13%; ACT scores over 30: 39%.

Faculty *Total:* 424, 68% full-time, 76% with terminal degrees. *Student/faculty ratio:* 14:1.

Academics *Calendar:* 4 7-week terms. *Degrees:* bachelor's, master's, doctoral, and first professional. *Special study options:* accelerated degree program, advanced placement credit, cooperative education, distance learning, double majors, English as a second language, independent study, internships, off-campus study, part-time degree program, services for LD students, student-designed majors, study abroad, summer session for credit. *ROTC:* Army (b), Navy (c), Air Force (b). *Unusual degree programs:* 3-2 business administration; engineering.

Computers on Campus 500 computers/terminals and 775 ports are available on campus for general student use. Students can access the following: campus intranet, computer help desk, free student e-mail accounts, online (class) grades, online (class) registration, online (class) schedules, online course content. Campuswide network is available. 100% of college-owned or -operated housing units are wired for high-speed Internet access. Wireless service is available via entire campus.

Student Life *Housing options:* coed, men-only, women-only, disabled students. Campus housing is university owned. Freshman campus housing is guaranteed. *Activities and organizations:* drama/theater group, student-run newspaper, radio station, choral group, marching band, Student Government Association, Social Committee (Student Events Programming Board), Music Association (all music-performing groups), intramural and club sports, International Student Council, national fraternities, national sororities. *Campus security:* 24-hour emergency response devices and patrols, student patrols, late-night transport/escort service, controlled dormitory access. *Student services:* health clinic, personal/psychological counseling.

Athletics Member NCAA. All Division III. *Intercollegiate sports:* baseball M, basketball M/W, crew M/W, cross-country running M/W, field hockey W, football M, soccer M/W, softball W, swimming and diving M/W, track and field M/W, volleyball W, water polo M(c)/W(c), wrestling M. *Intramural sports:* baseball M/W, basketball M/W, bowling M/W, cheerleading M(c)/W(c), cross-country running M(c)/W(c), fencing M(c)/W(c), golf M(c)/W(c), ice hockey M(c)/W(c), lacrosse M(c)/W(c), racquetball M/W, rugby M(c)/W(c), sailing M(c)/W(c), skiing (cross-country) M(c)/W(c), skiing (downhill) M(c)/W(c), soccer M/W, softball M/W, squash M/W, swimming and diving M/W, table tennis M/W, tennis M(c)/W(c), track and field M/W, ultimate Frisbee M(c)/W(c), volleyball M(c)/W, water polo M(c)/W(c), wrestling M(c).

Standardized Tests *Required for some:* SAT or ACT (for admission), IELTS or TOEFL.

Costs (2012–13) *One-time required fee:* $200. *Comprehensive fee:* $53,526 includes full-time tuition ($40,634), mandatory fees ($600), and room and board ($12,292). Part-time tuition: $1060 per credit hour. Part-time tuition and fees vary according to course load. *College room only:* $7191. Room and board charges vary according to board plan and housing facility. *Payment plans:* tuition prepayment, installment, deferred payment. *Waivers:* employees or children of employees.

Financial Aid Of all full-time matriculated undergraduates who enrolled in 2010, 2,740 applied for aid, 2,470 were judged to have need, 958 had their need fully met. 658 Federal Work-Study jobs (averaging $1129). In 2010, 928 non-need-based awards were made. *Average percent of need met:* 73%. *Average financial aid package:* $30,237. *Average need-based loan:* $2787. *Average need-based gift aid:* $18,707. *Average non-need-based aid:* $16,005. *Financial aid deadline:* 2/1.

Applying *Options:* electronic application, early admission, early action, deferred entrance. *Application fee:* $60. *Required:* essay or personal statement, high school transcript, 2 letters of recommendation. *Required for some:* interview. *Application deadlines:* 2/1 (freshmen), 4/15 (transfers), 11/10 (early action). *Notification:* 4/1 (freshmen), continuous (transfers), 12/20 (early action).

Freshman Application Contact Mr. Edward J. Connor, Dean of Admissions, Worcester Polytechnic Institute, 100 Institute Road, Worcester, MA 01609-2280. *Phone:* 508-831-5286. *Fax:* 508-831-5875. *E-mail:* admissions@wpi.edu. *Web site:* http://www.wpi.edu/.

See below for display ad and page 1770 for the College Close-Up.

Worcester State University

Worcester, Massachusetts

- **State-supported** comprehensive, founded 1874, part of Massachusetts Public Higher Education System
- **Urban** 58-acre campus with easy access to Boston
- **Endowment** $10.2 million
- **Coed** 5,277 undergraduate students, 74% full-time, 60% women, 40% men
- **Moderately difficult** entrance level, 65% of applicants were admitted

Undergraduates 3,901 full-time, 1,376 part-time. Students come from 20 states and territories; 19 other countries; 3% are from out of state; 6% Black or African American, non-Hispanic/Latino; 7% Hispanic/Latino; 3% Asian, non-Hispanic/Latino; 0.1% Native Hawaiian or other Pacific Islander, non-Hispanic/Latino; 0.5% American Indian or Alaska Native, non-Hispanic/Latino; 1% Two or more races, non-Hispanic/Latino; 6% Race/ethnicity unknown; 0.9% international; 10% transferred in; 26% live on campus. *Retention:* 80% of full-time freshmen returned.

Freshmen *Admission:* 3,647 applied, 2,385 admitted, 796 enrolled. *Average high school GPA:* 3.06. *Test scores:* SAT critical reading scores over 500: 51%; SAT math scores over 500: 59%; SAT writing scores over 500: 49%; ACT scores over 18: 92%; SAT critical reading scores over 600: 10%; SAT math scores over 600: 12%; SAT writing scores over 600: 9%; ACT scores over 24: 26%; SAT critical reading scores over 700: 1%; SAT writing scores over 700: 1%; ACT scores over 30: 4%.

Faculty *Total:* 420, 45% full-time, 47% with terminal degrees. *Student/faculty ratio:* 17:1.

Academics *Calendar:* semesters. *Degrees:* bachelor's, master's, post-master's, and postbachelor's certificates. *Special study options:* academic remediation for entering students, accelerated degree program, adult/continuing education programs, advanced placement credit, distance learning, double majors, English as a second language, honors programs, independent study, internships, off-campus study, part-time degree program, services for LD students, study abroad, summer session for credit. *ROTC:* Army (c), Navy (c), Air Force (c).

Computers on Campus 500 computers/terminals and 1,700 ports are available on campus for general student use. Students can access the following: campus intranet, computer help desk, free student e-mail accounts, online (class) grades, online (class) registration, online (class) schedules. Campus-wide network is available. 100% of college-owned or -operated housing units are wired for high-speed Internet access. Wireless service is available via entire campus.

Student Life *Housing options:* coed, men-only, women-only, disabled students. Campus housing is university owned. *Activities and organizations:* drama/theater group, student-run newspaper, radio and television station, choral group, Senate, SEC (Student Events Committee), TWA (Third World Alliance), WSCW (radio station), Dance Company/Club. *Campus security:* 24-hour emergency response devices and patrols, late-night transport/escort service, controlled dormitory access, well-lit campus and limited access to campus at night. *Student services:* health clinic, personal/psychological counseling.

Athletics Member NCAA. All Division III. *Intercollegiate sports:* baseball M, basketball M/W, cross-country running M/W, field hockey W, football M, golf M, ice hockey M, lacrosse W, soccer M/W, softball W, tennis W, track and field M/W, volleyball W. *Intramural sports:* basketball M/W, cheerleading M/W, football M, skiing (downhill) M(c)/W(c), soccer M/W, softball M/W, ultimate Frisbee M/W, volleyball M(c)/W.

Standardized Tests *Required:* SAT or ACT (for admission).

Costs (2011–12) *Tuition:* state resident $970 full-time, $40 per credit part-time; nonresident $7050 full-time, $294 per credit part-time. Full-time tuition and fees vary according to class time, course load, degree level, and reciprocity agreements. Part-time tuition and fees vary according to class time, course load, degree level, and reciprocity agreements. *Required fees:* $6683 full-time, $278 per credit part-time. *Room and board:* $10,400; room only: $7420. Room and board charges vary according to board plan and housing facility. *Payment plan:* installment. *Waivers:* senior citizens and employees or children of employees.

Financial Aid Of all full-time matriculated undergraduates who enrolled in 2010, 2,981 applied for aid, 2,069 were judged to have need, 982 had their need fully met. 180 Federal Work-Study jobs (averaging $1500). In 2010, 80 non-need-based awards were made. *Average percent of need met:* 84%. *Average financial aid package:* $10,824. *Average need-based loan:* $2941. *Average need-based gift aid:* $5054. *Average non-need-based aid:* $2514. *Average indebtedness upon graduation:* $22,049. *Financial aid deadline:* 5/1.

Applying *Options:* electronic application, deferred entrance. *Application fee:* $40. *Required:* high school transcript, minimum 2.0 GPA. *Required for some:* essay or personal statement. *Application deadlines:* 2/1 (freshmen), 6/1 (transfers). *Notification:* continuous (freshmen), continuous (transfers).

Freshman Application Contact Ms. Sarah Whitney, Clerk of Admissions, Worcester State University, 486 Chandler Street, Administration Building, Worcester, MA 01602-2597. *Phone:* 508-929-8040. *Toll-free phone:* 866-WSC-CALL. *Fax:* 508-929-8183. *E-mail:* admissions@worcester.edu. *Web site:* http://www.worcester.edu/.

Zion Bible College

Haverhill, Massachusetts

Director of Admissions Helen Brouillette, Admissions Director, Zion Bible College, 320 South Main Street, Haverhill, MA 01835. *Phone:* 800-356-4014. *Toll-free phone:* 800-356-4014. *E-mail:* admissions@zbc.edu. *Web site:* http://www.zbc.edu/.

MICHIGAN

Adrian College

Adrian, Michigan

- **Independent** comprehensive, founded 1859, affiliated with United Methodist Church
- **Small-town** 100-acre campus with easy access to Detroit, Toledo
- **Coed** 1,677 undergraduate students, 96% full-time, 50% women, 50% men
- **Moderately difficult** entrance level, 64% of applicants were admitted

Undergraduates 1,605 full-time, 72 part-time. Students come from 28 states and territories; 4 other countries; 22% are from out of state; 8% Black or African American, non-Hispanic/Latino; 3% Hispanic/Latino; 0.3% Asian, non-Hispanic/Latino; 0.1% Native Hawaiian or other Pacific Islander, non-Hispanic/Latino; 0.2% American Indian or Alaska Native, non-Hispanic/Latino; 2% Two or more races, non-Hispanic/Latino; 5% Race/ethnicity unknown; 5% international; 15% transferred in. *Retention:* 75% of full-time freshmen returned.

Freshmen *Admission:* 3,263 applied, 2,101 admitted, 461 enrolled. *Test scores:* ACT scores over 18: 98%; ACT scores over 24: 42%; ACT scores over 30: 5%.

Faculty *Total:* 176, 51% full-time. *Student/faculty ratio:* 14:1.

Academics *Calendar:* semesters. *Degrees:* associate, bachelor's, and master's. *Special study options:* academic remediation for entering students, adult/continuing education programs, advanced placement credit, double majors, English as a second language, honors programs, independent study, internships, off-campus study, part-time degree program, services for LD students, student-designed majors, study abroad, summer session for credit. *ROTC:* Army (c). *Unusual degree programs:* 3-2 engineering with University of Detroit Mercy, Washington University in St. Louis.

Computers on Campus Students can access the following: campus intranet, computer help desk, free student e-mail accounts, online (class) grades, online (class) registration, online (class) schedules. Campuswide network is available. 100% of college-owned or -operated housing units are wired for high-speed Internet access. Wireless service is available via entire campus.

Student Life *Housing:* on-campus residence required through senior year. *Options:* coed, men-only, women-only, disabled students. Campus housing is university owned. Freshman campus housing is guaranteed. *Activities and organizations:* drama/theater group, student-run newspaper, radio station, choral group, marching band, Student Government Association, Adrian College Premedical Chapter of the American Medical Association, Adrian College Kinesiology Club, Campus Activities Network, national fraternities, national sororities. *Campus security:* 24-hour patrols, student patrols, late-night transport/escort service. *Student services:* health clinic, personal/psychological counseling.

Athletics Member NCAA. All Division III. *Intercollegiate sports:* baseball M, basketball M/W, bowling W, cross-country running M/W, football M, golf M/W, ice hockey M/W, lacrosse M/W, soccer M/W, softball W, tennis M/W, track and field M/W, volleyball W. *Intramural sports:* badminton M/W, basketball M/W, bowling M/W, cheerleading W(c), football M/W, golf M, ice hockey M(c), lacrosse M/W, racquetball M/W, soccer M/W, softball M/W, tennis M/W, volleyball M/W.

Standardized Tests *Required:* SAT or ACT (for admission). *Recommended:* ACT (for admission).

Costs (2011–12) *Comprehensive fee:* $35,786 includes full-time tuition ($27,050), mandatory fees ($390), and room and board ($8346). *College room only:* $4026. Room and board charges vary according to board plan and housing facility.

Financial Aid Of all full-time matriculated undergraduates who enrolled in 2010, 1,497 applied for aid, 1,417 were judged to have need, 176 had their need fully met. 872 Federal Work-Study jobs (averaging $1800). 228 state and other part-time jobs (averaging $1800). In 2010, 219 non-need-based awards were made. *Average percent of need met:* 78%. *Average financial aid package:* $23,280. *Average need-based loan:* $4260. *Average need-based gift aid:* $18,282. *Average non-need-based aid:* $11,869. *Average indebtedness upon graduation:* $17,000.

Applying *Options:* electronic application, deferred entrance. *Required:* high school transcript. *Required for some:* essay or personal statement. *Recommended:* interview. *Application deadlines:* 3/15 (freshmen), 3/15 (transfers). *Notification:* continuous (freshmen), continuous (transfers).

Freshman Application Contact Mr. Frank Hribar, Vice President for Enrollment, Adrian College, 110 S. Madison St., Adrian, MI 49221. *Phone:* 800-877-2246. *Toll-free phone:* 800-877-2246. *Fax:* 517-264-3331. *E-mail:* admissions@adrian.edu. *Web site:* http://www.adrian.edu/.

Albion College

Albion, Michigan

- **Independent Methodist** 4-year, founded 1835
- **Small-town** 565-acre campus with easy access to Detroit
- **Endowment** $168.7 million
- **Coed** 1,514 undergraduate students, 99% full-time, 49% women, 51% men
- **Moderately difficult** entrance level, 92% of applicants were admitted

Undergraduates 1,492 full-time, 22 part-time. Students come from 22 states and territories; 23 other countries; 8% are from out of state; 4% Black or African American, non-Hispanic/Latino; 3% Hispanic/Latino; 2% Asian, non-Hispanic/Latino; 0.1% Native Hawaiian or other Pacific Islander, non-Hispanic/Latino; 0.2% American Indian or Alaska Native, non-Hispanic/Latino; 3% Two or more races, non-Hispanic/Latino; 4% Race/ethnicity unknown; 4% international; 2% transferred in; 90% live on campus. *Retention:* 84% of full-time freshmen returned.

Freshmen *Admission:* 1,637 applied, 1,499 admitted, 376 enrolled. *Average high school GPA:* 3.39. *Test scores:* SAT critical reading scores over 500: 81%; SAT math scores over 500: 84%; SAT writing scores over 500: 75%; ACT scores over 18: 97%; SAT critical reading scores over 600: 45%; SAT math scores over 600: 59%; SAT writing scores over 600: 30%; ACT scores over 24: 59%; SAT critical reading scores over 700: 7%; SAT math scores over 700: 18%; SAT writing scores over 700: 8%; ACT scores over 30: 11%.

Faculty *Total:* 155, 65% full-time, 74% with terminal degrees. *Student/faculty ratio:* 13:1.

Academics *Calendar:* semesters. *Degree:* bachelor's. *Special study options:* advanced placement credit, double majors, honors programs, independent study, internships, off-campus study, part-time degree program, services for LD students, student-designed majors, study abroad, summer session for credit. *Unusual degree programs:* 3-2 engineering with Columbia University, University of Michigan, Case Western Reserve University, Michigan Technological University, Washington University in St. Louis; forestry with Duke University, Washington University in St. Louis; nursing with Case Western Reserve University; public policy studies with University of Michigan, fine arts with Bank Street College of Education.

Computers on Campus 524 computers/terminals and 2,000 ports are available on campus for general student use. Students can access the following: campus intranet, computer help desk, free student e-mail accounts, online (class) grades, online (class) registration, online (class) schedules, online student account and financial aid. Campuswide network is available. 100% of college-owned or -operated housing units are wired for high-speed Internet access. Wireless service is available via classrooms, computer centers, computer labs, dorm rooms, learning centers, libraries, student centers.

Student Life *Housing:* on-campus residence required through senior year. *Options:* coed, men-only, women-only, cooperative, disabled students. Campus housing is university owned. Freshman campus housing is guaranteed. *Activities and organizations:* drama/theater group, student-run newspaper, radio station, choral group, marching band, Greek Life (Fraternities and Sororities), Student Senate (Student Government), Umbrella (Diversity Groups), Union Board (Programming Board), Spiritual Life (Religious Centered groups), national fraternities, national sororities. *Campus security:* 24-hour

emergency response devices and patrols, student patrols, late-night transport/ escort service, controlled dormitory access. *Student services:* health clinic, personal/psychological counseling, women's center.

Athletics Member NCAA. All Division III. *Intercollegiate sports:* baseball M, basketball M/W, cross-country running M/W, equestrian sports M/W, football M, golf M/W, lacrosse M/W, soccer M/W, softball W, swimming and diving M/W, tennis M/W, track and field M/W, volleyball M(c)/W. *Intramural sports:* basketball M/W, cheerleading M(c)/W(c), equestrian sports M(c)/ W(c), football M/W, ice hockey M(c)/W(c), racquetball M/W, rugby M/W, sailing M(c)/W(c), soccer M/W, softball M/W, swimming and diving M/W, tennis M/W, ultimate Frisbee M/W, volleyball M/W, water polo M(c)/W(c).

Standardized Tests *Required:* SAT or ACT (for admission).

Costs (2011–12) *One-time required fee:* $185. *Comprehensive fee:* $41,922 includes full-time tuition ($32,100), mandatory fees ($562), and room and board ($9260). Full-time tuition and fees vary according to course load. Part-time tuition: $1365 per credit hour. Part-time tuition and fees vary according to course load. *Required fees:* $281 per term part-time. *College room only:* $4528. Room and board charges vary according to housing facility. *Payment plans:* installment, deferred payment. *Waivers:* employees or children of employees.

Financial Aid Of all full-time matriculated undergraduates who enrolled in 2011, 1,164 applied for aid, 1,025 were judged to have need, 206 had their need fully met. 478 Federal Work-Study jobs (averaging $1096). In 2011, 450 non-need-based awards were made. *Average percent of need met:* 83%. *Average financial aid package:* $26,383. *Average need-based loan:* $5213. *Average need-based gift aid:* $21,284. *Average non-need-based aid:* $14,680. *Average indebtedness upon graduation:* $33,319.

Applying *Options:* electronic application, early action, deferred entrance. *Application fee:* $40. *Required:* high school transcript, 1 letter of recommendation. *Recommended:* essay or personal statement, minimum 3.0 GPA, interview. *Application deadlines:* 8/1 (freshmen), 6/1 (transfers), 12/1 (early action). *Notification:* continuous (freshmen), continuous until 7/1 (transfers), 10/1 (early action).

Freshman Application Contact Albion College, 611 East Porter Street, Albion, MI 49224-1831. *Phone:* 517-629-0600. *Toll-free phone:* 800-858-6770. *Web site:* http://www.albion.edu/.

Alma College
Alma, Michigan

- **Independent Presbyterian** 4-year, founded 1886
- **Small-town** 125-acre campus
- **Endowment** $101.0 million
- **Coed** 1,417 undergraduate students, 97% full-time, 58% women, 42% men
- **Moderately difficult** entrance level, 73% of applicants were admitted

Undergraduates 1,378 full-time, 39 part-time. Students come from 27 states and territories; 16 other countries; 7% are from out of state; 2% Black or African American, non-Hispanic/Latino; 3% Hispanic/Latino; 2% Asian, non-Hispanic/Latino; 1% American Indian or Alaska Native, non-Hispanic/Latino; 0.5% Two or more races, non-Hispanic/Latino; 0.4% international; 2% transferred in; 90% live on campus. *Retention:* 85% of full-time freshmen returned.

Freshmen *Admission:* 1,893 applied, 1,379 admitted, 387 enrolled. *Average high school GPA:* 3.51. *Test scores:* SAT critical reading scores over 500: 73%; SAT math scores over 500: 77%; SAT writing scores over 500: 66%; ACT scores over 18: 100%; SAT critical reading scores over 600: 46%; SAT math scores over 600: 42%; SAT writing scores over 600: 35%; ACT scores over 24: 58%; SAT critical reading scores over 700: 27%; SAT math scores over 700: 15%; SAT writing scores over 700: 8%; ACT scores over 30: 6%.

Faculty *Total:* 155, 57% full-time, 65% with terminal degrees. *Student/faculty ratio:* 13:1.

Academics *Calendar:* 4-4-1. *Degree:* bachelor's. *Special study options:* academic remediation for entering students, advanced placement credit, double majors, honors programs, independent study, internships, off-campus study, services for LD students, student-designed majors, study abroad, summer session for credit. *ROTC:* Army (c). *Unusual degree programs:* 3-2 engineering with University of Michigan, Michigan Technological University; occupational therapy with Washington University in St. Louis.

Computers on Campus 298 computers/terminals are available on campus for general student use. Students can access the following: campus intranet, computer help desk, free student e-mail accounts, online (class) grades, online (class) registration, online (class) schedules. Campuswide network is available. 100% of college-owned or -operated housing units are wired for high-speed Internet access. Wireless service is available via classrooms, dorm rooms, libraries, student centers.

Student Life *Housing:* on-campus residence required through senior year. *Options:* coed. Campus housing is university owned. Freshman campus housing is guaranteed. *Activities and organizations:* drama/theater group, student-

run newspaper, radio station, choral group, marching band, Ambassadors, Alma College Union Board, New Life Campus Ministries, Student Congress, Alpha Phi Omega, national fraternities, national sororities. *Campus security:* 24-hour emergency response devices and patrols, controlled dormitory access. *Student services:* health clinic, personal/psychological counseling.

Athletics Member NCAA. All Division III. *Intercollegiate sports:* baseball M, basketball M/W, bowling W, cross-country running M/W, football M, golf M/W, lacrosse M/W, soccer M/W, softball W, swimming and diving M/W, tennis M/W, track and field M/W, volleyball W, wrestling M. *Intramural sports:* basketball M/W, cheerleading M(c)/W(c), lacrosse M(c)/W(c), skiing (downhill) M/W, softball M/W, ultimate Frisbee M/W, volleyball M/W.

Standardized Tests *Required:* SAT or ACT (for admission).

Costs (2011–12) *Comprehensive fee:* $38,070 includes full-time tuition ($28,980), mandatory fees ($250), and room and board ($8840). Part-time tuition: $1000 per credit hour. Part-time tuition and fees vary according to course load. *College room only:* $4420. Room and board charges vary according to board plan and housing facility. *Payment plans:* installment, deferred payment. *Waivers:* employees or children of employees.

Financial Aid Of all full-time matriculated undergraduates who enrolled in 2011, 1,286 applied for aid, 1,140 were judged to have need, 145 had their need fully met. 372 Federal Work-Study jobs (averaging $1232). In 2011, 239 non-need-based awards were made. *Average percent of need met:* 82%. *Average financial aid package:* $24,318. *Average need-based loan:* $3910. *Average need-based gift aid:* $18,996. *Average non-need-based aid:* $14,728. *Average indebtedness upon graduation:* $21,907.

Applying *Options:* electronic application, deferred entrance. *Application fee:* $25. *Required:* high school transcript, minimum 3.0 GPA. *Required for some:* essay or personal statement, 3 letters of recommendation. *Recommended:* interview. *Application deadlines:* rolling (freshmen), rolling (out-of-state freshmen), rolling (transfers). *Notification:* continuous (freshmen), continuous (out-of-state freshmen), continuous (transfers).

Freshman Application Contact Mr. Bob Garcia, Director of Admissions, Alma College, Admissions Office, Alma, MI 48801-1599. *Phone:* 800-321-2562. *Toll-free phone:* 800-321-ALMA. *Fax:* 989-463-7057. *E-mail:* admissions@alma.edu. *Web site:* http://www.alma.edu/.

Andrews University
Berrien Springs, Michigan

- **Independent Seventh-day Adventist** university, founded 1874
- **Small-town** 1650-acre campus
- **Endowment** $37.7 million
- **Coed** 1,929 undergraduate students, 90% full-time, 55% women, 45% men
- **Moderately difficult** entrance level, 36% of applicants were admitted

Undergraduates 1,727 full-time, 202 part-time. Students come from 53 states and territories; 54 other countries; 54% are from out of state; 25% Black or African American, non-Hispanic/Latino; 16% Hispanic/Latino; 9% Asian, non-Hispanic/Latino; 0.2% Native Hawaiian or other Pacific Islander, non-Hispanic/Latino; 0.4% American Indian or Alaska Native, non-Hispanic/Latino; 3% Two or more races, non-Hispanic/Latino; 1% Race/ethnicity unknown; 13% international; 9% transferred in; 61% live on campus. *Retention:* 78% of full-time freshmen returned.

Freshmen *Admission:* 2,487 applied, 897 admitted, 393 enrolled. *Average high school GPA:* 3.41. *Test scores:* SAT critical reading scores over 500: 61%; SAT writing scores over 500: 62%; ACT scores over 18: 91%; SAT critical reading scores over 600: 25%; SAT writing scores over 600: 16%; ACT scores over 24: 42%; SAT critical reading scores over 700: 6%; SAT writing scores over 700: 3%; ACT scores over 30: 8%.

Faculty *Total:* 301, 74% full-time, 59% with terminal degrees. *Student/faculty ratio:* 11:1.

Academics *Calendar:* semesters. *Degrees:* associate, bachelor's, master's, doctoral, post-master's, postbachelor's, and first professional certificates. *Special study options:* academic remediation for entering students, accelerated degree program, adult/continuing education programs, advanced placement credit, cooperative education, distance learning, double majors, English as a second language, freshman honors college, honors programs, internships, off-campus study, part-time degree program, student-designed majors, study abroad, summer session for credit. *Unusual degree programs:* 3-2 physical therapy and architecture.

Computers on Campus 130 computers/terminals are available on campus for general student use. Students can access the following: campus intranet, computer help desk, free student e-mail accounts, online (class) grades, online (class) registration, online (class) schedules, degree audit. Campuswide network is available. 99% of college-owned or -operated housing units are wired for high-speed Internet access. Wireless service is available via classrooms, computer centers, computer labs, learning centers, libraries, student centers.

Student Life *Housing:* on-campus residence required through senior year. *Options:* men-only, women-only. Campus housing is university owned. Freshman campus housing is guaranteed. *Activities and organizations:* drama/theater group, student-run newspaper, radio station, choral group. *Campus security:* 24-hour emergency response devices and patrols, controlled dormitory access. *Student services:* health clinic, personal/psychological counseling.

Athletics *Intramural sports:* basketball M/W, football M/W, golf M/W, gymnastics M/W, racquetball M/W, soccer M/W, softball M/W, volleyball M/W, water polo M/W.

Standardized Tests *Required:* SAT or ACT (for admission).

Costs (2011–12) *Comprehensive fee:* $30,802 includes full-time tuition ($22,680), mandatory fees ($748), and room and board ($7374). Full-time tuition and fees vary according to course load. Part-time tuition: $945 per credit hour. Part-time tuition and fees vary according to course load. *College room only:* $3854. Room and board charges vary according to board plan. *Payment plan:* installment. *Waivers:* senior citizens and employees or children of employees.

Financial Aid Of all full-time matriculated undergraduates who enrolled in 2011, 1,274 applied for aid, 1,179 were judged to have need, 130 had their need fully met. 663 Federal Work-Study jobs (averaging $946). 62 state and other part-time jobs (averaging $1042). In 2011, 567 non-need-based awards were made. *Average percent of need met:* 83%. *Average financial aid package:* $25,559. *Average need-based loan:* $4754. *Average need-based gift aid:* $8293. *Average non-need-based aid:* $7316. *Average indebtedness upon graduation:* $38,054.

Applying *Options:* electronic application, deferred entrance. *Application fee:* $30. *Required:* high school transcript, minimum 2.3 GPA, 2 letters of recommendation. *Application deadlines:* rolling (freshmen), rolling (transfers). *Notification:* continuous (freshmen), continuous (transfers).

Freshman Application Contact Shanna Leak, Undergraduate Admissions Coordinator, Andrews University, Berrien Springs, MI 49104. *Phone:* 800-253-2874. *Toll-free phone:* 800-253-2874. *Fax:* 269-471-3228. *E-mail:* enroll@andrews.edu. *Web site:* http://www.andrews.edu/.

Aquinas College
Grand Rapids, Michigan

- **Independent Roman Catholic** comprehensive, founded 1886
- **Suburban** 107-acre campus with easy access to Detroit, Chicago, Grand Rapids
- **Endowment** $32.2 million
- **Coed** 2,114 undergraduate students, 87% full-time, 64% women, 36% men
- **Moderately difficult** entrance level, 89% of applicants were admitted

Undergraduates 1,847 full-time, 267 part-time. Students come from 25 states and territories; 8 other countries; 6% are from out of state; 3% Black or African American, non-Hispanic/Latino; 5% Hispanic/Latino; 1% Asian, non-Hispanic/Latino; 0.4% American Indian or Alaska Native, non-Hispanic/Latino; 1% Two or more races, non-Hispanic/Latino; 2% Race/ethnicity unknown; 0.2% international; 4% transferred in; 46% live on campus. *Retention:* 75% of full-time freshmen returned.

Freshmen *Admission:* 2,637 applied, 2,334 admitted, 376 enrolled. *Average high school GPA:* 3.41. *Test scores:* ACT scores over 18: 96%; ACT scores over 24: 49%; ACT scores over 30: 4%.

Faculty *Total:* 251, 36% full-time, 39% with terminal degrees. *Student/faculty ratio:* 13:1.

Academics *Calendar:* semesters. *Degrees:* associate, bachelor's, and master's. *Special study options:* academic remediation for entering students, accelerated degree program, adult/continuing education programs, advanced placement credit, cooperative education, distance learning, double majors, external degree program, honors programs, independent study, internships, off-campus study, part-time degree program, services for LD students, student-designed majors, study abroad, summer session for credit. *ROTC:* Army (c).

Computers on Campus 210 computers/terminals are available on campus for general student use. Students can access the following: campus intranet, computer help desk, free student e-mail accounts, online (class) grades, online (class) registration, online (class) schedules. Campuswide network is available. 100% of college-owned or -operated housing units are wired for high-speed Internet access. Wireless service is available via classrooms, dorm rooms, learning centers, libraries, student centers.

Student Life *Housing:* on-campus residence required through sophomore year. *Options:* coed. Campus housing is university owned. Freshman applicants given priority for college housing. *Activities and organizations:* drama/theater group, student-run newspaper, radio station, choral group, Community Senate

Programming Board, The Saint (newspaper), Insignis Honors Group, Community Action Volunteers of Aquinas (CAVA), RHC. *Campus security:* 24-hour emergency response devices and patrols, student patrols, late-night transport/escort service, controlled dormitory access. *Student services:* health clinic, personal/psychological counseling, women's center.

Athletics Member NAIA. *Intercollegiate sports:* baseball M(s), basketball M(s)/W(s), bowling M, cross-country running M(s)/W(s), golf M(s)/W(s), lacrosse M(s)/W, soccer M(s)/W(s), softball W(s), tennis M(s)/W(s), track and field M(s)/W(s), volleyball W(s). *Intramural sports:* basketball M/W, football M/W, golf M, ice hockey M, skiing (cross-country) M/W, skiing (downhill) M/W, soccer M/W, softball M/W, tennis M/W, volleyball M/W.

Standardized Tests *Required:* SAT or ACT (for admission).

Costs (2012–13) *Comprehensive fee:* $33,060 includes full-time tuition ($25,070), mandatory fees ($180), and room and board ($7810). Full-time tuition and fees vary according to course load. Part-time tuition: $498 per credit hour. Part-time tuition and fees vary according to course load. *College room only:* $3644. Room and board charges vary according to board plan and housing facility. *Payment plans:* installment, deferred payment. *Waivers:* children of alumni and employees or children of employees.

Financial Aid Of all full-time matriculated undergraduates who enrolled in 2011, 1,375 applied for aid, 1,244 were judged to have need, 540 had their need fully met. In 2011, 218 non-need-based awards were made. *Average percent of need met:* 85%. *Average financial aid package:* $21,214. *Average need-based loan:* $4108. *Average need-based gift aid:* $17,106. *Average non-need-based aid:* $15,827. *Average indebtedness upon graduation:* $20,694. *Financial aid deadline:* 8/15.

Applying *Options:* electronic application, early admission, deferred entrance. *Required:* high school transcript, minimum 2.5 GPA. *Required for some:* essay or personal statement, interview. *Application deadlines:* rolling (freshmen), rolling (transfers).

Freshman Application Contact Ms. Rebecca Roberts, Admissions Office Applications Specialist, Aquinas College, 1607 Robinson Road, SE, Grand Rapids, MI 49506-1799. *Phone:* 616-632-2900. *Toll-free phone:* 800-678-9593. *Fax:* 616-732-4469. *E-mail:* admissions@aquinas.edu. *Web site:* http://www.aquinas.edu/.

See page 1058 for the College Close-Up.

The Art Institute of Michigan

Novi, Michigan

- **Proprietary** 4-year, part of Education Management Corporation
- **Coed**

Academics *Degrees:* diplomas, associate, and bachelor's.

Costs (2011–12) *Tuition:* Tuition cost varies by program. Prospective students should contact the school for current tuition costs. Other charges include a starting kit for all first-quarter students. Kits vary in price, depending on the program of study.

Freshman Application Contact The Art Institute of Michigan, 28125 Cabot Drive, Suite 120, Novi, MI 48377. *Phone:* 248-675-3800. *Toll-free phone:* 800-479-0087. *Web site:* http://www.artinstitutes.edu/detroit/.

See page 1110 for the College Close-Up.

The Art Institute of Michigan–Troy

Troy, Michigan

- **Proprietary** 4-year
- **Coed**

Academics *Degrees:* diplomas, associate, and bachelor's.

Costs (2011–12) *Tuition:* Tuition cost varies by program. Prospective students should contact the school for current tuition costs. Other charges include a starting kit for all first-quarter students. Kits vary in price, depending on the program of study.

Freshman Application Contact The Art Institute of Michigan–Troy, 1414 East Maple Avenue, Suite 150, Troy, MI 48083. *Phone:* 248-837-3200. *Toll-free phone:* 877-320-3275. *Web site:* http://www.artinstitutes.edu/troy.

See page 1112 for the College Close-Up.

Baker College of Allen Park

Allen Park, Michigan

- **Independent** 4-year, founded 2003, part of Baker College System
- **Suburban** 13-acre campus with easy access to Detroit
- **Coed, primarily women** 3,954 undergraduate students, 61% full-time, 72% women, 28% men
- **Minimally difficult** entrance level, 100% of applicants were admitted

Undergraduates 2,412 full-time, 1,542 part-time. Students come from 1 other state; 36% Black or African American, non-Hispanic/Latino; 5% Hispanic/

Latino; 0.5% Asian, non-Hispanic/Latino; 0.7% American Indian or Alaska Native, non-Hispanic/Latino; 0.9% Race/ethnicity unknown.

Freshmen *Admission:* 1,582 applied, 1,582 admitted.

Faculty *Total:* 88, 2% full-time, 13% with terminal degrees. *Student/faculty ratio:* 34:1.

Academics *Calendar:* quarters. *Degrees:* certificates, diplomas, associate, and bachelor's. *Special study options:* academic remediation for entering students, accelerated degree program, advanced placement credit, cooperative education, distance learning, double majors, external degree program, independent study, internships, off-campus study, part-time degree program, services for LD students, summer session for credit.

Computers on Campus 150 computers/terminals are available on campus for general student use. Students can access the following: computer help desk, free student e-mail accounts, online (class) registration. Campuswide network is available. Wireless service is available via entire campus.

Student Life *Housing:* college housing not available. *Campus security:* 24-hour patrols. *Student services:* personal/psychological counseling.

Standardized Tests *Recommended:* SAT or ACT (for admission).

Costs (2012–13) *Tuition:* $7740 full-time, $215 per quarter hour part-time. Full-time tuition and fees vary according to program. Part-time tuition and fees vary according to program. *Waivers:* employees or children of employees.

Applying *Options:* electronic application, deferred entrance. *Required:* high school transcript, interview. *Application deadline:* 9/24 (freshmen).

Freshman Application Contact Mr. Steve Peterson, Vice President of Admissions, Baker College of Allen Park, 4500 Enterprise Drive, Allen Park, MI 48101. *Phone:* 313-425-3700. *Toll-free phone:* 800-767-4120. *E-mail:* steve.peterson@baker.edu. *Web site:* http://www.baker.edu/.

Baker College of Auburn Hills

Auburn Hills, Michigan

- **Independent** 4-year, founded 1911, part of Baker College System
- **Urban** 10-acre campus with easy access to Detroit
- **Coed** 3,803 undergraduate students, 48% full-time, 72% women, 28% men
- **Minimally difficult** entrance level, 100% of applicants were admitted

Undergraduates 1,826 full-time, 1,977 part-time. Students come from 1 other state; 18% Black or African American, non-Hispanic/Latino; 3% Hispanic/Latino; 2% Asian, non-Hispanic/Latino; 0.7% American Indian or Alaska Native, non-Hispanic/Latino; 0.3% Race/ethnicity unknown.

Freshmen *Admission:* 1,358 applied, 1,358 admitted.

Faculty *Total:* 155, 7% full-time, 15% with terminal degrees. *Student/faculty ratio:* 41:1.

Academics *Calendar:* quarters. *Degrees:* certificates, diplomas, associate, bachelor's, and postbachelor's certificates. *Special study options:* academic remediation for entering students, accelerated degree program, advanced placement credit, cooperative education, distance learning, double majors, external degree program, independent study, internships, part-time degree program, services for LD students, summer session for credit.

Computers on Campus 110 computers/terminals are available on campus for general student use. Students can access the following: online (class) registration. Campuswide network is available.

Student Life *Housing:* college housing not available. *Activities and organizations:* Baker Business Club, Interior Design Society, Students Action in Engineering, Marketing Club. *Campus security:* 24-hour emergency response devices.

Standardized Tests *Recommended:* SAT or ACT (for admission).

Costs (2012–13) *Tuition:* $7740 full-time, $215 per quarter hour part-time. Full-time tuition and fees vary according to program. Part-time tuition and fees vary according to program. *Waivers:* employees or children of employees.

Applying *Options:* early admission, deferred entrance. *Application fee:* $20. *Required:* high school transcript. *Application deadlines:* rolling (freshmen), rolling (transfers).

Freshman Application Contact Ms. Nicole Chirco, Director of Admissions, Baker College of Auburn Hills, 1500 University Drive, Auburn Hills, MI 48326-1586. *Phone:* 248-340-0600. *Toll-free phone:* 888-429-0410. *Fax:* 248-340-0608. *Web site:* http://www.baker.edu/.

Baker College of Cadillac

Cadillac, Michigan

- **Independent** 4-year, founded 1986, part of Baker College System
- **Small-town** 40-acre campus
- **Coed** 1,639 undergraduate students, 61% full-time, 71% women, 29% men
- **Minimally difficult** entrance level, 100% of applicants were admitted

Undergraduates 1,000 full-time, 639 part-time. Students come from 4 states and territories; 0.2% Black or African American, non-Hispanic/Latino; 0.3%

Hispanic/Latino; 0.1% Asian, non-Hispanic/Latino; 0.1% American Indian or Alaska Native, non-Hispanic/Latino; 4% Race/ethnicity unknown. *Retention:* 69% of full-time freshmen returned.

Freshmen *Admission:* 580 applied, 580 admitted.

Faculty *Total:* 105, 4% full-time, 5% with terminal degrees. *Student/faculty ratio:* 42:1.

Academics *Calendar:* quarters. *Degrees:* certificates, diplomas, associate, and bachelor's. *Special study options:* academic remediation for entering students, advanced placement credit, cooperative education, distance learning, double majors, external degree program, independent study, internships, part-time degree program, services for LD students, summer session for credit.

Computers on Campus 100 computers/terminals are available on campus for general student use. Students can access the following: online (class) registration. Campuswide network is available.

Student Life *Housing:* college housing not available. *Campus security:* 24-hour emergency response devices.

Standardized Tests *Recommended:* SAT or ACT (for admission).

Costs (2012–13) *Tuition:* $7740 full-time, $215 per quarter hour part-time. Full-time tuition and fees vary according to program. Part-time tuition and fees vary according to program. *Waivers:* employees or children of employees.

Applying *Options:* early admission, deferred entrance. *Application fee:* $20. *Required:* high school transcript. *Recommended:* interview. *Application deadlines:* 9/24 (freshmen), rolling (transfers).

Freshman Application Contact Ms. Audrey Charmoli, Director of Admissions, Baker College of Cadillac, 9600 East 13th Street, Cadillac, MI 49601. *Phone:* 231-876-3100. *Toll-free phone:* 888-313-3463. *Fax:* 231-775-8505. *E-mail:* audrey.charmoli@baker.edu. *Web site:* http://www.baker.edu/.

Baker College of Clinton Township

Clinton Township, Michigan

- **Independent** 4-year, founded 1990, part of Baker College System
- **Urban** 30-acre campus with easy access to Detroit
- **Coed** 5,712 undergraduate students
- **Minimally difficult** entrance level, 100% of applicants were admitted

Undergraduates Students come from 2 states and territories; 25% Black or African American, non-Hispanic/Latino; 2% Hispanic/Latino; 1% Asian, non-Hispanic/Latino; 0.5% American Indian or Alaska Native, non-Hispanic/Latino; 3% Race/ethnicity unknown.

Freshmen *Admission:* 2,311 applied, 2,311 admitted.

Faculty *Total:* 208, 8% full-time, 12% with terminal degrees. *Student/faculty ratio:* 45:1.

Academics *Calendar:* quarters. *Degrees:* certificates, diplomas, associate, and bachelor's. *Special study options:* academic remediation for entering students, advanced placement credit, cooperative education, external degree program, internships, part-time degree program, services for LD students, summer session for credit.

Computers on Campus 127 computers/terminals are available on campus for general student use. Campuswide network is available.

Student Life *Housing:* college housing not available. *Campus security:* 24-hour emergency response devices and patrols, evening security guard. *Student services:* personal/psychological counseling.

Standardized Tests *Required for some:* SAT or ACT (for admission).

Costs (2012–13) *Tuition:* $7740 full-time, $215 per quarter hour part-time. Full-time tuition and fees vary according to program. Part-time tuition and fees vary according to program. *Waivers:* employees or children of employees.

Applying *Options:* electronic application, early admission, deferred entrance. *Application fee:* $20. *Required:* high school transcript. *Application deadlines:* rolling (freshmen), rolling (transfers).

Freshman Application Contact Ms. Annette Looser, Vice President for Admissions, Baker College of Clinton Township, 34401 South Gratiot Avenue, Clinton Township, MI 48035. *Phone:* 586-791-3000. *Toll-free phone:* 888-272-2842. *Fax:* 586-791-6811. *E-mail:* annette.looser@baker.edu. *Web site:* http://www.baker.edu/.

Baker College of Flint

Flint, Michigan

- **Independent** 4-year, founded 1911, part of Baker College System
- **Urban** 53-acre campus with easy access to Detroit
- **Coed** 6,329 undergraduate students, 57% full-time, 67% women, 33% men
- **Minimally difficult** entrance level, 100% of applicants were admitted

Undergraduates 3,607 full-time, 2,722 part-time. Students come from 5 states and territories; 1% are from out of state; 21% Black or African American, non-

Hispanic/Latino; 3% Hispanic/Latino; 0.3% Asian, non-Hispanic/Latino; 0.6% American Indian or Alaska Native, non-Hispanic/Latino; 0.7% Race/ethnicity unknown; 2% live on campus.

Freshmen *Admission:* 2,507 applied, 2,507 admitted.

Faculty *Total:* 315, 13% full-time, 12% with terminal degrees. *Student/faculty ratio:* 31:1.

Academics *Calendar:* quarters. *Degrees:* certificates, diplomas, associate, and bachelor's. *Special study options:* academic remediation for entering students, accelerated degree program, advanced placement credit, cooperative education, distance learning, double majors, external degree program, independent study, internships, part-time degree program, services for LD students, summer session for credit.

Computers on Campus 412 computers/terminals are available on campus for general student use. Campuswide network is available.

Student Life *Housing:* on-campus residence required for freshman year. *Options:* coed. Campus housing is university owned. *Activities and organizations:* Occupational Therapy Club, Interior Design Society, Medical Assistants Student Organization, Physical Therapist Assistant Club, Cyber Defense Team (2008 National Champions). *Campus security:* 24-hour patrols, late-night transport/escort service, controlled dormitory access, video monitoring of high traffic areas. *Student services:* personal/psychological counseling.

Standardized Tests *Recommended:* SAT or ACT (for admission).

Costs (2012–13) *Tuition:* $7740 full-time, $215 per quarter hour part-time. Full-time tuition and fees vary according to program. Part-time tuition and fees vary according to program. *Room only:* $3000. Room and board charges vary according to housing facility. *Waivers:* employees or children of employees.

Applying *Options:* early admission, deferred entrance. *Application fee:* $20. *Required:* high school transcript. *Application deadlines:* 9/20 (freshmen), 9/20 (transfers).

Freshman Application Contact Ms. Jodi Cunez, Vice President for Admissions, Baker College of Flint, 1050 West Bristol Road, Flint, MI 48507-5508. *Phone:* 810-766-4008. *Toll-free phone:* 800-964-4299. *Fax:* 810-766-4049. *Web site:* http://www.baker.edu/.

Baker College of Jackson

Jackson, Michigan

- **Independent** 4-year, founded 1994, part of Baker College System
- **Suburban** 42-acre campus with easy access to Lansing
- **Coed** 2,730 undergraduate students, 57% full-time, 75% women, 25% men
- **Minimally difficult** entrance level, 100% of applicants were admitted

Undergraduates 1,556 full-time, 1,174 part-time. Students come from 2 states and territories; 1% are from out of state; 9% Black or African American, non-Hispanic/Latino; 3% Hispanic/Latino; 0.4% Asian, non-Hispanic/Latino; 0.6% American Indian or Alaska Native, non-Hispanic/Latino; 0.4% Race/ethnicity unknown.

Freshmen *Admission:* 891 applied, 891 admitted.

Faculty *Total:* 85, 6% full-time, 13% with terminal degrees. *Student/faculty ratio:* 36:1.

Academics *Calendar:* quarters. *Degrees:* certificates, diplomas, associate, and bachelor's. *Special study options:* academic remediation for entering students, accelerated degree program, advanced placement credit, cooperative education, distance learning, double majors, external degree program, independent study, internships, part-time degree program, services for LD students, summer session for credit.

Computers on Campus 150 computers/terminals are available on campus for general student use. Students can access the following: online (class) registration. Campuswide network is available.

Student Life *Housing:* college housing not available. *Campus security:* 24-hour emergency response devices. *Student services:* personal/psychological counseling.

Standardized Tests *Recommended:* SAT or ACT (for admission).

Costs (2012–13) *Tuition:* $7740 full-time, $215 per quarter hour part-time. Full-time tuition and fees vary according to program. Part-time tuition and fees vary according to program. *Waivers:* employees or children of employees.

Applying *Options:* electronic application, early admission, deferred entrance. *Application fee:* $20. *Required:* high school transcript. *Application deadlines:* 9/19 (freshmen), rolling (transfers). *Notification:* continuous (freshmen).

Freshman Application Contact Mr. Kevin Pnacek, Vice President for Admissions, Baker College of Jackson, 2800 Springport Road, Jackson, MI 49202. *Phone:* 517-788-7800. *Toll-free phone:* 888-343-3683. *Fax:* 517-789-7331. *E-mail:* kevin.pnacek@baker.edu. *Web site:* http://www.baker.edu/.

Baker College of Muskegon
Muskegon, Michigan

- **Independent** 4-year, founded 1888, part of Baker College System
- **Suburban** 45-acre campus with easy access to Grand Rapids
- **Coed** 4,994 undergraduate students, 68% full-time, 70% women, 30% men
- **Minimally difficult** entrance level, 100% of applicants were admitted

Undergraduates 3,396 full-time, 1,598 part-time. Students come from 17 states and territories; 1% are from out of state; 12% Black or African American, non-Hispanic/Latino; 5% Hispanic/Latino; 0.5% Asian, non-Hispanic/Latino; 0.8% American Indian or Alaska Native, non-Hispanic/Latino; 0.5% Race/ethnicity unknown; 11% live on campus.
Freshmen *Admission:* 1,942 applied, 1,942 admitted.
Faculty *Total:* 177, 10% full-time, 8% with terminal degrees. *Student/faculty ratio:* 55:1.
Academics *Calendar:* quarters. *Degrees:* certificates, diplomas, associate, and bachelor's. *Special study options:* academic remediation for entering students, accelerated degree program, adult/continuing education programs, advanced placement credit, cooperative education, distance learning, double majors, external degree program, independent study, internships, part-time degree program, services for LD students, summer session for credit.
Computers on Campus 165 computers/terminals are available on campus for general student use. Students can access the following: free student e-mail accounts. Campuswide network is available.
Student Life *Housing:* on-campus residence required for freshman year. *Options:* coed, disabled students. Campus housing is university owned. Freshman applicants given priority for college housing. *Activities and organizations:* Accounting Club, Rehab Club, Travel Club, Culinary Club. *Campus security:* 24-hour emergency response devices and patrols, late-night transport/escort service, controlled dormitory access, 24-hour security camera surveillance. *Student services:* personal/psychological counseling.
Standardized Tests *Recommended:* SAT or ACT (for admission).
Costs (2012–13) *Tuition:* $7740 full-time, $215 per quarter hour part-time. Full-time tuition and fees vary according to program. Part-time tuition and fees vary according to program. *Waivers:* employees or children of employees.
Applying *Options:* electronic application, early admission, deferred entrance. *Application fee:* $20. *Required:* high school transcript. *Application deadlines:* 9/24 (freshmen), rolling (transfers). *Notification:* continuous (freshmen).
Freshman Application Contact Ms. Kathy Jacobson, Vice President of Admissions, Baker College of Muskegon, 1903 Marquette Avenue, Muskegon, MI 49442-3497. *Phone:* 231-777-5207. *Toll-free phone:* 800-937-0337. *Fax:* 231-777-5201. *E-mail:* kathy.jacobson@baker.edu. *Web site:* http://www.baker.edu/.

Baker College of Owosso
Owosso, Michigan

- **Independent** 4-year, founded 1984, part of Baker College System
- **Small-town** 52-acre campus
- **Coed** 3,078 undergraduate students, 64% full-time, 62% women, 38% men
- **Minimally difficult** entrance level, 100% of applicants were admitted

Undergraduates 1,969 full-time, 1,109 part-time. Students come from 4 states and territories; 93% Black or African American, non-Hispanic/Latino; 2% Hispanic/Latino; 0.2% Asian, non-Hispanic/Latino; 0.5% American Indian or Alaska Native, non-Hispanic/Latino; 0.2% Race/ethnicity unknown; 15% live on campus.
Freshmen *Admission:* 1,231 applied, 1,231 admitted.
Faculty *Total:* 144, 6% full-time, 15% with terminal degrees. *Student/faculty ratio:* 40:1.
Academics *Calendar:* quarters. *Degrees:* certificates, diplomas, associate, and bachelor's. *Special study options:* academic remediation for entering students, accelerated degree program, adult/continuing education programs, advanced placement credit, cooperative education, external degree program, internships, part-time degree program, services for LD students, summer session for credit.
Computers on Campus 210 computers/terminals are available on campus for general student use. Campuswide network is available.
Student Life *Housing options:* coed. *Activities and organizations:* student-run newspaper, Accounting Club, Travel Club, Management Club, Baker Health Information Management Club, RAD Club. *Campus security:* 24-hour emergency response devices and patrols, late-night transport/escort service, controlled dormitory access. *Student services:* personal/psychological counseling.
Standardized Tests *Recommended:* SAT or ACT (for admission).
Costs (2012–13) *Tuition:* $7740 full-time, $215 per quarter hour part-time. Full-time tuition and fees vary according to program. Part-time tuition and fees vary according to program. *Room only:* $3000. Room and board charges vary according to housing facility. *Waivers:* employees or children of employees.

Applying *Options:* early admission, deferred entrance. *Application fee:* $20. *Required:* high school transcript. *Application deadlines:* rolling (freshmen), rolling (transfers).
Freshman Application Contact Mr. Michael Konopacke, Vice President for Admissions, Baker College of Owosso, 1020 South Washington Street, Owosso, MI 48867-4400. *Phone:* 989-729-3350. *Toll-free phone:* 800-879-3797. *Fax:* 989-729-3441. *E-mail:* mike.konopacke@baker.edu. *Web site:* http://www.baker.edu/.

Baker College of Port Huron
Port Huron, Michigan

- **Independent** 4-year, founded 1990, part of Baker College System
- **Urban** 10-acre campus with easy access to Detroit
- **Coed** 1,453 undergraduate students, 68% full-time, 74% women, 26% men
- **Minimally difficult** entrance level, 100% of applicants were admitted

Undergraduates 988 full-time, 465 part-time. Students come from 1 other state; 3% Black or African American, non-Hispanic/Latino; 2% Hispanic/Latino; 0.2% Asian, non-Hispanic/Latino; 0.5% American Indian or Alaska Native, non-Hispanic/Latino; 4% Race/ethnicity unknown.
Freshmen *Admission:* 419 applied, 419 admitted.
Faculty *Total:* 126, 10% full-time, 7% with terminal degrees. *Student/faculty ratio:* 28:1.
Academics *Calendar:* quarters. *Degrees:* diplomas, associate, and bachelor's. *Special study options:* academic remediation for entering students, accelerated degree program, advanced placement credit, cooperative education, distance learning, double majors, external degree program, independent study, internships, part-time degree program, services for LD students, summer session for credit.
Computers on Campus 165 computers/terminals are available on campus for general student use. Students can access the following: online (class) registration, software. Campuswide network is available.
Student Life *Housing:* college housing not available. *Activities and organizations:* Travel Club, Student Association Dental Hygienists of America. *Campus security:* 24-hour emergency response devices, late-night transport/escort service. *Student services:* personal/psychological counseling.
Standardized Tests *Recommended:* SAT or ACT (for admission).
Costs (2012–13) *Tuition:* $7740 full-time, $215 per quarter hour part-time. Full-time tuition and fees vary according to program. Part-time tuition and fees vary according to program. *Waivers:* employees or children of employees.
Applying *Options:* early admission, deferred entrance. *Application fee:* $20. *Required:* high school transcript, interview. *Application deadlines:* 9/24 (freshmen), rolling (transfers). *Notification:* continuous (freshmen), continuous (transfers).
Freshman Application Contact Mr. Daniel Kenny, Vice President for Admissions, Baker College of Port Huron, 3403 Lapeer Road, Port Huron, MI 48060-2597. *Phone:* 810-985-7000. *Toll-free phone:* 888-262-2442. *Fax:* 810-985-7066. *E-mail:* kenny_d@porthuron.baker.edu. *Web site:* http://www.baker.edu/.

Calvin College
Grand Rapids, Michigan

- **Independent Christian Reformed** comprehensive, founded 1876
- **Suburban** 400-acre campus with easy access to Grand Rapids
- **Endowment** $111.1 million
- **Coed** 3,873 undergraduate students, 97% full-time, 53% women, 47% men
- **Moderately difficult** entrance level, 75% of applicants were admitted

Undergraduates 3,748 full-time, 125 part-time. Students come from 48 states and territories; 54 other countries; 43% are from out of state; 3% Black or African American, non-Hispanic/Latino; 3% Hispanic/Latino; 4% Asian, non-Hispanic/Latino; 0.5% American Indian or Alaska Native, non-Hispanic/Latino; 1% Two or more races, non-Hispanic/Latino; 2% Race/ethnicity unknown; 9% international; 3% transferred in; 60% live on campus. *Retention:* 87% of full-time freshmen returned.
Freshmen *Admission:* 3,182 applied, 2,395 admitted, 961 enrolled. *Average high school GPA:* 3.6. *Test scores:* SAT critical reading scores over 500: 76%; SAT math scores over 500: 83%; ACT scores over 18: 98%; SAT critical reading scores over 600: 42%; SAT math scores over 600: 55%; ACT scores over 24: 69%; SAT critical reading scores over 700: 13%; SAT math scores over 700: 15%; ACT scores over 30: 22%.
Faculty *Total:* 384, 81% full-time, 72% with terminal degrees. *Student/faculty ratio:* 11:1.
Academics *Calendar:* 4-1-4. *Degrees:* bachelor's and master's. *Special study options:* academic remediation for entering students, accelerated degree program, adult/continuing education programs, advanced placement credit, double

majors, honors programs, independent study, internships, off-campus study, part-time degree program, services for LD students, student-designed majors, study abroad, summer session for credit. *ROTC:* Army (c). *Unusual degree programs:* 3-2 occupational therapy with Washington University in St. Louis.

Computers on Campus 1,024 computers/terminals and 2,656 ports are available on campus for general student use. Students can access the following: computer help desk, free student e-mail accounts, online (class) grades, online (class) registration, online (class) schedules. Campuswide network is available. 100% of college-owned or -operated housing units are wired for high-speed Internet access. Wireless service is available via classrooms, computer centers, computer labs, dorm rooms, libraries, student centers.

Student Life *Housing:* on-campus residence required through sophomore year. *Options:* men-only, women-only. Campus housing is university owned. Freshman campus housing is guaranteed. *Activities and organizations:* drama/theater group, student-run newspaper, choral group, Social Justice Committee, Environmental Stewardship Coalition, Dance Guild, Chimes, Calvin Video Network. *Campus security:* 24-hour emergency response devices and patrols, student patrols, late-night transport/escort service, controlled dormitory access, crime prevention programs, crime alert bulletins. *Student services:* health clinic, personal/psychological counseling.

Athletics Member NCAA. All Division III. *Intercollegiate sports:* baseball M, basketball M/W, crew M(c)/W(c), cross-country running M/W, golf M/W, ice hockey M(c), lacrosse M/W, rock climbing M(c)/W(c), rugby M(c), soccer M/W, softball W, swimming and diving M/W, tennis M/W, track and field M/W, ultimate Frisbee M(c)/W(c), volleyball M(c)/W. *Intramural sports:* badminton M/W, basketball M/W, cross-country running M/W, football M/W, golf M/W, racquetball M/W, soccer M/W, softball M/W, swimming and diving M/W, tennis M/W, track and field M/W, volleyball M/W, water polo M/W.

Standardized Tests *Required:* SAT or ACT (for admission).

Costs (2011–12) *Comprehensive fee:* $34,325 includes full-time tuition ($25,340), mandatory fees ($225), and room and board ($8760). Full-time tuition and fees vary according to degree level and program. Part-time tuition: $610 per credit hour. Part-time tuition and fees vary according to course load and degree level. *Room and board:* Room and board charges vary according to board plan. *Payment plans:* tuition prepayment, installment. *Waivers:* employees or children of employees.

Financial Aid Of all full-time matriculated undergraduates who enrolled in 2011, 3,101 applied for aid, 2,509 were judged to have need, 495 had their need fully met. 1,127 Federal Work-Study jobs (averaging $1609). 1,045 state and other part-time jobs (averaging $1483). In 2011, 1026 non-need-based awards were made. *Average percent of need met:* 74%. *Average financial aid package:* $18,360. *Average need-based loan:* $6631. *Average need-based gift aid:* $11,587. *Average non-need-based aid:* $5558. *Average indebtedness upon graduation:* $32,957.

Applying *Options:* electronic application, deferred entrance. *Application fee:* $35. *Required:* essay or personal statement, high school transcript, minimum 2.5 GPA, 1 letter of recommendation. *Recommended:* interview. *Application deadlines:* 8/15 (freshmen), rolling (transfers). *Notification:* continuous (freshmen).

Freshman Application Contact Mr. Dale Kuiper, Director of Admissions and Financial Aid, Calvin College, 3201 Burton Street, SE, Grand Rapids, MI 49546. *Phone:* 616-526-6106. *Toll-free phone:* 800-688-0122. *Fax:* 616-526-6777. *E-mail:* admissions@calvin.edu. *Web site:* http://www.calvin.edu/.

See below for display ad and page 1242 for the College Close-Up.

Central Michigan University
Mount Pleasant, Michigan

- **State-supported** university, founded 1892
- **Small-town** 854-acre campus
- **Endowment** $85.5 million
- **Coed** 21,698 undergraduate students, 88% full-time, 55% women, 45% men
- **Moderately difficult** entrance level, 68% of applicants were admitted

Undergraduates 19,073 full-time, 2,625 part-time. Students come from 48 states and territories; 56 other countries; 3% are from out of state; 6% Black or African American, non-Hispanic/Latino; 2% Hispanic/Latino; 0.9% Asian, non-Hispanic/Latino; 0.6% American Indian or Alaska Native, non-Hispanic/Latino; 1% Two or more races, non-Hispanic/Latino; 7% Race/ethnicity unknown; 2% international; 6% transferred in; 33% live on campus. *Retention:* 76% of full-time freshmen returned.

Freshmen *Admission:* 18,509 applied, 12,670 admitted, 3,899 enrolled. *Average high school GPA:* 3.33. *Test scores:* SAT critical reading scores over 500: 63%; SAT math scores over 500: 52%; ACT scores over 18: 95%; SAT critical reading scores over 600: 18%; SAT math scores over 600: 25%; ACT scores over 24: 36%; SAT critical reading scores over 700: 2%; SAT math scores over 700: 2%; ACT scores over 30: 4%.

Faculty *Total:* 1,137, 68% full-time, 63% with terminal degrees. *Student/faculty ratio:* 22:1.

Academics *Calendar:* semesters. *Degrees:* bachelor's, master's, doctoral, post-master's, postbachelor's, and first professional certificates. *Special study*

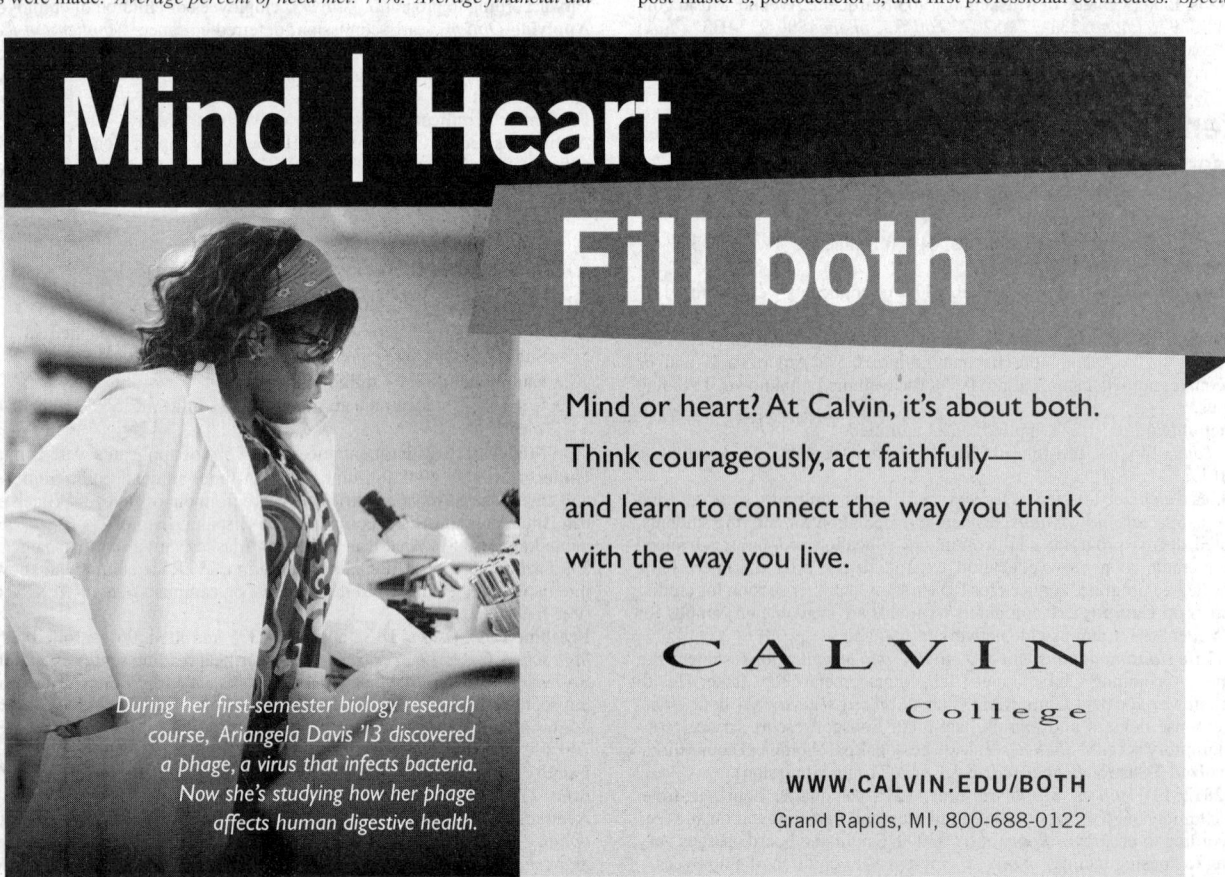

Mind | Heart
Fill both

Mind or heart? At Calvin, it's about both. Think courageously, act faithfully—and learn to connect the way you think with the way you live.

During her first-semester biology research course, Ariangela Davis '13 discovered a phage, a virus that infects bacteria. Now she's studying how her phage affects human digestive health.

CALVIN
College

WWW.CALVIN.EDU/BOTH

Grand Rapids, MI, 800-688-0122

options: academic remediation for entering students, accelerated degree program, adult/continuing education programs, advanced placement credit, distance learning, double majors, English as a second language, freshman honors college, honors programs, independent study, internships, off-campus study, part-time degree program, services for LD students, student-designed majors, study abroad, summer session for credit. *ROTC:* Army (b), Air Force (c). *Unusual degree programs:* 3-2 apparel product development and merchandising technology; computer science; economics; experimental psychology; geographic information science; human development and family studies; mathematics; political science.

Computers on Campus 3,000 computers/terminals and 10,000 ports are available on campus for general student use. Students can access the following: campus intranet, computer help desk, free student e-mail accounts, online (class) grades, online (class) registration, online (class) schedules, Blackboard. Campuswide network is available. 100% of college-owned or -operated housing units are wired for high-speed Internet access. Wireless service is available via entire campus.

Student Life *Housing:* on-campus residence required for freshman year. *Options:* coed, men-only, women-only, disabled students. Campus housing is university owned. Freshman campus housing is guaranteed. *Activities and organizations:* drama/theater group, student-run newspaper, radio and television station, choral group, marching band, Residence Hall Assembly, Student Government Association, High Adventure Club, Fellowship of Christian Athletes, College Republicans, national fraternities, national sororities. *Campus security:* 24-hour emergency response devices and patrols, student patrols, late-night transport/escort service, controlled dormitory access. *Student services:* health clinic, personal/psychological counseling, women's center, legal services.

Athletics Member NCAA. All Division I except football (Division I-A). *Intercollegiate sports:* baseball M(s), basketball M(s)/W(s), cross-country running M(s)/W(s), field hockey W(s), gymnastics W(s), soccer W(s), softball W(s), track and field M(s)/W(s), volleyball W(s), wrestling M(s). *Intramural sports:* archery M/W, baseball M(c), basketball M/W, bowling M/W, cheerleading W(c), cross-country running M/W, equestrian sports M(c)/W(c), football M/W, golf M(c)/W(c), ice hockey M(c)/W(c), lacrosse M(c)/W(c), racquetball M/W, rugby M(c)/W(c), skiing (downhill) M(c)/W(c), soccer M(c)/W(c), softball M/W, swimming and diving M(c)/W(c), table tennis M(c)/W(c), tennis M(c)/W(c), ultimate Frisbee M(c)/W(c), volleyball M(c)/W(c), water polo M(c)/W(c), weight lifting M(c)/W(c), wrestling M.

Standardized Tests *Required:* SAT or ACT (for admission). *Recommended:* ACT (for admission).

Costs (2011–12) *Tuition:* state resident $10,740 full-time, $358 per credit hour part-time; nonresident $23,670 full-time, $789 per credit hour part-time. Full-time tuition and fees vary according to location. Part-time tuition and fees vary according to location. *Room and board:* $8212; room only: $4106. Room and board charges vary according to board plan, housing facility, location, and student level. *Payment plan:* installment. *Waivers:* children of alumni, senior citizens, and employees or children of employees.

Financial Aid Of all full-time matriculated undergraduates who enrolled in 2010, 15,071 applied for aid, 11,834 were judged to have need, 6,535 had their need fully met. 921 Federal Work-Study jobs (averaging $1826). 4,086 state and other part-time jobs (averaging $2272). In 2010, 1460 non-need-based awards were made. *Average percent of need met:* 84%. *Average financial aid package:* $12,072. *Average need-based loan:* $6773. *Average need-based gift aid:* $5478. *Average non-need-based aid:* $3936. *Average indebtedness upon graduation:* $29,388.

Applying *Options:* electronic application, early admission, early action, deferred entrance. *Application fee:* $35. *Required:* high school transcript. *Required for some:* essay or personal statement, interview. *Application deadlines:* rolling (freshmen), rolling (transfers). *Notification:* continuous (freshmen), continuous (transfers).

Freshman Application Contact Central Michigan University, Mount Pleasant, MI 48859. *Phone:* 989-774-3076. *Toll-free phone:* 888-292-5366. *Web site:* http://www.cmich.edu.

Cleary University
Ann Arbor, Michigan

- **Independent** comprehensive, founded 1883
- **Suburban** 32-acre campus with easy access to Detroit, Ann Arbor
- **Endowment** $950,746
- **Coed** 618 undergraduate students, 42% full-time, 57% women, 43% men
- **Moderately difficult** entrance level, 58% of applicants were admitted

Undergraduates 257 full-time, 361 part-time. Students come from 11 states and territories; 2 other countries; 1% are from out of state; 8% Black or African American, non-Hispanic/Latino; 2% Hispanic/Latino; 0.5% Asian, non-Hispanic/Latino; 0.5% American Indian or Alaska Native, non-Hispanic/

Latino; 12% Race/ethnicity unknown; 16% transferred in. *Retention:* 75% of full-time freshmen returned.

Freshmen *Admission:* 33 applied, 19 admitted, 15 enrolled. *Test scores:* ACT scores over 18: 77%; ACT scores over 24: 27%.

Faculty *Total:* 86, 6% full-time, 19% with terminal degrees. *Student/faculty ratio:* 10:1.

Academics *Calendar:* quarters. *Degrees:* certificates, associate, bachelor's, and master's. *Special study options:* accelerated degree program, advanced placement credit, cooperative education, distance learning, double majors, independent study, internships, off-campus study, part-time degree program, summer session for credit.

Computers on Campus 50 computers/terminals are available on campus for general student use. Students can access the following: free student e-mail accounts, online (class) grades, online (class) schedules. Campuswide network is available. Wireless service is available via entire campus.

Student Life *Housing:* college housing not available. *Activities and organizations:* Cleary Professional Accounting Associates, Human Resources & Organizational Leadership Association, Event and Meeting Planning Student Association, Veterans Club, Accounting/Fraud Examiners Club. *Campus security:* 24-hour emergency response devices, access to facilities limited to authorized persons. *Student services:* personal/psychological counseling.

Athletics Member USCAA. *Intercollegiate sports:* cross-country running M(s)/W(s), golf M(s)/W(s).

Standardized Tests *Required:* SAT or ACT (for admission). *Required for some:* SAT Subject Tests (for admission).

Financial Aid Of all full-time matriculated undergraduates who enrolled in 2009, 391 applied for aid, 391 were judged to have need, 13 had their need fully met. In 2009, 60 non-need-based awards were made. *Average percent of need met:* 42%. *Average financial aid package:* $12,759. *Average need-based loan:* $1193. *Average need-based gift aid:* $1265. *Average non-need-based aid:* $2258. *Average indebtedness upon graduation:* $20,830. *Financial aid deadline:* 7/1.

Applying *Options:* electronic application, early admission, deferred entrance. *Application fee:* $25. *Required:* high school transcript, minimum 2.5 GPA. *Required for some:* essay or personal statement, First-Time/First Year Students: minimum ACT score of 19. Minimum high school GPA of 2.0 required for non-traditional and transfer students. *Recommended:* interview. *Application deadlines:* 8/15 (freshmen), rolling (transfers).

Freshman Application Contact Carrie Bonofiglio, Director of Admissions, Cleary University, 3750 Cleary Drive, Howell, MI 48843. *Phone:* 888-525-3279. *Toll-free phone:* 800-686-1883. *Fax:* 517-338-3336. *E-mail:* admissions@cleary.edu. *Web site:* http://www.cleary.edu/.

College for Creative Studies
Detroit, Michigan

- **Independent** comprehensive, founded 1926
- **Urban** 11-acre campus
- **Coed** 1,348 undergraduate students, 83% full-time, 48% women, 52% men
- **Moderately difficult** entrance level, 42% of applicants were admitted

Undergraduates 1,113 full-time, 235 part-time. 19% are from out of state; 8% Black or African American, non-Hispanic/Latino; 5% Hispanic/Latino; 4% Asian, non-Hispanic/Latino; 0.7% American Indian or Alaska Native, non-Hispanic/Latino; 3% Two or more races, non-Hispanic/Latino; 15% Race/ethnicity unknown; 7% international; 12% transferred in; 32% live on campus. *Retention:* 73% of full-time freshmen returned.

Freshmen *Admission:* 1,458 applied, 610 admitted, 235 enrolled. *Average high school GPA:* 3.16.

Faculty *Total:* 253, 19% full-time. *Student/faculty ratio:* 11:1.

Academics *Calendar:* semesters. *Degrees:* bachelor's, master's, and post-bachelor's certificates. *Special study options:* part-time degree program.

Computers on Campus Campuswide network is available.

Student Life *Housing options:* coed. Campus housing is university owned. *Campus security:* 24-hour patrols, late-night transport/escort service, controlled dormitory access.

Standardized Tests *Required:* SAT or ACT (for admission).

Costs (2011–12) *Comprehensive fee:* $40,485 includes full-time tuition ($31,440), mandatory fees ($1345), and room and board ($7700). Full-time tuition and fees vary according to course load. Part-time tuition: $1048 per credit hour. Part-time tuition and fees vary according to course load. *Room and board:* Room and board charges vary according to board plan and location. *Payment plans:* installment, deferred payment. *Waivers:* employees or children of employees.

Applying *Options:* electronic application, deferred entrance. *Application fee:* $35. *Required:* essay or personal statement, high school transcript, portfolio. *Required for some:* interview. *Recommended:* minimum 2.5 GPA. *Applica-*

tion deadlines: 7/1 (freshmen), rolling (transfers). *Notification:* continuous (freshmen).

Freshman Application Contact Office of Admissions, College for Creative Studies, 201 East Kirby, Detroit, MI 48202-4034. *Phone:* 800-952-2787. *Toll-free phone:* 800-952-ARTS. *Fax:* 313-872-2739. *E-mail:* admissions@collegeforcreativestudies.edu. *Web site:* http://www.collegeforcreativestudies.edu/.

Concordia University
Ann Arbor, Michigan

- **Independent** comprehensive, founded 1963, affiliated with Lutheran Church–Missouri Synod, part of Concordia University System
- **Suburban** 187-acre campus with easy access to Detroit
- **Endowment** $7.6 million
- **Coed** 509 undergraduate students, 93% full-time, 44% women, 56% men
- **Moderately difficult** entrance level, 56% of applicants were admitted

Undergraduates 474 full-time, 35 part-time. 10% Black or African American, non-Hispanic/Latino; 4% Hispanic/Latino; 1% Asian, non-Hispanic/Latino; 5% Two or more races, non-Hispanic/Latino; 1% Race/ethnicity unknown; 2% international; 9% transferred in; 79% live on campus. *Retention:* 58% of full-time freshmen returned.

Freshmen *Admission:* 837 applied, 467 admitted, 169 enrolled. *Average high school GPA:* 3.1. *Test scores:* ACT scores over 18: 90%; ACT scores over 24: 28%; ACT scores over 30: 7%.

Faculty *Total:* 124, 23% full-time, 23% with terminal degrees. *Student/faculty ratio:* 11:1.

Academics *Calendar:* semesters. *Degrees:* associate, bachelor's, master's, and postbachelor's certificates. *Special study options:* academic remediation for entering students, accelerated degree program, advanced placement credit, cooperative education, distance learning, double majors, English as a second language, independent study, internships, off-campus study, part-time degree program, services for LD students, student-designed majors, study abroad, summer session for credit. *ROTC:* Army (c), Air Force (c).

Computers on Campus 60 computers/terminals are available on campus for general student use. Students can access the following: campus intranet, computer help desk, free student e-mail accounts, online (class) grades, online (class) registration, online (class) schedules, online billing information. Campuswide network is available. 100% of college-owned or -operated housing units are wired for high-speed Internet access. Wireless service is available via entire campus.

Student Life *Housing:* on-campus residence required through sophomore year. *Options:* men-only, women-only. Campus housing is university owned. Freshman campus housing is guaranteed. *Activities and organizations:* drama/theater group, choral group, Student Activities Committee, Athletes in Action, Student Senate, Spiritual Life Committee, Off-campus ministries. *Campus security:* 24-hour emergency response devices and patrols, late-night transport/escort service, controlled dormitory access. *Student services:* personal/psychological counseling.

Athletics Member NAIA. *Intercollegiate sports:* baseball M(s), basketball M(s)/W(s), bowling M(s)/W(s), cheerleading W, cross-country running M(s)/W(s), football M(s), golf M(s)/W(s), soccer M(s)/W(s), softball W(s), track and field M(s)/W(s), volleyball W(s). *Intramural sports:* badminton M/W, basketball M/W, football M/W, golf M/W, softball M/W, table tennis M/W, ultimate Frisbee M/W, volleyball M/W.

Standardized Tests *Required:* SAT or ACT (for admission). *Recommended:* ACT (for admission).

Costs (2012–13) *Comprehensive fee:* $30,762 includes full-time tuition ($22,464) and room and board ($8298). Full-time tuition and fees vary according to location and program. Part-time tuition: $936 per credit hour. Part-time tuition and fees vary according to course load, location, and program. *Room and board:* Room and board charges vary according to housing facility. *Payment plan:* installment. *Waivers:* employees or children of employees.

Financial Aid Of all full-time matriculated undergraduates who enrolled in 2010, 392 applied for aid, 336 were judged to have need, 79 had their need fully met. 112 Federal Work-Study jobs (averaging $803). 68 state and other part-time jobs (averaging $1169). In 2010, 76 non-need-based awards were made. *Average percent of need met:* 74%. *Average financial aid package:* $16,032. *Average need-based loan:* $4636. *Average need-based gift aid:* $12,065. *Average non-need-based aid:* $6821. *Average indebtedness upon graduation:* $17,032.

Applying *Options:* electronic application, deferred entrance. *Application fee:* $25. *Required:* high school transcript. *Required for some:* essay or personal statement, 1 letter of recommendation, interview. *Recommended:* minimum 2.5 GPA. *Application deadlines:* rolling (freshmen), rolling (transfers).

Freshman Application Contact Mr. Ben Limback, Director of Admissions, Concordia University, 4090 Geddes Road, Ann Arbor, MI 48105-2797. *Phone:* 734-995-7311. *Toll-free phone:* 877-995-7520 (in-state); 877-955-

7520 (out-of-state). *Fax:* 734-995-4610. *E-mail:* admissions@cuaa.edu. *Web site:* http://www.cuaa.edu/.

Cornerstone University
Grand Rapids, Michigan

- **Independent nondenominational** comprehensive, founded 1941
- **Suburban** 132-acre campus
- **Endowment** $6.6 million
- **Coed** 2,125 undergraduate students, 80% full-time, 62% women, 38% men
- **Minimally difficult** entrance level, 63% of applicants were admitted

Undergraduates 1,693 full-time, 432 part-time. Students come from 34 states and territories; 12 other countries; 22% are from out of state; 10% Black or African American, non-Hispanic/Latino; 4% Hispanic/Latino; 0.3% Asian, non-Hispanic/Latino; 0.6% American Indian or Alaska Native, non-Hispanic/Latino; 1% Two or more races, non-Hispanic/Latino; 1% international; 3% transferred in; 62% live on campus. *Retention:* 74% of full-time freshmen returned.

Freshmen *Admission:* 2,062 applied, 1,293 admitted, 343 enrolled. *Average high school GPA:* 3.5. *Test scores:* SAT critical reading scores over 500: 79%; SAT math scores over 500: 70%; SAT writing scores over 500: 83%; ACT scores over 18: 96%; SAT critical reading scores over 600: 37%; SAT math scores over 600: 45%; SAT writing scores over 600: 28%; ACT scores over 24: 50%; SAT critical reading scores over 700: 9%; SAT math scores over 700: 6%; SAT writing scores over 700: 3%; ACT scores over 30: 10%.

Faculty *Total:* 114, 46% full-time, 32% with terminal degrees. *Student/faculty ratio:* 25:1.

Academics *Calendar:* semesters. *Degrees:* diplomas, associate, bachelor's, and master's. *Special study options:* academic remediation for entering students, accelerated degree program, adult/continuing education programs, advanced placement credit, distance learning, double majors, English as a second language, honors programs, independent study, internships, off-campus study, part-time degree program, services for LD students, study abroad, summer session for credit. *ROTC:* Army (c).

Computers on Campus 1,300 computers/terminals are available on campus for general student use. Students can access the following: campus intranet, computer help desk, free student e-mail accounts, online (class) grades, online (class) registration, online (class) schedules. Campuswide network is available. 100% of college-owned or -operated housing units are wired for high-speed Internet access. Wireless service is available via entire campus.

Student Life *Housing:* on-campus residence required through sophomore year. *Options:* men-only, women-only, disabled students. Campus housing is university owned. Freshman campus housing is guaranteed. *Activities and organizations:* drama/theater group, student-run newspaper, choral group, student government, Student Education Association, Breakpoint, Student Activities Council, International Justice Mission. *Campus security:* 24-hour emergency response devices and patrols, student patrols, late-night transport/escort service, controlled dormitory access. *Student services:* health clinic, personal/psychological counseling.

Athletics Member NAIA. *Intercollegiate sports:* basketball M(s)/W(s), cross-country running M(s)/W(s), golf M(s)/W, soccer M(s)/W(s), softball W(s), track and field M(s)/W(s), volleyball W(s). *Intramural sports:* basketball M/W, football M, soccer M/W, softball M/W, volleyball M/W.

Standardized Tests *Required:* SAT or ACT (for admission).

Costs (2011–12) *Comprehensive fee:* $29,702 includes full-time tuition ($21,818), mandatory fees ($570), and room and board ($7314). Full-time tuition and fees vary according to course load and reciprocity agreements. Part-time tuition: $836 per semester hour. Part-time tuition and fees vary according to course load. *Required fees:* $175 per term part-time. *Room and board:* Room and board charges vary according to board plan. *Payment plan:* installment. *Waivers:* employees or children of employees.

Financial Aid Of all full-time matriculated undergraduates who enrolled in 2010, 1,002 applied for aid, 915 were judged to have need, 127 had their need fully met. 237 Federal Work-Study jobs (averaging $825). In 2010, 174 non-need-based awards were made. *Average percent of need met:* 83%. *Average financial aid package:* $19,772. *Average need-based loan:* $4365. *Average need-based gift aid:* $12,708. *Average non-need-based aid:* $6742. *Average indebtedness upon graduation:* $29,510.

Applying *Options:* electronic application, deferred entrance. *Application fee:* $25. *Required:* essay or personal statement, high school transcript, minimum 2.5 GPA, 1 letter of recommendation, pastoral letter. *Recommended:* interview. *Application deadlines:* rolling (freshmen), rolling (transfers). *Notification:* continuous (freshmen), continuous (transfers).

Freshman Application Contact Office of Admissions, Cornerstone University, 1001 East Beltline Avenue, NE, Grand Rapids, MI 49525. *Phone:* 616-222-1426. *Toll-free phone:* 800-787-9778. *Fax:* 616-222-1400. *E-mail:* admissions@cornerstone.edu. *Web site:* http://www.cornerstone.edu/.

Davenport University

Grand Rapids, Michigan

- **Independent** comprehensive, founded 1866
- **Suburban** campus
- **Endowment** $16.4 million
- **Coed** 9,892 undergraduate students, 28% full-time, 63% women, 37% men
- **Minimally difficult** entrance level, 93% of applicants were admitted

Undergraduates 2,734 full-time, 7,158 part-time. Students come from 49 states and territories; 42 other countries; 2% are from out of state; 20% Black or African American, non-Hispanic/Latino; 3% Hispanic/Latino; 2% Asian, non-Hispanic/Latino; 0.1% Native Hawaiian or other Pacific Islander, non-Hispanic/Latino; 0.4% American Indian or Alaska Native, non-Hispanic/Latino; 2% Two or more races, non-Hispanic/Latino; 19% Race/ethnicity unknown; 0.9% international; 13% transferred in; 4% live on campus. *Retention:* 68% of full-time freshmen returned.

Freshmen *Admission:* 1,440 applied, 1,344 admitted, 817 enrolled.

Faculty *Total:* 1,069, 15% full-time, 21% with terminal degrees. *Student/faculty ratio:* 14:1.

Academics *Calendar:* semesters. *Degrees:* diplomas, associate, bachelor's, master's, post-master's, and postbachelor's certificates. *Special study options:* academic remediation for entering students, accelerated degree program, adult/continuing education programs, advanced placement credit, cooperative education, distance learning, English as a second language, independent study, internships, part-time degree program, services for LD students, study abroad, summer session for credit.

Computers on Campus 3,098 computers/terminals are available on campus for general student use. Students can access the following: campus intranet, computer help desk, free student e-mail accounts, online (class) grades, online (class) registration, online (class) schedules. Campuswide network is available. 100% of college-owned or -operated housing units are wired for high-speed Internet access. Wireless service is available via entire campus.

Student Life *Housing options:* coed. Campus housing is university owned. Freshman applicants given priority for college housing. *Activities and organizations:* student-run newspaper, Business Professionals of America, Delta Epsilon Chi, Student government, Health Occupations Students of America, Connect. *Campus security:* 24-hour emergency response devices and patrols, late-night transport/escort service, controlled dormitory access. *Student services:* personal/psychological counseling.

Athletics Member NAIA. *Intercollegiate sports:* baseball M(s), basketball M(s)/W(s), bowling M(s)/W(s), cheerleading W(s), cross-country running M(s)/W(s), golf M(s)/W(s), ice hockey M(s), lacrosse M(s)/W, rugby M(s), soccer M(s)/W(s), softball M/W(s), tennis M(s)/W(s), track and field M(s)/W(s), volleyball W(s).

Standardized Tests *Recommended:* SAT or ACT (for admission).

Costs (2011–12) *Comprehensive fee:* $20,798 includes full-time tuition ($12,096), mandatory fees ($290), and room and board ($8412). Full-time tuition and fees vary according to location and program. Part-time tuition: $504 per credit hour. Part-time tuition and fees vary according to location and program. *Room and board:* Room and board charges vary according to board plan and housing facility. *Payment plan:* installment. *Waivers:* employees or children of employees.

Applying *Options:* electronic application, deferred entrance. *Application fee:* $25. *Required:* high school transcript. *Recommended:* interview. *Application deadlines:* rolling (freshmen), rolling (out-of-state freshmen), rolling (transfers). *Notification:* continuous (freshmen), continuous (out-of-state freshmen), continuous (transfers).

Freshman Application Contact Mr. Daryl Kingrey, Executive Director of Admissions, Davenport University, 6191 Kraft Avenue SE, Grand Rapids, MI 49512. *Phone:* 616-451-3511. *Toll-free phone:* 800-925-3884 (in-state); 866-925-3884 (out-of-state). *E-mail:* heather.knechtel@davenport.edu. *Web site:* http://www.davenport.edu/.

DeVry University

Southfield, Michigan

Freshman Application Contact DeVry University, 26999 Central Park Boulevard, Suite 125, Southfield, MI 48076. *Toll-free phone:* 866-338-7941. *Web site:* http://www.devry.edu/.

Eastern Michigan University

Ypsilanti, Michigan

- **State-supported** comprehensive, founded 1849
- **Suburban** 460-acre campus with easy access to Detroit
- **Endowment** $48.2 million
- **Coed** 18,569 undergraduate students, 69% full-time, 57% women, 43% men
- **Moderately difficult** entrance level, 60% of applicants were admitted

Undergraduates 12,840 full-time, 5,729 part-time. Students come from 45 states and territories; 54 other countries; 8% are from out of state; 22% Black or African American, non-Hispanic/Latino; 3% Hispanic/Latino; 2% Asian, non-Hispanic/Latino; 0.1% Native Hawaiian or other Pacific Islander, non-Hispanic/Latino; 0.5% American Indian or Alaska Native, non-Hispanic/Latino; 1% Two or more races, non-Hispanic/Latino; 6% Race/ethnicity unknown; 2% international; 11% transferred in; 12% live on campus. *Retention:* 76% of full-time freshmen returned.

Freshmen *Admission:* 12,787 applied, 7,644 admitted, 2,176 enrolled. *Average high school GPA:* 3.11. *Test scores:* SAT critical reading scores over 500: 51%; SAT math scores over 500: 58%; SAT writing scores over 500: 47%; ACT scores over 18: 81%; SAT critical reading scores over 600: 18%; SAT math scores over 600: 21%; SAT writing scores over 600: 16%; ACT scores over 24: 26%; SAT critical reading scores over 700: 4%; SAT math scores over 700: 2%; SAT writing scores over 700: 4%; ACT scores over 30: 2%.

Faculty *Total:* 1,299, 60% full-time, 55% with terminal degrees. *Student/faculty ratio:* 18:1.

Academics *Calendar:* semesters. *Degrees:* bachelor's, master's, doctoral, post-master's, postbachelor's, and first professional certificates. *Special study options:* academic remediation for entering students, accelerated degree program, advanced placement credit, cooperative education, distance learning, double majors, English as a second language, external degree program, honors programs, independent study, internships, part-time degree program, services for LD students, student-designed majors, study abroad, summer session for credit. *ROTC:* Army (b), Navy (c), Air Force (c). *Unusual degree programs:* accounting, occupational therapy.

Computers on Campus 1,600 computers/terminals and 200 ports are available on campus for general student use. Students can access the following: campus intranet, computer help desk, free student e-mail accounts, online (class) grades, online (class) registration, online (class) schedules, Wireless internet connections are available for all students. Campuswide network is available. 100% of college-owned or -operated housing units are wired for high-speed Internet access. Wireless service is available via entire campus.

Student Life *Housing:* on-campus residence required through sophomore year. *Options:* coed, disabled students. Campus housing is university owned. *Activities and organizations:* drama/theater group, student-run newspaper, radio and television station, choral group, marching band, International Student Association, Golden Key International Honor Society, Psychology Club, Indian Student Association, GREEN (Gathering Resources to Educate about our Environment and Nature), national fraternities, national sororities. *Campus security:* 24-hour emergency response devices and patrols, student patrols, late-night transport/escort service, controlled dormitory access, bicycle patrols, local police in dormitories, self-defense education, lighted pathways, bike lock lease program. *Student services:* health clinic, personal/psychological counseling, women's center, legal services.

Athletics Member NCAA. All Division I except football (Division I-A). *Intercollegiate sports:* baseball M(s), basketball M(s)/W(s), crew W(s), cross-country running M(s)/W(s), golf M(s)/W(s), gymnastics W(s), soccer W(s), softball W(s), swimming and diving M(s)/W(s), tennis W(s), track and field M(s)/W(s), volleyball W(s), wrestling M(s). *Intramural sports:* badminton M/W, basketball M/W, bowling M/W, cross-country running M/W, golf M/W, ice hockey M(c), racquetball M/W, soccer M/W, softball M/W, swimming and diving M/W, table tennis M/W, tennis M/W, track and field M/W, ultimate Frisbee M(c)/W(c), volleyball M/W, weight lifting M(c)/W(c).

Standardized Tests *Required:* SAT or ACT (for admission).

Costs (2011–12) *One-time required fee:* $300. *Tuition:* state resident $7409 full-time, $247 per credit hour part-time; nonresident $21,821 full-time, $727 per credit hour part-time. Full-time tuition and fees vary according to course level and reciprocity agreements. Part-time tuition and fees vary according to course level and reciprocity agreements. *Required fees:* $1275 full-time, $39 per credit hour part-time, $46 per term part-time. *Room and board:* $7896; room only: $3766. Room and board charges vary according to board plan, housing facility, and location. *Payment plan:* installment. *Waivers:* employees or children of employees.

Financial Aid Of all full-time matriculated undergraduates who enrolled in 2009, 7,976 applied for aid, 6,864 were judged to have need, 85 had their need fully met. 908 Federal Work-Study jobs (averaging $1486). In 2009, 1090 non-need-based awards were made. *Average percent of need met:* 54%. *Average financial aid package:* $8767. *Average need-based loan:* $4437. *Average*

need-based gift aid: $4960. *Average non-need-based aid:* $4183. *Average indebtedness upon graduation:* $23,669.

Applying *Options:* electronic application, deferred entrance. *Application fee:* $30. *Required:* high school transcript, minimum 2.0 GPA. *Required for some:* 1 letter of recommendation, interview. *Application deadlines:* rolling (freshmen), rolling (out-of-state freshmen), rolling (transfers). *Notification:* continuous (freshmen), continuous (out-of-state freshmen), continuous (transfers).

Freshman Application Contact Eastern Michigan University, Ypsilanti, MI 48197. *Phone:* 734-487-3060. *Toll-free phone:* 800-GO TO EMU. *Web site:* http://www.emich.edu/.

Ferris State University
Big Rapids, Michigan

- **State-supported** comprehensive, founded 1884
- **Small-town** 880-acre campus with easy access to Grand Rapids
- **Endowment** $36.7 million
- **Coed** 13,350 undergraduate students, 69% full-time, 51% women, 49% men
- **Minimally difficult** entrance level, 77% of applicants were admitted

Undergraduates 9,276 full-time, 4,074 part-time. Students come from 44 states and territories; 30 other countries; 4% are from out of state; 6% Black or African American, non-Hispanic/Latino; 3% Hispanic/Latino; 1% Asian, non-Hispanic/Latino; 0.7% American Indian or Alaska Native, non-Hispanic/Latino; 2% Two or more races, non-Hispanic/Latino; 6% Race/ethnicity unknown; 1% international; 11% transferred in; 29% live on campus. *Retention:* 71% of full-time freshmen returned.

Freshmen *Admission:* 8,487 applied, 6,573 admitted, 2,114 enrolled. *Average high school GPA:* 3.2. *Test scores:* ACT scores over 18: 85%; ACT scores over 24: 33%; ACT scores over 30: 5%.

Faculty *Total:* 775, 62% full-time, 38% with terminal degrees. *Student/faculty ratio:* 16:1.

Academics *Calendar:* semesters. *Degrees:* certificates, associate, bachelor's, master's, doctoral, postbachelor's, and first professional certificates (associate degree). *Special study options:* academic remediation for entering students, accelerated degree program, adult/continuing education programs, advanced placement credit, cooperative education, distance learning, double majors, English as a second language, external degree program, freshman honors college, honors programs, independent study, internships, off-campus study, part-time degree program, services for LD students, student-designed majors, study abroad, summer session for credit. *ROTC:* Army (c).

Computers on Campus 1,195 computers/terminals are available on campus for general student use. Students can access the following: campus intranet, computer help desk, free student e-mail accounts, online (class) grades, online (class) registration, online (class) schedules. Campuswide network is available. 100% of college-owned or -operated housing units are wired for high-speed Internet access. Wireless service is available via entire campus.

Student Life *Housing:* on-campus residence required through sophomore year. *Options:* coed, disabled students. Campus housing is university owned. Freshman campus housing is guaranteed. *Activities and organizations:* drama/theater group, student-run newspaper, radio and television station, choral group, Student Government of Ferris State University, Intramural Sports Club, Entertainment Unlimited, Music Club, Crafter's Anonymous, national fraternities, national sororities. *Campus security:* 24-hour emergency response devices, student patrols, late-night transport/escort service, controlled dormitory access. *Student services:* health clinic, personal/psychological counseling.

Athletics Member NCAA. All Division II. *Intercollegiate sports:* basketball M(s)/W(s), cross-country running M(s)/W(s), football M(s), golf M(s)/W(s), ice hockey M(s), soccer W(s), softball W(s), tennis M(s)/W(s), track and field M(s)/W(s), volleyball W(s). *Intramural sports:* baseball M(c), basketball M/W, bowling M(c)/W(c), cheerleading M(c)/W(c), cross-country running M(c)/W(c), equestrian sports M(c)/W(c), football M/W, ice hockey M/W, lacrosse M(c)/W(c), rugby M(c)/W(c), soccer M/W, softball M/W, table tennis M(c)/W(c), tennis M(c)/W(c), ultimate Frisbee M(c)/W(c), volleyball M(c)/W(c).

Standardized Tests *Required:* SAT or ACT (for admission).

Costs (2011–12) *One-time required fee:* $162. *Tuition:* state resident $10,440 full-time, $348 per credit hour part-time; nonresident $15,660 full-time, $522 per credit hour part-time. Full-time tuition and fees vary according to location and program. Part-time tuition and fees vary according to location. *Room and board:* $9344. Room and board charges vary according to board plan and housing facility. *Payment plan:* deferred payment. *Waivers:* employees or children of employees.

Financial Aid Of all full-time matriculated undergraduates who enrolled in 2011, 8,440 applied for aid, 6,979 were judged to have need, 808 had their need fully met. 546 Federal Work-Study jobs (averaging $2050). In 2011, 845 non-need-based awards were made. *Average percent of need met:* 60%. *Average financial aid package:* $10,080. *Average need-based loan:* $4510. Aver-

age need-based gift aid: $4640. *Average non-need-based aid:* $4360. *Average indebtedness upon graduation:* $35,476.

Applying *Options:* electronic application. *Application fee:* $30. *Required:* high school transcript, minimum 2.5 GPA, SAT or ACT. *Application deadlines:* 8/1 (freshmen), 7/1 (transfers). *Notification:* continuous (freshmen), continuous (transfers).

Freshman Application Contact Mr. Jason Daday, Associate Director of Admissions, Ferris State University, 1201 South State Street, CSS201, Big Rapids, MI 49307-2742. *Phone:* 231-591-3106. *Toll-free phone:* 800-433-7747. *Fax:* 231-591-2242. *E-mail:* dadayja@ferris.edu. *Web site:* http://www.ferris.edu/.

Finlandia University
Hancock, Michigan

Freshman Application Contact Martin Kinard, Finlandia University, 601 Quincy Street, Hancock, MI 49930. *Phone:* 906-487-7352. *Toll-free phone:* 877-202-5491. *Fax:* 906-487-7383. *E-mail:* admissions@finlandia.edu. *Web site:* http://www.finlandia.edu/.

Grace Bible College
Grand Rapids, Michigan

- **Independent** 4-year, founded 1945, affiliated with Grace Gospel Fellowship
- **Suburban** 21-acre campus
- **Endowment** $319,000
- **Coed**
- **Minimally difficult** entrance level

Faculty *Student/faculty ratio:* 17:1.

Academics *Calendar:* semesters. *Degrees:* associate and bachelor's.

Student Life *Campus security:* student patrols, controlled dormitory access.

Athletics Member NCCAA.

Standardized Tests *Required:* SAT and SAT Subject Tests or ACT (for admission).

Costs (2011–12) *Comprehensive fee:* $21,100 includes full-time tuition ($14,850) and room and board ($6250). Part-time tuition: $495 per credit. Part-time tuition and fees vary according to course load. *College room only:* $3150. Room and board charges vary according to board plan and housing facility.

Financial Aid *Of all full-time matriculated undergraduates who enrolled in 2010,* 233 applied for aid, 221 were judged to have need, 16 had their need fully met. 52 Federal Work-Study jobs (averaging $430). *In 2010,* 18 non-need-based awards were made. *Average percent of need met:* 60. *Average financial aid package:* $9766. *Average need-based loan:* $3780. *Average need-based gift aid:* $4432. *Average non-need-based aid:* $2722. *Average indebtedness upon graduation:* $18,913.

Applying *Options:* electronic application, early admission, deferred entrance. *Required:* high school transcript, 2 letters of recommendation. *Required for some:* interview. *Recommended:* minimum 2.5 GPA.

Freshman Application Contact Mr. Kevin Gilliam, Director of Enrollment, Grace Bible College, 1101 Aldon Street, SW, PO Box 910, Grand Rapids, MI 49509. *Phone:* 616-538-2330 Ext. 239. *Toll-free phone:* 800-968-1887. *Fax:* 616-538-0599. *E-mail:* gbc@gbcol.edu. *Web site:* http://www.gbcol.edu/.

Grand Valley State University
Allendale, Michigan

- **State-supported** comprehensive, founded 1960
- **Small-town** 1337-acre campus with easy access to Grand Rapids
- **Endowment** $75.5 million
- **Coed** 21,236 undergraduate students, 87% full-time, 58% women, 42% men
- **Moderately difficult** entrance level, 83% of applicants were admitted

Undergraduates 18,488 full-time, 2,748 part-time. Students come from 45 states and territories; 69 other countries; 4% are from out of state; 5% Black or African American, non-Hispanic/Latino; 4% Hispanic/Latino; 2% Asian, non-Hispanic/Latino; 0.1% Native Hawaiian or other Pacific Islander, non-Hispanic/Latino; 0.5% American Indian or Alaska Native, non-Hispanic/Latino; 2% Two or more races, non-Hispanic/Latino; 0.9% Race/ethnicity unknown; 1% international; 9% transferred in; 31% live on campus. *Retention:* 82% of full-time freshmen returned.

Freshmen *Admission:* 16,697 applied, 13,877 admitted, 3,865 enrolled. *Average high school GPA:* 3.51. *Test scores:* SAT critical reading scores over 500: 66%; SAT math scores over 500: 82%; SAT writing scores over 500: 65%; ACT scores over 18: 97%; SAT critical reading scores over 600: 26%; SAT math scores over 600: 39%; SAT writing scores over 600: 20%; ACT scores

over 24: 51%; SAT critical reading scores over 700: 8%; SAT math scores over 700: 6%; SAT writing scores over 700: 5%; ACT scores over 30: 7%.

Faculty *Total:* 1,631, 65% full-time, 52% with terminal degrees. *Student/faculty ratio:* 17:1.

Academics *Calendar:* semesters. *Degrees:* certificates, bachelor's, master's, doctoral, post-master's, and postbachelor's certificates. *Special study options:* academic remediation for entering students, accelerated degree program, adult/continuing education programs, advanced placement credit, cooperative education, distance learning, double majors, English as a second language, freshman honors college, honors programs, independent study, internships, part-time degree program, services for LD students, study abroad, summer session for credit.

Computers on Campus 2,600 computers/terminals are available on campus for general student use. Students can access the following: campus intranet, computer help desk, free student e-mail accounts, online (class) grades, online (class) registration, online (class) schedules, transcript, degree audit, credit card payments. Campuswide network is available. 100% of college-owned or -operated housing units are wired for high-speed Internet access. Wireless service is available via entire campus.

Student Life *Housing options:* coed. Campus housing is university owned. Freshman campus housing is guaranteed. *Activities and organizations:* drama/theater group, student-run newspaper, radio and television station, choral group, marching band, Habitat for Humanity, Alternative Breaks, Hospitality and tourism Management Club, Dance Troupe, Colleges Against Cancer, national fraternities, national sororities. *Campus security:* 24-hour emergency response devices and patrols, student patrols, late-night transport/escort service, controlled dormitory access. *Student services:* health clinic, personal/psychological counseling, women's center.

Athletics Member NCAA. All Division II. *Intercollegiate sports:* baseball M(s), basketball M(s)/W(s), cheerleading M(c)/W(c), crew M(c)/W(c), cross-country running M(s)/W(s), football M(s), golf M(s)/W(s), ice hockey M(c), lacrosse M(c)/W, rugby M(c)/W(c), sailing M(c)/W(c), skiing (downhill) M(c)/W(c), soccer M(c)/W(s), softball W(s), swimming and diving M(s)/W(s), tennis M(s)/W(s), track and field M(s)/W(s), volleyball M(c)/W(s), water polo M(c)/W(c), wrestling M(c). *Intramural sports:* archery M/W, badminton M/W, basketball M/W, bowling M/W, cheerleading M/W, crew M/W, cross-country running M/W, fencing M/W, field hockey M/W, football M/W, golf M/W, gymnastics M/W, lacrosse M/W, racquetball M/W, skiing (cross-country) M/W, skiing (downhill) M/W, soccer M/W, softball M/W, squash M/W, swimming and diving M/W, tennis M/W, volleyball M/W, water polo M/W, weight lifting M/W, wrestling M.

Standardized Tests *Required:* SAT or ACT (for admission).

Costs (2011–12) *Tuition:* state resident $9716 full-time, $412 per credit hour part-time; nonresident $14,030 full-time, $588 per credit hour part-time. Full-time tuition and fees vary according to degree level, program, and student level. Part-time tuition and fees vary according to course load, degree level, program, and student level. *Room and board:* $7774; room only: $5344. Room and board charges vary according to board plan, housing facility, and location. *Payment plans:* installment, deferred payment. *Waivers:* employees or children of employees.

Financial Aid Of all full-time matriculated undergraduates who enrolled in 2011, 15,413 applied for aid, 12,204 were judged to have need, 1,457 had their need fully met. 1,872 Federal Work-Study jobs (averaging $2381). In 2011, 1953 non-need-based awards were made. *Average percent of need met:* 59%. *Average financial aid package:* $8684. *Average need-based loan:* $4500. *Average need-based gift aid:* $5661. *Average non-need-based aid:* $2531. *Average indebtedness upon graduation:* $26,912.

Applying *Options:* electronic application. *Application fee:* $30. *Required:* high school transcript. *Required for some:* essay or personal statement, interview. *Application deadlines:* 5/1 (freshmen), 7/24 (transfers). *Notification:* 5/1 (freshmen), continuous (transfers).

Freshman Application Contact Ms. Jodi Chycinski, Director of Admissions, Grand Valley State University, 1 Campus Drive, Allendale, MI 49401. *Phone:* 616-331-2025. *Toll-free phone:* 800-748-0246. *Fax:* 616-331-2000. *E-mail:* go2gvsu@gvsu.edu. *Web site:* http://www.gvsu.edu/.

Great Lakes Christian College

Lansing, Michigan

- **Independent** 4-year, founded 1949, affiliated with Christian Churches and Churches of Christ
- **Suburban** 47-acre campus
- **Endowment** $442,503
- **Coed** 225 undergraduate students, 74% full-time, 41% women, 59% men
- **Moderately difficult** entrance level

Undergraduates 166 full-time, 59 part-time. Students come from 4 states and territories; 3 other countries; 2% are from out of state. *Retention:* 53% of full-time freshmen returned.

Freshmen *Test scores:* ACT scores over 18: 79%; ACT scores over 24: 19%; ACT scores over 30: 2%.

Faculty *Total:* 23, 43% full-time, 30% with terminal degrees. *Student/faculty ratio:* 14:1.

Academics *Calendar:* semesters. *Degrees:* associate and bachelor's. *Special study options:* academic remediation for entering students, advanced placement credit, double majors, independent study, internships, off-campus study, part-time degree program, services for LD students.

Computers on Campus 24 computers/terminals and 190 ports are available on campus for general student use. Students can access the following: campus intranet, computer help desk, free student e-mail accounts, online (class) grades, online (class) schedules. Campuswide network is available. 100% of college-owned or -operated housing units are wired for high-speed Internet access. Wireless service is available via entire campus.

Student Life *Housing:* on-campus residence required through senior year. *Options:* men-only, women-only. Campus housing is university owned. *Activities and organizations:* drama/theater group, student-run newspaper, choral group. *Campus security:* controlled dormitory access, evening security patrols. *Student services:* personal/psychological counseling.

Athletics Member NCCAA. *Intercollegiate sports:* basketball M/W, soccer M, volleyball W.

Standardized Tests *Required:* SAT or ACT (for admission).

Costs (2011–12) *Comprehensive fee:* $21,712 includes full-time tuition ($12,672), mandatory fees ($1240), and room and board ($7800). Part-time tuition: $396 per credit. *Room and board:* Room and board charges vary according to board plan and housing facility. *Payment plan:* installment. *Waivers:* children of alumni and employees or children of employees.

Applying *Options:* electronic application. *Application fee:* $30. *Required:* essay or personal statement, high school transcript, minimum 2.3 GPA, 3 letters of recommendation. *Application deadlines:* 8/1 (freshmen), 8/1 (transfers). *Notification:* 8/15 (freshmen), continuous until 8/15 (transfers).

Freshman Application Contact Mrs. Judy Carter, Admissions Office Manager, Great Lakes Christian College, 6211 West Willow Highway, Lansing, MI 48917-1299. *Phone:* 517-321-0242 Ext. 221. *Toll-free phone:* 800-YES-GLCC. *Fax:* 517-321-5902. *E-mail:* jcarter@glcc.edu. *Web site:* http://www.glcc.edu/.

Hillsdale College

Hillsdale, Michigan

- **Independent** 4-year, founded 1844
- **Small-town** 200-acre campus
- **Endowment** $350.0 million
- **Coed** 1,457 undergraduate students, 96% full-time, 52% women, 48% men
- **Very difficult** entrance level, 42% of applicants were admitted

Undergraduates 1,406 full-time, 51 part-time. Students come from 48 states and territories; 8 other countries; 63% are from out of state; 2% transferred in; 75% live on campus. *Retention:* 98% of full-time freshmen returned.

Freshmen *Admission:* 2,207 applied, 925 admitted, 360 enrolled. *Average high school GPA:* 3.75. *Test scores:* SAT critical reading scores over 500: 100%; SAT math scores over 500: 100%; SAT writing scores over 500: 96%; ACT scores over 18: 100%; SAT critical reading scores over 600: 92%; SAT math scores over 600: 74%; SAT writing scores over 600: 75%; ACT scores over 24: 97%; SAT critical reading scores over 700: 45%; SAT math scores over 700: 26%; SAT writing scores over 700: 36%; ACT scores over 30: 49%.

Faculty *Total:* 163, 72% full-time, 88% with terminal degrees. *Student/faculty ratio:* 10:1.

Academics *Calendar:* semesters. *Degree:* bachelor's. *Special study options:* accelerated degree program, advanced placement credit, double majors, honors programs, independent study, internships, off-campus study, part-time degree program, study abroad, summer session for credit. *Unusual degree programs:* 3-2 engineering with Northwestern University, Trine University.

Computers on Campus 220 computers/terminals are available on campus for general student use. Students can access the following: computer help desk, free student e-mail accounts, online (class) grades, online (class) registration, online (class) schedules. Campuswide network is available. 100% of college-owned or -operated housing units are wired for high-speed Internet access. Wireless service is available via entire campus.

Student Life *Housing:* on-campus residence required through sophomore year. *Options:* men-only, women-only. Campus housing is university owned. Freshman campus housing is guaranteed. *Activities and organizations:* drama/theater group, student-run newspaper, choral group, Inter-Varsity Christian Fellowship, Varsity H-Club, Student Federation, Young Life, College Republicans, national fraternities, national sororities. *Campus security:* 24-hour emergency response devices and patrols, late-night transport/escort service, controlled dormitory access. *Student services:* health clinic, personal/psychological counseling.

Athletics Member NCAA. All Division II. *Intercollegiate sports:* baseball M(s), basketball M(s)/W(s), cheerleading M/W, cross-country running M(s)/W(s), equestrian sports W, football M(s), riflery M(s)/W(s), rugby M(c), soccer M/W, softball W(s), swimming and diving W(s), tennis W(s), track and field M(s)/W(s), volleyball W(s). *Intramural sports:* basketball M/W, bowling M/W, equestrian sports W(c), football M/W, ice hockey M(c), lacrosse M(c), racquetball M/W, riflery M(c)/W(c), skiing (downhill) M(c)/W(c), soccer M(c)/W(c), softball M/W, squash M/W, swimming and diving W, table tennis M/W, tennis M/W, track and field M/W, ultimate Frisbee M/W, volleyball M/W.

Standardized Tests *Required:* SAT or ACT (for admission). *Recommended:* SAT Subject Tests (for admission).

Costs (2012–13) *Comprehensive fee:* $30,570 includes full-time tuition ($21,390), mandatory fees ($540), and room and board ($8640). *College room only:* $4290. Room and board charges vary according to board plan. *Payment plans:* tuition prepayment, installment. *Waivers:* children of alumni and employees or children of employees.

Financial Aid Of all full-time matriculated undergraduates who enrolled in 2009, 672 applied for aid, 601 were judged to have need, 235 had their need fully met. In 2009, 641 non-need-based awards were made. *Average percent of need met:* 72%. *Average financial aid package:* $16,760. *Average need-based loan:* $5900. *Average need-based gift aid:* $7350. *Average non-need-based aid:* $9740. *Average indebtedness upon graduation:* $16,500. *Financial aid deadline:* 4/1.

Applying *Options:* electronic application, early admission, early decision, early action. *Required:* essay or personal statement, high school transcript, 2 letters of recommendation. *Required for some:* minimum 3.6 GPA, interview. *Recommended:* minimum 3.6 GPA, interview. *Application deadlines:* 2/15 (freshmen), 2/15 (out-of-state freshmen), 2/15 (transfers), 12/15 (early action). *Early decision deadline:* 11/15. *Notification:* 4/1 (freshmen), 4/1 (out-of-state freshmen), 4/1 (transfers), 12/1 (early decision), 2/15 (early action).

Freshman Application Contact Mr. Jeffrey S. Lantis, Director of Admissions, Hillsdale College, 33 East College Street, Hillsdale, MI 49242-1298. *Phone:* 517-607-2327. *Fax:* 517-607-2223. *E-mail:* admissions@hillsdale.edu. *Web site:* http://www.hillsdale.edu/.

See below for display ad and page 1364 for the College Close-Up.

Hope College
Holland, Michigan

- **Independent** 4-year, founded 1866, affiliated with Reformed Church in America
- **Suburban** 45-acre campus with easy access to Grand Rapids
- **Endowment** $153.8 million
- **Coed** 3,249 undergraduate students, 96% full-time, 62% women, 38% men
- **Moderately difficult** entrance level, 82% of applicants were admitted

Undergraduates 3,127 full-time, 122 part-time. Students come from 44 states and territories; 33 other countries; 31% are from out of state; 2% Black or African American, non-Hispanic/Latino; 5% Hispanic/Latino; 2% Asian, non-Hispanic/Latino; 0.2% American Indian or Alaska Native, non-Hispanic/Latino; 2% Two or more races, non-Hispanic/Latino; 2% international; 2% transferred in; 74% live on campus. *Retention:* 89% of full-time freshmen returned.

Freshmen *Admission:* 3,575 applied, 2,940 admitted, 848 enrolled. *Average high school GPA:* 3.75. *Test scores:* SAT critical reading scores over 500: 85%; SAT math scores over 500: 84%; ACT scores over 18: 100%; SAT critical reading scores over 600: 48%; SAT math scores over 600: 56%; ACT scores over 24: 77%; SAT critical reading scores over 700: 17%; SAT math scores over 700: 14%; ACT scores over 30: 25%.

Faculty *Total:* 316, 70% full-time, 60% with terminal degrees. *Student/faculty ratio:* 12:1.

Academics *Calendar:* semesters. *Degree:* bachelor's. *Special study options:* advanced placement credit, double majors, English as a second language, independent study, internships, off-campus study, part-time degree program, services for LD students, student-designed majors, study abroad, summer session for credit. *ROTC:* Army (c).

Computers on Campus 300 computers/terminals and 5,000 ports are available on campus for general student use. Students can access the following: campus intranet, computer help desk, free student e-mail accounts, online (class) grades, online (class) registration, online (class) schedules. Campus-wide network is available. 100% of college-owned or -operated housing units are wired for high-speed Internet access. Wireless service is available via entire campus.

Student Life *Housing:* on-campus residence required through junior year. *Options:* coed, men-only, women-only, disabled students. Campus housing is university owned and leased by the school. Freshman campus housing is guaranteed. *Activities and organizations:* drama/theater group, student-run news-

paper, radio station, choral group, Social Activities Committee, Greek Life, Dance Marathon, Hockey Club, Relay for Life, national fraternities, national sororities. *Campus security:* 24-hour emergency response devices and patrols, late-night transport/escort service, controlled dormitory access. *Student services:* health clinic, personal/psychological counseling.

Athletics Member NCAA. All Division III. *Intercollegiate sports:* baseball M, basketball M/W, cheerleading M/W, cross-country running M/W, football M, golf M/W, ice hockey M(c), lacrosse M/W, sailing M(c)/W(c), soccer M/W, softball W, swimming and diving M/W, tennis M/W, track and field M/W, volleyball W. *Intramural sports:* basketball M/W, bowling M/W, football M/W, racquetball M/W, soccer M/W, softball M/W, tennis M/W, ultimate Frisbee M/W, volleyball M/W, water polo M/W.

Standardized Tests *Required:* SAT or ACT (for admission).

Costs (2012–13) *Comprehensive fee:* $36,320 includes full-time tuition ($27,650), mandatory fees ($160), and room and board ($8510). Part-time tuition and fees vary according to course load. *College room only:* $3910. Room and board charges vary according to board plan. *Payment plan:* installment. *Waivers:* employees or children of employees.

Financial Aid Of all full-time matriculated undergraduates who enrolled in 2011, 2,267 applied for aid, 1,891 were judged to have need, 660 had their need fully met. 233 Federal Work-Study jobs (averaging $1421). 448 state and other part-time jobs (averaging $736). In 2011, 771 non-need-based awards were made. *Average percent of need met:* 82%. *Average financial aid package:* $23,081. *Average need-based loan:* $4675. *Average need-based gift aid:* $17,714. *Average non-need-based aid:* $7627. *Average indebtedness upon graduation:* $29,349.

Applying *Options:* electronic application, early admission, deferred entrance. *Application fee:* $50. *Required:* essay or personal statement, high school transcript. *Required for some:* 1 letter of recommendation. *Recommended:* interview. *Application deadlines:* rolling (freshmen), rolling (transfers). *Notification:* continuous (freshmen), continuous (transfers).

Freshman Application Contact Admissions Office, Hope College, 69 East 10th Street, PO Box 9000, Holland, MI 49422-9000. *Phone:* 616-395-7850. *Toll-free phone:* 800-968-7850. *E-mail:* admissions@hope.edu. *Web site:* http://www.hope.edu/.

ITT Technical Institute
Canton, Michigan

- **Proprietary** primarily 2-year, founded 2002, part of ITT Educational Services, Inc.
- **Coed**
- **Minimally difficult** entrance level

Academics *Calendar:* quarters. *Degrees:* associate and bachelor's.

Student Life *Housing:* college housing not available.

Freshman Application Contact Director of Recruitment, ITT Technical Institute, 1905 South Haggerty Road, Canton, MI 48188-2025. *Phone:* 784-397-7800. *Toll-free phone:* 800-247-4477. *Web site:* http://www.itt-tech.edu/.

ITT Technical Institute
Dearborn, Michigan

- **Proprietary** primarily 2-year, part of ITT Educational Services, Inc.
- **Coed**

Academics *Calendar:* quarters. *Degrees:* associate and bachelor's.

Freshman Application Contact Director of Recruitment, ITT Technical Institute, 19855 W. Outer Drive, Suite L10W, Dearborn, MI 48124. *Phone:* 313-278-5208. *Toll-free phone:* 800-605-0801. *Web site:* http://www.itt-tech.edu/.

ITT Technical Institute
Grand Rapids, Michigan

- **Proprietary** 4-year
- **Coed**
- **Minimally difficult** entrance level

Academics *Degrees:* associate and bachelor's.

Freshman Application Contact Director of Recruitment, ITT Technical Institute, 3518 Plainfield Avenue NE, Grand Rapids, MI 49525. *Phone:* 616-365-4800. *Toll-free phone:* 877-264-1715. *Web site:* http://www.itt-tech.edu/.

ITT Technical Institute
Southfield, Michigan

- **Proprietary** 4-year
- **Coed**
- **Minimally difficult** entrance level

Academics *Degrees:* associate and bachelor's.

Freshman Application Contact Director of Recruitment, ITT Technical Institute, 26700 Lahser Road, Suite 100, Southfield, MI 48033. *Phone:* 248-603-6100. *Toll-free phone:* 877-363-3221. *Web site:* http://www.itt-tech.edu/.

ITT Technical Institute
Swartz Creek, Michigan

- **Proprietary** primarily 2-year, founded 2005, part of ITT Educational Services, Inc.
- **Coed**
- **Minimally difficult** entrance level

Academics *Calendar:* quarters. *Degrees:* associate and bachelor's.

Freshman Application Contact Director of Recruitment, ITT Technical Institute, 6359 Miller Road, Swartz Creek, MI 48473. *Phone:* 810-628-2500. *Toll-free phone:* 800-514-6564. *Web site:* http://www.itt-tech.edu/.

ITT Technical Institute
Troy, Michigan

- **Proprietary** primarily 2-year, founded 1987, part of ITT Educational Services, Inc.
- **Coed**
- **Minimally difficult** entrance level

Academics *Calendar:* quarters. *Degrees:* associate and bachelor's.

Student Life *Housing:* college housing not available.

Freshman Application Contact Director of Recruitment, ITT Technical Institute, 1522 East Big Beaver Road, Troy, MI 48083-1905. *Phone:* 248-524-1800. *Toll-free phone:* 800-832-6817. *Fax:* 248-524-1965. *Web site:* http://www.itt-tech.edu/.

ITT Technical Institute
Wyoming, Michigan

- **Proprietary** primarily 2-year, part of ITT Educational Services, Inc.
- **Coed**
- **Minimally difficult** entrance level

Academics *Calendar:* quarters. *Degrees:* associate and bachelor's.

Student Life *Housing:* college housing not available.

Freshman Application Contact Director of Recruitment, ITT Technical Institute, 1980 Metro Court SW, Wyoming, MI 49519. *Phone:* 616-406-1200. *Toll-free phone:* 800-632-4676. *Web site:* http://www.itt-tech.edu/.

Kalamazoo College
Kalamazoo, Michigan

- **Independent** 4-year, founded 1833, affiliated with American Baptist Churches in the U.S.A.
- **Suburban** 60-acre campus with easy access to Grand Rapids
- **Endowment** $155.2 million
- **Coed** 1,403 undergraduate students, 99% full-time, 57% women, 43% men
- **Very difficult** entrance level, 69% of applicants were admitted

Undergraduates 1,387 full-time, 16 part-time. Students come from 36 states and territories; 31 other countries; 35% are from out of state; 4% Black or African American, non-Hispanic/Latino; 7% Hispanic/Latino; 4% Asian, non-Hispanic/Latino; 0.1% Native Hawaiian or other Pacific Islander, non-Hispanic/Latino; 0.6% American Indian or Alaska Native, non-Hispanic/Latino; 3% Two or more races, non-Hispanic/Latino; 7% Race/ethnicity unknown; 8% international; 0.8% transferred in; 70% live on campus. *Retention:* 90% of full-time freshmen returned.

Freshmen *Admission:* 2,225 applied, 1,531 admitted, 369 enrolled. *Average high school GPA:* 3.62. *Test scores:* SAT critical reading scores over 500: 86%; SAT math scores over 500: 86%; SAT writing scores over 500: 84%; ACT scores over 18: 99%; SAT critical reading scores over 600: 60%; SAT math scores over 600: 55%; SAT writing scores over 600: 53%; ACT scores over 24: 88%; SAT critical reading scores over 700: 20%; SAT math scores over 700: 14%; SAT writing scores over 700: 13%; ACT scores over 30: 30%. **Faculty** *Total:* 113, 85% full-time, 88% with terminal degrees. *Student/faculty ratio:* 14:1.

Academics *Calendar:* quarters. *Degree:* bachelor's. *Special study options:* advanced placement credit, double majors, independent study, internships, off-campus study, services for LD students, student-designed majors, study abroad. *ROTC:* Army (c). *Unusual degree programs:* 3-2 engineering with University of Michigan, Washington University in St. Louis.

Computers on Campus 250 computers/terminals are available on campus for general student use. Students can access the following: campus intranet, computer help desk, free student e-mail accounts, online (class) grades, online (class) registration, online (class) schedules, RCC - Residential computer consultant. Campuswide network is available. 100% of college-owned or -operated housing units are wired for high-speed Internet access. Wireless service is available via entire campus.

Student Life *Housing:* on-campus residence required through junior year. *Options:* coed, disabled students. Campus housing is university owned. Freshman campus housing is guaranteed. *Activities and organizations:* drama/theater group, student-run newspaper, radio station, choral group, Student Activities Committee, Student Commission, Frelon Dance Company, Environmental Student Organization, volunteer organization. *Campus security:* 24-hour emergency response devices and patrols, late-night transport/escort service, controlled dormitory access. *Student services:* health clinic, personal/psychological counseling.

Athletics Member NCAA. All Division III. *Intercollegiate sports:* baseball M, basketball M/W, cross-country running M/W, football M, golf M/W, soccer M/W, softball W, swimming and diving M/W, tennis M/W, volleyball W. *Intramural sports:* badminton M/W, basketball M/W, cheerleading W(c), lacrosse W(c), racquetball M/W, soccer M/W, softball M/W, table tennis M/W, tennis M/W, ultimate Frisbee M(c)/W(c), volleyball M/W.

Standardized Tests *Required:* SAT or ACT (for admission).

Costs (2011–12) *One-time required fee:* $100. *Comprehensive fee:* $43,899 includes full-time tuition ($35,508), mandatory fees ($312), and room and board ($8079). *College room only:* $3939. Room and board charges vary according to board plan. *Payment plan:* installment. *Waivers:* employees or children of employees.

Financial Aid Of all full-time matriculated undergraduates who enrolled in 2010, 883 applied for aid, 769 were judged to have need, 260 had their need fully met. In 2010, 543 non-need-based awards were made. *Average percent of need met:* 86%. *Average financial aid package:* $28,848. *Average need-based loan:* $5074. *Average need-based gift aid:* $19,121. *Average non-need-based aid:* $10,092.

Applying *Options:* electronic application, early decision, early action, deferred entrance. *Application fee:* $40. *Required:* essay or personal statement, high school transcript, 2 letters of recommendation, Common Application Supplement. *Recommended:* minimum 3.0 GPA, interview. *Application deadlines:* 2/1 (freshmen), 5/1 (transfers), 11/20 (early action). *Early decision deadline:* 11/10. *Notification:* 4/1 (freshmen), 5/15 (transfers), 11/20 (early decision), 12/20 (early action).

Freshman Application Contact Mrs. Kathy Gustafson, Records Associate, Kalamazoo College, Mandelle Hall, 1200 Academy Street, Kalamazoo, MI 49006-3295. *Phone:* 269-337-5759. *Toll-free phone:* 800-253-3602. *Fax:* 269-337-7390. *E-mail:* admission.records@kzoo.edu. *Web site:* http://www.kzoo.edu/.

Kettering University

Flint, Michigan

- **Independent** comprehensive, founded 1919
- **Urban** 85-acre campus with easy access to Detroit
- **Endowment** $65.9 million
- **Coed, primarily men** 1,745 undergraduate students, 98% full-time, 19% women, 81% men
- **Very difficult** entrance level, 62% of applicants were admitted

Undergraduates 1,706 full-time, 39 part-time. Students come from 44 states and territories; 11 other countries; 29% are from out of state; 4% Black or African American, non-Hispanic/Latino; 3% Hispanic/Latino; 2% Asian, non-Hispanic/Latino; 0.1% Native Hawaiian or other Pacific Islander, non-Hispanic/Latino; 0.3% American Indian or Alaska Native, non-Hispanic/Latino; 1% Two or more races, non-Hispanic/Latino; 8% Race/ethnicity unknown; 3% international; 2% transferred in; 34% live on campus. *Retention:* 89% of full-time freshmen returned.

Freshmen *Admission:* 1,770 applied, 1,098 admitted, 329 enrolled. *Average high school GPA:* 3.43. *Test scores:* SAT critical reading scores over 500: 88%; SAT math scores over 500: 96%; ACT scores over 18: 100%; SAT critical reading scores over 600: 46%; SAT math scores over 600: 76%; ACT scores over 24: 89%; SAT critical reading scores over 700: 6%; SAT math scores over 700: 22%; ACT scores over 30: 22%.

Faculty *Total:* 154, 79% full-time, 77% with terminal degrees. *Student/faculty ratio:* 13:1.

Academics *Calendar:* semesters (11 weeks of full-time study plus 12 weeks of paid co-op experience per semester). *Degrees:* bachelor's and master's. *Special study options:* advanced placement credit, cooperative education, distance

learning, double majors, independent study, internships, services for LD students, study abroad, summer session for credit.

Computers on Campus 450 computers/terminals and 800 ports are available on campus for general student use. Students can access the following: campus intranet, computer help desk, free student e-mail accounts, online (class) grades, online (class) registration, online (class) schedules. Campuswide network is available. 100% of college-owned or -operated housing units are wired for high-speed Internet access. Wireless service is available via classrooms, computer centers, computer labs, learning centers, libraries, student centers.

Student Life *Housing:* on-campus residence required for freshman year. *Options:* coed. Campus housing is university owned and is provided by a third party. Freshman campus housing is guaranteed. *Activities and organizations:* student-run newspaper, radio station, choral group, student government, Society of Automotive Engineers, Firebirds, Outdoors Club, International Club, national fraternities, national sororities. *Campus security:* 24-hour emergency response devices and patrols, late-night transport/escort service, controlled dormitory access, security card access to all campus buildings 24/7 except the campus center main entrance which is secure 11pm-7am.. *Student services:* health clinic, personal/psychological counseling, women's center.

Athletics *Intramural sports:* baseball M(c)/W(c), basketball M/W, bowling M/W, football M/W, golf M(c)/W(c), ice hockey M(c)/W(c), lacrosse M(c)/W(c), racquetball M/W, riflery M(c)/W(c), soccer M/W, softball M/W, squash M/W, table tennis M(c)/W(c), tennis M/W, ultimate Frisbee M(c)/W(c), volleyball M/W, water polo M/W.

Standardized Tests *Required:* SAT or ACT (for admission).

Costs (2012–13) *Comprehensive fee:* $40,606 includes full-time tuition ($33,946) and room and board ($6660). Part-time tuition: $1132 per credit. No tuition increase for student's term of enrollment. *College room only:* $4150. *Payment plan:* installment. *Waivers:* employees or children of employees.

Financial Aid Of all full-time matriculated undergraduates who enrolled in 2010, 1,327 applied for aid, 1,246 were judged to have need, 195 had their need fully met. 1,147 Federal Work-Study jobs (averaging $1165). In 2010, 598 non-need-based awards were made. *Average percent of need met:* 67%. *Average financial aid package:* $19,931. *Average need-based loan:* $4374. *Average need-based gift aid:* $15,347. *Average non-need-based aid:* $12,223. *Average indebtedness upon graduation:* $45,570.

Applying *Options:* electronic application, deferred entrance. *Application fee:* $35. *Required:* high school transcript. *Required for some:* essay or personal statement. *Recommended:* minimum 3.0 GPA, interview. *Application deadlines:* rolling (freshmen), rolling (out-of-state freshmen), rolling (transfers). *Notification:* continuous (freshmen), continuous (out-of-state freshmen), continuous (transfers).

Freshman Application Contact Ms. Karen Full, Director, International and Undergraduate Admissions, Kettering University, 1700 University Avenue, Flint, MI 48504-6214. *Phone:* 810-762-7496. *Toll-free phone:* 800-955-4464 Ext. 7865 (in-state); 800-955-4464 (out-of-state). *Fax:* 810-762-9837. *E-mail:* admissions@kettering.edu. *Web site:* http://www.kettering.edu/.

See page 1392 for the College Close-Up.

Kuyper College
Grand Rapids, Michigan

- **Independent Christian** 4-year, founded 1939
- **Suburban** 34-acre campus with easy access to Grand Rapids
- **Endowment** $7.4 million
- **Coed**
- **Moderately difficult** entrance level

Faculty *Student/faculty ratio:* 14:1.

Academics *Calendar:* semesters. *Degrees:* certificates, associate, bachelor's, and postbachelor's certificates.

Student Life *Campus security:* 24-hour emergency response devices, student patrols, late-night transport/escort service, controlled dormitory access.

Athletics Member NCCAA.

Standardized Tests *Required:* SAT or ACT (for admission).

Costs (2011–12) *Comprehensive fee:* $24,246 includes full-time tuition ($16,976), mandatory fees ($550), and room and board ($6720). Full-time tuition and fees vary according to course load. Part-time tuition: $810 per credit hour. Part-time tuition and fees vary according to course load. *Required fees:* $238 per year part-time. *Room and board:* Room and board charges vary according to board plan, housing facility, and student level.

Financial Aid *Of all full-time matriculated undergraduates who enrolled in 2010,* 284 applied for aid, 284 were judged to have need, 23 had their need fully met. 21 Federal Work-Study jobs (averaging $1192). 81 state and other part-time jobs (averaging $2000). *In 2010,* 27 non-need-based awards were made. *Average percent of need met:* 70. *Average financial aid package:* $10,658. *Average need-based loan:* $6236. *Average need-based gift aid:* $5833. *Average non-need-based aid:* $2708. *Average indebtedness upon graduation:* $18,709.

Applying *Options:* electronic application, deferred entrance. *Application fee:* $30. *Required:* essay or personal statement, high school transcript, minimum 2.5 GPA. *Recommended:* interview.

Freshman Application Contact Admissions Office, Kuyper College, 3333 East Beltline Avenue, NE, Grand Rapids, MI 49525. *Phone:* 616-222-3000 Ext. 632. *Fax:* 616-222-3045. *E-mail:* admissions@kuyper.edu. *Web site:* http://www.kuyper.edu/.

Lake Superior State University
Sault Sainte Marie, Michigan

- **State-supported** comprehensive, founded 1946
- **Small-town** 115-acre campus
- **Endowment** $8.2 million
- **Coed** 2,728 undergraduate students, 82% full-time, 51% women, 49% men
- **Moderately difficult** entrance level, 91% of applicants were admitted

Undergraduates 2,244 full-time, 484 part-time. Students come from 36 states and territories; 15 other countries; 8% are from out of state; 1% Black or African American, non-Hispanic/Latino; 2% Hispanic/Latino; 0.6% Asian, non-Hispanic/Latino; 8% American Indian or Alaska Native, non-Hispanic/Latino; 2% Race/ethnicity unknown; 8% international; 11% transferred in; 34% live on campus. *Retention:* 70% of full-time freshmen returned.

Freshmen *Admission:* 1,613 applied, 1,471 admitted, 499 enrolled. *Average high school GPA:* 3.22. *Test scores:* ACT scores over 18: 91%; ACT scores over 24: 34%; ACT scores over 30: 4%.

Faculty *Total:* 184, 63% full-time, 38% with terminal degrees. *Student/faculty ratio:* 17:1.

Academics *Calendar:* semesters. *Degrees:* certificates, associate, bachelor's, master's, and postbachelor's certificates. *Special study options:* advanced placement credit, cooperative education, distance learning, double majors, freshman honors college, honors programs, independent study, internships, off-campus study, part-time degree program, services for LD students, student-designed majors, study abroad, summer session for credit.

Computers on Campus 350 computers/terminals are available on campus for general student use. Students can access the following: campus intranet, computer help desk, free student e-mail accounts, online (class) grades, online (class) registration, online (class) schedules. Campuswide network is available. 100% of college-owned or -operated housing units are wired for high-speed Internet access. Wireless service is available via entire campus.

Student Life *Housing:* on-campus residence required through sophomore year. *Options:* coed, men-only, women-only. Campus housing is university owned. Freshman campus housing is guaranteed. *Activities and organizations:* drama/theater group, student-run newspaper, radio station, choral group, Students in Free Enterprise (SIFE), SAILS - Student Alumni Involved in Lake State, Fisheries and Wildlife, Harry Potter Club, Dance Company, national fraternities, national sororities. *Campus security:* 24-hour emergency response devices and patrols, student patrols, late-night transport/escort service. *Student services:* health clinic, personal/psychological counseling.

Athletics Member NCAA. All Division II except ice hockey (Division I). *Intercollegiate sports:* basketball M(s)/W(s), cross-country running M(s)/W(s), golf M(s)/W(s), ice hockey M(s), softball W(s), tennis M(s)/W(s), track and field M(s)/W(s), volleyball W(s). *Intramural sports:* basketball M/W, football M/W, ice hockey M, racquetball M/W, riflery M/W, soccer M/W, swimming and diving M/W, tennis M/W, volleyball M/W, water polo M/W, wrestling M(c).

Standardized Tests *Required:* SAT or ACT (for admission).

Costs (2011–12) *One-time required fee:* $125. *Tuition:* state resident $9264 full-time, $386 per credit hour part-time; nonresident $13,896 full-time, $579 per credit hour part-time. Full-time tuition and fees vary according to program and reciprocity agreements. Part-time tuition and fees vary according to course load, location, program, and reciprocity agreements. *Required fees:* $175 full-time. *Room and board:* $8319. Room and board charges vary according to board plan and housing facility. *Payment plans:* installment, deferred payment. *Waivers:* minority students, children of alumni, senior citizens, and employees or children of employees.

Financial Aid Of all full-time matriculated undergraduates who enrolled in 2010, 1,858 applied for aid, 1,638 were judged to have need, 251 had their need fully met. In 2010, 244 non-need-based awards were made. *Average percent of need met:* 63%. *Average financial aid package:* $9385. *Average need-based loan:* $4285. *Average need-based gift aid:* $6119. *Average non-need-based aid:* $3695. *Average indebtedness upon graduation:* $28,275.

Applying *Options:* electronic application, deferred entrance. *Application fee:* $35. *Required:* high school transcript. *Required for some:* SAT or ACT for students out of high school for less than 26 months or have less than 19 transferable credits. *Application deadlines:* rolling (freshmen), rolling (transfers). *Notification:* continuous (freshmen), continuous (transfers).

Freshman Application Contact Lake Superior State University, 650 West Easterday Avenue, Sault Sainte Marie, MI 49783. *Phone:* 906-635-2231. *Toll-free phone:* 888-800-LSSU Ext. 2231. *Web site:* http://www.lssu.edu/.

Lawrence Technological University
Southfield, Michigan

- **Independent** university, founded 1932
- **Suburban** 102-acre campus with easy access to Detroit
- **Endowment** $41.2 million
- **Coed** 3,056 undergraduate students, 48% full-time, 24% women, 76% men
- **Moderately difficult** entrance level, 51% of applicants were admitted

Undergraduates 1,455 full-time, 1,601 part-time. Students come from 23 states and territories; 26 other countries; 2% are from out of state; 8% Black or African American, non-Hispanic/Latino; 2% Hispanic/Latino; 28% Asian, non-Hispanic/Latino; 0.1% Native Hawaiian or other Pacific Islander, non-Hispanic/Latino; 0.3% American Indian or Alaska Native, non-Hispanic/Latino; 11% Race/ethnicity unknown; 3% international; 7% transferred in; 15% live on campus. *Retention:* 77% of full-time freshmen returned.

Freshmen *Admission:* 1,713 applied, 874 admitted, 269 enrolled. *Average high school GPA:* 3.34. *Test scores:* ACT scores over 18: 90%; ACT scores over 24: 61%; ACT scores over 30: 12%.

Faculty *Total:* 423, 27% full-time, 45% with terminal degrees. *Student/faculty ratio:* 11:1.

Academics *Calendar:* semesters. *Degrees:* certificates, associate, bachelor's, master's, doctoral, postbachelor's, and first professional certificates. *Special study options:* academic remediation for entering students, accelerated degree program, adult/continuing education programs, advanced placement credit, cooperative education, distance learning, double majors, English as a second language, honors programs, independent study, internships, off-campus study, part-time degree program, services for LD students, study abroad, summer session for credit. *ROTC:* Air Force (c).

Computers on Campus 120 computers/terminals and 3,146 ports are available on campus for general student use. Students can access the following: campus intranet, computer help desk, free student e-mail accounts, online (class) grades, online (class) registration, online (class) schedules, degree audit, Blackboard, SCT Banner (student information), Personal websites, Document collection. Campuswide network is available. 50% of college-owned or -operated housing units are wired for high-speed Internet access. Wireless service is available via entire campus.

Student Life *Housing options:* coed, disabled students. Campus housing is university owned. Freshman applicants given priority for college housing. *Activities and organizations:* drama/theater group, student-run newspaper, American Institute of Architecture Students, American Society of Mechanical Engineers, Institute of Electric and Electronic Engineers, American Society of Civil Engineers, student government, national fraternities, national sororities. *Campus security:* 24-hour emergency response devices and patrols, late-night transport/escort service, controlled dormitory access. *Student services:* personal/psychological counseling.

Athletics Member NAIA. *Intramural sports:* badminton M/W, basketball M/W, bowling M(c)/W(c), football M, golf M/W, ice hockey M(c), racquetball M/W, skiing (cross-country) M/W, skiing (downhill) M/W, soccer M(c)/W, softball M/W, table tennis M/W, tennis M/W, volleyball W(c), wrestling M.

Standardized Tests *Required:* ACT (preferred) (for admission).

Costs (2011–12) *Comprehensive fee:* $34,584 includes full-time tuition ($25,758), mandatory fees ($520), and room and board ($8306). Full-time tuition and fees vary according to course level, degree level, location, program, and student level. Part-time tuition: $859 per credit hour. Part-time tuition and fees vary according to course level, degree level, location, program, and student level. *Required fees:* $285 per term part-time. *College room only:* $4959. Room and board charges vary according to board plan and housing facility. *Payment plan:* installment. *Waivers:* employees or children of employees.

Financial Aid Of all full-time matriculated undergraduates who enrolled in 2010, 1,282 applied for aid, 1,020 were judged to have need, 97 had their need fully met. 47 Federal Work-Study jobs (averaging $2471). In 2010, 195 non-need-based awards were made. *Average percent of need met:* 66%. *Average financial aid package:* $21,548. *Average need-based loan:* $8244. *Average need-based gift aid:* $12,400. *Average non-need-based aid:* $9979. *Average indebtedness upon graduation:* $46,677.

Applying *Options:* electronic application, early admission, deferred entrance. *Application fee:* $30. *Required:* high school transcript, minimum 2.5 GPA. *Required for some:* essay or personal statement, minimum 2.8 GPA, 1 letter of recommendation, interview. *Application deadlines:* 8/15 (freshmen), 8/15 (transfers). *Notification:* continuous until 8/26 (freshmen), 8/26 (transfers).

Freshman Application Contact Jane Rohrback, Director of Admissions, Lawrence Technological University, 21000 West Ten Mile Road, Southfield,

MI 48075. *Phone:* 248-204-3160. *Toll-free phone:* 800-225-5588. *Fax:* 248-204-2228. *E-mail:* admissions@ltu.edu. *Web site:* http://www.ltu.edu/.

See page 1400 for the College Close-Up.

Madonna University
Livonia, Michigan

- **Independent Roman Catholic** comprehensive, founded 1947
- **Suburban** 49-acre campus with easy access to Detroit
- **Endowment** $29.0 million
- **Coed** 3,171 undergraduate students, 51% full-time, 73% women, 27% men
- **Moderately difficult** entrance level, 65% of applicants were admitted

Undergraduates 1,632 full-time, 1,539 part-time. Students come from 8 states and territories; 23 other countries; 2% are from out of state; 15% Black or African American, non-Hispanic/Latino; 3% Hispanic/Latino; 1% Asian, non-Hispanic/Latino; 0.2% Native Hawaiian or other Pacific Islander, non-Hispanic/Latino; 0.5% American Indian or Alaska Native, non-Hispanic/Latino; 1% Two or more races, non-Hispanic/Latino; 0.5% Race/ethnicity unknown; 4% international; 18% transferred in; 6% live on campus. *Retention:* 82% of full-time freshmen returned.

Freshmen *Admission:* 834 applied, 544 admitted, 183 enrolled. *Average high school GPA:* 3.3. *Test scores:* SAT critical reading scores over 500: 50%; SAT math scores over 500: 75%; SAT writing scores over 500: 75%; ACT scores over 18: 95%; SAT critical reading scores over 600: 50%; SAT math scores over 600: 25%; SAT writing scores over 600: 50%; ACT scores over 24: 38%; SAT critical reading scores over 700: 25%; SAT writing scores over 700: 25%; ACT scores over 30: 2%.

Faculty *Total:* 420, 30% full-time, 97% with terminal degrees. *Student/faculty ratio:* 10:1.

Academics *Calendar:* semesters. *Degrees:* certificates, diplomas, associate, bachelor's, master's, doctoral, post-master's, and postbachelor's certificates. *Special study options:* academic remediation for entering students, accelerated degree program, adult/continuing education programs, advanced placement credit, cooperative education, distance learning, double majors, English as a second language, independent study, internships, off-campus study, part-time degree program, services for LD students, student-designed majors, study abroad, summer session for credit. *ROTC:* Army (c).

Computers on Campus 199 computers/terminals and 199 ports are available on campus for general student use. Students can access the following: computer help desk, free student e-mail accounts, online (class) grades, online (class) registration, online (class) schedules, online payments, online statements, online Unofficial Transcripts. Campuswide network is available. 100% of college-owned or -operated housing units are wired for high-speed Internet access. Wireless service is available via classrooms, computer labs, dorm rooms, learning centers, libraries, student centers.

Student Life *Housing options:* men-only, women-only. Campus housing is university owned. Freshman campus housing is guaranteed. *Activities and organizations:* drama/theater group, student-run newspaper, radio station, choral group, Campus Ministry, Red Cross Club, Madonna University Nursing Student Association, Broadcast & Film Club, Society of Future Teachers. *Campus security:* 24-hour emergency response devices and patrols, late-night transport/escort service, controlled dormitory access. *Student services:* personal/psychological counseling.

Athletics Member NAIA. *Intercollegiate sports:* baseball M(s), basketball M(s)/W(s), cross-country running M(s)/W(s), golf M(s)/W(s), soccer M(s)/W(s), softball W(s), volleyball W(s). *Intramural sports:* basketball M/W, volleyball M/W.

Standardized Tests *Required:* SAT or ACT (for admission).

Costs (2011–12) *Comprehensive fee:* $22,130 includes full-time tuition ($14,580), mandatory fees ($120), and room and board ($7430). Full-time tuition and fees vary according to course load. Part-time tuition: $486 per credit hour. Part-time tuition and fees vary according to course load. *Required fees:* $60 per term part-time. *College room only:* $3392. Room and board charges vary according to board plan. *Payment plan:* deferred payment. *Waivers:* senior citizens and employees or children of employees.

Financial Aid Of all full-time matriculated undergraduates who enrolled in 2007, 862 applied for aid, 698 were judged to have need, 122 had their need fully met. In 2007, 172 non-need-based awards were made. *Average percent of need met:* 56%. *Average financial aid package:* $7396. *Average need-based loan:* $3862. *Average need-based gift aid:* $4508. *Average non-need-based aid:* $2427.

Applying *Options:* electronic application, deferred entrance. *Application fee:* $25. *Required:* essay or personal statement, high school transcript, minimum 2.8 GPA. *Required for some:* 2 letters of recommendation. *Recommended:* interview. *Application deadlines:* rolling (freshmen), rolling (transfers). *Notification:* continuous (freshmen), continuous (transfers).

Freshman Application Contact Mr. Mike Quattro, Director of Enrollment Management, Madonna University, 36600 Schoolcraft Road, Livonia, MI 48150-1173. *Phone:* 734-432-5341. *Toll-free phone:* 800-852-4951. *Fax:* 734-432-5424. *E-mail:* admissions@madonna.edu. *Web site:* http://www.madonna.edu/.

Marygrove College
Detroit, Michigan

Freshman Application Contact Mr. John Ambrose, Director of Undergraduate Admissions, Marygrove College, Admissions Office, Detroit, MI 48221-2599. *Phone:* 313-927-1236. *Toll-free phone:* 866-313-1297. *Fax:* 313-927-1345. *E-mail:* info@marygrove.edu. *Web site:* http://www.marygrove.edu/.

Michigan Jewish Institute
Oak Park, Michigan

Freshman Application Contact Mr. Dov Stein, Michigan Jewish Institute, 25401 Coolidge Highway, Oak Park, MI 48237. *Phone:* 248-414-6900 Ext. 103. *Toll-free phone:* 888-INFO-MJI. *Fax:* 248-414-6907. *E-mail:* dstein@mji.edu. *Web site:* http://www.mji.edu/.

Michigan State University
East Lansing, Michigan

- **State-supported** university, founded 1855
- **Suburban** 5192-acre campus with easy access to Detroit
- **Endowment** $1.4 billion
- **Coed** 36,675 undergraduate students, 91% full-time, 51% women, 49% men
- **Moderately difficult** entrance level, 73% of applicants were admitted

Undergraduates 33,412 full-time, 3,263 part-time. Students come from 55 states and territories; 96 other countries; 9% are from out of state; 7% Black or African American, non-Hispanic/Latino; 3% Hispanic/Latino; 4% Asian, non-Hispanic/Latino; 0.1% Native Hawaiian or other Pacific Islander, non-Hispanic/Latino; 0.4% American Indian or Alaska Native, non-Hispanic/Latino; 2% Two or more races, non-Hispanic/Latino; 1% Race/ethnicity unknown; 10% international; 4% transferred in; 42% live on campus. *Retention:* 91% of full-time freshmen returned.

Freshmen *Admission:* 28,416 applied, 20,728 admitted, 7,984 enrolled. *Average high school GPA:* 3.61. *Test scores:* SAT critical reading scores over 500: 57%; SAT math scores over 500: 86%; SAT writing scores over 500: 60%; ACT scores over 18: 98%; SAT critical reading scores over 600: 26%; SAT math scores over 600: 55%; SAT writing scores over 600: 25%; ACT scores over 24: 72%; SAT critical reading scores over 700: 8%; SAT math scores over 700: 17%; SAT writing scores over 700: 5%; ACT scores over 30: 13%.

Faculty *Total:* 2,937, 86% full-time, 89% with terminal degrees. *Student/faculty ratio:* 16:1.

Academics *Calendar:* semesters. *Degrees:* certificates, bachelor's, master's, doctoral, post-master's, and first professional certificates. *Special study options:* academic remediation for entering students, accelerated degree program, adult/continuing education programs, advanced placement credit, cooperative education, distance learning, double majors, English as a second language, freshman honors college, honors programs, independent study, internships, off-campus study, part-time degree program, services for LD students, student-designed majors, study abroad, summer session for credit. *ROTC:* Army (b), Air Force (b). *Unusual degree programs:* 3-2 engineering.

Computers on Campus 2,100 computers/terminals are available on campus for general student use. Students can access the following: campus intranet, computer help desk, free student e-mail accounts, online (class) grades, online (class) registration, online (class) schedules. Campuswide network is available. 100% of college-owned or -operated housing units are wired for high-speed Internet access. Wireless service is available via classrooms, computer centers, computer labs, dorm rooms, learning centers, libraries, student centers.

Student Life *Housing:* on-campus residence required for freshman year. *Options:* coed, women-only, cooperative, disabled students. Campus housing is university owned. Freshman campus housing is guaranteed. *Activities and organizations:* drama/theater group, student-run newspaper, radio and television station, choral group, marching band, national fraternities, national sororities. *Campus security:* 24-hour emergency response devices and patrols, late-night transport/escort service, controlled dormitory access, self-defense workshops. *Student services:* health clinic, personal/psychological counseling, women's center, legal services.

Athletics Member NCAA. All Division I except football (Division I-A). *Intercollegiate sports:* archery M(c)/W(c), baseball M(s), basketball M(s)/W(s), cheerleading M/W, crew M(c)/W(s), cross-country running M(s)/W(s), equestrian sports M(c)/W(c), fencing M(c)/W(c), field hockey W(s), golf M(s)/

W(s), gymnastics W(s), ice hockey M(s)/W(c), lacrosse M(c)/W(c), riflery M(c)/W(c), rugby M(c)/W(c), sailing M(c)/W(c), skiing (cross-country) M(c)/W(c), skiing (downhill) M(c)/W(c), soccer M(s)/W(s), softball W(s), swimming and diving M(s)/W(s), table tennis M/W, tennis M(s)/W(s), track and field M(s)/W(s), volleyball M(c)/W(s), water polo M(c)/W(c), wrestling M(s). *Intramural sports:* archery M/W, badminton M/W, baseball M, basketball M/W, bowling M/W, cheerleading W(c), cross-country running M/W, fencing M/W, field hockey W, football M/W, golf M/W, ice hockey M/W, lacrosse M/W, racquetball M/W, riflery M/W, rugby M/W, sailing M/W, skiing (cross-country) M/W, skiing (downhill) M/W, soccer M/W, softball M/W, squash M/W, swimming and diving M/W, table tennis M(c)/W(c), tennis M/W, track and field M/W, ultimate Frisbee M(c)/W(c), volleyball M/W, water polo M/W, weight lifting M/W, wrestling M.

Standardized Tests *Required:* SAT or ACT (for admission). *Recommended:* SAT and SAT Subject Tests or ACT (for admission).

Costs (2011–12) *Tuition:* state resident $12,203 full-time, $407 per credit hour part-time; nonresident $31,148 full-time, $1038 per credit hour part-time. Full-time tuition and fees vary according to course load, program, and student level. Part-time tuition and fees vary according to course load, program, and student level. *Room and board:* $8154; room only: $3368. Room and board charges vary according to board plan and housing facility. *Payment plan:* deferred payment. *Waivers:* employees or children of employees.

Financial Aid Of all full-time matriculated undergraduates who enrolled in 2011, 21,625 applied for aid, 17,038 were judged to have need, 2,543 had their need fully met. 1,120 Federal Work-Study jobs (averaging $1650). In 2011, 1364 non-need-based awards were made. *Average percent of need met:* 62%. *Average financial aid package:* $11,322. *Average need-based loan:* $4299. *Average need-based gift aid:* $8621. *Average non-need-based aid:* $7821. *Average indebtedness upon graduation:* $23,725.

Applying *Options:* electronic application, early action. *Application fee:* $50. *Required:* essay or personal statement, high school transcript. *Application deadlines:* rolling (freshmen), rolling (out-of-state freshmen), rolling (transfers). *Notification:* continuous (freshmen), continuous (out-of-state freshmen), continuous (transfers).

Freshman Application Contact James Cotter, Director of Admissions, Michigan State University, 250 Administration Building, East Lansing, MI 48824. *Phone:* 517-355-8332. *Fax:* 517-353-1647. *E-mail:* admis@msu.edu. *Web site:* http://www.msu.edu/.

Michigan Technological University
Houghton, Michigan

- **State-supported** university, founded 1885
- **Small-town** 925-acre campus
- **Coed** 5,731 undergraduate students, 93% full-time, 25% women, 75% men
- **Moderately difficult** entrance level, 75% of applicants were admitted

Undergraduates 5,318 full-time, 413 part-time. 22% are from out of state; 1% Black or African American, non-Hispanic/Latino; 2% Hispanic/Latino; 0.9% Asian, non-Hispanic/Latino; 0.1% Native Hawaiian or other Pacific Islander, non-Hispanic/Latino; 0.7% American Indian or Alaska Native, non-Hispanic/Latino; 1% Two or more races, non-Hispanic/Latino; 3% Race/ethnicity unknown; 7% international; 4% transferred in; 45% live on campus. *Retention:* 83% of full-time freshmen returned.

Freshmen *Admission:* 4,573 applied, 3,441 admitted, 1,161 enrolled. *Average high school GPA:* 3.62. *Test scores:* SAT critical reading scores over 500: 90%; SAT math scores over 500: 91%; SAT writing scores over 500: 82%; ACT scores over 18: 100%; SAT critical reading scores over 600: 59%; SAT math scores over 600: 72%; SAT writing scores over 600: 41%; ACT scores over 24: 77%; SAT critical reading scores over 700: 12%; SAT math scores over 700: 25%; SAT writing scores over 700: 3%; ACT scores over 30: 21%.

Faculty *Total:* 469, 87% full-time, 81% with terminal degrees. *Student/faculty ratio:* 13:1.

Academics *Calendar:* semesters. *Degrees:* certificates, associate, bachelor's, master's, doctoral, postbachelor's, and first professional certificates. *Special study options:* advanced placement credit, cooperative education, distance learning, double majors, English as a second language, honors programs, independent study, internships, off-campus study, part-time degree program, services for LD students, study abroad, summer session for credit. *ROTC:* Army (b), Air Force (b). *Unusual degree programs:* 3-2 engineering; forestry.

Computers on Campus Students can access the following: online (class) registration. Campuswide network is available.

Student Life *Housing:* on-campus residence required for freshman year. *Options:* coed, disabled students. Campus housing is university owned. Freshman campus housing is guaranteed. *Activities and organizations:* drama/theater group, student-run newspaper, radio station, choral group, national fraternities, national sororities. *Campus security:* 24-hour emergency response devices and patrols, late-night transport/escort service, controlled dormitory access. *Student services:* health clinic, personal/psychological counseling.

Athletics Member NCAA. All Division II except ice hockey (Division I). *Intercollegiate sports:* basketball M(s)/W(s), cross-country running M/W, fencing M(c)/W(c), football M(s), ice hockey M(s)/W(c), racquetball M(c)/W(c), riflery M(c)/W(c), skiing (cross-country) M/W, skiing (downhill) M(c)/W(c), soccer M(c)/W(c), squash M(c)/W(c), swimming and diving M(c)/W(c), table tennis M(c)/W(c), tennis M/W(s), track and field M/W, volleyball W(s), water polo M(c)/W(c). *Intramural sports:* badminton M/W, basketball M/W, bowling M/W, cross-country running M/W, football M/W, golf M/W, ice hockey M/W, racquetball M/W, riflery M/W, skiing (cross-country) M(c)/W(c), soccer M/W, softball M/W, squash M/W, swimming and diving M/W, table tennis M/W, tennis M/W, track and field M(c)/W(c), volleyball M/W(c), water polo M/W, weight lifting M/W, wrestling M.

Standardized Tests *Required:* SAT or ACT (for admission).

Costs (2011–12) *Tuition:* state resident $12,615 full-time, $421 per credit hour part-time; nonresident $25,710 full-time, $857 per credit hour part-time. Full-time tuition and fees vary according to course load and program. Part-time tuition and fees vary according to course load and program. *Required fees:* $238 full-time, $119 per term part-time. *Room and board:* $8648; room only: $4618. Room and board charges vary according to board plan and housing facility. *Payment plans:* installment, deferred payment. *Waivers:* children of alumni, senior citizens, and employees or children of employees.

Financial Aid Of all full-time matriculated undergraduates who enrolled in 2011, 4,121 applied for aid, 3,447 were judged to have need, 537 had their need fully met. In 2011, 1138 non-need-based awards were made. *Average percent of need met:* 70%. *Average financial aid package:* $11,903. *Average need-based loan:* $4554. *Average need-based gift aid:* $5675. *Average non-need-based aid:* $4931. *Average indebtedness upon graduation:* $33,141.

Applying *Options:* electronic application, deferred entrance. *Required:* high school transcript. *Recommended:* minimum 2.8 GPA, interview. *Application deadlines:* rolling (freshmen), rolling (transfers). *Notification:* continuous (freshmen), continuous (transfers).

Freshman Application Contact Ms. Allison Carter, Director of Admissions, Michigan Technological University, 1400 Townsend Drive, Houghton, MI 49931-1295. *Phone:* 906-487-1888. *Toll-free phone:* 888-MTU-1885. *Fax:* 906-487-2125. *E-mail:* mtu4u@mtu.edu. *Web site:* http://www.mtu.edu/.

See page 1448 for the College Close-Up.

Northern Michigan University
Marquette, Michigan

- **State-supported** comprehensive, founded 1899
- **Small-town** 300-acre campus
- **Coed** 8,615 undergraduate students, 91% full-time, 54% women, 46% men
- **Minimally difficult** entrance level, 72% of applicants were admitted

Undergraduates 7,827 full-time, 788 part-time. 19% are from out of state; 2% Black or African American, non-Hispanic/Latino; 0.5% Hispanic/Latino; 0.6% Asian, non-Hispanic/Latino; 0.1% Native Hawaiian or other Pacific Islander, non-Hispanic/Latino; 2% American Indian or Alaska Native, non-Hispanic/Latino; 2% Two or more races, non-Hispanic/Latino; 4% Race/ethnicity unknown; 0.1% international; 7% transferred in; 38% live on campus. *Retention:* 73% of full-time freshmen returned.

Freshmen *Admission:* 6,298 applied, 4,546 admitted, 1,331 enrolled. *Average high school GPA:* 3.14. *Test scores:* ACT scores over 18: 87%; ACT scores over 24: 34%; ACT scores over 30: 4%.

Faculty *Total:* 496, 63% full-time, 50% with terminal degrees. *Student/faculty ratio:* 21:1.

Academics *Calendar:* semesters. *Degrees:* certificates, diplomas, associate, bachelor's, master's, post-master's, and postbachelor's certificates. *Special study options:* adult/continuing education programs, part-time degree program. ROTC: Army (b).

Computers on Campus Students can access the following: campus intranet, computer help desk, free student e-mail accounts, online (class) grades, online (class) registration, online (class) schedules. Campuswide network is available. 100% of college-owned or -operated housing units are wired for high-speed Internet access. Wireless service is available via entire campus.

Student Life *Housing:* on-campus residence required through sophomore year. *Options:* coed, disabled students. Campus housing is university owned. Freshman campus housing is guaranteed. *Campus security:* 24-hour emergency response devices and patrols, student patrols, late-night transport/escort service.

Athletics Member NCAA. All Division II except ice hockey (Division I). *Intercollegiate sports:* crew M(c)/W(c), cross-country running W(s), football M(s), golf M(s), ice hockey M(s)/W(c), lacrosse M(c), rugby M(c)/W(c), skiing (cross-country) M(s)/W(s), skiing (downhill) M(c)/W(c), soccer M(c)/W(s), track and field M(c)/W(s), ultimate Frisbee M/W, volleyball W(s). *Intramural sports:* badminton M/W, basketball M/W, cheerleading M/W, foot-

ball M/W, ice hockey M/W, racquetball M/W, soccer M/W, softball M/W, table tennis M/W, ultimate Frisbee M/W, volleyball M/W, water polo M/W.

Standardized Tests *Required:* SAT or ACT (for admission).

Costs (2011–12) *One-time required fee:* $225. *Tuition:* state resident $7776 full-time, $324 per credit hour part-time; nonresident $12,504 full-time, $521 per credit hour part-time. Full-time tuition and fees vary according to program. Part-time tuition and fees vary according to program. *Required fees:* $638 full-time, $32 per term part-time. *Room and board:* $8174; room only: $4110. Room and board charges vary according to board plan and housing facility. *Payment plans:* installment, deferred payment. *Waivers:* senior citizens and employees or children of employees.

Financial Aid Of all full-time matriculated undergraduates who enrolled in 2010, 7,071 applied for aid, 4,977 were judged to have need, 608 had their need fully met. In 2010, 336 non-need-based awards were made. *Average percent of need met:* 63%. *Average financial aid package:* $9155. *Average need-based loan:* $3998. *Average need-based gift aid:* $4944. *Average non-need-based aid:* $2748. *Average indebtedness upon graduation:* $29,343.

Applying *Options:* electronic application, deferred entrance. *Application fee:* $30. *Required:* high school transcript. *Required for some:* minimum 2.3 GPA. *Application deadlines:* rolling (freshmen), rolling (transfers). *Notification:* continuous (freshmen), continuous (transfers).

Freshman Application Contact Ms. Gerri Daniels, Director of Admissions, Northern Michigan University, 1401 Presque Isle Avenue, Marquette, MI 49855. *Phone:* 906-227-2650. *Toll-free phone:* 800-682-9797. *Fax:* 906-227-1747. *E-mail:* admiss@nmu.edu. *Web site:* http://www.nmu.edu/.

Northwood University, Michigan Campus
Midland, Michigan

- **Independent** comprehensive, founded 1959
- **Small-town** 434-acre campus
- **Endowment** $31.1 million
- **Coed** 1,630 undergraduate students, 96% full-time, 38% women, 62% men
- **Moderately difficult** entrance level, 68% of applicants were admitted

Undergraduates 1,561 full-time, 69 part-time. Students come from 21 states and territories; 24 other countries; 11% are from out of state; 10% Black or African American, non-Hispanic/Latino; 2% Hispanic/Latino; 0.5% Asian, non-Hispanic/Latino; 1% Race/ethnicity unknown; 11% international; 13% transferred in; 36% live on campus. *Retention:* 78% of full-time freshmen returned.

Freshmen *Admission:* 1,466 applied, 998 admitted, 321 enrolled. *Average high school GPA:* 3.25. *Test scores:* SAT math scores over 500: 47%; ACT scores over 18: 87%; SAT math scores over 600: 20%; ACT scores over 24: 22%; SAT writing scores over 700: 15%; ACT scores over 30: 1%.

Faculty *Total:* 131, 39% full-time, 25% with terminal degrees. *Student/faculty ratio:* 23:1.

Academics *Calendar:* quarters. *Degrees:* associate, bachelor's, and master's. *Special study options:* academic remediation for entering students, accelerated degree program, adult/continuing education programs, advanced placement credit, cooperative education, distance learning, double majors, English as a second language, external degree program, honors programs, independent study, internships, off-campus study, part-time degree program, services for LD students, study abroad, summer session for credit.

Computers on Campus 215 computers/terminals are available on campus for general student use. Students can access the following: campus intranet, computer help desk, free student e-mail accounts, online (class) grades, online (class) registration, online (class) schedules. Campuswide network is available. 100% of college-owned or -operated housing units are wired for high-speed Internet access. Wireless service is available via entire campus.

Student Life *Housing:* on-campus residence required for freshman year. *Options:* men-only, women-only. Campus housing is university owned. Freshman campus housing is guaranteed. *Activities and organizations:* drama/theater group, student-run newspaper, choral group, Student Senate, intramural sports/club sports, campus art, Northwood University International Auto Show (NUTAS), national fraternities, national sororities. *Campus security:* 24-hour emergency response devices and patrols, late-night transport/escort service, controlled dormitory access. *Student services:* health clinic, personal/psychological counseling.

Athletics Member NCAA. All Division II. *Intercollegiate sports:* baseball M(s), basketball M(s)/W(s), cheerleading M(s)/W(s), cross-country running M(s)/W(s), football M(s)/W(s), golf M(s)/W(s), soccer M(s)/W(s), softball W(s), tennis M(s)/W(s), track and field M(s)/W(s), volleyball W(s). *Intramural sports:* badminton M/W, baseball M(c), basketball M/W, football M, ice hockey M(c), lacrosse M(c), soccer M(c)/W, softball M/W, table tennis M/W, tennis M/W, ultimate Frisbee M/W, volleyball M/W.

Standardized Tests *Required:* SAT or ACT (for admission).

Costs (2012–13) *Comprehensive fee:* $29,766 includes full-time tuition ($20,040), mandatory fees ($956), and room and board ($8770). Part-time tuition: $776 per credit hour. *College room only:* $4570. Room and board charges vary according to board plan. *Waivers:* employees or children of employees.

Financial Aid Of all full-time matriculated undergraduates who enrolled in 2010, 1,204 applied for aid, 1,075 were judged to have need, 220 had their need fully met. In 2010, 239 non-need-based awards were made. *Average percent of need met:* 60%. *Average financial aid package:* $17,072. *Average need-based loan:* $4333. *Average need-based gift aid:* $5414. *Average non-need-based aid:* $7058. *Average indebtedness upon graduation:* $31,590.

Applying *Options:* electronic application, early admission, deferred entrance. *Application fee:* $25. *Required:* essay or personal statement, high school transcript. *Recommended:* 1 letter of recommendation, interview. *Application deadlines:* rolling (freshmen), rolling (transfers). *Notification:* continuous (freshmen), continuous (transfers).

Freshman Application Contact Mr. Greg Stiffler, Director of Admission, Northwood University, Michigan Campus, 4000 Whiting Drive, Midland, MI 48640. *Phone:* 989-837-4273. *Toll-free phone:* 800-457-7878. *Fax:* 989-837-4490. *E-mail:* miadmit@northwood.edu. *Web site:* http://www.northwood.edu/.

Oakland University
Rochester, Michigan

- **State-supported** university, founded 1957
- **Suburban** 1444-acre campus with easy access to Detroit
- **Endowment** $50.9 million
- **Coed** 15,838 undergraduate students, 74% full-time, 60% women, 40% men
- **Moderately difficult** entrance level, 68% of applicants were admitted

Undergraduates 11,673 full-time, 4,165 part-time. Students come from 37 states and territories; 44 other countries; 1% are from out of state; 9% Black or African American, non-Hispanic/Latino; 2% Hispanic/Latino; 4% Asian, non-Hispanic/Latino; 0.1% Native Hawaiian or other Pacific Islander, non-Hispanic/Latino; 0.3% American Indian or Alaska Native, non-Hispanic/Latino; 1% Two or more races, non-Hispanic/Latino; 6% Race/ethnicity unknown; 0.9% international; 12% transferred in; 15% live on campus. *Retention:* 73% of full-time freshmen returned.

Freshmen *Admission:* 10,272 applied, 6,941 admitted, 2,361 enrolled. *Average high school GPA:* 3.26. *Test scores:* ACT scores over 18: 90%; ACT scores over 24: 37%; ACT scores over 30: 6%.

Faculty *Total:* 1,085, 49% full-time, 57% with terminal degrees. *Student/faculty ratio:* 21:1.

Academics *Calendar:* semesters. *Degrees:* bachelor's, master's, doctoral, post-master's, postbachelor's, and first professional certificates. *Special study options:* academic remediation for entering students, accelerated degree program, advanced placement credit, cooperative education, distance learning, double majors, English as a second language, honors programs, independent study, internships, off-campus study, part-time degree program, services for LD students, student-designed majors, study abroad, summer session for credit. *ROTC:* Air Force (c).

Computers on Campus Students can access the following: computer help desk, free student e-mail accounts, online (class) grades, online (class) registration, online (class) schedules. Campuswide network is available. 100% of college-owned or -operated housing units are wired for high-speed Internet access. Wireless service is available via entire campus.

Student Life *Housing options:* coed, cooperative, disabled students. Campus housing is university owned. Freshman applicants given priority for college housing. *Activities and organizations:* drama/theater group, student-run newspaper, radio and television station, choral group, American Marketing Association (AMA), International Allies Organization, Psi Chi - Psychology Student Association, Student Michigan Education Association (SMEA), Student Nurses Association of Oakland University (SNAOU), national fraternities, national sororities. *Campus security:* 24-hour emergency response devices and patrols, student patrols, late-night transport/escort service, controlled dormitory access, security lighting, self-defense classes. *Student services:* health clinic, personal/psychological counseling.

Athletics Member NCAA. All Division I except ice hockey (Division III). *Intercollegiate sports:* baseball M(s), basketball M(s)/W(s), cross-country running M(s)/W(s), golf M(s)/W(s), ice hockey M, soccer M(s)/W(s), softball W(s), swimming and diving M(s)/W(s), tennis W(s), track and field M/W, volleyball W(s). *Intramural sports:* basketball M/W, bowling M/W, equestrian sports M(c)/W(c), fencing M(c)/W(c), ice hockey M(c), lacrosse M(c)/W(c), rugby M(c), soccer M/W, tennis M(c)/W(c), volleyball M/W, water polo M(c)/W(c), wrestling M(c).

Standardized Tests *Required for some:* ACT (for admission). *Recommended:* SAT or ACT (for admission).

Costs (2011–12) *Tuition:* state resident $9938 full-time, $331 per credit hour part-time; nonresident $23,190 full-time, $773 per credit hour part-time. Full-time tuition and fees vary according to program and student level. Part-time tuition and fees vary according to program and student level. *Room and board:* $7986. Room and board charges vary according to housing facility. *Payment plans:* installment, deferred payment. *Waivers:* senior citizens and employees or children of employees.

Financial Aid Of all full-time matriculated undergraduates who enrolled in 2010, 8,463 applied for aid, 7,044 were judged to have need, 512 had their need fully met. In 2010, 1204 non-need-based awards were made. *Average percent of need met:* 73%. *Average financial aid package:* $12,277. *Average need-based loan:* $8633. *Average need-based gift aid:* $4913. *Average non-need-based aid:* $2668. *Average indebtedness upon graduation:* $24,317.

Applying *Options:* electronic application, deferred entrance. *Required:* high school transcript, minimum 2.5 GPA. *Required for some:* minimum 3.0 GPA, interview, audition. *Application deadlines:* rolling (freshmen), rolling (transfers). *Notification:* continuous (freshmen), continuous (transfers).

Freshman Application Contact Ms. Eleanor L Reynolds, Interim Assistant Vice President, Student Affairs, Oakland University, Rochester, MI 48309-4401. *Phone:* 248-370-3364. *Toll-free phone:* 800-OAK-UNIV. *Fax:* 248-370-4462. *E-mail:* ouinfo@oakland.edu. *Web site:* http://www.oakland.edu/.

Olivet College
Olivet, Michigan

Freshman Application Contact Olivet College, 320 South Main Street, Olivet, MI 49076-9701. *Phone:* 269-749-7635. *Toll-free phone:* 800-456-7189. *Web site:* http://www.olivetcollege.edu/.

Rochester College
Rochester Hills, Michigan

Freshman Application Contact Mr. Larry Norman, Dean of Admissions, Rochester College, 800 West Avon Road, Rochester Hills, MI 48307-2764. *Phone:* 248-218-2190. *Toll-free phone:* 800-521-6010. *Fax:* 248-218-2035. *E-mail:* admissions@rc.edu. *Web site:* http://www.rc.edu/.

Sacred Heart Major Seminary
Detroit, Michigan

- **Independent Roman Catholic** comprehensive, founded 1919
- **Urban** 24-acre campus
- **Coed** 264 undergraduate students, 22% full-time, 42% women, 58% men
- **Moderately difficult** entrance level, 100% of applicants were admitted

Undergraduates 57 full-time, 207 part-time. 4% are from out of state; 4% Black or African American, non-Hispanic/Latino; 5% Hispanic/Latino; 1% American Indian or Alaska Native, non-Hispanic/Latino; 13% Race/ethnicity unknown; 3% international; 10% transferred in; 17% live on campus. *Retention:* 100% of full-time freshmen returned.

Freshmen *Admission:* 4 applied, 4 admitted, 3 enrolled. *Average high school GPA:* 3.48. *Test scores:* ACT scores over 18: 100%; ACT scores over 24: 67%.

Faculty *Total:* 75, 39% full-time, 44% with terminal degrees. *Student/faculty ratio:* 6:1.

Academics *Calendar:* semesters. *Degrees:* diplomas, associate, bachelor's, master's, and postbachelor's certificates. *Special study options:* part-time degree program.

Student Life *Housing:* on-campus residence required through senior year. *Options:* Campus housing is university owned. Freshman campus housing is guaranteed. *Activities and organizations:* choral group. *Student services:* personal/psychological counseling.

Standardized Tests *Required:* SAT or ACT (for admission).

Costs (2011–12) *Comprehensive fee:* $24,708 includes full-time tuition ($15,927), mandatory fees ($100), and room and board ($8681). Part-time tuition: $373 per credit hour. *Required fees:* $50 per term part-time. *Payment plans:* installment, deferred payment. *Waivers:* employees or children of employees.

Financial Aid Of all full-time matriculated undergraduates who enrolled in 2010, 203 applied for aid, 203 were judged to have need. *Average percent of need met:* 70%. *Average financial aid package:* $2725.

Applying *Options:* early admission, deferred entrance. *Application fee:* $30. *Required:* essay or personal statement, high school transcript, minimum 2.0 GPA, 1 letter of recommendation, interview. *Application deadlines:* 8/15 (freshmen), 8/15 (transfers). *Notification:* 8/22 (freshmen), 8/22 (transfers).

Freshman Application Contact Fr. Michael Byrnes, Vice Rector, Sacred Heart Major Seminary, 2701 Chicago Boulevard, Detroit, MI 48206. *Phone:* 313-883-8552. *Fax:* 313-868-6400. *Web site:* http://www.shms.edu/.

Saginaw Valley State University
University Center, Michigan

- **State-supported** comprehensive, founded 1963
- **Small-town** 782-acre campus
- **Coed** 9,117 undergraduate students, 86% full-time, 57% women, 43% men
- **Moderately difficult** entrance level, 80% of applicants were admitted

Undergraduates 7,800 full-time, 1,317 part-time. Students come from 19 states and territories; 27 other countries; 0.7% are from out of state; 10% Black or African American, non-Hispanic/Latino; 3% Hispanic/Latino; 0.8% Asian, non-Hispanic/Latino; 0.1% Native Hawaiian or other Pacific Islander, non-Hispanic/Latino; 0.4% American Indian or Alaska Native, non-Hispanic/Latino; 1% Two or more races, non-Hispanic/Latino; 4% Race/ethnicity unknown; 5% international; 7% transferred in; 29% live on campus. *Retention:* 70% of full-time freshmen returned.

Freshmen *Admission:* 6,811 applied, 5,442 admitted, 1,776 enrolled. *Average high school GPA:* 3.2. *Test scores:* ACT scores over 18: 76%; ACT scores over 24: 29%; ACT scores over 30: 5%.

Faculty *Total:* 597, 50% full-time. *Student/faculty ratio:* 20:1.

Academics *Calendar:* semesters plus summer session. *Degrees:* bachelor's, master's, and post-master's certificates. *Special study options:* academic remediation for entering students, accelerated degree program, adult/continuing education programs, advanced placement credit, cooperative education, distance learning, double majors, English as a second language, honors programs, independent study, internships, part-time degree program, services for LD students, student-designed majors, study abroad, summer session for credit.

Computers on Campus 1,033 computers/terminals are available on campus for general student use. Students can access the following: computer help desk, free student e-mail accounts, online (class) grades, online (class) registration, online (class) schedules. Campuswide network is available. Wireless service is available via dorm rooms, libraries, student centers.

Student Life *Housing options:* men-only, women-only, disabled students. Campus housing is university owned. Freshman campus housing is guaranteed. *Activities and organizations:* drama/theater group, student-run newspaper, choral group, marching band, His House Christian Fellowship, Criminal Justice Society, Delta Sigma Pi, Alpha Phi Omega, International Students Club, national fraternities, national sororities. *Campus security:* 24-hour emergency response devices and patrols, student patrols, late-night transport/escort service, controlled dormitory access, rape prevention program. *Student services:* health clinic, personal/psychological counseling.

Athletics Member NCAA. All Division II. *Intercollegiate sports:* baseball M(s), basketball M(s)/W(s), bowling M(s), cheerleading M/W, cross-country running M(s)/W(s), equestrian sports M(c)/W(c), football M(s), golf M(s), gymnastics M(c)/W, ice hockey M(c), lacrosse M(c)/W(c), rugby M(c)/W(c), soccer M(s)/W(s), softball W(s), tennis M(c)/W(s), track and field M(s)/W(s), ultimate Frisbee M(c)/W(c), volleyball W(s), wrestling M(c). *Intramural sports:* badminton M/W, basketball M/W, football M/W, golf M/W, soccer M/W, softball M/W, tennis M/W, volleyball M/W.

Standardized Tests *Required:* ACT (for admission).

Costs (2012–13) *Tuition:* state resident $7578 full-time, $246 per credit hour part-time; nonresident $19,740 full-time, $597 per credit hour part-time. Full-time tuition and fees vary according to course level, course load, location, and program. Part-time tuition and fees vary according to course level, course load, location, and program. *Required fees:* $438 full-time, $15 part-time. *Room and board:* $8220; room only: $4110. Room and board charges vary according to board plan, housing facility, and student level. *Payment plan:* installment. *Waivers:* employees or children of employees.

Financial Aid Of all full-time matriculated undergraduates who enrolled in 2009, 6,168 applied for aid, 4,295 were judged to have need, 728 had their need fully met. In 2009, 705 non-need-based awards were made. *Average percent of need met:* 62%. *Average financial aid package:* $7086. *Average need-based loan:* $3816. *Average need-based gift aid:* $3432. *Average non-need-based aid:* $3745. *Average indebtedness upon graduation:* $23,555.

Applying *Options:* electronic application, deferred entrance. *Application fee:* $25. *Required:* high school transcript. *Recommended:* minimum 2.5 GPA. *Application deadlines:* rolling (freshmen), rolling (transfers). *Notification:* continuous (freshmen), continuous (transfers).

Freshman Application Contact Jennifer Pahl, Director of Admissions, Saginaw Valley State University, 7400 Bay Road, University Center, MI 48710-0001. *Phone:* 989-964-4200. *Toll-free phone:* 800-968-9500. *Fax:* 989-790-0180. *E-mail:* admissions@svsu.edu. *Web site:* http://www.svsu.edu/.

Siena Heights University
Adrian, Michigan

- **Independent Roman Catholic** comprehensive, founded 1919
- **Small-town** 140-acre campus with easy access to Detroit
- **Endowment** $7.7 million
- **Coed** 2,322 undergraduate students, 52% full-time, 58% women, 42% men
- **Moderately difficult** entrance level, 55% of applicants were admitted

Undergraduates 1,217 full-time, 1,105 part-time. Students come from 8 states and territories; 43 other countries; 5% are from out of state; 12% Black or African American, non-Hispanic/Latino; 5% Hispanic/Latino; 2% Asian, non-Hispanic/Latino; 0.1% Native Hawaiian or other Pacific Islander, non-Hispanic/Latino; 0.4% American Indian or Alaska Native, non-Hispanic/Latino; 2% Two or more races, non-Hispanic/Latino; 9% Race/ethnicity unknown; 0.6% international; 21% transferred in; 53% live on campus. *Retention:* 66% of full-time freshmen returned.

Freshmen *Admission:* 1,728 applied, 959 admitted, 302 enrolled. *Average high school GPA:* 3.4. *Test scores:* ACT scores over 18: 77%; ACT scores over 24: 19%; ACT scores over 30: 2%.

Faculty *Total:* 216, 31% full-time. *Student/faculty ratio:* 13:1.

Academics *Calendar:* semesters. *Degrees:* associate, bachelor's, and master's. *Special study options:* academic remediation for entering students, accelerated degree program, adult/continuing education programs, advanced placement credit, cooperative education, distance learning, double majors, English as a second language, independent study, internships, off-campus study, part-time degree program, services for LD students, student-designed majors, study abroad, summer session for credit.

Computers on Campus 75 computers/terminals are available on campus for general student use. Students can access the following: campus intranet, computer help desk, free student e-mail accounts, online (class) grades, online (class) registration, online (class) schedules. Campuswide network is available. 100% of college-owned or -operated housing units are wired for high-speed Internet access. Wireless service is available via entire campus.

Student Life *Housing:* on-campus residence required through junior year. *Options:* coed. Campus housing is university owned and is provided by a third party. Freshman campus housing is guaranteed. *Activities and organizations:* drama/theater group, student-run newspaper, choral group, marching band, International Club, Residence Hall Counsel, Student Senate, Sport Management Association, Gay Straight Alliance, national fraternities, national sororities. *Campus security:* 24-hour patrols, student patrols, late-night transport/escort service. *Student services:* health clinic, personal/psychological counseling.

Athletics Member NAIA. *Intercollegiate sports:* baseball M(s), basketball M(s)/W(s), bowling M(s)/W(s), cheerleading M/W, cross-country running M(s)/W(s), football M(s), golf M(s)/W(s), lacrosse M(s)/W(s), soccer M(s)/W(s), softball W(s), track and field M(s)/W(s), volleyball M(s)/W(s). *Intramural sports:* basketball M/W, softball M/W, volleyball M/W.

Standardized Tests *Required:* SAT or ACT (for admission).

Costs (2012–13) *Comprehensive fee:* $29,362 includes full-time tuition ($20,532), mandatory fees ($620), and room and board ($8210). Full-time tuition and fees vary according to location. Part-time tuition: $5100 per year. Part-time tuition and fees vary according to location. *Required fees:* $125 per term part-time. *Room and board:* Room and board charges vary according to board plan, housing facility, and location. *Payment plan:* installment. *Waivers:* senior citizens and employees or children of employees.

Financial Aid In 2002, 166 non-need-based awards were made. *Average percent of need met:* 66%. *Average financial aid package:* $12,200. *Average indebtedness upon graduation:* $13,500.

Applying *Options:* electronic application, deferred entrance. *Required:* high school transcript, minimum 2.5 GPA, Transfer GPA Requirement is 2.0 Minimum. *Required for some:* essay or personal statement, interview. *Application deadlines:* rolling (freshmen), rolling (out-of-state freshmen), rolling (transfers).

Freshman Application Contact Ms. Sara Johnson, Director of Admissions, Siena Heights University, 1247 East Siena Heights Drive, Adrian, MI 49221. *Phone:* 517-264-7185. *Toll-free phone:* 800-521-0009. *Fax:* 517-264-7745. *E-mail:* sjohnson@sienaheights.edu. *Web site:* http://www.sienaheights.edu/.

South University
Novi, Michigan

- **Proprietary** comprehensive, part of Education Management Corporation
- **Coed**

Academics *Degrees:* associate, bachelor's, and master's.

Costs (2011–12) *Tuition:* Information about tuition and fees can be obtained by contacting the South University Admissions Office.

Freshman Application Contact South University, 41555 Twelve Mile Road, Novi, MI 48377. *Phone:* 248-675-0200. *Toll-free phone:* 877-693-2085. *Web site:* http://www.southuniversity.edu/novi.aspx.

See page 1604 for the College Close-Up.

Spring Arbor University
Spring Arbor, Michigan

- **Independent Free Methodist** comprehensive, founded 1873
- **Rural** 100-acre campus
- **Endowment** $10.3 million
- **Coed** 3,100 undergraduate students, 70% full-time, 69% women, 31% men
- **Moderately difficult** entrance level, 74% of applicants were admitted

Undergraduates 2,167 full-time, 933 part-time. Students come from 30 states and territories; 9 other countries; 13% are from out of state; 12% Black or African American, non-Hispanic/Latino; 3% Hispanic/Latino; 0.7% Asian, non-Hispanic/Latino; 0.5% American Indian or Alaska Native, non-Hispanic/Latino; 1% Two or more races, non-Hispanic/Latino; 4% Race/ethnicity unknown; 1% international; 3% transferred in; 72% live on campus. *Retention:* 73% of full-time freshmen returned.

Freshmen *Admission:* 2,849 applied, 2,096 admitted, 404 enrolled. *Average high school GPA:* 3.38. *Test scores:* SAT critical reading scores over 500: 61%; SAT math scores over 500: 66%; SAT writing scores over 500: 68%; ACT scores over 18: 90%; SAT critical reading scores over 600: 29%; SAT math scores over 600: 22%; SAT writing scores over 600: 22%; ACT scores over 24: 41%; SAT critical reading scores over 700: 5%; SAT math scores over 700: 5%; SAT writing scores over 700: 10%; ACT scores over 30: 4%.

Faculty *Total:* 143, 58% full-time, 43% with terminal degrees. *Student/faculty ratio:* 15:1.

Academics *Calendar:* 4-1-4. *Degrees:* associate, bachelor's, master's, and postbachelor's certificates. *Special study options:* academic remediation for entering students, accelerated degree program, adult/continuing education programs, advanced placement credit, distance learning, double majors, English as a second language, honors programs, independent study, internships, off-campus study, part-time degree program, services for LD students, student-designed majors, study abroad, summer session for credit. *ROTC:* Army (b), Air Force (c). *Unusual degree programs:* 3-2 engineering with University of Michigan.

Computers on Campus 251 computers/terminals and 1,193 ports are available on campus for general student use. Students can access the following: campus intranet, computer help desk, free student e-mail accounts, online (class) grades, online (class) registration, online (class) schedules. Campuswide network is available. 100% of college-owned or -operated housing units are wired for high-speed Internet access. Wireless service is available via entire campus.

Student Life *Housing:* on-campus residence required through senior year. *Options:* men-only, women-only, disabled students. Campus housing is university owned. Freshman campus housing is guaranteed. *Activities and organizations:* drama/theater group, student-run newspaper, radio and television station, choral group, Inter-faith Shelter Ministries, Band of Brothers, Action Jackson, Circle of Sisters, Heartside Homeless. *Campus security:* 24-hour emergency response devices and patrols, student patrols, late-night transport/escort service, controlled dormitory access. *Student services:* health clinic, personal/psychological counseling.

Athletics Member NAIA, NCCAA. *Intercollegiate sports:* baseball M(s), basketball M(s)/W(s), cross-country running M(s)/W(s), golf M(s)/W(s), soccer M(s)/W(s), softball W(s), tennis M(s)/W(s), track and field M(s)/W(s), volleyball W(s). *Intramural sports:* basketball M/W, field hockey M, football M/W, soccer M/W, softball M/W, table tennis M/W, tennis M/W, ultimate Frisbee M/W, volleyball M/W.

Standardized Tests *Required:* SAT or ACT (for admission). *Recommended:* ACT (for admission).

Costs (2011–12) *Comprehensive fee:* $29,090 includes full-time tuition ($20,980), mandatory fees ($540), and room and board ($7570). Full-time tuition and fees vary according to course load, degree level, and program. Part-time tuition: $520 per credit hour. Part-time tuition and fees vary according to course load, degree level, program, and reciprocity agreements. *Required fees:* $225 per term part-time. *College room only:* $3550. Room and board charges vary according to board plan and housing facility. *Payment plan:* installment. *Waivers:* employees or children of employees.

Financial Aid Of all full-time matriculated undergraduates who enrolled in 2010, 1,428 applied for aid, 1,308 were judged to have need, 217 had their need fully met. 445 Federal Work-Study jobs (averaging $913). *Average percent of need met:* 80%. *Average financial aid package:* $18,866. *Average need-based loan:* $4471. *Average need-based gift aid:* $12,389. *Average indebtedness upon graduation:* $28,212.

Applying *Options:* electronic application, early admission, deferred entrance. *Application fee:* $30. *Required:* high school transcript. *Required for some:* essay or personal statement, interview. *Recommended:* minimum 2.6 GPA, Guidance counselor's form and ACT score of 20 or SAT score of 930 recommended. *Application deadlines:* 8/1 (freshmen), 8/1 (out-of-state freshmen), rolling (transfers). *Notification:* continuous (freshmen), continuous (out-of-state freshmen), continuous (transfers).

Freshman Application Contact Mr. Randy Comfort, Executive Director of Admissions, Spring Arbor University, 106 East Main Street, Spring Arbor, MI 49283-9799. *Phone:* 517-750-1200 Ext. 1468. *Toll-free phone:* 800-968-0011. *Fax:* 517-750-6620. *E-mail:* admissions@arbor.edu. *Web site:* http://www.arbor.edu/.

University of Detroit Mercy
Detroit, Michigan

Freshman Application Contact Office of Admissions, University of Detroit Mercy, 4001 West McNichols Road, Detroit, MI 48221-3038. *Phone:* 313-993-1245. *Toll-free phone:* 800-635-5020. *Fax:* 313-993-3326. *E-mail:* admissions@udmercy.edu. *Web site:* http://www.udmercy.edu/.

University of Michigan
Ann Arbor, Michigan

- **State-supported** university, founded 1817
- **Small-town** 3177-acre campus
- **Endowment** $7.7 billion
- **Coed** 27,407 undergraduate students, 97% full-time, 49% women, 51% men
- **Very difficult** entrance level, 41% of applicants were admitted

Undergraduates 26,538 full-time, 869 part-time. Students come from 56 states and territories; 93 other countries; 36% are from out of state; 4% Black or African American, non-Hispanic/Latino; 4% Hispanic/Latino; 12% Asian, non-Hispanic/Latino; 0.2% American Indian or Alaska Native, non-Hispanic/Latino; 3% Two or more races, non-Hispanic/Latino; 4% Race/ethnicity unknown; 6% international; 3% transferred in; 37% live on campus. *Retention:* 96% of full-time freshmen returned.

Freshmen *Admission:* 39,584 applied, 16,073 admitted, 6,236 enrolled. *Average high school GPA:* 3.79. *Test scores:* SAT critical reading scores over 500: 97%; SAT math scores over 500: 99%; SAT writing scores over 500: 98%; ACT scores over 18: 100%; SAT critical reading scores over 600: 78%; SAT math scores over 600: 92%; SAT writing scores over 600: 84%; ACT scores over 24: 95%; SAT critical reading scores over 700: 27%; SAT math scores over 700: 52%; SAT writing scores over 700: 38%; ACT scores over 30: 54%.

Faculty *Total:* 3,139, 81% full-time, 88% with terminal degrees. *Student/faculty ratio:* 16:1.

Academics *Calendar:* trimesters. *Degrees:* bachelor's, master's, doctoral, post-master's, postbachelor's, and first professional certificates. *Special study options:* accelerated degree program, adult/continuing education programs, advanced placement credit, cooperative education, distance learning, double majors, freshman honors college, honors programs, independent study, internships, off-campus study, part-time degree program, services for LD students, student-designed majors, study abroad, summer session for credit. *ROTC:* Army (b), Navy (b), Air Force (b). *Unusual degree programs:* 3-2 business administration; engineering; music; art and design.

Computers on Campus 2,529 computers/terminals are available on campus for general student use. Students can access the following: campus intranet, computer help desk, free student e-mail accounts, online (class) grades, online (class) registration, online (class) schedules, file storage. Campuswide network is available. 97% of college-owned or -operated housing units are wired for high-speed Internet access. Wireless service is available via entire campus.

Student Life *Housing options:* coed, women-only, cooperative. Campus housing is university owned. Freshman campus housing is guaranteed. *Activities and organizations:* drama/theater group, student-run newspaper, radio and television station, choral group, marching band, Hillel Society, K-Grams (Kids' Program), M-Powered Entrepreneurial Club, Dance Marathon, Alternative Spring Break, national fraternities, national sororities. *Campus security:* 24-hour emergency response devices and patrols, student patrols, late-night transport/escort service, controlled dormitory access, Safewalk, Night Owl ride service. *Student services:* health clinic, personal/psychological counseling, women's center, legal services.

Athletics Member NCAA. All Division I except football (Division I-AA). *Intercollegiate sports:* baseball M(s), basketball M(s)/W(s), crew M(c), cross-country running M(s)/W(s), field hockey W(s), golf M(s)/W(s), gymnastics M(s)/W(s), ice hockey M(s), soccer M(s)/W(s), softball W(s), swimming and diving M(s)/W(s), tennis M(s)/W(s), track and field M(s)/W(s), volleyball W(s), water polo W(s), wrestling M(s). *Intramural sports:* badminton M/W, baseball M(c)/W(c), basketball M/W, crew M(c)/W(c), fencing M(c)/W(c),

field hockey M(c)/W(c), golf M/W, gymnastics W(c), ice hockey M(c)/W(c), lacrosse M(c)/W(c), racquetball M/W, riflery M(c)/W(c), rugby M(c)/W(c), sailing M(c)/W(c), soccer M(c)/W(c), softball M(c)/W(c), swimming and diving M(c)/W(c), table tennis M/W, tennis M(c)/W(c), track and field M/W, ultimate Frisbee M(c)/W(c), volleyball M/W, water polo M(c)/W(c), wrestling M(c).

Standardized Tests *Required:* SAT or ACT (for admission). *Required for some:* SAT Subject Tests (for admission).

Costs (2011–12) *Tuition:* state resident $13,243 full-time, $489 per credit hour part-time; nonresident $38,915 full-time, $1537 per credit hour part-time. Full-time tuition and fees vary according to course load, program, and student level. Part-time tuition and fees vary according to course load, program, and student level. *Required fees:* $194 full-time, $97 per term part-time. *Room and board:* $9468. Room and board charges vary according to board plan and housing facility. *Payment plan:* installment.

Financial Aid Of all full-time matriculated undergraduates who enrolled in 2010, 15,883 applied for aid, 12,400 were judged to have need, 11,160 had their need fully met. 2,955 Federal Work-Study jobs (averaging $1639). In 2010, 9124 non-need-based awards were made. *Average percent of need met:* 90%. *Average financial aid package:* $13,681. *Average need-based loan:* $4260. *Average need-based gift aid:* $12,188. *Average non-need-based aid:* $5885. *Average indebtedness upon graduation:* $27,644. *Financial aid deadline:* 5/31.

Applying *Options:* electronic application, early action, deferred entrance. *Application fee:* $65. *Required:* essay or personal statement, high school transcript. *Required for some:* interview, audition for School of Music, Theatre and Dance; portfolio for School of Art and Design. *Application deadlines:* 2/1 (freshmen), 2/1 (out-of-state freshmen), 2/1 (transfers), 10/31 (early action). *Notification:* continuous (freshmen), continuous (out-of-state freshmen), continuous (transfers), 12/22 (early action).

Freshman Application Contact University of Michigan, Ann Arbor, MI 48109. *Phone:* 734-764-7433. *Web site:* http://www.umich.edu/.

University of Michigan–Dearborn

Dearborn, Michigan

- **State-supported** comprehensive, founded 1959, part of University of Michigan System
- **Suburban** 210-acre campus with easy access to Detroit
- **Coed** 7,188 undergraduate students, 68% full-time, 52% women, 48% men
- **Moderately difficult** entrance level, 59% of applicants were admitted

Undergraduates 4,879 full-time, 2,309 part-time. 11% Black or African American, non-Hispanic/Latino; 5% Hispanic/Latino; 6% Asian, non-Hispanic/Latino; 0.4% American Indian or Alaska Native, non-Hispanic/Latino; 7% Two or more races, non-Hispanic/Latino; 0.7% international; 12% transferred in. *Retention:* 82% of full-time freshmen returned.

Freshmen *Admission:* 4,684 applied, 2,769 admitted, 954 enrolled. *Average high school GPA:* 3.54. *Test scores:* ACT scores over 18: 100%; ACT scores over 24: 53%; ACT scores over 30: 8%.

Faculty *Total:* 539, 58% full-time, 63% with terminal degrees. *Student/faculty ratio:* 16:1.

Academics *Calendar:* semesters. *Degrees:* bachelor's, master's, doctoral, and first professional. *Special study options:* adult/continuing education programs, part-time degree program. *ROTC:* Army (b).

Computers on Campus Students can access the following: computer help desk, free student e-mail accounts, online (class) grades, online (class) registration, online (class) schedules, tuition and application payments accepted online. Campuswide network is available. Wireless service is available via entire campus.

Student Life *Housing:* college housing not available. *Campus security:* 24-hour emergency response devices and patrols, late-night transport/escort service.

Athletics Member NAIA. *Intercollegiate sports:* basketball M(s)/W(s), bowling M(c)/W(c), cheerleading M(c)/W(c), cross-country running M(c)/W(c), ice hockey M(c), rugby M(c), soccer M(c)/W(c), softball W(s), ultimate Frisbee M(c), volleyball W(s). *Intramural sports:* basketball M/W, cross-country running M(c)/W(c), fencing M(c)/W(c), volleyball M/W.

Standardized Tests *Required:* SAT or ACT (for admission).

Costs (2011–12) *Tuition:* state resident $9522 full-time, $377 per credit hour part-time; nonresident $21,500 full-time, $856 per credit hour part-time. Full-time tuition and fees vary according to course level, course load, degree level, program, and student level. Part-time tuition and fees vary according to course level, course load, degree level, program, and student level. *Required fees:* $585 full-time, $237 per term part-time. *Payment plan:* installment. *Waivers:* senior citizens and employees or children of employees.

Financial Aid Of all full-time matriculated undergraduates who enrolled in 2010, 3,704 applied for aid, 3,059 were judged to have need, 934 had their need fully met. 140 Federal Work-Study jobs (averaging $2300). In 2010, 494 non-need-based awards were made. *Average percent of need met:* 78%. *Average financial aid package:* $10,259. *Average need-based loan:* $4400. *Average need-based gift aid:* $5939. *Average non-need-based aid:* $4849. *Average indebtedness upon graduation:* $21,649.

Applying *Options:* electronic application, deferred entrance. *Application fee:* $30. *Required:* high school transcript, minimum 3.0 GPA. *Required for some:* interview. *Application deadlines:* rolling (freshmen), rolling (transfers). *Notification:* continuous (freshmen), continuous (transfers).

Freshman Application Contact Ms. Deb Peffer, Interim Director of Admissions, University of Michigan–Dearborn, 4901 Evergreen Road, Room 1145 UC, Dearborn, MI 48128-1491. *Phone:* 313-593-5100. *Fax:* 313-436-9167. *E-mail:* admissions@umd.umich.edu. *Web site:* http://www.umd.umich.edu/.

University of Michigan–Flint

Flint, Michigan

- **State-supported** comprehensive, founded 1956, part of University of Michigan System
- **Urban** 72-acre campus with easy access to Detroit, Lansing
- **Endowment** $79.2 million
- **Coed** 6,959 undergraduate students, 65% full-time, 61% women, 39% men
- **Moderately difficult** entrance level, 71% of applicants were admitted

Undergraduates 4,516 full-time, 2,443 part-time. Students come from 33 states and territories; 26 other countries; 1% are from out of state; 13% Black or African American, non-Hispanic/Latino; 4% Hispanic/Latino; 1% Asian, non-Hispanic/Latino; 0.1% Native Hawaiian or other Pacific Islander, non-Hispanic/Latino; 0.8% American Indian or Alaska Native, non-Hispanic/Latino; 2% Two or more races, non-Hispanic/Latino; 4% Race/ethnicity unknown; 3% international; 14% transferred in; 5% live on campus. *Retention:* 70% of full-time freshmen returned.

Freshmen *Admission:* 3,164 applied, 2,232 admitted, 686 enrolled. *Average high school GPA:* 3.32. *Test scores:* SAT critical reading scores over 500: 63%; SAT math scores over 500: 82%; SAT writing scores over 500: 67%; ACT scores over 18: 88%; SAT critical reading scores over 600: 45%; SAT math scores over 600: 73%; SAT writing scores over 600: 34%; ACT scores over 24: 33%; SAT critical reading scores over 700: 18%; SAT writing scores over 700: 9%; ACT scores over 30: 5%.

Faculty *Total:* 530, 52% full-time, 47% with terminal degrees. *Student/faculty ratio:* 17:1.

Academics *Calendar:* semesters. *Degrees:* bachelor's, master's, doctoral, and post-master's certificates. *Special study options:* academic remediation for entering students, accelerated degree program, adult/continuing education programs, advanced placement credit, cooperative education, distance learning, double majors, English as a second language, honors programs, independent study, internships, off-campus study, part-time degree program, services for LD students, student-designed majors, study abroad, summer session for credit. *ROTC:* Army (c), Navy (c), Air Force (c). *Unusual degree programs:* 3-2 business administration.

Computers on Campus 770 computers/terminals are available on campus for general student use. Campus access the following: campus intranet, computer help desk, free student e-mail accounts, online (class) grades, online (class) registration, online (class) schedules. Campuswide network is available. 100% of college-owned or -operated housing units are wired for high-speed Internet access. Wireless service is available via entire campus.

Student Life *Housing options:* coed. Campus housing is university owned. *Activities and organizations:* drama/theater group, student-run newspaper, choral group, International Student Organization, Muslim Student Association, Kappa Sigma Fraternity, Inter-Varsity Christian Fellowship, national fraternities, national sororities. *Campus security:* 24-hour emergency response devices and patrols, student patrols, late-night transport/escort service, controlled dormitory access. *Student services:* health clinic, personal/psychological counseling, women's center.

Athletics *Intramural sports:* basketball M/W, bowling M/W, cheerleading M(c)/W(c), football M(c), golf M/W, ice hockey M(c), soccer M/W, table tennis M/W, tennis M(c)/W(c), ultimate Frisbee M(c)/W(c), volleyball M/W, wrestling M(c)/W(c).

Standardized Tests *Required:* SAT or ACT (for admission).

Costs (2011–12) *One-time required fee:* $30. *Tuition:* state resident $8778 full-time, $346 per credit hour part-time; nonresident $17,130 full-time, $692 per credit hour part-time. Full-time tuition and fees vary according to course level, course load, degree level, program, and student level. Part-time tuition and fees vary according to course level, course load, degree level, program, and student level. *Required fees:* $406 full-time, $155 per term part-time. *Room and board:* $7287. Room and board charges vary according to board plan. *Payment plan:* installment. *Waivers:* senior citizens.

Financial Aid Of all full-time matriculated undergraduates who enrolled in 2010, 3,813 applied for aid, 3,315 were judged to have need, 201 had their need fully met. 240 Federal Work-Study jobs (averaging $2506). In 2010, 121 non-need-based awards were made. *Average percent of need met:* 77%. *Average financial aid package:* $12,092. *Average need-based loan:* $4198. *Average need-based gift aid:* $6066. *Average non-need-based aid:* $3244. *Average indebtedness upon graduation:* $25,652.

Applying *Options:* electronic application, deferred entrance. *Application fee:* $30. *Required:* high school transcript. *Application deadlines:* rolling (freshmen), rolling (out-of-state freshmen), 8/19 (transfers). *Notification:* continuous (freshmen), continuous (out-of-state freshmen), continuous (transfers).

Freshman Application Contact University of Michigan–Flint, 303 East Kearsley Street, Flint, MI 48502-1950. *Phone:* 810-762-3300. *Toll-free phone:* 800-942-5636. *Web site:* http://www.umflint.edu/.

University of Phoenix–Detroit Campus

Southfield, Michigan

Admissions Office Contact University of Phoenix–Detroit Campus, 26999 Central Park Boulevard, Suite 100, Southfield, MI 48076. *Toll-free phone:* 866-766-0766. *Web site:* http://www.phoenix.edu/.

University of Phoenix–Metro Detroit Campus

Troy, Michigan

Freshman Application Contact Marc Booker, Sr. Director, Office of Admissions and Evaluation, University of Phoenix–Metro Detroit Campus, 4035 South Riverpoint Parkway, Mail Stop CF-L101, Phoenix, AZ 85040. *Phone:* 602-557-4609. *Toll-free phone:* 866-766-0766. *Fax:* 480-643-1156. *Web site:* http://www.phoenix.edu/.

University of Phoenix–West Michigan Campus

Walker, Michigan

Freshman Application Contact Marc Booker, Sr. Director, Office of Admissions and Evaluation, University of Phoenix–West Michigan Campus, 4035 South Riverpoint Parkway, Mail Stop CF-L101, Phoenix, AZ 85040. *Phone:* 602-557-4609. *Toll-free phone:* 866-766-0766. *Fax:* 480-643-1156. *Web site:* http://www.phoenix.edu/.

Walsh College of Accountancy and Business Administration

Troy, Michigan

Application Contact Walsh College of Accountancy and Business Administration, 3838 Livernois Road, PO Box 7006, Troy, MI 48007-7006. *Phone:* 248-823-1344. *Toll-free phone:* 800-925-7401. *Web site:* http://www.walshcollege.edu/.

Wayne State University

Detroit, Michigan

- **State-supported** university, founded 1868
- **Urban** 210-acre campus with easy access to Detroit
- **Endowment** $230.5 million
- **Coed** 20,589 undergraduate students, 63% full-time, 58% women, 42% men
- **Minimally difficult** entrance level, 76% of applicants were admitted

Undergraduates 12,909 full-time, 7,680 part-time. Students come from 43 states and territories; 41 other countries; 1% are from out of state; 28% Black or African American, non-Hispanic/Latino; 3% Hispanic/Latino; 7% Asian, non-Hispanic/Latino; 0.4% American Indian or Alaska Native, non-Hispanic/Latino; 1% Two or more races, non-Hispanic/Latino; 8% Race/ethnicity unknown; 3% international; 10% transferred in; 10% live on campus. *Retention:* 77% of full-time freshmen returned.

Freshmen *Admission:* 9,468 applied, 7,150 admitted, 2,466 enrolled. *Average high school GPA:* 3.27. *Test scores:* ACT scores over 18: 81%; ACT scores over 24: 37%; ACT scores over 30: 7%.

Faculty *Total:* 1,872, 55% full-time. *Student/faculty ratio:* 16:1.

Academics *Calendar:* semesters. *Degrees:* certificates, bachelor's, master's, doctoral, post-master's, postbachelor's, and first professional certificates. *Special study options:* academic remediation for entering students, accelerated degree program, adult/continuing education programs, advanced placement credit, cooperative education, distance learning, double majors, English as a second language, freshman honors college, honors programs, independent study, internships, off-campus study, part-time degree program, services for LD students, study abroad, summer session for credit. *ROTC:* Army (b), Air Force (c).

Computers on Campus 2,877 computers/terminals are available on campus for general student use. Students can access the following: computer help desk, free student e-mail accounts, online (class) grades, online (class) registration, online (class) schedules. Campuswide network is available. 100% of college-owned or -operated housing units are wired for high-speed Internet access. Wireless service is available via entire campus.

Student Life *Housing options:* coed, women-only, disabled students. Campus housing is university owned. Freshman applicants given priority for college housing. *Activities and organizations:* student-run newspaper, choral group, marching band, Muslim Students Association, Honors Students Association, Indian Students Association, American Medical Students Association-Pre-Med Chapter, national fraternities, national sororities. *Campus security:* 24-hour emergency response devices and patrols, late-night transport/escort service, controlled dormitory access. *Student services:* health clinic, personal/psychological counseling, legal services.

Athletics Member NCAA. All Division II except men's and women's fencing (Division I). *Intercollegiate sports:* baseball M(s), basketball M(s)/W(s), cross-country running M(s)/W(s), fencing M(s)/W(s), football M(s), golf M(s), softball W(s), swimming and diving M(s)/W(s), tennis M(s)/W(s), volleyball W(s). *Intramural sports:* badminton M/W, basketball M/W, field hockey M/W, football M/W, ice hockey M(c), lacrosse M(c)/W(c), racquetball M/W, rock climbing M/W, rugby M(c)/W(c), soccer M/W, softball M/W, table tennis M/W, tennis M/W, ultimate Frisbee M/W, volleyball M/W, weight lifting M/W.

Standardized Tests *Required:* SAT or ACT (for admission).

Costs (2011–12) *Tuition:* state resident $8612 full-time, $287 per credit hour part-time; nonresident $19,724 full-time, $657 per credit hour part-time. Full-time tuition and fees vary according to course load, program, reciprocity agreements, and student level. Part-time tuition and fees vary according to course load, program, reciprocity agreements, and student level. *Required fees:* $1197 full-time, $27 per credit hour part-time, $200 per semester part-time. *Room and board:* $8696; room only: $5696. Room and board charges vary according to board plan and housing facility. *Payment plan:* installment. *Waivers:* senior citizens and employees or children of employees.

Financial Aid Of all full-time matriculated undergraduates who enrolled in 2010, 10,933 applied for aid, 9,967 were judged to have need, 9,748 had their need fully met. 283 Federal Work-Study jobs (averaging $2650). In 2010, 1559 non-need-based awards were made. *Average percent of need met:* 69%. *Average financial aid package:* $16,101. *Average need-based loan:* $4460. *Average need-based gift aid:* $6653. *Average non-need-based aid:* $4330. *Average indebtedness upon graduation:* $22,420. *Financial aid deadline:* 4/30.

Applying *Options:* electronic application, deferred entrance. *Required:* high school transcript, minimum 2.0 GPA. *Required for some:* ACT. *Application deadlines:* 8/26 (freshmen), 8/26 (out-of-state freshmen), 8/26 (transfers). *Notification:* continuous until 8/26 (freshmen), continuous until 8/26 (out-of-state freshmen), continuous until 8/26 (transfers).

Freshman Application Contact Ms. La Joyce Brown, Associate Director, Recruitment and Outreach, Wayne State University, 42 West Warren, Undergraduate Admissions, Student Development and Campus Life, Detroit 48202. *Phone:* 313-577-4906. *Toll-free phone:* 877-WSU-INFO. *E-mail:* admissions@wayne.edu. *Web site:* http://www.wayne.edu/.

Western Michigan University

Kalamazoo, Michigan

- **State-supported** university, founded 1903
- **Urban** 1200-acre campus
- **Endowment** $198.4 million
- **Coed** 20,054 undergraduate students, 85% full-time, 49% women, 51% men
- **Moderately difficult** entrance level, 83% of applicants were admitted

Undergraduates 16,995 full-time, 3,059 part-time. Students come from 46 states and territories; 62 other countries; 7% are from out of state; 10% Black or African American, non-Hispanic/Latino; 4% Hispanic/Latino; 1% Asian, non-Hispanic/Latino; 0.1% Native Hawaiian or other Pacific Islander, non-Hispanic/Latino; 0.4% American Indian or Alaska Native, non-Hispanic/Latino; 3% Two or more races, non-Hispanic/Latino; 1% Race/ethnicity unknown; 3% international; 9% transferred in; 27% live on campus. *Retention:* 74% of full-time freshmen returned.

Freshmen *Admission:* 14,413 applied, 11,986 admitted, 3,166 enrolled. *Average high school GPA:* 3.27. *Test scores:* ACT scores over 18: 87%; ACT scores over 24: 32%; ACT scores over 30: 3%.

Faculty *Total:* 1,437, 64% full-time. *Student/faculty ratio:* 19:1.

Academics *Calendar:* semesters. *Degrees:* bachelor's, master's, doctoral, post-master's, postbachelor's, and first professional certificates. *Special study options:* academic remediation for entering students, accelerated degree program, adult/continuing education programs, advanced placement credit, cooperative education, distance learning, double majors, English as a second language, freshman honors college, honors programs, independent study, internships, off-campus study, part-time degree program, services for LD students, student-designed majors, study abroad, summer session for credit. *ROTC:* Army (b).

Computers on Campus 2,244 computers/terminals are available on campus for general student use. Students can access the following: computer help desk, free student e-mail accounts, online (class) grades, online (class) registration, online (class) schedules. Campuswide network is available. 50% of college-owned or -operated housing units are wired for high-speed Internet access. Wireless service is available via entire campus.

Student Life *Housing options:* coed, men-only, women-only, disabled students. Campus housing is university owned. Freshman campus housing is guaranteed. *Activities and organizations:* drama/theater group, student-run newspaper, radio station, choral group, marching band, Campus Activities Board, Western Student Association, Young Black Male Support Network, Drive Safe Kalamazoo, Alternative Spring Break, national fraternities, national sororities. *Campus security:* 24-hour emergency response devices and patrols, student patrols, late-night transport/escort service, controlled dormitory access. *Student services:* health clinic, personal/psychological counseling, women's center, legal services.

Athletics Member NCAA. All Division I except football (Division I-A). *Intercollegiate sports:* baseball M(s), basketball M(s)/W(s), cross-country running W(s), golf W(s), gymnastics W(s), ice hockey M(s), soccer M(s)/W(s), softball W(s), tennis M(s)/W(s), track and field W(s), volleyball W(s). *Intramural sports:* badminton M/W, baseball M(c)/W(c), basketball M/W, bowling M(c)/W(c), cheerleading W(c), football M/W, golf M/W, ice hockey M/W, lacrosse M(c)/W(c), racquetball M/W, rugby M(c)/W(c), sailing M(c)/W(c), skiing (downhill) M(c)/W(c), soccer M/W, softball M/W, swimming and diving M(c)/W(c), table tennis M/W, tennis M/W, ultimate Frisbee M/W, volleyball M/W.

Standardized Tests *Required:* SAT or ACT (for admission).

Costs (2011–12) *One-time required fee:* $300. *Tuition:* state resident $8762 full-time, $303 per credit hour part-time; nonresident $21,494 full-time, $743 per credit hour part-time. Full-time tuition and fees vary according to course load, location, program, and student level. Part-time tuition and fees vary according to course load, location, program, and student level. *Required fees:* $844 full-time, $228 per term part-time. *Room and board:* $8249; room only: $4255. Room and board charges vary according to board plan. *Payment plan:* installment. *Waivers:* senior citizens and employees or children of employees.

Financial Aid Of all full-time matriculated undergraduates who enrolled in 2010, 14,254 applied for aid, 12,057 were judged to have need, 4,830 had their need fully met. In 2010, 639 non-need-based awards were made. *Average percent of need met:* 82%. *Average financial aid package:* $13,808. *Average need-based loan:* $4295. *Average need-based gift aid:* $5402. *Average non-need-based aid:* $3307. *Average indebtedness upon graduation:* $27,642.

Applying *Options:* electronic application. *Application fee:* $35. *Required:* high school transcript. *Required for some:* interview. *Application deadlines:* rolling (freshmen), 8/1 (transfers). *Notification:* continuous (freshmen), continuous (transfers).

Freshman Application Contact Western Michigan University, 1903 West Michigan Avenue, Kalamazoo, MI 49008. *Phone:* 269-387-2000. *Web site:* http://www.wmich.edu/.

Yeshiva Gedolah of Greater Detroit
Oak Park, Michigan

Director of Admissions Rabbi P. Rushnawitz, Director, Yeshiva Gedolah of Greater Detroit, 24600 Greenfield, Oak Park, MI 48237-1544.

MINNESOTA

Academy College
Minneapolis, Minnesota

Freshman Application Contact Ms. Tracey Schantz, Director, Academy College, Bloomington, MN 55420. *Phone:* 952-851-0066. *Toll-free phone:*

800-292-9149. *Fax:* 952-851-0094. *E-mail:* admissions@academycollege.edu. *Web site:* http://www.academycollege.edu/.

Argosy University, Twin Cities
Eagan, Minnesota

Freshman Application Contact Argosy University, Twin Cities, 1515 Central Parkway, Eagan, MN 55121. *Phone:* 651-846-2882. *Toll-free phone:* 888-844-2004. *Web site:* http://www.argosy.edu/twincities/.

See page 1064 for the College Close-Up.

The Art Institutes International Minnesota
Minneapolis, Minnesota

- **Proprietary** 4-year, founded 1964, part of Education Management Corporation
- **Urban** campus
- **Coed**

Academics *Calendar:* quarters. *Degrees:* diplomas, associate, and bachelor's.

Costs (2011–12) *Tuition:* Tuition cost varies by program. Prospective students should contact the school for current tuition costs. Other charges include a starting kit for all first-quarter students. Kits vary in price, depending on the program of study.

Freshman Application Contact The Art Institutes International Minnesota, 15 South 9th Street, Minneapolis, MN 55402. *Phone:* 612-332-3361. *Toll-free phone:* 800-777-3643. *Web site:* http://www.artinstitutes.edu/minneapolis/.

See page 1150 for the College Close-Up.

Augsburg College
Minneapolis, Minnesota

- **Independent Lutheran** comprehensive, founded 1869
- **Urban** 23-acre campus with easy access to Minneapolis-St. Paul
- **Endowment** $28.2 million
- **Coed**
- **Moderately difficult** entrance level

Faculty *Student/faculty ratio:* 16:1.

Academics *Calendar:* semesters for undergraduate programs; trimesters for graduate programs and weekend college. *Degrees:* certificates, bachelor's, master's, doctoral, post-master's, and postbachelor's certificates.

Student Life *Campus security:* 24-hour emergency response devices and patrols, student patrols, late-night transport/escort service, controlled dormitory access.

Athletics Member NCAA. All Division III.

Standardized Tests *Recommended:* SAT or ACT (for admission).

Costs (2011–12) *Comprehensive fee:* $38,490 includes full-time tuition ($29,794), mandatory fees ($624), and room and board ($8072). Full-time tuition and fees vary according to location. Part-time tuition: $3599 per course. Part-time tuition and fees vary according to course load and location. *College room only:* $4116. Room and board charges vary according to board plan and housing facility.

Financial Aid *Of all full-time matriculated undergraduates who enrolled in 2010,* 2,338 applied for aid, 2,033 were judged to have need, 233 had their need fully met. 363 Federal Work-Study jobs (averaging $2850). 818 state and other part-time jobs (averaging $2843). *In 2010,* 292 non-need-based awards were made. *Average percent of need met:* 67. *Average financial aid package:* $20,143. *Average need-based loan:* $4902. *Average need-based gift aid:* $16,115. *Average non-need-based aid:* $8739. *Average indebtedness upon graduation:* $24,311. *Financial aid deadline:* 8/15.

Applying *Options:* electronic application, deferred entrance. *Application fee:* $25. *Required:* essay or personal statement, high school transcript, minimum 2.5 GPA, interview. *Required for some:* 2 letters of recommendation.

Freshman Application Contact Ms. Carrie Carroll, Assistant Vice President for Admissions, Augsburg College, 2211 Riverside Avenue, Minneapolis, MN 55454-1351. *Phone:* 612-330-1001. *Toll-free phone:* 800-788-5678. *Fax:* 612-330-1590. *E-mail:* admissions@augsburg.edu. *Web site:* http://www.augsburg.edu/.

Bemidji State University
Bemidji, Minnesota

- **State-supported** comprehensive, founded 1919, part of Minnesota State Colleges and Universities System
- **Small-town** 89-acre campus
- **Coed** 4,981 undergraduate students, 75% full-time, 54% women, 46% men
- **Moderately difficult** entrance level, 90% of applicants were admitted

Undergraduates 3,751 full-time, 1,230 part-time. 9% are from out of state; 1% Black or African American, non-Hispanic/Latino; 2% Hispanic/Latino; 0.7% Asian, non-Hispanic/Latino; 0.1% Native Hawaiian or other Pacific Islander, non-Hispanic/Latino; 3% American Indian or Alaska Native, non-Hispanic/Latino; 2% Two or more races, non-Hispanic/Latino; 1% Race/ethnicity unknown; 3% international; 6% transferred in; 44% live on campus. *Retention:* 68% of full-time freshmen returned.

Freshmen *Admission:* 2,085 applied, 1,886 admitted, 840 enrolled. *Average high school GPA:* 3.14. *Test scores:* ACT scores over 18: 89%; ACT scores over 24: 27%; ACT scores over 30: 1%.

Faculty *Total:* 271, 59% full-time, 49% with terminal degrees. *Student/faculty ratio:* 21:1.

Academics *Calendar:* semesters. *Degrees:* certificates, associate, bachelor's, master's, and postbachelor's certificates. *Special study options:* adult/continuing education programs, part-time degree program.

Computers on Campus Students can access the following: computer help desk, free student e-mail accounts, online (class) grades, online (class) registration, online (class) schedules. Wireless service is available via entire campus.

Student Life *Housing options:* coed, disabled students. Campus housing is university owned. Freshman applicants given priority for college housing. *Campus security:* 24-hour emergency response devices and patrols, late-night transport/escort service, controlled dormitory access.

Athletics Member NCAA. All Division II except men's and women's ice hockey (Division I). *Intercollegiate sports:* baseball M(s), basketball M(s)/W(s), cross-country running W(s), football M(s), golf M(s)/W(s), ice hockey M(s)/W(s), soccer W(s), softball W(s), tennis W(s), track and field W(s), volleyball W(s). *Intramural sports:* basketball M/W, football M, ice hockey M/W, soccer M/W, softball M/W, volleyball M/W.

Standardized Tests *Required:* ACT (for admission), SAT or ACT (for admission).

Costs (2011–12) *Tuition:* state resident $6840 full-time, $228 per credit part-time; nonresident $6840 full-time, $228 per credit part-time. Full-time tuition and fees vary according to course load, location, program, and reciprocity agreements. Part-time tuition and fees vary according to course load, location, program, and reciprocity agreements. *Required fees:* $956 full-time, $32 per credit part-time. *Room and board:* $6690; room only: $4210. Room and board charges vary according to board plan and housing facility. *Payment plan:* installment. *Waivers:* senior citizens and employees or children of employees.

Financial Aid Of all full-time matriculated undergraduates who enrolled in 2011, 3,058 applied for aid, 2,454 were judged to have need, 393 had their need fully met. 275 Federal Work-Study jobs (averaging $1463). 109 state and other part-time jobs (averaging $1317). In 2011, 581 non-need-based awards were made. *Average percent of need met:* 65%. *Average financial aid package:* $8829. *Average need-based loan:* $3985. *Average need-based gift aid:* $5274. *Average non-need-based aid:* $9220. *Average indebtedness upon graduation:* $26,930.

Applying *Options:* electronic application, deferred entrance. *Application fee:* $20. *Required:* high school transcript. *Required for some:* essay or personal statement, interview. *Application deadlines:* rolling (freshmen), rolling (transfers). *Notification:* continuous (freshmen), continuous (transfers).

Freshman Application Contact Bemidji State University, 1500 Birchmont Drive, NE, Bemidji, MN 56601-2699. *Phone:* 218-755-2602. *Toll-free phone:* 800-475-2001. *Web site:* http://www.bemidjistate.edu/.

Bethany Lutheran College
Mankato, Minnesota

- **Independent Lutheran** 4-year, founded 1927
- **Small-town** 50-acre campus with easy access to Minneapolis-St. Paul
- **Endowment** $37.0 million
- **Coed** 612 undergraduate students, 95% full-time, 55% women, 45% men
- **Moderately difficult** entrance level, 84% of applicants were admitted

Undergraduates 582 full-time, 30 part-time. Students come from 24 states and territories; 9 other countries; 28% are from out of state; 2% Black or African American, non-Hispanic/Latino; 3% Hispanic/Latino; 1% Asian, non-Hispanic/Latino; 1% Two or more races, non-Hispanic/Latino; 11% Race/ethnicity unknown; 1% international; 6% transferred in; 67% live on campus. *Retention:* 71% of full-time freshmen returned.

Freshmen *Admission:* 452 applied, 381 admitted, 162 enrolled. *Average high school GPA:* 3.39. *Test scores:* ACT scores over 18: 94%; ACT scores over 24: 50%; ACT scores over 30: 9%.

Faculty *Total:* 65, 58% full-time, 34% with terminal degrees. *Student/faculty ratio:* 11:1.

Academics *Calendar:* semesters. *Degree:* bachelor's. *Special study options:* academic remediation for entering students, advanced placement credit, cooperative education, double majors, independent study, internships, services for LD students, student-designed majors, study abroad. *ROTC:* Army (c). *Unusual degree programs:* 3-2 engineering with University of Minnesota-Twin Cities.

Computers on Campus 100 computers/terminals are available on campus for general student use. Students can access the following: computer help desk, free student e-mail accounts, online (class) grades, online (class) registration, online (class) schedules. Campuswide network is available. 100% of college-owned or -operated housing units are wired for high-speed Internet access. Wireless service is available via entire campus.

Student Life *Housing:* on-campus residence required through sophomore year. *Options:* men-only, women-only. Campus housing is university owned. Freshman campus housing is guaranteed. *Activities and organizations:* drama/theater group, student-run newspaper, television station, choral group, Bethany Activities Committee, Student Senate, Scholastic Leadership Society, PAMA (Promoting Awareness, spurring Motivation, and encouraging Action), Bethany Society of Royal Scientists. *Campus security:* 24-hour emergency response devices and patrols, late-night transport/escort service, controlled dormitory access. *Student services:* personal/psychological counseling.

Athletics Member NCAA. All Division III. *Intercollegiate sports:* baseball M, basketball M/W, cross-country running M/W, equestrian sports M(c)/W(c), golf M/W, soccer M/W, softball W, tennis M/W, track and field M(c)/W(c), volleyball W. *Intramural sports:* basketball M/W, football M/W, racquetball M/W, table tennis M/W, ultimate Frisbee M/W, volleyball M/W.

Standardized Tests *Required:* SAT or ACT (for admission).

Costs (2012–13) *One-time required fee:* $130. *Comprehensive fee:* $30,250 includes full-time tuition ($22,810), mandatory fees ($330), and room and board ($7110). Part-time tuition: $960 per credit. Part-time tuition and fees vary according to course load. *Required fees:* $130 part-time. *College room only:* $3310. Room and board charges vary according to board plan and housing facility. *Payment plan:* installment. *Waivers:* senior citizens and employees or children of employees.

Financial Aid Of all full-time matriculated undergraduates who enrolled in 2010, 552 applied for aid, 500 were judged to have need, 90 had their need fully met. 29 Federal Work-Study jobs (averaging $1269). 262 state and other part-time jobs (averaging $729). In 2010, 83 non-need-based awards were made. *Average percent of need met:* 81%. *Average financial aid package:* $17,595. *Average need-based loan:* $5173. *Average need-based gift aid:* $12,759. *Average non-need-based aid:* $5348. *Average indebtedness upon graduation:* $28,391.

Applying *Options:* electronic application. *Required:* essay or personal statement, high school transcript, minimum 2.4 GPA. *Required for some:* interview. *Recommended:* minimum 3.2 GPA, interview. *Application deadline:* 7/1 (freshmen). *Notification:* continuous (transfers).

Freshman Application Contact Mr. Don Westphal, Dean of Admissions, Bethany Lutheran College, 700 Luther Drive, Mankato, MN 56001. *Phone:* 507-344-7320. *Toll-free phone:* 800-944-3066. *Fax:* 507-344-7376. *E-mail:* dwestpha@blc.edu. *Web site:* http://www.blc.edu/.

Bethel University
St. Paul, Minnesota

- **Independent** comprehensive, founded 1871, affiliated with Baptist General Conference
- **Suburban** 247-acre campus with easy access to Minneapolis-St. Paul
- **Endowment** $25.3 million
- **Coed** 3,486 undergraduate students, 81% full-time, 61% women, 39% men
- **Moderately difficult** entrance level, 82% of applicants were admitted

Undergraduates 2,815 full-time, 671 part-time. Students come from 44 states and territories; 6 other countries; 22% are from out of state; 5% Black or African American, non-Hispanic/Latino; 2% Hispanic/Latino; 2% Asian, non-Hispanic/Latino; 0.1% Native Hawaiian or other Pacific Islander, non-Hispanic/Latino; 0.1% American Indian or Alaska Native, non-Hispanic/Latino; 2% Two or more races, non-Hispanic/Latino; 6% Race/ethnicity unknown; 0.3% international; 4% transferred in; 69% live on campus. *Retention:* 85% of full-time freshmen returned.

Freshmen *Admission:* 2,314 applied, 1,905 admitted, 680 enrolled. *Average high school GPA:* 3.5. *Test scores:* SAT critical reading scores over 500: 76%; SAT math scores over 500: 81%; ACT scores over 18: 97%; SAT critical reading scores over 600: 47%; SAT math scores over 600: 41%; ACT scores over

24: 64%; SAT critical reading scores over 700: 14%; SAT math scores over 700: 12%; ACT scores over 30: 16%.

Faculty *Total:* 308, 60% full-time, 59% with terminal degrees. *Student/faculty ratio:* 12:1.

Academics *Calendar:* 4-1-4. *Degrees:* associate, bachelor's, master's, doctoral, post-master's, postbachelor's, and first professional certificates. *Special study options:* academic remediation for entering students, accelerated degree program, adult/continuing education programs, advanced placement credit, double majors, honors programs, independent study, internships, off-campus study, part-time degree program, services for LD students, student-designed majors, study abroad, summer session for credit. *ROTC:* Army (c), Air Force (c). *Unusual degree programs:* 3-2 engineering with University of Minnesota; other institutions by arrangement.

Computers on Campus 460 computers/terminals are available on campus for general student use. Students can access the following: campus intranet, computer help desk, free student e-mail accounts, online (class) grades, online (class) registration, online (class) schedules. Campuswide network is available. 100% of college-owned or -operated housing units are wired for high-speed Internet access. Wireless service is available via classrooms, computer centers, computer labs, dorm rooms, learning centers, libraries, student centers.

Student Life *Housing:* on-campus residence required through sophomore year. *Options:* coed, disabled students. Campus housing is university owned. Freshman campus housing is guaranteed. *Activities and organizations:* drama/theater group, student-run newspaper, radio station, choral group, campus ministries small groups, Pre-Medical Club, College Democrats/College Republicans, Student Activities, Tri Beta (biology honors society). *Campus security:* 24-hour emergency response devices and patrols, student patrols, late-night transport/escort service, controlled dormitory access, video surveillance for residents halls, academic buildings, and parking lots. *Student services:* health clinic, personal/psychological counseling.

Athletics Member NCAA. All Division III. *Intercollegiate sports:* baseball M, basketball M/W, cross-country running M/W, football M, golf M/W, ice hockey M/W, soccer M/W, softball W, tennis M/W, track and field M/W, volleyball M(c)/W. *Intramural sports:* badminton M/W, basketball M/W, football M, ice hockey M(c), lacrosse M(c)/W(c), rugby M(c), softball M/W, volleyball W.

Standardized Tests *Required:* SAT or ACT (for admission).

Costs (2011–12) *Comprehensive fee:* $37,990 includes full-time tuition ($29,320), mandatory fees ($140), and room and board ($8530). Part-time tuition: $1225 per credit. Part-time tuition and fees vary according to course load. *College room only:* $4900. Room and board charges vary according to board plan. *Payment plans:* tuition prepayment, installment. *Waivers:* employees or children of employees.

Financial Aid Of all full-time matriculated undergraduates who enrolled in 2010, 2,241 applied for aid, 1,974 were judged to have need, 325 had their need fully met. 300 Federal Work-Study jobs (averaging $2500). 1,300 state and other part-time jobs (averaging $2500). In 2010, 547 non-need-based awards were made. *Average percent of need met:* 74%. *Average financial aid package:* $20,453. *Average need-based loan:* $4373. *Average need-based gift aid:* $14,976. *Average non-need-based aid:* $6883. *Average indebtedness upon graduation:* $33,246.

Applying *Options:* electronic application, early admission, deferred entrance. *Required:* essay or personal statement, high school transcript, rank in upper 50% of high school class. *Required for some:* 2 letters of recommendation. *Recommended:* minimum 2.5 GPA, interview. *Application deadlines:* rolling (freshmen), rolling (out-of-state freshmen), rolling (transfers). *Notification:* continuous (freshmen), continuous (out-of-state freshmen), continuous (transfers).

Freshman Application Contact Office of Admissions, Bethel University, 3900 Bethel Drive, St. Paul, MN 55112. *Phone:* 651-638-6242. *Toll-free phone:* 800-255-8706 Ext. 6242. *Fax:* 651-635-1490. *E-mail:* buadmissions-cas@bethel.edu. *Web site:* http://www.bethel.edu/.

Brown College

Mendota Heights, Minnesota

Freshman Application Contact Mr. Mark Fredrichs, Registrar, Brown College, 1440 Northland Drive, Mendota Heights, MN 55120. *Phone:* 651-905-3400. *Toll-free phone:* 866-551-0049. *Fax:* 651-905-3550. *Web site:* http://www.browncollege.edu/.

Capella University

Minneapolis, Minnesota

- **Proprietary** upper-level, founded 1993
- **Urban** campus
- **Coed** 7,487 undergraduate students, 15% full-time, 65% women, 35% men
- **Minimally difficult** entrance level

Undergraduates 1,156 full-time, 6,331 part-time. 28% Black or African American, non-Hispanic/Latino; 5% Hispanic/Latino; 1% Asian, non-Hispanic/Latino; 0.4% Native Hawaiian or other Pacific Islander, non-Hispanic/Latino; 0.5% American Indian or Alaska Native, non-Hispanic/Latino; 2% Two or more races, non-Hispanic/Latino; 25% Race/ethnicity unknown; 0.2% international.

Academics *Calendar:* quarters. *Degrees:* certificates, bachelor's, master's, doctoral, post-master's, postbachelor's, and first professional certificates (offers only distance learning degree programs). *Special study options:* accelerated degree program, adult/continuing education programs, advanced placement credit, distance learning, double majors, independent study, internships, off-campus study, part-time degree program, services for LD students, summer session for credit.

Computers on Campus Students can access the following: online (class) grades, online (class) registration, online (class) schedules.

Financial Aid *Average percent of need met:* 90%. *Average financial aid package:* $10,500. *Average indebtedness upon graduation:* $8000.

Applying *Options:* electronic application. *Application fee:* $50. *Application deadline:* rolling (transfers). *Notification:* continuous (transfers).

Application Contact Enrollment Services, Capella University, 225 South Sixth Street, Capella Tower, 9th Floor, Minneapolis, MN 55402. *Phone:* 866-2837921. *Toll-free phone:* 866-283-7921. *Fax:* 612-977-5060. *E-mail:* info@capella.edu. *Web site:* http://www.capella.edu/.

Carleton College

Northfield, Minnesota

- **Independent** 4-year, founded 1866
- **Small-town** 955-acre campus with easy access to Minneapolis-St. Paul
- **Endowment** $653.5 million
- **Coed** 2,018 undergraduate students, 99% full-time, 52% women, 48% men
- **Very difficult** entrance level, 31% of applicants were admitted

Undergraduates 2,002 full-time, 16 part-time. Students come from 50 states and territories; 42 other countries; 78% are from out of state; 4% Black or African American, non-Hispanic/Latino; 6% Hispanic/Latino; 7% Asian, non-Hispanic/Latino; 0.1% Native Hawaiian or other Pacific Islander, non-Hispanic/Latino; 0.1% American Indian or Alaska Native, non-Hispanic/Latino; 5% Two or more races, non-Hispanic/Latino; 2% Race/ethnicity unknown; 8% international; 0.6% transferred in; 94% live on campus. *Retention:* 96% of full-time freshmen returned.

Freshmen *Admission:* 4,988 applied, 1,546 admitted, 519 enrolled. *Test scores:* SAT critical reading scores over 500: 99%; SAT math scores over 500: 100%; SAT writing scores over 500: 99%; ACT scores over 18: 100%; SAT critical reading scores over 600: 90%; SAT math scores over 600: 96%; SAT writing scores over 600: 92%; ACT scores over 24: 97%; SAT critical reading scores over 700: 57%; SAT math scores over 700: 57%; SAT writing scores over 700: 53%; ACT scores over 30: 73%.

Faculty *Total:* 243, 91% full-time, 95% with terminal degrees. *Student/faculty ratio:* 9:1.

Academics *Calendar:* three courses for each of three terms. *Degree:* bachelor's. *Special study options:* accelerated degree program, advanced placement credit, double majors, independent study, internships, off-campus study, services for LD students, student-designed majors, study abroad. *Unusual degree programs:* 3-2 engineering with Columbia University, Washington University in St. Louis.

Computers on Campus 388 computers/terminals and 220 ports are available on campus for general student use. Students can access the following: campus intranet, computer help desk, free student e-mail accounts, online (class) grades, online (class) registration, online (class) schedules. Campuswide network is available. 100% of college-owned or -operated housing units are wired for high-speed Internet access. Wireless service is available via classrooms, computer centers, computer labs, dorm rooms, learning centers, libraries, student centers.

Student Life *Housing:* on-campus residence required through senior year. *Options:* coed, disabled students. Campus housing is university owned. Freshman campus housing is guaranteed. *Activities and organizations:* drama/theater group, student-run newspaper, radio station, choral group, CANOE (Carleton Association of Nature and Outdoor Enthusiasts), Farm Club, Ebony II, WHIMS (Women in Math and Science), Amnesty International. *Campus*

security: 24-hour emergency response devices and patrols, student patrols, late-night transport/escort service, controlled dormitory access, Emergency Notification Service (cell phone text and email alerts). *Student services:* health clinic, personal/psychological counseling, women's center.

Athletics Member NCAA. All Division III. *Intercollegiate sports:* badminton M(c)/W(c), baseball M, basketball M/W, crew M(c)/W(c), cross-country running M/W, equestrian sports M(c)/W(c), fencing M(c)/W(c), field hockey W(c), football M, golf M/W, gymnastics W(c), ice hockey M(c)/W(c), lacrosse M(c)/W(c), rugby M(c)/W(c), sailing M(c)/W(c), skiing (cross-country) M(c)/W(c), skiing (downhill) M(c)/W(c), soccer M/W, softball W, swimming and diving M/W, tennis M/W, track and field M/W, ultimate Frisbee M(c)/W(c), volleyball M(c)/W, water polo M(c)/W(c). *Intramural sports:* badminton M/W, basketball M/W, soccer M/W, softball M/W, table tennis M/W, tennis M/W, ultimate Frisbee M/W, volleyball M/W.

Standardized Tests *Required:* SAT or ACT (for admission). *Recommended:* SAT Subject Tests (for admission).

Costs (2011–12) *Comprehensive fee:* $54,180 includes full-time tuition ($42,690), mandatory fees ($252), and room and board ($11,238). *College room only:* $5904. Room and board charges vary according to board plan. *Payment plans:* tuition prepayment, installment. *Waivers:* employees or children of employees.

Financial Aid Of all full-time matriculated undergraduates who enrolled in 2010, 1,729 applied for aid, 1,119 were judged to have need, 1,119 had their need fully met. 384 Federal Work-Study jobs (averaging $2493). 1,275 state and other part-time jobs (averaging $2511). In 2010, 122 non-need-based awards were made. *Average percent of need met:* 100%. *Average financial aid package:* $36,318. *Average need-based loan:* $5809. *Average need-based gift aid:* $30,260. *Average non-need-based aid:* $2617. *Average indebtedness upon graduation:* $19,341. *Financial aid deadline:* 2/15.

Applying *Options:* electronic application, early admission, early decision, deferred entrance. *Application fee:* $30. *Required:* essay or personal statement, high school transcript, 2 letters of recommendation, common application supplement. *Recommended:* interview. *Application deadlines:* 1/15 (freshmen), 3/31 (transfers). *Early decision deadline:* 11/15 (for plan 1), 1/15 (for plan 2). *Notification:* 4/15 (freshmen), 5/15 (transfers), 12/15 (early decision plan 1), 2/15 (early decision plan 2). **Freshman Application Contact** Carleton College, One North College Street, Northfield, MN 55057-4001. *Phone:* 507-222-4190. *Toll-free phone:* 800-995-2275. *Web site:* http://www.carleton.edu/.

College of Saint Benedict
Saint Joseph, Minnesota

- **Independent Roman Catholic** 4-year, founded 1887
- **Small-town** 800-acre campus with easy access to Minneapolis-St. Paul
- **Endowment** $44.6 million
- **Women only** 2,086 undergraduate students, 98% full-time
- **Moderately difficult** entrance level, 73% of applicants were admitted

Undergraduates 2,041 full-time, 45 part-time. Students come from 33 states and territories; 24 other countries; 16% are from out of state; 1% Black or African American, non-Hispanic/Latino; 3% Hispanic/Latino; 5% Asian, non-Hispanic/Latino; 0.5% American Indian or Alaska Native, non-Hispanic/Latino; 0.1% Two or more races, non-Hispanic/Latino; 6% international; 2% transferred in; 80% live on campus. *Retention:* 89% of full-time freshmen returned. **Freshmen** *Admission:* 1,972 applied, 1,444 admitted, 525 enrolled. *Average high school GPA:* 3.72. *Test scores:* SAT critical reading scores over 500: 79%; SAT math scores over 500: 81%; SAT writing scores over 500: 89%; ACT scores over 18: 100%; SAT critical reading scores over 600: 40%; SAT math scores over 600: 43%; SAT writing scores over 600: 43%; ACT scores over 24: 68%; SAT critical reading scores over 700: 17%; SAT math scores over 700: 12%; SAT writing scores over 700: 15%; ACT scores over 30: 13%. **Faculty** *Total:* 198, 86% full-time, 76% with terminal degrees. *Student/faculty ratio:* 11:1.

Academics *Calendar:* semesters. *Degrees:* bachelor's (coordinate with Saint John's University for men). *Special study options:* advanced placement credit, double majors, English as a second language, honors programs, independent study, internships, off-campus study, services for LD students, student-designed majors, study abroad. *ROTC:* Army (c). *Unusual degree programs:* 3-2 engineering with University of Minnesota.

Computers on Campus 940 computers/terminals and 3,000 ports are available on campus for general student use. Students can access the following: campus intranet, computer help desk, free student e-mail accounts, online (class) grades, online (class) registration, online (class) schedules, online student accounts. Campuswide network is available. 100% of college-owned or -operated housing units are wired for high-speed Internet access. Wireless service is available via entire campus.

Student Life *Housing:* on-campus residence required through senior year. *Options:* women-only, disabled students. Campus housing is university owned.

Freshman campus housing is guaranteed. *Activities and organizations:* drama/theater group, student-run newspaper, radio station, choral group, China Cross Cultural Communications Club, Outskirts Snow Club, Nutrition Club, Magis, AKS Sorority. *Campus security:* 24-hour emergency response devices and patrols, student patrols, late-night transport/escort service, controlled dormitory access, well-lit pathways, closed circuit TV monitors. *Student services:* health clinic, personal/psychological counseling, women's center.

Athletics Member NCAA. All Division III. *Intercollegiate sports:* basketball W, crew W(c), cross-country running W, golf W, ice hockey W, lacrosse W(c), riflery W(c), rugby W(c), soccer W, softball W, swimming and diving W, tennis W, track and field W, ultimate Frisbee W(c), volleyball W, water polo W(c). *Intramural sports:* badminton W, basketball W, football W, golf W(c), racquetball W, rock climbing W(c), skiing (cross-country) W(c), skiing (downhill) W(c), soccer W, softball W, table tennis W, tennis W, volleyball W.

Standardized Tests *Required:* SAT or ACT (for admission).

Costs (2011–12) *Comprehensive fee:* $43,264 includes full-time tuition ($33,458), mandatory fees ($850), and room and board ($8956). Part-time tuition: $1394 per credit hour. Part-time tuition and fees vary according to course load. *College room only:* $4312. Room and board charges vary according to board plan and housing facility. *Payment plan:* installment.

Financial Aid Of all full-time matriculated undergraduates who enrolled in 2011, 1,563 applied for aid, 1,398 were judged to have need, 487 had their need fully met. 558 Federal Work-Study jobs (averaging $2193). 960 state and other part-time jobs (averaging $2426). In 2011, 510 non-need-based awards were made. *Average percent of need met:* 86%. *Average financial aid package:* $26,629. *Average need-based loan:* $4950. *Average need-based gift aid:* $20,138. *Average non-need-based aid:* $12,740.

Applying *Options:* electronic application, early action, deferred entrance. *Required:* essay or personal statement, high school transcript, 1 letter of recommendation. *Recommended:* minimum 3.0 GPA, interview. *Application deadlines:* rolling (freshmen), rolling (transfers), 11/15 (early action). *Notification:* continuous (freshmen), continuous (transfers), 12/15 (early action). **Freshman Application Contact** Ms. Karen Backes, Dean of Admissions, College of Saint Benedict, 37 South College Avenue, St. Joseph, MN 56374. *Phone:* 320-363-5055. *Toll-free phone:* 800-544-1489. *Fax:* 320-363-5650. *E-mail:* admissions@csbsju.edu. *Web site:* http://www.csbsju.edu/.

The College of St. Scholastica
Duluth, Minnesota

- **Independent** comprehensive, founded 1912, affiliated with Roman Catholic Church
- **Suburban** 186-acre campus
- **Endowment** $21.2 million
- **Coed** 2,856 undergraduate students, 89% full-time, 68% women, 32% men
- **Moderately difficult** entrance level, 80% of applicants were admitted

Undergraduates 2,556 full-time, 300 part-time. Students come from 30 states and territories; 38 other countries; 13% are from out of state; 2% Black or African American, non-Hispanic/Latino; 1% Hispanic/Latino; 1% Asian, non-Hispanic/Latino; 2% American Indian or Alaska Native, non-Hispanic/Latino; 1% Two or more races, non-Hispanic/Latino; 7% Race/ethnicity unknown; 4% international; 13% transferred in; 51% live on campus. *Retention:* 84% of full-time freshmen returned. **Freshmen** *Admission:* 2,000 applied, 1,606 admitted, 596 enrolled. *Average high school GPA:* 3.46. *Test scores:* SAT critical reading scores over 500: 47%; SAT math scores over 500: 61%; SAT writing scores over 500: 41%; ACT scores over 18: 95%; SAT critical reading scores over 600: 22%; SAT math scores over 600: 18%; SAT writing scores over 600: 8%; ACT scores over 24: 49%; SAT critical reading scores over 700: 4%; SAT math scores over 700: 7%; SAT writing scores over 700: 4%; ACT scores over 30: 6%. **Faculty** *Total:* 361, 48% full-time. *Student/faculty ratio:* 14:1.

Academics *Calendar:* semesters. *Degrees:* certificates, bachelor's, master's, doctoral, post-master's, and postbachelor's certificates. *Special study options:* accelerated degree program, adult/continuing education programs, advanced placement credit, distance learning, double majors, external degree program, honors programs, independent study, internships, off-campus study, part-time degree program, services for LD students, student-designed majors, study abroad, summer session for credit. *ROTC:* Air Force (c). *Unusual degree programs:* 3-2 occupational therapy.

Computers on Campus 394 computers/terminals are available on campus for general student use. Students can access the following: campus intranet, computer help desk, free student e-mail accounts, online (class) grades, online (class) registration, online (class) schedules, student account information and transcripts online. Campuswide network is available. 100% of college-owned or -operated housing units are wired for high-speed Internet access. Wireless service is available via classrooms, computer centers, computer labs, dorm rooms, learning centers, libraries, student centers.

Student Life *Housing:* on-campus residence required through sophomore year. *Options:* coed, disabled students. Campus housing is university owned. Freshman campus housing is guaranteed. *Activities and organizations:* drama/theater group, student-run newspaper, television station, choral group, Campus Activity Board, Inter-Varsity, Habitat for Humanity, SHIMA, Volunteers Involved Through Action. *Campus security:* 24-hour emergency response devices and patrols, late-night transport/escort service, controlled dormitory access, student door monitor at night. *Student services:* health clinic, personal/psychological counseling.

Athletics Member NCAA. All Division III. *Intercollegiate sports:* baseball M, basketball M/W, cross-country running M/W, football M, ice hockey M/W, skiing (cross-country) M/W, soccer M/W, softball W, tennis M/W, track and field M/W, volleyball W. *Intramural sports:* basketball M/W, football M/W, ice hockey W(c), soccer M/W, tennis M/W, volleyball M/W.

Standardized Tests *Required:* SAT or ACT (for admission).

Costs (2011–12) *Comprehensive fee:* $37,222 includes full-time tuition ($29,328), mandatory fees ($178), and room and board ($7716). Full-time tuition and fees vary according to class time. Part-time tuition and fees vary according to class time and course load. *College room only:* $4376. Room and board charges vary according to board plan and housing facility. *Payment plan:* installment. *Waivers:* senior citizens and employees or children of employees.

Financial Aid Of all full-time matriculated undergraduates who enrolled in 2011, 2,176 applied for aid, 2,023 were judged to have need, 414 had their need fully met. In 2011, 135 non-need-based awards were made. *Average percent of need met:* 69%. *Average financial aid package:* $19,697. *Average need-based loan:* $4544. *Average need-based gift aid:* $6659. *Average non-need-based aid:* $10,858. *Average indebtedness upon graduation:* $41,282.

Applying *Options:* electronic application, early admission, deferred entrance. *Application fee:* $25. *Required:* high school transcript. *Required for some:* minimum 2.0 GPA, interview. *Recommended:* interview. *Application deadlines:* rolling (freshmen), rolling (transfers). *Notification:* continuous (freshmen), continuous (transfers).

Freshman Application Contact Mr. Eric Berg, Vice President for Enrollment Management, The College of St. Scholastica, 1200 Kenwood Avenue, Duluth, MN 55811-4199. *Phone:* 218-723-6053. *Toll-free phone:* 800-249-6412. *E-mail:* admissions@css.edu. *Web site:* http://www.css.edu/.

College of Visual Arts
St. Paul, Minnesota

Freshman Application Contact Anne White, Director for Student Life, College of Visual Arts, 344 Summit Avenue, St. Paul, MN 55102-2124. *Phone:* 651-757-4049. *Toll-free phone:* 800-224-1536. *Fax:* 651-757-4010. *E-mail:* awhite@cva.edu. *Web site:* http://www.cva.edu/.

Concordia College
Moorhead, Minnesota

- **Independent** comprehensive, founded 1891, affiliated with Evangelical Lutheran Church in America
- **Small-town** 113-acre campus
- **Endowment** $83.4 million
- **Coed** 2,746 undergraduate students, 98% full-time, 62% women, 38% men
- **Moderately difficult** entrance level, 95% of applicants were admitted

Undergraduates 2,698 full-time, 48 part-time. Students come from 35 states and territories; 36 other countries; 29% are from out of state; 2% Black or African American, non-Hispanic/Latino; 1% Hispanic/Latino; 2% Asian, non-Hispanic/Latino; 0.3% American Indian or Alaska Native, non-Hispanic/Latino; 1% Two or more races, non-Hispanic/Latino; 6% Race/ethnicity unknown; 3% international; 3% transferred in; 63% live on campus. *Retention:* 85% of full-time freshmen returned.

Freshmen *Admission:* 2,150 applied, 2,033 admitted, 722 enrolled. *Average high school GPA:* 3.59. *Test scores:* SAT critical reading scores over 500: 84%; SAT math scores over 500: 85%; ACT scores over 18: 98%; SAT critical reading scores over 600: 51%; SAT math scores over 600: 59%; ACT scores over 24: 64%; SAT critical reading scores over 700: 10%; SAT math scores over 700: 6%; ACT scores over 30: 14%.

Faculty *Total:* 257, 70% full-time, 68% with terminal degrees. *Student/faculty ratio:* 13:1.

Academics *Calendar:* semesters. *Degrees:* bachelor's and master's. *Special study options:* advanced placement credit, cooperative education, distance learning, double majors, honors programs, independent study, internships, off-campus study, part-time degree program, services for LD students, student-designed majors, study abroad, summer session for credit. *ROTC:* Army (c), Air Force (c). *Unusual degree programs:* 3-2 engineering with Institute of Technology (IT) at the University of Minnesota.

Computers on Campus 570 computers/terminals and 87 ports are available on campus for general student use. Students can access the following: campus intranet, computer help desk, free student e-mail accounts, online (class) grades, online (class) registration, online (class) schedules, online degree audit. Campuswide network is available. 100% of college-owned or -operated housing units are wired for high-speed Internet access. Wireless service is available via entire campus.

Student Life *Housing:* on-campus residence required through sophomore year. *Options:* coed, women-only. Campus housing is university owned. Freshman applicants given priority for college housing. *Activities and organizations:* drama/theater group, student-run newspaper, radio and television station, choral group, Campus Service Commission, Habitat for Humanity, Lead Now, Colleges Against Cancer (Relay for Life), Campus Ministry Commission. *Campus security:* 24-hour emergency response devices and patrols, late-night transport/escort service, controlled dormitory access, well-lighted campus. *Student services:* health clinic, personal/psychological counseling, women's center.

Athletics Member NCAA. All Division III. *Intercollegiate sports:* baseball M, basketball M/W, cheerleading W(c), cross-country running M/W, football M, golf M/W, ice hockey M/W, soccer M/W, softball W, swimming and diving W, tennis M/W, track and field M/W, volleyball M(c)/W, wrestling M. *Intramural sports:* badminton M(c)/W(c), basketball M/W, bowling M(c)/W(c), football M, ice hockey M(c), lacrosse M(c)/W(c), rugby W(c), skiing (cross-country) M(c)/W(c), skiing (downhill) M(c)/W(c), tennis M(c)/W(c), ultimate Frisbee M(c)/W(c), volleyball M/W.

Standardized Tests *Required:* SAT or ACT (for admission).

Costs (2012–13) *Comprehensive fee:* $37,860 includes full-time tuition ($30,650), mandatory fees ($210), and room and board ($7000). Full-time tuition and fees vary according to course load and degree level. Part-time tuition: $1205 per credit hour. Part-time tuition and fees vary according to course load and degree level. *Required fees:* $105 part-time. *College room only:* $3060. Room and board charges vary according to board plan and housing facility. *Payment plan:* installment. *Waivers:* employees or children of employees.

Financial Aid Of all full-time matriculated undergraduates who enrolled in 2010, 2,301 applied for aid, 2,038 were judged to have need, 348 had their need fully met. 1,525 Federal Work-Study jobs (averaging $1766). 1,022 state and other part-time jobs (averaging $2254). In 2010, 609 non-need-based awards were made. *Average percent of need met:* 87%. *Average financial aid package:* $22,477. *Average need-based loan:* $7802. *Average need-based gift aid:* $14,835. *Average non-need-based aid:* $10,323. *Average indebtedness upon graduation:* $35,240.

Applying *Options:* electronic application, early admission, deferred entrance. *Application fee:* $20. *Required:* high school transcript, 2 letters of recommendation. *Application deadlines:* rolling (freshmen), rolling (transfers). *Notification:* continuous (freshmen), continuous (transfers).

Freshman Application Contact Mr. Scott D. Ellingson, Director of Admissions, Concordia College, 901 8th Street South, Moorhead, MN 56562. *Phone:* 218-299-3004. *Toll-free phone:* 800-699-9897. *Fax:* 218-299-4720. *E-mail:* sellings@cord.edu. *Web site:* http://www.concordiacollege.edu/.

Concordia University, St. Paul
St. Paul, Minnesota

- **Independent** comprehensive, founded 1893, affiliated with Lutheran Church–Missouri Synod
- **Urban** 37-acre campus
- **Endowment** $21.7 million
- **Coed** 1,692 undergraduate students, 60% full-time, 59% women, 41% men
- **Minimally difficult** entrance level, 56% of applicants were admitted

Undergraduates 1,018 full-time, 674 part-time. Students come from 42 states and territories; 4 other countries; 17% are from out of state; 12% Black or African American, non-Hispanic/Latino; 4% Hispanic/Latino; 6% Asian, non-Hispanic/Latino; 0.2% Native Hawaiian or other Pacific Islander, non-Hispanic/Latino; 0.4% American Indian or Alaska Native, non-Hispanic/Latino; 3% Two or more races, non-Hispanic/Latino; 5% Race/ethnicity unknown; 0.2% international; 6% transferred in; 26% live on campus. *Retention:* 66% of full-time freshmen returned.

Freshmen *Admission:* 1,062 applied, 600 admitted, 197 enrolled. *Average high school GPA:* 3.12. *Test scores:* ACT scores over 18: 81%; ACT scores over 24: 30%; ACT scores over 30: 3%.

Faculty *Total:* 331, 24% full-time, 41% with terminal degrees. *Student/faculty ratio:* 15:1.

Academics *Calendar:* semesters. *Degrees:* certificates, associate, bachelor's, master's, and postbachelor's certificates. *Special study options:* academic remediation for entering students, accelerated degree program, adult/continuing education programs, advanced placement credit, distance learning, double

majors, honors programs, independent study, internships, off-campus study, part-time degree program, services for LD students, student-designed majors, study abroad, summer session for credit. *ROTC:* Army (c), Navy (c), Air Force (c).

Computers on Campus Students can access the following: campus intranet, computer help desk, free student e-mail accounts, online (class) grades, online (class) registration, online (class) schedules. Campuswide network is available. 100% of college-owned or -operated housing units are wired for high-speed Internet access. Wireless service is available via entire campus.

Student Life *Housing:* on-campus residence required for freshman year. *Options:* coed, men-only, women-only, disabled students. Campus housing is university owned. Freshman campus housing is guaranteed. *Activities and organizations:* drama/theater group, student-run newspaper, television station, choral group. *Campus security:* 24-hour emergency response devices and patrols, student patrols, late-night transport/escort service, controlled dormitory access. *Student services:* health clinic, personal/psychological counseling.

Athletics Member NCAA. All Division II. *Intercollegiate sports:* baseball M(s), basketball M(s)/W(s), cross-country running M(s)/W(s), football M(s), golf M(s)/W(s), soccer W(s), softball W(s), track and field M(s)/W(s), volleyball W(s). *Intramural sports:* basketball M/W, football M/W, lacrosse W, racquetball M/W, softball M/W, volleyball M/W.

Standardized Tests *Required:* ACT (for admission).

Costs (2012–13) *Comprehensive fee:* $37,450 includes full-time tuition ($29,700) and room and board ($7750). Full-time tuition and fees vary according to program. Part-time tuition: $625 per credit. Part-time tuition and fees vary according to course load and program. *Room and board:* Room and board charges vary according to housing facility. *Payment plan:* installment. *Waivers:* employees or children of employees.

Financial Aid Of all full-time matriculated undergraduates who enrolled in 2011, 869 applied for aid, 771 were judged to have need, 120 had their need fully met. 46 Federal Work-Study jobs (averaging $2380). 29 state and other part-time jobs (averaging $2255). In 2011, 79 non-need-based awards were made. *Average percent of need met:* 72%. *Average financial aid package:* $17,470. *Average need-based loan:* $4336. *Average need-based gift aid:* $16,283. *Average non-need-based aid:* $8210. *Average indebtedness upon graduation:* $30,944.

Applying *Options:* electronic application, early admission, deferred entrance. *Application fee:* $30. *Required:* high school transcript, 2 letters of recommendation. *Required for some:* essay or personal statement. *Recommended:* minimum 2.0 GPA. *Application deadlines:* 8/1 (freshmen), 8/1 (transfers). *Notification:* continuous (freshmen), continuous (transfers).

Freshman Application Contact Kristin Schoon, Director of Undergraduate Admission, Concordia University, St. Paul, 275 Syndicate North, St. Paul, MN 55104-5494. *Phone:* 651-641-8230. *Toll-free phone:* 800-333-4705. *Fax:* 651-603-6320. *E-mail:* admission@csp.edu. *Web site:* http://www.csp.edu/.

Crossroads College
Rochester, Minnesota

Freshman Application Contact Mr. Scott Klaehn, Director of Admissions, Crossroads College, 920 Mayowood Road, SW, Rochester, MN 55902-2382. *Phone:* 507-288-4563 Ext. 304. *Toll-free phone:* 800-456-7651. *Fax:* 507-288-9046. *E-mail:* admissions@crossroadscollege.edu. *Web site:* http://www.crossroadscollege.edu/.

Crown College
St. Bonifacius, Minnesota

- **Independent** comprehensive, founded 1916, affiliated with The Christian and Missionary Alliance
- **Small-town** 215-acre campus with easy access to Minneapolis-St. Paul
- **Endowment** $6.5 million
- **Coed** 1,030 undergraduate students, 79% full-time, 57% women, 43% men
- **Minimally difficult** entrance level, 78% of applicants were admitted

Undergraduates 814 full-time, 216 part-time. Students come from 34 states and territories; 13 other countries; 31% are from out of state; 4% Black or African American, non-Hispanic/Latino; 2% Hispanic/Latino; 7% Asian, non-Hispanic/Latino; 0.2% Native Hawaiian or other Pacific Islander, non-Hispanic/Latino; 0.7% American Indian or Alaska Native, non-Hispanic/Latino; 0.9% Two or more races, non-Hispanic/Latino; 7% Race/ethnicity unknown; 1% international; 5% transferred in; 79% live on campus. *Retention:* 63% of full-time freshmen returned.

Freshmen *Admission:* 453 applied, 352 admitted, 158 enrolled. *Average high school GPA:* 3.36. *Test scores:* SAT critical reading scores over 500: 78%; SAT math scores over 500: 63%; ACT scores over 18: 95%; SAT critical reading scores over 600: 32%; SAT math scores over 600: 27%; ACT scores over

24: 44%; SAT critical reading scores over 700: 5%; SAT math scores over 700: 9%; ACT scores over 30: 4%.

Faculty *Total:* 151, 23% full-time, 15% with terminal degrees. *Student/faculty ratio:* 14:1.

Academics *Calendar:* semesters. *Degrees:* certificates, associate, bachelor's, master's, and postbachelor's certificates. *Special study options:* academic remediation for entering students, accelerated degree program, adult/continuing education programs, advanced placement credit, distance learning, double majors, English as a second language, external degree program, honors programs, independent study, internships, part-time degree program, services for LD students, study abroad, summer session for credit. *ROTC:* Army (c).

Computers on Campus 95 computers/terminals are available on campus for general student use. Students can access the following: campus intranet, computer help desk, free student e-mail accounts, online (class) registration. Campuswide network is available. 95% of college-owned or -operated housing units are wired for high-speed Internet access. Wireless service is available via classrooms, computer labs, dorm rooms, libraries, student centers.

Student Life *Housing:* on-campus residence required through senior year. *Options:* men-only, women-only. Campus housing is university owned. Freshman campus housing is guaranteed. *Activities and organizations:* drama/theater group, student-run newspaper, radio station, choral group, Hmong Student Fellowship, Global Impact Team, Student Activities Board, Student Senate, Storm Chaser Newspaper. *Campus security:* 24-hour emergency response devices, student patrols, late-night transport/escort service, controlled dormitory access. *Student services:* health clinic, personal/psychological counseling.

Athletics Member NCAA. All Division III. *Intercollegiate sports:* baseball M, basketball M/W, cross-country running M/W, football M, golf M, soccer M/W, softball W, volleyball W. *Intramural sports:* basketball M/W, track and field M(c)/W(c), volleyball M/W.

Standardized Tests *Required:* SAT or ACT (for admission).

Costs (2012–13) *Comprehensive fee:* $29,580 includes full-time tuition ($22,100) and room and board ($7480). Full-time tuition and fees vary according to course load and program. Part-time tuition: $920 per credit. Part-time tuition and fees vary according to course load and program. *College room only:* $3890. Room and board charges vary according to board plan and housing facility. *Payment plan:* installment. *Waivers:* employees or children of employees.

Financial Aid Of all full-time matriculated undergraduates who enrolled in 2010, 546 applied for aid, 510 were judged to have need, 47 had their need fully met. 98 Federal Work-Study jobs (averaging $1881). 61 state and other part-time jobs (averaging $679). In 2010, 36 non-need-based awards were made. *Average percent of need met:* 62%. *Average financial aid package:* $15,563. *Average need-based loan:* $4640. *Average need-based gift aid:* $6017. *Average non-need-based aid:* $7675. *Average indebtedness upon graduation:* $38,042. *Financial aid deadline:* 8/1.

Applying *Options:* electronic application, early admission, deferred entrance. *Application fee:* $20. *Required:* essay or personal statement, high school transcript, minimum 2.0 GPA. *Required for some:* interview. *Application deadlines:* rolling (freshmen), rolling (out-of-state freshmen), rolling (transfers). *Notification:* continuous (freshmen), continuous (out-of-state freshmen), continuous (transfers).

Freshman Application Contact Mr. Bret Hyder, Assistant Director of Admissions, Crown College, 8700 College View Drive, St. Bonifacius, MN 55375-9001. *Phone:* 952-446-4142. *Toll-free phone:* 800-68-CROWN. *Fax:* 952-446-4149. *E-mail:* admissions@crown.edu. *Web site:* http://www.crown.edu/.

DeVry University
Edina, Minnesota

Freshman Application Contact DeVry University, 7700 France Avenue South, Suite 575, Edina, MN 55435. *Toll-free phone:* 866-338-7941. *Web site:* http://www.devry.edu/.

Dunwoody College of Technology
Minneapolis, Minnesota

Freshman Application Contact Bonney Bielen, Director of Admissions and Student Services, Dunwoody College of Technology, 818 Dunwoody Boulevard, Minneapolis, MN 55403. *Phone:* 612-374-5800. *Toll-free phone:* 800-292-4625. *Web site:* http://www.dunwoody.edu/.

Globe University–Minneapolis
Minneapolis, Minnesota

- **Proprietary** comprehensive, part of Globe Education Network (GEN) which is composed of Globe University, Minnesota School of Business,

Broadview University, The Institute of Production and Recording and Minnesota School of Cosmetology
- **Urban** campus
- **Coed** 188 undergraduate students, 31% full-time, 53% women, 47% men

Undergraduates 59 full-time, 129 part-time. Students come from 1 other state; 26% Black or African American, non-Hispanic/Latino; 4% Hispanic/Latino; 2% Asian, non-Hispanic/Latino; 2% American Indian or Alaska Native, non-Hispanic/Latino; 4% Two or more races, non-Hispanic/Latino; 7% Race/ethnicity unknown; 14% international; 28% transferred in. *Retention:* 25% of full-time freshmen returned.

Freshmen *Admission:* 27 enrolled.

Faculty *Total:* 30, 27% full-time, 50% with terminal degrees. *Student/faculty ratio:* 14:1.

Academics *Degrees:* diplomas, associate, bachelor's, master's, and doctoral. *Special study options:* academic remediation for entering students, accelerated degree program, adult/continuing education programs, advanced placement credit, internships, part-time degree program, services for LD students, summer session for credit.

Computers on Campus 46 computers/terminals and 64 ports are available on campus for general student use. Students can access the following: computer help desk, free student e-mail accounts, online (class) grades, online (class) registration, online (class) schedules. Campuswide network is available. Wireless service is available via entire campus.

Student Life *Housing:* college housing not available. *Campus security:* 24-hour emergency response devices, late-night transport/escort service.

Standardized Tests *Required:* AccuPlacer is required of all applicants unless documentation of a minimum ACT composite score of 21 or documentation of a minimum composite score of 1485 on the SAT is presented (for admission).

Applying *Options:* electronic application. *Application fee:* $50. *Required:* high school transcript, interview. *Required for some:* essay or personal statement, 2 letters of recommendation, GED certificate in lieu of high school transcript. *Application deadlines:* rolling (freshmen), rolling (out-of-state freshmen), rolling (transfers). *Notification:* continuous (freshmen), continuous (out-of-state freshmen), continuous (transfers).

Freshman Application Contact Globe University–Minneapolis, 80 South 8th Street, Suite 51, Minneapolis, MN 55402. *Phone:* 612-455-3000. *Web site:* http://www.globeuniversity.edu/.

Globe University–Woodbury

Woodbury, Minnesota

- **Proprietary** comprehensive, founded 1885, part of Globe Education Network (GEN) which is composed of Globe University, Minnesota School of Business, Broadview University, The Institute of Production and Recording and Minnesota School of Cosmetology
- **Suburban** 5-acre campus with easy access to Minneapolis-St. Paul
- **Coed** 1,499 undergraduate students, 35% full-time, 71% women, 29% men

Undergraduates 518 full-time, 981 part-time. Students come from 12 states and territories; 6% are from out of state; 7% Black or African American, non-Hispanic/Latino; 3% Hispanic/Latino; 5% Asian, non-Hispanic/Latino; 0.3% Native Hawaiian or other Pacific Islander, non-Hispanic/Latino; 1% American Indian or Alaska Native, non-Hispanic/Latino; 2% Two or more races, non-Hispanic/Latino; 9% Race/ethnicity unknown; 1% international; 22% transferred in. *Retention:* 38% of full-time freshmen returned.

Freshmen *Admission:* 171 enrolled.

Faculty *Total:* 159, 14% full-time, 20% with terminal degrees. *Student/faculty ratio:* 15:1.

Academics *Calendar:* quarters. *Degrees:* diplomas, associate, bachelor's, master's, and doctoral. *Special study options:* academic remediation for entering students, accelerated degree program, adult/continuing education programs, advanced placement credit, internships, part-time degree program, services for LD students, summer session for credit.

Computers on Campus 95 computers/terminals and 251 ports are available on campus for general student use. Students can access the following: computer help desk, free student e-mail accounts, online (class) grades, online (class) registration, online (class) schedules. Campuswide network is available. Wireless service is available via entire campus.

Student Life *Campus security:* 24-hour emergency response devices, late-night transport/escort service.

Standardized Tests *Required:* AccuPlacer is required of all applicants unless documentation of a minimum ACT composite score of 21 or documentation of a minimum composite score of 1485 on the SAT is presented (for admission).

Applying *Options:* electronic application. *Application fee:* $50. *Required:* high school transcript, interview. *Required for some:* essay or personal statement, 2 letters of recommendation, GED certificate in lieu of high school transcript. *Application deadlines:* rolling (freshmen), rolling (out-of-state

freshmen), rolling (transfers). *Notification:* continuous (freshmen), continuous (out-of-state freshmen), continuous (transfers).

Freshman Application Contact Globe University–Woodbury, 8089 Globe Drive, Woodbury, MN 55125. *Phone:* 651-730-5100. *Toll-free phone:* 800-231-0660. *Web site:* http://www.globeuniversity.edu/.

Gustavus Adolphus College

St. Peter, Minnesota

- **Independent** 4-year, founded 1862, affiliated with Evangelical Lutheran Church in America
- **Small-town** 340-acre campus with easy access to Minneapolis-St. Paul
- **Endowment** $108.9 million
- **Coed** 2,471 undergraduate students, 99% full-time, 56% women, 44% men
- **Very difficult** entrance level, 64% of applicants were admitted

Undergraduates 2,436 full-time, 35 part-time. Students come from 41 states and territories; 20 other countries; 17% are from out of state; 3% Black or African American, non-Hispanic/Latino; 3% Hispanic/Latino; 5% Asian, non-Hispanic/Latino; 0.4% American Indian or Alaska Native, non-Hispanic/Latino; 1% Two or more races, non-Hispanic/Latino; 0.3% Race/ethnicity unknown; 2% international; 1% transferred in; 95% live on campus. *Retention:* 93% of full-time freshmen returned.

Freshmen *Admission:* 4,818 applied, 3,088 admitted, 733 enrolled. *Average high school GPA:* 3.64. *Test scores:* ACT scores over 18: 100%; ACT scores over 24: 88%; ACT scores over 30: 25%.

Faculty *Total:* 269, 75% full-time, 77% with terminal degrees. *Student/faculty ratio:* 11:1.

Academics *Calendar:* 4-1-4. *Degree:* bachelor's. *Special study options:* accelerated degree program, advanced placement credit, cooperative education, double majors, honors programs, independent study, internships, off-campus study, services for LD students, student-designed majors, study abroad, summer session for credit. *ROTC:* Army (c). *Unusual degree programs:* 3-2 engineering with Minnesota State University, Mankato; University of Minnesota; social work; occupational therapy with Washington University in St. Louis.

Computers on Campus 440 computers/terminals and 5,000 ports are available on campus for general student use. Students can access the following: computer help desk, free student e-mail accounts, online (class) grades, online (class) registration, online (class) schedules. Campuswide network is available. 100% of college-owned or -operated housing units are wired for high-speed Internet access. Wireless service is available via entire campus.

Student Life *Housing:* on-campus residence required through senior year. *Options:* coed. Campus housing is university owned. Freshman campus housing is guaranteed. *Activities and organizations:* drama/theater group, student-run newspaper, radio and television station, choral group, Proclaim, Big Partner/Little Partner, Study Buddies, I am...We are, Pound Pals, national fraternities, national sororities. *Campus security:* 24-hour emergency response devices and patrols, late-night transport/escort service, controlled dormitory access. *Student services:* health clinic, personal/psychological counseling, women's center.

Athletics Member NCAA. All Division III. *Intercollegiate sports:* baseball M, basketball M/W, cross-country running M/W, football M, golf M/W, gymnastics W, ice hockey M/W, lacrosse M(c), rugby M(c)/W(c), skiing (cross-country) M/W, soccer M/W, softball W, swimming and diving M/W, tennis M/W, track and field M/W, ultimate Frisbee M(c)/W(c), volleyball M(c)/W. *Intramural sports:* badminton M/W, basketball M/W, football M/W, golf M/W, ice hockey M/W, racquetball M/W, rugby M/W, skiing (cross-country) M/W, skiing (downhill) M/W, soccer M/W, softball M/W, swimming and diving M/W, tennis M/W, track and field M/W, ultimate Frisbee M/W, volleyball M/W, water polo M/W, weight lifting M/W.

Standardized Tests *Recommended:* SAT or ACT (for admission).

Costs (2011–12) *One-time required fee:* $420. *Comprehensive fee:* $44,177 includes full-time tuition ($35,100), mandatory fees ($377), and room and board ($8700). Part-time tuition: $4790 per credit hour. *College room only:* $5600. Room and board charges vary according to board plan and housing facility. *Payment plans:* tuition prepayment, installment.

Financial Aid Of all full-time matriculated undergraduates who enrolled in 2010, 1,947 applied for aid, 1,798 were judged to have need, 988 had their need fully met. In 2010, 672 non-need-based awards were made. *Average percent of need met:* 93%. *Average financial aid package:* $26,967. *Average need-based loan:* $3758. *Average need-based gift aid:* $21,786. *Average non-need-based aid:* $10,229. *Average indebtedness upon graduation:* $25,694. *Financial aid deadline:* 4/15.

Applying *Options:* electronic application, early admission, early action, deferred entrance. *Required:* essay or personal statement, high school transcript, 1 letter of recommendation. *Recommended:* interview. *Application*

deadlines: 4/1 (freshmen), rolling (transfers), 11/1 (early action). *Notification:* continuous (freshmen), continuous (transfers), 11/20 (early action).
Freshman Application Contact Dr. Tom M. Crady, Vice President for Enrollment Management, Gustavus Adolphus College, 800 West College Avenue, St. Peter, MN 56082-1498. *Phone:* 507-933-7676. *Toll-free phone:* 800-GUSTAVU(S). *Fax:* 507-933-7474. *E-mail:* admission@gac.edu. *Web site:* http://www.gustavus.edu/.

Hamline University
St. Paul, Minnesota

- **Independent** comprehensive, founded 1854, affiliated with United Methodist Church
- **Urban** 60-acre campus with easy access to Minneapolis-St. Paul
- **Endowment** $75.1 million
- **Coed** 2,016 undergraduate students, 94% full-time, 57% women, 43% men
- **Moderately difficult** entrance level, 71% of applicants were admitted

Undergraduates 1,900 full-time, 116 part-time. Students come from 38 states and territories; 56 other countries; 17% are from out of state; 7% Black or African American, non-Hispanic/Latino; 5% Hispanic/Latino; 6% Asian, non-Hispanic/Latino; 0.6% American Indian or Alaska Native, non-Hispanic/Latino; 4% Two or more races, non-Hispanic/Latino; 4% Race/ethnicity unknown; 3% international; 6% transferred in; 42% live on campus. *Retention:* 80% of full-time freshmen returned.
Freshmen *Admission:* 2,982 applied, 2,131 admitted, 515 enrolled. *Average high school GPA:* 3.45. *Test scores:* SAT critical reading scores over 500: 67%; SAT math scores over 500: 69%; SAT writing scores over 500: 67%; ACT scores over 18: 96%; SAT critical reading scores over 600: 34%; SAT math scores over 600: 33%; SAT writing scores over 600: 26%; ACT scores over 24: 57%; SAT critical reading scores over 700: 9%; SAT math scores over 700: 5%; SAT writing scores over 700: 5%; ACT scores over 30: 13%.
Faculty *Total:* 485, 40% full-time, 47% with terminal degrees. *Student/faculty ratio:* 12:1.
Academics *Calendar:* 4-1-4. *Degrees:* bachelor's, master's, doctoral, postmaster's, postbachelor's, and first professional certificates. *Special study options:* advanced placement credit, double majors, English as a second language, honors programs, independent study, internships, off-campus study, part-time degree program, services for LD students, student-designed majors, study abroad, summer session for credit. *ROTC:* Army (c), Air Force (c). *Unusual degree programs:* 3-2 engineering with University of Minnesota, Washington University in St. Louis.
Computers on Campus 300 computers/terminals and 500 ports are available on campus for general student use. Students can access the following: campus intranet, computer help desk, free student e-mail accounts, online (class) grades, online (class) registration, online (class) schedules. Campuswide network is available. 99% of college-owned or -operated housing units are wired for high-speed Internet access. Wireless service is available via entire campus.
Student Life *Housing options:* coed, men-only, women-only, disabled students. Campus housing is university owned. Freshman campus housing is guaranteed. *Activities and organizations:* drama/theater group, student-run newspaper, radio and television station, choral group, Student Congress (HUSC), Hand in Hand (elementary school mentoring program), Residence Hall Association, PRIDE, Hamline Oracle (student newspaper), national fraternities. *Campus security:* 24-hour emergency response devices and patrols, late-night transport/escort service, controlled dormitory access, Security cameras on campus and in residence halls. Security officers are trained as first responders. *Student services:* health clinic, personal/psychological counseling, women's center.
Athletics Member NCAA. All Division III. *Intercollegiate sports:* baseball M, basketball M/W, cheerleading W(c), cross-country running M/W, football M, gymnastics W, ice hockey M/W, lacrosse M(c)/W(c), soccer M/W, softball W, swimming and diving M/W, tennis M/W, track and field M/W, ultimate Frisbee M(c)/W(c), volleyball W. *Intramural sports:* basketball M/W, football M/W, racquetball M/W, rock climbing M(c)/W(c), soccer M/W, volleyball M/W.
Standardized Tests *Required:* SAT or ACT (for admission).
Costs (2012–13) *Comprehensive fee:* $42,288 includes full-time tuition ($33,236), mandatory fees ($352), and room and board ($8700). Part-time tuition: $1040 per credit. Part-time tuition and fees vary according to course load. *Required fees:* $320 per year part-time. *College room only:* $4500. Room and board charges vary according to housing facility. *Payment plans:* installment, deferred payment. *Waivers:* children of alumni and employees or children of employees.
Financial Aid Of all full-time matriculated undergraduates who enrolled in 2011, 1,809 applied for aid, 1,551 were judged to have need, 241 had their need fully met. 475 Federal Work-Study jobs (averaging $2309). 795 state and other part-time jobs (averaging $2209). In 2011, 235 non-need-based awards

were made. *Average percent of need met:* 78%. *Average financial aid package:* $24,995. *Average need-based loan:* $4658. *Average need-based gift aid:* $18,992. *Average non-need-based aid:* $11,897. *Average indebtedness upon graduation:* $34,599.
Applying *Options:* electronic application, early admission, early action, deferred entrance. *Required:* essay or personal statement, high school transcript, 1 letter of recommendation, ACT or SAT. *Recommended:* interview. *Application deadlines:* rolling (freshmen), rolling (out-of-state freshmen), rolling (transfers), 12/1 (early action). *Notification:* continuous (freshmen), continuous (out-of-state freshmen), continuous (transfers), 1/15 (early action).
Freshman Application Contact Mr. Milyon Trulove, Director of Admission, Hamline University, 1536 Hewitt Avenue, MS-C1930, St. Paul, MN 55104. *Phone:* 651-523-2207. *Toll-free phone:* 800-753-9753. *Fax:* 651-523-2458. *E-mail:* admission@hamline.edu. *Web site:* http://www.hamline.edu/.

Herzing University
Minneapolis, Minnesota

Freshman Application Contact Ms. Shelly Larson, Director of Admissions, Herzing University, 5700 West Broadway, Minneapolis, MN 55428. *Phone:* 763-231-3155. *Toll-free phone:* 800-596-0724. *Fax:* 763-535-9205. *E-mail:* info@mpls.herzing.edu. *Web site:* http://www.herzing.edu/.

ITT Technical Institute
Brooklyn Center, Minnesota

- **Proprietary** primarily 2-year, part of ITT Educational Services, Inc.
- **Coed**

Academics *Calendar:* quarters. *Degrees:* associate and bachelor's.
Freshman Application Contact Director of Recruitment, ITT Technical Institute, 6120 Earle Brown Drive, Suite 100, Brooklyn Center, MN 55430. *Phone:* 763-549-5900. *Toll-free phone:* 800-216-8883. *Web site:* http://www.itt-tech.edu/.

ITT Technical Institute
Eden Prairie, Minnesota

- **Proprietary** primarily 2-year, founded 2003, part of ITT Educational Services, Inc.
- **Coed**
- **Minimally difficult** entrance level

Academics *Calendar:* quarters. *Degrees:* associate and bachelor's.
Freshman Application Contact Director of Recruitment, ITT Technical Institute, 8911 Columbine Road, Eden Prairie, MN 55347. *Phone:* 952-914-5300. *Toll-free phone:* 888-488-9646. *Web site:* http://www.itt-tech.edu/.

Macalester College
St. Paul, Minnesota

- **Independent Presbyterian** 4-year, founded 1874
- **Urban** 53-acre campus
- **Endowment** $654.2 million
- **Coed** 2,005 undergraduate students, 99% full-time, 59% women, 41% men
- **Very difficult** entrance level, 35% of applicants were admitted

Undergraduates 1,978 full-time, 27 part-time. Students come from 89 other countries; 81% are from out of state; 3% Black or African American, non-Hispanic/Latino; 6% Hispanic/Latino; 6% Asian, non-Hispanic/Latino; 0.5% American Indian or Alaska Native, non-Hispanic/Latino; 0.2% Two or more races, non-Hispanic/Latino; 12% international; 0.9% transferred in; 62% live on campus. *Retention:* 94% of full-time freshmen returned.
Freshmen *Admission:* 6,111 applied, 2,137 admitted, 478 enrolled. *Test scores:* SAT critical reading scores over 500: 100%; SAT math scores over 500: 100%; SAT writing scores over 500: 100%; ACT scores over 18: 100%; SAT critical reading scores over 600: 89%; SAT math scores over 600: 88%; SAT writing scores over 600: 91%; ACT scores over 24: 99%; SAT critical reading scores over 700: 51%; SAT math scores over 700: 35%; SAT writing scores over 700: 39%; ACT scores over 30: 57%.
Faculty *Total:* 233, 73% full-time, 85% with terminal degrees. *Student/faculty ratio:* 10:1.
Academics *Calendar:* semesters. *Degree:* bachelor's. *Special study options:* advanced placement credit, double majors, honors programs, independent study, internships, off-campus study, part-time degree program, services for LD students, student-designed majors, study abroad. *ROTC:* Army (c), Navy (c), Air Force (c). *Unusual degree programs:* 3-2 engineering with Washington University in St. Louis, University of Minnesota; architecture with Washington University in St. Louis.

Computers on Campus 486 computers/terminals and 2,500 ports are available on campus for general student use. Students can access the following: campus intranet, computer help desk, free student e-mail accounts, online (class) grades, online (class) registration, online (class) schedules, Web space, online course management (LMS), shared calendars, Room and Board transactions. Campuswide network is available. 100% of college-owned or -operated housing units are wired for high-speed Internet access. Wireless service is available via entire campus.

Student Life *Housing:* on-campus residence required through sophomore year. *Options:* coed, men-only, women-only, cooperative. Campus housing is university owned. Freshman campus housing is guaranteed. *Activities and organizations:* drama/theater group, student-run newspaper, radio station, choral group, Community Service Organization, Outing Club (outdoor recreation), Multicultural Organization, International Organization, campus publications. *Campus security:* 24-hour emergency response devices and patrols, late-night transport/escort service. *Student services:* health clinic, personal/psychological counseling.

Athletics Member NCAA. All Division III. *Intercollegiate sports:* baseball M, basketball M/W, crew M(c)/W(c), cross-country running M/W, football M, golf M/W, ice hockey M(c)/W(c), lacrosse W(c), rugby M(c)/W(c), skiing (cross-country) M(c)/W(c), soccer M/W, softball W, swimming and diving M/W, tennis M/W, track and field M/W, ultimate Frisbee M(c)/W(c), volleyball M(c)/W, water polo M(c)/W. *Intramural sports:* basketball M/W, racquetball M/W, soccer M/W, softball M/W, table tennis M/W, ultimate Frisbee M/W.

Standardized Tests *Required:* SAT or ACT (for admission).

Costs (2012–13) *Comprehensive fee:* $53,419 includes full-time tuition ($43,472), mandatory fees ($221), and room and board ($9726). Full-time tuition and fees vary according to course load. Part-time tuition and fees vary according to course load. *College room only:* $5214. Room and board charges vary according to board plan and housing facility. *Payment plan:* installment. *Waivers:* employees or children of employees.

Financial Aid Of all full-time matriculated undergraduates who enrolled in 2011, 1,541 applied for aid, 1,390 were judged to have need, 1,390 had their need fully met. In 2011, 87 non-need-based awards were made. *Average percent of need met:* 100%. *Average financial aid package:* $35,580. *Average need-based loan:* $4284. *Average need-based gift aid:* $30,331. *Average non-need-based aid:* $9330. *Average indebtedness upon graduation:* $21,123. *Financial aid deadline:* 3/1.

Applying *Options:* electronic application, early admission, early decision, deferred entrance. *Application fee:* $40. *Required:* essay or personal statement, high school transcript, 2 letters of recommendation. *Recommended:* interview. *Application deadlines:* 1/15 (freshmen), 4/15 (transfers). *Early decision deadline:* 11/15 (for plan 1), 1/3 (for plan 2). *Notification:* 3/30 (freshmen), 5/15 (transfers), 12/15 (early decision plan 1), 2/7 (early decision plan 2).

Freshman Application Contact Mr. Lorne T. Robinson, Dean of Admissions and Financial Aid, Macalester College, 1600 Grand Avenue, St. Paul, MN 55105-1899. *Phone:* 651-696-6357. *Toll-free phone:* 800-231-7974. *Fax:* 651-696-6724. *E-mail:* admissions@macalester.edu. *Web site:* http://www.macalester.edu/.

Martin Luther College
New Ulm, Minnesota

- **Independent** comprehensive, founded 1995, affiliated with Wisconsin Evangelical Lutheran Synod
- **Small-town** 50-acre campus
- **Coed** 730 undergraduate students, 93% full-time, 51% women, 49% men
- **Moderately difficult** entrance level, 95% of applicants were admitted

Undergraduates 679 full-time, 51 part-time. 83% are from out of state; 0.3% Black or African American, non-Hispanic/Latino; 0.7% Hispanic/Latino; 0.4% Asian, non-Hispanic/Latino; 0.4% American Indian or Alaska Native, non-Hispanic/Latino; 0.7% Two or more races, non-Hispanic/Latino; 0.1% Race/ethnicity unknown; 1% international; 2% transferred in; 87% live on campus. *Retention:* 84% of full-time freshmen returned.

Freshmen *Admission:* 223 applied, 212 admitted, 172 enrolled. *Average high school GPA:* 3.55. *Test scores:* ACT scores over 18: 99%; ACT scores over 24: 61%; ACT scores over 30: 11%.

Faculty *Total:* 73, 67% full-time, 44% with terminal degrees. *Student/faculty ratio:* 12:1.

Academics *Calendar:* semesters. *Degrees:* certificates, diplomas, bachelor's, and master's.

Computers on Campus Campuswide network is available.

Student Life *Housing:* on-campus residence required through junior year. *Options:* men-only, women-only. Campus housing is university owned. *Activities and organizations:* drama/theater group, choral group. *Student services:* health clinic, personal/psychological counseling.

Athletics Member NCAA, NAIA. All NCAA Division III. *Intercollegiate sports:* baseball M, basketball M/W, cross-country running M/W, football M, golf M, soccer M/W, softball W, tennis M/W, track and field M/W, volleyball W. *Intramural sports:* badminton M/W, basketball M/W, bowling M/W, football M, soccer M/W, softball M/W, tennis M/W, volleyball M/W.

Standardized Tests *Required:* ACT (for admission).

Costs (2011–12) *Comprehensive fee:* $15,710 includes full-time tuition ($11,320) and room and board ($4390). *Payment plan:* installment.

Financial Aid Of all full-time matriculated undergraduates who enrolled in 2010, 620 applied for aid, 545 were judged to have need, 64 had their need fully met. In 2010, 104 non-need-based awards were made. *Average percent of need met:* 66%. *Average financial aid package:* $8720. *Average need-based loan:* $4163. *Average need-based gift aid:* $5910. *Average non-need-based aid:* $2020. *Average indebtedness upon graduation:* $21,799. *Financial aid deadline:* 4/15.

Applying *Options:* deferred entrance. *Required:* high school transcript, minimum 2.0 GPA. *Application deadlines:* 5/1 (freshmen), 5/1 (transfers). *Notification:* continuous (freshmen), continuous (transfers).

Freshman Application Contact Prof. Ronald Brutlag, Director of Admissions, Martin Luther College, 1995 Luther Court, New Ulm, MN 56073. *Phone:* 507-354-8221 Ext. 280. *Toll-free phone:* 877-MLC-1995. *E-mail:* brutlaro@mlc-wels.edu. *Web site:* http://www.mlc-wels.edu/.

McNally Smith College of Music
Saint Paul, Minnesota

- **Proprietary** comprehensive, founded 1985
- **Urban** 1-acre campus with easy access to Minneapolis-St. Paul
- **Coed** 680 undergraduate students, 90% full-time, 21% women, 79% men
- **Moderately difficult** entrance level

Undergraduates 611 full-time, 69 part-time. Students come from 36 states and territories; 12 other countries; 42% are from out of state; 16% transferred in; 15% live on campus. *Retention:* 80% of full-time freshmen returned.

Freshmen *Admission:* 133 enrolled.

Faculty *Total:* 112, 45% full-time. *Student/faculty ratio:* 10:1.

Academics *Calendar:* semesters. *Degrees:* diplomas, associate, bachelor's, and master's. *Special study options:* academic remediation for entering students, advanced placement credit, cooperative education, distance learning, double majors, independent study, internships, off-campus study, part-time degree program, services for LD students, study abroad, summer session for credit.

Computers on Campus 40 computers/terminals are available on campus for general student use. Students can access the following: campus intranet, computer help desk, free student e-mail accounts, online (class) grades, online (class) registration, online (class) schedules. Campuswide network is available. Wireless service is available via entire campus.

Student Life *Housing options:* coed. Campus housing is leased by the school. Freshman applicants given priority for college housing. *Activities and organizations:* student-run newspaper, choral group, Student Advisory Board, Audio Engineering Society, Minnesota Songwriters Association, Jazz Club, intramural sports. *Campus security:* 24-hour emergency response devices and patrols, late-night transport/escort service. *Student services:* personal/psychological counseling.

Standardized Tests *Required for some:* ACT (for admission). *Recommended:* ACT (for admission).

Costs (2011–12) *Comprehensive fee:* $29,820 includes full-time tuition ($22,620), mandatory fees ($2200), and room and board ($5000). Full-time tuition and fees vary according to course load and degree level. Part-time tuition: $870 per credit. Part-time tuition and fees vary according to course load and degree level. No tuition increase for student's term of enrollment. *Required fees:* $450 per term part-time. *Room and board:* Room and board charges vary according to board plan and housing facility. *Payment plans:* tuition prepayment, installment, deferred payment. *Waivers:* employees or children of employees.

Financial Aid Of all full-time matriculated undergraduates who enrolled in 2009, 40 Federal Work-Study jobs (averaging $1500). 19 state and other part-time jobs (averaging $1124). *Financial aid deadline:* 8/1.

Applying *Options:* electronic application. *Application fee:* $75. *Required:* essay or personal statement, high school transcript, minimum 2.0 GPA, 2 letters of recommendation, interview. *Required for some:* audition. *Recommended:* minimum 2.5 GPA. *Application deadline:* 8/1 (freshmen). *Notification:* 8/1 (freshmen).

Freshman Application Contact Mrs. Katie Marshall, Admissions Representative, McNally Smith College of Music, 19 Exchange Street East, St. Paul, MN 55101. *Phone:* 651-361-3451. *Toll-free phone:* 800-594-9500. *Fax:* 651-291-0366. *E-mail:* katie.marshall@mcnallysmith.edu. *Web site:* http://www.mcnallysmith.edu/.

Metropolitan State University
St. Paul, Minnesota

- **State-supported** comprehensive, founded 1971, part of Minnesota State Colleges and Universities System
- **Urban** campus with easy access to Minneapolis-St. Paul
- **Endowment** $2.4 million
- **Coed** 7,266 undergraduate students, 36% full-time, 56% women, 44% men
- **Minimally difficult** entrance level

Undergraduates 2,643 full-time, 4,623 part-time. 14% Black or African American, non-Hispanic/Latino; 5% Hispanic/Latino; 10% Asian, non-Hispanic/Latino; 0.1% Native Hawaiian or other Pacific Islander, non-Hispanic/Latino; 0.5% American Indian or Alaska Native, non-Hispanic/Latino; 4% Two or more races, non-Hispanic/Latino; 4% Race/ethnicity unknown; 1% international. *Retention:* 64% of full-time freshmen returned.
Freshmen *Admission:* 72 enrolled.
Faculty *Student/faculty ratio:* 17:1.
Academics *Calendar:* semesters. *Degrees:* certificates, bachelor's, master's, doctoral, and postbachelor's certificates (offers primarily part-time evening degree programs). *Special study options:* adult/continuing education programs, advanced placement credit, distance learning, double majors, English as a second language, external degree program, independent study, internships, off-campus study, part-time degree program, student-designed majors, study abroad, summer session for credit.
Computers on Campus Students can access the following: computer help desk, free student e-mail accounts, online (class) grades, online (class) registration, online (class) schedules. Campuswide network is available. Wireless service is available via entire campus.
Student Life *Housing:* college housing not available. *Activities and organizations:* drama/theater group, student-run newspaper. *Campus security:* 24-hour emergency response devices, late-night transport/escort service. *Student services:* personal/psychological counseling.
Standardized Tests *Recommended:* SAT or ACT (for admission).
Costs (2011–12) *Tuition:* state resident $6028 full-time, $201 per credit part-time; nonresident $12,299 full-time, $410 per credit hour part-time. Full-time tuition and fees vary according to degree level, program, and reciprocity agreements. Part-time tuition and fees vary according to degree level, program, and reciprocity agreements. *Required fees:* $313 full-time, $10 per credit hour part-time. *Waivers:* senior citizens and employees or children of employees.
Applying *Options:* electronic application, deferred entrance. *Application fee:* $20. *Required:* high school transcript, minimum 2.0 GPA. *Application deadlines:* 6/15 (freshmen), 6/15 (transfers).
Freshman Application Contact Mr. Daryl Johnson, Director, Metropolitan State University, 700 East 7th Street, St. Paul, MN 55106. *Phone:* 651-793-1227. *Fax:* 651-793-1546. *E-mail:* daryl.johnson@metrostate.edu. *Web site:* http://www.metrostate.edu/.

Minneapolis College of Art and Design
Minneapolis, Minnesota

- **Independent** comprehensive, founded 1886
- **Urban** 7-acre campus
- **Endowment** $25.9 million
- **Coed**
- **Moderately difficult** entrance level

Faculty *Student/faculty ratio:* 13:1.
Academics *Calendar:* semesters. *Degrees:* bachelor's, master's, and postbachelor's certificates.
Student Life *Campus security:* 24-hour emergency response devices and patrols, late-night transport/escort service, controlled dormitory access.
Standardized Tests *Required:* SAT or ACT (for admission).
Costs (2011–12) *Tuition:* $30,385 full-time, $1266 per credit part-time. Part-time tuition and fees vary according to course load. *Required fees:* $200 full-time, $100 per term part-time. *Room only:* $4540. Room and board charges vary according to housing facility.
Financial Aid *Of all full-time matriculated undergraduates who enrolled in 2011,* 548 applied for aid, 495 were judged to have need, 40 had their need fully met. 70 Federal Work-Study jobs (averaging $2208). 39 state and other part-time jobs (averaging $2057). *In 2011,* 56 non-need-based awards were made. *Average percent of need met:* 65. *Average financial aid package:* $18,514. *Average need-based loan:* $4945. *Average need-based gift aid:* $13,419. *Average non-need-based aid:* $8295. *Average indebtedness upon graduation:* $43,035. *Financial aid deadline:* 4/1.
Applying *Options:* electronic application. *Application fee:* $50. *Required:* essay or personal statement, high school transcript, 1 letter of recommendation.

Required for some: portfolio of visual artwork. *Recommended:* minimum 2.8 GPA, interview.
Freshman Application Contact Minneapolis College of Art and Design, 2501 Stevens Avenue, Minneapolis, MN 55404-4347. *Phone:* 612-874-3762. *Toll-free phone:* 800-874-6223. *Web site:* http://www.mcad.edu/.

Minnesota School of Business–Blaine
Blaine, Minnesota

- **Proprietary** 4-year, part of Globe Education Network (GEN) which is composed of Globe University, Minnesota School of Business, Broadview University, The Institute of Production and Recording and Minnesota School of Cosmetology
- **Suburban** 7-acre campus with easy access to Minneapolis-St. Paul
- **Coed, primarily women** 1,012 undergraduate students, 29% full-time, 74% women, 26% men

Undergraduates 290 full-time, 722 part-time. Students come from 3 states and territories; 0.1% are from out of state; 1% Black or African American, non-Hispanic/Latino; 2% Hispanic/Latino; 3% Asian, non-Hispanic/Latino; 0.1% Native Hawaiian or other Pacific Islander, non-Hispanic/Latino; 0.8% American Indian or Alaska Native, non-Hispanic/Latino; 0.7% Two or more races, non-Hispanic/Latino; 12% Race/ethnicity unknown; 14% transferred in. *Retention:* 48% of full-time freshmen returned.
Freshmen *Admission:* 96 enrolled.
Faculty *Total:* 132, 12% full-time, 22% with terminal degrees. *Student/faculty ratio:* 11:1.
Academics *Degrees:* diplomas, associate, and bachelor's. *Special study options:* academic remediation for entering students, accelerated degree program, adult/continuing education programs, advanced placement credit, internships, part-time degree program, services for LD students, summer session for credit.
Computers on Campus 104 computers/terminals and 96 ports are available on campus for general student use. Students can access the following: computer help desk, free student e-mail accounts, online (class) grades, online (class) registration, online (class) schedules. Campuswide network is available. Wireless service is available via entire campus.
Student Life *Housing:* college housing not available. *Campus security:* 24-hour emergency response devices, late-night transport/escort service.
Applying *Options:* electronic application. *Application fee:* $50. *Required:* high school transcript, interview. *Required for some:* essay or personal statement, 2 letters of recommendation, GED certificate in lieu of high school transcript. *Application deadlines:* rolling (freshmen), rolling (out-of-state freshmen), rolling (transfers). *Notification:* continuous (freshmen), continuous (out-of-state freshmen), continuous (transfers).
Freshman Application Contact Minnesota School of Business–Blaine, 3680 Pheasant Ridge Drive NE, Blaine, MN 55449. *Phone:* 763-225-8000. *Web site:* http://www.msbcollege.edu/oncampus/blaine/.

Minnesota School of Business–Brooklyn Center
Brooklyn Center, Minnesota

- **Proprietary** primarily 2-year, founded 1989, part of Globe Education Network (GEN) which is composed of Globe University, Minnesota School of Business, Broadview University, The Institute of Production and Recording and Minnesota School of Cosmetology
- **Suburban** 4-acre campus with easy access to Minneapolis-St. Paul
- **Coed** 620 undergraduate students, 23% full-time, 68% women, 32% men
- **68%** of applicants were admitted

Undergraduates 145 full-time, 475 part-time. Students come from 2 states and territories; 0.2% are from out of state; 22% Black or African American, non-Hispanic/Latino; 1% Hispanic/Latino; 7% Asian, non-Hispanic/Latino; 1% American Indian or Alaska Native, non-Hispanic/Latino; 2% Two or more races, non-Hispanic/Latino; 40% Race/ethnicity unknown; 14% transferred in. *Retention:* 38% of full-time freshmen returned.
Freshmen *Admission:* 675 applied, 457 admitted, 48 enrolled.
Faculty *Total:* 100, 15% full-time, 14% with terminal degrees. *Student/faculty ratio:* 10:1.
Academics *Calendar:* quarters. *Degrees:* diplomas, associate, and bachelor's. *Special study options:* academic remediation for entering students, accelerated degree program, adult/continuing education programs, advanced placement credit, internships, part-time degree program, services for LD students, summer session for credit.
Computers on Campus 97 computers/terminals and 32 ports are available on campus for general student use. Students can access the following: computer help desk, free student e-mail accounts, online (class) grades, online (class)

registration, online (class) schedules. Campuswide network is available. Wireless service is available via entire campus.

Student Life *Housing:* college housing not available. *Campus security:* 24-hour emergency response devices, late-night transport/escort service.

Standardized Tests *Required:* AccuPlacer is required of all applicants unless documentation of a minimum ACT composite score of 21 or documentation of a minimum composite score of 1485 on the SAT is presented (for admission).

Applying *Options:* electronic application. *Application fee:* $50. *Required:* high school transcript, interview. *Required for some:* essay or personal statement, 2 letters of recommendation. *Application deadlines:* rolling (freshmen), rolling (out-of-state freshmen), rolling (transfers). *Notification:* continuous (freshmen), continuous (out-of-state freshmen), continuous (transfers).

Freshman Application Contact Minnesota School of Business–Brooklyn Center, 5910 Shingle Creek Parkway, Brooklyn Center, MN 55430. *Phone:* 763-566-7777. *Web site:* http://www.msbcollege.edu/.

Minnesota School of Business– Elk River

Elk River, Minnesota

- **Proprietary** 4-year, part of Globe Education Network (GEN) which is composed of Globe University, Minnesota School of Business, Broadview University, The Institute of Production and Recording and Minnesota School of Cosmetology
- **Suburban** 4-acre campus with easy access to Minneapolis-St. Paul
- **Coed** 545 undergraduate students, 32% full-time, 74% women, 26% men

Undergraduates 175 full-time, 370 part-time. Students come from 1 other state; 1% Black or African American, non-Hispanic/Latino; 0.9% Hispanic/Latino; 0.7% Asian, non-Hispanic/Latino; 1% American Indian or Alaska Native, non-Hispanic/Latino; 2% Two or more races, non-Hispanic/Latino; 10% Race/ethnicity unknown; 22% transferred in. *Retention:* 57% of full-time freshmen returned.

Freshmen *Admission:* 79 enrolled.

Faculty *Total:* 48, 21% full-time, 19% with terminal degrees. *Student/faculty ratio:* 16:1.

Academics *Degrees:* diplomas, associate, and bachelor's. *Special study options:* academic remediation for entering students, accelerated degree program, adult/continuing education programs, advanced placement credit, internships, part-time degree program, services for LD students, summer session for credit.

Computers on Campus 65 computers/terminals and 128 ports are available on campus for general student use. Students can access the following: computer help desk, free student e-mail accounts, online (class) grades, online (class) registration, online (class) schedules. Campuswide network is available. Wireless service is available via entire campus.

Student Life *Housing:* college housing not available. *Campus security:* 24-hour emergency response devices, late-night transport/escort service.

Standardized Tests *Required:* AccuPlacer is required of all applicants unless documentation of a minimum ACT composite score of 21 or documentation of a minimum composite score of 1485 on the SAT is presented (for admission).

Applying *Options:* electronic application. *Application fee:* $50. *Required:* high school transcript, interview, High school transcript or GED required of all applicants. *Required for some:* essay or personal statement, 2 letters of recommendation. *Application deadlines:* rolling (freshmen), rolling (out-of-state freshmen), rolling (transfers). *Notification:* continuous (freshmen), continuous (out-of-state freshmen), continuous (transfers).

Freshman Application Contact Minnesota School of Business–Elk River, 11500 193rd Avenue NW, Elk River, MN 55330. *Phone:* 763-367-7000. *Web site:* http://www.msbcollege.edu/locations/minnesota/elk-river/.

Minnesota School of Business– Lakeville

Lakeville, Minnesota

- **Proprietary** 4-year, part of Globe Education Network (GEN) which is composed of Globe University, Minnesota School of Business, Broadview University, The Institute of Production and Recording and Minnesota School of Cosmetology
- **Small-town** 3-acre campus with easy access to Minneapolis-St. Paul
- **Coed** 255 undergraduate students, 45% full-time, 65% women, 35% men

Undergraduates 114 full-time, 141 part-time. Students come from 1 other state; 2% Black or African American, non-Hispanic/Latino; 4% Hispanic/Latino; 4% Asian, non-Hispanic/Latino; 2% Two or more races, non-Hispanic/

Latino; 12% Race/ethnicity unknown; 0.4% international; 29% transferred in. *Retention:* 86% of full-time freshmen returned.

Freshmen *Admission:* 35 enrolled.

Faculty *Total:* 36, 25% full-time, 31% with terminal degrees. *Student/faculty ratio:* 11:1.

Academics *Degrees:* diplomas, associate, and bachelor's. *Special study options:* academic remediation for entering students, accelerated degree program, adult/continuing education programs, advanced placement credit, internships, part-time degree program, services for LD students, summer session for credit.

Computers on Campus 49 computers/terminals and 224 ports are available on campus for general student use. Students can access the following: computer help desk, free student e-mail accounts, online (class) grades, online (class) registration, online (class) schedules. Campuswide network is available. Wireless service is available via entire campus.

Student Life *Housing:* college housing not available. *Campus security:* 24-hour emergency response devices, late-night transport/escort service.

Standardized Tests *Required:* AccuPlacer is required of all applicants unless documentation of a minimum ACT composite score of 21 or documentation of a minimum composite score of 1485 on the SAT is presented (for admission).

Applying *Options:* electronic application. *Application fee:* $50. *Required:* high school transcript, interview. *Required for some:* essay or personal statement, 2 letters of recommendation, GED certificate in lieu of high school transcript. *Application deadlines:* rolling (freshmen), rolling (out-of-state freshmen), rolling (transfers). *Notification:* continuous (freshmen), continuous (out-of-state freshmen), continuous (transfers).

Freshman Application Contact Minnesota School of Business–Lakeville, 17685 Juniper Path, Lakeville, MN 55044. *Phone:* 952-892-9000. *Web site:* http://www.msbcollege.edu/.

Minnesota School of Business– Moorhead

Moorhead, Minnesota

- **Proprietary** 4-year, part of Globe Education Network (GEN) which is composed of Globe University, Minnesota School of Business, Broadview University, The Institute of Production and Recording and Minnesota School of Cosmetology
- **Small-town** 5-acre campus
- **Coed** 318 undergraduate students, 57% full-time, 79% women, 21% men

Undergraduates 180 full-time, 138 part-time. Students come from 3 states and territories; 6% are from out of state; 1% Black or African American, non-Hispanic/Latino; 2% Hispanic/Latino; 0.3% Asian, non-Hispanic/Latino; 2% American Indian or Alaska Native, non-Hispanic/Latino; 3% Two or more races, non-Hispanic/Latino; 4% Race/ethnicity unknown; 16% transferred in. *Retention:* 46% of full-time freshmen returned.

Freshmen *Admission:* 35 enrolled.

Faculty *Total:* 40, 23% full-time, 43% with terminal degrees. *Student/faculty ratio:* 12:1.

Academics *Degrees:* diplomas, associate, and bachelor's. *Special study options:* academic remediation for entering students, accelerated degree program, adult/continuing education programs, advanced placement credit, internships, part-time degree program, services for LD students, summer session for credit.

Computers on Campus 59 computers/terminals and 192 ports are available on campus for general student use. Students can access the following: computer help desk, free student e-mail accounts, online (class) grades, online (class) registration, online (class) schedules. Campuswide network is available. Wireless service is available via entire campus.

Student Life *Housing:* college housing not available. *Campus security:* 24-hour emergency response devices, late-night transport/escort service.

Standardized Tests *Required:* AccuPlacer is required of all applicants unless documentation of a minimum ACT composite score of 21 or documentation of a minimum composite score of 1485 on the SAT is presented (for admission).

Applying *Options:* electronic application. *Application fee:* $50. *Required:* high school transcript, interview, High school transcript or GED required of all applicants. *Required for some:* essay or personal statement, 2 letters of recommendation. *Application deadlines:* rolling (freshmen), rolling (out-of-state freshmen), rolling (transfers). *Notification:* continuous (freshmen), continuous (out-of-state freshmen), continuous (transfers).

Freshman Application Contact Minnesota School of Business–Moorhead, 2777 34th Street South, Moorhead, MN 56560. *Phone:* 218-422-1000. *Web site:* http://www.msbcollege.edu/.

Minnesota School of Business–Plymouth

Minneapolis, Minnesota

- **Proprietary** primarily 2-year, founded 2002, part of Globe Education Network (GEN) which is composed of Globe University, Minnesota School of Business, Broadview University, The Institute of Production and Recording and Minnesota School of Cosmetology
- **Suburban** 7-acre campus with easy access to Minneapolis-St. Paul
- **Coed** 487 undergraduate students, 23% full-time, 74% women, 26% men

Undergraduates 114 full-time, 373 part-time. Students come from 1 other state; 6% Black or African American, non-Hispanic/Latino; 2% Hispanic/Latino; 0.8% Asian, non-Hispanic/Latino; 0.2% Native Hawaiian or other Pacific Islander, non-Hispanic/Latino; 0.8% American Indian or Alaska Native, non-Hispanic/Latino; 2% Two or more races, non-Hispanic/Latino; 11% Race/ethnicity unknown; 14% transferred in. *Retention:* 44% of full-time freshmen returned.

Freshmen *Admission:* 40 enrolled.

Faculty *Total:* 36, 22% full-time, 47% with terminal degrees. *Student/faculty ratio:* 21:1.

Academics *Calendar:* quarters. *Degrees:* diplomas, associate, and bachelor's. *Special study options:* academic remediation for entering students, accelerated degree program, adult/continuing education programs, advanced placement credit, internships, part-time degree program, services for LD students, summer session for credit.

Computers on Campus 39 computers/terminals and 96 ports are available on campus for general student use. Students can access the following: computer help desk, free student e-mail accounts, online (class) grades, online (class) registration, online (class) schedules. Campuswide network is available. Wireless service is available via entire campus.

Student Life *Housing:* college housing not available. *Campus security:* 24-hour emergency response devices, late-night transport/escort service.

Standardized Tests *Required:* AccuPlacer is required of all applicants unless documentation of a minimum ACT composite score of 21 or documentation of a minimum composite score of 1485 on the SAT is presented (for admission).

Applying *Options:* electronic application. *Application fee:* $50. *Required:* high school transcript, interview, High school transcript or GED required of all applicants. *Required for some:* essay or personal statement, 2 letters of recommendation. *Application deadlines:* rolling (freshmen), rolling (out-of-state freshmen), rolling (transfers). *Notification:* continuous (freshmen), continuous (out-of-state freshmen), continuous (transfers).

Freshman Application Contact Minnesota School of Business–Plymouth, Plymouth, MN 55447. *Phone:* 763-476-2000. *Fax:* 763-476-1000. *Web site:* http://www.msbcollege.edu/.

Minnesota School of Business–Richfield

Richfield, Minnesota

- **Proprietary** primarily 2-year, founded 1877, part of Globe Education Network (GEN) which is composed of Globe University, Minnesota School of Business, Broadview University, The Institute of Production and Recording and Minnesota School of Cosmetology
- **Urban** 3-acre campus with easy access to Minneapolis-St. Paul
- **Coed** 1,738 undergraduate students, 30% full-time, 64% women, 36% men

Undergraduates 524 full-time, 1,214 part-time. Students come from 9 states and territories; 1% are from out of state; 9% Black or African American, non-Hispanic/Latino; 2% Hispanic/Latino; 3% Asian, non-Hispanic/Latino; 0.1% Native Hawaiian or other Pacific Islander, non-Hispanic/Latino; 1% American Indian or Alaska Native, non-Hispanic/Latino; 2% Two or more races, non-Hispanic/Latino; 12% Race/ethnicity unknown; 0.2% international; 18% transferred in. *Retention:* 28% of full-time freshmen returned.

Freshmen *Admission:* 144 enrolled.

Faculty *Total:* 177, 12% full-time, 15% with terminal degrees. *Student/faculty ratio:* 16:1.

Academics *Calendar:* quarters. *Degrees:* diplomas, associate, bachelor's, and master's. *Special study options:* academic remediation for entering students, accelerated degree program, adult/continuing education programs, advanced placement credit, internships, part-time degree program, services for LD students, summer session for credit.

Computers on Campus 73 computers/terminals and 192 ports are available on campus for general student use. Students can access the following: computer help desk, free student e-mail accounts, online (class) grades, online (class) registration, online (class) schedules. Campuswide network is available. Wireless service is available via entire campus.

Student Life *Housing:* college housing not available. *Campus security:* 24-hour emergency response devices, late-night transport/escort service.

Standardized Tests *Required:* AccuPlacer is required of all applicants unless documentation of a minimum ACT composite score of 21 or documentation of a minimum composite score of 1485 on the SAT is presented (for admission).

Costs (2011–12) *Waivers:* employees or children of employees.

Applying *Options:* electronic application. *Application fee:* $50. *Required:* high school transcript, interview, High school transcript or GED required of all applicants. Application fee for Nursing Program is $100. *Required for some:* essay or personal statement, 2 letters of recommendation. *Application deadlines:* rolling (freshmen), rolling (out-of-state freshmen), rolling (transfers). *Notification:* continuous (freshmen), continuous (out-of-state freshmen), continuous (transfers).

Freshman Application Contact Minnesota School of Business–Richfield, 1401 West 76th Street, Suite 500, Richfield, MN 55423. *Phone:* 612-861-2000. *Toll-free phone:* 800-752-4223. *Web site:* http://www.msbcollege.edu/.

Minnesota School of Business–Rochester

Rochester, Minnesota

- **Proprietary** comprehensive, part of Globe Education Network (GEN) which is composed of Globe University, Minnesota School of Business, Broadview University, The Institute of Production and Recording and Minnesota School of Cosmetology
- **Small-town** 5-acre campus
- **Coed** 650 undergraduate students, 49% full-time, 72% women, 28% men

Undergraduates 316 full-time, 334 part-time. Students come from 2 states and territories; 1% are from out of state; 0.9% Black or African American, non-Hispanic/Latino; 2% Hispanic/Latino; 2% Asian, non-Hispanic/Latino; 0.3% American Indian or Alaska Native, non-Hispanic/Latino; 1% Two or more races, non-Hispanic/Latino; 22% Race/ethnicity unknown; 0.2% international; 14% transferred in. *Retention:* 50% of full-time freshmen returned.

Freshmen *Admission:* 54 enrolled.

Faculty *Total:* 39, 31% full-time, 26% with terminal degrees. *Student/faculty ratio:* 23:1.

Academics *Calendar:* quarters. *Degrees:* diplomas, associate, bachelor's, and master's. *Special study options:* academic remediation for entering students, accelerated degree program, adult/continuing education programs, advanced placement credit, internships, part-time degree program, services for LD students, summer session for credit.

Computers on Campus 97 computers/terminals and 64 ports are available on campus for general student use. Students can access the following: computer help desk, free student e-mail accounts, online (class) grades, online (class) registration, online (class) schedules. Campuswide network is available. Wireless service is available via entire campus.

Student Life *Housing:* college housing not available. *Campus security:* 24-hour emergency response devices, late-night transport/escort service.

Standardized Tests *Required:* AccuPlacer is required of all applicants unless documentation of a minimum ACT composite score of 21 or documentation of a minimum composite score of 1485 on the SAT is presented (for admission).

Applying *Options:* electronic application. *Application fee:* $50. *Required:* high school transcript, interview, High school transcript or GED required of all applicants. *Required for some:* essay or personal statement, 2 letters of recommendation. *Application deadlines:* rolling (freshmen), rolling (out-of-state freshmen), rolling (transfers). *Notification:* continuous (freshmen), continuous (out-of-state freshmen), continuous (transfers).

Freshman Application Contact Minnesota School of Business–Rochester, 2521 Pennington Drive, NW, Rochester, MN 55901. *Phone:* 507-586-9500. *Toll-free phone:* 888-662-8772. *Web site:* http://www.msbcollege.edu/.

Minnesota School of Business–St. Cloud

Waite Park, Minnesota

- **Proprietary** primarily 2-year, founded 2004, part of Globe Education Network (GEN) which is composed of Globe University, Minnesota School of Business, Broadview University, The Institute of Production and Recording and Minnesota School of Cosmetology
- **Small-town** 2-acre campus
- **Coed** 921 undergraduate students, 51% full-time, 72% women, 28% men

Undergraduates 468 full-time, 453 part-time. Students come from 1 other state; 2% Black or African American, non-Hispanic/Latino; 1% Hispanic/Latino; 1% Asian, non-Hispanic/Latino; 0.8% American Indian or Alaska Native, non-Hispanic/Latino; 0.8% Two or more races, non-Hispanic/Latino;

7% Race/ethnicity unknown; 0.1% international; 16% transferred in. *Retention:* 47% of full-time freshmen returned.

Freshmen *Admission:* 109 enrolled.

Faculty *Total:* 61, 30% full-time, 20% with terminal degrees. *Student/faculty ratio:* 22:1.

Academics *Calendar:* quarters. *Degrees:* diplomas, associate, and bachelor's. *Special study options:* academic remediation for entering students, accelerated degree program, adult/continuing education programs, advanced placement credit, internships, part-time degree program, services for LD students, summer session for credit.

Computers on Campus 116 computers/terminals and 128 ports are available on campus for general student use. Students can access the following: computer help desk, free student e-mail accounts, online (class) grades, online (class) registration, online (class) schedules. Campuswide network is available. Wireless service is available via entire campus.

Student Life *Housing:* college housing not available. *Campus security:* 24-hour emergency response devices, late-night transport/escort service.

Standardized Tests *Required:* AccuPlacer is required of all applicants unless documentation of a minimum ACT composite score of 21 or documentation of a minimum composite score of 1485 on the SAT is presented (for admission).

Applying *Options:* electronic application. *Application fee:* $50. *Required:* high school transcript, interview, High school transcript or GED required of all applicants. *Required for some:* essay or personal statement, 2 letters of recommendation. *Application deadlines:* rolling (freshmen), rolling (out-of-state freshmen), rolling (transfers). *Notification:* continuous (freshmen), continuous (out-of-state freshmen), continuous (transfers).

Freshman Application Contact Minnesota School of Business–St. Cloud, 1201 2nd Street South, Waite Park, MN 56387. *Phone:* 320-257-2000. *Toll-free phone:* 866-403-3333. *Web site:* http://www.msbcollege.edu/.

Minnesota School of Business–Shakopee

Shakopee, Minnesota

- **Proprietary** primarily 2-year, founded 2004, part of Globe Education Network (GEN) which is composed of Globe University, Minnesota School of Business, Broadview University, The Institute of Production and Recording and Minnesota School of Cosmetology
- **Suburban** 1-acre campus
- **Coed** 390 undergraduate students, 39% full-time, 81% women, 19% men

Undergraduates 154 full-time, 236 part-time. Students come from 1 other state; 2% Black or African American, non-Hispanic/Latino; 3% Hispanic/Latino; 4% Asian, non-Hispanic/Latino; 1% American Indian or Alaska Native, non-Hispanic/Latino; 1% Two or more races, non-Hispanic/Latino; 9% Race/ethnicity unknown; 0.8% international; 14% transferred in. *Retention:* 20% of full-time freshmen returned.

Freshmen *Admission:* 35 enrolled.

Faculty *Total:* 36, 36% full-time, 36% with terminal degrees. *Student/faculty ratio:* 15:1.

Academics *Calendar:* quarters. *Degrees:* diplomas, associate, and bachelor's. *Special study options:* academic remediation for entering students, accelerated degree program, adult/continuing education programs, advanced placement credit, internships, part-time degree program, services for LD students, summer session for credit.

Computers on Campus 53 computers/terminals and 32 ports are available on campus for general student use. Students can access the following: computer help desk, free student e-mail accounts, online (class) grades, online (class) registration, online (class) schedules. Campuswide network is available. Wireless service is available via entire campus.

Student Life *Housing:* college housing not available. *Campus security:* 24-hour emergency response devices, late-night transport/escort service.

Standardized Tests *Required:* AccuPlacer is required of all applicants unless documentation of a minimum ACT composite score of 21 or documentation of a minimum composite score of 1485 on the SAT is presented (for admission).

Applying *Options:* electronic application. *Application fee:* $50. *Required:* high school transcript, interview, High school transcript or GED required of all applicants. *Required for some:* essay or personal statement, 2 letters of recommendation. *Application deadlines:* rolling (freshmen), rolling (out-of-state freshmen), rolling (transfers). *Notification:* continuous (freshmen), continuous (out-of-state freshmen), continuous (transfers).

Freshman Application Contact Minnesota School of Business–Shakopee, 1200 Shakopee Town Square, Shakopee, MN 55379. *Phone:* 952-345-1200. *Toll-free phone:* 866-766-1200. *Web site:* http://www.msbcollege.edu/.

Minnesota State University Mankato

Mankato, Minnesota

- **State-supported** university, founded 1868, part of Minnesota State Colleges and Universities System
- **Small-town** 303-acre campus with easy access to Minneapolis-St. Paul
- **Coed** 13,683 undergraduate students, 86% full-time, 51% women, 48% men
- **Moderately difficult** entrance level

Undergraduates 11,700 full-time, 1,952 part-time. Students come from 45 states and territories; 76 other countries; 13% are from out of state; 5% Black or African American, non-Hispanic/Latino; 1% Hispanic/Latino; 3% Asian, non-Hispanic/Latino; 0.1% Native Hawaiian or other Pacific Islander, non-Hispanic/Latino; 0.4% American Indian or Alaska Native, non-Hispanic/Latino; 4% Race/ethnicity unknown; 4% international; 7% transferred in; 25% live on campus. *Retention:* 77% of full-time freshmen returned.

Freshmen *Admission:* 2,532 enrolled. *Test scores:* ACT scores over 18: 91%; ACT scores over 24: 30%; ACT scores over 30: 2%.

Faculty *Total:* 761, 66% full-time, 56% with terminal degrees. *Student/faculty ratio:* 23:1.

Academics *Calendar:* semesters. *Degrees:* certificates, associate, bachelor's, master's, doctoral, and post-master's certificates. *Special study options:* academic remediation for entering students, accelerated degree program, adult/continuing education programs, advanced placement credit, cooperative education, distance learning, double majors, English as a second language, external degree program, honors programs, independent study, internships, off-campus study, part-time degree program, services for LD students, student-designed majors, study abroad, summer session for credit. *ROTC:* Army (b).

Computers on Campus 900 computers/terminals are available on campus for general student use. Students can access the following: campus intranet, computer help desk, free student e-mail accounts, online (class) grades, online (class) registration, online (class) schedules. Campuswide network is available. Wireless service is available via entire campus.

Student Life *Housing options:* coed. Campus housing is university owned and leased by the school. Freshman applicants given priority for college housing. *Activities and organizations:* drama/theater group, student-run newspaper, radio station, choral group, national fraternities, national sororities. *Campus security:* 24-hour emergency response devices and patrols, student patrols, late-night transport/escort service, Night Owl security program in residence halls, closed circuit cameras in parking lots. *Student services:* health clinic, personal/psychological counseling, women's center, legal services.

Athletics Member NCAA. All Division II except men's and women's ice hockey (Division I). *Intercollegiate sports:* baseball M(s), basketball M(s)/W(s), cheerleading M/W, cross-country running M(s)/W(s), football M(s), golf M(s)/W(s), ice hockey M(s)/W(s), soccer W(s), softball W(s), swimming and diving W(s), tennis M(s)/W(s), track and field M(s)/W(s), volleyball W(s), wrestling M(s). *Intramural sports:* archery M/W, basketball M/W, fencing M/W, football M, golf M/W, ice hockey M/W, lacrosse M/W, racquetball M/W, rock climbing M/W, rugby M/W, sailing M/W, skiing (downhill) M/W, soccer M/W, softball M/W, swimming and diving W, table tennis W, tennis M/W, track and field M/W, volleyball M/W, wrestling M.

Standardized Tests *Required:* SAT or ACT (for admission).

Costs (2011–12) *Tuition:* state resident $6350 full-time, $250 per credit hour part-time; nonresident $13,472 full-time, $537 per credit hour part-time. Full-time tuition and fees vary according to course load, location, and reciprocity agreements. Part-time tuition and fees vary according to course load, location, and reciprocity agreements. *Required fees:* $798 full-time, $33 per credit hour part-time. *Room and board:* $6470. Room and board charges vary according to board plan and housing facility. *Payment plan:* installment.

Financial Aid Of all full-time matriculated undergraduates who enrolled in 2010, 9,221 applied for aid, 6,738 were judged to have need, 4,108 had their need fully met. 526 Federal Work-Study jobs (averaging $3558). 436 state and other part-time jobs (averaging $3434). In 2010, 202 non-need-based awards were made. *Average percent of need met:* 81%. *Average financial aid package:* $8423. *Average need-based loan:* $4343. *Average need-based gift aid:* $5216. *Average non-need-based aid:* $1522. *Average indebtedness upon graduation:* $27,086.

Applying *Options:* electronic application, early admission, deferred entrance. *Application fee:* $20. *Required:* high school transcript. *Required for some:* essay or personal statement, 3 letters of recommendation, personal statement. *Application deadlines:* rolling (freshmen), rolling (transfers). *Notification:* continuous (freshmen), continuous (transfers).

Freshman Application Contact Office of Admissions, Minnesota State University Mankato, 122 Taylor Center, Mankato, MN 56001. *Phone:* 507-389-1822. *Toll-free phone:* 800-722-0544. *Fax:* 507-389-1511. *E-mail:* admissions@mnsu.edu. *Web site:* http://www.mnsu.edu/.

Minnesota State University Moorhead
Moorhead, Minnesota

- **State-supported** comprehensive, founded 1885, part of Minnesota State Colleges and Universities System
- **Urban** 119-acre campus
- **Endowment** $6.6 million
- **Coed** 6,790 undergraduate students, 82% full-time, 58% women, 42% men
- **Moderately difficult** entrance level, 63% of applicants were admitted

Undergraduates 5,569 full-time, 1,221 part-time. Students come from 31 states and territories; 60 other countries; 37% are from out of state; 2% Black or African American, non-Hispanic/Latino; 1% Hispanic/Latino; 1% Asian, non-Hispanic/Latino; 0.8% American Indian or Alaska Native, non-Hispanic/Latino; 3% Two or more races, non-Hispanic/Latino; 6% Race/ethnicity unknown; 6% international; 9% transferred in; 27% live on campus. *Retention:* 67% of full-time freshmen returned.

Freshmen *Admission:* 4,174 applied, 2,622 admitted, 1,078 enrolled. *Test scores:* SAT critical reading scores over 500: 74%; SAT math scores over 500: 64%; ACT scores over 18: 95%; SAT critical reading scores over 600: 11%; SAT math scores over 600: 18%; ACT scores over 24: 33%; SAT critical reading scores over 700: 5%; ACT scores over 30: 2%.

Faculty *Total:* 462, 59% full-time.

Academics *Calendar:* semesters. *Degrees:* certificates, associate, bachelor's, master's, doctoral, post-master's, and postbachelor's certificates. *Special study options:* academic remediation for entering students, adult/continuing education programs, advanced placement credit, distance learning, double majors, honors programs, independent study, internships, off-campus study, part-time degree program, services for LD students, student-designed majors, study abroad, summer session for credit. *ROTC:* Army (c), Air Force (c).

Computers on Campus 1,088 computers/terminals are available on campus for general student use. Students can access the following: computer help desk, free student e-mail accounts, online (class) grades, online (class) registration, online (class) schedules. Campuswide network is available. 100% of college-owned or -operated housing units are wired for high-speed Internet access. Wireless service is available via entire campus.

Student Life *Housing options:* coed, men-only, women-only, disabled students. Campus housing is university owned. *Activities and organizations:* drama/theater group, student-run newspaper, radio and television station, choral group, Student Senate, Sci-Fi Club, Pi Sigma Pi, Campus Crusade for Christ, Dragons 4 Wellness, national sororities. *Campus security:* 24-hour emergency response devices and patrols, student patrols, late-night transport/escort service, controlled dormitory access. *Student services:* health clinic, personal/psychological counseling, women's center.

Athletics Member NCAA. All Division II. *Intercollegiate sports:* basketball M/W, cross-country running M/W, football M, golf W, soccer W, softball W, swimming and diving W, tennis W, track and field M/W, volleyball W, wrestling M. *Intramural sports:* badminton M/W, basketball M/W, bowling M/W, football M, golf W, ice hockey M, racquetball M/W, soccer M/W, softball M/W, swimming and diving M/W, ultimate Frisbee M/W, volleyball M/W.

Standardized Tests *Required:* SAT or ACT (for admission).

Costs (2011–12) *Tuition:* state resident $6568 full-time, $212 per credit hour part-time; nonresident $6568 full-time, $212 per credit hour part-time. Full-time tuition and fees vary according to course load, degree level, program, and reciprocity agreements. Part-time tuition and fees vary according to course load, degree level, program, and reciprocity agreements. *Required fees:* $810 full-time, $38 per credit hour part-time. *Room and board:* $6726; room only: $4144. Room and board charges vary according to board plan and housing facility. *Payment plan:* installment. *Waivers:* senior citizens and employees or children of employees.

Financial Aid Of all full-time matriculated undergraduates who enrolled in 2010, 5,240 applied for aid, 4,077 were judged to have need. 243 Federal Work-Study jobs (averaging $2395), 209 state and other part-time jobs (averaging $2226). *Average financial aid package:* $5533. *Average need-based loan:* $4096. *Average need-based gift aid:* $4032. *Average indebtedness upon graduation:* $29,410.

Applying *Options:* electronic application, early admission, deferred entrance. *Application fee:* $20. *Required:* high school transcript. *Application deadlines:* 8/1 (freshmen), 8/1 (out-of-state freshmen), 8/1 (transfers).

Freshman Application Contact Ms. Sarah Nissen, Interim Director of Admissions, Minnesota State University Moorhead, Owens Hall, Moorhead, MN 56563-0002. *Phone:* 218-477-2549. *Toll-free phone:* 800-593-7246. *Fax:* 218-477-4374. *E-mail:* dragon@mnstate.edu. *Web site:* http://www.mnstate.edu/.

National American University
Roseville, Minnesota

Director of Admissions Mr. Steve Grunlan, Director of Admissions, National American University, 1500 West Highway 36, Roseville, MN 55113. *Phone:* 651-644-1265. *Web site:* http://www.national.edu/.

North Central University
Minneapolis, Minnesota

Freshman Application Contact Ms. Sigi Shawa, Assistant Director, North Central University, 910 Elliot Avenue, Minneapolis, MN 55404-1322. *Phone:* 612-343-4460. *Toll-free phone:* 800-289-6222. *Fax:* 612-343-4146. *E-mail:* admissions@northcentral.edu. *Web site:* http://www.northcentral.edu/.

Northwestern College
St. Paul, Minnesota

- **Independent nondenominational** comprehensive, founded 1902
- **Suburban** 107-acre campus with easy access to Minneapolis-St. Paul
- **Endowment** $14.5 million
- **Coed** 2,184 undergraduate students, 84% full-time, 58% women, 42% men
- **Moderately difficult** entrance level

Undergraduates 1,825 full-time, 359 part-time. Students come from 38 states and territories; 12 other countries; 25% are from out of state; 5% Black or African American, non-Hispanic/Latino; 2% Hispanic/Latino; 5% Asian, non-Hispanic/Latino; 0.6% American Indian or Alaska Native, non-Hispanic/Latino; 1% Two or more races, non-Hispanic/Latino; 2% Race/ethnicity unknown; 0.6% international; 8% transferred in; 66% live on campus. *Retention:* 76% of full-time freshmen returned.

Freshmen *Admission:* 1,289 applied, 460 enrolled. *Average high school GPA:* 3.45. *Test scores:* SAT critical reading scores over 500: 75%; SAT math scores over 500: 71%; ACT scores over 18: 93%; SAT critical reading scores over 600: 43%; SAT math scores over 600: 32%; ACT scores over 24: 52%; SAT critical reading scores over 700: 25%; SAT math scores over 700: 4%; ACT scores over 30: 11%.

Faculty *Total:* 198, 48% full-time, 50% with terminal degrees. *Student/faculty ratio:* 13:1.

Academics *Calendar:* semesters. *Degrees:* certificates, associate, bachelor's, master's, and postbachelor's certificates. *Special study options:* academic remediation for entering students, adult/continuing education programs, advanced placement credit, distance learning, double majors, honors programs, independent study, internships, off-campus study, part-time degree program, services for LD students, student-designed majors, study abroad, summer session for credit. *ROTC:* Army (c), Air Force (c). *Unusual degree programs:* 3-2 engineering with University of Minnesota-Twin Cities.

Computers on Campus 200 computers/terminals and 1,350 ports are available on campus for general student use. Students can access the following: campus intranet, computer help desk, free student e-mail accounts, online (class) grades, online (class) registration, online (class) schedules, network file space, personal web site, integrated student portal, b/w and color printing, virtual labs. Campuswide network is available. 100% of college-owned or -operated housing units are wired for high-speed Internet access. Wireless service is available via classrooms, computer centers, computer labs, dorm rooms, learning centers, libraries, student centers.

Student Life *Housing:* on-campus residence required through junior year. *Options:* men-only, women-only, disabled students. Campus housing is university owned. Freshman campus housing is guaranteed. *Activities and organizations:* drama/theater group, student-run newspaper, radio and television station, choral group, Northwestern Student Association (student government), The Gathering (religious group), Student Missions Fellowship, Guardian Angels, Outreach Ministries. *Campus security:* 24-hour emergency response devices and patrols, late-night transport/escort service, controlled dormitory access, gated access to main campus, emergency notification system. *Student services:* health clinic, personal/psychological counseling.

Athletics Member NCAA, NCCAA. All NCAA Division III. *Intercollegiate sports:* baseball M, basketball M/W, cross-country running M/W, football M, golf M/W, ice hockey M(c), soccer M/W, softball W, tennis M/W, track and field M/W, volleyball M(c)/W. *Intramural sports:* basketball M/W, football M/W, softball M/W, table tennis M/W, tennis M/W, volleyball M/W.

Standardized Tests *Required:* SAT or ACT (for admission).

Costs (2012–13) *Comprehensive fee:* $35,170 includes full-time tuition ($26,740), mandatory fees ($220), and room and board ($8210). Full-time tuition and fees vary according to course load. Part-time tuition: $1140 per semester hour. Part-time tuition and fees vary according to course load. *Required fees:* $65 per term part-time. *College room only:* $4820. Room and

board charges vary according to board plan. *Payment plan:* installment. *Waivers:* children of alumni and employees or children of employees.

Financial Aid Of all full-time matriculated undergraduates who enrolled in 2009, 1,721 applied for aid, 1,461 were judged to have need, 82 had their need fully met. 185 Federal Work-Study jobs (averaging $1935). 281 state and other part-time jobs (averaging $1997). In 2009, 233 non-need-based awards were made. *Average percent of need met:* 70%. *Average financial aid package:* $18,160. *Average need-based loan:* $4503. *Average need-based gift aid:* $13,525. *Average non-need-based aid:* $6433. *Average indebtedness upon graduation:* $25,707.

Applying *Options:* electronic application, early admission, deferred entrance. *Required:* essay or personal statement, high school transcript, minimum 2.0 GPA, 2 letters of recommendation, lifestyle agreement, statement of Christian faith. *Required for some:* interview. *Recommended:* minimum 3.0 GPA. *Application deadlines:* 8/1 (freshmen), 8/1 (out-of-state freshmen), 8/1 (transfers). *Notification:* continuous (freshmen), continuous (out-of-state freshmen), continuous (transfers).

Freshman Application Contact Mr. Kenneth K. Faffler, Director of Admissions, Northwestern College, Officer of Admissions, 3003 Snelling Avenue North, 212 Nazareth Hall, St. Paul, MN 55113-1598. *Phone:* 651-631-5111. *Toll-free phone:* 800-827-6827. *Fax:* 651-631-5680. *E-mail:* admissions@nwc.edu. *Web site:* http://www.nwc.edu/.

Oak Hills Christian College
Bemidji, Minnesota

- **Independent interdenominational** 4-year, founded 1946
- **Rural** 180-acre campus
- **Endowment** $371,108
- **Coed**
- **Minimally difficult** entrance level

Faculty *Student/faculty ratio:* 13:1.

Academics *Calendar:* semesters. *Degrees:* certificates, diplomas, associate, and bachelor's.

Student Life *Campus security:* controlled dormitory access, evening patrols by trained security personnel.

Standardized Tests *Required:* SAT or ACT (for admission).

Costs (2011–12) *Comprehensive fee:* $19,850 includes full-time tuition ($14,420), mandatory fees ($250), and room and board ($5180). Part-time tuition: $600 per credit. Part-time tuition and fees vary according to course load. No tuition increase for student's term of enrollment. *College room only:* $2072. Room and board charges vary according to board plan and housing facility.

Financial Aid *Of all full-time matriculated undergraduates who enrolled in 2002,* 138 applied for aid, 131 were judged to have need, 9 had their need fully met. 22 Federal Work-Study jobs (averaging $1234). 54 state and other part-time jobs (averaging $2188). *In 2002,* 7 non-need-based awards were made. *Average percent of need met:* 73. *Average financial aid package:* $9306. *Average need-based loan:* $3099. *Average need-based gift aid:* $6455. *Average non-need-based aid:* $2610. *Average indebtedness upon graduation:* $20,233.

Applying *Options:* electronic application, deferred entrance. *Application fee:* $25. *Required:* essay or personal statement, high school transcript, minimum 2.0 GPA, 2 letters of recommendation. *Required for some:* interview.

Freshman Application Contact Shelly Fast, Assistant Director of Admissions, Oak Hills Christian College, 1600 Oak Hills Road SW, Bemidji, MN 56601. *Phone:* 218-751-8670 Ext. 1285. *Toll-free phone:* 888-751-8670 Ext. 1285. *Fax:* 218-751-8825. *E-mail:* admissions@oakhills.edu. *Web site:* http://www.oakhills.edu/.

Rasmussen College Blaine
Blaine, Minnesota

- **Proprietary** 4-year, part of Rasmussen College System
- **Suburban** campus
- **Coed** 446 undergraduate students
- **Minimally difficult** entrance level

Faculty *Student/faculty ratio:* 22:1.

Academics *Degrees:* certificates, diplomas, associate, and bachelor's. *Special study options:* academic remediation for entering students, accelerated degree program, adult/continuing education programs, distance learning, double majors, internships, part-time degree program, summer session for credit.

Computers on Campus 81 computers/terminals are available on campus for general student use. Students can access the following: computer help desk, free student e-mail accounts, online (class) grades, online (class) schedules. Campuswide network is available. Wireless service is available via entire campus.

Student Life *Housing:* college housing not available.

Standardized Tests *Required:* Internal Exam (for admission).

Costs (2012–13) *Tuition:* $14,220 full-time. Full-time tuition and fees vary according to course level, course load, degree level, location, and program. Part-time tuition and fees vary according to course level, course load, degree level, location, and program. *Required fees:* $40 full-time. *Payment plans:* installment, deferred payment. *Waivers:* employees or children of employees.

Applying *Options:* electronic application, early admission, deferred entrance. *Application fee:* $40. *Required:* high school transcript, minimum 2.0 GPA, interview. *Application deadlines:* rolling (freshmen), rolling (transfers).

Freshman Application Contact Susan Hammerstrom, Director of Admissions, Rasmussen College Blaine, 3629 95th Avenue NE, Blaine, MN 55014. *Phone:* 763-795-4720. *Toll-free phone:* 888-549-6755. *E-mail:* susan.hammerstrom@rasmussen.edu. *Web site:* http://www.rasmussen.edu/.

Rasmussen College Bloomington
Bloomington, Minnesota

- **Proprietary** primarily 2-year, founded 1904, part of Rasmussen College System
- **Suburban** campus
- **Coed** 611 undergraduate students
- **Minimally difficult** entrance level

Faculty *Student/faculty ratio:* 22:1.

Academics *Calendar:* quarters. *Degrees:* certificates, diplomas, associate, and bachelor's. *Special study options:* academic remediation for entering students, accelerated degree program, adult/continuing education programs, distance learning, double majors, internships, part-time degree program, summer session for credit.

Computers on Campus 68 computers/terminals are available on campus for general student use. Students can access the following: computer help desk, free student e-mail accounts, online (class) grades, online (class) schedules. Campuswide network is available. Wireless service is available via entire campus.

Student Life *Housing:* college housing not available.

Standardized Tests *Required:* Internal Exam (for admission).

Costs (2012–13) *Tuition:* $14,220 full-time. Full-time tuition and fees vary according to course level, course load, degree level, location, and program. Part-time tuition and fees vary according to course level, course load, degree level, location, and program. *Required fees:* $40 full-time. *Payment plans:* installment, deferred payment. *Waivers:* employees or children of employees.

Financial Aid Of all full-time matriculated undergraduates who enrolled in 2010, 3 state and other part-time jobs (averaging $4338).

Applying *Options:* electronic application, early admission, deferred entrance. *Application fee:* $40. *Required:* high school transcript, minimum 2.0 GPA, interview. *Application deadlines:* rolling (freshmen), rolling (transfers).

Freshman Application Contact Susan Hammerstrom, Director of Admissions, Rasmussen College Bloomington, 440 West 78th Street, Bloomington, MN 55345. *Phone:* 952-545-2000. *Toll-free phone:* 888-549-6755. *Web site:* http://www.rasmussen.edu/.

Rasmussen College Brooklyn Park
Brooklyn Park, Minnesota

- **Proprietary** primarily 2-year, part of Rasmussen College System
- **Suburban** campus
- **Coed** 1,015 undergraduate students
- **Minimally difficult** entrance level

Faculty *Student/faculty ratio:* 22:1.

Academics *Degrees:* certificates, diplomas, associate, and bachelor's. *Special study options:* academic remediation for entering students, accelerated degree program, adult/continuing education programs, distance learning, double majors, internships, part-time degree program, summer session for credit.

Computers on Campus 80 computers/terminals are available on campus for general student use. Students can access the following: computer help desk, free student e-mail accounts, online (class) grades, online (class) schedules. Campuswide network is available. Wireless service is available via entire campus.

Student Life *Housing:* college housing not available.

Standardized Tests *Required:* Internal Exam (for admission).

Costs (2012–13) *Tuition:* $14,220 full-time. Full-time tuition and fees vary according to course level, course load, degree level, location, and program. Part-time tuition and fees vary according to course level, course load, degree level, location, and program. *Required fees:* $40 full-time. *Payment plans:* installment, deferred payment. *Waivers:* employees or children of employees.

Applying *Options:* electronic application, early admission, deferred entrance. *Application fee:* $40. *Required:* high school transcript, minimum 2.0 GPA, interview. *Application deadlines:* rolling (freshmen), rolling (transfers).

Freshman Application Contact Susan Hammerstrom, Director of Admissions, Rasmussen College Brooklyn Park, 8301 93rd Avenue North, Brooklyn Park, MN 55445-1512. *Phone:* 763-493-4500. *Toll-free phone:* 888-549-6755. *E-mail:* susan.hammerstrom@rasmussen.edu. *Web site:* http://www.rasmussen.edu/.

Rasmussen College Eagan

Eagan, Minnesota

- **Proprietary** primarily 2-year, founded 1904, part of Rasmussen College System
- **Suburban** campus
- **Coed, primarily women** 923 undergraduate students
- **Minimally difficult** entrance level

Faculty *Student/faculty ratio:* 22:1.

Academics *Calendar:* quarters. *Degrees:* certificates, diplomas, associate, and bachelor's. *Special study options:* academic remediation for entering students, accelerated degree program, adult/continuing education programs, distance learning, double majors, internships, part-time degree program, summer session for credit.

Computers on Campus 93 computers/terminals are available on campus for general student use. Students can access the following: computer help desk, free student e-mail accounts, online (class) grades, online (class) schedules. Campuswide network is available. Wireless service is available via entire campus.

Student Life *Housing:* college housing not available.

Standardized Tests *Required:* Internal Exam (for admission).

Costs (2012–13) *Tuition:* $14,220 full-time. Full-time tuition and fees vary according to course level, course load, degree level, location, and program. Part-time tuition and fees vary according to course level, course load, degree level, location, and program. *Required fees:* $40 full-time. *Payment plans:* installment, deferred payment. *Waivers:* employees or children of employees.

Applying *Options:* electronic application, early admission, deferred entrance. *Application fee:* $40. *Required:* high school transcript, minimum 2.0 GPA, interview. *Application deadlines:* rolling (freshmen), rolling (transfers).

Freshman Application Contact Susan Hammerstrom, Director of Admissions, Rasmussen College Eagan, 3500 Federal Drive, Eagan, MN 55122-1346. *Phone:* 651-687-9000. *Toll-free phone:* 888-549-6755. *E-mail:* susan.hammerstrom@rasmussen.edu. *Web site:* http://www.rasmussen.edu/.

Rasmussen College Lake Elmo/Woodbury

Lake Elmo, Minnesota

- **Proprietary** primarily 2-year, part of Rasmussen College System
- **Suburban** campus
- **Coed** 735 undergraduate students
- **Minimally difficult** entrance level

Faculty *Student/faculty ratio:* 22:1.

Academics *Degrees:* certificates, diplomas, associate, and bachelor's. *Special study options:* academic remediation for entering students, accelerated degree program, adult/continuing education programs, distance learning, double majors, internships, part-time degree program, summer session for credit.

Computers on Campus 85 computers/terminals are available on campus for general student use. Students can access the following: computer help desk, free student e-mail accounts, online (class) grades, online (class) schedules. Campuswide network is available. Wireless service is available via entire campus.

Student Life *Housing:* college housing not available.

Standardized Tests *Required:* Internal Exam (for admission).

Costs (2012–13) *Tuition:* $14,220 full-time. Full-time tuition and fees vary according to course level, course load, degree level, location, and program. Part-time tuition and fees vary according to course level, course load, degree level, location, and program. *Required fees:* $40 full-time. *Payment plans:* installment, deferred payment. *Waivers:* employees or children of employees.

Applying *Options:* electronic application, early admission, deferred entrance. *Application fee:* $40. *Required:* high school transcript, minimum 2.0 GPA, interview. *Application deadlines:* rolling (freshmen), rolling (transfers).

Freshman Application Contact Susan Hammerstrom, Director of Admissions, Rasmussen College Lake Elmo/Woodbury, 8565 Eagle Point Circle, Lake Elmo, MN 55042. *Phone:* 651-259-6600. *Toll-free phone:* 888-

549-6755. *E-mail:* susan.hammerstrom@rasmussen.edu. *Web site:* http://www.rasmussen.edu/.

Rasmussen College Mankato

Mankato, Minnesota

- **Proprietary** primarily 2-year, founded 1904, part of Rasmussen College System
- **Suburban** campus
- **Coed, primarily women** 797 undergraduate students
- **Minimally difficult** entrance level

Faculty *Student/faculty ratio:* 22:1.

Academics *Calendar:* quarters. *Degrees:* certificates, diplomas, associate, and bachelor's. *Special study options:* academic remediation for entering students, accelerated degree program, adult/continuing education programs, distance learning, double majors, internships, part-time degree program, summer session for credit.

Computers on Campus 116 computers/terminals are available on campus for general student use. Students can access the following: computer help desk, free student e-mail accounts, online (class) grades, online (class) schedules. Campuswide network is available. Wireless service is available via entire campus.

Student Life *Housing:* college housing not available.

Standardized Tests *Required:* Internal Exam (for admission).

Costs (2012–13) *Tuition:* $14,220 full-time. Full-time tuition and fees vary according to course level, course load, degree level, location, and program. Part-time tuition and fees vary according to course level, course load, degree level, location, and program. *Required fees:* $40 full-time. *Payment plans:* installment, deferred payment. *Waivers:* employees or children of employees.

Financial Aid Of all full-time matriculated undergraduates who enrolled in 2010, 15 Federal Work-Study jobs (averaging $4000). 13 state and other part-time jobs (averaging $4000).

Applying *Options:* electronic application, early admission, deferred entrance. *Application fee:* $40. *Required:* high school transcript, minimum 2.0 GPA, interview. *Application deadlines:* rolling (freshmen), rolling (transfers).

Freshman Application Contact Susan Hammerstrom, Director of Admissions, Rasmussen College Mankato, 130 Saint Andrews Drive, Mankato, MN 56001. *Phone:* 507-625-6556. *Toll-free phone:* 888-549-6755. *E-mail:* susan.hammerstrom@rasmussen.edu. *Web site:* http://www.rasmussen.edu/.

Rasmussen College Moorhead

Moorhead, Minnesota

- **Proprietary** primarily 2-year, part of Rasmussen College System
- **Suburban** campus
- **Coed** 525 undergraduate students
- **Minimally difficult** entrance level

Faculty *Student/faculty ratio:* 22:1.

Academics *Degrees:* certificates, diplomas, associate, and bachelor's. *Special study options:* academic remediation for entering students, accelerated degree program, adult/continuing education programs, distance learning, double majors, internships, part-time degree program, summer session for credit.

Computers on Campus 31 computers/terminals are available on campus for general student use. Students can access the following: computer help desk, free student e-mail accounts, online (class) grades, online (class) schedules. Campuswide network is available. Wireless service is available via entire campus.

Student Life *Housing:* college housing not available.

Standardized Tests *Required:* Internal Exam (for admission).

Costs (2012–13) *Tuition:* $14,220 full-time. Full-time tuition and fees vary according to course level, course load, degree level, location, and program. Part-time tuition and fees vary according to course level, course load, degree level, location, and program. *Required fees:* $40 full-time. *Payment plans:* installment, deferred payment. *Waivers:* employees or children of employees.

Applying *Options:* electronic application, early admission, deferred entrance. *Application fee:* $40. *Required:* high school transcript, minimum 2.0 GPA, interview. *Application deadlines:* rolling (freshmen), rolling (transfers).

Freshman Application Contact Susan Hammerstrom, Director of Admissions, Rasmussen College Moorhead, 1250 29th Avenue South, Moorhead, MN 56560. *Phone:* 218-304-6200. *Toll-free phone:* 888-549-6755. *E-mail:* susan.hammerstrom@rasmussen.edu. *Web site:* http://www.rasmussen.edu/.

Rasmussen College St. Cloud
St. Cloud, Minnesota

- **Proprietary** primarily 2-year, founded 1904, part of Rasmussen College System
- **Suburban** campus
- **Coed, primarily women** 1,017 undergraduate students
- **Minimally difficult** entrance level

Faculty *Student/faculty ratio:* 22:1.

Academics *Calendar:* quarters. *Degrees:* certificates, diplomas, associate, and bachelor's. *Special study options:* academic remediation for entering students, accelerated degree program, adult/continuing education programs, distance learning, double majors, internships, part-time degree program, summer session for credit.

Computers on Campus 91 computers/terminals are available on campus for general student use. Students can access the following: computer help desk, free student e-mail accounts, online (class) grades, online (class) schedules. Campuswide network is available. Wireless service is available via entire campus.

Student Life *Housing:* college housing not available.

Standardized Tests *Required:* Internal Exam (for admission).

Costs (2012–13) *Tuition:* $14,220 full-time. Full-time tuition and fees vary according to course level, course load, degree level, location, and program. Part-time tuition and fees vary according to course level, course load, degree level, location, and program. *Required fees:* $40 full-time. *Payment plans:* installment, deferred payment. *Waivers:* employees or children of employees.

Financial Aid Of all full-time matriculated undergraduates who enrolled in 2010, 34 Federal Work-Study jobs (averaging $866). 51 state and other part-time jobs (averaging $700).

Applying *Options:* electronic application, early admission, deferred entrance. *Application fee:* $40. *Required:* high school transcript, minimum 2.0 GPA, interview. *Application deadlines:* rolling (freshmen), rolling (transfers).

Freshman Application Contact Susan Hammerstrom, Director of Admissions, Rasmussen College St. Cloud, 226 Park Avenue South, St. Cloud, MN 56301-3713. *Phone:* 320-251-5600. *Toll-free phone:* 888-549-6755. *E-mail:* susan.hammerstrom@rasmussen.edu. *Web site:* http://www.rasmussen.edu/.

Rochester Community and Technical College
Rochester, Minnesota

Director of Admissions Mr. Troy Tynsky, Director of Admissions, Rochester Community and Technical College, 851 30th Avenue, SE, Rochester, MN 55904-4999. *Phone:* 507-280-3509. *Web site:* http://www.rctc.edu/.

St. Catherine University
St. Paul, Minnesota

- **Independent Roman Catholic** comprehensive, founded 1905
- **Urban** 110-acre campus with easy access to Minneapolis
- **Undergraduate: women only; graduate: coed** 3,826 undergraduate students, 65% full-time, 97% women, 3% men
- **Moderately difficult** entrance level, 52% of applicants were admitted

Undergraduates 2,486 full-time, 1,340 part-time. 10% are from out of state; 11% Black or African American, non-Hispanic/Latino; 4% Hispanic/Latino; 11% Asian, non-Hispanic/Latino; 0.1% Native Hawaiian or other Pacific Islander, non-Hispanic/Latino; 1% American Indian or Alaska Native, non-Hispanic/Latino; 1% Two or more races, non-Hispanic/Latino; 4% Race/ethnicity unknown; 1% international; 20% transferred in; 41% live on campus. *Retention:* 84% of full-time freshmen returned.

Freshmen *Admission:* 2,808 applied, 1,451 admitted, 463 enrolled. *Average high school GPA:* 3.57. *Test scores:* ACT scores over 18: 100%; ACT scores over 24: 53%; ACT scores over 30: 4%.

Faculty *Total:* 458, 64% full-time, 64% with terminal degrees. *Student/faculty ratio:* 12:1.

Academics *Calendar:* 4-1-4. *Degrees:* certificates, associate, bachelor's, master's, doctoral, post-master's, and postbachelor's certificates. *Special study options:* adult/continuing education programs, part-time degree program. *ROTC:* Army (c), Air Force (c).

Computers on Campus Students can access the following: campus intranet, computer help desk, free student e-mail accounts, online (class) grades, online (class) registration, online (class) schedules, transcript. Campuswide network is available. Wireless service is available via entire campus.

Student Life *Housing options:* women-only. Campus housing is university owned. Freshman campus housing is guaranteed. *Campus security:* 24-hour

emergency response devices and patrols, student patrols, late-night transport/escort service, controlled dormitory access.

Athletics Member NCAA. All Division III. *Intercollegiate sports:* basketball W, cross-country running W, ice hockey W, soccer W, softball W, swimming and diving W, tennis W, track and field W, volleyball W. *Intramural sports:* basketball W, cheerleading W, cross-country running W, football W, golf W, lacrosse W, racquetball W, soccer W, softball W, swimming and diving W, tennis W, track and field W, volleyball W.

Standardized Tests *Required:* SAT or ACT (for admission).

Costs (2011–12) *One-time required fee:* $100. *Comprehensive fee:* $39,642 includes full-time tuition ($31,360), mandatory fees ($280), and room and board ($8002). Full-time tuition and fees vary according to class time and degree level. Part-time tuition: $980 per credit hour. Part-time tuition and fees vary according to class time and degree level. *Required fees:* $980 per credit hour part-time, $140 per term part-time. *College room only:* $4490. Room and board charges vary according to board plan and housing facility. *Payment plan:* installment. *Waivers:* senior citizens and employees or children of employees.

Financial Aid Of all full-time matriculated undergraduates who enrolled in 2010, 1,764 applied for aid, 1,649 were judged to have need, 185 had their need fully met. In 2010, 99 non-need-based awards were made. *Average percent of need met:* 84%. *Average financial aid package:* $25,790. *Average need-based loan:* $4620. *Average need-based gift aid:* $10,830. *Average non-need-based aid:* $8170. *Average indebtedness upon graduation:* $33,610.

Applying *Options:* deferred entrance. *Required:* high school transcript, 1 letter of recommendation. *Required for some:* essay or personal statement, interview. *Recommended:* interview. *Application deadlines:* rolling (freshmen), rolling (transfers). *Notification:* continuous (freshmen), continuous (transfers).

Freshman Application Contact Ms. Cory Piper-Hauswirth, Associate Director of Admission and Financial Aid, St. Catherine University, 2004 Randolph Avenue, St. Paul, MN 55105. *Phone:* 651-690-6047. *Toll-free phone:* 800-945-4599. *E-mail:* stkate@stkate.edu. *Web site:* http://www.stkate.edu/.

St. Cloud State University
St. Cloud, Minnesota

Freshman Application Contact Mr. Richard Shearer, Director of Admissions, St. Cloud State University, 115 AS Building, 720 4th Avenue South, St. Cloud, MN 56301-4498. *Phone:* 320-308-2244. *Toll-free phone:* 877-654-7278. *Fax:* 320-308-2243. *E-mail:* scsu4u@stcloudstate.edu. *Web site:* http://www.stcloudstate.edu/.

Saint John's University
Collegeville, Minnesota

- **Independent Roman Catholic** comprehensive, founded 1857
- **Rural** 2500-acre campus with easy access to Minneapolis-St. Paul
- **Endowment** $144.1 million
- **Men only** 1,890 undergraduate students, 98% full-time
- **Moderately difficult** entrance level, 74% of applicants were admitted

Undergraduates 1,856 full-time, 34 part-time. Students come from 37 states and territories; 30 other countries; 16% are from out of state; 3% Black or African American, non-Hispanic/Latino; 3% Hispanic/Latino; 3% Asian, non-Hispanic/Latino; 0.2% Native Hawaiian or other Pacific Islander, non-Hispanic/Latino; 0.8% American Indian or Alaska Native, non-Hispanic/Latino; 0.1% Two or more races, non-Hispanic/Latino; 7% international; 2% transferred in; 87% live on campus. *Retention:* 91% of full-time freshmen returned.

Freshmen *Admission:* 1,647 applied, 1,225 admitted, 494 enrolled. *Average high school GPA:* 3.51. *Test scores:* SAT critical reading scores over 500: 61%; SAT math scores over 500: 73%; SAT writing scores over 500: 65%; ACT scores over 18: 99%; SAT critical reading scores over 600: 32%; SAT math scores over 600: 39%; SAT writing scores over 600: 32%; ACT scores over 24: 68%; SAT critical reading scores over 700: 16%; SAT math scores over 700: 13%; SAT writing scores over 700: 3%; ACT scores over 30: 18%.

Faculty *Total:* 180, 86% full-time, 76% with terminal degrees. *Student/faculty ratio:* 11:1.

Academics *Calendar:* semesters. *Degrees:* bachelor's and master's (coordinate with College of Saint Benedict for women). *Special study options:* advanced placement credit, double majors, English as a second language, honors programs, independent study, internships, off-campus study, services for LD students, student-designed majors, study abroad. *ROTC:* Army (b). *Unusual degree programs:* 3-2 engineering with University of Minnesota.

Computers on Campus 940 computers/terminals and 3,000 ports are available on campus for general student use. Students can access the following: campus intranet, computer help desk, free student e-mail accounts, online (class) grades, online (class) registration, online (class) schedules, online student accounts. Campuswide network is available. 100% of college-owned or -

operated housing units are wired for high-speed Internet access. Wireless service is available via entire campus.

Student Life *Housing:* on-campus residence required through senior year. *Options:* men-only, disabled students. Campus housing is university owned. Freshman campus housing is guaranteed. *Activities and organizations:* drama/theater group, student-run newspaper, radio station, choral group, China Cross Cultural Communications Club, Outskirts Snow Club, Nutrition Club, Magis, Joints Events Council. *Campus security:* 24-hour emergency response devices and patrols, student patrols, late-night transport/escort service, controlled dormitory access, well-lit pathways, 911 center on campus, closed circuit TV monitors. *Student services:* health clinic, personal/psychological counseling.

Athletics Member NCAA. All Division III. *Intercollegiate sports:* baseball M, basketball M, crew M(c), cross-country running M, football M, golf M, ice hockey M, lacrosse M(c), riflery M(c), rugby M(c), soccer M, swimming and diving M, tennis M, track and field M, ultimate Frisbee M(c), volleyball M(c), water polo M(c), wrestling M. *Intramural sports:* basketball M, football M, racquetball M, rock climbing M(c), skiing (cross-country) M(c), skiing (downhill) M(c), soccer M, softball M, table tennis M, ultimate Frisbee M, volleyball M.

Standardized Tests *Required:* SAT or ACT (for admission).

Costs (2011–12) *Comprehensive fee:* $41,950 includes full-time tuition ($33,022), mandatory fees ($584), and room and board ($8344). Part-time tuition: $1376 per credit hour. Part-time tuition and fees vary according to course load. *College room only:* $4200. Room and board charges vary according to board plan and housing facility. *Payment plan:* installment.

Financial Aid Of all full-time matriculated undergraduates who enrolled in 2011, 1,363 applied for aid, 1,180 were judged to have need, 479 had their need fully met. 299 Federal Work-Study (averaging $2638). 810 state and other part-time jobs (averaging $2695). In 2011, 525 non-need-based awards were made. *Average percent of need met:* 87%. *Average financial aid package:* $24,885. *Average need-based loan:* $4048. *Average need-based gift aid:* $20,228. *Average non-need-based aid:* $12,406.

Applying *Options:* electronic application, early action, deferred entrance. *Required:* essay or personal statement, high school transcript, 1 letter of recommendation. *Recommended:* minimum 3.0 GPA, interview. *Application deadlines:* rolling (freshmen), rolling (transfers), 11/15 (early action). *Notification:* continuous (freshmen), continuous (transfers), 12/15 (early action).

Freshman Application Contact Mr. Matt Beirne, Director of Admission, Saint John's University, PO Box 7155, Collegeville, MN 56321-7155. *Phone:* 320-363-5055. *Toll-free phone:* 800-544-1489. *Fax:* 320-363-5650. *E-mail:* admissions@csbsju.edu. *Web site:* http://www.csbsju.edu/.

Saint Mary's University of Minnesota
Winona, Minnesota

- **Independent Roman Catholic** comprehensive, founded 1912
- **Small-town** 350-acre campus
- **Endowment** $45.2 million
- **Coed** 2,061 undergraduate students, 70% full-time, 54% women, 46% men
- **Moderately difficult** entrance level, 72% of applicants were admitted

Undergraduates 1,434 full-time, 627 part-time. Students come from 25 states and territories; 17 other countries; 37% are from out of state; 6% Black or African American, non-Hispanic/Latino; 4% Hispanic/Latino; 2% Asian, non-Hispanic/Latino; 0.0% Native Hawaiian or other Pacific Islander, non-Hispanic/Latino; 0.0% American Indian or Alaska Native, non-Hispanic/Latino; 0.2% Two or more races, non-Hispanic/Latino; 25% Race/ethnicity unknown; 2% international; 8% transferred in; 89% live on campus. *Retention:* 77% of full-time freshmen returned.

Freshmen *Admission:* 1,708 applied, 1,228 admitted, 373 enrolled. *Average high school GPA:* 3.26. *Test scores:* SAT critical reading scores over 500: 54%; SAT math scores over 500: 38%; ACT scores over 18: 94%; SAT critical reading scores over 600: 13%; SAT math scores over 600: 17%; ACT scores over 24: 39%; SAT critical reading scores over 700: 3%; SAT math scores over 700: 7%; ACT scores over 30: 6%.

Faculty *Total:* 578, 18% full-time, 46% with terminal degrees. *Student/faculty ratio:* 16:1.

Academics *Calendar:* semesters. *Degrees:* certificates, diplomas, bachelor's, master's, doctoral, post-master's, postbachelor's, and first professional certificates. *Special study options:* academic remediation for entering students, accelerated degree program, adult/continuing education programs, advanced placement credit, cooperative education, distance learning, double majors, English as a second language, honors programs, independent study, internships, off-campus study, part-time degree program, services for LD students, student-designed majors, study abroad, summer session for credit. *ROTC:* Army (c).

Computers on Campus 200 computers/terminals and 50 ports are available on campus for general student use. Students can access the following: campus

intranet, computer help desk, free student e-mail accounts, online (class) grades, online (class) registration, online (class) schedules. Campuswide network is available. 100% of college-owned or -operated housing units are wired for high-speed Internet access. Wireless service is available via computer centers, computer labs, dorm rooms, libraries, student centers.

Student Life *Housing:* on-campus residence required through sophomore year. *Options:* coed, men-only, women-only, disabled students. Campus housing is university owned. Freshman campus housing is guaranteed. *Activities and organizations:* drama/theater group, student-run newspaper, radio station, choral group, Student Activity Committee, Habitat for Humanity, Serving Others United in Love (Soul) - Mission Trips, Colleges Against Cancer, concert choir/chamber singers, national fraternities, national sororities. *Campus security:* 24-hour emergency response devices and patrols, late-night transport/escort service, controlled dormitory access. *Student services:* health clinic, personal/psychological counseling.

Athletics Member NCAA. All Division III. *Intercollegiate sports:* baseball M, basketball M/W, cross-country running M/W, golf M/W, ice hockey M/W, soccer M/W, softball W, swimming and diving M/W, tennis M/W, track and field M/W, volleyball W. *Intramural sports:* basketball M/W, cheerleading W(c), fencing M(c)/W(c), field hockey M/W, football M/W, ice hockey M, lacrosse M(c)/W(c), rugby M(c), skiing (downhill) M(c)/W(c), soccer M/W, softball M/W, tennis M/W, ultimate Frisbee M/W, volleyball M/W, water polo M(c)/W(c).

Standardized Tests *Required:* SAT or ACT (for admission).

Costs (2012–13) *Comprehensive fee:* $35,760 includes full-time tuition ($27,820), mandatory fees ($500), and room and board ($7440). Full-time tuition and fees vary according to course load. Part-time tuition: $930 per credit. Part-time tuition and fees vary according to course load. *Required fees:* $500 per year part-time. *College room only:* $4160. Room and board charges vary according to board plan and housing facility. *Payment plan:* installment. *Waivers:* employees or children of employees.

Financial Aid Of all full-time matriculated undergraduates who enrolled in 2011, 1,199 applied for aid, 1,093 were judged to have need, 125 had their need fully met. 145 Federal Work-Study jobs (averaging $1613). 324 state and other part-time jobs (averaging $1660). In 2011, 264 non-need-based awards were made. *Average percent of need met:* 76%. *Average financial aid package:* $18,884. *Average need-based loan:* $4498. *Average need-based gift aid:* $15,318. *Average non-need-based aid:* $10,902. *Average indebtedness upon graduation:* $31,031.

Applying *Options:* electronic application, early admission, deferred entrance. *Application fee:* $25. *Required:* essay or personal statement, high school transcript, minimum 2.5 GPA. *Required for some:* interview. *Recommended:* 2 letters of recommendation. *Application deadlines:* 5/1 (freshmen), rolling (transfers). *Notification:* continuous (freshmen), continuous (transfers).

Freshman Application Contact Ms. Brandi DeFries, Admissions Director, Saint Mary's University of Minnesota, 700 Terrace Heights, Winona, MN 55987-1399. *Phone:* 507-457-1700. *Toll-free phone:* 800-635-5987. *Fax:* 507-457-1722. *E-mail:* admission@smumn.edu. *Web site:* http://www.smumn.edu/.

St. Olaf College
Northfield, Minnesota

- **Independent Lutheran** 4-year, founded 1874
- **Small-town** 300-acre campus with easy access to Minneapolis-St. Paul
- **Endowment** $342.7 million
- **Coed** 3,179 undergraduate students, 98% full-time, 56% women, 44% men
- **Very difficult** entrance level, 53% of applicants were admitted

Undergraduates 3,113 full-time, 66 part-time. Students come from 47 states and territories; 44 other countries; 49% are from out of state; 2% Black or African American, non-Hispanic/Latino; 3% Hispanic/Latino; 5% Asian, non-Hispanic/Latino; 0.1% Native Hawaiian or other Pacific Islander, non-Hispanic/Latino; 0.2% American Indian or Alaska Native, non-Hispanic/Latino; 3% Two or more races, non-Hispanic/Latino; 0.9% Race/ethnicity unknown; 4% international; 1% transferred in; 91% live on campus. *Retention:* 94% of full-time freshmen returned.

Freshmen *Admission:* 4,181 applied, 2,214 admitted, 739 enrolled. *Average high school GPA:* 3.65. *Test scores:* SAT critical reading scores over 500: 91%; SAT math scores over 500: 95%; SAT writing scores over 500: 95%; ACT scores over 18: 99%; SAT critical reading scores over 600: 74%; SAT math scores over 600: 76%; SAT writing scores over 600: 71%; ACT scores over 24: 91%; SAT critical reading scores over 700: 35%; SAT math scores over 700: 35%; SAT writing scores over 700: 30%; ACT scores over 30: 51%.

Faculty *Total:* 333, 65% full-time, 79% with terminal degrees. *Student/faculty ratio:* 12:1.

Academics *Calendar:* 4-1-4. *Degree:* bachelor's. *Special study options:* advanced placement credit, double majors, English as a second language, inde-

pendent study, internships, off-campus study, part-time degree program, services for LD students, student-designed majors, study abroad, summer session for credit. *Unusual degree programs:* 3-2 engineering with Washington University in St. Louis and University of Minnesota in Minneapolis.

Computers on Campus 902 computers/terminals and 3,300 ports are available on campus for general student use. Students can access the following: campus intranet, computer help desk, free student e-mail accounts, online (class) grades, online (class) registration, online (class) schedules. Campuswide network is available. 100% of college-owned or -operated housing units are wired for high-speed Internet access. Wireless service is available via entire campus.

Student Life *Housing:* on-campus residence required through senior year. *Options:* coed, disabled students. Campus housing is university owned. Freshman campus housing is guaranteed. *Activities and organizations:* drama/theater group, student-run newspaper, radio and television station, choral group, Student Government Association, Ultimate Frisbee Teams, Ole Spring Relief, Taiko Drumming, SELAH. *Campus security:* 24-hour emergency response devices and patrols, late-night transport/escort service, controlled dormitory access, lighted pathways and sidewalks, first-year only dorms, quiet halls. *Student services:* health clinic, personal/psychological counseling.

Athletics Member NCAA. All Division III. *Intercollegiate sports:* baseball M, basketball M/W, cross-country running M/W, football M, golf M/W, ice hockey M/W, skiing (cross-country) M/W, skiing (downhill) M/W, soccer M/W, softball W, swimming and diving M/W, tennis M/W, track and field M/W, volleyball W, wrestling M. *Intramural sports:* badminton M(c)/W(c), basketball M/W, bowling M/W, crew M(c)/W(c), equestrian sports M(c)/W(c), fencing M(c)/W(c), field hockey M, football M/W, golf M/W, ice hockey M(c), lacrosse M(c)/W(c), rugby M(c)/W(c), skiing (cross-country) M/W, skiing (downhill) M(c)/W(c), soccer M/W, softball M/W, swimming and diving M/W, table tennis M/W, tennis M/W, ultimate Frisbee M/W, volleyball M(c)/W.

Standardized Tests *Required:* SAT or ACT (for admission).

Costs (2011–12) *Comprehensive fee:* $46,950 includes full-time tuition ($38,150) and room and board ($8800). Full-time tuition and fees vary according to course load. Part-time tuition: $4770 per course. Part-time tuition and fees vary according to course load. *College room only:* $4110. Room and board charges vary according to board plan and housing facility. *Payment plan:* installment. *Waivers:* senior citizens and employees or children of employees.

Financial Aid Of all full-time matriculated undergraduates who enrolled in 2011, 2,817 applied for aid, 2,072 were judged to have need, 2,072 had their need fully met. 965 Federal Work-Study jobs (averaging $1915). 1,327 state and other part-time jobs (averaging $1755). In 2011, 593 non-need-based awards were made. *Average percent of need met:* 100%. *Average financial aid package:* $30,911. *Average need-based loan:* $4862. *Average need-based gift aid:* $25,267. *Average non-need-based aid:* $11,052. *Average indebtedness upon graduation:* $25,440. *Financial aid deadline:* 3/1.

Applying *Options:* electronic application, early decision, deferred entrance. *Application fee:* $40. *Required:* essay or personal statement, high school transcript, 1 letter of recommendation. *Recommended:* interview. *Application deadlines:* 1/15 (freshmen), 2/1 (transfers). *Early decision deadline:* 11/15 (for plan 1), 1/15 (for plan 2). *Notification:* 3/15 (freshmen), 3/15 (transfers), 12/15 (early decision plan 1), 2/15 (early decision plan 2).

Freshman Application Contact Derek Gueldenzoph, Dean of Admissions, St. Olaf College, 1520 St. Olaf Avenue, Northfield, MN 55057. *Phone:* 507-786-3025. *Toll-free phone:* 800-800-3025. *Fax:* 507-786-3832. *E-mail:* admissions@stolaf.edu. *Web site:* http://www.stolaf.edu/.

Southwest Minnesota State University

Marshall, Minnesota

- **State-supported** comprehensive, founded 1963, part of Minnesota State Colleges and Universities System
- **Small-town** 216-acre campus
- **Coed** 6,160 undergraduate students, 34% full-time, 58% women, 42% men
- **Minimally difficult** entrance level, 80% of applicants were admitted

Undergraduates 2,107 full-time, 4,053 part-time. Students come from 26 states and territories; 25 other countries; 20% are from out of state; 4% Black or African American, non-Hispanic/Latino; 2% Hispanic/Latino; 2% Asian, non-Hispanic/Latino; 0.7% American Indian or Alaska Native, non-Hispanic/Latino; 0.6% Race/ethnicity unknown; 4% international; 3% transferred in; 40% live on campus. *Retention:* 70% of full-time freshmen returned.

Freshmen *Admission:* 1,455 applied, 1,167 admitted, 408 enrolled. *Test scores:* ACT scores over 18: 87%; ACT scores over 24: 26%; ACT scores over 30: 2%.

Faculty *Total:* 180, 66% full-time, 61% with terminal degrees. *Student/faculty ratio:* 18:1.

Academics *Calendar:* semesters. *Degrees:* associate, bachelor's, master's, and postbachelor's certificates. *Special study options:* academic remediation for entering students, accelerated degree program, adult/continuing education programs, advanced placement credit, distance learning, double majors, English as a second language, external degree program, freshman honors college, honors programs, independent study, internships, off-campus study, part-time degree program, services for LD students, student-designed majors, study abroad, summer session for credit.

Computers on Campus 420 computers/terminals and 500 ports are available on campus for general student use. Students can access the following: campus intranet, computer help desk, free student e-mail accounts, online (class) grades, online (class) registration, online (class) schedules. Campuswide network is available. 100% of college-owned or -operated housing units are wired for high-speed Internet access. Wireless service is available via classrooms, computer centers, computer labs, dorm rooms, learning centers, libraries, student centers.

Student Life *Housing:* on-campus residence required for freshman year. *Options:* coed, men-only, women-only, disabled students. Campus housing is university owned. *Activities and organizations:* drama/theater group, student-run newspaper, radio and television station, choral group, marching band, Students in Free Enterprise (SIFE), Society of Leadership & Success, Family and Child Educators (FACE), Habitat for Humanity, Education Minnesota Student Program. *Campus security:* 24-hour emergency response devices and patrols, student patrols, late-night transport/escort service, controlled dormitory access. *Student services:* health clinic, personal/psychological counseling, women's center.

Athletics Member NCAA. All Division II. *Intercollegiate sports:* baseball M(s), basketball M(s)/W(s), football M(s), golf W(s), soccer W(s), softball W(s), tennis W(s), volleyball W(s), wrestling M(s). *Intramural sports:* badminton M/W, basketball M/W, football M, ice hockey M, racquetball M/W, softball M/W, tennis M/W, volleyball M/W.

Standardized Tests *Required:* SAT or ACT (for admission). *Recommended:* ACT (for admission).

Costs (2011–12) *Tuition:* state resident $6679 full-time, $216 per credit part-time; nonresident $6679 full-time, $216 per credit part-time. Full-time tuition and fees vary according to course load, location, program, and reciprocity agreements. Part-time tuition and fees vary according to location, program, and reciprocity agreements. *Required fees:* $1064 full-time, $41 per credit part-time. *Room and board:* $6944; room only: $4164. Room and board charges vary according to board plan and housing facility. *Payment plan:* installment. *Waivers:* senior citizens and employees or children of employees.

Financial Aid Of all full-time matriculated undergraduates who enrolled in 2011, 1,809 applied for aid, 1,503 were judged to have need, 209 had their need fully met. 101 Federal Work-Study jobs (averaging $2271). 139 state and other part-time jobs (averaging $2136). In 2011, 268 non-need-based awards were made. *Average percent of need met:* 53%. *Average financial aid package:* $8151. *Average need-based loan:* $4039. *Average need-based gift aid:* $4917. *Average non-need-based aid:* $2676. *Average indebtedness upon graduation:* $26,394.

Applying *Options:* electronic application, early admission, deferred entrance. *Application fee:* $20. *Required:* high school transcript, minimum 3.0 GPA, top half of graduating class or 21 ACT. *Required for some:* interview. *Application deadlines:* 9/1 (freshmen), 9/1 (out-of-state freshmen), 9/1 (transfers).

Freshman Application Contact Mr. Andrew Hlubeck, Director of Admissions, Southwest Minnesota State University, Southwest Minnesota State University, 1501 State Street, Marshall, MN 56258. *Phone:* 507-537-6286. *Toll-free phone:* 800-642-0684. *Fax:* 507-537-7145. *E-mail:* andrew.hlubek@smsu.edu. *Web site:* http://www.smsu.edu/.

University of Minnesota, Crookston

Crookston, Minnesota

- **State-supported** 4-year, founded 1966, part of University of Minnesota System
- **Rural** 237-acre campus
- **Endowment** $10.7 million
- **Coed** 2,653 undergraduate students, 51% full-time, 52% women, 48% men
- **Moderately difficult** entrance level, 74% of applicants were admitted

Undergraduates 1,340 full-time, 1,313 part-time. Students come from 38 states and territories; 32 other countries; 26% are from out of state; 3% Black or African American, non-Hispanic/Latino; 1% Hispanic/Latino; 2% Asian, non-Hispanic/Latino; 0.1% Native Hawaiian or other Pacific Islander, non-Hispanic/Latino; 0.9% American Indian or Alaska Native, non-Hispanic/Latino; 1% Two or more races, non-Hispanic/Latino; 24% Race/ethnicity unknown; 6% international; 9% transferred in; 39% live on campus.

Freshmen *Admission:* 862 applied, 636 admitted, 268 enrolled. *Average high school GPA:* 3.17. *Test scores:* ACT scores over 18: 94%; ACT scores over 24: 28%; ACT scores over 30: 3%.

Academics *Calendar:* semesters. *Degree:* bachelor's. *Special study options:* academic remediation for entering students, advanced placement credit, distance learning, double majors, English as a second language, external degree program, honors programs, independent study, internships, off-campus study, part-time degree program, services for LD students, student-designed majors, study abroad, summer session for credit. *ROTC:* Air Force (c).

Computers on Campus 25 computers/terminals are available on campus for general student use. Students can access the following: campus intranet, computer help desk, free student e-mail accounts, online (class) grades, online (class) registration, online (class) schedules, personal Web pages. Campuswide network is available. 100% of college-owned or -operated housing units are wired for high-speed Internet access. Wireless service is available via entire campus.

Student Life *Housing options:* coed, disabled students. Campus housing is university owned. Freshman applicants given priority for college housing. *Activities and organizations:* drama/theater group, choral group, Students in Free Enterprise (SIFE), Natural Resources Club, Horseman's Association, Multicultural and International Club, Ag-Arama Planning Club, national fraternities. *Campus security:* 24-hour emergency response devices, student patrols, controlled dormitory access. *Student services:* health clinic, personal/psychological counseling, women's center.

Athletics Member NCAA. All Division II. *Intercollegiate sports:* baseball M(s), basketball M(s)/W(s), equestrian sports W(s), football M(s), golf M(s)/W(s), soccer W(s), softball W(s), tennis W(s), volleyball W(s). *Intramural sports:* basketball M/W, football M/W, golf M/W, ice hockey M(c), racquetball M/W, soccer M(c)/W, softball M/W, table tennis M/W, tennis M/W, volleyball M/W.

Standardized Tests *Required:* SAT or ACT (for admission). *Recommended:* ACT (for admission).

Costs (2011–12) *Tuition:* state resident $9694 full-time, $373 per semester hour part-time; nonresident $9694 full-time, $373 per semester hour part-time. Full-time tuition and fees vary according to course load and reciprocity agreements. Part-time tuition and fees vary according to course load and reciprocity agreements. No tuition increase for student's term of enrollment. *Required fees:* $1402 full-time. *Room and board:* $6764; room only: $3180. Room and board charges vary according to board plan and housing facility. *Payment plan:* installment. *Waivers:* senior citizens.

Financial Aid Of all full-time matriculated undergraduates who enrolled in 2010, 970 applied for aid, 849 were judged to have need, 217 had their need fully met. 186 Federal Work-Study jobs (averaging $1000). 81 state and other part-time jobs (averaging $1000). In 2010, 84 non-need-based awards were made. *Average percent of need met:* 75%. *Average financial aid package:* $11,848. *Average need-based loan:* $4920. *Average need-based gift aid:* $7743. *Average non-need-based aid:* $2411. *Average indebtedness upon graduation:* $25,852.

Applying *Options:* electronic application, deferred entrance. *Application fee:* $30. *Required:* high school transcript, minimum 2.0 GPA, ACT composite 21 or SAT 980. *Application deadlines:* rolling (freshmen), rolling (out-of-state freshmen), rolling (transfers). *Notification:* continuous (freshmen), continuous (out-of-state freshmen), continuous (transfers).

Freshman Application Contact Ms. Amber Schultz, Director of Admissions, University of Minnesota, Crookston, 2900 University Avenue, Crookston, MN 56716-5001. *Phone:* 218-281-8569. *Toll-free phone:* 800-862-6466. *Fax:* 218-281-8575. *E-mail:* evan0331@umn.edu. *Web site:* http://www.umcrookston.edu/.

University of Minnesota, Duluth

Duluth, Minnesota

- **State-supported** comprehensive, founded 1947, part of University of Minnesota System
- **Suburban** 250-acre campus
- **Coed** 10,680 undergraduate students, 89% full-time, 47% women, 53% men
- **Moderately difficult** entrance level, 76% of applicants were admitted

Undergraduates 9,528 full-time, 1,152 part-time. Students come from 39 states and territories; 28 other countries; 16% are from out of state; 2% Black or African American, non-Hispanic/Latino; 1% Hispanic/Latino; 3% Asian, non-Hispanic/Latino; 0.2% Native Hawaiian or other Pacific Islander, non-Hispanic/Latino; 1% American Indian or Alaska Native, non-Hispanic/Latino;

4% Race/ethnicity unknown; 2% international; 5% transferred in; 32% live on campus. *Retention:* 78% of full-time freshmen returned.

Freshmen *Admission:* 7,456 applied, 5,694 admitted, 2,105 enrolled. *Average high school GPA:* 3.42. *Test scores:* SAT critical reading scores over 500: 55%; SAT math scores over 500: 75%; SAT writing scores over 500: 62%; ACT scores over 18: 98%; SAT critical reading scores over 600: 24%; SAT math scores over 600: 29%; SAT writing scores over 600: 21%; ACT scores over 24: 52%; SAT critical reading scores over 700: 2%; SAT math scores over 700: 8%; SAT writing scores over 700: 4%; ACT scores over 30: 5%.

Faculty *Total:* 566, 78% full-time. *Student/faculty ratio:* 21:1.

Academics *Calendar:* semesters. *Degrees:* bachelor's, master's, doctoral, and postbachelor's certificates. *Special study options:* academic remediation for entering students, adult/continuing education programs, advanced placement credit, cooperative education, distance learning, double majors, English as a second language, external degree program, honors programs, independent study, internships, off-campus study, part-time degree program, services for LD students, student-designed majors, study abroad, summer session for credit. *ROTC:* Air Force (b).

Computers on Campus 465 computers/terminals are available on campus for general student use. Students can access the following: campus intranet, computer help desk, free student e-mail accounts, online (class) grades, online (class) registration, online (class) schedules. Campuswide network is available. 100% of college-owned or -operated housing units are wired for high-speed Internet access. Wireless service is available via entire campus.

Student Life *Housing options:* coed, men-only, women-only, disabled students. Campus housing is university owned. Freshman applicants given priority for college housing. *Activities and organizations:* drama/theater group, student-run newspaper, radio station, choral group, marching band, national fraternities, national sororities. *Campus security:* 24-hour emergency response devices and patrols, late-night transport/escort service. *Student services:* health clinic, personal/psychological counseling, women's center.

Athletics Member NCAA. All Division II except men's and women's ice hockey (Division I). *Intercollegiate sports:* baseball M(s), basketball M(s)/W(s), cheerleading W(c), crew M(c)/W(c), cross-country running M(s)/W(s), football M(s), ice hockey M(s)/W(s), lacrosse M(s)(c)/W(c), rock climbing M(c)/W(c), rugby M(c)/W(c), skiing (cross-country) M(c)/W(c), skiing (downhill) M(c)/W(c), soccer M(c)/W(s), softball W(s), swimming and diving M(c)/W(c), tennis W(s), track and field M(s)/W(s), ultimate Frisbee M(c)/W(c), volleyball M(c)/W(s). *Intramural sports:* badminton M/W, basketball M/W, bowling M/W, football M/W, golf M/W, ice hockey M/W, rugby M/W, sailing M/W, skiing (cross-country) M/W, skiing (downhill) M/W, soccer M/W, softball M/W, table tennis M/W, tennis M/W, ultimate Frisbee M/W, volleyball M/W, water polo M/W.

Standardized Tests *Required:* SAT or ACT (for admission).

Costs (2011–12) *Tuition:* state resident $11,322 full-time, $435 per credit part-time; nonresident $13,832 full-time, $532 per credit part-time. Full-time tuition and fees vary according to course load and reciprocity agreements. Part-time tuition and fees vary according to course load and reciprocity agreements. *Required fees:* $1321 full-time, $63 per credit part-time. *Room and board:* $6614. Room and board charges vary according to board plan and housing facility. *Payment plan:* installment. *Waivers:* employees or children of employees.

Financial Aid Of all full-time matriculated undergraduates who enrolled in 2009, 7,447 applied for aid, 5,713 were judged to have need, 1,285 had their need fully met. In 2009, 873 non-need-based awards were made. *Average percent of need met:* 75%. *Average financial aid package:* $10,655. *Average need-based loan:* $4651. *Average need-based gift aid:* $6922. *Average non-need-based aid:* $3122. *Average indebtedness upon graduation:* $30,098.

Applying *Options:* electronic application. *Application fee:* $35. *Required:* high school transcript. *Application deadlines:* 12/15 (freshmen), 8/1 (transfers). *Notification:* continuous (freshmen), continuous (transfers).

Freshman Application Contact Office of Admissions, University of Minnesota, Duluth, 25 Solon Campus Center, 1117 University Drive, Duluth, MN 55812-3000. *Phone:* 218-726-7171. *Toll-free phone:* 800-232-1339. *Fax:* 218-726-7040. *E-mail:* umdadmis@d.umn.edu. *Web site:* http://www.d.umn.edu/.

University of Minnesota, Morris

Morris, Minnesota

Freshman Application Contact University of Minnesota, Morris, 600 East 4th Street, Morris, MN 56267-2134. *Phone:* 320-539-6035. *Toll-free phone:* 800-992-8863. *Fax:* 320-589-1673. *E-mail:* admissions@morris.umn.edu. *Web site:* http://www.mrs.umn.edu/.

University of Minnesota, Twin Cities Campus
Minneapolis, Minnesota

- **State-supported** comprehensive, founded 1851, part of University of Minnesota System
- **Urban** 2000-acre campus
- **Coed** 34,812 undergraduate students, 84% full-time, 52% women, 48% men
- **Moderately difficult** entrance level, 47% of applicants were admitted

Undergraduates 29,194 full-time, 5,618 part-time. Students come from 51 states and territories; 87 other countries; 25% are from out of state; 4% Black or African American, non-Hispanic/Latino; 3% Hispanic/Latino; 8% Asian, non-Hispanic/Latino; 0.1% Native Hawaiian or other Pacific Islander, non-Hispanic/Latino; 0.4% American Indian or Alaska Native, non-Hispanic/Latino; 2% Two or more races, non-Hispanic/Latino; 1% Race/ethnicity unknown; 8% international; 6% transferred in; 21% live on campus. *Retention:* 90% of full-time freshmen returned.

Freshmen *Admission:* 39,720 applied, 18,505 admitted, 5,368 enrolled. *Test scores:* SAT critical reading scores over 500: 86%; SAT math scores over 500: 96%; SAT writing scores over 500: 87%; ACT scores over 18: 99%; SAT critical reading scores over 600: 60%; SAT math scores over 600: 80%; SAT writing scores over 600: 58%; ACT scores over 24: 88%; SAT critical reading scores over 700: 22%; SAT math scores over 700: 40%; SAT writing scores over 700: 16%; ACT scores over 30: 28%.

Faculty *Total:* 2,700, 69% full-time, 69% with terminal degrees. *Student/faculty ratio:* 21:1.

Academics *Calendar:* semesters. *Degrees:* certificates, diplomas, bachelor's, master's, doctoral, post-master's, postbachelor's, and first professional certificates. *Special study options:* academic remediation for entering students, accelerated degree program, adult/continuing education programs, advanced placement credit, cooperative education, distance learning, double majors, English as a second language, external degree program, freshman honors college, honors programs, independent study, internships, off-campus study, part-time degree program, services for LD students, student-designed majors, study abroad, summer session for credit. *ROTC:* Army (b), Navy (b), Air Force (b).

Computers on Campus Students can access the following: computer help desk, free student e-mail accounts, online (class) grades, online (class) registration, online (class) schedules. Campuswide network is available.

Student Life *Housing options:* coed, cooperative, disabled students. Campus housing is university owned. Freshman campus housing is guaranteed. *Activities and organizations:* drama/theater group, student-run newspaper, radio and television station, choral group, marching band, student government, national fraternities, national sororities. *Campus security:* 24-hour emergency response devices and patrols, student patrols, late-night transport/escort service, controlled dormitory access, safety/security orientation, security lighting. *Student services:* health clinic, personal/psychological counseling, women's center, legal services.

Athletics Member NCAA. All Division I except football (Division I-A). *Intercollegiate sports:* baseball M(s), basketball M(s)/W(s), cross-country running M(s)/W(s), golf M(s)/W(s), gymnastics M(s)/W(s), ice hockey M(s)/W(s), soccer W(s), softball W(s), swimming and diving M(s)/W(s), tennis M(s)/W(s), track and field M(s)/W(s), volleyball W(s), wrestling M(s). *Intramural sports:* baseball M/W, basketball M/W, bowling M/W, crew M/W, football M/W, golf M/W, ice hockey M/W, rugby M/W, skiing (cross-country) M/W, skiing (downhill) M/W, soccer M/W, softball M/W, tennis M/W, volleyball M/W, water polo M/W, wrestling M/W.

Standardized Tests *Required:* SAT or ACT (for admission).

Costs (2011–12) *Tuition:* state resident $11,650 full-time, $448 per credit part-time; nonresident $16,650 full-time, $640 per credit part-time. Full-time tuition and fees vary according to program and reciprocity agreements. Part-time tuition and fees vary according to course load, program, and reciprocity agreements. *Required fees:* $1348 full-time. *Room and board:* $7834; room only: $4394. Room and board charges vary according to board plan, housing facility, and location. *Payment plan:* installment. *Waivers:* senior citizens.

Financial Aid Of all full-time matriculated undergraduates who enrolled in 2011, 20,384 applied for aid, 15,400 were judged to have need, 4,858 had their need fully met. In 2011, 4636 non-need-based awards were made. *Average percent of need met:* 75%. *Average financial aid package:* $13,157. *Average need-based loan:* $5919. *Average need-based gift aid:* $8087. *Average non-need-based aid:* $4658. *Average indebtedness upon graduation:* $28,407.

Applying *Options:* electronic application, early admission, deferred entrance. *Application fee:* $45. *Required:* high school transcript. *Recommended:* minimum 2.0 GPA. *Application deadlines:* rolling (freshmen), rolling (transfers). *Notification:* continuous (freshmen), continuous (transfers).

Freshman Application Contact Rachelle Hernandez, Associate Director of Admissions, University of Minnesota, Twin Cities Campus, 240 Williamson, Minneapolis, MN 55455-0213. *Phone:* 612-625-2008. *Toll-free phone:* 800-752-1000. *Fax:* 612-626-1693. *E-mail:* admissions@tc.umn.edu. *Web site:* http://www.umn.edu/tc/.

University of Phoenix–Minneapolis/St. Louis Park Campus
St. Louis Park, Minnesota

Admissions Office Contact University of Phoenix–Minneapolis/St. Louis Park Campus, 435 Ford Road Suite #1000, St. Louis Park, MN 55426. *Toll-free phone:* 866-766-0766. *Web site:* http://www.phoenix.edu/.

University of St. Thomas
St. Paul, Minnesota

- **Independent Roman Catholic** university, founded 1885
- **Urban** 78-acre campus with easy access to Minneapolis
- **Coed** 6,176 undergraduate students, 96% full-time, 47% women, 53% men
- **Moderately difficult** entrance level, 25% of applicants were admitted

Undergraduates 5,902 full-time, 274 part-time. 16% are from out of state; 3% Black or African American, non-Hispanic/Latino; 4% Hispanic/Latino; 5% Asian, non-Hispanic/Latino; 0.1% American Indian or Alaska Native, non-Hispanic/Latino; 3% Two or more races, non-Hispanic/Latino; 2% Race/ethnicity unknown; 2% international; 4% transferred in; 41% live on campus. *Retention:* 88% of full-time freshmen returned.

Freshmen *Admission:* 5,250 applied, 1,324 admitted, 1,324 enrolled. *Average high school GPA:* 3.56. *Test scores:* SAT critical reading scores over 500: 77%; SAT math scores over 500: 85%; ACT scores over 18: 100%; SAT critical reading scores over 600: 43%; SAT math scores over 600: 44%; ACT scores over 24: 71%; SAT critical reading scores over 700: 9%; SAT math scores over 700: 9%; ACT scores over 30: 15%.

Faculty *Student/faculty ratio:* 15:1.

Academics *Calendar:* 4-1-4. *Degrees:* certificates, bachelor's, master's, doctoral, post-master's, postbachelor's, and first professional certificates. *Special study options:* advanced placement credit, double majors, English as a second language, honors programs, independent study, internships, off-campus study, part-time degree program, services for LD students, student-designed majors, study abroad, summer session for credit. *ROTC:* Army (c), Navy (c), Air Force (b). *Unusual degree programs:* 3-2 engineering with University of Notre Dame, Washington University in St. Louis, University of Minnesota-Twin Cities, Kettering University.

Computers on Campus Students can access the following: online (class) registration. Campuswide network is available.

Student Life *Housing options:* men-only, women-only. Campus housing is university owned. Freshman applicants given priority for college housing. *Activities and organizations:* drama/theater group, student-run newspaper, radio and television station, choral group. *Campus security:* 24-hour emergency response devices and patrols, late-night transport/escort service, controlled dormitory access. *Student services:* health clinic, personal/psychological counseling, women's center, legal services.

Athletics Member NCAA. All Division III. *Intercollegiate sports:* baseball M, basketball M/W, crew M(c)/W(c), cross-country running M/W, football M, golf M/W, ice hockey M/W, lacrosse M(c)/W(c), skiing (downhill) M(c)/W(c), soccer M/W, softball W, swimming and diving M/W, tennis M/W, track and field M/W, volleyball W. *Intramural sports:* basketball M/W, golf M/W, racquetball M/W, soccer M/W, softball M/W, squash M/W, table tennis M/W, tennis M/W, volleyball M/W.

Standardized Tests *Required:* SAT or ACT (for admission).

Costs (2011–12) *Comprehensive fee:* $40,701 includes full-time tuition ($31,504), mandatory fees ($569), and room and board ($8628). Full-time tuition and fees vary according to course load, degree level, and program. Part-time tuition: $985 per credit hour. Part-time tuition and fees vary according to course load, degree level, and program. *College room only:* $5490. Room and board charges vary according to board plan and housing facility. *Waivers:* senior citizens and employees or children of employees.

Financial Aid Of all full-time matriculated undergraduates who enrolled in 2011, 4,306 applied for aid, 3,436 were judged to have need, 567 had their need fully met. 1,343 Federal Work-Study jobs (averaging $2889). 945 state and other part-time jobs (averaging $2759). In 2011, 644 non-need-based awards were made. *Average percent of need met:* 83%. *Average financial aid package:* $22,435. *Average need-based loan:* $7946. *Average need-based gift aid:* $16,260. *Average non-need-based aid:* $12,933. *Average indebtedness upon graduation:* $31,073.

Applying *Options:* electronic application, deferred entrance. *Required:* essay or personal statement, high school transcript. *Recommended:* interview. *Application deadlines:* rolling (freshmen), rolling (transfers). *Notification:* continuous (freshmen), continuous (transfers).

Freshman Application Contact University of St. Thomas, 2115 Summit Avenue, St. Paul, MN 55105-1096. *Phone:* 651-962-6150. *Toll-free phone:* 800-328-6819. *Web site:* http://www.stthomas.edu/.

Walden University

Minneapolis, Minnesota

- **Proprietary** upper-level, founded 1970, part of Laureate
- **Coed** 8,741 undergraduate students, 10% full-time, 75% women, 25% men
- 96% of applicants were admitted

Undergraduates 858 full-time, 7,883 part-time. Students come from 52 states and territories; 53 other countries; 98% are from out of state; 37% Black or African American, non-Hispanic/Latino; 5% Hispanic/Latino; 1% Asian, non-Hispanic/Latino; 0.2% Native Hawaiian or other Pacific Islander, non-Hispanic/Latino; 0.6% American Indian or Alaska Native, non-Hispanic/Latino; 2% Two or more races, non-Hispanic/Latino; 5% Race/ethnicity unknown; 10% international; 23% transferred in.

Freshmen *Admission:* 521 applied, 500 admitted.

Faculty *Total:* 2,535, 9% full-time, 86% with terminal degrees.

Academics *Calendar:* quarter/semester depending on program. *Degrees:* bachelor's, master's, doctoral, post-master's, postbachelor's, and first professional certificates. *Special study options:* academic remediation for entering students, accelerated degree program, distance learning, freshman honors college, internships, off-campus study, part-time degree program, services for LD students, student-designed majors, study abroad, summer session for credit.

Computers on Campus Students can access the following: free student e-mail accounts, online (class) grades, online (class) registration, online (class) schedules.

Student Life *Student services:* personal/psychological counseling, legal services.

Costs (2011–12) *Tuition:* $12,600 full-time, $280 per credit hour part-time. Full-time tuition and fees vary according to course level, course load, and program. Part-time tuition and fees vary according to course level, course load, and program. *Required fees:* $210 full-time, $70 per term part-time. *Payment plan:* installment. *Waivers:* employees or children of employees.

Financial Aid Of all full-time matriculated undergraduates who enrolled in 2009, 908 applied for aid, 878 were judged to have need, 7 had their need fully met. In 2009, 17 non-need-based awards were made. *Average percent of need met:* 26%. *Average financial aid package:* $6301. *Average need-based loan:* $3755. *Average need-based gift aid:* $3222. *Average non-need-based aid:* $1225.

Applying *Options:* electronic application. *Application fee:* $50. *Application deadline:* rolling (transfers). *Notification:* continuous (transfers).

Application Contact Walden University, 155 Fifth Avenue South, Minneapolis, MN 55401. *Phone:* 800-925-3368. *Toll-free phone:* 866-492-5336. *Web site:* http://www.waldenu.edu/.

Winona State University

Winona, Minnesota

- **State-supported** comprehensive, founded 1858, part of Minnesota State Colleges and Universities System
- **Small-town** 40-acre campus
- **Endowment** $15.0 million
- **Coed** 8,435 undergraduate students, 91% full-time, 60% women, 40% men
- **Moderately difficult** entrance level, 69% of applicants were admitted

Undergraduates 7,660 full-time, 775 part-time. 33% are from out of state; 2% Black or African American, non-Hispanic/Latino; 2% Hispanic/Latino; 2% Asian, non-Hispanic/Latino; 0.1% Native Hawaiian or other Pacific Islander, non-Hispanic/Latino; 0.1% American Indian or Alaska Native, non-Hispanic/Latino; 2% Two or more races, non-Hispanic/Latino; 2% Race/ethnicity unknown; 3% international; 7% transferred in; 93% live on campus. *Retention:* 78% of full-time freshmen returned.

Freshmen *Admission:* 6,528 applied, 4,506 admitted, 1,874 enrolled. *Average high school GPA:* 3.3. *Test scores:* SAT critical reading scores over 500: 55%; SAT math scores over 500: 73%; ACT scores over 18: 99%; SAT critical reading scores over 600: 9%; SAT math scores over 600: 18%; ACT scores over 24: 39%; ACT scores over 30: 2%.

Faculty *Total:* 556, 53% full-time, 43% with terminal degrees. *Student/faculty ratio:* 22:1.

Academics *Calendar:* semesters. *Degrees:* associate, bachelor's, master's, doctoral, post-master's, and postbachelor's certificates. *Special study options:* academic remediation for entering students, accelerated degree program, adult/continuing education programs, advanced placement credit, distance learning, double majors, English as a second language, external degree program, honors programs, independent study, internships, off-campus study, part-time degree

program, services for LD students, student-designed majors, study abroad, summer session for credit. *ROTC:* Army (c).

Computers on Campus 8,500 computers/terminals and 19,500 ports are available on campus for general student use. Students can access the following: campus intranet, computer help desk, free student e-mail accounts, online (class) grades, online (class) registration, online (class) schedules. Campus-wide network is available. 100% of college-owned or -operated housing units are wired for high-speed Internet access. Wireless service is available via entire campus.

Student Life *Housing options:* coed, men-only, women-only, disabled students. Campus housing is university owned and leased by the school. Freshman campus housing is guaranteed. *Activities and organizations:* drama/theater group, student-run newspaper, radio and television station, choral group, marching band, University Program Activities Committee, Student Senate, Residence Hall Association, Inter Varsity, national fraternities, national sororities. *Campus security:* 24-hour emergency response devices and patrols, student patrols, late-night transport/escort service, controlled dormitory access, security cameras. *Student services:* health clinic, personal/psychological counseling, women's center, legal services.

Athletics Member NCAA. All Division II. *Intercollegiate sports:* baseball M(s), basketball M(s)/W(s), bowling M(c)/W(c), cross-country running M/W(s), fencing M(c)/W(c), football M(s), golf M(s)/W(s), gymnastics W, rugby M(c)/W(c), skiing (downhill) M(c)/W(c), soccer M(c)/W(s), softball W(s), tennis W(s), track and field W(s), ultimate Frisbee M(c)/W(c), volleyball M(c)/W(s), wrestling M(c). *Intramural sports:* archery M/W, badminton M/W, baseball M, basketball M/W, bowling M/W, cross-country running M/W, fencing M/W, field hockey M/W, football M/W, golf M/W, ice hockey M/W, racquetball M/W, riflery M/W, rugby M/W, skiing (cross-country) M/W, skiing (downhill) M/W, soccer M/W, softball M/W, track and field W, volleyball M/W, weight lifting M/W, wrestling M.

Standardized Tests *Required:* SAT or ACT (for admission).

Costs (2011–12) *Tuition:* state resident $6660 full-time, $220 per credit part-time; nonresident $11,780 full-time, $392 per credit part-time. Full-time tuition and fees vary according to location and reciprocity agreements. Part-time tuition and fees vary according to course load, location, and reciprocity agreements. *Required fees:* $1860 full-time. *Room and board:* $7540. Room and board charges vary according to board plan, housing facility, and location. *Payment plan:* installment. *Waivers:* employees or children of employees.

Financial Aid Of all full-time matriculated undergraduates who enrolled in 2010, 5,098 applied for aid, 3,901 were judged to have need, 353 had their need fully met. 174 Federal Work-Study jobs (averaging $1939). 315 state and other part-time jobs (averaging $1996). In 2010, 944 non-need-based awards were made. *Average percent of need met:* 40%. *Average financial aid package:* $7260. *Average need-based loan:* $4141. *Average need-based gift aid:* $4922. *Average non-need-based aid:* $2430. *Average indebtedness upon graduation:* $31,275.

Applying *Options:* electronic application, early admission, early action, deferred entrance. *Application fee:* $20. *Required:* high school transcript, class rank. *Required for some:* essay or personal statement, minimum 3.0 GPA, interview. *Application deadlines:* 3/5 (freshmen), 7/15 (transfers). *Notification:* continuous (freshmen), continuous (transfers).

Freshman Application Contact Carl Stange, Director of Admissions, Winona State University, 170 West Sanborn, Winona, MN 55987. *Phone:* 507-457-5100. *Toll-free phone:* 800-DIAL WSU. *Fax:* 507-457-5620. *E-mail:* admissions@winona.edu. *Web site:* http://www.winona.edu/.

MISSISSIPPI

Alcorn State University

Alcorn State, Mississippi

- **State-supported** comprehensive, founded 1871, part of Mississippi Institutions of Higher Learning
- **Rural** 1756-acre campus
- **Endowment** $8.8 million
- **Coed** 3,296 undergraduate students, 89% full-time, 66% women, 34% men
- **Moderately difficult** entrance level, 36% of applicants were admitted

Undergraduates 2,946 full-time, 350 part-time. Students come from 35 states and territories; 16 other countries; 12% are from out of state; 93% Black or African American, non-Hispanic/Latino; 0.8% Hispanic/Latino; 0.1% Asian, non-Hispanic/Latino; 0.1% American Indian or Alaska Native, non-Hispanic/Latino; 0.8% Two or more races, non-Hispanic/Latino; 1% international; 8% transferred in; 46% live on campus. *Retention:* 67% of full-time freshmen returned.

Freshmen *Admission:* 4,535 applied, 1,652 admitted, 687 enrolled. *Average high school GPA:* 2.91. *Test scores:* SAT critical reading scores over 500: 20%; SAT math scores over 500: 27%; ACT scores over 18: 45%; SAT critical reading scores over 600: 3%; SAT math scores over 600: 10%; ACT scores over 24: 5%.
Faculty *Total:* 199, 82% full-time, 63% with terminal degrees. *Student/faculty ratio:* 20:1.
Academics *Calendar:* semesters. *Degrees:* associate, bachelor's, master's, and post-master's certificates. *Special study options:* academic remediation for entering students, accelerated degree program, adult/continuing education programs, advanced placement credit, cooperative education, distance learning, double majors, honors programs, independent study, internships, off-campus study, part-time degree program, study abroad, summer session for credit. *ROTC:* Army (b).
Computers on Campus 500 computers/terminals and 2,500 ports are available on campus for general student use. Students can access the following: campus intranet, computer help desk, free student e-mail accounts, online (class) grades, online (class) registration, online (class) schedules. Campuswide network is available. 100% of college-owned or -operated housing units are wired for high-speed Internet access. Wireless service is available via classrooms, computer centers, computer labs, learning centers, libraries, student centers.
Student Life *Housing options:* men-only, women-only. Campus housing is university owned. Freshman campus housing is guaranteed. *Activities and organizations:* drama/theater group, student-run newspaper, radio and television station, choral group, marching band, marching band, Gospel Choir, interfaith choir, national fraternities, national sororities. *Campus security:* 24-hour emergency response devices and patrols, late-night transport/escort service. *Student services:* health clinic, personal/psychological counseling.
Athletics Member NCAA. All Division I. *Intercollegiate sports:* baseball M(s), basketball M(s)/W(s), cross-country running M(s)/W(s), football M(s), golf M(s)/W(s), soccer W(s), softball W(s), tennis M(s)/W(s), track and field M(s)/W(s), volleyball W(s). *Intramural sports:* basketball M/W, football M.
Standardized Tests *Required:* SAT or ACT (for admission).
Costs (2011–12) *Tuition:* state resident $5256 full-time, $219 per credit hour part-time; nonresident $12,914 full-time, $538 per credit hour part-time. Full-time tuition and fees vary according to course load. Part-time tuition and fees vary according to course load. *Room and board:* $7592. *Payment plan:* installment. *Waivers:* employees or children of employees.
Financial Aid Of all full-time matriculated undergraduates who enrolled in 2010, 1,324 applied for aid, 1,279 were judged to have need, 109 had their need fully met. 213 Federal Work-Study jobs (averaging $964). In 2010, 535 non-need-based awards were made. *Average percent of need met:* 40%. *Average financial aid package:* $9873. *Average need-based loan:* $3773. *Average need-based gift aid:* $5356. *Average non-need-based aid:* $5493. *Average indebtedness upon graduation:* $19,838.
Applying *Options:* electronic application, early admission, deferred entrance. *Required:* high school transcript, minimum 2.0 GPA. *Application deadlines:* rolling (freshmen), rolling (transfers). *Notification:* continuous (freshmen), continuous (transfers).
Freshman Application Contact Mr. Emanuel Barnes, Director of Admissions, Alcorn State University, 1000 ASU Drive, #300, Alcorn State, MS 39096-7500. *Phone:* 601-877-6147. *Toll-free phone:* 800-222-6790. *Fax:* 601-877-6347. *E-mail:* ebarnes@alcorn.edu. *Web site:* http://www.alcorn.edu/.

Belhaven University
Jackson, Mississippi

- **Independent Presbyterian** comprehensive, founded 1883
- **Urban** 42-acre campus
- **Endowment** $4.9 million
- **Coed** 2,345 undergraduate students, 93% full-time, 66% women, 34% men
- **Moderately difficult** entrance level, 50% of applicants were admitted

Undergraduates 2,191 full-time, 154 part-time. Students come from 42 states and territories; 22 other countries; 46% are from out of state; 27% Black or African American, non-Hispanic/Latino; 5% Hispanic/Latino; 2% Asian, non-Hispanic/Latino; 0.4% Native Hawaiian or other Pacific Islander, non-Hispanic/Latino; 0.7% American Indian or Alaska Native, non-Hispanic/Latino; 2% Two or more races, non-Hispanic/Latino; 18% transferred in; 44% live on campus. *Retention:* 63% of full-time freshmen returned.
Freshmen *Admission:* 1,412 applied, 712 admitted, 206 enrolled. *Average high school GPA:* 3.3. *Test scores:* SAT critical reading scores over 500: 66%; SAT math scores over 500: 48%; ACT scores over 18: 94%; SAT critical reading scores over 600: 30%; SAT math scores over 600: 18%; ACT scores over 24: 37%; SAT critical reading scores over 700: 7%; SAT math scores over 700: 2%; ACT scores over 30: 6%.

Faculty *Total:* 173, 40% full-time, 29% with terminal degrees. *Student/faculty ratio:* 9:1.
Academics *Calendar:* semesters. *Degrees:* certificates, associate, bachelor's, and master's. *Special study options:* academic remediation for entering students, accelerated degree program, adult/continuing education programs, advanced placement credit, distance learning, double majors, English as a second language, honors programs, independent study, internships, off-campus study, part-time degree program, student-designed majors, study abroad, summer session for credit. *ROTC:* Army (c), Air Force (c). *Unusual degree programs:* 3-2 engineering with Mississippi State University.
Computers on Campus 36 computers/terminals are available on campus for general student use. Students can access the following: campus intranet, computer help desk, free student e-mail accounts, online (class) grades, online (class) registration, online (class) schedules. Campuswide network is available. 100% of college-owned or -operated housing units are wired for high-speed Internet access. Wireless service is available via classrooms, computer labs, dorm rooms, libraries, student centers.
Student Life *Housing:* on-campus residence required through sophomore year. *Options:* men-only, women-only. Campus housing is university owned. Freshman campus housing is guaranteed. *Activities and organizations:* drama/theater group, student-run newspaper, choral group, marching band, Belhaven Activities Team, intramurals, Reformed University Fellowship, Quartertone, Sports Medicine: Exercise Science Club. *Campus security:* 24-hour emergency response devices and patrols, late-night transport/escort service, controlled dormitory access. *Student services:* health clinic, personal/psychological counseling.
Athletics Member NAIA. *Intercollegiate sports:* baseball M(s), basketball M(s)/W(s), cross-country running M(s)/W(s), football M(s), golf M(s)/W(s), soccer M(s)/W(s), softball W(s), tennis M(s)/W(s), volleyball W(s). *Intramural sports:* basketball M/W, football M/W, soccer M/W, softball M/W, volleyball M/W.
Standardized Tests *Required:* SAT or ACT (for admission).
Costs (2012–13) *Comprehensive fee:* $26,090 includes full-time tuition ($19,200) and room and board ($6890). Part-time tuition: $375 per credit hour. Part-time tuition and fees vary according to course load. *Required fees:* $375 per credit hour part-time. *Room and board:* Room and board charges vary according to housing facility. *Payment plan:* installment. *Waivers:* employees or children of employees.
Financial Aid Of all full-time matriculated undergraduates who enrolled in 2009, 742 applied for aid, 667 were judged to have need, 81 had their need fully met. 148 Federal Work-Study jobs (averaging $1743). In 2009, 95 non-need-based awards were made. *Average percent of need met:* 61%. *Average financial aid package:* $14,653. *Average need-based loan:* $4342. *Average need-based gift aid:* $10,710. *Average non-need-based aid:* $6318. *Average indebtedness upon graduation:* $32,728.
Applying *Options:* electronic application, early admission, deferred entrance. *Application fee:* $25. *Required:* high school transcript, minimum 2.0 GPA, 1 letter of recommendation. *Required for some:* essay or personal statement, interview. *Application deadlines:* rolling (freshmen), rolling (out-of-state freshmen), rolling (transfers). *Notification:* continuous (freshmen), continuous (out-of-state freshmen), continuous (transfers).
Freshman Application Contact Ms. Suzanne T. Sullivan, Director of Admission, Belhaven University, 1500 Peachtree Street, Jackson, MS 39202. *Phone:* 601-968-5940. *Toll-free phone:* 800-960-5940. *Fax:* 601-968-8946. *E-mail:* admission@belhaven.edu. *Web site:* http://www.belhaven.edu/.

Blue Mountain College
Blue Mountain, Mississippi

- **Independent Southern Baptist** comprehensive, founded 1873
- **Rural** 44-acre campus with easy access to Memphis
- **Endowment** $10.5 million
- **Coed** 542 undergraduate students, 92% full-time, 58% women, 42% men
- **Moderately difficult** entrance level, 50% of applicants were admitted

Undergraduates 501 full-time, 41 part-time. Students come from 17 states and territories; 3 other countries; 16% are from out of state; 13% Black or African American, non-Hispanic/Latino; 0.9% Hispanic/Latino; 0.2% Asian, non-Hispanic/Latino; 0.6% international; 18% transferred in; 50% live on campus. *Retention:* 68% of full-time freshmen returned.
Freshmen *Admission:* 329 applied, 163 admitted, 88 enrolled. *Average high school GPA:* 3.3. *Test scores:* ACT scores over 18: 78%; ACT scores over 24: 19%.
Faculty *Total:* 43, 72% full-time, 70% with terminal degrees. *Student/faculty ratio:* 15:1.
Academics *Calendar:* semesters. *Degrees:* bachelor's and master's. *Special study options:* academic remediation for entering students, accelerated degree program, advanced placement credit, distance learning, double majors, honors

programs, internships, part-time degree program, summer session for credit. *Unusual degree programs:* 3-2 nursing with Union University.

Computers on Campus 43 computers/terminals are available on campus for general student use. Students can access the following: computer help desk, free student e-mail accounts, online (class) grades, online (class) registration, online (class) schedules. Campuswide network is available. 100% of college-owned or -operated housing units are wired for high-speed Internet access. Wireless service is available via classrooms, computer centers, computer labs, dorm rooms, learning centers, libraries, student centers.

Student Life *Housing:* on-campus residence required through junior year. *Options:* men-only, women-only. Campus housing is university owned. *Activities and organizations:* drama/theater group, choral group, Baptist Student Union, Student Body Association, Intramural Association, Ministerial Association, Mississippi Association of Educators/Student Program. *Campus security:* 24-hour emergency response devices and patrols.

Athletics Member NAIA. *Intercollegiate sports:* baseball M(s), basketball M(s)/W(s), cross-country running M(s)/W(s), golf M(s)/W(s), softball W(s). *Intramural sports:* basketball M/W, football M, soccer M, softball M/W, swimming and diving M/W, table tennis M/W, tennis W, track and field M/W, ultimate Frisbee M, volleyball M/W.

Standardized Tests *Required:* SAT or ACT (for admission).

Costs (2012–13) *Comprehensive fee:* $13,230 includes full-time tuition ($8250), mandatory fees ($980), and room and board ($4000). Full-time tuition and fees vary according to course load and degree level. Part-time tuition and fees vary according to course load and degree level. *Room and board:* Room and board charges vary according to board plan. *Payment plans:* installment, deferred payment. *Waivers:* employees or children of employees.

Financial Aid Of all full-time matriculated undergraduates who enrolled in 2010, 506 applied for aid, 336 were judged to have need, 273 had their need fully met. 70 Federal Work-Study jobs (averaging $935). 38 state and other part-time jobs (averaging $1100). In 2010, 273 non-need-based awards were made. *Average percent of need met:* 45%. *Average financial aid package:* $8577. *Average need-based loan:* $4750. *Average need-based gift aid:* $3923. *Average indebtedness upon graduation:* $4966.

Applying *Options:* electronic application, deferred entrance. *Application fee:* $10. *Required for some:* high school transcript. *Recommended:* minimum 2.0 GPA. *Application deadlines:* rolling (freshmen), rolling (out-of-state freshmen), rolling (transfers). *Notification:* continuous (freshmen), continuous (out-of-state freshmen), continuous (transfers).

Freshman Application Contact Miss Maria Teel, Director of Admissions, Blue Mountain College, PO Box 160, Blue Mountain, MS 38610-0160. *Phone:* 662-685-4771 Ext. 176. *Toll-free phone:* 800-235-0136. *Fax:* 662-685-4776. *E-mail:* mteel@bmc.edu. *Web site:* http://www.bmc.edu/.

Delta State University
Cleveland, Mississippi

- **State-supported** comprehensive, founded 1924, part of Mississippi Institutions of Higher Learning
- **Small-town** 274-acre campus
- **Endowment** $18.1 million
- **Coed** 2,880 undergraduate students, 81% full-time, 62% women, 38% men
- **Noncompetitive** entrance level, 58% of applicants were admitted

Undergraduates 2,333 full-time, 547 part-time. Students come from 26 states and territories; 22 other countries; 8% are from out of state; 39% Black or African American, non-Hispanic/Latino; 1% Hispanic/Latino; 1% Asian, non-Hispanic/Latino; 0.1% American Indian or Alaska Native, non-Hispanic/Latino; 0.1% Two or more races, non-Hispanic/Latino; 0.1% Race/ethnicity unknown; 2% international; 17% transferred in; 28% live on campus. *Retention:* 61% of full-time freshmen returned.

Freshmen *Admission:* 720 applied, 418 admitted, 333 enrolled. *Average high school GPA:* 3.23. *Test scores:* SAT critical reading scores over 500: 43%; SAT math scores over 500: 43%; ACT scores over 18: 77%; SAT critical reading scores over 600: 7%; SAT math scores over 600: 14%; ACT scores over 24: 20%; ACT scores over 30: 1%.

Faculty *Total:* 259, 71% full-time, 58% with terminal degrees. *Student/faculty ratio:* 19:1.

Academics *Calendar:* semesters. *Degrees:* bachelor's, master's, doctoral, post-master's, and first professional certificates. *Special study options:* academic remediation for entering students, adult/continuing education programs, advanced placement credit, cooperative education, distance learning, double majors, freshman honors college, honors programs, independent study, internships, part-time degree program, services for LD students, summer session for credit. *ROTC:* Army (b).

Computers on Campus 533 computers/terminals are available on campus for general student use. Students can access the following: campus intranet, computer help desk, free student e-mail accounts, online (class) grades, online

(class) registration, online (class) schedules. Campuswide network is available. 100% of college-owned or -operated housing units are wired for high-speed Internet access. Wireless service is available via classrooms, computer centers, dorm rooms, libraries, student centers.

Student Life *Housing:* on-campus residence required for freshman year. *Options:* men-only, women-only, disabled students. Campus housing is university owned. Freshman campus housing is guaranteed. *Activities and organizations:* drama/theater group, student-run newspaper, choral group, marching band, Student Government Association, Student Alumni Association, Baptist Student Union, Union Program Council, Delta Volunteers, national fraternities, national sororities. *Campus security:* 24-hour emergency response devices and patrols, late-night transport/escort service, controlled dormitory access. *Student services:* health clinic, personal/psychological counseling.

Athletics Member NCAA. All Division II. *Intercollegiate sports:* baseball M(s), basketball M(s)/W(s), cheerleading M(s)/W(s), cross-country running W(s), football M(s), golf M(s), soccer M(s)/W(s), softball W(s), swimming and diving M(s)/W(s), tennis M(s)/W(s). *Intramural sports:* archery M/W, badminton M/W, basketball M/W, bowling M/W, cross-country running M/W, football M/W, golf M/W, racquetball M/W, soccer M/W, softball M/W, swimming and diving M/W, table tennis M/W, tennis M/W, ultimate Frisbee M/W, volleyball M/W.

Standardized Tests *Required:* ACT (for admission). *Recommended:* SAT or ACT (for admission).

Costs (2011–12) *Tuition:* state resident $5288 full-time, $220 per credit hour part-time; nonresident $13,688 full-time, $570 per credit hour part-time. Part-time tuition and fees vary according to course load. *Room and board:* $6026. Room and board charges vary according to housing facility. *Payment plan:* installment. *Waivers:* children of alumni, senior citizens, and employees or children of employees.

Financial Aid Of all full-time matriculated undergraduates who enrolled in 2010, 1,937 applied for aid, 1,713 were judged to have need. 279 Federal Work-Study jobs (averaging $1850). 265 state and other part-time jobs (averaging $1168). *Average financial aid package:* $9518. *Average need-based gift aid:* $4852. *Average indebtedness upon graduation:* $19,717.

Applying *Options:* electronic application, deferred entrance. *Application fee:* $25. *Required:* high school transcript, minimum 2.0 GPA. *Required for some:* interview for art, music majors. *Application deadlines:* rolling (freshmen), rolling (out-of-state freshmen), rolling (transfers). *Notification:* continuous (freshmen), continuous (out-of-state freshmen), continuous (transfers).

Freshman Application Contact Delta State University, Highway 8 West, Cleveland, MS 38733-0001. *Phone:* 662-846-4655. *Toll-free phone:* 800-468-6378. *Web site:* http://www.deltastate.edu/.

ITT Technical Institute
Madison, Mississippi

- **Proprietary** 4-year, part of ITT Educational Services, Inc.
- **Coed**
- **Minimally difficult** entrance level

Academics *Calendar:* quarters. *Degrees:* associate and bachelor's.
Student Life *Housing:* college housing not available.
Freshman Application Contact Director of Recruitment, ITT Technical Institute, 382 Galleria Parkway, Suite 100, Madison, MS 39110. *Phone:* 601-607-4500. *Toll-free phone:* 800-209-2521. *Web site:* http://www.itt-tech.edu/.

Jackson State University
Jackson, Mississippi

Freshman Application Contact Mrs. Linda Rush, Director, Marketing and Recruitment, Jackson State University, PO Box 17330, 1400 John R. Lynch Street, Jackson, MS 39217. *Phone:* 601-979-2911. *Toll-free phone:* 800-848-6817. *E-mail:* schatman@ccaix.jsums.edu. *Web site:* http://www.jsums.edu/.

Millsaps College
Jackson, Mississippi

- **Independent United Methodist** comprehensive, founded 1890
- **Urban** 100-acre campus
- **Endowment** $97.5 million
- **Coed** 910 undergraduate students, 98% full-time, 49% women, 51% men
- **Moderately difficult** entrance level, 61% of applicants were admitted

Undergraduates 889 full-time, 21 part-time. Students come from 28 states and territories; 23 other countries; 57% are from out of state; 9% Black or African American, non-Hispanic/Latino; 3% Hispanic/Latino; 5% Asian, non-Hispanic/Latino; 0.1% Native Hawaiian or other Pacific Islander, non-Hispanic/Latino; 0.9% American Indian or Alaska Native, non-Hispanic/Latino; 0.6% Two or more races, non-Hispanic/Latino; 3% Race/ethnicity unknown; 3%

international; 3% transferred in; 86% live on campus. *Retention:* 88% of full-time freshmen returned.

Freshmen *Admission:* 1,779 applied, 1,077 admitted, 224 enrolled. *Average high school GPA:* 3.53. *Test scores:* SAT critical reading scores over 500: 80%; SAT math scores over 500: 83%; SAT writing scores over 500: 50%; ACT scores over 18: 100%; SAT critical reading scores over 600: 44%; SAT math scores over 600: 45%; SAT writing scores over 600: 17%; ACT scores over 24: 72%; SAT critical reading scores over 700: 9%; SAT math scores over 700: 9%; ACT scores over 30: 17%.

Faculty *Total:* 118, 82% full-time, 80% with terminal degrees. *Student/faculty ratio:* 9:1.

Academics *Calendar:* semesters. *Degrees:* bachelor's and master's. *Special study options:* accelerated degree program, advanced placement credit, double majors, honors programs, independent study, internships, off-campus study, part-time degree program, services for LD students, student-designed majors, study abroad, summer session for credit. *ROTC:* Army (c), Air Force (c). *Unusual degree programs:* 3-2 engineering with Auburn University, Columbia University, Vanderbilt University; nursing with University of Mississippi Medical Center School of Nursing, Vanderbilt University.

Computers on Campus 150 computers/terminals are available on campus for general student use. Students can access the following: campus intranet, computer help desk, free student e-mail accounts, online (class) grades, online (class) registration, online (class) schedules, online transcripts. Campuswide network is available. 100% of college-owned or -operated housing units are wired for high-speed Internet access. Wireless service is available via entire campus.

Student Life *Housing:* on-campus residence required through sophomore year. *Options:* coed, men-only, women-only, disabled students. Campus housing is university owned. Freshman campus housing is guaranteed. *Activities and organizations:* drama/theater group, student-run newspaper, choral group, Campus Ministry Team, Student Body Association, SAPS (Campus Programming Board), Inter-fraternity/Panhellenic Councils, intramural sports, national fraternities, national sororities. *Campus security:* 24-hour emergency response devices and patrols, student patrols, late-night transport/escort service, controlled dormitory access, self-defense education, lighted pathways. *Student services:* health clinic, personal/psychological counseling.

Athletics Member NCAA. All Division III. *Intercollegiate sports:* baseball M, basketball M/W, cross-country running M/W, football M, golf M/W, lacrosse M/W, soccer M/W, softball W, tennis M/W, track and field M/W, volleyball W. *Intramural sports:* basketball M/W, bowling M/W, cheerleading W(c), fencing M(c)/W(c), football M/W, golf M/W, lacrosse W(c), racquetball M/W, soccer M/W, softball M/W, table tennis M/W, tennis M/W, ultimate Frisbee M(c)/W(c), volleyball M/W.

Standardized Tests *Required:* SAT or ACT (for admission).

Costs (2011–12) *Comprehensive fee:* $39,794 includes full-time tuition ($27,650), mandatory fees ($1832), and room and board ($10,312). Part-time tuition: $856 per credit hour. Part-time tuition and fees vary according to course load. *Required fees:* $32 per credit hour part-time. *College room only:* $5820. Room and board charges vary according to housing facility. *Payment plan:* installment. *Waivers:* employees or children of employees.

Financial Aid Of all full-time matriculated undergraduates who enrolled in 2011, 642 applied for aid, 529 were judged to have need, 167 had their need fully met. In 2011, 333 non-need-based awards were made. *Average percent of need met:* 81%. *Average financial aid package:* $26,145. *Average need-based loan:* $4769. *Average need-based gift aid:* $20,433. *Average non-need-based aid:* $17,132. *Average indebtedness upon graduation:* $25,902.

Applying *Options:* electronic application, early admission, early decision, early action, deferred entrance. *Required:* essay or personal statement, high school transcript, minimum 2.5 GPA, 1 letter of recommendation, secondary school report. *Required for some:* interview. *Application deadlines:* 2/1 (freshmen), 2/1 (out-of-state freshmen), 7/1 (transfers), 12/1 (early action). *Early decision deadline:* 11/15. *Notification:* continuous until 10/15 (freshmen), continuous until 10/15 (out-of-state freshmen), continuous until 10/15 (transfers), 12/1 (early decision).

Freshman Application Contact Mr. Michael Thorp, Dean of Admissions and Financial Aid, Millsaps College, 1701 North State Street, Jackson, MS 39210-0001. *Phone:* 601-974-1050. *Toll-free phone:* 800-352-1050. *Fax:* 601-974-1059. *E-mail:* admissions@millsaps.edu. *Web site:* http://www.millsaps.edu/.

Mississippi College
Clinton, Mississippi

- **Independent Southern Baptist** comprehensive, founded 1826, part of Mississippi Baptist Convention
- **Suburban** 474-acre campus with easy access to Jackson
- **Endowment** $60.7 million
- **Coed** 3,200 undergraduate students, 87% full-time, 60% women, 40% men
- **Moderately difficult** entrance level, 45% of applicants were admitted

Undergraduates 2,791 full-time, 409 part-time. Students come from 33 states and territories; 10 other countries; 22% are from out of state; 24% Black or African American, non-Hispanic/Latino; 1% Hispanic/Latino; 1% Asian, non-Hispanic/Latino; 0.6% American Indian or Alaska Native, non-Hispanic/Latino; 4% Race/ethnicity unknown; 4% international; 12% transferred in; 52% live on campus. *Retention:* 76% of full-time freshmen returned.

Freshmen *Admission:* 1,821 applied, 816 admitted, 518 enrolled. *Average high school GPA:* 3.44. *Test scores:* SAT critical reading scores over 500: 73%; SAT math scores over 500: 75%; ACT scores over 18: 98%; SAT critical reading scores over 600: 38%; SAT math scores over 600: 21%; ACT scores over 24: 51%; SAT critical reading scores over 700: 12%; SAT math scores over 700: 3%; ACT scores over 30: 12%.

Faculty *Total:* 457, 42% full-time, 63% with terminal degrees. *Student/faculty ratio:* 13:1.

Academics *Calendar:* semesters. *Degrees:* bachelor's, master's, doctoral, post-master's, postbachelor's, and first professional certificates. *Special study options:* academic remediation for entering students, accelerated degree program, adult/continuing education programs, advanced placement credit, cooperative education, distance learning, double majors, English as a second language, honors programs, independent study, internships, part-time degree program, services for LD students, study abroad, summer session for credit. *ROTC:* Army (b), Air Force (b). *Unusual degree programs:* 3-2 engineering with Auburn University, University of Mississippi; law, medicine with University of Mississippi.

Computers on Campus 463 computers/terminals and 1,200 ports are available on campus for general student use. Students can access the following: campus intranet, computer help desk, free student e-mail accounts, online (class) grades, online (class) registration, online (class) schedules. Campuswide network is available. 100% of college-owned or -operated housing units are wired for high-speed Internet access. Wireless service is available via classrooms, computer centers, computer labs, dorm rooms, learning centers, libraries, student centers.

Student Life *Housing:* on-campus residence required through senior year. *Options:* men-only, women-only, disabled students. Campus housing is university owned. Freshman applicants given priority for college housing. *Activities and organizations:* drama/theater group, student-run newspaper, radio station, choral group, marching band, Baptist Student Union, Nenamoosha Social Tribe, Laguna Social Tribe, Civitan Service Club, Shawreth Service Club. *Campus security:* 24-hour emergency response devices and patrols, late-night transport/escort service, controlled dormitory access. *Student services:* health clinic, personal/psychological counseling.

Athletics Member NCAA. All Division III. *Intercollegiate sports:* baseball M, basketball M/W, cross-country running M/W, football M, golf M, soccer M/W, softball W, tennis M/W, track and field M/W, volleyball W. *Intramural sports:* badminton M/W, basketball M/W, cheerleading M/W, equestrian sports W, field hockey M/W, football M/W, soccer M/W, softball M/W, table tennis M/W, tennis M/W, volleyball M/W.

Standardized Tests *Required:* SAT or ACT (for admission).

Costs (2012–13) *Comprehensive fee:* $21,380 includes full-time tuition ($13,720), mandatory fees ($710), and room and board ($6950). Full-time tuition and fees vary according to course load. Part-time tuition: $430 per credit hour. Part-time tuition and fees vary according to course load. *Required fees:* $193 per term part-time. *College room only:* $5150. Room and board charges vary according to housing facility. *Payment plan:* installment. *Waivers:* employees or children of employees.

Financial Aid Of all full-time matriculated undergraduates who enrolled in 2010, 2,529 applied for aid, 1,605 were judged to have need, 458 had their need fully met. 258 Federal Work-Study jobs (averaging $1105). In 2010, 907 non-need-based awards were made. *Average percent of need met:* 75%. *Average financial aid package:* $16,449. *Average need-based loan:* $7663. *Average need-based gift aid:* $9312. *Average non-need-based aid:* $9850. *Average indebtedness upon graduation:* $24,800.

Applying *Options:* electronic application, early admission, early decision, deferred entrance. *Required:* high school transcript. *Required for some:* 2 letters of recommendation. *Recommended:* minimum 2.0 GPA, interview. *Application deadlines:* rolling (freshmen), rolling (transfers). *Early decision deadline:* 12/1. *Notification:* continuous (freshmen), continuous (out-of-state freshmen), continuous (transfers), 12/15 (early decision).

Freshman Application Contact Mr. Kyle Brantley, Director of Admissions, Mississippi College, Box 4026, 200 South Capitol Street, Clinton, MS 39058-0001. *Phone:* 601-925-3800. *Toll-free phone:* 800-738-1236. *Fax:* 601-925-3804. *E-mail:* enrollment-services@mc.edu. *Web site:* http://www.mc.edu/.

Mississippi State University
Mississippi State, Mississippi

- **State-supported** university, founded 1878, part of Mississippi Institutions of Higher Learning
- **Small-town** 4200-acre campus
- **Endowment** $326.3 million
- **Coed** 16,312 undergraduate students, 92% full-time, 48% women, 52% men
- **Moderately difficult** entrance level, 68% of applicants were admitted.

Undergraduates 14,949 full-time, 1,363 part-time. Students come from 52 states and territories; 55 other countries; 21% are from out of state; 23% Black or African American, non-Hispanic/Latino; 2% Hispanic/Latino; 1% Asian, non-Hispanic/Latino; 0.1% Native Hawaiian or other Pacific Islander, non-Hispanic/Latino; 0.5% American Indian or Alaska Native, non-Hispanic/Latino; 1% Two or more races, non-Hispanic/Latino; 1% Race/ethnicity unknown; 2% international; 11% transferred in; 25% live on campus. *Retention:* 83% of full-time freshmen returned.
Freshmen *Admission:* 9,864 applied, 6,684 admitted, 2,898 enrolled. *Average high school GPA:* 3.28. *Test scores:* SAT critical reading scores over 500: 69%; SAT math scores over 500: 73%; ACT scores over 18: 90%; SAT critical reading scores over 600: 29%; SAT math scores over 600: 38%; ACT scores over 24: 47%; SAT critical reading scores over 700: 7%; SAT math scores over 700: 8%; ACT scores over 30: 10%.
Faculty *Total:* 963, 87% full-time, 74% with terminal degrees. *Student/faculty ratio:* 20:1.
Academics *Calendar:* semesters. *Degrees:* associate, bachelor's, master's, doctoral, post-master's, and first professional certificates. *Special study options:* academic remediation for entering students, accelerated degree program, adult/continuing education programs, advanced placement credit, cooperative education, distance learning, double majors, English as a second language, freshman honors college, honors programs, independent study, internships, off-campus study, part-time degree program, services for LD students, student-designed majors, study abroad, summer session for credit. *ROTC:* Army (b), Air Force (b).
Computers on Campus 1,000 computers/terminals and 1,000 ports are available on campus for general student use. Students can access the following: campus intranet, computer help desk, free student e-mail accounts, online (class) grades, online (class) registration, online (class) schedules, campuswide wireless Internet access. Campuswide network is available. 100% of college-owned or -operated housing units are wired for high-speed Internet access. Wireless service is available via entire campus.
Student Life *Housing:* on-campus residence required for freshman year. *Options:* coed, men-only, women-only, disabled students. Campus housing is university owned. *Activities and organizations:* drama/theater group, student-run newspaper, radio and television station, choral group, marching band, Student Association, Black Student Alliance, Residence Hall Association, Fashion Board, Campus Activities Board, national fraternities, national sororities. *Campus security:* 24-hour emergency response devices and patrols, late-night transport/escort service, controlled dormitory access, bicycle patrols, crime prevention program, RAD program, general law enforcement services. *Student services:* health clinic, personal/psychological counseling.
Athletics Member NCAA. All Division I except football (Division I-A). *Intercollegiate sports:* baseball M(s), basketball M(s)/W(s), cheerleading M(s)/W(s), cross-country running M(s)/W(s), golf M(s)/W(s), soccer W(s), softball W(s), tennis M(s)/W(s), track and field M(s)/W(s), volleyball W(s). *Intramural sports:* badminton M(c)/W(c), basketball M/W, bowling M/W, cross-country running M(c)/W(c), fencing M(c)/W(c), football M/W, golf M/W, ice hockey M(c), lacrosse M(c), racquetball M/W, riflery M/W, rugby M(c)/W(c), soccer M(c)/W(c), softball M(c)/W(c), swimming and diving M(c)/W(c), table tennis M(c)/W(c), tennis M(c)/W(c), ultimate Frisbee M/W, volleyball M(c)/W(c), water polo M/W.
Standardized Tests *Required:* SAT or ACT (for admission).
Costs (2012–13) *Tuition:* state resident $5805 full-time, $242 per credit hour part-time; nonresident $14,670 full-time, $612 per credit hour part-time. Part-time tuition and fees vary according to course load. *Room and board:* $8162; room only: $4612. Room and board charges vary according to board plan, housing facility, and student level. *Payment plans:* tuition prepayment, installment. *Waivers:* children of alumni, senior citizens, and employees or children of employees.
Financial Aid Of all full-time matriculated undergraduates who enrolled in 2010, 9,856 applied for aid, 8,419 were judged to have need, 2,195 had their need fully met. 924 Federal Work-Study jobs (averaging $3489). In 2010,

2570 non-need-based awards were made. *Average percent of need met:* 65%. *Average financial aid package:* $12,558. *Average need-based loan:* $4006. *Average need-based gift aid:* $5810. *Average non-need-based aid:* $2998. *Average indebtedness upon graduation:* $26,008.
Applying *Options:* electronic application. *Application fee:* $40. *Required:* high school transcript, minimum 2.0 GPA. *Application deadlines:* 8/1 (freshmen), 8/1 (transfers). *Notification:* continuous (freshmen), continuous (transfers).
Freshman Application Contact Ms. Cheryl Dill, Associate Director of Admissions and Scholarships, Mississippi State University, PO Box 6334, Mississippi State, MS 39762. *Phone:* 662-325-2224. *Fax:* 662-325-1MSU. *E-mail:* admit@msstate.edu. *Web site:* http://www.msstate.edu/.

Mississippi University for Women
Columbus, Mississippi

- **State-supported** comprehensive, founded 1884, part of Mississippi Institutions of Higher Learning
- **Small-town** 110-acre campus
- **Endowment** $39.2 million
- **Coed, primarily women** 2,478 undergraduate students, 78% full-time, 83% women, 17% men
- **Moderately difficult** entrance level, 44% of applicants were admitted

Undergraduates 1,937 full-time, 541 part-time. Students come from 21 states and territories; 8 other countries; 9% are from out of state; 39% Black or African American, non-Hispanic/Latino; 0.7% Hispanic/Latino; 2% Asian, non-Hispanic/Latino; 0.2% American Indian or Alaska Native, non-Hispanic/Latino; 1% international; 19% transferred in; 28% live on campus. *Retention:* 75% of full-time freshmen returned.
Freshmen *Admission:* 1,360 applied, 603 admitted, 181 enrolled. *Average high school GPA:* 3.37. *Test scores:* ACT scores over 18: 82%; ACT scores over 24: 31%; ACT scores over 30: 2%.
Faculty *Total:* 202, 67% full-time, 49% with terminal degrees. *Student/faculty ratio:* 14:1.
Academics *Calendar:* semesters. *Degrees:* associate, bachelor's, master's, and post-master's certificates. *Special study options:* academic remediation for entering students, adult/continuing education programs, advanced placement credit, distance learning, double majors, freshman honors college, honors programs, independent study, internships, off-campus study, part-time degree program, services for LD students, study abroad, summer session for credit. *ROTC:* Army (c), Air Force (c). *Unusual degree programs:* 3-2 engineering with Auburn University, Mississippi State University.
Computers on Campus 352 computers/terminals and 1,220 ports are available on campus for general student use. Students can access the following: campus intranet, computer help desk, free student e-mail accounts, online (class) grades, online (class) registration, online (class) schedules, various software packages. Campuswide network is available. 100% of college-owned or -operated housing units are wired for high-speed Internet access. Wireless service is available via entire campus.
Student Life *Housing options:* men-only, women-only, disabled students. Campus housing is university owned. Freshman campus housing is guaranteed. *Activities and organizations:* drama/theater group, student-run newspaper, radio station, choral group, Student Government Association, Toastmasters, Class Council, Modeling Squad, Student Programming Board, national fraternities, national sororities. *Campus security:* 24-hour emergency response devices and patrols, late-night transport/escort service, controlled dormitory access. *Student services:* health clinic, personal/psychological counseling, women's center.
Athletics *Intramural sports:* badminton M/W, basketball M/W, equestrian sports M/W, football M/W, golf M/W, racquetball M/W, soccer M/W, softball M/W, table tennis M/W, tennis M/W, track and field M/W, ultimate Frisbee M/W, volleyball M/W.
Standardized Tests *Required for some:* SAT or ACT (for admission). *Recommended:* SAT or ACT (for admission).
Costs (2012–13) *Tuition:* state resident $5120 full-time, $213 per credit hour part-time; nonresident $13,950 full-time, $581 per credit hour part-time. Part-time tuition and fees vary according to course load. *Room and board:* $5668; room only: $3354. Room and board charges vary according to housing facility. *Payment plan:* installment. *Waivers:* employees or children of employees.
Financial Aid Of all full-time matriculated undergraduates who enrolled in 2010, 1,553 applied for aid, 1,385 were judged to have need, 1,005 had their need fully met. 52 Federal Work-Study jobs (averaging $2193). 201 state and other part-time jobs (averaging $1652). In 2010, 234 non-need-based awards were made. *Average percent of need met:* 69%. *Average financial aid package:* $9155. *Average need-based loan:* $5259. *Average need-based gift aid:* $5795. *Average non-need-based aid:* $4982. *Average indebtedness upon graduation:* $19,734.

Applying *Options:* electronic application, early admission. *Required:* high school transcript. *Required for some:* minimum 2.0 GPA, interview, rank in upper 50% of high school class. *Application deadlines:* rolling (freshmen), rolling (out-of-state freshmen), rolling (transfers). *Notification:* continuous (freshmen), continuous (out-of-state freshmen), continuous (transfers).
Freshman Application Contact Mississippi University for Women, 1100 College Street, MUW-1600, Columbus, MS 39701-9998. *Phone:* 662-329-7106. *Toll-free phone:* 877-GO 2 THE W. *Web site:* http://www.muw.edu/.

Mississippi Valley State University
Itta Bena, Mississippi

- **State-supported** comprehensive, founded 1946, part of Mississippi Institutions of Higher Learning
- **Small-town** 450-acre campus
- **Endowment** $1.7 million
- **Coed** 2,090 undergraduate students, 82% full-time, 61% women, 39% men
- **Minimally difficult** entrance level, 16% of applicants were admitted

Undergraduates 1,709 full-time, 381 part-time. Students come from 28 states and territories; 6 other countries; 14% are from out of state; 90% Black or African American, non-Hispanic/Latino; 0.8% Hispanic/Latino; 5% Race/ethnicity unknown; 10% transferred in; 43% live on campus. *Retention:* 62% of full-time freshmen returned.
Freshmen *Admission:* 4,278 applied, 690 admitted, 328 enrolled. *Average high school GPA:* 2.75. *Test scores:* ACT scores over 18: 39%; ACT scores over 24: 3%.
Faculty *Total:* 160, 81% full-time, 58% with terminal degrees. *Student/faculty ratio:* 15:1.
Academics *Calendar:* semesters. *Degrees:* bachelor's and master's. *Special study options:* academic remediation for entering students, cooperative education, distance learning, double majors, freshman honors college, honors programs, internships, part-time degree program, summer session for credit. *ROTC:* Army (b).
Computers on Campus 285 computers/terminals are available on campus for general student use. Students can access the following: computer help desk, free student e-mail accounts, online (class) registration. Campuswide network is available.
Student Life *Housing options:* men-only, women-only. Campus housing is university owned. *Activities and organizations:* drama/theater group, student-run newspaper, radio and television station, choral group, marching band, Student Government Association, Baptist Student Union, Black Student Fellowship, National Education Association, national fraternities, national sororities. *Campus security:* 24-hour emergency response devices and patrols, controlled dormitory access. *Student services:* health clinic, personal/psychological counseling.
Athletics Member NCAA. All Division I except football (Division I-AA). *Intercollegiate sports:* baseball M(s), basketball M(s)/W(s), bowling W, cross-country running M(s)/W(s), golf M(s)/W(s), softball W(s), tennis M(s)/W(s), track and field M(s)/W(s). *Intramural sports:* baseball M, basketball M/W, cross-country running M/W, football M, golf M/W, softball M/W, tennis M/W, track and field M/W.
Standardized Tests *Required:* SAT or ACT (for admission).
Costs (2011–12) *Tuition:* state resident $5232 full-time, $218 per credit hour part-time; nonresident $13,080 full-time, $327 per credit hour part-time. *Required fees:* $150 full-time. *Room and board:* $6200; room only: $2800. *Payment plan:* installment. *Waivers:* children of alumni and employees or children of employees.
Applying *Options:* deferred entrance. *Required:* high school transcript. *Required for some:* 2.5 letters of recommendation. *Recommended:* interview. *Application deadlines:* rolling (freshmen), rolling (transfers). *Notification:* continuous (freshmen), continuous (transfers).
Freshman Application Contact Mississippi Valley State University, 14000 Highway 82 West, Itta Bena, MS 38941-1400. *Phone:* 662-254-3345. *Toll-free phone:* 800-844-6885. *Web site:* http://www.mvsu.edu/.

Rust College
Holly Springs, Mississippi

- **Independent United Methodist** 4-year, founded 1866
- **Rural** 126-acre campus with easy access to Memphis
- **Endowment** $21.4 million
- **Coed** 922 undergraduate students, 88% full-time, 63% women, 37% men
- **Minimally difficult** entrance level, 7% of applicants were admitted

Undergraduates 810 full-time, 112 part-time. Students come from 27 states and territories; 8 other countries; 50% are from out of state; 93% Black or Afri-

can American, non-Hispanic/Latino; 0.2% Asian, non-Hispanic/Latino; 0.8% Race/ethnicity unknown; 5% international; 4% transferred in; 67% live on campus. *Retention:* 53% of full-time freshmen returned.
Freshmen *Admission:* 3,983 applied, 264 admitted, 264 enrolled. *Average high school GPA:* 2.7. *Test scores:* ACT scores over 18: 23%; ACT scores over 24: 1%.
Faculty *Total:* 50, 96% full-time, 54% with terminal degrees. *Student/faculty ratio:* 17:1.
Academics *Calendar:* semesters. *Degrees:* associate and bachelor's. *Special study options:* academic remediation for entering students, accelerated degree program, adult/continuing education programs, advanced placement credit, distance learning, double majors, honors programs, independent study, internships, part-time degree program, study abroad, summer session for credit.
Computers on Campus 220 computers/terminals are available on campus for general student use. Students can access the following: campus intranet, computer help desk, free student e-mail accounts, online (class) grades. Campuswide network is available. 100% of college-owned or -operated housing units are wired for high-speed Internet access. Wireless service is available via computer centers, computer labs, dorm rooms, libraries.
Student Life *Housing:* on-campus residence required for freshman year. *Options:* men-only, women-only. Campus housing is university owned. Freshman campus housing is guaranteed. *Activities and organizations:* drama/theater group, student-run newspaper, radio and television station, choral group, marching band, A Cappella Choir, BSU (Baptist Student Union), DOBSAC (Division of Business Students' Advisory Council), MAE (Mississippi Association for Educators), Pre-Alumni Council, national fraternities, national sororities. *Campus security:* 24-hour emergency response devices and patrols, late-night transport/escort service, controlled dormitory access. *Student services:* health clinic, personal/psychological counseling.
Athletics Member NCAA. All Division III. *Intercollegiate sports:* baseball M, basketball M/W, cheerleading M/W, cross-country running M/W, softball W, tennis M/W, track and field M/W, volleyball M/W. *Intramural sports:* badminton M/W, basketball M/W, football M/W, swimming and diving M/W, volleyball M/W.
Standardized Tests *Required:* ACT (for admission).
Costs (2011–12) *Comprehensive fee:* $11,800 includes full-time tuition ($8100) and room and board ($3700). Full-time tuition and fees vary according to course load. Part-time tuition: $346 per credit hour. Part-time tuition and fees vary according to course load. *College room only:* $1670. *Payment plan:* installment. *Waivers:* senior citizens and employees or children of employees.
Financial Aid Of all full-time matriculated undergraduates who enrolled in 2004, 806 applied for aid, 806 were judged to have need, 481 had their need fully met. 492 Federal Work-Study jobs (averaging $714). 189 state and other part-time jobs (averaging $546). In 2004, 112 non-need-based awards were made. *Average percent of need met:* 60%. *Average financial aid package:* $5067. *Average need-based loan:* $2158. *Average need-based gift aid:* $4281. *Average non-need-based aid:* $2795. *Average indebtedness upon graduation:* $9314.
Applying *Application fee:* $10. *Required:* high school transcript, minimum 2.2 GPA, 2 letters of recommendation. *Application deadlines:* rolling (freshmen), rolling (out-of-state freshmen), rolling (transfers). *Notification:* continuous (freshmen), continuous (out-of-state freshmen), continuous (transfers).
Freshman Application Contact Mr. Johnny B. McDonald, Director of Enrollment Services, Rust College, 150 Rust Avenue, Holly Springs, MS 38635-2328. *Phone:* 601-252-8000 Ext. 4065. *Toll-free phone:* 888-886-8492 Ext. 4065. *Fax:* 662-252-8895. *E-mail:* admissions@rustcollege.edu. *Web site:* http://www.rustcollege.edu/.

Southeastern Baptist College
Laurel, Mississippi

Freshman Application Contact Mrs. Emma Bond, Director of Admissions, Southeastern Baptist College, 4229 Highway 15 North, Laurel, MS 39440-1096. *Phone:* 601-426-6346.

Strayer University - Jackson Campus
Jackson, Mississippi

- **Proprietary** comprehensive
- **Coed**

Academics *Degrees:* certificates, diplomas, associate, bachelor's, and master's.
Freshman Application Contact Strayer University - Jackson Campus, 460 Briarwood Drive, Suite 200, Jackson, MS 39206. *Web site:* http://www.strayer.edu/jackson.

Tougaloo College

Tougaloo, Mississippi

Freshman Application Contact Ms. Juno Jacobs, Director of Admissions, Tougaloo College, 500 West County Line Road, Tougaloo, MS 39174. *Phone:* 601-977-7765. *Toll-free phone:* 888-42GALOO. *Fax:* 601-977-4501. *E-mail:* jjacobs@tougaloo.edu. *Web site:* http://www.tougaloo.edu/.

University of Mississippi

Oxford, Mississippi

- **State-supported** university, founded 1844, part of Mississippi Institutions of Higher Learning
- **Small-town** 3340-acre campus with easy access to Memphis
- **Endowment** $469.0 million
- **Coed** 15,346 undergraduate students, 93% full-time, 55% women, 46% men
- **Moderately difficult** entrance level, 79% of applicants were admitted

Undergraduates 14,296 full-time, 1,077 part-time. Students come from 53 states and territories; 90 other countries; 32% are from out of state; 17% Black or African American, non-Hispanic/Latino; 2% Hispanic/Latino; 1% Asian, non-Hispanic/Latino; 0.1% Native Hawaiian or other Pacific Islander, non-Hispanic/Latino; 0.4% American Indian or Alaska Native, non-Hispanic/Latino; 1% Two or more races, non-Hispanic/Latino; 0.2% Race/ethnicity unknown; 1% international; 10% transferred in. *Retention:* 81% of full-time freshmen returned.

Freshmen *Admission:* 13,321 applied, 10,524 admitted, 3,569 enrolled. *Average high school GPA:* 3.35. *Test scores:* SAT critical reading scores over 500: 63%; SAT math scores over 500: 65%; ACT scores over 18: 94%; SAT critical reading scores over 600: 23%; SAT math scores over 600: 24%; ACT scores over 24: 49%; SAT critical reading scores over 700: 6%; SAT math scores over 700: 3%; ACT scores over 30: 12%.

Faculty *Total:* 922, 84% full-time, 77% with terminal degrees. *Student/faculty ratio:* 19:1.

Academics *Calendar:* semesters. *Degrees:* bachelor's, master's, doctoral, post-master's, and first professional certificates. *Special study options:* academic remediation for entering students, accelerated degree program, adult/continuing education programs, advanced placement credit, cooperative education, distance learning, double majors, English as a second language, freshman honors college, honors programs, independent study, internships, part-time degree program, services for LD students, student-designed majors, study abroad, summer session for credit. *ROTC:* Army (b), Navy (b), Air Force (b).

Computers on Campus Students can access the following: campus intranet, computer help desk, free student e-mail accounts, online (class) grades, online (class) registration, online (class) schedules, application for admission, registration for orientation. Campuswide network is available. 100% of college-owned or -operated housing units are wired for high-speed Internet access. Wireless service is available via classrooms, computer centers, computer labs, learning centers, libraries, student centers.

Student Life *Housing:* on-campus residence required for freshman year. *Options:* men-only, women-only. Campus housing is university owned, leased by the school and is provided by a third party. Freshman campus housing is guaranteed. *Activities and organizations:* drama/theater group, student-run newspaper, radio and television station, choral group, marching band, Associated Student Body, Gospel Choir, sport clubs, Black Student Union, Student Programming Board, national fraternities, national sororities. *Campus security:* 24-hour emergency response devices and patrols, late-night transport/escort service, controlled dormitory access, crime prevention programs. *Student services:* health clinic, personal/psychological counseling, women's center.

Athletics Member NCAA. All Division I except football (Division I-A). *Intercollegiate sports:* baseball M(s), basketball M(s)/W(s), cheerleading M(s)/W(s), cross-country running M(s)/W(s), fencing M(c)/W(c), golf M(s)/W(s), ice hockey M, lacrosse M/W, riflery W(s), rugby M(c), soccer M(c)/W(s), softball W(s), tennis M(s)/W(s), track and field M(s)/W(s), volleyball M(c)/W(s). *Intramural sports:* badminton M/W, basketball M/W, bowling M/W, crew M(c)/W(c), football M/W, golf M/W, racquetball M/W, riflery M(c), soccer M/W, softball M/W, swimming and diving M/W, table tennis M(c)/W(c), tennis M/W, track and field M/W, ultimate Frisbee M/W, volleyball M/W, water polo M/W.

Standardized Tests *Required:* SAT or ACT (for admission).

Costs (2011–12) *Tuition:* state resident $5790 full-time, $241 per credit hour part-time; nonresident $14,796 full-time, $616 per credit hour part-time. Full-time tuition and fees vary according to course load and program. Part-time tuition and fees vary according to course load and program. *Room and board:* $8390. Room and board charges vary according to board plan, housing facility, and location. *Payment plan:* tuition prepayment. *Waivers:* children of alumni, senior citizens, and employees or children of employees.

Financial Aid Of all full-time matriculated undergraduates who enrolled in 2010, 8,798 applied for aid, 6,921 were judged to have need, 741 had their need fully met. 410 Federal Work-Study jobs (averaging $1650). In 2010, 2247 non-need-based awards were made. *Average percent of need met:* 74%. *Average financial aid package:* $7769. *Average need-based loan:* $4562. *Average need-based gift aid:* $7074. *Average non-need-based aid:* $4938. *Average indebtedness upon graduation:* $21,393.

Applying *Options:* electronic application. *Application fee:* $50. *Required:* high school transcript, minimum 2.0 GPA. *Application deadlines:* rolling (freshmen), rolling (out-of-state freshmen), rolling (transfers). *Notification:* continuous (freshmen), continuous (out-of-state freshmen), continuous (transfers).

Freshman Application Contact Mr. Jody Lowe, Associate Director of Enrollment Services, University of Mississippi, 145 Martindale Student Services Center, University, MS 38677. *Phone:* 662-915-7226. *Toll-free phone:* 800-653-6477. *Fax:* 662-915-5869. *E-mail:* admissions@olemiss.edu. *Web site:* http://www.olemiss.edu/.

University of Mississippi Medical Center

Jackson, Mississippi

Application Contact Ms. Barbara Westerfield, Director of Student Records and Registrar, University of Mississippi Medical Center, 2500 North State Street, Jackson, MS 39216-4505. *Phone:* 601-984-1080. *Fax:* 601-984-1079. *Web site:* http://www.umc.edu/.

University of Southern Mississippi

Hattiesburg, Mississippi

- **State-supported** university, founded 1910, part of Mississippi Institutions of Higher Learning
- **Suburban** 1090-acre campus with easy access to New Orleans
- **Coed** 13,618 undergraduate students, 83% full-time, 62% women, 38% men
- **Moderately difficult** entrance level, 63% of applicants were admitted

Undergraduates 11,296 full-time, 2,322 part-time. Students come from 45 states and territories; 32 other countries; 11% are from out of state; 31% Black or African American, non-Hispanic/Latino; 3% Hispanic/Latino; 1% Asian, non-Hispanic/Latino; 0.1% Native Hawaiian or other Pacific Islander, non-Hispanic/Latino; 0.4% American Indian or Alaska Native, non-Hispanic/Latino; 0.9% Two or more races, non-Hispanic/Latino; 5% Race/ethnicity unknown; 0.6% international; 13% transferred in; 45% live on campus. *Retention:* 72% of full-time freshmen returned.

Freshmen *Admission:* 6,426 applied, 4,060 admitted, 1,727 enrolled. *Average high school GPA:* 3.15. *Test scores:* SAT critical reading scores over 500: 67%; SAT math scores over 500: 68%; ACT scores over 18: 87%; SAT critical reading scores over 600: 17%; SAT math scores over 600: 24%; ACT scores over 24: 34%; SAT critical reading scores over 700: 5%; SAT math scores over 700: 8%; ACT scores over 30: 6%.

Faculty *Total:* 842, 80% full-time, 62% with terminal degrees. *Student/faculty ratio:* 17:1.

Academics *Calendar:* semesters. *Degrees:* certificates, bachelor's, master's, doctoral, post-master's, and first professional certificates. *Special study options:* academic remediation for entering students, accelerated degree program, advanced placement credit, cooperative education, distance learning, double majors, English as a second language, honors programs, independent study, internships, off-campus study, part-time degree program, services for LD students, study abroad, summer session for credit. *ROTC:* Army (c), Air Force (b).

Computers on Campus 600 computers/terminals and 2,933 ports are available on campus for general student use. Students can access the following: campus intranet, computer help desk, free student e-mail accounts, online (class) grades, online (class) registration, online (class) schedules. Campuswide network is available. 95% of college-owned or -operated housing units are wired for high-speed Internet access. Wireless service is available via entire campus.

Student Life *Housing options:* men-only, women-only, disabled students. Campus housing is university owned. Freshman applicants given priority for college housing. *Activities and organizations:* drama/theater group, student-run newspaper, radio station, choral group, marching band, Southern Miss Activities Council, Residence Halls Associations, Student Government Association, Baptist Student Union, African American Student Organization, national fraternities, national sororities. *Campus security:* 24-hour emergency response devices and patrols, late-night transport/escort service, controlled dormitory access. *Student services:* health clinic, personal/psychological counseling, women's center, legal services.

Athletics Member NCAA. All Division I. *Intercollegiate sports:* baseball M(s), basketball M(s)/W(s), cheerleading M/W, cross-country running W(s), football M(s)/W(s), golf M(s)/W(s), soccer W(s), softball W(s), tennis M(s)/W(s), track and field M(s)/W(s), volleyball W(s). *Intramural sports:* badminton M/W, basketball M/W, bowling M/W, fencing M/W, racquetball M/W, riflery M/W, rugby M, soccer M/W, softball M/W, table tennis M/W, tennis M/W, track and field M/W, ultimate Frisbee M/W, volleyball M/W.

Standardized Tests *Required:* SAT or ACT (for admission).

Costs (2012–13) *Tuition:* state resident $5834 full-time, $244 per credit hour part-time; nonresident $13,790 full-time, $576 per credit hour part-time. Part-time tuition and fees vary according to course load and degree level. *Room and board:* $6634. Room and board charges vary according to board plan and housing facility. *Payment plan:* installment. *Waivers:* children of alumni, senior citizens, and employees or children of employees.

Financial Aid Of all full-time matriculated undergraduates who enrolled in 2010, 9,128 applied for aid, 8,130 were judged to have need, 1,707 had their need fully met. In 2010, 552 non-need-based awards were made. *Average percent of need met:* 75%. *Average financial aid package:* $12,199. *Average need-based loan:* $4391. *Average need-based gift aid:* $406. *Average non-need-based aid:* $3905. *Average indebtedness upon graduation:* $23,975.

Applying *Options:* electronic application, early admission. *Application fee:* $35. *Required:* high school transcript, minimum 2.0 GPA. *Application deadlines:* 7/1 (freshmen), 7/1 (transfers).

Freshman Application Contact Mr. Jason Beverly, Senior Admissions Counselor, University of Southern Mississippi, 118 College Drive, #5166, Hattiesburg, MS 39406-1000. *Phone:* 601-266-5000. *Fax:* 601-266-5148. *E-mail:* admissions@usm.edu. *Web site:* http://www.usm.edu/.

William Carey University

Hattiesburg, Mississippi

Freshman Application Contact Mr. William N. Curry, Dean of Enrollment Management, William Carey University, 498 Tuscan Avenue, Hattiesburg, MS 39401-5499. *Phone:* 601-318-6051. *Toll-free phone:* 800-962-5991. *Fax:* 601-318-6154. *E-mail:* admissions@wmcarey.edu. *Web site:* http://www.wmcarey.edu/.

MISSOURI

Avila University

Kansas City, Missouri

- **Independent Roman Catholic** comprehensive, founded 1916
- **Suburban** 50-acre campus
- **Coed** 1,219 undergraduate students, 81% full-time, 63% women, 37% men
- **Minimally difficult** entrance level, 53% of applicants were admitted

Undergraduates 988 full-time, 231 part-time. Students come from 23 states and territories; 16 other countries; 32% are from out of state; 18% Black or African American, non-Hispanic/Latino; 6% Hispanic/Latino; 1% Asian, non-Hispanic/Latino; 0.4% Native Hawaiian or other Pacific Islander, non-Hispanic/Latino; 1% American Indian or Alaska Native, non-Hispanic/Latino; 2% Two or more races, non-Hispanic/Latino; 4% international; 13% transferred in; 28% live on campus. *Retention:* 65% of full-time freshmen returned.

Freshmen *Admission:* 1,170 applied, 619 admitted, 138 enrolled. *Average high school GPA:* 3.26. *Test scores:* SAT critical reading scores over 500: 40%; SAT math scores over 500: 40%; ACT scores over 18: 93%; SAT critical reading scores over 600: 30%; SAT math scores over 600: 20%; ACT scores over 24: 35%; SAT math scores over 700: 10%; ACT scores over 30: 2%.

Faculty *Total:* 200, 32% full-time, 43% with terminal degrees. *Student/faculty ratio:* 14:1.

Academics *Calendar:* semesters. *Degrees:* bachelor's, master's, and post-bachelor's certificates. *Special study options:* academic remediation for entering students, accelerated degree program, adult/continuing education programs, advanced placement credit, cooperative education, distance learning, double majors, English as a second language, independent study, internships, off-campus study, part-time degree program, services for LD students, study abroad, summer session for credit. *ROTC:* Army (c). *Unusual degree programs:* 3-2 occupational therapy, physical therapy, law with Rockhurst University, University of Missouri-Kansas City.

Computers on Campus 180 computers/terminals and 225 ports are available on campus for general student use. Students can access the following: campus intranet, computer help desk, free student e-mail accounts, online (class) grades, online (class) registration, online (class) schedules. Campuswide net-

work is available. 100% of college-owned or -operated housing units are wired for high-speed Internet access. Wireless service is available via entire campus.

Student Life *Housing:* on-campus residence required through sophomore year. *Options:* coed, men-only, women-only. Campus housing is university owned. Freshman campus housing is guaranteed. *Activities and organizations:* drama/theater group, student-run newspaper, choral group, Avila Ambassadors, Avila Student Nurses Association, Campus Ministries, Saudi Arabian Student Association, Avila University Theatre Company. *Campus security:* 24-hour emergency response devices, student patrols, late-night transport/escort service, controlled dormitory access. *Student services:* health clinic, personal/psychological counseling.

Athletics Member NAIA. *Intercollegiate sports:* baseball M(s), basketball M(s)/W(s), cheerleading W(s), cross-country running M(s)/W(s), football M(s), golf M(s)/W(s), soccer M(s)/W(s), softball W(s), volleyball W(s). *Intramural sports:* bowling M/W, table tennis M/W.

Standardized Tests *Required:* SAT or ACT (for admission).

Costs (2012–13) *Comprehensive fee:* $30,900 includes full-time tuition ($23,200), mandatory fees ($850), and room and board ($6850). Full-time tuition and fees vary according to course load and program. Part-time tuition and fees vary according to course load and program. No tuition increase for student's term of enrollment. *College room only:* $3350. Room and board charges vary according to board plan and housing facility. *Payment plans:* installment, deferred payment. *Waivers:* children of alumni, senior citizens, and employees or children of employees.

Financial Aid Of all full-time matriculated undergraduates who enrolled in 2008, 1,927 applied for aid, 1,852 were judged to have need, 1,846 had their need fully met. 161 Federal Work-Study jobs (averaging $903). 55 state and other part-time jobs (averaging $885). In 2008, 60 non-need-based awards were made. *Average percent of need met:* 35%. *Average financial aid package:* $12,976. *Average need-based loan:* $5465. *Average need-based gift aid:* $7854. *Average non-need-based aid:* $9152. *Average indebtedness upon graduation:* $16,508.

Applying *Options:* electronic application, early admission. *Required:* high school transcript, minimum 2.5 GPA, secondary school report. *Required for some:* essay or personal statement. *Recommended:* interview. *Application deadlines:* 8/15 (freshmen), 8/15 (transfers). *Notification:* 8/15 (freshmen), 8/15 (transfers).

Freshman Application Contact Ms. Bethany Bauer, Associate Director of Admissions, Avila University, 11901 Wornall Road, Kansas City, MO 64145. *Phone:* 816-501-2400. *Toll-free phone:* 800-GO-AVILA. *Fax:* 816-501-2453. *E-mail:* bethany.bauer@avila.edu. *Web site:* http://www.avila.edu/.

Baptist Bible College

Springfield, Missouri

Freshman Application Contact Mr. Terry Allcorn, Director of Admissions, Baptist Bible College, 628 East Kearney Street, Springfield, MO 65803-3498. *Phone:* 417-268-6000. *Toll-free phone:* 800-228-5754. *Fax:* 417-268-6694. *Web site:* http://www.gobbc.edu/.

Brown Mackie College–St. Louis

Fenton, Missouri

- **Proprietary** primarily 2-year, part of Education Management Corporation
- **Coed**

Academics *Degrees:* diplomas, associate, and bachelor's.

Costs (2011–12) *Tuition:* Tuition varies by program. Students should contact Brown Mackie College for tuition information.

Freshman Application Contact Brown Mackie College–St. Louis, #2 Soccer Park Road, Fenton, MO 63026. *Phone:* 636-651-3290. *Web site:* http://www.brownmackie.edu/st-louis/.

See page 1220 for the College Close-Up.

Calvary Bible College and Theological Seminary

Kansas City, Missouri

- **Independent nondenominational** comprehensive, founded 1932
- **Suburban** 55-acre campus
- **Coed** 283 undergraduate students, 62% full-time, 47% women, 53% men
- **Minimally difficult** entrance level, 83% of applicants were admitted

Undergraduates 175 full-time, 108 part-time. 56% are from out of state; 10% Black or African American, non-Hispanic/Latino; 4% Hispanic/Latino; 0.7% Asian, non-Hispanic/Latino; 1% American Indian or Alaska Native, non-Hispanic/Latino; 1% Two or more races, non-Hispanic/Latino; 0.7% Race/ethnic-

ity unknown; 0.7% international; 20% transferred in. *Retention:* 70% of full-time freshmen returned.

Freshmen *Admission:* 52 applied, 43 admitted, 33 enrolled. *Test scores:* SAT critical reading scores over 500: 100%; ACT scores over 18: 82%; ACT scores over 24: 21%.

Academics *Calendar:* semesters. *Degrees:* certificates, diplomas, associate, bachelor's, and master's. *Special study options:* academic remediation for entering students, adult/continuing education programs, advanced placement credit, distance learning, double majors, external degree program, independent study, internships, part-time degree program, services for LD students, student-designed majors, summer session for credit. *ROTC:* Army (c).

Computers on Campus 23 computers/terminals are available on campus for general student use. Students can access the following: campus intranet, computer help desk, free student e-mail accounts, online (class) grades, online (class) registration, online (class) schedules. Wireless service is available via entire campus.

Student Life *Housing:* on-campus residence required through senior year. *Options:* men-only, women-only. Campus housing is university owned. Freshman campus housing is guaranteed. *Activities and organizations:* drama/theater group, student-run radio station, choral group, Missions Encounter, Masterworks (Fine Arts). *Campus security:* late-night transport/escort service, night patrols by trained security personnel. *Student services:* personal/psychological counseling.

Athletics Member NCCAA. *Intercollegiate sports:* basketball M/W, soccer M, volleyball W. *Intramural sports:* basketball M/W, racquetball M/W, tennis M/W, volleyball M/W, weight lifting M/W.

Standardized Tests *Required:* SAT or ACT (for admission).

Costs (2012–13) *Comprehensive fee:* $15,536 includes full-time tuition ($9920), mandatory fees ($816), and room and board ($4800). Part-time tuition: $310 per credit. No tuition increase for student's term of enrollment. *Required fees:* $29 per credit part-time, $120 per term part-time. *Room and board:* Room and board charges vary according to housing facility. *Payment plan:* installment. *Waivers:* employees or children of employees.

Financial Aid *Financial aid deadline:* 4/1.

Applying *Options:* electronic application. *Application fee:* $25. *Required:* essay or personal statement, high school transcript, 2 letters of recommendation, statement of faith. *Application deadlines:* 7/15 (freshmen), 7/15 (transfers).

Freshman Application Contact Bob Crank, Director of Admissions, Calvary Bible College and Theological Seminary, 15800 Calvary Road, Kansas City, MO 64147-1341. *Phone:* 816-322-0110 Ext. 1321. *Toll-free phone:* 800-326-3960. *Fax:* 816-331-4474. *E-mail:* admissions@calvary.edu. *Web site:* http://www.calvary.edu/.

Central Bible College
Springfield, Missouri

Director of Admissions James Bell, Executive Director for Enrollment Services, Central Bible College, 3000 North Grant Avenue, Springfield, MO 65803-1096. *Phone:* 417-833-2551 Ext. 1290. *Toll-free phone:* 800-831-4222. *E-mail:* jbell@cbcag.edu. *Web site:* http://www.cbcag.edu/.

Central Christian College of the Bible
Moberly, Missouri

Freshman Application Contact Mr. Aaron Merritt, Director of Admissions, Central Christian College of the Bible, 911 Urbandale Drive East, Moberly, MO 65270-1997. *Phone:* 660-263-3900. *Toll-free phone:* 888-263-3900. *Fax:* 660-263-3936. *E-mail:* admissions@cccb.edu. *Web site:* http://www.cccb.edu/.

Central Methodist University
Fayette, Missouri

- **Independent Methodist** comprehensive, founded 1854
- **Small-town** 80-acre campus
- **Endowment** $27.4 million
- **Coed** 1,172 undergraduate students, 94% full-time, 50% women, 50% men
- **Moderately difficult** entrance level, 63% of applicants were admitted

Undergraduates 1,103 full-time, 69 part-time. Students come from 30 states and territories; 22 other countries; 11% are from out of state; 6% Black or African American, non-Hispanic/Latino; 2% Hispanic/Latino; 0.9% Asian, non-Hispanic/Latino; 0.4% Native Hawaiian or other Pacific Islander, non-Hispanic/Latino; 0.6% American Indian or Alaska Native, non-Hispanic/Latino; 0.2% Two or more races, non-Hispanic/Latino; 7% Race/ethnicity unknown; 3% international; 8% transferred in; 60% live on campus. *Retention:* 62% of full-time freshmen returned.

Freshmen *Admission:* 1,261 applied, 795 admitted, 281 enrolled. *Average high school GPA:* 3.42. *Test scores:* ACT scores over 18: 97%; ACT scores over 24: 32%; ACT scores over 30: 2%.

Faculty *Total:* 110, 55% full-time, 35% with terminal degrees. *Student/faculty ratio:* 15:1.

Academics *Calendar:* semesters. *Degrees:* associate, bachelor's, and master's. *Special study options:* accelerated degree program, adult/continuing education programs, distance learning, double majors, honors programs, independent study, internships, off-campus study, part-time degree program, services for LD students, study abroad, summer session for credit. *ROTC:* Army (c), Air Force (c). *Unusual degree programs:* 3-2 engineering with University of Missouri-Rolla.

Computers on Campus 72 computers/terminals are available on campus for general student use. Students can access the following: campus intranet, computer help desk, free student e-mail accounts, online (class) grades, online (class) schedules. Campuswide network is available. 100% of college-owned or -operated housing units are wired for high-speed Internet access. Wireless service is available via classrooms, computer centers, computer labs, learning centers, libraries, student centers.

Student Life *Housing:* on-campus residence required through senior year. *Options:* coed, men-only, women-only. Campus housing is university owned. Freshman applicants given priority for college housing. *Activities and organizations:* drama/theater group, student-run newspaper, radio and television station, choral group, marching band, Student Government Association, Students in Free Enterprise (SIFE), Alpha Phi Omega, Beta Beta Beta, Campus Ministries, national fraternities. *Campus security:* 24-hour emergency response devices, late-night transport/escort service, controlled dormitory access. *Student services:* health clinic, personal/psychological counseling.

Athletics Member NAIA. *Intercollegiate sports:* baseball M(s), basketball M(s)/W(s), cross-country running M(s)/W(s), football M(s), soccer M(s)/W(s), softball W(s), track and field M(s)/W(s), volleyball W(s). *Intramural sports:* basketball M/W, football M/W, racquetball M/W, soccer M/W, softball M/W, tennis M/W, track and field M/W, volleyball M/W, water polo M/W.

Standardized Tests *Required:* SAT or ACT (for admission). *Recommended:* ACT (for admission).

Costs (2011–12) *One-time required fee:* $100. *Comprehensive fee:* $26,610 includes full-time tuition ($19,400), mandatory fees ($730), and room and board ($6480). Full-time tuition and fees vary according to location. Part-time tuition: $185 per credit hour. Part-time tuition and fees vary according to course load and location. *Required fees:* $32 per credit hour part-time. *College room only:* $3240. Room and board charges vary according to board plan and housing facility. *Payment plan:* installment. *Waivers:* employees or children of employees.

Financial Aid Of all full-time matriculated undergraduates who enrolled in 2011, 918 applied for aid, 861 were judged to have need, 13 had their need fully met. 173 Federal Work-Study jobs (averaging $1024). 113 state and other part-time jobs (averaging $1042). In 2011, 165 non-need-based awards were made. *Average percent of need met:* 57%. *Average financial aid package:* $17,628. *Average need-based loan:* $4010. *Average need-based gift aid:* $4742. *Average non-need-based aid:* $7817. *Average indebtedness upon graduation:* $23,287.

Applying *Options:* electronic application, deferred entrance. *Application fee:* $20. *Required:* high school transcript, minimum 2.5 GPA. *Required for some:* 2 letters of recommendation. *Application deadlines:* rolling (freshmen), rolling (transfers). *Notification:* continuous (freshmen), continuous (transfers).

Freshman Application Contact Mr. Larry Anderson, Director of Admissions, Central Methodist University, 411 Central Methodist Square, Fayette, MO 65248-1198. *Phone:* 660-248-6247. *Toll-free phone:* 888-CMU-1854 (in-state); 877-CMU-1854 (out-of-state). *Fax:* 660-248-1872. *E-mail:* admissions@centralmethodist.edu. *Web site:* http://www.centralmethodist.edu/.

Chamberlain College of Nursing
St. Louis, Missouri

- **Proprietary** 4-year, founded 1889, part of DeVry Inc.
- **Urban** campus
- **Coed** 7,952 undergraduate students, 16% full-time, 93% women, 7% men
- **Moderately difficult** entrance level

Undergraduates 1,278 full-time, 6,674 part-time. 91% are from out of state; 16% Black or African American, non-Hispanic/Latino; 4% Hispanic/Latino; 3% Asian, non-Hispanic/Latino; 0.6% Native Hawaiian or other Pacific Islander, non-Hispanic/Latino; 0.4% American Indian or Alaska Native, non-Hispanic/Latino; 0.9% Two or more races, non-Hispanic/Latino; 15% Race/ethnicity unknown; 0.5% international.

Freshmen *Admission:* 14 enrolled.

Faculty *Total:* 246, 19% full-time. *Student/faculty ratio:* 31:1.

Academics *Calendar:* semesters. *Degree:* bachelor's. *Special study options:* part-time degree program.
Student Life *Campus security:* 24-hour patrols, late-night transport/escort service, controlled dormitory access.
Standardized Tests *Required:* SAT or ACT (for admission).
Costs (2011–12) *Tuition:* $15,600 full-time, $590 per credit hour part-time. Full-time tuition and fees vary according to course load and program. Part-time tuition and fees vary according to course load and program.
Applying *Application fee:* $95. *Required:* essay or personal statement, high school transcript. *Required for some:* interview. *Application deadlines:* rolling (freshmen), rolling (transfers). *Notification:* continuous (freshmen), continuous (transfers).
Freshman Application Contact Admissions, Chamberlain College of Nursing, 11830 Westline Industrial Drive, Suite 106, St. Louis, MO 63146. *Phone:* 314-991-6200. *Toll-free phone:* 888-556-8CCN. *Web site:* http://www.chamberlain.edu/.

City Vision College
Kansas City, Missouri
- **Independent Christian** upper-level
- **Coed** 67 undergraduate students, 45% full-time, 66% women, 34% men

Undergraduates 30 full-time, 37 part-time. Students come from 31 states and territories; 1 other country; 3% are from out of state; 37% Black or African American, non-Hispanic/Latino; 4% Hispanic/Latino; 3% American Indian or Alaska Native, non-Hispanic/Latino; 4% Race/ethnicity unknown; 34% transferred in.
Faculty *Total:* 18, 11% with terminal degrees. *Student/faculty ratio:* 6:1.
Academics *Degree:* certificates and bachelor's. *Special study options:* adult/continuing education programs, distance learning, double majors, internships, part-time degree program, summer session for credit.
Computers on Campus Students can access the following: computer help desk, online (class) grades, online (class) registration, online (class) schedules, All the course materials, weekly outlines, lectures and assignments. All the courses are online based.
Costs (2012–13) *Tuition:* $6000 full-time, $3000 per year part-time. Full-time tuition and fees vary according to course load. Part-time tuition and fees vary according to course load. *Waivers:* employees or children of employees.
Applying *Options:* electronic application. *Application fee:* $25. *Application deadline:* rolling (transfers). *Notification:* continuous (transfers).
Application Contact City Vision College, PO Box 413188, Kansas City, MO 64141-3188. *Phone:* 816-960-2008 Ext. 5. *Web site:* http://www.cityvision.edu/.

College of the Ozarks
Point Lookout, Missouri
- **Independent Presbyterian** 4-year, founded 1906
- **Small-town** 1000-acre campus
- **Endowment** $337.6 million
- **Coed** 1,374 undergraduate students, 99% full-time, 57% women, 43% men
- **Moderately difficult** entrance level, 9% of applicants were admitted

Undergraduates 1,359 full-time, 15 part-time. Students come from 28 states and territories; 14 other countries; 18% are from out of state; 0.7% Black or African American, non-Hispanic/Latino; 2% Hispanic/Latino; 0.6% Asian, non-Hispanic/Latino; 0.1% Native Hawaiian or other Pacific Islander, non-Hispanic/Latino; 0.6% American Indian or Alaska Native, non-Hispanic/Latino; 2% Two or more races, non-Hispanic/Latino; 1% international; 3% transferred in; 86% live on campus. *Retention:* 86% of full-time freshmen returned.
Freshmen *Admission:* 3,299 applied, 295 admitted, 281 enrolled. *Average high school GPA:* 3.58. *Test scores:* ACT scores over 18: 96%; ACT scores over 24: 35%; ACT scores over 30: 2%.
Faculty *Total:* 135, 64% full-time, 44% with terminal degrees. *Student/faculty ratio:* 13:1.
Academics *Calendar:* semesters. *Degree:* bachelor's. *Special study options:* academic remediation for entering students, advanced placement credit, double majors, independent study, internships, off-campus study, services for LD students, student-designed majors. *ROTC:* Army (b). *Unusual degree programs:* 3-2 engineering with Missouri University Science and Technology; law with University of Missouri, Medical Technology with Cox Medical Center.
Computers on Campus 164 computers/terminals and 1,097 ports are available on campus for general student use. Students can access the following: campus intranet, computer help desk, free student e-mail accounts, online (class) grades, online (class) registration, online (class) schedules. Campus-wide network is available. 100% of college-owned or -operated housing units

are wired for high-speed Internet access. Wireless service is available via classrooms, dorm rooms, libraries, student centers.
Student Life *Housing:* on-campus residence required through senior year. *Options:* men-only, women-only. Campus housing is university owned. *Activities and organizations:* drama/theater group, student-run newspaper, radio station, choral group, Students in Free Enterprise (SIFE), Student Senate, Baptist Student Union, Aggie Club, Business Undergraduate Society. *Campus security:* 24-hour emergency response devices and patrols, controlled dormitory access, front gate closed 6 p.m. to 5 a.m., Security checks cars for proper credentials for entry. *Student services:* health clinic, personal/psychological counseling.
Athletics Member NAIA. *Intercollegiate sports:* baseball M(s), basketball M(s)/W(s), cheerleading M/W, volleyball W(s). *Intramural sports:* basketball M/W, football M, racquetball M/W, softball M/W, tennis M/W, volleyball M/W.
Standardized Tests *Required:* SAT or ACT (for admission).
Costs (2012–13) *Comprehensive fee:* includes mandatory fees ($430) and room and board ($5900). Part-time tuition: $295 per credit hour. Part-time tuition and fees vary according to course load. Each student participates in the on-campus work program for 15 hours per week and two forty-hour work weeks. Earnings from participation in the work program, plus any federal and/or state aid for which students qualify, plus a College of the Ozarks Cost of Education Scholarship combine to meet each students full tuition charge. *Required fees:* $430 per year part-time. *College room only:* $2900. *Payment plan:* installment.
Financial Aid Of all full-time matriculated undergraduates who enrolled in 2011, 1,337 applied for aid, 1,289 were judged to have need, 375 had their need fully met. 777 Federal Work-Study jobs (averaging $4638). 580 state and other part-time jobs (averaging $1957). In 2011, 82 non-need-based awards were made. *Average percent of need met:* 85%. *Average financial aid package:* $18,686. *Average need-based gift aid:* $14,692. *Average non-need-based aid:* $14,077. *Average indebtedness upon graduation:* $7062.
Applying *Options:* electronic application. *Required:* high school transcript, 2 letters of recommendation, interview, medical history, financial statement. *Recommended:* minimum 3.0 GPA. *Application deadlines:* 2/15 (freshmen), 2/15 (transfers). *Notification:* continuous (freshmen), continuous (transfers).
Freshman Application Contact Mrs. Gayle Groves, Admissions Secretary, College of the Ozarks, PO Box 17, Point Lookout, MO 65726. *Phone:* 417-690-2636. *Toll-free phone:* 800-222-0525. *Fax:* 417-335-2618. *E-mail:* admiss4@cofo.edu. *Web site:* http://www.cofo.edu/.

Colorado Technical University North Kansas City
North Kansas City, Missouri
Director of Admissions Angela Vietti, Director of Admissions, Colorado Technical University North Kansas City, 520 East 19th Avenue, North Kansas City, MO 64116. *Phone:* 888-404-7555. *E-mail:* avietti@kc.coloradotech.edu. *Web site:* http://kc.coloradotech.edu/.

Columbia College
Columbia, Missouri
- **Independent** comprehensive, founded 1851, affiliated with Christian Church (Disciples of Christ)
- **Urban** 33-acre campus
- **Endowment** $81.6 million
- **Coed** 980 undergraduate students, 78% full-time, 59% women, 41% men
- **Moderately difficult** entrance level

Undergraduates 769 full-time, 211 part-time. Students come from 17 states and territories; 34 other countries; 11% are from out of state; 5% Black or African American, non-Hispanic/Latino; 3% Hispanic/Latino; 0.9% Asian, non-Hispanic/Latino; 0.1% Native Hawaiian or other Pacific Islander, non-Hispanic/Latino; 0.9% American Indian or Alaska Native, non-Hispanic/Latino; 2% Two or more races, non-Hispanic/Latino; 7% Race/ethnicity unknown; 10% international; 14% transferred in; 32% live on campus. *Retention:* 66% of full-time freshmen returned.
Freshmen *Admission:* 731 applied, 124 enrolled. *Average high school GPA:* 3.4. *Test scores:* SAT critical reading scores over 500: 56%; SAT math scores over 500: 67%; ACT scores over 18: 92%; SAT critical reading scores over 600: 11%; SAT math scores over 600: 33%; ACT scores over 24: 47%; SAT math scores over 700: 11%; ACT scores over 30: 8%.
Faculty *Total:* 121, 57% full-time, 50% with terminal degrees. *Student/faculty ratio:* 11:1.
Academics *Calendar:* semesters. *Degrees:* associate, bachelor's, and master's (offers continuing education program with significant enrollment not reflected in profile). *Special study options:* adult/continuing education programs,

advanced placement credit, distance learning, double majors, English as a second language, external degree program, honors programs, independent study, internships, off-campus study, part-time degree program, services for LD students, student-designed majors, study abroad, summer session for credit. *ROTC:* Army (c), Navy (c), Air Force (c). *Unusual degree programs:* 3-2 MAT/DayStar.

Computers on Campus 160 computers/terminals are available on campus for general student use. Students can access the following: campus intranet, computer help desk, free student e-mail accounts, online (class) grades, online (class) registration, online (class) schedules. Campuswide network is available. 100% of college-owned or -operated housing units are wired for high-speed Internet access. Wireless service is available via entire campus.

Student Life *Housing:* on-campus residence required through sophomore year. *Options:* coed, women-only, disabled students. Campus housing is university owned. Freshman campus housing is guaranteed. *Activities and organizations:* drama/theater group, choral group, Elysium Players, Student Government Association, International Club, Chi Alpha Christian Fellowship, The Pride. *Campus security:* 24-hour emergency response devices and patrols, late-night transport/escort service, controlled dormitory access. *Student services:* health clinic, personal/psychological counseling.

Athletics Member NAIA. *Intercollegiate sports:* basketball M(s)/W(s), soccer M(s), softball W(s), volleyball W(s). *Intramural sports:* basketball M/W, football M/W, soccer M/W, softball M/W, volleyball M/W.

Standardized Tests *Required:* SAT or ACT (for admission).

Costs (2012–13) *Comprehensive fee:* $24,204 includes full-time tuition ($17,950) and room and board ($6254). Full-time tuition and fees vary according to class time, course load, degree level, and program. Part-time tuition: $354 per credit hour. Part-time tuition and fees vary according to class time, course load, degree level, and location. *College room only:* $3892. Room and board charges vary according to board plan and housing facility. *Payment plans:* installment, deferred payment. *Waivers:* children of alumni, senior citizens, and employees or children of employees.

Financial Aid Of all full-time matriculated undergraduates who enrolled in 2010, 600 applied for aid, 547 were judged to have need, 58 had their need fully met. 264 Federal Work-Study jobs (averaging $1092). 264 state and other part-time jobs (averaging $1141). In 2010, 59 non-need-based awards were made. *Average percent of need met:* 56%. *Average financial aid package:* $11,652. *Average need-based loan:* $3956. *Average need-based gift aid:* $4935. *Average non-need-based aid:* $9564. *Average indebtedness upon graduation:* $15,493.

Applying *Options:* electronic application, deferred entrance. *Application fee:* $35. *Required:* high school transcript, minimum 2.5 GPA. *Required for some:* essay or personal statement, interview. *Application deadlines:* 8/8 (freshmen), 8/8 (transfers). *Notification:* continuous (freshmen), continuous (transfers).

Freshman Application Contact Daniel Kruse, Admissions Counselor, Columbia College, 1001 Rogers Street, Columbia, MO 65216. *Phone:* 573-875-7358. *Toll-free phone:* 800-231-2391. *Fax:* 573-875-7506. *E-mail:* admissions@ccis.edu. *Web site:* http://www.ccis.edu/.

Conception Seminary College

Conception, Missouri

Freshman Application Contact Br. Etienne Huard OSB, Director of Recruitment and Admissions, Conception Seminary College, PO Box 502, Conception, MO 64433-0502. *Phone:* 660-944-2886. *Fax:* 660-944-2829. *E-mail:* vocations@conception.edu. *Web site:* http://www.conception.edu/.

Cox College

Springfield, Missouri

Freshman Application Contact Cox College, 1423 North Jefferson, Springfield, MO 65802. *Phone:* 417-269-3083. *Toll-free phone:* 866-898-5355. *Web site:* http://www.coxcollege.edu/.

Culver-Stockton College

Canton, Missouri

- **Independent** 4-year, founded 1853, affiliated with Christian Church (Disciples of Christ)
- **Rural** 143-acre campus
- **Endowment** $21.4 million
- **Coed** 752 undergraduate students, 93% full-time, 52% women, 48% men
- **Moderately difficult** entrance level, 61% of applicants were admitted

Undergraduates 701 full-time, 51 part-time. Students come from 27 states and territories; 12 other countries; 50% are from out of state; 10% Black or African American, non-Hispanic/Latino; 3% Hispanic/Latino; 0.4% Asian, non-Hispanic/Latino; 0.5% Native Hawaiian or other Pacific Islander, non-Hispanic/Latino; 0.8% American Indian or Alaska Native, non-Hispanic/

Latino; 0.8% Two or more races, non-Hispanic/Latino; 2% international; 7% transferred in; 75% live on campus. *Retention:* 65% of full-time freshmen returned.

Freshmen *Admission:* 1,448 applied, 880 admitted, 198 enrolled. *Average high school GPA:* 3.11. *Test scores:* SAT critical reading scores over 500: 26%; SAT math scores over 500: 37%; ACT scores over 18: 89%; SAT critical reading scores over 600: 13%; SAT math scores over 600: 13%; ACT scores over 24: 25%; ACT scores over 30: 1%.

Faculty *Total:* 82, 59% full-time, 46% with terminal degrees. *Student/faculty ratio:* 13:1.

Academics *Calendar:* semesters. *Degree:* bachelor's. *Special study options:* academic remediation for entering students, adult/continuing education programs, advanced placement credit, distance learning, double majors, honors programs, independent study, internships, off-campus study, part-time degree program, services for LD students, student-designed majors, study abroad, summer session for credit. *Unusual degree programs:* 3-2 occupational therapy with Washington University in St. Louis.

Computers on Campus 100 computers/terminals and 50 ports are available on campus for general student use. Students can access the following: campus intranet, computer help desk, free student e-mail accounts, online (class) grades, online (class) registration, online (class) schedules. Campuswide network is available. 100% of college-owned or -operated housing units are wired for high-speed Internet access. Wireless service is available via entire campus.

Student Life *Housing:* on-campus residence required through senior year. *Options:* coed. Campus housing is university owned. Freshman campus housing is guaranteed. *Activities and organizations:* drama/theater group, student-run newspaper, radio station, choral group, Up til Dawn (benefiting St. Jude's Hospital), Interfraternity Council/Panhellenic Council, Student Government Association, Students in Free Enterprise (SIFE), Campus Programming Council, national fraternities, national sororities. *Campus security:* 24-hour emergency response devices and patrols, late-night transport/escort service, controlled dormitory access, lighted pathways/sidewalks; self defense education is currently offered on campus. *Student services:* personal/psychological counseling.

Athletics Member NAIA. *Intercollegiate sports:* baseball M(s), basketball M(s)/W(s), cheerleading M(s)/W(s), cross-country running M(s)/W(s), football M(s), golf M(s)/W(s), soccer M(s)/W(s), softball W(s), track and field M(s)/W(s), volleyball W(s). *Intramural sports:* basketball M/W, bowling M/W, football M/W, golf M/W, racquetball M/W, softball M/W, volleyball M/W.

Standardized Tests *Required:* SAT or ACT (for admission).

Costs (2012–13) *One-time required fee:* $200. *Comprehensive fee:* $30,150 includes full-time tuition ($22,250), mandatory fees ($300), and room and board ($7600). Part-time tuition: $515 per credit hour. *Required fees:* $13 per credit hour part-time. *College room only:* $3400. Room and board charges vary according to board plan. *Payment plan:* installment. *Waivers:* senior citizens and employees or children of employees.

Financial Aid Of all full-time matriculated undergraduates who enrolled in 2011, 632 applied for aid, 595 were judged to have need, 102 had their need fully met. 80 Federal Work-Study jobs (averaging $993). 266 state and other part-time jobs (averaging $1196). In 2011, 78 non-need-based awards were made. *Average percent of need met:* 75%. *Average financial aid package:* $19,484. *Average need-based loan:* $4148. *Average need-based gift aid:* $15,772. *Average non-need-based aid:* $12,708. *Average indebtedness upon graduation:* $28,975. *Financial aid deadline:* 6/1.

Applying *Options:* electronic application, deferred entrance. *Required:* high school transcript, minimum 2.0 GPA. *Recommended:* essay or personal statement, 1 letter of recommendation, interview. *Application deadlines:* rolling (freshmen), rolling (transfers). *Notification:* continuous (freshmen), continuous (transfers).

Freshman Application Contact Misty McBee, Director of Admission, Culver-Stockton College, One College Hill, Canton, MO 63435-1299. *Phone:* 573-288-6507. *Toll-free phone:* 800-537-1883. *Fax:* 573-288-6618. *E-mail:* admissions@culver.edu. *Web site:* http://www.culver.edu/.

DeVry University

Kansas City, Missouri

- **Proprietary** comprehensive, founded 1931, part of DeVry University
- **Urban** campus
- **Coed** 922 undergraduate students, 46% full-time, 33% women, 67% men
- **Minimally difficult** entrance level

Undergraduates 424 full-time, 498 part-time. 37% are from out of state; 18% Black or African American, non-Hispanic/Latino; 4% Hispanic/Latino; 2% Asian, non-Hispanic/Latino; 0.7% American Indian or Alaska Native, non-Hispanic/Latino; 2% Two or more races, non-Hispanic/Latino; 7% Race/ethnicity unknown; 0.3% international; 20% transferred in.

Freshmen *Admission:* 123 enrolled.

Faculty *Total:* 76, 33% full-time. *Student/faculty ratio:* 17:1.

Academics *Calendar:* semesters. *Degrees:* associate, bachelor's, master's, and postbachelor's certificates. *Special study options:* adult/continuing education programs, part-time degree program.
Computers on Campus Students can access the following: online (class) registration.
Student Life *Housing:* college housing not available.
Costs (2011–12) *Tuition:* $15,294 full-time, $597 per credit hour part-time. Full-time tuition and fees vary according to course load. Part-time tuition and fees vary according to course load. *Required fees:* $80 full-time, $40 per term part-time. *Payment plans:* installment, deferred payment. *Waivers:* employees or children of employees.
Financial Aid Of all full-time matriculated undergraduates who enrolled in 2007, 294 applied for aid, 281 were judged to have need, 12 had their need fully met. In 2007, 30 non-need-based awards were made. *Average percent of need met:* 40%. *Average financial aid package:* $11,948. *Average need-based loan:* $8396. *Average need-based gift aid:* $5419. *Average non-need-based aid:* $13,609. *Average indebtedness upon graduation:* $8969.
Applying *Application fee:* $50. *Required:* high school transcript, interview. *Application deadlines:* rolling (freshmen), rolling (transfers). *Notification:* continuous (freshmen), continuous (transfers).
Freshman Application Contact DeVry University, 11224 Holmes Road, Kansas City, MO 64131. *Phone:* 816-943-7300. *Toll-free phone:* 866-338-7941. *Web site:* http://www.devry.edu/.

DeVry University
Kansas City, Missouri

Admissions Office Contact DeVry University, City Center Square, 1100 Main Street, Suite 118, Kansas City, MO 64105-2112. *Toll-free phone:* 866-338-7941. *Web site:* http://www.devry.edu/.

DeVry University
St. Louis, Missouri

Admissions Office Contact DeVry University, 1801 Park 270 Drive, Suite 260, St. Louis, MO 63146-4020. *Toll-free phone:* 866-338-7941. *Web site:* http://www.devry.edu/.

Drury University
Springfield, Missouri

- **Independent** comprehensive, founded 1873
- **Urban** 80-acre campus
- **Endowment** $68.0 million
- **Coed** 1,618 undergraduate students, 98% full-time, 54% women, 46% men
- **Moderately difficult** entrance level, 73% of applicants were admitted

Undergraduates 1,580 full-time, 38 part-time. Students come from 30 states and territories; 38 other countries; 18% are from out of state; 3% Black or African American, non-Hispanic/Latino; 2% Hispanic/Latino; 3% Asian, non-Hispanic/Latino; 0.6% American Indian or Alaska Native, non-Hispanic/Latino; 0.1% Race/ethnicity unknown; 7% international; 7% transferred in; 53% live on campus. *Retention:* 83% of full-time freshmen returned.
Freshmen *Admission:* 1,554 applied, 1,134 admitted, 352 enrolled. *Average high school GPA:* 3.78. *Test scores:* ACT scores over 18: 99%; ACT scores over 24: 71%; ACT scores over 30: 16%.
Faculty *Total:* 181, 75% full-time, 76% with terminal degrees. *Student/faculty ratio:* 12:1.
Academics *Calendar:* semesters. *Degrees:* bachelor's and master's (also offers evening program with significant enrollment not reflected in profile). *Special study options:* academic remediation for entering students, accelerated degree program, adult/continuing education programs, advanced placement credit, cooperative education, distance learning, double majors, English as a second language, honors programs, independent study, internships, off-campus study, part-time degree program, services for LD students, student-designed majors, study abroad, summer session for credit. *ROTC:* Army (c). *Unusual degree programs:* 3-2 engineering with Washington University in St. Louis; international management with American Graduate School of International Management, occupational therapy with Washington University in St. Louis.
Computers on Campus 389 computers/terminals are available on campus for general student use. Students can access the following: campus intranet, computer help desk, free student e-mail accounts, online (class) grades, online (class) registration, online (class) schedules, digital imaging lab, online bill payment/student information. Campuswide network is available. 100% of college-owned or -operated housing units are wired for high-speed Internet access. Wireless service is available via entire campus.
Student Life *Housing:* on-campus residence required through sophomore year. *Options:* coed, men-only, women-only. Campus housing is university owned

and leased by the school. Freshman campus housing is guaranteed. *Activities and organizations:* drama/theater group, student-run newspaper, radio and television station, choral group, Drury Volunteer Corps (DVC), International Student Association, Lambda Chi Alpha, Zeta Tau Alpha, Kappa Delta, national fraternities, national sororities. *Campus security:* 24-hour emergency response devices and patrols, student patrols, late-night transport/escort service, controlled dormitory access, security cameras in parking areas, police substation on campus, well-lit campus. *Student services:* health clinic, personal/psychological counseling.
Athletics Member NCAA. All Division II. *Intercollegiate sports:* baseball M(s), basketball M(s)/W(s), cheerleading M(s)/W(s), cross-country running M(s)/W(s), golf M(s)/W(s), soccer M(s)/W(s), softball W(s), swimming and diving M(s)/W(s), tennis M(s)/W(s), track and field M(s)/W(s), volleyball W(s). *Intramural sports:* basketball M/W, cross-country running M(c)/W(c), football M/W, ice hockey M(c), soccer M/W, softball M/W, tennis M/W, ultimate Frisbee M/W, volleyball M/W.
Standardized Tests *Required:* SAT or ACT (for admission).
Costs (2012–13) *One-time required fee:* $150. *Comprehensive fee:* $29,355 includes full-time tuition ($21,000), mandatory fees ($575), and room and board ($7780). Full-time tuition and fees vary according to class time. Part-time tuition and fees vary according to class time. *Room and board:* Room and board charges vary according to board plan and housing facility. *Payment plans:* tuition prepayment, installment, deferred payment. *Waivers:* minority students, children of alumni, and employees or children of employees.
Financial Aid Of all full-time matriculated undergraduates who enrolled in 2010, 1,571 applied for aid, 1,540 were judged to have need, 1,292 had their need fully met. 454 Federal Work-Study jobs (averaging $2663). In 2010, 78 non-need-based awards were made. *Average percent of need met:* 82%. *Average financial aid package:* $8055. *Average need-based loan:* $6500. *Average need-based gift aid:* $6990. *Average non-need-based aid:* $4735. *Average indebtedness upon graduation:* $20,500.
Applying *Options:* electronic application, deferred entrance. *Application fee:* $25. *Required:* essay or personal statement, high school transcript, minimum 2.7 GPA, 1 letter of recommendation. *Recommended:* interview. *Application deadlines:* 8/1 (freshmen), rolling (transfers). *Notification:* continuous (freshmen), continuous (transfers).
Freshman Application Contact Ms. Dawn Hiles, Dean of Enrollment Management, Drury University, 900 North Benton Ave., Springfield, MO 65802. *Phone:* 417-873-7614. *Toll-free phone:* 800-922-2274. *Fax:* 417-866-3873. *E-mail:* druryad@drury.edu. *Web site:* http://www.drury.edu/.

Evangel University
Springfield, Missouri

- **Independent** comprehensive, founded 1955, affiliated with Assemblies of God
- **Urban** 80-acre campus
- **Coed** 1,897 undergraduate students, 91% full-time, 56% women, 44% men
- **Moderately difficult** entrance level, 70% of applicants were admitted

Undergraduates 1,729 full-time, 168 part-time. 4% Black or African American, non-Hispanic/Latino; 4% Hispanic/Latino; 1% Asian, non-Hispanic/Latino; 1% American Indian or Alaska Native, non-Hispanic/Latino; 3% Two or more races, non-Hispanic/Latino; 8% Race/ethnicity unknown; 0.5% international; 7% transferred in.
Freshmen *Admission:* 1,237 applied, 861 admitted, 409 enrolled.
Academics *Calendar:* semesters. *Degrees:* associate, bachelor's, and master's. *ROTC:* Army (c).
Computers on Campus Students can access the following: computer help desk, free student e-mail accounts, online (class) grades, online (class) registration, online (class) schedules, online payment. Campuswide network is available. Wireless service is available via classrooms, computer labs, learning centers, libraries, student centers.
Student Life *Housing:* on-campus residence required through senior year. *Options:* coed, men-only, women-only. Campus housing is university owned. *Campus security:* 24-hour emergency response devices and patrols, student patrols, late-night transport/escort service, controlled dormitory access.
Athletics Member NAIA. *Intercollegiate sports:* baseball M(s), basketball M(s)/W(s), cross-country running M(s)/W(s), football M(s), golf M(s)/W(s), softball W(s), tennis M(s)/W(s), track and field M(s)/W(s), volleyball W(s). *Intramural sports:* baseball M, basketball M/W, football M, golf M/W, soccer M/W, softball W, tennis M/W, volleyball W.
Standardized Tests *Required:* SAT or ACT (for admission).
Costs (2011–12) *Comprehensive fee:* $24,310 includes full-time tuition ($16,910), mandatory fees ($1090), and room and board ($6310). Full-time tuition and fees vary according to course load. Part-time tuition: $705 per credit hour. Part-time tuition and fees vary according to course load. *College*

room only: $3260. Room and board charges vary according to board plan. *Payment plan:* installment. *Waivers:* employees or children of employees.

Financial Aid Of all full-time matriculated undergraduates who enrolled in 2010, 1,506 applied for aid, 1,381 were judged to have need, 97 had their need fully met. 1,127 Federal Work-Study jobs (averaging $1694). 134 state and other part-time jobs (averaging $1985). In 2010, 118 non-need-based awards were made. *Average percent of need met:* 57%. *Average financial aid package:* $13,973. *Average need-based loan:* $4598. *Average need-based gift aid:* $8888. *Average non-need-based aid:* $3850. *Average indebtedness upon graduation:* $33,209.

Applying *Options:* electronic application, deferred entrance. *Application fee:* $25. *Required:* essay or personal statement, high school transcript, interview. *Recommended:* minimum 2.0 GPA. *Application deadline:* rolling (freshmen). *Notification:* continuous (freshmen).

Freshman Application Contact Evangel University, 1111 North Glenstone, Springfield, MO 65802. *Phone:* 417-865-2811 Ext. 7205. *Toll-free phone:* 800-382-6435. *Fax:* 417-865-9599. *E-mail:* admissions@evangel.edu. *Web site:* http://www.evangel.edu/.

Everest College
Springfield, Missouri

Freshman Application Contact Admissions Office, Everest College, 1010 West Sunshine, Springfield, MO 65807-2488. *Phone:* 417-864-7220. *Toll-free phone:* 888-741-4270. *Fax:* 417-864-5697. *Web site:* http://www.everest.edu/campus/springfield/.

Fontbonne University
St. Louis, Missouri

- **Independent Roman Catholic** comprehensive, founded 1917
- **Suburban** 13-acre campus with easy access to St. Louis
- **Endowment** $20.3 million
- **Coed** 1,515 undergraduate students, 74% full-time, 67% women, 33% men
- **Moderately difficult** entrance level, 63% of applicants were admitted

Undergraduates 1,116 full-time, 399 part-time. Students come from 21 states and territories; 16 other countries; 15% are from out of state; 24% Black or African American, non-Hispanic/Latino; 2% Hispanic/Latino; 1% Asian, non-Hispanic/Latino; 0.1% American Indian or Alaska Native, non-Hispanic/Latino; 0.1% Two or more races, non-Hispanic/Latino; 1% Race/ethnicity unknown; 5% international; 13% transferred in; 23% live on campus. *Retention:* 70% of full-time freshmen returned.

Freshmen *Admission:* 632 applied, 400 admitted, 142 enrolled. *Average high school GPA:* 3.35. *Test scores:* ACT scores over 18: 72%; ACT scores over 24: 27%; ACT scores over 30: 4%.

Faculty *Total:* 276, 29% full-time, 29% with terminal degrees. *Student/faculty ratio:* 11:1.

Academics *Calendar:* semesters. *Degrees:* certificates, bachelor's, master's, and postbachelor's certificates. *Special study options:* academic remediation for entering students, accelerated degree program, adult/continuing education programs, advanced placement credit, cooperative education, distance learning, double majors, English as a second language, honors programs, independent study, internships, off-campus study, part-time degree program, services for LD students, student-designed majors, study abroad, summer session for credit. *ROTC:* Army (c), Air Force (c). *Unusual degree programs:* 3-2 engineering with Washington University in St. Louis; social work with Washington University in St. Louis; Saint Louis University; occupational therapy with Washington University in St. Louis.

Computers on Campus 285 computers/terminals are available on campus for general student use. Students can access the following: campus intranet, computer help desk, free student e-mail accounts, online (class) grades, online (class) registration, online (class) schedules. Campuswide network is available. Wireless service is available via entire campus.

Student Life *Housing options:* coed, men-only, women-only, disabled students. Campus housing is university owned. Freshman campus housing is guaranteed. *Activities and organizations:* drama/theater group, student-run newspaper, choral group, Future Teachers Association, Students for the Enhancement of Black Awareness, Fontbonne Athletic Association, Fontbonne in Service and Humility, Student Government Association. *Campus security:* 24-hour patrols, late-night transport/escort service, controlled dormitory access. *Student services:* health clinic, personal/psychological counseling.

Athletics Member NCAA, NAIA. All NCAA Division III. *Intercollegiate sports:* baseball M, basketball M/W, bowling W, cheerleading W, cross-country running M/W, field hockey W, golf M/W, lacrosse M/W, soccer M/W, softball W, tennis M/W, track and field M/W, volleyball M/W. *Intramural sports:* basketball M/W, bowling M, soccer M, volleyball M/W.

Standardized Tests *Required:* SAT or ACT (for admission).

Costs (2011–12) *Comprehensive fee:* $28,200 includes full-time tuition ($20,060), mandatory fees ($360), and room and board ($7780). Full-time tuition and fees vary according to program. Part-time tuition: $558 per credit hour. Part-time tuition and fees vary according to program. *Required fees:* $18 per credit hour part-time. *Room and board:* Room and board charges vary according to board plan and housing facility.

Financial Aid In 2003, 502 non-need-based awards were made. *Average percent of need met:* 86%. *Average financial aid package:* $15,600.

Applying *Options:* electronic application, early admission, deferred entrance. *Application fee:* $25. *Required:* high school transcript, minimum 2.5 GPA. *Required for some:* essay or personal statement. *Recommended:* 2 letters of recommendation, interview. *Application deadlines:* rolling (freshmen), rolling (transfers). *Notification:* continuous (freshmen), continuous (transfers).

Freshman Application Contact Dr. Greg Taylor, Executive Vice President, Fontbonne University, 6800 Wydown Boulevard, St. Louis, MO 63105. *Phone:* 314-889-1400. *Toll-free phone:* 800-205-5862. *Fax:* 314-889-1451. *E-mail:* gtaylor@fontbonne.edu. *Web site:* http://www.fontbonne.edu/.

Global University
Springfield, Missouri

Freshman Application Contact Rev. Todd Waggoner, Enrollment and International Student Services Director, Global University, 1211 South Glenstone Avenue, Springfield, MO 65804. *Phone:* 417-862-9533 Ext. 2335. *Toll-free phone:* 800-443-1083. *Fax:* 417-863-9621. *E-mail:* twaggoner@globaluniversity.edu. *Web site:* http://www.globaluniversity.edu/.

Goldfarb School of Nursing at Barnes-Jewish College
St. Louis, Missouri

- **Independent** comprehensive, founded 1902
- **Urban** campus
- **Endowment** $21.0 million
- **Coed, primarily women** 580 undergraduate students, 84% full-time, 89% women, 11% men

Undergraduates 486 full-time, 94 part-time. Students come from 8 states and territories; 2 other countries; 25% are from out of state; 7% Black or African American, non-Hispanic/Latino; 2% Hispanic/Latino; 2% Asian, non-Hispanic/Latino; 1% Native Hawaiian or other Pacific Islander, non-Hispanic/Latino; 0.3% American Indian or Alaska Native, non-Hispanic/Latino; 2% Two or more races, non-Hispanic/Latino; 5% Race/ethnicity unknown; 100% transferred in.

Faculty *Total:* 52, 73% full-time, 63% with terminal degrees. *Student/faculty ratio:* 11:1.

Academics *Calendar:* trimesters. *Degrees:* bachelor's, master's, doctoral, and post-master's certificates. *Special study options:* accelerated degree program, advanced placement credit, independent study, off-campus study, services for LD students, summer session for credit.

Computers on Campus 160 computers/terminals are available on campus for general student use. Students can access the following: campus intranet, computer help desk, free student e-mail accounts, software, research databases. Campuswide network is available. Wireless service is available via entire campus.

Student Life *Housing:* college housing not available. *Activities and organizations:* student-run newspaper, Student Nurses Association. *Campus security:* 24-hour patrols, late-night transport/escort service. *Student services:* health clinic, personal/psychological counseling.

Costs (2012–13) *Tuition:* $18,090 full-time, $603 per credit hour part-time. Full-time tuition and fees vary according to course load and degree level. Part-time tuition and fees vary according to course load and degree level. *Required fees:* $1100 full-time. *Payment plan:* installment.

Financial Aid Of all full-time matriculated undergraduates who enrolled in 2003, 150 applied for aid, 150 were judged to have need, 21 had their need fully met. 10 Federal Work-Study jobs (averaging $3300). In 2003, 21 non-need-based awards were made. *Average financial aid package:* $16,000. *Average need-based loan:* $4000. *Average need-based gift aid:* $4000. *Average non-need-based aid:* $9000. *Average indebtedness upon graduation:* $10,000.

Applying *Options:* deferred entrance. *Application fee:* $50. *Application deadline:* rolling (transfers). *Notification:* continuous (transfers).

Freshman Application Contact Goldfarb School of Nursing at Barnes-Jewish College, 4483 Duncan Avenue, St. Louis, MO 63110. *Phone:* 314-362-9155. *Toll-free phone:* 800-832-9009. *Web site:* http://www.barnesjewishcollege.edu/.

Graceland University
Independence, Missouri

Freshman Application Contact Admissions, Graceland University, 1401 West Truman Road, Independence, MO 64050-3434. *Phone:* 816-833-0524. *Toll-free phone:* 866-GRACELAND. *E-mail:* gic@graceland.edu. *Web site:* http://www.graceland.edu/.

Grantham University
Kansas City, Missouri

Freshman Application Contact Mr. Matthew Hawes, Vice President of Enrollment Management, Grantham University, 7200 NW 86th Street, Kansas City, MO 64153. *Phone:* 800-955-2527. *Toll-free phone:* 800-955-2527. *Fax:* 816-595-5757. *E-mail:* admissions@grantham.edu. *Web site:* http://www.grantham.edu/.

Hannibal-LaGrange University
Hannibal, Missouri

- **Independent Southern Baptist** comprehensive, founded 1858
- **Small-town** 110-acre campus
- **Coed** 1,107 undergraduate students, 81% full-time, 63% women, 37% men
- **Minimally difficult** entrance level

Undergraduates 895 full-time, 212 part-time. Students come from 26 states and territories; 26 other countries; 29% are from out of state; 5% Black or African American, non-Hispanic/Latino; 3% Hispanic/Latino; 0.2% Asian, non-Hispanic/Latino; 0.3% Native Hawaiian or other Pacific Islander, non-Hispanic/Latino; 0.3% American Indian or Alaska Native, non-Hispanic/Latino; 1% Two or more races, non-Hispanic/Latino; 1% Race/ethnicity unknown; 6% international; 18% transferred in; 44% live on campus. *Retention:* 62% of full-time freshmen returned.
Freshmen *Admission:* 160 enrolled.
Faculty *Total:* 146, 41% full-time, 14% with terminal degrees. *Student/faculty ratio:* 13:1.
Academics *Calendar:* semesters. *Degrees:* certificates, associate, bachelor's, and master's. *Special study options:* academic remediation for entering students, accelerated degree program, adult/continuing education programs, advanced placement credit, distance learning, double majors, English as a second language, honors programs, independent study, internships, off-campus study, part-time degree program, services for LD students, student-designed majors, study abroad, summer session for credit.
Computers on Campus 90 computers/terminals are available on campus for general student use. Students can access the following: free student e-mail accounts, online (class) grades, online (class) registration, online (class) schedules. Campuswide network is available. Wireless service is available via classrooms, computer centers, computer labs, learning centers, libraries, student centers.
Student Life *Housing:* on-campus residence required through junior year. *Options:* men-only, women-only. Campus housing is university owned. Freshman applicants given priority for college housing. *Activities and organizations:* drama/theater group, student-run newspaper, choral group, Phi Beta Lambda, student government, Student Teachers Organization, Phi Beta Delta, Alpha Tau Beta, national fraternities, national sororities. *Campus security:* 24-hour emergency response devices and patrols, controlled dormitory access. *Student services:* health clinic.
Athletics Member NAIA. *Intercollegiate sports:* baseball M(s), basketball M(s)/W(s), cheerleading M(s)/W(s), cross-country running M(s)/W(s), golf M(s)/W(s), soccer M(s)/W(s), softball W(s), track and field M(s)/W(s), volleyball M(s)/W(s), wrestling M(s). *Intramural sports:* basketball M/W, bowling M/W, racquetball M/W, table tennis M/W, ultimate Frisbee M/W, volleyball M/W.
Standardized Tests *Required:* SAT or ACT (for admission).
Costs (2012–13) *Comprehensive fee:* $24,370 includes full-time tuition ($17,150), mandatory fees ($650), and room and board ($6570). Full-time tuition and fees vary according to course load, degree level, program, and reciprocity agreements. Part-time tuition and fees vary according to course load, degree level, program, and reciprocity agreements. *Room and board:* Room and board charges vary according to housing facility. *Payment plan:* installment. *Waivers:* employees or children of employees.
Financial Aid Of all full-time matriculated undergraduates who enrolled in 2010, 80 Federal Work-Study jobs (averaging $750).
Applying *Options:* electronic application, early admission, deferred entrance. *Application fee:* $25. *Required:* high school transcript, minimum 2.0 GPA. *Required for some:* GED. *Application deadlines:* 9/10 (freshmen), 8/10 (out-of-state freshmen), rolling (transfers). *Notification:* continuous until 9/10 (freshmen), 9/10 (out-of-state freshmen), continuous (transfers).

Freshman Application Contact Dr. Raymond Carty, Vice President for Enrollment Management, Hannibal-LaGrange University, 2800 Palmyra Road, Hannibal, MO 63401-1999. *Phone:* 573-629-2278. *Toll-free phone:* 800-HLG-1119. *E-mail:* admissio@hlg.edu. *Web site:* http://www.hlg.edu/.

Harris-Stowe State University
St. Louis, Missouri

Freshman Application Contact Meghan Sprung, Assistant Director of Admissions, Harris-Stowe State University, 3026 Laclede Avenue, St. Louis, MO 63103. *Phone:* 314-340-3300. *Fax:* 314-340-3555. *E-mail:* admissions@hssu.edu. *Web site:* http://www.hssu.edu/.

Hickey College
St. Louis, Missouri

- **Private** 4-year, founded 1933
- **Suburban** campus with easy access to St. Louis
- **Coed** 461 undergraduate students
- 64% of applicants were admitted

Freshmen *Admission:* 1,171 applied, 751 admitted.
Academics *Calendar:* semesters. *Degrees:* diplomas, associate, and bachelor's. *Special study options:* accelerated degree program, internships.
Freshman Application Contact Admissions Office, Hickey College, 940 West Port Plaza, Suite 101, St. Louis, MO 63146. *Phone:* 314-434-2212. *Toll-free phone:* 800-777-1544. *Web site:* http://www.hickeycollege.edu/.

See page 498 for display ad and page 1362 for the College Close-Up.

ITT Technical Institute
Arnold, Missouri

- **Proprietary** primarily 2-year, founded 1997, part of ITT Educational Services, Inc.
- **Coed**
- **Minimally difficult** entrance level

Academics *Calendar:* quarters. *Degrees:* associate and bachelor's.
Student Life *Housing:* college housing not available.
Freshman Application Contact Director of Recruitment, ITT Technical Institute, 1930 Meyer Drury Drive, Arnold, MO 63010. *Phone:* 636-464-6600. *Toll-free phone:* 888-488-1082. *Web site:* http://www.itt-tech.edu/.

ITT Technical Institute
Earth City, Missouri

- **Proprietary** primarily 2-year, founded 1936, part of ITT Educational Services, Inc.
- **Suburban** campus
- **Coed**
- **Minimally difficult** entrance level

Academics *Calendar:* quarters. *Degrees:* associate and bachelor's.
Student Life *Housing:* college housing not available.
Freshman Application Contact Director of Recruitment, ITT Technical Institute, 3640 Corporate Trail Drive, Earth City, MO 63045. *Phone:* 314-298-7800. *Toll-free phone:* 800-235-5488. *Web site:* http://www.itt-tech.edu/.

ITT Technical Institute
Kansas City, Missouri

- **Proprietary** primarily 2-year, founded 2004, part of ITT Educational Services, Inc.
- **Coed**
- **Minimally difficult** entrance level

Academics *Calendar:* quarters. *Degrees:* associate and bachelor's.
Freshman Application Contact Director of Recruitment, ITT Technical Institute, 9150 East 41st Terrace, Kansas City, MO 64133. *Phone:* 816-276-1400. *Toll-free phone:* 877-488-1442. *Web site:* http://www.itt-tech.edu/.

ITT Technical Institute
Springfield, Missouri

- **Proprietary** 4-year, part of ITT Educational Services, Inc.
- **Coed**
- **Minimally difficult** entrance level

Academics *Calendar:* quarters. *Degrees:* associate and bachelor's.

Freshman Application Contact Director of Recruitment, ITT Technical Institute, 3216 South National Avenue, Springfield, MO 65807. *Phone:* 417-877-4800. *Toll-free phone:* 877-219-4387. *Web site:* http://www.itt-tech.edu/.

Kansas City Art Institute
Kansas City, Missouri

- **Independent** 4-year, founded 1885
- **Urban** 18-acre campus
- **Endowment** $43.7 million
- **Coed** 777 undergraduate students, 99% full-time, 60% women, 40% men
- **Moderately difficult** entrance level, 67% of applicants were admitted

Undergraduates 771 full-time, 6 part-time. Students come from 37 states and territories; 2 other countries; 60% are from out of state; 4% Black or African American, non-Hispanic/Latino; 7% Hispanic/Latino; 3% Asian, non-Hispanic/Latino; 1% American Indian or Alaska Native, non-Hispanic/Latino; 2% Two or more races, non-Hispanic/Latino; 15% Race/ethnicity unknown; 0.5% international; 1% transferred in; 25% live on campus. *Retention:* 78% of full-time freshmen returned.

Freshmen *Admission:* 650 applied, 433 admitted, 196 enrolled. *Average high school GPA:* 3.2. *Test scores:* SAT critical reading scores over 500: 82%; SAT math scores over 500: 61%; SAT writing scores over 500: 54%; ACT scores over 18: 91%; SAT critical reading scores over 600: 32%; SAT math scores over 600: 10%; SAT writing scores over 600: 29%; ACT scores over 24: 45%; SAT math scores over 700: 3%; ACT scores over 30: 4%.

Faculty *Total:* 104, 49% full-time, 81% with terminal degrees.

Academics *Calendar:* semesters. *Degree:* bachelor's. *Special study options:* academic remediation for entering students, advanced placement credit, cooperative education, double majors, English as a second language, independent study, internships, off-campus study, services for LD students, summer session for credit.

Computers on Campus 145 computers/terminals and 1,000 ports are available on campus for general student use. Students can access the following: campus intranet, computer help desk, free student e-mail accounts, online (class) registration. Campuswide network is available. 95% of college-owned or -operated housing units are wired for high-speed Internet access. Wireless service is available via classrooms, computer centers, computer labs, learning centers, libraries, student centers.

Student Life *Housing:* on-campus residence required for freshman year. *Options:* coed. Campus housing is university owned. Freshman applicants given priority for college housing. *Activities and organizations:* Student Assembly (council), Ethnic Student Association. *Campus security:* 24-hour emergency response devices and patrols, late-night transport/escort service, controlled dormitory access. *Student services:* personal/psychological counseling.

Standardized Tests *Required:* SAT or ACT (for admission).

Costs (2012–13) *Comprehensive fee:* $41,364 includes full-time tuition ($31,992) and room and board ($9372).

Financial Aid Of all full-time matriculated undergraduates who enrolled in 2011, 705 applied for aid, 662 were judged to have need, 80 had their need fully met. 115 Federal Work-Study jobs (averaging $1109). 190 state and other part-time jobs (averaging $1000). In 2011, 129 non-need-based awards were made. *Average percent of need met:* 64%. *Average financial aid package:* $21,559. *Average need-based loan:* $4579. *Average need-based gift aid:* $17,458. *Average non-need-based aid:* $12,561. *Average indebtedness upon graduation:* $26,149.

Applying *Options:* electronic application, deferred entrance. *Application fee:* $35. *Required:* essay or personal statement, high school transcript, minimum 2.5 GPA, 2 letters of recommendation, portfolio, statement of purpose. *Recommended:* interview. *Application deadlines:* rolling (freshmen), rolling (transfers). *Notification:* 8/1 (freshmen), continuous until 8/1 (transfers).

Freshman Application Contact Mr. Gerald Valet, Director of Admission Technology, Kansas City Art Institute, 4415 Warwick Boulevard, Kansas City, MO 64111-1874. *Phone:* 816-474-5224. *Toll-free phone:* 800-522-5224. *Fax:* 816-802-3309. *E-mail:* admiss@kcai.edu. *Web site:* http://www.kcai.edu/.

Lincoln University
Jefferson City, Missouri

- **State-supported** comprehensive, founded 1866, part of Missouri Coordinating Board for Higher Education
- **Small-town** 170-acre campus
- **Endowment** $1.5 million
- **Coed** 3,192 undergraduate students, 69% full-time, 59% women, 41% men
- **Noncompetitive** entrance level, 51% of applicants were admitted

Undergraduates 2,213 full-time, 979 part-time. Students come from 37 states and territories; 17 other countries; 17% are from out of state; 49% Black or African American, non-Hispanic/Latino; 2% Hispanic/Latino; 0.6% Asian,

non-Hispanic/Latino; 0.1% Native Hawaiian or other Pacific Islander, non-Hispanic/Latino; 0.4% American Indian or Alaska Native, non-Hispanic/Latino; 1% Race/ethnicity unknown; 2% international; 7% transferred in; 27% live on campus. *Retention:* 49% of full-time freshmen returned.

Freshmen *Admission:* 2,947 applied, 1,510 admitted, 634 enrolled. *Average high school GPA:* 2.54. *Test scores:* SAT math scores over 500: 12%; ACT scores over 18: 35%; ACT scores over 24: 6%.

Faculty *Total:* 244, 60% full-time. *Student/faculty ratio:* 15:1.

Academics *Calendar:* semesters. *Degrees:* associate, bachelor's, master's, and post-master's certificates. *Special study options:* academic remediation for entering students, accelerated degree program, adult/continuing education programs, advanced placement credit, distance learning, double majors, honors programs, independent study, internships, off-campus study, part-time degree program, services for LD students, study abroad, summer session for credit. *ROTC:* Army (b), Navy (c), Air Force (c).

Computers on Campus 250 computers/terminals and 1,100 ports are available on campus for general student use. Students can access the following: campus intranet, computer help desk, free student e-mail accounts, online (class) grades, online (class) registration, online (class) schedules. Campuswide network is available. 100% of college-owned or -operated housing units are wired for high-speed Internet access. Wireless service is available via entire campus.

Student Life *Housing:* on-campus residence required through sophomore year. *Options:* coed, men-only, women-only. Campus housing is university owned. *Activities and organizations:* drama/theater group, student-run newspaper, radio and television station, choral group, marching band, Student Government Association (SGA), Lincoln University Band, Alpha Kappa Mu, ROTC, Dedicated Individuals Vastly Affecting Society (DIVAS), national fraternities, national sororities. *Campus security:* 24-hour emergency response devices and patrols, student patrols, late-night transport/escort service, controlled dormitory access, security-related training upon request, Operation ID-ent, Timely Warnings, text message safety alerts, webpage with helpful tips. *Student services:* health clinic, personal/psychological counseling, women's center.

Athletics Member NCAA. All Division II. *Intercollegiate sports:* baseball M(s), basketball M(s)/W(s), cheerleading W(s), cross-country running W(s), football M(s), golf M(s)/W(s), softball W(s), tennis W(s), track and field M(s)/W(s). *Intramural sports:* basketball M/W, bowling M/W, volleyball M/W, weight lifting M/W.

Standardized Tests *Required:* SAT or ACT (for admission).

Costs (2011–12) *Tuition:* state resident $5964 full-time, $199 per credit hour part-time; nonresident $11,451 full-time, $382 per credit hour part-time. Full-time tuition and fees vary according to location and reciprocity agreements. Part-time tuition and fees vary according to location and reciprocity agreements. *Required fees:* $514 full-time, $15 per credit hour part-time, $32 per term part-time. *Room and board:* $8404. Room and board charges vary according to board plan and housing facility. *Payment plans:* installment, deferred payment. *Waivers:* employees or children of employees.

Financial Aid Of all full-time matriculated undergraduates who enrolled in 2011, 1,935 applied for aid, 1,788 were judged to have need, 147 had their need fully met. 141 Federal Work-Study jobs (averaging $1680). 153 state and other part-time jobs (averaging $2240). In 2011, 1 non-need-based awards were made. *Average percent of need met:* 64%. *Average financial aid package:* $9245. *Average need-based loan:* $3930. *Average need-based gift aid:* $5238. *Average non-need-based aid:* $2259. *Average indebtedness upon graduation:* $26,224.

Applying *Options:* electronic application, deferred entrance. *Application fee:* $20. *Required:* high school transcript. *Required for some:* minimum 2.0 GPA, audition for sacred music and music education. *Application deadlines:* 7/15 (freshmen), 7/15 (out-of-state freshmen), 7/15 (transfers). *Notification:* continuous (freshmen), continuous (out-of-state freshmen), continuous (transfers).

Freshman Application Contact Roxanne Seidner, Interim Director of Admissions, Lincoln University, Office of Admissions, 820 Chestnut Street, B-7 Young Hall, Jefferson City, MO 65102-0029. *Phone:* 573-681-5599. *Toll-free phone:* 800-521-5052. *Fax:* 573-681-5889. *E-mail:* enroll@lincolnu.edu. *Web site:* http://www.lincolnu.edu/.

Lindenwood University
St. Charles, Missouri

- **Independent Presbyterian** comprehensive, founded 1827
- **Suburban** 500-acre campus with easy access to St. Louis
- **Endowment** $113.3 million
- **Coed** 7,811 undergraduate students, 90% full-time, 56% women, 44% men
- **Moderately difficult** entrance level, 53% of applicants were admitted

Undergraduates 7,028 full-time, 783 part-time. Students come from 45 states and territories; 86 other countries; 27% are from out of state; 16% Black or African American, non-Hispanic/Latino; 0.5% Asian, non-Hispanic/Latino; 0.2% Native Hawaiian or other Pacific Islander, non-Hispanic/Latino; 0.6% American Indian or Alaska Native, non-Hispanic/Latino; 3% Two or more races, non-Hispanic/Latino; 6% Race/ethnicity unknown; 10% international;

61% transferred in; 54% live on campus. *Retention:* 71% of full-time freshmen returned.

Freshmen *Admission:* 3,335 applied, 1,780 admitted, 1,027 enrolled. *Average high school GPA:* 3.2. *Test scores:* SAT critical reading scores over 500: 47%; SAT math scores over 500: 59%; SAT writing scores over 500: 80%; ACT scores over 18: 88%; SAT critical reading scores over 600: 15%; SAT math scores over 600: 18%; SAT writing scores over 600: 40%; ACT scores over 24: 30%; SAT critical reading scores over 700: 3%; SAT math scores over 700: 5%; ACT scores over 30: 3%.

Faculty *Total:* 736, 33% full-time, 48% with terminal degrees. *Student/faculty ratio:* 18:1.

Academics *Calendar:* 4-1-4 for daytime programs; quarters and trimesters for evening programs. *Degrees:* bachelor's, master's, doctoral, post-master's, postbachelor's, and first professional certificates. *Special study options:* academic remediation for entering students, accelerated degree program, adult/continuing education programs, advanced placement credit, distance learning, double majors, English as a second language, external degree program, freshman honors college, honors programs, independent study, internships, off-campus study, part-time degree program, services for LD students, student-designed majors, study abroad, summer session for credit. *ROTC:* Army (b). *Unusual degree programs:* 3-2 engineering with University of Missouri-Columbia.

Computers on Campus 200 computers/terminals and 7,500 ports are available on campus for general student use. Students can access the following: campus intranet, computer help desk, free student e-mail accounts, online (class) grades, online (class) registration, online (class) schedules, Blackboard. Campuswide network is available. 100% of college-owned or -operated housing units are wired for high-speed Internet access. Wireless service is available via classrooms, computer centers, computer labs, learning centers, libraries, student centers.

Student Life *Housing:* on-campus residence required through senior year. *Options:* men-only, women-only. Campus housing is university owned. Freshman applicants given priority for college housing. *Activities and organizations:* drama/theater group, student-run newspaper, radio and television station, choral group, marching band, A Cross Between Campus Ministry, Campus YMCA, Delta Zeta, Tri Sigma, Intervaristy, national fraternities, national sororities. *Campus security:* 24-hour emergency response devices and patrols, late-night transport/escort service, controlled dormitory access. *Student services:* health clinic, personal/psychological counseling.

Athletics Member USCAA. *Intercollegiate sports:* baseball M(s), basketball M(s)/W(s), bowling M(s)/W(s), cheerleading M(s)/W(s), cross-country running M(s)/W(s), field hockey W(s), football M(s), golf M(s)/W(s), ice hockey M(s)/W(s), lacrosse M(s)/W(s), riflery M(s)/W(s), rugby M(s)/W(s), soccer M(s)/W(s), softball W(s), swimming and diving M(s)/W(s), table tennis M(s)/W(s), tennis M(s)/W(s), track and field M(s)/W(s), volleyball M(s)/W(s), water polo M(s)/W(s), weight lifting M(s)/W(s), wrestling M(s)/W(s).

Standardized Tests *Required:* SAT or ACT (for admission).

Costs (2011–12) *Comprehensive fee:* $21,360 includes full-time tuition ($13,650), mandatory fees ($350), and room and board ($7360). Full-time tuition and fees vary according to program. Part-time tuition: $395 per credit hour. Part-time tuition and fees vary according to course load. *College room only:* $4080. *Payment plans:* installment, deferred payment. *Waivers:* senior citizens and employees or children of employees.

Financial Aid Of all full-time matriculated undergraduates who enrolled in 2011, 5,201 applied for aid, 4,587 were judged to have need, 3,263 had their need fully met. In 2011, 1200 non-need-based awards were made. *Average percent of need met:* 90%. *Average financial aid package:* $9549. *Average need-based loan:* $4364. *Average need-based gift aid:* $5471. *Average non-need-based aid:* $3366.

Applying *Options:* electronic application, deferred entrance. *Application fee:* $30. *Required:* high school transcript, minimum 2.5 GPA, Personal resume indicating community service, youth leadership, clubs, organizations, and non-academic experience. *Recommended:* essay or personal statement, 3 letters of recommendation, interview. *Application deadlines:* rolling (freshmen), rolling (transfers). *Notification:* continuous (freshmen), continuous (transfers).

Freshman Application Contact Lindenwood University, 209 South Kingshighway, St. Charles, MO 63301-1695. *Phone:* 636-949-4949. *Web site:* http://www.lindenwood.edu/.

See page 499 for display ad and page 1414 for the College Close-Up.

Logan University–College of Chiropractic
Chesterfield, Missouri

- **Independent** upper-level, founded 1935
- **Suburban** 111-acre campus with easy access to St. Louis
- **Endowment** $13.9 million
- **Coed** 66 undergraduate students, 76% full-time, 36% women, 64% men
- **Moderately difficult** entrance level, 98% of applicants were admitted

Undergraduates 50 full-time, 16 part-time. 3% Black or African American, non-Hispanic/Latino; 1% Hispanic/Latino; 1% Two or more races, non-Hispanic/Latino; 16% Race/ethnicity unknown; 1% international.

Freshmen *Admission:* 171 applied, 168 admitted.

Faculty *Total:* 101, 46% full-time. *Student/faculty ratio:* 12:1.

Academics *Calendar:* trimesters. *Degrees:* bachelor's, master's, and doctoral. *Special study options:* adult/continuing education programs, advanced placement credit, distance learning, independent study, internships, part-time degree program, services for LD students.

Computers on Campus 95 computers/terminals are available on campus for general student use. Students can access the following: computer help desk, free student e-mail accounts, online (class) grades, online (class) registration, online (class) schedules, on-line classes, course homepages, wireless technologies, Academic Software Solutions for teaching and learning, library resources, academic records access. Campuswide network is available. Wireless service is available via classrooms, computer centers, computer labs, learning centers, libraries, student centers.

Student Life *Housing:* college housing not available. *Activities and organizations:* Pi Kappa Chi, Lambda Kappa Chi, Chiro Sigma, Student American Chiropractic Association, Omega Sigma Pi, national fraternities, national sororities. *Campus security:* 24-hour patrols, late-night transport/escort service. *Student services:* health clinic, personal/psychological counseling.

Athletics *Intercollegiate sports:* basketball M(c)/W(c), golf M(c), soccer M(c), tennis M(c). *Intramural sports:* basketball M/W, football M, ice hockey M, softball M/W, volleyball M/W.

Costs (2012–13) *Tuition:* $6300 full-time, $175 per credit hour part-time. *Required fees:* $390 full-time, $130 per term part-time. *Waivers:* employees or children of employees.

Financial Aid Of all full-time matriculated undergraduates who enrolled in 1999, 160 applied for aid, 160 were judged to have need, 130 had their need fully met. 130 Federal Work-Study jobs (averaging $2693). *Average percent of need met:* 100%. *Average need-based loan:* $3500. *Average need-based gift aid:* $3000.

Applying *Options:* electronic application, deferred entrance. *Application fee:* $50. *Application deadline:* rolling (transfers). *Notification:* continuous (transfers).

Application Contact Logan University–College of Chiropractic, 1851 Schoettler Road, Chesterfield, MO 63006-1065. *Phone:* 636-227-2100. *Toll-free phone:* 800-533-9210. *Fax:* 636-207-2425. *E-mail:* loganadm@logan.edu. *Web site:* http://www.logan.edu/.

Maryville University of Saint Louis
St. Louis, Missouri

- **Independent** comprehensive, founded 1872
- **Suburban** 130-acre campus with easy access to St. Louis
- **Endowment** $36.5 million
- **Coed** 3,035 undergraduate students, 57% full-time, 74% women, 26% men
- **Moderately difficult** entrance level, 67% of applicants were admitted

Undergraduates 1,741 full-time, 1,294 part-time. Students come from 31 states and territories; 25 other countries; 15% are from out of state; 8% Black or African American, non-Hispanic/Latino; 2% Hispanic/Latino; 1% Asian, non-Hispanic/Latino; 0.2% Native Hawaiian or other Pacific Islander, non-Hispanic/Latino; 0.4% American Indian or Alaska Native, non-Hispanic/Latino; 1% Two or more races, non-Hispanic/Latino; 10% Race/ethnicity unknown; 2% international; 14% transferred in; 22% live on campus. *Retention:* 82% of full-time freshmen returned.

Freshmen *Admission:* 1,234 applied, 832 admitted, 354 enrolled. *Average high school GPA:* 3.59. *Test scores:* ACT scores over 18: 99%; ACT scores over 24: 69%; ACT scores over 30: 4%.

Faculty *Total:* 421, 25% full-time, 48% with terminal degrees. *Student/faculty ratio:* 12:1.

Academics *Calendar:* semesters. *Degrees:* bachelor's, master's, doctoral, postbachelor's, and first professional certificates. *Special study options:* accelerated degree program, adult/continuing education programs, advanced placement credit, cooperative education, distance learning, double majors, honors programs, independent study, internships, off-campus study, part-time degree

program, services for LD students, study abroad, summer session for credit. *ROTC:* Army (c). *Unusual degree programs:* 3-2 business administration; engineering with Washington University in St. Louis; social work with Saint Louis University; education.

Computers on Campus 490 computers/terminals are available on campus for general student use. Students can access the following: campus intranet, computer help desk, free student e-mail accounts, online (class) grades, online (class) registration, online (class) schedules, specialized software, university catalog. Campuswide network is available. 100% of college-owned or -operated housing units are wired for high-speed Internet access. Wireless service is available via entire campus.

Student Life *Housing options:* coed. Campus housing is university owned. *Activities and organizations:* drama/theater group, student-run newspaper, choral group, Campus Activities Board, Physical Therapy Club, Student Nurses Association, Community Service Club. *Campus security:* 24-hour emergency response devices and patrols, late-night transport/escort service, controlled dormitory access, video security system in residence halls, self-defense and education programs. *Student services:* health clinic, personal/psychological counseling.

Athletics Member NCAA. All Division II. *Intercollegiate sports:* baseball M(s), basketball M(s)/W(s), cross-country running M(s)/W(s), golf M(s)/W(s), soccer M(s)/W(s), softball W(s), tennis M(s)/W(s), track and field M(s)/W(s), volleyball W(s), wrestling M(s). *Intramural sports:* basketball M/W, cheerleading M/W, football M/W, soccer M/W, softball W, volleyball M/W.

Standardized Tests *Required:* SAT or ACT (for admission).

Costs (2011–12) *Comprehensive fee:* $31,774 includes full-time tuition ($21,922), mandatory fees ($960), and room and board ($8892). Full-time tuition and fees vary according to course load. Part-time tuition: $658 per credit hour. Part-time tuition and fees vary according to class time. *Required fees:* $234 per term part-time. *Room and board:* Room and board charges vary according to board plan and housing facility. *Payment plans:* installment, deferred payment. *Waivers:* senior citizens and employees or children of employees.

Financial Aid Of all full-time matriculated undergraduates who enrolled in 2011, 1,448 applied for aid, 1,310 were judged to have need, 174 had their need fully met. 257 Federal Work-Study jobs (averaging $839). 169 state and other part-time jobs (averaging $2760). In 2011, 243 non-need-based awards were made. *Average percent of need met:* 47%. *Average financial aid package:* $16,339. *Average need-based loan:* $3898. *Average need-based gift aid:* $12,745. *Average non-need-based aid:* $8770. *Average indebtedness upon graduation:* $26,669.

Applying *Options:* electronic application, deferred entrance. *Application fee:* $30. *Required:* high school transcript, minimum 2.5 GPA. *Required for some:* essay or personal statement, interview, audition, portfolio. *Application deadlines:* 8/15 (freshmen), rolling (transfers). *Notification:* continuous (freshmen), continuous (transfers).

Freshman Application Contact Ms. Shani Lenore-Jenkins, Assistant Vice President of Enrollment, Maryville University of Saint Louis, 650 Maryville University Drive, St. Louis, MO 63141-7299. *Phone:* 314-529-9350. *Toll-free phone:* 800-627-9855. *Fax:* 314-529-9927. *E-mail:* admissions@maryville.edu. *Web site:* http://www.maryville.edu/.

Messenger College

Joplin, Missouri

Freshman Application Contact Ron Cannon, Vice President of Academic Affairs, Messenger College, 300 East 50th Street, Joplin, MO 64804. *Phone:* 417-624-7070 Ext. 108. *Toll-free phone:* 800-385-8940. *Fax:* 417-624-5070. *E-mail:* info@messengercollege.edu. *Web site:* http://www.messengercollege.edu/.

Metro Business College

Cape Girardeau, Missouri

Director of Admissions Ms. Kyla Evans, Admissions Director, Metro Business College, 1732 North Kingshighway, Cape Girardeau, MO 63701. *Phone:* 573-334-9181. *Toll-free phone:* 888-206-4545. *Fax:* 573-334-0617. *Web site:* http://www.metrobusinesscollege.edu/.

Missouri Baptist University

St. Louis, Missouri

- **Independent Southern Baptist** comprehensive, founded 1964
- **Suburban** 65-acre campus with easy access to Saint Louis
- **Endowment** $2.9 million
- **Coed** 3,831 undergraduate students, 37% full-time, 60% women, 40% men
- **Moderately difficult** entrance level, 58% of applicants were admitted

Undergraduates 1,425 full-time, 2,406 part-time. Students come from 29 states and territories; 17 other countries; 15% are from out of state; 9% Black or African American, non-Hispanic/Latino; 3% Hispanic/Latino; 0.5% Asian, non-Hispanic/Latino; 0.6% American Indian or Alaska Native, non-Hispanic/Latino; 0.8% Two or more races, non-Hispanic/Latino; 10% Race/ethnicity unknown; 2% international; 7% transferred in; 14% live on campus. *Retention:* 66% of full-time freshmen returned.

Freshmen *Admission:* 740 applied, 432 admitted, 238 enrolled.

Faculty *Total:* 300, 25% full-time, 26% with terminal degrees. *Student/faculty ratio:* 10:1.

Academics *Calendar:* semesters. *Degrees:* certificates, associate, bachelor's, master's, doctoral, post-master's, and postbachelor's certificates. *Special study options:* academic remediation for entering students, accelerated degree program, adult/continuing education programs, advanced placement credit, distance learning, double majors, independent study, internships, off-campus study, part-time degree program, services for LD students, student-designed majors, study abroad, summer session for credit. *ROTC:* Army (c). *Unusual degree programs:* 3-2 engineering with University of Missouri-Columbia.

Computers on Campus 122 computers/terminals are available on campus for general student use. Students can access the following: campus intranet, computer help desk, free student e-mail accounts, online (class) grades, online (class) schedules. Campuswide network is available. 100% of college-owned or -operated housing units are wired for high-speed Internet access. Wireless service is available via entire campus.

Student Life *Housing options:* men-only, women-only. Campus housing is university owned. *Activities and organizations:* drama/theater group, student-run radio station, choral group, Baptist Collegiate Ministry, Students in Free Enterprise (SIFE), Missouri State Teacher's Association, Fellowship of Christian Athletes, Ministerial Alliance. *Campus security:* 24-hour emergency response devices and patrols, late-night transport/escort service, controlled dormitory access, self-defense classes. *Student services:* personal/psychological counseling.

Athletics Member NAIA. *Intercollegiate sports:* baseball M(s), basketball M(s)/W(s), bowling M(s)(c)/W(c), cheerleading M/W, cross-country running M(s)/W(s), golf M(s)/W, lacrosse M(s)(c)/W(s)(c), soccer M(s)/W(s), softball W(s), tennis M(s)/W(s), track and field M(s)/W(s), volleyball M(s)/W(s), wrestling M(s)/W(s). *Intramural sports:* basketball M/W, football M/W, soccer M/W, softball M/W, volleyball M/W.

Standardized Tests *Required for some:* SAT or ACT (for admission).

Costs (2012–13) *Comprehensive fee:* $28,884 includes full-time tuition ($19,730), mandatory fees ($924), and room and board ($8230). Full-time tuition and fees vary according to course load and location. Part-time tuition: $680 per credit. Part-time tuition and fees vary according to course load and location. *Required fees:* $22 per credit part-time, $30 per term part-time. *Room and board:* Room and board charges vary according to board plan and housing facility. *Payment plan:* installment. *Waivers:* children of alumni, senior citizens, and employees or children of employees.

Financial Aid Of all full-time matriculated undergraduates who enrolled in 2009, 65 state and other part-time jobs (averaging $4819). In 2009, 277 non-need-based awards were made. *Average financial aid package:* $13,290. *Average need-based loan:* $4442. *Average need-based gift aid:* $5411. *Average non-need-based aid:* $6718.

Applying *Options:* electronic application. *Application fee:* $30. *Required:* high school transcript, minimum 2.0 GPA, 1 letter of recommendation. *Application deadlines:* rolling (freshmen), rolling (transfers). *Notification:* continuous (freshmen), continuous (transfers).

Freshman Application Contact Mr. Aaron Black, Director of Admissions, Missouri Baptist University, One College Park Drive, St. Louis, MO 63141-8660. *Phone:* 877-434-1115. *Toll-free phone:* 877-434-1115 Ext. 2290. *Fax:* 314-434-7596. *E-mail:* admissions@mobap.edu. *Web site:* http://www.mobap.edu/.

Missouri College

St. Louis, Missouri

Director of Admissions Mr. Doug Brinker, Admissions Director, Missouri College, 10121 Manchester Road, St. Louis, MO 63122-1583. *Phone:* 314-821-7700. *Toll-free phone:* 800-216-6732. *Fax:* 314-821-0891. *Web site:* http://www.mocollege.com/.

Missouri Southern State University

Joplin, Missouri

- **State-supported** comprehensive, founded 1937

- **Small-town** 350-acre campus

- **Coed** 5,536 undergraduate students, 73% full-time, 57% women, 43% men

- **Moderately difficult** entrance level, 97% of applicants were admitted

Undergraduates 4,039 full-time, 1,497 part-time. 4% Black or African American, non-Hispanic/Latino; 3% Hispanic/Latino; 1% Asian, non-Hispanic/Latino; 0.1% Native Hawaiian or other Pacific Islander, non-Hispanic/Latino; 3% American Indian or Alaska Native, non-Hispanic/Latino; 0.7% Two or more races, non-Hispanic/Latino; 5% Race/ethnicity unknown; 2% international; 8% transferred in. *Retention:* 60% of full-time freshmen returned.

Freshmen *Admission:* 1,691 applied, 1,632 admitted, 775 enrolled.

Faculty *Total:* 306, 67% full-time. *Student/faculty ratio:* 18:1.

Academics *Calendar:* semesters. *Degrees:* certificates, associate, bachelor's, and master's. *Special study options:* academic remediation for entering students, accelerated degree program, adult/continuing education programs, advanced placement credit, cooperative education, distance learning, double majors, English as a second language, honors programs, independent study, internships, off-campus study, part-time degree program, services for LD students, study abroad, summer session for credit.

Computers on Campus Students can access the following: campus intranet, computer help desk, free student e-mail accounts, online (class) grades, online (class) registration, online (class) schedules. Campuswide network is available. Wireless service is available via entire campus.

Student Life *Housing:* on-campus residence required for freshman year. *Options:* coed, men-only, women-only. Campus housing is university owned. Freshman campus housing is guaranteed. *Activities and organizations:* drama/theater group, student-run newspaper, radio and television station, choral group, marching band, national fraternities, national sororities. *Campus security:* 24-hour emergency response devices and patrols, late-night transport/escort service, controlled dormitory access, security at campus events, emergency vehicle assistance, safety awareness information to students. *Student services:* health clinic, personal/psychological counseling.

Athletics Member NCAA. All Division II. *Intercollegiate sports:* baseball M(s), basketball M(s)/W(s), cross-country running M(s)/W(s), football M(s), golf M(s), soccer M(s)/W(s), softball W(s), tennis W(s), track and field M(s)/W(s), volleyball W(s). *Intramural sports:* baseball M/W, basketball M/W, football M/W, golf M/W, racquetball M/W, soccer M/W, softball M/W, swimming and diving M/W, table tennis M/W, tennis M/W, ultimate Frisbee M/W, volleyball M/W.

Standardized Tests *Required:* SAT or ACT (for admission), SAT and SAT Subject Tests or ACT (for admission). *Required for some:* Michigan Test of English Language Proficiency. *Recommended:* ACT (for admission).

Costs (2012–13) *Tuition:* state resident $4564 full-time, $143 per credit hour part-time; nonresident $9128 full-time, $297 per credit hour part-time. Full-time tuition and fees vary according to course load. *Required fees:* $526 full-time. *Room and board:* $5976. Room and board charges vary according to board plan and housing facility. *Waivers:* senior citizens and employees or children of employees.

Financial Aid Of all full-time matriculated undergraduates who enrolled in 2009, 2,553 applied for aid, 2,099 were judged to have need, 262 had their need fully met. In 2009, 308 non-need-based awards were made. *Average percent of need met:* 54%. *Average financial aid package:* $10,772. *Average need-based loan:* $2861. *Average need-based gift aid:* $4158. *Average non-need-based aid:* $3844. *Average indebtedness upon graduation:* $16,772.

Applying *Options:* electronic application, deferred entrance. *Application fee:* $25. *Required:* high school transcript, class rank. *Required for some:* 2 letters of recommendation. *Application deadlines:* 8/1 (freshmen), 8/1 (transfers). *Notification:* continuous (freshmen), continuous (transfers).

Freshman Application Contact Mr. Derek Skaggs, Director of Enrollment Services, Missouri Southern State University, 3950 East Newman Road, Joplin, MO 64801-1595. *Phone:* 417-625-9537. *Toll-free phone:* 866-818-MSSU. *Fax:* 417-659-4429. *E-mail:* admissions@mssu.edu. *Web site:* http://www.mssu.edu/.

Missouri State University

Springfield, Missouri

- **State-supported** comprehensive, founded 1905

- **Suburban** 225-acre campus

- **Endowment** $61.2 million

- **Coed** 17,187 undergraduate students, 79% full-time, 56% women, 44% men

- **Moderately difficult** entrance level, 83% of applicants were admitted

Undergraduates 13,508 full-time, 3,679 part-time. Students come from 50 states and territories; 77 other countries; 8% are from out of state; 4% Black or African American, non-Hispanic/Latino; 3% Hispanic/Latino; 1% Asian, non-Hispanic/Latino; 0.2% Native Hawaiian or other Pacific Islander, non-Hispanic/Latino; 0.7% American Indian or Alaska Native, non-Hispanic/Latino; 2% Two or more races, non-Hispanic/Latino; 3% Race/ethnicity unknown; 4% international; 10% transferred in; 18% live on campus. *Retention:* 75% of full-time freshmen returned.

Freshmen *Admission:* 7,072 applied, 5,876 admitted, 2,599 enrolled. *Average high school GPA:* 3.57. *Test scores:* SAT critical reading scores over 500: 83%; SAT math scores over 500: 64%; ACT scores over 18: 98%; SAT critical reading scores over 600: 34%; SAT math scores over 600: 29%; ACT scores over 24: 50%; SAT critical reading scores over 700: 6%; SAT math scores over 700: 4%; ACT scores over 30: 9%.

Faculty *Total:* 1,031, 68% full-time, 61% with terminal degrees. *Student/faculty ratio:* 21:1.

Academics *Calendar:* semesters. *Degrees:* bachelor's, master's, doctoral, post-master's, and postbachelor's certificates. *Special study options:* accelerated degree program, advanced placement credit, cooperative education, distance learning, double majors, English as a second language, freshman honors college, honors programs, independent study, internships, off-campus study, part-time degree program, services for LD students, student-designed majors, study abroad, summer session for credit. *ROTC:* Army (b).

Computers on Campus 1,940 computers/terminals and 2,096 ports are available on campus for general student use. Students can access the following: campus intranet, computer help desk, free student e-mail accounts, online (class) grades, online (class) registration, online (class) schedules. Campuswide network is available. 100% of college-owned or -operated housing units are wired for high-speed Internet access. Wireless service is available via classrooms, computer centers, computer labs, learning centers, libraries, student centers.

Student Life *Housing:* on-campus residence required for freshman year. *Options:* coed, disabled students. Campus housing is university owned. Freshman campus housing is guaranteed. *Activities and organizations:* drama/theater group, student-run newspaper, radio and television station, choral group, marching band, Residence Hall Association, Campus Ministries, Fraternity & Sorority Life, Student Government Association, Student Activities Council, national fraternities, national sororities. *Campus security:* 24-hour emergency response devices and patrols, late-night transport/escort service, controlled dormitory access, on-campus police substation. *Student services:* health clinic, personal/psychological counseling, legal services.

Athletics Member NCAA. All Division I except football (Division I-AA). *Intercollegiate sports:* baseball M(s), basketball M(s)/W(s), bowling M(c)/W(c), cross-country running M(s)/W(s), equestrian sports M(c)/W(c), field hockey W(s), golf M(s)/W(s), ice hockey M(c), lacrosse M(c), racquetball M(c)/W(c), soccer M(s)/W(s), softball W(s), swimming and diving M(s)/W(s), track and field W(s), ultimate Frisbee M(c)/W(c), volleyball M(c)/W(s), wrestling M(c). *Intramural sports:* basketball M/W, bowling M/W, football M/W, golf M/W, racquetball M/W, soccer M/W, softball M/W, table tennis M/W, tennis M/W, track and field W, ultimate Frisbee M/W, volleyball M/W, weight lifting M/W.

Standardized Tests *Required:* SAT or ACT (for admission).

Costs (2012–13) *Tuition:* state resident $5820 full-time, $194 per credit hour part-time; nonresident $11,640 full-time, $388 per credit hour part-time. Full-time tuition and fees vary according to course level, location, and program. Part-time tuition and fees vary according to course level, course load, location, and program. *Required fees:* $778 full-time. *Room and board:* $6580. Room and board charges vary according to board plan and housing facility. *Payment plans:* tuition prepayment, installment, deferred payment. *Waivers:* children of alumni, senior citizens, and employees or children of employees.

Financial Aid Of all full-time matriculated undergraduates who enrolled in 2011, 10,457 applied for aid, 8,218 were judged to have need, 1,182 had their need fully met. In 2011, 1291 non-need-based awards were made. *Average percent of need met:* 56%. *Average financial aid package:* $7974. *Average need-based loan:* $3922. *Average need-based gift aid:* $4828. *Average non-need-based aid:* $4180. *Average indebtedness upon graduation:* $19,977.

Applying *Options:* electronic application, deferred entrance. *Application fee:* $35. *Required:* high school transcript. *Required for some:* essay or personal statement, interview. *Application deadlines:* 7/20 (freshmen), 7/20 (transfers). *Notification:* continuous (freshmen), continuous (transfers).

Freshman Application Contact Ms. Jill Duncan, Associate Director of Admissions and Recruitment, Missouri State University, 901 South National Avenue, Springfield, MO 65897. *Phone:* 417-836-5517. *Toll-free phone:* 800-492-7900. *Fax:* 417-836-5137. *E-mail:* info@missouristate.edu. *Web site:* http://www.missouristate.edu/.

Missouri Tech

St. Louis, Missouri

Freshman Application Contact Mr. Bob Honaker, Director of Admissions, Missouri Tech, 1167 Corporate Lake Drive, St. Louis, MO 63132. *Phone:* 314-569-3600. *Toll-free phone:* 800-960-TECH. *Fax:* 314-569-1167. *Web site:* http://www.motech.edu/.

Missouri University of Science and Technology

Rolla, Missouri

- **State-supported** university, founded 1870, part of University of Missouri System
- **Small-town** 284-acre campus
- **Endowment** $133.9 million
- **Coed, primarily men** 5,672 undergraduate students, 91% full-time, 23% women, 77% men
- **Very difficult** entrance level, 90% of applicants were admitted

Undergraduates 5,143 full-time, 529 part-time. 29% are from out of state; 5% Black or African American, non-Hispanic/Latino; 2% Hispanic/Latino; 2% Asian, non-Hispanic/Latino; 0.2% Native Hawaiian or other Pacific Islander, non-Hispanic/Latino; 0.5% American Indian or Alaska Native, non-Hispanic/Latino; 0.9% Two or more races, non-Hispanic/Latino; 5% Race/ethnicity unknown; 5% international; 6% transferred in; 51% live on campus. *Retention:* 83% of full-time freshmen returned.

Freshmen *Admission:* 2,779 applied, 2,495 admitted, 1,096 enrolled. *Average high school GPA:* 3.53. *Test scores:* SAT critical reading scores over 500: 91%; SAT math scores over 500: 97%; ACT scores over 18: 100%; SAT critical reading scores over 600: 62%; SAT math scores over 600: 75%; ACT scores over 24: 90%; SAT critical reading scores over 700: 21%; SAT math scores over 700: 34%; ACT scores over 30: 34%.

Faculty *Total:* 455, 80% full-time, 79% with terminal degrees. *Student/faculty ratio:* 17:1.

Academics *Calendar:* semesters. *Degrees:* certificates, bachelor's, master's, doctoral, postbachelor's, and first professional certificates. *Special study options:* academic remediation for entering students, accelerated degree program, adult/continuing education programs, advanced placement credit, cooperative education, distance learning, double majors, English as a second language, freshman honors college, honors programs, independent study, internships, off-campus study, part-time degree program, services for LD students, study abroad, summer session for credit. *ROTC:* Army (b), Navy (c), Air Force (b).

Computers on Campus 980 computers/terminals and 4,500 ports are available on campus for general student use. Students can access the following: campus intranet, computer help desk, free student e-mail accounts, online (class) grades, online (class) registration, online (class) schedules. Campus-wide network is available. 100% of college-owned or -operated housing units are wired for high-speed Internet access. Wireless service is available via entire campus.

Student Life *Housing:* on-campus residence required through sophomore year. *Options:* coed, men-only, women-only, cooperative, disabled students. Campus housing is university owned, leased by the school and is provided by a third party. Freshman campus housing is guaranteed. *Activities and organizations:* drama/theater group, student-run newspaper, radio station, choral group, marching band, student government, Student Union Board, Residence Hall Association, academic organizations, service organizations, national fraternities, national sororities. *Campus security:* 24-hour emergency response devices and patrols, student patrols, late-night transport/escort service, controlled dormitory access, crime prevention programs. *Student services:* health clinic, personal/psychological counseling.

Athletics Member NCAA. All Division II. *Intercollegiate sports:* baseball M(s), basketball M(s)/W(s), cross-country running M(s)/W(s), football M(s), soccer M(s)/W(s), softball W(s), swimming and diving M(s), track and field M(s)/W(s), volleyball W(s). *Intramural sports:* badminton M/W, basketball M/W, bowling M/W, cross-country running M/W, football M/W, golf M/W, racquetball M/W, soccer M/W, softball M/W, swimming and diving M/W, table tennis M/W, tennis M/W, track and field M/W, ultimate Frisbee M/W, volleyball M/W, weight lifting M/W.

Standardized Tests *Required:* SAT or ACT (for admission). *Recommended:* ACT (for admission).

Costs (2011–12) *Tuition:* state resident $7848 full-time, $262 per credit hour part-time; nonresident $20,643 full-time, $688 per credit hour part-time. Full-time tuition and fees vary according to course load, degree level, and program. Part-time tuition and fees vary according to course load, degree level, and program. *Required fees:* $1245 full-time, $262 per credit hour part-time. *Room and board:* $8520; room only: $5415. Room and board charges vary according to board plan, housing facility, and location. *Payment plan:* installment. *Waivers:* employees or children of employees.

Financial Aid Of all full-time matriculated undergraduates who enrolled in 2010, 4,603 applied for aid, 3,704 were judged to have need, 2,306 had their need fully met. 103 Federal Work-Study jobs (averaging $2519). In 2010, 542 non-need-based awards were made. *Average percent of need met:* 61%. *Average financial aid package:* $10,760. *Average need-based loan:* $3000. *Average need-based gift aid:* $6906. *Average non-need-based aid:* $4326. *Average indebtedness upon graduation:* $21,700.

Applying *Options:* electronic application, early admission, deferred entrance. *Application fee:* $45. *Required:* high school transcript. *Recommended:* essay or personal statement. *Application deadlines:* 7/1 (freshmen), 7/1 (transfers). *Notification:* continuous (freshmen), continuous (transfers).

Freshman Application Contact Admissions Office, Missouri University of Science and Technology, 300 West 13th Street, 106 Parker Hall, Rolla, MO 65401. *Phone:* 573-341-4165. *Toll-free phone:* 800-522-0938. *Fax:* 573-341-4082. *E-mail:* admissions@mst.edu. *Web site:* http://www.mst.edu/.

Missouri Valley College

Marshall, Missouri

Freshman Application Contact Ms. Debi Bultmann, Admissions Office Manager, Missouri Valley College, 500 East College, Marshall, MO 65340-3197. *Phone:* 660-831-4125. *Fax:* 660-831-4233. *E-mail:* admissions@moval.edu. *Web site:* http://www.moval.edu/.

Missouri Western State University

St. Joseph, Missouri

- **State-supported** comprehensive, founded 1915
- **Suburban** 744-acre campus with easy access to Kansas City
- **Endowment** $6.3 million
- **Coed** 6,099 undergraduate students, 71% full-time, 57% women, 43% men
- **Noncompetitive** entrance level, 100% of applicants were admitted

Undergraduates 4,320 full-time, 1,779 part-time. Students come from 32 states and territories; 6 other countries; 9% are from out of state; 9% Black or African American, non-Hispanic/Latino; 1% Hispanic/Latino; 0.5% Asian, non-Hispanic/Latino; 0.1% Native Hawaiian or other Pacific Islander, non-Hispanic/Latino; 1% American Indian or Alaska Native, non-Hispanic/Latino; 3% Two or more races, non-Hispanic/Latino; 4% Race/ethnicity unknown; 0.6% international; 7% transferred in; 21% live on campus. *Retention:* 62% of full-time freshmen returned.

Freshmen *Admission:* 1,098 applied, 1,098 admitted, 1,150 enrolled. *Test scores:* ACT scores over 18: 70%; ACT scores over 24: 23%; ACT scores over 30: 2%.

Faculty *Total:* 383, 49% full-time, 48% with terminal degrees. *Student/faculty ratio:* 20:1.

Academics *Calendar:* semesters. *Degrees:* certificates, associate, bachelor's, master's, and postbachelor's certificates. *Special study options:* academic remediation for entering students, accelerated degree program, adult/continuing education programs, advanced placement credit, distance learning, double majors, English as a second language, freshman honors college, honors programs, independent study, internships, off-campus study, part-time degree program, services for LD students, student-designed majors, study abroad, summer session for credit. *ROTC:* Army (b).

Computers on Campus 618 computers/terminals are available on campus for general student use. Students can access the following: campus intranet, computer help desk, free student e-mail accounts, online (class) grades, online (class) registration, online (class) schedules, Personal online storage. Campus-wide network is available. 100% of college-owned or -operated housing units are wired for high-speed Internet access. Wireless service is available via entire campus.

Student Life *Housing:* on-campus residence required for freshman year. *Options:* coed, disabled students. Campus housing is university owned. *Activities and organizations:* drama/theater group, student-run newspaper, choral group, marching band, national fraternities, national sororities. *Campus security:* 24-hour emergency response devices and patrols, student patrols, late-night transport/escort service, controlled dormitory access. *Student services:* health clinic, personal/psychological counseling, women's center.

Athletics Member NCAA. All Division II. *Intercollegiate sports:* baseball M(s), basketball M(s)/W(s), football M(s), golf M(s)/W(s), soccer W(s), soft-

ball W(s), tennis W(s), volleyball W(s). *Intramural sports:* badminton M/W, basketball M/W, bowling M/W, football M/W, golf M/W, racquetball M/W, soccer M/W, tennis M/W, ultimate Frisbee M/W, volleyball M/W.

Standardized Tests *Required:* SAT or ACT (for admission).

Costs (2012–13) *Tuition:* state resident $5473 full-time, $182 per credit hour part-time; nonresident $10,571 full-time, $352 per credit hour part-time. Full-time tuition and fees vary according to location and program. Part-time tuition and fees vary according to location and program. *Required fees:* $568 full-time. *Room and board:* $6796. Room and board charges vary according to board plan and housing facility. *Payment plan:* installment. *Waivers:* senior citizens and employees or children of employees.

Financial Aid Of all full-time matriculated undergraduates who enrolled in 2011, 3,957 applied for aid, 3,202 were judged to have need, 283 had their need fully met. 294 Federal Work-Study jobs (averaging $1471). 857 state and other part-time jobs (averaging $1695). In 2011, 406 non-need-based awards were made. *Average percent of need met:* 65%. *Average financial aid package:* $7949. *Average need-based loan:* $3720. *Average need-based gift aid:* $5319. *Average non-need-based aid:* $3041. *Average indebtedness upon graduation:* $21,674.

Applying *Options:* electronic application, early admission. *Application fee:* $15. *Required:* high school transcript. *Application deadlines:* 5/1 (freshmen), 6/1 (transfers). *Notification:* continuous (freshmen), continuous (transfers).

Freshman Application Contact Mr. Howard McCauley, Dean of Enrollment Management, Missouri Western State University, 4525 Downs Drive, St. Joseph, MO 64507-2294. *Phone:* 816-271-4266. *Toll-free phone:* 800-662-7041. *Fax:* 816-271-5833. *E-mail:* admission@missouriwestern.edu. *Web site:* http://www.missouriwestern.edu/.

National American University

Kansas City, Missouri

Director of Admissions Admissions Office, National American University, 7490 Northwest 87th Street, Kansas City, MO 64153. *Phone:* 816-412-5500. *E-mail:* zradmissions@national.edu. *Web site:* http://www.national.edu/.

Northwest Missouri State University

Maryville, Missouri

- **State-supported** comprehensive, founded 1905, part of Missouri Coordinating Board for Higher Education
- **Small-town** 370-acre campus with easy access to Kansas City
- **Coed** 6,281 undergraduate students, 88% full-time, 56% women, 44% men
- **Moderately difficult** entrance level, 86% of applicants were admitted

Undergraduates 5,555 full-time, 726 part-time. Students come from 37 states and territories; 27 other countries; 25% are from out of state; 6% Black or African American, non-Hispanic/Latino; 2% Hispanic/Latino; 0.6% Asian, non-Hispanic/Latino; 0.1% Native Hawaiian or other Pacific Islander, non-Hispanic/Latino; 0.2% American Indian or Alaska Native, non-Hispanic/Latino; 2% Two or more races, non-Hispanic/Latino; 3% Race/ethnicity unknown; 2% international; 5% transferred in; 42% live on campus. *Retention:* 69% of full-time freshmen returned.

Freshmen *Admission:* 4,607 applied, 3,959 admitted, 1,595 enrolled. *Average high school GPA:* 3.32. *Test scores:* SAT critical reading scores over 500: 67%; SAT math scores over 500: 66%; ACT scores over 18: 91%; SAT critical reading scores over 600: 33%; SAT math scores over 600: 23%; ACT scores over 24: 33%; SAT math scores over 700: 3%; ACT scores over 30: 2%.

Faculty *Total:* 324, 82% full-time, 52% with terminal degrees. *Student/faculty ratio:* 22:1.

Academics *Calendar:* trimesters. *Degrees:* certificates, bachelor's, master's, post-master's, and postbachelor's certificates. *Special study options:* academic remediation for entering students, advanced placement credit, distance learning, double majors, English as a second language, honors programs, independent study, internships, off-campus study, part-time degree program, services for LD students, study abroad, summer session for credit. *ROTC:* Army (b).

Computers on Campus 7,550 computers/terminals and 12,608 ports are available on campus for general student use. Students can access the following: campus intranet, computer help desk, free student e-mail accounts, online (class) grades, online (class) registration, online (class) schedules, online courses with library and databases. Campuswide network is available. 100% of college-owned or -operated housing units are wired for high-speed Internet access. Wireless service is available via classrooms, computer centers, computer labs, dorm rooms, learning centers, libraries, student centers.

Student Life *Housing:* on-campus residence required for freshman year. *Options:* coed, disabled students. Campus housing is university owned. Freshman campus housing is guaranteed. *Activities and organizations:* drama/theater group, student-run newspaper, radio and television station, choral group, marching band, student government, Residence Hall Association, Greek Life, national fraternities, national sororities. *Campus security:* 24-hour emergency response devices and patrols, student patrols, late-night transport/escort service, controlled dormitory access, security personnel are all police officers. *Student services:* health clinic, personal/psychological counseling, women's center.

Athletics Member NCAA. All Division II. *Intercollegiate sports:* baseball M(s), basketball M(s)/W(s), cheerleading M(s)/W(s), cross-country running M(s)/W(s), football M(s), golf W(s), soccer W(s), softball W(s), tennis M(s)/W(s), track and field M(s)/W(s), volleyball W(s). *Intramural sports:* badminton M/W, basketball M/W, cross-country running M/W, football M/W, golf M/W, racquetball M/W, skiing (cross-country) M/W, soccer W(c), softball W, swimming and diving M/W, table tennis M/W, tennis M/W, track and field M/W, volleyball M/W, wrestling M(c).

Standardized Tests *Required:* SAT or ACT (for admission).

Costs (2011–12) *One-time required fee:* $140. *Tuition:* state resident $5027 full-time, $163 per credit hour part-time; nonresident $10,889 full-time, $363 per credit hour part-time. Full-time tuition and fees vary according to course load, location, and reciprocity agreements. Part-time tuition and fees vary according to course load and location. *Required fees:* $2408 full-time, $80 per credit hour part-time. *Room and board:* $8272; room only: $5246. Room and board charges vary according to board plan and housing facility. *Payment plans:* installment, deferred payment. *Waivers:* senior citizens and employees or children of employees.

Financial Aid Of all full-time matriculated undergraduates who enrolled in 2010, 4,726 applied for aid, 3,712 were judged to have need, 2,049 had their need fully met. 650 Federal Work-Study jobs (averaging $1045). 1,302 state and other part-time jobs (averaging $1603). In 2010, 498 non-need-based awards were made. *Average percent of need met:* 70%. *Average financial aid package:* $7131. *Average need-based loan:* $4096. *Average need-based gift aid:* $5526. *Average non-need-based aid:* $2229. *Average indebtedness upon graduation:* $22,555.

Applying *Options:* electronic application, deferred entrance. *Application fee:* $25. *Required:* high school transcript, minimum 2.0 GPA. *Required for some:* interview. *Application deadlines:* rolling (freshmen), rolling (out-of-state freshmen), rolling (transfers). *Notification:* continuous (freshmen), continuous (out-of-state freshmen), continuous (transfers).

Freshman Application Contact Ms. Tammi Grow, Associate Director of Admission, Northwest Missouri State University, 800 University Drive, Maryville, MO 64468-6001. *Phone:* 660-562-1146. *Toll-free phone:* 800-633-1175. *Fax:* 660-562-1146. *E-mail:* admissions@nwmissouri.edu. *Web site:* http://www.nwmissouri.edu/.

Ozark Christian College

Joplin, Missouri

Freshman Application Contact Mr. Troy B. Nelson, Executive Director of Admissions, Ozark Christian College, 1111 North Main Street, Joplin, MO 64801-4804. *Phone:* 417-624-2518. *Toll-free phone:* 800-299-4622. *Fax:* 417-624-0090. *E-mail:* occadmin@occ.edu. *Web site:* http://www.occ.edu/.

Park University

Parkville, Missouri

- **Independent** comprehensive, founded 1875
- **Suburban** 800-acre campus with easy access to Kansas City
- **Endowment** $42.5 million
- **Coed** 1,640 undergraduate students, 72% full-time, 56% women, 44% men
- **Moderately difficult** entrance level, 76% of applicants were admitted

Undergraduates 1,173 full-time, 467 part-time. Students come from 49 states and territories; 96 other countries; 20% are from out of state; 9% Black or African American, non-Hispanic/Latino; 4% Hispanic/Latino; 1% Asian, non-Hispanic/Latino; 0.7% American Indian or Alaska Native, non-Hispanic/Latino; 3% Two or more races, non-Hispanic/Latino; 16% international; 17% transferred in; 20% live on campus. *Retention:* 67% of full-time freshmen returned.

Freshmen *Admission:* 552 applied, 417 admitted, 180 enrolled. *Average high school GPA:* 3.3. *Test scores:* ACT scores over 18: 91%; ACT scores over 24: 38%; ACT scores over 30: 7%.

Faculty *Total:* 168, 49% full-time. *Student/faculty ratio:* 12:1.

Academics *Calendar:* semesters. *Degrees:* associate, bachelor's, master's, and postbachelor's certificates. *Special study options:* academic remediation for entering students, adult/continuing education programs, advanced placement credit, distance learning, double majors, English as a second language, external degree program, honors programs, independent study, internships, off-campus study, part-time degree program, services for LD students, student-designed majors, summer session for credit. *ROTC:* Army (b).

Computers on Campus 143 computers/terminals are available on campus for general student use. Students can access the following: online (class) registration. Campuswide network is available.

Student Life *Housing:* on-campus residence required through junior year. *Options:* coed. Campus housing is university owned. Freshman campus housing is guaranteed. *Activities and organizations:* drama/theater group, student-run newspaper, radio station, choral group, World Student Union, Student Senate, Radio Club, Latin American Student Organization, marketing club. *Campus security:* 24-hour patrols, student patrols, late-night transport/escort service. *Student services:* health clinic, personal/psychological counseling.

Athletics Member NAIA. *Intercollegiate sports:* baseball M(s), basketball M(s)/W(s), cross-country running M(s)/W(s), golf W(s), soccer M(s)/W(s), softball W(s), track and field M(s)/W(s), volleyball M(s)/W(s). *Intramural sports:* basketball M/W, softball M/W, volleyball M/W.

Standardized Tests *Required:* SAT or ACT (for admission).

Costs (2011–12) *Comprehensive fee:* $15,850 includes full-time tuition ($9240), mandatory fees ($100), and room and board ($6510). Full-time tuition and fees vary according to course load. Part-time tuition: $330 per credit hour. Part-time tuition and fees vary according to course load. *Room and board:* Room and board charges vary according to housing facility.

Financial Aid Of all full-time matriculated undergraduates who enrolled in 2007, 3,967 applied for aid, 2,767 were judged to have need, 3,171 had their need fully met. 209 Federal Work-Study jobs (averaging $2875). 103 state and other part-time jobs (averaging $2675). In 2007, 281 non-need-based awards were made. *Average percent of need met:* 84%. *Average financial aid package:* $3811. *Average need-based loan:* $1478. *Average need-based gift aid:* $1713. *Average non-need-based aid:* $3690. *Average indebtedness upon graduation:* $12,800.

Applying *Options:* electronic application, early admission, deferred entrance. *Application fee:* $25. *Required:* high school transcript, minimum 2.0 GPA. *Required for some:* 2 letters of recommendation, interview. *Recommended:* essay or personal statement. *Application deadlines:* 8/1 (freshmen), 8/1 (transfers). *Notification:* continuous (freshmen), continuous (transfers).

Freshman Application Contact Cathy Colapietro, Director of Admissions and Student Financial Services, Park University, 8700 NW River Park Drive, Campus Box 1, Parkville, MO 64152. *Phone:* 816-584-6728. *Toll-free phone:* 800-745-7275. *Fax:* 816-741-4462. *E-mail:* admissions@mail.park.edu. *Web site:* http://www.park.edu/.

Ranken Technical College
St. Louis, Missouri

Director of Admissions Ms. Elizabeth Keserauskis, Director of Admissions, Ranken Technical College, 4431 Finney Avenue, St. Louis, MO 63113. *Phone:* 314-371-0233 Ext. 4811. *Toll-free phone:* 866-4-RANKEN. *Web site:* http://www.ranken.edu/.

Research College of Nursing
Kansas City, Missouri

- **Independent** comprehensive, founded 1980, part of Rockhurst University
- **Urban** 66-acre campus with easy access to Kansas City
- **Coed, primarily women** 262 undergraduate students, 100% full-time, 92% women, 8% men
- **Moderately difficult** entrance level, 68% of applicants were admitted

Undergraduates 262 full-time. Students come from 7 states and territories; 7% Black or African American, non-Hispanic/Latino; 4% Hispanic/Latino; 2% Asian, non-Hispanic/Latino; 0.4% Native Hawaiian or other Pacific Islander, non-Hispanic/Latino; 0.4% American Indian or Alaska Native, non-Hispanic/Latino; 0.4% Two or more races, non-Hispanic/Latino; 13% Race/ethnicity unknown; 2% transferred in.

Freshmen *Admission:* 244 applied, 165 admitted, 50 enrolled. *Average high school GPA:* 3.46.

Faculty *Total:* 29, 90% full-time, 14% with terminal degrees. *Student/faculty ratio:* 7:1.

Academics *Calendar:* semesters. *Degrees:* bachelor's and master's (bachelor's degree offered jointly with Rockhurst College). *Special study options:* accelerated degree program, advanced placement credit, double majors, honors programs, independent study, services for LD students, study abroad, summer session for credit. *ROTC:* Army (c).

Computers on Campus 125 computers/terminals are available on campus for general student use. Students can access the following: online (class) registration. Campuswide network is available.

Student Life *Housing options:* coed, men-only, women-only. Campus housing is university owned. Freshman campus housing is guaranteed. *Activities and organizations:* drama/theater group, student-run newspaper, radio station, choral group, national fraternities, national sororities. *Campus security:* 24-hour

emergency response devices and patrols, late-night transport/escort service, controlled dormitory access. *Student services:* health clinic, personal/psychological counseling.

Athletics Member NCAA. All Division II. *Intercollegiate sports:* baseball M(s), basketball M(s)/W(s), golf M(s)/W(s), soccer M(s)/W(s), softball W(s), tennis M(s)/W(s), volleyball W(s). *Intramural sports:* badminton M/W, basketball M/W, cross-country running M/W, field hockey M/W, football M/W, golf M/W, lacrosse M/W, racquetball M/W, rugby M/W, soccer M/W, softball M/W, table tennis M/W, tennis M/W, volleyball M/W, weight lifting M.

Standardized Tests *Required:* SAT or ACT (for admission).

Costs (2011–12) *One-time required fee:* $500. *Comprehensive fee:* $36,400 includes full-time tuition ($27,770), mandatory fees ($740), and room and board ($7890). Part-time tuition: $925 per credit hour. Part-time tuition and fees vary according to class time. *College room only:* $4590. Room and board charges vary according to board plan, housing facility, and location. *Payment plans:* installment, deferred payment. *Waivers:* senior citizens and employees or children of employees.

Applying *Options:* electronic application, deferred entrance. *Required:* high school transcript, 1 letter of recommendation, ACT or SAT. *Recommended:* minimum 2.8 GPA, interview. *Application deadlines:* 6/30 (freshmen), 2/15 (transfers). *Notification:* 8/15 (freshmen), 6/20 (out-of-state freshmen), 3/15 (transfers).

Freshman Application Contact Research College of Nursing, 2252 East Meyer Boulevard, Kansas City, MO 64132. *Phone:* 816-995-2820. *Web site:* http://www.researchcollege.edu/.

Rockhurst University
Kansas City, Missouri

- **Independent Roman Catholic (Jesuit)** comprehensive, founded 1910
- **Urban** 35-acre campus
- **Endowment** $32.7 million
- **Coed** 2,130 undergraduate students, 65% full-time, 61% women, 39% men
- **Moderately difficult** entrance level, 76% of applicants were admitted

Undergraduates 1,375 full-time, 755 part-time. Students come from 26 states and territories; 18 other countries; 29% are from out of state; 6% Black or African American, non-Hispanic/Latino; 7% Hispanic/Latino; 3% Asian, non-Hispanic/Latino; 0.3% Native Hawaiian or other Pacific Islander, non-Hispanic/Latino; 0.7% American Indian or Alaska Native, non-Hispanic/Latino; 0.2% Two or more races, non-Hispanic/Latino; 6% Race/ethnicity unknown; 1% international; 3% transferred in; 53% live on campus. *Retention:* 82% of full-time freshmen returned.

Freshmen *Admission:* 2,113 applied, 1,609 admitted, 326 enrolled. *Average high school GPA:* 3.5. *Test scores:* SAT critical reading scores over 500: 80%; SAT math scores over 500: 76%; ACT scores over 18: 98%; SAT critical reading scores over 600: 36%; SAT math scores over 600: 28%; ACT scores over 24: 63%; ACT scores over 30: 14%.

Faculty *Total:* 233, 54% full-time, 64% with terminal degrees. *Student/faculty ratio:* 12:1.

Academics *Calendar:* semesters. *Degrees:* certificates, bachelor's, master's, doctoral, and postbachelor's certificates. *Special study options:* academic remediation for entering students, accelerated degree program, advanced placement credit, cooperative education, distance learning, double majors, freshman honors college, honors programs, independent study, internships, off-campus study, part-time degree program, services for LD students, study abroad, summer session for credit. *ROTC:* Army (c).

Computers on Campus 240 computers/terminals are available on campus for general student use. Students can access the following: campus intranet, computer help desk, free student e-mail accounts, online (class) grades, online (class) registration, online (class) schedules. Campuswide network is available. 100% of college-owned or -operated housing units are wired for high-speed Internet access. Wireless service is available via entire campus.

Student Life *Housing:* on-campus residence required through sophomore year. *Options:* coed, men-only, women-only, disabled students. Campus housing is university owned. Freshman campus housing is guaranteed. *Activities and organizations:* drama/theater group, student-run newspaper, choral group, Student Activities Board, Student Senate, Delta Sigma Pi Business Fraternity, Student Organization of Latinos, Rockhurst University Players (theatre troupe), national fraternities, national sororities. *Campus security:* 24-hour emergency response devices and patrols, late-night transport/escort service, controlled dormitory access, closed-circuit TV monitors. *Student services:* health clinic, personal/psychological counseling.

Athletics Member NCAA. All Division II. *Intercollegiate sports:* baseball M(s), basketball M(s)/W(s), golf M(s)/W(s), soccer M(s)/W(s), softball W(s), tennis M(s)/W(s), volleyball W(s). *Intramural sports:* basketball M/W, cheerleading M/W, field hockey W, football M/W, ice hockey M, lacrosse M, soccer M/W, softball M/W, tennis M/W, ultimate Frisbee M/W, volleyball M/W.

Standardized Tests *Required:* SAT or ACT (for admission).

Costs (2011–12) *One-time required fee:* $210. *Comprehensive fee:* $36,260 includes full-time tuition ($27,700), mandatory fees ($740), and room and board ($7820). Full-time tuition and fees vary according to class time and course load. Part-time tuition: $925 per credit hour. Part-time tuition and fees vary according to class time and course load. *Required fees:* $25 per credit hour part-time. *College room only:* $4820. Room and board charges vary according to board plan and housing facility. *Payment plans:* installment, deferred payment. *Waivers:* senior citizens and employees or children of employees.

Financial Aid Of all full-time matriculated undergraduates who enrolled in 2011, 1,195 applied for aid, 1,193 were judged to have need, 330 had their need fully met. In 2011, 160 non-need-based awards were made. *Average percent of need met:* 97%. *Average financial aid package:* $27,619. *Average need-based loan:* $1164. *Average need-based gift aid:* $8127. *Average non-need-based aid:* $13,899. *Average indebtedness upon graduation:* $21,085.

Applying *Options:* electronic application, deferred entrance. *Application fee:* $25. *Required:* high school transcript, minimum 2.0 GPA, 1 letter of recommendation. *Required for some:* essay or personal statement, interview. *Application deadlines:* 6/30 (freshmen), rolling (transfers). *Notification:* continuous (freshmen), continuous (transfers).

Freshman Application Contact Kyle Johnson, Director of Freshman Admissions, Rockhurst University, 1100 Rockhurst Road, Kansas City, MO 64110-2561. *Phone:* 816-501-4100. *Toll-free phone:* 800-842-6776. *Fax:* 816-501-4142. *E-mail:* admission@rockhurst.edu. *Web site:* http://www.rockhurst.edu/.

Saint Louis Christian College

Florissant, Missouri

- **Independent Christian** 4-year, founded 1956
- **Suburban** 20-acre campus with easy access to St. Louis
- **Endowment** $1.0 million
- **Coed** 288 undergraduate students, 75% full-time, 43% women, 57% men
- **Minimally difficult** entrance level, 61% of applicants were admitted

Undergraduates 217 full-time, 71 part-time. Students come from 18 states and territories; 1 other country; 37% are from out of state; 34% Black or African American, non-Hispanic/Latino; 2% Hispanic/Latino; 0.3% Asian, non-Hispanic/Latino; 0.7% American Indian or Alaska Native, non-Hispanic/Latino; 1% Two or more races, non-Hispanic/Latino; 2% international; 143% transferred in; 54% live on campus. *Retention:* 43% of full-time freshmen returned.

Freshmen *Admission:* 152 applied, 92 admitted, 25 enrolled. *Average high school GPA:* 2.7. *Test scores:* ACT scores over 18: 74%; ACT scores over 24: 28%.

Faculty *Total:* 36, 33% full-time, 22% with terminal degrees. *Student/faculty ratio:* 15:1.

Academics *Calendar:* semesters. *Degrees:* associate and bachelor's. *Special study options:* academic remediation for entering students, accelerated degree program, adult/continuing education programs, advanced placement credit, double majors, English as a second language, internships, part-time degree program, services for LD students, study abroad, summer session for credit.

Computers on Campus 11 computers/terminals are available on campus for general student use. Students can access the following: free student e-mail accounts, online (class) schedules. Campuswide network is available. Wireless service is available via classrooms, computer labs, libraries, student centers.

Student Life *Housing options:* men-only, women-only. Campus housing is university owned. *Activities and organizations:* drama/theater group, choral group, World Christians Unlimited, Drama Club, pep band. *Campus security:* 24-hour emergency response devices and patrols, controlled dormitory access, night security. *Student services:* personal/psychological counseling.

Athletics Member NCCAA. *Intercollegiate sports:* baseball M, basketball M/W, cross-country running W, ultimate Frisbee M(s)/W(s), volleyball W(s). *Intramural sports:* basketball M/W, ultimate Frisbee M/W, volleyball M/W.

Standardized Tests *Required:* SAT or ACT (for admission).

Costs (2012–13) *Comprehensive fee:* $25,080 includes full-time tuition ($14,880), mandatory fees ($1300), and room and board ($8900). *Room and board:* Room and board charges vary according to housing facility. *Waivers:* employees or children of employees.

Financial Aid Of all full-time matriculated undergraduates who enrolled in 2011, 194 applied for aid, 188 were judged to have need, 14 had their need fully met. 14 Federal Work-Study jobs (averaging $1475). In 2011, 28 non-need-based awards were made. *Average percent of need met:* 73%. *Average financial aid package:* $18,141. *Average need-based loan:* $3251. *Average need-based gift aid:* $14,810. *Average non-need-based aid:* $9792. *Average indebtedness upon graduation:* $20,217.

Applying *Options:* electronic application, early admission. *Required:* essay or personal statement, high school transcript, 2 letters of recommendation.

Required for some: interview. *Recommended:* minimum 2.0 GPA. *Application deadlines:* 8/7 (freshmen), 8/7 (transfers). *Notification:* continuous (freshmen), continuous (transfers).

Freshman Application Contact Carrie Chapman, Admissions Director, Saint Louis Christian College, 1360 Grandview Drive, Florissant, MO 63033. *Phone:* 314-837-6777 Ext. 1303. *Toll-free phone:* 800-887-SLCC. *E-mail:* cchapman@slcconline.edu. *Web site:* http://www.slcconline.edu/.

St. Louis College of Pharmacy

St. Louis, Missouri

- **Independent** comprehensive, founded 1864
- **Urban** 5-acre campus with easy access to St. Louis
- **Endowment** $111.8 million
- **Coed** 693 undergraduate students, 100% full-time, 59% women, 41% men
- **Moderately difficult** entrance level, 61% of applicants were admitted

Undergraduates 693 full-time. Students come from 27 states and territories; 1 other country; 53% are from out of state; 4% Black or African American, non-Hispanic/Latino; 1% Hispanic/Latino; 23% Asian, non-Hispanic/Latino; 0.1% Native Hawaiian or other Pacific Islander, non-Hispanic/Latino; 0.6% American Indian or Alaska Native, non-Hispanic/Latino; 1% Two or more races, non-Hispanic/Latino; 2% Race/ethnicity unknown; 0.4% international; 6% transferred in; 40% live on campus. *Retention:* 91% of full-time freshmen returned.

Freshmen *Admission:* 589 applied, 361 admitted, 252 enrolled. *Average high school GPA:* 3.7. *Test scores:* ACT scores over 18: 100%; ACT scores over 24: 93%; ACT scores over 30: 18%.

Faculty *Total:* 135, 59% full-time, 73% with terminal degrees. *Student/faculty ratio:* 17:1.

Academics *Calendar:* semesters. *Degree:* doctoral. *Special study options:* academic remediation for entering students, advanced placement credit, internships, summer session for credit. *ROTC:* Army (c), Navy (c), Air Force (c).

Computers on Campus 6 computers/terminals and 2,200 ports are available on campus for general student use. Students can access the following: campus intranet, computer help desk, free student e-mail accounts, online (class) grades, online (class) registration, online (class) schedules. Campuswide network is available. 100% of college-owned or -operated housing units are wired for high-speed Internet access. Wireless service is available via entire campus.

Student Life *Housing options:* coed. Campus housing is university owned. Freshman applicants given priority for college housing. *Activities and organizations:* drama/theater group, student-run newspaper, choral group, Outdoor Club, Student Body Union, International Student Organization, Student ambassadors, Student Organization for Drug and Alcohol Awareness, national fraternities, national sororities. *Campus security:* 24-hour emergency response devices and patrols, late-night transport/escort service, controlled dormitory access. *Student services:* personal/psychological counseling.

Athletics Member NAIA. *Intercollegiate sports:* basketball M/W, cross-country running M/W, tennis M/W, track and field M/W, volleyball W. *Intramural sports:* basketball M/W, cheerleading W, cross-country running M/W, football M/W, golf M/W, soccer M/W, softball M/W, table tennis M/W, tennis M/W, volleyball M/W, weight lifting M/W.

Standardized Tests *Required:* SAT or ACT (for admission).

Costs (2011–12) *Comprehensive fee:* $32,604 includes full-time tuition ($23,698), mandatory fees ($270), and room and board ($8636). Full-time tuition and fees vary according to student level. Part-time tuition: $825 per credit. *College room only:* $4975. Room and board charges vary according to housing facility. *Payment plan:* installment. *Waivers:* employees or children of employees.

Financial Aid Of all full-time matriculated undergraduates who enrolled in 2011, 606 applied for aid, 535 were judged to have need, 46 had their need fully met. 294 Federal Work-Study jobs (averaging $937). In 2011, 138 non-need-based awards were made. *Average percent of need met:* 46%. *Average financial aid package:* $13,637. *Average need-based loan:* $5383. *Average need-based gift aid:* $8978. *Average non-need-based aid:* $6063. *Average indebtedness upon graduation:* $106,759.

Applying *Options:* electronic application, early decision. *Application fee:* $50. *Required:* essay or personal statement, high school transcript, minimum 3.0 GPA, 2 letters of recommendation, letter of reference from science teacher. *Required for some:* interview. *Application deadlines:* 2/1 (freshmen), 2/1 (transfers). *Early decision deadline:* 12/15. *Notification:* 3/1 (freshmen), 5/1 (transfers), 1/15 (early decision).

Freshman Application Contact Connie Horrall, Administrative Assistant, St. Louis College of Pharmacy, 4588 Parkview Place, St. Louis, MO 63110-1088. *Phone:* 314-446-8328. *Toll-free phone:* 800-278-5267 (in-state); 800-278-267 (out-of-state). *Fax:* 314-446-8310. *E-mail:* chorrall@stlcop.edu. *Web site:* http://www.stlcop.edu/.

See next page for display ad and page 1560 for the College Close-Up.

Are you inquisitive, interested in health and wellness, love math and science, and enjoy helping people?

Earn a degree that allows you to benefit individuals and the community. Become an integral part of a close-knit campus with nearly 50 student organizations. Take advantage of the surrounding world class medical community, the expertise of faculty, and all St. Louis has to offer.

St. Louis College *of* Pharmacy

EST. 1864

4588 Parkview Place
St. Louis, MO 63110-1088
314.367.8700 1.800.2STLCOP
www.stlcop.edu

Saint Louis University

St. Louis, Missouri

- **Independent Roman Catholic (Jesuit)** university, founded 1818
- **Urban** 268-acre campus
- **Endowment** $880.3 million
- **Coed** 8,670 undergraduate students, 89% full-time, 59% women, 41% men
- **Moderately difficult** entrance level, 61% of applicants were admitted

Undergraduates 7,716 full-time, 954 part-time. Students come from 48 states and territories; 46 other countries; 59% are from out of state; 7% Black or African American, non-Hispanic/Latino; 4% Hispanic/Latino; 7% Asian, non-Hispanic/Latino; 0.2% American Indian or Alaska Native, non-Hispanic/Latino; 4% Two or more races, non-Hispanic/Latino; 5% Race/ethnicity unknown; 8% international; 5% transferred in; 52% live on campus. *Retention:* 86% of full-time freshmen returned.

Freshmen *Admission:* 13,389 applied, 8,202 admitted, 1,798 enrolled. *Average high school GPA:* 3.76. *Test scores:* SAT critical reading scores over 500: 87%; SAT math scores over 500: 89%; ACT scores over 18: 100%; SAT critical reading scores over 600: 51%; SAT math scores over 600: 56%; ACT scores over 24: 86%; SAT critical reading scores over 700: 11%; SAT math scores over 700: 17%; ACT scores over 30: 29%.

Faculty *Total:* 1,286, 58% full-time, 60% with terminal degrees. *Student/faculty ratio:* 12:1.

Academics *Calendar:* semesters. *Degrees:* certificates, bachelor's, master's, doctoral, post-master's, postbachelor's, and first professional certificates. *Special study options:* academic remediation for entering students, accelerated degree program, adult/continuing education programs, advanced placement credit, cooperative education, distance learning, double majors, English as a second language, honors programs, independent study, internships, off-campus study, part-time degree program, services for LD students, student-designed majors, study abroad, summer session for credit. *ROTC:* Army (c), Air Force (b).

Computers on Campus 581 computers/terminals and 5,050 ports are available on campus for general student use. Students can access the following: campus intranet, computer help desk, free student e-mail accounts, online (class) grades, online (class) registration, online (class) schedules. Campus-wide network is available. 100% of college-owned or -operated housing units are wired for high-speed Internet access. Wireless service is available via entire campus.

Student Life *Housing:* on-campus residence required through sophomore year. *Options:* coed, men-only, women-only, disabled students. Campus housing is university owned and leased by the school. Freshman campus housing is guaranteed. *Activities and organizations:* drama/theater group, student-run newspaper, radio and television station, choral group, Alpha Phi Omega, Oriflamme, Student Activities Board, Interfraternity Council, Panhellenic Council, national fraternities, national sororities. *Campus security:* 24-hour emergency response devices and patrols, late-night transport/escort service, controlled dormitory access, crime prevention program, bicycle patrols, pamphlets, posters, films, identification of valuables, video cameras. *Student services:* health clinic, personal/psychological counseling, women's center.

Athletics Member NCAA. All Division I. *Intercollegiate sports:* badminton M(c)/W(c), baseball M(s), basketball M(s)/W(s), bowling M(c)/W(c), crew M(c)/W(c), cross-country running M(s)/W(s), fencing M(c)/W(c), field hockey W(s), golf M(c)/W(c), ice hockey M(c), lacrosse M(c)/W(c), racquetball M(c)/W(c), rugby M(c)/W(c), soccer M(s)/W(s), softball W(s), swimming and diving M(s)/W(s), table tennis M(c)/W(c), tennis M(s)/W(s), track and field M(s)/W(s), ultimate Frisbee M(c)/W(c), volleyball M(c)/W(s), water polo M(c). *Intramural sports:* badminton M/W, basketball M/W, bowling M/W, football M/W, golf M/W, racquetball M/W, soccer M/W, softball M/W, squash M/W, swimming and diving M/W, table tennis M/W, tennis M/W, ultimate Frisbee M/W, volleyball M/W.

Standardized Tests *Required:* SAT or ACT (for admission).

Costs (2011–12) *Comprehensive fee:* $43,418 includes full-time tuition ($33,470), mandatory fees ($516), and room and board ($9432). Full-time tuition and fees vary according to location and program. Part-time tuition: $1170 per credit hour. Part-time tuition and fees vary according to location and program. *Required fees:* $148 per term part-time. *College room only:* $5334. Room and board charges vary according to board plan, housing facility, and location. *Payment plan:* installment. *Waivers:* children of alumni and employees or children of employees.

Financial Aid Of all full-time matriculated undergraduates who enrolled in 2010, 4,808 applied for aid, 4,309 were judged to have need, 594 had their need fully met. 895 Federal Work-Study jobs (averaging $2318). 79 state and other part-time jobs (averaging $1714). In 2010, 1930 non-need-based awards were made. *Average percent of need met:* 65%. *Average financial aid package:* $25,328. *Average need-based loan:* $4977. *Average need-based gift aid:*

$18,010. *Average non-need-based aid:* $10,939. *Average indebtedness upon graduation:* $36,601.

Applying *Options:* electronic application, deferred entrance. *Application fee:* $25. *Required:* essay or personal statement, high school transcript, minimum 2.5 GPA, secondary school report form. *Recommended:* 2 letters of recommendation, interview. *Application deadlines:* 8/1 (freshmen), 8/1 (out-of-state freshmen), 8/1 (transfers). *Notification:* 9/15 (freshmen), 9/15 (out-of-state freshmen), continuous until 9/15 (transfers).

Freshman Application Contact Jean M. Gilman, Dean of Undergraduate Admission, Saint Louis University, 221 North Grand Boulevard, DuBourg Hall, Room 100, St. Louis, MO 63103-2097. *Phone:* 314-977-2500. *Toll-free phone:* 800-758-3678. *Fax:* 314-977-7136. *E-mail:* admitme@slu.edu. *Web site:* http://www.slu.edu/.

Saint Luke's College of Health Sciences

Kansas City, Missouri

- **Independent Episcopal** upper-level, founded 1903
- **Urban** 3-acre campus
- **Endowment** $2.8 million
- **Coed, primarily women**
- **Very difficult** entrance level

Faculty *Student/faculty ratio:* 8:1.

Academics *Calendar:* semesters. *Degree:* bachelor's.

Student Life *Campus security:* 24-hour emergency response devices and patrols.

Costs (2011–12) *Tuition:* $387 per credit part-time.

Financial Aid *Of all full-time matriculated undergraduates who enrolled in 2011,* 158 applied for aid, 154 were judged to have need, 5 had their need fully met. 3 Federal Work-Study jobs (averaging $2000). *In 2011,* 5 non-need-based awards were made. *Average percent of need met:* 60. *Average financial aid package:* $13,000. *Average need-based loan:* $5500. *Average need-based gift aid:* $2000. *Average non-need-based aid:* $2000.

Applying *Options:* electronic application, early admission. *Application fee:* $35.

Application Contact Mrs. Jennifer Wright, Student Services Associate, Saint Luke's College of Health Sciences, 8320 Ward Parkway, Suite 300, Kansas City, MO 64114. *Phone:* 816-932-8629. *Fax:* 816-932-9064. *Web site:* http://www.saintlukescollege.edu/.

Sanford-Brown College

Fenton, Missouri

Director of Admissions Ms. Judy Wilga, Director of Admissions, Sanford-Brown College, 1203 Smizer Mill Road, Fenton, MO 63026. *Phone:* 636-349-4900 Ext. 102. *Toll-free phone:* 800-769-2433 (in-state); 888-769-2433 (out-of-state). *Fax:* 636-349-9170. *Web site:* http://www.sanford-brown.edu/.

Southeast Missouri State University

Cape Girardeau, Missouri

- **State-supported** comprehensive, founded 1873, part of Missouri Coordinating Board for Higher Education
- **Small-town** 400-acre campus
- **Endowment** $57.9 million
- **Coed** 10,386 undergraduate students, 78% full-time, 58% women, 42% men
- **Moderately difficult** entrance level, 97% of applicants were admitted

Undergraduates 8,130 full-time, 2,256 part-time. Students come from 35 states and territories; 51 other countries; 13% are from out of state; 9% Black or African American, non-Hispanic/Latino; 1% Hispanic/Latino; 0.8% Asian, non-Hispanic/Latino; 0.4% American Indian or Alaska Native, non-Hispanic/Latino; 0.2% Two or more races, non-Hispanic/Latino; 4% Race/ethnicity unknown; 6% international; 7% transferred in; 31% live on campus. *Retention:* 71% of full-time freshmen returned.

Freshmen *Admission:* 4,161 applied, 4,050 admitted, 1,904 enrolled. *Average high school GPA:* 3.33. *Test scores:* SAT critical reading scores over 500: 54%; SAT math scores over 500: 63%; ACT scores over 18: 96%; SAT critical reading scores over 600: 22%; SAT math scores over 600: 29%; ACT scores over 24: 40%; SAT critical reading scores over 700: 5%; SAT math scores over 700: 5%; ACT scores over 30: 5%.

Faculty *Total:* 582, 68% full-time, 56% with terminal degrees. *Student/faculty ratio:* 21:1.

Academics *Calendar:* semesters. *Degrees:* certificates, associate, bachelor's, master's, post-master's, and postbachelor's certificates. *Special study options:*

academic remediation for entering students, accelerated degree program, adult/continuing education programs, advanced placement credit, distance learning, double majors, English as a second language, honors programs, independent study, internships, part-time degree program, services for LD students, student-designed majors, study abroad, summer session for credit. *ROTC:* Air Force (b).

Computers on Campus 1,241 computers/terminals are available on campus for general student use. Students can access the following: campus intranet, computer help desk, free student e-mail accounts, online (class) grades, online (class) registration, online (class) schedules. Campuswide network is available. 100% of college-owned or -operated housing units are wired for high-speed Internet access. Wireless service is available via classrooms, computer centers, computer labs, dorm rooms, learning centers, libraries, student centers.

Student Life *Housing:* on-campus residence required through sophomore year. *Options:* coed, men-only, women-only, disabled students. Campus housing is university owned. *Activities and organizations:* drama/theater group, student-run newspaper, radio and television station, choral group, marching band, Student Government, Panhellenic Council, Interfraternity Council, Residence Hall Association, Student Activities Council, national fraternities, national sororities. *Campus security:* 24-hour emergency response devices and patrols, late-night transport/escort service, controlled dormitory access. *Student services:* health clinic, personal/psychological counseling.

Athletics Member NCAA. All Division I. *Intercollegiate sports:* baseball M(s), basketball M(s)/W(s), cheerleading M(s)/W(s), cross-country running M(s)/W(s), football M(s), gymnastics W(s), soccer W(s), softball W(s), tennis W(s), track and field M(s)/W(s), volleyball W(s). *Intramural sports:* badminton M/W, baseball M(c)/W(c), basketball M/W, bowling M/W, equestrian sports M(c)/W(c), fencing M(c)/W(c), football M/W, golf M/W, racquetball M/W, rock climbing M(c)/W(c), rugby M(c)/W(c), soccer M/W, softball M/W, swimming and diving M/W, table tennis M/W, tennis M/W, ultimate Frisbee M/W, volleyball M(c)/W(c), wrestling M/W.

Standardized Tests *Required:* SAT or ACT (for admission).

Costs (2011–12) *Tuition:* state resident $5634 full-time, $188 per credit hour part-time; nonresident $10,674 full-time, $356 per credit hour part-time. Full-time tuition and fees vary according to course load and location. Part-time tuition and fees vary according to course load and location. *Required fees:* $921 full-time, $31 per credit hour part-time. *Room and board:* $7715; room only: $5145. Room and board charges vary according to board plan and housing facility. *Payment plans:* installment, deferred payment. *Waivers:* senior citizens and employees or children of employees.

Financial Aid Of all full-time matriculated undergraduates who enrolled in 2010, 6,058 applied for aid, 4,881 were judged to have need, 626 had their need fully met. 359 Federal Work-Study jobs (averaging $1913). 1,730 state and other part-time jobs (averaging $1890). In 2010, 1110 non-need-based awards were made. *Average percent of need met:* 61%. *Average financial aid package:* $8441. *Average need-based loan:* $3977. *Average need-based gift aid:* $5528. *Average non-need-based aid:* $4214. *Average indebtedness upon graduation:* $23,417.

Applying *Options:* electronic application, deferred entrance. *Application fee:* $30. *Required:* high school transcript, minimum 2.0 GPA. *Application deadlines:* 6/1 (freshmen), 6/1 (out-of-state freshmen), 6/1 (transfers). *Notification:* continuous (freshmen), continuous (out-of-state freshmen), continuous (transfers).

Freshman Application Contact Southeast Missouri State University, One University Plaza, Cape Girardeau, MO 63701-4799. *Phone:* 573-651-2590. *Web site:* http://www.semo.edu/.

Southwest Baptist University

Bolivar, Missouri

- **Independent Southern Baptist** comprehensive, founded 1878
- **Small-town** 152-acre campus
- **Endowment** $21.0 million
- **Coed** 2,872 undergraduate students, 69% full-time, 64% women, 36% men
- **Moderately difficult** entrance level, 92% of applicants were admitted

Undergraduates 1,986 full-time, 886 part-time. Students come from 41 states and territories; 18 other countries; 27% are from out of state; 4% Black or African American, non-Hispanic/Latino; 2% Hispanic/Latino; 1% Asian, non-Hispanic/Latino; 1% American Indian or Alaska Native, non-Hispanic/Latino; 17% Race/ethnicity unknown; 1% international; 4% transferred in; 65% live on campus. *Retention:* 62% of full-time freshmen returned.

Freshmen *Admission:* 1,617 applied, 1,493 admitted, 470 enrolled. *Average high school GPA:* 3.4. *Test scores:* SAT critical reading scores over 500: 48%; SAT math scores over 500: 65%; SAT critical reading scores over 600: 13%; SAT math scores over 600: 25%; SAT critical reading scores over 700: 3%; SAT math scores over 700: 5%.

Faculty *Total:* 260, 45% full-time, 40% with terminal degrees. *Student/faculty ratio:* 13:1.

Academics *Calendar:* 4-1-4. *Degrees:* associate, bachelor's, master's, doctoral, and post-master's certificates. *Special study options:* academic remediation for entering students, advanced placement credit, cooperative education, distance learning, double majors, honors programs, independent study, internships, off-campus study, part-time degree program, services for LD students, student-designed majors, study abroad, summer session for credit. *ROTC:* Army (c).

Computers on Campus 321 computers/terminals are available on campus for general student use. Students can access the following: computer help desk, free student e-mail accounts, online (class) grades, online (class) registration, online (class) schedules. Campuswide network is available. 90% of college-owned or -operated housing units are wired for high-speed Internet access. Wireless service is available via entire campus.

Student Life *Housing:* on-campus residence required through junior year. *Options:* men-only, women-only, disabled students. Campus housing is university owned. Freshman campus housing is guaranteed. *Activities and organizations:* drama/theater group, student-run newspaper, choral group, Students in Free Enterprise (SIFE), Student Government Association, Fellowship of Christian Athletes, Student Missouri State Teachers Association, PSY CHI. *Campus security:* 24-hour emergency response devices and patrols, controlled dormitory access. *Student services:* health clinic, personal/psychological counseling.

Athletics Member NCAA. All Division II. *Intercollegiate sports:* baseball M(s), basketball M(s)/W(s), cheerleading M/W, cross-country running M(s)/W(s), football M(s), golf M(s), soccer M/W(s), softball W(s), tennis M(s)/W(s), track and field M(s)/W(s), volleyball W(s). *Intramural sports:* basketball M/W, football M/W, soccer M/W, softball M/W, table tennis M/W, volleyball M/W.

Standardized Tests *Required:* SAT or ACT (for admission).

Costs (2011–12) *Comprehensive fee:* $24,250 includes full-time tuition ($17,400), mandatory fees ($800), and room and board ($6050). Full-time tuition and fees vary according to course load and location. Part-time tuition and fees vary according to course load and location. *College room only:* $3000. Room and board charges vary according to board plan and housing facility. *Payment plan:* installment. *Waivers:* employees or children of employees.

Financial Aid Of all full-time matriculated undergraduates who enrolled in 2011, 1,936 applied for aid, 1,567 were judged to have need, 262 had their need fully met. 354 Federal Work-Study jobs (averaging $1812). In 2011, 324 non-need-based awards were made. *Average percent of need met:* 69%. *Average financial aid package:* $14,771. *Average need-based loan:* $4179. *Average need-based gift aid:* $4839. *Average non-need-based aid:* $8546.

Applying *Options:* electronic application. *Application fee:* $30. *Required:* high school transcript, minimum 2.5 GPA. *Required for some:* 3 letters of recommendation. *Recommended:* essay or personal statement, interview. *Application deadlines:* rolling (freshmen), rolling (transfers). *Notification:* continuous (freshmen), continuous (transfers).

Freshman Application Contact Mr. Darren Crowder, Director of Admissions, Southwest Baptist University, 1600 University Avenue, Bolivar, MO 65613-2597. *Phone:* 417-328-1817. *Toll-free phone:* 800-526-5859. *Fax:* 417-328-1808. *E-mail:* dcrowder@sbuniv.edu. *Web site:* http://www.sbuniv.edu/.

Stephens College
Columbia, Missouri

- **Independent** comprehensive, founded 1833
- **Urban** 86-acre campus
- **Endowment** $36.7 million
- **Coed, primarily women** 783 undergraduate students, 78% full-time, 97% women, 3% men
- **Moderately difficult** entrance level, 58% of applicants were admitted

Undergraduates 608 full-time, 175 part-time. Students come from 47 states and territories; 1 other country; 46% are from out of state; 13% Black or African American, non-Hispanic/Latino; 3% Hispanic/Latino; 0.4% Asian, non-Hispanic/Latino; 0.1% Native Hawaiian or other Pacific Islander, non-Hispanic/Latino; 1% American Indian or Alaska Native, non-Hispanic/Latino; 6% Two or more races, non-Hispanic/Latino; 0.7% Race/ethnicity unknown; 6% transferred in; 66% live on campus. *Retention:* 65% of full-time freshmen returned.

Freshmen *Admission:* 718 applied, 414 admitted, 169 enrolled. *Average high school GPA:* 3.33. *Test scores:* SAT critical reading scores over 500: 69%; SAT math scores over 500: 48%; SAT writing scores over 500: 69%; ACT scores over 18: 89%; SAT critical reading scores over 600: 19%; SAT math scores over 600: 18%; SAT writing scores over 600: 17%; ACT scores over 24: 38%; SAT critical reading scores over 700: 6%; ACT scores over 30: 4%.

Faculty *Total:* 97, 57% full-time, 35% with terminal degrees. *Student/faculty ratio:* 13:1.

Academics *Calendar:* semesters. *Degrees:* certificates, associate, bachelor's, master's, post-master's, and postbachelor's certificates. *Special study options:* academic remediation for entering students, accelerated degree program, adult/continuing education programs, advanced placement credit, cooperative education, distance learning, double majors, external degree program, freshman honors college, honors programs, independent study, internships, off-campus study, part-time degree program, services for LD students, student-designed majors, study abroad, summer session for credit. *ROTC:* Army (c), Navy (c), Air Force (c). *Unusual degree programs:* 3-2 occupational therapy with Washington University in St. Louis.

Computers on Campus 107 computers/terminals and 1 port are available on campus for general student use. Students can access the following: computer help desk, free student e-mail accounts, online (class) grades, online (class) schedules. Campuswide network is available. 100% of college-owned or -operated housing units are wired for high-speed Internet access. Wireless service is available via entire campus.

Student Life *Housing:* on-campus residence required through senior year. *Options:* women-only. Campus housing is university owned and is provided by a third party. Freshman campus housing is guaranteed. *Activities and organizations:* drama/theater group, student-run newspaper, radio station, choral group, IFA, Warehouse Theatre, Student government, Public Relations Student Society of America (PRSSA), national sororities. *Campus security:* 24-hour emergency response devices and patrols, student patrols, late-night transport/escort service, controlled dormitory access. *Student services:* health clinic, personal/psychological counseling.

Athletics Member NAIA. *Intercollegiate sports:* basketball W(s), cross-country running W(s), golf W(s), softball W(s), tennis W(s), volleyball W(s). *Intramural sports:* equestrian sports W(c).

Standardized Tests *Required:* SAT or ACT (for admission).

Costs (2011–12) *One-time required fee:* $200. *Comprehensive fee:* $33,590 includes full-time tuition ($26,420) and room and board ($7170). Full-time tuition and fees vary according to course load, degree level, program, and reciprocity agreements. Part-time tuition: $734 per credit hour. Part-time tuition and fees vary according to course load, degree level, and program. *College room only:* $4770. Room and board charges vary according to board plan and housing facility. *Payment plan:* installment. *Waivers:* employees or children of employees.

Financial Aid Of all full-time matriculated undergraduates who enrolled in 2011, 593 applied for aid, 587 were judged to have need, 98 had their need fully met. 82 Federal Work-Study jobs (averaging $1100). 125 state and other part-time jobs (averaging $110). In 2011, 59 non-need-based awards were made. *Average percent of need met:* 79%. *Average financial aid package:* $21,065. *Average need-based loan:* $4639. *Average need-based gift aid:* $16,978. *Average non-need-based aid:* $8846. *Average indebtedness upon graduation:* $18,175.

Applying *Options:* electronic application, deferred entrance. *Application fee:* $25. *Required:* essay or personal statement, high school transcript, minimum 2.0 GPA. *Required for some:* 1 letter of recommendation, audition mandatory for dance, recommended for theater. *Recommended:* minimum 2.5 GPA, interview. *Notification:* continuous until 9/15 (freshmen), continuous until 9/15 (transfers).

Freshman Application Contact Mr. Chris Collier, Director of Enrollment Management, Stephens College, 1200 East Broadway, Box 2121, Columbia, MO 65215-0002. *Phone:* 573-876-7207. *Toll-free phone:* 800-876-7207. *Fax:* 573-876-7237. *E-mail:* apply@stephens.edu. *Web site:* http://www.stephens.edu/.

Stevens Institute of Business & Arts
St. Louis, Missouri

- **Proprietary** 4-year, founded 1947
- **Urban** campus
- **Coed, primarily women** 187 undergraduate students, 72% full-time, 96% women, 11% men
- **Moderately difficult** entrance level, 86% of applicants were admitted

Undergraduates 134 full-time, 66 part-time. Students come from 2 states and territories; 25% are from out of state. *Retention:* 100% of full-time freshmen returned.

Freshmen *Admission:* 22 applied, 19 admitted. *Average high school GPA:* 2.8.

Faculty *Total:* 22, 32% full-time, 14% with terminal degrees. *Student/faculty ratio:* 10:1.

Academics *Calendar:* quarters. *Degrees:* diplomas, associate, and bachelor's. *Special study options:* academic remediation for entering students, accelerated degree program, adult/continuing education programs, advanced placement credit, cooperative education, honors programs, independent study, internships, part-time degree program, summer session for credit.

Computers on Campus 45 computers/terminals are available on campus for general student use. Students can access the following: campus intranet, free student e-mail accounts, online (class) schedules, wireless Internet. Campuswide network is available. Wireless service is available via entire campus.

Student Life *Housing:* college housing not available. *Campus security:* 24-hour emergency response devices, late-night transport/escort service. *Student services:* personal/psychological counseling.

Standardized Tests *Required for some:* SAT or ACT (for admission).

Costs (2012–13) *Tuition:* $225 per quarter hour part-time. No tuition increase for student's term of enrollment. *Payment plan:* installment. *Waivers:* employees or children of employees.

Applying *Application fee:* $15. *Required:* essay or personal statement, high school transcript, interview. *Required for some:* minimum 2.8 GPA. *Application deadlines:* rolling (freshmen), rolling (out-of-state freshmen), rolling (transfers). *Notification:* continuous (freshmen), continuous (out-of-state freshmen), continuous (transfers).

Freshman Application Contact Mr. John Willmon, Director of Admissions, Stevens Institute of Business & Arts, 1521 Washington Avenue, St. Louis, MO 63102. *Phone:* 314-421-0949 Ext. 1119. *Toll-free phone:* 800-871-0949. *Fax:* 314-421-0304. *E-mail:* admission@siba.edu. *Web site:* http://www.siba.edu/.

Truman State University
Kirksville, Missouri

- **State-supported** comprehensive, founded 1867
- **Small-town** 140-acre campus
- **Endowment** $26.5 million
- **Coed** 5,780 undergraduate students, 95% full-time, 59% women, 41% men
- **Moderately difficult** entrance level, 75% of applicants were admitted

Undergraduates 5,481 full-time, 299 part-time. Students come from 39 states and territories; 44 other countries; 16% are from out of state; 4% Black or African American, non-Hispanic/Latino; 3% Hispanic/Latino; 2% Asian, non-Hispanic/Latino; 0.5% American Indian or Alaska Native, non-Hispanic/Latino; 1% Two or more races, non-Hispanic/Latino; 3% Race/ethnicity unknown; 5% international; 4% transferred in; 49% live on campus. *Retention:* 86% of full-time freshmen returned.

Freshmen *Admission:* 4,569 applied, 3,428 admitted, 1,378 enrolled. *Average high school GPA:* 3.77. *Test scores:* SAT critical reading scores over 500: 93%; SAT math scores over 500: 93%; ACT scores over 18: 100%; SAT critical reading scores over 600: 57%; SAT math scores over 600: 43%; ACT scores over 24: 85%; SAT critical reading scores over 700: 14%; SAT math scores over 700: 14%; ACT scores over 30: 27%.

Faculty *Total:* 370, 86% full-time, 78% with terminal degrees. *Student/faculty ratio:* 17:1.

Academics *Calendar:* semesters. *Degrees:* bachelor's and master's. *Special study options:* advanced placement credit, cooperative education, double majors, honors programs, independent study, internships, off-campus study, part-time degree program, services for LD students, student-designed majors, study abroad, summer session for credit. *ROTC:* Army (b). *Unusual degree programs:* 3-2 engineering with Missouri University of Science and Technology, University of Missouri–Columbia.

Computers on Campus 738 computers/terminals and 3,690 ports are available on campus for general student use. Students can access the following: campus intranet, computer help desk, free student e-mail accounts, online (class) grades, online (class) registration, online (class) schedules. Campuswide network is available. 100% of college-owned or -operated housing units are wired for high-speed Internet access. Wireless service is available via entire campus.

Student Life *Housing:* on-campus residence required for freshman year. *Options:* coed, disabled students. Campus housing is university owned. Freshman campus housing is guaranteed. *Activities and organizations:* drama/theater group, student-run newspaper, radio and television station, choral group, marching band, Alpha Phi Omega (national coed service fraternity), Campus Christian Fellowship (CCF), Alpha Sigma Gamma (service sorority), Sigma Sigma Sigma (national social sorority) — 132, American Medical Student Association (AMSA), national fraternities, national sororities. *Campus security:* 24-hour emergency response devices and patrols, student patrols, late-night transport/escort service, controlled dormitory access, patrols by commissioned officers, perimeter access system, dual 911 call center for campus & community, emergency text messaging system. *Student services:* health clinic, personal/psychological counseling, women's center.

Athletics Member NCAA. All Division II. *Intercollegiate sports:* baseball M(s), basketball M(s)/W(s), bowling M(c)/W(c), cheerleading M(c)/W(c), cross-country running M(s)/W(s), equestrian sports M(c)/W(c), football M(s), golf W(s), lacrosse W(c), riflery M(c)/W(c), rugby M(c)/W(c), soccer M(s)/W(s), softball W(s), swimming and diving M/W(s), tennis M(s)/W(s), track

and field M(s)/W(s), ultimate Frisbee M(c)/W(c), volleyball M(c)/W(s), weight lifting M(c)/W(c), wrestling M(s). *Intramural sports:* badminton M/W, basketball M/W, cross-country running M/W, football M/W, rock climbing M/W, skiing (cross-country) M(c)/W(c), skiing (downhill) M(c)/W(c), soccer M/W, softball M/W, swimming and diving M/W, table tennis M/W, tennis M/W, track and field M/W, ultimate Frisbee M/W, volleyball M/W.

Standardized Tests *Required:* SAT or ACT (for admission).

Costs (2011–12) *One-time required fee:* $305. *Tuition:* state resident $6772 full-time, $282 per credit hour part-time; nonresident $12,316 full-time, $513 per credit hour part-time. Full-time tuition and fees vary according to course load, degree level, and program. Part-time tuition and fees vary according to course load, degree level, and program. *Required fees:* $240 full-time. *Room and board:* $7254. Room and board charges vary according to housing facility. *Payment plan:* installment. *Waivers:* senior citizens and employees or children of employees.

Financial Aid Of all full-time matriculated undergraduates who enrolled in 2010, 3,802 applied for aid, 2,764 were judged to have need, 986 had their need fully met. 422 Federal Work-Study jobs (averaging $1632), 1,443 state and other part-time jobs (averaging $1234). In 2010, 1948 non-need-based awards were made. *Average percent of need met:* 85%. *Average financial aid package:* $10,906. *Average need-based loan:* $4260. *Average need-based gift aid:* $6770. *Average non-need-based aid:* $5500. *Average indebtedness upon graduation:* $20,777.

Applying *Options:* electronic application, deferred entrance. *Required:* essay or personal statement, high school transcript, official college entrance exam scores required, activities list/resume recommended. *Recommended:* minimum 3.0 GPA, interview. *Application deadlines:* rolling (freshmen), rolling (out-of-state freshmen), rolling (transfers). *Notification:* continuous until 9/15 (freshmen), continuous until 9/15 (out-of-state freshmen), continuous (transfers).

Freshman Application Contact Melody Chambers, Director of Admissions, Truman State University, Ruth Towne Museum and Visitors Center, 100 East Normal Avenue, Kirksville, MO 63501-4221. *Phone:* 660-785-4114. *Toll-free phone:* 800-892-7792. *Fax:* 660-785-7456. *E-mail:* mchamber@truman.edu. *Web site:* http://www.truman.edu/.

See page 1646 for the College Close-Up.

University of Central Missouri
Warrensburg, Missouri

- **State-supported** comprehensive, founded 1871
- **Small-town** 1561-acre campus with easy access to Kansas City
- **Endowment** $27.8 million
- **Coed** 9,466 undergraduate students, 85% full-time, 55% women, 45% men
- **Moderately difficult** entrance level, 80% of applicants were admitted

Undergraduates 8,009 full-time, 1,457 part-time. Students come from 42 states and territories; 47 other countries; 6% are from out of state; 8% Black or African American, non-Hispanic/Latino; 2% Hispanic/Latino; 0.3% Asian, non-Hispanic/Latino; 0.2% Native Hawaiian or other Pacific Islander, non-Hispanic/Latino; 0.4% American Indian or Alaska Native, non-Hispanic/Latino; 2% Two or more races, non-Hispanic/Latino; 11% Race/ethnicity unknown; 3% international; 10% transferred in; 33% live on campus. *Retention:* 72% of full-time freshmen returned.

Freshmen *Admission:* 4,410 applied, 3,523 admitted, 1,689 enrolled. *Average high school GPA:* 3.23. *Test scores:* ACT scores over 18: 89%; ACT scores over 24: 29%; ACT scores over 30: 2%.

Faculty *Total:* 459. *Student/faculty ratio:* 17:1.

Academics *Calendar:* semesters. *Degrees:* associate, bachelor's, master's, post-master's, and postbachelor's certificates. *Special study options:* academic remediation for entering students, adult/continuing education programs, advanced placement credit, cooperative education, distance learning, double majors, English as a second language, honors programs, internships, off-campus study, part-time degree program, services for LD students, student-designed majors, study abroad, summer session for credit. *ROTC:* Army (b), Air Force (c). *Unusual degree programs:* 3-2 engineering with University of Missouri–Columbia, University of Missouri–Rolla, University of Missouri–Kansas City; law, medical.

Computers on Campus 6,395 computers/terminals and 19,008 ports are available on campus for general student use. Students can access the following: campus intranet, computer help desk, free student e-mail accounts, online (class) grades, online (class) registration, online (class) schedules. Campuswide network is available. 100% of college-owned or -operated housing units are wired for high-speed Internet access. Wireless service is available via classrooms, computer centers, computer labs, dorm rooms, learning centers, libraries, student centers.

Student Life *Housing:* on-campus residence required for freshman year. *Options:* coed, women-only, disabled students. Campus housing is university

owned. Freshman campus housing is guaranteed. *Activities and organizations:* drama/theater group, student-run newspaper, radio and television station, choral group, marching band, Roaring Red (Student Booster Club), Greek Organization, Campus Christian House, BSU (Baptist Student Union), International Student Organization, national fraternities, national sororities. *Campus security:* 24-hour emergency response devices and patrols, student patrols, late-night transport/escort service, controlled dormitory access, canine patrol. *Student services:* health clinic, personal/psychological counseling, women's center.

Athletics Member NCAA. All Division II. *Intercollegiate sports:* baseball M(s), basketball M(s)/W(s), bowling M(c)/W(c), cross-country running M(s)/W(s), football M(s), golf M(s), rock climbing M(c)/W(c), soccer M(c)/W(s), softball W(s), track and field M(s)/W(s), volleyball W(s), wrestling M(s). *Intramural sports:* archery M, badminton M/W, basketball M/W, bowling M/W, cheerleading M/W, cross-country running M/W, football M/W, golf M/W, racquetball M/W, riflery M/W, rock climbing M/W, soccer M/W, softball M/W, swimming and diving M/W, table tennis M/W, tennis M/W, track and field M/W, volleyball M/W, water polo M/W, weight lifting M, wrestling M.

Standardized Tests *Required:* SAT or ACT (for admission).

Costs (2011–12) *Tuition:* state resident $6945 full-time, $232 per credit hour part-time; nonresident $13,050 full-time, $435 per credit hour part-time. Full-time tuition and fees vary according to course load and location. Part-time tuition and fees vary according to course load and location. *Required fees:* $840 full-time, $28 per credit hour part-time. *Room and board:* $7094; room only: $4656. Room and board charges vary according to board plan and housing facility. *Payment plans:* installment, deferred payment. *Waivers:* children of alumni, senior citizens, and employees or children of employees.

Financial Aid Of all full-time matriculated undergraduates who enrolled in 2010, 4,917 applied for aid, 3,106 were judged to have need, 346 had their need fully met. 330 Federal Work-Study jobs (averaging $1576). 1,165 state and other part-time jobs (averaging $1913). In 2010, 966 non-need-based awards were made. *Average percent of need met:* 84%. *Average financial aid package:* $10,020. *Average need-based loan:* $4224. *Average need-based gift aid:* $4195. *Average non-need-based aid:* $8975. *Average indebtedness upon graduation:* $23,323.

Applying *Options:* electronic application, deferred entrance. *Application fee:* $30. *Required:* high school transcript, rank in upper two-thirds of high school class. *Application deadlines:* rolling (freshmen), rolling (transfers). *Notification:* continuous (freshmen), continuous (transfers).

Freshman Application Contact Ms. Ann Nordyke, Director of Admissions, University of Central Missouri, 1400 Ward Edwards, Warrensburg, MO 64093. *Phone:* 660-543-4170. *Toll-free phone:* 800-729-8266. *Fax:* 660-543-8517. *E-mail:* admit@ucmo.edu. *Web site:* http://www.ucmo.edu/.

University of Missouri

Columbia, Missouri

- **State-supported** university, founded 1839, part of University of Missouri System
- **Suburban** 1250-acre campus
- **Endowment** $585.5 million
- **Coed** 26,024 undergraduate students, 94% full-time, 52% women, 48% men
- **Moderately difficult** entrance level, 82% of applicants were admitted

Undergraduates 24,413 full-time, 1,611 part-time. Students come from 52 states and territories; 89 other countries; 19% are from out of state; 8% Black or African American, non-Hispanic/Latino; 3% Hispanic/Latino; 2% Asian, non-Hispanic/Latino; 0.4% American Indian or Alaska Native, non-Hispanic/Latino; 1% Two or more races, non-Hispanic/Latino; 2% Race/ethnicity unknown; 3% international; 6% transferred in; 27% live on campus. *Retention:* 85% of full-time freshmen returned.

Freshmen *Admission:* 18,103 applied, 14,924 admitted, 6,138 enrolled. *Test scores:* SAT critical reading scores over 500: 86%; SAT math scores over 500: 83%; ACT scores over 18: 99%; SAT critical reading scores over 600: 52%; SAT math scores over 600: 50%; ACT scores over 24: 71%; SAT critical reading scores over 700: 13%; SAT math scores over 700: 11%; ACT scores over 30: 16%.

Faculty *Total:* 1,438, 92% full-time, 92% with terminal degrees. *Student/faculty ratio:* 20:1.

Academics *Calendar:* semesters. *Degrees:* bachelor's, master's, doctoral, post-master's, and first professional certificates. *Special study options:* accelerated degree program, adult/continuing education programs, advanced placement credit, cooperative education, distance learning, double majors, English as a second language, external degree program, freshman honors college, honors programs, independent study, internships, off-campus study, part-time degree program, services for LD students, student-designed majors, study abroad, summer session for credit. *ROTC:* Army (b), Navy (b), Air Force (b).

Unusual degree programs: 3-2 accountancy, physical therapy, occupational therapy.

Computers on Campus 1,168 computers/terminals are available on campus for general student use. Students can access the following: computer help desk, free student e-mail accounts, online (class) grades, online (class) registration, online (class) schedules. Campuswide network is available. 90% of college-owned or -operated housing units are wired for high-speed Internet access. Wireless service is available via classrooms, computer centers, computer labs, dorm rooms, learning centers, libraries, student centers.

Student Life *Housing:* on-campus residence required for freshman year. *Options:* coed, men-only, women-only, disabled students. Campus housing is university owned. Freshman campus housing is guaranteed. *Activities and organizations:* drama/theater group, student-run newspaper, radio and television station, choral group, marching band, Academic organizations, Greek organizations, religious organizations, sports clubs, Student Governance, national fraternities, national sororities. *Campus security:* 24-hour emergency response devices and patrols, late-night transport/escort service, controlled dormitory access. *Student services:* health clinic, personal/psychological counseling, women's center, legal services.

Athletics Member NCAA. All Division I except football (Division I-A). *Intercollegiate sports:* baseball M(s), basketball M(s)/W(s), cross-country running M(s)/W(s), golf M(s)/W(s), gymnastics W(s), soccer W(s), softball W(s), swimming and diving M(s)/W(s), tennis W(s), track and field M(s)/W(s), volleyball W(s), wrestling M(s). *Intramural sports:* archery M(c)/W(c), badminton W(c), baseball M(c), basketball M(c)/W(c), bowling M(c)/W(c), fencing M(c)/W(c), field hockey W(c), ice hockey M(c), lacrosse M(c)/W(c), racquetball M(c)/W(c), rugby M(c)/W(c), soccer M(c)/W(c), softball W(c), swimming and diving M(c)/W(c), table tennis M(c)/W(c), tennis M(c)/W(c), ultimate Frisbee M(c)/W(c), volleyball M(c)/W(c), water polo M(c)/W(c), weight lifting M(c)/W(c).

Standardized Tests *Required:* SAT or ACT (for admission). *Recommended:* ACT (for admission).

Costs (2011–12) *Tuition:* state resident $7848 full-time, $262 per credit hour part-time; nonresident $20,643 full-time, $688 per credit hour part-time. Full-time tuition and fees vary according to course load, program, and reciprocity agreements. Part-time tuition and fees vary according to course load, program, and reciprocity agreements. *Required fees:* $1141 full-time. *Room and board:* $8643. Room and board charges vary according to board plan and housing facility. *Payment plan:* installment. *Waivers:* senior citizens and employees or children of employees.

Financial Aid Of all full-time matriculated undergraduates who enrolled in 2011, 16,967 applied for aid, 12,452 were judged to have need, 1,772 had their need fully met. In 2011, 4067 non-need-based awards were made. *Average percent of need met:* 80%. *Average financial aid package:* $13,342. *Average need-based loan:* $4459. *Average need-based gift aid:* $7438. *Average non-need-based aid:* $3541. *Average indebtedness upon graduation:* $23,588.

Applying *Options:* electronic application, deferred entrance. *Application fee:* $50. *Required:* high school transcript, specific high school curriculum. *Application deadlines:* rolling (freshmen), rolling (transfers). *Notification:* continuous (freshmen), continuous (transfers).

Freshman Application Contact Ms. Barbara Rupp, Director of Admissions, University of Missouri, 230 Jesse Hall, Columbia, MO 65211. *Phone:* 573-882-7786. *Toll-free phone:* 800-225-6075. *Fax:* 573-882-7887. *E-mail:* mu4u@missouri.edu. *Web site:* http://www.missouri.edu/.

University of Missouri–Kansas City

Kansas City, Missouri

- **State-supported** university, founded 1929, part of University of Missouri System
- **Urban** 191-acre campus with easy access to Kansas City
- **Endowment** $209.1 million
- **Coed** 10,134 undergraduate students, 68% full-time, 58% women, 42% men
- **Moderately difficult** entrance level, 33% of applicants were admitted

Undergraduates 6,850 full-time, 3,284 part-time. Students come from 42 states and territories; 38 other countries; 23% are from out of state; 14% Black or African American, non-Hispanic/Latino; 5% Hispanic/Latino; 5% Asian, non-Hispanic/Latino; 0.2% Native Hawaiian or other Pacific Islander, non-Hispanic/Latino; 0.4% American Indian or Alaska Native, non-Hispanic/Latino; 2% Two or more races, non-Hispanic/Latino; 8% Race/ethnicity unknown; 4% international; 14% transferred in; 10% live on campus. *Retention:* 74% of full-time freshmen returned.

Freshmen *Admission:* 4,206 applied, 1,392 admitted, 1,159 enrolled. *Average high school GPA:* 3.25. *Test scores:* SAT critical reading scores over 500: 78%; SAT math scores over 500: 70%; ACT scores over 18: 88%; SAT critical reading scores over 600: 54%; SAT math scores over 600: 54%; ACT scores

over 24: 49%; SAT critical reading scores over 700: 10%; SAT math scores over 700: 29%; ACT scores over 30: 14%.

Faculty *Total:* 1,185, 63% full-time, 71% with terminal degrees. *Student/faculty ratio:* 13:1.

Academics *Calendar:* semesters. *Degrees:* bachelor's, master's, doctoral, post-master's, and first professional certificates. *Special study options:* accelerated degree program, adult/continuing education programs, advanced placement credit, cooperative education, distance learning, double majors, English as a second language, honors programs, independent study, internships, off-campus study, part-time degree program, services for LD students, student-designed majors, study abroad, summer session for credit. *ROTC:* Army (b), Air Force (c).

Computers on Campus 400 computers/terminals are available on campus for general student use. Students can access the following: campus intranet, computer help desk, free student e-mail accounts, online (class) grades, online (class) registration, online (class) schedules. Campuswide network is available. 100% of college-owned or -operated housing units are wired for high-speed Internet access. Wireless service is available via classrooms, computer labs, dorm rooms, libraries, student centers.

Student Life *Housing options:* coed, disabled students. Campus housing is university owned. *Activities and organizations:* drama/theater group, student-run newspaper, radio station, choral group, Activities and Programs Council, International Student Council, Alpha Phi Omega, Omicron Delta Kappa, Greek Organizations, national fraternities, national sororities. *Campus security:* 24-hour emergency response devices and patrols, late-night transport/escort service, controlled dormitory access. *Student services:* health clinic, personal/psychological counseling, women's center, legal services.

Athletics Member NCAA. All Division I. *Intercollegiate sports:* basketball M(s)/W(s), cross-country running M(s)/W(s), golf M(s)/W(s), soccer M(s)/W(s), softball W(s), tennis M(s)/W(s), track and field M(s)/W(s), volleyball W(s). *Intramural sports:* badminton M/W, basketball M/W, football M/W, racquetball M/W, soccer M/W, softball M/W, swimming and diving M/W, table tennis M/W, volleyball M/W.

Standardized Tests *Required:* SAT or ACT (for admission).

Costs (2012–13) *Tuition:* state resident $7968 full-time, $266 per credit hour part-time; nonresident $20,502 full-time, $683 per credit hour part-time. Full-time tuition and fees vary according to course load and program. Part-time tuition and fees vary according to course load and program. *Required fees:* $1252 full-time, $64 per credit hour part-time. *Room and board:* $11,428. Room and board charges vary according to board plan and housing facility. *Payment plan:* installment. *Waivers:* employees or children of employees.

Financial Aid Of all full-time matriculated undergraduates who enrolled in 2010, 5,290 applied for aid, 4,811 were judged to have need, 242 had their need fully met. In 2010, 586 non-need-based awards were made. *Average percent of need met:* 46%. *Average financial aid package:* $8790. *Average need-based loan:* $4580. *Average need-based gift aid:* $4515. *Average non-need-based aid:* $6444. *Average indebtedness upon graduation:* $25,374.

Applying *Options:* electronic application, deferred entrance. *Application fee:* $45. *Required:* high school transcript. *Required for some:* essay or personal statement, interview. *Application deadlines:* rolling (freshmen), rolling (transfers). *Notification:* continuous (freshmen), continuous (transfers).

Freshman Application Contact Ms. Sara Bedwell, Associate Director of Recruitment, University of Missouri–Kansas City, Office of Admissions, 5100 Rockhill Road, Kansas City, MO 64110-2499. *Phone:* 816-235-1111. *Toll-free phone:* 800-775-8652. *Fax:* 816-235-5544. *E-mail:* admit@umkc.edu. *Web site:* http://www.umkc.edu/.

University of Missouri–St. Louis

St. Louis, Missouri

- **State-supported** university, founded 1963, part of University of Missouri System
- **Suburban** 350-acre campus
- **Endowment** $55.9 million
- **Coed** 13,159 undergraduate students, 46% full-time, 59% women, 41% men
- **Moderately difficult** entrance level, 69% of applicants were admitted

Undergraduates 6,014 full-time, 7,145 part-time. Students come from 43 states and territories; 45 other countries; 10% are from out of state; 16% Black or African American, non-Hispanic/Latino; 2% Hispanic/Latino; 4% Asian, non-Hispanic/Latino; 0.2% American Indian or Alaska Native, non-Hispanic/Latino; 0.9% Two or more races, non-Hispanic/Latino; 7% Race/ethnicity unknown; 3% international; 13% transferred in; 8% live on campus. *Retention:* 78% of full-time freshmen returned.

Freshmen *Admission:* 1,769 applied, 1,222 admitted, 504 enrolled. *Test scores:* SAT math scores over 500: 67%; ACT scores over 18: 97%; SAT math

scores over 600: 39%; ACT scores over 24: 48%; SAT math scores over 700: 11%; ACT scores over 30: 7%.

Faculty *Total:* 889, 53% full-time, 52% with terminal degrees. *Student/faculty ratio:* 18:1.

Academics *Calendar:* semesters. *Degrees:* bachelor's, master's, doctoral, post-master's, postbachelor's, and first professional certificates. *Special study options:* accelerated degree program, adult/continuing education programs, advanced placement credit, cooperative education, distance learning, double majors, English as a second language, freshman honors college, honors programs, independent study, internships, off-campus study, part-time degree program, services for LD students, student-designed majors, study abroad, summer session for credit. *ROTC:* Army (c), Air Force (c). *Unusual degree programs:* 3-2 engineering with Washington University; economics, history, philosophy, political science and sociology.

Computers on Campus 1,326 computers/terminals and 1,326 ports are available on campus for general student use. Students can access the following: campus intranet, computer help desk, free student e-mail accounts, online (class) grades, online (class) registration, online (class) schedules. Campuswide network is available. 90% of college-owned or -operated housing units are wired for high-speed Internet access. Wireless service is available via classrooms, computer centers, computer labs, dorm rooms, learning centers, libraries, student centers.

Student Life *Housing options:* coed, women-only, disabled students. Campus housing is university owned and is provided by a third party. *Activities and organizations:* drama/theater group, student-run newspaper, radio station, choral group, Student Government Association, Associated Black Collegians, Pierre laclede Honors College Student Association, Residence Hall Association, UMSL Radio Station, national fraternities, national sororities. *Campus security:* 24-hour emergency response devices and patrols, late-night transport/escort service, controlled dormitory access. *Student services:* health clinic, personal/psychological counseling, women's center.

Athletics Member NCAA. All Division II. *Intercollegiate sports:* baseball M(s), basketball M(s)/W(s), cheerleading W, golf M(s)/W(s), ice hockey M(c), soccer M(s)/W(s), softball W(s), table tennis M(c)/W(c), tennis M(s)/W(s), volleyball W(s). *Intramural sports:* badminton M/W, basketball M/W, bowling M/W, football M/W, golf M/W, racquetball M/W, rock climbing M/W, skiing (downhill) M/W, soccer M/W, softball M/W, table tennis M/W, tennis M/W, volleyball M/W, weight lifting M/W.

Standardized Tests *Required:* SAT or ACT (for admission).

Costs (2011–12) *Tuition:* state resident $7737 full-time, $258 per credit hour part-time; nonresident $19,905 full-time, $664 per credit hour part-time. Full-time tuition and fees vary according to course load, program, and reciprocity agreements. Part-time tuition and fees vary according to course load, program, and reciprocity agreements. *Required fees:* $1301 full-time, $50 per credit hour part-time. *Room and board:* $8404; room only: $5044. Room and board charges vary according to board plan and housing facility. *Payment plan:* installment. *Waivers:* senior citizens and employees or children of employees.

Financial Aid Of all full-time matriculated undergraduates who enrolled in 2011, 4,629 applied for aid, 4,268 were judged to have need, 252 had their need fully met. 66 Federal Work-Study jobs (averaging $3478). In 2011, 456 non-need-based awards were made. *Average percent of need met:* 46%. *Average financial aid package:* $9059. *Average need-based loan:* $4571. *Average need-based gift aid:* $6091. *Average non-need-based aid:* $4831. *Average indebtedness upon graduation:* $25,504.

Applying *Options:* electronic application. *Application fee:* $35. *Required:* high school transcript, CBHE core requirements. *Required for some:* essay or personal statement, 2 letters of recommendation, interview. *Application deadlines:* 8/23 (freshmen), 8/23 (out-of-state freshmen), rolling (transfers). *Notification:* continuous until 10/1 (freshmen), continuous until 10/1 (out-of-state freshmen), continuous (transfers).

Freshman Application Contact Mr. Andrew L. Griffin, Associate Director of Admissions, University of Missouri–St. Louis, 351 Millennium Student Center, One University Boulevard, St. Louis, MO 63121-4400. *Phone:* 314-516-6941. *Toll-free phone:* 888-GO2-UMSL (in-state); 888-GO2-USML (out-of-state). *Fax:* 314-516-5310. *E-mail:* askdrew@umsl.edu. *Web site:* http://www.umsl.edu/.

University of Phoenix–Kansas City Campus

Kansas City, Missouri

Freshman Application Contact Marc Booker, Sr. Director, Office of Admissions and Evaluation, University of Phoenix–Kansas City Campus, 4035 South Riverpoint Parkway, Mail Stop CF-L101, Phoenix, AZ 85040. *Phone:* 602-557-4609. *Toll-free phone:* 866-766-0766. *Fax:* 480-643-1156. *Web site:* http://www.phoenix.edu/.

University of Phoenix–St. Louis Campus

St. Louis, Missouri

Freshman Application Contact Marc Booker, Sr. Director, Office of Admissions and Evaluation, University of Phoenix–St. Louis Campus, 4035 South Riverpoint Parkway, Mail Stop CF-L101, Phoenix, AZ 85040. *Phone:* 602-557-4609. *Toll-free phone:* 866-766-0766. *Fax:* 480-643-1156. *Web site:* http://www.phoenix.edu/.

University of Phoenix–Springfield Campus

Springfield, Missouri

Freshman Application Contact Marc Booker, Sr. Director, Office of Admissions and Evaluation, University of Phoenix–Springfield Campus, 4035 South Riverpoint Parkway, Mail Stop CF-L101, Phoenix, AZ 85040. *Phone:* 602-557-4609. *Toll-free phone:* 866-766-0766. *Fax:* 480-643-1156. *Web site:* http://www.phoenix.edu/.

Vatterott College

St. Ann, Missouri

Director of Admissions Ann Farajallah, Director of Admissions, Vatterott College, 3925 Industrial Drive, St. Ann, MO 63074-1807. *Phone:* 314-264-1020. *Toll-free phone:* 888-553-6627. *Web site:* http://www.vatterott-college.edu/.

Vatterott College

Sunset Hills, Missouri

Director of Admissions Director of Admission, Vatterott College, 12970 Maurer Industrial Drive, St. Louis, MO 63127. *Phone:* 314-843-4200. *Toll-free phone:* 888-553-6627. *Fax:* 314-843-1709. *Web site:* http://www.vatterott-college.edu/.

Washington University in St. Louis

St. Louis, Missouri

- **Independent** university, founded 1853
- **Suburban** 169-acre campus
- **Endowment** $5.3 billion
- **Coed** 7,239 undergraduate students, 88% full-time, 52% women, 48% men
- **Most difficult** entrance level, 17% of applicants were admitted

Undergraduates 6,372 full-time, 867 part-time. Students come from 54 states and territories; 60 other countries; 92% are from out of state; 6% Black or African American, non-Hispanic/Latino; 5% Hispanic/Latino; 15% Asian, non-Hispanic/Latino; 0.1% American Indian or Alaska Native, non-Hispanic/Latino; 3% Two or more races, non-Hispanic/Latino; 7% Race/ethnicity unknown; 7% international; 0.7% transferred in; 78% live on campus. *Retention:* 97% of full-time freshmen returned.
Freshmen *Admission:* 28,823 applied, 4,763 admitted, 1,488 enrolled. *Test scores:* SAT critical reading scores over 500: 100%; SAT math scores over 500: 100%; ACT scores over 18: 100%; SAT critical reading scores over 600: 98%; SAT math scores over 600: 99%; ACT scores over 24: 100%; SAT critical reading scores over 700: 71%; SAT math scores over 700: 81%; ACT scores over 30: 95%.
Faculty *Total:* 1,089, 86% full-time, 84% with terminal degrees. *Student/faculty ratio:* 7:1.
Academics *Calendar:* semesters. *Degrees:* certificates, bachelor's, master's, doctoral, post-master's, postbachelor's, and first professional certificates. *Special study options:* accelerated degree program, adult/continuing education programs, advanced placement credit, cooperative education, double majors, English as a second language, independent study, internships, off-campus study, part-time degree program, services for LD students, student-designed majors, study abroad, summer session for credit. *ROTC:* Army (b), Air Force (c). *Unusual degree programs:* 3-2 business administration; engineering; social work; art, occupational therapy, physical therapy.
Computers on Campus 2,500 computers/terminals are available on campus for general student use. Students can access the following: campus intranet, computer help desk, free student e-mail accounts, online (class) grades, online (class) registration, online (class) schedules. Campuswide network is available. 90% of college-owned or -operated housing units are wired for high-speed Internet access. Wireless service is available via classrooms, computer centers, computer labs, dorm rooms, learning centers, libraries, student centers.

Student Life *Housing:* on-campus residence required for freshman year. *Options:* coed, men-only, women-only, cooperative. Campus housing is university owned. Freshman campus housing is guaranteed. *Activities and organizations:* drama/theater group, student-run newspaper, radio and television station, choral group, national fraternities, national sororities. *Campus security:* 24-hour emergency response devices and patrols, student patrols, late-night transport/escort service, controlled dormitory access. *Student services:* health clinic, personal/psychological counseling, women's center.
Athletics Member NCAA. All Division III. *Intercollegiate sports:* baseball M, basketball M/W, crew M(c)/W(c), cross-country running M/W, equestrian sports M(c)/W(c), fencing M(c)/W(c), field hockey W(c), football M, golf M(c)/W, gymnastics M(c)/W(c), ice hockey M(c), lacrosse M(c)/W(c), rugby M(c)/W(c), sailing M(c)/W(c), soccer M/W, softball W, swimming and diving M/W, table tennis M(c)/W(c), tennis M/W, track and field M/W, ultimate Frisbee M(c)/W(c), volleyball M(c)/W, water polo M(c)/W(c). *Intramural sports:* badminton M/W, basketball M/W, bowling M/W, cross-country running M/W, football M/W, golf M/W, racquetball M/W, soccer M(c)/W(c), softball M/W, swimming and diving M/W, table tennis M/W, tennis M/W, track and field M/W, ultimate Frisbee M/W, volleyball M/W, water polo M/W.
Standardized Tests *Required:* SAT or ACT (for admission).
Costs (2012–13) *Comprehensive fee:* $57,285 includes full-time tuition ($42,500), mandatory fees ($1205), and room and board ($13,580). *College room only:* $9162. Room and board charges vary according to board plan and housing facility. *Payment plans:* tuition prepayment, installment. *Waivers:* employees or children of employees.
Financial Aid Of all full-time matriculated undergraduates who enrolled in 2011, 4,273 applied for aid, 2,524 were judged to have need, 2,487 had their need fully met. 1,088 Federal Work-Study jobs (averaging $1913). In 2011, 936 non-need-based awards were made. *Average percent of need met:* 100%. *Average financial aid package:* $33,619. *Average need-based loan:* $6353. *Average need-based gift aid:* $30,317. *Average non-need-based aid:* $6720. *Financial aid deadline:* 2/1.
Applying *Options:* electronic application, early admission, early decision, deferred entrance. *Application fee:* $55. *Required:* essay or personal statement, high school transcript, 2 letters of recommendation. *Recommended:* minimum 3.0 GPA, Portfolios are required for students applying to the College of Art. Portfolios are strongly encouraged for students applying to the College of Architecture. *Application deadlines:* 1/15 (freshmen), 4/15 (transfers). *Early decision deadline:* 11/15. *Notification:* 4/1 (freshmen), continuous (transfers), 12/15 (early decision).
Freshman Application Contact Ms. Julie Shimabukuro, Director of Admissions, Washington University in St. Louis, Campus Box 1089, One Brookings Drive, St. Louis, MO 63130-4899. *Phone:* 314-935-6000. *Toll-free phone:* 800-638-0700. *Fax:* 314-935-4290. *E-mail:* admissions@wustl.edu. *Web site:* http://www.wustl.edu/.

Webster University

St. Louis, Missouri

- **Independent** comprehensive, founded 1915
- **Suburban** 47-acre campus with easy access to St. Louis
- **Endowment** $87.6 million
- **Coed** 2,995 undergraduate students, 81% full-time, 56% women, 44% men
- **Moderately difficult** entrance level, 59% of applicants were admitted

Undergraduates 2,415 full-time, 580 part-time. Students come from 41 states and territories; 36 other countries; 18% are from out of state; 10% Black or African American, non-Hispanic/Latino; 4% Hispanic/Latino; 2% Asian, non-Hispanic/Latino; 0.1% American Indian or Alaska Native, non-Hispanic/Latino; 0.7% Two or more races, non-Hispanic/Latino; 10% Race/ethnicity unknown; 1% international; 13% transferred in; 23% live on campus. *Retention:* 80% of full-time freshmen returned.
Freshmen *Admission:* 1,733 applied, 1,014 admitted, 480 enrolled. *Average high school GPA:* 3.49. *Test scores:* ACT scores over 18: 95%; ACT scores over 24: 54%; ACT scores over 30: 8%.
Faculty *Total:* 904, 20% full-time, 28% with terminal degrees. *Student/faculty ratio:* 9:1.
Academics *Calendar:* semesters. *Degrees:* certificates, bachelor's, master's, doctoral, post-master's, and postbachelor's certificates. *Special study options:* academic remediation for entering students, accelerated degree program, adult/continuing education programs, advanced placement credit, cooperative education, distance learning, double majors, English as a second language, independent study, internships, off-campus study, part-time degree program, services for LD students, student-designed majors, study abroad, summer session for credit. *ROTC:* Army (c), Air Force (c). *Unusual degree programs:* 3-2 engineering with University of Missouri-Columbia, Washington University in St. Louis; architecture with Washington University in St. Louis, Athletic Training with Saint Louis University, Chiropractic with Logan College of Chi-

ropractic, Occupational Therapy with Washington University School of Medicine.

Computers on Campus 661 computers/terminals and 250 ports are available on campus for general student use. Students can access the following: campus intranet, computer help desk, free student e-mail accounts, online (class) grades, online (class) registration, online (class) schedules. Campuswide network is available. 100% of college-owned or -operated housing units are wired for high-speed Internet access. Wireless service is available via entire campus.

Student Life *Housing:* on-campus residence required for freshman year. *Options:* coed. Campus housing is university owned. Freshman applicants given priority for college housing. *Activities and organizations:* drama/theater group, student-run newspaper, radio and television station, choral group, Student Government Association, Habitat for Humanity, International Student Association, Marketing Communications Club, Residential Housing Association, national sororities. *Campus security:* 24-hour emergency response devices and patrols, student patrols, late-night transport/escort service, controlled dormitory access. *Student services:* health clinic, personal/psychological counseling, women's center.

Athletics Member NCAA. All Division III. *Intercollegiate sports:* baseball M, basketball M/W, cross-country running M/W, golf M, soccer M/W, softball W, tennis M/W, track and field M/W, volleyball W. *Intramural sports:* bowling M/W, cheerleading M(c)/W(c), football M/W, soccer M(c)/W(c), swimming and diving M(c)/W(c), volleyball M/W.

Standardized Tests *Required:* SAT or ACT (for admission).

Costs (2011–12) *Comprehensive fee:* $32,020 includes full-time tuition ($22,340) and room and board ($9680). Full-time tuition and fees vary according to program. Part-time tuition: $570 per credit hour. Part-time tuition and fees vary according to location. *College room only:* $5360. Room and board charges vary according to board plan and housing facility. *Payment plan:* installment. *Waivers:* employees or children of employees.

Financial Aid Of all full-time matriculated undergraduates who enrolled in 2011, 2,078 applied for aid, 1,846 were judged to have need, 81 had their need fully met. 960 Federal Work-Study jobs (averaging $2153). 838 state and other part-time jobs (averaging $1086). In 2011, 148 non-need-based awards were made. *Average percent of need met:* 61%. *Average financial aid package:* $23,376. *Average need-based loan:* $4592. *Average need-based gift aid:* $7403. *Average non-need-based aid:* $6520. *Average indebtedness upon graduation:* $27,159.

Applying *Options:* electronic application, early admission, deferred entrance. *Application fee:* $35. *Required:* essay or personal statement, high school transcript, minimum 2.5 GPA, 1 letter of recommendation. *Required for some:* minimum 3.0 GPA, audition. *Recommended:* minimum 3.0 GPA, interview. *Application deadlines:* 6/1 (freshmen), 6/1 (out-of-state freshmen), 8/1 (transfers). *Notification:* continuous (freshmen), continuous (out-of-state freshmen), continuous (transfers).

Freshman Application Contact Mr. Andrew Laue, Associate Director of Undergraduate Admission, Webster University, 470 East Lockwood Avenue, St. Louis, MO 63119-3194. *Phone:* 314-246-7712. *Toll-free phone:* 800-75-ENROL. *Fax:* 314-246-7122. *E-mail:* lauear@webster.edu. *Web site:* http://www.webster.edu/.

Westminster College

Fulton, Missouri

- **Independent** 4-year, founded 1851, affiliated with Presbyterian Church
- **Small-town** 80-acre campus
- **Endowment** $45.1 million
- **Coed** 1,102 undergraduate students, 99% full-time, 45% women, 55% men
- **Moderately difficult** entrance level, 71% of applicants were admitted

Undergraduates 1,088 full-time, 14 part-time. Students come from 25 states and territories; 65 other countries; 20% are from out of state; 6% Black or African American, non-Hispanic/Latino; 3% Hispanic/Latino; 2% Asian, non-Hispanic/Latino; 0.2% Native Hawaiian or other Pacific Islander, non-Hispanic/Latino; 3% American Indian or Alaska Native, non-Hispanic/Latino; 0.6% Two or more races, non-Hispanic/Latino; 2% Race/ethnicity unknown; 16% international; 5% transferred in; 85% live on campus. *Retention:* 81% of full-time freshmen returned.

Freshmen *Admission:* 1,387 applied, 978 admitted, 254 enrolled. *Average high school GPA:* 3.43. *Test scores:* SAT critical reading scores over 500: 46%; SAT math scores over 500: 59%; SAT writing scores over 500: 54%; ACT scores over 18: 99%; SAT critical reading scores over 600: 32%; SAT math scores over 600: 27%; SAT writing scores over 600: 19%; ACT scores over 24: 66%; SAT critical reading scores over 700: 5%; SAT math scores over 700: 11%; SAT writing scores over 700: 3%; ACT scores over 30: 12%.

Faculty *Total:* 95, 66% full-time, 63% with terminal degrees. *Student/faculty ratio:* 15:1.

Academics *Calendar:* semesters. *Degree:* bachelor's. *Special study options:* academic remediation for entering students, advanced placement credit, cooperative education, double majors, English as a second language, honors programs, independent study, internships, off-campus study, part-time degree program, services for LD students, student-designed majors, study abroad, summer session for credit. *ROTC:* Army (c), Air Force (c). *Unusual degree programs:* 3-2 engineering with Washington University in St. Louis, University of Missouri-Columbia; nursing with Golfarb School of Nursing at Barnes-Jewish College in St. Louis.

Computers on Campus 188 computers/terminals are available on campus for general student use. Students can access the following: campus intranet, computer help desk, free student e-mail accounts, online (class) grades, online (class) registration, online (class) schedules. Campuswide network is available. 100% of college-owned or -operated housing units are wired for high-speed Internet access. Wireless service is available via entire campus.

Student Life *Housing:* on-campus residence required through junior year. *Options:* coed, men-only, women-only. Campus housing is university owned. Freshman campus housing is guaranteed. *Activities and organizations:* drama/theater group, student-run newspaper, choral group, Student Government Association, Environmentally Concerned Students, International Student Club, Habitat for Humanity, Little Brother/Little Sister, national fraternities, national sororities. *Campus security:* 24-hour emergency response devices and patrols, late-night transport/escort service, controlled dormitory access, well-lit campus. *Student services:* health clinic, personal/psychological counseling, women's center.

Athletics Member NCAA. All Division III. *Intercollegiate sports:* baseball M, basketball M/W, cross-country running M/W, football M, golf M/W, soccer M/W, softball M/W, tennis M/W, track and field M/W, volleyball W. *Intramural sports:* basketball M/W, football M, table tennis M/W, volleyball M/W.

Standardized Tests *Required:* SAT or ACT (for admission).

Costs (2011–12) *Comprehensive fee:* $28,560 includes full-time tuition ($19,750), mandatory fees ($820), and room and board ($7990). Part-time tuition: $800 per credit hour. *College room only:* $4190. Room and board charges vary according to board plan and housing facility. *Payment plan:* installment. *Waivers:* children of alumni and employees or children of employees.

Financial Aid Of all full-time matriculated undergraduates who enrolled in 2011, 846 applied for aid, 683 were judged to have need, 319 had their need fully met. 561 Federal Work-Study jobs (averaging $1351). 263 state and other part-time jobs (averaging $2014). In 2011, 382 non-need-based awards were made. *Average percent of need met:* 82%. *Average financial aid package:* $18,345. *Average need-based loan:* $4239. *Average need-based gift aid:* $13,440. *Average non-need-based aid:* $9215. *Average indebtedness upon graduation:* $20,745.

Applying *Options:* electronic application, early admission, deferred entrance. *Required:* high school transcript, 1 letter of recommendation. *Required for some:* interview. *Recommended:* essay or personal statement, minimum 2.5 GPA. *Notification:* 8/1 (freshmen), continuous (transfers).

Freshman Application Contact Mr. George Wolf, Vice President and Dean of Enrollment Services, Westminster College, 501 Westminster Avenue, Fulton, MO 65251-1299. *Phone:* 573-592-5251. *Toll-free phone:* 800-475-3361. *Fax:* 573-592-5255. *E-mail:* admissions@westminster-mo.edu. *Web site:* http://www.westminster-mo.edu/.

William Jewell College

Liberty, Missouri

- **Independent** 4-year, founded 1849
- **Suburban** 200-acre campus with easy access to Kansas City
- **Endowment** $64.4 million
- **Coed** 1,060 undergraduate students, 95% full-time, 59% women, 41% men
- **Moderately difficult** entrance level, 54% of applicants were admitted

Undergraduates 1,012 full-time, 48 part-time. Students come from 32 states and territories; 12 other countries; 34% are from out of state; 4% Black or African American, non-Hispanic/Latino; 4% Hispanic/Latino; 2% Asian, non-Hispanic/Latino; 0.9% American Indian or Alaska Native, non-Hispanic/Latino; 3% Two or more races, non-Hispanic/Latino; 2% Race/ethnicity unknown; 3% international; 3% transferred in; 81% live on campus. *Retention:* 75% of full-time freshmen returned.

Freshmen *Admission:* 3,333 applied, 1,803 admitted, 270 enrolled. *Average high school GPA:* 3.69. *Test scores:* SAT critical reading scores over 500: 73%; SAT math scores over 500: 88%; ACT scores over 18: 99%; SAT critical reading scores over 600: 35%; SAT math scores over 600: 35%; ACT scores over 24: 71%; SAT critical reading scores over 700: 3%; ACT scores over 30: 15%.

Faculty *Total:* 147, 46% full-time, 46% with terminal degrees. *Student/faculty ratio:* 11:1.

Academics *Calendar:* semesters. *Degrees:* bachelor's (also offers evening program with significant enrollment not reflected in profile). *Special study options:* academic remediation for entering students, accelerated degree program, advanced placement credit, cooperative education, double majors, honors programs, independent study, internships, off-campus study, services for LD students, student-designed majors, study abroad, summer session for credit. *ROTC:* Army (c). *Unusual degree programs:* 3-2 engineering with Washington University in St. Louis, University of Kansas, Vanderbilt University, Columbia University, Missouri University of Science and Technology; forestry with Duke University; occupational therapy with Washington University in St. Louis.

Computers on Campus 260 computers/terminals are available on campus for general student use. Students can access the following: campus intranet, computer help desk, free student e-mail accounts, online (class) grades, online (class) registration, online (class) schedules. Campuswide network is available. 100% of college-owned or -operated housing units are wired for high-speed Internet access. Wireless service is available via classrooms, dorm rooms, learning centers, libraries, student centers.

Student Life *Housing:* on-campus residence required through senior year. *Options:* coed, men-only, women-only, disabled students. Campus housing is university owned. Freshman campus housing is guaranteed. *Activities and organizations:* drama/theater group, student-run newspaper, radio station, choral group, College Union Activities, intramurals, Mosaic, Students in Free Enterprise (SIFE), Student Senate, national fraternities, national sororities. *Campus security:* 24-hour emergency response devices and patrols, late-night transport/escort service, controlled dormitory access. *Student services:* health clinic, personal/psychological counseling.

Athletics Member NCAA. All Division II. *Intercollegiate sports:* baseball M(s), basketball M(s)/W(s), cheerleading M(s)/W(s), cross-country running M(s)/W(s), football M(s), golf M(s)/W(s), soccer M(s)/W(s), softball W(s), swimming and diving M(s)/W(s), tennis M(s)/W(s), track and field M(s)/W(s), volleyball W(s). *Intramural sports:* racquetball M/W, soccer M/W, softball M/W, tennis M/W, ultimate Frisbee M/W, volleyball M/W.

Standardized Tests *Required:* SAT or ACT (for admission).

Costs (2012–13) *Comprehensive fee:* $38,290 includes full-time tuition ($30,200), mandatory fees ($300), and room and board ($7790). Full-time tuition and fees vary according to class time, course load, program, and student level. Part-time tuition: $870 per credit. *Room and board:* Room and board charges vary according to board plan and housing facility. *Payment plan:* installment. *Waivers:* employees or children of employees.

Financial Aid Of all full-time matriculated undergraduates who enrolled in 2011, 840 applied for aid, 776 were judged to have need, 130 had their need fully met. 488 Federal Work-Study jobs (averaging $1509). In 2011, 226 non-need-based awards were made. *Average percent of need met:* 67%. *Average financial aid package:* $19,118. *Average need-based loan:* $4776. *Average need-based gift aid:* $19,113. *Average non-need-based aid:* $12,213. *Average indebtedness upon graduation:* $29,444.

Applying *Options:* electronic application, deferred entrance. *Application fee:* $25. *Required:* essay or personal statement, high school transcript. *Required for some:* interview. *Recommended:* interview. *Application deadlines:* 8/15 (freshmen), rolling (transfers). *Notification:* continuous (transfers).

Freshman Application Contact Mr. Clint Chapman, Dean of Admission, William Jewell College, 500 College Hill, Liberty, MO 64068-1843. *Phone:* 816-415-7872. *Toll-free phone:* 888-2JEWELL. *Fax:* 816-415-5040. *E-mail:* chapmanc@william.jewell.edu. *Web site:* http://www.jewell.edu/.

William Woods University

Fulton, Missouri

- **Independent** comprehensive, founded 1870, affiliated with Christian Church (Disciples of Christ)
- **Rural** campus with easy access to St. Louis
- **Coed** 1,036 undergraduate students, 84% full-time, 73% women, 27% men
- **Moderately difficult** entrance level, 80% of applicants were admitted

Undergraduates 872 full-time, 164 part-time. 34% are from out of state; 4% Black or African American, non-Hispanic/Latino; 0.6% Hispanic/Latino; 0.7% Asian, non-Hispanic/Latino; 0.5% American Indian or Alaska Native, non-Hispanic/Latino; 3% Two or more races, non-Hispanic/Latino; 7% Race/ethnicity unknown; 0.1% international; 11% transferred in; 75% live on campus. *Retention:* 74% of full-time freshmen returned.

Freshmen *Admission:* 753 applied, 602 admitted, 182 enrolled. *Average high school GPA:* 3.5. *Test scores:* SAT critical reading scores over 500: 67%; SAT math scores over 500: 64%; SAT writing scores over 500: 60%; ACT scores over 18: 94%; SAT critical reading scores over 600: 29%; SAT math scores over 600: 22%; SAT writing scores over 600: 20%; ACT scores over 24: 36%; SAT critical reading scores over 700: 2%; SAT math scores over 700: 2%; ACT scores over 30: 4%.

Faculty *Total:* 357, 20% full-time, 32% with terminal degrees. *Student/faculty ratio:* 12:1.

Academics *Calendar:* semesters. *Degrees:* associate, bachelor's, master's, and post-master's certificates. *Special study options:* academic remediation for entering students, accelerated degree program, adult/continuing education programs, advanced placement credit, double majors, honors programs, independent study, internships, off-campus study, part-time degree program, student-designed majors, study abroad, summer session for credit. *ROTC:* Army (c), Navy (c), Air Force (c).

Computers on Campus Students can access the following: campus intranet, computer help desk, free student e-mail accounts, online (class) grades, online (class) registration, online (class) schedules. Campuswide network is available. 100% of college-owned or -operated housing units are wired for high-speed Internet access. Wireless service is available via classrooms, computer labs, learning centers, libraries.

Student Life *Housing:* on-campus residence required through senior year. *Options:* coed, men-only, women-only. Campus housing is university owned. Freshman campus housing is guaranteed. *Campus security:* 24-hour emergency response devices and patrols, late-night transport/escort service, controlled dormitory access.

Athletics Member NAIA. *Intercollegiate sports:* baseball M(s), basketball M(s)/W(s), cross-country running M(s)/W(s), golf M(s)/W(s), soccer M(s)/W(s), softball W(s), track and field M(s)/W(s), volleyball M(s)/W(s). *Intramural sports:* badminton M/W, baseball M, basketball M/W, equestrian sports M/W, football M/W, rugby M/W, softball M/W, table tennis M/W, tennis M/W, volleyball M/W, weight lifting M/W.

Standardized Tests *Required:* SAT or ACT (for admission).

Costs (2011–12) *Comprehensive fee:* $26,500 includes full-time tuition ($18,450), mandatory fees ($550), and room and board ($7500). Full-time tuition and fees vary according to degree level and program. Part-time tuition: $585 per credit hour. Part-time tuition and fees vary according to course load, degree level, and program. *Required fees:* $15 per term part-time. *Room and board:* Room and board charges vary according to board plan and housing facility. *Payment plan:* installment. *Waivers:* children of alumni, senior citizens, and employees or children of employees.

Financial Aid Of all full-time matriculated undergraduates who enrolled in 2011, 800 applied for aid, 711 were judged to have need, 147 had their need fully met. In 2011, 236 non-need-based awards were made. *Average percent of need met:* 55%. *Average financial aid package:* $14,416. *Average need-based loan:* $4193. *Average need-based gift aid:* $10,713. *Average non-need-based aid:* $7170. *Average indebtedness upon graduation:* $22,032.

Applying *Options:* deferred entrance. *Application fee:* $25. *Required:* high school transcript, minimum 2.5 GPA, 16 hours college preparatory units. *Required for some:* essay or personal statement, 2 letters of recommendation. *Recommended:* interview. *Application deadlines:* 8/15 (freshmen), rolling (transfers). *Notification:* continuous (freshmen), continuous (transfers).

Freshman Application Contact Ms. Sharon Horn, Admissions Data Analyst, William Woods University, One University Avenue, Fulton, MO 65251. *Phone:* 573-592-4221. *Toll-free phone:* 800-995-3159 Ext. 4221. *Fax:* 573-592-1146. *E-mail:* admissions@williamwoods.edu. *Web site:* http://www.williamwoods.edu/.

MONTANA

Carroll College

Helena, Montana

- **Independent Roman Catholic** 4-year, founded 1909
- **Small-town** campus
- **Coed** 1,436 undergraduate students, 93% full-time, 58% women, 42% men
- **Moderately difficult** entrance level, 72% of applicants were admitted

Undergraduates 1,330 full-time, 106 part-time. Students come from 20 states and territories; 11 other countries; 47% are from out of state; 0.5% Black or African American, non-Hispanic/Latino; 3% Hispanic/Latino; 1% Asian, non-Hispanic/Latino; 0.4% Native Hawaiian or other Pacific Islander, non-Hispanic/Latino; 1% American Indian or Alaska Native, non-Hispanic/Latino; 0.4% Two or more races, non-Hispanic/Latino; 11% Race/ethnicity unknown; 1% international; 6% transferred in. *Retention:* 78% of full-time freshmen returned.

Freshmen *Admission:* 1,588 applied, 1,141 admitted, 345 enrolled. *Average high school GPA:* 3.49. *Test scores:* SAT critical reading scores over 500: 76%; SAT math scores over 500: 76%; SAT writing scores over 500: 69%; ACT scores over 18: 98%; SAT critical reading scores over 600: 32%; SAT math scores over 600: 33%; SAT writing scores over 600: 26%; ACT scores

over 24: 60%; SAT critical reading scores over 700: 4%; SAT math scores over 700: 4%; SAT writing scores over 700: 3%; ACT scores over 30: 6%.

Faculty *Total:* 143, 59% full-time. *Student/faculty ratio:* 13:1.

Academics *Calendar:* semesters. *Degrees:* associate and bachelor's. *Special study options:* accelerated degree program, adult/continuing education programs, advanced placement credit, cooperative education, double majors, English as a second language, freshman honors college, honors programs, independent study, internships, part-time degree program, student-designed majors, study abroad, summer session for credit. *ROTC:* Army (b). *Unusual degree programs:* 3-2 engineering with Columbia University, University of Southern California, University of Notre Dame, Montana State University, Gonzaga University, Montana College of Mineral Science and Technology, University of Minnesota.

Computers on Campus Students can access the following: campus intranet, computer help desk, free student e-mail accounts, online (class) grades, online (class) registration, online (class) schedules, online book order. Campuswide network is available.

Student Life *Housing:* on-campus residence required through sophomore year. *Options:* coed. Campus housing is university owned. Freshman campus housing is guaranteed. *Activities and organizations:* student-run newspaper, student government, Carroll Outreach Team, Carroll Adventure and Mountaineering Program, Up 'Til Dawn, Engineers Without Borders. *Campus security:* late-night transport/escort service, controlled dormitory access. *Student services:* health clinic, personal/psychological counseling.

Athletics Member NAIA. *Intercollegiate sports:* basketball M(s)/W(s), cheerleading M(s)/W(s), cross-country running M(s)/W(s), football M(s), golf M(s)/W(s), soccer W(s), track and field M(s)/W(s), volleyball W(s).

Standardized Tests *Required:* SAT or ACT (for admission). *Required for some:* SAT Subject Tests (for admission).

Costs (2011–12) *Comprehensive fee:* $32,948 includes full-time tuition ($24,648), mandatory fees ($550), and room and board ($7750). Full-time tuition and fees vary according to course load. Part-time tuition: $1027 per credit hour. Part-time tuition and fees vary according to course load. *Required fees:* $138 per term part-time. *Room and board:* Room and board charges vary according to board plan and housing facility. *Payment plan:* installment. *Waivers:* senior citizens and employees or children of employees.

Financial Aid Of all full-time matriculated undergraduates who enrolled in 2010, 990 applied for aid, 863 were judged to have need, 168 had their need fully met. 242 Federal Work-Study jobs (averaging $2094). In 2010, 384 non-need-based awards were made. *Average percent of need met:* 76%. *Average*

financial aid package: $19,272. *Average need-based loan:* $4338. *Average need-based gift aid:* $13,059. *Average non-need-based aid:* $8558. *Average indebtedness upon graduation:* $29,122.

Applying *Options:* electronic application, deferred entrance. *Required:* essay or personal statement, high school transcript. *Required for some:* interview. *Recommended:* interview. *Notification:* continuous (freshmen), continuous (transfers).

Freshman Application Contact Director of Admission, Carroll College, 1601 North Benton Avenue, Helena, MT 59625-0002. *Phone:* 406-447-4384. *Toll-free phone:* 800-992-3648. *E-mail:* admission@carroll.edu. *Web site:* http://www.carroll.edu/.

See below for display ad and page 1244 for the College Close-Up.

Montana State University
Bozeman, Montana

- **State-supported** university, founded 1893, part of Montana University System
- **Small-town** 1781-acre campus
- **Endowment** $85.5 million
- **Coed** 12,188 undergraduate students, 82% full-time, 46% women, 54% men
- **Moderately difficult** entrance level, 60% of applicants were admitted

Undergraduates 10,033 full-time, 2,155 part-time. Students come from 50 states and territories; 70 other countries; 33% are from out of state; 0.7% Black or African American, non-Hispanic/Latino; 3% Hispanic/Latino; 0.8% Asian, non-Hispanic/Latino; 2% American Indian or Alaska Native, non-Hispanic/Latino; 3% Two or more races, non-Hispanic/Latino; 0.9% Race/ethnicity unknown; 3% international; 7% transferred in; 25% live on campus. *Retention:* 74% of full-time freshmen returned.

Freshmen *Admission:* 9,871 applied, 5,938 admitted, 2,669 enrolled. *Average high school GPA:* 3.28. *Test scores:* SAT critical reading scores over 500: 75%; SAT math scores over 500: 76%; SAT writing scores over 500: 67%; ACT scores over 18: 94%; SAT critical reading scores over 600: 36%; SAT math scores over 600: 38%; SAT writing scores over 600: 27%; ACT scores over 24: 56%; SAT critical reading scores over 700: 7%; SAT math scores over 700: 7%; SAT writing scores over 700: 4%; ACT scores over 30: 12%.

Faculty *Total:* 880, 65% full-time, 57% with terminal degrees. *Student/faculty ratio:* 17:1.

Academics *Calendar:* semesters. *Degrees:* certificates, associate, bachelor's, master's, doctoral, post-master's, and first professional certificates. *Special study options:* academic remediation for entering students, adult/continuing education programs, advanced placement credit, distance learning, double majors, English as a second language, honors programs, independent study, internships, off-campus study, part-time degree program, services for LD students, student-designed majors, study abroad, summer session for credit. *ROTC:* Army (b), Air Force (b).

Computers on Campus 850 computers/terminals are available on campus for general student use. Students can access the following: computer help desk, free student e-mail accounts, online (class) registration, online (class) schedules. Campuswide network is available. 100% of college-owned or -operated housing units are wired for high-speed Internet access. Wireless service is available via entire campus.

Student Life *Housing:* on-campus residence required for freshman year. *Options:* coed, men-only, women-only. Campus housing is university owned. Freshman campus housing is guaranteed. *Activities and organizations:* drama/theater group, student-run newspaper, radio and television station, choral group, marching band, Spurs, Inter-Varsity Christian Fellowship, Campus Crusade for Christ, Fangs, Mortar Board, national fraternities, national sororities. *Campus security:* 24-hour emergency response devices and patrols, student patrols, late-night transport/escort service, 24-hour residence hall monitoring. *Student services:* health clinic, personal/psychological counseling, women's center, legal services.

Athletics Member NCAA. All Division I except football (Division I-AA). *Intercollegiate sports:* basketball M(s)/W(s), cheerleading M(s)/W(s), cross-country running M(s)/W(s), golf W(s), skiing (cross-country) M(s)/W(s), skiing (downhill) M(s)/W(s), tennis M(s)/W(s), track and field M(s)/W(s), volleyball W(s). *Intramural sports:* archery W, badminton M/W, baseball M, basketball M/W, bowling M/W, cross-country running M/W, fencing M/W, football M, golf M/W, gymnastics M/W, racquetball M/W, rugby M/W, skiing (cross-country) M/W, skiing (downhill) M/W, soccer M/W, softball M/W, swimming and diving M/W, table tennis M/W, tennis M/W, track and field M/W, ultimate Frisbee M/W, volleyball M/W, water polo M/W, weight lifting M/W, wrestling M.

Standardized Tests *Required:* SAT or ACT (for admission).

Costs (2011–12) *Tuition:* state resident $5077 full-time, $212 per credit part-time; nonresident $17,714 full-time, $738 per credit part-time. Full-time tuition and fees vary according to course load, degree level, and program. Part-time tuition and fees vary according to course load, degree level, and program. *Required fees:* $1395 full-time, $105 per credit part-time. *Room and board:* $7840. Room and board charges vary according to board plan and housing facility. *Payment plans:* installment, deferred payment. *Waivers:* minority students, senior citizens, and employees or children of employees.

Financial Aid Of all full-time matriculated undergraduates who enrolled in 2010, 6,411 applied for aid, 5,169 were judged to have need, 195 had their need fully met. In 2010, 279 non-need-based awards were made. *Average percent of need met:* 74%. *Average financial aid package:* $12,062. *Average need-based loan:* $4413. *Average need-based gift aid:* $5504. *Average non-need-based aid:* $1674. *Average indebtedness upon graduation:* $25,682.

Applying *Options:* electronic application, early admission, deferred entrance. *Application fee:* $30. *Required:* high school transcript, minimum 2.5 GPA. *Application deadlines:* rolling (freshmen), rolling (out-of-state freshmen), rolling (transfers). *Notification:* continuous (freshmen), continuous (out-of-state freshmen), continuous (transfers).

Freshman Application Contact Ms. Ronda Russell, Director of New Student Services, Montana State University, PO Box 172190, Bozeman, MT 59717-2190. *Phone:* 406-994-2452. *Toll-free phone:* 888-MSU-CATS. *Fax:* 406-994-1923. *E-mail:* admissions@montana.edu. *Web site:* http://www.montana.edu/.

Montana State University Billings

Billings, Montana

- **State-supported** comprehensive, founded 1927, part of Montana University System
- **Urban** 92-acre campus
- **Endowment** $15.6 million
- **Coed** 4,719 undergraduate students, 72% full-time, 61% women, 39% men
- **Moderately difficult** entrance level, 99% of applicants were admitted

Undergraduates 3,412 full-time, 1,307 part-time. Students come from 45 states and territories; 12 other countries; 8% are from out of state; 0.6% Black or African American, non-Hispanic/Latino; 4% Hispanic/Latino; 0.8% Asian, non-Hispanic/Latino; 0.1% Native Hawaiian or other Pacific Islander, non-Hispanic/Latino; 7% American Indian or Alaska Native, non-Hispanic/Latino; 0.7% Two or more races, non-Hispanic/Latino; 0.9% Race/ethnicity unknown; 2% international; 10% transferred in; 18% live on campus. *Retention:* 56% of full-time freshmen returned.

Freshmen *Admission:* 1,523 applied, 1,515 admitted, 865 enrolled. *Average high school GPA:* 3.2. *Test scores:* SAT critical reading scores over 500: 60%; SAT math scores over 500: 56%; ACT scores over 18: 86%; SAT critical reading scores over 600: 26%; SAT math scores over 600: 18%; ACT scores over 24: 26%; SAT critical reading scores over 700: 2%; ACT scores over 30: 2%.

Faculty *Total:* 343, 45% full-time. *Student/faculty ratio:* 19:1.

Academics *Calendar:* semesters. *Degrees:* certificates, associate, bachelor's, master's, and postbachelor's certificates. *Special study options:* academic remediation for entering students, accelerated degree program, adult/continuing education programs, advanced placement credit, cooperative education, distance learning, double majors, English as a second language, external degree program, honors programs, independent study, internships, off-campus study, part-time degree program, services for LD students, study abroad, summer session for credit. *ROTC:* Army (b).

Computers on Campus 1,500 computers/terminals and 1,500 ports are available on campus for general student use. Students can access the following: campus intranet, computer help desk, free student e-mail accounts, online (class) grades, online (class) registration, online (class) schedules, online degree programs. Campuswide network is available. 95% of college-owned or -operated housing units are wired for high-speed Internet access. Wireless service is available via classrooms, computer labs, dorm rooms, libraries, student centers.

Student Life *Housing:* on-campus residence required for freshman year. *Options:* coed, men-only, women-only, disabled students. Campus housing is university owned. Freshman applicants given priority for college housing. *Activities and organizations:* drama/theater group, student-run newspaper, radio station, choral group, Art Student League, Band Club, Inter-Varsity Christian Fellowship, Residence Hall Association, Student Council for Exceptional Children. *Campus security:* 24-hour emergency response devices and patrols, late-night transport/escort service, controlled dormitory access. *Student services:* health clinic, personal/psychological counseling, women's center, legal services.

Athletics Member NCAA. All Division II. *Intercollegiate sports:* baseball M, basketball M(s)/W(s), cross-country running M(s)/W(s), golf M/W, soccer M(s)/W(s), softball W, tennis M(s)/W(s), volleyball W(s). *Intramural sports:* baseball M/W, basketball M/W, bowling M/W, cheerleading M/W, cross-country running M/W, football M/W, golf M/W, racquetball M/W, skiing (cross-country) M/W, soccer M/W, softball M/W, swimming and diving M/W, table tennis M/W, tennis M/W, track and field M/W, volleyball M/W.

Standardized Tests *Required:* SAT or ACT (for admission).

Costs (2011–12) *Tuition:* state resident $4187 full-time, $140 per credit hour part-time; nonresident $15,961 full-time, $486 per credit hour part-time. Full-time tuition and fees vary according to course load, degree level, and location. Part-time tuition and fees vary according to course load, degree level, and location. *Required fees:* $1283 full-time. *Room and board:* $5960. Room and board charges vary according to board plan and housing facility. *Payment plan:* installment. *Waivers:* senior citizens and employees or children of employees.

Financial Aid Of all full-time matriculated undergraduates who enrolled in 2010, 2,749 applied for aid, 2,308 were judged to have need, 82 had their need fully met. 245 Federal Work-Study jobs (averaging $1280). 68 state and other part-time jobs (averaging $1675). In 2010, 82 non-need-based awards were made. *Average percent of need met:* 72%. *Average financial aid package:* $9930. *Average need-based loan:* $3507. *Average need-based gift aid:* $5104. *Average non-need-based aid:* $2348. *Average indebtedness upon graduation:* $28,447.

Applying *Options:* electronic application, early admission, deferred entrance. *Application fee:* $30. *Required:* high school transcript, minimum 2.5 GPA. *Application deadlines:* 7/1 (freshmen), rolling (transfers). *Notification:* continuous (freshmen), continuous (transfers).

Freshman Application Contact Ms. Shelly Andersen, Associate Director of Admissions, Montana State University Billings, 1500 University Drive, Billings, MT 59101. *Phone:* 406-657-2158. *Toll-free phone:* 800-565-6782. *Fax:* 406-657-2302. *E-mail:* sandersen@msubillings.edu. *Web site:* http://www.msubillings.edu/.

Montana State University–Northern
Havre, Montana

- **State-supported** comprehensive, founded 1929, part of Montana University System
- **Small-town** campus
- **Coed** 1,208 undergraduate students, 76% full-time, 50% women, 50% men
- **Moderately difficult** entrance level, 64% of applicants were admitted

Undergraduates 923 full-time, 285 part-time. 89% are from out of state; 0.9% Black or African American, non-Hispanic/Latino; 2% Hispanic/Latino; 1% Asian, non-Hispanic/Latino; 13% American Indian or Alaska Native, non-Hispanic/Latino; 6% Race/ethnicity unknown; 1% international; 15% transferred in; 22% live on campus. *Retention:* 58% of full-time freshmen returned.

Freshmen *Admission:* 378 applied, 242 admitted, 228 enrolled. *Average high school GPA:* 2.79. *Test scores:* SAT critical reading scores over 500: 41%; SAT math scores over 500: 47%; SAT writing scores over 500: 41%; ACT scores over 18: 66%; SAT critical reading scores over 600: 6%; SAT math scores over 600: 6%; SAT writing scores over 600: 6%; ACT scores over 24: 11%.

Faculty *Total:* 96, 65% full-time, 23% with terminal degrees. *Student/faculty ratio:* 15:1.

Academics *Calendar:* semesters. *Degrees:* certificates, diplomas, associate, bachelor's, and master's. *Special study options:* adult/continuing education programs, part-time degree program.

Computers on Campus Students can access the following: online (class) registration. Campuswide network is available.

Student Life *Housing:* on-campus residence required for freshman year. *Options:* coed.

Athletics Member NAIA. *Intercollegiate sports:* basketball M(s)/W(s), football M(s), golf W(s), volleyball W(s), wrestling M(s). *Intramural sports:* basketball M/W, bowling M/W, football M/W, golf M/W, gymnastics M/W, racquetball M/W, skiing (cross-country) M/W, skiing (downhill) M/W, soccer M/W, softball M/W, swimming and diving M/W, table tennis M/W, tennis M/W, track and field M/W, volleyball M/W, water polo M/W, weight lifting M/W.

Standardized Tests *Required:* SAT or ACT (for admission).

Costs (2012–13) *Tuition:* state resident $3765 full-time, $232 per credit hour part-time; nonresident $14,943 full-time, $635 per credit hour part-time. Full-time tuition and fees vary according to course level, course load, degree level, location, reciprocity agreements, and student level. Part-time tuition and fees vary according to course level, course load, degree level, location, reciprocity agreements, and student level. *Required fees:* $1305 full-time. *Room and board:* $6275; room only: $2147. Room and board charges vary according to board plan.

Financial Aid Of all full-time matriculated undergraduates who enrolled in 2010, 837 applied for aid, 749 were judged to have need, 17 had their need fully met. In 2010, 22 non-need-based awards were made. *Average percent of need met:* 63%. *Average financial aid package:* $10,428. *Average need-based loan:* $3956. *Average need-based gift aid:* $5282. *Average non-need-based aid:* $1735. *Average indebtedness upon graduation:* $20,350.

Applying *Options:* early admission, deferred entrance. *Application fee:* $30. *Required:* high school transcript. *Required for some:* minimum 2.0 GPA. *Application deadlines:* rolling (freshmen), rolling (transfers). *Notification:* continuous (freshmen), continuous (transfers).

Freshman Application Contact Montana State University–Northern, PO Box 7751, Havre, MT 59501-7751. *Phone:* 406-265-3704. *Toll-free phone:* 800-662-6132. *Web site:* http://www.msun.edu/.

Montana Tech of The University of Montana
Butte, Montana

- **State-supported** comprehensive, founded 1895, part of Montana University System
- **Small-town** 56-acre campus
- **Endowment** $25.4 million
- **Coed** 2,651 undergraduate students, 83% full-time, 41% women, 59% men
- **Moderately difficult** entrance level, 89% of applicants were admitted

Undergraduates 2,198 full-time, 453 part-time. Students come from 36 states and territories; 9 other countries; 12% are from out of state; 0.8% Black or African American, non-Hispanic/Latino; 2% Hispanic/Latino; 0.9% Asian, non-Hispanic/Latino; 2% American Indian or Alaska Native, non-Hispanic/Latino; 8% Race/ethnicity unknown; 7% international; 7% transferred in; 11% live on campus. *Retention:* 68% of full-time freshmen returned.

Freshmen *Admission:* 858 applied, 763 admitted, 486 enrolled. *Average high school GPA:* 3.39. *Test scores:* SAT critical reading scores over 500: 68%; SAT math scores over 500: 80%; SAT writing scores over 500: 59%; ACT scores over 18: 98%; SAT critical reading scores over 600: 24%; SAT math scores over 600: 42%; SAT writing scores over 600: 17%; ACT scores over 24: 56%; SAT critical reading scores over 700: 4%; SAT math scores over 700: 3%; SAT writing scores over 700: 1%; ACT scores over 30: 9%.

Faculty *Total:* 212, 63% full-time. *Student/faculty ratio:* 15:1.

Academics *Calendar:* semesters. *Degrees:* certificates, diplomas, associate, bachelor's, master's, and postbachelor's certificates. *Special study options:* academic remediation for entering students, adult/continuing education programs, advanced placement credit, cooperative education, distance learning, double majors, external degree program, honors programs, independent study, internships, part-time degree program, services for LD students, student-designed majors, summer session for credit. *Unusual degree programs:* engineering.

Computers on Campus 541 computers/terminals are available on campus for general student use. Students can access the following: campus intranet, computer help desk, free student e-mail accounts, online (class) grades, online (class) registration, online (class) schedules. Campuswide network is available. 100% of college-owned or -operated housing units are wired for high-speed Internet access. Wireless service is available via entire campus.

Student Life *Housing:* on-campus residence required for freshman year. *Options:* coed, disabled students. Campus housing is university owned. Freshman campus housing is guaranteed. *Activities and organizations:* student-run newspaper, radio station, choral group, Circle K, Ski/Snowboard Club, Health Physical Education Recreation Hooligans , Hockey Club, Dance Club. *Campus security:* 24-hour patrols, controlled dormitory access. *Student services:* health clinic, personal/psychological counseling.

Athletics Member NAIA. *Intercollegiate sports:* basketball M(s)/W(s), football M(s), golf M(s)/W(s), volleyball W(s). *Intramural sports:* basketball M/W, cheerleading M(c)/W(c), football M/W, ice hockey M(c)/W(c), racquetball M/W, rugby M(c)/W(c), skiing (cross-country) M(c)/W(c), skiing (downhill) M(c)/W(c), softball M(c)/W(c), volleyball M/W.

Standardized Tests *Required:* SAT or ACT (for admission).

Costs (2012–13) *Tuition:* state resident $4930 full-time, $273 per credit part-time; nonresident $16,606 full-time, $760 per credit part-time. Full-time tuition and fees vary according to course load, degree level, location, program, and student level. Part-time tuition and fees vary according to course load, degree level, location, program, and student level. *Required fees:* $1490 full-time. *Room and board:* $7266; room only: $3234. Room and board charges vary according to board plan. *Payment plans:* installment, deferred payment. *Waivers:* employees or children of employees.

Financial Aid Of all full-time matriculated undergraduates who enrolled in 2010, 1,636 applied for aid, 1,324 were judged to have need, 535 had their need fully met. In 2010, 249 non-need-based awards were made. *Average percent of need met:* 81%. *Average financial aid package:* $10,184. *Average need-based loan:* $3740. *Average need-based gift aid:* $5511. *Average non-need-based aid:* $2971. *Average indebtedness upon graduation:* $23,000.

Applying *Options:* electronic application, deferred entrance. *Application fee:* $30. *Required:* high school transcript, proof of immunization. *Required for some:* minimum 2.5 GPA. *Application deadlines:* rolling (freshmen), rolling (transfers). *Notification:* continuous (freshmen), continuous (transfers).

Freshman Application Contact Montana Tech of The University of Montana, 1300 West Park Street, Butte, MT 59701-8997. *Phone:* 406-496-4568. *Toll-free phone:* 800-445-TECH. *Web site:* http://www.mtech.edu/.

Rocky Mountain College
Billings, Montana

- **Independent interdenominational** comprehensive, founded 1878
- **Urban** 60-acre campus
- **Endowment** $21.7 million
- **Coed** 965 undergraduate students, 96% full-time, 51% women, 49% men
- **Moderately difficult** entrance level, 58% of applicants were admitted

Undergraduates 929 full-time, 36 part-time. Students come from 42 states and territories; 20 other countries; 43% are from out of state; 1% Black or African American, non-Hispanic/Latino; 4% Hispanic/Latino; 1% Asian, non-Hispanic/Latino; 0.2% Native Hawaiian or other Pacific Islander, non-Hispanic/Latino; 2% American Indian or Alaska Native, non-Hispanic/Latino; 1% Two or more races, non-Hispanic/Latino; 2% Race/ethnicity unknown; 5% international; 8% transferred in; 50% live on campus. *Retention:* 70% of full-time freshmen returned.

Freshmen *Admission:* 1,327 applied, 766 admitted, 228 enrolled. *Average high school GPA:* 3.43. *Test scores:* SAT critical reading scores over 500: 52%; SAT math scores over 500: 69%; SAT writing scores over 500: 47%; ACT scores over 18: 96%; SAT critical reading scores over 600: 12%; SAT math scores over 600: 18%; SAT writing scores over 600: 12%; ACT scores over 24: 46%; ACT scores over 30: 3%.

Faculty *Total:* 120, 53% full-time, 46% with terminal degrees. *Student/faculty ratio:* 12:1.

Academics *Calendar:* semesters. *Degrees:* associate, bachelor's, and master's. *Special study options:* academic remediation for entering students, accelerated degree program, adult/continuing education programs, advanced placement credit, distance learning, double majors, English as a second language, honors programs, independent study, internships, off-campus study, part-time degree program, services for LD students, student-designed majors, study abroad, summer session for credit. *ROTC:* Army (b). *Unusual degree programs:* 3-2 athletic training with Montana State University Billings.

Computers on Campus 129 computers/terminals are available on campus for general student use. Students can access the following: campus intranet, computer help desk, free student e-mail accounts, online (class) grades, online (class) registration, online (class) schedules. Campuswide network is available. 100% of college-owned or -operated housing units are wired for high-speed Internet access. Wireless service is available via entire campus.

Student Life *Housing:* on-campus residence required through sophomore year. *Options:* coed, disabled students. Campus housing is university owned. Freshman campus housing is guaranteed. *Activities and organizations:* drama/theater group, student-run newspaper, choral group, Outdoor Recreation/Climbing Club, Students in Free Enterprise (SIFE), Flight Team/Club, Residence Hall Association, OISTERS, Organization of Interested Students Toward Environmentally Responsible Solutions. *Campus security:* 24-hour emergency response devices, student patrols, late-night transport/escort service, controlled dormitory access, security cameras. *Student services:* health clinic, personal/psychological counseling.

Athletics Member NAIA. *Intercollegiate sports:* basketball M(s)/W(s), cheerleading W(s), cross-country running M(s)/W(s), equestrian sports M(c)/W(c), football M(s), golf M(s)/W(s), skiing (downhill) M(s)/W(s), soccer M(s)/W(s), volleyball W(s). *Intramural sports:* basketball M/W, football M, golf M/W, racquetball M/W, skiing (downhill) M/W, soccer M/W, softball M/W, tennis M/W, volleyball M/W.

Standardized Tests *Required:* SAT or ACT (for admission).

Costs (2012–13) *Comprehensive fee:* $30,014 includes full-time tuition ($22,442), mandatory fees ($450), and room and board ($7122). Full-time tuition and fees vary according to course load, degree level, and program. Part-time tuition: $935 per credit. Part-time tuition and fees vary according to course load, degree level, and program. *College room only:* $3362. Room and board charges vary according to board plan and housing facility. *Payment plan:* installment. *Waivers:* employees or children of employees.

Financial Aid Of all full-time matriculated undergraduates who enrolled in 2011, 768 applied for aid, 688 were judged to have need, 126 had their need fully met. 177 Federal Work-Study jobs (averaging $773). 182 state and other part-time jobs (averaging $1928). In 2011, 180 non-need-based awards were made. *Average percent of need met:* 74%. *Average financial aid package:* $19,087. *Average need-based loan:* $4479. *Average need-based gift aid:* $13,861. *Average non-need-based aid:* $9807. *Average indebtedness upon graduation:* $25,623.

Applying *Options:* electronic application, early admission, early action, deferred entrance. *Application fee:* $35. *Required:* high school transcript, minimum 2.5 GPA. *Required for some:* essay or personal statement, 2 letters of recommendation, interview. *Application deadlines:* rolling (freshmen), rolling (transfers). *Notification:* continuous (freshmen), continuous (transfers).

Freshman Application Contact Kelly Edwards, Rocky Mountain College, 1511 Poly Drive, Vice President for Enrollment Services, Director of Admissions, Billings, MT 59102. *Phone:* 406-657-1026. *Toll-free phone:* 800-877-6259. *Fax:* 406-259-9751. *E-mail:* admissions@rocky.edu. *Web site:* http://www.rocky.edu/.

Salish Kootenai College
Pablo, Montana

Freshman Application Contact Ms. Jackie Moran, Admissions Officer, Salish Kootenai College, PO Box 70, Pablo, MT 59855-0117. *Phone:* 406-275-4866. *Fax:* 406-275-4810. *E-mail:* jackie_moran@skc.edu. *Web site:* http://www.skc.edu/.

University of Great Falls
Great Falls, Montana

- **Independent Roman Catholic** comprehensive, founded 1932
- **Urban** 40-acre campus
- **Coed** 1,005 undergraduate students, 67% full-time, 66% women, 34% men
- **Noncompetitive** entrance level, 27% of applicants were admitted

Undergraduates 674 full-time, 331 part-time. 43% are from out of state; 2% Black or African American, non-Hispanic/Latino; 4% Hispanic/Latino; 2% Asian, non-Hispanic/Latino; 0.5% Native Hawaiian or other Pacific Islander,

non-Hispanic/Latino; 3% American Indian or Alaska Native, non-Hispanic/Latino; 3% Two or more races, non-Hispanic/Latino; 6% Race/ethnicity unknown; 16% transferred in; 34% live on campus. *Retention:* 52% of full-time freshmen returned.

Freshmen *Admission:* 723 applied, 198 admitted, 169 enrolled. *Average high school GPA:* 3.23. *Test scores:* SAT writing scores over 500: 39%; ACT scores over 18: 82%; SAT writing scores over 600: 12%; ACT scores over 24: 30%; ACT scores over 30: 2%.

Faculty *Total:* 114, 37% full-time, 39% with terminal degrees. *Student/faculty ratio:* 13:1.

Academics *Calendar:* semesters. *Degrees:* certificates, associate, bachelor's, and master's. *Special study options:* adult/continuing education programs, part-time degree program.

Computers on Campus Students can access the following: campus intranet, computer help desk, free student e-mail accounts, online (class) grades, online (class) registration, online (class) schedules. Campuswide network is available. Wireless service is available via classrooms, computer centers, computer labs, dorm rooms, learning centers, libraries, student centers.

Student Life *Housing:* on-campus residence required through sophomore year. *Options:* coed. Campus housing is university owned and leased by the school. Freshman campus housing is guaranteed. *Campus security:* 24-hour emergency response devices and patrols, late-night transport/escort service, controlled dormitory access.

Athletics Member NAIA. *Intercollegiate sports:* basketball M(s)/W(s), cheerleading M(s)/W(s), cross-country running M/W, equestrian sports M(s)/W(s), golf M(s)/W(s), soccer M(s)/W(s), softball W, track and field M(s)/W(s), volleyball W(s), wrestling M(s). *Intramural sports:* basketball M/W, equestrian sports M/W(c), football M/W, golf M/W, skiing (downhill) M/W, soccer M/W, softball W, table tennis M/W, track and field M/W, ultimate Frisbee M/W, volleyball M/W, wrestling M.

Standardized Tests *Required:* SAT or ACT (for admission). *Recommended:* SAT Subject Tests (for admission).

Costs (2011–12) *One-time required fee:* $150. *Comprehensive fee:* $26,502 includes full-time tuition ($18,480), mandatory fees ($1100), and room and board ($6922). Full-time tuition and fees vary according to course load. Part-time tuition: $586 per credit hour. Part-time tuition and fees vary according to course load, location, and program. *College room only:* $3722. Room and board charges vary according to housing facility.

Financial Aid Of all full-time matriculated undergraduates who enrolled in 2011, 593 applied for aid, 551 were judged to have need, 10 had their need fully met. In 2011, 59 non-need-based awards were made. *Average percent of need met:* 67%. *Average financial aid package:* $16,200. *Average need-based loan:* $3976. *Average need-based gift aid:* $8980. *Average non-need-based aid:* $6223.

Applying *Options:* electronic application, early admission, deferred entrance. *Application fee:* $35. *Required:* high school transcript. *Recommended:* essay or personal statement, interview. *Application deadlines:* 9/1 (freshmen), rolling (transfers). *Notification:* continuous (freshmen), continuous (transfers).

Freshman Application Contact Kelly Braun, Assistant Director of Admissions, University of Great Falls, 1301 20th Street South, Great Falls, MT 59405. *Phone:* 406-791-5202 Ext. 5211. *Toll-free phone:* 800-856-9544. *Fax:* 406-791-5209. *E-mail:* enroll@ugf.edu. *Web site:* http://www.ugf.edu/.

The University of Montana
Missoula, Montana

Freshman Application Contact Ms. Juana Alcala, Manager, Enrollment Services, The University of Montana, Missoula, MT 59812-0002. *Phone:* 406-243-6266. *Toll-free phone:* 800-462-8636. *Fax:* 406-243-5711. *E-mail:* admiss@umontana.edu. *Web site:* http://www.umt.edu/.

The University of Montana Western
Dillon, Montana

- **State-supported** 4-year, founded 1893, part of Montana University System
- **Small-town** 30-acre campus
- **Endowment** $3.5 million
- **Coed** 1,379 undergraduate students, 86% full-time, 58% women, 42% men
- **Minimally difficult** entrance level, 75% of applicants were admitted

Undergraduates 1,185 full-time, 194 part-time. Students come from 35 states and territories; 3 other countries; 22% are from out of state; 0.9% Black or African American, non-Hispanic/Latino; 2% Hispanic/Latino; 0.2% Asian, non-Hispanic/Latino; 2% Native Hawaiian or other Pacific Islander, non-Hispanic/Latino; 2% American Indian or Alaska Native, non-Hispanic/Latino; 0.9% Two or more races, non-Hispanic/Latino; 4% Race/ethnicity unknown;

0.1% international; 10% transferred in; 25% live on campus. *Retention:* 70% of full-time freshmen returned.

Freshmen *Admission:* 522 applied, 393 admitted, 264 enrolled. *Average high school GPA:* 3. *Test scores:* SAT critical reading scores over 500: 40%; SAT math scores over 500: 40%; ACT scores over 18: 72%; SAT critical reading scores over 600: 18%; SAT math scores over 600: 19%; ACT scores over 24: 19%; SAT critical reading scores over 700: 1%; SAT math scores over 700: 1%; ACT scores over 30: 3%.

Faculty *Total:* 91, 76% full-time, 67% with terminal degrees. *Student/faculty ratio:* 18:1.

Academics *Calendar:* semesters. *Degrees:* certificates, associate, bachelor's, and postbachelor's certificates. *Special study options:* academic remediation for entering students, advanced placement credit, cooperative education, distance learning, double majors, honors programs, independent study, internships, off-campus study, part-time degree program, services for LD students, study abroad, summer session for credit.

Computers on Campus 140 computers/terminals are available on campus for general student use. Students can access the following: computer help desk, free student e-mail accounts, online (class) grades, online (class) registration, online (class) schedules. Campuswide network is available. Wireless service is available via entire campus.

Student Life *Housing:* on-campus residence required for freshman year. *Options:* coed, men-only, women-only, disabled students. Campus housing is university owned. Freshman campus housing is guaranteed. *Activities and organizations:* drama/theater group, student-run radio station, choral group, Chi Alpha, Equestrian, Humans in Performance, Polynesian Club, Rodeo Club. *Campus security:* 24-hour emergency response devices and patrols, student patrols, late-night transport/escort service. *Student services:* health clinic, personal/psychological counseling.

Athletics Member NAIA. *Intercollegiate sports:* basketball M(s)/W(s), equestrian sports M(s)/W(s), football M(s), volleyball W(s). *Intramural sports:* basketball M/W, equestrian sports M(c)/W(c), football M/W, racquetball M/W, rock climbing M(c)/W(c), rugby M(c)/W(c), skiing (downhill) M(c)/W(c), softball M/W, ultimate Frisbee M/W, volleyball M/W, wrestling M(c).

Standardized Tests *Required:* SAT or ACT (for admission).

Costs (2011–12) *Tuition:* state resident $2942 full-time, $123 per credit hour part-time; nonresident $11,903 full-time, $529 per credit hour part-time. Full-time tuition and fees vary according to course load, location, program, reciprocity agreements, and student level. Part-time tuition and fees vary according to course load, location, program, reciprocity agreements, and student level. *Required fees:* $15 per credit hour part-time, $122 per term part-time. *Room and board:* $5834; room only: $2264. Room and board charges vary according to housing facility. *Payment plan:* deferred payment. *Waivers:* senior citizens and employees or children of employees.

Financial Aid Of all full-time matriculated undergraduates who enrolled in 2008, 881 applied for aid, 741 were judged to have need, 20 had their need fully met. 79 Federal Work-Study jobs (averaging $2808). 126 state and other part-time jobs (averaging $2382). In 2008, 5 non-need-based awards were made. *Average percent of need met:* 17%. *Average financial aid package:* $2858. *Average need-based loan:* $3774. *Average need-based gift aid:* $2525. *Average non-need-based aid:* $1786. *Average indebtedness upon graduation:* $21,969.

Applying *Options:* electronic application, early admission, deferred entrance. *Application fee:* $30. *Required:* high school transcript, MMR, ACT or SAT, high school self report form. *Application deadlines:* rolling (freshmen), rolling (transfers). *Notification:* continuous (freshmen), continuous (transfers).

Freshman Application Contact Mrs. Janet Jones, Admissions Evaluator, The University of Montana Western, 710 South Atlantic, Dillon, MT 59725. *Phone:* 406-683-7331. *Toll-free phone:* 877-683-7331. *E-mail:* j_jones@umwestern.edu. *Web site:* http://www.umwestern.edu/.

NEBRASKA

Bellevue University

Bellevue, Nebraska

- **Independent** comprehensive, founded 1965
- **Suburban** 50-acre campus with easy access to Omaha
- **Endowment** $43.6 million
- **Coed** 6,828 undergraduate students, 73% full-time, 48% women, 52% men
- **Noncompetitive** entrance level

Undergraduates 4,978 full-time, 1,850 part-time. Students come from 53 states and territories; 34 other countries; 50% are from out of state; 13% Black or African American, non-Hispanic/Latino; 7% Hispanic/Latino; 2% Asian, non-Hispanic/Latino; 0.4% Native Hawaiian or other Pacific Islander, non-

Hispanic/Latino; 0.7% American Indian or Alaska Native, non-Hispanic/Latino; 1% Two or more races, non-Hispanic/Latino; 18% Race/ethnicity unknown; 2% international. *Retention:* 50% of full-time freshmen returned.

Freshmen *Admission:* 139 enrolled.

Faculty *Total:* 411, 22% full-time, 29% with terminal degrees. *Student/faculty ratio:* 40:1.

Academics *Calendar:* semesters for day division, trimesters for evening division. *Degrees:* bachelor's, master's, and doctoral. *Special study options:* academic remediation for entering students, accelerated degree program, adult/continuing education programs, advanced placement credit, distance learning, double majors, English as a second language, external degree program, independent study, internships, off-campus study, part-time degree program, services for LD students, study abroad, summer session for credit. *ROTC:* Army (c), Air Force (c).

Computers on Campus 470 computers/terminals are available on campus for general student use. Students can access the following: campus intranet, computer help desk, free student e-mail accounts, online (class) registration. Campuswide network is available. Wireless service is available via entire campus.

Student Life *Housing:* college housing not available. *Activities and organizations:* International Student Organization, Multicultural Club, Student Advisory Council, Student Veterans Organization, Institute of Management Accountants. *Campus security:* 24-hour emergency response devices.

Athletics Member NAIA.

Costs (2012–13) *Tuition:* $7500 full-time, $250 per credit hour part-time. Full-time tuition and fees vary according to course load. Part-time tuition and fees vary according to course load. *Required fees:* $200 full-time, $100 per term part-time. *Payment plan:* installment. *Waivers:* employees or children of employees.

Financial Aid Of all full-time matriculated undergraduates who enrolled in 2003, 2,477 applied for aid, 2,477 were judged to have need. 44 Federal Work-Study jobs (averaging $1793). In 2003, 912 non-need-based awards were made. *Average financial aid package:* $4107. *Average need-based loan:* $3326. *Average need-based gift aid:* $2325. *Average non-need-based aid:* $1134.

Applying *Options:* electronic application, deferred entrance. *Application fee:* $50. *Required:* high school transcript. *Application deadlines:* rolling (freshmen), rolling (transfers).

Freshman Application Contact Nick Baker, Director of Undergraduate Enrollment, Bellevue University, 1000 Galvin Road South, Bellevue, NE 68005-3098. *Phone:* 402-557-7250. *Toll-free phone:* 800-756-7920. *E-mail:* nick.baker@bellevue.edu. *Web site:* http://www.bellevue.edu/.

Chadron State College

Chadron, Nebraska

Freshman Application Contact Ms. Tena Cook, Director of Admissions, Chadron State College, 1000 Main Street, Chadron, NE 69337-2690. *Phone:* 308-432-6263. *Toll-free phone:* 800-242-3766. *Fax:* 308-432-6229. *E-mail:* inquire@csc.edu. *Web site:* http://www.csc.edu/.

Clarkson College

Omaha, Nebraska

- **Independent** comprehensive, founded 1888
- **Urban** 3-acre campus
- **Endowment** $937,115
- **Coed, primarily women** 658 undergraduate students, 100% full-time, 90% women, 10% men
- **Moderately difficult** entrance level, 55% of applicants were admitted

Undergraduates 658 full-time. Students come from 33 states and territories; 33% are from out of state; 438% transferred in; 14% live on campus. *Retention:* 85% of full-time freshmen returned.

Freshmen *Admission:* 87 applied, 48 admitted, 39 enrolled. *Test scores:* ACT scores over 18: 91%; ACT scores over 24: 30%.

Faculty *Total:* 101, 48% full-time. *Student/faculty ratio:* 8:1.

Academics *Calendar:* semesters. *Degrees:* certificates, associate, bachelor's, master's, and post-master's certificates. *Special study options:* accelerated degree program, adult/continuing education programs, advanced placement credit, cooperative education, distance learning, double majors, external degree program, independent study, internships, part-time degree program, study abroad, summer session for credit. *ROTC:* Army (c), Air Force (c).

Computers on Campus 40 computers/terminals are available on campus for general student use. Students can access the following: campus intranet, computer help desk, free student e-mail accounts, online (class) grades, online (class) registration, online (class) schedules. Campuswide network is available. 100% of college-owned or -operated housing units are wired for high-speed Internet access. Wireless service is available via entire campus.

Student Life *Housing options:* coed. Campus housing is university owned. *Activities and organizations:* student-run newspaper, Student Nurses Association, Radiology Student Association, Student Government Association, Student Ambassadors, Physical Therapist Assistant Student Association. *Campus security:* 24-hour emergency response devices and patrols, student patrols, late-night transport/escort service, controlled dormitory access. *Student services:* health clinic, personal/psychological counseling.

Athletics *Intramural sports:* bowling M/W, volleyball M/W.

Standardized Tests *Required for some:* SAT or ACT (for admission).

Financial Aid Of all full-time matriculated undergraduates who enrolled in 2001, 109 applied for aid, 94 were judged to have need, 22 had their need fully met. 40 Federal Work-Study jobs (averaging $2500). In 2001, 15 non-need-based awards were made. *Average percent of need met:* 71%. *Average financial aid package:* $8291. *Average need-based loan:* $3365. *Average need-based gift aid:* $5434. *Average non-need-based aid:* $4374. *Average indebtedness upon graduation:* $13,931.

Applying *Options:* electronic application, deferred entrance. *Application fee:* $35. *Required:* essay or personal statement, high school transcript, minimum 2.5 GPA. *Required for some:* minimum 3.0 GPA, 2 letters of recommendation. *Recommended:* minimum 3.0 GPA. *Application deadlines:* rolling (freshmen), rolling (out-of-state freshmen), rolling (transfers). *Notification:* continuous (freshmen), continuous (out-of-state freshmen), continuous (transfers).

Freshman Application Contact Clarkson College, 101 South 42nd Street, Omaha, NE 68131-2739. *Phone:* 402-552-3100. *Toll-free phone:* 800-647-5500. *Web site:* http://www.clarksoncollege.edu/.

College of Saint Mary
Omaha, Nebraska

- **Independent Roman Catholic** comprehensive, founded 1923
- **Urban** 25-acre campus
- **Endowment** $6.8 million
- **Women only** 820 undergraduate students, 80% full-time
- **Minimally difficult** entrance level, 46% of applicants were admitted

Undergraduates 659 full-time, 161 part-time. Students come from 22 states and territories; 7 other countries; 14% are from out of state; 8% Black or African American, non-Hispanic/Latino; 12% Hispanic/Latino; 1% Asian, non-Hispanic/Latino; 0.4% Native Hawaiian or other Pacific Islander, non-Hispanic/Latino; 0.5% American Indian or Alaska Native, non-Hispanic/Latino; 1% Two or more races, non-Hispanic/Latino; 2% Race/ethnicity unknown; 0.5% international; 15% transferred in; 34% live on campus. *Retention:* 60% of full-time freshmen returned.

Freshmen *Admission:* 398 applied, 184 admitted, 88 enrolled. *Average high school GPA:* 3.36. *Test scores:* ACT scores over 18: 99%; ACT scores over 24: 27%.

Faculty *Total:* 169, 36% full-time, 36% with terminal degrees. *Student/faculty ratio:* 9:1.

Academics *Calendar:* semesters. *Degrees:* certificates, associate, bachelor's, master's, doctoral, postbachelor's, and first professional certificates. *Special study options:* academic remediation for entering students, accelerated degree program, advanced placement credit, distance learning, double majors, honors programs, independent study, internships, part-time degree program, services for LD students, study abroad, summer session for credit. *ROTC:* Army (c), Air Force (c). *Unusual degree programs:* 3-2 engineering with University of Nebraska - Omaha.

Computers on Campus 170 computers/terminals and 300 ports are available on campus for general student use. Students can access the following: campus intranet, computer help desk, free student e-mail accounts, online (class) grades, online (class) registration, online (class) schedules. Campuswide network is available. 100% of college-owned or -operated housing units are wired for high-speed Internet access. Wireless service is available via entire campus.

Student Life *Housing:* on-campus residence required through sophomore year. *Options:* women-only. Campus housing is university owned. Freshman campus housing is guaranteed. *Activities and organizations:* drama/theater group, choral group, Students Against Violence (SAV), Campus Activities Board, Student Education Association of Nebraska, Student Occupational Therapy Club, Student Nurses Association. *Campus security:* 24-hour emergency response devices and patrols, late-night transport/escort service, controlled dormitory access, surveillance cameras at residence hall entrances; CSM Alert Text Message System. *Student services:* health clinic, personal/psychological counseling.

Athletics Member NAIA. *Intercollegiate sports:* basketball W(s), cross-country running W(s), golf W(s), soccer W(s), softball W(s), swimming and diving W(s), volleyball W(s). *Intramural sports:* basketball W, bowling W, volleyball W, water polo W.

Standardized Tests *Required:* Students graduating high school within the past five years with less than 12 transfer credits are required to submit ACT scores. The minimum ACT score for admission is 18 (for admission).

Costs (2012–13) *Comprehensive fee:* $32,110 includes full-time tuition ($24,830), mandatory fees ($480), and room and board ($6800). Full-time tuition and fees vary according to location and program. Part-time tuition: $825 per credit. Part-time tuition and fees vary according to class time, course load, location, and program. *Required fees:* $16 per credit part-time. *Payment plans:* installment, deferred payment. *Waivers:* senior citizens and employees or children of employees.

Financial Aid Of all full-time matriculated undergraduates who enrolled in 2011, 677 applied for aid, 648 were judged to have need, 43 had their need fully met. 177 Federal Work-Study jobs (averaging $1533). 9 state and other part-time jobs (averaging $7144). In 2011, 28 non-need-based awards were made. *Average percent of need met:* 61%. *Average financial aid package:* $17,126. *Average need-based loan:* $5803. *Average need-based gift aid:* $11,563. *Average non-need-based aid:* $7422. *Average indebtedness upon graduation:* $31,327.

Applying *Options:* electronic application. *Application fee:* $30. *Required:* high school transcript, minimum 2.0 GPA. *Required for some:* essay or personal statement, 2 letters of recommendation, interview. *Application deadlines:* rolling (freshmen), rolling (transfers). *Notification:* continuous (freshmen), continuous (transfers).

Freshman Application Contact Ms. Jamie Hilz, High School Admissions Counselor, College of Saint Mary, 7000 Mercy Road, Omaha, NE 68106. *Phone:* 402-399-2425. *Toll-free phone:* 800-926-5534. *Fax:* 402-399-2412. *E-mail:* enroll@csm.edu. *Web site:* http://www.csm.edu/.

Concordia University, Nebraska
Seward, Nebraska

- **Independent** comprehensive, founded 1894, affiliated with Lutheran Church–Missouri Synod
- **Small-town** 120-acre campus with easy access to Omaha
- **Endowment** $34.6 million
- **Coed** 1,552 undergraduate students, 74% full-time, 52% women, 48% men
- **Moderately difficult** entrance level, 69% of applicants were admitted

Undergraduates 1,153 full-time, 399 part-time. Students come from 41 states and territories; 8 other countries; 53% are from out of state; 3% Black or African American, non-Hispanic/Latino; 2% Hispanic/Latino; 0.5% Asian, non-Hispanic/Latino; 0.5% Native Hawaiian or other Pacific Islander, non-Hispanic/Latino; 0.2% American Indian or Alaska Native, non-Hispanic/Latino; 1% Two or more races, non-Hispanic/Latino; 3% Race/ethnicity unknown; 0.7% international; 3% transferred in; 71% live on campus. *Retention:* 81% of full-time freshmen returned.

Freshmen *Admission:* 1,397 applied, 959 admitted, 315 enrolled. *Average high school GPA:* 3.54. *Test scores:* SAT critical reading scores over 500: 68%; SAT math scores over 500: 75%; ACT scores over 18: 97%; SAT critical reading scores over 600: 25%; SAT math scores over 600: 32%; ACT scores over 24: 54%; SAT critical reading scores over 700: 4%; SAT math scores over 700: 7%; ACT scores over 30: 9%.

Faculty *Total:* 178, 33% full-time, 42% with terminal degrees. *Student/faculty ratio:* 14:1.

Academics *Calendar:* 4-4-1. *Degrees:* certificates, bachelor's, master's, and postbachelor's certificates. *Special study options:* academic remediation for entering students, accelerated degree program, adult/continuing education programs, advanced placement credit, distance learning, double majors, English as a second language, independent study, internships, off-campus study, part-time degree program, services for LD students, study abroad, summer session for credit. *ROTC:* Army (c), Air Force (c).

Computers on Campus 220 computers/terminals and 1,508 ports are available on campus for general student use. Students can access the following: campus intranet, computer help desk, free student e-mail accounts, online (class) grades, online (class) registration, online (class) schedules, academic plans, human resource data. Campuswide network is available. 100% of college-owned or -operated housing units are wired for high-speed Internet access. Wireless service is available via entire campus.

Student Life *Housing:* on-campus residence required through junior year. *Options:* men-only, women-only, disabled students. Campus housing is university owned. Freshman campus housing is guaranteed. *Activities and organizations:* drama/theater group, student-run newspaper, choral group, Student Activities Council, Musical Groups, Curtain/Drama Club, Student Senate, Concordia Youth Ministry. *Campus security:* 24-hour emergency response devices and patrols, controlled dormitory access. *Student services:* health clinic, personal/psychological counseling.

Athletics Member NAIA. *Intercollegiate sports:* baseball M(s), basketball M(s)/W(s), cross-country running M(s)/W(s), football M(s), golf M(s)/W(s), soccer M(s)/W(s), softball W(s), tennis M(s)/W(s), track and field M(s)/W(s), volleyball W(s), wrestling M(s). *Intramural sports:* badminton M/W, basket-

ball M/W, bowling M/W, cross-country running M/W, soccer M/W, softball M/W, table tennis M/W, tennis M/W, volleyball M/W.

Standardized Tests *Required:* SAT or ACT (for admission).

Costs (2012–13) *Comprehensive fee:* $30,240 includes full-time tuition ($23,550), mandatory fees ($250), and room and board ($6440). Part-time tuition: $735 per credit hour. *College room only:* $2650. Room and board charges vary according to board plan and housing facility. *Payment plan:* installment. *Waivers:* employees or children of employees.

Financial Aid Of all full-time matriculated undergraduates who enrolled in 2010, 984 applied for aid, 863 were judged to have need, 223 had their need fully met. 111 Federal Work-Study jobs (averaging $917). In 2010, 124 non-need-based awards were made. *Average percent of need met:* 78%. *Average financial aid package:* $17,502. *Average need-based loan:* $4420. *Average need-based gift aid:* $13,518. *Average non-need-based aid:* $10,575. *Average indebtedness upon graduation:* $22,586.

Applying *Options:* deferred entrance. *Required:* high school transcript. *Recommended:* interview. *Application deadlines:* 8/1 (freshmen), 8/1 (transfers). *Notification:* continuous (freshmen), continuous (transfers).

Freshman Application Contact Mr. Aaron W. Roberts, Director of Undergraduate Recruitment, Concordia University, Nebraska, 800 North Columbia Avenue, Seward, NE 68434-1556. *Phone:* 800-535-5494 Ext. 7233. *Toll-free phone:* 800-535-5494. *Fax:* 402-643-4073. *E-mail:* admiss@cune.edu. *Web site:* http://www.cune.edu/.

Creative Center

Omaha, Nebraska

- **Proprietary** primarily 2-year, founded 1993
- **Urban** 2-acre campus
- **Coed**

Faculty *Total:* 18, 22% full-time. *Student/faculty ratio:* 13:1.

Academics *Calendar:* semesters. *Degrees:* associate and bachelor's. *Special study options:* distance learning, part-time degree program, services for LD students.

Computers on Campus 8 computers/terminals are available on campus for general student use. Students can access the following: computer help desk. Campuswide network is available. Wireless service is available via entire campus.

Student Life *Housing:* college housing not available.

Costs (2011–12) *Tuition:* $23,600 full-time. Full-time tuition and fees vary according to course load, program, and student level. Part-time tuition and fees vary according to course load, program, and student level.

Applying *Application fee:* $100. *Required:* essay or personal statement, high school transcript, 1 letter of recommendation, interview, portfolio. *Application deadlines:* rolling (freshmen), rolling (out-of-state freshmen), rolling (transfers). *Notification:* continuous (freshmen), continuous (out-of-state freshmen), continuous (transfers).

Freshman Application Contact Mr. Richard Caldwell, Director of Admissions, Creative Center, 10850 Emmet Street, Omaha, NE 68164. *Phone:* 402-898-1000 Ext. 216. *Toll-free phone:* 888-898-1789. *Fax:* 402-898-1301. *E-mail:* rich_c@creativecenter.edu. *Web site:* http://www.creativecenter.edu/.

Creighton University

Omaha, Nebraska

- **Independent Roman Catholic (Jesuit)** university, founded 1878
- **Urban** 130-acre campus with easy access to Omaha
- **Endowment** $300.4 million
- **Coed** 4,153 undergraduate students, 94% full-time, 60% women, 40% men
- **Moderately difficult** entrance level, 78% of applicants were admitted

Undergraduates 3,907 full-time, 246 part-time. Students come from 54 states and territories; 38 other countries; 66% are from out of state; 3% Black or African American, non-Hispanic/Latino; 6% Hispanic/Latino; 10% Asian, non-Hispanic/Latino; 0.3% Native Hawaiian or other Pacific Islander, non-Hispanic/Latino; 0.7% American Indian or Alaska Native, non-Hispanic/Latino; 3% Two or more races, non-Hispanic/Latino; 2% Race/ethnicity unknown; 2% international; 1% transferred in; 56% live on campus. *Retention:* 88% of full-time freshmen returned.

Freshmen *Admission:* 5,104 applied, 3,971 admitted, 978 enrolled. *Average high school GPA:* 3.77. *Test scores:* SAT critical reading scores over 500: 83%; SAT math scores over 500: 90%; SAT writing scores over 500: 82%; ACT scores over 18: 99%; SAT critical reading scores over 600: 41%; SAT math scores over 600: 54%; SAT writing scores over 600: 37%; ACT scores over 24: 82%; SAT critical reading scores over 700: 10%; SAT math scores over 700: 13%; SAT writing scores over 700: 7%; ACT scores over 30: 28%.

Faculty *Total:* 772, 68% full-time, 69% with terminal degrees. *Student/faculty ratio:* 12:1.

Academics *Calendar:* semesters. *Degrees:* certificates, diplomas, associate, bachelor's, master's, doctoral, post-master's, postbachelor's, and first professional certificates. *Special study options:* academic remediation for entering students, accelerated degree program, adult/continuing education programs, advanced placement credit, distance learning, double majors, English as a second language, external degree program, freshman honors college, honors programs, independent study, internships, off-campus study, part-time degree program, services for LD students, study abroad, summer session for credit. *ROTC:* Army (b), Air Force (c). *Unusual degree programs:* 3-2 engineering with University of Detroit Mercy.

Computers on Campus 550 computers/terminals are available on campus for general student use. Students can access the following: campus intranet, computer help desk, free student e-mail accounts, online (class) grades, online (class) registration, online (class) schedules, financial aid information. Campuswide network is available. 100% of college-owned or -operated housing units are wired for high-speed Internet access. Wireless service is available via entire campus.

Student Life *Housing:* on-campus residence required through sophomore year. *Options:* coed, women-only, disabled students. Campus housing is university owned. Freshman campus housing is guaranteed. *Activities and organizations:* drama/theater group, student-run newspaper, choral group, Birdcage (Athletic Boosters), Pre-Medical Society, Student Nurses Association, Alpha Kappa Psi (business majors), Omicron Delta Kappa (Greek Leadership), national fraternities, national sororities. *Campus security:* 24-hour emergency response devices and patrols, student patrols, late-night transport/escort service, controlled dormitory access. *Student services:* health clinic, personal/psychological counseling, women's center.

Athletics Member NCAA. All Division I. *Intercollegiate sports:* baseball M(s), basketball M(s)/W(s), crew W(s), cross-country running M(s)/W(s), golf M(s)/W(s), soccer M(s)/W(s), softball W(s), tennis M(s)/W(s), volleyball W(s). *Intramural sports:* basketball M/W, crew M(c), football M/W, golf M/W, lacrosse M(c), racquetball M/W, rugby M(c), soccer M/W, tennis M/W, ultimate Frisbee M/W, volleyball M/W, weight lifting M(c)/W(c).

Standardized Tests *Required:* SAT or ACT (for admission).

Costs (2011–12) *Comprehensive fee:* $41,132 includes full-time tuition ($30,484), mandatory fees ($1410), and room and board ($9238). Full-time tuition and fees vary according to course load, degree level, program, and reciprocity agreements. Part-time tuition: $952 per credit hour. Part-time tuition and fees vary according to course load, degree level, program, and reciprocity agreements. *Required fees:* $136 per degree program part-time. *College room only:* $5262. Room and board charges vary according to board plan and housing facility. *Payment plan:* installment. *Waivers:* adult students and employees or children of employees.

Financial Aid Of all full-time matriculated undergraduates who enrolled in 2011, 2,769 applied for aid, 2,362 were judged to have need, 874 had their need fully met. 936 Federal Work-Study jobs (averaging $2045). In 2011, 1138 non-need-based awards were made. *Average percent of need met:* 88%. *Average financial aid package:* $26,320. *Average need-based loan:* $5775. *Average need-based gift aid:* $20,850. *Average non-need-based aid:* $13,561. *Average indebtedness upon graduation:* $33,901.

Applying *Options:* electronic application, deferred entrance. *Application fee:* $40. *Required:* essay or personal statement, high school transcript, minimum 2.8 GPA, 1 letter of recommendation. *Application deadlines:* 2/15 (freshmen), 8/1 (transfers). *Notification:* continuous (freshmen), continuous (transfers).

Freshman Application Contact Ms. Sarah Richardson, Director of Admissions and Scholarships, Creighton University, 2500 California Plaza, Omaha, NE 68178-0001. *Phone:* 402-280-2703. *Toll-free phone:* 800-282-5835. *Fax:* 402-280-2685. *E-mail:* williampierce@creighton.edu. *Web site:* http://www.creighton.edu/.

Doane College

Crete, Nebraska

- **Independent** comprehensive, founded 1872, affiliated with United Church of Christ
- **Small-town** 300-acre campus with easy access to Omaha
- **Endowment** $78.3 million
- **Coed** 1,066 undergraduate students, 99% full-time, 52% women, 48% men
- **Moderately difficult** entrance level, 78% of applicants were admitted

Undergraduates 1,059 full-time, 7 part-time. Students come from 28 states and territories; 6 other countries; 18% are from out of state; 3% Black or African American, non-Hispanic/Latino; 5% Hispanic/Latino; 1% Asian, non-Hispanic/Latino; 0.3% Native Hawaiian or other Pacific Islander, non-Hispanic/Latino; 0.4% American Indian or Alaska Native, non-Hispanic/Latino; 1% Two or more races, non-Hispanic/Latino; 2% Race/ethnicity unknown; 1%

international; 3% transferred in; 82% live on campus. *Retention:* 74% of full-time freshmen returned.

Freshmen *Admission:* 1,462 applied, 1,144 admitted, 291 enrolled. *Average high school GPA:* 3.47. *Test scores:* ACT scores over 18: 93%; ACT scores over 24: 45%; ACT scores over 30: 6%.

Faculty *Total:* 117, 62% full-time. *Student/faculty ratio:* 12:1.

Academics *Calendar:* 4-1-4. *Degrees:* bachelor's and master's (non-traditional undergraduate programs and graduate programs offered at Lincoln campus). *Special study options:* advanced placement credit, cooperative education, double majors, English as a second language, honors programs, independent study, internships, off-campus study, student-designed majors, study abroad, summer session for credit. *ROTC:* Army (c), Air Force (c). *Unusual degree programs:* 3-2 engineering with Columbia University, Washington University in St. Louis; forestry with Duke University; environmental studies with Duke University.

Computers on Campus 250 computers/terminals and 1,000 ports are available on campus for general student use. Students can access the following: campus intranet, computer help desk, free student e-mail accounts, online (class) grades, online (class) registration, online (class) schedules. Campus-wide network is available. 100% of college-owned or -operated housing units are wired for high-speed Internet access. Wireless service is available via entire campus.

Student Life *Housing:* on-campus residence required through senior year. *Options:* coed, women-only. Campus housing is university owned. Freshman campus housing is guaranteed. *Activities and organizations:* drama/theater group, student-run newspaper, radio and television station, choral group, marching band, Student Activities Council, Hansen Leadership Program, band/choir, Doane Ambassadors, Doane Art League. *Campus security:* 24-hour emergency response devices and patrols, student patrols, late-night transport/escort service, controlled dormitory access, evening patrols by trained security personnel. *Student services:* health clinic, personal/psychological counseling.

Athletics Member NAIA. *Intercollegiate sports:* baseball M(s), basketball M(s)/W(s), cross-country running M(s)/W(s), football M(s), golf M(s)/W(s), soccer M(s)/W(s), softball W(s), tennis M/W, track and field M(s)/W(s), volleyball W(s). *Intramural sports:* baseball M(c)/W(c), basketball M/W, bowling M/W, football M/W, golf M/W, ice hockey M, racquetball M(c)/W(c), softball M/W, swimming and diving M/W, table tennis M(c)/W(c), tennis M/W, volleyball M/W, water polo M/W.

Standardized Tests *Required:* SAT or ACT (for admission).

Costs (2011–12) *Comprehensive fee:* $30,240 includes full-time tuition ($22,970), mandatory fees ($620), and room and board ($6650). Full-time tuition and fees vary according to location. Part-time tuition: $770 per credit hour. Part-time tuition and fees vary according to course load and location. *Room and board:* Room and board charges vary according to board plan, housing facility, and location. *Payment plan:* installment. *Waivers:* senior citizens and employees or children of employees.

Financial Aid Of all full-time matriculated undergraduates who enrolled in 2011, 957 applied for aid, 833 were judged to have need, 272 had their need fully met. In 2011, 78 non-need-based awards were made. *Average percent of need met:* 87%. *Average financial aid package:* $18,855. *Average need-based loan:* $4626. *Average need-based gift aid:* $13,999. *Average non-need-based aid:* $10,641. *Average indebtedness upon graduation:* $20,784.

Applying *Options:* electronic application, early admission, deferred entrance. *Required:* high school transcript, 2 letters of recommendation. *Required for some:* interview. *Recommended:* minimum 2.0 GPA. *Application deadlines:* rolling (freshmen), rolling (transfers). *Notification:* continuous (freshmen), continuous (transfers).

Freshman Application Contact Doane College, 1014 Boswell Avenue, Crete, NE 68333-2430. *Phone:* 800-333-6263. *Toll-free phone:* 800-333-6263. *Web site:* http://www.doane.edu/.

Grace University
Omaha, Nebraska

Freshman Application Contact Angela Wayman, Director of Admissions, Grace University, 1311 South Ninth Street, Omaha, NE 68108. *Phone:* 402-449-2831. *Toll-free phone:* 800-383-1422. *Fax:* 402-341-9587. *E-mail:* admissions@graceuniversity.com. *Web site:* http://www.graceuniversity.edu/.

Hastings College
Hastings, Nebraska

Freshman Application Contact Ms. Mary Molliconi, Director of Admissions, Hastings College, 710 North Turner Avenue, Hastings, NE 68901-7621. *Phone:* 402-461-7320. *Toll-free phone:* 800-532-7642. *Fax:* 402-461-7490. *E-mail:* mmolliconi@hastings.edu. *Web site:* http://www.hastings.edu/.

ITT Technical Institute
Omaha, Nebraska

- **Proprietary** primarily 2-year, founded 1991, part of ITT Educational Services, Inc.
- **Urban** campus
- **Coed**
- **Minimally difficult** entrance level

Academics *Calendar:* quarters. *Degrees:* associate and bachelor's.

Student Life *Housing:* college housing not available.

Freshman Application Contact Director of Recruitment, ITT Technical Institute, 9814 M Street, Omaha, NE 68127-2056. *Phone:* 402-331-2900. *Toll-free phone:* 800-677-9260. *Web site:* http://www.itt-tech.edu/.

Kaplan University, Lincoln
Lincoln, Nebraska

Freshman Application Contact Kaplan University, Lincoln, 1821 K Street, Lincoln, NE 68501-2826. *Phone:* 402-474-5315. *Toll-free phone:* 866-527-5268 (in-state); 800-527-5268 (out-of-state). *Web site:* http://www.lincoln.kaplanuniversity.edu/.

Kaplan University, Omaha
Omaha, Nebraska

Freshman Application Contact Kaplan University, Omaha, 5425 North 103rd Street, Omaha, NE 68134. *Phone:* 402-572-8500. *Toll-free phone:* 866-527-5268 (in-state); 800-527-5268 (out-of-state). *Web site:* http://www.omaha.kaplanuniversity.edu/.

Midland University
Fremont, Nebraska

Freshman Application Contact Mr. Todd Hansen, Associate Director of Admissions, Midland University, Fremont, NE 68025-4200. *Phone:* 402-941-6504. *Toll-free phone:* 800-642-8382 Ext. 6501. *Fax:* 402-941-6513. *E-mail:* admissions@mlc.edu. *Web site:* http://www.midlandu.edu/.

Nebraska Christian College
Papillion, Nebraska

Freshman Application Contact Ms. Alisha Livengood, Associate Director of Admissions, Nebraska Christian College, 12550 South 114th Steet, Papillion, NE 68046. *Phone:* 402-935-9407. *Web site:* http://www.nechristian.edu/.

Nebraska Methodist College
Omaha, Nebraska

Freshman Application Contact Sara Bonney, Director of Enrollment Services, Nebraska Methodist College, 720 North 87th Street, Omaha, NE 68114. *Phone:* 402-354-7111. *Toll-free phone:* 800-335-5510. *Fax:* 402-354-7020. *E-mail:* sara.bonney@methodistcollege.edu. *Web site:* http://www.methodistcollege.edu/.

Nebraska Wesleyan University
Lincoln, Nebraska

- **Independent United Methodist** comprehensive, founded 1887
- **Suburban** 50-acre campus with easy access to Omaha
- **Endowment** $48.1 million
- **Coed** 1,781 undergraduate students, 89% full-time, 60% women, 40% men
- **Moderately difficult** entrance level, 82% of applicants were admitted

Undergraduates 1,578 full-time, 203 part-time. Students come from 31 states and territories; 17 other countries; 12% are from out of state; 2% Black or African American, non-Hispanic/Latino; 3% Hispanic/Latino; 2% Asian, non-Hispanic/Latino; 0.2% Native Hawaiian or other Pacific Islander, non-Hispanic/Latino; 0.5% American Indian or Alaska Native, non-Hispanic/Latino; 1% Two or more races, non-Hispanic/Latino; 6% Race/ethnicity unknown; 4% transferred in; 65% live on campus. *Retention:* 79% of full-time freshmen returned.

Freshmen *Admission:* 1,459 applied, 1,196 admitted, 360 enrolled. *Average high school GPA:* 3.64. *Test scores:* ACT scores over 18: 100%; ACT scores over 24: 66%; ACT scores over 30: 11%.

Faculty *Total:* 160, 64% full-time, 71% with terminal degrees. *Student/faculty ratio:* 14:1.

Academics *Calendar:* semesters. *Degrees:* certificates, bachelor's, master's, post-master's, and postbachelor's certificates. *Special study options:* accelerated degree program, adult/continuing education programs, advanced placement credit, double majors, independent study, internships, off-campus study, part-time degree program, services for LD students, study abroad, summer session for credit. *ROTC:* Army (c), Air Force (c). *Unusual degree programs:* 3-2 engineering with Washington University in St. Louis, Columbia University, University of Nebraska-Lincoln.

Computers on Campus 360 computers/terminals are available on campus for general student use. Students can access the following: computer help desk, free student e-mail accounts, online (class) grades, online (class) registration, online (class) schedules. Campuswide network is available. Wireless service is available via classrooms, computer centers, computer labs, learning centers, libraries, student centers.

Student Life *Housing:* on-campus residence required through junior year. *Options:* coed, women-only. Campus housing is university owned. Freshman campus housing is guaranteed. *Activities and organizations:* drama/theater group, student-run newspaper, choral group, national fraternities, national sororities. *Campus security:* 24-hour emergency response devices, late-night transport/escort service, controlled dormitory access. *Student services:* health clinic, personal/psychological counseling, women's center.

Athletics Member NCAA, NAIA. All NCAA Division III. *Intercollegiate sports:* baseball M, basketball M/W, cheerleading W, cross-country running M/W, football M, golf M/W, soccer M/W, softball W, tennis M/W, track and field M/W, volleyball W. *Intramural sports:* basketball M/W, bowling M/W, football M/W, racquetball M/W, soccer M/W, softball M/W, tennis M/W, ultimate Frisbee M/W, volleyball M/W, weight lifting M/W.

Standardized Tests *Required:* SAT or ACT (for admission).

Costs (2011–12) *One-time required fee:* $120. *Comprehensive fee:* $31,328 includes full-time tuition ($24,256), mandatory fees ($400), and room and board ($6672). Part-time tuition: $913 per credit hour. *College room only:* $3796. Room and board charges vary according to board plan and housing facility. *Payment plan:* installment. *Waivers:* senior citizens and employees or children of employees.

Financial Aid Of all full-time matriculated undergraduates who enrolled in 2011, 1,215 applied for aid, 1,071 were judged to have need, 217 had their need fully met. 129 Federal Work-Study jobs (averaging $868). 431 state and other part-time jobs (averaging $1551). In 2011, 344 non-need-based awards were made. *Average percent of need met:* 69%. *Average financial aid package:* $17,243. *Average need-based loan:* $4630. *Average need-based gift aid:* $12,523. *Average non-need-based aid:* $9199. *Average indebtedness upon graduation:* $25,490.

Applying *Options:* electronic application, deferred entrance. *Application fee:* $20. *Required:* high school transcript. *Required for some:* essay or personal statement. *Recommended:* interview. *Application deadlines:* 8/15 (freshmen), 8/15 (transfers). *Notification:* continuous (freshmen).

Freshman Application Contact Mr. David Duzik, Director of Admissions, Nebraska Wesleyan University, 5000 Saint Paul Avenue, Lincoln, NE 68504. *Phone:* 402-465-2144. *Toll-free phone:* 800-541-3818. *Fax:* 402-465-2177. *E-mail:* admissions@nebrwesleyan.edu. *Web site:* http://www.nebrwesleyan.edu/.

Peru State College
Peru, Nebraska

- **State-supported** comprehensive, founded 1867, part of Nebraska State College System
- **Rural** 104-acre campus
- **Coed** 2,094 undergraduate students, 57% full-time, 59% women, 41% men
- **Noncompetitive** entrance level, 49% of applicants were admitted

Undergraduates 1,192 full-time, 902 part-time. 5% Black or African American, non-Hispanic/Latino; 4% Hispanic/Latino; 1% Asian, non-Hispanic/Latino; 0.1% Native Hawaiian or other Pacific Islander, non-Hispanic/Latino; 1% American Indian or Alaska Native, non-Hispanic/Latino; 1% Two or more races, non-Hispanic/Latino; 3% Race/ethnicity unknown; 9% transferred in; 33% live on campus.

Freshmen *Admission:* 869 applied, 422 admitted, 174 enrolled. *Test scores:* ACT scores over 18: 74%; ACT scores over 24: 16%; ACT scores over 30: 1%.

Faculty *Total:* 109, 43% full-time. *Student/faculty ratio:* 24:1.

Academics *Calendar:* semesters. *Degrees:* bachelor's and master's. *Special study options:* academic remediation for entering students, accelerated degree program, adult/continuing education programs, advanced placement credit, cooperative education, distance learning, double majors, external degree program, freshman honors college, honors programs, internships, off-campus study, part-time degree program, services for LD students, summer session for credit. *ROTC:* Army (c), Air Force (c).

Computers on Campus 125 computers/terminals are available on campus for general student use. Students can access the following: campus intranet, free student e-mail accounts, online (class) grades, online (class) registration, online (class) schedules. Campuswide network is available. 100% of college-owned or -operated housing units are wired for high-speed Internet access. Wireless service is available via entire campus.

Student Life *Housing:* on-campus residence required through sophomore year. *Options:* coed, men-only, women-only. Campus housing is university owned. Freshman campus housing is guaranteed. *Activities and organizations:* drama/theater group, student-run newspaper, choral group, marching band, Campus Activities Board, Black Student Union, Peru Student Education Association (PSEA), Phi Beta Lambda (PBL), Pilot Club. *Campus security:* 24-hour emergency response devices and patrols, late-night transport/escort service. *Student services:* health clinic.

Athletics Member NAIA. *Intercollegiate sports:* baseball M(s), basketball M(s)/W(s), cheerleading W(s), cross-country running W(s), football M(s), golf W(s), softball W(s), volleyball W(s). *Intramural sports:* basketball M/W, football M/W, softball M/W, volleyball M/W.

Standardized Tests *Required for some:* SAT or ACT (for admission).

Costs (2011–12) *Tuition:* state resident $4058 full-time, $135 per credit hour part-time; nonresident $4058 full-time, $135 per credit hour part-time. Full-time tuition and fees vary according to course level, course load, and location. Part-time tuition and fees vary according to course level, course load, and location. *Required fees:* $1313 full-time. *Room and board:* $5820; room only: $3012. Room and board charges vary according to board plan and housing facility. *Payment plan:* deferred payment. *Waivers:* employees or children of employees.

Applying *Options:* electronic application. *Required:* high school transcript. *Application deadlines:* rolling (freshmen), rolling (out-of-state freshmen), rolling (transfers). *Notification:* continuous (freshmen), continuous (out-of-state freshmen), continuous (transfers).

Freshman Application Contact Ms. Micki Willis, Vice President for Enrollment Management and Student Affairs, Peru State College, PO Box 10, Peru, NE 68421. *Phone:* 402-872-2221. *Toll-free phone:* 800-742-4412 (in-state); 800-741-4412 (out-of-state). *Fax:* 402-872-2296. *E-mail:* mwillis@peru.edu. *Web site:* http://www.peru.edu/.

St. Gregory the Great Seminary
Seward, Nebraska

- **Independent Roman Catholic** 4-year
- **Small-town** 60-acre campus
- **Men only**
- **100%** of applicants were admitted

Academics *Degrees:* bachelor's and postbachelor's certificates.

Standardized Tests *Required:* SAT or ACT (for admission).

Costs (2011–12) *Comprehensive fee:* $13,500 includes full-time tuition ($7800) and room and board ($5700).

Applying *Required:* essay or personal statement, high school transcript, 3 letters of recommendation, interview, Church documents, letter of sponsorship from diocese.

Freshman Application Contact Rev. Peter M. Mitchell, Dean of Men, St. Gregory the Great Seminary, 800 Fletcher Road, Seward, NE 68434. *Phone:* 402-643-4052. *Fax:* 402-643-6964. *E-mail:* sggs@stgregoryseminary.edu. *Web site:* http://www.stgregoryseminary.edu/.

Union College
Lincoln, Nebraska

- **Independent Seventh-day Adventist** comprehensive, founded 1891
- **Suburban** 26-acre campus with easy access to Omaha
- **Endowment** $12.8 million
- **Coed** 810 undergraduate students, 83% full-time, 59% women, 41% men
- **Moderately difficult** entrance level, 53% of applicants were admitted

Undergraduates 673 full-time, 137 part-time. Students come from 47 states and territories; 30 other countries; 72% are from out of state; 6% Black or African American, non-Hispanic/Latino; 13% Hispanic/Latino; 3% Asian, non-Hispanic/Latino; 0.6% Native Hawaiian or other Pacific Islander, non-Hispanic/Latino; 0.3% American Indian or Alaska Native, non-Hispanic/Latino; 2% Two or more races, non-Hispanic/Latino; 2% Race/ethnicity unknown; 6% international; 10% transferred in; 74% live on campus. *Retention:* 80% of full-time freshmen returned.

Freshmen *Admission:* 1,002 applied, 534 admitted, 160 enrolled. *Average high school GPA:* 3.2. *Test scores:* SAT math scores over 500: 56%; SAT writing scores over 500: 67%; ACT scores over 18: 79%; SAT math scores over 600: 22%; SAT writing scores over 600: 33%; ACT scores over 24: 31%; SAT math scores over 700: 11%; SAT writing scores over 700: 11%; ACT scores over 30: 3%.

Faculty *Total:* 114, 51% full-time, 27% with terminal degrees. *Student/faculty ratio:* 10:1.

Academics *Calendar:* semesters. *Degrees:* associate, bachelor's, and master's. *Special study options:* accelerated degree program, adult/continuing education programs, advanced placement credit, cooperative education, double majors, English as a second language, honors programs, independent study, internships, off-campus study, part-time degree program, services for LD students, student-designed majors, study abroad, summer session for credit.

Computers on Campus 85 computers/terminals are available on campus for general student use. Students can access the following: free student e-mail accounts, online (class) grades, online (class) registration, online (class) schedules. Campuswide network is available. 100% of college-owned or -operated housing units are wired for high-speed Internet access. Wireless service is available via entire campus.

Student Life *Housing:* on-campus residence required through junior year. *Options:* men-only, women-only. Campus housing is university owned. Freshman campus housing is guaranteed. *Activities and organizations:* drama/theater group, student-run newspaper, choral group. *Campus security:* 24-hour emergency response devices, student patrols, late-night transport/escort service. *Student services:* health clinic, personal/psychological counseling.

Athletics *Intercollegiate sports:* basketball M/W, golf M, volleyball W. *Intramural sports:* badminton M/W, basketball M/W, football M/W, golf M/W, gymnastics M(c)/W(c), soccer M(c)/W(c), softball M/W, tennis M/W, ultimate Frisbee M/W, volleyball M/W.

Standardized Tests *Required:* SAT or ACT (for admission).

Costs (2012–13) *Comprehensive fee:* $26,100 includes full-time tuition ($18,990), mandatory fees ($890), and room and board ($6220). Full-time tuition and fees vary according to course load, degree level, and program. Part-time tuition: $792 per credit hour. Part-time tuition and fees vary according to program. *College room only:* $3520. Room and board charges vary according to housing facility. *Payment plan:* installment. *Waivers:* employees or children of employees.

Financial Aid *Financial aid deadline:* 7/31.

Applying *Options:* electronic application. *Required:* high school transcript, minimum 2.5 GPA, 3 letters of recommendation. *Required for some:* essay or personal statement, interview. *Application deadlines:* rolling (freshmen), rolling (transfers). *Notification:* continuous (freshmen), continuous (transfers).

Freshman Application Contact Jennifer Enos, Admissions Assistant Director, Union College, 3800 South 48th Street, Lincoln, NE 68506. *Phone:* 402-486-2600 Ext. 2052. *Toll-free phone:* 800-228-4600. *Fax:* 402-486-2895. *E-mail:* ucenroll@ucollege.edu. *Web site:* http://www.ucollege.edu/.

University of Nebraska at Kearney
Kearney, Nebraska

- **State-supported** comprehensive, founded 1903, part of University of Nebraska System
- **Small-town** 235-acre campus
- **Coed** 5,442 undergraduate students, 88% full-time, 54% women, 46% men
- **Moderately difficult** entrance level, 86% of applicants were admitted

Undergraduates 4,762 full-time, 680 part-time. 8% are from out of state; 1% Black or African American, non-Hispanic/Latino; 7% Hispanic/Latino; 0.7% Asian, non-Hispanic/Latino; 0.2% American Indian or Alaska Native, non-Hispanic/Latino; 1% Two or more races, non-Hispanic/Latino; 3% Race/ethnicity unknown; 6% international; 8% transferred in; 49% live on campus. *Retention:* 77% of full-time freshmen returned.

Freshmen *Admission:* 2,615 applied, 2,258 admitted, 1,074 enrolled. *Average high school GPA:* 3.24. *Test scores:* SAT critical reading scores over 500: 62%; SAT math scores over 500: 57%; ACT scores over 18: 92%; SAT critical reading scores over 600: 24%; SAT math scores over 600: 19%; ACT scores over 24: 39%; SAT critical reading scores over 700: 10%; ACT scores over 30: 6%.

Faculty *Total:* 422, 73% full-time, 60% with terminal degrees. *Student/faculty ratio:* 16:1.

Academics *Calendar:* semesters. *Degrees:* bachelor's, master's, and post-master's certificates. *Special study options:* part-time degree program. *ROTC:* Army (b).

Computers on Campus Students can access the following: computer help desk, free student e-mail accounts, online (class) grades, online (class) registration, online (class) schedules, online degree audit, online personal information update, online bill viewing and payment, online financial aid awards and acceptance. Campuswide network is available. Wireless service is available via entire campus.

Student Life *Housing:* on-campus residence required for freshman year. *Options:* coed. Campus housing is university owned. Freshman campus housing is guaranteed. *Campus security:* 24-hour emergency response devices and patrols, late-night transport/escort service.

Athletics Member NCAA. All Division II. *Intercollegiate sports:* baseball M(s), basketball M(s)/W(s), cross-country running M(s)/W(s), football M(s), golf M(s)/W(s), soccer W, softball W(s), swimming and diving W(s), tennis M(s)/W(s), track and field M(s)/W(s), volleyball W(s), wrestling M(s). *Intramural sports:* badminton M/W, basketball M/W, cross-country running M/W, football M/W, golf M/W, racquetball M/W, soccer M/W, softball M/W, tennis M/W, volleyball M/W, water polo M/W, wrestling M/W.

Standardized Tests *Required:* SAT and SAT Subject Tests or ACT (for admission).

Costs (2011–12) *Tuition:* state resident $5048 full-time, $168 per credit hour part-time; nonresident $10,350 full-time, $345 per credit hour part-time. Full-time tuition and fees vary according to course level, course load, degree level, and location. Part-time tuition and fees vary according to course level, course load, degree level, and location. *Required fees:* $1151 full-time, $24 per credit hour part-time, $219 per term part-time. *Room and board:* $7558; room only: $3822. Room and board charges vary according to board plan and housing facility. *Payment plan:* installment. *Waivers:* employees or children of employees.

Financial Aid Of all full-time matriculated undergraduates who enrolled in 2011, 3,369 applied for aid, 2,836 were judged to have need, 943 had their need fully met. In 2011, 179 non-need-based awards were made. *Average percent of need met:* 74%. *Average financial aid package:* $9889. *Average need-based loan:* $3945. *Average need-based gift aid:* $6024. *Average non-need-based aid:* $2209.

Applying *Options:* electronic application. *Application fee:* $45. *Required:* high school transcript, rank in upper 50% of high school class. *Application deadlines:* 9/1 (freshmen), rolling (transfers). *Notification:* continuous (freshmen), continuous (transfers).

Freshman Application Contact Mr. Dusty Newton, Director of Admissions, University of Nebraska at Kearney, 905 West 25th Street, Kearney, NE 68849-0001. *Phone:* 308-865-8702. *Toll-free phone:* 800-532-7639. *Fax:* 308-865-8987. *E-mail:* admissionsug@unk.edu. *Web site:* http://www.unk.edu/.

University of Nebraska at Omaha
Omaha, Nebraska

- **State-supported** university, founded 1908, part of University of Nebraska System
- **Urban** 503-acre campus
- **Coed** 11,964 undergraduate students, 78% full-time, 52% women, 48% men
- **Minimally difficult** entrance level, 76% of applicants were admitted

Undergraduates 9,328 full-time, 2,636 part-time. Students come from 43 states and territories; 79 other countries; 7% are from out of state; 6% Black or African American, non-Hispanic/Latino; 6% Hispanic/Latino; 2% Asian, non-Hispanic/Latino; 0.1% Native Hawaiian or other Pacific Islander, non-Hispanic/Latino; 0.5% American Indian or Alaska Native, non-Hispanic/Latino; 2% Two or more races, non-Hispanic/Latino; 4% Race/ethnicity unknown; 3% international; 9% transferred in; 13% live on campus. *Retention:* 73% of full-time freshmen returned.

Freshmen *Admission:* 4,625 applied, 3,503 admitted, 1,785 enrolled. *Average high school GPA:* 3.4. *Test scores:* ACT scores over 18: 89%; ACT scores over 24: 39%; ACT scores over 30: 7%.

Faculty *Total:* 939, 51% full-time, 54% with terminal degrees. *Student/faculty ratio:* 18:1.

Academics *Calendar:* semesters. *Degrees:* bachelor's, master's, doctoral, post-master's, and postbachelor's certificates. *Special study options:* adult/continuing education programs, advanced placement credit, cooperative education, distance learning, double majors, English as a second language, honors programs, independent study, internships, off-campus study, part-time degree program, services for LD students, student-designed majors, study abroad, summer session for credit. *ROTC:* Army (c), Air Force (b).

Computers on Campus 2,000 computers/terminals are available on campus for general student use. Students can access the following: computer help desk, free student e-mail accounts, online (class) grades, online (class) registration, online (class) schedules. Campuswide network is available. 100% of college-owned or -operated housing units are wired for high-speed Internet access. Wireless service is available via classrooms, computer centers, computer labs, dorm rooms, learning centers, libraries, student centers.

Student Life *Housing options:* coed. Campus housing is university owned and leased by the school. *Activities and organizations:* drama/theater group, student-run newspaper, radio and television station, choral group, marching band, Student Programming Board-Maverick Productions, student government, Greek Life, Emerging Leaders, PRSSA - Public Relations student society of America, national fraternities, national sororities. *Campus security:* 24-hour emergency response devices and patrols, late-night transport/escort service, controlled dormitory access. *Student services:* health clinic, personal/psychological counseling, women's center, legal services.

Athletics Member NCAA. All Division I. *Intercollegiate sports:* baseball M(s), basketball M(s)/W(s), golf M(s)/W(s), ice hockey M(s), soccer M(s)/W(s), softball W(s), swimming and diving W(s), tennis M(s)/W(s), volleyball W(s). *Intramural sports:* bowling M/W, fencing M/W, field hockey M/W, golf M/W, lacrosse M/W, racquetball M/W, riflery M/W, rugby M/W, soccer M/W, softball M/W, track and field M/W, ultimate Frisbee M/W, volleyball M/W.

Standardized Tests *Required:* SAT or ACT (for admission).

Costs (2011–12) *Tuition:* state resident $5693 full-time, $190 per credit hour part-time; nonresident $16,785 full-time, $560 per credit hour part-time. Full-time tuition and fees vary according to course load and reciprocity agreements. Part-time tuition and fees vary according to course load and reciprocity agreements. *Required fees:* $1334 full-time. *Room and board:* $8858; room only: $6460. Room and board charges vary according to board plan and housing facility. *Payment plans:* installment, deferred payment. *Waivers:* children of alumni, senior citizens, and employees or children of employees.

Financial Aid Of all full-time matriculated undergraduates who enrolled in 2010, 6,904 applied for aid, 6,347 were judged to have need. 450 Federal Work-Study jobs (averaging $1817). In 2010, 450 non-need-based awards were made. *Average financial aid package:* $6121. *Average need-based loan:* $3792. *Average need-based gift aid:* $5087. *Average non-need-based aid:* $1817. *Average indebtedness upon graduation:* $23,500.

Applying *Options:* electronic application, deferred entrance. *Application fee:* $45. *Required:* high school transcript. *Application deadlines:* 8/1 (freshmen), 8/1 (transfers). *Notification:* continuous (freshmen), continuous (transfers).

Freshman Application Contact University of Nebraska at Omaha, 6001 Dodge Street, Omaha, NE 68182. *Phone:* 402-554-2416. *Toll-free phone:* 800-858-8648. *Web site:* http://www.unomaha.edu/.

University of Nebraska–Lincoln
Lincoln, Nebraska

- **State-supported** university, founded 1869, part of University of Nebraska System
- **Urban** 624-acre campus with easy access to Omaha
- **Endowment** $1.2 billion
- **Coed** 19,345 undergraduate students, 93% full-time, 46% women, 54% men
- **Moderately difficult** entrance level, 59% of applicants were admitted

Undergraduates 18,039 full-time, 1,306 part-time. Students come from 51 states and territories; 92 other countries; 16% are from out of state; 2% Black or African American, non-Hispanic/Latino; 4% Hispanic/Latino; 2% Asian, non-Hispanic/Latino; 0.1% Native Hawaiian or other Pacific Islander, non-Hispanic/Latino; 0.3% American Indian or Alaska Native, non-Hispanic/Latino; 1% Two or more races, non-Hispanic/Latino; 3% Race/ethnicity unknown; 4% international; 5% transferred in; 41% live on campus. *Retention:* 84% of full-time freshmen returned.

Freshmen *Admission:* 10,022 applied, 5,943 admitted, 4,093 enrolled. *Test scores:* SAT critical reading scores over 500: 79%; SAT math scores over 500: 83%; ACT scores over 18: 99%; SAT critical reading scores over 600: 48%; SAT math scores over 600: 52%; ACT scores over 24: 63%; SAT critical reading scores over 700: 16%; SAT math scores over 700: 19%; ACT scores over 30: 18%.

Faculty *Total:* 1,060, 99% full-time, 97% with terminal degrees. *Student/faculty ratio:* 21:1.

Academics *Calendar:* semesters. *Degrees:* associate, bachelor's, master's, doctoral, post-master's, postbachelor's, and first professional certificates. *Special study options:* accelerated degree program, adult/continuing education programs, advanced placement credit, cooperative education, distance learning, double majors, English as a second language, honors programs, independent study, internships, off-campus study, part-time degree program, services for LD students, student-designed majors, study abroad, summer session for credit. *ROTC:* Army (b), Navy (b), Air Force (b).

Computers on Campus 600 computers/terminals are available on campus for general student use. Students can access the following: campus intranet, computer help desk, free student e-mail accounts, online (class) grades, online (class) registration, online (class) schedules. Campuswide network is available. 100% of college-owned or -operated housing units are wired for high-speed Internet access. Wireless service is available via entire campus.

Student Life *Housing:* on-campus residence required for freshman year. *Options:* coed, women-only, cooperative, disabled students. Campus housing is university owned. Freshman campus housing is guaranteed. *Activities and organizations:* drama/theater group, student-run newspaper, radio and television station, choral group, marching band, Student Alumni Association, University Ambassadors, University Program Council, Golden Key Honor Society, national fraternities, national sororities. *Campus security:* 24-hour emergency response devices and patrols, late-night transport/escort service,

controlled dormitory access. *Student services:* health clinic, personal/psychological counseling, women's center, legal services.

Athletics Member NCAA. All Division I except football (Division I-A). *Intercollegiate sports:* baseball M(s), basketball M(s)/W(s), bowling W(s), cross-country running M(s)/W(s), golf M(s)/W(s), gymnastics M(s)/W(s), riflery W(s), soccer W(s), softball W(s), swimming and diving W(s), tennis M(s)/W(s), track and field M(s)/W(s), volleyball W(s), wrestling M(s). *Intramural sports:* baseball M(c)/W(c), basketball M/W, bowling M(c), crew M(c)/W(c), cross-country running M/W, golf M/W, ice hockey M(c)/W(c), lacrosse M(c)/W(c), racquetball M(c)/W(c), riflery M(c)/W(c), rock climbing M(c)/W(c), rugby M(c)/W(c), soccer M(c)/W(c), softball M(c)/W(c), swimming and diving M(c)/W(c), table tennis M(c)/W(c), tennis M(c)/W(c), track and field M/W, ultimate Frisbee M(c)/W(c), volleyball M(c)/W(c), water polo M(c), weight lifting M/W.

Standardized Tests *Required:* SAT or ACT (for admission). *Recommended:* ACT (for admission).

Costs (2011–12) *Tuition:* state resident $6248 full-time, $208 per semester hour part-time; nonresident $18,533 full-time, $618 per semester hour part-time. Full-time tuition and fees vary according to course load, program, and reciprocity agreements. Part-time tuition and fees vary according to course load, program, and reciprocity agreements. *Required fees:* $1315 full-time, $10 per semester hour part-time, $288 per term part-time. *Room and board:* $8647. Room and board charges vary according to board plan and housing facility. *Payment plan:* installment. *Waivers:* employees or children of employees.

Financial Aid Of all full-time matriculated undergraduates who enrolled in 2010, 11,155 applied for aid, 8,442 were judged to have need, 1,359 had their need fully met. 1,176 Federal Work-Study jobs (averaging $2103). In 2010, 3366 non-need-based awards were made. *Average percent of need met:* 83%. *Average financial aid package:* $11,532. *Average need-based loan:* $4149. *Average need-based gift aid:* $7331. *Average non-need-based aid:* $6231. *Average indebtedness upon graduation:* $21,604.

Applying *Options:* electronic application. *Application fee:* $45. *Required:* high school transcript. *Required for some:* rank in upper 50% of high school class. *Application deadlines:* 5/1 (freshmen), 5/1 (transfers). *Notification:* continuous (freshmen), continuous (transfers).

Freshman Application Contact Ms. Amber Hunter, Associate Dean - Enrollment Management, University of Nebraska–Lincoln, 1410 Q Street, Lincoln, NE 68588-0417. *Phone:* 402-472-2023. *Toll-free phone:* 800-742-8800. *Fax:* 402-472-0670. *E-mail:* admissions@unl.edu. *Web site:* http://www.unl.edu/.

University of Nebraska Medical Center
Omaha, Nebraska

- **State-supported** upper-level, founded 1869, part of University of Nebraska System
- **Urban** 16-acre campus
- **Endowment** $11.9 million
- **Coed** 1,013 undergraduate students, 88% full-time, 87% women, 13% men

Undergraduates 895 full-time, 118 part-time. Students come from 20 states and territories; 10 other countries; 10% are from out of state; 1% Black or African American, non-Hispanic/Latino; 3% Hispanic/Latino; 2% Asian, non-Hispanic/Latino; 0.1% Native Hawaiian or other Pacific Islander, non-Hispanic/Latino; 0.6% American Indian or Alaska Native, non-Hispanic/Latino; 0.8% Race/ethnicity unknown; 1% international; 42% transferred in.

Faculty *Total:* 1,232, 83% full-time, 87% with terminal degrees. *Student/faculty ratio:* 3:1.

Academics *Calendar:* semesters. *Degrees:* bachelor's, master's, doctoral, post-master's, postbachelor's, and first professional certificates. *Special study options:* accelerated degree program, distance learning, honors programs, off-campus study, part-time degree program, services for LD students, summer session for credit. *ROTC:* Army (c), Air Force (c).

Computers on Campus 120 computers/terminals are available on campus for general student use. Students can access the following: campus intranet, computer help desk, free student e-mail accounts, online (class) grades, online (class) registration, online (class) schedules, various software packages. Campuswide network is available. Wireless service is available via classrooms, computer centers, computer labs, libraries, student centers.

Student Life *Housing:* college housing not available. *Activities and organizations:* student government, Toastmasters, Student Alliance for Global Health, Christian Medical Society, Student Research Group, national fraternities, national sororities. *Campus security:* 24-hour emergency response devices and patrols, late-night transport/escort service. *Student services:* health clinic, personal/psychological counseling.

Costs (2011–12) *Tuition:* state resident $7924 full-time, $209 per semester hour part-time; nonresident $22,648 full-time, $618 per semester hour part-time. Full-time tuition and fees vary according to location and program. Part-time tuition and fees vary according to location and program. *Required fees:* $500 full-time, $150 per year part-time. *Payment plan:* installment.

Financial Aid Of all full-time matriculated undergraduates who enrolled in 2008, 863 applied for aid, 729 were judged to have need, 103 had their need fully met. 53 Federal Work-Study jobs (averaging $663). In 2008, 181 non-need-based awards were made. *Average percent of need met:* 56%. *Average financial aid package:* $8239. *Average need-based loan:* $4871. *Average need-based gift aid:* $4760. *Average non-need-based aid:* $8607. *Average indebtedness upon graduation:* $29,188.

Applying *Options:* electronic application, deferred entrance. *Application fee:* $45. *Application deadline:* rolling (transfers).

Application Contact University of Nebraska Medical Center, Nebraska Medical Center, Omaha, NE 68198. *Toll-free phone:* 800-626-8431 Ext. 6468. *Web site:* http://www.unmc.edu/.

University of Phoenix–Omaha Campus

Omaha, Nebraska

Admissions Office Contact University of Phoenix–Omaha Campus, 13321 California Street, Suite 200, Omaha, NE 68154-5240. *Toll-free phone:* 866-766-0766. *Web site:* http://www.phoenix.edu/.

Wayne State College

Wayne, Nebraska

- **State-supported** comprehensive, founded 1910, part of Nebraska State College System
- **Small-town** 128-acre campus
- **Endowment** $12.1 million
- **Coed** 2,994 undergraduate students, 91% full-time, 56% women, 44% men
- **Noncompetitive** entrance level, 100% of applicants were admitted

Undergraduates 2,717 full-time, 277 part-time. Students come from 32 states and territories; 16 other countries; 14% are from out of state; 3% Black or African American, non-Hispanic/Latino; 5% Hispanic/Latino; 0.4% Asian, non-Hispanic/Latino; 0.1% Native Hawaiian or other Pacific Islander, non-Hispanic/Latino; 0.7% American Indian or Alaska Native, non-Hispanic/Latino; 1% Two or more races, non-Hispanic/Latino; 8% Race/ethnicity unknown; 0.5% international; 7% transferred in; 46% live on campus. *Retention:* 68% of full-time freshmen returned.

Freshmen *Admission:* 2,043 applied, 2,043 admitted, 682 enrolled. *Average high school GPA:* 3.24. *Test scores:* ACT scores over 18: 82%; ACT scores over 24: 31%; ACT scores over 30: 3%.

Faculty *Total:* 215, 57% full-time, 53% with terminal degrees. *Student/faculty ratio:* 20:1.

Academics *Calendar:* semesters. *Degrees:* bachelor's, master's, and post-master's certificates. *Special study options:* adult/continuing education programs, advanced placement credit, cooperative education, distance learning, double majors, honors programs, independent study, internships, off-campus study, part-time degree program, services for LD students, student-designed majors, study abroad, summer session for credit. *ROTC:* Army (b).

Computers on Campus 365 computers/terminals are available on campus for general student use. Students can access the following: campus intranet, computer help desk, free student e-mail accounts, online (class) grades, online (class) registration, online (class) schedules. Campuswide network is available. 100% of college-owned or -operated housing units are wired for high-speed Internet access. Wireless service is available via classrooms, computer centers, computer labs, learning centers, libraries, student centers.

Student Life *Housing:* on-campus residence required for freshman year. *Options:* coed. Campus housing is university owned. Freshman campus housing is guaranteed. *Activities and organizations:* drama/theater group, student-run newspaper, radio and television station, choral group, marching band, national fraternities, national sororities. *Campus security:* 24-hour emergency response devices and patrols, student patrols, late-night transport/escort service, controlled dormitory access. *Student services:* health clinic, personal/psychological counseling.

Athletics Member NCAA. All Division II. *Intercollegiate sports:* baseball M(s), basketball M(s)/W(s), cheerleading M(c)/W(c), cross-country running M(s)/W(s), football M(s), golf M(s)/W(s), rugby M(c)/W(c), soccer M(c)/

W(s), softball W(s), track and field M(s)/W(s), volleyball W(s), wrestling M(c). *Intramural sports:* archery M/W, badminton M/W, basketball M/W, bowling M/W, football M/W, golf M/W, racquetball M/W, softball M/W, swimming and diving M/W, table tennis M/W, tennis M/W, track and field M/W, volleyball M/W, weight lifting M/W, wrestling M.

Standardized Tests *Recommended:* SAT or ACT (for admission).

Costs (2011–12) *Tuition:* state resident $4058 full-time, $135 per credit hour part-time; nonresident $8115 full-time, $271 per credit hour part-time. Full-time tuition and fees vary according to course level and course load. Part-time tuition and fees vary according to course level and course load. *Required fees:* $1260 full-time, $50 per credit hour part-time. *Room and board:* $5740; room only: $2770. Room and board charges vary according to board plan and housing facility. *Payment plan:* installment. *Waivers:* employees or children of employees.

Financial Aid Of all full-time matriculated undergraduates who enrolled in 2011, 2,368 applied for aid, 1,898 were judged to have need, 817 had their need fully met. In 2011, 235 non-need-based awards were made. *Average percent of need met:* 58%. *Average financial aid package:* $8022. *Average need-based loan:* $3821. *Average need-based gift aid:* $3941. *Average non-need-based aid:* $3111.

Applying *Options:* electronic application, deferred entrance. *Required:* high school transcript. *Application deadlines:* rolling (freshmen), rolling (out-of-state freshmen), rolling (transfers). *Notification:* continuous (freshmen), continuous (out-of-state freshmen), continuous (transfers).

Freshman Application Contact Mr. Kevin Halle, Director of Admissions, Wayne State College, 1111 Main Street, Wayne, NE 68787. *Phone:* 402-375-7234. *Toll-free phone:* 866-WSC-CATS. *Fax:* 402-375-7204. *E-mail:* admit1@wsc.edu. *Web site:* http://www.wsc.edu/.

York College

York, Nebraska

Freshman Application Contact Ms. Janae Parsons, York College, 1125 East 8th Street, York, NE 68467-2699. *Phone:* 402-363-5627. *Toll-free phone:* 800-950-9675. *Fax:* 402-363-5623. *E-mail:* enroll@york.edu. *Web site:* http://www.york.edu/.

NEVADA

The Art Institute of Las Vegas

Henderson, Nevada

- **Proprietary** 4-year, founded 2002, part of Education Management Corporation
- **Suburban** campus
- **Coed**

Academics *Calendar:* quarters. *Degrees:* diplomas, associate, and bachelor's.

Costs (2011–12) *Tuition:* Tuition cost varies by program. Prospective students should contact the school for current tuition costs. Other charges include a starting kit for all first-quarter students. Kits vary in price, depending on the program of study.

Freshman Application Contact The Art Institute of Las Vegas, 2350 Corporate Circle Drive, Henderson, NV 89074. *Phone:* 702-369-9944. *Toll-free phone:* 800-833-2678. *Web site:* http://www.artinstitutes.edu/lasvegas/.

See page 1108 for the College Close-Up.

College of Southern Nevada

North Las Vegas, Nevada

Freshman Application Contact Admissions and Records, College of Southern Nevada, 3200 East Cheyenne Avenue, North Las Vegas, NV 89030-4296. *Phone:* 702-651-4060. *Web site:* http://www.csn.edu/.

DeVry University

Henderson, Nevada

Freshman Application Contact DeVry University, 2490 Paseo Verde Parkway, Henderson, NV 89074-7120. *Toll-free phone:* 866-338-7941. *Web site:* http://www.devry.edu/.

Great Basin College

Elko, Nevada

- **State-supported** primarily 2-year, founded 1967, part of University and Community College System of Nevada
- **Small-town** 45-acre campus
- **Endowment** $187,761
- **Coed**
- **Noncompetitive** entrance level

Faculty *Student/faculty ratio:* 15:1.

Academics *Calendar:* semesters. *Degrees:* certificates, associate, bachelor's, and postbachelor's certificates.

Student Life *Campus security:* late-night transport/escort service, evening patrols by trained security personnel.

Costs (2011–12) *Tuition:* state resident $2243 full-time, $69 per credit hour part-time; nonresident $8738 full-time, $146 per credit hour part-time. Full-time tuition and fees vary according to course level. Part-time tuition and fees vary according to course level. *Required fees:* $6 per credit hour part-time. *Room only:* $2299. Room and board charges vary according to housing facility.

Financial Aid *Of all full-time matriculated undergraduates who enrolled in 2010,* 35 Federal Work-Study jobs (averaging $1000). 50 state and other part-time jobs (averaging $1800).

Applying *Options:* electronic application, early admission, deferred entrance. *Application fee:* $10.

Freshman Application Contact Ms. Janice King, Director of Admissions and Registrar, Great Basin College, 1500 College Parkway, Elko, NV 89801-3348. *Phone:* 775-753-2361. *Fax:* 775-753-2311. *E-mail:* janicek@gwmail.gbcnv.edu. *Web site:* http://www.gbcnv.edu/.

ITT Technical Institute

Henderson, Nevada

- **Proprietary** primarily 2-year, founded 1997, part of ITT Educational Services, Inc.
- **Coed**
- **Minimally difficult** entrance level

Academics *Degrees:* associate and bachelor's.

Student Life *Housing:* college housing not available.

Financial Aid Of all full-time matriculated undergraduates who enrolled in 2010, 6 Federal Work-Study jobs (averaging $5000).

Freshman Application Contact Director of Recruitment, ITT Technical Institute, 168 North Gibson Road, Henderson, NV 89014. *Phone:* 702-558-5404. *Toll-free phone:* 800-488-8459. *Web site:* http://www.itt-tech.edu/.

ITT Technical Institute

North Las Vegas, Nevada

- **Proprietary** primarily 2-year, part of ITT Educational Services, Inc.
- **Coed**

Academics *Calendar:* quarters. *Degrees:* associate and bachelor's.

Freshman Application Contact Director of Recruitment, ITT Technical Institute, 3825 W. Cheyenne Avenue, Suite 600, North Las Vegas, NV 89032. *Phone:* 702-240-0967. *Toll-free phone:* 877-832-8442. *Web site:* http://www.itt-tech.edu/.

Morrison University

Reno, Nevada

Freshman Application Contact Mr. Charles Timinsky, Director of Enrollment, Morrison University, 10315 Professional Circle, Suite 201, Reno, NV 89521. *Phone:* 775-850-0700 Ext. 101. *Toll-free phone:* 866-381-6050. *Fax:* 775-850-0711. *E-mail:* ctiminsky@morrison.neumont.edu. *Web site:* http://anthem.edu/morrison/.

Nevada State College at Henderson

Henderson, Nevada

- **State-supported** 4-year, founded 2002, part of Nevada System of Higher Education
- **Suburban** 520-acre campus with easy access to Las Vegas
- **Coed**
- **Minimally difficult** entrance level

Faculty *Student/faculty ratio:* 28:1.

Academics *Calendar:* semesters. *Degree:* bachelor's.

Student Life *Campus security:* private contracted security patrols.

Applying *Options:* electronic application. *Application fee:* $30. *Required:* high school transcript, minimum 2.0 GPA.

Freshman Application Contact Ms. Patricia Ring, Registrar, Nevada State College at Henderson, Office of Admissions and Records, 1125 Nevada State Drive, Henderson, NV 89002. *Phone:* 702-992-2114. *Fax:* 702-992-2111. *E-mail:* admissions@nsc.nevada.edu. *Web site:* http://www.nsc.nevada.edu/.

Pima Medical Institute

Las Vegas, Nevada

- **Proprietary** primarily 2-year, founded 2003, part of Vocational Training Institutes, Inc.
- **Urban** campus
- **Coed**
- **Moderately difficult** entrance level

Academics *Calendar:* modular. *Degrees:* certificates, associate, and bachelor's.

Standardized Tests *Required:* Wonderlic Scholastic Level Exam (for admission).

Applying *Required:* interview. *Required for some:* essay or personal statement, high school transcript.

Freshman Application Contact Admissions Office, Pima Medical Institute, 3333 East Flamingo Road, Las Vegas, NV 89121. *Phone:* 702-458-9650 Ext. 202. *Toll-free phone:* 800-477-PIMA. *Web site:* http://www.pmi.edu/.

Sierra Nevada College

Incline Village, Nevada

- **Independent** comprehensive, founded 1969
- **Small-town** 20-acre campus with easy access to Reno
- **Endowment** $4.0 million
- **Coed** 520 undergraduate students, 98% full-time, 42% women, 58% men
- **Moderately difficult** entrance level, 69% of applicants were admitted

Undergraduates 510 full-time, 10 part-time. Students come from 34 states and territories; 12 other countries; 81% are from out of state; 1% Black or African American, non-Hispanic/Latino; 5% Hispanic/Latino; 2% Asian, non-Hispanic/Latino; 1% Native Hawaiian or other Pacific Islander, non-Hispanic/Latino; 3% American Indian or Alaska Native, non-Hispanic/Latino; 8% Race/ethnicity unknown; 0.6% international; 20% transferred in; 28% live on campus. *Retention:* 65% of full-time freshmen returned.

Freshmen *Admission:* 423 applied, 293 admitted, 103 enrolled. *Average high school GPA:* 3.05.

Faculty *Total:* 123, 20% full-time, 61% with terminal degrees. *Student/faculty ratio:* 9:1.

Academics *Calendar:* semesters. *Degrees:* bachelor's and master's. *Special study options:* academic remediation for entering students, accelerated degree program, adult/continuing education programs, advanced placement credit, cooperative education, double majors, English as a second language, honors programs, independent study, internships, part-time degree program, services for LD students, student-designed majors, study abroad, summer session for credit. *Unusual degree programs:* 3-2 Master of Teaching, elementary or secondary education.

Computers on Campus 50 computers/terminals are available on campus for general student use. Students can access the following: computer help desk, free student e-mail accounts, online (class) grades, online (class) schedules. Campuswide network is available. 100% of college-owned or -operated housing units are wired for high-speed Internet access. Wireless service is available via entire campus.

Student Life *Housing:* on-campus residence required for freshman year. *Options:* coed. Campus housing is university owned. Freshman campus housing is guaranteed. *Activities and organizations:* drama/theater group, student-run newspaper, choral group, Film Club, International Club, Sustainability Club, Rock Climbing Club, First Generation Club. *Campus security:* 24-hour emergency response devices and patrols, controlled dormitory access. *Student services:* health clinic, personal/psychological counseling.

Athletics *Intercollegiate sports:* rock climbing M/W, skiing (downhill) M(s)/W(s). *Intramural sports:* rock climbing M/W, skiing (downhill) M/W, soccer M/W, softball M/W, volleyball M/W.

Standardized Tests *Required:* SAT or ACT (for admission).

Costs (2011–12) *Comprehensive fee:* $34,985 includes full-time tuition ($24,720), mandatory fees ($515), and room and board ($9750). Full-time tuition and fees vary according to course load, degree level, location, and program. Part-time tuition: $1030 per credit hour. Part-time tuition and fees vary according to course load, degree level, location, and program. *Required fees:* $165 per term part-time. *Room and board:* Room and board charges vary according to board plan. *Payment plan:* installment. *Waivers:* employees or children of employees.

Financial Aid Of all full-time matriculated undergraduates who enrolled in 2011, 335 applied for aid, 308 were judged to have need, 17 had their need fully met. 208 Federal Work-Study jobs (averaging $648). In 2011, 21 non-need-based awards were made. *Average percent of need met:* 55%. *Average financial aid package:* $20,549. *Average need-based loan:* $4750. *Average need-based gift aid:* $10,410. *Average non-need-based aid:* $8619. *Average indebtedness upon graduation:* $14,918.

Applying *Options:* electronic application, early admission, deferred entrance. *Required:* essay or personal statement, high school transcript, minimum 2.6 GPA. *Recommended:* interview. *Application deadlines:* rolling (freshmen), rolling (transfers). *Notification:* continuous (freshmen), continuous (transfers).

Freshman Application Contact Sierra Nevada College, 999 Tahoe Boulevard, Incline Village, NV 89451. *Phone:* 866-412-4636. *Fax:* 775-831-6223. *E-mail:* admissions@sierranevada.edu. *Web site:* http://www.sierranevada.edu/.

University of Nevada, Las Vegas
Las Vegas, Nevada

- **State-supported** university, founded 1957, part of Nevada System of Higher Education
- **Urban** campus
- **Coed** 22,138 undergraduate students, 72% full-time, 55% women, 45% men
- **Moderately difficult** entrance level, 82% of applicants were admitted

Undergraduates 16,036 full-time, 6,102 part-time. 14% are from out of state; 8% Black or African American, non-Hispanic/Latino; 19% Hispanic/Latino; 16% Asian, non-Hispanic/Latino; 2% Native Hawaiian or other Pacific Islander, non-Hispanic/Latino; 0.6% American Indian or Alaska Native, non-Hispanic/Latino; 5% Two or more races, non-Hispanic/Latino; 2% Race/ethnicity unknown; 4% international; 11% transferred in; 4% live on campus. *Retention:* 76% of full-time freshmen returned.

Freshmen *Admission:* 5,801 applied, 4,746 admitted, 2,870 enrolled. *Average high school GPA:* 3.22. *Test scores:* SAT critical reading scores over 500: 50%; SAT math scores over 500: 53%; ACT scores over 18: 86%; SAT critical reading scores over 600: 13%; SAT math scores over 600: 18%; ACT scores over 24: 33%; SAT critical reading scores over 700: 2%; SAT math scores over 700: 3%; ACT scores over 30: 4%.

Faculty *Total:* 1,259, 62% full-time. *Student/faculty ratio:* 22:1.

Academics *Calendar:* semesters. *Degrees:* certificates, bachelor's, master's, doctoral, post-master's, postbachelor's, and first professional certificates. *Special study options:* adult/continuing education programs, part-time degree program. *ROTC:* Army (b), Air Force (b).

Computers on Campus Students can access the following: computer help desk, free student e-mail accounts, online (class) grades, online (class) registration, online (class) schedules. Campuswide network is available. 100% of college-owned or -operated housing units are wired for high-speed Internet access. Wireless service is available via entire campus.

Student Life *Housing options:* coed, disabled students. Campus housing is university owned. Freshman applicants given priority for college housing. *Campus security:* 24-hour emergency response devices and patrols, late-night transport/escort service, controlled dormitory access.

Athletics Member NCAA. All Division I except football (Division I-A). *Intercollegiate sports:* baseball M(s), basketball M(s)/W(s), cheerleading M(s)/W(s), cross-country running W(s), golf M(s), soccer M(s)/W(s), softball W(s), swimming and diving M(s)/W(s), tennis M(s)/W(s), track and field W(s), volleyball W(s). *Intramural sports:* badminton M/W, basketball M/W, bowling M/W, football M/W, golf M/W, racquetball M/W, soccer M/W, softball M/W, swimming and diving M/W, tennis M/W, volleyball M/W.

Standardized Tests *Recommended:* SAT or ACT (for admission).

Costs (2012–13) *Tuition:* state resident $6089 full-time, $192 per credit hour part-time; nonresident $19,999 full-time, $380 per credit hour part-time. Full-time tuition and fees vary according to course level and program. Part-time tuition and fees vary according to course level and program. *Required fees:* $616 full-time. *Room and board:* $10,524; room only: $5880. Room and board charges vary according to board plan. *Payment plan:* deferred payment. *Waivers:* children of alumni and employees or children of employees.

Financial Aid Of all full-time matriculated undergraduates who enrolled in 2010, 10,547 applied for aid, 8,942 were judged to have need, 1,228 had their need fully met. In 2010, 459 non-need-based awards were made. *Average percent of need met:* 56%. *Average financial aid package:* $8965. *Average need-based loan:* $4135. *Average need-based gift aid:* $4572. *Average non-need-based aid:* $3211. *Average indebtedness upon graduation:* $17,165.

Applying *Options:* electronic application, early admission, deferred entrance. *Application fee:* $60. *Required:* high school transcript, minimum 3.0 GPA. *Required for some:* 2 letters of recommendation. *Application deadlines:* 7/1 (freshmen), 7/1 (transfers). *Notification:* continuous (freshmen), continuous (transfers).

Freshman Application Contact Director of Admissions, University of Nevada, Las Vegas, 4505 Maryland Parkway, Box 451021, Las Vegas, NV 89154-1021. *Phone:* 702-774-8658. *Fax:* 702-774-8008. *E-mail:* admissions@unlv.edu. *Web site:* http://www.unlv.edu/.

See page 1688 for the College Close-Up.

University of Nevada, Reno
Reno, Nevada

- **State-supported** university, founded 1874, part of Nevada System of Higher Education
- **Urban** 200-acre campus
- **Endowment** $235.4 million
- **Coed** 14,820 undergraduate students, 81% full-time, 53% women, 47% men
- **Moderately difficult** entrance level, 86% of applicants were admitted

Undergraduates 11,993 full-time, 2,827 part-time. Students come from 46 states and territories; 43 other countries; 22% are from out of state; 3% Black or African American, non-Hispanic/Latino; 12% Hispanic/Latino; 6% Asian, non-Hispanic/Latino; 0.3% Native Hawaiian or other Pacific Islander, non-Hispanic/Latino; 1% American Indian or Alaska Native, non-Hispanic/Latino; 5% Two or more races, non-Hispanic/Latino; 2% Race/ethnicity unknown; 2% international; 8% transferred in; 14% live on campus. *Retention:* 78% of full-time freshmen returned.

Freshmen *Admission:* 7,182 applied, 6,191 admitted, 2,880 enrolled. *Average high school GPA:* 3.3. *Test scores:* SAT critical reading scores over 500: 62%; SAT math scores over 500: 65%; SAT writing scores over 500: 55%; ACT scores over 18: 90%; SAT critical reading scores over 600: 18%; SAT math scores over 600: 24%; SAT writing scores over 600: 13%; ACT scores over 24: 42%; SAT critical reading scores over 700: 2%; SAT math scores over 700: 3%; SAT writing scores over 700: 1%; ACT scores over 30: 6%.

Faculty *Total:* 566, 96% full-time, 89% with terminal degrees. *Student/faculty ratio:* 26:1.

Academics *Calendar:* semesters. *Degrees:* associate, bachelor's, master's, doctoral, post-master's, postbachelor's, and first professional certificates. *Special study options:* academic remediation for entering students, adult/continuing education programs, advanced placement credit, distance learning, double majors, English as a second language, honors programs, independent study, internships, off-campus study, part-time degree program, services for LD students, study abroad, summer session for credit. *ROTC:* Army (b). *Unusual degree programs:* 3-2 biotechnology.

Computers on Campus 725 computers/terminals are available on campus for general student use. Students can access the following: computer help desk, free student e-mail accounts, online (class) grades, online (class) registration, online (class) schedules. Campuswide network is available. 100% of college-owned or -operated housing units are wired for high-speed Internet access. Wireless service is available via entire campus.

Student Life *Housing options:* coed, men-only, women-only, disabled students. Campus housing is university owned. Freshman applicants given priority for college housing. *Activities and organizations:* drama/theater group, student-run newspaper, radio station, choral group, marching band, Intervarsity Christian Fellowship, Student Ambassadors, Young Democrats, Asian American Association, Blue Crew, national fraternities, national sororities. *Campus security:* 24-hour emergency response devices and patrols, late-night transport/escort service, controlled dormitory access. *Student services:* health clinic, personal/psychological counseling, women's center, legal services.

Athletics Member NCAA. All Division I except football (Division I-A). *Intercollegiate sports:* baseball M(s), basketball M(s)/W(s), cheerleading M(c)/W(c), cross-country running M(s), golf M(s)/W(s), riflery M(s)/W(s), soccer W(s), softball W(s), swimming and diving W(s), tennis M(s)/W(s), track and field W(s), volleyball W(s). *Intramural sports:* basketball M/W, bowling M/W, cross-country running M/W, equestrian sports M/W, football M, golf M/W, racquetball M/W, rock climbing M/W, rugby M/W, skiing (cross-country) M/W, skiing (downhill) M/W, soccer M/W, softball M/W, swimming and diving M/W, table tennis M/W, tennis M/W, track and field M/W, ultimate Frisbee M/W, volleyball M/W, water polo M/W.

Standardized Tests *Required for some:* SAT or ACT (for admission).

Costs (2012–13) *Tuition:* state resident $5678 full-time, $189 per credit hour part-time; nonresident $19,273 full-time, $205 per credit hour part-time. Full-time tuition and fees vary according to course level, course load, and program. Part-time tuition and fees vary according to course level, course load, and program. *Required fees:* $758 full-time, $55 per term part-time. *Room and board:* $9518. Room and board charges vary according to board plan and housing facility.

Financial Aid Of all full-time matriculated undergraduates who enrolled in 2010, 6,918 applied for aid, 5,434 were judged to have need, 1,055 had their need fully met. In 2010, 3569 non-need-based awards were made. *Average percent of need met:* 63%. *Average financial aid package:* $9925. *Average*

need-based loan: $4389. *Average need-based gift aid:* $6257. *Average non-need-based aid:* $2784. *Average indebtedness upon graduation:* $18,420.
Applying *Options:* electronic application, early admission, deferred entrance. *Application fee:* $60. *Required:* high school transcript, minimum 3.0 GPA. *Application deadlines:* 5/31 (freshmen), rolling (transfers). *Notification:* continuous (freshmen), continuous (transfers).
Freshman Application Contact Dr. Steve Maples, Director of Undergraduate Admissions, University of Nevada, Reno, Mail Stop 120, Reno, NV 89557. *Phone:* 775-784-4700. *Toll-free phone:* 866-263-8232. *Fax:* 775-784-4283. *E-mail:* asknevada@unr.edu. *Web site:* http://www.unr.edu/.

University of Phoenix–Las Vegas Campus
Las Vegas, Nevada

Freshman Application Contact Marc Booker, Sr. Director, Office of Admissions and Evaluation, University of Phoenix–Las Vegas Campus, 4305 South Riverpoint Parkway, Mail Stop CF-L101, Phoenix, AZ 85040. *Phone:* 602-557-4609. *Toll-free phone:* 866-766-0766. *Fax:* 480-643-1156. *Web site:* http://www.phoenix.edu/.

University of Phoenix–Northern Nevada Campus
Reno, Nevada

Freshman Application Contact Marc Booker, Sr. Director, Office of Admissions and Evaluation, University of Phoenix–Northern Nevada Campus, 4035 South Riverpoint Parkway, Mail Stop CF-L101, Phoenix, AZ 85040. *Phone:* 602-557-4609. *Toll-free phone:* 866-766-0766. *Fax:* 480-643-1156. *Web site:* http://www.phoenix.edu/.

Western Nevada College
Carson City, Nevada

Freshman Application Contact Admissions and Records, Western Nevada College, 2201 West College Parkway, Carson City, NV 89703. *Phone:* 775-445-2377. *Fax:* 775-445-3147. *E-mail:* wncc_aro@wncc.edu. *Web site:* http://www.wnc.edu/.

NEW HAMPSHIRE

Chester College of New England
Chester, New Hampshire

- **Independent** 4-year, founded 1965
- **Rural** 75-acre campus with easy access to Boston
- **Coed**
- **Moderately difficult** entrance level

Undergraduates *Retention:* 80% of full-time freshmen returned.
Academics *Calendar:* semesters. *Degree:* diplomas and bachelor's. *Special study options:* academic remediation for entering students, adult/continuing education programs, advanced placement credit, cooperative education, double majors, English as a second language, independent study, internships, part-time degree program, student-designed majors, study abroad, summer session for credit.
Computers on Campus Campuswide network is available.
Student Life *Housing options:* coed. Campus housing is university owned. Freshman campus housing is guaranteed. *Activities and organizations:* drama/theater group, student-run newspaper, choral group. *Campus security:* late-night transport/escort service, controlled dormitory access, regular patrols by trained security personnel. *Student services:* personal/psychological counseling.
Standardized Tests *Required:* SAT or ACT (for admission).
Costs (2012–13) *Comprehensive fee:* $29,490 includes full-time tuition ($19,470), mandatory fees ($850), and room and board ($9170).
Financial Aid Of all full-time matriculated undergraduates who enrolled in 2006, 148 applied for aid, 140 were judged to have need. In 2006, 8 non-need-based awards were made. *Average percent of need met:* 25%. *Average financial aid package:* $7200. *Average need-based loan:* $3713. *Average need-based gift aid:* $2545. *Average non-need-based aid:* $2312. *Average indebtedness upon graduation:* $32,915.
Applying *Options:* electronic application, deferred entrance. *Application fee:* $45. *Required:* essay or personal statement, high school transcript, minimum

2.0 GPA, 2 letters of recommendation, interview. *Recommended:* minimum 3.0 GPA, Art and/ or writing portfolio. *Application deadlines:* 2/1 (freshmen), 2/1 (out-of-state freshmen), 3/1 (transfers). *Notification:* continuous (freshmen), continuous (out-of-state freshmen), continuous (transfers).
Freshman Application Contact Michael Hayes, Director of Admissions, Chester College of New England, 40 Chester Street, Chester, NH 03036. *Phone:* 603-887-7400. *Toll-free phone:* 800-974-6372. *Fax:* 603-887-1777. *E-mail:* admissions@chestercollege.edu. *Web site:* http://www.chestercollege.edu/.

Colby-Sawyer College
New London, New Hampshire

Freshman Application Contact Director of Admissions and Financial Aid, Colby-Sawyer College, 541 Main Street, New London, NH 03257-4648. *Phone:* 603-526-3700. *Toll-free phone:* 800-272-1015. *Fax:* 603-526-3452. *E-mail:* admissions@colby-sawyer.edu. *Web site:* http://www.colby-sawyer.edu/.

College of Saint Mary Magdalen
Warner, New Hampshire

Freshman Application Contact Admissions Director, College of Saint Mary Magdalen, 511 Kearsarge Mountain Road, Warner, NH 03278. *Phone:* 603-456-2656. *Toll-free phone:* 877-498-1723. *Fax:* 603-456-2660. *E-mail:* admissions@magdalen.edu. *Web site:* http://www.magdalen.edu/.

Daniel Webster College
Nashua, New Hampshire

- **Independent** comprehensive, founded 1965
- **Suburban** 59-acre campus with easy access to Boston
- **Coed** 648 undergraduate students, 88% full-time, 22% women, 78% men
- **Moderately difficult** entrance level

Undergraduates 573 full-time, 75 part-time. Students come from 22 states and territories; 15 other countries; 62% are from out of state; 3% Black or African American, non-Hispanic/Latino; 3% Hispanic/Latino; 2% Asian, non-Hispanic/Latino; 0.3% American Indian or Alaska Native, non-Hispanic/Latino; 0.5% Two or more races, non-Hispanic/Latino; 37% Race/ethnicity unknown; 10% transferred in; 51% live on campus. *Retention:* 63% of full-time freshmen returned.
Freshmen *Admission:* 118 enrolled. *Average high school GPA:* 2.77.
Faculty *Total:* 79, 39% full-time, 25% with terminal degrees. *Student/faculty ratio:* 13:1.
Academics *Calendar:* semesters. *Degrees:* bachelor's and master's. *Special study options:* academic remediation for entering students, accelerated degree program, advanced placement credit, distance learning, double majors, independent study, internships, off-campus study, part-time degree program, summer session for credit. *ROTC:* Army (c), Air Force (c).
Computers on Campus 50 computers/terminals and 535 ports are available on campus for general student use. Students can access the following: campus intranet, computer help desk, free student e-mail accounts, online (class) grades, online (class) registration, online (class) schedules. Campuswide network is available. 100% of college-owned or -operated housing units are wired for high-speed Internet access. Wireless service is available via entire campus.
Student Life *Housing:* on-campus residence required through sophomore year. *Options:* coed, men-only, disabled students. Campus housing is university owned. Freshman campus housing is guaranteed. *Activities and organizations:* drama/theater group, Student Activity Board, Gaming Guild, SATCA (Student Air Traffic Controllers Association), AIAA (American Institute of Aeronautics and Astronautics), Culinary Club. *Campus security:* 24-hour emergency response devices and patrols, controlled dormitory access. *Student services:* health clinic, personal/psychological counseling.
Athletics Member NCAA. All Division III. *Intercollegiate sports:* baseball M, basketball M/W, cross-country running M/W, field hockey W, golf M, ice hockey M(c), lacrosse M/W, soccer M/W, softball W, volleyball M/W. *Intramural sports:* basketball M/W, football M/W, ultimate Frisbee M/W, volleyball M/W.
Standardized Tests *Required:* SAT or ACT (for admission).
Costs (2012–13) *Comprehensive fee:* $25,380 includes full-time tuition ($15,090) and room and board ($10,290). Full-time tuition and fees vary according to course load. Part-time tuition: $503 per credit. Part-time tuition and fees vary according to course load. *College room only:* $5050. Room and board charges vary according to board plan and housing facility. *Payment plan:* installment. *Waivers:* employees or children of employees.
Financial Aid Of all full-time matriculated undergraduates who enrolled in 2006, 567 applied for aid, 566 were judged to have need. 369 Federal Work-Study jobs (averaging $2000). In 2006, 31 non-need-based awards were made.

Average percent of need met: 72%. *Average financial aid package:* $15,371. *Average need-based loan:* $4257. *Average need-based gift aid:* $6114. *Average non-need-based aid:* $8287. *Average indebtedness upon graduation:* $45,000.

Applying *Options:* electronic application, early admission, deferred entrance. *Required:* high school transcript. *Recommended:* interview. *Application deadlines:* rolling (freshmen), rolling (out-of-state freshmen), rolling (transfers). *Notification:* continuous (freshmen), continuous (out-of-state freshmen), continuous (transfers).

Freshman Application Contact Mr. Martin Nilsson, Director of Admissions, Daniel Webster College, 20 University Drive, Nashua, NH 03063-1300. *Phone:* 800-794-6188. *Toll-free phone:* 800-325-6876. *E-mail:* nilsson@dwc.edu. *Web site:* http://www.dwc.edu/.

Dartmouth College
Hanover, New Hampshire

- **Independent** university, founded 1769
- **Small-town** 265-acre campus
- **Coed** 4,194 undergraduate students, 99% full-time, 49% women, 51% men
- **Most difficult** entrance level, 10% of applicants were admitted

Undergraduates 4,147 full-time, 47 part-time. Students come from 54 states and territories; 60 other countries; 96% are from out of state; 8% Black or African American, non-Hispanic/Latino; 9% Hispanic/Latino; 14% Asian, non-Hispanic/Latino; 0.1% Native Hawaiian or other Pacific Islander, non-Hispanic/Latino; 3% American Indian or Alaska Native, non-Hispanic/Latino; 3% Two or more races, non-Hispanic/Latino; 8% Race/ethnicity unknown; 7% international; 0.4% transferred in; 85% live on campus. *Retention:* 98% of full-time freshmen returned.

Freshmen *Admission:* 22,385 applied, 2,270 admitted, 1,112 enrolled. *Test scores:* SAT critical reading scores over 500: 100%; SAT math scores over 500: 100%; SAT writing scores over 500: 100%; SAT critical reading scores over 600: 91%; SAT math scores over 600: 97%; SAT writing scores over 600: 94%; SAT critical reading scores over 700: 69%; SAT math scores over 700: 69%; SAT writing scores over 700: 72%.

Faculty *Total:* 682, 79% full-time, 90% with terminal degrees. *Student/faculty ratio:* 8:1.

Academics *Calendar:* quarters. *Degrees:* bachelor's, master's, doctoral, and first professional. *Special study options:* advanced placement credit, double majors, honors programs, independent study, internships, off-campus study, services for LD students, student-designed majors, study abroad, summer session for credit. *ROTC:* Army (c). *Unusual degree programs:* 3-2 engineering.

Computers on Campus 200 computers/terminals are available on campus for general student use. Students can access the following: campus intranet, computer help desk, free student e-mail accounts, online (class) grades, online (class) registration, online (class) schedules. Campuswide network is available. 100% of college-owned or -operated housing units are wired for high-speed Internet access. Wireless service is available via entire campus.

Student Life *Housing:* on-campus residence required for freshman year. *Options:* coed, cooperative. Campus housing is university owned. Freshman campus housing is guaranteed. *Activities and organizations:* drama/theater group, student-run newspaper, radio and television station, choral group, marching band, Dartmouth Student Assembly, Dartmouth Outing Club, national fraternities, national sororities. *Campus security:* 24-hour emergency response devices and patrols, student patrols, late-night transport/escort service, controlled dormitory access. *Student services:* health clinic, personal/psychological counseling, women's center.

Athletics Member NCAA. All Division I except football (Division I-AA). *Intercollegiate sports:* badminton M(c)/W(c), baseball M, basketball M/W, cheerleading M(c)/W(c), crew M/W, cross-country running M/W, equestrian sports M/W, fencing M(c)/W(c), field hockey W, golf M/W, gymnastics M(c)/W(c), ice hockey M/W, lacrosse M/W, rugby M(c)/W(c), sailing M/W, skiing (cross-country) M/W, skiing (downhill) M/W, soccer M/W, softball W, squash M/W, swimming and diving M/W, table tennis M(c)/W(c), tennis M/W, track and field M/W, ultimate Frisbee M(c)/W(c), volleyball M(c)/W, water polo M(c)/W(c), wrestling M(c). *Intramural sports:* baseball M, basketball M/W, cross-country running M/W, football M/W, golf M/W, ice hockey M/W, lacrosse M/W, racquetball M/W, riflery M/W, rugby M/W, skiing (cross-country) M/W, skiing (downhill) M/W, soccer M/W, softball M/W, squash M/W, swimming and diving M/W, table tennis M/W, tennis M/W, track and field M/W, volleyball M/W, water polo M/W, weight lifting M/W, wrestling M.

Standardized Tests *Required:* SAT or ACT (for admission), SAT Subject Tests (for admission).

Costs (2011–12) *One-time required fee:* $280. *Comprehensive fee:* $55,365 includes full-time tuition ($41,736), mandatory fees ($1260), and room and board ($12,369). *College room only:* $7395. Room and board charges vary according to board plan. *Payment plans:* tuition prepayment, installment.

Financial Aid Of all full-time matriculated undergraduates who enrolled in 2011, 2,429 applied for aid, 2,127 were judged to have need, 2,127 had their need fully met. *Average percent of need met:* 100%. *Average financial aid package:* $41,339. *Average need-based loan:* $3586. *Average need-based gift aid:* $38,188. *Average indebtedness upon graduation:* $16,615. *Financial aid deadline:* 2/1.

Applying *Options:* electronic application, early admission, early decision, deferred entrance. *Application fee:* $75. *Required:* essay or personal statement, high school transcript, 2 letters of recommendation, peer evaluation. *Recommended:* interview. *Application deadlines:* 1/1 (freshmen), 3/1 (transfers). *Early decision deadline:* 11/1. *Notification:* 4/1 (freshmen), 5/15 (transfers), 12/15 (early decision).

Freshman Application Contact Maria Laskaris, Dean of Admissions and Financial Aid, Dartmouth College, 6016 McNutt Hall, Hanover, NH 03755. *Phone:* 603-646-2875. *E-mail:* admissions.reply@dartmouth.edu. *Web site:* http://www.dartmouth.edu/.

Franklin Pierce University
Rindge, New Hampshire

- **Independent** university, founded 1962
- **Rural** 1000-acre campus
- **Endowment** $7.7 million
- **Coed**
- **Minimally difficult** entrance level

Faculty *Student/faculty ratio:* 14:1.

Academics *Calendar:* differs by branch and program. *Degrees:* certificates, associate, bachelor's, master's, doctoral, and post-master's certificates (profile does not reflect significant enrollment at 6 continuing education sites; master's degree is only offered at these sites).

Student Life *Campus security:* 24-hour emergency response devices and patrols, student patrols, late-night transport/escort service, controlled dormitory access.

Athletics Member NCAA. All Division II.

Standardized Tests *Required:* SAT or ACT (for admission).

Costs (2011–12) *One-time required fee:* $250. *Comprehensive fee:* $40,070 includes full-time tuition ($28,250), mandatory fees ($1200), and room and board ($10,620). Full-time tuition and fees vary according to course load, degree level, and location. Part-time tuition: $945 per credit hour. Part-time tuition and fees vary according to course load, degree level, and location. *College room only:* $6200. Room and board charges vary according to board plan, housing facility, and student level.

Financial Aid Of all full-time matriculated undergraduates who enrolled in 2011, 1,057 applied for aid, 971 were judged to have need, 175 had their need fully met. 627 Federal Work-Study jobs (averaging $1509). 167 state and other part-time jobs (averaging $500). In 2011, 168 non-need-based awards were made. *Average percent of need met:* 74. *Average financial aid package:* $23,055. *Average need-based loan:* $5127. *Average need-based gift aid:* $17,882. *Average non-need-based aid:* $11,561. *Average indebtedness upon graduation:* $44,702.

Applying *Options:* electronic application, early admission, deferred entrance. *Application fee:* $40. *Required:* essay or personal statement, high school transcript, 1 letter of recommendation. *Required for some:* minimum 2.0 GPA. *Recommended:* minimum 2.2 GPA, interview.

Freshman Application Contact Office of Admissions, Franklin Pierce University, 40 University Drive, Rindge, NH 03461. *Phone:* 603-899-4050. *Toll-free phone:* 800-437-0048. *Fax:* 603-899-4394. *E-mail:* admissions@franklinpierce.edu. *Web site:* http://www.franklinpierce.edu/.

Granite State College
Concord, New Hampshire

- **State and locally supported** comprehensive, founded 1972, part of University System of New Hampshire
- **Suburban** campus
- **Endowment** $2.1 million
- **Coed** 1,669 undergraduate students, 49% full-time, 71% women, 29% men
- **Noncompetitive** entrance level, 100% of applicants were admitted

Undergraduates 820 full-time, 849 part-time. Students come from 23 states and territories; 10% are from out of state; 1% Black or African American, non-Hispanic/Latino; 2% Hispanic/Latino; 0.6% Asian, non-Hispanic/Latino; 0.1% Native Hawaiian or other Pacific Islander, non-Hispanic/Latino; 0.4% American Indian or Alaska Native, non-Hispanic/Latino; 2% Two or more races, non-Hispanic/Latino; 8% Race/ethnicity unknown; 14% transferred in. *Retention:* 78% of full-time freshmen returned.

Freshmen *Admission:* 187 applied, 187 admitted, 90 enrolled.

Faculty *Total:* 169, 0.6% full-time, 39% with terminal degrees. *Student/faculty ratio:* 10:1.

Academics *Calendar:* trimesters. *Degrees:* associate, bachelor's, master's, and postbachelor's certificates (offers primarily part-time degree programs; courses offered at 50 locations in New Hampshire). *Special study options:* academic remediation for entering students, accelerated degree program, adult/continuing education programs, advanced placement credit, cooperative education, distance learning, double majors, independent study, internships, off-campus study, part-time degree program, services for LD students, student-designed majors, summer session for credit. *ROTC:* Army (c), Air Force (c).

Computers on Campus 150 computers/terminals are available on campus for general student use. Students can access the following: campus intranet, computer help desk, free student e-mail accounts, online (class) grades, online (class) registration, online (class) schedules. Campuswide network is available. Wireless service is available via entire campus.

Student Life *Housing:* college housing not available. *Activities and organizations:* Alumni Learner Association, Green Team. *Campus security:* UNH Alert, a system that provides emergency notifications via text and voice messages.

Costs (2011–12) *Tuition:* state resident $6600 full-time, $275 per credit part-time; nonresident $6840 full-time, $285 per credit part-time. *Required fees:* $70 per term part-time. *Payment plan:* deferred payment. *Waivers:* senior citizens and employees or children of employees.

Applying *Options:* electronic application. *Application fee:* $45. *Required for some:* high school transcript, self-certify high school graduate or GED. *Application deadlines:* rolling (freshmen), rolling (out-of-state freshmen), rolling (transfers). *Notification:* continuous (freshmen), continuous (out-of-state freshmen), continuous (transfers).

Freshman Application Contact Ms. Ruth Nawn, Associate Director of Admissions, Granite State College, 8 Old Suncook Road, Concord, NH 03301. *Phone:* 603-513-1339. *Toll-free phone:* 888-228-3000. *Fax:* 603-513-1386. *E-mail:* ruth.nawn@granite.edu. *Web site:* http://www.granite.edu/.

Hesser College, Concord

Concord, New Hampshire

- **Proprietary** primarily 2-year
- **Coed**

Academics *Degrees:* diplomas, associate, and bachelor's.

Freshman Application Contact Hesser College, Concord, 16 Foundry Street, Concord, NH 03301. *Phone:* 603-225-9200. *Toll-free phone:* 800-935-1824. *Web site:* http://www.hesser.edu/.

Hesser College, Manchester

Manchester, New Hampshire

- **Proprietary** primarily 2-year, founded 1900
- **Urban** campus
- **Coed**

Academics *Calendar:* semesters. *Degrees:* diplomas, associate, and bachelor's.

Financial Aid Of all full-time matriculated undergraduates who enrolled in 2010, 700 Federal Work-Study jobs (averaging $1000).

Freshman Application Contact Hesser College, Manchester, 3 Sundial Avenue, Manchester, NH 03103. *Phone:* 603-668-6660. *Toll-free phone:* 800-935-1824. *Web site:* http://www.hesser.edu/.

Hesser College, Nashua

Nashua, New Hampshire

- **Proprietary** primarily 2-year
- **Coed**

Academics *Degrees:* diplomas, associate, and bachelor's.

Freshman Application Contact Hesser College, Nashua, 410 Amherst Street, Nashua, NH 03063. *Phone:* 603-883-0404. *Toll-free phone:* 800-935-1824. *Web site:* http://www.hesser.edu/.

Hesser College, Portsmouth

Portsmouth, New Hampshire

- **Proprietary** primarily 2-year
- **Coed**

Academics *Degrees:* diplomas, associate, and bachelor's.

Freshman Application Contact Hesser College, Portsmouth, 170 Commerce Way, Portsmouth, NH 03801. *Phone:* 603-436-5300. *Toll-free phone:* 800-935-1824. *Web site:* http://www.hesser.edu/.

Hesser College, Salem

Salem, New Hampshire

- **Proprietary** primarily 2-year
- **Coed**

Academics *Degrees:* diplomas, associate, and bachelor's.

Freshman Application Contact Hesser College, Salem, 11 Manor Parkway, Salem, NH 03079. *Phone:* 603-898-3480. *Toll-free phone:* 800-935-1824. *Web site:* http://www.hesser.edu/.

Keene State College

Keene, New Hampshire

- **State-supported** comprehensive, founded 1909, part of University System of New Hampshire
- **Small-town** 160-acre campus
- **Coed** 5,109 undergraduate students, 95% full-time, 57% women, 43% men
- **75% of applicants were admitted**

Undergraduates 4,848 full-time, 261 part-time. Students come from 25 states and territories; 4 other countries; 47% are from out of state; 0.6% Black or African American, non-Hispanic/Latino; 3% Hispanic/Latino; 0.7% Asian, non-Hispanic/Latino; 0.2% American Indian or Alaska Native, non-Hispanic/Latino; 1% Two or more races, non-Hispanic/Latino; 8% Race/ethnicity unknown; 0.1% international; 4% transferred in; 54% live on campus. *Retention:* 79% of full-time freshmen returned.

Freshmen *Admission:* 6,887 applied, 5,152 admitted, 1,262 enrolled. *Average high school GPA:* 3.04. *Test scores:* SAT critical reading scores over 500: 50%; SAT math scores over 500: 51%; SAT writing scores over 500: 50%; ACT scores over 18: 85%; SAT critical reading scores over 600: 11%; SAT math scores over 600: 10%; SAT writing scores over 600: 10%; ACT scores over 24: 24%; SAT critical reading scores over 700: 1%; SAT math scores over 700: 1%; SAT writing scores over 700: 1%; ACT scores over 30: 1%.

Faculty *Total:* 464, 44% full-time, 39% with terminal degrees. *Student/faculty ratio:* 17:1.

Academics *Calendar:* semesters. *Degrees:* certificates, associate, bachelor's, master's, post-master's, and postbachelor's certificates. *Special study options:* advanced placement credit, cooperative education, double majors, English as a second language, freshman honors college, honors programs, independent study, internships, off-campus study, part-time degree program, services for LD students, student-designed majors, study abroad, summer session for credit. *ROTC:* Air Force (c). *Unusual degree programs:* 3-2 engineering with Clarkson University, University of New Hampshire.

Computers on Campus 600 computers/terminals are available on campus for general student use. Students can access the following: campus intranet, computer help desk, free student e-mail accounts, online (class) grades, online (class) registration, online (class) schedules, student web pages. Campuswide network is available. 100% of college-owned or -operated housing units are wired for high-speed Internet access. Wireless service is available via classrooms, computer centers, computer labs, dorm rooms, learning centers, libraries, student centers.

Student Life *Housing:* on-campus residence required through sophomore year. *Options:* coed, women-only, disabled students. Campus housing is university owned. Freshman campus housing is guaranteed. *Activities and organizations:* drama/theater group, student-run newspaper, radio and television station, choral group, Social Activities Council, Concerned Students Coalition, Pride, Habitat for Humanity, sports clubs, national fraternities, national sororities. *Campus security:* 24-hour emergency response devices and patrols, late-night transport/escort service, controlled dormitory access. *Student services:* health clinic, personal/psychological counseling, women's center.

Athletics Member NCAA. All Division III. *Intercollegiate sports:* baseball M, basketball M/W, cheerleading W, cross-country running M/W, field hockey W, lacrosse M/W, rugby M(c)/W(c), skiing (downhill) M(c)/W(c), soccer M/W, softball W, swimming and diving M/W, track and field M/W, ultimate Frisbee M(c)/W(c), volleyball W. *Intramural sports:* badminton M/W, basketball M/W, bowling M/W, cheerleading M/W, fencing M(c), football M/W, racquetball M/W, soccer M/W, softball M/W, squash M/W, tennis M/W, volleyball M/W, water polo M/W.

Standardized Tests *Required:* SAT or ACT (for admission).

Costs (2012–13) *Tuition:* state resident $10,410 full-time; nonresident $17,310 full-time. Part-time tuition and fees vary according to course load. *Required fees:* $2366 full-time. *Room and board:* $8762. Room and board charges vary according to board plan and housing facility. *Payment plan:* installment. *Waivers:* employees or children of employees.

Financial Aid Of all full-time matriculated undergraduates who enrolled in 2010, 4,004 applied for aid, 3,101 were judged to have need, 472 had their need fully met. 1,471 Federal Work-Study jobs (averaging $2133). 709 state and other part-time jobs (averaging $1165). In 2010, 281 non-need-based

awards were made. *Average percent of need met:* 69%. *Average financial aid package:* $10,185. *Average need-based loan:* $4417. *Average need-based gift aid:* $6282. *Average non-need-based aid:* $2706. *Average indebtedness upon graduation:* $30,715. *Financial aid deadline:* 3/1.

Applying *Options:* electronic application, deferred entrance. *Application fee:* $50. *Required:* essay or personal statement, high school transcript, 1 letter of recommendation. *Application deadlines:* 4/1 (freshmen), rolling (transfers). *Notification:* continuous (freshmen), continuous (transfers).

Freshman Application Contact Ms. Margaret Richmond, Director of Admissions, Keene State College, 229 Main Street, Keene, NH 03435-2604. *Phone:* 603-358-2273. *Toll-free phone:* 800-KSC-1909. *Fax:* 603-358-2767. *E-mail:* admissions@keene.edu. *Web site:* http://www.keene.edu/.

New England College
Henniker, New Hampshire

- **Independent** comprehensive, founded 1946
- **Small-town** 225-acre campus with easy access to Boston
- **Endowment** $6.8 million
- **Coed** 961 undergraduate students, 93% full-time, 47% women, 53% men
- **Minimally difficult** entrance level, 77% of applicants were admitted

Undergraduates 896 full-time, 65 part-time. Students come from 28 states and territories; 23 other countries; 66% are from out of state; 5% Black or African American, non-Hispanic/Latino; 4% Hispanic/Latino; 2% Asian, non-Hispanic/Latino; 0.3% American Indian or Alaska Native, non-Hispanic/Latino; 17% Race/ethnicity unknown; 7% international; 8% transferred in; 58% live on campus. *Retention:* 58% of full-time freshmen returned.

Freshmen *Admission:* 1,985 applied, 1,523 admitted, 265 enrolled. *Average high school GPA:* 2.63. *Test scores:* SAT critical reading scores over 500: 28%; SAT math scores over 500: 39%; SAT writing scores over 500: 30%; ACT scores over 18: 80%; SAT critical reading scores over 600: 4%; SAT math scores over 600: 6%; SAT writing scores over 600: 6%; ACT scores over 24: 20%; SAT math scores over 700: 1%; SAT writing scores over 700: 1%.

Faculty *Total:* 164, 39% full-time, 43% with terminal degrees. *Student/faculty ratio:* 11:1.

Academics *Calendar:* semesters. *Degrees:* associate, bachelor's, master's, and doctoral. *Special study options:* academic remediation for entering students, accelerated degree program, adult/continuing education programs, advanced placement credit, distance learning, double majors, English as a second language, honors programs, independent study, internships, off-campus study, part-time degree program, services for LD students, student-designed majors, study abroad, summer session for credit. *ROTC:* Army (c), Air Force (c). *Unusual degree programs:* 3-2 engineering with Clarkson University; nursing with Mass College of Pharmacy.

Computers on Campus 171 computers/terminals and 350 ports are available on campus for general student use. Students can access the following: campus intranet, computer help desk, free student e-mail accounts, online (class) grades, online (class) registration, online (class) schedules. Campuswide network is available. 100% of college-owned or -operated housing units are wired for high-speed Internet access. Wireless service is available via entire campus.

Student Life *Housing:* on-campus residence required through sophomore year. *Options:* coed. Campus housing is university owned. *Activities and organizations:* drama/theater group, student-run newspaper, radio station, Student Senate, Campus Activities Board, Role Playing Association, International Student Association, Political Science Club, national fraternities, national sororities. *Campus security:* 24-hour emergency response devices and patrols, student patrols, late-night transport/escort service, controlled dormitory access, Emergency Text System. *Student services:* health clinic, personal/psychological counseling, women's center.

Athletics Member NCAA. All Division III. *Intercollegiate sports:* baseball M, basketball M/W, cross-country running M/W, field hockey W, ice hockey M/W, lacrosse M/W, soccer M/W, softball W. *Intramural sports:* basketball M/W, cheerleading W, golf M/W, ice hockey M/W, lacrosse M/W, rugby M/W, soccer M/W, softball W, table tennis M/W, tennis M/W, ultimate Frisbee M/W, volleyball M/W.

Costs (2012–13) *Comprehensive fee:* $42,354 includes full-time tuition ($30,100), mandatory fees ($300), and room and board ($11,954). Full-time tuition and fees vary according to class time, course load, degree level, location, program, and reciprocity agreements. Part-time tuition: $369 per semester hour. Part-time tuition and fees vary according to class time, course load, degree level, location, and program. *College room only:* $5528. Room and board charges vary according to board plan and housing facility. *Payment plan:* installment. *Waivers:* children of alumni, adult students, senior citizens, and employees or children of employees.

Financial Aid Of all full-time matriculated undergraduates who enrolled in 2011, 722 applied for aid, 689 were judged to have need, 140 had their need fully met. 192 Federal Work-Study jobs (averaging $1783). 30 state and other part-time jobs (averaging $1262). In 2011, 191 non-need-based awards were

---

made. *Average percent of need met:* 75%. *Average financial aid package:* $26,957. *Average need-based loan:* $5322. *Average need-based gift aid:* $17,253. *Average non-need-based aid:* $12,328. *Average indebtedness upon graduation:* $43,808.

Applying *Options:* electronic application, deferred entrance. *Application fee:* $30. *Required:* essay or personal statement, high school transcript, 3 letters of recommendation. *Recommended:* interview. *Application deadlines:* 9/7 (freshmen), 9/7 (out-of-state freshmen), 9/7 (transfers). *Notification:* continuous (freshmen), continuous (out-of-state freshmen), continuous (transfers).

Freshman Application Contact Valerie Salyer, Senior Associate Director of Undergraduate Admissions, New England College, 102 Bridge Street, Henniker, NH 03242. *Phone:* 603-428 2223. *Toll-free phone:* 800-521-7642. *Fax:* 603-428 3155. *E-mail:* vsalyer@nec.edu. *Web site:* http://www.nec.edu/.

New Hampshire Institute of Art
Manchester, New Hampshire

- **Proprietary** 4-year, founded 1898
- **Urban** campus with easy access to Boston
- **Endowment** $220.1 million
- **Coed**
- **Moderately difficult** entrance level

Faculty *Student/faculty ratio:* 12:1.

Academics *Calendar:* semesters. *Degrees:* certificates, bachelor's, and post-bachelor's certificates.

Student Life *Campus security:* late-night transport/escort service, controlled dormitory access.

Standardized Tests *Recommended:* SAT and SAT Subject Tests or ACT (for admission).

Costs (2011–12) *Tuition:* $18,610 full-time, $1779 per course part-time. Part-time tuition and fees vary according to course load. *Required fees:* $1935 full-time, $245 per course part-time, $205 per term part-time. *Room only:* $7550. Room and board charges vary according to housing facility.

Applying *Options:* electronic application, early action, deferred entrance. *Application fee:* $25. *Required:* essay or personal statement, high school transcript, 2 letters of recommendation, interview, portfolio review. *Recommended:* interview.

Freshman Application Contact Ms. Amanda Abbott, Assistant Director of Enrollment, New Hampshire Institute of Art, 148 Concord Street, Manchester, NH 03104-4158. *Phone:* 866-241-4918 Ext. 576. *Toll-free phone:* 866-241-4918. *Fax:* 603-647-0658. *E-mail:* aabbott@nhia.edu. *Web site:* http://www.nhia.edu/.

Plymouth State University
Plymouth, New Hampshire

- **State-supported** comprehensive, founded 1871, part of University System of New Hampshire
- **Small-town** 170-acre campus
- **Endowment** $8.7 million
- **Coed** 4,455 undergraduate students, 93% full-time, 47% women, 53% men
- **Moderately difficult** entrance level, 74% of applicants were admitted

Undergraduates 4,148 full-time, 307 part-time. Students come from 29 states and territories; 13 other countries; 41% are from out of state; 1% Black or African American, non-Hispanic/Latino; 2% Hispanic/Latino; 0.9% Asian, non-Hispanic/Latino; 0.2% American Indian or Alaska Native, non-Hispanic/Latino; 1% Two or more races, non-Hispanic/Latino; 14% Race/ethnicity unknown; 0.8% international; 7% transferred in; 58% live on campus. *Retention:* 74% of full-time freshmen returned.

Freshmen *Admission:* 5,279 applied, 3,898 admitted, 1,017 enrolled. *Average high school GPA:* 2.86. *Test scores:* SAT critical reading scores over 500: 40%; SAT math scores over 500: 44%; ACT scores over 18: 77%; SAT critical reading scores over 600: 9%; SAT math scores over 600: 7%; ACT scores over 24: 12%; SAT critical reading scores over 700: 1%.

Faculty *Total:* 418, 45% full-time, 51% with terminal degrees. *Student/faculty ratio:* 16:1.

Academics *Calendar:* semesters. *Degrees:* certificates, bachelor's, master's, doctoral, post-master's, postbachelor's, and first professional certificates. *Special study options:* adult/continuing education programs, advanced placement credit, double majors, English as a second language, honors programs, independent study, internships, off-campus study, part-time degree program, services for LD students, student-designed majors, study abroad, summer session for credit. *ROTC:* Army (c), Air Force (c).

Computers on Campus 900 computers/terminals are available on campus for general student use. Students can access the following: campus intranet, computer help desk, free student e-mail accounts, online (class) grades, online (class) registration, online (class) schedules, degree audit, academic history,

account status. Campuswide network is available. 100% of college-owned or -operated housing units are wired for high-speed Internet access. Wireless service is available via entire campus.

Student Life *Housing:* on-campus residence required for freshman year. *Options:* coed. Campus housing is university owned. Freshman applicants given priority for college housing. *Activities and organizations:* drama/theater group, student-run newspaper, radio station, choral group, Programming Activities in College Environment, Student Senate, alternative spring break, Childhood Studies Club, Health, Physical Ed, and Recreation Club, national sororities. *Campus security:* 24-hour emergency response devices and patrols, student patrols, late-night transport/escort service, controlled dormitory access, shuttle bus service, crime prevention programs, self-defense education. *Student services:* health clinic, personal/psychological counseling, women's center.

Athletics Member NCAA. All Division III. *Intercollegiate sports:* baseball M, basketball M/W, cheerleading M(c)/W, field hockey W, football M, ice hockey M/W, lacrosse M/W, skiing (downhill) M/W, soccer M/W, softball W, swimming and diving W, tennis W, volleyball M(c)/W, wrestling M. *Intramural sports:* basketball M/W, rugby M(c)/W(c), soccer M/W, softball M/W, table tennis M/W, ultimate Frisbee M/W, volleyball M/W.

Standardized Tests *Required:* SAT or ACT (for admission).

Costs (2011–12) *One-time required fee:* $198. *Tuition:* state resident $9110 full-time, $380 per credit hour part-time; nonresident $16,570 full-time, $690 per credit hour part-time. Full-time tuition and fees vary according to reciprocity agreements. Part-time tuition and fees vary according to course load and reciprocity agreements. *Required fees:* $2408 full-time, $103 per credit hour part-time. *Room and board:* $9290; room only: $6280. Room and board charges vary according to board plan and housing facility. *Payment plan:* installment. *Waivers:* senior citizens and employees or children of employees.

Financial Aid Of all full-time matriculated undergraduates who enrolled in 2010, 3,463 applied for aid, 2,441 were judged to have need, 810 had their need fully met. 1,855 Federal Work-Study jobs (averaging $2031). In 2010, 355 non-need-based awards were made. *Average percent of need met:* 60%. *Average financial aid package:* $9525. *Average need-based loan:* $4180. *Average need-based gift aid:* $6789. *Average non-need-based aid:* $2954. *Average indebtedness upon graduation:* $31,145.

Applying *Options:* electronic application, deferred entrance. *Application fee:* $50. *Required:* essay or personal statement, high school transcript, 1 letter of recommendation. *Required for some:* interview. *Application deadlines:* 4/1 (freshmen), 4/1 (transfers). *Notification:* continuous until 11/1 (freshmen), continuous until 11/1 (transfers).

Freshman Application Contact Mr. Eugene Fahey, Senior Associate Director of Admission, Plymouth State University, 17 High Street, MSC #52, Plymouth, NH 03264-1595. *Phone:* 603-535-2237. *Toll-free phone:* 800-842-6900. *Fax:* 603-535-2714. *E-mail:* plymouthadmit@plymouth.edu. *Web site:* http://www.plymouth.edu/.

Rivier College

Nashua, New Hampshire

- **Independent Roman Catholic** comprehensive, founded 1933
- **Suburban** 68-acre campus with easy access to Boston
- **Coed** 1,437 undergraduate students, 64% full-time, 84% women, 16% men
- **Moderately difficult** entrance level, 81% of applicants were admitted

Undergraduates 917 full-time, 520 part-time. Students come from 18 states and territories; 4 other countries; 38% are from out of state; 2% Black or African American, non-Hispanic/Latino; 5% Hispanic/Latino; 2% Asian, non-Hispanic/Latino; 0.5% American Indian or Alaska Native, non-Hispanic/Latino; 0.1% Two or more races, non-Hispanic/Latino; 16% Race/ethnicity unknown; 8% transferred in; 42% live on campus. *Retention:* 78% of full-time freshmen returned.

Freshmen *Admission:* 680 applied, 548 admitted, 201 enrolled. *Average high school GPA:* 3. *Test scores:* SAT critical reading scores over 500: 30%; SAT math scores over 500: 32%; SAT writing scores over 500: 31%; SAT critical reading scores over 600: 5%; SAT math scores over 600: 4%; SAT writing scores over 600: 4%.

Faculty *Total:* 193, 37% full-time, 40% with terminal degrees. *Student/faculty ratio:* 17:1.

Academics *Calendar:* semesters. *Degrees:* certificates, associate, bachelor's, master's, doctoral, post-master's, postbachelor's, and first professional certificates. *Special study options:* advanced placement credit, distance learning, double majors, independent study, internships, off-campus study, part-time degree program, services for LD students, summer session for credit. *ROTC:* Air Force (c).

Computers on Campus 173 computers/terminals are available on campus for general student use. Students can access the following: campus intranet, computer help desk, free student e-mail accounts, online (class) grades, online (class) registration, online (class) schedules. Campuswide network is available. Wireless service is available via entire campus.

Student Life *Housing options:* coed. Campus housing is university owned. Freshman campus housing is guaranteed. *Activities and organizations:* drama/ theater group, choral group, Student Government Association, Student Program Board, Rivier Theater Company, Student Nurses Association, Student Business Association. *Campus security:* 24-hour emergency response devices and patrols, late-night transport/escort service, controlled dormitory access. *Student services:* health clinic, personal/psychological counseling.

Athletics Member NCAA. All Division III. *Intercollegiate sports:* baseball M, basketball M/W, cross-country running M/W, field hockey W, lacrosse M/W, soccer M/W, softball W, volleyball M/W. *Intramural sports:* basketball M/W, volleyball M/W.

Standardized Tests *Required:* SAT or ACT (for admission). *Required for some:* nursing exam.

Costs (2011–12) *One-time required fee:* $175. *Comprehensive fee:* $35,533 includes full-time tuition ($25,410), mandatory fees ($325), and room and board ($9798). Full-time tuition and fees vary according to program. Part-time tuition: $847 per credit. Part-time tuition and fees vary according to class time, course load, and program. *Required fees:* $25 per year part-time. *College room only:* $5400. Room and board charges vary according to board plan and housing facility. *Payment plans:* installment, deferred payment. *Waivers:* senior citizens and employees or children of employees.

Financial Aid Of all full-time matriculated undergraduates who enrolled in 2010, 888 applied for aid, 822 were judged to have need, 70 had their need fully met. In 2010, 105 non-need-based awards were made. *Average percent of need met:* 59%. *Average financial aid package:* $14,850. *Average need-based loan:* $4378. *Average need-based gift aid:* $10,806. *Average non-need-based aid:* $5066. *Average indebtedness upon graduation:* $43,189.

Applying *Options:* electronic application, early action, deferred entrance. *Application fee:* $25. *Required:* essay or personal statement, high school transcript, 1 letter of recommendation. *Required for some:* interview. *Recommended:* minimum 2.3 GPA, interview. *Application deadlines:* rolling (freshmen), rolling (transfers), 11/15 (early action). *Notification:* continuous (freshmen), continuous (transfers), 12/1 (early action).

Freshman Application Contact David Boisvert, Vice President of Enrollment, Rivier College, 420 South Main Street, Nashua, NH 03060. *Phone:* 603-897-8507. *Toll-free phone:* 800-44RIVIER. *Fax:* 603-891-1799. *E-mail:* rivadmit@rivier.edu. *Web site:* http://www.rivier.edu/.

See page 1524 for the College Close-Up.

Saint Anselm College
Manchester, New Hampshire

- **Independent Roman Catholic** 4-year, founded 1889
- **Suburban** 450-acre campus with easy access to Boston
- **Endowment** $94.3 million
- **Coed** 1,899 undergraduate students, 97% full-time, 58% women, 42% men
- **Moderately difficult** entrance level, 71% of applicants were admitted

Undergraduates 1,850 full-time, 49 part-time. Students come from 24 states and territories; 3 other countries; 78% are from out of state; 2% Black or African American, non-Hispanic/Latino; 3% Hispanic/Latino; 1% Asian, non-Hispanic/Latino; 0.1% Native Hawaiian or other Pacific Islander, non-Hispanic/Latino; 0.2% American Indian or Alaska Native, non-Hispanic/Latino; 1% Two or more races, non-Hispanic/Latino; 9% Race/ethnicity unknown; 0.4% international; 0.8% transferred in; 91% live on campus. *Retention:* 85% of full-time freshmen returned.

Freshmen *Admission:* 4,134 applied, 2,953 admitted, 550 enrolled. *Average high school GPA:* 3.23. *Test scores:* SAT critical reading scores over 500: 78%; SAT math scores over 500: 83%; SAT writing scores over 500: 80%; ACT scores over 18: 100%; SAT critical reading scores over 600: 29%; SAT math scores over 600: 32%; SAT writing scores over 600: 30%; ACT scores over 24: 81%; SAT critical reading scores over 700: 3%; SAT math scores over 700: 2%; SAT writing scores over 700: 3%; ACT scores over 30: 1%.

Faculty *Total:* 205, 69% full-time, 71% with terminal degrees. *Student/faculty ratio:* 11:1.

Academics *Calendar:* semesters. *Degree:* bachelor's. *Special study options:* advanced placement credit, honors programs, independent study, internships, off-campus study, part-time degree program, services for LD students, study abroad, summer session for credit. *ROTC:* Army (c), Air Force (c). *Unusual degree programs:* 3-2 engineering with University of Massachusetts Lowell, Catholic University of America, University of Notre Dame, Manhattan College.

Computers on Campus 400 computers/terminals are available on campus for general student use. Students can access the following: campus intranet, computer help desk, free student e-mail accounts, online (class) registration, online (class) schedules. Campuswide network is available. Wireless service is available via classrooms, computer centers, computer labs, dorm rooms, learning centers, libraries, student centers.

1889

Founded in 1889 as a Benedictine, Catholic, liberal arts college dedicated to undergraduate education. Located on 400 acres overlooking Manchester, New Hampshire, Saint Anselm seeks to provide and educational experience that promotes the intelectual, spiritual and personal growth of its students.

For more information, contact:

Office of Admission
Saint Anselm College
School College or University
100 SaintAnselm Drive
Manchester, NH, 03102-1310
Phone: 603.641.7500
Fax: 603.641.7550
E-mail admission@anselm.edu

www.anselm.edu

Student Life *Housing options:* coed, men-only, women-only. Campus housing is university owned. Freshman campus housing is guaranteed. *Activities and organizations:* drama/theater group, student-run newspaper, radio station, choral group, Center for Volunteers, Anselmian Abbey Players, Knights of Columbus, spring break alternative, International Relations Club. *Campus security:* 24-hour emergency response devices and patrols, late-night transport/escort service, controlled dormitory access. *Student services:* health clinic, personal/ psychological counseling.

Athletics Member NCAA. All Division II. *Intercollegiate sports:* baseball M, basketball M(s)/W(s), cheerleading W(c), cross-country running M/W, field hockey W, football M, golf M, ice hockey M/W, lacrosse M/W, rugby M(c)/ W(c), skiing (downhill) M/W, soccer M/W, softball W, tennis M/W, volleyball W. *Intramural sports:* basketball M/W, football M/W, ice hockey M/W, racquetball M/W, skiing (cross-country) M/W, soccer M/W, softball M/W, swimming and diving M(c)/W(c), tennis M/W, track and field M(c)/W(c), ultimate Frisbee M/W, volleyball M/W, weight lifting M/W.

Standardized Tests *Required for some:* SAT or ACT (for admission).

Costs (2012–13) *Tuition:* $3150 per course part-time. *Room only:* Room and board charges vary according to housing facility. *Payment plan:* installment. *Waivers:* employees or children of employees.

Financial Aid Of all full-time matriculated undergraduates who enrolled in 2011, 1,597 applied for aid, 1,387 were judged to have need, 217 had their need fully met. 1,176 Federal Work-Study jobs (averaging $1484). 8 state and other part-time jobs (averaging $2000). In 2011, 333 non-need-based awards were made. *Average percent of need met:* 81%. *Average financial aid package:* $24,781. *Average need-based loan:* $5704. *Average non-need-based aid:* $9979. *Average indebtedness upon graduation:* $38,356. *Financial aid deadline:* 3/15.

Applying *Options:* electronic application, early admission, early action, deferred entrance. *Application fee:* $55. *Required:* essay or personal statement, high school transcript, 2 letters of recommendation. *Recommended:* interview. *Application deadlines:* 2/15 (freshmen), rolling (transfers), 11/15 (early action). *Notification:* continuous (freshmen), continuous (transfers), 1/ 15 (early action).

Freshman Application Contact Saint Anselm College, 100 Saint Anselm Drive, Manchester, NH 03102-1310. *Phone:* 603-641-7500. *Toll-free phone:* 888-4ANSELM. *Web site:* http://www.anselm.edu/.

See page 535 for display ad and page 1540 for the College Close-Up.

Southern New Hampshire University
Manchester, New Hampshire

- **Independent** comprehensive, founded 1932
- **Suburban** 300-acre campus with easy access to Boston
- **Coed** 7,351 undergraduate students, 59% full-time, 58% women, 42% men
- **Moderately difficult** entrance level, 87% of applicants were admitted

Undergraduates 4,311 full-time, 3,040 part-time. 0.8% Black or African American, non-Hispanic/Latino; 0.8% Hispanic/Latino; 0.5% Asian, non-Hispanic/Latino; 0.2% American Indian or Alaska Native, non-Hispanic/Latino; 66% Race/ethnicity unknown; 4% international; 71% live on campus. *Retention:* 71% of full-time freshmen returned.

Freshmen *Admission:* 3,994 applied, 3,483 admitted, 1,078 enrolled. *Average high school GPA:* 3. *Test scores:* SAT critical reading scores over 500: 44%; SAT math scores over 500: 53%; SAT writing scores over 500: 43%; SAT critical reading scores over 600: 7%; SAT math scores over 600: 9%; SAT writing scores over 600: 4%.

Faculty *Total:* 870, 13% full-time, 31% with terminal degrees. *Student/faculty ratio:* 21:1.

Academics *Calendar:* semesters. *Degrees:* certificates, associate, bachelor's, master's, doctoral, post-master's, postbachelor's, and first professional certificates. *Special study options:* academic remediation for entering students, accelerated degree program, adult/continuing education programs, advanced placement credit, cooperative education, distance learning, double majors, English as a second language, honors programs, independent study, internships, off-campus study, part-time degree program, services for LD students, study abroad, summer session for credit. *ROTC:* Army (c), Air Force (c). *Unusual degree programs:* 3-2 business administration.

Computers on Campus 557 computers/terminals and 1,500 ports are available on campus for general student use. Students can access the following: campus intranet, computer help desk, free student e-mail accounts, online (class) grades, online (class) registration, online (class) schedules. Campus-wide network is available. 100% of college-owned or -operated housing units are wired for high-speed Internet access. Wireless service is available via entire campus.

Student Life *Housing options:* coed, disabled students. Campus housing is university owned. *Activities and organizations:* drama/theater group, student-run newspaper, radio and television station, choral group, Coordinators of Activities and Programming Events (CAPE), International Student Associa-

tion, Radio SNHU, Outing Club, Outreach Association, national fraternities, national sororities. *Campus security:* 24-hour emergency response devices and patrols, student patrols, late-night transport/escort service, controlled dormitory access. *Student services:* health clinic, personal/psychological counseling.

Athletics Member NCAA. All Division II. *Intercollegiate sports:* baseball M(s), basketball M(s)/W(s), cheerleading M/W, cross-country running M(s)/W(s), golf M, ice hockey M, lacrosse M(s)/W(s), soccer M(s)/W(s), softball W(s), tennis M(s)/W(s), volleyball W(s). *Intramural sports:* badminton M/W, basketball M/W, crew M(c)/W(c), field hockey M(c)/W(c), football M, ice hockey M(c), racquetball M/W, skiing (cross-country) M/W, soccer M/W, softball W, table tennis M/W, tennis M/W, ultimate Frisbee M/W, volleyball W.

Standardized Tests *Recommended:* SAT or ACT (for admission).

Costs (2012–13) *Comprehensive fee:* $38,950 includes full-time tuition ($27,720), mandatory fees ($330), and room and board ($10,900). Full-time tuition and fees vary according to class time and course load. Part-time tuition and fees vary according to class time, location, and program. *Room and board:* Room and board charges vary according to housing facility. *Waivers:* senior citizens and employees or children of employees.

Financial Aid Of all full-time matriculated undergraduates who enrolled in 2007, 1,560 applied for aid, 1,392 were judged to have need, 173 had their need fully met. In 2007, 330 non-need-based awards were made. *Average percent of need met:* 69%. *Average financial aid package:* $15,514. *Average need-based loan:* $5174. *Average need-based gift aid:* $10,223. *Average non-need-based aid:* $3599.

Applying *Options:* electronic application, early action, deferred entrance. *Application fee:* $50. *Required:* essay or personal statement, high school transcript, minimum 2.0 GPA, 1 letter of recommendation. *Recommended:* interview. *Application deadlines:* rolling (freshmen), rolling (transfers), 11/15 (early action). *Notification:* continuous (freshmen), continuous (transfers), 12/15 (early action).

Freshman Application Contact Mr. Steve Soba, Assistant VP for Undergraduate Day Admission, Southern New Hampshire University, 2500 North River Road, Manchester, NH 03106-1045. *Phone:* 603-645-9611. *Toll-free phone:* 888-327-7648. *Fax:* 603-645-9693. *E-mail:* s.soba@snhu.edu. *Web site:* http://www.snhu.edu/.

See page 1594 for the College Close-Up.

Thomas More College of Liberal Arts
Merrimack, New Hampshire

- **Independent** 4-year, founded 1978, affiliated with Roman Catholic Church
- **Small-town** 14-acre campus with easy access to Boston
- **Coed** 99 undergraduate students, 100% full-time, 49% women, 51% men
- **Moderately difficult** entrance level, 70% of applicants were admitted

Undergraduates 99 full-time. Students come from 24 states and territories; 4 other countries; 84% are from out of state; 9% transferred in; 97% live on campus. *Retention:* 85% of full-time freshmen returned.

Freshmen *Admission:* 100 applied, 70 admitted, 24 enrolled. *Average high school GPA:* 3.33. *Test scores:* SAT critical reading scores over 500: 95%; SAT math scores over 500: 73%; ACT scores over 18: 100%; SAT critical reading scores over 600: 64%; SAT math scores over 600: 27%; ACT scores over 24: 100%; SAT critical reading scores over 700: 23%.

Faculty *Total:* 13. *Student/faculty ratio:* 12:1.

Academics *Calendar:* semesters. *Degree:* bachelor's. *Special study options:* independent study, study abroad.

Computers on Campus 6 computers/terminals are available on campus for general student use.

Student Life *Housing:* on-campus residence required through senior year. *Options:* men-only, women-only. Campus housing is university owned. Freshman campus housing is guaranteed. *Activities and organizations:* drama/theater group, choral group. *Campus security:* student patrols, late-night transport/escort service. *Student services:* personal/psychological counseling.

Standardized Tests *Recommended:* SAT or ACT (for admission).

Financial Aid Of all full-time matriculated undergraduates who enrolled in 2010, 78 applied for aid, 78 were judged to have need, 2 had their need fully met. 46 state and other part-time jobs (averaging $65,300). In 2010, 10 non-need-based awards were made. *Average percent of need met:* 75%. *Average financial aid package:* $18,556. *Average need-based loan:* $4220. *Average need-based gift aid:* $9178. *Average non-need-based aid:* $6135. *Average indebtedness upon graduation:* $18,355.

Applying *Options:* electronic application. *Required:* essay or personal statement, high school transcript, 2 letters of recommendation. *Required for some:* interview. *Application deadlines:* rolling (freshmen), rolling (transfers). *Notification:* continuous (freshmen), continuous (transfers).

Freshman Application Contact Teddy Sifert, Director of Admissions, Thomas More College of Liberal Arts, 6 Manchester Street, Merrimack, NH 03054-4818. *Toll-free phone:* 800-880-8308. *Fax:* 603-880-9280. *E-mail:*

admissions@thomasmorecollege.edu. *Web site:* http://www.thomasmorecollege.edu/.

University of New Hampshire
Durham, New Hampshire

- **State-supported** university, founded 1866, part of University System of New Hampshire
- **Small-town** 2600-acre campus with easy access to Boston
- **Endowment** $222.2 million
- **Coed** 12,609 undergraduate students, 96% full-time, 54% women, 46% men
- **Moderately difficult** entrance level, 74% of applicants were admitted

Undergraduates 12,109 full-time, 500 part-time. Students come from 42 states and territories; 29 other countries; 40% are from out of state; 1% Black or African American, non-Hispanic/Latino; 2% Hispanic/Latino; 2% Asian, non-Hispanic/Latino; 0.3% American Indian or Alaska Native, non-Hispanic/Latino; 2% Two or more races, non-Hispanic/Latino; 6% Race/ethnicity unknown; 0.8% international; 4% transferred in; 59% live on campus. *Retention:* 87% of full-time freshmen returned.

Freshmen *Admission:* 17,344 applied, 12,863 admitted, 2,949 enrolled. *Test scores:* SAT critical reading scores over 500: 74%; SAT math scores over 500: 80%; SAT writing scores over 500: 76%; ACT scores over 18: 98%; SAT critical reading scores over 600: 24%; SAT math scores over 600: 33%; SAT writing scores over 600: 24%; ACT scores over 24: 57%; SAT critical reading scores over 700: 3%; SAT math scores over 700: 3%; SAT writing scores over 700: 2%; ACT scores over 30: 7%.

Faculty *Total:* 1,027, 60% full-time, 61% with terminal degrees. *Student/faculty ratio:* 18:1.

Academics *Calendar:* semesters. *Degrees:* associate, bachelor's, master's, doctoral, post-master's, postbachelor's, and first professional certificates. *Special study options:* accelerated degree program, advanced placement credit, cooperative education, distance learning, double majors, English as a second language, honors programs, independent study, internships, off-campus study, part-time degree program, services for LD students, student-designed majors, study abroad, summer session for credit. *ROTC:* Army (b), Air Force (b). *Unusual degree programs:* 3-2 business administration; social work; accounting, biochemistry, occupational therapy.

Computers on Campus 448 computers/terminals are available on campus for general student use. Students can access the following: campus intranet, computer help desk, free student e-mail accounts, online (class) grades, online (class) registration, online (class) schedules. Campuswide network is available. 100% of college-owned or -operated housing units are wired for high-speed Internet access. Wireless service is available via classrooms, computer centers, computer labs, dorm rooms, libraries, student centers.

Student Life *Housing options:* coed, disabled students. Campus housing is university owned. Freshman campus housing is guaranteed. *Activities and organizations:* drama/theater group, student-run newspaper, radio station, choral group, marching band, Campus Activity Board, The Outing Club, SCOPE (Student Committee on Popular Entertainment), Best Buddies, Memorial Union Student Organization, national fraternities, national sororities. *Campus security:* 24-hour emergency response devices and patrols, student patrols, late-night transport/escort service, controlled dormitory access, lighted pathways and sidewalks. *Student services:* health clinic, personal/psychological counseling, women's center, legal services.

Athletics Member NCAA. All Division I except football (Division I-AA). *Intercollegiate sports:* archery M(c)/W(c), baseball M(c), basketball M(s)/W(s), crew M(c)/W(c), cross-country running M(s)/W(s), fencing M(c)/W(c), field hockey W(s), golf M(c)/W(c), gymnastics W(s), ice hockey M(s)/W(s), lacrosse M(c)/W(s), riflery M(c)/W(c), rock climbing M(c)/W(c), rugby M(c)/W(c), sailing M(c)/W(c), skiing (cross-country) M(s)/W(s), skiing (downhill) M(s)/W(s), soccer M(s)/W(s), softball W(c), swimming and diving W(s), tennis M(c)/W(c), track and field M(s)/W(s), ultimate Frisbee M(c)/W(c), volleyball M(c)/W(s), wrestling M(c). *Intramural sports:* basketball M/W, field hockey W, football M/W, ice hockey M/W, racquetball M/W, soccer M/W, softball M/W, table tennis M/W, tennis M/W, volleyball M/W, water polo M/W.

Standardized Tests *Required:* SAT or ACT (for admission).

Costs (2011–12) *Tuition:* state resident $12,060 full-time, $503 per credit hour part-time; nonresident $25,380 full-time, $1058 per credit hour part-time. Full-time tuition and fees vary according to degree level and program. Part-time tuition and fees vary according to course load, degree level, and program. *Required fees:* $3190 full-time, $797 per term part-time. *Room and board:* $9452; room only: $5844. Room and board charges vary according to board plan and housing facility. *Payment plan:* installment. *Waivers:* employees or children of employees.

Financial Aid Of all full-time matriculated undergraduates who enrolled in 2010, 9,233 applied for aid, 7,706 were judged to have need, 1,100 had their

need fully met. 5,191 Federal Work-Study jobs (averaging $2530). 2,644 state and other part-time jobs (averaging $1757). In 2010, 1933 non-need-based awards were made. *Average percent of need met:* 78%. *Average financial aid package:* $20,723. *Average need-based loan:* $3313. *Average need-based gift aid:* $3955. *Average non-need-based aid:* $8280. *Average indebtedness upon graduation:* $34,194.

Applying *Options:* electronic application, early action, deferred entrance. *Application fee:* $50. *Required:* essay or personal statement, high school transcript, 1 letter of recommendation. *Recommended:* minimum 3.0 GPA. *Application deadlines:* 2/1 (freshmen), 2/1 (out-of-state freshmen), 3/1 (transfers), 11/15 (early action). *Notification:* 4/15 (freshmen), 4/15 (out-of-state freshmen), 4/15 (transfers), 1/15 (early action).

Freshman Application Contact Admissions Office, University of New Hampshire, 3 Garrison Avenue, Durham, NH 03824. *Phone:* 603-862-1360. *Fax:* 603-862-0077. *E-mail:* admissions@unh.edu. *Web site:* http://www.unh.edu/.

See below for display ad and page 1692 for the College Close-Up.

University of New Hampshire at Manchester

Manchester, New Hampshire

- **State-supported** comprehensive, founded 1967, part of University System of New Hampshire
- **Urban** campus with easy access to Boston
- **Coed** 846 undergraduate students, 78% full-time, 52% women, 48% men
- **Moderately difficult** entrance level, 48% of applicants were admitted

Undergraduates 663 full-time, 183 part-time. 1% Black or African American, non-Hispanic/Latino; 3% Hispanic/Latino; 2% Asian, non-Hispanic/Latino; 0.1% Native Hawaiian or other Pacific Islander, non-Hispanic/Latino; 0.1% American Indian or Alaska Native, non-Hispanic/Latino; 0.9% Two or more races, non-Hispanic/Latino; 13% Race/ethnicity unknown; 0.1% international.

Freshmen *Admission:* 207 applied, 99 admitted, 99 enrolled. *Test scores:* SAT math scores over 500: 57%; SAT math scores over 600: 15%; SAT math scores over 700: 3%.

Faculty *Total:* 98, 37% full-time, 76% with terminal degrees. *Student/faculty ratio:* 12:1.

Academics *Calendar:* semesters. *Degrees:* certificates, associate, bachelor's, and master's. *Special study options:* academic remediation for entering students, adult/continuing education programs, advanced placement credit, double majors, independent study, internships, off-campus study, part-time degree program, services for LD students, student-designed majors, study abroad, summer session for credit. *ROTC:* Army (c), Air Force (c). *Unusual degree programs:* 3-2 pharmacy program with Massachusetts College of Pharmacy and Health Sciences.

Computers on Campus 47 computers/terminals are available on campus for general student use. Students can access the following: online (class) registration. Campuswide network is available. Wireless service is available via entire campus.

Student Life *Housing:* college housing not available. *Activities and organizations:* student-run radio station, Student Council. *Campus security:* 24-hour emergency response devices, late-night transport/escort service.

Standardized Tests *Required:* SAT or ACT (for admission).

Costs (2011–12) *Tuition:* state resident $12,060 full-time, $503 per credit hour part-time; nonresident $25,380 full-time, $1058 per credit hour part-time. Full-time tuition and fees vary according to course load and program. Part-time tuition and fees vary according to course load and program. *Required fees:* $505 full-time. *Payment plan:* installment. *Waivers:* senior citizens and employees or children of employees.

Financial Aid Of all full-time matriculated undergraduates who enrolled in 2010, 660 applied for aid, 545 were judged to have need, 46 had their need fully met. 169 Federal Work-Study jobs (averaging $2286). In 2010, 6 non-need-based awards were made. *Average percent of need met:* 64%. *Average financial aid package:* $12,263. *Average need-based loan:* $3781. *Average need-based gift aid:* $1400. *Average non-need-based aid:* $433. *Average indebtedness upon graduation:* $21,824.

Applying *Options:* electronic application, deferred entrance. *Application fee:* $45. *Required:* essay or personal statement, high school transcript, 1 letter of recommendation. *Recommended:* interview. *Application deadlines:* 6/15 (freshmen), 6/15 (transfers). *Notification:* continuous (freshmen), continuous (transfers).

Freshman Application Contact Ms. Donna Lukasiak, Senior Assistant Director Admissions, University of New Hampshire at Manchester, 400 Commercial Street, Manchester, NH 03101. *Phone:* 603-641-4150. *Fax:* 603-641-4342. *E-mail:* unhm@unh.edu. *Web site:* http://www.unhm.unh.edu/.

NEW JERSEY

Berkeley College
Woodland Park, New Jersey

Freshman Application Contact Berkeley College, 44 Rifle Camp Road, Woodland Park, NJ 07424-3353. *Phone:* 973-278-5400. *Toll-free phone:* 800-446-5400. *Web site:* http://www.berkeleycollege.edu/.

Beth Medrash Govoha
Lakewood, New Jersey

Director of Admissions Director of Admissions, Beth Medrash Govoha, 617 Sixth Street, Lakewood, NJ 08701-2797. *Phone:* 908-367-1060 Ext. 4224.

Bloomfield College
Bloomfield, New Jersey

- **Independent** comprehensive, founded 1868, affiliated with Presbyterian Church (U.S.A.)
- **Suburban** 12-acre campus with easy access to New York City
- **Endowment** $10.1 million
- **Coed** 2,131 undergraduate students, 87% full-time, 64% women, 36% men
- **Moderately difficult** entrance level, 50% of applicants were admitted

Undergraduates 1,851 full-time, 280 part-time. Students come from 19 states and territories; 36 other countries; 5% are from out of state; 52% Black or African American, non-Hispanic/Latino; 18% Hispanic/Latino; 3% Asian, non-Hispanic/Latino; 0.4% American Indian or Alaska Native, non-Hispanic/Latino; 0.3% Two or more races, non-Hispanic/Latino; 9% Race/ethnicity unknown; 2% international; 12% transferred in; 24% live on campus. *Retention:* 66% of full-time freshmen returned.

Freshmen *Admission:* 3,673 applied, 1,854 admitted, 392 enrolled. *Average high school GPA:* 2.63. *Test scores:* SAT critical reading scores over 500: 15%; SAT math scores over 500: 14%; SAT critical reading scores over 600: 2%; SAT math scores over 600: 3%.

Faculty *Total:* 239, 29% full-time, 31% with terminal degrees. *Student/faculty ratio:* 15:1.

Academics *Calendar:* semesters. *Degrees:* certificates, bachelor's, master's, and postbachelor's certificates. *Special study options:* academic remediation for entering students, accelerated degree program, advanced placement credit, distance learning, double majors, English as a second language, freshman honors college, honors programs, independent study, internships, off-campus study, part-time degree program, services for LD students, student-designed majors, study abroad, summer session for credit. *ROTC:* Army (c).

Computers on Campus 630 computers/terminals and 50 ports are available on campus for general student use. Students can access the following: computer help desk, free student e-mail accounts, online (class) grades, online (class) schedules. Campuswide network is available. 100% of college-owned or -operated housing units are wired for high-speed Internet access. Wireless service is available via classrooms, computer centers, dorm rooms, learning centers, libraries, student centers.

Student Life *Housing options:* coed. Campus housing is university owned and is provided by a third party. *Activities and organizations:* drama/theater group, student-run radio station, First Ladies, Team Infinite, Lambda Theta Alpha, Gentlemen's Club, Iota Phi Theta/ Chi Phi Sigma/Zeta Phi Beta, national fraternities, national sororities. *Campus security:* 24-hour emergency response devices and patrols, late-night transport/escort service, security cameras in high-traffic areas. *Student services:* health clinic, personal/psychological counseling.

Athletics Member NCAA. All Division II. *Intercollegiate sports:* baseball M(s), basketball M(s)/W(s), cross-country running M(s)/W(s), soccer M(s)/W(s), softball W(s), tennis M(s), volleyball W(s). *Intramural sports:* basketball M/W, volleyball M/W.

Standardized Tests *Required:* SAT or ACT (for admission).

Costs (2011–12) *Comprehensive fee:* $34,300 includes full-time tuition ($22,500), mandatory fees ($1200), and room and board ($10,600). Part-time tuition: $2450 per course. Part-time tuition and fees vary according to course load. *College room only:* $5300. Room and board charges vary according to housing facility. *Payment plans:* installment, deferred payment. *Waivers:* senior citizens and employees or children of employees.

Financial Aid Of all full-time matriculated undergraduates who enrolled in 2011, 1,714 applied for aid, 1,626 were judged to have need, 33 had their need fully met. 579 Federal Work-Study jobs (averaging $2177). In 2011, 66 non-need-based awards were made. *Average percent of need met:* 51%. *Average financial aid package:* $20,690. *Average need-based loan:* $4051. *Average need-based gift aid:* $14,453. *Average non-need-based aid:* $13,616. *Average indebtedness upon graduation:* $32,698. *Financial aid deadline:* 6/1.

Applying *Options:* electronic application, early action, deferred entrance. *Application fee:* $40. *Required:* essay or personal statement, high school transcript, minimum 2.5 GPA, 2 letters of recommendation, graded essay/term paper or personal essay. *Required for some:* interview. *Application deadlines:* 8/1 (freshmen), 8/1 (out-of-state freshmen), 8/1 (transfers), 12/15 (early action). *Notification:* continuous until 10/1 (freshmen), continuous until 10/1 (out-of-state freshmen), continuous until 10/1 (transfers), 12/23 (early action).

Freshman Application Contact Ms. Nicole Cibelli, Director of Admissions, Bloomfield College, Office of Enrollment Management and Admission, Bloomfield, NJ 07003-9981. *Phone:* 973-748-9000 Ext. 390. *Toll-free phone:* 800-848-4555 Ext. 230. *Fax:* 973-748-0916. *E-mail:* nicole_cibelli@bloomfield.edu. *Web site:* http://www.bloomfield.edu/.

Caldwell College
Caldwell, New Jersey

- **Independent Roman Catholic** comprehensive, founded 1939
- **Suburban** 70-acre campus with easy access to New York City
- **Endowment** $6.0 million
- **Coed** 1,647 undergraduate students, 76% full-time, 67% women, 33% men
- **Moderately difficult** entrance level, 63% of applicants were admitted

Undergraduates 1,250 full-time, 397 part-time. Students come from 19 states and territories; 17 other countries; 7% are from out of state; 16% Black or African American, non-Hispanic/Latino; 14% Hispanic/Latino; 2% Asian, non-Hispanic/Latino; 0.1% Native Hawaiian or other Pacific Islander, non-Hispanic/Latino; 0.1% American Indian or Alaska Native, non-Hispanic/Latino; 1% Two or more races, non-Hispanic/Latino; 15% Race/ethnicity unknown; 5% international; 4% transferred in; 31% live on campus. *Retention:* 76% of full-time freshmen returned.

Freshmen *Admission:* 1,687 applied, 1,057 admitted, 306 enrolled. *Test scores:* SAT critical reading scores over 500: 29%; SAT math scores over 500: 31%; ACT scores over 18: 71%; SAT critical reading scores over 600: 4%; SAT math scores over 600: 11%; ACT scores over 24: 18%; SAT math scores over 700: 4%.

Faculty *Total:* 216, 38% full-time. *Student/faculty ratio:* 13:1.

Academics *Calendar:* semesters. *Degrees:* bachelor's, master's, doctoral, post-master's, postbachelor's, and first professional certificates. *Special study options:* academic remediation for entering students, accelerated degree program, adult/continuing education programs, advanced placement credit, cooperative education, distance learning, double majors, English as a second language, external degree program, honors programs, independent study, internships, off-campus study, part-time degree program, services for LD students, student-designed majors, study abroad, summer session for credit. *ROTC:* Army (c). *Unusual degree programs:* 3-2 business administration; social work with Rutgers University; counseling psychology, education (MA in curriculum and instruction), occupational therapy (Columbia University), athletic training (Seton Hall University).

Computers on Campus 284 computers/terminals and 796 ports are available on campus for general student use. Students can access the following: campus intranet, computer help desk, free student e-mail accounts, online (class) grades, online (class) registration, online (class) schedules. Campuswide network is available. 100% of college-owned or -operated housing units are wired for high-speed Internet access. Wireless service is available via classrooms, dorm rooms, learning centers, libraries.

Student Life *Housing options:* coed. Campus housing is university owned. Freshman applicants given priority for college housing. *Activities and organizations:* drama/theater group, student-run newspaper, choral group, Black Student Union, Latino American Student Organization, Autism Awareness Club, Martial Arts Club, Marketing Club, national fraternities, national sororities. *Campus security:* 24-hour patrols, late-night transport/escort service, controlled dormitory access, dusk-to-dawn patrols by trained security personnel. *Student services:* health clinic, personal/psychological counseling.

Athletics Member NCAA. All Division II. *Intercollegiate sports:* baseball M(s), basketball M(s)/W(s), cross-country running W(s), golf M, soccer M(s)/W(s), softball W(s), tennis M/W, track and field W, volleyball W. *Intramural sports:* basketball M/W, cheerleading W(c), football M/W, soccer M/W, softball W.

Standardized Tests *Required:* SAT or ACT (for admission).

Costs (2011–12) *Comprehensive fee:* $36,330 includes full-time tuition ($25,990), mandatory fees ($900), and room and board ($9440). Part-time tuition: $712 per credit hour. Part-time tuition and fees vary according to course load and degree level. *Required fees:* $100 per semester part-time. *Room and board:* Room and board charges vary according to board plan and housing facility. *Payment plan:* installment. *Waivers:* children of alumni, adult students, senior citizens, and employees or children of employees.

Financial Aid Of all full-time matriculated undergraduates who enrolled in 2011, 1,063 applied for aid, 979 were judged to have need, 93 had their need fully met. 168 Federal Work-Study jobs (averaging $696). 104 state and other part-time jobs (averaging $4562). In 2011, 206 non-need-based awards were made. *Average percent of need met:* 70%. *Average financial aid package:* $19,853. *Average need-based loan:* $3936. *Average need-based gift aid:* $16,494. *Average non-need-based aid:* $14,511. *Average indebtedness upon graduation:* $24,196.

Applying *Options:* electronic application, early admission, early action, deferred entrance. *Application fee:* $40. *Required:* essay or personal statement, high school transcript, 2 letters of recommendation. *Recommended:* minimum 3.0 GPA, interview. *Application deadlines:* rolling (freshmen), rolling (out-of-state freshmen), rolling (transfers), 12/1 (early action). *Notification:* continuous (freshmen), continuous (out-of-state freshmen), continuous (transfers), 12/31 (early action).

Freshman Application Contact Mr. Stephen Quinn, Executive Director of Undergraduate Admissions, Caldwell College, 120 Bloomfield Avenue, Caldwell, NJ 07006. *Phone:* 973-618-3320. *Fax:* 973-618-3600. *E-mail:* squinn@caldwell.edu. *Web site:* http://www.caldwell.edu/.

Centenary College

Hackettstown, New Jersey

- **Independent** comprehensive, founded 1867, affiliated with United Methodist Church
- **Suburban** campus
- **Coed** 1,915 undergraduate students, 94% full-time, 62% women, 38% men
- **Moderately difficult** entrance level, 88% of applicants were admitted

Undergraduates 1,800 full-time, 115 part-time. 16% are from out of state; 9% Black or African American, non-Hispanic/Latino; 6% Hispanic/Latino; 2% Asian, non-Hispanic/Latino; 0.1% American Indian or Alaska Native, non-Hispanic/Latino; 1% Two or more races, non-Hispanic/Latino; 15% Race/ethnicity unknown; 3% international; 9% transferred in; 56% live on campus. *Retention:* 76% of full-time freshmen returned.

Freshmen *Admission:* 1,060 applied, 930 admitted, 306 enrolled. *Average high school GPA:* 2.7. *Test scores:* SAT critical reading scores over 500: 27%; SAT math scores over 500: 30%; ACT scores over 18: 76%; SAT critical reading scores over 600: 5%; SAT math scores over 600: 4%; ACT scores over 24: 13%.

Faculty *Total:* 222, 34% full-time. *Student/faculty ratio:* 19:1.

Academics *Calendar:* semesters. *Degrees:* associate, bachelor's, master's, and postbachelor's certificates. *Special study options:* adult/continuing education programs, part-time degree program.

Computers on Campus Students can access the following: campus intranet, computer help desk, free student e-mail accounts, online (class) grades, online (class) registration, online (class) schedules. Campuswide network is available. Wireless service is available via entire campus.

Student Life *Housing options:* coed, women-only. Campus housing is university owned. Freshman applicants given priority for college housing. *Campus security:* 24-hour emergency response devices and patrols, late-night transport/escort service, controlled dormitory access.

Athletics Member NCAA. All Division III. *Intercollegiate sports:* baseball M, basketball M/W, cheerleading W(c), cross-country running M/W, equestrian sports M(c)/W(c), golf M, lacrosse M/W, soccer M/W, softball W, volleyball W, wrestling M.

Standardized Tests *Required:* SAT or ACT (for admission).

Costs (2011–12) *Comprehensive fee:* $38,610 includes full-time tuition ($27,660), mandatory fees ($1230), and room and board ($9720). Full-time tuition and fees vary according to program. Part-time tuition: $535 per credit. Part-time tuition and fees vary according to program. *Required fees:* $30 per term part-time. *Room and board:* Room and board charges vary according to board plan. *Payment plan:* installment.

Financial Aid Of all full-time matriculated undergraduates who enrolled in 2008, 1,165 applied for aid, 1,025 were judged to have need, 191 had their need fully met. 239 Federal Work-Study jobs (averaging $645). 276 state and other part-time jobs (averaging $480). In 2008, 389 non-need-based awards were made. *Average percent of need met:* 67%. *Average financial aid package:* $17,741. *Average need-based loan:* $5625. *Average need-based gift aid:* $13,066. *Average non-need-based aid:* $7453. *Average indebtedness upon graduation:* $20,649.

Applying *Options:* electronic application, deferred entrance. *Application fee:* $30. *Required:* essay or personal statement, high school transcript. *Required for some:* interview. *Recommended:* interview. *Application deadlines:* rolling (freshmen), rolling (transfers). *Notification:* continuous (freshmen), continuous (transfers).

Freshman Application Contact Centenary College, 400 Jefferson Street, Hackettstown, NJ 07840-2100. *Phone:* 908-852-1400. *Toll-free phone:* 800-236-8679. *Web site:* http://www.centenarycollege.edu/.

The College of New Jersey

Ewing, New Jersey

- **State-supported** comprehensive, founded 1855
- **Suburban** 255-acre campus with easy access to Philadelphia
- **Endowment** $23.6 million
- **Coed** 6,504 undergraduate students, 97% full-time, 56% women, 44% men
- **Very difficult** entrance level, 46% of applicants were admitted

Undergraduates 6,339 full-time, 165 part-time. Students come from 27 states and territories; 5 other countries; 6% are from out of state; 6% Black or African American, non-Hispanic/Latino; 10% Hispanic/Latino; 8% Asian, non-Hispanic/Latino; 0.3% Native Hawaiian or other Pacific Islander, non-Hispanic/Latino; 0.1% American Indian or Alaska Native, non-Hispanic/Latino; 2% Two or more races, non-Hispanic/Latino; 9% Race/ethnicity unknown; 0.3% international; 4% transferred in; 60% live on campus. *Retention:* 95% of full-time freshmen returned.

Freshmen *Admission:* 10,150 applied, 4,710 admitted, 1,371 enrolled. *Test scores:* SAT critical reading scores over 500: 92%; SAT math scores over 500: 95%; SAT writing scores over 500: 93%; SAT critical reading scores over 600: 53%; SAT math scores over 600: 69%; SAT writing scores over 600: 57%; SAT critical reading scores over 700: 11%; SAT math scores over 700: 19%; SAT writing scores over 700: 14%.

Faculty *Total:* 754, 47% full-time, 55% with terminal degrees. *Student/faculty ratio:* 13:1.

Academics *Calendar:* semesters. *Degrees:* bachelor's, master's, post-master's, and postbachelor's certificates. *Special study options:* academic remediation for entering students, accelerated degree program, advanced placement credit, double majors, honors programs, independent study, internships, off-campus study, part-time degree program, services for LD students, student-designed majors, study abroad, summer session for credit. *ROTC:* Army (c), Air Force (c). *Unusual degree programs:* 3-2 education of the deaf and hard of hearing and elementary education; special education and liberal arts.

Computers on Campus 631 computers/terminals are available on campus for general student use. Students can access the following: campus intranet, computer help desk, free student e-mail accounts, online (class) grades, online (class) registration, online (class) schedules. Campuswide network is available. 100% of college-owned or -operated housing units are wired for high-speed Internet access. Wireless service is available via classrooms, computer labs, learning centers, libraries, student centers.

Student Life *Housing:* on-campus residence required for freshman year. *Options:* coed, disabled students. Campus housing is university owned. Freshman campus housing is guaranteed. *Activities and organizations:* drama/theater group, student-run newspaper, radio and television station, choral group, Student Government Association, College Union Board, Inter-Greek Council, The Signal, national fraternities, national sororities. *Campus security:* 24-hour emergency response devices and patrols, student patrols, late-night transport/escort service, controlled dormitory access. *Student services:* health clinic, personal/psychological counseling, women's center, legal services.

Athletics Member NCAA. All Division III. *Intercollegiate sports:* baseball M, basketball M/W, cross-country running M/W, field hockey W, football M, lacrosse W, soccer M/W, softball W, swimming and diving M/W, tennis M/W, track and field M/W, wrestling M. *Intramural sports:* baseball M(c), basketball M(c)/W, bowling M(c)/W(c), cheerleading M(c)/W(c), crew M(c)/W(c), fencing M(c)/W(c), field hockey M/W, football M/W, golf M(c)/W(c), ice hockey M(c), lacrosse M(c)/W(c), racquetball M/W, rugby M(c)/W(c), skiing (cross-country) M(c)/W(c), skiing (downhill) M(c)/W(c), soccer M(c)/W(c), softball M/W(c), swimming and diving M(c)/W(c), table tennis M(c)/W(c), tennis M(c)/W(c), ultimate Frisbee M(c)/W(c), volleyball M(c)/W(c), water polo M(c)/W(c).

Standardized Tests *Required:* SAT or ACT (for admission).

Costs (2011–12) *Tuition:* state resident $9760 full-time, $346 per credit hour part-time; nonresident $19,569 full-time, $693 per credit hour part-time. Part-time tuition and fees vary according to course load. *Required fees:* $4127 full-time, $164 per credit hour part-time. *Room and board:* $10,677; room only: $7772. Room and board charges vary according to board plan. *Payment plan:* installment. *Waivers:* senior citizens and employees or children of employees.

Financial Aid Of all full-time matriculated undergraduates who enrolled in 2011, 4,616 applied for aid, 3,265 were judged to have need, 458 had their need fully met. 171 Federal Work-Study jobs (averaging $1412). In 2011, 730 non-need-based awards were made. *Average percent of need met:* 48%. *Average financial aid package:* $10,197. *Average need-based loan:* $4550. *Average need-based gift aid:* $10,196. *Average non-need-based aid:* $4171. *Average indebtedness upon graduation:* $32,754.

Applying *Options:* electronic application, early admission, early decision, deferred entrance. *Application fee:* $75. *Required:* essay or personal statement, high school transcript. *Required for some:* interview, art portfolio or music audition. *Recommended:* minimum 2.5 GPA, 3 letters of recommendation. *Application deadlines:* 1/15 (freshmen), 1/15 (transfers). *Early decision deadline:* 11/15. *Notification:* continuous (freshmen), continuous (transfers), 12/15 (early decision).

Freshman Application Contact Ms. Grecia Montero, Director of Admissions, The College of New Jersey, PO Box 7718, Ewing, NJ 08628. *Phone:* 609-771-2131. *Fax:* 609-637-5174. *E-mail:* admiss@tcnj.edu. *Web site:* http://www.tcnj.edu/.

See below for display ad and page 1270 for the College Close-Up.

College of Saint Elizabeth
Morristown, New Jersey

- **Independent Roman Catholic** comprehensive, founded 1899
- **Suburban** 188-acre campus with easy access to New York City
- **Endowment** $20.9 million
- **Coed, primarily women** 1,181 undergraduate students, 51% full-time, 91% women, 9% men
- **Moderately difficult** entrance level, 12% of applicants were admitted

Undergraduates 604 full-time, 577 part-time. Students come from 7 states and territories; 43 other countries; 3% are from out of state; 21% Black or African American, non-Hispanic/Latino; 15% Hispanic/Latino; 5% Asian, non-Hispanic/Latino; 0.1% Native Hawaiian or other Pacific Islander, non-Hispanic/Latino; 0.1% American Indian or Alaska Native, non-Hispanic/Latino; 0.4% Two or more races, non-Hispanic/Latino; 14% Race/ethnicity unknown; 6% international; 2% transferred in; 70% live on campus. *Retention:* 64% of full-time freshmen returned.

Freshmen *Admission:* 1,486 applied, 180 admitted, 180 enrolled. *Test scores:* SAT critical reading scores over 500: 23%; SAT math scores over 500: 22%; SAT writing scores over 500: 25%; SAT critical reading scores over 600: 5%; SAT math scores over 600: 6%; SAT writing scores over 600: 7%; SAT critical reading scores over 700: 1%; SAT math scores over 700: 1%; SAT writing scores over 700: 2%.

Faculty *Total:* 222, 32% full-time. *Student/faculty ratio:* 9:1.

Academics *Calendar:* semesters. *Degrees:* certificates, bachelor's, master's, doctoral, postbachelor's, and first professional certificates (also offers coed adult undergraduate degree program and coed graduate programs). *Special*

study options: academic remediation for entering students, accelerated degree program, advanced placement credit, distance learning, double majors, English as a second language, honors programs, independent study, internships, off-campus study, part-time degree program, services for LD students, student-designed majors, study abroad, summer session for credit. *Unusual degree programs:* 3-2 business administration; counseling psychology.

Computers on Campus 127 computers/terminals and 20 ports are available on campus for general student use. Students can access the following: campus intranet, computer help desk, free student e-mail accounts, online (class) grades, online (class) registration, online (class) schedules. Campuswide network is available. 100% of college-owned or -operated housing units are wired for high-speed Internet access. Wireless service is available via classrooms, computer labs, dorm rooms, libraries.

Student Life *Housing options:* women-only. Campus housing is university owned. Freshman campus housing is guaranteed. *Activities and organizations:* drama/theater group, student-run newspaper, choral group, Student Government Association, Students Take Action Committee, International/Intercultural Club, College Activities Board, Campus Ministry. *Campus security:* 24-hour emergency response devices and patrols, late-night transport/escort service, controlled dormitory access. *Student services:* health clinic, personal/psychological counseling.

Athletics Member NCAA. All Division III. *Intercollegiate sports:* basketball W, equestrian sports W, soccer W, softball W, swimming and diving W, tennis W, volleyball W. *Intramural sports:* volleyball W.

Standardized Tests *Required:* SAT or ACT (for admission).

Costs (2011–12) *Comprehensive fee:* $39,781 includes full-time tuition ($26,440), mandatory fees ($1781), and room and board ($11,560). Full-time tuition and fees vary according to degree level. Part-time tuition: $704 per credit hour. Part-time tuition and fees vary according to course load, degree level, location, and reciprocity agreements. *Required fees:* $73 per credit hour part-time. *Payment plan:* installment. *Waivers:* children of alumni, senior citizens, and employees or children of employees.

Financial Aid Of all full-time matriculated undergraduates who enrolled in 2009, 576 applied for aid, 576 were judged to have need, 68 had their need fully met. 120 Federal Work-Study jobs (averaging $949). In 2009, 25 non-need-based awards were made. *Average percent of need met:* 73%. *Average financial aid package:* $21,992. *Average need-based loan:* $5005. *Average need-based gift aid:* $16,489. *Average non-need-based aid:* $9942.

Applying *Options:* electronic application, early admission, deferred entrance. *Application fee:* $35. *Required:* high school transcript, minimum 2.0 GPA, 2 letters of recommendation. *Recommended:* essay or personal statement, inter-

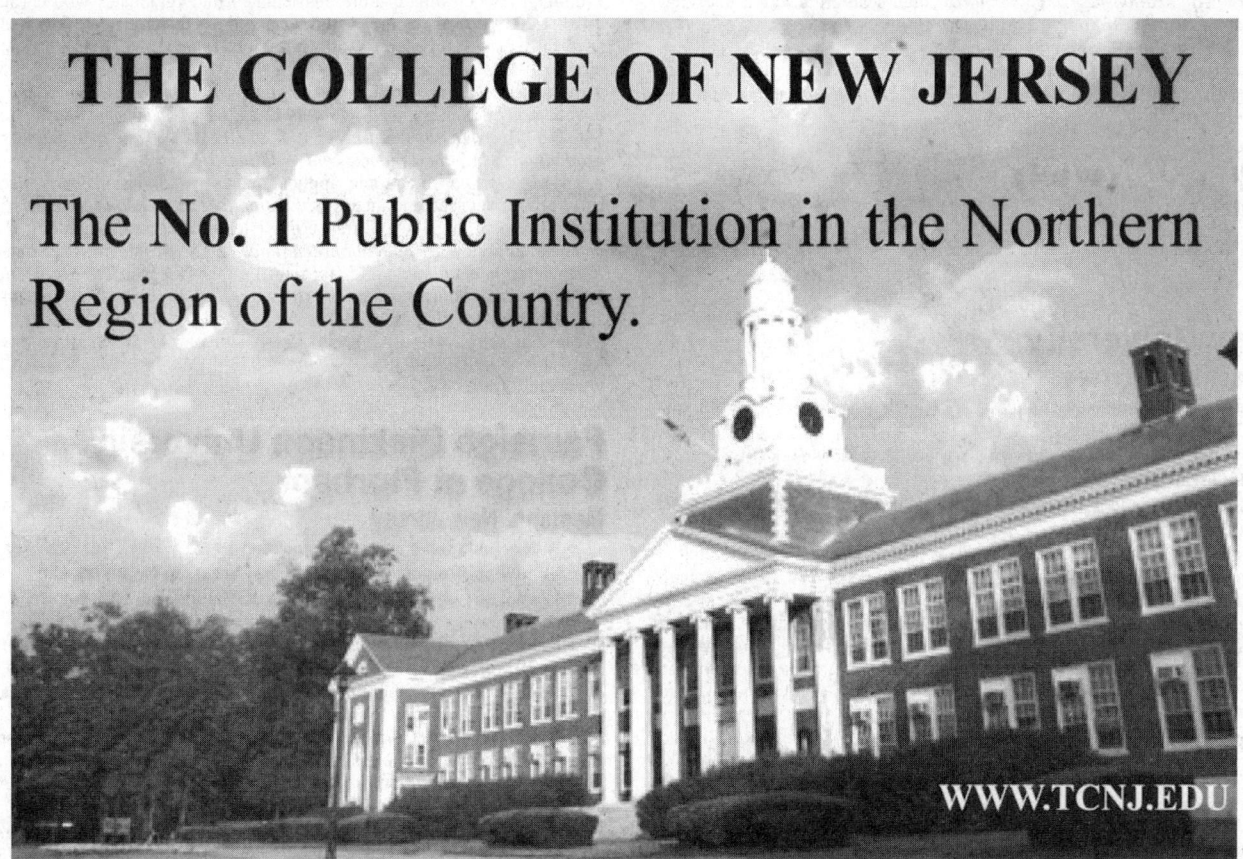

THE COLLEGE OF NEW JERSEY

The **No. 1** Public Institution in the Northern Region of the Country.

WWW.TCNJ.EDU

view. *Application deadlines:* 8/15 (freshmen), rolling (transfers). *Notification:* 11/15 (freshmen), continuous (transfers).

Freshman Application Contact Ms. Donna Tatarka, Dean of Admissions, College of Saint Elizabeth, 2 Convent Road, Morristown, NJ 07960-6989. *Phone:* 973-290-4700. *Toll-free phone:* 800-210-7900. *Fax:* 973-290-4710. *E-mail:* apply@csa.edu. *Web site:* http://www.cse.edu/.

DeVry University

North Brunswick, New Jersey

- **Proprietary** comprehensive, founded 1969, part of DeVry University
- **Urban** campus
- **Coed** 1,571 undergraduate students, 45% full-time, 29% women, 71% men
- **Minimally difficult** entrance level

Undergraduates 708 full-time, 863 part-time. 7% are from out of state; 21% Black or African American, non-Hispanic/Latino; 20% Hispanic/Latino; 6% Asian, non-Hispanic/Latino; 0.5% Native Hawaiian or other Pacific Islander, non-Hispanic/Latino; 0.3% American Indian or Alaska Native, non-Hispanic/Latino; 1% Two or more races, non-Hispanic/Latino; 13% Race/ethnicity unknown; 1% international; 18% transferred in.

Freshmen *Admission:* 279 enrolled.

Faculty *Total:* 153, 25% full-time. *Student/faculty ratio:* 15:1.

Academics *Calendar:* semesters. *Degrees:* associate, bachelor's, and master's. *Special study options:* adult/continuing education programs, part-time degree program.

Computers on Campus Students can access the following: online (class) registration.

Student Life *Housing:* college housing not available.

Costs (2011–12) *Tuition:* $15,294 full-time, $580 per credit hour part-time. Full-time tuition and fees vary according to course load. Part-time tuition and fees vary according to course load. *Required fees:* $80 full-time, $40 per term part-time. *Payment plans:* installment, deferred payment. *Waivers:* employees or children of employees.

Financial Aid Of all full-time matriculated undergraduates who enrolled in 2007, 449 applied for aid, 430 were judged to have need, 9 had their need fully met. In 2007, 50 non-need-based awards were made. *Average percent of need met:* 34%. *Average financial aid package:* $12,399. *Average need-based loan:* $6629. *Average need-based gift aid:* $8242. *Average non-need-based aid:* $11,630. *Average indebtedness upon graduation:* $24,045.

Applying *Application fee:* $50. *Required:* high school transcript, interview. *Application deadlines:* rolling (freshmen), rolling (transfers). *Notification:* continuous (freshmen), continuous (transfers).

Freshman Application Contact DeVry University, 630 US Highway 1, North Brunswick, NJ 08902-3362. *Phone:* 732-729-3532. *Toll-free phone:* 866-338-7941. *Web site:* http://www.devry.edu/.

DeVry University

Paramus, New Jersey

Admissions Office Contact DeVry University, 35 Plaza, 81 East State Route 4, Suite 102, Paramus, NJ 07652. *Toll-free phone:* 866-338-7941. *Web site:* http://www.devry.edu/.

Drew University

Madison, New Jersey

- **Independent** university, founded 1867, affiliated with United Methodist Church
- **Suburban** 186-acre campus with easy access to New York City
- **Endowment** $210.0 million
- **Coed** 1,725 undergraduate students, 96% full-time, 60% women, 40% men
- **Moderately difficult** entrance level, 84% of applicants were admitted

Undergraduates 1,662 full-time, 63 part-time. Students come from 35 states and territories; 24 other countries; 36% are from out of state; 9% Black or African American, non-Hispanic/Latino; 14% Hispanic/Latino; 5% Asian, non-Hispanic/Latino; 0.3% American Indian or Alaska Native, non-Hispanic/Latino; 2% Two or more races, non-Hispanic/Latino; 10% Race/ethnicity unknown; 2% international; 3% transferred in; 82% live on campus. *Retention:* 79% of full-time freshmen returned.

Freshmen *Admission:* 4,195 applied, 3,527 admitted, 454 enrolled. *Average high school GPA:* 3.42. *Test scores:* SAT math scores over 500: 76%; SAT writing scores over 500: 80%; ACT scores over 18: 93%; SAT math scores over 600: 34%; SAT writing scores over 600: 34%; ACT scores over 24: 61%; SAT math scores over 700: 5%; SAT writing scores over 700: 8%; ACT scores over 30: 14%.

Faculty *Total:* 293, 58% full-time. *Student/faculty ratio:* 10:1.

Academics *Calendar:* semesters. *Degrees:* bachelor's, master's, doctoral, post-master's, postbachelor's, and first professional certificates. *Special study options:* academic remediation for entering students, accelerated degree program, adult/continuing education programs, advanced placement credit, double majors, external degree program, honors programs, independent study, internships, off-campus study, part-time degree program, services for LD students, student-designed majors, study abroad, summer session for credit. *Unusual degree programs:* 3-2 engineering with Columbia University, Washington University, Stevens Institute of Technology.

Computers on Campus 200 computers/terminals are available on campus for general student use. Students can access the following: campus intranet, computer help desk, free student e-mail accounts, online (class) grades, online (class) registration, online (class) schedules. Campuswide network is available. 100% of college-owned or -operated housing units are wired for high-speed Internet access. Wireless service is available via entire campus.

Student Life *Housing options:* coed, disabled students. Campus housing is university owned. Freshman campus housing is guaranteed. *Activities and organizations:* drama/theater group, student-run newspaper, radio and television station, choral group, New Social Engine, Student Government Association, D.U.D.S.-Drew University Dramatic Society, University Program Board, Kuumba Pan African Student Association. *Campus security:* 24-hour emergency response devices and patrols, late-night transport/escort service, controlled dormitory access. *Student services:* health clinic, personal/psychological counseling.

Athletics Member NCAA. All Division III. *Intercollegiate sports:* baseball M, basketball M/W, cross-country running M/W, equestrian sports M/W, fencing M/W, field hockey W, lacrosse M/W, rugby M(c)/W(c), soccer M/W, softball W, swimming and diving M/W, tennis M/W. *Intramural sports:* basketball M/W, football M/W, racquetball M/W, soccer M/W, softball M/W, squash M/W, table tennis M/W, ultimate Frisbee M/W, volleyball M/W.

Standardized Tests *Recommended:* SAT and ACT scores are optional and are considered if submitted. SAT subject tests are not used.

Costs (2011–12) *One-time required fee:* $325. *Comprehensive fee:* $52,154 includes full-time tuition ($40,122), mandatory fees ($882), and room and board ($11,150). Full-time tuition and fees vary according to course load. Part-time tuition: $1672 per credit hour. Part-time tuition and fees vary according to course load. *College room only:* $7208. Room and board charges vary according to board plan and housing facility. *Payment plans:* tuition prepayment, installment, deferred payment. *Waivers:* senior citizens and employees or children of employees.

Financial Aid Of all full-time matriculated undergraduates who enrolled in 2010, 1,225 applied for aid, 1,060 were judged to have need, 119 had their need fully met. 316 Federal Work-Study jobs (averaging $1041). 35 state and other part-time jobs (averaging $9753). In 2010, 545 non-need-based awards were made. *Average percent of need met:* 76%. *Average financial aid package:* $30,342. *Average need-based loan:* $4764. *Average need-based gift aid:* $25,208. *Average non-need-based aid:* $12,121. *Average indebtedness upon graduation:* $21,303. *Financial aid deadline:* 2/15.

Applying *Options:* electronic application, early admission, early decision, early action, deferred entrance. *Application fee:* $50. *Required:* essay or personal statement, high school transcript, 1 letter of recommendation. *Recommended:* interview. *Application deadlines:* 2/15 (freshmen), 6/1 (transfers). *Early decision deadline:* 11/15 (for plan 1), 1/15 (for plan 2). *Notification:* 3/15 (freshmen), continuous until 4/1 (transfers), 12/24 (early decision plan 1), 2/15 (early decision plan 2).

Freshman Application Contact Drew University, 36 Madison Avenue, Madison, NJ 07940-1493. *Phone:* 973-408-3739. *Web site:* http://www.drew.edu/.

Fairleigh Dickinson University, College at Florham

Madison, New Jersey

- **Independent** comprehensive, founded 1942
- **Suburban** 178-acre campus with easy access to New York City
- **Coed** 2,401 undergraduate students, 93% full-time, 55% women, 45% men
- **Moderately difficult** entrance level, 66% of applicants were admitted

Undergraduates 2,223 full-time, 178 part-time. Students come from 29 states and territories; 12 other countries; 16% are from out of state; 11% Black or African American, non-Hispanic/Latino; 11% Hispanic/Latino; 4% Asian, non-Hispanic/Latino; 1% American Indian or Alaska Native, non-Hispanic/Latino; 0.2% Two or more races, non-Hispanic/Latino; 9% Race/ethnicity unknown; 0.6% international; 5% transferred in; 61% live on campus. *Retention:* 72% of full-time freshmen returned.

Freshmen *Admission:* 4,332 applied, 2,851 admitted, 587 enrolled. *Average high school GPA:* 3.14. *Test scores:* SAT critical reading scores over 500:

55%; SAT math scores over 500: 59%; SAT writing scores over 500: 55%; SAT critical reading scores over 600: 15%; SAT math scores over 600: 17%; SAT writing scores over 600: 16%; SAT critical reading scores over 700: 1%; SAT math scores over 700: 1%; SAT writing scores over 700: 2%.

Faculty *Total:* 394, 33% full-time. *Student/faculty ratio:* 12:1.

Academics *Calendar:* semesters. *Degrees:* bachelor's, master's, post-master's, and postbachelor's certificates. *Special study options:* academic remediation for entering students, accelerated degree program, adult/continuing education programs, advanced placement credit, cooperative education, distance learning, double majors, honors programs, independent study, internships, off-campus study, part-time degree program, services for LD students, study abroad, summer session for credit. *ROTC:* Army (c), Air Force (c).

Computers on Campus 150 computers/terminals are available on campus for general student use. Students can access the following: computer help desk, free student e-mail accounts, online (class) grades, online (class) registration, online (class) schedules. Campuswide network is available. 100% of college-owned or -operated housing units are wired for high-speed Internet access. Wireless service is available via entire campus.

Student Life *Housing options:* coed, disabled students. Campus housing is university owned. Freshman applicants given priority for college housing. *Activities and organizations:* drama/theater group, student-run newspaper, radio station, choral group, Student Government Association, Florham Programming Committee, Green Club, Association of Black Collegians, Latin American Student Organization, national fraternities, national sororities. *Campus security:* 24-hour emergency response devices and patrols, late-night transport/escort service, controlled dormitory access, trained law enforcement personnel on staff. *Student services:* health clinic, personal/psychological counseling.

Athletics Member NCAA. All Division III. *Intercollegiate sports:* baseball M, basketball M/W, cross-country running M/W, field hockey W, football M, golf M/W, lacrosse M/W, soccer M/W, softball W, swimming and diving M/W, tennis M/W, volleyball W. *Intramural sports:* basketball M/W, football M/W, soccer M/W, softball M/W, volleyball M/W, weight lifting M/W.

Standardized Tests *Required:* SAT or ACT (for admission).

Costs (2011–12) *Comprehensive fee:* $46,664 includes full-time tuition ($34,082), mandatory fees ($920), and room and board ($11,662). Part-time tuition: $887 per credit. *College room only:* $7710. Room and board charges vary according to board plan and housing facility. *Payment plans:* installment, deferred payment. *Waivers:* senior citizens and employees or children of employees.

Financial Aid Of all full-time matriculated undergraduates who enrolled in 2007, 1,788 applied for aid, 1,568 were judged to have need. In 2007, 213 non-need-based awards were made. *Average financial aid package:* $17,400. *Average need-based loan:* $4001. *Average need-based gift aid:* $9956. *Average non-need-based aid:* $6501.

Applying *Options:* electronic application. *Application fee:* $40. *Required:* high school transcript, 2 letters of recommendation. *Application deadlines:* rolling (freshmen), rolling (transfers). *Notification:* continuous (freshmen), continuous (transfers).

Freshman Application Contact Fairleigh Dickinson University, College at Florham, 285 Madison Avenue, Madison, NJ 07940-1099. *Toll-free phone:* 800-338-8803. *Web site:* http://www.fdu.edu/.

Fairleigh Dickinson University, Metropolitan Campus

Teaneck, New Jersey

- **Independent** comprehensive, founded 1942
- **Suburban** 88-acre campus with easy access to New York City
- **Coed** 6,636 undergraduate students, 42% full-time, 61% women, 39% men
- **Moderately difficult** entrance level, 62% of applicants were admitted

Undergraduates 2,777 full-time, 3,859 part-time. Students come from 32 states and territories; 60 other countries; 14% are from out of state; 14% Black or African American, non-Hispanic/Latino; 33% Hispanic/Latino; 6% Asian, non-Hispanic/Latino; 0.4% American Indian or Alaska Native, non-Hispanic/Latino; 0.1% Two or more races, non-Hispanic/Latino; 10% Race/ethnicity unknown; 7% international; 7% transferred in; 20% live on campus. *Retention:* 72% of full-time freshmen returned.

Freshmen *Admission:* 6,466 applied, 4,038 admitted, 712 enrolled. *Average high school GPA:* 3.18. *Test scores:* SAT critical reading scores over 500: 45%; SAT math scores over 500: 54%; SAT writing scores over 500: 44%; SAT critical reading scores over 600: 8%; SAT math scores over 600: 16%; SAT writing scores over 600: 10%; SAT critical reading scores over 700: 1%; SAT math scores over 700: 2%; SAT writing scores over 700: 1%.

Faculty *Total:* 771, 25% full-time. *Student/faculty ratio:* 14:1.

Academics *Calendar:* semesters. *Degrees:* certificates, associate, bachelor's, master's, doctoral, post-master's, and postbachelor's certificates. *Special*

---

study options: academic remediation for entering students, accelerated degree program, adult/continuing education programs, advanced placement credit, cooperative education, distance learning, double majors, English as a second language, honors programs, independent study, internships, off-campus study, part-time degree program, services for LD students, student-designed majors, study abroad, summer session for credit. *ROTC:* Army (c), Air Force (c).

Computers on Campus 225 computers/terminals are available on campus for general student use. Students can access the following: computer help desk, free student e-mail accounts, online (class) grades, online (class) registration, online (class) schedules. Campuswide network is available. 100% of college-owned or -operated housing units are wired for high-speed Internet access. Wireless service is available via entire campus.

Student Life *Housing options:* coed, men-only, women-only. Campus housing is university owned. *Activities and organizations:* drama/theater group, student-run newspaper, radio station, choral group, Student Government Association, Student Program Board, International Student Association, Greek Life, Spectrum (LGBT), national fraternities, national sororities. *Campus security:* 24-hour emergency response devices and patrols, late-night transport/escort service, controlled dormitory access, trained law enforcement personnel on staff. *Student services:* health clinic, personal/psychological counseling, women's center.

Athletics Member NCAA. All Division I. *Intercollegiate sports:* baseball M(s), basketball M(s)/W(s), bowling W(s), cross-country running M(s)/W(s), fencing W(s), golf M(s)/W(s), soccer M(s)/W(s), softball W(s), tennis M(s)/W(s), track and field M(s)/W(s), volleyball W(s). *Intramural sports:* badminton M/W, basketball M/W, football M/W, rugby M(c)/W(c), soccer M/W, table tennis M/W, tennis M/W, volleyball M/W.

Standardized Tests *Required:* SAT or ACT (for admission).

Costs (2011–12) *Comprehensive fee:* $44,584 includes full-time tuition ($31,618), mandatory fees ($920), and room and board ($12,046). Part-time tuition: $887 per credit. *College room only:* $8094. Room and board charges vary according to board plan and housing facility. *Payment plans:* installment, deferred payment. *Waivers:* senior citizens and employees or children of employees.

Financial Aid Of all full-time matriculated undergraduates who enrolled in 2007, 1,671 applied for aid, 1,549 were judged to have need. In 2007, 117 non-need-based awards were made. *Average financial aid package:* $18,283. *Average need-based loan:* $3808. *Average need-based gift aid:* $8702. *Average non-need-based aid:* $6403.

Applying *Options:* electronic application, early admission. *Application fee:* $40. *Required:* high school transcript, 2 letters of recommendation. *Required for some:* interview. *Application deadlines:* rolling (freshmen), rolling (transfers). *Notification:* continuous (freshmen), continuous (transfers).

Freshman Application Contact Fairleigh Dickinson University, Metropolitan Campus, 1000 River Road, Teaneck, NJ 07666-1914. *Toll-free phone:* 800-338-8803. *Web site:* http://www.fdu.edu/.

Felician College

Lodi, New Jersey

- **Independent Roman Catholic** comprehensive, founded 1942
- **Suburban** 37-acre campus with easy access to New York City
- **Endowment** $4.8 million
- **Coed** 1,931 undergraduate students, 81% full-time, 73% women, 27% men
- **Moderately difficult** entrance level, 81% of applicants were admitted

Undergraduates 1,555 full-time, 376 part-time. Students come from 10 states and territories; 23 other countries; 6% are from out of state; 13% Black or African American, non-Hispanic/Latino; 19% Hispanic/Latino; 7% Asian, non-Hispanic/Latino; 0.5% Native Hawaiian or other Pacific Islander, non-Hispanic/Latino; 0.5% American Indian or Alaska Native, non-Hispanic/Latino; 0.3% Two or more races, non-Hispanic/Latino; 29% Race/ethnicity unknown; 2% international; 6% transferred in; 20% live on campus. *Retention:* 70% of full-time freshmen returned.

Freshmen *Admission:* 2,119 applied, 1,722 admitted, 344 enrolled. *Average high school GPA:* 3.1. *Test scores:* SAT critical reading scores over 500: 21%; SAT math scores over 500: 25%; SAT writing scores over 500: 24%; ACT scores over 18: 47%; SAT critical reading scores over 600: 4%; SAT math scores over 600: 6%; SAT writing scores over 600: 6%; ACT scores over 24: 9%; SAT critical reading scores over 700: 1%; SAT math scores over 700: 1%; SAT writing scores over 700: 2%; ACT scores over 30: 3%.

Faculty *Total:* 241, 48% full-time. *Student/faculty ratio:* 12:1.

Academics *Calendar:* semesters. *Degrees:* certificates, associate, bachelor's, master's, post-master's, and postbachelor's certificates. *Special study options:* academic remediation for entering students, accelerated degree program, adult/continuing education programs, advanced placement credit, cooperative education, distance learning, double majors, English as a second language, honors programs, independent study, internships, off-campus study, part-time degree

program, services for LD students, student-designed majors, study abroad, summer session for credit.

Computers on Campus 100 computers/terminals are available on campus for general student use. Students can access the following: computer help desk, free student e-mail accounts, online (class) grades, online (class) registration, online (class) schedules. Campuswide network is available. 100% of college-owned or -operated housing units are wired for high-speed Internet access. Wireless service is available via dorm rooms, learning centers, libraries, student centers.

Student Life *Housing options:* coed, men-only, women-only, disabled students. Campus housing is university owned. Freshman applicants given priority for college housing. *Activities and organizations:* drama/theater group, student-run radio station, choral group, Student Nurses Association, Zeta Alpha Zeta teaching sorority, Campus Activity Board, Students In Free Enterprise (SIFE), Student Government Association. *Campus security:* 24-hour patrols, student patrols, late-night transport/escort service. *Student services:* health clinic, personal/psychological counseling.

Athletics Member NCAA, NAIA. All NCAA Division II. *Intercollegiate sports:* baseball M(s), basketball M(s)/W(s), cross-country running M(s)/W(s), golf M(s), soccer M(s)/W(s), softball W(s), volleyball W(s). *Intramural sports:* soccer M/W, softball W, volleyball M/W, weight lifting M/W.

Standardized Tests *Required:* SAT or ACT (for admission). *Required for some:* ACT (for admission), SAT Subject Tests (for admission).

Costs (2012–13) *Comprehensive fee:* $40,800 includes full-time tuition ($27,800), mandatory fees ($1600), and room and board ($11,400). Full-time tuition and fees vary according to program. Part-time tuition: $915 per credit hour. Part-time tuition and fees vary according to course load and program. *Room and board:* Room and board charges vary according to housing facility. *Payment plan:* installment. *Waivers:* employees or children of employees.

Financial Aid Of all full-time matriculated undergraduates who enrolled in 2010, 1,169 applied for aid, 980 were judged to have need, 85 had their need fully met. 88 Federal Work-Study jobs (averaging $1352). 90 state and other part-time jobs (averaging $2652). In 2010, 73 non-need-based awards were made. *Average need-based loan:* $5217. *Average need-based gift aid:* $12,249. *Average non-need-based aid:* $18,968. *Average indebtedness upon graduation:* $22,963.

Applying *Options:* deferred entrance. *Application fee:* $30. *Required:* high school transcript, minimum 2.0 GPA. *Required for some:* essay or personal statement, interview. *Application deadlines:* rolling (freshmen), rolling (transfers). *Notification:* continuous (freshmen), continuous (transfers).

Freshman Application Contact College Admissions Office, Felician College, 262 South Main Street, Lodi, NJ 07644-2117. *Phone:* 201-559-6131. *Fax:* 201-559-6138. *E-mail:* admissions@felician.edu. *Web site:* http://www.felician.edu/.

See below for display ad and page 1324 for the College Close-Up.

Georgian Court University
Lakewood, New Jersey

- **Independent Roman Catholic** comprehensive, founded 1908
- **Suburban** 156-acre campus with easy access to New York City, Philadelphia
- **Coed, primarily women** 1,772 undergraduate students, 79% full-time, 91% women, 9% men
- **Moderately difficult** entrance level, 66% of applicants were admitted

Undergraduates 1,393 full-time, 379 part-time. 4% are from out of state; 14% Black or African American, non-Hispanic/Latino; 10% Hispanic/Latino; 2% Asian, non-Hispanic/Latino; 0.1% Native Hawaiian or other Pacific Islander, non-Hispanic/Latino; 0.3% American Indian or Alaska Native, non-Hispanic/Latino; 2% Two or more races, non-Hispanic/Latino; 12% Race/ethnicity unknown; 0.3% international; 13% transferred in; 25% live on campus. *Retention:* 65% of full-time freshmen returned.

Freshmen *Admission:* 1,134 applied, 743 admitted, 244 enrolled. *Average high school GPA:* 3.22.

Faculty *Total:* 272, 39% full-time, 49% with terminal degrees. *Student/faculty ratio:* 13:1.

Academics *Calendar:* semesters. *Degrees:* certificates, bachelor's, master's, post-master's, and postbachelor's certificates. *Special study options:* adult/continuing education programs, part-time degree program.

Computers on Campus Students can access the following: campus intranet, computer help desk, free student e-mail accounts, online (class) grades, online (class) registration, online (class) schedules. Campuswide network is available. 100% of college-owned or -operated housing units are wired for high-speed Internet access. Wireless service is available via classrooms, computer centers, computer labs, dorm rooms, learning centers, libraries, student centers.

Student Life *Housing options:* women-only. Campus housing is university owned. Freshman campus housing is guaranteed. *Campus security:* 24-hour emergency response devices and patrols, late-night transport/escort service, controlled dormitory access.

Athletics Member NCAA. All Division II. *Intercollegiate sports:* basketball W(s), cross-country running W(s), lacrosse W(s), soccer W(s), softball W(s), tennis W(s), track and field W(s), volleyball W(s).

Standardized Tests *Required:* SAT or ACT (for admission).

Costs (2011–12) *Comprehensive fee:* $38,234 includes full-time tuition ($26,740), mandatory fees ($1244), and room and board ($10,250). Part-time tuition: $611 per credit hour. Part-time tuition and fees vary according to location. *Payment plan:* installment. *Waivers:* employees or children of employees.

Financial Aid Of all full-time matriculated undergraduates who enrolled in 2011, 1,295 applied for aid, 1,201 were judged to have need, 334 had their need fully met. In 2011, 102 non-need-based awards were made. *Average percent of need met:* 83%. *Average financial aid package:* $24,201. *Average need-based loan:* $7936. *Average need-based gift aid:* $14,817. *Average non-need-based aid:* $8996. *Average indebtedness upon graduation:* $33,888. *Financial aid deadline:* 8/1.

Applying *Options:* electronic application, early action, deferred entrance. *Application fee:* $40. *Required:* high school transcript, minimum 2.5 GPA, 2 letters of recommendation. *Recommended:* essay or personal statement, interview. *Application deadlines:* 8/1 (freshmen), 8/1 (transfers), 11/15 (early action). *Notification:* continuous (transfers), 12/30 (early action).

Freshman Application Contact Ms. Maria Colon, Assistant Director of Undergraduate Admissions, Georgian Court University, 900 Lakewood Avenue. *Phone:* 732-987-2760. *Toll-free phone:* 800-458-8422. *Fax:* 732-987-2000. *E-mail:* admissions@georgian.edu. *Web site:* http://www.georgian.edu/.

Kean University
Union, New Jersey

- **State-supported** comprehensive, founded 1855, part of New Jersey State College System
- **Suburban** 186-acre campus with easy access to New York City
- **Endowment** $13.0 million
- **Coed** 13,462 undergraduate students, 78% full-time, 60% women, 40% men
- **Moderately difficult** entrance level, 70% of applicants were admitted

Undergraduates 10,492 full-time, 2,970 part-time. Students come from 23 states and territories; 53 other countries; 2% are from out of state; 18% Black or African American, non-Hispanic/Latino; 23% Hispanic/Latino; 6% Asian, non-Hispanic/Latino; 0.4% Native Hawaiian or other Pacific Islander, non-Hispanic/Latino; 0.1% American Indian or Alaska Native, non-Hispanic/Latino; 1% Two or more races, non-Hispanic/Latino; 8% Race/ethnicity unknown; 1% international; 13% transferred in; 15% live on campus. *Retention:* 80% of full-time freshmen returned.

Freshmen *Admission:* 6,085 applied, 4,283 admitted, 1,837 enrolled. *Average high school GPA:* 3. *Test scores:* SAT critical reading scores over 500: 25%; SAT math scores over 500: 36%; SAT critical reading scores over 600: 3%; SAT math scores over 600: 6%.

Faculty *Total:* 1,461, 23% full-time. *Student/faculty ratio:* 18:1.

Academics *Calendar:* semesters. *Degrees:* bachelor's, master's, doctoral, post-master's, and first professional certificates. *Special study options:* academic remediation for entering students, accelerated degree program, adult/continuing education programs, advanced placement credit, cooperative education, distance learning, double majors, English as a second language, honors programs, independent study, internships, off-campus study, part-time degree program, services for LD students, study abroad, summer session for credit. *ROTC:* Army (c), Air Force (c). *Unusual degree programs:* 3-2 public administration; occupational therapy; science and technology; instruction & curriculum; biology/physician's assistant; health information management or psychology/psychiatric rehabilitation; DPT: UMDNJ; MD: Drexel University; DPM: New York College of Podiatric Medicine.

Computers on Campus 1,700 computers/terminals and 2,000 ports are available on campus for general student use. Students can access the following: free student e-mail accounts, online (class) grades, online (class) registration, online (class) schedules. Campuswide network is available. 100% of college-owned or -operated housing units are wired for high-speed Internet access. Wireless service is available via entire campus.

Student Life *Housing options:* coed, disabled students. Campus housing is university owned. Freshman applicants given priority for college housing. *Activities and organizations:* drama/theater group, student-run newspaper, radio station, choral group, Student Organization of Kean University, Graduate and Part-time Student Council, Lambda Alpha Sigma - Honor Society, Operation Smile, Speech Language Hearing Association, national fraternities, national sororities. *Campus security:* 24-hour emergency response devices and patrols, student patrols, late-night transport/escort service, controlled dormitory access, 24-hour patrols by campus police. *Student services:* health clinic, personal/psychological counseling.

Athletics Member NCAA. All Division III. *Intercollegiate sports:* baseball M, basketball M/W, field hockey W, football M, lacrosse M/W, soccer M/W, softball W, tennis W, volleyball M/W. *Intramural sports:* basketball M/W, soccer M/W, softball M/W, tennis M/W, volleyball M/W, weight lifting M/W.

Standardized Tests *Required:* SAT or ACT (for admission).

Costs (2011–12) *Tuition:* state resident $6662 full-time, $260 per credit part-time; nonresident $12,474 full-time, $440 per credit part-time. Part-time tuition and fees vary according to course load. *Required fees:* $3538 full-time, $130 per credit part-time. *Room and board:* $13,528; room only: $10,490. Room and board charges vary according to board plan, housing facility, and student level. *Payment plan:* installment. *Waivers:* senior citizens and employees or children of employees.

Financial Aid Of all full-time matriculated undergraduates who enrolled in 2011, 8,503 applied for aid, 7,428 were judged to have need, 701 had their need fully met. 395 Federal Work-Study jobs (averaging $1777). In 2011, 66 non-need-based awards were made. *Average percent of need met:* 82%. *Average financial aid package:* $9474. *Average need-based loan:* $4437. *Average need-based gift aid:* $7147. *Average non-need-based aid:* $4281. *Average indebtedness upon graduation:* $25,119.

Applying *Options:* electronic application. *Application fee:* $75. *Required:* essay or personal statement, high school transcript, minimum 2.8 GPA. *Required for some:* interview. *Recommended:* 2 letters of recommendation. *Application deadlines:* 5/31 (freshmen), 7/6 (transfers). *Notification:* continuous (freshmen), continuous (transfers).

Freshman Application Contact Ms. Valerie Winslow, Director of Undergraduate Admissions, Kean University, 1000 Morris Avenue, Union, NJ 07083. *Phone:* 908-737-7100. *Fax:* 908-737-7105. *E-mail:* admitme@kean.edu. *Web site:* http://www.kean.edu/.

Monmouth University
West Long Branch, New Jersey

- **Independent** comprehensive, founded 1933
- **Suburban** 156-acre campus with easy access to New York City, Philadelphia
- **Endowment** $61.6 million
- **Coed** 4,700 undergraduate students, 93% full-time, 58% women, 42% men
- **Moderately difficult** entrance level, 63% of applicants were admitted

Undergraduates 4,375 full-time, 325 part-time. Students come from 25 states and territories; 20 other countries; 13% are from out of state; 4% Black or African American, non-Hispanic/Latino; 7% Hispanic/Latino; 2% Asian, non-Hispanic/Latino; 0.1% Native Hawaiian or other Pacific Islander, non-Hispanic/Latino; 0.1% American Indian or Alaska Native, non-Hispanic/Latino; 2% Two or more races, non-Hispanic/Latino; 4% Race/ethnicity unknown; 0.8% international; 7% transferred in; 46% live on campus. *Retention:* 80% of full-time freshmen returned.

Freshmen *Admission:* 6,491 applied, 4,110 admitted, 944 enrolled. *Average high school GPA:* 3.4. *Test scores:* SAT critical reading scores over 500: 66%; SAT math scores over 500: 78%; SAT writing scores over 500: 77%; ACT scores over 18: 98%; SAT critical reading scores over 600: 13%; SAT math scores over 600: 20%; SAT writing scores over 600: 16%; ACT scores over 24: 44%; SAT critical reading scores over 700: 1%; SAT math scores over 700: 1%; SAT writing scores over 700: 1%; ACT scores over 30: 1%.

Faculty *Total:* 603, 43% full-time, 49% with terminal degrees. *Student/faculty ratio:* 15:1.

Academics *Calendar:* semesters. *Degrees:* certificates, associate, bachelor's, master's, doctoral, post-master's, and postbachelor's certificates. *Special study options:* academic remediation for entering students, accelerated degree program, advanced placement credit, cooperative education, distance learning, double majors, honors programs, independent study, internships, part-time degree program, services for LD students, student-designed majors, study abroad, summer session for credit. *ROTC:* Army (c), Air Force (c).

Computers on Campus 422 computers/terminals are available on campus for general student use. Students can access the following: computer help desk, free student e-mail accounts, online (class) grades, online (class) registration, online (class) schedules. Campuswide network is available. 85% of college-owned or -operated housing units are wired for high-speed Internet access. Wireless service is available via classrooms, computer centers, computer labs, dorm rooms, learning centers, libraries, student centers.

Student Life *Housing options:* coed. Campus housing is university owned and leased by the school. Freshman campus housing is guaranteed. *Activities and organizations:* drama/theater group, student-run newspaper, radio and television station, choral group, radio station WMCX 88.9 FM, Student Government Association, student newspaper (Outlook), Student Activities Board, Shadows (yearbook), national fraternities, national sororities. *Campus security:* 24-hour emergency response devices and patrols, late-night transport/escort service,

controlled dormitory access. *Student services:* health clinic, personal/psychological counseling, women's center, legal services.

Athletics Member NCAA. All Division I except football (Division I-AA). *Intercollegiate sports:* baseball M(s), basketball M(s)/W(s), bowling M(c)/W(s), cross-country running M(s)/W(s), field hockey W(s), golf M(s)/W(s), ice hockey M(c), lacrosse W(s), sailing M(c)/W(c), soccer M(s)/W(s), softball W(s), tennis M(s)/W(s), track and field M(s)/W(s). *Intramural sports:* badminton M/W, basketball M/W, cheerleading M(c)/W(c), field hockey W(c), football W, soccer M/W, softball M/W, volleyball M/W.

Standardized Tests *Required:* SAT or ACT (for admission).

Costs (2011–12) *One-time required fee:* $200. *Comprehensive fee:* $38,459 includes full-time tuition ($27,372), mandatory fees ($628), and room and board ($10,459). Part-time tuition: $793 per credit. Part-time tuition and fees vary according to course load. *Required fees:* $157 per term part-time. *College room only:* $5932. Room and board charges vary according to board plan and housing facility. *Payment plan:* installment. *Waivers:* senior citizens and employees or children of employees.

Financial Aid Of all full-time matriculated undergraduates who enrolled in 2011, 3,078 applied for aid, 3,078 were judged to have need, 189 had their need fully met. 896 Federal Work-Study jobs (averaging $2031). In 2011, 1119 non-need-based awards were made. *Average percent of need met:* 67%. *Average financial aid package:* $19,017. *Average need-based loan:* $4708. *Average need-based gift aid:* $10,700. *Average non-need-based aid:* $8325. *Average indebtedness upon graduation:* $34,859.

Applying *Options:* electronic application, early action, deferred entrance. *Application fee:* $50. *Required:* high school transcript. *Required for some:* essay or personal statement, 2 letters of recommendation, interview. *Recommended:* resume of activities including community involvement and leadership positions. *Application deadlines:* 3/1 (freshmen), 7/15 (transfers), 12/1 (early action). *Notification:* 4/1 (freshmen), continuous (transfers), 1/15 (early action).

Freshman Application Contact Ms. Victoria Bobik, Director of Undergraduate Admission, Monmouth University, 400 Cedar Avenue, West Long Branch, NJ 07764-1898. *Phone:* 732-571-3456. *Toll-free phone:* 800-543-9671. *Fax:* 732-263-5166. *E-mail:* admission@monmouth.edu. *Web site:* http://www.monmouth.edu/.

See page 1464 for the College Close-Up.

Montclair State University
Montclair, New Jersey

- **State-supported** comprehensive, founded 1908
- **Suburban** 275-acre campus with easy access to New York City
- **Coed** 14,139 undergraduate students, 86% full-time, 61% women, 39% men
- **Moderately difficult** entrance level, 47% of applicants were admitted

Undergraduates 12,113 full-time, 2,026 part-time. Students come from 79 other countries; 3% are from out of state; 9% transferred in; 26% live on campus. *Retention:* 82% of full-time freshmen returned.

Freshmen *Admission:* 13,469 applied, 6,332 admitted, 2,114 enrolled. *Test scores:* SAT critical reading scores over 500: 43%; SAT math scores over 500: 44%; SAT writing scores over 500: 48%; SAT critical reading scores over 600: 8%; SAT math scores over 600: 10%; SAT writing scores over 600: 8%; SAT critical reading scores over 700: 1%; SAT math scores over 700: 1%; SAT writing scores over 700: 1%.

Faculty *Total:* 1,489, 37% full-time, 38% with terminal degrees. *Student/faculty ratio:* 17:1.

Academics *Calendar:* semesters. *Degrees:* bachelor's, master's, doctoral, postbachelor's, and first professional certificates. *Special study options:* academic remediation for entering students, accelerated degree program, adult/continuing education programs, advanced placement credit, cooperative education, double majors, English as a second language, freshman honors college, honors programs, independent study, internships, off-campus study, part-time degree program, services for LD students, study abroad, summer session for credit. *ROTC:* Army (b), Navy (b), Air Force (b).

Computers on Campus 218 computers/terminals are available on campus for general student use. Students can access the following: campus intranet, computer help desk, free student e-mail accounts, online (class) grades, online (class) registration, online (class) schedules. Campuswide network is available. 20% of college-owned or -operated housing units are wired for high-speed Internet access. Wireless service is available via entire campus.

Student Life *Housing options:* coed, women-only. Campus housing is university owned and is provided by a third party. Freshman applicants given priority for college housing. *Activities and organizations:* drama/theater group, student-run newspaper, radio station, choral group, Latin American Student Organization, Campus Recreation, MSU Gamers, Unified Asian American Student Organization, Human Relations and Leadership Association, national fraternities, national sororities. *Campus security:* 24-hour emergency response

devices and patrols, late-night transport/escort service, controlled dormitory access, video surveillance, student escorts. *Student services:* health clinic, personal/psychological counseling, women's center.

Athletics Member NCAA. All Division III. *Intercollegiate sports:* baseball M, basketball M/W, field hockey W, football M, golf M/W, lacrosse M/W, soccer M/W, softball W, swimming and diving M/W, track and field M/W, volleyball W. *Intramural sports:* badminton M(c)/W(c), baseball M, basketball M/W, bowling M/W, football M, ice hockey M(c), rugby M(c), softball M/W, volleyball M/W.

Standardized Tests *Required:* SAT or ACT (for admission).

Costs (2011–12) *Tuition:* state resident $7690 full-time, $256 per credit part-time; nonresident $16,438 full-time, $548 per credit part-time. *Required fees:* $2956 full-time, $93 per credit part-time, $157 per term part-time. *Room and board:* $11,264; room only: $7814. Room and board charges vary according to board plan and housing facility. *Payment plan:* installment. *Waivers:* senior citizens and employees or children of employees.

Financial Aid Of all full-time matriculated undergraduates who enrolled in 2010, 9,045 applied for aid, 7,633 were judged to have need, 1,418 had their need fully met. In 2010, 354 non-need-based awards were made. *Average percent of need met:* 74%. *Average financial aid package:* $9110. *Average need-based loan:* $4472. *Average need-based gift aid:* $7969. *Average non-need-based aid:* $6017. *Average indebtedness upon graduation:* $28,070.

Applying *Options:* electronic application, deferred entrance. *Application fee:* $60. *Required:* essay or personal statement, high school transcript. *Required for some:* interview. *Application deadlines:* 3/1 (freshmen), 6/15 (transfers). *Notification:* continuous (freshmen), continuous (transfers).

Freshman Application Contact Jason Langdon, Director of Admissions, Montclair State University, One Normal Avenue, Montclair, NJ 07043-1624. *Phone:* 973-655-5116. *Fax:* 973-655-7700. *E-mail:* undergraduate.admissions@montclair.edu. *Web site:* http://www.montclair.edu/.

New Jersey City University
Jersey City, New Jersey

- **State-supported** comprehensive, founded 1927
- **Urban** 51-acre campus with easy access to New York City
- **Endowment** $3.3 million
- **Coed** 6,639 undergraduate students, 74% full-time, 60% women, 40% men
- **Moderately difficult** entrance level, 43% of applicants were admitted

Undergraduates 4,907 full-time, 1,732 part-time. Students come from 16 states and territories; 15 other countries; 1% are from out of state; 20% Black or African American, non-Hispanic/Latino; 37% Hispanic/Latino; 8% Asian, non-Hispanic/Latino; 0.2% American Indian or Alaska Native, non-Hispanic/Latino; 0.5% Two or more races, non-Hispanic/Latino; 9% Race/ethnicity unknown; 1% international; 15% transferred in; 4% live on campus. *Retention:* 70% of full-time freshmen returned.

Freshmen *Admission:* 4,399 applied, 1,893 admitted, 772 enrolled. *Test scores:* SAT critical reading scores over 500: 20%; SAT critical reading scores over 600: 3%.

Faculty *Total:* 694, 35% full-time, 31% with terminal degrees. *Student/faculty ratio:* 21:1.

Academics *Calendar:* semesters. *Degrees:* certificates, bachelor's, master's, post-master's, and postbachelor's certificates. *Special study options:* academic remediation for entering students, accelerated degree program, adult/continuing education programs, advanced placement credit, cooperative education, distance learning, double majors, English as a second language, honors programs, independent study, internships, off-campus study, part-time degree program, services for LD students, study abroad, summer session for credit.

Computers on Campus 704 computers/terminals are available on campus for general student use. Students can access the following: free student e-mail accounts, online (class) grades, online (class) registration, online (class) schedules. Campuswide network is available. Wireless service is available via learning centers, student centers.

Student Life *Housing options:* coed. Campus housing is university owned. *Activities and organizations:* drama/theater group, student-run newspaper, radio station, choral group, International Student Association, Black Freedom Society, Latin Power Association, national fraternities. *Campus security:* 24-hour emergency response devices and patrols, late-night transport/escort service. *Student services:* health clinic, personal/psychological counseling, women's center, legal services.

Athletics Member NCAA. All Division III. *Intercollegiate sports:* baseball M, basketball M/W, bowling W, cross-country running W, soccer M/W, softball W, track and field M/W, volleyball M/W. *Intramural sports:* basketball M/W, bowling W, soccer M/W, softball M/W, swimming and diving M/W, table tennis M/W, tennis M/W, volleyball M/W, weight lifting M/W.

Standardized Tests *Required:* SAT (for admission).

Costs (2012–13) *Tuition:* state resident $236 per credit hour part-time; nonresident $498 per credit hour part-time. Full-time tuition and fees vary according to program. Part-time tuition and fees vary according to course load. *Payment plan:* deferred payment. *Waivers:* senior citizens and employees or children of employees.

Financial Aid Of all full-time matriculated undergraduates who enrolled in 2011, 4,359 applied for aid, 4,161 were judged to have need, 253 had their need fully met. In 2011, 45 non-need-based awards were made. *Average percent of need met:* 59%. *Average financial aid package:* $19,099. *Average need-based loan:* $12,659. *Average need-based gift aid:* $7716. *Average non-need-based aid:* $6414. *Average indebtedness upon graduation:* $17,310.

Applying *Options:* electronic application, early admission, deferred entrance. *Application fee:* $50. *Required:* essay or personal statement, high school transcript, minimum 2.0 GPA. *Required for some:* interview. *Recommended:* 1 letter of recommendation. *Application deadlines:* 4/1 (freshmen), rolling (transfers). *Notification:* continuous (freshmen).

Freshman Application Contact Mr. Jose Balda, Director of Admissions, New Jersey City University, 2039 Kennedy Loulevard, Jersey City, NJ 07305. *Phone:* 201-200-3234. *Toll-free phone:* 888-441-NJCU. *E-mail:* admissions@njcu.edu. *Web site:* http://www.njcu.edu/.

New Jersey Institute of Technology
Newark, New Jersey

- **State-supported** university, founded 1881
- **Urban** 48-acre campus with easy access to New York City
- **Endowment** $67.5 million
- **Coed**
- **Moderately difficult** entrance level

Faculty *Student/faculty ratio:* 15:1.

Academics *Calendar:* semesters. *Degrees:* bachelor's, master's, doctoral, postbachelor's, and first professional certificates.

Student Life *Campus security:* 24-hour emergency response devices and patrols, late-night transport/escort service, controlled dormitory access, bicycle patrols.

Athletics Member NCAA. All Division I.

Standardized Tests *Required:* SAT or ACT (for admission).

Costs (2011–12) *Tuition:* state resident $11,756 full-time, $447 per credit part-time; nonresident $23,116 full-time, $988 per credit part-time. Full-time tuition and fees vary according to course load and degree level. Part-time tuition and fees vary according to course load and degree level. *Required fees:* $2218 full-time, $110 per credit part-time. *Room and board:* $10,486; room only: $8000. Room and board charges vary according to board plan and housing facility. *Payment plans:* installment, deferred payment.

Financial Aid *Of all full-time matriculated undergraduates who enrolled in 2010,* 3,606 applied for aid, 3,291 were judged to have need, 281 had their need fully met. 285 Federal Work-Study jobs (averaging $1215). 375 state and other part-time jobs (averaging $754). *In 2010,* 177 non-need-based awards were made. *Average percent of need met:* 68. *Average financial aid package:* $14,090. *Average need-based loan:* $4915. *Average need-based gift aid:* $11,805. *Average non-need-based aid:* $10,164. *Average indebtedness upon graduation:* $26,045.

Applying *Options:* electronic application, early admission, deferred entrance. *Application fee:* $70. *Required:* high school transcript. *Required for some:* essay or personal statement, interview. *Recommended:* 1 letter of recommendation.

Freshman Application Contact Mr. Stephen M. Eck, Director of University Admissions, New Jersey Institute of Technology, University Heights, Newark, NJ 07102. *Phone:* 973-596-3306. *Toll-free phone:* 800-925-NJIT. *Fax:* 973-596-3461. *E-mail:* admissions@njit.edu. *Web site:* http://www.njit.edu/.

Princeton University
Princeton, New Jersey

- **Independent** university, founded 1746
- **Suburban** 600-acre campus with easy access to New York City, Philadelphia
- **Endowment** $16.5 billion
- **Coed** 5,249 undergraduate students, 99% full-time, 49% women, 51% men
- **Most difficult** entrance level, 8% of applicants were admitted

Undergraduates 5,173 full-time, 76 part-time. Students come from 52 states and territories; 95 other countries; 84% are from out of state; 7% Black or African American, non-Hispanic/Latino; 8% Hispanic/Latino; 18% Asian, non-Hispanic/Latino; 0.1% Native Hawaiian or other Pacific Islander, non-Hispanic/Latino; 0.3% American Indian or Alaska Native, non-Hispanic/Latino; 4% Two or more races, non-Hispanic/Latino; 3% Race/ethnicity unknown;

11% international; 97% live on campus. *Retention:* 98% of full-time freshmen returned.

Freshmen *Admission:* 27,189 applied, 2,300 admitted, 1,298 enrolled. *Average high school GPA:* 3.89. *Test scores:* SAT critical reading scores over 500: 99%; SAT math scores over 500: 100%; SAT writing scores over 500: 101%; ACT scores over 18: 100%; SAT critical reading scores over 600: 97%; SAT math scores over 600: 99%; SAT writing scores over 600: 99%; ACT scores over 24: 100%; SAT critical reading scores over 700: 76%; SAT math scores over 700: 81%; SAT writing scores over 700: 80%; ACT scores over 30: 88%.

Faculty *Total:* 1,082, 79% full-time, 86% with terminal degrees. *Student/faculty ratio:* 6:1.

Academics *Calendar:* semesters. *Degrees:* bachelor's, master's, doctoral, and first professional. *Special study options:* adult/continuing education programs, advanced placement credit, independent study, off-campus study, services for LD students, student-designed majors, study abroad. *ROTC:* Army (b), Navy (c).

Computers on Campus 500 computers/terminals and 17,000 ports are available on campus for general student use. Students can access the following: campus intranet, computer help desk, free student e-mail accounts, online (class) grades, online (class) registration, online (class) schedules, academic applications and courseware, printing, network file space, Web site hosting, media lab, broadcast center. Campuswide network is available. 100% of college-owned or -operated housing units are wired for high-speed Internet access. Wireless service is available via entire campus.

Student Life *Housing:* on-campus residence required through sophomore year. *Options:* coed, men-only, women-only, disabled students. Campus housing is university owned. Freshman campus housing is guaranteed. *Activities and organizations:* drama/theater group, student-run newspaper, radio station, choral group, marching band. *Campus security:* 24-hour emergency response devices and patrols, student patrols, late-night transport/escort service, controlled dormitory access. *Student services:* health clinic, personal/psychological counseling, women's center, legal services.

Athletics Member NCAA. All Division I except football (Division I-AA). *Intercollegiate sports:* baseball M, basketball M/W, crew M/W, cross-country running M/W, fencing M/W, field hockey W, golf M/W, ice hockey M/W, lacrosse M/W, soccer M/W, softball W, squash M/W, swimming and diving M/W, tennis M/W, track and field M/W, volleyball M/W, water polo M/W, wrestling M. *Intramural sports:* badminton M(c)/W(c), baseball M(c), basketball M(c)/W(c), cheerleading M(c)/W(c), cross-country running M(c)/W(c), equestrian sports M(c)/W(c), fencing M(c)/W(c), field hockey W(c), ice hockey M(c)/W(c), lacrosse M(c)/W(c), rugby M(c)/W(c), sailing M(c)/W(c), skiing (downhill) M(c)/W(c), soccer M(c)/W(c), softball W(c), squash M(c)/W(c), swimming and diving M(c)/W(c), table tennis M(c)/W(c), tennis M(c)/W(c), ultimate Frisbee M(c)/W(c), volleyball M(c)/W(c).

Standardized Tests *Required:* SAT or ACT (for admission).

Costs (2012–13) *Comprehensive fee:* $52,145 includes full-time tuition ($38,650), mandatory fees ($865), and room and board ($12,630). *College room only:* $6950. Room and board charges vary according to board plan. *Payment plans:* installment, deferred payment. *Waivers:* employees or children of employees.

Financial Aid Of all full-time matriculated undergraduates who enrolled in 2010, 3,259 applied for aid, 3,056 were judged to have need, 3,056 had their need fully met. 715 Federal Work-Study jobs (averaging $818). 1,487 state and other part-time jobs (averaging $1437). *Average percent of need met:* 100%. *Average financial aid package:* $37,692. *Average need-based gift aid:* $35,665. *Average indebtedness upon graduation:* $5330.

Applying *Options:* electronic application, early action, deferred entrance. *Application fee:* $65. *Required:* essay or personal statement, high school transcript, 3 letters of recommendation. *Recommended:* interview. *Application deadlines:* 1/1 (freshmen), 11/1 (early action). *Notification:* 3/3 (freshmen).

Freshman Application Contact Ms. Janet Rapelye, Dean of Admission, Princeton University, PO Box 430, Princeton, NJ 08542-0430. *Phone:* 609-258-3060. *Fax:* 609-258-6743. *E-mail:* uaoffice@princeton.edu. *Web site:* http://www.princeton.edu/.

Rabbi Jacob Joseph School

Edison, New Jersey

Admissions Office Contact Rabbi Jacob Joseph School, One Plainfield Ave, Edison, NJ 08817.

Rabbinical College of America

Morristown, New Jersey

Director of Admissions Sharon Miller, Registrar, Rabbinical College of America, 226 Sussex Avenue, PO Box 1996, Morristown, NJ 07962-1996. *Phone:* 973-267-9404. *E-mail:* rca079@aol.com.

Ramapo College of New Jersey

Mahwah, New Jersey

- **State-supported** comprehensive, founded 1969, part of New Jersey State College System
- **Suburban** 300-acre campus with easy access to New York City
- **Endowment** $12.2 million
- **Coed** 5,715 undergraduate students, 90% full-time, 58% women, 42% men
- **Moderately difficult** entrance level, 50% of applicants were admitted

Undergraduates 5,122 full-time, 593 part-time. Students come from 18 states and territories; 27 other countries; 4% are from out of state; 5% Black or African American, non-Hispanic/Latino; 11% Hispanic/Latino; 5% Asian, non-Hispanic/Latino; 0.4% Native Hawaiian or other Pacific Islander, non-Hispanic/Latino; 0.2% American Indian or Alaska Native, non-Hispanic/Latino; 1% Two or more races, non-Hispanic/Latino; 4% Race/ethnicity unknown; 0.7% international; 10% transferred in; 53% live on campus. *Retention:* 86% of full-time freshmen returned.

Freshmen *Admission:* 5,091 applied, 2,561 admitted, 895 enrolled. *Average high school GPA:* 3.3. *Test scores:* SAT critical reading scores over 500: 75%; SAT math scores over 500: 85%; SAT writing scores over 500: 78%; SAT critical reading scores over 600: 26%; SAT math scores over 600: 39%; SAT writing scores over 600: 27%; SAT critical reading scores over 700: 3%; SAT math scores over 700: 4%; SAT writing scores over 700: 4%.

Faculty *Total:* 481, 46% full-time. *Student/faculty ratio:* 17:1.

Academics *Calendar:* semesters. *Degrees:* certificates, bachelor's, and master's. *Special study options:* academic remediation for entering students, accelerated degree program, adult/continuing education programs, advanced placement credit, cooperative education, distance learning, double majors, external degree program, freshman honors college, honors programs, independent study, internships, off-campus study, part-time degree program, services for LD students, student-designed majors, study abroad, summer session for credit. *ROTC:* Air Force (c). *Unusual degree programs:* 3-2 biology, and chemistry with Rutgers, The State University of New Jersey; NY University College of Dentistry; SUNY State College of Optometry. RCNJ confers BSN & MSN degrees here on campus (with clinical internships at Valley Hospital, Englewood Hospital & Medical Center, and other state hospitals).

Computers on Campus 1,058 computers/terminals and 1,500 ports are available on campus for general student use. Students can access the following: campus intranet, computer help desk, free student e-mail accounts, online (class) grades, online (class) registration, online (class) schedules. Campuswide network is available. 100% of college-owned or -operated housing units are wired for high-speed Internet access. Wireless service is available via classrooms, computer centers, computer labs, learning centers, libraries, student centers.

Student Life *Housing options:* coed, disabled students. Campus housing is university owned. Freshman campus housing is guaranteed. *Activities and organizations:* drama/theater group, student-run newspaper, radio and television station, choral group, NORML, 1 Step, Biology & BioChemistry Club, Campus Crusade for Christ, Culture Club, national fraternities, national sororities. *Campus security:* 24-hour emergency response devices and patrols, late-night transport/escort service, controlled dormitory access, surveillance cameras, patrols by trained security personnel. *Student services:* health clinic, personal/psychological counseling, women's center.

Athletics Member NCAA. All Division III. *Intercollegiate sports:* baseball M, basketball M/W, cross-country running M/W, field hockey W, lacrosse W, soccer M/W, softball W, swimming and diving M/W, tennis M/W, track and field M/W, volleyball W. *Intramural sports:* basketball M/W, bowling M/W, football M/W, rock climbing M/W, soccer M/W, softball M/W, table tennis M/W, ultimate Frisbee M/W, volleyball M/W.

Standardized Tests *Required:* SAT (for admission). *Required for some:* ACT (for admission).

Costs (2011–12) *Tuition:* state resident $8187 full-time, $256 per credit part-time; nonresident $16,374 full-time, $512 per credit part-time. Full-time tuition and fees vary according to degree level and reciprocity agreements. Part-time tuition and fees vary according to degree level and reciprocity agreements. *Required fees:* $4571 full-time, $143 per credit part-time. *Room and board:* $10,510; room only: $7860. Room and board charges vary according to board plan and housing facility. *Payment plan:* installment. *Waivers:* senior citizens and employees or children of employees.

Financial Aid Of all full-time matriculated undergraduates who enrolled in 2011, 3,324 applied for aid, 2,588 were judged to have need, 120 had their need fully met. 102 Federal Work-Study jobs (averaging $1835). 742 state and other part-time jobs (averaging $2076). In 2011, 301 non-need-based awards were made. *Average percent of need met:* 62%. *Average financial aid package:* $11,842. *Average need-based loan:* $4680. *Average need-based gift aid:* $10,096. *Average non-need-based aid:* $11,082. *Average indebtedness upon graduation:* $28,955.

Applying *Options:* electronic application, early admission, early action, deferred entrance. *Application fee:* $60. *Required:* essay or personal statement, high school transcript. *Recommended:* minimum 3.0 GPA. *Application deadlines:* 3/1 (freshmen), 5/1 (transfers). *Notification:* continuous until 3/15 (freshmen), continuous until 7/1 (transfers).

Freshman Application Contact Michael DiBartolomeo, Associate Director for Freshmen Admissions, Ramapo College of New Jersey, Office of Admissions, 505 Ramapo Valley Road, Mahwah, NJ 07430-1680. *Phone:* 201-684-7300. *Toll-free phone:* 800-9RAMAPO. *Fax:* 201-684-7964. *E-mail:* admissions@ramapo.edu. *Web site:* http://www.ramapo.edu/.

The Richard Stockton College of New Jersey
Pomona, New Jersey

- **State-supported** comprehensive, founded 1969, part of New Jersey State College System
- **Suburban** 2000-acre campus with easy access to Philadelphia
- **Endowment** $14.0 million
- **Coed** 7,240 undergraduate students, 91% full-time, 58% women, 42% men
- **Very difficult** entrance level, 65% of applicants were admitted

Undergraduates 6,584 full-time, 656 part-time. Students come from 15 states and territories; 10 other countries; 1% are from out of state; 7% Black or African American, non-Hispanic/Latino; 8% Hispanic/Latino; 5% Asian, non-Hispanic/Latino; 0.2% Native Hawaiian or other Pacific Islander, non-Hispanic/Latino; 0.2% American Indian or Alaska Native, non-Hispanic/Latino; 2% Two or more races, non-Hispanic/Latino; 1% Race/ethnicity unknown; 0.3% international; 15% transferred in; 35% live on campus. *Retention:* 84% of full-time freshmen returned.

Freshmen *Admission:* 5,089 applied, 3,284 admitted, 973 enrolled. *Test scores:* SAT critical reading scores over 500: 64%; SAT math scores over 500: 73%; SAT writing scores over 500: 62%; ACT scores over 18: 86%; SAT critical reading scores over 600: 16%; SAT math scores over 600: 27%; SAT writing scores over 600: 13%; ACT scores over 24: 23%; SAT critical reading scores over 700: 1%; SAT math scores over 700: 3%; SAT writing scores over 700: 1%; ACT scores over 30: 2%.

Faculty *Total:* 601, 47% full-time, 64% with terminal degrees. *Student/faculty ratio:* 18:1.

Academics *Calendar:* semesters. *Degrees:* certificates, bachelor's, master's, doctoral, and postbachelor's certificates. *Special study options:* academic remediation for entering students, accelerated degree program, adult/continuing education programs, advanced placement credit, distance learning, honors programs, independent study, internships, off-campus study, part-time degree program, services for LD students, student-designed majors, study abroad, summer session for credit. *ROTC:* Army (c). *Unusual degree programs:* 3-2 business administration; engineering with New Jersey Institute of Technology; Rutgers, The State University of New Jersey; criminal justice/public health with University of Medicine and Dentistry of NJ; medical technology with University of Delaware.

Computers on Campus 930 computers/terminals and 2,400 ports are available on campus for general student use. Students can access the following: campus intranet, computer help desk, free student e-mail accounts, online (class) grades, online (class) registration, online (class) schedules. Campus-wide network is available. 100% of college-owned or -operated housing units are wired for high-speed Internet access. Wireless service is available via entire campus.

Student Life *Housing options:* coed. Campus housing is university owned. Freshman campus housing is guaranteed. *Activities and organizations:* drama/theater group, student-run newspaper, radio and television station, choral group, Multi-Cultural Connection, Stockton Entertainment Team, Los Latinos Unidos, Unified Black Student Society, Stockton Action Volunteers for the Environment, national fraternities, national sororities. *Campus security:* 24-hour emergency response devices and patrols, late-night transport/escort service, controlled dormitory access, on-campus sworn/commissioned police force. *Student services:* health clinic, personal/psychological counseling, women's center.

Athletics Member NCAA. All Division III. *Intercollegiate sports:* baseball M, basketball M/W, cheerleading M/W, crew W, cross-country running M/W, field hockey W, lacrosse M, soccer M/W, softball W, tennis W, track and field M/W, volleyball W. *Intramural sports:* basketball M/W, bowling M(c)/W(c), crew M(c), fencing M(c)/W(c), golf M(c)/W(c), ice hockey M(c), skiing (downhill) M(c)/W(c), soccer M/W, softball M/W, table tennis M/W, ultimate Frisbee M(c)/W(c), volleyball M(c)/W(c).

Standardized Tests *Required:* SAT or ACT (for admission).

Costs (2011–12) *Tuition:* state resident $7717 full-time, $297 per credit hour part-time; nonresident $13,923 full-time, $536 per credit hour part-time. Part-time tuition and fees vary according to course load. *Required fees:* $4246 full-time, $163 per credit hour part-time, $70 per term part-time. *Room and board:* $10,477; room only: $7236. Room and board charges vary according to board

plan and housing facility. *Payment plans:* installment, deferred payment. *Waivers:* senior citizens and employees or children of employees.

Financial Aid Of all full-time matriculated undergraduates who enrolled in 2011, 5,607 applied for aid, 4,887 were judged to have need, 1,159 had their need fully met. 192 Federal Work-Study jobs (averaging $1775) and 973 state and other part-time jobs (averaging $1642). In 2011, 396 non-need-based awards were made. *Average percent of need met:* 66%. *Average financial aid package:* $16,070. *Average need-based loan:* $4559. *Average need-based gift aid:* $7834. *Average non-need-based aid:* $6817. *Average indebtedness upon graduation:* $32,255.

Applying *Options:* electronic application, early admission. *Application fee:* $50. *Required:* high school transcript, minimum 2.0 GPA. *Recommended:* essay or personal statement, minimum 3.0 GPA, 3 letters of recommendation. *Application deadlines:* 5/1 (freshmen), 6/1 (transfers). *Notification:* 5/15 (freshmen), continuous until 6/15 (transfers).

Freshman Application Contact The Richard Stockton College of New Jersey, PO Box 195, Jimmie Leeds Road, Pomona, NJ 08240-0195. *Phone:* 609-652-4261. *Web site:* http://www.stockton.edu/.

See page 549 for display ad and page 1518 for the College Close-Up.

Rider University
Lawrenceville, New Jersey

- **Independent** comprehensive, founded 1865
- **Suburban** 280-acre campus with easy access to New York City, Philadelphia
- **Endowment** $46.8 million
- **Coed** 4,651 undergraduate students, 85% full-time, 59% women, 41% men
- **Moderately difficult** entrance level, 73% of applicants were admitted

Undergraduates 3,935 full-time, 716 part-time. Students come from 38 states and territories; 65 other countries; 21% are from out of state; 10% Black or African American, non-Hispanic/Latino; 9% Hispanic/Latino; 4% Asian, non-Hispanic/Latino; 0.1% Native Hawaiian or other Pacific Islander, non-Hispanic/Latino; 0.3% American Indian or Alaska Native, non-Hispanic/Latino; 0.9% Two or more races, non-Hispanic/Latino; 9% Race/ethnicity unknown; 2% international; 6% transferred in; 57% live on campus. *Retention:* 83% of full-time freshmen returned.

Freshmen *Admission:* 7,947 applied, 5,827 admitted, 941 enrolled. *Average high school GPA:* 3.27. *Test scores:* SAT critical reading scores over 500: 60%; SAT math scores over 500: 65%; SAT writing scores over 500: 59%; ACT scores over 18: 85%; SAT critical reading scores over 600: 16%; SAT math scores over 600: 20%; SAT writing scores over 600: 18%; ACT scores over 24: 33%; SAT critical reading scores over 700: 2%; SAT math scores over 700: 2%; SAT writing scores over 700: 2%; ACT scores over 30: 2%.

Faculty *Total:* 612, 41% full-time, 67% with terminal degrees. *Student/faculty ratio:* 13:1.

Academics *Calendar:* semesters. *Degrees:* certificates, associate, bachelor's, master's, and post-master's certificates. *Special study options:* academic remediation for entering students, adult/continuing education programs, advanced placement credit, cooperative education, distance learning, double majors, English as a second language, honors programs, independent study, internships, part-time degree program, services for LD students, study abroad, summer session for credit. *ROTC:* Army (c).

Computers on Campus 300 computers/terminals are available on campus for general student use. Students can access the following: computer help desk, free student e-mail accounts, online (class) grades, online (class) registration, online (class) schedules. Campuswide network is available. 100% of college-owned or -operated housing units are wired for high-speed Internet access. Wireless service is available via entire campus.

Student Life *Housing options:* coed, women-only, disabled students. Campus housing is university owned. Freshman applicants given priority for college housing. *Activities and organizations:* drama/theater group, student-run newspaper, radio and television station, choral group, Student Government Association, Greek Council, Association of Commuter Students, Black Student Union, Residence Hall Association, national fraternities, national sororities. *Campus security:* 24-hour emergency response devices and patrols, student patrols, late-night transport/escort service, controlled dormitory access. *Student services:* health clinic, personal/psychological counseling.

Athletics Member NCAA. All Division I. *Intercollegiate sports:* baseball M(s), basketball M(s)/W(s), cheerleading M/W, cross-country running M(s)/W(s), field hockey W(s), golf M(s), soccer M(s)/W(s), softball W(s), swimming and diving M(s)/W(s), tennis M(s)/W(s), track and field M(s)/W(s), volleyball W(s), wrestling M(s). *Intramural sports:* basketball M/W, cheerleading M/W, equestrian sports W(c), golf M, ice hockey M(c), lacrosse M(c)/W, soccer M/W, softball M/W, track and field M/W, volleyball M/W, water polo M/W.

Standardized Tests *Required:* SAT or ACT (for admission).

Costs (2011–12) *Comprehensive fee:* $43,740 includes full-time tuition ($31,330), mandatory fees ($600), and room and board ($11,810). Full-time tuition and fees vary according to course load and program. Part-time tuition: $560 per credit. Part-time tuition and fees vary according to course load and program. *Required fees:* $35 per course part-time. *College room only:* $7330. Room and board charges vary according to board plan, housing facility, and location. *Payment plan:* installment. *Waivers:* employees or children of employees.

Financial Aid Of all full-time matriculated undergraduates who enrolled in 2011, 3,203 applied for aid, 2,886 were judged to have need, 492 had their need fully met. In 2011, 772 non-need-based awards were made. *Average percent of need met:* 69%. *Average financial aid package:* $22,113. *Average need-based loan:* $42,414. *Average need-based gift aid:* $16,470. *Average non-need-based aid:* $12,448. *Average indebtedness upon graduation:* $35,449.

Applying *Options:* electronic application, early admission, early action, deferred entrance. *Application fee:* $50. *Required:* essay or personal statement, high school transcript, 2 letters of recommendation. *Required for some:* interview. *Application deadlines:* rolling (freshmen), rolling (transfers), 11/15 (early action). *Notification:* continuous (freshmen), continuous (transfers), 12/15 (early action).

Freshman Application Contact Mr. William Larrousse, Director of Admissions, Rider University, 2083 Lawrenceville Road, Lawrenceville, NJ 08648. *Phone:* 609-896-5177. *Toll-free phone:* 800-257-9026. *Fax:* 609-895-6645. *E-mail:* wlarrousse@rider.edu. *Web site:* http://www.rider.edu/.

Rowan University
Glassboro, New Jersey

- **State-supported** comprehensive, founded 1923, part of New Jersey State College System
- **Suburban** 800-acre campus with easy access to Philadelphia
- **Endowment** $150.4 million
- **Coed** 10,438 undergraduate students, 85% full-time, 52% women, 48% men
- **Moderately difficult** entrance level, 58% of applicants were admitted

Undergraduates 8,909 full-time, 1,529 part-time. Students come from 24 states and territories; 17 other countries; 2% are from out of state; 8% Black or African American, non-Hispanic/Latino; 9% Hispanic/Latino; 4% Asian, non-Hispanic/Latino; 0.2% Native Hawaiian or other Pacific Islander, non-Hispanic/Latino; 1% American Indian or Alaska Native, non-Hispanic/Latino; 0.8% Two or more races, non-Hispanic/Latino; 0.6% Race/ethnicity unknown; 0.6% international; 11% transferred in; 38% live on campus. *Retention:* 86% of full-time freshmen returned.

Freshmen *Admission:* 7,285 applied, 4,239 admitted, 1,584 enrolled. *Average high school GPA:* 3.46. *Test scores:* SAT critical reading scores over 500: 72%; SAT math scores over 500: 80%; SAT writing scores over 500: 67%; SAT critical reading scores over 600: 21%; SAT math scores over 600: 33%; SAT writing scores over 600: 19%; SAT critical reading scores over 700: 3%; SAT math scores over 700: 4%; SAT writing scores over 700: 2%.

Faculty *Total:* 1,049, 37% full-time, 43% with terminal degrees. *Student/faculty ratio:* 16:1.

Academics *Calendar:* semesters. *Degrees:* certificates, bachelor's, master's, doctoral, and postbachelor's certificates. *Special study options:* academic remediation for entering students, adult/continuing education programs, advanced placement credit, cooperative education, distance learning, double majors, English as a second language, freshman honors college, honors programs, independent study, internships, off-campus study, part-time degree program, services for LD students, study abroad, summer session for credit. *ROTC:* Army (c). *Unusual degree programs:* 3-2 mathematics and computer science.

Computers on Campus 1,200 computers/terminals and 2,500 ports are available on campus for general student use. Students can access the following: campus intranet, computer help desk, free student e-mail accounts, online (class) grades, online (class) registration, online (class) schedules, online library. Campuswide network is available. 100% of college-owned or -operated housing units are wired for high-speed Internet access. Wireless service is available via entire campus.

Student Life *Housing:* on-campus residence required through sophomore year. *Options:* coed, men-only, women-only, disabled students. Campus housing is university owned and leased by the school. Freshman campus housing is guaranteed. *Activities and organizations:* drama/theater group, student-run newspaper, radio and television station, choral group, Kappa Delta Pi, Public Relations Student Society of America, Student University Programmes, Rowan Television Network, Elementary Education Club, national fraternities, national sororities. *Campus security:* 24-hour emergency response devices and patrols, student patrols, late-night transport/escort service, controlled dormitory access, EMS Service including 2 ambulances. Security and Campus

Police trained as Police Officers in NJ. *Student services:* health clinic, personal/psychological counseling, legal services.

Athletics Member NCAA. All Division III. *Intercollegiate sports:* baseball M, basketball M/W, cross-country running M/W, field hockey W, football M, lacrosse W, soccer M/W, softball W, swimming and diving M/W, track and field M/W, volleyball W. *Intramural sports:* basketball M/W, bowling M/W, cheerleading W(c), field hockey W(c), football M/W, golf M/W, ice hockey M(c), lacrosse M(c)/W, racquetball M/W, rock climbing M(c), rugby M, skiing (downhill) M(c)/W(c), soccer M/W, softball M/W, table tennis M/W, tennis M(c)/W(c), ultimate Frisbee M(c)/W(c), volleyball M/W, water polo M/W, wrestling M(c).

Standardized Tests *Required:* SAT or ACT (for admission).

Costs (2012–13) *Tuition:* state resident $8646 full-time, $332 per credit part-time; nonresident $16,226 full-time, $625 per credit part-time. Full-time tuition and fees vary according to course load, degree level, and program. Part-time tuition and fees vary according to course load, degree level, and program. *Required fees:* $3372 full-time, $144 per credit hour part-time. *Room and board:* $10,450; room only: $6690. Room and board charges vary according to board plan and housing facility. *Payment plan:* deferred payment. *Waivers:* employees or children of employees.

Financial Aid Of all full-time matriculated undergraduates who enrolled in 2010, 6,988 applied for aid, 5,557 were judged to have need, 840 had their need fully met. 426 Federal Work-Study jobs (averaging $1478). 1,032 state and other part-time jobs (averaging $1305). In 2010, 468 non-need-based awards were made. *Average percent of need met:* 80%. *Average financial aid package:* $9337. *Average need-based loan:* $4252. *Average need-based gift aid:* $8620. *Average non-need-based aid:* $5414. *Average indebtedness upon graduation:* $31,895.

Applying *Options:* electronic application, early admission, deferred entrance. *Application fee:* $65. *Required:* high school transcript. *Required for some:* interview. *Recommended:* minimum 2.0 GPA. *Application deadlines:* 3/1 (freshmen), 3/1 (transfers). *Notification:* continuous (freshmen), continuous (transfers).

Freshman Application Contact Mr. Albert Betts, Director of Admissions, Rowan University, 201 Mullica Hill Road, Glassboro, NJ 08028. *Phone:* 856-256-4200. *Toll-free phone:* 800-447-1165 (in-state); 800-447-1165N (out-of-state). *Fax:* 856-256-4430. *E-mail:* admissions@rowan.edu. *Web site:* http://www.rowan.edu/.

See page 1534 for the College Close-Up.

Rutgers, The State University of New Jersey, Camden

Camden, New Jersey

- **State-supported** university, founded 1927, part of Rutgers, The State University of New Jersey
- **Urban** 34-acre campus with easy access to Philadelphia
- **Endowment** $508.8 million
- **Coed** 4,653 undergraduate students, 82% full-time, 55% women, 45% men
- **Moderately difficult** entrance level, 54% of applicants were admitted

Undergraduates 3,800 full-time, 853 part-time. Students come from 25 states and territories; 12 other countries; 4% are from out of state; 18% Black or African American, non-Hispanic/Latino; 10% Hispanic/Latino; 8% Asian, non-Hispanic/Latino; 0.3% Native Hawaiian or other Pacific Islander, non-Hispanic/Latino; 0.2% American Indian or Alaska Native, non-Hispanic/Latino; 3% Two or more races, non-Hispanic/Latino; 2% Race/ethnicity unknown; 0.6% international; 17% transferred in; 10% live on campus. *Retention:* 83% of full-time freshmen returned.

Freshmen *Admission:* 5,791 applied, 3,115 admitted, 536 enrolled. *Test scores:* SAT critical reading scores over 500: 72%; SAT writing scores over 500: 70%; SAT critical reading scores over 600: 22%; SAT writing scores over 600: 22%; SAT critical reading scores over 700: 2%; SAT writing scores over 700: 2%.

Faculty *Total:* 522, 54% full-time, 99% with terminal degrees. *Student/faculty ratio:* 11:1.

Academics *Calendar:* semesters. *Degrees:* bachelor's, master's, doctoral, and first professional. *Special study options:* academic remediation for entering students, accelerated degree program, advanced placement credit, cooperative education, distance learning, double majors, English as a second language, freshman honors college, honors programs, independent study, internships, part-time degree program, services for LD students, student-designed majors, study abroad, summer session for credit. *ROTC:* Army (c), Air Force (c). *Unusual degree programs:* 3-2 business administration; engineering; medical technology with approved hospital; African-American studies, general science, childhood studies, English, history, liberal studies, psychology; biology, chemistry and mathematics with the Graduate School-Camden.

Computers on Campus 184 computers/terminals are available on campus for general student use. Students can access the following: campus intranet, computer help desk, free student e-mail accounts, online (class) grades, online (class) registration, online (class) schedules, online grade reports. Campuswide network is available. 100% of college-owned or -operated housing units are wired for high-speed Internet access. Wireless service is available via classrooms, computer centers, computer labs, dorm rooms, learning centers, libraries, student centers.

Student Life *Housing options:* coed, disabled students. Campus housing is university owned. *Activities and organizations:* drama/theater group, student-run radio station. *Campus security:* 24-hour emergency response devices and patrols, student patrols, late-night transport/escort service, controlled dormitory access.

Athletics Member NCAA. All Division III. *Intercollegiate sports:* baseball M, basketball M/W, crew M/W, cross-country running W, golf M, lacrosse W, soccer M/W, softball W, track and field M/W, volleyball W. *Intramural sports:* baseball M, basketball M/W, cheerleading W, crew M, golf M, ice hockey M, lacrosse M, racquetball M, soccer M, tennis M, track and field M, ultimate Frisbee M/W, volleyball M/W.

Standardized Tests *Required:* SAT or ACT (for admission).

Costs (2011–12) *Tuition:* state resident $10,104 full-time, $325 per credit part-time; nonresident $22,766 full-time, $725 per credit part-time. Part-time tuition and fees vary according to course load. *Required fees:* $2511 full-time, $1089 per year part-time. *Room and board:* $10,226; room only: $7706. Room and board charges vary according to board plan and housing facility.

Financial Aid Of all full-time matriculated undergraduates who enrolled in 2011, 3,201 applied for aid, 2,765 were judged to have need, 307 had their need fully met. 229 Federal Work-Study jobs (averaging $1520). 450 state and other part-time jobs (averaging $1976). In 2011, 75 non-need-based awards were made. *Average percent of need met:* 56%. *Average financial aid package:* $12,297. *Average need-based loan:* $4464. *Average need-based gift aid:* $9467. *Average non-need-based aid:* $3692. *Average indebtedness upon graduation:* $25,516.

Applying *Options:* electronic application. *Application fee:* $65. *Required:* high school transcript. *Application deadlines:* 12/1 (freshmen), 1/15 (transfers). *Notification:* 2/28 (freshmen), 5/15 (transfers).

Freshman Application Contact Rutgers, The State University of New Jersey, Camden, 406 Penn Street, Camden, NJ 08102-1401. *Phone:* 856-225-6104. *Web site:* http://www.rutgers.edu/.

Rutgers, The State University of New Jersey, Newark

Newark, New Jersey

- **State-supported** university, founded 1892, part of Rutgers, The State University of New Jersey
- **Urban** 38-acre campus
- **Endowment** $508.8 million
- **Coed** 7,465 undergraduate students, 81% full-time, 53% women, 47% men
- **Moderately difficult** entrance level, 54% of applicants were admitted

Undergraduates 6,021 full-time, 1,444 part-time. Students come from 29 states and territories; 45 other countries; 4% are from out of state; 18% Black or African American, non-Hispanic/Latino; 22% Hispanic/Latino; 23% Asian, non-Hispanic/Latino; 0.8% Native Hawaiian or other Pacific Islander, non-Hispanic/Latino; 0.1% American Indian or Alaska Native, non-Hispanic/Latino; 3% Two or more races, non-Hispanic/Latino; 3% Race/ethnicity unknown; 2% international; 12% transferred in; 17% live on campus. *Retention:* 83% of full-time freshmen returned.

Freshmen *Admission:* 11,352 applied, 6,135 admitted, 986 enrolled. *Test scores:* SAT critical reading scores over 500: 60%; SAT math scores over 500: 80%; SAT writing scores over 500: 68%; SAT critical reading scores over 600: 17%; SAT math scores over 600: 32%; SAT writing scores over 600: 20%; SAT critical reading scores over 700: 2%; SAT math scores over 700: 4%; SAT writing scores over 700: 3%.

Faculty *Total:* 788, 63% full-time, 99% with terminal degrees. *Student/faculty ratio:* 10:1.

Academics *Calendar:* semesters. *Degrees:* bachelor's, master's, doctoral, and first professional. *Special study options:* academic remediation for entering students, accelerated degree program, adult/continuing education programs, advanced placement credit, cooperative education, distance learning, double majors, English as a second language, freshman honors college, honors programs, independent study, internships, off-campus study, part-time degree program, services for LD students, student-designed majors, study abroad, summer session for credit. *ROTC:* Army (b), Air Force (b). *Unusual degree programs:* 3-2 business administration; engineering; nursing.

Computers on Campus 708 computers/terminals are available on campus for general student use. Students can access the following: computer help desk, free student e-mail accounts, online (class) grades, online (class) schedules, online grade reports. Campuswide network is available. Wireless service is available via classrooms, computer centers, computer labs, dorm rooms, learning centers, libraries, student centers.

Student Life *Housing options:* coed. Campus housing is university owned. *Activities and organizations:* drama/theater group, student-run newspaper, radio station, choral group. *Campus security:* 24-hour emergency response devices and patrols, student patrols, late-night transport/escort service, controlled dormitory access.

Athletics Member NCAA. All Division III except volleyball (Division I). *Intercollegiate sports:* baseball M, basketball M/W, cross-country running M/W, soccer M/W, tennis M/W, track and field M, volleyball M/W. *Intramural sports:* baseball M/W, basketball M/W, racquetball M/W, rock climbing M/W, soccer M/W, swimming and diving M/W, weight lifting M/W.

Standardized Tests *Required:* SAT or ACT (for admission).

Costs (2011–12) *Tuition:* state resident $10,104 full-time, $325 per credit part-time; nonresident $22,766 full-time, $738 per credit part-time. Part-time tuition and fees vary according to course load. *Required fees:* $2190 full-time, $805 per year part-time. *Room and board:* $12,013; room only: $7513. Room and board charges vary according to board plan and housing facility. *Payment plan:* installment.

Financial Aid Of all full-time matriculated undergraduates who enrolled in 2011, 4,681 applied for aid, 4,368 were judged to have need, 378 had their need fully met. 482 Federal Work-Study jobs (averaging $1257). 803 state and other part-time jobs (averaging $1496). In 2011, 41 non-need-based awards were made. *Average percent of need met:* 57%. *Average financial aid package:* $13,205. *Average need-based loan:* $4478. *Average need-based gift aid:* $10,197. *Average non-need-based aid:* $9074. *Average indebtedness upon graduation:* $21,863.

Applying *Options:* electronic application. *Application fee:* $65. *Required:* high school transcript. *Application deadlines:* 12/1 (freshmen), 1/15 (transfers). *Notification:* 2/28 (freshmen), 5/15 (transfers).

Freshman Application Contact Mr. Jason Hand, Director of Admissions, Rutgers, The State University of New Jersey, Newark, 249 University Avenue, Newark, NJ 07102. *Phone:* 973-353-5205. *Fax:* 973-353-1440. *E-mail:* admissions@ugadm.rutgers.edu. *Web site:* http://www.rutgers.edu/.

Rutgers, The State University of New Jersey, New Brunswick

Piscataway, New Jersey

- **State-supported** university, founded 1766, part of Rutgers, The State University of New Jersey
- **Urban** 2683-acre campus with easy access to New York City
- **Endowment** $508.8 million
- **Coed** 31,268 undergraduate students, 95% full-time, 49% women, 51% men
- **Moderately difficult** entrance level, 61% of applicants were admitted

Undergraduates 29,752 full-time, 1,516 part-time. Students come from 52 states and territories; 72 other countries; 7% are from out of state; 8% Black or African American, non-Hispanic/Latino; 11% Hispanic/Latino; 25% Asian, non-Hispanic/Latino; 0.4% Native Hawaiian or other Pacific Islander, non-Hispanic/Latino; 0.1% American Indian or Alaska Native, non-Hispanic/Latino; 3% Two or more races, non-Hispanic/Latino; 2% Race/ethnicity unknown; 2% international; 7% transferred in; 45% live on campus. *Retention:* 91% of full-time freshmen returned.

Freshmen *Admission:* 28,602 applied, 17,487 admitted, 6,075 enrolled. *Test scores:* SAT critical reading scores over 500: 86%; SAT math scores over 500: 93%; SAT writing scores over 500: 90%; SAT critical reading scores over 600: 39%; SAT math scores over 600: 60%; SAT writing scores over 600: 46%; SAT critical reading scores over 700: 8%; SAT math scores over 700: 18%; SAT writing scores over 700: 11%.

Faculty *Total:* 2,745, 63% full-time, 99% with terminal degrees. *Student/faculty ratio:* 15:1.

Academics *Calendar:* semesters. *Degrees:* bachelor's, master's, doctoral, post-master's, postbachelor's, and first professional certificates. *Special study options:* academic remediation for entering students, accelerated degree program, advanced placement credit, cooperative education, distance learning, double majors, English as a second language, honors programs, independent study, internships, part-time degree program, student-designed majors, study abroad. *ROTC:* Army (b), Air Force (b). *Unusual degree programs:* 3-2 business administration; engineering; University of Medicine and Dentistry of New Jersey, Robert Wood Johnson Medical School.

Computers on Campus 1,450 computers/terminals are available on campus for general student use. Students can access the following: campus intranet,

computer help desk, free student e-mail accounts, online (class) grades, online (class) registration, online (class) schedules, online grade reports. Campuswide network is available. Wireless service is available via entire campus.

Student Life *Housing options:* coed, men-only, women-only, cooperative. Campus housing is university owned. *Activities and organizations:* drama/theater group, student-run newspaper, radio and television station, choral group, marching band, national fraternities, national sororities. *Campus security:* 24-hour emergency response devices and patrols, student patrols, late-night transport/escort service, controlled dormitory access. *Student services:* health clinic, personal/psychological counseling, women's center.

Athletics Member NCAA. All Division I except football (Division I-A). *Intercollegiate sports:* baseball M, basketball M/W, crew M/W, cross-country running M/W, fencing M/W, golf M/W, gymnastics W, lacrosse M/W, soccer M/W, softball W, swimming and diving M/W, tennis M/W, track and field M/W, volleyball M/W, wrestling M. *Intramural sports:* badminton M/W, baseball M(c), basketball M/W, bowling M/W, cross-country running M/W, equestrian sports M(c)/W(c), field hockey W(c), football M, golf M/W, ice hockey M(c), lacrosse M/W, racquetball M/W, rugby M(c)/W(c), sailing M(c)/W(c), skiing (cross-country) M(c)/W(c), skiing (downhill) M(c)/W(c), soccer M/W, softball M/W, squash M(c)/W(c), swimming and diving M/W, table tennis M(c)/W(c), tennis M/W, track and field M/W, volleyball M/W, water polo M/W, wrestling M.

Standardized Tests *Required:* SAT or ACT (for admission).

Costs (2011–12) *Tuition:* state resident $10,104 full-time, $325 per credit part-time; nonresident $22,766 full-time, $738 per credit part-time. *Required fees:* $2651 full-time, $747 per year part-time. *Room and board:* $11,262; room only: $7042. Room and board charges vary according to board plan and housing facility. *Payment plan:* installment. *Waivers:* employees or children of employees.

Financial Aid Of all full-time matriculated undergraduates who enrolled in 2011, 25,577 applied for aid, 17,762 were judged to have need, 2,285 had their need fully met. 2,580 Federal Work-Study jobs (averaging $1208). 6,051 state and other part-time jobs (averaging $1604). In 2011, 703 non-need-based awards were made. *Average percent of need met:* 52%. *Average financial aid package:* $13,372. *Average need-based loan:* $4417. *Average need-based gift aid:* $9955. *Average non-need-based aid:* $8473. *Average indebtedness upon graduation:* $23,320.

Applying *Options:* electronic application. *Application fee:* $65. *Required:* high school transcript. *Required for some:* interview. *Recommended:* essay or personal statement. *Application deadlines:* 12/1 (freshmen), 1/15 (transfers). *Notification:* 2/28 (freshmen), 5/15 (transfers).

Freshman Application Contact Rutgers, The State University of New Jersey, New Brunswick, 65 Davidson Road, Room 202, Piscataway, NJ 08854-8097. *Phone:* 732-445-4636. *Web site:* http://www.rutgers.edu/.

Saint Peter's College
Jersey City, New Jersey

- **Independent Roman Catholic (Jesuit)** comprehensive, founded 1872
- **Urban** 15-acre campus with easy access to New York City
- **Coed** 2,344 undergraduate students, 86% full-time, 59% women, 41% men
- **Moderately difficult** entrance level, 67% of applicants were admitted

Undergraduates 2,011 full-time, 333 part-time. 14% are from out of state; 27% Black or African American, non-Hispanic/Latino; 26% Hispanic/Latino; 11% Asian, non-Hispanic/Latino; 0.2% Native Hawaiian or other Pacific Islander, non-Hispanic/Latino; 0.6% American Indian or Alaska Native, non-Hispanic/Latino; 1% Two or more races, non-Hispanic/Latino; 2% Race/ethnicity unknown; 3% international; 6% transferred in; 34% live on campus. *Retention:* 74% of full-time freshmen returned.

Freshmen *Admission:* 2,779 applied, 1,861 admitted, 422 enrolled. *Average high school GPA:* 3.21. *Test scores:* SAT critical reading scores over 500: 34%; SAT math scores over 500: 35%; SAT writing scores over 500: 32%; ACT scores over 18: 54%; SAT critical reading scores over 600: 8%; SAT math scores over 600: 10%; SAT writing scores over 600: 8%; ACT scores over 24: 12%; SAT math scores over 700: 1%; SAT writing scores over 700: 1%.

Faculty *Total:* 283, 41% full-time, 58% with terminal degrees. *Student/faculty ratio:* 12:1.

Academics *Calendar:* semesters. *Degrees:* certificates, associate, bachelor's, master's, and doctoral. *Special study options:* academic remediation for entering students, accelerated degree program, adult/continuing education programs, advanced placement credit, cooperative education, distance learning, double majors, honors programs, independent study, internships, off-campus study, part-time degree program, services for LD students, student-designed majors, study abroad, summer session for credit. *ROTC:* Army (b), Air Force (c). *Unusual degree programs:* 3-2 medical technology, cytotechnology, toxicology with University of Medicine and Dentistry of New Jersey.

Computers on Campus 150 computers/terminals are available on campus for general student use. Students can access the following: campus intranet, computer help desk, free student e-mail accounts, online (class) grades, online (class) schedules. Campuswide network is available. Wireless service is available via entire campus.

Student Life *Housing options:* coed, women-only. Campus housing is university owned. Freshman campus housing is guaranteed. *Activities and organizations:* drama/theater group, student-run newspaper, radio station, choral group, Caribbean Culture Club, Black Action Committee, Asian American Student Union, Argus Eyes Dramatic Society, Voices of Praise Gospel Choir. *Campus security:* 24-hour emergency response devices and patrols, late-night transport/escort service, controlled dormitory access, ID checks at residence halls and library. *Student services:* health clinic, personal/psychological counseling.

Athletics Member NCAA. All Division I. *Intercollegiate sports:* baseball M(s), basketball M(s)/W(s), bowling M/W, cross-country running M(s)/W(s), golf M(s), soccer M(s)/W(s), softball W(s), swimming and diving M(s)/W(s), tennis M(s)/W(s), track and field M(s)/W(s), volleyball W(s). *Intramural sports:* badminton M/W, basketball M/W, bowling M/W, football M/W, golf M/W, racquetball M/W, soccer M/W, softball M/W, squash M/W, swimming and diving M/W, table tennis M/W, tennis M/W, track and field M/W, volleyball M/W, water polo M/W, weight lifting M/W.

Standardized Tests *Required:* SAT or ACT (for admission).

Costs (2011–12) *One-time required fee:* $290. *Comprehensive fee:* $42,492 includes full-time tuition ($28,900), mandatory fees ($900), and room and board ($12,692). Full-time tuition and fees vary according to class time and course load. Part-time tuition: $970 per credit. Part-time tuition and fees vary according to class time and course load. *Required fees:* $8 per credit part-time. *Room and board:* Room and board charges vary according to board plan, housing facility, and student level.

Financial Aid Of all full-time matriculated undergraduates who enrolled in 2008, 1,999 applied for aid, 1,698 were judged to have need, 255 had their need fully met. 244 Federal Work-Study jobs (averaging $1976). In 2008, 272 non-need-based awards were made. *Average percent of need met:* 77%. *Average financial aid package:* $22,083. *Average need-based loan:* $3932. *Average need-based gift aid:* $16,453. *Average non-need-based aid:* $13,962. *Average indebtedness upon graduation:* $19,553.

Applying *Options:* early admission, deferred entrance. *Required:* essay or personal statement, high school transcript, minimum 2.0 GPA, 2 letters of recommendation. *Required for some:* interview. *Recommended:* interview. *Application deadlines:* rolling (freshmen), 8/1 (transfers). *Notification:* continuous (freshmen).

Freshman Application Contact Saint Peter's College, 2641 Kennedy Boulevard, Jersey City, NJ 07306-5997. *Phone:* 201-761-7106. *Toll-free phone:* 888-SPC-9933. *Web site:* http://www.spc.edu/.

Seton Hall University
South Orange, New Jersey

Freshman Application Contact Mr. Peter Nacy, Assistant Vice President for Admissions, Seton Hall University, Enrollment Management, South Orange, NJ 07079-2697. *Phone:* 973-275-2498. *Toll-free phone:* 800-THE HALL. *Fax:* 973-275-2040. *E-mail:* thehall@shu.edu. *Web site:* http://www.shu.edu/.

Somerset Christian College
Zarephath, New Jersey

Freshman Application Contact Ms. Linda Aarni, Senior Admissions Counselor, Somerset Christian College, 10 College Way, PO Box 9035, Zarephath, NJ 08890-9035. *Phone:* 732-356-1595. *Toll-free phone:* 800-234-9305. *Fax:* 732-356-4846. *E-mail:* info@somerset.edu. *Web site:* http://www.somerset.edu/.

See page 554 for display ad and page 1590 for the College Close-Up.

Stevens Institute of Technology
Hoboken, New Jersey

- **Independent** university, founded 1870
- **Urban** 55-acre campus with easy access to New York City
- **Endowment** $144.0 million
- **Coed** 2,427 undergraduate students, 100% full-time, 25% women, 75% men
- **Very difficult** entrance level, 42% of applicants were admitted

Undergraduates 2,421 full-time, 6 part-time. Students come from 47 states and territories; 60 other countries; 35% are from out of state; 3% Black or African American, non-Hispanic/Latino; 9% Hispanic/Latino; 10% Asian, non-Hispanic/Latino; 0.1% American Indian or Alaska Native, non-Hispanic/

Latino; 14% Race/ethnicity unknown; 7% international; 3% transferred in; 85% live on campus. *Retention:* 92% of full-time freshmen returned.

Freshmen *Admission:* 3,600 applied, 1,500 admitted, 559 enrolled. *Average high school GPA:* 3.8. *Test scores:* SAT critical reading scores over 500: 97%; SAT math scores over 500: 100%; SAT writing scores over 500: 95%; ACT scores over 18: 100%; SAT critical reading scores over 600: 58%; SAT math scores over 600: 91%; SAT writing scores over 600: 60%; ACT scores over 24: 100%; SAT critical reading scores over 700: 15%; SAT math scores over 700: 37%; SAT writing scores over 700: 15%; ACT scores over 30: 44%.

Faculty *Total:* 406, 58% full-time. *Student/faculty ratio:* 8:1.

Academics *Calendar:* semesters. *Degrees:* bachelor's, master's, doctoral, postbachelor's, and first professional certificates. *Special study options:* accelerated degree program, advanced placement credit, cooperative education, double majors, honors programs, independent study, internships, off-campus study, services for LD students, summer session for credit. *ROTC:* Army (c), Air Force (c). *Unusual degree programs:* 3-2 engineering with New York University.

Computers on Campus 500 computers/terminals and 3,800 ports are available on campus for general student use. Students can access the following: campus intranet, computer help desk, free student e-mail accounts, online (class) grades, online (class) registration, online (class) schedules, online account information, debit dining program, laundry status. Campuswide network is available. 100% of college-owned or -operated housing units are wired for high-speed Internet access. Wireless service is available via entire campus.

Student Life *Housing:* on-campus residence required for freshman year. *Options:* coed, women-only. Campus housing is university owned and leased by the school. Freshman campus housing is guaranteed. *Activities and organizations:* drama/theater group, student-run newspaper, radio and television station, choral group, Drama Society, Student Council, APO Service Fraternity, Jazz Band, Ethnic Student Association, national fraternities, national sororities. *Campus security:* 24-hour emergency response devices and patrols, late-night transport/escort service, controlled dormitory access. *Student services:* health clinic, personal/psychological counseling, women's center.

Athletics Member NCAA. All Division III. *Intercollegiate sports:* baseball M, basketball M/W, cross-country running M/W, equestrian sports W, fencing M/W, field hockey W, golf M, lacrosse M/W, soccer M/W, softball W, swimming and diving M/W, tennis M/W, track and field M/W, volleyball M/W, wrestling M. *Intramural sports:* archery M/W, badminton M/W, baseball M, basketball M/W, bowling M(c)/W(c), cheerleading W(c), football M/W, ice hockey M(c), racquetball M/W, sailing M(c)/W(c), skiing (cross-country) M(c)/W(c), skiing (downhill) M(c)/W(c), soccer M/W, softball M, squash M/W, table tennis M/W, tennis M/W, ultimate Frisbee M/W, volleyball M/W, weight lifting M(c)/W(c).

Standardized Tests *Required:* SAT or ACT (for admission). *Required for some:* SAT Subject Tests (for admission).

Costs (2011–12) *Comprehensive fee:* $55,122 includes full-time tuition ($40,300), mandatory fees ($1482), and room and board ($13,340). Part-time tuition: $1344 per credit. *Required fees:* $741 per term part-time. *Room and board:* Room and board charges vary according to board plan and housing facility.

Financial Aid Of all full-time matriculated undergraduates who enrolled in 2005, 1,645 applied for aid, 1,431 were judged to have need, 245 had their need fully met. 818 Federal Work-Study jobs (averaging $1269). In 2005, 296 non-need-based awards were made. *Average percent of need met:* 85%. *Average financial aid package:* $21,139. *Average need-based loan:* $4203. *Average need-based gift aid:* $12,871. *Average non-need-based aid:* $9973. *Average indebtedness upon graduation:* $14,113.

Applying *Options:* electronic application, early admission, early decision, deferred entrance. *Application fee:* $55. *Required:* essay or personal statement, high school transcript, 2 letters of recommendation, interview. *Application deadlines:* 2/1 (freshmen), 7/1 (transfers). *Early decision deadline:* 11/15 (for plan 1), 1/15 (for plan 2). *Notification:* 3/15 (freshmen), continuous (transfers), 12/15 (early decision plan 1), 2/15 (early decision plan 2).

Freshman Application Contact Mr. Daniel Gallagher, Dean of University Admissions, Stevens Institute of Technology, Castle Point on Hudson, Hoboken, NJ 07030. *Phone:* 201-216-5197. *Toll-free phone:* 800-458-5323. *E-mail:* admissions@stevens.edu. *Web site:* http://www.stevens.edu/.

Strayer University - Cherry Hill Campus

Cherry Hill, New Jersey

- **Proprietary** comprehensive
- **Coed**

Academics *Degrees:* bachelor's and master's.

Freshman Application Contact Strayer University - Cherry Hill Campus, 2201 Route 38, Suite 100, Cherry Hill, NJ 08002. *Web site:* http://www.strayer.edu/cherry_hill/.

Strayer University - Lawrenceville Campus

Lawrenceville, New Jersey
- **Proprietary** comprehensive
- **Coed**

Academics *Degrees:* bachelor's and master's.
Freshman Application Contact Strayer University - Lawrenceville Campus, 3150 Brunswick Pike, Suite 100, Lawrenceville, NJ 08648. *Web site:* http://www.strayer.edu/lawrenceville.

Strayer University - Piscataway Campus

Piscataway, New Jersey
- **Proprietary** comprehensive
- **Coed**

Academics *Degrees:* bachelor's and master's.
Freshman Application Contact Strayer University - Piscataway Campus, 242 Old New Brunswick Road, Suite 220, Piscataway, NJ 08854. *Web site:* http://www.strayer.edu/piscataway.

Strayer University - Willingboro Campus

Willingboro, New Jersey
- **Proprietary** comprehensive
- **Coed**

Academics *Degrees:* bachelor's and master's.
Freshman Application Contact Strayer University - Willingboro Campus, 300 Willingboro Parkway, Willingboro Town Center, Suite 125, Willingboro, NJ 08046. *Web site:* http://www.strayer.edu/willingboro.

Talmudical Academy of New Jersey

Adelphia, New Jersey

Director of Admissions Director of Admissions, Talmudical Academy of New Jersey, 868 Route 524, Adelphia, NJ 07710. *Phone:* 201-431-1600.

Thomas Edison State College

Trenton, New Jersey
- **State-supported** comprehensive, founded 1972
- **Urban** 2-acre campus with easy access to Philadelphia
- **Coed** 19,140 undergraduate students, 41% women, 59% men
- **Noncompetitive** entrance level

Undergraduates 19,140 part-time. Students come from 56 states and territories; 64 other countries; 63% are from out of state; 17% Black or African American, non-Hispanic/Latino; 10% Hispanic/Latino; 3% Asian, non-Hispanic/Latino; 0.7% Native Hawaiian or other Pacific Islander, non-Hispanic/Latino; 0.8% American Indian or Alaska Native, non-Hispanic/Latino; 0.3% Two or more races, non-Hispanic/Latino; 8% Race/ethnicity unknown; 1% international.
Academics *Calendar:* continuous. *Degrees:* certificates, associate, bachelor's, master's, post-master's, and postbachelor's certificates (offers only distance learning degree programs). *Special study options:* accelerated degree program, adult/continuing education programs, advanced placement credit, distance learning, double majors, external degree program, independent study, part-time degree program, services for LD students, student-designed majors, summer session for credit.
Computers on Campus Students can access the following: online (class) grades, online (class) registration, online (class) schedules, undergraduate and Nursing students are able to schedule appointments online with their advisors. Campuswide network is available. Wireless service is available via entire campus.
Student Life *Housing:* college housing not available. *Campus security:* 24-hour emergency response devices and patrols, late-night transport/escort service, security officer from 7 am to 11 pm, local police patrol.
Costs (2012–13) *Tuition:* state resident $5322 full-time, $157 per credit hour part-time; nonresident $7837 full-time, $212 per credit hour part-time. Part-time tuition and fees vary according to program and student level. There are two tuition plans available. Students may choose either the Comprehensive Plan: $5322 per year (state residents and military personnel), $7837 (non-resident), which covers up to 36 credits per year for all credit-earning options, or the Enrolled Options Plan: $1533 per year (state residents and military person-

nel), $2858 (non-resident) and $4011 (international) for annual enrollment tuition and a technology services fee($113); tests, portfolios, courses and other fees at additional cost. *Required fees:* $113 per year part-time. *Waivers:* employees or children of employees.
Applying *Options:* electronic application. *Application fee:* $75. *Required:* age 21 or older and a high school graduate. *Application deadlines:* rolling (freshmen), rolling (out-of-state freshmen), rolling (transfers).
Freshman Application Contact Mr. David Hoftiezer, Director of Admissions, Thomas Edison State College, 101 West State Street, Trenton, NJ 08608. *Phone:* 888-442-8372. *Toll-free phone:* 888-442-8372. *Fax:* 609-984-8447. *E-mail:* admissions@tesc.edu. *Web site:* http://www.tesc.edu/.

University of Medicine and Dentistry of New Jersey

Newark, New Jersey
- **State-supported** comprehensive, founded 1970, part of The School of Health Related Professions is one of 8 schools within the University of Medicine and Dentistry of New Jersey
- **Rural** campus with easy access to New York City, Philadelphia and Newark
- **Coed** 568 undergraduate students, 43% full-time, 83% women, 17% men

Undergraduates 245 full-time, 323 part-time. Students come from 27 states and territories; 9 other countries; 20% are from out of state; 13% Black or African American, non-Hispanic/Latino; 11% Hispanic/Latino; 8% Asian, non-Hispanic/Latino; 0.4% Native Hawaiian or other Pacific Islander, non-Hispanic/Latino; 0.2% American Indian or Alaska Native, non-Hispanic/Latino; 24% Race/ethnicity unknown; 2% international.
Faculty *Total:* 434, 33% full-time, 38% with terminal degrees. *Student/faculty ratio:* 10:1.
Academics *Calendar:* semesters. *Degrees:* certificates, diplomas, associate, bachelor's, master's, doctoral, post-master's, postbachelor's, and first professional certificates. *Special study options:* academic remediation for entering students, accelerated degree program, distance learning, external degree program, honors programs, independent study, internships, off-campus study, part-time degree program, services for LD students, summer session for credit. *Unusual degree programs:* 3-2 health professions.
Computers on Campus 120 computers/terminals are available on campus for general student use. Students can access the following: campus intranet, computer help desk, free student e-mail accounts, online (class) grades, online (class) registration, online (class) schedules. Campuswide network is available. Wireless service is available via entire campus.
Student Life *Housing options:* coed. Campus housing is university owned. *Activities and organizations:* Student Leadership Council, Student Senate. *Campus security:* 24-hour emergency response devices and patrols. *Student services:* health clinic, personal/psychological counseling.
Applying *Options:* electronic application, early admission, deferred entrance. *Required for some:* essay or personal statement, interview.
Freshman Application Contact Student Contact, University of Medicine and Dentistry of New Jersey, 65 Bergen Street, PO Box 1709, Newark, NJ 07107-1709. *Phone:* 973-972-5454. *Web site:* http://www.umdnj.edu/.

University of Phoenix–Jersey City Campus

Jersey City, New Jersey

Admissions Office Contact University of Phoenix–Jersey City Campus, 100 Town Square Place, Jersey City, NJ 07310. *Toll-free phone:* 866-766-0766. *Web site:* http://www.phoenix.edu/.

William Paterson University of New Jersey

Wayne, New Jersey
- **State-supported** comprehensive, founded 1855, part of New Jersey State College System
- **Suburban** 370-acre campus with easy access to New York City
- **Endowment** $8.5 million
- **Coed** 10,085 undergraduate students, 83% full-time, 54% women, 45% men
- **Moderately difficult** entrance level, 71% of applicants were admitted

Undergraduates 8,376 full-time, 1,641 part-time. Students come from 44 states and territories; 37 other countries; 2% are from out of state; 14% Black or African American, non-Hispanic/Latino; 22% Hispanic/Latino; 7% Asian, non-Hispanic/Latino; 0.2% American Indian or Alaska Native, non-Hispanic/

Latino; 1% Two or more races, non-Hispanic/Latino; 6% Race/ethnicity unknown; 0.8% international; 13% transferred in; 24% live on campus. *Retention:* 76% of full-time freshmen returned.

Freshmen *Admission:* 10,112 applied, 7,148 admitted, 1,397 enrolled. *Test scores:* SAT critical reading scores over 500: 50%; SAT math scores over 500: 57%; SAT critical reading scores over 600: 10%; SAT math scores over 600: 10%.

Faculty *Total:* 1,134, 34% full-time. *Student/faculty ratio:* 16:1.

Academics *Calendar:* semesters. *Degrees:* bachelor's, master's, doctoral, post-master's, and postbachelor's certificates. *Special study options:* academic remediation for entering students, accelerated degree program, adult/continuing education programs, advanced placement credit, distance learning, double majors, English as a second language, freshman honors college, honors programs, independent study, internships, off-campus study, part-time degree program, services for LD students, study abroad, summer session for credit. *ROTC:* Air Force (c).

Computers on Campus 700 computers/terminals are available on campus for general student use. Students can access the following: campus intranet, computer help desk, free student e-mail accounts, online (class) grades, online (class) registration, online (class) schedules. Campuswide network is available. 100% of college-owned or -operated housing units are wired for high-speed Internet access. Wireless service is available via entire campus.

Student Life *Housing options:* coed, disabled students. Campus housing is university owned, leased by the school and is provided by a third party. *Activities and organizations:* drama/theater group, student-run newspaper, radio and television station, choral group, 720 Modeling Group, Organization of Latin American Students (OLAS), Young Democratic Socialists, WPBN (TV Club), Honors College Club, national fraternities, national sororities. *Campus security:* 24-hour emergency response devices and patrols, student patrols, controlled dormitory access. *Student services:* health clinic, personal/psychological counseling, women's center, legal services.

Athletics Member NCAA. All Division III. *Intercollegiate sports:* baseball M, basketball M/W, bowling M(c)/W(c), field hockey W, football M, golf M, ice hockey M(c), skiing (downhill) M(c)/W(c), soccer M/W, softball W, swimming and diving M/W, volleyball W. *Intramural sports:* basketball M, equestrian sports M/W, football M, golf M, racquetball M/W, softball M/W, tennis M(c)/W(c), volleyball M/W, wrestling M.

Standardized Tests *Required:* SAT or ACT (for admission).

Costs (2011–12) *Tuition:* state resident $6967 full-time, $223 per credit hour part-time; nonresident $14,131 full-time, $458 per credit hour part-time. Full-time tuition and fees vary according to location and program. Part-time tuition

and fees vary according to course load, location, and program. *Required fees:* $4497 full-time, $145 per credit hour part-time. *Room and board:* $10,500; room only: $6800. Room and board charges vary according to board plan and housing facility. *Payment plan:* installment. *Waivers:* senior citizens and employees or children of employees.

Financial Aid *Average indebtedness upon graduation:* $29,314.

Applying *Options:* electronic application, early admission, early decision, deferred entrance. *Application fee:* $50. *Required:* high school transcript. *Required for some:* essay or personal statement, interview, portfolio for art, audition for music. *Recommended:* minimum 2.0 GPA. *Application deadlines:* 5/1 (freshmen), 6/1 (transfers). *Notification:* continuous (freshmen), continuous (transfers).

Freshman Application Contact Mr. Anthony Leckey, Associate Director of Admissions, William Paterson University of New Jersey, 300 Pompton Road, Wayne, NJ 07470-8420. *Phone:* 973-720-2903. *Toll-free phone:* 877-WPU-EXCEL. *Fax:* 973-720-2910. *E-mail:* admissions@wpunj.edu. *Web site:* http://www.wpunj.edu/.

See below for display ad and page 1766 for the College Close-Up.

NEW MEXICO

Brookline College
Albuquerque, New Mexico

- **Proprietary** 4-year
- **Urban** campus with easy access to Albuquerque
- **Coed**
- **Noncompetitive** entrance level

Faculty *Student/faculty ratio:* 18:1.

Academics *Calendar:* continuous. *Degrees:* diplomas, associate, and bachelor's.

Student Life *Campus security:* 24-hour emergency response devices.

Costs (2011–12) *Tuition:* $13,750 full-time. Full-time tuition and fees vary according to degree level and program. No tuition increase for student's term of enrollment.

Applying *Options:* electronic application. *Required:* interview.

WILLIAM PATERSON UNIVERSITY
wpunj.edu/undergraduate

Jonathan Ledesma
Major: Political Science

Christine Kelly,
Associate Professor,
Political Science,
College of Humanities
and Social Sciences

Your next mentor.

At William Paterson University, enterprising students and expert faculty have one big thing in common: a belief that we're all in this together. Just ask Jonathan. He'll tell you that Professor Christine Kelly's passion for political science inspired him to take what he learned to a whole new level.

Make your reservation online at
wpunj.edu/openhouse

LEARN FROM EXPERIENCE
AT WILLIAM PATERSON UNIVERSITY.

PLAN YOUR NEXT MOVE AT wpunj.edu/undergraduate

Freshman Application Contact Mr. Andrew Webb, Campus Director, Brookline College, 4201 Central Avenue NW, Suite J, Albuquerque, NM 87105. *Phone:* 505-880-2877. *Toll-free phone:* 888-660-2428. *Fax:* 505-352-0199. *E-mail:* awebb@brooklinecollege.edu. *Web site:* http://brooklinecollege.edu/.

Brown Mackie College–Albuquerque

Albuquerque, New Mexico

- **Proprietary** primarily 2-year, part of Education Management Corporation
- **Coed**

Academics *Degrees:* associate and bachelor's.

Costs (2011–12) *Tuition:* Tuition varies by program. Students should contact Brown Mackie College for tuition information.

Freshman Application Contact Brown Mackie College–Albuquerque, 10500 Cooper Avenue NE, Albuquerque, NM 87123. *Phone:* 505-559-5200. *Toll-free phone:* 877-271-3488. *Web site:* http://www.brownmackie.edu/.

See page 1188 for the College Close-Up.

Eastern New Mexico University

Portales, New Mexico

- **State-supported** comprehensive, founded 1934
- **Rural** 400-acre campus
- **Endowment** $7.3 million
- **Coed** 4,406 undergraduate students, 63% full-time, 56% women, 44% men
- **Noncompetitive** entrance level, 63% of applicants were admitted

Undergraduates 2,768 full-time, 1,638 part-time. Students come from 49 states and territories; 20 other countries; 24% are from out of state; 5% Black or African American, non-Hispanic/Latino; 33% Hispanic/Latino; 0.9% Asian, non-Hispanic/Latino; 0.1% Native Hawaiian or other Pacific Islander, non-Hispanic/Latino; 2% American Indian or Alaska Native, non-Hispanic/Latino; 2% Two or more races, non-Hispanic/Latino; 4% Race/ethnicity unknown; 3% international; 11% transferred in; 26% live on campus. *Retention:* 52% of full-time freshmen returned.

Freshmen *Admission:* 2,176 applied, 1,368 admitted, 690 enrolled. *Average high school GPA:* 3.21. *Test scores:* SAT critical reading scores over 500: 40%; ACT scores over 18: 74%; SAT critical reading scores over 600: 18%; ACT scores over 24: 19%; SAT critical reading scores over 700: 1%; ACT scores over 30: 1%.

Faculty *Total:* 340, 43% full-time, 42% with terminal degrees. *Student/faculty ratio:* 18:1.

Academics *Calendar:* semesters. *Degrees:* associate, bachelor's, and master's. *Special study options:* academic remediation for entering students, accelerated degree program, adult/continuing education programs, advanced placement credit, cooperative education, distance learning, double majors, English as a second language, independent study, internships, part-time degree program, services for LD students, student-designed majors, summer session for credit. *Unusual degree programs:* 3-2 chemistry (qualified undergraduate students entering the chemistry program will be allowed to apply to the Graduate School during the last semester of the junior year to take a limited number of graduate courses for credit at the 500 level leading to a B.S. and an M.S. in 5-5.5 years total).

Computers on Campus 513 computers/terminals are available on campus for general student use. Students can access the following: campus intranet, computer help desk, free student e-mail accounts, online (class) grades, online (class) registration, online (class) schedules, WIFI in most buildings. Campus-wide network is available. 100% of college-owned or -operated housing units are wired for high-speed Internet access. Wireless service is available via entire campus.

Student Life *Housing:* on-campus residence required for freshman year. *Options:* coed, women-only, disabled students. Campus housing is university owned. Freshman campus housing is guaranteed. *Activities and organizations:* drama/theater group, student-run newspaper, radio and television station, choral group, marching band, Student Government, Student Activities Board, Residence Hall Association, IFC (Inter-Fraternity Council)Panhellenic Council, national fraternities, national sororities. *Campus security:* 24-hour emergency response devices and patrols, late-night transport/escort service, controlled dormitory access, University Emergency Notification System; security cameras; security lights. *Student services:* health clinic, personal/psychological counseling.

Athletics Member NCAA. All Division II. *Intercollegiate sports:* baseball M(s), basketball M(s)/W(s), cross-country running M(s)/W(s), football M(s), soccer M(s)/W(s), softball W(s), track and field M(s)/W(s), volleyball W(s). *Intramural sports:* badminton M/W, basketball M/W, cross-country running M/W, football M/W, racquetball M/W, soccer M/W, softball M/W, volleyball M/W, water polo M/W.

Standardized Tests *Required for some:* SAT or ACT (for admission).

Costs (2011–12) *Tuition:* state resident $2839 full-time, $118 per credit hour part-time; nonresident $8350 full-time, $348 per credit hour part-time. Full-time tuition and fees vary according to course load and reciprocity agreements. Part-time tuition and fees vary according to course load. *Required fees:* $1308 full-time, $55 per credit hour part-time. *Room and board:* $5830; room only: $2802. Room and board charges vary according to gender, housing facility, location, and student level. *Payment plan:* installment. *Waivers:* senior citizens and employees or children of employees.

Financial Aid Of all full-time matriculated undergraduates who enrolled in 2009, 1,540 applied for aid, 1,540 were judged to have need, 1,540 had their need fully met. In 2009, 8 non-need-based awards were made. *Average percent of need met:* 47%. *Average financial aid package:* $8869. *Average need-based loan:* $4082. *Average need-based gift aid:* $4442. *Average non-need-based aid:* $2293. *Average indebtedness upon graduation:* $11,769.

Applying *Options:* electronic application. *Required:* official transcripts from any post-secondary institution attended - must be in good standing with all institutions. *Required for some:* high school transcript, minimum 2.5 GPA. *Application deadlines:* 8/24 (freshmen), 8/24 (out-of-state freshmen), 8/24 (transfers).

Freshman Application Contact Mr. Cody Spitz, Director, Enrollment Services, Eastern New Mexico University, Station #7 ENMU, Portales, NM 88130. *Phone:* 575-562-2178. *Toll-free phone:* 800-367-3668. *Fax:* 575-562-2118. *E-mail:* cody.spitz@enmu.edu. *Web site:* http://www.enmu.edu/.

Institute of American Indian Arts

Santa Fe, New Mexico

Director of Admissions Myra Garro, Manager of Enrollment and Admissions, Institute of American Indian Arts, 83 Avan Nu Po Road, Santa Fe, NM 87508. *Phone:* 505-424-2328. *Web site:* http://www.iaia.edu/.

ITT Technical Institute

Albuquerque, New Mexico

- **Proprietary** primarily 2-year, founded 1989, part of ITT Educational Services, Inc.
- **Coed**
- **Minimally difficult** entrance level

Academics *Calendar:* quarters. *Degrees:* associate and bachelor's.

Student Life *Housing:* college housing not available.

Freshman Application Contact Director of Recruitment, ITT Technical Institute, 5100 Masthead Street, NE, Albuquerque, NM 87109. *Phone:* 505-828-1114. *Toll-free phone:* 800-636-1114. *Web site:* http://www.itt-tech.edu/.

National American University

Albuquerque, New Mexico

Freshman Application Contact National American University, 4775 Indian School, NE, Suite 200, Albuquerque, NM 87110. *Phone:* 505-265-7517. *Toll-free phone:* 800-895-9904. *Web site:* http://www.national.edu/.

National College of Midwifery

Taos, New Mexico

Director of Admissions Ms. Beth Enson, Dean of Students, National College of Midwifery, 209 State Road 240, Taos, NM 87571. *Phone:* 505-758-8914. *E-mail:* info@midwiferycollege.org. *Web site:* http://www.midwiferycollege.org/.

New Mexico Highlands University

Las Vegas, New Mexico

- **State-supported** comprehensive, founded 1893
- **Small-town** campus
- **Endowment** $1.8 million
- **Coed** 2,338 undergraduate students, 72% full-time, 59% women, 41% men
- **Minimally difficult** entrance level, 100% of applicants were admitted

Undergraduates 1,675 full-time, 663 part-time. Students come from 39 states and territories; 13 other countries; 18% are from out of state; 7% Black or African American, non-Hispanic/Latino; 56% Hispanic/Latino; 0.4% Asian, non-Hispanic/Latino; 0.3% Native Hawaiian or other Pacific Islander, non-Hispanic/Latino; 7% American Indian or Alaska Native, non-Hispanic/Latino; 2% Two or more races, non-Hispanic/Latino; 2% Race/ethnicity unknown; 7%

international; 17% transferred in; 27% live on campus. *Retention:* 48% of full-time freshmen returned.

Freshmen *Admission:* 1,981 applied, 1,981 admitted, 419 enrolled. *Average high school GPA:* 2.97. *Test scores:* ACT scores over 18: 44%; ACT scores over 24: 4%.

Faculty *Total:* 298, 48% full-time, 39% with terminal degrees. *Student/faculty ratio:* 14:1.

Academics *Calendar:* semesters. *Degrees:* associate, bachelor's, and master's. *Special study options:* academic remediation for entering students, accelerated degree program, advanced placement credit, cooperative education, distance learning, double majors, honors programs, independent study, internships, off-campus study, part-time degree program, services for LD students, summer session for credit.

Computers on Campus 500 computers/terminals are available on campus for general student use. Students can access the following: online (class) registration. Campuswide network is available.

Student Life *Housing options:* coed, disabled students. Campus housing is university owned. *Activities and organizations:* drama/theater group, student-run radio station, choral group, marching band, Vatos Rugby, Fire Escape Club, MeChA, NMHU Cheerleaders, NMHU Student Ambassadors, national fraternities, national sororities. *Campus security:* 24-hour emergency response devices and patrols, late-night transport/escort service, controlled dormitory access. *Student services:* health clinic, personal/psychological counseling, women's center.

Athletics Member NCAA. All Division II. *Intercollegiate sports:* baseball M(s), basketball M(s)/W(s), cross-country running M(s)/W(s), football M(s), soccer W(s), softball W(s), track and field M/W, volleyball W(s). *Intramural sports:* badminton M/W, basketball M/W, football M, golf M/W, racquetball M/W, rugby M, skiing (cross-country) M/W, skiing (downhill) M/W, softball W, swimming and diving M/W, table tennis M/W, tennis M/W, volleyball M/W, weight lifting M/W.

Standardized Tests *Recommended:* SAT or ACT (for admission), COMPASS.

Costs (2011–12) *One-time required fee:* $20. *Tuition:* state resident $3264 full-time, $136 per credit hour part-time; nonresident $5328 full-time, $222 per credit hour part-time. Full-time tuition and fees vary according to course load and location. Part-time tuition and fees vary according to course load and location. *Room and board:* $7873; room only: $4410. Room and board charges vary according to board plan and housing facility. *Payment plan:* installment. *Waivers:* senior citizens and employees or children of employees.

Applying *Options:* electronic application, early admission, deferred entrance. *Application fee:* $15. *Required:* high school transcript, minimum 2.0 GPA. *Required for some:* 2 letters of recommendation, interview. *Application deadlines:* rolling (freshmen), rolling (out-of-state freshmen), rolling (transfers). *Notification:* continuous (freshmen), continuous (out-of-state freshmen), continuous (transfers).

Freshman Application Contact Ms. Fidel Trujillo, Vice President for Student Affairs, New Mexico Highlands University, Box 9000, Las Vegas, NM 87701. *Phone:* 505-454-3566. *Toll-free phone:* 800-338-6648. *E-mail:* judycordova@nmhu.edu. *Web site:* http://www.nmhu.edu/.

New Mexico Institute of Mining and Technology
Socorro, New Mexico

- **State-supported** university, founded 1889
- **Small-town** 320-acre campus with easy access to Albuquerque
- **Endowment** $29.3 million
- **Coed** 1,454 undergraduate students, 85% full-time, 32% women, 68% men
- **Moderately difficult** entrance level, 70% of applicants were admitted

Undergraduates 1,243 full-time, 211 part-time. Students come from 37 states and territories; 8 other countries; 17% are from out of state; 2% Black or African American, non-Hispanic/Latino; 25% Hispanic/Latino; 3% Asian, non-Hispanic/Latino; 0.1% Native Hawaiian or other Pacific Islander, non-Hispanic/Latino; 3% American Indian or Alaska Native, non-Hispanic/Latino; 2% Two or more races, non-Hispanic/Latino; 0.8% international; 6% transferred in; 49% live on campus. *Retention:* 71% of full-time freshmen returned.

Freshmen *Admission:* 612 applied, 431 admitted, 324 enrolled. *Average high school GPA:* 3.68. *Test scores:* SAT critical reading scores over 500: 90%; SAT math scores over 500: 97%; ACT scores over 18: 100%; SAT critical reading scores over 600: 50%; SAT math scores over 600: 63%; ACT scores over 24: 71%; SAT critical reading scores over 700: 14%; SAT math scores over 700: 17%; ACT scores over 30: 18%.

Faculty *Total:* 178, 69% full-time. *Student/faculty ratio:* 11:1.

Academics *Calendar:* semesters. *Degrees:* associate, bachelor's, master's, doctoral, and first professional. *Special study options:* accelerated degree program, advanced placement credit, cooperative education, distance learning,

double majors, independent study, internships, services for LD students, student-designed majors, summer session for credit. *Unusual degree programs:* 3-2 engineering; earth sciences.

Computers on Campus 225 computers/terminals are available on campus for general student use. Students can access the following: computer help desk, free student e-mail accounts, online (class) registration, online (class) schedules. Campuswide network is available. Wireless service is available via computer centers, learning centers, student centers.

Student Life *Housing options:* coed, men-only, women-only. Campus housing is university owned. *Activities and organizations:* drama/theater group, student-run newspaper, radio station, choral group, Search and Rescue, Society for Creative Anachronism, Amateur Astronomers, Ski Club. *Campus security:* 24-hour emergency response devices and patrols, late-night transport/escort service. *Student services:* health clinic, personal/psychological counseling.

Athletics *Intercollegiate sports:* golf M(c)/W(c), rugby M(c)/W(c), soccer M(c)/W(c). *Intramural sports:* badminton M/W, basketball M/W, soccer M/W, softball M/W, volleyball M/W.

Standardized Tests *Required:* SAT or ACT (for admission). *Recommended:* ACT (for admission).

Costs (2011–12) *Tuition:* state resident $4643 full-time, $193 per credit hour part-time; nonresident $15,095 full-time, $629 per credit hour part-time. Full-time tuition and fees vary according to reciprocity agreements. Part-time tuition and fees vary according to course load. *Required fees:* $658 full-time, $18 per credit hour part-time, $67 per term part-time. *Room and board:* $6108. Room and board charges vary according to board plan and housing facility. *Waivers:* senior citizens and employees or children of employees.

Financial Aid Of all full-time matriculated undergraduates who enrolled in 2011, 1,139 applied for aid, 612 were judged to have need, 180 had their need fully met. 181 Federal Work-Study jobs (averaging $2783). 66 state and other part-time jobs (averaging $1987). In 2011, 473 non-need-based awards were made. *Average percent of need met:* 80%. *Average financial aid package:* $11,047. *Average need-based loan:* $4076. *Average need-based gift aid:* $5579. *Average non-need-based aid:* $6569. *Average indebtedness upon graduation:* $17,765.

Applying *Options:* electronic application, deferred entrance. *Application fee:* $15. *Required:* high school transcript, minimum 2.5 GPA. *Required for some:* 2 letters of recommendation. *Recommended:* interview. *Application deadlines:* 8/1 (freshmen), 8/1 (transfers). *Notification:* continuous (freshmen), continuous (transfers).

Freshman Application Contact Mr. Mike Kloeppel, Director of Admissions, New Mexico Institute of Mining and Technology, 801 Leroy Place, Socorro, NM 87801. *Phone:* 575-835-5424. *Toll-free phone:* 800-428-TECH. *Fax:* 575-835-5989. *E-mail:* admission@admin.nmt.edu. *Web site:* http://www.nmt.edu/.

New Mexico State University
Las Cruces, New Mexico

- **State-supported** university, founded 1888, part of New Mexico State University System
- **Suburban** 900-acre campus with easy access to El Paso
- **Endowment** $82.7 million
- **Coed** 14,495 undergraduate students, 77% full-time, 54% women, 46% men
- **Moderately difficult** entrance level, 80% of applicants were admitted

Undergraduates 11,232 full-time, 3,263 part-time. Students come from 50 states and territories; 57 other countries; 21% are from out of state; 3% Black or African American, non-Hispanic/Latino; 49% Hispanic/Latino; 1% Asian, non-Hispanic/Latino; 0.2% Native Hawaiian or other Pacific Islander, non-Hispanic/Latino; 3% American Indian or Alaska Native, non-Hispanic/Latino; 0.9% Two or more races, non-Hispanic/Latino; 5% Race/ethnicity unknown; 3% international; 5% transferred in; 18% live on campus. *Retention:* 71% of full-time freshmen returned.

Freshmen *Admission:* 7,321 applied, 5,867 admitted, 2,163 enrolled. *Average high school GPA:* 3.36. *Test scores:* SAT critical reading scores over 500: 37%; SAT math scores over 500: 42%; SAT writing scores over 500: 33%; ACT scores over 18: 79%; SAT critical reading scores over 600: 9%; SAT math scores over 600: 11%; SAT writing scores over 600: 7%; ACT scores over 24: 28%; SAT critical reading scores over 700: 1%; SAT math scores over 700: 1%; SAT writing scores over 700: 1%; ACT scores over 30: 2%.

Faculty *Total:* 975, 69% full-time, 64% with terminal degrees. *Student/faculty ratio:* 19:1.

Academics *Calendar:* semesters. *Degrees:* associate, bachelor's, master's, doctoral, post-master's, postbachelor's, and first professional certificates. *Special study options:* academic remediation for entering students, accelerated degree program, adult/continuing education programs, advanced placement credit, cooperative education, distance learning, double majors, English as a second language, honors programs, independent study, internships, off-campus

study, part-time degree program, services for LD students, student-designed majors, study abroad, summer session for credit. *ROTC:* Army (b), Air Force (b).

Computers on Campus 604 computers/terminals are available on campus for general student use. Students can access the following: campus intranet, computer help desk, free student e-mail accounts, online (class) grades, online (class) registration, online (class) schedules, online financial aid, wireless is available in many areas, scholarship application ("scholar dollars"), academic records personal information update, a content learning management system, academic calendar, STAR degree audit. Campuswide network is available. 100% of college-owned or -operated housing units are wired for high-speed Internet access. Wireless service is available via entire campus.

Student Life *Housing options:* coed, disabled students. Campus housing is university owned. *Activities and organizations:* drama/theater group, student-run newspaper, radio and television station, choral group, marching band, Pride Marching Band, Kappa Sigma (Social Fraternity), Blue Wings, Gamma Beta Phi, Chi Omega (social sorority), national fraternities, national sororities. *Campus security:* 24-hour emergency response devices and patrols, late-night transport/escort service, controlled dormitory access. *Student services:* health clinic, personal/psychological counseling, legal services.

Athletics Member NCAA. All Division I except football (Division I-A). *Intercollegiate sports:* baseball M(s), basketball M(s)/W(s), cross-country running M(s)/W(s), equestrian sports M/W, golf M(s)/W(s), softball W(s), swimming and diving W(s), tennis M(s)/W(s), track and field W(s), volleyball W(s). *Intramural sports:* archery M/W, badminton M/W, baseball M, basketball M/W, bowling M(c)/W(c), cheerleading M/W, football M/W, golf M/W, racquetball M/W, rock climbing M(c)/W(c), rugby M(c)/W(c), skiing (downhill) M(c)/W(c), soccer M(c)/W(c), softball M/W, tennis M/W, ultimate Frisbee M(c)/W(c), volleyball M(c)/W(c), water polo M/W, weight lifting M(c)/W(c), wrestling M.

Standardized Tests *Required:* SAT or ACT (for admission).

Costs (2011–12) *Tuition:* state resident $4553 full-time, $243 per credit hour part-time; nonresident $16,994 full-time, $761 per credit hour part-time. *Required fees:* $1274 full-time, $53 per credit hour part-time. *Room and board:* $6620; room only: $3830. Room and board charges vary according to board plan and housing facility. *Payment plans:* installment, deferred payment. *Waivers:* senior citizens and employees or children of employees.

Financial Aid Of all full-time matriculated undergraduates who enrolled in 2011, 8,022 applied for aid, 7,027 were judged to have need, 1,154 had their need fully met. 780 Federal Work-Study jobs (averaging $2811). 893 state and other part-time jobs (averaging $3693). In 2011, 712 non-need-based awards were made. *Average percent of need met:* 65%. *Average financial aid package:* $10,797. *Average need-based loan:* $4013. *Average need-based gift aid:* $7633. *Average non-need-based aid:* $1361.

Applying *Options:* electronic application, early admission, deferred entrance. *Application fee:* $20. *Required:* high school transcript, minimum 2.0 GPA. *Application deadlines:* 8/19 (freshmen), 8/14 (transfers). *Notification:* continuous (freshmen), continuous (transfers).

Freshman Application Contact Valerie Pickett, Director of Admissions, New Mexico State University, Box 30001, MSC 3A, Las Cruces, NM 88003-8001. *Phone:* 575-646-3121. *Toll-free phone:* 800-662-6678. *Fax:* 575-646-6330. *E-mail:* admssions@nmsu.edu. *Web site:* http://www.nmsu.edu/.

Northern New Mexico College
Espalfnola, New Mexico

Freshman Application Contact Mr. Mike L. Costello, Registrar, Northern New Mexico College, 921 Paseo de O|fnate, Espa|fnola, NM 87532. *Phone:* 505-747-2193. *Fax:* 505-747-2191. *E-mail:* dms@nnmc.edu. *Web site:* http://www.nnmc.edu/.

Pima Medical Institute
Albuquerque, New Mexico

- **Proprietary** primarily 2-year, founded 1985, part of Vocational Training Institutes, Inc.
- **Urban** campus
- **Coed**
- **Minimally difficult** entrance level

Academics *Calendar:* modular. *Degrees:* certificates, associate, and bachelor's.

Standardized Tests *Required:* Wonderlic Scholastic Level Exam (for admission).

Financial Aid *Of all full-time matriculated undergraduates who enrolled in 2010,* 6 Federal Work-Study jobs.

Applying *Options:* early admission. *Required:* interview. *Required for some:* high school transcript.

Freshman Application Contact Admissions Office, Pima Medical Institute, 4400 Cutler Avenue NE, Albuquerque, NM 87110. *Phone:* 505-881-1234. *Toll-free phone:* 800-477-PIMA (in-state); 888-477-PIMA (out-of-state). *Fax:* 505-881-5329. *Web site:* http://www.pmi.edu/.

St. John's College
Santa Fe, New Mexico

- **Independent** comprehensive, founded 1964
- **Suburban** 250-acre campus with easy access to Albuquerque
- **Endowment** $129.9 million
- **Coed** 365 undergraduate students, 99% full-time, 41% women, 59% men
- **Very difficult** entrance level, 86% of applicants were admitted

Undergraduates 361 full-time, 4 part-time. Students come from 24 other countries; 91% are from out of state; 1% Black or African American, non-Hispanic/Latino; 9% Hispanic/Latino; 3% Asian, non-Hispanic/Latino; 0.5% American Indian or Alaska Native, non-Hispanic/Latino; 5% Two or more races, non-Hispanic/Latino; 3% Race/ethnicity unknown; 12% international; 5% transferred in; 71% live on campus. *Retention:* 69% of full-time freshmen returned.

Freshmen *Admission:* 263 applied, 227 admitted, 99 enrolled. *Test scores:* SAT critical reading scores over 500: 93%; SAT math scores over 500: 88%; ACT scores over 18: 95%; SAT critical reading scores over 600: 76%; SAT math scores over 600: 64%; ACT scores over 24: 87%; SAT critical reading scores over 700: 37%; SAT math scores over 700: 32%; ACT scores over 30: 29%.

Faculty *Total:* 63, 100% full-time, 78% with terminal degrees. *Student/faculty ratio:* 6:1.

Academics *Calendar:* semesters. *Degrees:* bachelor's and master's. *Special study options:* internships, off-campus study, summer session for credit.

Computers on Campus 30 computers/terminals are available on campus for general student use. Students can access the following: computer help desk, free student e-mail accounts. Campuswide network is available. 100% of college-owned or -operated housing units are wired for high-speed Internet access. Wireless service is available via classrooms, computer centers, computer labs, dorm rooms, learning centers, student centers.

Student Life *Housing:* on-campus residence required through senior year. *Options:* coed, men-only, women-only, disabled students. Campus housing is university owned. Freshman campus housing is guaranteed. *Activities and organizations:* drama/theater group, student-run newspaper, Iron Bookworm Workout, Chrysostomos (Theater), Jazz Dance, Student Government/Student Committee on Instruction, Intramural Sports. *Campus security:* 24-hour emergency response devices and patrols, late-night transport/escort service, controlled dormitory access. *Student services:* health clinic, personal/psychological counseling.

Athletics *Intercollegiate sports:* fencing M/W. *Intramural sports:* badminton M/W, basketball M/W, cross-country running M/W, fencing M/W, ice hockey M/W, racquetball M/W, rock climbing M/W, skiing (cross-country) M/W, skiing (downhill) M/W, soccer M/W, softball M/W, squash M/W, table tennis M/W, tennis M/W, ultimate Frisbee M/W, volleyball M/W.

Standardized Tests *Required for some:* SAT (for admission).

Costs (2012–13) *Comprehensive fee:* $54,998 includes full-time tuition ($44,554), mandatory fees ($450), and room and board ($9994). Part-time tuition: $1272 per credit. *College room only:* $4997. Room and board charges vary according to board plan. *Payment plans:* tuition prepayment, installment. *Waivers:* employees or children of employees.

Financial Aid Of all full-time matriculated undergraduates who enrolled in 2010, 328 applied for aid, 318 were judged to have need, 286 had their need fully met. 151 Federal Work-Study jobs (averaging $304,879). 10 state and other part-time jobs (averaging $27,520). *Average percent of need met:* 93%. *Average financial aid package:* $33,266. *Average need-based loan:* $5375. *Average need-based gift aid:* $23,989. *Average indebtedness upon graduation:* $26,414.

Applying *Options:* electronic application. *Required:* essay or personal statement, high school transcript, 2 letters of recommendation. *Required for some:* interview. *Recommended:* 3 letters of recommendation, interview.

Freshman Application Contact Mr. Larry Clendenin, Director of Admissions, St. John's College, 1160 Camino Cruz Blanca, Santa Fe, NM 87505. *Phone:* 505-984-6060. *Toll-free phone:* 800-331-5232. *Fax:* 505-984-6162. *E-mail:* admissions@sjcsf.edu. *Web site:* http://www.stjohnscollege.edu/.

Santa Fe University of Art and Design
Santa Fe, New Mexico

Freshman Application Contact Ms. Jackie Donohoe, Santa Fe University of Art and Design, 1600 Saint Michael's Drive, Santa Fe, NM 87505-7634.

Phone: 505-473-6133. *Toll-free phone:* 800-456-2673. *Fax:* 505-473-6129. *E-mail:* admissions@csf.edu. *Web site:* http://www.santafeuniversity.edu/.

University of New Mexico

Albuquerque, New Mexico

- **State-supported** university, founded 1889
- **Urban** 769-acre campus with easy access to Albuquerque
- **Endowment** $336.0 million
- **Coed**
- **Moderately difficult** entrance level, 64% of applicants were admitted

Undergraduates Students come from 52 states and territories; 63 other countries; 11% are from out of state. *Retention:* 74% of full-time freshmen returned.

Freshmen *Admission:* 11,410 applied, 7,288 admitted. *Average high school GPA:* 3.18. *Test scores:* SAT critical reading scores over 500: 68%; SAT math scores over 500: 64%; ACT scores over 18: 89%; SAT critical reading scores over 600: 28%; SAT math scores over 600: 25%; ACT scores over 24: 36%; SAT critical reading scores over 700: 6%; SAT math scores over 700: 3%; ACT scores over 30: 5%.

Faculty *Total:* 1,481, 65% full-time, 68% with terminal degrees. *Student/faculty ratio:* 23:1.

Academics *Calendar:* semesters. *Degrees:* certificates, associate, bachelor's, master's, doctoral, post-master's, and first professional certificates. *Special study options:* academic remediation for entering students, accelerated degree program, adult/continuing education programs, advanced placement credit, cooperative education, distance learning, double majors, English as a second language, honors programs, independent study, internships, off-campus study, part-time degree program, services for LD students, student-designed majors, study abroad, summer session for credit. *ROTC:* Army (b), Navy (b), Air Force (b). *Unusual degree programs:* 3-2 business administration; engineering; Latin American studies, business.

Computers on Campus 766 computers/terminals are available on campus for general student use. Students can access the following: computer help desk, free student e-mail accounts, online (class) grades, online (class) registration, online (class) schedules. Campuswide network is available. 100% of college-owned or -operated housing units are wired for high-speed Internet access. Wireless service is available via entire campus.

Student Life *Housing options:* coed, disabled students. Campus housing is university owned. *Activities and organizations:* drama/theater group, student-run newspaper, radio and television station, choral group, marching band, Associated Students of UNM, Graduate and Professional Students Association, Golden Key National Honor Society, national fraternities, national sororities. *Campus security:* 24-hour emergency response devices and patrols, student patrols, late-night transport/escort service, controlled dormitory access. *Student services:* health clinic, personal/psychological counseling, women's center.

Athletics Member NCAA. All Division I except football (Division I-A). *Intercollegiate sports:* baseball M, basketball M(s)/W(s), cross-country running M(s)/W(s), golf M(s)/W(s), skiing (cross-country) M(s)/W(s), skiing (downhill) M(s)/W(s), soccer M(s)/W(s), softball W(s), swimming and diving W(s), tennis M(s)/W(s), track and field M(s)/W(s), volleyball W(s). *Intramural sports:* basketball M/W, bowling M/W, cheerleading W(c), cross-country running M/W, fencing M/W, football M/W, golf M/W, ice hockey M(c)/W(c), racquetball M/W, rugby M(c)/W(c), skiing (downhill) M/W, soccer M/W, softball M/W, swimming and diving W, table tennis M/W, tennis M/W, ultimate Frisbee M(c)/W(c), volleyball M/W, water polo M/W, wrestling M(c).

Standardized Tests *Required:* SAT or ACT (for admission).

Costs (2011–12) *Tuition:* state resident $5809 full-time, $242 per credit hour part-time; nonresident $19,918 full-time, $830 per credit hour part-time. Full-time tuition and fees vary according to program. Part-time tuition and fees vary according to course load and program. *Room and board:* $8068. Room and board charges vary according to board plan and housing facility. *Payment plan:* installment. *Waivers:* senior citizens and employees or children of employees.

Applying *Options:* electronic application, early admission, deferred entrance. *Application fee:* $20. *Required:* high school transcript, minimum 2.4 GPA. *Required for some:* essay or personal statement, interview. *Application deadlines:* rolling (freshmen), rolling (transfers). *Notification:* continuous (freshmen), continuous (transfers).

Freshman Application Contact Mr. Matthew Hulett, Director of Admissions and Recruitment Services, University of New Mexico, Office of Admissions, PO Box 4895, Albuquerque, NM 87196-4895. *Phone:* 505-277-8900. *Toll-free phone:* 800-CALL-UNM. *Fax:* 505-277-6686. *E-mail:* apply@unm.edu. *Web site:* http://www.unm.edu/.

University of New Mexico–Gallup

Gallup, New Mexico

Director of Admissions Ms. Pearl A. Morris, Admissions Representative, University of New Mexico–Gallup, 200 College Road, Gallup, NM 87301-5603. *Phone:* 505-863-7576. *Web site:* http://www.gallup.unm.edu/.

University of Phoenix–New Mexico Campus

Albuquerque, New Mexico

Freshman Application Contact Marc Booker, Sr. Director, Office of Admissions and Evaluation, University of Phoenix–New Mexico Campus, 4035 South Riverpoint Parkway, Mail Stop CF-L101, Phoenix, AZ 85040. *Phone:* 602-557-4609. *Toll-free phone:* 866-766-0766. *Fax:* 480-643-1156. *Web site:* http://www.phoenix.edu/.

University of the Southwest

Hobbs, New Mexico

- **Independent Christian** comprehensive, founded 1962
- **Small-town** 162-acre campus
- **Endowment** $4.5 million
- **Coed** 322 undergraduate students, 83% full-time, 51% women, 49% men
- **Moderately difficult** entrance level, 50% of applicants were admitted

Undergraduates 266 full-time, 56 part-time. Students come from 16 states and territories; 2 other countries; 53% are from out of state; 14% Black or African American, non-Hispanic/Latino; 43% Hispanic/Latino; 0.6% Asian, non-Hispanic/Latino; 0.9% Native Hawaiian or other Pacific Islander, non-Hispanic/Latino; 0.9% American Indian or Alaska Native, non-Hispanic/Latino; 16% Race/ethnicity unknown; 0.6% international; 29% transferred in; 55% live on campus. *Retention:* 45% of full-time freshmen returned.

Freshmen *Admission:* 171 applied, 85 admitted, 98 enrolled. *Average high school GPA:* 3.2. *Test scores:* SAT critical reading scores over 500: 20%; SAT math scores over 500: 29%; ACT scores over 18: 48%; SAT math scores over 600: 6%; ACT scores over 24: 3%.

Faculty *Total:* 43, 33% full-time, 44% with terminal degrees. *Student/faculty ratio:* 15:1.

Academics *Calendar:* semesters. *Degrees:* bachelor's and master's. *Special study options:* advanced placement credit, distance learning, double majors, internships, part-time degree program, services for LD students, summer session for credit.

Computers on Campus 65 computers/terminals are available on campus for general student use. Students can access the following: campus intranet, computer help desk, free student e-mail accounts, online (class) grades, online (class) registration, online (class) schedules. Campuswide network is available. 100% of college-owned or -operated housing units are wired for high-speed Internet access. Wireless service is available via entire campus.

Student Life *Housing:* on-campus residence required through sophomore year. *Options:* coed. Campus housing is university owned. Freshman applicants given priority for college housing. *Activities and organizations:* Student Government Association (SGA), Students in Free Enterprise (SIFE), Southwest Association of Future Educators, Fellowship of Christian Athletes, BEST. *Campus security:* student patrols, controlled dormitory access, night Security. *Student services:* personal/psychological counseling.

Athletics Member NAIA. *Intercollegiate sports:* baseball M(s), basketball M(s)/W(s), cross-country running M(s)/W(s), soccer M(s)/W(s), softball W(s), tennis M(s)/W(s), track and field M(s)/W(s), volleyball W(s). *Intramural sports:* badminton M/W, basketball M/W, soccer M/W, table tennis M/W, volleyball M/W.

Standardized Tests *Required:* SAT or ACT (for admission).

Costs (2012–13) *One-time required fee:* $300. *Comprehensive fee:* $18,905 includes full-time tuition ($12,240), mandatory fees ($25), and room and board ($6640). Full-time tuition and fees vary according to course load. Part-time tuition: $510 per semester hour. Part-time tuition and fees vary according to course load. *College room only:* $3720. Room and board charges vary according to board plan and housing facility. *Payment plan:* installment. *Waivers:* employees or children of employees.

Financial Aid Of all full-time matriculated undergraduates who enrolled in 2011, 282 applied for aid, 234 were judged to have need, 38 had their need fully met. 22 Federal Work-Study jobs (averaging $1663). 18 state and other part-time jobs (averaging $1751). In 2011, 48 non-need-based awards were made. *Average percent of need met:* 70%. *Average financial aid package:* $6687. *Average need-based loan:* $3815. *Average need-based gift aid:* $3948. *Average non-need-based aid:* $1219. *Average indebtedness upon graduation:* $23,159.

Applying *Options:* electronic application, early admission, deferred entrance. *Application fee:* $25. *Required:* high school transcript, minimum 2.0 GPA. *Application deadlines:* rolling (freshmen), rolling (transfers). *Notification:* continuous (freshmen), continuous (transfers).

Freshman Application Contact Ashley Taylor, Admissions Coordinator, University of the Southwest, 6610 North Lovington Highway, Hobbs, NM 88240. *Phone:* 575-492-2121. *Toll-free phone:* 800-530-4400. *Fax:* 575-392-6006. *E-mail:* ataylor@usw.edu. *Web site:* http://www.usw.edu/.

Western New Mexico University

Silver City, New Mexico

Freshman Application Contact Mr. Dan Tressler, Director of Admissions, Western New Mexico University, PO Box 680, Silver City, NM 88062-0680. *Phone:* 505-538-6106. *Toll-free phone:* 800-872-WNMU. *Fax:* 505-538-6127. *E-mail:* tresslerd@wnmu.edu. *Web site:* http://www.wnmu.edu/.

NEW YORK

Adelphi University

Garden City, New York

- **Independent** university, founded 1896
- **Suburban** 75-acre campus with easy access to New York City
- **Endowment** $127.4 million
- **Coed** 5,021 undergraduate students, 89% full-time, 69% women, 31% men
- **Moderately difficult** entrance level, 69% of applicants were admitted

Undergraduates 4,474 full-time, 547 part-time. Students come from 40 states and territories; 45 other countries; 8% are from out of state; 11% Black or African American, non-Hispanic/Latino; 10% Hispanic/Latino; 6% Asian, non-Hispanic/Latino; 0.3% Native Hawaiian or other Pacific Islander, non-Hispanic/Latino; 0.3% American Indian or Alaska Native, non-Hispanic/Latino; 2% Two or more races, non-Hispanic/Latino; 11% Race/ethnicity unknown; 3% international; 10% transferred in; 24% live on campus. *Retention:* 81% of full-time freshmen returned.

Freshmen *Admission:* 8,278 applied, 5,730 admitted, 988 enrolled. *Average high school GPA:* 3.4. *Test scores:* SAT critical reading scores over 500: 70%; SAT math scores over 500: 78%; SAT writing scores over 500: 77%; ACT scores over 18: 97%; SAT critical reading scores over 600: 21%; SAT math scores over 600: 28%; SAT writing scores over 600: 26%; ACT scores over 24: 47%; SAT critical reading scores over 700: 2%; SAT math scores over 700: 4%; SAT writing scores over 700: 3%; ACT scores over 30: 9%.

Faculty *Total:* 975, 32% full-time. *Student/faculty ratio:* 13:1.

Academics *Calendar:* semesters. *Degrees:* associate, bachelor's, master's, doctoral, post-master's, postbachelor's, and first professional certificates. *Special study options:* accelerated degree program, advanced placement credit, cooperative education, distance learning, double majors, English as a second language, freshman honors college, honors programs, independent study, internships, part-time degree program, services for LD students, student-designed majors, study abroad, summer session for credit. *ROTC:* Army (c), Air Force (c). *Unusual degree programs:* 3-2 engineering with Columbia University, Rensselaer Polytechnic University, Stevens Institute of Technology; physical therapy with New York Medical College; Tufts University; New York University College of Dentistry; New York Law School; SUNY College of Optometry; Columbia University; osteopathic with Touro College; New York College of Podiatric Medicine.

Computers on Campus 880 computers/terminals are available on campus for general student use. Students can access the following: computer help desk, free student e-mail accounts, online (class) grades, online (class) registration, online (class) schedules, payment, drop/add classes, check application status. Campuswide network is available. 100% of college-owned or -operated housing units are wired for high-speed Internet access. Wireless service is available via entire campus.

Student Life *Housing options:* coed, disabled students. Campus housing is university owned. Freshman applicants given priority for college housing. *Activities and organizations:* drama/theater group, student-run newspaper, radio station, choral group, Student Activities Board, C. A. L. I. B. E. R. (Cause to Achieve Leadership, Intelligence, Brotherhood, Excellence, and Respect), Circle K International, Future Teachers Association, Adelphi Christian Fellowship, national fraternities, national sororities. *Campus security:* 24-hour emergency response devices and patrols, late-night transport/escort service, controlled dormitory access. *Student services:* health clinic, personal/psychological counseling.

Athletics Member NCAA. All Division II except soccer (Division I). *Intercollegiate sports:* baseball M(s), basketball M(s)/W(s), bowling W(s), cross-country running M(s)/W(s), field hockey W(s), golf M(s), lacrosse M(s)/W(s),

RISE AND SHINE

ADELPHI UNIVERSITY ADELPHI.EDU/SUCCESS

soccer M(s)/W(s), softball W(s), swimming and diving M(s)/W(s), tennis M(s)/W(s), track and field M(s)/W(s), volleyball W(s). *Intramural sports:* badminton M/W, basketball M/W, cheerleading W, equestrian sports M(c)/W(c), fencing M(c)/W(c), football M/W, soccer M/W, ultimate Frisbee M(c)/W(c), volleyball M/W, water polo M(c)/W.

Standardized Tests *Required for some:* SAT or ACT (for admission).

Costs (2012–13) *Comprehensive fee:* $39,880 includes full-time tuition ($27,010), mandatory fees ($1450), and room and board ($11,420). Full-time tuition and fees vary according to course level, course load, location, program, and student level. Part-time tuition: $835 per credit hour. Part-time tuition and fees vary according to course level, course load, location, program, and student level. *College room only:* $8170. Room and board charges vary according to board plan and housing facility. *Payment plans:* tuition prepayment, installment, deferred payment. *Waivers:* children of alumni, senior citizens, and employees or children of employees.

Financial Aid Of all full-time matriculated undergraduates who enrolled in 2011, 3,666 applied for aid, 3,281 were judged to have need, 30 had their need fully met. In 2011, 774 non-need-based awards were made. *Average percent of need met:* 25%. *Average financial aid package:* $20,475. *Average need-based loan:* $4591. *Average need-based gift aid:* $7096. *Average non-need-based aid:* $11,281. *Average indebtedness upon graduation:* $32,527.

Applying *Options:* electronic application, early action, deferred entrance. *Application fee:* $40. *Required:* essay or personal statement, high school transcript. *Required for some:* 2 letters of recommendation, interview, auditions/portfolios for performing and fine arts. *Recommended:* minimum 3.4 GPA, interview. *Application deadlines:* rolling (freshmen), rolling (transfers), 12/1 (early action). *Notification:* continuous (freshmen), continuous (transfers), 12/31 (early action).

Freshman Application Contact Ms. Christine Murphy, Director of Admissions, Adelphi University, Levermore Hall 110, 1 South Avenue, PO Box 701, Garden City, NY 11530-0701. *Phone:* 516-877-3050. *Toll-free phone:* 800-ADELPHI. *Fax:* 516-877-3039. *E-mail:* admissions@adelphi.edu. *Web site:* http://www.adelphi.edu/.

See page 561 for display ad and page 1046 for the College Close-Up.

Albany College of Pharmacy and Health Sciences
Albany, New York

- **Independent** comprehensive, founded 1881
- **Urban** 28-acre campus
- **Coed** 1,079 undergraduate students, 98% full-time, 59% women, 41% men
- **Very difficult** entrance level, 64% of applicants were admitted

Undergraduates 1,059 full-time, 20 part-time. Students come from 26 states and territories; 18 other countries; 33% are from out of state; 4% Black or African American, non-Hispanic/Latino; 3% Hispanic/Latino; 16% Asian, non-Hispanic/Latino; 0.3% Native Hawaiian or other Pacific Islander, non-Hispanic/Latino; 0.2% American Indian or Alaska Native, non-Hispanic/Latino; 1% Two or more races, non-Hispanic/Latino; 4% Race/ethnicity unknown; 6% international; 14% transferred in; 45% live on campus. *Retention:* 82% of full-time freshmen returned.

Freshmen *Admission:* 1,437 applied, 921 admitted, 212 enrolled. *Average high school GPA:* 3.7. *Test scores:* SAT critical reading scores over 500: 87%; SAT math scores over 500: 96%; SAT writing scores over 500: 87%; ACT scores over 18: 100%; SAT critical reading scores over 600: 34%; SAT math scores over 600: 58%; SAT writing scores over 600: 28%; ACT scores over 24: 79%; SAT critical reading scores over 700: 3%; SAT math scores over 700: 9%; SAT writing scores over 700: 4%; ACT scores over 30: 11%.

Faculty *Total:* 148, 74% full-time, 76% with terminal degrees. *Student/faculty ratio:* 13:1.

Academics *Calendar:* semesters. *Degrees:* bachelor's, master's, and doctoral. *Special study options:* advanced placement credit, off-campus study, services for LD students, summer session for credit. *ROTC:* Army (c), Navy (c), Air Force (c).

Computers on Campus 30 computers/terminals are available on campus for general student use. Students can access the following: campus intranet, computer help desk, free student e-mail accounts, online (class) grades, online (class) registration, online (class) schedules. Campuswide network is available. 100% of college-owned or -operated housing units are wired for high-speed Internet access. Wireless service is available via entire campus.

Student Life *Housing:* on-campus residence required through sophomore year. *Options:* coed. Campus housing is university owned and is provided by a third party. Freshman campus housing is guaranteed. *Activities and organizations:* student-run newspaper, choral group, American Pharmacy Association-Student Chapter, Orthodox Christian Student Association, Student Government Association, Colleges Against Cancer, national fraternities, national sororities.

Campus security: 24-hour emergency response devices and patrols, controlled dormitory access. *Student services:* health clinic, personal/psychological counseling.

Athletics *Intercollegiate sports:* basketball M/W, cross-country running M/W, soccer M/W. *Intramural sports:* basketball M/W, football M/W, golf M(c)/W(c), lacrosse M(c), tennis M(c)/W(c), ultimate Frisbee M/W, volleyball M/W.

Standardized Tests *Required:* SAT or ACT (for admission).

Costs (2011–12) *Comprehensive fee:* $36,490 includes full-time tuition ($25,700), mandatory fees ($1230), and room and board ($9560). Full-time tuition and fees vary according to degree level. Part-time tuition: $855 per credit hour. Part-time tuition and fees vary according to course load and degree level. *College room only:* $6300. Room and board charges vary according to board plan, housing facility, and location. *Payment plan:* installment. *Waivers:* employees or children of employees.

Financial Aid Of all full-time matriculated undergraduates who enrolled in 2002, 567 applied for aid, 498 were judged to have need, 186 had their need fully met. 202 Federal Work-Study jobs (averaging $450). 12 state and other part-time jobs (averaging $432). In 2002, 74 non-need-based awards were made. *Average percent of need met:* 78%. *Average financial aid package:* $12,320. *Average need-based loan:* $8238. *Average need-based gift aid:* $5247. *Average non-need-based aid:* $8933. *Average indebtedness upon graduation:* $9397.

Applying *Options:* electronic application, early decision. *Application fee:* $75. *Required:* essay or personal statement, high school transcript, 2 letters of recommendation. *Required for some:* interview. *Recommended:* minimum 3.0 GPA. *Application deadlines:* 2/1 (freshmen), 2/1 (transfers). *Early decision deadline:* 11/1. *Notification:* 3/15 (freshmen), 3/15 (transfers), 12/15 (early decision).

Freshman Application Contact Mr. Matthew Stever, Director of Admissions, Albany College of Pharmacy and Health Sciences, 106 New Scotland Avenue, Albany, NY 12208. *Phone:* 518-694-7221. *Toll-free phone:* 888-203-8010. *Fax:* 518-694-7322. *E-mail:* admissions@acphs.edu. *Web site:* http://www.acphs.edu/.

Alfred University
Alfred, New York

- **Independent** university, founded 1836
- **Rural** 232-acre campus
- **Coed** 1,953 undergraduate students, 97% full-time, 49% women, 51% men
- **Moderately difficult** entrance level, 72% of applicants were admitted

Undergraduates 1,895 full-time, 58 part-time. 23% are from out of state; 7% Black or African American, non-Hispanic/Latino; 6% Hispanic/Latino; 1% Asian, non-Hispanic/Latino; 0.1% American Indian or Alaska Native, non-Hispanic/Latino; 1% Two or more races, non-Hispanic/Latino; 14% Race/ethnicity unknown; 2% international; 4% transferred in; 76% live on campus. *Retention:* 76% of full-time freshmen returned.

Freshmen *Admission:* 3,025 applied, 2,187 admitted, 560 enrolled. *Average high school GPA:* 3.09. *Test scores:* SAT critical reading scores over 500: 67%; SAT math scores over 500: 79%; SAT writing scores over 500: 54%; ACT scores over 18: 98%; SAT critical reading scores over 600: 21%; SAT math scores over 600: 28%; SAT writing scores over 600: 14%; ACT scores over 24: 54%; SAT critical reading scores over 700: 4%; SAT math scores over 700: 3%; SAT writing scores over 700: 2%; ACT scores over 30: 8%.

Faculty *Total:* 201, 80% full-time. *Student/faculty ratio:* 13:1.

Academics *Calendar:* semesters. *Degrees:* bachelor's, master's, doctoral, post-master's, and first professional certificates. *ROTC:* Army (c).

Computers on Campus Students can access the following: computer help desk, free student e-mail accounts, online (class) grades, online (class) registration, online (class) schedules, online bill pay. Campuswide network is available. 100% of college-owned or -operated housing units are wired for high-speed Internet access. Wireless service is available via classrooms, computer labs, dorm rooms, libraries, student centers.

Student Life *Housing:* on-campus residence required through junior year. *Options:* coed. Campus housing is university owned. Freshman campus housing is guaranteed. *Campus security:* 24-hour emergency response devices, student patrols, late-night transport/escort service, all dormitories are key-only access, but not electronic.

Athletics Member NCAA. All Division III. *Intercollegiate sports:* basketball M/W, cross-country running M/W, equestrian sports M/W, football M, lacrosse M/W, skiing (downhill) M/W, soccer M/W, softball W, swimming and diving M/W, tennis M/W, track and field M/W, volleyball W. *Intramural sports:* baseball M(c), basketball M/W, cheerleading W(c), football M/W, golf M/W, ice hockey M(c), lacrosse M/W, racquetball M/W, rugby M(c)/W(c), skiing (cross-country) M/W, soccer M/W, softball M/W, squash M/W, tennis M/W, ultimate Frisbee M(c)/W(c), volleyball M/W.

Standardized Tests *Required:* SAT or ACT (for admission).

Costs (2012–13) *Comprehensive fee:* $39,292 includes full-time tuition ($26,884), mandatory fees ($910), and room and board ($11,498). Full-time tuition and fees vary according to program. Part-time tuition: $872 per credit hour. Part-time tuition and fees vary according to course load. *Required fees:* $152 per term part-time. *Room and board:* Room and board charges vary according to board plan and housing facility. *Payment plans:* tuition prepayment, installment, deferred payment. *Waivers:* employees or children of employees.

Financial Aid Of all full-time matriculated undergraduates who enrolled in 2010, 1,654 applied for aid, 1,499 were judged to have need, 234 had their need fully met. In 2010, 111 non-need-based awards were made. *Average percent of need met:* 84%. *Average financial aid package:* $23,086. *Average need-based loan:* $5615. *Average need-based gift aid:* $16,820. *Average non-need-based aid:* $9188. *Average indebtedness upon graduation:* $31,159. *Financial aid deadline:* 3/15.

Applying *Options:* early admission, early decision, deferred entrance. *Application fee:* $50. *Required:* essay or personal statement, high school transcript, 1 letter of recommendation. *Required for some:* interview, portfolio. *Recommended:* interview. *Application deadlines:* 8/1 (freshmen), 8/1 (transfers). *Early decision deadline:* 12/1. *Notification:* continuous (freshmen), continuous (transfers), 12/15 (early decision).

Freshman Application Contact Mr. Jeremy C. Spencer, Director of Admissions, Alfred University, Alumni Hall, Alfred, NY 14802-1205. *Phone:* 607-871-2115. *Toll-free phone:* 800-541-9229. *Fax:* 607-871-2198. *E-mail:* admissions@alfred.edu. *Web site:* http://www.alfred.edu/.

Bard College
Annandale-on-Hudson, New York

- **Independent** comprehensive, founded 1860
- **Rural** 600-acre campus
- **Coed** 1,982 undergraduate students, 96% full-time, 58% women, 42% men
- **Very difficult** entrance level, 35% of applicants were admitted

Undergraduates 1,910 full-time, 72 part-time. Students come from 49 states and territories; 64 other countries; 65% are from out of state; 3% Black or African American, non-Hispanic/Latino; 2% Hispanic/Latino; 3% Asian, non-Hispanic/Latino; 0.4% American Indian or Alaska Native, non-Hispanic/Latino; 20% Race/ethnicity unknown; 13% international; 3% transferred in; 74% live on campus. *Retention:* 88% of full-time freshmen returned.

Freshmen *Admission:* 5,670 applied, 1,960 admitted, 486 enrolled. *Average high school GPA:* 3.5.

Faculty *Total:* 257, 60% full-time, 91% with terminal degrees. *Student/faculty ratio:* 10:1.

Academics *Calendar:* semesters. *Degrees:* associate, bachelor's, master's, doctoral, and first professional. *Special study options:* adult/continuing education programs, advanced placement credit, double majors, independent study, internships, off-campus study, part-time degree program, services for LD students, student-designed majors, study abroad, summer session for credit. *Unusual degree programs:* 3-2 business administration; engineering with Columbia University, Washington University in St. Louis, Dartmouth College; forestry with Duke University; social work; teaching.

Computers on Campus 425 computers/terminals are available on campus for general student use. Students can access the following: campus intranet, computer help desk, free student e-mail accounts, online (class) grades, online (class) registration, online (class) schedules. Campuswide network is available. 100% of college-owned or -operated housing units are wired for high-speed Internet access. Wireless service is available via classrooms, computer centers, computer labs, dorm rooms, libraries, student centers.

Student Life *Housing:* on-campus residence required through sophomore year. *Options:* coed, women-only, cooperative. Campus housing is university owned. Freshman campus housing is guaranteed. *Activities and organizations:* drama/theater group, student-run newspaper, radio station, choral group, Student government, Debate Team, Queer-Straight Alliance, International Student Organization / Black Student Organization / Anti—Racist Discourse, Free Press (student newspaper). *Campus security:* 24-hour emergency response devices and patrols, student patrols, late-night transport/escort service, controlled dormitory access. *Student services:* health clinic, personal/psychological counseling, legal services.

Athletics Member NCAA, NAIA. All NCAA Division III. *Intercollegiate sports:* baseball M, basketball M/W, cross-country running M/W, lacrosse M/W, soccer M/W, squash M, swimming and diving M/W, tennis M/W, track and field M/W, volleyball M/W. *Intramural sports:* badminton M/W, baseball M(c)/W(c), basketball M/W, bowling M/W, equestrian sports M(c)/W(c), fencing M(c)/W(c), golf M/W, rugby M(c)/W(c), soccer M/W, softball M/W, squash M/W, swimming and diving M(c)/W(c), table tennis M/W, tennis M/W, ultimate Frisbee M(c)/W(c), volleyball M/W.

Costs (2011–12) *One-time required fee:* $1370. *Comprehensive fee:* $55,592 includes full-time tuition ($42,476), mandatory fees ($830), and room and board ($12,286). Part-time tuition: $1328 per credit. *Room and board:* Room and board charges vary according to housing facility. *Payment plans:* tuition prepayment, installment. *Waivers:* employees or children of employees.

Financial Aid Of all full-time matriculated undergraduates who enrolled in 2011, 1,346 applied for aid, 1,237 were judged to have need, 646 had their need fully met. 795 Federal Work-Study jobs (averaging $1490). 61 state and other part-time jobs (averaging $1640). In 2011, 43 non-need-based awards were made. *Average percent of need met:* 87%. *Average financial aid package:* $37,948. *Average need-based loan:* $4986. *Average need-based gift aid:* $30,018. *Average non-need-based aid:* $16,761. *Average indebtedness upon graduation:* $26,897. *Financial aid deadline:* 2/15.

Applying *Options:* electronic application, early admission, early action, deferred entrance. *Application fee:* $50. *Required:* essay or personal statement, high school transcript, minimum 3.0 GPA, 3 letters of recommendation. *Required for some:* interview. *Recommended:* interview. *Application deadlines:* 1/1 (freshmen), 3/15 (transfers), 11/1 (early action). *Notification:* 4/1 (freshmen), 5/15 (transfers), 1/1 (early action).

Freshman Application Contact Ms. Mary Backlund, Director of Admissions, Bard College, PO Box 5000, 51 Ravine Road, Annandale-on-Hudson, NY 12504-5000. *Phone:* 845-758-7472. *Fax:* 845-758-5208. *E-mail:* admission@bard.edu. *Web site:* http://www.bard.edu/.

Barnard College
New York, New York

- **Independent** 4-year, founded 1889, part of Columbia University
- **Urban** 4-acre campus
- **Women only** 2,445 undergraduate students, 98% full-time
- **Most difficult** entrance level, 25% of applicants were admitted

Undergraduates 2,389 full-time, 56 part-time. 66% are from out of state; 5% Black or African American, non-Hispanic/Latino; 9% Hispanic/Latino; 17% Asian, non-Hispanic/Latino; 0.2% Native Hawaiian or other Pacific Islander, non-Hispanic/Latino; 0.1% American Indian or Alaska Native, non-Hispanic/Latino; 0.3% Race/ethnicity unknown; 6% international; 1% transferred in; 89% live on campus. *Retention:* 94% of full-time freshmen returned.

Freshmen *Admission:* 5,153 applied, 1,282 admitted, 612 enrolled. *Average high school GPA:* 3.78. *Test scores:* SAT critical reading scores over 500: 98%; SAT math scores over 500: 99%; SAT writing scores over 500: 100%; ACT scores over 18: 100%; SAT critical reading scores over 600: 86%; SAT math scores over 600: 84%; SAT writing scores over 600: 90%; ACT scores over 24: 97%; SAT critical reading scores over 700: 40%; SAT math scores over 700: 32%; SAT writing scores over 700: 53%; ACT scores over 30: 60%.

Faculty *Total:* 335, 61% full-time, 70% with terminal degrees. *Student/faculty ratio:* 10:1.

Academics *Calendar:* semesters. *Degree:* bachelor's. *ROTC:* Air Force (c).

Computers on Campus Students can access the following: campus intranet, computer help desk, free student e-mail accounts, online (class) grades, online (class) registration, online (class) schedules. Campuswide network is available. 100% of college-owned or -operated housing units are wired for high-speed Internet access. Wireless service is available via computer centers, computer labs, dorm rooms, libraries, student centers.

Student Life *Housing options:* women-only, disabled students. Campus housing is university owned and leased by the school. Freshman campus housing is guaranteed. *Campus security:* 24-hour emergency response devices and patrols, late-night transport/escort service, gated campus with permanent security posts.

Athletics Member NCAA. All Division I. *Intercollegiate sports:* archery W, basketball W, crew W, cross-country running W, equestrian sports W(c), fencing W, field hockey W, golf W, ice hockey W(c), lacrosse W, rugby W(c), sailing W(c), skiing (downhill) W(c), soccer W, softball W, squash W(c), swimming and diving W, tennis W, track and field W, volleyball W. *Intramural sports:* archery W, badminton W, basketball W, equestrian sports W, ice hockey W, rugby W, sailing W, soccer W, squash W, tennis W, volleyball W, water polo W.

Standardized Tests *Required:* SAT with writing and two subject tests or ACT with writing (for admission).

Costs (2011–12) *Comprehensive fee:* $55,566 includes full-time tuition ($40,422), mandatory fees ($1762), and room and board ($13,382). Part-time tuition: $1347 per credit. *College room only:* $8000. Room and board charges vary according to board plan and housing facility. *Payment plans:* tuition prepayment, installment, deferred payment. *Waivers:* employees or children of employees.

Financial Aid Of all full-time matriculated undergraduates who enrolled in 2011, 1,114 applied for aid, 983 were judged to have need, 983 had their need fully met. 374 Federal Work-Study jobs (averaging $1711). 556 state and other part-time jobs (averaging $1684). *Average percent of need met:* 100%. *Aver-*

age financial aid package: $39,696. *Average need-based loan:* $4534. *Average need-based gift aid:* $35,335. *Average indebtedness upon graduation:* $17,360. *Financial aid deadline:* 2/15.

Applying *Options:* early admission, early decision, deferred entrance. *Application fee:* $55. *Required:* essay or personal statement, high school transcript, 3 letters of recommendation, Common Application with Barnard supplement. *Recommended:* interview. *Application deadlines:* 1/1 (freshmen), 4/1 (transfers). *Early decision deadline:* 11/15. *Notification:* 4/1 (freshmen), 5/15 (transfers), 12/15 (early decision).

Freshman Application Contact Ms. Jennifer Gill Fondiller, Dean of Admissions, Barnard College, 3009 Broadway, New York, NY 10027-6598. *Phone:* 212-854-2014. *Fax:* 212-854-6220. *E-mail:* admissions@barnard.edu. *Web site:* http://www.barnard.edu/.

See below for display ad and page 1162 for the College Close-Up.

Beis Medrash Heichal Dovid

Far Rockaway, New York

Admissions Office Contact Beis Medrash Heichal Dovid, 257 Beach 17th Street, Far Rockaway, NY 11691.

Berkeley College–New York City Campus

New York, New York

Freshman Application Contact Berkeley College–New York City Campus, 3 East 43rd Street, New York, NY 10017-4604. *Phone:* 212-986-4343. *Toll-free phone:* 800-446-5400. *Web site:* http://www.berkeleycollege.edu/.

Berkeley College–Westchester Campus

White Plains, New York

Freshman Application Contact Director of Admissions, Berkeley College–Westchester Campus, White Plains, NY 10601. *Phone:* 914-694-1122. *Toll-free phone:* 800-446-5400. *Fax:* 914-328-9469. *E-mail:* info@berkeleycollege.edu. *Web site:* http://www.berkeleycollege.edu/.

Bernard M. Baruch College of the City University of New York

New York, New York

- **State and locally supported** comprehensive, founded 1919, part of City University of New York System
- **Urban** campus
- **Coed** 14,266 undergraduate students, 74% full-time, 51% women, 49% men
- **Very difficult** entrance level, 22% of applicants were admitted

Undergraduates 10,574 full-time, 3,692 part-time. 4% are from out of state; 10% Black or African American, non-Hispanic/Latino; 14% Hispanic/Latino; 34% Asian, non-Hispanic/Latino; 0.1% American Indian or Alaska Native, non-Hispanic/Latino; 11% international; 15% transferred in. *Retention:* 89% of full-time freshmen returned.

Freshmen *Admission:* 19,283 applied, 4,325 admitted, 1,311 enrolled. *Average high school GPA:* 3.14. *Test scores:* SAT critical reading scores over 500: 78%; SAT math scores over 500: 97%; SAT critical reading scores over 600: 30%; SAT math scores over 600: 68%; SAT critical reading scores over 700: 4%; SAT math scores over 700: 21%.

Faculty *Total:* 1,043, 45% full-time, 75% with terminal degrees. *Student/faculty ratio:* 18:1.

Academics *Calendar:* semesters. *Degrees:* bachelor's, master's, and post-master's certificates. *Special study options:* accelerated degree program, adult/continuing education programs, advanced placement credit, distance learning, double majors, English as a second language, freshman honors college, honors programs, independent study, internships, part-time degree program, services for LD students, student-designed majors, study abroad, summer session for credit. *ROTC:* Army (c).

Computers on Campus 1,300 computers/terminals are available on campus for general student use. Students can access the following: campus intranet, computer help desk, free student e-mail accounts, online (class) grades, online (class) registration, online (class) schedules. Campuswide network is available. Wireless service is available via classrooms, computer centers, computer labs, learning centers, libraries, student centers.

Student Life *Activities and organizations:* drama/theater group, student-run newspaper, radio station, choral group, Accounting Society, Caribbean Students Association, Association of Latino Professionals in Finance and Accounting, Golden Key International Honor Society, Helpline, national fra-

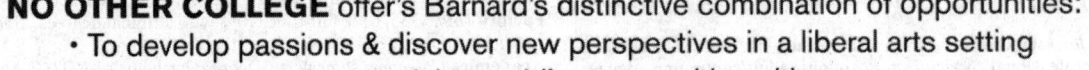

ternities, national sororities. *Campus security:* 24-hour emergency response devices and patrols, late-night transport/escort service, controlled access by ID card. *Student services:* health clinic, personal/psychological counseling, legal services.

Athletics Member NCAA. All Division III. *Intercollegiate sports:* baseball M, basketball M/W, cheerleading M/W, cross-country running M/W, soccer M, softball W, swimming and diving M/W, tennis M/W, volleyball M/W. *Intramural sports:* archery M(c)/W(c), badminton M/W, basketball M/W, cross-country running M/W, racquetball M/W, swimming and diving M/W, table tennis M/W, volleyball M/W.

Standardized Tests *Required:* SAT or ACT (for admission).

Costs (2011–12) *Tuition:* state resident $5130 full-time, $215 per credit hour part-time; nonresident $13,800 full-time, $460 per credit hour part-time. Full-time tuition and fees vary according to course load. Part-time tuition and fees vary according to course load. *Required fees:* $480 full-time, $150 per term part-time. *Room only:* $10,776. Room and board charges vary according to housing facility. *Payment plans:* installment, deferred payment. *Waivers:* senior citizens and employees or children of employees.

Financial Aid Of all full-time matriculated undergraduates who enrolled in 2009, 8,812 applied for aid, 8,012 were judged to have need, 1,179 had their need fully met. 675 Federal Work-Study jobs (averaging $800). 755 state and other part-time jobs (averaging $1200). In 2009, 80 non-need-based awards were made. *Average percent of need met:* 76%. *Average financial aid package:* $6598. *Average need-based loan:* $5000. *Average need-based gift aid:* $4958. *Average non-need-based aid:* $4600. *Average indebtedness upon graduation:* $14,265.

Applying *Options:* electronic application, early admission, deferred entrance. *Application fee:* $65. *Required:* high school transcript, minimum 2.5 GPA, 16 academic units. *Required for some:* interview. *Application deadlines:* 2/1 (freshmen), 2/1 (transfers). *Notification:* 5/15 (freshmen), continuous until 5/1 (transfers).

Freshman Application Contact Bernard M. Baruch College of the City University of New York, 1 Bernard Baruch Way, New York, NY 10010-5585. *Phone:* 646-312-1400. *Web site:* http://www.baruch.cuny.edu/.

Beth HaMedrash Shaarei Yosher Institute
Brooklyn, New York

Director of Admissions Director of Admissions, Beth HaMedrash Shaarei Yosher Institute, 4102-10 Sixteenth Avenue, Brooklyn, NY 11204. *Phone:* 718-854-2290.

Beth Hatalmud Rabbinical College
Brooklyn, New York

Director of Admissions Rabbi Osina, Director of Admissions, Beth Hatalmud Rabbinical College, 2127 Eighty-second Street, Brooklyn, NY 11214. *Phone:* 718-259-2525.

Boricua College
New York, New York

Freshman Application Contact Mrs. Miriam Pfeffer, Director of Student Services, Boricua College, 186 North 6th Street, Brooklyn, NY 11211. *Phone:* 718-782-2200. *Fax:* 718-782-2025. *E-mail:* mpfeffer@boricuacollege.edu. *Web site:* http://www.boricuacollege.edu/.

Briarcliffe College
Bethpage, New York

Freshman Application Contact Admissions Office, Briarcliffe College, 1055 Stewart Avenue, Bethpage, NY 11714. *Phone:* 516-918-3600. *Toll-free phone:* 888-349-4999 (in-state); 888-348-4999 (out-of-state). *Fax:* 516-470-6020. *Web site:* http://www.briarcliffe.edu/.

Brooklyn College of the City University of New York
Brooklyn, New York

Freshman Application Contact Office of Admissions, Brooklyn College of the City University of New York, 2900 Bedford Avenue, West Quad Building, Room 222, Brooklyn, NY 11210-2889. *Phone:* 718-951-5001. *Fax:* 718-951-4506. *E-mail:* adminqry@brooklyn.cuny.edu. *Web site:* http://www.brooklyn.cuny.edu/.

Bryant & Stratton College - Amherst Campus
Clarence, New York

Freshman Application Contact Mr. Brian K. Dioguardi, Director of Admissions, Bryant & Stratton College - Amherst Campus, Audubon Business Center, 40 Hazelwood Drive, Amherst, NY 14228. *Phone:* 716-691-0012. *Fax:* 716-691-0012. *E-mail:* bkdioguardi@bryantstratton.edu. *Web site:* http://www.bryantstratton.edu/.

Bryant & Stratton College - Buffalo Campus
Buffalo, New York

Freshman Application Contact Mr. Philip J. Struebel, Director of Admissions, Bryant & Stratton College - Buffalo Campus, 465 Main Street, Suite 400, Buffalo, NY 14203. *Phone:* 716-884-9120. *Fax:* 716-884-0091. *E-mail:* pjstruebel@bryantstratton.edu. *Web site:* http://www.bryantstratton.edu/.

Bryant & Stratton College - Southtowns Campus
Orchard Park, New York

Freshman Application Contact Bryant & Stratton College - Southtowns Campus, 200 Redtail, Orchard Park, NY 14127. *Phone:* 716-677-9500. *Web site:* http://www.bryantstratton.edu/.

Buffalo State College, State University of New York
Buffalo, New York

- **State-supported** comprehensive, founded 1867, part of State University of New York System
- **Urban** 115-acre campus
- **Endowment** $22.7 million
- **Coed** 10,012 undergraduate students, 88% full-time, 58% women, 42% men
- **Moderately difficult** entrance level, 45% of applicants were admitted

Undergraduates 8,811 full-time, 1,201 part-time. Students come from 31 states and territories; 53 other countries; 1% are from out of state; 16% Black or African American, non-Hispanic/Latino; 7% Hispanic/Latino; 2% Asian, non-Hispanic/Latino; 0.1% Native Hawaiian or other Pacific Islander, non-Hispanic/Latino; 0.6% American Indian or Alaska Native, non-Hispanic/Latino; 2% Two or more races, non-Hispanic/Latino; 8% Race/ethnicity unknown; 1% international; 14% transferred in; 25% live on campus. *Retention:* 75% of full-time freshmen returned.

Freshmen *Admission:* 11,431 applied, 5,185 admitted, 1,404 enrolled. *Average high school GPA:* 3.15. *Test scores:* SAT critical reading scores over 500: 43%; SAT math scores over 500: 49%; SAT critical reading scores over 600: 7%; SAT math scores over 600: 8%.

Faculty *Total:* 810, 50% full-time, 61% with terminal degrees. *Student/faculty ratio:* 17:1.

Academics *Calendar:* semesters. *Degrees:* bachelor's, master's, and post-master's certificates. *Special study options:* academic remediation for entering students, adult/continuing education programs, advanced placement credit, cooperative education, distance learning, double majors, English as a second language, freshman honors college, honors programs, independent study, internships, off-campus study, part-time degree program, services for LD students, study abroad, summer session for credit. *ROTC:* Army (c). *Unusual degree programs:* 3-2 engineering with State University of New York at Binghamton, Clarkson University, State University of New York at Buffalo.

Computers on Campus 1,700 computers/terminals are available on campus for general student use. Students can access the following: computer help desk, free student e-mail accounts, online (class) registration, online (class) schedules. Campuswide network is available. Wireless service is available via classrooms, libraries, student centers.

Student Life *Housing:* on-campus residence required through sophomore year. *Options:* coed. Campus housing is university owned. Freshman campus housing is guaranteed. *Activities and organizations:* drama/theater group, student-run newspaper, radio station, choral group, United Student Government, African-American Student Organization, Caribbean Student Organization, The Record, WBNY radio, national fraternities, national sororities. *Campus security:* 24-hour emergency response devices and patrols, student patrols, late-

night transport/escort service, controlled dormitory access. *Student services:* health clinic, personal/psychological counseling, women's center, legal services.

Athletics Member NCAA. All Division III. *Intercollegiate sports:* baseball M(c), basketball M/W, bowling M(c)/W(c), cheerleading W(c), cross-country running M/W, fencing M(c), football M, ice hockey M/W, lacrosse M(c)/W, rugby M(c)/W(c), skiing (cross-country) M(c)/W(c), skiing (downhill) M(c)/W(c), soccer M/W, softball W, swimming and diving M/W, tennis W, track and field M/W, volleyball M(c)/W. *Intramural sports:* basketball M, football M, racquetball M/W, softball M/W, volleyball M/W, water polo M(c)/W(c).

Standardized Tests *Required:* SAT and SAT Subject Tests or ACT (for admission). *Recommended:* SAT (for admission).

Costs (2011–12) *Tuition:* state resident $5270 full-time, $220 per credit hour part-time; nonresident $14,320 full-time, $597 per credit hour part-time. Part-time tuition and fees vary according to course load. *Required fees:* $1083 full-time, $45 per credit hour part-time. *Room and board:* $10,240; room only: $6338. Room and board charges vary according to board plan, housing facility, and student level. *Payment plan:* installment. *Waivers:* employees or children of employees.

Financial Aid Of all full-time matriculated undergraduates who enrolled in 2009, 7,805 applied for aid, 7,805 were judged to have need, 4,449 had their need fully met. In 2009, 375 non-need-based awards were made. *Average percent of need met:* 67%. *Average financial aid package:* $12,248. *Average need-based loan:* $4592. *Average need-based gift aid:* $5760. *Average non-need-based aid:* $2074. *Average indebtedness upon graduation:* $22,565. *Financial aid deadline:* 5/1.

Applying *Options:* electronic application, early admission, early decision, deferred entrance. *Application fee:* $40. *Required:* high school transcript, minimum 3.0 GPA. *Required for some:* essay or personal statement, interview. *Application deadlines:* rolling (freshmen), rolling (transfers). *Early decision deadline:* 11/15. *Notification:* continuous (freshmen), continuous (transfers), 12/15 (early decision).

Freshman Application Contact Ms. Carmella Thompson, Director of Admissions, Buffalo State College, State University of New York, 110 Moot Hall, Buffalo, NY 14222. *Phone:* 716-878-4017. *Fax:* 716-878-6100. *E-mail:* admissions@buffalostate.edu. *Web site:* http://www.buffalostate.edu/.

Canisius College

Buffalo, New York

- **Independent Roman Catholic (Jesuit)** comprehensive, founded 1870
- **Urban** 36-acre campus
- **Endowment** $88.4 million
- **Coed** 3,381 undergraduate students, 90% full-time, 49% women, 51% men
- **Moderately difficult** entrance level, 75% of applicants were admitted

Undergraduates 3,028 full-time, 353 part-time. Students come from 32 states and territories; 28 other countries; 6% are from out of state; 5% Black or African American, non-Hispanic/Latino; 2% Hispanic/Latino; 2% Asian, non-Hispanic/Latino; 0.3% American Indian or Alaska Native, non-Hispanic/Latino; 1% Two or more races, non-Hispanic/Latino; 8% Race/ethnicity unknown; 4% international; 5% transferred in; 42% live on campus. *Retention:* 84% of full-time freshmen returned.

Freshmen *Admission:* 4,348 applied, 3,258 admitted, 814 enrolled. *Average high school GPA:* 3.55. *Test scores:* SAT critical reading scores over 500: 75%; SAT math scores over 500: 80%; ACT scores over 18: 100%; SAT critical reading scores over 600: 29%; SAT math scores over 600: 33%; ACT scores over 24: 67%; SAT critical reading scores over 700: 4%; SAT math scores over 700: 3%; ACT scores over 30: 13%.

Faculty *Total:* 546, 43% full-time, 53% with terminal degrees. *Student/faculty ratio:* 11:1.

Academics *Calendar:* semesters. *Degrees:* associate, bachelor's, master's, and post-master's certificates. *Special study options:* academic remediation for entering students, adult/continuing education programs, advanced placement credit, cooperative education, distance learning, double majors, English as a second language, honors programs, independent study, internships, off-campus study, part-time degree program, services for LD students, study abroad, summer session for credit. *ROTC:* Army (b). *Unusual degree programs:* 3-2 business administration with BA/BS MBA program enables a qualified student in most majors to earn an undergraduate degree and an MBA within a five-year period; engineering with Physics Engineering with SUNY Buffalo (UB).

Computers on Campus 700 computers/terminals are available on campus for general student use. Students can access the following: computer help desk, free student e-mail accounts, online (class) grades, online (class) registration, online (class) schedules, online accounts. Campuswide network is available. 100% of college-owned or -operated housing units are wired for high-speed Internet access. Wireless service is available via entire campus.

Student Life *Housing:* on-campus residence required through sophomore year. *Options:* coed, disabled students. Campus housing is university owned. Freshman applicants given priority for college housing. *Activities and organizations:* drama/theater group, student-run newspaper, radio and television station, choral group, Campus Programming Board, Undergraduate Student Association, Afro-American Society, Residence Hall Association, Student Association, national fraternities, national sororities. *Campus security:* 24-hour emergency response devices and patrols, late-night transport/escort service, controlled dormitory access, crime prevention programs, closed-circuit television monitors, emergency call boxes across campus. *Student services:* health clinic, personal/psychological counseling.

Athletics Member NCAA. All Division I. *Intercollegiate sports:* baseball M(s), basketball M(s)/W(s), cross-country running M(s)/W(s), equestrian sports W(c), golf M(s), ice hockey M(s), lacrosse M(s)/W(s), rugby M(c)/W(c), soccer M(s)/W(s), softball W(s), swimming and diving M(s)/W(s), volleyball M(c)/W(s). *Intramural sports:* badminton M/W, basketball M/W, bowling M/W, cheerleading M(c)/W(c), crew M(c)/W(c), field hockey M/W, ice hockey M(c)/W(c), lacrosse M(c), racquetball M/W, riflery M(c)/W(c), skiing (downhill) M/W, soccer M/W, softball M(c)/W(c), tennis M/W, track and field M/W, ultimate Frisbee M/W, volleyball M/W.

Standardized Tests *Required:* SAT or ACT (for admission).

Costs (2011–12) *Comprehensive fee:* $39,672 includes full-time tuition ($29,600), mandatory fees ($1057), and room and board ($9015). Full-time tuition and fees vary according to course load and degree level. Part-time tuition: $845 per credit hour. Part-time tuition and fees vary according to course load and degree level. *Required fees:* $21 per credit hour part-time, $33 per term part-time. *College room only:* $6670. Room and board charges vary according to board plan and housing facility. *Payment plans:* installment, deferred payment. *Waivers:* employees or children of employees.

Financial Aid Of all full-time matriculated undergraduates who enrolled in 2010, 2,501 applied for aid, 2,358 were judged to have need, 551 had their need fully met. 556 Federal Work-Study jobs (averaging $1739). In 2010, 544 non-need-based awards were made. *Average percent of need met:* 81%. *Average financial aid package:* $25,536. *Average need-based loan:* $4297. *Average need-based gift aid:* $19,366. *Average non-need-based aid:* $14,220. *Average indebtedness upon graduation:* $33,918.

Applying *Options:* electronic application, early admission, deferred entrance. *Application fee:* $40. *Required:* high school transcript, minimum 2.0 GPA. *Required for some:* interview. *Recommended:* essay or personal statement, 1 letter of recommendation, interview. *Application deadlines:* 5/1 (freshmen), rolling (transfers). *Notification:* continuous (freshmen), continuous (transfers).

Freshman Application Contact Ms. Molly Strasser, Director of Admissions, Canisius College, 2001 Main Street, Buffalo, NY 14208-1098. *Phone:* 716-888-2200. *Toll-free phone:* 800-843-1517. *Fax:* 716-888-3230. *E-mail:* admissions@canisius.edu. *Web site:* http://www.canisius.edu/.

Cazenovia College

Cazenovia, New York

- **Independent** 4-year, founded 1824
- **Small-town** 40-acre campus with easy access to Syracuse
- **Endowment** $30.0 million
- **Coed**
- **Minimally difficult** entrance level

Faculty *Student/faculty ratio:* 12:1.

Academics *Calendar:* semesters. *Degrees:* certificates, associate, and bachelor's.

Student Life *Campus security:* 24-hour emergency response devices and patrols, late-night transport/escort service, controlled dormitory access.

Athletics Member NCAA. All Division III.

Standardized Tests *Recommended:* SAT or ACT (for admission).

Costs (2011–12) *Comprehensive fee:* $38,206 includes full-time tuition ($26,288), mandatory fees ($448), and room and board ($11,470). Full-time tuition and fees vary according to class time, course load, and program. Part-time tuition: $558 per credit hour. Part-time tuition and fees vary according to class time and course load. *Room and board:* Room and board charges vary according to board plan and housing facility.

Financial Aid *Of all full-time matriculated undergraduates who enrolled in 2010,* 881 applied for aid, 831 were judged to have need, 145 had their need fully met. *In 2010,* 91 non-need-based awards were made. *Average percent of need met:* 75. *Average financial aid package:* $21,982. *Average need-based loan:* $4405. *Average need-based gift aid:* $16,350. *Average non-need-based aid:* $12,359.

Applying *Options:* electronic application, deferred entrance. *Application fee:* $30. *Required:* high school transcript, 1 letter of recommendation. *Recommended:* essay or personal statement, minimum 2.0 GPA, interview, portfolio for art and design students.

Freshman Application Contact Office of Admission and Enrollment Services, Cazenovia College, 3 Sullivan Street, Cazenovia, NY 13035. *Phone:* 315-655-7208. *Toll-free phone:* 800-654-3210. *Fax:* 315-655-4860. *E-mail:* admission@cazenovia.edu. *Web site:* http://www.cazenovia.edu/.

Central Yeshiva Tomchei Tmimim-Lubavitch
Brooklyn, New York

Director of Admissions Director of Admissions, Central Yeshiva Tomchei Tmimim-Lubavitch, 841-853 Ocean Parkway, Brooklyn, NY 11230. *Phone:* 718-859-7600.

City College of the City University of New York
New York, New York

- **State and locally supported** comprehensive, founded 1847, part of City University of New York System
- **Urban** 35-acre campus with easy access to New York City
- **Coed** 13,315 undergraduate students, 74% full-time, 52% women, 48% men
- **Moderately difficult** entrance level, 32% of applicants were admitted

Undergraduates 9,867 full-time, 3,448 part-time. Students come from 130 other countries; 4% are from out of state; 21% Black or African American, non-Hispanic/Latino; 32% Hispanic/Latino; 18% Asian, non-Hispanic/Latino; 0.2% American Indian or Alaska Native, non-Hispanic/Latino; 9% international; 10% transferred in; 1% live on campus. *Retention:* 85% of full-time freshmen returned.

Freshmen *Admission:* 23,250 applied, 7,540 admitted, 1,519 enrolled. *Test scores:* SAT critical reading scores over 500: 51%; SAT math scores over 500: 80%; SAT critical reading scores over 600: 19%; SAT math scores over 600: 35%; SAT critical reading scores over 700: 5%; SAT math scores over 700: 10%.

Faculty *Total:* 1,490, 36% full-time, 38% with terminal degrees. *Student/faculty ratio:* 16:1.

Academics *Calendar:* semesters. *Degrees:* bachelor's, master's, doctoral, and post-master's certificates. *Special study options:* academic remediation for entering students, accelerated degree program, adult/continuing education programs, advanced placement credit, cooperative education, English as a second language, freshman honors college, honors programs, independent study, internships, off-campus study, part-time degree program, services for LD students, student-designed majors, study abroad, summer session for credit. *ROTC:* Army (c), Air Force (c). *Unusual degree programs:* 3-2 optometry with State University of New York Optometry.

Computers on Campus 3,000 computers/terminals are available on campus for general student use. Students can access the following: campus intranet, computer help desk, free student e-mail accounts, online (class) grades, online (class) registration, online (class) schedules. Campuswide network is available. 100% of college-owned or -operated housing units are wired for high-speed Internet access. Wireless service is available via entire campus.

Student Life *Housing options:* coed. Campus housing is provided by a third party. *Activities and organizations:* drama/theater group, student-run newspaper, radio station, choral group, LAESA-SHPE, NSBE, BSA, Salsa-Mambo, IVCF, national fraternities. *Campus security:* 24-hour patrols, late-night transport/escort service, controlled dormitory access. *Student services:* health clinic, personal/psychological counseling.

Athletics Member NCAA. All Division III. *Intercollegiate sports:* baseball M, basketball M/W, cross-country running M/W, fencing W, lacrosse M, soccer M/W, softball W, tennis M/W, track and field M/W, volleyball W. *Intramural sports:* basketball M/W, fencing W, soccer M, softball W, tennis M/W, track and field M/W, volleyball W.

Standardized Tests *Required:* SAT or ACT (for admission).

Costs (2012–13) *Tuition:* state resident $5131 full-time; nonresident $13,800 full-time. Full-time tuition and fees vary according to course load and program. Part-time tuition and fees vary according to course load and program. *Room and board:* Room and board charges vary according to housing facility. *Payment plan:* deferred payment. *Waivers:* senior citizens.

Financial Aid Of all full-time matriculated undergraduates who enrolled in 2010, 8,997 applied for aid, 8,854 were judged to have need, 7,201 had their need fully met. In 2010, 873 non-need-based awards were made. *Average percent of need met:* 83%. *Average financial aid package:* $9246. *Average need-based loan:* $4226. *Average need-based gift aid:* $7632. *Average non-need-based aid:* $2640. *Average indebtedness upon graduation:* $15,780.

Applying *Options:* early admission, deferred entrance. *Application fee:* $65. *Required:* high school transcript. *Required for some:* essay or personal state-ment, creative challenge for Architecture, supplemental application for Engineering. *Application deadlines:* 2/1 (freshmen), 2/1 (transfers). *Notification:* continuous until 2/1 (freshmen), continuous until 3/1 (transfers).

Freshman Application Contact City College of the City University of New York, 160 Convent Avenue, New York, NY 10031-9198. *Phone:* 212-650-6977. *Web site:* http://www.ccny.cuny.edu/.

Clarkson University
Potsdam, New York

- **Independent** university, founded 1896
- **Small-town** 640-acre campus
- **Endowment** $165.1 million
- **Coed** 3,018 undergraduate students, 99% full-time, 28% women, 72% men
- **Very difficult** entrance level, 77% of applicants were admitted

Undergraduates 2,997 full-time, 21 part-time. Students come from 35 states and territories; 30 other countries; 26% are from out of state; 3% Black or African American, non-Hispanic/Latino; 4% Hispanic/Latino; 3% Asian, non-Hispanic/Latino; 0.4% American Indian or Alaska Native, non-Hispanic/Latino; 2% Two or more races, non-Hispanic/Latino; 0.7% Race/ethnicity unknown; 4% international; 3% transferred in; 82% live on campus. *Retention:* 87% of full-time freshmen returned.

Freshmen *Admission:* 4,686 applied, 3,630 admitted, 851 enrolled. *Average high school GPA:* 3.53. *Test scores:* SAT critical reading scores over 500: 76%; SAT math scores over 500: 91%; SAT writing scores over 500: 70%; ACT scores over 18: 99%; SAT critical reading scores over 600: 32%; SAT math scores over 600: 54%; SAT writing scores over 600: 21%; ACT scores over 24: 68%; SAT critical reading scores over 700: 4%; SAT math scores over 700: 10%; SAT writing scores over 700: 2%; ACT scores over 30: 11%.

Faculty *Total:* 270, 79% full-time, 75% with terminal degrees. *Student/faculty ratio:* 15:1.

Academics *Calendar:* semesters. *Degrees:* bachelor's, master's, doctoral, and first professional. *Special study options:* accelerated degree program, advanced placement credit, cooperative education, distance learning, double majors, English as a second language, honors programs, independent study, off-campus study, part-time degree program, services for LD students, student-designed majors, study abroad, summer session for credit. *ROTC:* Army (b), Air Force (b). *Unusual degree programs:* 3-2 engineering.

Computers on Campus 350 computers/terminals and 10,000 ports are available on campus for general student use. Students can access the following: campus intranet, computer help desk, free student e-mail accounts, online (class) grades, online (class) registration, online (class) schedules. Campuswide network is available. 100% of college-owned or -operated housing units are wired for high-speed Internet access. Wireless service is available via classrooms, computer centers, computer labs, learning centers, libraries, student centers.

Student Life *Housing:* on-campus residence required through senior year. *Options:* coed, men-only, women-only, disabled students. Campus housing is university owned. Freshman campus housing is guaranteed. *Activities and organizations:* drama/theater group, student-run newspaper, radio and television station, choral group, Ski Club, Outing Club, Pep Band, Ultimate Frisbee Club, Sports Car Club, national fraternities, national sororities. *Campus security:* 24-hour emergency response devices and patrols, late-night transport/escort service, controlled dormitory access. *Student services:* health clinic, personal/psychological counseling, legal services.

Athletics Member NCAA. All Division III except men's and women's ice hockey (Division I). *Intercollegiate sports:* baseball M, basketball M/W, cross-country running M/W, golf M, ice hockey M(s)/W(s), lacrosse M/W, skiing (cross-country) M/W, skiing (downhill) M/W, soccer M/W, swimming and diving M/W, volleyball W. *Intramural sports:* basketball M/W, bowling M(c)/W(c), crew M(c)/W(c), football M/W, golf M(c), ice hockey M/W, lacrosse M(c)/W(c), racquetball M(c)/W(c), rugby M(c)/W(c), skiing (cross-country) M(c)/W(c), skiing (downhill) M(c)/W(c), soccer M/W, softball M/W, tennis M(c), ultimate Frisbee M(c)/W(c), volleyball M/W.

Standardized Tests *Required:* SAT or ACT (for admission). *Recommended:* SAT Subject Tests (for admission).

Costs (2012–13) *Comprehensive fee:* $51,144 includes full-time tuition ($37,770), mandatory fees ($840), and room and board ($12,534). Full-time tuition and fees vary according to course load. Part-time tuition: $1259 per credit. Part-time tuition and fees vary according to course load. *College room only:* $6640. Room and board charges vary according to board plan and housing facility. *Payment plans:* tuition prepayment, installment. *Waivers:* employees or children of employees.

Financial Aid Of all full-time matriculated undergraduates who enrolled in 2011, 2,677 applied for aid, 2,541 were judged to have need, 484 had their need fully met. 1,693 Federal Work-Study jobs (averaging $1600). 61 state and other part-time jobs (averaging $9217). In 2011, 383 non-need-based awards

were made. *Average percent of need met:* 88%. *Average financial aid package:* $34,002. *Average need-based loan:* $4486. *Average need-based gift aid:* $24,507. *Average non-need-based aid:* $14,026. *Average indebtedness upon graduation:* $32,362. *Financial aid deadline:* 3/1.

Applying *Options:* electronic application, early admission, early decision, deferred entrance. *Application fee:* $50. *Required:* essay or personal statement, high school transcript, 2 letters of recommendation, SAT or ACT. *Recommended:* interview. *Application deadline:* 1/15 (freshmen). *Early decision deadline:* 12/1. *Notification:* continuous (freshmen), continuous (transfers), 1/1 (early decision).

Freshman Application Contact Mr. Brian T. Grant, Dean of Admissions, Clarkson University, Holcroft House, CU Box 5605, Potsdam, NY 13699. *Phone:* 315-268-6480. *Toll-free phone:* 800-527-6577. *Fax:* 315-268-7647. *E-mail:* admission@clarkson.edu. *Web site:* http://www.clarkson.edu/.

See below for display ad and page 1264 for the College Close-Up.

Colgate University

Hamilton, New York

- **Independent** comprehensive, founded 1819
- **Rural** 515-acre campus with easy access to Syracuse, NY and Utica, NY
- **Endowment** $693.4 million
- **Coed** 2,947 undergraduate students, 99% full-time, 53% women, 47% men
- **Most difficult** entrance level, 29% of applicants were admitted

Undergraduates 2,926 full-time, 21 part-time. Students come from 47 states and territories; 42 other countries; 73% are from out of state; 5% Black or African American, non-Hispanic/Latino; 8% Hispanic/Latino; 3% Asian, non-Hispanic/Latino; 0.2% Native Hawaiian or other Pacific Islander, non-Hispanic/Latino; 0.4% American Indian or Alaska Native, non-Hispanic/Latino; 3% Two or more races, non-Hispanic/Latino; 4% Race/ethnicity unknown; 7% international; 0.1% transferred in; 91% live on campus. *Retention:* 95% of full-time freshmen returned.

Freshmen *Admission:* 7,835 applied, 2,305 admitted, 764 enrolled. *Average high school GPA:* 3.64. *Test scores:* SAT critical reading scores over 500: 99%; SAT math scores over 500: 99%; SAT writing scores over 500: 98%; ACT scores over 18: 100%; SAT critical reading scores over 600: 82%; SAT math scores over 600: 88%; SAT writing scores over 600: 84%; ACT scores over 24: 96%; SAT critical reading scores over 700: 39%; SAT math scores over 700: 42%; SAT writing scores over 700: 40%; ACT scores over 30: 77%.

Faculty *Total:* 343, 84% full-time, 93% with terminal degrees. *Student/faculty ratio:* 9:1.

Academics *Calendar:* semesters. *Degrees:* bachelor's and master's. *Special study options:* advanced placement credit, double majors, honors programs, independent study, internships, off-campus study, services for LD students, student-designed majors, study abroad. *ROTC:* Army (c). *Unusual degree programs:* 3-2 engineering with Rensselaer Polytechnic Institute, Columbia University, Washington University in St. Louis.

Computers on Campus Students can access the following: campus intranet, computer help desk, free student e-mail accounts, online (class) registration, online (class) schedules, software applications. Campuswide network is available. 100% of college-owned or -operated housing units are wired for high-speed Internet access. Wireless service is available via entire campus.

Student Life *Housing:* on-campus residence required through junior year. *Options:* coed, men-only, women-only, cooperative. Campus housing is university owned. Freshman campus housing is guaranteed. *Activities and organizations:* drama/theater group, student-run newspaper, radio and television station, choral group, COVE, student government, cultural/ethnic interest groups, student publications, Outdoor Education, national fraternities, national sororities. *Campus security:* 24-hour emergency response devices and patrols, student patrols, late-night transport/escort service, controlled dormitory access. *Student services:* health clinic, personal/psychological counseling, women's center, legal services.

Athletics Member NCAA. All Division I except football (Division I-AA). *Intercollegiate sports:* baseball M(c), basketball M(s)/W(s), cheerleading M(c)/W(c), crew M/W, cross-country running M/W, equestrian sports M(c)/W(c), fencing M(c)/W(c), field hockey W(s), golf M/W(c), ice hockey M(s)/W(s), lacrosse M(s)/W(s), rugby M(c)/W(c), sailing M(c)/W(c), skiing (downhill) M(c)/W(c), soccer M(s)/W(s), softball W(s), squash M(c)/W(c), swimming and diving M/W, table tennis M(c)/W(c), tennis M/W, track and field M/W, volleyball M(c)/W(s), water polo M(c)/W(c), wrestling M(c)/W(c). *Intramural sports:* basketball M/W, bowling M/W, football M/W, golf M/W, ice hockey M/W, racquetball M/W, riflery M/W, soccer M/W, softball M/W, squash M/W, tennis M/W, ultimate Frisbee M/W, volleyball M/W.

Standardized Tests *Required:* SAT or ACT (for admission). *Recommended:* SAT and SAT Subject Tests or ACT (for admission).

Costs (2011–12) *One-time required fee:* $50. *Comprehensive fee:* $53,570 includes full-time tuition ($42,625), mandatory fees ($295), and room and board ($10,650). Full-time tuition and fees vary according to course load. Part-time tuition: $5328 per course. Part-time tuition and fees vary according to course load. *College room only:* $5140. Room and board charges vary accord-

ing to board plan and housing facility. *Payment plans:* tuition prepayment, installment, deferred payment. *Waivers:* employees or children of employees.
Financial Aid Of all full-time matriculated undergraduates who enrolled in 2011, 1,176 applied for aid, 1,047 were judged to have need, 1,047 had their need fully met. 524 Federal Work-Study jobs (averaging $2078). 334 state and other part-time jobs (averaging $1947). *Average percent of need met:* 100%. *Average financial aid package:* $40,866. *Average need-based loan:* $4025. *Average need-based gift aid:* $36,192. *Average indebtedness upon graduation:* $19,721. *Financial aid deadline:* 1/15.
Applying *Options:* electronic application, early decision, deferred entrance. *Application fee:* $60. *Required:* essay or personal statement, high school transcript, 3 letters of recommendation. *Application deadlines:* 1/15 (freshmen), 1/15 (out-of-state freshmen), 3/15 (transfers). *Early decision deadline:* 11/15 (for plan 1), 1/15 (for plan 2). *Notification:* 4/1 (freshmen), 5/1 (transfers), 12/15 (early decision plan 1), rolling (early decision plan 2).
Freshman Application Contact Mr. Gary L. Ross, Dean of Admission, Colgate University, Colgate Office of Admission, 13 Oak Drive, Hamilton, NY 13346-1383. *Phone:* 315-228-7401. *Fax:* 315-228-7544. *E-mail:* admission@colgate.edu. *Web site:* http://www.colgate.edu/.

The College at Brockport, State University of New York

Brockport, New York

- **State-supported** comprehensive, founded 1867, part of State University of New York System
- **Small-town** 454-acre campus with easy access to Rochester
- **Coed** 7,167 undergraduate students, 90% full-time, 55% women, 45% men
- **Moderately difficult** entrance level, 46% of applicants were admitted

Undergraduates 6,454 full-time, 713 part-time. 1% are from out of state; 7% Black or African American, non-Hispanic/Latino; 4% Hispanic/Latino; 2% Asian, non-Hispanic/Latino; 0.2% Native Hawaiian or other Pacific Islander, non-Hispanic/Latino; 0.6% American Indian or Alaska Native, non-Hispanic/Latino; 6% Race/ethnicity unknown; 13% transferred in; 37% live on campus. *Retention:* 84% of full-time freshmen returned.
Freshmen *Admission:* 8,575 applied, 3,956 admitted, 1,050 enrolled. *Average high school GPA:* 3.5. *Test scores:* SAT critical reading scores over 500: 65%; SAT math scores over 500: 75%; SAT writing scores over 500: 54%; SAT critical reading scores over 600: 15%; SAT math scores over 600: 19%; SAT writing scores over 600: 10%; SAT critical reading scores over 700: 1%; SAT math scores over 700: 1%; SAT writing scores over 700: 1%.
Faculty *Total:* 595, 56% full-time, 59% with terminal degrees. *Student/faculty ratio:* 17:1.
Academics *Calendar:* semesters. *Degrees:* bachelor's, master's, and post-master's certificates. *Special study options:* academic remediation for entering students, accelerated degree program, advanced placement credit, cooperative education, distance learning, double majors, freshman honors college, honors programs, independent study, internships, off-campus study, part-time degree program, services for LD students, student-designed majors, study abroad, summer session for credit. *ROTC:* Army (b), Navy (c), Air Force (c).
Computers on Campus Students can access the following: campus intranet, computer help desk, free student e-mail accounts, online (class) registration, online (class) schedules. Campuswide network is available. 100% of college-owned or -operated housing units are wired for high-speed Internet access. Wireless service is available via entire campus.
Student Life *Housing:* on-campus residence required through sophomore year. *Options:* coed, disabled students. Campus housing is university owned. Freshman campus housing is guaranteed. *Activities and organizations:* drama/theater group, student-run newspaper, radio and television station, choral group, fine arts clubs, Organization for Students of African Descent, Communication Club, student radio station, sports clubs, national fraternities, national sororities. *Campus security:* 24-hour emergency response devices and patrols, student patrols, late-night transport/escort service, controlled dormitory access. *Student services:* health clinic, personal/psychological counseling, women's center, legal services.
Athletics Member NCAA. All Division III. *Intercollegiate sports:* baseball M, basketball M/W, cross-country running M/W, field hockey W, football M, gymnastics W, ice hockey M, lacrosse M/W, soccer M/W, softball W, swimming and diving M/W, tennis W, track and field M/W, volleyball W, wrestling M. *Intramural sports:* badminton M/W, basketball M/W, bowling M/W, cheerleading M/W, football M/W, golf M(c), ice hockey W(c), racquetball M/W, rugby M/W, soccer M/W, softball M/W, table tennis M/W, tennis M/W, ultimate Frisbee M/W, volleyball M/W.
Standardized Tests *Required:* SAT or ACT (for admission).
Costs (2011–12) *Tuition:* state resident $5270 full-time; nonresident $14,320 full-time. Part-time tuition and fees vary according to course load. *Required fees:* $1238 full-time. *Room and board:* $10,320. Room and board charges

vary according to board plan and housing facility. *Payment plans:* installment, deferred payment. *Waivers:* senior citizens and employees or children of employees.
Financial Aid Of all full-time matriculated undergraduates who enrolled in 2011, 4,807 applied for aid, 4,000 were judged to have need, 535 had their need fully met. 523 Federal Work-Study jobs (averaging $2037). 1,692 state and other part-time jobs (averaging $1258). In 2011, 133 non-need-based awards were made. *Average percent of need met:* 68%. *Average financial aid package:* $9385. *Average need-based loan:* $4745. *Average need-based gift aid:* $5151. *Average non-need-based aid:* $4090. *Average indebtedness upon graduation:* $26,785.
Applying *Options:* electronic application, deferred entrance. *Application fee:* $50. *Required:* essay or personal statement, high school transcript, 1 letter of recommendation, SAT or ACT. *Required for some:* interview. *Recommended:* minimum 3.1 GPA. *Application deadlines:* rolling (freshmen), 8/1 (transfers). *Notification:* continuous (freshmen), continuous (transfers).
Freshman Application Contact The College at Brockport, State University of New York, 350 New Campus Drive, Brockport, NY 14420-2997. *Phone:* 585-395-2751. *Web site:* http://www.brockport.edu/.

College of Mount Saint Vincent

Riverdale, New York

- **Independent** comprehensive, founded 1911
- **Suburban** 70-acre campus with easy access to New York City
- **Coed** 1,655 undergraduate students, 84% full-time, 73% women, 27% men
- **Moderately difficult** entrance level, 67% of applicants were admitted

Undergraduates 1,394 full-time, 261 part-time. Students come from 22 states and territories; 6 other countries; 10% are from out of state; 15% Black or African American, non-Hispanic/Latino; 32% Hispanic/Latino; 3% Asian, non-Hispanic/Latino; 6% Native Hawaiian or other Pacific Islander, non-Hispanic/Latino; 0.2% American Indian or Alaska Native, non-Hispanic/Latino; 5% Two or more races, non-Hispanic/Latino; 8% Race/ethnicity unknown; 0.7% international; 6% transferred in; 44% live on campus. *Retention:* 74% of full-time freshmen returned.
Freshmen *Admission:* 3,184 applied, 2,120 admitted, 438 enrolled. *Average high school GPA:* 2.9. *Test scores:* SAT critical reading scores over 500: 33%; SAT math scores over 500: 32%; SAT writing scores over 500: 33%; ACT scores over 18: 87%; SAT critical reading scores over 600: 4%; SAT math scores over 600: 5%; SAT writing scores over 600: 4%; ACT scores over 24: 27%; SAT critical reading scores over 700: 1%; SAT writing scores over 700: 1%.
Faculty *Total:* 213, 36% full-time. *Student/faculty ratio:* 13:1.
Academics *Calendar:* semesters. *Degrees:* bachelor's, master's, and post-master's certificates. *Special study options:* academic remediation for entering students, accelerated degree program, adult/continuing education programs, advanced placement credit, double majors, honors programs, independent study, internships, part-time degree program, services for LD students, study abroad, summer session for credit. *ROTC:* Air Force (c). *Unusual degree programs:* 3-2 occupational therapy with Columbia University, physical therapy with New York Medical College.
Computers on Campus 249 computers/terminals and 1,355 ports are available on campus for general student use. Students can access the following: campus intranet, computer help desk, free student e-mail accounts, online (class) grades, online (class) registration, online (class) schedules. Campuswide network is available. 100% of college-owned or -operated housing units are wired for high-speed Internet access. Wireless service is available via classrooms, computer centers, computer labs, dorm rooms, libraries, student centers.
Student Life *Housing options:* coed, disabled students. Campus housing is university owned. Freshman campus housing is guaranteed. *Activities and organizations:* drama/theater group, student-run newspaper, radio and television station, choral group, Casa Latina, Players, Dance Club, Student Nurse Association. *Campus security:* 24-hour emergency response devices and patrols, late-night transport/escort service, controlled dormitory access, emergency call boxes. *Student services:* health clinic, personal/psychological counseling.
Athletics Member NCAA. All Division III. *Intercollegiate sports:* baseball M, basketball M/W, cheerleading W, cross-country running M/W, lacrosse M/W, soccer M/W, softball W, swimming and diving M/W, tennis M/W, track and field M/W, volleyball M/W. *Intramural sports:* basketball M.
Standardized Tests *Required:* SAT or ACT (for admission).
Costs (2011–12) *Comprehensive fee:* $38,610 includes full-time tuition ($26,500), mandatory fees ($1310), and room and board ($10,800). Part-time tuition: $760 per credit. *Required fees:* $250 per term part-time. *Room and board:* Room and board charges vary according to housing facility. *Payment plan:* installment. *Waivers:* employees or children of employees.

Financial Aid Of all full-time matriculated undergraduates who enrolled in 2004, 1,019 applied for aid, 881 were judged to have need. *Average percent of need met:* 74%. *Average financial aid package:* $17,000. *Average need-based loan:* $4100. *Average need-based gift aid:* $7500. *Average indebtedness upon graduation:* $17,000.

Applying *Options:* electronic application, early admission, early action, deferred entrance. *Application fee:* $35. *Required:* essay or personal statement, high school transcript, minimum 2.0 GPA. *Required for some:* interview. *Recommended:* 2 letters of recommendation, interview. *Application deadlines:* rolling (freshmen), rolling (transfers), 11/15 (early action). *Notification:* continuous (freshmen), continuous (transfers), 12/1 (early action).

Freshman Application Contact Ms. Brenda Nelson, Associate Director of Admissions, College of Mount Saint Vincent, 6301 Riverdale Avenue, Riverdale, NY 10471-1093. *Phone:* 718-405-3223. *Toll-free phone:* 800-665-CMSV. *Fax:* 718-549-7945. *E-mail:* brenda.nelson@mountsaintvincent.edu. *Web site:* http://www.mountsaintvincent.edu/.

The College of New Rochelle

New Rochelle, New York

Freshman Application Contact Ms. Bridget Kennedy, Assistant Director, Enrollment Management, The College of New Rochelle, 29 Castle Place, New Rochelle, NY 10805-2339. *Phone:* 914-654-5452. *Toll-free phone:* 800-933-5923. *Fax:* 914-654-5464. *E-mail:* admission@cnr.edu. *Web site:* http://www.cnr.edu/.

See below for display ad and page 1272 for the College Close-Up.

The College of Saint Rose

Albany, New York

- **Independent** comprehensive, founded 1920
- **Urban** 46-acre campus
- **Endowment** $31.7 million
- **Coed** 2,931 undergraduate students, 94% full-time, 68% women, 32% men
- **Moderately difficult** entrance level, 60% of applicants were admitted

Undergraduates 2,757 full-time, 174 part-time. Students come from 24 states and territories; 27 other countries; 8% are from out of state; 6% Black or African American, non-Hispanic/Latino; 5% Hispanic/Latino; 2% Asian, non-His-

panic/Latino; 0.1% Native Hawaiian or other Pacific Islander, non-Hispanic/Latino; 0.4% American Indian or Alaska Native, non-Hispanic/Latino; 3% Two or more races, non-Hispanic/Latino; 6% Race/ethnicity unknown; 1% international; 9% transferred in; 42% live on campus. *Retention:* 78% of full-time freshmen returned.

Freshmen *Admission:* 5,198 applied, 3,143 admitted, 595 enrolled. *Average high school GPA:* 3.4. *Test scores:* SAT critical reading scores over 500: 63%; SAT math scores over 500: 64%; ACT scores over 18: 97%; SAT critical reading scores over 600: 17%; SAT math scores over 600: 17%; ACT scores over 24: 37%; SAT critical reading scores over 700: 2%; SAT math scores over 700: 1%; ACT scores over 30: 4%.

Faculty *Student/faculty ratio:* 14:1.

Academics *Calendar:* semesters. *Degrees:* certificates, bachelor's, master's, post-master's, and postbachelor's certificates. *Special study options:* academic remediation for entering students, accelerated degree program, advanced placement credit, double majors, external degree program, independent study, internships, off-campus study, part-time degree program, services for LD students, student-designed majors, study abroad, summer session for credit. *ROTC:* Army (c), Navy (c), Air Force (c). *Unusual degree programs:* 3-2 engineering with Alfred University, Clarkson University, Union College (NY), Rensselaer Polytechnic Institute.

Computers on Campus 665 computers/terminals and 3,968 ports are available on campus for general student use. Students can access the following: computer help desk, free student e-mail accounts, online (class) grades, online (class) registration, online (class) schedules. Campuswide network is available. 100% of college-owned or -operated housing units are wired for high-speed Internet access. Wireless service is available via entire campus.

Student Life *Housing options:* coed, men-only, women-only. Campus housing is university owned and leased by the school. Freshman applicants given priority for college housing. *Activities and organizations:* drama/theater group, student-run newspaper, radio and television station, choral group, Student Association, Student Events Board, Spectrum-ALANA Student Union, Environmental Club, Music & Entertainment Industry Student Association. *Campus security:* 24-hour emergency response devices and patrols, late-night transport/escort service, controlled dormitory access. *Student services:* health clinic, personal/psychological counseling.

Athletics Member NCAA. All Division II. *Intercollegiate sports:* baseball M(s), basketball M(s)/W(s), cross-country running M/W, golf M, lacrosse M(s), soccer M(s)/W(s), softball W(s), swimming and diving M(s)/W(s), tennis W, track and field M(s)/W(s), volleyball W(s). *Intramural sports:* basket-

ball M/W, cheerleading M(c)/W(c), soccer M/W, softball M/W, ultimate Frisbee M/W, volleyball M/W.

Standardized Tests *Required:* SAT or ACT (for admission).

Costs (2012–13) *Comprehensive fee:* $37,606 includes full-time tuition ($25,722), mandatory fees ($900), and room and board ($10,984). Full-time tuition and fees vary according to class time and course load. Part-time tuition: $856 per credit hour. Part-time tuition and fees vary according to class time and course load. *Required fees:* $26 part-time, $75 part-time. *College room only:* $5440. Room and board charges vary according to board plan and housing facility. *Payment plan:* installment. *Waivers:* employees or children of employees.

Financial Aid Of all full-time matriculated undergraduates who enrolled in 2010, 2,602 applied for aid, 2,561 were judged to have need, 39 had their need fully met. In 2010, 204 non-need-based awards were made. *Average percent of need met:* 38%. *Average financial aid package:* $11,935. *Average need-based gift aid:* $8068. *Average non-need-based aid:* $11,552.

Applying *Options:* electronic application, early admission, early action, deferred entrance. *Application fee:* $40. *Required:* essay or personal statement, high school transcript, 1 letter of recommendation. *Required for some:* interview. *Recommended:* minimum 3.0 GPA. *Application deadlines:* 5/1 (freshmen), 5/1 (transfers), 12/1 (early action). *Notification:* continuous (freshmen), continuous (transfers), 12/15 (early action).

Freshman Application Contact Mr. Jeremy Bogan, Assistant Vice President of Undergraduate Admissions, The College of Saint Rose, 1001 Madison Avenue, Albany, NY 12203. *Phone:* 518-454-5154. *Toll-free phone:* 800-637-8556. *Fax:* 518-454-2013. *E-mail:* admit@strose.edu. *Web site:* http://www.strose.edu/.

See below for display ad and page 1274 for the College Close-Up.

College of Staten Island of the City University of New York

Staten Island, New York

- **State and locally supported** comprehensive, founded 1955, part of City University of New York
- **Urban** 204-acre campus with easy access to New York City
- **Coed** 13,156 undergraduate students, 73% full-time, 57% women, 43% men
- **Moderately difficult** entrance level, 100% of applicants were admitted

Undergraduates 9,639 full-time, 3,517 part-time. 1% are from out of state; 8% Black or African American, non-Hispanic/Latino; 14% Hispanic/Latino; 9% Asian, non-Hispanic/Latino; 0.2% Native Hawaiian or other Pacific Islander, non-Hispanic/Latino; 0.2% American Indian or Alaska Native, non-Hispanic/Latino; 0.7% Two or more races, non-Hispanic/Latino; 25% Race/ethnicity unknown; 3% international; 6% transferred in. *Retention:* 83% of full-time freshmen returned.

Freshmen *Admission:* 10,985 applied, 10,985 admitted, 2,459 enrolled. *Average high school GPA:* 2.98. *Test scores:* SAT critical reading scores over 500: 43%; SAT math scores over 500: 60%; SAT writing scores over 500: 44%; SAT critical reading scores over 600: 12%; SAT math scores over 600: 15%; SAT writing scores over 600: 10%; SAT critical reading scores over 700: 2%; SAT math scores over 700: 2%; SAT writing scores over 700: 1%.

Faculty *Total:* 1,256, 27% full-time, 50% with terminal degrees. *Student/faculty ratio:* 18:1.

Academics *Calendar:* semesters. *Degrees:* certificates, associate, bachelor's, master's, doctoral, post-master's, and first professional certificates. *Special study options:* academic remediation for entering students, accelerated degree program, adult/continuing education programs, advanced placement credit, cooperative education, distance learning, double majors, English as a second language, freshman honors college, honors programs, independent study, internships, off-campus study, part-time degree program, services for LD students, student-designed majors, study abroad, summer session for credit.

Computers on Campus Students can access the following: campus intranet, computer help desk, free student e-mail accounts, online (class) grades, online (class) registration, online (class) schedules. Campuswide network is available.

100% of college-owned or -operated housing units are wired for high-speed Internet access. Wireless service is available via entire campus.

Student Life *Campus security:* 24-hour emergency response devices and patrols, late-night transport/escort service, emergency call boxes, blue light system, bicycle patrols, radar-controlled traffic monitoring, lighted pathways.

Athletics Member NCAA. All Division III. *Intercollegiate sports:* baseball M, basketball M/W, cheerleading M(c)/W(c), cross-country running M/W, soccer M/W, softball W, swimming and diving M/W, tennis M/W, track and field M(c)/W(c), volleyball W. *Intramural sports:* basketball M/W, racquetball M/W, tennis M/W, volleyball M/W.

Standardized Tests *Required:* SAT or ACT (for admission).

Costs (2011–12) *Tuition:* state resident $5130 full-time, $215 per credit part-time; nonresident $13,800 full-time, $460 per credit part-time. *Required fees:* $428 full-time, $128 per term part-time. *Payment plan:* installment.

Financial Aid Of all full-time matriculated undergraduates who enrolled in 2011, 5,393 applied for aid, 4,507 were judged to have need, 126 had their need fully met. 348 Federal Work-Study jobs (averaging $1417). In 2011, 266 non-need-based awards were made. *Average percent of need met:* 55%. *Average financial aid package:* $7204. *Average need-based loan:* $4900. *Average need-based gift aid:* $6341. *Average non-need-based aid:* $1560.

Applying *Options:* electronic application, deferred entrance. *Application fee:* $65. *Required:* high school transcript, minimum 2.0 GPA. *Required for some:* essay or personal statement, interview. *Application deadlines:* 2/1 (freshmen), 2/1 (out-of-state freshmen), rolling (transfers). *Notification:* continuous (freshmen), continuous (transfers).

Freshman Application Contact Mr. Emmanuel Esperance Jr., Director of Recruitment and Admissions, College of Staten Island of the City University of New York, 2800 Victory Boulevard, Building 2A Room 103, Staten Island, NY 10314. *Phone:* 718-982-2010. *Fax:* 718-982-2500. *E-mail:* admissions@cuny.csi.edu. *Web site:* http://www.csi.cuny.edu/.

See page 574 for display ad and page 1276 for the College Close-Up.

Columbia University

New York, New York

Freshman Application Contact Columbia University, 116th Street and Broadway, New York, NY 10027. *Phone:* 212-854-1222. *Web site:* http://www.columbia.edu/.

See page 1282 for the College Close-Up.

Columbia University, School of General Studies

New York, New York

- **Independent** 4-year, founded 1754, part of Columbia University
- **Urban** 36-acre campus
- **Endowment** $6.5 billion
- **Coed** 1,499 undergraduate students, 62% full-time, 45% women, 55% men
- **Most difficult** entrance level, 35% of applicants were admitted

Undergraduates 929 full-time, 570 part-time. Students come from 82 other countries; 43% are from out of state; 5% Black or African American, non-Hispanic/Latino; 8% Hispanic/Latino; 6% Asian, non-Hispanic/Latino; 0.9% American Indian or Alaska Native, non-Hispanic/Latino; 28% Race/ethnicity unknown; 15% international; 718% transferred in; 32% live on campus.

Freshmen *Admission:* 321 applied, 113 admitted, 55 enrolled.

Faculty *Total:* 1,823, 79% full-time. *Student/faculty ratio:* 6:1.

Academics *Calendar:* semesters. *Degrees:* bachelor's and postbachelor's certificates. *Special study options:* adult/continuing education programs, advanced placement credit, double majors, external degree program, independent study, internships, off-campus study, part-time degree program, services for LD students, student-designed majors, study abroad, summer session for credit. *ROTC:* Army (c), Navy (b), Air Force (c). *Unusual degree programs:* 3-2 business administration with Columbia University, Graduate School of Business; engineering with Columbia University, School of Engineering and Applied Science; social work with Columbia University School of Social Work; international affairs, public policy and administration with Columbia University, School of International and Public Affairs; public health with Columbia University, School of Public Health.

Computers on Campus 768 computers/terminals are available on campus for general student use. Students can access the following: campus intranet, computer help desk, free student e-mail accounts, online (class) grades, online (class) registration, online (class) schedules. Campuswide network is available. 100% of college-owned or -operated housing units are wired for high-speed Internet access. Wireless service is available via entire campus.

Student Life *Housing options:* coed, cooperative. Campus housing is university owned, leased by the school and is provided by a third party. *Activities and organizations:* drama/theater group, student-run newspaper, radio and television station, choral group, marching band, Columbia Dramatists, writers

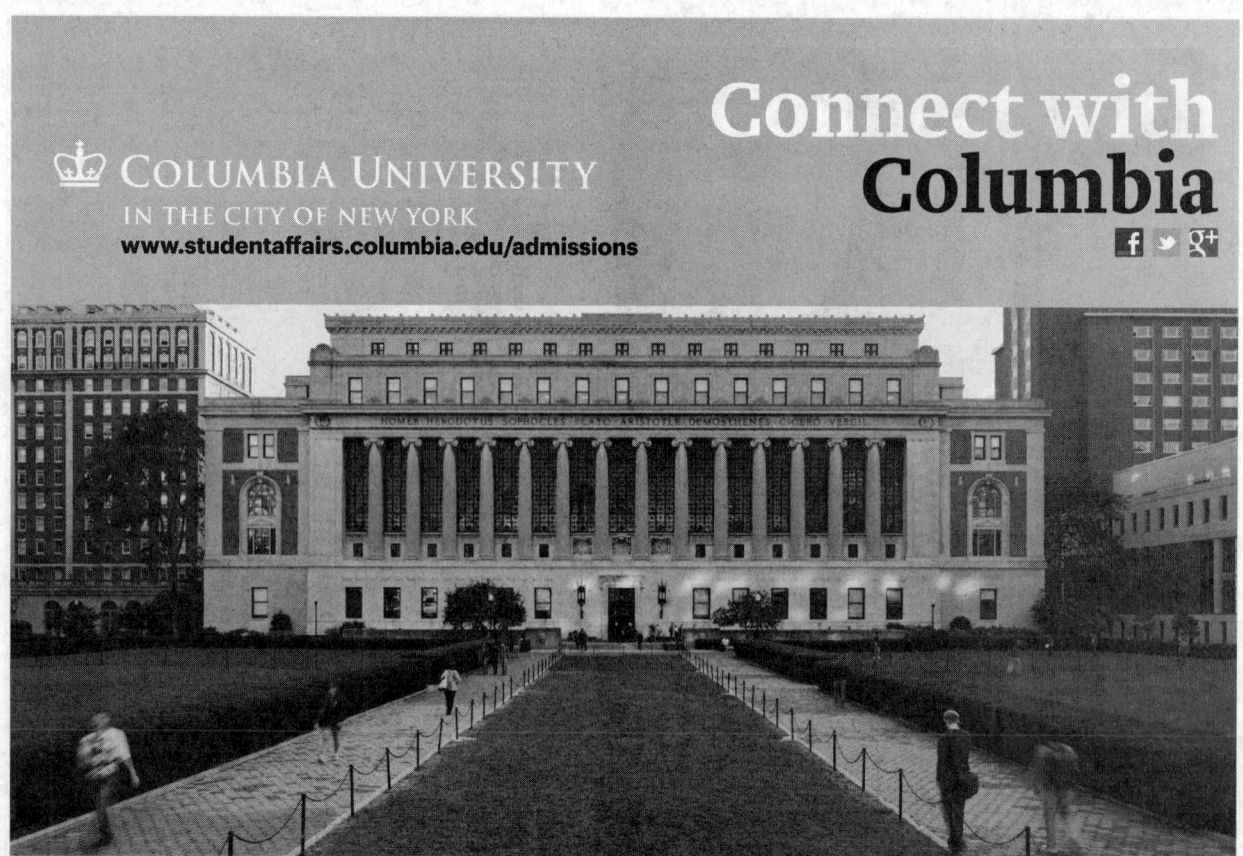

club, General Studies Student Council, The Observer, national fraternities, national sororities. *Campus security:* 24-hour emergency response devices and patrols, late-night transport/escort service. *Student services:* health clinic, personal/psychological counseling, women's center.

Athletics Member NCAA. All Division I except football (Division I-AA). *Intercollegiate sports:* archery W, badminton M(c)/W(c), baseball M, basketball M/W, crew M/W, cross-country running M/W, equestrian sports W(c), fencing M/W, field hockey W(c), golf M, gymnastics W, ice hockey M(c)/W(c), lacrosse M(c), racquetball M(c)/W(c), rugby M(c)/W(c), sailing M(c)/W(c), skiing (downhill) M(c)/W(c), soccer M/W, squash M(c)/W(c), swimming and diving M/W, table tennis M(c)/W(c), tennis M/W, track and field M/W, volleyball W, water polo M(c)/W(c), wrestling M. *Intramural sports:* football M/W, soccer M/W, volleyball M/W.

Standardized Tests *Required:* SAT or ACT (for admission).

Costs (2011–12) *Comprehensive fee:* $54,083 includes full-time tuition ($41,760), mandatory fees ($2198), and room and board ($10,125). Full-time tuition and fees vary according to course load, program, and student level. Part-time tuition: $1392 per credit hour. Part-time tuition and fees vary according to course load, program, and student level. *College room only:* $5850. Room and board charges vary according to board plan and housing facility. *Payment plans:* tuition prepayment, installment. *Waivers:* employees or children of employees.

Financial Aid *Financial aid deadline:* 6/1.

Applying *Options:* electronic application, early action, deferred entrance. *Application fee:* $75. *Required:* essay or personal statement, high school transcript, 2 letters of recommendation. *Required for some:* interview. *Application deadlines:* 6/1 (freshmen), 6/1 (transfers), 3/1 (early action). *Notification:* continuous (freshmen), continuous (transfers), 5/1 (early action).

Freshman Application Contact Mr. Curtis M. Rodgers, Dean of Enrollment Management, Columbia University, School of General Studies, 2970 Broadway, 408 Lewisohn Hall, MC 4101, New York, NY 10027. *Phone:* 212-854-2772. *Toll-free phone:* 800-895-1169. *Fax:* 212-854-6316. *E-mail:* gsdegree@columbia.edu. *Web site:* http://www.gs.columbia.edu/.

See below for display ad and page 1284 for the College Close-Up.

Concordia College–New York

Bronxville, New York

- **Independent Lutheran** comprehensive, founded 1881, part of Concordia University System
- **Suburban** 33-acre campus with easy access to New York City
- **Endowment** $6.4 million
- **Coed** 715 undergraduate students, 82% full-time, 65% women, 35% men
- **Moderately difficult** entrance level, 69% of applicants were admitted

Undergraduates 587 full-time, 128 part-time. Students come from 46 states and territories; 35 other countries; 29% are from out of state; 16% Black or African American, non-Hispanic/Latino; 16% Hispanic/Latino; 1% Asian, non-Hispanic/Latino; 0.4% Native Hawaiian or other Pacific Islander, non-Hispanic/Latino; 1% American Indian or Alaska Native, non-Hispanic/Latino; 3% Two or more races, non-Hispanic/Latino; 5% Race/ethnicity unknown; 11% international; 6% transferred in; 68% live on campus. *Retention:* 73% of full-time freshmen returned.

Freshmen *Admission:* 1,010 applied, 700 admitted, 138 enrolled. *Average high school GPA:* 2.86. *Test scores:* SAT critical reading scores over 500: 36%; SAT math scores over 500: 40%; SAT writing scores over 500: 35%; ACT scores over 18: 66%; SAT critical reading scores over 600: 8%; SAT math scores over 600: 9%; SAT writing scores over 600: 6%; ACT scores over 24: 21%; SAT critical reading scores over 700: 1%; SAT math scores over 700: 1%; ACT scores over 30: 3%.

Faculty *Total:* 77, 43% full-time, 79% with terminal degrees. *Student/faculty ratio:* 12:1.

Academics *Calendar:* semesters. *Degrees:* associate, bachelor's, and master's. *Special study options:* academic remediation for entering students, accelerated degree program, adult/continuing education programs, advanced placement credit, distance learning, double majors, English as a second language, honors programs, independent study, internships, off-campus study, part-time degree program, services for LD students, student-designed majors, study abroad. *ROTC:* Army (c), Air Force (c).

Computers on Campus 50 computers/terminals are available on campus for general student use. Students can access the following: campus intranet, computer help desk, free student e-mail accounts, online (class) grades, online (class) registration, online (class) schedules. Campuswide network is available. Wireless service is available via entire campus.

Student Life *Housing:* on-campus residence required for freshman year. *Options:* men-only, women-only. Campus housing is university owned. Fresh-

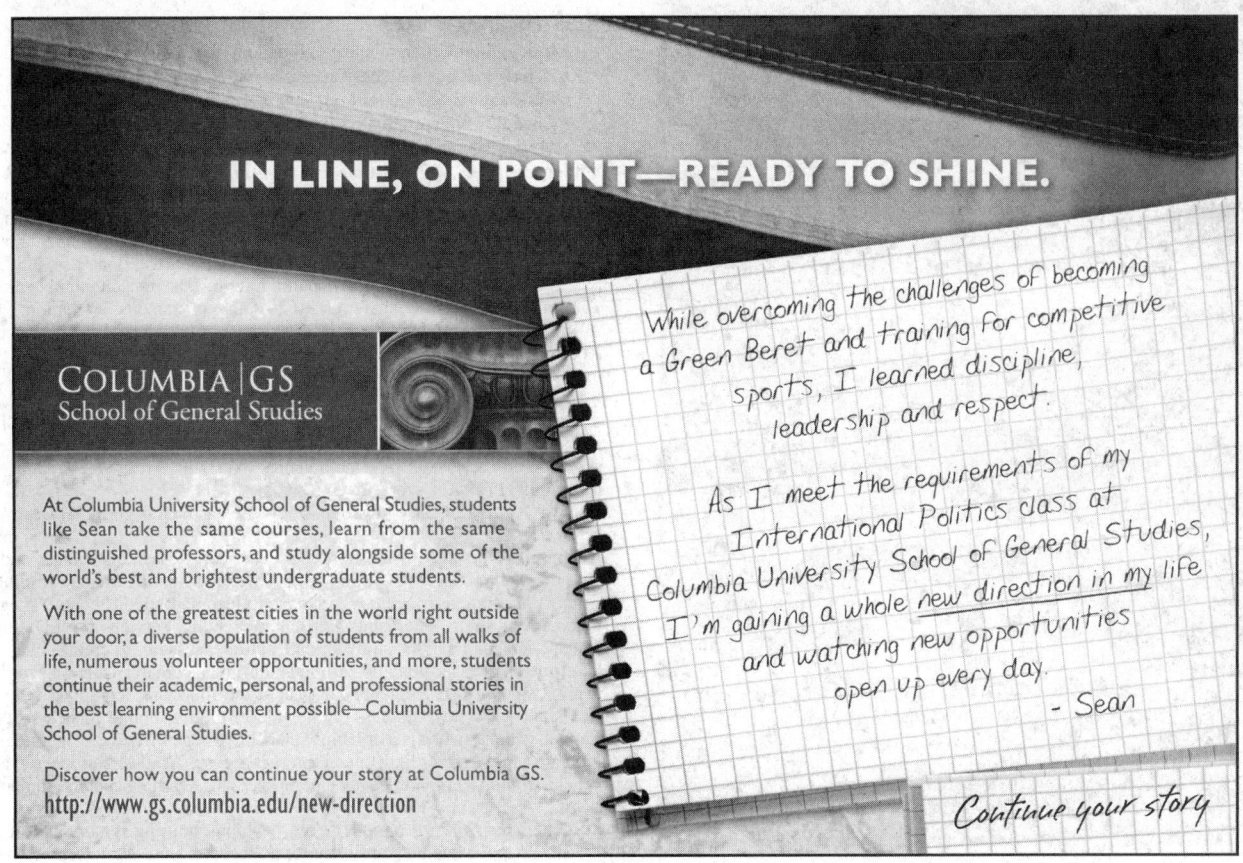

man campus housing is guaranteed. *Activities and organizations:* drama/theater group, student-run newspaper, choral group, Campus Christian Ministries, Drama Club, Student Government Association, International and Afro/Latin American Club, Yearbook and newspaper. *Campus security:* 24-hour emergency response devices and patrols, late-night transport/escort service, controlled dormitory access. *Student services:* health clinic, personal/psychological counseling.

Athletics Member NCAA. All Division II. *Intercollegiate sports:* baseball M(s), basketball M(s)/W(s), cross-country running M(s)/W(s), golf M, soccer M(s)/W(s), softball W(s), tennis M(s)/W(s), volleyball W(s). *Intramural sports:* basketball M/W, cheerleading W, football M/W, racquetball M/W, softball M/W, squash M/W, tennis M/W, ultimate Frisbee M/W, volleyball W.

Standardized Tests *Required:* SAT or ACT (for admission).

Costs (2012–13) *Comprehensive fee:* $37,200 includes full-time tuition ($26,500), mandatory fees ($950), and room and board ($9750). Full-time tuition and fees vary according to course load and program. Part-time tuition and fees vary according to course load and program. *Room and board:* Room and board charges vary according to board plan. *Payment plan:* installment. *Waivers:* senior citizens and employees or children of employees.

Financial Aid Of all full-time matriculated undergraduates who enrolled in 2008, 533 applied for aid, 448 were judged to have need, 89 had their need fully met. In 2008, 100 non-need-based awards were made. *Average percent of need met:* 71%. *Average financial aid package:* $22,309. *Average need-based loan:* $4133. *Average need-based gift aid:* $11,129. *Average non-need-based aid:* $6170. *Average indebtedness upon graduation:* $24,153.

Applying *Options:* electronic application, early admission, early action, deferred entrance. *Application fee:* $50. *Required:* essay or personal statement, high school transcript, 1 letter of recommendation, Common Application Supplement. *Required for some:* interview. *Recommended:* minimum 2.7 GPA. *Application deadlines:* 3/15 (freshmen), 7/15 (transfers), 11/15 (early action). *Notification:* continuous until 4/15 (freshmen), continuous until 8/15 (transfers), 12/1 (early action).

Freshman Application Contact Mr. Robert Piurowski, Director of Admission, Concordia College–New York, 171 White Plains Rd, Bronxville, NY 10708. *Phone:* 914-337-9300 Ext. 2155. *Toll-free phone:* 800-YES-COLLEGE. *Fax:* 914-395-4636. *E-mail:* admission@concordia-ny.edu. *Web site:* http://www.concordia-ny.edu/.

Cooper Union for the Advancement of Science and Art

New York, New York

- **Independent** comprehensive, founded 1859
- **Urban** campus with easy access to New York City
- **Endowment** $579.2 million
- **Coed** 927 undergraduate students, 97% full-time, 38% women, 62% men
- **Most difficult** entrance level, 8% of applicants were admitted

Undergraduates 902 full-time, 25 part-time. Students come from 38 states and territories; 30 other countries; 46% are from out of state; 6% Black or African American, non-Hispanic/Latino; 9% Hispanic/Latino; 18% Asian, non-Hispanic/Latino; 0.2% Native Hawaiian or other Pacific Islander, non-Hispanic/Latino; 0.9% American Indian or Alaska Native, non-Hispanic/Latino; 5% Two or more races, non-Hispanic/Latino; 9% Race/ethnicity unknown; 15% international; 4% transferred in; 20% live on campus. *Retention:* 96% of full-time freshmen returned.

Freshmen *Admission:* 3,415 applied, 264 admitted, 201 enrolled. *Average high school GPA:* 3.6. *Test scores:* SAT critical reading scores over 500: 96%; SAT math scores over 500: 95%; SAT writing scores over 500: 93%; SAT critical reading scores over 600: 82%; SAT math scores over 600: 83%; SAT writing scores over 600: 79%; ACT scores over 24: 100%; SAT critical reading scores over 700: 37%; SAT math scores over 700: 61%; SAT writing scores over 700: 37%; ACT scores over 30: 60%.

Faculty *Total:* 229, 23% full-time, 49% with terminal degrees. *Student/faculty ratio:* 9:1.

Academics *Calendar:* semesters. *Degrees:* certificates, bachelor's, and master's (also offers master's program primarily made up of currently-enrolled students). *Special study options:* advanced placement credit, honors programs, independent study, internships, off-campus study, services for LD students, student-designed majors, study abroad, summer session for credit.

Computers on Campus 400 computers/terminals are available on campus for general student use. Students can access the following: computer help desk, free student e-mail accounts, online (class) grades, online (class) schedules. Campuswide network is available. 100% of college-owned or -operated housing units are wired for high-speed Internet access. Wireless service is available via classrooms, computer centers, computer labs, learning centers, student centers.

Student Life *Housing options:* coed. Campus housing is university owned. Freshman applicants given priority for college housing. *Activities and organi-*

zations: drama/theater group, student-run newspaper, choral group, South Asian Society, Pro Musica, Chinese Student Association, Drama Society, Outdoors Club; Intervarsity Christian Fellowship, national fraternities, national sororities. *Campus security:* 24-hour emergency response devices and patrols, controlled dormitory access, security guards. *Student services:* personal/psychological counseling.

Athletics *Intercollegiate sports:* badminton M/W, basketball M/W(c), cross-country running M/W, soccer M/W, tennis M/W, volleyball M/W. *Intramural sports:* basketball M/W, bowling M/W, fencing M(c)/W(c), golf M/W, sailing M/W, skiing (downhill) M/W, soccer M(c)/W(c), softball M/W, swimming and diving M/W, table tennis M(c)/W(c), tennis M/W, ultimate Frisbee M(c)/W(c), volleyball M/W.

Standardized Tests *Required:* SAT or ACT (for admission). *Required for some:* SAT Subject Tests (for admission).

Costs (2011–12) *Comprehensive fee:* $52,850 includes full-time tuition ($37,500), mandatory fees ($1650), and room and board ($13,700). *College room only:* $9700. Room and board charges vary according to board plan and housing facility.

Financial Aid Of all full-time matriculated undergraduates who enrolled in 2010, 421 applied for aid, 254 were judged to have need, 135 had their need fully met. 54 Federal Work-Study jobs (averaging $844). 652 state and other part-time jobs (averaging $1238). In 2010, 637 non-need-based awards were made. *Average percent of need met:* 92%. *Average financial aid package:* $35,000. *Average need-based loan:* $3624. *Average need-based gift aid:* $40,984. *Average non-need-based aid:* $35,000. *Average indebtedness upon graduation:* $13,721. *Financial aid deadline:* 6/1.

Applying *Options:* electronic application, early admission, early decision, deferred entrance. *Application fee:* $65. *Required:* essay or personal statement, high school transcript, minimum 2.0 GPA. *Required for some:* minimum 3.5 GPA, 3 letters of recommendation, interview, portfolio, home examination for art and architecture applicants. *Recommended:* minimum 3.0 GPA. *Application deadlines:* 1/1 (freshmen), 1/1 (transfers). *Early decision deadline:* 12/1 (for plan 1), 12/1 (for plan 2). *Notification:* 4/1 (freshmen), 5/1 (transfers), 12/24 (early decision plan 1), 2/1 (early decision plan 2).

Freshman Application Contact Mr. Mitchell L. Lipton, Dean of Admissions and Records and Registrar, Cooper Union for the Advancement of Science and Art, 30 Cooper Square, New York, NY 10003. *Phone:* 212-353-4120. *Fax:* 212-353-4342. *E-mail:* admissions@cooper.edu. *Web site:* http://www.cooper.edu/.

Cornell University
Ithaca, New York

- **Independent** university, founded 1865
- **Small-town** 745-acre campus with easy access to Syracuse
- **Endowment** $5.1 million
- **Coed** 14,167 undergraduate students, 100% full-time, 50% women, 50% men
- **Most difficult** entrance level, 18% of applicants were admitted

Undergraduates 14,167 full-time. Students come from 54 states and territories; 82 other countries; 65% are from out of state; 6% Black or African American, non-Hispanic/Latino; 9% Hispanic/Latino; 16% Asian, non-Hispanic/Latino; 0.1% Native Hawaiian or other Pacific Islander, non-Hispanic/Latino; 0.3% American Indian or Alaska Native, non-Hispanic/Latino; 4% Two or more races, non-Hispanic/Latino; 10% Race/ethnicity unknown; 9% international; 4% transferred in; 57% live on campus. *Retention:* 97% of full-time freshmen returned.

Freshmen *Admission:* 36,387 applied, 6,538 admitted, 3,307 enrolled. *Test scores:* SAT critical reading scores over 500: 99%; SAT math scores over 500: 100%; ACT scores over 18: 100%; SAT critical reading scores over 600: 87%; SAT math scores over 600: 94%; ACT scores over 24: 99%; SAT critical reading scores over 700: 42%; SAT math scores over 700: 65%; ACT scores over 30: 75%.

Faculty *Total:* 1,827, 90% full-time, 91% with terminal degrees. *Student/faculty ratio:* 9:1.

Academics *Calendar:* semesters. *Degrees:* bachelor's, master's, doctoral, and first professional. *Special study options:* academic remediation for entering students, accelerated degree program, advanced placement credit, cooperative education, distance learning, double majors, English as a second language, honors programs, independent study, internships, off-campus study, services for LD students, student-designed majors, study abroad, summer session for credit. *ROTC:* Army (b), Navy (b), Air Force (b).

Computers on Campus 2,650 computers/terminals and 1,000 ports are available on campus for general student use. Students can access the following: campus intranet, computer help desk, free student e-mail accounts, online (class) grades, online (class) registration. Campuswide network is available. 100% of college-owned or -operated housing units are wired for high-speed Internet access. Wireless service is available via entire campus.

Student Life *Housing options:* coed, men-only, women-only, cooperative, disabled students. Campus housing is university owned. Freshman campus housing is guaranteed. *Activities and organizations:* drama/theater group, student-run newspaper, radio and television station, choral group, marching band, national fraternities, national sororities. *Campus security:* 24-hour emergency response devices and patrols, late-night transport/escort service, controlled dormitory access, indoor and outdoor emergency phones. *Student services:* health clinic, personal/psychological counseling, women's center.

Athletics Member NCAA. All Division I except football (Division I-AA). *Intercollegiate sports:* baseball M, basketball M/W, crew M/W, cross-country running M/W, equestrian sports W, fencing W, field hockey W, golf M, gymnastics W, ice hockey M/W, lacrosse M/W, soccer M/W, softball W, squash M/W, swimming and diving M/W, table tennis M(c)/W(c), tennis M/W, track and field M/W, ultimate Frisbee M(c)/W(c), volleyball M(c)/W, water polo M(c)/W(c), wrestling M. *Intramural sports:* archery M(c)/W(c), badminton M/W, baseball M(c), basketball M/W, bowling M/W, cheerleading M(c)/W(c), cross-country running M(c)/W(c), equestrian sports M(c)/W(c), fencing M(c)/W(c), field hockey W(c), football M/W, golf M/W, gymnastics M(c)/W(c), ice hockey M/W, lacrosse W(c), rugby M(c)/W(c), sailing M(c)/W(c), skiing (cross-country) M(c)/W(c), skiing (downhill) M(c)/W(c), soccer M/W, softball M/W, squash M/W, table tennis M/W, tennis M/W, ultimate Frisbee M/W, volleyball M/W, water polo M(c)/W(c), wrestling M(c)/W(c).

Standardized Tests *Required:* SAT or ACT (for admission). *Required for some:* SAT Subject Tests (for admission).

Costs (2011–12) *Comprehensive fee:* $54,701 includes full-time tuition ($41,325), mandatory fees ($216), and room and board ($13,160). Full-time tuition and fees vary according to degree level. *College room only:* $7800. Room and board charges vary according to board plan and housing facility. *Payment plan:* installment. *Waivers:* employees or children of employees.

Financial Aid Of all full-time matriculated undergraduates who enrolled in 2011, 8,014 applied for aid, 7,047 were judged to have need, 7,074 had their need fully met. 5,180 Federal Work-Study jobs (averaging $1780). 1,415 state and other part-time jobs (averaging $1500). *Average percent of need met:* 100%. *Average financial aid package:* $39,095. *Average need-based loan:* $3510. *Average need-based gift aid:* $33,961. *Average indebtedness upon graduation:* $19,180. *Financial aid deadline:* 2/15.

Applying *Options:* electronic application, early decision, deferred entrance. *Application fee:* $75. *Required:* essay or personal statement, high school transcript, 2 letters of recommendation. *Required for some:* interview. *Application deadlines:* 1/2 (freshmen), 3/1 (transfers). *Early decision deadline:* 11/1. *Notification:* 3/31 (freshmen), continuous until 6/15 (transfers), 12/15 (early decision).

Freshman Application Contact Mr. Jason C. Locke, Director of Undergraduate Admissions, Cornell University, Ithaca, NY 14853-0001. *Phone:* 607-255-1446. *Fax:* 607-255-0659. *E-mail:* admissions@cornell.edu. *Web site:* http://www.cornell.edu/.

The Culinary Institute of America
Hyde Park, New York

- **Independent** 4-year, founded 1946
- **Suburban** 170-acre campus
- **Endowment** $92.2 million
- **Coed** 2,807 undergraduate students, 100% full-time, 46% women, 54% men
- **Moderately difficult** entrance level, 81% of applicants were admitted

Undergraduates 2,807 full-time. Students come from 55 states and territories; 39 other countries; 4% Black or African American, non-Hispanic/Latino; 9% Hispanic/Latino; 11% Asian, non-Hispanic/Latino; 0.4% Native Hawaiian or other Pacific Islander, non-Hispanic/Latino; 0.3% American Indian or Alaska Native, non-Hispanic/Latino; 2% Two or more races, non-Hispanic/Latino; 3% Race/ethnicity unknown; 4% international; 79% live on campus. *Retention:* 91% of full-time freshmen returned.

Freshmen *Admission:* 940 applied, 758 admitted, 570 enrolled. *Average high school GPA:* 3.2. *Test scores:* SAT critical reading scores over 500: 59%; SAT math scores over 500: 66%; ACT scores over 18: 94%; SAT critical reading scores over 600: 21%; SAT math scores over 600: 16%; ACT scores over 24: 41%; SAT critical reading scores over 700: 2%; SAT math scores over 700: 4%; ACT scores over 30: 6%.

Faculty *Total:* 184, 84% full-time. *Student/faculty ratio:* 17:1.

Academics *Calendar:* semesters plus 18 or 21 week externship program. *Degrees:* certificates, associate, and bachelor's. *Special study options:* academic remediation for entering students, honors programs, internships, off-campus study, services for LD students.

Computers on Campus 218 computers/terminals are available on campus for general student use. Students can access the following: campus intranet, computer help desk, free student e-mail accounts, online (class) grades, online (class) registration, online (class) schedules, online course guides. Campus-

wide network is available. 100% of college-owned or -operated housing units are wired for high-speed Internet access. Wireless service is available via entire campus. **Student Life** *Housing options:* coed. Campus housing is university owned. Freshman campus housing is guaranteed. *Activities and organizations:* student-run newspaper, choral group, Alliance, Baking and Pastry Society, Global Culinary Society, Eta Sigma Delta Honor Society, Chips Supporting Agriculture. *Campus security:* 24-hour emergency response devices and patrols, late-night transport/escort service, controlled dormitory access. *Student services:* health clinic, personal/psychological counseling. **Athletics** *Intercollegiate sports:* basketball M/W, cross-country running M/W, soccer M/W, tennis M/W, volleyball M/W. *Intramural sports:* basketball M/W, cross-country running M/W, football M/W, soccer M/W, softball M/W, swimming and diving M/W, tennis M/W, volleyball M/W. **Standardized Tests** *Recommended:* SAT or ACT (for admission). **Financial Aid** Of all full-time matriculated undergraduates who enrolled in 2008, 2,600 applied for aid, 2,340 were judged to have need, 134 had their need fully met. 900 Federal Work-Study jobs (averaging $435). In 2008, 238 non-need-based awards were made. *Average percent of need met:* 44%. *Average financial aid package:* $13,805. *Average need-based loan:* $4032. *Average need-based gift aid:* $3500. *Average non-need-based aid:* $2500. *Average indebtedness upon graduation:* $29,351. *Financial aid deadline:* 2/15. **Applying** *Options:* electronic application, deferred entrance. *Application fee:* $50. *Required:* essay or personal statement, high school transcript, 1 letter of recommendation. *Required for some:* Affidavit of Support. *Application deadline:* rolling (freshmen). *Notification:* continuous (transfers). **Freshman Application Contact** Ms. Rachel Birchwood, Director of Admissions, The Culinary Institute of America, 1946 Campus Drive, Hyde Park, NY 12538. *Phone:* 845-451-1459. *Toll-free phone:* 800-CULINARY. *Fax:* 845-451-1068. *E-mail:* admissions@culinary.edu. *Web site:* http://www.ciachef.edu/.

See page 1286 for the College Close-Up.

Daemen College
Amherst, New York

- **Independent** comprehensive, founded 1947
- **Suburban** 35-acre campus with easy access to Buffalo
- **Endowment** $7.1 million
- **Coed** 2,156 undergraduate students, 77% full-time, 72% women, 28% men
- **Moderately difficult** entrance level, 59% of applicants were admitted

Undergraduates 1,654 full-time, 502 part-time. Students come from 9 other countries; 10% Black or African American, non-Hispanic/Latino; 4% Hispanic/Latino; 2% Asian, non-Hispanic/Latino; 0.1% Native Hawaiian or other Pacific Islander, non-Hispanic/Latino; 0.2% American Indian or Alaska Native, non-Hispanic/Latino; 0.5% Two or more races, non-Hispanic/Latino; 4% Race/ethnicity unknown; 3% international; 14% transferred in. *Retention:* 81% of full-time freshmen returned. **Freshmen** *Admission:* 2,372 applied, 1,405 admitted, 435 enrolled. *Average high school GPA:* 3.59. *Test scores:* SAT critical reading scores over 500: 54%; SAT math scores over 500: 61%; SAT writing scores over 500: 48%; ACT scores over 18: 94%; SAT critical reading scores over 600: 12%; SAT math scores over 600: 18%; SAT writing scores over 600: 10%; ACT scores over 24: 39%; SAT math scores over 700: 1%; SAT writing scores over 700: 1%; ACT scores over 30: 3%. **Faculty** *Total:* 291, 41% full-time, 43% with terminal degrees. *Student/faculty ratio:* 14:1. **Academics** *Calendar:* semesters. *Degrees:* certificates, bachelor's, master's, doctoral, and post-master's certificates. *Special study options:* academic remediation for entering students, accelerated degree program, adult/continuing education programs, advanced placement credit, double majors, honors programs, independent study, internships, off-campus study, part-time degree program, services for LD students, student-designed majors, study abroad, summer session for credit. *ROTC:* Army (c). *Unusual degree programs:* 3-2 physician assistant studies; professional accountancy; health care studies/athletic training. **Computers on Campus** 146 computers/terminals are available on campus for general student use. Students can access the following: campus intranet, computer help desk, free student e-mail accounts, online (class) grades, online (class) registration, online (class) schedules. Campuswide network is available. 100% of college-owned or -operated housing units are wired for high-speed Internet access. Wireless service is available via classrooms, dorm rooms, learning centers, libraries, student centers. **Student Life** *Housing:* on-campus residence required for freshman year. *Options:* coed. Campus housing is university owned. Freshman campus housing is guaranteed. *Activities and organizations:* student-run newspaper, Students Without Borders, Step Team, Ski Club, Multi-Cultural Association.

Campus security: 24-hour emergency response devices and patrols, late-night transport/escort service, 24-hour security cameras. *Student services:* personal/psychological counseling.

Athletics Member NAIA. *Intercollegiate sports:* basketball M(s)/W(s), cross-country running M(s)/W(s), golf M(s), soccer M(s)/W(s), track and field M(s)/W(s), volleyball W(s). *Intramural sports:* basketball M/W, cheerleading W(c), softball M/W, ultimate Frisbee M/W, volleyball M(c)/W.

Standardized Tests *Recommended:* SAT or ACT (for admission).

Costs (2011–12) *Comprehensive fee:* $32,610 includes full-time tuition ($21,800), mandatory fees ($510), and room and board ($10,300). Full-time tuition and fees vary according to location and reciprocity agreements. Part-time tuition: $725 per credit hour. Part-time tuition and fees vary according to course load, location, and reciprocity agreements. *Required fees:* $6 per credit hour part-time, $70 per term part-time. *Room and board:* Room and board charges vary according to board plan and housing facility. *Payment plans:* installment, deferred payment. *Waivers:* senior citizens and employees or children of employees.

Financial Aid Of all full-time matriculated undergraduates who enrolled in 2009, 1,380 applied for aid, 1,205 were judged to have need, 421 had their need fully met. 265 Federal Work-Study jobs (averaging $1456). 327 state and other part-time jobs (averaging $1464). In 2009, 241 non-need-based awards were made. *Average percent of need met:* 80%. *Average financial aid package:* $16,217. *Average need-based loan:* $4837. *Average need-based gift aid:* $16,528. *Average non-need-based aid:* $9388. *Average indebtedness upon graduation:* $27,444.

Applying *Options:* electronic application, early admission, deferred entrance. *Application fee:* $25. *Required:* essay or personal statement, high school transcript, minimum 2.0 GPA, 1 letter of recommendation. *Required for some:* 3 letters of recommendation, interview, high school transcript, class rank, writing sample-test optional. *Application deadlines:* rolling (freshmen), rolling (out-of-state freshmen), rolling (transfers). *Notification:* continuous (freshmen), continuous (out-of-state freshmen), continuous (transfers).

Freshman Application Contact Daemen College, 4380 Main Street, Amherst, NY 14226-3592. *Phone:* 716-839-8225. *Toll-free phone:* 800-462-7652. *Fax:* 716-839-8229. *E-mail:* admissions@daemen.edu. *Web site:* http://www.daemen.edu/.

See page 1290 for the College Close-Up.

Darkei Noam Rabbinical College
Brooklyn, New York

Director of Admissions Rabbi Pinchas Horowitz, Director of Admissions, Darkei Noam Rabbinical College, 2822 Avenue J, Brooklyn, NY 11210. *Phone:* 718-338-6464.

Davis College
Johnson City, New York

Freshman Application Contact Admissions Coordinator, Davis College, 400 Riverside Drive, Johnson City, NY 13790. *Phone:* 607-729-1581 Ext. 406. *Toll-free phone:* 877-949-3248. *Fax:* 607-798-7754. *E-mail:* admissions@davisny.edu. *Web site:* http://www.davisny.edu/.

DeVry College of New York
New York, New York

- **Proprietary** comprehensive, founded 1998, part of DeVry University
- **Urban** campus
- **Coed** 1,321 undergraduate students, 57% full-time, 28% women, 72% men
- **Minimally difficult** entrance level

Undergraduates 759 full-time, 562 part-time. 8% are from out of state; 32% Black or African American, non-Hispanic/Latino; 30% Hispanic/Latino; 7% Asian, non-Hispanic/Latino; 0.6% Native Hawaiian or other Pacific Islander, non-Hispanic/Latino; 0.3% American Indian or Alaska Native, non-Hispanic/Latino; 1% Two or more races, non-Hispanic/Latino; 14% Race/ethnicity unknown; 3% international; 19% transferred in.

Freshmen *Admission:* 220 enrolled.

Faculty *Total:* 93, 40% full-time. *Student/faculty ratio:* 24:1.

Academics *Calendar:* semesters. *Degrees:* associate, bachelor's, master's, and postbachelor's certificates. *Special study options:* adult/continuing education programs, part-time degree program.

Student Life *Housing:* college housing not available.

Costs (2011–12) *Tuition:* $15,294 full-time, $597 per credit hour part-time. Full-time tuition and fees vary according to course load. Part-time tuition and fees vary according to course load. *Required fees:* $80 full-time, $40 per term part-time. *Payment plans:* installment, deferred payment. *Waivers:* employees or children of employees.

Financial Aid Of all full-time matriculated undergraduates who enrolled in 2007, 387 applied for aid, 371 were judged to have need, 8 had their need fully met. In 2007, 19 non-need-based awards were made. *Average percent of need met: 5%. Average financial aid package: $15,942. Average need-based loan: $8712. Average need-based gift aid: $7343. Average non-need-based aid: $11,806. Average indebtedness upon graduation: $29,136.*
Applying *Application fee:* $50. *Required:* high school transcript, interview. *Application deadlines:* rolling (freshmen), rolling (transfers). *Notification:* continuous (freshmen), continuous (transfers).
Freshman Application Contact DeVry College of New York, 180 Madison Avenue, Suite 900, New York, NY 10016-5267. *Phone:* 212-312-4300. *Toll-free phone:* 866-338-7941. *Web site:* http://www.devry.edu/.

Dominican College
Orangeburg, New York

- **Independent** comprehensive, founded 1952
- **Suburban** 70-acre campus with easy access to New York City
- **Endowment** $892,984
- **Coed** 1,643 undergraduate students, 84% full-time, 67% women, 33% men
- **Noncompetitive** entrance level, 71% of applicants were admitted

Undergraduates 1,377 full-time, 266 part-time. Students come from 23 states and territories; 15 other countries; 26% are from out of state; 14% Black or African American, non-Hispanic/Latino; 17% Hispanic/Latino; 8% Asian, non-Hispanic/Latino; 0.2% American Indian or Alaska Native, non-Hispanic/Latino; 3% Two or more races, non-Hispanic/Latino; 23% Race/ethnicity unknown; 0.9% international; 11% transferred in; 42% live on campus. *Retention:* 67% of full-time freshmen returned.
Freshmen *Admission:* 1,594 applied, 1,126 admitted, 352 enrolled. *Average high school GPA:* 2.67. *Test scores:* SAT critical reading scores over 500: 25%; SAT math scores over 500: 25%; SAT writing scores over 500: 22%; ACT scores over 18: 78%; SAT critical reading scores over 600: 3%; SAT math scores over 600: 6%; SAT writing scores over 600: 3%; ACT scores over 24: 11%; SAT critical reading scores over 700: 1%; SAT math scores over 700: 1%; SAT writing scores over 700: 1%.
Faculty *Total:* 233, 31% full-time, 31% with terminal degrees. *Student/faculty ratio:* 15:1.
Academics *Calendar:* semesters. *Degrees:* certificates, associate, bachelor's, master's, and doctoral. *Special study options:* academic remediation for enter-

ing students, accelerated degree program, adult/continuing education programs, advanced placement credit, cooperative education, distance learning, double majors, freshman honors college, honors programs, independent study, internships, off-campus study, part-time degree program, services for LD students, summer session for credit. *Unusual degree programs:* 3-2 occupational therapy.
Computers on Campus 150 computers/terminals are available on campus for general student use. Students can access the following: campus intranet, free student e-mail accounts, online (class) schedules, Web portal, Black Board. Campuswide network is available. 100% of college-owned or -operated housing units are wired for high-speed Internet access. Wireless service is available via entire campus.
Student Life *Housing options:* coed. Campus housing is university owned. Freshman campus housing is guaranteed. *Activities and organizations:* drama/theater group, student-run newspaper, radio station, choral group, Student Government Association, Business Club, Aquin Players, school newspaper, Nursing Association. *Campus security:* 24-hour emergency response devices and patrols, student patrols, late-night transport/escort service, controlled dormitory access. *Student services:* health clinic, personal/psychological counseling.
Athletics Member NCAA, NAIA. All NCAA Division II. *Intercollegiate sports:* baseball M(s), basketball M(s)/W(s), cross-country running W(s), golf M(s), lacrosse M(s)/W(s), soccer M(s)/W(s), softball W(s), track and field W(s), volleyball W(s). *Intramural sports:* basketball M/W, crew M(c)/W(c), volleyball M/W.
Standardized Tests *Required:* SAT or ACT (for admission).
Costs (2011–12) *Comprehensive fee:* $33,920 includes full-time tuition ($22,200), mandatory fees ($740), and room and board ($10,980). Full-time tuition and fees vary according to degree level. Part-time tuition: $670 per credit hour. Part-time tuition and fees vary according to degree level and program. *Room and board:* Room and board charges vary according to board plan and housing facility. *Payment plans:* installment, deferred payment. *Waivers:* senior citizens and employees or children of employees.
Financial Aid Of all full-time matriculated undergraduates who enrolled in 2009, 1,343 applied for aid, 1,232 were judged to have need, 132 had their need fully met. 217 Federal Work-Study jobs (averaging $1200). 73 state and other part-time jobs (averaging $3000). In 2009, 108 non-need-based awards were made. *Average percent of need met:* 59%. *Average financial aid package:* $15,385. *Average need-based loan:* $4270. *Average need-based gift aid:* $12,101. *Average non-need-based aid:* $6662. *Average indebtedness upon graduation:* $18,398.

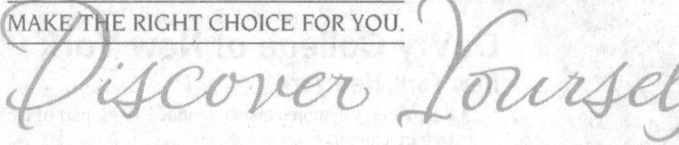
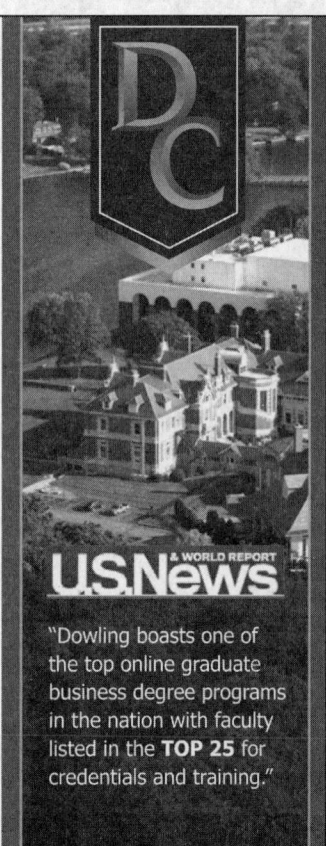

Applying *Options:* electronic application, deferred entrance. *Application fee:* $35. *Required:* high school transcript. *Required for some:* essay or personal statement, interview. *Recommended:* interview. *Application deadlines:* rolling (freshmen), rolling (transfers). *Notification:* continuous (freshmen), continuous (transfers).
Freshman Application Contact Ms. Joyce Elbe, Director of Admissions, Dominican College, 470 Western Highway, Orangeburg, NY 10962-1210. *Phone:* 845-359-7901. *Toll-free phone:* 866-432-4636. *Fax:* 845-365-3150. *E-mail:* admissions@dc.edu. *Web site:* http://www.dc.edu/.

Dowling College
Oakdale, New York

- **Independent** comprehensive, founded 1955
- **Suburban** 157-acre campus with easy access to New York City
- **Coed** 2,883 undergraduate students, 66% full-time, 55% women, 45% men
- **Moderately difficult** entrance level, 79% of applicants were admitted

Undergraduates 1,910 full-time, 973 part-time. 6% are from out of state; 8% Black or African American, non-Hispanic/Latino; 7% Hispanic/Latino; 1% Asian, non-Hispanic/Latino; 0.1% American Indian or Alaska Native, non-Hispanic/Latino; 35% Race/ethnicity unknown; 3% international; 9% transferred in; 13% live on campus. *Retention:* 65% of full-time freshmen returned.
Freshmen *Admission:* 2,495 applied, 1,962 admitted, 358 enrolled.
Faculty *Total:* 431, 27% full-time, 45% with terminal degrees. *Student/faculty ratio:* 15:1.
Academics *Calendar:* semesters. *Degrees:* bachelor's, master's, doctoral, post-master's, and postbachelor's certificates. *Special study options:* academic remediation for entering students, accelerated degree program, advanced placement credit, cooperative education, distance learning, double majors, English as a second language, honors programs, independent study, internships, off-campus study, part-time degree program, services for LD students, student-designed majors, study abroad, summer session for credit. *ROTC:* Army (c), Air Force (c).
Computers on Campus 317 computers/terminals and 89 ports are available on campus for general student use. Students can access the following: campus intranet, computer help desk, free student e-mail accounts, online (class) grades, online (class) registration, online (class) schedules. Campuswide network is available. 100% of college-owned or -operated housing units are wired for high-speed Internet access. Wireless service is available via entire campus.

Student Life *Housing options:* coed. Campus housing is university owned. *Activities and organizations:* drama/theater group, student-run newspaper, radio station, choral group, Student Government Association, Dormitory Councils, Aviation Organization, Student Newspaper. *Campus security:* 24-hour emergency response devices and patrols, late-night transport/escort service, controlled dormitory access. *Student services:* health clinic, personal/psychological counseling.
Athletics Member NCAA. All Division II. *Intercollegiate sports:* baseball M(s), basketball M(s)/W(s), cheerleading W(c), crew M(s)(c)/W(s), cross-country running M(s)/W(s), equestrian sports W(c), golf M(s), lacrosse M(s)/W(s), soccer M(s)/W(s), softball W(s), tennis M(s)/W(s), volleyball W(s).
Standardized Tests *Recommended:* SAT or ACT (for admission).
Costs (2011–12) *Comprehensive fee:* $36,758 includes full-time tuition ($24,118), mandatory fees ($1790), and room and board ($10,850). Full-time tuition and fees vary according to course load and degree level. Part-time tuition: $809 per credit. Part-time tuition and fees vary according to course load and degree level. *Required fees:* $566 per term part-time. *Room and board:* Room and board charges vary according to housing facility and location. *Payment plans:* installment, deferred payment. *Waivers:* minority students, children of alumni, adult students, senior citizens, and employees or children of employees.
Financial Aid Of all full-time matriculated undergraduates who enrolled in 2010, 1,543 applied for aid, 1,543 were judged to have need, 168 had their need fully met. 313 Federal Work-Study jobs (averaging $1599), 59 state and other part-time jobs (averaging $1536). In 2010, 239 non-need-based awards were made. *Average percent of need met:* 94%. *Average financial aid package:* $15,570. *Average need-based loan:* $4200. *Average need-based gift aid:* $8270. *Average non-need-based aid:* $5770. *Average indebtedness upon graduation:* $22,177.
Applying *Options:* electronic application, early action, deferred entrance. *Application fee:* $35. *Required:* essay or personal statement, high school transcript, minimum 2.0 GPA, 1 letter of recommendation. *Recommended:* minimum 2.5 GPA. *Application deadlines:* rolling (freshmen), rolling (out-of-state freshmen), rolling (transfers), 12/31 (early action). *Notification:* continuous (freshmen), continuous (out-of-state freshmen), continuous (transfers), 1/31 (early action).
Freshman Application Contact Ms. Ronnie Lee Macdonald, Vice President for Enrollment and Student Services, Dowling College, 150 Idle Hour Boulevard, Oakdale, NY 11769. *Phone:* 631-244-3480. *Toll-free phone:* 800-DOWLING. *Fax:* 631-244-1059. *Web site:* http://www.dowling.edu/.

See page 578 for display ad and page 1304 for the College Close-Up.

D'Youville College

Buffalo, New York

Freshman Application Contact D'Youville College, 320 Porter Avenue, Buffalo, NY 14201-1084. *Phone:* 716-829-7600. *Toll-free phone:* 800-777-3921. *Web site:* http://www.dyc.edu/.

See page 579 for display ad and page 1308 for the College Close-Up.

Elmira College

Elmira, New York

- **Independent** comprehensive, founded 1855
- **Suburban** 55-acre campus
- **Coed** 1,406 undergraduate students, 83% full-time, 72% women, 28% men
- **Moderately difficult** entrance level, 75% of applicants were admitted

Undergraduates 1,161 full-time, 245 part-time. Students come from 35 states and territories; 31 other countries; 53% are from out of state; 3% Black or African American, non-Hispanic/Latino; 2% Hispanic/Latino; 1% Asian, non-Hispanic/Latino; 0.5% American Indian or Alaska Native, non-Hispanic/Latino; 0.7% Two or more races, non-Hispanic/Latino; 16% Race/ethnicity unknown; 4% international; 3% transferred in; 94% live on campus. *Retention:* 71% of full-time freshmen returned.

Freshmen *Admission:* 2,424 applied, 1,829 admitted, 349 enrolled. *Average high school GPA:* 3.36. *Test scores:* SAT critical reading scores over 500: 65%; SAT math scores over 500: 65%; ACT scores over 18: 98%; SAT critical reading scores over 600: 23%; SAT math scores over 600: 23%; ACT scores over 24: 53%; SAT critical reading scores over 700: 3%; SAT math scores over 700: 2%; ACT scores over 30: 8%.

Faculty *Total:* 221, 42% full-time. *Student/faculty ratio:* 11:1.

Academics *Calendar:* 4-4-1. *Degrees:* associate, bachelor's, and master's. *Special study options:* accelerated degree program, adult/continuing education programs, advanced placement credit, distance learning, double majors, English as a second language, independent study, internships, off-campus study, part-time degree program, services for LD students, student-designed majors, study abroad, summer session for credit. *ROTC:* Army (b), Air Force (c).

Unusual degree programs: 3-2 chemical engineering with Clarkson University.

Computers on Campus 173 computers/terminals are available on campus for general student use. Students can access the following: campus intranet, computer help desk, free student e-mail accounts, online (class) grades, online (class) schedules. Campuswide network is available. 100% of college-owned or -operated housing units are wired for high-speed Internet access. Wireless service is available via classrooms, computer centers, computer labs, dorm rooms, libraries, student centers.

Student Life *Housing:* on-campus residence required through senior year. *Options:* coed, women-only, cooperative, disabled students. Campus housing is university owned. Freshman campus housing is guaranteed. *Activities and organizations:* drama/theater group, student-run newspaper, radio station, choral group, student radio station, Student Activities Board, College Republicans and Democrats, Ski Club, Habitat for Humanity. *Campus security:* 24-hour patrols, late-night transport/escort service, 24-hour locked residence hall entrances. *Student services:* health clinic, personal/psychological counseling.

Athletics Member NCAA. All Division III. *Intercollegiate sports:* basketball M/W, cheerleading W, field hockey W, golf M/W, ice hockey M/W, lacrosse M/W, soccer M/W, softball W, tennis M/W, volleyball M/W. *Intramural sports:* badminton M/W, basketball M/W, equestrian sports M/W, football M/W, ice hockey M/W, lacrosse M/W, racquetball M/W, rock climbing M/W, skiing (cross-country) M/W, skiing (downhill) M/W, soccer M/W, softball M/W, swimming and diving M/W, table tennis M/W, tennis M/W, ultimate Frisbee M/W, volleyball M/W.

Standardized Tests *Required:* SAT or ACT (for admission).

Costs (2011–12) *Comprehensive fee:* $48,450 includes full-time tuition ($35,550), mandatory fees ($1400), and room and board ($11,500). Part-time tuition: $315 per credit hour. Part-time tuition and fees vary according to course load and degree level. *Room and board:* Room and board charges vary according to housing facility. *Payment plans:* tuition prepayment, installment. *Waivers:* employees or children of employees.

Financial Aid Of all full-time matriculated undergraduates who enrolled in 2011, 978 applied for aid, 912 were judged to have need, 172 had their need fully met. 309 Federal Work-Study jobs (averaging $1000). 221 state and other part-time jobs (averaging $1200). In 2011, 220 non-need-based awards were made. *Average percent of need met:* 80%. *Average financial aid package:*

$28,180. *Average need-based loan:* $4148. *Average need-based gift aid:* $24,357. *Average non-need-based aid:* $20,640. *Average indebtedness upon graduation:* $26,528.
Applying *Options:* electronic application, early decision, deferred entrance. *Application fee:* $50. *Required:* essay or personal statement, high school transcript, minimum 2.0 GPA, 1 letter of recommendation. *Required for some:* interview. *Recommended:* interview. *Application deadlines:* 3/31 (freshmen), rolling (transfers). *Early decision deadline:* 11/15 (for plan 1), 1/15 (for plan 2). *Notification:* continuous until 4/30 (freshmen), continuous (transfers), 12/15 (early decision plan 1), 1/31 (early decision plan 2).
Freshman Application Contact Mr. Brett Moore, Director of Admissions, Elmira College, One Park Place, Elmira, NY 14901. *Phone:* 607-735-1724. *Toll-free phone:* 800-935-6472. *Fax:* 607-735-1718. *E-mail:* admissions@elmira.edu. *Web site:* http://www.elmira.edu/.

See page 580 for display ad and page 1316 for the College Close-Up.

Eugene Lang College The New School for Liberal Arts

New York, New York

- **Independent** 4-year, founded 1978, part of The New School
- **Urban** 5-acre campus with easy access to New York City
- **Coed**
- **Very difficult** entrance level

Faculty *Student/faculty ratio:* 14:1.
Academics *Calendar:* semesters. *Degree:* bachelor's.
Student Life *Campus security:* 24-hour emergency response devices, controlled dormitory access, 24-hour desk attendants in residence halls.
Costs (2011–12) *Comprehensive fee:* $52,150 includes full-time tuition ($36,970), mandatory fees ($270), and room and board ($14,910). Part-time tuition: $1255 per credit. Part-time tuition and fees vary according to course load. *College room only:* $14,360. Room and board charges vary according to board plan and housing facility.
Financial Aid *Of all full-time matriculated undergraduates who enrolled in 2010,* 1,061 applied for aid, 842 were judged to have need, 121 had their need fully met. *In 2010,* 39 non-need-based awards were made. *Average percent of need met:* 80. *Average financial aid package:* $34,210. *Average need-based loan:* $8390. *Average need-based gift aid:* $22,555. *Average non-need-based aid:* $2925. *Average indebtedness upon graduation:* $30,830.
Applying *Options:* electronic application, early decision, deferred entrance. *Application fee:* $50. *Required:* essay or personal statement, high school transcript, interview, counselor evaluation, teacher evaluation. *Recommended:* minimum 3.0 GPA.
Freshman Application Contact Eugene Lang College The New School for Liberal Arts, 65 West 11th Street, New York, NY 10011-8601. *Phone:* 212-229-5665. *Toll-free phone:* 800-292-3040. *Web site:* http://www.newschool.edu/lang.

See page 1476 for the College Close-Up.

Excelsior College

Albany, New York

- **Independent** comprehensive, founded 1970
- **Suburban** campus with easy access to Albany, NY
- **Coed** 32,093 undergraduate students, 55% women, 45% men

Undergraduates 32,093 part-time. Students come from 52 states and territories; 20 other countries; 87% are from out of state; 21% Black or African American, non-Hispanic/Latino; 8% Hispanic/Latino; 3% Asian, non-Hispanic/Latino; 0.5% Native Hawaiian or other Pacific Islander, non-Hispanic/Latino; 0.7% American Indian or Alaska Native, non-Hispanic/Latino; 2% Two or more races, non-Hispanic/Latino; 3% Race/ethnicity unknown; 18% transferred in.
Faculty *Student/faculty ratio:* 6:1.
Academics *Calendar:* continuous. *Degrees:* certificates, associate, bachelor's, master's, post-master's, and postbachelor's certificates (offers only external degree programs). *Special study options:* accelerated degree program, adult/continuing education programs, advanced placement credit, distance learning, external degree program, honors programs, independent study, off-campus study, part-time degree program, services for LD students, student-designed majors. *Unusual degree programs:* 3-2 nursing.
Computers on Campus Students can access the following: computer help desk, online (class) grades, online (class) registration, online (class) schedules. Campuswide network is available.
Costs (2012–13) *Tuition:* $355 per credit hour part-time. *Payment plan:* installment. *Waivers:* employees or children of employees.

Applying *Options:* electronic application. *Application fee:* $75. *Required for some:* college transcripts. *Application deadlines:* rolling (freshmen), rolling (transfers). *Notification:* continuous (freshmen), continuous (transfers). **Freshman Application Contact** Admissions, Excelsior College, 7 Columbia Circle, Albany, NY 12203-5159. *Phone:* 518-464-8500. *Toll-free phone:* 888-647-2388. *Fax:* 518-464-8777. *E-mail:* admissions@excelsior.edu. *Web site:* http://www.excelsior.edu/.

Farmingdale State College

Farmingdale, New York

- **State-supported** 4-year, founded 1912, part of State University of New York System
- **Small-town** 380-acre campus with easy access to New York City
- **Endowment** $5.6 million
- **Coed** 7,633 undergraduate students, 70% full-time, 42% women, 58% men
- **Moderately difficult** entrance level, 47% of applicants were admitted

Undergraduates 5,377 full-time, 2,256 part-time. Students come from 12 states and territories; 21 other countries; 1% are from out of state; 6% Black or African American, non-Hispanic/Latino; 6% Hispanic/Latino; 3% Asian, non-Hispanic/Latino; 0.1% American Indian or Alaska Native, non-Hispanic/Latino; 47% Race/ethnicity unknown; 1% international; 14% transferred in; 7% live on campus. *Retention:* 84% of full-time freshmen returned.

Freshmen *Admission:* 5,373 applied, 2,520 admitted, 939 enrolled. *Average high school GPA:* 3.24. *Test scores:* SAT critical reading scores over 500: 45%; SAT math scores over 500: 70%; SAT critical reading scores over 600: 6%; SAT math scores over 600: 18%; SAT math scores over 700: 1%.

Faculty *Total:* 569, 34% full-time, 33% with terminal degrees. *Student/faculty ratio:* 19:1.

Academics *Calendar:* semesters. *Degrees:* certificates, associate, and bachelor's. *Special study options:* academic remediation for entering students, advanced placement credit, distance learning, double majors, internships, part-time degree program, services for LD students, study abroad, summer session for credit.

Computers on Campus 950 computers/terminals are available on campus for general student use. Students can access the following: free student e-mail accounts, online (class) registration, online (class) schedules. Campuswide network is available. Wireless service is available via entire campus.

Student Life *Housing options:* coed. Campus housing is university owned. *Activities and organizations:* drama/theater group, student-run newspaper, radio station, Liberal Arts Club, Campus Activities Board, Farmingdale Student Government, student radio station, Rambler Newspaper. *ampus security:*

24-hour emergency response devices and patrols, controlled dormitory access. *Student services:* health clinic, personal/psychological counseling.

Athletics Member NCAA. All Division III except basketball (Division II), lacrosse (Division II), volleyball (Division II). *Intercollegiate sports:* baseball M, basketball M/W, cross-country running M/W, golf M, ice hockey M(c), lacrosse M/W, soccer M/W, softball W, tennis M/W, track and field M/W, volleyball W. *Intramural sports:* basketball M/W, football M, golf M/W, racquetball M/W, soccer M/W, softball M/W, squash M/W, swimming and diving M/W, table tennis M(c)/W(c), tennis M/W, ultimate Frisbee M(c)/W(c), volleyball M/W, weight lifting M(c)/W(c).

Standardized Tests *Required:* SAT or ACT (for admission).

Costs (2011–12) *Tuition:* state resident $5270 full-time, $220 per credit part-time; nonresident $14,320 full-time, $597 per credit part-time. Part-time tuition and fees vary according to course load. *Required fees:* $1164 full-time, $46 per credit part-time. *Room and board:* $11,440. Room and board charges vary according to board plan and location. *Payment plan:* installment.

Financial Aid Of all full-time matriculated undergraduates who enrolled in 2011, 3,748 applied for aid, 2,902 were judged to have need, 341 had their need fully met. 163 Federal Work-Study jobs (averaging $4307). In 2011, 26 non-need-based awards were made. *Average percent of need met:* 57%. *Average financial aid package:* $6986. *Average need-based loan:* $4154. *Average need-based gift aid:* $5590. *Average non-need-based aid:* $758. *Average indebtedness upon graduation:* $16,482.

Applying *Options:* electronic application, early admission. *Application fee:* $50. *Required:* high school transcript, minimum 2.0 GPA. *Required for some:* interview, portfolio for graphic arts / advertising. *Application deadlines:* rolling (freshmen), rolling (transfers). *Notification:* continuous (freshmen), continuous (transfers).

Freshman Application Contact Farmingdale State College, 2350 Broadhollow Road, Farmingdale, NY 11735. *Phone:* 631-420-2457. *Toll-free phone:* 877-4-FARMINGDALE. *Web site:* http://www.farmingdale.edu/.

Fashion Institute of Technology

New York, New York

- **State and locally supported** comprehensive, founded 1944, part of State University of New York System
- **Urban** 5-acre campus with easy access to New York City
- **Endowment** $25.9 million
- **Coed, primarily women** 10,023 undergraduate students, 71% full-time, 84% women, 16% men
- **Moderately difficult** entrance level, 43% of applicants were admitted

Undergraduates 7,141 full-time, 2,882 part-time. 29% are from out of state; 7% transferred in; 24% live on campus. *Retention:* 87% of full-time freshmen returned.

Freshmen *Admission:* 4,417 applied, 1,916 admitted, 1,156 enrolled.

Faculty *Total:* 977, 24% full-time. *Student/faculty ratio:* 17:1.

Academics *Calendar:* semesters. *Degrees:* certificates, associate, bachelor's, and master's. *Special study options:* academic remediation for entering students, adult/continuing education programs, advanced placement credit, distance learning, English as a second language, honors programs, internships, part-time degree program, services for LD students, study abroad, summer session for credit.

Computers on Campus 1,300 computers/terminals are available on campus for general student use. Students can access the following: campus intranet, computer help desk, free student e-mail accounts, online (class) grades, online (class) registration, online (class) schedules. Campuswide network is available. 100% of college-owned or -operated housing units are wired for high-speed Internet access. Wireless service is available via classrooms, computer centers, computer labs, dorm rooms, learning centers, libraries, student centers.

Student Life *Housing options:* coed, women-only. Campus housing is university owned and is provided by a third party. Freshman applicants given priority for college housing. *Activities and organizations:* drama/theater group, student-run newspaper, radio and television station, choral group, FITSA/Student Government, Merchandising Society/Style Shop, Delta Epilson Chi: Promoting Leadership in Marketing, Merchandising, and Advertising, PRSSA: Public Relations Student Society of America, Student Ambassadors. *Campus security:* 24-hour emergency response devices and patrols, late-night transport/escort service, controlled dormitory access. *Student services:* health clinic, personal/psychological counseling.

Athletics Member NJCAA. *Intercollegiate sports:* cheerleading M/W, cross-country running M/W, soccer W, swimming and diving M/W, table tennis M/W, tennis W, track and field M/W, volleyball W. *Intramural sports:* basketball M/W, table tennis M/W, tennis M/W, volleyball M/W.

Costs (2011–12) *Tuition:* state resident $5168 full-time, $215 per credit hour part-time; nonresident $13,550 full-time, $565 per credit hour part-time. Full-time tuition and fees vary according to degree level. Part-time tuition and fees vary according to degree level. *Required fees:* $435 full-time, $40 per credit hour part-time, $93 per term part-time. *Room and board:* $12,190. Room and board charges vary according to board plan and housing facility. *Payment plan:* installment. *Waivers:* employees or children of employees.

Financial Aid Of all full-time matriculated undergraduates who enrolled in 2009, 4,507 applied for aid, 3,512 were judged to have need, 459 had their need fully met. 553 Federal Work-Study jobs (averaging $1479). In 2009, 170 non-need-based awards were made. *Average percent of need met:* 63%. *Average financial aid package:* $11,305. *Average need-based loan:* $4298. *Average need-based gift aid:* $5355. *Average non-need-based aid:* $1676. *Average indebtedness upon graduation:* $24,143.

Applying *Options:* electronic application. *Application fee:* $50. *Required:* essay or personal statement, high school transcript. *Required for some:* portfolio for art and design programs. *Application deadlines:* 2/1 (freshmen), 2/1 (transfers). *Notification:* continuous until 4/1 (freshmen), continuous until 4/1 (transfers).

Freshman Application Contact Ms. Laura Arbrogast, Director of Admissions, Fashion Institute of Technology, Seventh Avenue at 27th Street, New York, NY 10001-5992. *Phone:* 212-217-3760. *Fax:* 212-217-3761. *E-mail:* fitinfo@fitnyc.edu. *Web site:* http://www.fitnyc.edu/.

See page 582 for display ad and page 1322 for the College Close-Up.

Five Towns College

Dix Hills, New York

- **Independent** comprehensive, founded 1972
- **Suburban** 40-acre campus with easy access to New York City
- **Coed** 990 undergraduate students, 97% full-time, 34% women, 66% men
- **Moderately difficult** entrance level, 61% of applicants were admitted

Undergraduates 956 full-time, 34 part-time. Students come from 12 states and territories; 2 other countries; 10% are from out of state; 23% Black or African American, non-Hispanic/Latino; 14% Hispanic/Latino; 3% Asian, non-Hispanic/Latino; 0.2% American Indian or Alaska Native, non-Hispanic/Latino; 0.2% Race/ethnicity unknown; 0.3% international; 10% transferred in; 20% live on campus.

Freshmen *Admission:* 634 applied, 388 admitted, 232 enrolled. *Average high school GPA:* 2.7. *Test scores:* ACT scores over 18: 86%; ACT scores over 24: 9%.

Faculty *Total:* 213, 16% full-time. *Student/faculty ratio:* 21:1.

Academics *Calendar:* semesters. *Degrees:* associate, bachelor's, master's, and doctoral. *Special study options:* academic remediation for entering students, adult/continuing education programs, advanced placement credit, independent study, internships, off-campus study, part-time degree program, services for LD students, summer session for credit.

Computers on Campus 110 computers/terminals are available on campus for general student use. Students can access the following: campus intranet, free student e-mail accounts, online (class) grades. Campuswide network is available. 100% of college-owned or -operated housing units are wired for high-speed Internet access. Wireless service is available via entire campus.

Student Life *Housing options:* coed. Campus housing is university owned. Freshman applicants given priority for college housing. *Activities and organizations:* drama/theater group, student-run newspaper, radio station, choral group, Film Video Club, Audio Club, Music Business Club, Hip Hop Club, yearbook. *Campus security:* 24-hour emergency response devices and patrols, late-night transport/escort service, controlled dormitory access. *Student services:* personal/psychological counseling.

Standardized Tests *Required:* SAT or ACT (for admission).

Costs (2011–12) *Comprehensive fee:* $32,230 includes full-time tuition ($19,200), mandatory fees ($370), and room and board ($12,660). Full-time tuition and fees vary according to course level, degree level, program, and student level. Part-time tuition: $800 per credit. Part-time tuition and fees vary according to course level, course load, degree level, program, and student level. *Required fees:* $60 per term part-time. *College room only:* $8060. Room and board charges vary according to board plan. *Payment plan:* installment. *Waivers:* employees or children of employees.

Financial Aid Of all full-time matriculated undergraduates who enrolled in 2009, 939 applied for aid, 791 were judged to have need, 466 had their need fully met. 95 Federal Work-Study jobs (averaging $1387). In 2009, 69 non-need-based awards were made. *Average percent of need met:* 48%. *Average financial aid package:* $8100. *Average need-based loan:* $3700. *Average need-based gift aid:* $5500. *Average non-need-based aid:* $2400. *Average indebtedness upon graduation:* $19,000.

Applying *Options:* early decision, deferred entrance. *Application fee:* $35. *Required:* essay or personal statement, high school transcript, minimum 2.3 GPA, 2 letters of recommendation, immunization records and an audition for Music or Theatre students. *Required for some:* interview. *Application dead-*

lines: rolling (freshmen), rolling (transfers). *Early decision deadline:* 12/1. *Notification:* continuous (freshmen), continuous (transfers), rolling (early decision).

Freshman Application Contact Mr. Jerry Cohen, Dean of Enrollment, Five Towns College, 305 North Service Road, Dix Hills, NY 11746-6055. *Phone:* 631-424-7000 Ext. 2110. *Fax:* 631-656-2172. *E-mail:* jcohen@ftc.edu. *Web site:* http://www.ftc.edu/.

See page 583 for display ad and page 1330 for the College Close-Up.

Fordham University
New York, New York

- **Independent Roman Catholic (Jesuit)** university, founded 1841
- **Urban** 85-acre campus with easy access to New York City
- **Endowment** $458.0 million
- **Coed** 8,427 undergraduate students, 93% full-time, 53% women, 47% men
- **Very difficult** entrance level, 42% of applicants were admitted

Undergraduates 7,812 full-time, 615 part-time. Students come from 44 states and territories; 69 other countries; 52% are from out of state; 5% Black or African American, non-Hispanic/Latino; 14% Hispanic/Latino; 8% Asian, non-Hispanic/Latino; 0.2% American Indian or Alaska Native, non-Hispanic/Latino; 2% Two or more races, non-Hispanic/Latino; 6% Race/ethnicity unknown; 4% international; 4% transferred in; 49% live on campus. *Retention:* 88% of full-time freshmen returned.

Freshmen *Admission:* 31,792 applied, 13,478 admitted, 1,986 enrolled. *Average high school GPA:* 3.52. *Test scores:* SAT critical reading scores over 500: 93%; SAT math scores over 500: 97%; SAT writing scores over 500: 95%; ACT scores over 18: 99%; SAT critical reading scores over 600: 62%; SAT math scores over 600: 69%; SAT writing scores over 600: 67%; ACT scores over 24: 93%; SAT critical reading scores over 700: 17%; SAT math scores over 700: 16%; SAT writing scores over 700: 18%; ACT scores over 30: 28%.

Faculty *Total:* 1,510, 46% full-time, 63% with terminal degrees. *Student/faculty ratio:* 13:1.

Academics *Calendar:* semesters. *Degrees:* bachelor's, master's, doctoral, post-master's, and first professional certificates (branch locations at Rose Hill and Lincoln Center). *Special study options:* accelerated degree program, adult/continuing education programs, advanced placement credit, double majors, English as a second language, honors programs, independent study, internships, off-campus study, part-time degree program, services for LD students,

student-designed majors, study abroad, summer session for credit. *ROTC:* Army (b), Navy (c), Air Force (c). *Unusual degree programs:* 3-2 business administration; engineering with Columbia University, Case Western Reserve University; social work; education, law, religion.

Computers on Campus 1,400 computers/terminals are available on campus for general student use. Students can access the following: free student e-mail accounts, online (class) registration. Campuswide network is available. Wireless service is available via entire campus.

Student Life *Housing options:* coed, disabled students. Campus housing is university owned. *Activities and organizations:* drama/theater group, student-run newspaper, radio station, choral group, marching band, United Student Government, Commuting Student Association, Residence Hall Association, Ambassador Program (Admission Department Student Tour Guides). *Campus security:* 24-hour emergency response devices and patrols, student patrols, late-night transport/escort service, controlled dormitory access, security at each campus entrance and at residence halls. *Student services:* health clinic, personal/psychological counseling.

Athletics Member NCAA. All Division I except football (Division I-AA). *Intercollegiate sports:* baseball M(s), basketball M(s)/W(s), cheerleading M(c)/W(c), crew M(c)/W(s), golf M, ice hockey M(c), lacrosse M(c)/W(c), rugby M(c)/W(c), sailing M(c)/W(c), soccer M(s)/W(s), softball W(s), squash M, swimming and diving M(s)/W(s), tennis M(s)/W(s), track and field M(s)/W(s), ultimate Frisbee M(c)/W(c), volleyball W(s), water polo M(s). *Intramural sports:* badminton M/W, baseball M, basketball M/W, cross-country running M/W, fencing M/W, field hockey M/W, football M/W, golf W, racquetball M/W, skiing (cross-country) M/W, skiing (downhill) M/W, soccer M/W, softball M/W, squash M/W, swimming and diving M/W, tennis M/W, volleyball M/W.

Standardized Tests *Required:* SAT or ACT (for admission). *Recommended:* SAT Subject Tests (for admission).

Costs (2011–12) *Comprehensive fee:* $54,161 includes full-time tuition ($39,235) and room and board ($14,926). Full-time tuition and fees vary according to student level. Part-time tuition: $798 per credit hour. Part-time tuition and fees vary according to course load. *Room and board:* Room and board charges vary according to board plan, housing facility, and location. *Payment plan:* installment. *Waivers:* employees or children of employees.

Financial Aid Of all full-time matriculated undergraduates who enrolled in 2009, 6,253 applied for aid, 4,773 were judged to have need, 1,236 had their need fully met. 1,189 Federal Work-Study jobs (averaging $2752). In 2009, 1301 non-need-based awards were made. *Average percent of need met:* 75%. *Average financial aid package:* $26,057. *Average need-based loan:* $8964. *Average need-based gift aid:* $18,140. *Average non-need-based aid:* $10,264. *Average indebtedness upon graduation:* $33,365. *Financial aid deadline:* 2/1.

Applying *Options:* electronic application, early admission, early action, deferred entrance. *Application fee:* $70. *Required:* essay or personal statement, high school transcript, 1 letter of recommendation. *Application deadlines:* 1/15 (freshmen), 6/1 (transfers), 11/1 (early action). *Notification:* 4/1 (freshmen), continuous (transfers), 12/25 (early action).

Freshman Application Contact Mr. John Buckley, Associate Vice President of Enrollment, Fordham University, 441 East Fordham Road, New York, NY 10458. *Phone:* 718-817-4000. *Toll-free phone:* 800-FORDHAM. *Fax:* 718-367-9404. *E-mail:* enroll@fordham.edu. *Web site:* http://www.fordham.edu/.

See page 584 for display ad and page 1336 for the College Close-Up.

Globe Institute of Technology

New York, New York

Freshman Application Contact Mr. Michael Scalice, Admissions Director, Globe Institute of Technology, 500 7th Avenue, New York, NY 10018. *Phone:* 212-349-4330 Ext. 1624. *Toll-free phone:* 888-51-GLOBE (in-state); 800-51-GLOBE (out-of-state). *Fax:* 212-227-5920. *E-mail:* admissions@globe.edu. *Web site:* http://www.globe.edu/.

Hamilton College

Clinton, New York

- **Independent** 4-year, founded 1812
- **Small-town** 1300-acre campus
- **Endowment** $657.5 million
- **Coed** 1,864 undergraduate students, 99% full-time, 53% women, 47% men
- **Very difficult** entrance level, 27% of applicants were admitted

Undergraduates 1,844 full-time, 20 part-time. Students come from 48 states and territories; 38 other countries; 67% are from out of state; 4% Black or Afri-

can American, non-Hispanic/Latino; 6% Hispanic/Latino; 6% Asian, non-Hispanic/Latino; 0.3% American Indian or Alaska Native, non-Hispanic/Latino; 2% Two or more races, non-Hispanic/Latino; 12% Race/ethnicity unknown; 5% international; 1% transferred in; 98% live on campus. *Retention:* 94% of full-time freshmen returned.

Freshmen *Admission:* 5,265 applied, 1,441 admitted, 481 enrolled. *Test scores:* SAT critical reading scores over 500: 99%; SAT math scores over 500: 100%; SAT writing scores over 500: 99%; ACT scores over 18: 100%; SAT critical reading scores over 600: 90%; SAT math scores over 600: 90%; SAT writing scores over 600: 89%; ACT scores over 24: 94%; SAT critical reading scores over 700: 47%; SAT math scores over 700: 49%; SAT writing scores over 700: 50%; ACT scores over 30: 62%.

Faculty *Total:* 219, 84% full-time, 86% with terminal degrees. *Student/faculty ratio:* 9:1.

Academics *Calendar:* semesters. *Degree:* bachelor's. *Special study options:* accelerated degree program, adult/continuing education programs, advanced placement credit, double majors, English as a second language, independent study, internships, off-campus study, part-time degree program, services for LD students, student-designed majors, study abroad. *ROTC:* Army (c), Air Force (c). *Unusual degree programs:* 3-2 engineering with Columbia University, Dartmouth College, Rensselaer Polytechnic Institute, Washington University in St. Louis.

Computers on Campus 878 computers/terminals and 3,000 ports are available on campus for general student use. Students can access the following: campus intranet, computer help desk, free student e-mail accounts, online (class) grades, online (class) registration, online (class) schedules. Campuswide network is available. 100% of college-owned or -operated housing units are wired for high-speed Internet access. Wireless service is available via entire campus.

Student Life *Housing:* on-campus residence required through senior year. *Options:* coed, cooperative, disabled students. Campus housing is university owned. Freshman campus housing is guaranteed. *Activities and organizations:* drama/theater group, student-run newspaper, radio station, choral group, WHCL (Hamilton College Radio), People Who Like To Do Fun Things, Yoga Club, Operation Smile, Hamilton eSports Team, national fraternities, national sororities. *Campus security:* 24-hour emergency response devices and patrols, late-night transport/escort service, controlled dormitory access, student safety program. *Student services:* health clinic, personal/psychological counseling, women's center.

Athletics Member NCAA. All Division III. *Intercollegiate sports:* baseball M, basketball M/W, crew M/W, cross-country running M/W, equestrian sports M(c)/W(c), fencing M(c)/W(c), field hockey W, football M, golf M/W(c), ice hockey M/W, lacrosse M/W, rugby M(c)/W(c), sailing M(c)/W(c), skiing (cross-country) M(c)/W(c), skiing (downhill) M(c)/W(c), soccer M/W, softball W, squash M/W, swimming and diving M/W, tennis M/W, track and field M/W, ultimate Frisbee M(c)/W(c), volleyball M(c)/W, water polo M(c). *Intramural sports:* badminton M/W, basketball M/W, football M/W, golf M/W, ice hockey M/W, racquetball M/W, skiing (cross-country) M/W, soccer M/W, softball M/W, squash M/W, tennis M/W, volleyball M/W, water polo M/W.

Standardized Tests *Required:* SAT and SAT Subject Tests or ACT (for admission).

Costs (2011–12) *Comprehensive fee:* $53,470 includes full-time tuition ($42,220), mandatory fees ($420), and room and board ($10,830). Part-time tuition: $5278 per course. *College room only:* $5920. Room and board charges vary according to board plan. *Payment plan:* installment. *Waivers:* employees or children of employees.

Financial Aid Of all full-time matriculated undergraduates who enrolled in 2011, 888 applied for aid, 822 were judged to have need, 822 had their need fully met. 543 Federal Work-Study jobs (averaging $1636). 56 state and other part-time jobs (averaging $1809). *Average percent of need met:* 100%. *Average financial aid package:* $38,085. *Average need-based loan:* $3873. *Average need-based gift aid:* $33,795. *Average indebtedness upon graduation:* $20,262. *Financial aid deadline:* 2/8.

Applying *Options:* electronic application, early decision, deferred entrance. *Application fee:* $60. *Required:* essay or personal statement, high school transcript, 1 letter of recommendation. *Recommended:* interview. *Application deadlines:* 1/1 (freshmen), 4/15 (transfers). *Early decision deadline:* 11/15 (for plan 1), 1/1 (for plan 2). *Notification:* 4/1 (freshmen), 5/15 (transfers), 12/15 (early decision plan 1), 2/15 (early decision plan 2).

Freshman Application Contact Ms. Monica Inzer, Vice President and Dean of Admission and Financial Aid, Hamilton College, 198 College Hill Road, Clinton, NY 13323. *Phone:* 800-843-2655. *Toll-free phone:* 800-843-2655. *Fax:* 315-859-4457. *E-mail:* admission@hamilton.edu. *Web site:* http://www.hamilton.edu/.

Hartwick College

Oneonta, New York

- **Independent** 4-year, founded 1797
- **Small-town** 425-acre campus with easy access to Albany, NY
- **Endowment** $61.2 million
- **Coed** 1,578 undergraduate students, 96% full-time, 58% women, 42% men
- **Moderately difficult** entrance level, 77% of applicants were admitted

Undergraduates 1,520 full-time, 58 part-time. Students come from 32 states and territories; 18 other countries; 27% are from out of state; 5% Black or African American, non-Hispanic/Latino; 6% Hispanic/Latino; 2% Asian, non-Hispanic/Latino; 0.1% American Indian or Alaska Native, non-Hispanic/Latino; 19% Race/ethnicity unknown; 2% international; 2% transferred in; 75% live on campus. *Retention:* 77% of full-time freshmen returned.

Freshmen *Admission:* 4,897 applied, 3,774 admitted, 489 enrolled. *Average high school GPA:* 3.2. *Test scores:* SAT critical reading scores over 500: 82%; SAT math scores over 500: 83%; SAT writing scores over 500: 73%; ACT scores over 18: 99%; SAT critical reading scores over 600: 30%; SAT math scores over 600: 33%; SAT writing scores over 600: 24%; ACT scores over 24: 68%; SAT critical reading scores over 700: 4%; SAT math scores over 700: 2%; SAT writing scores over 700: 4%; ACT scores over 30: 12%.

Faculty *Total:* 183, 57% full-time, 55% with terminal degrees. *Student/faculty ratio:* 11:1.

Academics *Calendar:* 4-1-4. *Degree:* bachelor's. *Special study options:* accelerated degree program, advanced placement credit, double majors, honors programs, independent study, internships, off-campus study, part-time degree program, services for LD students, student-designed majors, study abroad, summer session for credit. *Unusual degree programs:* 3-2 engineering with Clarkson University, Columbia University.

Computers on Campus 80 computers/terminals are available on campus for general student use. Students can access the following: computer help desk, free student e-mail accounts, online (class) grades, online (class) registration, online (class) schedules. Campuswide network is available. 100% of college-owned or -operated housing units are wired for high-speed Internet access. Wireless service is available via entire campus.

Student Life *Housing:* on-campus residence required through junior year. *Options:* coed. Campus housing is university owned. Freshman campus housing is guaranteed. *Activities and organizations:* drama/theater group, student-run newspaper, radio station, choral group, Student Union, student radio station, Student Senate, Hilltops campus newspaper, Cardboard Alley Players, national fraternities, national sororities. *Campus security:* 24-hour emergency response devices and patrols, late-night transport/escort service, controlled dormitory access. *Student services:* health clinic, personal/psychological counseling, women's center.

Athletics Member NCAA. All Division III except soccer (Division I), water polo (Division I). *Intercollegiate sports:* basketball M/W, cheerleading W, cross-country running M/W, equestrian sports W, field hockey W, football M, ice hockey M(c), lacrosse M/W, rugby M(c), soccer M(s)/W, swimming and diving M/W, tennis M/W, volleyball W, water polo M(c)/W(s). *Intramural sports:* basketball M/W, cross-country running M/W, football M, golf M/W, racquetball M/W, soccer M/W, squash M/W, swimming and diving M/W, table tennis M/W, tennis M/W, track and field M/W, volleyball M/W, water polo M/W.

Standardized Tests *Required for some:* SAT or ACT (for admission).

Costs (2011–12) *One-time required fee:* $400. *Comprehensive fee:* $45,665 includes full-time tuition ($35,240), mandatory fees ($800), and room and board ($9625). Part-time tuition: $1115 per credit hour. *College room only:* $4985. Room and board charges vary according to board plan and housing facility. *Payment plan:* installment. *Waivers:* employees or children of employees.

Financial Aid Of all full-time matriculated undergraduates who enrolled in 2010, 586 Federal Work-Study jobs (averaging $710,000).

Applying *Options:* electronic application, early admission, early decision, deferred entrance. *Required:* high school transcript, audition for music program; portfolio for Art majors; SAT scores required of Nursing majors. *Recommended:* minimum 2.5 GPA. *Application deadlines:* rolling (freshmen), 8/1 (transfers). *Early decision deadline:* 11/1. *Notification:* continuous (freshmen), continuous until 8/15 (transfers), 12/1 (early decision plan 1), rolling (early decision plan 2).

Freshman Application Contact Mr. Jonathan Kent, Director of Admissions, Hartwick College, PO Box 4022, Oneonta, NY 13820-4022. *Phone:* 607-431-4150. *Toll-free phone:* 888-HARTWICK. *Fax:* 607-431-4102. *E-mail:* admissions@hartwick.edu. *Web site:* http://www.hartwick.edu/.

Hilbert College

Hamburg, New York

- **Independent** comprehensive, founded 1957
- **Small-town** 40-acre campus with easy access to Buffalo
- **Endowment** $3.4 million
- **Coed** 1,068 undergraduate students, 86% full-time, 58% women, 42% men
- **Minimally difficult** entrance level, 69% of applicants were admitted

Undergraduates 915 full-time, 153 part-time. Students come from 5 states and territories; 3 other countries; 1% are from out of state; 10% Black or African American, non-Hispanic/Latino; 3% Hispanic/Latino; 0.5% Asian, non-Hispanic/Latino; 0.1% Native Hawaiian or other Pacific Islander, non-Hispanic/Latino; 1% American Indian or Alaska Native, non-Hispanic/Latino; 0.9% Two or more races, non-Hispanic/Latino; 19% Race/ethnicity unknown; 0.1% international; 32% transferred in; 28% live on campus. *Retention:* 66% of full-time freshmen returned.

Freshmen *Admission:* 1,124 applied, 777 admitted, 228 enrolled. *Average high school GPA:* 3. *Test scores:* SAT critical reading scores over 500: 26%; SAT math scores over 500: 31%; ACT scores over 18: 80%; SAT critical reading scores over 600: 2%; SAT math scores over 600: 6%; ACT scores over 24: 21%.

Faculty *Total:* 126, 37% full-time, 29% with terminal degrees. *Student/faculty ratio:* 13:1.

Academics *Calendar:* semesters. *Degrees:* associate, bachelor's, and master's. *Special study options:* academic remediation for entering students, advanced placement credit, cooperative education, distance learning, honors programs, independent study, internships, part-time degree program, services for LD students, study abroad, summer session for credit. *ROTC:* Army (c).

Computers on Campus 146 computers/terminals are available on campus for general student use. Students can access the following: campus intranet, computer help desk, free student e-mail accounts, online (class) grades, online (class) registration, online (class) schedules. Campuswide network is available. 100% of college-owned or -operated housing units are wired for high-speed Internet access. Wireless service is available via entire campus.

Student Life *Housing options:* coed. Campus housing is university owned and leased by the school. Freshman applicants given priority for college housing. *Activities and organizations:* drama/theater group, student-run newspaper, radio station, Student Government Association, Student Business and Accounting Association, SADD, Students in Free Enterprise (SIFE), Criminal Justice Association. *Campus security:* 24-hour emergency response devices and patrols, student patrols, late-night transport/escort service, controlled dormitory access. *Student services:* health clinic, personal/psychological counseling.

Athletics Member NCAA. All Division III. *Intercollegiate sports:* baseball M, basketball M/W, cross-country running M/W, golf M, lacrosse M/W, soccer M/W, softball W, volleyball M/W. *Intramural sports:* baseball M, basketball M/W, bowling M/W, cheerleading W, football M/W, golf M, ice hockey M(c), lacrosse W(c), skiing (downhill) M(c)/W(c), soccer M/W, softball W, table tennis M/W, ultimate Frisbee M/W, volleyball M/W.

Standardized Tests *Recommended:* SAT or ACT (for admission).

Costs (2012–13) *One-time required fee:* $40. *Comprehensive fee:* $28,190 includes full-time tuition ($19,000), mandatory fees ($620), and room and board ($8570). Full-time tuition and fees vary according to course load. Part-time tuition: $460 per credit. Part-time tuition and fees vary according to course load. *Required fees:* $15 per credit part-time, $55 per term part-time. *College room only:* $4350. Room and board charges vary according to board plan and housing facility. *Payment plan:* installment. *Waivers:* minority students, children of alumni, adult students, senior citizens, and employees or children of employees.

Financial Aid Of all full-time matriculated undergraduates who enrolled in 2007, 797 applied for aid, 707 were judged to have need, 192 had their need fully met. 67 Federal Work-Study jobs (averaging $1547). In 2007, 103 non-need-based awards were made. *Average percent of need met:* 74%. *Average financial aid package:* $11,096. *Average need-based loan:* $4947. *Average need-based gift aid:* $6690. *Average non-need-based aid:* $10,870. *Average indebtedness upon graduation:* $24,444. *Financial aid deadline:* 5/1.

Applying *Options:* electronic application, deferred entrance. *Application fee:* $25. *Required:* high school transcript. *Required for some:* interview. *Recommended:* essay or personal statement, interview. *Application deadlines:* rolling (freshmen), rolling (transfers). *Notification:* continuous (freshmen), continuous (transfers).

Freshman Application Contact Mr. Timothy Lee, Director of Admissions, Hilbert College, 5200 South Park Avenue, Hamburg, NY 14075-1597. *Phone:* 716-649-7900. *Toll-free phone:* 800-649-8003. *Fax:* 716-649-0702. *E-mail:* tlee@hilbert.edu. *Web site:* http://www.hilbert.edu/.

Hobart and William Smith Colleges

Geneva, New York

- **Independent** comprehensive, founded 1822
- **Small-town** 200-acre campus with easy access to Rochester, Syracuse
- **Endowment** $182.8 million
- **Coed** 2,234 undergraduate students, 100% full-time, 56% women, 44% men
- **Very difficult** entrance level, 60% of applicants were admitted

Undergraduates 2,225 full-time, 9 part-time. Students come from 39 states and territories; 25 other countries; 56% are from out of state; 5% Black or African American, non-Hispanic/Latino; 5% Hispanic/Latino; 3% Asian, non-Hispanic/Latino; 0.9% American Indian or Alaska Native, non-Hispanic/Latino; 20% Race/ethnicity unknown; 4% international; 0.5% transferred in; 90% live on campus. *Retention:* 87% of full-time freshmen returned.
Freshmen *Admission:* 4,454 applied, 2,656 admitted, 681 enrolled. *Average high school GPA:* 3.55. *Test scores:* SAT critical reading scores over 500: 97%; SAT math scores over 500: 97%; ACT scores over 18: 100%; SAT critical reading scores over 600: 55%; SAT math scores over 600: 59%; ACT scores over 24: 91%; SAT critical reading scores over 700: 9%; SAT math scores over 700: 10%; ACT scores over 30: 22%.
Faculty *Total:* 214, 89% full-time, 96% with terminal degrees. *Student/faculty ratio:* 11:1.
Academics *Calendar:* semesters. *Degrees:* bachelor's, master's, and post-bachelor's certificates. *Special study options:* accelerated degree program, adult/continuing education programs, advanced placement credit, double majors, English as a second language, honors programs, independent study, internships, off-campus study, services for LD students, student-designed majors, study abroad. *Unusual degree programs:* 3-2 business administration with Clarkson University, Rochester Institute of Technology; engineering with Columbia University, Rensselaer Polytechnic Institute, Dartmouth College; architecture with Washington University in St. Louis.
Computers on Campus 115 computers/terminals and 7,942 ports are available on campus for general student use. Students can access the following: campus intranet, computer help desk, free student e-mail accounts, online (class) grades, online (class) registration, online (class) schedules. Campus-wide network is available. 100% of college-owned or -operated housing units are wired for high-speed Internet access. Wireless service is available via entire campus.
Student Life *Housing:* on-campus residence required through junior year. *Options:* coed, men-only, women-only, cooperative. Campus housing is university owned. Freshman campus housing is guaranteed. *Activities and organizations:* drama/theater group, student-run newspaper, radio station, choral group, Student Life and Leadership, student government, campus publications, Service Network, sports clubs, national fraternities. *Campus security:* 24-hour emergency response devices and patrols, late-night transport/escort service, controlled dormitory access. *Student services:* health clinic, personal/psychological counseling, women's center, legal services.
Athletics Member NCAA. All Division III except lacrosse (Division I). *Intercollegiate sports:* basketball M/W, crew M/W, cross-country running M/W, equestrian sports M(c)/W(c), field hockey W, football M, golf M/W, ice hockey M/W(c), lacrosse M/W, rock climbing M(c)/W(c), rugby M(c)/W(c), sailing M/W, skiing (downhill) M(c)/W(c), soccer M/W, squash M/W, swimming and diving W, tennis M/W, ultimate Frisbee M(c)/W(c). *Intramural sports:* badminton M/W, baseball M, basketball M/W, fencing M/W, football M, golf M/W, ice hockey M/W, lacrosse M/W, racquetball M/W, skiing (cross-country) M/W, skiing (downhill) M/W, soccer M/W, softball M/W, squash M/W, swimming and diving M/W, table tennis M/W, tennis M/W, track and field M/W, ultimate Frisbee M/W, volleyball M/W, water polo M/W, weight lifting M/W.
Standardized Tests *Required for some:* SAT or ACT (for admission).
Costs (2011–12) *Comprehensive fee:* $53,767 includes full-time tuition ($42,014), mandatory fees ($901), and room and board ($10,852). *Room and board:* Room and board charges vary according to board plan. *Payment plans:* tuition prepayment, installment. *Waivers:* employees or children of employees.
Financial Aid Of all full-time matriculated undergraduates who enrolled in 2009, 1,581 applied for aid, 1,329 were judged to have need, 1,106 had their need fully met. 901 Federal Work-Study jobs (averaging $1752), 423 state and other part-time jobs (averaging $1896). In 2009, 396 non-need-based awards were made. *Average percent of need met:* 78%. *Average financial aid package:* $29,446. *Average need-based loan:* $4211. *Average need-based gift aid:* $25,001. *Average non-need-based aid:* $14,182. *Average indebtedness upon graduation:* $29,932. *Financial aid deadline:* 3/15.
Applying *Options:* electronic application, early admission, early decision, deferred entrance. *Application fee:* $45. *Required:* essay or personal statement, high school transcript, 1 letter of recommendation. *Recommended:* interview. *Application deadlines:* 2/1 (freshmen), 7/1 (transfers). *Early decision deadline:* 11/15 (for plan 1), 1/1 (for plan 2). *Notification:* 4/1 (freshmen), continuous (transfers), 12/15 (early decision plan 1), 2/1 (early decision plan 2).
Freshman Application Contact Hobart and William Smith Colleges, Geneva, NY 14456-3397. *Phone:* 315-781-3622. *Toll-free phone:* 800-852-2256. *Web site:* http://www.hws.edu/.

Hofstra University

Hempstead, New York

- **Independent** university, founded 1935
- **Suburban** 240-acre campus with easy access to New York City
- **Endowment** $278.3 million
- **Coed** 7,183 undergraduate students, 92% full-time, 53% women, 47% men
- **Moderately difficult** entrance level, 59% of applicants were admitted

Undergraduates 6,636 full-time, 547 part-time. Students come from 47 states and territories; 50 other countries; 36% are from out of state; 9% Black or African American, non-Hispanic/Latino; 11% Hispanic/Latino; 6% Asian, non-Hispanic/Latino; 0.3% Native Hawaiian or other Pacific Islander, non-Hispanic/Latino; 0.2% American Indian or Alaska Native, non-Hispanic/Latino; 2% Two or more races, non-Hispanic/Latino; 5% Race/ethnicity unknown; 2% international; 7% transferred in; 49% live on campus. *Retention:* 80% of full-time freshmen returned.
Freshmen *Admission:* 21,376 applied, 12,576 admitted, 1,675 enrolled. *Average high school GPA:* 3.51. *Test scores:* SAT critical reading scores over 500: 91%; SAT math scores over 500: 95%; ACT scores over 18: 99%; SAT critical reading scores over 600: 38%; SAT math scores over 600: 46%; ACT scores over 24: 74%; SAT critical reading scores over 700: 5%; SAT math scores over 700: 6%; ACT scores over 30: 9%.
Faculty *Total:* 1,114, 47% full-time, 65% with terminal degrees. *Student/faculty ratio:* 14:1.
Academics *Calendar:* 4-1-4. *Degrees:* certificates, bachelor's, master's, doctoral, post-master's, postbachelor's, and first professional certificates. *Special study options:* accelerated degree program, advanced placement credit, distance learning, double majors, English as a second language, external degree program, freshman honors college, honors programs, independent study, internships, part-time degree program, services for LD students, student-designed majors, study abroad, summer session for credit. *ROTC:* Army (b). *Unusual degree programs:* 3-2 business administration; BS/MS in Physician Assistant Studies; BA/MS and BS/MS in Computer Science; BA/JD LEAP Program.
Computers on Campus 1,628 computers/terminals and 1,900 ports are available on campus for general student use. Students can access the following: campus intranet, computer help desk, free student e-mail accounts, online (class) grades, online (class) registration, online (class) schedules, Gmail/Google Apps for students; Emergency Notification System; Online course management system; online card services balance update; online e-portfolio. Campuswide network is available. 100% of college-owned or -operated housing units are wired for high-speed Internet access. Wireless service is available via entire campus.
Student Life *Housing options:* coed, disabled students. Campus housing is university owned. Freshman applicants given priority for college housing. *Activities and organizations:* drama/theater group, student-run newspaper, radio and television station, choral group, Inter Fraternal and Sororal Council, Danceworks, APHOS (Association of Pre-Health Oriented students), Zarb Asian Students Association (graduate club), Phi Eta Sigma Honor Society, national fraternities, national sororities. *Campus security:* 24-hour emergency response devices and patrols, student patrols, late-night transport/escort service, controlled dormitory access, residence halls - security cameras/card access to entry (monitored 24/7); bike patrol; and motorist assistance program. *Student services:* health clinic, personal/psychological counseling.
Athletics Member NCAA. All Division I. *Intercollegiate sports:* baseball M(s), basketball M(s)/W(s), cross-country running M(s)/W(s), field hockey W(s), golf M(s)/W(s), lacrosse M(s)/W(s), soccer M(s)/W(s), softball W(s), tennis M(s)/W(s), volleyball W(s), wrestling M(s). *Intramural sports:* badminton M/W, baseball M(c), basketball M/W, crew M(c)/W(c), cross-country running M(c)/W(c), equestrian sports M(c)/W(c), football M/W, ice hockey M(c), lacrosse M(c)/W(c), rugby M(c)/W(c), soccer M/W, softball M/W, table tennis M/W, tennis M/W, track and field W(c), ultimate Frisbee M/W, volleyball M/W.
Standardized Tests *Required for some:* SAT or ACT (for admission). *Recommended:* SAT Subject Tests (for admission).
Costs (2011–12) *Comprehensive fee:* $46,090 includes full-time tuition ($33,100), mandatory fees ($1050), and room and board ($11,940). Full-time tuition and fees vary according to course load and program. Part-time tuition: $990 per credit hour. Part-time tuition and fees vary according to course load and program. No tuition increase for student's term of enrollment. *Required*

fees: $155 per term part-time. *College room only:* $8150. Room and board charges vary according to board plan and housing facility. *Payment plan:* installment. *Waivers:* senior citizens and employees or children of employees. **Financial Aid** Of all full-time matriculated undergraduates who enrolled in 2011, 5,181 applied for aid, 4,398 were judged to have need, 845 had their need fully met. 1,403 Federal Work-Study jobs (averaging $3024). 1,514 state and other part-time jobs (averaging $2960). In 2011, 1302 non-need-based awards were made. *Average percent of need met:* 60%. *Average financial aid package:* $22,000. *Average need-based loan:* $5000. *Average need-based gift aid:* $13,000. *Average non-need-based aid:* $11,000.
Applying *Options:* electronic application, early admission, early action, deferred entrance. *Application fee:* $70. *Required:* essay or personal statement, high school transcript, minimum 2.5 GPA, 2 letters of recommendation, proof of degree required for all; TOEFL required for international students. *Required for some:* interview. *Application deadlines:* rolling (freshmen), 12/15 (early action). *Notification:* 2/1 (freshmen), continuous (transfers), 1/15 (early action).
Freshman Application Contact Sunil Samuel, Director of Admissions, Hofstra University, 100 Hofstra University, Hempstead, NY 11549. *Phone:* 516-463-6700. *Toll-free phone:* 800-HOFSTRA. *Fax:* 516-463-5100. *E-mail:* admission@hofstra.edu. *Web site:* http://www.hofstra.edu/.

See page 589 for display ad and page 1366 for the College Close-Up.

Holy Trinity Orthodox Seminary
Jordanville, New York

- **Independent Russian Orthodox** 5-year, founded 1948
- **Rural** 900-acre campus
- **Men only** 29 undergraduate students, 100% full-time
- **Noncompetitive** entrance level, 100% of applicants were admitted

Undergraduates 29 full-time. 95% live on campus.
Freshmen *Admission:* 12 applied, 12 admitted, 11 enrolled.
Faculty *Total:* 15. *Student/faculty ratio:* 2:1.
Academics *Calendar:* semesters. *Degree:* certificates and bachelor's. *Special study options:* accelerated degree program, distance learning, English as a second language.
Computers on Campus 8 computers/terminals are available on campus for general student use. Campuswide network is available.
Student Life *Housing options:* men-only. Campus housing is university owned. *Activities and organizations:* student-run newspaper, choral group,

Student Union. *Campus security:* 24-hour emergency response devices. *Student services:* health clinic, personal/psychological counseling.
Costs (2012–13) *Comprehensive fee:* $8000 includes full-time tuition ($5500) and room and board ($2500).
Applying *Options:* deferred entrance. *Required:* essay or personal statement, high school transcript, 1 letter of recommendation, interview, Orthodoxy/Orthodox baptism, entrance exam required. Recommendation from spiritual father or parish priest necessary. *Application deadlines:* 5/1 (freshmen), 5/1 (out-of-state freshmen), 5/1 (transfers).
Freshman Application Contact Ephraim Willmarth, Administrative Assistant, Holy Trinity Orthodox Seminary, PO Box 36, Jordanville, NY 13361. *Phone:* 315-858-0945. *Fax:* 315-858-0945. *E-mail:* ejwillmarth@hts.edu. *Web site:* http://www.hts.edu/.

Houghton College
Houghton, New York

- **Independent Wesleyan** comprehensive, founded 1883
- **Rural** 1300-acre campus with easy access to Buffalo, Rochester
- **Endowment** $39.7 million
- **Coed** 1,268 undergraduate students, 94% full-time, 65% women, 35% men
- **Moderately difficult** entrance level, 72% of applicants were admitted

Undergraduates 1,187 full-time, 81 part-time. Students come from 37 states and territories; 32 other countries; 41% are from out of state; 3% Black or African American, non-Hispanic/Latino; 2% Hispanic/Latino; 1% Asian, non-Hispanic/Latino; 0.8% American Indian or Alaska Native, non-Hispanic/Latino; 1% Two or more races, non-Hispanic/Latino; 1% Race/ethnicity unknown; 6% international; 4% transferred in; 88% live on campus. *Retention:* 86% of full-time freshmen returned.
Freshmen *Admission:* 1,085 applied, 777 admitted, 266 enrolled. *Average high school GPA:* 3.57. *Test scores:* SAT critical reading scores over 500: 83%; SAT math scores over 500: 80%; SAT writing scores over 500: 75%; ACT scores over 18: 97%; SAT critical reading scores over 600: 44%; SAT math scores over 600: 42%; SAT writing scores over 600: 31%; ACT scores over 24: 65%; SAT critical reading scores over 700: 12%; SAT math scores over 700: 5%; SAT writing scores over 700: 6%; ACT scores over 30: 8%.
Faculty *Total:* 135, 61% full-time, 65% with terminal degrees. *Student/faculty ratio:* 11:1.

Academics *Calendar:* semesters. *Degrees:* associate, bachelor's, and master's. *Special study options:* accelerated degree program, adult/continuing education programs, advanced placement credit, distance learning, double majors, honors programs, independent study, internships, off-campus study, services for LD students, study abroad, summer session for credit. *ROTC:* Army (c). *Unusual degree programs:* 3-2 engineering with Clarkson University.

Computers on Campus 30 computers/terminals and 820 ports are available on campus for general student use. Students can access the following: campus intranet, computer help desk, free student e-mail accounts, online (class) grades, online (class) registration, online (class) schedules. Campuswide network is available. 100% of college-owned or -operated housing units are wired for high-speed Internet access. Wireless service is available via entire campus.

Student Life *Housing:* on-campus residence required through sophomore year. *Options:* men-only, women-only, cooperative. Campus housing is university owned. Freshman campus housing is guaranteed. *Activities and organizations:* drama/theater group, student-run newspaper, choral group, Student Government Association, Global Christian Fellowship, Allegany County Outreach, Drama Clubs, Intercultural Student Association. *Campus security:* 24-hour patrols, late-night transport/escort service, controlled dormitory access, phone connection to security patrols. *Student services:* health clinic, personal/psychological counseling.

Athletics Member NCAA, NAIA, NCCAA. All NCAA Division III. *Intercollegiate sports:* baseball M, basketball M/W, cross-country running M/W, field hockey W, golf M/W, lacrosse M/W, soccer M/W, softball W, tennis M/W, track and field M/W, volleyball W. *Intramural sports:* baseball M, basketball M/W, equestrian sports M/W, football M, racquetball M/W, rock climbing M/W, skiing (cross-country) M/W, skiing (downhill) M/W, soccer M/W, swimming and diving M/W, table tennis M/W, ultimate Frisbee M(c)/W(c), volleyball M/W, water polo M/W.

Standardized Tests *Required for some:* SAT or ACT (for admission). *Recommended:* SAT or ACT (for admission).

Costs (2011–12) *Comprehensive fee:* $33,644 includes full-time tuition ($25,994), mandatory fees ($100), and room and board ($7550). Part-time tuition: $1092 per credit hour. *College room only:* $4050. Room and board charges vary according to board plan, gender, housing facility, and student level. *Payment plan:* installment. *Waivers:* employees or children of employees.

Financial Aid Of all full-time matriculated undergraduates who enrolled in 2010, 1,054 applied for aid, 993 were judged to have need, 176 had their need fully met. 744 Federal Work-Study jobs (averaging $2127). 1 state and other part-time job (averaging $2250). In 2010, 169 non-need-based awards were made. *Average percent of need met:* 79%. *Average financial aid package:* $21,540. *Average need-based loan:* $5350. *Average need-based gift aid:* $15,315. *Average non-need-based aid:* $9743. *Average indebtedness upon graduation:* $23,010.

Applying *Options:* electronic application, early action, deferred entrance. *Application fee:* $40. *Required:* high school transcript, 1 letter of recommendation. *Required for some:* essay or personal statement. *Recommended:* essay or personal statement, interview. *Application deadlines:* rolling (freshmen), rolling (transfers), 12/1 (early action). *Notification:* continuous (freshmen), continuous (transfers), 1/15 (early action).

Freshman Application Contact Mr. Matthew Reitnour, Director of Admission, Houghton College, PO Box 128, Houghton, NY 14744. *Phone:* 585-567-9353. *Toll-free phone:* 800-777-2556. *Fax:* 585-567-9522. *E-mail:* admission@houghton.edu. *Web site:* http://www.houghton.edu/.

See page 1372 for the College Close-Up.

Hunter College of the City University of New York

New York, New York

- **State and locally supported** comprehensive, founded 1870, part of City University of New York System
- **Urban** campus
- **Endowment** $54.7 million
- **Coed** 16,345 undergraduate students, 71% full-time, 66% women, 34% men
- **Moderately difficult** entrance level, 27% of applicants were admitted

Undergraduates 11,548 full-time, 4,797 part-time. Students come from 38 states and territories; 147 other countries; 4% are from out of state; 11% Black or African American, non-Hispanic/Latino; 18% Hispanic/Latino; 24% Asian, non-Hispanic/Latino; 0.2% American Indian or Alaska Native, non-Hispanic/Latino; 7% international; 11% transferred in; 1% live on campus. *Retention:* 85% of full-time freshmen returned.

Freshmen *Admission:* 30,529 applied, 8,315 admitted, 2,177 enrolled. *Average high school GPA:* 3. *Test scores:* SAT critical reading scores over 500: 78%; SAT math scores over 500: 92%; SAT critical reading scores over 600:

29%; SAT math scores over 600: 43%; SAT critical reading scores over 700: 7%; SAT math scores over 700: 9%.

Faculty *Total:* 1,873, 37% full-time, 44% with terminal degrees. *Student/faculty ratio:* 15:1.

Academics *Calendar:* semesters. *Degrees:* bachelor's, master's, and post-master's certificates. *Special study options:* advanced placement credit, distance learning, double majors, English as a second language, freshman honors college, honors programs, independent study, internships, off-campus study, part-time degree program, services for LD students, student-designed majors, study abroad, summer session for credit. *Unusual degree programs:* 3-2 anthropology, economics, English, history, mathematics, music, physics, sociology.

Computers on Campus 1,280 computers/terminals are available on campus for general student use. Students can access the following: computer help desk, free student e-mail accounts, online (class) registration, online (class) schedules. Campuswide network is available.

Student Life *Housing options:* coed. *Activities and organizations:* drama/theater group, student-run newspaper, radio and television station, choral group. *Campus security:* 24-hour emergency response devices and patrols. *Student services:* personal/psychological counseling, women's center.

Athletics Member NCAA. All Division III. *Intercollegiate sports:* basketball M/W, cross-country running M/W, fencing M/W, gymnastics W, soccer M, swimming and diving W, tennis M/W, track and field M/W, volleyball M/W, wrestling M. *Intramural sports:* basketball M/W, cross-country running M/W, gymnastics M/W, racquetball M/W, rugby M, soccer M/W, swimming and diving M/W, tennis M/W, volleyball M/W.

Standardized Tests *Required:* SAT or ACT (for admission).

Costs (2012–13) *Tuition:* state resident $215 per credit part-time; nonresident $460 per credit part-time. Full-time tuition and fees vary according to degree level and program. Part-time tuition and fees vary according to degree level and program. *Required fees:* $184 part-time. *Payment plan:* installment.

Financial Aid Of all full-time matriculated undergraduates who enrolled in 2010, 8,235 applied for aid, 6,996 were judged to have need, 1,028 had their need fully met. In 2010, 788 non-need-based awards were made. *Average percent of need met:* 76%. *Average financial aid package:* $5094. *Average need-based loan:* $3338. *Average need-based gift aid:* $4178. *Average non-need-based aid:* $2487. *Average indebtedness upon graduation:* $9000.

Applying *Options:* early admission. *Application fee:* $65. *Required:* high school transcript. *Application deadlines:* 3/15 (freshmen), 3/15 (transfers). *Notification:* continuous (freshmen), continuous (transfers).

Freshman Application Contact Mr. William Zlata, Director of Admissions, Hunter College of the City University of New York, 695 Park Avenue, New York, NY 10065-5085. *Phone:* 212-772-4490. *Fax:* 212-650-3472. *E-mail:* bill.zlata@hunter.cuny.edu. *Web site:* http://www.hunter.cuny.edu/.

See page 1374 for the College Close-Up.

Iona College

New Rochelle, New York

- **Independent** comprehensive, founded 1940, affiliated with Roman Catholic Church
- **Suburban** 35-acre campus with easy access to New York City
- **Endowment** $49.7 million
- **Coed** 3,189 undergraduate students, 97% full-time, 57% women, 43% men
- **Moderately difficult** entrance level, 72% of applicants were admitted

Undergraduates 3,097 full-time, 92 part-time. Students come from 40 states and territories; 32 other countries; 23% are from out of state; 6% Black or African American, non-Hispanic/Latino; 16% Hispanic/Latino; 2% Asian, non-Hispanic/Latino; 0.3% American Indian or Alaska Native, non-Hispanic/Latino; 1% Two or more races, non-Hispanic/Latino; 9% Race/ethnicity unknown; 2% international; 3% transferred in; 39% live on campus. *Retention:* 84% of full-time freshmen returned.

Freshmen *Admission:* 7,884 applied, 5,697 admitted, 812 enrolled. *Average high school GPA:* 2.95. *Test scores:* SAT critical reading scores over 500: 45%; SAT math scores over 500: 51%; ACT scores over 18: 88%; SAT critical reading scores over 600: 10%; SAT math scores over 600: 10%; ACT scores over 24: 26%; SAT critical reading scores over 700: 1%; SAT math scores over 700: 1%; ACT scores over 30: 2%.

Faculty *Total:* 372, 50% full-time. *Student/faculty ratio:* 15:1.

Academics *Calendar:* semesters. *Degrees:* certificates, bachelor's, master's, post-master's, and postbachelor's certificates. *Special study options:* accelerated degree program, adult/continuing education programs, advanced placement credit, distance learning, double majors, honors programs, independent study, internships, off-campus study, part-time degree program, services for LD students, study abroad, summer session for credit. *ROTC:* Army (c), Air Force (c). *Unusual degree programs:* 3-2 chemistry and education, chemistry

and computer science, criminal justice, computer science, English, history, psychology.

Computers on Campus 623 computers/terminals and 10,000 ports are available on campus for general student use. Students can access the following: campus intranet, computer help desk, free student e-mail accounts, online (class) grades, online (class) registration, online (class) schedules, Bill Payment. Campuswide network is available. 100% of college-owned or -operated housing units are wired for high-speed Internet access. Wireless service is available via entire campus.

Student Life *Housing options:* coed, disabled students. Campus housing is university owned and leased by the school. Freshman applicants given priority for college housing. *Activities and organizations:* drama/theater group, student-run newspaper, radio and television station, choral group, marching band, Student Government Association, Gales Activities Board, Council for Greek Governance, Council of Multicultural Leaders, The Ionian - Student Newspaper, national fraternities, national sororities. *Campus security:* 24-hour emergency response devices and patrols, controlled dormitory access. *Student services:* health clinic, personal/psychological counseling.

Athletics Member NCAA. All Division I. *Intercollegiate sports:* baseball M(s), basketball M(s)/W(s), crew M/W, cross-country running M(s)/W(s), golf M(s), lacrosse W(s), soccer M(s)/W(s), softball W(s), swimming and diving M(s)/W(s), track and field M(s)/W(s), volleyball W(s), water polo M/W(s). *Intramural sports:* basketball M/W, cheerleading M(c)/W(c), rugby M(c)/W(c), soccer M/W, table tennis M/W, ultimate Frisbee M/W, volleyball M/W.

Standardized Tests *Required:* SAT or ACT (for admission).

Costs (2012–13) *Comprehensive fee:* $43,978 includes full-time tuition ($29,490), mandatory fees ($2000), and room and board ($12,488). Part-time tuition: $980 per credit. Part-time tuition and fees vary according to course load. *Required fees:* $500 per term part-time. *Room and board:* Room and board charges vary according to housing facility. *Payment plans:* installment, deferred payment. *Waivers:* children of alumni, senior citizens, and employees or children of employees.

Financial Aid Of all full-time matriculated undergraduates who enrolled in 2011, 3,028 applied for aid, 2,452 were judged to have need, 473 had their need fully met. 479 Federal Work-Study jobs (averaging $1094). 300 state and other part-time jobs (averaging $1075). In 2011, 529 non-need-based awards were made. *Average percent of need met:* 27%. *Average financial aid package:* $19,091. *Average need-based loan:* $3204. *Average need-based gift aid:* $5812. *Average non-need-based aid:* $12,015. *Average indebtedness upon graduation:* $21,794. *Financial aid deadline:* 4/15.

Applying *Options:* electronic application, early action, deferred entrance. *Application fee:* $50. *Required:* essay or personal statement, high school transcript, 2 letters of recommendation, SAT or ACT required. *Required for some:* interview. *Application deadlines:* 2/15 (freshmen), 8/15 (transfers), 12/1 (early action). *Notification:* continuous (freshmen), continuous (transfers), 12/21 (early action).

Freshman Application Contact Mr. Kevin Cavanagh, Assistant Vice President for College Admissions, Iona College, Admissions, 715 North Avenue, New Rochelle, NY 10801. *Phone:* 914-633-2502. *Toll-free phone:* 800-231-IONA. *Fax:* 914-637-2778. *E-mail:* icad@iona.edu. *Web site:* http://www.iona.edu/.

Ithaca College
Ithaca, New York

- **Independent** comprehensive, founded 1892
- **Small-town** 669-acre campus with easy access to Syracuse
- **Endowment** $208.5 million
- **Coed** 6,276 undergraduate students, 98% full-time, 57% women, 43% men
- **Moderately difficult** entrance level, 68% of applicants were admitted

Undergraduates 6,173 full-time, 103 part-time. Students come from 52 states and territories; 64 other countries; 56% are from out of state; 4% Black or African American, non-Hispanic/Latino; 6% Hispanic/Latino; 3% Asian, non-Hispanic/Latino; 0.1% Native Hawaiian or other Pacific Islander, non-Hispanic/Latino; 0.2% American Indian or Alaska Native, non-Hispanic/Latino; 3% Two or more races, non-Hispanic/Latino; 13% Race/ethnicity unknown; 2% international; 2% transferred in; 69% live on campus. *Retention:* 83% of full-time freshmen returned.

Freshmen *Admission:* 13,436 applied, 9,163 admitted, 1,625 enrolled. *Test scores:* SAT critical reading scores over 500: 83%; SAT math scores over 500: 86%; SAT writing scores over 500: 86%; SAT critical reading scores over 600: 39%; SAT math scores over 600: 43%; SAT writing scores over 600: 40%; SAT critical reading scores over 700: 6%; SAT math scores over 700: 6%; SAT writing scores over 700: 6%.

Faculty *Total:* 701, 68% full-time, 86% with terminal degrees. *Student/faculty ratio:* 12:1.

Academics *Calendar:* semesters. *Degrees:* certificates, bachelor's, master's, and doctoral. *Special study options:* accelerated degree program, adult/continuing education programs, advanced placement credit, distance learning, double majors, freshman honors college, honors programs, independent study, internships, off-campus study, part-time degree program, services for LD students, student-designed majors, study abroad, summer session for credit. *ROTC:* Army (c), Air Force (c). *Unusual degree programs:* 3-2 engineering with Cornell University, Rensselaer Polytechnic Institute, Clarkson University, State University of New York at Binghamton.

Computers on Campus 640 computers/terminals and 20 ports are available on campus for general student use. Students can access the following: campus intranet, computer help desk, free student e-mail accounts, online (class) grades, online (class) registration, online (class) schedules. Campuswide network is available. 100% of college-owned or -operated housing units are wired for high-speed Internet access. Wireless service is available via entire campus.

Student Life *Housing:* on-campus residence required through junior year. *Options:* coed, women-only, disabled students. Campus housing is university owned and leased by the school. Freshman campus housing is guaranteed. *Activities and organizations:* drama/theater group, student-run newspaper, radio and television station, choral group, Student Government Association, African-Latino Society, Residence Hall Association, Habitat for Humanity, Senior Class, national fraternities, national sororities. *Campus security:* 24-hour emergency response devices and patrols, student patrols, late-night transport/escort service, controlled dormitory access. *Student services:* health clinic, personal/psychological counseling.

Athletics Member NCAA. All Division III. *Intercollegiate sports:* baseball M, basketball M/W, crew M/W, cross-country running M/W, field hockey W, football M, golf W, gymnastics W, lacrosse M/W, soccer M/W, softball W, swimming and diving M/W, tennis M/W, track and field M/W, volleyball W, wrestling M. *Intramural sports:* basketball M/W, crew M(c)/W(c), equestrian sports M(c)/W(c), football M, golf M/W, ice hockey M(c), lacrosse M(c)/W(c), rugby M(c)/W(c), skiing (downhill) M(c)/W(c), soccer M/W, softball M/W, squash M(c)/W(c), tennis M/W, ultimate Frisbee M(c)/W(c), volleyball M/W.

Standardized Tests *Required:* SAT or ACT (for admission).

Costs (2011–12) *Comprehensive fee:* $48,132 includes full-time tuition ($35,278) and room and board ($12,854). Part-time tuition: $1175 per credit hour. *College room only:* $6874. Room and board charges vary according to board plan and housing facility. *Payment plan:* installment. *Waivers:* children of alumni and employees or children of employees.

Financial Aid Of all full-time matriculated undergraduates who enrolled in 2011, 4,871 applied for aid, 4,288 were judged to have need, 2,048 had their need fully met. 3,265 Federal Work-Study jobs (averaging $2356). 1,627 state and other part-time jobs (averaging $2401). In 2011, 1205 non-need-based awards were made. *Average percent of need met:* 87%. *Average financial aid package:* $29,473. *Average need-based loan:* $6301. *Average need-based gift aid:* $19,988. *Average non-need-based aid:* $10,086.

Applying *Options:* electronic application, early admission, early decision, deferred entrance. *Application fee:* $60. *Required:* essay or personal statement, high school transcript, 1 letter of recommendation. *Required for some:* audition for some programs. *Recommended:* minimum 3.0 GPA. *Application deadlines:* 2/1 (freshmen), 3/1 (transfers). *Early decision deadline:* 11/1. *Notification:* 4/15 (freshmen), continuous (transfers), 12/15 (early decision).

Freshman Application Contact Mr. Gerard Turbide, Director of Admission, Ithaca College, 953 Danby Road, Ithaca, NY 14850-7002. *Phone:* 607-274-3124. *Toll-free phone:* 800-429-4274. *Fax:* 607-274-1900. *E-mail:* admission@ithaca.edu. *Web site:* http://www.ithaca.edu/.

Jamestown Business College
Jamestown, New York

- **Proprietary** primarily 2-year, founded 1886
- **Small-town** 1-acre campus
- **Coed** 317 undergraduate students, 96% full-time, 70% women, 30% men
- **Minimally difficult** entrance level, 98% of applicants were admitted

Undergraduates 304 full-time, 13 part-time. Students come from 2 states and territories; 11% are from out of state; 2% Black or African American, non-Hispanic/Latino; 4% Hispanic/Latino; 0.6% Asian, non-Hispanic/Latino; 0.3% Native Hawaiian or other Pacific Islander, non-Hispanic/Latino; 2% American Indian or Alaska Native, non-Hispanic/Latino; 0.6% Two or more races, non-Hispanic/Latino; 2% Race/ethnicity unknown; 13% transferred in.

Freshmen *Admission:* 101 applied, 99 admitted, 70 enrolled.

Faculty *Total:* 17, 41% full-time, 6% with terminal degrees. *Student/faculty ratio:* 32:1.

Academics *Calendar:* quarters. *Degrees:* certificates, associate, and bachelor's. *Special study options:* advanced placement credit, double majors, internships, part-time degree program, summer session for credit.

Computers on Campus 98 computers/terminals are available on campus for general student use. Students can access the following: campus intranet, free

student e-mail accounts, online (class) grades, online (class) schedules. Campuswide network is available. Wireless service is available via entire campus. **Student Life** *Housing:* college housing not available. *Campus security:* 24-hour emergency response devices.

Athletics *Intramural sports:* basketball M(c)/W(c), racquetball M(c)/W(c), softball M(c)/W(c), swimming and diving M(c)/W(c), table tennis M(c)/W(c), tennis M(c)/W(c), volleyball M(c)/W(c), weight lifting M(c)/W(c).

Costs (2012–13) *One-time required fee:* $25. *Tuition:* $10,500 full-time, $292 per credit hour part-time. *Required fees:* $900 full-time, $150 per term part-time. *Waivers:* employees or children of employees.

Applying *Application fee:* $25. *Required:* essay or personal statement, high school transcript, interview. *Application deadlines:* rolling (freshmen), rolling (transfers).

Freshman Application Contact Mrs. Brenda Salemme, Director of Admissions and Placement, Jamestown Business College, 7 Fairmount Avenue, Box 429, Jamestown, NY 14702-0429. *Phone:* 716-664-5100. *Fax:* 716-664-3144. *E-mail:* brendasalemme@jamestownbusinesscollege.edu. *Web site:* http://www.jbcny.org/.

The Jewish Theological Seminary
New York, New York

Freshman Application Contact Mr. Sergio Lineberge, List College Admissions Coordinator, The Jewish Theological Seminary, 3080 Broadway, New York, NY 10027. *Phone:* 212-678-8820. *E-mail:* lcadmissions@jtsa.edu. *Web site:* http://www.jtsa.edu/.

John Jay College of Criminal Justice of the City University of New York
New York, New York

- **State and locally supported** comprehensive, founded 1964, part of City University of New York System
- **Urban** campus with easy access to New York City
- **Coed** 12,887 undergraduate students, 77% full-time, 56% women, 44% men
- **Moderately difficult** entrance level, 13% of applicants were admitted

Undergraduates 9,935 full-time, 2,952 part-time. Students come from 26 states and territories; 139 other countries; 4% are from out of state; 22% Black or African American, non-Hispanic/Latino; 40% Hispanic/Latino; 10% Asian, non-Hispanic/Latino; 0.3% American Indian or Alaska Native, non-Hispanic/Latino; 3% international; 11% transferred in. *Retention:* 78% of full-time freshmen returned.

Freshmen *Admission:* 13,858 applied, 1,766 admitted, 1,766 enrolled. *Average high school GPA:* 2.72. *Test scores:* SAT critical reading scores over 500: 27%; SAT math scores over 500: 34%; SAT critical reading scores over 600: 4%; SAT math scores over 600: 4%.

Academics *Calendar:* semesters. *Degrees:* certificates, associate, bachelor's, and master's. *Special study options:* academic remediation for entering students, advanced placement credit, cooperative education, distance learning, double majors, English as a second language, honors programs, independent study, internships, off-campus study, part-time degree program, services for LD students, student-designed majors, study abroad, summer session for credit. *ROTC:* Air Force (c). *Unusual degree programs:* 3-2 public management, law enforcement.

Computers on Campus 1,900 computers/terminals are available on campus for general student use. Students can access the following: campus intranet, computer help desk, free student e-mail accounts, online (class) grades, online (class) registration, online (class) schedules. Campuswide network is available. Wireless service is available via classrooms, computer centers, computer labs, learning centers, libraries, student centers.

Student Life *Housing:* college housing not available. *Activities and organizations:* drama/theater group, student-run newspaper, radio station, choral group, JJC Debate Team, Universal Image Dance Group, Environmental Club, Justice in Action Club, Artist United. *Campus security:* 24-hour emergency response devices and patrols. *Student services:* health clinic, personal/psychological counseling, women's center, legal services.

Athletics Member NCAA. All Division III. *Intercollegiate sports:* baseball M, basketball M/W, cross-country running M/W, soccer M/W, softball W, swimming and diving W, tennis M/W, volleyball W. *Intramural sports:* baseball M, basketball M/W, cross-country running M/W, riflery M/W, soccer M/W, softball M/W, swimming and diving M/W, tennis M/W, track and field M/W, volleyball M/W, weight lifting M/W.

Standardized Tests *Required:* SAT or ACT (for admission).

Costs (2011–12) *Tuition:* state resident $5130 full-time, $215 per credit part-time; nonresident $13,800 full-time, $460 per credit part-time. Full-time tuition and fees vary according to course load and program. Part-time tuition

and fees vary according to course load and program. *Required fees:* $330 full-time, $40 per term part-time. *Payment plan:* installment. *Waivers:* senior citizens.

Financial Aid Of all full-time matriculated undergraduates who enrolled in 2011, 8,662 applied for aid, 7,393 were judged to have need. *Average percent of need met:* 85%. *Average financial aid package:* $10,150. *Average need-based loan:* $3500. *Average need-based gift aid:* $3175. *Average indebtedness upon graduation:* $11,890.

Applying *Application fee:* $65. *Required:* high school transcript, minimum 2.0 GPA, high school diploma and minimum SAT score of 1100. *Application deadlines:* 5/31 (freshmen), rolling (transfers). *Notification:* continuous until 1/15 (freshmen), continuous (transfers).

Freshman Application Contact John Jay College of Criminal Justice of the City University of New York, 899 Tenth Avenue, New York, NY 10019-1093. *Phone:* 212-237-8878. *Toll-free phone:* 877-JOHNJAY. *Web site:* http://www.jjay.cuny.edu/.

The Juilliard School
New York, New York

- **Independent** comprehensive, founded 1905
- **Urban** campus
- **Coed** 684 undergraduate students, 76% full-time, 46% women, 54% men
- **Most difficult** entrance level, 6% of applicants were admitted

Undergraduates 521 full-time, 163 part-time. 85% are from out of state; 5% Black or African American, non-Hispanic/Latino; 6% Hispanic/Latino; 12% Asian, non-Hispanic/Latino; 7% Two or more races, non-Hispanic/Latino; 0.8% Race/ethnicity unknown; 24% international; 4% transferred in; 55% live on campus.

Freshmen *Admission:* 2,566 applied, 153 admitted, 101 enrolled.

Faculty *Total:* 307, 40% full-time. *Student/faculty ratio:* 4:1.

Academics *Calendar:* semesters. *Degrees:* diplomas, bachelor's, master's, doctoral, and post-master's certificates. *Special study options:* adult/continuing education programs.

Computers on Campus Campuswide network is available.

Student Life *Housing:* on-campus residence required for freshman year. *Options:* coed. Campus housing is university owned. Freshman campus housing is guaranteed. *Campus security:* 24-hour emergency response devices and patrols, controlled dormitory access, electronically operated main building entrances.

Financial Aid Of all full-time matriculated undergraduates who enrolled in 2010, 461 applied for aid, 403 were judged to have need, 86 had their need fully met. In 2010, 29 non-need-based awards were made. *Average percent of need met:* 75%. *Average financial aid package:* $28,300. *Average need-based loan:* $4977. *Average need-based gift aid:* $24,303. *Average non-need-based aid:* $14,280. *Average indebtedness upon graduation:* $20,382. *Financial aid deadline:* 3/1.

Applying *Options:* electronic application. *Application fee:* $110. *Required:* essay or personal statement, high school transcript, audition. *Application deadlines:* 12/1 (freshmen), 12/1 (transfers). *Notification:* 4/1 (freshmen), 4/1 (transfers).

Freshman Application Contact Ms. Lee Cioppa, Associate Dean for Admissions, The Juilliard School, 60 Lincoln Center Plaza, New York, NY 10023-6588. *Phone:* 212-799-5000. *Fax:* 212-724-0263. *E-mail:* admissions@juilliard.edu. *Web site:* http://www.juilliard.edu/.

Kehilath Yakov Rabbinical Seminary
Ossining, New York

Director of Admissions Admissions Officer, Kehilath Yakov Rabbinical Seminary, 340 Illington Road, Ossining, NY 10562. *Phone:* 718-963-1212.

Keuka College
Keuka Park, New York

- **Independent** comprehensive, founded 1890, affiliated with American Baptist Churches in the U.S.A.
- **Rural** 173-acre campus with easy access to Rochester
- **Endowment** $7.0 million
- **Coed** 1,702 undergraduate students, 72% full-time, 75% women, 25% men
- **Moderately difficult** entrance level, 77% of applicants were admitted

Undergraduates 1,229 full-time, 473 part-time. Students come from 22 states and territories; 4 other countries; 6% are from out of state; 6% Black or African American, non-Hispanic/Latino; 2% Hispanic/Latino; 2% Asian, non-Hispanic/Latino; 0.7% American Indian or Alaska Native, non-Hispanic/Latino; 0.3% Two or more races, non-Hispanic/Latino; 15% Race/ethnicity unknown;

2% international; 5% transferred in; 81% live on campus. *Retention:* 70% of full-time freshmen returned.

Freshmen *Admission:* 840 applied, 646 admitted, 265 enrolled. *Average high school GPA:* 3.1. *Test scores:* SAT critical reading scores over 500: 38%; SAT math scores over 500: 41%; SAT writing scores over 500: 27%; ACT scores over 18: 86%; SAT critical reading scores over 600: 6%; SAT math scores over 600: 9%; SAT writing scores over 600: 5%; ACT scores over 24: 24%; SAT math scores over 700: 1%; ACT scores over 30: 4%.

Faculty *Total:* 223, 35% full-time, 46% with terminal degrees. *Student/faculty ratio:* 14:1.

Academics *Calendar:* 4-1-4. *Degrees:* bachelor's and master's. *Special study options:* academic remediation for entering students, accelerated degree program, adult/continuing education programs, advanced placement credit, cooperative education, double majors, independent study, internships, off-campus study, part-time degree program, services for LD students, student-designed majors, study abroad, summer session for credit. *Unusual degree programs:* 3-2 occupational therapy.

Computers on Campus 256 computers/terminals are available on campus for general student use. Campuswide network is available.

Student Life *Housing options:* coed, women-only, cooperative. Campus housing is university owned. Freshman campus housing is guaranteed. *Activities and organizations:* drama/theater group, student-run newspaper, radio station, choral group, Student Senate, Campus Activities Board, OTTERS (occupational therapy club), Education Club, BAKU. *Campus security:* 24-hour emergency response devices and patrols, late-night transport/escort service. *Student services:* health clinic, personal/psychological counseling.

Athletics Member NCAA. All Division III. *Intercollegiate sports:* baseball M, basketball M/W, cross-country running M/W, golf W, lacrosse M, soccer M/W, softball W, swimming and diving W, track and field M, volleyball W. *Intramural sports:* badminton M/W, basketball M/W, cheerleading M/W, crew M/W, lacrosse W, skiing (cross-country) M/W, skiing (downhill) M/W, soccer M/W, softball M/W, table tennis M/W, tennis M/W, volleyball W, water polo M/W.

Standardized Tests *Recommended:* SAT or ACT (for admission).

Costs (2012–13) *Comprehensive fee:* $34,980 includes full-time tuition ($24,310), mandatory fees ($790), and room and board ($9880). Full-time tuition and fees vary according to degree level and program. Part-time tuition: $810 per credit hour. Part-time tuition and fees vary according to program. *Required fees:* $700 per year part-time. *College room only:* $4690. Room and board charges vary according to board plan and housing facility. *Payment plan:* installment. *Waivers:* employees or children of employees.

Financial Aid Of all full-time matriculated undergraduates who enrolled in 2011, 1,420 applied for aid, 1,351 were judged to have need, 180 had their need fully met. In 2011, 55 non-need-based awards were made. *Average percent of need met:* 68%. *Average financial aid package:* $16,004. *Average need-based loan:* $5046. *Average need-based gift aid:* $12,158. *Average non-need-based aid:* $10,402. *Average indebtedness upon graduation:* $19,507.

Applying *Options:* electronic application, early admission, deferred entrance. *Application fee:* $30. *Required:* essay or personal statement, high school transcript, 1 letter of recommendation. *Required for some:* interview. *Recommended:* minimum 2.8 GPA, interview. *Application deadlines:* rolling (freshmen), rolling (transfers).

Freshman Application Contact Gary Boyer, Director of Admissions, Keuka College, Wagner House, Keuka Park, NY 14478. *Phone:* 315-279-5254. *Toll-free phone:* 800-33-KEUKA. *Fax:* 315-279-5386. *E-mail:* admissions@mail.keuka.edu. *Web site:* http://www.keuka.edu/.

The King's College

New York, New York

- **Independent nondenominational** 4-year, founded 1939
- **Urban** campus
- **Endowment** $755,106
- **Coed** 465 undergraduate students, 97% full-time, 58% women, 42% men
- **Moderately difficult** entrance level, 67% of applicants were admitted

Undergraduates 453 full-time, 12 part-time. Students come from 51 states and territories; 10 other countries; 93% are from out of state; 3% Black or African American, non-Hispanic/Latino; 6% Hispanic/Latino; 2% Asian, non-Hispanic/Latino; 2% Native Hawaiian or other Pacific Islander, non-Hispanic/Latino; 0.6% American Indian or Alaska Native, non-Hispanic/Latino; 5% Two or more races, non-Hispanic/Latino; 3% Race/ethnicity unknown; 2% international; 11% transferred in; 76% live on campus. *Retention:* 68% of full-time freshmen returned.

Freshmen *Admission:* 3,388 applied, 2,255 admitted, 162 enrolled. *Average high school GPA:* 3.61. *Test scores:* SAT critical reading scores over 500: 99%; SAT math scores over 500: 84%; ACT scores over 18: 100%; SAT critical reading scores over 600: 63%; SAT math scores over 600: 35%; ACT

scores over 24: 78%; SAT critical reading scores over 700: 14%; SAT math scores over 700: 2%; ACT scores over 30: 15%.

Faculty *Total:* 43, 56% full-time, 74% with terminal degrees. *Student/faculty ratio:* 14:1.

Academics *Calendar:* semesters. *Degree:* bachelor's. *Special study options:* advanced placement credit, distance learning, independent study, internships, summer session for credit.

Computers on Campus 14 computers/terminals are available on campus for general student use. Students can access the following: computer help desk, free student e-mail accounts, online (class) grades, online (class) registration, online (class) schedules. Campuswide network is available. 100% of college-owned or -operated housing units are wired for high-speed Internet access. Wireless service is available via entire campus.

Student Life *Housing options:* men-only, women-only. Campus housing is leased by the school. Freshman campus housing is guaranteed. *Activities and organizations:* drama/theater group, student-run newspaper, choral group, King's Debate Society, King's Theater, sports clubs, King's Dancers, The Tent. *Campus security:* 24-hour emergency response devices. *Student services:* personal/psychological counseling.

Athletics *Intramural sports:* baseball M, basketball M/W, cross-country running M/W, golf M, soccer M/W, ultimate Frisbee M/W, volleyball W.

Standardized Tests *Required:* SAT or ACT (for admission).

Costs (2012–13) *Tuition:* $28,890 full-time, $1204 per credit hour part-time. Full-time tuition and fees vary according to course load. Part-time tuition and fees vary according to course load. *Required fees:* $350 full-time, $175 per term part-time. *Room only:* $11,600. Room and board charges vary according to location. *Payment plans:* installment, deferred payment. *Waivers:* employees or children of employees.

Financial Aid Of all full-time matriculated undergraduates who enrolled in 2009, 233 applied for aid, 200 were judged to have need, 32 had their need fully met. In 2009, 85 non-need-based awards were made. *Average percent of need met:* 66%. *Average financial aid package:* $19,256. *Average need-based loan:* $4210. *Average need-based gift aid:* $16,119. *Average non-need-based aid:* $11,413. *Average indebtedness upon graduation:* $16,102.

Applying *Options:* electronic application, early action, deferred entrance. *Application fee:* $30. *Required:* high school transcript. *Recommended:* high school transcript, minimum 3.0 GPA, interview. *Application deadlines:* rolling (freshmen), rolling (out-of-state freshmen), rolling (transfers), 11/15 (early action). *Notification:* continuous (freshmen), continuous (out-of-state freshmen), continuous (transfers), 12/15 (early action).

Freshman Application Contact The King's College, 350 Fifth Avenue, 15th Floor Empire State Building, New York, NY 10118. *Phone:* 212-659-7217. *Toll-free phone:* 888-969-7200 Ext. 3610. *Web site:* http://www.tkc.edu/.

Kol Yaakov Torah Center

Monsey, New York

Freshman Application Contact Assistant Director of Admissions, Kol Yaakov Torah Center, 29 West Maple Avenue, Monsey, NY 10952-2954. *Phone:* 914-425-3871. *E-mail:* horizonss@aol.com.

Lehman College of the City University of New York

Bronx, New York

- **State and locally supported** comprehensive, founded 1931, part of City University of New York System
- **Urban** 37-acre campus
- **Endowment** $7.1 million
- **Coed** 9,863 undergraduate students, 59% full-time, 69% women, 31% men
- **Moderately difficult** entrance level, 20% of applicants were admitted

Undergraduates 5,784 full-time, 4,079 part-time. Students come from 14 states and territories; 36 other countries; 1% are from out of state; 31% Black or African American, non-Hispanic/Latino; 50% Hispanic/Latino; 5% Asian, non-Hispanic/Latino; 4% international; 15% transferred in. *Retention:* 79% of full-time freshmen returned.

Freshmen *Admission:* 15,348 applied, 3,124 admitted, 626 enrolled. *Test scores:* SAT critical reading scores over 500: 33%; SAT math scores over 500: 41%; SAT writing scores over 500: 32%; SAT critical reading scores over 600: 6%; SAT math scores over 600: 7%; SAT writing scores over 600: 6%; SAT critical reading scores over 700: 1%; SAT math scores over 700: 1%; SAT writing scores over 700: 2%.

Faculty *Total:* 912, 40% full-time, 42% with terminal degrees. *Student/faculty ratio:* 13:1.

Academics *Calendar:* semesters. *Degrees:* certificates, bachelor's, master's, and post-master's certificates. *Special study options:* adult/continuing educa-

tion programs, advanced placement credit, cooperative education, distance learning, double majors, English as a second language, freshman honors college, honors programs, independent study, internships, off-campus study, part-time degree program, services for LD students, student-designed majors, study abroad, summer session for credit. *ROTC:* Army (c). *Unusual degree programs:* 3-2 mathematics.

Computers on Campus 800 computers/terminals are available on campus for general student use. Students can access the following: campus intranet, computer help desk, free student e-mail accounts, online (class) grades, online (class) registration, online (class) schedules. Campuswide network is available. Wireless service is available via entire campus.

Student Life *Housing options:* Campus housing is university owned. *Activities and organizations:* drama/theater group, student-run newspaper, radio and television station, choral group, Club Mac, African Students Association, Dominican Student Association, The Sociology Club, Club Live. *Campus security:* 24-hour emergency response devices and patrols, student patrols, late-night transport/escort service. *Student services:* health clinic, personal/psychological counseling, women's center.

Athletics Member NCAA. All Division III. *Intercollegiate sports:* baseball M, basketball M/W, cross-country running M/W, racquetball M/W, soccer M/W, softball M/W, swimming and diving M/W, table tennis M/W, tennis M/W, track and field M/W, volleyball M/W, water polo M, wrestling M. *Intramural sports:* badminton M/W, baseball M/W, basketball M/W, cross-country running M/W, racquetball M/W, soccer M, softball M/W, swimming and diving M/W, tennis M/W, volleyball M/W, wrestling M.

Standardized Tests *Required:* SAT or ACT (for admission).

Costs (2011–12) *Tuition:* state resident $5130 full-time, $215 per credit part-time; nonresident $11,040 full-time, $460 per credit part-time. *Required fees:* $378 full-time. *Room only:* $8085. *Payment plan:* installment.

Financial Aid Of all full-time matriculated undergraduates who enrolled in 2011, 5,115 applied for aid, 5,115 were judged to have need, 116 had their need fully met. In 2011, 174 non-need-based awards were made. *Average percent of need met:* 65%. *Average financial aid package:* $3850. *Average need-based loan:* $1756. *Average need-based gift aid:* $1740. *Average non-need-based aid:* $1240. *Average indebtedness upon graduation:* $12,800.

Applying *Options:* deferred entrance. *Application fee:* $65. *Required:* high school transcript, minimum 3.0 GPA. *Required for some:* essay or personal statement, interview. *Application deadlines:* rolling (freshmen), rolling (transfers). *Notification:* continuous (freshmen), continuous (transfers).

Freshman Application Contact Ms. Laurie Austin, Director of Admissions, Lehman College of the City University of New York, 250 Bedford Park Boulevard West, Bronx, NY 10468. *Phone:* 718-960-8706. *Toll-free phone:* 877-LEHMAN1. *Fax:* 718-960-8712. *E-mail:* enroll@lehman.cuny.edu. *Web site:* http://www.lehman.cuny.edu/.

Le Moyne College

Syracuse, New York

- **Independent Roman Catholic (Jesuit)** comprehensive, founded 1946
- **Suburban** 161-acre campus
- **Endowment** $124.2 million
- **Coed** 2,871 undergraduate students, 84% full-time, 61% women, 39% men
- **Moderately difficult** entrance level, 62% of applicants were admitted

Undergraduates 2,414 full-time, 457 part-time. Students come from 25 states and territories; 28 other countries; 6% are from out of state; 5% Black or African American, non-Hispanic/Latino; 5% Hispanic/Latino; 2% Asian, non-Hispanic/Latino; 0.6% American Indian or Alaska Native, non-Hispanic/Latino; 2% Two or more races, non-Hispanic/Latino; 4% Race/ethnicity unknown; 0.4% international; 7% transferred in; 50% live on campus. *Retention:* 83% of full-time freshmen returned.

Freshmen *Admission:* 5,772 applied, 3,559 admitted, 639 enrolled. *Average high school GPA:* 3.37. *Test scores:* SAT critical reading scores over 500: 70%; SAT math scores over 500: 77%; ACT scores over 18: 96%; SAT critical reading scores over 600: 24%; SAT math scores over 600: 30%; ACT scores over 24: 45%; SAT critical reading scores over 700: 1%; SAT math scores over 700: 2%; ACT scores over 30: 7%.

Faculty *Total:* 366, 42% full-time, 58% with terminal degrees. *Student/faculty ratio:* 12:1.

Academics *Calendar:* semesters. *Degrees:* bachelor's, master's, and post-master's certificates. *Special study options:* academic remediation for entering students, accelerated degree program, adult/continuing education programs, advanced placement credit, double majors, honors programs, independent study, internships, off-campus study, part-time degree program, services for LD students, study abroad, summer session for credit. *ROTC:* Army (c), Air Force (c). *Unusual degree programs:* 3-2 engineering with Manhattan College, Clarkson University, University of Detroit Mercy, Syracuse University.

Computers on Campus 330 computers/terminals and 330 ports are available on campus for general student use. Students can access the following: campus intranet, computer help desk, free student e-mail accounts, online (class) grades, online (class) registration, online (class) schedules, ECHO (campuswide portal), some virtual access from off campus. Campuswide network is available. 100% of college-owned or -operated housing units are wired for high-speed Internet access. Wireless service is available via classrooms, computer centers, computer labs, dorm rooms, learning centers, libraries, student centers.

Student Life *Housing:* on-campus residence required through senior year. *Options:* coed, women-only, disabled students. Campus housing is university owned. Freshman campus housing is guaranteed. *Activities and organizations:* drama/theater group, student-run newspaper, radio and television station, choral group, Student Programming Board, Outing Club, performing arts groups, Student Dancers, New Student Orientation Committee. *Campus security:* 24-hour emergency response devices and patrols, late-night transport/escort service, controlled dormitory access, lighted pathways, closed-circuit security cameras, and emergency code blue phones. *Student services:* health clinic, personal/psychological counseling.

Athletics Member NCAA. All Division II. *Intercollegiate sports:* baseball M(s), basketball M(s)/W(s), cross-country running M(s)/W(s), golf M(s)/W(s), lacrosse M(s)/W(s), soccer M(s)/W(s), softball W(s), swimming and diving M(s)/W(s), tennis M(s)/W(s), volleyball W(s). *Intramural sports:* basketball M/W, field hockey W(c), football M, ice hockey M(c), racquetball M/W, rugby M(c)/W(c), soccer M/W, softball M/W, volleyball M/W.

Standardized Tests *Required:* SAT or ACT (for admission).

Costs (2012–13) *Comprehensive fee:* $40,780 includes full-time tuition ($28,470), mandatory fees ($990), and room and board ($11,320). Part-time tuition: $597 per credit hour. Part-time tuition and fees vary according to class time and course load. *College room only:* $7180. Room and board charges vary according to board plan and housing facility. *Payment plans:* installment, deferred payment. *Waivers:* employees or children of employees.

Financial Aid Of all full-time matriculated undergraduates who enrolled in 2009, 2,134 applied for aid, 1,983 were judged to have need, 501 had their need fully met. 357 Federal Work-Study jobs (averaging $995). 512 state and other part-time jobs (averaging $985). In 2009, 195 non-need-based awards were made. *Average percent of need met:* 76%. *Average financial aid package:* $20,065. *Average need-based loan:* $4499. *Average need-based gift aid:* $15,652. *Average non-need-based aid:* $5414. *Average indebtedness upon graduation:* $25,587.

Applying *Options:* electronic application, early admission, deferred entrance. *Application fee:* $35. *Required:* essay or personal statement, high school transcript, 2 letters of recommendation. *Recommended:* interview. *Application deadlines:* 2/1 (freshmen), 8/1 (transfers). *Notification:* continuous until 12/1 (freshmen), continuous (transfers).

Freshman Application Contact Mr. Dennis J. Nicholson, Dean of Admission, Le Moyne College, 1419 Salt Springs Road, Syracuse, NY 13214-1301. *Phone:* 315-445-4300. *Toll-free phone:* 800-333-4733. *Fax:* 315-445-4711. *E-mail:* admission@lemoyne.edu. *Web site:* http://www.lemoyne.edu/.

See page 596 for display ad and page 1404 for the College Close-Up.

LIM College

New York, New York

Freshman Application Contact Ms. Kristina Ortiz, Assistant Dean of Admissions, LIM College, 12 East 53rd Street, New York, NY 10022. *Phone:* 212-752-1530 Ext. 217. *Toll-free phone:* 800-677-1323. *Fax:* 212-317-8602. *E-mail:* admissions@limcollege.edu. *Web site:* http://www.limcollege.edu/.

See page 595 for display as and page 1410 for the College Close-Up.

LIU Global

Brooklyn, New York

Freshman Application Contact LIU Global, 9 Hanover Place, 4th Floor, Brooklyn, NY 11201. *Phone:* 718-780-4320. *Toll-free phone:* 800-LIU-PLAN. *Web site:* http://www.liu.edu/globalcollege/.

Long Island University–Brentwood Campus

Brentwood, New York

- **Independent** upper-level, founded 1959, part of Long Island University
- **Suburban** 172-acre campus with easy access to Manhattan
- **Endowment** $74.0 million
- **Coed** 29 undergraduate students, 41% full-time, 52% women, 48% men

Undergraduates 12 full-time, 17 part-time. Students come from 1 other state; 21% Black or African American, non-Hispanic/Latino; 10% Hispanic/Latino; 10% Race/ethnicity unknown; 17% transferred in.

Faculty *Total:* 75, 27% full-time, 91% with terminal degrees. *Student/faculty ratio:* 6:1.

Academics *Calendar:* semesters. *Degrees:* bachelor's, master's, and post-master's certificates. *Special study options:* advanced placement credit, independent study, internships, part-time degree program, services for LD students, summer session for credit.

Computers on Campus 50 computers/terminals and 80 ports are available on campus for general student use. Students can access the following: campus intranet, computer help desk, free student e-mail accounts, online (class) grades, online (class) registration, online (class) schedules. Campuswide network is available. Wireless service is available via entire campus.

Student Life *Housing:* college housing not available. *Campus security:* evening security guards.

Costs (2011–12) *Tuition:* $30,046 full-time, $938 per credit part-time. Full-time tuition and fees vary according to course load. Part-time tuition and fees vary according to course load. *Required fees:* $1380 full-time, $345 per term part-time. *Payment plan:* installment. *Waivers:* senior citizens and employees or children of employees.

Applying *Options:* electronic application. *Application fee:* $30. *Application deadline:* rolling (transfers). *Notification:* continuous (transfers).

Application Contact Long Island University–Brentwood Campus, 100 Second Avenue, Brentwood, NY 11717. *Phone:* 631-273-5112 Ext. 202. *Web site:* http://www.liu.edu/.

Long Island University–Brooklyn Campus

Brooklyn, New York

- **Independent** university, founded 1926
- **Urban** 10-acre campus
- **Coed** 5,194 undergraduate students, 85% full-time, 72% women, 28% men
- **Moderately difficult** entrance level, 84% of applicants were admitted

Undergraduates 4,436 full-time, 758 part-time. Students come from 44 states and territories; 28 other countries; 14% are from out of state; 35% Black or African American, non-Hispanic/Latino; 12% Hispanic/Latino; 15% Asian, non-Hispanic/Latino; 0.5% American Indian or Alaska Native, non-Hispanic/Latino; 0.3% Two or more races, non-Hispanic/Latino; 16% Race/ethnicity unknown; 1% international; 12% transferred in; 15% live on campus. *Retention:* 64% of full-time freshmen returned.

Freshmen *Admission:* 4,268 applied, 3,578 admitted, 1,046 enrolled. *Average high school GPA:* 2.8. *Test scores:* SAT critical reading scores over 500: 23%; SAT math scores over 500: 35%; ACT scores over 18: 66%; SAT critical reading scores over 600: 3%; SAT math scores over 600: 12%; ACT scores over 24: 22%; SAT math scores over 700: 2%.

Faculty *Total:* 789, 39% full-time. *Student/faculty ratio:* 15:1.

Academics *Calendar:* semesters. *Degrees:* associate, bachelor's, master's, doctoral, post-master's, postbachelor's, and first professional certificates. *Special study options:* academic remediation for entering students, accelerated degree program, advanced placement credit, cooperative education, distance learning, double majors, English as a second language, honors programs, independent study, internships, services for LD students, student-designed majors, study abroad, summer session for credit. *Unusual degree programs:* 3-2 physical therapy.

Computers on Campus 300 computers/terminals are available on campus for general student use. Students can access the following: campus intranet, computer help desk, free student e-mail accounts, online (class) grades, online (class) registration, online (class) schedules. Campuswide network is available. 100% of college-owned or -operated housing units are wired for high-speed Internet access. Wireless service is available via entire campus.

Student Life *Housing options:* coed, disabled students. Campus housing is university owned. Freshman applicants given priority for college housing. *Activities and organizations:* drama/theater group, student-run newspaper,

radio and television station, choral group, The Student Government Association, The American Pharmacists Association - Academy of Student Pharmacists, Hillel Jewish Students Organization, Student Activities Board, The Society of Health Systems Pharmacists, national fraternities, national sororities. *Campus security:* 24-hour emergency response devices and patrols, controlled dormitory access, lighted pathways/sidewalks. *Student services:* health clinic, personal/psychological counseling.

Athletics Member NCAA. All Division I. *Intercollegiate sports:* baseball M(s), basketball M(s)/W(s), cross-country running M(s)/W(s), golf M(s)/W(s), lacrosse W(s), soccer M(s)/W(s), softball W(s), tennis W(s), track and field M(s)/W(s), volleyball W(s).

Standardized Tests *Required:* SAT or ACT (for admission).

Costs (2011–12) *Comprehensive fee:* $41,590 includes full-time tuition ($28,140), mandatory fees ($1510), and room and board ($11,940). Full-time tuition and fees vary according to program. Part-time tuition: $938 per credit. Part-time tuition and fees vary according to program. *Required fees:* $400 per term part-time. *Room and board:* Room and board charges vary according to board plan and housing facility. *Payment plan:* installment. *Waivers:* employees or children of employees.

Financial Aid Of all full-time matriculated undergraduates who enrolled in 2011, 4,126 applied for aid, 3,947 were judged to have need, 271 had their need fully met. In 2011, 215 non-need-based awards were made. *Average percent of need met:* 56%. *Average financial aid package:* $16,409. *Average need-based loan:* $4230. *Average need-based gift aid:* $9120. *Average non-need-based aid:* $5511.

Applying *Options:* electronic application, deferred entrance. *Application fee:* $40. *Required:* essay or personal statement, high school transcript, minimum 2.0 GPA, 3 letters of recommendation. *Required for some:* minimum 3.0 GPA. *Recommended:* minimum 2.5 GPA, interview. *Application deadlines:* 9/1 (freshmen), rolling (transfers). *Notification:* continuous (freshmen), continuous (transfers).

Freshman Application Contact Richard Sunday, Senior Associate Dean of Admissions, Long Island University–Brooklyn Campus, 1 University Plaza, Brooklyn, NY 11201. *Phone:* 718-488-1011. *Toll-free phone:* 800-LIU-PLAN. *E-mail:* admissions@brooklyn.liu.edu. *Web site:* http://www.liu.edu/.

Long Island University–C. W. Post Campus

Brookville, New York

- **Independent** comprehensive, founded 1954
- **Suburban** 308-acre campus with easy access to New York City
- **Coed** 8,467 undergraduate students, 47% full-time, 70% women, 30% men
- **Moderately difficult** entrance level, 81% of applicants were admitted

Undergraduates 4,007 full-time, 4,460 part-time. Students come from 50 states and territories; 26 other countries; 8% are from out of state; 11% Black or African American, non-Hispanic/Latino; 10% Hispanic/Latino; 4% Asian, non-Hispanic/Latino; 0.5% American Indian or Alaska Native, non-Hispanic/Latino; 0.3% Two or more races, non-Hispanic/Latino; 15% Race/ethnicity unknown; 9% international; 6% transferred in; 36% live on campus. *Retention:* 68% of full-time freshmen returned.

Freshmen *Admission:* 7,372 applied, 5,948 admitted, 943 enrolled. *Average high school GPA:* 3. *Test scores:* SAT critical reading scores over 500: 42%; SAT math scores over 500: 47%; SAT writing scores over 500: 41%; ACT scores over 18: 89%; SAT critical reading scores over 600: 8%; SAT math scores over 600: 12%; SAT writing scores over 600: 10%; ACT scores over 24: 34%; SAT critical reading scores over 700: 1%; SAT math scores over 700: 1%; SAT writing scores over 700: 1%; ACT scores over 30: 1%.

Faculty *Total:* 822, 37% full-time. *Student/faculty ratio:* 12:1.

Academics *Calendar:* semesters. *Degrees:* associate, bachelor's, master's, doctoral, post-master's, postbachelor's, and first professional certificates. *Special study options:* academic remediation for entering students, accelerated degree program, advanced placement credit, cooperative education, double majors, English as a second language, honors programs, independent study, internships, off-campus study, part-time degree program, services for LD students, student-designed majors, study abroad, summer session for credit. *ROTC:* Army (c). *Unusual degree programs:* 3-2 respiratory therapy and pharmacy with Long Island University, Brooklyn Campus.

Computers on Campus 500 computers/terminals are available on campus for general student use. Students can access the following: campus intranet, computer help desk, free student e-mail accounts, online (class) grades, online (class) registration, online (class) schedules. Campuswide network is available. 100% of college-owned or -operated housing units are wired for high-speed Internet access. Wireless service is available via entire campus.

Student Life *Housing options:* coed, disabled students. Campus housing is university owned. Freshman campus housing is guaranteed. *Activities and organizations:* drama/theater group, student-run newspaper, radio and televi-

sion station, choral group, Student Government Association, Association for Campus Programming, African People's Organization, Resident Student Association, Post TV and Newman, national fraternities, national sororities. *Campus security:* 24-hour emergency response devices and patrols, late-night transport/escort service, controlled dormitory access, lighted pathways/sidewalks. *Student services:* health clinic, personal/psychological counseling.

Athletics Member NCAA. All Division II. *Intercollegiate sports:* baseball M(s), basketball M(s)/W(s), crew M(c)/W(c), cross-country running M(s)/W(s), equestrian sports M(c)/W(c), field hockey W(s), football M(s), lacrosse M(s)/W(s), soccer M(s)/W(s), softball W(s), swimming and diving W(s), tennis W(s), volleyball W(s).

Standardized Tests *Required:* SAT or ACT (for admission).

Costs (2011–12) *Comprehensive fee:* $43,486 includes full-time tuition ($30,046), mandatory fees ($1600), and room and board ($11,840). Part-time tuition: $938 per credit. *Required fees:* $430 per term part-time. *Room and board:* Room and board charges vary according to board plan and housing facility. *Payment plan:* installment. *Waivers:* employees or children of employees.

Financial Aid Of all full-time matriculated undergraduates who enrolled in 2011, 3,257 applied for aid, 2,744 were judged to have need, 713 had their need fully met. In 2011, 523 non-need-based awards were made. *Average percent of need met:* 68%. *Average financial aid package:* $18,043. *Average need-based loan:* $4439. *Average need-based gift aid:* $8324. *Average non-need-based aid:* $11,136. *Financial aid deadline:* 3/1.

Applying *Options:* electronic application, deferred entrance. *Application fee:* $40. *Required:* essay or personal statement, high school transcript, minimum 2.5 GPA, letters of recommendation. *Required for some:* interview. *Application deadlines:* 9/4 (freshmen), rolling (transfers). *Notification:* continuous (freshmen), continuous (transfers).

Freshman Application Contact Ms. Joanne Graziano, Executive Director of Admissions and Recruitment, Long Island University–C. W. Post Campus, 720 Northern Boulevard, Brookville, NY 11548-1300. *Phone:* 516-299-2900. *Toll-free phone:* 800-LIU-PLAN. *Fax:* 516-299-2137. *E-mail:* enroll@cwpost.liu.edu. *Web site:* http://www.liu.edu/.

Machzikei Hadath Rabbinical College
Brooklyn, New York

Director of Admissions Rabbi Abraham M. Lezerowitz, Director of Admissions, Machzikei Hadath Rabbinical College, 5407 Sixteenth Avenue, Brooklyn, NY 11204-1805. *Phone:* 718-854-8777.

Manhattan College
Riverdale, New York

- **Independent** comprehensive, founded 1853, affiliated with Roman Catholic Church
- **Urban** 31-acre campus with easy access to New York City
- **Endowment** $55.8 million
- **Coed** 3,237 undergraduate students, 93% full-time, 45% women, 55% men
- **Moderately difficult** entrance level, 69% of applicants were admitted

Undergraduates 3,006 full-time, 231 part-time. Students come from 35 states and territories; 22 other countries; 27% are from out of state; 3% Black or African American, non-Hispanic/Latino; 15% Hispanic/Latino; 4% Asian, non-Hispanic/Latino; 0.1% American Indian or Alaska Native, non-Hispanic/Latino; 1% Two or more races, non-Hispanic/Latino; 13% Race/ethnicity unknown; 3% international; 4% transferred in; 64% live on campus. *Retention:* 83% of full-time freshmen returned.

Freshmen *Admission:* 6,253 applied, 4,335 admitted, 802 enrolled. *Average high school GPA:* 3.3. *Test scores:* SAT critical reading scores over 500: 67%; SAT math scores over 500: 78%; ACT scores over 18: 97%; SAT critical reading scores over 600: 19%; SAT math scores over 600: 34%; ACT scores over 24: 54%; SAT critical reading scores over 700: 1%; SAT math scores over 700: 4%; ACT scores over 30: 5%.

Faculty *Total:* 401, 51% full-time, 65% with terminal degrees. *Student/faculty ratio:* 12:1.

Academics *Calendar:* semesters. *Degrees:* bachelor's, master's, and post-master's certificates. *Special study options:* accelerated degree program, adult/continuing education programs, advanced placement credit, cooperative education, distance learning, double majors, English as a second language, honors programs, independent study, internships, off-campus study, part-time degree program, services for LD students, student-designed majors, study abroad, summer session for credit. *ROTC:* Army (c), Air Force (b). *Unusual degree programs:* business administration; engineering; education.

Computers on Campus 350 computers/terminals and 600 ports are available on campus for general student use. Students can access the following: campus intranet, computer help desk, free student e-mail accounts, online (class)

grades, online (class) registration, online (class) schedules, course management system. Campuswide network is available. 100% of college-owned or -operated housing units are wired for high-speed Internet access. Wireless service is available via entire campus.

Student Life *Housing options:* coed, disabled students. Campus housing is university owned. Freshman campus housing is guaranteed. *Activities and organizations:* drama/theater group, student-run newspaper, radio station, choral group, marching band, Society of Hispanic Professional Engineers, Gaelic Society, Student Government, LaSallian Collegians (Community Service Group), Manhattan College Players (Theater/Drama group), national fraternities, national sororities. *Campus security:* 24-hour emergency response devices and patrols, late-night transport/escort service, controlled dormitory access. *Student services:* health clinic, personal/psychological counseling.

Athletics Member NCAA. All Division I. *Intercollegiate sports:* baseball M(s), basketball M(s)/W(s), cheerleading M/W, crew M(c)/W(c), cross-country running M(s)/W(s), golf M(s), lacrosse M(s)/W(s), rugby M(c), soccer M(s)/W(s), softball W(s), swimming and diving M(s)/W(s), tennis W(s), track and field M(s)/W(s), volleyball W(s). *Intramural sports:* baseball M, basketball M/W, cross-country running M/W, equestrian sports M/W, soccer M/W, softball M/W, swimming and diving W, track and field M/W, volleyball M/W.

Standardized Tests *Required:* SAT or ACT (for admission).

Costs (2012–13) *Comprehensive fee:* $44,995 includes full-time tuition ($30,100), mandatory fees ($2675), and room and board ($12,220). Full-time tuition and fees vary according to course load, program, and student level. Part-time tuition: $820 per credit. Part-time tuition and fees vary according to course load. *Room and board:* Room and board charges vary according to board plan. *Payment plans:* installment, deferred payment. *Waivers:* employees or children of employees.

Financial Aid Of all full-time matriculated undergraduates who enrolled in 2011, 2,438 applied for aid, 2,121 were judged to have need, 285 had their need fully met. In 2011, 869 non-need-based awards were made. *Average percent of need met:* 65%. *Average financial aid package:* $18,918. *Average need-based loan:* $4456. *Average need-based gift aid:* $13,947. *Average non-need-based aid:* $8573. *Average indebtedness upon graduation:* $31,912.

Applying *Options:* electronic application, early admission, early decision, deferred entrance. *Application fee:* $60. *Required:* essay or personal statement, high school transcript, minimum 3.0 GPA, 1 letter of recommendation. *Required for some:* interview. *Recommended:* minimum 3.0 GPA. *Application deadlines:* 4/15 (freshmen), 7/1 (transfers). *Early decision deadline:* 11/15. *Notification:* continuous until 4/15 (freshmen), continuous until 8/15 (transfers), 12/1 (early decision).

Freshman Application Contact Mr. William Bisset, Vice President for Enrollment Management, Manhattan College, 4513 Manhattan College Parkway, Riverdale, NY 10471. *Phone:* 718-862-7200. *Toll-free phone:* 800-622-9235. *Fax:* 718-862-8019. *E-mail:* admit@manhattan.edu. *Web site:* http://www.manhattan.edu/.

See page 598 for display ad and page 1430 for the College Close-Up.

Manhattan School of Music
New York, New York

Freshman Application Contact Amy Anderson, Associate Dean for Enrollment Management, Manhattan School of Music, 120 Claremont Avenue, New York, NY 10027-4698. *Phone:* 917-493-4501. *Fax:* 212-749-3025. *E-mail:* admission@msmnyc.edu. *Web site:* http://www.msmnyc.edu/.

Manhattanville College
Purchase, New York

- **Independent** comprehensive, founded 1841
- **Suburban** 100-acre campus with easy access to New York City
- **Endowment** $10.4 million
- **Coed** 1,736 undergraduate students, 95% full-time, 64% women, 36% men
- **Moderately difficult** entrance level, 60% of applicants were admitted

Undergraduates 1,644 full-time, 92 part-time. Students come from 39 states and territories; 53 other countries; 39% are from out of state; 10% Black or African American, non-Hispanic/Latino; 17% Hispanic/Latino; 3% Asian, non-Hispanic/Latino; 0.5% American Indian or Alaska Native, non-Hispanic/Latino; 15% Race/ethnicity unknown; 11% international; 3% transferred in; 78% live on campus. *Retention:* 69% of full-time freshmen returned.

Freshmen *Admission:* 4,772 applied, 2,863 admitted, 534 enrolled. *Average high school GPA:* 3.

Faculty *Total:* 340, 30% full-time. *Student/faculty ratio:* 11:1.

Academics *Calendar:* semesters. *Degrees:* bachelor's, master's, doctoral, post-master's, and postbachelor's certificates. *Special study options:* academic remediation for entering students, accelerated degree program, adult/continuing education programs, advanced placement credit, distance learning, double

majors, English as a second language, honors programs, independent study, internships, off-campus study, part-time degree program, services for LD students, student-designed majors, study abroad, summer session for credit. *Unusual degree programs:* 3-2 business administration; education.

Computers on Campus 240 computers/terminals are available on campus for general student use. Students can access the following: computer help desk, free student e-mail accounts, online (class) grades, online (class) registration, online (class) schedules. Campuswide network is available. 100% of college-owned or -operated housing units are wired for high-speed Internet access. Wireless service is available via classrooms, computer centers, computer labs, libraries, student centers.

Student Life *Housing options:* coed, disabled students. Campus housing is university owned. Freshman campus housing is guaranteed. *Activities and organizations:* drama/theater group, student-run newspaper, radio and television station, choral group, Latin American Student Organization, International Student Organization, Black Student Union, WMVL (radio station), Connie Hogarth Center. *Campus security:* 24-hour emergency response devices and patrols, late-night transport/escort service, controlled dormitory access. *Student services:* health clinic, personal/psychological counseling, women's center.

Athletics Member NCAA. All Division III. *Intercollegiate sports:* baseball M, basketball M/W, field hockey W, golf M, ice hockey M/W, lacrosse M/W, soccer M/W, softball W, swimming and diving W, tennis M/W, volleyball W. *Intramural sports:* basketball M/W, cheerleading M/W.

Costs (2012–13) *Comprehensive fee:* $49,710 includes full-time tuition ($34,020), mandatory fees ($1350), and room and board ($14,340). Part-time tuition: $790 per credit. Part-time tuition and fees vary according to program. *Required fees:* $60 part-time. *College room only:* $8680. Room and board charges vary according to board plan. *Payment plans:* installment, deferred payment. *Waivers:* senior citizens and employees or children of employees.

Financial Aid Of all full-time matriculated undergraduates who enrolled in 2009, 1,234 applied for aid, 1,131 were judged to have need, 111 had their need fully met. 275 Federal Work-Study jobs (averaging $1300). 265 state and other part-time jobs (averaging $1300). In 2009, 480 non-need-based awards were made. *Average percent of need met:* 96%. *Average financial aid package:* $26,779. *Average need-based loan:* $4523. *Average need-based gift aid:* $17,427. *Average non-need-based aid:* $18,753.

Applying *Options:* electronic application, early admission, early decision, deferred entrance. *Application fee:* $75. *Required:* essay or personal statement, high school transcript, minimum 2.0 GPA, 2 letters of recommendation. *Recommended:* minimum 3.0 GPA, interview. *Application deadlines:* 3/1 (freshmen), 3/1 (transfers). *Notification:* continuous (freshmen), continuous (transfers).

Freshman Application Contact Ms. Kathy Fitzgerald, Director of Admissions, Manhattanville College, 2900 Purchase Street, Purchase, NY 10577. *Phone:* 914-323-5124. *Toll-free phone:* 800-328-4553. *Fax:* 914-694-1732. *E-mail:* admissions@mville.edu. *Web site:* http://www.manhattanville.edu/.

Mannes College The New School for Music

New York, New York

- **Independent** comprehensive, founded 1916, part of The New School
- **Urban** campus with easy access to Manhattan
- **Coed**
- **Very difficult** entrance level

Faculty *Student/faculty ratio:* 6:1.

Academics *Calendar:* semesters. *Degrees:* diplomas, bachelor's, master's, post-master's, and postbachelor's certificates.

Student Life *Campus security:* 24-hour emergency response devices, controlled dormitory access.

Costs (2011–12) *Comprehensive fee:* $51,120 includes full-time tuition ($35,940), mandatory fees ($270), and room and board ($14,910). Part-time tuition: $1175 per credit. Part-time tuition and fees vary according to course load. *College room only:* $14,360. Room and board charges vary according to board plan and housing facility.

Financial Aid *Of all full-time matriculated undergraduates who enrolled in 2010,* 52 applied for aid, 48 were judged to have need, 6 had their need fully met. *In 2010,* 3 non-need-based awards were made. *Average percent of need met:* 53. *Average financial aid package:* $20,135. *Average need-based loan:* $8695. *Average need-based gift aid:* $14,825. *Average non-need-based aid:* $12,910. *Average indebtedness upon graduation:* $33,060.

Applying *Options:* electronic application. *Application fee:* $100. *Required:* essay or personal statement, high school transcript, 1 letter of recommendation, interview, audition, written test.

Freshman Application Contact Mannes College The New School for Music, 150 West 85th Street, New York, NY 10024-4402. *Phone:* 212-580-0210 Ext. 4862. *Toll-free phone:* 800-292-3040. *Web site:* http://www.mannes.edu/.

See page 581 for display ad and page 1476 for the College Close-Up.

Maria College

Albany, New York

- **Independent** 4-year, founded 1958
- **Urban** 9-acre campus
- **Coed** 905 undergraduate students, 27% full-time, 86% women, 14% men
- **Minimally difficult** entrance level, 21% of applicants were admitted

Undergraduates 242 full-time, 663 part-time. 3% are from out of state; 16% Black or African American, non-Hispanic/Latino; 3% Hispanic/Latino; 3% Asian, non-Hispanic/Latino; 0.2% Native Hawaiian or other Pacific Islander, non-Hispanic/Latino; 0.4% American Indian or Alaska Native, non-Hispanic/Latino; 0.6% Two or more races, non-Hispanic/Latino; 0.8% Race/ethnicity unknown. *Retention:* 54% of full-time freshmen returned.

Freshmen *Admission:* 341 applied, 71 admitted, 46 enrolled. *Test scores:* SAT critical reading scores over 500: 39%; SAT math scores over 500: 33%.

Faculty *Total:* 89, 34% full-time, 12% with terminal degrees. *Student/faculty ratio:* 12:1.

Academics *Calendar:* semesters. *Degrees:* certificates, associate, and bachelor's. *Special study options:* academic remediation for entering students, adult/continuing education programs, advanced placement credit, distance learning, independent study, off-campus study, part-time degree program, services for LD students, summer session for credit. *ROTC:* Air Force (c).

Computers on Campus 78 computers/terminals are available on campus for general student use. Students can access the following: campus intranet, online (class) grades, online (class) registration, online (class) schedules. Campuswide network is available. Wireless service is available via entire campus.

Student Life *Housing:* college housing not available. *Campus security:* late-night transport/escort service. *Student services:* personal/psychological counseling.

Standardized Tests *Required:* SAT or ACT (for admission).

Financial Aid Of all full-time matriculated undergraduates who enrolled in 2010, 25 Federal Work-Study jobs (averaging $1000).

Applying *Options:* electronic application, early admission. *Application fee:* $35. *Required:* essay or personal statement, high school transcript, minimum 2.0 GPA, 1 letter of recommendation, interview. *Application deadlines:* 8/25 (freshmen), 8/25 (transfers).

Freshman Application Contact Ms. Laurie A. Gilmore, Director of Admissions, Maria College, 700 New Scotland Avenue, Albany, NY 12208-1798. *Phone:* 518-438-3111. *Fax:* 518-453-1366. *E-mail:* admissions@mariacollege.edu. *Web site:* http://www.mariacollege.edu/.

Marist College

Poughkeepsie, New York

- **Independent** comprehensive, founded 1929
- **Suburban** 180-acre campus with easy access to Albany, New York City
- **Endowment** $118.6 million
- **Coed**
- **Very difficult** entrance level

Faculty *Student/faculty ratio:* 15:1.

Academics *Calendar:* semesters. *Degrees:* certificates, bachelor's, master's, and postbachelor's certificates.

Student Life *Campus security:* 24-hour emergency response devices and patrols, student patrols, late-night transport/escort service, controlled dormitory access, night residence hall monitors.

Athletics Member NCAA. All Division I except football (Division I-AA).

Costs (2011–12) *One-time required fee:* $90. *Comprehensive fee:* $40,900 includes full-time tuition ($28,300), mandatory fees ($500), and room and board ($12,100). Part-time tuition: $634 per credit. *Required fees:* $40 per term part-time. *Room and board:* Room and board charges vary according to board plan and housing facility.

Financial Aid *Of all full-time matriculated undergraduates who enrolled in 2011,* 3,548 applied for aid, 2,855 were judged to have need. *In 2011,* 1081 non-need-based awards were made. *Average percent of need met:* 41. *Average financial aid package:* $18,773. *Average need-based loan:* $4615. *Average need-based gift aid:* $13,352. *Average non-need-based aid:* $7308. *Average indebtedness upon graduation:* $32,507. *Financial aid deadline:* 5/1.

Applying *Options:* electronic application, early admission, early decision, early action, deferred entrance. *Application fee:* $50. *Required:* essay or personal statement, high school transcript, 2 letters of recommendation.

Freshman Application Contact Mr. Kenton Rinehart, Dean of Undergraduate Admissions, Marist College, 3399 North Road, Poughkeepsie, NY 12601. *Phone:* 845-575-3226. *Toll-free phone:* 800-436-5483. *Fax:* 845-575-3215. *E-mail:* admission@marist.edu. *Web site:* http://www.marist.edu/.

Marymount Manhattan College

New York, New York

- **Independent** 4-year, founded 1936
- **Urban** 3-acre campus
- **Endowment** $14.0 million
- **Coed** 1,953 undergraduate students, 87% full-time, 76% women, 24% men
- **Moderately difficult** entrance level, 79% of applicants were admitted

Undergraduates 1,707 full-time, 246 part-time. Students come from 45 states and territories; 38 other countries; 56% are from out of state; 6% Black or African American, non-Hispanic/Latino; 15% Hispanic/Latino; 4% Asian, non-Hispanic/Latino; 0.3% Native Hawaiian or other Pacific Islander, non-Hispanic/Latino; 1% American Indian or Alaska Native, non-Hispanic/Latino; 4% international; 8% transferred in; 36% live on campus. *Retention:* 67% of full-time freshmen returned.

Freshmen *Admission:* 3,664 applied, 2,892 admitted, 439 enrolled. *Average high school GPA:* 3.21. *Test scores:* SAT critical reading scores over 500: 77%; SAT math scores over 500: 57%; SAT writing scores over 500: 70%; ACT scores over 18: 96%; SAT critical reading scores over 600: 32%; SAT math scores over 600: 14%; SAT writing scores over 600: 21%; ACT scores over 24: 52%; SAT critical reading scores over 700: 3%; SAT math scores over 700: 1%; SAT writing scores over 700: 3%; ACT scores over 30: 5%.

Faculty *Total:* 318, 32% full-time, 61% with terminal degrees. *Student/faculty ratio:* 10:1.

Academics *Calendar:* semesters plus summer and January mini-semesters. *Degrees:* associate and bachelor's. *Special study options:* academic remediation for entering students, accelerated degree program, adult/continuing education programs, advanced placement credit, distance learning, double majors, honors programs, independent study, internships, off-campus study, part-time degree program, services for LD students, study abroad, summer session for credit. *Unusual degree programs:* computer science with Polytechnic University.

Computers on Campus 152 computers/terminals are available on campus for general student use. Students can access the following: campus intranet, computer help desk, free student e-mail accounts, online (class) grades, online (class) registration, online (class) schedules. Campuswide network is available. 100% of college-owned or -operated housing units are wired for high-speed Internet access. Wireless service is available via classrooms, computer centers, computer labs, dorm rooms, learning centers, libraries, student centers.

Student Life *Housing options:* coed. Campus housing is university owned and leased by the school. Freshman applicants given priority for college housing. *Activities and organizations:* drama/theater group, student-run newspaper, radio station, choral group, Education Club, African-American Heritage Club, Asian-American Heritage Club, Latino Heritage Club, Business Club. *Campus security:* 24-hour emergency response devices and patrols, student patrols, 24-hour security in residence halls. *Student services:* personal/psychological counseling.

Athletics *Intramural sports:* softball M/W.

Standardized Tests *Required:* SAT or ACT (for admission).

Costs (2011–12) *Comprehensive fee:* $38,738 includes full-time tuition ($23,542), mandatory fees ($1166), and room and board ($14,030). Part-time tuition: $75 per credit hour. *Required fees:* $420 per term part-time. *College room only:* $11,930. *Payment plan:* installment. *Waivers:* senior citizens and employees or children of employees.

Financial Aid Of all full-time matriculated undergraduates who enrolled in 2009, 1,303 applied for aid, 1,073 were judged to have need, 32 had their need fully met. In 2009, 294 non-need-based awards were made. *Average percent of need met:* 47%. *Average financial aid package:* $13,251. *Average need-based loan:* $4236. *Average need-based gift aid:* $9454. *Average non-need-based aid:* $5119. *Average indebtedness upon graduation:* $15,988.

Applying *Options:* electronic application, deferred entrance. *Application fee:* $60. *Required:* essay or personal statement, high school transcript, minimum 2.0 GPA, 2 letters of recommendation. *Required for some:* audition for dance and theater programs. *Recommended:* interview. *Application deadlines:* rolling (freshmen), rolling (transfers). *Notification:* continuous (freshmen), continuous (transfers).

Freshman Application Contact Mr. James Rogers, Dean of Admissions, Marymount Manhattan College, 221 East 71st Street, New York, NY 10021. *Phone:* 212-517-0430. *Toll-free phone:* 800-MARYMOUNT. *Fax:* 212-517-0448. *E-mail:* admissions@mmm.edu. *Web site:* http://www.mmm.edu/.

See page 600 for display ad and page 1434 for the College Close-Up.

Medaille College

Buffalo, New York

- **Independent** comprehensive, founded 1875
- **Urban** 13-acre campus
- **Endowment** $941,453
- **Coed** 1,797 undergraduate students, 92% full-time, 64% women, 36% men
- **Moderately difficult** entrance level, 68% of applicants were admitted

Undergraduates 1,660 full-time, 137 part-time. Students come from 19 states and territories; 2 other countries; 4% are from out of state; 16% Black or African American, non-Hispanic/Latino; 5% Hispanic/Latino; 3% Asian, non-Hispanic/Latino; 3% Native Hawaiian or other Pacific Islander, non-Hispanic/Latino; 1% American Indian or Alaska Native, non-Hispanic/Latino; 11% Race/ethnicity unknown; 0.2% international; 12% transferred in; 23% live on campus. *Retention:* 65% of full-time freshmen returned.

Freshmen *Admission:* 1,438 applied, 984 admitted, 375 enrolled. *Test scores:* SAT critical reading scores over 500: 24%; SAT math scores over 500: 27%; SAT critical reading scores over 600: 3%; SAT math scores over 600: 5%.

Faculty *Total:* 277, 29% full-time. *Student/faculty ratio:* 17:1.

Academics *Calendar:* semesters (modular courses available for evening studies and weekend college program). *Degrees:* certificates, associate, bachelor's, master's, and post-master's certificates. *Special study options:* academic remediation for entering students, accelerated degree program, adult/continuing education programs, advanced placement credit, double majors, honors programs, independent study, internships, off-campus study, part-time degree program, services for LD students, student-designed majors, summer session for credit. *ROTC:* Army (c). *Unusual degree programs:* 3-2 business administration; sport management.

Computers on Campus 120 computers/terminals are available on campus for general student use. Students can access the following: campus intranet, computer help desk, free student e-mail accounts, online (class) grades, online (class) registration, online (class) schedules. Campuswide network is available. 100% of college-owned or -operated housing units are wired for high-speed Internet access. Wireless service is available via entire campus.

Student Life *Housing options:* coed, men-only, women-only, disabled students. Campus housing is university owned. *Activities and organizations:* drama/theater group, student-run newspaper, radio and television station, student government, Club Green, Dance Team, WMCB The Lizard (college radio station), ice hockey club. *Campus security:* 24-hour emergency response devices and patrols, late-night transport/escort service, controlled dormitory access. *Student services:* health clinic, personal/psychological counseling.

Athletics Member NCAA. All Division III. *Intercollegiate sports:* baseball M, basketball M/W, bowling W, cross-country running M/W, golf M, lacrosse M/W, soccer M/W, softball W, volleyball M/W. *Intramural sports:* basketball M/W, soccer M/W, softball M/W, table tennis M/W, tennis M/W, volleyball M/W, weight lifting M/W.

Standardized Tests *Required:* SAT or ACT (for admission). *Recommended:* SAT (for admission).

Costs (2011–12) *Comprehensive fee:* $31,842 includes full-time tuition ($21,598) and room and board ($10,244). Full-time tuition and fees vary according to location. Part-time tuition: $761 per credit hour. Part-time tuition and fees vary according to course load. *Room and board:* Room and board charges vary according to housing facility. *Payment plan:* installment. *Waivers:* adult students, senior citizens, and employees or children of employees.

Financial Aid Of all full-time matriculated undergraduates who enrolled in 2010, 1,722 applied for aid, 1,586 were judged to have need, 43 had their need fully met. 234 Federal Work-Study jobs (averaging $1451). In 2010, 52 non-need-based awards were made. *Average percent of need met:* 58%. *Average financial aid package:* $14,241. *Average need-based loan:* $4882. *Average need-based gift aid:* $8500. *Average non-need-based aid:* $7529.

Applying *Options:* electronic application, early admission, deferred entrance. *Application fee:* $25. *Required:* high school transcript, interview. *Required for some:* essay or personal statement, 2.5 high school GPA for veterinary technology and elementary teacher education majors. *Recommended:* essay or personal statement, minimum 2.0 GPA, 1 letter of recommendation. *Application deadlines:* 8/1 (freshmen), rolling (transfers). *Notification:* continuous (freshmen), continuous (transfers).

Freshman Application Contact Mr. Greg Florczak, Director of Undergraduate Admissions, Medaille College, Office of Admissions, Buffalo, NY 14214. *Phone:* 716-880-2200. *Toll-free phone:* 800-292-1582. *Fax:* 716-880-2007. *E-mail:* admissionsug@medaille.edu. *Web site:* http://www.medaille.edu/.

THIS IS YOUR 10AM CLASS.

THIS IS YOUR INTERNSHIP.

THIS IS YOUR BACKYARD.

Visit us at www.mmm.edu or call 1-800-MARYMOUNT

This is MarymountManhattan
a college of the liberal arts

Medgar Evers College of the City University of New York

Brooklyn, New York

- **State and locally supported** 4-year, founded 1969, part of City University of New York System
- **Urban** 8-acre campus
- **Endowment** $515,142
- **Coed** 6,966 undergraduate students, 65% full-time, 74% women, 26% men
- **Noncompetitive** entrance level, 100% of applicants were admitted

Undergraduates 4,561 full-time, 2,405 part-time. Students come from 7 states and territories; 77 other countries; 1% are from out of state; 86% Black or African American, non-Hispanic/Latino; 8% Hispanic/Latino; 1% Asian, non-Hispanic/Latino; 0.1% American Indian or Alaska Native, non-Hispanic/Latino; 0.8% Two or more races, non-Hispanic/Latino; 1% Race/ethnicity unknown; 1% international; 9% transferred in. *Retention:* 62% of full-time freshmen returned.

Freshmen *Admission:* 8,042 applied, 8,042 admitted, 1,201 enrolled. *Test scores:* SAT critical reading scores over 500: 9%; SAT math scores over 500: 7%; SAT critical reading scores over 600: 1%; SAT math scores over 600: 1%.

Faculty *Total:* 498, 36% full-time, 38% with terminal degrees. *Student/faculty ratio:* 19:1.

Academics *Calendar:* semesters. *Degrees:* certificates, associate, and bachelor's. *Special study options:* academic remediation for entering students, adult/continuing education programs, advanced placement credit, cooperative education, double majors, English as a second language, external degree program, honors programs, independent study, internships, off-campus study, part-time degree program, services for LD students, study abroad, summer session for credit.

Computers on Campus 120 computers/terminals are available on campus for general student use. Students can access the following: free student e-mail accounts, online (class) grades, online (class) registration, online (class) schedules. Campuswide network is available. Wireless service is available via entire campus.

Student Life *Housing:* college housing not available. *Activities and organizations:* drama/theater group, student-run newspaper, radio and television station, choral group, American Marketing Association, Drama Students Association, Rising Stars, Medgar Evers College Society of Public Administrators, National Society of Black Accountants. *Campus security:* 24-hour patrols. *Student services:* women's center, legal services.

Athletics Member NCAA. All Division III. *Intercollegiate sports:* basketball M/W, cross-country running M/W, soccer M/W, tennis W, track and field M/W, volleyball M/W. *Intramural sports:* basketball M/W, tennis W.

Standardized Tests *Recommended:* SAT and SAT Subject Tests or ACT (for admission).

Costs (2012–13) *Tuition:* state resident $5130 full-time, $215 per credit part-time; nonresident $13,800 full-time, $460 per credit part-time. Full-time tuition and fees vary according to course load. Part-time tuition and fees vary according to course load. *Required fees:* $302 full-time, $101 per term part-time. *Payment plans:* installment, deferred payment.

Financial Aid Of all full-time matriculated undergraduates who enrolled in 2009, 289 Federal Work-Study jobs (averaging $1071). *Average financial aid package:* $3835. *Average need-based loan:* $1758. *Average need-based gift aid:* $3572.

Applying *Options:* electronic application, deferred entrance. *Application fee:* $65. *Required:* high school transcript. *Application deadlines:* rolling (freshmen), rolling (transfers). *Notification:* continuous (freshmen), continuous (transfers).

Freshman Application Contact Ms. Julie M. Augustin, Director of Admissions, Medgar Evers College of the City University of New York, 1650 Bedford Avenue, Brooklyn, NY 11225. *Phone:* 718-270-6021. *Fax:* 718-270-6411. *E-mail:* jaugustin@mec.cuny.edu. *Web site:* http://www.mec.cuny.edu/.

Mercy College

Dobbs Ferry, New York

- **Independent** comprehensive, founded 1951
- **Suburban** 45-acre campus with easy access to New York City
- **Endowment** $31.1 million
- **Coed** 7,968 undergraduate students, 68% full-time, 67% women, 33% men
- **Moderately difficult** entrance level, 64% of applicants were admitted

Undergraduates 5,451 full-time, 2,517 part-time. Students come from 35 states and territories; 23 other countries; 7% are from out of state; 26% Black or African American, non-Hispanic/Latino; 31% Hispanic/Latino; 3% Asian, non-Hispanic/Latino; 0.1% Native Hawaiian or other Pacific Islander, non-Hispanic/Latino; 0.4% American Indian or Alaska Native, non-Hispanic/Latino; 1% Two or more races, non-Hispanic/Latino; 11% Race/ethnicity unknown; 0.5% international; 13% transferred in; 3% live on campus. *Retention:* 68% of full-time freshmen returned.

Freshmen *Admission:* 6,687 applied, 4,286 admitted, 1,192 enrolled. *Average high school GPA:* 2.7.

Faculty *Total:* 1,047, 19% full-time. *Student/faculty ratio:* 18:1.

Academics *Calendar:* semesters. *Degrees:* certificates, associate, bachelor's, master's, doctoral, post-master's, and postbachelor's certificates. *Special study options:* academic remediation for entering students, accelerated degree program, adult/continuing education programs, advanced placement credit, cooperative education, distance learning, double majors, honors programs, independent study, internships, off-campus study, part-time degree program, services for LD students, study abroad, summer session for credit. *ROTC:* Army (c), Air Force (c). *Unusual degree programs:* 3-2 education, accounting.

Computers on Campus 186 computers/terminals are available on campus for general student use. Students can access the following: campus intranet, computer help desk, free student e-mail accounts, online (class) grades, online (class) registration, online (class) schedules. Campuswide network is available. 100% of college-owned or -operated housing units are wired for high-speed Internet access. Wireless service is available via entire campus.

Student Life *Housing options:* coed, disabled students. Campus housing is university owned and leased by the school. Freshman applicants given priority for college housing. *Activities and organizations:* student-run newspaper, PACT, Honors, Mercy Gives Back, Model United Nations. *Campus security:* 24-hour emergency response devices and patrols, late-night transport/escort service, controlled dormitory access. *Student services:* health clinic, personal/psychological counseling.

Athletics Member NCAA. All Division II. *Intercollegiate sports:* baseball M(s), basketball M(s)/W(s), field hockey W(s), lacrosse M(s)/W(s), soccer M(s)/W(s), softball W(s), volleyball W(s). *Intramural sports:* baseball M, basketball M/W, softball W.

Standardized Tests *Recommended:* SAT (for admission), ACT (for admission), SAT or ACT (for admission), SAT and SAT Subject Tests or ACT (for admission), SAT Subject Tests (for admission).

Costs (2012–13) *Comprehensive fee:* $29,740 includes full-time tuition ($16,996), mandatory fees ($560), and room and board ($12,184). Full-time tuition and fees vary according to course load. Part-time tuition: $715 per credit. Part-time tuition and fees vary according to course load. *Required fees:* $140 per term part-time. *College room only:* $8734. Room and board charges vary according to board plan and housing facility. *Payment plan:* installment. *Waivers:* employees or children of employees.

Financial Aid Of all full-time matriculated undergraduates who enrolled in 2009, 3,515 applied for aid, 3,484 were judged to have need, 53 had their need fully met. In 2009, 60 non-need-based awards were made. *Average percent of need met:* 47%. *Average financial aid package:* $12,164. *Average need-based loan:* $4103. *Average need-based gift aid:* $8609. *Average non-need-based aid:* $3385. *Average indebtedness upon graduation:* $23,307.

Applying *Options:* electronic application, deferred entrance. *Application fee:* $40. *Required:* high school transcript, minimum 2.5 GPA. *Required for some:* essay or personal statement, interview. *Application deadlines:* rolling (freshmen), rolling (out-of-state freshmen), rolling (transfers). *Notification:* continuous (freshmen), continuous (out-of-state freshmen), continuous (transfers).

Freshman Application Contact Mrs. Tara Fay-Reilly, Senior Director of Admissions, Mercy College, 555 Broadway, Dobbs Ferry, NY 10522-1189. *Phone:* 914-674-7762 Ext. 7762. *Toll-free phone:* 800-MERCY-NY. *Fax:* 914-674-7608. *E-mail:* admissions@mercy.edu. *Web site:* http://www.mercy.edu/.

Mesivta of Eastern Parkway–Yeshiva Zichron Meilech

Brooklyn, New York

Director of Admissions Rabbi Joseph Halberstadt, Dean, Mesivta of Eastern Parkway–Yeshiva Zichron Meilech, 510 Dahill Road, Brooklyn, NY 11218-5559. *Phone:* 718-438-1002.

Mesivta Tifereth Jerusalem of America

New York, New York

Director of Admissions Rabbi Fishellis, Director of Admissions, Mesivta Tifereth Jerusalem of America, 145 East Broadway, New York, NY 10002-6301. *Phone:* 212-964-2830.

Mesivta Torah Vodaath Rabbinical Seminary

Brooklyn, New York

Director of Admissions Rabbi Issac Braun, Administrator, Mesivta Torah Vodaath Rabbinical Seminary, 425 East Ninth Street, Brooklyn, NY 11218-5299. *Phone:* 718-941-8000.

Metropolitan College of New York

New York, New York

Freshman Application Contact Metropolitan College of New York, 431 Canal Street, New York, NY 10013. *Phone:* 212-343-1234 Ext. 2700. *Toll-free phone:* 800-33-THINK Ext. 5001. *Fax:* 212-343-8470. *Web site:* http://www.metropolitan.edu/.

Mirrer Yeshiva

Brooklyn, New York

Director of Admissions Director of Admissions, Mirrer Yeshiva, 1795 Ocean Parkway, Brooklyn, NY 11223-2010. *Phone:* 718-645-0536.

Molloy College

Rockville Centre, New York

- **Independent** comprehensive, founded 1955
- **Suburban** 30-acre campus with easy access to New York City
- **Endowment** $24.1 million
- **Coed** 3,414 undergraduate students, 77% full-time, 76% women, 24% men
- **Moderately difficult** entrance level, 47% of applicants were admitted

Undergraduates 2,636 full-time, 778 part-time. Students come from 10 states and territories; 6 other countries; 14% Black or African American, non-Hispanic/Latino; 12% Hispanic/Latino; 7% Asian, non-Hispanic/Latino; 0.6% Native Hawaiian or other Pacific Islander, non-Hispanic/Latino; 0.1% American Indian or Alaska Native, non-Hispanic/Latino; 1% Two or more races, non-Hispanic/Latino; 1% Race/ethnicity unknown; 0.2% international; 15%

transferred in; 3% live on campus. *Retention:* 88% of full-time freshmen returned.

Freshmen *Admission:* 1,793 applied, 836 admitted, 403 enrolled. *Test scores:* SAT critical reading scores over 500: 63%; SAT math scores over 500: 72%; SAT writing scores over 500: 59%; ACT scores over 18: 100%; SAT critical reading scores over 600: 17%; SAT math scores over 600: 23%; SAT writing scores over 600: 16%; ACT scores over 24: 63%; SAT critical reading scores over 700: 1%; SAT math scores over 700: 2%; SAT writing scores over 700: 1%; ACT scores over 30: 21%.

Faculty *Total:* 653, 27% full-time, 33% with terminal degrees. *Student/faculty ratio:* 10:1.

Academics *Calendar:* 4-1-4. *Degrees:* associate, bachelor's, master's, doctoral, post-master's, and first professional certificates. *Special study options:* academic remediation for entering students, adult/continuing education programs, advanced placement credit, cooperative education, double majors, English as a second language, honors programs, internships, part-time degree program, services for LD students, study abroad, summer session for credit. *ROTC:* Army (c), Navy (c), Air Force (c).

Computers on Campus 400 computers/terminals are available on campus for general student use. Students can access the following: computer help desk, free student e-mail accounts, online (class) grades, online (class) registration, online (class) schedules. Campuswide network is available. Wireless service is available via entire campus.

Student Life *Housing options:* coed. Campus housing is university owned. Freshman applicants given priority for college housing. *Activities and organizations:* drama/theater group, student-run newspaper, choral group, Nursing Student Association, African-American Caribbean Organization, Gaelic Society, Education Club, International Society. *Campus security:* 24-hour emergency response devices and patrols, late-night transport/escort service. *Student services:* health clinic, personal/psychological counseling, women's center, legal services.

Athletics Member NCAA. All Division II. *Intercollegiate sports:* baseball M(s), basketball M(s)/W(s), cross-country running M(s)/W(s), equestrian sports W, lacrosse M(s)/W(s), rugby M/W, soccer M(s)/W(s), softball W(s), tennis W(s), track and field M(s)/W(s), volleyball W(s). *Intramural sports:* cheerleading W, rugby M/W, ultimate Frisbee M/W.

Standardized Tests *Required:* SAT or ACT (for admission).

Costs (2011–12) *Comprehensive fee:* $36,180 includes full-time tuition ($22,290), mandatory fees ($1010), and room and board ($12,880). Full-time tuition and fees vary according to degree level. Part-time tuition: $735 per credit. Part-time tuition and fees vary according to degree level. *College room*

only: $9090. Room and board charges vary according to board plan. *Payment plan:* installment. *Waivers:* employees or children of employees.

Financial Aid Of all full-time matriculated undergraduates who enrolled in 2010, 2,075 applied for aid, 1,796 were judged to have need, 194 had their need fully met. 182 Federal Work-Study jobs (averaging $1704). In 2010, 179 non-need-based awards were made. *Average percent of need met: 53%. Average financial aid package:* $13,218. *Average need-based loan:* $5794. *Average need-based gift aid:* $9169. *Average non-need-based aid:* $6399. *Average indebtedness upon graduation:* $29,823. *Financial aid deadline:* 5/1.

Applying *Options:* electronic application, early admission, early action, deferred entrance. *Application fee:* $30. *Required for some:* essay or personal statement, high school transcript, 1 letter of recommendation. *Recommended:* interview. *Application deadlines:* rolling (freshmen), rolling (transfers). *Notification:* continuous (freshmen), continuous (transfers).

Freshman Application Contact Ms. Marguerite Lane, Director of Admissions, Molloy College, 1000 Hempstead Avenue, PO Box 5002, Rockville Centre, NY 11571-5002. *Phone:* 516-678-5000 Ext. 6240. *Toll-free phone:* 888-4MOLLOY. *Fax:* 516-256-2247. *E-mail:* admissions@molloy.edu. *Web site:* http://www.molloy.edu/.

See page 1462 for the College Close-Up.

Monroe College
Bronx, New York

Freshman Application Contact Monroe College, Monroe College Way, Bronx, NY 10468-5407. *Phone:* 718-933-6700 Ext. 8246. *Toll-free phone:* 800-55MONROE. *Web site:* http://www.monroecollege.edu/.

Monroe College
New Rochelle, New York

Freshman Application Contact Ms. Lisa Scorca, High School Admissions, Monroe College, 434 Main Street, New Rochelle, NY 10801. *Phone:* 914-654-3200. *Toll-free phone:* 800-55MONROE. *E-mail:* lscorca@monroecollege.edu. *Web site:* http://www.monroecollege.edu/.

Morrisville State College
Morrisville, New York

- **State-supported** 4-year, founded 1908, part of State University of New York System
- **Rural** 185-acre campus with easy access to Syracuse
- **Coed** 3,432 undergraduate students, 82% full-time, 48% women, 52% men
- **Moderately difficult** entrance level, 75% of applicants were admitted

Undergraduates 2,802 full-time, 630 part-time. Students come from 27 states and territories; 12 other countries; 5% are from out of state; 6% transferred in; 73% live on campus.

Freshmen *Admission:* 3,579 applied, 2,683 admitted, 1,277 enrolled. *Average high school GPA:* 2.9. *Test scores:* SAT critical reading scores over 500: 47%; SAT math scores over 500: 59%; SAT critical reading scores over 600: 9%; SAT math scores over 600: 9%.

Faculty *Total:* 261, 51% full-time, 17% with terminal degrees. *Student/faculty ratio:* 13:1.

Academics *Calendar:* semesters. *Degrees:* certificates, associate, and bachelor's. *Special study options:* academic remediation for entering students, advanced placement credit, cooperative education, distance learning, double majors, honors programs, internships, off-campus study, part-time degree program, services for LD students, student-designed majors, summer session for credit. *ROTC:* Army (c).

Computers on Campus 90 computers/terminals are available on campus for general student use. Students can access the following: campus intranet, computer help desk, free student e-mail accounts, online (class) grades, online (class) registration, online (class) schedules, various software applications. Campuswide network is available. 100% of college-owned or -operated housing units are wired for high-speed Internet access. Wireless service is available via entire campus.

Student Life *Housing:* on-campus residence required for freshman year. *Options:* coed, disabled students. Campus housing is university owned. Freshman campus housing is guaranteed. *Activities and organizations:* drama/theater group, student-run newspaper, radio station, choral group, marching band, African Student Union Black Alliance, Student Government Organization, Agriculture Club, Latino-American Student Association, WCVM (student radio station). *Campus security:* 24-hour emergency response devices and patrols, late-night transport/escort service, controlled dormitory access. *Student services:* health clinic, personal/psychological counseling, legal services.

Athletics Member NCAA. All Division III. *Intercollegiate sports:* basketball M/W, cross-country running M/W, equestrian sports M/W, field hockey W, football M, ice hockey M, lacrosse M/W, soccer M/W, softball W, volleyball W. *Intramural sports:* badminton M/W, basketball M/W, ice hockey M/W, soccer M/W, tennis M/W, ultimate Frisbee M/W, volleyball M/W, weight lifting M/W.

Standardized Tests *Required for some:* SAT or ACT (for admission).

Costs (2011–12) *Tuition:* state resident $5270 full-time, $220 per credit hour part-time; nonresident $9740 full-time, $406 per credit hour part-time. Full-time tuition and fees vary according to degree level. Part-time tuition and fees vary according to course load. *Required fees:* $1202 full-time. *Room and board:* $9980; room only: $5600. Room and board charges vary according to board plan and housing facility. *Payment plans:* installment, deferred payment.

Financial Aid Of all full-time matriculated undergraduates who enrolled in 2009, 2,785 applied for aid, 2,515 were judged to have need, 32 had their need fully met. 160 Federal Work-Study jobs (averaging $1740). In 2009, 60 non-need-based awards were made. *Average financial aid package:* $9249. *Average need-based loan:* $3659. *Average need-based gift aid:* $5900. *Average non-need-based aid:* $1597. *Average indebtedness upon graduation:* $21,067.

Applying *Options:* electronic application, deferred entrance. *Application fee:* $50. *Required:* high school transcript. *Recommended:* essay or personal statement, minimum 2.0 GPA, 2 letters of recommendation, interview. *Application deadlines:* rolling (freshmen), rolling (out-of-state freshmen), rolling (transfers). *Notification:* continuous (freshmen), continuous (out-of-state freshmen), continuous (transfers).

Freshman Application Contact Morrisville State College, PO Box 901, Morrisville, NY 13408-0901. *Phone:* 315-684-6046. *Toll-free phone:* 800-258-0111. *Web site:* http://www.morrisville.edu/.

Mount Saint Mary College
Newburgh, New York

- **Independent** comprehensive, founded 1960
- **Suburban** 86-acre campus with easy access to New York City
- **Endowment** $4.7 million
- **Coed** 2,347 undergraduate students, 82% full-time, 73% women, 27% men
- **Moderately difficult** entrance level, 81% of applicants were admitted

Undergraduates 1,929 full-time, 418 part-time. Students come from 14 states and territories; 24 other countries; 12% are from out of state; 7% Black or African American, non-Hispanic/Latino; 12% Hispanic/Latino; 2% Asian, non-Hispanic/Latino; 0.4% Native Hawaiian or other Pacific Islander, non-Hispanic/Latino; 0.7% American Indian or Alaska Native, non-Hispanic/Latino; 1% Two or more races, non-Hispanic/Latino; 8% Race/ethnicity unknown; 10% transferred in; 44% live on campus. *Retention:* 68% of full-time freshmen returned.

Freshmen *Admission:* 3,347 applied, 2,711 admitted, 454 enrolled. *Average high school GPA:* 3.1. *Test scores:* SAT critical reading scores over 500: 47%; SAT math scores over 500: 56%; SAT writing scores over 500: 49%; ACT scores over 18: 91%; SAT critical reading scores over 600: 7%; SAT math scores over 600: 11%; SAT writing scores over 600: 6%; ACT scores over 24: 27%; SAT math scores over 700: 1%; ACT scores over 30: 1%.

Faculty *Total:* 276, 32% full-time, 41% with terminal degrees. *Student/faculty ratio:* 15:1.

Academics *Calendar:* semesters. *Degrees:* certificates, bachelor's, master's, and post-master's certificates. *Special study options:* academic remediation for entering students, accelerated degree program, adult/continuing education programs, advanced placement credit, cooperative education, distance learning, double majors, freshman honors college, honors programs, independent study, internships, off-campus study, part-time degree program, services for LD students, student-designed majors, study abroad, summer session for credit. *Unusual degree programs:* 3-2 social work with Fordham University; publishing, counseling with Pace University.

Computers on Campus 576 computers/terminals are available on campus for general student use. Students can access the following: campus intranet, computer help desk, free student e-mail accounts, online (class) grades, online (class) registration, online (class) schedules, Intranet. Campuswide network is available. 100% of college-owned or -operated housing units are wired for high-speed Internet access. Wireless service is available via entire campus.

Student Life *Housing:* on-campus residence required through sophomore year. *Options:* coed, men-only, women-only, disabled students. Campus housing is university owned. Freshman applicants given priority for college housing. *Activities and organizations:* drama/theater group, student-run newspaper, radio station, choral group, Student Government Association, Delta Leadership Society, Big Brothers/Big Sisters, Black and Latin Student Unions, Habitat for Humanity. *Campus security:* 24-hour emergency response devices and patrols, student patrols, late-night transport/escort service, controlled dormitory access,

monitored surveillance cameras in all residence halls. *Student services:* health clinic, personal/psychological counseling.

Athletics Member NCAA. All Division III. *Intercollegiate sports:* baseball M, basketball M/W, cross-country running M/W, lacrosse M/W, soccer M/W, softball W, swimming and diving M/W, tennis M/W, track and field M/W, volleyball W. *Intramural sports:* basketball M/W, bowling M/W, cheerleading W(c), football M, golf M/W, soccer M/W, softball M/W, swimming and diving M/W, table tennis M/W, volleyball M/W.

Standardized Tests *Required:* SAT or ACT (for admission).

Costs (2012–13) *Comprehensive fee:* $38,150 includes full-time tuition ($24,390), mandatory fees ($950), and room and board ($12,810). Full-time tuition and fees vary according to class time, location, and program. Part-time tuition: $813 per credit hour. Part-time tuition and fees vary according to class time, location, and program. *College room only:* $7420. Room and board charges vary according to board plan and housing facility. *Payment plan:* installment. *Waivers:* employees or children of employees.

Financial Aid Of all full-time matriculated undergraduates who enrolled in 2011, 1,756 applied for aid, 1,550 were judged to have need, 266 had their need fully met. 298 Federal Work-Study jobs (averaging $1331). In 2011, 239 non-need-based awards were made. *Average percent of need met:* 60%. *Average financial aid package:* $15,138. *Average need-based loan:* $4174. *Average need-based gift aid:* $11,586. *Average non-need-based aid:* $7858. *Average indebtedness upon graduation:* $35,185. *Financial aid deadline:* 3/1.

Applying *Options:* electronic application, early admission, deferred entrance. *Application fee:* $45. *Required:* essay or personal statement, high school transcript. *Required for some:* 2 letters of recommendation, interview. *Recommended:* minimum 3.0 GPA, 2 letters of recommendation, interview. *Application deadline:* 8/15 (freshmen). *Notification:* continuous (freshmen).

Freshman Application Contact Ms. Michelle Taylor, Director of Admissions, Mount Saint Mary College, 330 Powell Avenue, Newburgh, NY 12550-3494. *Phone:* 845-569-3248. *Toll-free phone:* 888-937-6762. *Fax:* 845-562-6762. *E-mail:* admissions@msmc.edu. *Web site:* http://www.msmc.edu/.

Nazareth College of Rochester
Rochester, New York

- **Independent** comprehensive, founded 1924
- **Suburban** 150-acre campus
- **Endowment** $48.1 million
- **Coed** 2,178 undergraduate students, 93% full-time, 75% women, 25% men
- **Moderately difficult** entrance level, 70% of applicants were admitted

Undergraduates 2,018 full-time, 160 part-time. Students come from 22 states and territories; 21 other countries; 8% are from out of state; 5% Black or African American, non-Hispanic/Latino; 4% Hispanic/Latino; 2% Asian, non-Hispanic/Latino; 0.4% American Indian or Alaska Native, non-Hispanic/Latino; 0.7% Two or more races, non-Hispanic/Latino; 13% Race/ethnicity unknown; 2% international; 7% transferred in; 55% live on campus. *Retention:* 82% of full-time freshmen returned.

Freshmen *Admission:* 2,976 applied, 2,081 admitted, 439 enrolled. *Average high school GPA:* 3.5. *Test scores:* SAT critical reading scores over 500: 86%; SAT math scores over 500: 89%; ACT scores over 18: 100%; SAT critical reading scores over 600: 43%; SAT math scores over 600: 41%; ACT scores over 24: 75%; SAT critical reading scores over 700: 7%; SAT math scores over 700: 4%; ACT scores over 30: 8%.

Faculty *Total:* 493, 32% full-time, 37% with terminal degrees. *Student/faculty ratio:* 10:1.

Academics *Calendar:* semesters. *Degrees:* bachelor's, master's, doctoral, and post-master's certificates. *Special study options:* academic remediation for entering students, adult/continuing education programs, advanced placement credit, cooperative education, double majors, English as a second language, honors programs, independent study, internships, off-campus study, part-time degree program, services for LD students, study abroad, summer session for credit. *ROTC:* Army (c), Air Force (c).

Computers on Campus 240 computers/terminals are available on campus for general student use. Students can access the following: computer help desk, free student e-mail accounts, online (class) grades, online (class) registration, online (class) schedules. Campuswide network is available. 100% of college-owned or -operated housing units are wired for high-speed Internet access. Wireless service is available via classrooms, computer centers, dorm rooms, libraries, student centers.

Student Life *Housing:* on-campus residence required through sophomore year. *Options:* coed, disabled students. Campus housing is university owned. Freshman campus housing is guaranteed. *Activities and organizations:* drama/theater group, student-run newspaper, radio station, choral group, Student Activities Council, intramurals and recreation, Theater League, Center for Spirituality Council, NAZ Ultimate Frisbee. *Campus security:* 24-hour emer-

gency response devices and patrols, student patrols, late-night transport/escort service, controlled dormitory access, alarm system, security beeper, lighted pathways. *Student services:* health clinic, personal/psychological counseling, women's center.

Athletics Member NCAA. All Division III. *Intercollegiate sports:* basketball M/W, cross-country running M/W, equestrian sports M/W, field hockey W, golf M/W, ice hockey M, lacrosse M/W, soccer M/W, softball W, swimming and diving M/W, tennis M/W, track and field M/W, volleyball M/W. *Intramural sports:* basketball M/W, crew W(c), racquetball M/W, soccer M/W, ultimate Frisbee M/W, volleyball M/W.

Costs (2012–13) *Comprehensive fee:* $38,366 includes full-time tuition ($26,048), mandatory fees ($1174), and room and board ($11,144). Full-time tuition and fees vary according to course load and program. Part-time tuition: $621 per credit hour. *Required fees:* $25 per term part-time. *Room and board:* Room and board charges vary according to board plan and housing facility. *Waivers:* minority students, children of alumni, and employees or children of employees.

Financial Aid Of all full-time matriculated undergraduates who enrolled in 2010, 1,828 applied for aid, 1,681 were judged to have need, 271 had their need fully met. 1,041 Federal Work-Study jobs (averaging $2026). In 2010, 324 non-need-based awards were made. *Average percent of need met:* 71%. *Average financial aid package:* $19,195. *Average need-based loan:* $4864. *Average need-based gift aid:* $13,921. *Average non-need-based aid:* $15,652. *Average indebtedness upon graduation:* $32,957.

Applying *Options:* electronic application, early admission, early decision, early action, deferred entrance. *Application fee:* $45. *Required:* essay or personal statement, high school transcript, 1 letter of recommendation. *Required for some:* audition/portfolio review. *Recommended:* interview. *Application deadlines:* 2/15 (freshmen), 5/15 (transfers), 12/15 (early action). *Early decision deadline:* 11/15. *Notification:* continuous until 3/1 (freshmen), continuous until 2/15 (transfers), 12/15 (early decision), 1/15 (early action).

Freshman Application Contact Mr. Thomas DaRin, Vice President for Enrollment Management, Nazareth College of Rochester, 4245 East Avenue, Rochester, NY 14618-3790. *Phone:* 585-389-2860. *Toll-free phone:* 800-462-3944. *Fax:* 585-389-2826. *E-mail:* admissions@naz.edu. *Web site:* http://www.naz.edu/.

The New School for General Studies
New York, New York

- **Independent** upper-level, founded 1919, part of The New School
- **Urban** campus with easy access to Manhattan
- **Coed**
- **Moderately difficult** entrance level

Academics *Calendar:* semesters. *Degrees:* certificates, bachelor's, master's, and postbachelor's certificates.

Student Life *Campus security:* 24-hour emergency response devices, controlled dormitory access, trained security personnel in central buildings.

Costs (2011–12) *Comprehensive fee:* $39,540 includes full-time tuition ($24,360), mandatory fees ($270), and room and board ($14,910). Part-time tuition: $1015 per credit. Part-time tuition and fees vary according to course load. *College room only:* $14,360. Room and board charges vary according to board plan and housing facility.

Financial Aid Of all full-time matriculated undergraduates who enrolled in 2010, 264 applied for aid, 246 were judged to have need, 8 had their need fully met. In 2010, 4 non-need-based awards were made. *Average percent of need met:* 67. *Average financial aid package:* $23,660. *Average need-based loan:* $11,430. *Average need-based gift aid:* $10,805. *Average non-need-based aid:* $6625.

Applying *Options:* electronic application, deferred entrance. *Application fee:* $50.

Application Contact Ms. Cory Meyers, Assistant Director of Admissions, The New School for General Studies, 72 Fifth Avenue, Room 304, New York, NY 10011. *Phone:* 212-229-5630. *Toll-free phone:* 800-292-3040. *Fax:* 212-627-2695. *E-mail:* nsadmissions@newschool.edu. *Web site:* http://www.newschool.edu/generalstudies/.

See page 581 for display ad and page 1476 for the College Close-Up.

The New School for Jazz and Contemporary Music
New York, New York

- **Independent** 4-year, founded 1986, part of The New School
- **Urban** campus with easy access to Manhattan
- **Coed**
- **Very difficult** entrance level

Faculty *Student/faculty ratio:* 11:1.

Academics *Calendar:* semesters. *Degree:* bachelor's.

Student Life *Campus security:* 24-hour emergency response devices, controlled dormitory access.

Costs (2011–12) *Comprehensive fee:* $52,150 includes full-time tuition ($36,970), mandatory fees ($270), and room and board ($14,910). Part-time tuition: $1255 per credit. Part-time tuition and fees vary according to course load. *College room only:* $14,360. Room and board charges vary according to board plan and housing facility.

Financial Aid *Of all full-time matriculated undergraduates who enrolled in 2010,* 109 applied for aid, 99 were judged to have need, 13 had their need fully met. *In 2010,* 4 non-need-based awards were made. *Average percent of need met:* 70. *Average financial aid package:* $24,691. *Average need-based loan:* $10,169. *Average need-based gift aid:* $17,942. *Average non-need-based aid:* $14,735. *Average indebtedness upon graduation:* $25,735.

Applying *Options:* electronic application, deferred entrance. *Application fee:* $100. *Required:* essay or personal statement, high school transcript, 1 letter of recommendation, audition, pre-screen tape/CD.

Freshman Application Contact Ms. Terri Lucas, Jazz Admissions, The New School for Jazz and Contemporary Music, 55 West 13th Street, 5th Floor, New York, NY 10011. *Phone:* 212-229-5896. *Toll-free phone:* 800-292-3040. *Fax:* 212-229-8936. *E-mail:* jazzadm@newschool.edu. *Web site:* http://www.jazz.newschool.edu/.

See page 581 for display ad and page 1476 for the College Close-Up.

New York City College of Technology of the City University of New York
Brooklyn, New York

- **State and locally supported** 4-year, founded 1946, part of City University of New York System
- **Urban** campus
- **Coed** 15,961 undergraduate students, 62% full-time, 46% women, 54% men
- **Noncompetitive** entrance level, 87% of applicants were admitted

Undergraduates 9,856 full-time, 6,105 part-time. Students come from 15 states and territories; 134 other countries; 34% Black or African American, non-Hispanic/Latino; 29% Hispanic/Latino; 16% Asian, non-Hispanic/Latino; 0.4% Native Hawaiian or other Pacific Islander, non-Hispanic/Latino; 0.3% American Indian or Alaska Native, non-Hispanic/Latino; 0.6% Two or more races, non-Hispanic/Latino; 5% international; 7% transferred in. *Retention:* 74% of full-time freshmen returned.

Freshmen *Admission:* 16,848 applied, 14,696 admitted, 3,127 enrolled.

Faculty *Total:* 1,230, 32% full-time, 35% with terminal degrees. *Student/faculty ratio:* 18:1.

Academics *Calendar:* semesters. *Degrees:* certificates, associate, and bachelor's. *Special study options:* academic remediation for entering students, accelerated degree program, adult/continuing education programs, advanced placement credit, distance learning, English as a second language, freshman honors college, honors programs, independent study, internships, off-campus study, part-time degree program, services for LD students, student-designed majors, study abroad, summer session for credit.

Computers on Campus 340 computers/terminals are available on campus for general student use. Students can access the following: campus intranet, computer help desk, free student e-mail accounts, online (class) grades, online (class) registration, online (class) schedules. Campuswide network is available. Wireless service is available via classrooms, computer centers, computer labs, learning centers, libraries, student centers.

Student Life *Housing:* college housing not available. *Activities and organizations:* drama/theater group, student-run newspaper, choral group, International Business Organization (IBO), NYCCT - Mock Trial Club, Chess Club, Women in Islam, ASCE-Student Chapter of American Society of Civil Engineering. *Campus security:* 24-hour emergency response devices and patrols. *Student services:* health clinic, personal/psychological counseling, women's center.

Athletics *Intramural sports:* basketball M/W, soccer M/W, table tennis M/W, volleyball M/W, weight lifting M/W.

Standardized Tests *Required for some:* SAT or ACT (for admission).

Costs (2012–13) *Tuition:* state resident $5130 full-time, $215 per credit part-time; nonresident $13,800 full-time, $460 per credit part-time. *Required fees:* $339 full-time, $85 per term part-time. *Payment plan:* installment. *Waivers:* employees or children of employees.

Financial Aid *Of all full-time matriculated undergraduates who enrolled in 2011,* 8,570 applied for aid, 8,169 were judged to have need, 185 had their need fully met. *In 2011,* 146 non-need-based awards were made. *Average percent of need met:* 59%. *Average financial aid package:* $7869. *Average need-based loan:* $4482. *Average need-based gift aid:* $7651. *Average non-need-based aid:* $63. *Financial aid deadline:* 4/30.

Applying *Options:* electronic application, deferred entrance. *Application fee:* $65. *Required:* high school transcript. *Application deadlines:* 2/1 (freshmen), 2/1 (transfers). *Notification:* continuous until 2/1 (freshmen), 4/1 (transfers).

Freshman Application Contact Alexis Chaconis, Director of Admissions, New York City College of Technology of the City University of New York, 300 Jay Street, Brooklyn, NY 11201-2983. *Phone:* 718-260-5500. *E-mail:* achaconis@citytech.cuny.edu. *Web site:* http://www.citytech.cuny.edu/.

New York College of Health Professions
Syosset, New York

Director of Admissions Ms. Mary Rodas, Associate Director of Admissions, New York College of Health Professions, 6801 Jericho Turnpike, Syosset, NY 11791-4413. *Toll-free phone:* 800-922-7337 Ext. 351. *E-mail:* rdodas@nycollege.edu. *Web site:* http://www.nycollege.edu/.

New York Institute of Technology
Old Westbury, New York

- **Independent** university, founded 1955
- **Suburban** 1050-acre campus with easy access to New York City
- **Endowment** $51.7 million
- **Coed** 4,977 undergraduate students, 83% full-time, 39% women, 61% men
- **Moderately difficult** entrance level, 69% of applicants were admitted

Undergraduates 4,111 full-time, 866 part-time. Students come from 38 states and territories; 82 other countries; 12% are from out of state; 9% Black or African American, non-Hispanic/Latino; 12% Hispanic/Latino; 14% Asian, non-Hispanic/Latino; 0.2% Native Hawaiian or other Pacific Islander, non-Hispanic/Latino; 0.5% American Indian or Alaska Native, non-Hispanic/Latino; 0.9% Two or more races, non-Hispanic/Latino; 26% Race/ethnicity unknown; 11% international; 9% transferred in; 14% live on campus. *Retention:* 71% of full-time freshmen returned.

Freshman *Admission:* 5,529 applied, 3,804 admitted, 860 enrolled. *Average high school GPA:* 3.43. *Test scores:* SAT critical reading scores over 500: 71%; SAT math scores over 500: 90%; ACT scores over 18: 98%; SAT critical reading scores over 600: 19%; SAT math scores over 600: 41%; ACT scores over 24: 60%; SAT critical reading scores over 700: 3%; SAT math scores over 700: 9%; ACT scores over 30: 16%.

Faculty *Total:* 1,260, 22% full-time. *Student/faculty ratio:* 11:1.

Academics *Calendar:* semesters. *Degrees:* certificates, associate, bachelor's, master's, doctoral, post-master's, and postbachelor's certificates. *Special study options:* academic remediation for entering students, accelerated degree program, adult/continuing education programs, advanced placement credit, cooperative education, distance learning, double majors, English as a second language, external degree program, honors programs, independent study, internships, off-campus study, part-time degree program, services for LD students, student-designed majors, study abroad, summer session for credit. *ROTC:* Army (b), Air Force (b). *Unusual degree programs:* 3-2 occupational therapy, physical therapy, communication arts, architectural technology/energy management, architectural technology/MBA, mechanical engineering/energy management.

Computers on Campus 1,386 computers/terminals are available on campus for general student use. Students can access the following: e-mail. Campuswide network is available. 100% of college-owned or -operated housing units are wired for high-speed Internet access. Wireless service is available via classrooms, computer centers, computer labs, libraries.

Student Life *Housing options:* coed. Campus housing is university owned and is provided by a third party. Freshman campus housing is guaranteed. *Activities and organizations:* drama/theater group, student-run newspaper, radio and television station, choral group, national fraternities, national sororities. *Campus security:* 24-hour emergency response devices and patrols, late-night transport/escort service, controlled dormitory access. *Student services:* health clinic, personal/psychological counseling, women's center.

Athletics Member NCAA. All Division II except baseball (Division I). *Intercollegiate sports:* baseball M(s), basketball M(s)/W(s), cross-country running M(s)/W(s), lacrosse M(s), soccer M(s)/W(s), softball W(s), tennis M(s)/W(s), volleyball W(s). *Intramural sports:* basketball M/W, soccer M/W, softball W, tennis M/W, volleyball W.

Standardized Tests *Required:* SAT or ACT (for admission).

Costs (2011–12) *Comprehensive fee:* $39,964 includes full-time tuition ($26,430), mandatory fees ($860), and room and board ($12,674). Full-time tuition and fees vary according to course load and program. Part-time tuition: $895 per credit hour. Part-time tuition and fees vary according to course load. *Required fees:* $375 per term part-time. *Room and board:* Room and board charges vary according to board plan, housing facility, and location. *Payment*

plan: installment. *Waivers:* senior citizens and employees or children of employees.

Financial Aid Of all full-time matriculated undergraduates who enrolled in 2011, 3,137 applied for aid, 2,932 were judged to have need. In 2011, 419 non-need-based awards were made. *Average financial aid package:* $21,387. *Average need-based loan:* $5456. *Average need-based gift aid:* $6219. *Average non-need-based aid:* $12,993.

Applying *Options:* electronic application, deferred entrance. *Application fee:* $50. *Required:* essay or personal statement, 2 letters of recommendation. *Required for some:* high school transcript, interview. *Application deadlines:* rolling (freshmen), rolling (transfers). *Notification:* continuous (freshmen), continuous (transfers).

Freshman Application Contact Ms. Doreen Meyer, Director of Financial Aid, New York Institute of Technology, PO Box 8000, Old Westbury, NY 11568. *Phone:* 516-686-1083. *Toll-free phone:* 800-345-NYIT. *Fax:* 516-686-7613. *E-mail:* admissions@nyit.edu. *Web site:* http://www.nyit.edu/.

New York School of Interior Design

New York, New York

- **Independent** comprehensive, founded 1916
- **Urban** 1-acre campus
- **Endowment** $3.1 million
- **Coed, primarily women** 558 undergraduate students, 30% full-time, 89% women, 11% men
- **Moderately difficult** entrance level, 32% of applicants were admitted

Undergraduates 166 full-time, 392 part-time. Students come from 24 states and territories; 28 other countries; 27% are from out of state; 3% Black or African American, non-Hispanic/Latino; 9% Hispanic/Latino; 10% Asian, non-Hispanic/Latino; 1% Two or more races, non-Hispanic/Latino; 22% Race/ethnicity unknown; 6% international; 11% transferred in; 5% live on campus. *Retention:* 93% of full-time freshmen returned.

Freshmen *Admission:* 188 applied, 60 admitted, 17 enrolled. *Average high school GPA:* 2.97. *Test scores:* SAT critical reading scores over 500: 31%; SAT math scores over 500: 23%; SAT writing scores over 500: 8%; SAT math scores over 600: 8%.

Faculty *Total:* 109, 7% full-time, 61% with terminal degrees. *Student/faculty ratio:* 7:1.

Academics *Calendar:* semesters. *Degrees:* certificates, associate, bachelor's, and master's. *Special study options:* adult/continuing education programs, advanced placement credit, English as a second language, external degree program, independent study, internships, part-time degree program, services for LD students, summer session for credit.

Computers on Campus 135 computers/terminals are available on campus for general student use. Students can access the following: free student e-mail accounts, online (class) grades, online (class) registration, online (class) schedules. Campuswide network is available. Wireless service is available via classrooms, libraries.

Student Life *Housing options:* coed. Campus housing is leased by the school and is provided by a third party. *Activities and organizations:* American Society of Interior Designers, Contract Club, Student Council. *Campus security:* security during school hours.

Standardized Tests *Required for some:* SAT or ACT (for admission).

Costs (2012–13) *Tuition:* $27,324 full-time, $828 per credit part-time. Full-time tuition and fees vary according to course load. Part-time tuition and fees vary according to course load. *Required fees:* $570 full-time, $570 per term part-time. *Room only:* $14,400. *Payment plan:* installment. *Waivers:* employees or children of employees.

Financial Aid Of all full-time matriculated undergraduates who enrolled in 2011, 99 applied for aid, 95 were judged to have need, 1 had their need fully met. 25 Federal Work-Study jobs (averaging $1770). In 2011, 4 non-need-based awards were made. *Average percent of need met:* 29%. *Average financial aid package:* $10,186. *Average need-based loan:* $3854. *Average need-based gift aid:* $7768. *Average non-need-based aid:* $9500. *Average indebtedness upon graduation:* $15,458.

Applying *Options:* electronic application, deferred entrance. *Application fee:* $55. *Required:* essay or personal statement, high school transcript, minimum 2.8 GPA, 2 letters of recommendation, portfolio. *Application deadlines:* 2/1 (freshmen), 2/1 (transfers). *Notification:* 4/1 (freshmen), 4/1 (transfers).

Freshman Application Contact Audrey Zahor, Admissions Associate, New York School of Interior Design, 170 East 70th Street, New York, NY 10021-5110. *Phone:* 212-472-1500 Ext. 204. *Toll-free phone:* 800-336-9743 Ext. 204. *Fax:* 212-472-1867. *E-mail:* admissions@nysid.edu. *Web site:* http://www.nysid.edu/.

See page 1478 for the College Close-Up.

New York University

New York, New York

- **Independent** university, founded 1831
- **Urban** campus
- **Endowment** $2.7 billion
- **Coed** 22,280 undergraduate students, 94% full-time, 60% women, 40% men
- **Most difficult** entrance level, 33% of applicants were admitted

Undergraduates 21,025 full-time, 1,255 part-time. Students come from 52 states and territories; 94 other countries; 65% are from out of state; 4% Black or African American, non-Hispanic/Latino; 9% Hispanic/Latino; 19% Asian, non-Hispanic/Latino; 0.1% Native Hawaiian or other Pacific Islander, non-Hispanic/Latino; 0.4% American Indian or Alaska Native, non-Hispanic/Latino; 2% Two or more races, non-Hispanic/Latino; 14% Race/ethnicity unknown; 10% international; 4% transferred in; 47% live on campus. *Retention:* 92% of full-time freshmen returned.

Freshmen *Admission:* 41,243 applied, 13,487 admitted, 4,870 enrolled. *Average high school GPA:* 3.6. *Test scores:* SAT critical reading scores over 500: 99%; SAT math scores over 500: 99%; SAT writing scores over 500: 99%; ACT scores over 18: 100%; SAT critical reading scores over 600: 87%; SAT math scores over 600: 86%; SAT writing scores over 600: 89%; ACT scores over 24: 99%; SAT critical reading scores over 700: 34%; SAT math scores over 700: 42%; SAT writing scores over 700: 42%; ACT scores over 30: 57%.

Faculty *Total:* 6,120, 40% full-time, 72% with terminal degrees. *Student/faculty ratio:* 11:1.

Academics *Calendar:* semesters. *Degrees:* certificates, associate, bachelor's, master's, doctoral, post-master's, postbachelor's, and first professional certificates. *Special study options:* accelerated degree program, adult/continuing education programs, advanced placement credit, double majors, honors programs, independent study, internships, off-campus study, part-time degree program, services for LD students, student-designed majors, study abroad, summer session for credit. *ROTC:* Army (c), Air Force (c). *Unusual degree programs:* 3-2 engineering with NYU-Polytechnic.

Computers on Campus 4,500 computers/terminals are available on campus for general student use. Students can access the following: computer help desk, free student e-mail accounts, online (class) grades, online (class) registration, online (class) schedules. Campuswide network is available. 100% of college-owned or -operated housing units are wired for high-speed Internet access. Wireless service is available via classrooms, computer labs, learning centers, libraries, student centers.

Student Life *Housing options:* coed, disabled students. Campus housing is university owned and leased by the school. Freshman campus housing is guaranteed. *Activities and organizations:* drama/theater group, student-run newspaper, radio and television station, choral group, Inter-Varsity Christian Fellowship, Asian Cultural Union, Hillel, Latinos Unidos Con Honor y Amistad (LUCHA), South Asian Student Association (SHRUTI), national fraternities, national sororities. *Campus security:* 24-hour emergency response devices and patrols, student patrols, late-night transport/escort service, controlled dormitory access, 24-hour security in residence halls. *Student services:* health clinic, personal/psychological counseling, women's center.

Athletics Member NCAA. All Division III. *Intercollegiate sports:* baseball M(c), basketball M/W, cheerleading M/W, crew M(c)/W(c), cross-country running M/W, equestrian sports M(c)/W(c), fencing M/W, golf M/W, ice hockey M(c), lacrosse M(c)/W(c), soccer M/W, softball W(c), swimming and diving M/W, tennis M/W, track and field M/W, ultimate Frisbee M(c)/W(c), volleyball M/W, wrestling M. *Intramural sports:* badminton M(c)/W(c), basketball M/W, bowling M/W, ice hockey M(c), lacrosse M(c)/W(c), racquetball M/W, soccer M/W, softball M(c)/W(c), squash M/W, table tennis M(c)/W(c), tennis M/W, volleyball M/W, water polo M/W(c).

Standardized Tests *Required:* SAT or ACT (for admission), Three SAT subject tests or three Advanced Placement Exam scores. These scores must be submitted in the form of: one in literature or the humanities; one in math or science; and one test of the student's choice in any subject (for admission). *Recommended:* SAT and SAT Subject Tests or ACT (for admission).

Costs (2011–12) *Comprehensive fee:* $56,788 includes full-time tuition ($39,344), mandatory fees ($2262), and room and board ($15,182). Full-time tuition and fees vary according to course load and program. Part-time tuition: $1220 per credit. Part-time tuition and fees vary according to program. *Required fees:* $61 per credit part-time, $418 per credit part-time. *Room and board:* Room and board charges vary according to board plan and housing facility. *Payment plans:* tuition prepayment, installment, deferred payment. *Waivers:* employees or children of employees.

Financial Aid Of all full-time undergraduates who enrolled in 2010, 12,585 applied for aid, 11,255 were judged to have need, 655 had their need fully met. 8,505 Federal Work-Study jobs (averaging $3382). In 2010, 1234 non-need-based awards were made. *Average percent of need met:* 59%. *Average financial aid package:* $25,165. *Average need-based loan:* $5113.

Average need-based gift aid: $18,703. *Average non-need-based aid:* $7253. *Average indebtedness upon graduation:* $36,351. *Financial aid deadline:* 2/15.

Applying *Options:* electronic application, early decision, deferred entrance. *Application fee:* $70. *Required:* essay or personal statement, high school transcript, 1 letter of recommendation. *Required for some:* An audition or a portfolio is required for some specific programs. *Application deadlines:* 1/1 (freshmen), 1/1 (out-of-state freshmen), 4/1 (transfers). *Early decision deadline:* 11/1 (for plan 1), 1/1 (for plan 2). *Notification:* 4/1 (freshmen), 4/1 (out-of-state freshmen), 12/15 (early decision plan 1), 3/15 (early decision plan 2). **Freshman Application Contact** Kristy Materasso, Undergraduate Admissions Processing Center, New York University, 665 Broadway, 11th Floor, New York, NY 10011. *Phone:* 212-998-4500. *Fax:* 212-995-4902. *E-mail:* admissions@nyu.edu. *Web site:* http://www.nyu.edu/.

Niagara University

Niagara Falls, New York

- **Independent** comprehensive, founded 1856, affiliated with Roman Catholic Church
- **Suburban** 160-acre campus with easy access to Buffalo, Toronto
- **Endowment** $77.5 million
- **Coed** 3,303 undergraduate students, 88% full-time, 62% women, 38% men
- **Moderately difficult** entrance level, 76% of applicants were admitted

Undergraduates 2,894 full-time, 409 part-time. Students come from 31 states and territories; 12 other countries; 8% are from out of state; 4% Black or African American, non-Hispanic/Latino; 3% Hispanic/Latino; 1% Asian, non-Hispanic/Latino; 0.1% Native Hawaiian or other Pacific Islander, non-Hispanic/Latino; 0.6% American Indian or Alaska Native, non-Hispanic/Latino; 0.3% Two or more races, non-Hispanic/Latino; 5% Race/ethnicity unknown; 18% international; 6% transferred in; 51% live on campus. *Retention:* 81% of full-time freshmen returned.

Freshmen *Admission:* 3,241 applied, 2,456 admitted, 631 enrolled. *Average high school GPA:* 3.3. *Test scores:* SAT critical reading scores over 500: 50%; SAT math scores over 500: 59%; ACT scores over 18: 90%; SAT critical reading scores over 600: 9%; SAT math scores over 600: 16%; ACT scores over 24: 39%; SAT critical reading scores over 700: 1%; SAT math scores over 700: 1%; ACT scores over 30: 4%.

Faculty *Total:* 350, 46% full-time, 43% with terminal degrees. *Student/faculty ratio:* 12:1.

Academics *Calendar:* semesters. *Degrees:* associate, bachelor's, master's, doctoral, post-master's, postbachelor's, and first professional certificates. *Special study options:* academic remediation for entering students, accelerated degree program, advanced placement credit, cooperative education, double majors, English as a second language, freshman honors college, honors programs, internships, off-campus study, part-time degree program, services for LD students, study abroad, summer session for credit. *ROTC:* Army (b).

Computers on Campus 175 computers/terminals are available on campus for general student use. Students can access the following: campus intranet, computer help desk, free student e-mail accounts, online (class) grades, online (class) registration, online (class) schedules. Campuswide network is available. 100% of college-owned or -operated housing units are wired for high-speed Internet access. Wireless service is available via classrooms, computer centers, computer labs, libraries, student centers.

Student Life *Housing:* on-campus residence required through sophomore year. *Options:* coed, women-only. Campus housing is university owned. Freshman campus housing is guaranteed. *Activities and organizations:* drama/theater group, student-run newspaper, radio station, choral group, Niagara University Community Action Program, student government, Programming Board, national fraternities. *Campus security:* 24-hour emergency response devices and patrols, late-night transport/escort service, controlled dormitory access, 24-hour escort service. *Student services:* health clinic, personal/psychological counseling.

Athletics Member NCAA. All Division I. *Intercollegiate sports:* baseball M(s), basketball M(s)/W(s), cross-country running M(s)/W(s), golf M(s)/W(s), ice hockey M(s)/W(s), lacrosse M/W(s), soccer M(s)/W(s), softball W(s), swimming and diving M(s)/W(s), tennis M(s)/W(s), volleyball W(s). *Intramural sports:* basketball M/W, ice hockey M/W, lacrosse M/W, racquetball M/W, rugby M(c)/W(c), skiing (downhill) M(c)/W(c), soccer M/W, softball M/W, volleyball M/W, water polo M/W.

Standardized Tests *Required:* SAT or ACT (for admission).

Costs (2011–12) *Comprehensive fee:* $37,400 includes full-time tuition ($25,300), mandatory fees ($1100), and room and board ($11,000). Part-time tuition: $845 per credit hour. *Payment plans:* installment, deferred payment. *Waivers:* senior citizens and employees or children of employees.

Financial Aid Of all full-time matriculated undergraduates who enrolled in 2011, 2,263 applied for aid, 2,084 were judged to have need, 1,135 had their

need fully met. 389 Federal Work-Study jobs (averaging $2863). 34 state and other part-time jobs (averaging $5460). In 2011, 472 non-need-based awards were made. *Average percent of need met:* 82%. *Average financial aid package:* $21,170. *Average need-based loan:* $4683. *Average need-based gift aid:* $16,996. *Average non-need-based aid:* $10,900. *Average indebtedness upon graduation:* $26,406.

Applying *Options:* electronic application, early admission, deferred entrance. *Application fee:* $30. *Required:* high school transcript. *Recommended:* minimum 3.0 GPA, 3 letters of recommendation, interview. *Application deadlines:* 8/1 (freshmen), 8/15 (transfers).

Freshman Application Contact Ms. Christine M. McDermott, Associate Director of Admissions, Niagara University, Niagara University, NY 14109. *Phone:* 716-286-8700 Ext. 8715. *Toll-free phone:* 800-462-2111. *Fax:* 716-286-8733. *E-mail:* admissions@niagara.edu. *Web site:* http://www.niagara.edu/.

See page 1480 for the College Close-Up.

Nyack College
Nyack, New York

- **Independent** comprehensive, founded 1882, affiliated with The Christian and Missionary Alliance
- **Suburban** 125-acre campus with easy access to New York City
- **Coed** 2,040 undergraduate students, 86% full-time, 60% women, 40% men
- 96% of applicants were admitted

Undergraduates 1,754 full-time, 286 part-time. Students come from 36 states and territories; 48 other countries; 31% are from out of state; 34% Black or African American, non-Hispanic/Latino; 26% Hispanic/Latino; 9% Asian, non-Hispanic/Latino; 0.3% Native Hawaiian or other Pacific Islander, non-Hispanic/Latino; 0.1% American Indian or Alaska Native, non-Hispanic/Latino; 3% Two or more races, non-Hispanic/Latino; 0.6% Race/ethnicity unknown; 4% international; 13% transferred in; 70% live on campus. *Retention:* 66% of full-time freshmen returned.

Freshmen *Admission:* 691 applied, 666 admitted, 303 enrolled. *Average high school GPA:* 2.76. *Test scores:* SAT critical reading scores over 500: 29%; SAT math scores over 500: 30%; ACT scores over 18: 75%; SAT critical reading scores over 600: 6%; SAT math scores over 600: 6%; ACT scores over 24: 17%; SAT critical reading scores over 700: 1%; ACT scores over 30: 4%.

Faculty *Total:* 305, 36% full-time, 37% with terminal degrees. *Student/faculty ratio:* 14:1.

Academics *Calendar:* semesters. *Degrees:* associate, bachelor's, master's, and doctoral. *Special study options:* academic remediation for entering students, accelerated degree program, adult/continuing education programs, advanced placement credit, distance learning, double majors, English as a second language, honors programs, independent study, internships, off-campus study, part-time degree program, services for LD students, study abroad, summer session for credit. *Unusual degree programs:* 3-2 education (BS./MS childhood special education).

Computers on Campus 130 computers/terminals are available on campus for general student use. Students can access the following: campus intranet, computer help desk, free student e-mail accounts, online (class) grades, online (class) registration, online (class) schedules. Campuswide network is available. 98% of college-owned or -operated housing units are wired for high-speed Internet access. Wireless service is available via entire campus.

Student Life *Housing:* on-campus residence required through sophomore year. *Options:* men-only, women-only, disabled students. Campus housing is university owned. Freshman campus housing is guaranteed. *Activities and organizations:* drama/theater group, student-run newspaper, radio station, choral group. *Campus security:* 24-hour emergency response devices and patrols, late-night transport/escort service. *Student services:* health clinic, personal/psychological counseling.

Athletics Member NCAA, NCCAA. All NCAA Division II. *Intercollegiate sports:* baseball M(s), basketball M(s)/W(s), cheerleading M(s)/W(s), cross-country running M(s)/W(s), golf M(s), soccer M(s)/W(s), softball W(s), volleyball W(s).

Standardized Tests *Required for some:* SAT or ACT (for admission).

Costs (2012–13) *One-time required fee:* $100. *Comprehensive fee:* $30,900 includes full-time tuition ($22,250), mandatory fees ($250), and room and board ($8400). Part-time tuition: $927 per credit hour. *Required fees:* $75 per term part-time. *Room and board:* Room and board charges vary according to board plan and housing facility. *Payment plan:* installment. *Waivers:* employees or children of employees.

Financial Aid Of all full-time matriculated undergraduates who enrolled in 2010, 1,413 applied for aid, 1,347 were judged to have need, 109 had their need fully met. 202 Federal Work-Study jobs (averaging $1069). 56 state and other part-time jobs (averaging $1559). In 2010, 183 non-need-based awards were made. *Average percent of need met:* 63%. *Average financial aid pack-*

age: $18,009. *Average need-based loan:* $4564. *Average need-based gift aid:* $12,526. *Average non-need-based aid:* $7161. *Average indebtedness upon graduation:* $35,725.

Applying *Options:* electronic application, deferred entrance. *Application fee:* $25. *Required:* essay or personal statement, high school transcript, minimum 2.0 GPA, 1 letter of recommendation, Signed statement of faith and community life form. *Required for some:* interview. *Application deadlines:* rolling (freshmen), rolling (out-of-state freshmen), rolling (transfers). *Notification:* continuous (freshmen), continuous (out-of-state freshmen), continuous (transfers).

Freshman Application Contact Dinesh Mahtani, Director of Admissions, Nyack College, 1 South Boulevard, Nyack, NY 10960-3698. *Phone:* 845-675-4401. *Toll-free phone:* 800-33-NYACK. *Fax:* 845-358-3047. *E-mail:* admissions@nyack.edu. *Web site:* http://www.nyack.edu/.

Ohr Hameir Theological Seminary
Cortlandt Manor, New York

Director of Admissions Director of Admissions, Ohr Hameir Theological Seminary, 141 Furnace Woods Road, Cortlandt Manor, NY 10567. *Phone:* 914-736-1500.

Ohr Somayach/Joseph Tanenbaum Educational Center
Monsey, New York

- **Independent Jewish** comprehensive, founded 1979
- **Small-town** 7-acre campus with easy access to New York City
- **Men only** 65 undergraduate students, 100% full-time
- **Moderately difficult** entrance level, 65% of applicants were admitted

Undergraduates 65 full-time. Students come from 10 states and territories; 6 other countries; 39% are from out of state; 6% transferred in.
Freshmen *Admission:* 100 applied, 65 admitted, 15 enrolled.
Faculty *Total:* 16, 50% full-time.
Academics *Calendar:* semesters. *Degree:* bachelor's and doctoral. *Special study options:* academic remediation for entering students, adult/continuing education programs, honors programs, internships, part-time degree program, services for LD students, summer session for credit.

Student Life *Housing:* on-campus residence required through senior year. *Options:* men-only. Campus housing is university owned. *Campus security:* 24-hour emergency response devices and patrols, controlled dormitory access. *Student services:* personal/psychological counseling.
Applying *Options:* early admission. *Required:* interview. *Required for some:* essay or personal statement. *Recommended:* high school transcript. *Application deadlines:* rolling (freshmen), rolling (transfers).
Freshman Application Contact Ohr Somayach/Joseph Tanenbaum Educational Center, PO Box 334, 244 Route 306, Monsey, NY 10952-0334. *Phone:* 845-425-1370 Ext. 22. *Web site:* http://ohr.edu/.

Pace University
New York, New York

- **Independent** university, founded 1906
- **Urban** campus with easy access to New York City
- **Endowment** $126.5 million
- **Coed** 8,025 undergraduate students, 86% full-time, 59% women, 41% men
- **Moderately difficult** entrance level, 84% of applicants were admitted

Undergraduates 6,870 full-time, 1,155 part-time. Students come from 54 states and territories; 100 other countries; 34% are from out of state; 11% Black or African American, non-Hispanic/Latino; 15% Hispanic/Latino; 10% Asian, non-Hispanic/Latino; 0.2% Native Hawaiian or other Pacific Islander, non-Hispanic/Latino; 0.4% American Indian or Alaska Native, non-Hispanic/Latino; 3% Two or more races, non-Hispanic/Latino; 9% Race/ethnicity unknown; 7% international; 6% transferred in; 43% live on campus. *Retention:* 79% of full-time freshmen returned.
Freshmen *Admission:* 11,778 applied, 9,918 admitted, 1,594 enrolled. *Average high school GPA:* 3.2. *Test scores:* SAT critical reading scores over 500: 75%; SAT math scores over 500: 79%; ACT scores over 18: 99%; SAT critical reading scores over 600: 23%; SAT math scores over 600: 28%; ACT scores over 24: 55%; SAT critical reading scores over 700: 2%; SAT math scores over 700: 3%; ACT scores over 30: 2%.
Faculty *Total:* 1,279, 35% full-time, 46% with terminal degrees. *Student/faculty ratio:* 14:1.
Academics *Calendar:* semesters. *Degrees:* certificates, associate, bachelor's, master's, doctoral, post-master's, postbachelor's, and first professional certificates. *Special study options:* academic remediation for entering students, accelerated degree program, adult/continuing education programs, advanced

placement credit, cooperative education, distance learning, double majors, English as a second language, freshman honors college, honors programs, independent study, internships, part-time degree program, study abroad, summer session for credit. *ROTC:* Army (c), Air Force (c). *Unusual degree programs:* 3-2 engineering with Manhattan College, Rensselaer Polytechnic Institute; occupational therapy with Columbia University College of Physicians and Surgeons, physical therapy with New York Medical College, podiatry with the New York College of Podiatric Medicine.

Computers on Campus 268 computers/terminals are available on campus for general student use. Students can access the following: computer help desk, free student e-mail accounts, online (class) registration, online (class) schedules. Campuswide network is available. 100% of college-owned or -operated housing units are wired for high-speed Internet access. Wireless service is available via classrooms, computer centers, computer labs, libraries, student centers.

Student Life *Housing options:* coed. Campus housing is university owned and leased by the school. *Activities and organizations:* drama/theater group, student-run newspaper, radio and television station, choral group, Black Student Union, Beta Alpha Psi, OLAS (Organization of Latin American Students), Pace Board, Lubin Business Association, national fraternities, national sororities. *Campus security:* 24-hour emergency response devices and patrols, late-night transport/escort service, controlled dormitory access. *Student services:* health clinic, personal/psychological counseling.

Athletics Member NCAA. All Division II. *Intercollegiate sports:* baseball M(s), basketball M(s)/W(s), cheerleading W, cross-country running M(s)/W(s), equestrian sports W, football M, golf M(s), lacrosse M(s), soccer W(s), softball W(s), swimming and diving M/W, tennis M(s)/W(s), track and field M(s)/W(s), volleyball W(s). *Intramural sports:* badminton M/W, soccer M/W, softball M/W, volleyball M/W.

Standardized Tests *Required:* SAT or ACT (for admission).

Costs (2011–12) *Comprehensive fee:* $47,142 includes full-time tuition ($33,962), mandatory fees ($1070), and room and board ($12,110). Part-time tuition: $974 per credit. Part-time tuition and fees vary according to course load. *Room and board:* Room and board charges vary according to board plan, housing facility, and location. *Payment plan:* installment. *Waivers:* senior citizens and employees or children of employees.

Financial Aid Of all full-time matriculated undergraduates who enrolled in 2011, 5,630 applied for aid, 5,281 were judged to have need, 475 had their need fully met. 1,075 Federal Work-Study jobs (averaging $3614). In 2011, 1243 non-need-based awards were made. *Average percent of need met:* 71%. *Average financial aid package:* $27,632. *Average need-based loan:* $4586. *Average need-based gift aid:* $23,043. *Average non-need-based aid:* $12,269. *Average indebtedness upon graduation:* $36,666.

Applying *Options:* electronic application, early action, deferred entrance. *Application fee:* $50. *Required:* essay or personal statement, high school transcript, 2 letters of recommendation. *Recommended:* minimum 3.0 GPA, interview. *Application deadlines:* 2/15 (freshmen), rolling (transfers), 11/30 (early action). *Notification:* continuous (freshmen), continuous (transfers), 1/1 (early action).

Freshman Application Contact Ms. Donna J. Grand Pre, Dean of Admissions, Pace University, One Pace Plaza, 163 William Street, New York, NY 10038. *Phone:* 212-346-1794. *Toll-free phone:* 800-874-7223. *Fax:* 212-346-1821. *E-mail:* dgrandpre@pace.edu. *Web site:* http://www.pace.edu/.

See page 609 for display ad and page 1498 for the College Close-Up.

Parsons The New School for Design
New York, New York

- **Independent** comprehensive, founded 1896, part of The New School
- **Urban** 2-acre campus with easy access to Manhattan
- **Coed**
- **Very difficult** entrance level

Faculty *Student/faculty ratio:* 9:1.

Academics *Calendar:* semesters. *Degrees:* certificates, associate, bachelor's, and master's.

Student Life *Campus security:* 24-hour emergency response devices, controlled dormitory access.

Standardized Tests *Required:* SAT or ACT (for admission).

Costs (2011–12) *Comprehensive fee:* $52,340 includes full-time tuition ($36,970), mandatory fees ($460), and room and board ($14,910). Part-time tuition: $1255 per credit. Part-time tuition and fees vary according to course load. *College room only:* $14,360. Room and board charges vary according to board plan and housing facility.

Financial Aid *Of all full-time matriculated undergraduates who enrolled in 2010,* 2,078 applied for aid, 1,940 were judged to have need, 193 had their need fully met. *In 2010,* 96 non-need-based awards were made. *Average percent of need met:* 63. *Average financial aid package:* $27,120. *Average need-based loan:* $10,395. *Average need-based gift aid:* $17,805. *Average non-need-based aid:* $4150. *Average indebtedness upon graduation:* $38,290.

Applying *Options:* electronic application, early action, deferred entrance. *Application fee:* $50. *Required:* high school transcript, portfolio, home examination. *Required for some:* essay or personal statement, interview. *Recommended:* minimum 3.0 GPA.

Freshman Application Contact Director of Admissions, Parsons The New School for Design, 65 Fifth Avenue, New York, NY 10011-8878. *Phone:* 212-229-8989. *Toll-free phone:* 800-292-3040. *Fax:* 212-229-8975. *E-mail:* thinkparsons@newschool.edu. *Web site:* http://www.parsons.edu/.

See page 581 for display ad and page 1476 for the College Close-Up.

Paul Smith's College
Paul Smiths, New York

Freshman Application Contact Admissions Office, Paul Smith's College, Routes 86 and 30, PO Box 265, Paul Smiths, NY 12970. *Phone:* 518-327-6227. *Toll-free phone:* 800-421-2605. *Fax:* 518-327-6016. *E-mail:* admissions@paulsmiths.edu. *Web site:* http://www.paulsmiths.edu/.

Plaza College
Jackson Heights, New York

Freshman Application Contact Dean Rose Ann Black, Dean of Administration, Plaza College, 74-09 37th Avenue, Jackson Heights, NY 11372. *Phone:* 718-779-1430. *E-mail:* info@plazacollege.edu. *Web site:* http://www.plazacollege.edu/.

Polytechnic Institute of NYU
Brooklyn, New York

- **Independent** university, founded 1854
- **Urban** 3-acre campus
- **Endowment** $112.8 million
- **Coed** 1,939 undergraduate students, 94% full-time, 22% women, 78% men
- **Very difficult** entrance level, 68% of applicants were admitted

Undergraduates 1,832 full-time, 107 part-time. Students come from 34 states and territories; 25 other countries; 15% are from out of state; 8% Black or African American, non-Hispanic/Latino; 11% Hispanic/Latino; 34% Asian, non-Hispanic/Latino; 0.2% American Indian or Alaska Native, non-Hispanic/Latino; 8% Race/ethnicity unknown; 11% international; 3% transferred in; 24% live on campus. *Retention:* 84% of full-time freshmen returned.

Freshmen *Admission:* 3,116 applied, 2,124 admitted, 416 enrolled. *Average high school GPA:* 3.5. *Test scores:* SAT critical reading scores over 500: 100%; SAT math scores over 500: 100%; SAT writing scores over 500: 96%; ACT scores over 18: 100%; SAT critical reading scores over 600: 57%; SAT math scores over 600: 96%; SAT writing scores over 600: 53%; ACT scores over 24: 96%; SAT critical reading scores over 700: 9%; SAT math scores over 700: 46%; SAT writing scores over 700: 9%; ACT scores over 30: 46%.

Faculty *Total:* 369, 42% full-time, 68% with terminal degrees. *Student/faculty ratio:* 13:1.

Academics *Calendar:* semesters. *Degrees:* bachelor's, master's, doctoral, postbachelor's, and first professional certificates. *Special study options:* academic remediation for entering students, accelerated degree program, advanced placement credit, cooperative education, distance learning, double majors, honors programs, internships, part-time degree program, study abroad, summer session for credit. *ROTC:* Army (c), Air Force (c).

Computers on Campus 1,334 computers/terminals are available on campus for general student use. Students can access the following: campus intranet, computer help desk, free student e-mail accounts, online (class) grades, online (class) registration, online (class) schedules. Campuswide network is available. 100% of college-owned or -operated housing units are wired for high-speed Internet access. Wireless service is available via entire campus.

Student Life *Housing options:* coed. Campus housing is university owned. Freshman applicants given priority for college housing. *Activities and organizations:* student-run newspaper, National Society of Black Engineers, Society of Hispanic Professional Engineers, Association for Computing Machinery, Alpha Phi Omega, Chinese Student Society, national fraternities, national sororities. *Campus security:* 24-hour patrols, controlled dormitory access. *Student services:* health clinic, personal/psychological counseling, women's center.

Athletics Member NCAA. All Division III. *Intercollegiate sports:* baseball M, basketball M/W, cross-country running M/W, soccer M/W, softball W, tennis M/W, volleyball M/W. *Intramural sports:* badminton M/W, basketball M/W, bowling M/W, football M/W, golf M(c)/W(c), soccer M/W, table tennis M(c)/W(c), volleyball M/W, weight lifting M(c)/W(c).

Standardized Tests *Required:* SAT or ACT (for admission). *Recommended:* SAT Subject Tests (for admission).

Costs (2011–12) *Comprehensive fee:* $47,962 includes full-time tuition ($36,684), mandatory fees ($1198), and room and board ($10,080). Full-time tuition and fees vary according to course load. Part-time tuition: $1166 per credit. Part-time tuition and fees vary according to course load. *Required fees:* $374 per term part-time. *College room only:* $7950. Room and board charges vary according to housing facility. *Payment plans:* installment, deferred payment. *Waivers:* employees or children of employees.

Financial Aid Of all full-time matriculated undergraduates who enrolled in 2010, 1,607 applied for aid, 1,297 were judged to have need, 550 had their need fully met. In 2010, 299 non-need-based awards were made. *Average percent of need met:* 88%. *Average financial aid package:* $26,575. *Average need-based loan:* $4518. *Average need-based gift aid:* $15,151. *Average non-need-based aid:* $17,228. *Average indebtedness upon graduation:* $24,862.

Applying *Options:* electronic application, early admission, deferred entrance. *Application fee:* $65. *Required:* essay or personal statement, high school transcript, 2 letters of recommendation. *Recommended:* interview. *Application deadlines:* 2/1 (freshmen), rolling (transfers).

Freshman Application Contact Joy Colelli, Dean of Admissions and New Students, Polytechnic Institute of NYU, Six Metrotech Center, Brooklyn, NY 11201-2990. *Phone:* 718-260-5917. *Toll-free phone:* 800-POLYTECH. *Fax:* 718-260-3446. *E-mail:* uadmit@poly.edu. *Web site:* http://www.poly.edu/.

Pratt Institute
Brooklyn, New York

- **Independent** comprehensive, founded 1887
- **Urban** 25-acre campus
- **Coed** 3,021 undergraduate students, 95% full-time, 63% women, 37% men
- **Very difficult** entrance level, 60% of applicants were admitted

Undergraduates 2,873 full-time, 148 part-time. 69% are from out of state; 4% Black or African American, non-Hispanic/Latino; 9% Hispanic/Latino; 18% Asian, non-Hispanic/Latino; 0.1% Native Hawaiian or other Pacific Islander, non-Hispanic/Latino; 0.1% American Indian or Alaska Native, non-Hispanic/Latino; 3% Two or more races, non-Hispanic/Latino; 1% Race/ethnicity unknown; 17% international; 5% transferred in; 53% live on campus. *Retention:* 83% of full-time freshmen returned.

Freshmen *Admission:* 4,247 applied, 2,541 admitted, 608 enrolled. *Average high school GPA:* 3.58. *Test scores:* SAT critical reading scores over 500: 86%; SAT math scores over 500: 90%; SAT writing scores over 500: 93%; ACT scores over 18: 100%; SAT critical reading scores over 600: 48%; SAT math scores over 600: 59%; SAT writing scores over 600: 52%; ACT scores over 24: 88%; SAT critical reading scores over 700: 9%; SAT math scores over 700: 12%; SAT writing scores over 700: 8%; ACT scores over 30: 16%.

Faculty *Total:* 1,005, 13% full-time. *Student/faculty ratio:* 11:1.

Academics *Calendar:* semesters plus optional May term and summer session. *Degrees:* associate, bachelor's, master's, and post-master's certificates. *Special study options:* part-time degree program.

Computers on Campus Students can access the following: online (class) registration. Campuswide network is available.

Student Life *Housing options:* coed, disabled students. Campus housing is university owned. Freshman campus housing is guaranteed. *Campus security:* 24-hour emergency response devices and patrols, late-night transport/escort service.

Athletics Member NCAA. All Division III. *Intercollegiate sports:* basketball M, cross-country running M/W, soccer M/W, tennis M/W, track and field M/W, volleyball W. *Intramural sports:* badminton M/W, basketball M, field hockey M, football M, golf M, lacrosse M/W, volleyball M, weight lifting M/W.

Standardized Tests *Required:* SAT or ACT (for admission). *Required for some:* SAT Subject Tests (for admission).

Costs (2012–13) *Comprehensive fee:* $51,598 includes full-time tuition ($39,282), mandatory fees ($1810), and room and board ($10,506). Part-time tuition: $1267 per credit. *College room only:* $6726. Room and board charges vary according to board plan and housing facility.

Financial Aid Of all full-time matriculated undergraduates who enrolled in 2010, 1,827 applied for aid, 1,674 were judged to have need. In 2010, 469 non-need-based awards were made. *Average financial aid package:* $18,914. *Average need-based loan:* $7891. *Average need-based gift aid:* $11,148. *Average non-need-based aid:* $10,527. *Financial aid deadline:* 2/1.

Applying *Options:* electronic application, early action, deferred entrance. *Application fee:* $50. *Required:* essay or personal statement, high school transcript, 1 letter of recommendation. *Required for some:* portfolio. *Recommended:* minimum 3.0 GPA. *Application deadlines:* 1/5 (freshmen), 2/1 (transfers), 11/1 (early action). *Notification:* 4/1 (freshmen), 4/1 (transfers), 12/22 (early action).

Freshman Application Contact Ms. Olga Burger, Visit Coordinator, Pratt Institute, 200 Willoughby Avenue, DeKalb Hall, Brooklyn, NY 11205. *Phone:* 718-636-3779. *Toll-free phone:* 800-331-0834. *Fax:* 718-636-3670. *E-mail:* visit@pratt.edu. *Web site:* http://www.pratt.edu/.

See page 1506 for the College Close-Up.

Purchase College, State University of New York

Purchase, New York

- **State-supported** comprehensive, founded 1967, part of State University of New York System
- **Small-town** 500-acre campus with easy access to New York City
- **Coed** 4,148 undergraduate students, 90% full-time, 56% women, 44% men
- **Moderately difficult** entrance level, 34% of applicants were admitted

Undergraduates 3,740 full-time, 408 part-time. Students come from 42 states and territories; 24 other countries; 18% are from out of state; 6% Black or African American, non-Hispanic/Latino; 14% Hispanic/Latino; 2% Asian, non-Hispanic/Latino; 0.1% American Indian or Alaska Native, non-Hispanic/Latino; 7% Two or more races, non-Hispanic/Latino; 18% Race/ethnicity unknown; 2% international; 9% transferred in; 67% live on campus. *Retention:* 81% of full-time freshmen returned.

Freshmen *Admission:* 8,949 applied, 3,011 admitted, 797 enrolled. *Average high school GPA:* 3.16. *Test scores:* SAT critical reading scores over 500: 79%; SAT math scores over 500: 68%; SAT writing scores over 500: 75%; ACT scores over 18: 96%; SAT critical reading scores over 600: 33%; SAT math scores over 600: 18%; SAT writing scores over 600: 25%; ACT scores over 24: 51%; SAT critical reading scores over 700: 5%; SAT math scores over 700: 2%; SAT writing scores over 700: 3%; ACT scores over 30: 8%.

Faculty *Total:* 388, 43% full-time, 52% with terminal degrees. *Student/faculty ratio:* 16:1.

Academics *Calendar:* semesters. *Degrees:* certificates, bachelor's, master's, and post-master's certificates. *Special study options:* academic remediation for entering students, adult/continuing education programs, advanced placement credit, double majors, English as a second language, independent study, internships, off-campus study, part-time degree program, services for LD students, student-designed majors, study abroad, summer session for credit.

Computers on Campus 600 computers/terminals and 3,500 ports are available on campus for general student use. Students can access the following: campus intranet, computer help desk, free student e-mail accounts, online (class) grades, online (class) registration, online (class) schedules. Campuswide network is available. 100% of college-owned or -operated housing units are wired for high-speed Internet access. Wireless service is available via classrooms, computer centers, computer labs, learning centers, libraries, student centers.

Student Life *Housing options:* coed. Campus housing is university owned. Freshman applicants given priority for college housing. *Activities and organizations:* drama/theater group, student-run newspaper, radio and television station, choral group, Student Union, WPUR radio station, Latinos Unidos, Gay/Lesbian/Bisexual/Transgender Union, Organization of African People in America. *Campus security:* 24-hour emergency response devices and patrols, late-night transport/escort service, controlled dormitory access, 24-hour patrols by police officers. *Student services:* health clinic, personal/psychological counseling, women's center, legal services.

Athletics Member NCAA. All Division III except golf (Division I), swimming and diving (Division I). *Intercollegiate sports:* baseball M, basketball M/W, cross-country running M/W, golf M, soccer M/W, softball W, swimming and diving M/W, tennis M/W, volleyball M/W. *Intramural sports:* badminton M/W, basketball M/W, bowling M/W, cross-country running M/W, fencing M/W, football M/W, golf M/W, racquetball M/W, skiing (cross-country) M/W, skiing (downhill) M/W, soccer M/W, softball M/W, squash M/W, swimming and diving M/W, table tennis M/W, tennis M/W, volleyball M/W, water polo M/W, weight lifting M/W.

Standardized Tests *Required:* SAT or ACT (for admission). *Recommended:* SAT (for admission).

Costs (2012–13) *One-time required fee:* $200. *Tuition:* state resident $5270 full-time, $220 per credit part-time; nonresident $14,320 full-time, $597 per credit hour part-time. Full-time tuition and fees vary according to program. Part-time tuition and fees vary according to course load and program. *Required fees:* $1559 full-time, $65 per credit hour part-time. *Room and board:* $11,058; room only: $7060. Room and board charges vary according to board plan and housing facility. *Payment plan:* installment. *Waivers:* employees or children of employees.

Financial Aid Of all full-time matriculated undergraduates who enrolled in 2011, 2,884 applied for aid, 2,280 were judged to have need, 73 had their need fully met. In 2011, 106 non-need-based awards were made. *Average percent of need met:* 56%. *Average financial aid package:* $9864. *Average need-based loan:* $4692. *Average need-based gift aid:* $6077. *Average non-need-based aid:* $2374. *Average indebtedness upon graduation:* $25,812.

Applying *Options:* electronic application, early admission, early action, deferred entrance. *Application fee:* $40. *Required:* high school transcript, minimum 3.0 GPA. *Required for some:* essay or personal statement, 1 letter of recommendation, interview, audition, portfolio. *Application deadlines:* 7/15 (freshmen), rolling (transfers), 11/15 (early action). *Notification:* continuous until 5/1 (freshmen), continuous (transfers), 12/15 (early action).

Freshman Application Contact Stephanie McCaine, Director of Admissions, Purchase College, State University of New York, 735 Anderson Hill Road, Purchase, NY 10577-1400. *Phone:* 914-251-6300. *Fax:* 914-251-6314. *E-mail:* admission@purchase.edu. *Web site:* http://www.purchase.edu/.

Queens College of the City University of New York

Flushing, New York

- **State and locally supported** comprehensive, founded 1937, part of City University of New York System
- **Urban** 77-acre campus with easy access to New York City
- **Coed** 16,559 undergraduate students, 69% full-time, 58% women, 42% men
- **Very difficult** entrance level, 31% of applicants were admitted

Undergraduates 11,377 full-time, 5,182 part-time. Students come from 15 states and territories; 170 other countries; 1% are from out of state; 8% Black or African American, non-Hispanic/Latino; 17% Hispanic/Latino; 24% Asian, non-Hispanic/Latino; 0.1% American Indian or Alaska Native, non-Hispanic/Latino; 5% international; 13% transferred in; 3% live on campus. *Retention:* 88% of full-time freshmen returned.

Freshmen *Admission:* 18,722 applied, 5,746 admitted, 1,444 enrolled. *Average high school GPA:* 3.7. *Test scores:* SAT critical reading scores over 500: 73%; SAT math scores over 500: 91%; SAT critical reading scores over 600: 20%; SAT math scores over 600: 32%; SAT critical reading scores over 700: 3%; SAT math scores over 700: 4%.

Faculty *Total:* 1,464, 41% full-time, 54% with terminal degrees. *Student/faculty ratio:* 16:1.

Academics *Calendar:* semesters. *Degrees:* bachelor's, master's, post-master's, and postbachelor's certificates. *Special study options:* accelerated degree program, adult/continuing education programs, advanced placement credit, double majors, English as a second language, honors programs, independent study, internships, off-campus study, part-time degree program, services for LD students, student-designed majors, study abroad, summer session for credit. *ROTC:* Army (c), Navy (c). *Unusual degree programs:* chemistry, biochemistry, computer science, physics, political science, music, philosophy.

Computers on Campus 2,500 computers/terminals are available on campus for general student use. Students can access the following: campus intranet, computer help desk, free student e-mail accounts, online (class) grades, online (class) registration, online (class) schedules. Campuswide network is available. Wireless service is available via entire campus.

Student Life *Housing options:* coed. Campus housing is university owned. *Activities and organizations:* drama/theater group, student-run newspaper, radio station, choral group, Alliance of Latin American Students, Black Student Union, Caribbean Student Association, Hillel-Jewish Student Organization, India Cultural Exchange, national fraternities, national sororities. *Campus security:* 24-hour emergency response devices and patrols. *Student services:* health clinic, personal/psychological counseling.

Athletics Member NCAA. All Division II. *Intercollegiate sports:* baseball M(s), basketball M(s)/W(s), cross-country running M(s)/W(s), fencing W(s), lacrosse W(s), soccer M(s)/W(s), softball W(s), swimming and diving M(s)/W(s), table tennis W, tennis M(s)/W(s), track and field M(s)/W(s), volleyball W(s), water polo M(s). *Intramural sports:* basketball M/W, cross-country running M/W, football M/W, soccer M/W, softball M/W, table tennis M/W, tennis M/W, track and field M/W, volleyball M/W.

Standardized Tests *Required:* SAT or ACT (for admission). *Required for some:* SAT Subject Tests (for admission). *Recommended:* SAT Subject Tests (for admission).

Costs (2012–13) *Tuition:* state resident $5130 full-time, $215 per credit part-time; nonresident $13,800 full-time, $460 per credit part-time. *Required fees:* $477 full-time. *Room and board:* $11,840. Room and board charges vary according to board plan and housing facility. *Payment plan:* installment. *Waivers:* senior citizens.

Financial Aid Of all full-time matriculated undergraduates who enrolled in 2010, 11,756 applied for aid, 9,071 were judged to have need, 7,141 had their need fully met. 519,700 Federal Work-Study jobs (averaging $456). In 2010, 165 non-need-based awards were made. *Average percent of need met:* 95%. *Average financial aid package:* $8000. *Average need-based loan:* $4900. *Average need-based gift aid:* $4800. *Average non-need-based aid:* $8300. *Average indebtedness upon graduation:* $17,700.

Applying *Options:* electronic application, deferred entrance. *Application fee:* $65. *Required:* high school transcript, minimum 3.0 GPA. *Application deadline:* 5/15 (freshmen). *Notification:* 5/30 (freshmen).

Freshman Application Contact Queens College of the City University of New York, 65-30 Kissena Boulevard, Flushing, NY 11367-1597. *Phone:* 718-997-5600. *Web site:* http://www.qc.cuny.edu/.

See below for display ad and page 1510 for the College Close-Up.

Rabbinical Academy Mesivta Rabbi Chaim Berlin

Brooklyn, New York

Director of Admissions Executive Administrator, Rabbinical Academy Mesivta Rabbi Chaim Berlin, 1605 Coney Island Avenue, Brooklyn, NY 11230-4715. *Phone:* 718-377-0777. *Fax:* 718-338-5578.

Rabbinical College Beth Shraga

Monsey, New York

Director of Admissions Rabbi Sydney Schiff, Director of Admissions, Rabbinical College Beth Shraga, 28 Saddle River Road, Monsey, NY 10952-3035.

Rabbinical College Bobover Yeshiva B'nei Zion

Brooklyn, New York

Director of Admissions Director of Admissions, Rabbinical College Bobover Yeshiva B'nei Zion, 1577 Forty-eighth Street, Brooklyn, NY 11219. *Phone:* 718-438-2018.

Rabbinical College Ch'san Sofer

Brooklyn, New York

Director of Admissions Director of Admissions, Rabbinical College Ch'san Sofer, 1876 Fiftieth Street, Brooklyn, NY 11204. *Phone:* 718-236-1171.

Rabbinical College of Long Island

Long Beach, New York

Director of Admissions Director of Admissions, Rabbinical College of Long Island, 205 West Beech Street, Long Beach, NY 11561-3305. *Phone:* 516-431-7414.

Rabbinical College of Ohr Shimon Yisroel

Brooklyn, New York

Admissions Office Contact Rabbinical College of Ohr Shimon Yisroel, 215-217 Hewes Street, Brooklyn, NY 11211.

Rabbinical Seminary Adas Yereim

Brooklyn, New York

Director of Admissions Director of Admissions, Rabbinical Seminary Adas Yereim, 185 Wilson Street, Brooklyn, NY 11211-7206. *Phone:* 718-388-1751.

Rabbinical Seminary M'kor Chaim

Brooklyn, New York

Director of Admissions Director of Admissions, Rabbinical Seminary M'kor Chaim, 1571 Fifty-fifth Street, Brooklyn, NY 11219. *Phone:* 718-851-0183.

Rabbinical Seminary of America

Flushing, New York

Director of Admissions Rabbi Abraham Semmel, Director of Admissions, Rabbinical Seminary of America, 76-01 147th Street, Flushing, NY 11367. *Phone:* 718-268-4700.

Affordable Tuition
Priceless Education

It's impossible to calculate the value of learning with a caring faculty mentor. In addition to an award-winning faculty, at Queens College you'll find honors programs, career-enhancing internships, research and study abroad opportunities, and over 100 clubs and sports teams—all on our beautiful, 77-acre campus.

www.qc.cuny.edu/Pet

QUEENS COLLEGE   CUNY The City University of New York

Undergraduate | Graduate | Professional & Continuing Studies   65-30 Kissena Blvd. | Flushing, NY 11367 | 718.997.5600

Rensselaer Polytechnic Institute

Troy, New York

- **Independent** university, founded 1824
- **Suburban** 284-acre campus with easy access to Albany, NY
- **Endowment** $629.7 million
- **Coed** 5,322 undergraduate students, 100% full-time, 29% women, 71% men
- **Very difficult** entrance level, 40% of applicants were admitted

Undergraduates 5,299 full-time, 23 part-time. Students come from 47 states and territories; 28 other countries; 62% are from out of state; 2% Black or African American, non-Hispanic/Latino; 6% Hispanic/Latino; 10% Asian, non-Hispanic/Latino; 0.1% Native Hawaiian or other Pacific Islander, non-Hispanic/Latino; 0.1% American Indian or Alaska Native, non-Hispanic/Latino; 5% Two or more races, non-Hispanic/Latino; 1% Race/ethnicity unknown; 5% international; 2% transferred in; 63% live on campus. *Retention:* 93% of full-time freshmen returned.

Freshmen *Admission:* 14,584 applied, 5,779 admitted, 1,186 enrolled. *Test scores:* SAT critical reading scores over 500: 99%; SAT math scores over 500: 100%; SAT writing scores over 500: 98%; ACT scores over 18: 100%; SAT critical reading scores over 600: 81%; SAT math scores over 600: 96%; SAT writing scores over 600: 74%; ACT scores over 24: 93%; SAT critical reading scores over 700: 30%; SAT math scores over 700: 59%; SAT writing scores over 700: 26%; ACT scores over 30: 34%.

Faculty *Total:* 482, 78% full-time, 90% with terminal degrees. *Student/faculty ratio:* 15:1.

Academics *Calendar:* semesters. *Degrees:* bachelor's, master's, doctoral, and first professional. *Special study options:* accelerated degree program, adult/continuing education programs, advanced placement credit, cooperative education, double majors, English as a second language, honors programs, independent study, internships, off-campus study, part-time degree program, services for LD students, student-designed majors, study abroad, summer session for credit. *ROTC:* Army (c), Navy (b), Air Force (b). *Unusual degree programs:* 3-2 engineering.

Computers on Campus Students can access the following: campus intranet, computer help desk, free student e-mail accounts, online (class) grades, online (class) registration, online (class) schedules, billing, downloadable software, web pages. Campuswide network is available. 100% of college-owned or -operated housing units are wired for high-speed Internet access. Wireless service is available via entire campus.

Student Life *Housing:* on-campus residence required through sophomore year. *Options:* coed, disabled students. Campus housing is university owned. Freshman campus housing is guaranteed. *Activities and organizations:* drama/theater group, student-run newspaper, radio and television station, choral group, Red Army Spirit Club, Outing Club, Indian Student Association, Chinese American Student Association, pep band, national fraternities, national sororities. *Campus security:* 24-hour emergency response devices and patrols, late-night transport/escort service, controlled dormitory access, campus foot patrols at night. *Student services:* health clinic, personal/psychological counseling, women's center, legal services.

Athletics Member NCAA. All Division III except men's and women's ice hockey (Division I). *Intercollegiate sports:* archery M(c)/W(c), badminton M(c)/W(c), baseball M/W(c), basketball M/W, crew M(c)/W(c), cross-country running M/W, equestrian sports M(c)/W(c), fencing M(c)/W(c), field hockey W, football M, golf M, ice hockey M(s)/W(s), lacrosse M/W, racquetball M(c)/W(c), riflery M(c)/W(c), rugby M(c)/W(c), sailing M(c)/W(c), skiing (cross-country) M(c)/W(c), soccer M/W, softball W, squash M(c)/W(c), swimming and diving M/W, table tennis M(c)/W(c), tennis M/W, track and field M/W, ultimate Frisbee M(c)/W(c), volleyball M(c)/W(c), water polo M(c)/W(c), weight lifting M(c)/W(c). *Intramural sports:* basketball M/W, bowling M(c)/W(c), cheerleading W, ice hockey M/W, lacrosse M(c), racquetball M/W, rock climbing M(c)/W(c), skiing (downhill) M/W, soccer M/W, softball M/W, swimming and diving M/W, table tennis M/W, tennis M(c)/W(c), ultimate Frisbee M/W, volleyball M/W, wrestling M.

Standardized Tests *Required:* SAT or ACT (for admission). *Required for some:* SAT and SAT Subject Tests or ACT (for admission).

Costs (2011–12) *Comprehensive fee:* $54,679 includes full-time tuition ($41,600), mandatory fees ($1104), and room and board ($11,975). Part-time tuition: $1733 per credit hour. *College room only:* $6840. Room and board charges vary according to board plan and location. *Payment plan:* installment. *Waivers:* employees or children of employees.

Financial Aid Of all full-time matriculated undergraduates who enrolled in 2011, 3,751 applied for aid, 3,381 were judged to have need, 883 had their need fully met. 1,387 Federal Work-Study jobs (averaging $1913). In 2011, 1586 non-need-based awards were made. *Average percent of need met:* 80%. *Average financial aid package:* $31,830. *Average need-based loan:* $5486. *Average need-based gift aid:* $23,722. *Average non-need-based aid:* $12,945. *Average indebtedness upon graduation:* $29,625.

Applying *Options:* electronic application, early admission, early decision, deferred entrance. *Application fee:* $70. *Required:* high school transcript. *Required for some:* essay or personal statement, portfolio for Electronic Arts. *Recommended:* 1 letter of recommendation. *Application deadline:* 1/15 (freshmen). *Early decision deadline:* 11/1 (for plan 1), 12/15 (for plan 2). *Notification:* 3/12 (freshmen), continuous (transfers), 12/10 (early decision plan 1), 1/14 (early decision plan 2).

Freshman Application Contact Mr. Paul Marthers, Vice President for Enrollment, Rensselaer Polytechnic Institute, 110 8th Street, Troy, NY 12180. *Phone:* 518-276-6216. *Fax:* 518-276-4072. *E-mail:* admissions@rpi.edu. *Web site:* http://www.rpi.edu/.

Roberts Wesleyan College

Rochester, New York

- **Independent** comprehensive, founded 1866, affiliated with Free Methodist Church of North America
- **Suburban** 188-acre campus
- **Endowment** $16.4 million
- **Coed** 1,400 undergraduate students, 90% full-time, 70% women, 30% men
- **Moderately difficult** entrance level, 51% of applicants were admitted

Undergraduates 1,256 full-time, 144 part-time. Students come from 27 states and territories; 16 other countries; 10% are from out of state; 11% Black or African American, non-Hispanic/Latino; 4% Hispanic/Latino; 0.9% Asian, non-Hispanic/Latino; 0.4% American Indian or Alaska Native, non-Hispanic/Latino; 2% Two or more races, non-Hispanic/Latino; 3% Race/ethnicity unknown; 2% international; 7% transferred in; 65% live on campus. *Retention:* 73% of full-time freshmen returned.

Freshmen *Admission:* 1,834 applied, 940 admitted, 261 enrolled. *Average high school GPA:* 3.4. *Test scores:* SAT critical reading scores over 500: 66%; SAT math scores over 500: 70%; SAT writing scores over 500: 55%; ACT scores over 18: 97%; SAT critical reading scores over 600: 32%; SAT math scores over 600: 27%; SAT writing scores over 600: 22%; ACT scores over 24: 45%; SAT critical reading scores over 700: 4%; SAT math scores over 700: 4%; SAT writing scores over 700: 5%; ACT scores over 30: 11%.

Faculty *Total:* 255, 40% full-time, 38% with terminal degrees. *Student/faculty ratio:* 11:1.

Academics *Calendar:* semesters. *Degrees:* associate, bachelor's, and master's. *Special study options:* academic remediation for entering students, accelerated degree program, advanced placement credit, cooperative education, double majors, English as a second language, honors programs, independent study, internships, off-campus study, services for LD students, student-designed majors, study abroad, summer session for credit. *ROTC:* Army (b), Air Force (c). *Unusual degree programs:* 3-2 engineering with Clarkson University, Rensselaer Polytechnic Institute, Rochester Institute of Technology.

Computers on Campus 250 computers/terminals are available on campus for general student use. Students can access the following: campus intranet, computer help desk, free student e-mail accounts, online (class) grades, online (class) registration, online (class) schedules. Campuswide network is available. 100% of college-owned or -operated housing units are wired for high-speed Internet access. Wireless service is available via student centers.

Student Life *Housing:* on-campus residence required through senior year. *Options:* men-only, women-only. Campus housing is university owned. Freshman campus housing is guaranteed. *Activities and organizations:* drama/theater group, student-run newspaper, choral group, Intramurals, Foot of the Cross, Fellowship of Christian Athletes, Nursing Club, Drama Club. *Campus security:* 24-hour emergency response devices and patrols, student patrols, late-night transport/escort service, controlled dormitory access, 24-hour Resident Life staff on-call. *Student services:* health clinic, personal/psychological counseling.

Athletics Member NAIA, NCCAA. *Intercollegiate sports:* basketball M(s)/W(s), cross-country running M(s)/W(s), golf M(s)/W(s), soccer M(s)/W(s), tennis M(s)/W(s), track and field M(s)/W(s), volleyball W(s). *Intramural sports:* basketball M/W, football M/W, racquetball M/W, skiing (downhill) M/W, soccer M/W, softball M/W, table tennis M/W, tennis M/W, ultimate Frisbee M/W, volleyball M/W, water polo M/W.

Standardized Tests *Required:* SAT or ACT (for admission).

Costs (2012–13) *One-time required fee:* $375. *Comprehensive fee:* $35,588 includes full-time tuition ($25,350), mandatory fees ($974), and room and board ($9264). Part-time tuition and fees vary according to course load. *College room only:* $5932. Room and board charges vary according to board plan and housing facility.

Financial Aid Of all full-time matriculated undergraduates who enrolled in 2010, 1,325 applied for aid, 1,257 were judged to have need, 102 had their need fully met. 751 Federal Work-Study jobs (averaging $1857). 30 state and other part-time jobs (averaging $2016). In 2010, 157 non-need-based awards were made. *Average percent of need met:* 66%. *Average financial aid pack-*

age: $17,170. *Average need-based loan:* $5011. *Average need-based gift aid:* $12,198. *Average non-need-based aid:* $5453. *Average indebtedness upon graduation:* $36,486.

Applying *Options:* electronic application, early admission, deferred entrance. *Application fee:* $35. *Required:* essay or personal statement, high school transcript, 1 letter of recommendation. *Recommended:* minimum 2.7 GPA, 2 letters of recommendation, interview. *Application deadlines:* 2/1 (freshmen), rolling (transfers).

Freshman Application Contact Ms. Linda Kurtz Hoffman, Associate Vice President for Undergraduate Admissions, Roberts Wesleyan College, 2301 Westside Drive, Rochester, NY 14624-1997. *Phone:* 585-594-6400. *Toll-free phone:* 800-777-4RWC. *Fax:* 585-594-6371. *E-mail:* admissions@roberts.edu. *Web site:* http://www.roberts.edu/.

Rochester Institute of Technology

Rochester, New York

- **Independent** comprehensive, founded 1829
- **Suburban** 1300-acre campus with easy access to Buffalo
- **Endowment** $640.8 million
- **Coed** 14,653 undergraduate students, 91% full-time, 32% women, 68% men
- **Moderately difficult** entrance level, 59% of applicants were admitted

Undergraduates 13,349 full-time, 1,304 part-time. Students come from 52 states and territories; 102 other countries; 45% are from out of state; 5% Black or African American, non-Hispanic/Latino; 5% Hispanic/Latino; 5% Asian, non-Hispanic/Latino; 0.1% Native Hawaiian or other Pacific Islander, non-Hispanic/Latino; 0.4% American Indian or Alaska Native, non-Hispanic/Latino; 1% Two or more races, non-Hispanic/Latino; 16% Race/ethnicity unknown; 5% international; 6% transferred in; 68% live on campus. *Retention:* 91% of full-time freshmen returned.

Freshmen *Admission:* 15,806 applied, 9,266 admitted, 2,986 enrolled. *Average high school GPA:* 3.7. *Test scores:* SAT critical reading scores over 500: 89%; SAT math scores over 500: 94%; SAT writing scores over 500: 80%; ACT scores over 18: 100%; SAT critical reading scores over 600: 47%; SAT math scores over 600: 64%; SAT writing scores over 600: 38%; ACT scores over 24: 86%; SAT critical reading scores over 700: 11%; SAT math scores over 700: 18%; SAT writing scores over 700: 6%; ACT scores over 30: 29%.

Faculty *Total:* 1,475, 65% full-time, 45% with terminal degrees. *Student/faculty ratio:* 12:1.

Academics *Calendar:* quarters. *Degrees:* certificates, associate, bachelor's, master's, doctoral, post-master's, postbachelor's, and first professional certificates. *Special study options:* accelerated degree program, adult/continuing education programs, advanced placement credit, cooperative education, distance learning, double majors, English as a second language, honors programs, independent study, internships, off-campus study, part-time degree program, services for LD students, student-designed majors, study abroad, summer session for credit. *ROTC:* Army (b), Navy (c), Air Force (b).

Computers on Campus 2,500 computers/terminals are available on campus for general student use. Students can access the following: campus intranet, computer help desk, free student e-mail accounts, online (class) grades, online (class) registration, student account information. Campuswide network is available. 100% of college-owned or -operated housing units are wired for high-speed Internet access. Wireless service is available via classrooms, computer centers, computer labs, learning centers, libraries, student centers.

Student Life *Housing:* on-campus residence required for freshman year. *Options:* coed, men-only, women-only, disabled students. Campus housing is university owned. Freshman campus housing is guaranteed. *Activities and organizations:* drama/theater group, student-run newspaper, radio station, choral group, national fraternities, national sororities. *Campus security:* 24-hour emergency response devices and patrols, student patrols, late-night transport/escort service. *Student services:* health clinic, personal/psychological counseling, women's center, legal services.

Athletics Member NCAA. All Division III except ice hockey (Division I). *Intercollegiate sports:* baseball M, basketball M/W, bowling M(c)/W(c), cheerleading M(c)/W(c), crew M/W, cross-country running M/W, equestrian sports M(c)/W(c), fencing M(c)/W(c), field hockey W(c), ice hockey M/W, lacrosse M/W, skiing (downhill) M(c)/W(c), soccer M/W, softball W, swimming and diving M/W, tennis M/W, track and field M/W, ultimate Frisbee M(c)/W(c), volleyball M(c)/W, water polo M(c)/W(c), wrestling M. *Intramural sports:* badminton M/W, basketball M/W, bowling M/W, football M, golf M/W, ice hockey M/W, lacrosse M(c), racquetball M/W, rock climbing M(c)/W(c), soccer M/W, softball M/W, table tennis M/W, tennis M/W, volleyball M/W.

Standardized Tests *Required:* SAT or ACT (for admission).

Costs (2011–12) *Comprehensive fee:* $42,450 includes full-time tuition ($31,584), mandatory fees ($453), and room and board ($10,413). Full-time tuition and fees vary according to course load. Part-time tuition and fees vary according to class time and course load. *College room only:* $6096. Room and board charges vary according to board plan and housing facility. *Payment*

plans: tuition prepayment, installment, deferred payment. *Waivers:* employees or children of employees.

Financial Aid Of all full-time matriculated undergraduates who enrolled in 2010, 9,357 applied for aid, 8,558 were judged to have need, 7,100 had their need fully met. In 2010, 1400 non-need-based awards were made. *Average percent of need met:* 88%. *Average financial aid package:* $22,600. *Average need-based loan:* $5500. *Average need-based gift aid:* $17,000. *Average non-need-based aid:* $9000.

Applying *Options:* electronic application, early admission, early decision, deferred entrance. *Application fee:* $50. *Required:* essay or personal statement, high school transcript. *Required for some:* portfolio of original artwork required. *Recommended:* minimum 3.0 GPA, 1 letter of recommendation, interview. *Application deadline:* 2/1 (freshmen). *Early decision deadline:* 12/1. *Notification:* 3/15 (freshmen), continuous (transfers), 1/15 (early decision).

Freshman Application Contact Dr. Daniel Shelley, Assistant Vice President, Rochester Institute of Technology, 60 Lomb Memorial Drive, Rochester, NY 14623-5604. *Phone:* 585-475-6631. *Fax:* 585-475-7424. *E-mail:* admissions@rit.edu. *Web site:* http://www.rit.edu/.

See page 1530 for the College Close-Up.

Russell Sage College
Troy, New York

- **Independent** 4-year, founded 1916, part of The Sage Colleges
- **Urban** 8-acre campus
- **Endowment** $21.8 million
- **Women only** 789 undergraduate students, 94% full-time
- **Moderately difficult** entrance level, 69% of applicants were admitted

Undergraduates 745 full-time, 44 part-time. Students come from 15 states and territories; 2 other countries; 9% are from out of state; 10% Black or African American, non-Hispanic/Latino; 4% Hispanic/Latino; 2% Asian, non-Hispanic/Latino; 0.1% Native Hawaiian or other Pacific Islander, non-Hispanic/Latino; 0.4% American Indian or Alaska Native, non-Hispanic/Latino; 2% Two or more races, non-Hispanic/Latino; 12% Race/ethnicity unknown; 0.3% international; 14% transferred in; 51% live on campus. *Retention:* 81% of full-time freshmen returned.

Freshmen *Admission:* 718 applied, 494 admitted, 153 enrolled. *Average high school GPA:* 3.16. *Test scores:* SAT critical reading scores over 500: 55%; SAT math scores over 500: 48%; ACT scores over 18: 83%; SAT critical reading scores over 600: 19%; SAT math scores over 600: 13%; ACT scores over 24: 46%; SAT critical reading scores over 700: 1%; SAT math scores over 700: 5%; ACT scores over 30: 3%.

Faculty *Total:* 115, 53% full-time, 58% with terminal degrees. *Student/faculty ratio:* 10:1.

Academics *Calendar:* semesters. *Degree:* bachelor's. *Special study options:* academic remediation for entering students, accelerated degree program, advanced placement credit, cooperative education, distance learning, double majors, honors programs, independent study, internships, off-campus study, services for LD students, student-designed majors, study abroad, summer session for credit. *ROTC:* Army (c), Air Force (c). *Unusual degree programs:* 3-2 business administration with Sage Graduate School; engineering with Rensselaer Polytechnic Institute; nursing with Sage Graduate School; occupational therapy and physical therapy with Sage Graduate School.

Computers on Campus 165 computers/terminals are available on campus for general student use. Students can access the following: campus intranet, computer help desk, free student e-mail accounts, online (class) grades, online (class) registration, online (class) schedules. Campuswide network is available. 100% of college-owned or -operated housing units are wired for high-speed Internet access. Wireless service is available via classrooms, computer labs, learning centers, libraries.

Student Life *Housing options:* women-only. Campus housing is university owned. Freshman campus housing is guaranteed. *Activities and organizations:* drama/theater group, student-run newspaper, choral group, student government, Sage Recreation Association, Physical Therapy Club, Crew Club, Black-Latin Student Alliance. *Campus security:* 24-hour emergency response devices and patrols, late-night transport/escort service, controlled dormitory access. *Student services:* health clinic, personal/psychological counseling, women's center.

Athletics Member NCAA. All Division III. *Intercollegiate sports:* basketball W, lacrosse W, soccer W, softball W, tennis W, volleyball W. *Intramural sports:* cheerleading W(c), crew W(c), ice hockey W, track and field W(c).

Standardized Tests *Required for some:* SAT or ACT (for admission).

Costs (2011–12) *Comprehensive fee:* $38,675 includes full-time tuition ($27,000), mandatory fees ($1000), and room and board ($10,675). Part-time tuition: $900 per credit hour. *College room only:* $5625. Room and board charges vary according to board plan. *Payment plans:* installment, deferred payment. *Waivers:* senior citizens and employees or children of employees.

Financial Aid Of all full-time matriculated undergraduates who enrolled in 2011, 725 applied for aid, 691 were judged to have need, 282 had their need fully met. 362 Federal Work-Study jobs (averaging $1942). 78 state and other part-time jobs (averaging $1926). In 2011, 27 non-need-based awards were made. *Average financial aid package:* $28,941. *Average need-based loan:* $4852. *Average need-based gift aid:* $12,662. *Average non-need-based aid:* $9574. *Average indebtedness upon graduation:* $26,159.

Applying *Options:* electronic application, early admission, early action, deferred entrance. *Application fee:* $30. *Required:* essay or personal statement, high school transcript, minimum 2.5 GPA, 2 letters of recommendation. *Recommended:* interview. *Application deadlines:* rolling (freshmen), rolling (transfers). *Notification:* continuous (freshmen), continuous (transfers).

Freshman Application Contact Mr. Andrew Palumbo, Director of Undergraduate Admission, Russell Sage College, 140 New Scotland Avenue, Albany, NY 12208. *Phone:* 518-292-1926. *Toll-free phone:* 888-VERY-SAGE (in-state); 888-VERY SAGE (out-of-state). *Fax:* 518-292-1912. *E-mail:* paluma@sage.edu. *Web site:* http://www.sage.edu/rsc/.

Sage College of Albany
Albany, New York

- **Independent** 4-year, founded 1957, part of The Sage Colleges
- **Urban** 15-acre campus
- **Endowment** $21.8 million
- **Coed** 901 undergraduate students, 74% full-time, 61% women, 39% men
- **Minimally difficult** entrance level, 58% of applicants were admitted

Undergraduates 667 full-time, 234 part-time. Students come from 12 states and territories; 3 other countries; 5% are from out of state; 16% Black or African American, non-Hispanic/Latino; 9% Hispanic/Latino; 2% Asian, non-Hispanic/Latino; 0.5% Native Hawaiian or other Pacific Islander, non-Hispanic/Latino; 0.5% American Indian or Alaska Native, non-Hispanic/Latino; 2% Two or more races, non-Hispanic/Latino; 13% Race/ethnicity unknown; 0.3% international; 17% transferred in; 53% live on campus. *Retention:* 68% of full-time freshmen returned.

Freshmen *Admission:* 1,083 applied, 629 admitted, 154 enrolled. *Average high school GPA:* 2.9. *Test scores:* SAT critical reading scores over 500: 42%; SAT math scores over 500: 38%; ACT scores over 18: 77%; SAT critical reading scores over 600: 6%; SAT math scores over 600: 8%; ACT scores over 24: 18%.

Faculty *Total:* 102, 41% full-time, 57% with terminal degrees. *Student/faculty ratio:* 13:1.

Academics *Calendar:* semesters. *Degree:* bachelor's. *Special study options:* academic remediation for entering students, accelerated degree program, adult/continuing education programs, advanced placement credit, cooperative education, distance learning, honors programs, independent study, internships, off-campus study, part-time degree program, services for LD students, student-designed majors, study abroad, summer session for credit. *ROTC:* Army (c), Air Force (c). *Unusual degree programs:* 3-2 business administration with Sage Graduate School; clinical biology and cytotechnology with Albany College of Pharmacy.

Computers on Campus 205 computers/terminals are available on campus for general student use. Students can access the following: campus intranet, computer help desk, free student e-mail accounts, online (class) grades, online (class) registration. Campuswide network is available. 100% of college-owned or -operated housing units are wired for high-speed Internet access. Wireless service is available via classrooms, computer labs, learning centers, libraries, student centers.

Student Life *Housing options:* coed, women-only. Campus housing is university owned. Freshman applicants given priority for college housing. *Activities and organizations:* Sage African, Latino, Asian, and Native American, VIBE, College Republicans, Love Your College Experience, Sage GEMS. *Campus security:* 24-hour emergency response devices and patrols, late-night transport/escort service, controlled dormitory access, 24-hour security cameras. *Student services:* health clinic, personal/psychological counseling.

Athletics Member NCAA. All Division III. *Intercollegiate sports:* basketball M/W, cross-country running M, golf M, lacrosse W, soccer M/W, softball W, tennis M/W, volleyball M/W. *Intramural sports:* badminton M/W, cheerleading W(c), crew M(c)/W(c), football M/W, ice hockey M(c)/W(c), skiing (cross-country) M(c).

Standardized Tests *Required for some:* SAT or ACT (for admission).

Costs (2011–12) *Comprehensive fee:* $38,675 includes full-time tuition ($27,000), mandatory fees ($1000), and room and board ($10,675). Part-time tuition: $900 per credit hour. *College room only:* $5625. Room and board charges vary according to board plan. *Payment plans:* installment, deferred payment. *Waivers:* employees or children of employees.

Financial Aid Of all full-time matriculated undergraduates who enrolled in 2011, 601 applied for aid, 589 were judged to have need, 247 had their need fully met. 357 Federal Work-Study jobs (averaging $1942). 21 state and other

part-time jobs (averaging $1800). In 2011, 8 non-need-based awards were made. *Average financial aid package:* $29,793. *Average need-based loan:* $4607. *Average need-based gift aid:* $15,509. *Average non-need-based aid:* $7425. *Average indebtedness upon graduation:* $28,112.

Applying *Options:* electronic application, deferred entrance. *Application fee:* $30. *Required:* essay or personal statement, high school transcript, minimum 2.5 GPA, 2 letters of recommendation, portfolio for fine arts program. *Recommended:* interview. *Application deadlines:* rolling (freshmen), 8/1 (transfers). *Notification:* 8/15 (freshmen), continuous until 8/15 (transfers).

Freshman Application Contact Mr. Andrew Palumbo, Director of Undergraduate Admission, Sage College of Albany, 140 New Scotland Avenue, Albany, NY 12208. *Phone:* 518-292-1730. *Toll-free phone:* 888-VERY-SAGE. *Fax:* 518-292-1912. *E-mail:* scaadm@sage.edu. *Web site:* http://www.sage.edu/.

St. Bonaventure University

St. Bonaventure, New York

- **Independent** comprehensive, founded 1858, affiliated with Roman Catholic Church
- **Small-town** 500-acre campus
- **Endowment** $48.0 million
- **Coed** 1,959 undergraduate students, 96% full-time, 52% women, 48% men
- **Moderately difficult** entrance level, 80% of applicants were admitted

Undergraduates 1,890 full-time, 69 part-time. Students come from 33 states and territories; 34 other countries; 25% are from out of state; 4% Black or African American, non-Hispanic/Latino; 4% Hispanic/Latino; 2% Asian, non-Hispanic/Latino; 1% Native Hawaiian or other Pacific Islander, non-Hispanic/Latino; 0.5% American Indian or Alaska Native, non-Hispanic/Latino; 0.3% Two or more races, non-Hispanic/Latino; 17% Race/ethnicity unknown; 2% international; 4% transferred in; 75% live on campus. *Retention:* 80% of full-time freshmen returned.

Freshmen *Admission:* 2,545 applied, 2,045 admitted, 489 enrolled. *Average high school GPA:* 3.18. *Test scores:* SAT critical reading scores over 500: 63%; SAT math scores over 500: 68%; SAT writing scores over 500: 58%; ACT scores over 18: 93%; SAT critical reading scores over 600: 21%; SAT math scores over 600: 24%; SAT writing scores over 600: 17%; ACT scores over 24: 48%; SAT critical reading scores over 700: 4%; SAT math scores over 700: 4%; SAT writing scores over 700: 3%; ACT scores over 30: 7%.

Faculty *Total:* 223, 69% full-time, 54% with terminal degrees. *Student/faculty ratio:* 13:1.

Academics *Calendar:* semesters. *Degrees:* bachelor's, master's, post-master's, and postbachelor's certificates. *Special study options:* accelerated degree program, advanced placement credit, distance learning, double majors, honors programs, independent study, internships, off-campus study, part-time degree program, services for LD students, student-designed majors, study abroad, summer session for credit. *ROTC:* Army (b). *Unusual degree programs:* 3-2 business administration.

Computers on Campus 220 computers/terminals and 2,500 ports are available on campus for general student use. Students can access the following: campus intranet, computer help desk, free student e-mail accounts, online (class) grades, online (class) registration, online (class) schedules. Campus-wide network is available. 100% of college-owned or -operated housing units are wired for high-speed Internet access. Wireless service is available via entire campus.

Student Life *Housing:* on-campus residence required for freshman year. *Options:* coed, disabled students. Campus housing is university owned. Freshman campus housing is guaranteed. *Activities and organizations:* drama/theater group, student-run newspaper, radio and television station, choral group, Student Government Association, Bona Responds, BV newspaper, Students for the Mountain, Student Ambassadors. *Campus security:* 24-hour emergency response devices and patrols, late-night transport/escort service, controlled dormitory access. *Student services:* health clinic, personal/psychological counseling.

Athletics Member NCAA. All Division I. *Intercollegiate sports:* baseball M(s), basketball M(s)/W(s), cross-country running M(s)/W(s), field hockey W(c), golf M(s), lacrosse M(c)/W(s), rugby M(c)/W(c), soccer M(s)/W(s), softball W(s), swimming and diving M(s)/W(s), tennis M(s)/W(s). *Intramural sports:* basketball M/W, football M/W, golf M/W, ice hockey M(c), racquetball M/W, soccer M(c)/W(c), softball M/W, table tennis M/W, tennis M/W, volleyball M/W.

Standardized Tests *Required:* SAT or ACT (for admission). *Required for some:* SAT Subject Tests (for admission).

Costs (2011–12) *Comprehensive fee:* $37,932 includes full-time tuition ($26,925), mandatory fees ($965), and room and board ($10,042). Part-time tuition: $805 per credit hour. Part-time tuition and fees vary according to course load. *College room only:* $5422. Room and board charges vary accord-

ing to board plan and housing facility. *Waivers:* senior citizens and employees or children of employees.

Financial Aid Of all full-time matriculated undergraduates who enrolled in 2010, 1,684 applied for aid, 1,493 were judged to have need, 379 had their need fully met. 381 Federal Work-Study jobs (averaging $841). 350 state and other part-time jobs (averaging $936). In 2010, 435 non-need-based awards were made. *Average percent of need met:* 77%. *Average financial aid package:* $23,814. *Average need-based loan:* $4472. *Average need-based gift aid:* $17,378. *Average non-need-based aid:* $10,319. *Average indebtedness upon graduation:* $34,622.

Applying *Options:* electronic application, deferred entrance. *Application fee:* $30. *Required:* high school transcript, 1 letter of recommendation. *Required for some:* essay or personal statement. *Recommended:* essay or personal statement, minimum 3.0 GPA, 3 letters of recommendation, interview. *Application deadlines:* 7/1 (freshmen), 8/15 (transfers). *Notification:* continuous until 10/15 (freshmen), continuous until 10/1 (transfers).

Freshman Application Contact Monica Emery, Director of Recruitment, St. Bonaventure University, 3261 West State Road, St. Bonaventure, NY 14778. *Phone:* 716-375-2400. *Toll-free phone:* 800-462-5050. *Fax:* 716-375-4005. *E-mail:* memery@sbu.edu. *Web site:* http://www.sbu.edu/.

See page 1542 for the College Close-Up.

St. Francis College

Brooklyn Heights, New York

Freshman Application Contact Office of Admissions, St. Francis College, 180 Remsen Street, Brooklyn Heights, NY 11201-4398. *Phone:* 718-489-5200. *Fax:* 718-802-0453. *E-mail:* mmichalski@stfranciscollege.edu. *Web site:* http://www.stfranciscollege.edu/.

See below for display ad and page 1544 for the College Close-Up.

St. John Fisher College

Rochester, New York

- **Independent** comprehensive, founded 1948, affiliated with Roman Catholic Church
- **Suburban** 154-acre campus
- **Endowment** $51.4 million
- **Coed** 2,871 undergraduate students, 93% full-time, 58% women, 42% men
- **Moderately difficult** entrance level, 66% of applicants were admitted

Undergraduates 2,672 full-time, 199 part-time. Students come from 19 states and territories; 6 other countries; 2% are from out of state; 4% Black or African American, non-Hispanic/Latino; 4% Hispanic/Latino; 2% Asian, non-Hispanic/Latino; 3% American Indian or Alaska Native, non-Hispanic/Latino; 0.8% Two or more races, non-Hispanic/Latino; 4% Race/ethnicity unknown; 0.2% international; 9% transferred in; 49% live on campus. *Retention:* 83% of full-time freshmen returned.

Freshmen *Admission:* 3,460 applied, 2,300 admitted, 555 enrolled. *Average high school GPA:* 3.5. *Test scores:* SAT critical reading scores over 500: 66%; SAT math scores over 500: 81%; SAT writing scores over 500: 58%; ACT scores over 18: 100%; SAT critical reading scores over 600: 19%; SAT math scores over 600: 29%; SAT writing scores over 600: 15%; ACT scores over 24: 59%; SAT critical reading scores over 700: 2%; SAT math scores over 700: 2%; SAT writing scores over 700: 1%; ACT scores over 30: 7%.

Faculty *Total:* 423, 51% full-time, 45% with terminal degrees. *Student/faculty ratio:* 11:1.

Academics *Calendar:* semesters. *Degrees:* certificates, bachelor's, master's, doctoral, post-master's, postbachelor's, and first professional certificates. *Special study options:* academic remediation for entering students, accelerated degree program, adult/continuing education programs, advanced placement credit, distance learning, double majors, honors programs, independent study, internships, off-campus study, part-time degree program, services for LD students, student-designed majors, study abroad, summer session for credit. *ROTC:* Army (c), Navy (c), Air Force (c). *Unusual degree programs:* 3-2 engineering with Clarkson University, Manhattan College, Rensselaer Polytechnic Institute, Columbia University, University of Detroit Mercy, University of Rochester, S.U.N.Y. at Buffalo.

Computers on Campus 550 computers/terminals and 1,875 ports are available on campus for general student use. Students can access the following: campus intranet, computer help desk, free student e-mail accounts, online

(class) grades, online (class) registration, online (class) schedules. Campus-wide network is available. 100% of college-owned or -operated housing units are wired for high-speed Internet access. Wireless service is available via entire campus.

Student Life *Housing options:* coed, women-only, disabled students. Campus housing is university owned. Freshman campus housing is guaranteed. *Activities and organizations:* drama/theater group, student-run newspaper, television station, choral group, student government, Student Activities Board, Commuter Council, Resident Student Association, Teddi Dance for Love. *Campus security:* 24-hour emergency response devices and patrols, late-night transport/escort service, controlled dormitory access. *Student services:* health clinic, personal/psychological counseling.

Athletics Member NCAA. All Division III. *Intercollegiate sports:* baseball M, basketball M/W, cross-country running M/W, field hockey W, football M, golf M/W, lacrosse M/W, soccer M/W, softball W, tennis M/W, track and field M/W, volleyball W. *Intramural sports:* basketball M/W, cheerleading W(c), crew M(c)/W(c), equestrian sports M(c)/W(c), ice hockey M(c)/W(c), rugby M(c)/W(c), soccer M/W, volleyball M.

Standardized Tests *Required:* SAT or ACT (for admission).

Costs (2011–12) *Comprehensive fee:* $36,770 includes full-time tuition ($25,790), mandatory fees ($470), and room and board ($10,510). Part-time tuition: $700 per credit hour. Part-time tuition and fees vary according to course load. *Required fees:* $25 per term part-time. *College room only:* $6810. Room and board charges vary according to board plan. *Payment plans:* installment, deferred payment. *Waivers:* employees or children of employees.

Financial Aid Of all full-time matriculated undergraduates who enrolled in 2011, 2,470 applied for aid, 2,223 were judged to have need, 897 had their need fully met. 1,362 Federal Work-Study jobs (averaging $1438). In 2011, 419 non-need-based awards were made. *Average percent of need met:* 81%. *Average financial aid package:* $19,708. *Average need-based loan:* $4764. *Average need-based gift aid:* $14,173. *Average non-need-based aid:* $8764. *Average indebtedness upon graduation:* $36,602.

Applying *Options:* electronic application, early decision, deferred entrance. *Application fee:* $30. *Required:* essay or personal statement, high school transcript, minimum 3.0 GPA, 1 letter of recommendation. *Recommended:* interview. *Application deadlines:* rolling (freshmen), rolling (transfers). *Early decision deadline:* 12/1. *Notification:* continuous until 12/1 (freshmen), continuous until 9/1 (transfers), 12/15 (early decision).

Freshman Application Contact Mrs. Stacy A. Ledermann, Director of Freshmen Admissions, St. John Fisher College, 3690 East Avenue, Rochester,

NY 14618. *Phone:* 585-385-8064. *Toll-free phone:* 800-444-4640. *Fax:* 585-385-8386. *E-mail:* admissions@sjfc.edu. *Web site:* http://www.sjfc.edu/.

See below for display ad and page 1548 for the College Close-Up.

St. John's University
Queens, New York

- **Independent** university, founded 1870, affiliated with Roman Catholic Church
- **Urban** 105-acre campus with easy access to New York City
- **Endowment** $359.5 million
- **Coed** 15,766 undergraduate students, 73% full-time, 54% women, 46% men
- **Moderately difficult** entrance level, 49% of applicants were admitted

Undergraduates 11,440 full-time, 4,326 part-time. Students come from 47 states and territories; 90 other countries; 28% are from out of state; 19% Black or African American, non-Hispanic/Latino; 16% Hispanic/Latino; 18% Asian, non-Hispanic/Latino; 0.4% Native Hawaiian or other Pacific Islander, non-Hispanic/Latino; 0.1% American Indian or Alaska Native, non-Hispanic/Latino; 3% Two or more races, non-Hispanic/Latino; 2% Race/ethnicity unknown; 5% international; 4% transferred in; 31% live on campus. *Retention:* 79% of full-time freshmen returned.

Freshmen *Admission:* 52,972 applied, 25,998 admitted, 2,763 enrolled. *Average high school GPA:* 3.2. *Test scores:* SAT critical reading scores over 500: 66%; SAT math scores over 500: 70%; ACT scores over 18: 99%; SAT critical reading scores over 600: 21%; SAT math scores over 600: 29%; ACT scores over 24: 54%; SAT critical reading scores over 700: 3%; SAT math scores over 700: 8%; ACT scores over 30: 14%.

Faculty *Total:* 1,490, 42% full-time, 53% with terminal degrees. *Student/faculty ratio:* 18:1.

Academics *Calendar:* semesters. *Degrees:* certificates, associate, bachelor's, master's, doctoral, post-master's, postbachelor's, and first professional certificates. *Special study options:* accelerated degree program, adult/continuing education programs, advanced placement credit, distance learning, double majors, English as a second language, honors programs, independent study, internships, off-campus study, part-time degree program, services for LD students, study abroad, summer session for credit. *ROTC:* Army (b). *Unusual degree programs:* 3-2 engineering with Manhattan College.

Computers on Campus 12,959 computers/terminals and 302 ports are available on campus for general student use. Students can access the following:

Teaching is what we do best.

St. John Fisher College in Rochester, NY, offers students access to an outstanding faculty—caring and competent men and women who help students develop critical-thinking skills, a foundation in the liberal arts, and proficiency in a major. Our goal is to help students reach their goals.

Visit our impressive campus and see for yourself!

ST. JOHN FISHER COLLEGE

www.sjfc.edu/freshman

campus intranet, computer help desk, free student e-mail accounts, online (class) grades, online (class) registration, online (class) schedules, various software packages. Campuswide network is available. 100% of college-owned or -operated housing units are wired for high-speed Internet access. Wireless service is available via entire campus.

Student Life *Housing options:* coed. Campus housing is university owned and leased by the school. Freshman applicants given priority for college housing. *Activities and organizations:* drama/theater group, student-run newspaper, radio and television station, choral group, Student Government, Incorporated, Student Programming Board, Haraya (Pan-African Students Coalition), American Pharmaceutical Association, Muslim Student Organization, national fraternities, national sororities. *Campus security:* 24-hour emergency response devices and patrols, student patrols, late-night transport/escort service, controlled dormitory access, Emergency Notification System. *Student services:* health clinic, personal/psychological counseling.

Athletics Member NCAA. All Division I. *Intercollegiate sports:* baseball M(s), basketball M(s)/W(s), cross-country running W(s), fencing M(s)/W(s), golf M(s)/W(s), lacrosse M(s), soccer M(s)/W(s), softball W(s), tennis M(s)/W(s), track and field W(s), volleyball W(s). *Intramural sports:* badminton M/W, basketball M/W, bowling M(c)/W(c), cheerleading M/W, fencing M/W, football M/W, racquetball M/W, soccer M/W, softball M/W, table tennis M/W, tennis M/W, ultimate Frisbee M/W, volleyball M(c)/W(c), weight lifting M/W.

Standardized Tests *Required:* SAT or ACT (for admission).

Costs (2011–12) *Comprehensive fee:* $48,175 includes full-time tuition ($33,125), mandatory fees ($750), and room and board ($14,300). Full-time tuition and fees vary according to course load, program, and student level. Part-time tuition: $1104 per credit. Part-time tuition and fees vary according to course load, program, and student level. *Required fees:* $278 per term part-time. *College room only:* $8900. Room and board charges vary according to board plan, housing facility, and location. *Payment plan:* installment. *Waivers:* senior citizens and employees or children of employees.

Financial Aid Of all full-time matriculated undergraduates who enrolled in 2010, 10,019 applied for aid, 9,534 were judged to have need, 902 had their need fully met. 945 Federal Work-Study jobs (averaging $2678). In 2010, 333 non-need-based awards were made. *Average percent of need met:* 62%. *Average financial aid package:* $24,655. *Average need-based loan:* $4801. *Average need-based gift aid:* $12,689. *Average non-need-based aid:* $11,917. *Average indebtedness upon graduation:* $35,451.

Applying *Options:* electronic application, early admission, deferred entrance. *Application fee:* $50. *Required:* high school transcript. *Required for some:* essay or personal statement, 2 letters of recommendation, interview. *Recommended:* essay or personal statement, minimum 3.0 GPA. *Application deadlines:* rolling (freshmen), rolling (out-of-state freshmen), rolling (transfers). *Notification:* continuous (freshmen), continuous (out-of-state freshmen), continuous (transfers).

Freshman Application Contact Mrs. Karen Vahey, Admission Director, St. John's University, 8000 Utopia Parkway, Queens, NY 11439. *Phone:* 718-990-2000. *Toll-free phone:* 888-9STJOHNS. *Fax:* 718-990-2096. *E-mail:* admhelp@stjohns.edu. *Web site:* http://www.stjohns.edu/.

St. Joseph's College, Long Island Campus

Patchogue, New York

- **Independent** comprehensive, founded 1916
- **Suburban** 51-acre campus with easy access to New York City
- **Endowment** $35.0 million
- **Coed** 3,778 undergraduate students, 80% full-time, 71% women, 29% men
- **Moderately difficult** entrance level, 78% of applicants were admitted

Undergraduates 3,020 full-time, 758 part-time. Students come from 8 states and territories; 2 other countries; 4% Black or African American, non-Hispanic/Latino; 8% Hispanic/Latino; 2% Asian, non-Hispanic/Latino; 0.1% Native Hawaiian or other Pacific Islander, non-Hispanic/Latino; 0.2% American Indian or Alaska Native, non-Hispanic/Latino; 2% Two or more races, non-Hispanic/Latino; 11% Race/ethnicity unknown; 13% transferred in. *Retention:* 89% of full-time freshmen returned.

Freshmen *Admission:* 1,425 applied, 1,116 admitted, 448 enrolled. *Average high school GPA:* 3.39. *Test scores:* SAT critical reading scores over 500: 69%; SAT math scores over 500: 72%; SAT writing scores over 500: 67%; ACT scores over 18: 98%; SAT critical reading scores over 600: 15%; SAT math scores over 600: 21%; SAT writing scores over 600: 15%; ACT scores over 24: 38%; SAT critical reading scores over 700: 1%; SAT math scores over 700: 2%; SAT writing scores over 700: 1%; ACT scores over 30: 1%.

Faculty *Total:* 435, 27% full-time, 30% with terminal degrees. *Student/faculty ratio:* 16:1.

Academics *Calendar:* 4-1-4. *Degrees:* certificates, bachelor's, master's, and postbachelor's certificates. *Special study options:* accelerated degree program,

adult/continuing education programs, advanced placement credit, cooperative education, distance learning, double majors, honors programs, independent study, internships, off-campus study, part-time degree program, services for LD students, study abroad, summer session for credit. *Unusual degree programs:* 3-2 business administration; math education.

Computers on Campus 257 computers/terminals are available on campus for general student use. Students can access the following: campus intranet, computer help desk, free student e-mail accounts, online (class) grades, online (class) registration, online (class) schedules. Campuswide network is available. Wireless service is available via classrooms, computer centers, computer labs, learning centers, libraries, student centers.

Student Life *Housing:* college housing not available. *Activities and organizations:* drama/theater group, student-run newspaper, choral group, Admissions Club, Science Club, Dramatics, Shild Study Club, Dance Team, national fraternities, national sororities. *Campus security:* 24-hour emergency response devices and patrols, late-night transport/escort service. *Student services:* health clinic, personal/psychological counseling.

Athletics Member NCAA. All Division III. *Intercollegiate sports:* baseball M, basketball M/W, cross-country running M/W, equestrian sports W, golf M, lacrosse W, soccer M/W, softball W, swimming and diving W, tennis M/W, track and field M/W, volleyball W. *Intramural sports:* cheerleading M(c)/W(c), equestrian sports M(c)/W(c), golf M(c)/W(c), lacrosse M(c).

Standardized Tests *Required:* SAT or ACT (for admission).

Costs (2011–12) *Tuition:* $17,800 full-time, $580 per credit hour part-time. Full-time tuition and fees vary according to course load, degree level, and program. Part-time tuition and fees vary according to course load, degree level, and program. *Required fees:* $625 full-time, $96 per semester part-time. *Payment plans:* installment, deferred payment. *Waivers:* senior citizens and employees or children of employees.

Financial Aid Of all full-time matriculated undergraduates who enrolled in 2011, 2,913 applied for aid, 2,383 were judged to have need, 540 had their need fully met. 79 Federal Work-Study jobs (averaging $2841). 129 state and other part-time jobs (averaging $4294). In 2011, 522 non-need-based awards were made. *Average percent of need met:* 68%. *Average financial aid package:* $11,725. *Average need-based loan:* $4071. *Average need-based gift aid:* $8262. *Average non-need-based aid:* $7530. *Average indebtedness upon graduation:* $24,793.

Applying *Options:* electronic application, early admission, deferred entrance. *Application fee:* $25. *Required:* essay or personal statement, high school transcript, minimum 2.8 GPA. *Recommended:* 2 letters of recommendation, interview. *Application deadlines:* 8/15 (freshmen), 8/15 (transfers). *Notification:* continuous until 11/1 (freshmen), continuous until 11/1 (transfers).

Freshman Application Contact Ms. Gigi Lamens, Associate Vice President for Enrollment Management, St. Joseph's College, Long Island Campus, 155 West Roe Boulevard, Patchogue, NY 11772-2399. *Phone:* 631-687-4500. *E-mail:* glamens@sjcny.edu. *Web site:* http://www.sjcny.edu/.

St. Joseph's College, New York

Brooklyn, New York

- **Independent** comprehensive, founded 1916
- **Urban** 5-acre campus
- **Endowment** $10.5 million
- **Coed** 1,261 undergraduate students, 75% full-time, 72% women, 28% men
- **Moderately difficult** entrance level, 72% of applicants were admitted

Undergraduates 943 full-time, 318 part-time. Students come from 14 states and territories; 14 other countries; 3% are from out of state; 32% Black or African American, non-Hispanic/Latino; 17% Hispanic/Latino; 6% Asian, non-Hispanic/Latino; 0.1% Native Hawaiian or other Pacific Islander, non-Hispanic/Latino; 0.3% American Indian or Alaska Native, non-Hispanic/Latino; 2% Two or more races, non-Hispanic/Latino; 6% Race/ethnicity unknown; 0.1% international; 11% transferred in; 1% live on campus. *Retention:* 82% of full-time freshmen returned.

Freshmen *Admission:* 1,012 applied, 732 admitted, 208 enrolled. *Average high school GPA:* 3.12. *Test scores:* SAT critical reading scores over 500: 41%; SAT math scores over 500: 46%; SAT writing scores over 500: 43%; ACT scores over 18: 82%; SAT critical reading scores over 600: 7%; SAT math scores over 600: 11%; SAT writing scores over 600: 9%; ACT scores over 24: 24%; SAT critical reading scores over 700: 1%; SAT writing scores over 700: 1%.

Faculty *Total:* 181, 33% full-time, 34% with terminal degrees. *Student/faculty ratio:* 11:1.

Academics *Calendar:* semesters. *Degrees:* certificates, bachelor's, master's, and postbachelor's certificates. *Special study options:* adult/continuing education programs, advanced placement credit, cooperative education, distance learning, double majors, honors programs, independent study, internships,

part-time degree program, study abroad, summer session for credit. *Unusual degree programs:* 3-2 business administration.

Computers on Campus 222 computers/terminals are available on campus for general student use. Students can access the following: campus intranet, computer help desk, free student e-mail accounts, online (class) grades, online (class) registration, online (class) schedules. Campuswide network is available. Wireless service is available via classrooms, computer centers, computer labs, learning centers, libraries, student centers.

Student Life *Housing:* college housing not available. *Options:* coed. Campus housing is leased by the school. *Activities and organizations:* drama/theater group, student-run newspaper, choral group, Admissions Club, Science Club, dramatics, Child Study Club, Dance Team, national fraternities, national sororities. *Campus security:* 24-hour emergency response devices and patrols, late-night transport/escort service, Emergency Notification System via cell phones. *Student services:* health clinic, personal/psychological counseling.

Athletics Member NCAA, USCAA. All Division III. *Intercollegiate sports:* baseball M, basketball M/W, cross-country running M/W, soccer M, softball W, swimming and diving W, tennis M/W, volleyball M/W. *Intramural sports:* basketball M/W, bowling M/W, golf M(c), soccer W(c), table tennis M/W, ultimate Frisbee M/W, wrestling M(c).

Standardized Tests *Required:* SAT or ACT (for admission).

Costs (2011–12) *Tuition:* $17,800 full-time, $580 per credit hour part-time. Full-time tuition and fees vary according to course load, degree level, and program. Part-time tuition and fees vary according to course load, degree level, and program. *Required fees:* $625 full-time, $96 per semester part-time. *Payment plans:* installment, deferred payment. *Waivers:* senior citizens and employees or children of employees.

Financial Aid Of all full-time matriculated undergraduates who enrolled in 2011, 898 applied for aid, 789 were judged to have need, 107 had their need fully met. 106 Federal Work-Study jobs (averaging $140). 20 state and other part-time jobs (averaging $1367). In 2011, 123 non-need-based awards were made. *Average percent of need met:* 65%. *Average financial aid package:* $13,600. *Average need-based loan:* $3720. *Average need-based gift aid:* $10,537. *Average non-need-based aid:* $8621. *Average indebtedness upon graduation:* $22,888.

Applying *Options:* electronic application, early admission, deferred entrance. *Application fee:* $25. *Required:* high school transcript, minimum 2.5 GPA. *Required for some:* interview. *Recommended:* essay or personal statement, 2 letters of recommendation. *Application deadlines:* 8/15 (freshmen), 8/15 (transfers).

Freshman Application Contact Mr. Michael Learmond, Director of Admissions Operation, St. Joseph's College, New York, 245 Clinton Avenue, Brooklyn, NY 11205-3688. *Phone:* 718-940-5828. *E-mail:* mlearmond@sjcny.edu. *Web site:* http://www.sjcny.edu/.

See below for display ad and page 1552 for the College Close-Up.

St. Lawrence University
Canton, New York

- **Independent** comprehensive, founded 1856
- **Small-town** 1000-acre campus
- **Endowment** $239.8 million
- **Coed** 2,361 undergraduate students, 99% full-time, 54% women, 46% men
- **Very difficult** entrance level, 43% of applicants were admitted

Undergraduates 2,335 full-time, 26 part-time. Students come from 40 states and territories; 45 other countries; 56% are from out of state; 3% Black or African American, non-Hispanic/Latino; 4% Hispanic/Latino; 1% Asian, non-Hispanic/Latino; 0.1% Native Hawaiian or other Pacific Islander, non-Hispanic/Latino; 0.3% American Indian or Alaska Native, non-Hispanic/Latino; 2% Two or more races, non-Hispanic/Latino; 1% Race/ethnicity unknown; 6% international; 0.7% transferred in; 97% live on campus. *Retention:* 90% of full-time freshmen returned.

Freshmen *Admission:* 4,273 applied, 1,855 admitted, 645 enrolled. *Average high school GPA:* 3.52. *Test scores:* SAT critical reading scores over 500: 97%; SAT math scores over 500: 97%; SAT writing scores over 500: 94%; ACT scores over 18: 99%; SAT critical reading scores over 600: 62%; SAT math scores over 600: 69%; SAT writing scores over 600: 62%; ACT scores over 24: 92%; SAT critical reading scores over 700: 12%; SAT math scores over 700: 9%; SAT writing scores over 700: 12%; ACT scores over 30: 22%.

Faculty *Total:* 192, 89% full-time, 91% with terminal degrees. *Student/faculty ratio:* 12:1.

Academics *Calendar:* semesters. *Degrees:* bachelor's, master's, and post-master's certificates. *Special study options:* advanced placement credit, double majors, independent study, internships, off-campus study, part-time degree program, services for LD students, student-designed majors, study abroad, summer session for credit. *ROTC:* Army (c), Air Force (c). *Unusual degree programs:* 3-2 business administration with Clarkson University, Union College, Rochester Institute of Technology; engineering with Columbia University, Clarkson University, Rensselaer Polytechnic Institute, University of

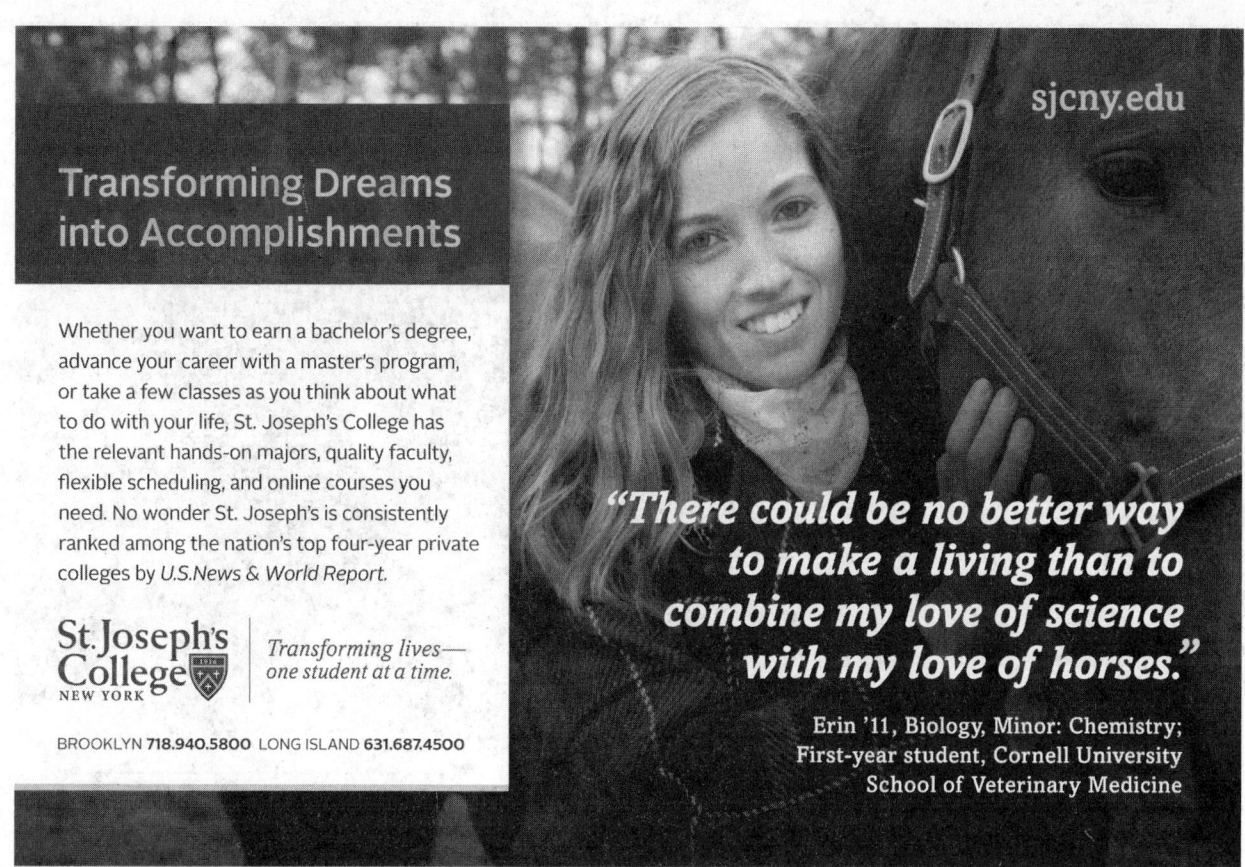

Rochester, University of Southern California; nursing with New York University; physician assistant program at Clarkson University, early assurance program for medical school at Syracuse, SUNY Buffalo, SUNY Buffalo School of Dentistry.

Computers on Campus 681 computers/terminals are available on campus for general student use. Students can access the following: computer help desk, free student e-mail accounts, online (class) grades, online (class) registration, online (class) schedules. Campuswide network is available. 100% of college-owned or -operated housing units are wired for high-speed Internet access. Wireless service is available via entire campus.

Student Life *Housing:* on-campus residence required through senior year. *Options:* coed, women-only, disabled students. Campus housing is university owned. Freshman campus housing is guaranteed. *Activities and organizations:* drama/theater group, student-run newspaper, radio station, choral group, Outing Club, student newspaper, student government, Circle K, Habitat for Humanity, national fraternities, national sororities. *Campus security:* 24-hour emergency response devices and patrols, student patrols, late-night transport/escort service, controlled dormitory access. *Student services:* health clinic, personal/psychological counseling, women's center.

Athletics Member NCAA. All Division III except men's and women's ice hockey (Division I). *Intercollegiate sports:* baseball M, basketball M/W, crew M/W, cross-country running M/W, equestrian sports M/W, field hockey W, football M, golf M/W, ice hockey M(s)/W(s), lacrosse M/W, skiing (cross-country) M/W, skiing (downhill) M/W, soccer M/W, softball W, squash M/W, swimming and diving M/W, tennis M/W, track and field M/W, volleyball W. *Intramural sports:* basketball M/W, football M, ice hockey M/W, skiing (cross-country) M/W, soccer M/W, softball W, ultimate Frisbee M/W, volleyball M/W.

Costs (2011–12) *Comprehensive fee:* $53,730 includes full-time tuition ($42,420), mandatory fees ($305), and room and board ($11,005). *College room only:* $5925. Room and board charges vary according to board plan. *Payment plan:* installment. *Waivers:* employees or children of employees.

Financial Aid Of all full-time matriculated undergraduates who enrolled in 2011, 1,696 applied for aid, 1,504 were judged to have need, 565 had their need fully met. 875 Federal Work-Study jobs (averaging $1569). 353 state and other part-time jobs (averaging $1536). In 2011, 504 non-need-based awards were made. *Average percent of need met:* 89%. *Average financial aid package:* $37,945. *Average need-based loan:* $4541. *Average need-based gift aid:* $28,278. *Average non-need-based aid:* $17,381. *Average indebtedness upon graduation:* $26,270. *Financial aid deadline:* 2/1.

Applying *Options:* electronic application, early admission, early decision, deferred entrance. *Application fee:* $60. *Required:* essay or personal statement, high school transcript, 2 letters of recommendation. *Recommended:* minimum 2.0 GPA, interview. *Application deadlines:* 2/1 (freshmen), 4/1 (transfers). *Early decision deadline:* 11/15. *Notification:* 3/31 (freshmen), 5/1 (transfers), 12/15 (early decision).

Freshman Application Contact Mr. Jeffery Rickey, Vice President and Dean of Admissions and Financial Aid, St. Lawrence University, 23 Romoda Drive, Canton, NY 13617-1455. *Phone:* 315-229-5261. *Toll-free phone:* 800-285-1856. *Fax:* 315-229-5818. *E-mail:* jrickey@stlawu.edu. *Web site:* http://www.stlawu.edu/.

See below for display ad and page 1556 for the College Close-Up.

St. Thomas Aquinas College
Sparkill, New York

- **Independent** comprehensive, founded 1952
- **Suburban** 46-acre campus with easy access to New York City
- **Endowment** $23.1 million
- **Coed** 1,843 undergraduate students, 69% full-time, 55% women, 45% men
- **Moderately difficult** entrance level, 81% of applicants were admitted

Undergraduates 1,277 full-time, 566 part-time. Students come from 14 states and territories; 8 other countries; 16% are from out of state; 6% Black or African American, non-Hispanic/Latino; 15% Hispanic/Latino; 3% Asian, non-Hispanic/Latino; 0.3% American Indian or Alaska Native, non-Hispanic/Latino; 0.8% Two or more races, non-Hispanic/Latino; 8% Race/ethnicity unknown; 0.9% international; 5% transferred in; 30% live on campus. *Retention:* 76% of full-time freshmen returned.

Freshmen *Admission:* 1,669 applied, 1,350 admitted, 304 enrolled. *Average high school GPA:* 3.23. *Test scores:* SAT critical reading scores over 500: 33%; SAT math scores over 500: 37%; SAT writing scores over 500: 33%; ACT scores over 18: 77%; SAT critical reading scores over 600: 9%; SAT math scores over 600: 10%; SAT writing scores over 600: 7%; ACT scores over 24: 20%; SAT critical reading scores over 700: 1%; SAT math scores over 700: 1%; SAT writing scores over 700: 1%; ACT scores over 30: 4%.

Faculty *Total:* 129, 50% full-time, 47% with terminal degrees. *Student/faculty ratio:* 18:1.

Academics *Calendar:* semesters. *Degrees:* associate, bachelor's, master's, post-master's, and postbachelor's certificates. *Special study options:* academic

remediation for entering students, accelerated degree program, adult/continuing education programs, advanced placement credit, double majors, freshman honors college, honors programs, independent study, internships, off-campus study, part-time degree program, services for LD students, study abroad, summer session for credit. *ROTC:* Air Force (c). *Unusual degree programs:* 3-2 engineering with George Washington University, Manhattan College; social work with New York University School of Social Work; physical therapy with New York Medical College.

Computers on Campus 200 computers/terminals are available on campus for general student use. Students can access the following: campus intranet, computer help desk, free student e-mail accounts, online (class) grades, online (class) registration, online (class) schedules. Campuswide network is available. 100% of college-owned or -operated housing units are wired for high-speed Internet access. Wireless service is available via entire campus.

Student Life *Housing options:* men-only, women-only, disabled students. Campus housing is university owned. Freshman campus housing is guaranteed. *Activities and organizations:* drama/theater group, student-run newspaper, radio station, choral group, Spartan Volunteers, Campus Activities Board, WSTK campus radio, Bowling Club, Laetare Players, national fraternities. *Campus security:* 24-hour emergency response devices and patrols, student patrols, late-night transport/escort service, controlled dormitory access. *Student services:* health clinic, personal/psychological counseling.

Athletics Member NCAA, NAIA. All NCAA Division II. *Intercollegiate sports:* baseball M(s), basketball M(s)/W(s), cross-country running M(s)/W(s), golf M/W, lacrosse W, soccer M(s)/W(s), softball W(s), tennis M/W, volleyball W(s). *Intramural sports:* basketball M/W, volleyball M/W.

Standardized Tests *Required:* SAT or ACT (for admission).

Costs (2011–12) *Comprehensive fee:* $34,370 includes full-time tuition ($23,220), mandatory fees ($500), and room and board ($10,650). Part-time tuition: $745 per credit hour. *College room only:* $2875. Room and board charges vary according to board plan and housing facility. *Payment plan:* installment. *Waivers:* employees or children of employees.

Applying *Options:* electronic application, early decision, early action, deferred entrance. *Application fee:* $30. *Required:* high school transcript, minimum 2.0 GPA. *Required for some:* 3 letters of recommendation. *Recommended:* essay or personal statement, 2 letters of recommendation, interview. *Application deadlines:* rolling (freshmen), rolling (transfers), 12/15 (early action). *Early decision deadline:* 12/1. *Notification:* 10/1 (freshmen), continuous (transfers), 1/15 (early decision), 1/15 (early action).

Freshman Application Contact Ms. Danielle Mac Kay, Director of Admissions, St. Thomas Aquinas College, 125 Route 340, Sparkill, NY 10976.

Phone: 845-398-4100. *Toll-free phone:* 800-999-STAC. *Fax:* 845-398-4114. *E-mail:* dmackay@stac.edu. *Web site:* http://www.stac.edu/.

See below for display ad and page 1568 for the College Close-Up.

Sarah Lawrence College
Bronxville, New York

- **Independent** comprehensive, founded 1926
- **Suburban** 44-acre campus with easy access to New York City
- **Coed** 1,413 undergraduate students, 97% full-time, 72% women, 28% men
- **Very difficult** entrance level, 61% of applicants were admitted

Undergraduates 1,369 full-time, 44 part-time. 78% are from out of state; 4% Black or African American, non-Hispanic/Latino; 8% Hispanic/Latino; 7% Asian, non-Hispanic/Latino; 0.7% Native Hawaiian or other Pacific Islander, non-Hispanic/Latino; 0.6% American Indian or Alaska Native, non-Hispanic/Latino; 4% Race/ethnicity unknown; 6% international; 3% transferred in; 85% live on campus. *Retention:* 89% of full-time freshmen returned.

Freshmen *Admission:* 2,012 applied, 1,225 admitted, 374 enrolled. *Average high school GPA:* 3.6.

Faculty *Total:* 311, 35% full-time. *Student/faculty ratio:* 9:1.

Academics *Calendar:* semesters. *Degrees:* bachelor's, master's, and post-master's certificates. *Special study options:* adult/continuing education programs, part-time degree program.

Computers on Campus Students can access the following: campus intranet, computer help desk, free student e-mail accounts. Campuswide network is available. 100% of college-owned or -operated housing units are wired for high-speed Internet access. Wireless service is available via classrooms, computer centers, computer labs, dorm rooms, libraries, student centers.

Student Life *Housing:* on-campus residence required for freshman year. *Options:* coed, men-only, women-only. Campus housing is university owned. Freshman campus housing is guaranteed. *Campus security:* 24-hour emergency response devices and patrols, late-night transport/escort service, controlled dormitory access.

Athletics *Intercollegiate sports:* basketball M, crew M/W, cross-country running M/W, equestrian sports M/W, soccer M, softball W, swimming and diving W, tennis M/W, volleyball W. *Intramural sports:* basketball W, cross-country running M(c)/W(c), fencing M(c)/W(c), soccer W(c), squash M(c)/W(c), swimming and diving M(c), ultimate Frisbee M/W.

Costs (2012–13) *Comprehensive fee:* $56,248 includes full-time tuition ($45,900), mandatory fees ($1024), and room and board ($9324). Full-time tuition and fees vary according to course load. Part-time tuition and fees vary according to course load. *College room only:* $4520. Room and board charges vary according to board plan. *Payment plan:* installment. *Waivers:* employees or children of employees.

Financial Aid Of all full-time matriculated undergraduates who enrolled in 2011, 1,051 applied for aid, 966 were judged to have need, 308 had their need fully met. 702 Federal Work-Study jobs (averaging $1603). 8 state and other part-time jobs (averaging $1688). In 2011, 52 non-need-based awards were made. *Average percent of need met:* 89%. *Average financial aid package:* $33,525. *Average need-based loan:* $4293. *Average need-based gift aid:* $31,076. *Average non-need-based aid:* $7910. *Average indebtedness upon graduation:* $18,360. *Financial aid deadline:* 2/1.

Applying *Options:* early admission, early decision, deferred entrance. *Required:* essay or personal statement, high school transcript, 3 letters of recommendation. *Recommended:* minimum 3.0 GPA, interview. *Application deadlines:* 1/1 (freshmen), 4/1 (transfers). *Early decision deadline:* 11/1 (for plan 1), 1/1 (for plan 2). *Notification:* 4/1 (freshmen), 5/1 (transfers), 12/15 (early decision plan 1), 2/15 (early decision plan 2).

Freshman Application Contact Mr. Stephen M. Schierloh, Director of Admission, Sarah Lawrence College, 1 Mead Way, Bronxville, NY 10708-5999. *Phone:* 914-395-2510. *Toll-free phone:* 800-888-2858. *Fax:* 914-395-2515. *E-mail:* slcadmit@sarahlawrence.edu. *Web site:* http://www.sarahlawrence.edu/.

School of Visual Arts

New York, New York

- **Proprietary** comprehensive, founded 1947
- **Urban** 1-acre campus
- **Coed**
- **Moderately difficult** entrance level

Faculty *Student/faculty ratio:* 10:1.

Academics *Calendar:* semesters. *Degrees:* bachelor's and master's.

Student Life *Campus security:* 24-hour patrols.

Standardized Tests *Required:* SAT or ACT (for admission).

Costs (2011–12) *Comprehensive fee:* $45,250 includes full-time tuition ($29,550) and room and board ($15,700). Part-time tuition: $985 per credit hour. *College room only:* $12,800. Room and board charges vary according to housing facility.

Financial Aid *Of all full-time matriculated undergraduates who enrolled in 2010,* 2,060 applied for aid, 1,877 were judged to have need, 14 had their need fully met. *In 2010,* 240 non-need-based awards were made. *Average percent of need met:* 38. *Average financial aid package:* $13,361. *Average need-based loan:* $4593. *Average need-based gift aid:* $9468. *Average non-need-based aid:* $7545. *Average indebtedness upon graduation:* $41,495. *Financial aid deadline:* 3/1.

Applying *Options:* electronic application, deferred entrance. *Application fee:* $50. *Required:* essay or personal statement, high school transcript, minimum 2.5 GPA, portfolio. *Recommended:* interview.

Freshman Application Contact Admissions Office, School of Visual Arts, 209 East 23rd Street, New York, NY 10010. *Phone:* 212-592-2100. *Toll-free phone:* 800-436-4204. *Fax:* 212-592-2116. *E-mail:* admissions@sva.edu. *Web site:* http://www.sva.edu/.

Sh'or Yoshuv Rabbinical College

Lawrence, New York

Director of Admissions Rabbi Moshe Rubin, Registrar, Sh'or Yoshuv Rabbinical College, 1 Cedarlawn Avenue, Lawrence, NY 11559-1714. *Phone:* 516-239-9002 Ext. 124. *Fax:* 516-977-1282. *E-mail:* mrubin@shoryoshuv.org. *Web site:* http://www.shoryoshuv.org/.

Siena College

Loudonville, New York

- **Independent Roman Catholic** comprehensive, founded 1937
- **Suburban** 175-acre campus
- **Endowment** $131.9 million
- **Coed** 3,292 undergraduate students, 95% full-time, 52% women, 48% men
- **Moderately difficult** entrance level, 48% of applicants were admitted

Undergraduates 3,132 full-time, 160 part-time. Students come from 31 states and territories; 11 other countries; 18% are from out of state; 3% Black or Afri-

can American, non-Hispanic/Latino; 5% Hispanic/Latino; 3% Asian, non-Hispanic/Latino; 0.1% Native Hawaiian or other Pacific Islander, non-Hispanic/Latino; 0.2% American Indian or Alaska Native, non-Hispanic/Latino; 2% Two or more races, non-Hispanic/Latino; 1% Race/ethnicity unknown; 1% international; 4% transferred in; 79% live on campus. *Retention:* 85% of full-time freshmen returned.

Freshmen *Admission:* 9,723 applied, 4,714 admitted, 782 enrolled. *Average high school GPA:* 3.5. *Test scores:* SAT critical reading scores over 500: 81%; SAT math scores over 500: 88%; SAT writing scores over 500: 77%; ACT scores over 18: 99%; SAT critical reading scores over 600: 34%; SAT math scores over 600: 45%; SAT writing scores over 600: 28%; ACT scores over 24: 78%; SAT critical reading scores over 700: 3%; SAT math scores over 700: 7%; SAT writing scores over 700: 4%; ACT scores over 30: 7%.

Faculty *Total:* 353, 62% full-time, 72% with terminal degrees. *Student/faculty ratio:* 12:1.

Academics *Calendar:* semesters. *Degrees:* certificates, bachelor's, and master's. *Special study options:* accelerated degree program, advanced placement credit, double majors, English as a second language, honors programs, independent study, internships, off-campus study, part-time degree program, services for LD students, study abroad, summer session for credit. *ROTC:* Army (b), Navy (c), Air Force (c).

Computers on Campus 359 computers/terminals and 5,291 ports are available on campus for general student use. Students can access the following: campus intranet, computer help desk, free student e-mail accounts, online (class) grades, online (class) registration, online (class) schedules. Campus-wide network is available. 100% of college-owned or -operated housing units are wired for high-speed Internet access. Wireless service is available via classrooms, computer centers, computer labs, dorm rooms, learning centers, libraries, student centers.

Student Life *Housing:* on-campus residence required through senior year. *Options:* coed, disabled students. Campus housing is university owned. Freshman applicants given priority for college housing. *Activities and organizations:* drama/theater group, student-run newspaper, radio and television station, choral group, Dog Pound (sports spirit group), Mentoring Program, Outing Club, READ for the Stars, Accounting student Association, national fraternities, national sororities. *Campus security:* 24-hour emergency response devices and patrols, late-night transport/escort service, controlled dormitory access, call boxes in parking lots and on roadways. *Student services:* health clinic, personal/psychological counseling, women's center, legal services.

Athletics Member NCAA. All Division I. *Intercollegiate sports:* baseball M(s), basketball M(s)/W(s), cheerleading W(c), cross-country running M(s)/W(s), equestrian sports M(c)/W(c), field hockey W(s), golf M(s)/W(s), ice hockey M(c), lacrosse M(s)/W(s), rugby M(c)/W(c), soccer M(s)/W(s), softball W(s), squash M, swimming and diving W(s), tennis M(s)/W(s), track and field M(c)/W(c), volleyball M(c)/W(s), water polo W(s). *Intramural sports:* basketball M/W, cheerleading W, golf M, soccer M/W, softball M/W, volleyball M/W.

Standardized Tests *Required:* SAT or ACT (for admission).

Costs (2012–13) *One-time required fee:* $250. *Comprehensive fee:* $40,885 includes full-time tuition ($28,665), mandatory fees ($250), and room and board ($11,970). Full-time tuition and fees vary according to student level. Part-time tuition: $500 per credit. Part-time tuition and fees vary according to student level. *Required fees:* $500 per credit part-time, $60 per term part-time. *College room only:* $7055. Room and board charges vary according to board plan and housing facility. *Payment plan:* installment. *Waivers:* employees or children of employees.

Financial Aid Of all full-time matriculated undergraduates who enrolled in 2010, 2,641 applied for aid, 2,271 were judged to have need, 335 had their need fully met. 500 Federal Work-Study jobs (averaging $712). In 2010, 223 non-need-based awards were made. *Average percent of need met:* 70%. *Average financial aid package:* $18,100. *Average need-based loan:* $4622. *Average need-based gift aid:* $13,800. *Average non-need-based aid:* $6900. *Average indebtedness upon graduation:* $29,700.

Applying *Options:* electronic application, early admission, early decision, early action, deferred entrance. *Application fee:* $50. *Required:* essay or personal statement, high school transcript, 1 letter of recommendation. *Required for some:* interview. *Recommended:* interview. *Application deadlines:* 2/15 (freshmen), 8/15 (transfers), 12/1 (early action). *Early decision deadline:* 12/1. *Notification:* 3/15 (freshmen), continuous (transfers), 12/15 (early decision), 1/1 (early action).

Freshman Application Contact Ms. Heather Renault, Director of Admissions, Siena College, 515 Loudon Road, Loudonville, NY 12211-1462. *Phone:* 518-783-2426. *Toll-free phone:* 888-AT-SIENA. *Fax:* 518-783-2436. *E-mail:* admit@siena.edu. *Web site:* http://www.siena.edu/.

Skidmore College
Saratoga Springs, New York

- **Independent** comprehensive, founded 1903
- **Small-town** 800-acre campus with easy access to Albany, NY
- **Coed** 2,689 undergraduate students, 98% full-time, 61% women, 39% men
- **Very difficult** entrance level, 42% of applicants were admitted

Undergraduates 2,648 full-time, 41 part-time. Students come from 47 states and territories; 51 other countries; 66% are from out of state; 3% Black or African American, non-Hispanic/Latino; 7% Hispanic/Latino; 5% Asian, non-Hispanic/Latino; 0.3% Native Hawaiian or other Pacific Islander, non-Hispanic/Latino; 5% Two or more races, non-Hispanic/Latino; 7% Race/ethnicity unknown; 4% international; 1% transferred in; 85% live on campus. *Retention:* 95% of full-time freshmen returned.

Freshmen *Admission:* 5,780 applied, 2,431 admitted, 663 enrolled. *Test scores:* SAT critical reading scores over 500: 91%; SAT math scores over 500: 95%; SAT writing scores over 500: 95%; ACT scores over 18: 100%; SAT critical reading scores over 600: 66%; SAT math scores over 600: 68%; SAT writing scores over 600: 69%; ACT scores over 24: 92%; SAT critical reading scores over 700: 19%; SAT math scores over 700: 16%; SAT writing scores over 700: 21%; ACT scores over 30: 34%.

Faculty *Total:* 339, 70% full-time, 73% with terminal degrees. *Student/faculty ratio:* 9:1.

Academics *Calendar:* semesters plus optional 6-week internship period. *Degrees:* bachelor's and master's. *Special study options:* accelerated degree program, adult/continuing education programs, advanced placement credit, double majors, honors programs, independent study, internships, off-campus study, services for LD students, student-designed majors, study abroad, summer session for credit. *ROTC:* Army (c), Air Force (c). *Unusual degree programs:* 3-2 business administration with Clarkson University, Union College; engineering with Dartmouth College, Clarkson University; nursing with New York University.

Computers on Campus 600 computers/terminals are available on campus for general student use. Students can access the following: campus intranet, computer help desk, free student e-mail accounts, online (class) grades, online (class) registration, online (class) schedules. Campuswide network is available. 100% of college-owned or -operated housing units are wired for high-speed Internet access. Wireless service is available via classrooms, computer centers, computer labs, dorm rooms, learning centers, libraries, student centers.

Student Life *Housing:* on-campus residence required through sophomore year. *Options:* coed, women-only, disabled students. Campus housing is university owned. Freshman campus housing is guaranteed. *Activities and organizations:* drama/theater group, student-run newspaper, radio and television station, choral group, Student Government Association, student radio station, Student Volunteer Bureau, Outing Club, Skidmore News. *Campus security:* 24-hour emergency response devices and patrols, late-night transport/escort service, controlled dormitory access, well-lit campus. *Student services:* health clinic, personal/psychological counseling.

Athletics Member NCAA. All Division III. *Intercollegiate sports:* baseball M, basketball M/W, crew M/W, equestrian sports W, field hockey W, golf M, ice hockey M, lacrosse M/W, soccer M/W, softball W, swimming and diving M/W, tennis M/W, volleyball W. *Intramural sports:* basketball M/W, football M/W, racquetball M/W, soccer M/W, softball M/W, tennis M/W, volleyball M/W.

Standardized Tests *Required:* SAT or ACT (for admission). *Recommended:* SAT Subject Tests (for admission).

Costs (2011–12) *Comprehensive fee:* $53,684 includes full-time tuition ($41,520), mandatory fees ($860), and room and board ($11,304). Full-time tuition and fees vary according to course load. Part-time tuition: $1384 per credit. Part-time tuition and fees vary according to course load. *Required fees:* $25 per term part-time. *College room only:* $6684. Room and board charges vary according to board plan and housing facility. *Payment plans:* tuition prepayment, installment. *Waivers:* senior citizens and employees or children of employees.

Financial Aid Of all full-time matriculated undergraduates who enrolled in 2011, 1,309 applied for aid, 1,238 were judged to have need, 1,100 had their need fully met. In 2011, 35 non-need-based awards were made. *Average percent of need met:* 93%. *Average financial aid package:* $33,400. *Average need-based loan:* $4211. *Average need-based gift aid:* $31,789. *Average non-need-based aid:* $10,000. *Average indebtedness upon graduation:* $21,000. *Financial aid deadline:* 2/1.

Applying *Options:* electronic application, early admission, early decision, deferred entrance. *Application fee:* $65. *Required:* essay or personal statement, high school transcript, 2 letters of recommendation. *Recommended:* interview. *Application deadlines:* 1/15 (freshmen), 4/1 (transfers). *Early decision deadline:* 11/15 (for plan 1), 1/15 (for plan 2). *Notification:* 4/1 (freshmen), 12/15 (early decision plan 1), 2/15 (early decision plan 2).

Freshman Application Contact Ms. Mary Lou Bates, Dean of Admissions and Financial Aid, Skidmore College, 815 North Broadway, Saratoga Springs, NY 12866-1632. *Phone:* 518-580-5570. *Toll-free phone:* 800-867-6007. *Fax:* 518-580-5584. *E-mail:* admissions@skidmore.edu. *Web site:* http://www.skidmore.edu/.

See page 626 for display ad and page 1586 for the College Close-Up.

State University of New York at Binghamton
Binghamton, New York

- **State-supported** university, founded 1946, part of State University of New York System
- **Suburban** 930-acre campus
- **Endowment** $64.1 million
- **Coed** 11,861 undergraduate students, 97% full-time, 47% women, 53% men
- **Very difficult** entrance level, 41% of applicants were admitted

Undergraduates 11,464 full-time, 397 part-time. Students come from 43 states and territories; 93 other countries; 13% are from out of state; 5% Black or African American, non-Hispanic/Latino; 9% Hispanic/Latino; 13% Asian, non-Hispanic/Latino; 0.1% Native Hawaiian or other Pacific Islander, non-Hispanic/Latino; 0.1% American Indian or Alaska Native, non-Hispanic/Latino; 1% Two or more races, non-Hispanic/Latino; 10% Race/ethnicity unknown; 10% international; 7% transferred in; 61% live on campus. *Retention:* 91% of full-time freshmen returned.

Freshmen *Admission:* 28,101 applied, 11,440 admitted, 2,516 enrolled. *Average high school GPA:* 3.6. *Test scores:* SAT critical reading scores over 500: 98%; SAT math scores over 500: 100%; SAT writing scores over 500: 99%; ACT scores over 18: 100%; SAT critical reading scores over 600: 75%; SAT math scores over 600: 87%; SAT writing scores over 600: 78%; ACT scores over 24: 98%; SAT critical reading scores over 700: 18%; SAT math scores over 700: 33%; SAT writing scores over 700: 23%; ACT scores over 30: 41%.

Faculty *Total:* 848, 68% full-time. *Student/faculty ratio:* 20:1.

Academics *Calendar:* semesters. *Degrees:* bachelor's, master's, doctoral, post-master's, and first professional certificates. *Special study options:* accelerated degree program, adult/continuing education programs, advanced placement credit, distance learning, double majors, English as a second language, honors programs, independent study, internships, off-campus study, part-time degree program, services for LD students, student-designed majors, study abroad, summer session for credit. *ROTC:* Army (c), Air Force (c). *Unusual degree programs:* 3-2 business administration; engineering; anthropology; art history; Asian & Asian American studies; biology; chemistry; computer science; economics; education; French; geography; geology; Italian; mathematics; materials science; philosophy, politics, & law; physics; political science; public administration; Spanish; systems science;theatre.

Computers on Campus 1,190 computers/terminals and 40,000 ports are available on campus for general student use. Students can access the following: campus intranet, computer help desk, free student e-mail accounts, online (class) grades, online (class) registration, online (class) schedules, course management system, personal Web space, wiki, virtual desktop. Campuswide network is available. 100% of college-owned or -operated housing units are wired for high-speed Internet access. Wireless service is available via entire campus.

Student Life *Housing:* on-campus residence required for freshman year. *Options:* coed, disabled students. Campus housing is university owned and is provided by a third party. Freshman campus housing is guaranteed. *Activities and organizations:* drama/theater group, student-run newspaper, radio and television station, choral group, intramurals, club sports, Student Association, cultural organizations, Peer Counseling/Mentoring/Volunteering Program, national fraternities, national sororities. *Campus security:* 24-hour emergency response devices and patrols, student patrols, late-night transport/escort service, controlled dormitory access, safety programs, well-lit campus, self-defense education, secured campus entrance 12 am-5 am, emergency phones, emergency text messages. *Student services:* health clinic, personal/psychological counseling, women's center, legal services.

Athletics Member NCAA. All Division I. *Intercollegiate sports:* baseball M(s), basketball M(s)/W(s), cross-country running M(s)/W(s), golf M(s), lacrosse M(s)/W(s), soccer M(s)/W(s), softball W(s), swimming and diving M(s)/W(s), tennis M(s)/W(s), track and field M(s)/W(s), volleyball W(s), wrestling M(s). *Intramural sports:* badminton M(c)/W(c), baseball M(c), basketball M/W, bowling M/W, cheerleading M/W, crew M(c)/W(c), cross-country running M(c)/W(c), equestrian sports M(c)/W(c), fencing M(c)/W(c), field hockey M(c)/W(c), golf M(c)/W(c), gymnastics M(c)/W(c), ice hockey M(c)/W(c), lacrosse M(c)/W(c), racquetball M/W, rugby M(c)/W(c), skiing (downhill) M(c)/W(c), soccer M/W, softball M/W, swimming and diving M(c)/W(c), table tennis M(c)/W(c), tennis M/W, ultimate Frisbee M(c)/W(c), volleyball M/W, water polo M(c)/W(c).

SKIDMORE
C O L L E G E

"**Creative Thought Matters** *actually* has *sentimental* value to *me*. I asked my *Mother* if she remembered **THE SLOGAN** from SKIDMORE, **Creative Thought Matters**. She answered as if it was the **stupidest** question I'd ever asked, '*Of course! It's why you went to Skidmore.*'"

2008 Skidmore graduate

"**Creative Thought Matters** is *more* than just a **theme** for me. It really **captures** what makes SKIDMORE *unique....* SKIDMORE understands that learning does not (*and should not*) *exist* in neat little **silos,** which I think helps GRADUATES **thrive** in a **complex,** INTERCONNECTED WORLD."

2007 Skidmore graduate

Skidmore College Office of Admissions
Saratoga Springs, New York
www.skidmore.edu

Creative Thought Matters

Standardized Tests *Required:* SAT or ACT (for admission).

Costs (2011–12) *Tuition:* state resident $5270 full-time, $220 per credit hour part-time; nonresident $13,380 full-time, $558 per credit hour part-time. Full-time tuition and fees vary according to program. Part-time tuition and fees vary according to course load and program. *Required fees:* $1946 full-time, $85 per credit hour part-time, $24 per term part-time. *Room and board:* $11,810; room only: $7528. Room and board charges vary according to board plan and housing facility.

Financial Aid Of all full-time matriculated undergraduates who enrolled in 2011, 7,822 applied for aid, 5,668 were judged to have need, 689 had their need fully met. 331 Federal Work-Study jobs (averaging $1451). In 2011, 237 non-need-based awards were made. *Average percent of need met:* 72%. *Average financial aid package:* $11,582. *Average need-based loan:* $5515. *Average need-based gift aid:* $6779. *Average non-need-based aid:* $6335. *Average indebtedness upon graduation:* $22,634.

Applying *Options:* electronic application, early admission, early action, deferred entrance. *Application fee:* $50. *Required:* essay or personal statement, high school transcript, 1 letter of recommendation. *Required for some:* portfolio, audition. *Application deadlines:* 1/15 (freshmen), 1/15 (out-of-state freshmen), rolling (transfers), 11/15 (early action). *Notification:* 4/1 (freshmen), 4/1 (out-of-state freshmen), continuous (transfers), 1/15 (early action).

Freshman Application Contact Sandra Starke, Vice Provost for Enrollment Management, State University of New York at Binghamton, Binghamton University, PO Box 6001, Binghamton, NY 13902-6001. *Phone:* 607-777-2171. *Fax:* 607-777-4445. *E-mail:* admit@binghamton.edu. *Web site:* http://www.binghamton.edu/.

State University of New York at Fredonia
Fredonia, New York

- **State-supported** comprehensive, founded 1826, part of State University of New York System
- **Small-town** 249-acre campus with easy access to Buffalo
- **Endowment** $24.0 million
- **Coed** 5,393 undergraduate students, 97% full-time, 56% women, 44% men
- **Moderately difficult** entrance level, 50% of applicants were admitted

Undergraduates 5,242 full-time, 151 part-time. Students come from 27 states and territories; 14 other countries; 2% are from out of state; 3% Black or African American, non-Hispanic/Latino; 4% Hispanic/Latino; 1% Asian, non-Hispanic/Latino; 0.1% Native Hawaiian or other Pacific Islander, non-Hispanic/Latino; 0.5% American Indian or Alaska Native, non-Hispanic/Latino; 1% Two or more races, non-Hispanic/Latino; 4% Race/ethnicity unknown; 1% international; 9% transferred in; 53% live on campus. *Retention:* 83% of full-time freshmen returned.

Freshmen *Admission:* 6,696 applied, 3,319 admitted, 1,124 enrolled. *Average high school GPA:* 3.4. *Test scores:* SAT critical reading scores over 500: 65%; SAT math scores over 500: 71%; ACT scores over 18: 97%; SAT critical reading scores over 600: 19%; SAT math scores over 600: 22%; ACT scores over 24: 53%; SAT critical reading scores over 700: 1%; SAT math scores over 700: 1%; ACT scores over 30: 6%.

Faculty *Total:* 482, 52% full-time, 54% with terminal degrees. *Student/faculty ratio:* 17:1.

Academics *Calendar:* semesters. *Degrees:* bachelor's, master's, and post-master's certificates. *Special study options:* accelerated degree program, adult/continuing education programs, advanced placement credit, distance learning, double majors, honors programs, independent study, internships, off-campus study, part-time degree program, services for LD students, student-designed majors, study abroad, summer session for credit. *Unusual degree programs:* 3-2 business administration with Clarkson University, State University of New York at Buffalo, University of Pittsburgh; engineering with Clarkson University, State University of New York at Buffalo, Case Western Reserve, Columbia University, Cornell University, Louisiana Technical University, New York State College of Ceramics at Alfred, Ohio State University.

Computers on Campus 500 computers/terminals are available on campus for general student use. Students can access the following: campus intranet, computer help desk, free student e-mail accounts, online (class) grades, online (class) registration, online (class) schedules. Campuswide network is available. 100% of college-owned or -operated housing units are wired for high-speed Internet access. Wireless service is available via entire campus.

Student Life *Housing:* on-campus residence required through sophomore year. *Options:* coed, men-only, women-only. Campus housing is university owned. Freshman campus housing is guaranteed. *Activities and organizations:* drama/theater group, student-run newspaper, radio and television station, choral group, Student Association, Undergraduate Alumni Council, Communication Club, ethnic organizations, spectrum entertainment board, national fraternities,

national sororities. *Campus security:* 24-hour emergency response devices and patrols, late-night transport/escort service, controlled dormitory access. *Student services:* health clinic, personal/psychological counseling, legal services.

Athletics Member NCAA. All Division III. *Intercollegiate sports:* baseball M, basketball M/W, cheerleading M/W, cross-country running M/W, field hockey M(c)/W(c), ice hockey M, lacrosse W, soccer M/W, softball W, swimming and diving M/W, tennis M/W, track and field M/W, volleyball M/W. *Intramural sports:* basketball M/W, cross-country running M/W, ice hockey M(c), lacrosse M, racquetball M/W, rock climbing M/W, rugby M(c)/W(c), skiing (cross-country) M/W, skiing (downhill) M/W, soccer M/W, softball W, squash M/W, tennis M/W, ultimate Frisbee M/W, volleyball M(c)/W, water polo M/W.

Standardized Tests *Required:* SAT or ACT (for admission).

Costs (2011–12) *Tuition:* state resident $5270 full-time, $220 per credit hour part-time; nonresident $14,320 full-time, $597 per credit hour part-time. Full-time tuition and fees vary according to course load and program. Part-time tuition and fees vary according to course load and program. *Required fees:* $1418 full-time, $59 per credit hour part-time. *Room and board:* $10,290; room only: $6250. Room and board charges vary according to board plan and housing facility. *Payment plan:* installment.

Financial Aid Of all full-time matriculated undergraduates who enrolled in 2011, 4,482 applied for aid, 3,538 were judged to have need, 208 had their need fully met. 241 Federal Work-Study jobs (averaging $1467). In 2011, 264 non-need-based awards were made. *Average percent of need met:* 61%. *Average financial aid package:* $9323. *Average need-based loan:* $4892. *Average need-based gift aid:* $4494. *Average non-need-based aid:* $2227. *Average indebtedness upon graduation:* $26,192.

Applying *Options:* electronic application, early admission, early decision, deferred entrance. *Application fee:* $50. *Required:* essay or personal statement, high school transcript, 1 letter of recommendation. *Required for some:* interview, Audition for music, dance and theater programs: portfolio for visual arts and technical theatre programs. *Application deadlines:* rolling (freshmen), rolling (transfers). *Early decision deadline:* 11/1. *Notification:* continuous (freshmen), continuous (transfers), 12/1 (early decision).

Freshman Application Contact Office of Admissions, State University of New York at Fredonia, 178 Central Avenue, Fredonia, NY 14063. *Phone:* 716-673-3251. *Toll-free phone:* 800-252-1212. *Fax:* 716-673-3249. *E-mail:* admissions@fredonia.edu. *Web site:* http://www.fredonia.edu/.

State University of New York at New Paltz

New Paltz, New York

- **State-supported** comprehensive, founded 1828, part of State University of New York System
- **Small-town** 216-acre campus
- **Coed** 6,814 undergraduate students, 92% full-time, 63% women, 37% men
- **Very difficult** entrance level, 40% of applicants were admitted

Undergraduates 6,301 full-time, 513 part-time. Students come from 23 states and territories; 47 other countries; 4% are from out of state; 5% Black or African American, non-Hispanic/Latino; 12% Hispanic/Latino; 4% Asian, non-Hispanic/Latino; 0.1% Native Hawaiian or other Pacific Islander, non-Hispanic/Latino; 0.1% American Indian or Alaska Native, non-Hispanic/Latino; 2% Two or more races, non-Hispanic/Latino; 9% Race/ethnicity unknown; 4% international; 9% transferred in. *Retention:* 88% of full-time freshmen returned.

Freshmen *Admission:* 14,161 applied, 5,690 admitted, 1,162 enrolled. *Test scores:* SAT critical reading scores over 500: 83%; SAT math scores over 500: 87%; SAT writing scores over 500: 83%; ACT scores over 18: 98%; SAT critical reading scores over 600: 33%; SAT math scores over 600: 32%; SAT writing scores over 600: 32%; ACT scores over 24: 68%; SAT critical reading scores over 700: 4%; SAT math scores over 700: 2%; SAT writing scores over 700: 4%; ACT scores over 30: 3%.

Faculty *Total:* 650, 50% full-time, 55% with terminal degrees. *Student/faculty ratio:* 17:1.

Academics *Calendar:* semesters. *Degrees:* bachelor's, master's, and post-master's certificates. *Special study options:* academic remediation for entering students, adult/continuing education programs, advanced placement credit, cooperative education, distance learning, double majors, English as a second language, honors programs, independent study, internships, off-campus study, part-time degree program, services for LD students, student-designed majors, study abroad, summer session for credit. *Unusual degree programs:* 3-2 forestry with State University of New York College of Environmental Science and Forestry.

Computers on Campus Students can access the following: campus intranet, computer help desk, free student e-mail accounts, online (class) grades, online (class) registration, online (class) schedules. Campuswide network is available.

100% of college-owned or -operated housing units are wired for high-speed Internet access. Wireless service is available via classrooms, dorm rooms, libraries, student centers.

Student Life *Housing:* on-campus residence required for freshman year. *Options:* coed, men-only, women-only, disabled students. Campus housing is university owned. Freshman campus housing is guaranteed. *Activities and organizations:* drama/theater group, student-run newspaper, radio and television station, choral group, Student Association, Residence Hall Student Association, intramurals and club sports, Outing Club, national fraternities, national sororities. *Campus security:* 24-hour emergency response devices and patrols, late-night transport/escort service, controlled dormitory access, safety seminars, RAD Women's Self Defense. *Student services:* health clinic, personal/psychological counseling, legal services.

Athletics Member NCAA. All Division III. *Intercollegiate sports:* baseball M, basketball M/W, cross-country running M/W, equestrian sports W(c), fencing M(c)/W(c), field hockey W, ice hockey M(c), lacrosse M(c)/W, racquetball M(c)/W(c), rugby M(c)/W(c), skiing (cross-country) M/W, soccer M/W, softball W, squash W, swimming and diving M/W, tennis M/W, track and field M(c)/W(c), ultimate Frisbee M(c)/W(c), volleyball M/W. *Intramural sports:* badminton M/W, basketball M/W, cheerleading M(c)/W(c), field hockey M/W, golf M/W, racquetball M/W, soccer M/W, softball M/W, swimming and diving M(c)/W(c), tennis M/W, volleyball M/W.

Standardized Tests *Required:* SAT or ACT (for admission).

Costs (2011–12) *Tuition:* state resident $5270 full-time, $220 per credit hour part-time; nonresident $14,320 full-time, $597 per credit hour part-time. *Required fees:* $1188 full-time, $34 per credit hour part-time, $184 per term part-time. *Room and board:* $9950. Room and board charges vary according to board plan. *Payment plan:* installment.

Financial Aid Of all full-time matriculated undergraduates who enrolled in 2011, 4,721 applied for aid, 3,359 were judged to have need, 314 had their need fully met. 1,250 Federal Work-Study jobs (averaging $1000). 915 state and other part-time jobs (averaging $826). In 2011, 28 non-need-based awards were made. *Average percent of need met:* 58%. *Average financial aid package:* $9498. *Average need-based loan:* $4548. *Average need-based gift aid:* $4565. *Average non-need-based aid:* $2385. *Average indebtedness upon graduation:* $31,278.

Applying *Options:* electronic application, early admission, early action. *Application fee:* $50. *Required:* essay or personal statement, high school transcript, 1 letter of recommendation. *Required for some:* portfolio for art program, audition for music and theater programs. *Application deadlines:* 4/1 (freshmen), 4/1 (transfers), 11/15 (early action). *Notification:* continuous (freshmen), continuous (transfers), 12/15 (early action).

Freshman Application Contact Ms. Kimberly A. Strano, Director of Freshman Admissions, State University of New York at New Paltz, 1 Hawk Drive, New Paltz, NY 12561-2499. *Phone:* 845-257-3200. *Fax:* 845-257-3209. *E-mail:* admissions@newpaltz.edu. *Web site:* http://www.newpaltz.edu/.

State University of New York at Oswego

Oswego, New York

- **State-supported** comprehensive, founded 1861, part of State University of New York System
- **Small-town** 696-acre campus with easy access to Syracuse
- **Endowment** $11.5 million
- **Coed** 7,379 undergraduate students, 95% full-time, 52% women, 48% men
- **Moderately difficult** entrance level, 48% of applicants were admitted

Undergraduates 6,992 full-time, 387 part-time. Students come from 27 states and territories; 13 other countries; 2% are from out of state; 5% Black or African American, non-Hispanic/Latino; 6% Hispanic/Latino; 2% Asian, non-Hispanic/Latino; 0.1% Native Hawaiian or other Pacific Islander, non-Hispanic/Latino; 0.3% American Indian or Alaska Native, non-Hispanic/Latino; 2% Two or more races, non-Hispanic/Latino; 0.5% Race/ethnicity unknown; 1% international; 11% transferred in; 57% live on campus. *Retention:* 79% of full-time freshmen returned.

Freshmen *Admission:* 9,743 applied, 4,707 admitted, 1,336 enrolled. *Average high school GPA:* 3.5. *Test scores:* SAT critical reading scores over 500: 80%; SAT math scores over 500: 85%; ACT scores over 18: 100%; SAT critical reading scores over 600: 20%; SAT math scores over 600: 24%; ACT scores over 24: 47%; SAT critical reading scores over 700: 2%; SAT math scores over 700: 2%; ACT scores over 30: 2%.

Faculty *Total:* 562, 56% full-time, 59% with terminal degrees. *Student/faculty ratio:* 19:1.

Academics *Calendar:* semesters. *Degrees:* bachelor's, master's, and post-master's certificates. *Special study options:* accelerated degree program, adult/

continuing education programs, advanced placement credit, cooperative education, distance learning, double majors, English as a second language, freshman honors college, honors programs, independent study, internships, off-campus study, part-time degree program, services for LD students, study abroad, summer session for credit. *ROTC:* Army (c). *Unusual degree programs:* 3-2 engineering with Clarkson University, Case Western Reserve University, State University of New York at Binghamton.

Computers on Campus 1,050 computers/terminals are available on campus for general student use. Students can access the following: campus intranet, computer help desk, free student e-mail accounts, online (class) grades, online (class) registration, online (class) schedules. Campuswide network is available. 100% of college-owned or -operated housing units are wired for high-speed Internet access. Wireless service is available via classrooms, computer centers, computer labs, dorm rooms, learning centers, libraries, student centers.

Student Life *Housing:* on-campus residence required through sophomore year. *Options:* coed, disabled students. Campus housing is university owned. Freshman campus housing is guaranteed. *Activities and organizations:* drama/theater group, student-run newspaper, radio and television station, choral group, club/intramural sports, student radio/television stations (WNYO and WTOP), Outing/Recreation Club, Dance Organization (Del Sarte), Financial Management Association, national fraternities, national sororities. *Campus security:* 24-hour emergency response devices and patrols, controlled dormitory access. *Student services:* health clinic, personal/psychological counseling, women's center, legal services.

Athletics Member NCAA. All Division III. *Intercollegiate sports:* baseball M, basketball M/W, crew M(c)/W(c), cross-country running M/W, field hockey W, golf M, ice hockey M/W, lacrosse M/W, soccer M/W, softball W, swimming and diving M/W, tennis M/W, track and field M/W, volleyball W, wrestling M. *Intramural sports:* badminton M/W, basketball M/W, cheerleading W(c), equestrian sports M(c)/W(c), fencing M(c)/W(c), field hockey W(c), football M/W, golf M/W, gymnastics M(c)/W(c), ice hockey M(c)/W(c), racquetball M/W, rock climbing M(c)/W(c), rugby M(c)/W(c), skiing (cross-country) M(c)/W(c), skiing (downhill) M(c)/W(c), soccer M/W, softball M/W, swimming and diving M/W, table tennis M/W, tennis M/W, ultimate Frisbee M(c)/W(c), volleyball M(c)/W, water polo M/W.

Standardized Tests *Required:* SAT or ACT (for admission).

Costs (2011–12) *Tuition:* state resident $5270 full-time, $220 per credit hour part-time; nonresident $14,320 full-time, $597 per credit hour part-time. Full-time tuition and fees vary according to degree level. *Required fees:* $1240 full-time, $52 per credit hour part-time. *Room and board:* $12,310; room only:

$7890. Room and board charges vary according to board plan and housing facility. *Payment plan:* installment.

Financial Aid Of all full-time matriculated undergraduates who enrolled in 2011, 6,057 applied for aid, 4,791 were judged to have need, 488 had their need fully met. 481 Federal Work-Study jobs (averaging $1080). 1,490 state and other part-time jobs (averaging $1688). In 2011, 595 non-need-based awards were made. *Average percent of need met:* 82%. *Average financial aid package:* $7761. *Average need-based loan:* $4488. *Average need-based gift aid:* $5911. *Average non-need-based aid:* $3705. *Average indebtedness upon graduation:* $26,123.

Applying *Options:* electronic application, early admission, early decision, deferred entrance. *Application fee:* $50. *Required:* high school transcript. *Recommended:* essay or personal statement, interview. *Application deadlines:* rolling (freshmen), rolling (transfers). *Early decision deadline:* 11/15. *Notification:* 1/15 (freshmen), 1/15 (transfers), 12/15 (early decision).

Freshman Application Contact Dr. Joseph Grant, Vice President for Student Affairs and Enrollment, State University of New York at Oswego, 7060 State Route 104, Oswego, NY 13126. *Phone:* 315-312-2250. *Fax:* 315-312-3260. *E-mail:* admiss@oswego.edu. *Web site:* http://www.oswego.edu/.

See below for display ad and page 1618 for the College Close-Up.

State University of New York at Plattsburgh

Plattsburgh, New York

- **State-supported** comprehensive, founded 1889, part of State University of New York System
- **Small-town** 265-acre campus with easy access to Montreal
- **Endowment** $14.1 million
- **Coed** 5,822 undergraduate students, 93% full-time, 55% women, 45% men
- **Moderately difficult** entrance level, 48% of applicants were admitted

Undergraduates 5,438 full-time, 384 part-time. Students come from 26 states and territories; 61 other countries; 4% are from out of state; 5% Black or African American, non-Hispanic/Latino; 7% Hispanic/Latino; 2% Asian, non-Hispanic/Latino; 0.1% Native Hawaiian or other Pacific Islander, non-Hispanic/Latino; 0.4% American Indian or Alaska Native, non-Hispanic/Latino; 2% Two or more races, non-Hispanic/Latino; 4% Race/ethnicity unknown; 6%

international; 12% transferred in; 44% live on campus. *Retention:* 81% of full-time freshmen returned.

Freshmen *Admission:* 7,368 applied, 3,541 admitted, 961 enrolled. *Average high school GPA:* 3.24. *Test scores:* SAT critical reading scores over 500: 67%; SAT math scores over 500: 77%; ACT scores over 18: 99%; SAT critical reading scores over 600: 18%; SAT math scores over 600: 19%; ACT scores over 24: 40%; SAT critical reading scores over 700: 2%; SAT math scores over 700: 2%; ACT scores over 30: 2%.

Faculty *Total:* 504, 56% full-time, 57% with terminal degrees. *Student/faculty ratio:* 17:1.

Academics *Calendar:* semesters plus 2 5-week summer sessions and 1 winter session. *Degrees:* certificates, bachelor's, master's, and post-master's certificates. *Special study options:* academic remediation for entering students, accelerated degree program, adult/continuing education programs, advanced placement credit, cooperative education, distance learning, double majors, English as a second language, honors programs, independent study, internships, off-campus study, part-time degree program, services for LD students, student-designed majors, study abroad, summer session for credit. *ROTC:* Army (b).

Computers on Campus 343 computers/terminals and 8 ports are available on campus for general student use. Students can access the following: campus intranet, computer help desk, free student e-mail accounts, online (class) grades, online (class) registration, online (class) schedules. Campuswide network is available. 100% of college-owned or -operated housing units are wired for high-speed Internet access. Wireless service is available via classrooms, computer labs, dorm rooms, learning centers, libraries, student centers.

Student Life *Housing:* on-campus residence required through sophomore year. *Options:* coed, disabled students. Campus housing is university owned. Freshman campus housing is guaranteed. *Activities and organizations:* drama/theater group, student-run newspaper, radio and television station, choral group, Student Association, Honor Societies, Student Media Organizations, service/leadership organizations, intramural and recreational sports, national fraternities, national sororities. *Campus security:* 24-hour emergency response devices and patrols, late-night transport/escort service, controlled dormitory access. *Student services:* health clinic, personal/psychological counseling, women's center, legal services.

Athletics Member NCAA. All Division III. *Intercollegiate sports:* baseball M, basketball M/W, cross-country running M/W, ice hockey M/W, lacrosse M, soccer M/W, softball W, tennis W, track and field W, volleyball W. *Intramural sports:* basketball M/W, cheerleading M(c)/W(c), field hockey M/W, football M, ice hockey M(c)/W(c), racquetball M/W, rock climbing M(c)/W(c), rugby M(c)/W(c), soccer M/W, softball M/W, tennis M/W, ultimate Frisbee M/W, volleyball M/W.

Standardized Tests *Required:* SAT or ACT (for admission).

Costs (2011–12) *Tuition:* state resident $5270 full-time, $220 per credit hour part-time; nonresident $14,320 full-time, $597 per credit hour part-time. Part-time tuition and fees vary according to course load. *Required fees:* $1212 full-time, $50 per credit hour part-time. *Room and board:* $9550. Room and board charges vary according to board plan. *Payment plans:* installment, deferred payment. *Waivers:* employees or children of employees.

Financial Aid Of all full-time matriculated undergraduates who enrolled in 2011, 4,471 applied for aid, 3,491 were judged to have need, 619 had their need fully met. 532 Federal Work-Study jobs (averaging $1931). In 2011, 1380 non-need-based awards were made. *Average percent of need met:* 84%. *Average financial aid package:* $11,502. *Average need-based loan:* $7216. *Average need-based gift aid:* $5879. *Average non-need-based aid:* $5958. *Average indebtedness upon graduation:* $25,362.

Applying *Options:* electronic application, early admission, early decision, deferred entrance. *Application fee:* $50. *Required:* essay or personal statement, high school transcript, minimum 2.5 GPA, 1 letter of recommendation. *Required for some:* minimum 3.4 GPA. *Recommended:* minimum 3.0 GPA, interview. *Application deadline:* rolling (transfers). *Notification:* continuous (freshmen), continuous (transfers).

Freshman Application Contact Mrs. Carrie Woodward, Assistant Director for Freshman Admissions, State University of New York at Plattsburgh, 101 Broad Street, Plattsburgh, NY 12901. *Phone:* 888-673-0012. *Toll-free phone:* 888-673-0012. *Fax:* 518-564-2045. *E-mail:* carrie.woodward@plattsburgh.edu. *Web site:* http://www.plattsburgh.edu/.

State University of New York College at Cortland

Cortland, New York

- **State-supported** comprehensive, founded 1868, part of State University of New York System

- **Small-town** 191-acre campus with easy access to Syracuse

- **Coed** 6,371 undergraduate students, 98% full-time, 57% women, 43% men

- **Moderately difficult** entrance level, 41% of applicants were admitted

Undergraduates 6,241 full-time, 130 part-time. 3% are from out of state; 3% Black or African American, non-Hispanic/Latino; 8% Hispanic/Latino; 1% Asian, non-Hispanic/Latino; 0.3% American Indian or Alaska Native, non-Hispanic/Latino; 1% Two or more races, non-Hispanic/Latino; 9% Race/ethnicity unknown; 0.5% international; 10% transferred in; 50% live on campus. *Retention:* 85% of full-time freshmen returned.

Freshmen *Admission:* 12,348 applied, 5,057 admitted, 1,202 enrolled. *Average high school GPA:* 3.45. *Test scores:* SAT critical reading scores over 500: 80%; SAT math scores over 500: 64%; SAT critical reading scores over 600: 23%; SAT math scores over 600: 10%; SAT critical reading scores over 700: 1%.

Faculty *Total:* 622, 46% full-time, 44% with terminal degrees. *Student/faculty ratio:* 17:1.

Academics *Calendar:* semesters. *Degrees:* bachelor's, master's, post-master's, and postbachelor's certificates. *Special study options:* adult/continuing education programs, off-campus study. *ROTC:* Army (c), Air Force (c). *Unusual degree programs:* 3-2 engineering with State University of New York at Buffalo, State University of New York at Stony Brook, Alfred University, Clarkson University, State University of New York at Binghamton, Case Western Reserve University; forestry with Duke University, State University of New York College of Environmental Science and Forestry.

Computers on Campus Campuswide network is available.

Student Life *Housing options:* coed, cooperative, disabled students. Campus housing is university owned. *Campus security:* 24-hour emergency response devices and patrols, late-night transport/escort service.

Athletics Member NCAA. All Division III. *Intercollegiate sports:* baseball M, basketball M/W, cross-country running M/W, field hockey W, football M/W(c), golf W, gymnastics W, ice hockey M/W(c), lacrosse M/W, racquetball M(c)/W(c), rugby M(c)/W(c), soccer M/W, softball W, swimming and diving M/W, tennis W, track and field M/W, volleyball M(c)/W, wrestling M. *Intramural sports:* archery M/W, badminton M/W, baseball M, basketball M/W, bowling M/W, cross-country running M/W, fencing M/W, field hockey W, football M/W, golf M/W, gymnastics W, ice hockey M, lacrosse M/W, racquetball M/W, rugby M/W, skiing (cross-country) M/W, skiing (downhill) M/W, soccer M/W, softball M/W, squash M/W, swimming and diving M/W, table tennis M/W, tennis M/W, track and field M/W, volleyball M/W, weight lifting M/W, wrestling M.

Standardized Tests *Required:* SAT or ACT (for admission).

Costs (2011–12) *Tuition:* state resident $5270 full-time, $220 per credit hour part-time; nonresident $14,320 full-time, $597 per credit hour part-time. Full-time tuition and fees vary according to degree level. Part-time tuition and fees vary according to degree level. *Required fees:* $1304 full-time, $74 per credit hour part-time. *Room and board:* $11,060; room only: $6730. Room and board charges vary according to board plan and housing facility. *Payment plan:* installment.

Financial Aid Of all full-time matriculated undergraduates who enrolled in 2010, 5,115 applied for aid, 3,834 were judged to have need, 375 had their need fully met. In 2010, 151 non-need-based awards were made. *Average percent of need met:* 69%. *Average financial aid package:* $12,500. *Average need-based loan:* $4330. *Average need-based gift aid:* $5192. *Average non-need-based aid:* $2724. *Average indebtedness upon graduation:* $26,303.

Applying *Options:* early admission, early action, deferred entrance. *Application fee:* $50. *Required:* essay or personal statement, high school transcript, minimum 2.3 GPA, 1 letter of recommendation. *Recommended:* minimum 3.0 GPA, 3 letters of recommendation, interview. *Application deadlines:* rolling (freshmen), rolling (transfers), 11/15 (early action). *Notification:* continuous (freshmen), continuous (transfers), 1/1 (early action).

Freshman Application Contact Director of Admission, State University of New York College at Cortland, PO Box 2000, Cortland, NY 13045. *Phone:* 607-753-4711. *Fax:* 607-753-5998. *E-mail:* admissions@cortland.edu. *Web site:* http://www.cortland.edu/.

State University of New York College at Geneseo

Geneseo, New York

- **State-supported** comprehensive, founded 1871, part of State University of New York system
- **Small-town** 220-acre campus with easy access to Rochester
- **Endowment** $15.6 million
- **Coed** 5,485 undergraduate students, 98% full-time, 57% women, 43% men
- **Very difficult** entrance level, 43% of applicants were admitted

Undergraduates 5,371 full-time, 114 part-time. Students come from 29 states and territories; 36 other countries; 2% are from out of state; 2% Black or African American, non-Hispanic/Latino; 5% Hispanic/Latino; 6% Asian, non-Hispanic/Latino; 0.1% Native Hawaiian or other Pacific Islander, non-Hispanic/Latino; 0.2% American Indian or Alaska Native, non-Hispanic/Latino; 2% Two or more races, non-Hispanic/Latino; 5% Race/ethnicity unknown; 4% international; 7% transferred in; 53% live on campus. *Retention:* 91% of full-time freshmen returned.

Freshmen *Admission:* 9,569 applied, 4,136 admitted, 1,010 enrolled. *Average high school GPA:* 3.7. *Test scores:* SAT critical reading scores over 500: 92%; SAT math scores over 500: 94%; ACT scores over 18: 100%; SAT critical reading scores over 600: 73%; SAT math scores over 600: 76%; ACT scores over 24: 94%; SAT critical reading scores over 700: 24%; SAT math scores over 700: 20%; ACT scores over 30: 31%.

Faculty *Total:* 352, 68% full-time, 68% with terminal degrees. *Student/faculty ratio:* 20:1.

Academics *Calendar:* semesters. *Degrees:* bachelor's and master's. *Special study options:* advanced placement credit, double majors, English as a second language, honors programs, independent study, internships, off-campus study, part-time degree program, services for LD students, study abroad, summer session for credit. *ROTC:* Army (c), Air Force (c). *Unusual degree programs:* 3-2 business administration with Syracuse University, State University of New York at Buffalo, State University of New York at Binghamton, Rochester Institute of Technology, Clarkson University, Alfred University, Union College; engineering with Columbia University, Case Western Reserve University, Alfred University, Clarkson University, Syracuse University, The Pennsylvania State University, University of Rochester, SUNY Binghamton, SUNY Buffalo, Rochester Institute of Technology; nursing with Johns Hopkins School of Nursing; optometry with State University of New York College of Optometry; dental with State University of New York at Buffalo.

Computers on Campus 544 computers/terminals and 136 ports are available on campus for general student use. Students can access the following: campus intranet, computer help desk, free student e-mail accounts, online (class) grades, online (class) registration, online (class) schedules. Campuswide network is available. 100% of college-owned or -operated housing units are wired for high-speed Internet access. Wireless service is available via entire campus.

Student Life *Housing:* on-campus residence required through sophomore year. *Options:* coed, disabled students. Campus housing is university owned. Freshman campus housing is guaranteed. *Activities and organizations:* drama/theater group, student-run newspaper, radio and television station, choral group, Korean-American Student Association, Inter-Varsity Christian Fellowship, Alpha Phi Omega, Ski & Snowboarding Club, Orchesis Dance Club, national fraternities, national sororities. *Campus security:* 24-hour emergency response devices and patrols, student patrols, late-night transport/escort service, controlled dormitory access. *Student services:* health clinic, personal/psychological counseling, women's center, legal services.

Athletics Member NCAA. All Division III. *Intercollegiate sports:* baseball M(c), basketball M/W, cheerleading M(c)/W(c), crew M(c)/W(c), cross-country running M/W, equestrian sports W, fencing M(c)/W(c), field hockey W, ice hockey M/W(c), lacrosse M/W, rugby M(c)/W(c), skiing (downhill) M(c)/W(c), soccer M/W, softball W, swimming and diving M/W, tennis M(c)/W, track and field M/W, ultimate Frisbee M(c)/W(c), volleyball M(c)/W, water polo M(c)/W(c). *Intramural sports:* badminton M/W, basketball M/W, football M/W, racquetball M/W, skiing (downhill) M/W, soccer M/W, softball M/W, squash M/W, table tennis M/W, tennis M/W, ultimate Frisbee M/W, volleyball M/W.

Standardized Tests *Required:* SAT or ACT (for admission).

Costs (2011–12) *Tuition:* state resident $5270 full-time, $220 per credit hour part-time; nonresident $14,320 full-time, $597 per credit hour part-time. Part-time tuition and fees vary according to course load. *Required fees:* $1463 full-time, $61 per credit hour part-time. *Room and board:* $10,476. Room and board charges vary according to board plan and housing facility. *Payment plans:* installment, deferred payment.

Financial Aid Of all full-time matriculated undergraduates who enrolled in 2010, 3,764 applied for aid, 2,371 were judged to have need, 1,776 had their need fully met. In 2010, 532 non-need-based awards were made. *Average percent of need met:* 75%. *Average financial aid package:* $8686. *Average need-based loan:* $4513. *Average need-based gift aid:* $4376. *Average non-need-based aid:* $1920. *Average indebtedness upon graduation:* $21,200. *Financial aid deadline:* 2/15.

Applying *Options:* electronic application, early admission, early decision, deferred entrance. *Application fee:* $50. *Required:* essay or personal statement, high school transcript. *Recommended:* minimum 3.5 GPA, 1 letter of recommendation, interview. *Application deadlines:* 1/1 (freshmen), 2/15 (transfers). *Early decision deadline:* 11/15. *Notification:* 3/1 (freshmen), 2/15 (transfers), 12/15 (early decision).

Freshman Application Contact Ms. Kris Shay, Director of Admissions, State University of New York College at Geneseo, 1 College Circle, Geneseo, NY 14454-1401. *Phone:* 585-245-5571. *Toll-free phone:* 866-245-5211. *Fax:* 585-245-5550. *E-mail:* admissions@geneseo.edu. *Web site:* http://www.geneseo.edu/.

State University of New York College at Old Westbury

Old Westbury, New York

- **State-supported** comprehensive, founded 1965, part of State University of New York System
- **Suburban** 604-acre campus with easy access to New York City
- **Coed** 4,230 undergraduate students, 84% full-time, 58% women, 42% men
- **Moderately difficult** entrance level, 45% of applicants were admitted

Undergraduates 3,561 full-time, 669 part-time. Students come from 15 states and territories; 60 other countries; 1% are from out of state; 30% Black or African American, non-Hispanic/Latino; 20% Hispanic/Latino; 8% Asian, non-Hispanic/Latino; 0.3% Native Hawaiian or other Pacific Islander, non-Hispanic/Latino; 0.2% American Indian or Alaska Native, non-Hispanic/Latino; 2% Two or more races, non-Hispanic/Latino; 4% Race/ethnicity unknown; 0.7% international; 18% transferred in; 23% live on campus. *Retention:* 76% of full-time freshmen returned.

Freshmen *Admission:* 3,914 applied, 1,755 admitted, 400 enrolled. *Average high school GPA:* 3.3. *Test scores:* SAT math scores over 500: 53%; SAT writing scores over 500: 33%; ACT scores over 18: 93%; SAT math scores over 600: 9%; SAT writing scores over 600: 4%; ACT scores over 24: 21%.

Faculty *Total:* 308, 46% full-time, 50% with terminal degrees. *Student/faculty ratio:* 19:1.

Academics *Calendar:* semesters. *Degrees:* certificates, bachelor's, master's, and post-master's certificates. *Special study options:* academic remediation for entering students, advanced placement credit, distance learning, double majors, English as a second language, freshman honors college, honors programs, independent study, internships, off-campus study, part-time degree program, services for LD students, study abroad, summer session for credit. *ROTC:* Army (c), Air Force (c). *Unusual degree programs:* 3-2 engineering with State University of New York at Stony Brook; biological sciences/Doctor of Osteopathic Medicine with NY College of Osteopathic Medicine.

Computers on Campus 462 computers/terminals and 700 ports are available on campus for general student use. Students can access the following: campus intranet, free student e-mail accounts, online (class) grades, online (class) registration, financial aid, billing information, grades. Campuswide network is available. 100% of college-owned or -operated housing units are wired for high-speed Internet access. Wireless service is available via entire campus.

Student Life *Housing options:* coed. Campus housing is university owned. Freshman campus housing is guaranteed. *Activities and organizations:* drama/theater group, student-run newspaper, radio station, choral group, Student Government Association, Alianza Latina, PRIDE, Step Tunes, Anime Magna Games Club, national fraternities, national sororities. *Campus security:* 24-hour emergency response devices and patrols, student patrols, late-night transport/escort service, controlled dormitory access. *Student services:* health clinic, personal/psychological counseling, women's center.

Athletics Member NCAA. All Division III. *Intercollegiate sports:* baseball M, basketball M/W, cross-country running M/W, golf M, lacrosse W, soccer M/W, softball W, swimming and diving M/W, volleyball W. *Intramural sports:* badminton M/W, basketball M/W, cheerleading M(c)/W(c), equestrian sports M(c)/W(c), football M/W, racquetball M/W, soccer M/W, softball W, squash M/W, ultimate Frisbee M/W, weight lifting M/W.

Standardized Tests *Required:* SAT or ACT (for admission).

Costs (2011–12) *Tuition:* state resident $5270 full-time, $220 per credit part-time; nonresident $14,320 full-time, $597 per credit part-time. Part-time tuition and fees vary according to course load. *Required fees:* $1054 full-time, $21 per credit part-time, $143 per credit part-time. *Room and board:* $9700; room only: $6600. Room and board charges vary according to board plan. *Payment plan:* installment. *Waivers:* senior citizens.

Financial Aid Of all full-time matriculated undergraduates who enrolled in 2011, 2,231 applied for aid, 2,228 were judged to have need, 2,228 had their need fully met. 337 Federal Work-Study jobs (averaging $887). *Average per-*

cent of need met: 50%. *Average financial aid package:* $8265. *Average need-based loan:* $4415. *Average need-based gift aid:* $5616. *Average indebtedness upon graduation:* $17,722.

Applying *Options:* electronic application, early admission, early decision, deferred entrance. *Application fee:* $50. *Required:* essay or personal statement, high school transcript, 2 letters of recommendation. *Required for some:* interview. *Application deadlines:* rolling (freshmen), 12/15 (transfers). *Early decision deadline:* 11/1. *Notification:* continuous (freshmen), continuous (transfers), 12/15 (early decision).

Freshman Application Contact State University of New York College at Old Westbury, PO Box 307, Old Westbury, NY 11568. *Phone:* 516-876-3073. *Fax:* 516-876-3307. *E-mail:* enroll@oldwestbury.edu. *Web site:* http://www.oldwestbury.edu/.

State University of New York College at Oneonta
Oneonta, New York

- **State-supported** comprehensive, founded 1889, part of State University of New York
- **Small-town** 250-acre campus
- **Endowment** $37.8 million
- **Coed** 5,852 undergraduate students, 98% full-time, 59% women, 41% men
- **Very difficult** entrance level, 43% of applicants were admitted

Undergraduates 5,738 full-time, 114 part-time. Students come from 11 states and territories; 17 other countries; 1% are from out of state; 3% Black or African American, non-Hispanic/Latino; 4% Hispanic/Latino; 2% Asian, non-Hispanic/Latino; 0.2% American Indian or Alaska Native, non-Hispanic/Latino; 5% Two or more races, non-Hispanic/Latino; 3% Race/ethnicity unknown; 2% international; 8% transferred in; 59% live on campus. *Retention:* 84% of full-time freshmen returned.

Freshmen *Admission:* 12,338 applied, 5,359 admitted, 1,172 enrolled. *Average high school GPA:* 3.6. *Test scores:* SAT critical reading scores over 500: 78%; SAT math scores over 500: 86%; ACT scores over 18: 99%; SAT critical reading scores over 600: 17%; SAT math scores over 600: 26%; ACT scores over 24: 56%; SAT critical reading scores over 700: 1%; SAT math scores over 700: 1%; ACT scores over 30: 2%.

Faculty *Total:* 483, 52% full-time. *Student/faculty ratio:* 18:1.

Academics *Calendar:* semesters. *Degrees:* bachelor's, master's, post-master's, and postbachelor's certificates. *Special study options:* academic remediation for entering students, adult/continuing education programs, advanced placement credit, distance learning, double majors, English as a second language, honors programs, independent study, internships, off-campus study, part-time degree program, services for LD students, study abroad, summer session for credit. *Unusual degree programs:* 3-2 business administration with State University of New York at Binghamton, Clarkson University, Rochester Institute of Technology, Union College; engineering with University at Buffalo, the State University of New York; Alfred University; Clarkson University; Rensselaer Polytechnic Institute; Syracuse University; accounting at State University of New York at Binghamton, fashion with Fashion Institute of Technology, American Intercontinental University in London.

Computers on Campus 700 computers/terminals are available on campus for general student use. Students can access the following: campus intranet, computer help desk, free student e-mail accounts, online (class) grades, online (class) registration, online (class) schedules, Digital video/audio editing suites, presentation rehearsal room using lecture capture software, large format printing, network file storage space. Campuswide network is available. 100% of college-owned or -operated housing units are wired for high-speed Internet access. Wireless service is available via entire campus.

Student Life *Housing:* on-campus residence required through sophomore year. *Options:* coed. Campus housing is university owned. Freshman campus housing is guaranteed. *Activities and organizations:* drama/theater group, student-run newspaper, radio and television station, choral group, Center for Social Responsibility and Community, Music Industry Club, Terpsichorean Dance Company, student government, Zombie Defense Corps, national fraternities, national sororities. *Campus security:* 24-hour emergency response devices and patrols, late-night transport/escort service, controlled dormitory access, Oneonta Emergency Squad: an organization of student volunteers with first responder credentials, e.g., EMT training, CPR certification. *Student services:* health clinic, personal/psychological counseling, women's center.

Athletics Member NCAA. All Division III. *Intercollegiate sports:* baseball M, basketball M/W, cheerleading W(c), cross-country running M/W, fencing M(c)/W(c), field hockey W, ice hockey M(c), lacrosse M/W, rugby W(c), soccer M/W, softball W, swimming and diving M/W, tennis M/W, track and field M/W, volleyball W, wrestling M. *Intramural sports:* badminton M(c)/W(c), basketball M/W, equestrian sports M(c)/W(c), football M, racquetball M(c)/

W(c), skiing (downhill) M(c)/W(c), soccer M/W, softball M/W, ultimate Frisbee M/W, volleyball M/W.

Standardized Tests *Required:* SAT or ACT (for admission).

Costs (2012–13) *Tuition:* state resident $5270 full-time, $220 per semester hour part-time; nonresident $14,320 full-time, $597 per semester hour part-time. Part-time tuition and fees vary according to course load. *Required fees:* $1326 full-time, $38 per semester hour part-time. *Room and board:* $10,164; room only: $6314. Room and board charges vary according to housing facility. *Payment plan:* installment. *Waivers:* employees or children of employees.

Financial Aid Of all full-time matriculated undergraduates who enrolled in 2011, 4,577 applied for aid, 3,361 were judged to have need, 1,540 had their need fully met. 343 Federal Work-Study jobs (averaging $1133). In 2011, 690 non-need-based awards were made. *Average percent of need met:* 36%. *Average financial aid package:* $15,540. *Average need-based loan:* $2022. *Average need-based gift aid:* $5320. *Average non-need-based aid:* $2618. *Average indebtedness upon graduation:* $13,697.

Applying *Options:* electronic application, early admission, early action, deferred entrance. *Application fee:* $50. *Required:* essay or personal statement, high school transcript. *Recommended:* minimum 3.0 GPA, 3 letters of recommendation. *Application deadlines:* rolling (freshmen), rolling (transfers), 11/15 (early action). *Notification:* continuous (freshmen), continuous (transfers), 12/15 (early action).

Freshman Application Contact Ms. Karen Brown, Director of Admissions, State University of New York College at Oneonta, Alumni Hall 116, Oneonta, NY 13820-4015. *Phone:* 607-436-2524. *Toll-free phone:* 800-SUNY-123. *Fax:* 607-436-3074. *E-mail:* admissions@oneonta.edu. *Web site:* http://www.oneonta.edu/.

State University of New York College at Potsdam
Potsdam, New York

- **State-supported** comprehensive, founded 1816, part of State University of New York System
- **Small-town** 240-acre campus
- **Coed** 3,958 undergraduate students, 97% full-time, 58% women, 42% men
- **Moderately difficult** entrance level, 63% of applicants were admitted

Undergraduates 3,834 full-time, 124 part-time. Students come from 43 states and territories; 19 other countries; 4% Black or African American, non-Hispanic/Latino; 6% Hispanic/Latino; 1% Asian, non-Hispanic/Latino; 0.1% Native Hawaiian or other Pacific Islander, non-Hispanic/Latino; 1% American Indian or Alaska Native, non-Hispanic/Latino; 2% Two or more races, non-Hispanic/Latino; 6% Race/ethnicity unknown; 2% international; 10% transferred in; 94% live on campus. *Retention:* 77% of full-time freshmen returned.

Freshmen *Admission:* 5,099 applied, 3,237 admitted, 897 enrolled. *Average high school GPA:* 3.4.

Faculty *Total:* 363, 70% full-time, 56% with terminal degrees. *Student/faculty ratio:* 14:1.

Academics *Calendar:* semesters. *Degrees:* bachelor's and master's. *Special study options:* advanced placement credit, distance learning, double majors, honors programs, independent study, internships, off-campus study, part-time degree program, services for LD students, student-designed majors, study abroad, summer session for credit. *ROTC:* Army (c), Air Force (c). *Unusual degree programs:* 3-2 engineering with Clarkson University, SUNY IT; geology, physics, computer science, chemistry and mathematics with Clarkson University.

Computers on Campus 608 computers/terminals and 80 ports are available on campus for general student use. Students can access the following: campus intranet, computer help desk, free student e-mail accounts, online (class) grades, online (class) registration, online (class) schedules, online access to financial aid status, unofficial transcripts, billing, meal plan and housing sign ups,225 wireless hot spots with 95 on campus and 130 in the residence halls. Campuswide network is available. 100% of college-owned or -operated housing units are wired for high-speed Internet access. Wireless service is available via classrooms, computer centers, computer labs, dorm rooms, learning centers, libraries, student centers.

Student Life *Housing:* on-campus residence required through sophomore year. *Options:* coed, disabled students. Campus housing is university owned. Freshman campus housing is guaranteed. *Activities and organizations:* drama/theater group, student-run newspaper, radio station, choral group, Student Government Association, Crane Student Association, Student Entertainment Services (Programming Board), WALH Radio, The Racquette Student Newspaper, national fraternities, national sororities. *Campus security:* 24-hour emergency response devices and patrols, late-night transport/escort service, controlled dormitory access, educational programs, campus rescue squad, portable jump start packets, vehicle lock outs and parking management. *Student*

services: health clinic, personal/psychological counseling, women's center, legal services.

Athletics Member NCAA. All Division III. *Intercollegiate sports:* basketball M/W, cross-country running M/W, equestrian sports W, golf M, ice hockey M/W, lacrosse M/W, soccer M/W, swimming and diving M/W, track and field M(c)/W(c), volleyball W. *Intramural sports:* archery M(c)/W(c), basketball M/W, bowling M(c)/W(c), cheerleading M(c)/W(c), football M/W, racquetball M/W, soccer M/W, softball M/W.

Standardized Tests *Required for some:* SAT or ACT (for admission).

Costs (2011–12) *Tuition:* state resident $5270 full-time, $220 per credit hour part-time; nonresident $14,320 full-time, $597 per credit hour part-time. *Required fees:* $1236 full-time. *Room and board:* $9830; room only: $5770. Room and board charges vary according to board plan and housing facility. *Payment plan:* installment. *Waivers:* employees or children of employees.

Financial Aid Of all full-time matriculated undergraduates who enrolled in 2011, 3,543 applied for aid, 2,741 were judged to have need, 1,289 had their need fully met. 277 Federal Work-Study jobs (averaging $1127). In 2011, 287 non-need-based awards were made. *Average percent of need met:* 88%. *Average financial aid package:* $12,453. *Average need-based loan:* $4613. *Average need-based gift aid:* $6038. *Average non-need-based aid:* $2217. *Average indebtedness upon graduation:* $19,247. *Financial aid deadline:* 5/1.

Applying *Options:* electronic application, early admission, deferred entrance. *Application fee:* $50. *Required:* high school transcript, minimum 2.5 GPA, audition for music program. *Required for some:* essay or personal statement, minimum 2.0 GPA, interview. *Application deadlines:* rolling (freshmen), rolling (transfers). *Notification:* continuous (freshmen), continuous (transfers).

Freshman Application Contact Mr. Thomas Nesbitt, Director of Admissions, State University of New York College at Potsdam, 44 Pierrepont Avenue, Potsdam, NY 13676. *Phone:* 315-267-2180. *Toll-free phone:* 877-POTSDAM. *Fax:* 315-267-2163. *E-mail:* admissions@potsdam.edu. *Web site:* http://www.potsdam.edu/.

State University of New York College of Agriculture and Technology at Cobleskill

Cobleskill, New York

Freshman Application Contact State University of New York College of Agriculture and Technology at Cobleskill, Cobleskill, NY 12043. *Phone:* 518-255-5525. *Toll-free phone:* 800-295-8988. *Web site:* http://www.cobleskill.edu/.

State University of New York College of Environmental Science and Forestry

Syracuse, New York

- **State-supported** university, founded 1911, part of State University of New York System
- **Urban** 17-acre campus
- **Endowment** $18.9 million
- **Coed** 1,744 undergraduate students, 93% full-time, 44% women, 56% men
- **Very difficult** entrance level, 47% of applicants were admitted

Undergraduates 1,628 full-time, 116 part-time. Students come from 38 states and territories; 11 other countries; 12% are from out of state; 2% Black or African American, non-Hispanic/Latino; 3% Hispanic/Latino; 4% Asian, non-Hispanic/Latino; 0.4% American Indian or Alaska Native, non-Hispanic/Latino; 2% international; 14% transferred in; 40% live on campus. *Retention:* 82% of full-time freshmen returned.

Freshmen *Admission:* 1,865 applied, 872 admitted, 287 enrolled. *Average high school GPA:* 3.8. *Test scores:* SAT critical reading scores over 500: 92%; SAT math scores over 500: 96%; ACT scores over 18: 100%; SAT critical reading scores over 600: 41%; SAT math scores over 600: 52%; ACT scores over 24: 77%; SAT critical reading scores over 700: 7%; SAT math scores over 700: 8%; ACT scores over 30: 12%.

Faculty *Total:* 177, 82% full-time, 84% with terminal degrees. *Student/faculty ratio:* 13:1.

Academics *Calendar:* semesters. *Degrees:* associate, bachelor's, master's, doctoral, postbachelor's, and first professional certificates. *Special study options:* accelerated degree program, adult/continuing education programs, advanced placement credit, cooperative education, distance learning, double majors, English as a second language, honors programs, independent study, internships, off-campus study, part-time degree program, services for LD stu-

dents, study abroad, summer session for credit. *ROTC:* Army (c), Air Force (c).

Computers on Campus 350 computers/terminals and 2,250 ports are available on campus for general student use. Students can access the following: campus intranet, computer help desk, free student e-mail accounts, online (class) grades, online (class) registration, online (class) schedules. Campus-wide network is available. 100% of college-owned or -operated housing units are wired for high-speed Internet access. Wireless service is available via classrooms, computer centers, computer labs, dorm rooms, libraries, student centers.

Student Life *Housing:* on-campus residence required for freshman year. *Options:* coed, disabled students. Campus housing is university owned and is provided by a third party. Freshman campus housing is guaranteed. *Activities and organizations:* drama/theater group, student-run newspaper, choral group, marching band, Bob Marshall/Outing Club, Forestry Club, Student Environmental Action Coalition, Student Green Campus Initiative, Recycling Club, national fraternities, national sororities. *Campus security:* 24-hour emergency response devices and patrols, late-night transport/escort service, controlled dormitory access. *Student services:* health clinic, personal/psychological counseling, women's center, legal services.

Athletics Member USCAA. *Intercollegiate sports:* basketball M, cross-country running M/W, golf M/W, soccer M/W. *Intramural sports:* archery M/W, badminton M/W, baseball M/W, basketball M/W, bowling M/W, cheerleading M/W, crew M/W, cross-country running M/W, equestrian sports M/W, fencing M/W, field hockey W, football M, gymnastics M/W, ice hockey M/W, lacrosse M/W, racquetball M/W, riflery M, rugby M/W, sailing M/W, skiing (cross-country) M/W, skiing (downhill) M/W, soccer M/W, softball M/W, squash M/W, swimming and diving M/W, table tennis M/W, tennis M/W, track and field M/W, ultimate Frisbee M/W, volleyball M/W, weight lifting M/W.

Standardized Tests *Required:* SAT or ACT (for admission). *Recommended:* SAT Subject Tests (for admission).

Costs (2012–13) *Tuition:* state resident $5270 full-time, $220 per credit hour part-time; nonresident $14,320 full-time, $597 per credit hour part-time. Full-time tuition and fees vary according to location. Part-time tuition and fees vary according to course load and location. *Required fees:* $971 full-time, $43 per credit hour part-time. *Room and board:* $14,032. Room and board charges vary according to board plan, housing facility, and location. *Payment plans:* installment, deferred payment.

Financial Aid Of all full-time matriculated undergraduates who enrolled in 2011, 1,389 applied for aid, 975 were judged to have need, 887 had their need fully met. 190 Federal Work-Study jobs (averaging $1750). 175 state and other part-time jobs (averaging $1500). In 2011, 85 non-need-based awards were made. *Average percent of need met:* 90%. *Average financial aid package:* $13,000. *Average need-based loan:* $5500. *Average need-based gift aid:* $5000. *Average non-need-based aid:* $2820. *Average indebtedness upon graduation:* $23,982.

Applying *Options:* electronic application, early admission, early decision, deferred entrance. *Application fee:* $50. *Required:* essay or personal statement, high school transcript, minimum 3.0 GPA, supplemental application. *Recommended:* 1 letter of recommendation, interview. *Application deadlines:* 1/15 (freshmen), 1/15 (out-of-state freshmen), 3/1 (transfers). *Early decision deadline:* 12/1. *Notification:* continuous (freshmen), continuous (out-of-state freshmen), continuous (transfers), rolling (early decision).

Freshman Application Contact Ms. Susan Sanford, Director of Admissions, State University of New York College of Environmental Science and Forestry, Office of Undergraduate Admissions, 106 Bray Hall, 1 Forestry Drive, Syracuse, NY 13210-2779. *Phone:* 315-470-6600. *Fax:* 315-470-6933. *E-mail:* esfinfo@esf.edu. *Web site:* http://www.esf.edu/.

See page 633 for display ad and page 1620 for the College Close-Up.

State University of New York College of Technology at Alfred

Alfred, New York

- **State-supported** primarily 2-year, founded 1908, part of The State University of New York System
- **Rural** 1084-acre campus
- **Endowment** $3.6 million
- **Coed** 3,617 undergraduate students, 91% full-time, 38% women, 62% men
- **Moderately difficult** entrance level, 55% of applicants were admitted

Undergraduates 3,279 full-time, 338 part-time. Students come from 35 states and territories; 19 other countries; 7% are from out of state; 9% Black or African American, non-Hispanic/Latino; 5% Hispanic/Latino; 2% Asian, non-Hispanic/Latino; 0.1% Native Hawaiian or other Pacific Islander, non-Hispanic/Latino; 0.3% American Indian or Alaska Native, non-Hispanic/Latino; 2% Two or more races, non-Hispanic/Latino; 4% Race/ethnicity unknown; 7%

transferred in; 74% live on campus. *Retention:* 81% of full-time freshmen returned.

Freshmen *Admission:* 3,890 applied, 2,136 admitted, 1,082 enrolled. *Average high school GPA:* 3.3.

Faculty *Total:* 219, 83% full-time, 21% with terminal degrees. *Student/faculty ratio:* 18:1.

Academics *Calendar:* semesters. *Degrees:* certificates, associate, and bachelor's. *Special study options:* academic remediation for entering students, adult/continuing education programs, advanced placement credit, cooperative education, distance learning, double majors, English as a second language, honors programs, independent study, internships, off-campus study, part-time degree program, services for LD students, student-designed majors, study abroad, summer session for credit. *ROTC:* Army (c).

Computers on Campus 100 computers/terminals are available on campus for general student use. Students can access the following: campus intranet, computer help desk, free student e-mail accounts, online (class) grades, online (class) registration, online (class) schedules. Campuswide network is available. 100% of college-owned or -operated housing units are wired for high-speed Internet access. Wireless service is available via entire campus.

Student Life *Housing options:* coed, men-only, women-only, disabled students. Campus housing is university owned. Freshman campus housing is guaranteed. *Activities and organizations:* drama/theater group, student-run newspaper, radio station, choral group, Outdoor Recreation Club, International Club, intramural Sports, Pioneer Woodsmen Team, Black Student Union. *Campus security:* 24-hour emergency response devices and patrols, late-night transport/escort service, controlled dormitory access, residence hall entrance guards. *Student services:* health clinic, personal/psychological counseling.

Athletics Member NJCAA. *Intercollegiate sports:* baseball M, basketball M(s)/W(s), cross-country running M/W, equestrian sports M/W, football M(s), lacrosse M(s), soccer M/W, softball W, swimming and diving M/W, track and field M/W, volleyball W, wrestling M. *Intramural sports:* basketball M/W, football M(c), golf M/W, ice hockey M(c)/W(c), lacrosse M(c)/W(c), rock climbing M/W, soccer M/W, softball M/W, swimming and diving M(c)/W(c), tennis M/W, ultimate Frisbee M/W, volleyball M/W.

Standardized Tests *Required for some:* SAT or ACT (for admission). *Recommended:* SAT or ACT (for admission).

Costs (2012–13) *Tuition:* state resident $5570 full-time, $220 per credit hour part-time; nonresident $10,714 full-time, $406 per credit hour part-time. Full-time tuition and fees vary according to course load and degree level. Part-time tuition and fees vary according to course load and degree level. *Required fees:* $1272 full-time, $53 per credit hour part-time, $5 per credit hour part-time. *Room and board:* $10,450; room only: $6100. Room and board charges vary according to board plan and housing facility. *Payment plan:* installment. *Waivers:* employees or children of employees.

Financial Aid Of all full-time matriculated undergraduates who enrolled in 2010, 3,084 applied for aid, 2,722 were judged to have need, 256 had their need fully met. 228 Federal Work-Study jobs (averaging $861). In 2010, 99 non-need-based awards were made. *Average percent of need met:* 57%. *Average financial aid package:* $9568. *Average need-based loan:* $3760. *Average need-based gift aid:* $5759. *Average non-need-based aid:* $4307. *Average indebtedness upon graduation:* $29,772.

Applying *Options:* electronic application. *Application fee:* $50. *Required:* high school transcript, minimum 2.0 GPA. *Recommended:* essay or personal statement, interview. *Application deadlines:* rolling (freshmen), rolling (out-of-state freshmen), rolling (transfers). *Notification:* continuous (freshmen), continuous (out-of-state freshmen), continuous (transfers).

Freshman Application Contact Mrs. Deborah Goodrich, Associate Vice President for Enrollment Management, State University of New York College of Technology at Alfred, Huntington Administration Building, 10 Upper College Drive, Alfred, NY 14802. *Phone:* 607-587-4215. *Toll-free phone:* 800-4-ALFRED. *Fax:* 607-587-4299. *E-mail:* admissions@alfredstate.edu. *Web site:* http://www.alfredstate.edu/.

State University of New York College of Technology at Canton

Canton, New York

- **State-supported** comprehensive, founded 1906, part of State University of New York System
- **Small-town** 555-acre campus
- **Endowment** $6.5 million
- **Coed** 3,881 undergraduate students, 76% full-time, 52% women, 48% men
- **Minimally difficult** entrance level, 74% of applicants were admitted

Undergraduates 2,952 full-time, 929 part-time. Students come from 29 states and territories; 10 other countries; 3% are from out of state; 21% Black or African American, non-Hispanic/Latino; 2% Hispanic/Latino; 0.7% Asian, non-

Hispanic/Latino; 0.1% Native Hawaiian or other Pacific Islander, non-Hispanic/Latino; 2% American Indian or Alaska Native, non-Hispanic/Latino; 2% Two or more races, non-Hispanic/Latino; 16% Race/ethnicity unknown; 0.1% international; 11% transferred in; 37% live on campus. *Retention:* 75% of full-time freshmen returned.

Freshmen *Admission:* 3,856 applied, 2,841 admitted, 953 enrolled. *Test scores:* SAT critical reading scores over 500: 27%; SAT math scores over 500: 29%; SAT writing scores over 500: 15%; ACT scores over 18: 71%; SAT critical reading scores over 600: 1%; SAT math scores over 600: 5%; ACT scores over 24: 14%.

Faculty *Total:* 205, 57% full-time, 26% with terminal degrees. *Student/faculty ratio:* 21:1.

Academics *Calendar:* semesters. *Degrees:* certificates, associate, bachelor's, and master's. *Special study options:* academic remediation for entering students, advanced placement credit, distance learning, independent study, internships, off-campus study, services for LD students, student-designed majors, summer session for credit. *ROTC:* Army (c), Air Force (c).

Computers on Campus 635 computers/terminals are available on campus for general student use. Students can access the following: campus intranet, computer help desk, free student e-mail accounts, online (class) grades, online (class) registration, online (class) schedules, bill payment. Campuswide network is available. 100% of college-owned or -operated housing units are wired for high-speed Internet access. Wireless service is available via classrooms, computer labs, dorm rooms, libraries, student centers.

Student Life *Housing:* on-campus residence required through junior year. *Options:* coed, disabled students. Campus housing is university owned. Freshman campus housing is guaranteed. *Activities and organizations:* drama/theater group, student-run newspaper, radio station, choral group, Criminal Justice, Student Cooperative Alliance, Automotive Club, Gaming Club, African Student Union, national fraternities, national sororities. *Campus security:* 24-hour emergency response devices and patrols, late-night transport/escort service, controlled dormitory access. *Student services:* health clinic, personal/psychological counseling.

Athletics Member NAIA, USCAA. *Intercollegiate sports:* baseball M, basketball M/W, cross-country running M/W, golf M, ice hockey M, lacrosse M/W, soccer M/W, softball W. *Intramural sports:* basketball M/W, soccer M/W, volleyball M/W.

Standardized Tests *Required for some:* SAT or ACT (for admission).

Costs (2012–13) *One-time required fee:* $90. *Tuition:* state resident $5570 full-time, $220 per credit hour part-time; nonresident $10,324 full-time, $597 per credit hour part-time. Full-time tuition and fees vary according to degree level, location, and program. Part-time tuition and fees vary according to degree level, location, and program. *Required fees:* $1400 full-time, $58 per credit hour part-time, $5 per term part-time. *Room and board:* $10,952; room only: $6510. Room and board charges vary according to board plan and housing facility. *Payment plans:* installment, deferred payment. *Waivers:* employees or children of employees.

Applying *Options:* electronic application, early admission, deferred entrance. *Application fee:* $40. *Required:* high school transcript. *Required for some:* essay or personal statement, interview. *Recommended:* minimum 2.0 GPA. *Application deadlines:* rolling (freshmen), rolling (transfers). *Notification:* continuous (freshmen), continuous (transfers).

Freshman Application Contact Ms. Nicole Campbell, Director of Admissions, State University of New York College of Technology at Canton, Cornell Drive, Canton, NY 13617. *Phone:* 315-386-7123. *Toll-free phone:* 800-388-7123. *Fax:* 315-386-7929. *E-mail:* admissions@canton.edu. *Web site:* http://www.canton.edu/.

State University of New York College of Technology at Delhi

Delhi, New York

- **State-supported** 4-year, founded 1913, part of State University of New York System
- **Rural** 405-acre campus
- **Endowment** $2.9 million
- **Coed** 3,430 undergraduate students, 81% full-time, 52% women, 48% men
- **Moderately difficult** entrance level, 57% of applicants were admitted

Undergraduates 2,779 full-time, 651 part-time. Students come from 24 states and territories; 6 other countries; 3% are from out of state; 13% Black or African American, non-Hispanic/Latino; 10% Hispanic/Latino; 3% Asian, non-Hispanic/Latino; 0.6% American Indian or Alaska Native, non-Hispanic/Latino; 7% Race/ethnicity unknown; 1% international; 10% transferred in; 48% live on campus. *Retention:* 77% of full-time freshmen returned.

Freshmen *Admission:* 5,122 applied, 2,907 admitted, 910 enrolled. *Average high school GPA:* 3.3. *Test scores:* SAT critical reading scores over 500: 37%; SAT math scores over 500: 44%; SAT critical reading scores over 600: 5%; SAT math scores over 600: 6%.

Faculty *Total:* 225, 55% full-time, 18% with terminal degrees. *Student/faculty ratio:* 19:1.

Academics *Calendar:* semesters. *Degrees:* certificates, associate, and bachelor's. *Special study options:* academic remediation for entering students, advanced placement credit, distance learning, English as a second language, honors programs, internships, off-campus study, part-time degree program, services for LD students, student-designed majors, summer session for credit.

Computers on Campus 350 computers/terminals are available on campus for general student use. Students can access the following: campus intranet, computer help desk, free student e-mail accounts, online (class) grades, online (class) registration, online (class) schedules. Campuswide network is available. 100% of college-owned or -operated housing units are wired for high-speed Internet access. Wireless service is available via entire campus.

Student Life *Housing:* on-campus residence required through sophomore year. *Options:* coed, women-only. Campus housing is university owned and is provided by a third party. *Activities and organizations:* drama/theater group, student-run newspaper, radio station, choral group, Latin American Student Organization, Hotel Sales Management Association, student radio station, Phi Theta Kappa, Student Programming Board, national fraternities. *Campus security:* 24-hour emergency response devices and patrols, late-night transport/escort service, controlled dormitory access. *Student services:* health clinic, personal/psychological counseling.

Athletics Member NAIA, NJCAA. *Intercollegiate sports:* basketball M/W, cross-country running M/W, golf M/W, lacrosse M, soccer M/W, softball W, swimming and diving M/W, tennis M/W, track and field M/W, volleyball W. *Intramural sports:* basketball M/W, bowling M/W, cross-country running M/W, football M/W, golf M/W, racquetball M/W, skiing (cross-country) M/W, skiing (downhill) M/W, swimming and diving M/W, tennis M/W, volleyball M/W, weight lifting M/W.

Standardized Tests *Required for some:* SAT or ACT (for admission).

Financial Aid Of all full-time matriculated undergraduates who enrolled in 2010, 2,443 applied for aid, 2,416 were judged to have need. 96 Federal Work-Study jobs (averaging $1080).

Applying *Options:* electronic application, early admission, deferred entrance. *Application fee:* $50. *Required:* high school transcript. *Required for some:* minimum 2.0 GPA, some Bachelor degree programs require Associate degree for admission; BSN program requires RN license. *Recommended:* interview. *Application deadlines:* rolling (freshmen), rolling (transfers). *Notification:* continuous (freshmen), continuous (transfers).

Freshman Application Contact Mr. Robert Mazzei, State University of New York College of Technology at Delhi, 2 Main St - Stop 2, Delhi, NY 13753. *Phone:* 607-746-4550. *Toll-free phone:* 800-96-DELHI. *Fax:* 607-746-4104. *E-mail:* mazzeirw@delhi.edu. *Web site:* http://www.delhi.edu/.

State University of New York Downstate Medical Center

Brooklyn, New York

- **State-supported** upper-level, founded 1858, part of State University of New York System
- **Urban** campus
- **Coed**
- **Moderately difficult** entrance level

Academics *Calendar:* semesters. *Degrees:* bachelor's, master's, doctoral, post-master's, postbachelor's, and first professional certificates.

Student Life *Campus security:* late-night transport/escort service.

Costs (2011–12) *Tuition:* state resident $5270 full-time, $220 per credit hour part-time; nonresident $14,320 full-time, $597 per credit hour part-time. Full-time tuition and fees vary according to course load, degree level, and program. Part-time tuition and fees vary according to course load, degree level, and program. *Required fees:* $519 full-time, $21 per credit hour part-time. *Room only:* $12,134. Room and board charges vary according to housing facility.

Financial Aid *Of all full-time matriculated undergraduates who enrolled in 2005,* 302 applied for aid, 302 were judged to have need. 40 Federal Work-Study jobs (averaging $1000). *Average percent of need met:* 50. *Average financial aid package:* $12,500. *Average need-based loan:* $4186. *Average need-based gift aid:* $2729.

Applying *Application fee:* $30.

Application Contact Admissions Office, State University of New York Downstate Medical Center, 450 Clarkson Avenue, Brooklyn, NY 11203-2446. *Phone:* 718-270-2446. *Fax:* 718-270-7592. *E-mail:* admissions@downstate.edu. *Web site:* http://www.downstate.edu/.

State University of New York Empire State College

Saratoga Springs, New York

- **State-supported** comprehensive, founded 1971, part of State University of New York System
- **Small-town** campus
- **Endowment** $14.4 million
- **Coed** 10,983 undergraduate students, 40% full-time, 61% women, 39% men
- **Minimally difficult** entrance level, 80% of applicants were admitted

Undergraduates 4,364 full-time, 6,619 part-time. Students come from 51 states and territories; 24 other countries; 9% are from out of state; 18% Black or African American, non-Hispanic/Latino; 5% Hispanic/Latino; 2% Asian, non-Hispanic/Latino; 1% American Indian or Alaska Native, non-Hispanic/Latino; 0.8% Two or more races, non-Hispanic/Latino; 7% Race/ethnicity unknown; 21% transferred in.

Freshmen *Admission:* 1,555 applied, 1,249 admitted, 466 enrolled.

Faculty *Total:* 1,404, 14% full-time. *Student/faculty ratio:* 9:1.

Academics *Calendar:* continuous. *Degrees:* associate, bachelor's, master's, and postbachelor's certificates (branch locations at 7 regional centers with 35 auxiliary units). *Special study options:* adult/continuing education programs, advanced placement credit, cooperative education, distance learning, external degree program, independent study, off-campus study, part-time degree program, services for LD students, student-designed majors, summer session for credit.

Computers on Campus 100 computers/terminals are available on campus for general student use. Students can access the following: online (class) registration. Campuswide network is available.

Student Life *Housing:* college housing not available.

Costs (2011–12) *Tuition:* state resident $5270 full-time, $220 per credit hour part-time; nonresident $14,320 full-time, $597 per credit hour part-time. Full-time tuition and fees vary according to course level, location, and program. Part-time tuition and fees vary according to course level, location, and program. *Required fees:* $345 full-time, $7 per credit hour part-time, $115 per term part-time.

Applying *Options:* electronic application, early admission. *Required:* essay or personal statement, high school transcript. *Required for some:* interview. *Application deadlines:* rolling (freshmen), rolling (transfers). *Notification:* continuous (transfers).

Freshman Application Contact Ms. Jennifer D'Agostino, Director of Admissions, State University of New York Empire State College, Two Union Avenue, Saratoga Springs, NY 12866. *Phone:* 518-587-2100 Ext. 2214. *Toll-free phone:* 800-847-3000. *Fax:* 518-587-9759. *E-mail:* Jennifer.D'Agostino@esc.edu. *Web site:* http://www.esc.edu/.

State University of New York Institute of Technology

Utica, New York

Freshman Application Contact Amy Stokes, State University of New York Institute of Technology, PO Box 3050, Utica, NY 13504-3050. *Phone:* 315-792-7500. *Toll-free phone:* 866-2-SUNYIT. *Fax:* 315-792-7837. *E-mail:* admissions@sunyit.edu. *Web site:* http://www.sunyit.edu/.

See page 1622 for the College Close-Up.

State University of New York Maritime College

Throggs Neck, New York

- **State-supported** comprehensive, founded 1874, part of State University of New York System
- **Suburban** 56-acre campus with easy access to New York City
- **Endowment** $4.1 million
- **Coed, primarily men** 1,661 undergraduate students, 95% full-time, 11% women, 89% men
- **Very difficult** entrance level, 67% of applicants were admitted

Undergraduates 1,573 full-time, 88 part-time. Students come from 32 states and territories; 16 other countries; 26% are from out of state; 4% Black or African American, non-Hispanic/Latino; 8% Hispanic/Latino; 3% Asian, non-Hispanic/Latino; 0.2% American Indian or Alaska Native, non-Hispanic/Latino; 22% Race/ethnicity unknown; 4% international; 5% transferred in; 78% live on campus. *Retention:* 80% of full-time freshmen returned.

Freshmen *Admission:* 1,348 applied, 907 admitted, 367 enrolled. *Test scores:* SAT critical reading scores over 500: 60%; SAT math scores over 500: 81%;

ACT scores over 18: 95%; SAT critical reading scores over 600: 15%; SAT math scores over 600: 30%; ACT scores over 24: 42%; SAT critical reading scores over 700: 2%; SAT math scores over 700: 3%; ACT scores over 30: 4%.
Faculty *Total:* 148, 64% full-time, 34% with terminal degrees. *Student/faculty ratio:* 14:1.
Academics *Calendar:* semesters plus 2-month summer sea term. *Degrees:* associate, bachelor's, and master's. *Special study options:* academic remediation for entering students, accelerated degree program, adult/continuing education programs, advanced placement credit, cooperative education, distance learning, double majors, English as a second language, honors programs, independent study, internships, services for LD students, summer session for credit. *ROTC:* Army (c), Navy (b).
Computers on Campus 110 computers/terminals are available on campus for general student use. Students can access the following: computer help desk, free student e-mail accounts, online (class) grades, online (class) registration, online (class) schedules. Campuswide network is available. Wireless service is available via classrooms, computer centers, dorm rooms, libraries.
Student Life *Housing:* on-campus residence required through senior year. *Options:* coed. Campus housing is university owned. *Activities and organizations:* choral group, marching band, student government, Maritime Activities and Programs, Campus Crusade for Christ, The Propeller Club, Chorale. *Campus security:* 24-hour emergency response devices and patrols, student patrols, late-night transport/escort service, controlled dormitory access. *Student services:* health clinic, personal/psychological counseling.
Athletics Member NCAA. All Division III. *Intercollegiate sports:* baseball M, basketball M/W, crew W, cross-country running M/W, football M, ice hockey M, lacrosse M/W, riflery M/W, soccer M/W, softball W, swimming and diving M/W, volleyball W. *Intramural sports:* basketball M/W, cross-country running M/W, football M, rugby M, sailing M/W, soccer M/W, softball M/W, volleyball M/W.
Standardized Tests *Required:* SAT or ACT (for admission).
Costs (2011–12) *Tuition:* state resident $5270 full-time, $220 per credit hour part-time; nonresident $14,320 full-time, $597 per credit hour part-time. Full-time tuition and fees vary according to degree level and program. Part-time tuition and fees vary according to course load, degree level, and program. *Required fees:* $1187 full-time, $49 per credit hour part-time. *Room and board:* $10,090; room only: $6340. Room and board charges vary according to board plan and housing facility. *Payment plan:* installment. *Waivers:* employees or children of employees.
Financial Aid Of all full-time matriculated undergraduates who enrolled in 2010, 805 applied for aid, 774 were judged to have need, 259 had their need fully met. In 2010, 88 non-need-based awards were made. *Average percent of need met:* 76%. *Average financial aid package:* $9374. *Average need-based loan:* $4676. *Average need-based gift aid:* $6570. *Average non-need-based aid:* $2808. *Financial aid deadline:* 7/15.
Applying *Options:* electronic application, deferred entrance. *Application fee:* $40. *Required for some:* interview. *Recommended:* essay or personal statement, high school transcript, minimum 3.0 GPA, 1 letter of recommendation. *Application deadlines:* rolling (freshmen), rolling (transfers). *Notification:* continuous (freshmen), continuous (transfers).
Freshman Application Contact Mr. Jonathan White, Dean of Admissions, State University of New York Maritime College, 6 Pennyfield Avenue, Throggs Neck, NY 10465. *Phone:* 718-409-7222. *Fax:* 718-409-7465. *E-mail:* jwhite@sunymaritime.edu. *Web site:* http://www.sunymaritime.edu/.

State University of New York Upstate Medical University

Syracuse, New York

- **State-supported** upper-level, founded 1950, part of State University of New York System
- **Urban** 25-acre campus
- **Endowment** $60.1 million
- **Coed** 296 undergraduate students, 72% full-time, 71% women, 29% men
- **Moderately difficult** entrance level, 34% of applicants were admitted

Undergraduates 213 full-time, 83 part-time. Students come from 8 states and territories; 7% are from out of state; 4% Black or African American, non-Hispanic/Latino; 5% Hispanic/Latino; 3% Asian, non-Hispanic/Latino; 0.3% Native Hawaiian or other Pacific Islander, non-Hispanic/Latino; 0.3% American Indian or Alaska Native, non-Hispanic/Latino; 4% Two or more races, non-Hispanic/Latino; 6% Race/ethnicity unknown; 3% international; 43% transferred in; 50% live on campus.
Freshmen *Admission:* 477 applied, 163 admitted.
Faculty *Total:* 54, 87% full-time, 96% with terminal degrees.
Academics *Calendar:* semesters. *Degrees:* bachelor's, master's, doctoral, post-master's, and first professional certificates. *Special study options:* distance learning, internships, off-campus study, part-time degree program, services for LD students, summer session for credit. *ROTC:* Army (c).

Computers on Campus 150 computers/terminals are available on campus for general student use. Students can access the following: campus intranet, computer help desk, free student e-mail accounts, online (class) grades, online (class) registration, online (class) schedules. Campuswide network is available. 100% of college-owned or -operated housing units are wired for high-speed Internet access. Wireless service is available via entire campus.
Student Life *Housing options:* coed. Campus housing is university owned. *Activities and organizations:* choral group, Upstate Student Government, Campus Activities Governing Board, Emergency Medicine Interest Group, Family Medicine Student Organization, Student National Medical Association. *Campus security:* 24-hour emergency response devices and patrols, late-night transport/escort service, controlled dormitory access. *Student services:* health clinic, personal/psychological counseling.
Athletics *Intramural sports:* basketball M/W, racquetball M/W, soccer M/W, tennis M/W, volleyball M/W.
Costs (2011–12) *Tuition:* state resident $5270 full-time, $220 per credit part-time; nonresident $14,320 full-time, $597 per credit part-time. Full-time tuition and fees vary according to course load and program. Part-time tuition and fees vary according to course load and program. *Required fees:* $610 full-time, $27 per credit hour part-time, $33 per term part-time. *Room and board:* $10,710; room only: $6750. Room and board charges vary according to housing facility. *Payment plan:* installment.
Financial Aid Of all full-time matriculated undergraduates who enrolled in 2009, 227 applied for aid, 227 were judged to have need. *Average percent of need met:* 86%. *Average financial aid package:* $11,847. *Average need-based loan:* $11,128. *Average need-based gift aid:* $1608.
Applying *Options:* electronic application, early admission, deferred entrance. *Application fee:* $50. *Application deadline:* rolling (transfers).
Application Contact Mrs. Donna L. Vavonese, Associate Director of Admissions, State University of New York Upstate Medical University, Weiskotten Hall, 766 Irving Avenue, Syracuse, NY 13210. *Phone:* 315-464-4570. *Toll-free phone:* 800-736-2171. *Fax:* 315-464-8867. *E-mail:* admiss@upstate.edu. *Web site:* http://www.upstate.edu/.

Stony Brook University, State University of New York

Stony Brook, New York

- **State-supported** university, founded 1957, part of State University of New York
- **Suburban** 1450-acre campus with easy access to New York City
- **Endowment** $110.3 million
- **Coed** 15,926 undergraduate students, 92% full-time, 47% women, 53% men
- **Very difficult** entrance level, 39% of applicants were admitted

Undergraduates 14,715 full-time, 1,211 part-time. Students come from 48 states and territories; 111 other countries; 7% are from out of state; 6% Black or African American, non-Hispanic/Latino; 10% Hispanic/Latino; 24% Asian, non-Hispanic/Latino; 0.1% Native Hawaiian or other Pacific Islander, non-Hispanic/Latino; 0.1% American Indian or Alaska Native, non-Hispanic/Latino; 1% Two or more races, non-Hispanic/Latino; 13% Race/ethnicity unknown; 9% international; 8% transferred in; 59% live on campus. *Retention:* 92% of full-time freshmen returned.
Freshmen *Admission:* 26,911 applied, 10,536 admitted, 2,521 enrolled. *Average high school GPA:* 3.6. *Test scores:* SAT critical reading scores over 500: 86%; SAT math scores over 500: 95%; SAT writing scores over 500: 86%; ACT scores over 18: 99%; SAT critical reading scores over 600: 47%; SAT math scores over 600: 73%; SAT writing scores over 600: 46%; ACT scores over 24: 87%; SAT critical reading scores over 700: 8%; SAT math scores over 700: 24%; SAT writing scores over 700: 9%; ACT scores over 30: 20%.
Faculty *Total:* 1,448, 65% full-time. *Student/faculty ratio:* 18:1.
Academics *Calendar:* semesters. *Degrees:* bachelor's, master's, doctoral, post-master's, postbachelor's, and first professional certificates. *Special study options:* academic remediation for entering students, adult/continuing education programs, advanced placement credit, cooperative education, distance learning, double majors, English as a second language, freshman honors college, honors programs, independent study, internships, off-campus study, part-time degree program, services for LD students, student-designed majors, study abroad, summer session for credit. *ROTC:* Army (c). *Unusual degree programs:* 3-2 business administration; engineering; applied math and statistics BS/MPH, pharmacology BS/MPH, women's students BA/MPH, earth and space sciences BA/MPH, occupational therapy BS/MS, linguistics BA/TESOL MA, political science BA/public policy MA, Masters in Adolescent Ed in combination with a variety of academic programs.
Computers on Campus 2,600 computers/terminals are available on campus for general student use. Students can access the following: campus intranet, computer help desk, free student e-mail accounts, online (class) grades, online

(class) registration, online (class) schedules. Campuswide network is available. 100% of college-owned or -operated housing units are wired for high-speed Internet access. Wireless service is available via entire campus.

Student Life *Housing options:* coed. Campus housing is university owned. Freshman campus housing is guaranteed. *Activities and organizations:* drama/theater group, student-run newspaper, radio and television station, choral group, marching band, Inter Fraternity and Sorority Council, Residence Hall Association, Commuter Student Association, Student Activities Board, Chinese Association at Stony Brook, national fraternities, national sororities. *Campus security:* 24-hour emergency response devices and patrols, late-night transport/escort service, controlled dormitory access. *Student services:* health clinic, personal/psychological counseling, women's center, legal services.

Athletics Member NCAA. All Division I. *Intercollegiate sports:* baseball M(s), basketball M(s)/W(s), cross-country running M(s)/W(s), football M(s), lacrosse M(s)/W(s), soccer M(s)/W(s), softball W(s), swimming and diving M(s)/W(s), tennis M(s)/W(s), track and field M(s)/W(s), volleyball W(s). *Intramural sports:* badminton M(c)/W(c), basketball M/W, bowling M/W, cheerleading W, crew M(c)/W(c), equestrian sports M(c)/W(c), fencing M(c)/W(c), golf M, ice hockey M(c), racquetball M/W, rugby M(c)/W(c), soccer M/W, softball M/W, squash M(c)/W(c), table tennis M(c)/W(c), tennis M(c)/W(c), ultimate Frisbee M(c)/W(c), volleyball M/W.

Standardized Tests *Required:* SAT or ACT (for admission).

Costs (2011–12) *Tuition:* state resident $4970 full-time; nonresident $13,380 full-time. Full-time tuition and fees vary according to course load. Part-time tuition and fees vary according to course load. *Required fees:* $1610 full-time. *Room and board:* $10,142; room only: $6442. Room and board charges vary according to board plan and housing facility. *Payment plan:* installment.

Financial Aid Of all full-time matriculated undergraduates who enrolled in 2011, 10,538 applied for aid, 8,725 were judged to have need, 1,699 had their need fully met. 557 Federal Work-Study jobs (averaging $1975). 1,642 state and other part-time jobs (averaging $2238). In 2011, 1130 non-need-based awards were made. *Average percent of need met:* 72%. *Average financial aid package:* $12,739. *Average need-based loan:* $5353. *Average need-based gift aid:* $7621. *Average non-need-based aid:* $3766. *Average indebtedness upon graduation:* $20,371.

Applying *Options:* electronic application, deferred entrance. *Application fee:* $50. *Required:* essay or personal statement, high school transcript, minimum 3.0 GPA, 1 letter of recommendation. *Required for some:* audition. *Recommended:* interview. *Application deadlines:* 1/15 (freshmen), 3/1 (transfers). *Notification:* 4/1 (freshmen), continuous (transfers).

Freshman Application Contact Ms. Judith Burke-Berhanan, Director of Undergraduate Admissions, Stony Brook University, State University of New York, Admissions Office, 118 Administration Building, Stony Brook, NY 11794-1901. *Phone:* 631-632-6868. *Fax:* 631-632-9898. *E-mail:* enroll@stonybrook.edu. *Web site:* http://www.sunysb.edu/.

See below for display ad and page 1628 for the College Close-Up.

Swedish Institute, College of Health Sciences
New York, New York

Freshman Application Contact Admissions Advisor, Swedish Institute, College of Health Sciences, 226 West 26th Street, New York, NY 10001. *Phone:* 212-914-5900 Ext. 125. *E-mail:* admissions@swedishinstitute.edu. *Web site:* http://www.swedishinstitute.org/.

Syracuse University
Syracuse, New York

- **Independent** university, founded 1870
- **Urban** 200-acre campus with easy access to Syracuse
- **Endowment** $913.7 million
- **Coed** 14,671 undergraduate students, 95% full-time, 56% women, 44% men
- **Moderately difficult** entrance level, 49% of applicants were admitted

Undergraduates 13,987 full-time, 684 part-time. Students come from 49 states and territories; 77 other countries; 54% are from out of state; 8% Black or African American, non-Hispanic/Latino; 9% Hispanic/Latino; 9% Asian, non-Hispanic/Latino; 0.1% Native Hawaiian or other Pacific Islander, non-Hispanic/Latino; 0.7% American Indian or Alaska Native, non-Hispanic/Latino; 2% Two or more races, non-Hispanic/Latino; 7% Race/ethnicity unknown; 8% international; 3% transferred in; 75% live on campus. *Retention:* 92% of full-time freshmen returned.

Freshmen *Admission:* 25,884 applied, 12,779 admitted, 3,410 enrolled. *Average high school GPA:* 3.6. *Test scores:* SAT critical reading scores over 500: 81%; SAT math scores over 500: 89%; SAT writing scores over 500: 85%; ACT scores over 18: 98%; SAT critical reading scores over 600: 34%; SAT math scores over 600: 52%; SAT writing scores over 600: 42%; ACT scores

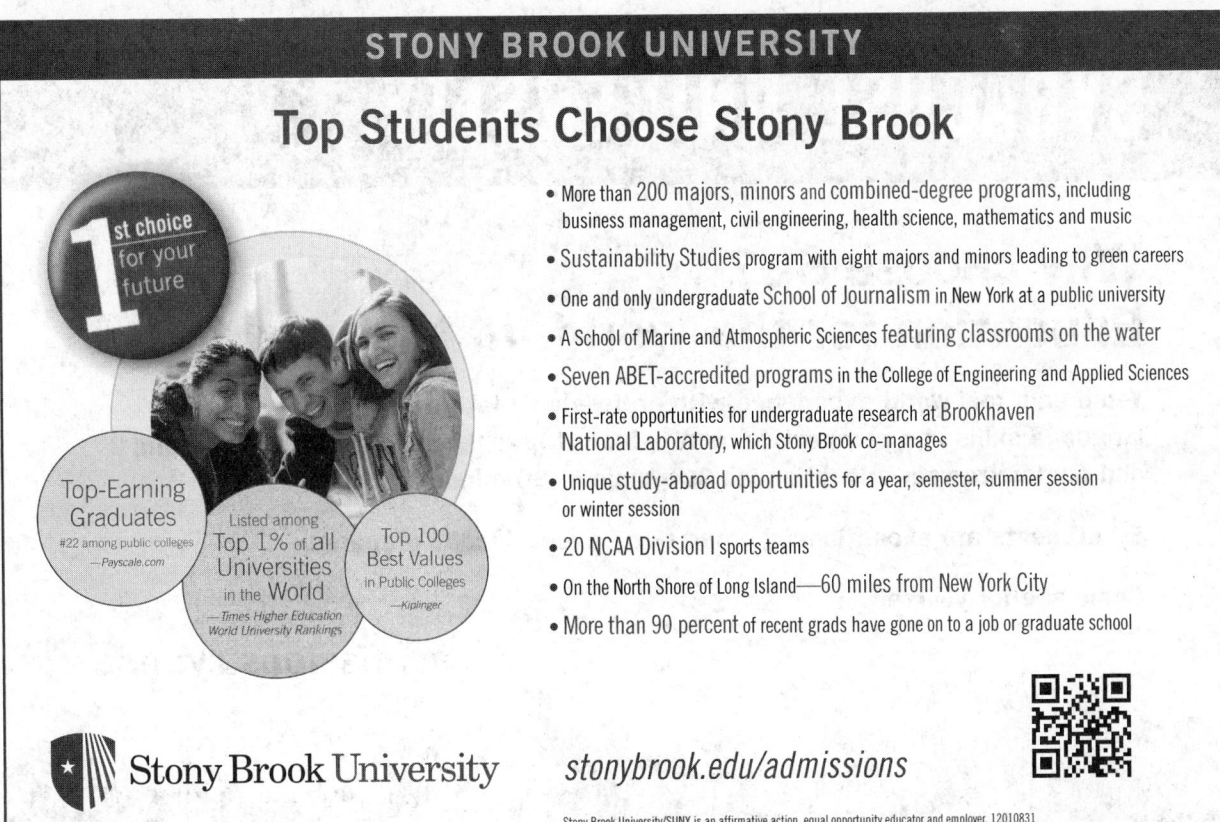

over 24: 74%; SAT critical reading scores over 700: 5%; SAT math scores over 700: 10%; SAT writing scores over 700: 7%; ACT scores over 30: 14%.

Faculty *Total:* 1,559, 63% full-time. *Student/faculty ratio:* 16:1.

Academics *Calendar:* semesters. *Degrees:* certificates, associate, bachelor's, master's, doctoral, post-master's, postbachelor's, and first professional certificates. *Special study options:* academic remediation for entering students, accelerated degree program, adult/continuing education programs, advanced placement credit, cooperative education, distance learning, double majors, English as a second language, freshman honors college, honors programs, independent study, internships, off-campus study, part-time degree program, services for LD students, student-designed majors, study abroad, summer session for credit. *ROTC:* Army (b), Air Force (b).

Computers on Campus 3,500 computers/terminals and 678 ports are available on campus for general student use. Students can access the following: campus intranet, computer help desk, free student e-mail accounts, online (class) grades, online (class) registration, online (class) schedules, online services, networked client and server computing. Campuswide network is available. 100% of college-owned or -operated housing units are wired for high-speed Internet access. Wireless service is available via classrooms, computer centers, computer labs, dorm rooms, learning centers, libraries, student centers.

Student Life *Housing:* on-campus residence required through sophomore year. *Options:* coed, disabled students. Campus housing is university owned. Freshman campus housing is guaranteed. *Activities and organizations:* drama/theater group, student-run newspaper, radio and television station, choral group, marching band, University Union, Citrus TV, Danceworks, Habitat for Humanity, Student Association, national fraternities, national sororities. *Campus security:* 24-hour emergency response devices and patrols, student patrols, late-night transport/escort service, controlled dormitory access, crisis alert notification system, outdoor emergency sirens, off-campus patrols in student rental neighborhoods. *Student services:* health clinic, personal/psychological counseling, women's center, legal services.

Athletics Member NCAA. All Division I except football (Division I-A). *Intercollegiate sports:* badminton M(c)/W(c), baseball M(c), basketball M(s)/W(s), bowling M(c)/W(c), cheerleading M/W, crew M(s)/W(s), cross-country running M(s)/W(s), equestrian sports M(c)/W(c), fencing M(c)/W(c), field hockey W(s), gymnastics M(c)/W(c), ice hockey M(c)/W(s), lacrosse M(s)/W(s), rugby M(c)/W(c), sailing M(c)/W(c), skiing (downhill) M(c)/W(c), soccer M(s)/W(s), softball W(s), tennis M(c)/W(s), track and field M(s)/W(s), volleyball M(c)/W(s), water polo M(c)/W(c), wrestling M(c). *Intramural sports:* basketball M/W, field hockey M(c)/W(c), football M/W, golf M(c)/W(c), ice

hockey M/W, lacrosse M(c)/W(c), racquetball M/W, soccer M/W, softball M/W, swimming and diving M(c)/W(c), tennis M/W, ultimate Frisbee M(c)/W(c), volleyball M/W.

Standardized Tests *Required:* SAT or ACT (for admission).

Costs (2011–12) *Comprehensive fee:* $50,921 includes full-time tuition ($36,300), mandatory fees ($1367), and room and board ($13,254). Full-time tuition and fees vary according to course load. Part-time tuition: $1580 per credit hour. Part-time tuition and fees vary according to course load. *College room only:* $7004. Room and board charges vary according to board plan and housing facility. *Payment plan:* installment. *Waivers:* employees or children of employees.

Financial Aid Of all full-time matriculated undergraduates who enrolled in 2011, 9,418 applied for aid, 8,038 were judged to have need, 5,220 had their need fully met. In 2011, 1465 non-need-based awards were made. *Average percent of need met:* 92%. *Average financial aid package:* $32,760. *Average need-based loan:* $7400. *Average need-based gift aid:* $23,580. *Average non-need-based aid:* $8940. *Average indebtedness upon graduation:* $32,663. *Financial aid deadline:* 2/1.

Applying *Options:* electronic application, early admission, early decision, deferred entrance. *Application fee:* $70. *Required:* essay or personal statement, high school transcript, 2 letters of recommendation, Visit the Apply to SU link at admissions.syr.edu for information about all application requirements. *Application deadline:* 1/1 (freshmen). *Early decision deadline:* 11/15.

Freshman Application Contact Office of Admissions, Syracuse University, 100 Crouse-Hinds Hall, 900 South Crouse Avenue, Syracuse, NY 13244-2130. *Phone:* 315-443-3611. *Fax:* 315-443-4226. *E-mail:* orange@syr.edu. *Web site:* http://www.syr.edu.

See below for display ad and page 1634 for the College Close-Up.

Talmudical Institute of Upstate New York

Rochester, New York

Director of Admissions Rabbi Menachem Davidowitz, Director of Admissions, Talmudical Institute of Upstate New York, 769 Park Avenue, Rochester, NY 14607-3046. *Phone:* 716-473-2810. *E-mail:* yeshiva@tiuny.org. *Web site:* http://www.tiuny.org/.

Talmudical Seminary Oholei Torah
Brooklyn, New York

Director of Admissions Rabbi Yisroel Friedman, Director of Academic Affairs, Talmudical Seminary Oholei Torah, 667 Eastern Parkway, Brooklyn, NY 11213-3310. *Phone:* 718-363-2034. *E-mail:* info@oholeitorah.com.

Torah Temimah Talmudical Seminary
Brooklyn, New York

Director of Admissions Principal, Torah Temimah Talmudical Seminary, 507 Ocean Parkway, Brooklyn, NY 11218-5913. *Phone:* 718-853-8500.

Touro College
New York, New York

- **Independent** comprehensive, founded 1971
- **Urban** campus
- **Coed** 8,150 undergraduate students
- **Moderately difficult** entrance level, 57% of applicants were admitted

Freshmen *Admission:* 2,576 applied, 1,465 admitted.

Academics *Calendar:* semesters. *Degrees:* certificates, associate, bachelor's, master's, doctoral, and post-master's certificates. *Special study options:* academic remediation for entering students, accelerated degree program, advanced placement credit, distance learning, double majors, English as a second language, external degree program, freshman honors college, honors programs, independent study, internships, part-time degree program, services for LD students, student-designed majors, study abroad, summer session for credit. *Unusual degree programs:* 3-2 physical therapy, occupational therapy, physician assistant.

Computers on Campus Students can access the following: free student e-mail accounts, online (class) grades, online (class) registration, online (class) schedules. Campuswide network is available.

Student Life *Housing options:* Campus housing is university owned. *Activities and organizations:* student-run newspaper. *Campus security:* 24-hour emergency response devices and patrols. *Student services:* personal/psychological counseling.

Standardized Tests *Recommended:* SAT or ACT (for admission).

Costs (2012–13) *Comprehensive fee:* $25,770 includes full-time tuition ($14,800), mandatory fees ($570), and room and board ($10,400). Full-time tuition and fees vary according to degree level, location, and program. Part-time tuition and fees vary according to degree level, location, and program. *College room only:* $7300. Room and board charges vary according to housing facility.

Financial Aid Of all full-time matriculated undergraduates who enrolled in 2002, 5,940 applied for aid, 5,940 were judged to have need. *Average percent of need met:* 90%. *Average financial aid package:* $9000. *Average need-based loan:* $4275. *Average non-need-based aid:* $1500. *Average indebtedness upon graduation:* $17,000.

Applying *Options:* early admission, deferred entrance. *Application fee:* $50. *Required:* high school transcript. *Required for some:* minimum 3.0 GPA, 2 letters of recommendation, interview. *Recommended:* essay or personal statement, 1 letter of recommendation. *Application deadlines:* rolling (freshmen), rolling (out-of-state freshmen), rolling (transfers). *Notification:* continuous (freshmen), continuous (out-of-state freshmen), continuous (transfers).

Freshman Application Contact Mr. David Luk, Associate Director of Admissions, Touro College, 27-33 West 23rd Street, New York, NY 10010. *Phone:* 212-463-0400 Ext. 5644. *Fax:* 212-627-9542. *E-mail:* david.luk@touro.edu. *Web site:* http://www.touro.edu/.

Union College
Schenectady, New York

- **Independent** 4-year, founded 1795
- **Urban** 100-acre campus
- **Endowment** $327.8 million
- **Coed** 2,220 undergraduate students, 99% full-time, 47% women, 53% men
- **Very difficult** entrance level, 43% of applicants were admitted

Undergraduates 2,194 full-time, 26 part-time. Students come from 38 states and territories; 39 other countries; 58% are from out of state; 5% Black or African American, non-Hispanic/Latino; 6% Hispanic/Latino; 6% Asian, non-Hispanic/Latino; 0.3% American Indian or Alaska Native, non-Hispanic/Latino; 1% Two or more races, non-Hispanic/Latino; 0.3% Race/ethnicity unknown; 5% international; 1% transferred in; 87% live on campus. *Retention:* 94% of full-time freshmen returned.

Freshmen *Admission:* 5,151 applied, 2,197 admitted, 572 enrolled. *Average high school GPA:* 3.49. *Test scores:* SAT critical reading scores over 500: 98%; SAT math scores over 500: 100%; SAT writing scores over 500: 98%; ACT scores over 18: 100%; SAT critical reading scores over 600: 74%; SAT

math scores over 600: 85%; SAT writing scores over 600: 76%; ACT scores over 24: 100%; SAT critical reading scores over 700: 18%; SAT math scores over 700: 30%; SAT writing scores over 700: 20%; ACT scores over 30: 46%.

Faculty *Total:* 237, 85% full-time, 89% with terminal degrees. *Student/faculty ratio:* 10:1.

Academics *Calendar:* trimesters. *Degree:* bachelor's. *Special study options:* accelerated degree program, advanced placement credit, double majors, honors programs, independent study, internships, off-campus study, student-designed majors, study abroad, summer session for credit. *ROTC:* Army (c), Navy (c), Air Force (c).

Computers on Campus 541 computers/terminals and 3,032 ports are available on campus for general student use. Students can access the following: campus intranet, computer help desk, free student e-mail accounts, online (class) grades, online (class) registration, online (class) schedules, multimedia lab. Campuswide network is available. 100% of college-owned or -operated housing units are wired for high-speed Internet access. Wireless service is available via classrooms, computer centers, computer labs, learning centers, libraries, student centers.

Student Life *Housing:* on-campus residence required through senior year. *Options:* coed. Campus housing is university owned. Freshman campus housing is guaranteed. *Activities and organizations:* drama/theater group, student-run newspaper, radio and television station, choral group, U-Program (Programming Board), speaker's forum, student newspaper, Concert Committee, ski club, national fraternities, national sororities. *Campus security:* 24-hour emergency response devices and patrols, late-night transport/escort service, controlled dormitory access, awareness programs, bicycle patrol, shuttle service. *Student services:* health clinic, personal/psychological counseling, women's center.

Athletics Member NCAA. All Division III except men's and women's ice hockey (Division I). *Intercollegiate sports:* baseball M, basketball M/W, cheerleading M(c)/W(c), crew M/W, cross-country running M/W, fencing M(c)/W(c), field hockey W, football M, golf M(c)/W(c), ice hockey M/W, lacrosse M/W, rugby M(c)/W(c), soccer M/W, softball W, swimming and diving M/W, tennis M/W, track and field M/W, ultimate Frisbee M(c)/W(c), volleyball W. *Intramural sports:* basketball M/W, football M/W, ice hockey M(c), lacrosse M(c)/W, racquetball M/W, rock climbing M(c)/W(c), skiing (downhill) M(c)/W(c), soccer M/W, softball M/W, squash M/W, tennis M/W, volleyball M/W, water polo M/W.

Standardized Tests *Required for some:* SAT or ACT (for admission), SAT and SAT Subject Tests or ACT (for admission).

Costs (2011–12) *Comprehensive fee:* $54,273. *Payment plan:* installment. *Waivers:* senior citizens and employees or children of employees.

Financial Aid Of all full-time matriculated undergraduates who enrolled in 2010, 1,307 applied for aid, 1,113 were judged to have need, 1,078 had their need fully met. In 2010, 335 non-need-based awards were made. *Average percent of need met:* 97%. *Average financial aid package:* $34,600. *Average need-based loan:* $4167. *Average need-based gift aid:* $29,907. *Average non-need-based aid:* $10,538. *Average indebtedness upon graduation:* $25,621. *Financial aid deadline:* 2/1.

Applying *Options:* electronic application, early admission, early decision, deferred entrance. *Application fee:* $50. *Required:* essay or personal statement, high school transcript, 2 letters of recommendation. *Recommended:* interview. *Application deadlines:* 1/15 (freshmen), 5/1 (transfers). *Early decision deadline:* 11/15 (for plan 1), 1/15 (for plan 2). *Notification:* 4/1 (freshmen), continuous (transfers), 12/15 (early decision plan 1), 2/1 (early decision plan 2).

Freshman Application Contact Union College, Grant Hall, 807 Union Street, Schenectady, NY 12308. *Phone:* 518-388-6112. *Toll-free phone:* 888-843-6688. *Fax:* 518-388-6986. *E-mail:* admissions@union.edu. *Web site:* http://www.union.edu/.

See page 639 for display ad and page 1648 for the College Close-Up.

United States Merchant Marine Academy

Kings Point, New York

- **Federally supported** comprehensive, founded 1943
- **Suburban** 82-acre campus with easy access to New York City
- **Coed** 1,058 undergraduate students, 100% full-time, 13% women, 87% men
- **Very difficult** entrance level, 14% of applicants were admitted

Undergraduates 1,058 full-time. Students come from 52 states and territories; 4 other countries; 89% are from out of state; 100% live on campus. *Retention:* 92% of full-time freshmen returned.

Freshmen *Admission:* 2,076 applied, 285 admitted, 285 enrolled. *Average high school GPA:* 3.6. *Test scores:* SAT critical reading scores over 500: 99%; SAT math scores over 500: 100%; ACT scores over 18: 100%; SAT critical reading scores over 600: 43%; SAT math scores over 600: 76%; ACT scores

over 24: 98%; SAT critical reading scores over 700: 9%; SAT math scores over 700: 17%; ACT scores over 30: 14%.

Faculty *Total:* 89.

Academics *Calendar:* trimesters. *Degrees:* bachelor's and master's. *Special study options:* honors programs, internships.

Computers on Campus 1,200 computers/terminals are available on campus for general student use. Students can access the following: campus intranet, computer help desk, free student e-mail accounts, engineering and economics software. Campuswide network is available.

Student Life *Housing:* on-campus residence required through senior year. *Options:* coed. Campus housing is university owned. Freshman campus housing is guaranteed. *Activities and organizations:* drama/theater group, student-run newspaper, choral group, marching band, Regimental Band, CFC, Neuman Club, Honor Guard. *Campus security:* 24-hour patrols. *Student services:* health clinic, personal/psychological counseling.

Athletics Member NCAA. All Division III. *Intercollegiate sports:* baseball M, basketball M/W, crew M/W, cross-country running M/W, football M, golf M/W, ice hockey M(c), lacrosse M, rugby M(c), sailing M, soccer M, softball W, swimming and diving M, tennis M/W, track and field M/W, volleyball W, wrestling M. *Intramural sports:* basketball M/W, bowling M/W, crew M/W, cross-country running M/W, football M, golf M/W, lacrosse M, racquetball M/W, riflery M/W, rugby M, sailing M/W, skiing (cross-country) M/W, skiing (downhill) M/W, soccer M/W, softball M/W, swimming and diving M/W, tennis M/W, track and field M/W, volleyball M/W, water polo M, wrestling M.

Standardized Tests *Required:* SAT or ACT (for admission).

Costs (2011–12) *Tuition:* Full-time tuition and fees vary according to student level. Tuition, room and board, and medical and dental care are provided by the U.S. government. Each midshipman receives a monthly stipend while assigned aboard ship for training. Entering freshmen are required to pay fees for laptop, equipment, and activity fees. *Required fees:* $2905 full-time.

Applying *Options:* electronic application. *Required:* essay or personal statement, high school transcript, 3 letters of recommendation, SAT or ACT. *Recommended:* interview. *Application deadlines:* 3/1 (freshmen), 3/1 (transfers). *Notification:* continuous until 4/1 (freshmen), continuous until 4/1 (transfers).

Freshman Application Contact Capt. Robert E. Johnson, Director of Admissions and Financial Aid, United States Merchant Marine Academy, 300 Steamboat Road, Kings Point, NY 11024-1699. *Phone:* 516-726-5641. *Toll-free phone:* 866-546-4778. *Fax:* 516-773-5390. *E-mail:* admissions@usmma.edu. *Web site:* http://www.usmma.edu/.

See page 1654 for the College Close-Up.

United States Military Academy
West Point, New York

- **Federally supported** 4-year, founded 1802
- **Small-town** 16,080-acre campus with easy access to New York City
- **Endowment** $187.7 million
- **Coed** 4,624 undergraduate students, 100% full-time, 16% women, 84% men
- **Most difficult** entrance level, 11% of applicants were admitted

Undergraduates 4,624 full-time. Students come from 55 states and territories; 30 other countries; 93% are from out of state; 7% Black or African American, non-Hispanic/Latino; 9% Hispanic/Latino; 5% Asian, non-Hispanic/Latino; 0.4% Native Hawaiian or other Pacific Islander, non-Hispanic/Latino; 0.7% American Indian or Alaska Native, non-Hispanic/Latino; 4% Two or more races, non-Hispanic/Latino; 0.9% Race/ethnicity unknown; 1% international; 100% live on campus. *Retention:* 94% of full-time freshmen returned.

Freshmen *Admission:* 13,954 applied, 1,473 admitted, 1,231 enrolled. *Test scores:* SAT critical reading scores over 500: 94%; SAT math scores over 500: 96%; SAT writing scores over 500: 91%; ACT scores over 18: 100%; SAT critical reading scores over 600: 61%; SAT math scores over 600: 71%; SAT writing scores over 600: 52%; ACT scores over 24: 87%; SAT critical reading scores over 700: 18%; SAT math scores over 700: 23%; SAT writing scores over 700: 13%; ACT scores over 30: 38%.

Faculty *Total:* 613, 100% full-time, 46% with terminal degrees. *Student/faculty ratio:* 8:1.

Academics *Calendar:* semesters. *Degree:* bachelor's. *Special study options:* academic remediation for entering students, advanced placement credit, double majors, honors programs, independent study, off-campus study, study abroad, summer session for credit.

Computers on Campus 900 computers/terminals are available on campus for general student use. Students can access the following: computer help desk, free student e-mail accounts, online (class) grades, online (class) registration, online (class) schedules. Campuswide network is available. 100% of college-owned or -operated housing units are wired for high-speed Internet access. Wireless service is available via entire campus.

Student Life *Housing:* on-campus residence required through senior year. *Options:* coed. Campus housing is university owned. Freshman campus housing is guaranteed. *Activities and organizations:* drama/theater group, student-run radio station, choral group, Asian-Pacific Club, Officers' Christian Fellowship, Spirit Support Group, Fellowship of Christian Athletes, Philosophy Forum. *Campus security:* 24-hour emergency response devices and patrols, late-night transport/escort service. *Student services:* health clinic, personal/psychological counseling, legal services.

Athletics Member NCAA. All Division I except football (Division I-A). *Intercollegiate sports:* baseball M, basketball M/W, cheerleading M/W, crew M(c)/W(c), cross-country running M/W, equestrian sports M(c)/W(c), fencing M(c)/W(c), golf M, gymnastics M, ice hockey M, lacrosse M/W(c), racquetball M(c)/W(c), riflery M/W, rock climbing M(c)/W(c), rugby M(c)/W(c), sailing M(c)/W(c), skiing (cross-country) M(c)/W(c), skiing (downhill) M(c)/W(c), soccer M/W, softball W, swimming and diving M/W, tennis M/W, track and field M/W, volleyball M(c)/W, water polo M(c), weight lifting M(c)/W(c), wrestling M. *Intramural sports:* basketball M/W, bowling M(c)/W(c), football M, rugby M/W, soccer M/W, squash M/W, swimming and diving M/W, ultimate Frisbee M/W, wrestling M.

Standardized Tests *Required:* SAT or ACT (for admission).

Costs (2011–12) *Comprehensive fee:* Tuition is covered by a full scholarship for all students who attend West Point. All students are on Active Duty Status as members of the U.S. Army and receive an annual salary of approximately $10,150. Room and board, medical and dental care are provided for by the U.S. Army; however, a one-time deposit of $2,000 is required upon admission in order to defray the initial cost of uniforms, books, supplies, equipment and fees. A cadet's salary pays for uniforms, activities, services, books, sundries, and other personal services they are permitted.

Applying *Options:* electronic application. *Required:* essay or personal statement, high school transcript, 4 letters of recommendation, You must obtain nominations from an approved source, pass a Department of Defense qualifying medical examination, must be at least 17 but not yet 23 years of age by July 1 of year of entry, and be an unmarried U.S. citizen (foreign nationals with approval) with no parental obligations. *Recommended:* interview. *Application deadline:* 2/28 (freshmen). *Notification:* 5/1 (freshmen).

Freshman Application Contact Col. Deborah J. McDonald, Director of Admissions, United States Military Academy, 600 Thayer Road, West Point, NY 10996. *Phone:* 845-938-4041. *E-mail:* 8dad@sunams.usma.army.mil. *Web site:* http://www.usma.edu/.

United Talmudical Seminary
Brooklyn, New York

Director of Admissions Director of Admissions, United Talmudical Seminary, 191 Rodney Street, Brooklyn, NY 11211. *Phone:* 718-963-9770.

University at Albany, State University of New York
Albany, New York

- **State-supported** university, founded 1844, part of State University of New York System
- **Suburban** 560-acre campus
- **Endowment** $27.7 million
- **Coed** 12,797 undergraduate students, 94% full-time, 49% women, 51% men
- **Very difficult** entrance level, 51% of applicants were admitted

Undergraduates 11,967 full-time, 830 part-time. Students come from 38 states and territories; 53 other countries; 5% are from out of state; 11% Black or African American, non-Hispanic/Latino; 11% Hispanic/Latino; 7% Asian, non-Hispanic/Latino; 0.2% Native Hawaiian or other Pacific Islander, non-Hispanic/Latino; 0.3% American Indian or Alaska Native, non-Hispanic/Latino; 2% Two or more races, non-Hispanic/Latino; 7% Race/ethnicity unknown; 4% international; 11% transferred in; 57% live on campus. *Retention:* 84% of full-time freshmen returned.

Freshmen *Admission:* 21,054 applied, 10,810 admitted, 2,422 enrolled. *Average high school GPA:* 3.3. *Test scores:* SAT critical reading scores over 500: 75%; SAT math scores over 500: 85%; ACT scores over 18: 99%; SAT critical reading scores over 600: 20%; SAT math scores over 600: 29%; ACT scores over 24: 56%; SAT critical reading scores over 700: 2%; SAT math scores over 700: 3%; ACT scores over 30: 4%.

Faculty *Total:* 1,267, 47% full-time. *Student/faculty ratio:* 19:1.

Academics *Calendar:* semesters. *Degrees:* bachelor's, master's, doctoral, post-master's, postbachelor's, and first professional certificates. *Special study options:* accelerated degree program, advanced placement credit, distance learning, double majors, English as a second language, freshman honors college, honors programs, independent study, internships, off-campus study, part-

time degree program, services for LD students, student-designed majors, study abroad, summer session for credit. *ROTC:* Army (b), Air Force (c). *Unusual degree programs:* 3-2 business administration; engineering with Rensselaer Polytechnic Institute, State University of New York at Binghamton, State University of New York at New Paltz, Clarkson University.

Computers on Campus 500 computers/terminals are available on campus for general student use. Students can access the following: campus intranet, computer help desk, free student e-mail accounts, online (class) grades, online (class) registration, online (class) schedules. Campuswide network is available. 100% of college-owned or -operated housing units are wired for high-speed Internet access. Wireless service is available via classrooms, computer centers, computer labs, dorm rooms, libraries, student centers.

Student Life *Housing:* on-campus residence required through sophomore year. *Options:* coed. Campus housing is university owned. Freshman campus housing is guaranteed. *Activities and organizations:* drama/theater group, student-run newspaper, radio and television station, choral group, intramural athletics, cultural organizations, political organizations, community service, national fraternities, national sororities. *Campus security:* 24-hour emergency response devices and patrols, late-night transport/escort service, controlled dormitory access, Five Quad Ambulance Service; On-Campus Dead Car Battery Assistance. *Student services:* health clinic, personal/psychological counseling, legal services.

Athletics Member NCAA. All Division I. *Intercollegiate sports:* baseball M(s), basketball M(s)/W(s), crew M/W, cross-country running M(s)/W(s), field hockey W(s), football M(s), golf W(s), lacrosse M(s)/W(s), rock climbing M/W, soccer M(s)/W(s), softball W(s), tennis W(s), track and field M(s)/W(s), volleyball W(s). *Intramural sports:* badminton M/W, baseball M, basketball M/W, equestrian sports W, fencing M/W, football M(c), ice hockey M, lacrosse M, racquetball M/W, rugby M/W, skiing (cross-country) M/W, skiing (downhill) M/W, soccer M/W, softball W, tennis M/W, track and field M/W, ultimate Frisbee M/W, volleyball M/W, wrestling M.

Standardized Tests *Required:* SAT or ACT (for admission).

Costs (2012–13) *Tuition:* state resident $5570 full-time, $232 per credit hour part-time; nonresident $16,190 full-time, $675 per credit hour part-time. Part-time tuition and fees vary according to course load. *Required fees:* $1902 full-time. *Room and board:* $11,276; room only: $6976. Room and board charges vary according to board plan and housing facility.

Financial Aid Of all full-time matriculated undergraduates who enrolled in 2011, 9,310 applied for aid, 7,257 were judged to have need, 300 had their need fully met. 771 Federal Work-Study jobs (averaging $1555). 227 state and other part-time jobs (averaging $5906). In 2011, 456 non-need-based awards were made. *Average percent of need met:* 64%. *Average financial aid package:* $9553. *Average need-based loan:* $4364. *Average need-based gift aid:* $6544. *Average non-need-based aid:* $3920. *Average indebtedness upon graduation:* $23,039.

Applying *Options:* electronic application, early admission, early action, deferred entrance. *Application fee:* $50. *Required:* essay or personal statement, high school transcript, 1 letter of recommendation. *Required for some:* portfolio, audition. *Application deadlines:* 3/1 (freshmen), 3/1 (out-of-state freshmen), 8/1 (transfers), 11/15 (early action). *Notification:* continuous (freshmen), continuous (transfers), 1/15 (early action).

Freshman Application Contact University at Albany, State University of New York, 1400 Washington Avenue, Albany, NY 12222-0001. *Phone:* 518-442-5435. *Web site:* http://www.albany.edu/.

University at Buffalo, the State University of New York

Buffalo, New York

- **State-supported** university, founded 1846, part of State University of New York System
- **Suburban** 1350-acre campus
- **Endowment** $494.8 million
- **Coed** 19,334 undergraduate students, 91% full-time, 46% women, 54% men
- **Moderately difficult** entrance level, 53% of applicants were admitted

Undergraduates 17,664 full-time, 1,670 part-time. Students come from 44 states and territories; 88 other countries; 4% are from out of state; 7% Black or African American, non-Hispanic/Latino; 7% Hispanic/Latino; 11% Asian, non-Hispanic/Latino; 0.1% Native Hawaiian or other Pacific Islander, non-Hispanic/Latino; 0.6% American Indian or Alaska Native, non-Hispanic/Latino; 5% Race/ethnicity unknown; 16% international; 10% transferred in; 35% live on campus. *Retention:* 88% of full-time freshmen returned.

Freshmen *Admission:* 21,357 applied, 11,363 admitted, 3,255 enrolled. *Average high school GPA:* 3.3. *Test scores:* SAT critical reading scores over 500: 78%; SAT math scores over 500: 92%; ACT scores over 18: 99%; SAT critical reading scores over 600: 29%; SAT math scores over 600: 54%; ACT scores over 24: 71%; SAT critical reading scores over 700: 5%; SAT math scores over 700: 12%; ACT scores over 30: 13%.

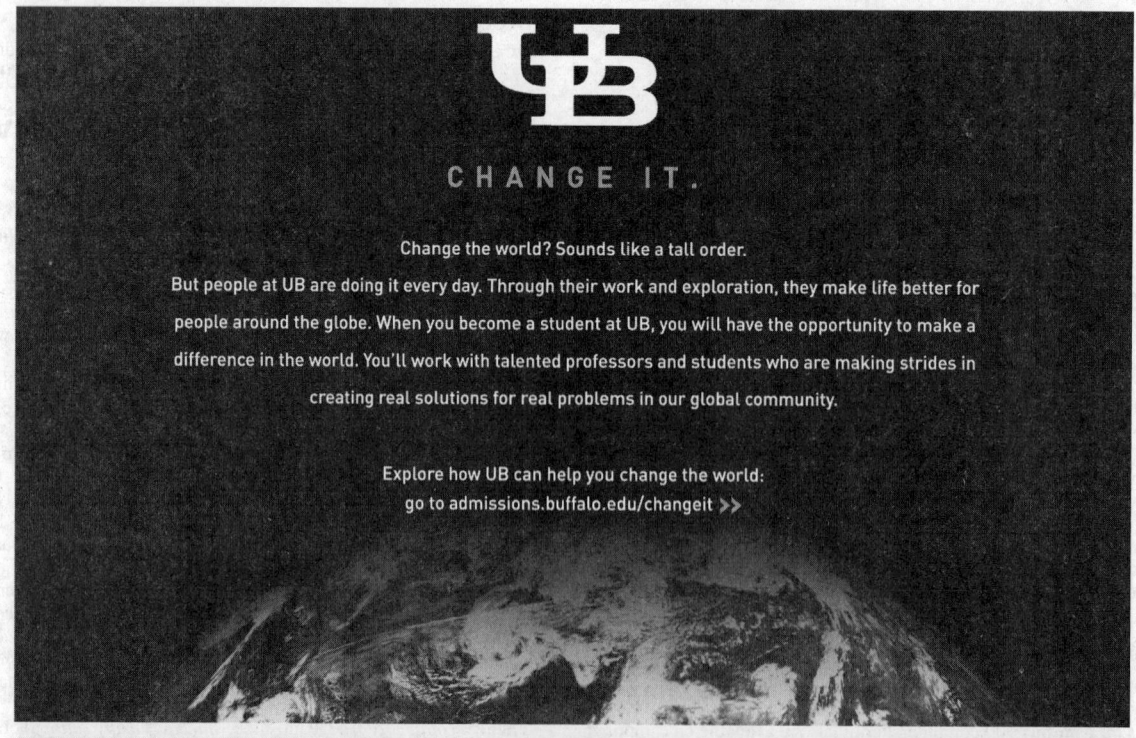

Faculty *Total:* 1,676, 69% full-time, 83% with terminal degrees. *Student/faculty ratio:* 15:1.

Academics *Calendar:* semesters. *Degrees:* bachelor's, master's, doctoral, post-master's, and first professional certificates. *Special study options:* academic remediation for entering students, accelerated degree program, advanced placement credit, cooperative education, distance learning, double majors, English as a second language, freshman honors college, honors programs, independent study, internships, off-campus study, part-time degree program, services for LD students, student-designed majors, study abroad, summer session for credit. *ROTC:* Army (c). *Unusual degree programs:* 3-2 business administration; engineering; nursing; social work; law.

Computers on Campus 2,300 computers/terminals are available on campus for general student use. Students can access the following: campus intranet, computer help desk, free student e-mail accounts, online (class) grades, online (class) registration, online (class) schedules. Campuswide network is available. 100% of college-owned or -operated housing units are wired for high-speed Internet access. Wireless service is available via entire campus.

Student Life *Housing options:* coed, disabled students. Campus housing is university owned. Freshman campus housing is guaranteed. *Activities and organizations:* drama/theater group, student-run newspaper, radio and television station, choral group, marching band, national fraternities, national sororities. *Campus security:* 24-hour emergency response devices and patrols, student patrols, late-night transport/escort service, controlled dormitory access, self-defense and awareness programs, security cameras. *Student services:* health clinic, personal/psychological counseling, legal services.

Athletics Member NCAA. All Division I except football (Division I-A). *Intercollegiate sports:* baseball M(s), basketball M(s)/W(s), crew W(s), cross-country running M(s)/W(s), soccer M(s)/W(s), softball W(s), swimming and diving M(s)/W(s), tennis M(s)/W(s), track and field M(s)/W(s), volleyball W(s), wrestling M(s). *Intramural sports:* badminton M(c)/W(c), baseball M(c), basketball M/W, crew M(c), cross-country running M(c)/W(c), equestrian sports M(c)/W(c), field hockey W(c), gymnastics M(c)/W(c), ice hockey M(c)/W(c), lacrosse M(c)/W(c), racquetball M/W, rock climbing M(c)/W(c), rugby M(c)/W(c), skiing (cross-country) M(c)/W(c), skiing (downhill) M(c)/W(c), soccer M(c)/W(c), softball M/W, tennis M(c)/W(c), track and field M(c)/W(c), ultimate Frisbee M(c)/W(c), volleyball M(c)/W(c), wrestling M(c).

Standardized Tests *Required:* SAT or ACT (for admission).

Costs (2011–12) *Tuition:* state resident $5270 full-time, $220 per credit hour part-time; nonresident $14,720 full-time, $613 per credit hour part-time. Part-time tuition and fees vary according to course load. *Required fees:* $2212 full-time, $92 per credit hour part-time. *Room and board:* $10,728; room only: $6228. Room and board charges vary according to board plan and housing facility. *Payment plan:* installment. *Waivers:* minority students.

Financial Aid Of all full-time matriculated undergraduates who enrolled in 2010, 13,020 applied for aid, 10,248 were judged to have need, 9,947 had their need fully met. 1,100 Federal Work-Study jobs (averaging $1479). 2,305 state and other part-time jobs (averaging $3545). In 2010, 221 non-need-based awards were made. *Average percent of need met:* 66%. *Average financial aid package:* $7261. *Average need-based loan:* $4424. *Average need-based gift aid:* $5136. *Average non-need-based aid:* $5585. *Average indebtedness upon graduation:* $17,760.

Applying *Options:* electronic application, early admission, early decision. *Application fee:* $50. *Required:* essay or personal statement, high school transcript, 1 letter of recommendation. *Required for some:* Architecture requires a portfolio and Dance, Music Theatre, Theatre and Music require an audition. *Early decision deadline:* 11/1. *Notification:* continuous (freshmen), continuous (transfers), 12/15 (early decision).

Freshman Application Contact Ms. Patricia Armstrong, Director of Admissions, University at Buffalo, the State University of New York, 12 Capen Hall, North Campus, Buffalo, NY 14260-1660. *Phone:* 716-645-6900. *Toll-free phone:* 888-UB-ADMIT. *Fax:* 716-645-6411. *E-mail:* ub-admissions@buffalo.edu. *Web site:* http://www.buffalo.edu/.

See page 1656 for the College Close-Up.

University of Rochester

Rochester, New York

- **Independent** university, founded 1850
- **Suburban** 655-acre campus
- **Endowment** $1.5 billion
- **Coed** 5,643 undergraduate students, 95% full-time, 51% women, 49% men
- **Very difficult** entrance level, 37% of applicants were admitted

Undergraduates 5,373 full-time, 270 part-time. Students come from 50 states and territories; 75 other countries; 61% are from out of state; 4% Black or African American, non-Hispanic/Latino; 5% Hispanic/Latino; 11% Asian, non-Hispanic/Latino; 0.1% Native Hawaiian or other Pacific Islander, non-Hispanic/Latino; 0.2% American Indian or Alaska Native, non-Hispanic/Latino;

3% Two or more races, non-Hispanic/Latino; 6% Race/ethnicity unknown; 11% international; 2% transferred in; 83% live on campus. *Retention:* 95% of full-time freshmen returned.

Freshmen *Admission:* 13,678 applied, 5,001 admitted, 1,267 enrolled. *Average high school GPA:* 3.8.

Faculty *Student/faculty ratio:* 9:1.

Academics *Calendar:* semesters plus optional summer term. *Degrees:* bachelor's, master's, doctoral, post-master's, postbachelor's, and first professional certificates. *Special study options:* accelerated degree program, advanced placement credit, cooperative education, double majors, English as a second language, honors programs, independent study, internships, off-campus study, part-time degree program, services for LD students, student-designed majors, study abroad, summer session for credit. *ROTC:* Army (c), Navy (b), Air Force (c). *Unusual degree programs:* 3-2 business administration; engineering; nursing; business, computer science, engineering, public health, optics, human development, neuroscience, medical physics, and physics and astronomy.

Computers on Campus 450 computers/terminals and 4,000 ports are available on campus for general student use. Students can access the following: computer help desk, free student e-mail accounts, online (class) grades, online (class) registration, online (class) schedules. Campuswide network is available. 100% of college-owned or -operated housing units are wired for high-speed Internet access. Wireless service is available via classrooms, computer centers, computer labs, learning centers, libraries, student centers.

Student Life *Housing:* on-campus residence required through sophomore year. *Options:* coed. Campus housing is university owned and leased by the school. Freshman campus housing is guaranteed. *Activities and organizations:* drama/theater group, student-run newspaper, radio and television station, choral group, marching band, Campus Activities Board, Black Students' Union, Grassroots (environmental group), Women's Caucus, American Sign Language Club, national fraternities, national sororities. *Campus security:* 24-hour emergency response devices and patrols, student patrols, late-night transport/escort service, controlled dormitory access. *Student services:* health clinic, personal/psychological counseling, women's center, legal services.

Athletics Member NCAA. All Division III except squash (Division I). *Intercollegiate sports:* badminton M(c)/W(c), baseball M, basketball M/W, crew M(c)/W, cross-country running M/W, equestrian sports M(c)/W(c), field hockey W, football M, golf M, ice hockey M(c)/W(c), lacrosse M(c)/W, rugby M(c)/W(c), skiing (downhill) M(c)/W(c), soccer M/W, softball W, squash M, swimming and diving M/W, tennis M/W, track and field M/W, ultimate Frisbee M(c)/W(c), volleyball M(c)/W, water polo M(c)/W(c). *Intramural sports:* archery M(c)/W(c), basketball M/W, cheerleading M(c)/W(c), fencing M(c)/W(c), football M/W, gymnastics M(c)/W(c), sailing M(c)/W(c), soccer M/W, softball M/W, tennis M/W, ultimate Frisbee M/W, volleyball M/W.

Standardized Tests *Required:* SAT or ACT (for admission). *Required for some:* SAT and SAT Subject Tests or ACT (for admission). *Recommended:* SAT Subject Tests (for admission).

Costs (2011–12) *One-time required fee:* $12. *Comprehensive fee:* $53,946 includes full-time tuition ($41,040), mandatory fees ($786), and room and board ($12,120). Part-time tuition: $1284 per credit hour. Part-time tuition and fees vary according to course load. *College room only:* $7350. Room and board charges vary according to board plan. *Payment plans:* tuition prepayment, installment. *Waivers:* employees or children of employees.

Financial Aid Of all full-time matriculated undergraduates who enrolled in 2011, 2,994 applied for aid, 2,649 were judged to have need, 334 had their need fully met. 1,602 Federal Work-Study jobs (averaging $2075). In 2011, 1337 non-need-based awards were made. *Average percent of need met:* 97%. *Average financial aid package:* $34,781. *Average need-based loan:* $4944. *Average need-based gift aid:* $29,699. *Average non-need-based aid:* $11,432. *Average indebtedness upon graduation:* $28,100.

Applying *Options:* electronic application, early admission, early decision, deferred entrance. *Application fee:* $60. *Required:* essay or personal statement, high school transcript. *Required for some:* Audition is required for music programs at Eastman School of Music. *Recommended:* 2 letters of recommendation, interview. *Application deadlines:* 1/1 (freshmen), 1/1 (out-of-state freshmen), 3/15 (transfers). *Early decision deadline:* 11/1. *Notification:* 4/1 (freshmen), 4/1 (out-of-state freshmen), 3/1 (transfers), 12/15 (early decision).

Freshman Application Contact Office of Admissions, University of Rochester, PO Box 270251, 300 Wilson Boulevard, Rochester, NY 14627-0251. *Phone:* 585-275-3221. *Toll-free phone:* 888-822-2256. *Fax:* 585-461-4595. *E-mail:* admit@admissions.rochester.edu. *Web site:* http://www.rochester.edu/.

U.T.A. Mesivta of Kiryas Joel

Monroe, New York

Admissions Office Contact U.T.A. Mesivta of Kiryas Joel, 9 Nickelsburg Road, Unit 312, Monroe, NY 10950.

Utica College

Utica, New York

- **Independent** comprehensive, founded 1946
- **Suburban** 128-acre campus
- **Endowment** $18.4 million
- **Coed** 2,697 undergraduate students, 79% full-time, 59% women, 41% men
- **Moderately difficult** entrance level, 78% of applicants were admitted

Undergraduates 2,132 full-time, 565 part-time. Students come from 43 states and territories; 21% are from out of state; 11% Black or African American, non-Hispanic/Latino; 7% Hispanic/Latino; 2% Asian, non-Hispanic/Latino; 0.2% Native Hawaiian or other Pacific Islander, non-Hispanic/Latino; 0.4% American Indian or Alaska Native, non-Hispanic/Latino; 2% Two or more races, non-Hispanic/Latino; 3% Race/ethnicity unknown; 3% international; 7% transferred in; 48% live on campus. *Retention:* 63% of full-time freshmen returned.

Freshmen *Admission:* 3,605 applied, 2,823 admitted, 532 enrolled. *Average high school GPA:* 3.01. *Test scores:* SAT critical reading scores over 500: 36%; SAT math scores over 500: 48%; SAT writing scores over 500: 31%; ACT scores over 18: 84%; SAT critical reading scores over 600: 5%; SAT math scores over 600: 8%; SAT writing scores over 600: 3%; ACT scores over 24: 25%; SAT critical reading scores over 700: 1%; SAT math scores over 700: 1%; ACT scores over 30: 1%.

Faculty *Total:* 363, 41% full-time. *Student/faculty ratio:* 11:1.

Academics *Calendar:* semesters. *Degrees:* certificates, bachelor's, master's, doctoral, and postbachelor's certificates. *Special study options:* academic remediation for entering students, accelerated degree program, adult/continuing education programs, advanced placement credit, distance learning, double majors, honors programs, independent study, internships, off-campus study, part-time degree program, services for LD students, study abroad, summer session for credit. *ROTC:* Army (b), Air Force (c). *Unusual degree programs:* 3-2 engineering with Syracuse University.

Computers on Campus 430 computers/terminals are available on campus for general student use. Students can access the following: computer help desk, free student e-mail accounts, online (class) grades, online (class) registration, online (class) schedules. Campuswide network is available. 100% of college-owned or -operated housing units are wired for high-speed Internet access. Wireless service is available via classrooms, libraries, student centers.

Student Life *Housing:* on-campus residence required through sophomore year. *Options:* coed, disabled students. Campus housing is university owned. Freshman campus housing is guaranteed. *Activities and organizations:* drama/theater group, student-run newspaper, radio station, choral group, Physical Therapy Society, Student Nurses Association, Kappa Delta Pi, Student Senate, Utica College Honor Association, national fraternities, national sororities. *Campus security:* 24-hour emergency response devices and patrols, late-night transport/escort service, controlled dormitory access. *Student services:* health clinic, personal/psychological counseling, women's center.

Athletics Member NCAA. All Division III except track and field (Division II). *Intercollegiate sports:* baseball M, basketball M/W, field hockey W, football M, golf M/W, ice hockey M/W, lacrosse M/W, soccer M/W, softball W, swimming and diving M/W, tennis M/W, track and field M/W, volleyball W, water polo W. *Intramural sports:* basketball M/W, bowling M/W, cheerleading M(c)/W(c), fencing M(c)/W(c), racquetball M/W, soccer M/W, softball M/W, tennis M/W, volleyball M/W, water polo M/W.

Standardized Tests *Required for some:* SAT or ACT (for admission).

Costs (2011–12) *Comprehensive fee:* $41,646 includes full-time tuition ($29,476), mandatory fees ($520), and room and board ($11,650). Full-time tuition and fees vary according to class time and course load. Part-time tuition: $995 per credit hour. Part-time tuition and fees vary according to class time and course load. *Room and board:* Room and board charges vary according to board plan and housing facility. *Payment plans:* installment, deferred payment. *Waivers:* senior citizens and employees or children of employees.

Financial Aid Of all full-time matriculated undergraduates who enrolled in 2011, 1,952 applied for aid, 1,859 were judged to have need, 179 had their need fully met. In 2011, 124 non-need-based awards were made. *Average percent of need met:* 67%. *Average financial aid package:* $22,591. *Average need-based loan:* $4363. *Average need-based gift aid:* $6264. *Average non-need-based aid:* $10,857. *Average indebtedness upon graduation:* $39,000.

Applying *Options:* electronic application, deferred entrance. *Application fee:* $40. *Required:* essay or personal statement, high school transcript, minimum 2.0 GPA, 1 letter of recommendation. *Required for some:* minimum 3.0 GPA. *Recommended:* interview. *Application deadlines:* rolling (freshmen), rolling (transfers). *Notification:* 9/1 (freshmen), continuous (transfers).

Freshman Application Contact Utica College, 1600 Burrstone Road, Utica, NY 13502-4892. *Phone:* 315-792-3006. *Toll-free phone:* 800-782-8884. *Web site:* http://www.utica.edu/.

See page 1728 for the College Close-Up.

Vassar College

Poughkeepsie, New York

- **Independent** 4-year, founded 1861
- **Suburban** 1000-acre campus with easy access to New York City
- **Endowment** $814.1 million
- **Coed** 2,386 undergraduate students, 98% full-time, 56% women, 44% men
- **Very difficult** entrance level, 23% of applicants were admitted

Undergraduates 2,345 full-time, 41 part-time. Students come from 52 states and territories; 58 other countries; 74% are from out of state; 5% Black or African American, non-Hispanic/Latino; 10% Hispanic/Latino; 9% Asian, non-Hispanic/Latino; 0.1% American Indian or Alaska Native, non-Hispanic/Latino; 5% Two or more races, non-Hispanic/Latino; 6% international; 0.4% transferred in; 95% live on campus. *Retention:* 98% of full-time freshmen returned.

Freshmen *Admission:* 7,985 applied, 1,798 admitted, 670 enrolled. *Average high school GPA:* 3.8. *Test scores:* SAT critical reading scores over 500: 100%; SAT math scores over 500: 100%; SAT writing scores over 500: 100%; ACT scores over 18: 100%; SAT critical reading scores over 600: 96%; SAT math scores over 600: 94%; SAT writing scores over 600: 94%; ACT scores over 24: 100%; SAT critical reading scores over 700: 57%; SAT math scores over 700: 44%; SAT writing scores over 700: 57%; ACT scores over 30: 79%.

Faculty *Total:* 323, 87% full-time, 85% with terminal degrees. *Student/faculty ratio:* 8:1.

Academics *Calendar:* semesters. *Degrees:* bachelor's and master's. *Special study options:* advanced placement credit, cooperative education, double majors, independent study, internships, off-campus study, part-time degree program, services for LD students, student-designed majors, study abroad. *Unusual degree programs:* 3-2 engineering with Dartmouth College.

Computers on Campus 300 computers/terminals are available on campus for general student use. Students can access the following: campus intranet, computer help desk, free student e-mail accounts, online (class) grades, online (class) registration, online (class) schedules, Ethernet. Campuswide network is available. 100% of college-owned or -operated housing units are wired for high-speed Internet access. Wireless service is available via entire campus.

Student Life *Housing:* on-campus residence required through senior year. *Options:* coed, women-only, cooperative. Campus housing is university owned. Freshman campus housing is guaranteed. *Activities and organizations:* drama/theater group, student-run newspaper, radio station, choral group, Student Association, WVKR radio station, VICE (programming social events), Vassar Greens, Ultimate Frisbee. *Campus security:* 24-hour emergency response devices and patrols, student patrols, late-night transport/escort service, controlled dormitory access. *Student services:* health clinic, personal/psychological counseling, women's center.

Athletics Member NCAA. All Division III. *Intercollegiate sports:* baseball M, basketball M/W, crew M(c)/W(c), cross-country running M/W, fencing M/W, field hockey W, golf W, lacrosse M/W, rugby M(c)/W(c), soccer M/W, squash M(c)/W(c), swimming and diving M/W, tennis M/W, track and field M/W, volleyball M/W. *Intramural sports:* badminton M(c)/W(c), equestrian sports M(c)/W(c), sailing M(c)/W(c), skiing (cross-country) M(c)/W(c), skiing (downhill) M(c)/W(c), ultimate Frisbee M(c)/W(c).

Standardized Tests *Required:* SAT and SAT Subject Tests or ACT (for admission).

Costs (2011–12) *One-time required fee:* $70. *Comprehensive fee:* $55,135 includes full-time tuition ($44,050), mandatory fees ($655), and room and board ($10,430). Part-time tuition: $5220 per unit. Part-time tuition and fees vary according to course load. *College room only:* $5660. Room and board charges vary according to board plan and housing facility. *Payment plan:* installment. *Waivers:* employees or children of employees.

Financial Aid Of all full-time matriculated undergraduates who enrolled in 2011, 1,736 applied for aid, 1,563 were judged to have need, 1,563 had their need fully met. 1,026 Federal Work-Study jobs (averaging $1830). 397 state and other part-time jobs (averaging $1871). *Average percent of need met:* 100%. *Average financial aid package:* $42,523. *Average need-based loan:* $2542. *Average need-based gift aid:* $38,285. *Average indebtedness upon graduation:* $18,150. *Financial aid deadline:* 2/15.

Applying *Options:* electronic application, early decision, deferred entrance. *Application fee:* $65. *Required:* essay or personal statement, high school transcript, 2 letters of recommendation. *Application deadlines:* 1/1 (freshmen), 4/1 (transfers). *Early decision deadline:* 11/15. *Notification:* 4/1 (freshmen), 5/10 (transfers), 12/15 (early decision).

Freshman Application Contact Dr. David M. Borus, Dean of Admission and Financial Aid, Vassar College, 124 Raymond Avenue, Poughkeepsie, NY 12604. *Phone:* 845-437-7300. *Toll-free phone:* 800-827-7270. *Fax:* 845-437-7063. *E-mail:* admissions@vassar.edu. *Web site:* http://www.vassar.edu/.

Vaughn College of Aeronautics and Technology

Flushing, New York

- **Independent** comprehensive, founded 1932
- **Urban** 6-acre campus with easy access to New York City
- **Endowment** $21.3 million
- **Coed, primarily men** 1,664 undergraduate students, 72% full-time, 13% women, 87% men
- **Moderately difficult** entrance level, 83% of applicants were admitted

Undergraduates 1,206 full-time, 458 part-time. Students come from 24 states and territories; 8 other countries; 13% are from out of state; 20% Black or African American, non-Hispanic/Latino; 35% Hispanic/Latino; 12% Asian, non-Hispanic/Latino; 0.8% Native Hawaiian or other Pacific Islander, non-Hispanic/Latino; 0.9% American Indian or Alaska Native, non-Hispanic/Latino; 3% Two or more races, non-Hispanic/Latino; 8% Race/ethnicity unknown; 3% international; 9% live on campus. *Retention:* 73% of full-time freshmen returned.

Freshmen *Admission:* 626 applied, 521 admitted, 308 enrolled. *Average high school GPA:* 3.2. *Test scores:* SAT critical reading scores over 500: 47%; SAT math scores over 500: 79%; ACT scores over 18: 100%; SAT critical reading scores over 600: 9%; SAT math scores over 600: 17%; ACT scores over 24: 34%.

Faculty *Total:* 162, 22% full-time, 20% with terminal degrees. *Student/faculty ratio:* 18:1.

Academics *Calendar:* semesters. *Degrees:* certificates, associate, bachelor's, and master's. *Special study options:* academic remediation for entering students, advanced placement credit, cooperative education, distance learning, double majors, independent study, internships, part-time degree program, summer session for credit. *ROTC:* Army (c), Air Force (c).

Computers on Campus 225 ports are available on campus for general student use. Students can access the following: campus intranet, computer help desk, free student e-mail accounts, online (class) grades, online (class) registration, online (class) schedules, Vaughn Student Portal. Campuswide network is available. 100% of college-owned or -operated housing units are wired for high-speed Internet access. Wireless service is available via entire campus.

Student Life *Housing options:* coed, disabled students. Campus housing is university owned. Freshman applicants given priority for college housing. *Activities and organizations:* American Association of Airport Executives, Women in Aviation-International, Institute of Electrical and Electronics Engineers, Robotics Club, Red Tail Pilots Club. *Campus security:* 24-hour emergency response devices and patrols, student patrols, late-night transport/escort service, controlled dormitory access. *Student services:* personal/psychological counseling.

Athletics *Intercollegiate sports:* basketball M, soccer M, tennis W, track and field M/W. *Intramural sports:* basketball M, soccer M, tennis W.

Standardized Tests *Required for some:* SAT and SAT Subject Tests or ACT (for admission).

Costs (2012–13) *One-time required fee:* $160. *Comprehensive fee:* $30,930 includes full-time tuition ($18,900), mandatory fees ($600), and room and board ($11,430). Full-time tuition and fees vary according to course load and program. Part-time tuition: $630 per credit. Part-time tuition and fees vary according to course load and program. *College room only:* $9030. Room and board charges vary according to board plan. *Payment plan:* installment. *Waivers:* employees or children of employees.

Financial Aid Of all full-time matriculated undergraduates who enrolled in 2008, 704 applied for aid, 704 were judged to have need, 476 had their need fully met. 25 Federal Work-Study jobs (averaging $3000). In 2008, 145 non-need-based awards were made. *Average percent of need met:* 82%. *Average financial aid package:* $18,030. *Average need-based loan:* $1770. *Average need-based gift aid:* $2950. *Average non-need-based aid:* $2000. *Average indebtedness upon graduation:* $17,125.

Applying *Options:* electronic application. *Application fee:* $40. *Required:* high school transcript. *Recommended:* essay or personal statement, 2 letters of recommendation, interview. *Application deadlines:* rolling (freshmen), rolling (out-of-state freshmen), rolling (transfers). *Notification:* continuous (freshmen), continuous (out-of-state freshmen), continuous (transfers).

Freshman Application Contact Mr. Celso Alvarez, Director of Admissions, Vaughn College of Aeronautics and Technology, Vaughn College, 8601 23rd Avenue, Flushing, NY 11369. *Phone:* 718-429.6600 Ext. 117. *Toll-free phone:* 866-6VAUGHN. *Fax:* 718-779.2231. *E-mail:* celso.alvarez@vaughn.edu. *Web site:* http://www.vaughn.edu/.

See page 646 for display ad and page 1732 for the College Close-Up.

Villa Maria College of Buffalo
Buffalo, New York

- **Independent** 4-year, founded 1960, affiliated with Roman Catholic Church
- **Suburban** 9-acre campus
- **Endowment** $1.1 million
- **Coed** 457 undergraduate students, 81% full-time, 65% women, 35% men
- **Minimally difficult** entrance level, 70% of applicants were admitted

Undergraduates 372 full-time, 85 part-time. Students come from 5 states and territories; 2 other countries; 1% are from out of state; 16% Black or African American, non-Hispanic/Latino; 4% Hispanic/Latino; 1% Asian, non-Hispanic/Latino; 1% American Indian or Alaska Native, non-Hispanic/Latino; 2% Two or more races, non-Hispanic/Latino; 0.4% Race/ethnicity unknown; 13% transferred in; 7% live on campus. *Retention:* 68% of full-time freshmen returned.

Freshmen *Admission:* 306 applied, 215 admitted, 91 enrolled. *Average high school GPA:* 2.96.

Faculty *Total:* 81, 37% full-time, 38% with terminal degrees. *Student/faculty ratio:* 12:1.

Academics *Calendar:* semesters. *Degrees:* associate and bachelor's. *Special study options:* academic remediation for entering students, advanced placement credit, cooperative education, independent study, internships, off-campus study, part-time degree program, services for LD students, summer session for credit.

Computers on Campus 250 computers/terminals are available on campus for general student use. Students can access the following: computer help desk, free student e-mail accounts, online (class) grades, online (class) registration, online (class) schedules. Campuswide network is available. Wireless service is available via libraries, student centers.

Student Life *Housing:* college housing not available. *Options:* Campus housing is provided by a third party. *Activities and organizations:* choral group, Design and Beyond, Teachers Love Children, Multicultural Club, Phi Theta Kappa, Helping Adults New Dreams Succeed. *Campus security:* late-night transport/escort service, security guard during hours of operation. *Student services:* health clinic, personal/psychological counseling.

Costs (2012–13) *Tuition:* $16,800 full-time, $560 per credit part-time. Full-time tuition and fees vary according to degree level, program, and reciprocity agreements. Part-time tuition and fees vary according to course load, degree level, program, and reciprocity agreements. *Required fees:* $350 full-time, $275 per year part-time. *Payment plan:* installment. *Waivers:* employees or children of employees.

Financial Aid Of all full-time matriculated undergraduates who enrolled in 2010, 470 applied for aid, 468 were judged to have need, 18 had their need fully met. 59 Federal Work-Study jobs (averaging $535). In 2010, 11 non-need-based awards were made. *Average percent of need met:* 54%. *Average financial aid package:* $7965. *Average need-based gift aid:* $941. *Average non-need-based aid:* $1868. *Average indebtedness upon graduation:* $30,353.

Applying *Options:* electronic application, deferred entrance. *Required:* essay or personal statement, high school transcript, interview, writing sample, portfolio review, music audition. *Required for some:* writing sample, portfolio review, music audition. *Application deadlines:* rolling (freshmen), rolling (out-of-state freshmen), rolling (transfers). *Notification:* continuous (freshmen), continuous (out-of-state freshmen), continuous (transfers).

Freshman Application Contact Mr. Kevin Donovan, Director of Admissions, Villa Maria College of Buffalo, Buffalo, NY 14211. *Phone:* 716-896-0700 Ext. 1802. *Fax:* 716-896-0705. *E-mail:* admissions@villa.edu. *Web site:* http://www.villa.edu/.

Wagner College
Staten Island, New York

- **Independent** comprehensive, founded 1883
- **Urban** 105-acre campus with easy access to New York City
- **Endowment** $64.4 million
- **Coed** 1,856 undergraduate students, 95% full-time, 64% women, 36% men
- **Moderately difficult** entrance level, 69% of applicants were admitted

Undergraduates 1,759 full-time, 97 part-time. Students come from 40 states and territories; 19 other countries; 48% are from out of state; 6% Black or African American, non-Hispanic/Latino; 8% Hispanic/Latino; 2% Asian, non-Hispanic/Latino; 0.2% Native Hawaiian or other Pacific Islander, non-Hispanic/Latino; 0.1% American Indian or Alaska Native, non-Hispanic/Latino; 2% Two or more races, non-Hispanic/Latino; 10% Race/ethnicity unknown; 2% international; 5% transferred in; 68% live on campus. *Retention:* 79% of full-time freshmen returned.

Freshmen *Admission:* 3,001 applied, 2,079 admitted, 470 enrolled. *Average high school GPA:* 3.6. *Test scores:* SAT critical reading scores over 500: 91%;

SAT math scores over 500: 90%; SAT writing scores over 500: 89%; ACT scores over 18: 99%; SAT critical reading scores over 600: 48%; SAT math scores over 600: 48%; SAT writing scores over 600: 47%; ACT scores over 24: 88%; SAT critical reading scores over 700: 7%; SAT math scores over 700: 5%; SAT writing scores over 700: 6%; ACT scores over 30: 7%.

Faculty *Total:* 261, 37% full-time. *Student/faculty ratio:* 14:1.

Academics *Calendar:* semesters. *Degrees:* bachelor's, master's, and post-master's certificates. *Special study options:* adult/continuing education programs, advanced placement credit, double majors, honors programs, independent study, internships, off-campus study, part-time degree program, services for LD students, student-designed majors, study abroad, summer session for credit. *ROTC:* Army (c). *Unusual degree programs:* 3-2 accounting.

Computers on Campus 230 computers/terminals are available on campus for general student use. Students can access the following: campus intranet, computer help desk, free student e-mail accounts, online (class) grades, online (class) registration, online (class) schedules. Campuswide network is available. 100% of college-owned or -operated housing units are wired for high-speed Internet access. Wireless service is available via entire campus.

Student Life *Housing options:* coed. Campus housing is university owned and leased by the school. Freshman campus housing is guaranteed. *Activities and organizations:* drama/theater group, student-run newspaper, radio station, choral group, Student Government Association, Student Activities Board, Wagner College Theatre, Wagner College Choir, student newspaper, national fraternities, national sororities. *Campus security:* 24-hour emergency response devices and patrols, late-night transport/escort service, controlled dormitory access. *Student services:* health clinic, personal/psychological counseling.

Athletics Member NCAA. All Division I except football (Division I-AA). *Intercollegiate sports:* baseball M(s), basketball M(s)/W(s), cross-country running M(s)/W(s), golf M(s)/W(s), ice hockey M(c), lacrosse M(s)/W(s), soccer W(s), softball W(s), swimming and diving W(s), tennis M(s)/W(s), track and field M(s)/W(s), water polo W(s). *Intramural sports:* basketball M/W, bowling M/W, football M, rugby M, soccer M/W, softball M/W, table tennis M/W, tennis M/W, ultimate Frisbee M/W, volleyball M/W.

Standardized Tests *Required for some:* SAT or ACT (for admission), SAT Subject Tests (for admission).

Costs (2012–13) *Comprehensive fee:* $48,600 includes full-time tuition ($37,240), mandatory fees ($200), and room and board ($11,160). Full-time tuition and fees vary according to course load. Part-time tuition: $4655 per unit. Part-time tuition and fees vary according to course load. *Waivers:* employees or children of employees.

Financial Aid Of all full-time matriculated undergraduates who enrolled in 2010, 1,292 applied for aid, 1,099 were judged to have need, 258 had their need fully met. 687 Federal Work-Study jobs (averaging $1576). In 2010, 449 non-need-based awards were made. *Average percent of need met:* 73%. *Average financial aid package:* $22,354. *Average need-based loan:* $4688. *Average need-based gift aid:* $17,672. *Average non-need-based aid:* $11,880. *Average indebtedness upon graduation:* $36,988.

Applying *Options:* electronic application, early decision, deferred entrance. *Application fee:* $50. *Required:* essay or personal statement, high school transcript, minimum 2.5 GPA, 2 letters of recommendation. *Required for some:* interview. *Recommended:* minimum 3.0 GPA, interview. *Application deadlines:* 2/15 (freshmen), 2/15 (out-of-state freshmen), 5/1 (transfers). *Early decision deadline:* 12/15. *Notification:* continuous until 2/15 (freshmen), continuous until 2/15 (out-of-state freshmen), continuous until 5/15 (transfers), 1/2 (early decision).

Freshman Application Contact Mr. Robert Herr, Dean of Admissions, Wagner College, One Campus Road, Pape Admissions Building, Staten Island, NY 10301. *Phone:* 718-420-4242. *Toll-free phone:* 800-221-1010. *Fax:* 718-390-3105. *E-mail:* robert.herr@wagner.edu. *Web site:* http://www.wagner.edu/.

Webb Institute

Glen Cove, New York

- **Independent** 4-year, founded 1889
- **Suburban** 26-acre campus with easy access to New York City
- **Endowment** $50.2 million
- **Coed** 81 undergraduate students, 100% full-time, 16% women, 84% men
- **Most difficult** entrance level, 37% of applicants were admitted

Undergraduates 81 full-time. Students come from 21 states and territories; 4 other countries; 62% are from out of state; 2% Hispanic/Latino; 11% Asian, non-Hispanic/Latino; 2% Two or more races, non-Hispanic/Latino; 5% transferred in; 100% live on campus. *Retention:* 83% of full-time freshmen returned.

Freshmen *Admission:* 73 applied, 27 admitted, 22 enrolled. *Average high school GPA:* 4. *Test scores:* SAT critical reading scores over 500: 100%; SAT

WEBB INSTITUTE

For more information, contact:

William G. Murray, Director of Enrollment Management
Office of Admissions
298 Crescent Beach Road
Glen Cove, New York 11542
E-mail: admissions@webb-institute.edu

Web site: www.webb-institute.edu

math scores over 500: 100%; SAT writing scores over 500: 100%; SAT critical reading scores over 600: 100%; SAT math scores over 600: 100%; SAT writing scores over 600: 82%; SAT critical reading scores over 700: 32%; SAT math scores over 700: 82%; SAT writing scores over 700: 32%.

Faculty *Total:* 12, 83% full-time, 58% with terminal degrees. *Student/faculty ratio:* 7:1.

Academics *Calendar:* semesters. *Degree:* bachelor's. *Special study options:* cooperative education, double majors, independent study, internships, services for LD students, study abroad.

Computers on Campus 25 computers/terminals are available on campus for general student use. Students can access the following: campus intranet, computer help desk, free student e-mail accounts. Campuswide network is available. 100% of college-owned or -operated housing units are wired for high-speed Internet access. Wireless service is available via entire campus.

Student Life *Housing:* on-campus residence required through senior year. *Options:* coed, men-only, women-only. Campus housing is university owned. Freshman campus housing is guaranteed. *Activities and organizations:* choral group, Student Organization, Society of Naval Architects and Marine Engineers, American Society of Naval Engineers, Society of Women Engineers, Marine Technology Society. *Campus security:* 24-hour emergency response devices and patrols, controlled dormitory access. *Student services:* personal/psychological counseling.

Athletics *Intercollegiate sports:* basketball M/W, cross-country running M/W, sailing M/W, soccer M/W, tennis M/W, volleyball M/W. *Intramural sports:* ultimate Frisbee M/W.

Standardized Tests *Required:* SAT (for admission), SAT Subject Tests (for admission).

Costs (2012–13) *Comprehensive fee:* includes room and board ($13,200). All students admitted receive a four-year, full tuition scholarship.

Financial Aid Of all full-time matriculated undergraduates who enrolled in 2011, 17 applied for aid, 17 were judged to have need. *Average financial aid package:* $4500. *Average need-based gift aid:* $5500. *Average indebtedness upon graduation:* $4500.

Applying *Options:* early decision. *Application fee:* $25. *Required:* high school transcript, minimum 3.5 GPA, 2 letters of recommendation, interview, proof of U.S. citizenship or permanent residency status. *Application deadlines:* 2/15 (freshmen), 2/15 (transfers). *Early decision deadline:* 10/15. *Notification:* 4/30 (freshmen), continuous until 4/30 (transfers), 12/15 (early decision).

Freshman Application Contact Webb Institute, Crescent Beach Road, Glen Cove, NY 11542-1398. *Phone:* 516-671-2213. *Fax:* 516-674-9838. *E-mail:* admissions@webb-institute.edu. *Web site:* http://www.webb-institute.edu/.

See page 647 for display as and page 1746 for the College Close-Up.

Wells College

Aurora, New York

- **Independent** 4-year, founded 1868
- **Rural** 365-acre campus with easy access to Syracuse
- **Endowment** $22.3 million
- **Coed, primarily women** 507 undergraduate students, 98% full-time, 69% women, 31% men
- **Moderately difficult** entrance level, 79% of applicants were admitted

Undergraduates 497 full-time, 10 part-time. Students come from 29 states and territories; 7 other countries; 33% are from out of state; 9% Black or African American, non-Hispanic/Latino; 7% Hispanic/Latino; 2% Asian, non-Hispanic/Latino; 0.4% Native Hawaiian or other Pacific Islander, non-Hispanic/Latino; 0.4% American Indian or Alaska Native, non-Hispanic/Latino; 2% Two or more races, non-Hispanic/Latino; 13% Race/ethnicity unknown; 1% international; 3% transferred in; 84% live on campus. *Retention:* 69% of full-time freshmen returned.

Freshmen *Admission:* 1,610 applied, 1,264 admitted, 137 enrolled. *Average high school GPA:* 3.5. *Test scores:* SAT critical reading scores over 500: 68%; SAT math scores over 500: 66%; SAT writing scores over 500: 60%; ACT scores over 18: 100%; SAT critical reading scores over 600: 29%; SAT math scores over 600: 20%; SAT writing scores over 600: 20%; ACT scores over 24: 55%; SAT critical reading scores over 700: 4%; SAT math scores over 700: 2%; SAT writing scores over 700: 2%; ACT scores over 30: 10%.

Faculty *Total:* 74, 61% full-time, 81% with terminal degrees. *Student/faculty ratio:* 10:1.

Academics *Calendar:* semesters. *Degree:* bachelor's. *Special study options:* accelerated degree program, adult/continuing education programs, advanced placement credit, double majors, English as a second language, independent study, internships, off-campus study, part-time degree program, services for LD students, student-designed majors, study abroad. *ROTC:* Army (c), Air Force (c). *Unusual degree programs:* 3-2 engineering with Columbia University, Clarkson University, and Cornell University; community health with University of Rochester, education with University of Rochester.

Computers on Campus 96 computers/terminals and 1,224 ports are available on campus for general student use. Students can access the following: campus intranet, computer help desk, free student e-mail accounts, online (class) grades, online (class) registration, online (class) schedules. Campuswide network is available. 100% of college-owned or -operated housing units are wired for high-speed Internet access. Wireless service is available via classrooms, dorm rooms, learning centers, libraries, student centers.

Student Life *Housing:* on-campus residence required through senior year. *Options:* coed, women-only. Campus housing is university owned. Freshman campus housing is guaranteed. *Activities and organizations:* drama/theater group, student-run newspaper, choral group, Programming Board, POWER, SAGA, choral groups, SIFE. *Campus security:* 24-hour emergency response devices and patrols, late-night transport/escort service, controlled dormitory access. *Student services:* health clinic, personal/psychological counseling, women's center.

Athletics Member NCAA. All Division III. *Intercollegiate sports:* basketball M/W, cross-country running M/W, field hockey W, golf M/W, lacrosse M/W, soccer M/W, softball W, swimming and diving M/W, tennis W, volleyball M/W. *Intramural sports:* basketball M/W, field hockey W, football W, golf M/W, sailing M/W, skiing (cross-country) M/W, skiing (downhill) M/W, soccer M/W, swimming and diving M/W, tennis W, ultimate Frisbee M/W, volleyball W.

Standardized Tests *Required:* SAT or ACT (for admission).

Costs (2011–12) *Comprehensive fee:* $43,180 includes full-time tuition ($30,680), mandatory fees ($1500), and room and board ($11,000). *Payment plan:* installment. *Waivers:* senior citizens and employees or children of employees.

Financial Aid Of all full-time matriculated undergraduates who enrolled in 2011, 438 applied for aid, 426 were judged to have need, 70 had their need fully met. 63 Federal Work-Study jobs (averaging $1600). 343 state and other part-time jobs (averaging $1600). In 2011, 45 non-need-based awards were made. *Average percent of need met:* 81%. *Average financial aid package:* $28,027. *Average need-based loan:* $4811. *Average need-based gift aid:* $23,656. *Average non-need-based aid:* $13,535. *Average indebtedness upon graduation:* $26,062.

Applying *Options:* electronic application, early admission, early decision, early action, deferred entrance. *Application fee:* $40. *Required:* essay or personal statement, high school transcript, 2 letters of recommendation. *Recommended:* minimum 3.0 GPA, interview. *Application deadlines:* 3/1 (freshmen), rolling (transfers), 12/15 (early action). *Early decision deadline:* 12/15. *Notification:* 4/1 (freshmen), continuous (transfers), 1/15 (early decision), 2/1 (early action).

Freshman Application Contact Ms. Susan Raith Sloan, Director of Admission, Wells College, 170 Main Street, Aurora, NY 13026. *Phone:* 315-364-3264. *Toll-free phone:* 800-952-9355. *Fax:* 315-364-3227. *E-mail:* admissions@wells.edu. *Web site:* http://www.wells.edu/.

See page 648 for display ad and page 1748 for the College Close-Up.

Yeshiva and Kolel Bais Medrash Elyon

Monsey, New York

Admissions Office Contact Yeshiva and Kolel Bais Medrash Elyon, 73 Main Street, Monsey, NY 10952.

Yeshiva and Kollel Harbotzas Torah

Brooklyn, New York

Admissions Office Contact Yeshiva and Kollel Harbotzas Torah, 1049 East 15th Street, Brooklyn, NY 11230.

Yeshiva Derech Chaim

Brooklyn, New York

Director of Admissions Administrator, Yeshiva Derech Chaim, 1573 39th Street, Brooklyn, NY 11218. *Phone:* 718-438-5476.

Yeshiva D'Monsey Rabbinical College

Monsey, New York

Admissions Office Contact Yeshiva D'Monsey Rabbinical College, 2 Roman Boulevard, Monsey, NY 10952.

Yeshiva Gedolah Imrei Yosef D'Spinka

Brooklyn, New York

Admissions Office Contact Yeshiva Gedolah Imrei Yosef D'Spinka, 1466 56th Street, Brooklyn, NY 11219.

Yeshiva Karlin Stolin Rabbinical Institute

Brooklyn, New York

Director of Admissions Director of Admissions, Yeshiva Karlin Stolin Rabbinical Institute, 1818 Fifty-fourth Street, Brooklyn, NY 11204. *Phone:* 718-232-7800 Ext. 26.

Yeshiva of Nitra Rabbinical College

Mount Kisco, New York

Director of Admissions Administrator, Yeshiva of Nitra Rabbinical College, Pines Bridge Road, Mount Kisco, NY 10549. *Phone:* 718-384-5460. *Fax:* 718-387-9400.

Yeshiva of the Telshe Alumni

Riverdale, New York

Admissions Office Contact Yeshiva of the Telshe Alumni, 4904 Independence Avenue, Riverdale, NY 10471.

Yeshiva Shaarei Torah of Rockland

Suffern, New York

Admissions Office Contact Yeshiva Shaarei Torah of Rockland, 91 West Carlton Road, Suffern, NY 10901.

Yeshiva Shaar Hatorah Talmudic Research Institute

Kew Gardens, New York

Director of Admissions Assistant Dean, Yeshiva Shaar Hatorah Talmudic Research Institute, 117-06 84th Avenue, Kew Gardens, NY 11418-1469. *Phone:* 718-846-1940.

Yeshivas Novominsk

Brooklyn, New York

Admissions Office Contact Yeshivas Novominsk, 1569 47th Street, Brooklyn, NY 11219.

Yeshivath Viznitz

Monsey, New York

Director of Admissions Registrar, Yeshivath Viznitz, 25 Phyllis Terrace, Monsey, NY 10952. *Phone:* 914-356-1010.

Yeshivath Zichron Moshe

South Fallsburg, New York

Director of Admissions Rabbi Abba Gorelick, Dean, Yeshivath Zichron Moshe, Laurel Park Road, South Fallsburg, NY 12779. *Phone:* 914-434-5240.

Yeshivat Mikdash Melech

Brooklyn, New York

Director of Admissions Rabbi S. Beyda, Director of Admissions, Yeshivat Mikdash Melech, 1326 Ocean Parkway, Brooklyn, NY 11230-5601. *Phone:* 718-339-1090. *E-mail:* mikdashmelech@verizon.net. *Web site:* http://mikdashmelech.com/.

Yeshiva University

New York, New York

- **Independent** university, founded 1886
- **Urban** campus
- **Coed** 2,786 undergraduate students, 97% full-time, 47% women, 53% men
- **Moderately difficult** entrance level, 70% of applicants were admitted

Undergraduates 2,703 full-time, 83 part-time. 65% are from out of state; 0.9% Hispanic/Latino; 0.1% Asian, non-Hispanic/Latino; 0.1% American Indian or Alaska Native, non-Hispanic/Latino; 1% Two or more races, non-Hispanic/Latino; 0.6% Race/ethnicity unknown; 6% international; 1% transferred in; 78% live on campus. *Retention:* 89% of full-time freshmen returned.
Freshmen *Admission:* 1,818 applied, 1,265 admitted, 915 enrolled. *Average high school GPA:* 3.47. *Test scores:* SAT critical reading scores over 500: 90%; SAT math scores over 500: 90%; SAT writing scores over 500: 91%; ACT scores over 18: 100%; SAT critical reading scores over 600: 55%; SAT math scores over 600: 57%; SAT writing scores over 600: 53%; ACT scores over 24: 65%; SAT critical reading scores over 700: 20%; SAT math scores over 700: 20%; SAT writing scores over 700: 18%; ACT scores over 30: 21%.
Faculty *Total:* 1,327, 77% full-time. *Student/faculty ratio:* 6:1.
Academics *Calendar:* semesters. *Degrees:* associate, bachelor's, master's, doctoral, post-master's, postbachelor's, and first professional certificates (Yeshiva College and Stern College for Women are coordinate undergraduate colleges of arts and sciences for men and women, respectively. Sy Syms School of Business offers programs at both campuses). *Special study options:* advanced placement credit, double majors, honors programs, independent study, internships, off-campus study, student-designed majors, study abroad, summer session for credit.
Student Life *Housing options:* men-only, women-only. *Activities and organizations:* drama/theater group, student-run newspaper, radio station, choral group. *Campus security:* 24-hour emergency response devices and patrols, late-night transport/escort service.
Athletics Member NCAA. All Division III. *Intercollegiate sports:* baseball M, basketball M/W, cross-country running M/W, fencing M/W, golf M, soccer M/W, tennis M/W, volleyball M, wrestling M. *Intramural sports:* basketball M/W, fencing M/W, swimming and diving M/W, table tennis M, volleyball M/W.
Standardized Tests *Required:* SAT or ACT (for admission).
Costs (2011–12) *Comprehensive fee:* $45,850 includes full-time tuition ($34,200), mandatory fees ($1000), and room and board ($10,650). Full-time tuition and fees vary according to student level. Part-time tuition: $1180 per credit hour. *Payment plan:* installment. *Waivers:* employees or children of employees.
Financial Aid Of all full-time matriculated undergraduates who enrolled in 2009, 1,832 applied for aid, 1,498 were judged to have need, 332 had their need fully met. In 2009, 323 non-need-based awards were made. *Average percent of need met:* 86%. *Average financial aid package:* $27,434. *Average need-based loan:* $6136. *Average need-based gift aid:* $20,988. *Average non-need-based aid:* $18,543. *Average indebtedness upon graduation:* $21,654.
Applying *Options:* early admission, deferred entrance. *Application fee:* $65. *Required:* essay or personal statement, high school transcript, 2 letters of recommendation, interview. *Application deadlines:* 2/1 (freshmen), rolling (transfers). *Notification:* 4/1 (freshmen).
Freshman Application Contact Yeshiva University, 500 West 185th Street, New York, NY 10033-3201. *Phone:* 212-960-5277. *Web site:* http://www.yu.edu/.

York College of the City University of New York

Jamaica, New York

- **State and locally supported** comprehensive, founded 1967, part of City University of New York System
- **Urban** 50-acre campus with easy access to New York City
- **Coed** 8,210 undergraduate students, 62% full-time, 66% women, 34% men
- **Moderately difficult** entrance level, 51% of applicants were admitted

Undergraduates 5,121 full-time, 3,089 part-time. Students come from 4 states and territories; 131 other countries; 0.4% are from out of state; 38% Black or African American, non-Hispanic/Latino; 19% Hispanic/Latino; 16% Asian, non-Hispanic/Latino; 0.9% American Indian or Alaska Native, non-Hispanic/Latino; 22% Race/ethnicity unknown; 12% transferred in. *Retention:* 77% of full-time freshmen returned.
Freshmen *Admission:* 13,129 applied, 6,751 admitted, 955 enrolled. *Test scores:* SAT critical reading scores over 500: 14%; SAT math scores over 500: 22%; SAT critical reading scores over 600: 2%; SAT math scores over 600: 3%.
Faculty *Total:* 548, 39% full-time. *Student/faculty ratio:* 18:1.
Academics *Calendar:* semesters. *Degrees:* bachelor's and master's. *Special study options:* adult/continuing education programs, advanced placement credit, cooperative education, double majors, English as a second language, honors programs, independent study, internships, off-campus study, part-time degree program, services for LD students, study abroad, summer session for credit. *ROTC:* Army (b). *Unusual degree programs:* 3-2 occupational therapy.
Computers on Campus 650 computers/terminals and 844 ports are available on campus for general student use. Students can access the following: computer help desk, free student e-mail accounts, online (class) registration, online (class) schedules. Campuswide network is available. Wireless service is available via entire campus.
Student Life *Housing:* college housing not available. *Activities and organizations:* drama/theater group, student-run newspaper, television station, choral group, Haitian Students Association, Caribbean Students Association, Haitian Cultural Association, Latin Caucus, Muslim Student Association. *Campus security:* 24-hour emergency response devices and patrols, late-night transport/escort service. *Student services:* health clinic, personal/psychological counseling, women's center.
Athletics Member NCAA. All Division III. *Intercollegiate sports:* baseball M/W, basketball M/W, cross-country running M/W, soccer M, softball W, swimming and diving M/W, tennis M, track and field M/W, volleyball M/W. *Intramural sports:* basketball M/W, cross-country running M/W, soccer M, softball W, swimming and diving M/W, table tennis M/W, tennis M, track and field M/W, volleyball M/W.
Standardized Tests *Required:* SAT or ACT (for admission).
Costs (2012–13) *Tuition:* state resident $5130 full-time, $215 per credit part-time; nonresident $13,800 full-time, $460 per credit part-time. No tuition increase for student's term of enrollment. *Required fees:* $366 full-time. *Payment plan:* installment. *Waivers:* senior citizens and employees or children of employees.
Financial Aid Of all full-time matriculated undergraduates who enrolled in 2011, 4,335 applied for aid, 3,896 were judged to have need, 16 had their need fully met. 1,737 Federal Work-Study jobs (averaging $1160). In 2011, 52 non-need-based awards were made. *Average percent of need met:* 10%. *Average financial aid package:* $1819. *Average need-based loan:* $2225. *Average need-based gift aid:* $800. *Average non-need-based aid:* $1084. *Average indebtedness upon graduation:* $2996. *Financial aid deadline:* 6/30.
Applying *Options:* electronic application, early admission, deferred entrance. *Application fee:* $65. *Required:* high school transcript, minimum 2.5 GPA. *Required for some:* minimum 2.8 GPA. *Recommended:* minimum 3.0 GPA. *Application deadlines:* rolling (freshmen), rolling (out-of-state freshmen), rolling (transfers). *Notification:* continuous (freshmen), continuous (out-of-state freshmen), continuous (transfers).
Freshman Application Contact Ms. Laura Bruno, Acting Associate Director of Admissions, York College of the City University of New York, 94-20 Guy R. Brewer Boulevard, Jamaica, NY 11451. *Phone:* 718-262-2165. *Fax:* 718-262-2601. *E-mail:* lbruno@york.cuny.edu. *Web site:* http://www.york.cuny.edu/.

NORTH CAROLINA

Apex School of Theology

Durham, North Carolina

- **Independent interdenominational** comprehensive, founded 1995
- **Suburban** campus
- **Coed** 529 undergraduate students, 85% full-time, 67% women, 33% men
- **Moderately difficult** entrance level, 83% of applicants were admitted

Undergraduates 452 full-time, 77 part-time. Students come from 1 other state; 95% Black or African American, non-Hispanic/Latino; 2% Hispanic/Latino. *Retention:* 92% of full-time freshmen returned.
Freshmen *Admission:* 362 applied, 300 admitted.
Faculty *Total:* 41, 34% full-time, 59% with terminal degrees. *Student/faculty ratio:* 17:1.
Academics *Calendar:* semesters. *Degrees:* associate, bachelor's, master's, doctoral, and first professional. *Special study options:* distance learning, double majors, independent study, internships.
Student Life *Housing:* college housing not available. *Activities and organizations:* student-run newspaper, choral group.
Costs (2012–13) *Tuition:* $4800 full-time, $200 per credit hour part-time. No tuition increase for student's term of enrollment. *Required fees:* $200 full-time. *Payment plan:* installment.

Applying *Options:* electronic application. *Application fee:* $25. *Required:* essay or personal statement, high school transcript, letters of recommendation. **Freshman Application Contact** Dr. Henry D. Wells Jr., Registrar, Apex School of Theology, 2945 South Miami Boulevard, Suite 114, Durham, NC 27703. *Phone:* 919-572-1625. *Fax:* 919-572-1762. *E-mail:* registrar@apexsot.edu. *Web site:* http://www.apexsot.edu/.

Appalachian State University
Boone, North Carolina

- **State-supported** comprehensive, founded 1899, part of University of North Carolina System
- **Small-town** 411-acre campus
- **Endowment** $69.6 million
- **Coed** 15,460 undergraduate students, 95% full-time, 52% women, 48% men
- **Moderately difficult** entrance level, 62% of applicants were admitted

Undergraduates 14,704 full-time, 756 part-time. Students come from 46 states and territories; 54 other countries; 9% are from out of state; 3% Black or African American, non-Hispanic/Latino; 3% Hispanic/Latino; 1% Asian, non-Hispanic/Latino; 0.3% American Indian or Alaska Native, non-Hispanic/Latino; 2% Two or more races, non-Hispanic/Latino; 2% Race/ethnicity unknown; 0.5% international; 6% transferred in; 35% live on campus. *Retention:* 88% of full-time freshmen returned.

Freshmen *Admission:* 12,959 applied, 8,006 admitted, 2,972 enrolled. *Average high school GPA:* 3.94. *Test scores:* SAT critical reading scores over 500: 84%; SAT math scores over 500: 90%; SAT writing scores over 500: 77%; ACT scores over 18: 99%; SAT critical reading scores over 600: 34%; SAT math scores over 600: 37%; SAT writing scores over 600: 24%; ACT scores over 24: 57%; SAT critical reading scores over 700: 4%; SAT math scores over 700: 3%; SAT writing scores over 700: 2%; ACT scores over 30: 7%.

Faculty *Total:* 1,180, 74% full-time, 92% with terminal degrees. *Student/faculty ratio:* 17:1.

Academics *Calendar:* semesters. *Degrees:* bachelor's, master's, doctoral, post-master's, postbachelor's, and first professional certificates. *Special study options:* academic remediation for entering students, adult/continuing education programs, advanced placement credit, distance learning, double majors, English as a second language, honors programs, independent study, internships, off-campus study, part-time degree program, services for LD students, student-designed majors, study abroad, summer session for credit. *ROTC:* Army (b). *Unusual degree programs:* 3-2 engineering with Auburn University, Clemson University.

Computers on Campus 1,800 computers/terminals are available on campus for general student use. Students can access the following: campus intranet, computer help desk, free student e-mail accounts, online (class) grades, online (class) registration, online (class) schedules. Campuswide network is available. 100% of college-owned or -operated housing units are wired for high-speed Internet access. Wireless service is available via entire campus.

Student Life *Housing:* on-campus residence required for freshman year. *Options:* coed, men-only, women-only, disabled students. Campus housing is university owned. Freshman campus housing is guaranteed. *Activities and organizations:* drama/theater group, student-run newspaper, radio station, choral group, marching band, Appalachian Intramural Recreation Sports Association, Appalachian State Fly-Fishing Club, Health Professions Club, Invisible Children at Appalachian State, APPS Special Events, national fraternities, national sororities. *Campus security:* 24-hour emergency response devices and patrols, late-night transport/escort service, controlled dormitory access. *Student services:* health clinic, personal/psychological counseling, women's center, legal services.

Athletics Member NCAA, NAIA. All NCAA Division I except football (Division I-AA). *Intercollegiate sports:* baseball M(s), basketball M(s)/W(s), cross-country running M(s)/W(s), field hockey W(s), golf M(s)/W(s), soccer M(s)/W(s), softball W(s), tennis M(s)/W(s), track and field M(s)/W(s), volleyball W(s), wrestling M(s). *Intramural sports:* badminton M/W, baseball M(c), basketball M/W, bowling M/W, cross-country running M/W, equestrian sports M(c)/W(c), fencing M(c)/W(c), football M/W, golf M/W, ice hockey M(c)/W(c), lacrosse M(c)/W(c), racquetball M(c)/W(c), rugby M(c)/W(c), skiing (downhill) M(c)/W(c), soccer M/W(c), swimming and diving M(c)/W(c), table tennis M/W, ultimate Frisbee M(c)/W(c), volleyball M/W(c).

Standardized Tests *Required:* SAT or ACT (for admission).

Costs (2011–12) *Tuition:* state resident $3153 full-time, $107 per credit hour part-time; nonresident $15,201 full-time, $514 per credit hour part-time. Part-time tuition and fees vary according to course load. *Required fees:* $2385 full-time, $13 per credit hour part-time. *Room and board:* $6810; room only: $3800. Room and board charges vary according to board plan and housing facility. *Payment plan:* installment. *Waivers:* employees or children of employees.

Financial Aid Of all full-time matriculated undergraduates who enrolled in 2011, 7,324 applied for aid, 7,102 were judged to have need, 2,810 had their

need fully met. 298 Federal Work-Study jobs (averaging $1654). In 2011, 448 non-need-based awards were made. *Average percent of need met:* 74%. *Average financial aid package:* $8864. *Average need-based loan:* $4144. *Average need-based gift aid:* $7226. *Average non-need-based aid:* $2566. *Average indebtedness upon graduation:* $17,155.

Applying *Options:* electronic application, deferred entrance. *Application fee:* $55. *Required:* high school transcript. *Application deadline:* rolling (transfers). *Notification:* continuous (transfers).

Freshman Application Contact Mr. Lloyd M Scott, Director of Admissions, Appalachian State University, ASU Box 32004, Boone, NC 28608. *Phone:* 828-262-2120. *Fax:* 828-262-3296. *E-mail:* admissions@appstate.edu. *Web site:* http://www.appstate.edu/.

The Art Institute of Charlotte
Charlotte, North Carolina

- **Proprietary** 4-year, founded 1973, part of Education Management Corporation
- **Suburban** campus
- **Coed**

Academics *Calendar:* quarters. *Degrees:* certificates, associate, and bachelor's. *Special study options:* summer session for credit.

Costs (2011–12) *Tuition:* Tuition cost varies by program. Prospective students should contact the school for current tuition costs. Other charges include a starting kit for all first-quarter students. Kits vary in price, depending on the program of study.

Freshman Application Contact The Art Institute of Charlotte, Three LakePointe Plaza, 2110 Water Ridge Parkway, Charlotte, NC 28217. *Phone:* 704-357-8020. *Toll-free phone:* 800-872-4417. *Web site:* http://www.artinstitutes.edu/charlotte/.

See page 1090 for the College Close-Up.

The Art Institute of Raleigh-Durham
Durham, North Carolina

- **Proprietary** 4-year, founded 2008, part of Education Management Corporation
- **Coed**

Academics *Degrees:* certificates, associate, and bachelor's.

Costs (2011–12) *Tuition:* Tuition cost varies by program. Prospective students should contact the school for current tuition costs. Other charges include a starting kit for all first-quarter students. Kits vary in price, depending on the program of study.

Freshman Application Contact The Art Institute of Raleigh-Durham, 410 Blackwell Street, Suite 200, Durham, NC 27701. *Phone:* 919-317-3050. *Toll-free phone:* 888-245-9593. *Web site:* http://www.artinstitutes.edu/raleigh-durham.

See page 1124 for the College Close-Up.

Barton College
Wilson, North Carolina

- **Independent** comprehensive, founded 1902, affiliated with Christian Church (Disciples of Christ)
- **Small-town** 76-acre campus with easy access to Raleigh-Durham
- **Coed** 2,521 undergraduate students, 89% full-time, 87% women, 13% men
- **Minimally difficult** entrance level, 52% of applicants were admitted

Undergraduates 2,244 full-time, 277 part-time. Students come from 26 states and territories; 9 other countries; 11% are from out of state; 26% Black or African American, non-Hispanic/Latino; 3% Hispanic/Latino; 0.7% Asian, non-Hispanic/Latino; 0.4% Native Hawaiian or other Pacific Islander, non-Hispanic/Latino; 0.3% American Indian or Alaska Native, non-Hispanic/Latino; 3% Two or more races, non-Hispanic/Latino; 5% Race/ethnicity unknown; 2% international; 49% live on campus. *Retention:* 68% of full-time freshmen returned.

Freshmen *Admission:* 2,598 applied, 1,352 admitted, 1,578 enrolled. *Average high school GPA:* 3.04. *Test scores:* SAT critical reading scores over 500: 30%; SAT math scores over 500: 39%; ACT scores over 18: 85%; SAT critical reading scores over 600: 4%; SAT math scores over 600: 5%; ACT scores over 24: 4%.

Faculty *Total:* 108, 65% full-time, 47% with terminal degrees. *Student/faculty ratio:* 12:1.

Academics *Calendar:* 4-1-4. *Degrees:* bachelor's and master's. *Special study options:* academic remediation for entering students, adult/continuing education programs, advanced placement credit, cooperative education, double majors, English as a second language, honors programs, independent study,

internships, part-time degree program, services for LD students, summer session for credit.

Computers on Campus 125 computers/terminals are available on campus for general student use. Students can access the following: campus intranet, computer help desk, free student e-mail accounts, student picture directory. Campuswide network is available. 100% of college-owned or -operated housing units are wired for high-speed Internet access. Wireless service is available via computer centers, computer labs, learning centers, libraries, student centers.

Student Life *Housing:* on-campus residence required through sophomore year. *Options:* coed, women-only. Campus housing is university owned. Freshman campus housing is guaranteed. *Activities and organizations:* drama/theater group, student-run newspaper, television station, choral group, Barton College Association of Nurses, Students in Free Enterprise (SIFE), Stage and Script, Campus Activities Board, College Habitat for Humanity, national fraternities, national sororities. *Campus security:* 24-hour emergency response devices, late-night transport/escort service, controlled dormitory access, city police sub-station on campus. *Student services:* health clinic, personal/psychological counseling.

Athletics Member NCAA. All Division II. *Intercollegiate sports:* baseball M(s), basketball M(s)/W(s), cross-country running M(s)/W(s), golf M(s)/W(s), soccer M(s)/W(s), softball W(s), tennis M(s)/W(s), track and field M(s)/W(s), volleyball M(s)/W(s). *Intramural sports:* archery M/W, badminton M/W, baseball M/W, basketball M/W, cheerleading M/W, football M/W, golf M/W, soccer M/W, softball M/W, swimming and diving M/W, table tennis M/W, tennis M/W, volleyball M/W, weight lifting M/W.

Standardized Tests *Required:* SAT or ACT (for admission).

Costs (2011–12) *Comprehensive fee:* $30,614 includes full-time tuition ($21,258), mandatory fees ($1724), and room and board ($7632). Full-time tuition and fees vary according to class time, course load, and program. Part-time tuition: $897 per credit hour. Part-time tuition and fees vary according to class time, course load, and program. *College room only:* $3461. Room and board charges vary according to housing facility. *Payment plan:* installment. *Waivers:* children of alumni, adult students, senior citizens, and employees or children of employees.

Financial Aid Of all full-time matriculated undergraduates who enrolled in 2009, 791 applied for aid, 740 were judged to have need, 74 had their need fully met. In 2009, 116 non-need-based awards were made. *Average percent of need met:* 67%. *Average financial aid package:* $19,289. *Average need-based loan:* $5318. *Average need-based gift aid:* $6134. *Average non-need-based aid:* $4837. *Average indebtedness upon graduation:* $28,343.

Applying *Options:* electronic application, deferred entrance. *Application fee:* $25. *Required:* high school transcript. *Recommended:* minimum 2.3 GPA, interview. *Application deadlines:* rolling (freshmen), rolling (transfers). *Notification:* continuous (freshmen), continuous (transfers).

Freshman Application Contact Barton College, PO Box 5000, Wilson, NC 27893-7000. *Phone:* 800-345-4973. *Toll-free phone:* 800-345-4973. *Web site:* http://www.barton.edu/.

Belmont Abbey College

Belmont, North Carolina

- **Independent Roman Catholic** 4-year, founded 1876
- **Small-town** 650-acre campus with easy access to Charlotte
- **Endowment** $5.8 million
- **Coed** 1,711 undergraduate students, 93% full-time, 62% women, 38% men
- **Moderately difficult** entrance level, 63% of applicants were admitted

Undergraduates 1,587 full-time, 124 part-time. Students come from 41 states and territories; 17 other countries; 27% are from out of state; 28% Black or African American, non-Hispanic/Latino; 3% Hispanic/Latino; 1% Asian, non-Hispanic/Latino; 0.2% Native Hawaiian or other Pacific Islander, non-Hispanic/Latino; 0.3% American Indian or Alaska Native, non-Hispanic/Latino; 0.1% Two or more races, non-Hispanic/Latino; 33% Race/ethnicity unknown; 2% international; 11% transferred in; 48% live on campus. *Retention:* 64% of full-time freshmen returned.

Freshmen *Admission:* 1,987 applied, 1,252 admitted, 263 enrolled. *Average high school GPA:* 3.08. *Test scores:* SAT critical reading scores over 500: 50%; SAT math scores over 500: 51%; ACT scores over 18: 76%; SAT critical reading scores over 600: 19%; SAT math scores over 600: 16%; ACT scores over 24: 22%; SAT critical reading scores over 700: 6%; SAT math scores over 700: 3%; ACT scores over 30: 3%.

Faculty *Total:* 145, 50% full-time, 46% with terminal degrees. *Student/faculty ratio:* 17:1.

Academics *Calendar:* semesters. *Degree:* bachelor's. *Special study options:* accelerated degree program, adult/continuing education programs, advanced placement credit, cooperative education, double majors, external degree program, freshman honors college, honors programs, independent study, intern-

ships, off-campus study, part-time degree program, services for LD students, study abroad, summer session for credit. *ROTC:* Army (c), Air Force (c).

Computers on Campus 125 computers/terminals are available on campus for general student use. Students can access the following: computer help desk, free student e-mail accounts, online (class) grades, online (class) registration, online (class) schedules. Campuswide network is available. 100% of college-owned or -operated housing units are wired for high-speed Internet access. Wireless service is available via classrooms, computer labs, libraries, student centers.

Student Life *Housing:* on-campus residence required through senior year. *Options:* coed, men-only, women-only. Campus housing is university owned and leased by the school. Freshman campus housing is guaranteed. *Activities and organizations:* drama/theater group, student-run newspaper, radio station, choral group, Abbey Ambassadors, Abbey Players, The Crusader, Greek Life (fraternities and sororities), national fraternities, national sororities. *Campus security:* 24-hour emergency response devices and patrols, late-night transport/escort service. *Student services:* health clinic, personal/psychological counseling.

Athletics Member NCAA. All Division II. *Intercollegiate sports:* baseball M(s), basketball M(s)/W(s), cheerleading M/W, cross-country running M(s)/W(s), golf M(s)/W(s), lacrosse M(s)/W(s), soccer M(s)/W(s), softball W(s), tennis M(s)/W(s), track and field M(s)/W(s), volleyball M(s)/W(s), wrestling M(s). *Intramural sports:* badminton M/W, basketball M/W, crew M/W, cross-country running M/W, football M/W, rugby M(c), soccer M/W, softball M/W, table tennis M/W, tennis M/W, ultimate Frisbee M/W, volleyball M/W, weight lifting M, wrestling M.

Standardized Tests *Required for some:* SAT or ACT (for admission).

Costs (2011–12) *One-time required fee:* $400. *Comprehensive fee:* $36,585 includes full-time tuition ($26,182) and room and board ($10,403). Full-time tuition and fees vary according to class time, course load, location, program, and reciprocity agreements. Part-time tuition: $873 per credit hour. Part-time tuition and fees vary according to class time, course load, location, and reciprocity agreements. *College room only:* $6137. Room and board charges vary according to board plan, housing facility, and location. *Payment plans:* installment, deferred payment. *Waivers:* senior citizens and employees or children of employees.

Financial Aid Of all full-time matriculated undergraduates who enrolled in 2010, 1,583 applied for aid, 1,443 were judged to have need, 146 had their need fully met. 98 Federal Work-Study jobs (averaging $1063). In 2010, 286 non-need-based awards were made. *Average percent of need met:* 56%. *Average financial aid package:* $13,988. *Average need-based loan:* $4049. *Average need-based gift aid:* $10,246. *Average non-need-based aid:* $10,628. *Average indebtedness upon graduation:* $21,602.

Applying *Options:* electronic application, deferred entrance. *Application fee:* $35. *Required:* high school transcript, minimum 2.3 GPA. *Required for some:* essay or personal statement, 2 letters of recommendation. *Recommended:* interview. *Application deadlines:* 8/1 (freshmen), 8/15 (transfers). *Notification:* continuous (freshmen), continuous (transfers).

Freshman Application Contact Danielle Blanchard, Assistant Director of Admission, Belmont Abbey College, 100 Belmont-Mt. Holly Road, Belmont, NC 28012-1802. *Phone:* 704-461-6668. *Toll-free phone:* 888-BAC-0110. *E-mail:* danielleblanchard@bac.edu. *Web site:* http://www.belmontabbeycollege.edu/.

Bennett College for Women

Greensboro, North Carolina

- **Independent United Methodist** 4-year, founded 1873
- **Urban** 55-acre campus
- **Endowment** $12.3 million
- **Women only** 736 undergraduate students, 91% full-time
- **Moderately difficult** entrance level, 63% of applicants were admitted

Undergraduates 672 full-time, 64 part-time. Students come from 31 states and territories; 2 other countries; 61% are from out of state; 93% Black or African American, non-Hispanic/Latino; 3% Hispanic/Latino; 0.3% Asian, non-Hispanic/Latino; 0.3% American Indian or Alaska Native, non-Hispanic/Latino; 3% Two or more races, non-Hispanic/Latino; 0.1% Race/ethnicity unknown; 0.3% international; 2% transferred in; 65% live on campus. *Retention:* 73% of full-time freshmen returned.

Freshmen *Admission:* 1,433 applied, 900 admitted, 158 enrolled. *Average high school GPA:* 2.61.

Faculty *Total:* 89, 69% full-time, 54% with terminal degrees. *Student/faculty ratio:* 10:1.

Academics *Calendar:* semesters. *Degree:* bachelor's. *Special study options:* academic remediation for entering students, advanced placement credit, cooperative education, double majors, honors programs, independent study, internships, off-campus study, part-time degree program, services for LD students, study abroad. *ROTC:* Army (c), Air Force (c). *Unusual degree programs:* 3-2

engineering with North Carolina Agricultural and Technical State University; nursing with Howard University.

Computers on Campus Students can access the following: campus intranet, computer help desk, free student e-mail accounts, online (class) grades, online (class) registration, online (class) schedules. Campuswide network is available. Wireless service is available via classrooms, dorm rooms, learning centers, libraries.

Student Life *Housing:* on-campus residence required through sophomore year. *Options:* women-only. Campus housing is university owned. Freshman campus housing is guaranteed. *Activities and organizations:* drama/theater group, student-run newspaper, choral group, Christian Fellowship, Pre-Alumnae Council, Belles of Harmony, NAACP, National Council of Negro Women, national sororities. *Campus security:* 24-hour patrols, late-night transport/escort service, controlled dormitory access. *Student services:* health clinic, personal/psychological counseling, women's center, legal services.

Athletics Member USCAA. *Intercollegiate sports:* basketball W. *Intramural sports:* golf W, soccer W, softball W.

Standardized Tests *Recommended:* SAT or ACT (for admission).

Costs (2011–12) *One-time required fee:* $225. *Comprehensive fee:* $24,222 includes full-time tuition ($14,614), mandatory fees ($2180), and room and board ($7428). Part-time tuition: $609 per credit hour. Part-time tuition and fees vary according to course load. *Required fees:* $900 per term part-time. *College room only:* $3698. Room and board charges vary according to housing facility. *Payment plan:* installment. *Waivers:* employees or children of employees.

Financial Aid Of all full-time matriculated undergraduates who enrolled in 2011, 664 applied for aid, 643 were judged to have need, 22 had their need fully met. In 2011, 7 non-need-based awards were made. *Average percent of need met:* 47%. *Average financial aid package:* $13,092. *Average need-based loan:* $4170. *Average need-based gift aid:* $9402. *Average non-need-based aid:* $4714. *Financial aid deadline:* 3/15.

Applying *Options:* electronic application, deferred entrance. *Application fee:* $35. *Required:* essay or personal statement, high school transcript, minimum 2.0 GPA, 2 letters of recommendation. *Required for some:* interview. *Application deadlines:* rolling (freshmen), rolling (out-of-state freshmen), rolling (transfers). *Notification:* continuous (freshmen), continuous (out-of-state freshmen), continuous (transfers).

Freshman Application Contact Ms. Taunya Monroe, Interim Director of Admissions, Bennett College for Women, 900 East Washington Street, Campus Box H, Greensboro, NC 27401. *Phone:* 336-517-2161. *Toll-free phone:* 800-413-5323. *E-mail:* tmonroe@bennett.edu. *Web site:* http://www.bennett.edu/.

Brevard College

Brevard, North Carolina

- **Independent United Methodist** 4-year, founded 1853
- **Small-town** 120-acre campus
- **Endowment** $21.8 million
- **Coed** 627 undergraduate students, 98% full-time, 41% women, 59% men
- **Minimally difficult** entrance level, 55% of applicants were admitted

Undergraduates 613 full-time, 14 part-time. Students come from 34 states and territories; 10 other countries; 48% are from out of state; 11% Black or African American, non-Hispanic/Latino; 0.5% Hispanic/Latino; 0.2% Asian, non-Hispanic/Latino; 1% American Indian or Alaska Native, non-Hispanic/Latino; 0.8% Two or more races, non-Hispanic/Latino; 5% Race/ethnicity unknown; 5% international; 7% transferred in; 79% live on campus. *Retention:* 65% of full-time freshmen returned.

Freshmen *Admission:* 1,329 applied, 734 admitted, 190 enrolled. *Average high school GPA:* 2.93. *Test scores:* SAT critical reading scores over 500: 38%; SAT math scores over 500: 47%; ACT scores over 18: 76%; SAT critical reading scores over 600: 7%; SAT math scores over 600: 8%; ACT scores over 24: 16%; SAT critical reading scores over 700: 1%; SAT math scores over 700: 1%; ACT scores over 30: 2%.

Faculty *Total:* 86, 62% full-time, 59% with terminal degrees. *Student/faculty ratio:* 10:1.

Academics *Calendar:* semesters. *Degree:* bachelor's. *Special study options:* academic remediation for entering students, advanced placement credit, double majors, honors programs, independent study, internships, part-time degree program, services for LD students, student-designed majors, study abroad.

Computers on Campus 100 computers/terminals are available on campus for general student use. Students can access the following: campus intranet, computer help desk, free student e-mail accounts, online (class) grades, online (class) schedules. Campuswide network is available. 100% of college-owned or -operated housing units are wired for high-speed Internet access. Wireless service is available via learning centers, libraries, student centers.

Student Life *Housing:* on-campus residence required through senior year. *Options:* coed, men-only, women-only, disabled students. Campus housing is university owned. Freshman campus housing is guaranteed. *Activities and organizations:* drama/theater group, student-run newspaper, choral group, Fine Arts organizations, Omicron Delta Kappa, Fellowship of Christian Athletes, BC Greens, Business Club. *Campus security:* 24-hour emergency response devices and patrols. *Student services:* health clinic, personal/psychological counseling, women's center.

Athletics Member NCAA. All Division II. *Intercollegiate sports:* baseball M(s), basketball M(s)/W(s), cheerleading W(s), cross-country running M(s)/W(s), football M(s), golf M(s)/W(s), soccer M(s)/W(s), softball W(s), tennis M(s)/W(s), track and field M(s)/W(s), volleyball W(s). *Intramural sports:* badminton M/W, basketball M/W, bowling M/W, fencing M(c)/W(c), football M/W, soccer M/W, softball M/W, tennis M/W, track and field M/W, ultimate Frisbee M/W, volleyball M/W, weight lifting M/W.

Standardized Tests *Required:* SAT or ACT (for admission).

Costs (2012–13) *Comprehensive fee:* $32,100 includes full-time tuition ($23,900) and room and board ($8200). Full-time tuition and fees vary according to course load. Part-time tuition: $850 per credit hour. Part-time tuition and fees vary according to course load. *Room and board:* Room and board charges vary according to board plan and housing facility. *Payment plan:* installment. *Waivers:* senior citizens and employees or children of employees.

Financial Aid Of all full-time matriculated undergraduates who enrolled in 2010, 558 applied for aid, 370 were judged to have need, 147 had their need fully met. 66 Federal Work-Study jobs (averaging $1000). In 2010, 377 non-need-based awards were made. *Average percent of need met:* 61%. *Average financial aid package:* $16,585. *Average need-based loan:* $4260. *Average need-based gift aid:* $14,287. *Average non-need-based aid:* $7909. *Average indebtedness upon graduation:* $23,016.

Applying *Options:* electronic application, deferred entrance. *Required:* essay or personal statement, high school transcript, minimum 2.0 GPA. *Required for some:* interview, students in music require auditions, music tests; students in art require portfolio. *Application deadlines:* rolling (freshmen), rolling (out-of-state freshmen), rolling (transfers). *Notification:* continuous (freshmen), continuous (out-of-state freshmen), continuous (transfers).

Freshman Application Contact Ms. Jessica Coye, Admissions, Brevard College, One Brevard College Drive, Brevard, NC 28712. *Phone:* 828-884-8291. *Toll-free phone:* 800-527-9090. *Fax:* 828-884-3790. *E-mail:* admissions@brevard.edu. *Web site:* http://www.brevard.edu/.

Cabarrus College of Health Sciences

Concord, North Carolina

Freshman Application Contact Mr. Mark Ellison, Director of Admissions, Cabarrus College of Health Sciences, 401 Medical Park Drive, Concord, NC 28025-2077. *Phone:* 704-403-1616. *Fax:* 704-403-2077. *E-mail:* mellison@cabarruscollege.edu. *Web site:* http://www.cabarruscollege.edu/.

Campbell University

Buies Creek, North Carolina

Freshman Application Contact Ms. Peggy Mason, Director of Admissions, Campbell University, PO Box 546, 450 Leslie Campbell Avenue, Buies Creek, NC 27506. *Phone:* 910-893-1290. *Toll-free phone:* 800-334-4111. *Fax:* 910-893-1288. *E-mail:* adm@mailcenter.campbell.edu. *Web site:* http://www.campbell.edu/.

Carolina Christian College

Winston-Salem, North Carolina

- **Independent nondenominational** comprehensive, founded 1949
- **Small-town** 2-acre campus
- **Endowment** $250,000
- **Coed** 70 undergraduate students, 96% full-time, 51% women, 49% men
- **Noncompetitive** entrance level, 68% of applicants were admitted

Undergraduates 67 full-time, 3 part-time. Students come from 1 other state; 92% Black or African American, non-Hispanic/Latino; 4% Hispanic/Latino; 1% Asian, non-Hispanic/Latino. *Retention:* 90% of full-time freshmen returned.

Freshmen *Admission:* 22 applied, 15 admitted, 9 enrolled. *Average high school GPA:* 2.6.

Faculty *Total:* 12, 17% full-time, 50% with terminal degrees. *Student/faculty ratio:* 13:1.

Academics *Calendar:* semesters. *Degrees:* associate, bachelor's, and master's. *Special study options:* accelerated degree program, adult/continuing education programs, external degree program, part-time degree program.

Computers on Campus 8 computers/terminals and 8 ports are available on campus for general student use. Wireless service is available via entire campus.

Student Life *Housing:* college housing not available. *Campus security:* 24-hour emergency response devices. *Student services:* personal/psychological counseling.

Costs (2012–13) *Tuition:* $7000 full-time, $875 per course part-time. *Required fees:* $200 full-time. *Payment plan:* installment. *Waivers:* employees or children of employees.

Financial Aid Of all full-time matriculated undergraduates who enrolled in 2011, 64 applied for aid, 60 were judged to have need, 50 had their need fully met. In 2011, 4 non-need-based awards were made. *Average percent of need met:* 85%. *Average financial aid package:* $9500. *Average need-based gift aid:* $1500. *Average non-need-based aid:* $3500. *Average indebtedness upon graduation:* $6500.

Applying *Options:* electronic application. *Application fee:* $50. *Required:* essay or personal statement, high school transcript, 2 letters of recommendation, interview. *Application deadlines:* rolling (freshmen), rolling (out-of-state freshmen), rolling (transfers). *Notification:* continuous (freshmen), continuous (out-of-state freshmen), continuous (transfers).

Freshman Application Contact Carolina Christian College, 4209 Indiana Avenue, PO Box 777, Winston-Salem, NC 27102-0777. *Phone:* 336-744-0900 Ext. 106. *Web site:* http://www.carolina.edu/.

Catawba College
Salisbury, North Carolina

- **Independent** comprehensive, founded 1851, affiliated with United Church of Christ
- **Small-town** 210-acre campus with easy access to Charlotte
- **Coed** 1,305 undergraduate students, 94% full-time, 52% women, 48% men
- **Moderately difficult** entrance level, 42% of applicants were admitted

Undergraduates 1,226 full-time, 79 part-time. Students come from 31 states and territories; 9 other countries; 24% are from out of state; 20% Black or African American, non-Hispanic/Latino; 3% Hispanic/Latino; 0.8% Asian, non-Hispanic/Latino; 0.1% Native Hawaiian or other Pacific Islander, non-Hispanic/Latino; 0.6% American Indian or Alaska Native, non-Hispanic/Latino; 1% Two or more races, non-Hispanic/Latino; 0.1% Race/ethnicity unknown; 2% international; 7% transferred in; 72% live on campus. *Retention:* 71% of full-time freshmen returned.

Freshmen *Admission:* 2,427 applied, 1,010 admitted, 312 enrolled. *Average high school GPA:* 3.42. *Test scores:* SAT critical reading scores over 500: 42%; SAT math scores over 500: 45%; SAT critical reading scores over 600: 9%; SAT math scores over 600: 14%; SAT critical reading scores over 700: 2%; SAT math scores over 700: 1%.

Faculty *Total:* 106, 63% full-time, 59% with terminal degrees. *Student/faculty ratio:* 16:1.

Academics *Calendar:* semesters. *Degrees:* bachelor's and master's. *Special study options:* advanced placement credit, double majors, honors programs, independent study, internships, part-time degree program, services for LD students, student-designed majors, study abroad, summer session for credit. *ROTC:* Army (c).

Computers on Campus 97 computers/terminals are available on campus for general student use. Students can access the following: campus intranet, computer help desk, free student e-mail accounts, online (class) grades, online (class) registration, online (class) schedules. Campuswide network is available. 100% of college-owned or -operated housing units are wired for high-speed Internet access. Wireless service is available via entire campus.

Student Life *Housing:* on-campus residence required through senior year. *Options:* coed, men-only, women-only. Campus housing is university owned. Freshman campus housing is guaranteed. *Activities and organizations:* drama/theater group, student-run newspaper, choral group, Volunteer Catawba, Catawba Ambassadors (admissions guides), Blue Masque (drama), Fellowship of Christian Athletes, Wigwam Productions (student activities board). *Campus security:* 24-hour emergency response devices and patrols, late-night transport/escort service, controlled dormitory access. *Student services:* health clinic, personal/psychological counseling.

Athletics Member NCAA. All Division II. *Intercollegiate sports:* baseball M(s), basketball M(s)/W(s), cheerleading M(s)/W(s), cross-country running M(s)/W(s), football M(s), golf M(s)/W(s), lacrosse M(s)/W(s), soccer M(s)/W(s), softball W(s), swimming and diving M(s)/W(s), tennis M(s)/W(s), volleyball W(s). *Intramural sports:* basketball M/W, football M/W, racquetball M/W, soccer M/W, tennis M/W, volleyball M/W, weight lifting M/W.

Standardized Tests *Required:* SAT or ACT (for admission).

Costs (2011–12) *Comprehensive fee:* $33,860 includes full-time tuition ($25,160) and room and board ($8700). Part-time tuition: $655 per credit hour. *Required fees:* $50 per term part-time. *Payment plan:* installment. *Waivers:* employees or children of employees.

Financial Aid Of all full-time matriculated undergraduates who enrolled in 2010, 1,038 applied for aid, 971 were judged to have need, 193 had their need

fully met. 195 Federal Work-Study jobs (averaging $1633). In 2010, 69 non-need-based awards were made. *Average percent of need met:* 80%. *Average financial aid package:* $19,968. *Average need-based loan:* $4053. *Average need-based gift aid:* $5727. *Average non-need-based aid:* $11,053. *Average indebtedness upon graduation:* $27,907.

Applying *Options:* electronic application, early admission, deferred entrance. *Application fee:* $25. *Required:* essay or personal statement, high school transcript, minimum 2.0 GPA, 2 letters of recommendation. *Recommended:* interview. *Application deadlines:* rolling (freshmen), rolling (transfers). *Notification:* continuous (freshmen), continuous (transfers).

Freshman Application Contact Catawba College, 2300 West Innes Street, Salisbury, NC 28144-2488. *Phone:* 704-637-4414. *Toll-free phone:* 800-CATAWBA. *Web site:* http://www.catawba.edu/.

Chowan University
Murfreesboro, North Carolina

Freshman Application Contact Chowan University, One University Place, Murfreesboro, NC 27855. *Phone:* 252-398-6298. *Toll-free phone:* 888-4-CHOWAN. *Web site:* http://www.chowan.edu/.

Davidson College
Davidson, North Carolina

- **Independent Presbyterian** 4-year, founded 1837
- **Small-town** 665-acre campus with easy access to Charlotte
- **Endowment** $509.6 million
- **Coed** 1,756 undergraduate students, 100% full-time, 49% women, 51% men
- **Very difficult** entrance level, 28% of applicants were admitted

Undergraduates 1,755 full-time, 1 part-time. Students come from 46 states and territories; 42 other countries; 79% are from out of state; 7% Black or African American, non-Hispanic/Latino; 5% Hispanic/Latino; 4% Asian, non-Hispanic/Latino; 0.1% Native Hawaiian or other Pacific Islander, non-Hispanic/Latino; 0.3% American Indian or Alaska Native, non-Hispanic/Latino; 2% Two or more races, non-Hispanic/Latino; 6% Race/ethnicity unknown; 5% international; 0.5% transferred in; 90% live on campus. *Retention:* 96% of full-time freshmen returned.

Freshmen *Admission:* 4,309 applied, 1,208 admitted, 488 enrolled. *Average high school GPA:* 4.1. *Test scores:* SAT critical reading scores over 500: 99%; SAT math scores over 500: 99%; SAT writing scores over 500: 99%; ACT scores over 18: 99%; SAT critical reading scores over 600: 86%; SAT math scores over 600: 92%; SAT writing scores over 600: 88%; ACT scores over 24: 97%; SAT critical reading scores over 700: 43%; SAT math scores over 700: 36%; SAT writing scores over 700: 43%; ACT scores over 30: 69%.

Faculty *Total:* 167, 97% full-time, 95% with terminal degrees. *Student/faculty ratio:* 11:1.

Academics *Calendar:* semesters. *Degree:* bachelor's. *Special study options:* advanced placement credit, double majors, honors programs, independent study, off-campus study, services for LD students, student-designed majors, study abroad. *ROTC:* Army (b), Air Force (c). *Unusual degree programs:* 3-2 engineering with Columbia University, Washington University in St. Louis.

Computers on Campus 142 computers/terminals are available on campus for general student use. Students can access the following: campus intranet, computer help desk, free student e-mail accounts, online (class) grades, online (class) registration, online (class) schedules. Campuswide network is available. 100% of college-owned or -operated housing units are wired for high-speed Internet access. Wireless service is available via entire campus.

Student Life *Housing:* on-campus residence required through senior year. *Options:* coed, cooperative. Campus housing is university owned. Freshman campus housing is guaranteed. *Activities and organizations:* drama/theater group, student-run newspaper, radio station, choral group, Inter-Varsity Christian Fellowship, Dean Rusk Program Student Advisory Council, music organizations, Community Service Council, Student Government Association, national fraternities, national sororities. *Campus security:* 24-hour emergency response devices and patrols, late-night transport/escort service, controlled dormitory access. *Student services:* health clinic, personal/psychological counseling, women's center.

Athletics Member NCAA. All Division I except football (Division I-AA). *Intercollegiate sports:* baseball M(s), basketball M(s)/W(s), crew M(c)/W(c), cross-country running M(s)/W(s), fencing M(c)/W(c), field hockey W(s), golf M(s), lacrosse W(s), rugby M(c), sailing M(c)/W(c), soccer M(s)/W(s), swimming and diving M(s)/W(s), tennis M(s)/W(s), track and field M(s)/W(s), ultimate Frisbee M(c)/W(c), volleyball W(s), weight lifting M(c)/W(c), wrestling M(s). *Intramural sports:* basketball M/W, equestrian sports W(c), field hockey M(c)/W(c), football M/W, lacrosse M(c)/W(c), soccer M(c)/W(c), softball M/W, swimming and diving M(c)/W(c), tennis M(c)/W(c), volleyball M/W(c), water polo M(c).

Standardized Tests *Required:* SAT or ACT (for admission). *Recommended:* SAT and SAT Subject Tests or ACT (for admission).

Costs (2011–12) *Comprehensive fee:* $49,723 includes full-time tuition ($38,481), mandatory fees ($385), and room and board ($10,857). *College room only:* $5733. Room and board charges vary according to board plan. *Waivers:* employees or children of employees.

Financial Aid Of all full-time matriculated undergraduates who enrolled in 2010, 853 applied for aid, 775 were judged to have need, 775 had their need fully met. 292 Federal Work-Study jobs (averaging $1509). 117 state and other part-time jobs (averaging $1543). In 2010, 144 non-need-based awards were made. *Average percent of need met:* 100%. *Average financial aid package:* $32,071. *Average need-based loan:* $3113. *Average need-based gift aid:* $27,829. *Average non-need-based aid:* $19,915. *Average indebtedness upon graduation:* $24,972. *Financial aid deadline:* 3/15.

Applying *Options:* electronic application, early admission, early decision, deferred entrance. *Application fee:* $50. *Required:* essay or personal statement, high school transcript, 3 letters of recommendation. *Recommended:* interview. *Application deadlines:* 1/2 (freshmen), 3/15 (transfers). *Early decision deadline:* 11/15 (for plan 1), 1/2 (for plan 2). *Notification:* 4/1 (freshmen), 5/15 (transfers), 12/15 (early decision plan 1), 2/1 (early decision plan 2).

Freshman Application Contact Mr. Christopher J. Gruber, Vice President and Dean of Admission and Financial Aid, Davidson College, Box 7156, Davidson, NC 28035-7156. *Phone:* 704-894-2230. *Toll-free phone:* 800-768-0380. *Fax:* 704-894-2016. *E-mail:* admission@davidson.edu. *Web site:* http://www.davidson.edu/.

DeVry University

Charlotte, North Carolina

Freshman Application Contact DeVry University, 2015 Ayrsley Town Boulevard, Suite 109, Charlotte, NC 28273-4068. *Toll-free phone:* 866-338-7941. *Web site:* http://www.devry.edu/.

Duke University

Durham, North Carolina

Freshman Application Contact Mr. Christoph Guttentag, Director of Admissions, Duke University, Durham, NC 27708-0586. *Phone:* 919-684-3214. *E-mail:* askduke@admiss.duke.edu. *Web site:* http://www.duke.edu/.

East Carolina University

Greenville, North Carolina

- **State-supported** university, founded 1907, part of University of North Carolina System
- **Urban** 1386-acre campus
- **Endowment** $130.5 million
- **Coed** 21,589 undergraduate students, 86% full-time, 58% women, 42% men
- **Moderately difficult** entrance level, 61% of applicants were admitted

Undergraduates 18,606 full-time, 2,983 part-time. Students come from 50 states and territories; 38 other countries; 12% are from out of state; 15% Black or African American, non-Hispanic/Latino; 3% Hispanic/Latino; 2% Asian, non-Hispanic/Latino; 0.1% Native Hawaiian or other Pacific Islander, non-Hispanic/Latino; 0.5% American Indian or Alaska Native, non-Hispanic/Latino; 2% Two or more races, non-Hispanic/Latino; 4% Race/ethnicity unknown; 0.5% international; 6% transferred in; 24% live on campus. *Retention:* 81% of full-time freshmen returned.

Freshmen *Admission:* 15,299 applied, 9,283 admitted, 3,891 enrolled. *Average high school GPA:* 3.62. *Test scores:* SAT critical reading scores over 500: 56%; SAT math scores over 500: 70%; SAT writing scores over 500: 45%; ACT scores over 18: 96%; SAT critical reading scores over 600: 9%; SAT math scores over 600: 13%; SAT writing scores over 600: 6%; ACT scores over 24: 26%; SAT critical reading scores over 700: 1%; SAT math scores over 700: 1%; ACT scores over 30: 1%.

Faculty *Total:* 1,463, 82% full-time, 73% with terminal degrees. *Student/faculty ratio:* 18:1.

Academics *Calendar:* semesters. *Degrees:* certificates, bachelor's, master's, doctoral, post-master's, postbachelor's, and first professional certificates. *Special study options:* accelerated degree program, adult/continuing education programs, advanced placement credit, cooperative education, distance learning, double majors, honors programs, independent study, internships, off-campus study, part-time degree program, services for LD students, student-designed majors, study abroad, summer session for credit. *ROTC:* Army (b), Air Force (b). *Unusual degree programs:* 3-2 business administration.

Computers on Campus 2,625 computers/terminals and 2,625 ports are available on campus for general student use. Students can access the following: campus intranet, computer help desk, free student e-mail accounts, online (class) grades, online (class) registration, online (class) schedules. Campus-wide network is available. 100% of college-owned or -operated housing units are wired for high-speed Internet access. Wireless service is available via entire campus.

Student Life *Housing options:* coed, women-only, disabled students. Campus housing is university owned. *Activities and organizations:* drama/theater group, student-run newspaper, radio and television station, choral group, marching band, Student Government Association, Student Union, Residence Hall Association, Student Pirate Club, Black Student Union, national fraternities, national sororities. *Campus security:* 24-hour emergency response devices and patrols, student patrols, late-night transport/escort service, controlled dormitory access, Operation ID, Staff and Faculty Eyes, Campus Community Watch program. *Student services:* health clinic, personal/psychological counseling, legal services.

Athletics Member NCAA. All Division I except football (Division I-A). *Intercollegiate sports:* baseball M(s), basketball M(s)/W(s), cross-country running M(s)/W(s), golf M(s)/W(s), soccer M(s)/W(s), softball W(s), swimming and diving M(s)/W(s), tennis M(s)/W(s), track and field M(s)/W(s), volleyball W(s). *Intramural sports:* badminton M/W, baseball M(c), basketball M/W, bowling M/W, equestrian sports M(c)/W(c), fencing M(c)/W(c), field hockey M(c)/W(c), football M/W, golf M/W, ice hockey M(c), lacrosse M(c)/W(c), racquetball M/W, rugby M(c)/W(c), skiing (downhill) M(c)/W(c), soccer M/W, softball M/W, swimming and diving M(c)/W(c), tennis M/W, ultimate Frisbee M/W, volleyball M/W.

Standardized Tests *Required:* SAT or ACT (for admission).

Costs (2011–12) *Tuition:* state resident $3348 full-time, $419 per course part-time; nonresident $15,927 full-time, $1991 per course part-time. Full-time tuition and fees vary according to location. Part-time tuition and fees vary according to course load and location. *Required fees:* $2016 full-time, $252 per course part-time. *Room and board:* $7950; room only: $4550. Room and board charges vary according to board plan and housing facility. *Payment plans:* installment, deferred payment. *Waivers:* senior citizens and employees or children of employees.

Financial Aid Of all full-time matriculated undergraduates who enrolled in 2011, 13,249 applied for aid, 10,655 were judged to have need, 1,096 had their need fully met. 436 Federal Work-Study jobs (averaging $3700). 1,745 state and other part-time jobs (averaging $3000). In 2011, 425 non-need-based awards were made. *Average percent of need met:* 67%. *Average financial aid package:* $9383. *Average need-based loan:* $4252. *Average need-based gift aid:* $7069. *Average non-need-based aid:* $3072. *Average indebtedness upon graduation:* $17,805.

Applying *Options:* electronic application, early admission, deferred entrance. *Application fee:* $70. *Required:* high school transcript, minimum 2.0 GPA. *Application deadlines:* 3/15 (freshmen), 3/15 (out-of-state freshmen), 4/15 (transfers). *Notification:* continuous (freshmen), continuous (out-of-state freshmen), continuous (transfers).

Freshman Application Contact Undergraduate Admission, East Carolina University, Whichard Building 106, East Fifth St., Greenville, NC 27858-4353. *Phone:* 252-328-6640. *E-mail:* admis@ecu.edu. *Web site:* http://www.ecu.edu/.

ECPI College of Technology

Charlotte, North Carolina

Admissions Office Contact ECPI College of Technology, 4800 Airport Center Parkway, Charlotte, NC 28208. *Toll-free phone:* 866-708-6167. *Web site:* http://www.ecpi.edu/.

ECPI College of Technology

Greensboro, North Carolina

Admissions Office Contact ECPI College of Technology, 7802 Airport Center Drive, Greensboro, NC 27409. *Toll-free phone:* 866-708-6170. *Web site:* http://www.ecpi.edu/.

ECPI College of Technology

Raleigh, North Carolina

Freshman Application Contact Ms. Susan Wells, Campus President, ECPI College of Technology, 4101 Doie Cope Road, Raleigh, NC 27613. *Phone:* 919-571-0057. *Toll-free phone:* 800-986-1200. *Fax:* 919-571-0780. *E-mail:* swells@ecpi.edu. *Web site:* http://www.ecpi.edu/.

Elizabeth City State University

Elizabeth City, North Carolina

- **State-supported** comprehensive, founded 1891, part of University of North Carolina System
- **Small-town** 200-acre campus with easy access to Norfolk
- **Coed** 2,837 undergraduate students, 90% full-time, 61% women, 39% men
- **Moderately difficult** entrance level, 50% of applicants were admitted

Undergraduates 2,540 full-time, 297 part-time. Students come from 5 other countries; 13% are from out of state; 74% Black or African American, non-Hispanic/Latino; 0.9% Hispanic/Latino; 0.5% Asian, non-Hispanic/Latino; 0.5% American Indian or Alaska Native, non-Hispanic/Latino; 10% Race/ethnicity unknown; 0.4% international; 6% transferred in; 53% live on campus. *Retention:* 77% of full-time freshmen returned.

Freshmen *Admission:* 2,894 applied, 1,458 admitted, 392 enrolled. *Average high school GPA:* 2.92. *Test scores:* SAT critical reading scores over 500: 11%; SAT math scores over 500: 12%; SAT writing scores over 500: 7%; ACT scores over 18: 25%; SAT critical reading scores over 600: 1%; SAT math scores over 600: 1%; SAT writing scores over 600: 1%.

Faculty *Total:* 241, 63% full-time, 54% with terminal degrees. *Student/faculty ratio:* 16:1.

Academics *Calendar:* semesters. *Degrees:* bachelor's and master's. *Special study options:* academic remediation for entering students, adult/continuing education programs, advanced placement credit, cooperative education, distance learning, double majors, honors programs, independent study, internships, off-campus study, part-time degree program, services for LD students, study abroad, summer session for credit. *ROTC:* Army (b).

Computers on Campus 1,035 computers/terminals and 1,200 ports are available on campus for general student use. Students can access the following: campus intranet, computer help desk, free student e-mail accounts, online (class) registration, online (class) schedules. Campuswide network is available. 100% of college-owned or -operated housing units are wired for high-speed Internet access. Wireless service is available via entire campus.

Student Life *Housing options:* coed, men-only, women-only. Campus housing is university owned and leased by the school. Freshman campus housing is guaranteed. *Activities and organizations:* drama/theater group, student-run newspaper, choral group, marching band, Vans (Vikings Assisting New Students), Student Activities Committee, Vike Nu' Fashion Troupe, Pep Squad, Essence of Praise, national fraternities, national sororities. *Campus security:* 24-hour emergency response devices and patrols. *Student services:* health clinic, personal/psychological counseling.

Athletics Member NCAA. All Division II. *Intercollegiate sports:* baseball M(s), basketball M(s)/W(s), bowling W(s), cheerleading W, cross-country running M/W, football M(s), golf M(s), softball W(s), tennis W(s), volleyball W(s).

Standardized Tests *Required:* SAT or ACT (for admission). *Recommended:* SAT (for admission).

Costs (2011–12) *Tuition:* state resident $2348 full-time; nonresident $12,091 full-time. *Room and board:* $5657; room only: $3287. Room and board charges vary according to housing facility. *Payment plan:* installment.

Financial Aid Of all full-time matriculated undergraduates who enrolled in 2009, 2,711 applied for aid, 2,711 were judged to have need. *Average need-based loan:* $5036. *Average need-based gift aid:* $6482. *Average indebtedness upon graduation:* $3846.

Applying *Options:* electronic application, deferred entrance. *Application fee:* $30. *Required:* high school transcript, minimum 2.3 GPA. *Application deadlines:* 5/8 (freshmen), 5/8 (transfers). *Notification:* continuous (freshmen), continuous (transfers).

Freshman Application Contact Elizabeth City State University, 1704 Weeksville Road, Elizabeth City, NC 27909-7806. *Toll-free phone:* 800-347-3278. *Web site:* http://www.ecsu.edu/.

Elon University

Elon, North Carolina

- **Independent** comprehensive, founded 1889, affiliated with United Church of Christ
- **Suburban** 600-acre campus with easy access to Raleigh
- **Endowment** $122.9 million
- **Coed** 5,225 undergraduate students, 98% full-time, 59% women, 41% men
- **Moderately difficult** entrance level, 58% of applicants were admitted

Undergraduates 5,103 full-time, 122 part-time. Students come from 48 states and territories; 57 other countries; 80% are from out of state; 6% Black or Afri-

can American, non-Hispanic/Latino; 4% Hispanic/Latino; 2% Asian, non-Hispanic/Latino; 0.1% Native Hawaiian or other Pacific Islander, non-Hispanic/Latino; 0.2% American Indian or Alaska Native, non-Hispanic/Latino; 1% Two or more races, non-Hispanic/Latino; 4% Race/ethnicity unknown; 1% international; 2% transferred in; 60% live on campus. *Retention:* 90% of full-time freshmen returned.

Freshmen *Admission:* 9,079 applied, 5,252 admitted, 1,417 enrolled. *Average high school GPA:* 3.96. *Test scores:* SAT critical reading scores over 500: 92%; SAT math scores over 500: 93%; SAT writing scores over 500: 93%; ACT scores over 18: 100%; SAT critical reading scores over 600: 56%; SAT math scores over 600: 60%; SAT writing scores over 600: 61%; ACT scores over 24: 86%; SAT critical reading scores over 700: 11%; SAT math scores over 700: 12%; SAT writing scores over 700: 14%; ACT scores over 30: 19%.

Faculty *Total:* 522, 70% full-time, 72% with terminal degrees. *Student/faculty ratio:* 13:1.

Academics *Calendar:* semesters 3-week winter term. *Degrees:* bachelor's, master's, and doctoral. *Special study options:* accelerated degree program, advanced placement credit, double majors, English as a second language, honors programs, independent study, internships, off-campus study, part-time degree program, services for LD students, student-designed majors, study abroad, summer session for credit. *ROTC:* Army (b), Air Force (c). *Unusual degree programs:* 3-2 engineering with North Carolina State University, North Carolina Agricultural and Technical State University, Virginia Polytechnic Institute and State University, Washington University, Columbia University, University of South Carolina, Georgia Tech, Notre Dame.

Computers on Campus 1,200 computers/terminals and 12,000 ports are available on campus for general student use. Students can access the following: computer help desk, free student e-mail accounts, online (class) grades, online (class) registration, online (class) schedules. Campuswide network is available. 100% of college-owned or -operated housing units are wired for high-speed Internet access. Wireless service is available via entire campus.

Student Life *Housing:* on-campus residence required through sophomore year. *Options:* coed, men-only, women-only. Campus housing is university owned and leased by the school. Freshman campus housing is guaranteed. *Activities and organizations:* drama/theater group, student-run newspaper, radio and television station, choral group, marching band, Elon volunteers, student media, intramural athletics, religious life, Habitat for Humanity, national fraternities, national sororities. *Campus security:* 24-hour emergency response devices and patrols, late-night transport/escort service, controlled dormitory access. *Student services:* health clinic, personal/psychological counseling, women's center.

Athletics Member NCAA. All Division I except football (Division I-AA). *Intercollegiate sports:* baseball M(s), basketball M(s)/W(s), cheerleading M/W, cross-country running M(s)/W(s), equestrian sports M(c)/W(c), field hockey W(c), golf M(s)/W(s), lacrosse M(c)/W(c), rugby M(c)/W(c), skiing (downhill) M(c)/W(c), soccer M(s)/W(s), softball W(s), swimming and diving M(c)/W(c), tennis M(s)/W(s), track and field W(s), ultimate Frisbee M(c)/W(c), volleyball W(s). *Intramural sports:* basketball M/W, bowling M/W, football M/W, golf M/W, racquetball M/W, soccer M/W, softball M/W, table tennis M/W, tennis M/W, volleyball M/W.

Standardized Tests *Required:* SAT or ACT (for admission).

Costs (2011–12) *Comprehensive fee:* $36,971 includes full-time tuition ($27,534), mandatory fees ($347), and room and board ($9090). Part-time tuition: $864 per hour. Part-time tuition and fees vary according to course load. *College room only:* $4440. Room and board charges vary according to board plan and housing facility. *Payment plan:* installment. *Waivers:* employees or children of employees.

Financial Aid Of all full-time matriculated undergraduates who enrolled in 2011, 2,533 applied for aid, 1,880 were judged to have need. 1,255 Federal Work-Study jobs (averaging $2382). In 2011, 1631 non-need-based awards were made. *Average percent of need met:* 70%. *Average financial aid package:* $17,320. *Average need-based loan:* $4756. *Average need-based gift aid:* $13,212. *Average non-need-based aid:* $5545. *Average indebtedness upon graduation:* $27,417.

Applying *Options:* electronic application, early admission, early decision, early action, deferred entrance. *Application fee:* $50. *Required:* essay or personal statement, high school transcript, minimum 2.7 GPA. *Required for some:* interview. *Application deadlines:* 1/10 (freshmen), rolling (transfers), 11/10 (early action). *Early decision deadline:* 11/1. *Notification:* 3/15 (freshmen), continuous (transfers), 12/1 (early decision), 12/20 (early action).

Freshman Application Contact Ms. Melinda Wood, Associate Director of Admissions and Director of Applications, Elon University, 100 Campus Box, Elon, NC 27244. *Phone:* 336-278-3566. *Toll-free phone:* 800-334-8448. *Fax:* 336-278-7699. *E-mail:* admissions@elon.edu. *Web site:* http://www.elon.edu/.

Fayetteville State University

Fayetteville, North Carolina

- **State-supported** comprehensive, founded 1867, part of University of North Carolina System
- **Urban** 156-acre campus with easy access to Raleigh
- **Endowment** $13.6 million
- **Coed** 5,162 undergraduate students, 77% full-time, 67% women, 33% men
- **Minimally difficult** entrance level, 64% of applicants were admitted

Undergraduates 3,977 full-time, 1,185 part-time. Students come from 35 states and territories; 6 other countries; 5% are from out of state; 70% Black or African American, non-Hispanic/Latino; 5% Hispanic/Latino; 1% Asian, non-Hispanic/Latino; 0.1% Native Hawaiian or other Pacific Islander, non-Hispanic/Latino; 2% American Indian or Alaska Native, non-Hispanic/Latino; 0.6% Two or more races, non-Hispanic/Latino; 5% Race/ethnicity unknown; 0.7% international; 13% transferred in; 29% live on campus. *Retention:* 70% of full-time freshmen returned.

Freshmen *Admission:* 3,062 applied, 1,970 admitted, 655 enrolled. *Average high school GPA:* 2.92.

Faculty *Total:* 331, 85% full-time, 79% with terminal degrees. *Student/faculty ratio:* 16:1.

Academics *Calendar:* semesters. *Degrees:* bachelor's, master's, doctoral, and first professional. *Special study options:* academic remediation for entering students, accelerated degree program, adult/continuing education programs, advanced placement credit, cooperative education, distance learning, double majors, honors programs, independent study, internships, part-time degree program, services for LD students, study abroad, summer session for credit. *ROTC:* Army (c), Air Force (b). *Unusual degree programs:* 3-2 engineering with North Carolina State University.

Computers on Campus 600 computers/terminals and 1,800 ports are available on campus for general student use. Students can access the following: campus intranet, computer help desk, free student e-mail accounts, online (class) grades, online (class) registration, online (class) schedules. Campuswide network is available. 100% of college-owned or -operated housing units are wired for high-speed Internet access. Wireless service is available via classrooms, computer centers, computer labs, learning centers, libraries, student centers.

Student Life *Housing options:* coed, men-only, women-only, disabled students. Campus housing is university owned. Freshman applicants given priority for college housing. *Activities and organizations:* drama/theater group, student-run newspaper, choral group, marching band, Student Government Association, Student Activities Council, Pan-Hellenic Council, Residence Hall Association, Illusions and Black Millennium Modeling Clubs, national fraternities, national sororities. *Campus security:* 24-hour emergency response devices and patrols, late-night transport/escort service, controlled dormitory access. *Student services:* health clinic, personal/psychological counseling.

Athletics Member NCAA. All Division II. *Intercollegiate sports:* basketball M(s), bowling W(s), cheerleading M/W, cross-country running M/W, football M(s)/W(s), golf M(s), softball W(s), tennis W(s), volleyball W(s). *Intramural sports:* basketball M/W, football M/W, soccer M/W, softball M/W, volleyball M/W.

Standardized Tests *Required:* SAT or ACT (for admission).

Costs (2012–13) *Tuition:* state resident $2427 full-time; nonresident $13,039 full-time. Full-time tuition and fees vary according to course load, degree level, location, and program. Part-time tuition and fees vary according to course level, course load, degree level, location, and program. *Required fees:* $2032 full-time. *Room and board:* $5500. Room and board charges vary according to board plan and housing facility. *Payment plan:* installment. *Waivers:* senior citizens and employees or children of employees.

Financial Aid Of all full-time matriculated undergraduates who enrolled in 2010, 4,022 applied for aid, 3,712 were judged to have need, 758 had their need fully met. In 2010, 129 non-need-based awards were made. *Average percent of need met:* 80%. *Average financial aid package:* $9586. *Average need-based loan:* $3824. *Average need-based gift aid:* $6380. *Average non-need-based aid:* $495. *Financial aid deadline:* 3/1.

Applying *Options:* electronic application, early admission, early decision, early action, deferred entrance. *Application fee:* $35. *Required:* high school transcript, minimum 2.0 GPA. *Recommended:* essay or personal statement. *Application deadlines:* 6/30 (freshmen), 6/30 (transfers). *Notification:* continuous (freshmen), continuous (transfers).

Freshman Application Contact Fayetteville State University, 1200 Murchison Road, Fayetteville, NC 28301-4298. *Phone:* 910-672-1371. *Toll-free phone:* 800-222-2594. *Fax:* 910-672-1414. *Web site:* http://www.uncfsu.edu/.

Gardner-Webb University

Boiling Springs, North Carolina

- **Independent Baptist** comprehensive, founded 1905
- **Small-town** 250-acre campus with easy access to Charlotte
- **Endowment** $49.0 million
- **Coed** 2,774 undergraduate students, 84% full-time, 66% women, 34% men
- **Moderately difficult** entrance level, 59% of applicants were admitted

Undergraduates 2,319 full-time, 455 part-time. Students come from 38 states and territories; 12 other countries; 21% are from out of state; 20% Black or African American, non-Hispanic/Latino; 2% Hispanic/Latino; 0.9% Asian, non-Hispanic/Latino; 0.4% American Indian or Alaska Native, non-Hispanic/Latino; 8% Race/ethnicity unknown; 1% international; 16% transferred in; 36% live on campus. *Retention:* 65% of full-time freshmen returned.

Freshmen *Admission:* 4,544 applied, 2,696 admitted, 453 enrolled. *Average high school GPA:* 3.54. *Test scores:* SAT critical reading scores over 500: 55%; SAT math scores over 500: 46%; ACT scores over 18: 84%; SAT critical reading scores over 600: 19%; SAT math scores over 600: 14%; ACT scores over 24: 31%; SAT critical reading scores over 700: 1%; SAT math scores over 700: 1%; ACT scores over 30: 2%.

Faculty *Total:* 422, 36% full-time. *Student/faculty ratio:* 13:1.

Academics *Calendar:* semesters. *Degrees:* associate, bachelor's, master's, and doctoral. *Special study options:* academic remediation for entering students, accelerated degree program, adult/continuing education programs, advanced placement credit, cooperative education, distance learning, double majors, English as a second language, honors programs, independent study, internships, off-campus study, part-time degree program, services for LD students, study abroad, summer session for credit. *ROTC:* Army (b), Air Force (c). *Unusual degree programs:* 3-2 Bachelor of Music/MBA.

Computers on Campus 100 computers/terminals are available on campus for general student use. Students can access the following: campus intranet, free student e-mail accounts, online (class) grades, online (class) registration, online (class) schedules. Campuswide network is available. 100% of college-owned or -operated housing units are wired for high-speed Internet access. Wireless service is available via entire campus.

Student Life *Housing:* on-campus residence required through junior year. *Options:* men-only, women-only, disabled students. Campus housing is university owned. Freshman campus housing is guaranteed. *Activities and organizations:* drama/theater group, student-run newspaper, radio station, choral group, marching band, Campus Ministries United, Student Government Association, Dawg Pound, Honors Student Association, International Club. *Campus security:* 24-hour emergency response devices and patrols, student patrols, late-night transport/escort service, controlled dormitory access. *Student services:* personal/psychological counseling.

Athletics Member NCAA. All Division I except football (Division I-AA). *Intercollegiate sports:* baseball M(s), basketball M(s)/W(s), cheerleading M(s)/W(s), cross-country running M(s)/W(s), golf M(s)/W(s), soccer M(s)/W(s), swimming and diving M(s)/W(s), tennis M(s)/W(s), track and field M(s)/W(s), volleyball W(s), wrestling M(s). *Intramural sports:* badminton M/W, baseball M/W, basketball M/W, football M/W, racquetball M/W, soccer M/W, softball M/W, swimming and diving M/W, table tennis M/W, tennis M/W, ultimate Frisbee M/W, volleyball M/W.

Standardized Tests *Required:* SAT or ACT (for admission).

Costs (2011–12) *One-time required fee:* $100. *Comprehensive fee:* $31,080 includes full-time tuition ($23,120), mandatory fees ($390), and room and board ($7570). Full-time tuition and fees vary according to degree level and program. Part-time tuition: $372 per credit hour. Part-time tuition and fees vary according to course load. *College room only:* $3890. Room and board charges vary according to board plan and housing facility. *Payment plan:* installment. *Waivers:* employees or children of employees.

Financial Aid Of all full-time matriculated undergraduates who enrolled in 2010, 1,379 applied for aid, 1,257 were judged to have need, 184 had their need fully met. In 2010, 274 non-need-based awards were made. *Average percent of need met:* 87%. *Average financial aid package:* $20,710. *Average need-based loan:* $4122. *Average need-based gift aid:* $8728. *Average non-need-based aid:* $7371.

Applying *Options:* electronic application. *Application fee:* $40. *Required:* high school transcript, minimum 2.5 GPA, SAT or ACT. *Required for some:* 2 letters of recommendation, interview. *Recommended:* essay or personal statement, 2 letters of recommendation. *Application deadlines:* rolling (freshmen), rolling (out-of-state freshmen), rolling (transfers). *Notification:* continuous (freshmen), continuous (out-of-state freshmen), continuous (transfers).

Freshman Application Contact Mrs. Kristen Setzer, Associate Vice President of Undergraduate Admissions, Gardner-Webb University, PO Box 817, 110 South Main Street, Boiling Springs, NC 28017. *Phone:* 704-406-4491. *Toll-free phone:* 800-253-6472. *Fax:* 704-406-4488. *E-mail:* admissions@gardner-webb.edu. *Web site:* http://www.gardner-webb.edu/.

Greensboro College

Greensboro, North Carolina

- **Independent United Methodist** comprehensive, founded 1838
- **Urban** 75-acre campus with easy access to Charlotte
- **Coed**
- **Moderately difficult** entrance level

Faculty *Student/faculty ratio:* 13:1.

Academics *Calendar:* semesters. *Degrees:* certificates, bachelor's, master's, and postbachelor's certificates.

Student Life *Campus security:* 24-hour patrols, late-night transport/escort service, controlled dormitory access.

Athletics Member NCAA. All Division III.

Standardized Tests *Required:* SAT or ACT (for admission).

Costs (2011–12) *Comprehensive fee:* $34,100 includes full-time tuition ($24,700), mandatory fees ($300), and room and board ($9100). Full-time tuition and fees vary according to course load, degree level, and program. Part-time tuition: $680 per credit hour. Part-time tuition and fees vary according to course load, degree level, and program. *College room only:* $4400. Room and board charges vary according to board plan and housing facility.

Applying *Options:* electronic application, early admission, early action, deferred entrance. *Application fee:* $35. *Required:* high school transcript. *Required for some:* 2 letters of recommendation, interview. *Recommended:* essay or personal statement, interview.

Freshman Application Contact Ms. Colleen Murphy, Vice President for Enrollment Management and Marketing, Greensboro College, 815 West Market Street, Greensboro, NC 27401-1875. *Phone:* 336-272-7102. *Toll-free phone:* 800-346-8226. *Fax:* 336-378-0154. *E-mail:* admissions@greensborocollege.edu. *Web site:* http://www.greensboro.edu/.

Guilford College

Greensboro, North Carolina

- **Independent** 4-year, founded 1837, affiliated with Society of Friends
- **Suburban** 340-acre campus
- **Endowment** $67.7 million
- **Coed** 2,739 undergraduate students, 83% full-time, 58% women, 42% men
- **Moderately difficult** entrance level, 64% of applicants were admitted

Undergraduates 2,272 full-time, 467 part-time. Students come from 43 states and territories; 13 other countries; 28% are from out of state; 26% Black or African American, non-Hispanic/Latino; 4% Hispanic/Latino; 2% Asian, non-Hispanic/Latino; 0.1% Native Hawaiian or other Pacific Islander, non-Hispanic/Latino; 0.5% American Indian or Alaska Native, non-Hispanic/Latino; 3% Two or more races, non-Hispanic/Latino; 0.9% Race/ethnicity unknown; 0.7% international; 1% transferred in; 76% live on campus. *Retention:* 76% of full-time freshmen returned.

Freshmen *Admission:* 3,054 applied, 1,963 admitted, 376 enrolled. *Average high school GPA:* 3.19. *Test scores:* SAT critical reading scores over 500: 69%; SAT math scores over 500: 71%; SAT writing scores over 500: 61%; ACT scores over 18: 90%; SAT critical reading scores over 600: 36%; SAT math scores over 600: 24%; SAT writing scores over 600: 26%; ACT scores over 24: 49%; SAT critical reading scores over 700: 7%; SAT math scores over 700: 2%; SAT writing scores over 700: 3%; ACT scores over 30: 7%.

Faculty *Total:* 214, 58% full-time, 73% with terminal degrees. *Student/faculty ratio:* 16:1.

Academics *Calendar:* semesters. *Degree:* certificates and bachelor's. *Special study options:* academic remediation for entering students, accelerated degree program, adult/continuing education programs, advanced placement credit, cooperative education, double majors, English as a second language, honors programs, independent study, internships, off-campus study, part-time degree program, services for LD students, student-designed majors, study abroad, summer session for credit. *ROTC:* Army (c), Navy (c), Air Force (c). *Unusual degree programs:* 3-2 environmental studies, physician assistant.

Computers on Campus 275 computers/terminals are available on campus for general student use. Students can access the following: computer help desk, free student e-mail accounts, online (class) grades, online (class) registration, online (class) schedules, network storage. Campuswide network is available. 100% of college-owned or -operated housing units are wired for high-speed Internet access. Wireless service is available via libraries, student centers.

Student Life *Housing:* on-campus residence required through junior year. *Options:* coed, men-only, women-only, cooperative, disabled students. Campus housing is university owned. Freshman campus housing is guaranteed. *Activities and organizations:* drama/theater group, student-run newspaper, radio station, choral group, student government, student radio station, student newspaper, Project Community, African-American Cultural Society. *Campus security:* 24-hour emergency response devices and patrols, student patrols,

late-night transport/escort service, controlled dormitory access. *Student services:* health clinic, personal/psychological counseling, women's center.

Athletics Member NCAA. All Division III. *Intercollegiate sports:* baseball M, basketball M/W, cross-country running M/W, football M, golf M, lacrosse M/W, rugby M/W, soccer M/W, softball W, swimming and diving W, tennis M/W, volleyball W. *Intramural sports:* archery M(c)/W(c), badminton M(c)/W(c), basketball M(c)/W(c), bowling M(c)/W(c), cheerleading W(c), football M(c), rugby M(c)/W(c), soccer M(c)/W(c), softball W(c), table tennis M(c)/W(c), tennis M(c)/W(c), ultimate Frisbee M(c)/W(c), volleyball M(c)/W(c), water polo M(c)/W(c).

Standardized Tests *Recommended:* SAT or ACT (for admission).

Costs (2011–12) *Comprehensive fee:* $38,700 includes full-time tuition ($30,100), mandatory fees ($330), and room and board ($8270). Part-time tuition: $923 per credit hour. Part-time tuition and fees vary according to course load. *Room and board:* Room and board charges vary according to board plan and housing facility. *Payment plan:* installment. *Waivers:* employees or children of employees.

Financial Aid Of all full-time matriculated undergraduates who enrolled in 2009, 1,994 applied for aid, 1,598 were judged to have need, 293 had their need fully met. 213 Federal Work-Study jobs (averaging $1993). 121 state and other part-time jobs (averaging $1588). In 2009, 139 non-need-based awards were made. *Average percent of need met:* 91%. *Average financial aid package:* $21,918. *Average need-based loan:* $5126. *Average need-based gift aid:* $7857. *Average non-need-based aid:* $7307. *Average indebtedness upon graduation:* $24,580.

Applying *Options:* electronic application, early admission, early action, deferred entrance. *Application fee:* $25. *Required:* essay or personal statement, high school transcript, minimum 2.0 GPA. *Recommended:* minimum 3.0 GPA, 2 letters of recommendation, interview. *Application deadlines:* 2/15 (freshmen), 4/1 (transfers), 1/15 (early action). *Notification:* 4/1 (freshmen), continuous until 5/1 (transfers), 2/15 (early action).

Freshman Application Contact Andrew Strickler, Associate Director of Admissions, Guilford College, 5800 West Friendly Avenue, Greensboro, NC 27410. *Phone:* 336-316-2100. *Toll-free phone:* 800-992-7759. *Fax:* 336-316-2954. *E-mail:* admission@guilford.edu. *Web site:* http://www.guilford.edu/.

See page 659 for display ad and page 1352 for the College Close-Up.

Heritage Bible College

Dunn, North Carolina

Freshman Application Contact Mrs. Traci Newton, Director of Recruitment and Marketing, Heritage Bible College, PO Box 1628, Dunn, NC 28335-1628. *Phone:* 910-892-3178 Ext. 239. *Toll-free phone:* 800-297-6351. *Fax:* 910-891-1660. *E-mail:* tnewton@heritagebiblecollege.edu. *Web site:* http://www.heritagebiblecollege.edu/.

High Point University

High Point, North Carolina

Freshman Application Contact Ms. Beth McCarthy, Director of Admissions, High Point University, University Station, Montlieu Avenue, High Point, NC 27262-3598. *Phone:* 336-841-9148. *Toll-free phone:* 800-345-6993. *Fax:* 336-888-6382. *E-mail:* jmcilrat@highpoint.edu. *Web site:* http://www.highpoint.edu/.

ITT Technical Institute

Cary, North Carolina

- **Proprietary** primarily 2-year, part of ITT Educational Services, Inc.
- **Coed**
- **Minimally difficult** entrance level

Academics *Degrees:* associate and bachelor's.

Student Life *Housing:* college housing not available.

Freshman Application Contact Director of Recruitment, ITT Technical Institute, 5520 Dillard Drive, Suite 100, Cary, NC 27518. *Phone:* 919-233-2520. *Toll-free phone:* 877-203-5533. *Web site:* http://www.itt-tech.edu/.

ITT Technical Institute

Charlotte, North Carolina

- **Proprietary** 4-year, part of ITT Educational Services, Inc.
- **Coed**
- **Minimally difficult** entrance level

Academics *Calendar:* quarters. *Degrees:* associate and bachelor's.

Freshman Application Contact Director of Recruitment, ITT Technical Institute, 10926 David Taylor Drive, Suite 100, Charlotte, NC 28262. *Phone:* 704-548-2300. *Toll-free phone:* 877-243-7685. *Web site:* http://www.itt-tech.edu/.

ITT Technical Institute

Charlotte, North Carolina

- **Proprietary** primarily 2-year
- **Coed**
- **Minimally difficult** entrance level

Academics *Degrees:* associate and bachelor's.

Student Life *Housing:* college housing not available.

Freshman Application Contact Director of Recruitment, ITT Technical Institute, 4135 Southstream Boulevard, Suite 200, Charlotte, NC 28217. *Phone:* 704-423-3100. *Toll-free phone:* 800-488-0173. *Web site:* http://www.itt-tech.edu/.

ITT Technical Institute

Durham, North Carolina

- **Proprietary** 4-year
- **Coed**
- **Minimally difficult** entrance level

Academics *Degrees:* associate and bachelor's.

Freshman Application Contact Director of Recruitment, ITT Technical Institute, 3518 Westgate Drive, Suite 150, Durham, NC 27707. *Phone:* 919-401-1400. *Toll-free phone:* 877-452-8662. *Web site:* http://www.itt-tech.edu/.

ITT Technical Institute

High Point, North Carolina

- **Proprietary** primarily 2-year, founded 2007, part of ITT Educational Services, Inc.
- **Coed**
- **Minimally difficult** entrance level

Academics *Calendar:* quarters. *Degrees:* associate and bachelor's.

Student Life *Housing:* college housing not available.

Freshman Application Contact Director of Recruitment, ITT Technical Institute, 4050 Piedmont Parkway, Suite 110, High Point, NC 27265. *Phone:* 336-819-5900. *Toll-free phone:* 877-536-5231. *Web site:* http://www.itt-tech.edu/.

Johnson & Wales University - Charlotte Campus

Charlotte, North Carolina

- **Independent** 4-year, founded 2004
- **Coed**
- **Moderately difficult** entrance level

Faculty *Student/faculty ratio:* 27:1.

Academics *Calendar:* quarters. *Degrees:* associate and bachelor's.

Student Life *Campus security:* 24-hour emergency response devices and patrols, late-night transport/escort service, controlled dormitory access.

Standardized Tests *Required for some:* SAT or ACT (for admission).

Costs (2011–12) *One-time required fee:* $300. *Comprehensive fee:* $35,421 includes full-time tuition ($23,955), mandatory fees ($1152), and room and board ($10,314). *Room and board:* Room and board charges vary according to board plan, housing facility, and location.

Financial Aid *Of all full-time matriculated undergraduates who enrolled in 2010,* 2,294 applied for aid, 2,107 were judged to have need, 332 had their need fully met. *In 2010,* 299 non-need-based awards were made. *Average percent of need met:* 72. *Average financial aid package:* $18,403. *Average need-based loan:* $5089. *Average need-based gift aid:* $8161. *Average non-need-based aid:* $5457.

Applying *Options:* electronic application, early admission, deferred entrance. *Required:* high school transcript. *Required for some:* interview. *Recommended:* minimum 2.0 GPA.

Freshman Application Contact Joseph Campos, Director of Admissions, Johnson & Wales University - Charlotte Campus, 801 West Trade Street, Charlotte, NC 28202. *Phone:* 980-598-1100. *Toll-free phone:* 866-598-2427. *Fax:* 980-598-1111. *E-mail:* clt@admissions.jwu.edu. *Web site:* http://www.jwu.edu/charlotte/.

Johnson C. Smith University

Charlotte, North Carolina

- **Independent** 4-year, founded 1867
- **Urban** 100-acre campus with easy access to Atlanta
- **Endowment** $50.4 million
- **Coed** 1,543 undergraduate students, 97% full-time, 60% women, 40% men
- **Moderately difficult** entrance level, 30% of applicants were admitted

Undergraduates 1,496 full-time, 47 part-time. Students come from 31 states and territories; 7 other countries; 53% are from out of state; 80% Black or African American, non-Hispanic/Latino; 2% Hispanic/Latino; 0.3% Native Hawaiian or other Pacific Islander, non-Hispanic/Latino; 0.6% Two or more races, non-Hispanic/Latino; 13% Race/ethnicity unknown; 3% international; 9% transferred in; 60% live on campus. *Retention:* 74% of full-time freshmen returned.

Freshmen *Admission:* 5,099 applied, 1,507 admitted, 373 enrolled. *Average high school GPA:* 2.91. *Test scores:* SAT critical reading scores over 500: 21%; SAT math scores over 500: 20%; ACT scores over 18: 58%; SAT critical reading scores over 600: 3%; SAT math scores over 600: 4%; ACT scores over 24: 7%.

Faculty *Total:* 144, 65% full-time, 59% with terminal degrees. *Student/faculty ratio:* 14:1.

Academics *Calendar:* semesters. *Degree:* bachelor's. *Special study options:* adult/continuing education programs, advanced placement credit, cooperative education, double majors, honors programs, independent study, internships, off-campus study, part-time degree program, services for LD students, student-designed majors, study abroad, summer session for credit. *ROTC:* Army (b), Air Force (c).

Computers on Campus 335 computers/terminals are available on campus for general student use. Students can access the following: campus intranet, computer help desk, free student e-mail accounts, online (class) grades, online (class) registration, online (class) schedules. Campuswide network is available. 100% of college-owned or -operated housing units are wired for high-speed Internet access. Wireless service is available via entire campus.

Student Life *Housing:* on-campus residence required for freshman year. *Options:* coed, men-only, women-only. Campus housing is university owned. Freshman campus housing is guaranteed. *Activities and organizations:* drama/theater group, student-run newspaper, choral group, marching band, Student Government Association, Golden Bull Activities Committee, Black Ink Monks Poetry Society, National Pan-Hellenic Council, Student Ambassadors, national fraternities, national sororities. *Campus security:* 24-hour emergency response devices and patrols, late-night transport/escort service, controlled dormitory access. *Student services:* health clinic, personal/psychological counseling.

Athletics Member NCAA. All Division II. *Intercollegiate sports:* basketball M(s)/W(s), bowling W(s), cheerleading W(c), cross-country running M(s)/W(s), football M(s), golf M(s), softball W(s), tennis M(s)/W(s), track and field M(s)/W(s), volleyball W(s).

Standardized Tests *Required:* SAT or ACT (for admission).

Costs (2011–12) *Comprehensive fee:* $24,130 includes full-time tuition ($14,730), mandatory fees ($2638), and room and board ($6762). Full-time tuition and fees vary according to course load. Part-time tuition: $398 per credit hour. Part-time tuition and fees vary according to course load. *Required fees:* $364 per term part-time. *College room only:* $3892. Room and board charges vary according to board plan and housing facility. *Payment plan:* installment. *Waivers:* children of alumni and employees or children of employees.

Financial Aid Of all full-time matriculated undergraduates who enrolled in 2011, 1,319 applied for aid, 1,276 were judged to have need, 69 had their need fully met. 366 Federal Work-Study jobs (averaging $1395). In 2011, 72 non-need-based awards were made. *Average percent of need met:* 51%. *Average financial aid package:* $13,943. *Average need-based loan:* $4913. *Average need-based gift aid:* $9508. *Average non-need-based aid:* $17,478. *Average indebtedness upon graduation:* $46,673.

Applying *Options:* electronic application, early admission, deferred entrance. *Application fee:* $25. *Required:* essay or personal statement, high school transcript, 2 letters of recommendation. *Notification:* continuous (freshmen), continuous (out-of-state freshmen), continuous (transfers).

Freshman Application Contact Mr. Dwight Sanchez, Interim Senior Associate Director of Admissions, Johnson C. Smith University, 100 Beatties Ford Road, Charlotte, NC 28216. *Phone:* 704-378-3500. *Toll-free phone:* 800-782-7303. *Fax:* 704-378-1242. *E-mail:* dsanchez@jcsu.edu. *Web site:* http://www.jcsu.edu/.

Laurel University

High Point, North Carolina

Freshman Application Contact Jeremy Reese, Admissions Officer, Laurel University, 2314 North Centennial Street, High Point, NC 27265-3197. *Phone:* 336-887-3000 Ext. 127. *Toll-free phone:* 855-LaurelU. *E-mail:* admissions@laureluniversity.edu. *Web site:* http://www.laureluniversity.edu/.

Lees-McRae College

Banner Elk, North Carolina

- **Independent** 4-year, founded 1900, affiliated with Presbyterian Church (U.S.A.)
- **Rural** 460-acre campus
- **Coed** 890 undergraduate students, 99% full-time, 62% women, 38% men
- **Minimally difficult** entrance level, 87% of applicants were admitted

Undergraduates 883 full-time, 7 part-time. Students come from 34 states and territories; 14 other countries; 34% are from out of state; 7% Black or African American, non-Hispanic/Latino; 0.9% Hispanic/Latino; 0.1% Asian, non-Hispanic/Latino; 0.3% Two or more races, non-Hispanic/Latino; 42% Race/ethnicity unknown; 3% international; 5% transferred in; 63% live on campus. *Retention:* 67% of full-time freshmen returned.

Freshmen *Admission:* 1,242 applied, 1,077 admitted, 207 enrolled. *Average high school GPA:* 3.16. *Test scores:* SAT critical reading scores over 500: 35%; SAT math scores over 500: 35%; SAT writing scores over 500: 23%; ACT scores over 18: 69%; SAT critical reading scores over 600: 9%; SAT math scores over 600: 8%; SAT writing scores over 600: 6%; ACT scores over 24: 16%; SAT critical reading scores over 700: 2%; SAT writing scores over 700: 1%; ACT scores over 30: 3%.

Faculty *Total:* 99, 46% full-time, 36% with terminal degrees. *Student/faculty ratio:* 14:1.

Academics *Calendar:* semesters. *Degree:* bachelor's. *Special study options:* academic remediation for entering students, accelerated degree program, adult/continuing education programs, advanced placement credit, double majors, English as a second language, honors programs, independent study, internships, off-campus study, part-time degree program, services for LD students, student-designed majors, study abroad, summer session for credit.

Computers on Campus Students can access the following: computer help desk, free student e-mail accounts, online (class) registration, online (class) schedules. Campuswide network is available.

Student Life *Housing:* on-campus residence required through sophomore year. *Options:* coed, men-only, women-only. Campus housing is university owned. Freshman campus housing is guaranteed. *Activities and organizations:* drama/theater group, Student Government Association. *Campus security:* 24-hour patrols. *Student services:* health clinic.

Athletics Member NCAA. All Division II. *Intercollegiate sports:* basketball M(s)/W(s), cross-country running M(s)/W(s), lacrosse M(s)/W(s), soccer M(s)/W(s), softball W(s), tennis M(s)/W(s), track and field M(s)/W(s), volleyball M(s)/W(s). *Intramural sports:* basketball M/W, cross-country running M/W, lacrosse M(c), skiing (downhill) M/W, soccer M/W, softball M/W, swimming and diving M/W, tennis M/W, track and field M/W, volleyball M/W.

Standardized Tests *Required:* SAT or ACT (for admission).

Costs (2012–13) *Comprehensive fee:* $32,950 includes full-time tuition ($23,950), mandatory fees ($500), and room and board ($8500). Full-time tuition and fees vary according to course load, location, and reciprocity agreements. Part-time tuition: $650 per credit hour. Part-time tuition and fees vary according to course load, location, and reciprocity agreements. *Required fees:* $650 per credit hour part-time. *Room and board:* Room and board charges vary according to housing facility. *Payment plan:* installment. *Waivers:* employees or children of employees.

Financial Aid Of all full-time matriculated undergraduates who enrolled in 2009, 741 applied for aid, 647 were judged to have need, 26 had their need fully met. In 2009, 51 non-need-based awards were made. *Average percent of need met:* 74%. *Average financial aid package:* $12,600. *Average need-based loan:* $5000. *Average need-based gift aid:* $9700. *Average non-need-based aid:* $5600.

Applying *Options:* electronic application. *Application fee:* $35. *Required:* high school transcript, minimum 2.0 GPA. *Required for some:* interview. *Recommended:* essay or personal statement. *Application deadlines:* rolling (freshmen), rolling (out-of-state freshmen), rolling (transfers). *Notification:* continuous (freshmen), continuous (out-of-state freshmen), continuous (transfers).

Freshman Application Contact Mrs. Ginger Hansen, Lees-McRae College, PO Box 128, Banner Elk, NC 28604. *Phone:* 800-280-4562. *Toll-free phone:* 800-280-4562. *Fax:* 828-898-8707. *E-mail:* admissions@lmc.edu. *Web site:* http://www.lmc.edu/.

Lenoir-Rhyne University

Hickory, North Carolina

- **Independent Lutheran** comprehensive, founded 1891

- **Small-town** campus

- **Coed** 1,595 undergraduate students, 92% full-time, 62% women, 38% men

- **Moderately difficult** entrance level, 87% of applicants were admitted

Undergraduates 1,463 full-time, 132 part-time. 18% are from out of state; 28% Black or African American, non-Hispanic/Latino; 8% Hispanic/Latino; 1% Asian, non-Hispanic/Latino; 0.4% Native Hawaiian or other Pacific Islander, non-Hispanic/Latino; 0.8% American Indian or Alaska Native, non-Hispanic/Latino; 2% Two or more races, non-Hispanic/Latino; 2% Race/ethnicity unknown; 4% international; 6% transferred in; 56% live on campus. *Retention:* 65% of full-time freshmen returned.

Freshmen *Admission:* 3,336 applied, 2,888 admitted, 400 enrolled. *Average high school GPA:* 3.59. *Test scores:* SAT critical reading scores over 500: 45%; SAT math scores over 500: 55%; ACT scores over 18: 80%; SAT critical reading scores over 600: 11%; SAT math scores over 600: 15%; ACT scores over 24: 34%; SAT critical reading scores over 700: 1%; SAT math scores over 700: 2%; ACT scores over 30: 1%.

Faculty *Total:* 178, 52% full-time, 57% with terminal degrees. *Student/faculty ratio:* 14:1.

Academics *Calendar:* semesters. *Degrees:* bachelor's, master's, and post-bachelor's certificates. *Special study options:* adult/continuing education programs, part-time degree program. *ROTC:* Army (c), Air Force (c).

Computers on Campus Students can access the following: campus intranet, computer help desk, free student e-mail accounts. Campuswide network is available. 100% of college-owned or -operated housing units are wired for high-speed Internet access. Wireless service is available via entire campus.

Student Life *Housing:* on-campus residence required through junior year. *Options:* coed. Campus housing is university owned. Freshman campus housing is guaranteed. *Campus security:* 24-hour emergency response devices and patrols, late-night transport/escort service, controlled dormitory access.

Athletics Member NCAA. All Division II. *Intercollegiate sports:* baseball M(s), basketball M(s)/W(s), cheerleading M(s)/W(s), cross-country running M(s)/W(s), football M(s), golf M(s)/W(s), soccer M(s)/W(s), softball W(s), swimming and diving W(s), tennis M(s)/W(s), track and field M(s)/W(s), volleyball W(s). *Intramural sports:* basketball M/W, football M/W, lacrosse M, soccer M/W, softball M/W, ultimate Frisbee M/W.

Standardized Tests *Required:* SAT or ACT (for admission).

Costs (2012–13) *Comprehensive fee:* $37,514 includes full-time tuition ($27,718) and room and board ($9796). Part-time tuition: $1100 per credit hour. Part-time tuition and fees vary according to class time.

Financial Aid Of all full-time matriculated undergraduates who enrolled in 2011, 1,371 applied for aid, 1,280 were judged to have need, 334 had their need fully met. In 2011, 146 non-need-based awards were made. *Average percent of need met:* 82%. *Average financial aid package:* $26,212. *Average need-based loan:* $4338. *Average need-based gift aid:* $21,803. *Average non-need-based aid:* $10,887. *Average indebtedness upon graduation:* $23,600.

Applying *Options:* early admission, early action, deferred entrance. *Application fee:* $35. *Required:* high school transcript, minimum 2.5 GPA. *Recommended:* interview. *Application deadlines:* 8/1 (freshmen), rolling (transfers), 8/15 (early action). *Notification:* continuous (freshmen), continuous (transfers).

Freshman Application Contact Lenoir-Rhyne University, 625 7th Avenue NE, Hickory, NC 28601. *Phone:* 828-328-7300. *Toll-free phone:* 800-277-5721. *Web site:* http://www.lr.edu/.

Livingstone College

Salisbury, North Carolina

Freshman Application Contact Livingstone College, 701 West Monroe Street, Salifbury, NC 28144. *Phone:* 704-216-6001. *Toll-free phone:* 800-835-3435. *Fax:* 704-216-6215. *E-mail:* admissions@livingstone.edu. *Web site:* http://www.livingstone.edu/.

Mars Hill College

Mars Hill, North Carolina

- **Independent Baptist** comprehensive, founded 1856

- **Small-town** 194-acre campus

- **Endowment** $43.8 million

- **Coed** 1,281 undergraduate students, 92% full-time, 50% women, 50% men

- **Moderately difficult** entrance level, 68% of applicants were admitted

Undergraduates 1,175 full-time, 106 part-time. Students come from 34 states and territories; 16 other countries; 28% are from out of state; 17% Black or African American, non-Hispanic/Latino; 3% Hispanic/Latino; 0.9% Asian, non-Hispanic/Latino; 0.1% Native Hawaiian or other Pacific Islander, non-Hispanic/Latino; 2% American Indian or Alaska Native, non-Hispanic/Latino; 3% Race/ethnicity unknown; 4% international; 9% transferred in; 64% live on campus. *Retention:* 60% of full-time freshmen returned.

Freshmen *Admission:* 2,356 applied, 1,597 admitted, 394 enrolled. *Average high school GPA:* 3.13. *Test scores:* SAT critical reading scores over 500: 33%; SAT math scores over 500: 39%; ACT scores over 18: 64%; SAT critical reading scores over 600: 6%; SAT math scores over 600: 12%; ACT scores over 24: 19%; SAT math scores over 700: 1%; ACT scores over 30: 1%.

Faculty *Total:* 135, 56% full-time. *Student/faculty ratio:* 12:1.

Academics *Calendar:* semesters. *Degrees:* bachelor's and master's. *Special study options:* academic remediation for entering students, accelerated degree program, adult/continuing education programs, advanced placement credit, cooperative education, double majors, English as a second language, honors programs, independent study, internships, part-time degree program, services for LD students, student-designed majors, study abroad, summer session for credit.

Computers on Campus 188 computers/terminals are available on campus for general student use. Students can access the following: campus intranet, computer help desk, free student e-mail accounts, online (class) grades, online (class) registration, online (class) schedules. Campuswide network is available. 100% of college-owned or -operated housing units are wired for high-speed Internet access. Wireless service is available via entire campus.

Student Life *Housing:* on-campus residence required through sophomore year. *Options:* men-only, women-only. Campus housing is university owned. Freshman campus housing is guaranteed. *Activities and organizations:* drama/theater group, student-run newspaper, choral group, marching band, Student Government Association, Fellowship of Christian Athletes, Christian Student Movement, Fraternity/Sorority, Athletic Trainers Association, national fraternities, national sororities. *Campus security:* 24-hour emergency response devices and patrols, late-night transport/escort service, controlled dormitory access. *Student services:* health clinic, personal/psychological counseling.

Athletics Member NCAA. All Division II. *Intercollegiate sports:* baseball M(s), basketball M(s)/W(s), cheerleading M(s)/W(s), cross-country running M(s)/W(s), football M(s), golf M(s)/W(s), lacrosse M(s), soccer M(s)/W(s), softball W(s), swimming and diving M(s)/W(s), tennis M(s)/W(s), track and field M(s)/W(s), volleyball W(s). *Intramural sports:* basketball M/W, football M/W, rock climbing M/W, skiing (downhill) M(c)/W(c), soccer M/W, track and field M(c)/W(c), ultimate Frisbee M/W, volleyball M/W, water polo M/W, weight lifting M/W.

Standardized Tests *Required:* SAT or ACT (for admission).

Costs (2011–12) *Comprehensive fee:* $31,400 includes full-time tuition ($21,100), mandatory fees ($2218), and room and board ($8082). Part-time tuition: $775 per credit hour. *Required fees:* $95 per credit hour part-time. *Room and board:* Room and board charges vary according to board plan and housing facility. *Payment plan:* installment. *Waivers:* employees or children of employees.

Financial Aid Of all full-time matriculated undergraduates who enrolled in 2010, 2,256 applied for aid, 1,007 were judged to have need, 164 had their need fully met. 252 Federal Work-Study jobs (averaging $1354). In 2010, 141 non-need-based awards were made. *Average percent of need met:* 73%. *Average financial aid package:* $17,195. *Average need-based loan:* $3988. *Average need-based gift aid:* $13,790. *Average non-need-based aid:* $8631. *Average indebtedness upon graduation:* $27,775.

Applying *Options:* electronic application, early admission, deferred entrance. *Application fee:* $25. *Required:* high school transcript, minimum 2.0 GPA. *Required for some:* interview. *Recommended:* essay or personal statement, minimum 3.0 GPA. *Application deadlines:* rolling (freshmen), rolling (transfers).

Freshman Application Contact Dr. Craig Goforth, Dean of Admissions and Financial Aid, Mars Hill College, PO Box 370, Mars Hill, NC 28754. *Phone:* 828-689-1201. *Toll-free phone:* 866-MHC-4-YOU. *Fax:* 828-689-1473. *E-mail:* ehoffmeyer@mhc.edu. *Web site:* http://www.mhc.edu/.

Meredith College

Raleigh, North Carolina

- **Independent** comprehensive, founded 1891
- **Urban** 225-acre campus
- **Endowment** $80.4 million
- **Undergraduate: women only; graduate: coed** 1,707 undergraduate students, 93% full-time, 100% women, 0% men
- **Moderately difficult** entrance level, 61% of applicants were admitted

Undergraduates 1,590 full-time, 117 part-time. Students come from 30 states and territories; 16 other countries; 11% are from out of state; 12% Black or African American, non-Hispanic/Latino; 3% Hispanic/Latino; 2% Asian, non-Hispanic/Latino; 1% Two or more races, non-Hispanic/Latino; 3% Race/ethnicity unknown; 3% international; 5% transferred in; 60% live on campus. *Retention:* 77% of full-time freshmen returned.

Freshmen *Admission:* 1,599 applied, 976 admitted, 398 enrolled. *Average high school GPA:* 3.05. *Test scores:* SAT critical reading scores over 500: 54%; SAT math scores over 500: 53%; ACT scores over 18: 83%; SAT critical reading scores over 600: 13%; SAT math scores over 600: 15%; ACT scores over 24: 25%; SAT critical reading scores over 700: 2%; SAT math scores over 700: 1%; ACT scores over 30: 6%.

Faculty *Total:* 207, 58% full-time, 67% with terminal degrees. *Student/faculty ratio:* 11:1.

Academics *Calendar:* semesters. *Degrees:* bachelor's, master's, and post-bachelor's certificates. *Special study options:* academic remediation for entering students, accelerated degree program, advanced placement credit, cooperative education, double majors, honors programs, independent study, internships, off-campus study, part-time degree program, services for LD students, student-designed majors, study abroad, summer session for credit. *ROTC:* Army (c), Air Force (c). *Unusual degree programs:* engineering with North Carolina State University.

Computers on Campus 140 computers/terminals are available on campus for general student use. Students can access the following: free student e-mail accounts, online (class) registration, laptop computers for full-time students. Campuswide network is available. 100% of college-owned or -operated housing units are wired for high-speed Internet access. Wireless service is available via classrooms, computer centers, computer labs, dorm rooms, learning centers, libraries, student centers.

Student Life *Housing:* on-campus residence required through sophomore year. *Options:* women-only. Campus housing is university owned. Freshman campus housing is guaranteed. *Activities and organizations:* drama/theater group, student-run newspaper, choral group, Student Government Association, Entertainment Association, Recreation Association, Class Organizations, choral groups. *Campus security:* 24-hour emergency response devices and patrols, late-night transport/escort service, controlled dormitory access, self-defense instruction. *Student services:* health clinic, personal/psychological counseling.

Athletics Member NCAA. All Division III. *Intercollegiate sports:* basketball W, cross-country running W, lacrosse W, soccer W, softball W, tennis W, volleyball W. *Intramural sports:* swimming and diving W(c).

Standardized Tests *Required:* SAT or ACT (for admission). *Required for some:* SAT Subject Tests (for admission).

Costs (2011–12) *Comprehensive fee:* $35,720 includes full-time tuition ($27,770) and room and board ($7950). Full-time tuition and fees vary according to course load. Part-time tuition and fees vary according to course load. *Waivers:* employees or children of employees.

Financial Aid Of all full-time matriculated undergraduates who enrolled in 2010, 1,087 applied for aid, 972 were judged to have need, 139 had their need fully met. In 2010, 82 non-need-based awards were made. *Average percent of need met:* 71%. *Average financial aid package:* $19,325. *Average need-based loan:* $4495. *Average need-based gift aid:* $15,324. *Average non-need-based aid:* $7123. *Average indebtedness upon graduation:* $33,691.

Applying *Options:* electronic application, early admission, early decision, deferred entrance. *Application fee:* $40. *Required:* high school transcript, minimum 2.0 GPA, 2 letters of recommendation. *Required for some:* essay or personal statement, interview. *Application deadlines:* 2/15 (freshmen), 2/15 (transfers). *Early decision deadline:* 10/15. *Notification:* continuous (freshmen), continuous (transfers), 11/1 (early decision).

Freshman Application Contact Dr. Daniel Green, Associate Vice President for Enrollment Management, Meredith College, 3800 Hillsborough Street, Raleigh, NC 27807-5298. *Phone:* 919-760-8026. *Toll-free phone:* 800-MEREDITH. *Fax:* 919-760-2298. *E-mail:* admissions@meredith.edu. *Web site:* http://www.meredith.edu/.

Methodist University

Fayetteville, North Carolina

- **Independent United Methodist** comprehensive, founded 1956
- **Suburban** 600-acre campus with easy access to Raleigh-Durham
- **Endowment** $13.9 million
- **Coed**
- **Moderately difficult** entrance level

Faculty *Student/faculty ratio:* 12:1.

Academics *Calendar:* semesters. *Degrees:* associate, bachelor's, and master's.

Student Life *Campus security:* 24-hour emergency response devices and patrols, student patrols, late-night transport/escort service, controlled dormitory access, regular patrol by county sheriff department.

Athletics Member NCAA. All Division III.

Standardized Tests *Required:* SAT or ACT (for admission).

Costs (2011–12) *Comprehensive fee:* $35,146 includes full-time tuition ($25,160), mandatory fees ($465), and room and board ($9521). Full-time tuition and fees vary according to class time. Part-time tuition and fees vary according to class time and course load. *College room only:* $4785. Room and board charges vary according to housing facility.

Financial Aid *Of all full-time matriculated undergraduates who enrolled in 2010,* 1,911 applied for aid, 1,486 were judged to have need, 133 had their need fully met. 959 Federal Work-Study jobs (averaging $230). 131 state and other part-time jobs (averaging $2052). *In 2010,* 274 non-need-based awards were made. *Average percent of need met:* 67. *Average financial aid package:* $19,006. *Average need-based loan:* $4016. *Average need-based gift aid:* $8486. *Average non-need-based aid:* $9097. *Average indebtedness upon graduation:* $25,432.

Applying *Options:* deferred entrance. *Application fee:* $25. *Required:* high school transcript. *Required for some:* essay or personal statement, interview. *Recommended:* interview.

Freshman Application Contact Mr. Jamie Legg, Director of Admissions, Methodist University, 5400 Ramset Street, Fayetteville, NC 28311-1496. *Phone:* 910-630-7027. *Toll-free phone:* 800-488-7110 Ext. 7027. *Fax:* 910-630-7285. *E-mail:* admissions@methodist.edu. *Web site:* http://www.methodist.edu/.

Mid-Atlantic Christian University

Elizabeth City, North Carolina

- **Independent Christian** 4-year, founded 1948
- **Small-town** 19-acre campus with easy access to Norfolk
- **Endowment** $2.6 million
- **Coed** 169 undergraduate students, 78% full-time, 44% women, 56% men
- **Minimally difficult** entrance level, 34% of applicants were admitted

Undergraduates 131 full-time, 38 part-time. Students come from 16 states and territories; 1 other country; 39% are from out of state; 19% Black or African American, non-Hispanic/Latino; 4% Hispanic/Latino; 8% transferred in; 52% live on campus. *Retention:* 63% of full-time freshmen returned.

Freshmen *Admission:* 114 applied, 39 admitted, 27 enrolled. *Average high school GPA:* 2.88. *Test scores:* SAT critical reading scores over 500: 47%; SAT math scores over 500: 27%; ACT scores over 18: 50%; SAT critical reading scores over 600: 16%; SAT math scores over 600: 11%; ACT scores over 24: 50%; ACT scores over 30: 50%.

Faculty *Total:* 41, 22% full-time, 46% with terminal degrees.

Academics *Calendar:* semesters. *Degrees:* certificates, associate, bachelor's, and postbachelor's certificates. *Special study options:* academic remediation for entering students, advanced placement credit, distance learning, double majors, internships, part-time degree program. *ROTC:* Army (c).

Computers on Campus 24 computers/terminals are available on campus for general student use. Students can access the following: free student e-mail accounts. Campuswide network is available. 100% of college-owned or -operated housing units are wired for high-speed Internet access. Wireless service is available via entire campus.

Student Life *Housing:* on-campus residence required through senior year. *Options:* men-only, women-only. Campus housing is university owned. Freshman campus housing is guaranteed. *Activities and organizations:* choral group, Student Advisory Council, Counseling Club, choral group. *Campus security:* 24-hour emergency response devices, controlled dormitory access. *Student services:* personal/psychological counseling.

Athletics *Intercollegiate sports:* basketball M/W. *Intramural sports:* basketball M/W, golf M/W, soccer M/W, softball M/W, table tennis M/W, tennis M/W, volleyball M/W.

Standardized Tests *Required:* SAT or ACT (for admission).

Costs (2012–13) *Comprehensive fee:* $19,260 includes full-time tuition ($11,680) and room and board ($7580). Full-time tuition and fees vary according to program. Part-time tuition: $365 per credit hour. Part-time tuition and

fees vary according to program. *College room only:* $4000. Room and board charges vary according to housing facility. *Payment plan:* deferred payment. *Waivers:* children of alumni, senior citizens, and employees or children of employees.

Financial Aid Of all full-time matriculated undergraduates who enrolled in 2010, 135 applied for aid, 127 were judged to have need, 9 had their need fully met. 20 Federal Work-Study jobs (averaging $551). In 2010, 5 non-need-based awards were made. *Average percent of need met:* 50%. *Average financial aid package:* $9433. *Average need-based loan:* $4159. *Average need-based gift aid:* $5482. *Average non-need-based aid:* $3746. *Average indebtedness upon graduation:* $35,030.

Applying *Options:* electronic application, early admission, deferred entrance. *Application fee:* $35. *Required:* essay or personal statement, high school transcript, minimum 2.0 GPA, 1 letter of recommendation, reference from church or character reference. *Required for some:* interview. *Application deadlines:* 8/1 (freshmen), 8/1 (transfers). *Notification:* continuous (freshmen), continuous (transfers).

Freshman Application Contact Mrs. Julie A. Fields, Mid-Atlantic Christian University, 715 North Poindexter Street, Elizabeth City, NC 27909-4054. *Phone:* 252-334-2028. *Toll-free phone:* 866-996-MACU. *Fax:* 252-334-2064. *E-mail:* julie.fields@macuniversity.edu. *Web site:* http://www.macuniversity.edu/.

Montreat College

Montreat, North Carolina

- **Independent** comprehensive, founded 1916, affiliated with Presbyterian Church (U.S.A.)
- **Small-town** 112-acre campus
- **Coed** 703 undergraduate students, 91% full-time, 58% women, 42% men
- **Moderately difficult** entrance level, 51% of applicants were admitted

Undergraduates 643 full-time, 60 part-time. 21% are from out of state; 21% Black or African American, non-Hispanic/Latino; 2% Hispanic/Latino; 0.3% Asian, non-Hispanic/Latino; 0.9% American Indian or Alaska Native, non-Hispanic/Latino; 2% Two or more races, non-Hispanic/Latino; 16% Race/ethnicity unknown; 2% international; 5% transferred in; 43% live on campus. *Retention:* 51% of full-time freshmen returned.

Freshmen *Admission:* 553 applied, 280 admitted, 84 enrolled. *Average high school GPA:* 3.19. *Test scores:* SAT critical reading scores over 500: 40%; SAT math scores over 500: 57%; ACT scores over 18: 74%; SAT critical reading scores over 600: 10%; SAT math scores over 600: 10%; ACT scores over 24: 34%; ACT scores over 30: 3%.

Faculty *Total:* 69, 49% full-time, 49% with terminal degrees. *Student/faculty ratio:* 9:1.

Academics *Calendar:* semesters. *Degrees:* certificates, associate, bachelor's, and master's. *Special study options:* adult/continuing education programs, part-time degree program.

Computers on Campus Students can access the following: campus intranet, computer help desk, free student e-mail accounts, online (class) grades, online (class) schedules. Campuswide network is available. 100% of college-owned or -operated housing units are wired for high-speed Internet access. Wireless service is available via entire campus.

Student Life *Housing:* on-campus residence required through sophomore year. *Options:* men-only, women-only. Campus housing is university owned. Freshman campus housing is guaranteed. *Activities and organizations:* drama/theater group, student-run newspaper, choral group. *Campus security:* 24-hour emergency response devices and patrols, controlled dormitory access. *Student services:* health clinic, personal/psychological counseling.

Athletics Member NAIA. *Intercollegiate sports:* baseball M(s), basketball M(s)/W(s), cross-country running M(s)/W(s), golf M(s), soccer M(s)/W(s), softball W(s), tennis M(s)/W(s), track and field M(s)/W(s), volleyball W(s). *Intramural sports:* basketball M/W, football M, softball M/W, table tennis M/W, tennis M/W, ultimate Frisbee M/W, volleyball M/W.

Standardized Tests *Required:* SAT or ACT (for admission).

Costs (2012–13) *Comprehensive fee:* $30,692 includes full-time tuition ($22,684), mandatory fees ($514), and room and board ($7494). Part-time tuition: $600 per credit. *Room and board:* Room and board charges vary according to board plan.

Financial Aid Of all full-time matriculated undergraduates who enrolled in 2010, 745 applied for aid, 688 were judged to have need, 92 had their need fully met. *Average percent of need met:* 69%. *Average financial aid package:* $11,664. *Average need-based loan:* $4446.

Applying *Options:* early admission, deferred entrance. *Required:* essay or personal statement, high school transcript, minimum 2.8 GPA. *Required for some:* 1 letter of recommendation, interview. *Application deadlines:* 8/15 (freshmen), 8/15 (out-of-state freshmen), rolling (transfers). *Notification:* continuous (freshmen), continuous (out-of-state freshmen), continuous (transfers).

Freshman Application Contact Mr. Joey Higgins, Director of Admissions, Montreat College, PO Box 1267, Montreat, NC 28757. *Phone:* 828-669-8012 Ext. 3782. *Toll-free phone:* 800-622-6968. *Fax:* 828-669-0120. *E-mail:* admissions@montreat.edu. *Web site:* http://www.montreat.edu/.

Mount Olive College

Mount Olive, North Carolina

- **Independent Free Will Baptist** 4-year, founded 1951
- **Small-town** 123-acre campus with easy access to Raleigh
- **Coed**
- **Minimally difficult** entrance level

Faculty *Student/faculty ratio:* 26:1.

Academics *Calendar:* semester or continuous accelerated programs. *Degrees:* associate and bachelor's.

Student Life *Campus security:* overnight security patrols; weekend patrols.

Athletics Member NCAA. All Division II.

Standardized Tests *Required for some:* SAT or ACT required for those under 21.

Costs (2011–12) *Comprehensive fee:* $22,800 includes full-time tuition ($16,300) and room and board ($6500). Part-time tuition: $395 per credit hour. *Room and board:* Room and board charges vary according to board plan.

Financial Aid Of all full-time matriculated undergraduates who enrolled in 2010, 3,275 applied for aid, 3,064 were judged to have need, 293 had their need fully met. *In 2010,* 10 non-need-based awards were made. *Average percent of need met:* 54. *Average financial aid package:* $10,301. *Average need-based loan:* $4451. *Average need-based gift aid:* $6486. *Average non-need-based aid:* $2452. *Average indebtedness upon graduation:* $21,042.

Applying *Options:* electronic application, deferred entrance. *Application fee:* $20. *Required:* high school transcript. *Recommended:* 2 letters of recommendation, interview.

Freshman Application Contact Mount Olive College, 634 Henderson Street, Mount Olive, NC 28365. *Phone:* 919-658-2502 Ext. 3009. *Toll-free phone:* 800-653-0854. *Web site:* http://www.moc.edu/.

New Life Theological Seminary

Charlotte, North Carolina

Freshman Application Contact New Life Theological Seminary, PO Box 790106, Charlotte, NC 28206-7901. *Phone:* 704-334-6882 Ext. 08. *Web site:* http://www.nlts.org/.

North Carolina Agricultural and Technical State University

Greensboro, North Carolina

- **State-supported** university, founded 1891, part of University of North Carolina System
- **Suburban** 200-acre campus with easy access to Charlotte
- **Coed** 9,206 undergraduate students, 90% full-time, 54% women, 46% men
- **Moderately difficult** entrance level, 66% of applicants were admitted

Undergraduates 8,278 full-time, 928 part-time. 86% Black or African American, non-Hispanic/Latino; 1% Hispanic/Latino; 0.8% Asian, non-Hispanic/Latino; 0.4% American Indian or Alaska Native, non-Hispanic/Latino; 0.1% Two or more races, non-Hispanic/Latino; 2% Race/ethnicity unknown; 1% international; 41% live on campus. *Retention:* 74% of full-time freshmen returned.

Freshmen *Admission:* 6,692 applied, 4,446 admitted, 1,875 enrolled. *Average high school GPA:* 3.13. *Test scores:* SAT critical reading scores over 500: 17%; SAT math scores over 500: 22%; SAT writing scores over 500: 12%; ACT scores over 18: 62%; SAT critical reading scores over 600: 2%; SAT math scores over 600: 4%; SAT writing scores over 600: 1%; ACT scores over 24: 10%; ACT scores over 30: 1%.

Faculty *Total:* 674, 79% full-time, 69% with terminal degrees.

Academics *Calendar:* semesters. *Degrees:* bachelor's, master's, doctoral, and first professional. *Special study options:* academic remediation for entering students, accelerated degree program, adult/continuing education programs, advanced placement credit, cooperative education, distance learning, double majors, honors programs, internships, off-campus study, part-time degree program, study abroad, summer session for credit. *ROTC:* Army (b), Air Force (b).

Computers on Campus Students can access the following: computer help desk, free student e-mail accounts, online (class) grades, online (class) registration, online (class) schedules. Campuswide network is available.

Student Life *Housing options:* coed, men-only, women-only. Campus housing is university owned and is provided by a third party. Freshman applicants given

priority for college housing. *Activities and organizations:* drama/theater group, student-run newspaper, radio and television station, choral group, marching band, student government, national fraternities, national sororities. *Campus security:* 24-hour emergency response devices and patrols, late-night transport/escort service, controlled dormitory access. *Student services:* health clinic, personal/psychological counseling.

Athletics Member NCAA. All Division I. *Intercollegiate sports:* baseball M(s), basketball M(s)/W(s), bowling W(s), cross-country running M(s)/W(s), football M(s), softball W(s), swimming and diving W(s), tennis W(s), track and field M(s)/W(s), volleyball W(s). *Intramural sports:* baseball M, basketball M/W, football M, golf M/W, soccer M/W, volleyball M/W.

Standardized Tests *Required:* SAT or ACT (for admission).

Costs (2011–12) *One-time required fee:* $140. *Tuition:* state resident $2791 full-time; nonresident $12,425 full-time. Full-time tuition and fees vary according to course load and student level. Part-time tuition and fees vary according to course load and student level. *Required fees:* $1887 full-time. *Room and board:* $7225; room only: $4625. Room and board charges vary according to board plan and housing facility. *Waivers:* employees or children of employees.

Financial Aid Of all full-time matriculated undergraduates who enrolled in 2010, 7,701 applied for aid, 6,954 were judged to have need, 365 had their need fully met. In 2010, 307 non-need-based awards were made. *Average percent of need met:* 82%. *Average financial aid package:* $13,583. *Average need-based loan:* $3939. *Average need-based gift aid:* $5741. *Average non-need-based aid:* $4610. *Average indebtedness upon graduation:* $7095.

Applying *Options:* early admission, deferred entrance. *Application fee:* $45. *Required:* high school transcript, minimum 2.0 GPA. *Application deadlines:* rolling (freshmen), rolling (out-of-state freshmen), rolling (transfers). *Notification:* continuous (freshmen), continuous (out-of-state freshmen), continuous (transfers).

Freshman Application Contact Ms. Keyana Scales, Director of Admissions, North Carolina Agricultural and Technical State University, North Carolina Agricultural & Technical State University (Webb Hall), 1601 East Market Street, Greensboro, NC 27411. *Phone:* 336-334-7946. *Toll-free phone:* 800-443-8964. *Fax:* 336-334-7478. *E-mail:* uadmit@ncat.edu. *Web site:* http://www.ncat.edu/.

North Carolina Central University
Durham, North Carolina

- **State-supported** comprehensive, founded 1910, part of University of North Carolina System
- **Urban** 115-acre campus with easy access to Raleigh
- **Endowment** $19.3 million
- **Coed** 6,416 undergraduate students, 83% full-time, 67% women, 33% men
- **Minimally difficult** entrance level, 52% of applicants were admitted

Undergraduates 5,327 full-time, 1,089 part-time. Students come from 35 states and territories; 29 other countries; 11% are from out of state; 84% Black or African American, non-Hispanic/Latino; 4% Hispanic/Latino; 1% Asian, non-Hispanic/Latino; 0.4% American Indian or Alaska Native, non-Hispanic/Latino; 1% Two or more races, non-Hispanic/Latino; 5% Race/ethnicity unknown; 0.4% international; 7% transferred in; 39% live on campus. *Retention:* 68% of full-time freshmen returned.

Freshmen *Admission:* 9,240 applied, 4,782 admitted, 1,258 enrolled. *Average high school GPA:* 3.01. *Test scores:* SAT critical reading scores over 500: 14%; SAT math scores over 500: 16%; SAT writing scores over 500: 10%; ACT scores over 18: 41%; SAT critical reading scores over 600: 2%; SAT math scores over 600: 2%; SAT writing scores over 600: 2%; ACT scores over 24: 5%.

Faculty *Total:* 608, 71% full-time, 63% with terminal degrees. *Student/faculty ratio:* 15:1.

Academics *Calendar:* semesters. *Degrees:* bachelor's, master's, and doctoral. *Special study options:* academic remediation for entering students, accelerated degree program, adult/continuing education programs, advanced placement credit, cooperative education, distance learning, double majors, English as a second language, external degree program, honors programs, independent study, internships, off-campus study, part-time degree program, services for LD students, study abroad, summer session for credit. *ROTC:* Army (c), Air Force (c).

Computers on Campus 3,700 ports are available on campus for general student use. Students can access the following: campus intranet, computer help desk, free student e-mail accounts, online (class) grades, online (class) registration, online (class) schedules. Campuswide network is available. 100% of college-owned or -operated housing units are wired for high-speed Internet access. Wireless service is available via entire campus.

Student Life *Housing options:* coed, women-only. Campus housing is university owned and leased by the school. Freshman applicants given priority for

college housing. *Activities and organizations:* drama/theater group, student-run newspaper, choral group, marching band, national fraternities, national sororities. *Campus security:* 24-hour emergency response devices and patrols, student patrols, late-night transport/escort service, controlled dormitory access. *Student services:* health clinic, personal/psychological counseling, women's center.

Athletics Member NCAA, NAIA. All NCAA Division I. *Intercollegiate sports:* baseball M(s), basketball M(s)/W(s), bowling M(s)/W(s), cross-country running M(s)/W(s), football M(s), golf M(s)/W(s), softball W(s), tennis M(s)/W(s), track and field M(s)/W(s), volleyball W(s). *Intramural sports:* basketball M/W, football M, soccer M, volleyball W.

Standardized Tests *Required:* SAT or ACT (for admission).

Costs (2011–12) *Tuition:* state resident $2952 full-time; nonresident $13,525 full-time. Part-time tuition and fees vary according to course load. *Required fees:* $2737 full-time. *Room and board:* $9421. Room and board charges vary according to board plan, housing facility, and location. *Payment plan:* installment. *Waivers:* employees or children of employees.

Financial Aid Of all full-time matriculated undergraduates who enrolled in 2009, 4,893 applied for aid, 4,561 were judged to have need, 332 had their need fully met. In 2009, 43 non-need-based awards were made. *Average percent of need met:* 68%. *Average financial aid package:* $12,324. *Average need-based loan:* $3854. *Average need-based gift aid:* $6944. *Average non-need-based aid:* $2669.

Applying *Options:* electronic application, deferred entrance. *Application fee:* $40. *Required:* high school transcript, minimum 2.3 GPA, University of North Carolina System minimum course requirements. *Application deadlines:* 8/1 (freshmen), 8/1 (transfers). *Notification:* continuous until 10/15 (freshmen), continuous until 10/15 (transfers).

Freshman Application Contact Mr. Anthony Brooks, Undergraduate Director of Admissions, North Carolina Central University, 1801 Fayetteville Street, McDougald House, Durham, NC 27707. *Phone:* 919-530-6298. *Toll-free phone:* 877-667-7533. *Fax:* 919-530-7625. *E-mail:* admissions@nccu.edu. *Web site:* http://www.nccu.edu/.

North Carolina State University
Raleigh, North Carolina

- **State-supported** university, founded 1887, part of University of North Carolina System
- **Urban** 2110-acre campus
- **Endowment** $617.6 million
- **Coed** 25,176 undergraduate students, 88% full-time, 44% women, 56% men
- **Very difficult** entrance level, 52% of applicants were admitted

Undergraduates 22,069 full-time, 3,107 part-time. Students come from 52 states and territories; 71 other countries; 8% are from out of state; 8% Black or African American, non-Hispanic/Latino; 4% Hispanic/Latino; 5% Asian, non-Hispanic/Latino; 0.5% American Indian or Alaska Native, non-Hispanic/Latino; 2% Two or more races, non-Hispanic/Latino; 3% Race/ethnicity unknown; 2% international; 4% transferred in; 32% live on campus. *Retention:* 91% of full-time freshmen returned.

Freshmen *Admission:* 19,863 applied, 10,395 admitted, 4,697 enrolled. *Average high school GPA:* 4.28. *Test scores:* SAT critical reading scores over 500: 88%; SAT math scores over 500: 95%; SAT writing scores over 500: 82%; ACT scores over 18: 98%; SAT critical reading scores over 600: 40%; SAT math scores over 600: 59%; SAT writing scores over 600: 32%; ACT scores over 24: 73%; SAT critical reading scores over 700: 6%; SAT math scores over 700: 13%; SAT writing scores over 700: 4%; ACT scores over 30: 17%.

Faculty *Total:* 1,881, 92% full-time, 86% with terminal degrees. *Student/faculty ratio:* 18:1.

Academics *Calendar:* semesters. *Degrees:* certificates, associate, bachelor's, master's, doctoral, post-master's, postbachelor's, and first professional certificates. *Special study options:* academic remediation for entering students, accelerated degree program, adult/continuing education programs, advanced placement credit, cooperative education, distance learning, double majors, English as a second language, honors programs, independent study, internships, off-campus study, part-time degree program, services for LD students, student-designed majors, study abroad, summer session for credit. *ROTC:* Army (b), Navy (b), Air Force (b).

Computers on Campus 3,024 computers/terminals are available on campus for general student use. Students can access the following: campus intranet, computer help desk, free student e-mail accounts, online (class) grades, online (class) registration, online (class) schedules, course materials, online homework submission, online testing/quizzes, financial aid/cashier's office account balances, wiki space, blogging service, Web space, online storage space, on-site OS and virus removal, online/hybrid courses. Campuswide network is available. 100% of college-owned or -operated housing units are wired for high-speed Internet access. Wireless service is available via classrooms, com-

puter centers, computer labs, dorm rooms, learning centers, libraries, student centers.

Student Life *Housing options:* coed, men-only, women-only, disabled students. Campus housing is university owned. Freshman applicants given priority for college housing. *Activities and organizations:* drama/theater group, student-run newspaper, radio and television station, choral group, marching band, Student Wolfpack Club, Inter-Fraternity Council, Panhellenic Association, Campus Crusade for Christ, Mechanical and Aerospace Engineering Graduate Student Association, national fraternities, national sororities. *Campus security:* 24-hour emergency response devices and patrols, student patrols, late-night transport/escort service, controlled dormitory access. *Student services:* health clinic, personal/psychological counseling, women's center, legal services.

Athletics Member NCAA. All Division I except football (Division I-A). *Intercollegiate sports:* badminton M(c)/W(c), baseball M(s), basketball M(s)/W(s), bowling M(c)/W(c), cheerleading M(s)/W(s), crew M(c)/W(c), cross-country running M(s)/W(s), equestrian sports M(c)/W(c), fencing M/W, field hockey M(c)/W(c), golf M(s)/W(s), gymnastics W(s), ice hockey M(c)/W(c), lacrosse M(c)/W(c), racquetball M(c)/W(c), riflery M(s)/W(s), rugby M(c)/W(c), sailing M(c)/W(c), skiing (downhill) M(c)/W(c), soccer M(s)/W(s), softball W(s), swimming and diving M(s)/W(s), table tennis M(c)/W(c), tennis M(s)/W(s), track and field M(s)/W(s), ultimate Frisbee M(c)/W(c), volleyball M(c)/W(s), water polo M(c)/W(c), wrestling M(s). *Intramural sports:* badminton M/W, baseball M, basketball M/W, bowling M/W, cheerleading W(c), crew M/W, cross-country running M/W, equestrian sports M/W, fencing M/W, field hockey W, football M/W, golf M/W, gymnastics W, ice hockey M, lacrosse M/W, racquetball M/W, rugby M/W, sailing M/W, skiing (downhill) M/W, soccer M/W, softball M/W, swimming and diving M/W, table tennis M/W, tennis M/W, track and field M/W, volleyball M/W, water polo M/W, wrestling M.

Standardized Tests *Required:* SAT or ACT (for admission). *Recommended:* SAT Subject Tests (for admission).

Costs (2011–12) *Tuition:* state resident $5153 full-time; nonresident $17,988 full-time. Full-time tuition and fees vary according to degree level, location, and program. Part-time tuition and fees vary according to course load, degree level, location, and program. *Required fees:* $1865 full-time. *Room and board:* $8536; room only: $5176. Room and board charges vary according to board plan and housing facility. *Payment plan:* installment. *Waivers:* employees or children of employees.

Financial Aid Of all full-time matriculated undergraduates who enrolled in 2011, 14,529 applied for aid, 11,011 were judged to have need, 3,813 had their need fully met. In 2011, 822 non-need-based awards were made. *Average percent of need met:* 83%. *Average financial aid package:* $11,794. *Average need-based loan:* $3867. *Average need-based gift aid:* $8623. *Average non-need-based aid:* $5697. *Average indebtedness upon graduation:* $17,317.

Applying *Options:* electronic application, early action, deferred entrance. *Application fee:* $70. *Required:* high school transcript. *Required for some:* interview. *Recommended:* essay or personal statement. *Application deadlines:* 2/1 (freshmen), 4/1 (transfers). *Notification:* continuous (freshmen), continuous (transfers).

Freshman Application Contact Mr. Thomas Griffin, Director of Undergraduate Admissions, North Carolina State University, Box 7103, Raleigh, NC 27695. *Phone:* 919-515-2434. *Fax:* 919-515-5039. *E-mail:* undergrad_admissions@ncsu.edu. *Web site:* http://www.ncsu.edu/.

North Carolina Wesleyan College
Rocky Mount, North Carolina

- **Independent** 4-year, founded 1956, affiliated with United Methodist Church
- **Suburban** 200-acre campus
- **Endowment** $9.9 million
- **Coed** 1,402 undergraduate students, 79% full-time, 62% women, 38% men
- **Moderately difficult** entrance level, 54% of applicants were admitted

Undergraduates 1,105 full-time, 297 part-time. Students come from 20 states and territories; 11 other countries; 12% are from out of state; 52% Black or African American, non-Hispanic/Latino; 2% Hispanic/Latino; 0.1% Asian, non-Hispanic/Latino; 0.1% Native Hawaiian or other Pacific Islander, non-Hispanic/Latino; 1% American Indian or Alaska Native, non-Hispanic/Latino; 1% Two or more races, non-Hispanic/Latino; 9% Race/ethnicity unknown; 4% international; 2% transferred in; 41% live on campus. *Retention:* 51% of full-time freshmen returned.

Freshmen *Admission:* 1,501 applied, 804 admitted, 194 enrolled. *Average high school GPA:* 2.99. *Test scores:* SAT critical reading scores over 500: 24%; SAT math scores over 500: 15%; SAT critical reading scores over 600: 4%; SAT math scores over 600: 1%.

Faculty *Total:* 189, 24% full-time, 33% with terminal degrees. *Student/faculty ratio:* 15:1.

Academics *Calendar:* semesters. *Degrees:* bachelor's (also offers adult part-time degree program with significant enrollment not reflected in profile). *Special study options:* academic remediation for entering students, accelerated degree program, adult/continuing education programs, advanced placement credit, cooperative education, distance learning, double majors, honors programs, independent study, internships, part-time degree program, services for LD students, summer session for credit. *ROTC:* Army (b).

Computers on Campus 199 computers/terminals are available on campus for general student use. Students can access the following: campus intranet, computer help desk, free student e-mail accounts, online (class) grades, online (class) schedules. Campuswide network is available.

Student Life *Housing:* on-campus residence required through sophomore year. *Options:* coed, men-only, women-only, disabled students. Campus housing is university owned. Freshman campus housing is guaranteed. *Activities and organizations:* drama/theater group, student-run newspaper, choral group, Refuge Campus Ministry, NCWC Cheerleaders, Voices of Triumph, Campus Crusade for Christ, Visions of Beauty, national fraternities, national sororities. *Campus security:* 24-hour emergency response devices and patrols, late-night transport/escort service, controlled dormitory access. *Student services:* health clinic, personal/psychological counseling.

Athletics Member NCAA. All Division III. *Intercollegiate sports:* baseball M, basketball M/W, football M, golf M, lacrosse W, soccer M/W, softball W, tennis M/W, volleyball W. *Intramural sports:* basketball M/W, football M/W, lacrosse M/W, softball M/W, table tennis M/W, tennis·M/W, volleyball M/W.

Standardized Tests *Required:* SAT or ACT (for admission).

Costs (2012–13) *Comprehensive fee:* $34,636 includes full-time tuition ($25,710), mandatory fees ($500), and room and board ($8426). Full-time tuition and fees vary according to location. Part-time tuition and fees vary according to course load and location. *College room only:* $4038. Room and board charges vary according to housing facility. *Payment plan:* installment. *Waivers:* employees or children of employees.

Financial Aid Of all full-time matriculated undergraduates who enrolled in 2008, 956 applied for aid, 788 were judged to have need, 360 had their need fully met. 323 Federal Work-Study jobs (averaging $1438). 67 state and other part-time jobs (averaging $565). In 2008, 46 non-need-based awards were made. *Average percent of need met:* 70%. *Average financial aid package:* $12,524. *Average need-based loan:* $3898. *Average need-based gift aid:* $6696. *Average non-need-based aid:* $7876. *Average indebtedness upon graduation:* $7269.

Applying *Options:* electronic application. *Application fee:* $45. *Required:* high school transcript. *Required for some:* essay or personal statement, interview. *Recommended:* minimum 2.0 GPA, 2 letters of recommendation, interview. *Application deadlines:* rolling (freshmen), 7/15 (transfers). *Notification:* continuous (freshmen), continuous (transfers).

Freshman Application Contact Ms. Heather Johnson, Associate Director of Admissions, North Carolina Wesleyan College, 3400 North Wesleyan Boulevard, Rocky Mount, NC 27804. *Phone:* 252-985-5200. *Toll-free phone:* 800-488-6292. *Fax:* 252-985-5295. *E-mail:* hjohnson@ncwc.edu. *Web site:* http://www.ncwc.edu/.

Pfeiffer University
Misenheimer, North Carolina

Freshman Application Contact Ms. Diane Martin, Associate Director of Admissions, Pfeiffer University, PO Box 960, Highway 52 North, Misenheimer, NC 28109. *Phone:* 704-463-3052. *Toll-free phone:* 800-338-2060. *Fax:* 704-463-1363. *E-mail:* admiss@pfeiffer.edu. *Web site:* http://www.pfeiffer.edu/.

Piedmont International University
Winston-Salem, North Carolina

- **Independent Baptist** comprehensive, founded 1947
- **Urban** 12-acre campus
- **Coed** 274 undergraduate students, 72% full-time, 46% women, 54% men
- **Noncompetitive** entrance level, 48% of applicants were admitted

Undergraduates 197 full-time, 77 part-time. Students come from 21 states and territories; 4 other countries; 29% are from out of state; 5% Black or African American, non-Hispanic/Latino; 2% Hispanic/Latino; 0.7% Asian, non-Hispanic/Latino; 0.7% Native Hawaiian or other Pacific Islander, non-Hispanic/Latino; 0.4% American Indian or Alaska Native, non-Hispanic/Latino; 0.4% Two or more races, non-Hispanic/Latino; 50% transferred in; 33% live on campus. *Retention:* 57% of full-time freshmen returned.

Freshmen *Admission:* 111 applied, 53 admitted, 39 enrolled. *Average high school GPA:* 3.57.

Academics *Calendar:* semesters. *Degrees:* certificates, associate, bachelor's, master's, doctoral, and first professional. *Special study options:* academic remediation for entering students, adult/continuing education programs, advanced placement credit, double majors, internships, part-time degree program, study abroad, summer session for credit.
Computers on Campus Campuswide network is available.
Student Life *Housing options:* men-only, women-only. Campus housing is university owned. *Activities and organizations:* choral group. *Campus security:* 24-hour emergency response devices, student patrols, late-night transport/ escort service, controlled dormitory access, security guards on duty from dusk until dawn.
Athletics Member NCCAA. *Intercollegiate sports:* basketball M/W, soccer M, volleyball W. *Intramural sports:* basketball M, soccer M/W, table tennis M/W, volleyball M/W.
Standardized Tests *Required:* SAT or ACT (for admission).
Costs (2012–13) *Comprehensive fee:* $19,605 includes full-time tuition ($12,340), mandatory fees ($855), and room and board ($6410). Part-time tuition and fees vary according to course load. *Payment plan:* installment. *Waivers:* employees or children of employees.
Financial Aid *Financial aid deadline:* 8/31.
Applying *Options:* electronic application, early admission, early action, deferred entrance. *Application fee:* $55. *Required:* essay or personal statement, high school transcript, 2 letters of recommendation, medical history, proof of immunization. *Recommended:* minimum 2.0 GPA, interview. *Application deadlines:* rolling (freshmen), rolling (transfers), 11/1 (early action). *Notification:* continuous (transfers), 12/1 (early action).
Freshman Application Contact Ms. Samantha Stevenson, Undergraduate Admissions Counselor, Piedmont International University, 420 South Broad Street, Winston-Salem, NC 27101. *Phone:* 336-714-7963. *Toll-free phone:* 800-937-5097. *Fax:* 336-725-5522. *E-mail:* stevensons@piedmontU.edu. *Web site:* http://www.pbc.edu/.

Queens University of Charlotte
Charlotte, North Carolina

- **Independent Presbyterian** comprehensive, founded 1857
- **Suburban** 30-acre campus
- **Endowment** $83.3 million
- **Coed** 1,956 undergraduate students, 75% full-time, 75% women, 25% men
- **Moderately difficult** entrance level, 74% of applicants were admitted

Undergraduates 1,460 full-time, 496 part-time. Students come from 29 states and territories; 19 other countries; 16% Black or African American, non-Hispanic/Latino; 3% Hispanic/Latino; 2% Asian, non-Hispanic/Latino; 0.6% American Indian or Alaska Native, non-Hispanic/Latino; 2% Two or more races, non-Hispanic/Latino; 1% Race/ethnicity unknown; 8% international; 8% transferred in; 72% live on campus. *Retention:* 70% of full-time freshmen returned.
Freshmen *Admission:* 2,199 applied, 1,618 admitted, 359 enrolled. *Average high school GPA:* 3.56. *Test scores:* SAT critical reading scores over 500: 60%; SAT math scores over 500: 63%; SAT writing scores over 500: 59%; ACT scores over 18: 94%; SAT critical reading scores over 600: 21%; SAT math scores over 600: 19%; SAT writing scores over 600: 15%; ACT scores over 24: 42%; SAT critical reading scores over 700: 3%; SAT math scores over 700: 2%; SAT writing scores over 700: 2%; ACT scores over 30: 2%.
Faculty *Total:* 258, 48% full-time, 48% with terminal degrees. *Student/faculty ratio:* 12:1.
Academics *Calendar:* semesters. *Degrees:* associate, bachelor's, master's, and postbachelor's certificates. *Special study options:* adult/continuing education programs, advanced placement credit, double majors, honors programs, independent study, internships, off-campus study, part-time degree program, study abroad, summer session for credit. *ROTC:* Army (c), Air Force (c).
Computers on Campus 125 computers/terminals are available on campus for general student use. Students can access the following: campus intranet, computer help desk, free student e-mail accounts, online (class) grades, online (class) registration, online (class) schedules. Campuswide network is available. 100% of college-owned or -operated housing units are wired for high-speed Internet access. Wireless service is available via entire campus.
Student Life *Housing:* on-campus residence required through sophomore year. *Options:* coed. Campus housing is university owned. Freshman campus housing is guaranteed. *Activities and organizations:* drama/theater group, student-run newspaper, choral group, Senate, College Union Board, Admissions Ambassadors, Students for Black Awareness, International Club, national fraternities, national sororities. *Campus security:* 24-hour emergency response devices and patrols, late-night transport/escort service, controlled dormitory access. *Student services:* health clinic, personal/psychological counseling.
Athletics Member NCAA. All Division II. *Intercollegiate sports:* basketball M(s)/W(s), cheerleading M(s)/W(s), cross-country running M(s)/W(s), golf

M(s)/W(s), lacrosse M(s)/W(s), soccer M(s)/W(s), softball W(s), swimming and diving M(s)/W(s), tennis M(s)/W(s), volleyball W(s). *Intramural sports:* basketball M/W, soccer M/W, softball M/W, tennis M/W, volleyball M/W.
Standardized Tests *Required:* SAT or ACT (for admission).
Costs (2011–12) *Comprehensive fee:* $34,588 includes full-time tuition ($25,356), mandatory fees ($40), and room and board ($9192). Part-time tuition: $425 per credit hour. *Room and board:* Room and board charges vary according to board plan and housing facility. *Payment plan:* installment. *Waivers:* employees or children of employees.
Financial Aid Of all full-time matriculated undergraduates who enrolled in 2011, 1,111 applied for aid, 966 were judged to have need, 217 had their need fully met. In 2011, 360 non-need-based awards were made. *Average percent of need met:* 67%. *Average financial aid package:* $18,055. *Average need-based loan:* $4193. *Average need-based gift aid:* $14,332. *Average non-need-based aid:* $9773. *Average indebtedness upon graduation:* $27,832.
Applying *Options:* electronic application, deferred entrance. *Application fee:* $40. *Required:* high school transcript, minimum 2.5 GPA. *Required for some:* essay or personal statement. *Recommended:* interview. *Application deadlines:* rolling (freshmen), rolling (out-of-state freshmen), rolling (transfers). *Notification:* continuous (freshmen), continuous (out-of-state freshmen), continuous (transfers).
Freshman Application Contact Queens University of Charlotte, 1900 Selwyn Avenue, Harris Welcome Center - MSC 1428, Charlotte, NC 28274. *Phone:* 704-337-2212. *Toll-free phone:* 800-849-0202. *Fax:* 704-337-2403. *E-mail:* admissions@queens.edu. *Web site:* http://www.queens.edu/.

St. Andrews University
Laurinburg, North Carolina

- **Independent Presbyterian** 4-year, founded 1958
- **Small-town** 600-acre campus
- **Coed** 458 undergraduate students, 96% full-time, 52% women, 48% men
- **Moderately difficult** entrance level, 74% of applicants were admitted

Undergraduates 439 full-time, 19 part-time. 59% are from out of state; 16% Black or African American, non-Hispanic/Latino; 2% Hispanic/Latino; 1% Asian, non-Hispanic/Latino; 2% American Indian or Alaska Native, non-Hispanic/Latino; 0.9% Race/ethnicity unknown; 5% international; 10% transferred in; 85% live on campus.
Freshmen *Admission:* 599 applied, 442 admitted, 142 enrolled. *Average high school GPA:* 3. *Test scores:* SAT critical reading scores over 500: 34%; SAT math scores over 500: 48%; SAT writing scores over 500: 35%; ACT scores over 18: 64%; SAT critical reading scores over 600: 6%; SAT math scores over 600: 7%; SAT writing scores over 600: 5%; ACT scores over 24: 10%.
Faculty *Total:* 55, 51% full-time, 55% with terminal degrees. *Student/faculty ratio:* 8:1.
Academics *Calendar:* semesters. *Degree:* bachelor's. *Special study options:* adult/continuing education programs, part-time degree program.
Computers on Campus Students can access the following: campus intranet, computer help desk, free student e-mail accounts. Campuswide network is available. Wireless service is available via classrooms, libraries, student centers.
Student Life *Housing:* on-campus residence required through senior year. *Options:* coed, men-only, women-only. Campus housing is university owned. *Campus security:* 24-hour emergency response devices and patrols, late-night transport/escort service.
Athletics Member NCAA. All Division II. *Intercollegiate sports:* baseball M(s), basketball M(s)/W(s), cross-country running M(s)/W(s), equestrian sports M(s)/W(s), golf M(s)/W(s), lacrosse M(s)/W(s), soccer M(s)/W(s), softball W(s), wrestling M. *Intramural sports:* basketball M/W, football M/W, rugby M(c)/W(c), softball M/W, table tennis M/W, volleyball M/W.
Standardized Tests *Required:* SAT or ACT (for admission).
Costs (2011–12) *Comprehensive fee:* $30,552 includes full-time tuition ($21,614) and room and board ($8938). Full-time tuition and fees vary according to course load and location. Part-time tuition and fees vary according to location. *Room and board:* Room and board charges vary according to housing facility. *Payment plan:* installment. *Waivers:* adult students, senior citizens, and employees or children of employees.
Financial Aid Of all full-time matriculated undergraduates who enrolled in 2010, 435 applied for aid, 347 were judged to have need, 75 had their need fully met. 196 Federal Work-Study jobs (averaging $1800). 19 state and other part-time jobs (averaging $1800). In 2010, 77 non-need-based awards were made. *Average percent of need met:* 75%. *Average financial aid package:* $18,461. *Average need-based loan:* $4374. *Average need-based gift aid:* $14,177. *Average non-need-based aid:* $5270. *Average indebtedness upon graduation:* $22,599.
Applying *Options:* electronic application, deferred entrance. *Application fee:* $30. *Required:* high school transcript. *Required for some:* essay or personal statement, interview. *Recommended:* minimum 2.0 GPA. *Application dead-*

lines: rolling (freshmen), rolling (transfers). *Notification:* continuous (freshmen), continuous (transfers).

Freshman Application Contact Kristen Simmons, Director of Admissions, St. Andrews University, 1700 Dogwood Mile, Laurinburg, NC 28352. *Phone:* 910-277-5555. *Toll-free phone:* 800-763-0198. *Fax:* 910-277-5087. *E-mail:* admission@sapc.edu. *Web site:* http://www.sapc.edu/.

See below for display ad and page 1538 for the College Close-Up.

Saint Augustine's College
Raleigh, North Carolina

- **Independent Episcopal** 4-year, founded 1867
- **Urban** 122-acre campus
- **Endowment** $17.7 million
- **Coed** 1,506 undergraduate students, 97% full-time, 49% women, 51% men
- **Moderately difficult** entrance level, 69% of applicants were admitted

Undergraduates 1,466 full-time, 40 part-time. Students come from 33 states and territories; 10 other countries; 45% are from out of state; 97% Black or African American, non-Hispanic/Latino; 0.5% Hispanic/Latino; 0.6% Race/ethnicity unknown; 2% international; 4% transferred in; 79% live on campus. *Retention:* 51% of full-time freshmen returned.

Freshmen *Admission:* 2,796 applied, 1,928 admitted, 461 enrolled. *Average high school GPA:* 2.37.

Faculty *Total:* 151, 56% full-time, 37% with terminal degrees. *Student/faculty ratio:* 14:1.

Academics *Calendar:* semesters. *Degree:* bachelor's. *Special study options:* accelerated degree program, adult/continuing education programs, advanced placement credit, cooperative education, double majors, freshman honors college, honors programs, independent study, internships, off-campus study, part-time degree program, services for LD students, study abroad, summer session for credit. *ROTC:* Army (b), Air Force (c).

Computers on Campus 193 computers/terminals and 1,825 ports are available on campus for general student use. Students can access the following: campus intranet, computer help desk, free student e-mail accounts, online (class) grades, online (class) registration, online (class) schedules. Campus-wide network is available. 100% of college-owned or -operated housing units are wired for high-speed Internet access. Wireless service is available via entire campus.

Student Life *Housing:* on-campus residence required through sophomore year. *Options:* men-only, women-only. Campus housing is university owned and leased by the school. Freshman campus housing is guaranteed. *Activities and organizations:* drama/theater group, choral group, marching band, Campus Activity Board, Christian Fellowship Organization, Collegiate 100 Black Men of America, Student Government Association/Student Leaders, Falcon Fanatic Pep Squad, national fraternities, national sororities. *Campus security:* 24-hour emergency response devices and patrols, RAVE - Emergency Notification System. *Student services:* health clinic, personal/psychological counseling.

Athletics Member NCAA. All Division II. *Intercollegiate sports:* baseball M(s), basketball M(s)/W(s), bowling W(s), cheerleading W(s), cross-country running M(s)/W(s), football M(s), golf M(s), softball W(s), tennis M(s)/W(s), track and field M(s)/W(s), volleyball W(s).

Standardized Tests *Required:* SAT or ACT (for admission).

Costs (2011–12) *Comprehensive fee:* $24,500 includes full-time tuition ($12,364), mandatory fees ($4796), and room and board ($7340). Full-time tuition and fees vary according to course load. Part-time tuition: $515 per credit hour. Part-time tuition and fees vary according to course load. *Required fees:* $200 per credit hour part-time. *College room only:* $3036. Room and board charges vary according to housing facility. *Payment plans:* installment, deferred payment. *Waivers:* employees or children of employees.

Financial Aid Of all full-time matriculated undergraduates who enrolled in 2011, 1,432 applied for aid, 1,355 were judged to have need, 40 had their need fully met. 327 Federal Work-Study jobs (averaging $2500). 4 state and other part-time jobs (averaging $2500). In 2011, 34 non-need-based awards were made. *Average percent of need met:* 96%. *Average financial aid package:* $3850. *Average need-based loan:* $2167. *Average need-based gift aid:* $2069. *Average non-need-based aid:* $2028. *Average indebtedness upon graduation:* $12,652.

Applying *Options:* electronic application, deferred entrance. *Application fee:* $25. *Required:* high school transcript, minimum 2.0 GPA, 2 letters of recommendation, medical history, social security card, background check. *Required for some:* essay or personal statement, interview. *Recommended:* minimum 2.5 GPA. *Application deadlines:* rolling (freshmen), rolling (out-of-state freshmen), rolling (transfers). *Notification:* continuous (freshmen), continuous (out-of-state freshmen), continuous (transfers).

Freshman Application Contact Mr. Jorge E. Sousa, Director of Admissions, Saint Augustine's College, 1315 Oakwood Avenue, Raleigh, NC 27610-2298. *Phone:* 919-516-4012. *Toll-free phone:* 800-948-1126. *Fax:* 919-516-5804. *E-mail:* jesousa@st-aug.edu. *Web site:* http://www.st-aug.edu/.

Salem College

Winston-Salem, North Carolina

Freshman Application Contact Dean Katherine Knapp Watts, Dean of Admissions and Financial Aid, Salem College, Single Sisters House, 601 South Church Street, Winston-Salem, NC 27101. *Phone:* 336-721-2621. *Toll-free phone:* 800-327-2536. *Fax:* 336-917-5572. *E-mail:* admissions@salem.edu. *Web site:* http://www.salem.edu/.

Shaw University

Raleigh, North Carolina

- **Independent Baptist** comprehensive, founded 1865
- **Urban** 30-acre campus
- **Coed** 2,265 undergraduate students, 90% full-time, 60% women, 40% men
- **Minimally difficult** entrance level, 48% of applicants were admitted

Undergraduates 2,046 full-time, 219 part-time. Students come from 28 states and territories; 15 other countries; 29% are from out of state; 84% Black or African American, non-Hispanic/Latino; 0.4% Hispanic/Latino; 0.1% American Indian or Alaska Native, non-Hispanic/Latino; 12% Race/ethnicity unknown; 2% international; 5% transferred in; 43% live on campus. *Retention:* 49% of full-time freshmen returned.

Freshmen *Admission:* 6,763 applied, 3,259 admitted, 548 enrolled. *Average high school GPA:* 2.31.

Faculty *Total:* 227, 47% full-time, 51% with terminal degrees. *Student/faculty ratio:* 16:1.

Academics *Calendar:* semesters. *Degrees:* associate, bachelor's, and master's. *Special study options:* academic remediation for entering students, accelerated degree program, adult/continuing education programs, advanced placement credit, distance learning, double majors, honors programs, independent study, internships, off-campus study, part-time degree program, services for LD students, student-designed majors, study abroad, summer session for credit. *ROTC:* Army (c), Air Force (c).

Computers on Campus Students can access the following: computer help desk, free student e-mail accounts, online (class) grades, online (class) registration, online (class) schedules. Campuswide network is available. Wireless service is available via classrooms, computer centers, computer labs, learning centers, libraries, student centers.

Student Life *Housing:* on-campus residence required for freshman year. *Options:* men-only, women-only. Campus housing is university owned. *Activities and organizations:* drama/theater group, student-run newspaper, radio station, choral group, marching band, Student Government Association, choir, University band, Shaw Players, academic clubs, national fraternities, national sororities. *Campus security:* 24-hour emergency response devices and patrols, late-night transport/escort service, 24-hour electronic surveillance cameras. *Student services:* health clinic, personal/psychological counseling.

Athletics Member NCAA. All Division II. *Intercollegiate sports:* baseball M(s), basketball M(s)/W(s), bowling W(s), cross-country running M(s)/W(s), football M(s), golf M, softball W(s), tennis M(s)/W(s), track and field M(s)/W(s), volleyball W(s). *Intramural sports:* basketball M/W, football M, tennis M/W, volleyball M/W.

Standardized Tests *Required:* SAT or ACT (for admission).

Costs (2011–12) *Comprehensive fee:* $20,788 includes full-time tuition ($10,440), mandatory fees ($2788), and room and board ($7560). Part-time tuition: $435 per credit hour. *College room only:* $3570. *Payment plans:* installment, deferred payment. *Waivers:* employees or children of employees.

Financial Aid Of all full-time matriculated undergraduates who enrolled in 2005, 2,197 applied for aid, 2,068 were judged to have need, 201 had their need fully met. 347 Federal Work-Study jobs (averaging $1120). In 2005, 117 non-need-based awards were made. *Average percent of need met:* 63%. *Average financial aid package:* $8992. *Average need-based loan:* $3394. *Average need-based gift aid:* $5898. *Average non-need-based aid:* $9333. *Average indebtedness upon graduation:* $15,982. *Financial aid deadline:* 6/1.

Applying *Options:* electronic application, early admission, deferred entrance. *Application fee:* $25. *Required:* essay or personal statement, high school transcript, minimum 2.0 GPA. *Application deadline:* 7/30 (freshmen). *Notification:* continuous (freshmen).

Freshman Application Contact Mr. Sherlock McDougald, Director of Admissions and Recruitment, Shaw University, 118 East South Street, Raleigh, NC 27601-2399. *Phone:* 919-546-8423. *Toll-free phone:* 800-214-6683. *Fax:* 919-546-8271. *E-mail:* sherlock@shawu.edu. *Web site:* http://www.shawu.edu/.

South College–Asheville

Asheville, North Carolina

Freshman Application Contact Director of Admissions, South College–Asheville, 1567 Patton Avenue, Asheville, NC 28806. *Phone:* 828-277-5521. *Fax:* 828-277-6151. *Web site:* http://www.southcollegenc.edu.

Southeastern Baptist Theological Seminary

Wake Forest, North Carolina

- **Independent Southern Baptist** comprehensive, founded 1950
- **Small-town** 300-acre campus with easy access to Raleigh
- **Coed** 519 undergraduate students, 48% full-time, 41% women, 59% men
- **Minimally difficult** entrance level, 97% of applicants were admitted

Undergraduates 250 full-time, 269 part-time. Students come from 32 states and territories; 3 other countries; 15% are from out of state; 3% Black or African American, non-Hispanic/Latino; 2% Hispanic/Latino; 94% American Indian or Alaska Native, non-Hispanic/Latino; 0.8% Race/ethnicity unknown; 1% international.

Freshmen *Admission:* 172 applied, 166 admitted, 67 enrolled.

Faculty *Total:* 85, 74% full-time, 80% with terminal degrees. *Student/faculty ratio:* 17:1.

Academics *Calendar:* semesters. *Degrees:* certificates, associate, bachelor's, and master's. *Special study options:* academic remediation for entering students, adult/continuing education programs, distance learning, double majors, independent study, internships, off-campus study, part-time degree program, summer session for credit.

Computers on Campus 7 computers/terminals are available on campus for general student use. Students can access the following: campus intranet, free student e-mail accounts, online (class) grades, online (class) registration, online (class) schedules. Campuswide network is available. Wireless service is available via classrooms, libraries, student centers.

Student Life *Housing options:* men-only, women-only. Campus housing is university owned and leased by the school. *Activities and organizations:* drama/theater group, choral group. *Campus security:* 24-hour emergency response devices and patrols, late-night transport/escort service. *Student services:* health clinic, personal/psychological counseling, women's center.

Athletics *Intramural sports:* basketball M/W, football M, golf M, racquetball M, table tennis M, tennis M, volleyball M, weight lifting M.

Standardized Tests *Required:* SAT or ACT (for admission).

Costs (2011–12) *Tuition:* $6168 full-time, $257 per credit hour part-time. Full-time tuition and fees vary according to course load, degree level, location, and program. Part-time tuition and fees vary according to course load, degree level, location, and program. *Required fees:* $190 full-time, $190 per term part-time. *Room only:* $1935. Room and board charges vary according to housing facility. *Payment plan:* installment.

Applying *Application fee:* $25. *Required:* essay or personal statement, high school transcript. *Required for some:* interview. *Application deadlines:* 7/20 (freshmen), 7/20 (transfers). *Notification:* continuous until 8/20 (freshmen), continuous until 8/20 (transfers).

Freshman Application Contact Mrs. Audrey Greeson, Admissions Counselor, Southeastern Baptist Theological Seminary, PO Box 1889, Wake Forest, NC 27588-1889. *Phone:* 800-284-6317. *Toll-free phone:* 800-284-6317. *Web site:* http://www.sebts.edu/.

Strayer University - Greensboro Campus

Greensboro, North Carolina

- **Proprietary** comprehensive
- **Coed**

Academics *Degrees:* associate, bachelor's, master's, and postbachelor's certificates.

Freshman Application Contact Strayer University - Greensboro Campus, 4900 Koger Boulevard, Suite 400, Greensboro, NC 27407. *Web site:* http://www.strayer.edu/greensboro.

Strayer University - Huntersville Campus

Huntersville, North Carolina

- **Proprietary** comprehensive
- **Coed**

Academics *Degrees:* associate, bachelor's, master's, and postbachelor's certificates.

Freshman Application Contact Strayer University - Huntersville Campus, 13620 Reese Boulevard, Suite 130, Huntersville, NC 28078. *Web site:* http://www.strayer.edu/huntersville/.

Strayer University - North Charlotte Campus

Charlotte, North Carolina

- **Proprietary** comprehensive
- **Coed**

Academics *Degrees:* associate, bachelor's, master's, and postbachelor's certificates.

Freshman Application Contact Strayer University - North Charlotte Campus, 8335 IBM Drive, Suite 150, Charlotte, NC 28262. *Web site:* http://www.strayer.edu/north_charlotte.

Strayer University - North Raleigh Campus

Raleigh, North Carolina

- **Proprietary** comprehensive
- **Coed**

Academics *Degrees:* associate, bachelor's, master's, and postbachelor's certificates.

Freshman Application Contact Strayer University - North Raleigh Campus, 3200 Spring Forest Road, Suite 214, Raleigh, NC 27616. *Web site:* http://www.strayer.edu/north_raleigh.

Strayer University - RTP Campus

Morrisville, North Carolina

- **Proprietary** comprehensive
- **Coed**

Academics *Degrees:* associate, bachelor's, master's, and postbachelor's certificates.

Freshman Application Contact Strayer University - RTP Campus, 4 Copley Parkway, Morrisville, NC 27560. *Web site:* http://www.strayer.edu/rtp_campus/.

Strayer University - South Charlotte Campus

Charlotte, North Carolina

- **Proprietary** comprehensive
- **Coed**

Academics *Degrees:* associate, bachelor's, master's, and postbachelor's certificates.

Freshman Application Contact Strayer University - South Charlotte Campus, 9101 Kings Parade Boulevard, Suite 200, Charlotte, NC 28273. *Web site:* http://www.strayer.edu/south_charlotte.

Strayer University - South Raleigh Campus

Raleigh, North Carolina

- **Proprietary** comprehensive
- **Coed**

Academics *Degrees:* associate, bachelor's, master's, and postbachelor's certificates.

Freshman Application Contact Strayer University - South Raleigh Campus, 3421 Olympia Drive, Raleigh, NC 27603. *Web site:* http://www.strayer.edu/south_raleigh.

The University of North Carolina at Asheville

Asheville, North Carolina

- **State-supported** comprehensive, founded 1927, part of University of North Carolina System
- **Suburban** 365-acre campus
- **Endowment** $27.8 million
- **Coed** 3,814 undergraduate students, 82% full-time, 56% women, 44% men
- **Moderately difficult** entrance level, 68% of applicants were admitted

Undergraduates 3,124 full-time, 690 part-time. Students come from 40 states and territories; 24 other countries; 12% are from out of state; 3% Black or African American, non-Hispanic/Latino; 4% Hispanic/Latino; 1% Asian, non-Hispanic/Latino; 0.1% Native Hawaiian or other Pacific Islander, non-Hispanic/Latino; 0.3% American Indian or Alaska Native, non-Hispanic/Latino; 2% Two or more races, non-Hispanic/Latino; 3% Race/ethnicity unknown; 0.9% international; 9% transferred in; 33% live on campus. *Retention:* 81% of full-time freshmen returned.

Freshmen *Admission:* 2,947 applied, 2,018 admitted, 540 enrolled. *Average high school GPA:* 3.99. *Test scores:* SAT critical reading scores over 500: 91%; SAT math scores over 500: 89%; SAT writing scores over 500: 82%; ACT scores over 18: 97%; SAT critical reading scores over 600: 47%; SAT math scores over 600: 41%; SAT writing scores over 600: 36%; ACT scores over 24: 82%; SAT critical reading scores over 700: 12%; SAT math scores over 700: 4%; SAT writing scores over 700: 8%; ACT scores over 30: 14%.

Faculty *Total:* 276, 76% full-time, 76% with terminal degrees. *Student/faculty ratio:* 14:1.

Academics *Calendar:* semesters. *Degrees:* bachelor's, master's, and postbachelor's certificates. *Special study options:* academic remediation for entering students, adult/continuing education programs, advanced placement credit, distance learning, double majors, honors programs, independent study, internships, off-campus study, part-time degree program, services for LD students, student-designed majors, study abroad, summer session for credit. *Unusual degree programs:* 3-2 chemistry and textile chemistry with North Carolina State University.

Computers on Campus 400 computers/terminals are available on campus for general student use. Students can access the following: computer help desk, free student e-mail accounts, online (class) grades, online (class) registration, online (class) schedules. Campuswide network is available. 100% of college-owned or -operated housing units are wired for high-speed Internet access. Wireless service is available via classrooms, computer centers, computer labs, learning centers, libraries, student centers.

Student Life *Housing:* on-campus residence required for freshman year. *Options:* coed, men-only, women-only, disabled students. Campus housing is university owned. Freshman campus housing is guaranteed. *Activities and organizations:* drama/theater group, student-run newspaper, radio station, choral group, Student Government Association, Underdog Productions, Residence Hall Association, African-American Association, Active Students for a Healthy Environment, national fraternities, national sororities. *Campus security:* 24-hour emergency response devices and patrols, late-night transport/escort service, dorm entrances secured at night. *Student services:* health clinic, personal/psychological counseling, women's center.

Athletics Member NCAA. All Division I. *Intercollegiate sports:* baseball M(s), basketball M(s)/W(s), cheerleading M/W, cross-country running M(s)/W(s), soccer M(s)/W(s), tennis M(s)/W(s), track and field M(s)/W(s), volleyball W(s). *Intramural sports:* badminton M/W, basketball M/W, equestrian sports M(c)/W(c), fencing M(c)/W(c), football M/W, racquetball M/W, rugby M(c)/W(c), soccer M/W, swimming and diving M(c)/W(c), tennis M/W, ultimate Frisbee M(c)/W(c), volleyball M/W, water polo M/W.

Standardized Tests *Required:* SAT or ACT (for admission).

Costs (2011–12) *Tuition:* state resident $3166 full-time; nonresident $16,798 full-time. Full-time tuition and fees vary according to course load. Part-time tuition and fees vary according to course load. *Required fees:* $2227 full-time. *Room and board:* $7302; room only: $4160. Room and board charges vary according to housing facility. *Payment plan:* installment. *Waivers:* employees or children of employees.

Financial Aid Of all full-time matriculated undergraduates who enrolled in 2011, 2,282 applied for aid, 1,678 were judged to have need, 657 had their need fully met. 46 Federal Work-Study jobs (averaging $2614). In 2011, 116 non-need-based awards were made. *Average percent of need met:* 80%. *Average financial aid package:* $11,299. *Average need-based loan:* $4427. *Average need-based gift aid:* $5929. *Average non-need-based aid:* $3060. *Average indebtedness upon graduation:* $16,252.

Applying *Options:* electronic application, early action, deferred entrance. *Application fee:* $50. *Required:* essay or personal statement, high school transcript, 1 letter of recommendation, minimum course requirement. *Required for some:* interview. *Application deadlines:* 2/15 (freshmen), 4/15 (transfers), 11/

15 (early action). *Notification:* 3/15 (freshmen), continuous (transfers), 12/15 (early action).

Freshman Application Contact Ms. Leigh McBride, Associate Director of Admissions, The University of North Carolina at Asheville, University Dining Hall, CPO # 1320, Asheville, NC 28804-8510. *Phone:* 828-251-6481. *Toll-free phone:* 800-531-9842. *Fax:* 828-251-6482. *E-mail:* admissions@unca.edu. *Web site:* http://www.unca.edu/.

The University of North Carolina at Chapel Hill

Chapel Hill, North Carolina

- **State-supported** university, founded 1789, part of University of North Carolina System
- **Suburban** 729-acre campus with easy access to Raleigh-Durham
- **Endowment** $2.2 billion
- **Coed** 18,430 undergraduate students, 95% full-time, 58% women, 42% men
- **Very difficult** entrance level, 33% of applicants were admitted

Undergraduates 17,437 full-time, 993 part-time. Students come from 51 states and territories; 60 other countries; 18% are from out of state; 9% Black or African American, non-Hispanic/Latino; 9% Hispanic/Latino; 7% Asian, non-Hispanic/Latino; 0.2% Native Hawaiian or other Pacific Islander, non-Hispanic/Latino; 0.6% American Indian or Alaska Native, non-Hispanic/Latino; 2% Two or more races, non-Hispanic/Latino; 3% Race/ethnicity unknown; 3% international; 4% transferred in; 46% live on campus. *Retention:* 97% of full-time freshmen returned.

Freshmen *Admission:* 22,652 applied, 7,469 admitted, 4,026 enrolled. *Average high school GPA:* 4.5. *Test scores:* SAT critical reading scores over 500: 97%; SAT math scores over 500: 98%; SAT writing scores over 500: 95%; ACT scores over 18: 99%; SAT critical reading scores over 600: 73%; SAT math scores over 600: 81%; SAT writing scores over 600: 70%; ACT scores over 24: 93%; SAT critical reading scores over 700: 26%; SAT math scores over 700: 30%; SAT writing scores over 700: 25%; ACT scores over 30: 49%.

Faculty *Total:* 1,810, 92% full-time, 89% with terminal degrees. *Student/faculty ratio:* 14:1.

Academics *Calendar:* semesters. *Degrees:* certificates, bachelor's, master's, doctoral, post-master's, postbachelor's, and first professional certificates. *Special study options:* advanced placement credit, distance learning, double majors, English as a second language, honors programs, independent study, internships, off-campus study, part-time degree program, services for LD students, student-designed majors, study abroad, summer session for credit. *ROTC:* Army (b), Navy (b), Air Force (b).

Computers on Campus 867 computers/terminals and 9,999 ports are available on campus for general student use. Students can access the following: computer help desk, free student e-mail accounts, online (class) grades, online (class) registration, online (class) schedules. Campuswide network is available. 100% of college-owned or -operated housing units are wired for high-speed Internet access. Wireless service is available via entire campus.

Student Life *Housing:* on-campus residence required for freshman year. *Options:* coed, men-only, women-only, disabled students. Campus housing is university owned. Freshman campus housing is guaranteed. *Activities and organizations:* drama/theater group, student-run newspaper, radio and television station, choral group, marching band, Campus Y, Carolina Athletic Association, Campus Crusade for Christ (Cornerstone), Residence Hall Association, Out-of-State Students Association, national fraternities, national sororities. *Campus security:* 24-hour emergency response devices and patrols, student patrols, late-night transport/escort service, controlled dormitory access, crime prevention initiatives (date rape, violence, larcen, etc.), campus-wide emergency alert system, cell phone/GPS security options. *Student services:* health clinic, personal/psychological counseling, women's center, legal services.

Athletics Member NCAA. All Division I except football (Division I-A). *Intercollegiate sports:* baseball M(s), basketball M(s)/W(s), crew W(s), cross-country running M(s)/W(s), fencing M/W, field hockey W(s), golf M(s)/W(s), gymnastics W(s), lacrosse M(s)/W(s), racquetball M(c)/W(c), soccer M(s)/W(s), softball W(s), swimming and diving M(s)/W(s), tennis M(s)/W(s), track and field M(s)/W(s), ultimate Frisbee M(c)/W(c), volleyball M(c)/W(c), water polo M(c)/W(c), wrestling M(s). *Intramural sports:* badminton M/W, baseball M(c), basketball M(c)/W(c), cheerleading W(c), crew M(c), cross-country running M(c)/W(c), equestrian sports W(c), field hockey M(c)/W(c), football M(c), golf M(c)/W(c), gymnastics M(c)/W(c), ice hockey M(c), lacrosse M(c)/W(c), racquetball M/W, rugby M(c)/W(c), sailing M(c)/W(c), skiing (downhill) M(c)/W(c), soccer M(c)/W(c), softball M/W(c), swimming and diving M(c)/W(c), table tennis M/W, tennis M(c)/W(c), track and field M(c)/W(c), ultimate Frisbee M/W, volleyball M/W, water polo M/W, wrestling M(c).

Standardized Tests *Required:* SAT or ACT (for admission).

Costs (2011–12) *Tuition:* state resident $5128 full-time; nonresident $24,953 full-time. Full-time tuition and fees vary according to program. Part-time tuition and fees vary according to course load and program. *Required fees:* $1881 full-time. *Room and board:* $9470; room only: $5520. Room and board charges vary according to board plan, housing facility, and location. *Payment plan:* installment. *Waivers:* employees or children of employees.

Financial Aid Of all full-time matriculated undergraduates who enrolled in 2010, 9,650 applied for aid, 7,273 were judged to have need, 6,315 had their need fully met. 1,730 Federal Work-Study jobs (averaging $2014). In 2010, 688 non-need-based awards were made. *Average percent of need met:* 100%. *Average financial aid package:* $15,271. *Average need-based loan:* $4270. *Average need-based gift aid:* $12,574. *Average non-need-based aid:* $6336. *Average indebtedness upon graduation:* $17,525.

Applying *Options:* electronic application, early action, deferred entrance. *Application fee:* $80. *Required:* essay or personal statement, high school transcript, 1 letter of recommendation, counselor's statement. *Application deadlines:* 1/5 (freshmen), 3/1 (transfers), 10/15 (early action). *Notification:* 3/31 (freshmen), 4/15 (transfers), 1/31 (early action).

Freshman Application Contact The University of North Carolina at Chapel Hill, Chapel Hill, NC 27599. *Phone:* 919-966-3621. *Web site:* http://www.unc.edu/.

The University of North Carolina at Charlotte

Charlotte, North Carolina

- **State-supported** university, founded 1946, part of University of North Carolina System
- **Suburban** 1000-acre campus
- **Endowment** $140.9 million
- **Coed** 20,283 undergraduate students, 85% full-time, 50% women, 50% men
- **Moderately difficult** entrance level, 70% of applicants were admitted

Undergraduates 17,243 full-time, 3,040 part-time. Students come from 46 states and territories; 73 other countries; 7% are from out of state; 17% Black or African American, non-Hispanic/Latino; 6% Hispanic/Latino; 5% Asian, non-Hispanic/Latino; 0.1% Native Hawaiian or other Pacific Islander, non-Hispanic/Latino; 0.5% American Indian or Alaska Native, non-Hispanic/Latino; 2% Two or more races, non-Hispanic/Latino; 4% Race/ethnicity unknown; 3% international; 12% transferred in; 25% live on campus. *Retention:* 77% of full-time freshmen returned.

Freshmen *Admission:* 12,306 applied, 8,570 admitted, 3,169 enrolled. *Average high school GPA:* 3.66. *Test scores:* SAT critical reading scores over 500: 64%; SAT math scores over 500: 76%; ACT scores over 18: 96%; SAT critical reading scores over 600: 14%; SAT math scores over 600: 23%; ACT scores over 24: 30%; SAT critical reading scores over 700: 1%; SAT math scores over 700: 2%; ACT scores over 30: 4%.

Faculty *Total:* 1,368, 73% full-time, 71% with terminal degrees. *Student/faculty ratio:* 19:1.

Academics *Calendar:* semesters. *Degrees:* bachelor's, master's, doctoral, post-master's, postbachelor's, and first professional certificates. *Special study options:* accelerated degree program, adult/continuing education programs, advanced placement credit, cooperative education, distance learning, double majors, English as a second language, freshman honors college, honors programs, independent study, internships, off-campus study, part-time degree program, services for LD students, study abroad, summer session for credit. *ROTC:* Army (b), Air Force (b).

Computers on Campus 1,500 computers/terminals are available on campus for general student use. Students can access the following: computer help desk, free student e-mail accounts, online (class) grades, online (class) registration, online (class) schedules. Campuswide network is available. 100% of college-owned or -operated housing units are wired for high-speed Internet access. Wireless service is available via classrooms, computer centers, computer labs, learning centers, libraries, student centers.

Student Life *Housing options:* coed, men-only, women-only, disabled students. Campus housing is university owned. *Activities and organizations:* drama/theater group, student-run newspaper, radio and television station, choral group, Student Government Association, Student Alumni Ambassadors, Black Student Union, 49er Social and Ballroom Dance, Feminist Student Union, national fraternities, national sororities. *Campus security:* 24-hour emergency response devices and patrols, late-night transport/escort service, controlled dormitory access. *Student services:* health clinic, personal/psychological counseling.

Athletics Member NCAA. All Division I. *Intercollegiate sports:* baseball M(s), basketball M(s)/W(s), cheerleading M/W, cross-country running M(s)/W(s), golf M(s), soccer M(s)/W(s), softball W(s), tennis M(s)/W(s), track and field M(s)/W(s), volleyball W(s). *Intramural sports:* archery M(c)/W(c), bad-

minton M(c)/W(c), baseball M(c)/W(c), basketball M/W, bowling M(c)/W(c), fencing M(c)/W(c), football M/W, golf M/W, ice hockey M(c)/W(c), lacrosse M(c)/W(c), racquetball M(c)/W(c), rock climbing M/W, rugby M(c)/W(c), soccer M(c)/W(c), softball M(c)/W(c), swimming and diving M(c)/W(c), table tennis M/W, tennis M(c)/W(c), track and field M/W, ultimate Frisbee M(c)/W(c), volleyball M(c)/W(c), water polo M/W, wrestling M(c)/W(c).

Standardized Tests *Required:* SAT or ACT (for admission).

Costs (2011–12) *Tuition:* state resident $3242 full-time; nonresident $15,007 full-time. Full-time tuition and fees vary according to course load and program. Part-time tuition and fees vary according to course load and program. *Required fees:* $2198 full-time. *Room and board:* $7742; room only: $4202. Room and board charges vary according to board plan and housing facility. *Payment plan:* installment. *Waivers:* senior citizens and employees or children of employees.

Financial Aid Of all full-time matriculated undergraduates who enrolled in 2009, 11,301 applied for aid, 8,557 were judged to have need, 1,493 had their need fully met. In 2009, 263 non-need-based awards were made. *Average percent of need met:* 71%. *Average financial aid package:* $9203. *Average need-based loan:* $4000. *Average need-based gift aid:* $6234. *Average non-need-based aid:* $2190. *Average indebtedness upon graduation:* $17,472.

Applying *Options:* electronic application, early admission, early action. *Application fee:* $50. *Required:* high school transcript, minimum 2.0 GPA, medical history, no criminal record. *Required for some:* interview. *Application deadlines:* 7/1 (freshmen), 7/1 (out-of-state freshmen), 7/1 (transfers), 10/15 (early action). *Notification:* continuous (freshmen), continuous (out-of-state freshmen), continuous (transfers), 12/15 (early action).

Freshman Application Contact Ms. Claire Kirby, Director of Admissions, The University of North Carolina at Charlotte, 9201 University City Boulevard, 1st Floor, Cato Hall, Charlotte, NC 28223-0001. *Phone:* 704-687-2213. *Fax:* 704-687-6483. *E-mail:* unccadm@uncc.edu. *Web site:* http://www.uncc.edu/.

The University of North Carolina at Greensboro

Greensboro, North Carolina

- **State-supported** university, founded 1891, part of University of North Carolina System
- **Urban** 357-acre campus
- **Endowment** $171.8 million
- **Coed**
- **Moderately difficult** entrance level

Faculty *Student/faculty ratio:* 17:1.

Academics *Calendar:* semesters. *Degrees:* bachelor's, master's, doctoral, post-master's, postbachelor's, and first professional certificates.

Student Life *Campus security:* 24-hour emergency response devices and patrols, student patrols, late-night transport/escort service, controlled dormitory access.

Athletics Member NCAA. All Division I.

Standardized Tests *Required:* SAT or ACT (for admission).

Costs (2011–12) *Tuition:* state resident $3454 full-time, $432 per course part-time; nonresident $15,979 full-time, $1997 per course part-time. Part-time tuition and fees vary according to course load. *Required fees:* $1821 full-time, $65 per course part-time. *Room and board:* $6840; room only: $4040. Room and board charges vary according to board plan and housing facility.

Financial Aid *Of all full-time matriculated undergraduates who enrolled in 2011,* 10,470 applied for aid, 10,159 were judged to have need, 1,629 had their need fully met. *In 2011,* 303 non-need-based awards were made. *Average percent of need met:* 53. *Average financial aid package:* $9510. *Average need-based loan:* $4170. *Average need-based gift aid:* $5640. *Average non-need-based aid:* $3057. *Average indebtedness upon graduation:* $24,064.

Applying *Options:* electronic application, early admission, early action, deferred entrance. *Application fee:* $45. *Required:* high school transcript, minimum 2.0 GPA.

Freshman Application Contact The University of North Carolina at Greensboro, Armfield-Preyer Admissions and Visitor Center, 1400 Spring Garden Street, Greensboro, NC 27412. *Phone:* 336-334-5243. *Fax:* 336-334-4180. *E-mail:* admissions@uncg.edu. *Web site:* http://www.uncg.edu/.

The University of North Carolina at Pembroke

Pembroke, North Carolina

- **State-supported** comprehensive, founded 1887, part of University of North Carolina System
- **Rural** 161-acre campus
- **Endowment** $11.8 million
- **Coed**
- **Moderately difficult** entrance level

Faculty *Student/faculty ratio:* 16:1.

Academics *Calendar:* semesters. *Degrees:* bachelor's and master's.

Student Life *Campus security:* 24-hour emergency response devices and patrols, late-night transport/escort service, controlled dormitory access.

Athletics Member NCAA. All Division II.

Standardized Tests *Required:* SAT or ACT (for admission).

Costs (2011–12) *Tuition:* state resident $2813 full-time; nonresident $12,020 full-time. Full-time tuition and fees vary according to course load and location. Part-time tuition and fees vary according to course load and location. *Required fees:* $1855 full-time. *Room and board:* $6830; room only: $5500. Room and board charges vary according to board plan and housing facility.

Financial Aid *Of all full-time matriculated undergraduates who enrolled in 2011,* 3,879 applied for aid, 3,447 were judged to have need, 615 had their need fully met. 122 Federal Work-Study jobs (averaging $1609). *In 2011,* 10 non-need-based awards were made. *Average percent of need met:* 76. *Average financial aid package:* $10,169. *Average need-based loan:* $3891. *Average need-based gift aid:* $6064. *Average non-need-based aid:* $672.

Applying *Options:* electronic application, deferred entrance. *Application fee:* $40. *Required:* high school transcript. *Required for some:* 1 letter of recommendation, interview. *Recommended:* essay or personal statement, minimum 2.0 GPA.

Freshman Application Contact Ms. Jennifer McNeil, Associate Director of Admissions, The University of North Carolina at Pembroke, PO Box 1510, Pembroke, NC 28372-1510. *Phone:* 910-521-6507. *Toll-free phone:* 800-949-UNCP. *Fax:* 910-521-6497. *E-mail:* jennifer.mcneill@uncp.edu. *Web site:* http://www.uncp.edu/.

University of North Carolina School of the Arts

Winston-Salem, North Carolina

- **State-supported** comprehensive, founded 1963, part of University of North Carolina System
- **Urban** 57-acre campus
- **Endowment** $16.8 million
- **Coed** 772 undergraduate students, 98% full-time, 39% women, 61% men
- **Very difficult** entrance level, 64% of applicants were admitted

Undergraduates 755 full-time, 17 part-time. Students come from 38 states and territories; 29 other countries; 49% are from out of state; 9% Black or African American, non-Hispanic/Latino; 7% Hispanic/Latino; 1% Asian, non-Hispanic/Latino; 0.3% American Indian or Alaska Native, non-Hispanic/Latino; 2% Two or more races, non-Hispanic/Latino; 4% Race/ethnicity unknown; 1% international; 7% transferred in; 55% live on campus. *Retention:* 85% of full-time freshmen returned.

Freshmen *Admission:* 624 applied, 402 admitted, 185 enrolled. *Average high school GPA:* 3.3.

Faculty *Total:* 170, 77% full-time, 56% with terminal degrees. *Student/faculty ratio:* 7:1.

Academics *Calendar:* trimesters. *Degrees:* diplomas, bachelor's, master's, and post-master's certificates. *Special study options:* academic remediation for entering students, advanced placement credit, English as a second language, independent study, internships, services for LD students, summer session for credit.

Computers on Campus 60 computers/terminals are available on campus for general student use. Students can access the following: computer help desk, free student e-mail accounts, online (class) grades. Campuswide network is available. Wireless service is available via entire campus.

Student Life *Housing:* on-campus residence required through sophomore year. *Options:* coed. Campus housing is university owned. Freshman campus housing is guaranteed. *Activities and organizations:* drama/theater group, student-run newspaper, choral group, Pride (gay/lesbian organization), Appreciation of Black Artists. *Campus security:* 24-hour emergency response devices and patrols, controlled dormitory access. *Student services:* health clinic, personal/psychological counseling.

Standardized Tests *Required:* SAT or ACT (for admission).

Costs (2011–12) *Tuition:* state resident $4716 full-time, $180 per credit part-time; nonresident $17,665 full-time, $695 per credit part-time. Full-time tuition and fees vary according to program. Part-time tuition and fees vary according to course load. *Required fees:* $2192 full-time. *Room and board:* $7922; room only: $3900. Room and board charges vary according to board plan and housing facility. *Payment plan:* installment.

Financial Aid Of all full-time matriculated undergraduates who enrolled in 2009, 519 applied for aid, 405 were judged to have need, 67 had their need fully met. 108 Federal Work-Study jobs (averaging $460). In 2009, 108 non-need-based awards were made. *Average percent of need met:* 89%. *Average financial aid package:* $15,093. *Average need-based loan:* $4167. *Average need-based gift aid:* $7404. *Average non-need-based aid:* $3960. *Average indebtedness upon graduation:* $22,173.

Applying *Options:* electronic application. *Application fee:* $60. *Required:* high school transcript, 2 letters of recommendation, audition. *Required for some:* essay or personal statement, interview. *Application deadlines:* 3/1 (freshmen), rolling (transfers). *Notification:* continuous (freshmen), continuous (transfers).

Freshman Application Contact University of North Carolina School of the Arts, 1533 South Main Street, PO Box 12189, Winston-Salem, NC 27127-2188. *Phone:* 336-770-3290. *Web site:* http://www.uncsa.edu/.

The University of North Carolina Wilmington

Wilmington, North Carolina

- **State-supported** comprehensive, founded 1947, part of University of North Carolina System
- **Urban** 656-acre campus
- **Endowment** $62.8 million
- **Coed** 11,902 undergraduate students, 88% full-time, 60% women, 40% men
- **Moderately difficult** entrance level, 53% of applicants were admitted

Undergraduates 10,457 full-time, 1,445 part-time. Students come from 47 states and territories; 62 other countries; 14% are from out of state; 4% Black or African American, non-Hispanic/Latino; 5% Hispanic/Latino; 2% Asian, non-Hispanic/Latino; 0.2% Native Hawaiian or other Pacific Islander, non-Hispanic/Latino; 0.6% American Indian or Alaska Native, non-Hispanic/Latino; 2% Two or more races, non-Hispanic/Latino; 2% Race/ethnicity unknown; 0.6% international; 13% transferred in; 35% live on campus. *Retention:* 86% of full-time freshmen returned.

Freshmen *Admission:* 10,339 applied, 5,471 admitted, 1,980 enrolled. *Average high school GPA:* 3.97. *Test scores:* SAT critical reading scores over 500: 95%; SAT math scores over 500: 96%; SAT writing scores over 500: 85%; ACT scores over 18: 99%; SAT critical reading scores over 600: 39%; SAT math scores over 600: 48%; SAT writing scores over 600: 28%; ACT scores over 24: 60%; SAT critical reading scores over 700: 4%; SAT math scores over 700: 3%; SAT writing scores over 700: 2%; ACT scores over 30: 5%.

Faculty *Total:* 964, 62% full-time, 67% with terminal degrees. *Student/faculty ratio:* 16:1.

Academics *Calendar:* semesters. *Degrees:* bachelor's, master's, doctoral, post-master's, postbachelor's, and first professional certificates. *Special study options:* academic remediation for entering students, accelerated degree program, advanced placement credit, cooperative education, distance learning, double majors, English as a second language, honors programs, independent study, internships, off-campus study, services for LD students, study abroad, summer session for credit.

Computers on Campus 1,650 computers/terminals and 3,481 ports are available on campus for general student use. Students can access the following: campus intranet, computer help desk, free student e-mail accounts, online (class) grades, online (class) registration, online (class) schedules. Campus-wide network is available. 100% of college-owned or -operated housing units are wired for high-speed Internet access. Wireless service is available via entire campus.

Student Life *Housing options:* coed, women-only, disabled students. Campus housing is university owned and is provided by a third party. Freshman applicants given priority for college housing. *Activities and organizations:* drama/theater group, student-run newspaper, radio and television station, choral group, Student Government Association, Association of Campus Entertainment, Residence Hall Association, national fraternities, national sororities. *Campus security:* 24-hour emergency response devices and patrols, late-night transport/escort service, controlled dormitory access. *Student services:* health clinic, personal/psychological counseling, women's center, legal services.

Athletics Member NCAA. All Division I. *Intercollegiate sports:* baseball M(s), basketball M(s)/W(s), cheerleading M/W(s), cross-country running M(s)/W(s), golf M(s)/W(s), soccer M(s)/W(s), softball W(s), swimming and diving M(s)/W(s), tennis M(s)/W(s), track and field M(s)/W(s), volleyball

W(s). *Intramural sports:* baseball M(c), basketball W, crew M(c)/W(c), field hockey W(c), golf M/W, gymnastics W(c), ice hockey M, lacrosse M(c)/W(c), sailing M(c)/W(c), soccer M/W, softball M/W, swimming and diving M(c)/W(c), tennis M(c)/W(c), ultimate Frisbee M(c)/W(c), volleyball M/W.

Standardized Tests *Required:* SAT or ACT (for admission).

Costs (2011–12) *Tuition:* state resident $3225 full-time; nonresident $15,046 full-time. Full-time tuition and fees vary according to course load. Part-time tuition and fees vary according to course load. *Required fees:* $2446 full-time. *Room and board:* $7900; room only: $4400. Room and board charges vary according to board plan and housing facility. *Payment plan:* installment. *Waivers:* employees or children of employees.

Financial Aid Of all full-time matriculated undergraduates who enrolled in 2011, 7,821 applied for aid, 5,411 were judged to have need, 2,029 had their need fully met. In 2011, 296 non-need-based awards were made. *Average percent of need met:* 75%. *Average financial aid package:* $10,606. *Average need-based loan:* $4251. *Average need-based gift aid:* $5321. *Average non-need-based aid:* $2550. *Average indebtedness upon graduation:* $23,481.

Applying *Options:* electronic application, early admission, early action, deferred entrance. *Application fee:* $60. *Required:* essay or personal statement, high school transcript. *Application deadlines:* 2/1 (freshmen), 3/1 (transfers), 11/1 (early action). *Notification:* 4/1 (freshmen), continuous (transfers), 1/20 (early action).

Freshman Application Contact Dr. Terrence M. Curran, Associate Provost, The University of North Carolina Wilmington, 601 South College Road, Wilmington, NC 28403-3297. *Phone:* 910-962-3876. *Fax:* 910-962-3922. *E-mail:* admissions@uncw.edu. *Web site:* http://www.uncw.edu/.

University of Phoenix–Charlotte Campus

Charlotte, North Carolina

Freshman Application Contact Marc Booker, Sr. Director, Office of Admissions and Evaluation, University of Phoenix–Charlotte Campus, 4035 South Riverpoint Parkway, Mail Stop CF-L101, Phoenix, AZ 85040. *Phone:* 602-557-4609. *Toll-free phone:* 866-766-0766. *Fax:* 480-643-1156. *Web site:* http://www.phoenix.edu/.

University of Phoenix–Raleigh Campus

Raleigh, North Carolina

Freshman Application Contact Marc Booker, Sr. Director, Office of Admissions and Evaluation, University of Phoenix–Raleigh Campus, 4035 South Riverpoint Parkway, Mail Stop CF-L101, Phoenix, AZ 85040. *Phone:* 602-557-4609. *Toll-free phone:* 866-766-0766. *Fax:* 480-643-1156. *Web site:* http://www.phoenix.edu/.

Wake Forest University

Winston-Salem, North Carolina

- **Independent** university, founded 1834
- **Suburban** 340-acre campus
- **Coed** 4,775 undergraduate students, 99% full-time, 52% women, 48% men
- **Very difficult** entrance level, 40% of applicants were admitted

Undergraduates 4,720 full-time, 55 part-time. 75% are from out of state; 8% Black or African American, non-Hispanic/Latino; 5% Hispanic/Latino; 5% Asian, non-Hispanic/Latino; 0.4% American Indian or Alaska Native, non-Hispanic/Latino; 2% Two or more races, non-Hispanic/Latino; 0.4% Race/ethnicity unknown; 2% international; 1% transferred in; 71% live on campus. *Retention:* 93% of full-time freshmen returned.

Freshmen *Admission:* 9,869 applied, 3,933 admitted, 1,237 enrolled. *Test scores:* SAT critical reading scores over 500: 96%; SAT math scores over 500: 98%; ACT scores over 18: 100%; SAT critical reading scores over 600: 80%; SAT math scores over 600: 83%; ACT scores over 24: 93%; SAT critical reading scores over 700: 25%; SAT math scores over 700: 31%; ACT scores over 30: 58%.

Faculty *Total:* 639, 81% full-time. *Student/faculty ratio:* 11:1.

Academics *Calendar:* semesters. *Degrees:* bachelor's, master's, doctoral, and first professional. *Special study options:* advanced placement credit, double majors, honors programs, independent study, internships, part-time degree program, services for LD students, study abroad, summer session for credit. *ROTC:* Army (b). *Unusual degree programs:* 3-2 engineering.

Computers on Campus Students can access the following: campus intranet, computer help desk, free student e-mail accounts, online (class) grades, online (class) registration, online (class) schedules, financial information online,

advanced placement credit, double majors, honors programs, independent study, internships, off-campus study, part-time degree program, services for LD students, study abroad, summer session for credit. *ROTC:* Army (c), Air Force (c).

Computers on Campus 80 computers/terminals are available on campus for general student use. Students can access the following: campus intranet, computer help desk, free student e-mail accounts, online (class) grades, online (class) registration, online (class) schedules. Campuswide network is available. 100% of college-owned or -operated housing units are wired for high-speed Internet access. Wireless service is available via classrooms, dorm rooms, learning centers, libraries, student centers.

Student Life *Housing:* on-campus residence required through senior year. *Options:* men-only, women-only. Campus housing is university owned. Freshman campus housing is guaranteed. *Activities and organizations:* drama/theater group, student-run newspaper, television station, choral group, marching band, national fraternities, national sororities. *Campus security:* 24-hour emergency response devices and patrols, late-night transport/escort service, controlled dormitory access. *Student services:* health clinic, personal/psychological counseling.

Athletics Member NCAA. All Division II. *Intercollegiate sports:* baseball M(s), basketball M(s)/W(s), cross-country running M(s)/W, football M(s), golf M(s)/W(s), lacrosse M(s), soccer M(s)/W, softball W(s), swimming and diving M(s)/W(s), tennis M(s)/W(s), track and field M/W, volleyball W(s). *Intramural sports:* basketball M/W, bowling M/W, cross-country running M, football M/W, golf M/W, racquetball M/W, swimming and diving M/W, table tennis M/W, tennis M/W, track and field M/W, volleyball M/W, water polo M/W, weight lifting M/W.

Standardized Tests *Required:* SAT or ACT (for admission).

Costs (2012–13) *Comprehensive fee:* $33,165 includes full-time tuition ($22,540), mandatory fees ($1305), and room and board ($9320). Part-time tuition: $750 per hour. Part-time tuition and fees vary according to course load. *Room and board:* Room and board charges vary according to board plan. *Payment plan:* installment. *Waivers:* employees or children of employees.

Financial Aid Of all full-time matriculated undergraduates who enrolled in 2011, 1,507 applied for aid, 1,375 were judged to have need, 380 had their need fully met. 293 Federal Work-Study jobs (averaging $900). 330 state and other part-time jobs (averaging $1019). In 2011, 357 non-need-based awards

were made. *Average percent of need met:* 83%. *Average financial aid package:* $20,367. *Average need-based loan:* $3946. *Average need-based gift aid:* $16,479. *Average non-need-based aid:* $10,766. *Average indebtedness upon graduation:* $24,298.

Applying *Options:* electronic application, early admission, deferred entrance. *Application fee:* $30. *Required:* high school transcript, minimum 2.0 GPA. *Recommended:* minimum 3.0 GPA, interview. *Application deadlines:* rolling (freshmen), rolling (transfers). *Notification:* continuous (freshmen), continuous (transfers).

Freshman Application Contact Director of Student Recruitment, Wingate University, PO Box 159, Wingate, NC 28174. *Phone:* 704-233-8000. *Toll-free phone:* 800-755-5550. *Fax:* 704-233-8110. *E-mail:* admit@wingate.edu. *Web site:* http://www.wingate.edu/.

Winston-Salem State University

Winston-Salem, North Carolina

Freshman Application Contact Ms. Tomikia LeGrande, Assistant Vice Chancellor for Enrollment Services, Winston-Salem State University, 601 Martin Luther King, Jr. Drive, Thompson Center, Winston-Salem, NC 27110. *Phone:* 336-750-2070. *Toll-free phone:* 800-257-4052. *Fax:* 336-750-2079. *E-mail:* Legrandet@wssu.edu. *Web site:* http://www.wssu.edu/.

NORTH DAKOTA

Bismarck State College

Bismarck, North Dakota

Freshman Application Contact Greg Sturm, Dean of Admissions and Enrollment Services, Bismarck State College, PO Box 5587, Bismarck, ND 58506-5587. *Phone:* 701-224-5426. *Toll-free phone:* 800-445-5073. *Fax:* 701-224-5643. *E-mail:* gregory.sturm@bsc.nodak.edu. *Web site:* http://www.bismarckstate.edu/.

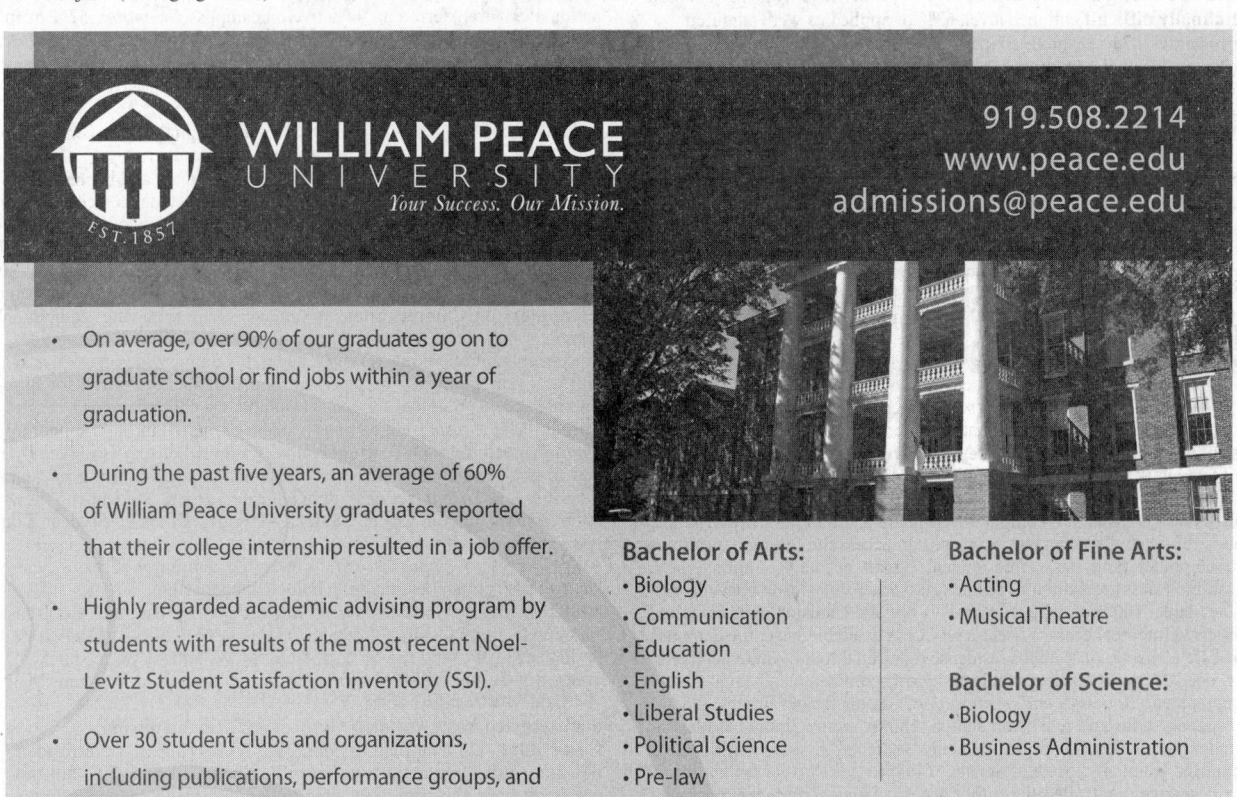

Dickinson State University

Dickinson, North Dakota

- **State-supported** 4-year, founded 1918, part of North Dakota University System
- **Small-town** 132-acre campus
- **Endowment** $9.9 million
- **Coed**
- **Minimally difficult** entrance level

Faculty *Student/faculty ratio:* 17:1.

Academics *Calendar:* semesters. *Degrees:* certificates, associate, and bachelor's.

Student Life *Campus security:* 24-hour emergency response devices and patrols, late-night transport/escort service.

Athletics Member NAIA.

Standardized Tests *Required:* SAT or ACT (for admission).

Costs (2011–12) *Tuition:* state resident $5608 full-time; nonresident $12,978 full-time. *Room only:* $1774. Room and board charges vary according to board plan.

Financial Aid *Of all full-time matriculated undergraduates who enrolled in 2010,* 1,147 applied for aid, 901 were judged to have need, 872 had their need fully met. *In 2010,* 502 non-need-based awards were made. *Average percent of need met:* 35. *Average financial aid package:* $7577. *Average need-based loan:* $3799. *Average need-based gift aid:* $4020. *Average non-need-based aid:* $1491. *Average indebtedness upon graduation:* $18,837.

Applying *Options:* electronic application, early admission, deferred entrance. *Application fee:* $35. *Required:* high school transcript, medical history, proof of measles-rubella shot.

Freshman Application Contact Mr. Norman Coley, Director of Enrollment Services, Dickinson State University, Campus Box 169, Dickinson, ND 58601. *Phone:* 701-483-2175. *Toll-free phone:* 800-279-4295. *Fax:* 701-483-2409. *E-mail:* dsu.hawks@dsu.nodak.edu. *Web site:* http://www.dickinsonstate.edu.

Jamestown College

Jamestown, North Dakota

- **Independent Presbyterian** comprehensive, founded 1883
- **Small-town** 110-acre campus
- **Endowment** $23.6 million
- **Coed** 932 undergraduate students, 94% full-time, 53% women, 47% men
- **Minimally difficult** entrance level, 63% of applicants were admitted

Undergraduates 875 full-time, 57 part-time. Students come from 36 states and territories; 13 other countries; 51% are from out of state; 2% Black or African American, non-Hispanic/Latino; 3% Hispanic/Latino; 0.9% Asian, non-Hispanic/Latino; 0.9% Native Hawaiian or other Pacific Islander, non-Hispanic/Latino; 0.8% American Indian or Alaska Native, non-Hispanic/Latino; 7% international; 6% transferred in; 69% live on campus. *Retention:* 73% of full-time freshmen returned.

Freshmen *Admission:* 797 applied, 502 admitted, 238 enrolled. *Average high school GPA:* 3.39. *Test scores:* SAT critical reading scores over 500: 37%; SAT math scores over 500: 50%; ACT scores over 18: 90%; SAT critical reading scores over 600: 8%; SAT math scores over 600: 15%; ACT scores over 24: 36%; SAT math scores over 700: 2%; ACT scores over 30: 5%.

Faculty *Total:* 84, 71% full-time, 42% with terminal degrees. *Student/faculty ratio:* 13:1.

Academics *Calendar:* semesters. *Degrees:* bachelor's and master's. *Special study options:* advanced placement credit, cooperative education, double majors, honors programs, independent study, internships, part-time degree program, services for LD students, student-designed majors, study abroad, summer session for credit. *Unusual degree programs:* 3-2 engineering with North Dakota State University, University of North Dakota, South Dakota State University, Washington University in St. Louis.

Computers on Campus 300 computers/terminals and 600 ports are available on campus for general student use. Students can access the following: campus intranet, computer help desk, free student e-mail accounts, online (class) grades, online (class) registration, online (class) schedules. Campuswide network is available. 100% of college-owned or -operated housing units are wired for high-speed Internet access. Wireless service is available via entire campus.

Student Life *Housing:* on-campus residence required through sophomore year. *Options:* coed. Campus housing is university owned. Freshman campus housing is guaranteed. *Activities and organizations:* drama/theater group, student-run newspaper, radio and television station, choral group, Jimmie Ambassadors, Student Activities Committee, Nursing Students' Association, Building 28-Habitat for Humanity, Student Senate. *Campus security:* late-night transport/escort service, controlled dormitory access. *Student services:* personal/psychological counseling.

Athletics Member NAIA. *Intercollegiate sports:* baseball M(s), basketball M(s)/W(s), cross-country running M(s)/W(s), football M(s), golf M(s)/W(s),

soccer M(s)/W(s), softball W(s), track and field M(s)/W(s), volleyball W(s), wrestling M(s)/W(s). *Intramural sports:* basketball M/W, football M/W, soccer M(c)/W(c), volleyball M/W.

Standardized Tests *Required:* SAT or ACT (for admission).

Costs (2012–13) *Comprehensive fee:* $23,900 includes full-time tuition ($17,450), mandatory fees ($420), and room and board ($6030). Full-time tuition and fees vary according to course load and program. Part-time tuition and fees vary according to course load and program. *College room only:* $2674. *Payment plan:* installment. *Waivers:* employees or children of employees.

Financial Aid *Of all full-time matriculated undergraduates who enrolled in 2011,* 916 applied for aid, 625 were judged to have need, 128 had their need fully met. 243 Federal Work-Study jobs (averaging $913). 73 state and other part-time jobs (averaging $784). In 2011, 273 non-need-based awards were made. *Average percent of need met:* 75%. *Average financial aid package:* $12,763. *Average need-based loan:* $4004. *Average need-based gift aid:* $9475. *Average non-need-based aid:* $6022. *Average indebtedness upon graduation:* $28,726.

Applying *Options:* electronic application, deferred entrance. *Application fee:* $35. *Required:* high school transcript, 1 letter of recommendation. *Recommended:* minimum 2.5 GPA. *Application deadlines:* rolling (freshmen), rolling (out-of-state freshmen), rolling (transfers).

Freshman Application Contact Jamestown College, 6000 College Lane, Jamestown, ND 58405. *Phone:* 701-252-3467 Ext. 5512. *Toll-free phone:* 800-336-2554. *Web site:* http://www.jc.edu/.

Mayville State University

Mayville, North Dakota

- **State-supported** 4-year, founded 1889, part of North Dakota University System
- **Rural** 60-acre campus
- **Coed** 970 undergraduate students, 59% full-time, 56% women, 44% men
- **Noncompetitive** entrance level, 60% of applicants were admitted

Undergraduates 568 full-time, 402 part-time. Students come from 37 states and territories; 4 other countries; 36% are from out of state; 4% Black or African American, non-Hispanic/Latino; 4% Hispanic/Latino; 1% Asian, non-Hispanic/Latino; 2% Native Hawaiian or other Pacific Islander, non-Hispanic/Latino; 2% American Indian or Alaska Native, non-Hispanic/Latino; 1% Two or more races, non-Hispanic/Latino; 0.2% Race/ethnicity unknown; 4% international; 9% transferred in; 44% live on campus. *Retention:* 52% of full-time freshmen returned.

Freshmen *Admission:* 302 applied, 181 admitted, 149 enrolled. *Test scores:* ACT scores over 18: 65%; ACT scores over 24: 18%; ACT scores over 30: 1%.

Faculty *Total:* 76, 53% full-time, 26% with terminal degrees. *Student/faculty ratio:* 14:1.

Academics *Calendar:* semesters. *Degrees:* associate and bachelor's. *Special study options:* academic remediation for entering students, accelerated degree program, adult/continuing education programs, advanced placement credit, cooperative education, distance learning, double majors, internships, off-campus study, part-time degree program, services for LD students, student-designed majors, summer session for credit. *ROTC:* Army (c), Air Force (c).

Computers on Campus Students can access the following: campus intranet, computer help desk, free student e-mail accounts, online (class) grades, online (class) registration, online (class) schedules. Campuswide network is available. 100% of college-owned or -operated housing units are wired for high-speed Internet access. Wireless service is available via entire campus.

Student Life *Housing:* on-campus residence required through sophomore year. *Options:* coed, men-only, women-only. Campus housing is university owned and is provided by a third party. Freshman campus housing is guaranteed. *Activities and organizations:* drama/theater group, student-run newspaper, radio station, choral group, Student Activities Council, Student Education Association, Health and Physical Education Club, Campus Crusade, Student Ambassadors. *Campus security:* controlled dormitory access. *Student services:* health clinic, personal/psychological counseling.

Athletics Member NAIA. *Intercollegiate sports:* baseball M(s), basketball M(s)/W(s), football M(s), softball W(s), volleyball W(s). *Intramural sports:* basketball M/W, bowling M/W, football M/W, golf M/W, ice hockey M, racquetball M/W, soccer M/W, softball M/W, table tennis M/W, tennis M/W, track and field M/W, volleyball M/W.

Standardized Tests *Required:* SAT or ACT (for admission).

Costs (2011–12) *One-time required fee:* $35. *Tuition:* state resident $4375 full-time, $182 per credit hour part-time; nonresident $6502 full-time, $273 per credit hour part-time. Full-time tuition and fees vary according to course load and reciprocity agreements. Part-time tuition and fees vary according to course load and reciprocity agreements. *Required fees:* $1709 full-time, $71 per credit hour part-time. *Room and board:* $4632; room only: $1742. Room

and board charges vary according to board plan and housing facility. *Payment plan:* installment. *Waivers:* minority students, senior citizens, and employees or children of employees.

Financial Aid Of all full-time matriculated undergraduates who enrolled in 2011, 471 applied for aid, 372 were judged to have need, 369 had their need fully met. 58 Federal Work-Study jobs (averaging $1200). In 2011, 249 non-need-based awards were made. *Average percent of need met:* 56%. *Average financial aid package:* $8245. *Average need-based loan:* $4072. *Average need-based gift aid:* $4289. *Average non-need-based aid:* $808. *Average indebtedness upon graduation:* $27,552.

Applying *Options:* electronic application, deferred entrance. *Application fee:* $35. *Required:* high school transcript, minimum 2.0 GPA. *Application deadlines:* rolling (freshmen), rolling (out-of-state freshmen), rolling (transfers). *Notification:* continuous until 1/1 (freshmen), continuous (out-of-state freshmen), continuous until 1/1 (transfers).

Freshman Application Contact Jim Morowski, Director of Freshmen Enrollment Services, Mayville State University, 330 3rd Street, NE, Mayville, ND 58257-1299. *Phone:* 701-788-4842. *Toll-free phone:* 800-437-4104. *Fax:* 701-788-4748. *E-mail:* james.morowski@mayvillestate.edu. *Web site:* http://www.mayvillestate.edu/.

Medcenter One College of Nursing
Bismarck, North Dakota

- **Independent** upper-level, founded 1988
- **Small-town** 15-acre campus
- **Endowment** $791,956
- **Coed, primarily women** 92 undergraduate students, 98% full-time, 86% women, 14% men
- **Moderately difficult** entrance level, 49% of applicants were admitted

Undergraduates 90 full-time, 2 part-time. Students come from 3 states and territories; 4 other countries; 3% are from out of state; 4% Black or African American, non-Hispanic/Latino; 1% Hispanic/Latino; 2% Asian, non-Hispanic/Latino; 3% Two or more races, non-Hispanic/Latino; 2% Race/ethnicity unknown; 52% transferred in.

Freshmen *Admission:* 108 applied, 53 admitted.

Faculty *Total:* 13, 77% full-time, 8% with terminal degrees. *Student/faculty ratio:* 8:1.

Academics *Calendar:* semesters. *Degree:* bachelor's. *Special study options:* independent study, internships.

Computers on Campus 25 computers/terminals are available on campus for general student use. Students can access the following: campus intranet, free student e-mail accounts. Campuswide network is available. Wireless service is available via entire campus.

Student Life *Housing:* college housing not available. *Activities and organizations:* Student Body Organization, Student Nurses Association. *Campus security:* late-night transport/escort service. *Student services:* personal/psychological counseling.

Costs (2012–13) *One-time required fee:* $275. *Tuition:* $10,312 full-time, $430 per credit part-time. Part-time tuition and fees vary according to course load. *Required fees:* $855 full-time, $71 per credit part-time.

Financial Aid Of all full-time matriculated undergraduates who enrolled in 2011, 78 applied for aid, 60 were judged to have need, 40 had their need fully met. 6 Federal Work-Study jobs (averaging $1200). In 2011, 4 non-need-based awards were made. *Average percent of need met:* 92%. *Average financial aid package:* $13,553. *Average need-based loan:* $4467. *Average need-based gift aid:* $3881. *Average non-need-based aid:* $650.

Applying *Options:* early admission. *Application fee:* $40. *Application deadline:* 11/1 (transfers). *Notification:* continuous (transfers).

Application Contact Ms. Mary Smith, Director of Student Services, Medcenter One College of Nursing, 512 North 7th Street, Bismarck, ND 58501-4494. *Phone:* 701-323-6271. *Fax:* 701-323-6289. *E-mail:* msmith@mohs.org. *Web site:* http://www.medcenterone.com/collegeofnursing/index.asp.

Minot State University
Minot, North Dakota

- **State-supported** comprehensive, founded 1913, part of North Dakota University System
- **Small-town** 103-acre campus
- **Endowment** $2.4 million
- **Coed** 3,367 undergraduate students, 67% full-time, 61% women, 39% men
- **Moderately difficult** entrance level, 58% of applicants were admitted

Undergraduates 2,255 full-time, 1,112 part-time. Students come from 54 states and territories; 23 other countries; 27% are from out of state; 3% Black or African American, non-Hispanic/Latino; 2% Hispanic/Latino; 0.7% Asian,

non-Hispanic/Latino; 3% American Indian or Alaska Native, non-Hispanic/Latino; 1% Two or more races, non-Hispanic/Latino; 2% Race/ethnicity unknown; 15% international; 8% transferred in; 18% live on campus. *Retention:* 63% of full-time freshmen returned.

Freshmen *Admission:* 1,163 applied, 672 admitted, 460 enrolled. *Average high school GPA:* 3.35. *Test scores:* ACT scores over 18: 89%; ACT scores over 24: 29%; ACT scores over 30: 2%.

Faculty *Total:* 304, 60% full-time, 35% with terminal degrees. *Student/faculty ratio:* 14:1.

Academics *Calendar:* semesters. *Degrees:* certificates, associate, bachelor's, master's, post-master's, and postbachelor's certificates. *Special study options:* academic remediation for entering students, accelerated degree program, advanced placement credit, cooperative education, distance learning, double majors, English as a second language, honors programs, independent study, internships, part-time degree program, services for LD students, student-designed majors, study abroad, summer session for credit.

Computers on Campus 450 computers/terminals are available on campus for general student use. Students can access the following: campus intranet, computer help desk, free student e-mail accounts, online (class) grades, online (class) registration, online (class) schedules. Campuswide network is available. Wireless service is available via entire campus.

Student Life *Housing:* on-campus residence required for freshman year. *Options:* coed, men-only, women-only. Campus housing is university owned. Freshman campus housing is guaranteed. *Activities and organizations:* drama/theater group, student-run newspaper, radio and television station, choral group, marching band, Residence Hall Association, Student Government Association, Beavers on Business, Student Social Work Organization, National Student Speech and Hearing Association. *Campus security:* controlled dormitory access, patrols by trained security personnel. *Student services:* health clinic, personal/psychological counseling, women's center.

Athletics Member NCAA, NAIA, NCCAA. All NCAA Division II. *Intercollegiate sports:* baseball M(s), basketball M(s)/W(s), cheerleading W, cross-country running M(s)/W(s), football M(s), golf M/W, ice hockey M(c), soccer W, softball W(s), track and field M(s)/W(s), volleyball W(s), wrestling M. *Intramural sports:* basketball M/W, racquetball M/W, softball M/W, volleyball M/W.

Standardized Tests *Required:* SAT or ACT (for admission).

Costs (2012–13) *Tuition:* state resident $4587 full-time, $240 per credit hour part-time; nonresident $4587 full-time, $240 per credit hour part-time. Full-time tuition and fees vary according to class time, course load, degree level, location, program, and reciprocity agreements. Part-time tuition and fees vary according to class time, course load, degree level, location, program, and reciprocity agreements. *Required fees:* $1175 full-time, $49 per credit hour part-time, $49 per credit hour part-time. *Room and board:* $5762; room only: $3250. Room and board charges vary according to board plan and housing facility. *Payment plan:* installment. *Waivers:* minority students, children of alumni, senior citizens, and employees or children of employees.

Financial Aid Of all full-time matriculated undergraduates who enrolled in 2010, 1,412 applied for aid, 1,026 were judged to have need, 1,004 had their need fully met. In 2010, 546 non-need-based awards were made. *Average percent of need met:* 48%. *Average financial aid package:* $8000. *Average need-based loan:* $4233. *Average need-based gift aid:* $4720. *Average non-need-based aid:* $932. *Average indebtedness upon graduation:* $20,804.

Applying *Options:* electronic application, deferred entrance. *Application fee:* $35. *Required:* high school transcript. *Required for some:* minimum 2.5 GPA. *Application deadlines:* rolling (freshmen), rolling (out-of-state freshmen), rolling (transfers). *Notification:* continuous (freshmen), continuous (out-of-state freshmen), continuous (transfers).

Freshman Application Contact Mr. Kevin Harmon, Vice President of Enrollment Management, Minot State University, 500 University Avenue West, Minot, ND 58707-0002. *Phone:* 701-858-3126. *Toll-free phone:* 800-777-0750 Ext. 3350. *Fax:* 701-858-3825. *E-mail:* askmsu@minotstateu.edu. *Web site:* http://www.minotstateu.edu/.

North Dakota State University
Fargo, North Dakota

- **State-supported** university, founded 1890, part of North Dakota University System
- **Urban** 2100-acre campus
- **Endowment** $370,017
- **Coed** 11,911 undergraduate students, 90% full-time, 43% women, 57% men
- **Moderately difficult** entrance level, 86% of applicants were admitted

Undergraduates 10,675 full-time, 1,236 part-time. Students come from 47 states and territories; 80 other countries; 56% are from out of state; 2% Black or African American, non-Hispanic/Latino; 1% Hispanic/Latino; 1% Asian, non-Hispanic/Latino; 0.1% Native Hawaiian or other Pacific Islander, non-

Hispanic/Latino; 0.7% American Indian or Alaska Native, non-Hispanic/Latino; 1% Two or more races, non-Hispanic/Latino; 1% Race/ethnicity unknown; 5% international; 6% transferred in; 26% live on campus. *Retention:* 76% of full-time freshmen returned.

Freshmen *Admission:* 5,096 applied, 4,383 admitted, 2,247 enrolled. *Average high school GPA:* 3.39. *Test scores:* SAT critical reading scores over 500: 68%; SAT math scores over 500: 80%; ACT scores over 18: 97%; SAT critical reading scores over 600: 30%; SAT math scores over 600: 38%; ACT scores over 24: 50%; SAT critical reading scores over 700: 4%; SAT math scores over 700: 12%; ACT scores over 30: 8%.

Faculty *Total:* 812, 78% full-time, 72% with terminal degrees. *Student/faculty ratio:* 18:1.

Academics *Calendar:* semesters. *Degrees:* certificates, bachelor's, master's, doctoral, post-master's, postbachelor's, and first professional certificates. *Special study options:* academic remediation for entering students, advanced placement credit, cooperative education, distance learning, double majors, honors programs, independent study, internships, off-campus study, part-time degree program, services for LD students, student-designed majors, study abroad, summer session for credit. *ROTC:* Army (b), Air Force (b).

Computers on Campus 500 computers/terminals are available on campus for general student use. Students can access the following: computer help desk, free student e-mail accounts, online (class) grades, online (class) registration, online (class) schedules. Campuswide network is available. Wireless service is available via classrooms, computer centers, computer labs, dorm rooms, libraries, student centers.

Student Life *Housing:* on-campus residence required for freshman year. *Options:* coed, men-only, women-only, disabled students. Campus housing is university owned. Freshman campus housing is guaranteed. *Activities and organizations:* drama/theater group, student-run newspaper, radio and television station, choral group, marching band, Saddle and Sirloin, Students Today, Leaders Forever, International Student Association, Chi Alpha Christian Organization, fraternities/sororities, national fraternities, national sororities. *Campus security:* 24-hour emergency response devices and patrols, student patrols, late-night transport/escort service, controlled dormitory access. *Student services:* health clinic, personal/psychological counseling.

Athletics Member NCAA. All Division I. *Intercollegiate sports:* baseball M(s), basketball M(s)/W(s), bowling M(c)/W(c), cheerleading M(c)/W(c), cross-country running M(s)/W(s), equestrian sports M(c)/W(c), football M(s), golf M/W(s), ice hockey M(c)/W(c), lacrosse M(c)/W(c), riflery M(c)/W(c), rugby M(c)/W(c), soccer M(c)/W(s), softball W(s), track and field M(s)/W(s), volleyball M(c)/W(s), wrestling M(s). *Intramural sports:* basketball M/W, football M/W, softball M/W, volleyball M/W, wrestling M.

Standardized Tests *Required:* SAT or ACT (for admission).

Costs (2011–12) *One-time required fee:* $95. *Tuition:* state resident $6135 full-time, $256 per credit hour part-time; nonresident $16,381 full-time, $683 per credit hour part-time. Full-time tuition and fees vary according to reciprocity agreements and student level. Part-time tuition and fees vary according to course load, reciprocity agreements, and student level. *Required fees:* $1040 full-time, $43 per credit hour part-time. *Room and board:* $6722; room only: $3162. Room and board charges vary according to board plan and housing facility. *Payment plan:* installment. *Waivers:* minority students, children of alumni, senior citizens, and employees or children of employees.

Financial Aid Of all full-time matriculated undergraduates who enrolled in 2007, 7,109 applied for aid, 4,917 were judged to have need, 980 had their need fully met. In 2007, 1763 non-need-based awards were made. *Average percent of need met:* 3%. *Average financial aid package:* $7030. *Average need-based loan:* $4378. *Average need-based gift aid:* $3419. *Average non-need-based aid:* $1533.

Applying *Options:* electronic application. *Application fee:* $35. *Required:* high school transcript, minimum 2.5 GPA. *Application deadlines:* 8/15 (freshmen), 8/15 (transfers). *Notification:* continuous (freshmen), continuous (transfers).

Freshman Application Contact Jobey Lichtblau, Director of Admission, North Dakota State University, PO Box 5454, Fargo, ND 58105-5454. *Phone:* 701-231-8643. *Toll-free phone:* 800-488-NDSU. *Fax:* 701-231-8802. *E-mail:* ndsu.admission@ndsu.edu. *Web site:* http://www.ndsu.edu/.

Rasmussen College Bismarck
Bismarck, North Dakota

- **Proprietary** primarily 2-year, part of Rasmussen College System
- **Suburban** campus
- **Coed** 289 undergraduate students
- **Minimally difficult** entrance level

Faculty *Student/faculty ratio:* 22:1.

Academics *Degrees:* certificates, diplomas, associate, and bachelor's. *Special study options:* academic remediation for entering students, accelerated degree

program, adult/continuing education programs, distance learning, double majors, internships, part-time degree program, summer session for credit.

Computers on Campus 67 computers/terminals are available on campus for general student use. Students can access the following: computer help desk, free student e-mail accounts, online (class) grades, online (class) schedules. Campuswide network is available. Wireless service is available via entire campus.

Student Life *Housing:* college housing not available.

Standardized Tests *Required:* Internal Exam (for admission).

Costs (2012–13) *Tuition:* $12,600 full-time. Full-time tuition and fees vary according to course level, course load, degree level, location, and program. Part-time tuition and fees vary according to course level, course load, degree level, location, and program. *Required fees:* $40 full-time. *Payment plans:* installment, deferred payment. *Waivers:* employees or children of employees.

Applying *Options:* electronic application, early admission, deferred entrance. *Application fee:* $40. *Required:* high school transcript, minimum 2.0 GPA, interview. *Application deadlines:* rolling (freshmen), rolling (transfers).

Freshman Application Contact Susan Hammerstrom, Director of Admissions, Rasmussen College Bismarck, 1701 East Century Avenue, Bismarck, ND 58503. *Phone:* 701-530-9600. *Toll-free phone:* 888-549-6755. *E-mail:* susan.hammerstrom@rasmussen.edu. *Web site:* http://www.rasmussen.edu/.

Rasmussen College Fargo
Fargo, North Dakota

- **Proprietary** primarily 2-year, founded 1902, part of Rasmussen College System
- **Suburban** campus
- **Coed** 418 undergraduate students
- **Minimally difficult** entrance level

Faculty *Student/faculty ratio:* 22:1.

Academics *Calendar:* quarters. *Degrees:* certificates, diplomas, associate, and bachelor's. *Special study options:* academic remediation for entering students, accelerated degree program, adult/continuing education programs, distance learning, double majors, internships, part-time degree program, summer session for credit.

Computers on Campus 87 computers/terminals are available on campus for general student use. Students can access the following: computer help desk, free student e-mail accounts, online (class) grades, online (class) schedules. Campuswide network is available. Wireless service is available via entire campus.

Student Life *Housing:* college housing not available.

Standardized Tests *Required:* Internal Exam (for admission).

Costs (2012–13) *Tuition:* $12,600 full-time. Full-time tuition and fees vary according to course level, course load, degree level, location, and program. Part-time tuition and fees vary according to course level, course load, degree level, location, and program. *Required fees:* $40 full-time. *Payment plans:* installment, deferred payment. *Waivers:* employees or children of employees.

Applying *Options:* electronic application, early admission, deferred entrance. *Application fee:* $40. *Required:* high school transcript, minimum 2.0 GPA, interview. *Application deadlines:* rolling (freshmen), rolling (transfers).

Freshman Application Contact Susan Hammerstrom, Director of Admissions, Rasmussen College Fargo, 4012 19th Avenue, SW, Fargo, ND 58103. *Phone:* 701-277-3889. *Toll-free phone:* 888-549-6755. *E-mail:* susan.hammerstrom@rasmussen.edu. *Web site:* http://www.rasmussen.edu/.

Trinity Bible College
Ellendale, North Dakota

Director of Admissions Rev. Steve Tvedt, Vice President of College Relations, Trinity Bible College, 50 South 6th Avenue, Ellendale, ND 58436-7150. *Phone:* 701-349-3621 Ext. 2045. *Toll-free phone:* 800-523-1603. *Web site:* http://www.trinitybiblecollege.edu/.

University of Mary
Bismarck, North Dakota

- **Independent Roman Catholic** comprehensive, founded 1959
- **Rural** 107-acre campus
- **Endowment** $23.4 million
- **Coed** 2,130 undergraduate students, 77% full-time, 61% women, 39% men
- **Minimally difficult** entrance level, 75% of applicants were admitted

Undergraduates 1,633 full-time, 497 part-time. Students come from 34 states and territories; 13 other countries; 31% are from out of state; 3% Black or African American, non-Hispanic/Latino; 2% Hispanic/Latino; 0.7% Asian, non-

Hispanic/Latino; 0.5% Native Hawaiian or other Pacific Islander, non-Hispanic/Latino; 4% American Indian or Alaska Native, non-Hispanic/Latino; 0.9% Two or more races, non-Hispanic/Latino; 4% Race/ethnicity unknown; 1% international; 13% transferred in; 35% live on campus. *Retention:* 72% of full-time freshmen returned.

Freshmen *Admission:* 1,001 applied, 753 admitted, 374 enrolled. *Average high school GPA:* 3.36. *Test scores:* SAT critical reading scores over 500: 46%; SAT math scores over 500: 65%; ACT scores over 18: 94%; SAT critical reading scores over 600: 19%; SAT math scores over 600: 23%; ACT scores over 24: 37%; ACT scores over 30: 5%.

Faculty *Total:* 257, 39% full-time, 37% with terminal degrees. *Student/faculty ratio:* 17:1.

Academics *Calendar:* 4-4-1. *Degrees:* bachelor's, master's, and doctoral. *Special study options:* academic remediation for entering students, accelerated degree program, adult/continuing education programs, advanced placement credit, cooperative education, distance learning, double majors, external degree program, honors programs, independent study, internships, off-campus study, part-time degree program, services for LD students, student-designed majors, study abroad, summer session for credit. *Unusual degree programs:* 3-2 engineering with University of Minnesota; occupational therapy.

Computers on Campus 100 computers/terminals and 1,000 ports are available on campus for general student use. Students can access the following: campus intranet, computer help desk, free student e-mail accounts, online (class) grades, online (class) registration, online (class) schedules. Campus-wide network is available. 100% of college-owned or -operated housing units are wired for high-speed Internet access. Wireless service is available via classrooms, computer labs, dorm rooms, libraries.

Student Life *Housing:* on-campus residence required through sophomore year. *Options:* coed, men-only, women-only. Campus housing is university owned. Freshman campus housing is guaranteed. *Activities and organizations:* drama/theater group, student-run newspaper, choral group, Collegians for Life, Nursing Students Association, Student Occupational Therapy, UMPHERD, Pre-PT Club. *Campus security:* 24-hour emergency response devices and patrols, late-night transport/escort service, controlled dormitory access. *Student services:* health clinic, personal/psychological counseling.

Athletics Member NCAA. All Division II. *Intercollegiate sports:* baseball M(s), basketball M(s)/W(s), cross-country running M(s)/W(s), football M(s), golf M/W(s), soccer M(s)/W(s), softball W(s), tennis M/W(s), track and field M(s)/W(s), volleyball W(s), wrestling M(s). *Intramural sports:* badminton M/W, basketball M/W, bowling M/W, cheerleading M(c)/W(c), golf M/W, racquetball M/W, soccer M/W, softball M/W, swimming and diving M/W, table tennis M/W, tennis M/W, ultimate Frisbee M/W, volleyball M/W, water polo M/W, weight lifting M/W.

Standardized Tests *Required:* SAT or ACT (for admission).

Costs (2011–12) *Comprehensive fee:* $18,898 includes full-time tuition ($13,200), mandatory fees ($368), and room and board ($5330). Full-time tuition and fees vary according to course load, degree level, and program. Part-time tuition: $435 per credit hour. Part-time tuition and fees vary according to course load, degree level, and program. *College room only:* $2450. Room and board charges vary according to board plan and housing facility. *Payment plan:* installment. *Waivers:* senior citizens and employees or children of employees.

Financial Aid Of all full-time matriculated undergraduates who enrolled in 2010, 1,513 applied for aid, 1,264 were judged to have need, 640 had their need fully met. 155 Federal Work-Study jobs (averaging $1224). 60 state and other part-time jobs (averaging $1725). In 2010, 414 non-need-based awards were made. *Average percent of need met:* 70%. *Average financial aid package:* $11,057. *Average need-based loan:* $4418. *Average need-based gift aid:* $3904. *Average non-need-based aid:* $4163. *Average indebtedness upon graduation:* $24,749.

Applying *Options:* electronic application, early admission, deferred entrance. *Application fee:* $25. *Required:* high school transcript, 2.0 College Prep GPA. *Required for some:* essay or personal statement, interview. *Recommended:* minimum 2.5 GPA, 2 letters of recommendation. *Application deadlines:* rolling (freshmen), rolling (transfers).

Freshman Application Contact Mike Heitkamp, University of Mary, 7500 University Drive, Bismarck, ND 58504-9652. *Phone:* 701-355-8191. *Toll-free phone:* 800-288-6279. *Fax:* 701-255-7687. *E-mail:* mcheitkamp@umary.edu. *Web site:* http://www.umary.edu/.

University of North Dakota
Grand Forks, North Dakota

- **State-supported** university, founded 1883, part of North Dakota University System
- **Urban** 550-acre campus
- **Endowment** $13.1 million
- **Coed** 11,522 undergraduate students, 81% full-time, 45% women, 55% men
- **Minimally difficult** entrance level, 43% of applicants were admitted

Undergraduates 9,334 full-time, 2,188 part-time. Students come from 44 other countries; 57% are from out of state; 2% Black or African American, non-Hispanic/Latino; 2% Hispanic/Latino; 1% Asian, non-Hispanic/Latino; 0.1% Native Hawaiian or other Pacific Islander, non-Hispanic/Latino; 2% American Indian or Alaska Native, non-Hispanic/Latino; 2% Two or more races, non-Hispanic/Latino; 4% Race/ethnicity unknown; 6% international; 8% transferred in; 32% live on campus. *Retention:* 77% of full-time freshmen returned.

Freshmen *Admission:* 4,857 applied, 2,091 admitted, 2,091 enrolled. *Average high school GPA:* 3.36. *Test scores:* ACT scores over 18: 95%; ACT scores over 24: 45%; ACT scores over 30: 6%.

Faculty *Total:* 703, 91% full-time, 74% with terminal degrees.

Academics *Calendar:* semesters. *Degrees:* certificates, diplomas, bachelor's, master's, doctoral, postbachelor's, and first professional certificates. *Special study options:* accelerated degree program, adult/continuing education programs, advanced placement credit, cooperative education, distance learning, double majors, English as a second language, honors programs, independent study, internships, off-campus study, part-time degree program, services for LD students, student-designed majors, study abroad, summer session for credit. *ROTC:* Army (b), Air Force (b). *Unusual degree programs:* 3-2 engineering; applied economics, counseling, chemistry, public administration.

Computers on Campus 1,500 computers/terminals and 400 ports are available on campus for general student use. Students can access the following: campus intranet, computer help desk, free student e-mail accounts, online (class) grades, online (class) registration, online (class) schedules. Campus-wide network is available. 100% of college-owned or -operated housing units are wired for high-speed Internet access. Wireless service is available via classrooms, computer centers, computer labs, dorm rooms, learning centers, libraries, student centers.

Student Life *Housing options:* coed, men-only, women-only, disabled students. Campus housing is university owned and leased by the school. *Activities and organizations:* drama/theater group, student-run newspaper, radio and television station, choral group, marching band, Student Government, Greek Life, Association of Residence Halls, University of North Dakota Indian Association, NoDak Nation Student Athletic Boosters, national fraternities, national sororities. *Campus security:* 24-hour emergency response devices and patrols, student patrols, late-night transport/escort service, controlled dormitory access, emergency telephones. *Student services:* health clinic, personal/psychological counseling, women's center, legal services.

Athletics Member NCAA. All Division I. *Intercollegiate sports:* baseball M(s), basketball M(s)/W(s), cross-country running M(s)/W(s), football M(s), golf M(s)/W(s), ice hockey M(s)/W(s), soccer W(s), softball W(s), swimming and diving M(s)/W(s), tennis W(s), track and field M(s)/W(s), volleyball W(s). *Intramural sports:* basketball M/W, ice hockey M/W, soccer M/W, softball M/W, ultimate Frisbee M/W, volleyball M/W.

Standardized Tests *Required:* SAT or ACT (for admission). *Recommended:* ACT (for admission).

Costs (2011–12) *Tuition:* state resident $5793 full-time, $241 per credit hour part-time; nonresident $15,468 full-time, $645 per credit hour part-time. Full-time tuition and fees vary according to degree level, program, and reciprocity agreements. Part-time tuition and fees vary according to course load, degree level, program, and reciprocity agreements. *Required fees:* $1299 full-time. *Room and board:* $6100; room only: $2410. Room and board charges vary according to board plan and housing facility. *Payment plan:* deferred payment. *Waivers:* minority students, adult students, senior citizens, and employees or children of employees.

Financial Aid Of all full-time matriculated undergraduates who enrolled in 2010, 6,433 applied for aid, 4,458 were judged to have need, 4,297 had their need fully met. In 2010, 2343 non-need-based awards were made. *Average percent of need met:* 44%. *Average financial aid package:* $9517. *Average need-based loan:* $5047. *Average need-based gift aid:* $4195. *Average non-need-based aid:* $1668. *Average indebtedness upon graduation:* $31,384.

Applying *Options:* electronic application, deferred entrance. *Application fee:* $35. *Required:* high school transcript. *Recommended:* minimum 2.5 GPA. *Application deadline:* rolling (transfers). *Notification:* continuous (transfers).

Freshman Application Contact Deborah Melby, Director of Admissions, University of North Dakota, Stop 8357, 205 Twamley Hall, 264 Centennial Drive, Grand Forks, ND 58202. *Phone:* 701-777-3821. *Toll-free phone:* 800-

CALL-UND. *Fax:* 701-777-2721. *E-mail:* und.enrollmentservices@und.edu. *Web site:* http://www.und.nodak.edu/.

Valley City State University

Valley City, North Dakota

- **State-supported** comprehensive, founded 1890, part of North Dakota University System
- **Small-town** 55-acre campus
- **Coed**
- **Noncompetitive** entrance level

Undergraduates 33% live on campus.

Freshmen *Average high school GPA:* 3.02. *Test scores:* SAT critical reading scores over 500: 39%; SAT math scores over 500: 47%; ACT scores over 18: 78%; SAT critical reading scores over 600: 11%; SAT math scores over 600: 6%; ACT scores over 24: 18%; ACT scores over 30: 2%.

Faculty *Total:* 112, 60% full-time, 46% with terminal degrees. *Student/faculty ratio:* 13:1.

Academics *Calendar:* semesters. *Degrees:* bachelor's and master's. *Special study options:* academic remediation for entering students, cooperative education, distance learning, double majors, internships, off-campus study, part-time degree program, services for LD students, student-designed majors, study abroad, summer session for credit.

Computers on Campus 990 computers/terminals are available on campus for general student use. Students can access the following: campus intranet, computer help desk, free student e-mail accounts, online (class) grades, online (class) registration, online (class) schedules. Campuswide network is available. 100% of college-owned or -operated housing units are wired for high-speed Internet access. Wireless service is available via entire campus.

Student Life *Housing:* on-campus residence required for freshman year. *Options:* coed, men-only, women-only. Campus housing is university owned. Freshman campus housing is guaranteed. *Activities and organizations:* drama/theater group, choral group, departmental clubs, Fellowship of Christian Athletes, intramural sports, VCAB, Viking Ambassadors. *Campus security:* controlled dormitory access, security cameras throughout campus. *Student services:* health clinic, personal/psychological counseling.

Athletics Member NAIA. *Intercollegiate sports:* baseball M(s), basketball M(s)/W(s), cross-country running M(s)/W(s), football M(s), golf M(s)/W(s), softball W(s), tennis M(c)/W(c), track and field M(s)/W(s), volleyball W(s). *Intramural sports:* basketball M/W, bowling M/W, cross-country running M/W, football M/W, golf M/W, ice hockey M/W, racquetball M/W, skiing (cross-country) M/W, soccer M/W, softball M/W, tennis M/W, track and field M/W, volleyball M/W.

Standardized Tests *Required for some:* SAT or ACT (for admission).

Costs (2012–13) *Tuition:* state resident $4544 full-time; nonresident $12,131 full-time. Full-time tuition and fees vary according to course load, location, program, and reciprocity agreements. Part-time tuition and fees vary according to course load, location, program, and reciprocity agreements. *Required fees:* $1653 full-time. *Room and board:* $5610; room only: $1960. Room and board charges vary according to board plan and housing facility. *Payment plan:* installment. *Waivers:* employees or children of employees.

Financial Aid Of all full-time matriculated undergraduates who enrolled in 2011, 581 applied for aid, 441 were judged to have need, 432 had their need fully met. 34 Federal Work-Study jobs (averaging $2400). In 2011, 286 non-need-based awards were made. *Average percent of need met:* 67%. *Average financial aid package:* $8335. *Average need-based loan:* $3939. *Average need-based gift aid:* $4515. *Average non-need-based aid:* $1735. *Average indebtedness upon graduation:* $24,514.

Applying *Options:* electronic application, early admission, deferred entrance. *Application fee:* $35. *Required:* high school transcript. *Application deadlines:* rolling (freshmen), rolling (transfers). *Notification:* continuous (freshmen), continuous (transfers).

Freshman Application Contact Ms. Kaleen Peterson, Admission Counselor, Valley City State University, 101 College Street Southwest, Valley City, ND 58072. *Phone:* 701-845-7115. *Toll-free phone:* 800-532-8641 Ext. 7101. *Fax:* 701-845-7299. *E-mail:* kaleen.peterson@vcsu.edu. *Web site:* http://www.vcsu.edu/.

OHIO

Akron Institute of Herzing University

Akron, Ohio

Admissions Office Contact Akron Institute of Herzing University, 1600 South Arlington Street, Suite 100, Akron, OH 44306. *Toll-free phone:* 800-311-0512. *Web site:* http://www.akroninstitute.com/.

Allegheny Wesleyan College

Salem, Ohio

Director of Admissions Admissions Office, Allegheny Wesleyan College, 2161 Woodsdale Road, Salem, OH 44460. *Phone:* 330-337-6403. *Toll-free phone:* 800-292-3153. *E-mail:* college@awc.edu. *Web site:* http://www.awc.edu/.

Antioch University Midwest

Yellow Springs, Ohio

- **Independent** upper-level, founded 1988, part of Antioch University
- **Small-town** 100-acre campus with easy access to Dayton
- **Coed** 142 undergraduate students, 46% full-time, 69% women, 31% men
- **Noncompetitive** entrance level

Undergraduates 66 full-time, 76 part-time. Students come from 1 other state; 18% Black or African American, non-Hispanic/Latino; 1% Hispanic/Latino; 2% Asian, non-Hispanic/Latino; 4% American Indian or Alaska Native, non-Hispanic/Latino; 6% Race/ethnicity unknown; 20% transferred in.

Faculty *Total:* 67, 27% full-time. *Student/faculty ratio:* 8:1.

Academics *Calendar:* quarters. *Degrees:* certificates, bachelor's, master's, post-master's, and postbachelor's certificates. *Special study options:* accelerated degree program, adult/continuing education programs, advanced placement credit, cooperative education, distance learning, double majors, independent study, internships, off-campus study, part-time degree program, summer session for credit.

Computers on Campus 32 computers/terminals are available on campus for general student use. Students can access the following: campus intranet, computer help desk, free student e-mail accounts, online (class) grades, online (class) registration, online (class) schedules, online bill pay, and online view of financial aid award letter. Campuswide network is available. Wireless service is available via entire campus.

Student Life *Housing:* college housing not available. *Campus security:* 24-hour emergency response devices. *Student services:* personal/psychological counseling.

Costs (2011–12) *Tuition:* $21,184 full-time, $331 per credit hour part-time. *Required fees:* $600 full-time. *Waivers:* employees or children of employees.

Financial Aid Of all full-time matriculated undergraduates who enrolled in 2010, 122 applied for aid, 118 were judged to have need. 10 Federal Work-Study jobs (averaging $5149). *Average percent of need met:* 35%. *Average financial aid package:* $11,000. *Average need-based loan:* $6500. *Average need-based gift aid:* $4500. *Average indebtedness upon graduation:* $40,000.

Applying *Options:* electronic application, deferred entrance. *Application fee:* $45. *Application deadline:* rolling (transfers).

Application Contact Antioch University Midwest, 900 Dayton Street, Yellow Springs, OH 45387-1609. *Phone:* 937-769-1823. *Web site:* http://midwest.antioch.edu/.

Art Academy of Cincinnati

Cincinnati, Ohio

Freshman Application Contact Mr. John J. Wadell, Director of Admissions, Art Academy of Cincinnati, 1212 Jackson Street, Cincinnati, OH 45202-7106. *Phone:* 513-562-8744. *Toll-free phone:* 800-323-5692. *Fax:* 513-562-8778. *E-mail:* admissions@artacademy.edu. *Web site:* http://www.artacademy.edu/.

The Art Institute of Ohio–Cincinnati

Cincinnati, Ohio

- **Proprietary** primarily 2-year, part of Education Management Corporation
- **Urban** campus
- **Coed**

Academics *Calendar:* continuous. *Degrees:* diplomas, associate, and bachelor's.

Costs (2011–12) *Tuition:* Tuition cost varies by program. Prospective students should contact the school for current tuition costs. Other charges include a

starting kit for all first-quarter students. Kits vary in price, depending on the program of study.
Freshman Application Contact The Art Institute of Ohio–Cincinnati, 8845 Governors Hill Drive, Cincinnati, OH 45249-3317. *Phone:* 513-833-2400. *Toll-free phone:* 866-613-5184. *Web site:* http://www.artinstitutes.edu/cincinnati/.

See page 1114 for the College Close-Up.

Ashland University
Ashland, Ohio

- **Independent** comprehensive, founded 1878, affiliated with Brethren Church
- **Small-town** 135-acre campus with easy access to Cleveland
- **Endowment** $39.4 million
- **Coed** 3,146 undergraduate students, 83% full-time, 54% women, 46% men
- **Moderately difficult** entrance level, 77% of applicants were admitted

Undergraduates 2,622 full-time, 524 part-time. Students come from 31 states and territories; 19 other countries; 10% are from out of state; 3% transferred in; 72% live on campus. *Retention:* 69% of full-time freshmen returned.
Freshmen *Admission:* 3,530 applied, 2,722 admitted, 675 enrolled. *Average high school GPA:* 3.37. *Test scores:* SAT critical reading scores over 500: 59%; SAT math scores over 500: 58%; ACT scores over 18: 96%; SAT critical reading scores over 600: 18%; SAT math scores over 600: 22%; ACT scores over 24: 40%; SAT critical reading scores over 700: 1%; SAT math scores over 700: 2%; ACT scores over 30: 4%.
Faculty *Total:* 591, 46% full-time, 56% with terminal degrees. *Student/faculty ratio:* 13:1.
Academics *Calendar:* semesters. *Degrees:* certificates, diplomas, associate, bachelor's, master's, doctoral, post-master's, postbachelor's, and first professional certificates. *Special study options:* academic remediation for entering students, accelerated degree program, adult/continuing education programs, advanced placement credit, cooperative education, distance learning, double majors, English as a second language, honors programs, independent study, internships, off-campus study, part-time degree program, services for LD students, student-designed majors, study abroad, summer session for credit. *ROTC:* Army (c).
Computers on Campus 760 computers/terminals are available on campus for general student use. Students can access the following: campus intranet, computer help desk, free student e-mail accounts, online (class) grades, online (class) registration, online (class) schedules. Campuswide network is available. 100% of college-owned or -operated housing units are wired for high-speed Internet access. Wireless service is available via classrooms, computer centers, computer labs, learning centers, libraries, student centers.
Student Life *Housing:* on-campus residence required through junior year. *Options:* coed, men-only, women-only, disabled students. Campus housing is university owned. Freshman campus housing is guaranteed. *Activities and organizations:* drama/theater group, student-run newspaper, radio and television station, choral group, marching band, Campus Activity Board, Fellowship of Christian Athletes, Hope Fellowship, intramurals, Community Care, national fraternities, national sororities. *Campus security:* 24-hour emergency response devices and patrols, student patrols, late-night transport/escort service, controlled dormitory access. *Student services:* health clinic, personal/psychological counseling, women's center.
Athletics Member NCAA. All Division II. *Intercollegiate sports:* baseball M(s), basketball M(s)/W(s), cross-country running M(s)/W(s), football M(s), golf M(s)/W(s), soccer M(s)/W(s), softball M/W(s), swimming and diving M(s)/W(s), tennis W, track and field M(s)/W(s), volleyball W(s), wrestling M(s). *Intramural sports:* badminton M/W, baseball M(c), basketball M/W, bowling M/W, cross-country running M/W, field hockey M/W, football M, golf M/W, lacrosse M(c), racquetball M/W, rugby M(c)/W(c), skiing (downhill) M(c)/W(c), soccer M/W, softball M(c)/W(c), swimming and diving M/W, table tennis M/W, tennis M/W, track and field M/W, ultimate Frisbee M/W, volleyball M(c)/W(c), weight lifting M(c)/W(c), wrestling M.
Standardized Tests *Required:* SAT or ACT (for admission).
Costs (2011–12) *Comprehensive fee:* $37,934 includes full-time tuition ($27,654), mandatory fees ($928), and room and board ($9352). Full-time tuition and fees vary according to location and program. Part-time tuition: $848 per semester hour. Part-time tuition and fees vary according to course load, location, and program. *Required fees:* $23 per semester hour part-time. *College room only:* $5022. Room and board charges vary according to board plan and housing facility. *Payment plan:* installment. *Waivers:* children of alumni, senior citizens, and employees or children of employees.
Financial Aid Of all full-time matriculated undergraduates who enrolled in 2011, 2,332 applied for aid, 1,933 were judged to have need, 1,740 had their need fully met. 1,391 Federal Work-Study jobs (averaging $2604). In 2011, 223 non-need-based awards were made. *Average percent of need met:* 90%.

Average financial aid package: $24,904. *Average need-based loan:* $4823. *Average need-based gift aid:* $17,836. *Average non-need-based aid:* $10,292. *Average indebtedness upon graduation:* $39,399.
Applying *Options:* electronic application, deferred entrance. *Required:* high school transcript, minimum 2.5 GPA. *Application deadlines:* rolling (freshmen), rolling (out-of-state freshmen), rolling (transfers). *Notification:* continuous (freshmen), continuous (transfers).
Freshman Application Contact Mr. W.C. Vance, Director of Admission, Ashland University, 401 College Avenue, Ashland, OH 44805. *Phone:* 419-289-5052. *Toll-free phone:* 800-882-1548. *Fax:* 419-289-5999. *E-mail:* enrollme@ashland.edu. *Web site:* http://www.exploreashland.com/.

Baldwin-Wallace College
Berea, Ohio

- **Independent Methodist** comprehensive, founded 1845
- **Suburban** 120-acre campus with easy access to Cleveland
- **Endowment** $119.7 million
- **Coed** 3,518 undergraduate students, 86% full-time, 56% women, 44% men
- **Moderately difficult** entrance level, 63% of applicants were admitted

Undergraduates 3,018 full-time, 500 part-time. Students come from 38 states and territories; 13 other countries; 15% are from out of state; 8% Black or African American, non-Hispanic/Latino; 4% Hispanic/Latino; 0.9% Asian, non-Hispanic/Latino; 0.1% Native Hawaiian or other Pacific Islander, non-Hispanic/Latino; 0.1% American Indian or Alaska Native, non-Hispanic/Latino; 3% Two or more races, non-Hispanic/Latino; 0.6% Race/ethnicity unknown; 1% international; 6% transferred in; 60% live on campus. *Retention:* 81% of full-time freshmen returned.
Freshmen *Admission:* 3,748 applied, 2,372 admitted, 665 enrolled. *Average high school GPA:* 3.43. *Test scores:* SAT critical reading scores over 500: 65%; SAT math scores over 500: 64%; SAT writing scores over 500: 62%; ACT scores over 18: 93%; SAT critical reading scores over 600: 30%; SAT math scores over 600: 31%; SAT writing scores over 600: 23%; ACT scores over 24: 50%; SAT critical reading scores over 700: 5%; SAT math scores over 700: 5%; SAT writing scores over 700: 2%; ACT scores over 30: 7%.
Faculty *Total:* 397, 42% full-time, 43% with terminal degrees. *Student/faculty ratio:* 15:1.
Academics *Calendar:* semesters. *Degrees:* certificates, bachelor's, and master's. *Special study options:* academic remediation for entering students, accelerated degree program, adult/continuing education programs, advanced placement credit, distance learning, double majors, English as a second language, honors programs, independent study, internships, off-campus study, part-time degree program, services for LD students, student-designed majors, study abroad, summer session for credit. *ROTC:* Army (c), Air Force (c). *Unusual degree programs:* 3-2 engineering with Case Western Reserve University and Columbia University; social work with Case Western Reserve University; MBA programs in accounting, computer information systems, computer science, and human resources.
Computers on Campus 583 computers/terminals and 100 ports are available on campus for general student use. Students can access the following: campus intranet, computer help desk, free student e-mail accounts, online (class) grades, online (class) registration, online (class) schedules. Campuswide network is available. 100% of college-owned or -operated housing units are wired for high-speed Internet access. Wireless service is available via entire campus.
Student Life *Housing:* on-campus residence required through sophomore year. *Options:* coed, disabled students. Campus housing is university owned. Freshman campus housing is guaranteed. *Activities and organizations:* drama/theater group, student-run newspaper, radio and television station, choral group, marching band, Circle K, Student Senate, Dance Marathon, Campus Crusade, Black Student Alliance, national fraternities, national sororities. *Campus security:* 24-hour emergency response devices and patrols, student patrols, late-night transport/escort service, controlled dormitory access. *Student services:* health clinic, personal/psychological counseling, women's center.
Athletics Member NCAA. All Division III. *Intercollegiate sports:* baseball M, basketball M/W, cross-country running M/W, football M, golf M/W, soccer M/W, softball W, swimming and diving M/W, tennis M/W, track and field M/W, volleyball W, wrestling M. *Intramural sports:* archery M(c)/W(c), badminton M/W, basketball M/W, cheerleading W(c), crew M(c)/W(c), fencing M(c)/W(c), football M/W, golf M/W, gymnastics W(c), lacrosse M(c)/W(c), racquetball M/W, skiing (cross-country) M(c)/W(c), skiing (downhill) M(c)/W(c), soccer M/W, softball M/W, table tennis M(c)/W(c), tennis M/W, volleyball M/W, water polo M(c)/W(c), wrestling M.
Standardized Tests *Required for some:* SAT or ACT (for admission).
Costs (2011–12) *Comprehensive fee:* $33,742 includes full-time tuition ($26,396) and room and board ($7346). Full-time tuition and fees vary according to class time, course level, course load, degree level, program, and reciprocity agreements. Part-time tuition: $820 per semester hour. Part-time tuition

and fees vary according to class time, course level, course load, degree level, program, and reciprocity agreements. *College room only:* $4240. *Payment plans:* installment, deferred payment. *Waivers:* children of alumni and employees or children of employees.

Financial Aid Of all full-time matriculated undergraduates who enrolled in 2011, 2,671 applied for aid, 2,497 were judged to have need, 760 had their need fully met. 900 Federal Work-Study jobs (averaging $750). 400 state and other part-time jobs (averaging $500). In 2011, 502 non-need-based awards were made. *Average percent of need met:* 86%. *Average financial aid package:* $21,623. *Average need-based loan:* $4267. *Average need-based gift aid:* $15,696. *Average non-need-based aid:* $9585. *Average indebtedness upon graduation:* $31,241. *Financial aid deadline:* 9/1.

Applying *Options:* electronic application, deferred entrance. *Application fee:* $25. *Required:* essay or personal statement, high school transcript, 1 letter of recommendation. *Recommended:* minimum 3.2 GPA, interview. *Application deadlines:* 3/1 (freshmen), 8/1 (transfers). *Notification:* continuous (freshmen), continuous (transfers).

Freshman Application Contact Patricia Skrha, Director of Undergraduate Admission, Baldwin-Wallace College, Bonds Administration Building, 275 Eastland Road, Berea, OH 44017. *Phone:* 440-826-2222. *Toll-free phone:* 877-BW-APPLY. *Fax:* 440-826-3830. *E-mail:* admission@bw.edu. *Web site:* http://www.bw.edu/.

See below for display ad and page 1158 for the College Close-Up.

Bluffton University

Bluffton, Ohio

- **Independent Mennonite** comprehensive, founded 1899
- **Small-town** 65-acre campus with easy access to Toledo
- **Endowment** $19.5 million
- **Coed** 1,115 undergraduate students, 80% full-time, 54% women, 46% men
- **Moderately difficult** entrance level, 64% of applicants were admitted

Undergraduates 895 full-time, 220 part-time. Students come from 20 states and territories; 9 other countries; 25% are from out of state; 8% Black or African American, non-Hispanic/Latino; 3% Hispanic/Latino; 0.3% Asian, non-Hispanic/Latino; 0.2% American Indian or Alaska Native, non-Hispanic/Latino; 1% Two or more races, non-Hispanic/Latino; 3% Race/ethnicity unknown; 1% international; 3% transferred in; 95% live on campus. *Retention:* 64% of full-time freshmen returned.

Freshmen *Admission:* 1,915 applied, 1,226 admitted, 250 enrolled. *Average high school GPA:* 3.3. *Test scores:* SAT critical reading scores over 500: 55%; SAT math scores over 500: 50%; ACT scores over 18: 89%; SAT critical reading scores over 600: 11%; SAT math scores over 600: 15%; ACT scores over 24: 29%; SAT critical reading scores over 700: 2%; ACT scores over 30: 3%.

Faculty *Total:* 112, 56% full-time, 55% with terminal degrees. *Student/faculty ratio:* 13:1.

Academics *Calendar:* semesters. *Degrees:* bachelor's and master's. *Special study options:* academic remediation for entering students, accelerated degree program, adult/continuing education programs, advanced placement credit, distance learning, double majors, honors programs, independent study, internships, off-campus study, part-time degree program, services for LD students, student-designed majors, study abroad, summer session for credit.

Computers on Campus 170 computers/terminals and 1,300 ports are available on campus for general student use. Students can access the following: campus intranet, computer help desk, free student e-mail accounts, online (class) grades, online (class) registration, online (class) schedules. Campus-wide network is available. 100% of college-owned or -operated housing units are wired for high-speed Internet access. Wireless service is available via classrooms, computer centers, computer labs, dorm rooms, libraries, student centers.

Student Life *Housing:* on-campus residence required through senior year. *Options:* coed, men-only, women-only. Campus housing is university owned. Freshman campus housing is guaranteed. *Activities and organizations:* drama/theater group, student-run newspaper, radio station, choral group, Brothers and Sisters in Christ, Campus Government, Student Union Board, music groups/chorale, chapel service. *Campus security:* 24-hour emergency response devices, controlled dormitory access, night security guards. *Student services:* health clinic, personal/psychological counseling.

Athletics Member NCAA. All Division III. *Intercollegiate sports:* baseball M, basketball M/W, cheerleading W, cross-country running M/W, football M, soccer M/W, softball W, tennis M/W, track and field M/W, volleyball W. *Intramural sports:* basketball M/W, bowling M/W, football M/W, softball M/W, ultimate Frisbee M, volleyball M/W.

Standardized Tests *Required:* SAT or ACT (for admission).

Costs (2012–13) *Comprehensive fee:* $36,436 includes full-time tuition ($26,976), mandatory fees ($450), and room and board ($9010). Full-time tuition and fees vary according to course load and reciprocity agreements. Part-time tuition: $1124 per credit hour. Part-time tuition and fees vary according to course load. *Required fees:* $113 per term part-time. *Room and board:* Room

and board charges vary according to board plan and housing facility. *Payment plan:* installment. *Waivers:* employees or children of employees.

Financial Aid Of all full-time matriculated undergraduates who enrolled in 2011, 736 applied for aid, 704 were judged to have need, 326 had their need fully met. 624 Federal Work-Study jobs (averaging $2316). 157 state and other part-time jobs (averaging $2439). In 2011, 73 non-need-based awards were made. *Average percent of need met:* 90%. *Average financial aid package:* $24,242. *Average need-based loan:* $5014. *Average need-based gift aid:* $17,215. *Average non-need-based aid:* $11,919. *Average indebtedness upon graduation:* $34,225. *Financial aid deadline:* 10/1.

Applying *Options:* electronic application, deferred entrance. *Application fee:* $20. *Required:* high school transcript, minimum 2.3 GPA, 1 letter of recommendation, rank in upper 50% of high school class or 19 on ACT. *Required for some:* essay or personal statement. *Recommended:* interview. *Application deadlines:* 8/15 (freshmen), rolling (transfers). *Notification:* continuous (freshmen), continuous (transfers).

Freshman Application Contact Mr. Chris Jebsen, Director of Admissions, Bluffton University, 1 University Drive, Bluffton, OH 45817. *Phone:* 419-358-3254. *Toll-free phone:* 800-488-3257. *Fax:* 419-358-3081. *E-mail:* admissions@bluffton.edu. *Web site:* http://www.bluffton.edu/.

Bowling Green State University

Bowling Green, Ohio

- **State-supported** university, founded 1910
- **Small-town** 1338-acre campus with easy access to Toledo
- **Endowment** $141.6 million
- **Coed** 15,064 undergraduate students, 92% full-time, 55% women, 45% men
- **Moderately difficult** entrance level, 76% of applicants were admitted

Undergraduates 13,891 full-time, 1,173 part-time. Students come from 52 states and territories; 35 other countries; 11% are from out of state; 11% Black or African American, non-Hispanic/Latino; 4% Hispanic/Latino; 1% Asian, non-Hispanic/Latino; 0.1% Native Hawaiian or other Pacific Islander, non-Hispanic/Latino; 0.4% American Indian or Alaska Native, non-Hispanic/Latino; 1% Two or more races, non-Hispanic/Latino; 3% Race/ethnicity unknown; 2% international; 4% transferred in; 45% live on campus. *Retention:* 72% of full-time freshmen returned.

Freshmen *Admission:* 16,217 applied, 12,251 admitted, 3,861 enrolled. *Average high school GPA:* 3.2. *Test scores:* SAT critical reading scores over 500: 53%; SAT math scores over 500: 51%; SAT writing scores over 500: 44%; ACT scores over 18: 90%; SAT critical reading scores over 600: 16%; SAT math scores over 600: 16%; SAT writing scores over 600: 11%; ACT scores over 24: 33%; SAT critical reading scores over 700: 2%; SAT math scores over 700: 1%; SAT writing scores over 700: 2%; ACT scores over 30: 3%.

Faculty *Total:* 1,087, 76% full-time. *Student/faculty ratio:* 18:1.

Academics *Calendar:* semesters. *Degrees:* bachelor's, master's, doctoral, post-master's, postbachelor's, and first professional certificates. *Special study options:* academic remediation for entering students, accelerated degree program, adult/continuing education programs, advanced placement credit, cooperative education, distance learning, double majors, English as a second language, honors programs, independent study, internships, off-campus study, part-time degree program, services for LD students, student-designed majors, study abroad, summer session for credit. *ROTC:* Army (b), Air Force (b).

Computers on Campus 1,500 computers/terminals and 500 ports are available on campus for general student use. Students can access the following: computer help desk, free student e-mail accounts, online (class) grades, online (class) registration, online (class) schedules, wireless networking, ePortfolio, MyFiles, Bursar billing information and payment, online mid-term grade reporting, view and change personal information, order official and unofficial transcripts, check meal plan balance, apply for graduation. Campuswide network is available. 100% of college-owned or -operated housing units are wired for high-speed Internet access. Wireless service is available via classrooms, computer centers, computer labs, dorm rooms, learning centers, libraries, student centers.

Student Life *Housing:* on-campus residence required through sophomore year. *Options:* coed, disabled students. Campus housing is university owned. Freshman campus housing is guaranteed. *Activities and organizations:* drama/theater group, student-run newspaper, radio station, choral group, marching band, Dance Marathon, University Activities Organization, BG Undead, Men's Rugby, Black Student Union, national fraternities, national sororities. *Campus security:* 24-hour emergency response devices and patrols, student patrols, late-night transport/escort service, controlled dormitory access. *Student services:* health clinic, personal/psychological counseling, women's center, legal services.

Athletics Member NCAA. All Division I. *Intercollegiate sports:* baseball M(s), basketball M(s)/W(s), cross-country running M(s)/W(s), football M(s),

golf M(s)/W(s), gymnastics W(s), ice hockey M(s), soccer M(s)/W(s), softball W(s), swimming and diving W(s), tennis W(s), track and field W(s), volleyball W(s). *Intramural sports:* badminton M/W, baseball M, basketball M/W, bowling M(c)/W(c), cross-country running M(c)/W(c), equestrian sports M(c)/W(c), football M/W, golf M/W, gymnastics M(c)/W(c), ice hockey M(c), lacrosse M(c)/W(c), racquetball M/W, rugby M(c)/W(c), sailing M(c)/W(c), skiing (downhill) M(c)/W(c), soccer M/W, softball W, swimming and diving M(c)/W(c), tennis M(c)/W, track and field M(c)/W, ultimate Frisbee M/W, volleyball M/W, water polo M/W, wrestling M(c)/W(c).

Standardized Tests *Required:* SAT or ACT (for admission).

Costs (2011–12) *Tuition:* state resident $8614 full-time, $359 per credit hour part-time; nonresident $15,922 full-time, $664 per credit hour part-time. Full-time tuition and fees vary according to course load and location. Part-time tuition and fees vary according to course load and location. *Required fees:* $1430 full-time, $59 per credit hour part-time. *Room and board:* $7794. Room and board charges vary according to board plan and housing facility. *Payment plan:* installment. *Waivers:* senior citizens and employees or children of employees.

Financial Aid Of all full-time matriculated undergraduates who enrolled in 2010, 10,941 applied for aid, 9,727 were judged to have need, 940 had their need fully met. 827 Federal Work-Study jobs (averaging $1177). In 2010, 1922 non-need-based awards were made. *Average percent of need met:* 73%. *Average financial aid package:* $13,973. *Average need-based loan:* $7485. *Average need-based gift aid:* $6502. *Average non-need-based aid:* $3896. *Average indebtedness upon graduation:* $33,083.

Applying *Options:* electronic application, deferred entrance. *Application fee:* $45. *Required:* high school transcript. *Required for some:* interview. *Application deadlines:* 7/15 (freshmen), 7/15 (out-of-state freshmen), 7/15 (transfers). *Notification:* continuous (freshmen), continuous (out-of-state freshmen), continuous (transfers).

Freshman Application Contact Mr. Gary Swegan, Assistant Vice President/Director of Admissions, Bowling Green State University, Admissions Office, 110 McFall, Bowling Green, OH 43403. *Phone:* 419-372-BGSU. *Fax:* 419-372-6955. *E-mail:* choosebgsu@bgsu.edu. *Web site:* http://www.bgsu.edu/.

Bowling Green State University-Firelands College

Huron, Ohio

Freshman Application Contact Debralee Divers, Director of Admissions and Financial Aid, Bowling Green State University-Firelands College, One University Drive, Huron, OH 44839-9791. *Phone:* 419-433-5560. *Toll-free phone:* 800-322-4787. *Fax:* 419-372-0604. *E-mail:* divers@bgsu.edu. *Web site:* http://www.firelands.bgsu.edu/.

Brown Mackie College–Akron

Akron, Ohio

- **Proprietary** 2-year, founded 1968, part of Education Management Corporation
- **Suburban** campus
- **Coed**

Academics *Calendar:* quarters. *Degree:* certificates, diplomas, and associate.

Costs (2011–12) *Tuition:* Tuition varies by program. Students should contact Brown Mackie College for tuition information.

Freshman Application Contact Brown Mackie College–Akron, 755 White Pond Drive, Suite 101, Akron, OH 44320. *Phone:* 330-869-3600. *Web site:* http://www.brownmackie.edu/akron/.

See page 1186 for the College Close-Up.

Brown Mackie College–Cincinnati

Cincinnati, Ohio

- **Proprietary** 2-year, founded 1927, part of Education Management Corporation
- **Suburban** campus
- **Coed**

Academics *Calendar:* quarters. *Degree:* certificates, diplomas, and associate.

Costs (2011–12) *Tuition:* Tuition varies by program. Students should contact Brown Mackie College for tuition information.

Freshman Application Contact Brown Mackie College–Cincinnati, 1011 Glendale-Milford Road, Cincinnati, OH 45215. *Phone:* 513-771-2424. *Toll-free phone:* 800-888-1445. *Web site:* http://www.brownmackie.edu/cincinnati/

See page 1194 for the College Close-Up.

Brown Mackie College–Findlay
Findlay, Ohio

- **Proprietary** 2-year, founded 1929, part of Education Management Corporation
- **Rural** campus
- **Coed**

Academics *Calendar:* continuous. *Degree:* diplomas and associate.

Costs (2011–12) *Tuition:* Tuition varies by program. Students should contact Brown Mackie College for tuition information.

Freshman Application Contact Brown Mackie College–Findlay, 1700 Fostoria Avenue, Suite 100, Findlay, OH 45840. *Phone:* 419-423-2211. *Toll-free phone:* 800-842-3687. *Web site:* http://www.brownmackie.edu/findlay/.

See page 1198 for the College Close-Up.

Brown Mackie College–North Canton
Canton, Ohio

- **Proprietary** 2-year, founded 1929, part of Education Management Corporation
- **Suburban** campus
- **Coed**

Academics *Calendar:* quarters. *Degree:* diplomas and associate.

Costs (2011–12) *Tuition:* Tuition varies by program. Students should contact Brown Mackie College for tuition information.

Freshman Application Contact Brown Mackie College–North Canton, 4300 Munson Street NW, Canton, OH 44718-3674. *Phone:* 330-494-1214. *Web site:* http://www.brownmackie.edu/northcanton/.

See page 1214 for the College Close-Up.

Bryant & Stratton College
Cleveland, Ohio

Freshman Application Contact Bryant & Stratton College, Cleveland, OH 44114-3203. *Phone:* 216-771-1700. *Fax:* 216-771-7787. *Web site:* http://www.bryantstratton.edu/.

Bryant & Stratton College - Eastlake Campus
Eastlake, Ohio

Freshman Application Contact Ms. Melanie Pettit, Director of Admissions, Bryant & Stratton College - Eastlake Campus, 35350 Curtis Boulevard, Eastlake, OH 44095. *Phone:* 440-510-1112. *Web site:* http://www.bryantstratton.edu/.

Bryant & Stratton College - Parma Campus
Parma, Ohio

Freshman Application Contact Bryant & Stratton College - Parma Campus, 12955 Snow Road, Parma, OH 44130-1013. *Phone:* 216-265-3151. *Toll-free phone:* 866-948-0571. *Web site:* http://www.bryantstratton.edu/.

Capital University
Columbus, Ohio

- **Independent** comprehensive, founded 1830, affiliated with Evangelical Lutheran Church in America
- **Suburban** 48-acre campus with easy access to Columbus
- **Endowment** $61.9 million
- **Coed** 2,682 undergraduate students, 89% full-time, 59% women, 41% men
- **Moderately difficult** entrance level, 76% of applicants were admitted

Undergraduates 2,397 full-time, 285 part-time. Students come from 33 states and territories; 15 other countries; 9% are from out of state; 9% Black or African American, non-Hispanic/Latino; 3% Hispanic/Latino; 1% Asian, non-Hispanic/Latino; 0.2% Native Hawaiian or other Pacific Islander, non-Hispanic/Latino; 0.2% American Indian or Alaska Native, non-Hispanic/Latino; 3% Two or more races, non-Hispanic/Latino; 3% Race/ethnicity unknown; 1% international; 3% transferred in; 54% live on campus. *Retention:* 74% of full-time freshmen returned.

Freshmen *Admission:* 3,631 applied, 2,760 admitted, 626 enrolled. *Average high school GPA:* 3.45. *Test scores:* SAT critical reading scores over 500:

71%; SAT math scores over 500: 70%; SAT writing scores over 500: 62%; ACT scores over 18: 98%; SAT critical reading scores over 600: 30%; SAT math scores over 600: 23%; SAT writing scores over 600: 19%; ACT scores over 24: 55%; SAT critical reading scores over 700: 2%; SAT math scores over 700: 1%; SAT writing scores over 700: 1%; ACT scores over 30: 10%.

Faculty *Total:* 429, 44% full-time, 49% with terminal degrees. *Student/faculty ratio:* 11:1.

Academics *Calendar:* semesters. *Degrees:* bachelor's, master's, and doctoral. *Special study options:* accelerated degree program, adult/continuing education programs, advanced placement credit, cooperative education, double majors, English as a second language, external degree program, freshman honors college, honors programs, independent study, internships, off-campus study, part-time degree program, services for LD students, student-designed majors, study abroad, summer session for credit. *ROTC:* Army (b), Air Force (c). *Unusual degree programs:* 3-2 engineering with Washington University in St. Louis, Case Western Reserve University; occupational therapy with Washington University in St. Louis, University of Indianapolis.

Computers on Campus 397 computers/terminals and 1,350 ports are available on campus for general student use. Students can access the following: campus intranet, computer help desk, free student e-mail accounts, online (class) grades, online (class) registration, online (class) schedules. Campus-wide network is available. 100% of college-owned or -operated housing units are wired for high-speed Internet access. Wireless service is available via entire campus.

Student Life *Housing:* on-campus residence required through sophomore year. *Options:* coed, disabled students. Campus housing is university owned. Freshman campus housing is guaranteed. *Activities and organizations:* drama/theater group, student-run newspaper, radio station, choral group, Campus Crusade for Christ, student government, University Programming, College Republicans, American Marketing Association, national fraternities, national sororities. *Campus security:* 24-hour emergency response devices and patrols, late-night transport/escort service, controlled dormitory access. *Student services:* health clinic, personal/psychological counseling.

Athletics Member NCAA. All Division III. *Intercollegiate sports:* baseball M, basketball M/W, cross-country running M/W, football M, golf M/W, soccer M/W, softball W, tennis M/W, track and field M/W, volleyball W. *Intramural sports:* basketball M/W, bowling M/W, cheerleading M(c)/W(c), football M/W, lacrosse M(c)/W(c), skiing (downhill) M(c)/W(c), softball M/W, swimming and diving M(c)/W(c), volleyball M/W.

Standardized Tests *Required:* SAT or ACT (for admission).

Costs (2011–12) *Comprehensive fee:* $38,630 includes full-time tuition ($30,450) and room and board ($8180). Full-time tuition and fees vary according to course load. Part-time tuition: $1015 per credit hour. Part-time tuition and fees vary according to course load. *Room and board:* Room and board charges vary according to board plan and housing facility. *Payment plan:* installment. *Waivers:* senior citizens and employees or children of employees.

Financial Aid Of all full-time matriculated undergraduates who enrolled in 2010, 2,096 applied for aid, 1,959 were judged to have need, 799 had their need fully met. In 2010, 435 non-need-based awards were made. *Average percent of need met:* 88%. *Average financial aid package:* $25,328. *Average need-based loan:* $3991. *Average need-based gift aid:* $5665. *Average non-need-based aid:* $14,000. *Average indebtedness upon graduation:* $34,225.

Applying *Options:* electronic application, deferred entrance. *Application fee:* $25. *Required:* high school transcript, minimum 2.6 GPA. *Required for some:* 1 letter of recommendation, audition for Conservatory of Music. *Recommended:* interview. *Application deadlines:* 5/1 (freshmen), rolling (transfers). *Notification:* 9/30 (freshmen), continuous (transfers).

Freshman Application Contact Ms. Amanda Steiner, Director of Admission, Capital University, 1 College and Main, Columbus, OH 43209. *Phone:* 614-236-6574. *Toll-free phone:* 866-544-6175. *Fax:* 614-236-6926. *E-mail:* asteiner@capital.edu. *Web site:* http://www.capital.edu/.

Case Western Reserve University
Cleveland, Ohio

- **Independent** university, founded 1826
- **Urban** 155-acre campus
- **Endowment** $1.7 billion
- **Coed** 4,016 undergraduate students, 97% full-time, 44% women, 56% men
- **Very difficult** entrance level, 51% of applicants were admitted

Undergraduates 3,895 full-time, 121 part-time. Students come from 47 states and territories; 30 other countries; 54% are from out of state; 5% Black or African American, non-Hispanic/Latino; 3% Hispanic/Latino; 17% Asian, non-Hispanic/Latino; 0.1% Native Hawaiian or other Pacific Islander, non-Hispanic/Latino; 0.2% American Indian or Alaska Native, non-Hispanic/Latino; 2% Two or more races, non-Hispanic/Latino; 12% Race/ethnicity unknown;

7% international; 1% transferred in; 79% live on campus. *Retention:* 93% of full-time freshmen returned.

Freshmen *Admission:* 13,543 applied, 6,944 admitted, 902 enrolled. *Test scores:* SAT critical reading scores over 500: 94%; SAT math scores over 500: 100%; SAT writing scores over 500: 99%; ACT scores over 18: 100%; SAT critical reading scores over 600: 73%; SAT math scores over 600: 91%; SAT writing scores over 600: 74%; ACT scores over 24: 100%; SAT critical reading scores over 700: 26%; SAT math scores over 700: 51%; SAT writing scores over 700: 25%; ACT scores over 30: 61%.

Faculty *Total:* 956, 79% full-time, 87% with terminal degrees. *Student/faculty ratio:* 9:1.

Academics *Calendar:* semesters. *Degrees:* bachelor's, master's, doctoral, postbachelor's, and first professional certificates. *Special study options:* accelerated degree program, adult/continuing education programs, advanced placement credit, cooperative education, double majors, English as a second language, honors programs, independent study, internships, off-campus study, part-time degree program, services for LD students, student-designed majors, study abroad, summer session for credit. *ROTC:* Army (c), Air Force (c). *Unusual degree programs:* 3-2 engineering.

Computers on Campus 219 computers/terminals and 1,000 ports are available on campus for general student use. Students can access the following: campus intranet, computer help desk, free student e-mail accounts, online (class) grades, online (class) registration, online (class) schedules, software library, online reference databases, electronic books and journals, research computing, training. Campuswide network is available. 100% of college-owned or -operated housing units are wired for high-speed Internet access. Wireless service is available via entire campus.

Student Life *Housing:* on-campus residence required through sophomore year. *Options:* coed. Campus housing is university owned. Freshman campus housing is guaranteed. *Activities and organizations:* drama/theater group, student-run newspaper, radio station, choral group, marching band, student radio station, Habitat for Humanity, international student groups, music/dance groups, Alpha Phi Omega (national service organization), national fraternities, national sororities. *Campus security:* 24-hour emergency response devices and patrols, student patrols, late-night transport/escort service, controlled dormitory access, crime prevention programs. *Student services:* health clinic, personal/psychological counseling, women's center, legal services.

Athletics Member NCAA. All Division III. *Intercollegiate sports:* archery M(c)/W(c), baseball M, basketball M/W, cheerleading M(c)/W(c), crew M(c)/W(c), cross-country running M/W, fencing M(c)/W(c), football M, ice hockey M(c)/W(c), soccer M/W, softball W, swimming and diving M/W, tennis M/W, track and field M/W, ultimate Frisbee M(c)/W(c), volleyball M(c)/W(c), wrestling M. *Intramural sports:* badminton M/W, basketball M/W, bowling M/W, cross-country running M/W, football M/W, golf M/W, racquetball M/W, soccer M/W, softball M/W, squash M/W, swimming and diving M/W, table tennis M/W, tennis M/W, track and field M/W, ultimate Frisbee M/W, volleyball M/W, water polo M/W, weight lifting M/W, wrestling M.

Standardized Tests *Required:* SAT or ACT (for admission).

Costs (2011–12) *One-time required fee:* $450. *Comprehensive fee:* $51,058 includes full-time tuition ($38,760), mandatory fees ($360), and room and board ($11,938). Part-time tuition: $1615 per credit hour. Part-time tuition and fees vary according to course load. *College room only:* $6870. Room and board charges vary according to board plan, housing facility, and student level. *Payment plan:* installment. *Waivers:* employees or children of employees.

Financial Aid Of all full-time matriculated undergraduates who enrolled in 2011, 2,688 applied for aid, 2,426 were judged to have need, 1,994 had their need fully met. 1,633 Federal Work-Study jobs (averaging $3089). In 2011, 753 non-need-based awards were made. *Average percent of need met:* 81%. *Average financial aid package:* $33,200. *Average need-based loan:* $7577. *Average need-based gift aid:* $24,639. *Average non-need-based aid:* $18,976. *Average indebtedness upon graduation:* $39,886.

Applying *Options:* electronic application, early admission, early action, deferred entrance. *Required:* essay or personal statement, high school transcript, 1 letter of recommendation. *Recommended:* interview. *Application deadlines:* 1/15 (freshmen), 5/15 (transfers), 11/1 (early action). *Notification:* 3/20 (freshmen), continuous until 7/1 (transfers), 12/15 (early action).

Freshman Application Contact Mr. Robert McCullough, Director of Undergraduate Admission, Case Western Reserve University, 10900 Euclid Avenue, Cleveland, OH 44106. *Phone:* 216-368-4450. *Fax:* 216-368-5111. *E-mail:* admission@case.edu. *Web site:* http://www.case.edu/.

See page 1248 for the College Close-Up.

Cedarville University
Cedarville, Ohio

- **Independent Baptist** comprehensive, founded 1887
- **Rural** 400-acre campus with easy access to Columbus, Dayton
- **Endowment** $20.3 million
- **Coed** 3,220 undergraduate students, 94% full-time, 54% women, 46% men
- **Moderately difficult** entrance level, 75% of applicants were admitted

Undergraduates 3,021 full-time, 199 part-time. Students come from 49 states and territories; 16 other countries; 64% are from out of state; 2% Black or African American, non-Hispanic/Latino; 2% Hispanic/Latino; 1% Asian, non-Hispanic/Latino; 0.1% Native Hawaiian or other Pacific Islander, non-Hispanic/Latino; 0.3% American Indian or Alaska Native, non-Hispanic/Latino; 0.5% Two or more races, non-Hispanic/Latino; 4% Race/ethnicity unknown; 1% international; 3% transferred in; 77% live on campus. *Retention:* 85% of full-time freshmen returned.

Freshmen *Admission:* 3,143 applied, 2,369 admitted, 851 enrolled. *Average high school GPA:* 3.64. *Test scores:* SAT critical reading scores over 500: 89%; SAT math scores over 500: 84%; SAT writing scores over 500: 81%; ACT scores over 18: 100%; SAT critical reading scores over 600: 47%; SAT math scores over 600: 48%; SAT writing scores over 600: 40%; ACT scores over 24: 76%; SAT critical reading scores over 700: 13%; SAT math scores over 700: 10%; SAT writing scores over 700: 10%; ACT scores over 30: 19%.

Faculty *Total:* 311, 69% full-time, 47% with terminal degrees. *Student/faculty ratio:* 13:1.

Academics *Calendar:* semesters. *Degrees:* certificates, bachelor's, and master's. *Special study options:* academic remediation for entering students, accelerated degree program, adult/continuing education programs, advanced placement credit, distance learning, double majors, honors programs, independent study, internships, off-campus study, part-time degree program, services for LD students, study abroad, summer session for credit. *ROTC:* Army (c), Air Force (c).

Computers on Campus 3,000 computers/terminals are available on campus for general student use. Students can access the following: campus intranet, computer help desk, free student e-mail accounts, online (class) grades, online (class) registration, online (class) schedules, over 150 software packages. Campuswide network is available. Wireless service is available via entire campus.

Student Life *Housing:* on-campus residence required through senior year. *Options:* men-only, women-only, disabled students. Campus housing is university owned. Freshman campus housing is guaranteed. *Activities and organizations:* drama/theater group, student-run newspaper, radio station, choral group, Students in Free Enterprise, Christian Pharmacist Association, Society of Automotive Engineers - SAE, Christian Nursing Association, Cedarville Men's Rugby. *Campus security:* 24-hour emergency response devices and patrols, student patrols, late-night transport/escort service, controlled dormitory access. *Student services:* health clinic, personal/psychological counseling.

Athletics Member NCCAA. *Intercollegiate sports:* baseball M(s), basketball M(s)/W(s), cheerleading M/W, cross-country running M(s)/W(s), golf M(s), soccer M(s)/W(s), softball W(s), tennis M(s)/W(s), track and field M(s)/W(s), volleyball W(s). *Intramural sports:* badminton M/W, basketball M/W, bowling M/W, cross-country running M/W, football M/W, golf M/W, racquetball M/W, rock climbing M/W, skiing (downhill) M/W, soccer M/W, softball M/W, table tennis M/W, tennis M/W, ultimate Frisbee M/W, volleyball M/W.

Standardized Tests *Required:* SAT or ACT (for admission). *Recommended:* SAT and SAT Subject Tests or ACT (for admission).

Costs (2012–13) *Comprehensive fee:* $31,036 includes full-time tuition ($25,496) and room and board ($5540). Part-time tuition: $965 per credit. Part-time tuition and fees vary according to course load. *College room only:* $3140. Room and board charges vary according to board plan. *Payment plan:* installment. *Waivers:* senior citizens and employees or children of employees.

Financial Aid Of all full-time matriculated undergraduates who enrolled in 2011, 2,324 applied for aid, 2,011 were judged to have need, 377 had their need fully met. 606 Federal Work-Study jobs (averaging $459). 1,631 state and other part-time jobs (averaging $1065). In 2011, 427 non-need-based awards were made. *Average percent of need met:* 38%. *Average financial aid package:* $21,547. *Average need-based loan:* $5382. *Average need-based gift aid:* $4424. *Average non-need-based aid:* $14,233. *Average indebtedness upon graduation:* $27,279.

Applying *Options:* electronic application, early admission, deferred entrance. *Application fee:* $30. *Required:* essay or personal statement, high school transcript, minimum 3.0 GPA, 2 letters of recommendation, Clear testimony of faith in Jesus Christ and evidence of consistent Christian lifestyle. *Required for some:* interview. *Application deadlines:* rolling (freshmen), rolling (transfers). *Notification:* continuous (freshmen), continuous (transfers).

Freshman Application Contact Mr. Mark Weinstein, Director of Admissions, Cedarville University, 251 North Main Street, Cedarville, OH 45314-0601. *Phone:* 937-766-7700. *Toll-free phone:* 800-CEDARVILLE. *Fax:* 937-766-7575. *E-mail:* admiss@cedarville.edu. *Web site:* http://www.cedarville.edu/.

Central State University
Wilberforce, Ohio

- **State-supported** comprehensive, founded 1887, part of Ohio Board of Regents
- **Rural** 60-acre campus with easy access to Dayton
- **Coed** 2,458 undergraduate students, 92% full-time, 51% women, 49% men
- **Minimally difficult** entrance level, 22% of applicants were admitted

Undergraduates 2,255 full-time, 203 part-time. Students come from 32 states and territories; 3 other countries; 42% are from out of state; 95% Black or African American, non-Hispanic/Latino; 0.7% Hispanic/Latino; 0.1% Asian, non-Hispanic/Latino; 0.2% American Indian or Alaska Native, non-Hispanic/Latino; 0.3% Two or more races, non-Hispanic/Latino; 2% Race/ethnicity unknown; 0.2% international; 8% transferred in; 59% live on campus. *Retention:* 55% of full-time freshmen returned.

Freshmen *Admission:* 8,637 applied, 1,934 admitted, 722 enrolled. *Average high school GPA:* 2.4. *Test scores:* SAT critical reading scores over 500: 8%; SAT math scores over 500: 6%; ACT scores over 18: 24%; SAT critical reading scores over 600: 1%; ACT scores over 24: 2%.

Faculty *Total:* 224, 49% full-time, 38% with terminal degrees. *Student/faculty ratio:* 16:1.

Academics *Calendar:* semesters. *Degrees:* bachelor's and master's. *Special study options:* adult/continuing education programs, cooperative education, double majors, honors programs, independent study, internships, off-campus study, part-time degree program, services for LD students, study abroad, summer session for credit. *ROTC:* Army (b).

Computers on Campus 555 computers/terminals and 160 ports are available on campus for general student use. Students can access the following: campus intranet, computer help desk, free student e-mail accounts, online (class) grades, online (class) registration, online (class) schedules. Campuswide network is available. 100% of college-owned or -operated housing units are wired for high-speed Internet access. Wireless service is available via classrooms, computer centers, computer labs, dorm rooms, learning centers, libraries, student centers.

Student Life *Housing:* on-campus residence required for freshman year. *Options:* coed, men-only, women-only. Campus housing is university owned and leased by the school. Freshman campus housing is guaranteed. *Activities and organizations:* drama/theater group, student-run newspaper, radio and television station, choral group, marching band, Student Ambassadors, student government, Make it Happen (Inter-Faith), Daughters of Nia Anaya (Social Group), Evolutions (Modeling Troupe), national fraternities, national sororities. *Campus security:* 24-hour emergency response devices and patrols, controlled dormitory access. *Student services:* health clinic, personal/psychological counseling.

Athletics Member NCAA. All Division II. *Intercollegiate sports:* basketball M(s)/W(s), cheerleading M(s)/W(s), cross-country running M(s)/W(s), golf M(s)/W(s), tennis M(s)/W(s), track and field M(s)/W(s), volleyball W(s). *Intramural sports:* basketball M/W, bowling M/W, softball M/W, tennis M/W.

Standardized Tests *Required:* SAT or ACT (for admission). *Recommended:* ACT (for admission).

Costs (2011–12) *Tuition:* state resident $3430 full-time, $234 per credit hour part-time; nonresident $10,406 full-time, $547 per credit hour part-time. Full-time tuition and fees vary according to course load. Part-time tuition and fees vary according to course load. *Required fees:* $2242 full-time. *Room and board:* $8484; room only: $4560. Room and board charges vary according to board plan. *Payment plans:* installment, deferred payment. *Waivers:* senior citizens and employees or children of employees.

Financial Aid Of all full-time matriculated undergraduates who enrolled in 2008, 1,899 applied for aid, 1,799 were judged to have need. 408 Federal Work-Study jobs (averaging $1720). In 2008, 33 non-need-based awards were made. *Average non-need-based aid:* $5125.

Applying *Options:* electronic application. *Application fee:* $20. *Required:* high school transcript. *Required for some:* essay or personal statement, minimum 2.0 GPA, 2 letters of recommendation, 2.5 high school GPA for nonresidents. *Recommended:* interview. *Application deadlines:* 6/15 (freshmen), 6/15 (transfers). *Notification:* continuous (freshmen), continuous (transfers).

Freshman Application Contact Ms. Robin Rucker, Director, Admissions, Central State University, PO Box 1004, 1400 Blush Row Road, Wilberforce, OH 45384. *Phone:* 937-376-6580. *Toll-free phone:* 800-388-CSU1 (in-state); 800-388-2781 (out-of-state). *Fax:* 937-376-6648. *E-mail:* admissions@centralstate.edu. *Web site:* http://www.centralstate.edu/.

Chamberlain College of Nursing
Columbus, Ohio

- **Proprietary** 4-year
- **Coed** 610 undergraduate students, 44% full-time, 89% women, 11% men

Undergraduates 267 full-time, 343 part-time. 1% are from out of state; 10% Black or African American, non-Hispanic/Latino; 2% Hispanic/Latino; 2% Asian, non-Hispanic/Latino; 0.7% American Indian or Alaska Native, non-Hispanic/Latino; 2% Two or more races, non-Hispanic/Latino; 42% transferred in.
Freshmen *Admission:* 14 enrolled.
Faculty *Total:* 86, 21% full-time. *Student/faculty ratio:* 9:1.
Academics *Calendar:* semesters.
Standardized Tests *Required:* SAT or ACT (for admission).
Freshman Application Contact Admissions, Chamberlain College of Nursing, 1350 Alum Creek Drive, Columbus, OH 43209. *Phone:* 614-252-8890. *Toll-free phone:* 888-556-8CCN. *Web site:* http://www.chamberlain.edu/.

Chancellor University
Cleveland, Ohio

Director of Admissions Vice President for Enrollment Management, Chancellor University, 3921 Chester Avenue, Cleveland, OH 44114-4624. *Phone:* 216-523-3806 Ext. 805. *Toll-free phone:* 888-316-9377. *E-mail:* admissions@myers.edu. *Web site:* http://www.chancelloru.edu/.

Cincinnati Christian University
Cincinnati, Ohio

- **Independent** comprehensive, founded 1924, affiliated with Church of Christ
- **Urban** 40-acre campus with easy access to Cincinnati
- **Coed** 722 undergraduate students, 85% full-time, 43% women, 57% men
- **Minimally difficult** entrance level, 74% of applicants were admitted

Undergraduates 613 full-time, 109 part-time. 33% are from out of state; 12% Black or African American, non-Hispanic/Latino; 0.8% Hispanic/Latino; 0.1% Asian, non-Hispanic/Latino; 0.1% American Indian or Alaska Native, non-Hispanic/Latino; 0.7% Two or more races, non-Hispanic/Latino; 13% Race/ethnicity unknown; 1% international; 9% transferred in; 39% live on campus. *Retention:* 62% of full-time freshmen returned.
Freshmen *Admission:* 192 applied, 143 admitted, 121 enrolled. *Average high school GPA:* 3.07. *Test scores:* SAT critical reading scores over 500: 53%; SAT math scores over 500: 43%; SAT writing scores over 500: 43%; ACT scores over 18: 82%; SAT critical reading scores over 600: 10%; SAT math scores over 600: 10%; SAT writing scores over 600: 10%; ACT scores over 24: 26%; SAT critical reading scores over 700: 3%; SAT math scores over 700: 7%; SAT writing scores over 700: 3%; ACT scores over 30: 2%.
Faculty *Total:* 91, 35% full-time, 44% with terminal degrees. *Student/faculty ratio:* 15:1.
Academics *Calendar:* semesters. *Degrees:* associate, bachelor's, and master's. *Special study options:* academic remediation for entering students, adult/continuing education programs, advanced placement credit, cooperative education, distance learning, double majors, independent study, internships, off-campus study, part-time degree program, services for LD students, summer session for credit.
Computers on Campus 45 computers/terminals are available on campus for general student use. Students can access the following: campus intranet, computer help desk, free student e-mail accounts, online (class) grades, online (class) registration, online (class) schedules. Campuswide network is available. Wireless service is available via classrooms, computer labs, libraries, student centers.
Student Life *Housing:* on-campus residence required through junior year. *Options:* men-only, women-only. Campus housing is university owned. Freshman campus housing is guaranteed. *Activities and organizations:* drama/theater group, choral group. *Campus security:* 24-hour emergency response devices and patrols, student patrols, late-night transport/escort service, controlled dormitory access. *Student services:* health clinic, personal/psychological counseling.
Athletics Member NAIA. *Intercollegiate sports:* basketball M(s), cross-country running M(s)/W(s), golf M(s), soccer M(s)/W(s), volleyball W(s). *Intramural sports:* soccer M/W, volleyball M/W.
Standardized Tests *Required:* SAT or ACT (for admission).
Costs (2012–13) *Comprehensive fee:* $21,826 includes full-time tuition ($14,766), mandatory fees ($500), and room and board ($6560). Full-time tuition and fees vary according to course load and student level. Part-time tuition: $527 per credit. Part-time tuition and fees vary according to course load and student level. *College room only:* $2820. Room and board charges

vary according to board plan, housing facility, and student level. *Payment plan:* installment. *Waivers:* employees or children of employees.
Financial Aid Of all full-time matriculated undergraduates who enrolled in 2010, 623 applied for aid, 577 were judged to have need, 40 had their need fully met. In 2010, 60 non-need-based awards were made. *Average percent of need met:* 50%. *Average financial aid package:* $9589. *Average need-based loan:* $3761. *Average need-based gift aid:* $6770. *Average non-need-based aid:* $5353. *Average indebtedness upon graduation:* $31,969.
Applying *Options:* electronic application, early admission, deferred entrance. *Application fee:* $40. *Required:* essay or personal statement, high school transcript, 1 letter of recommendation. *Recommended:* minimum 2.0 GPA, interview. *Application deadlines:* 8/1 (freshmen), 8/1 (transfers). *Notification:* continuous (freshmen), continuous (transfers).
Freshman Application Contact Cincinnati Christian University, 2700 Glenway Avenue, PO Box 04320, Cincinnati, OH 45204-3200. *Phone:* 513-244-8485. *Toll-free phone:* 800-949-4228 (in-state); 800-949-4CCU (out-of-state). *Web site:* http://www.ccuniversity.edu/.

Cincinnati College of Mortuary Science
Cincinnati, Ohio

- **Independent** 4-year, founded 1882
- **Urban** 10-acre campus
- **Coed**

Faculty *Student/faculty ratio:* 33:1.
Academics *Calendar:* quarters. *Degrees:* associate and bachelor's.
Standardized Tests *Required:* SAT or ACT (for admission).
Applying *Options:* deferred entrance. *Application fee:* $40. *Required:* high school transcript, minimum 2.0 GPA.
Freshman Application Contact Cincinnati College of Mortuary Science, 645 West North Bend Road, Cincinnati, OH 45224-1462. *Phone:* 513-761-2020. *Toll-free phone:* 888-377-8433. *Fax:* 513-761-3333. *Web site:* http://www.ccms.edu/.

The Cleveland Institute of Art
Cleveland, Ohio

- **Independent** 4-year, founded 1882
- **Urban** 5-acre campus
- **Endowment** $26.7 million
- **Coed** 546 undergraduate students, 99% full-time, 54% women, 46% men
- **Moderately difficult** entrance level, 71% of applicants were admitted

Undergraduates 539 full-time, 7 part-time. Students come from 33 states and territories; 9 other countries; 30% are from out of state; 10% Black or African American, non-Hispanic/Latino; 3% Hispanic/Latino; 4% Asian, non-Hispanic/Latino; 0.4% American Indian or Alaska Native, non-Hispanic/Latino; 3% Two or more races, non-Hispanic/Latino; 2% international; 5% transferred in; 21% live on campus. *Retention:* 79% of full-time freshmen returned.
Freshmen *Admission:* 615 applied, 435 admitted, 127 enrolled. *Average high school GPA:* 3.06. *Test scores:* SAT critical reading scores over 500: 56%; SAT math scores over 500: 52%; SAT writing scores over 500: 55%; ACT scores over 18: 85%; SAT critical reading scores over 600: 21%; SAT math scores over 600: 14%; SAT writing scores over 600: 18%; ACT scores over 24: 34%; SAT critical reading scores over 700: 1%; SAT math scores over 700: 2%; SAT writing scores over 700: 2%; ACT scores over 30: 3%.
Faculty *Total:* 98, 52% full-time, 69% with terminal degrees. *Student/faculty ratio:* 8:1.
Academics *Calendar:* semesters. *Degree:* bachelor's. *Special study options:* academic remediation for entering students, advanced placement credit, double majors, independent study, internships, off-campus study, part-time degree program, services for LD students, study abroad.
Computers on Campus 80 computers/terminals are available on campus for general student use. Students can access the following: campus intranet, free student e-mail accounts, online (class) grades, online (class) registration, online (class) schedules, Wireless Internet access available throughout campus. Campuswide network is available. 100% of college-owned or -operated housing units are wired for high-speed Internet access. Wireless service is available via entire campus.
Student Life *Housing:* on-campus residence required for freshman year. *Options:* coed. Campus housing is leased by the school. Freshman applicants given priority for college housing. *Activities and organizations:* marching band, Campus Activities Board, Student Independent Exhibition, Artists for Christ, Student Leadership Council, Community Service Club, national fraternities, national sororities. *Campus security:* 24-hour emergency response devices and patrols, late-night transport/escort service, controlled dormitory

access. *Student services:* health clinic, personal/psychological counseling, women's center, legal services.

Athletics *Intramural sports:* basketball M/W, cross-country running M/W, football M/W, golf M/W, ice hockey M/W, racquetball M/W, soccer M/W, softball M/W, swimming and diving M/W, tennis M/W, track and field M/W, ultimate Frisbee M/W, volleyball M/W.

Standardized Tests *Required:* SAT or ACT (for admission).

Costs (2012–13) *Comprehensive fee:* $46,855 includes full-time tuition ($32,960), mandatory fees ($2185), and room and board ($11,710). Full-time tuition and fees vary according to program, reciprocity agreements, and student level. Part-time tuition: $1375 per credit hour. Part-time tuition and fees vary according to course load, program, reciprocity agreements, and student level. *Required fees:* $142 per credit hour part-time, $105 per term part-time. *College room only:* $6710. Room and board charges vary according to board plan. *Payment plan:* installment. *Waivers:* employees or children of employees.

Financial Aid Of all full-time matriculated undergraduates who enrolled in 2011, 488 applied for aid, 470 were judged to have need, 26 had their need fully met. 381 Federal Work-Study jobs (averaging $2461). In 2011, 59 non-need-based awards were made. *Average percent of need met:* 61%. *Average financial aid package:* $24,550. *Average need-based loan:* $4642. *Average need-based gift aid:* $18,521. *Average non-need-based aid:* $10,426. *Average indebtedness upon graduation:* $38,259.

Applying *Options:* electronic application, early action, deferred entrance. *Application fee:* $30. *Required:* essay or personal statement, high school transcript, minimum 2.0 GPA, 1 letter of recommendation, portfolio. *Recommended:* interview. *Application deadlines:* 3/1 (freshmen), 6/1 (transfers). *Notification:* continuous (freshmen), continuous (transfers).

Freshman Application Contact Office of Admissions, The Cleveland Institute of Art, 11141 East Boulevard, Cleveland, OH 44106-1700. *Phone:* 216-421-7418. *Toll-free phone:* 800-223-4700. *Fax:* 216-754-3634. *E-mail:* admissions@cia.edu. *Web site:* http://www.cia.edu/.

Cleveland Institute of Music
Cleveland, Ohio

Freshman Application Contact Mr. William Fay, Director of Admission, Cleveland Institute of Music, 11021 East Boulevard, Cleveland, OH 44106-1776. *Phone:* 216-795-3107. *Fax:* 216-791-1530. *E-mail:* william.fay@case.edu. *Web site:* http://www.cim.edu/.

Cleveland State University
Cleveland, Ohio

- **State-supported** university, founded 1964, part of University System of Ohio
- **Urban** 82-acre campus
- **Endowment** $57.1 million
- **Coed** 11,729 undergraduate students, 71% full-time, 55% women, 45% men
- **Moderately difficult** entrance level, 47% of applicants were admitted

Undergraduates 8,361 full-time, 3,368 part-time. Students come from 34 states and territories; 12 other countries; 3% are from out of state; 22% Black or African American, non-Hispanic/Latino; 4% Hispanic/Latino; 2% Asian, non-Hispanic/Latino; 0.1% Native Hawaiian or other Pacific Islander, non-Hispanic/Latino; 0.3% American Indian or Alaska Native, non-Hispanic/Latino; 2% Two or more races, non-Hispanic/Latino; 5% Race/ethnicity unknown; 3% international; 13% transferred in; 9% live on campus. *Retention:* 66% of full-time freshmen returned.

Freshmen *Admission:* 5,113 applied, 2,389 admitted, 1,375 enrolled. *Average high school GPA:* 3.15. *Test scores:* SAT critical reading scores over 500: 55%; SAT math scores over 500: 55%; ACT scores over 18: 83%; SAT critical reading scores over 600: 19%; SAT math scores over 600: 18%; ACT scores over 24: 30%; SAT critical reading scores over 700: 2%; SAT math scores over 700: 3%; ACT scores over 30: 3%.

Faculty *Total:* 1,032, 51% full-time, 51% with terminal degrees. *Student/faculty ratio:* 18:1.

Academics *Calendar:* semesters. *Degrees:* bachelor's, master's, doctoral, post-master's, postbachelor's, and first professional certificates. *Special study options:* academic remediation for entering students, accelerated degree program, adult/continuing education programs, advanced placement credit, cooperative education, distance learning, double majors, English as a second language, freshman honors college, honors programs, independent study, internships, off-campus study, part-time degree program, services for LD students, student-designed majors, study abroad, summer session for credit. *ROTC:* Army (c), Air Force (c).

Computers on Campus 736 computers/terminals are available on campus for general student use. Students can access the following: campus intranet, computer help desk, free student e-mail accounts, online (class) grades, online (class) registration, online (class) schedules, each general purpose computer lab has a scanner and printer, and students are allowed free black and white printing up to 2,000 pages per semester. Campuswide network is available. 100% of college-owned or -operated housing units are wired for high-speed Internet access. Wireless service is available via entire campus.

Student Life *Housing options:* coed, disabled students. Campus housing is university owned. Freshman campus housing is guaranteed. *Activities and organizations:* drama/theater group, student-run newspaper, radio station, choral group, Friends of India, Chinese Students and Scholars Association, Chi Sigma Iota, Student Nurses Association, Engineers Without Borders, national fraternities, national sororities. *Campus security:* 24-hour emergency response devices and patrols, student patrols, late-night transport/escort service, controlled dormitory access, Campus Watch, CSU Alert Notification System, Community Emergency and Response Team (CERT). *Student services:* health clinic, personal/psychological counseling, women's center.

Athletics Member NCAA. All Division I. *Intercollegiate sports:* basketball M(s)/W(s), cheerleading M/W, cross-country running W(s), fencing M(s)/W(s), golf M(s)/W, soccer M(s)/W, softball W(s), swimming and diving M(s)/W(s), tennis M/W(s), track and field W(s), volleyball W(s), wrestling M(s). *Intramural sports:* baseball M(c), basketball M/W, crew M(c)/W(c), cross-country running M/W, fencing M/W, golf M/W, ice hockey M(c), rock climbing M(c)/W(c), rugby M(c), soccer M(c)/W(c), track and field M/W, ultimate Frisbee M/W, volleyball W, wrestling M.

Standardized Tests *Required:* SAT or ACT (for admission).

Costs (2012–13) *Tuition:* state resident $8952 full-time, $373 per credit hour part-time; nonresident $11,972 full-time, $499 per credit hour part-time. Full-time tuition and fees vary according to course load, degree level, and program. Part-time tuition and fees vary according to course load, degree level, and program. *Required fees:* $50 full-time, $25 per term part-time. *Room and board:* $11,848; room only: $7648. Room and board charges vary according to board plan and housing facility. *Payment plan:* installment. *Waivers:* senior citizens and employees or children of employees.

Financial Aid Of all full-time matriculated undergraduates who enrolled in 2011, 7,291 applied for aid, 6,795 were judged to have need, 315 had their need fully met. 492 Federal Work-Study jobs (averaging $3736). In 2011, 331 non-need-based awards were made. *Average percent of need met:* 41%. *Average financial aid package:* $8755. *Average need-based loan:* $4354. *Average need-based gift aid:* $5971. *Average non-need-based aid:* $4702. *Average indebtedness upon graduation:* $19,199.

Applying *Options:* electronic application, early action, deferred entrance. *Application fee:* $30. *Required:* high school transcript, minimum 2.3 GPA, minimum ACT score of 16 or SAT of 770. *Application deadlines:* 5/15 (freshmen), 5/15 (transfers), 5/1 (early action). *Notification:* continuous (freshmen), continuous (transfers).

Freshman Application Contact Undergraduate Admissions Office, Cleveland State University, 2121 Euclid Avenue, RW 204, Cleveland, OH 44115. *Phone:* 216-687-2100. *Toll-free phone:* 888-CSU-OHIO. *E-mail:* admissions@csuohio.edu. *Web site:* http://www.csuohio.edu/.

College of Mount St. Joseph
Cincinnati, Ohio

- **Independent Roman Catholic** comprehensive, founded 1920
- **Suburban** 92-acre campus
- **Endowment** $27.4 million
- **Coed** 1,889 undergraduate students, 68% full-time, 65% women, 35% men
- **Moderately difficult** entrance level, 63% of applicants were admitted

Undergraduates 1,278 full-time, 611 part-time. Students come from 21 states and territories; 1 other country; 17% are from out of state; 10% Black or African American, non-Hispanic/Latino; 1% Hispanic/Latino; 0.3% Asian, non-Hispanic/Latino; 0.1% Native Hawaiian or other Pacific Islander, non-Hispanic/Latino; 0.3% American Indian or Alaska Native, non-Hispanic/Latino; 1% Two or more races, non-Hispanic/Latino; 2% Race/ethnicity unknown; 0.1% international; 7% transferred in; 21% live on campus. *Retention:* 69% of full-time freshmen returned.

Freshmen *Admission:* 1,621 applied, 1,021 admitted, 300 enrolled. *Average high school GPA:* 3.3. *Test scores:* SAT critical reading scores over 500: 48%; SAT math scores over 500: 51%; ACT scores over 18: 93%; SAT critical reading scores over 600: 8%; SAT math scores over 600: 11%; ACT scores over 24: 37%; SAT critical reading scores over 700: 1%; SAT math scores over 700: 1%; ACT scores over 30: 2%.

Faculty *Total:* 247, 50% full-time, 48% with terminal degrees. *Student/faculty ratio:* 11:1.

Academics *Calendar:* semesters. *Degrees:* certificates, associate, bachelor's, master's, doctoral, and postbachelor's certificates. *Special study options:* academic remediation for entering students, accelerated degree program,

advanced placement credit, cooperative education, distance learning, double majors, honors programs, independent study, internships, off-campus study, part-time degree program, services for LD students, study abroad, summer session for credit. *ROTC:* Army (c), Air Force (c).

Computers on Campus 202 computers/terminals are available on campus for general student use. Students can access the following: computer help desk, free student e-mail accounts, online (class) grades, online (class) registration, online (class) schedules. Campuswide network is available. 100% of college-owned or -operated housing units are wired for high-speed Internet access. Wireless service is available via entire campus.

Student Life *Housing:* on-campus residence required through sophomore year. *Options:* coed, disabled students. Campus housing is university owned. Freshman applicants given priority for college housing. *Activities and organizations:* drama/theater group, student-run newspaper, choral group, Student Government Association, Black Student Union, Campus Ministry Leadership Team, Campus Activities Board, Campus Ambassadors. *Campus security:* 24-hour emergency response devices and patrols, late-night transport/escort service. *Student services:* health clinic, personal/psychological counseling.

Athletics Member NCAA. All Division III. *Intercollegiate sports:* baseball M, basketball M/W, cheerleading W, cross-country running M/W, football M, golf M/W, lacrosse M/W, soccer M/W, softball W, tennis M/W, track and field M/W, volleyball M/W, wrestling M. *Intramural sports:* basketball M/W, football M/W, racquetball M/W, soccer M/W, softball M/W, tennis M/W, volleyball M/W.

Standardized Tests *Required:* SAT or ACT (for admission).

Costs (2012–13) *One-time required fee:* $150. *Comprehensive fee:* $32,960 includes full-time tuition ($24,200), mandatory fees ($900), and room and board ($7860). Full-time tuition and fees vary according to course load and reciprocity agreements. Part-time tuition: $495 per credit. Part-time tuition and fees vary according to course load and reciprocity agreements. *College room only:* $3880. Room and board charges vary according to board plan and housing facility. *Payment plans:* installment, deferred payment. *Waivers:* senior citizens and employees or children of employees.

Financial Aid Of all full-time matriculated undergraduates who enrolled in 2010, 1,153 applied for aid, 1,025 were judged to have need, 190 had their need fully met. 41 Federal Work-Study jobs (averaging $1488). 94 state and other part-time jobs (averaging $1476). In 2010, 204 non-need-based awards were made. *Average percent of need met:* 73%. *Average financial aid package:* $17,208. *Average need-based loan:* $4559. *Average need-based gift aid:* $13,091. *Average non-need-based aid:* $10,634. *Average indebtedness upon graduation:* $40,797.

Applying *Options:* electronic application, deferred entrance. *Application fee:* $25. *Required:* high school transcript. *Required for some:* essay or personal statement, 2 letters of recommendation, interview. *Recommended:* minimum 2.0 GPA. *Application deadlines:* 8/15 (freshmen), 8/1 (transfers). *Notification:* continuous (freshmen), continuous (transfers).

Freshman Application Contact Peggy Minnich, Director of Admission, College of Mount St. Joseph, 5701 Delhi Road, Cincinnati, OH 45233-1670. *Phone:* 513-244-4531. *Toll-free phone:* 800-654-9314. *Fax:* 513-244-4629. *E-mail:* admissions@mail.msj.edu. *Web site:* http://www.msj.edu/.

The College of Wooster
Wooster, Ohio

- **Independent** 4-year, founded 1866, affiliated with Presbyterian Church (U.S.A.)
- **Small-town** 240-acre campus with easy access to Cleveland
- **Endowment** $247.5 million
- **Coed** 2,033 undergraduate students, 97% full-time, 54% women, 46% men
- **Moderately difficult** entrance level, 61% of applicants were admitted

Undergraduates 1,982 full-time, 51 part-time. Students come from 47 states and territories; 41 other countries; 62% are from out of state; 8% Black or African American, non-Hispanic/Latino; 3% Hispanic/Latino; 3% Asian, non-Hispanic/Latino; 0.1% Native Hawaiian or other Pacific Islander, non-Hispanic/Latino; 1% American Indian or Alaska Native, non-Hispanic/Latino; 9% Race/ethnicity unknown; 6% international; 0.7% transferred in; 96% live on campus. *Retention:* 90% of full-time freshmen returned.

Freshmen *Admission:* 4,893 applied, 2,968 admitted, 571 enrolled. *Average high school GPA:* 3.61. *Test scores:* SAT critical reading scores over 500: 90%; SAT math scores over 500: 91%; SAT writing scores over 500: 91%; ACT scores over 18: 99%; SAT critical reading scores over 600: 61%; SAT math scores over 600: 54%; SAT writing scores over 600: 53%; ACT scores over 24: 80%; SAT critical reading scores over 700: 18%; SAT math scores over 700: 12%; SAT writing scores over 700: 14%; ACT scores over 30: 25%.

Faculty *Total:* 179, 79% full-time, 83% with terminal degrees. *Student/faculty ratio:* 11:1.

Academics *Calendar:* semesters. *Degree:* bachelor's. *Special study options:* advanced placement credit, double majors, independent study, internships, off-campus study, services for LD students, student-designed majors, study abroad. *Unusual degree programs:* 3-2 engineering with Case Western

Reserve University, Washington University in St. Louis, University of Michigan; forestry with Duke University; nursing with Case Western Reserve University; social work with Case Western Reserve University; dentistry with Case Western Reserve University, architecture with Washington University in St. Louis.

Computers on Campus 450 computers/terminals and 3,000 ports are available on campus for general student use. Students can access the following: campus intranet, computer help desk, free student e-mail accounts, online (class) grades, online (class) registration, online (class) schedules, learning management system, campus blogging site, campus wiki site. Campuswide network is available. 100% of college-owned or -operated housing units are wired for high-speed Internet access. Wireless service is available via entire campus.

Student Life *Housing:* on-campus residence required through senior year. *Options:* coed, women-only. Campus housing is university owned. Freshman campus housing is guaranteed. *Activities and organizations:* drama/theater group, student-run newspaper, radio station, choral group, marching band, Volunteer Network, International Student Association, Inter-Greek Council, Wooster Activities Crew, Women's Athletic and Recreation Association. *Campus security:* 24-hour emergency response devices and patrols, student patrols, late-night transport/escort service, controlled dormitory access. *Student services:* health clinic, personal/psychological counseling, women's center.

Athletics Member NCAA. All Division III. *Intercollegiate sports:* badminton M(c)/W(c), baseball M, basketball M/W, cheerleading W(c), cross-country running M/W, equestrian sports M(c)/W(c), field hockey W, football M, golf M/W, ice hockey M(c)/W(c), lacrosse M/W, rugby M(c)/W(c), soccer M/W, softball M, swimming and diving M/W, tennis M/W, track and field M/W, ultimate Frisbee M(c)/W(c), volleyball M(c)/W. *Intramural sports:* badminton M/W, basketball M/W, bowling M/W, football M, golf M/W, soccer M/W, softball M/W, table tennis M/W, tennis M/W, track and field M/W, ultimate Frisbee M/W, volleyball M/W.

Standardized Tests *Required:* SAT or ACT (for admission).

Costs (2012–13) *Comprehensive fee:* $49,400 includes full-time tuition ($39,500), mandatory fees ($310), and room and board ($9590). Full-time tuition and fees vary according to course load. Part-time tuition: $1230 per credit. Part-time tuition and fees vary according to course load. *College room only:* $4440. Room and board charges vary according to board plan and housing facility. *Payment plan:* installment. *Waivers:* employees or children of employees.

Financial Aid Of all full-time matriculated undergraduates who enrolled in 2011, 1,317 applied for aid, 1,176 were judged to have need, 747 had their need fully met. 830 Federal Work-Study jobs (averaging $1500). 48 state and other part-time jobs (averaging $1967). In 2011, 721 non-need-based awards were made. *Average percent of need met:* 92%. *Average financial aid package:* $32,002. *Average need-based loan:* $3623. *Average need-based gift aid:* $25,215. *Average non-need-based aid:* $17,826. *Average indebtedness upon graduation:* $25,163.

Applying *Options:* electronic application, early admission, early decision, early action, deferred entrance. *Application fee:* $40. *Required:* essay or personal statement, high school transcript, SAT or ACT. *Recommended:* interview. *Application deadlines:* 2/15 (freshmen), 6/1 (transfers), 11/15 (early action). *Early decision deadline:* 11/15. *Notification:* 3/15 (freshmen), continuous (transfers), 12/1 (early decision), 12/31 (early action).

Freshman Application Contact Ms. Jennifer Winge, Dean of Admissions, The College of Wooster, 1189 Beall Avenue, Wooster, OH 44691-2363. *Phone:* 330-263-2270. *Toll-free phone:* 800-877-9905. *Fax:* 330-263-2621. *E-mail:* admissions@wooster.edu. *Web site:* http://www.wooster.edu/.

See page 689 for display ad and page 1278 for the College Close-Up.

Columbus College of Art & Design
Columbus, Ohio

- **Independent** comprehensive, founded 1879
- **Urban** 17-acre campus
- **Endowment** $7.5 million
- **Coed** 1,425 undergraduate students, 90% full-time, 61% women, 39% men
- **Moderately difficult** entrance level, 85% of applicants were admitted

Undergraduates 1,278 full-time, 147 part-time. Students come from 38 states and territories; 22 other countries; 23% are from out of state; 8% Black or African American, non-Hispanic/Latino; 4% Hispanic/Latino; 4% Asian, non-Hispanic/Latino; 0.1% American Indian or Alaska Native, non-Hispanic/Latino; 5% Two or more races, non-Hispanic/Latino; 2% Race/ethnicity unknown; 5% international; 0.4% transferred in; 32% live on campus. *Retention:* 79% of full-time freshmen returned.

Freshmen *Admission:* 627 applied, 536 admitted, 136 enrolled. *Average high school GPA:* 3.11. *Test scores:* SAT critical reading scores over 500: 64%;

SAT math scores over 500: 46%; SAT writing scores over 500: 51%; ACT scores over 18: 83%; SAT critical reading scores over 600: 18%; SAT math scores over 600: 11%; SAT writing scores over 600: 17%; ACT scores over 24: 31%; SAT critical reading scores over 700: 3%; SAT writing scores over 700: 1%; ACT scores over 30: 3%.

Faculty *Total:* 201, 36% full-time, 43% with terminal degrees. *Student/faculty ratio:* 12:1.

Academics *Calendar:* semesters. *Degrees:* bachelor's and master's. *Special study options:* academic remediation for entering students, advanced placement credit, distance learning, double majors, English as a second language, honors programs, independent study, internships, off-campus study, part-time degree program, services for LD students, study abroad, summer session for credit.

Computers on Campus 485 computers/terminals are available on campus for general student use. Students can access the following: campus intranet, computer help desk, free student e-mail accounts, online (class) grades, online (class) registration, online (class) schedules, online library. Campuswide network is available. 100% of college-owned or -operated housing units are wired for high-speed Internet access. Wireless service is available via classrooms, computer centers, computer labs, dorm rooms, learning centers, libraries, student centers.

Student Life *Housing:* on-campus residence required for freshman year. *Options:* coed, disabled students. Campus housing is university owned. Freshman campus housing is guaranteed. *Activities and organizations:* Student Government Association, Gay Straight Student Alliance, Sanctuary, Black Student Leadership Association, Student Programming Board. *Campus security:* 24-hour emergency response devices and patrols, late-night transport/escort service, controlled dormitory access. *Student services:* personal/psychological counseling.

Athletics *Intramural sports:* basketball M/W, soccer M/W, ultimate Frisbee M/W.

Standardized Tests *Required:* SAT or ACT (for admission).

Costs (2011–12) *Comprehensive fee:* $36,542 includes full-time tuition ($26,112), mandatory fees ($1020), and room and board ($9410). Full-time tuition and fees vary according to course load. Part-time tuition: $1088 per credit hour. Part-time tuition and fees vary according to course load. *Required fees:* $180 per term part-time. *Room and board:* Room and board charges vary according to board plan, housing facility, and student level. *Payment plans:* installment, deferred payment. *Waivers:* employees or children of employees.

Financial Aid Of all full-time matriculated undergraduates who enrolled in 2011, 1,190 applied for aid, 1,089 were judged to have need, 93 had their need fully met. 164 Federal Work-Study jobs (averaging $3150). 198 state and other part-time jobs (averaging $3150). In 2011, 190 non-need-based awards were made. *Average percent of need met:* 54%. *Average financial aid package:* $18,135. *Average need-based loan:* $5842. *Average need-based gift aid:* $12,739. *Average non-need-based aid:* $9613. *Average indebtedness upon graduation:* $38,179.

Applying *Options:* electronic application, deferred entrance. *Application fee:* $30. *Required:* essay or personal statement, high school transcript, minimum 2.0 GPA, 1 letter of recommendation, portfolio. *Recommended:* interview. *Application deadlines:* rolling (freshmen), rolling (transfers). *Notification:* continuous (freshmen), continuous (transfers).

Freshman Application Contact Columbus College of Art & Design, 60 Cleveland Avenue, Columbus, OH 43215-1758. *Phone:* 614-224-9101. *Toll-free phone:* 877-997-2223. *Fax:* 614-232-8344. *E-mail:* admissions@ccad.edu. *Web site:* http://www.ccad.edu/.

Defiance College
Defiance, Ohio

- **Independent** comprehensive, founded 1850, affiliated with United Church of Christ
- **Small-town** 150-acre campus with easy access to Toledo
- **Coed** 998 undergraduate students, 81% full-time, 48% women, 52% men
- **Moderately difficult** entrance level, 67% of applicants were admitted

Undergraduates 805 full-time, 193 part-time. Students come from 26 states and territories; 4 other countries; 27% are from out of state; 10% Black or African American, non-Hispanic/Latino; 5% Hispanic/Latino; 0.6% Asian, non-Hispanic/Latino; 1% American Indian or Alaska Native, non-Hispanic/Latino; 0.1% Two or more races, non-Hispanic/Latino; 0.2% Race/ethnicity unknown; 0.5% international; 4% transferred in; 44% live on campus. *Retention:* 59% of full-time freshmen returned.

Freshmen *Admission:* 1,854 applied, 1,248 admitted, 300 enrolled. *Average high school GPA:* 3.02. *Test scores:* SAT critical reading scores over 500: 37%; SAT math scores over 500: 43%; SAT writing scores over 500: 26%; ACT scores over 18: 81%; SAT critical reading scores over 600: 4%; SAT math scores over 600: 7%; SAT writing scores over 600: 3%; ACT scores over 24: 23%; ACT scores over 30: 1%.

Faculty *Total:* 107, 38% full-time, 56% with terminal degrees. *Student/faculty ratio:* 12:1.

Academics *Calendar:* semesters. *Degrees:* associate, bachelor's, and master's. *Special study options:* academic remediation for entering students, adult/continuing education programs, advanced placement credit, cooperative education, distance learning, double majors, honors programs, independent study, internships, off-campus study, part-time degree program, services for LD students, student-designed majors, study abroad, summer session for credit.

Computers on Campus 200 computers/terminals are available on campus for general student use. Students can access the following: campus intranet, computer help desk, free student e-mail accounts, online (class) grades, online (class) schedules. Campuswide network is available. 100% of college-owned or -operated housing units are wired for high-speed Internet access. Wireless service is available via classrooms, computer centers, computer labs, learning centers, libraries, student centers.

Student Life *Housing:* on-campus residence required through junior year. *Options:* coed. Campus housing is university owned. Freshman campus housing is guaranteed. *Activities and organizations:* drama/theater group, student-run newspaper, choral group, Campus Activities Board, Criminal Justice Society, Student Senate, Black Action Student Association, DC Players, national sororities. *Campus security:* late-night transport/escort service, controlled dormitory access. *Student services:* health clinic, personal/psychological counseling.

Athletics Member NCAA. All Division III. *Intercollegiate sports:* baseball M, basketball M/W, cross-country running M/W, football M, golf M/W, lacrosse M/W, soccer M/W, softball W, swimming and diving M/W, tennis M/W, track and field M/W, volleyball W. *Intramural sports:* baseball M, basketball M/W, cheerleading M/W, field hockey M/W, football M/W, racquetball M/W, soccer M/W, softball M/W, volleyball M/W, weight lifting M, wrestling M(c).

Standardized Tests *Required:* SAT or ACT (for admission).

Costs (2011–12) *One-time required fee:* $75. *Comprehensive fee:* $34,340 includes full-time tuition ($25,300), mandatory fees ($590), and room and board ($8450). Full-time tuition and fees vary according to program. Part-time tuition: $410 per credit hour. Part-time tuition and fees vary according to course load. *Required fees:* $85 per term part-time. *College room only:* $4680. Room and board charges vary according to board plan and housing facility. *Payment plan:* installment. *Waivers:* senior citizens and employees or children of employees.

Financial Aid Of all full-time matriculated undergraduates who enrolled in 2010, 729 applied for aid, 702 were judged to have need, 71 had their need fully met. 535 Federal Work-Study jobs (averaging $2438). 30 state and other part-time jobs (averaging $2527). In 2010, 58 non-need-based awards were made. *Average percent of need met:* 71%. *Average financial aid package:* $20,818. *Average need-based loan:* $4523. *Average need-based gift aid:* $6970. *Average non-need-based aid:* $8826. *Average indebtedness upon graduation:* $31,410.

Applying *Options:* electronic application, deferred entrance. *Application fee:* $25. *Required:* high school transcript, minimum 2.3 GPA. *Required for some:* essay or personal statement, interview. *Recommended:* interview. *Application deadlines:* 8/15 (freshmen), 8/15 (transfers). *Notification:* continuous (freshmen), continuous (transfers).

Freshman Application Contact Mr. Brad Harsha, Director of Admissions, Defiance College, 701 North Clinton Street, Defiance, OH 43512. *Phone:* 419-783-2365. *Toll-free phone:* 800-520-4632. *Fax:* 419-783-2468. *E-mail:* bharsha@defiance.edu. *Web site:* http://www.defiance.edu/.

Denison University
Granville, Ohio

- **Independent** 4-year, founded 1831
- **Small-town** 800-acre campus with easy access to Columbus
- **Endowment** $585.0 million
- **Coed** 2,275 undergraduate students, 99% full-time, 56% women, 44% men
- **Very difficult** entrance level, 49% of applicants were admitted

Undergraduates 2,257 full-time, 18 part-time. Students come from 51 states and territories; 36 other countries; 73% are from out of state; 7% Black or African American, non-Hispanic/Latino; 4% Hispanic/Latino; 3% Asian, non-Hispanic/Latino; 0.2% American Indian or Alaska Native, non-Hispanic/Latino; 4% Two or more races, non-Hispanic/Latino; 0.3% Race/ethnicity unknown; 6% international; 0.9% transferred in; 98% live on campus. *Retention:* 89% of full-time freshmen returned.

Freshmen *Admission:* 4,723 applied, 2,326 admitted, 623 enrolled. *Average high school GPA:* 3.5. *Test scores:* SAT critical reading scores over 500: 98%; SAT math scores over 500: 99%; ACT scores over 18: 100%; SAT critical reading scores over 600: 76%; SAT math scores over 600: 69%; ACT scores over 24: 97%; SAT critical reading scores over 700: 25%; SAT math scores over 700: 20%; ACT scores over 30: 48%.

Faculty *Total:* 223, 92% full-time, 95% with terminal degrees. *Student/faculty ratio:* 10:1.

Academics *Calendar:* semesters plus optional May term. *Degree:* bachelor's. *Special study options:* advanced placement credit, double majors, honors programs, independent study, internships, off-campus study, part-time degree program, services for LD students, student-designed majors, study abroad. *ROTC:* Army (c). *Unusual degree programs:* 3-2 engineering with Case Western Reserve University, Columbia University, Rensselaer Polytechnic Institute, Washington University in St. Louis; forestry with Duke University; natural resources with University of Michigan; occupational therapy with Washington University in St. Louis; environmental management, dentistry with Case Western Reserve University; medical technology with Rochester General Hospital.
Computers on Campus Students can access the following: campus intranet, computer help desk, free student e-mail accounts, online (class) grades, online (class) registration, online (class) schedules. Campuswide network is available. Wireless service is available via entire campus.
Student Life *Housing:* on-campus residence required through senior year. *Options:* coed, men-only, women-only, cooperative. Campus housing is university owned. Freshman campus housing is guaranteed. *Activities and organizations:* drama/theater group, student-run newspaper, radio and television station, choral group, Community Association, Black Student Union, International Student Association, Student Activities Committee, national fraternities, national sororities. *Campus security:* 24-hour emergency response devices and patrols, student patrols, late-night transport/escort service, controlled dormitory access, security lighting, escort service. *Student services:* health clinic, personal/psychological counseling, women's center.
Athletics Member NCAA. All Division III. *Intercollegiate sports:* baseball M, basketball M/W, crew M(c), cross-country running M/W, equestrian sports M(c)/W(c), field hockey W, football M, golf M, ice hockey M(c), lacrosse M/W, riflery M(c)/W(c), rugby M(c)/W(c), sailing M(c)/W(c), skiing (downhill) M(c)/W(c), soccer M/W, softball W, squash M(c)/W(c), swimming and diving M/W, tennis M/W, track and field M/W, volleyball W. *Intramural sports:* badminton M(c)/W(c), basketball M/W, cheerleading M/W, crew W(c), fencing M(c)/W(c), football M/W, golf M/W, lacrosse M(c), racquetball M/W, soccer M/W, softball M/W, squash M/W, table tennis M/W, tennis M/W, ultimate Frisbee M/W, volleyball M(c)/W, water polo M/W, weight lifting M/W.
Standardized Tests *Required for some:* SAT or ACT (for admission).
Costs (2012–13) *Comprehensive fee:* $52,640 includes full-time tuition ($41,380), mandatory fees ($900), and room and board ($10,360). Part-time tuition: $1290 per credit. Part-time tuition and fees vary according to course load. *Required fees:* $660 per term part-time. *College room only:* $5700. Room and board charges vary according to board plan and housing facility. *Payment plan:* installment. *Waivers:* employees or children of employees.
Financial Aid Of all full-time matriculated undergraduates who enrolled in 2011, 1,301 applied for aid, 1,115 were judged to have need, 387 had their need fully met. In 2011, 1032 non-need-based awards were made. *Average percent of need met:* 96%. *Average financial aid package:* $35,182. *Average need-based loan:* $4584. *Average need-based gift aid:* $28,999. *Average non-need-based aid:* $16,283.
Applying *Options:* early admission, early decision, deferred entrance. *Application fee:* $40. *Required:* essay or personal statement, high school transcript, 2 letters of recommendation. *Recommended:* interview. *Application deadlines:* 1/15 (freshmen), 6/1 (transfers). *Early decision deadline:* 11/15 (for plan 1), 1/15 (for plan 2). *Notification:* 4/1 (freshmen), continuous (transfers), 1/1 (early decision). **Freshman Application Contact** Mr. Perry Robinson, Director of Admissions, Denison University, Granville, OH 43023. *Phone:* 740-587-6276. *Toll-free phone:* 800-DENISON. *E-mail:* admissions@denison.edu. *Web site:* http://www.denison.edu/.

See page 691 for display ad and page 1296 for the College Close-Up.

DeVry University
Columbus, Ohio

- **Proprietary** comprehensive, founded 1952, part of DeVry University
- **Urban** campus
- **Coed** 2,677 undergraduate students, 40% full-time, 45% women, 55% men
- **Minimally difficult** entrance level

Undergraduates 1,059 full-time, 1,618 part-time. 2% are from out of state; 21% Black or African American, non-Hispanic/Latino; 3% Hispanic/Latino; 1% Asian, non-Hispanic/Latino; 0.1% Native Hawaiian or other Pacific Islander, non-Hispanic/Latino; 0.4% American Indian or Alaska Native, non-Hispanic/Latino; 1% Two or more races, non-Hispanic/Latino; 9% Race/ethnicity unknown; 0.2% international; 24% transferred in.
Freshmen *Admission:* 317 enrolled.
Faculty *Total:* 102, 36% full-time. *Student/faculty ratio:* 30:1.
Academics *Calendar:* semesters. *Degrees:* associate, bachelor's, master's, and postbachelor's certificates. *Special study options:* adult/continuing education programs, part-time degree program.

Student Life *Housing:* college housing not available.
Costs (2011–12) *Tuition:* $15,294 full-time, $597 per credit hour part-time. Full-time tuition and fees vary according to course load. Part-time tuition and fees vary according to course load. *Required fees:* $80 full-time, $40 per term part-time. *Payment plans:* installment, deferred payment. *Waivers:* employees or children of employees.
Financial Aid Of all full-time matriculated undergraduates who enrolled in 2007, 853 applied for aid, 826 were judged to have need, 35 had their need fully met. In 2007, 53 non-need-based awards were made. *Average percent of need met:* 46%. *Average financial aid package:* $14,130. *Average need-based loan:* $7868. *Average need-based gift aid:* $7762. *Average non-need-based aid:* $13,228. *Average indebtedness upon graduation:* $40,467.
Applying *Application fee:* $50. *Required:* high school transcript, interview. *Application deadlines:* rolling (freshmen), rolling (transfers). *Notification:* continuous (freshmen), continuous (transfers).
Freshman Application Contact DeVry University, 1350 Alum Creek Drive, Columbus, OH 43209-2705. *Phone:* 614-253-7291. *Toll-free phone:* 866-338-7941. *Web site:* http://www.devry.edu/.

DeVry University
Columbus, Ohio

Admissions Office Contact DeVry University, 8800 Lyra Drive, Columbus, OH 43240. *Toll-free phone:* 866-338-7941. *Web site:* http://www.devry.edu/.

DeVry University
Seven Hills, Ohio

Admissions Office Contact DeVry University, The Genesis Building, 6000 Lombardo Center, Suite 200, Seven Hills, OH 44131. *Toll-free phone:* 866-338-7941. *Web site:* http://www.devry.edu/.

Franciscan University of Steubenville
Steubenville, Ohio

- **Independent Roman Catholic** comprehensive, founded 1946
- **Suburban** campus
- **Coed** 2,131 undergraduate students, 93% full-time, 61% women, 39% men
- **Moderately difficult** entrance level, 76% of applicants were admitted

Undergraduates 1,979 full-time, 152 part-time. 79% are from out of state; 0.4% Black or African American, non-Hispanic/Latino; 8% Hispanic/Latino; 1% Asian, non-Hispanic/Latino; 0.1% Native Hawaiian or other Pacific Islander, non-Hispanic/Latino; 0.2% American Indian or Alaska Native, non-Hispanic/Latino; 1% Two or more races, non-Hispanic/Latino; 8% Race/ethnicity unknown; 1% international; 8% transferred in; 74% live on campus. *Retention:* 85% of full-time freshmen returned.
Freshmen *Admission:* 1,739 applied, 1,329 admitted, 449 enrolled. *Average high school GPA:* 3.68. *Test scores:* SAT critical reading scores over 500: 93%; SAT math scores over 500: 84%; SAT writing scores over 500: 84%; ACT scores over 18: 100%; SAT critical reading scores over 600: 53%; SAT math scores over 600: 33%; SAT writing scores over 600: 41%; ACT scores over 24: 71%; SAT critical reading scores over 700: 13%; SAT math scores over 700: 4%; SAT writing scores over 700: 6%; ACT scores over 30: 19%.
Faculty *Total:* 223, 52% full-time, 52% with terminal degrees. *Student/faculty ratio:* 15:1.
Academics *Calendar:* semesters. *Degrees:* associate, bachelor's, and master's. *Special study options:* adult/continuing education programs, part-time degree program. *ROTC:* Army (b), Air Force (c).
Computers on Campus Students can access the following: campus intranet, computer help desk, free student e-mail accounts, online (class) grades, online (class) registration, online (class) schedules. Campuswide network is available. 100% of college-owned or -operated housing units are wired for high-speed Internet access. Wireless service is available via classrooms, computer centers, computer labs, dorm rooms, libraries, student centers.
Student Life *Housing:* on-campus residence required through junior year. *Options:* men-only, women-only. Campus housing is university owned. Freshman applicants given priority for college housing. *Campus security:* 24-hour emergency response devices and patrols, student patrols, late-night transport/escort service.
Athletics Member NCAA. All Division III. *Intercollegiate sports:* baseball M, basketball M/W, cross-country running M/W, rugby M(c), soccer M/W, softball W, tennis M/W, track and field M/W, volleyball W. *Intramural sports:* basketball M/W, football M/W, racquetball M/W, soccer M/W, softball M/W, ultimate Frisbee M/W, volleyball M/W, weight lifting M/W.
Standardized Tests *Required:* SAT or ACT (for admission).
Costs (2012–13) *Comprehensive fee:* $29,580 includes full-time tuition ($21,740), mandatory fees ($440), and room and board ($7400). Part-time

tuition: $725 per credit hour. Part-time tuition and fees vary according to class time and course load. *College room only:* $4280. Room and board charges vary according to board plan.

Financial Aid Of all full-time matriculated undergraduates who enrolled in 2009, 1,577 applied for aid, 1,324 were judged to have need, 183 had their need fully met. In 2009, 232 non-need-based awards were made. *Average percent of need met:* 60%. *Average financial aid package:* $12,549. *Average need-based loan:* $4311. *Average need-based gift aid:* $8177. *Average non-need-based aid:* $4094. *Average indebtedness upon graduation:* $30,180.

Applying *Options:* deferred entrance. *Application fee:* $20. *Required:* essay or personal statement, high school transcript, minimum 2.4 GPA. *Required for some:* 3 letters of recommendation. *Recommended:* interview. *Application deadlines:* rolling (freshmen), rolling (transfers). *Notification:* continuous (freshmen), continuous (transfers).

Freshman Application Contact Mrs. Margaret Weber, Director of Admissions, Franciscan University of Steubenville, 1235 University Boulevard, Steubenville, OH 43952-1763. *Phone:* 740-283-6226. *Toll-free phone:* 800-783-6220. *Fax:* 740-284-5456. *E-mail:* admissions@franciscan.edu. *Web site:* http://www.franciscan.edu/.

Franklin University

Columbus, Ohio

- **Independent** comprehensive, founded 1902
- **Urban** 14-acre campus
- **Coed** 6,439 undergraduate students, 38% full-time, 60% women, 40% men
- **Noncompetitive** entrance level

Undergraduates 2,456 full-time, 3,983 part-time. Students come from 48 states and territories; 89 other countries; 24% are from out of state; 25% Black or African American, non-Hispanic/Latino; 1% Hispanic/Latino; 2% Asian, non-Hispanic/Latino; 1% American Indian or Alaska Native, non-Hispanic/Latino; 3% Race/ethnicity unknown; 1% international; 20% transferred in. *Retention:* 31% of full-time freshmen returned.

Freshmen *Admission:* 420 enrolled.

Faculty *Total:* 766, 8% full-time. *Student/faculty ratio:* 16:1.

Academics *Calendar:* trimesters. *Degrees:* associate, bachelor's, master's, and post-master's certificates. *Special study options:* academic remediation for entering students, accelerated degree program, adult/continuing education programs, advanced placement credit, cooperative education, distance learning, double majors, English as a second language, independent study, internships, off-campus study, part-time degree program, services for LD students, student-designed majors, study abroad, summer session for credit. *ROTC:* Army (c), Air Force (c).

Computers on Campus Students can access the following: online (class) registration. Campuswide network is available.

Student Life *Housing:* college housing not available. *Campus security:* 24-hour patrols, security personnel during operating hours.

Costs (2011–12) *One-time required fee:* $25. *Tuition:* $13,500 full-time, $375 per credit hour part-time. Full-time tuition and fees vary according to program. Part-time tuition and fees vary according to program. *Payment plans:* installment, deferred payment. *Waivers:* employees or children of employees.

Financial Aid Of all full-time matriculated undergraduates who enrolled in 2003, 1,135 applied for aid, 1,071 were judged to have need. 29 Federal Work-Study jobs (averaging $7702). In 2003, 108 non-need-based awards were made. *Average need-based loan:* $5091. *Average need-based gift aid:* $4436. *Average non-need-based aid:* $2211.

Applying *Options:* electronic application, deferred entrance. *Required for some:* high school transcript. *Application deadlines:* rolling (freshmen), rolling (transfers). *Notification:* continuous (transfers).

Freshman Application Contact Franklin University, 201 South Grant Avenue, Columbus, OH 43215-5399. *Toll-free phone:* 877-341-6300. *Web site:* http://www.franklin.edu/.

God's Bible School and College

Cincinnati, Ohio

Freshman Application Contact Steve Buckland, Director of Financial Aid and Admissions, God's Bible School and College, 1810 Young Street, Cincinnati, OH 45202-6838. *Phone:* 513-721-7944 Ext. 1161. *Toll-free phone:* 800-486-4637. *Fax:* 513-763-6649. *E-mail:* sbuckland@gbs.edu. *Web site:* http://www.gbs.edu/.

Heidelberg University

Tiffin, Ohio

- **Independent** comprehensive, founded 1850, affiliated with United Church of Christ
- **Small-town** 115-acre campus with easy access to Cleveland, Columbus, Detroit
- **Endowment** $32.1 million
- **Coed** 1,113 undergraduate students, 93% full-time, 49% women, 51% men
- **Moderately difficult** entrance level, 64% of applicants were admitted

Undergraduates 1,033 full-time, 80 part-time. Students come from 25 states and territories; 12 other countries; 15% are from out of state; 9% Black or African American, non-Hispanic/Latino; 2% Hispanic/Latino; 0.4% Asian, non-Hispanic/Latino; 0.2% American Indian or Alaska Native, non-Hispanic/Latino; 1% Two or more races, non-Hispanic/Latino; 8% Race/ethnicity unknown; 2% international; 4% transferred in; 85% live on campus. *Retention:* 65% of full-time freshmen returned.

Freshmen *Admission:* 2,043 applied, 1,307 admitted, 282 enrolled. *Average high school GPA:* 3.2. *Test scores:* SAT critical reading scores over 500: 36%; SAT math scores over 500: 61%; SAT writing scores over 500: 37%; ACT scores over 18: 87%; SAT critical reading scores over 600: 16%; SAT math scores over 600: 22%; SAT writing scores over 600: 8%; ACT scores over 24: 27%; SAT critical reading scores over 700: 4%; SAT math scores over 700: 2%; SAT writing scores over 700: 4%; ACT scores over 30: 3%.

Faculty *Total:* 150, 42% full-time, 57% with terminal degrees. *Student/faculty ratio:* 13:1.

Academics *Calendar:* semesters. *Degrees:* bachelor's and master's. *Special study options:* academic remediation for entering students, accelerated degree program, adult/continuing education programs, advanced placement credit, double majors, English as a second language, honors programs, independent study, internships, off-campus study, part-time degree program, services for LD students, student-designed majors, study abroad, summer session for credit. *ROTC:* Army (c), Air Force (c). *Unusual degree programs:* 3-2 nursing with Ursuline - Breen School of Nursing.

Computers on Campus 125 computers/terminals are available on campus for general student use. Students can access the following: computer help desk, free student e-mail accounts, online (class) grades, online (class) registration, online (class) schedules. Campuswide network is available. 100% of college-owned or -operated housing units are wired for high-speed Internet access. Wireless service is available via classrooms, computer centers, computer labs, learning centers, libraries, student centers.

Student Life *Housing:* on-campus residence required through junior year. *Options:* coed, women-only, cooperative. Campus housing is university owned and leased by the school. Freshman campus housing is guaranteed. *Activities and organizations:* drama/theater group, student-run newspaper, radio and television station, choral group, Alpha Phi Omega, BERG Events Council, Student Senate, Campus Fellowship, Black Student Union/World Student Union. *Campus security:* 24-hour emergency response devices and patrols, student patrols, late-night transport/escort service, controlled dormitory access. *Student services:* health clinic, personal/psychological counseling.

Athletics Member NCAA. All Division III. *Intercollegiate sports:* baseball M, basketball M/W, cross-country running M/W, football M, golf M/W, soccer M/W, softball W, tennis M/W, track and field M/W, volleyball M/W, wrestling M. *Intramural sports:* archery M/W, badminton M/W, cheerleading M/W, football M, golf M/W, racquetball M/W, skiing (cross-country) M/W, softball W, table tennis M/W.

Standardized Tests *Required:* SAT or ACT (for admission).

Costs (2012–13) *Comprehensive fee:* $33,556 includes full-time tuition ($24,000), mandatory fees ($582), and room and board ($8974). Full-time tuition and fees vary according to course load, degree level, and location. Part-time tuition and fees vary according to course load, degree level, and location. *College room only:* $4248. Room and board charges vary according to housing facility and location. *Payment plan:* installment. *Waivers:* employees or children of employees.

Financial Aid Of all full-time matriculated undergraduates who enrolled in 2011, 953 applied for aid, 898 were judged to have need, 164 had their need fully met. 623 Federal Work-Study jobs (averaging $1867). 89 state and other part-time jobs (averaging $1911). In 2011, 118 non-need-based awards were made. *Average percent of need met:* 74%. *Average financial aid package:* $19,960. *Average need-based loan:* $4666. *Average need-based gift aid:* $14,400. *Average non-need-based aid:* $13,871. *Average indebtedness upon graduation:* $36,706.

Applying *Options:* electronic application, deferred entrance. *Application fee:* $25. *Required:* high school transcript, minimum 2.5 GPA. *Recommended:* essay or personal statement, interview. *Application deadlines:* 8/15 (freshmen), 8/15 (out-of-state freshmen), 8/15 (transfers). *Notification:* 8/15 (freshmen), 8/15 (transfers).

Freshman Application Contact Mr. Jason Miller, Interim Director of Admission, Heidelberg University, 310 East Market Street, Tiffin, OH 44883. *Phone:* 419-448-2330. *Toll-free phone:* 800-434-3352. *Fax:* 419-448-2334. *E-mail:* jmiller7@heidelberg.edu. *Web site:* http://www.heidelberg.edu/.

Herzing University
Toledo, Ohio

Admissions Office Contact Herzing University, 5212 Hill Avenue, Toledo, OH 43615. *Toll-free phone:* 800-596-0724. *Web site:* http://www.herzing.edu/toledo.

Hiram College
Hiram, Ohio

Freshman Application Contact Mr. Sherman C. Dean II, Director of Admission, Hiram College, PO Box 96, Hiram, OH 44234. *Phone:* 330-569-5169. *Toll-free phone:* 800-362-5280. *Fax:* 330-569-5944. *E-mail:* admission@hiram.edu. *Web site:* http://www.hiram.edu/.

ITT Technical Institute
Akron, Ohio

- **Proprietary** primarily 2-year
- **Coed**
- **Minimally difficult** entrance level

Academics *Degrees:* associate and bachelor's.
Freshman Application Contact Director of Recruitment, ITT Technical Institute, 3428 West Market Street, Akron, OH 44333. *Phone:* 330-865-8600. *Toll-free phone:* 877-818-0154. *Web site:* http://www.itt-tech.edu/.

ITT Technical Institute
Columbus, Ohio

- **Proprietary** primarily 2-year, part of ITT Educational Services, Inc.
- **Coed**
- **Minimally difficult** entrance level

Academics *Calendar:* quarters. *Degrees:* associate and bachelor's.
Freshman Application Contact Director of Recruitment, ITT Technical Institute, 4717 Hilton Corporate Drive, Columbus, OH 43232. *Phone:* 614-868-2000. *Toll-free phone:* 877-233-8864. *Web site:* http://www.itt-tech.edu/.

ITT Technical Institute
Dayton, Ohio

- **Proprietary** primarily 2-year, founded 1935, part of ITT Educational Services, Inc.
- **Suburban** campus
- **Coed**
- **Minimally difficult** entrance level

Academics *Calendar:* quarters. *Degrees:* associate and bachelor's.
Student Life *Housing:* college housing not available.
Freshman Application Contact Director of Recruitment, ITT Technical Institute, 3325 Stop 8 Road, Dayton, OH 45414. *Phone:* 937-264-7700. *Toll-free phone:* 800-568-3241. *Web site:* http://www.itt-tech.edu/.

ITT Technical Institute
Hilliard, Ohio

- **Proprietary** primarily 2-year, founded 2003, part of ITT Educational Services, Inc.
- **Coed**
- **Minimally difficult** entrance level

Academics *Calendar:* quarters. *Degrees:* associate and bachelor's.
Freshman Application Contact Director of Recruitment, ITT Technical Institute, 3781 Park Mill Run Drive, Hilliard, OH 43026. *Phone:* 614-771-4888. *Toll-free phone:* 888-483-4888. *Web site:* http://www.itt-tech.edu/.

ITT Technical Institute
Maumee, Ohio

- **Proprietary** primarily 2-year
- **Coed**

Academics *Degrees:* associate and bachelor's.
Student Life *Housing:* college housing not available.

Freshman Application Contact Director of Recruitment, ITT Technical Institute, 1656 Henthorne Drive, Suite B, Maumee, OH 43537. *Phone:* 419-861-6500. *Toll-free phone:* 877-205-4639. *Web site:* http://www.itt-tech.edu/.

ITT Technical Institute
Norwood, Ohio

- **Proprietary** primarily 2-year, founded 1995, part of ITT Educational Services, Inc.
- **Coed**
- **Minimally difficult** entrance level

Academics *Calendar:* quarters. *Degrees:* associate and bachelor's.
Student Life *Housing:* college housing not available.
Freshman Application Contact Director of Recruitment, ITT Technical Institute, 4750 Wesley Avenue, Norwood, OH 45212. *Phone:* 513-531-8300. *Toll-free phone:* 800-314-8324. *Web site:* http://www.itt-tech.edu/.

ITT Technical Institute
Strongsville, Ohio

- **Proprietary** primarily 2-year, founded 1994, part of ITT Educational Services, Inc.
- **Coed**
- **Minimally difficult** entrance level

Academics *Calendar:* quarters. *Degrees:* associate and bachelor's.
Student Life *Housing:* college housing not available.
Freshman Application Contact Director of Recruitment, ITT Technical Institute, 14955 Sprague Road, Strongsville, OH 44136. *Phone:* 440-234-9091. *Toll-free phone:* 800-331-1488. *Web site:* http://www.itt-tech.edu/.

ITT Technical Institute
Warrensville Heights, Ohio

- **Proprietary** primarily 2-year, founded 2005
- **Coed**
- **Minimally difficult** entrance level

Academics *Calendar:* quarters. *Degrees:* associate and bachelor's.
Student Life *Housing:* college housing not available.
Freshman Application Contact Director of Recruitment, ITT Technical Institute, 4700 Richmond Road, Warrensville Heights, OH 44128. *Phone:* 216-896-6500. *Toll-free phone:* 800-741-3494. *Web site:* http://www.itt-tech.edu/.

ITT Technical Institute
Youngstown, Ohio

- **Proprietary** primarily 2-year, founded 1967, part of ITT Educational Services, Inc.
- **Suburban** campus
- **Coed**
- **Minimally difficult** entrance level

Academics *Calendar:* quarters. *Degrees:* associate and bachelor's.
Student Life *Housing:* college housing not available.
Financial Aid Of all full-time matriculated undergraduates who enrolled in 2010, 5 Federal Work-Study jobs (averaging $3979).
Freshman Application Contact Director of Recruitment, ITT Technical Institute, 1030 North Meridian Road, Youngstown, OH 44509-4098. *Phone:* 330-270-1600. *Toll-free phone:* 800-832-5001. *Web site:* http://www.itt-tech.edu/.

John Carroll University
University Heights, Ohio

- **Independent Roman Catholic (Jesuit)** comprehensive, founded 1886
- **Suburban** 60-acre campus with easy access to Cleveland
- **Endowment** $167.4 million
- **Coed** 2,956 undergraduate students, 98% full-time, 49% women, 51% men
- **Moderately difficult** entrance level, 84% of applicants were admitted

Undergraduates 2,910 full-time, 46 part-time. Students come from 37 states and territories; 9 other countries; 30% are from out of state; 5% Black or African American, non-Hispanic/Latino; 4% Hispanic/Latino; 2% Asian, non-Hispanic/Latino; 0.1% American Indian or Alaska Native, non-Hispanic/Latino; 2% Two or more races, non-Hispanic/Latino; 4% Race/ethnicity unknown; 3% transferred in; 59% live on campus. *Retention:* 89% of full-time freshmen returned.

Freshmen *Admission:* 3,309 applied, 2,772 admitted, 746 enrolled. *Average high school GPA:* 3.39. *Test scores:* SAT critical reading scores over 500: 71%; SAT math scores over 500: 73%; SAT writing scores over 500: 74%; ACT scores over 18: 99%; SAT critical reading scores over 600: 27%; SAT math scores over 600: 28%; SAT writing scores over 600: 24%; ACT scores over 24: 58%; SAT critical reading scores over 700: 4%; SAT math scores over 700: 4%; SAT writing scores over 700: 2%; ACT scores over 30: 12%.

Faculty *Total:* 353, 54% full-time, 71% with terminal degrees. *Student/faculty ratio:* 13:1.

Academics *Calendar:* semesters. *Degrees:* bachelor's, master's, and post-master's certificates. *Special study options:* advanced placement credit, cooperative education, double majors, honors programs, independent study, internships, off-campus study, part-time degree program, services for LD students, student-designed majors, study abroad, summer session for credit. *ROTC:* Army (b). *Unusual degree programs:* 3-2 engineering with Case Western Reserve University; nursing with Joint BA/BSN degree program with Ursuline College.

Computers on Campus 411 computers/terminals and 500 ports are available on campus for general student use. Students can access the following: campus intranet, computer help desk, free student e-mail accounts, online (class) grades, online (class) registration, online (class) schedules, campus portal, course management site, online financial aid and billing; online course sites; online housing selection. Campuswide network is available. 100% of college-owned or -operated housing units are wired for high-speed Internet access. Wireless service is available via entire campus.

Student Life *Housing:* on-campus residence required through sophomore year. *Options:* coed, cooperative. Campus housing is university owned. Freshman campus housing is guaranteed. *Activities and organizations:* drama/theater group, student-run newspaper, radio and television station, choral group, Community Outreach/Volunteer Service Organization, Student Union, Club Sports, Fraternities and Sororities, Carroll News, national fraternities, national sororities. *Campus security:* 24-hour emergency response devices and patrols, late-night transport/escort service, Distinctive Student EMS program fully staffed. *Student services:* health clinic, personal/psychological counseling, women's center.

Athletics Member NCAA. All Division III. *Intercollegiate sports:* baseball M, basketball M/W, cheerleading W(c), crew M(c)/W(c), cross-country running M/W, field hockey W(c), football M, golf M/W, ice hockey M(c), lacrosse M(c)/W(c), rugby M(c)/W(c), sailing M(c)/W(c), skiing (cross-country) M(c)/W(c), skiing (downhill) M(c)/W(c), soccer M/W, softball W, swimming and diving M/W, tennis M/W, track and field M/W, ultimate Frisbee M(c), volleyball M(c)/W, wrestling M. *Intramural sports:* basketball M/W, football M/W, golf M/W, racquetball M/W, rock climbing M/W, soccer M/W, softball M/W, swimming and diving M/W, table tennis M/W, tennis M/W, ultimate Frisbee M/W, volleyball M/W, water polo M/W.

Standardized Tests *Required:* SAT or ACT (for admission).

Costs (2012–13) *One-time required fee:* $325. *Comprehensive fee:* $42,790 includes full-time tuition ($32,130), mandatory fees ($1050), and room and board ($9610). Part-time tuition: $980 per credit. Part-time tuition and fees vary according to course load. *Room and board:* Room and board charges vary according to board plan and housing facility. *Payment plans:* installment, deferred payment. *Waivers:* senior citizens and employees or children of employees.

Financial Aid Of all full-time matriculated undergraduates who enrolled in 2010, 2,479 applied for aid, 2,217 were judged to have need, 988 had their need fully met. 744 Federal Work-Study jobs (averaging $2200). 209 state and other part-time jobs (averaging $1188). In 2010, 539 non-need-based awards were made. *Average percent of need met:* 81%. *Average financial aid package:* $24,817. *Average need-based loan:* $3935. *Average need-based gift aid:* $19,554. *Average non-need-based aid:* $10,222. *Average indebtedness upon graduation:* $30,422. *Financial aid deadline:* 3/15.

Applying *Options:* electronic application, early admission, early action, deferred entrance. *Required:* essay or personal statement, high school transcript, 1 letter of recommendation. *Required for some:* 2 letters of recommendation, interview. *Application deadlines:* 2/1 (freshmen), rolling (transfers), 12/1 (early action). *Notification:* continuous (freshmen), 12/20 (early action).

Freshman Application Contact Mr. Steven P. Vitatoe, Executive Director of Enrollment, John Carroll University, 20700 North Park Boulevard, University Heights, OH 44118. *Phone:* 216-397-4294. *Toll-free phone:* 888-335-6800. *Fax:* 216-397-4981. *E-mail:* svitatoe@jcu.edu. *Web site:* http://www.jcu.edu/.

Kent State University

Kent, Ohio

- **State-supported** university, founded 1910, part of Kent State University System
- **Suburban** 1347-acre campus with easy access to Cleveland
- **Endowment** $90.5 million
- **Coed** 22,260 undergraduate students, 87% full-time, 59% women, 41% men
- **Moderately difficult** entrance level, 87% of applicants were admitted

Undergraduates 19,320 full-time, 2,940 part-time. Students come from 50 states and territories; 64 other countries; 10% are from out of state; 9% Black or African American, non-Hispanic/Latino; 3% Hispanic/Latino; 1% Asian, non-Hispanic/Latino; 0.0% Native Hawaiian or other Pacific Islander, non-Hispanic/Latino; 0.3% American Indian or Alaska Native, non-Hispanic/Latino; 1% Two or more races, non-Hispanic/Latino; 3% Race/ethnicity unknown; 5% international; 6% transferred in; 29% live on campus. *Retention:* 75% of full-time freshmen returned.

Freshmen *Admission:* 13,980 applied, 12,231 admitted, 4,331 enrolled. *Average high school GPA:* 3.22. *Test scores:* SAT critical reading scores over 500: 55%; SAT math scores over 500: 59%; SAT writing scores over 500: 49%; ACT scores over 18: 93%; SAT critical reading scores over 600: 15%; SAT math scores over 600: 18%; SAT writing scores over 600: 14%; ACT scores over 24: 34%; SAT critical reading scores over 700: 3%; SAT math scores over 700: 3%; SAT writing scores over 700: 1%; ACT scores over 30: 4%.

Faculty *Total:* 1,592, 55% full-time. *Student/faculty ratio:* 21:1.

Academics *Calendar:* semesters. *Degrees:* certificates, associate, bachelor's, master's, doctoral, post-master's, postbachelor's, and first professional certificates. *Special study options:* academic remediation for entering students, accelerated degree program, adult/continuing education programs, advanced placement credit, cooperative education, distance learning, double majors, English as a second language, external degree program, freshman honors college, honors programs, independent study, internships, off-campus study, part-time degree program, services for LD students, student-designed majors, study abroad, summer session for credit. *ROTC:* Army (b), Air Force (b).

Computers on Campus 2,000 computers/terminals and 1,200 ports are available on campus for general student use. Students can access the following: computer help desk, free student e-mail accounts, online (class) grades, online (class) registration, online (class) schedules. Campuswide network is available. 100% of college-owned or -operated housing units are wired for high-speed Internet access. Wireless service is available via entire campus.

Student Life *Housing:* on-campus residence required through sophomore year. *Options:* coed, men-only, women-only, disabled students. Campus housing is university owned. Freshman campus housing is guaranteed. *Activities and organizations:* drama/theater group, student-run newspaper, radio and television station, choral group, marching band, Commuter & Off-Campus Student Organization (COSO), Fashion Student Organization (FSO), Public Relations Students Society of America (PRSSA), Habitat for Humanity, Relay for Life, national fraternities, national sororities. *Campus security:* 24-hour emergency response devices and patrols, student patrols, late-night transport/escort service, controlled dormitory access, campus police and fire department, electronic locks on computer labs, studios and laboratory research areas. *Student services:* health clinic, personal/psychological counseling, women's center, legal services.

Athletics Member NCAA. All Division I. *Intercollegiate sports:* baseball M(s), basketball M(s)/W(s), cross-country running M(s)/W(s), field hockey W(s), football M(s), golf M(s)/W(s), gymnastics W(s), soccer W(s), softball W(s), track and field M(s)/W(s), volleyball W(s), wrestling M(s). *Intramural sports:* badminton M(c)/W(c), baseball M(c), basketball M/W, bowling M(c)/W(c), equestrian sports M(c)/W(c), fencing M(c)/W(c), field hockey W(c), football M/W, golf M(c)/W(c), gymnastics M(c)/W(c), ice hockey M(c), lacrosse M(c), racquetball M(c)/W(c), rugby M(c)/W(c), sailing M(c)/W(c), skiing (downhill) M(c)/W(c), soccer M(c)/W(c), softball M/W, swimming and diving M(c)/W(c), table tennis M/W, tennis M/W, ultimate Frisbee M/W, volleyball M(c)/W(c), water polo M/W, wrestling M.

Standardized Tests *Required:* SAT or ACT (for admission).

Costs (2011–12) *Tuition:* state resident $9346 full-time, $425 per credit hour part-time; nonresident $17,306 full-time, $787 per credit hour part-time. Full-time tuition and fees vary according to course load. Part-time tuition and fees vary according to course load. *Room and board:* $8830; room only: $5440. Room and board charges vary according to board plan and housing facility. *Payment plans:* installment, deferred payment. *Waivers:* senior citizens and employees or children of employees.

Financial Aid Of all full-time matriculated undergraduates who enrolled in 2011, 14,592 applied for aid, 12,705 were judged to have need, 4,795 had their need fully met. 386 Federal Work-Study jobs (averaging $2900). In 2011, 2082 non-need-based awards were made. *Average percent of need met:* 49%. *Average financial aid package:* $8994. *Average need-based loan:* $4012.

Average need-based gift aid: $5465. *Average non-need-based aid:* $4174. *Average indebtedness upon graduation:* $29,842.

Applying *Options:* electronic application, early admission. *Application fee:* $40. *Required:* high school transcript, minimum 2.5 GPA. *Application deadlines:* rolling (freshmen), rolling (transfers). *Notification:* continuous (freshmen), continuous (transfers).

Freshman Application Contact Mr. Christopher Buttenschon, Assistant Director of Admissions, Kent State University, 161 Michael Schwartz Center, Kent, OH 44242-0001. *Phone:* 330-672-2444. *Toll-free phone:* 800-988-KENT. *Fax:* 330-672-2499. *E-mail:* admissions@kent.edu. *Web site:* http://www.kent.edu/.

See below for display ad and page 1390 for the College Close-Up.

Kent State University at Ashtabula

Ashtabula, Ohio

- **State-supported** primarily 2-year, founded 1958, part of Kent State University System
- **Small-town** 120-acre campus with easy access to Cleveland
- **Coed** 2,451 undergraduate students, 50% full-time, 66% women, 34% men
- **Noncompetitive** entrance level, 99% of applicants were admitted

Undergraduates 1,227 full-time, 1,224 part-time. Students come from 12 states and territories; 1 other country; 2% are from out of state; 6% Black or African American, non-Hispanic/Latino; 3% Hispanic/Latino; 0.7% Asian, non-Hispanic/Latino; 0.5% American Indian or Alaska Native, non-Hispanic/Latino; 1% Two or more races, non-Hispanic/Latino; 3% Race/ethnicity unknown; 10% transferred in. *Retention:* 49% of full-time freshmen returned.

Freshmen *Admission:* 607 applied, 603 admitted, 419 enrolled. *Average high school GPA:* 2.68. *Test scores:* ACT scores over 18: 69%; ACT scores over 24: 10%; ACT scores over 30: 2%.

Faculty *Total:* 126, 41% full-time. *Student/faculty ratio:* 18:1.

Academics *Calendar:* semesters. *Degrees:* certificates, associate, and bachelor's (also offers some upper-level and graduate courses). *Special study*

options: academic remediation for entering students, advanced placement credit, distance learning, double majors, independent study, part-time degree program, services for LD students, student-designed majors, study abroad, summer session for credit.

Computers on Campus 70 computers/terminals and 175 ports are available on campus for general student use. Students can access the following: computer help desk, free student e-mail accounts, online (class) grades, online (class) registration, online (class) schedules. Campuswide network is available. Wireless service is available via entire campus.

Student Life *Housing:* college housing not available. *Activities and organizations:* student government, student veterans association, Student Nurses Association, Student Occupational Therapy Association (SOTA), Media Club. *Campus security:* 24-hour emergency response devices.

Standardized Tests *Required for some:* SAT or ACT (for admission). *Recommended:* SAT or ACT (for admission).

Costs (2011–12) *Tuition:* state resident $5288 full-time, $241 per credit hour part-time; nonresident $13,248 full-time, $603 per credit hour part-time. Full-time tuition and fees vary according to course level and course load. Part-time tuition and fees vary according to course level and course load. *Payment plans:* installment, deferred payment. *Waivers:* senior citizens and employees or children of employees.

Financial Aid Of all full-time matriculated undergraduates who enrolled in 2011, 880 applied for aid, 852 were judged to have need, 182 had their need fully met. In 2011, 7 non-need-based awards were made. *Average percent of need met:* 44%. *Average financial aid package:* $7753. *Average need-based loan:* $3568. *Average need-based gift aid:* $4829. *Average non-need-based aid:* $1426.

Applying *Options:* electronic application, early admission, deferred entrance. *Application fee:* $30. *Required:* high school transcript. *Application deadlines:* rolling (freshmen), rolling (transfers). *Notification:* continuous (freshmen), continuous (transfers).

Freshman Application Contact Kent State University at Ashtabula, 3300 Lake Road West, Ashtabula, OH 44004-2299. *Phone:* 440-964-4217. *Web site:* http://www.ashtabula.kent.edu/.

Kent State University at East Liverpool
East Liverpool, Ohio

- **State-supported** primarily 2-year, founded 1967, part of Kent State University System
- **Small-town** 4-acre campus with easy access to Pittsburgh
- **Coed** 1,491 undergraduate students, 59% full-time, 68% women, 32% men
- **Noncompetitive** entrance level, 96% of applicants were admitted

Undergraduates 883 full-time, 608 part-time. Students come from 8 states and territories; 2 other countries; 5% are from out of state; 4% Black or African American, non-Hispanic/Latino; 1% Hispanic/Latino; 0.3% Asian, non-Hispanic/Latino; 0.1% Native Hawaiian or other Pacific Islander, non-Hispanic/Latino; 0.3% American Indian or Alaska Native, non-Hispanic/Latino; 0.8% Two or more races, non-Hispanic/Latino; 3% Race/ethnicity unknown; 0.1% international; 6% transferred in. *Retention:* 54% of full-time freshmen returned.

Freshmen *Admission:* 211 applied, 203 admitted, 146 enrolled. *Average high school GPA:* 2.86. *Test scores:* SAT critical reading scores over 500: 67%; SAT math scores over 500: 67%; SAT writing scores over 500: 100%; ACT scores over 18: 52%; SAT critical reading scores over 600: 67%; SAT math scores over 600: 33%; SAT writing scores over 600: 67%; ACT scores over 24: 7%; SAT critical reading scores over 700: 33%.

Faculty *Total:* 77, 34% full-time. *Student/faculty ratio:* 18:1.

Academics *Calendar:* semesters. *Degrees:* certificates, associate, and bachelor's (also offers some upper-level and graduate courses). *Special study options:* academic remediation for entering students, accelerated degree program, adult/continuing education programs, advanced placement credit, distance learning, double majors, freshman honors college, honors programs, independent study, internships, part-time degree program, services for LD students, student-designed majors, study abroad, summer session for credit.

Computers on Campus 72 computers/terminals are available on campus for general student use. Students can access the following: computer help desk, free student e-mail accounts, online (class) grades, online (class) registration, online (class) schedules. Campuswide network is available. Wireless service is available via entire campus.

Student Life *Housing:* college housing not available. *Activities and organizations:* student-run newspaper, Student Government, Student Nurses Association, Environmental Club, Occupational Therapist Assistant Club, Physical Therapist Assistant Club. *Campus security:* student patrols, late-night transport/escort service.

Standardized Tests *Required for some:* SAT or ACT (for admission). *Recommended:* SAT or ACT (for admission).

Costs (2011–12) *Tuition:* state resident $5288 full-time, $241 per credit hour part-time; nonresident $13,248 full-time, $603 per credit hour part-time. Full-time tuition and fees vary according to course level and course load. Part-time tuition and fees vary according to course level and course load. *Payment plans:* installment, deferred payment. *Waivers:* senior citizens and employees or children of employees.

Financial Aid Of all full-time matriculated undergraduates who enrolled in 2011, 473 applied for aid, 451 were judged to have need, 94 had their need fully met. In 2011, 1 non-need-based awards were made. *Average percent of need met:* 45%. *Average financial aid package:* $7873. *Average need-based loan:* $3481. *Average need-based gift aid:* $4787. *Average non-need-based aid:* $500.

Applying *Options:* electronic application, early admission, deferred entrance. *Application fee:* $30. *Required:* high school transcript. *Application deadlines:* rolling (freshmen), rolling (transfers). *Notification:* continuous (freshmen), continuous (transfers).

Freshman Application Contact Kent State University at East Liverpool, 400 East 4th Street, East Liverpool, OH 43920-3497. *Phone:* 330-382-7415. *Web site:* http://www.eliv.kent.edu/.

Kent State University at Geauga
Burton, Ohio

- **State-supported** 4-year, founded 1964, part of Kent State University System
- **Rural** 87-acre campus with easy access to Cleveland
- **Coed** 2,577 undergraduate students, 57% full-time, 66% women, 34% men
- **Noncompetitive** entrance level

Undergraduates 1,465 full-time, 1,112 part-time. Students come from 12 states and territories; 6 other countries; 1% are from out of state; 9% Black or African American, non-Hispanic/Latino; 2% Hispanic/Latino; 1% Asian, non-Hispanic/Latino; 0.1% Native Hawaiian or other Pacific Islander, non-His-

panic/Latino; 0.5% American Indian or Alaska Native, non-Hispanic/Latino; 1% Two or more races, non-Hispanic/Latino; 4% Race/ethnicity unknown; 0.5% international; 4% transferred in. *Retention:* 60% of full-time freshmen returned.

Freshmen *Admission:* 264 enrolled. *Average high school GPA:* 2.52. *Test scores:* SAT critical reading scores over 500: 41%; SAT math scores over 500: 38%; SAT writing scores over 500: 23%; ACT scores over 18: 67%; SAT critical reading scores over 600: 6%; SAT math scores over 600: 16%; SAT writing scores over 600: 7%; ACT scores over 24: 12%; ACT scores over 30: 2%.

Faculty *Total:* 126, 22% full-time. *Student/faculty ratio:* 20:1.

Academics *Calendar:* semesters. *Degrees:* certificates, associate, and bachelor's. *Special study options:* academic remediation for entering students, accelerated degree program, advanced placement credit, distance learning, double majors, internships, part-time degree program, services for LD students, student-designed majors, summer session for credit.

Computers on Campus 270 computers/terminals and 110 ports are available on campus for general student use. Students can access the following: campus intranet, computer help desk, free student e-mail accounts, online (class) grades, online (class) registration, online (class) schedules. Campuswide network is available. Wireless service is available via entire campus.

Student Life *Housing:* college housing not available. *Activities and organizations:* Student Ambassadors, Campus Crusade for Christ, Gaia Society. *Campus security:* 24-hour emergency response devices.

Standardized Tests *Required for some:* SAT or ACT (for admission). *Recommended:* SAT or ACT (for admission).

Costs (2011–12) *Tuition:* state resident $5288 full-time, $241 per credit hour part-time; nonresident $13,248 full-time, $603 per credit hour part-time. Full-time tuition and fees vary according to course level and course load. Part-time tuition and fees vary according to course level and course load. *Payment plans:* installment, deferred payment. *Waivers:* senior citizens and employees or children of employees.

Financial Aid Of all full-time matriculated undergraduates who enrolled in 2011, 546 applied for aid, 499 were judged to have need, 154 had their need fully met. In 2011, 4 non-need-based awards were made. *Average percent of need met:* 45%. *Average financial aid package:* $6890. *Average need-based loan:* $3603. *Average need-based gift aid:* $4308. *Average non-need-based aid:* $1981.

Applying *Options:* electronic application, deferred entrance. *Application fee:* $30. *Required:* high school transcript. *Application deadlines:* rolling (freshmen), rolling (transfers). *Notification:* continuous (freshmen), continuous (transfers).

Freshman Application Contact Thomas Hoiles, Kent State University at Geauga, 14111 Claridon-Troy Road, Burton, OH 44021. *Phone:* 440-834-4187. *Fax:* 440-834-8846. *E-mail:* thoiles@kent.edu. *Web site:* http://www.geauga.kent.edu/.

Kent State University at Salem
Salem, Ohio

- **State-supported** primarily 2-year, founded 1966, part of Kent State University System
- **Rural** 98-acre campus
- **Coed** 2,018 undergraduate students, 68% full-time, 71% women, 29% men
- **Noncompetitive** entrance level, 97% of applicants were admitted

Undergraduates 1,373 full-time, 645 part-time. Students come from 11 states and territories; 4 other countries; 2% are from out of state; 3% Black or African American, non-Hispanic/Latino; 2% Hispanic/Latino; 0.5% Asian, non-Hispanic/Latino; 0.6% American Indian or Alaska Native, non-Hispanic/Latino; 0.7% Two or more races, non-Hispanic/Latino; 3% Race/ethnicity unknown; 0.2% international; 8% transferred in. *Retention:* 54% of full-time freshmen returned.

Freshmen *Admission:* 418 applied, 405 admitted, 267 enrolled. *Average high school GPA:* 2.84. *Test scores:* SAT critical reading scores over 500: 67%; SAT math scores over 500: 33%; SAT writing scores over 500: 33%; ACT scores over 18: 71%; ACT scores over 24: 12%.

Faculty *Total:* 133, 34% full-time. *Student/faculty ratio:* 17:1.

Academics *Calendar:* semesters. *Degrees:* certificates, associate, and bachelor's (also offers some upper-level and graduate courses). *Special study options:* academic remediation for entering students, accelerated degree program, adult/continuing education programs, advanced placement credit, cooperative education, distance learning, double majors, freshman honors college, honors programs, independent study, internships, part-time degree program, services for LD students, student-designed majors, summer session for credit.

Computers on Campus Students can access the following: computer help desk, free student e-mail accounts, online (class) grades, online (class) registration, online (class) schedules. Campuswide network is available. Wireless service is available via entire campus.

Student Life *Housing:* college housing not available. *Activities and organizations:* choral group, Honors Club, Human Services Technology Club, Radiologic Technology Club, Student Government Organization, Students for Professional Nursing. *Campus security:* 24-hour emergency response devices, late-night transport/escort service. *Student services:* personal/psychological counseling.

Athletics *Intramural sports:* basketball M/W, skiing (downhill) M/W, table tennis M/W, tennis M/W, volleyball M/W.

Standardized Tests *Required for some:* SAT or ACT (for admission). *Recommended:* SAT or ACT (for admission).

Costs (2011–12) *Tuition:* state resident $5288 full-time, $241 per credit hour part-time; nonresident $13,248 full-time, $603 per credit hour part-time. Full-time tuition and fees vary according to course level and course load. Part-time tuition and fees vary according to course level and course load. *Payment plans:* installment, deferred payment. *Waivers:* senior citizens and employees or children of employees.

Financial Aid Of all full-time matriculated undergraduates who enrolled in 2011, 894 applied for aid, 844 were judged to have need, 228 had their need fully met. In 2011, 9 non-need-based awards were made. *Average percent of need met:* 45%. *Average financial aid package:* $7217. *Average need-based loan:* $3496. *Average need-based gift aid:* $4489. *Average non-need-based aid:* $979.

Applying *Options:* electronic application, early admission, deferred entrance. *Application fee:* $30. *Required:* high school transcript. *Required for some:* essay or personal statement. *Application deadlines:* rolling (freshmen), rolling (transfers). *Notification:* continuous (freshmen), continuous (transfers).

Freshman Application Contact Kristin Toothman, Kent State University at Salem, 2491 State Route 45 South, Salem, OH 44460-9412. *Phone:* 330-337-4226. *E-mail:* ktoothm@kent.edu. *Web site:* http://www.salem.kent.edu/.

Kent State University at Stark
Canton, Ohio

- **State-supported** comprehensive, founded 1967, part of Kent State University System
- **Suburban** 200-acre campus with easy access to Cleveland
- **Coed** 4,868 undergraduate students, 66% full-time, 60% women, 40% men
- **Noncompetitive** entrance level, 94% of applicants were admitted

Undergraduates 3,193 full-time, 1,675 part-time. Students come from 14 states and territories; 5 other countries; 1% are from out of state; 8% Black or African American, non-Hispanic/Latino; 2% Hispanic/Latino; 0.7% Asian, non-Hispanic/Latino; 0.5% American Indian or Alaska Native, non-Hispanic/Latino; 1% Two or more races, non-Hispanic/Latino; 3% Race/ethnicity unknown; 0.1% international; 10% transferred in. *Retention:* 62% of full-time freshmen returned.

Freshmen *Admission:* 1,060 applied, 992 admitted, 736 enrolled. *Average high school GPA:* 2.78. *Test scores:* SAT critical reading scores over 500: 50%; SAT math scores over 500: 38%; SAT writing scores over 500: 47%; ACT scores over 18: 75%; SAT critical reading scores over 600: 19%; SAT math scores over 600: 13%; SAT writing scores over 600: 7%; ACT scores over 24: 15%.

Faculty *Total:* 262, 40% full-time. *Student/faculty ratio:* 21:1.

Academics *Calendar:* semesters. *Degrees:* certificates, associate, bachelor's, and master's (also offers some graduate courses). *Special study options:* academic remediation for entering students, adult/continuing education programs, advanced placement credit, distance learning, double majors, honors programs, independent study, internships, off-campus study, part-time degree program, services for LD students, student-designed majors, study abroad, summer session for credit.

Computers on Campus 575 computers/terminals are available on campus for general student use. Students can access the following: campus intranet, computer help desk, free student e-mail accounts, online (class) grades, online (class) registration, online (class) schedules. Campuswide network is available. Wireless service is available via entire campus.

Student Life *Housing:* college housing not available. *Activities and organizations:* drama/theater group, choral group, Club Sunaarashi (Japanese Animation, Magic the Gathering, and Dungeons and Dragons), Rooted in Faith-Bible Club (non-denominational), Kent State Stark Education Association (KSSEA), SCRUBS (nursing organization), Ohio Collegiate Music Education Association (OCMEA). *Campus security:* 24-hour emergency response devices, late-night transport/escort service. *Student services:* personal/psychological counseling.

Standardized Tests *Required for some:* SAT or ACT (for admission). *Recommended:* SAT or ACT (for admission).

Costs (2011–12) *Tuition:* state resident $5288 full-time, $241 per credit hour part-time; nonresident $13,248 full-time, $603 per credit hour part-time. Full-time tuition and fees vary according to course level and course load. Part-time

tuition and fees vary according to course level and course load. *Payment plans:* installment, deferred payment. *Waivers:* senior citizens and employees or children of employees.

Financial Aid Of all full-time matriculated undergraduates who enrolled in 2011, 2,344 applied for aid, 2,140 were judged to have need, 632 had their need fully met. In 2011, 39 non-need-based awards were made. *Average percent of need met:* 49%. *Average financial aid package:* $7146. *Average need-based loan:* $3593. *Average need-based gift aid:* $4354. *Average non-need-based aid:* $2201.

Applying *Options:* electronic application, early admission, deferred entrance. *Application fee:* $30. *Required:* high school transcript. *Application deadlines:* rolling (freshmen), rolling (transfers). *Notification:* continuous (freshmen), continuous (transfers).

Freshman Application Contact Eleanor Kuder, Kent State University at Stark, 6000 Frank Avenue, NW, Canton, OH 44720-7599. *Phone:* 330-244-3252. *E-mail:* ekuder@kent.edu. *Web site:* http://www.stark.kent.edu/.

Kent State University at Trumbull
Warren, Ohio

- **State-supported** primarily 2-year, founded 1954, part of Kent State University System
- **Suburban** 200-acre campus with easy access to Cleveland
- **Coed** 3,205 undergraduate students, 61% full-time, 64% women, 36% men
- **Noncompetitive** entrance level, 99% of applicants were admitted

Undergraduates 1,971 full-time, 1,234 part-time. Students come from 16 states and territories; 3 other countries; 1% are from out of state; 12% Black or African American, non-Hispanic/Latino; 2% Hispanic/Latino; 0.7% Asian, non-Hispanic/Latino; 0.2% American Indian or Alaska Native, non-Hispanic/Latino; 1% Two or more races, non-Hispanic/Latino; 3% Race/ethnicity unknown; 0.4% international; 7% transferred in. *Retention:* 49% of full-time freshmen returned.

Freshmen *Admission:* 513 applied, 507 admitted, 392 enrolled. *Average high school GPA:* 2.65. *Test scores:* SAT critical reading scores over 500: 33%; SAT math scores over 500: 50%; SAT writing scores over 500: 17%; ACT scores over 18: 70%; SAT math scores over 600: 17%; ACT scores over 24: 12%; ACT scores over 30: 1%.

Faculty *Total:* 128, 45% full-time. *Student/faculty ratio:* 22:1.

Academics *Calendar:* semesters. *Degrees:* certificates, associate, and bachelor's (also offers some upper-level and graduate courses). *Special study options:* academic remediation for entering students, adult/continuing education programs, advanced placement credit, distance learning, double majors, freshman honors college, honors programs, independent study, internships, part-time degree program, services for LD students, student-designed majors, study abroad, summer session for credit.

Computers on Campus 300 computers/terminals are available on campus for general student use. Students can access the following: computer help desk, free student e-mail accounts, online (class) grades, online (class) registration, online (class) schedules. Campuswide network is available. Wireless service is available via entire campus.

Student Life *Housing:* college housing not available. *Activities and organizations:* drama/theater group, National Student Nurses Association, Spot On Improv Group, Amnesty International, Campus Crusade for Christ, Student Veteran Organization. *Campus security:* 24-hour emergency response devices, late-night transport/escort service, patrols by trained security personnel during open hours. *Student services:* personal/psychological counseling.

Standardized Tests *Required for some:* SAT or ACT (for admission). *Recommended:* SAT or ACT (for admission).

Costs (2011–12) *Tuition:* state resident $5288 full-time, $241 per credit hour part-time; nonresident $13,248 full-time, $603 per credit hour part-time. Full-time tuition and fees vary according to course level and course load. Part-time tuition and fees vary according to course level and course load. *Payment plans:* installment, deferred payment. *Waivers:* senior citizens and employees or children of employees.

Financial Aid Of all full-time matriculated undergraduates who enrolled in 2011, 1,253 applied for aid, 1,198 were judged to have need, 292 had their need fully met. In 2011, 6 non-need-based awards were made. *Average percent of need met:* 45%. *Average financial aid package:* $7686. *Average need-based loan:* $3615. *Average need-based gift aid:* $4803. *Average non-need-based aid:* $1167.

Applying *Options:* electronic application, deferred entrance. *Application fee:* $30. *Required:* high school transcript. *Application deadlines:* rolling (freshmen), rolling (transfers). *Notification:* continuous (freshmen), continuous (transfers).

Freshman Application Contact Kent State University at Trumbull, Warren, OH 44483. *Phone:* 330-675-8935. *Web site:* http://www.trumbull.kent.edu/.

Kent State University at Tuscarawas

New Philadelphia, Ohio

- **State-supported** primarily 2-year, founded 1962, part of Kent State University System
- **Small-town** 172-acre campus with easy access to Cleveland
- **Coed** 2,659 undergraduate students, 57% full-time, 60% women, 40% men
- **Noncompetitive** entrance level, 96% of applicants were admitted

Undergraduates 1,510 full-time, 1,149 part-time. Students come from 7 states and territories; 4 other countries; 1% are from out of state; 2% Black or African American, non-Hispanic/Latino; 0.9% Hispanic/Latino; 0.4% Asian, non-Hispanic/Latino; 0.1% Native Hawaiian or other Pacific Islander, non-Hispanic/Latino; 0.3% American Indian or Alaska Native, non-Hispanic/Latino; 0.8% Two or more races, non-Hispanic/Latino; 3% Race/ethnicity unknown; 0.2% international; 7% transferred in. *Retention:* 62% of full-time freshmen returned.

Freshmen *Admission:* 542 applied, 519 admitted, 401 enrolled. *Average high school GPA:* 2.81. *Test scores:* ACT scores over 18: 80%; ACT scores over 24: 21%; ACT scores over 30: 1%.

Faculty *Total:* 139, 39% full-time. *Student/faculty ratio:* 20:1.

Academics *Calendar:* semesters. *Degrees:* certificates, associate, and bachelor's (also offers some upper-level and graduate courses). *Special study options:* academic remediation for entering students, accelerated degree program, adult/continuing education programs, advanced placement credit, distance learning, double majors, freshman honors college, honors programs, independent study, internships, part-time degree program, services for LD students, student-designed majors, study abroad, summer session for credit.

Computers on Campus 194 computers/terminals are available on campus for general student use. Students can access the following: computer help desk, free student e-mail accounts, online (class) grades, online (class) registration, online (class) schedules. Campuswide network is available. Wireless service is available via entire campus.

Student Life *Housing:* college housing not available. *Activities and organizations:* drama/theater group, choral group, Society of Manufacturing Engineers, IEEE, Animation Imagineers, Justice Studies Club, Student Activities Council.

Athletics *Intramural sports:* basketball M/W, volleyball M/W.

Standardized Tests *Required for some:* SAT or ACT (for admission). *Recommended:* SAT or ACT (for admission).

Costs (2011–12) *Tuition:* state resident $5288 full-time, $241 per credit hour part-time; nonresident $13,248 full-time, $603 per credit hour part-time. Full-time tuition and fees vary according to course level and course load. Part-time tuition and fees vary according to course level and course load. *Payment plans:* installment, deferred payment. *Waivers:* senior citizens and employees or children of employees.

Financial Aid Of all full-time matriculated undergraduates who enrolled in 2011, 1,137 applied for aid, 1,075 were judged to have need, 244 had their need fully met. In 2011, 7 non-need-based awards were made. *Average percent of need met:* 47%. *Average financial aid package:* $7391. *Average need-based loan:* $3423. *Average need-based gift aid:* $4577. *Average non-need-based aid:* $1111.

Applying *Options:* electronic application, early admission, deferred entrance. *Application fee:* $30. *Required:* high school transcript. *Application deadlines:* rolling (freshmen), rolling (transfers). *Notification:* continuous (freshmen), continuous (transfers).

Freshman Application Contact Mrs. Laurie R. Donley, Director of Enrollment Management and Student Services, Kent State University at Tuscarawas, 330 University Drive Northeast, New Philadelphia, OH 44663-9403. *Phone:* 330-339-3391 Ext. 47425. *Fax:* 330-339-3321. *E-mail:* ldonley@kent.edu. *Web site:* http://www.tusc.kent.edu/.

Kenyon College

Gambier, Ohio

- **Independent** 4-year, founded 1824
- **Rural** 1200-acre campus with easy access to Columbus
- **Endowment** $175.0 million
- **Coed** 1,657 undergraduate students, 99% full-time, 54% women, 46% men
- **Very difficult** entrance level, 33% of applicants were admitted

Undergraduates 1,648 full-time, 9 part-time. Students come from 49 states and territories; 40 other countries; 84% are from out of state; 3% Black or African American, non-Hispanic/Latino; 5% Hispanic/Latino; 6% Asian, non-Hispanic/Latino; 0.9% American Indian or Alaska Native, non-Hispanic/Latino; 0.3% Two or more races, non-Hispanic/Latino; 2% Race/ethnicity unknown; 3% international; 1% transferred in; 98% live on campus. *Retention:* 94% of full-time freshmen returned.

Freshmen *Admission:* 4,272 applied, 1,429 admitted, 468 enrolled. *Average high school GPA:* 3.9. *Test scores:* SAT critical reading scores over 500: 100%; SAT math scores over 500: 100%; SAT writing scores over 500: 99%; ACT scores over 18: 100%; SAT critical reading scores over 600: 90%; SAT math scores over 600: 82%; SAT writing scores over 600: 88%; ACT scores over 24: 97%; SAT critical reading scores over 700: 42%; SAT math scores over 700: 24%; SAT writing scores over 700: 48%; ACT scores over 30: 60%.

Faculty *Total:* 166, 94% full-time, 99% with terminal degrees. *Student/faculty ratio:* 10:1.

Academics *Calendar:* semesters. *Degree:* bachelor's. *Special study options:* accelerated degree program, advanced placement credit, double majors, honors programs, independent study, off-campus study, services for LD students, student-designed majors, study abroad. *Unusual degree programs:* 3-2 engineering with Washington University in St. Louis, Case Western Reserve University, Rensselaer Polytechnic Institute; environmental science with Duke University, education with The Bank Street College of Education.

Computers on Campus 450 computers/terminals are available on campus for general student use. Students can access the following: campus intranet, computer help desk, free student e-mail accounts, online (class) grades, online (class) schedules, commercial databases. Campuswide network is available. 99% of college-owned or -operated housing units are wired for high-speed Internet access. Wireless service is available via entire campus.

Student Life *Housing:* on-campus residence required through senior year. *Options:* coed, women-only, disabled students. Campus housing is university owned. Freshman campus housing is guaranteed. *Activities and organizations:* drama/theater group, student-run newspaper, radio station, choral group, student theater organizations, student radio station, musical groups, intramural sports and clubs, national fraternities, national sororities. *Campus security:* 24-hour emergency response devices and patrols, student patrols, late-night transport/escort service, controlled dormitory access. *Student services:* health clinic, personal/psychological counseling, women's center.

Athletics Member NCAA. All Division III. *Intercollegiate sports:* baseball M, basketball M/W, cross-country running M/W, field hockey W, football M, golf M, lacrosse M/W, soccer M/W, softball W, swimming and diving M/W, tennis M/W, track and field M/W, volleyball W. *Intramural sports:* archery M(c)/W(c), baseball M(c), basketball M/W, equestrian sports M(c)/W(c), fencing M(c)/W(c), football M/W, lacrosse M(c), racquetball M/W, rugby M(c)/W(c), soccer M, softball M/W, squash M(c)/W(c), tennis M/W, ultimate Frisbee M(c)/W(c), volleyball M/W.

Standardized Tests *Required:* SAT or ACT (for admission).

Costs (2012–13) *Comprehensive fee:* $54,760 includes full-time tuition ($42,780), mandatory fees ($1640), and room and board ($10,340). *Payment plan:* installment. *Waivers:* employees or children of employees.

Financial Aid Of all full-time matriculated undergraduates who enrolled in 2011, 811 applied for aid, 718 were judged to have need, 433 had their need fully met. 229 Federal Work-Study jobs (averaging $1286). 143 state and other part-time jobs (averaging $1236). In 2011, 213 non-need-based awards were made. *Average percent of need met:* 98%. *Average financial aid package:* $36,603. *Average need-based loan:* $4964. *Average need-based gift aid:* $32,723. *Average non-need-based aid:* $11,392. *Average indebtedness upon graduation:* $19,480.

Applying *Options:* electronic application, early admission, early decision, deferred entrance. *Application fee:* $50. *Required:* essay or personal statement, high school transcript, counselor recommendation. *Recommended:* minimum 3.5 GPA, 2 letters of recommendation, interview. *Application deadlines:* 1/15 (freshmen), 4/15 (transfers). *Early decision deadline:* 11/15 (for plan 1), 1/15 (for plan 2). *Notification:* 4/1 (freshmen), 5/15 (transfers), 12/15 (early decision plan 1), 2/1 (early decision plan 2).

Freshman Application Contact Ms. Jennifer Delahunty, Dean of Admissions, Kenyon College, Ransom Hall, Gambier, OH 43022. *Phone:* 740-427-5776. *Toll-free phone:* 800-848-2468. *Fax:* 740-427-5770. *E-mail:* admissions@kenyon.edu. *Web site:* http://www.kenyon.edu/.

Kettering College of Medical Arts

Kettering, Ohio

Freshman Application Contact Mrs. Becky McDonald, Director of Enrollment Services, Kettering College of Medical Arts, 3737 Southern Boulevard, Kettering, OH 45429-1299. *Phone:* 937-395-8628. *Toll-free phone:* 800-433-5262. *Fax:* 937-296-4238. *Web site:* http://www.kcma.edu/.

Lake Erie College
Painesville, Ohio

- **Independent** comprehensive, founded 1856
- **Suburban** 48-acre campus with easy access to Cleveland
- **Endowment** $33.5 million
- **Coed** 981 undergraduate students, 93% full-time, 49% women, 51% men
- **Moderately difficult** entrance level, 59% of applicants were admitted

Undergraduates 912 full-time, 69 part-time. Students come from 29 states and territories; 6 other countries; 23% are from out of state; 7% Black or African American, non-Hispanic/Latino; 2% Hispanic/Latino; 0.6% Asian, non-Hispanic/Latino; 0.3% American Indian or Alaska Native, non-Hispanic/Latino; 3% Two or more races, non-Hispanic/Latino; 1% Race/ethnicity unknown; 2% international; 6% transferred in; 55% live on campus. *Retention:* 62% of full-time freshmen returned.

Freshmen *Admission:* 1,456 applied, 860 admitted, 210 enrolled. *Average high school GPA:* 3.12. *Test scores:* SAT critical reading scores over 500: 47%; SAT math scores over 500: 59%; SAT writing scores over 500: 43%; ACT scores over 18: 91%; SAT critical reading scores over 600: 13%; SAT math scores over 600: 23%; SAT writing scores over 600: 17%; ACT scores over 24: 27%; SAT critical reading scores over 700: 3%; SAT math scores over 700: 3%; SAT writing scores over 700: 1%; ACT scores over 30: 4%.

Faculty *Total:* 116, 40% full-time, 46% with terminal degrees. *Student/faculty ratio:* 14:1.

Academics *Calendar:* semesters. *Degrees:* bachelor's, master's, and post-bachelor's certificates. *Special study options:* academic remediation for entering students, accelerated degree program, adult/continuing education programs, advanced placement credit, cooperative education, double majors, honors programs, independent study, internships, off-campus study, part-time degree program, services for LD students, student-designed majors, study abroad, summer session for credit.

Computers on Campus 75 computers/terminals are available on campus for general student use. Students can access the following: campus intranet, computer help desk, free student e-mail accounts, online (class) grades, online (class) registration, online (class) schedules. Campuswide network is available. 100% of college-owned or -operated housing units are wired for high-speed Internet access. Wireless service is available via entire campus.

Student Life *Housing:* on-campus residence required through sophomore year. *Options:* coed, women-only. Campus housing is university owned and leased by the school. Freshman campus housing is guaranteed. *Activities and organizations:* drama/theater group, choral group, marching band, Student Athlete Advisory Committee, Intercollegiate Horse Show Association, Gamma Phi Beta Sorority, Spanish Club, Student Government Association, national fraternities, national sororities. *Campus security:* 24-hour emergency response devices and patrols, late-night transport/escort service. *Student services:* health clinic.

Athletics Member NCAA. All Division II. *Intercollegiate sports:* baseball M(s), basketball M(s)/W(s), cross-country running M(s)/W(s), football M(s), golf M(s)/W(s), lacrosse M(s)/W(s), soccer M(s)/W(s), softball W(s), swimming and diving M(s)/W(s), tennis M(s)/W(s), track and field M(s)/W(s), volleyball W(s), wrestling M(s). *Intramural sports:* basketball M/W, cheerleading W(c), equestrian sports M(c)/W(c), football M/W, soccer M/W, softball M/W, ultimate Frisbee M/W, volleyball M/W.

Standardized Tests *Recommended:* SAT or ACT (for admission), AP, CLEP, Institutional Exam.

Costs (2012–13) *Comprehensive fee:* $35,704 includes full-time tuition ($25,976), mandatory fees ($1392), and room and board ($8336). Full-time tuition and fees vary according to course load, degree level, and program. Part-time tuition: $688 per credit hour. Part-time tuition and fees vary according to course load, degree level, and program. *Required fees:* $51 per credit hour part-time. *College room only:* $4054. Room and board charges vary according to board plan. *Payment plan:* installment. *Waivers:* senior citizens and employees or children of employees.

Financial Aid Of all full-time matriculated undergraduates who enrolled in 2011, 817 applied for aid, 770 were judged to have need, 126 had their need fully met. In 2011, 6 non-need-based awards were made. *Average percent of need met:* 70%. *Average financial aid package:* $19,789. *Average need-based loan:* $4365. *Average need-based gift aid:* $15,972. *Average non-need-based aid:* $6848. *Average indebtedness upon graduation:* $34,691.

Applying *Options:* electronic application, deferred entrance. *Application fee:* $30. *Required:* essay or personal statement, high school transcript, minimum 2.5 GPA, SAT or ACT Tests. *Required for some:* high school transcript. *Recommended:* interview. *Application deadlines:* 8/1 (freshmen), 8/1 (out-of-state freshmen), rolling (transfers). *Notification:* continuous (freshmen), continuous (out-of-state freshmen), continuous (transfers).

Freshman Application Contact Mr. Chris Harris, Dean of Admissions and Financial Aid, Lake Erie College, 391 West Washington Street, Painesville, OH 44077-3389. *Phone:* 800-916-0904. *Toll-free phone:* 800-916-0904.

Fax: 440-375-7058. *E-mail:* admissions@lec.edu. *Web site:* http://www.lec.edu/.

Laura and Alvin Siegal College of Judaic Studies
Beachwood, Ohio

Freshman Application Contact Ms. Ruth Kronick, Director of Student Services, Laura and Alvin Siegal College of Judaic Studies, 26500 Shaker Boulevard, Beachwood, OH 44122. *Phone:* 216-464-4050 Ext. 101. *Fax:* 216-464-5827. *E-mail:* admissions@siegalcollege.edu. *Web site:* http://www.siegalcollege.edu/.

Lourdes University
Sylvania, Ohio

- **Independent Roman Catholic** comprehensive, founded 1958
- **Suburban** 113-acre campus with easy access to Toledo
- **Endowment** $7.7 million
- **Coed** 2,208 undergraduate students, 52% full-time, 76% women, 24% men
- **Minimally difficult** entrance level, 74% of applicants were admitted

Undergraduates 1,142 full-time, 1,066 part-time. Students come from 14 states and territories; 11% are from out of state; 16% Black or African American, non-Hispanic/Latino; 6% Hispanic/Latino; 0.4% Asian, non-Hispanic/Latino; 0.1% Native Hawaiian or other Pacific Islander, non-Hispanic/Latino; 0.1% American Indian or Alaska Native, non-Hispanic/Latino; 2% Two or more races, non-Hispanic/Latino; 16% Race/ethnicity unknown; 0.1% international; 14% transferred in; 10% live on campus. *Retention:* 55% of full-time freshmen returned.

Freshmen *Admission:* 894 applied, 664 admitted, 215 enrolled. *Average high school GPA:* 2.95.

Faculty *Total:* 257, 37% full-time, 32% with terminal degrees. *Student/faculty ratio:* 12:1.

Academics *Calendar:* semesters. *Degrees:* certificates, associate, bachelor's, master's, and postbachelor's certificates. *Special study options:* academic remediation for entering students, adult/continuing education programs, advanced placement credit, distance learning, double majors, independent study, internships, part-time degree program, services for LD students, student-designed majors, study abroad, summer session for credit. *ROTC:* Army (c), Air Force (c).

Computers on Campus 180 computers/terminals are available on campus for general student use. Students can access the following: computer help desk, free student e-mail accounts, online (class) grades, online (class) registration, online (class) schedules, Sakai/eLearning, LiveText ePortfolio system, RRS news feeds, Facebook, Twitter, online polls, webcasting, panopto, ploycom. Campuswide network is available. 100% of college-owned or -operated housing units are wired for high-speed Internet access. Wireless service is available via entire campus.

Student Life *Housing:* on-campus residence required through junior year. *Options:* coed. Campus housing is university owned. Freshman applicants given priority for college housing. *Activities and organizations:* drama/theater group, choral group, Student Government Association, Drama Society, Student Nurses Association, Orbis Ars, Pre-Art Therapy Association. *Campus security:* 24-hour emergency response devices and patrols, late-night transport/escort service, controlled dormitory access. *Student services:* personal/psychological counseling.

Athletics Member NAIA. *Intercollegiate sports:* baseball M(s), basketball M(s)/W(s), golf M(s)/W(s), softball W(s), volleyball M(s)/W(s). *Intramural sports:* basketball M/W, bowling M/W, golf M/W, ice hockey M/W, soccer M/W, tennis M/W, volleyball M/W.

Costs (2011–12) *Comprehensive fee:* $23,670 includes full-time tuition ($14,520), mandatory fees ($1950), and room and board ($7200). Full-time tuition and fees vary according to course load. Part-time tuition: $484 per credit hour. Part-time tuition and fees vary according to course load. *Required fees:* $65 per credit hour part-time. *College room only:* $4200. Room and board charges vary according to board plan and housing facility. *Payment plans:* installment, deferred payment. *Waivers:* senior citizens and employees or children of employees.

Financial Aid Of all full-time matriculated undergraduates who enrolled in 2011, 1,079 applied for aid, 980 were judged to have need. 124 Federal Work-Study jobs (averaging $1694). 200 state and other part-time jobs (averaging $1000). *Average financial aid package:* $11,278. *Average need-based loan:* $3842. *Average need-based gift aid:* $6119.

Applying *Options:* electronic application, early admission, deferred entrance. *Application fee:* $25. *Required:* high school transcript. *Application deadlines:* rolling (freshmen), rolling (out-of-state freshmen), rolling (transfers). *Notifi-*

cation: continuous (freshmen), continuous (out-of-state freshmen), continuous (transfers).

Freshman Application Contact Ms. Amy Mergen, Dean of Enrollment, Lourdes University, 6832 Convent Boulevard, Sylvania, OH 43560. *Phone:* 419-885-5291. *Toll-free phone:* 800-878-3210. *Fax:* 419-824-3916. *E-mail:* AdmissionsLCAdmits@lourdes.edu. *Web site:* http://www.lourdes.edu/.

Malone University

Canton, Ohio

- **Independent** comprehensive, founded 1892, affiliated with Evangelical Friends Church–Eastern Region
- **Suburban** 96-acre campus with easy access to Cleveland
- **Endowment** $14.9 million
- **Coed** 1,953 undergraduate students, 88% full-time, 58% women, 42% men
- **Moderately difficult** entrance level, 75% of applicants were admitted

Undergraduates 1,714 full-time, 239 part-time. Students come from 30 states and territories; 17 other countries; 13% are from out of state; 8% Black or African American, non-Hispanic/Latino; 2% Hispanic/Latino; 0.5% Asian, non-Hispanic/Latino; 0.1% Native Hawaiian or other Pacific Islander, non-Hispanic/Latino; 1% Two or more races, non-Hispanic/Latino; 0.3% Race/ethnicity unknown; 1% international; 6% transferred in; 56% live on campus. *Retention:* 71% of full-time freshmen returned.

Freshmen *Admission:* 1,600 applied, 1,201 admitted, 362 enrolled. *Average high school GPA:* 3.3. *Test scores:* SAT critical reading scores over 500: 48%; SAT math scores over 500: 57%; ACT scores over 18: 92%; SAT critical reading scores over 600: 22%; SAT math scores over 600: 15%; ACT scores over 24: 44%; SAT math scores over 700: 1%; ACT scores over 30: 3%.

Faculty *Total:* 235, 46% full-time, 42% with terminal degrees. *Student/faculty ratio:* 13:1.

Academics *Calendar:* semesters. *Degrees:* bachelor's, master's, and post-bachelor's certificates. *Special study options:* academic remediation for entering students, accelerated degree program, adult/continuing education programs, advanced placement credit, distance learning, double majors, honors programs, independent study, internships, off-campus study, part-time degree program, services for LD students, student-designed majors, study abroad, summer session for credit. *ROTC:* Army (c), Air Force (c).

Computers on Campus 232 computers/terminals and 250 ports are available on campus for general student use. Students can access the following: campus intranet, computer help desk, free student e-mail accounts, online (class) grades, online (class) registration, online (class) schedules, online advising, online financial aid information, and online credit card payments. Campuswide network is available. 100% of college-owned or -operated housing units are wired for high-speed Internet access. Wireless service is available via entire campus.

Student Life *Housing:* on-campus residence required through junior year. *Options:* men-only, women-only, disabled students. Campus housing is university owned. Freshman applicants given priority for college housing. *Activities and organizations:* drama/theater group, student-run newspaper, radio and television station, choral group, marching band, Celebration Worship Services, Student Activities Council, Student Senate, be: Justice, intramural athletics. *Campus security:* 24-hour emergency response devices and patrols, late-night transport/escort service, controlled dormitory access. *Student services:* health clinic, personal/psychological counseling.

Athletics Member NCCAA. *Intercollegiate sports:* baseball M(s), basketball M(s)/W(s), cheerleading M/W, cross-country running M(s)/W(s), football M(s), golf M(s)/W(s), soccer M(s)/W(s), softball W(s), swimming and diving M(s)/W(s), tennis M(s)/W(s), track and field M(s)/W(s), volleyball W(s). *Intramural sports:* basketball M/W, bowling M/W, football M/W, lacrosse M(c)/W(c), skiing (cross-country) M/W, soccer M/W, softball M/W, table tennis M/W, ultimate Frisbee M(c)/W(c), volleyball M/W, weight lifting M/W.

Standardized Tests *Required:* SAT or ACT (for admission).

Costs (2011–12) *Comprehensive fee:* $31,510 includes full-time tuition ($22,832), mandatory fees ($588), and room and board ($8090). Part-time tuition: $435 per credit hour. Part-time tuition and fees vary according to course load. *Required fees:* $147 per term part-time. *College room only:* $4222. Room and board charges vary according to board plan. *Payment plan:* installment. *Waivers:* senior citizens and employees or children of employees.

Financial Aid Of all full-time matriculated undergraduates who enrolled in 2011, 1,446 applied for aid, 1,347 were judged to have need, 199 had their need fully met. 386 Federal Work-Study jobs (averaging $2011). In 2011, 194 non-need-based awards were made. *Average percent of need met:* 73%. *Average financial aid package:* $19,427. *Average need-based loan:* $4680. *Average need-based gift aid:* $14,963. *Average non-need-based aid:* $9192. *Average indebtedness upon graduation:* $32,029. *Financial aid deadline:* 7/31.

Applying *Options:* electronic application, early admission, deferred entrance. *Application fee:* $20. *Required:* high school transcript, minimum 2.0 GPA. *Required for some:* essay or personal statement. *Recommended:* interview. *Application deadlines:* rolling (freshmen), rolling (out-of-state freshmen), rolling (transfers). *Notification:* continuous (freshmen), continuous (out-of-state freshmen), continuous (transfers).

Freshman Application Contact Mr. David L. Kleffman, Director of Admissions, Malone University, Malone University, 2600 Cleveland Avenue NW, Canton, OH 44709-3897. *Phone:* 330-471-8145. *Toll-free phone:* 800-521-1146. *Fax:* 330-471-8149. *E-mail:* admissions@malone.edu. *Web site:* http://www.malone.edu/.

Marietta College

Marietta, Ohio

- **Independent** comprehensive, founded 1835
- **Small-town** 90-acre campus
- **Endowment** $63.4 million
- **Coed** 1,480 undergraduate students, 95% full-time, 46% women, 54% men
- **Moderately difficult** entrance level, 70% of applicants were admitted

Undergraduates 1,406 full-time, 74 part-time. Students come from 42 states and territories; 17 other countries; 36% are from out of state; 5% Black or African American, non-Hispanic/Latino; 2% Hispanic/Latino; 0.6% Asian, non-Hispanic/Latino; 0.1% Native Hawaiian or other Pacific Islander, non-Hispanic/Latino; 0.3% American Indian or Alaska Native, non-Hispanic/Latino; 1% Two or more races, non-Hispanic/Latino; 7% Race/ethnicity unknown; 12% international; 2% transferred in; 80% live on campus. *Retention:* 78% of full-time freshmen returned.

Freshmen *Admission:* 4,099 applied, 2,871 admitted, 362 enrolled. *Average high school GPA:* 3.45. *Test scores:* SAT critical reading scores over 500: 66%; SAT math scores over 500: 75%; SAT writing scores over 500: 61%; ACT scores over 18: 98%; SAT critical reading scores over 600: 30%; SAT math scores over 600: 35%; SAT writing scores over 600: 25%; ACT scores over 24: 52%; SAT critical reading scores over 700: 7%; SAT math scores over 700: 6%; SAT writing scores over 700: 5%; ACT scores over 30: 6%.

Faculty *Total:* 147, 74% full-time, 84% with terminal degrees. *Student/faculty ratio:* 12:1.

Academics *Calendar:* semesters. *Degrees:* certificates, associate, bachelor's, and master's. *Special study options:* academic remediation for entering students, accelerated degree program, adult/continuing education programs, advanced placement credit, double majors, English as a second language, honors programs, independent study, internships, off-campus study, part-time degree program, services for LD students, student-designed majors, study abroad, summer session for credit. *Unusual degree programs:* 3-2 engineering with University of Pennsylvania, Columbia University, Case Western Reserve University, Washington University in St. Louis.

Computers on Campus 400 computers/terminals are available on campus for general student use. Students can access the following: campus intranet, computer help desk, free student e-mail accounts, online (class) grades, online (class) schedules. Campuswide network is available. 100% of college-owned or -operated housing units are wired for high-speed Internet access. Wireless service is available via classrooms, computer centers, computer labs, dorm rooms, learning centers, libraries, student centers.

Student Life *Housing:* on-campus residence required through senior year. *Options:* coed, men-only, women-only, disabled students. Campus housing is university owned, leased by the school and is provided by a third party. Freshman campus housing is guaranteed. *Activities and organizations:* drama/theater group, student-run newspaper, radio and television station, choral group, Student Programming Board, student government, Society of Petroleum Engineers, Inter-Varsity Christian Fellowship, Arts and Humanities Council, national fraternities, national sororities. *Campus security:* 24-hour emergency response devices and patrols, student patrols, late-night transport/escort service, controlled dormitory access. *Student services:* health clinic, personal/psychological counseling.

Athletics Member NCAA. All Division III. *Intercollegiate sports:* baseball M, basketball M/W, cheerleading W(c), crew M/W, cross-country running M/W, football M, lacrosse M(c), soccer M/W, softball W, tennis M/W, track and field M/W, volleyball W, wrestling M(c)/W(c). *Intramural sports:* badminton M/W, basketball M/W, bowling M/W, cross-country running M/W, football M/W, golf M/W, racquetball M/W, rock climbing M/W, soccer M/W, softball M/W, swimming and diving M/W, tennis M/W, ultimate Frisbee M/W, volleyball M/W, weight lifting M.

Standardized Tests *Required:* SAT or ACT (for admission). *Recommended:* SAT Subject Tests (for admission).

Costs (2011–12) *Comprehensive fee:* $38,780 includes full-time tuition ($28,950), mandatory fees ($740), and room and board ($9090). Full-time tuition and fees vary according to course load and degree level. Part-time

tuition: $960 per credit hour. Part-time tuition and fees vary according to course load and degree level. *College room only:* $5040. Room and board charges vary according to board plan and housing facility.

Financial Aid Of all full-time matriculated undergraduates who enrolled in 2011, 1,168 applied for aid, 1,060 were judged to have need, 327 had their need fully met. 914 Federal Work-Study jobs (averaging $1977). In 2011, 206 non-need-based awards were made. *Average percent of need met:* 87%. *Average financial aid package:* $24,703. *Average need-based loan:* $4178. *Average need-based gift aid:* $14,372. *Average non-need-based aid:* $11,215. *Average indebtedness upon graduation:* $32,127.

Applying *Options:* electronic application, early admission, deferred entrance. *Application fee:* $25. *Required:* essay or personal statement, high school transcript, minimum 2.0 GPA, 1 letter of recommendation. *Recommended:* minimum 3.0 GPA, interview. *Application deadlines:* 5/1 (freshmen), rolling (transfers). *Notification:* continuous until 5/1 (freshmen), continuous (transfers).

Freshman Application Contact Mr. Jason Turley, Director of Admission, Marietta College, 215 Fifth Street, Marietta, OH 45750. *Phone:* 740-376-4600. *Toll-free phone:* 800-331-7896. *Fax:* 740-376-8888. *E-mail:* admit@marietta.edu. *Web site:* http://www.marietta.edu/.

Mercy College of Ohio

Toledo, Ohio

- **Independent** 4-year, founded 1993, affiliated with Roman Catholic Church
- **Urban** campus with easy access to Detroit
- **Endowment** $9.5 million
- **Coed, primarily women** 1,210 undergraduate students, 37% full-time, 86% women, 14% men
- **Moderately difficult** entrance level, 75% of applicants were admitted

Undergraduates 453 full-time, 757 part-time. Students come from 4 states and territories; 25% are from out of state; 7% Black or African American, non-Hispanic/Latino; 4% Hispanic/Latino; 0.8% Asian, non-Hispanic/Latino; 0.6% American Indian or Alaska Native, non-Hispanic/Latino; 2% Two or more races, non-Hispanic/Latino; 2% Race/ethnicity unknown; 21% transferred in; 3% live on campus. *Retention:* 77% of full-time freshmen returned.

Freshmen *Admission:* 87 applied, 65 admitted, 40 enrolled.

Faculty *Total:* 159, 41% full-time, 16% with terminal degrees. *Student/faculty ratio:* 11:1.

Academics *Calendar:* semesters. *Degrees:* certificates, associate, and bachelor's. *Special study options:* academic remediation for entering students, advanced placement credit, distance learning, double majors, independent study, internships, part-time degree program, services for LD students, summer session for credit.

Computers on Campus 40 computers/terminals and 40 ports are available on campus for general student use. Students can access the following: free student e-mail accounts, online (class) grades, online (class) registration, online (class) schedules, billing and payment, degree audit, and transcripts. Campuswide network is available. Wireless service is available via entire campus.

Student Life *Housing options:* coed. Campus housing is leased by the school. *Activities and organizations:* Student Senate, intramural sports, Student Nurses Association, Phi Theta Kappa. *Campus security:* 24-hour patrols, late-night transport/escort service, controlled dormitory access. *Student services:* personal/psychological counseling.

Standardized Tests *Required for some:* SAT or ACT (for admission), SAT and SAT Subject Tests or ACT (for admission).

Financial Aid Of all full-time matriculated undergraduates who enrolled in 2010, 473 applied for aid, 438 were judged to have need, 40 had their need fully met. 28 Federal Work-Study jobs (averaging $1235). In 2010, 8 non-need-based awards were made. *Average percent of need met:* 38%. *Average financial aid package:* $8553. *Average need-based loan:* $4154. *Average need-based gift aid:* $3999. *Average non-need-based aid:* $2780. *Average indebtedness upon graduation:* $22,460.

Applying *Options:* electronic application, deferred entrance. *Application fee:* $25. *Required:* high school transcript, minimum 2.3 GPA. *Application deadlines:* rolling (freshmen), rolling (transfers). *Notification:* continuous (freshmen), continuous (transfers).

Freshman Application Contact Admissions Counselor, Mercy College of Ohio, 2221 Madison Avenue, Toledo, OH 43604. *Phone:* 419-251-1313. *Toll-free phone:* 888-80-MERCY. *Fax:* 419-251-1462. *E-mail:* admissions@mercycollege.edu. *Web site:* http://www.mercycollege.edu/.

Miami University

Oxford, Ohio

- **State-related** university, founded 1809, part of Miami University System
- **Small-town** 2000-acre campus with easy access to Cincinnati
- **Endowment** $167.7 million
- **Coed** 14,936 undergraduate students, 97% full-time, 52% women, 48% men
- **Moderately difficult** entrance level, 74% of applicants were admitted

Undergraduates 14,544 full-time, 392 part-time. Students come from 47 states and territories; 50 other countries; 30% are from out of state; 5% Black or African American, non-Hispanic/Latino; 3% Hispanic/Latino; 2% Asian, non-Hispanic/Latino; 0.1% Native Hawaiian or other Pacific Islander, non-Hispanic/Latino; 0.4% American Indian or Alaska Native, non-Hispanic/Latino; 1% Two or more races, non-Hispanic/Latino; 1% Race/ethnicity unknown; 5% international; 2% transferred in; 52% live on campus. *Retention:* 89% of full-time freshmen returned.

Freshmen *Admission:* 18,482 applied, 13,702 admitted, 3,581 enrolled. *Average high school GPA:* 3.65. *Test scores:* SAT critical reading scores over 500: 86%; SAT math scores over 500: 95%; ACT scores over 18: 100%; SAT critical reading scores over 600: 40%; SAT math scores over 600: 60%; ACT scores over 24: 82%; SAT critical reading scores over 700: 7%; SAT math scores over 700: 13%; ACT scores over 30: 18%.

Faculty *Total:* 1,134, 75% full-time, 76% with terminal degrees. *Student/faculty ratio:* 17:1.

Academics *Calendar:* semesters. *Degrees:* certificates, associate, bachelor's, master's, doctoral, post-master's, and first professional certificates. *Special study options:* advanced placement credit, cooperative education, distance learning, double majors, English as a second language, honors programs, independent study, internships, off-campus study, services for LD students, student-designed majors, study abroad, summer session for credit. *ROTC:* Army (c), Navy (b), Air Force (b). *Unusual degree programs:* 3-2 engineering with Case Western Reserve University, Columbia University; forestry with Duke University.

Computers on Campus 400 computers/terminals and 11,200 ports are available on campus for general student use. Students can access the following: campus intranet, computer help desk, free student e-mail accounts, online (class) grades, online (class) registration, online (class) schedules. Campuswide network is available. 100% of college-owned or -operated housing units are wired for high-speed Internet access. Wireless service is available via entire campus.

Student Life *Housing:* on-campus residence required through sophomore year. *Options:* coed, men-only, women-only, disabled students. Campus housing is university owned. Freshman campus housing is guaranteed. *Activities and organizations:* drama/theater group, student-run newspaper, radio and television station, choral group, marching band, Associated Student Government, Campus Crusade for Christ, College Democrats/College Republicans, Fraternities and Sororities, Red Alert, national fraternities, national sororities. *Campus security:* 24-hour emergency response devices and patrols, student patrols, late-night transport/escort service, controlled dormitory access. *Student services:* health clinic, personal/psychological counseling, women's center.

Athletics Member NCAA. All Division I except football (Division I-A). *Intercollegiate sports:* baseball M(s)/W(s), basketball M(s)/W(s), cross-country running M(s)/W(s), equestrian sports M(c)/W(c), fencing M(c)/W(c), field hockey M(c)/W(s), golf M(s), gymnastics M(c)/W(c), ice hockey M(s)/W(c), lacrosse M(c)/W(c), rugby M(c)/W(c), sailing M(c)/W(c), soccer M(c)/W(s), softball M(s)/W(s), swimming and diving M(s)/W(s), tennis M(c)/W(s), track and field M(s)/W(s), ultimate Frisbee M(c)/W(c), volleyball M(c)/W(s), water polo M(c)/W(c), weight lifting M(c)/W(c), wrestling M(c)/W(c). *Intramural sports:* badminton M(c)/W(c), baseball M/W, basketball M/W, golf M(c)/W(c), ice hockey M/W, racquetball M/W, soccer M/W, softball M/W, ultimate Frisbee M/W, volleyball M/W.

Standardized Tests *Required:* SAT or ACT (for admission).

Costs (2011–12) *Tuition:* state resident $12,625 full-time; nonresident $27,797 full-time. Full-time tuition and fees vary according to location and program. Part-time tuition and fees vary according to course load, location, and program. *Required fees:* $588 full-time. *Room and board:* $10,640; room only: $5098. Room and board charges vary according to board plan and housing facility. *Payment plan:* installment. *Waivers:* employees or children of employees.

Financial Aid Of all full-time matriculated undergraduates who enrolled in 2011, 8,761 applied for aid, 6,576 were judged to have need, 1,081 had their need fully met. 819 Federal Work-Study jobs (averaging $2180). In 2011, 2669 non-need-based awards were made. *Average percent of need met:* 59%. *Average financial aid package:* $12,097. *Average need-based loan:* $4518. *Average need-based gift aid:* $5463. *Average non-need-based aid:* $5250. *Average indebtedness upon graduation:* $27,178.

Applying *Options:* electronic application, early decision, early action, deferred entrance. *Application fee:* $50. *Required:* essay or personal statement, high

school transcript, 1 letter of recommendation. *Application deadlines:* 2/1 (freshmen), 6/1 (transfers), 12/1 (early action). *Early decision deadline:* 11/1. *Notification:* 3/15 (freshmen), continuous (transfers), 12/15 (early decision), 2/1 (early action).
Freshman Application Contact Office of Admissions, Miami University, 301 South Campus Avenue, Oxford, OH 45056. *Phone:* 513-529-2531. *Fax:* 513-529-1550. *E-mail:* admission@muohio.edu. *Web site:* http://www.muohio.edu/.

Miami University Hamilton
Hamilton, Ohio

Freshman Application Contact Mr. Archie Nelson, Director of Admission and Financial Aid, Miami University Hamilton, 1601 Peck Boulevard, Hamilton, OH 45011-3399. *Phone:* 513-785-3111. *Fax:* 513-785-1807. *E-mail:* nelsona3@muohio.edu. *Web site:* http://www.ham.muohio.edu/.

Miami University–Middletown Campus
Middletown, Ohio

Freshman Application Contact Diane Cantonwine, Assistant Director of Admission and Financial Aid, Miami University–Middletown Campus, 4200 East University Boulevard, Middletown, OH 45042-3497. *Phone:* 513-727-3346. *Toll-free phone:* 866-426-4643. *Fax:* 513-727-3223. *E-mail:* cantondm@muohio.edu. *Web site:* http://www.mid.muohio.edu/.

Mount Carmel College of Nursing
Columbus, Ohio

- **Independent** comprehensive, founded 1903
- **Urban** campus with easy access to Columbus
- **Endowment** $824,552
- **Coed, primarily women** 809 undergraduate students, 81% full-time, 89% women, 11% men
- **Moderately difficult** entrance level, 75% of applicants were admitted

Undergraduates 654 full-time, 155 part-time. Students come from 5 states and territories; 1% are from out of state; 5% Black or African American, non-Hispanic/Latino; 1% Hispanic/Latino; 1% Asian, non-Hispanic/Latino; 0.1% Native Hawaiian or other Pacific Islander, non-Hispanic/Latino; 0.2% American Indian or Alaska Native, non-Hispanic/Latino; 2% Two or more races, non-Hispanic/Latino; 1% Race/ethnicity unknown; 16% transferred in; 8% live on campus. *Retention:* 87% of full-time freshmen returned.
Freshmen *Admission:* 171 applied, 129 admitted, 91 enrolled. *Average high school GPA:* 3.61. *Test scores:* ACT scores over 18: 98%; ACT scores over 24: 33%.
Faculty *Total:* 89, 49% full-time, 13% with terminal degrees. *Student/faculty ratio:* 15:1.
Academics *Calendar:* semesters. *Degrees:* bachelor's, master's, and post-master's certificates. *Special study options:* accelerated degree program, adult/continuing education programs, advanced placement credit, distance learning, honors programs, off-campus study, summer session for credit. *ROTC:* Army (c), Navy (c), Air Force (c).
Computers on Campus 70 computers/terminals are available on campus for general student use. Students can access the following: campus intranet, computer help desk, free student e-mail accounts, online (class) grades, online (class) registration, online (class) schedules. Campuswide network is available. Wireless service is available via entire campus.
Student Life *Housing:* on-campus residence required through sophomore year. *Options:* coed. Campus housing is provided by a third party. Freshman applicants given priority for college housing. *Activities and organizations:* Student Nurses Association, Campus Ministry, Sigma Theta Tau, Student Government. *Campus security:* 24-hour emergency response devices and patrols, late-night transport/escort service, controlled dormitory access. *Student services:* health clinic, personal/psychological counseling.
Athletics *Intramural sports:* basketball W(c), softball W(c), volleyball M(c)/W(c).
Standardized Tests *Required for some:* SAT or ACT (for admission).
Costs (2011–12) *One-time required fee:* $225. *Tuition:* $9527 full-time, $333 per semester hour part-time. Full-time tuition and fees vary according to course level, course load, and student level. Part-time tuition and fees vary according to course level, course load, and student level. Tuition and fees are for full-time, first-time freshman students taking non-nursing courses. Nursing courses carry a higher tuition charge. Current average annual tuition (including nursing and non-nursing courses) is $15,727; current average annual fees are $794. *Required fees:* $732 full-time, $276 per term part-time. *Room only:*

$4500. *Payment plan:* installment. *Waivers:* employees or children of employees.
Financial Aid Of all full-time matriculated undergraduates who enrolled in 2011, 588 applied for aid, 588 were judged to have need. In 2011, 5 non-need-based awards were made. *Average percent of need met:* 65%. *Average financial aid package:* $13,500. *Average need-based loan:* $4427. *Average need-based gift aid:* $1700. *Average non-need-based aid:* $2200. *Average indebtedness upon graduation:* $8675.
Applying *Application fee:* $30. *Required:* essay or personal statement, high school transcript, activities/interests resume. *Required for some:* interview. *Recommended:* minimum 3.0 GPA. *Application deadlines:* 4/1 (freshmen), 4/1 (out-of-state freshmen), 4/1 (transfers). *Notification:* continuous (freshmen), continuous (out-of-state freshmen), continuous (transfers).
Freshman Application Contact Kim Campbell, Direct, Admissions and Recruitment, Mount Carmel College of Nursing, 127 South Davis Avenue, Columbus, OH 43222-1504. *Phone:* 614-234-1085. *Toll-free phone:* 800-556-6942. *Fax:* 614-234-5427. *E-mail:* kcampbell@mccn.edu. *Web site:* http://www.mccn.edu/.

Mount Vernon Nazarene University
Mount Vernon, Ohio

- **Independent Nazarene** comprehensive, founded 1964
- **Small-town** 406-acre campus with easy access to Columbus
- **Endowment** $14.7 million
- **Coed** 1,948 undergraduate students, 87% full-time, 63% women, 37% men
- **Moderately difficult** entrance level, 72% of applicants were admitted

Undergraduates 1,698 full-time, 250 part-time. Students come from 25 states and territories; 6 other countries; 8% are from out of state; 3% Black or African American, non-Hispanic/Latino; 2% Hispanic/Latino; 0.6% Asian, non-Hispanic/Latino; 0.1% Native Hawaiian or other Pacific Islander, non-Hispanic/Latino; 0.2% American Indian or Alaska Native, non-Hispanic/Latino; 1% Two or more races, non-Hispanic/Latino; 0.5% international; 2% transferred in; 78% live on campus. *Retention:* 71% of full-time freshmen returned.
Freshmen *Admission:* 1,034 applied, 748 admitted, 354 enrolled. *Average high school GPA:* 3.34. *Test scores:* SAT critical reading scores over 500: 72%; SAT math scores over 500: 62%; ACT scores over 18: 90%; SAT critical reading scores over 600: 29%; SAT math scores over 600: 25%; ACT scores over 24: 47%; SAT critical reading scores over 700: 7%; ACT scores over 30: 4%.
Faculty *Total:* 241, 43% full-time, 38% with terminal degrees. *Student/faculty ratio:* 14:1.
Academics *Calendar:* 4-1-4. *Degrees:* associate, bachelor's, and master's. *Special study options:* academic remediation for entering students, adult/continuing education programs, advanced placement credit, distance learning, double majors, honors programs, independent study, internships, off-campus study, part-time degree program, services for LD students, study abroad, summer session for credit. *Unusual degree programs:* 3-2 engineering with Olivet Nazarene University; pre-occupational therapy/physician assistant with Chatham University.
Computers on Campus 232 computers/terminals and 1,200 ports are available on campus for general student use. Students can access the following: campus intranet, computer help desk, free student e-mail accounts, online (class) grades, online (class) schedules. Campuswide network is available. 100% of college-owned or -operated housing units are wired for high-speed Internet access. Wireless service is available via classrooms, computer centers, computer labs, learning centers, libraries, student centers.
Student Life *Housing:* on-campus residence required through senior year. *Options:* men-only, women-only, disabled students. Campus housing is university owned. Freshman campus housing is guaranteed. *Activities and organizations:* drama/theater group, student-run newspaper, radio station, choral group, campus ministry groups, Student Government Association, Student Education Association, Drama Club, music department ensembles. *Campus security:* 24-hour emergency response devices and patrols, late-night transport/escort service, controlled dormitory access. *Student services:* health clinic, personal/psychological counseling.
Athletics Member NAIA, NCCAA. *Intercollegiate sports:* baseball M(s), basketball M(s)/W(s), cross-country running M(s)/W(s), golf M(s)/W(s), soccer M(s)/W(s), softball W(s), volleyball W(s). *Intramural sports:* basketball M/W, bowling M/W, cheerleading M(c)/W(c), football M/W, soccer M/W, softball M/W, table tennis M/W, ultimate Frisbee M/W, volleyball M/W.
Standardized Tests *Required:* SAT or ACT (for admission).
Costs (2012–13) *Comprehensive fee:* $29,590 includes full-time tuition ($22,890) and room and board ($6700). Full-time tuition and fees vary according to course load, program, and reciprocity agreements. Part-time tuition: $636 per credit hour. Part-time tuition and fees vary according to course load, program, and reciprocity agreements. *College room only:* $3740. *Payment*

plan: installment. *Waivers:* senior citizens and employees or children of employees.

Financial Aid Of all full-time matriculated undergraduates who enrolled in 2011, 1,547 applied for aid, 1,333 were judged to have need, 176 had their need fully met. 277 Federal Work-Study jobs (averaging $1834). 250 state and other part-time jobs (averaging $1760). In 2011, 71 non-need-based awards were made. *Average percent of need met:* 66%. *Average financial aid package:* $16,738. *Average need-based loan:* $4062. *Average need-based gift aid:* $10,307. *Average non-need-based aid:* $7209. *Average indebtedness upon graduation:* $32,046.

Applying *Options:* electronic application, deferred entrance. *Application fee:* $25. *Required:* essay or personal statement, high school transcript, minimum 2.5 GPA, 2 letters of recommendation. *Application deadline:* 7/15 (freshmen). *Notification:* 9/1 (freshmen), continuous (transfers).

Freshman Application Contact Mr. James Smith, Director of Admissions and Student Recruitment, Mount Vernon Nazarene University, 800 Martinsburg Road, Mount Vernon, OH 43050. *Phone:* 740-392-6868 Ext. 4516. *Toll-free phone:* 866-462-6868. *Fax:* 740-393-0511. *E-mail:* admissions@mvnu.edu. *Web site:* http://www.mvnu.edu/.

Muskingum University

New Concord, Ohio

Freshman Application Contact Mrs. Beth DaLonzo, Director of Admission, Muskingum University, 163 Stormont Street, New Concord, OH 43762. *Phone:* 740-826-8137. *Toll-free phone:* 800-752-6082. *Fax:* 740-826-8100. *E-mail:* adminfo@muskingum.edu. *Web site:* http://www.muskingum.edu/.

Notre Dame College

South Euclid, Ohio

Freshman Application Contact Mr. David Armstrong, Dean of Admissions, Notre Dame College, 4545 College Road, South Euclid, OH 44121-4293. *Phone:* 216-373-5214. *Toll-free phone:* 877-NDC-OHIO. *Fax:* 216-381-3802. *E-mail:* admissinos@ndc.edu. *Web site:* http://www.notredamecollege.edu/.

See page 706 for display ad and page 1490 for the College Close-Up.

Oberlin College

Oberlin, Ohio

- **Independent** comprehensive, founded 1833
- **Small-town** 440-acre campus with easy access to Cleveland
- **Endowment** $603.4 million
- **Coed**
- **Very difficult** entrance level

Faculty *Student/faculty ratio:* 9:1.

Academics *Calendar:* 4-1-4. *Degrees:* diplomas, bachelor's, master's, and postbachelor's certificates.

Student Life *Campus security:* 24-hour emergency response devices and patrols, student patrols, late-night transport/escort service, controlled dormitory access, crime prevention programs.

Athletics Member NCAA. All Division III.

Standardized Tests *Required:* SAT or ACT (for admission). *Recommended:* SAT Subject Tests (for admission).

Costs (2011–12) *Comprehensive fee:* $54,760 includes full-time tuition ($42,842), mandatory fees ($368), and room and board ($11,550). Part-time tuition: $1780 per credit hour. *College room only:* $6000. Room and board charges vary according to board plan and housing facility.

Financial Aid *Of all full-time matriculated undergraduates who enrolled in 2011,* 1,805 applied for aid, 1,595 were judged to have need, 1,595 had their need fully met. 1,500 Federal Work-Study jobs (averaging $2200). 600 state and other part-time jobs (averaging $2200). *In 2011,* 895 non-need-based awards were made. *Average percent of need met:* 100. *Average financial aid package:* $33,387. *Average need-based loan:* $4896. *Average need-based gift aid:* $28,813. *Average non-need-based aid:* $10,917.

Applying *Options:* electronic application, early admission, early decision, deferred entrance. *Application fee:* $35. *Required:* essay or personal statement, high school transcript, 2 letters of recommendation. *Required for some:* interview, audition for applicants to the Conservatory of Music.

Freshman Application Contact Ms. Debra Chermonte, Dean of Admissions and Financial Aid, Oberlin College, Admissions Office, Carnegie Building, Oberlin, OH 44074-1090. *Phone:* 440-775-8411. *Toll-free phone:* 800-622-OBIE. *Fax:* 440-775-6905. *E-mail:* college.admissions@oberlin.edu. *Web site:* http://www.oberlin.edu/.

Ohio Christian University

Circleville, Ohio

Director of Admissions Mike Egenreider, Associate Vice President for Enrollment, Ohio Christian University, 1476 Lancaster Pike, PO Box 458, Circleville, OH 43113-9487. *Phone:* 740-477-7741. *Toll-free phone:* 877-762-8669. *E-mail:* enroll@ohiochristian.edu. *Web site:* http://www.ohiochristian.edu/.

Ohio Dominican University

Columbus, Ohio

Freshman Application Contact Ms. Nicole A. Evans, Director of Admissions, Ohio Dominican University, 1216 Sunbury Road, Columbus, OH 43219. *Phone:* 614-251-4500. *Toll-free phone:* 800-955-6446. *Fax:* 614-251-0156. *E-mail:* admissions@ohiodominican.edu. *Web site:* http://www.ohiodominican.edu/.

Ohio Northern University

Ada, Ohio

- **Independent** comprehensive, founded 1871, affiliated with United Methodist Church
- **Small-town** 340-acre campus
- **Endowment** $143.1 million
- **Coed** 2,601 undergraduate students, 86% full-time, 47% women, 53% men
- **Moderately difficult** entrance level, 82% of applicants were admitted

Undergraduates 2,231 full-time, 370 part-time. Students come from 42 states and territories; 18 other countries; 14% are from out of state; 4% Black or African American, non-Hispanic/Latino; 2% Hispanic/Latino; 1% Asian, non-Hispanic/Latino; 0.1% Native Hawaiian or other Pacific Islander, non-Hispanic/Latino; 0.1% American Indian or Alaska Native, non-Hispanic/Latino; 2% Two or more races, non-Hispanic/Latino; 4% international; 2% transferred in; 68% live on campus. *Retention:* 88% of full-time freshmen returned.

Freshmen *Admission:* 3,136 applied, 2,575 admitted, 686 enrolled. *Test scores:* SAT critical reading scores over 500: 83%; SAT math scores over 500: 88%; SAT writing scores over 500: 81%; ACT scores over 18: 100%; SAT critical reading scores over 600: 41%; SAT math scores over 600: 59%; SAT writing scores over 600: 37%; ACT scores over 24: 78%; SAT critical reading scores over 700: 7%; SAT math scores over 700: 13%; SAT writing scores over 700: 4%; ACT scores over 30: 24%.

Faculty *Total:* 308, 73% full-time, 70% with terminal degrees. *Student/faculty ratio:* 12:1.

Academics *Calendar:* quarters. *Degrees:* bachelor's, master's, doctoral, and postbachelor's certificates. *Special study options:* academic remediation for entering students, advanced placement credit, cooperative education, distance learning, double majors, English as a second language, honors programs, independent study, internships, off-campus study, part-time degree program, services for LD students, study abroad, summer session for credit. *ROTC:* Army (c), Air Force (c).

Computers on Campus 533 computers/terminals and 3,000 ports are available on campus for general student use. Students can access the following: campus intranet, computer help desk, free student e-mail accounts, online (class) grades, online (class) registration, online (class) schedules. Campus-wide network is available. 100% of college-owned or -operated housing units are wired for high-speed Internet access. Wireless service is available via entire campus.

Student Life *Housing:* on-campus residence required through junior year. *Options:* coed, men-only, women-only, disabled students. Campus housing is university owned. Freshman campus housing is guaranteed. *Activities and organizations:* drama/theater group, student-run newspaper, radio and television station, choral group, marching band, Habitat for Humanity, Student Planning Committee, Student Senate, Northern Christian Fellowship, marching band, national fraternities, national sororities. *Campus security:* 24-hour emergency response devices and patrols, late-night transport/escort service, controlled dormitory access. *Student services:* health clinic, personal/psychological counseling, legal services.

Athletics Member NCAA. All Division III. *Intercollegiate sports:* baseball M, basketball M/W, cross-country running M/W, football M, golf M/W, soccer M/W, softball W, swimming and diving M/W, tennis M/W, track and field M/W, volleyball M(c)/W, wrestling M. *Intramural sports:* badminton M/W, basketball M/W, cheerleading M(c)/W(c), lacrosse M(c), rugby M(c)/W(c), skiing (downhill) M(c)/W(c), soccer M/W, softball M/W, swimming and diving M/W, table tennis M/W, tennis M/W, ultimate Frisbee M(c)/W(c), volleyball M/W, water polo W(c).

Standardized Tests *Required:* SAT or ACT (for admission).

Costs (2012–13) *Comprehensive fee:* $45,898 includes full-time tuition ($35,438), mandatory fees ($240), and room and board ($10,220). Full-time tuition and fees vary according to course load, degree level, and program. Part-time tuition and fees vary according to course load, degree level, and program. *Required fees:* $1477 per semester hour part-time. *Room and board:* Room and board charges vary according to board plan, housing facility, and student level. *Payment plan:* installment. *Waivers:* minority students, children of alumni, and employees or children of employees.

Financial Aid Of all full-time matriculated undergraduates who enrolled in 2010, 2,199 applied for aid, 1,821 were judged to have need, 252 had their need fully met. 1,354 Federal Work-Study jobs (averaging $1487). 169 state and other part-time jobs (averaging $2050). In 2010, 342 non-need-based awards were made. *Average percent of need met:* 76%. *Average financial aid package:* $26,304. *Average need-based loan:* $4605. *Average need-based gift aid:* $21,219. *Average non-need-based aid:* $17,001. *Average indebtedness upon graduation:* $48,886.

Applying *Options:* electronic application, deferred entrance. *Application fee:* $30. *Required:* essay or personal statement, high school transcript, 1 letter of recommendation. *Recommended:* minimum 2.5 GPA, 2 letters of recommendation, interview. *Application deadlines:* 8/1 (freshmen), 8/1 (transfers). *Notification:* continuous (freshmen), continuous (transfers).

Freshman Application Contact Ms. Deborah Miller, Director of Admissions, Ohio Northern University, 525 South Main Street, Ada, OH 45810-1599. *Phone:* 419-772-2260 Ext. 2464. *Toll-free phone:* 888-408-4ONU. *Fax:* 419-772-2821. *E-mail:* admissions-ug@onu.edu. *Web site:* http://www.onu.edu/.

See below for display ad and page 1492 for the College Close-Up.

The Ohio State University

Columbus, Ohio

- **State-supported** university, founded 1870, part of Ohio State University System
- **Urban** 3469-acre campus with easy access to Columbus
- **Endowment** $1.9 billion
- **Coed** 42,082 undergraduate students, 92% full-time, 47% women, 53% men
- **Very difficult** entrance level, 68% of applicants were admitted

Undergraduates 38,523 full-time, 3,559 part-time. Students come from 56 states and territories; 63 other countries; 11% are from out of state; 6% Black or African American, non-Hispanic/Latino; 3% Hispanic/Latino; 5% Asian, non-Hispanic/Latino; 0.3% American Indian or Alaska Native, non-Hispanic/Latino; 0.6% Two or more races, non-Hispanic/Latino; 2% Race/ethnicity unknown; 5% international; 5% transferred in; 25% live on campus. *Retention:* 93% of full-time freshmen returned.

Freshmen *Admission:* 24,302 applied, 16,531 admitted, 6,672 enrolled. *Test scores:* SAT critical reading scores over 500: 85%; SAT math scores over 500: 96%; SAT writing scores over 500: 88%; ACT scores over 18: 100%; SAT critical reading scores over 600: 51%; SAT math scores over 600: 75%; SAT writing scores over 600: 46%; ACT scores over 24: 91%; SAT critical reading scores over 700: 12%; SAT math scores over 700: 28%; SAT writing scores over 700: 9%; ACT scores over 30: 31%.

Faculty *Total:* 4,632, 73% full-time, 72% with terminal degrees. *Student/faculty ratio:* 19:1.

Academics *Calendar:* quarters. *Degrees:* certificates, associate, bachelor's, master's, doctoral, post-master's, postbachelor's, and first professional certificates. *Special study options:* academic remediation for entering students, accelerated degree program, adult/continuing education programs, advanced placement credit, cooperative education, distance learning, double majors, English as a second language, freshman honors college, honors programs, independent study, internships, off-campus study, part-time degree program, services for LD students, student-designed majors, study abroad, summer session for credit. *ROTC:* Army (b), Navy (b), Air Force (b). *Unusual degree programs:* 3-2 business administration.

Computers on Campus 675 computers/terminals are available on campus for general student use. Students can access the following: campus intranet, computer help desk, free student e-mail accounts, online (class) grades, online (class) registration, online (class) schedules, students can apply for admission, register, check grades, pay fees and obtain library resources, including books, online. Campuswide network is available. 100% of college-owned or -operated housing units are wired for high-speed Internet access. Wireless service is available via entire campus.

Student Life *Housing:* on-campus residence required for freshman year. *Options:* coed, women-only, cooperative, disabled students. Campus housing is university owned. Freshman campus housing is guaranteed. *Activities and organizations:* drama/theater group, student-run newspaper, radio and television station, choral group, marching band, African Student Union, Bisexual, Gay and Lesbian Alliance, Campus Crusade for Christ, University Wide Council of Hispanic Organizations, Asian-American Association, national fraternities, national sororities. *Campus security:* 24-hour emergency response devices and patrols, student patrols, late-night transport/escort service, controlled dormitory access, dorm entrances locked after 9 pm, lighted pathways

Notre Dame College

Experience the Excitement!

■ Stimulating academics with programs that help you achieve your potential and build your future

■ More than 30 career-focused majors and programs including Nursing, Education, Intelligence Studies, Criminal Justice, International Business and Sports Management

Notre Dame College is one of the best colleges and universities in the Midwest according to The Princeton Review.

■ Exceptional faculty, personal attention, small classes – a great liberal arts education in the Catholic tradition of the Sisters of Notre Dame

■ Beautiful 48-acre suburban campus just minutes from Cleveland's vibrant cultural, entertainment, medical and research centers, and major corporations

■ Big-time athletics in a small-college setting with 22 intercollegiate sports for men and women

■ Nationally recognized Academic Support Center for Students with Learning Differences

Plan now to continue your education and your life at Notre Dame College. Contact us for more information or an appointment at 877.NDC.OHIO, ext. 5355, or *admissions@ndc.edu.*

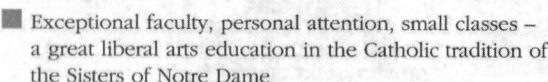

NOTRE DAME
COLLEGE

4545 College Road, South Euclid, Ohio 44121-4293
1.877.NDC.OHIO NotreDameCollege.edu
Changing the World...One Student at a Time

---

and sidewalks, self-defense education. *Student services:* health clinic, personal/psychological counseling, women's center, legal services.

Athletics Member NCAA. All Division I except football (Division I-A). *Intercollegiate sports:* baseball M(s), basketball M(s)/W(s), cheerleading M/W, cross-country running M(s)/W(s), fencing M(s)/W(s), field hockey W(s), golf M(s)/W(s), gymnastics M(s)/W(s), ice hockey M(s)/W(s), lacrosse M(s)/W(s), riflery M/W, soccer M(s)/W(s), softball W(s), swimming and diving M(s)/W(s), tennis M(s)/W(s), track and field M(s)/W(s), volleyball M(s)/W(s), wrestling M(s). *Intramural sports:* badminton M(c)/W(c), baseball M(c), basketball M/W, bowling M(c)/W(c), crew M(c)/W, cross-country running M/W, equestrian sports M(c)/W(c), fencing M(c)/W(c), field hockey W, football M/W, golf M/W, gymnastics M(c)/W(c), ice hockey M(c)/W(c), lacrosse M(c)/W(c), racquetball M(c)/W(c), riflery M(c)/W(c), rock climbing M/W, rugby M(c)/W(c), sailing M(c)/W(c), skiing (downhill) M(c)/W(c), soccer M(c)/W(c), softball W(c), squash M(c)/W(c), swimming and diving M(c)/W(c), table tennis M/W, tennis M/W, track and field M(c)/W(c), ultimate Frisbee M(c)/W(c), volleyball M(c)/W(c), water polo M(c)/W(c), weight lifting M/W, wrestling M/W.

Standardized Tests *Required:* SAT or ACT (for admission).

Costs (2011–12) *Tuition:* state resident $9309 full-time, $259 per quarter hour part-time; nonresident $24,204 full-time, $672 per quarter hour part-time. Full-time tuition and fees vary according to course load, location, program, and reciprocity agreements. Part-time tuition and fees vary according to course load, location, program, and reciprocity agreements. *Required fees:* $426 full-time. *Room and board:* $9180; room only: $6585. Room and board charges vary according to board plan, housing facility, and location. *Payment plan:* installment. *Waivers:* senior citizens and employees or children of employees.

Financial Aid Of all full-time matriculated undergraduates who enrolled in 2011, 27,096 applied for aid, 21,958 were judged to have need, 2,793 had their need fully met. 3,022 Federal Work-Study jobs (averaging $2027). 188 state and other part-time jobs (averaging $2465). In 2011, 6698 non-need-based awards were made. *Average percent of need met:* 55%. *Average financial aid package:* $10,616. *Average need-based loan:* $4754. *Average need-based gift aid:* $7887. *Average non-need-based aid:* $4888. *Average indebtedness upon graduation:* $24,840.

Applying *Options:* electronic application. *Application fee:* $40. *Required:* essay or personal statement, high school transcript. *Application deadlines:* 2/1 (freshmen), 2/1 (out-of-state freshmen), 6/1 (transfers). *Notification:* 11/15 (freshmen), 11/15 (out-of-state freshmen).

Freshman Application Contact Dr. Mabel Freeman, Assistant Vice President for Undergraduate Admissions and First Year Experience, The Ohio State University, 110 Enarson Hall, 154 West 12th Avenue, Columbus, OH 43210. *Phone:* 614-292-3980. *Fax:* 614-292-4818. *E-mail:* askabuckeye@osu.edu. *Web site:* http://www.osu.edu/.

The Ohio State University at Lima
.Lima, Ohio

• **State-supported** comprehensive, founded 1960, part of The Ohio State University
• **Suburban** 565-acre campus
• **Coed** 1,240 undergraduate students, 86% full-time, 53% women, 47% men
• **Noncompetitive** entrance level, 99% of applicants were admitted

Undergraduates 1,066 full-time, 174 part-time. Students come from 3 states and territories; 4% Black or African American, non-Hispanic/Latino; 3% Hispanic/Latino; 0.9% Asian, non-Hispanic/Latino; 0.3% American Indian or Alaska Native, non-Hispanic/Latino; 2% Two or more races, non-Hispanic/Latino; 1% Race/ethnicity unknown; 0.1% international; 5% transferred in. *Retention:* 60% of full-time freshmen returned.

Freshmen *Admission:* 1,185 applied, 1,169 admitted, 462 enrolled. *Test scores:* SAT critical reading scores over 500: 44%; SAT math scores over 500: 59%; SAT writing scores over 500: 39%; ACT scores over 18: 90%; SAT critical reading scores over 600: 3%; SAT math scores over 600: 28%; SAT writing scores over 600: 8%; ACT scores over 24: 31%; ACT scores over 30: 1%.

Faculty *Total:* 87, 45% full-time, 44% with terminal degrees. *Student/faculty ratio:* 20:1.

Academics *Calendar:* quarters. *Degrees:* associate, bachelor's, and master's. *Special study options:* academic remediation for entering students, accelerated degree program, adult/continuing education programs, advanced placement credit, cooperative education, distance learning, double majors, English as a second language, freshman honors college, honors programs, independent study, internships, off-campus study, part-time degree program, services for LD students, student-designed majors, study abroad, summer session for credit. *ROTC:* Army (c), Navy (c), Air Force (c).

Computers on Campus 150 computers/terminals are available on campus for general student use. Students can access the following: campus intranet, computer help desk, free student e-mail accounts, online (class) grades, online

(class) registration, online (class) schedules. Campuswide network is available. Wireless service is available via entire campus.

Student Life *Housing:* college housing not available. *Activities and organizations:* choral group, Student Senate, Psychology Club, Honors Club, Aggies, Newman Catholic Association. *Campus security:* 24-hour emergency response devices and patrols, student patrols, late-night transport/escort service, lighted pathways/sidewalks. *Student services:* personal/psychological counseling.

Athletics *Intramural sports:* baseball M(c), basketball M(c)/W(c), football M/W, golf M(c)/W(c), soccer M/W, volleyball M(c)/W(c).

Standardized Tests *Required:* SAT or ACT (for admission).

Costs (2011–12) *Tuition:* state resident $6903 full-time, $176 per credit hour part-time; nonresident $21,798 full-time, $590 per credit hour part-time. Full-time tuition and fees vary according to course load, location, and student level. Part-time tuition and fees vary according to course load, location, and student level. *Required fees:* $426 full-time. *Payment plan:* installment. *Waivers:* senior citizens and employees or children of employees.

Applying *Options:* electronic application. *Application fee:* $60. *Required:* essay or personal statement, high school transcript. *Application deadline:* 7/7 (freshmen). *Notification:* 11/15 (freshmen).

Freshman Application Contact Ms. Garlene Smithson, Director of Admissions, The Ohio State University at Lima, 4240 Campus Drive, Lima, OH 45804. *Phone:* 419-995-8434. *Fax:* 419-995-8483. *E-mail:* admissions@lima.ohio-state.edu. *Web site:* http://lima.osu.edu/.

The Ohio State University at Marion

Marion, Ohio

- **State-supported** comprehensive, founded 1958, part of The Ohio State University
- **Small-town** 188-acre campus with easy access to Columbus
- **Coed** 1,441 undergraduate students, 77% full-time, 53% women, 47% men
- **Noncompetitive** entrance level, 98% of applicants were admitted

Undergraduates 1,108 full-time, 333 part-time. Students come from 5 states and territories; 1 other country; 10% Black or African American, non-Hispanic/Latino; 2% Hispanic/Latino; 4% Asian, non-Hispanic/Latino; 0.1% Native Hawaiian or other Pacific Islander, non-Hispanic/Latino; 0.5% American Indian or Alaska Native, non-Hispanic/Latino; 2% Two or more races, non-Hispanic/Latino; 2% Race/ethnicity unknown; 0.1% international; 4% transferred in. *Retention:* 67% of full-time freshmen returned.

Freshmen *Admission:* 964 applied, 944 admitted, 473 enrolled. *Test scores:* SAT critical reading scores over 500: 60%; SAT math scores over 500: 72%; SAT writing scores over 500: 54%; ACT scores over 18: 85%; SAT critical reading scores over 600: 11%; SAT math scores over 600: 24%; SAT writing scores over 600: 8%; ACT scores over 24: 34%; SAT math scores over 700: 2%; ACT scores over 30: 2%.

Faculty *Total:* 101, 36% full-time, 36% with terminal degrees. *Student/faculty ratio:* 21:1.

Academics *Calendar:* quarters. *Degrees:* associate, bachelor's, and master's. *Special study options:* academic remediation for entering students, accelerated degree program, adult/continuing education programs, advanced placement credit, cooperative education, distance learning, double majors, English as a second language, freshman honors college, honors programs, independent study, internships, off-campus study, part-time degree program, services for LD students, student-designed majors, study abroad, summer session for credit. *ROTC:* Army (c), Navy (c), Air Force (c).

Computers on Campus 128 computers/terminals are available on campus for general student use. Students can access the following: campus intranet, computer help desk, free student e-mail accounts, online (class) grades, online (class) registration, online (class) schedules. Campuswide network is available. Wireless service is available via classrooms, libraries.

Student Life *Activities and organizations:* choral group. *Campus security:* 24-hour emergency response devices. *Student services:* personal/psychological counseling.

Athletics Member USCAA. *Intercollegiate sports:* basketball M, golf M, volleyball W. *Intramural sports:* cheerleading M(c)/W(c), rugby M(c)/W(c), skiing (downhill) M(c)/W(c), soccer M(c)/W(c), softball M(c)/W(c), table tennis M/W.

Standardized Tests *Required:* SAT or ACT (for admission).

Costs (2011–12) *Tuition:* state resident $6903 full-time, $176 per credit hour part-time; nonresident $21,798 full-time, $590 per credit hour part-time. Full-time tuition and fees vary according to course load and student level. Part-time tuition and fees vary according to course load and student level. *Payment plan:* installment. *Waivers:* senior citizens and employees or children of employees.

Applying *Options:* electronic application. *Application fee:* $60. *Required:* essay or personal statement, high school transcript. *Application deadlines:* 7/1 (freshmen), 7/1 (out-of-state freshmen), 6/1 (transfers). *Notification:* 11/15 (freshmen), 11/15 (out-of-state freshmen).

Freshman Application Contact Mr. Matthew Moreau, Admissions and Financial Aid Coordinator, The Ohio State University at Marion, 1465 Mount Vernon Avenue, Marion, OH 43302. *Phone:* 740-725-6337. *Fax:* 740-386-2439. *E-mail:* moreau.1@osu.edu. *Web site:* http://osumarion.osu.edu/.

The Ohio State University–Mansfield Campus

Mansfield, Ohio

- **State-supported** comprehensive, founded 1958, part of The Ohio State University
- **Small-town** 640-acre campus with easy access to Columbus, Cleveland
- **Coed** 1,310 undergraduate students, 83% full-time, 54% women, 46% men
- **Noncompetitive** entrance level, 99% of applicants were admitted

Undergraduates 1,083 full-time, 227 part-time. Students come from 4 states and territories; 7% Black or African American, non-Hispanic/Latino; 2% Hispanic/Latino; 1% Asian, non-Hispanic/Latino; 0.1% Native Hawaiian or other Pacific Islander, non-Hispanic/Latino; 0.3% American Indian or Alaska Native, non-Hispanic/Latino; 1% Two or more races, non-Hispanic/Latino; 1% Race/ethnicity unknown; 4% transferred in; 16% live on campus. *Retention:* 71% of full-time freshmen returned.

Freshmen *Admission:* 1,500 applied, 1,484 admitted, 502 enrolled. *Test scores:* SAT critical reading scores over 500: 60%; SAT math scores over 500: 59%; SAT writing scores over 500: 46%; ACT scores over 18: 94%; SAT critical reading scores over 600: 17%; SAT math scores over 600: 15%; SAT writing scores over 600: 6%; ACT scores over 24: 41%; SAT math scores over 700: 2%; ACT scores over 30: 2%.

Faculty *Total:* 95, 43% full-time, 42% with terminal degrees. *Student/faculty ratio:* 20:1.

Academics *Calendar:* quarters. *Degrees:* associate, bachelor's, and master's. *Special study options:* academic remediation for entering students, accelerated degree program, adult/continuing education programs, advanced placement credit, cooperative education, distance learning, double majors, English as a second language, freshman honors college, honors programs, independent study, internships, off-campus study, part-time degree program, services for LD students, student-designed majors, study abroad, summer session for credit. *ROTC:* Army (c), Navy (c), Air Force (c).

Computers on Campus 235 computers/terminals are available on campus for general student use. Students can access the following: campus intranet, computer help desk, free student e-mail accounts, online (class) grades, online (class) registration, online (class) schedules. Campuswide network is available. 100% of college-owned or -operated housing units are wired for high-speed Internet access. Wireless service is available via computer centers, libraries, student centers.

Student Life *Housing options:* coed, disabled students. Campus housing is university owned. *Activities and organizations:* drama/theater group, choral group, Campus Activities Board, Campus Crusader for Christ, Club Ed, Multicultural Student Association, Psychology Student Association. *Campus security:* 24-hour emergency response devices and patrols. *Student services:* personal/psychological counseling.

Athletics *Intramural sports:* baseball M(c), basketball M(c)/W(c), bowling M/W, cheerleading M(c)/W(c), football M/W, golf M/W, soccer M(c), softball M/W, table tennis M/W, tennis M/W, volleyball M/W(c).

Standardized Tests *Required:* SAT or ACT (for admission).

Costs (2011–12) *Tuition:* state resident $6903 full-time, $176 per credit hour part-time; nonresident $21,798 full-time, $590 per credit hour part-time. Full-time tuition and fees vary according to course load, location, and student level. Part-time tuition and fees vary according to course load, location, and student level. *Room and board:* $7589. Room and board charges vary according to housing facility. *Payment plan:* installment. *Waivers:* senior citizens and employees or children of employees.

Applying *Options:* electronic application. *Application fee:* $60. *Required:* essay or personal statement, high school transcript. *Application deadlines:* 7/1 (freshmen), 7/1 (out-of-state freshmen). *Notification:* 11/15 (freshmen), 11/15 (out-of-state freshmen).

Freshman Application Contact Mr. Henry D. Thomas, Coordinator of Admissions and Financial Aid, The Ohio State University–Mansfield Campus, 1760 University Drive, Mansfield, OH 44906. *Phone:* 419-755-4225. *Fax:* 419-755-4241. *E-mail:* admissions@mansfield.ohio-state.edu. *Web site:* http://www.mansfield.osu.edu/.

The Ohio State University–Newark Campus

Newark, Ohio

- **State-supported** comprehensive, founded 1957, part of The Ohio State University
- **Small-town** 106-acre campus with easy access to Columbus
- **Coed** 2,568 undergraduate students, 86% full-time, 52% women, 48% men
- **Noncompetitive** entrance level, 99% of applicants were admitted

Undergraduates 2,216 full-time, 352 part-time. Students come from 10 states and territories; 14% Black or African American, non-Hispanic/Latino; 2% Hispanic/Latino; 3% Asian, non-Hispanic/Latino; 0.1% Native Hawaiian or other Pacific Islander, non-Hispanic/Latino; 0.4% American Indian or Alaska Native, non-Hispanic/Latino; 3% Two or more races, non-Hispanic/Latino; 2% Race/ethnicity unknown; 5% transferred in; 7% live on campus. *Retention:* 63% of full-time freshmen returned.

Freshmen *Admission:* 3,174 applied, 3,145 admitted, 1,270 enrolled. *Test scores:* SAT critical reading scores over 500: 52%; SAT math scores over 500: 62%; SAT writing scores over 500: 40%; ACT scores over 18: 85%; SAT critical reading scores over 600: 11%; SAT math scores over 600: 19%; SAT writing scores over 600: 5%; ACT scores over 24: 29%; SAT critical reading scores over 700: 1%; SAT math scores over 700: 1%; SAT writing scores over 700: 1%; ACT scores over 30: 1%.

Faculty *Total:* 140, 38% full-time, 37% with terminal degrees. *Student/faculty ratio:* 28:1.

Academics *Calendar:* quarters. *Degrees:* associate, bachelor's, and master's. *Special study options:* academic remediation for entering students, accelerated degree program, adult/continuing education programs, advanced placement credit, cooperative education, distance learning, double majors, English as a second language, freshman honors college, honors programs, independent study, internships, off-campus study, part-time degree program, services for LD students, student-designed majors, study abroad, summer session for credit. *ROTC:* Army (b), Navy (c), Air Force (c).

Computers on Campus 132 computers/terminals are available on campus for general student use. Students can access the following: campus intranet, computer help desk, free student e-mail accounts, online (class) grades, online (class) registration, online (class) schedules. Campuswide network is available. 100% of college-owned or -operated housing units are wired for high-speed Internet access. Wireless service is available via entire campus.

Student Life *Housing options:* coed. Campus housing is university owned. *Activities and organizations:* choral group. *Campus security:* 24-hour emergency response devices and patrols, late-night transport/escort service, self-defense education. *Student services:* personal/psychological counseling.

Athletics *Intramural sports:* baseball M(c), basketball M(c)/W(c), football M(c)/W(c), golf M(c)/W(c), soccer M(c)/W(c), softball W(c), volleyball M(c)/W(c), weight lifting M(c)/W(c).

Standardized Tests *Required:* SAT or ACT (for admission).

Costs (2011–12) *Tuition:* state resident $6903 full-time, $176 per credit hour part-time; nonresident $21,798 full-time, $590 per credit hour part-time. Full-time tuition and fees vary according to course load and student level. Part-time tuition and fees vary according to course load and student level. *Room and board:* $7185; room only: $6075. Room and board charges vary according to housing facility. *Payment plan:* installment. *Waivers:* employees or children of employees.

Applying *Options:* electronic application. *Application fee:* $60. *Required:* essay or personal statement, high school transcript. *Application deadlines:* 7/1 (freshmen), 7/1 (out-of-state freshmen), 6/1 (transfers). *Notification:* 11/15 (freshmen), 11/15 (out-of-state freshmen).

Freshman Application Contact Ms. Ann Donahue, Director of Enrollment, The Ohio State University–Newark Campus, 1179 University Drive, Newark, OH 43055. *Phone:* 740-366-9333. *Fax:* 740-364-9645. *E-mail:* barclay.3@osu.edu. *Web site:* http://www.newark.osu.edu/.

Ohio University

Athens, Ohio

- **State-supported** university, founded 1804, part of Ohio Board of Regents, University System of Ohio
- **Small-town** 1773-acre campus
- **Endowment** $336.0 million
- **Coed** 21,655 undergraduate students, 79% full-time, 58% women, 42% men
- **Moderately difficult** entrance level, 86% of applicants were admitted

Undergraduates 17,143 full-time, 4,512 part-time. Students come from 49 states and territories; 55 other countries; 13% are from out of state; 5% Black

or African American, non-Hispanic/Latino; 2% Hispanic/Latino; 0.7% Asian, non-Hispanic/Latino; 0.1% Native Hawaiian or other Pacific Islander, non-Hispanic/Latino; 0.2% American Indian or Alaska Native, non-Hispanic/Latino; 2% Two or more races, non-Hispanic/Latino; 1% Race/ethnicity unknown; 4% international; 2% transferred in; 40% live on campus. *Retention:* 80% of full-time freshmen returned.

Freshmen *Admission:* 13,251 applied, 11,415 admitted, 3,886 enrolled. *Average high school GPA:* 3.33. *Test scores:* SAT critical reading scores over 500: 68%; SAT math scores over 500: 68%; SAT writing scores over 500: 62%; ACT scores over 18: 98%; SAT critical reading scores over 600: 26%; SAT math scores over 600: 23%; SAT writing scores over 600: 19%; ACT scores over 24: 46%; SAT critical reading scores over 700: 5%; SAT math scores over 700: 3%; SAT writing scores over 700: 3%; ACT scores over 30: 7%.

Faculty *Total:* 1,163, 75% full-time, 79% with terminal degrees. *Student/faculty ratio:* 20:1.

Academics *Calendar:* quarters. *Degrees:* associate, bachelor's, master's, doctoral, and first professional. *Special study options:* academic remediation for entering students, accelerated degree program, adult/continuing education programs, advanced placement credit, cooperative education, distance learning, double majors, English as a second language, external degree program, freshman honors college, honors programs, independent study, internships, off-campus study, part-time degree program, services for LD students, student-designed majors, study abroad, summer session for credit. *ROTC:* Army (b), Air Force (b).

Computers on Campus 1,000 computers/terminals and 22,000 ports are available on campus for general student use. Students can access the following: campus intranet, computer help desk, free student e-mail accounts, online (class) grades, online (class) registration, online (class) schedules. Campuswide network is available. 100% of college-owned or -operated housing units are wired for high-speed Internet access. Wireless service is available via entire campus.

Student Life *Housing:* on-campus residence required through sophomore year. *Options:* coed, women-only, disabled students. Campus housing is university owned. Freshman campus housing is guaranteed. *Activities and organizations:* drama/theater group, student-run newspaper, radio and television station, choral group, marching band, Alpha Phi Omega, Golden Key Honor Society, International Student Union, Kappa Delta Pi, Campus Crusade for Christ, national fraternities, national sororities. *Campus security:* 24-hour emergency response devices and patrols, student patrols, late-night transport/escort service, controlled dormitory access, electronic dormitory access is being phased in gradually as part of renovations. *Student services:* health clinic, personal/psychological counseling, women's center, legal services.

Athletics Member NCAA. All Division I except football (Division I-A). *Intercollegiate sports:* baseball M(s), basketball M(s)/W(s), cheerleading M/W, cross-country running M(s)/W(s), field hockey W(s), golf M(s)/W(s), ice hockey M(c), soccer W(s), softball W(s), swimming and diving W(s), track and field W(s), volleyball W(s), wrestling M(s). *Intramural sports:* badminton M/W, basketball M/W, crew M(c)/W(c), equestrian sports M(c)/W(c), fencing M(c)/W(c), field hockey M(c)/W(c), golf M/W, gymnastics M(c)/W(c), lacrosse M(c)/W(c), racquetball M/W, rugby M(c)/W(c), soccer M(c)/W(c), softball M/W, tennis M(c)/W(c), ultimate Frisbee M(c)/W(c), volleyball M(c)/W(c), water polo M(c)/W, wrestling M(c)/W(c).

Standardized Tests *Required:* SAT or ACT (for admission).

Costs (2011–12) *Tuition:* state resident $9936 full-time, $314 per quarter hour part-time; nonresident $18,900 full-time, $609 per quarter hour part-time. Full-time tuition and fees vary according to degree level, location, program, and reciprocity agreements. Part-time tuition and fees vary according to course load, degree level, location, program, and reciprocity agreements. *Room and board:* $9753; room only: $5457. Room and board charges vary according to board plan. *Payment plan:* installment. *Waivers:* senior citizens and employees or children of employees.

Financial Aid Of all full-time matriculated undergraduates who enrolled in 2010, 13,179 applied for aid, 10,059 were judged to have need, 1,284 had their need fully met. In 2010, 1888 non-need-based awards were made. *Average percent of need met:* 56%. *Average financial aid package:* $8969. *Average need-based loan:* $4414. *Average need-based gift aid:* $7724. *Average non-need-based aid:* $3642. *Average indebtedness upon graduation:* $25,330.

Applying *Options:* electronic application, early admission, deferred entrance. *Application fee:* $45. *Required:* high school transcript. *Required for some:* essay or personal statement, 2 letters of recommendation, interview, Auditions required for music and dance; interview and portfolio reviews for visual communication, and application supplement for Honors Tutorial College. *Recommended:* 2 letters of recommendation. *Application deadlines:* 2/1 (freshmen), 2/1 (out-of-state freshmen), 6/15 (transfers). *Notification:* continuous (freshmen), continuous (out-of-state freshmen), continuous (transfers).

Freshman Application Contact Undergraduate Admissions, Ohio University, Athens, OH 45701-2979. *Phone:* 740-593-4100. *Fax:* 740-593-0560. *E-mail:* admissions@ohio.edu. *Web site:* http://www.ohio.edu/.

Ohio University–Chillicothe

Chillicothe, Ohio

- **State-supported** comprehensive, founded 1946, part of Ohio Board of Regents
- **Small-town** 124-acre campus with easy access to Columbus
- **Coed** 2,350 undergraduate students
- **Noncompetitive** entrance level

Academics *Calendar:* quarters. *Degrees:* associate, bachelor's, and master's (offers first 2 years of most bachelor's degree programs available at the main campus in Athens; also offers several bachelor's degree programs that can be completed at this campus and several programs exclusive to this campus; also offers some graduate programs). *Special study options:* academic remediation for entering students, adult/continuing education programs, advanced placement credit, distance learning, external degree program, internships, part-time degree program, services for LD students, study abroad, summer session for credit.

Computers on Campus Students can access the following: online (class) registration. Campuswide network is available.

Student Life *Housing:* college housing not available. *Activities and organizations:* drama/theater group. *Campus security:* 24-hour emergency response devices, patrols by city police. *Student services:* personal/psychological counseling.

Athletics *Intramural sports:* baseball M(c), basketball M(c)/W(c), golf M(c), softball W(c), tennis M(c)/W(c), volleyball M(c)/W(c).

Standardized Tests *Required:* COMPASS (for admission).

Financial Aid Of all full-time matriculated undergraduates who enrolled in 2010, 1,649 applied for aid, 1,535 were judged to have need, 78 had their need fully met. 15 Federal Work-Study jobs (averaging $1842). In 2010, 16 non-need-based awards were made. *Average percent of need met:* 55%. *Average financial aid package:* $8544. *Average need-based loan:* $3827. *Average need-based gift aid:* $8438. *Average non-need-based aid:* $3651. *Average indebtedness upon graduation:* $25,330.

Applying *Options:* early admission, deferred entrance. *Required:* high school transcript. *Application deadlines:* 9/1 (freshmen), 9/1 (transfers). *Notification:* continuous (freshmen), continuous (transfers).

Freshman Application Contact Thomas Eveland, Manager, Recruitment and Admissions, Ohio University–Chillicothe, 101 University Drive, Chillicothe, OH 45601. *Phone:* 740-774-7241. *Toll-free phone:* 877-462-6824. *Fax:* 740-774-7214. *E-mail:* evelandt@ohio.edu. *Web site:* http://www.chillicothe.ohiou.edu/.

Ohio University–Eastern

St. Clairsville, Ohio

Director of Admissions N. Kip Howard, Assistant Vice President for Enrollment Services/Director of Admissions, Ohio University–Eastern, 45425 National Road, St. Clairsville, OH 43950-9724. *Phone:* 740-593-4120. *Toll-free phone:* 800-648-3331. *E-mail:* howardn@ohio.edu. *Web site:* http://www.eastern.ohiou.edu/.

Ohio University–Lancaster

Lancaster, Ohio

Director of Admissions Pat Fox, Enrollment Manager, Ohio University–Lancaster, 1570 Granville Pike, Lancaster, OH 43130-1097. *Phone:* 740-654-6711 Ext. 215. *Toll-free phone:* 888-446-4468. *E-mail:* fox@ohio.edu. *Web site:* http://www.ohiou.edu/lancaster/.

Ohio University–Southern Campus

Ironton, Ohio

Director of Admissions Linda Harlow, Admission, Registration and Records Coordinator, Ohio University–Southern Campus, 1804 Liberty Avenue, Ironton, OH 45638-2214. *Phone:* 740-533-4584. *Toll-free phone:* 800-626-0513. *E-mail:* harlow@ohio.edu. *Web site:* http://www.ohiou.edu/.

Ohio University–Zanesville

Zanesville, Ohio

- **State-supported** 4-year, founded 1946
- **Rural** 179-acre campus with easy access to Columbus
- **Coed** 2,106 undergraduate students, 52% full-time, 70% women, 30% men
- **Noncompetitive** entrance level, 89% of applicants were admitted

Undergraduates 1,091 full-time, 1,015 part-time. Students come from 2 states and territories; 1 other country; 1% are from out of state; 4% Black or African American, non-Hispanic/Latino; 1% Hispanic/Latino; 0.4% Asian, non-Hispanic/Latino; 0.4% American Indian or Alaska Native, non-Hispanic/Latino; 4% Two or more races, non-Hispanic/Latino; 1% Race/ethnicity unknown; 0.9% international. *Retention:* 55% of full-time freshmen returned.

Freshmen *Admission:* 556 applied, 496 admitted, 288 enrolled.

Faculty *Total:* 130, 24% full-time, 25% with terminal degrees. *Student/faculty ratio:* 23:1.

Academics *Calendar:* quarters. *Degrees:* associate and bachelor's (offers first 2 years of most bachelor's degree programs available at the main campus in Athens; also offers several bachelor's degree programs that can be completed at this campus; also offers some graduate courses). *Special study options:* academic remediation for entering students, adult/continuing education programs, advanced placement credit, distance learning, double majors, external degree program, independent study, off-campus study, part-time degree program, services for LD students, student-designed majors, study abroad, summer session for credit.

Computers on Campus 200 computers/terminals are available on campus for general student use. Students can access the following: computer help desk, free student e-mail accounts, online (class) grades, online (class) registration, online (class) schedules. Campuswide network is available.

Student Life *Activities and organizations:* drama/theater group, student-run newspaper, radio station, Student Senate, Student Nurses Association, Good Intentions Group, Green Bobcats, Habitat for Humanity Club. *Campus security:* student patrols, late-night transport/escort service, night security. *Student services:* personal/psychological counseling.

Athletics *Intercollegiate sports:* baseball M, basketball M/W, golf M/W, softball W, volleyball M/W.

Standardized Tests *Required for some:* SAT or ACT (for admission).

Costs (2011–12) *Tuition:* state resident $4728 full-time; nonresident $9051 full-time. Full-time tuition and fees vary according to student level. Part-time tuition and fees vary according to student level. *Payment plan:* installment. *Waivers:* senior citizens and employees or children of employees.

Financial Aid Of all full-time matriculated undergraduates who enrolled in 2010, 1,118 applied for aid, 994 were judged to have need, 123 had their need fully met. 19 Federal Work-Study jobs (averaging $1802). In 2010, 88 non-need-based awards were made. *Average percent of need met:* 63%. *Average financial aid package:* $8176. *Average need-based loan:* $3931. *Average need-based gift aid:* $7531. *Average non-need-based aid:* $2122. *Average indebtedness upon graduation:* $25,330.

Applying *Options:* electronic application. *Application fee:* $20. *Required:* high school transcript. *Application deadlines:* rolling (freshmen), rolling (transfers).

Freshman Application Contact Mrs. Karen Ragsdale, Administrative Associate, Ohio University–Zanesville, Office of Student Services, 1425 Newark Road, Zanesville, OH 43701. *Phone:* 740-588-1440. *Fax:* 740-588-1444. *E-mail:* ouzservices@ohio.edu. *Web site:* http://www.zanesville.ohiou.edu/.

Ohio Wesleyan University

Delaware, Ohio

- **Independent United Methodist** 4-year, founded 1842
- **Small-town** 200-acre campus with easy access to Columbus
- **Coed** 1,829 undergraduate students, 99% full-time, 56% women, 44% men
- **Very difficult** entrance level, 70% of applicants were admitted

Undergraduates 1,815 full-time, 14 part-time. 47% are from out of state; 4% Black or African American, non-Hispanic/Latino; 2% Hispanic/Latino; 2% Asian, non-Hispanic/Latino; 78% Native Hawaiian or other Pacific Islander, non-Hispanic/Latino; 0.3% American Indian or Alaska Native, non-Hispanic/Latino; 2% Two or more races, non-Hispanic/Latino; 2% Race/ethnicity unknown; 8% international; 1% transferred in; 84% live on campus. *Retention:* 82% of full-time freshmen returned.

Freshmen *Admission:* 4,226 applied, 2,950 admitted, 483 enrolled. *Average high school GPA:* 3.44. *Test scores:* SAT critical reading scores over 500: 80%; SAT math scores over 500: 82%; SAT writing scores over 500: 80%; ACT scores over 18: 98%; SAT critical reading scores over 600: 49%; SAT math scores over 600: 42%; SAT writing scores over 600: 39%; ACT scores over 24: 68%; SAT critical reading scores over 700: 11%; SAT math scores over 700: 12%; SAT writing scores over 700: 8%; ACT scores over 30: 20%.

Faculty *Total:* 220, 63% full-time. *Student/faculty ratio:* 11:1.

Academics *Calendar:* semesters. *Degree:* bachelor's.

Computers on Campus Campuswide network is available.

Student Life *Housing:* on-campus residence required through senior year. *Options:* coed, women-only. Campus housing is university owned. Freshman campus housing is guaranteed. *Campus security:* 24-hour emergency response devices and patrols, late-night transport/escort service, controlled dormitory access.

The Opposite of Ordinary

93 majors, sequences, and courses of study

Comprehensive academic and pre-professional programs

Internationally focused curriculum

Community building through leadership and service

Unwavering commitment to linking theory to practice in every field of study

Ohio Wesleyan University

choose.owu.edu

Athletics Member NCAA. All Division III. *Intercollegiate sports:* baseball M, basketball M/W, cross-country running M/W, equestrian sports M(c)/W(c), field hockey W, football M, golf M, ice hockey M(c)/W(c), lacrosse M/W, rugby M(c)/W(c), sailing M(c)/W(c), soccer M/W, softball W, swimming and diving M/W, tennis M/W, track and field M/W, ultimate Frisbee M(c)/W(c), volleyball M(c)/W. *Intramural sports:* badminton M/W, basketball M/W, football M/W, golf M/W, lacrosse M/W, racquetball M/W, skiing (cross-country) M/W, skiing (downhill) M/W, soccer M/W, softball M/W, squash M/W, swimming and diving M/W, tennis M/W, track and field M/W, volleyball M/W, water polo M/W.

Standardized Tests *Required:* SAT or ACT (for admission).

Costs (2011–12) *Comprehensive fee:* $47,604 includes full-time tuition ($37,580), mandatory fees ($240), and room and board ($9784). *College room only:* $5320. Room and board charges vary according to board plan. *Payment plan:* installment.

Financial Aid Of all full-time matriculated undergraduates who enrolled in 2010, 1,310 applied for aid, 1,133 were judged to have need, 277 had their need fully met. In 2010, 670 non-need-based awards were made. *Average percent of need met:* 83%. *Average financial aid package:* $29,125. *Average need-based loan:* $5125. *Average need-based gift aid:* $28,530. *Average non-need-based aid:* $18,140. *Average indebtedness upon graduation:* $30,900. *Financial aid deadline:* 5/1.

Applying *Options:* early admission, early action, deferred entrance. *Application fee:* $35. *Required:* essay or personal statement, high school transcript, minimum 2.5 GPA, 1 letter of recommendation. *Recommended:* 2 letters of recommendation, interview. *Application deadlines:* 3/1 (freshmen), rolling (transfers), 12/15 (early action). *Notification:* continuous (transfers), 1/15 (early action).

Freshman Application Contact Ms. Carol DelPropost, Assistant Vice President of Admission and Financial Aid, Ohio Wesleyan University, 61 South Sandusky Street, Delaware, OH 43015. *Phone:* 740-368-3059. *Toll-free phone:* 800-922-8953. *Fax:* 740-368-3314. *E-mail:* cjdelpro@owu.edu. *Web site:* http://www.owu.edu/.

See page 1494 for the College Close-Up.

Otterbein University
Westerville, Ohio

- **Independent United Methodist** comprehensive, founded 1847
- **Suburban** 142-acre campus with easy access to Columbus
- **Endowment** $70.0 million
- **Coed** 2,575 undergraduate students, 89% full-time, 63% women, 37% men
- **Moderately difficult** entrance level, 79% of applicants were admitted

Undergraduates 2,282 full-time, 293 part-time. Students come from 40 states and territories; 10 other countries; 10% are from out of state; 7% Black or African American, non-Hispanic/Latino; 0.8% Hispanic/Latino; 1% Asian, non-Hispanic/Latino; 0.2% Native Hawaiian or other Pacific Islander, non-Hispanic/Latino; 0.5% American Indian or Alaska Native, non-Hispanic/Latino; 0.9% Two or more races, non-Hispanic/Latino; 6% Race/ethnicity unknown; 1% international; 4% transferred in; 61% live on campus. *Retention:* 75% of full-time freshmen returned.

Freshmen *Admission:* 3,190 applied, 2,525 admitted, 638 enrolled. *Average high school GPA:* 3.5. *Test scores:* SAT critical reading scores over 500: 70%; SAT math scores over 500: 71%; SAT writing scores over 500: 64%; ACT scores over 18: 96%; SAT critical reading scores over 600: 30%; SAT math scores over 600: 26%; SAT writing scores over 600: 24%; ACT scores over 24: 51%; SAT critical reading scores over 700: 7%; SAT math scores over 700: 1%; SAT writing scores over 700: 3%; ACT scores over 30: 5%.

Faculty *Total:* 337, 52% full-time. *Student/faculty ratio:* 11:1.

Academics *Calendar:* quarters. *Degrees:* bachelor's, master's, doctoral, and post-master's certificates. *Special study options:* academic remediation for entering students, adult/continuing education programs, advanced placement credit, double majors, English as a second language, honors programs, internships, off-campus study, part-time degree program, services for LD students, student-designed majors, study abroad, summer session for credit. *ROTC:* Army (c). *Unusual degree programs:* 3-2 engineering with Case Western Reserve University, Washington University in St. Louis.

Computers on Campus 146 computers/terminals are available on campus for general student use. Students can access the following: campus intranet, computer help desk, free student e-mail accounts, online (class) grades, online (class) registration, online (class) schedules. Campuswide network is available. 100% of college-owned or -operated housing units are wired for high-speed Internet access. Wireless service is available via entire campus.

Student Life *Housing:* on-campus residence required through junior year. *Options:* coed, men-only, women-only. Campus housing is university owned. Freshman applicants given priority for college housing. *Activities and organizations:* drama/theater group, student-run newspaper, radio and television sta-

tion, choral group, marching band, musical groups, Honoraries, academic interest clubs, Governance, national fraternities. *Campus security:* 24-hour emergency response devices and patrols, student patrols, late-night transport/escort service, controlled dormitory access, 24-hour locked residence hall entrances. *Student services:* health clinic, personal/psychological counseling.

Athletics Member NCAA. All Division III. *Intercollegiate sports:* baseball M, basketball M/W, cheerleading M/W, cross-country running M/W, equestrian sports M/W, football M, golf M/W, lacrosse M/W, soccer M/W, softball W, tennis M/W, track and field M/W, volleyball W. *Intramural sports:* basketball M/W, football M, racquetball M/W, soccer M/W, softball M/W, ultimate Frisbee M/W, volleyball M/W.

Standardized Tests *Required:* SAT or ACT (for admission).

Costs (2011–12) *Comprehensive fee:* $37,802 includes full-time tuition ($29,550) and room and board ($8252). Full-time tuition and fees vary according to course load and program. Part-time tuition: $530 per credit hour. Part-time tuition and fees vary according to course load and program. *College room only:* $4276. Room and board charges vary according to housing facility. *Payment plan:* installment. *Waivers:* employees or children of employees.

Financial Aid Of all full-time matriculated undergraduates who enrolled in 2008, 2,006 applied for aid, 1,788 were judged to have need, 144 had their need fully met. 500 Federal Work-Study jobs (averaging $1000). 250 state and other part-time jobs (averaging $1000). In 2008, 405 non-need-based awards were made. *Average percent of need met:* 72%. *Average financial aid package:* $16,337. *Average need-based loan:* $4496. *Average need-based gift aid:* $14,473. *Average non-need-based aid:* $8843.

Applying *Options:* electronic application, deferred entrance. *Application fee:* $25. *Required:* high school transcript. *Required for some:* essay or personal statement, 1 letter of recommendation. *Recommended:* minimum 2.5 GPA, interview. *Application deadlines:* 3/1 (freshmen), rolling (transfers). *Notification:* continuous (freshmen), continuous (transfers).

Freshman Application Contact Mr. Ben Shoemaker, Interim Director of Admissions, Otterbein University, 1 South Grove Street, Office Of Admission, Westerville, OH 43081-9924. *Phone:* 614-823-1500. *Toll-free phone:* 800-488-8144. *Fax:* 614-823-1200. *E-mail:* uotterb@otterbein.edu. *Web site:* http://www.otterbein.edu/.

Pontifical College Josephinum

Columbus, Ohio

Freshman Application Contact Mrs. Arminda Crawford, Secretary for Admissions, Pontifical College Josephinum, 7825 North High Street, Columbus, OH 43235. *Phone:* 614-985-2241. *Toll-free phone:* 888-252-5812. *Fax:* 614-885-2307. *E-mail:* acrawford@pcj.edu. *Web site:* http://www.pcj.edu/.

Rabbinical College of Telshe

Wickliffe, Ohio

Freshman Application Contact Admissions Office, Rabbinical College of Telshe, 28400 Euclid Avenue, Wickliffe, OH 44092-2523. *Phone:* 440-943-5300.

Shawnee State University

Portsmouth, Ohio

- **State-supported** comprehensive, founded 1986
- **Small-town** 52-acre campus
- **Endowment** $13.6 million
- **Coed** 4,618 undergraduate students, 85% full-time, 58% women, 42% men
- **Noncompetitive** entrance level, 85% of applicants were admitted

Undergraduates 3,913 full-time, 705 part-time. Students come from 21 states and territories; 18 other countries; 11% are from out of state; 5% Black or African American, non-Hispanic/Latino; 0.6% Hispanic/Latino; 0.4% Asian, non-Hispanic/Latino; 0.1% Native Hawaiian or other Pacific Islander, non-Hispanic/Latino; 0.8% American Indian or Alaska Native, non-Hispanic/Latino; 1% Two or more races, non-Hispanic/Latino; 7% Race/ethnicity unknown; 0.7% international; 6% transferred in; 22% live on campus. *Retention:* 53% of full-time freshmen returned.

Freshmen *Admission:* 4,451 applied, 3,766 admitted, 1,187 enrolled. *Test scores:* SAT critical reading scores over 500: 45%; SAT math scores over 500: 42%; ACT scores over 18: 71%; SAT critical reading scores over 600: 16%; SAT math scores over 600: 16%; ACT scores over 24: 19%; ACT scores over 30: 1%.

Faculty *Total:* 316, 46% full-time. *Student/faculty ratio:* 21:1.

Academics *Calendar:* semesters. *Degrees:* certificates, associate, bachelor's, and master's. *Special study options:* academic remediation for entering students, accelerated degree program, adult/continuing education programs, advanced placement credit, distance learning, double majors, English as a second language, honors programs, independent study, internships, off-campus study, part-time degree program, services for LD students, student-designed majors, study abroad, summer session for credit. *Unusual degree programs:* psychology (MOT).

Computers on Campus 620 computers/terminals are available on campus for general student use. Students can access the following: campus intranet, computer help desk, free student e-mail accounts, online (class) grades, online (class) registration, online (class) schedules, financial aid, student billing, courses, student service portal. Campuswide network is available. 100% of college-owned or -operated housing units are wired for high-speed Internet access. Wireless service is available via entire campus.

Student Life *Housing:* on-campus residence required for freshman year. *Options:* coed. Campus housing is university owned and leased by the school. Freshman applicants given priority for college housing. *Activities and organizations:* drama/theater group, student-run newspaper, choral group, campus ministry, Health Executives and Administrators Learning Society, Student Programming Board, Student Government Association, national fraternities. *Campus security:* 24-hour emergency response devices and patrols. *Student services:* health clinic, personal/psychological counseling, women's center.

Athletics Member NAIA. *Intercollegiate sports:* baseball M(s), basketball M(s)/W(s), cross-country running M(s)/W(s), golf M(s), soccer M(s)/W(s), softball W, tennis W(s), volleyball W(s). *Intramural sports:* basketball M/W, bowling M/W, golf M/W, racquetball M/W, softball M, swimming and diving M/W, table tennis M/W, tennis M/W, volleyball M/W.

Standardized Tests *Required for some:* ACT (for admission). *Recommended:* ACT (for admission).

Costs (2011–12) *Tuition:* state resident $5718 full-time, $238 per credit hour part-time; nonresident $10,524 full-time, $438 per credit hour part-time. Full-time tuition and fees vary according to course load and reciprocity agreements. Part-time tuition and fees vary according to course load and reciprocity agreements. *Required fees:* $1044 full-time, $44 per credit hour part-time. *Room and board:* $8494; room only: $5292. Room and board charges vary according to board plan and housing facility. *Payment plan:* installment. *Waivers:* senior citizens and employees or children of employees.

Applying *Options:* electronic application, deferred entrance. *Required:* high school transcript. *Required for some:* interview. *Application deadlines:* rolling (freshmen), rolling (out-of-state freshmen), rolling (transfers). *Notification:* continuous (freshmen), continuous (out-of-state freshmen), continuous (transfers).

Freshman Application Contact Shawnee State University, 940 Second Street, Portsmouth, OH 45662-4344. *Phone:* 740-351-3610 Ext. 610. *Toll-free phone:* 800-959-2SSU. *Web site:* http://www.shawnee.edu/.

South University

Cleveland, Ohio

Admissions Office Contact South University, 4743 Richmond Road, Cleveland, OH 44128. *Toll-free phone:* 855-398-9280. *Web site:* http://www.southuniversity.edu/cleveland.aspx.

See page 1596 for the College Close-Up.

Strayer University - Akron Campus

Akron, Ohio

- **Proprietary** comprehensive
- **Coed**

Academics *Degrees:* certificates, diplomas, associate, bachelor's, master's, and postbachelor's certificates.

Freshman Application Contact Strayer University - Akron Campus, 51 Park West Boulevard, Akron, OH 44320. *Web site:* http://strayer.edu/akron.

Strayer University - Cincinnati Campus

Cincinnati, Ohio

- **Proprietary** comprehensive
- **Coed**

Academics *Degrees:* certificates, diplomas, associate, bachelor's, master's, and postbachelor's certificates.

Freshman Application Contact Strayer University - Cincinnati Campus, 2135 Dana Avenue, Suite 300, Cincinnati, OH 45207. *Web site:* http://www.strayer.edu/cincinnati.

Strayer University - Columbus Campus

Columbus, Ohio

- **Proprietary** comprehensive
- **Coed**

Academics *Degrees:* certificates, diplomas, associate, bachelor's, master's, and postbachelor's certificates.

Freshman Application Contact Strayer University - Columbus Campus, 8425 Pulsar Place, Suite 400, Columbus, OH 43240. *Web site:* http://www.strayer.edu/columbus/.

Strayer University - Fairborn Campus

Fairborn, Ohio

- **Proprietary** comprehensive
- **Coed**

Academics *Degrees:* certificates, diplomas, associate, bachelor's, master's, and postbachelor's certificates.

Freshman Application Contact Strayer University - Fairborn Campus, 2600 Paramount Place, Suite 300, Fairborn, OH 45324. *Web site:* http://www.strayer.edu/fairborn.

Strayer University - Fairview Park Campus

Fairview Park, Ohio

- **Proprietary** comprehensive
- **Coed**

Academics *Degrees:* certificates, diplomas, associate, bachelor's, master's, and postbachelor's certificates.

Freshman Application Contact Strayer University - Fairview Park Campus, 22730 Fairview Center Drive, Suite 150, Fairview Park, OH 44126-3616. *Web site:* http://strayer.edu/fairview_park.

Strayer University - Mason Campus

Mason, Ohio

- **Proprietary** comprehensive
- **Coed**

Academics *Degrees:* certificates, diplomas, associate, bachelor's, master's, and postbachelor's certificates.

Freshman Application Contact Strayer University - Mason Campus, 4605 Duke Drive, Suite 700, Mason, OH 45040. *Web site:* http://www.strayer.edu/mason/.

Temple Baptist College

Cincinnati, Ohio

Admissions Office Contact Temple Baptist College, 11965 Kenn Road, Cincinnati, OH 45240. *Web site:* http://www.templebaptistcollege.com/.

Tiffin University

Tiffin, Ohio

- **Independent** comprehensive, founded 1888
- **Small-town** 110-acre campus with easy access to Toledo
- **Endowment** $5.3 million
- **Coed** 5,663 undergraduate students, 43% full-time, 63% women, 37% men
- **Moderately difficult** entrance level, 51% of applicants were admitted

Undergraduates 2,455 full-time, 3,208 part-time. Students come from 50 states and territories; 29 other countries; 51% are from out of state; 30% Black or African American, non-Hispanic/Latino; 4% Hispanic/Latino; 0.5% Asian, non-Hispanic/Latino; 0.1% Native Hawaiian or other Pacific Islander, non-Hispanic/Latino; 0.5% American Indian or Alaska Native, non-Hispanic/Latino; 22% Race/ethnicity unknown; 1% international; 4% transferred in; 18% live on campus. *Retention:* 69% of full-time freshmen returned.

Freshmen *Admission:* 7,082 applied, 3,615 admitted, 1,682 enrolled. *Average high school GPA:* 3.01. *Test scores:* SAT critical reading scores over 500: 34%; SAT math scores over 500: 40%; ACT scores over 18: 77%; SAT critical reading scores over 600: 6%; SAT math scores over 600: 7%; ACT scores over 24: 19%; SAT critical reading scores over 700: 1%; ACT scores over 30: 1%.

Faculty *Total:* 446, 17% full-time, 29% with terminal degrees. *Student/faculty ratio:* 21:1.

Academics *Calendar:* semesters. *Degrees:* certificates, associate, bachelor's, master's, post-master's, and postbachelor's certificates. *Special study options:* academic remediation for entering students, accelerated degree program, adult/continuing education programs, advanced placement credit, distance learning, double majors, English as a second language, external degree program, freshman honors college, honors programs, independent study, internships, off-campus study, services for LD students, study abroad, summer session for credit. *ROTC:* Army (c), Air Force (c).

Computers on Campus 270 computers/terminals are available on campus for general student use. Students can access the following: campus intranet, computer help desk, free student e-mail accounts, online (class) grades, online (class) registration, online (class) schedules. Campuswide network is available. 100% of college-owned or -operated housing units are wired for high-speed Internet access. Wireless service is available via classrooms, computer centers, computer labs, dorm rooms, learning centers, libraries, student centers.

Student Life *Housing:* on-campus residence required through sophomore year. *Options:* coed, men-only, women-only, disabled students. Campus housing is university owned and leased by the school. Freshman campus housing is guaranteed. *Activities and organizations:* drama/theater group, student-run newspaper, choral group, marching band, Student Government Association, H2O, International Student Association, Global Affairs Organization, Circle K, national fraternities, national sororities. *Campus security:* 24-hour emergency response devices, student patrols, late-night transport/escort service, controlled dormitory access. *Student services:* health clinic, personal/psychological counseling, women's center.

Athletics Member NCAA. All Division II. *Intercollegiate sports:* baseball M(s), basketball M(s)/W(s), cheerleading M(s)/W(s), cross-country running M(s)/W(s), equestrian sports M(s)/W(s), football M(s), golf M(s)/W(s), lacrosse W(s), soccer M(s)/W(s), softball W(s), tennis M(s)/W(s), track and field M(s)/W(s), volleyball W(s), wrestling M(s). *Intramural sports:* basketball M/W, bowling M/W, equestrian sports M(c)/W(c), football M, rugby M(c), soccer M/W, softball M/W, table tennis M/W, tennis M/W, ultimate Frisbee M/W, volleyball M/W, weight lifting M/W.

Standardized Tests *Required for some:* SAT or ACT (for admission).

Costs (2012–13) *Comprehensive fee:* $29,092 includes full-time tuition ($19,890) and room and board ($9202). Full-time tuition and fees vary according to course load, degree level, location, and program. Part-time tuition: $663 per credit. Part-time tuition and fees vary according to course load, degree level, location, and program. *College room only:* $4736. Room and board charges vary according to board plan and housing facility. *Payment plan:* installment. *Waivers:* senior citizens and employees or children of employees.

Financial Aid Of all full-time matriculated undergraduates who enrolled in 2011, 2,299 applied for aid, 2,177 were judged to have need, 186 had their need fully met. 190 Federal Work-Study jobs (averaging $2663). *Average percent of need met:* 60%. *Average financial aid package:* $14,589. *Average need-based loan:* $4822. *Average need-based gift aid:* $9772. *Average indebtedness upon graduation:* $25,246.

Applying *Options:* electronic application. *Application fee:* $20. *Required:* high school transcript. *Required for some:* essay or personal statement, interview. *Recommended:* minimum 3.0 GPA. *Application deadline:* rolling (freshmen). *Notification:* continuous (transfers).

Freshman Application Contact Mr. Jeremy Marinis, Director of Undergraduate Admissions, Tiffin University, 155 Miami Street, Tiffin, OH 44883. *Phone:* 419-448-3301. *Toll-free phone:* 800-968-6446. *Fax:* 419-443-5006. *E-mail:* marinisjj@tiffin.edu. *Web site:* http://www.tiffin.edu/.

Tri-State Bible College

South Point, Ohio

- **Independent nondenominational** comprehensive, founded 1970
- **Suburban** 4-acre campus
- **Coed** 65 undergraduate students

Academics *Calendar:* semesters. *Degrees:* associate, bachelor's, and master's.

Applying *Application fee:* $25.

Freshman Application Contact Tri-State Bible College, 506 Margaret Street, PO Box 445, South Point, OH 45680-8402. *Phone:* 740-377-2520. *Web site:* http://www.tsbc.edu/.

Union Institute & University

Cincinnati, Ohio

- **Independent** university, founded 1969
- **Urban** 5-acre campus with easy access to Cincinnati
- **Endowment** $696,114
- **Coed** 1,162 undergraduate students, 60% full-time, 55% women, 45% men
- **Noncompetitive** entrance level

Undergraduates 694 full-time, 468 part-time. Students come from 39 states and territories; 1 other country; 12% are from out of state; 28% Black or African American, non-Hispanic/Latino; 14% Hispanic/Latino; 1% Asian, non-Hispanic/Latino; 0.4% Native Hawaiian or other Pacific Islander, non-Hispanic/Latino; 0.5% American Indian or Alaska Native, non-Hispanic/Latino; 2% Two or more races, non-Hispanic/Latino; 19% Race/ethnicity unknown; 29% transferred in. *Retention:* 71% of full-time freshmen returned.
Freshmen *Admission:* 18 enrolled.
Faculty *Total:* 353, 9% full-time, 52% with terminal degrees. *Student/faculty ratio:* 9:1.
Academics *Calendar:* trimesters some programs offer split (8wk) sessions. *Degrees:* bachelor's, master's, doctoral, post-master's, and first professional certificates. *Special study options:* academic remediation for entering students, accelerated degree program, adult/continuing education programs, advanced placement credit, distance learning, double majors, external degree program, independent study, internships, off-campus study, part-time degree program, services for LD students, student-designed majors, summer session for credit.
Computers on Campus 80 computers/terminals are available on campus for general student use. Students can access the following: computer help desk, free student e-mail accounts, online (class) grades, online (class) registration, online (class) schedules, CampusWeb-online access to basic information and grades. Campuswide network is available. Wireless service is available via classrooms, computer labs, libraries.
Student Life *Campus security:* 24-hour emergency response devices, late-night transport/escort service, security personnel on site during business and class hours.
Costs (2011–12) *Tuition:* $11,352 full-time, $473 per semester hour part-time. *Required fees:* $240 full-time, $60 per term part-time. *Payment plan:* installment. *Waivers:* employees or children of employees.
Applying *Options:* electronic application, deferred entrance. *Required:* essay or personal statement, recommendation from program faculty. *Required for some:* high school transcript, 1 letter of recommendation. *Recommended:* interview. *Application deadlines:* rolling (freshmen), rolling (out-of-state freshmen), rolling (transfers). *Notification:* continuous (freshmen), continuous (out-of-state freshmen), continuous (transfers).
Freshman Application Contact Union Institute & University, 440 East McMillan Street, Cincinnati, OH 45206-1925. *Phone:* 513-487-1173. *Toll-free phone:* 800-486-3116. *Web site:* http://www.myunion.edu/.

The University of Akron

Akron, Ohio

- **State-supported** university, founded 1870
- **Urban** 223-acre campus with easy access to Cleveland
- **Endowment** $193.2 million
- **Coed** 22,966 undergraduate students, 78% full-time, 48% women, 52% men
- **Moderately difficult** entrance level, 74% of applicants were admitted

Undergraduates 17,916 full-time, 5,050 part-time. Students come from 37 states and territories; 52 other countries; 3% are from out of state; 17% Black or African American, non-Hispanic/Latino; 2% Hispanic/Latino; 2% Asian, non-Hispanic/Latino; 0.1% Native Hawaiian or other Pacific Islander, non-Hispanic/Latino; 0.2% American Indian or Alaska Native, non-Hispanic/Latino; 2% Two or more races, non-Hispanic/Latino; 3% Race/ethnicity unknown; 1% international; 5% transferred in; 15% live on campus. *Retention:* 71% of full-time freshmen returned.
Freshmen *Admission:* 14,413 applied, 10,673 admitted, 4,627 enrolled. *Average high school GPA:* 2.97. *Test scores:* SAT critical reading scores over 500: 54%; SAT math scores over 500: 57%; ACT scores over 18: 76%; SAT critical reading scores over 600: 17%; SAT math scores over 600: 25%; ACT scores over 24: 28%; SAT critical reading scores over 700: 3%; SAT math scores over 700: 4%; ACT scores over 30: 4%.
Faculty *Total:* 1,756, 44% full-time, 52% with terminal degrees. *Student/faculty ratio:* 21:1.
Academics *Calendar:* semesters. *Degrees:* certificates, associate, bachelor's, master's, doctoral, post-master's, postbachelor's, and first professional certificates. *Special study options:* academic remediation for entering students, accelerated degree program, adult/continuing education programs, advanced

placement credit, cooperative education, distance learning, double majors, English as a second language, external degree program, freshman honors college, honors programs, independent study, internships, part-time degree program, services for LD students, student-designed majors, study abroad, summer session for credit. *ROTC:* Army (b), Air Force (c). *Unusual degree programs:* 3-2 accounting, BSMD (NEOUCOM), mathematics.
Computers on Campus 3,100 computers/terminals and 16,000 ports are available on campus for general student use. Students can access the following: campus intranet, computer help desk, free student e-mail accounts, online (class) grades, online (class) registration, online (class) schedules, library laptops for student checkout. Campuswide network is available. 100% of college-owned or -operated housing units are wired for high-speed Internet access. Wireless service is available via entire campus.
Student Life *Housing:* on-campus residence required for freshman year. *Options:* coed, men-only, women-only. Campus housing is university owned. Freshman applicants given priority for college housing. *Activities and organizations:* drama/theater group, student-run newspaper, radio and television station, choral group, marching band, Associated Student Government, Residence Hall Program Board, American Society of Mechanical Engineers, national fraternities, national sororities. *Campus security:* 24-hour emergency response devices and patrols, student patrols, late-night transport/escort service, controlled dormitory access. *Student services:* health clinic, personal/psychological counseling, women's center, legal services.
Athletics Member NCAA. All Division I except football (Division I-A). *Intercollegiate sports:* baseball M(s), basketball M(s)/W(s), cheerleading M/W, cross-country running M(s)/W(s), golf M(s)/W(s), riflery M/W(s), soccer M(s)/W(s), softball W(s), swimming and diving W(s), tennis W(s), track and field M(s)/W(s), volleyball W(s). *Intramural sports:* badminton M/W, basketball M/W, bowling M/W, cross-country running M/W, golf M/W, racquetball M/W, skiing (cross-country) M/W, skiing (downhill) M/W, soccer M/W, softball M/W, swimming and diving M/W, table tennis M/W, track and field M/W, volleyball W, wrestling M.
Standardized Tests *Required:* SAT or ACT (for admission).
Costs (2012–13) *Tuition:* state resident $8004 full-time; nonresident $15,927 full-time. Full-time tuition and fees vary according to course load, degree level, and location. Part-time tuition and fees vary according to course load, degree level, and location. *Required fees:* $1541 full-time. *Room and board:* $9586; room only: $6122. Room and board charges vary according to board plan and housing facility. *Payment plan:* installment. *Waivers:* senior citizens and employees or children of employees.
Financial Aid Of all full-time matriculated undergraduates who enrolled in 2011, 15,320 applied for aid, 12,749 were judged to have need, 2,954 had their need fully met. 452 Federal Work-Study jobs (averaging $1675). 3,015 state and other part-time jobs (averaging $1988). In 2011, 1538 non-need-based awards were made. *Average percent of need met:* 67%. *Average financial aid package:* $7545. *Average need-based loan:* $3826. *Average need-based gift aid:* $4559. *Average non-need-based aid:* $4004. *Average indebtedness upon graduation:* $22,096.
Applying *Options:* electronic application, early action, deferred entrance. *Application fee:* $40. *Required:* high school transcript. *Required for some:* essay or personal statement, 3 letters of recommendation, interview. *Application deadlines:* 8/11 (freshmen), rolling (transfers), 11/1 (early action). *Notification:* 9/15 (freshmen), continuous (transfers).
Freshman Application Contact The University of Akron, 302 Buchtel Common, Akron, OH 44325. *Phone:* 330-972-7100. *Toll-free phone:* 800-655-4884. *Web site:* http://www.uakron.edu/.

The University of Akron–Wayne College

Orrville, Ohio

- **State-supported** primarily 2-year, founded 1972, part of The University of Akron
- **Rural** 157-acre campus
- **Coed** 2,502 undergraduate students, 53% full-time, 61% women, 39% men
- **Noncompetitive** entrance level, 91% of applicants were admitted

Undergraduates 1,327 full-time, 1,175 part-time. Students come from 5 states and territories; 2 other countries; 8% Black or African American, non-Hispanic/Latino; 1% Hispanic/Latino; 0.6% Asian, non-Hispanic/Latino; 0.4% American Indian or Alaska Native, non-Hispanic/Latino; 1% Two or more races, non-Hispanic/Latino; 3% Race/ethnicity unknown; 3% transferred in. *Retention:* 48% of full-time freshmen returned.
Freshmen *Admission:* 859 applied, 780 admitted, 389 enrolled. *Average high school GPA:* 3.16. *Test scores:* ACT scores over 18: 69%; ACT scores over 24: 15%; ACT scores over 30: 1%.
Faculty *Total:* 174, 16% full-time, 22% with terminal degrees. *Student/faculty ratio:* 23:1.

Academics *Calendar:* semesters. *Degrees:* certificates, associate, and bachelor's. *Special study options:* academic remediation for entering students, adult/continuing education programs, advanced placement credit, cooperative education, distance learning, double majors, English as a second language, honors programs, independent study, internships, off-campus study, summer session for credit. *ROTC:* Army (c), Air Force (c).

Computers on Campus 240 computers/terminals are available on campus for general student use. Students can access the following: campus intranet, computer help desk, free student e-mail accounts, online (class) grades, online (class) registration, online (class) schedules. Campuswide network is available. Wireless service is available via entire campus.

Student Life *Housing:* college housing not available. *Campus security:* 24-hour emergency response devices, late-night transport/escort service. *Student services:* personal/psychological counseling.

Athletics *Intercollegiate sports:* basketball M/W, cheerleading W, golf M, volleyball W. *Intramural sports:* basketball M/W, golf M, volleyball M/W.

Standardized Tests *Required for some:* SAT or ACT (for admission), ACT COMPASS. *Recommended:* SAT or ACT (for admission), ACT COMPASS.

Costs (2011–12) *Tuition:* state resident $5740 full-time; nonresident $13,526 full-time. Full-time tuition and fees vary according to course load and location. Part-time tuition and fees vary according to course load and location. *Required fees:* $170 full-time. *Payment plan:* installment. *Waivers:* employees or children of employees.

Financial Aid Of all full-time matriculated undergraduates who enrolled in 2010, 8 Federal Work-Study jobs (averaging $2200).

Applying *Options:* electronic application, early admission, deferred entrance. *Application fee:* $40. *Required for some:* high school transcript. *Application deadlines:* 8/30 (freshmen), 8/30 (transfers). *Notification:* continuous until 8/30 (freshmen), continuous until 8/30 (transfers).

Freshman Application Contact Ms. Alicia Broadus, Student Services Counselor, The University of Akron–Wayne College, Orrville, OH 44667. *Phone:* 800-221-8308 Ext. 8901. *Toll-free phone:* 800-221-8308. *Fax:* 330-684-8989. *E-mail:* wayneadmissions@uakron.edu. *Web site:* http://www.wayne.uakron.edu/.

University of Cincinnati

Cincinnati, Ohio

- **State-supported** university, founded 1819, part of University System of Ohio
- **Urban** 137-acre campus with easy access to Cincinnati
- **Endowment** $831.7 million
- **Coed** 22,893 undergraduate students, 85% full-time, 51% women, 49% men
- **Moderately difficult** entrance level, 65% of applicants were admitted

Undergraduates 19,371 full-time, 3,522 part-time. Students come from 52 states and territories; 108 other countries; 14% are from out of state; 8% Black or African American, non-Hispanic/Latino; 2% Hispanic/Latino; 3% Asian, non-Hispanic/Latino; 0.3% American Indian or Alaska Native, non-Hispanic/Latino; 1% Two or more races, non-Hispanic/Latino; 4% Race/ethnicity unknown; 3% international; 5% transferred in; 20% live on campus. *Retention:* 85% of full-time freshmen returned.

Freshmen *Admission:* 17,020 applied, 11,020 admitted, 4,300 enrolled. *Average high school GPA:* 3.43. *Test scores:* SAT critical reading scores over 500: 76%; SAT math scores over 500: 82%; SAT writing scores over 500: 68%; ACT scores over 18: 100%; SAT critical reading scores over 600: 33%; SAT math scores over 600: 42%; SAT writing scores over 600: 25%; ACT scores over 24: 63%; SAT critical reading scores over 700: 7%; SAT math scores over 700: 9%; SAT writing scores over 700: 5%; ACT scores over 30: 12%.

Faculty *Total:* 1,201, 97% full-time, 77% with terminal degrees. *Student/faculty ratio:* 18:1.

Academics *Calendar:* quarters. *Degrees:* certificates, associate, bachelor's, master's, doctoral, post-master's, postbachelor's, and first professional certificates. *Special study options:* academic remediation for entering students, accelerated degree program, adult/continuing education programs, advanced placement credit, cooperative education, distance learning, double majors, English as a second language, honors programs, independent study, internships, off-campus study, part-time degree program, services for LD students, study abroad, summer session for credit. *ROTC:* Army (b), Air Force (b).

Computers on Campus Students can access the following: campus intranet, computer help desk, free student e-mail accounts, online (class) grades, online (class) registration, online (class) schedules. Campuswide network is available. 100% of college-owned or -operated housing units are wired for high-speed Internet access. Wireless service is available via entire campus.

Student Life *Housing:* on-campus residence required for freshman year. *Options:* coed, men-only, women-only, disabled students. Campus housing is university owned, leased by the school and is provided by a third party. Fresh-

man campus housing is guaranteed. *Activities and organizations:* drama/theater group, student-run newspaper, radio station, choral group, marching band, Navigators, Criminal Justice Society, Serve Beyond Cincinnati, United Black Student Association, Engineering Tribunal, national fraternities, national sororities. *Campus security:* 24-hour emergency response devices and patrols, late-night transport/escort service, controlled dormitory access. *Student services:* health clinic, personal/psychological counseling, women's center.

Athletics Member NCAA. All Division I except football (Division I-A). *Intercollegiate sports:* baseball M(s), basketball M(s)/W(s), cheerleading M/W, cross-country running M(s)/W(s), golf M(s)/W(s), lacrosse W(s), soccer M(s)/W(s), swimming and diving M(s)/W(s), tennis W(s), track and field M(s)/W(s), volleyball W(s). *Intramural sports:* badminton M(c)/W(c), baseball M(c)/W(c), basketball M/W, bowling M(c)/W(c), crew M/W, fencing M(c)/W(c), football M(c)/W(c), golf M(c)/W(c), gymnastics W, ice hockey M(c), lacrosse M(c)/W(c), racquetball M/W, riflery M(c)/W(c), rugby M, soccer M/W, softball M/W, squash M/W, swimming and diving M/W, table tennis M(c)/W(c), tennis M(c)/W(c), track and field M(c)/W(c), ultimate Frisbee M(c)/W(c), volleyball M/W, water polo M(c)/W(c), weight lifting M, wrestling M(c)/W(c).

Standardized Tests *Required:* SAT or ACT (for admission).

Costs (2011–12) *Tuition:* state resident $8805 full-time; $245 per credit hour part-time; nonresident $23,328 full-time, $648 per credit hour part-time. Full-time tuition and fees vary according to course load, degree level, location, program, and reciprocity agreements. Part-time tuition and fees vary according to course load, degree level, location, program, and reciprocity agreements. *Required fees:* $1614 full-time, $45 per credit hour part-time. *Room and board:* $9780; room only: $5799. Room and board charges vary according to board plan and housing facility. *Payment plan:* installment. *Waivers:* employees or children of employees.

Financial Aid Of all full-time matriculated undergraduates who enrolled in 2011, 14,063 applied for aid, 11,794 were judged to have need, 602 had their need fully met. 1,270 Federal Work-Study jobs (averaging $2499). In 2011, 2869 non-need-based awards were made. *Average percent of need met:* 66%. *Average financial aid package:* $8354. *Average need-based loan:* $4610. *Average need-based gift aid:* $5342. *Average non-need-based aid:* $5325. *Average indebtedness upon graduation:* $27,593.

Applying *Options:* electronic application, deferred entrance. *Application fee:* $50. *Required:* essay or personal statement, high school transcript, minimum 2.7 GPA. *Required for some:* 2 letters of recommendation, audition. *Application deadlines:* 7/1 (freshmen), rolling (transfers). *Notification:* continuous (freshmen), continuous (transfers).

Freshman Application Contact Dr. Thomas Canepa EdD, Associate Vice President, Admissions, University of Cincinnati, Office of Admissions, PO Box210091, Cincinnati, OH 45221-0091. *Phone:* 513-556-1100. *Fax:* 513-556-1105. *E-mail:* admissions@uc.edu. *Web site:* http://www.uc.edu/.

University of Dayton

Dayton, Ohio

- **Independent Roman Catholic** university, founded 1850
- **Suburban** 373-acre campus with easy access to Cincinnati
- **Endowment** $423.4 million
- **Coed** 7,843 undergraduate students, 93% full-time, 49% women, 51% men
- **Moderately difficult** entrance level, 77% of applicants were admitted

Undergraduates 7,292 full-time, 551 part-time. Students come from 50 states and territories; 50 other countries; 41% are from out of state; 4% Black or African American, non-Hispanic/Latino; 3% Hispanic/Latino; 1% Asian, non-Hispanic/Latino; 0.4% American Indian or Alaska Native, non-Hispanic/Latino; 0.5% Two or more races, non-Hispanic/Latino; 3% Race/ethnicity unknown; 4% international; 2% transferred in; 75% live on campus. *Retention:* 86% of full-time freshmen returned.

Freshmen *Admission:* 11,567 applied, 8,931 admitted, 1,954 enrolled. *Average high school GPA:* 3.55. *Test scores:* SAT critical reading scores over 500: 80%; SAT math scores over 500: 85%; SAT writing scores over 500: 76%; ACT scores over 18: 100%; SAT critical reading scores over 600: 33%; SAT math scores over 600: 41%; SAT writing scores over 600: 29%; ACT scores over 24: 77%; SAT critical reading scores over 700: 4%; SAT math scores over 700: 6%; SAT writing scores over 700: 4%; ACT scores over 30: 16%.

Faculty *Total:* 955, 51% full-time. *Student/faculty ratio:* 15:1.

Academics *Calendar:* semesters plus 2 6-week summer terms. *Degrees:* bachelor's, master's, doctoral, post-master's, postbachelor's, and first professional certificates. *Special study options:* academic remediation for entering students, accelerated degree program, adult/continuing education programs, advanced placement credit, cooperative education, distance learning, double majors, English as a second language, honors programs, independent study, internships, off-campus study, part-time degree program, services for LD students, student-designed majors, study abroad, summer session for credit.

ROTC: Army (b), Air Force (c). *Unusual degree programs:* 3-2 business administration; engineering.

Computers on Campus Students can access the following: campus intranet, computer help desk, free student e-mail accounts, online (class) grades, online (class) registration, online (class) schedules, applications, admission/enrollment status, virtual orientation, online digital resources, online courses, assistive technology, learning management system, multimedia labs, payment, cyber cafes, centrally-licensed, downloadable software and training. Campuswide network is available. 100% of college-owned or -operated housing units are wired for high-speed Internet access. Wireless service is available via entire campus.

Student Life *Housing:* on-campus residence required through sophomore year. *Options:* coed, men-only, women-only, disabled students. Campus housing is university owned. Freshman campus housing is guaranteed. *Activities and organizations:* drama/theater group, student-run newspaper, radio and television station, choral group, marching band, Student Government Association, marching band, Red Scare (basketball student cheering section), Campus Connection, Habitat for Humanity, national fraternities, national sororities. *Campus security:* 24-hour emergency response devices and patrols, student patrols, late-night transport/escort service, controlled dormitory access. *Student services:* health clinic, personal/psychological counseling, women's center.

Athletics Member NCAA. All Division I except football (Division I-AA). *Intercollegiate sports:* baseball M(s), basketball M(s)/W(s), cheerleading M/W, crew W, cross-country running M(s)/W(s), golf M(s)/W, soccer M(s)/W(s), softball W(s), tennis M(s)/W(s), track and field W(s), volleyball W(s). *Intramural sports:* badminton M/W, baseball M(c), basketball M/W, bowling M(c)/W(c), crew M(c), fencing M(c)/W(c), field hockey W(c), football M/W, golf M/W, gymnastics M(c)/W(c), ice hockey M(c), lacrosse M(c)/W(c), racquetball M/W, rugby M(c)/W(c), soccer M(c)/W(c), softball M/W, tennis M/W, track and field M(c), ultimate Frisbee M(c)/W(c), volleyball M(c)/W(c), water polo M(c)/W(c), wrestling M(c)/W(c).

Standardized Tests *Required:* SAT or ACT (for admission).

Costs (2011–12) *Comprehensive fee:* $41,590 includes full-time tuition ($30,340), mandatory fees ($1300), and room and board ($9950). Full-time tuition and fees vary according to program. Part-time tuition: $1011 per credit hour. Part-time tuition and fees vary according to course load and program. *Required fees:* $650 per term part-time. *College room only:* $6220. Room and board charges vary according to board plan and housing facility. *Payment plans:* installment, deferred payment. *Waivers:* senior citizens and employees or children of employees.

Financial Aid Of all full-time matriculated undergraduates who enrolled in 2011, 5,036 applied for aid, 3,967 were judged to have need, 1,866 had their need fully met. 1,492 Federal Work-Study jobs (averaging $2369). 4,051 state and other part-time jobs (averaging $2360). In 2011, 2724 non-need-based awards were made. *Average percent of need met:* 79%. *Average financial aid package:* $22,051. *Average need-based loan:* $4396. *Average need-based gift aid:* $15,608. *Average non-need-based aid:* $10,828. *Average indebtedness upon graduation:* $36,331.

Applying *Options:* electronic application, early action, deferred entrance. *Required:* essay or personal statement, high school transcript, 1 letter of recommendation. *Required for some:* audition required for music, music therapy, music education programs. *Recommended:* interview. *Application deadlines:* 6/15 (transfers), 12/15 (early action). *Notification:* continuous (transfers), 1/15 (early action).

Freshman Application Contact Mr. Robert Durkle, Assistant Vice President of Enrollment Management, University of Dayton, 300 College Park, Dayton, OH 45469-1300. *Phone:* 937-229-4411. *Toll-free phone:* 800-837-7433. *Fax:* 937-229-4729. *E-mail:* admission@udayton.edu. *Web site:* http://www.udayton.edu/.

The University of Findlay
Findlay, Ohio

- **Independent** comprehensive, founded 1882, affiliated with Church of God
- **Urban** 390-acre campus with easy access to Toledo
- **Endowment** $25.5 million
- **Coed** 4,063 undergraduate students, 63% full-time, 62% women, 38% men
- **Moderately difficult** entrance level, 69% of applicants were admitted

Undergraduates 2,559 full-time, 1,504 part-time. Students come from 45 states and territories; 34 other countries; 19% are from out of state; 3% Black or African American, non-Hispanic/Latino; 2% Hispanic/Latino; 1% Asian, non-Hispanic/Latino; 0.3% American Indian or Alaska Native, non-Hispanic/Latino; 1% Two or more races, non-Hispanic/Latino; 7% Race/ethnicity unknown; 4% international; 2% transferred in; 40% live on campus. *Retention:* 78% of full-time freshmen returned.

Freshmen *Admission:* 2,570 applied, 1,769 admitted, 587 enrolled. *Average high school GPA:* 3.3. *Test scores:* SAT critical reading scores over 500: 68%; SAT math scores over 500: 66%; SAT writing scores over 500: 66%; ACT

scores over 18: 93%; SAT critical reading scores over 600: 23%; SAT math scores over 600: 22%; SAT writing scores over 600: 20%; ACT scores over 24: 42%; SAT critical reading scores over 700: 4%; SAT math scores over 700: 2%; SAT writing scores over 700: 2%; ACT scores over 30: 8%.

Faculty *Total:* 288, 70% full-time, 50% with terminal degrees. *Student/faculty ratio:* 14:1.

Academics *Calendar:* semesters. *Degrees:* certificates, associate, bachelor's, master's, and doctoral. *Special study options:* academic remediation for entering students, accelerated degree program, adult/continuing education programs, advanced placement credit, cooperative education, distance learning, double majors, English as a second language, honors programs, independent study, internships, off-campus study, part-time degree program, services for LD students, student-designed majors, study abroad, summer session for credit. *ROTC:* Army (c), Air Force (c). *Unusual degree programs:* 3-2 nursing with Mount Carmel College of Nursing.

Computers on Campus 274 computers/terminals are available on campus for general student use. Students can access the following: campus intranet, computer help desk, free student e-mail accounts, online (class) grades, online (class) registration, online (class) schedules. Campuswide network is available. 100% of college-owned or -operated housing units are wired for high-speed Internet access. Wireless service is available via entire campus.

Student Life *Housing:* on-campus residence required through junior year. *Options:* coed, men-only, women-only, disabled students. Campus housing is university owned. Freshman campus housing is guaranteed. *Activities and organizations:* drama/theater group, student-run newspaper, radio and television station, choral group, marching band, Campus Program Board, Pre-Vet Club, Horse Club, Circle K, International Club, national fraternities, national sororities. *Campus security:* 24-hour emergency response devices and patrols, late-night transport/escort service. *Student services:* health clinic, personal/psychological counseling, women's center.

Athletics Member NCAA. All Division II. *Intercollegiate sports:* baseball M(s), basketball M(s)/W(s), cheerleading M/W, cross-country running M(s)/W(s), equestrian sports W, football M(s), golf M(s)/W(s), soccer M(s)/W(s), softball W(s), swimming and diving M(s)/W(s), tennis M(s)/W(s), track and field M(s)/W(s), volleyball W(s), water polo M(c)/W(c), wrestling M(s). *Intramural sports:* basketball M/W, bowling M/W, golf M/W, lacrosse M(c), soccer M/W, softball M/W, tennis M/W, volleyball M/W, water polo M/W.

Standardized Tests *Required:* SAT or ACT (for admission).

Costs (2011–12) *Comprehensive fee:* $37,178 includes full-time tuition ($27,290), mandatory fees ($814), and room and board ($9074). Part-time tuition: $605 per semester hour. Part-time tuition and fees vary according to course load and program. *Required fees:* $714 per term part-time. *College room only:* $4528. *Payment plan:* installment. *Waivers:* children of alumni, senior citizens, and employees or children of employees.

Financial Aid Of all full-time matriculated undergraduates who enrolled in 2011, 2,235 applied for aid, 1,970 were judged to have need, 31 had their need fully met. In 2011, 273 non-need-based awards were made. *Average percent of need met:* 57%. *Average financial aid package:* $20,859. *Average need-based loan:* $5055. *Average need-based gift aid:* $2635. *Average non-need-based aid:* $11,850. *Average indebtedness upon graduation:* $38,022.

Applying *Options:* electronic application, deferred entrance. *Required:* essay or personal statement, high school transcript, minimum 2.3 GPA. *Required for some:* interview. *Application deadlines:* rolling (freshmen), rolling (transfers). *Notification:* continuous (freshmen), continuous (transfers).

Freshman Application Contact Dr. Donna Gruber, Director of Undergraduate Admissions, The University of Findlay, 1000 North Main Street, Findlay, OH 45840-3653. *Phone:* 419-434-4540. *Toll-free phone:* 800-548-0932. *Fax:* 419-434-4898. *E-mail:* admissions@findlay.edu. *Web site:* http://www.findlay.edu/.

See page 715 for display ad and page 1668 for the College Close-Up.

University of Mount Union

Alliance, Ohio

- **Independent United Methodist** comprehensive, founded 1846
- **Suburban** 122-acre campus with easy access to Cleveland
- **Endowment** $133.2 million
- **Coed** 2,174 undergraduate students, 98% full-time, 48% women, 52% men
- **Moderately difficult** entrance level, 73% of applicants were admitted

Undergraduates 2,131 full-time, 43 part-time. Students come from 31 states and territories; 21 other countries; 13% are from out of state; 6% Black or African American, non-Hispanic/Latino; 1% Hispanic/Latino; 0.8% Asian, non-Hispanic/Latino; 0.2% American Indian or Alaska Native, non-Hispanic/Latino; 4% Two or more races, non-Hispanic/Latino; 3% Race/ethnicity

unknown; 3% international; 2% transferred in; 76% live on campus. *Retention:* 72% of full-time freshmen returned.

Freshmen *Admission:* 2,579 applied, 1,880 admitted, 618 enrolled. *Average high school GPA:* 3.19. *Test scores:* SAT critical reading scores over 500: 48%; SAT math scores over 500: 59%; ACT scores over 18: 93%; SAT critical reading scores over 600: 10%; SAT math scores over 600: 17%; ACT scores over 24: 36%; SAT math scores over 700: 2%; ACT scores over 30: 3%.

Faculty *Total:* 236, 53% full-time, 52% with terminal degrees. *Student/faculty ratio:* 13:1.

Academics *Calendar:* semesters. *Degrees:* bachelor's and master's. *Special study options:* accelerated degree program, adult/continuing education programs, advanced placement credit, cooperative education, distance learning, double majors, English as a second language, honors programs, independent study, internships, off-campus study, part-time degree program, services for LD students, student-designed majors, study abroad, summer session for credit. *ROTC:* Army (b), Air Force (c).

Computers on Campus 265 computers/terminals and 6,000 ports are available on campus for general student use. Students can access the following: campus intranet, computer help desk, free student e-mail accounts, online (class) grades, online (class) registration, online (class) schedules. Campuswide network is available. 100% of college-owned or -operated housing units are wired for high-speed Internet access. Wireless service is available via entire campus.

Student Life *Housing:* on-campus residence required through sophomore year. *Options:* coed, men-only, women-only, disabled students. Campus housing is university owned. Freshman campus housing is guaranteed. *Activities and organizations:* drama/theater group, student-run newspaper, radio and television station, choral group, marching band, Alpha Phi Omega, Student Senate, FCA Fellowship of Christian Athletes, Black Student Union, Raider Programming Board, national fraternities, national sororities. *Campus security:* 24-hour emergency response devices and patrols, late-night transport/escort service, controlled dormitory access, 24-hour locked residence hall entrances, outside phones. *Student services:* health clinic, personal/psychological counseling.

Athletics Member NCAA. All Division III. *Intercollegiate sports:* baseball M, basketball M/W, cheerleading W, cross-country running M/W, football M, golf M/W, soccer M/W, softball W, swimming and diving M/W, tennis M/W, track and field M/W, volleyball W, wrestling M. *Intramural sports:* archery M/W, badminton M/W, basketball M/W, bowling M/W, football M, golf M/W, gymnastics M/W, lacrosse M/W, racquetball M/W, soccer M/W, softball M/W, swimming and diving M/W, tennis M/W, track and field M/W, volleyball M/W, weight lifting M/W.

Standardized Tests *Required:* SAT or ACT (for admission).

Costs (2011–12) *Comprehensive fee:* $33,850 includes full-time tuition ($25,400), mandatory fees ($300), and room and board ($8150). Full-time tuition and fees vary according to course load and degree level. Part-time tuition: $1065 per credit hour. Part-time tuition and fees vary according to course load. *Room and board:* Room and board charges vary according to board plan and housing facility. *Payment plans:* tuition prepayment, installment. *Waivers:* children of alumni, senior citizens, and employees or children of employees.

Financial Aid Of all full-time matriculated undergraduates who enrolled in 2011, 1,925 applied for aid, 1,799 were judged to have need, 149 had their need fully met. 1,513 Federal Work-Study jobs (averaging $1258). 288 state and other part-time jobs (averaging $1554). In 2011, 324 non-need-based awards were made. *Average percent of need met:* 73%. *Average financial aid package:* $19,520. *Average need-based loan:* $5309. *Average need-based gift aid:* $13,988. *Average non-need-based aid:* $8887. *Average indebtedness upon graduation:* $34,586.

Applying *Options:* electronic application, early admission, deferred entrance. *Required:* essay or personal statement, high school transcript, minimum 2.0 GPA, 1 letter of recommendation. *Recommended:* interview. *Application deadlines:* rolling (freshmen), rolling (transfers). *Notification:* continuous (freshmen), continuous (transfers).

Freshman Application Contact Ms. Grace Chalker, Director of Admissions, University of Mount Union, 1972 Clark Avenue, Alliance, OH 44601. *Phone:* 330-823-2587. *Toll-free phone:* 800-334-6682 (in-state); 800-992-6682 (out-of-state). *Fax:* 330-823-5097. *E-mail:* admission@mountunion.edu. *Web site:* http://www.mountunion.edu/.

University of Northwestern Ohio

Lima, Ohio

Freshman Application Contact Mr. Dan Klopp, Vice President for Enrollment Management, University of Northwestern Ohio, 1441 North Cable Road, Lima, OH 45805-1498. *Phone:* 419-227-3141. *Fax:* 419-229-6926. *E-mail:* klopp_d@unoh.edu. *Web site:* http://www.unoh.edu/.

University of Phoenix–Cincinnati Campus

West Chester, Ohio

Freshman Application Contact Marc Booker, Sr. Director, Office of Admissions and Evaluation, University of Phoenix–Cincinnati Campus, 4035 South Riverpoint Parkway, Mail Stop CF-L101, Phoenix, AZ 85040. *Phone:* 602-557-4609. *Toll-free phone:* 866-766-0766. *Fax:* 480-643-1156. *Web site:* http://www.phoenix.edu/.

University of Phoenix–Cleveland Campus

Independence, Ohio

Freshman Application Contact Marc Booker, Sr. Director, Office of Admissions and Evaluation, University of Phoenix–Cleveland Campus, 4035 South Riverpoint Parkway, Mail Stop CF-L101, Phoenix, AZ 85040. *Phone:* 602-557-4609. *Toll-free phone:* 866-766-0766. *Fax:* 480-643-1156. *Web site:* http://www.phoenix.edu/.

University of Phoenix–Columbus Ohio Campus

Columbus, Ohio

Freshman Application Contact Marc Booker, Sr. Director, Office of Admissions and Evaluation, University of Phoenix–Columbus Ohio Campus, 4035 South Riverpoint Parkway, Mall Stop CF-L101, Phoenix, AZ 85040. *Phone:* 602-557-4609. *Toll-free phone:* 866-766-0766. *Fax:* 480-643-1156. *Web site:* http://www.phoenix.edu/.

University of Rio Grande

Rio Grande, Ohio

- **Independent** comprehensive, founded 1876
- **Rural** 170-acre campus
- **Endowment** $18.1 million
- **Coed** 2,169 undergraduate students, 77% full-time, 59% women, 41% men
- **Noncompetitive** entrance level, 67% of applicants were admitted

Undergraduates 1,674 full-time, 495 part-time. Students come from 7 states and territories; 7 other countries; 2% are from out of state; 6% transferred in; 20% live on campus. *Retention:* 59% of full-time freshmen returned.
Freshmen *Admission:* 3,310 applied, 2,229 admitted, 311 enrolled. *Average high school GPA:* 3.06. *Test scores:* ACT scores over 18: 71%; ACT scores over 24: 11%; ACT scores over 30: 1%.
Faculty *Total:* 150, 60% full-time, 27% with terminal degrees. *Student/faculty ratio:* 15:1.
Academics *Calendar:* semesters. *Degrees:* certificates, associate, bachelor's, and master's. *Special study options:* academic remediation for entering students, accelerated degree program, adult/continuing education programs, advanced placement credit, cooperative education, distance learning, double majors, English as a second language, freshman honors college, honors programs, independent study, internships, part-time degree program, services for LD students, student-designed majors, study abroad, summer session for credit. *ROTC:* Army (c).
Computers on Campus 300 computers/terminals are available on campus for general student use. Students can access the following: computer help desk, free student e-mail accounts, online (class) grades, online (class) registration, online (class) schedules. Campuswide network is available. Wireless service is available via dorm rooms, libraries, student centers.
Student Life *Housing options:* coed, men-only, women-only. Campus housing is university owned. *Activities and organizations:* drama/theater group, student-run newspaper, radio and television station, choral group, student government, Honoraries, Bible studies, Students in Free Enterprise (SIFE), national fraternities. *Campus security:* 24-hour emergency response devices and patrols, late-night transport/escort service, controlled dormitory access. *Student services:* health clinic, personal/psychological counseling.
Athletics Member NAIA. *Intercollegiate sports:* archery M, baseball M(s), basketball M(s)/W(s), cross-country running M(s)/W(s), soccer M(s)/W, softball W(s), track and field M(s)/W(s), volleyball W(s). *Intramural sports:* basketball M/W, football M, golf M, gymnastics W, racquetball M/W, soccer M/W, table tennis M/W, tennis M/W, volleyball M/W.
Standardized Tests *Recommended:* ACT (for admission).
Costs (2011–12) *Comprehensive fee:* $27,740 includes full-time tuition ($19,520) and room and board ($8220). Full-time tuition and fees vary according to course level, course load, degree level, program, reciprocity agreements, and student level. Part-time tuition: $818 per credit hour. Part-time tuition and fees vary according to course level, course load, degree level, program, reciprocity agreements, and student level. *Room and board:* Room and board charges vary according to board plan, housing facility, and student level.
Financial Aid Of all full-time matriculated undergraduates who enrolled in 2009, 1,146 applied for aid, 1,138 were judged to have need, 856 had their need fully met. *Average percent of need met:* 91%. *Average financial aid package:* $12,420. *Average need-based gift aid:* $4836. *Average indebtedness upon graduation:* $18,689.
Applying *Options:* electronic application. *Application fee:* $25. *Required:* high school transcript, medical history. *Application deadlines:* rolling (freshmen), rolling (transfers). *Notification:* continuous (freshmen), continuous (transfers).
Freshman Application Contact Ms. Alicia Martin, Director of Admissions, University of Rio Grande, PO Box 500, Rio Grande, OH 45674. *Phone:* 740-245-7208. *Toll-free phone:* 800-282-7201. *Fax:* 740-245-7260. *E-mail:* admissions@rio.edu. *Web site:* http://www.rio.edu/.

The University of Toledo

Toledo, Ohio

- **State-supported** university, founded 1872
- **Urban** 813-acre campus with easy access to Detroit
- **Endowment** $165.1 million
- **Coed** 17,844 undergraduate students, 81% full-time, 50% women, 50% men
- **Noncompetitive** entrance level, 96% of applicants were admitted

Undergraduates 14,517 full-time, 3,327 part-time. Students come from 41 states and territories; 90 other countries; 12% are from out of state; 17% Black or African American, non-Hispanic/Latino; 4% Hispanic/Latino; 2% Asian, non-Hispanic/Latino; 0.1% Native Hawaiian or other Pacific Islander, non-Hispanic/Latino; 0.2% American Indian or Alaska Native, non-Hispanic/Latino; 2% Two or more races, non-Hispanic/Latino; 4% Race/ethnicity unknown; 4% international; 6% transferred in; 21% live on campus. *Retention:* 65% of full-time freshmen returned.
Freshmen *Admission:* 11,633 applied, 11,131 admitted, 3,894 enrolled. *Average high school GPA:* 3.09. *Test scores:* ACT scores over 18: 80%; ACT scores over 24: 33%; ACT scores over 30: 4%.
Faculty *Total:* 1,319, 65% full-time, 56% with terminal degrees. *Student/faculty ratio:* 19:1.
Academics *Calendar:* semesters. *Degrees:* certificates, associate, bachelor's, master's, doctoral, post-master's, postbachelor's, and first professional certificates. *Special study options:* academic remediation for entering students, adult/continuing education programs, advanced placement credit, cooperative education, distance learning, double majors, English as a second language, honors programs, independent study, internships, off-campus study, part-time degree program, services for LD students, student-designed majors, study abroad, summer session for credit. *ROTC:* Army (b), Air Force (c).
Computers on Campus 5,000 computers/terminals and 7,450 ports are available on campus for general student use. Students can access the following: campus intranet, computer help desk, free student e-mail accounts, online (class) grades, online (class) registration, online (class) schedules, online transcripts, student account. Campuswide network is available. 100% of college-owned or -operated housing units are wired for high-speed Internet access. Wireless service is available via classrooms, libraries, student centers.
Student Life *Housing:* on-campus residence required for freshman year. *Options:* coed, disabled students. Campus housing is university owned. *Activities and organizations:* drama/theater group, student-run newspaper, radio station, choral group, marching band, student government, University YMCA, Newman Club, International Student Association, Campus Activities and Programming, national fraternities, national sororities. *Campus security:* 24-hour emergency response devices and patrols, student patrols, late-night transport/escort service, controlled dormitory access, bicycle patrols by security staff, crime prevention officer. *Student services:* health clinic, personal/psychological counseling, women's center, legal services.
Athletics Member NCAA. All Division I except football (Division I-A). *Intercollegiate sports:* baseball M(s), basketball M(s)/W(s), cross-country running M(s)/W(s), golf M(s)/W(s), soccer W(s), softball W(s), swimming and diving W(s), tennis M(s)/W(s), track and field W(s), volleyball W(s). *Intramural sports:* badminton M/W, basketball M/W, bowling M/W, cheerleading W, crew M(c)/W(c), fencing M(c)/W(c), football M/W, golf M/W, lacrosse M/W, racquetball M/W, sailing M(c)/W(c), skiing (cross-country) M(c)/W(c), skiing (downhill) M(c)/W(c), soccer M(c)/W(c), softball M/W, swimming and diving M/W, table tennis M/W, tennis M/W, track and field M/W, volleyball M/W, water polo M/W, weight lifting M/W, wrestling M.
Standardized Tests *Required:* SAT or ACT (for admission).

Costs (2011–12) *Tuition:* state resident $7598 full-time, $317 per semester hour part-time; nonresident $16,718 full-time, $697 per semester hour part-time. Full-time tuition and fees vary according to course load, program, and reciprocity agreements. Part-time tuition and fees vary according to course load, program, and reciprocity agreements. *Required fees:* $1190 full-time, $50 per semester hour part-time. *Room and board:* $9708; room only: $6478. Room and board charges vary according to board plan and housing facility.
Financial Aid Of all full-time matriculated undergraduates who enrolled in 2011, 12,124 applied for aid, 10,311 were judged to have need, 1,329 had their need fully met. 304 Federal Work-Study jobs (averaging $2762). In 2011, 2662 non-need-based awards were made. *Average percent of need met:* 57%. *Average financial aid package:* $10,231. *Average need-based loan:* $4119. *Average need-based gift aid:* $7489. *Average non-need-based aid:* $5756. *Average indebtedness upon graduation:* $28,438.
Applying *Options:* electronic application, deferred entrance. *Application fee:* $40. *Required:* high school transcript. *Required for some:* minimum 2.0 GPA, CORE high school curriculum. *Application deadlines:* rolling (freshmen), rolling (transfers). *Notification:* continuous (freshmen), continuous (transfers).
Freshman Application Contact Catherine Kwapich, Director of Undergraduate Admissions, The University of Toledo, 2801 West Bancroft, Toledo, OH 43606-3390. *Phone:* 419-530-5704. *Toll-free phone:* 800-5TOLEDO. *Fax:* 419-530-1202. *E-mail:* cathi.kwapich@utoledo.edu. *Web site:* http://www.utoledo.edu/.

Urbana University
Urbana, Ohio

Freshman Application Contact Ms. Paula Brown, Director of Admissions, Urbana University, 579 College Way, Urbana, OH 43078. *Phone:* 937-484-1356. *Toll-free phone:* 800-7-URBANA. *Fax:* 937-652-6871. *E-mail:* admiss@urbana.edu. *Web site:* http://www.urbana.edu/.

Ursuline College
Pepper Pike, Ohio

- **Independent Roman Catholic** comprehensive, founded 1871
- **Suburban** 112-acre campus with easy access to Cleveland
- **Endowment** $34.0 million
- **Coed, primarily women** 953 undergraduate students, 61% full-time, 91% women, 9% men
- **Minimally difficult** entrance level, 57% of applicants were admitted

Undergraduates 585 full-time, 368 part-time. Students come from 19 states and territories; 9 other countries; 32% are from out of state; 28% Black or African American, non-Hispanic/Latino; 2% Hispanic/Latino; 1% Asian, non-Hispanic/Latino; 0.4% American Indian or Alaska Native, non-Hispanic/Latino; 2% Two or more races, non-Hispanic/Latino; 0.1% Race/ethnicity unknown; 1% international; 16% transferred in; 17% live on campus. *Retention:* 72% of full-time freshmen returned.
Freshmen *Admission:* 457 applied, 260 admitted, 78 enrolled. *Average high school GPA:* 3.23. *Test scores:* SAT critical reading scores over 500: 34%; SAT math scores over 500: 38%; SAT writing scores over 500: 38%; ACT scores over 18: 90%; SAT critical reading scores over 600: 3%; SAT math scores over 600: 13%; SAT writing scores over 600: 3%; ACT scores over 24: 29%; SAT math scores over 700: 3%.
Faculty *Total:* 215, 32% full-time, 36% with terminal degrees. *Student/faculty ratio:* 9:1.
Academics *Calendar:* semesters. *Degrees:* certificates, bachelor's, master's, doctoral, post-master's, and postbachelor's certificates (applications from men are also accepted). *Special study options:* academic remediation for entering students, accelerated degree program, adult/continuing education programs, advanced placement credit, cooperative education, distance learning, double majors, independent study, internships, off-campus study, part-time degree program, services for LD students, summer session for credit. *ROTC:* Army (c). *Unusual degree programs:* 3-2 pharmacy with University of Toledo.
Computers on Campus 72 computers/terminals are available on campus for general student use. Students can access the following: campus intranet, computer help desk, free student e-mail accounts, online (class) grades, online (class) registration, online (class) schedules. Campuswide network is available. 100% of college-owned or -operated housing units are wired for high-speed Internet access. Wireless service is available via classrooms, computer centers, computer labs, libraries.
Student Life *Housing options:* coed, women-only. Campus housing is university owned. *Activities and organizations:* drama/theater group, choral group, Student Government Association, Student Nurses of Ursuline College, Fashion Focus, Students United for Black Awareness, Drama Club. *Campus security:* 24-hour emergency response devices and patrols, late-night transport/escort service, controlled dormitory access. *Student services:* personal/psychological counseling.

Athletics *Intercollegiate sports:* basketball W(s), bowling W(s), cross-country running W(s), golf W(s), soccer W(s), softball W(s), swimming and diving W(s), tennis W(s), track and field W(s), volleyball W(s).
Standardized Tests *Required:* SAT or ACT (for admission).
Costs (2011–12) *Comprehensive fee:* $33,198 includes full-time tuition ($24,660), mandatory fees ($250), and room and board ($8288). Full-time tuition and fees vary according to location. Part-time tuition: $822 per credit hour. Part-time tuition and fees vary according to location. *Required fees:* $85 per term part-time. *College room only:* $4234. Room and board charges vary according to board plan and housing facility. *Payment plan:* installment. *Waivers:* employees or children of employees.
Financial Aid Of all full-time matriculated undergraduates who enrolled in 2010, 697 applied for aid, 665 were judged to have need, 44 had their need fully met. In 2010, 41 non-need-based awards were made. *Average percent of need met:* 63%. *Average financial aid package:* $15,913. *Average need-based loan:* $5711. *Average need-based gift aid:* $11,790. *Average non-need-based aid:* $4979. *Average indebtedness upon graduation:* $26,701.
Applying *Options:* electronic application, deferred entrance. *Application fee:* $25. *Required:* essay or personal statement, high school transcript. *Required for some:* essay or personal statement, 1 letter of recommendation. *Recommended:* minimum 2.0 GPA, interview. *Application deadlines:* 2/1 (freshmen), 2/1 (out-of-state freshmen), rolling (transfers). *Notification:* continuous (freshmen), continuous (out-of-state freshmen), continuous (transfers).
Freshman Application Contact Ursuline College, 2550 Lander Road, Pepper Pike, OH 44124-4398. *Phone:* 440-449-4203. *Toll-free phone:* 888-URSULINE. *Web site:* http://www.ursuline.edu/.

Walsh University
North Canton, Ohio

- **Independent Roman Catholic** comprehensive, founded 1958
- **Small-town** 134-acre campus with easy access to Cleveland
- **Endowment** $12.5 million
- **Coed** 2,389 undergraduate students, 80% full-time, 63% women, 37% men
- **Moderately difficult** entrance level, 77% of applicants were admitted

Undergraduates 1,917 full-time, 472 part-time. Students come from 17 states and territories; 14 other countries; 3% are from out of state; 5% Black or African American, non-Hispanic/Latino; 1% Hispanic/Latino; 0.5% Asian, non-Hispanic/Latino; 0.1% Native Hawaiian or other Pacific Islander, non-Hispanic/Latino; 0.1% American Indian or Alaska Native, non-Hispanic/Latino; 2% Two or more races, non-Hispanic/Latino; 11% Race/ethnicity unknown; 1% international; 9% transferred in; 54% live on campus. *Retention:* 75% of full-time freshmen returned.
Freshmen *Admission:* 1,650 applied, 1,269 admitted, 512 enrolled. *Average high school GPA:* 3.45. *Test scores:* SAT critical reading scores over 500: 47%; SAT math scores over 500: 56%; ACT scores over 18: 94%; SAT critical reading scores over 600: 10%; SAT math scores over 600: 19%; ACT scores over 24: 33%; SAT critical reading scores over 700: 2%; SAT math scores over 700: 2%; ACT scores over 30: 3%.
Faculty *Total:* 314, 36% full-time, 36% with terminal degrees. *Student/faculty ratio:* 14:1.
Academics *Calendar:* semesters. *Degrees:* associate, bachelor's, master's, and doctoral. *Special study options:* academic remediation for entering students, accelerated degree program, adult/continuing education programs, advanced placement credit, distance learning, double majors, English as a second language, external degree program, honors programs, independent study, internships, off-campus study, part-time degree program, services for LD students, study abroad, summer session for credit. *Unusual degree programs:* 3-2 behavioral science/counseling; biology/physical therapy, theology.
Computers on Campus 335 computers/terminals and 1,000 ports are available on campus for general student use. Students can access the following: computer help desk, free student e-mail accounts, online (class) grades, online (class) registration, online (class) schedules. Campuswide network is available. 100% of college-owned or -operated housing units are wired for high-speed Internet access. Wireless service is available via entire campus.
Student Life *Housing:* on-campus residence required through senior year. *Options:* coed, men-only, women-only, disabled students. Campus housing is university owned. Freshman campus housing is guaranteed. *Activities and organizations:* drama/theater group, student-run newspaper, radio station, choral group, marching band, student government, University Programming Board, Business and Communication Club, Behavioral Science Club, Education Club. *Campus security:* 24-hour emergency response devices and patrols, late-night transport/escort service, controlled dormitory access. *Student services:* health clinic, personal/psychological counseling.
Athletics Member NCAA, NAIA. All NCAA Division II. *Intercollegiate sports:* baseball M(s), basketball M(s)/W(s), cheerleading W, cross-country running M(s)/W(s), football M(s), golf M(s)/W(s), lacrosse M(s)/W(s), soccer

M(s)/W(s), softball W(s), tennis M(s)/W(s), track and field M(s)/W(s), volleyball W(s). *Intramural sports:* basketball M/W, bowling M/W, football M, golf M/W, skiing (downhill) M(c)/W(c), soccer M/W, table tennis M/W, tennis M/W, ultimate Frisbee M(c)/W(c), volleyball M/W.

Standardized Tests *Required:* SAT or ACT (for admission).

Costs (2011–12) *One-time required fee:* $215. *Comprehensive fee:* $32,225 includes full-time tuition ($22,500), mandatory fees ($1085), and room and board ($8640). Full-time tuition and fees vary according to location. Part-time tuition: $750 per semester hour. Part-time tuition and fees vary according to course load and location. *Required fees:* $35 per semester hour part-time. *College room only:* $4570. Room and board charges vary according to board plan and housing facility. *Payment plan:* installment. *Waivers:* children of alumni, senior citizens, and employees or children of employees.

Financial Aid Of all full-time matriculated undergraduates who enrolled in 2010, 1,726 applied for aid, 1,661 were judged to have need, 798 had their need fully met. In 2010, 180 non-need-based awards were made. *Average percent of need met:* 71%. *Average financial aid package:* $18,133. *Average need-based loan:* $4850. *Average need-based gift aid:* $6844. *Average non-need-based aid:* $9372. *Average indebtedness upon graduation:* $24,753.

Applying *Options:* electronic application, early admission, deferred entrance. *Application fee:* $25. *Required:* high school transcript, minimum 2.4 GPA. *Required for some:* essay or personal statement, minimum 3.0 GPA, 2 letters of recommendation. *Recommended:* interview. *Application deadlines:* rolling (freshmen), rolling (out-of-state freshmen), rolling (transfers). *Notification:* continuous (freshmen), continuous (out-of-state freshmen), continuous (transfers).

Freshman Application Contact Mr. Brett Freshour, Vice President for Enrollment Management, Walsh University, 2020 East Maple, North Canton, OH 44720. *Phone:* 330-490-7171. *Toll-free phone:* 800-362-9846 (in-state); 800-362-8846 (out-of-state). *Fax:* 330-490-7165. *E-mail:* admissions@walsh.edu. *Web site:* http://www.walsh.edu/.

See below for display ad and page 1740 for the College Close-Up.

Wilberforce University
Wilberforce, Ohio

Freshman Application Contact Wilberforce University, 1055 North Bickett Road, Wilberforce, OH 45384. *Phone:* 937-708-5789. *Toll-free phone:* 800-367-8568. *Web site:* http://www.wilberforce.edu/.

Wilmington College
Wilmington, Ohio

- **Independent Friends** comprehensive, founded 1870
- **Small-town** campus
- **Coed** 1,432 undergraduate students, 82% full-time, 54% women, 46% men
- **Moderately difficult** entrance level

Undergraduates 1,179 full-time, 253 part-time. 6% are from out of state; 11% Black or African American, non-Hispanic/Latino; 0.6% Hispanic/Latino; 0.4% Asian, non-Hispanic/Latino; 0.7% American Indian or Alaska Native, non-Hispanic/Latino; 3% Two or more races, non-Hispanic/Latino; 11% Race/ethnicity unknown; 1% international; 5% transferred in; 80% live on campus. *Retention:* 67% of full-time freshmen returned.

Freshmen *Admission:* 1,651 applied, 296 enrolled. *Average high school GPA:* 3.2. *Test scores:* SAT critical reading scores over 500: 44%; SAT math scores over 500: 51%; ACT scores over 18: 84%; SAT critical reading scores over 600: 12%; SAT math scores over 600: 14%; ACT scores over 24: 22%; SAT critical reading scores over 700: 4%; ACT scores over 30: 2%.

Faculty *Total:* 119, 55% full-time. *Student/faculty ratio:* 14:1.

Academics *Calendar:* semesters. *Degrees:* bachelor's and master's. *Special study options:* adult/continuing education programs, part-time degree program. *ROTC:* Army (c).

Computers on Campus Students can access the following: online (class) registration, OhioLink. Campuswide network is available.

Student Life *Housing:* on-campus residence required through senior year. *Options:* coed, men-only, women-only. Campus housing is university owned. *Campus security:* 24-hour emergency response devices and patrols, late-night transport/escort service, controlled dormitory access.

Athletics Member NCAA. All Division III. *Intercollegiate sports:* baseball M, basketball M/W, cross-country running M/W, football M, golf M/W, soccer M/W, softball W, swimming and diving M/W, tennis M/W, track and field M/W, volleyball W, wrestling M. *Intramural sports:* basketball M/W, football M, racquetball M/W, soccer M/W, softball M/W, squash M/W, swimming and diving M/W, table tennis M/W, volleyball M/W.

Standardized Tests *Recommended:* SAT or ACT (for admission).

Costs (2011–12) *Comprehensive fee:* $35,710 includes full-time tuition ($26,340), mandatory fees ($500), and room and board ($8870). Part-time tuition and fees vary according to course load. *Room and board:* Room and

board charges vary according to board plan and housing facility. *Payment plan:* installment. *Waivers:* employees or children of employees.

Financial Aid Of all full-time matriculated undergraduates who enrolled in 2008, 1,096 applied for aid, 1,021 were judged to have need, 306 had their need fully met. In 2008, 138 non-need-based awards were made. *Average percent of need met:* 81%. *Average financial aid package:* $21,500. *Average need-based loan:* $6000. *Average need-based gift aid:* $14,300. *Average non-need-based aid:* $7300.

Applying *Options:* deferred entrance. *Required:* high school transcript. *Recommended:* minimum 2.5 GPA, 1 letter of recommendation, interview. *Application deadline:* 8/1 (freshmen). *Notification:* continuous (freshmen).

Freshman Application Contact Ms. Tina Garland, Director of Admission and Financial Aid, Wilmington College, 1870 Quaker Way, Wilmington, OH 45177. *Phone:* 937-382-6661 Ext. 426. *Toll-free phone:* 800-341-9318. *Fax:* 937-383-8542. *E-mail:* admissions@wilmington.edu. *Web site:* http://www.wilmington.edu/.

Wittenberg University
Springfield, Ohio

- **Independent** comprehensive, founded 1845, affiliated with Evangelical Lutheran Church
- **Suburban** 114-acre campus with easy access to Columbus, Dayton
- **Endowment** $96.1 million
- **Coed** 1,901 undergraduate students, 94% full-time, 56% women, 44% men
- **Moderately difficult** entrance level, 85% of applicants were admitted

Undergraduates 1,792 full-time, 109 part-time. Students come from 41 states and territories; 25 other countries; 30% are from out of state; 6% Black or African American, non-Hispanic/Latino; 3% Hispanic/Latino; 1% Asian, non-Hispanic/Latino; 3% Two or more races, non-Hispanic/Latino; 3% Race/ethnicity unknown; 2% international; 2% transferred in; 85% live on campus. *Retention:* 79% of full-time freshmen returned.

Freshmen *Admission:* 4,412 applied, 3,735 admitted, 535 enrolled. *Average high school GPA:* 3.48. *Test scores:* SAT critical reading scores over 500: 78%; SAT math scores over 500: 80%; ACT scores over 18: 99%; SAT critical reading scores over 600: 33%; SAT math scores over 600: 38%; ACT scores over 24: 71%; SAT critical reading scores over 700: 7%; SAT math scores over 700: 4%; ACT scores over 30: 20%.

Faculty *Total:* 200, 71% full-time, 78% with terminal degrees. *Student/faculty ratio:* 11:1.

Academics *Calendar:* semesters. *Degrees:* bachelor's and master's. *Special study options:* academic remediation for entering students, adult/continuing education programs, advanced placement credit, cooperative education, double majors, English as a second language, freshman honors college, honors programs, independent study, internships, off-campus study, part-time degree program, student-designed majors, study abroad, summer session for credit. *ROTC:* Army (c), Air Force (c). *Unusual degree programs:* 3-2 engineering with Georgia Institute of Technology, Washington University in St. Louis, Case Western Reserve University; forestry with Duke University; nursing with Case Western Reserve University, Johns Hopkins University; occupational therapy with Washington University in St. Louis.

Computers on Campus 900 computers/terminals and 1,200 ports are available on campus for general student use. Students can access the following: computer help desk, free student e-mail accounts, online (class) grades, online (class) registration, online (class) schedules. Campuswide network is available. Wireless service is available via entire campus.

Student Life *Housing:* on-campus residence required through sophomore year. *Options:* coed, women-only. Campus housing is university owned, leased by the school and is provided by a third party. Freshman campus housing is guaranteed. *Activities and organizations:* drama/theater group, student-run newspaper, radio station, choral group, Student Senate, Union Board, Choirs, Weaver Chapel Association, national fraternities, national sororities. *Campus security:* 24-hour emergency response devices and patrols, student patrols, late-night transport/escort service, controlled dormitory access, crime prevention programs. *Student services:* health clinic, personal/psychological counseling, women's center.

Athletics Member NCAA. All Division III. *Intercollegiate sports:* baseball M, basketball M/W, crew M(c)/W(c), cross-country running M/W, field hockey W, football M, golf M/W, lacrosse M/W, rugby M(c)/W(c), soccer M/W, softball W, swimming and diving M/W, tennis M/W, track and field M/W, volleyball M(c)/W. *Intramural sports:* basketball M/W, football M, golf M/W, sailing M/W, soccer M/W, softball M/W, swimming and diving M/W, tennis M/W, track and field M/W, volleyball M/W.

Standardized Tests *Recommended:* Test scores are optional.

Costs (2012–13) *Comprehensive fee:* $47,766 includes full-time tuition ($37,230), mandatory fees ($800), and room and board ($9736). Part-time tuition and fees vary according to course load. *College room only:* $5056.

Room and board charges vary according to board plan and housing facility. *Payment plan:* installment. *Waivers:* minority students, children of alumni, adult students, senior citizens, and employees or children of employees.

Financial Aid Of all full-time matriculated undergraduates who enrolled in 2010, 1,546 applied for aid, 1,357 were judged to have need, 369 had their need fully met. 570 Federal Work-Study jobs (averaging $2612), 560 state and other part-time jobs (averaging $2316). In 2010, 433 non-need-based awards were made. *Average percent of need met:* 83%. *Average financial aid package:* $28,460. *Average need-based loan:* $4187. *Average need-based gift aid:* $22,549. *Average non-need-based aid:* $15,163. *Average indebtedness upon graduation:* $29,506.

Applying *Options:* electronic application, early admission, early decision, early action, deferred entrance. *Application fee:* $40. *Required:* essay or personal statement, high school transcript, interview. *Application deadlines:* rolling (transfers), 12/1 (early action). *Early decision deadline:* 11/15. *Notification:* continuous (freshmen), continuous (transfers), 12/15 (early decision), 1/1 (early action).

Freshman Application Contact Ms. Karen Hunt, Director of Admission, Wittenberg University, PO Box 720, Springfield, OH 45501-0720. *Phone:* 877-206-0332 Ext. 6377. *Toll-free phone:* 800-677-7558 Ext. 6314. *Fax:* 937-327-6379. *E-mail:* admission@wittenberg.edu. *Web site:* http://www.wittenberg.edu/.

Wright State University
Dayton, Ohio

- **State-supported** university, founded 1964, part of University System of Ohio
- **Suburban** 557-acre campus with easy access to Columbus
- **Endowment** $82.3 million
- **Coed** 14,408 undergraduate students, 84% full-time, 54% women, 46% men
- **Minimally difficult** entrance level, 75% of applicants were admitted

Undergraduates 12,039 full-time, 2,369 part-time. Students come from 46 states and territories; 45 other countries; 3% are from out of state; 15% Black or African American, non-Hispanic/Latino; 3% Hispanic/Latino; 2% Asian, non-Hispanic/Latino; 0.1% Native Hawaiian or other Pacific Islander, non-Hispanic/Latino; 0.3% American Indian or Alaska Native, non-Hispanic/Latino; 3% Two or more races, non-Hispanic/Latino; 0.9% Race/ethnicity unknown; 3% international; 8% transferred in; 20% live on campus. *Retention:* 62% of full-time freshmen returned.

Freshmen *Admission:* 8,333 applied, 6,273 admitted, 2,713 enrolled. *Average high school GPA:* 3.02. *Test scores:* SAT critical reading scores over 500: 54%; SAT math scores over 500: 51%; SAT writing scores over 500: 43%; ACT scores over 18: 77%; SAT critical reading scores over 600: 18%; SAT math scores over 600: 18%; SAT writing scores over 600: 13%; ACT scores over 24: 27%; SAT critical reading scores over 700: 3%; SAT math scores over 700: 1%; SAT writing scores over 700: 1%; ACT scores over 30: 3%.

Faculty *Total:* 658, 99% full-time. *Student/faculty ratio:* 24:1.

Academics *Calendar:* quarters. *Degrees:* associate, bachelor's, master's, doctoral, post-master's, postbachelor's, and first professional certificates. *Special study options:* academic remediation for entering students, adult/continuing education programs, advanced placement credit, cooperative education, distance learning, double majors, English as a second language, freshman honors college, honors programs, independent study, internships, off-campus study, part-time degree program, services for LD students, student-designed majors, study abroad, summer session for credit. *ROTC:* Army (b), Air Force (b).

Computers on Campus 1,700 computers/terminals are available on campus for general student use. Students can access the following: campus intranet, computer help desk, free student e-mail accounts, online (class) grades, online (class) registration, online (class) schedules, Student web pages permitted. Campuswide network is available. 100% of college-owned or -operated housing units are wired for high-speed Internet access. Wireless service is available via entire campus.

Student Life *Housing options:* coed, disabled students. Campus housing is university owned and leased by the school. *Activities and organizations:* drama/theater group, student-run newspaper, radio and television station, choral group, student government, National Association for the Advancement of Colored People, Interfraternity Council, Panhellenic Council, Golden Key International Honor Society, national fraternities, national sororities. *Campus security:* 24-hour emergency response devices and patrols, student patrols, late-night transport/escort service, controlled dormitory access. *Student services:* health clinic, personal/psychological counseling, women's center, legal services.

Athletics Member NCAA. All Division I. *Intercollegiate sports:* baseball M(s), basketball M(s)/W(s), cross-country running M(s)/W(s), golf M(s), soccer M(s)/W(s), softball W(s), swimming and diving M(s)/W(s), tennis M(s)/W(s), track and field W(s), volleyball W(s). *Intramural sports:* badminton M/

W, baseball M/W, basketball M/W, bowling M/W, cheerleading M/W, football M/W, gymnastics M/W, ice hockey M, lacrosse M, racquetball M(c)/W(c), rugby M(c)/W(c), skiing (downhill) M(c)/W(c), soccer M/W, softball M/W, squash M/W, table tennis M(c), tennis M/W, ultimate Frisbee M/W, volleyball M(c)/W, wrestling M.

Standardized Tests *Required:* SAT or ACT (for admission).

Costs (2011–12) *Tuition:* state resident $8070 full-time, $243 per credit hour part-time; nonresident $15,633 full-time, $475 per credit hour part-time. Full-time tuition and fees vary according to course load. Part-time tuition and fees vary according to course load. *Room and board:* $8387; room only: $6012. Room and board charges vary according to housing facility and location. *Payment plan:* installment. *Waivers:* senior citizens and employees or children of employees.

Financial Aid Of all full-time matriculated undergraduates who enrolled in 2011, 9,849 applied for aid, 8,789 were judged to have need, 619 had their need fully met. 1,451 Federal Work-Study jobs (averaging $3166). In 2011, 863 non-need-based awards were made. *Average percent of need met:* 50%. *Average financial aid package:* $9459. *Average need-based loan:* $4400. *Average need-based gift aid:* $5686. *Average non-need-based aid:* $4043. *Average indebtedness upon graduation:* $27,119.

Applying *Options:* electronic application, early admission, deferred entrance. *Application fee:* $30. *Required:* high school transcript. *Recommended:* minimum 2.0 GPA. *Application deadlines:* rolling (freshmen), rolling (transfers). *Notification:* continuous (freshmen), continuous (out-of-state freshmen), continuous (transfers).

Freshman Application Contact Ms. Cathy Davis, Assistant Vice President for Undergraduate Admissions, Wright State University, 3640 Colonel Glenn Highway, E148 Student Union, Dayton, OH 45435. *Phone:* 937-775-5700. *Toll-free phone:* 800-247-1770. *Fax:* 937-775-5795. *E-mail:* admissions@wright.edu. *Web site:* http://www.wright.edu/.

Xavier University
Cincinnati, Ohio

- **Independent Roman Catholic** comprehensive, founded 1831
- **Urban** 180-acre campus
- **Endowment** $120.8 million
- **Coed** 4,540 undergraduate students, 88% full-time, 53% women, 47% men
- **Moderately difficult** entrance level, 70% of applicants were admitted

Undergraduates 4,008 full-time, 532 part-time. Students come from 45 states and territories; 36 other countries; 43% are from out of state; 10% Black or African American, non-Hispanic/Latino; 4% Hispanic/Latino; 2% Asian, non-Hispanic/Latino; 0.3% American Indian or Alaska Native, non-Hispanic/Latino; 1% Two or more races, non-Hispanic/Latino; 2% Race/ethnicity unknown; 3% international; 2% transferred in; 50% live on campus. *Retention:* 84% of full-time freshmen returned.

Freshmen *Admission:* 9,783 applied, 6,865 admitted, 1,123 enrolled. *Average high school GPA:* 3.53. *Test scores:* SAT critical reading scores over 500: 72%; SAT math scores over 500: 76%; ACT scores over 18: 99%; SAT critical reading scores over 600: 27%; SAT math scores over 600: 28%; ACT scores over 24: 65%; SAT critical reading scores over 700: 3%; SAT math scores over 700: 3%; ACT scores over 30: 12%.

Faculty *Total:* 666, 52% full-time, 38% with terminal degrees. *Student/faculty ratio:* 12:1.

Academics *Calendar:* semesters. *Degrees:* certificates, associate, bachelor's, master's, and doctoral. *Special study options:* academic remediation for entering students, adult/continuing education programs, advanced placement credit, cooperative education, double majors, English as a second language, honors programs, independent study, internships, off-campus study, part-time degree program, services for LD students, study abroad, summer session for credit. *ROTC:* Army (b), Air Force (c). *Unusual degree programs:* 3-2 forestry with Duke University; environmental management, accounting.

Computers on Campus 340 computers/terminals and 10,128 ports are available on campus for general student use. Students can access the following: campus intranet, computer help desk, free student e-mail accounts, online (class) grades, online (class) registration, online (class) schedules. Campus-wide network is available. 100% of college-owned or -operated housing units are wired for high-speed Internet access. Wireless service is available via entire campus.

Student Life *Housing:* on-campus residence required through sophomore year. *Options:* coed, disabled students. Campus housing is university owned. Freshman campus housing is guaranteed. *Activities and organizations:* drama/theater group, student-run newspaper, television station, choral group, Student Government Association, Black Student Association, X-treme Fans, Alternative Spring Break, Club Sports. *Campus security:* 24-hour emergency response devices and patrols, late-night transport/escort service, controlled

dormitory access, campus-wide shuttle service. *Student services:* health clinic, personal/psychological counseling, women's center.

Athletics Member NCAA. All Division I. *Intercollegiate sports:* baseball M(s), basketball M(s)/W(s), cheerleading M(c)/W(c), crew M(c)/W(c), cross-country running M(s)/W(s), equestrian sports M(c)/W(c), fencing M(c)/W(c), field hockey M(c)/W(c), football M(c), golf M(s)/W(s), gymnastics M(c)/W(c), ice hockey M(c)/W(c), lacrosse M(c)/W(c), racquetball M(c)/W(c), rugby M(c)/W(c), soccer M(s)/W(s), softball M(c)/W(c), swimming and diving M(s)/W(s), tennis M(s)/W(s), track and field M(s)/W(s), ultimate Frisbee M(c)/W(c), volleyball M(c)/W(s), water polo M(c)/W(c). *Intramural sports:* baseball M(c), basketball M/W, bowling M/W, cross-country running M(c)/W(c), football M/W, golf M(c), racquetball M/W, soccer M(c)/W(c), softball W, swimming and diving M(c)/W(c), tennis M/W, volleyball M/W.

Standardized Tests *Required:* SAT or ACT (for admission).

Costs (2011–12) *Comprehensive fee:* $41,080 includes full-time tuition ($30,230), mandatory fees ($930), and room and board ($9920). Full-time tuition and fees vary according to course load and program. Part-time tuition: $590 per credit hour. Part-time tuition and fees vary according to course load and program. *Required fees:* $9 per term part-time. *College room only:* $5600. Room and board charges vary according to board plan and housing facility. *Payment plan:* installment. *Waivers:* adult students and senior citizens.

Financial Aid Of all full-time matriculated undergraduates who enrolled in 2011, 2,895 applied for aid, 2,442 were judged to have need, 501 had their need fully met. 631 Federal Work-Study jobs (averaging $2225). 23 state and other part-time jobs (averaging $1932). In 2011, 1273 non-need-based awards were made. *Average percent of need met:* 71%. *Average financial aid package:* $19,394. *Average need-based loan:* $4472. *Average need-based gift aid:* $14,658. *Average non-need-based aid:* $12,167. *Average indebtedness upon graduation:* $29,121.

Applying *Options:* electronic application, deferred entrance. *Application fee:* $35. *Required:* essay or personal statement, high school transcript, 1 letter of recommendation. *Required for some:* minimum 3.0 GPA, interview. *Application deadlines:* 2/1 (freshmen), rolling (transfers). *Notification:* 10/15 (freshmen), continuous (transfers).

Freshman Application Contact Xavier University, 3800 Victory Parkway, Cincinnati, OH 45207-5311. *Phone:* 513-745-3301. *Toll-free phone:* 877-XUADMIT. *E-mail:* xuadmit@xavier.edu. *Web site:* http://www.xu.edu/.

Youngstown State University
Youngstown, Ohio

- **State-supported** comprehensive, founded 1908
- **Urban** 200-acre campus with easy access to Cleveland, Pittsburgh
- **Endowment** $185.8 million
- **Coed** 13,358 undergraduate students, 78% full-time, 52% women, 48% men
- **Noncompetitive** entrance level, 86% of applicants were admitted

Undergraduates 10,363 full-time, 2,995 part-time. Students come from 35 states and territories; 58 other countries; 10% are from out of state; 17% Black or African American, non-Hispanic/Latino; 3% Hispanic/Latino; 1% Asian, non-Hispanic/Latino; 0.3% American Indian or Alaska Native, non-Hispanic/Latino; 0.8% Two or more races, non-Hispanic/Latino; 5% Race/ethnicity unknown; 0.7% international; 5% transferred in; 10% live on campus. *Retention:* 65% of full-time freshmen returned.

Freshmen *Admission:* 5,274 applied, 4,530 admitted, 2,571 enrolled. *Average high school GPA:* 2.88. *Test scores:* SAT critical reading scores over 500: 40%; SAT math scores over 500: 43%; SAT writing scores over 500: 34%; ACT scores over 18: 69%; SAT critical reading scores over 600: 17%; SAT math scores over 600: 15%; SAT writing scores over 600: 10%; ACT scores over 24: 22%; SAT critical reading scores over 700: 3%; SAT math scores over 700: 3%; SAT writing scores over 700: 1%; ACT scores over 30: 4%.

Faculty *Total:* 1,066, 41% full-time, 44% with terminal degrees. *Student/faculty ratio:* 19:1.

Academics *Calendar:* semesters. *Degrees:* certificates, diplomas, associate, bachelor's, master's, doctoral, post-master's, postbachelor's, and first professional certificates. *Special study options:* academic remediation for entering students, accelerated degree program, adult/continuing education programs, advanced placement credit, cooperative education, distance learning, double majors, English as a second language, honors programs, independent study, internships, off-campus study, part-time degree program, services for LD students, student-designed majors, study abroad, summer session for credit. *ROTC:* Army (b), Air Force (c). *Unusual degree programs:* 3-2 BS/MS Program in Chemistry; BS/MD Program.

Computers on Campus 170 computers/terminals are available on campus for general student use. Students can access the following: campus intranet, computer help desk, free student e-mail accounts, online (class) grades, online (class) registration, online (class) schedules. Campuswide network is available.

100% of college-owned or -operated housing units are wired for high-speed Internet access. Wireless service is available via entire campus.

Student Life *Housing options:* coed, women-only. Campus housing is university owned and is provided by a third party. *Activities and organizations:* drama/theater group, student-run newspaper, radio station, choral group, marching band, student government, Omicron Delta Kappa, Golden Key Society, Fraternities/Sororities (IFC, NPHC and Panhellenic Council, history club, national fraternities, national sororities. *Campus security:* 24-hour emergency response devices and patrols, student patrols, late-night transport/escort service, controlled dormitory access, residence hall patrols. *Student services:* health clinic, personal/psychological counseling.

Athletics Member NCAA. All Division I except football (Division I-AA). *Intercollegiate sports:* baseball M(s), basketball M(s)/W(s), cross-country running M(s)/W(s), golf M(s)/W(s), soccer W(s), softball W(s), swimming and diving W(s), tennis M(s)/W(s), track and field M(s)/W(s), volleyball W(s). *Intramural sports:* badminton M/W, basketball M/W, bowling M(c)/W(c), football M/W, ice hockey M(c), racquetball M/W, rock climbing M/W, rugby M, soccer M/W, softball M/W, table tennis M/W, tennis M/W, ultimate Frisbee M/W, volleyball M/W, weight lifting M/W.

Standardized Tests *Required:* SAT or ACT (for admission).

Costs (2011–12) *Tuition:* state resident $7222 full-time, $301 per credit part-time; nonresident $13,179 full-time, $549 per credit part-time. Full-time tuition and fees vary according to course load. Part-time tuition and fees vary according to course load. *Required fees:* $229 full-time, $10 per credit part-time. *Room and board:* $7900. Room and board charges vary according to board plan and housing facility. *Payment plan:* installment. *Waivers:* senior citizens and employees or children of employees.

Financial Aid Of all full-time matriculated undergraduates who enrolled in 2010, 9,418 applied for aid, 8,490 were judged to have need, 620 had their need fully met. In 2010, 719 non-need-based awards were made. *Average percent of need met:* 31%. *Average financial aid package:* $8699. *Average need-based loan:* $3823. *Average need-based gift aid:* $5516. *Average non-need-based aid:* $2772.

Applying *Options:* electronic application, early admission, deferred entrance. *Application fee:* $30. *Required:* high school transcript. *Required for some:* interview. *Application deadlines:* 8/1 (freshmen), 8/1 (transfers). *Notification:* continuous (freshmen), continuous (transfers).

Freshman Application Contact Ms. Sue Davis, Director of Undergraduate Admissions, Youngstown State University, One University Plaza, Youngstown, OH 44555-0001. *Phone:* 330-941-2000. *Toll-free phone:* 877-468-6978. *Fax:* 330-941-3674. *E-mail:* enroll@ysu.edu. *Web site:* http://www.ysu.edu/.

OKLAHOMA

Bacone College

Muskogee, Oklahoma

Freshman Application Contact Bacone College, 2299 Old Bacone Road, Muskogee, OK 74403-1597. *Phone:* 918-781-7342. *Toll-free phone:* 888-682-5514 Ext. 7340. *Web site:* http://www.bacone.edu/.

Brown Mackie College–Tulsa

Tulsa, Oklahoma

- **Proprietary** primarily 2-year, part of Education Management Corporation
- **Coed**

Academics *Degrees:* diplomas, associate, and bachelor's.

Costs (2011–12) *Tuition:* Tuition varies by program. Students should contact Brown Mackie College for tuition information.

Freshman Application Contact Brown Mackie College–Tulsa, 4608 South Garnett, Suite 110, Tulsa, OK 74146. *Phone:* 918-628-3700. *Toll-free phone:* 888-794-8411. *Web site:* http://www.brownmackie.edu/tulsa/.

See page 1228 for the College Close-Up.

Cameron University

Lawton, Oklahoma

- **State-supported** comprehensive, founded 1908, part of Oklahoma State Regents for Higher Education
- **Small-town** 360-acre campus
- **Endowment** $15.5 million
- **Coed** 5,943 undergraduate students, 66% full-time, 61% women, 39% men
- **Noncompetitive** entrance level, 99% of applicants were admitted

Undergraduates 3,913 full-time, 2,030 part-time. Students come from 39 states and territories; 42 other countries; 5% are from out of state; 16% Black or African American, non-Hispanic/Latino; 6% Hispanic/Latino; 2% Asian, non-Hispanic/Latino; 0.7% Native Hawaiian or other Pacific Islander, non-Hispanic/Latino; 7% American Indian or Alaska Native, non-Hispanic/Latino; 7% Race/ethnicity unknown; 5% international; 8% transferred in; 10% live on campus. *Retention:* 52% of full-time freshmen returned.

Freshmen *Admission:* 1,490 applied, 1,479 admitted, 1,096 enrolled. *Average high school GPA:* 3.08. *Test scores:* ACT scores over 18: 65%; ACT scores over 24: 16%; ACT scores over 30: 1%.

Faculty *Total:* 326, 53% full-time, 46% with terminal degrees. *Student/faculty ratio:* 22:1.

Academics *Calendar:* semesters. *Degrees:* associate, bachelor's, master's, and post-master's certificates. *Special study options:* academic remediation for entering students, accelerated degree program, adult/continuing education programs, advanced placement credit, distance learning, double majors, honors programs, independent study, internships, off-campus study, part-time degree program, services for LD students, student-designed majors, study abroad, summer session for credit. *ROTC:* Army (b).

Computers on Campus 277 computers/terminals are available on campus for general student use. Students can access the following: computer help desk, free student e-mail accounts, online (class) grades, online (class) schedules, online courses, student information system, library. Campuswide network is available. 100% of college-owned or -operated housing units are wired for high-speed Internet access. Wireless service is available via classrooms, computer centers, computer labs, dorm rooms, learning centers, libraries, student centers.

Student Life *Housing options:* coed, men-only, women-only. Campus housing is university owned. *Activities and organizations:* drama/theater group, student-run newspaper, television station, choral group, Student Government Association, Programming Activities Council, Nigerian Student Association, International Club, Greek Life, national fraternities, national sororities. *Campus security:* 24-hour emergency response devices and patrols, late-night transport/escort service, controlled dormitory access. *Student services:* health clinic, personal/psychological counseling.

Athletics Member NCAA. All Division II. *Intercollegiate sports:* baseball M(s), basketball M(s)/W(s), cross-country running M(s), golf M(s)/W(s), softball W(s), tennis M(s)/W(s), volleyball W(s). *Intramural sports:* archery M/W, badminton M/W, basketball M/W, bowling M/W, golf M/W, racquetball M/W, soccer M/W, swimming and diving M/W, table tennis M/W, tennis M/W, volleyball M/W.

Standardized Tests *Required:* SAT or ACT (for admission).

Costs (2011–12) *Tuition:* state resident $3105 full-time, $104 per credit hour part-time; nonresident $9713 full-time, $324 per credit hour part-time. Full-time tuition and fees vary according to course load, location, and program. Part-time tuition and fees vary according to course load, location, and program. *Required fees:* $1485 full-time, $50 per credit hour part-time. *Room and board:* $3754. Room and board charges vary according to board plan and housing facility. *Payment plan:* installment. *Waivers:* employees or children of employees.

Financial Aid Of all full-time matriculated undergraduates who enrolled in 2010, 2,851 applied for aid, 2,441 were judged to have need, 953 had their need fully met. 68 Federal Work-Study jobs (averaging $2011). 215 state and other part-time jobs (averaging $5162). In 2010, 223 non-need-based awards were made. *Average percent of need met:* 62%. *Average financial aid package:* $8176. *Average need-based loan:* $3698. *Average need-based gift aid:* $5774. *Average non-need-based aid:* $1262. *Average indebtedness upon graduation:* $7805.

Applying *Options:* electronic application, deferred entrance. *Application fee:* $15. *Required for some:* high school transcript, minimum 2.7 GPA, rank in top 50 percentile of high school graduating class. *Application deadlines:* rolling (freshmen), rolling (out-of-state freshmen), rolling (transfers). *Notification:* continuous (freshmen), continuous (out-of-state freshmen), continuous (transfers).

Freshman Application Contact Mr. Nate Todd, Coordinator of Prospective Student Services, Cameron University, Admissions, 2800 West Gore Boulevard, Lawton, OK 73505-6377. *Phone:* 580-581-5496. *Toll-free phone:*

888-454-7600. *Fax:* 580-581-5514. *E-mail:* admissions@cameron.edu. *Web site:* http://www.cameron.edu/.

DeVry University
Oklahoma City, Oklahoma

Freshman Application Contact DeVry University, Lakepointe Towers, 4013 Northwest Expressway Street, Suite 100, Oklahoma City, OK 73116. *Toll-free phone:* 866-338-7941. *Web site:* http://www.devry.edu/.

East Central University
Ada, Oklahoma

- **State-supported** comprehensive, founded 1909, part of Oklahoma State Regents for Higher Education
- **Small-town** 140-acre campus with easy access to Oklahoma City
- **Endowment** $25.0 million
- **Coed** 3,880 undergraduate students, 81% full-time, 58% women, 42% men
- **Minimally difficult** entrance level, 92% of applicants were admitted

Undergraduates 3,161 full-time, 719 part-time. Students come from 32 states and territories; 37 other countries; 7% are from out of state; 4% Black or African American, non-Hispanic/Latino; 4% Hispanic/Latino; 0.3% Asian, non-Hispanic/Latino; 0.2% Native Hawaiian or other Pacific Islander, non-Hispanic/Latino; 18% American Indian or Alaska Native, non-Hispanic/Latino; 7% Two or more races, non-Hispanic/Latino; 2% Race/ethnicity unknown; 5% international; 10% transferred in; 29% live on campus. *Retention:* 65% of full-time freshmen returned.

Freshmen *Admission:* 946 applied, 869 admitted, 622 enrolled. *Average high school GPA:* 3.31. *Test scores:* SAT critical reading scores over 500: 19%; SAT math scores over 500: 64%; ACT scores over 18: 83%; SAT math scores over 600: 33%; ACT scores over 24: 23%; SAT math scores over 700: 8%; ACT scores over 30: 2%.

Faculty *Total:* 270, 63% full-time, 44% with terminal degrees. *Student/faculty ratio:* 18:1.

Academics *Calendar:* semesters. *Degrees:* bachelor's and master's. *Special study options:* academic remediation for entering students, adult/continuing education programs, advanced placement credit, distance learning, double majors, honors programs, independent study, internships, off-campus study, part-time degree program, services for LD students, study abroad, summer session for credit.

Computers on Campus 677 computers/terminals are available on campus for general student use. Students can access the following: campus intranet, computer help desk, free student e-mail accounts, online (class) grades, online (class) registration, online (class) schedules. Campuswide network is available. Wireless service is available via entire campus.

Student Life *Housing:* on-campus residence required for freshman year. *Options:* coed, women-only, disabled students. Campus housing is university owned. *Activities and organizations:* drama/theater group, student-run newspaper, choral group, marching band, BACCHUS, Fellowship of Christian Athletes, Human Resources, national fraternities, national sororities. *Campus security:* 24-hour emergency response devices and patrols, student patrols, late-night transport/escort service, agreements with all local, state, federal, and tribal police departments for added crime and violation prevention. *Student services:* health clinic, personal/psychological counseling.

Athletics Member NCAA, NAIA. All NCAA Division II. *Intercollegiate sports:* baseball M(s), basketball M(s)/W(s), cheerleading M/W, cross-country running M(s)/W(s), football M(s), golf M(s)/W, soccer W(s), softball W(s), tennis M(s)/W(s), track and field M/W, volleyball W(s). *Intramural sports:* basketball M/W, football M/W, racquetball M/W, soccer M/W, softball M/W, tennis M/W, volleyball M/W.

Standardized Tests *Required:* SAT or ACT (for admission). *Recommended:* ACT (for admission).

Costs (2011–12) *Tuition:* state resident $3444 full-time, $115 per semester hour part-time; nonresident $10,076 full-time, $336 per semester hour part-time. No tuition increase for student's term of enrollment. *Required fees:* $1259 full-time, $39 per semester hour part-time, $48 per term part-time. *Room and board:* $4574; room only: $1762. Room and board charges vary according to board plan and housing facility. *Waivers:* senior citizens and employees or children of employees.

Financial Aid Of all full-time matriculated undergraduates who enrolled in 2006, 2,396 applied for aid, 2,085 were judged to have need, 756 had their need fully met. 175 Federal Work-Study jobs (averaging $2349). 232 state and other part-time jobs (averaging $572). In 2006, 542 non-need-based awards were made. *Average percent of need met:* 70%. *Average financial aid package:* $7597. *Average need-based loan:* $3835. *Average need-based gift aid:*

$3420. *Average non-need-based aid:* $1567. *Average indebtedness upon graduation:* $19,190.

Applying *Options:* electronic application, early admission. *Application fee:* $20. *Required:* high school transcript. *Required for some:* minimum 2.7 GPA, rank in upper 50% of high school class. *Notification:* continuous (freshmen), continuous (transfers).

Freshman Application Contact Ms. Julie Coble, Freshman Admissions Officer, East Central University, PMBJ8, 1100 East 14th Street, Ada, OK 74820-6999. *Phone:* 580-310-5233 Ext. 233. *Fax:* 580-310-5432. *E-mail:* jcoble@ecok.edu. *Web site:* http://www.ecok.edu/.

Hillsdale Free Will Baptist College
Moore, Oklahoma

- **Independent Free Will Baptist** comprehensive, founded 1959
- **Suburban** 41-acre campus with easy access to Oklahoma City
- **Coed** 202 undergraduate students, 96% full-time, 35% women, 65% men
- **Noncompetitive** entrance level, 21% of applicants were admitted

Undergraduates 193 full-time, 9 part-time. 15% Black or African American, non-Hispanic/Latino; 3% Hispanic/Latino; 10% American Indian or Alaska Native, non-Hispanic/Latino; 0.5% Race/ethnicity unknown; 1% international. *Retention:* 60% of full-time freshmen returned.

Freshmen *Admission:* 258 applied, 54 admitted, 48 enrolled. *Test scores:* ACT scores over 18: 70%; ACT scores over 24: 19%.

Faculty *Total:* 49, 29% full-time, 16% with terminal degrees. *Student/faculty ratio:* 7:1.

Academics *Calendar:* semesters. *Degrees:* associate, bachelor's, and master's. *Special study options:* academic remediation for entering students, accelerated degree program, adult/continuing education programs, advanced placement credit, English as a second language, independent study, internships, part-time degree program, summer session for credit.

Computers on Campus 22 computers/terminals are available on campus for general student use. Students can access the following: campus intranet, free student e-mail accounts. Campuswide network is available.

Student Life *Housing:* on-campus residence required through sophomore year. *Options:* men-only, women-only. Campus housing is university owned. *Activities and organizations:* drama/theater group, choral group. *Campus security:* 24-hour emergency response devices, controlled dormitory access. *Student services:* personal/psychological counseling.

Athletics Member NCCAA. *Intercollegiate sports:* baseball M, basketball M/W, cross-country running M/W, soccer M, softball W, volleyball W. *Intramural sports:* basketball M/W, volleyball M/W.

Standardized Tests *Required:* SAT or ACT (for admission).

Costs (2012–13) *Comprehensive fee:* $16,650 includes full-time tuition ($8900), mandatory fees ($1825), and room and board ($5925). Full-time tuition and fees vary according to course load. Part-time tuition: $370 per credit hour. Part-time tuition and fees vary according to course load. *Required fees:* $232 per term part-time. *College room only:* $2472. Room and board charges vary according to board plan and housing facility. *Payment plan:* installment. *Waivers:* children of alumni, senior citizens, and employees or children of employees.

Financial Aid Of all full-time matriculated undergraduates who enrolled in 2010, 172 applied for aid, 143 were judged to have need, 19 had their need fully met. 48 Federal Work-Study jobs (averaging $994). In 2010, 70 non-need-based awards were made. *Average percent of need met:* 49%. *Average financial aid package:* $9253. *Average need-based loan:* $3017. *Average need-based gift aid:* $3821. *Average non-need-based aid:* $3113. *Average indebtedness upon graduation:* $23,822.

Applying *Options:* electronic application, early admission, deferred entrance. *Application fee:* $20. *Required:* high school transcript, 2 letters of recommendation. *Required for some:* interview. *Recommended:* minimum 2.0 GPA.

Freshman Application Contact Hillsdale Free Will Baptist College, PO Box 7208, Moore, OK 73160. *Phone:* 405-912-9007. *Fax:* 405-912-9050. *E-mail:* recruitment@hc.edu. *Web site:* http://www.hc.edu/.

ITT Technical Institute
Oklahoma City, Oklahoma

- **Proprietary** 4-year, founded 2006, part of ITT Educational Services, Inc.
- **Coed**
- **Minimally difficult** entrance level

Academics *Calendar:* quarters. *Degrees:* associate and bachelor's.

Student Life *Housing:* college housing not available.

Freshman Application Contact Director of Recruitment, ITT Technical Institute, 50 Penn Place Office Tower, 1900 Northwest Expressway, Suite 305R, Oklahoma City, OK 73118. *Phone:* 405-810-4100. *Toll-free phone:* 800-518-1612. *Web site:* http://www.itt-tech.edu/.

ITT Technical Institute

Tulsa, Oklahoma

- **Proprietary** primarily 2-year, founded 2005
- **Coed**
- **Minimally difficult** entrance level

Academics *Calendar:* quarters. *Degrees:* associate and bachelor's.
Student Life *Housing:* college housing not available.
Freshman Application Contact Director of Recruitment, ITT Technical Institute, 4500 South 129th East Avenue, Suite 152, Tulsa, OK 74134. *Phone:* 918-615-3900. *Toll-free phone:* 800-514-6535. *Web site:* http://www.itt-tech.edu/.

Langston University

Langston, Oklahoma

Freshman Application Contact Maurice Osborne, Assistant Director of Admission, Langston University, PO Box 667, Langston, OK 73050. *Phone:* 405-466-2984. *Web site:* http://www.langston.edu/.

Mid-America Christian University

Oklahoma City, Oklahoma

Freshman Application Contact Mid-America Christian University, 3500 Southwest 119th Street, Oklahoma City, OK 73170-4504. *Phone:* 405-392-3180. *Toll-free phone:* 888-436-3035. *Web site:* http://www.macu.edu/.

Northeastern State University

Tahlequah, Oklahoma

- **State-supported** comprehensive, founded 1846, part of Regional University System of Oklahoma
- **Small-town** 160-acre campus with easy access to Tulsa
- **Endowment** $12.8 million
- **Coed** 8,116 undergraduate students, 73% full-time, 61% women, 39% men
- **Moderately difficult** entrance level, 54% of applicants were admitted

Undergraduates 5,904 full-time, 2,212 part-time. Students come from 29 states and territories; 56 other countries; 6% are from out of state; 6% Black or African American, non-Hispanic/Latino; 2% Hispanic/Latino; 2% Asian, non-Hispanic/Latino; 29% American Indian or Alaska Native, non-Hispanic/Latino; 0.2% Race/ethnicity unknown; 2% international; 12% transferred in; 19% live on campus. *Retention:* 65% of full-time freshmen returned.
Freshmen *Admission:* 2,540 applied, 1,377 admitted, 953 enrolled. *Average high school GPA:* 3.23. *Test scores:* ACT scores over 18: 77%; ACT scores over 24: 20%; ACT scores over 30: 2%.
Faculty *Total:* 513, 56% full-time, 53% with terminal degrees. *Student/faculty ratio:* 20:1.
Academics *Calendar:* semesters. *Degrees:* bachelor's, master's, doctoral, post-master's, and postbachelor's certificates. *Special study options:* academic remediation for entering students, adult/continuing education programs, advanced placement credit, cooperative education, distance learning, double majors, honors programs, independent study, internships, part-time degree program, services for LD students, student-designed majors, summer session for credit. *ROTC:* Army (b).
Computers on Campus 1,160 computers/terminals and 1,200 ports are available on campus for general student use. Students can access the following: campus intranet, computer help desk, free student e-mail accounts, online (class) grades, online (class) schedules. Campuswide network is available. 100% of college-owned or -operated housing units are wired for high-speed Internet access. Wireless service is available via computer centers, computer labs, libraries, student centers.
Student Life *Housing:* on-campus residence required for freshman year. *Options:* coed, women-only, disabled students. Campus housing is university owned. Freshman applicants given priority for college housing. *Activities and organizations:* drama/theater group, student-run newspaper, television station, choral group, marching band, national fraternities, national sororities. *Campus security:* 24-hour emergency response devices and patrols, late-night transport/escort service, controlled dormitory access. *Student services:* health clinic, personal/psychological counseling.
Athletics Member NCAA. All Division II. *Intercollegiate sports:* baseball M(s), basketball M(s)/W(s), football M(s), golf M(s)/W(s), soccer M(s)/W(s), softball W(s), tennis W(s). *Intramural sports:* basketball M/W, football M/W, golf M/W, racquetball M/W, soccer M/W, softball M/W, tennis M/W, volleyball M/W.
Standardized Tests *Required:* ACT (for admission).

Costs (2011–12) *Tuition:* state resident $3495 full-time, $117 per credit hour part-time; nonresident $10,020 full-time, $334 per credit hour part-time. Full-time tuition and fees vary according to course load and program. Part-time tuition and fees vary according to course load and program. *Required fees:* $1107 full-time, $37 per credit hour part-time. *Room and board:* $5220. Room and board charges vary according to board plan and housing facility. *Waivers:* senior citizens and employees or children of employees.
Financial Aid Of all full-time matriculated undergraduates who enrolled in 2010, 5,177 applied for aid, 3,449 were judged to have need, 2,209 had their need fully met. In 2010, 443 non-need-based awards were made. *Average percent of need met:* 80%. *Average financial aid package:* $12,445. *Average need-based loan:* $3573. *Average need-based gift aid:* $5823. *Average non-need-based aid:* $3316. *Average indebtedness upon graduation:* $22,306.
Applying *Options:* deferred entrance. *Application fee:* $25. *Required:* high school transcript, minimum 2.7 GPA, upper 50% of class or minimum ACT composite of 20. *Required for some:* interview. *Application deadlines:* 8/1 (freshmen), 8/1 (transfers). *Notification:* continuous (freshmen), continuous (transfers).
Freshman Application Contact Ms. Dawn Cain, Director of Admissions, Northeastern State University, 600 N Grand Ave, Tahlequah, OK 74464. *Phone:* 918-444-2211. *Toll-free phone:* 800-722-9614. *Fax:* 918-458-2342. *E-mail:* cain@nsuok.edu. *Web site:* http://www.nsuok.edu/.

Northwestern Oklahoma State University

Alva, Oklahoma

- **State-supported** comprehensive, founded 1897, part of Oklahoma State Regents for Higher Education
- **Rural** 70-acre campus
- **Endowment** $19.4 million
- **Coed** 2,092 undergraduate students, 82% full-time, 55% women, 45% men
- **Moderately difficult** entrance level, 100% of applicants were admitted

Undergraduates 1,715 full-time, 377 part-time. Students come from 39 states and territories; 14 other countries; 21% are from out of state; 5% Black or African American, non-Hispanic/Latino; 6% Hispanic/Latino; 0.3% Asian, non-Hispanic/Latino; 0.2% Native Hawaiian or other Pacific Islander, non-Hispanic/Latino; 6% American Indian or Alaska Native, non-Hispanic/Latino; 8% Race/ethnicity unknown; 2% international; 11% transferred in; 30% live on campus. *Retention:* 53% of full-time freshmen returned.
Freshmen *Admission:* 882 applied, 882 admitted, 403 enrolled. *Average high school GPA:* 3.28. *Test scores:* ACT scores over 18: 72%; ACT scores over 24: 20%; ACT scores over 30: 2%.
Faculty *Total:* 166, 46% full-time, 33% with terminal degrees. *Student/faculty ratio:* 17:1.
Academics *Calendar:* semesters. *Degrees:* bachelor's, master's, post-master's, and postbachelor's certificates. *Special study options:* academic remediation for entering students, adult/continuing education programs, advanced placement credit, cooperative education, distance learning, honors programs, independent study, internships, off-campus study, part-time degree program, services for LD students, study abroad, summer session for credit.
Computers on Campus 260 computers/terminals are available on campus for general student use. Students can access the following: campus intranet, computer help desk, free student e-mail accounts, online (class) grades, online (class) registration, online (class) schedules. Campuswide network is available. 100% of college-owned or -operated housing units are wired for high-speed Internet access. Wireless service is available via classrooms, computer centers, computer labs, learning centers, libraries, student centers.
Student Life *Housing:* on-campus residence required for freshman year. *Options:* men-only, women-only. Campus housing is university owned. Freshman campus housing is guaranteed. *Activities and organizations:* drama/theater group, student-run newspaper, radio and television station, choral group, marching band, Student Government Association, Aggie Club, Phi Beta Lambda, Baptist Student Union. *Campus security:* 24-hour emergency response devices and patrols, late-night transport/escort service. *Student services:* personal/psychological counseling.
Athletics Member NAIA. *Intercollegiate sports:* baseball M(s), basketball M(s)/W(s), cheerleading M(s)/W(s), cross-country running M(s)/W(s), football M(s), golf M(s)/W(s), soccer W(s), softball W(s). *Intramural sports:* basketball M/W, football M, racquetball M/W, softball M/W, ultimate Frisbee M/W, volleyball M/W.
Standardized Tests *Required:* SAT or ACT (for admission).
Costs (2011–12) *Tuition:* state resident $3968 full-time; nonresident $9518 full-time. Full-time tuition and fees vary according to course load, degree level, location, and program. Part-time tuition and fees vary according to course load, degree level, location, and program. *Required fees:* $623 full-

time. *Room and board:* $3700; room only: $1300. Room and board charges vary according to board plan. *Payment plan:* installment. *Waivers:* senior citizens and employees or children of employees.

Financial Aid Of all full-time matriculated undergraduates who enrolled in 2011, 1,056 applied for aid, 900 were judged to have need. 90 Federal Work-Study jobs (averaging $1505). 194 state and other part-time jobs (averaging $1433). *Average indebtedness upon graduation:* $14,812.

Applying *Options:* electronic application, early admission. *Application fee:* $15. *Required:* high school transcript. *Required for some:* essay or personal statement, minimum 2.7 GPA, 3 letters of recommendation. *Application deadlines:* rolling (freshmen), rolling (transfers). *Notification:* continuous (freshmen), continuous (transfers).

Freshman Application Contact Mr. Matt Adair, Director of Recruitment, Northwestern Oklahoma State University, 709 Oklahoma Boulevard, Alva, OK 73717-2799. *Phone:* 580-327-8545. *Fax:* 580-327-8699. *E-mail:* wmadair@nwosu.edu. *Web site:* http://www.nwosu.edu/.

Oklahoma Baptist University

Shawnee, Oklahoma

Freshman Application Contact Oklahoma Baptist University, 500 West University, Shawnee, OK 74804. *Phone:* 405-878-2033. *Toll-free phone:* 800-654-3285. *Web site:* http://www.okbu.edu/.

Oklahoma Christian University

Oklahoma City, Oklahoma

- **Independent** comprehensive, founded 1950, affiliated with Church of Christ
- **Suburban** 200-acre campus
- **Endowment** $59.4 million
- **Coed** 1,854 undergraduate students, 96% full-time, 49% women, 51% men
- **Noncompetitive** entrance level, 55% of applicants were admitted

Undergraduates 1,777 full-time, 77 part-time. Students come from 42 states and territories; 38 other countries; 58% are from out of state; 5% Black or African American, non-Hispanic/Latino; 4% Hispanic/Latino; 2% Asian, non-Hispanic/Latino; 0.1% Native Hawaiian or other Pacific Islander, non-Hispanic/Latino; 4% American Indian or Alaska Native, non-Hispanic/Latino; 5% Race/ethnicity unknown; 9% international; 6% transferred in; 78% live on campus. *Retention:* 72% of full-time freshmen returned.

Freshmen *Admission:* 1,786 applied, 991 admitted, 465 enrolled. *Average high school GPA:* 3.42. *Test scores:* SAT critical reading scores over 500: 59%; SAT math scores over 500: 66%; ACT scores over 18: 88%; SAT critical reading scores over 600: 32%; SAT math scores over 600: 29%; ACT scores over 24: 52%; SAT critical reading scores over 700: 8%; SAT math scores over 700: 9%; ACT scores over 30: 14%.

Faculty *Total:* 207, 54% full-time, 68% with terminal degrees. *Student/faculty ratio:* 13:1.

Academics *Calendar:* semesters. *Degrees:* bachelor's and master's. *Special study options:* academic remediation for entering students, accelerated degree program, advanced placement credit, distance learning, double majors, English as a second language, honors programs, independent study, internships, off-campus study, services for LD students, study abroad, summer session for credit. *ROTC:* Army (c), Air Force (c).

Computers on Campus 101 computers/terminals and 450 ports are available on campus for general student use. Students can access the following: campus intranet, computer help desk, free student e-mail accounts, online (class) grades, online (class) registration, online (class) schedules. Campuswide network is available. 100% of college-owned or -operated housing units are wired for high-speed Internet access. Wireless service is available via entire campus.

Student Life *Housing:* on-campus residence required through senior year. *Options:* men-only, women-only, disabled students. Campus housing is university owned. Freshman campus housing is guaranteed. *Activities and organizations:* drama/theater group, student-run newspaper, radio and television station, choral group, Outreach, Wishing Well Project, Acting on Aids, Young Republicans, College Democrats. *Campus security:* 24-hour emergency response devices and patrols, late-night transport/escort service, controlled dormitory access. *Student services:* health clinic, personal/psychological counseling.

Athletics Member NAIA. *Intercollegiate sports:* baseball M(s), basketball M(s)/W(s), cross-country running M(s)/W(s), golf M(s), soccer M(s)/W(s), softball W(s), tennis M(s)/W(s), track and field M(s)/W(s). *Intramural sports:* baseball M/W, basketball M/W, bowling M/W, cheerleading M/W, cross-country running M/W, football M/W, golf M/W, soccer M/W, softball M/W, swimming and diving M/W, table tennis M/W, tennis M/W, track and field M/W, volleyball M/W.

Standardized Tests *Required:* SAT or ACT (for admission).

Costs (2012–13) *Comprehensive fee:* $24,975 includes full-time tuition ($18,800) and room and board ($6175). Full-time tuition and fees vary according to course load. Part-time tuition: $783 per credit hour. Part-time tuition and fees vary according to course load. *College room only:* $3575. Room and board charges vary according to board plan and housing facility. *Payment plan:* installment. *Waivers:* employees or children of employees.

Financial Aid Of all full-time matriculated undergraduates who enrolled in 2009, 1,906 applied for aid, 1,272 were judged to have need, 265 had their need fully met. 589 Federal Work-Study jobs (averaging $1557). In 2009, 423 non-need-based awards were made. *Average percent of need met:* 55%. *Average financial aid package:* $15,613. *Average need-based loan:* $3877. *Average need-based gift aid:* $2506. *Average non-need-based aid:* $3941. *Average indebtedness upon graduation:* $22,333. *Financial aid deadline:* 8/31.

Applying *Options:* electronic application, early admission, deferred entrance. *Application fee:* $25. *Required:* high school transcript, 1 letter of recommendation. *Application deadlines:* rolling (freshmen), rolling (transfers). *Notification:* continuous (freshmen), continuous (transfers).

Freshman Application Contact Mr. Michael Mitchell, Director, Admissions and Recruiting, Oklahoma Christian University, Box 11000, Oklahoma City, OK 73136-1100. *Phone:* 405-425-5065. *Toll-free phone:* 800-877-5010. *Fax:* 405-425-5208. *E-mail:* info@oc.edu. *Web site:* http://www.oc.edu/.

Oklahoma City University

Oklahoma City, Oklahoma

- **Independent United Methodist** comprehensive, founded 1904
- **Urban** 104-acre campus with easy access to Oklahoma City
- **Endowment** $83.5 million
- **Coed** 2,227 undergraduate students, 84% full-time, 63% women, 37% men
- **Moderately difficult** entrance level, 74% of applicants were admitted

Undergraduates 1,861 full-time, 366 part-time. Students come from 41 states and territories; 56 other countries; 42% are from out of state; 7% Black or African American, non-Hispanic/Latino; 6% Hispanic/Latino; 2% Asian, non-Hispanic/Latino; 0.2% Native Hawaiian or other Pacific Islander, non-Hispanic/Latino; 3% American Indian or Alaska Native, non-Hispanic/Latino; 5% Two or more races, non-Hispanic/Latino; 2% Race/ethnicity unknown; 16% international; 11% transferred in; 58% live on campus. *Retention:* 79% of full-time freshmen returned.

Freshmen *Admission:* 1,329 applied, 977 admitted, 331 enrolled. *Average high school GPA:* 3.56. *Test scores:* SAT critical reading scores over 500: 80%; SAT math scores over 500: 79%; ACT scores over 18: 99%; SAT critical reading scores over 600: 35%; SAT math scores over 600: 37%; ACT scores over 24: 72%; SAT critical reading scores over 700: 9%; SAT math scores over 700: 3%; ACT scores over 30: 14%.

Faculty *Total:* 343, 63% full-time, 71% with terminal degrees. *Student/faculty ratio:* 11:1.

Academics *Calendar:* semesters. *Degrees:* bachelor's, master's, doctoral, and first professional. *Special study options:* academic remediation for entering students, accelerated degree program, adult/continuing education programs, advanced placement credit, cooperative education, distance learning, double majors, English as a second language, honors programs, independent study, internships, off-campus study, part-time degree program, services for LD students, study abroad, summer session for credit. *ROTC:* Army (c), Air Force (c). *Unusual degree programs:* 3-2 Oklahoma City University School of Law - combined Bachelor's and JD degrees.

Computers on Campus 369 computers/terminals and 6,828 ports are available on campus for general student use. Students can access the following: campus intranet, computer help desk, free student e-mail accounts, online (class) grades, online (class) registration, online (class) schedules. Campuswide network is available. 100% of college-owned or -operated housing units are wired for high-speed Internet access. Wireless service is available via entire campus.

Student Life *Housing options:* men-only, women-only. Campus housing is university owned. Freshman applicants given priority for college housing. *Activities and organizations:* drama/theater group, student-run newspaper, choral group, Tri-Beta, Student Nursing Association, Fellowship of Christian Athletes, Multicultural Student Association, Student Government Association, national fraternities, national sororities. *Campus security:* 24-hour emergency response devices and patrols, student patrols, late-night transport/escort service, controlled dormitory access, Operation ID; Emergency Electronic Network. *Student services:* health clinic, personal/psychological counseling.

Athletics Member NAIA. *Intercollegiate sports:* baseball M(s), basketball M(s)/W(s), cheerleading M(s)/W(s), crew M(s)/W(s), golf M(s)/W(s), sailing M(c)/W(c), soccer M(s)/W(s), softball W(s), track and field M(s)/W(s), volleyball W(s), wrestling M(s)/W(s). *Intramural sports:* basketball M/W, fencing M/W, football M, golf M/W, softball M/W, table tennis M/W, volleyball M/W.

Standardized Tests *Required:* SAT or ACT (for admission).

Costs (2012–13) *Comprehensive fee:* $37,360 includes full-time tuition ($24,740), mandatory fees ($3450), and room and board ($9170). Part-time tuition: $840 per credit hour. No tuition increase for student's term of enrollment. *College room only:* $5090. Room and board charges vary according to board plan and housing facility. *Payment plans:* installment, deferred payment. *Waivers:* employees or children of employees.

Financial Aid Of all full-time matriculated undergraduates who enrolled in 2010, 1,425 applied for aid, 1,312 were judged to have need, 726 had their need fully met. 363 Federal Work-Study jobs (averaging $1362). 270 state and other part-time jobs (averaging $1692). In 2010, 349 non-need-based awards were made. *Average percent of need met:* 56%. *Average financial aid package:* $17,823. *Average need-based loan:* $5128. *Average need-based gift aid:* $14,465. *Average non-need-based aid:* $14,174. *Average indebtedness upon graduation:* $19,470.

Applying *Options:* electronic application, early decision, deferred entrance. *Application fee:* $50. *Required:* essay or personal statement, high school transcript, minimum 3.0 GPA, 2 letters of recommendation. *Required for some:* interview, audition for music and dance programs. *Recommended:* interview. *Application deadlines:* 3/1 (freshmen), rolling (out-of-state freshmen), rolling (transfers). *Early decision deadline:* 11/15. *Notification:* continuous until 4/30 (freshmen), continuous (out-of-state freshmen), continuous until 4/30 (transfers), 12/30 (early decision).

Freshman Application Contact Ms. Michelle cook, Director of Undergraduate Admissions, Admissions Operations and Visitor Services, Oklahoma City University, 2501 North Blackwelder, Oklahoma City, OK 73106. *Phone:* 405-208-5055. *Toll-free phone:* 800-633-7242. *Fax:* 405-208-5032. *E-mail:* mlockhart@okcu.edu. *Web site:* http://www.okcu.edu/.

Oklahoma Panhandle State University
Goodwell, Oklahoma

- **State-supported** 4-year, founded 1909, part of Oklahoma State Regents for Higher Education
- **Rural** 40-acre campus
- **Coed**
- **Noncompetitive** entrance level

Faculty *Student/faculty ratio:* 16:1.
Academics *Calendar:* semesters. *Degrees:* associate and bachelor's.
Student Life *Campus security:* safety bars over door latches.
Athletics Member NCAA. All Division II.
Standardized Tests *Recommended:* SAT or ACT (for admission).
Applying *Options:* electronic application. *Required:* high school transcript.
Freshman Application Contact Mr. Bobby Jenkins, Registrar and Director of Admissions, Oklahoma Panhandle State University, PO Box 430, 323 Eagle Boulevard, Goodwell, OK 73939-0430. *Phone:* 580-349-1376. *Toll-free phone:* 800-664-6778. *Fax:* 580-349-1371. *E-mail:* opsu@opsu.edu. *Web site:* http://www.opsu.edu/.

Oklahoma State University
Stillwater, Oklahoma

- **State-supported** university, founded 1890, part of Oklahoma State University
- **Small-town** 840-acre campus with easy access to Oklahoma City, Tulsa
- **Endowment** $531.9 million
- **Coed** 71,247 undergraduate students, 96% full-time, 86% women, 14% men
- **Moderately difficult** entrance level, 82% of applicants were admitted

Undergraduates 68,663 full-time, 2,584 part-time. Students come from 51 states and territories; 63 other countries; 22% are from out of state; 5% Black or African American, non-Hispanic/Latino; 4% Hispanic/Latino; 1% Asian, non-Hispanic/Latino; 7% American Indian or Alaska Native, non-Hispanic/Latino; 6% Two or more races, non-Hispanic/Latino; 1% Race/ethnicity unknown; 2% international; 2% transferred in; 44% live on campus. *Retention:* 80% of full-time freshmen returned.
Freshmen *Admission:* 9,914 applied, 8,099 admitted, 3,896 enrolled. *Average high school GPA:* 3.48. *Test scores:* SAT critical reading scores over 500: 72%; SAT math scores over 500: 79%; ACT scores over 18: 97%; SAT critical reading scores over 600: 27%; SAT math scores over 600: 38%; ACT scores over 24: 63%; SAT critical reading scores over 700: 5%; SAT math scores over 700: 7%; ACT scores over 30: 14%.
Faculty *Total:* 1,300, 76% full-time, 71% with terminal degrees. *Student/faculty ratio:* 19:1.
Academics *Calendar:* semesters. *Degrees:* bachelor's, master's, doctoral, post-master's, postbachelor's, and first professional certificates. *Special study options:* academic remediation for entering students, accelerated degree program, advanced placement credit, distance learning, double majors, English as a second language, freshman honors college, honors programs, independent study, internships, off-campus study, part-time degree program, services for LD students, student-designed majors, study abroad, summer session for credit. *ROTC:* Army (b), Air Force (b).
Computers on Campus Students can access the following: campus intranet, computer help desk, free student e-mail accounts, online (class) grades, online (class) registration, online (class) schedules. Campuswide network is available. Wireless service is available via classrooms, computer centers, computer labs, libraries, student centers.
Student Life *Housing:* on-campus residence required for freshman year. *Options:* coed, men-only, women-only, disabled students. Campus housing is university owned. Freshman campus housing is guaranteed. *Activities and organizations:* drama/theater group, student-run newspaper, radio and television station, choral group, marching band, national fraternities, national sororities. *Campus security:* 24-hour emergency response devices and patrols, student patrols, controlled dormitory access. *Student services:* health clinic, personal/psychological counseling, women's center.
Athletics Member NCAA. All Division I. *Intercollegiate sports:* baseball M(s), basketball M(s)/W(s), cross-country running M(s)/W(s), equestrian sports W(s), football M(s), golf M(s)/W(s), soccer W(s), softball W(s), tennis M(s)/W(s), track and field M(s)/W(s), wrestling M(s).
Standardized Tests *Required:* SAT or ACT (for admission).
Costs (2012–13) *One-time required fee:* $95. *Tuition:* state resident $4304 full-time, $143 per credit hour part-time; nonresident $15,621 full-time, $522 per credit hour part-time. Full-time tuition and fees vary according to program and student level. Part-time tuition and fees vary according to program and student level. *Required fees:* $93 per credit hour part-time. *Room and board:* $6680; room only: $3600. Room and board charges vary according to board plan and housing facility. *Payment plan:* installment. *Waivers:* children of alumni.
Financial Aid Of all full-time matriculated undergraduates who enrolled in 2010, 10,398 applied for aid, 8,422 were judged to have need, 1,077 had their need fully met. 463 Federal Work-Study jobs (averaging $2339). 3,493 state and other part-time jobs (averaging $2468). In 2010, 3885 non-need-based awards were made. *Average percent of need met:* 77%. *Average financial aid package:* $12,596. *Average need-based loan:* $4109. *Average need-based gift aid:* $6766. *Average non-need-based aid:* $4730. *Average indebtedness upon graduation:* $21,204.
Applying *Options:* electronic application, deferred entrance. *Application fee:* $40. *Required:* high school transcript, minimum 3.0 GPA, class rank. *Required for some:* essay or personal statement, interview. *Application deadlines:* rolling (freshmen), rolling (out-of-state freshmen), rolling (transfers). *Notification:* continuous (freshmen), continuous (out-of-state freshmen), continuous (transfers).
Freshman Application Contact Oklahoma State University, Stillwater, OK 74078. *Phone:* 405-744-3087. *Toll-free phone:* 800-233-5019 Ext. 1 (in-state); 800-852-1255 (out-of-state). *Web site:* http://www.okstate.edu/.

Oklahoma State University, Oklahoma City
Oklahoma City, Oklahoma

- **State-supported** primarily 2-year, founded 1961, part of Oklahoma State University
- **Urban** 110-acre campus
- **Coed** 7,721 undergraduate students
- **Noncompetitive** entrance level, 100% of applicants were admitted

Undergraduates Students come from 9 states and territories; 8 other countries; 1% are from out of state. *Retention:* 34% of full-time freshmen returned.
Freshmen *Admission:* 1,087 applied, 1,087 admitted.
Faculty *Total:* 381, 22% full-time. *Student/faculty ratio:* 20:1.
Academics *Calendar:* semesters. *Degrees:* certificates, associate, and bachelor's. *Special study options:* academic remediation for entering students, advanced placement credit, cooperative education, distance learning, double majors, honors programs, independent study, part-time degree program, services for LD students, study abroad, summer session for credit.
Computers on Campus 800 computers/terminals are available on campus for general student use. Campuswide network is available.
Student Life *Housing:* college housing not available. *Activities and organizations:* Phi Theta Kappa, Deaf/Hearing Social Club, American Criminal Justice Association, Horticulture Club, Vet-Tech Club. *Campus security:* 24-hour patrols, late-night transport/escort service.
Costs (2011–12) *Tuition:* state resident $2534 full-time, $106 per credit hour part-time; nonresident $6836 full-time, $285 per credit hour part-time. Full-time tuition and fees vary according to course level, degree level, and program. Part-time tuition and fees vary according to course level, degree level, and program. No tuition increase for student's term of enrollment. *Required fees:* $30 full-time. *Payment plan:* installment. *Waivers:* senior citizens and employees or children of employees.

Applying *Options:* electronic application, early admission. *Required:* high school transcript. *Application deadlines:* rolling (freshmen), rolling (transfers). *Notification:* continuous (freshmen), continuous (transfers).

Freshman Application Contact Mr. Kyle Williams, Director, Enrollment Management, Oklahoma State University, Oklahoma City, 900 North Portland, AD202, Oklahoma City, OK 73107. *Phone:* 405-945-9152. *Toll-free phone:* 800-560-4099. *E-mail:* wilkylw@osuokc.edu. *Web site:* http://www.osuokc.edu/.

Oklahoma Wesleyan University

Bartlesville, Oklahoma

- **Independent** comprehensive, founded 1909, affiliated with Wesleyan Church
- **Small-town** 127-acre campus with easy access to Tulsa
- **Endowment** $2.8 million
- **Coed**
- **Minimally difficult** entrance level

Faculty *Student/faculty ratio:* 19:1.

Academics *Calendar:* semesters. *Degrees:* certificates, diplomas, associate, bachelor's, and master's.

Student Life *Campus security:* 24-hour emergency response devices, student patrols.

Athletics Member NAIA, NCCAA.

Standardized Tests *Required:* SAT or ACT (for admission).

Costs (2011–12) *Comprehensive fee:* $27,034 includes full-time tuition ($19,060), mandatory fees ($1100), and room and board ($6874). Full-time tuition and fees vary according to course load. Part-time tuition: $755 per credit hour. *Required fees:* $55 per credit hour part-time, $60 per term part-time. *College room only:* $3634. Room and board charges vary according to board plan and housing facility. *Payment plans:* installment, deferred payment.

Financial Aid *Of all full-time matriculated undergraduates who enrolled in 2011,* 557 applied for aid, 499 were judged to have need, 65 had their need fully met. 120 Federal Work-Study jobs (averaging $1774). 43 state and other part-time jobs (averaging $1846). *In 2011,* 73 non-need-based awards were made. *Average percent of need met:* 64. *Average financial aid package:* $13,658. *Average need-based loan:* $4362. *Average need-based gift aid:* $9892. *Average non-need-based aid:* $5211. *Average indebtedness upon graduation:* $18,051.

Applying *Options:* electronic application. *Application fee:* $25. *Required:* high school transcript, ACT score 18 or higher. *Recommended:* minimum 2.0 GPA.

Freshman Application Contact Jennifer Weaver, Enrollment Counselor, Oklahoma Wesleyan University, 2201 Silver Lake Drive, Bartlesville, OK 74006. *Phone:* 866-222-8226. *Toll-free phone:* 866-222-8226. *Fax:* 918-335-6229. *E-mail:* admissions@okwu.edu. *Web site:* http://www.okwu.edu/.

Oral Roberts University

Tulsa, Oklahoma

- **Independent interdenominational** comprehensive, founded 1963
- **Urban** 263-acre campus
- **Coed** 2,676 undergraduate students, 88% full-time, 59% women, 41% men
- **Moderately difficult** entrance level, 59% of applicants were admitted

Undergraduates 2,355 full-time, 321 part-time. 15% Black or African American, non-Hispanic/Latino; 6% Hispanic/Latino; 0.5% Asian, non-Hispanic/Latino; 2% Native Hawaiian or other Pacific Islander, non-Hispanic/Latino; 2% American Indian or Alaska Native, non-Hispanic/Latino; 3% Two or more races, non-Hispanic/Latino; 11% Race/ethnicity unknown; 5% international.

Freshmen *Admission:* 1,163 applied, 690 admitted, 470 enrolled.

Faculty *Total:* 263, 65% full-time, 47% with terminal degrees. *Student/faculty ratio:* 15:1.

Academics *Calendar:* semesters. *Degrees:* bachelor's, master's, doctoral, and first professional. *Special study options:* adult/continuing education programs, external degree program, part-time degree program. *ROTC:* Air Force (c).

Computers on Campus Students can access the following: free student e-mail accounts, online (class) registration. Campuswide network is available.

Student Life *Housing:* on-campus residence required through senior year. *Options:* men-only, women-only. *Campus security:* 24-hour emergency response devices and patrols, late-night transport/escort service.

Athletics Member NCAA. All Division I. *Intercollegiate sports:* baseball M(s), basketball M(s)/W(s), cross-country running M(s)/W(s), golf M(s)/W(s), soccer M(s)/W(s), tennis M(s)/W(s), track and field M(s)/W(s), volleyball W(s), wrestling M. *Intramural sports:* badminton M/W, basketball M/W, bowling M/W, cross-country running M/W, football M/W, golf M/W, racquet-

ball M/W, softball M/W, swimming and diving M/W, table tennis M/W, tennis M/W, volleyball M/W.

Standardized Tests *Required:* SAT or ACT (for admission).

Costs (2011–12) *Comprehensive fee:* $29,350 includes full-time tuition ($20,060), mandatory fees ($696), and room and board ($8594). Full-time tuition and fees vary according to degree level. Part-time tuition: $838 per credit hour. Part-time tuition and fees vary according to degree level. *Required fees:* $201 per hour part-time. *Room and board:* Room and board charges vary according to board plan and housing facility.

Financial Aid Of all full-time matriculated undergraduates who enrolled in 2008, 1,978 applied for aid, 1,738 were judged to have need, 643 had their need fully met. In 2008, 501 non-need-based awards were made. *Average percent of need met:* 86%. *Average financial aid package:* $18,229. *Average need-based loan:* $10,159. *Average need-based gift aid:* $9304. *Average non-need-based aid:* $7151. *Average indebtedness upon graduation:* $34,555.

Applying *Options:* early action, deferred entrance. *Application fee:* $35. *Required:* essay or personal statement, high school transcript, minimum 2.0 GPA, 1 letter of recommendation, proof of immunization. *Required for some:* interview. *Recommended:* interview. *Application deadlines:* rolling (freshmen), rolling (transfers). *Notification:* continuous (freshmen), continuous (transfers).

Freshman Application Contact Chris Belcher, Director of Admissions, Oral Roberts University, 7777 South Lewis Avenue, Tulsa, OK 74171. *Phone:* 918-495-6529. *Toll-free phone:* 800-678-8876. *Fax:* 918-495-6222. *E-mail:* admissions@oru.edu. *Web site:* http://www.oru.edu/.

Rogers State University

Claremore, Oklahoma

- **State-supported** 4-year, founded 1909, part of Oklahoma State Regents for Higher Education
- **Small-town** 40-acre campus with easy access to Tulsa
- **Endowment** $7.3 million
- **Coed** 4,632 undergraduate students, 62% full-time, 63% women, 37% men
- **Noncompetitive** entrance level, 54% of applicants were admitted

Undergraduates 2,854 full-time, 1,778 part-time. Students come from 34 states and territories; 29 other countries; 4% are from out of state; 3% Black or African American, non-Hispanic/Latino; 4% Hispanic/Latino; 1% Asian, non-Hispanic/Latino; 0.1% Native Hawaiian or other Pacific Islander, non-Hispanic/Latino; 13% American Indian or Alaska Native, non-Hispanic/Latino; 16% Two or more races, non-Hispanic/Latino; 0.2% Race/ethnicity unknown; 1% international; 10% transferred in; 6% live on campus. *Retention:* 55% of full-time freshmen returned.

Freshmen *Admission:* 1,925 applied, 1,043 admitted, 888 enrolled. *Average high school GPA:* 3.11. *Test scores:* ACT scores over 18: 75%; ACT scores over 24: 18%; ACT scores over 30: 1%.

Faculty *Total:* 268, 39% full-time, 37% with terminal degrees. *Student/faculty ratio:* 22:1.

Academics *Calendar:* semesters. *Degrees:* associate and bachelor's. *Special study options:* academic remediation for entering students, adult/continuing education programs, advanced placement credit, cooperative education, distance learning, double majors, honors programs, independent study, internships, off-campus study, part-time degree program, services for LD students, study abroad, summer session for credit.

Computers on Campus 237 computers/terminals are available on campus for general student use. Students can access the following: computer help desk, free student e-mail accounts, online (class) grades, online (class) registration, online (class) schedules, software to support courses. Campuswide network is available. 100% of college-owned or -operated housing units are wired for high-speed Internet access. Wireless service is available via classrooms, computer labs, learning centers, libraries, student centers.

Student Life *Housing options:* coed. Campus housing is university owned. *Activities and organizations:* drama/theater group, student-run newspaper, radio station, choral group, Student Veterans Association, Baptist Collegiate Ministry, Campus Crusade for Christ, Community Counseling Student Association, Student Nursing Association, national fraternities, national sororities. *Campus security:* 24-hour emergency response devices and patrols, student patrols, late-night transport/escort service, controlled dormitory access, trained security personnel, trained police officers. *Student services:* health clinic, personal/psychological counseling.

Athletics Member NAIA. *Intercollegiate sports:* baseball M(s), basketball M(s)/W(s), cheerleading M(s)/W(s), cross-country running M(s)/W(s), golf M(s)/W(s), soccer M(s)/W(s), softball W(s). *Intramural sports:* basketball M/W, soccer M/W, softball M/W, table tennis M/W, volleyball M/W.

Standardized Tests *Required:* SAT or ACT (for admission). *Required for some:* ACT COMPASS. *Recommended:* ACT (for admission).

Costs (2012–13) *Tuition:* state resident $3023 full-time, $101 per credit hour part-time; nonresident $9068 full-time, $302 per credit hour part-time. Full-time tuition and fees vary according to course load, location, program, and student level. Part-time tuition and fees vary according to course load, location, program, and student level. *Required fees:* $1754 full-time, $57 per credit hour part-time, $15 per term part-time. *Room and board:* $6540; room only: $5940. Room and board charges vary according to housing facility. *Payment plan:* installment. *Waivers:* senior citizens and employees or children of employees.

Financial Aid Of all full-time matriculated undergraduates who enrolled in 2011, 1,997 applied for aid, 1,740 were judged to have need, 142 had their need fully met. 45 Federal Work-Study jobs (averaging $2553). 300 state and other part-time jobs (averaging $1798). In 2011, 43 non-need-based awards were made. *Average percent of need met:* 48%. *Average financial aid package:* $8457. *Average need-based loan:* $3919. *Average need-based gift aid:* $5458. *Average non-need-based aid:* $4306. *Average indebtedness upon graduation:* $18,989.

Applying *Options:* electronic application. *Required:* high school transcript. *Required for some:* minimum 2.8 GPA, Baccalaureate degree programs require 20 ACT composite or 2.75 GPA and top 50% rank for admission; Associate degree programs have an open admission policy. *Application deadlines:* rolling (freshmen), rolling (out-of-state freshmen), rolling (transfers).

Freshman Application Contact Ms. Julie Rampey, Director of Admissions, Rogers State University, 1701 West Will Rogers Boulevard, Claremore, OK 74017. *Phone:* 918-343-7546. *Toll-free phone:* 800-256-7511. *Fax:* 918-343-7595. *E-mail:* info@rsu.edu. *Web site:* http://www.rsu.edu/.

St. Gregory's University
Shawnee, Oklahoma

Freshman Application Contact Director of Admissions, St. Gregory's University, 1900 West MacArthur Drive, Shawnee, OK 74804. *Phone:* 405-878-5447. *Toll-free phone:* 888-STGREGS. *Fax:* 405-878-5198. *E-mail:* admissions@stgregorys.edu. *Web site:* http://www.stgregorys.edu/.

Southeastern Oklahoma State University
Durant, Oklahoma

- **State-supported** comprehensive, founded 1909, part of Oklahoma State Regents for Higher Education
- **Small-town** 177-acre campus
- **Endowment** $12.0 million
- **Coed** 3,709 undergraduate students, 78% full-time, 56% women, 44% men
- **Moderately difficult** entrance level, 78% of applicants were admitted

Undergraduates 2,887 full-time, 822 part-time. Students come from 36 states and territories; 41 other countries; 24% are from out of state; 6% Black or African American, non-Hispanic/Latino; 3% Hispanic/Latino; 0.9% Asian, non-Hispanic/Latino; 0.4% Native Hawaiian or other Pacific Islander, non-Hispanic/Latino; 30% American Indian or Alaska Native, non-Hispanic/Latino; 3% international; 11% transferred in; 17% live on campus. *Retention:* 54% of full-time freshmen returned.

Freshmen *Admission:* 1,143 applied, 886 admitted, 635 enrolled. *Average high school GPA:* 3.25. *Test scores:* ACT scores over 18: 75%; ACT scores over 24: 16%; ACT scores over 30: 2%.

Faculty *Total:* 262, 54% full-time, 52% with terminal degrees. *Student/faculty ratio:* 19:1.

Academics *Calendar:* semesters. *Degrees:* bachelor's, master's, and post-master's certificates. *Special study options:* academic remediation for entering students, accelerated degree program, adult/continuing education programs, advanced placement credit, distance learning, double majors, honors programs, independent study, internships, off-campus study, part-time degree program, services for LD students, summer session for credit.

Computers on Campus 598 computers/terminals and 598 ports are available on campus for general student use. Students can access the following: campus intranet, computer help desk, free student e-mail accounts, online (class) grades, online (class) registration, online (class) schedules, campus Blackboard classes. Campuswide network is available. 100% of college-owned or -operated housing units are wired for high-speed Internet access. Wireless service is available via classrooms, computer labs, dorm rooms, learning centers, libraries, student centers.

Student Life *Housing:* on-campus residence required for freshman year. *Options:* coed, men-only, women-only, disabled students. Campus housing is university owned. Freshman campus housing is guaranteed. *Activities and organizations:* drama/theater group, student-run newspaper, radio station, choral group, marching band, Baptist Collegiate Ministries, Fellowship of Chris-

tian Athletes, Wesley Foundation, Resident Hall Association, national fraternities, national sororities. *Campus security:* 24-hour emergency response devices and patrols, late-night transport/escort service, controlled dormitory access. *Student services:* health clinic, personal/psychological counseling.

Athletics Member NCAA. All Division II. *Intercollegiate sports:* baseball M(s), basketball M(s)/W(s), cross-country running W(s), football M(s), golf M(s), softball W(s), tennis M(s)/W(s), volleyball W(s). *Intramural sports:* basketball M/W, football M.

Standardized Tests *Required:* SAT or ACT (for admission).

Costs (2011–12) *Tuition:* state resident $4127 full-time, $138 per credit hour part-time; nonresident $11,340 full-time, $378 per credit hour part-time. Full-time tuition and fees vary according to course level. Part-time tuition and fees vary according to course level and course load. *Required fees:* $667 full-time, $23 per credit hour part-time. *Room and board:* $4760; room only: $2090. Room and board charges vary according to board plan and housing facility. *Payment plan:* installment. *Waivers:* minority students, children of alumni, senior citizens, and employees or children of employees.

Financial Aid Of all full-time matriculated undergraduates who enrolled in 2010, 2,459 applied for aid, 2,229 were judged to have need, 649 had their need fully met. 657 Federal Work-Study jobs (averaging $1666). 712 state and other part-time jobs (averaging $1260). In 2010, 5 non-need-based awards were made. *Average percent of need met:* 34%. *Average financial aid package:* $9769. *Average need-based loan:* $1796. *Average need-based gift aid:* $1503. *Average non-need-based aid:* $550. *Average indebtedness upon graduation:* $14,808.

Applying *Application fee:* $20. *Required:* high school transcript. *Required for some:* interview. *Application deadlines:* rolling (freshmen), rolling (transfers). *Notification:* continuous (freshmen), continuous (transfers).

Freshman Application Contact Southeastern Oklahoma State University, 1405 North 4th Avenue, Durant, OK 74701-0609. *Phone:* 580-745-2060. *Toll-free phone:* 800-435-1327. *Web site:* http://www.se.edu/.

Southern Nazarene University
Bethany, Oklahoma

- **Independent Nazarene** comprehensive, founded 1899
- **Suburban** 40-acre campus with easy access to Oklahoma City
- **Endowment** $19.9 million
- **Coed**
- **Noncompetitive** entrance level

Faculty *Student/faculty ratio:* 18:1.

Academics *Calendar:* semesters. *Degrees:* associate, bachelor's, and master's.

Student Life *Campus security:* 24-hour emergency response devices, student patrols, late-night transport/escort service, controlled dormitory access.

Athletics Member NAIA.

Standardized Tests *Required:* SAT or ACT (for admission). *Recommended:* ACT (for admission).

Costs (2011–12) *Comprehensive fee:* $27,394 includes full-time tuition ($19,170), mandatory fees ($624), and room and board ($7600). Part-time tuition: $639 per credit. Part-time tuition and fees vary according to course load. *Room and board:* Room and board charges vary according to board plan and housing facility. *Payment plans:* tuition prepayment, installment, deferred payment.

Financial Aid *Of all full-time matriculated undergraduates who enrolled in 2009,* 1,485 applied for aid, 1,366 were judged to have need. 104 Federal Work-Study jobs (averaging $2125). 115 state and other part-time jobs (averaging $3000).

Applying *Options:* electronic application, deferred entrance. *Application fee:* $35. *Required:* high school transcript, minimum 2.0 GPA, 2 letters of recommendation, interview.

Freshman Application Contact Mr. Todd Brant, Director of Recruitment, Southern Nazarene University, 6729 Northwest 39th Expressway, Bethany, OK 73008. *Phone:* 405-491-6324. *Toll-free phone:* 800-648-9899. *Fax:* 405-491-6320. *E-mail:* admiss@snu.edu. *Web site:* http://www.snu.edu/.

Southwestern Christian University
Bethany, Oklahoma

- **Independent** comprehensive, founded 1946, affiliated with Pentecostal Holiness Church
- **Suburban** 7-acre campus with easy access to Oklahoma City
- **Coed** 325 undergraduate students
- **Minimally difficult** entrance level

Undergraduates Students come from 12 other countries; 50% live on campus.

Freshmen *Admission:* 171 admitted. *Average high school GPA:* 3.22.

Faculty *Student/faculty ratio:* 15:1.

Academics *Calendar:* semesters. *Degrees:* certificates, associate, bachelor's, and master's. *Special study options:* academic remediation for entering students, advanced placement credit, distance learning, double majors, internships, off-campus study, part-time degree program, summer session for credit. *ROTC:* Army (c).

Computers on Campus 12 computers/terminals are available on campus for general student use. Students can access the following: campus intranet, free student e-mail accounts, online (class) grades, online (class) registration, online (class) schedules. Campuswide network is available. 100% of college-owned or -operated housing units are wired for high-speed Internet access. Wireless service is available via entire campus.

Student Life *Housing options:* men-only, women-only. Campus housing is university owned. *Activities and organizations:* drama/theater group, choral group. *Campus security:* 24-hour emergency response devices and patrols, student patrols. *Student services:* personal/psychological counseling.

Athletics Member NAIA, NCCAA. *Intercollegiate sports:* basketball M(s)/W(s), bowling M(s)/W(s), cheerleading W(s), crew M(s)/W(s), cross-country running M(s)/W(s), golf M(s)/W(s), soccer M(s)/W(s), softball W(s), tennis M(s)/W(s), track and field M(s)/W(s), volleyball W(s). *Intramural sports:* basketball M/W, bowling M/W, football M/W, golf M/W, soccer M/W, softball M/W, table tennis M/W, tennis M/W, ultimate Frisbee M/W, volleyball M/W.

Standardized Tests *Required:* SAT or ACT (for admission).

Costs (2012–13) *Comprehensive fee:* $16,560 includes full-time tuition ($11,060), mandatory fees ($500), and room and board ($5000). Full-time tuition and fees vary according to class time, course load, location, and program. Part-time tuition: $395 per credit hour. Part-time tuition and fees vary according to class time, course load, location, and program. *Required fees:* $250 per term part-time. *Room and board:* Room and board charges vary according to housing facility. *Payment plan:* deferred payment.

Financial Aid Of all full-time matriculated undergraduates who enrolled in 2008, 177 applied for aid, 170 were judged to have need, 61 had their need fully met. 60 Federal Work-Study jobs (averaging $1500). 10 state and other part-time jobs (averaging $1000). In 2008, 12 non-need-based awards were made. *Average percent of need met:* 71%. *Average financial aid package:* $9000. *Average need-based loan:* $4000. *Average need-based gift aid:* $2500. *Average non-need-based aid:* $2000. *Average indebtedness upon graduation:* $17,000.

Applying *Options:* electronic application, early admission, deferred entrance. *Required:* essay or personal statement, high school transcript, minimum 2.5 GPA, 19 ACT or 900 SAT, top 50% rank in class. *Recommended:* interview. *Application deadlines:* rolling (freshmen), rolling (out-of-state freshmen), rolling (transfers). *Notification:* continuous (freshmen), continuous (out-of-state freshmen), continuous (transfers).

Freshman Application Contact Jessie Burpo, Admissions Counselor, Southwestern Christian University, PO Box 340, Bethany, OK 73008-0340. *Phone:* 405-789-7661 Ext. 3432. *Fax:* 405-495-0078. *E-mail:* admissions@swcu.edu. *Web site:* http://www.swcu.edu/.

Southwestern Oklahoma State University
Weatherford, Oklahoma

- **State-supported** comprehensive, founded 1901
- **Small-town** campus
- **Coed** 4,517 undergraduate students, 82% full-time, 58% women, 42% men
- **Minimally difficult** entrance level, 92% of applicants were admitted

Undergraduates 3,699 full-time, 818 part-time. 13% are from out of state; 6% Black or African American, non-Hispanic/Latino; 6% Hispanic/Latino; 2% Asian, non-Hispanic/Latino; 0.4% Native Hawaiian or other Pacific Islander, non-Hispanic/Latino; 6% American Indian or Alaska Native, non-Hispanic/Latino; 4% Two or more races, non-Hispanic/Latino; 0.9% Race/ethnicity unknown; 2% international; 10% transferred in; 24% live on campus. *Retention:* 57% of full-time freshmen returned.

Freshmen *Admission:* 1,717 applied, 1,585 admitted, 953 enrolled. *Average high school GPA:* 3.34. *Test scores:* ACT scores over 18: 80%; ACT scores over 24: 28%; ACT scores over 30: 4%.

Faculty *Total:* 234, 92% full-time. *Student/faculty ratio:* 21:1.

Academics *Calendar:* semesters. *Degrees:* associate, bachelor's, master's, and doctoral. *Special study options:* adult/continuing education programs, part-time degree program.

Student Life *Housing options:* men-only, women-only. Campus housing is university owned. Freshman campus housing is guaranteed. *Campus security:* late-night transport/escort service, controlled dormitory access, 20-hour campus emergency security.

Athletics Member NCAA. All Division II. *Intercollegiate sports:* baseball M(s), basketball M(s)/W(s), cheerleading M/W, cross-country running W(s), equestrian sports M(s)/W(s), football M(s), golf M(s)/W(s), soccer W(s), soft-

ball W(s). *Intramural sports:* basketball M/W, bowling M/W, football M/W, softball M/W, volleyball M/W, weight lifting M.

Standardized Tests *Required:* SAT or ACT (for admission). *Recommended:* ACT (for admission).

Costs (2011–12) *Tuition:* state resident $3660 full-time, $122 per credit hour part-time; nonresident $9720 full-time, $324 per credit hour part-time. Full-time tuition and fees vary according to program. Part-time tuition and fees vary according to program. *Required fees:* $930 full-time, $31 per credit hour part-time. *Room and board:* $4360; room only: $1700. Room and board charges vary according to board plan.

Financial Aid Of all full-time matriculated undergraduates who enrolled in 2011, 2,888 applied for aid, 2,462 were judged to have need, 898 had their need fully met. In 2011, 1388 non-need-based awards were made. *Average percent of need met:* 92%. *Average financial aid package:* $5290. *Average need-based loan:* $1855. *Average need-based gift aid:* $1645. *Average non-need-based aid:* $465. *Average indebtedness upon graduation:* $18,190. *Financial aid deadline:* 3/1.

Applying *Options:* deferred entrance. *Application fee:* $15. *Required:* high school transcript, minimum 2.0 GPA. *Application deadline:* rolling (freshmen). *Notification:* continuous (freshmen).

Freshman Application Contact Ms. Connie Phillips, Admission Counselor, Southwestern Oklahoma State University, 100 Campus Drive, Weatherford, OK 73096-3098. *Phone:* 580-774-3009. *Fax:* 580-774-3795. *E-mail:* ropers@swosu.edu. *Web site:* http://www.swosu.edu/.

Spartan College of Aeronautics and Technology
Tulsa, Oklahoma

Freshman Application Contact Mr. Mark Fowler, Vice President of Student Records and Finance, Spartan College of Aeronautics and Technology, 8820 East Pine Street, PO Box 582833, Tulsa, OK 74158-2833. *Phone:* 918-836-6886. *Toll-free phone:* 800-331-1204 (in-state); 800-331-124 (out-of-state). *Web site:* http://www.spartan.edu/.

University of Central Oklahoma
Edmond, Oklahoma

Freshman Application Contact Ms. Linda Lofton, Director, Admissions and Records Processing, University of Central Oklahoma, Office of Enrollment Services, 100 North University Drive, Box 151, Edmond, OK 73034-5209. *Phone:* 405-974-2338 Ext. 2338. *Fax:* 405-341-4964. *E-mail:* admituco@uco.edu. *Web site:* http://www.uco.edu/.

University of Oklahoma
Norman, Oklahoma

- **State-supported** university, founded 1890
- **Suburban** 3914-acre campus with easy access to Oklahoma City
- **Endowment** $804.9 million
- **Coed** 20,495 undergraduate students, 87% full-time, 50% women, 50% men
- **Moderately difficult** entrance level, 82% of applicants were admitted

Undergraduates 17,787 full-time, 2,708 part-time. Students come from 54 states and territories; 100 other countries; 32% are from out of state; 5% Black or African American, non-Hispanic/Latino; 6% Hispanic/Latino; 6% Asian, non-Hispanic/Latino; 0.2% Native Hawaiian or other Pacific Islander, non-Hispanic/Latino; 5% American Indian or Alaska Native, non-Hispanic/Latino; 4% Two or more races, non-Hispanic/Latino; 7% Race/ethnicity unknown; 4% international; 7% transferred in; 35% live on campus. *Retention:* 85% of full-time freshmen returned.

Freshmen *Admission:* 11,456 applied, 9,377 admitted, 4,053 enrolled. *Average high school GPA:* 3.63. *Test scores:* SAT critical reading scores over 500: 81%; SAT math scores over 500: 89%; ACT scores over 18: 99%; SAT critical reading scores over 600: 42%; SAT math scores over 600: 50%; ACT scores over 24: 72%; SAT critical reading scores over 700: 15%; SAT math scores over 700: 14%; ACT scores over 30: 20%.

Faculty *Total:* 1,374, 84% full-time, 80% with terminal degrees. *Student/faculty ratio:* 18:1.

Academics *Calendar:* semesters. *Degrees:* bachelor's, master's, doctoral, postbachelor's, and first professional certificates. *Special study options:* academic remediation for entering students, accelerated degree program, adult/continuing education programs, advanced placement credit, cooperative education, distance learning, double majors, English as a second language, external degree program, freshman honors college, honors programs, independent study, internships, off-campus study, part-time degree program, services for LD students, student-designed majors, study abroad, summer session for

credit. *ROTC:* Army (b), Navy (b), Air Force (b). *Unusual degree programs:* 3-2 business administration; engineering; English, mathematics/biostatistics, computer science.

Computers on Campus 4,500 computers/terminals and 2,200 ports are available on campus for general student use. Students can access the following: campus intranet, computer help desk, free student e-mail accounts, online (class) grades, online (class) registration, online (class) schedules. Campuswide network is available. 100% of college-owned or -operated housing units are wired for high-speed Internet access. Wireless service is available via entire campus.

Student Life *Housing:* on-campus residence required for freshman year. *Options:* coed, men-only, women-only, disabled students. Campus housing is university owned. Freshman campus housing is guaranteed. *Activities and organizations:* drama/theater group, student-run newspaper, radio and television station, choral group, marching band, Campus Activities Council, University of Oklahoma Student Association, OU Cousins, Fraternities/Sororities, The Big Event, national fraternities, national sororities. *Campus security:* 24-hour emergency response devices and patrols, student patrols, late-night transport/escort service, controlled dormitory access, crime prevention programs, police bicycle patrols, self-defense classes. *Student services:* health clinic, personal/psychological counseling, women's center, legal services.

Athletics Member NCAA. All Division I except football (Division I-A). *Intercollegiate sports:* baseball M(s), basketball M(s)/W(s), cheerleading M(s)/W(s), crew W(s), cross-country running M(s)/W(s), golf M(s)/W(s), gymnastics M(s)/W(s), soccer W(s), softball W(s), tennis M(s)/W(s), track and field M(s)/W(s), volleyball W(s), wrestling M(s). *Intramural sports:* badminton M/W, basketball M/W, crew M(c)/W(c), equestrian sports M(c)/W(c), field hockey M(c)/W(c), golf M/W, ice hockey M(c), lacrosse M(c)/W(c), racquetball M/W, rugby M(c)/W(c), sailing M(c)/W(c), soccer M, swimming and diving M/W, table tennis M/W, tennis M/W, ultimate Frisbee M(c)/W(c), volleyball M/W, water polo M/W.

Standardized Tests *Required:* SAT or ACT (for admission).

Costs (2011–12) *Tuition:* state resident $3849 full-time, $128 per credit hour part-time; nonresident $14,802 full-time, $493 per credit hour part-time. Full-time tuition and fees vary according to course load, location, program, and reciprocity agreements. Part-time tuition and fees vary according to course load, location, program, and reciprocity agreements. No tuition increase for student's term of enrollment. *Required fees:* $3276 full-time, $101 per credit hour part-time, $127 per term part-time. *Room and board:* $8060; room only: $4412. Room and board charges vary according to board plan and housing facility. *Payment plans:* tuition prepayment, installment. *Waivers:* senior citizens and employees or children of employees.

Financial Aid Of all full-time matriculated undergraduates who enrolled in 2010, 10,686 applied for aid, 8,345 were judged to have need, 6,855 had their need fully met. 545 Federal Work-Study jobs (averaging $2991). In 2010, 1849 non-need-based awards were made. *Average percent of need met:* 85%. *Average financial aid package:* $11,603. *Average need-based loan:* $4179. *Average need-based gift aid:* $5920. *Average non-need-based aid:* $2032. *Average indebtedness upon graduation:* $23,707.

Applying *Options:* electronic application. *Application fee:* $40. *Required:* high school transcript, 15 specified curricular units. *Application deadlines:* 4/1 (freshmen), 4/1 (out-of-state freshmen), 4/1 (transfers). *Notification:* continuous (freshmen), continuous (out-of-state freshmen), continuous (transfers).

Freshman Application Contact Mr. Andy Roop, Executive Director of Recruitment Services, University of Oklahoma, 550 Parrington Oval, Norman, OK 73019-3032. *Phone:* 405-325-2151. *Toll-free phone:* 800-234-6868. *Fax:* 405-325-7478. *E-mail:* ou-pss@ou.edu. *Web site:* http://www.ou.edu/.

University of Oklahoma Health Sciences Center

Oklahoma City, Oklahoma

- **State-supported** upper-level, founded 1890, part of University of Oklahoma
- **Urban** 200-acre campus with easy access to Oklahoma City
- **Endowment** $1.2 billion
- **Coed** 925 undergraduate students, 93% full-time, 89% women, 11% men

Undergraduates 864 full-time, 61 part-time. Students come from 41 states and territories; 27 other countries; 13% are from out of state; 1% Black or African American, non-Hispanic/Latino; 1% Hispanic/Latino; 3% Asian, non-Hispanic/Latino; 3% American Indian or Alaska Native, non-Hispanic/Latino; 2% Two or more races, non-Hispanic/Latino; 29% Race/ethnicity unknown; 0.9% international; 37% transferred in; 17% live on campus.

Faculty *Total:* 444, 74% full-time, 75% with terminal degrees. *Student/faculty ratio:* 10:1.

Academics *Calendar:* semesters. *Degrees:* bachelor's, master's, doctoral, post-master's, postbachelor's, and first professional certificates. *Special study options:* advanced placement credit, distance learning, honors programs,

internships, part-time degree program, summer session for credit. *ROTC:* Army (c), Air Force (c).

Computers on Campus 140 computers/terminals are available on campus for general student use. Students can access the following: campus intranet, computer help desk, free student e-mail accounts, online (class) grades, online (class) registration, online (class) schedules, online bursar bill and payment. Campuswide network is available. 100% of college-owned or -operated housing units are wired for high-speed Internet access. Wireless service is available via classrooms, computer centers, computer labs, learning centers, libraries, student centers.

Student Life *Housing options:* coed, disabled students. Campus housing is university owned. *Activities and organizations:* student-run newspaper, Health Sciences Center Student Association, College of Nursing Student Association, College of Medicine Student Association, Pharmacy Student Counsel, College of Allied Health Student Association. *Campus security:* 24-hour emergency response devices and patrols, late-night transport/escort service. *Student services:* health clinic, personal/psychological counseling, women's center.

Costs (2011–12) *Tuition:* state resident $3849 full-time, $128 per credit hour part-time; nonresident $14,802 full-time, $493 per credit hour part-time. Full-time tuition and fees vary according to course load, degree level, program, and student level. Part-time tuition and fees vary according to course load, degree level, program, and student level. *Required fees:* $2080 full-time, $53 per credit hour part-time, $238 per term part-time. *Payment plan:* installment. *Waivers:* employees or children of employees.

Applying *Options:* electronic application, deferred entrance. *Application deadline:* rolling (transfers). *Notification:* continuous (transfers).

Application Contact University of Oklahoma Health Sciences Center, PO Box 26901, Oklahoma City, OK 73190. *Phone:* 405-271-2359 Ext. 48916. *Web site:* http://www.ouhsc.edu/.

University of Phoenix–Oklahoma City Campus

Oklahoma City, Oklahoma

Freshman Application Contact Marc Booker, Sr. Director, Office of Admissions and Evaluation, University of Phoenix–Oklahoma City Campus, 4035 South Riverpoint Parkway, Mail Stop CF-L101, Phoenix, AZ 85040-1958. *Phone:* 602-557-4609. *Toll-free phone:* 866-766-0766. *Fax:* 480-643-1156. *Web site:* http://www.phoenix.edu/.

University of Phoenix–Tulsa Campus

Tulsa, Oklahoma

Freshman Application Contact Marc Booker, Sr. Director, Office of Admissions and Evaluation, University of Phoenix–Tulsa Campus, 4615 East Elwood Street, Mail Stop AA-K101, Phoenix, AZ 85040-1958. *Phone:* 602-557-4609. *Toll-free phone:* 866-766-0766. *Fax:* 480-643-1156. *Web site:* http://www.phoenix.edu/.

University of Science and Arts of Oklahoma

Chickasha, Oklahoma

- **State-supported** 4-year, founded 1908, part of Oklahoma State Regents for Higher Education
- **Small-town** 75-acre campus with easy access to Oklahoma City
- **Endowment** $8.3 million
- **Coed** 1,033 undergraduate students, 87% full-time, 62% women, 38% men
- **Moderately difficult** entrance level, 27% of applicants were admitted

Undergraduates 895 full-time, 138 part-time. Students come from 23 states and territories; 17 other countries; 8% are from out of state; 5% Black or African American, non-Hispanic/Latino; 5% Hispanic/Latino; 0.8% Asian, non-Hispanic/Latino; 13% American Indian or Alaska Native, non-Hispanic/Latino; 5% international; 15% transferred in; 52% live on campus. *Retention:* 63% of full-time freshmen returned.

Freshmen *Admission:* 866 applied, 236 admitted, 207 enrolled. *Average high school GPA:* 3.4. *Test scores:* ACT scores over 18: 95%; ACT scores over 24: 44%; ACT scores over 30: 8%.

Faculty *Total:* 87, 62% full-time, 59% with terminal degrees. *Student/faculty ratio:* 14:1.

Academics *Calendar:* trimesters. *Degree:* bachelor's. *Special study options:* academic remediation for entering students, accelerated degree program, advanced placement credit, double majors, independent study, internships, off-campus study, part-time degree program, services for LD students, student-designed majors, summer session for credit.

Computers on Campus 175 computers/terminals are available on campus for general student use. Students can access the following: computer help desk, free student e-mail accounts, online (class) schedules, personal Web space. Campuswide network is available. 100% of college-owned or -operated housing units are wired for high-speed Internet access. Wireless service is available via entire campus.

Student Life *Housing:* on-campus residence required for freshman year. *Options:* coed. Campus housing is university owned and is provided by a third party. Freshman campus housing is guaranteed. *Activities and organizations:* drama/theater group, student-run newspaper, television station, choral group, Student Activities Council, Volunteer Action Council, Baptist Student Union, Intertribal Heritage Club, Psychology Club, national fraternities. *Campus security:* 24-hour emergency response devices and patrols, controlled dormitory access. *Student services:* health clinic, personal/psychological counseling.

Athletics Member NAIA. *Intercollegiate sports:* baseball M(s), basketball M(s)/W(s), cheerleading M(s)/W(s), soccer M(s)/W(s), softball W(s). *Intramural sports:* basketball M/W, football M/W, golf M/W, softball M/W, volleyball M/W.

Standardized Tests *Required:* SAT or ACT (for admission).

Costs (2011–12) *Tuition:* state resident $3870 full-time, $129 per credit hour part-time; nonresident $10,830 full-time, $361 per credit hour part-time. No tuition increase for student's term of enrollment. *Required fees:* $1170 full-time, $39 per credit hour part-time. *Room and board:* $4990; room only: $2600. Room and board charges vary according to board plan and housing facility. *Payment plan:* installment. *Waivers:* senior citizens and employees or children of employees.

Financial Aid Of all full-time matriculated undergraduates who enrolled in 2011, 712 applied for aid, 611 were judged to have need, 81 had their need fully met. 170 Federal Work-Study jobs (averaging $1561). In 2011, 107 non-need-based awards were made. *Average percent of need met:* 67%. *Average financial aid package:* $9088. *Average need-based loan:* $2989. *Average need-based gift aid:* $7161. *Average non-need-based aid:* $1750. *Average indebtedness upon graduation:* $17,757.

Applying *Options:* electronic application, deferred entrance. *Application fee:* $25. *Required for some:* high school transcript, minimum 3.0 GPA, graduation in top 25% of high school class. *Recommended:* graduation in top 25% of high school class. *Application deadlines:* 9/2 (freshmen), 9/2 (out-of-state freshmen), 9/2 (transfers). *Notification:* continuous until 1/2 (freshmen), continuous until 1/2 (out-of-state freshmen), continuous (transfers).

Freshman Application Contact Ms. Kellee Johnson, Director of Admissions, University of Science and Arts of Oklahoma, 1727 West Alabama, Chickasha,

OK 73018-5322. *Phone:* 405-574-1357. *Toll-free phone:* 800-933-8726. *Fax:* 405-574-1220. *E-mail:* usao-admissions@usao.edu. *Web site:* http://www.usao.edu/.

University of Tulsa
Tulsa, Oklahoma

- **Independent** university, founded 1894, affiliated with Presbyterian Church (U.S.A.)
- **Urban** 209-acre campus with easy access to Oklahoma City
- **Endowment** $817.3 million
- **Coed** 3,004 undergraduate students, 96% full-time, 45% women, 55% men
- **Very difficult** entrance level, 41% of applicants were admitted

Undergraduates 2,875 full-time, 129 part-time. Students come from 41 states and territories; 55 other countries; 44% are from out of state; 6% Black or African American, non-Hispanic/Latino; 4% Hispanic/Latino; 3% Asian, non-Hispanic/Latino; 4% American Indian or Alaska Native, non-Hispanic/Latino; 2% Two or more races, non-Hispanic/Latino; 2% Race/ethnicity unknown; 18% international; 4% transferred in; 74% live on campus. *Retention:* 86% of full-time freshmen returned.

Freshmen *Admission:* 6,257 applied, 2,564 admitted, 617 enrolled. *Average high school GPA:* 3.78. *Test scores:* SAT critical reading scores over 500: 92%; SAT math scores over 500: 91%; ACT scores over 18: 100%; SAT critical reading scores over 600: 61%; SAT math scores over 600: 67%; ACT scores over 24: 80%; SAT critical reading scores over 700: 24%; SAT math scores over 700: 23%; ACT scores over 30: 37%.

Faculty *Total:* 412, 76% full-time, 96% with terminal degrees. *Student/faculty ratio:* 11:1.

Academics *Calendar:* semesters. *Degrees:* bachelor's, master's, doctoral, postbachelor's, and first professional certificates. *Special study options:* accelerated degree program, adult/continuing education programs, advanced placement credit, double majors, English as a second language, honors programs, independent study, internships, part-time degree program, services for LD students, student-designed majors, study abroad, summer session for credit. *ROTC:* Air Force (c). *Unusual degree programs:* 3-2 business administration.

Computers on Campus 900 computers/terminals are available on campus for general student use. Students can access the following: campus intranet, computer help desk, free student e-mail accounts, online (class) grades, online (class) registration, online (class) schedules. Campuswide network is available.

100% of college-owned or -operated housing units are wired for high-speed Internet access. Wireless service is available via entire campus.
Student Life *Housing:* on-campus residence required through sophomore year. *Options:* coed, men-only, women-only, disabled students. Campus housing is university owned. Freshman campus housing is guaranteed. *Activities and organizations:* drama/theater group, student-run newspaper, radio and television station, choral group, marching band, Student Association, Residence Hall Association, Pre-Professional organizations, Intramural sports, Greek life, national fraternities, national sororities. *Campus security:* 24-hour emergency response devices and patrols, late-night transport/escort service, controlled dormitory access. *Student services:* health clinic, personal/psychological counseling, women's center.
Athletics Member NCAA. All Division I except football (Division I-A). *Intercollegiate sports:* basketball M(s)/W(s), crew W(s), cross-country running M(s)/W(s), golf M(s)/W(s), soccer M(s)/W(s), softball W(s), tennis M(s)/W(s), track and field M(s)/W(s), volleyball W(s). *Intramural sports:* badminton M/W, basketball M/W, bowling M/W, crew M(c), cross-country running M/W, fencing M(c)/W(c), football M/W, golf M/W, racquetball M/W, rugby M(c), soccer M/W, softball M/W, squash M/W, swimming and diving M/W, table tennis M/W, tennis M/W, track and field M/W, volleyball M/W, water polo M/W, weight lifting M/W.
Standardized Tests *Required:* SAT or ACT (for admission).
Costs (2011–12) *One-time required fee:* $425. *Comprehensive fee:* $40,640 includes full-time tuition ($30,866), mandatory fees ($260), and room and board ($9514). Full-time tuition and fees vary according to course load. Part-time tuition: $1108 per credit. Part-time tuition and fees vary according to course load. *College room only:* $5260. Room and board charges vary according to board plan and housing facility. *Payment plans:* tuition prepayment, installment. *Waivers:* employees or children of employees.
Financial Aid Of all full-time matriculated undergraduates who enrolled in 2011, 2,499 applied for aid, 1,220 were judged to have need, 508 had their need fully met. In 2011, 1080 non-need-based awards were made. *Average percent of need met:* 80%. *Average financial aid package:* $27,670. *Average need-based loan:* $5202. *Average need-based gift aid:* $6372. *Average non-need-based aid:* $15,158. *Average indebtedness upon graduation:* $36,470.
Applying *Options:* electronic application, early admission, early action, deferred entrance. *Application fee:* $35. *Required:* essay or personal statement, high school transcript, 1 letter of recommendation, interview. *Recommended:* minimum 3.0 GPA. *Application deadlines:* rolling (freshmen), rolling (out-of-state freshmen), rolling (transfers), 11/1 (early action). *Notification:* continuous (freshmen), continuous (out-of-state freshmen), continuous (transfers), 11/22 (early action).
Freshman Application Contact Mr. Earl Johnson, Dean of Admission, University of Tulsa, 800 South Tucker Drive, Tulsa, OK 74104. *Phone:* 918-631-2307. *Toll-free phone:* 800-331-3050. *Fax:* 918-631-5003. *E-mail:* admission@utulsa.edu. *Web site:* http://www.utulsa.edu/.

See page 731 for display ad and page 1722 for the College Close-Up.

OREGON

The Art Institute of Portland
Portland, Oregon

- **Proprietary** 4-year, founded 1963, part of Education Management Corporation
- **Urban** campus
- **Coed**

Academics *Calendar:* quarters. *Degrees:* diplomas, associate, and bachelor's.
Costs (2011–12) *Tuition:* Tuition cost varies by program. Prospective students should contact the school for current tuition costs. Other charges include a starting kit for all first-quarter students. Kits vary in price, depending on the program of study.
Freshman Application Contact The Art Institute of Portland, 1122 NW Davis Street, Portland, OR 97209. *Phone:* 503-228-6528. *Toll-free phone:* 888-228-6528. *Web site:* http://www.artinstitutes.edu/portland/.

See page 1122 for the College Close-Up.

Birthingway College of Midwifery
Portland, Oregon

Director of Admissions Director of Admission, Birthingway College of Midwifery, 12113 SE Foster Road, Portland, OR 97299. *Phone:* 503-760-3131. *E-mail:* info@birthingway.edu. *Web site:* http://www.birthingway.edu/.

Concordia University
Portland, Oregon

Freshman Application Contact Ms. Bobi Swan, Dean of Admission, Concordia University, 2811 Northeast Holman, Portland, OR 97211-6099. *Phone:* 503-493-6526. *Toll-free phone:* 800-321-9371. *Fax:* 503-280-8531. *E-mail:* admissions@cu-portland.edu. *Web site:* http://www.cu-portland.edu/.

Corban University
Salem, Oregon

- **Independent Christian** comprehensive, founded 1935
- **Suburban** 145-acre campus with easy access to Portland
- **Endowment** $1.6 million
- **Coed** 985 undergraduate students, 87% full-time, 63% women, 37% men
- **Moderately difficult** entrance level, 43% of applicants were admitted

Undergraduates 854 full-time, 131 part-time. Students come from 20 states and territories; 4 other countries; 39% are from out of state; 2% Black or African American, non-Hispanic/Latino; 5% Hispanic/Latino; 4% Asian, non-Hispanic/Latino; 2% Native Hawaiian or other Pacific Islander, non-Hispanic/Latino; 3% American Indian or Alaska Native, non-Hispanic/Latino; 0.2% Two or more races, non-Hispanic/Latino; 5% Race/ethnicity unknown; 2% international; 6% transferred in; 51% live on campus. *Retention:* 78% of full-time freshmen returned.
Freshmen *Admission:* 2,551 applied, 1,104 admitted, 275 enrolled. *Average high school GPA:* 3.58. *Test scores:* SAT critical reading scores over 500: 74%; SAT math scores over 500: 61%; SAT writing scores over 500: 62%; ACT scores over 18: 93%; SAT critical reading scores over 600: 29%; SAT math scores over 600: 21%; SAT writing scores over 600: 19%; ACT scores over 24: 56%; SAT critical reading scores over 700: 5%; SAT math scores over 700: 4%; SAT writing scores over 700: 2%; ACT scores over 30: 5%.
Faculty *Total:* 117, 40% full-time, 32% with terminal degrees. *Student/faculty ratio:* 14:1.
Academics *Calendar:* semesters. *Degrees:* certificates, associate, bachelor's, master's, doctoral, and postbachelor's certificates. *Special study options:* accelerated degree program, adult/continuing education programs, advanced placement credit, cooperative education, distance learning, double majors, freshman honors college, honors programs, independent study, internships, off-campus study, services for LD students, student-designed majors, study abroad, summer session for credit. *ROTC:* Army (c), Air Force (c).
Computers on Campus 64 computers/terminals are available on campus for general student use. Students can access the following: computer help desk, free student e-mail accounts, online (class) grades, online (class) schedules. Campuswide network is available. 100% of college-owned or -operated housing units are wired for high-speed Internet access. Wireless service is available via computer centers, computer labs, dorm rooms, learning centers, libraries, student centers.
Student Life *Housing:* on-campus residence required through sophomore year. *Options:* men-only, women-only, disabled students. Campus housing is university owned. Freshman campus housing is guaranteed. *Activities and organizations:* drama/theater group, student-run newspaper, choral group, Student Fellowship Groups, Poetry Club, Worship Teams, Drama Club, Westrek Hiking Club. *Campus security:* 24-hour emergency response devices and patrols, student patrols, late-night transport/escort service, controlled dormitory access. *Student services:* health clinic, personal/psychological counseling.
Athletics Member NAIA, NCCAA. *Intercollegiate sports:* baseball M(s), basketball M(s)/W(s), cross-country running M(s)/W(s), golf M(s)/W(s), soccer M(s)/W(s), softball W(s), track and field M(s)/W(s), volleyball W(s). *Intramural sports:* basketball M/W, football M, soccer M/W, softball W, volleyball M/W.
Standardized Tests *Required:* SAT or ACT (for admission).
Costs (2011–12) *One-time required fee:* $100. *Comprehensive fee:* $33,425 includes full-time tuition ($24,975), mandatory fees ($470), and room and board ($7980). Full-time tuition and fees vary according to program and reciprocity agreements. Part-time tuition: $1041 per credit hour. Part-time tuition and fees vary according to course load, program, and reciprocity agreements. *Room and board:* Room and board charges vary according to board plan. *Payment plan:* installment. *Waivers:* senior citizens and employees or children of employees.
Financial Aid Of all full-time matriculated undergraduates who enrolled in 2011, 741 applied for aid, 699 were judged to have need, 71 had their need fully met. In 2011, 108 non-need-based awards were made. *Average percent of need met:* 63%. *Average financial aid package:* $18,670. *Average need-based loan:* $4273. *Average need-based gift aid:* $15,327. *Average non-need-based aid:* $7448. *Average indebtedness upon graduation:* $27,756.
Applying *Options:* electronic application. *Application fee:* $35. *Required:* essay or personal statement, high school transcript, minimum 2.7 GPA, 3 let-

ters of recommendation. *Application deadlines:* 8/1 (freshmen), 8/1 (transfers). *Notification:* continuous (freshmen).

Freshman Application Contact Ms. Heidi Stowman, Director of Admissions, Corban University, 5000 Deer Park Drive, SE, Salem, OR 97301-9392. *Phone:* 503-375-7115. *Toll-free phone:* 800-845-3005. *Fax:* 503-585-4316. *E-mail:* admissions@corban.edu. *Web site:* http://www.corban.edu/.

DeVry University

Portland, Oregon

Freshman Application Contact DeVry University, 9755 Southwest Barnes Road, Suite 150, Portland, OR 97225-6651. *Toll-free phone:* 866-338-7941. *Web site:* http://www.devry.edu/.

Eastern Oregon University

La Grande, Oregon

- **State-supported** comprehensive, founded 1929, part of Oregon University System
- **Rural** 121-acre campus
- **Coed** 3,900 undergraduate students, 61% full-time, 61% women, 39% men
- **Moderately difficult** entrance level, 65% of applicants were admitted

Undergraduates 2,392 full-time, 1,508 part-time. Students come from 49 states and territories; 20 other countries; 29% are from out of state; 2% Black or African American, non-Hispanic/Latino; 5% Hispanic/Latino; 2% Asian, non-Hispanic/Latino; 1% Native Hawaiian or other Pacific Islander, non-Hispanic/Latino; 2% American Indian or Alaska Native, non-Hispanic/Latino; 1% Two or more races, non-Hispanic/Latino; 5% Race/ethnicity unknown; 1% international; 13% transferred in; 12% live on campus. *Retention:* 72% of full-time freshmen returned.

Freshmen *Admission:* 1,296 applied, 843 admitted, 385 enrolled. *Average high school GPA:* 3.24. *Test scores:* SAT critical reading scores over 500: 46%; SAT math scores over 500: 43%; SAT writing scores over 500: 33%; ACT scores over 18: 84%; SAT critical reading scores over 600: 10%; SAT math scores over 600: 7%; SAT writing scores over 600: 6%; ACT scores over 24: 24%; SAT critical reading scores over 700: 1%; SAT math scores over 700: 1%.

Faculty *Total:* 128, 91% full-time, 78% with terminal degrees. *Student/faculty ratio:* 24:1.

Academics *Calendar:* quarters. *Degrees:* certificates, associate, bachelor's, and master's. *Special study options:* adult/continuing education programs, advanced placement credit, cooperative education, distance learning, double majors, external degree program, honors programs, independent study, internships, off-campus study, part-time degree program, services for LD students, student-designed majors, study abroad, summer session for credit. *ROTC:* Army (b). *Unusual degree programs:* 3-2 nursing with Oregon Health Sciences University; agriculture with Oregon State University.

Computers on Campus Students can access the following: free student e-mail accounts, online (class) grades, online (class) registration, online (class) schedules. Campuswide network is available. Wireless service is available via entire campus.

Student Life *Housing:* on-campus residence required for freshman year. *Options:* coed. Campus housing is university owned. *Activities and organizations:* drama/theater group, student-run newspaper, radio station, choral group, Outdoor Club, Island Magic, student radio station, intramurals, student government. *Campus security:* controlled dormitory access. *Student services:* health clinic, personal/psychological counseling, women's center.

Athletics Member NCAA, NAIA. All NCAA Division III. *Intercollegiate sports:* basketball M/W, cross-country running M/W, football M, skiing (cross-country) M(c)/W(c), skiing (downhill) M(c)/W(c), soccer W, track and field M/W, volleyball W. *Intramural sports:* basketball M/W, football M, racquetball M/W, soccer W, softball M/W, volleyball W.

Standardized Tests *Required:* SAT or ACT (for admission).

Costs (2011–12) *Tuition:* state resident $5603 full-time, $125 per credit hour part-time; nonresident $5603 full-time, $125 per credit hour part-time. Full-time tuition and fees vary according to course load and location. Part-time tuition and fees vary according to course load and location. *Required fees:* $1443 full-time. *Room and board:* $8100; room only: $4800. Room and board charges vary according to board plan and housing facility. *Waivers:* senior citizens and employees or children of employees.

Financial Aid Of all full-time matriculated undergraduates who enrolled in 2010, 1,988 applied for aid, 1,795 were judged to have need, 700 had their need fully met. In 2010, 25 non-need-based awards were made. *Average percent of need met:* 50%. *Average financial aid package:* $9242. *Average need-based loan:* $3693. *Average need-based gift aid:* $5308. *Average non-need-based aid:* $1204.

Applying *Options:* electronic application, early admission, early action, deferred entrance. *Required:* high school transcript, minimum 3.0 GPA. *Required for some:* essay or personal statement, 2 letters of recommendation. *Application deadlines:* 8/15 (freshmen), rolling (transfers), 12/1 (early action). *Notification:* continuous (freshmen), 1/15 (early action).

Freshman Application Contact Tyler Dubsky, Assistant Director of Admissions, Eastern Oregon University, Eastern Oregon University, La Grande, OR. *Phone:* 541-962-3085. *Toll-free phone:* 800-452-8639. *Fax:* 541-962-3418. *E-mail:* admissions@eou.edu. *Web site:* http://www.eou.edu/.

George Fox University

Newberg, Oregon

- **Independent Friends** university, founded 1891
- **Small-town** 108-acre campus with easy access to Portland
- **Endowment** $18.6 million
- **Coed** 2,177 undergraduate students, 87% full-time, 59% women, 41% men
- **Moderately difficult** entrance level, 80% of applicants were admitted

Undergraduates 1,900 full-time, 277 part-time. Students come from 34 states and territories; 28 other countries; 32% are from out of state; 2% Black or African American, non-Hispanic/Latino; 7% Hispanic/Latino; 4% Asian, non-Hispanic/Latino; 0.5% Native Hawaiian or other Pacific Islander, non-Hispanic/Latino; 0.9% American Indian or Alaska Native, non-Hispanic/Latino; 3% Two or more races, non-Hispanic/Latino; 5% Race/ethnicity unknown; 6% international; 5% transferred in; 54% live on campus. *Retention:* 80% of full-time freshmen returned.

Freshmen *Admission:* 2,547 applied, 2,028 admitted, 457 enrolled. *Average high school GPA:* 3.61. *Test scores:* SAT critical reading scores over 500: 74%; SAT math scores over 500: 73%; SAT writing scores over 500: 68%; ACT scores over 18: 91%; SAT critical reading scores over 600: 38%; SAT math scores over 600: 34%; SAT writing scores over 600: 28%; ACT scores over 24: 49%; SAT critical reading scores over 700: 7%; SAT math scores over 700: 3%; SAT writing scores over 700: 4%; ACT scores over 30: 10%.

Faculty *Total:* 388, 45% full-time, 50% with terminal degrees. *Student/faculty ratio:* 13:1.

Academics *Calendar:* semesters. *Degrees:* bachelor's, master's, doctoral, post-master's, and postbachelor's certificates. *Special study options:* academic remediation for entering students, accelerated degree program, adult/continuing education programs, advanced placement credit, distance learning, double majors, English as a second language, honors programs, independent study, internships, off-campus study, part-time degree program, services for LD students, student-designed majors, study abroad, summer session for credit. *ROTC:* Air Force (c). *Unusual degree programs:* 3-2 engineering.

Computers on Campus 130 computers/terminals are available on campus for general student use. Students can access the following: campus intranet, computer help desk, free student e-mail accounts, online (class) grades, online (class) registration, online (class) schedules, online acceptance of financial aid. Campuswide network is available. 100% of college-owned or -operated housing units are wired for high-speed Internet access. Wireless service is available via classrooms, computer centers, computer labs, dorm rooms, learning centers, libraries, student centers.

Student Life *Housing:* on-campus residence required through junior year. *Options:* men-only, women-only, disabled students. Campus housing is university owned. Freshman applicants given priority for college housing. *Activities and organizations:* drama/theater group, student-run newspaper, radio station, choral group, student government, Christian Ministries, Orientation Committee, Outdoor Club and Bruin Ambassadors, Blue Zone. *Campus security:* 24-hour emergency response devices and patrols, student patrols, late-night transport/escort service, controlled dormitory access, parking lot cameras, and video surveillance of key buildings. *Student services:* health clinic, personal/psychological counseling.

Athletics Member NCAA. All Division III. *Intercollegiate sports:* baseball M, basketball M/W, cross-country running M/W, football M, golf M/W, lacrosse W, soccer M/W, softball W, tennis M/W, track and field M/W, volleyball W. *Intramural sports:* badminton M/W, basketball M/W, football M/W, golf M/W, racquetball M/W, rock climbing M/W, soccer M/W, table tennis M/W, tennis M/W, volleyball M/W.

Standardized Tests *Required:* SAT or ACT (for admission).

Costs (2011–12) *Comprehensive fee:* $38,430 includes full-time tuition ($29,050), mandatory fees ($330), and room and board ($9050). Part-time tuition: $880 per semester hour. Part-time tuition and fees vary according to course load. *College room only:* $5300. Room and board charges vary according to board plan. *Payment plan:* installment. *Waivers:* senior citizens and employees or children of employees.

Financial Aid Of all full-time matriculated undergraduates who enrolled in 2011, 1,579 applied for aid, 1,459 were judged to have need, 515 had their need fully met. In 2011, 91 non-need-based awards were made. *Average per-*

cent of need met: 86%. *Average financial aid package:* $26,813. *Average need-based loan:* $3728. *Average need-based gift aid:* $9906. *Average non-need-based aid:* $7281. *Average indebtedness upon graduation:* $25,766.

Applying *Options:* electronic application, early action, deferred entrance. *Application fee:* $40. *Required:* essay or personal statement, high school transcript, 2 letters of recommendation. *Required for some:* interview. *Recommended:* minimum 2.6 GPA, interview. *Application deadlines:* rolling (freshmen), 6/1 (transfers), 12/1 (early action). *Notification:* continuous until 10/1 (freshmen), continuous (transfers), 12/15 (early action).

Freshman Application Contact Mr. Ryan Dougherty, Director of Undergraduate Admissions, George Fox University, 414 North Meridian Street, Newberg, OR 97132. *Phone:* 503-554-2240. *Toll-free phone:* 800-765-4369. *Fax:* 503-554-3110. *E-mail:* admissions@georgefox.edu. *Web site:* http://www.georgefox.edu/.

Gutenberg College
Eugene, Oregon

Freshman Application Contact Mr. Terry Stollar, Director of Admissions and Development, Gutenberg College, 1883 University Street, Eugene, OR 97403. *Phone:* 541-736-9071. *Fax:* 541-683-6997. *E-mail:* tstollar@gutenberg.edu. *Web site:* http://www.gutenberg.edu/.

ITT Technical Institute
Portland, Oregon

- **Proprietary** primarily 2-year, founded 1971, part of ITT Educational Services, Inc.
- **Urban** campus
- **Coed**
- **Minimally difficult** entrance level

Academics *Calendar:* quarters. *Degrees:* associate and bachelor's.

Student Life *Housing:* college housing not available.

Financial Aid Of all full-time matriculated undergraduates who enrolled in 2010, 15 Federal Work-Study jobs (averaging $5000).

Freshman Application Contact Director of Recruitment, ITT Technical Institute, 9500 Northeast Cascades Parkway, Portland, OR 97220. *Phone:* 503-255-6500. *Toll-free phone:* 800-234-5488. *Web site:* http://www.itt-tech.edu/.

ITT Technical Institute
Salem, Oregon

- **Proprietary** 4-year
- **Coed**
- **Minimally difficult** entrance level

Academics *Degrees:* associate and bachelor's.

Freshman Application Contact Director of Recruiting, ITT Technical Institute, 4825 Commercial Street SE, Suite 100, Salem, OR 97302-2177. *Phone:* 503-579-2300. *Toll-free phone:* 877-273-7397. *Web site:* http://www.itt-tech.edu/.

Lewis & Clark College
Portland, Oregon

- **Independent** comprehensive, founded 1867
- **Suburban** 137-acre campus with easy access to Portland
- **Endowment** $201.6 million
- **Coed** 2,141 undergraduate students, 99% full-time, 58% women, 42% men
- **Very difficult** entrance level, 66% of applicants were admitted

Undergraduates 2,111 full-time, 30 part-time. Students come from 51 states and territories; 46 other countries; 81% are from out of state; 2% Black or African American, non-Hispanic/Latino; 7% Hispanic/Latino; 4% Asian, non-Hispanic/Latino; 0.1% Native Hawaiian or other Pacific Islander, non-Hispanic/Latino; 0.8% American Indian or Alaska Native, non-Hispanic/Latino; 5% Two or more races, non-Hispanic/Latino; 14% Race/ethnicity unknown; 5% international; 2% transferred in; 65% live on campus. *Retention:* 88% of full-time freshmen returned.

Freshmen *Admission:* 5,950 applied, 3,928 admitted, 606 enrolled. *Average high school GPA:* 3.71. *Test scores:* SAT critical reading scores over 500: 97%; SAT math scores over 500: 97%; SAT writing scores over 500: 98%; ACT scores over 18: 100%; SAT critical reading scores over 600: 82%; SAT math scores over 600: 70%; SAT writing scores over 600: 74%; ACT scores over 24: 95%; SAT critical reading scores over 700: 31%; SAT math scores over 700: 15%; SAT writing scores over 700: 20%; ACT scores over 30: 38%.

Faculty *Total:* 374, 61% full-time, 81% with terminal degrees. *Student/faculty ratio:* 12:1.

Academics *Calendar:* semesters. *Degrees:* bachelor's, master's, doctoral, post-master's, and first professional certificates. *Special study options:* accel-

LEWIS & CLARK COLLEGE

For more information, contact:

Emily A. Decker
Office of Admissions
0615 SW Palatine Hill Road
Portland, Oregon 97219
E-mail: admiss@lclark.edu

www.lclark.edu

erated degree program, advanced placement credit, double majors, English as a second language, honors programs, independent study, internships, off-campus study, services for LD students, student-designed majors, study abroad, summer session for credit. *Unusual degree programs:* 3-2 engineering with Columbia University, Washington University in St. Louis, University of Southern California, Oregon Health Sciences University.

Computers on Campus Students can access the following: campus intranet, computer help desk, free student e-mail accounts, online (class) grades, online (class) registration, online (class) schedules. Campuswide network is available. 100% of college-owned or -operated housing units are wired for high-speed Internet access. Wireless service is available via classrooms, computer centers, computer labs, dorm rooms, learning centers, libraries, student centers.

Student Life *Housing:* on-campus residence required through sophomore year. *Options:* coed, women-only. Campus housing is university owned. Freshman campus housing is guaranteed. *Activities and organizations:* drama/theater group, student-run newspaper, radio and television station, choral group. *Campus security:* 24-hour emergency response devices and patrols, student patrols, late-night transport/escort service, controlled dormitory access. *Student services:* health clinic, personal/psychological counseling, women's center.

Athletics Member NCAA. All Division III. *Intercollegiate sports:* baseball M, basketball M/W, crew M/W, cross-country running M/W, football M, golf M/W, lacrosse M(c)/W(c), soccer M(c)/W, softball W, swimming and diving M/W, tennis M/W, track and field M/W, volleyball W. *Intramural sports:* badminton M/W, basketball M/W, cross-country running M/W, fencing M(c)/W(c), football M/W, rock climbing M(c)/W(c), rugby M(c)/W(c), sailing M(c)/W(c), skiing (cross-country) M/W, skiing (downhill) M/W, soccer W(c), softball M/W, swimming and diving M/W, table tennis M/W, tennis M/W, ultimate Frisbee M(c)/W(c), volleyball M/W, water polo M/W.

Standardized Tests *Required:* SAT or ACT, or academic portfolio. Students may apply via Portfolio Path where test scores are optional (for admission). *Required for some:* SAT or ACT (for admission).

Costs (2012–13) *Comprehensive fee:* $50,688 includes full-time tuition ($39,970), mandatory fees ($360), and room and board ($10,358). *College room only:* $5450. Room and board charges vary according to board plan and housing facility. *Payment plan:* installment. *Waivers:* employees or children of employees.

Financial Aid Of all full-time matriculated undergraduates who enrolled in 2011, 1,383 applied for aid, 1,240 were judged to have need, 466 had their need fully met. In 2011, 314 non-need-based awards were made. *Average percent of need met:* 89%. *Average financial aid package:* $31,841. *Average*

need-based loan: $4980. *Average need-based gift aid:* $26,166. *Average non-need-based aid:* $10,631. *Average indebtedness upon graduation:* $22,956.

Applying *Options:* electronic application, early action, deferred entrance. *Application fee:* $50. *Required:* essay or personal statement, high school transcript, minimum 2.0 GPA, "portfolio path" applicants submit samples of writing. *Required for some:* 4 letters of recommendation. *Recommended:* minimum 3.0 GPA, interview. *Application deadlines:* 1/15 (freshmen), 1/15 (out-of-state freshmen), rolling (transfers), 11/1 (early action). *Notification:* 4/1 (freshmen), 4/1 (out-of-state freshmen), continuous (transfers), 1/1 (early action).

Freshman Application Contact Lisa Meyer, Dean of Admissions and Financial Aid, Lewis & Clark College, 0615 SW Palatine Hill Road, Portland, OR 97219. *Phone:* 503-768-7040. *Toll-free phone:* 800-444-4111. *Fax:* 503-768-7055. *E-mail:* admissions@lclark.edu. *Web site:* http://www.lclark.edu/.

See page 1406 for the College Close-Up.

Linfield College
McMinnville, Oregon

- **Independent American Baptist Churches in the USA** 4-year, founded 1849
- **Small-town** 193-acre campus with easy access to Portland
- **Endowment** $83.9 million
- **Coed** 1,727 undergraduate students, 98% full-time, 61% women, 39% men
- **Moderately difficult** entrance level, 76% of applicants were admitted

Undergraduates 1,692 full-time, 35 part-time. Students come from 20 states and territories; 24 other countries; 45% are from out of state; 2% Black or African American, non-Hispanic/Latino; 7% Hispanic/Latino; 7% Asian, non-Hispanic/Latino; 0.2% Native Hawaiian or other Pacific Islander, non-Hispanic/Latino; 1% American Indian or Alaska Native, non-Hispanic/Latino; 6% Two or more races, non-Hispanic/Latino; 6% Race/ethnicity unknown; 4% international; 3% transferred in; 74% live on campus. *Retention:* 84% of full-time freshmen returned.

Freshmen *Admission:* 2,376 applied, 1,811 admitted, 459 enrolled. *Average high school GPA:* 3.6. *Test scores:* SAT critical reading scores over 500: 71%; SAT math scores over 500: 79%; SAT writing scores over 500: 68%; ACT scores over 18: 97%; SAT critical reading scores over 600: 29%; SAT math scores over 600: 32%; SAT writing scores over 600: 23%; ACT scores over 24:

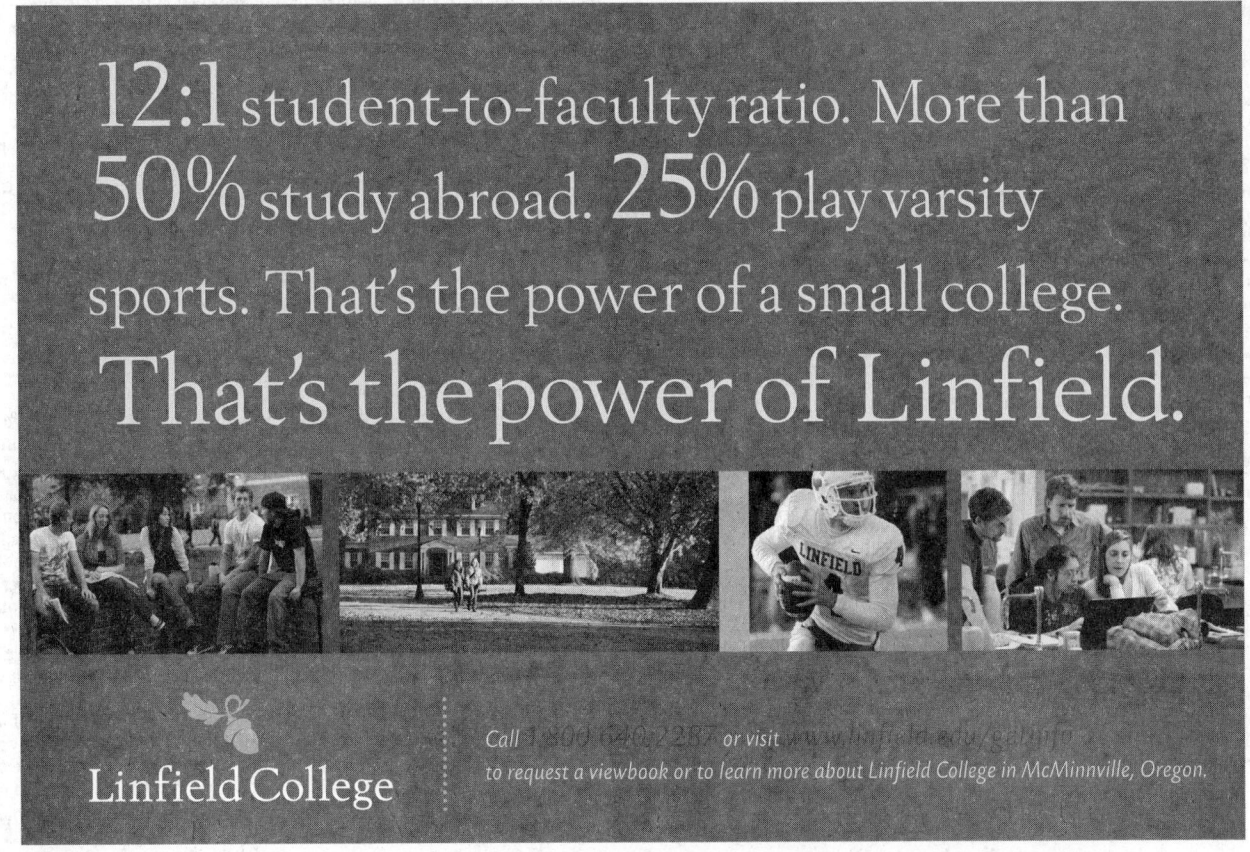

63%; SAT critical reading scores over 700: 3%; SAT math scores over 700: 4%; SAT writing scores over 700: 3%; ACT scores over 30: 14%.

Faculty *Total:* 194, 60% full-time, 69% with terminal degrees. *Student/faculty ratio:* 12:1.

Academics *Calendar:* 4-1-4. *Degrees:* bachelor's and postbachelor's certificates. *Special study options:* accelerated degree program, adult/continuing education programs, advanced placement credit, distance learning, double majors, English as a second language, external degree program, independent study, internships, off-campus study, part-time degree program, services for LD students, student-designed majors, study abroad, summer session for credit. *ROTC:* Air Force (c). *Unusual degree programs:* 3-2 engineering with Washington State University, Oregon State University, University of Southern California.

Computers on Campus 250 computers/terminals are available on campus for general student use. Students can access the following: computer help desk, free student e-mail accounts, online (class) grades, online (class) registration, online (class) schedules. Campuswide network is available. 100% of college-owned or -operated housing units are wired for high-speed Internet access. Wireless service is available via classrooms, computer centers, computer labs, dorm rooms, learning centers, libraries, student centers.

Student Life *Housing:* on-campus residence required through junior year. *Options:* coed, men-only, women-only, disabled students. Campus housing is university owned. Freshman campus housing is guaranteed. *Activities and organizations:* drama/theater group, student-run newspaper, radio station, choral group, Fellowship of Christian Athletes, Linfield Ultimate Players Association, Hawaiian Club, International Club, Outdoor Club, national fraternities, national sororities. *Campus security:* 24-hour emergency response devices and patrols, late-night transport/escort service, controlled dormitory access. *Student services:* health clinic, personal/psychological counseling.

Athletics Member NCAA. All Division III. *Intercollegiate sports:* baseball M, basketball M/W, cross-country running M/W, football M, golf M/W, lacrosse W, soccer M/W, softball W, swimming and diving M/W, tennis M/W, track and field M/W, volleyball W. *Intramural sports:* basketball M/W, bowling M/W, soccer M/W, softball M/W, volleyball M/W.

Standardized Tests *Required:* SAT or ACT (for admission).

Costs (2011–12) *Comprehensive fee:* $41,506 includes full-time tuition ($32,100), mandatory fees ($316), and room and board ($9090). Full-time tuition and fees vary according to location. Part-time tuition: $1000 per semester hour. Part-time tuition and fees vary according to course load and location. *College room only:* $4980. Room and board charges vary according to board plan, housing facility, and location. *Payment plan:* installment. *Waivers:* senior citizens and employees or children of employees.

Financial Aid Of all full-time matriculated undergraduates who enrolled in 2011, 1,370 applied for aid, 1,201 were judged to have need, 239 had their need fully met. 889 Federal Work-Study jobs (averaging $2337). 571 state and other part-time jobs (averaging $2253). In 2011, 334 non-need-based awards were made. *Average percent of need met:* 83%. *Average financial aid package:* $24,767. *Average need-based loan:* $4799. *Average need-based gift aid:* $10,816. *Average non-need-based aid:* $13,421. *Average indebtedness upon graduation:* $29,754.

Applying *Options:* electronic application, early action, deferred entrance. *Required:* essay or personal statement, high school transcript, 1 letter of recommendation. *Recommended:* interview. *Application deadlines:* 2/15 (freshmen), 4/15 (transfers), 11/15 (early action). *Notification:* 4/1 (freshmen), 5/15 (transfers), 1/15 (early action).

Freshman Application Contact Ms. Lisa Knodle-Bragiel, Director of Admission, Linfield College, 900 SE Baker Street, McMinnville, OR 97128. *Phone:* 503-883-2213. *Toll-free phone:* 800-640-2287. *Fax:* 503-883-2472. *E-mail:* admission@linfield.edu. *Web site:* http://www.linfield.edu/.

See page 735 for display ad and page 1416 for the College Close-Up.

Marylhurst University
Marylhurst, Oregon

- **Independent Roman Catholic** comprehensive, founded 1893
- **Suburban** 63-acre campus with easy access to Portland
- **Endowment** $15.2 million
- **Coed, primarily women** 839 undergraduate students, 27% full-time, 71% women, 29% men
- **Noncompetitive** entrance level, 70% of applicants were admitted

Undergraduates 228 full-time, 611 part-time. Students come from 33 states and territories; 15 other countries; 23% are from out of state; 4% Black or African American, non-Hispanic/Latino; 5% Hispanic/Latino; 3% Asian, non-Hispanic/Latino; 0.8% Native Hawaiian or other Pacific Islander, non-Hispanic/Latino; 0.5% American Indian or Alaska Native, non-Hispanic/Latino; 3% Two or more races, non-Hispanic/Latino; 3% Race/ethnicity unknown; 7% international; 16% transferred in. *Retention:* 66% of full-time freshmen returned.

Freshmen *Admission:* 33 applied, 23 admitted, 15 enrolled.

Faculty *Total:* 263, 21% full-time, 34% with terminal degrees. *Student/faculty ratio:* 7:1.

Academics *Calendar:* quarters. *Degrees:* bachelor's, master's, post-master's, and postbachelor's certificates. *Special study options:* accelerated degree program, adult/continuing education programs, advanced placement credit, distance learning, double majors, English as a second language, independent study, internships, off-campus study, part-time degree program, services for LD students, student-designed majors, study abroad, summer session for credit.

Computers on Campus 50 computers/terminals are available on campus for general student use. Students can access the following: campus intranet, computer help desk, online (class) grades, online (class) registration, online (class) schedules. Campuswide network is available. Wireless service is available via entire campus.

Student Life *Housing:* college housing not available. *Activities and organizations:* student-run newspaper, choral group, Marylhurst's Writer's Club, Marylhurst Gerontology Association, Solutions: Marylhurst Mediation Resource, Marylhurst S.A.F.E. Community: Sexual Acceptance for Everyone, LABY: Labyrinth Alliance Balances You. *Campus security:* security is available during campus hours. *Student services:* personal/psychological counseling.

Costs (2011–12) *Tuition:* $18,405 full-time, $409 per credit hour part-time. Full-time tuition and fees vary according to course load and program. Part-time tuition and fees vary according to course load and program. *Payment plan:* installment. *Waivers:* senior citizens and employees or children of employees.

Financial Aid Of all full-time matriculated undergraduates who enrolled in 2010, 339 applied for aid, 312 were judged to have need, 8 had their need fully met. 41 Federal Work-Study jobs (averaging $3955). In 2010, 30 non-need-based awards were made. *Average percent of need met:* 48%. *Average financial aid package:* $10,399. *Average need-based loan:* $4510. *Average need-based gift aid:* $7613. *Average non-need-based aid:* $1713. *Average indebtedness upon graduation:* $10,278.

Applying *Options:* electronic application, deferred entrance. *Application fee:* $40. *Required:* essay or personal statement, high school transcript, minimum 2.5 GPA. *Required for some:* 2 letters of recommendation, interview. *Application deadlines:* rolling (freshmen), rolling (transfers). *Notification:* continuous (freshmen), continuous (transfers).

Freshman Application Contact Chris Sweet, Director of Admissions, Marylhurst University, 17600 Pacific Highway, PO Box 261, Marylhurst, OR 97036-0261. *Phone:* 503-699-6267. *Toll-free phone:* 800-634-9982. *Fax:* 503-699-6320. *E-mail:* admissions@marylhurst.edu. *Web site:* http://www.marylhurst.edu/.

Mount Angel Seminary
Saint Benedict, Oregon

Director of Admissions Registrar/Admissions Officer, Mount Angel Seminary, Saint Benedict, OR 97373. *Phone:* 503-845-3951 Ext. 14. *E-mail:* admissions@mtangel.edu. *Web site:* http://www.mountangelabbey.org/seminary/.

Multnomah University
Portland, Oregon

- **Independent interdenominational** comprehensive, founded 1936
- **Urban** 22-acre campus
- **Endowment** $6.6 million
- **Coed** 583 undergraduate students, 84% full-time, 42% women, 58% men
- **Moderately difficult** entrance level, 73% of applicants were admitted

Undergraduates 490 full-time, 93 part-time. Students come from 25 states and territories; 4 other countries; 49% are from out of state; 3% Black or African American, non-Hispanic/Latino; 5% Hispanic/Latino; 2% Asian, non-Hispanic/Latino; 0.5% Native Hawaiian or other Pacific Islander, non-Hispanic/Latino; 0.5% American Indian or Alaska Native, non-Hispanic/Latino; 3% Two or more races, non-Hispanic/Latino; 4% Race/ethnicity unknown; 0.7% international; 12% transferred in; 48% live on campus. *Retention:* 62% of full-time freshmen returned.

Freshmen *Admission:* 135 applied, 99 admitted, 65 enrolled. *Average high school GPA:* 3.48. *Test scores:* SAT critical reading scores over 500: 63%; SAT math scores over 500: 59%; SAT writing scores over 500: 49%; ACT scores over 18: 63%; SAT critical reading scores over 600: 30%; SAT math scores over 600: 15%; SAT writing scores over 600: 23%; ACT scores over 24: 38%; SAT critical reading scores over 700: 8%; SAT math scores over 700: 2%.

Faculty *Total:* 90, 37% full-time, 52% with terminal degrees. *Student/faculty ratio:* 16:1.

Academics *Calendar:* semesters. *Degrees:* bachelor's and master's. *Special study options:* academic remediation for entering students, adult/continuing education programs, advanced placement credit, double majors, internships, part-time degree program, services for LD students, summer session for credit.

Computers on Campus 44 computers/terminals are available on campus for general student use. Students can access the following: campus intranet, computer help desk, free student e-mail accounts, online (class) grades, online (class) registration, online (class) schedules. Campuswide network is available. 80% of college-owned or -operated housing units are wired for high-speed Internet access. Wireless service is available via entire campus.

Student Life *Housing:* on-campus residence required through junior year. *Options:* men-only, women-only. Campus housing is university owned. Freshman campus housing is guaranteed. *Activities and organizations:* drama/theater group, choral group, Acting for Life, Prayer for the Persecuted, Community Response Team, MU Snow Club, Student World Outreach Team. *Campus security:* 24-hour emergency response devices and patrols, late-night transport/escort service, controlled dormitory access. *Student services:* health clinic, personal/psychological counseling.

Athletics Member NCCAA. *Intercollegiate sports:* basketball M, volleyball W. *Intramural sports:* basketball M/W, soccer M/W, ultimate Frisbee M/W, volleyball M/W.

Standardized Tests *Required:* SAT or ACT (for admission).

Costs (2011–12) *Comprehensive fee:* $26,900 includes full-time tuition ($19,990), mandatory fees ($250), and room and board ($6660). Full-time tuition and fees vary according to course load. Part-time tuition: $625 per credit hour. Part-time tuition and fees vary according to course load. *Required fees:* $55 per term part-time. *Room and board:* Room and board charges vary according to board plan and housing facility. *Payment plan:* installment. *Waivers:* employees or children of employees.

Financial Aid Of all full-time matriculated undergraduates who enrolled in 2009, 503 applied for aid, 441 were judged to have need, 11 had their need fully met. 75 Federal Work-Study jobs (averaging $1500). In 2009, 36 non-need-based awards were made. *Average percent of need met:* 50%. *Average financial aid package:* $9211. *Average need-based loan:* $4094. *Average need-based gift aid:* $5846. *Average non-need-based aid:* $1848. *Average indebtedness upon graduation:* $21,020.

Applying *Options:* electronic application, deferred entrance. *Application fee:* $40. *Required:* essay or personal statement, high school transcript, minimum 2.5 GPA, 2 letters of recommendation. *Application deadlines:* 8/15 (freshmen), 8/30 (transfers). *Notification:* continuous (freshmen), continuous (transfers).

Freshman Application Contact Ms. Erin Kascel, Admissions Assistant, Multnomah University, 8435 Northeast Glisan Street, Portland, OR 97220-5898. *Phone:* 503-251-6489. *Toll-free phone:* 877-251-6560. *Fax:* 503-254-1268. *E-mail:* admiss@multnomah.edu. *Web site:* http://www.multnomah.edu/.

New Hope Christian College
Eugene, Oregon

- **Independent** 4-year, founded 1925, affiliated with Open Bible Standard Churches
- **Suburban** 40-acre campus
- **Coed** 143 undergraduate students, 94% full-time, 39% women, 61% men
- **Minimally difficult** entrance level, 22% of applicants were admitted

Undergraduates 134 full-time, 9 part-time. 3% Black or African American, non-Hispanic/Latino; 3% Hispanic/Latino; 1% Asian, non-Hispanic/Latino; 0.7% Native Hawaiian or other Pacific Islander, non-Hispanic/Latino; 9% Two or more races, non-Hispanic/Latino; 1% international; 20% transferred in. *Retention:* 60% of full-time freshmen returned.

Freshmen *Admission:* 165 applied, 37 admitted, 38 enrolled.

Faculty *Total:* 25, 36% full-time, 28% with terminal degrees. *Student/faculty ratio:* 11:1.

Academics *Calendar:* semesters. *Degree:* bachelor's. *Special study options:* part-time degree program.

Computers on Campus Students can access the following: campus intranet, free student e-mail accounts, online (class) grades. Campuswide network is available. Wireless service is available via dorm rooms, student centers.

Student Life *Housing:* on-campus residence required through junior year. *Options:* men-only, women-only. Campus housing is university owned. Freshman campus housing is guaranteed. *Campus security:* 24-hour emergency response devices, student patrols, controlled dormitory access.

Athletics *Intercollegiate sports:* basketball M, soccer M/W, volleyball M/W. *Intramural sports:* basketball M/W, soccer M/W, ultimate Frisbee M/W, volleyball M/W.

Costs (2011–12) *Comprehensive fee:* $19,450 includes full-time tuition ($12,000), mandatory fees ($1190), and room and board ($6260). Full-time tuition and fees vary according to location. Part-time tuition: $500 per credit

hour. Part-time tuition and fees vary according to class time, course load, and location. *College room only:* $2500. Room and board charges vary according to housing facility. *Payment plans:* tuition prepayment, installment. *Waivers:* senior citizens and employees or children of employees.

Financial Aid Of all full-time matriculated undergraduates who enrolled in 2011, 80 applied for aid, 80 were judged to have need. In 2011, 8 non-need-based awards were made. *Average percent of need met:* 50%. *Average financial aid package:* $14,000. *Average need-based loan:* $3500. *Average need-based gift aid:* $6500. *Average non-need-based aid:* $1900. *Financial aid deadline:* 9/1.

Applying *Options:* electronic application, deferred entrance. *Application fee:* $35. *Required:* essay or personal statement, high school transcript, minimum 2.0 GPA, 2 letters of recommendation. *Application deadlines:* 8/1 (freshmen), rolling (transfers). *Notification:* continuous (freshmen), continuous (transfers).

Freshman Application Contact Sarah Slater, Director of Admissions, New Hope Christian College, 2155 Bailey Hill Road, Eugene, OR 97405. *Phone:* 541-485-1780 Ext. 3115. *Toll-free phone:* 800-322-2638. *Fax:* 541-343-5801. *E-mail:* sarahslater@newhope.edu. *Web site:* http://www.newhope.edu/.

Northwest Christian University
Eugene, Oregon

- **Independent Christian** comprehensive, founded 1895
- **Urban** 8-acre campus with easy access to Portland
- **Endowment** $10.8 million
- **Coed** 479 undergraduate students, 81% full-time, 62% women, 38% men
- **Moderately difficult** entrance level, 66% of applicants were admitted

Undergraduates 386 full-time, 93 part-time. Students come from 14 states and territories; 10% are from out of state; 2% Black or African American, non-Hispanic/Latino; 5% Hispanic/Latino; 2% Asian, non-Hispanic/Latino; 1% American Indian or Alaska Native, non-Hispanic/Latino; 10% Race/ethnicity unknown; 9% transferred in. *Retention:* 60% of full-time freshmen returned.

Freshmen *Admission:* 256 applied, 168 admitted, 75 enrolled. *Average high school GPA:* 3.43. *Test scores:* SAT critical reading scores over 500: 43%; SAT math scores over 500: 48%; SAT writing scores over 500: 34%; ACT scores over 18: 76%; SAT critical reading scores over 600: 11%; SAT math scores over 600: 8%; SAT writing scores over 600: 2%; ACT scores over 24: 24%.

Faculty *Total:* 28, 93% full-time, 68% with terminal degrees. *Student/faculty ratio:* 18:1.

Academics *Calendar:* quarters. *Degrees:* certificates, associate, bachelor's, master's, and postbachelor's certificates. *Special study options:* academic remediation for entering students, accelerated degree program, adult/continuing education programs, advanced placement credit, distance learning, double majors, independent study, internships, off-campus study, part-time degree program, services for LD students, student-designed majors, study abroad, summer session for credit.

Computers on Campus 60 computers/terminals are available on campus for general student use. Students can access the following: campus intranet, computer help desk, free student e-mail accounts, online (class) grades, online (class) schedules. Campuswide network is available. 100% of college-owned or -operated housing units are wired for high-speed Internet access. Wireless service is available via entire campus.

Student Life *Housing:* on-campus residence required for freshman year. *Options:* coed, men-only, women-only. Campus housing is university owned. Freshman campus housing is guaranteed. *Activities and organizations:* drama/theater group, student-run newspaper, choral group, Community Life Groups, Circle K, Believers Building Bonds through Boardgames, Parable. *Campus security:* 24-hour emergency response devices and patrols, late-night transport/escort service, controlled dormitory access, late-night patrols by trained security personnel. *Student services:* personal/psychological counseling.

Athletics Member NAIA. *Intercollegiate sports:* basketball M(s)/W(s), cross-country running M(s)/W(s), golf M(s)/W(s), soccer M(s)/W(s), softball W(s), track and field M(s)/W(s), volleyball W(s). *Intramural sports:* badminton M/W, basketball M/W, football M, skiing (downhill) M/W, ultimate Frisbee M/W, volleyball M/W.

Standardized Tests *Required:* SAT or ACT (for admission).

Costs (2012–13) *Comprehensive fee:* $32,480 includes full-time tuition ($24,780), mandatory fees ($100), and room and board ($7600). Full-time tuition and fees vary according to course load. Part-time tuition: $825 per credit. Part-time tuition and fees vary according to course load. *Required fees:* $100 per year part-time. *Room and board:* Room and board charges vary according to board plan and housing facility. *Payment plans:* installment, deferred payment. *Waivers:* employees or children of employees.

Financial Aid Of all full-time matriculated undergraduates who enrolled in 2010, 305 applied for aid, 284 were judged to have need, 48 had their need fully met. 70 Federal Work-Study jobs (averaging $945). 66 state and other part-time jobs (averaging $900). In 2010, 24 non-need-based awards were

made. *Average percent of need met:* 75%. *Average financial aid package:* $19,742. *Average need-based loan:* $4921. *Average need-based gift aid:* $14,974. *Average non-need-based aid:* $6729. *Average indebtedness upon graduation:* $22,818.

Applying *Options:* electronic application, deferred entrance. *Required:* essay or personal statement, high school transcript, minimum 2.5 GPA. *Application deadlines:* rolling (freshmen), rolling (out-of-state freshmen), rolling (transfers). *Notification:* continuous (freshmen), continuous (out-of-state freshmen), continuous (transfers).

Freshman Application Contact Kacie Gerdrum, Associate Director of Undergraduate Admissions, Northwest Christian University, 828 East 11th Avenue, Eugene, OR 97401-3745. *Phone:* 541-684-7201. *Toll-free phone:* 877-463-6622. *Fax:* 541-684-7317. *E-mail:* admissions@nwcu.edu. *Web site:* http://www.nwcu.edu/.

Oregon College of Art & Craft
Portland, Oregon

- **Independent** 4-year, founded 1907
- **Urban** 10-acre campus with easy access to Portland
- **Endowment** $4.4 million
- **Coed** 151 undergraduate students, 74% full-time, 73% women, 27% men
- **Moderately difficult** entrance level, 92% of applicants were admitted

Undergraduates 112 full-time, 39 part-time. Students come from 20 states and territories; 28% are from out of state; 5% Hispanic/Latino; 2% Asian, non-Hispanic/Latino; 2% Native Hawaiian or other Pacific Islander, non-Hispanic/Latino; 3% American Indian or Alaska Native, non-Hispanic/Latino; 8% Two or more races, non-Hispanic/Latino; 11% Race/ethnicity unknown; 21% transferred in; 5% live on campus. *Retention:* 65% of full-time freshmen returned.

Freshmen *Admission:* 60 applied, 55 admitted, 26 enrolled. *Average high school GPA:* 3.

Faculty *Total:* 30, 33% full-time, 83% with terminal degrees. *Student/faculty ratio:* 7:1.

Academics *Calendar:* semesters. *Degrees:* certificates, bachelor's, and post-bachelor's certificates. *Special study options:* adult/continuing education programs, advanced placement credit, independent study, internships, off-campus study, part-time degree program, services for LD students, study abroad.

Computers on Campus 15 computers/terminals are available on campus for general student use. Students can access the following: free student e-mail accounts. Campuswide network is available. 100% of college-owned or -operated housing units are wired for high-speed Internet access. Wireless service is available via entire campus.

Student Life *Housing options:* coed. Campus housing is university owned. Freshman applicants given priority for college housing. *Activities and organizations:* student-run newspaper, Student Commonwealth. *Campus security:* 24-hour emergency response devices. *Student services:* personal/psychological counseling.

Standardized Tests *Recommended:* SAT (for admission), ACT (for admission).

Financial Aid Of all full-time matriculated undergraduates who enrolled in 2011, 95 applied for aid, 93 were judged to have need, 1 had their need fully met. 85 Federal Work-Study jobs (averaging $200). 86 state and other part-time jobs (averaging $600). In 2011, 16 non-need-based awards were made. *Average percent of need met:* 28%. *Average financial aid package:* $22,082. *Average need-based loan:* $4879. *Average need-based gift aid:* $4582. *Average non-need-based aid:* $7269.

Applying *Options:* electronic application, deferred entrance. *Application fee:* $35. *Required:* essay or personal statement, high school transcript, minimum 2.0 GPA, 2 letters of recommendation, A portfolio that includes 12 to 20 pieces of studio artwork on a CD with four drawings created from direct observation should be included. *Required for some:* interview. *Application deadlines:* rolling (freshmen), rolling (out-of-state freshmen), rolling (transfers). *Notification:* continuous (freshmen), continuous (out-of-state freshmen), continuous (transfers).

Freshman Application Contact Oregon College of Art & Craft, 8245 Southwest Barnes Road, Portland, OR 97225. *Phone:* 971-255-4192. *Toll-free phone:* 800-390-0632. *Web site:* http://www.ocac.edu/.

Oregon Health & Science University
Portland, Oregon

- **State-related** upper-level, founded 1974
- **Urban** 116-acre campus
- **Endowment** $257.9 million
- **Coed** 780 undergraduate students

Undergraduates 0.6% Black or African American, non-Hispanic/Latino; 5% Hispanic/Latino; 4% Asian, non-Hispanic/Latino; 0.3% Native Hawaiian or other Pacific Islander, non-Hispanic/Latino; 1% American Indian or Alaska Native, non-Hispanic/Latino; 3% Two or more races, non-Hispanic/Latino; 7% Race/ethnicity unknown; 0.9% international.

Faculty *Total:* 2,129.

Academics *Calendar:* quarters. *Degrees:* certificates, bachelor's, master's, doctoral, post-master's, postbachelor's, and first professional certificates. *Special study options:* accelerated degree program, advanced placement credit, distance learning, off-campus study, part-time degree program, summer session for credit. *ROTC:* Army (c).

Computers on Campus 45 computers/terminals are available on campus for general student use. Students can access the following: campus intranet, computer help desk, free student e-mail accounts, online (class) grades, online (class) schedules. Campuswide network is available. Wireless service is available via entire campus.

Student Life *Housing:* college housing not available. *Campus security:* 24-hour emergency response devices and patrols. *Student services:* health clinic, personal/psychological counseling, women's center.

Athletics *Intramural sports:* basketball M/W, soccer M/W, volleyball M/W.

Financial Aid Of all full-time matriculated undergraduates who enrolled in 2011, 302 applied for aid, 294 were judged to have need, 19 had their need fully met. 16 Federal Work-Study jobs (averaging $1333). In 2011, 1 non-need-based awards were made. *Average percent of need met:* 32%. *Average financial aid package:* $10,315. *Average need-based loan:* $5290. *Average need-based gift aid:* $8255. *Average non-need-based aid:* $4200.

Applying *Application fee:* $120. *Application deadline:* 2/1 (transfers). *Notification:* 4/1 (transfers).

Application Contact Jennifer Anderson, Director of Admissions, Oregon Health & Science University, 3181 Southwest Sam Jackson Park Road, Mail Code: 337A/SNADM, Portland, OR 97201-3098. *Phone:* 503-494-0647. *Fax:* 503-494-4350. *E-mail:* andersje@ohsu.edu. *Web site:* http://www.ohsu.edu/.

Oregon Institute of Technology
Klamath Falls, Oregon

- **State-supported** comprehensive, founded 1947, part of Oregon University System
- **Small-town** 173-acre campus
- **Coed** 3,881 undergraduate students, 55% full-time, 48% women, 52% men
- **Moderately difficult** entrance level, 93% of applicants were admitted

Undergraduates 2,148 full-time, 1,733 part-time. 25% are from out of state; 1% Black or African American, non-Hispanic/Latino; 6% Hispanic/Latino; 4% Asian, non-Hispanic/Latino; 0.6% Native Hawaiian or other Pacific Islander, non-Hispanic/Latino; 1% American Indian or Alaska Native, non-Hispanic/Latino; 5% Two or more races, non-Hispanic/Latino; 4% Race/ethnicity unknown; 2% international; 13% transferred in; 13% live on campus. *Retention:* 73% of full-time freshmen returned.

Freshmen *Admission:* 713 applied, 664 admitted, 318 enrolled. *Average high school GPA:* 3.41. *Test scores:* SAT critical reading scores over 500: 56%; SAT math scores over 500: 61%; ACT scores over 18: 86%; SAT critical reading scores over 600: 15%; SAT math scores over 600: 25%; ACT scores over 24: 43%; SAT critical reading scores over 700: 1%; SAT math scores over 700: 3%; ACT scores over 30: 9%.

Faculty *Total:* 257, 56% full-time. *Student/faculty ratio:* 20:1.

Academics *Calendar:* quarters. *Degrees:* certificates, associate, bachelor's, master's, and postbachelor's certificates. *Special study options:* academic remediation for entering students, advanced placement credit, cooperative education, distance learning, double majors, external degree program, internships, off-campus study, part-time degree program, services for LD students, study abroad, summer session for credit. *ROTC:* Army (c).

Computers on Campus Students can access the following: online (class) registration. Campuswide network is available.

Student Life *Housing options:* coed. Campus housing is university owned. *Activities and organizations:* student-run newspaper, radio and television station, choral group, Phi Delta Theta, Christian Fellowship, International Club, Society of Women Engineers, Association of Student Mechanical Engineers, national fraternities. *Campus security:* 24-hour emergency response devices and patrols, late-night transport/escort service. *Student services:* health clinic, personal/psychological counseling.

Athletics Member NAIA. *Intercollegiate sports:* baseball M, basketball M(s)/W, cross-country running M(s)/W(s), soccer W, softball W(s), track and field M(s)/W(s), volleyball W(s). *Intramural sports:* basketball M/W, bowling M/W, cheerleading M/W, cross-country running M/W, football M/W, golf M/W, lacrosse M, rugby M/W, soccer W, softball W, track and field M/W, volleyball M/W, water polo M/W.

Standardized Tests *Required:* SAT or ACT (for admission).

Financial Aid Of all full-time matriculated undergraduates who enrolled in 2009, 1,955 applied for aid, 1,734 were judged to have need, 441 had their

need fully met. In 2009, 53 non-need-based awards were made. *Average percent of need met:* 20%. *Average financial aid package:* $6600. *Average need-based loan:* $4219. *Average need-based gift aid:* $6001. *Average non-need-based aid:* $8475. *Average indebtedness upon graduation:* $21,733.

Applying *Options:* electronic application, deferred entrance. *Application fee:* $50. *Required:* high school transcript, minimum 3.0 GPA. *Application deadlines:* 10/1 (freshmen), rolling (transfers). *Notification:* continuous (freshmen), continuous (transfers).

Freshman Application Contact Oregon Institute of Technology, 3201 Campus Drive, Klamath Falls, OR 97601-8801. *Phone:* 541-885-1151. *Toll-free phone:* 800-422-2017. *Web site:* http://www.oit.edu/.

Oregon State University
Corvallis, Oregon

- **State-supported** university, founded 1868, part of Oregon University System
- **Small-town** 422-acre campus
- **Endowment** $372.3 million
- **Coed**
- **Moderately difficult** entrance level

Faculty *Student/faculty ratio:* 25:1.

Academics *Calendar:* quarters. *Degrees:* certificates, bachelor's, master's, doctoral, post-master's, postbachelor's, and first professional certificates.

Student Life *Campus security:* 24-hour emergency response devices and patrols, student patrols, late-night transport/escort service, controlled dormitory access, crime prevention office.

Athletics Member NCAA. All Division I except football (Division I-A).

Standardized Tests *Required:* SAT or ACT (for admission). *Required for some:* SAT Subject Tests (for admission).

Costs (2011–12) *Tuition:* state resident $6228 full-time, $173 per credit hour part-time; nonresident $19,944 full-time, $554 per credit hour part-time. Full-time tuition and fees vary according to course load. Part-time tuition and fees vary according to course load. *Required fees:* $1372 full-time. *Room and board:* $10,464. Room and board charges vary according to board plan and housing facility.

Financial Aid *Of all full-time matriculated undergraduates who enrolled in 2011,* 12,170 applied for aid, 9,862 were judged to have need, 1,322 had their need fully met. *In 2011,* 2088 non-need-based awards were made. *Average percent of need met:* 62. *Average financial aid package:* $10,380. *Average need-based loan:* $4790. *Average need-based gift aid:* $6593. *Average non-need-based aid:* $3252.

Applying *Options:* electronic application, early action, deferred entrance. *Application fee:* $50. *Required:* essay or personal statement, high school transcript, minimum 3.0 GPA.

Freshman Application Contact Oregon State University, Corvallis, OR 97331. *Phone:* 541-737-4411. *Toll-free phone:* 800-291-4192. *Web site:* http://www.oregonstate.edu/.

Oregon State University–Cascades
Bend, Oregon

Freshman Application Contact Admissions Department, Oregon State University–Cascades, 2600 Northwest College Way, Bend, OR 97701. *Phone:* 541-322-3150. *E-mail:* cascadeadmit@osucascades.edu. *Web site:* http://www.osucascades.edu/.

Pacific Northwest College of Art
Portland, Oregon

- **Independent** comprehensive, founded 1909
- **Urban** 2-acre campus with easy access to Portland
- **Endowment** $13.7 million
- **Coed** 521 undergraduate students, 92% full-time, 65% women, 35% men
- **Minimally difficult** entrance level, 51% of applicants were admitted

Undergraduates 477 full-time, 44 part-time. Students come from 29 states and territories; 4 other countries; 65% are from out of state; 2% Black or African American, non-Hispanic/Latino; 4% Hispanic/Latino; 3% Asian, non-Hispanic/Latino; 0.4% Native Hawaiian or other Pacific Islander, non-Hispanic/Latino; 2% American Indian or Alaska Native, non-Hispanic/Latino; 9% Two or more races, non-Hispanic/Latino; 0.8% Race/ethnicity unknown; 0.6% international; 13% transferred in; 16% live on campus. *Retention:* 70% of full-time freshmen returned.

Freshmen *Admission:* 425 applied, 215 admitted, 76 enrolled. *Average high school GPA:* 3.12.

Faculty *Total:* 101, 26% full-time, 87% with terminal degrees. *Student/faculty ratio:* 9:1.

Academics *Calendar:* semesters. *Degrees:* bachelor's and master's. *Special study options:* advanced placement credit, cooperative education, independent study, internships, off-campus study, part-time degree program, services for LD students, student-designed majors, study abroad, summer session for credit.

Computers on Campus 300 computers/terminals are available on campus for general student use. Students can access the following: campus intranet, computer help desk, free student e-mail accounts, online (class) grades, online (class) registration, online (class) schedules. Campuswide network is available. Wireless service is available via entire campus.

Student Life *Housing options:* Campus housing is leased by the school. Freshman applicants given priority for college housing. *Campus security:* 24-hour emergency response devices, late-night transport/escort service, entrance security guards during open hours. *Student services:* personal/psychological counseling.

Costs (2012–13) *Tuition:* $28,866 full-time, $1203 per credit part-time. Part-time tuition and fees vary according to course load. *Required fees:* $1118 full-time, $42 per credit part-time. *Room only:* $8500. *Payment plans:* installment, deferred payment. *Waivers:* employees or children of employees.

Financial Aid Of all full-time matriculated undergraduates who enrolled in 2006, 264 applied for aid, 238 were judged to have need, 13 had their need fully met. 33 Federal Work-Study jobs (averaging $1200). 33 state and other part-time jobs (averaging $1200). In 2006, 10 non-need-based awards were made. *Average percent of need met:* 54%. *Average financial aid package:* $11,845. *Average need-based loan:* $4040. *Average need-based gift aid:* $4699. *Average non-need-based aid:* $2442. *Average indebtedness upon graduation:* $22,155.

Applying *Options:* electronic application, deferred entrance. *Required:* essay or personal statement, high school transcript, portfolio of artwork. *Recommended:* minimum 2.0 GPA, interview. *Application deadlines:* rolling (freshmen), rolling (out-of-state freshmen), rolling (transfers). *Notification:* continuous (freshmen), continuous (out-of-state freshmen), continuous (transfers).

Freshman Application Contact Pacific Northwest College of Art, 1241 NW Johnson Street, Portland, OR 97209. *Phone:* 503-821-8926. *Web site:* http://www.pnca.edu/.

Pacific University
Forest Grove, Oregon

- **Independent** comprehensive, founded 1849
- **Small-town** 60-acre campus with easy access to Portland
- **Coed** 1,596 undergraduate students, 96% full-time, 58% women, 42% men
- **Moderately difficult** entrance level, 75% of applicants were admitted

Undergraduates 1,537 full-time, 59 part-time. 47% are from out of state; 2% Black or African American, non-Hispanic/Latino; 8% Hispanic/Latino; 14% Asian, non-Hispanic/Latino; 3% Native Hawaiian or other Pacific Islander, non-Hispanic/Latino; 0.9% American Indian or Alaska Native, non-Hispanic/Latino; 8% Two or more races, non-Hispanic/Latino; 7% Race/ethnicity unknown; 2% international; 5% transferred in; 60% live on campus. *Retention:* 75% of full-time freshmen returned.

Freshmen *Admission:* 2,499 applied, 1,880 admitted, 374 enrolled. *Average high school GPA:* 3.62. *Test scores:* SAT critical reading scores over 500: 71%; SAT math scores over 500: 85%; ACT scores over 18: 99%; SAT critical reading scores over 600: 27%; SAT math scores over 600: 31%; ACT scores over 24: 55%; SAT critical reading scores over 700: 3%; SAT math scores over 700: 4%; ACT scores over 30: 6%.

Academics *Calendar:* semesters. *Degrees:* bachelor's, master's, doctoral, post-master's, and postbachelor's certificates. *ROTC:* Army (c), Air Force (c).

Computers on Campus Students can access the following: campus intranet, computer help desk, free student e-mail accounts, online (class) grades, online (class) schedules, Web space, printing, student and academic information, WebCT, computer peripherals. Campuswide network is available. 100% of college-owned or -operated housing units are wired for high-speed Internet access. Wireless service is available via entire campus.

Student Life *Housing:* on-campus residence required through sophomore year. *Options:* coed, disabled students. Campus housing is university owned. Freshman campus housing is guaranteed. *Campus security:* 24-hour emergency response devices and patrols, late-night transport/escort service, controlled dormitory access.

Athletics Member NCAA, NAIA. All NCAA Division III. *Intercollegiate sports:* baseball M, basketball M/W, cross-country running M/W, football M, golf M/W, lacrosse M/W, soccer M/W, softball W, swimming and diving M/W, tennis M/W, track and field M/W, volleyball W, wrestling M/W. *Intramural sports:* basketball M/W, cheerleading M/W, crew M/W, football M/W, racquetball W, softball M/W, volleyball M/W.

Standardized Tests *Required:* SAT or ACT (for admission).

Costs (2011–12) *Comprehensive fee:* $42,820 includes full-time tuition ($32,850), mandatory fees ($762), and room and board ($9208). Part-time tuition: $1368 per credit hour. Part-time tuition and fees vary according to course load. *College room only:* $4644. Room and board charges varying to board plan and housing facility. *Payment plans:* installment, deferred payment. *Waivers:* employees or children of employees.

Financial Aid Of all full-time matriculated undergraduates who enrolled in 2011, 1,362 applied for aid, 1,256 were judged to have need, 186 had their need fully met. In 2011, 238 non-need-based awards were made. *Average percent of need met:* 80%. *Average financial aid package:* $25,528. *Average need-based loan:* $4554. *Average need-based gift aid:* $17,121. *Average non-need-based aid:* $11,216. *Average indebtedness upon graduation:* $29,303.

Applying *Options:* electronic application, deferred entrance. *Application fee:* $40. *Required:* essay or personal statement, high school transcript, minimum 3.0 GPA, 1 letter of recommendation. *Recommended:* interview. *Application deadlines:* 8/15 (freshmen), 8/15 (transfers). *Notification:* continuous (freshmen), continuous (transfers).

Freshman Application Contact Ms. Karen Dunston, Executive Director, Pacific University, 2043 College Way, Forest Grove, OR 97116-1797. *Phone:* 503-352-2218. *Toll-free phone:* 877-722-8648. *Fax:* 503-352-2975. *E-mail:* admissions@pacificu.edu. *Web site:* http://www.pacificu.edu/.

Pioneer Pacific College

Clackamas, Oregon

Freshman Application Contact Admissions Office, Pioneer Pacific College, 8800 SE Sunnyside Road, Clackamas, OR 97015. *Phone:* 503-654-8000. *Toll-free phone:* 866-772-4636. *E-mail:* inquiries@pioneerpacific.edu. *Web site:* http://www.pioneerpacific.edu/.

Pioneer Pacific College

Wilsonville, Oregon

Freshman Application Contact Ms. Kristin Lynn, Director of Admissions, Pioneer Pacific College, 27501 Southwest Parkway Avenue, Wilsonville, OR 97070. *Phone:* 866-772-4636. *Toll-free phone:* 866-PPC-INFO. *Fax:* 503-682-1514. *E-mail:* inquiries@pioneerpacific.edu. *Web site:* http://www.pioneerpacific.edu/.

Pioneer Pacific College–Eugene/Springfield Branch

Springfield, Oregon

Freshman Application Contact Admissions Office, Pioneer Pacific College–Eugene/Springfield Branch, 3800 Sports Way, Springfield, OR 97477. *Phone:* 541-684-4644. *Toll-free phone:* 866-772-4636. *E-mail:* inquiries@pioneerpacific.edu. *Web site:* http://www.pioneerpacific.edu/.

Portland State University

Portland, Oregon

- **State-supported** university, founded 1946, part of Oregon University System
- **Urban** 49-acre campus with easy access to Portland
- **Endowment** $62.9 million
- **Coed** 22,780 undergraduate students, 64% full-time, 53% women, 47% men
- **Moderately difficult** entrance level, 70% of applicants were admitted

Undergraduates 14,549 full-time, 8,231 part-time. Students come from 53 states and territories; 86 other countries; 12% are from out of state; 3% Black or African American, non-Hispanic/Latino; 8% Hispanic/Latino; 8% Asian, non-Hispanic/Latino; 0.8% Native Hawaiian or other Pacific Islander, non-Hispanic/Latino; 2% American Indian or Alaska Native, non-Hispanic/Latino; 4% Two or more races, non-Hispanic/Latino; 4% Race/ethnicity unknown; 4% international; 13% transferred in; 12% live on campus. *Retention:* 73% of full-time freshmen returned.

Freshmen *Admission:* 4,954 applied, 3,471 admitted, 1,354 enrolled. *Average high school GPA:* 3.39. *Test scores:* SAT critical reading scores over 500: 59%; SAT writing scores over 500: 50%; ACT scores over 18: 77%; SAT critical reading scores over 600: 18%; SAT writing scores over 600: 14%; ACT scores over 24: 33%; SAT critical reading scores over 700: 3%; SAT writing scores over 700: 1%; ACT scores over 30: 2%.

Faculty *Total:* 1,581, 56% full-time, 50% with terminal degrees. *Student/faculty ratio:* 16:1.

Academics *Calendar:* quarters. *Degrees:* certificates, bachelor's, master's, doctoral, postbachelor's, and first professional certificates. *Special study*

options: academic remediation for entering students, accelerated degree program, adult/continuing education programs, advanced placement credit, cooperative education, distance learning, double majors, English as a second language, freshman honors college, honors programs, independent study, internships, off-campus study, part-time degree program, services for LD students, study abroad, summer session for credit. *ROTC:* Army (b), Air Force (c).

Computers on Campus 1,000 computers/terminals are available on campus for general student use. Students can access the following: campus intranet, computer help desk, free student e-mail accounts, online (class) grades, online (class) registration, online (class) schedules. Campuswide network is available. Wireless service is available via entire campus.

Student Life *Housing options:* coed, disabled students. Campus housing is university owned. Freshman campus housing is guaranteed. *Activities and organizations:* drama/theater group, student-run newspaper, radio station, choral group, national fraternities, national sororities. *Campus security:* 24-hour emergency response devices and patrols, late-night transport/escort service, controlled dormitory access. *Student services:* health clinic, personal/psychological counseling, women's center, legal services.

Athletics Member NCAA. All Division I except football (Division I-AA). *Intercollegiate sports:* basketball M/W, cross-country running M/W, golf W, soccer W, softball W, tennis M/W, track and field M/W, volleyball W.

Standardized Tests *Required:* SAT or ACT (for admission).

Costs (2012–13) *One-time required fee:* $300. *Tuition:* state resident $6156 full-time; nonresident $21,375 full-time. Full-time tuition and fees vary according to program and reciprocity agreements. Part-time tuition and fees vary according to course level. *Required fees:* $1608 full-time. *Room and board:* $10,368; room only: $7311. Room and board charges vary according to board plan and housing facility. *Payment plan:* installment. *Waivers:* minority students, senior citizens, and employees or children of employees.

Financial Aid Of all full-time matriculated undergraduates who enrolled in 2010, 9,885 applied for aid, 8,737 were judged to have need, 539 had their need fully met. 1,421 Federal Work-Study jobs (averaging $2876). In 2010, 76 non-need-based awards were made. *Average percent of need met:* 80%. *Average financial aid package:* $12,986. *Average need-based loan:* $4505. *Average need-based gift aid:* $5447. *Average non-need-based aid:* $1176. *Average indebtedness upon graduation:* $26,287.

Applying *Options:* electronic application, early admission, deferred entrance. *Application fee:* $50. *Required:* high school transcript, minimum 3.0 GPA. *Application deadlines:* rolling (freshmen), rolling (out-of-state freshmen), rolling (transfers). *Notification:* continuous (freshmen), continuous (out-of-state freshmen), continuous (transfers).

Freshman Application Contact Melissa Trifiletti, Director of New Student Programs, Portland State University, PO Box 751, Portland, OR 97207. *Phone:* 503-725-5504. *Toll-free phone:* 800-547-8887. *Fax:* 503-725-5525. *E-mail:* mtrifi@pdx.edu. *Web site:* http://www.pdx.edu/.

Reed College

Portland, Oregon

- **Independent** comprehensive, founded 1908
- **Urban** 116-acre campus
- **Endowment** $373.7 million
- **Coed**
- **Most difficult** entrance level

Faculty *Student/faculty ratio:* 10:1.

Academics *Calendar:* semesters. *Degrees:* bachelor's and master's.

Student Life *Campus security:* 24-hour emergency response devices and patrols, student patrols, late-night transport/escort service, controlled dormitory access, 24-hour emergency dispatch.

Standardized Tests *Required:* SAT or ACT (for admission). *Recommended:* SAT Subject Tests (for admission).

Costs (2011–12) *Comprehensive fee:* $53,850 includes full-time tuition ($42,540), mandatory fees ($260), and room and board ($11,050). Part-time tuition: $1813 per semester hour. Part-time tuition and fees vary according to course load. *College room only:* $5750. Room and board charges varying to board plan and housing facility.

Financial Aid *Of all full-time matriculated undergraduates who enrolled in 2010,* 842 applied for aid, 757 were judged to have need, 747 had their need fully met. *Average percent of need met:* 100. *Average financial aid package:* $34,196. *Average need-based loan:* $5034. *Average need-based gift aid:* $32,548. *Average indebtedness upon graduation:* $16,910. *Financial aid deadline:* 2/1.

Applying *Options:* electronic application, early admission, early decision, deferred entrance. *Application fee:* $50. *Required:* essay or personal statement, high school transcript, 2 letters of recommendation. *Recommended:* interview.

Freshman Application Contact Mr. Keith Todd, Dean of Admission, Reed College, 3203 Southeast Woodstock Boulevard, Portland, OR 97202-8199. *Phone:* 503-777-7511. *Toll-free phone:* 800-547-4750. *Fax:* 503-777-7553. *E-mail:* admission@reed.edu. *Web site:* http://www.reed.edu/.

See below for display ad and page 1516 for the College Close-Up.

Southern Oregon University
Ashland, Oregon

- **State-supported** comprehensive, founded 1926, part of Oregon University System
- **Small-town** 175-acre campus
- **Endowment** $16.9 million
- **Coed** 5,998 undergraduate students, 66% full-time, 57% women, 43% men
- **Moderately difficult** entrance level, 94% of applicants were admitted

Undergraduates 3,941 full-time, 2,057 part-time. Students come from 45 states and territories; 33 other countries; 31% are from out of state; 2% Black or African American, non-Hispanic/Latino; 7% Hispanic/Latino; 2% Asian, non-Hispanic/Latino; 0.7% Native Hawaiian or other Pacific Islander, non-Hispanic/Latino; 1% American Indian or Alaska Native, non-Hispanic/Latino; 3% Two or more races, non-Hispanic/Latino; 24% Race/ethnicity unknown; 2% international; 13% transferred in; 24% live on campus. *Retention:* 69% of full-time freshmen returned.

Freshmen *Admission:* 1,447 applied, 1,356 admitted, 697 enrolled. *Average high school GPA:* 3.25. *Test scores:* SAT math scores over 500: 52%; SAT writing scores over 500: 46%; ACT scores over 18: 89%; SAT math scores over 600: 15%; SAT writing scores over 600: 14%; ACT scores over 24: 39%; SAT math scores over 700: 1%; SAT writing scores over 700: 1%; ACT scores over 30: 4%.

Faculty *Total:* 346, 59% full-time, 48% with terminal degrees. *Student/faculty ratio:* 20:1.

Academics *Calendar:* quarters. *Degrees:* bachelor's, master's, post-master's, and postbachelor's certificates. *Special study options:* academic remediation for entering students, accelerated degree program, adult/continuing education programs, advanced placement credit, cooperative education, distance learning, double majors, English as a second language, freshman honors college, honors programs, independent study, internships, off-campus study, part-time degree program, services for LD students, student-designed majors, study abroad, summer session for credit. *ROTC:* Army (b). *Unusual degree programs:* 3-2 engineering with Oregon State University.

Computers on Campus 750 computers/terminals are available on campus for general student use. Students can access the following: campus intranet, computer help desk, free student e-mail accounts, online (class) grades, online (class) registration, online (class) schedules, Online account information including bill payment, online employee records for student workers. Campus-wide network is available. 100% of college-owned or -operated housing units are wired for high-speed Internet access. Wireless service is available via classrooms, computer centers, computer labs, dorm rooms, learning centers, libraries, student centers.

Student Life *Housing:* on-campus residence required for freshman year. *Options:* coed, disabled students. Campus housing is university owned. Freshman campus housing is guaranteed. *Activities and organizations:* drama/theater group, student-run newspaper, radio and television station, choral group, Native American Student Union, International Student Association, Impact (religious club), Ho`opa`a Hawaii Club, Omicron Delta Kappa. *Campus security:* 24-hour emergency response devices and patrols, student patrols, late-night transport/escort service, controlled dormitory access. *Student services:* health clinic, personal/psychological counseling, women's center, legal services.

Athletics Member NAIA. *Intercollegiate sports:* basketball M(s)/W(s), cross-country running M(s)/W(s), football M(s), soccer W(s), softball W(s), track and field M(s)/W(s), volleyball W(s), wrestling M(s). *Intramural sports:* basketball M/W, bowling M/W, cheerleading M/W, crew M/W, football M/W, golf M/W, racquetball M/W, rugby M/W, sailing M/W, skiing (cross-country) M/W, soccer M/W, softball M/W, swimming and diving M/W, table tennis M/W, tennis M/W, track and field M/W, ultimate Frisbee M/W, volleyball M/W, water polo M/W.

Standardized Tests *Required:* SAT or ACT (for admission). *Required for some:* SAT Subject Tests (for admission).

Costs (2012–13) *Tuition:* state resident $5625 full-time, $125 per credit part-time; nonresident $18,900 full-time, $420 per credit part-time. Full-time tuition and fees vary according to course load and reciprocity agreements. Part-time tuition and fees vary according to course load and reciprocity agreements. *Required fees:* $530 full-time, $450 per term part-time. *Room and board:* $9918; room only: $5400. Room and board charges vary according to board plan and housing facility. *Payment plans:* installment, deferred payment. *Waivers:* senior citizens and employees or children of employees.

Financial Aid Of all full-time matriculated undergraduates who enrolled in 2009, 3,272 applied for aid, 2,860 were judged to have need, 273 had their

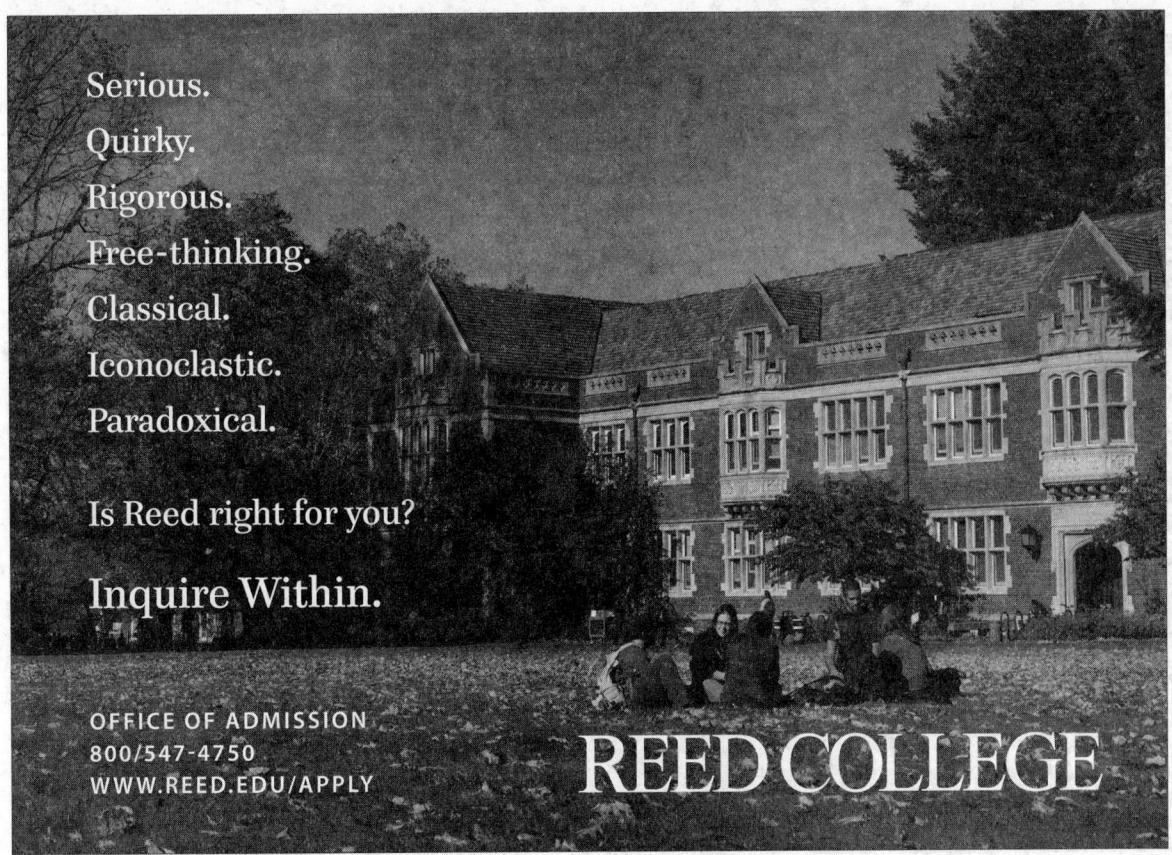

need fully met. 316 Federal Work-Study jobs (averaging $1047). In 2009, 297 non-need-based awards were made. *Average percent of need met:* 60%. *Average financial aid package:* $10,226. *Average need-based loan:* $4003. *Average need-based gift aid:* $7816. *Average non-need-based aid:* $8905. *Average indebtedness upon graduation:* $24,132.

Applying *Options:* electronic application, early admission, deferred entrance. *Application fee:* $50. *Required:* high school transcript, minimum 2.8 GPA. *Required for some:* essay or personal statement. *Application deadlines:* rolling (freshmen), rolling (transfers). *Notification:* continuous (freshmen), continuous (transfers).

Freshman Application Contact Mr. Mark Bottorff, Director of Admissions, Southern Oregon University, 1250 Siskiyou Boulevard, Ashland, OR 97520. *Phone:* 541-552-6411. *Fax:* 541-552-6614. *E-mail:* admissions@sou.edu. *Web site:* http://www.sou.edu/.

University of Oregon

Eugene, Oregon

- **State-supported** university, founded 1872, part of Oregon University System
- **Urban** 295-acre campus
- **Endowment** $436.7 million
- **Coed** 20,623 undergraduate students, 91% full-time, 51% women, 49% men
- **Moderately difficult** entrance level, 73% of applicants were admitted

Undergraduates 18,738 full-time, 1,885 part-time. Students come from 52 states and territories; 69 other countries; 37% are from out of state; 2% Black or African American, non-Hispanic/Latino; 6% Hispanic/Latino; 5% Asian, non-Hispanic/Latino; 0.7% Native Hawaiian or other Pacific Islander, non-Hispanic/Latino; 0.8% American Indian or Alaska Native, non-Hispanic/Latino; 4% Two or more races, non-Hispanic/Latino; 3% Race/ethnicity unknown; 8% international; 7% transferred in; 19% live on campus. *Retention:* 86% of full-time freshmen returned.

Freshmen *Admission:* 23,012 applied, 16,790 admitted, 4,167 enrolled. *Average high school GPA:* 3.59. *Test scores:* SAT critical reading scores over 500: 74%; SAT math scores over 500: 78%; SAT critical reading scores over 600: 30%; SAT math scores over 600: 33%; SAT critical reading scores over 700: 5%; SAT math scores over 700: 5%.

Faculty *Total:* 1,445, 69% full-time, 87% with terminal degrees. *Student/faculty ratio:* 20:1.

Academics *Calendar:* quarters. *Degrees:* bachelor's, master's, doctoral, post-bachelor's, and first professional certificates. *Special study options:* adult/continuing education programs, advanced placement credit, cooperative education, distance learning, double majors, English as a second language, honors programs, independent study, internships, off-campus study, part-time degree program, services for LD students, student-designed majors, study abroad, summer session for credit. *ROTC:* Army (b), Air Force (c). *Unusual degree programs:* 3-2 engineering with Oregon State University.

Computers on Campus 1,237 computers/terminals and 700 ports are available on campus for general student use. Students can access the following: campus intranet, computer help desk, free student e-mail accounts, online (class) grades, online (class) registration, online (class) schedules. Campus-wide network is available. 100% of college-owned or -operated housing units are wired for high-speed Internet access. Wireless service is available via entire campus.

Student Life *Housing options:* coed, cooperative. Campus housing is university owned. Freshman applicants given priority for college housing. *Activities and organizations:* drama/theater group, student-run newspaper, radio station, choral group, marching band, political and environmental action, cultural organizations, major-specific organizations, community service organizations, club sports, national fraternities, national sororities. *Campus security:* 24-hour emergency response devices and patrols, late-night transport/escort service, controlled dormitory access. *Student services:* health clinic, personal/psychological counseling, women's center, legal services.

Athletics Member NCAA. All Division I except football (Division I-A). *Intercollegiate sports:* baseball M(s), basketball M(s)/W(s), cross-country running M(s)/W(s), golf M(s)/W(s), lacrosse W(s), soccer W(s), softball W(s), tennis M(s)/W(s), track and field M(s)/W(s), volleyball W(s). *Intramural sports:* archery M(c)/W(c), badminton M/W, baseball M(c), basketball M/W, crew M(c)/W(c), cross-country running M/W, equestrian sports M(c)/W(c), fencing M(c)/W(c), football M/W, golf M/W, ice hockey M(c)/W(c), lacrosse M(c)/W(c), racquetball M/W, rugby M(c)/W(c), sailing M(c)/W(c), skiing (downhill) M(c)/W(c), soccer M(c)/W(c), softball W(c), swimming and diving M/W, table tennis M(c)/W(c), tennis M/W, track and field M(c)/W(c), ultimate Frisbee M(c)/W(c), volleyball M(c)/W(c), water polo M(c)/W(c).

Standardized Tests *Required:* SAT or ACT (for admission). *Required for some:* SAT and SAT Subject Tests or ACT (for admission).

Costs (2011–12) *One-time required fee:* $327. *Tuition:* state resident $7551 full-time, $168 per credit hour part-time; nonresident $26,415 full-time, $587 per credit hour part-time. Full-time tuition and fees vary according to course load. Part-time tuition and fees vary according to course load. *Required fees:*

$1238 full-time. *Room and board:* $9801. Room and board charges vary according to board plan and housing facility. *Payment plan:* installment. *Waivers:* employees or children of employees.

Financial Aid Of all full-time matriculated undergraduates who enrolled in 2011, 11,405 applied for aid, 8,889 were judged to have need, 833 had their need fully met. 3,308 Federal Work-Study jobs (averaging $1467). 330 state and other part-time jobs (averaging $1684). In 2011, 854 non-need-based awards were made. *Average percent of need met:* 50%. *Average financial aid package:* $9772. *Average need-based loan:* $4739. *Average need-based gift aid:* $5817. *Average non-need-based aid:* $3069. *Average indebtedness upon graduation:* $22,736.

Applying *Options:* electronic application, early action. *Application fee:* $50. *Required:* essay or personal statement, high school transcript, 15 college preparatory units required. *Required for some:* 2 letters of recommendation. *Recommended:* minimum 3.0 GPA. *Application deadlines:* 1/15 (freshmen), 5/15 (transfers), 11/1 (early action). *Notification:* 12/15 (freshmen), 12/15 (early action).

Freshman Application Contact University of Oregon, Eugene, OR 97403. *Phone:* 541-346-3201. *Toll-free phone:* 800-232-3825. *Web site:* http://www.uoregon.edu/.

See page 742 for display ad and page 1696 for the College Close-Up.

University of Phoenix–Oregon Campus
Tigard, Oregon

Freshman Application Contact Marc Booker, Sr. Director, Office of Admissions and Evaluation, University of Phoenix–Oregon Campus, 4035 South Riverpoint Parkway, Mail Stop CF-L101, Phoenix, AZ 85040. *Phone:* 602-557-4609. *Toll-free phone:* 866-766-0766. *Fax:* 480-643-1156. *Web site:* http://www.phoenix.edu/.

University of Portland
Portland, Oregon

- **Independent Roman Catholic** comprehensive, founded 1901
- **Urban** 125-acre campus
- **Endowment** $80.0 million
- **Coed** 3,321 undergraduate students, 97% full-time, 60% women, 40% men
- **Moderately difficult** entrance level, 65% of applicants were admitted

Undergraduates 3,212 full-time, 109 part-time. Students come from 39 states and territories; 19 other countries; 62% are from out of state; 1% Black or African American, non-Hispanic/Latino; 8% Hispanic/Latino; 10% Asian, non-Hispanic/Latino; 1% Native Hawaiian or other Pacific Islander, non-Hispanic/Latino; 0.4% American Indian or Alaska Native, non-Hispanic/Latino; 5% Two or more races, non-Hispanic/Latino; 7% Race/ethnicity unknown; 3% international; 3% transferred in; 57% live on campus. *Retention:* 89% of full-time freshmen returned.

Freshmen *Admission:* 8,156 applied, 5,300 admitted, 888 enrolled. *Average high school GPA:* 3.67. *Test scores:* SAT critical reading scores over 500: 91%; SAT math scores over 500: 91%; SAT critical reading scores over 600: 47%; SAT math scores over 600: 53%; SAT critical reading scores over 700: 12%; SAT math scores over 700: 10%.

Faculty *Total:* 321, 64% full-time, 61% with terminal degrees. *Student/faculty ratio:* 13:1.

Academics *Calendar:* semesters. *Degrees:* bachelor's, master's, doctoral, and post-master's certificates. *Special study options:* adult/continuing education programs, advanced placement credit, double majors, honors programs, independent study, internships, off-campus study, part-time degree program, services for LD students, study abroad, summer session for credit. *ROTC:* Army (b), Air Force (b).

Computers on Campus 575 computers/terminals and 1,950 ports are available on campus for general student use. Students can access the following: campus intranet, computer help desk, free student e-mail accounts, online (class) grades, online (class) registration, online (class) schedules. Campuswide network is available. 100% of college-owned or -operated housing units are wired for high-speed Internet access. Wireless service is available via entire campus.

Student Life *Housing:* on-campus residence required for freshman year. *Options:* coed, men-only, women-only. Campus housing is university owned. Freshman campus housing is guaranteed. *Activities and organizations:* drama/theater group, student-run newspaper, radio station, choral group, English Society, International Club, Hawaiian Club, rugby club, Social Science Club. *Campus security:* 24-hour emergency response devices and patrols, student patrols, late-night transport/escort service, controlled dormitory access. *Student services:* health clinic, personal/psychological counseling.

Athletics Member NCAA. All Division I. *Intercollegiate sports:* baseball M(s), basketball M(s)/W(s), crew W, cross-country running M(s)/W(s), rugby M(c), soccer M(s)/W(s), tennis M(s)/W(s), track and field M(s)/W(s), volleyball W(s). *Intramural sports:* basketball M/W, crew M/W, cross-country running M/W, football M/W, rugby M, skiing (cross-country) M/W, skiing (downhill) M/W, soccer M(c)/W, softball M/W, swimming and diving M/W, tennis M/W, track and field M/W, volleyball M/W, water polo M/W, weight lifting M/W.

Standardized Tests *Required:* SAT or ACT (for admission).

Costs (2011–12) *Comprehensive fee:* $44,954 includes full-time tuition ($33,640), mandatory fees ($1348), and room and board ($9966). Full-time tuition and fees vary according to program. Part-time tuition: $1055 per credit hour. Part-time tuition and fees vary according to course load and program. *College room only:* $5660. Room and board charges vary according to board plan and housing facility. *Payment plans:* installment, deferred payment. *Waivers:* employees or children of employees.

Financial Aid Of all full-time matriculated undergraduates who enrolled in 2011, 2,500 applied for aid, 2,144 were judged to have need, 151 had their need fully met. 495 Federal Work-Study jobs (averaging $971). 1,873 state and other part-time jobs (averaging $1335). In 2011, 858 non-need-based awards were made. *Average percent of need met:* 71%. *Average financial aid package:* $26,335. *Average need-based loan:* $4999. *Average need-based gift aid:* $19,753. *Average non-need-based aid:* $13,068. *Average indebtedness upon graduation:* $26,957.

Applying *Options:* electronic application, deferred entrance. *Application fee:* $50. *Required:* essay or personal statement, high school transcript, 1 letter of recommendation. *Application deadlines:* 6/1 (freshmen), 6/1 (transfers). *Notification:* continuous (freshmen), continuous (transfers).

Freshman Application Contact Mr. Jason McDonald, Dean of Admissions, University of Portland, 5000 North Willamette Boulevard, Portland, OR 97203-5798. *Phone:* 503-943-7147. *Toll-free phone:* 888-627-5601. *Fax:* 503-943-7315. *E-mail:* admissions@up.edu. *Web site:* http://www.up.edu/.

Warner Pacific College
Portland, Oregon

Freshman Application Contact Mrs. Shannon Mackey, Executive Director of Enrollment Management, Warner Pacific College, 2219 Southeast 68th Avenue, Portland, OR 97215. *Phone:* 503-517-1020. *Toll-free phone:* 800-804-1510. *Fax:* 503-517-1540. *E-mail:* admiss@warnerpacific.edu. *Web site:* http://www.warnerpacific.edu/.

Western Oregon University
Monmouth, Oregon

- **State-supported** comprehensive, founded 1856, part of Oregon University System
- **Rural** 157-acre campus with easy access to Portland
- **Coed** 5,428 undergraduate students, 86% full-time, 59% women, 41% men
- **Moderately difficult** entrance level, 88% of applicants were admitted

Undergraduates 4,688 full-time, 740 part-time. Students come from 33 states and territories; 22 other countries; 12% are from out of state; 3% Black or African American, non-Hispanic/Latino; 11% Hispanic/Latino; 2% Asian, non-Hispanic/Latino; 2% Native Hawaiian or other Pacific Islander, non-Hispanic/Latino; 2% American Indian or Alaska Native, non-Hispanic/Latino; 2% Two or more races, non-Hispanic/Latino; 2% Race/ethnicity unknown; 5% international; 11% transferred in. *Retention:* 68% of full-time freshmen returned.

Freshmen *Admission:* 2,693 applied, 2,362 admitted, 1,011 enrolled. *Average high school GPA:* 3.21. *Test scores:* SAT math scores over 500: 39%; SAT writing scores over 500: 28%; SAT math scores over 600: 7%; SAT writing scores over 600: 5%.

Faculty *Total:* 444, 46% full-time, 41% with terminal degrees. *Student/faculty ratio:* 19:1.

Academics *Calendar:* quarters. *Degrees:* bachelor's, master's, and postbachelor's certificates. *Special study options:* academic remediation for entering students, advanced placement credit, distance learning, double majors, English as a second language, freshman honors college, honors programs, independent study, internships, off-campus study, part-time degree program, services for LD students, student-designed majors, study abroad, summer session for credit. *ROTC:* Army (b), Navy (c). *Unusual degree programs:* nursing.

Computers on Campus 411 computers/terminals are available on campus for general student use. Students can access the following: computer help desk, free student e-mail accounts, online (class) grades, online (class) registration, online (class) schedules. Campuswide network is available. Wireless service is available via entire campus.

Student Life *Housing:* on-campus residence required for freshman year. *Options:* coed, disabled students. Campus housing is university owned. Fresh-

man applicants given priority for college housing. *Activities and organizations:* drama/theater group, student-run newspaper, television station, choral group, Model United Nations, Multicultural Student Union, Oregon Student Association, Alternative Spring Break (community service), M.E.Ch.A. *Campus security:* 24-hour emergency response devices and patrols, student patrols, late-night transport/escort service, controlled dormitory access. *Student services:* health clinic, personal/psychological counseling, women's center.

Athletics Member NCAA. All Division II. *Intercollegiate sports:* baseball M(s), basketball M(s)/W(s), cross-country running M(s)/W(s), football M(s), soccer W(s), softball W(s), track and field M(s)/W(s), volleyball W(s). *Intramural sports:* badminton M/W, basketball M/W, bowling M/W, cross-country running M(c)/W(c), football M/W, golf M/W, lacrosse M(c), racquetball M(c)/W(c), riflery M/W, rugby M(c)/W(c), skiing (downhill) M/W, soccer M(c)/W(c), softball M/W, swimming and diving M(c)/W(c), table tennis M/W, tennis M/W, track and field M/W, volleyball M(c)/W(c), water polo M(c)/W(c), weight lifting M/W, wrestling M.

Costs (2011–12) *One-time required fee:* $237. *Tuition:* state resident $6450 full-time, $148 per credit hour part-time; nonresident $18,360 full-time, $408 per credit hour part-time. Full-time tuition and fees vary according to course level, course load, degree level, reciprocity agreements, and student level. Part-time tuition and fees vary according to course level, course load, degree level, reciprocity agreements, and student level. No tuition increase for student's term of enrollment. *Required fees:* $1626 full-time. *Room and board:* $8620. Room and board charges vary according to board plan and housing facility. *Payment plan:* deferred payment. *Waivers:* employees or children of employees.

Financial Aid Of all full-time matriculated undergraduates who enrolled in 2011, 4,101 applied for aid, 3,594 were judged to have need, 382 had their need fully met. 794 Federal Work-Study jobs (averaging $1133). In 2011, 169 non-need-based awards were made. *Average percent of need met:* 59%. *Average financial aid package:* $8733. *Average need-based loan:* $4049. *Average need-based gift aid:* $5978. *Average non-need-based aid:* $1844. *Average indebtedness upon graduation:* $26,504.

Applying *Options:* electronic application, deferred entrance. *Application fee:* $50. *Required:* high school transcript, minimum 2.8 GPA, general college preparatory program completion. *Application deadlines:* rolling (freshmen), rolling (transfers). *Notification:* continuous (freshmen), continuous (transfers).

Freshman Application Contact Mr. Rob Findtner, Assistant Director of Admissions, Western Oregon University, 345 North Monmouth Avenue, Monmouth, OR 97361. *Phone:* 503-838-8211. *Toll-free phone:* 877-877-1593. *Fax:* 503-838-8067. *E-mail:* wolfgram@wou.edu. *Web site:* http://www.wou.edu/.

Willamette University

Salem, Oregon

- **Independent United Methodist** comprehensive, founded 1842
- **Urban** 72-acre campus with easy access to Portland
- **Endowment** $225.0 million
- **Coed** 2,099 undergraduate students, 94% full-time, 57% women, 43% men
- **Very difficult** entrance level, 57% of applicants were admitted

Undergraduates 1,973 full-time, 126 part-time. Students come from 46 states and territories; 38 other countries; 70% are from out of state; 2% Black or African American, non-Hispanic/Latino; 6% Hispanic/Latino; 6% Asian, non-Hispanic/Latino; 0.8% Native Hawaiian or other Pacific Islander, non-Hispanic/Latino; 0.9% American Indian or Alaska Native, non-Hispanic/Latino; 7% Two or more races, non-Hispanic/Latino; 13% Race/ethnicity unknown; 0.8% international; 1% transferred in; 71% live on campus. *Retention:* 88% of full-time freshmen returned.

Freshmen *Admission:* 8,175 applied, 4,685 admitted, 617 enrolled. *Average high school GPA:* 3.54. *Test scores:* SAT critical reading scores over 500: 92%; SAT math scores over 500: 93%; SAT writing scores over 500: 89%; ACT scores over 18: 100%; SAT critical reading scores over 600: 59%; SAT math scores over 600: 52%; SAT writing scores over 600: 50%; ACT scores over 24: 91%; SAT critical reading scores over 700: 15%; SAT math scores over 700: 9%; SAT writing scores over 700: 9%; ACT scores over 30: 28%.

Faculty *Total:* 337, 73% full-time, 91% with terminal degrees. *Student/faculty ratio:* 10:1.

Academics *Calendar:* semesters. *Degrees:* bachelor's, master's, and doctoral. *Special study options:* accelerated degree program, advanced placement credit, double majors, independent study, internships, off-campus study, part-time degree program, services for LD students, student-designed majors, study abroad. *ROTC:* Army (c), Air Force (c). *Unusual degree programs:* 3-2 engineering with University of Southern California, Washington University in St. Louis, Columbia University; forestry with Duke University.

Computers on Campus Students can access the following: online (class) registration. Campuswide network is available. 100% of college-owned or -operated housing units are wired for high-speed Internet access.

Student Life *Housing:* on-campus residence required through sophomore year. *Options:* coed. Campus housing is university owned. Freshman campus housing is guaranteed. *Activities and organizations:* drama/theater group, student-run newspaper, radio station, choral group, national fraternities, national sororities. *Campus security:* 24-hour emergency response devices and patrols, student patrols, late-night transport/escort service, controlled dormitory access. *Student services:* health clinic, personal/psychological counseling, women's center.

Athletics Member NCAA. All Division III. *Intercollegiate sports:* baseball M, basketball M/W, crew M/W, cross-country running M/W, football M, golf M/W, lacrosse M(c), soccer M/W, softball W, swimming and diving M/W, tennis M/W, track and field M/W, volleyball W. *Intramural sports:* badminton M/W, basketball M/W, bowling M/W, cross-country running M/W, football M/W, golf M/W, racquetball M/W, skiing (cross-country) M(c)/W(c), skiing (downhill) M(c)/W(c), soccer M/W, softball M/W, table tennis M/W, tennis M/W, ultimate Frisbee M/W, volleyball M/W, water polo M/W, weight lifting M/W.

Standardized Tests *Required:* SAT or ACT (for admission).

Costs (2011–12) *Comprehensive fee:* $48,362 includes full-time tuition ($38,800), mandatory fees ($212), and room and board ($9350). Full-time tuition and fees vary according to course load. Part-time tuition: $4850 per course. Part-time tuition and fees vary according to course load. *Room and board:* Room and board charges vary according to board plan and housing facility. *Payment plans:* tuition prepayment, installment. *Waivers:* employees or children of employees.

Financial Aid Of all full-time matriculated undergraduates who enrolled in 2011, 1,911 applied for aid, 1,261 were judged to have need, 493 had their need fully met. In 2011, 612 non-need-based awards were made. *Average percent of need met:* 87%. *Average financial aid package:* $31,350. *Average need-based loan:* $4710. *Average need-based gift aid:* $25,987. *Average non-need-based aid:* $13,951. *Average indebtedness upon graduation:* $25,932.

Applying *Options:* electronic application, early action, deferred entrance. *Application fee:* $50. *Required:* essay or personal statement, high school transcript, minimum 2.0 GPA, 1 letter of recommendation. *Required for some:* interview. *Recommended:* interview. *Application deadlines:* 2/1 (freshmen), 2/1 (transfers), 11/1 (early action). *Notification:* continuous until 4/1 (freshmen), 3/15 (transfers), 12/15 (early action).

Freshman Application Contact Teresa Hudkins, Director of Admission, Willamette University, 900 State Street, Salem, OR 97301. *Phone:* 877-542-2787. *Toll-free phone:* 877-542-2787. *Fax:* 503-375-5363. *E-mail:* libarts@willamette.edu. *Web site:* http://www.willamette.edu/.

PENNSYLVANIA

Albright College

Reading, Pennsylvania

- **Independent** comprehensive, founded 1856, affiliated with United Methodist Church
- **Suburban** 118-acre campus with easy access to Philadelphia
- **Endowment** $52.6 million
- **Coed** 2,317 undergraduate students, 99% full-time, 57% women, 43% men
- **Moderately difficult** entrance level, 49% of applicants were admitted

Undergraduates 2,299 full-time, 18 part-time. Students come from 23 states and territories; 17 other countries; 36% are from out of state; 13% Black or African American, non-Hispanic/Latino; 8% Hispanic/Latino; 2% Asian, non-Hispanic/Latino; 0.6% American Indian or Alaska Native, non-Hispanic/Latino; 1% Two or more races, non-Hispanic/Latino; 5% Race/ethnicity unknown; 3% international; 2% transferred in; 67% live on campus. *Retention:* 75% of full-time freshmen returned.

Freshmen *Admission:* 6,132 applied, 3,011 admitted, 519 enrolled. *Average high school GPA:* 3.35. *Test scores:* SAT critical reading scores over 500: 65%; SAT math scores over 500: 68%; SAT critical reading scores over 600: 17%; SAT math scores over 600: 20%; SAT critical reading scores over 700: 2%; SAT math scores over 700: 1%.

Faculty *Total:* 166, 69% full-time, 65% with terminal degrees. *Student/faculty ratio:* 13:1.

Academics *Calendar:* 4-1-4. *Degrees:* certificates, bachelor's, and master's. *Special study options:* accelerated degree program, advanced placement credit, double majors, English as a second language, honors programs, independent study, internships, off-campus study, part-time degree program, services for LD students, student-designed majors, study abroad, summer session for

credit. *ROTC:* Army (c). *Unusual degree programs:* 3-2 forestry with Duke University; environmental studies with Duke University.

Computers on Campus 458 computers/terminals are available on campus for general student use. Students can access the following: campus intranet, computer help desk, free student e-mail accounts, online (class) grades, online (class) registration, online (class) schedules, online financial statements, housing choices, course management systems. Campuswide network is available. 100% of college-owned or -operated housing units are wired for high-speed Internet access. Wireless service is available via entire campus.

Student Life *Housing:* on-campus residence required through sophomore year. *Options:* coed, men-only, women-only. Campus housing is university owned. Freshman campus housing is guaranteed. *Activities and organizations:* drama/theater group, student-run newspaper, radio station, choral group, Albright College Activities Council, Student Government Association, yearbook, newspaper, radio station, national fraternities, national sororities. *Campus security:* 24-hour emergency response devices and patrols, student patrols, late-night transport/escort service, controlled dormitory access, E2 Campus Text messaging, Rape Aggression Defense Training, Marked Patrol Cars, Partnership with Reading PD, PA State Police. *Student services:* health clinic, personal/psychological counseling, women's center.

Athletics Member NCAA. All Division III. *Intercollegiate sports:* badminton W(c), baseball M, basketball M/W, cheerleading M/W, cross-country running M/W, field hockey W, football M, golf M/W, lacrosse M/W, rugby M(c)/W(c), soccer M/W, softball W, swimming and diving M/W, tennis M/W, track and field M/W, ultimate Frisbee M(c)/W(c), volleyball W. *Intramural sports:* badminton W, basketball M/W, football M, racquetball M/W, soccer M/W, softball M/W, volleyball M/W.

Standardized Tests *Required:* students applying tests optional, must complete an on-campus admission interview (for admission). *Recommended:* SAT (for admission), ACT (for admission), SAT or ACT (for admission).

Costs (2011–12) *Comprehensive fee:* $43,190 includes full-time tuition ($33,190), mandatory fees ($800), and room and board ($9200). Full-time tuition and fees vary according to degree level. Part-time tuition: $4150 per course. Part-time tuition and fees vary according to degree level. *College room only:* $5110. Room and board charges vary according to board plan and housing facility. *Payment plan:* installment. *Waivers:* adult students, senior citizens, and employees or children of employees.

Applying *Options:* electronic application, early admission, deferred entrance. *Application fee:* $25. *Required:* essay or personal statement, high school transcript, 1 letter of recommendation, secondary school report (guidance department). *Recommended:* interview. *Application deadlines:* rolling (freshmen), rolling (transfers). *Notification:* continuous (freshmen), continuous (transfers).

Freshman Application Contact Mr. Gregory Eichhorn, Vice President for Enrollment Management, Albright College, PO Box 15234, 13th and Bern Streets, Reading, PA 19612-5234. *Phone:* 610-921-7260. *Toll-free phone:* 800-252-1856. *Fax:* 610-921-7294. *E-mail:* admission@albright.edu. *Web site:* http://www.albright.edu/.

Allegheny College
Meadville, Pennsylvania

- **Independent** 4-year, founded 1815
- **Suburban** 565-acre campus
- **Endowment** $153.5 million
- **Coed** 2,123 undergraduate students, 98% full-time, 53% women, 47% men
- **Very difficult** entrance level, 58% of applicants were admitted

Undergraduates 2,086 full-time, 37 part-time. Students come from 44 states and territories; 34 other countries; 45% are from out of state; 5% Black or African American, non-Hispanic/Latino; 5% Hispanic/Latino; 3% Asian, non-Hispanic/Latino; 0.1% American Indian or Alaska Native, non-Hispanic/Latino; 2% Two or more races, non-Hispanic/Latino; 0.4% Race/ethnicity unknown; 1% international; 1% transferred in; 90% live on campus. *Retention:* 87% of full-time freshmen returned.

Freshmen *Admission:* 4,770 applied, 2,747 admitted, 559 enrolled. *Average high school GPA:* 3.72. *Test scores:* SAT critical reading scores over 500: 87%; SAT math scores over 500: 87%; SAT writing scores over 500: 82%; ACT scores over 18: 100%; SAT critical reading scores over 600: 55%; SAT math scores over 600: 48%; SAT writing scores over 600: 42%; ACT scores over 24: 71%; SAT critical reading scores over 700: 12%; SAT math scores over 700: 7%; SAT writing scores over 700: 8%; ACT scores over 30: 16%.

Faculty *Total:* 196, 84% full-time, 83% with terminal degrees. *Student/faculty ratio:* 12:1.

Academics *Calendar:* semesters. *Degree:* bachelor's. *Special study options:* advanced placement credit, double majors, English as a second language, independent study, internships, off-campus study, services for LD students, student-designed majors, study abroad. *Unusual degree programs:* 3-2 engineering with Columbia University, Case Western Reserve University,

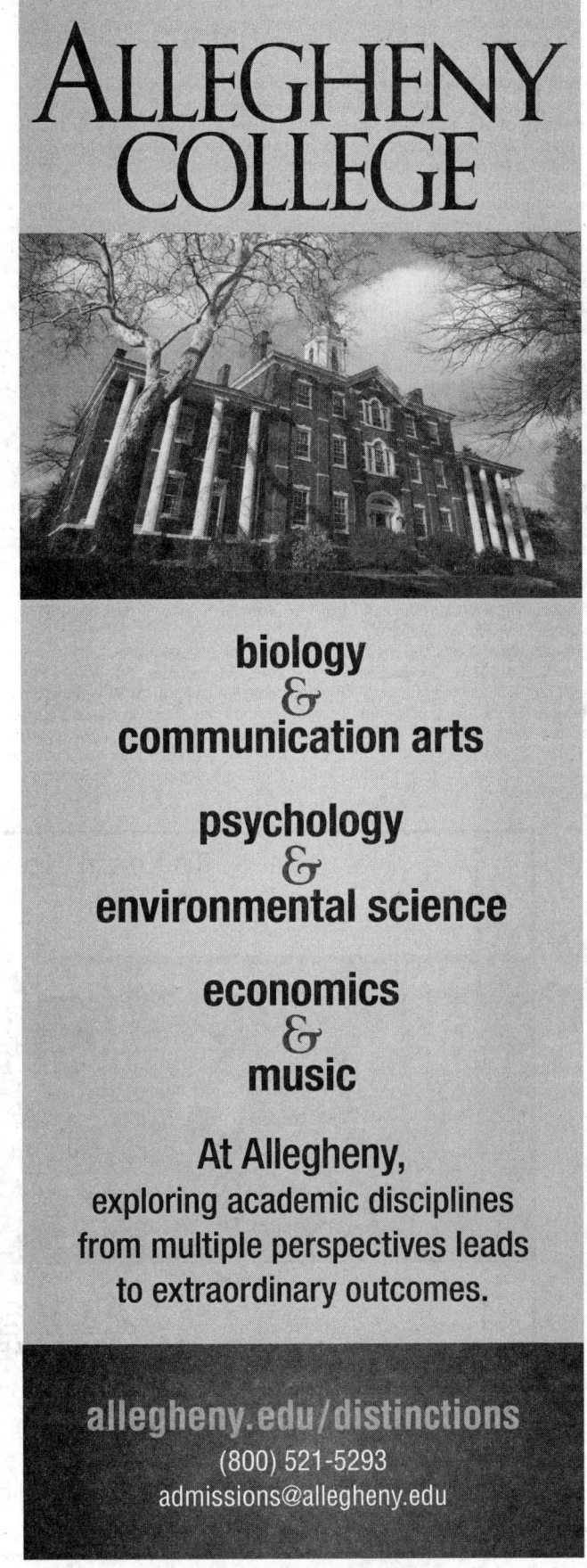

Duke University, Washington University, University of Pittsburgh; nursing with Case Western Reserve University; arts management, public policy and management, health care policy and management and information systems management at Carnegie Mellon University; physician assistant and occupational therapy at Chatham; osteopathic medicine at PCOM and LECOM; physical therapy 4-2 doctorate program at Chatham.

Computers on Campus 205 computers/terminals and 200 ports are available on campus for general student use. Students can access the following: campus intranet, computer help desk, free student e-mail accounts, online (class) grades, online (class) registration, online (class) schedules, online room selection, placement testing, course catalog, class lists, book buy, repair service, transcript review and ordering, billing, payroll time cards, internet kiosks, dataports for laptops, campus organizations, financial aid. Campuswide network is available. 100% of college-owned or -operated housing units are wired for high-speed Internet access. Wireless service is available via entire campus.

Student Life *Housing:* on-campus residence required through senior year. *Options:* coed, men-only, women-only, disabled students. Campus housing is university owned. Freshman campus housing is guaranteed. *Activities and organizations:* drama/theater group, student-run newspaper, radio and television station, choral group, student government, Gators Activity Programming, Alpha Phi Omega (service fraternity), Outing Club, Greek life, national fraternities, national sororities. *Campus security:* 24-hour emergency response devices and patrols, late-night transport/escort service, controlled dormitory access, local police patrol, emergency alert system, self defense education, TIPS Hotline - discriminatory harassment reporting. *Student services:* health clinic, personal/psychological counseling.

Athletics Member NCAA. All Division III. *Intercollegiate sports:* baseball M, basketball M/W, cheerleading M(c)/W(c), crew M(c)/W(c), cross-country running M/W, equestrian sports M(c)/W(c), fencing M(c)/W(c), football M, golf M/W, ice hockey M(c), lacrosse W, rugby M(c)/W(c), soccer M/W, softball W, swimming and diving M/W, tennis M/W, track and field M/W, ultimate Frisbee M(c)/W(c), volleyball M(c)/W. *Intramural sports:* basketball M/W, soccer M/W, volleyball M/W.

Standardized Tests *Required:* SAT or ACT (for admission).

Costs (2012–13) *Comprehensive fee:* $47,150 includes full-time tuition ($37,260), mandatory fees ($350), and room and board ($9540). Part-time tuition: $1553 per credit hour. Part-time tuition and fees vary according to course load. *Required fees:* $175 per term part-time. *College room only:* $5020. Room and board charges vary according to board plan and housing facility. *Payment plan:* installment. *Waivers:* employees or children of employees.

Financial Aid Of all full-time matriculated undergraduates who enrolled in 2011, 1,666 applied for aid, 1,477 were judged to have need, 475 had their need fully met. 1,220 Federal Work-Study jobs (averaging $2000). 94 state and other part-time jobs (averaging $4700). In 2011, 560 non-need-based awards were made. *Average percent of need met:* 89%. *Average financial aid package:* $29,742. *Average need-based loan:* $5008. *Average need-based gift aid:* $22,848. *Average non-need-based aid:* $13,008.

Applying *Options:* electronic application, early admission, early decision, deferred entrance. *Application fee:* $35. *Required:* essay or personal statement, high school transcript, 2 letters of recommendation, college preparatory program, standardized test scores, health examination. *Recommended:* interview. *Application deadlines:* 2/15 (freshmen), 7/1 (transfers). *Early decision deadline:* 11/15. *Notification:* 4/1 (freshmen), 8/1 (transfers), 12/15 (early decision).

Freshman Application Contact Ms. Linda Clune, Senior Associate Director of Admissions, Allegheny College, 520 North Main Street, Box 5, Meadville, PA 16335. *Phone:* 814-332-4351. *Toll-free phone:* 800-521-5293. *Fax:* 814-337-0431. *E-mail:* admissions@allegheny.edu. *Web site:* http://www.allegheny.edu/.

See page 745 for display ad and page 1048 for the College Close-Up.

Alvernia University
Reading, Pennsylvania

- **Independent Roman Catholic** comprehensive, founded 1958
- **Suburban** 121-acre campus with easy access to Philadelphia
- **Coed** 2,366 undergraduate students, 71% full-time, 70% women, 30% men
- **Moderately difficult** entrance level, 75% of applicants were admitted

Undergraduates 1,690 full-time, 676 part-time. 23% are from out of state; 10% Black or African American, non-Hispanic/Latino; 7% Hispanic/Latino; 1% Asian, non-Hispanic/Latino; 0.1% American Indian or Alaska Native, non-Hispanic/Latino; 1% Two or more races, non-Hispanic/Latino; 3% Race/ethnicity unknown; 0.2% international; 5% transferred in; 56% live on campus. *Retention:* 72% of full-time freshmen returned.

Freshmen *Admission:* 1,814 applied, 1,364 admitted, 376 enrolled. *Average high school GPA:* 3.2. *Test scores:* SAT critical reading scores over 500: 42%; SAT math scores over 500: 50%; SAT writing scores over 500: 35%; ACT scores over 18: 83%; SAT critical reading scores over 600: 9%; SAT math

scores over 600: 10%; SAT writing scores over 600: 6%; ACT scores over 24: 25%; ACT scores over 30: 1%.

Faculty *Total:* 324, 30% full-time, 35% with terminal degrees. *Student/faculty ratio:* 13:1.

Academics *Calendar:* semesters. *Degrees:* associate, bachelor's, master's, doctoral, and first professional. *Special study options:* adult/continuing education programs, part-time degree program. *ROTC:* Army (c).

Computers on Campus Students can access the following: computer help desk, free student e-mail accounts, online (class) grades, online (class) registration, online (class) schedules. Campuswide network is available. 100% of college-owned or -operated housing units are wired for high-speed Internet access. Wireless service is available via classrooms, computer centers, computer labs, dorm rooms, learning centers, libraries, student centers.

Student Life *Housing:* on-campus residence required for freshman year. *Options:* coed. Campus housing is university owned. Freshman campus housing is guaranteed. *Campus security:* 24-hour patrols, late-night transport/escort service, controlled dormitory access.

Athletics Member NCAA. All Division III. *Intercollegiate sports:* baseball M, basketball M/W, cross-country running M/W, field hockey W, golf M, ice hockey M(c), lacrosse M/W, soccer M/W, softball W, tennis M/W, track and field M/W, volleyball W. *Intramural sports:* basketball M/W, cheerleading W(c), soccer M/W.

Standardized Tests *Required:* SAT or ACT (for admission).

Costs (2012–13) *Comprehensive fee:* $37,960 includes full-time tuition ($27,400), mandatory fees ($550), and room and board ($10,010). Full-time tuition and fees vary according to class time and reciprocity agreements. Part-time tuition: $750 per credit hour. Part-time tuition and fees vary according to class time and course load. *College room only:* $5060. Room and board charges vary according to board plan and housing facility. *Payment plan:* installment. *Waivers:* senior citizens and employees or children of employees.

Financial Aid Of all full-time matriculated undergraduates who enrolled in 2010, 1,588 applied for aid, 1,464 were judged to have need, 141 had their need fully met. 213 Federal Work-Study jobs (averaging $968). 27 state and other part-time jobs (averaging $2677). In 2010, 163 non-need-based awards were made. *Average percent of need met:* 58%. *Average financial aid package:* $16,241. *Average need-based loan:* $4196. *Average need-based gift aid:* $12,182. *Average non-need-based aid:* $7785. *Average indebtedness upon graduation:* $37,773.

Applying *Options:* electronic application, deferred entrance. *Application fee:* $25. *Required:* essay or personal statement, high school transcript. *Required for some:* 2 letters of recommendation, interview. *Recommended:* minimum 2.0 GPA, 1 letter of recommendation. *Application deadlines:* rolling (freshmen), rolling (transfers). *Notification:* continuous (freshmen).

Freshman Application Contact Mr. John McCloskey, Vice President for Enrollment Management, Alvernia University, 400 Saint Bernardine Street, Reading, PA 19607-1799. *Phone:* 610-796-3005. *Toll-free phone:* 888-ALVERNIA. *Fax:* 610-796-2873. *E-mail:* admissions@alvernia.edu. *Web site:* http://www.alvernia.edu/.

See page 1050 for the College Close-Up.

Arcadia University
Glenside, Pennsylvania

- **Independent** comprehensive, founded 1853, affiliated with Presbyterian Church (U.S.A.)
- **Suburban** 71-acre campus with easy access to Philadelphia
- **Endowment** $55.5 million
- **Coed** 2,211 undergraduate students, 91% full-time, 71% women, 29% men
- **Moderately difficult** entrance level, 54% of applicants were admitted

Undergraduates 2,007 full-time, 204 part-time. Students come from 47 states and territories; 16 other countries; 30% are from out of state; 7% Black or African American, non-Hispanic/Latino; 5% Hispanic/Latino; 4% Asian, non-Hispanic/Latino; 0.3% American Indian or Alaska Native, non-Hispanic/Latino; 2% Two or more races, non-Hispanic/Latino; 14% Race/ethnicity unknown; 1% international; 7% transferred in; 53% live on campus. *Retention:* 78% of full-time freshmen returned.

Freshmen *Admission:* 7,673 applied, 4,108 admitted, 511 enrolled. *Average high school GPA:* 3.63. *Test scores:* SAT critical reading scores over 500: 79%; SAT math scores over 500: 80%; SAT writing scores over 500: 79%; ACT scores over 18: 98%; SAT critical reading scores over 600: 29%; SAT math scores over 600: 28%; SAT writing scores over 600: 28%; ACT scores over 24: 63%; SAT critical reading scores over 700: 4%; SAT math scores over 700: 2%; SAT writing scores over 700: 2%; ACT scores over 30: 11%.

Faculty *Total:* 479, 34% full-time. *Student/faculty ratio:* 11:1.

Academics *Calendar:* semesters. *Degrees:* bachelor's, master's, doctoral, postbachelor's, and first professional certificates. *Special study options:* accelerated degree program, advanced placement credit, cooperative education, distance learning, double majors, English as a second language, honors programs, independent study, internships, off-campus study, part-time degree program,

services for LD students, student-designed majors, study abroad, summer session for credit.

Computers on Campus 120 computers/terminals and 620 ports are available on campus for general student use. Students can access the following: campus intranet, computer help desk, free student e-mail accounts, online (class) grades, online (class) registration, online (class) schedules. Campuswide network is available.

Student Life *Housing options:* coed, women-only. Campus housing is university owned and leased by the school. Freshman campus housing is guaranteed. *Activities and organizations:* drama/theater group, student-run newspaper, radio station, choral group, Student Program Board, Residence Hall Council, student government, Arcadia Christian Fellowship, Student Alumni Association. *Campus security:* 24-hour emergency response devices and patrols, student patrols, late-night transport/escort service, controlled dormitory access. *Student services:* health clinic, personal/psychological counseling.

Athletics Member NCAA. All Division III. *Intercollegiate sports:* baseball M, basketball M/W, equestrian sports M/W, field hockey W, golf M/W, lacrosse W, soccer M/W, softball W, swimming and diving M/W, tennis M/W, volleyball W. *Intramural sports:* basketball M/W, cheerleading W(c), equestrian sports M/W, field hockey W, rock climbing M/W, soccer M/W, swimming and diving M, tennis M/W, volleyball M/W, weight lifting M/W.

Standardized Tests *Required:* SAT or ACT (for admission).

Costs (2011–12) *Comprehensive fee:* $45,790 includes full-time tuition ($33,490), mandatory fees ($660), and room and board ($11,640). Full-time tuition and fees vary according to course load, degree level, and program. Part-time tuition: $560 per credit. *Room and board:* Room and board charges vary according to board plan.

Financial Aid Of all full-time matriculated undergraduates who enrolled in 2011, 1,966 applied for aid, 1,765 were judged to have need, 234 had their need fully met. 1,289 Federal Work-Study jobs (averaging $1645). 150 state and other part-time jobs (averaging $1541). In 2011, 321 non-need-based awards were made. *Average percent of need met:* 70%. *Average financial aid package:* $23,875. *Average need-based loan:* $4164. *Average need-based gift aid:* $19,587. *Average non-need-based aid:* $14,367. *Average indebtedness upon graduation:* $40,287.

Applying *Options:* electronic application, deferred entrance. *Application fee:* $30. *Required:* essay or personal statement, high school transcript, 2 letters of recommendation. *Required for some:* portfolio, audition. *Recommended:* minimum 3.0 GPA, interview. *Application deadlines:* 3/1 (freshmen), 6/15 (transfers). *Notification:* continuous until 9/1 (freshmen), continuous until 9/1 (transfers).

Freshman Application Contact Colleen Pernicello, Director of Undergraduate Admissions, Arcadia University, 450 South Easton Road, Glenside, PA 19038. *Phone:* 215-572-2910. *Toll-free phone:* 877-ARCADIA. *Fax:* 215-572-4049. *E-mail:* admiss@arcadia.edu. *Web site:* http://www.arcadia.edu/.

See page 747 for display ad and page 1060 for the College Close-Up.

The Art Institute of Philadelphia
Philadelphia, Pennsylvania

- **Proprietary** 4-year, founded 1966, part of Education Management Corporation
- **Urban** campus
- **Coed**

Academics *Calendar:* quarters. *Degrees:* diplomas, associate, and bachelor's.

Costs (2011–12) *Tuition:* Tuition cost varies by program. Prospective students should contact the school for current tuition costs. Other charges include a starting kit for all first-quarter students. Kits vary in price, depending on the program of study.

Freshman Application Contact The Art Institute of Philadelphia, 1622 Chestnut Street, Philadelphia, PA 19103. *Phone:* 215-567-7080. *Toll-free phone:* 800-275-2474. *Web site:* http://www.artinstitutes.edu/philadelphia/.

See page 1116 for the College Close-Up.

The Art Institute of Pittsburgh
Pittsburgh, Pennsylvania

- **Proprietary** 4-year, founded 1921, part of Education Management Corporation
- **Urban** campus
- **Coed**

Academics *Calendar:* quarters. *Degrees:* certificates, diplomas, associate, and bachelor's.

Costs (2011–12) *Tuition:* Tuition cost varies by program. Prospective students should contact the school for current tuition costs. Other charges include a starting kit for all first-quarter students. Kits vary in price, depending on the program of study.

Freshman Application Contact The Art Institute of Pittsburgh, 420 Boulevard of the Allies, Pittsburgh, PA 15219. *Phone:* 412-263-6600. *Toll-free phone:* 800-275-2470. *Web site:* http://www.artinstitutes.edu/pittsburgh/.

See page 1120 for the College Close-Up.

The Art Institute of York–Pennsylvania
York, Pennsylvania

- **Proprietary** primarily 2-year, founded 1952, part of Education Management Corporation
- **Suburban** campus
- **Coed**

Academics *Calendar:* quarters. *Degrees:* associate and bachelor's.

Costs (2011–12) *Tuition:* Tuition cost varies by program. Prospective students should contact the school for current tuition costs. Other charges include a starting kit for all first-quarter students. Kits vary in price, depending on the program of study.

Freshman Application Contact The Art Institute of York–Pennsylvania, 1409 Williams Road, York, PA 17402-9012. *Phone:* 717-755-2300. *Toll-free phone:* 800-864-7725. *Web site:* http://www.artinstitutes.edu/york/.

See page 1146 for the College Close-Up.

Baptist Bible College of Pennsylvania
Clarks Summit, Pennsylvania

- **Independent Baptist** comprehensive, founded 1932
- **Suburban** 124-acre campus
- **Endowment** $2.1 million
- **Coed** 722 undergraduate students, 79% full-time, 50% women, 50% men
- **Minimally difficult** entrance level, 81% of applicants were admitted

Undergraduates 568 full-time, 154 part-time. Students come from 34 states and territories; 86 other countries; 51% are from out of state; 3% Black or African American, non-Hispanic/Latino; 2% Hispanic/Latino; 0.6% Asian, non-Hispanic/Latino; 0.1% Native Hawaiian or other Pacific Islander, non-Hispanic/Latino; 0.4% American Indian or Alaska Native, non-Hispanic/Latino; 1% Two or more races, non-Hispanic/Latino; 3% Race/ethnicity unknown; 0.1% international; 7% transferred in; 91% live on campus. *Retention:* 47% of full-time freshmen returned.

Freshmen *Admission:* 834 applied, 676 admitted, 115 enrolled. *Average high school GPA:* 3.31. *Test scores:* SAT critical reading scores over 500: 66%; SAT math scores over 500: 46%; SAT writing scores over 500: 56%; ACT scores over 18: 85%; SAT critical reading scores over 600: 22%; SAT math scores over 600: 14%; SAT writing scores over 600: 21%; ACT scores over 24: 31%; SAT critical reading scores over 700: 6%; SAT math scores over 700: 2%; SAT writing scores over 700: 2%; ACT scores over 30: 4%.

Faculty *Total:* 47, 87% full-time. *Student/faculty ratio:* 11:1.

Academics *Calendar:* semesters. *Degrees:* certificates, associate, bachelor's, master's, doctoral, and first professional. *Special study options:* academic remediation for entering students, adult/continuing education programs, advanced placement credit, distance learning, double majors, English as a second language, external degree program, independent study, internships, part-time degree program, student-designed majors, summer session for credit. *ROTC:* Army (c), Navy (c), Air Force (c).

Computers on Campus 25 computers/terminals are available on campus for general student use. Students can access the following: campus intranet, computer help desk, free student e-mail accounts, online (class) grades, online (class) registration, online (class) schedules. Campuswide network is available. 100% of college-owned or -operated housing units are wired for high-speed Internet access. Wireless service is available via classrooms, computer centers, computer labs, learning centers, libraries, student centers.

Student Life *Housing:* on-campus residence required through senior year. *Options:* men-only, women-only. Campus housing is university owned. Freshman campus housing is guaranteed. *Activities and organizations:* drama/theater group, choral group. *Campus security:* 24-hour patrols, student patrols, controlled dormitory access. *Student services:* health clinic, personal/psychological counseling.

Athletics Member NCAA, NCCAA. All NCAA Division III. *Intercollegiate sports:* baseball M, basketball M/W, cheerleading W, cross-country running M/W, golf M, soccer M/W, softball W, tennis W, track and field M/W, volleyball W. *Intramural sports:* basketball M, golf M, soccer M/W, softball M, volleyball W.

Standardized Tests *Required:* SAT or ACT (for admission).

Costs (2012–13) *Comprehensive fee:* $25,981 includes full-time tuition ($17,771), mandatory fees ($1260), and room and board ($6950). Part-time tuition: $592 per credit. *Required fees:* $42 per credit part-time. *College room only:* $2500. Room and board charges vary according to board plan. *Payment plan:* installment. *Waivers:* employees or children of employees.

Financial Aid Of all full-time matriculated undergraduates who enrolled in 2010, 480 applied for aid, 443 were judged to have need, 30 had their need fully met. 60 Federal Work-Study jobs (averaging $1582). In 2010, 70 non-need-based awards were made. *Average percent of need met:* 63%. *Average financial aid package:* $13,342. *Average need-based loan:* $3755. *Average need-based gift aid:* $5380. *Average non-need-based aid:* $4466. *Average indebtedness upon graduation:* $23,412.

Applying *Options:* electronic application, early admission, deferred entrance. *Application fee:* $40. *Required:* essay or personal statement, high school transcript, 3 letters of recommendation, Christian testimony. *Required for some:* interview. *Application deadlines:* 8/15 (freshmen), rolling (transfers). *Notification:* continuous (freshmen).

Freshman Application Contact Ms. Kellyn Lovell, Supervisor, Support Services, Baptist Bible College of Pennsylvania, 538 Venard Road, Clarks Summit, PA 18411-1297. *Phone:* 800-451-7664. *Toll-free phone:* 800-451-7664. *Fax:* 570-585-9271. *E-mail:* admissions@bbc.edu. *Web site:* http://www.bbc.edu/.

Bloomsburg University of Pennsylvania

Bloomsburg, Pennsylvania

- **State-supported** comprehensive, founded 1839, part of Pennsylvania State System of Higher Education
- **Rural** 282-acre campus
- **Endowment** $22.0 million
- **Coed** 9,256 undergraduate students, 94% full-time, 57% women, 43% men
- **Moderately difficult** entrance level, 63% of applicants were admitted

Undergraduates 8,686 full-time, 570 part-time. Students come from 26 states and territories; 21 other countries; 11% are from out of state; 7% Black or African American, non-Hispanic/Latino; 4% Hispanic/Latino; 0.9% Asian, non-Hispanic/Latino; 0.1% Native Hawaiian or other Pacific Islander, non-Hispanic/Latino; 0.1% American Indian or Alaska Native, non-Hispanic/Latino; 1% Two or more races, non-Hispanic/Latino; 4% Race/ethnicity unknown; 1% international; 5% transferred in; 48% live on campus. *Retention:* 80% of full-time freshmen returned.

Freshmen *Admission:* 11,423 applied, 7,188 admitted, 1,981 enrolled. *Average high school GPA:* 3.3. *Test scores:* SAT critical reading scores over 500: 49%; SAT math scores over 500: 59%; SAT writing scores over 500: 45%; ACT scores over 18: 90%; SAT critical reading scores over 600: 8%; SAT math scores over 600: 12%; SAT writing scores over 600: 7%; ACT scores over 24: 27%; SAT critical reading scores over 700: 1%.

Faculty *Total:* 490, 81% full-time, 69% with terminal degrees. *Student/faculty ratio:* 22:1.

Academics *Calendar:* semesters. *Degrees:* bachelor's, master's, doctoral, post-master's, and postbachelor's certificates. *Special study options:* academic remediation for entering students, advanced placement credit, cooperative education, distance learning, double majors, English as a second language, freshman honors college, honors programs, independent study, internships, off-campus study, part-time degree program, services for LD students, study abroad, summer session for credit. *ROTC:* Army (b), Air Force (c). *Unusual degree programs:* 3-2 engineering with Pennsylvania State University, Wilkes University.

Computers on Campus 1,557 computers/terminals are available on campus for general student use. Students can access the following: computer help desk, free student e-mail accounts, online (class) grades, online (class) registration, online (class) schedules. Campuswide network is available. 100% of college-owned or -operated housing units are wired for high-speed Internet access. Wireless service is available via entire campus.

Student Life *Housing:* on-campus residence required for freshman year. *Options:* coed. Campus housing is university owned and leased by the school. Freshman campus housing is guaranteed. *Activities and organizations:* drama/theater group, student-run newspaper, radio and television station, choral group, marching band, Living and Learning Communities, national fraternities, national sororities. *Campus security:* 24-hour emergency response devices and patrols, late-night transport/escort service, controlled dormitory access, monitored surveillance cameras. *Student services:* health clinic, personal/psychological counseling, women's center, legal services.

Athletics Member NCAA. All Division II except wrestling (Division I). *Intercollegiate sports:* baseball M(s), basketball M(s)/W(s), cross-country running M(s)/W(s), field hockey W(s), football M(s), lacrosse W(s), soccer M(s)/W(s),

softball W(s), swimming and diving M(s)/W(s), tennis M(s)/W(s), track and field M(s)/W(s), wrestling M(s). *Intramural sports:* baseball M(c), basketball M/W, bowling M(c)/W(c), cheerleading M(c)/W(c), cross-country running M(c)/W(c), equestrian sports M(c)/W(c), field hockey W, football M, ice hockey M(c), lacrosse M(c), racquetball M/W, rugby M(c)/W(c), skiing (downhill) M(c)/W(c), soccer M(c)/W(c), softball M/W, table tennis M(c)/W(c), tennis M(c)/W(c), ultimate Frisbee M(c)/W(c), volleyball M(c)/W(c), water polo M(c)/W(c), weight lifting M(c).

Standardized Tests *Required:* SAT or ACT (for admission).

Costs (2011–12) *Tuition:* state resident $6240 full-time, $260 per credit part-time; nonresident $15,600 full-time, $650 per credit part-time. Full-time tuition and fees vary according to course load. Part-time tuition and fees vary according to course load. *Required fees:* $1842 full-time, $69 per credit part-time, $40 per term part-time. *Room and board:* $7216; room only: $4464. Room and board charges vary according to board plan and housing facility. *Payment plan:* installment. *Waivers:* minority students, senior citizens, and employees or children of employees.

Financial Aid Of all full-time matriculated undergraduates who enrolled in 2011, 7,469 applied for aid, 5,431 were judged to have need, 647 had their need fully met. 768 Federal Work-Study jobs (averaging $2404). 980 state and other part-time jobs (averaging $3491). In 2011, 137 non-need-based awards were made. *Average percent of need met:* 57%. *Average financial aid package:* $8252. *Average need-based loan:* $4107. *Average need-based gift aid:* $5732. *Average non-need-based aid:* $1527. *Average indebtedness upon graduation:* $25,321.

Applying *Options:* electronic application, early admission, early action, deferred entrance. *Application fee:* $35. *Required:* high school transcript. *Application deadlines:* rolling (freshmen), rolling (transfers), 10/31 (early action). *Notification:* continuous until 10/1 (freshmen), continuous (out-of-state freshmen), continuous (transfers).

Freshman Application Contact Mr. Christopher Keller, Director of Admissions, Bloomsburg University of Pennsylvania, 104 Student Services Center, Bloomsburg, PA 17815-1905. *Phone:* 570-389-4316. *Fax:* 570-389-4741. *E-mail:* buadmiss@bloomu.edu. *Web site:* http://www.bloomu.edu/.

Bryn Athyn College of the New Church

Bryn Athyn, Pennsylvania

- **Independent Christian** comprehensive, founded 1876, affiliated with Church of the New Jerusalem, part of The Academy of the New Church
- **Suburban** 130-acre campus with easy access to Philadelphia
- **Endowment** $247.9 million
- **Coed** 238 undergraduate students, 97% full-time, 60% women, 40% men
- **Minimally difficult** entrance level, 44% of applicants were admitted

Undergraduates 231 full-time, 7 part-time. Students come from 16 states and territories; 12 other countries; 32% are from out of state; 12% Black or African American, non-Hispanic/Latino; 3% Hispanic/Latino; 1% Asian, non-Hispanic/Latino; 0.4% American Indian or Alaska Native, non-Hispanic/Latino; 0.9% Two or more races, non-Hispanic/Latino; 13% international; 6% transferred in; 74% live on campus. *Retention:* 72% of full-time freshmen returned.

Freshmen *Admission:* 833 applied, 370 admitted, 82 enrolled. *Average high school GPA:* 3.26. *Test scores:* SAT critical reading scores over 500: 63%; SAT math scores over 500: 51%; SAT writing scores over 500: 51%; ACT scores over 18: 73%; SAT critical reading scores over 600: 28%; SAT math scores over 600: 28%; SAT writing scores over 600: 19%; ACT scores over 24: 51%; SAT critical reading scores over 700: 13%; SAT math scores over 700: 3%; SAT writing scores over 700: 10%; ACT scores over 30: 28%.

Faculty *Total:* 43, 60% full-time, 49% with terminal degrees. *Student/faculty ratio:* 7:1.

Academics *Calendar:* trimesters. *Degrees:* associate, bachelor's, master's, and doctoral. *Special study options:* academic remediation for entering students, accelerated degree program, advanced placement credit, cooperative education, English as a second language, independent study, internships, part-time degree program, services for LD students, student-designed majors, study abroad. *ROTC:* Army (c), Air Force (c).

Computers on Campus 24 computers/terminals are available on campus for general student use. Students can access the following: computer help desk, free student e-mail accounts, online (class) registration, online (class) schedules. Campuswide network is available. 100% of college-owned or -operated housing units are wired for high-speed Internet access. Wireless service is available via entire campus.

Student Life *Housing options:* men-only, women-only. Campus housing is university owned. Freshman campus housing is guaranteed. *Activities and organizations:* drama/theater group, student-run newspaper, choral group, C.A.R.E. (Community Service), Social council, International Student Organization, Peer Advisory Council, Student government. *Campus security:* 24-hour emergency response devices, controlled dormitory access, 18-hour patrols

by trained personnel. *Student services:* health clinic, personal/psychological counseling.

Athletics *Intramural sports:* ice hockey M, lacrosse M, soccer M, tennis M/W, volleyball W.

Standardized Tests *Required:* SAT or ACT (for admission).

Costs (2012–13) *Comprehensive fee:* $26,649 includes full-time tuition ($15,712), mandatory fees ($1166), and room and board ($9771). Part-time tuition: $605 per credit hour. *Required fees:* $45 per credit hour part-time. *Room and board:* Room and board charges vary according to housing facility. *Payment plan:* installment. *Waivers:* senior citizens.

Financial Aid Of all full-time matriculated undergraduates who enrolled in 2008, 92 applied for aid, 66 were judged to have need, 30 had their need fully met. In 2008, 22 non-need-based awards were made. *Average percent of need met:* 95%. *Average financial aid package:* $9987. *Average need-based loan:* $3329. *Average need-based gift aid:* $8358. *Average non-need-based aid:* $2232. *Average indebtedness upon graduation:* $8299. *Financial aid deadline:* 7/1.

Applying *Options:* electronic application, deferred entrance. *Required:* essay or personal statement, high school transcript, minimum 2.0 GPA, 1 letter of recommendation, interest in the writings of Emanuel Swedenborg. *Required for some:* interview. *Application deadlines:* 7/1 (freshmen), 7/1 (transfers). *Notification:* continuous (freshmen), continuous (transfers).

Freshman Application Contact Admissions Office, Bryn Athyn College of the New Church, 2945 College Drive, Box 462, Bryn Athyn, PA 19009. *Phone:* 267-502-6000. *Toll-free phone:* 800-767-9552. *Fax:* 267-502-2593. *E-mail:* admissions@brynathyn.edu. *Web site:* http://www.brynathyn.edu/.

Bryn Mawr College

Bryn Mawr, Pennsylvania

- **Independent** university, founded 1885
- **Suburban** 135-acre campus with easy access to Philadelphia
- **Endowment** $671.1 million
- **Undergraduate: women only; graduate: coed** 1,313 undergraduate students, 98% full-time, 100% women
- **Most difficult** entrance level, 46% of applicants were admitted

Undergraduates 1,289 full-time, 24 part-time. Students come from 46 states and territories; 61 other countries; 86% are from out of state; 4% Black or African American, non-Hispanic/Latino; 9% Hispanic/Latino; 13% Asian, non-Hispanic/Latino; 0.1% Native Hawaiian or other Pacific Islander, non-His-

panic/Latino; 4% Two or more races, non-Hispanic/Latino; 16% Race/ethnicity unknown; 16% international; 0.8% transferred in; 95% live on campus. *Retention:* 90% of full-time freshmen returned.

Freshmen *Admission:* 2,335 applied, 1,080 admitted, 361 enrolled. *Test scores:* SAT critical reading scores over 500: 98%; SAT math scores over 500: 98%; SAT writing scores over 500: 99%; ACT scores over 18: 100%; SAT critical reading scores over 600: 79%; SAT math scores over 600: 77%; SAT writing scores over 600: 85%; ACT scores over 24: 91%; SAT critical reading scores over 700: 30%; SAT math scores over 700: 36%; SAT writing scores over 700: 34%; ACT scores over 30: 40%.

Faculty *Total:* 210, 75% full-time, 90% with terminal degrees. *Student/faculty ratio:* 8:1.

Academics *Calendar:* semesters. *Degrees:* bachelor's, master's, doctoral, postbachelor's, and first professional certificates. *Special study options:* academic remediation for entering students, accelerated degree program, advanced placement credit, double majors, independent study, internships, off-campus study, services for LD students, student-designed majors, study abroad, summer session for credit. *ROTC:* Air Force (c).

Computers on Campus 200 computers/terminals and 1,500 ports are available on campus for general student use. Students can access the following: online (class) registration. Campuswide network is available.

Student Life *Housing:* on-campus residence required for freshman year. *Options:* coed, women-only, cooperative. Campus housing is university owned. Freshman campus housing is guaranteed. *Activities and organizations:* drama/theater group, student-run newspaper, choral group, musical and theater groups, community service, Student Government Association, International Students Association, cultural groups. *Campus security:* 24-hour emergency response devices and patrols, late-night transport/escort service, controlled dormitory access, shuttle bus service, awareness programs, bicycle registration, security Web site. *Student services:* health clinic, personal/psychological counseling, women's center.

Athletics Member NCAA. All Division III. *Intercollegiate sports:* badminton W, basketball W, crew W, cross-country running W, field hockey W, lacrosse W, soccer W, swimming and diving W, tennis W, track and field W, volleyball W.

Standardized Tests *Required:* SAT and SAT Subject Tests or ACT (for admission).

Costs (2012–13) *Comprehensive fee:* $55,586 includes full-time tuition ($41,260), mandatory fees ($986), and room and board ($13,340). Part-time tuition: $5160 per course. *College room only:* $7620.

Financial Aid Of all full-time matriculated undergraduates who enrolled in 2011, 822 applied for aid, 760 were judged to have need, 760 had their need

fully met. 549 Federal Work-Study jobs (averaging $1956). 155 state and other part-time jobs (averaging $2041). In 2011, 99 non-need-based awards were made. *Average percent of need met:* 100%. *Average financial aid package:* $37,817. *Average need-based loan:* $4781. *Average need-based gift aid:* $32,303. *Average non-need-based aid:* $12,550. *Average indebtedness upon graduation:* $22,830. *Financial aid deadline:* 3/1.

Applying *Options:* electronic application, early admission, early decision, deferred entrance. *Application fee:* $50. *Required:* essay or personal statement, high school transcript, 3 letters of recommendation. *Recommended:* interview. *Application deadlines:* 1/15 (freshmen), 3/15 (transfers). *Early decision deadline:* 11/15 (for plan 1), 1/1 (for plan 2). *Notification:* 4/1 (freshmen), 6/1 (transfers), 12/15 (early decision plan 1), 2/1 (early decision plan 2).

Freshman Application Contact Ms. Laurie Koehler, Dean of Admissions, Bryn Mawr College, 101 North Merion Avenue, Bryn Mawr, PA 19010. *Phone:* 610-526-5152. *Toll-free phone:* 800-BMC-1885. *Fax:* 610-526-7471. *E-mail:* admissions@brynmawr.edu. *Web site:* http://www.brynmawr.edu/.

See page 1230 for the College Close-Up.

Bucknell University

Lewisburg, Pennsylvania

- **Independent** comprehensive, founded 1846
- **Small-town** 446-acre campus
- **Endowment** $575.4 million
- **Coed** 3,554 undergraduate students, 99% full-time, 52% women, 48% men
- **Most difficult** entrance level, 28% of applicants were admitted

Undergraduates 3,530 full-time, 24 part-time. Students come from 48 states and territories; 63 other countries; 76% are from out of state; 3% Black or African American, non-Hispanic/Latino; 4% Hispanic/Latino; 3% Asian, non-Hispanic/Latino; 0.1% American Indian or Alaska Native, non-Hispanic/Latino; 2% Two or more races, non-Hispanic/Latino; 3% Race/ethnicity unknown; 5% international; 0.8% transferred in; 86% live on campus. *Retention:* 94% of full-time freshmen returned.

Freshmen *Admission:* 7,940 applied, 2,188 admitted, 916 enrolled. *Average high school GPA:* 3.52. *Test scores:* SAT critical reading scores over 500: 95%; SAT math scores over 500: 99%; SAT writing scores over 500: 97%; ACT scores over 18: 100%; SAT critical reading scores over 600: 73%; SAT math scores over 600: 87%; SAT writing scores over 600: 77%; ACT scores over 24: 95%; SAT critical reading scores over 700: 21%; SAT math scores over 700: 37%; SAT writing scores over 700: 27%; ACT scores over 30: 44%.

Faculty *Total:* 379, 94% full-time, 93% with terminal degrees. *Student/faculty ratio:* 10:1.

Academics *Calendar:* semesters. *Degrees:* bachelor's and master's. *Special study options:* advanced placement credit, double majors, honors programs, independent study, internships, off-campus study, part-time degree program, services for LD students, student-designed majors, study abroad, summer session for credit. *ROTC:* Army (b). *Unusual degree programs:* 3-2 engineering; biology, chemistry.

Computers on Campus 970 computers/terminals and 153 ports are available on campus for general student use. Students can access the following: campus intranet, computer help desk, free student e-mail accounts, online (class) grades, online (class) registration, online (class) schedules. Campuswide network is available. 100% of college-owned or -operated housing units are wired for high-speed Internet access. Wireless service is available via entire campus.

Student Life *Housing:* on-campus residence required through senior year. *Options:* coed, men-only, cooperative, disabled students. Campus housing is university owned. Freshman campus housing is guaranteed. *Activities and organizations:* drama/theater group, student-run newspaper, radio station, choral group, Alpha Phi Omega, Outing Club, Activities and Campus Events, Catholic Campus Ministries, CALVIN and HOBBES, national fraternities, national sororities. *Campus security:* 24-hour emergency response devices and patrols, student patrols, late-night transport/escort service, controlled dormitory access, well-lit pathways, self-defense education, safety/security orientation. *Student services:* health clinic, personal/psychological counseling, women's center.

Athletics Member NCAA. All Division I except football (Division I-AA). *Intercollegiate sports:* baseball M, basketball M(s)/W(s), cheerleading M(c)/W(c), crew M(c)/W, cross-country running M/W(s), equestrian sports M(c)/W(c), field hockey W, golf M/W, ice hockey M(c), lacrosse M(s)/W(s), rock climbing M(c)/W(c), rugby M(c)/W(c), skiing (downhill) M(c)/W(c), soccer M(s)/W(s), softball W, squash M(c)/W(c), swimming and diving M(s)/W(s), tennis M/W, track and field M/W, ultimate Frisbee M(c)/W(c), volleyball M(c)/W, water polo M/W, weight lifting M(c)/W(c), wrestling M(s). *Intramural sports:* badminton M/W, basketball M/W, bowling M/W, cross-country running M/W, golf M/W, racquetball M/W, soccer M/W, softball M/W, squash M/W, table tennis M/W, tennis M/W, ultimate Frisbee M/W, volleyball M/W, weight lifting M, wrestling M.

Standardized Tests *Required:* SAT or ACT (for admission).

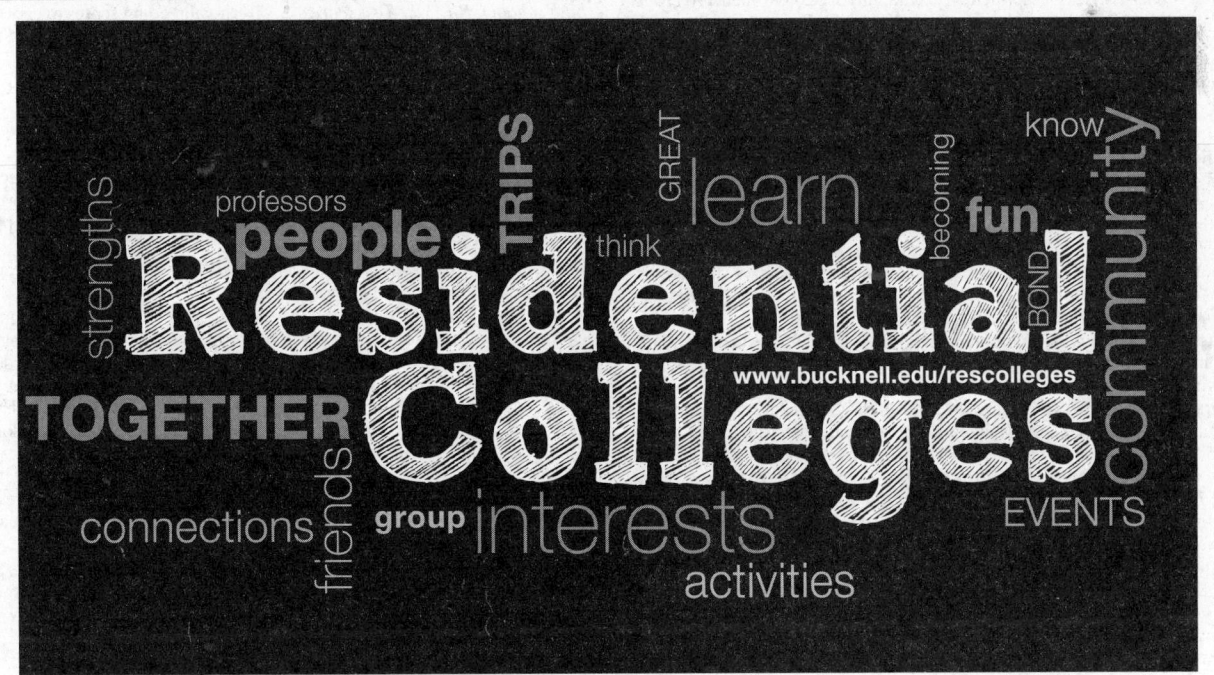

Find out more about how our first-year students form lasting connections with each other through our Residential Colleges program. www.bucknell.edu/rescolleges

Costs (2012–13) *Comprehensive fee:* $56,190 includes full-time tuition ($45,132), mandatory fees ($246), and room and board ($10,812). *College room only:* $6330. Room and board charges vary according to board plan and housing facility. *Payment plans:* tuition prepayment, installment. *Waivers:* employees or children of employees.

Financial Aid Of all full-time matriculated undergraduates who enrolled in 2011, 1,825 applied for aid, 1,556 were judged to have need, 1,462 had their need fully met. 700 Federal Work-Study jobs (averaging $1500). 50 state and other part-time jobs (averaging $1500). In 2011, 157 non-need-based awards were made. *Average percent of need met:* 95%. *Average financial aid package:* $26,000. *Average need-based loan:* $5300. *Average need-based gift aid:* $23,300. *Average non-need-based aid:* $12,855. *Average indebtedness upon graduation:* $20,149. *Financial aid deadline:* 1/15.

Applying *Options:* electronic application, early decision, deferred entrance. *Application fee:* $60. *Required:* essay or personal statement, high school transcript, 1 letter of recommendation. *Application deadlines:* 1/15 (freshmen), 3/15 (transfers). *Early decision deadline:* 11/15 (for plan 1), 1/15 (for plan 2). *Notification:* 4/1 (freshmen), 5/1 (transfers), 12/15 (early decision plan 1), 2/15 (early decision plan 2).

Freshman Application Contact Dean Robert Springall, Dean of Admissions, Bucknell University, Lewisburg, PA 17837. *Phone:* 570-577-1101. *Fax:* 570-577-3538. *E-mail:* admissions@bucknell.edu. *Web site:* http://www.bucknell.edu/.

See page 751 for display ad and page 1232 for the College Close-Up.

Cabrini College
Radnor, Pennsylvania

- **Independent Roman Catholic** comprehensive, founded 1957
- **Suburban** 112-acre campus with easy access to Philadelphia
- **Endowment** $12.7 million
- **Coed** 1,366 undergraduate students, 93% full-time, 63% women, 37% men
- **Moderately difficult** entrance level, 72% of applicants were admitted

Undergraduates 1,266 full-time, 100 part-time. Students come from 20 states and territories; 18 other countries; 39% are from out of state; 9% Black or African American, non-Hispanic/Latino; 6% Hispanic/Latino; 1% Asian, non-Hispanic/Latino; 0.7% Native Hawaiian or other Pacific Islander, non-Hispanic/Latino; 2% Two or more races, non-Hispanic/Latino; 6% Race/ethnicity unknown; 0.2% international; 5% transferred in; 56% live on campus. *Retention:* 73% of full-time freshmen returned.

Freshmen *Admission:* 2,397 applied, 1,720 admitted, 326 enrolled. *Average high school GPA:* 3.05. *Test scores:* SAT critical reading scores over 500: 29%; SAT math scores over 500: 28%; SAT writing scores over 500: 29%; SAT critical reading scores over 600: 5%; SAT math scores over 600: 7%; SAT writing scores over 600: 5%; SAT math scores over 700: 1%.

Faculty *Total:* 302, 24% full-time, 38% with terminal degrees. *Student/faculty ratio:* 14:1.

Academics *Calendar:* semesters. *Degrees:* bachelor's, master's, and post-bachelor's certificates. *Special study options:* academic remediation for entering students, adult/continuing education programs, advanced placement credit, cooperative education, double majors, honors programs, independent study, internships, off-campus study, part-time degree program, services for LD students, student-designed majors, study abroad, summer session for credit. *ROTC:* Army (c), Air Force (c). *Unusual degree programs:* 3-2 physical therapy, occupational therapy with Thomas Jefferson University.

Computers on Campus 575 computers/terminals and 2,922 ports are available on campus for general student use. Students can access the following: campus intranet, computer help desk, free student e-mail accounts, online (class) grades, online (class) registration, online (class) schedules, account balances and other services. Campuswide network is available. 100% of college-owned or -operated housing units are wired for high-speed Internet access. Wireless service is available via entire campus.

Student Life *Housing options:* coed, women-only, disabled students. Campus housing is university owned and leased by the school. Freshman applicants given priority for college housing. *Activities and organizations:* drama/theater group, student-run newspaper, radio station, choral group, Student Government Association, Campus Activities and Programming Board, Colleges Against Cancer/Relay for Life, Psychology Club, Habitat for Humanity. *Campus security:* 24-hour emergency response devices and patrols, student patrols, late-night transport/escort service, controlled dormitory access, resident assistants and directors on nightly duty. *Student services:* health clinic, personal/psychological counseling.

Athletics Member NCAA. All Division III. *Intercollegiate sports:* basketball M/W, cross-country running M/W, field hockey W, golf M, lacrosse M/W, soccer M/W, softball W, swimming and diving M/W, tennis M/W, volleyball W. *Intramural sports:* basketball M/W, cheerleading M(c)/W(c), football M/W, soccer M/W, squash M/W, ultimate Frisbee M/W, volleyball M/W.

Standardized Tests *Required:* SAT or ACT (for admission).

Costs (2012–13) *Comprehensive fee:* $40,860 includes full-time tuition ($28,090), mandatory fees ($910), and room and board ($11,860). Part-time tuition and fees vary according to course load. *Room and board:* Room and board charges vary according to board plan and housing facility. *Payment plan:* installment. *Waivers:* children of alumni, senior citizens, and employees or children of employees.

Financial Aid Of all full-time matriculated undergraduates who enrolled in 2011, 1,048 applied for aid, 976 were judged to have need, 189 had their need fully met. 171 Federal Work-Study jobs (averaging $996). In 2011, 176 non-need-based awards were made. *Average percent of need met:* 64%. *Average financial aid package:* $22,064. *Average need-based loan:* $4167. *Average need-based gift aid:* $8794. *Average non-need-based aid:* $11,106. *Average indebtedness upon graduation:* $31,556.

Applying *Options:* electronic application, deferred entrance. *Application fee:* $35. *Required:* high school transcript, minimum 2.0 GPA. *Recommended:* essay or personal statement, minimum 3.0 GPA, 3 letters of recommendation, interview. *Application deadlines:* rolling (freshmen), rolling (out-of-state freshmen), rolling (transfers).

Freshman Application Contact Mr. Eugene Soltys, Director of Admissions, Cabrini College, 610 King of Prussia Road, Radnor, PA 19087-3698. *Phone:* 610-902-8293. *Toll-free phone:* 800-848-1003. *Fax:* 610-902-8508. *E-mail:* admit@cabrini.edu. *Web site:* http://www.cabrini.edu/.

California University of Pennsylvania
California, Pennsylvania

- **State-supported** comprehensive, founded 1852, part of Pennsylvania State System of Higher Education
- **Small-town** 188-acre campus with easy access to Pittsburgh
- **Coed** 7,417 undergraduate students, 89% full-time, 52% women, 48% men
- **Moderately difficult** entrance level, 59% of applicants were admitted

Undergraduates 6,590 full-time, 827 part-time. 10% are from out of state; 7% Black or African American, non-Hispanic/Latino; 2% Hispanic/Latino; 0.4% Asian, non-Hispanic/Latino; 0.1% Native Hawaiian or other Pacific Islander, non-Hispanic/Latino; 0.1% American Indian or Alaska Native, non-Hispanic/Latino; 2% Two or more races, non-Hispanic/Latino; 8% Race/ethnicity unknown; 0.8% international; 9% transferred in; 30% live on campus. *Retention:* 73% of full-time freshmen returned.

Freshmen *Admission:* 4,400 applied, 2,602 admitted, 1,342 enrolled. *Average high school GPA:* 3.2. *Test scores:* SAT critical reading scores over 500: 34%; SAT math scores over 500: 36%; SAT writing scores over 500: 36%; SAT critical reading scores over 600: 5%; SAT math scores over 600: 6%; SAT writing scores over 600: 6%; SAT critical reading scores over 700: 1%; SAT math scores over 700: 1%; SAT writing scores over 700: 1%.

Faculty *Total:* 413, 60% full-time, 49% with terminal degrees. *Student/faculty ratio:* 19:1.

Academics *Calendar:* semesters. *Degrees:* certificates, associate, bachelor's, master's, post-master's, and postbachelor's certificates. *Special study options:* adult/continuing education programs, external degree program, part-time degree program. *ROTC:* Army (b).

Computers on Campus Students can access the following: online (class) registration. Campuswide network is available.

Student Life *Housing:* on-campus residence required through sophomore year. *Options:* coed, men-only, women-only, cooperative, disabled students. Campus housing is university owned, leased by the school and is provided by a third party. Freshman campus housing is guaranteed. *Activities and organizations:* drama/theater group, student-run newspaper, radio and television station, choral group, marching band, national fraternities, national sororities. *Campus security:* 24-hour emergency response devices and patrols, student patrols, late-night transport/escort service, residence hall entrances staffed 24/7, fire suppression and smoke detection systems, security staff are trained police officers. *Student services:* health clinic, personal/psychological counseling, women's center, legal services.

Athletics Member NCAA. All Division II. *Intercollegiate sports:* baseball M, basketball M/W, cross-country running M/W, football M, golf M/W, soccer M/W, softball W, swimming and diving W, tennis W, track and field M/W, volleyball W.

Standardized Tests *Required:* SAT or ACT (for admission).

Costs (2012–13) *Tuition:* state resident $6240 full-time, $260 per credit hour part-time; nonresident $9984 full-time, $416 per credit hour part-time. Full-time tuition and fees vary according to location and student level. Part-time tuition and fees vary according to location and student level. *Required fees:* $2774 full-time. *Room and board:* $9934; room only: $6592. Room and board charges vary according to board plan and housing facility. *Payment plan:* installment. *Waivers:* employees or children of employees.

Financial Aid Of all full-time matriculated undergraduates who enrolled in 2011, 5,090 applied for aid, 3,907 were judged to have need, 3,750 had their need fully met. In 2011, 81 non-need-based awards were made. *Average percent of need met:* 77%. *Average financial aid package:* $7212. *Average need-based loan:* $7212. *Average need-based gift aid:* $8645. *Average non-need-based aid:* $4500. *Average indebtedness upon graduation:* $24,251.

Applying *Options:* early admission, deferred entrance. *Application fee:* $25. *Required:* high school transcript. *Application deadlines:* 5/1 (freshmen), 5/1 (transfers). *Notification:* continuous (freshmen), continuous (transfers).

Freshman Application Contact Mr. William Edmonds, Dean of Enrollment Management and Academic Services, California University of Pennsylvania, 250 University Avenue, California, PA 15419. *Phone:* 724-938-4404. *Toll-free phone:* 888-412-0479. *Fax:* 724-938-4564. *Web site:* http://www.calu.edu/.

Carlow University

Pittsburgh, Pennsylvania

- **Independent Roman Catholic** comprehensive, founded 1929
- **Urban** 14-acre campus with easy access to Pittsburgh
- **Endowment** $12.9 million
- **Coed, primarily women** 1,986 undergraduate students, 56% full-time, 83% women, 17% men
- **Moderately difficult** entrance level, 65% of applicants were admitted

Undergraduates 1,103 full-time, 883 part-time. Students come from 15 states and territories; 8 other countries; 4% are from out of state; 17% Black or African American, non-Hispanic/Latino; 2% Hispanic/Latino; 1% Asian, non-Hispanic/Latino; 0.4% American Indian or Alaska Native, non-Hispanic/Latino; 1% Two or more races, non-Hispanic/Latino; 19% Race/ethnicity unknown; 0.1% international; 11% transferred in; 25% live on campus. *Retention:* 74% of full-time freshmen returned.

Freshmen *Admission:* 1,072 applied, 696 admitted, 224 enrolled. *Average high school GPA:* 3.33. *Test scores:* SAT critical reading scores over 500: 44%; SAT math scores over 500: 35%; SAT writing scores over 500: 39%; SAT critical reading scores over 600: 7%; SAT math scores over 600: 4%; SAT writing scores over 600: 5%; SAT critical reading scores over 700: 1%; SAT math scores over 700: 1%.

Faculty *Total:* 280, 33% full-time, 29% with terminal degrees. *Student/faculty ratio:* 10:1.

Academics *Calendar:* semesters. *Degrees:* bachelor's, master's, doctoral, post-master's, and postbachelor's certificates. *Special study options:* academic remediation for entering students, accelerated degree program, adult/continuing education programs, advanced placement credit, cooperative education, distance learning, double majors, honors programs, independent study, internships, off-campus study, part-time degree program, services for LD students, study abroad, summer session for credit. *ROTC:* Army (c), Navy (c), Air Force (c). *Unusual degree programs:* 3-2 engineering with Carnegie Mellon University (Math/Engineering, Chemistry/Chemical Engineering, Biology/Environmental Engineering); Duquesne University (Biology/Environmental Science & Management).

Computers on Campus 212 computers/terminals are available on campus for general student use. Students can access the following: campus intranet, computer help desk, free student e-mail accounts, online (class) grades, online (class) registration, online (class) schedules. Campuswide network is available. 100% of college-owned or -operated housing units are wired for high-speed Internet access. Wireless service is available via entire campus.

Student Life *Housing options:* men-only, women-only. Campus housing is university owned. *Activities and organizations:* drama/theater group, student-run newspaper, choral group, Student Government Association, Campus Activities, SPiRiT (Student Ambassadors), SNAP (Student Nursing Association), PSEA (School Education Association). *Campus security:* 24-hour emergency response devices and patrols, late-night transport/escort service, controlled dormitory access. *Student services:* health clinic, personal/psychological counseling.

Athletics Member NAIA. *Intercollegiate sports:* basketball W(s), soccer W(s), softball W(s), tennis W(s), volleyball W(s).

Standardized Tests *Required:* SAT or ACT (for admission).

Costs (2011–12) *Comprehensive fee:* $32,760 includes full-time tuition ($23,296), mandatory fees ($208), and room and board ($9256). Full-time tuition and fees vary according to course load, program, and reciprocity agreements. Part-time tuition: $738 per credit hour. Part-time tuition and fees vary according to course load, program, and reciprocity agreements. *College room only:* $4732. Room and board charges vary according to board plan. *Payment plans:* installment, deferred payment. *Waivers:* children of alumni, adult students, and employees or children of employees.

Financial Aid Of all full-time matriculated undergraduates who enrolled in 2003, 431 Federal Work-Study jobs (averaging $776).

Applying *Options:* electronic application, deferred entrance. *Application fee:* $20. *Required:* high school transcript. *Recommended:* essay or personal statement, minimum 2.5 GPA, interview. *Application deadlines:* rolling (freshmen), rolling (transfers). *Notification:* continuous (freshmen), continuous (transfers).

Freshman Application Contact Ms. Susan Winstel, Director of Admissions, Carlow University, 3333 Fifth Avenue, Pittsburgh, PA 15213. *Phone:* 412-578-6059. *Toll-free phone:* 800-333-CARLOW. *Fax:* 412-578-6668. *E-mail:* admissions@carlow.edu. *Web site:* http://www.carlow.edu/.

Carnegie Mellon University

Pittsburgh, Pennsylvania

- **Independent** university, founded 1900
- **Urban** 145-acre campus
- **Endowment** $1.0 billion
- **Coed** 6,281 undergraduate students, 97% full-time, 42% women, 58% men
- **Most difficult** entrance level, 30% of applicants were admitted

Undergraduates 6,093 full-time, 188 part-time. Students come from 52 states and territories; 70 other countries; 81% are from out of state; 5% Black or African American, non-Hispanic/Latino; 7% Hispanic/Latino; 22% Asian, non-Hispanic/Latino; 0.1% American Indian or Alaska Native, non-Hispanic/Latino; 3% Two or more races, non-Hispanic/Latino; 6% Race/ethnicity unknown; 17% international; 0.7% transferred in; 61% live on campus. *Retention:* 96% of full-time freshmen returned.

Freshmen *Admission:* 16,527 applied, 5,030 admitted, 1,436 enrolled. *Average high school GPA:* 3.64. *Test scores:* SAT critical reading scores over 500: 99%; SAT math scores over 500: 99%; SAT writing scores over 500: 99%; ACT scores over 18: 100%; SAT critical reading scores over 600: 88%; SAT math scores over 600: 96%; SAT writing scores over 600: 89%; ACT scores over 24: 97%; SAT critical reading scores over 700: 43%; SAT math scores over 700: 69%; SAT writing scores over 700: 48%; ACT scores over 30: 72%.

Faculty *Total:* 991, 92% full-time, 98% with terminal degrees. *Student/faculty ratio:* 12:1.

Academics *Calendar:* semesters. *Degrees:* bachelor's, master's, doctoral, post-master's, and first professional certificates. *Special study options:* advanced placement credit, cooperative education, distance learning, double majors, independent study, internships, off-campus study, part-time degree program, services for LD students, student-designed majors, study abroad, summer session for credit. *ROTC:* Army (b), Navy (b), Air Force (b). *Unusual degree programs:* 3-2 business administration; engineering; public management and policy.

Computers on Campus 497 computers/terminals are available on campus for general student use. Students can access the following: campus intranet, computer help desk, free student e-mail accounts, online (class) grades, online (class) registration, online (class) schedules. Campuswide network is available. 100% of college-owned or -operated housing units are wired for high-speed Internet access. Wireless service is available via entire campus.

Student Life *Housing:* on-campus residence required for freshman year. *Options:* coed, men-only, women-only, disabled students. Campus housing is university owned and leased by the school. Freshman campus housing is guaranteed. *Activities and organizations:* drama/theater group, student-run newspaper, radio and television station, choral group, marching band, Student Senate, Alpha Phi Omega, Tartan Club, Spirit Club, Greek Community, national fraternities, national sororities. *Campus security:* 24-hour emergency response devices and patrols, late-night transport/escort service, controlled dormitory access. *Student services:* health clinic, personal/psychological counseling, women's center, legal services.

Athletics Member NCAA. All Division III. *Intercollegiate sports:* badminton W(c), baseball M(c), basketball M/W, cheerleading M/W, crew M(c)/W(c), cross-country running M/W, fencing M(c)/W(c), football M, golf M, ice hockey M(c)/W(c), lacrosse M(c)/W(c), racquetball M(c)/W(c), rugby M(c)/W(c), soccer M/W, softball W(c), squash M(c)/W(c), swimming and diving M/W, tennis M/W, track and field M/W, ultimate Frisbee M(c)/W(c), volleyball M(c)/W, water polo M(c)/W(c). *Intramural sports:* badminton M/W, basketball M/W, bowling M/W, cross-country running M/W, fencing M/W, football M/W, golf M/W, racquetball M/W, soccer M/W, softball M/W, squash M/W, swimming and diving M/W, table tennis M/W, tennis M/W, track and field M/W, ultimate Frisbee M/W, volleyball M/W, water polo M/W.

Standardized Tests *Required:* SAT or ACT (for admission), SAT Subject Tests (for admission).

Costs (2011–12) *One-time required fee:* $198. *Comprehensive fee:* $54,922 includes full-time tuition ($43,160), mandatory fees ($652), and room and board ($11,110). Full-time tuition and fees vary according to student level. Part-time tuition and fees vary according to student level. *College room only:* $6550. Room and board charges vary according to board plan and housing facility.

Pennsylvania

Financial Aid Of all full-time matriculated undergraduates who enrolled in 2010, 3,428 applied for aid, 2,955 were judged to have need, 923 had their need fully met. In 2010, 436 non-need-based awards were made. *Average percent of need met:* 81%. *Average financial aid package:* $29,315. *Average need-based loan:* $4668. *Average need-based gift aid:* $24,819. *Average non-need-based aid:* $11,851. *Average indebtedness upon graduation:* $30,744. *Financial aid deadline:* 5/1.

Applying *Options:* electronic application, early admission, early decision, deferred entrance. *Application fee:* $70. *Required:* essay or personal statement, high school transcript, 2 letters of recommendation. *Required for some:* audition/portfolio required for certain majors/BFA. *Recommended:* interview. *Application deadlines:* 1/1 (freshmen), 3/1 (transfers). *Early decision deadline:* 11/1 (for plan 1), 12/1 (for plan 2). *Notification:* 4/15 (freshmen), 6/30 (transfers), 12/15 (early decision plan 1), 1/15 (early decision plan 2).

Freshman Application Contact Mr. Michael Steidel, Director of Admissions, Carnegie Mellon University, 5000 Forbes Avenue, Pittsburgh, PA 15213. *Phone:* 412-268-2082. *Fax:* 412-268-7838. *E-mail:* undergraduate-admissions@andrew.cmu.edu. *Web site:* http://www.cmu.edu/.

Cedar Crest College
Allentown, Pennsylvania

- **Independent** comprehensive, founded 1867, affiliated with United Church of Christ
- **Suburban** 84-acre campus with easy access to Philadelphia
- **Endowment** $19.8 million
- **Coed, primarily women** 1,403 undergraduate students, 52% full-time, 95% women, 5% men
- **Moderately difficult** entrance level, 62% of applicants were admitted

Undergraduates 733 full-time, 670 part-time. Students come from 22 states and territories; 15% are from out of state; 9% Black or African American, non-Hispanic/Latino; 10% Hispanic/Latino; 3% Asian, non-Hispanic/Latino; 0.3% Native Hawaiian or other Pacific Islander, non-Hispanic/Latino; 0.1% American Indian or Alaska Native, non-Hispanic/Latino; 2% Two or more races, non-Hispanic/Latino; 3% Race/ethnicity unknown; 0.7% international; 4% transferred in; 30% live on campus. *Retention:* 76% of full-time freshmen returned.

Freshmen *Admission:* 924 applied, 576 admitted, 118 enrolled. *Average high school GPA:* 3.07. *Test scores:* SAT critical reading scores over 500: 52%; SAT math scores over 500: 43%; SAT writing scores over 500: 39%; ACT scores over 18: 100%; SAT critical reading scores over 600: 19%; SAT math scores over 600: 8%; SAT writing scores over 600: 15%; ACT scores over 24: 22%; SAT critical reading scores over 700: 2%; SAT writing scores over 700: 1%; ACT scores over 30: 5%.

Faculty *Total:* 171, 49% full-time, 47% with terminal degrees. *Student/faculty ratio:* 10:1.

Academics *Calendar:* semesters. *Degrees:* certificates, bachelor's, master's, and postbachelor's certificates. *Special study options:* academic remediation for entering students, advanced placement credit, double majors, honors programs, independent study, internships, off-campus study, part-time degree program, services for LD students, student-designed majors, summer session for credit. *ROTC:* Army (c).

Computers on Campus 285 computers/terminals and 587 ports are available on campus for general student use. Students can access the following: campus intranet, computer help desk, free student e-mail accounts, online (class) grades, online (class) registration, online (class) schedules. Campuswide network is available. 100% of college-owned or -operated housing units are wired for high-speed Internet access. Wireless service is available via entire campus.

Student Life *Housing options:* women-only, disabled students. Campus housing is university owned. Freshman campus housing is guaranteed. *Activities and organizations:* drama/theater group, student-run newspaper, radio station, choral group, Alpha Phi Omega, Forensic Science Student Organization, Crestiad Student Newspaper, Student Activities Board, Student Government Association. *Campus security:* 24-hour emergency response devices and patrols, late-night transport/escort service, controlled dormitory access, crime prevention programs. *Student services:* health clinic, personal/psychological counseling.

Athletics Member NCAA. All Division III. *Intercollegiate sports:* basketball W, cross-country running W, equestrian sports W(c), field hockey W, lacrosse W, soccer W, softball W, tennis W, track and field W(c), volleyball W. *Intramural sports:* badminton W, basketball W, soccer W, softball W, tennis W, volleyball W.

Standardized Tests *Required:* SAT or ACT (for admission).

Costs (2011–12) *Comprehensive fee:* $39,914 includes full-time tuition ($29,710), mandatory fees ($400), and room and board ($9804). Full-time tuition and fees vary according to class time, course load, and program. Part-time tuition: $990 per credit hour. Part-time tuition and fees vary according to class time, course load, and program. *Required fees:* $100 per term part-time. *College room only:* $5160. Room and board charges vary according to board plan and housing facility. *Payment plans:* installment, deferred payment. *Waivers:* children of alumni and employees or children of employees.

Financial Aid Of all full-time matriculated undergraduates who enrolled in 2010, 659 applied for aid, 614 were judged to have need, 72 had their need fully met. 104 Federal Work-Study jobs (averaging $1500). In 2010, 65 non-need-based awards were made. *Average percent of need met:* 76%. *Average financial aid package:* $22,826. *Average need-based loan:* $4675. *Average need-based gift aid:* $18,215. *Average non-need-based aid:* $8719. *Average indebtedness upon graduation:* $32,225. *Financial aid deadline:* 5/1.

Applying *Options:* electronic application, early admission, deferred entrance. *Required:* essay or personal statement, high school transcript. *Required for some:* 2 letters of recommendation. *Recommended:* minimum 2.0 GPA, interview. *Application deadlines:* rolling (freshmen), rolling (transfers). *Notification:* continuous (freshmen), continuous (transfers).

Freshman Application Contact Andrea Stewart, Associate Director of Admissions, Cedar Crest College, 100 College Drive, Allentown, PA 18104. *Phone:* 610-606-4666. *Toll-free phone:* 800-360-1222. *E-mail:* astewart@cedarcrest.edu. *Web site:* http://www.cedarcrest.edu/.

See page 1252 for the College Close-Up.

Central Penn College
Summerdale, Pennsylvania

- **Proprietary** 4-year, founded 1881
- **Small-town** 35-acre campus with easy access to Harrisburg
- **Coed** 1,462 undergraduate students, 50% full-time, 66% women, 34% men
- **Minimally difficult** entrance level, 43% of applicants were admitted

Undergraduates 738 full-time, 724 part-time. Students come from 17 states and territories; 5% are from out of state; 20% Black or African American, non-Hispanic/Latino; 4% Hispanic/Latino; 1% Asian, non-Hispanic/Latino; 0.2% Native Hawaiian or other Pacific Islander, non-Hispanic/Latino; 0.3% American Indian or Alaska Native, non-Hispanic/Latino; 14% Race/ethnicity unknown; 1% transferred in; 16% live on campus. *Retention:* 68% of full-time freshmen returned.

Freshmen *Admission:* 2,987 applied, 1,298 admitted, 204 enrolled.

Faculty *Total:* 133, 21% full-time. *Student/faculty ratio:* 16:1.

Academics *Calendar:* quarters. *Degrees:* certificates, associate, and bachelor's. *Special study options:* academic remediation for entering students, adult/continuing education programs, advanced placement credit, distance learning, double majors, honors programs, independent study, internships, part-time degree program, study abroad, summer session for credit.

Computers on Campus 100 computers/terminals are available on campus for general student use. Students can access the following: campus intranet, computer help desk, free student e-mail accounts, online (class) grades, online (class) registration, online (class) schedules. Campuswide network is available. 100% of college-owned or -operated housing units are wired for high-speed Internet access. Wireless service is available via entire campus.

Student Life *Housing options:* men-only, women-only. Campus housing is university owned. Freshman applicants given priority for college housing. *Activities and organizations:* student-run newspaper, choral group, International Travel Club, Student Government Association, Toastmasters, Student Ambassadors. *Campus security:* 24-hour emergency response devices and patrols, late-night transport/escort service. *Student services:* personal/psychological counseling.

Athletics Member USCAA. *Intercollegiate sports:* basketball M/W, bowling M/W, golf M/W. *Intramural sports:* basketball M/W, football M/W, tennis M/W, volleyball M/W.

Standardized Tests *Recommended:* SAT or ACT (for admission).

Costs (2011–12) *Comprehensive fee:* $21,561 includes full-time tuition ($14,256), mandatory fees ($735), and room and board ($6570). Full-time tuition and fees vary according to course load and program. Part-time tuition: $396 per credit hour. Part-time tuition and fees vary according to course load and program. *Required fees:* $240 per term part-time. *College room only:* $4920. Room and board charges vary according to board plan and housing facility. *Payment plans:* installment, deferred payment. *Waivers:* employees or children of employees.

Financial Aid Of all full-time matriculated undergraduates who enrolled in 2006, 50 Federal Work-Study jobs (averaging $1500). *Financial aid deadline:* 5/1.

Applying *Options:* electronic application. *Required:* essay or personal statement, high school transcript, minimum 2.0 GPA, interview. *Required for some:* some majors have special requirements. *Application deadlines:* rolling (freshmen), rolling (out-of-state freshmen), rolling (transfers). *Notification:* continuous (freshmen), continuous (out-of-state freshmen), continuous (transfers).

Freshman Application Contact Ms. Stacy Scott, Director of Traditional Admissions, Central Penn College, College Hill and Valley Roads, Mechanicsburg, PA 17093. *Phone:* 717-728-2531. *Toll-free phone:* 800-759-2727. *Fax:* 717-728-2505. *E-mail:* stacyscott@centralpenn.edu. *Web site:* http://www.centralpenn.edu/.

Chatham University
Pittsburgh, Pennsylvania

- **Independent** university, founded 1869
- **Urban** 427-acre campus
- **Endowment** $61.2 million
- **Undergraduate: women only; graduate: coed** 903 undergraduate students, 72% full-time, 95% women, 5% men
- **Moderately difficult** entrance level, 62% of applicants were admitted

Undergraduates 654 full-time, 249 part-time. Students come from 31 states and territories; 28 other countries; 18% are from out of state; 13% Black or African American, non-Hispanic/Latino; 3% Hispanic/Latino; 2% Asian, non-Hispanic/Latino; 0.3% American Indian or Alaska Native, non-Hispanic/Latino; 2% Two or more races, non-Hispanic/Latino; 7% Race/ethnicity unknown; 8% international; 23% transferred in; 53% live on campus. *Retention:* 70% of full-time freshmen returned.

Freshmen *Admission:* 693 applied, 429 admitted, 130 enrolled. *Average high school GPA:* 3.48. *Test scores:* SAT critical reading scores over 500: 66%; SAT math scores over 500: 49%; SAT writing scores over 500: 60%; ACT scores over 18: 91%; SAT critical reading scores over 600: 27%; SAT math scores over 600: 12%; SAT writing scores over 600: 19%; ACT scores over 24: 48%; SAT critical reading scores over 700: 2%; SAT math scores over 700: 2%; SAT writing scores over 700: 1%; ACT scores over 30: 9%.

Faculty *Total:* 319, 31% full-time. *Student/faculty ratio:* 10:1.

Academics *Calendar:* 4-4-1. *Degrees:* bachelor's, master's, doctoral, post-master's, and postbachelor's certificates. *Special study options:* accelerated degree program, adult/continuing education programs, advanced placement credit, cooperative education, distance learning, double majors, English as a second language, honors programs, independent study, internships, off-campus study, part-time degree program, services for LD students, student-designed majors, study abroad, summer session for credit. *ROTC:* Army (c), Navy (c), Air Force (c). *Unusual degree programs:* 3-2 business administration; engineering with Carnegie Mellon University, Pennsylvania State University, University of Pittsburgh; arts management with Carnegie Mellon, biology, counseling psychology, film/digital technology, leadership/organizational transformation, occupational therapy, physician assistant studies, business, teaching, writing and creative writing, architecture (landscape and interior), global/public policy.

Computers on Campus 250 computers/terminals are available on campus for general student use. Students can access the following: campus intranet, computer help desk, free student e-mail accounts, online (class) grades, online (class) registration, online (class) schedules. Campuswide network is available. Wireless service is available via classrooms, computer centers, computer labs, learning centers, libraries.

Student Life *Housing:* on-campus residence required through sophomore year. *Options:* women-only. Campus housing is university owned. Freshman campus housing is guaranteed. *Activities and organizations:* drama/theater group, student-run newspaper, choral group, Chatham Student Government, Residence Hall Council, Chatham University Dance Team, Creative Writing Club & MFA Writing Council, Graduate Student Assembly. *Campus security:* 24-hour emergency response devices and patrols, late-night transport/escort service, controlled dormitory access, self-defense education, well-lighted pathways and sidewalks. *Student services:* health clinic, personal/psychological counseling.

Athletics Member NCAA. All Division III. *Intercollegiate sports:* basketball W, cross-country running W, ice hockey W, soccer W, softball W, swimming and diving W, tennis W, track and field W, volleyball W, water polo W. *Intramural sports:* badminton W, basketball W, bowling W, cross-country running W, football W, golf W, rock climbing W, skiing (downhill) W, soccer W, softball W, squash W, swimming and diving W, volleyball W, water polo W.

Costs (2012–13) *Comprehensive fee:* $41,224 includes full-time tuition ($30,382), mandatory fees ($1150), and room and board ($9692). Full-time tuition and fees vary according to student level. Part-time tuition: $737 per credit. Part-time tuition and fees vary according to course load. *College room only:* $4912. Room and board charges vary according to board plan and housing facility. *Payment plan:* installment. *Waivers:* employees or children of employees.

Financial Aid Of all full-time matriculated undergraduates who enrolled in 2009, 552 applied for aid, 517 were judged to have need, 80 had their need fully met. In 2009, 25 non-need-based awards were made. *Average percent of need met:* 66%. *Average financial aid package:* $15,515. *Average need-based loan:* $9265. *Average need-based gift aid:* $8645. *Average non-need-based aid:* $13,107.

Applying *Options:* electronic application, early admission, deferred entrance. *Application fee:* $35. *Required:* essay or personal statement, high school transcript, minimum 2.0 GPA, 1 letter of recommendation. *Recommended:* inter-

Grow your talents and discover new ones. Expand your mind and explore the world. You'll be amazed at the big thinking – and big opportunities – that unfold everyday at Chatham. Take classes in another country. Learn what it means to live green. Develop an entrepreneurial spirit. And get involved in the world on a more meaningful level. Small class sizes and dedicated professors let you soar and explore in unbelievable ways. Think you want to know more? Visit chatham.edu.

CHATHAM ADVANTAGES

- Experience a distinctive education built upon women's leadership, environmental awareness, and global understanding
- SAT/ACT optional admissions policy available for first-year students
- Nearly 95% of Chatham undergraduate students receive some form of merit or need-based scholarship
- All first-year students and transfers are provided with a new 13-inch MacBook Pro laptop computer for use in the classroom and throughout our wireless campus
- Most students have the opportunity to earn a bachelor's and a master's degree from Chatham in as few as five years from many of our graduate programs
- Study abroad almost anywhere in the world during Maymester term, a full term, or a full year

view. *Application deadlines:* 8/1 (freshmen), rolling (transfers). *Notification:* continuous (freshmen), continuous (transfers).
Freshman Application Contact Ms. Marylyn Scott, Director of Admissions, Chatham University, Woodland Road, Pittsburgh, PA 15232. *Phone:* 412-365-1295. *Toll-free phone:* 800-837-1290. *Fax:* 412-365-1609. *E-mail:* MSCOTT2@chatham.edu. *Web site:* http://www.chatham.edu/.

See page 1258 for the College Close-Up.

Chestnut Hill College
Philadelphia, Pennsylvania

- **Independent Roman Catholic** comprehensive, founded 1924
- **Suburban** 75-acre campus with easy access to Philadelphia
- **Endowment** $6.0 million
- **Coed** 1,548 undergraduate students, 81% full-time, 71% women, 29% men
- **Moderately difficult** entrance level, 64% of applicants were admitted

Undergraduates 1,255 full-time, 293 part-time. Students come from 22 states and territories; 46 other countries; 23% are from out of state; 32% Black or African American, non-Hispanic/Latino; 6% Hispanic/Latino; 3% Asian, non-Hispanic/Latino; 0.4% Native Hawaiian or other Pacific Islander, non-Hispanic/Latino; 0.2% American Indian or Alaska Native, non-Hispanic/Latino; 2% Two or more races, non-Hispanic/Latino; 9% Race/ethnicity unknown; 3% international; 5% transferred in; 32% live on campus. *Retention:* 75% of full-time freshmen returned.
Freshmen *Admission:* 2,294 applied, 1,467 admitted, 241 enrolled. *Average high school GPA:* 3.21. *Test scores:* SAT critical reading scores over 500: 42%; SAT math scores over 500: 37%; SAT writing scores over 500: 45%; ACT scores over 18: 85%; SAT critical reading scores over 600: 9%; SAT math scores over 600: 7%; SAT writing scores over 600: 5%; ACT scores over 24: 10%.
Faculty *Total:* 354, 24% full-time, 41% with terminal degrees. *Student/faculty ratio:* 10:1.
Academics *Calendar:* semesters. *Degrees:* certificates, associate, bachelor's, master's, doctoral, post-master's, and postbachelor's certificates (profile includes figures from both traditional and accelerated (part-time) programs). *Special study options:* academic remediation for entering students, adult/continuing education programs, advanced placement credit, distance learning, double majors, English as a second language, honors programs, independent study, internships, off-campus study, part-time degree program, services for LD students, student-designed majors, study abroad, summer session for credit. *Unusual degree programs:* 3-2 instructional technology, human services administration, counseling psychology, medical technology with Thomas Jefferson University, physician assistant with Arcadia University.
Computers on Campus 70 computers/terminals and 150 ports are available on campus for general student use. Students can access the following: campus intranet, computer help desk, free student e-mail accounts, online (class) grades, online (class) registration, online (class) schedules. Campuswide network is available. 90% of college-owned or -operated housing units are wired for high-speed Internet access. Wireless service is available via classrooms, dorm rooms.
Student Life *Housing options:* coed. Campus housing is university owned and leased by the school. Freshman campus housing is guaranteed. *Activities and organizations:* drama/theater group, student-run newspaper, radio and television station, choral group, Student Government, Mask and Foil Drama Club, African American Awareness Society, Campus Ministry Community Service Group, Business Club. *Campus security:* 24-hour emergency response devices and patrols, late-night transport/escort service, controlled dormitory access. *Student services:* health clinic, personal/psychological counseling.
Athletics Member NCAA. All Division II. *Intercollegiate sports:* baseball M(s), basketball M(s)/W(s), cross-country running M(s)/W(s), golf M(s), lacrosse M(s)/W(s), soccer M(s)/W(s), softball W(s), tennis M(s)/W(s), volleyball W(s).
Standardized Tests *Required:* SAT or ACT (for admission).
Costs (2012–13) *Tuition:* $29,995 full-time, $645 per credit part-time. *Required fees:* $100 full-time. *Room only:* Room and board charges vary according to housing facility. *Payment plans:* installment, deferred payment. *Waivers:* senior citizens and employees or children of employees.
Financial Aid Of all full-time matriculated undergraduates who enrolled in 2011, 1,064 applied for aid, 988 were judged to have need, 138 had their need fully met. In 2011, 4 non-need-based awards were made. *Average percent of need met:* 66%. *Average financial aid package:* $18,150. *Average need-based loan:* $4752. *Average need-based gift aid:* $14,439. *Average non-need-based aid:* $1832.
Applying *Options:* electronic application, deferred entrance. *Application fee:* $35. *Required:* high school transcript. *Required for some:* interview. *Recommended:* essay or personal statement, minimum 2.0 GPA. *Application deadlines:* rolling (freshmen), rolling (out-of-state freshmen), rolling (transfers).

Notification: continuous (freshmen), continuous (out-of-state freshmen), continuous (transfers).

Freshman Application Contact Ms. Stephanie Williams, Chestnut Hill College, 9601 Germantown Avenue, Philadelphia, PA 19118-2693. *Phone:* 215-248-7001. *Toll-free phone:* 800-248-0052. *Fax:* 215-248-7082. *E-mail:* williamss@chc.edu. *Web site:* http://www.chc.edu/.

See page 758 for display ad and page 1260 for the College Close-Up.

Cheyney University of Pennsylvania

Cheyney, Pennsylvania

- **State-supported** comprehensive, founded 1837, part of Pennsylvania State System of Higher Education
- **Suburban** 275-acre campus with easy access to Philadelphia
- **Coed** 1,141 undergraduate students, 96% full-time, 52% women, 48% men
- **Minimally difficult** entrance level, 81% of applicants were admitted

Undergraduates 1,099 full-time, 42 part-time. 21% are from out of state; 93% Black or African American, non-Hispanic/Latino; 2% Hispanic/Latino; 0.1% Native Hawaiian or other Pacific Islander, non-Hispanic/Latino; 0.1% American Indian or Alaska Native, non-Hispanic/Latino; 1% Two or more races, non-Hispanic/Latino; 3% Race/ethnicity unknown; 6% transferred in; 74% live on campus. *Retention:* 45% of full-time freshmen returned.

Freshmen *Admission:* 1,740 applied, 1,407 admitted, 234 enrolled. *Average high school GPA:* 2.5.

Faculty *Total:* 102, 74% full-time, 59% with terminal degrees. *Student/faculty ratio:* 13:1.

Academics *Calendar:* semesters. *Degrees:* associate, bachelor's, master's, and postbachelor's certificates. *Special study options:* academic remediation for entering students, adult/continuing education programs, cooperative education, distance learning, double majors, honors programs, independent study, internships, off-campus study, part-time degree program, services for LD students, study abroad, summer session for credit. *ROTC:* Army (c).

Computers on Campus Students can access the following: free student e-mail accounts, online (class) grades, online (class) registration, online (class) schedules, online tutorials, various software packages, online payment/online Praxis study guide. Campuswide network is available. Wireless service is available via classrooms, computer centers, computer labs, learning centers, libraries, student centers.

Student Life *Housing options:* coed, men-only, women-only. Campus housing is university owned. Freshman applicants given priority for college housing. *Activities and organizations:* drama/theater group, student-run newspaper, radio and television station, choral group, marching band, NAACP, Student Government Association, Alpha Kappa Alpha, Kappa Alpha Psi, Alpha Phi Alpha, national fraternities, national sororities. *Campus security:* 24-hour emergency response devices and patrols. *Student services:* health clinic, personal/psychological counseling.

Athletics Member NCAA. All Division II. *Intercollegiate sports:* basketball M(s)/W(s), bowling W(s), cross-country running M(s)/W(s), football M(s), track and field M(s)/W(s), volleyball W(s). *Intramural sports:* basketball M/W, football M.

Standardized Tests *Required:* SAT (for admission), ACT (for admission), SAT and SAT Subject Tests or ACT (for admission).

Costs (2011–12) *One-time required fee:* $150. *Tuition:* state resident $6240 full-time, $260 per credit hour part-time; nonresident $15,778 full-time, $650 per credit hour part-time. Full-time tuition and fees vary according to course load. Part-time tuition and fees vary according to course load. *Required fees:* $2164 full-time, $15 per credit part-time, $454 per term part-time. *Room and board:* $8910; room only: $5008. Room and board charges vary according to board plan. *Payment plan:* deferred payment. *Waivers:* senior citizens and employees or children of employees.

Financial Aid Of all full-time matriculated undergraduates who enrolled in 2003, 1,030 applied for aid, 1,005 were judged to have need, 451 had their need fully met. 215 Federal Work-Study jobs (averaging $1300). 133 state and other part-time jobs (averaging $600). *Average percent of need met:* 87%. *Average financial aid package:* $11,789. *Average need-based loan:* $3700. *Average need-based gift aid:* $1975. *Average non-need-based aid:* $10,000. *Average indebtedness upon graduation:* $21,000.

Applying *Options:* electronic application, deferred entrance. *Application fee:* $20. *Required:* essay or personal statement, high school transcript. *Required for some:* 3 letters of recommendation. *Recommended:* interview. *Application deadline:* 3/31 (freshmen). *Notification:* continuous (freshmen).

Freshman Application Contact Cheyney University of Pennsylvania, 1837 University Circle, PO Box 200, Cheyney, PA 19319. *Phone:* 610-399-2275. *Toll-free phone:* 800-CHEYNEY. *Web site:* http://www.cheyney.edu/.

See page 1262 for the College Close-Up.

I Am Confident
I Am Competent
I Am A Leader
I Am Cheyney

Our mission is to prepare confident; competent; reflective, visionary leaders; and responsible citizens.

Contact us today at **(800)CHEYNEY**
or visit us at **www.cheyney.edu**

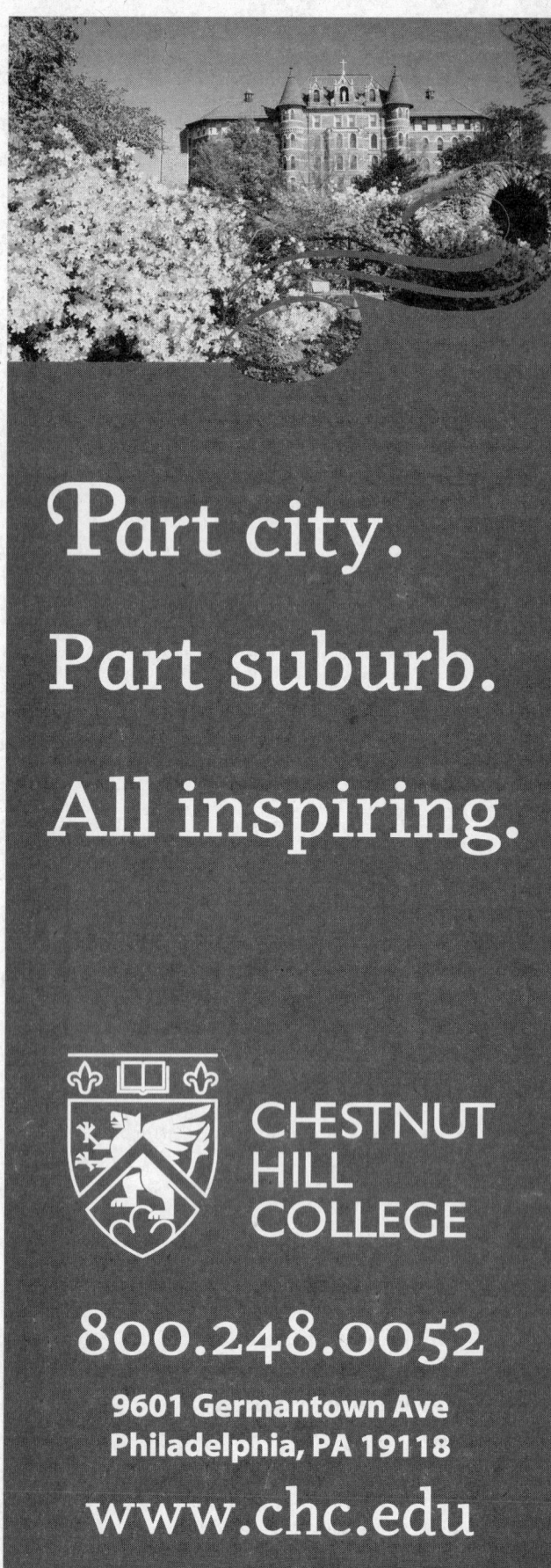

Clarion University of Pennsylvania
Clarion, Pennsylvania

- **State-supported** comprehensive, founded 1867, part of Pennsylvania State System of Higher Education
- **Rural** 100-acre campus
- **Endowment** $17.6 million
- **Coed** 5,876 undergraduate students, 86% full-time, 62% women, 38% men
- **Minimally difficult** entrance level, 71% of applicants were admitted

Undergraduates 5,030 full-time, 846 part-time. Students come from 37 states and territories; 17 other countries; 5% are from out of state; 6% Black or African American, non-Hispanic/Latino; 1% Hispanic/Latino; 0.6% Asian, non-Hispanic/Latino; 0.1% Native Hawaiian or other Pacific Islander, non-Hispanic/Latino; 0.2% American Indian or Alaska Native, non-Hispanic/Latino; 1% Two or more races, non-Hispanic/Latino; 3% Race/ethnicity unknown; 0.7% international; 6% transferred in; 33% live on campus. *Retention:* 70% of full-time freshmen returned.

Freshmen *Admission:* 3,795 applied, 2,700 admitted, 1,235 enrolled. *Average high school GPA:* 3.19. *Test scores:* SAT critical reading scores over 500: 33%; SAT math scores over 500: 34%; SAT writing scores over 500: 26%; SAT critical reading scores over 600: 7%; SAT math scores over 600: 7%; SAT writing scores over 600: 5%; SAT critical reading scores over 700: 1%; SAT math scores over 700: 1%.

Faculty *Total:* 343, 72% full-time, 58% with terminal degrees. *Student/faculty ratio:* 20:1.

Academics *Calendar:* semesters. *Degrees:* certificates, associate, bachelor's, master's, post-master's, and postbachelor's certificates. *Special study options:* academic remediation for entering students, accelerated degree program, adult/continuing education programs, advanced placement credit, cooperative education, distance learning, double majors, English as a second language, honors programs, independent study, internships, off-campus study, part-time degree program, services for LD students, study abroad, summer session for credit. *ROTC:* Army (c). *Unusual degree programs:* 3-2 engineering with University of Pittsburgh, Case Western Reserve University.

Computers on Campus 386 computers/terminals and 117 ports are available on campus for general student use. Students can access the following: campus intranet, computer help desk, free student e-mail accounts, online (class) grades, online (class) registration, online (class) schedules, Online Learning Management System, web-based personal disk space, other online student services (financial aid, billing etc.). Campuswide network is available. 100% of college-owned or -operated housing units are wired for high-speed Internet access. Wireless service is available via classrooms, computer centers, computer labs, learning centers, libraries, student centers.

Student Life *Housing:* on-campus residence required for freshman year. *Options:* coed, men-only, women-only. Campus housing is university owned. Freshman campus housing is guaranteed. *Activities and organizations:* drama/theater group, student-run newspaper, radio and television station, choral group, marching band, Circle K, Psychology Club, Council for Exceptional Children, Animae Club, Allies, national fraternities, national sororities. *Campus security:* 24-hour emergency response devices and patrols, student patrols, controlled dormitory access. *Student services:* health clinic, personal/psychological counseling, women's center.

Athletics Member NCAA. All Division II except wrestling (Division I). *Intercollegiate sports:* baseball M(s), basketball M(s)/W(s), cross-country running W(s), football M(s), golf M(s), soccer W(s), softball W(s), swimming and diving M(s)/W(s), tennis W(s), track and field W(s), volleyball W(s), wrestling M(s). *Intramural sports:* badminton M/W, basketball M/W, bowling M/W, cheerleading M/W, cross-country running W, equestrian sports M(c)/W(c), football M/W, golf M/W, racquetball M/W, rock climbing M/W, rugby M/W, soccer M/W, softball M/W, swimming and diving M/W, table tennis M/W, tennis M/W, track and field M/W, ultimate Frisbee M/W, volleyball M(c)/W, weight lifting M/W, wrestling M.

Standardized Tests *Required:* SAT or ACT (for admission). *Required for some:* International TOEFL or TSE or IELTS students.

Costs (2011–12) *One-time required fee:* $50. *Tuition:* state resident $6240 full-time, $260 per credit hour part-time; nonresident $12,480 full-time, $520 per credit hour part-time. Full-time tuition and fees vary according to course level and course load. Part-time tuition and fees vary according to course level and course load. *Required fees:* $2590 full-time, $178 per year part-time. *Room and board:* $6932; room only: $4702. Room and board charges vary according to board plan, housing facility, and location. *Payment plan:* installment. *Waivers:* senior citizens and employees or children of employees.

Financial Aid Of all full-time matriculated undergraduates who enrolled in 2010, 4,664 applied for aid, 4,098 were judged to have need, 429 had their need fully met. In 2010, 229 non-need-based awards were made. *Average percent of need met:* 63%. *Average financial aid package:* $8185. *Average need-based loan:* $4008. *Average need-based gift aid:* $5780. *Average non-need-*

based aid: $3226. *Average indebtedness upon graduation:* $3815. *Financial aid deadline:* 5/1.

Applying *Options:* deferred entrance. *Application fee:* $30. *Required:* high school transcript. *Required for some:* essay or personal statement, interview, NLN Test for ASN Program. *Recommended:* essay or personal statement, 2 letters of recommendation, interview. *Application deadlines:* rolling (freshmen), rolling (out-of-state freshmen), rolling (transfers). *Notification:* continuous (freshmen), continuous (out-of-state freshmen), continuous (transfers).

Freshman Application Contact Clarion University of Pennsylvania, 890 Wood Street, Clarion, PA 16214. *Phone:* 814-393-2306. *Toll-free phone:* 800-672-7171. *Web site:* http://www.clarion.edu/.

Curtis Institute of Music

Philadelphia, Pennsylvania

Director of Admissions Mr. Christopher Hodges, Admissions Officer, Curtis Institute of Music, 1726 Locust Street, Philadelphia, PA 19103-6107. *Phone:* 215-893-5262. *E-mail:* chris.hodges@curtis.edu. *Web site:* http://www.curtis.edu/.

Delaware Valley College

Doylestown, Pennsylvania

- **Independent** comprehensive, founded 1896
- **Suburban** 600-acre campus with easy access to Philadelphia
- **Endowment** $33.1 million
- **Coed** 1,983 undergraduate students, 86% full-time, 60% women, 40% men
- **Moderately difficult** entrance level, 74% of applicants were admitted

Undergraduates 1,712 full-time, 271 part-time. 37% are from out of state; 4% Black or African American, non-Hispanic/Latino; 3% Hispanic/Latino; 0.8% Asian, non-Hispanic/Latino; 0.1% Native Hawaiian or other Pacific Islander, non-Hispanic/Latino; 0.6% American Indian or Alaska Native, non-Hispanic/Latino; 6% Race/ethnicity unknown; 7% transferred in; 61% live on campus. *Retention:* 75% of full-time freshmen returned.

Freshmen *Admission:* 1,652 applied, 1,215 admitted, 424 enrolled. *Average high school GPA:* 3.51. *Test scores:* SAT critical reading scores over 500: 56%; SAT math scores over 500: 54%; SAT writing scores over 500: 48%; ACT scores over 18: 98%; SAT critical reading scores over 600: 12%; SAT math scores over 600: 14%; SAT writing scores over 600: 10%; ACT scores over 24: 50%; SAT critical reading scores over 700: 1%; SAT writing scores over 700: 1%; ACT scores over 30: 2%.

Faculty *Total:* 195, 43% full-time, 37% with terminal degrees. *Student/faculty ratio:* 15:1.

Academics *Calendar:* semesters. *Degrees:* certificates, associate, bachelor's, and master's. *Special study options:* academic remediation for entering students, accelerated degree program, adult/continuing education programs, advanced placement credit, distance learning, double majors, honors programs, independent study, internships, part-time degree program, services for LD students, study abroad, summer session for credit.

Computers on Campus Students can access the following: computer help desk, free student e-mail accounts, online (class) grades, online (class) registration. Campuswide network is available. Wireless service is available via classrooms, computer centers, dorm rooms, libraries, student centers.

Student Life *Housing options:* coed, women-only. Campus housing is university owned and is provided by a third party. Freshman applicants given priority for college housing. *Activities and organizations:* drama/theater group, student-run newspaper, radio station, choral group. *Campus security:* 24-hour patrols, late-night transport/escort service, controlled dormitory access. *Student services:* health clinic, personal/psychological counseling.

Athletics Member NCAA. All Division III. *Intercollegiate sports:* baseball M, basketball M/W, cheerleading W, cross-country running M/W, equestrian sports M/W, field hockey W, football M, golf M, soccer M/W, softball W, track and field M/W, volleyball W, wrestling M. *Intramural sports:* basketball M/W, cross-country running M/W, football M, golf M, lacrosse M, soccer M, softball M/W, volleyball M/W.

Standardized Tests *Required:* SAT or ACT (for admission).

Costs (2012–13) *Comprehensive fee:* $43,008 includes full-time tuition ($29,696), mandatory fees ($2050), and room and board ($11,262). Part-time tuition: $818 per credit. *College room only:* $5106.

Financial Aid Of all full-time matriculated undergraduates who enrolled in 2011, 1,474 applied for aid, 1,375 were judged to have need, 221 had their need fully met. In 2011, 281 non-need-based awards were made. *Average percent of need met:* 67%. *Average financial aid package:* $22,135. *Average need-based loan:* $4498. *Average need-based gift aid:* $14,498. *Average non-need-based aid:* $10,806. *Average indebtedness upon graduation:* $34,998. *Financial aid deadline:* 4/1.

Applying *Options:* electronic application, deferred entrance. *Application fee:* $50. *Required:* high school transcript, 1 letter of recommendation. *Required for some:* minimum 3.0 GPA. *Recommended:* minimum 2.8 GPA, interview. *Application deadline:* 5/1 (freshmen). *Notification:* continuous (freshmen).

Freshman Application Contact Mr. Dwayne Walker, Director of Admissions, Delaware Valley College, 700 East Butler Avenue, Doylestown, PA 18901-2697. *Phone:* 215-489-2372. *Toll-free phone:* 800-2DELVAL. *Fax:* 215-230-2968. *E-mail:* admitme@devalcol.edu. *Web site:* http://www.delval.edu/.

See page 759 for display ad and page 1294 for the College Close-Up.

DeSales University

Center Valley, Pennsylvania

- **Independent Roman Catholic** comprehensive, founded 1964
- **Suburban** 480-acre campus
- **Endowment** $47.4 million
- **Coed** 2,375 undergraduate students, 75% full-time, 59% women, 41% men
- **Moderately difficult** entrance level, 73% of applicants were admitted

Undergraduates 1,775 full-time, 600 part-time. 64% are from out of state; 3% Black or African American, non-Hispanic/Latino; 6% Hispanic/Latino; 2% Asian, non-Hispanic/Latino; 0.1% Native Hawaiian or other Pacific Islander, non-Hispanic/Latino; 0.6% American Indian or Alaska Native, non-Hispanic/Latino; 13% Race/ethnicity unknown; 3% transferred in; 67% live on campus. *Retention:* 81% of full-time freshmen returned.

Freshmen *Admission:* 2,207 applied, 1,603 admitted, 446 enrolled. *Average high school GPA:* 3.21. *Test scores:* SAT critical reading scores over 500: 70%; SAT math scores over 500: 69%; ACT scores over 18: 94%; SAT critical reading scores over 600: 23%; SAT math scores over 600: 26%; ACT scores over 24: 41%; SAT critical reading scores over 700: 3%; SAT math scores over 700: 3%; ACT scores over 30: 2%.

Faculty *Total:* 312, 33% full-time. *Student/faculty ratio:* 14:1.

Academics *Calendar:* semesters. *Degrees:* bachelor's, master's, doctoral, and post-master's certificates. *Special study options:* academic remediation for entering students, accelerated degree program, advanced placement credit, cooperative education, distance learning, double majors, English as a second language, external degree program, honors programs, independent study, internships, off-campus study, part-time degree program, services for LD students, student-designed majors, study abroad, summer session for credit. *ROTC:* Army (c). *Unusual degree programs:* physician assistant studies, MACJ, MBA/Accounting.

Computers on Campus 250 computers/terminals and 250 ports are available on campus for general student use. Students can access the following: computer help desk, free student e-mail accounts, online (class) grades, online (class) registration, online (class) schedules. Campuswide network is available.

100% of college-owned or -operated housing units are wired for high-speed Internet access. Wireless service is available via classrooms, computer centers, computer labs, learning centers, libraries, student centers.

Student Life *Housing:* on-campus residence required for freshman year. *Options:* men-only, women-only, disabled students. Campus housing is university owned. Freshman campus housing is guaranteed. *Activities and organizations:* drama/theater group, student-run newspaper, radio and television station, choral group, marching band, Best Buddies, Student Night Life, National Science Club, Colleges Against Cancer, Sports Management Society. *Campus security:* 24-hour emergency response devices and patrols, late-night transport/escort service, controlled dormitory access. *Student services:* personal/psychological counseling.

Athletics Member NCAA. All Division III. *Intercollegiate sports:* baseball M, basketball M, cross-country running M, field hockey W, golf M, lacrosse M, soccer M/W, softball W, track and field M/W, volleyball W. *Intramural sports:* basketball M/W, cheerleading W(c), fencing M(c), ice hockey M(c), lacrosse M(c)/W, rugby M(c), soccer M/W, softball M/W, swimming and diving M(c), tennis M(c), ultimate Frisbee M/W, volleyball M/W.

Standardized Tests *Required:* SAT or ACT (for admission).

Costs (2011–12) *Comprehensive fee:* $39,224 includes full-time tuition ($28,000), mandatory fees ($1094), and room and board ($10,130). Part-time tuition: $1170 per credit hour. *Room and board:* Room and board charges vary according to board plan and housing facility. *Payment plan:* installment. *Waivers:* senior citizens and employees or children of employees.

Financial Aid Of all full-time matriculated undergraduates who enrolled in 2011, 1,563 applied for aid, 1,417 were judged to have need, 265 had their need fully met. 110 Federal Work-Study jobs (averaging $2137). 68 state and other part-time jobs (averaging $1980). In 2011, 289 non-need-based awards were made. *Average percent of need met:* 68%. *Average financial aid package:* $20,491. *Average need-based loan:* $4559. *Average need-based gift aid:* $16,236. *Average non-need-based aid:* $9780. *Average indebtedness upon graduation:* $32,078. *Financial aid deadline:* 5/1.

Applying *Options:* electronic application. *Required:* essay or personal statement, high school transcript. *Recommended:* interview. *Application deadline:* 8/1 (freshmen).

Freshman Application Contact Mr. Derrick Wetzel, Director of Admissions, DeSales University, 2755 Station Avenue, Center Valley, PA 18034-9568. *Phone:* 610-282-4443. *Fax:* 610-282-0131. *E-mail:* derrick.wetzell@desales.edu. *Web site:* http://www.desales.edu/.

See page 1298 for the College Close-Up.

DeSales University exists to educate ...to educate the whole you ... to educate the whole you and develop character while giving you concentrated, career-centered study with a broad-based liberal arts foundation. With more than 30 majors of study, DeSales University offers uncommon solutions for seekers of educational excellence.

Join the fun and challenging experience at a university defined by the spirituality of St. Francis de Sales.

Allison '14
Theatre, Design & Technology Major

DeSales University

2755 Station Avenue • Center Valley, PA 18034 • www.desales.edu/admis • 877.4-DE SALES

DeVry University

Fort Washington, Pennsylvania

- **Proprietary** comprehensive, founded 2002, part of DeVry University
- **Coed** 837 undergraduate students, 46% full-time, 34% women, 66% men
- **Minimally difficult** entrance level

Undergraduates 387 full-time, 450 part-time. 11% are from out of state; 31% Black or African American, non-Hispanic/Latino; 9% Hispanic/Latino; 4% Asian, non-Hispanic/Latino; 0.2% Native Hawaiian or other Pacific Islander, non-Hispanic/Latino; 0.6% American Indian or Alaska Native, non-Hispanic/Latino; 1% Two or more races, non-Hispanic/Latino; 13% Race/ethnicity unknown; 0.6% international; 21% transferred in.

Freshmen *Admission:* 132 enrolled.

Faculty *Total:* 124, 16% full-time. *Student/faculty ratio:* 11:1.

Academics *Calendar:* semesters. *Degrees:* associate, bachelor's, and master's. *Special study options:* adult/continuing education programs, part-time degree program.

Student Life *Housing:* college housing not available.

Costs (2011–12) *Tuition:* $15,294 full-time, $597 per credit hour part-time. Full-time tuition and fees vary according to course load. Part-time tuition and fees vary according to course load. *Required fees:* $80 full-time, $40 per term part-time. *Payment plans:* installment, deferred payment. *Waivers:* employees or children of employees.

Financial Aid Of all full-time matriculated undergraduates who enrolled in 2007, 254 applied for aid, 244 were judged to have need, 2 had their need fully met. In 2007, 23 non-need-based awards were made. *Average percent of need met:* 34%. *Average financial aid package:* $12,114. *Average need-based loan:* $6836. *Average need-based gift aid:* $6835. *Average non-need-based aid:* $13,057. *Average indebtedness upon graduation:* $15,638.

Applying *Application fee:* $50. *Required:* high school transcript, interview. *Application deadlines:* rolling (freshmen), rolling (transfers). *Notification:* continuous (freshmen), continuous (transfers).

Freshman Application Contact DeVry University, 1140 Virginia Drive, Fort Washington, PA 19034. *Phone:* 215-591-5700. *Toll-free phone:* 866-338-7941. *Web site:* http://www.devry.edu/.

DeVry University

King of Prussia, Pennsylvania

Admissions Office Contact DeVry University, 150 Allendale Road, Buillding 3, Suite 3201, King of Prussia, PA 19406-2926. *Toll-free phone:* 866-338-7941. *Web site:* http://www.devry.edu/.

DeVry University

Philadelphia, Pennsylvania

Admissions Office Contact DeVry University, Philadelphia Downtown Center, 1800 JFK Boulevard, Suite 104, Philadelphia, PA 19103-7421. *Toll-free phone:* 866-338-7941. *Web site:* http://www.devry.edu/.

DeVry University

Pittsburgh, Pennsylvania

Admissions Office Contact DeVry University, FreeMarkets Center, 210 Sixth Avenue, Suite 200, Pittsburgh, PA 15222-2606. *Toll-free phone:* 866-338-7941. *Web site:* http://www.devry.edu/.

Dickinson College

Carlisle, Pennsylvania

- **Independent** 4-year, founded 1773
- **Suburban** 120-acre campus with easy access to Harrisburg
- **Endowment** $326.6 million
- **Coed** 2,397 undergraduate students, 99% full-time, 56% women, 44% men
- **Very difficult** entrance level, 42% of applicants were admitted

Undergraduates 2,364 full-time, 33 part-time. Students come from 39 states and territories; 46 other countries; 77% are from out of state; 4% Black or African American, non-Hispanic/Latino; 6% Hispanic/Latino; 3% Asian, non-Hispanic/Latino; 0.1% American Indian or Alaska Native, non-Hispanic/Latino; 2% Two or more races, non-Hispanic/Latino; 1% Race/ethnicity unknown; 7%

international; 0.6% transferred in; 94% live on campus. *Retention:* 90% of full-time freshmen returned.

Freshmen *Admission:* 6,063 applied, 2,543 admitted, 652 enrolled. *Test scores:* SAT critical reading scores over 500: 96%; SAT math scores over 500: 98%; SAT writing scores over 500: 98%; ACT scores over 18: 100%; SAT critical reading scores over 600: 77%; SAT math scores over 600: 73%; SAT writing scores over 600: 76%; ACT scores over 24: 95%; SAT critical reading scores over 700: 21%; SAT math scores over 700: 20%; SAT writing scores over 700: 22%; ACT scores over 30: 35%.

Faculty *Total:* 252, 83% full-time, 87% with terminal degrees. *Student/faculty ratio:* 10:1.

Academics *Calendar:* semesters. *Degree:* bachelor's. *Special study options:* accelerated degree program, adult/continuing education programs, advanced placement credit, double majors, English as a second language, independent study, internships, off-campus study, part-time degree program, services for LD students, student-designed majors, study abroad, summer session for credit. *ROTC:* Army (b). *Unusual degree programs:* 3-2 engineering with Case Western Reserve University; Rensselaer Polytechnic Institute; Columbia University's Fu Foundation School of Engineering and Applied Science; nursing with Johns Hopkins University School of Nursing; pre-law with the Dickinson School of Law of the Pennsylvania State University 3/3.

Computers on Campus 1,041 computers/terminals and 5,000 ports are available on campus for general student use. Students can access the following: campus intranet, computer help desk, free student e-mail accounts, online (class) grades, online (class) registration, online (class) schedules. Campus-wide network is available. 100% of college-owned or -operated housing units are wired for high-speed Internet access. Wireless service is available via classrooms, computer centers, computer labs, dorm rooms, libraries, student centers.

Student Life *Housing:* on-campus residence required through senior year. *Options:* coed, disabled students. Campus housing is university owned. Freshman campus housing is guaranteed. *Activities and organizations:* drama/theater group, student-run newspaper, radio station, choral group, Student Senate, Alpha Phi Omega, Multi-Organization Board, Hillel, Jive Turkeys (ultimate Frisbee), national fraternities, national sororities. *Campus security:* 24-hour emergency response devices and patrols, student patrols, late-night transport/escort service, controlled dormitory access. *Student services:* health clinic, personal/psychological counseling, women's center.

Athletics Member NCAA. All Division III. *Intercollegiate sports:* baseball M, basketball M/W, cheerleading M(c)/W(c), cross-country running M/W, equestrian sports M(c)/W(c), fencing M(c)/W(c), field hockey W, football M, golf M/W, ice hockey M(c)/W(c), lacrosse M/W, skiing (downhill) M(c)/W(c), soccer M/W, softball W, squash M(c)/W(c), swimming and diving M/W, tennis M/W, track and field M/W, ultimate Frisbee M(c)/W(c), volleyball M(c)/W. *Intramural sports:* badminton M/W, basketball M/W, field hockey W, football M, racquetball M/W, soccer M/W, softball M, tennis M/W, volleyball M/W.

Standardized Tests *Recommended:* SAT or ACT (for admission).

Costs (2011–12) *One-time required fee:* $25. *Comprehensive fee:* $53,860 includes full-time tuition ($42,610), mandatory fees ($450), and room and board ($10,800). Part-time tuition: $5330 per course. *Required fees:* $44 per course part-time. *College room only:* $5570. Room and board charges vary according to board plan and housing facility. *Payment plan:* installment. *Waivers:* senior citizens and employees or children of employees.

Financial Aid Of all full-time matriculated undergraduates who enrolled in 2011, 1,480 applied for aid, 1,324 were judged to have need, 954 had their need fully met. 919 Federal Work-Study jobs (averaging $2222). 182 state and other part-time jobs (averaging $3565). In 2011, 255 non-need-based awards were made. *Average percent of need met:* 96%. *Average financial aid package:* $35,211. *Average need-based loan:* $5505. *Average need-based gift aid:* $29,363. *Average non-need-based aid:* $10,874. *Average indebtedness upon graduation:* $26,928. *Financial aid deadline:* 2/1.

Applying *Options:* electronic application, early decision, early action, deferred entrance. *Application fee:* $65. *Required:* essay or personal statement, high school transcript, 2 letters of recommendation. *Recommended:* minimum 3.0 GPA, interview. *Application deadlines:* 2/1 (freshmen), 2/1 (out-of-state freshmen), 4/1 (transfers), 12/1 (early action). *Early decision deadline:* 11/15 (for plan 1), 1/15 (for plan 2). *Notification:* 3/20 (freshmen), 3/20 (out-of-state freshmen), continuous until 5/1 (transfers), 12/15 (early decision plan 1), 2/15 (early decision plan 2), 2/1 (early action).

Freshman Application Contact Stephanie Balmer, Vice President for Enrollment, Marketing and Communications and Dean of Admissions, Dickinson College, PO Box 1773, Admissions Office, Carlisle, PA 17013-2896. *Phone:* 717-245-1231. *Toll-free phone:* 800-644-1773. *Fax:* 717-245-1442. *E-mail:* admit@dickinson.edu. *Web site:* http://www.dickinson.edu/.

Drexel University
Philadelphia, Pennsylvania

- **Independent** university, founded 1891
- **Urban** 96-acre campus with easy access to Philadelphia
- **Coed** 15,047 undergraduate students, 82% full-time, 46% women, 54% men
- **Moderately difficult** entrance level, 58% of applicants were admitted

Undergraduates 12,332 full-time, 2,715 part-time. Students come from 53 states and territories; 134 other countries; 50% are from out of state; 8% Black or African American, non-Hispanic/Latino; 6% Hispanic/Latino; 12% Asian, non-Hispanic/Latino; 0.1% Native Hawaiian or other Pacific Islander, non-Hispanic/Latino; 0.7% American Indian or Alaska Native, non-Hispanic/Latino; 5% Race/ethnicity unknown; 9% international; 9% transferred in; 34% live on campus. *Retention:* 85% of full-time freshmen returned.

Freshmen *Admission:* 48,450 applied, 27,861 admitted, 3,141 enrolled. *Average high school GPA:* 3.44. *Test scores:* SAT critical reading scores over 500: 90%; SAT math scores over 500: 96%; SAT writing scores over 500: 87%; ACT scores over 18: 100%; SAT critical reading scores over 600: 43%; SAT math scores over 600: 65%; SAT writing scores over 600: 41%; ACT scores over 24: 75%; SAT critical reading scores over 700: 8%; SAT math scores over 700: 18%; SAT writing scores over 700: 8%; ACT scores over 30: 20%.

Faculty *Total:* 1,636, 62% full-time. *Student/faculty ratio:* 11:1.

Academics *Calendar:* quarters. *Degrees:* certificates, associate, bachelor's, master's, doctoral, post-master's, postbachelor's, and first professional certificates. *Special study options:* academic remediation for entering students, accelerated degree program, adult/continuing education programs, advanced placement credit, cooperative education, distance learning, double majors, English as a second language, freshman honors college, honors programs, independent study, internships, part-time degree program, services for LD students, student-designed majors, study abroad, summer session for credit. *ROTC:* Army (b), Navy (c), Air Force (c).

Computers on Campus 8,000 computers/terminals are available on campus for general student use. Students can access the following: campus intranet, computer help desk, free student e-mail accounts, online (class) grades, online (class) registration, online (class) schedules. Campuswide network is available. 100% of college-owned or -operated housing units are wired for high-speed Internet access. Wireless service is available via entire campus.

Student Life *Housing:* on-campus residence required for freshman year. *Options:* coed, disabled students. Freshman campus housing is guaranteed. *Activities and organizations:* drama/theater group, student-run newspaper, radio and television station, choral group, student government, Black Student Union, Society of Hispanic Professional Engineers, Society of Minority Engineers and Scientists, Campus Activities Board, national fraternities, national sororities. *Campus security:* 24-hour emergency response devices and patrols, late-night transport/escort service, controlled dormitory access. *Student services:* health clinic, personal/psychological counseling.

Athletics Member NCAA. All Division I. *Intercollegiate sports:* basketball M(s)/W(s), crew M(s)/W(s), field hockey W(s), golf M(s), lacrosse M(s)/W(s), soccer M(s)/W(s), softball W(s), swimming and diving M(s)/W(s), tennis M(s)/W(s), wrestling M(s). *Intramural sports:* badminton M/W, basketball M/W, fencing M/W, football M, ice hockey M, riflery M/W, sailing M/W, softball M, squash M/W, table tennis M/W, tennis M/W, volleyball M/W, water polo M/W.

Standardized Tests *Required:* SAT or ACT (for admission). *Recommended:* SAT (for admission).

Costs (2012–13) *Comprehensive fee:* $50,275 includes full-time tuition ($33,800), mandatory fees ($2300), and room and board ($14,175). Full-time tuition and fees vary according to course load, location, program, and student level. Part-time tuition: $930 per credit. Part-time tuition and fees vary according to course load and program. *College room only:* $8430. Room and board charges vary according to board plan and housing facility. *Payment plan:* installment. *Waivers:* children of alumni and employees or children of employees.

Financial Aid Of all full-time matriculated undergraduates who enrolled in 2008, 5,878 applied for aid, 5,833 were judged to have need, 1,826 had their need fully met. In 2008, 2086 non-need-based awards were made. *Average percent of need met:* 56%. *Average financial aid package:* $21,488. *Average need-based loan:* $12,875. *Average need-based gift aid:* $13,204. *Average non-need-based aid:* $11,641. *Financial aid deadline:* 3/1.

Applying *Options:* electronic application, deferred entrance. *Application fee:* $75. *Required:* essay or personal statement, high school transcript, minimum 2.0 GPA. *Recommended:* 2 letters of recommendation, interview. *Application deadlines:* 3/1 (freshmen), 8/15 (transfers). *Notification:* continuous (freshmen), continuous (transfers).

Freshman Application Contact Ms. Margaret Sparzani, Director of Freshman Admissions, Drexel University, 3141 Chestnut Street, Philadelphia, PA 19104-2875. *Phone:* 215-895-2400. *Toll-free phone:* 800-2-DREXEL. *Fax:* 215-895-5939. *E-mail:* enroll@drexel.edu. *Web site:* http://www.drexel.edu/.

See page 763 for display ad and page 1306 for the College Close-Up.

Duquesne University
Pittsburgh, Pennsylvania

- **Independent Roman Catholic** university, founded 1878
- **Urban** 50-acre campus with easy access to Pittsburgh
- **Endowment** $171.1 million
- **Coed** 5,677 undergraduate students, 96% full-time, 57% women, 43% men
- **Moderately difficult** entrance level, 70% of applicants were admitted

Undergraduates 5,475 full-time, 202 part-time. Students come from 47 states and territories; 49 other countries; 24% are from out of state; 5% Black or African American, non-Hispanic/Latino; 3% Hispanic/Latino; 2% Asian, non-Hispanic/Latino; 0.2% American Indian or Alaska Native, non-Hispanic/Latino; 1% Two or more races, non-Hispanic/Latino; 3% Race/ethnicity unknown; 3% international; 3% transferred in; 56% live on campus. *Retention:* 87% of full-time freshmen returned.

Freshmen *Admission:* 6,528 applied, 4,578 admitted, 1,343 enrolled. *Average high school GPA:* 3.64. *Test scores:* SAT critical reading scores over 500: 87%; SAT math scores over 500: 86%; SAT writing scores over 500: 82%; ACT scores over 18: 99%; SAT critical reading scores over 600: 30%; SAT math scores over 600: 36%; SAT writing scores over 600: 29%; ACT scores over 24: 65%; SAT critical reading scores over 700: 3%; SAT math scores over 700: 4%; SAT writing scores over 700: 4%; ACT scores over 30: 6%.

Faculty *Total:* 991, 49% full-time. *Student/faculty ratio:* 14:1.

Academics *Calendar:* semesters. *Degrees:* bachelor's, master's, doctoral, post-master's, postbachelor's, and first professional certificates. *Special study options:* academic remediation for entering students, accelerated degree program, adult/continuing education programs, advanced placement credit, distance learning, double majors, English as a second language, external degree program, freshman honors college, honors programs, independent study, internships, off-campus study, part-time degree program, services for LD students, student-designed majors, study abroad, summer session for credit. *ROTC:* Army (b), Navy (c), Air Force (c). *Unusual degree programs:* 3-2 engineering with Case Western Reserve University, University of Pittsburgh.

Computers on Campus 1,000 computers/terminals are available on campus for general student use. Students can access the following: campus intranet, computer help desk, free student e-mail accounts, online (class) grades, online (class) registration, online (class) schedules. Campuswide network is available. 100% of college-owned or -operated housing units are wired for high-speed Internet access. Wireless service is available via classrooms, computer centers, computer labs, learning centers, libraries, student centers.

Student Life *Housing:* on-campus residence required through sophomore year. *Options:* coed, men-only, women-only, disabled students. Campus housing is university owned. Freshman campus housing is guaranteed. *Activities and organizations:* drama/theater group, student-run newspaper, radio and television station, choral group, marching band, Duquesne University Volunteers (DUV), Red and Blue Crew, Student Government Association, Duquesne Program Council, Residence Hall Association, national fraternities, national sororities. *Campus security:* 24-hour emergency response devices and patrols, late-night transport/escort service, controlled dormitory access, cameras monitor exterior 24 hours/day; card access for buildings; 8 Code Blue Emergency service stations; outside warning system. *Student services:* health clinic, personal/psychological counseling.

Athletics Member NCAA. All Division I except football (Division I-AA). *Intercollegiate sports:* basketball M(s)/W(s), crew M(c)/W(s), cross-country running M(s)/W(s), ice hockey M(c), lacrosse W(s), soccer M(s)/W(s), swimming and diving W(s), tennis M(s)/W(s), track and field M(s)/W(s), volleyball W(s). *Intramural sports:* basketball M/W, equestrian sports W(c), football M/W, racquetball M/W, rugby M(c), skiing (downhill) M(c)/W(c), soccer M/W, volleyball M(c)/W.

Standardized Tests *Required:* SAT or ACT (for admission).

Costs (2011–12) *Comprehensive fee:* $38,477 includes full-time tuition ($26,413), mandatory fees ($2258), and room and board ($9806). Full-time tuition and fees vary according to program. Part-time tuition: $861 per credit. Part-time tuition and fees vary according to program. *Required fees:* $88 per credit part-time. *College room only:* $5348. Room and board charges vary according to board plan and housing facility. *Payment plans:* installment, deferred payment. *Waivers:* senior citizens and employees or children of employees.

Financial Aid Of all full-time matriculated undergraduates who enrolled in 2010, 4,636 applied for aid, 3,983 were judged to have need, 989 had their need fully met. 3,028 Federal Work-Study jobs (averaging $3114). In 2010, 1291 non-need-based awards were made. *Average percent of need met:* 79%.

COLLEGES AT-A-GLANCE

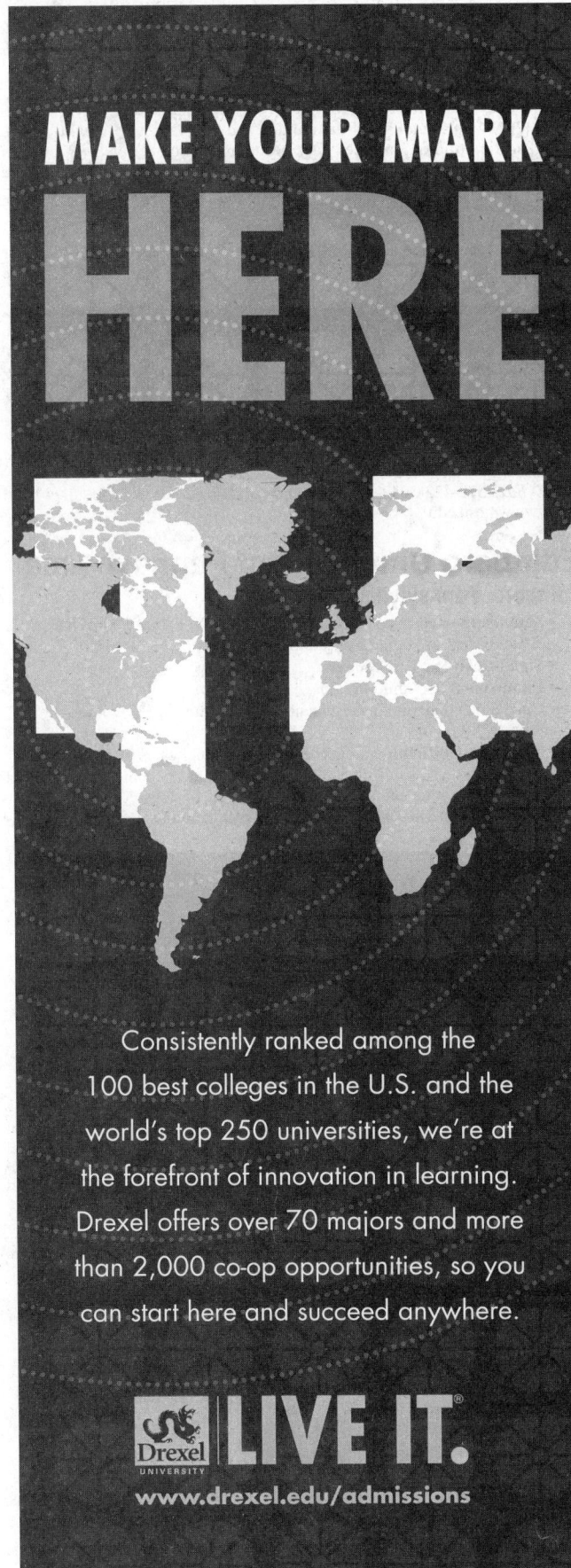

Average financial aid package: $21,376. *Average need-based loan:* $3183. *Average need-based gift aid:* $13,860. *Average non-need-based aid:* $8231. *Financial aid deadline:* 5/1.
Applying *Options:* electronic application, early admission, early decision, early action, deferred entrance. *Application fee:* $50. *Required:* essay or personal statement, high school transcript, 1 letter of recommendation. *Required for some:* audition for School of Music applicants. *Recommended:* minimum 3.0 GPA, interview. *Application deadlines:* 7/1 (freshmen), 7/1 (transfers), 12/1 (early action). *Early decision deadline:* 11/1. *Notification:* continuous until 10/1 (freshmen), 1/15 (early action).
Freshman Application Contact Ms. Debra Zugates, Director of Admissions, Duquesne University, Administration Building, 600 Forbes Avenue, Pittsburgh, PA 15282-0201. *Phone:* 412-396-5211. *Toll-free phone:* 800-456-0590. *Fax:* 412-396-5644. *E-mail:* admissions@duq.edu. *Web site:* http://www.duq.edu/.

Eastern University
St. Davids, Pennsylvania

- **Independent Christian** comprehensive, founded 1952
- **Suburban** 92-acre campus with easy access to Philadelphia
- **Coed** 2,713 undergraduate students
- **Moderately difficult** entrance level

Undergraduates 46% are from out of state. *Retention:* 74% of full-time freshmen returned.
Faculty *Student/faculty ratio:* 13:1.
Academics *Calendar:* semesters. *Degrees:* associate, bachelor's, master's, doctoral, and first professional. *Special study options:* academic remediation for entering students, accelerated degree program, adult/continuing education programs, advanced placement credit, English as a second language, honors programs, independent study, internships, off-campus study, part-time degree program, student-designed majors, study abroad, summer session for credit. *ROTC:* Army (c), Air Force (c).
Computers on Campus Campuswide network is available.
Student Life *Housing:* on-campus residence required through senior year. *Options:* coed. Campus housing is university owned and leased by the school. *Activities and organizations:* drama/theater group, student-run newspaper, radio station, choral group. *Campus security:* 24-hour emergency response devices and patrols, late-night transport/escort service, controlled dormitory access, emergency call boxes. *Student services:* health clinic, personal/psychological counseling, women's center.
Athletics Member NCAA. All Division III. *Intercollegiate sports:* baseball M, basketball M/W, field hockey W, golf M, lacrosse M/W, soccer M/W, softball W, tennis M/W, volleyball W.
Standardized Tests *Required:* SAT or ACT (for admission).
Costs (2011–12) *Comprehensive fee:* $35,230 includes full-time tuition ($25,800), mandatory fees ($100), and room and board ($9330). Full-time tuition and fees vary according to course load, degree level, and program. Part-time tuition: $540 per credit hour. Part-time tuition and fees vary according to course load, degree level, and program. *Required fees:* $50 per term part-time. *College room only:* $5080. Room and board charges vary according to board plan, housing facility, and location.
Applying *Options:* electronic application, early admission, deferred entrance. *Required:* essay or personal statement, high school transcript, minimum 2.0 GPA, 1 letter of recommendation. *Recommended:* minimum 3.0 GPA, 2 letters of recommendation, interview. *Application deadlines:* rolling (freshmen), rolling (transfers). *Notification:* continuous (freshmen), continuous (transfers).
Freshman Application Contact Mr. Michael Dziedziak, Director of Undergraduate Admissions, Eastern University, 1300 Eagle Road, St. Davids, PA 19087-3696. *Phone:* 610-341-1376. *Toll-free phone:* 800-452-0996. *Fax:* 610-341-1723. *E-mail:* ugadm@eastern.edu. *Web site:* http://www.eastern.edu/.

East Stroudsburg University of Pennsylvania
East Stroudsburg, Pennsylvania

- **State-supported** comprehensive, founded 1893, part of Pennsylvania State System of Higher Education
- **Small-town** 256-acre campus
- **Endowment** $10.3 million
- **Coed** 6,656 undergraduate students, 91% full-time, 55% women, 45% men
- **Moderately difficult** entrance level, 81% of applicants were admitted

Undergraduates 6,056 full-time, 600 part-time. Students come from 26 states and territories; 23 other countries; 25% are from out of state; 7% Black or African American, non-Hispanic/Latino; 4% Hispanic/Latino; 2% Asian, non-His-

panic/Latino; 4% Native Hawaiian or other Pacific Islander, non-Hispanic/Latino; 0.3% American Indian or Alaska Native, non-Hispanic/Latino; 0.9% Two or more races, non-Hispanic/Latino; 14% Race/ethnicity unknown; 0.8% international; 10% transferred in; 43% live on campus. *Retention:* 78% of full-time freshmen returned.

Freshmen *Admission:* 6,520 applied, 5,256 admitted, 1,412 enrolled. *Average high school GPA:* 3.1. *Test scores:* SAT critical reading scores over 500: 37%; SAT math scores over 500: 45%; SAT writing scores over 500: 35%; SAT critical reading scores over 600: 5%; SAT math scores over 600: 7%; SAT writing scores over 600: 5%; SAT math scores over 700: 1%.

Faculty *Total:* 319, 82% full-time, 74% with terminal degrees. *Student/faculty ratio:* 24:1.

Academics *Calendar:* semesters. *Degrees:* associate, bachelor's, and master's. *Special study options:* academic remediation for entering students, accelerated degree program, adult/continuing education programs, advanced placement credit, distance learning, double majors, honors programs, independent study, internships, off-campus study, part-time degree program, services for LD students, student-designed majors, study abroad, summer session for credit. *ROTC:* Army (b), Air Force (c). *Unusual degree programs:* 3-2 engineering with Pennsylvania State University-University Park Campus.

Computers on Campus 500 computers/terminals are available on campus for general student use. Students can access the following: campus intranet, computer help desk, free student e-mail accounts, online (class) grades, online (class) registration, online (class) schedules, Online classes. Students can connect through the wireless network. Campuswide network is available. 100% of college-owned or -operated housing units are wired for high-speed Internet access. Wireless service is available via classrooms, dorm rooms, libraries, student centers.

Student Life *Housing:* on-campus residence required for freshman year. *Options:* coed. Campus housing is university owned and is provided by a third party. Freshman campus housing is guaranteed. *Activities and organizations:* drama/theater group, student-run newspaper, radio station, choral group, marching band, Student Senate, Stage II, Council for Exceptional Children, United Campus Ministry/ESU Christian Fellowship, University Band/Vocal Performing Choirs, national fraternities, national sororities. *Campus security:* 24-hour emergency response devices and patrols, late-night transport/escort service, controlled dormitory access. *Student services:* health clinic, personal/psychological counseling, women's center.

Athletics Member NCAA. All Division II. *Intercollegiate sports:* baseball M(s), basketball M(s)/W(s), cross-country running M(s)/W(s), field hockey W(s), football M(s), golf W(s), lacrosse W(s), soccer M(s)/W(s), softball W(s), swimming and diving W(s), tennis W(s), track and field M(s)/W(s), volleyball W(s), wrestling M(s). *Intramural sports:* badminton M/W, basketball M/W, equestrian sports M/W, golf M/W, ice hockey M/W, lacrosse M, racquetball M/W, rugby M/W, soccer M/W, softball W, tennis M/W, track and field M/W, ultimate Frisbee M/W, volleyball M/W, water polo M/W.

Standardized Tests *Required:* SAT or ACT (for admission).

Costs (2012–13) *Tuition:* Full-time tuition and fees vary according to course load. Part-time tuition and fees vary according to course load. *Room and board:* Room and board charges vary according to board plan and housing facility. *Payment plans:* installment, deferred payment. *Waivers:* senior citizens and employees or children of employees.

Financial Aid Of all full-time matriculated undergraduates who enrolled in 2008, 4,144 applied for aid, 3,013 were judged to have need, 1,773 had their need fully met. In 2008, 1047 non-need-based awards were made. *Average percent of need met:* 83%. *Average financial aid package:* $5933. *Average need-based loan:* $4106. *Average need-based gift aid:* $4312. *Average non-need-based aid:* $10,063. *Average indebtedness upon graduation:* $25,887. *Financial aid deadline:* 3/1.

Applying *Options:* electronic application. *Application fee:* $45. *Required for some:* high school transcript. *Application deadlines:* 4/1 (freshmen), 5/1 (transfers). *Notification:* 5/1 (freshmen), continuous (transfers).

Freshman Application Contact Mr. Jeff Jones, Director of Admissions, East Stroudsburg University of Pennsylvania, 200 Prospect Street, East Stroudsburg, PA 18301. *Phone:* 570-422-3542. *Toll-free phone:* 877-230-5547. *Fax:* 570-422-3933. *E-mail:* undergrads@po-box.esu.edu. *Web site:* http://www4.esu.edu/.

Edinboro University of Pennsylvania
Edinboro, Pennsylvania

- **State-supported** comprehensive, founded 1857, part of Pennsylvania State System of Higher Education
- **Small-town** 585-acre campus
- **Endowment** $5.7 million
- **Coed** 6,649 undergraduate students, 91% full-time, 58% women, 42% men
- **Moderately difficult** entrance level, 75% of applicants were admitted

Undergraduates 6,024 full-time, 625 part-time. Students come from 38 states and territories; 28 other countries; 13% are from out of state; 7% Black or African American, non-Hispanic/Latino; 2% Hispanic/Latino; 0.7% Asian, non-

Hispanic/Latino; 0.2% Native Hawaiian or other Pacific Islander, non-Hispanic/Latino; 0.2% American Indian or Alaska Native, non-Hispanic/Latino; 2% Two or more races, non-Hispanic/Latino; 0.4% Race/ethnicity unknown; 1% international; 5% transferred in; 31% live on campus. *Retention:* 74% of full-time freshmen returned.

Freshmen *Admission:* 4,852 applied, 3,660 admitted, 1,512 enrolled. *Average high school GPA:* 3.2. *Test scores:* SAT critical reading scores over 500: 36%; SAT math scores over 500: 37%; ACT scores over 18: 65%; SAT critical reading scores over 600: 7%; SAT math scores over 600: 5%; ACT scores over 24: 19%; ACT scores over 30: 2%.

Faculty *Total:* 396, 82% full-time. *Student/faculty ratio:* 20:1.

Academics *Calendar:* semesters. *Degrees:* associate, bachelor's, master's, post-master's, and postbachelor's certificates. *Special study options:* academic remediation for entering students, adult/continuing education programs, advanced placement credit, distance learning, double majors, freshman honors college, honors programs, independent study, internships, off-campus study, part-time degree program, services for LD students, student-designed majors, study abroad, summer session for credit. *ROTC:* Army (b). *Unusual degree programs:* 3-2 engineering with Pennsylvania State University-University Park Campus, University of Pittsburgh, Case Western Reserve University, Pennsylvania State University at Erie, The Behrend College; pre-pharmacy (2+3 at Lake Erie College of Osteopathic Medicine and School of Pharmacy), MA Counseling (3-2 program for Criminal Justice Majors).

Computers on Campus 998 computers/terminals and 2,000 ports are available on campus for general student use. Students can access the following: campus intranet, computer help desk, free student e-mail accounts, online (class) grades, online (class) registration, online (class) schedules, software. Campuswide network is available. 100% of college-owned or -operated housing units are wired for high-speed Internet access. Wireless service is available via classrooms, computer centers, computer labs, dorm rooms, learning centers, libraries, student centers.

Student Life *Housing:* on-campus residence required through sophomore year. *Options:* coed, disabled students. Campus housing is university owned and is provided by a third party. Freshman campus housing is guaranteed. *Activities and organizations:* drama/theater group, student-run newspaper, radio and television station, choral group, marching band, Student Government Association, University Programming Board, Greek Life, Recreational Sports, Student Concert Series, national fraternities, national sororities. *Campus security:* 24-hour emergency response devices and patrols, controlled dormitory access, self-defense education. *Student services:* health clinic, personal/psychological counseling, women's center, legal services.

Athletics Member NCAA. All Division II except wrestling (Division I). *Intercollegiate sports:* basketball M(s)/W(s), cross-country running M(s)/W(s), football M(s), ice hockey M(c), lacrosse W(s), soccer W(s), softball W(s), swimming and diving M(s)/W(s), tennis M/W, track and field M(s)/W(s), volleyball W(s), wrestling M(s). *Intramural sports:* badminton M(c)/W(c), basketball M(c)/W(c), cheerleading W, equestrian sports M(c)/W(c), fencing M(c)/W(c), football M(c)/W(c), golf M(c)/W(c), ice hockey M(c)/W(c), racquetball M(c)/W(c), rock climbing M(c)/W(c), skiing (downhill) M(c)/W(c), soccer M(c)/W(c), softball M(c)/W(c), table tennis M(c)/W(c), tennis M(c)/W(c), track and field M(c)/W(c), ultimate Frisbee M(c)/W(c), volleyball M(c)/W(c), weight lifting M(c)/W(c), wrestling M.

Standardized Tests *Required:* SAT or ACT (for admission).

Costs (2011–12) *Tuition:* state resident $6240 full-time, $260 per credit hour part-time; nonresident $9868 full-time, $390 per credit hour part-time. Part-time tuition and fees vary according to course load. *Required fees:* $2119 full-time. *Room and board:* $8068; room only: $5200. Room and board charges vary according to board plan. *Waivers:* employees or children of employees.

Financial Aid Of all full-time matriculated undergraduates who enrolled in 2009, 5,343 applied for aid, 4,660 were judged to have need, 367 had their need fully met. In 2009, 331 non-need-based awards were made. *Average percent of need met:* 61%. *Average financial aid package:* $9012. *Average need-based loan:* $3751. *Average need-based gift aid:* $2864. *Average non-need-based aid:* $2200. *Average indebtedness upon graduation:* $18,726.

Applying *Options:* electronic application, deferred entrance. *Application fee:* $30. *Required:* high school transcript. *Required for some:* essay or personal statement, 1 letter of recommendation, interview, music auditions. *Recommended:* minimum 2.5 GPA. *Application deadline:* rolling (transfers). *Notification:* continuous (freshmen), continuous (transfers).

Freshman Application Contact Mr. Craig Grooms, Director of Undergraduate Admissions, Edinboro University of Pennsylvania, Academy Hall, Edinboro, PA 16444. *Phone:* 814-732-2761. *Toll-free phone:* 888-846-2676. *Fax:* 814-732-2420. *E-mail:* eup_admissions@edinboro.edu. *Web site:* http://www.edinboro.edu/.

See page 1312 for the College Close-Up.

Elizabethtown College
Elizabethtown, Pennsylvania

- **Independent** comprehensive, founded 1899, affiliated with Church of the Brethren
- **Small-town** 201-acre campus with easy access to Baltimore, Philadelphia
- **Endowment** $56.5 million
- **Coed** 2,356 undergraduate students, 79% full-time, 64% women, 36% men
- **Moderately difficult** entrance level, 66% of applicants were admitted

Undergraduates 1,854 full-time, 502 part-time. Students come from 30 states and territories; 23 other countries; 27% are from out of state; 4% Black or African American, non-Hispanic/Latino; 3% Hispanic/Latino; 2% Asian, non-Hispanic/Latino; 0.1% Native Hawaiian or other Pacific Islander, non-Hispanic/Latino; 0.3% American Indian or Alaska Native, non-Hispanic/Latino; 0.6% Two or more races, non-Hispanic/Latino; 0.1% Race/ethnicity unknown; 3% international; 2% transferred in; 75% live on campus. *Retention:* 84% of full-time freshmen returned.

Freshmen *Admission:* 3,665 applied, 2,411 admitted, 511 enrolled. *Test scores:* SAT critical reading scores over 500: 74%; SAT math scores over 500: 82%; ACT scores over 18: 96%; SAT critical reading scores over 600: 30%; SAT math scores over 600: 34%; ACT scores over 24: 55%; SAT critical reading scores over 700: 4%; SAT math scores over 700: 5%; ACT scores over 30: 9%.

Faculty *Total:* 250, 52% full-time, 54% with terminal degrees. *Student/faculty ratio:* 12:1.

Academics *Calendar:* semesters. *Degrees:* certificates, associate, bachelor's, master's, and postbachelor's certificates. *Special study options:* academic remediation for entering students, accelerated degree program, adult/continuing education programs, advanced placement credit, distance learning, double majors, English as a second language, external degree program, honors programs, independent study, internships, off-campus study, part-time degree program, services for LD students, study abroad, summer session for credit. *Unusual degree programs:* 3-2 engineering with Pennsylvania State University - University Park Campus; forestry with Duke University; allied health programs with Thomas Jefferson University, Widener University, University of Maryland at Baltimore.

Computers on Campus 200 computers/terminals and 200 ports are available on campus for general student use. Students can access the following: campus intranet, computer help desk, free student e-mail accounts, online (class) grades, online (class) registration, online (class) schedules, file space, personal web page, financial aid, student billing. Campuswide network is available. 100% of college-owned or -operated housing units are wired for high-speed Internet access. Wireless service is available via classrooms, computer centers, computer labs, dorm rooms, learning centers, libraries, student centers.

Student Life *Housing:* on-campus residence required through senior year. *Options:* coed, women-only, disabled students. Campus housing is university owned and leased by the school. Freshman campus housing is guaranteed. *Activities and organizations:* drama/theater group, student-run newspaper, radio and television station, choral group, Students in Free Enterprise (SIFE), Emotion Dance Club, Student Senate, Acappella groups, religious groups. *Campus security:* 24-hour emergency response devices and patrols, student patrols, late-night transport/escort service, controlled dormitory access, self-defense workshops, crime prevention program. *Student services:* personal/psychological counseling.

Athletics Member NCAA. All Division III. *Intercollegiate sports:* baseball M, basketball M/W, cross-country running M/W, field hockey W, golf M, lacrosse M/W, soccer M/W, softball W, swimming and diving M/W, tennis M/W, track and field M/W, volleyball W, wrestling M. *Intramural sports:* badminton M/W, basketball M/W, cheerleading M(c)/W(c), ice hockey M(c), racquetball M/W, soccer M/W, softball M/W, tennis M/W, volleyball M/W, water polo M/W.

Standardized Tests *Required:* SAT or ACT (for admission).

Costs (2012–13) *Comprehensive fee:* $45,600 includes full-time tuition ($36,550) and room and board ($9050). Full-time tuition and fees vary according to course load. Part-time tuition: $885 per credit hour. Part-time tuition and fees vary according to class time and course load. *Required fees:* $515 per credit hour part-time. *College room only:* $4400. Room and board charges vary according to board plan and housing facility. *Payment plan:* installment. *Waivers:* employees or children of employees.

Financial Aid Of all full-time matriculated undergraduates who enrolled in 2011, 1,603 applied for aid, 1,426 were judged to have need, 268 had their need fully met. 946 Federal Work-Study jobs (averaging $1285). In 2011, 380 non-need-based awards were made. *Average percent of need met:* 79%. *Average financial aid package:* $23,891. *Average need-based loan:* $4398. *Average need-based gift aid:* $19,456. *Average non-need-based aid:* $14,764.

Applying *Options:* electronic application, deferred entrance. *Application fee:* $30. *Required:* essay or personal statement, high school transcript, minimum

2.0 GPA, 2 letters of recommendation. *Required for some:* interview. *Recommended:* minimum 3.0 GPA, interview. *Application deadlines:* 3/1 (freshmen), 8/1 (transfers). *Notification:* continuous (freshmen), continuous (transfers). **Freshman Application Contact** Ms. Debra Murray, Director of Admissions, Elizabethtown College, One Alpha Drive, Elizabethtown, PA 17022. *Phone:* 717-361-1400. *Fax:* 717-361-1365. *E-mail:* admissions@etown.edu. *Web site:* http://www.etown.edu/.

See below for display ad and page 1314 for the College Close-Up.

Franklin & Marshall College
Lancaster, Pennsylvania

- **Independent** 4-year, founded 1787
- **Suburban** 209-acre campus with easy access to Philadelphia
- **Endowment** $315.4 million
- **Coed** 2,363 undergraduate students, 98% full-time, 52% women, 48% men
- **Very difficult** entrance level, 38% of applicants were admitted

Undergraduates 2,324 full-time, 39 part-time. Students come from 42 states and territories; 42 other countries; 72% are from out of state; 3% Black or African American, non-Hispanic/Latino; 6% Hispanic/Latino; 3% Asian, non-Hispanic/Latino; 2% Two or more races, non-Hispanic/Latino; 3% Race/ethnicity unknown; 9% international; 0.7% transferred in; 99% live on campus. *Retention:* 93% of full-time freshmen returned.

Freshmen *Admission:* 5,105 applied, 1,965 admitted, 597 enrolled. *Average high school GPA:* 3.54. *Test scores:* SAT critical reading scores over 500: 98%; SAT math scores over 500: 100%; ACT scores over 18: 100%; SAT critical reading scores over 600: 81%; SAT math scores over 600: 89%; ACT scores over 24: 100%; SAT critical reading scores over 700: 21%; SAT math scores over 700: 29%; ACT scores over 30: 52%.

Faculty *Total:* 268, 79% full-time, 89% with terminal degrees. *Student/faculty ratio:* 10:1.

Academics *Calendar:* semesters. *Degree:* bachelor's. *Special study options:* accelerated degree program, advanced placement credit, double majors, independent study, internships, off-campus study, services for LD students, student-designed majors, study abroad, summer session for credit. *ROTC:* Army

(c). *Unusual degree programs:* 3-2 engineering with Rensselaer Polytechnic Institute, Washington University in St. Louis, Columbia University, Case Western Reserve University, Penn State University College of Engineering; forestry with Duke University; environmental studies with Duke University.

Computers on Campus 125 computers/terminals are available on campus for general student use. Students can access the following: campus intranet, computer help desk, free student e-mail accounts, online (class) grades, online (class) registration, online (class) schedules, online degree audit, unofficial transcripts, course material. Campuswide network is available. 100% of college-owned or -operated housing units are wired for high-speed Internet access. Wireless service is available via entire campus.

Student Life *Housing:* on-campus residence required through senior year. *Options:* coed, disabled students. Campus housing is university owned and is provided by a third party. Freshman campus housing is guaranteed. *Activities and organizations:* drama/theater group, student-run newspaper, radio station, choral group, Intervarsity, Hillel, Mi Gente Latina, Cia Bella, F&M Players, national fraternities, national sororities. *Campus security:* 24-hour emergency response devices and patrols, late-night transport/escort service, controlled dormitory access, residence hall security, campus security connected to city police and fire company. *Student services:* health clinic, personal/psychological counseling, women's center.

Athletics Member NCAA. All Division III except wrestling (Division I). *Intercollegiate sports:* baseball M, basketball M/W, crew M(c)/W, cross-country running M/W, equestrian sports W(c), field hockey W, football M, golf M/W, ice hockey M(c), lacrosse M/W, rugby M(c)/W(c), soccer M/W, softball W, squash M/W, swimming and diving M/W, tennis M/W, track and field M/W, ultimate Frisbee M(c)/W(c), volleyball M(c)/W, wrestling M. *Intramural sports:* basketball M/W, football M; soccer M/W, softball M/W, squash M/W, tennis M/W, volleyball M/W, wrestling M.

Costs (2011–12) *One-time required fee:* $200. *Comprehensive fee:* $54,070 includes full-time tuition ($42,510), mandatory fees ($60), and room and board ($11,500). Part-time tuition: $5314 per course. *College room only:* $7330. Room and board charges vary according to board plan and housing facility. *Payment plans:* installment, deferred payment. *Waivers:* employees or children of employees.

Financial Aid Of all full-time matriculated undergraduates who enrolled in 2011, 1,306 applied for aid, 1,071 were judged to have need, 897 had their

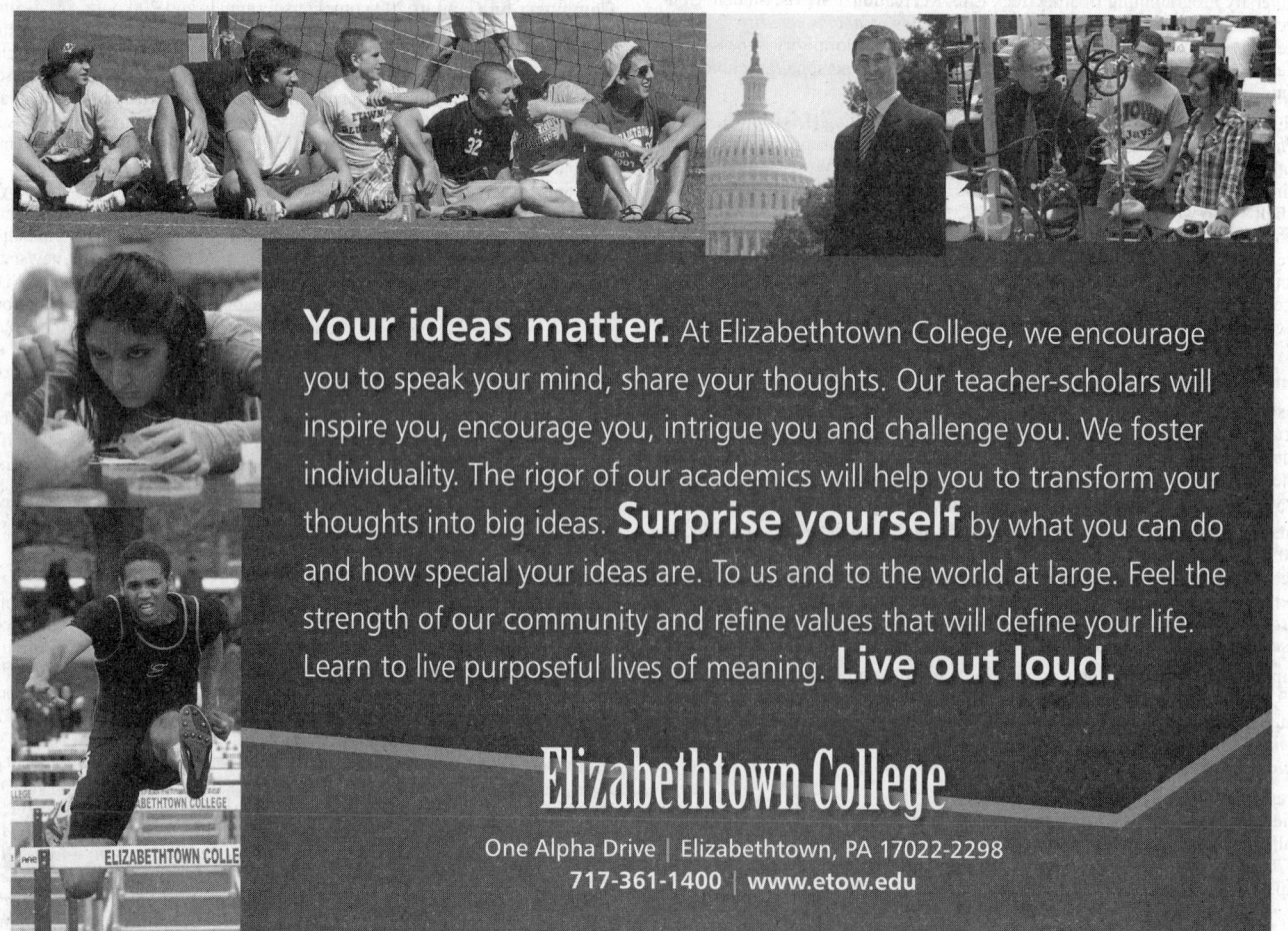

Your ideas matter. At Elizabethtown College, we encourage you to speak your mind, share your thoughts. Our teacher-scholars will inspire you, encourage you, intrigue you and challenge you. We foster individuality. The rigor of our academics will help you to transform your thoughts into big ideas. **Surprise yourself** by what you can do and how special your ideas are. To us and to the world at large. Feel the strength of our community and refine values that will define your life. Learn to live purposeful lives of meaning. **Live out loud.**

Elizabethtown College

One Alpha Drive | Elizabethtown, PA 17022-2298
717-361-1400 | www.etow.edu

need fully met. In 2011, 177 non-need-based awards were made. *Average percent of need met:* 98%. *Average financial aid package:* $34,998. *Average need-based loan:* $4236. *Average need-based gift aid:* $30,597. *Average non-need-based aid:* $11,222. *Average indebtedness upon graduation:* $31,617. *Financial aid deadline:* 2/15.

Applying *Options:* electronic application, early admission, early decision, deferred entrance. *Application fee:* $60. *Required:* essay or personal statement, high school transcript, 2 letters of recommendation, Common Application Supplement. *Required for some:* interview. *Application deadlines:* 2/1 (freshmen), 2/1 (out-of-state freshmen), 5/15 (transfers). *Early decision deadline:* 11/15 (for plan 1), 1/15 (for plan 2). *Notification:* 4/1 (freshmen), 4/1 (out-of-state freshmen), 12/15 (early decision plan 1), 2/15 (early decision plan 2).

Freshman Application Contact Julie Kerich, Director of Admissions, Franklin & Marshall College, PO Box 3003, Lancaster, PA 17604-3003. *Phone:* 717-358-47433. *Toll-free phone:* 877-678-9111. *Fax:* 717-291-4389. *E-mail:* julie.kerich@fandm.edu. *Web site:* http://www.fandm.edu/.

Gannon University

Erie, Pennsylvania

- **Independent Roman Catholic** university, founded 1925
- **Urban** 36-acre campus with easy access to Cleveland, Buffalo, Pittsburgh
- **Endowment** $40.4 million
- **Coed** 2,925 undergraduate students, 87% full-time, 59% women, 41% men
- **Moderately difficult** entrance level, 85% of applicants were admitted

Undergraduates 2,536 full-time, 389 part-time. Students come from 37 states and territories; 24 other countries; 24% are from out of state; 7% Black or African American, non-Hispanic/Latino; 2% Hispanic/Latino; 1% Asian, non-Hispanic/Latino; 0.5% American Indian or Alaska Native, non-Hispanic/Latino; 0.2% Two or more races, non-Hispanic/Latino; 3% Race/ethnicity unknown; 4% international; 4% transferred in; 46% live on campus. *Retention:* 79% of full-time freshmen returned.

Freshmen *Admission:* 3,633 applied, 3,095 admitted, 684 enrolled. *Average high school GPA:* 3.47. *Test scores:* SAT critical reading scores over 500: 58%; SAT math scores over 500: 64%; ACT scores over 18: 88%; SAT critical reading scores over 600: 14%; SAT math scores over 600: 18%; ACT scores over 24: 43%; SAT critical reading scores over 700: 1%; SAT math scores over 700: 2%; ACT scores over 30: 3%.

Faculty *Total:* 356, 55% full-time, 46% with terminal degrees. *Student/faculty ratio:* 14:1.

Academics *Calendar:* semesters plus 2 summer sessions. *Degrees:* certificates, associate, bachelor's, master's, doctoral, post-master's, postbachelor's, and first professional certificates. *Special study options:* academic remediation for entering students, accelerated degree program, adult/continuing education programs, advanced placement credit, cooperative education, distance learning, double majors, English as a second language, honors programs, independent study, internships, off-campus study, part-time degree program, services for LD students, study abroad, summer session for credit. *ROTC:* Army (b). *Unusual degree programs:* 3-2 business administration; engineering with University of Pittsburgh; occupational therapy, physician assistant.

Computers on Campus 380 computers/terminals and 1,425 ports are available on campus for general student use. Students can access the following: campus intranet, computer help desk, free student e-mail accounts, online (class) grades, online (class) registration, online (class) schedules. Campus-wide network is available. 100% of college-owned or -operated housing units are wired for high-speed Internet access. Wireless service is available via entire campus.

Student Life *Housing:* on-campus residence required through sophomore year. *Options:* coed, disabled students. Campus housing is university owned and leased by the school. Freshman campus housing is guaranteed. *Activities and organizations:* drama/theater group, student-run newspaper, radio station, choral group, Exercise Science Club, GU Habitat for Humanity, Phi Eta Sigma, Ski Club, GU Society of Physician Assistants, national fraternities, national sororities. *Campus security:* 24-hour emergency response devices and patrols, student patrols, late-night transport/escort service, controlled dormitory access, security cameras. *Student services:* health clinic, personal/psychological counseling.

Athletics Member NCAA. All Division II. *Intercollegiate sports:* baseball M(s), basketball M(s)/W(s), cheerleading M/W, cross-country running M(s)/W(s), football M(s), golf M(s)/W(s), lacrosse W(s), soccer M(s)/W(s), softball W(s), swimming and diving M(s)/W(s), volleyball W(s), water polo M(s)/W(s), wrestling M(s). *Intramural sports:* badminton M/W, basketball M/W, football M/W, racquetball M/W, soccer M/W, ultimate Frisbee M/W, volleyball M(c)/W, water polo M, weight lifting M, wrestling M.

Standardized Tests *Required:* SAT or ACT (for admission).

Costs (2012–13) *Comprehensive fee:* $37,106 includes full-time tuition ($25,980), mandatory fees ($546), and room and board ($10,580). Full-time

tuition and fees vary according to class time, course load, and program. Part-time tuition: $625 per credit hour. Part-time tuition and fees vary according to class time, course load, and program. *Required fees:* $18 per credit hour part-time. *College room only:* $5530. Room and board charges vary according to board plan and housing facility. *Payment plans:* installment, deferred payment. *Waivers:* senior citizens and employees or children of employees.

Financial Aid Of all full-time matriculated undergraduates who enrolled in 2011, 2,307 applied for aid, 2,142 were judged to have need, 511 had their need fully met. 587 Federal Work-Study jobs (averaging $2300). 177 state and other part-time jobs (averaging $2300). In 2011, 331 non-need-based awards were made. *Average percent of need met:* 81%. *Average financial aid package:* $20,989. *Average need-based loan:* $4487. *Average need-based gift aid:* $17,030. *Average non-need-based aid:* $9928. *Average indebtedness upon graduation:* $33,541.

Applying *Options:* electronic application, early admission, deferred entrance. *Application fee:* $25. *Required:* high school transcript, minimum 2.0 GPA. *Required for some:* minimum 3.0 GPA, 3 letters of recommendation, interview. *Recommended:* essay or personal statement, counselor's recommendation. *Application deadlines:* rolling (freshmen), rolling (transfers).

Freshman Application Contact Office of Admissions, Gannon University, 109 University Square, Erie, PA 16541. *Phone:* 814-871-7240. *Toll-free phone:* 800-GANNONU. *Fax:* 814-871-5803. *E-mail:* admissions@gannon.edu. *Web site:* http://www.gannon.edu/.

See page 1342 for the College Close-Up.

Geneva College
Beaver Falls, Pennsylvania

- **Independent** comprehensive, founded 1848, affiliated with Reformed Presbyterian Church of North America
- **Small-town** 55-acre campus with easy access to Pittsburgh
- **Endowment** $33.0 million
- **Coed** 1,367 undergraduate students, 98% full-time, 50% women, 50% men
- **Moderately difficult** entrance level, 79% of applicants were admitted

Undergraduates 1,339 full-time, 28 part-time. Students come from 38 states and territories; 9 other countries; 29% are from out of state; 3% Black or African American, non-Hispanic/Latino; 1% Hispanic/Latino; 1% Asian, non-Hispanic/Latino; 0.1% American Indian or Alaska Native, non-Hispanic/Latino; 2% Two or more races, non-Hispanic/Latino; 1% international; 4% transferred in; 65% live on campus. *Retention:* 75% of full-time freshmen returned.

Freshmen *Admission:* 1,373 applied, 1,084 admitted, 313 enrolled. *Average high school GPA:* 3.55. *Test scores:* SAT critical reading scores over 500: 72%; SAT math scores over 500: 68%; ACT scores over 18: 94%; SAT critical reading scores over 600: 28%; SAT math scores over 600: 23%; ACT scores over 24: 57%; SAT critical reading scores over 700: 5%; SAT math scores over 700: 4%; ACT scores over 30: 9%.

Faculty *Total:* 178, 48% full-time. *Student/faculty ratio:* 13:1.

Academics *Calendar:* semesters. *Degrees:* associate, bachelor's, and master's (also offers non-traditional programs in Philadelphia and western Pennsylvania with significant enrollment not reflected in profile). *Special study options:* academic remediation for entering students, accelerated degree program, adult/continuing education programs, advanced placement credit, cooperative education, double majors, English as a second language, honors programs, independent study, internships, off-campus study, part-time degree program, services for LD students, student-designed majors, study abroad, summer session for credit. *ROTC:* Army (c). *Unusual degree programs:* 3-2 nursing with Roberts Wesleyan College; Master's of Divinity with Reformed Presbyterian Theological Seminary.

Computers on Campus 150 computers/terminals and 400 ports are available on campus for general student use. Students can access the following: campus intranet, computer help desk, free student e-mail accounts, online (class) grades, online (class) registration, online (class) schedules. Campuswide network is available. 50% of college-owned or -operated housing units are wired for high-speed Internet access. Wireless service is available via entire campus.

Student Life *Housing:* on-campus residence required through senior year. *Options:* men-only, women-only. Campus housing is university owned. Freshman campus housing is guaranteed. *Activities and organizations:* drama/theater group, student-run newspaper, radio station, choral group, marching band, marching band, Genevans Choir, ministry groups, intermurals, discipleship groups. *Campus security:* 24-hour emergency response devices and patrols, late-night transport/escort service, controlled dormitory access. *Student services:* health clinic, personal/psychological counseling.

Athletics Member NCAA, NCCAA. All NCAA Division III. *Intercollegiate sports:* baseball M, basketball M/W, cross-country running M/W, football M, soccer M/W, softball W, tennis W, track and field M/W, volleyball M(c)/W. *Intramural sports:* basketball M/W, football M/W, golf M/W, ice hockey

M(c), racquetball M/W, rugby M(c)/W(c), skiing (downhill) M(c)/W(c), soccer M/W, softball M/W, table tennis M/W, ultimate Frisbee M/W, volleyball M/W.

Standardized Tests *Required:* SAT or ACT (for admission).

Costs (2011–12) *Comprehensive fee:* $31,890 includes full-time tuition ($23,330) and room and board ($8560). Full-time tuition and fees vary according to course load. Part-time tuition: $780 per credit hour. Part-time tuition and fees vary according to course load. *Room and board:* Room and board charges vary according to board plan. *Payment plan:* installment. *Waivers:* employees or children of employees.

Financial Aid Of all full-time matriculated undergraduates who enrolled in 2010, 1,367 applied for aid, 1,258 were judged to have need, 213 had their need fully met. 250 Federal Work-Study jobs (averaging $2000). In 2010, 200 non-need-based awards were made. *Average percent of need met:* 78%. *Average financial aid package:* $18,433. *Average need-based loan:* $4192. *Average need-based gift aid:* $14,096. *Average non-need-based aid:* $8179. *Average indebtedness upon graduation:* $24,000.

Applying *Options:* electronic application, early admission, early action, deferred entrance. *Application fee:* $40. *Required:* essay or personal statement, high school transcript, minimum 2.0 GPA. *Required for some:* interview. *Recommended:* minimum 3.0 GPA, 2 letters of recommendation, interview. *Application deadlines:* rolling (freshmen), rolling (transfers). *Notification:* continuous (freshmen), continuous (transfers).

Freshman Application Contact Mr. David Layton, Associate Vice President for Enrollment, Geneva College, 3200 College Avenue, Beaver Falls, PA 15010-3599. *Phone:* 724-847-6500. *Toll-free phone:* 800-847-8255. *E-mail:* admissions@geneva.edu. *Web site:* http://www.geneva.edu/.

Gettysburg College
Gettysburg, Pennsylvania

- **Independent** 4-year, founded 1832, affiliated with Evangelical Lutheran Church in America
- **Suburban** 200-acre campus with easy access to Baltimore and Washington, D.C.
- **Endowment** $245.9 million
- **Coed** 2,516 undergraduate students, 99% full-time, 52% women, 48% men
- **Most difficult** entrance level, 40% of applicants were admitted

Undergraduates 2,491 full-time, 25 part-time. Students come from 41 states and territories; 31 other countries; 75% are from out of state; 4% Black or African American, non-Hispanic/Latino; 4% Hispanic/Latino; 2% Asian, non-Hispanic/Latino; 0.2% American Indian or Alaska Native, non-Hispanic/Latino; 8% Race/ethnicity unknown; 2% international; 0.7% transferred in; 92% live on campus. *Retention:* 92% of full-time freshmen returned.

Freshmen *Admission:* 5,662 applied, 2,257 admitted, 732 enrolled. *Test scores:* SAT critical reading scores over 500: 100%; SAT math scores over 500: 100%; SAT critical reading scores over 600: 83%; SAT math scores over 600: 83%; SAT critical reading scores over 700: 18%; SAT math scores over 700: 14%.

Faculty *Total:* 292, 74% full-time, 80% with terminal degrees. *Student/faculty ratio:* 10:1.

Academics *Calendar:* semesters. *Degree:* bachelor's. *Special study options:* adult/continuing education programs, advanced placement credit, double majors, independent study, internships, off-campus study, student-designed majors, study abroad. *ROTC:* Army (c). *Unusual degree programs:* 3-2 engineering with Rensselaer Polytechnic Institute, Washington University, Columbia University; forestry with Duke University; nursing with Johns Hopkins University; optometry with State University of New York College of Optometry, Pennsylvania College of Optometry, physical therapy at Drexel University.

Computers on Campus 268 computers/terminals are available on campus for general student use. Students can access the following: campus intranet, computer help desk, free student e-mail accounts, online (class) grades, online (class) registration, online (class) schedules. Campuswide network is available. 100% of college-owned or -operated housing units are wired for high-speed Internet access. Wireless service is available via entire campus.

Student Life *Housing:* on-campus residence required through senior year. *Options:* coed, men-only, women-only. Campus housing is university owned. Freshman campus housing is guaranteed. *Activities and organizations:* drama/theater group, student-run newspaper, radio and television station, choral group, marching band, community service, music, athletics, student government, national fraternities, national sororities. *Campus security:* 24-hour emergency response devices and patrols, late-night transport/escort service, controlled dormitory access. *Student services:* health clinic, personal/psychological counseling, women's center.

Athletics Member NCAA. All Division III. *Intercollegiate sports:* baseball M, basketball M/W, cheerleading M/W, cross-country running M/W, equestrian sports M(c)/W(c), field hockey W, football M, golf M/W, ice hockey M(c), lacrosse M/W, rugby M(c)/W(c), soccer M/W, softball W, swimming and

diving M/W, tennis M/W, track and field M/W, ultimate Frisbee M(c)/W(c), volleyball W, wrestling M. *Intramural sports:* basketball M/W, fencing M(c)/W(c), football M/W, lacrosse W, soccer M/W, softball M/W, tennis M/W, volleyball M/W, water polo M/W.

Standardized Tests *Required:* SAT or ACT (for admission). *Recommended:* SAT Subject Tests (for admission).

Costs (2011–12) *Comprehensive fee:* $52,790 includes full-time tuition ($42,610) and room and board ($10,180). Full-time tuition and fees vary according to program. Part-time tuition and fees vary according to program. *College room only:* $5460. Room and board charges vary according to board plan and housing facility.

Financial Aid Of all full-time matriculated undergraduates who enrolled in 2011, 1,752 applied for aid, 1,528 were judged to have need, 1,414 had their need fully met. 568 Federal Work-Study jobs (averaging $932). 736 state and other part-time jobs (averaging $1200). In 2011, 320 non-need-based awards were made. *Average percent of need met:* 100%. *Average financial aid package:* $33,315. *Average need-based loan:* $4745. *Average need-based gift aid:* $28,379. *Average non-need-based aid:* $10,169. *Average indebtedness upon graduation:* $29,067. *Financial aid deadline:* 2/15.

Applying *Options:* electronic application, early admission, early decision, deferred entrance. *Application fee:* $55. *Required:* essay or personal statement, high school transcript, 2 letters of recommendation. *Recommended:* minimum 3.0 GPA, interview, extracurricular activities. *Application deadlines:* 2/1 (freshmen), 11/1 (transfers). *Early decision deadline:* 11/15 (for plan 1), 1/15 (for plan 2). *Notification:* 4/1 (freshmen), continuous (transfers), 12/15 (early decision plan 1), 2/15 (early decision plan 2).

Freshman Application Contact Ms. Gail Sweezey, Director of Admissions, Gettysburg College, 300 North Washington Street, Gettysburg, PA 17325. *Phone:* 717-337-6100. *Toll-free phone:* 800-431-0803. *Fax:* 717-337-6145. *E-mail:* admiss@gettysburg.edu. *Web site:* http://www.gettysburg.edu/.

Gratz College

Melrose Park, Pennsylvania

Freshman Application Contact Admissions, Gratz College, 7605 Old York Road, Melrose Park, PA 19027. *Phone:* 215-635-7300. *Toll-free phone:* 800-475-4635. *Fax:* 215-635-1046. *E-mail:* admissions@gratz.edu. *Web site:* http://www.gratzcollege.edu/.

Grove City College

Grove City, Pennsylvania

- **Independent Presbyterian** 4-year, founded 1876
- **Small-town** 180-acre campus with easy access to Pittsburgh
- **Endowment** $103.2 million
- **Coed** 2,461 undergraduate students, 99% full-time, 50% women, 50% men
- **Very difficult** entrance level, 76% of applicants were admitted

Undergraduates 2,434 full-time, 27 part-time. Students come from 45 states and territories; 10 other countries; 53% are from out of state; 0.6% Black or African American, non-Hispanic/Latino; 2% Hispanic/Latino; 2% Asian, non-Hispanic/Latino; 0.2% American Indian or Alaska Native, non-Hispanic/Latino; 0.7% Two or more races, non-Hispanic/Latino; 0.1% Race/ethnicity unknown; 0.8% international; 1% transferred in; 94% live on campus. *Retention:* 88% of full-time freshmen returned.

Freshmen *Admission:* 1,592 applied, 1,205 admitted, 617 enrolled. *Average high school GPA:* 3.71. *Test scores:* SAT critical reading scores over 500: 95%; SAT math scores over 500: 96%; ACT scores over 18: 100%; SAT critical reading scores over 600: 65%; SAT math scores over 600: 61%; ACT scores over 24: 89%; SAT critical reading scores over 700: 20%; SAT math scores over 700: 16%; ACT scores over 30: 31%.

Faculty *Total:* 217, 59% full-time, 65% with terminal degrees. *Student/faculty ratio:* 15:1.

Academics *Calendar:* semesters. *Degree:* bachelor's. *Special study options:* advanced placement credit, double majors, independent study, internships, student-designed majors, study abroad, summer session for credit. *ROTC:* Army (c). *Unusual degree programs:* 3-2 Lake Erie College of Osteopathic Medicine Doctor of Osteopathy Program.

Computers on Campus 50 computers/terminals are available on campus for general student use. Students can access the following: campus intranet, computer help desk, free student e-mail accounts, online (class) grades, online (class) registration, online (class) schedules. Campuswide network is available. 100% of college-owned or -operated housing units are wired for high-speed Internet access. Wireless service is available via classrooms, learning centers, student centers.

Student Life *Housing:* on-campus residence required through senior year. *Options:* men-only, women-only. Campus housing is university owned. Freshman campus housing is guaranteed. *Activities and organizations:* drama/theater group, student-run newspaper, radio and television station, choral group,

marching band, Salt Company, Warriors for Christ, Orientation Board, Orchesis, Touring Choir. *Campus security:* 24-hour emergency response devices and patrols, student patrols, late-night transport/escort service, controlled dormitory access, security cameras located around campus and in parking lots. *Student services:* health clinic, personal/psychological counseling.

Athletics Member NCAA. All Division III. *Intercollegiate sports:* baseball M, basketball M/W, cheerleading W, cross-country running M/W, football M, golf M/W, soccer M/W, softball W, swimming and diving M/W, tennis M/W, track and field M/W, volleyball W, water polo W. *Intramural sports:* badminton M/W, basketball M/W, bowling M/W, football M, golf M/W, racquetball M/W, soccer W, softball M/W, table tennis M/W, tennis M/W, ultimate Frisbee M/W, volleyball M/W, weight lifting M.

Standardized Tests *Required:* SAT or ACT (for admission).

Costs (2011–12) *Comprehensive fee:* $21,008 includes full-time tuition ($13,598) and room and board ($7410). Full-time tuition and fees vary according to course load. Part-time tuition: $425 per credit hour. *Room and board:* Room and board charges vary according to housing facility. *Payment plan:* installment. *Waivers:* employees or children of employees.

Financial Aid Of all full-time matriculated undergraduates who enrolled in 2011, 1,216 applied for aid, 1,019 were judged to have need, 70 had their need fully met. In 2011, 227 non-need-based awards were made. *Average percent of need met:* 49%. *Average financial aid package:* $6049. *Average need-based gift aid:* $6049. *Average non-need-based aid:* $2082. *Average indebtedness upon graduation:* $26,597. *Financial aid deadline:* 4/15.

Applying *Options:* electronic application, early admission, early decision, deferred entrance. *Application fee:* $50. *Required:* essay or personal statement, high school transcript, 2 letters of recommendation. *Recommended:* interview. *Application deadlines:* 2/1 (freshmen), 8/15 (transfers). *Early decision deadline:* 11/15. *Notification:* 3/15 (freshmen), continuous (transfers), 12/15 (early decision).

Freshman Application Contact Director of Admissions, Grove City College, 100 Campus Drive, Grove City, PA 16127-2104. *Phone:* 724-458-2100. *Fax:* 724-458-3395. *E-mail:* admissions@gcc.edu. *Web site:* http://www.gcc.edu/.

See page 769 for display ad and page 1350 for the College Close-Up.

Gwynedd-Mercy College
Gwynedd Valley, Pennsylvania

- **Independent Roman Catholic** comprehensive, founded 1948
- **Suburban** 170-acre campus with easy access to Philadelphia
- **Endowment** $7.4 million
- **Coed** 2,347 undergraduate students, 90% full-time, 75% women, 25% men
- **Moderately difficult** entrance level, 87% of applicants were admitted

Undergraduates 2,122 full-time, 225 part-time. Students come from 13 states and territories; 47 other countries; 10% are from out of state; 26% Black or African American, non-Hispanic/Latino; 3% Hispanic/Latino; 3% Asian, non-Hispanic/Latino; 0.3% American Indian or Alaska Native, non-Hispanic/Latino; 0.1% Race/ethnicity unknown; 0.1% international; 13% transferred in; 31% live on campus. *Retention:* 81% of full-time freshmen returned.

Freshmen *Admission:* 1,187 applied, 1,035 admitted, 298 enrolled. *Average high school GPA:* 3.23. *Test scores:* SAT math scores over 500: 39%; SAT writing scores over 500: 32%; SAT math scores over 600: 5%; SAT writing scores over 600: 4%; SAT math scores over 700: 1%.

Faculty *Total:* 272, 29% full-time, 29% with terminal degrees. *Student/faculty ratio:* 16:1.

Academics *Calendar:* semesters. *Degrees:* certificates, associate, bachelor's, master's, post-master's, and postbachelor's certificates. *Special study options:* academic remediation for entering students, accelerated degree program, adult/continuing education programs, advanced placement credit, cooperative education, double majors, English as a second language, freshman honors college, honors programs, independent study, internships, part-time degree program, summer session for credit.

Computers on Campus 218 computers/terminals are available on campus for general student use. Students can access the following: campus intranet, computer help desk, free student e-mail accounts, online (class) grades, online (class) registration, online (class) schedules. Campuswide network is available. 100% of college-owned or -operated housing units are wired for high-speed Internet access. Wireless service is available via classrooms, computer labs, libraries, student centers.

Student Life *Housing options:* coed, disabled students. Campus housing is university owned. Freshman applicants given priority for college housing. *Activities and organizations:* student-run newspaper, choral group, Voices of Gwynedd, Athletic Association, student government, Program Board, Peer Mentors. *Campus security:* 24-hour emergency response devices and patrols,

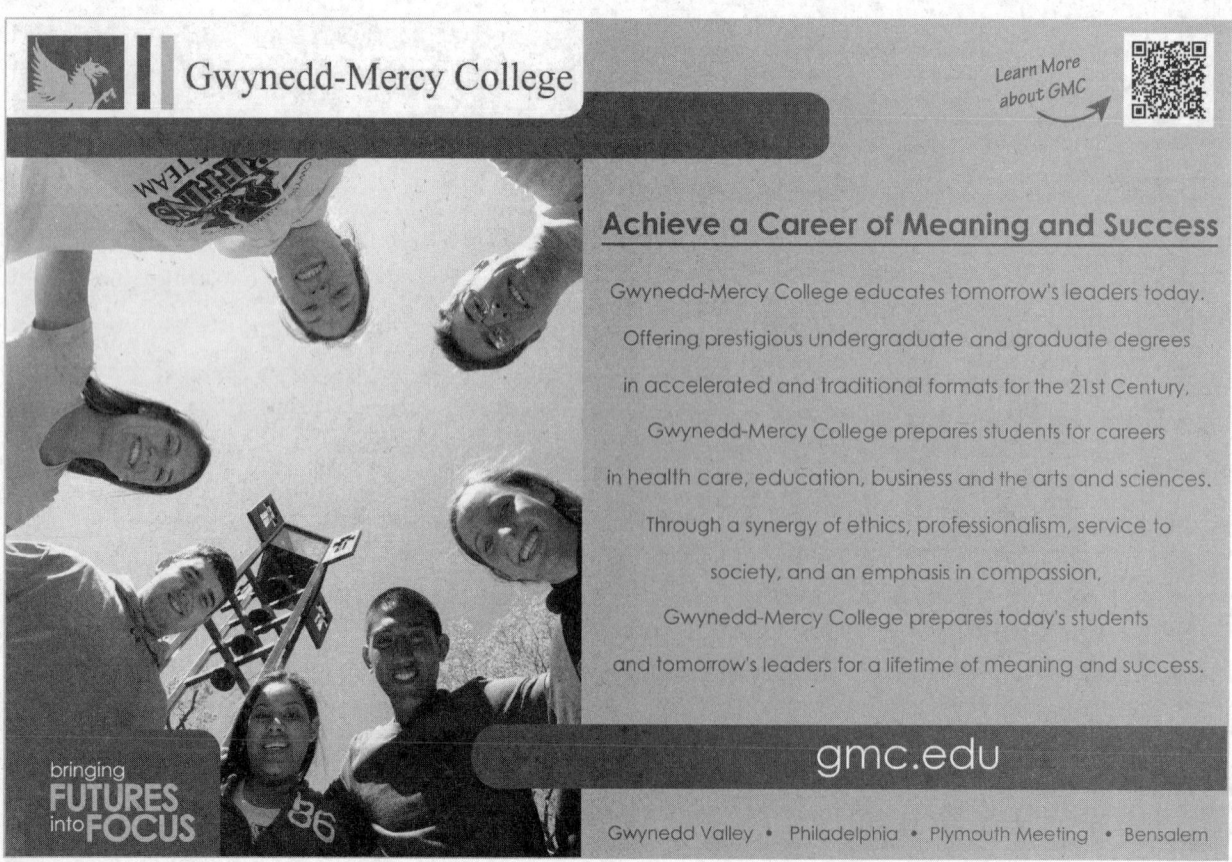

late-night transport/escort service. *Student services:* health clinic, personal/psychological counseling.

Athletics Member NCAA. All Division III. *Intercollegiate sports:* baseball M, basketball M/W, cheerleading W, cross-country running M/W, field hockey W, golf M, lacrosse M/W, soccer M/W, softball W, tennis M/W, track and field M/W, volleyball W.

Standardized Tests *Required:* SAT or ACT (for admission).

Costs (2012–13) *Comprehensive fee:* $38,190 includes full-time tuition ($27,740), mandatory fees ($600), and room and board ($9850). Full-time tuition and fees vary according to program. Part-time tuition: $600 per credit hour. Part-time tuition and fees vary according to program. *Room and board:* Room and board charges vary according to board plan and housing facility. *Payment plan:* installment. *Waivers:* employees or children of employees.

Financial Aid Of all full-time matriculated undergraduates who enrolled in 2010, 1,308 applied for aid, 1,164 were judged to have need, 128 had their need fully met. 194 Federal Work-Study jobs (averaging $928). In 2010, 175 non-need-based awards were made. *Average percent of need met:* 71%. *Average financial aid package:* $17,616. *Average need-based loan:* $4050. *Average need-based gift aid:* $14,042. *Average non-need-based aid:* $8925. *Average indebtedness upon graduation:* $34,520.

Applying *Options:* electronic application, deferred entrance. *Application fee:* $25. *Required:* high school transcript. *Required for some:* essay or personal statement, interview. *Application deadlines:* rolling (freshmen), rolling (out-of-state freshmen), 8/20 (transfers). *Notification:* continuous (freshmen), continuous (out-of-state freshmen), continuous (transfers).

Freshman Application Contact Ms. Michelle Diehl, Director of Admissions, Gwynedd-Mercy College, 1325 Sumneytown Pike, Gwynedd Valley, PA 19437-0901. *Phone:* 215-646-7300. *Toll-free phone:* 800-DIAL-GMC. *Fax:* 215-641-5556. *E-mail:* admissions@gmc.edu. *Web site:* http://www.gmc.edu/

See page 1354 for the College Close-Up.

Harrisburg University of Science and Technology

Harrisburg, Pennsylvania

- **Independent** comprehensive, founded 2005
- **Urban** campus
- **Coed** 223 undergraduate students, 91% full-time, 46% women, 54% men
- **Minimally difficult** entrance level

Undergraduates 202 full-time, 21 part-time. Students come from 5 states and territories; 1 other country; 5% are from out of state; 25% Black or African American, non-Hispanic/Latino; 9% Hispanic/Latino; 7% Asian, non-Hispanic/Latino; 0.4% American Indian or Alaska Native, non-Hispanic/Latino; 3% Race/ethnicity unknown; 5% transferred in; 30% live on campus. *Retention:* 60% of full-time freshmen returned.

Freshmen *Admission:* 91 enrolled. *Average high school GPA:* 2.79.

Faculty *Total:* 40, 30% full-time, 30% with terminal degrees. *Student/faculty ratio:* 11:1.

Academics *Calendar:* semesters. *Degrees:* certificates, bachelor's, master's, and postbachelor's certificates. *Special study options:* academic remediation for entering students, adult/continuing education programs, advanced placement credit, double majors, independent study, internships, part-time degree program, services for LD students, student-designed majors, summer session for credit.

Computers on Campus 10 computers/terminals and 80 ports are available on campus for general student use. Students can access the following: campus intranet, computer help desk, free student e-mail accounts. Campuswide network is available. Wireless service is available via entire campus.

Student Life *Housing:* on-campus residence required for freshman year. *Options:* coed. Campus housing is provided by a third party. Freshman campus housing is guaranteed. *Campus security:* 24-hour emergency response devices and patrols, trained security personnel during all university operating hours. *Student services:* personal/psychological counseling.

Standardized Tests *Recommended:* SAT or ACT (for admission).

Costs (2012–13) *Tuition:* Full-time tuition and fees vary according to degree level. Part-time tuition and fees vary according to course load and degree level. *Room only:* $6340. *Payment plans:* installment, deferred payment.

Financial Aid Of all full-time matriculated undergraduates who enrolled in 2011, 718 applied for aid, 664 were judged to have need, 22 had their need fully met. In 2011, 34 non-need-based awards were made. *Average percent of need met:* 46%. *Average financial aid package:* $10,798. *Average need-based loan:* $3751. *Average need-based gift aid:* $8859. *Average non-need-based aid:* $4331. *Average indebtedness upon graduation:* $27,150.

Applying *Options:* electronic application. *Required:* high school transcript. *Recommended:* essay or personal statement, interview. *Application deadline:* rolling (freshmen). *Notification:* continuous (freshmen).

Freshman Application Contact Harrisburg University of Science and Technology, 326 Market Street, Harrisburg, PA 17101. *Phone:* 717-901-5158. *Toll-free phone:* 866-HBG-UNIV. *Web site:* http://www.HarrisburgU.edu/.

Haverford College

Haverford, Pennsylvania

- **Independent** 4-year, founded 1833
- **Suburban** 200-acre campus with easy access to Philadelphia
- **Endowment** $402.7 million
- **Coed** 1,198 undergraduate students, 100% full-time, 54% women, 46% men
- **Most difficult** entrance level, 25% of applicants were admitted

Undergraduates 1,198 full-time. Students come from 44 states and territories; 35 other countries; 85% are from out of state; 7% Black or African American, non-Hispanic/Latino; 8% Hispanic/Latino; 10% Asian, non-Hispanic/Latino; 0.2% American Indian or Alaska Native, non-Hispanic/Latino; 7% Two or more races, non-Hispanic/Latino; 4% international; 0.2% transferred in; 98% live on campus. *Retention:* 96% of full-time freshmen returned.

Freshmen *Admission:* 3,470 applied, 870 admitted, 335 enrolled. *Test scores:* SAT critical reading scores over 500: 100%; SAT math scores over 500: 99%; SAT writing scores over 500: 100%; SAT critical reading scores over 600: 92%; SAT math scores over 600: 92%; SAT writing scores over 600: 97%; SAT critical reading scores over 700: 55%; SAT math scores over 700: 51%; SAT writing scores over 700: 55%.

Faculty *Total:* 138, 85% full-time, 93% with terminal degrees. *Student/faculty ratio:* 8:1.

Academics *Calendar:* semesters. *Degree:* bachelor's. *Special study options:* advanced placement credit, double majors, independent study, internships, off-campus study, services for LD students, student-designed majors, study abroad. *Unusual degree programs:* 3-2 engineering with California Institute of Technology.

Computers on Campus 300 computers/terminals and 1,600 ports are available on campus for general student use. Students can access the following: campus intranet, computer help desk, free student e-mail accounts, online (class) grades, online (class) registration, online (class) schedules. Campuswide network is available. 100% of college-owned or -operated housing units are wired for high-speed Internet access. Wireless service is available via entire campus.

Student Life *Housing:* on-campus residence required for freshman year. *Options:* coed, disabled students. Campus housing is university owned. Freshman campus housing is guaranteed. *Activities and organizations:* drama/theater group, student-run newspaper, radio station, choral group, Volunteer Programs, student government, choral groups, Multicultural Groups, Orientation Team/Residential Life Leaders. *Campus security:* 24-hour emergency response devices and patrols, late-night transport/escort service, controlled dormitory access. *Student services:* health clinic, personal/psychological counseling, women's center.

Athletics Member NCAA. All Division III. *Intercollegiate sports:* badminton W(c), baseball M, basketball M/W, crew M(c)/W(c), cross-country running M/W, fencing M/W, field hockey W, golf M(c)/W(c), lacrosse M/W, rugby M(c), soccer M/W, softball W, squash M/W, tennis M/W, track and field M/W, ultimate Frisbee M(c)/W(c), volleyball M(c)/W, wrestling M(c). *Intramural sports:* basketball M/W, ice hockey M(c)/W(c), sailing M(c)/W(c), soccer M/W, softball M/W, tennis M/W, volleyball W.

Standardized Tests *Required:* SAT and SAT Subject Tests or ACT (for admission).

Costs (2011–12) *One-time required fee:* $200. *Comprehensive fee:* $55,050 includes full-time tuition ($41,830), mandatory fees ($378), and room and board ($12,842). *College room only:* $7312. *Payment plans:* tuition prepayment, installment. *Waivers:* employees or children of employees.

Financial Aid Of all full-time matriculated undergraduates who enrolled in 2011, 687 applied for aid, 617 were judged to have need, 617 had their need fully met. *Average percent of need met:* 100%. *Average financial aid package:* $38,146. *Average need-based loan:* $1413. *Average need-based gift aid:* $37,515. *Average indebtedness upon graduation:* $16,525. *Financial aid deadline:* 2/1.

Applying *Options:* electronic application, early admission, early decision, deferred entrance. *Application fee:* $60. *Required:* essay or personal statement, 2 letters of recommendation. *Required for some:* high school transcript. *Recommended:* interview. *Application deadlines:* 1/15 (freshmen), 3/31 (transfers). *Early decision deadline:* 11/15. *Notification:* 4/15 (freshmen), 6/1 (transfers), 12/15 (early decision).

Freshman Application Contact Mr. Jess Lord, Dean of Admissions and Financial Aid, Haverford College, 370 Lancaster Avenue, Haverford, PA 19041-1392. *Phone:* 610-896-1350. *Fax:* 610-896-1338. *E-mail:* admitme@haverford.edu. *Web site:* http://www.haverford.edu/.

See page 1358 for the College Close-Up.

Holy Family University

Philadelphia, Pennsylvania

- **Independent Roman Catholic** comprehensive, founded 1954
- **Suburban** 47-acre campus with easy access to Philadelphia
- **Endowment** $15.2 million
- **Coed** 2,122 undergraduate students, 76% full-time, 73% women, 27% men
- **Moderately difficult** entrance level, 71% of applicants were admitted

Undergraduates 1,609 full-time, 513 part-time. Students come from 20 states and territories; 10 other countries; 17% are from out of state; 7% Black or African American, non-Hispanic/Latino; 6% Hispanic/Latino; 4% Asian, non-Hispanic/Latino; 0.1% Native Hawaiian or other Pacific Islander, non-Hispanic/Latino; 0.1% American Indian or Alaska Native, non-Hispanic/Latino; 17% Race/ethnicity unknown; 0.5% international; 9% transferred in; 15% live on campus. *Retention:* 79% of full-time freshmen returned.

Freshmen *Admission:* 1,270 applied, 896 admitted, 289 enrolled. *Average high school GPA:* 2.98. *Test scores:* SAT critical reading scores over 500: 32%; SAT math scores over 500: 27%; SAT writing scores over 500: 31%; SAT critical reading scores over 600: 3%; SAT math scores over 600: 4%; SAT writing scores over 600: 3%.

Faculty *Total:* 370, 25% full-time, 38% with terminal degrees. *Student/faculty ratio:* 12:1.

Academics *Calendar:* semesters. *Degrees:* certificates, associate, bachelor's, master's, doctoral, post-master's, postbachelor's, and first professional certificates. *Special study options:* academic remediation for entering students, accelerated degree program, adult/continuing education programs, advanced placement credit, cooperative education, double majors, English as a second language, freshman honors college, honors programs, independent study, internships, part-time degree program, services for LD students, study abroad, summer session for credit.

Computers on Campus 900 computers/terminals and 1,000 ports are available on campus for general student use. Students can access the following: campus intranet, computer help desk, free student e-mail accounts, online (class) grades, online (class) registration, online (class) schedules. Campus-wide network is available. 100% of college-owned or -operated housing units are wired for high-speed Internet access. Wireless service is available via entire campus.

Student Life *Housing options:* coed, cooperative, disabled students. Campus housing is university owned. Freshman applicants given priority for college housing. *Activities and organizations:* drama/theater group, student-run newspaper, television station, choral group, Students at Your Service (S.A.Y.S.), student government, Campus Ministry Team, Habitat for Humanity, Tri-lite. *Campus security:* 24-hour emergency response devices and patrols, late-night transport/escort service, controlled dormitory access, video surveillance. *Student services:* health clinic, personal/psychological counseling.

Athletics Member NCAA. All Division II. *Intercollegiate sports:* basketball M(s)/W(s), cheerleading W, cross-country running M(s)/W(s), golf M(s), lacrosse W(s), soccer M(s)/W(s), softball W(s), tennis W(s), track and field M(s)/W(s), volleyball W(s). *Intramural sports:* basketball M/W, football M, racquetball M/W, rugby M, table tennis M/W, ultimate Frisbee M/W, volleyball M/W.

Standardized Tests *Required:* SAT or ACT (for admission).

Costs (2011–12) *Comprehensive fee:* $36,300 includes full-time tuition ($23,900), mandatory fees ($650), and room and board ($11,750). Full-time tuition and fees vary according to course load and program. Part-time tuition: $515 per credit. Part-time tuition and fees vary according to course load and program. *Required fees:* $60 per term part-time. *College room only:* $6500. Room and board charges vary according to board plan and housing facility. *Payment plans:* installment, deferred payment. *Waivers:* senior citizens and employees or children of employees.

Financial Aid Of all full-time matriculated undergraduates who enrolled in 2009, 1,447 applied for aid, 1,284 were judged to have need, 216 had their need fully met. 324 Federal Work-Study jobs (averaging $1518). In 2009, 124 non-need-based awards were made. *Average percent of need met:* 71%. *Average financial aid package:* $16,005. *Average need-based loan:* $4351. *Average need-based gift aid:* $11,705. *Average non-need-based aid:* $8093. *Average indebtedness upon graduation:* $31,855.

Applying *Options:* electronic application, deferred entrance. *Application fee:* $25. *Required:* essay or personal statement, high school transcript, minimum 2.0 GPA, 2 letters of recommendation. *Recommended:* interview. *Application deadlines:* rolling (freshmen), rolling (out-of-state freshmen), rolling (transfers). *Notification:* continuous (freshmen), continuous (out-of-state freshmen), continuous (transfers).

Freshman Application Contact Ms. Lauren Campbell, Director of Admissions, Holy Family University, 9801 Frankford Avenue, Philadelphia, PA 19114-2009. *Phone:* 215-637-3050. *Fax:* 215-281-1022. *E-mail:* admissions@holyfamily.edu. *Web site:* http://www.holyfamily.edu/.

See page 1368 for the College Close-Up.

From the moment they step on campus and throughout their lives and careers as alumni, Holy Family students make an impact. Our focus on achievement—in our students and in ourselves—fosters an educational experience steeped in excellence, inspired by faith, and guided by values.

WHAT WILL YOUR IMPACT BE?

www.holyfamily.edu

Holy Family
UNIVERSITY

Immaculata University

Immaculata, Pennsylvania

- **Independent Roman Catholic** comprehensive, founded 1920
- **Suburban** 400-acre campus with easy access to Philadelphia
- **Coed, primarily women** 3,070 undergraduate students, 39% full-time, 78% women, 22% men
- **Moderately difficult** entrance level, 80% of applicants were admitted

Undergraduates 1,212 full-time, 1,858 part-time. 22% are from out of state; 17% Black or African American, non-Hispanic/Latino; 3% Hispanic/Latino; 3% Asian, non-Hispanic/Latino; 0.2% Native Hawaiian or other Pacific Islander, non-Hispanic/Latino; 0.3% American Indian or Alaska Native, non-Hispanic/Latino; 2% Two or more races, non-Hispanic/Latino; 2% Race/ethnicity unknown; 0.6% international; 3% transferred in; 17% live on campus. *Retention:* 83% of full-time freshmen returned.

Freshmen *Admission:* 1,426 applied, 1,140 admitted, 251 enrolled. *Average high school GPA:* 3.13. *Test scores:* SAT critical reading scores over 500: 34%; SAT math scores over 500: 36%; SAT writing scores over 500: 40%; ACT scores over 18: 71%; SAT critical reading scores over 600: 9%; SAT math scores over 600: 9%; SAT writing scores over 600: 11%; ACT scores over 24: 23%; SAT critical reading scores over 700: 1%.

Faculty *Total:* 408, 28% full-time, 36% with terminal degrees. *Student/faculty ratio:* 10:1.

Academics *Calendar:* semesters. *Degrees:* certificates, associate, bachelor's, master's, doctoral, and first professional. *ROTC:* Army (c).

Computers on Campus Campuswide network is available.

Student Life *Housing options:* coed, men-only, women-only, disabled students. Campus housing is university owned. Freshman campus housing is guaranteed. *Campus security:* 24-hour emergency response devices and patrols, late-night transport/escort service, controlled dormitory access.

Athletics Member NCAA. All Division III. *Intercollegiate sports:* basketball W, cross-country running W, field hockey W, lacrosse W, soccer W, softball W, tennis W, volleyball W. *Intramural sports:* archery W, badminton W, cheerleading W(c), equestrian sports W(c), fencing W, swimming and diving W.

Standardized Tests *Required:* SAT or ACT (for admission).

Costs (2011–12) *Comprehensive fee:* $40,310 includes full-time tuition ($28,850) and room and board ($11,460). Full-time tuition and fees vary according to student level. Part-time tuition: $455 per credit hour. No tuition increase for student's term of enrollment. *College room only:* $6160. Room and board charges vary according to board plan and housing facility. *Payment plan:* installment. *Waivers:* senior citizens and employees or children of employees.

Financial Aid Of all full-time matriculated undergraduates who enrolled in 2007, 810 applied for aid, 697 were judged to have need, 201 had their need fully met. *Average percent of need met:* 24%. *Average financial aid package:* $15,657. *Average need-based loan:* $4132. *Average need-based gift aid:* $5516. *Average non-need-based aid:* $6508.

Applying *Options:* electronic application. *Application fee:* $35. *Required:* high school transcript, minimum 2.0 GPA. *Required for some:* essay or personal statement. *Recommended:* minimum 3.0 GPA, interview. *Application deadlines:* rolling (freshmen), rolling (transfers). *Notification:* continuous (freshmen), continuous (transfers).

Freshman Application Contact Director of Admissions, Immaculata University, PO Box 642, Immaculata, PA 19345-0702. *Phone:* 610-647-4400 Ext. 3046. *Toll-free phone:* 877-428-6329. *Fax:* 610-640-0836. *E-mail:* admiss@immaculata.edu. *Web site:* http://www.immaculata.edu/.

See page 774 for display ad and page 1382 for the College Close-Up.

Indiana University of Pennsylvania

Indiana, Pennsylvania

- **State-supported** university, founded 1875, part of Pennsylvania State System of Higher Education
- **Small-town** 374-acre campus with easy access to Pittsburgh
- **Endowment** $47.1 million
- **Coed** 12,943 undergraduate students, 94% full-time, 57% women, 43% men
- **Moderately difficult** entrance level, 58% of applicants were admitted

Undergraduates 12,125 full-time, 818 part-time. Students come from 39 states and territories; 49 other countries; 7% are from out of state; 10% Black or African American, non-Hispanic/Latino; 3% Hispanic/Latino; 1% Asian, non-Hispanic/Latino; 0.2% American Indian or Alaska Native, non-Hispanic/Latino; 1% Two or more races, non-Hispanic/Latino; 2% Race/ethnicity unknown; 2% international; 6% transferred in; 85% live on campus. *Retention:* 77% of full-time freshmen returned.

Freshmen *Admission:* 12,735 applied, 7,428 admitted, 2,922 enrolled. *Test scores:* SAT critical reading scores over 500: 47%; SAT math scores over 500: 50%; SAT writing scores over 500: 40%; SAT critical reading scores over 600: 8%; SAT math scores over 600: 9%; SAT writing scores over 600: 6%; SAT critical reading scores over 700: 1%; SAT writing scores over 700: 1%.

Faculty *Total:* 703, 85% full-time. *Student/faculty ratio:* 19:1.

Academics *Calendar:* semesters. *Degrees:* certificates, associate, bachelor's, master's, doctoral, post-master's, postbachelor's, and first professional certificates. *Special study options:* academic remediation for entering students, accelerated degree program, adult/continuing education programs, advanced placement credit, cooperative education, distance learning, double majors, English as a second language, external degree program, freshman honors college, honors programs, independent study, internships, off-campus study, part-time degree program, services for LD students, study abroad, summer session for credit. *ROTC:* Army (b). *Unusual degree programs:* 3-2 engineering with Drexel University, University of Pittsburgh; forestry with Duke University; chiropractic with Logan College of Chiropractic, New York Chiropractic College, Parker College of Straight Chiropractic; dentistry with Temple University School of Dentistry; optometry with Pennsylvania College of Optometry.

Computers on Campus 1,754 computers/terminals and 2,263 ports are available on campus for general student use. Students can access the following: computer help desk, free student e-mail accounts, online (class) registration, online (class) schedules. Campuswide network is available. 100% of college-owned or -operated housing units are wired for high-speed Internet access. Wireless service is available via entire campus.

Student Life *Housing:* on-campus residence required for freshman year. *Options:* coed, women-only, disabled students. Campus housing is university owned and is provided by a third party. Freshman campus housing is guaranteed. *Activities and organizations:* drama/theater group, student-run newspaper, radio and television station, choral group, marching band, Student Government Association, Panhellenic Association, Interfraternity Council, NAACP, Alpha Phi Omega, national fraternities, national sororities. *Campus security:* 24-hour emergency response devices and patrols, late-night transport/escort service, controlled dormitory access. *Student services:* health clinic, personal/psychological counseling, women's center, legal services.

Athletics Member NCAA. All Division II. *Intercollegiate sports:* baseball M(s), basketball M(s)/W(s), cross-country running M(s)/W(s), field hockey W(s), football M(s), golf M(s), lacrosse W(s), soccer W(s), softball W(s), swimming and diving M(s)/W(s), tennis W(s), track and field M(s)/W(s), volleyball W(s). *Intramural sports:* basketball M/W, bowling M/W, cheerleading M(c)/W(c), equestrian sports M(c)/W(c), fencing M(c)/W(c), golf M/W, gymnastics M(c)/W(c), ice hockey M(c)/W(c), lacrosse M(c), racquetball M/W, riflery M(c)/W(c), rugby M(c)/W(c), sailing M(c)/W(c), skiing (downhill) M(c)/W(c), soccer M(c)/W, softball M/W, swimming and diving M(c)/W(c), tennis M(c)/W(c), track and field M/W, ultimate Frisbee M(c)/W(c), volleyball M(c)/W.

Standardized Tests *Required:* SAT or ACT (for admission).

Costs (2011–12) *Tuition:* state resident $6240 full-time, $260 per credit hour part-time; nonresident $15,600 full-time, $650 per credit hour part-time. Full-time tuition and fees vary according to course load and reciprocity agreements. Part-time tuition and fees vary according to course load and reciprocity agreements. *Required fees:* $2122 full-time, $49 per credit hour part-time, $200 per term part-time. *Room and board:* $9782; room only: $7260. Room and board charges vary according to board plan, housing facility, and location. *Payment plans:* installment, deferred payment. *Waivers:* senior citizens and employees or children of employees.

Financial Aid Of all full-time matriculated undergraduates who enrolled in 2010, 10,286 applied for aid, 8,623 were judged to have need, 559 had their need fully met. 959 Federal Work-Study jobs (averaging $2036). 1,809 state and other part-time jobs (averaging $2510). In 2010, 241 non-need-based awards were made. *Average percent of need met:* 61%. *Average financial aid package:* $9066. *Average need-based loan:* $4201. *Average need-based gift aid:* $5607. *Average non-need-based aid:* $1445. *Average indebtedness upon graduation:* $32,416. *Financial aid deadline:* 4/15.

Applying *Options:* electronic application, early admission, deferred entrance. *Application fee:* $45. *Required:* high school transcript. *Recommended:* essay or personal statement, 2 letters of recommendation. *Application deadlines:* rolling (freshmen), rolling (transfers). *Notification:* 9/1 (freshmen), continuous (transfers).

Freshman Application Contact Office of Admissions, Indiana University of Pennsylvania, 1011 South Drive, Sutton Hall 214, Indiana, PA 15705. *Phone:* 724-357-2230. *Toll-free phone:* 800-442-6830. *Fax:* 724-357-6281. *E-mail:* admissions-inquiry@iup.edu. *Web site:* http://www.iup.edu/.

Juniata College
Huntingdon, Pennsylvania

- **Independent** 4-year, founded 1876, affiliated with Church of the Brethren
- **Small-town** 110-acre campus
- **Endowment** $78.2 million
- **Coed** 1,619 undergraduate students, 95% full-time, 57% women, 43% men
- **Moderately difficult** entrance level, 71% of applicants were admitted

Undergraduates 1,530 full-time, 89 part-time. Students come from 29 states and territories; 43 other countries; 33% are from out of state; 2% Black or African American, non-Hispanic/Latino; 3% Hispanic/Latino; 2% Asian, non-Hispanic/Latino; 0.1% American Indian or Alaska Native, non-Hispanic/Latino; 2% Two or more races, non-Hispanic/Latino; 3% Race/ethnicity unknown; 9% international; 1% transferred in; 81% live on campus. *Retention:* 85% of full-time freshmen returned.

Freshmen *Admission:* 2,144 applied, 1,528 admitted, 363 enrolled. *Average high school GPA:* 3.75. *Test scores:* SAT critical reading scores over 500: 90%; SAT math scores over 500: 90%; SAT critical reading scores over 600: 48%; SAT math scores over 600: 49%; SAT critical reading scores over 700: 7%; SAT math scores over 700: 11%.

Faculty *Total:* 147, 71% full-time, 72% with terminal degrees. *Student/faculty ratio:* 13:1.

Academics *Calendar:* semesters. *Degree:* bachelor's. *Special study options:* accelerated degree program, advanced placement credit, double majors, English as a second language, freshman honors college, honors programs, independent study, internships, off-campus study, part-time degree program, services for LD students, student-designed majors, study abroad, summer session for credit. *Unusual degree programs:* 3-2 engineering with Columbia University, Penn State University, Washington University-St. Louis, Clarkson University; nursing with Case Western University, Johns Hopkins University.

Computers on Campus 340 computers/terminals and 500 ports are available on campus for general student use. Students can access the following: computer help desk, free student e-mail accounts, online (class) grades, online (class) registration, online (class) schedules. Campuswide network is available. 100% of college-owned or -operated housing units are wired for high-speed Internet access. Wireless service is available via classrooms, computer centers, computer labs, dorm rooms, learning centers, libraries, student centers.

Student Life *Housing:* on-campus residence required through senior year. *Options:* coed, women-only. Campus housing is university owned. Freshman campus housing is guaranteed. *Activities and organizations:* drama/theater group, student-run newspaper, radio and television station, choral group, student government, Juniata Activities Board (JAB), Colleges Against Cancer, habitat for Humanity, Model UN. *Campus security:* 24-hour emergency response devices and patrols, student patrols, late-night transport/escort service, controlled dormitory access, fire safety training, adopt-an-officer program, security web site, weather/terror alerts, travel forecast, crime statistics. *Student services:* health clinic, personal/psychological counseling, women's center.

Athletics Member NCAA. All Division III. *Intercollegiate sports:* baseball M, basketball M/W, cross-country running M/W, equestrian sports M(c)/W(c), field hockey W, football M, golf M(c)/W(c), lacrosse M(c), rugby M(c)/W(c), soccer M/W, softball W, swimming and diving W, tennis M/W, track and field M/W, ultimate Frisbee M(c)/W(c), volleyball M/W. *Intramural sports:* basketball M/W, cheerleading W(c), field hockey M(c)/W(c), lacrosse W(c), racquetball M(c)/W(c), skiing (downhill) M(c)/W(c), soccer M/W, volleyball M(c)/W(c).

Standardized Tests *Recommended:* SAT or ACT (for admission).

Costs (2012–13) *Comprehensive fee:* $45,580 includes full-time tuition ($35,040), mandatory fees ($740), and room and board ($9800). *College room only:* $5170. Room and board charges vary according to board plan. *Payment plan:* installment. *Waivers:* senior citizens and employees or children of employees.

Financial Aid Of all full-time matriculated undergraduates who enrolled in 2011, 1,184 applied for aid, 1,062 were judged to have need, 223 had their need fully met. 340 Federal Work-Study jobs (averaging $567). 368 state and other part-time jobs (averaging $965). In 2011, 406 non-need-based awards were made. *Average percent of need met:* 83%. *Average financial aid package:* $26,506. *Average need-based loan:* $4838. *Average need-based gift aid:* $21,165. *Average non-need-based aid:* $15,016. *Average indebtedness upon graduation:* $30,109. *Financial aid deadline:* 3/1.

Applying *Options:* electronic application, early admission, early decision, early action, deferred entrance. *Application fee:* $35. *Required:* essay or personal statement, high school transcript, minimum 3.0 GPA, 1 letter of recommendation. *Recommended:* interview. *Application deadlines:* 3/15 (freshmen), 6/15 (transfers), 1/1 (early action). *Early decision deadline:* 11/15.

Notification: continuous (freshmen), continuous (transfers), 12/23 (early decision), 1/30 (early action).
Freshman Application Contact Terri Bollman-Dalansky, Director of Admissions, Juniata College, 1700 Moore Street, Huntingdon, PA 16652-2119. *Phone:* 814-641-3424. *Toll-free phone:* 877-JUNIATA. *Fax:* 814-641-3100. *E-mail:* admissions@juniata.edu. *Web site:* http://www.juniata.edu/.

Keystone College
La Plume, Pennsylvania

- **Independent** 4-year, founded 1868
- **Small-town** 270-acre campus
- **Endowment** $7.1 million
- **Coed** 1,726 undergraduate students, 80% full-time, 61% women, 39% men
- **Minimally difficult** entrance level, 93% of applicants were admitted

Undergraduates 1,379 full-time, 347 part-time. Students come from 11 other countries; 13% are from out of state; 5% Black or African American, non-Hispanic/Latino; 3% Hispanic/Latino; 1% Asian, non-Hispanic/Latino; 0.1% Native Hawaiian or other Pacific Islander, non-Hispanic/Latino; 0.1% American Indian or Alaska Native, non-Hispanic/Latino; 0.6% Two or more races, non-Hispanic/Latino; 22% Race/ethnicity unknown; 0.5% international; 8% transferred in; 29% live on campus. *Retention:* 71% of full-time freshmen returned.

Freshmen *Admission:* 1,144 applied, 1,062 admitted, 350 enrolled. *Test scores:* SAT critical reading scores over 500: 24%; SAT math scores over 500: 24%; SAT writing scores over 500: 15%; ACT scores over 18: 50%; SAT critical reading scores over 600: 3%; SAT math scores over 600: 5%; SAT writing scores over 600: 2%; ACT scores over 24: 12%.

Faculty *Total:* 260, 26% full-time, 21% with terminal degrees. *Student/faculty ratio:* 11:1.

Academics *Calendar:* semesters. *Degrees:* certificates, associate, bachelor's, and postbachelor's certificates. *Special study options:* academic remediation for entering students, adult/continuing education programs, advanced placement credit, cooperative education, distance learning, double majors, English as a second language, honors programs, independent study, internships, part-time degree program, services for LD students, study abroad, summer session for credit. *ROTC:* Army (c), Air Force (c).

Computers on Campus 100 computers/terminals are available on campus for general student use. Students can access the following: campus intranet, computer help desk, free student e-mail accounts, online (class) grades, online (class) registration, online (class) schedules. Campuswide network is available. 100% of college-owned or -operated housing units are wired for high-speed Internet access. Wireless service is available via entire campus.

Student Life *Housing:* on-campus residence required for freshman year. *Options:* coed, women-only, disabled students. Campus housing is university owned. Freshman campus housing is guaranteed. *Activities and organizations:* drama/theater group, student-run newspaper, radio station, choral group, Art Society, Inter-Hall Council, O.P.E.N. (Opposing Prejudice Ending Negativity), S.M.A.R.T. (Sports Management and Recreation Team), Eco Club. *Campus security:* 24-hour emergency response devices and patrols, student patrols, late-night transport/escort service, controlled dormitory access. *Student services:* health clinic, personal/psychological counseling, women's center.

Athletics Member NCAA. All Division III. *Intercollegiate sports:* baseball M, basketball M/W, cross-country running M/W, field hockey W, golf M, soccer M/W, softball W, tennis M/W, track and field M/W, volleyball W. *Intramural sports:* basketball M/W, cheerleading M(c)/W(c), football M/W, skiing (downhill) M/W, soccer M/W, volleyball M/W, wrestling M(c).

Standardized Tests *Required:* SAT or ACT (for admission).

Costs (2011–12) *One-time required fee:* $300. *Comprehensive fee:* $28,820 includes full-time tuition ($18,770), mandatory fees ($850), and room and board ($9200). Part-time tuition: $400 per credit. Part-time tuition and fees vary according to course load. *Required fees:* $200 per term part-time. *College room only:* $4650. Room and board charges vary according to board plan and housing facility. *Payment plans:* installment, deferred payment. *Waivers:* senior citizens and employees or children of employees.

Financial Aid Of all full-time matriculated undergraduates who enrolled in 2010, 1,123 applied for aid, 1,123 were judged to have need, 352 had their need fully met. 202 Federal Work-Study jobs (averaging $1450). 50 state and other part-time jobs (averaging $1450). In 2010, 39 non-need-based awards were made. *Average percent of need met:* 77%. *Average financial aid package:* $22,554. *Average need-based loan:* $6500. *Average need-based gift aid:* $20,719. *Average non-need-based aid:* $11,868. *Average indebtedness upon graduation:* $24,750.

Applying *Options:* electronic application, early admission, deferred entrance. *Application fee:* $30. *Required:* essay or personal statement, high school transcript, 1 letter of recommendation. *Required for some:* interview, art portfolio for visual arts and art education. *Recommended:* interview. *Application deadlines:* 7/15 (freshmen), 8/1 (transfers). *Notification:* continuous (freshmen), continuous (transfers).

Freshman Application Contact Jessica Lopez, Senior Administrative Assistant, Keystone College, One College Green, PO Box 50, La Plume, PA 18440-1099. *Phone:* 570-945-8111. *Toll-free phone:* 877-4-COLLEGE. *Fax:* 570-945-7916. *E-mail:* admissions@keystone.edu. *Web site:* http://www.keystone.edu/.

See page 775 for display ad and page 1394 for the College Close-Up.

King's College

Wilkes-Barre, Pennsylvania

- **Independent Roman Catholic** comprehensive, founded 1946
- **Urban** 48-acre campus
- **Endowment** $55.6 million
- **Coed** 2,296 undergraduate students, 88% full-time, 50% women, 50% men
- **Moderately difficult** entrance level, 72% of applicants were admitted

Undergraduates 2,020 full-time, 276 part-time. Students come from 22 states and territories; 4 other countries; 29% are from out of state; 3% Black or African American, non-Hispanic/Latino; 5% Hispanic/Latino; 2% Asian, non-Hispanic/Latino; 0.2% American Indian or Alaska Native, non-Hispanic/Latino; 1% Two or more races, non-Hispanic/Latino; 9% Race/ethnicity unknown; 0.2% international; 5% transferred in; 54% live on campus. *Retention:* 79% of full-time freshmen returned.

Freshmen *Admission:* 2,561 applied, 1,850 admitted, 551 enrolled. *Average high school GPA:* 3.3. *Test scores:* SAT critical reading scores over 500: 58%; SAT math scores over 500: 59%; SAT writing scores over 500: 52%; SAT critical reading scores over 600: 16%; SAT math scores over 600: 19%; SAT writing scores over 600: 13%; SAT critical reading scores over 700: 2%; SAT math scores over 700: 1%; SAT writing scores over 700: 1%.

Faculty *Total:* 235, 56% full-time, 57% with terminal degrees. *Student/faculty ratio:* 13:1.

Academics *Calendar:* semesters. *Degrees:* certificates, associate, bachelor's, master's, and postbachelor's certificates. *Special study options:* accelerated degree program, adult/continuing education programs, advanced placement credit, distance learning, double majors, English as a second language, honors programs, independent study, internships, off-campus study, part-time degree program, services for LD students, student-designed majors, study abroad, summer session for credit. *ROTC:* Army (b), Air Force (c).

Computers on Campus 470 computers/terminals are available on campus for general student use. Students can access the following: computer help desk, free student e-mail accounts, online (class) grades, online (class) registration, online (class) schedules. Campuswide network is available. 100% of college-owned or -operated housing units are wired for high-speed Internet access. Wireless service is available via classrooms, computer labs, libraries, student centers.

Student Life *Housing:* on-campus residence required through sophomore year. *Options:* coed, men-only, women-only, cooperative, disabled students. Campus housing is university owned. Freshman campus housing is guaranteed. *Activities and organizations:* drama/theater group, student-run newspaper, radio station, choral group, Association of Campus Events, Student Government Association, Accounting Association, International/Multicultural Club, Biology Club. *Campus security:* 24-hour emergency response devices and patrols, student patrols, late-night transport/escort service, bicycle patrols. *Student services:* health clinic, personal/psychological counseling, women's center.

Athletics Member NCAA. All Division III. *Intercollegiate sports:* baseball M, basketball M/W, cheerleading M/W, cross-country running M/W, field hockey W, football M, golf M, lacrosse M/W, soccer M/W, softball W, swimming and diving M/W, tennis M/W, volleyball W, wrestling M. *Intramural sports:* basketball M/W, ice hockey M(c), soccer M/W, track and field M(c)/W(c).

Standardized Tests *Recommended:* SAT or ACT (for admission).

Costs (2011–12) *Comprehensive fee:* $38,150 includes full-time tuition ($27,680) and room and board ($10,470). Part-time tuition: $509 per credit hour. *College room only:* $5100. Room and board charges vary according to board plan. *Payment plans:* installment, deferred payment. *Waivers:* senior citizens and employees or children of employees.

Financial Aid Of all full-time matriculated undergraduates who enrolled in 2011, 1,849 applied for aid, 1,697 were judged to have need, 235 had their need fully met. 311 Federal Work-Study jobs (averaging $1280). 371 state and other part-time jobs (averaging $1020). In 2011, 314 non-need-based awards were made. *Average percent of need met:* 76%. *Average financial aid package:* $21,626. *Average need-based loan:* $4486. *Average need-based gift aid:* $16,671. *Average non-need-based aid:* $12,828. *Average indebtedness upon graduation:* $32,077.

Applying *Options:* electronic application, deferred entrance. *Application fee:* $30. *Required:* essay or personal statement, high school transcript. *Recommended:* interview. *Application deadlines:* rolling (freshmen), rolling (out-of-state freshmen), rolling (transfers). *Notification:* continuous (freshmen), continuous (out-of-state freshmen), continuous (transfers).

Freshman Application Contact Mr. James Anderson, Director of Admission, King's College, 133 North River Street, Wilkes-Barre, PA 18711-0801. *Phone:* 570-208-5858. *Toll-free phone:* 888-KINGSPA. *Fax:* 570-208-5971. *E-mail:* admissions@kings.edu. *Web site:* http://www.kings.edu/.

See page 1396 for the College Close-Up.

Kutztown University of Pennsylvania
Kutztown, Pennsylvania

- **State-supported** comprehensive, founded 1866, part of Pennsylvania State System of Higher Education
- **Rural** 289-acre campus with easy access to Philadelphia
- **Endowment** $15.1 million
- **Coed** 9,487 undergraduate students, 93% full-time, 57% women, 43% men
- **Moderately difficult** entrance level, 67% of applicants were admitted

Undergraduates 8,853 full-time, 634 part-time. Students come from 25 states and territories; 29 other countries; 11% are from out of state; 7% Black or African American, non-Hispanic/Latino; 6% Hispanic/Latino; 1% Asian, non-Hispanic/Latino; 0.3% American Indian or Alaska Native, non-Hispanic/Latino; 1% Two or more races, non-Hispanic/Latino; 2% Race/ethnicity unknown; 0.6% international; 6% transferred in; 48% live on campus. *Retention:* 77% of full-time freshmen returned.

Freshmen *Admission:* 10,087 applied, 6,760 admitted, 2,037 enrolled. *Average high school GPA:* 3.1. *Test scores:* SAT critical reading scores over 500: 39%; SAT math scores over 500: 39%; SAT writing scores over 500: 34%; ACT scores over 18: 74%; SAT critical reading scores over 600: 7%; SAT math scores over 600: 7%; SAT writing scores over 600: 5%; ACT scores over 24: 13%; SAT critical reading scores over 700: 1%.

Faculty *Total:* 461, 93% full-time, 78% with terminal degrees. *Student/faculty ratio:* 20:1.

Academics *Calendar:* semesters. *Degrees:* bachelor's, master's, and post-bachelor's certificates. *Special study options:* academic remediation for entering students, accelerated degree program, adult/continuing education programs, advanced placement credit, distance learning, double majors, honors programs, independent study, internships, off-campus study, part-time degree program, services for LD students, student-designed majors, study abroad, summer session for credit. *ROTC:* Army (c). *Unusual degree programs:* 3-2 engineering with Pennsylvania State University–University Park Campus.

Computers on Campus 1,075 computers/terminals and 100 ports are available on campus for general student use. Students can access the following: computer help desk, free student e-mail accounts, online (class) grades, online (class) registration, online (class) schedules. Campuswide network is available. 100% of college-owned or -operated housing units are wired for high-speed Internet access. Wireless service is available via classrooms, computer centers, computer labs, dorm rooms, learning centers, libraries, student centers.

Student Life *Housing options:* coed, women-only, cooperative. Campus housing is university owned and leased by the school. Freshman campus housing is guaranteed. *Activities and organizations:* drama/theater group, student-run newspaper, radio and television station, choral group, marching band, Student Government Board, Student Pennsylvania State Education Association, National Art Education Association, Residence Hall Association, Association of Campus Events, national fraternities, national sororities. *Campus security:* 24-hour emergency response devices and patrols, student patrols, late-night transport/escort service, secondary door electronic alarm system in residence halls, 24-hour student desk personnel at main entrance of residence halls. *Student services:* health clinic, personal/psychological counseling, women's center.

Athletics Member NCAA. All Division II. *Intercollegiate sports:* baseball M(s), basketball M(s)/W(s), bowling W(s), cheerleading W(c), cross-country running M(s)/W(s), equestrian sports M(c)/W(c), field hockey W(s), football M(s), golf W(s), ice hockey M(c), lacrosse M(c)/W(s), rugby M(c)/W(c), skiing (downhill) M(c)/W(c), soccer M(c)/W(s), softball W(s), swimming and diving M(c)/W(s), tennis M(s)/W(s), track and field M(s)/W(s), ultimate Frisbee M(c)/W(c), volleyball M(c)/W(s), wrestling M(s). *Intramural sports:* basketball M/W, fencing M/W, lacrosse W(c), rock climbing M/W, soccer M/W, softball M/W, swimming and diving M/W, tennis M/W, volleyball M/W.

Standardized Tests *Required:* SAT or ACT (for admission). *Required for some:* SAT Subject Tests (for admission).

Costs (2011–12) *One-time required fee:* $108. *Tuition:* state resident $6240 full-time, $260 per credit hour part-time; nonresident $15,600 full-time, $650 per credit hour part-time. Part-time tuition and fees vary according to course load. *Required fees:* $2119 full-time, $178 per credit hour part-time. *Room and board* $8536; room only: $5280. Room and board charges vary according to board plan and housing facility. *Payment plans:* installment, deferred payment. *Waivers:* senior citizens and employees or children of employees.

Financial Aid Of all full-time matriculated undergraduates who enrolled in 2010, 7,932 applied for aid, 6,211 were judged to have need, 2,437 had their need fully met. 399 Federal Work-Study jobs (averaging $831). 870 state and other part-time jobs (averaging $1830). In 2010, 217 non-need-based awards were made. *Average percent of need met:* 53%. *Average financial aid package:* $7891. *Average need-based loan:* $4083. *Average need-based gift aid:* $5393. *Average non-need-based aid:* $2080. *Average indebtedness upon graduation:* $25,250.

Applying *Options:* electronic application, early admission, deferred entrance. *Application fee:* $35. *Required:* high school transcript, minimum 2.0 GPA. *Required for some:* audition for music; portfolio and/or art test for arts. *Application deadlines:* rolling (freshmen), rolling (transfers). *Notification:* continuous (freshmen), continuous (transfers).

Freshman Application Contact Kutztown University of Pennsylvania, 15200 Kutztown Road, Kutztown, PA 19530-0730. *Phone:* 610-683-4060. *Toll-free phone:* 877-628-1915. *Web site:* http://www.kutztown.edu/.

Lafayette College
Easton, Pennsylvania

- **Independent** 4-year, founded 1826, affiliated with Presbyterian Church (U.S.A.)
- **Suburban** 340-acre campus with easy access to New York City, Philadelphia
- **Endowment** $700.0 million
- **Coed** 2,478 undergraduate students, 98% full-time, 47% women, 53% men
- **Most difficult** entrance level, 40% of applicants were admitted

Undergraduates 2,423 full-time, 55 part-time. Students come from 39 states and territories; 44 other countries; 69% are from out of state; 5% Black or African American, non-Hispanic/Latino; 5% Hispanic/Latino; 4% Asian, non-Hispanic/Latino; 0.1% Native Hawaiian or other Pacific Islander, non-Hispanic/Latino; 0.1% American Indian or Alaska Native, non-Hispanic/Latino; 2% Two or more races, non-Hispanic/Latino; 13% Race/ethnicity unknown; 6% international; 0.2% transferred in; 95% live on campus. *Retention:* 95% of full-time freshmen returned.

Freshmen *Admission:* 5,716 applied, 2,304 admitted, 638 enrolled. *Average high school GPA:* 3.47. *Test scores:* SAT critical reading scores over 500: 97%; SAT math scores over 500: 99%; SAT writing scores over 500: 97%; ACT scores over 18: 100%; SAT critical reading scores over 600: 71%; SAT math scores over 600: 83%; SAT writing scores over 600: 72%; ACT scores over 24: 95%; SAT critical reading scores over 700: 16%; SAT math scores over 700: 29%; SAT writing scores over 700: 21%; ACT scores over 30: 37%.

Faculty *Total:* 261, 82% full-time, 90% with terminal degrees. *Student/faculty ratio:* 10:1.

Academics *Calendar:* semesters plus interim January program. *Degree:* bachelor's. *Special study options:* academic remediation for entering students, accelerated degree program, advanced placement credit, honors programs, internships, off-campus study, part-time degree program, services for LD students, student-designed majors, study abroad, summer session for credit. *ROTC:* Army (c).

Computers on Campus 690 computers/terminals and 690 ports are available on campus for general student use. Students can access the following: online (class) registration. Campuswide network is available. Wireless service is available via entire campus.

Student Life *Housing:* on-campus residence required through senior year. *Options:* coed. Campus housing is university owned. Freshman campus housing is guaranteed. *Activities and organizations:* drama/theater group, student-run newspaper, radio station, choral group, Association of Biscer Collegians, International Student Association, Activities Forum, national fraternities, national sororities. *Campus security:* 24-hour emergency response devices and patrols, student patrols, late-night transport/escort service, controlled dormitory access. *Student services:* health clinic, personal/psychological counseling, women's center.

Athletics Member NCAA. All Division I except football (Division I-AA). *Intercollegiate sports:* baseball M, basketball M/W, crew M(c)/W(c), cross-country running M/W, equestrian sports M(c)/W(c), fencing M/W, field hockey W, golf M, ice hockey M(c), lacrosse M/W, rugby M(c)/W(c), skiing (downhill) M(c)/W(c), soccer M/W, softball W, squash M(c), swimming and diving M/W, tennis M/W, track and field M/W, weight lifting M(c)/W(c), wrestling M(c). *Intramural sports:* badminton M/W, baseball M, basketball M/W, bowling M/W, cross-country running M/W, fencing M/W, field hockey W, football M, golf M/W, lacrosse M/W, racquetball M/W, sailing M(c)/W(c), skiing (cross-country) M(c)/W(c), soccer M/W, softball M/W, squash M/W, swimming and diving M/W, table tennis M/W, tennis M/W, track and field M/W, volleyball M/W, weight lifting M/W, wrestling M.

Standardized Tests *Required:* SAT or ACT (for admission). *Recommended:* SAT Subject Tests (for admission).

Costs (2011–12) *One-time required fee:* $700. *Comprehensive fee:* $53,020 includes full-time tuition ($40,340), mandatory fees ($318), and room and

Launch your Life at Lafayette.

Make Big Use of Big Resources

What do you want to accomplish in the next four years? Lafayette has the muscle and energy to make it happen. One of the highest endowment-per-student rates in the nation means ample resources to bring the best faculty here and to fuel student research, study abroad, internships, and field work. Better still — Lafayette's ardent and unswerving devotion to undergraduates means all of our remarkable university-size resources are devoted entirely to students like you.

LAFAYETTE
COLLEGE
Admissions

Easton, Pennsylvania 18042-1773
610.330.5100 | www.lafayette.edu

---

board ($12,362). Full-time tuition and fees vary according to course load. Part-time tuition: $1795 per course. Part-time tuition and fees vary according to course load. *College room only:* $7580. Room and board charges vary according to board plan and student level. *Payment plans:* tuition prepayment, installment.

Financial Aid Of all full-time matriculated undergraduates who enrolled in 2011, 1,418 applied for aid, 1,041 were judged to have need, 912 had their need fully met. In 2011, 166 non-need-based awards were made. *Average percent of need met:* 99%. *Average financial aid package:* $36,700. *Average need-based loan:* $4176. *Average need-based gift aid:* $31,134. *Average non-need-based aid:* $19,756. *Average indebtedness upon graduation:* $24,441. *Financial aid deadline:* 3/1.

Applying *Options:* electronic application, early admission, early decision, deferred entrance. *Application fee:* $65. *Required:* essay or personal statement, high school transcript, 1 letter of recommendation. *Recommended:* interview. *Application deadlines:* 1/15 (freshmen), 5/1 (transfers). *Early decision deadline:* 2/1. *Notification:* 4/1 (freshmen), continuous (transfers), 3/1 (early decision).

Freshman Application Contact Mr. Matthew Hyde, Director of Admissions, Lafayette College, 118 Markle Hall, Easton, PA 18042-1798. *Phone:* 610-330-5100. *Fax:* 610-330-5355. *E-mail:* hydem@lafayette.edu. *Web site:* http://www.lafayette.edu/.

See page 1398 for the College Close-Up.

Lancaster Bible College
Lancaster, Pennsylvania

Freshman Application Contact Mrs. Joanne M. Roper, Associate Vice President for Admissions, Lancaster Bible College, PO Box 83403, Lancaster, PA 17608. *Phone:* 717-560-8271. *Toll-free phone:* 800-544-7335. *Fax:* 717-560-8213. *E-mail:* admissions@lbc.edu. *Web site:* http://www.lbc.edu/.

La Roche College
Pittsburgh, Pennsylvania

- **Independent** comprehensive, founded 1963, affiliated with Roman Catholic Church
- **Suburban** 43-acre campus
- **Endowment** $4.4 million
- **Coed** 1,312 undergraduate students, 83% full-time, 58% women, 42% men
- **Minimally difficult** entrance level, 51% of applicants were admitted

Undergraduates 1,091 full-time, 221 part-time. Students come from 19 states and territories; 31 other countries; 7% are from out of state; 8% Black or African American, non-Hispanic/Latino; 1% Hispanic/Latino; 1% Asian, non-Hispanic/Latino; 0.1% American Indian or Alaska Native, non-Hispanic/Latino; 0.7% Two or more races, non-Hispanic/Latino; 15% Race/ethnicity unknown; 10% international; 16% transferred in; 40% live on campus. *Retention:* 74% of full-time freshmen returned.

Freshmen *Admission:* 1,845 applied, 948 admitted, 262 enrolled. *Average high school GPA:* 3.12. *Test scores:* SAT critical reading scores over 500: 29%; SAT math scores over 500: 29%; SAT writing scores over 500: 26%; ACT scores over 18: 63%; SAT critical reading scores over 600: 3%; SAT math scores over 600: 3%; SAT writing scores over 600: 3%; ACT scores over 24: 16%; SAT math scores over 700: 1%.

Faculty *Total:* 178, 35% full-time, 33% with terminal degrees. *Student/faculty ratio:* 12:1.

Academics *Calendar:* semesters plus summer term. *Degrees:* certificates, associate, bachelor's, master's, and postbachelor's certificates. *Special study options:* academic remediation for entering students, accelerated degree program, adult/continuing education programs, advanced placement credit, distance learning, double majors, English as a second language, honors programs, independent study, internships, part-time degree program, services for LD students, student-designed majors, study abroad, summer session for credit. *ROTC:* Army (c), Air Force (c). *Unusual degree programs:* 3-2 engineering with University of Pittsburgh; physical therapy, physician's assistant, speech language pathologist, athletic trainer, occupational therapy with Duquesne University.

Computers on Campus 167 computers/terminals are available on campus for general student use. Students can access the following: campus intranet, computer help desk, free student e-mail accounts, online (class) grades, online (class) registration, online (class) schedules. Campuswide network is available. 100% of college-owned or -operated housing units are wired for high-speed Internet access. Wireless service is available via classrooms, computer labs, learning centers, libraries, student centers.

Student Life *Housing options:* coed. Campus housing is university owned. Freshman campus housing is guaranteed. *Activities and organizations:* drama/theater group, student-run newspaper, radio station, choral group, American

Society of Interior Design, student government, Visions (environmental club), Helping Hands. *Campus security:* 24-hour emergency response devices and patrols, student patrols, late-night transport/escort service, controlled dormitory access. *Student services:* health clinic, personal/psychological counseling.

Athletics Member NCAA. All Division III. *Intercollegiate sports:* baseball M, basketball M/W, cross-country running M/W, golf M, lacrosse M, soccer M/W, softball W, tennis W, volleyball W. *Intramural sports:* basketball M/W, weight lifting M/W.

Standardized Tests *Required:* SAT or ACT (for admission).

Costs (2011–12) *Comprehensive fee:* $32,342 includes full-time tuition ($22,430), mandatory fees ($730), and room and board ($9182). Full-time tuition and fees vary according to student level. Part-time tuition: $575 per credit hour. *College room only:* $5812. Room and board charges vary according to board plan and housing facility. *Payment plan:* installment. *Waivers:* senior citizens and employees or children of employees.

Financial Aid Of all full-time matriculated undergraduates who enrolled in 2011, 866 applied for aid, 803 were judged to have need, 324 had their need fully met. 182 Federal Work-Study jobs (averaging $1721). In 2011, 63 non-need-based awards were made. *Average percent of need met:* 95%. *Average financial aid package:* $24,403. *Average need-based loan:* $4218. *Average need-based gift aid:* $3355. *Average non-need-based aid:* $17,258. *Average indebtedness upon graduation:* $25,125.

Applying *Options:* electronic application, early admission, deferred entrance. *Application fee:* $50. *Required:* high school transcript, minimum 2.0 GPA, 2 letters of recommendation. *Recommended:* essay or personal statement, minimum 3.0 GPA, interview. *Application deadlines:* rolling (freshmen), rolling (transfers). *Notification:* 9/15 (freshmen).

Freshman Application Contact Mr. Stephen Steppe, Director of Admissions, La Roche College, 9000 Babcock Boulevard, Pittsburgh, PA 15237. *Phone:* 412-536-1275. *Toll-free phone:* 800-838-4LRC. *Fax:* 412-536-1048. *E-mail:* admissions@laroche.edu. *Web site:* http://www.laroche.edu/.

La Salle University

Philadelphia, Pennsylvania

- **Independent Roman Catholic** comprehensive, founded 1863
- **Urban** 130-acre campus with easy access to Philadelphia
- **Endowment** $73.3 million
- **Coed** 4,543 undergraduate students, 77% full-time, 64% women, 36% men
- **Moderately difficult** entrance level, 73% of applicants were admitted

Undergraduates 3,517 full-time, 1,026 part-time. Students come from 36 states and territories; 22 other countries; 39% are from out of state; 19% Black or African American, non-Hispanic/Latino; 12% Hispanic/Latino; 5% Asian, non-Hispanic/Latino; 0.1% Native Hawaiian or other Pacific Islander, non-Hispanic/Latino; 0.6% American Indian or Alaska Native, non-Hispanic/Latino; 7% Race/ethnicity unknown; 1% international; 3% transferred in; 58% live on campus. *Retention:* 81% of full-time freshmen returned.

Freshmen *Admission:* 5,838 applied, 4,279 admitted, 957 enrolled. *Average high school GPA:* 3.34. *Test scores:* SAT critical reading scores over 500: 46%; SAT math scores over 500: 37%; ACT scores over 18: 69%; SAT critical reading scores over 600: 11%; SAT math scores over 600: 4%; ACT scores over 24: 12%; SAT critical reading scores over 700: 2%; SAT math scores over 700: 1%; ACT scores over 30: 1%.

Faculty *Total:* 441, 53% full-time. *Student/faculty ratio:* 13:1.

Academics *Calendar:* semesters. *Degrees:* associate, bachelor's, master's, doctoral, post-master's, postbachelor's, and first professional certificates. *Special study options:* academic remediation for entering students, accelerated degree program, adult/continuing education programs, advanced placement credit, cooperative education, distance learning, double majors, English as a second language, freshman honors college, honors programs, independent study, internships, off-campus study, part-time degree program, services for LD students, student-designed majors, study abroad, summer session for credit. *ROTC:* Army (c), Air Force (c). *Unusual degree programs:* 3-2 business administration; 5-year BS/MS in speech-language-hearing science, 5-year BA/BS/MS in computer information science, 5-year BA/MA in history, and an occupational therapy program with Thomas Jefferson University.

Computers on Campus 1,100 computers/terminals are available on campus for general student use. Students can access the following: campus intranet, computer help desk, free student e-mail accounts, online (class) grades, online (class) registration, online (class) schedules, Blackboard Course Management System. Campuswide network is available. 100% of college-owned or -operated housing units are wired for high-speed Internet access. Wireless service is available via classrooms, computer centers, computer labs, dorm rooms, learning centers, libraries, student centers.

Student Life *Housing options:* coed, men-only, women-only, disabled students. Campus housing is university owned. Freshman campus housing is guaranteed. *Activities and organizations:* drama/theater group, student-run

newspaper, radio and television station, choral group, Student Government Association, Community service organization, La Salle Entertainment Organization, The Explorer (yearbook), The Masque (theater group), national fraternities, national sororities. *Campus security:* 24-hour emergency response devices and patrols, student patrols, late-night transport/escort service, controlled dormitory access. *Student services:* health clinic, personal/psychological counseling, women's center.

Athletics Member NCAA. All Division I. *Intercollegiate sports:* baseball M(s), basketball M(s)/W(s), cheerleading M/W, crew M(s)/W(s), cross-country running M(s)/W(s), field hockey W(s), golf M(s)/W(s), lacrosse W(s), soccer M(s)/W(s), softball W(s), swimming and diving M(s)/W(s), tennis M(s)/W(s), track and field M(s)/W(s), volleyball W(s). *Intramural sports:* cross-country running M(c)/W(c), equestrian sports W(c), ice hockey M(c), lacrosse M(c), rugby M(c)/W(c), swimming and diving M(c)/W(c), tennis M(c)/W(c), track and field M(c)/W(c), ultimate Frisbee M(c)/W(c), water polo M(c)/W(c).

Standardized Tests *Required:* SAT or ACT (for admission).

Costs (2011–12) *One-time required fee:* $150. *Comprehensive fee:* $46,820 includes full-time tuition ($34,840), mandatory fees ($300), and room and board ($11,680). Full-time tuition and fees vary according to course load and program. Part-time tuition: $475 per credit hour. Part-time tuition and fees vary according to course load and program. *Required fees:* $125 per term part-time. *College room only:* $6150. Room and board charges vary according to board plan and housing facility. *Payment plans:* installment, deferred payment. *Waivers:* employees or children of employees.

Financial Aid Of all full-time matriculated undergraduates who enrolled in 2010, 2,867 applied for aid, 2,562 were judged to have need, 409 had their need fully met. 416 Federal Work-Study jobs (averaging $1225). In 2010, 578 non-need-based awards were made. *Average percent of need met:* 73%. *Average financial aid package:* $24,987. *Average need-based loan:* $4687. *Average need-based gift aid:* $18,980. *Average non-need-based aid:* $13,296. *Average indebtedness upon graduation:* $40,615.

Applying *Options:* electronic application, early admission, early decision, early action, deferred entrance. *Application fee:* $35. *Required:* essay or personal statement, high school transcript, 1 letter of recommendation, SAT or ACT. *Recommended:* interview. *Application deadlines:* 8/15 (transfers), 11/15 (early action). *Notification:* continuous (freshmen), continuous (transfers), 12/15 (early action).

Freshman Application Contact Mr. James Plunkett, Executive Director of Undergraduate Admission, La Salle University, 1900 West Olney Avenue, Philadelphia, PA 19141-1199. *Phone:* 215-951-1500. *Toll-free phone:* 800-328-1910. *Fax:* 215-951-1656. *E-mail:* admiss@lasalle.edu. *Web site:* http://www.lasalle.edu/.

Lebanon Valley College

Annville, Pennsylvania

- **Independent United Methodist** comprehensive, founded 1866
- **Small-town** 340-acre campus
- **Endowment** $52.2 million
- **Coed** 1,785 undergraduate students, 91% full-time, 56% women, 44% men
- **Moderately difficult** entrance level, 67% of applicants were admitted

Undergraduates 1,630 full-time, 155 part-time. Students come from 18 states and territories; 2 other countries; 21% are from out of state; 2% Black or African American, non-Hispanic/Latino; 4% Hispanic/Latino; 1% Asian, non-Hispanic/Latino; 0.1% Native Hawaiian or other Pacific Islander, non-Hispanic/Latino; 0.1% American Indian or Alaska Native, non-Hispanic/Latino; 1% Two or more races, non-Hispanic/Latino; 3% Race/ethnicity unknown; 0.2% international; 2% transferred in; 76% live on campus. *Retention:* 86% of full-time freshmen returned.

Freshmen *Admission:* 3,534 applied, 2,385 admitted, 468 enrolled. *Test scores:* SAT critical reading scores over 500: 68%; SAT math scores over 500: 75%; SAT writing scores over 500: 65%; ACT scores over 18: 87%; SAT critical reading scores over 600: 25%; SAT math scores over 600: 30%; SAT writing scores over 600: 19%; ACT scores over 24: 40%; SAT critical reading scores over 700: 2%; SAT math scores over 700: 4%; SAT writing scores over 700: 2%; ACT scores over 30: 4%.

Faculty *Total:* 227, 45% full-time, 54% with terminal degrees. *Student/faculty ratio:* 13:1.

Academics *Calendar:* semesters. *Degrees:* certificates, associate, bachelor's, master's, doctoral, and postbachelor's certificates. *Special study options:* academic remediation for entering students, adult/continuing education programs, advanced placement credit, double majors, independent study, internships, off-campus study, part-time degree program, services for LD students, student-designed majors, study abroad, summer session for credit. *ROTC:* Army (c). *Unusual degree programs:* 3-2 engineering with Case Western Reserve University, The Pennsylvania State University.

Computers on Campus 189 computers/terminals are available on campus for general student use. Students can access the following: campus intranet, computer help desk, free student e-mail accounts, online (class) grades, online (class) registration, online (class) schedules. Campuswide network is available. 100% of college-owned or -operated housing units are wired for high-speed Internet access. Wireless service is available via classrooms, computer centers, computer labs, dorm rooms, learning centers, libraries, student centers.

Student Life *Housing:* on-campus residence required through senior year. *Options:* coed, women-only, disabled students. Campus housing is university owned. Freshman campus housing is guaranteed. *Activities and organizations:* drama/theater group, student-run newspaper, radio station, choral group, marching band, LVC PSEA, Corner Stone, College Against Cancer, Wig and Buckle Theater Group, Habitat for Humanity, national fraternities, national sororities. *Campus security:* 24-hour emergency response devices and patrols, late-night transport/escort service, controlled dormitory access, residence hall entrances locked 24 hours a day. *Student services:* health clinic, personal/psychological counseling, women's center.

Athletics Member NCAA. All Division III. *Intercollegiate sports:* baseball M, basketball M/W, cross-country running M/W, field hockey W, football M, golf M, ice hockey M(c), lacrosse M/W, soccer M/W, softball W, swimming and diving M/W, tennis M/W, track and field M/W, volleyball W. *Intramural sports:* basketball M/W, equestrian sports M(c), football M/W, racquetball M/W, rugby W(c), soccer M(c), softball M/W, table tennis M/W, ultimate Frisbee M(c)/W(c), volleyball M(c).

Costs (2011–12) *Comprehensive fee:* $42,000 includes full-time tuition ($32,490), mandatory fees ($710), and room and board ($8800). Part-time tuition: $520 per credit. Part-time tuition and fees vary according to class time and degree level. *College room only:* $4300. Room and board charges vary according to board plan and housing facility. *Payment plans:* tuition prepayment, installment. *Waivers:* senior citizens and employees or children of employees.

Financial Aid Of all full-time matriculated undergraduates who enrolled in 2011, 1,474 applied for aid, 1,359 were judged to have need, 289 had their need fully met. 994 Federal Work-Study jobs (averaging $1464). In 2011, 207 non-need-based awards were made. *Average percent of need met:* 76%. *Average financial aid package:* $23,978. *Average need-based loan:* $4428. *Average need-based gift aid:* $20,698. *Average non-need-based aid:* $13,261. *Average indebtedness upon graduation:* $36,780.

Applying *Options:* electronic application. *Application fee:* $30. *Required:* high school transcript. *Required for some:* essay or personal statement, audition for music majors. *Recommended:* 2 letters of recommendation, interview.

Application deadlines: rolling (freshmen), rolling (transfers). *Notification:* continuous (freshmen), continuous (transfers).
Freshman Application Contact Ms. Erin Sanno, Associate Director of Admission, Lebanon Valley College, 101 North College Avenue, Annville, PA 17003. *Phone:* 717-867-6181. *Toll-free phone:* 866-LVC-4ADM. *Fax:* 717-867-6026. *E-mail:* admission@lvc.edu. *Web site:* http://www.lvc.edu/.

See below for display ad and page 1402 for the College Close-Up.

Lehigh University
Bethlehem, Pennsylvania

- **Independent** university, founded 1865
- **Suburban** 1600-acre campus with easy access to Philadelphia
- **Endowment** $1.1 billion
- **Coed** 4,869 undergraduate students, 99% full-time, 42% women, 58% men
- **Most difficult** entrance level, 33% of applicants were admitted

Undergraduates 4,810 full-time, 59 part-time. Students come from 55 states and territories; 49 other countries; 75% are from out of state; 4% Black or African American, non-Hispanic/Latino; 8% Hispanic/Latino; 6% Asian, non-Hispanic/Latino; 0.1% Native Hawaiian or other Pacific Islander, non-Hispanic/Latino; 0.1% American Indian or Alaska Native, non-Hispanic/Latino; 2% Two or more races, non-Hispanic/Latino; 5% Race/ethnicity unknown; 5% international; 1% transferred in; 69% live on campus. *Retention:* 95% of full-time freshmen returned.

Freshmen *Admission:* 11,578 applied, 3,864 admitted, 1,207 enrolled. *Test scores:* SAT critical reading scores over 500: 95%; SAT math scores over 500: 100%; ACT scores over 18: 100%; SAT critical reading scores over 600: 67%; SAT math scores over 600: 90%; ACT scores over 24: 97%; SAT critical reading scores over 700: 16%; SAT math scores over 700: 43%; ACT scores over 30: 53%.

Faculty *Total:* 681, 71% full-time, 68% with terminal degrees. *Student/faculty ratio:* 10:1.

Academics *Calendar:* semesters. *Degrees:* bachelor's, master's, doctoral, post-master's, postbachelor's, and first professional certificates. *Special study options:* accelerated degree program, advanced placement credit, cooperative education, distance learning, double majors, English as a second language, external degree program, honors programs, independent study, internships, off-campus study, services for LD students, study abroad, summer session for credit. *ROTC:* Army (b). *Unusual degree programs:* 3-2 engineering; education.

Computers on Campus 638 computers/terminals are available on campus for general student use. Students can access the following: campus intranet, computer help desk, free student e-mail accounts, online (class) grades, online (class) registration, online (class) schedules. Campuswide network is available. 100% of college-owned or -operated housing units are wired for high-speed Internet access. Wireless service is available via classrooms, computer centers, computer labs, dorm rooms, learning centers, libraries, student centers.

Student Life *Housing:* on-campus residence required through sophomore year. *Options:* coed, disabled students. Campus housing is university owned. Freshman campus housing is guaranteed. *Activities and organizations:* drama/theater group, student-run newspaper, radio station, choral group, marching band, WLVR Radio Station, Association of Student Alumni, University Productions, Accounting Club, Phi Sigma Pi, national fraternities, national sororities. *Campus security:* 24-hour emergency response devices and patrols, student patrols, late-night transport/escort service, controlled dormitory access. *Student services:* health clinic, personal/psychological counseling, women's center.

Athletics Member NCAA. All Division I except football (Division I-AA). *Intercollegiate sports:* baseball M, basketball M(s)/W(s), cheerleading M(c)/W(c), crew M(c)/W(s), cross-country running M(s)/W(s), equestrian sports M(c)/W(c), fencing M(c)/W(c), field hockey W(s), golf M(s)/W(s), ice hockey M(c), lacrosse M(s)/W(s), rugby M(c)/W(c), skiing (downhill) M(c)/W(c), soccer M(s)/W(s), softball W(s), swimming and diving M(s)/W(s), tennis M(s)/W(s), track and field M(s)/W(s), volleyball M(c)/W(s), wrestling M(s). *Intramural sports:* badminton M(c)/W(c), baseball M(c), basketball M(c)/W(c), cross-country running M(c)/W(c), field hockey W(c), football M/W, golf M(c)/W(c), gymnastics M(c)/W(c), lacrosse M(c)/W(c), soccer M(c)/W(c), softball M/W, squash M(c), table tennis M(c)/W(c), tennis M(c)/W(c), ultimate Frisbee M(c)/W(c), volleyball M/W, water polo M(c)/W(c), wrestling M(c).

Standardized Tests *Required:* SAT or ACT (for admission).

Costs (2011–12) *Comprehensive fee:* $51,800 includes full-time tuition ($40,660), mandatory fees ($300), and room and board ($10,840). Part-time tuition: $1695 per credit hour. *College room only:* $6220. Room and board charges vary according to board plan and housing facility. *Payment plans:* tuition prepayment, installment. *Waivers:* employees or children of employees.

Financial Aid Of all full-time matriculated undergraduates who enrolled in 2011, 2,840 applied for aid, 2,149 were judged to have need, 1,487 had their need fully met. 1,102 Federal Work-Study jobs (averaging $1655). 56 state and other part-time jobs (averaging $1921). In 2011, 276 non-need-based awards were made. *Average percent of need met:* 96%. *Average financial aid package:* $36,064. *Average need-based loan:* $4341. *Average need-based gift aid:* $30,479. *Average non-need-based aid:* $10,409. *Average indebtedness upon graduation:* $29,668. *Financial aid deadline:* 2/15.

Applying *Options:* electronic application, early admission, early decision, deferred entrance. *Application fee:* $70. *Required:* essay or personal statement, high school transcript, 2 letters of recommendation. *Application deadlines:* 1/1 (freshmen), 4/1 (transfers). *Early decision deadline:* 11/15 (for plan 1), 1/15 (for plan 2). *Notification:* 4/1 (freshmen), 5/1 (transfers), 12/15 (early decision plan 1), 2/15 (early decision plan 2).

Freshman Application Contact Bruce Bunnick, Director of Admissions, Lehigh University, 27 Memorial Drive West, Bethlehem, PA 18015. *Phone:* 610-758-3100. *Fax:* 610-758-4361. *E-mail:* admissions@lehigh.edu. *Web site:* http://www.lehigh.edu/.

Lincoln University
Lincoln University, Pennsylvania

- **State-related** comprehensive, founded 1854
- **Rural** 422-acre campus with easy access to Philadelphia
- **Endowment** $21.7 million
- **Coed** 1,749 undergraduate students, 96% full-time, 58% women, 42% men
- **Moderately difficult** entrance level, 28% of applicants were admitted

Undergraduates 1,682 full-time, 67 part-time. Students come from 31 states and territories; 33 other countries; 56% are from out of state; 80% Black or African American, non-Hispanic/Latino; 0.7% Hispanic/Latino; 0.2% Asian, non-Hispanic/Latino; 0.2% American Indian or Alaska Native, non-Hispanic/Latino; 0.7% Two or more races, non-Hispanic/Latino; 15% Race/ethnicity unknown; 2% international; 3% transferred in; 96% live on campus. *Retention:* 57% of full-time freshmen returned.

Freshmen *Admission:* 6,171 applied, 1,719 admitted, 305 enrolled. *Average high school GPA:* 2.9.

Faculty *Total:* 197, 55% full-time. *Student/faculty ratio:* 16:1.

Academics *Calendar:* semesters. *Degrees:* bachelor's and master's. *Special study options:* academic remediation for entering students, accelerated degree program, advanced placement credit, cooperative education, double majors, honors programs, independent study, internships, off-campus study, part-time

degree program, student-designed majors, summer session for credit. *ROTC:* Army (c), Air Force (c). *Unusual degree programs:* 3-2 engineering.

Computers on Campus 167 computers/terminals are available on campus for general student use. Students can access the following: campus intranet, computer help desk, free student e-mail accounts, online (class) grades, online (class) registration, online (class) schedules. Campuswide network is available. Wireless service is available via entire campus.

Student Life *Housing options:* coed, men-only, women-only. Campus housing is university owned. Freshman applicants given priority for college housing. *Activities and organizations:* drama/theater group, student-run newspaper, radio and television station, choral group, marching band, The Gospel Ensemble, Ziana Fashion Club, We R One, Council of Independent Organizations, national fraternities, national sororities. *Campus security:* 24-hour emergency response devices and patrols, late-night transport/escort service, controlled dormitory access. *Student services:* health clinic, personal/psychological counseling, women's center.

Athletics Member NCAA. All Division II. *Intercollegiate sports:* baseball M, basketball M/W, bowling W, cross-country running M/W, football M, soccer M/W, softball W, tennis M/W, track and field M/W, volleyball W. *Intramural sports:* cheerleading W.

Standardized Tests *Required:* SAT or ACT (for admission).

Costs (2011–12) *Tuition:* state resident $6490 full-time, $387 per credit hour part-time; nonresident $11,456 full-time, $592 per credit hour part-time. Full-time tuition and fees vary according to student level. Part-time tuition and fees vary according to course load. *Required fees:* $2400 full-time. *Room and board:* $8404. Room and board charges vary according to board plan and housing facility. *Waivers:* children of alumni and employees or children of employees.

Financial Aid Of all full-time matriculated undergraduates who enrolled in 2009, 1,913 applied for aid, 1,797 were judged to have need, 51 had their need fully met. 146 Federal Work-Study jobs (averaging $1294). In 2009, 31 non-need-based awards were made. *Average percent of need met:* 49%. *Average financial aid package:* $9060. *Average need-based loan:* $3740. *Average need-based gift aid:* $5122. *Average non-need-based aid:* $3740. *Average indebtedness upon graduation:* $30,818. *Financial aid deadline:* 5/1.

Applying *Options:* electronic application, early admission, deferred entrance. *Application fee:* $20. *Required:* essay or personal statement, high school transcript, minimum 2.0 GPA, 2 letters of recommendation. *Recommended:* interview. *Application deadlines:* rolling (freshmen), rolling (transfers). *Notification:* continuous (transfers).

Freshman Application Contact Ms. Germel Eaton-Clarke, Interim Director of Admissions, Lincoln University, PO Box 179, Lincoln University, PA 19352. *Phone:* 484-365-7218. *Toll-free phone:* 800-790-0191. *Fax:* 484-365-8109. *E-mail:* admiss@lincoln.edu. *Web site:* http://www.lincoln.edu/.

Lock Haven University of Pennsylvania
Lock Haven, Pennsylvania

- **State-supported** comprehensive, founded 1870, part of Pennsylvania State System of Higher Education
- **Rural** 165-acre campus
- **Endowment** $8.7 million
- **Coed** 5,029 undergraduate students, 93% full-time, 57% women, 43% men
- **Moderately difficult** entrance level, 61% of applicants were admitted

Undergraduates 4,693 full-time, 336 part-time. Students come from 26 states and territories; 22 other countries; 7% are from out of state; 6% Black or African American, non-Hispanic/Latino; 2% Hispanic/Latino; 0.7% Asian, non-Hispanic/Latino; 0.2% American Indian or Alaska Native, non-Hispanic/Latino; 0.6% Two or more races, non-Hispanic/Latino; 0.5% Race/ethnicity unknown; 1% international; 6% transferred in; 37% live on campus. *Retention:* 69% of full-time freshmen returned.

Freshmen *Admission:* 5,072 applied, 3,118 admitted, 1,236 enrolled. *Average high school GPA:* 3.31. *Test scores:* SAT critical reading scores over 500: 35%; SAT math scores over 500: 41%; SAT writing scores over 500: 26%; ACT scores over 18: 70%; SAT critical reading scores over 600: 6%; SAT math scores over 600: 7%; SAT writing scores over 600: 3%; ACT scores over 24: 16%; ACT scores over 30: 1%.

Faculty *Total:* 250, 92% full-time, 71% with terminal degrees. *Student/faculty ratio:* 21:1.

Academics *Calendar:* semesters. *Degrees:* associate, bachelor's, and master's. *Special study options:* academic remediation for entering students, adult/continuing education programs, advanced placement credit, cooperative education, distance learning, double majors, English as a second language, freshman honors college, honors programs, independent study, internships, off-campus study, part-time degree program, services for LD students, student-

designed majors, study abroad, summer session for credit. *ROTC:* Army (b). *Unusual degree programs:* 3-2 engineering with Pennsylvania State University-University Park Campus; nursing with Clarion University of Pennsylvania.

Computers on Campus 290 computers/terminals are available on campus for general student use. Students can access the following: online (class) registration. Campuswide network is available.

Student Life *Housing:* on-campus residence required for freshman year. *Options:* coed. Campus housing is university owned and is provided by a third party. Freshman applicants given priority for college housing. *Activities and organizations:* drama/theater group, student-run newspaper, radio and television station, choral group, marching band, student government, Residence Hall Association, national fraternities, national sororities. *Campus security:* 24-hour emergency response devices and patrols, late-night transport/escort service, controlled dormitory access. *Student services:* health clinic, personal/psychological counseling, women's center.

Athletics Member NCAA. All Division II except field hockey (Division I), wrestling (Division I). *Intercollegiate sports:* baseball M(s), basketball M(s)/W(s), cross-country running M(s)/W(s), field hockey W(s), football M(s), lacrosse W(s), soccer M(s)/W(s), softball W(s), swimming and diving W(s), track and field M(s)/W(s), volleyball W(s), wrestling M(s). *Intramural sports:* badminton M/W, basketball M/W, cross-country running M/W, fencing M/W, field hockey W, football M, golf M/W, ice hockey M, lacrosse M/W, racquetball M/W, rugby M/W, skiing (cross-country) M/W, skiing (downhill) M/W, soccer M/W, softball M/W, swimming and diving M/W, tennis M/W, track and field M/W, ultimate Frisbee M/W, volleyball M/W, water polo M, weight lifting M/W, wrestling M.

Standardized Tests *Required:* SAT or ACT (for admission).

Costs (2011–12) *One-time required fee:* $25. *Tuition:* state resident $6240 full-time, $260 per credit hour part-time; nonresident $13,600 full-time, $567 per credit hour part-time. Full-time tuition and fees vary according to course load and location. Part-time tuition and fees vary according to course load and location. *Required fees:* $1999 full-time, $46 per credit hour part-time, $135 per term part-time. *Room and board:* $7056; room only: $4160. Room and board charges vary according to board plan and housing facility. *Payment plan:* installment. *Waivers:* minority students, senior citizens, and employees or children of employees.

Financial Aid Of all full-time matriculated undergraduates who enrolled in 2011, 4,355 applied for aid, 3,354 were judged to have need, 1,844 had their need fully met. 250 Federal Work-Study jobs (averaging $1230). 750 state and other part-time jobs (averaging $1190). In 2011, 79 non-need-based awards were made. *Average percent of need met:* 75%. *Average financial aid package:* $9481. *Average need-based loan:* $4372. *Average need-based gift aid:* $7858. *Average non-need-based aid:* $1144. *Average indebtedness upon graduation:* $23,707. *Financial aid deadline:* 3/15.

Applying *Options:* electronic application, deferred entrance. *Application fee:* $25. *Required:* high school transcript. *Required for some:* essay or personal statement. *Recommended:* interview. *Application deadlines:* rolling (freshmen), rolling (transfers). *Notification:* continuous (freshmen), continuous (transfers).

Freshman Application Contact Ms. Robin Rockey, Interim Director of Admissions, Lock Haven University of Pennsylvania, Office of Admission, DACC, Lock Haven, PA 17745. *Phone:* 570-484-2027. *Toll-free phone:* 800-332-8900 (in-state); 800-233-8978 (out-of-state). *Fax:* 570-484-2201. *E-mail:* admissions@lhup.edu. *Web site:* http://www.lhup.edu/.

Lycoming College
Williamsport, Pennsylvania

- **Independent United Methodist** 4-year, founded 1812
- **Small-town** 35-acre campus
- **Endowment** $152.3 million
- **Coed** 1,369 undergraduate students, 99% full-time, 56% women, 44% men
- **Moderately difficult** entrance level, 70% of applicants were admitted

Undergraduates 1,350 full-time, 19 part-time. Students come from 29 states and territories; 10 other countries; 34% are from out of state; 5% Black or African American, non-Hispanic/Latino; 3% Hispanic/Latino; 0.6% Asian, non-Hispanic/Latino; 0.1% Native Hawaiian or other Pacific Islander, non-Hispanic/Latino; 0.3% American Indian or Alaska Native, non-Hispanic/Latino; 2% Two or more races, non-Hispanic/Latino; 8% Race/ethnicity unknown; 2% international; 2% transferred in; 92% live on campus. *Retention:* 86% of full-time freshmen returned.

Freshmen *Admission:* 1,868 applied, 1,299 admitted, 416 enrolled. *Average high school GPA:* 3.47. *Test scores:* SAT critical reading scores over 500: 63%; SAT math scores over 500: 68%; SAT writing scores over 500: 54%; ACT scores over 18: 89%; SAT critical reading scores over 600: 20%; SAT math scores over 600: 22%; SAT writing scores over 600: 17%; ACT scores

over 24: 47%; SAT critical reading scores over 700: 3%; SAT math scores over 700: 2%; SAT writing scores over 700: 3%; ACT scores over 30: 7%.

Faculty *Total:* 119, 69% full-time, 69% with terminal degrees. *Student/faculty ratio:* 14:1.

Academics *Calendar:* semesters. *Degree:* bachelor's. *Special study options:* accelerated degree program, advanced placement credit, double majors, honors programs, independent study, internships, off-campus study, part-time degree program, services for LD students, student-designed majors, study abroad, summer session for credit. *ROTC:* Army (c). *Unusual degree programs:* 3-2 forestry with Duke University; environmental management with Duke University.

Computers on Campus 165 computers/terminals are available on campus for general student use. Students can access the following: campus intranet, computer help desk, free student e-mail accounts, online (class) grades, online (class) registration, online (class) schedules, Online financial aid, free printing up to a limit. Campuswide network is available. 100% of college-owned or -operated housing units are wired for high-speed Internet access. Wireless service is available via entire campus.

Student Life *Housing:* on-campus residence required through senior year. *Options:* coed, women-only. Campus housing is university owned. Freshman campus housing is guaranteed. *Activities and organizations:* drama/theater group, student-run newspaper, radio station, choral group, Campus Activities Board, Lycoming Dance Club, Habitat for Humanity, Circle K, United Campus Ministry, national fraternities, national sororities. *Campus security:* 24-hour emergency response devices and patrols, student patrols, late-night transport/escort service, controlled dormitory access. *Student services:* health clinic, personal/psychological counseling.

Athletics Member NCAA. All Division III. *Intercollegiate sports:* badminton M(c)/W(c), basketball M/W, cheerleading M(c)/W(c), crew M(c)/W(c), cross-country running M/W, equestrian sports M(c)/W(c), fencing M(c)/W(c), football M, golf M/W, lacrosse M/W, rugby M(c), soccer M/W, softball W, swimming and diving M/W, tennis M/W, ultimate Frisbee M(c)/W(c), volleyball W, water polo M(c)/W(c), wrestling M. *Intramural sports:* basketball M/W, football M/W, soccer M/W, softball M/W, table tennis M/W, volleyball M/W.

Standardized Tests *Recommended:* SAT or ACT (for admission).

Costs (2012–13) *One-time required fee:* $225. *Comprehensive fee:* $42,176 includes full-time tuition ($32,096), mandatory fees ($660), and room and board ($9420). Part-time tuition: $1003 per contact hour. Part-time tuition and fees vary according to course load. *Room and board:* Room and board charges vary according to board plan and housing facility. *Payment plan:* installment. *Waivers:* employees or children of employees.

Financial Aid Of all full-time matriculated undergraduates who enrolled in 2011, 1,233 applied for aid, 1,153 were judged to have need, 199 had their need fully met. 285 Federal Work-Study jobs (averaging $763). In 2011, 169 non-need-based awards were made. *Average percent of need met:* 80%. *Average financial aid package:* $26,072. *Average need-based loan:* $4529. *Average need-based gift aid:* $20,733. *Average non-need-based aid:* $14,593. *Average indebtedness upon graduation:* $28,464.

Applying *Options:* electronic application, deferred entrance. *Application fee:* $35. *Required:* essay or personal statement, high school transcript, 2 letters of recommendation. *Recommended:* minimum 2.3 GPA, interview. *Application deadlines:* 3/1 (freshmen), rolling (transfers). *Notification:* continuous (freshmen), continuous (transfers).

Freshman Application Contact Mr. James Spencer, Vice President of Admissions and Financial Aid, Lycoming College, 700 College Place, Williamsport, PA 17701. *Phone:* 570-321-4026. *Toll-free phone:* 800-345-3920 Ext. 4026. *Fax:* 570-321-4317. *E-mail:* admissions@lycoming.edu. *Web site:* http://www.lycoming.edu/.

Mansfield University of Pennsylvania
Mansfield, Pennsylvania

- **State-supported** comprehensive, founded 1857, part of Pennsylvania State System of Higher Education
- **Small-town** 174-acre campus
- **Coed** 2,876 undergraduate students, 93% full-time, 59% women, 41% men
- **Moderately difficult** entrance level, 77% of applicants were admitted

Undergraduates 2,667 full-time, 209 part-time. 19% are from out of state; 8% Black or African American, non-Hispanic/Latino; 2% Hispanic/Latino; 1% Asian, non-Hispanic/Latino; 0.5% American Indian or Alaska Native, non-Hispanic/Latino; 1% Two or more races, non-Hispanic/Latino; 6% Race/ethnicity unknown; 0.8% international; 8% transferred in; 54% live on campus. *Retention:* 72% of full-time freshmen returned.

Freshmen *Admission:* 2,340 applied, 1,798 admitted, 624 enrolled. *Average high school GPA:* 3.3. *Test scores:* SAT critical reading scores over 500: 40%; SAT math scores over 500: 40%; SAT writing scores over 500: 31%; SAT critical reading scores over 600: 11%; SAT math scores over 600: 8%; SAT writ-

ing scores over 600: 4%; SAT critical reading scores over 700: 2%; SAT math scores over 700: 1%.

Faculty *Total:* 178, 74% full-time. *Student/faculty ratio:* 19:1.

Academics *Calendar:* semesters. *Degrees:* associate, bachelor's, master's, and post-master's certificates. *Special study options:* adult/continuing education programs, part-time degree program. *ROTC:* Army (c).

Computers on Campus Students can access the following: campus intranet, computer help desk, free student e-mail accounts, online (class) grades, online (class) registration, online (class) schedules. Campuswide network is available. 100% of college-owned or -operated housing units are wired for high-speed Internet access. Wireless service is available via classrooms, computer centers, computer labs, dorm rooms, learning centers, libraries, student centers.

Student Life *Housing:* on-campus residence required through sophomore year. *Options:* coed. Campus housing is university owned. Freshman campus housing is guaranteed. *Campus security:* 24-hour emergency response devices and patrols, student patrols, late-night transport/escort service, controlled dormitory access.

Athletics Member NCAA. All Division II. *Intercollegiate sports:* baseball M(s), basketball M(s)/W(s), cross-country running M(s)/W(s), field hockey W(s), football M(c), soccer W(s), softball W(s), swimming and diving W, track and field M(s)/W(s). *Intramural sports:* badminton M/W, basketball M/W, bowling M/W, cheerleading W, cross-country running M/W, equestrian sports M/W, football M/W, golf M/W, racquetball M/W, skiing (cross-country) M/W, skiing (downhill) M/W, soccer M/W, softball M/W, swimming and diving M/W, tennis M/W, track and field M/W, volleyball M/W, water polo M/W, weight lifting M/W.

Standardized Tests *Required:* SAT or ACT (for admission).

Costs (2011–12) *Tuition:* state resident $6240 full-time, $260 per credit hour part-time; nonresident $10,296 full-time, $429 per credit hour part-time. Part-time tuition and fees vary according to course load. *Required fees:* $2414 full-time, $900 per year part-time. *Room and board:* $8078; room only: $5026. Room and board charges vary according to board plan. *Payment plans:* installment, deferred payment. *Waivers:* senior citizens and employees or children of employees.

Financial Aid Of all full-time matriculated undergraduates who enrolled in 2010, 2,454 applied for aid, 2,234 were judged to have need, 134 had their need fully met. *Average percent of need met:* 54%. *Average financial aid package:* $9305. *Average need-based loan:* $4331. *Average need-based gift aid:* $5612. *Average indebtedness upon graduation:* $23,216.

Applying *Options:* electronic application, early admission, deferred entrance. *Application fee:* $25. *Required:* high school transcript. *Required for some:*

interview. *Recommended:* essay or personal statement, minimum 2.5 GPA. *Application deadlines:* rolling (freshmen), rolling (transfers). *Notification:* continuous (freshmen), continuous (transfers).

Freshman Application Contact Mr. Brian Barden, Director of Admissions, Mansfield University of Pennsylvania, Academy Street, Mansfield, PA 16933. *Phone:* 570-662-4813. *Toll-free phone:* 800-577-6826. *E-mail:* admissions@mnsfld.edu. *Web site:* http://www.mansfield.edu/.

Marywood University
Scranton, Pennsylvania

- **Independent Roman Catholic** comprehensive, founded 1915
- **Suburban** 122-acre campus
- **Endowment** $38.5 million
- **Coed** 2,267 undergraduate students, 93% full-time, 70% women, 30% men
- **Moderately difficult** entrance level, 71% of applicants were admitted

Undergraduates 2,106 full-time, 161 part-time. 27% are from out of state; 1% Black or African American, non-Hispanic/Latino; 3% Hispanic/Latino; 2% Asian, non-Hispanic/Latino; 0.1% American Indian or Alaska Native, non-Hispanic/Latino; 0.1% Two or more races, non-Hispanic/Latino; 6% Race/ethnicity unknown; 0.7% international; 6% transferred in; 56% live on campus. *Retention:* 81% of full-time freshmen returned.

Freshmen *Admission:* 2,062 applied, 1,455 admitted, 458 enrolled. *Average high school GPA:* 3.21. *Test scores:* SAT critical reading scores over 500: 66%; SAT math scores over 500: 64%; SAT writing scores over 500: 63%; ACT scores over 18: 97%; SAT critical reading scores over 600: 14%; SAT math scores over 600: 16%; SAT writing scores over 600: 14%; ACT scores over 24: 29%; SAT critical reading scores over 700: 1%; SAT math scores over 700: 1%; SAT writing scores over 700: 3%; ACT scores over 30: 4%.

Faculty *Total:* 398, 38% full-time. *Student/faculty ratio:* 13:1.

Academics *Calendar:* semesters. *Degrees:* bachelor's, master's, doctoral, post-master's, postbachelor's, and first professional certificates. *Special study options:* adult/continuing education programs, advanced placement credit, double majors, English as a second language, honors programs, independent study, internships, off-campus study, part-time degree program, services for LD students, student-designed majors, study abroad, summer session for credit. *ROTC:* Army (c), Air Force (c). *Unusual degree programs:* 3-2 physician assistant, communication sciences disorders, criminal justice, biotechnology, health services administration.

Computers on Campus 460 computers/terminals are available on campus for general student use. Students can access the following: computer help desk, free student e-mail accounts, online (class) grades, online (class) registration, online (class) schedules. Campuswide network is available. 100% of college-owned or -operated housing units are wired for high-speed Internet access. Wireless service is available via entire campus.
Student Life *Housing:* on-campus residence required through sophomore year. *Options:* coed, men-only, women-only, disabled students. Campus housing is university owned. Freshman campus housing is guaranteed. *Activities and organizations:* drama/theater group, student-run newspaper, radio and television station, choral group, Anime and Japanese Club, Diversity United, Marywood Aviators, Marywood Players, International Club. *Campus security:* 24-hour emergency response devices and patrols, late-night transport/escort service, controlled dormitory access, apartments with deadbolts, self-defense education, lighted pathways, seminars on safety. *Student services:* health clinic, personal/psychological counseling.
Athletics Member NCAA. All Division III. *Intercollegiate sports:* baseball M, basketball M/W, cheerleading M(c)/W(c), cross-country running M/W, field hockey W, golf M, lacrosse M/W, skiing (cross-country) M(c)/W(c), soccer M/W, softball W, swimming and diving M/W, tennis M/W, track and field M(c)/W(c), volleyball W. *Intramural sports:* badminton M/W, basketball M/W, cross-country running M(c)/W(c), racquetball M/W, soccer M/W, softball M/W, table tennis M/W, tennis M/W, volleyball M/W, water polo M/W.
Standardized Tests *Required:* SAT or ACT (for admission).
Costs (2011–12) *Comprehensive fee:* $40,695 includes full-time tuition ($27,000), mandatory fees ($1175), and room and board ($12,520). Full-time tuition and fees vary according to course load. Part-time tuition: $600 per credit. Part-time tuition and fees vary according to course load. *Required fees:* $100 per term part-time. *College room only:* $7060. Room and board charges vary according to board plan and housing facility. *Payment plans:* installment, deferred payment. *Waivers:* senior citizens and employees or children of employees.
Financial Aid Of all full-time matriculated undergraduates who enrolled in 2011, 1,950 applied for aid, 1,846 were judged to have need, 341 had their need fully met. 639 Federal Work-Study jobs (averaging $1984). In 2011, 237 non-need-based awards were made. *Average percent of need met:* 75%. *Average financial aid package:* $20,765. *Average need-based loan:* $4570. *Average need-based gift aid:* $16,598. *Average non-need-based aid:* $12,496. *Average indebtedness upon graduation:* $38,965.
Applying *Options:* electronic application, early admission, deferred entrance. *Application fee:* $35. *Required:* high school transcript, 1 letter of recommendation. *Required for some:* essay or personal statement, interview, art majors require portfolio, music majors require audition. *Recommended:* essay or personal statement, interview. *Application deadlines:* rolling (freshmen), rolling (transfers). *Notification:* continuous (freshmen), continuous (transfers).
Freshman Application Contact Mr. Christian DiGregorio, Director of University Admissions, Marywood University, 2300 Adams Avenue, Scranton, PA 18509. *Phone:* 570-348-6234. *Toll-free phone:* 866-279-9663. *Fax:* 570-961-4763. *E-mail:* yourfuture@marywood.edu. *Web site:* http://www.marywood.edu/.

See page 1436 for the College Close-Up.

Mercyhurst College
Erie, Pennsylvania

- **Independent Roman Catholic** comprehensive, founded 1926
- **Suburban** 88-acre campus with easy access to Buffalo
- **Endowment** $26.9 million
- **Coed** 3,945 undergraduate students, 85% full-time, 59% women, 41% men
- **Moderately difficult** entrance level, 76% of applicants were admitted

Undergraduates 3,372 full-time, 573 part-time. Students come from 41 states and territories; 31 other countries; 45% are from out of state; 7% Black or African American, non-Hispanic/Latino; 2% Hispanic/Latino; 0.9% Asian, non-Hispanic/Latino; 0.3% American Indian or Alaska Native, non-Hispanic/Latino; 10% Race/ethnicity unknown; 5% international; 2% transferred in; 73% live on campus. *Retention:* 81% of full-time freshmen returned.
Freshmen *Admission:* 2,965 applied, 2,260 admitted, 671 enrolled. *Average high school GPA:* 3.3. *Test scores:* SAT critical reading scores over 500: 62%; SAT math scores over 500: 63%; ACT scores over 18: 94%; SAT critical reading scores over 600: 17%; SAT math scores over 600: 19%; ACT scores over 24: 41%; SAT critical reading scores over 700: 2%; SAT math scores over 700: 1%; ACT scores over 30: 5%.
Faculty *Total:* 339, 57% full-time, 32% with terminal degrees. *Student/faculty ratio:* 15:1.
Academics *Calendar:* 4-3-3. *Degrees:* certificates, associate, bachelor's, master's, and postbachelor's certificates. *Special study options:* academic remediation for entering students, accelerated degree program, adult/continuing

education programs, advanced placement credit, cooperative education, distance learning, double majors, honors programs, independent study, internships, off-campus study, part-time degree program, services for LD students, student-designed majors, study abroad, summer session for credit. *ROTC:* Army (c), Air Force (c). *Unusual degree programs:* business administration; law with Duquesne University; pre-med 2 + 3 with LECOM.
Computers on Campus 350 computers/terminals and 150 ports are available on campus for general student use. Students can access the following: campus intranet, computer help desk, free student e-mail accounts, online (class) grades, online (class) registration, online (class) schedules. Campuswide network is available. 100% of college-owned or -operated housing units are wired for high-speed Internet access. Wireless service is available via entire campus.
Student Life *Housing:* on-campus residence required through sophomore year. *Options:* coed, men-only, women-only. Campus housing is university owned and leased by the school. Freshman campus housing is guaranteed. *Activities and organizations:* drama/theater group, student-run newspaper, radio and television station, choral group, student government, chorus, Admission Ambassadors, Amnesty International, The Merciad. *Campus security:* 24-hour emergency response devices and patrols, campus-wide camera system. *Student services:* health clinic, personal/psychological counseling.
Athletics Member NCAA. All Division II except men's and women's ice hockey (Division I). *Intercollegiate sports:* baseball M(s), basketball M(s)/W(s), crew M(s)/W(s), cross-country running M(s)/W(s), field hockey W(s), football M(s), golf M(s)/W(s), ice hockey M(s)/W(s), lacrosse M(s)/W(s), soccer M(s)/W(s), softball W(s), tennis M(s)/W(s), volleyball W(s), water polo M(s)/W(s), wrestling M(s). *Intramural sports:* basketball M/W, football M, skiing (cross-country) M/W, skiing (downhill) M/W, volleyball M/W.
Standardized Tests *Required:* SAT or ACT (for admission). *Recommended:* SAT Subject Tests (for admission).
Costs (2011–12) *Comprehensive fee:* $38,796 includes full-time tuition ($25,860), mandatory fees ($1797), and room and board ($11,139). Full-time tuition and fees vary according to program. Part-time tuition: $862 per credit hour. Part-time tuition and fees vary according to class time, course load, degree level, and location. *College room only:* $5664. Room and board charges vary according to board plan, housing facility, and location. *Payment plan:* installment. *Waivers:* adult students and employees or children of employees.
Financial Aid Of all full-time matriculated undergraduates who enrolled in 2010, 2,022 applied for aid, 1,813 were judged to have need, 536 had their need fully met. 503 Federal Work-Study jobs (averaging $1195). 472 state and other part-time jobs (averaging $1196). In 2010, 357 non-need-based awards were made. *Average percent of need met:* 54%. *Average financial aid package:* $21,937. *Average need-based loan:* $3591. *Average need-based gift aid:* $11,011. *Average non-need-based aid:* $13,436. *Average indebtedness upon graduation:* $25,357. *Financial aid deadline:* 5/1.
Applying *Options:* electronic application, deferred entrance. *Application fee:* $30. *Required:* essay or personal statement, high school transcript. *Required for some:* 1 letter of recommendation. *Recommended:* interview. *Application deadlines:* rolling (freshmen), rolling (out-of-state freshmen), rolling (transfers). *Notification:* continuous until 11/1 (freshmen), continuous until 11/1 (out-of-state freshmen), continuous until 12/1 (transfers).
Freshman Application Contact Christopher Coons, Director of Undergraduate Admissions, Mercyhurst College, 501 East 38th Street, Erie, PA 16546-0001. *Phone:* 814-824-2202. *Toll-free phone:* 800-825-1926. *Fax:* 814-824-2071. *E-mail:* ccoons@mercyhurst.edu. *Web site:* http://www.mercyhurst.edu/.

See page 1442 for the College Close-Up.

Mercyhurst North East
North East, Pennsylvania

Director of Admissions Travis Lindahl, Director of Admissions, Mercyhurst North East, 16 West Division Street, North East, PA 16428. *Phone:* 814-725-6217. *Toll-free phone:* 866-846-6042. *Fax:* 814-725-6251. *E-mail:* neadmiss@mercyhurst.edu. *Web site:* http://northeast.mercyhurst.edu/.

Messiah College
Grantham, Pennsylvania

- **Independent interdenominational** comprehensive, founded 1909
- **Small-town** 485-acre campus
- **Endowment** $126.8 million
- **Coed** 2,805 undergraduate students, 97% full-time, 61% women, 39% men
- **Moderately difficult** entrance level, 64% of applicants were admitted

Undergraduates 2,733 full-time, 72 part-time. Students come from 34 states and territories; 32 other countries; 40% are from out of state; 2% Black or African American, non-Hispanic/Latino; 2% Hispanic/Latino; 1% Asian, non-His-

panic/Latino; 0.1% Native Hawaiian or other Pacific Islander, non-Hispanic/Latino; 0.1% American Indian or Alaska Native, non-Hispanic/Latino; 2% Two or more races, non-Hispanic/Latino; 4% Race/ethnicity unknown; 2% international; 3% transferred in; 88% live on campus. *Retention:* 83% of full-time freshmen returned.

Freshmen *Admission:* 3,154 applied, 2,032 admitted, 694 enrolled. *Average high school GPA:* 3.71. *Test scores:* SAT critical reading scores over 500: 85%; SAT math scores over 500: 84%; SAT writing scores over 500: 79%; ACT scores over 18: 98%; SAT critical reading scores over 600: 39%; SAT math scores over 600: 41%; SAT writing scores over 600: 34%; ACT scores over 24: 65%; SAT critical reading scores over 700: 9%; SAT math scores over 700: 9%; SAT writing scores over 700: 6%; ACT scores over 30: 21%.

Faculty *Total:* 288, 61% full-time, 59% with terminal degrees. *Student/faculty ratio:* 13:1.

Academics *Calendar:* semesters. *Degrees:* bachelor's, master's, and post-master's certificates. *Special study options:* accelerated degree program, adult/continuing education programs, advanced placement credit, cooperative education, distance learning, double majors, English as a second language, freshman honors college, honors programs, independent study, internships, off-campus study, part-time degree program, services for LD students, student-designed majors, study abroad, summer session for credit. *Unusual degree programs:* 3-2 biopsychology (BS)/EMOT in occupational therapy and health and exercise science (BA)/EMOT in occupational therapy with Thomas Jefferson University.

Computers on Campus 571 computers/terminals are available on campus for general student use. Students can access the following: campus intranet, computer help desk, free student e-mail accounts, online (class) grades, online (class) registration, online (class) schedules, access to software. Campuswide network is available. 100% of college-owned or -operated housing units are wired for high-speed Internet access. Wireless service is available via entire campus.

Student Life *Housing:* on-campus residence required through senior year. *Options:* coed, men-only, women-only, disabled students. Campus housing is university owned. Freshman campus housing is guaranteed. *Activities and organizations:* drama/theater group, student-run newspaper, radio station, choral group, Outreach teams, student government, choral groups and ensembles, Small Group Program, Outdoors Club. *Campus security:* 24-hour emergency response devices and patrols, student patrols, late-night transport/escort service, controlled dormitory access, bicycle patrols, security lighting, self-defense classes, prevention/awareness programs. *Student services:* health clinic, personal/psychological counseling.

Athletics Member NCAA. All Division III. *Intercollegiate sports:* baseball M, basketball M/W, cross-country running M/W, field hockey W, golf M, lacrosse M/W, soccer M/W, softball W, swimming and diving M/W, tennis M/W, track and field M/W, volleyball W, wrestling M. *Intramural sports:* basketball M/W, football M/W, ice hockey M(c), racquetball M/W, soccer M/W, softball M/W, ultimate Frisbee M/W, volleyball M/W.

Standardized Tests *Required for some:* SAT or ACT (for admission). *Recommended:* SAT or ACT (for admission).

Costs (2012–13) *Comprehensive fee:* $38,220 includes full-time tuition ($28,640), mandatory fees ($820), and room and board ($8760). Part-time tuition: $1195 per credit. *Room and board:* Room and board charges vary according to board plan, housing facility, and location. *Payment plan:* installment. *Waivers:* minority students, children of alumni, adult students, senior citizens, and employees or children of employees.

Financial Aid Of all full-time matriculated undergraduates who enrolled in 2011, 2,243 applied for aid, 1,970 were judged to have need, 406 had their need fully met. 840 Federal Work-Study jobs (averaging $2104). 796 state and other part-time jobs (averaging $1907). In 2011, 708 non-need-based awards were made. *Average percent of need met:* 71%. *Average financial aid package:* $19,724. *Average need-based loan:* $4658. *Average need-based gift aid:* $14,057. *Average non-need-based aid:* $10,719. *Average indebtedness upon graduation:* $34,833.

Applying *Options:* electronic application, deferred entrance. *Application fee:* $30. *Required:* essay or personal statement, high school transcript, 1 letter of recommendation. *Recommended:* interview. *Application deadlines:* rolling (freshmen), rolling (transfers). *Notification:* continuous (freshmen), continuous (transfers).

Freshman Application Contact Mr. John Chopka, Vice President for Enrollment Management, Messiah College, PO Box 3005, One College Avenue, Grantham, PA 17027. *Phone:* 717-691-6000. *Toll-free phone:* 800-233-4220. *Fax:* 717-791-2307. *E-mail:* admiss@messiah.edu. *Web site:* http://www.messiah.edu/.

See page 1444 for the College Close-Up.

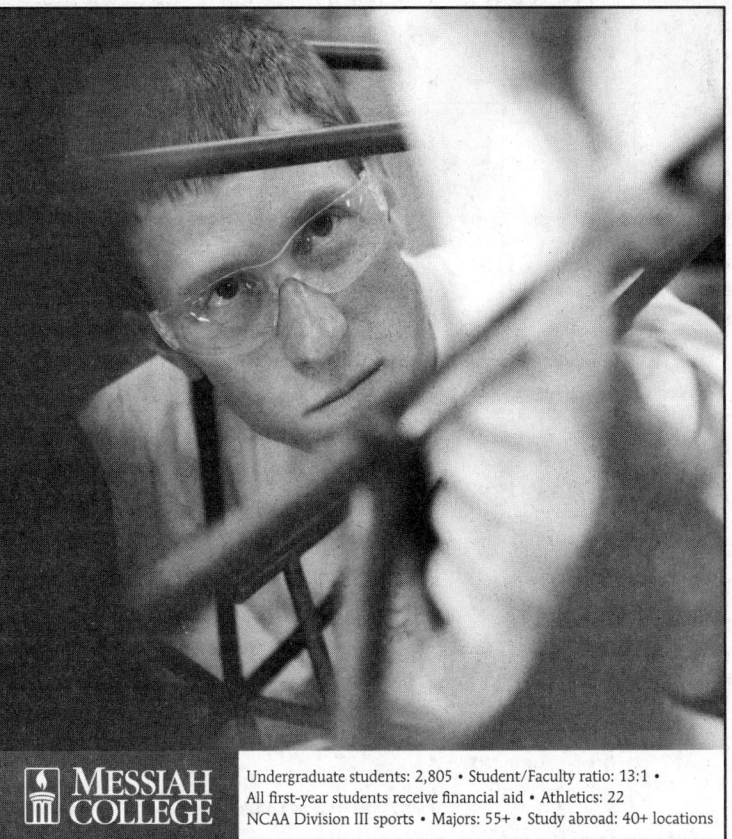

Millersville University of Pennsylvania
Millersville, Pennsylvania

- **State-supported** comprehensive, founded 1855, part of Pennsylvania State System of Higher Education
- **Small-town** 250-acre campus
- **Endowment** $2.3 million
- **Coed** 7,644 undergraduate students, 89% full-time, 56% women, 44% men
- **Moderately difficult** entrance level, 58% of applicants were admitted

Undergraduates 6,833 full-time, 811 part-time. Students come from 24 states and territories; 45 other countries; 4% are from out of state; 8% Black or African American, non-Hispanic/Latino; 6% Hispanic/Latino; 2% Asian, non-Hispanic/Latino; 0.1% Native Hawaiian or other Pacific Islander, non-Hispanic/Latino; 0.2% American Indian or Alaska Native, non-Hispanic/Latino; 1% Two or more races, non-Hispanic/Latino; 1% Race/ethnicity unknown; 0.5% international; 10% transferred in; 31% live on campus. *Retention:* 81% of full-time freshmen returned.

Freshmen *Admission:* 6,974 applied, 4,023 admitted, 1,304 enrolled. *Test scores:* SAT critical reading scores over 500: 61%; SAT math scores over 500: 65%; SAT writing scores over 500: 52%; ACT scores over 18: 90%; SAT critical reading scores over 600: 15%; SAT math scores over 600: 18%; SAT writing scores over 600: 10%; ACT scores over 24: 32%; SAT critical reading scores over 700: 1%; SAT math scores over 700: 1%; SAT writing scores over 700: 1%; ACT scores over 30: 3%.

Faculty *Total:* 431, 69% full-time, 77% with terminal degrees. *Student/faculty ratio:* 22:1.

Academics *Calendar:* 4-1-4. *Degrees:* associate, bachelor's, master's, postmaster's, and postbachelor's certificates. *Special study options:* academic remediation for entering students, accelerated degree program, adult/continuing education programs, advanced placement credit, cooperative education, distance learning, double majors, honors programs, independent study, internships, off-campus study, part-time degree program, services for LD students, study abroad, summer session for credit. *ROTC:* Army (b). *Unusual degree programs:* engineering with Pennsylvania State University and University of Southern California.

Computers on Campus 430 computers/terminals are available on campus for general student use. Students can access the following: computer help desk, free student e-mail accounts, online (class) grades, online (class) registration, online (class) schedules. Campuswide network is available. 100% of college-owned or -operated housing units are wired for high-speed Internet access. Wireless service is available via entire campus.

Student Life *Housing:* on-campus residence required through sophomore year. *Options:* coed. Campus housing is university owned. Freshman campus housing is guaranteed. *Activities and organizations:* drama/theater group, student-run newspaper, radio and television station, choral group, marching band, MUTV 99, University Christian Fellowship, Marching Band, University Activities Board (UAB), Student Senate, national fraternities, national sororities. *Campus security:* 24-hour emergency response devices and patrols, student patrols, late-night transport/escort service, controlled dormitory access, crime awareness programs, self-defense education, shuttle buses, lighted pathways / sidewalks. *Student services:* health clinic, personal/psychological counseling, women's center.

Athletics Member NCAA. All Division II except wrestling (Division I). *Intercollegiate sports:* baseball M(s), basketball M(s)/W(s), cheerleading W, cross-country running M(s)/W(s), field hockey W(s), football M(s), golf M(s), lacrosse W(s), soccer M(s)/W(s), softball W(s), swimming and diving W(s), tennis M(s)/W(s), track and field M(s)/W(s), volleyball W(s), wrestling M(s). *Intramural sports:* badminton M/W, basketball M/W, bowling M(c)/W(c), fencing M(c)/W(c), golf M/W, ice hockey M(c), lacrosse M(c), racquetball M/W, rock climbing M/W, rugby M(c)/W(c), soccer M/W, softball M/W, tennis M/W, ultimate Frisbee M/W, volleyball M(c)/W, water polo M(c)/W(c).

Standardized Tests *Required:* SAT or ACT (for admission).

Costs (2011–12) *Tuition:* state resident $6240 full-time, $260 per credit part-time; nonresident $15,600 full-time, $650 per credit part-time. Part-time tuition and fees vary according to course load. *Required fees:* $2121 full-time, $74 per credit part-time, $15 per credit part-time. *Room and board:* $8732; room only: $5076. Room and board charges vary according to board plan and housing facility. *Payment plan:* installment. *Waivers:* senior citizens and employees or children of employees.

Financial Aid Of all full-time matriculated undergraduates who enrolled in 2010, 5,637 applied for aid, 4,414 were judged to have need, 482 had their need fully met. 237 Federal Work-Study jobs (averaging $1187). 1,747 state and other part-time jobs (averaging $1449). In 2010, 137 non-need-based awards were made. *Average percent of need met:* 72%. *Average financial aid package:* $7957. *Average need-based loan:* $4171. *Average need-based gift aid:* $5370. *Average non-need-based aid:* $3149. *Average indebtedness upon graduation:* $28,444.

Applying *Options:* electronic application, early admission, deferred entrance. *Application fee:* $50. *Required:* high school transcript, minimum 2.0 GPA. *Required for some:* essay or personal statement, 1 letter of recommendation,

The "Ah-ha!" moment.

Millersville University
SEIZE THE OPPORTUNITY

www.millersville.edu

Millersville University is an Equal Opportunity/Affirmative Action institution. A member of the Pennsylvania State System of Higher Education.

interview. *Recommended:* essay or personal statement, 1 letter of recommendation. *Application deadlines:* rolling (freshmen), rolling (out-of-state freshmen), rolling (transfers). *Notification:* continuous (freshmen), continuous (out-of-state freshmen), continuous (transfers).

Freshman Application Contact Dr. Jose A. Aviles, Director of Admissions, Millersville University of Pennsylvania, PO Box 1002, Millersville, PA 17551-0302. *Phone:* 717-872-3371. *Toll-free phone:* 800-MU-ADMIT. *Fax:* 717-871-2147. *E-mail:* admissions@millersville.edu. *Web site:* http://www.millersville.edu/.

See page 1452 for the College Close-Up.

Misericordia University

Dallas, Pennsylvania

- **Independent Roman Catholic** comprehensive, founded 1924
- **Small-town** 120-acre campus
- **Endowment** $24.8 million
- **Coed, primarily women** 2,386 undergraduate students, 70% full-time, 71% women, 29% men
- **Moderately difficult** entrance level, 57% of applicants were admitted

Undergraduates 1,679 full-time, 707 part-time. Students come from 17 states and territories; 18% are from out of state; 1% Black or African American, non-Hispanic/Latino; 2% Hispanic/Latino; 0.7% Asian, non-Hispanic/Latino; 0.2% American Indian or Alaska Native, non-Hispanic/Latino; 0.5% Two or more races, non-Hispanic/Latino; 5% transferred in; 39% live on campus. *Retention:* 86% of full-time freshmen returned.

Freshmen *Admission:* 2,013 applied, 1,153 admitted, 368 enrolled. *Average high school GPA:* 3.33. *Test scores:* SAT critical reading scores over 500: 69%; SAT math scores over 500: 76%; ACT scores over 18: 99%; SAT critical reading scores over 600: 14%; SAT math scores over 600: 23%; ACT scores over 24: 51%; SAT critical reading scores over 700: 1%; SAT math scores over 700: 2%; ACT scores over 30: 3%.

Faculty *Total:* 316, 34% full-time, 36% with terminal degrees. *Student/faculty ratio:* 12:1.

Academics *Calendar:* semesters. *Degrees:* certificates, bachelor's, master's, doctoral, post-master's, and postbachelor's certificates. *Special study options:* academic remediation for entering students, accelerated degree program, adult/continuing education programs, advanced placement credit, cooperative education, distance learning, double majors, external degree program, honors programs, independent study, internships, off-campus study, part-time degree program, services for LD students, student-designed majors, study abroad, summer session for credit. *ROTC:* Army (c), Air Force (c). *Unusual degree programs:* 3-2 occupational therapy, speech-language pathology.

Computers on Campus 150 computers/terminals and 1,000 ports are available on campus for general student use. Students can access the following: campus intranet, computer help desk, free student e-mail accounts, online (class) grades, online (class) registration, online (class) schedules, student leadership transcript. Campuswide network is available. 100% of college-owned or -operated housing units are wired for high-speed Internet access. Wireless service is available via entire campus.

Student Life *Housing options:* coed. Campus housing is university owned. Freshman applicants given priority for college housing. *Activities and organizations:* drama/theater group, student-run newspaper, radio and television station, choral group, MSOTA, Peer Associates, Physical Therapy club, Varsity 'M' Club, Education Club. *Campus security:* 24-hour emergency response devices and patrols, late-night transport/escort service, controlled dormitory access. *Student services:* health clinic, personal/psychological counseling, women's center.

Athletics Member NCAA. All Division III except tennis (Division II). *Intercollegiate sports:* baseball M, basketball M/W, cross-country running M/W, field hockey W, football M, golf M/W, lacrosse M/W, soccer M/W, softball W, swimming and diving M/W, tennis M/W, track and field M/W, volleyball W. *Intramural sports:* basketball M/W, cross-country running M/W, football M/W, racquetball M/W, soccer M/W, softball M/W, tennis M/W, ultimate Frisbee M/W, volleyball M/W.

Standardized Tests *Required:* SAT or ACT (for admission).

Costs (2011–12) *Comprehensive fee:* $36,750 includes full-time tuition ($24,700), mandatory fees ($1290), and room and board ($10,760). Part-time tuition: $495 per credit. Part-time tuition and fees vary according to class time, degree level, and location. *College room only:* $6250. Room and board charges vary according to board plan and housing facility. *Payment plans:* installment, deferred payment. *Waivers:* employees or children of employees.

Financial Aid Of all full-time matriculated undergraduates who enrolled in 2011, 1,552 applied for aid, 1,396 were judged to have need, 340 had their need fully met. In 2011, 153 non-need-based awards were made. *Average percent of need met:* 78%. *Average financial aid package:* $18,695. *Average need-based loan:* $8755. *Average need-based gift aid:* $12,765. *Average non-need-based aid:* $7907. *Average indebtedness upon graduation:* $34,043.

Applying *Options:* electronic application, early admission, deferred entrance. *Application fee:* $25. *Required:* high school transcript. *Required for some:* essay or personal statement, minimum 2.0 GPA, 2 letters of recommendation.

Recommended: interview. *Application deadlines:* rolling (freshmen), rolling (transfers). *Notification:* continuous (freshmen), continuous (transfers).

Freshman Application Contact Mr. Glenn Bozinski, Director of Admissions, Misericordia University, 301 Lake Street, Dallas, PA 18612-1098. *Phone:* 570-675-6264. *Toll-free phone:* 866-262-6363. *Fax:* 570-674-6232. *E-mail:* admiss@misericordia.edu. *Web site:* http://www.misericordia.edu/.

See page 787 for display ad and page 1458 for the College Close-Up.

Moore College of Art & Design

Philadelphia, Pennsylvania

- **Independent** comprehensive, founded 1848
- **Urban** 3-acre campus with easy access to Philadelphia
- **Endowment** $10.3 million
- **Women only** 468 undergraduate students, 94% full-time
- **Moderately difficult** entrance level, 67% of applicants were admitted

Undergraduates 439 full-time, 29 part-time. Students come from 24 states and territories; 7 other countries; 45% are from out of state; 15% Black or African American, non-Hispanic/Latino; 4% Hispanic/Latino; 4% Asian, non-Hispanic/Latino; 0.6% Native Hawaiian or other Pacific Islander, non-Hispanic/Latino; 0.9% American Indian or Alaska Native, non-Hispanic/Latino; 4% Two or more races, non-Hispanic/Latino; 0.6% Race/ethnicity unknown; 3% international; 10% transferred in. *Retention:* 84% of full-time freshmen returned.

Freshmen *Admission:* 493 applied, 329 admitted, 94 enrolled. *Average high school GPA:* 3.23. *Test scores:* SAT critical reading scores over 500: 47%; SAT math scores over 500: 35%; ACT scores over 18: 58%; SAT critical reading scores over 600: 20%; SAT math scores over 600: 12%; ACT scores over 24: 25%; SAT critical reading scores over 700: 2%; SAT math scores over 700: 2%; ACT scores over 30: 8%.

Faculty *Total:* 136, 18% full-time, 42% with terminal degrees. *Student/faculty ratio:* 8:1.

Academics *Calendar:* semesters. *Degrees:* certificates, bachelor's, master's, and postbachelor's certificates. *Special study options:* academic remediation for entering students, advanced placement credit, cooperative education, double majors, independent study, internships, part-time degree program, services for LD students, study abroad, summer session for credit.

Computers on Campus Students can access the following: computer help desk, free student e-mail accounts, online (class) grades, online (class) registration. Wireless service is available via entire campus.

Student Life *Housing options:* women-only. Campus housing is university owned. Freshman campus housing is guaranteed. *Activities and organizations:* Student Government Association, Student Orientation Staff, yearbook, Residence Life Staff, Business Scholars in the Arts. *Campus security:* 24-hour patrols, late-night transport/escort service. *Student services:* health clinic, personal/psychological counseling.

Athletics *Intramural sports:* volleyball W.

Standardized Tests *Required for some:* SAT or ACT (for admission).

Financial Aid Of all full-time matriculated undergraduates who enrolled in 2006, 383 applied for aid, 357 were judged to have need, 9 had their need fully met. 87 Federal Work-Study jobs (averaging $1500). In 2006, 93 non-need-based awards were made. *Average percent of need met:* 45%. *Average financial aid package:* $14,823. *Average need-based loan:* $4355. *Average need-based gift aid:* $10,180. *Average non-need-based aid:* $9729. *Average indebtedness upon graduation:* $36,778.

Applying *Options:* electronic application, deferred entrance. *Application fee:* $40. *Required:* high school transcript, minimum 2.5 GPA, 1 letter of recommendation, interview, portfolio. *Required for some:* minimum 3.0 GPA. *Recommended:* essay or personal statement. *Application deadlines:* 8/15 (freshmen), rolling (transfers). *Notification:* continuous (freshmen), continuous (transfers).

Freshman Application Contact Ms. Heesung Lee, Director of Admissions, Moore College of Art & Design, 20th and The Parkway, Philadelphia, PA 19103. *Phone:* 215-965-4014. *Toll-free phone:* 800-523-2025. *Fax:* 215-965-8544. *E-mail:* enroll@moore.edu. *Web site:* http://www.moore.edu/.

Moravian College

Bethlehem, Pennsylvania

- **Independent** comprehensive, founded 1742, affiliated with Moravian Church
- **Suburban** 60-acre campus with easy access to Philadelphia
- **Endowment** $91.5 million
- **Coed** 1,737 undergraduate students, 88% full-time, 61% women, 39% men
- **Moderately difficult** entrance level, 80% of applicants were admitted

Undergraduates 1,533 full-time, 204 part-time. Students come from 19 states and territories; 12 other countries; 35% are from out of state; 4% Black or African American, non-Hispanic/Latino; 9% Hispanic/Latino; 2% Asian, non-Hispanic/Latino; 0.2% Native Hawaiian or other Pacific Islander, non-Hispanic/Latino; 0.1% American Indian or Alaska Native, non-Hispanic/Latino; 3% Two or more races, non-Hispanic/Latino; 0.3% Race/ethnicity unknown; 0.5% international; 5% transferred in; 76% live on campus. *Retention:* 78% of full-time freshmen returned.

Freshmen *Admission:* 1,940 applied, 1,546 admitted, 375 enrolled. *Average high school GPA:* 3.33. *Test scores:* SAT critical reading scores over 500: 61%; SAT math scores over 500: 66%; SAT writing scores over 500: 63%; SAT critical reading scores over 600: 21%; SAT math scores over 600: 22%; SAT writing scores over 600: 18%; SAT critical reading scores over 700: 2%; SAT math scores over 700: 3%; SAT writing scores over 700: 1%.

Faculty *Total:* 192, 59% full-time, 66% with terminal degrees. *Student/faculty ratio:* 11:1.

Academics *Calendar:* semesters. *Degrees:* bachelor's, master's, and postbachelor's certificates. *Special study options:* adult/continuing education programs, advanced placement credit, double majors, honors programs, independent study, internships, off-campus study, part-time degree program, services for LD students, student-designed majors, study abroad, summer session for credit. *ROTC:* Army (c). *Unusual degree programs:* 3-2 engineering with Washington University in St. Louis; Lehigh University; forestry with Duke University; occupational therapy with Thomas Jefferson University, Dental School, Temple University.

Computers on Campus 180 computers/terminals are available on campus for general student use. Students can access the following: campus intranet, computer help desk, free student e-mail accounts, online (class) grades, online (class) schedules. Campuswide network is available. 100% of college-owned or -operated housing units are wired for high-speed Internet access. Wireless service is available via entire campus.

Student Life *Housing:* on-campus residence required through senior year. *Options:* coed, men-only, women-only. Campus housing is university owned. Freshman campus housing is guaranteed. *Activities and organizations:* drama/theater group, student-run newspaper, radio station, choral group, marching band, Instilling Diversity Equality & Awareness (I.D.E.A.), United Student Government, Moravian College Choir, Habitat for Humanity, Christian Fellowship, national fraternities, national sororities. *Campus security:* 24-hour emergency response devices and patrols, late-night transport/escort service, controlled dormitory access. *Student services:* health clinic, personal/psychological counseling.

Athletics Member NCAA. All Division III. *Intercollegiate sports:* baseball M, basketball M/W, cheerleading W(c), cross-country running M/W, equestrian sports M(c)/W(c), field hockey W, football M, golf M, ice hockey M(c)/W(c), soccer M/W, softball W, tennis M/W, track and field M/W, volleyball W. *Intramural sports:* basketball M/W, volleyball M/W.

Standardized Tests *Recommended:* SAT (for admission), ACT (for admission), SAT or ACT (for admission), SAT and SAT Subject Tests or ACT (for admission).

Costs (2011–12) *Comprehensive fee:* $43,069 includes full-time tuition ($32,931), mandatory fees ($515), and room and board ($9623). Part-time tuition: $915 per credit hour. Part-time tuition and fees vary according to class time. *College room only:* $5406. Room and board charges vary according to board plan and housing facility. *Payment plan:* installment. *Waivers:* employees or children of employees.

Financial Aid Of all full-time matriculated undergraduates who enrolled in 2011, 1,351 applied for aid, 1,246 were judged to have need, 152 had their need fully met. 958 Federal Work-Study jobs (averaging $1851). 260 state and other part-time jobs (averaging $721). In 2011, 179 non-need-based awards were made. *Average percent of need met:* 75%. *Average financial aid package:* $24,978. *Average need-based loan:* $4702. *Average need-based gift aid:* $19,308. *Average non-need-based aid:* $10,023.

Applying *Options:* electronic application, early admission, early decision, early action, deferred entrance. *Application fee:* $40. *Required:* essay or personal statement, high school transcript, 3 letters of recommendation. *Recommended:* interview. *Application deadlines:* 3/1 (freshmen), 3/1 (transfers). *Early decision deadline:* 2/1. *Notification:* 3/15 (freshmen), continuous (transfers), 12/15 (early decision).

Freshman Application Contact Erika Mondok, Interim Director of Enrollment, Moravian College, 1200 Main Street, Bethlehem, PA 18018. *Phone:* 610-861-1325. *Toll-free phone:* 800-441-3191. *Fax:* 610-625-7930. *E-mail:* admissions@moravian.edu. *Web site:* http://www.moravian.edu/.

Mount Aloysius College

Cresson, Pennsylvania

- **Independent Roman Catholic** comprehensive, founded 1939
- **Small-town** 193-acre campus
- **Endowment** $19.5 million
- **Coed** 1,639 undergraduate students, 75% full-time, 70% women, 30% men
- **Minimally difficult** entrance level, 76% of applicants were admitted

Undergraduates 1,230 full-time, 409 part-time. Students come from 15 states and territories; 7 other countries; 4% are from out of state; 2% Black or African American, non-Hispanic/Latino; 0.5% Hispanic/Latino; 0.3% Asian, non-Hispanic/Latino; 0.1% American Indian or Alaska Native, non-Hispanic/Latino; 0.7% Two or more races, non-Hispanic/Latino; 21% Race/ethnicity unknown; 0.4% international; 7% transferred in; 32% live on campus. *Retention:* 62% of full-time freshmen returned.

Freshmen *Admission:* 1,323 applied, 1,004 admitted, 373 enrolled. *Average high school GPA:* 3.2. *Test scores:* SAT critical reading scores over 500: 32%; SAT math scores over 500: 28%; SAT writing scores over 500: 23%; ACT scores over 18: 71%; SAT critical reading scores over 600: 4%; SAT math scores over 600: 3%; SAT writing scores over 600: 1%; ACT scores over 24: 6%; ACT scores over 30: 1%.

Faculty *Total:* 180, 37% full-time, 22% with terminal degrees. *Student/faculty ratio:* 13:1.

Academics *Calendar:* semesters. *Degrees:* certificates, associate, bachelor's, and master's. *Special study options:* academic remediation for entering students, accelerated degree program, advanced placement credit, distance learning, double majors, external degree program, honors programs, independent study, internships, part-time degree program, student-designed majors, study abroad, summer session for credit.

Computers on Campus 120 computers/terminals and 20 ports are available on campus for general student use. Students can access the following: campus intranet, computer help desk, free student e-mail accounts, online (class) grades, online (class) registration, online (class) schedules. Campuswide network is available. 100% of college-owned or -operated housing units are wired for high-speed Internet access. Wireless service is available via entire campus.

Student Life *Housing:* on-campus residence required through sophomore year. *Options:* coed. Campus housing is university owned. Freshman campus housing is guaranteed. *Activities and organizations:* drama/theater group, student-run newspaper, choral group, Student Government, Campus Activity Board, Student Athletic Advisory Committee, Spirit Team, Dance Team. *Campus security:* 24-hour emergency response devices and patrols, student patrols, late-night transport/escort service, controlled dormitory access. *Student services:* health clinic, personal/psychological counseling.

Athletics Member NCAA. All Division III. *Intercollegiate sports:* baseball M, basketball M/W, cross-country running M/W, golf M/W, soccer M/W, softball W, tennis M/W, volleyball W. *Intramural sports:* basketball M/W, bowling M/W, cheerleading M(c)/W(c), football M/W, skiing (cross-country) M/W, skiing (downhill) M/W, table tennis M/W, ultimate Frisbee M/W, volleyball M/W, weight lifting M/W.

Standardized Tests *Required:* SAT or ACT (for admission).

Costs (2011–12) *Comprehensive fee:* $26,870 includes full-time tuition ($17,930), mandatory fees ($820), and room and board ($8120). Full-time tuition and fees vary according to program. Part-time tuition: $560 per credit. Part-time tuition and fees vary according to program. *Required fees:* $210 per term part-time. *College room only:* $4020. Room and board charges vary according to board plan. *Payment plan:* installment. *Waivers:* employees or children of employees.

Financial Aid Of all full-time matriculated undergraduates who enrolled in 2011, 1,230 applied for aid, 1,174 were judged to have need. 186 Federal Work-Study jobs (averaging $1400). In 2011, 56 non-need-based awards were made. *Average percent of need met:* 35%. *Average financial aid package:* $13,100. *Average need-based loan:* $4300. *Average need-based gift aid:* $5300. *Average non-need-based aid:* $3700. *Average indebtedness upon graduation:* $30,965.

Applying *Options:* electronic application, early admission, deferred entrance. *Application fee:* $30. *Required:* high school transcript. *Required for some:* essay or personal statement, interview. *Recommended:* interview. *Application deadlines:* rolling (freshmen), rolling (transfers). *Notification:* continuous (freshmen), continuous (transfers).

Freshman Application Contact Mr. Frank C. Crouse Jr., Vice President for Enrollment Management/Dean of Admissions, Mount Aloysius College, 7373 Admiral Peary Highway, Cresson, PA 16630-1999. *Phone:* 814-886-6383.

Toll-free phone: 888-823-2220. *Fax:* 814-886-6441. *E-mail:* admissions@mtaloy.edu. *Web site:* http://www.mtaloy.edu/.

See page 790 for display ad and page 1468 for the College Close-Up.

Muhlenberg College

Allentown, Pennsylvania

- **Independent** 4-year, founded 1848, affiliated with Lutheran Church
- **Suburban** 75-acre campus with easy access to Philadelphia
- **Endowment** $150.2 million
- **Coed** 2,483 undergraduate students, 94% full-time, 58% women, 42% men
- **Very difficult** entrance level, 43% of applicants were admitted

Undergraduates 2,342 full-time, 141 part-time. Students come from 38 states and territories; 6 other countries; 79% are from out of state; 3% Black or African American, non-Hispanic/Latino; 4% Hispanic/Latino; 3% Asian, non-Hispanic/Latino; 0.1% Native Hawaiian or other Pacific Islander, non-Hispanic/Latino; 0.3% American Indian or Alaska Native, non-Hispanic/Latino; 0.8% Two or more races, non-Hispanic/Latino; 1% Race/ethnicity unknown; 0.3% international; 0.4% transferred in; 91% live on campus. *Retention:* 90% of full-time freshmen returned.

Freshmen *Admission:* 4,876 applied, 2,109 admitted, 584 enrolled. *Average high school GPA:* 3.34. *Test scores:* SAT critical reading scores over 500: 95%; SAT math scores over 500: 94%; SAT writing scores over 500: 97%; ACT scores over 18: 100%; SAT critical reading scores over 600: 58%; SAT math scores over 600: 65%; SAT writing scores over 600: 66%; ACT scores over 24: 92%; SAT critical reading scores over 700: 12%; SAT math scores over 700: 16%; SAT writing scores over 700: 18%; ACT scores over 30: 26%.

Faculty *Total:* 275, 63% full-time, 64% with terminal degrees. *Student/faculty ratio:* 12:1.

Academics *Calendar:* semesters. *Degrees:* certificates, associate, and bachelor's. *Special study options:* accelerated degree program, adult/continuing education programs, advanced placement credit, double majors, honors programs, independent study, internships, off-campus study, part-time degree program, services for LD students, student-designed majors, study abroad, summer session for credit. *ROTC:* Army (c). *Unusual degree programs:* 3-2 engineering with Columbia University; forestry with Duke University.

Computers on Campus 490 computers/terminals and 100 ports are available on campus for general student use. Students can access the following: campus intranet, computer help desk, free student e-mail accounts, online (class) grades, online (class) registration, online (class) schedules. Campuswide network is available. 100% of college-owned or -operated housing units are wired for high-speed Internet access. Wireless service is available via classrooms, dorm rooms, libraries, student centers.

Student Life *Housing:* on-campus residence required for freshman year. *Options:* coed, women-only, disabled students. Campus housing is university owned and leased by the school. Freshman campus housing is guaranteed. *Activities and organizations:* drama/theater group, student-run newspaper, radio and television station, choral group, Theater Association, Environmental Action Team, Jefferson School Partnership, Select Choir, Habitat for Humanity, national fraternities, national sororities. *Campus security:* 24-hour emergency response devices and patrols, late-night transport/escort service, controlled dormitory access. *Student services:* health clinic, personal/psychological counseling.

Athletics Member NCAA. All Division III. *Intercollegiate sports:* baseball M, basketball M/W, cheerleading M/W, cross-country running M/W, field hockey W, football M, golf M/W, lacrosse M/W, soccer M/W, softball W, tennis M/W, track and field M/W, volleyball W, wrestling M. *Intramural sports:* basketball M/W, cross-country running M/W, football M/W, ice hockey M, racquetball M/W, rugby M/W, soccer M/W, softball M, swimming and diving M/W, tennis M/W, ultimate Frisbee M, volleyball M/W.

Standardized Tests *Required for some:* SAT or ACT (for admission).

Costs (2011–12) *Comprehensive fee:* $49,420 includes full-time tuition ($39,630), mandatory fees ($285), and room and board ($9505). Part-time tuition and fees vary according to program. *Room and board:* Room and board charges vary according to board plan, housing facility, and location. *Payment plan:* installment. *Waivers:* employees or children of employees.

Financial Aid Of all full-time matriculated undergraduates who enrolled in 2011, 1,486 applied for aid, 1,207 were judged to have need, 1,102 had their need fully met. In 2011, 687 non-need-based awards were made. *Average percent of need met:* 94%. *Average financial aid package:* $25,143. *Average need-based loan:* $4662. *Average need-based gift aid:* $22,081. *Average non-need-based aid:* $10,806. *Average indebtedness upon graduation:* $26,270. *Financial aid deadline:* 2/15.

Applying *Options:* electronic application, early admission, early decision, deferred entrance. *Application fee:* $50. *Required:* essay or personal statement, high school transcript, 2 letters of recommendation. *Required for some:* interview, graded paper. *Recommended:* interview. *Application deadlines:* 2/15 (freshmen), 6/15 (transfers). *Early decision deadline:* 2/1. *Notification:* 3/15 (freshmen), continuous until 7/1 (transfers).

Freshman Application Contact Mr. Christopher Hooker-Haring, Director of Undergraduate Admissions, Muhlenberg College, 2400 Chew Street, Allentown, PA 18104. *Phone:* 484-664-3245. *Fax:* 484-664-3234. *E-mail:* adm@muhlenberg.edu. *Web site:* http://www.muhlenberg.edu/.

See page 1470 for the College Close-Up.

Neumann University

Aston, Pennsylvania

- **Independent Roman Catholic** comprehensive, founded 1965
- **Suburban** 50-acre campus with easy access to Philadelphia
- **Endowment** $21.8 million
- **Coed** 2,617 undergraduate students, 82% full-time, 65% women, 35% men
- **Minimally difficult** entrance level, 90% of applicants were admitted

Undergraduates 2,144 full-time, 473 part-time. 23% are from out of state; 17% Black or African American, non-Hispanic/Latino; 3% Hispanic/Latino; 1% Asian, non-Hispanic/Latino; 0.1% Native Hawaiian or other Pacific Islander, non-Hispanic/Latino; 0.1% American Indian or Alaska Native, non-Hispanic/Latino; 1% Two or more races, non-Hispanic/Latino; 22% Race/ethnicity unknown; 1% international; 4% transferred in; 40% live on campus. *Retention:* 73% of full-time freshmen returned.

Freshmen *Admission:* 2,660 applied, 2,401 admitted, 575 enrolled. *Average high school GPA:* 2.87. *Test scores:* SAT math scores over 500: 20%; SAT math scores over 600: 3%.

Faculty *Total:* 321, 30% full-time, 38% with terminal degrees. *Student/faculty ratio:* 13:1.

Academics *Calendar:* semesters. *Degrees:* associate, bachelor's, master's, doctoral, post-master's, and postbachelor's certificates. *Special study options:* academic remediation for entering students, accelerated degree program, adult/continuing education programs, advanced placement credit, cooperative education, distance learning, double majors, freshman honors college, honors programs, independent study, internships, off-campus study, part-time degree program, services for LD students, student-designed majors, study abroad, summer session for credit. *ROTC:* Army (c).

Computers on Campus 1,500 computers/terminals and 1,500 ports are available on campus for general student use. Students can access the following: campus intranet, computer help desk, free student e-mail accounts, online (class) grades, online (class) schedules. Campuswide network is available.

100% of college-owned or -operated housing units are wired for high-speed Internet access. Wireless service is available via entire campus.

Student Life *Housing options:* coed. Campus housing is university owned and leased by the school. Freshman applicants given priority for college housing. *Activities and organizations:* drama/theater group, student-run newspaper, radio station, choral group, Student Government, Student Activities Board, Black Student Union, Boogie Knights, Neumann Media. *Campus security:* 24-hour emergency response devices and patrols, late-night transport/escort service, controlled dormitory access. *Student services:* health clinic, personal/psychological counseling.

Athletics Member NCAA. All Division III. *Intercollegiate sports:* baseball M, basketball M/W, cross-country running M/W, field hockey W, golf M, ice hockey M/W, lacrosse M/W, soccer M/W, softball W, tennis M/W, track and field M/W, volleyball W. *Intramural sports:* basketball M/W, cheerleading W(c), ice hockey M(c), lacrosse M, soccer M/W, softball W, tennis M/W, track and field M/W, volleyball W.

Standardized Tests *Required:* SAT or ACT (for admission).

Costs (2011–12) *Comprehensive fee:* $33,994 includes full-time tuition ($22,476), mandatory fees ($874), and room and board ($10,644). Part-time tuition: $513 per credit hour. *Required fees:* $37 per semester hour part-time. *College room only:* $6260. Room and board charges vary according to board plan. *Payment plan:* installment. *Waivers:* employees or children of employees.

Financial Aid Of all full-time matriculated undergraduates who enrolled in 2009, 1,820 applied for aid, 1,820 were judged to have need, 1,100 had their need fully met. 180 Federal Work-Study jobs (averaging $1400). *Average percent of need met:* 65%. *Average financial aid package:* $19,000. *Average need-based loan:* $5000. *Average need-based gift aid:* $11,000. *Average indebtedness upon graduation:* $30,000.

Applying *Options:* electronic application, deferred entrance. *Application fee:* $40. *Required:* high school transcript, minimum 2.0 GPA. *Recommended:* interview. *Application deadlines:* 4/1 (freshmen), rolling (transfers). *Notification:* continuous (freshmen), continuous (transfers).

Freshman Application Contact Mr. Dennis J. Murphy, Vice President for Enrollment Management, Neumann University, One Neumann Drive, Aston, PA 19014-1298. *Phone:* 610-361-2448. *Toll-free phone:* 800-963-8626. *Fax:* 610-558-5652. *E-mail:* neumann@neumann.edu. *Web site:* http://www.neumann.edu/.

See page 1472 for the College Close-Up.

Peirce College

Philadelphia, Pennsylvania

- **Independent** 4-year, founded 1865
- **Urban** 1-acre campus
- **Endowment** $16.8 million
- **Coed, primarily women** 2,276 undergraduate students, 32% full-time, 72% women, 28% men
- **Noncompetitive** entrance level

Undergraduates 725 full-time, 1,551 part-time. Students come from 27 states and territories; 26 other countries; 12% are from out of state; 65% Black or African American, non-Hispanic/Latino; 6% Hispanic/Latino; 1% Asian, non-Hispanic/Latino; 0.1% Native Hawaiian or other Pacific Islander, non-Hispanic/Latino; 0.4% American Indian or Alaska Native, non-Hispanic/Latino; 0.8% Two or more races, non-Hispanic/Latino; 2% Race/ethnicity unknown; 0.5% international. *Retention:* 100% of full-time freshmen returned.

Freshmen *Admission:* 127 enrolled.

Faculty *Total:* 158, 23% full-time, 30% with terminal degrees. *Student/faculty ratio:* 16:1.

Academics *Calendar:* semesters. *Degrees:* certificates, associate, and bachelor's. *Special study options:* accelerated degree program, adult/continuing education programs, advanced placement credit, cooperative education, distance learning, internships, part-time degree program, services for LD students, summer session for credit.

Computers on Campus 44 computers/terminals are available on campus for general student use. Students can access the following: campus intranet, computer help desk, free student e-mail accounts, online (class) grades, online (class) registration, online (class) schedules. Campuswide network is available. Wireless service is available via entire campus.

Student Life *Housing:* college housing not available. *Campus security:* 24-hour emergency response devices and patrols, late-night transport/escort service, 24-hour security cameras.

Costs (2011–12) *Tuition:* $14,850 full-time, $495 per credit part-time. Full-time tuition and fees vary according to course load. Part-time tuition and fees vary according to course load. *Required fees:* $1050 full-time, $105 per credit part-time. *Payment plan:* installment. *Waivers:* children of alumni and employees or children of employees.

Financial Aid Of all full-time matriculated undergraduates who enrolled in 2010, 707 applied for aid, 672 were judged to have need, 15 had their need fully met. 38 Federal Work-Study jobs (averaging $3390). In 2010, 25 non-need-based awards were made. *Average percent of need met:* 47%. *Average financial aid package:* $9844. *Average need-based loan:* $4698. *Average need-based gift aid:* $5990. *Average non-need-based aid:* $2659.

Applying *Options:* electronic application. *Application fee:* $50. *Required:* high school transcript. *Application deadlines:* rolling (freshmen), rolling (out-of-state freshmen), rolling (transfers). *Notification:* continuous (freshmen), continuous (out-of-state freshmen), continuous (transfers).

Freshman Application Contact Mr. Paul Ballentine, Supervisor, Admissions, Peirce College, 1420 Pine Street, Philadelphia, PA 19102. *Phone:* 215-670-9214. *Toll-free phone:* 888-467-3472. *Fax:* 215-670-9366. *E-mail:* info@peirce.edu. *Web site:* http://www.peirce.edu/.

Penn State Abington

Abington, Pennsylvania

- **State-related** 4-year, founded 1950, part of Pennsylvania State University
- **Small-town** campus
- **Coed** 3,371 undergraduate students, 82% full-time, 48% women, 52% men
- **Very difficult** entrance level, 78% of applicants were admitted

Undergraduates 2,763 full-time, 608 part-time. 6% are from out of state; 15% Black or African American, non-Hispanic/Latino; 8% Hispanic/Latino; 15% Asian, non-Hispanic/Latino; 0.1% Native Hawaiian or other Pacific Islander, non-Hispanic/Latino; 0.3% American Indian or Alaska Native, non-Hispanic/Latino; 2% Two or more races, non-Hispanic/Latino; 3% Race/ethnicity unknown; 2% international; 4% transferred in. *Retention:* 74% of full-time freshmen returned.

Freshmen *Admission:* 3,363 applied, 2,629 admitted, 811 enrolled. *Average high school GPA:* 3.04. *Test scores:* SAT critical reading scores over 500: 33%; SAT math scores over 500: 44%; SAT writing scores over 500: 31%; SAT critical reading scores over 600: 6%; SAT math scores over 600: 15%; SAT writing scores over 600: 5%; SAT critical reading scores over 700: 1%; SAT math scores over 700: 2%.

Faculty *Total:* 230, 47% full-time, 45% with terminal degrees. *Student/faculty ratio:* 20:1.

Academics *Calendar:* semesters. *Degrees:* certificates, associate, and bachelor's (enrollment figures include students enrolled at The Graduate School at Penn State who are taking courses at this location). *Special study options:* adult/continuing education programs, external degree program, part-time degree program. *ROTC:* Army (b), Air Force (c).

Computers on Campus Students can access the following: campus intranet, computer help desk, free student e-mail accounts, online (class) grades, online (class) registration, online (class) schedules. Campuswide network is available.

Student Life *Housing:* college housing not available. *Campus security:* 24-hour emergency response devices and patrols.

Athletics *Intercollegiate sports:* baseball M, basketball M/W, golf M, soccer M/W, softball W, tennis M/W, volleyball W. *Intramural sports:* basketball M/W, cross-country running M/W, football M, soccer M/W, softball M, tennis M/W, volleyball M/W.

Standardized Tests *Required:* SAT or ACT (for admission).

Costs (2011–12) *Tuition:* state resident $12,242 full-time, $495 per credit part-time; nonresident $18,682 full-time, $778 per credit part-time. Full-time tuition and fees vary according to course level, degree level, location, program, and student level. Part-time tuition and fees vary according to course level, course load, degree level, location, program, and student level. *Required fees:* $860 full-time. *Payment plans:* installment, deferred payment. *Waivers:* senior citizens and employees or children of employees.

Financial Aid Of all full-time matriculated undergraduates who enrolled in 2009, 2,217 applied for aid, 1,803 were judged to have need, 68 had their need fully met. In 2009, 85 non-need-based awards were made. *Average percent of need met:* 58%. *Average financial aid package:* $9852. *Average need-based loan:* $3937. *Average need-based gift aid:* $6978. *Average non-need-based aid:* $1795. *Average indebtedness upon graduation:* $31,135.

Applying *Options:* electronic application, early admission, deferred entrance. *Application fee:* $50. *Required:* high school transcript. *Required for some:* interview. *Recommended:* essay or personal statement. *Application deadlines:* rolling (freshmen), rolling (transfers). *Notification:* continuous (freshmen), continuous (transfers).

Freshman Application Contact Admissions Office, Penn State Abington, 1600 Woodland Road, Abington, PA 19001. *Phone:* 215-881-7600. *Fax:* 215-881-7655. *E-mail:* abingtonadmissions@psu.edu. *Web site:* http://www.abington.psu.edu/.

Penn State Altoona

Altoona, Pennsylvania

- **State-related** 4-year, founded 1939, part of Pennsylvania State University
- **Suburban** campus
- **Coed** 4,103 undergraduate students, 95% full-time, 47% women, 53% men
- **Very difficult** entrance level, 84% of applicants were admitted

Undergraduates 3,898 full-time, 205 part-time. 18% are from out of state; 7% Black or African American, non-Hispanic/Latino; 4% Hispanic/Latino; 2% Asian, non-Hispanic/Latino; 0.1% Native Hawaiian or other Pacific Islander, non-Hispanic/Latino; 0.1% American Indian or Alaska Native, non-Hispanic/Latino; 2% Two or more races, non-Hispanic/Latino; 1% Race/ethnicity unknown; 1% international; 2% transferred in; 23% live on campus. *Retention:* 86% of full-time freshmen returned.

Freshmen *Admission:* 6,083 applied, 5,138 admitted, 1,585 enrolled. *Average high school GPA:* 3.03. *Test scores:* SAT critical reading scores over 500: 47%; SAT math scores over 500: 58%; SAT writing scores over 500: 46%; SAT critical reading scores over 600: 7%; SAT math scores over 600: 15%; SAT writing scores over 600: 6%; SAT math scores over 700: 1%.

Faculty *Total:* 299, 58% full-time, 51% with terminal degrees. *Student/faculty ratio:* 19:1.

Academics *Calendar:* semesters. *Degrees:* certificates, associate, and bachelor's (enrollment figures include students enrolled at The Graduate School at Penn State who are taking courses at this location). *ROTC:* Army (c), Air Force (c).

Computers on Campus Students can access the following: campus intranet, computer help desk, free student e-mail accounts, online (class) grades, online (class) registration, online (class) schedules.

Student Life *Housing options:* coed, disabled students. Campus housing is university owned. *Campus security:* 24-hour emergency response devices and patrols, late-night transport/escort service.

Athletics Member NCAA. All Division III. *Intercollegiate sports:* baseball M, basketball M/W, cross-country running M/W, golf M/W, soccer M/W, softball W, swimming and diving M/W, tennis M/W. *Intramural sports:* badminton M/W, baseball M/W, basketball M/W, football M/W, golf M/W, racquetball M/W, soccer M/W, softball M/W, table tennis M/W, tennis M/W, track and field M/W, volleyball M/W, weight lifting M/W.

Standardized Tests *Required:* SAT or ACT (for admission).

Costs (2011–12) *Tuition:* state resident $12,776 full-time, $532 per credit part-time; nonresident $19,548 full-time, $815 per credit part-time. Full-time

tuition and fees vary according to course level, degree level, location, program, and student level. Part-time tuition and fees vary according to course level, course load, degree level, location, program, and student level. *Required fees:* $860 full-time. *Room and board:* $8940; room only: $4770. Room and board charges vary according to board plan, housing facility, and location. *Payment plans:* installment, deferred payment. *Waivers:* employees or children of employees.

Financial Aid Of all full-time matriculated undergraduates who enrolled in 2009, 3,238 applied for aid, 2,698 were judged to have need, 126 had their need fully met. In 2009, 120 non-need-based awards were made. *Average percent of need met:* 55%. *Average financial aid package:* $9298. *Average need-based loan:* $4083. *Average need-based gift aid:* $6126. *Average non-need-based aid:* $1473. *Average indebtedness upon graduation:* $31,135.

Applying *Options:* electronic application, early admission, deferred entrance. *Application fee:* $50. *Required:* high school transcript. *Required for some:* interview. *Recommended:* essay or personal statement. *Application deadlines:* rolling (freshmen), rolling (transfers). *Notification:* continuous (freshmen), continuous (transfers).

Freshman Application Contact Admissions Office, Penn State Altoona, 3000 Ivyside Park, Altoona, PA 16601-3760. *Phone:* 814-949-5466. *Toll-free phone:* 800-848-9843. *Fax:* 814-949-5564. *E-mail:* aaadmit@psu.edu. *Web site:* http://www.aa.psu.edu/.

Penn State Beaver

Monaca, Pennsylvania

- **State-related** primarily 2-year, founded 1964, part of Pennsylvania State University
- **Small-town** campus
- **Coed** 870 undergraduate students, 80% full-time, 46% women, 54% men
- **Moderately difficult** entrance level, 86% of applicants were admitted

Undergraduates 700 full-time, 170 part-time. 8% are from out of state; 11% Black or African American, non-Hispanic/Latino; 4% Hispanic/Latino; 2% Asian, non-Hispanic/Latino; 0.3% Native Hawaiian or other Pacific Islander, non-Hispanic/Latino; 0.1% American Indian or Alaska Native, non-Hispanic/Latino; 3% Two or more races, non-Hispanic/Latino; 2% Race/ethnicity unknown; 0.8% international; 6% transferred in; 23% live on campus. *Retention:* 71% of full-time freshmen returned.

Freshmen *Admission:* 737 applied, 637 admitted, 251 enrolled. *Average high school GPA:* 2.9. *Test scores:* SAT critical reading scores over 500: 38%; SAT math scores over 500: 45%; SAT writing scores over 500: 32%; SAT critical reading scores over 600: 9%; SAT math scores over 600: 15%; SAT writing scores over 600: 7%; SAT critical reading scores over 700: 3%; SAT math scores over 700: 2%; SAT writing scores over 700: 1%.

Faculty *Total:* 61, 56% full-time, 46% with terminal degrees. *Student/faculty ratio:* 18:1.

Academics *Calendar:* semesters. *Degrees:* certificates, associate, bachelor's, and master's. *Special study options:* adult/continuing education programs.

Student Life *Housing options:* coed, disabled students. Campus housing is university owned. Freshman campus housing is guaranteed.

Athletics Member NJCAA. *Intercollegiate sports:* baseball M, basketball M, softball M/W, volleyball W. *Intramural sports:* basketball M/W, cheerleading M(c)/W(c), cross-country running M/W, football M, golf M/W, soccer M/W, softball M/W, table tennis M/W.

Standardized Tests *Required:* SAT or ACT (for admission).

Costs (2011–12) *Tuition:* state resident $12,242 full-time, $495 per credit part-time; nonresident $18,682 full-time, $778 per credit part-time. Full-time tuition and fees vary according to course level, degree level, location, program, and student level. Part-time tuition and fees vary according to course level, course load, degree level, location, program, and student level. *Required fees:* $860 full-time. *Room and board:* $8940; room only: $4770. Room and board charges vary according to board plan, housing facility, and location. *Payment plans:* installment, deferred payment. *Waivers:* employees or children of employees.

Financial Aid Of all full-time matriculated undergraduates who enrolled in 2009, 573 applied for aid, 473 were judged to have need, 32 had their need fully met. In 2009, 48 non-need-based awards were made. *Average percent of need met:* 61%. *Average financial aid package:* $10,069. *Average need-based loan:* $3936. *Average need-based gift aid:* $6603. *Average non-need-based aid:* $2040. *Average indebtedness upon graduation:* $31,135.

Applying *Options:* electronic application, early admission, deferred entrance. *Application fee:* $50. *Required:* high school transcript. *Required for some:* interview. *Recommended:* essay or personal statement. *Application deadlines:* rolling (freshmen), rolling (transfers). *Notification:* continuous (freshmen), continuous (transfers).

Freshman Application Contact Admissions Office, Penn State Beaver, 100 University Drive, Monaca, PA 15061. *Phone:* 724-773-3800. *Fax:* 724-773-3658. *E-mail:* br-admissions@psu.edu. *Web site:* http://www.br.psu.edu/.

Penn State Berks

Reading, Pennsylvania

- **State-related** 4-year, founded 1924, part of Pennsylvania State University
- **Suburban** campus
- **Coed** 2,830 undergraduate students, 89% full-time, 44% women, 56% men
- **Very difficult** entrance level, 82% of applicants were admitted

Undergraduates 2,524 full-time, 306 part-time. 9% are from out of state; 8% Black or African American, non-Hispanic/Latino; 8% Hispanic/Latino; 4% Asian, non-Hispanic/Latino; 0.1% American Indian or Alaska Native, non-Hispanic/Latino; 2% Two or more races, non-Hispanic/Latino; 2% Race/ethnicity unknown; 1% international; 4% transferred in; 29% live on campus. *Retention:* 79% of full-time freshmen returned.

Freshmen *Admission:* 2,788 applied, 2,280 admitted, 855 enrolled. *Average high school GPA:* 2.95. *Test scores:* SAT critical reading scores over 500: 42%; SAT math scores over 500: 50%; SAT writing scores over 500: 36%; SAT critical reading scores over 600: 7%; SAT math scores over 600: 16%; SAT writing scores over 600: 4%; SAT math scores over 700: 1%.

Faculty *Total:* 217, 54% full-time, 41% with terminal degrees. *Student/faculty ratio:* 18:1.

Academics *Calendar:* semesters. *Degrees:* certificates, associate, and bachelor's (enrollment figures include students enrolled at The Graduate School at Penn State who are taking courses at this location). *Special study options:* adult/continuing education programs, part-time degree program. *ROTC:* Army (c).

Computers on Campus Students can access the following: campus intranet, computer help desk, free student e-mail accounts, online (class) grades, online (class) registration, online (class) schedules. Campuswide network is available.

Student Life *Housing options:* coed, disabled students. Campus housing is university owned. *Campus security:* 24-hour emergency response devices and patrols, late-night transport/escort service, controlled dormitory access.

Athletics Member NJCAA. *Intercollegiate sports:* baseball M, basketball M/W, cheerleading M/W, cross-country running M/W, golf M, soccer M/W, softball W, tennis M/W, volleyball W. *Intramural sports:* badminton M/W, basketball M/W, football M/W, golf M/W, table tennis M/W, volleyball M/W.

Standardized Tests *Required:* SAT or ACT (for admission).

Costs (2011–12) *Tuition:* state resident $12,776 full-time, $532 per credit part-time; nonresident $19,548 full-time, $815 per credit part-time. Full-time tuition and fees vary according to course level, degree level, location, program, and student level. Part-time tuition and fees vary according to course level, course load, degree level, location, program, and student level. *Required fees:* $860 full-time. *Room and board:* $9770; room only: $5600. Room and board charges vary according to board plan, housing facility, and location. *Payment plans:* installment, deferred payment. *Waivers:* employees or children of employees.

Financial Aid Of all full-time matriculated undergraduates who enrolled in 2009, 1,915 applied for aid, 1,513 were judged to have need, 54 had their need fully met. In 2009, 40 non-need-based awards were made. *Average percent of need met:* 55%. *Average financial aid package:* $9088. *Average need-based loan:* $4113. *Average need-based gift aid:* $6344. *Average non-need-based aid:* $1513. *Average indebtedness upon graduation:* $31,135.

Applying *Options:* electronic application, early admission, deferred entrance. *Application fee:* $50. *Required:* high school transcript. *Required for some:* interview. *Recommended:* essay or personal statement. *Application deadlines:* rolling (freshmen), rolling (transfers). *Notification:* continuous (freshmen), continuous (transfers).

Freshman Application Contact Admissions Office, Penn State Berks, Tulpehocken Road, PO Box 7009, Reading, PA 19610-6009. *Phone:* 610-396-6060. *Fax:* 610-396-6077. *E-mail:* admissionsbk@psu.edu. *Web site:* http://www.bk.psu.edu/.

Penn State Brandywine

Media, Pennsylvania

- **State-related** primarily 2-year, founded 1966, part of Pennsylvania State University
- **Small-town** campus
- **Coed** 1,628 undergraduate students, 85% full-time, 42% women, 58% men
- **Moderately difficult** entrance level, 83% of applicants were admitted

Undergraduates 1,390 full-time, 238 part-time. 5% are from out of state; 11% Black or African American, non-Hispanic/Latino; 4% Hispanic/Latino; 8% Asian, non-Hispanic/Latino; 0.1% Native Hawaiian or other Pacific Islander, non-Hispanic/Latino; 2% Two or more races, non-Hispanic/Latino; 3% Race/ethnicity unknown; 0.8% international; 5% transferred in. *Retention:* 72% of full-time freshmen returned.

Freshmen *Admission:* 1,260 applied, 1,050 admitted, 402 enrolled. *Average high school GPA:* 2.89. *Test scores:* SAT critical reading scores over 500: 37%; SAT math scores over 500: 46%; SAT writing scores over 500: 31%; SAT critical reading scores over 600: 6%; SAT math scores over 600: 14%; SAT writing scores over 600: 4%; SAT critical reading scores over 700: 1%; SAT math scores over 700: 2%; SAT writing scores over 700: 1%.

Faculty *Total:* 128, 44% full-time, 45% with terminal degrees. *Student/faculty ratio:* 18:1.

Academics *Calendar:* semesters. *Degrees:* certificates, associate, and bachelor's. *Special study options:* adult/continuing education programs. *ROTC:* Army (c), Air Force (c).

Computers on Campus Students can access the following: online (class) registration. Campuswide network is available.

Student Life *Housing:* college housing not available. *Campus security:* late-night transport/escort service, part-time trained security personnel.

Athletics Member NJCAA. *Intercollegiate sports:* baseball M, basketball M/W, soccer M/W, tennis M/W, volleyball W. *Intramural sports:* basketball M/W, cheerleading M(c)/W(c), golf M/W, ice hockey M(c)/W(c), lacrosse M/W, soccer M/W, softball W(c), tennis M/W, volleyball M(c)/W.

Standardized Tests *Required:* SAT or ACT (for admission).

Costs (2011–12) *Tuition:* state resident $12,242 full-time, $495 per credit part-time; nonresident $18,682 full-time, $778 per credit part-time. Full-time tuition and fees vary according to course level, degree level, location, program, and student level. Part-time tuition and fees vary according to course level, course load, degree level, location, program, and student level. *Required fees:* $860 full-time. *Payment plans:* installment, deferred payment. *Waivers:* employees or children of employees.

Financial Aid Of all full-time matriculated undergraduates who enrolled in 2009, 1,003 applied for aid, 750 were judged to have need, 33 had their need fully met. In 2009, 116 non-need-based awards were made. *Average percent of need met:* 58%. *Average financial aid package:* $9078. *Average need-based loan:* $3921. *Average need-based gift aid:* $6280. *Average non-need-based aid:* $2367. *Average indebtedness upon graduation:* $31,135.

Applying *Options:* electronic application, early admission, deferred entrance. *Application fee:* $50. *Required:* high school transcript. *Required for some:* interview. *Recommended:* essay or personal statement. *Application deadlines:* rolling (freshmen), rolling (transfers). *Notification:* continuous (freshmen), continuous (transfers).

Freshman Application Contact Admissions Office, Penn State Brandywine, 25 Yearsley Mill Road, Media, PA 19063-5596. *Phone:* 610-892-1200. *Fax:* 610-892-1320. *E-mail:* bwadmissions@psu.edu. *Web site:* http://www.brandywine.psu.edu/.

Penn State DuBois

DuBois, Pennsylvania

- **State-related** primarily 2-year, founded 1935, part of Pennsylvania State University
- **Small-town** campus
- **Coed** 795 undergraduate students, 76% full-time, 49% women, 51% men
- **Moderately difficult** entrance level, 88% of applicants were admitted

Undergraduates 602 full-time, 193 part-time. 3% are from out of state; 2% Black or African American, non-Hispanic/Latino; 2% Hispanic/Latino; 0.9% Asian, non-Hispanic/Latino; 0.2% Native Hawaiian or other Pacific Islander, non-Hispanic/Latino; 0.6% Two or more races, non-Hispanic/Latino; 1% Race/ethnicity unknown; 3% transferred in. *Retention:* 74% of full-time freshmen returned.

Freshmen *Admission:* 433 applied, 379 admitted, 165 enrolled. *Average high school GPA:* 2.88. *Test scores:* SAT critical reading scores over 500: 31%; SAT math scores over 500: 45%; SAT writing scores over 500: 21%; SAT critical reading scores over 600: 6%; SAT math scores over 600: 9%; SAT writing scores over 600: 1%; SAT math scores over 700: 1%.

Faculty *Total:* 76, 61% full-time, 46% with terminal degrees. *Student/faculty ratio:* 12:1.

Academics *Calendar:* semesters. *Degrees:* certificates, associate, bachelor's, and master's. *Special study options:* adult/continuing education programs.

Computers on Campus Students can access the following: online (class) registration. Campuswide network is available.

Student Life *Housing:* college housing not available.

Athletics Member NJCAA. *Intercollegiate sports:* basketball M, cross-country running M/W, golf M/W, volleyball W. *Intramural sports:* basketball M/W, football M, soccer M/W, table tennis M/W, volleyball M/W.

Standardized Tests *Required:* SAT or ACT (for admission).

Costs (2011–12) *Tuition:* state resident $12,242 full-time, $495 per credit part-time; nonresident $18,682 full-time, $778 per credit part-time. Full-time tuition and fees vary according to course level, degree level, location, program, and student level. Part-time tuition and fees vary according to course level, course load, degree level, location, program, and student level. *Required fees:*

$752 full-time. *Payment plans:* installment, deferred payment. *Waivers:* employees or children of employees.

Financial Aid Of all full-time matriculated undergraduates who enrolled in 2009, 642 applied for aid, 586 were judged to have need, 29 had their need fully met. In 2009, 4 non-need-based awards were made. *Average percent of need met:* 61%. *Average financial aid package:* $10,851. *Average need-based loan:* $3821. *Average need-based gift aid:* $6569. *Average non-need-based aid:* $2000. *Average indebtedness upon graduation:* $31,135.

Applying *Options:* electronic application, early admission, deferred entrance. *Application fee:* $50. *Required:* high school transcript. *Required for some:* interview. *Recommended:* essay or personal statement. *Application deadlines:* rolling (freshmen), rolling (transfers). *Notification:* continuous (freshmen), continuous (transfers).

Freshman Application Contact Admissions Office, Penn State DuBois, College Place, DuBois, PA 15801-3199. *Phone:* 814-375-4720. *Toll-free phone:* 800-346-7627. *Fax:* 814-375-4784. *E-mail:* duboisinfo@psi.edu. *Web site:* http://www.ds.psu.edu/.

Penn State Erie, The Behrend College

Erie, Pennsylvania

- **State-related** comprehensive, founded 1948, part of Pennsylvania State University
- **Suburban** 725-acre campus
- **Coed** 4,135 undergraduate students, 92% full-time, 36% women, 64% men
- **Very difficult** entrance level, 83% of applicants were admitted

Undergraduates 3,815 full-time, 320 part-time. 9% are from out of state; 3% Black or African American, non-Hispanic/Latino; 3% Hispanic/Latino; 2% Asian, non-Hispanic/Latino; 0.1% Native Hawaiian or other Pacific Islander, non-Hispanic/Latino; 0.1% American Indian or Alaska Native, non-Hispanic/Latino; 2% Two or more races, non-Hispanic/Latino; 2% Race/ethnicity unknown; 2% international; 2% transferred in; 40% live on campus. *Retention:* 82% of full-time freshmen returned.

Freshmen *Admission:* 3,367 applied, 2,778 admitted, 1,083 enrolled. *Average high school GPA:* 3.2. *Test scores:* SAT critical reading scores over 500: 57%; SAT math scores over 500: 70%; SAT writing scores over 500: 50%; SAT critical reading scores over 600: 16%; SAT math scores over 600: 28%; SAT writing scores over 600: 10%; SAT critical reading scores over 700: 1%; SAT math scores over 700: 2%; SAT writing scores over 700: 1%.

Faculty *Total:* 302, 77% full-time, 51% with terminal degrees. *Student/faculty ratio:* 16:1.

Academics *Calendar:* semesters. *Degrees:* certificates, associate, bachelor's, and master's. *Special study options:* adult/continuing education programs, part-time degree program. *ROTC:* Army (b).

Computers on Campus Students can access the following: campus intranet, computer help desk, free student e-mail accounts, online (class) grades, online (class) registration, online (class) schedules. Campuswide network is available.

Student Life *Housing options:* coed, men-only, women-only, disabled students. Campus housing is university owned. *Campus security:* 24-hour emergency response devices and patrols, student patrols, late-night transport/escort service, controlled dormitory access.

Athletics Member NCAA. All Division III. *Intercollegiate sports:* baseball M, basketball M/W, cheerleading M/W, cross-country running M/W, golf M/W, ice hockey M(c), lacrosse M(c), skiing (downhill) M(c)/W(c), soccer M/W, softball W, swimming and diving M/W, tennis M/W, track and field M/W, volleyball M(c)/W, water polo M/W. *Intramural sports:* badminton M/W, basketball M/W, bowling M/W, cross-country running M/W, football M/W, golf M/W, skiing (downhill) M/W, soccer M/W, softball M/W, swimming and diving M/W, table tennis M/W, tennis M/W, volleyball M/W.

Standardized Tests *Required:* SAT or ACT (for admission).

Costs (2011–12) *Tuition:* state resident $12,776 full-time, $532 per credit part-time; nonresident $19,548 full-time, $815 per credit part-time. Full-time tuition and fees vary according to course level, degree level, location, program, and student level. Part-time tuition and fees vary according to course level, course load, degree level, location, program, and student level. *Required fees:* $860 full-time. *Room and board:* $8940; room only: $4770. Room and board charges vary according to board plan, housing facility, and location. *Payment plans:* installment, deferred payment. *Waivers:* employees or children of employees.

Financial Aid Of all full-time matriculated undergraduates who enrolled in 2009, 3,418 applied for aid, 2,917 were judged to have need, 122 had their need fully met. In 2009, 65 non-need-based awards were made. *Average percent of need met:* 58%. *Average financial aid package:* $9651. *Average need-based loan:* $4454. *Average need-based gift aid:* $6176. *Average non-need-based aid:* $3967. *Average indebtedness upon graduation:* $31,135.

Applying *Options:* electronic application, early admission, deferred entrance. *Application fee:* $50. *Required:* high school transcript. *Required for some:*

interview. *Recommended:* essay or personal statement. *Application deadlines:* rolling (freshmen), rolling (transfers). *Notification:* continuous (freshmen), continuous (transfers).

Freshman Application Contact Admissions Office, Penn State Erie, The Behrend College, 4701 College Drive, Erie, PA 16563-0001. *Phone:* 814-898-6100. *Toll-free phone:* 866-374-3378. *Fax:* 814-898-6044. *E-mail:* behrend.admissions@psu.edu. *Web site:* http://www.pserie.psu.edu/.

Penn State Fayette, The Eberly Campus

Uniontown, Pennsylvania

- **State-related** primarily 2-year, founded 1934, part of Pennsylvania State University
- **Small-town** campus
- **Coed** 956 undergraduate students, 82% full-time, 57% women, 43% men
- **Moderately difficult** entrance level, 90% of applicants were admitted

Undergraduates 781 full-time, 175 part-time. 3% are from out of state; 5% Black or African American, non-Hispanic/Latino; 1% Hispanic/Latino; 0.6% Asian, non-Hispanic/Latino; 0.1% American Indian or Alaska Native, non-Hispanic/Latino; 2% Two or more races, non-Hispanic/Latino; 2% Race/ethnicity unknown; 0.9% international; 6% transferred in. *Retention:* 74% of full-time freshmen returned.

Freshmen *Admission:* 555 applied, 497 admitted, 232 enrolled. *Average high school GPA:* 2.99. *Test scores:* SAT critical reading scores over 500: 26%; SAT math scores over 500: 39%; SAT writing scores over 500: 22%; SAT critical reading scores over 600: 4%; SAT math scores over 600: 11%; SAT writing scores over 600: 3%; SAT critical reading scores over 700: 1%; SAT math scores over 700: 1%.

Faculty *Total:* 90, 61% full-time, 39% with terminal degrees. *Student/faculty ratio:* 13:1.

Academics *Calendar:* semesters. *Degrees:* certificates, associate, and bachelor's. *Special study options:* adult/continuing education programs. *ROTC:* Army (b).

Computers on Campus Students can access the following: online (class) registration. Campuswide network is available.

Student Life *Housing:* college housing not available. *Campus security:* student patrols, 8-hour patrols by trained security personnel.

Athletics Member NJCAA. *Intercollegiate sports:* baseball M, basketball M, softball W, volleyball W. *Intramural sports:* badminton M/W, basketball M/W, cheerleading M(c)/W(c), equestrian sports M(c)/W(c), football M/W, golf M(c)/W(c), softball M/W, tennis M/W, volleyball M/W, weight lifting M/W.

Standardized Tests *Required:* SAT or ACT (for admission).

Costs (2011–12) *Tuition:* state resident $12,242 full-time, $495 per credit part-time; nonresident $18,682 full-time, $778 per credit part-time. Full-time tuition and fees vary according to course level, degree level, location, program, and student level. Part-time tuition and fees vary according to course level, course load, degree level, location, program, and student level. *Required fees:* $798 full-time. *Payment plans:* installment, deferred payment. *Waivers:* employees or children of employees.

Financial Aid Of all full-time matriculated undergraduates who enrolled in 2009, 677 applied for aid, 615 were judged to have need, 36 had their need fully met. In 2009, 23 non-need-based awards were made. *Average percent of need met:* 60%. *Average financial aid package:* $10,051. *Average need-based loan:* $3893. *Average need-based gift aid:* $6339. *Average non-need-based aid:* $2304. *Average indebtedness upon graduation:* $31,135.

Applying *Options:* electronic application, early admission, deferred entrance. *Application fee:* $50. *Required:* high school transcript. *Required for some:* interview. *Recommended:* essay or personal statement. *Application deadlines:* rolling (freshmen), rolling (transfers). *Notification:* continuous (freshmen), continuous (transfers).

Freshman Application Contact Admissions Office, Penn State Fayette, The Eberly Campus, 1 University Drive, PO Box 519, Uniontown, PA 15401-0519. *Phone:* 724-430-4130. *Toll-free phone:* 877-568-4130. *Fax:* 724-430-4175. *E-mail:* feadm@psu.edu. *Web site:* http://www.fe.psu.edu/.

Penn State Greater Allegheny

McKeesport, Pennsylvania

- **State-related** primarily 2-year, founded 1947, part of Pennsylvania State University
- **Small-town** campus
- **Coed** 701 undergraduate students, 88% full-time, 47% women, 53% men
- **Moderately difficult** entrance level, 81% of applicants were admitted

Undergraduates 620 full-time, 81 part-time. 9% are from out of state; 29% Black or African American, non-Hispanic/Latino; 3% Hispanic/Latino; 2% Asian, non-Hispanic/Latino; 0.3% Native Hawaiian or other Pacific Islander,

non-Hispanic/Latino; 0.2% American Indian or Alaska Native, non-Hispanic/Latino; 3% Two or more races, non-Hispanic/Latino; 2% Race/ethnicity unknown; 3% international; 4% transferred in; 29% live on campus. *Retention:* 70% of full-time freshmen returned.

Freshmen *Admission:* 719 applied, 583 admitted, 234 enrolled. *Average high school GPA:* 2.82. *Test scores:* SAT critical reading scores over 500: 29%; SAT math scores over 500: 34%; SAT writing scores over 500: 19%; SAT critical reading scores over 600: 9%; SAT math scores over 600: 11%; SAT writing scores over 600: 4%; SAT critical reading scores over 700: 1%; SAT math scores over 700: 2%; SAT writing scores over 700: 1%.

Faculty *Total:* 69, 52% full-time, 46% with terminal degrees. *Student/faculty ratio:* 14:1.

Academics *Calendar:* semesters. *Degrees:* certificates, associate, bachelor's, and master's. *Special study options:* adult/continuing education programs.

Computers on Campus Students can access the following: online (class) registration. Campuswide network is available.

Student Life *Housing options:* coed, disabled students. Campus housing is university owned. Freshman campus housing is guaranteed. *Campus security:* 24-hour patrols, controlled dormitory access.

Athletics Member NJCAA. *Intercollegiate sports:* baseball M, basketball M, softball W, volleyball W. *Intramural sports:* basketball M/W, cheerleading M(c)/W(c), football M/W, ice hockey M(c), racquetball M/W, skiing (cross-country) M(c)/W(c), skiing (downhill) M(c)/W(c), soccer M(c)/W(c), softball M/W, tennis M/W, volleyball M/W.

Standardized Tests *Required:* SAT or ACT (for admission).

Costs (2011–12) *Tuition:* state resident $12,242 full-time, $495 per credit part-time; nonresident $18,682 full-time, $778 per credit part-time. Full-time tuition and fees vary according to course level, degree level, location, program, and student level. Part-time tuition and fees vary according to course level, course load, degree level, location, program, and student level. *Required fees:* $860 full-time. *Room and board:* $8940; room only: $4770. Room and board charges vary according to board plan, housing facility, and location. *Payment plans:* installment, deferred payment. *Waivers:* employees or children of employees.

Financial Aid Of all full-time matriculated undergraduates who enrolled in 2009, 544 applied for aid, 481 were judged to have need, 10 had their need fully met. In 2009, 27 non-need-based awards were made. *Average percent of need met:* 62%. *Average financial aid package:* $11,087. *Average need-based loan:* $3817. *Average need-based gift aid:* $7344. *Average non-need-based aid:* $3515. *Average indebtedness upon graduation:* $31,135.

Applying *Options:* electronic application, early admission, deferred entrance. *Application fee:* $50. *Required:* high school transcript. *Required for some:* interview. *Recommended:* essay or personal statement. *Application deadlines:* rolling (freshmen), rolling (transfers). *Notification:* continuous (freshmen), continuous (transfers).

Freshman Application Contact Admissions Office, Penn State Greater Allegheny, 4000 University Drive, McKeesport, PA 15132-7698. *Phone:* 412-675-9010. *Fax:* 412-675-9046. *E-mail:* psuga@psu.edu. *Web site:* http://www.ga.psu.edu/.

Penn State Harrisburg

Middletown, Pennsylvania

- **State-related** comprehensive, founded 1966, part of Pennsylvania State University
- **Small-town** campus
- **Coed** 3,167 undergraduate students, 84% full-time, 44% women, 56% men
- **Very difficult** entrance level, 79% of applicants were admitted

Undergraduates 2,667 full-time, 500 part-time. 14% are from out of state; 9% Black or African American, non-Hispanic/Latino; 6% Hispanic/Latino; 7% Asian, non-Hispanic/Latino; 0.2% Native Hawaiian or other Pacific Islander, non-Hispanic/Latino; 0.2% American Indian or Alaska Native, non-Hispanic/Latino; 2% Two or more races, non-Hispanic/Latino; 3% Race/ethnicity unknown; 3% international; 10% transferred in; 14% live on campus. *Retention:* 84% of full-time freshmen returned.

Freshmen *Admission:* 2,482 applied, 1,964 admitted, 543 enrolled. *Average high school GPA:* 3.08. *Test scores:* SAT critical reading scores over 500: 49%; SAT math scores over 500: 61%; SAT writing scores over 500: 46%; SAT critical reading scores over 600: 14%; SAT math scores over 600: 23%; SAT writing scores over 600: 9%; SAT critical reading scores over 700: 1%; SAT math scores over 700: 3%.

Faculty *Total:* 321, 64% full-time, 64% with terminal degrees. *Student/faculty ratio:* 14:1.

Academics *Calendar:* semesters. *Degrees:* certificates, associate, bachelor's, master's, doctoral, and first professional. *Special study options:* adult/continuing education programs, part-time degree program. *ROTC:* Army (c).

Computers on Campus Students can access the following: campus intranet, computer help desk, free student e-mail accounts, online (class) grades, online (class) registration, online (class) schedules. Campuswide network is available.

Student Life *Housing options:* disabled students. Campus housing is university owned. *Campus security:* 24-hour emergency response devices and patrols, student patrols, late-night transport/escort service, controlled dormitory access.

Athletics *Intercollegiate sports:* baseball M, basketball M/W, cross-country running M/W, golf M/W, soccer M/W, softball W, tennis M/W, volleyball W. *Intramural sports:* badminton M/W, basketball M/W, racquetball M/W, tennis M/W.

Standardized Tests *Required:* SAT or ACT (for admission).

Costs (2011–12) *Tuition:* state resident $12,776 full-time, $532 per credit part-time; nonresident $19,548 full-time, $815 per credit part-time. Full-time tuition and fees vary according to course level, degree level, location, program, and student level. Part-time tuition and fees vary according to course level, course load, degree level, location, program, and student level. *Required fees:* $852 full-time. *Room and board:* $10,210; room only: $6040. Room and board charges vary according to board plan, housing facility, and location. *Payment plans:* installment, deferred payment. *Waivers:* employees or children of employees.

Financial Aid Of all full-time matriculated undergraduates who enrolled in 2009, 1,743 applied for aid, 1,429 were judged to have need, 93 had their need fully met. In 2009, 32 non-need-based awards were made. *Average percent of need met:* 56%. *Average financial aid package:* $9974. *Average need-based loan:* $4565. *Average need-based gift aid:* $6524. *Average non-need-based aid:* $1272. *Average indebtedness upon graduation:* $31,135.

Applying *Options:* electronic application, early admission, deferred entrance. *Application fee:* $50. *Required:* high school transcript. *Required for some:* interview. *Recommended:* essay or personal statement. *Application deadlines:* rolling (freshmen), rolling (transfers). *Notification:* continuous (freshmen), continuous (transfers).

Freshman Application Contact Admissions Office, Penn State Harrisburg, 777 West Harrisburg Pike, Middletown, PA 17057-4898. *Phone:* 717-948-6250. *Toll-free phone:* 800-222-2056. *Fax:* 717-948-6325. *E-mail:* hbgadmit@psu.edu. *Web site:* http://www.hbg.psu.edu/.

Penn State Hazleton

Hazleton, Pennsylvania

- **State-related** primarily 2-year, founded 1934, part of Pennsylvania State University
- **Small-town** campus
- **Coed** 1,172 undergraduate students, 95% full-time, 46% women, 54% men
- **Moderately difficult** entrance level, 87% of applicants were admitted

Undergraduates 1,108 full-time, 64 part-time. 27% are from out of state; 13% Black or African American, non-Hispanic/Latino; 15% Hispanic/Latino; 4% Asian, non-Hispanic/Latino; 0.4% American Indian or Alaska Native, non-Hispanic/Latino; 2% Two or more races, non-Hispanic/Latino; 2% Race/ethnicity unknown; 1% international; 5% transferred in; 41% live on campus. *Retention:* 76% of full-time freshmen returned.

Freshmen *Admission:* 1,268 applied, 1,100 admitted, 458 enrolled. *Average high school GPA:* 2.83. *Test scores:* SAT critical reading scores over 500: 32%; SAT math scores over 500: 39%; SAT writing scores over 500: 27%; SAT critical reading scores over 600: 5%; SAT math scores over 600: 10%; SAT writing scores over 600: 2%; SAT math scores over 700: 1%.

Faculty *Total:* 83, 66% full-time, 48% with terminal degrees. *Student/faculty ratio:* 18:1.

Academics *Calendar:* semesters. *Degrees:* certificates, associate, and bachelor's. *Special study options:* adult/continuing education programs. *ROTC:* Army (b), Air Force (c).

Computers on Campus Students can access the following: online (class) registration. Campuswide network is available.

Student Life *Housing options:* coed. Campus housing is university owned. Freshman campus housing is guaranteed. *Campus security:* 24-hour patrols, late-night transport/escort service, controlled dormitory access.

Athletics Member NJCAA. *Intercollegiate sports:* baseball M, basketball M/W, cheerleading M/W, soccer M, softball W(s), tennis M/W, volleyball M/W. *Intramural sports:* basketball M/W, skiing (downhill) M(c)/W(c), soccer M/W, volleyball M/W.

Standardized Tests *Required:* SAT or ACT (for admission).

Costs (2011–12) *Tuition:* state resident $12,242 full-time, $495 per credit part-time; nonresident $18,682 full-time, $778 per credit part-time. Full-time tuition and fees vary according to course level, degree level, location, program, and student level. Part-time tuition and fees vary according to course level, course load, degree level, location, program, and student level. *Required fees:*

$806 full-time. *Room and board:* $8940; room only: $4770. Room and board charges vary according to board plan, housing facility, and location. *Payment plans:* installment, deferred payment. *Waivers:* employees or children of employees.

Financial Aid Of all full-time matriculated undergraduates who enrolled in 2009, 1,031 applied for aid, 886 were judged to have need, 30 had their need fully met. In 2009, 93 non-need-based awards were made. *Average percent of need met:* 55%. *Average financial aid package:* $9388. *Average need-based loan:* $3692. *Average need-based gift aid:* $6639. *Average non-need-based aid:* $2689. *Average indebtedness upon graduation:* $31,135.

Applying *Options:* electronic application, early admission, deferred entrance. *Application fee:* $50. *Required:* high school transcript. *Required for some:* interview. *Recommended:* essay or personal statement. *Application deadlines:* rolling (freshmen), rolling (transfers). *Notification:* continuous (freshmen), continuous (transfers).

Freshman Application Contact Admissions Office, Penn State Hazleton, Hazleton, PA 18202-1291. *Phone:* 570-450-3142. *Toll-free phone:* 800-279-8495. *Fax:* 570-450-3182. *E-mail:* admissions-hn@psu.edu. *Web site:* http://www.hn.psu.edu/.

Penn State Lehigh Valley

Fogelsville, Pennsylvania

- **State-related** primarily 2-year, founded 1912, part of Pennsylvania State University
- **Rural** campus
- **Coed** 915 undergraduate students, 81% full-time, 43% women, 57% men
- **Moderately difficult** entrance level, 87% of applicants were admitted

Undergraduates 738 full-time, 177 part-time. 4% are from out of state; 4% Black or African American, non-Hispanic/Latino; 14% Hispanic/Latino; 9% Asian, non-Hispanic/Latino; 0.1% Native Hawaiian or other Pacific Islander, non-Hispanic/Latino; 2% Two or more races, non-Hispanic/Latino; 2% Race/ethnicity unknown; 0.5% international; 6% transferred in. *Retention:* 76% of full-time freshmen returned.

Freshmen *Admission:* 951 applied, 831 admitted, 260 enrolled. *Average high school GPA:* 2.87. *Test scores:* SAT critical reading scores over 500: 47%; SAT math scores over 500: 51%; SAT writing scores over 500: 37%; SAT critical reading scores over 600: 12%; SAT math scores over 600: 14%; SAT writing scores over 600: 8%; SAT critical reading scores over 700: 3%; SAT math scores over 700: 2%.

Faculty *Total:* 89, 37% full-time, 42% with terminal degrees. *Student/faculty ratio:* 16:1.

Academics *Calendar:* semesters. *Degrees:* certificates, associate, and bachelor's (enrollment figures include students enrolled at The Graduate School at Penn State who are taking courses at this location). *Special study options:* adult/continuing education programs. *ROTC:* Army (c).

Computers on Campus Students can access the following: online (class) registration. Campuswide network is available.

Student Life *Housing:* college housing not available.

Athletics Member NJCAA. *Intercollegiate sports:* baseball M, basketball M/W, bowling M(c)/W(c), cheerleading M/W, cross-country running M/W, football M(c), golf M(c)/W(c), ice hockey M(c)/W(c), skiing (downhill) M(c)/W(c), soccer M(c)/W, tennis M/W, volleyball M(c)/W. *Intramural sports:* badminton M/W, basketball M/W, football M/W, golf M/W, soccer M/W, volleyball M/W.

Standardized Tests *Required:* SAT or ACT (for admission).

Costs (2011–12) *Tuition:* state resident $12,242 full-time, $495 per credit part-time; nonresident $18,682 full-time, $778 per credit part-time. Full-time tuition and fees vary according to course level, degree level, location, program, and student level. Part-time tuition and fees vary according to course level, course load, degree level, location, program, and student level. *Required fees:* $852 full-time. *Payment plans:* installment, deferred payment. *Waivers:* employees or children of employees.

Financial Aid Of all full-time matriculated undergraduates who enrolled in 2009, 478 applied for aid, 382 were judged to have need, 13 had their need fully met. In 2009, 40 non-need-based awards were made. *Average percent of need met:* 58%. *Average financial aid package:* $9147. *Average need-based loan:* $3877. *Average need-based gift aid:* $6720. *Average non-need-based aid:* $2129. *Average indebtedness upon graduation:* $31,135.

Applying *Options:* electronic application, early admission, deferred entrance. *Application fee:* $50. *Required:* high school transcript. *Application deadlines:* rolling (freshmen), rolling (transfers). *Notification:* continuous (freshmen), continuous (transfers).

Freshman Application Contact Admissions Office, Penn State Lehigh Valley, 2809 Saucon Valley Road, Fogelsville, PA 18051-9999. *Phone:* 610-285-5000. *Fax:* 610-285-5220. *E-mail:* admissions-lv@psu.edu. *Web site:* http://www.lv.psu.edu/.

Penn State Mont Alto

Mont Alto, Pennsylvania

- **State-related** primarily 2-year, founded 1929, part of Pennsylvania State University
- **Small-town** campus
- **Coed** 1,217 undergraduate students, 79% full-time, 58% women, 42% men
- **Moderately difficult** entrance level, 85% of applicants were admitted

Undergraduates 956 full-time, 261 part-time. 18% are from out of state; 12% Black or African American, non-Hispanic/Latino; 5% Hispanic/Latino; 2% Asian, non-Hispanic/Latino; 0.1% Native Hawaiian or other Pacific Islander, non-Hispanic/Latino; 0.1% American Indian or Alaska Native, non-Hispanic/Latino; 3% Two or more races, non-Hispanic/Latino; 1% Race/ethnicity unknown; 0.4% international; 5% transferred in; 35% live on campus. *Retention:* 76% of full-time freshmen returned.
Freshmen *Admission:* 947 applied, 803 admitted, 394 enrolled. *Average high school GPA:* 2.92. *Test scores:* SAT critical reading scores over 500: 35%; SAT math scores over 500: 38%; SAT writing scores over 500: 28%; SAT critical reading scores over 600: 6%; SAT math scores over 600: 10%; SAT writing scores over 600: 4%; SAT critical reading scores over 700: 1%.
Faculty *Total:* 114, 49% full-time, 32% with terminal degrees. *Student/faculty ratio:* 14:1.
Academics *Calendar:* semesters. *Degrees:* certificates, associate, and bachelor's. *Special study options:* adult/continuing education programs. *ROTC:* Army (c).
Computers on Campus Students can access the following: online (class) registration. Campuswide network is available.
Student Life *Housing options:* coed, disabled students. Campus housing is university owned. Freshman campus housing is guaranteed. *Campus security:* 24-hour patrols, controlled dormitory access.
Athletics Member NJCAA. *Intercollegiate sports:* basketball M/W, cheerleading M/W, cross-country running M/W, golf M/W, soccer M/W, softball W, tennis M/W, volleyball W. *Intramural sports:* badminton M/W, basketball M/W, cheerleading M(c)/W(c), racquetball M/W, soccer M/W, softball W, volleyball M/W.
Standardized Tests *Required:* SAT or ACT (for admission).
Costs (2011–12) *Tuition:* state resident $12,242 full-time, $495 per credit part-time; nonresident $18,682 full-time, $778 per credit part-time. Full-time tuition and fees vary according to course level, degree level, location, program, and student level. Part-time tuition and fees vary according to course level, course load, degree level, location, program, and student level. *Required fees:* $860 full-time. *Room and board:* $8940; room only: $4770. Room and board charges vary according to board plan, housing facility, and location. *Payment plans:* installment, deferred payment. *Waivers:* employees or children of employees.
Financial Aid Of all full-time matriculated undergraduates who enrolled in 2009, 774 applied for aid, 651 were judged to have need, 34 had their need fully met. In 2009, 47 non-need-based awards were made. *Average percent of need met:* 58%. *Average financial aid package:* $9783. *Average need-based loan:* $3768. *Average need-based gift aid:* $6075. *Average non-need-based aid:* $3204. *Average indebtedness upon graduation:* $31,135.
Applying *Options:* electronic application, early admission, deferred entrance. *Application fee:* $50. *Required:* high school transcript. *Required for some:* interview. *Recommended:* essay or personal statement. *Application deadlines:* rolling (freshmen), rolling (transfers). *Notification:* continuous (freshmen), continuous (transfers).
Freshman Application Contact Admissions Office, Penn State Mont Alto, 1 Campus Drive, Mont Alto, PA 17237-9703. *Phone:* 717-749-6130. *Toll-free phone:* 800-392-6173. *Fax:* 717-749-6132. *E-mail:* psuma@psu.edu. *Web site:* http://www.ma.psu.edu/.

Penn State New Kensington

New Kensington, Pennsylvania

- **State-related** primarily 2-year, founded 1958, part of Pennsylvania State University
- **Small-town** campus
- **Coed** 800 undergraduate students, 74% full-time, 42% women, 59% men
- **Moderately difficult** entrance level, 80% of applicants were admitted

Undergraduates 595 full-time, 205 part-time. 3% are from out of state; 5% Black or African American, non-Hispanic/Latino; 2% Hispanic/Latino; 0.7% Asian, non-Hispanic/Latino; 0.1% American Indian or Alaska Native, non-Hispanic/Latino; 0.7% Two or more races, non-Hispanic/Latino; 2% Race/ethnicity unknown; 5% transferred in. *Retention:* 74% of full-time freshmen returned.
Freshmen *Admission:* 528 applied, 422 admitted, 195 enrolled. *Average high school GPA:* 2.95. *Test scores:* SAT critical reading scores over 500: 34%;

SAT math scores over 500: 45%; SAT writing scores over 500: 25%; SAT critical reading scores over 600: 7%; SAT math scores over 600: 9%; SAT writing scores over 600: 2%; SAT math scores over 700: 1%.
Faculty *Total:* 79, 47% full-time, 44% with terminal degrees. *Student/faculty ratio:* 13:1.
Academics *Calendar:* semesters. *Degrees:* certificates, associate, bachelor's, and master's. *Special study options:* adult/continuing education programs, external degree program. *ROTC:* Air Force (c).
Computers on Campus Students can access the following: online (class) registration. Campuswide network is available.
Student Life *Campus security:* part-time trained security personnel.
Athletics Member NJCAA. *Intercollegiate sports:* baseball M, basketball M/W, cheerleading M/W, golf M/W, softball W, volleyball W. *Intramural sports:* badminton M/W, basketball M/W, bowling M/W, cheerleading M(c)/W(c), football M/W, ice hockey M(c)/W(c), racquetball M/W, skiing (downhill) M(c)/W(c), soccer M/W, softball W, volleyball M/W.
Standardized Tests *Required:* SAT or ACT (for admission).
Costs (2011–12) *Tuition:* state resident $12,242 full-time, $495 per credit part-time; nonresident $18,682 full-time, $778 per credit part-time. Full-time tuition and fees vary according to course level, degree level, location, program, and student level. Part-time tuition and fees vary according to course level, course load, degree level, location, program, and student level. *Required fees:* $806 full-time. *Payment plans:* installment, deferred payment. *Waivers:* employees or children of employees.
Financial Aid Of all full-time matriculated undergraduates who enrolled in 2009, 776 applied for aid, 720 were judged to have need, 30 had their need fully met. In 2009, 15 non-need-based awards were made. *Average percent of need met:* 58%. *Average financial aid package:* $10,943. *Average need-based loan:* $3996. *Average need-based gift aid:* $7125. *Average non-need-based aid:* $2132. *Average indebtedness upon graduation:* $31,135.
Applying *Options:* electronic application, early admission, deferred entrance. *Application fee:* $50. *Required:* high school transcript. *Required for some:* interview. *Recommended:* essay or personal statement. *Application deadlines:* rolling (freshmen), rolling (transfers). *Notification:* continuous (freshmen), continuous (transfers).
Freshman Application Contact Admissions Office, Penn State New Kensington, 3550 Seventh Street Road, New Kensington, PA 15068. *Phone:* 724-334-5466. *Toll-free phone:* 888-968-7297. *Fax:* 724-334-6111. *E-mail:* nkadmissions@psu.edu. *Web site:* http://www.nk.psu.edu/.

Penn State Schuylkill

Schuylkill Haven, Pennsylvania

- **State-related** primarily 2-year, founded 1934, part of Pennsylvania State University
- **Small-town** campus
- **Coed** 1,012 undergraduate students, 84% full-time, 53% women, 47% men
- **Moderately difficult** entrance level, 79% of applicants were admitted

Undergraduates 851 full-time, 161 part-time. 20% are from out of state; 30% Black or African American, non-Hispanic/Latino; 7% Hispanic/Latino; 2% Asian, non-Hispanic/Latino; 0.1% Native Hawaiian or other Pacific Islander, non-Hispanic/Latino; 0.1% American Indian or Alaska Native, non-Hispanic/Latino; 2% Two or more races, non-Hispanic/Latino; 2% Race/ethnicity unknown; 0.9% international; 3% transferred in; 30% live on campus. *Retention:* 71% of full-time freshmen returned.
Freshmen *Admission:* 834 applied, 663 admitted, 332 enrolled. *Average high school GPA:* 2.66. *Test scores:* SAT critical reading scores over 500: 26%; SAT math scores over 500: 22%; SAT writing scores over 500: 19%; SAT critical reading scores over 600: 2%; SAT math scores over 600: 4%; SAT writing scores over 600: 3%.
Faculty *Total:* 74, 61% full-time, 50% with terminal degrees. *Student/faculty ratio:* 17:1.
Academics *Calendar:* semesters. *Degrees:* certificates, associate, and bachelor's (bachelor's degree programs completed at the Harrisburg campus). *Special study options:* adult/continuing education programs.
Computers on Campus Students can access the following: online (class) registration. Campuswide network is available.
Student Life *Housing options:* disabled students. *Campus security:* 24-hour patrols, controlled dormitory access.
Athletics Member NJCAA. *Intercollegiate sports:* basketball M, cross-country running M/W, golf M, soccer M, softball W, volleyball W. *Intramural sports:* basketball M/W, football M, soccer M/W, softball M/W, table tennis M/W, volleyball M/W.
Standardized Tests *Required:* SAT or ACT (for admission).
Costs (2011–12) *Tuition:* state resident $12,242 full-time, $495 per credit part-time; nonresident $18,682 full-time, $778 per credit part-time. Full-time tuition and fees vary according to course level, degree level, location, program,

and student level. Part-time tuition and fees vary according to course level, course load, degree level, location, program, and student level. *Required fees:* $752 full-time. *Payment plans:* installment, deferred payment. *Waivers:* employees or children of employees.

Financial Aid Of all full-time matriculated undergraduates who enrolled in 2009, 776 applied for aid, 720 were judged to have need, 30 had their need fully met. In 2009, 15 non-need-based awards were made. *Average percent of need met:* 58%. *Average financial aid package:* $10,943. *Average need-based loan:* $3996. *Average need-based gift aid:* $7125. *Average non-need-based aid:* $2132. *Average indebtedness upon graduation:* $31,135.

Applying *Options:* electronic application, early admission, deferred entrance. *Application fee:* $50. *Required:* high school transcript. *Application deadlines:* rolling (freshmen), rolling (transfers). *Notification:* continuous (freshmen), continuous (transfers).

Freshman Application Contact Admissions Office, Penn State Schuylkill, 200 University Drive, Schuylkill Haven, PA 17972-2208. *Phone:* 570-385-6252. *Fax:* 570-385-6272. *E-mail:* sl-admissions@psu.edu. *Web site:* http://www.sl.psu.edu/.

Penn State Shenango

Sharon, Pennsylvania

- **State-related** primarily 2-year, founded 1965, part of Pennsylvania State University
- **Small-town** campus
- **Coed** 651 undergraduate students, 60% full-time, 63% women, 37% men
- **Moderately difficult** entrance level, 74% of applicants were admitted

Undergraduates 393 full-time, 258 part-time. 20% are from out of state; 7% Black or African American, non-Hispanic/Latino; 2% Hispanic/Latino; 0.4% Native Hawaiian or other Pacific Islander, non-Hispanic/Latino; 1% Two or more races, non-Hispanic/Latino; 3% Race/ethnicity unknown; 8% transferred in. *Retention:* 63% of full-time freshmen returned.

Freshmen *Admission:* 254 applied, 189 admitted, 101 enrolled. *Average high school GPA:* 2.83. *Test scores:* SAT critical reading scores over 500: 19%; SAT math scores over 500: 29%; SAT writing scores over 500: 13%; SAT critical reading scores over 600: 6%; SAT writing scores over 600: 3%.

Faculty *Total:* 68, 41% full-time, 40% with terminal degrees. *Student/faculty ratio:* 12:1.

Academics *Calendar:* semesters. *Degrees:* certificates, associate, and bachelor's. *Special study options:* adult/continuing education programs.

Computers on Campus Students can access the following: online (class) registration. Campuswide network is available.

Student Life *Housing:* college housing not available.

Athletics *Intramural sports:* basketball M(c)/W, bowling M/W, football M(c), golf M/W, softball M/W, tennis M/W, volleyball M/W.

Standardized Tests *Required:* SAT or ACT (for admission).

Costs (2011–12) *Tuition:* state resident $12,242 full-time, $495 per credit part-time; nonresident $18,682 full-time, $778 per credit part-time. Full-time tuition and fees vary according to course level, degree level, location, program, and student level. Part-time tuition and fees vary according to course level, course load, degree level, location, program, and student level. *Required fees:* $752 full-time. *Payment plans:* installment, deferred payment. *Waivers:* employees or children of employees.

Financial Aid Of all full-time matriculated undergraduates who enrolled in 2009, 438 applied for aid, 410 were judged to have need, 18 had their need fully met. In 2009, 10 non-need-based awards were made. *Average percent of need met:* 56%. *Average financial aid package:* $10,771. *Average need-based loan:* $3779. *Average need-based gift aid:* $6548. *Average non-need-based aid:* $2569. *Average indebtedness upon graduation:* $31,135.

Applying *Options:* electronic application, early admission, deferred entrance. *Application fee:* $50. *Required:* high school transcript. *Required for some:* interview. *Recommended:* essay or personal statement. *Application deadlines:* rolling (freshmen), rolling (transfers). *Notification:* continuous (freshmen), continuous (transfers).

Freshman Application Contact Admissions Office, Penn State Shenango, 147 Shenango Avenue, Sharon, PA 16146-1537. *Phone:* 724-983-2803. *Fax:* 724-983-2820. *E-mail:* psushenango@psu.edu. *Web site:* http://www.shenango.psu.edu/.

Penn State University Park

State College, Pennsylvania

- **State-related** university, founded 1855, part of Pennsylvania State University
- **Small-town** 8556-acre campus with easy access to Harrisburg
- **Endowment** $1.8 billion
- **Coed** 38,954 undergraduate students, 97% full-time, 46% women, 54% men
- **Very difficult** entrance level, 52% of applicants were admitted

Undergraduates 37,727 full-time, 1,227 part-time. Students come from 56 states and territories; 119 other countries; 29% are from out of state; 4% Black or African American, non-Hispanic/Latino; 5% Hispanic/Latino; 5% Asian, non-Hispanic/Latino; 0.0% Native Hawaiian or other Pacific Islander, non-Hispanic/Latino; 0.1% American Indian or Alaska Native, non-Hispanic/Latino; 2% Two or more races, non-Hispanic/Latino; 2% Race/ethnicity unknown; 7% international; 1% transferred in; 37% live on campus. *Retention:* 92% of full-time freshmen returned.

Freshmen *Admission:* 45,502 applied, 23,855 admitted, 7,366 enrolled. *Average high school GPA:* 3.54. *Test scores:* SAT math scores over 500: 93%; SAT writing scores over 500: 89%; SAT math scores over 600: 61%; SAT writing scores over 600: 47%; SAT math scores over 700: 15%; SAT writing scores over 700: 8%.

Faculty *Total:* 2,880, 86% full-time, 73% with terminal degrees. *Student/faculty ratio:* 17:1.

Academics *Calendar:* semesters. *Degrees:* certificates, associate, bachelor's, master's, doctoral, post-master's, postbachelor's, and first professional certificates. *Special study options:* academic remediation for entering students, accelerated degree program, adult/continuing education programs, advanced placement credit, cooperative education, distance learning, double majors, English as a second language, external degree program, freshman honors college, honors programs, independent study, internships, off-campus study, part-time degree program, services for LD students, student-designed majors, study abroad, summer session for credit. *ROTC:* Army (b), Navy (b), Air Force (b). *Unusual degree programs:* 3-2 engineering; geoscience.

Computers on Campus 6,150 computers/terminals and 23,225 ports are available on campus for general student use. Students can access the following: campus intranet, computer help desk, free student e-mail accounts, online (class) grades, online (class) registration, online (class) schedules. Campuswide network is available. 50% of college-owned or -operated housing units are wired for high-speed Internet access. Wireless service is available via classrooms, computer centers, computer labs, dorm rooms, learning centers, libraries, student centers.

Student Life *Housing:* on-campus residence required for freshman year. *Options:* coed, men-only, women-only, disabled students. Campus housing is university owned. Freshman campus housing is guaranteed. *Activities and organizations:* drama/theater group, student-run newspaper, radio and television station, choral group, marching band, national fraternities, national sororities. *Campus security:* 24-hour emergency response devices and patrols, student patrols, late-night transport/escort service, controlled dormitory access. *Student services:* health clinic, personal/psychological counseling, women's center.

Athletics Member NCAA, USCAA. All Division I except football (Division I-A). *Intercollegiate sports:* archery M(c)/W(c), badminton M(c)/W(c), baseball M(s)/W(c), basketball M(s)/W(s), bowling M(c), cheerleading M/W, cross-country running M(s)/W(s), equestrian sports M(c)/W(c), fencing M(s)/W(s), field hockey W(s), golf M(s)/W(s), gymnastics M(s)/W(s), ice hockey M(c)/W(c), lacrosse M(s)/W(s), rugby M(c)/W(c), skiing (downhill) M(c)/W(c), soccer M(s)/W(s), softball W, swimming and diving M(s)/W(s), table tennis M(c), tennis M(s)/W(s), track and field M(s)/W(s), volleyball M(s)/W(s), water polo M(c)/W(c), weight lifting M(c)/W(c), wrestling M(s). *Intramural sports:* basketball M/W, bowling M/W, crew M(c)/W(c), cross-country running M/W, fencing M(c)/W(c), field hockey W, football M, golf M/W, gymnastics M(c)/W(c), lacrosse M(c)/W(c), racquetball M/W, riflery M(c)/W(c), sailing M(c)/W(c), soccer M/W, softball M/W, squash M/W, tennis M/W, track and field M/W, ultimate Frisbee M(c)/W(c), volleyball M/W, wrestling M.

Standardized Tests *Required:* SAT or ACT (for admission).

Costs (2011–12) *Tuition:* state resident $15,124 full-time, $630 per credit part-time; nonresident $27,206 full-time, $1134 per credit part-time. Full-time tuition and fees vary according to course level, degree level, location, program, and student level. Part-time tuition and fees vary according to course level, course load, degree level, location, program, and student level. *Required fees:* $860 full-time. *Room and board:* $9420; room only: $4770. Room and board charges vary according to board plan, housing facility, and location. *Payment plans:* installment, deferred payment. *Waivers:* employees or children of employees.

Financial Aid Of all full-time matriculated undergraduates who enrolled in 2011, 24,696 applied for aid, 19,805 were judged to have need, 1,505 had their

need fully met. 908 Federal Work-Study jobs (averaging $1891). In 2011, 2733 non-need-based awards were made. *Average percent of need met:* 61%. *Average financial aid package:* $10,242. *Average need-based loan:* $4638. *Average need-based gift aid:* $6462. *Average non-need-based aid:* $3200. *Average indebtedness upon graduation:* $33,530.

Applying *Options:* electronic application, early admission, deferred entrance. *Application fee:* $50. *Required:* high school transcript. *Required for some:* interview. *Recommended:* essay or personal statement. *Application deadlines:* rolling (freshmen), rolling (transfers). *Notification:* continuous (freshmen), continuous (transfers).

Freshman Application Contact Anne L. Rohrbach, Director for Undergraduate Admissions, Penn State University Park, 201 Shields Building, Box 3000, University Park, PA 16804-3000. *Phone:* 814-865-4700. *Fax:* 814-863-7590. *E-mail:* admissions@psu.edu. *Web site:* http://www.psu.edu/.

Penn State Wilkes-Barre

Lehman, Pennsylvania

- **State-related** primarily 2-year, founded 1916, part of Pennsylvania State University
- **Rural** campus
- **Coed** 678 undergraduate students, 85% full-time, 35% women, 65% men
- **Moderately difficult** entrance level, 88% of applicants were admitted

Undergraduates 579 full-time, 99 part-time. 6% are from out of state; 5% Black or African American, non-Hispanic/Latino; 3% Hispanic/Latino; 2% Asian, non-Hispanic/Latino; 0.3% American Indian or Alaska Native, non-Hispanic/Latino; 2% Two or more races, non-Hispanic/Latino; 0.8% Race/ethnicity unknown; 0.5% international; 6% transferred in. *Retention:* 73% of full-time freshmen returned.

Freshmen *Admission:* 549 applied, 482 admitted, 191 enrolled. *Average high school GPA:* 3.01. *Test scores:* SAT critical reading scores over 500: 46%; SAT math scores over 500: 53%; SAT writing scores over 500: 36%; SAT critical reading scores over 600: 10%; SAT math scores over 600: 15%; SAT writing scores over 600: 5%; SAT critical reading scores over 700: 1%; SAT math scores over 700: 2%.

Faculty *Total:* 57, 60% full-time, 49% with terminal degrees. *Student/faculty ratio:* 15:1.

Academics *Calendar:* semesters. *Degrees:* certificates, associate, and bachelor's (enrollment figures include students enrolled at The Graduate School at Penn State who are taking courses at this location). *Special study options:* adult/continuing education programs. *ROTC:* Army (c), Air Force (c).

Computers on Campus Students can access the following: online (class) registration. Campuswide network is available.

Student Life *Housing:* college housing not available.

Athletics Member NJCAA. *Intercollegiate sports:* baseball M, basketball M, cross-country running M/W, golf M/W, soccer M/W, volleyball W. *Intramural sports:* basketball M/W, bowling M(c)/W(c), cheerleading M(c)/W(c), football M, racquetball M/W, softball W, volleyball M(c)/W.

Standardized Tests *Required:* SAT or ACT (for admission).

Costs (2011–12) *Tuition:* state resident $12,242 full-time, $495 per credit part-time; nonresident $18,682 full-time, $778 per credit part-time. Full-time tuition and fees vary according to course level, degree level, location, program, and student level. Part-time tuition and fees vary according to course level, course load, degree level, location, program, and student level. *Required fees:* $752 full-time. *Payment plans:* installment, deferred payment. *Waivers:* employees or children of employees.

Financial Aid Of all full-time matriculated undergraduates who enrolled in 2009, 495 applied for aid, 408 were judged to have need, 16 had their need fully met. In 2009, 40 non-need-based awards were made. *Average percent of need met:* 59%. *Average financial aid package:* $9495. *Average need-based loan:* $3920. *Average need-based gift aid:* $6367. *Average non-need-based aid:* $2415. *Average indebtedness upon graduation:* $31,135.

Applying *Options:* electronic application, early admission, deferred entrance. *Application fee:* $50. *Required:* high school transcript. *Required for some:* interview. *Recommended:* essay or personal statement. *Application deadlines:* rolling (freshmen), rolling (transfers). *Notification:* continuous (freshmen), continuous (transfers).

Freshman Application Contact Admissions Office, Penn State Wilkes-Barre, PO PSU, Lehman, PA 18627-0217. *Phone:* 570-675-9238. *Fax:* 570-675-9113. *E-mail:* wbadmissions@psu.edu. *Web site:* http://www.wb.psu.edu/.

Penn State Worthington Scranton

Dunmore, Pennsylvania

- **State-related** primarily 2-year, founded 1923, part of Pennsylvania State University
- **Small-town** campus
- **Coed** 1,270 undergraduate students, 80% full-time, 51% women, 49% men
- **Moderately difficult** entrance level, 82% of applicants were admitted

Undergraduates 1,011 full-time, 259 part-time. 2% are from out of state; 1% Black or African American, non-Hispanic/Latino; 4% Hispanic/Latino; 4% Asian, non-Hispanic/Latino; 0.2% American Indian or Alaska Native, non-Hispanic/Latino; 1% Two or more races, non-Hispanic/Latino; 2% Race/ethnicity unknown; 0.2% international; 3% transferred in. *Retention:* 71% of full-time freshmen returned.

Freshmen *Admission:* 799 applied, 653 admitted, 318 enrolled. *Average high school GPA:* 2.83. *Test scores:* SAT critical reading scores over 500: 38%; SAT math scores over 500: 41%; SAT writing scores over 500: 29%; SAT critical reading scores over 600: 7%; SAT math scores over 600: 6%; SAT writing scores over 600: 3%; SAT critical reading scores over 700: 1%.

Faculty *Total:* 100, 52% full-time, 40% with terminal degrees. *Student/faculty ratio:* 16:1.

Academics *Calendar:* semesters. *Degrees:* certificates, associate, and bachelor's. *Special study options:* adult/continuing education programs. *ROTC:* Army (c), Air Force (c).

Computers on Campus Students can access the following: online (class) registration. Campuswide network is available.

Student Life *Housing:* college housing not available.

Athletics Member NJCAA. *Intercollegiate sports:* baseball M, basketball M/W, cheerleading M/W, cross-country running M/W, soccer M, softball W, volleyball W. *Intramural sports:* basketball M/W, bowling M(c)/W(c), skiing (downhill) M(c)/W(c), soccer M/W, softball M/W, volleyball M/W(c), weight lifting M(c)/W(c).

Standardized Tests *Required:* SAT or ACT (for admission).

Costs (2011–12) *Tuition:* state resident $12,242 full-time, $495 per credit part-time; nonresident $18,682 full-time, $778 per credit part-time. Full-time tuition and fees vary according to course level, degree level, location, program, and student level. Part-time tuition and fees vary according to course level, course load, degree level, location, program, and student level. *Required fees:* $724 full-time. *Payment plans:* installment, deferred payment. *Waivers:* employees or children of employees.

Financial Aid Of all full-time matriculated undergraduates who enrolled in 2009, 904 applied for aid, 760 were judged to have need, 26 had their need fully met. In 2009, 54 non-need-based awards were made. *Average percent of need met:* 59%. *Average financial aid package:* $9067. *Average need-based loan:* $3888. *Average need-based gift aid:* $6009. *Average non-need-based aid:* $2838. *Average indebtedness upon graduation:* $31,135.

Applying *Options:* electronic application, early admission, deferred entrance. *Application fee:* $50. *Required:* high school transcript. *Required for some:* interview. *Recommended:* essay or personal statement. *Application deadlines:* rolling (freshmen), rolling (transfers). *Notification:* continuous (freshmen), continuous (transfers).

Freshman Application Contact Admissions Office, Penn State Worthington Scranton, 120 Ridge View Drive, Dunmore, PA 18512-1699. *Phone:* 570-963-2500. *Fax:* 570-963-2524. *E-mail:* wsadmissions@psu.edu. *Web site:* http://www.sn.psu.edu/.

Penn State York

York, Pennsylvania

- **State-related** primarily 2-year, founded 1926, part of Pennsylvania State University
- **Suburban** campus
- **Coed** 1,259 undergraduate students, 68% full-time, 44% women, 56% men
- **Moderately difficult** entrance level, 79% of applicants were admitted

Undergraduates 862 full-time, 397 part-time. 9% are from out of state; 8% Black or African American, non-Hispanic/Latino; 6% Hispanic/Latino; 5% Asian, non-Hispanic/Latino; 0.2% American Indian or Alaska Native, non-Hispanic/Latino; 3% Two or more races, non-Hispanic/Latino; 2% Race/ethnicity unknown; 4% international; 4% transferred in. *Retention:* 77% of full-time freshmen returned.

Freshmen *Admission:* 1,200 applied, 947 admitted, 282 enrolled. *Average high school GPA:* 2.92. *Test scores:* SAT critical reading scores over 500: 41%; SAT math scores over 500: 50%; SAT writing scores over 500: 34%; SAT critical reading scores over 600: 9%; SAT math scores over 600: 13%; SAT writing scores over 600: 8%; SAT critical reading scores over 700: 2%; SAT math scores over 700: 2%.

Faculty *Total:* 110, 51% full-time, 45% with terminal degrees. *Student/faculty ratio:* 14:1.

Academics *Calendar:* semesters. *Degrees:* certificates, associate, bachelor's, and master's (also offers up to 2 years of most bachelor's degree programs offered at University Park campus). *Special study options:* adult/continuing education programs.

Computers on Campus Students can access the following: online (class) registration. Campuswide network is available.

Student Life *Housing:* college housing not available.

Athletics Member NJCAA.

Standardized Tests *Required:* SAT or ACT (for admission).

Costs (2011–12) *Tuition:* state resident $12,242 full-time, $495 per credit part-time; nonresident $18,682 full-time, $778 per credit part-time. Full-time tuition and fees vary according to course level, degree level, location, program, and student level. Part-time tuition and fees vary according to course level, course load, degree level, location, program, and student level. *Required fees:* $724 full-time. *Payment plans:* installment, deferred payment. *Waivers:* employees or children of employees.

Financial Aid Of all full-time matriculated undergraduates who enrolled in 2009, 758 applied for aid, 597 were judged to have need, 33 had their need fully met. In 2009, 59 non-need-based awards were made. *Average percent of need met:* 58%. *Average financial aid package:* $9160. *Average need-based loan:* $3819. *Average need-based gift aid:* $5905. *Average non-need-based aid:* $2670. *Average indebtedness upon graduation:* $31,135.

Applying *Options:* electronic application, early admission, deferred entrance. *Application fee:* $50. *Required:* high school transcript. *Required for some:* interview. *Recommended:* essay or personal statement. *Application deadlines:* rolling (freshmen), rolling (transfers). *Notification:* continuous (freshmen), continuous (transfers).

Freshman Application Contact Admissions Office, Penn State York, 1031 Edgecomb Avenue, York, PA 17403-3398. *Phone:* 717-771-4040. *Toll-free phone:* 800-778-6227. *Fax:* 717-771-4005. *E-mail:* ykadmission@psu.edu. *Web site:* http://www.yk.psu.edu/.

Pennsylvania College of Art & Design
Lancaster, Pennsylvania

- **Independent** 4-year, founded 1982
- **Urban** campus with easy access to Philadelphia, Baltimore
- **Coed** 257 undergraduate students, 93% full-time, 66% women, 34% men
- **Moderately difficult** entrance level, 39% of applicants were admitted

Undergraduates 238 full-time, 19 part-time. Students come from 12 states and territories; 23% are from out of state; 4% Black or African American, non-Hispanic/Latino; 5% Hispanic/Latino; 2% Asian, non-Hispanic/Latino; 5% Two or more races, non-Hispanic/Latino; 6% Race/ethnicity unknown; 4% transferred in. *Retention:* 66% of full-time freshmen returned.

Freshmen *Admission:* 357 applied, 140 admitted, 64 enrolled. *Average high school GPA:* 3.01.

Faculty *Total:* 53, 28% full-time. *Student/faculty ratio:* 10:1.

Academics *Calendar:* semesters. *Degree:* certificates and bachelor's. *Special study options:* advanced placement credit, internships.

Computers on Campus 74 computers/terminals are available on campus for general student use. Students can access the following: campus intranet, computer help desk, free student e-mail accounts, online (class) grades, online (class) schedules. Campuswide network is available. Wireless service is available via entire campus.

Student Life *Housing:* college housing not available. *Activities and organizations:* Student Council, Anime Club, Student AIGA, Society of Illustrators - Student Group. *Campus security:* late-night transport/escort service, trained evening/weekend security personnel.

Standardized Tests *Recommended:* SAT (for admission), ACT (for admission).

Costs (2011–12) *Tuition:* $18,000 full-time, $750 per credit part-time. Part-time tuition and fees vary according to course load. *Required fees:* $980 full-time, $750 per credit part-time. *Payment plan:* installment. *Waivers:* employees or children of employees.

Applying *Options:* electronic application, deferred entrance. *Application fee:* $40. *Required:* essay or personal statement, high school transcript, minimum 2.5 GPA, interview, portfolio. *Required for some:* 2 letters of recommendation. *Application deadlines:* rolling (freshmen), rolling (transfers). *Notification:* continuous (freshmen), continuous (transfers).

Freshman Application Contact Admissions Department, Pennsylvania College of Art & Design, 204 North Prince Street, PO Box 59, Lancaster, PA 17608. *Phone:* 717-396-7833. *Fax:* 717-396-1339. *E-mail:* admissions@pcad.edu. *Web site:* http://www.pcad.edu/.

Pennsylvania College of Technology
Williamsport, Pennsylvania

- **State-related** 4-year, founded 1965
- **Small-town** 997-acre campus
- **Coed** 5,976 undergraduate students, 83% full-time, 37% women, 63% men
- **Noncompetitive** entrance level, 92% of applicants were admitted

Undergraduates 4,965 full-time, 1,011 part-time. Students come from 32 states and territories; 15 other countries; 10% are from out of state; 4% Black or African American, non-Hispanic/Latino; 2% Hispanic/Latino; 0.7% Asian, non-Hispanic/Latino; 0.2% Native Hawaiian or other Pacific Islander, non-Hispanic/Latino; 0.3% American Indian or Alaska Native, non-Hispanic/Latino; 1% Two or more races, non-Hispanic/Latino; 6% Race/ethnicity unknown; 0.6% international; 10% transferred in; 29% live on campus. *Retention:* 66% of full-time freshmen returned.

Freshmen *Admission:* 3,384 applied, 3,112 admitted, 1,228 enrolled.

Faculty *Total:* 480, 62% full-time. *Student/faculty ratio:* 18:1.

Academics *Calendar:* semesters. *Degrees:* certificates, associate, and bachelor's. *Special study options:* academic remediation for entering students, advanced placement credit, cooperative education, distance learning, English as a second language, independent study, internships, off-campus study, part-time degree program, services for LD students, student-designed majors, study abroad, summer session for credit. *ROTC:* Army (c).

Computers on Campus 1,794 computers/terminals are available on campus for general student use. Students can access the following: campus intranet, computer help desk, free student e-mail accounts, online (class) grades, online (class) registration, online (class) schedules. Campuswide network is available. 100% of college-owned or -operated housing units are wired for high-speed Internet access. Wireless service is available via entire campus.

Student Life *Housing options:* coed, disabled students. Campus housing is university owned. *Activities and organizations:* student-run radio station, Student Government Association, Residence Hall Association, Wildcats Event Board, Association of Computing Machinery, Campus Crusade for Christ, national fraternities. *Campus security:* 24-hour emergency response devices and patrols, late-night transport/escort service, controlled dormitory access. *Student services:* health clinic, personal/psychological counseling.

Athletics Member USCAA. *Intercollegiate sports:* archery M/W, baseball M, basketball M/W, bowling M/W, cross-country running M/W, golf M/W, soccer M/W, softball W, tennis M/W, volleyball M/W, wrestling M. *Intramural sports:* archery M/W, badminton M/W, basketball M/W, bowling M/W, football M/W, golf M/W, lacrosse M/W, racquetball M/W, soccer M/W, softball M/W, table tennis M/W, tennis M/W, ultimate Frisbee M/W, volleyball M/W, weight lifting M/W.

Standardized Tests *Required for some:* SAT (for admission).

Costs (2011–12) *Tuition:* state resident $11,370 full-time, $379 per credit part-time; nonresident $14,790 full-time, $493 per credit part-time. Full-time tuition and fees vary according to course load and program. Part-time tuition and fees vary according to course load and program. *Required fees:* $2220 full-time, $74 per credit part-time. *Room and board:* $9766; room only: $5666. Room and board charges vary according to board plan and housing facility. *Payment plan:* deferred payment. *Waivers:* employees or children of employees.

Financial Aid Of all full-time matriculated undergraduates who enrolled in 2010, 4,654 applied for aid, 4,606 were judged to have need. 158 Federal Work-Study jobs (averaging $1538). *Average financial aid package:* $8606. *Average need-based loan:* $3622. *Average need-based gift aid:* $6969.

Applying *Options:* electronic application, early admission, deferred entrance. *Application fee:* $50. *Required:* high school transcript. *Required for some:* college transcripts if transfer applicant. *Application deadlines:* 7/1 (freshmen), rolling (transfers).

Freshman Application Contact Mr. Dennis L. Correll, Associate Dean for Admissions/Financial Aid, Pennsylvania College of Technology, One College Avenue, DIF #119, Williamsport, PA 17701. *Phone:* 570-327-4761 Ext. 7337. *Toll-free phone:* 800-367-9222. *Fax:* 570-321-5551. *E-mail:* admissions@pct.edu. *Web site:* http://www.pct.edu/.

Philadelphia Biblical University
Langhorne, Pennsylvania

- **Independent nondenominational** comprehensive, founded 1913
- **Suburban** 105-acre campus with easy access to Philadelphia
- **Endowment** $9.6 million
- **Coed** 941 undergraduate students, 92% full-time, 53% women, 47% men
- **Moderately difficult** entrance level, 74% of applicants were admitted

Undergraduates 867 full-time, 74 part-time. Students come from 33 states and territories; 32 other countries; 44% are from out of state; 14% Black or African American, non-Hispanic/Latino; 5% Hispanic/Latino; 4% Asian, non-

Hispanic/Latino; 0.5% American Indian or Alaska Native, non-Hispanic/Latino; 2% Two or more races, non-Hispanic/Latino; 0.5% Race/ethnicity unknown; 2% international; 10% transferred in; 58% live on campus. *Retention:* 78% of full-time freshmen returned.

Freshmen *Admission:* 482 applied, 358 admitted, 148 enrolled. *Average high school GPA:* 3.3. *Test scores:* SAT critical reading scores over 500: 62%; SAT math scores over 500: 64%; ACT scores over 18: 72%; SAT critical reading scores over 600: 23%; SAT math scores over 600: 22%; ACT scores over 24: 44%; SAT critical reading scores over 700: 5%; SAT math scores over 700: 2%.

Faculty *Total:* 128, 39% full-time, 39% with terminal degrees. *Student/faculty ratio:* 13:1.

Academics *Calendar:* semesters. *Degrees:* certificates, bachelor's, master's, and postbachelor's certificates. *Special study options:* academic remediation for entering students, accelerated degree program, adult/continuing education programs, advanced placement credit, double majors, honors programs, internships, off-campus study, part-time degree program, services for LD students, study abroad, summer session for credit. *ROTC:* Air Force (c).

Computers on Campus 79 computers/terminals are available on campus for general student use. Students can access the following: campus intranet, computer help desk, free student e-mail accounts, online (class) grades, online (class) registration, online (class) schedules. Campuswide network is available. 100% of college-owned or -operated housing units are wired for high-speed Internet access. Wireless service is available via classrooms, computer labs, dorm rooms, learning centers, libraries.

Student Life *Housing:* on-campus residence required through senior year. *Options:* men-only, women-only, disabled students. Campus housing is university owned and leased by the school. Freshman campus housing is guaranteed. *Activities and organizations:* drama/theater group, student-run newspaper, choral group, Student Senate, Chi Beta Sigma (Social Work Club), Students in Free Enterprise, Student Missionary Fellowship, Culture & Arts Association. *Campus security:* 24-hour emergency response devices and patrols, student patrols, late-night transport/escort service, controlled dormitory access. *Student services:* health clinic, personal/psychological counseling.

Athletics Member NCAA, NCCAA. All NCAA Division III. *Intercollegiate sports:* baseball M, basketball M/W, cross-country running M/W, golf M, soccer M/W, softball W, tennis W, volleyball M/W. *Intramural sports:* basketball M/W, soccer M/W, tennis M/W, ultimate Frisbee M/W, volleyball M/W.

Standardized Tests *Required:* SAT or ACT (for admission).

Costs (2012–13) *Comprehensive fee:* $30,230 includes full-time tuition ($21,500), mandatory fees ($205), and room and board ($8525). Full-time tuition and fees vary according to course load and location. Part-time tuition: $638 per credit. Part-time tuition and fees vary according to course load and location. *College room only:* $4500. Room and board charges vary according to board plan and location. *Payment plan:* installment. *Waivers:* employees or children of employees.

Financial Aid Of all full-time matriculated undergraduates who enrolled in 2011, 758 applied for aid, 707 were judged to have need, 53 had their need fully met. 124 Federal Work-Study jobs. In 2011, 122 non-need-based awards were made. *Average percent of need met:* 68%. *Average financial aid package:* $17,009. *Average need-based loan:* $5154. *Average need-based gift aid:* $12,324. *Average non-need-based aid:* $7424. *Average indebtedness upon graduation:* $32,725.

Applying *Options:* electronic application, early admission, deferred entrance. *Application fee:* $25. *Required:* essay or personal statement, high school transcript, minimum 2.0 GPA. *Required for some:* interview. *Recommended:* interview. *Application deadlines:* rolling (freshmen), rolling (out-of-state freshmen), rolling (transfers). *Notification:* continuous (freshmen), continuous (out-of-state freshmen), continuous (transfers).

Freshman Application Contact Mr. Eric Rivera, Interim Director of Undergraduate Admissions, Philadelphia Biblical University, 200 Manor Avenue, Langhorne, PA 19047. *Phone:* 215-702-4250. *Toll-free phone:* 800-RUN-2-PBU. *Fax:* 215-702-4248. *E-mail:* admissions@pbu.edu. *Web site:* http://www.pbu.edu/.

Philadelphia University
Philadelphia, Pennsylvania

- **Independent** comprehensive, founded 1884
- **Suburban** 100-acre campus
- **Coed** 2,960 undergraduate students, 93% full-time, 65% women, 35% men
- **Moderately difficult** entrance level, 71% of applicants were admitted

Undergraduates 2,766 full-time, 194 part-time. 48% are from out of state; 11% Black or African American, non-Hispanic/Latino; 6% Hispanic/Latino; 4% Asian, non-Hispanic/Latino; 0.1% Native Hawaiian or other Pacific Islander, non-Hispanic/Latino; 0.2% American Indian or Alaska Native, non-Hispanic/Latino; 2% Two or more races, non-Hispanic/Latino; 9% Race/ethnicity unknown; 2% international; 5% transferred in; 49% live on campus. *Retention:* 71% of full-time freshmen returned.

Philadelphia University

Philadelphia University, founded in 1884, is a private university with 3,500 students enrolled in more than 60 undergraduate and graduate programs. As part of its core mission, the University focuses on professionally oriented programs that prepare students for successful careers, with a strong foundation in the liberal arts and an orientation toward interdisciplinary collaboration. Philadelphia University includes Schools of Architecture, Business Administration, Design and Engineering, Liberal Arts, and Science and Health.

PHILADELPHIA UNIVERSITY
Powered to Do
4201 Henry Avenue
Philadelphia, PA 19144-5497

Undergraduate Majors

Business
  Accounting+
  Finance+
  International Business+
  Management+
  Marketing+
Animation
Architecture *(five-year B.Arch)*
Biochemistry
Biology
Biopsychology
Chemistry
Construction Management
Engineering*
Environmental & Conservation Biology
Environmental Design and Visual Studies
  Architectural Design and Technology+
  Historic Preservation+
  Photography and New Media+
Environmental Sustainability
Fashion Design

Fashion Merchandising and Management
  Fashion Merchandising+
  Fashion Industry Management+
Graphic Design Communication
Health Sciences
Health Sciences/Occupational Therapy
  (joint B.S./M.S.)
Industrial Design
Interactive Design and Media
Interior Design
Landscape Architecture
Law and Society
Mechanical Engineering
Physician Assistant Studies
  (five-year B.S./M.S.)
Pre-Medical Studies
Professional Communication
Psychology
Psychology/Occupational Therapy *(joint B.S./M.S.)*
Textile Design
Textile Materials Technology

Engineering minors available: Architectural, Composites, Industrial, Textile
+ *denotes academic concentration*

Freshmen *Admission:* 4,136 applied, 2,929 admitted, 649 enrolled. *Average high school GPA:* 3.5. *Test scores:* SAT critical reading scores over 500: 65%; SAT math scores over 500: 77%; SAT writing scores over 500: 63%; SAT critical reading scores over 600: 17%; SAT math scores over 600: 27%; SAT writing scores over 600: 17%; SAT critical reading scores over 700: 3%; SAT math scores over 700: 2%; SAT writing scores over 700: 1%.

Faculty *Total:* 499, 23% full-time, 17% with terminal degrees. *Student/faculty ratio:* 13:1.

Academics *Calendar:* semesters. *Degrees:* certificates, associate, bachelor's, master's, doctoral, post-master's, postbachelor's, and first professional certificates. *Special study options:* adult/continuing education programs, part-time degree program.

Computers on Campus Students can access the following: online (class) registration. Campuswide network is available.

Student Life *Housing options:* coed, women-only, disabled students. Campus housing is university owned and leased by the school. Freshman campus housing is guaranteed. *Campus security:* 24-hour emergency response devices and patrols, late-night transport/escort service, controlled dormitory access.

Athletics Member NCAA. All Division II except soccer (Division I). *Intercollegiate sports:* baseball M(s), basketball M(s)/W(s), field hockey W(s), golf M(s), lacrosse W(s), soccer M(s)/W(s), softball W(s), tennis M(s)/W(s), volleyball W(s). *Intramural sports:* basketball M/W, cross-country running M/W, football M, skiing (downhill) M(c)/W(c), soccer M/W, softball M/W, swimming and diving M/W, table tennis M/W, tennis M/W, volleyball M/W, weight lifting M/W.

Standardized Tests *Required:* SAT or ACT (for admission).

Costs (2011–12) *Comprehensive fee:* $40,280 includes full-time tuition ($30,356), mandatory fees ($90), and room and board ($9834). Full-time tuition and fees vary according to degree level and program. Part-time tuition: $530 per credit hour. Part-time tuition and fees vary according to class time, course load, degree level, program, and reciprocity agreements. *College room only:* $4862. Room and board charges vary according to board plan and housing facility. *Payment plans:* installment, deferred payment. *Waivers:* employees or children of employees.

Financial Aid Of all full-time matriculated undergraduates who enrolled in 2010, 2,352 applied for aid, 2,093 were judged to have need, 189 had their need fully met. In 2010, 612 non-need-based awards were made. *Average percent of need met:* 76%. *Average financial aid package:* $23,477. *Average need-based loan:* $4730. *Average need-based gift aid:* $15,034. *Average non-need-based aid:* $6439. *Average indebtedness upon graduation:* $32,337. *Financial aid deadline:* 4/15.

Applying *Options:* electronic application, deferred entrance. *Application fee:* $40. *Required:* high school transcript. *Recommended:* essay or personal statement, 2 letters of recommendation, interview. *Application deadlines:* rolling (freshmen), rolling (transfers). *Notification:* continuous (freshmen).

Freshman Application Contact Ms. Christine Greb, Director of Admissions, Philadelphia University, School House Lane and Henry Avenue, Philadelphia, PA 19144-5497. *Phone:* 215-951-2800. *Fax:* 215-951-2907. *E-mail:* admissions@philau.edu. *Web site:* http://www.philau.edu/.

See page 801 for display ad and page 1502 for the College Close-Up.

Point Park University

Pittsburgh, Pennsylvania

- **Independent** comprehensive, founded 1960
- **Urban** campus
- **Endowment** $26.3 million
- **Coed** 3,382 undergraduate students, 78% full-time, 58% women, 42% men
- **Moderately difficult** entrance level, 75% of applicants were admitted

Undergraduates 2,639 full-time, 743 part-time. Students come from 47 states and territories; 23 other countries; 20% are from out of state; 18% Black or African American, non-Hispanic/Latino; 3% Hispanic/Latino; 0.7% Asian, non-Hispanic/Latino; 0.1% Native Hawaiian or other Pacific Islander, non-Hispanic/Latino; 0.2% American Indian or Alaska Native, non-Hispanic/Latino; 3% Two or more races, non-Hispanic/Latino; 0.6% Race/ethnicity unknown; 1% international; 15% transferred in; 25% live on campus. *Retention:* 75% of full-time freshmen returned.

Freshmen *Admission:* 3,357 applied, 2,503 admitted, 491 enrolled. *Average high school GPA:* 3.22. *Test scores:* SAT critical reading scores over 500: 61%; SAT math scores over 500: 47%; SAT writing scores over 500: 53%; ACT scores over 18: 93%; SAT critical reading scores over 600: 16%; SAT math scores over 600: 10%; SAT writing scores over 600: 13%; ACT scores over 24: 32%; SAT critical reading scores over 700: 2%; SAT math scores over 700: 1%; SAT writing scores over 700: 1%; ACT scores over 30: 6%.

Faculty *Total:* 433, 30% full-time. *Student/faculty ratio:* 14:1.

Academics *Calendar:* semesters. *Degrees:* certificates, associate, bachelor's, master's, and postbachelor's certificates. *Special study options:* academic

remediation for entering students, accelerated degree program, adult/continuing education programs, advanced placement credit, cooperative education, distance learning, double majors, English as a second language, honors programs, independent study, internships, off-campus study, part-time degree program, services for LD students, student-designed majors, study abroad, summer session for credit. *ROTC:* Army (c), Air Force (c).

Computers on Campus 262 computers/terminals and 112 ports are available on campus for general student use. Students can access the following: campus intranet, computer help desk, free student e-mail accounts, online (class) grades, online (class) registration, online (class) schedules. Campuswide network is available. 100% of college-owned or -operated housing units are wired for high-speed Internet access. Wireless service is available via classrooms, computer labs, libraries, student centers.

Student Life *Housing options:* coed, women-only, disabled students. Campus housing is university owned and leased by the school. Freshman campus housing is guaranteed. *Activities and organizations:* drama/theater group, student-run newspaper, radio and television station, Black Student Union, student radio station, Dance Club, The Body Christian Fellowship, College Students in Broadcasting. *Campus security:* 24-hour emergency response devices and patrols, late-night transport/escort service, controlled dormitory access, 24-hour security desk, video security. *Student services:* personal/psychological counseling.

Athletics Member NAIA. *Intercollegiate sports:* baseball M(s), basketball M(s)/W(s), cross-country running M(s)/W(s), golf M(s)/W(s), soccer M(s)/W(s), softball W(s), volleyball W(s). *Intramural sports:* basketball M, bowling M/W, football M, golf M, tennis M/W, volleyball M/W, weight lifting M/W.

Standardized Tests *Required:* SAT or ACT (for admission).

Costs (2011–12) *Comprehensive fee:* $33,440 includes full-time tuition ($22,900), mandatory fees ($820), and room and board ($9720). Full-time tuition and fees vary according to program. Part-time tuition: $650 per credit. Part-time tuition and fees vary according to program. *Required fees:* $35 per credit part-time. *College room only:* $4620. Room and board charges vary according to board plan and housing facility. *Payment plans:* installment, deferred payment. *Waivers:* employees or children of employees.

Financial Aid Of all full-time matriculated undergraduates who enrolled in 2011, 2,629 applied for aid, 2,407 were judged to have need, 299 had their need fully met. 246 Federal Work-Study jobs (averaging $2102). 269 state and other part-time jobs (averaging $3151). In 2011, 179 non-need-based awards were made. *Average percent of need met:* 62%. *Average financial aid package:* $16,469. *Average need-based loan:* $5088. *Average need-based gift aid:* $11,766. *Average non-need-based aid:* $7893. *Average indebtedness upon graduation:* $19,779. *Financial aid deadline:* 3/15.

Applying *Options:* electronic application, early admission, deferred entrance. *Application fee:* $40. *Required:* high school transcript. *Required for some:* 2 letters of recommendation, interview, audition. *Recommended:* essay or personal statement, minimum 2.5 GPA. *Application deadlines:* rolling (freshmen), rolling (transfers). *Notification:* continuous (freshmen), continuous (transfers).

Freshman Application Contact Point Park University, 201 Wood Street, Pittsburgh, PA 15222-1984. *Phone:* 412-392-3430. *Toll-free phone:* 800-321-0129. *Web site:* http://www.pointpark.edu/.

The Restaurant School at Walnut Hill College

Philadelphia, Pennsylvania

- **Proprietary** primarily 2-year, founded 1974
- **Urban** 2-acre campus
- **Coed** 402 undergraduate students, 100% full-time, 56% women, 44% men
- **97%** of applicants were admitted

Undergraduates 402 full-time. Students come from 4 other countries; 29% are from out of state; 14% Black or African American, non-Hispanic/Latino; 4% Hispanic/Latino; 2% Asian, non-Hispanic/Latino; 1% Two or more races, non-Hispanic/Latino; 32% Race/ethnicity unknown; 10% transferred in.

Freshmen *Admission:* 174 applied, 168 admitted, 278 enrolled.

Faculty *Total:* 19, 95% full-time. *Student/faculty ratio:* 22:1.

Academics *Calendar:* quarters. *Degrees:* associate and bachelor's. *Special study options:* internships, part-time degree program.

Computers on Campus 60 computers/terminals are available on campus for general student use. Students can access the following: campus intranet, computer help desk, free student e-mail accounts, online (class) grades, online (class) schedules, All students receive an IPad. Campuswide network is available. 100% of college-owned or -operated housing units are wired for high-speed Internet access. Wireless service is available via entire campus.

Student Life *Housing options:* coed. Campus housing is leased by the school. *Activities and organizations:* Wine Club, Book Club, Coffee & Tea Club, Craft

Club, Flair Bartending. *Campus security:* 24-hour emergency response devices and patrols, student patrols, controlled dormitory access.

Standardized Tests *Recommended:* SAT or ACT (for admission).

Costs (2012–13) *One-time required fee:* $200. *Tuition:* $17,850 full-time. *Required fees:* $3750 full-time. *Room only:* $4600. Room and board charges vary according to housing facility. *Payment plans:* installment, deferred payment.

Applying *Options:* electronic application, early admission, early decision, deferred entrance. *Application fee:* $50. *Required:* essay or personal statement, high school transcript, 2 letters of recommendation, interview. *Required for some:* entrance exam. *Recommended:* minimum 2.0 GPA. *Application deadline:* rolling (freshmen).

Freshman Application Contact Miss Toni Morelli, Director of Admissions, The Restaurant School at Walnut Hill College, 4207 Walnut Street, Philadelphia, PA 19104-3518. *Phone:* 267-295-2353. *Fax:* 215-222-4219. *E-mail:* tmorelli@walnuthillcollege.edu. *Web site:* http://www.walnuthillcollege.edu/.

Robert Morris University

Moon Township, Pennsylvania

- **Independent** university, founded 1921
- **Suburban** 230-acre campus with easy access to Pittsburgh
- **Endowment** $26.4 million
- **Coed** 3,921 undergraduate students, 89% full-time, 45% women, 55% men
- **Minimally difficult** entrance level, 79% of applicants were admitted

Undergraduates 3,474 full-time, 447 part-time. Students come from 38 states and territories; 39 other countries; 15% are from out of state; 8% Black or African American, non-Hispanic/Latino; 2% Hispanic/Latino; 1% Asian, non-Hispanic/Latino; 0.1% Native Hawaiian or other Pacific Islander, non-Hispanic/Latino; 0.2% American Indian or Alaska Native, non-Hispanic/Latino; 0.7% Two or more races, non-Hispanic/Latino; 6% Race/ethnicity unknown; 3% international; 9% transferred in; 43% live on campus. *Retention:* 81% of full-time freshmen returned.

Freshmen *Admission:* 5,354 applied, 4,233 admitted, 787 enrolled. *Average high school GPA:* 3.35. *Test scores:* SAT critical reading scores over 500: 50%; SAT math scores over 500: 60%; SAT writing scores over 500: 45%; ACT scores over 18: 98%; SAT critical reading scores over 600: 11%; SAT math scores over 600: 17%; SAT writing scores over 600: 9%; ACT scores over 24: 33%; SAT critical reading scores over 700: 1%; SAT math scores over 700: 1%; SAT writing scores over 700: 1%; ACT scores over 30: 5%.

Faculty *Total:* 409, 47% full-time, 58% with terminal degrees. *Student/faculty ratio:* 15:1.

Academics *Calendar:* semesters. *Degrees:* certificates, bachelor's, master's, doctoral, and postbachelor's certificates. *Special study options:* academic remediation for entering students, accelerated degree program, adult/continuing education programs, advanced placement credit, cooperative education, distance learning, double majors, honors programs, independent study, internships, off-campus study, part-time degree program, services for LD students, study abroad, summer session for credit. *ROTC:* Army (b), Air Force (c).

Computers on Campus 300 computers/terminals are available on campus for general student use. Students can access the following: campus intranet, computer help desk, free student e-mail accounts, online (class) grades, online (class) registration, online (class) schedules, online payment. Campuswide network is available. 100% of college-owned or -operated housing units are wired for high-speed Internet access. Wireless service is available via classrooms, computer centers, computer labs, learning centers, libraries, student centers.

Student Life *Housing:* on-campus residence required for freshman year. *Options:* coed, men-only, women-only, disabled students. Campus housing is university owned. Freshman applicants given priority for college housing. *Activities and organizations:* drama/theater group, student-run newspaper, radio and television station, choral group, marching band, Student Government Association, Residence Hall Association, R-MOVE, National Society of Collegiate Scholars, Black Student Union, national fraternities, national sororities. *Campus security:* 24-hour emergency response devices and patrols, late-night transport/escort service, controlled dormitory access. *Student services:* health clinic, personal/psychological counseling.

Athletics Member NCAA. All Division I. *Intercollegiate sports:* baseball M(c), basketball M(s)/W(s), cheerleading M(c)/W(c), crew W(s), field hockey W(s), football M(s), golf M(s)/W(s), ice hockey M(s)/W(s), lacrosse M(s)/W(s), soccer M(s)/W(s), softball W(s), tennis M(s)/W(s), track and field M(s)/W(s), volleyball W(s). *Intramural sports:* basketball M/W, bowling M(c)/W(c), football M, ice hockey M(c), rugby M(c), softball M/W, volleyball M(c)/W.

Standardized Tests *Required:* SAT or ACT (for admission).

Costs (2011–12) *Comprehensive fee:* $34,068 includes full-time tuition ($22,405), mandatory fees ($633), and room and board ($11,030). Full-time tuition and fees vary according to degree level and program. Part-time tuition: $745 per credit hour. Part-time tuition and fees vary according to course load, degree level, and program. *Required fees:* $30 per credit hour part-time. *Col-*

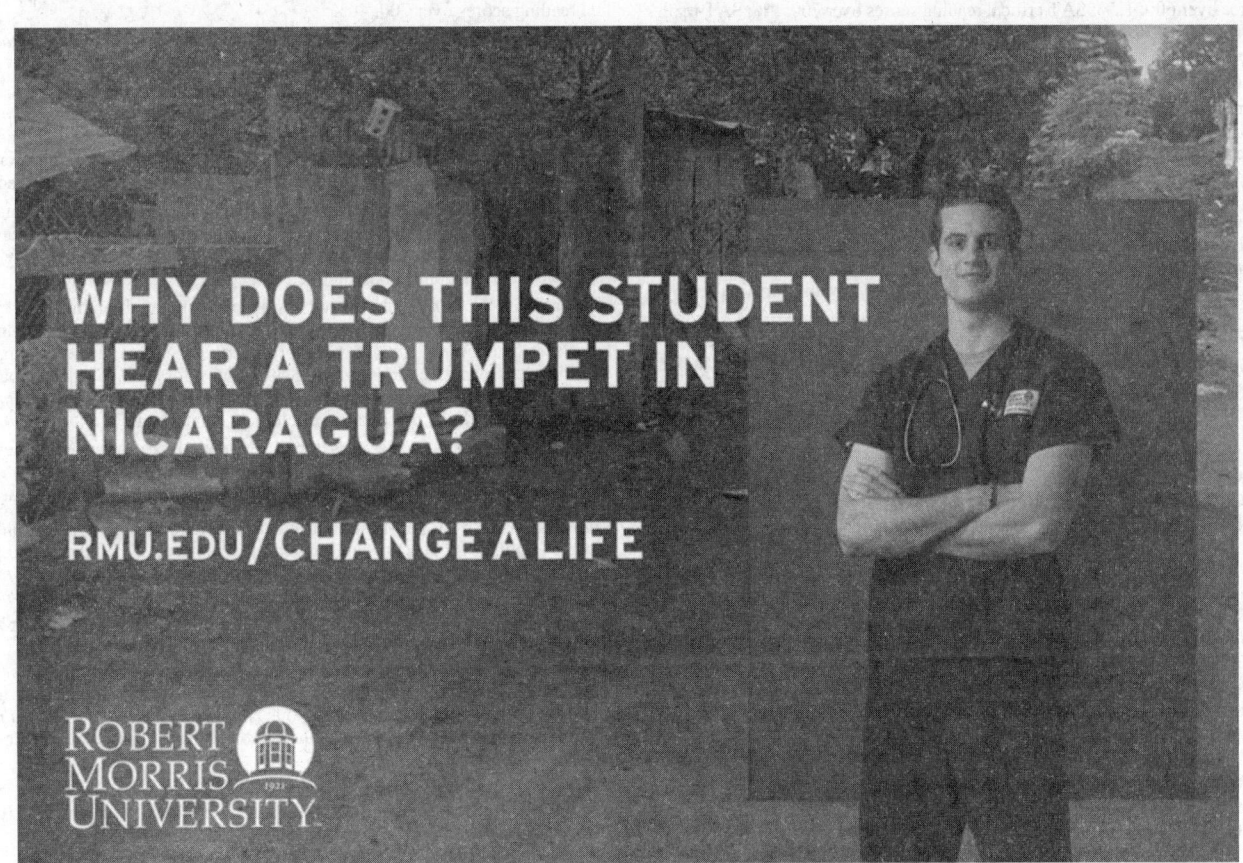

lege room only: $5240. Room and board charges vary according to board plan and housing facility. *Payment plans:* installment, deferred payment. *Waivers:* employees or children of employees.

Financial Aid Of all full-time matriculated undergraduates who enrolled in 2011, 2,989 applied for aid, 2,697 were judged to have need, 329 had their need fully met. In 2011, 536 non-need-based awards were made. *Average percent of need met:* 70%. *Average financial aid package:* $18,294. *Average need-based loan:* $5646. *Average need-based gift aid:* $12,039. *Average non-need-based aid:* $9735. *Average indebtedness upon graduation:* $42,477.

Applying *Options:* electronic application, deferred entrance. *Application fee:* $30. *Required:* high school transcript, minimum 2.5 GPA. *Required for some:* interview. *Recommended:* essay or personal statement, minimum 3.0 GPA, interview. *Application deadlines:* 7/1 (freshmen), 7/1 (transfers). *Notification:* continuous until 9/1 (freshmen), continuous (transfers).

Freshman Application Contact Enrollment Services Department, Robert Morris University, 6001 University Boulevard, Moon Township, PA 15108-1189. *Phone:* 412-397-5200. *Toll-free phone:* 800-762-0097. *Fax:* 412-397-2425. *E-mail:* admissionsoffice@rmu.edu. *Web site:* http://www.rmu.edu/.

See page 803 for display ad and page 1526 for the College Close-Up.

Rosemont College

Rosemont, Pennsylvania

- **Independent Roman Catholic** comprehensive, founded 1921
- **Suburban** 56-acre campus with easy access to Philadelphia
- **Endowment** $13.7 million
- **Coed** 519 undergraduate students, 83% full-time, 69% women, 31% men
- **Moderately difficult** entrance level, 54% of applicants were admitted

Undergraduates 431 full-time, 88 part-time. Students come from 12 states and territories; 13 other countries; 20% are from out of state; 40% Black or African American, non-Hispanic/Latino; 6% Hispanic/Latino; 4% Asian, non-Hispanic/Latino; 2% Two or more races, non-Hispanic/Latino; 9% Race/ethnicity unknown; 2% international; 5% transferred in; 70% live on campus. *Retention:* 67% of full-time freshmen returned.

Freshmen *Admission:* 1,032 applied, 553 admitted, 107 enrolled. *Average high school GPA:* 3.4. *Test scores:* SAT critical reading scores over 500: 39%; SAT math scores over 500: 37%; SAT writing scores over 500: 43%; SAT critical reading scores over 600: 15%; SAT math scores over 600: 7%; SAT writing scores over 600: 12%; SAT critical reading scores over 700: 2%; SAT math scores over 700: 2%; SAT writing scores over 700: 6%.

Faculty *Total:* 148, 19% full-time, 75% with terminal degrees. *Student/faculty ratio:* 10:1.

Academics *Calendar:* semesters. *Degrees:* bachelor's, master's, and post-bachelor's certificates. *Special study options:* academic remediation for entering students, accelerated degree program, adult/continuing education programs, advanced placement credit, double majors, English as a second language, honors programs, independent study, internships, off-campus study, part-time degree program, services for LD students, student-designed majors, study abroad, summer session for credit. *ROTC:* Army (c). *Unusual degree programs:* 3-2 nursing with Villanova University, Drexel University; counseling psychology, dentistry, art therapy, physical therapy, creative arts in therapy, nursing with Drexel University.

Computers on Campus 100 computers/terminals and 250 ports are available on campus for general student use. Students can access the following: campus intranet, computer help desk, free student e-mail accounts, online (class) grades, online (class) registration, online (class) schedules. Campuswide network is available. 100% of college-owned or -operated housing units are wired for high-speed Internet access. Wireless service is available via classrooms, computer centers, computer labs, dorm rooms, learning centers, libraries, student centers.

Student Life *Housing:* on-campus residence required through junior year. *Options:* coed, women-only. Campus housing is university owned. Freshman campus housing is guaranteed. *Activities and organizations:* drama/theater group, student-run newspaper, choral group, student government, Triad, Jest and Gesture, Best Buddies, Political Science Club. *Campus security:* 24-hour emergency response devices and patrols, late-night transport/escort service, controlled dormitory access. *Student services:* health clinic, personal/psychological counseling, women's center, legal services.

Athletics Member NCAA. All Division III. *Intercollegiate sports:* basketball M/W, cross-country running M/W, field hockey W, golf M, lacrosse M, soccer M/W, softball W, tennis M/W, volleyball W.

Standardized Tests *Required:* SAT or ACT (for admission).

Costs (2012–13) *Comprehensive fee:* $42,350 includes full-time tuition ($29,500), mandatory fees ($950), and room and board ($11,900). Part-time tuition: $1120 per credit hour. *Room and board:* Room and board charges vary

according to board plan and housing facility. *Payment plan:* installment. *Waivers:* senior citizens and employees or children of employees.

Financial Aid Of all full-time matriculated undergraduates who enrolled in 2009, 407 applied for aid, 393 were judged to have need, 42 had their need fully met. 65 Federal Work-Study jobs (averaging $1550). In 2009, 27 non-need-based awards were made. *Average percent of need met:* 71%. *Average financial aid package:* $22,845. *Average need-based loan:* $3330. *Average need-based gift aid:* $19,781. *Average non-need-based aid:* $10,657. *Average indebtedness upon graduation:* $21,490.

Applying *Options:* electronic application, early admission, deferred entrance. *Required:* essay or personal statement, high school transcript, 2 letters of recommendation. *Recommended:* minimum 3.0 GPA, interview. *Application deadlines:* rolling (freshmen), rolling (transfers). *Notification:* 8/1 (freshmen), continuous until 8/1 (transfers).

Freshman Application Contact Mr. Kevin McIntyre, Vice President for Enrollment Management, Rosemont College, 1400 Montgomery Avenue, Main Building, Rosemont, PA 19010. *Phone:* 610-527-0200 Ext. 2905. *Toll-free phone:* 888-2-ROSEMONT. *Fax:* 610-520-4399. *E-mail:* admissions@rosemont.edu. *Web site:* http://www.rosemont.edu/.

Saint Charles Borromeo Seminary, Overbrook

Wynnewood, Pennsylvania

- **Independent Roman Catholic** comprehensive, founded 1832
- **Suburban** 77-acre campus with easy access to Philadelphia
- **Coed, primarily men** 89 undergraduate students, 78% full-time, 15% women, 85% men
- **Moderately difficult** entrance level, 100% of applicants were admitted

Undergraduates 69 full-time, 20 part-time. Students come from 9 states and territories; 17% are from out of state; 7% Hispanic/Latino; 2% Asian, non-Hispanic/Latino; 7% transferred in; 94% live on campus. *Retention:* 76% of full-time freshmen returned.

Freshmen *Admission:* 9 applied, 9 admitted, 9 enrolled. *Test scores:* SAT critical reading scores over 500: 100%; SAT math scores over 500: 100%; SAT writing scores over 500: 100%; SAT critical reading scores over 600: 60%; SAT math scores over 600: 40%; SAT writing scores over 600: 60%; SAT critical reading scores over 700: 40%.

Faculty *Total:* 38, 50% full-time, 53% with terminal degrees. *Student/faculty ratio:* 8:1.

Academics *Calendar:* semesters. *Degrees:* certificates, bachelor's, master's, and postbachelor's certificates (also offers coed part-time programs). *Special study options:* academic remediation for entering students, accelerated degree program, adult/continuing education programs, advanced placement credit, English as a second language, independent study, summer session for credit.

Computers on Campus 60 computers/terminals are available on campus for general student use. Students can access the following: campus intranet, free student e-mail accounts. Campuswide network is available. Wireless service is available via classrooms, computer centers, computer labs, libraries.

Student Life *Housing:* on-campus residence required through senior year. *Options:* men-only. Campus housing is university owned. Freshman campus housing is guaranteed. *Activities and organizations:* drama/theater group, student-run newspaper, choral group, Seminarians for Life, Student Council. *Campus security:* 24-hour emergency response devices and patrols. *Student services:* health clinic, personal/psychological counseling.

Athletics *Intramural sports:* basketball M, football M, soccer M, volleyball M.

Standardized Tests *Recommended:* SAT or ACT (for admission).

Financial Aid Of all full-time matriculated undergraduates who enrolled in 2010, 54 applied for aid, 54 were judged to have need, 25 had their need fully met. In 2010, 25 non-need-based awards were made. *Average percent of need met:* 80%. *Average financial aid package:* $19,000. *Average need-based loan:* $5000. *Average need-based gift aid:* $5600. *Average non-need-based aid:* $20,790. *Average indebtedness upon graduation:* $19,000.

Applying *Options:* deferred entrance. *Required:* essay or personal statement, high school transcript, minimum 2.0 GPA, 3 letters of recommendation, interview, sponsorship by diocese or religious community. *Application deadlines:* 7/15 (freshmen), 7/15 (transfers). *Notification:* continuous (freshmen), continuous (transfers).

Freshman Application Contact Rev. Joseph W. Bongard, Vice Rector, Saint Charles Borromeo Seminary, Overbrook, 100 East Wynnewood Road, Wynnewood, PA 19096. *Phone:* 610-785-6271. *Fax:* 610-617-9267. *Web site:* http://www.scs.edu/.

Saint Francis University

Loretto, Pennsylvania

- **Independent Roman Catholic** comprehensive, founded 1847
- **Rural** 600-acre campus
- **Endowment** $34.2 million
- **Coed** 1,746 undergraduate students, 93% full-time, 60% women, 40% men
- **Moderately difficult** entrance level, 95% of applicants were admitted

Undergraduates 1,628 full-time, 118 part-time. Students come from 31 states and territories; 25% are from out of state; 6% Black or African American, non-Hispanic/Latino; 1% Hispanic/Latino; 0.7% Asian, non-Hispanic/Latino; 0.1% American Indian or Alaska Native, non-Hispanic/Latino; 5% Race/ethnicity unknown; 4% international; 2% transferred in; 88% live on campus. *Retention:* 84% of full-time freshmen returned.

Freshmen *Admission:* 1,358 applied, 1,293 admitted, 421 enrolled. *Average high school GPA:* 3.46. *Test scores:* SAT critical reading scores over 500: 57%; SAT math scores over 500: 64%; SAT writing scores over 500: 51%; ACT scores over 18: 85%; SAT critical reading scores over 600: 13%; SAT math scores over 600: 19%; SAT writing scores over 600: 14%; ACT scores over 24: 37%; SAT critical reading scores over 700: 1%; SAT math scores over 700: 1%; SAT writing scores over 700: 1%; ACT scores over 30: 5%.

Faculty *Total:* 192, 59% full-time. *Student/faculty ratio:* 15:1.

Academics *Calendar:* semesters. *Degrees:* certificates, associate, bachelor's, master's, doctoral, and first professional. *Special study options:* academic remediation for entering students, accelerated degree program, adult/continuing education programs, advanced placement credit, distance learning, double majors, external degree program, freshman honors college, honors programs, independent study, internships, off-campus study, part-time degree program, student-designed majors, study abroad, summer session for credit. *ROTC:* Army (b). *Unusual degree programs:* 3-2 engineering with Pennsylvania State University - University Park Campus, University of Pittsburgh, Clarkson University; forestry with Duke University; Pennsylvania College of Optometry, Lake Erie College of Osteopathic Medicine (LECOM), Temple University.

Computers on Campus 75 computers/terminals are available on campus for general student use. Students can access the following: campus intranet, computer help desk, free student e-mail accounts, online (class) grades, online (class) registration, online (class) schedules, wireless access throughout all of campus. Campuswide network is available. 95% of college-owned or -operated housing units are wired for high-speed Internet access. Wireless service is available via entire campus.

Student Life *Housing:* on-campus residence required through junior year. *Options:* men-only, women-only. Campus housing is university owned and leased by the school. Freshman campus housing is guaranteed. *Activities and organizations:* drama/theater group, student-run newspaper, radio station, choral group, marching band, Student Activities Organization, Club Baseball, Student Government Association, Best Buddies, Ultimate Frisbee Club, national fraternities, national sororities. *Campus security:* 24-hour emergency response devices and patrols, late-night transport/escort service, controlled dormitory access. *Student services:* health clinic, personal/psychological counseling.

Athletics Member NCAA. All Division I. *Intercollegiate sports:* basketball M(s)/W(s), bowling W, cross-country running M(s)/W(s), field hockey W(s), football M, golf M(s)/W(s), lacrosse W(s), soccer M(s)/W(s), softball W(s), swimming and diving M(s)/W(s), tennis M(s)/W(s), track and field M(s)/W(s), volleyball M(s)/W(s). *Intramural sports:* baseball M(c), basketball M/W, cheerleading M/W, cross-country running M/W, football M, golf M/W, lacrosse W, racquetball M/W, skiing (cross-country) M/W, skiing (downhill) M/W, soccer M/W, softball W, swimming and diving M/W, table tennis M/W, tennis M/W, track and field M/W, ultimate Frisbee M/W, volleyball M/W.

Standardized Tests *Required:* SAT or ACT (for admission).

Costs (2012–13) *One-time required fee:* $60. *Comprehensive fee:* $39,008 includes full-time tuition ($27,962), mandatory fees ($1050), and room and board ($9996). Full-time tuition and fees vary according to course load, degree level, program, and student level. Part-time tuition: $874 per credit hour. Part-time tuition and fees vary according to class time, degree level, and program. *Required fees:* $412 per credit hour part-time. *College room only:* $5024. Room and board charges vary according to board plan and housing facility. *Waivers:* employees or children of employees.

Financial Aid Of all full-time matriculated undergraduates who enrolled in 2011, 1,495 applied for aid, 1,360 were judged to have need, 270 had their need fully met. 258 Federal Work-Study jobs (averaging $1000). 840 state and other part-time jobs (averaging $1000). In 2011, 128 non-need-based awards were made. *Average percent of need met:* 61%. *Average financial aid package:* $18,848. *Average need-based loan:* $4415. *Average need-based gift aid:* $15,012. *Average non-need-based aid:* $9624. *Average indebtedness upon graduation:* $10,441.

Applying *Options:* electronic application, deferred entrance. *Application fee:* $30. *Required:* essay or personal statement, high school transcript, 1 letter of recommendation. *Required for some:* interview. *Recommended:* interview.

97% of Saint Francis University graduates are at work, or in graduate school just six months after graduation.

Reach higher. Go far.

SAINT FRANCIS UNIVERSITY
FOUNDED 1847

Application deadlines: rolling (freshmen), rolling (out-of-state freshmen), rolling (transfers). *Notification:* continuous (transfers).

Freshman Application Contact Robert Beener, Dean for Enrollment Management, Saint Francis University, PO Box 600, 117 Evergreen Drive, Loretto, PA 15940-0600. *Phone:* 814-472-3100. *Toll-free phone:* 866-DIAL-SFU. *E-mail:* rbeener@francis.edu. *Web site:* http://www.francis.edu/.

See page 805 for display ad and page 1546 for the College Close-Up.

Saint Joseph's University
Philadelphia, Pennsylvania

- **Independent Roman Catholic (Jesuit)** comprehensive, founded 1851
- **Suburban** 103-acre campus
- **Endowment** $173.1 million
- **Coed** 5,500 undergraduate students, 84% full-time, 52% women, 48% men
- **Moderately difficult** entrance level, 78% of applicants were admitted

Undergraduates 4,603 full-time, 897 part-time. Students come from 38 states and territories; 28 other countries; 54% are from out of state; 7% Black or African American, non-Hispanic/Latino; 4% Hispanic/Latino; 2% Asian, non-Hispanic/Latino; 0.1% Native Hawaiian or other Pacific Islander, non-Hispanic/Latino; 0.1% American Indian or Alaska Native, non-Hispanic/Latino; 1% Two or more races, non-Hispanic/Latino; 3% Race/ethnicity unknown; 1% international; 1% transferred in; 57% live on campus. *Retention:* 89% of full-time freshmen returned.

Freshmen *Admission:* 7,401 applied, 5,752 admitted, 1,133 enrolled. *Average high school GPA:* 3.46. *Test scores:* SAT critical reading scores over 500: 82%; SAT math scores over 500: 84%; ACT scores over 18: 99%; SAT critical reading scores over 600: 27%; SAT math scores over 600: 36%; ACT scores over 24: 58%; SAT critical reading scores over 700: 4%; SAT math scores over 700: 4%; ACT scores over 30: 7%.

Faculty *Total:* 774, 39% full-time. *Student/faculty ratio:* 13:1.

Academics *Calendar:* semesters. *Degrees:* certificates, associate, bachelor's, master's, doctoral, post-master's, postbachelor's, and first professional certificates. *Special study options:* accelerated degree program, adult/continuing education programs, advanced placement credit, cooperative education, distance learning, double majors, English as a second language, honors programs, independent study, internships, off-campus study, part-time degree program, services for LD students, student-designed majors, study abroad, summer session for credit. *ROTC:* Army (c), Navy (c), Air Force (b).

Computers on Campus 720 computers/terminals are available on campus for general student use. Students can access the following: campus intranet, computer help desk, free student e-mail accounts, online (class) grades, online (class) registration, online (class) schedules. Campuswide network is available. 100% of college-owned or -operated housing units are wired for high-speed Internet access. Wireless service is available via entire campus.

Student Life *Housing:* on-campus residence required through sophomore year. *Options:* coed, men-only, women-only, disabled students. Campus housing is university owned, leased by the school and is provided by a third party. Freshman campus housing is guaranteed. *Activities and organizations:* drama/theater group, student-run newspaper, radio station, choral group, Student Union Board, Hand-in-Hand, Collegiate Challenge, Appalachian Experience, Weekly Service, national fraternities, national sororities. *Campus security:* 24-hour emergency response devices and patrols, late-night transport/escort service, controlled dormitory access, 24-hour shuttle/escort service, bicycle patrols. *Student services:* health clinic, personal/psychological counseling.

Athletics Member NCAA. All Division I. *Intercollegiate sports:* baseball M(s), basketball M(s)/W(s), cheerleading M(c)/W(c), crew M(s)/W(s), cross-country running M(s)/W(s), field hockey W(s), golf M(s), lacrosse M(s)/W(s), soccer M(s)/W(s), softball W(s), tennis M(s)/W(s), track and field M(s)/W(s). *Intramural sports:* baseball M(c), basketball M(c)/W(c), field hockey W(c), football M/W, golf M(c)/W(c), ice hockey M(c), lacrosse M(c)/W(c), racquetball M/W, rugby M(c)/W(c), soccer M(c)/W(c), softball M/W, swimming and diving M(c)/W(c), tennis M(c)/W(c), ultimate Frisbee M(c)/W(c), volleyball M(c)/W(c), water polo M(c)/W(c).

Standardized Tests *Required:* SAT or ACT (for admission).

Costs (2011–12) *One-time required fee:* $225. *Comprehensive fee:* $48,846 includes full-time tuition ($36,480), mandatory fees ($160), and room and board ($12,206). Full-time tuition and fees vary according to course load. Part-time tuition: $480 per credit. *College room only:* $7650. Room and board charges vary according to board plan and housing facility. *Payment plans:* installment, deferred payment. *Waivers:* employees or children of employees.

Financial Aid Of all full-time matriculated undergraduates who enrolled in 2011, 3,285 applied for aid, 2,653 were judged to have need, 967 had their need fully met. In 2011, 1822 non-need-based awards were made. *Average percent of need met:* 79%. *Average financial aid package:* $20,329. *Average need-based loan:* $5500. *Average need-based gift aid:* $15,569. *Average non-need-based aid:* $10,425. *Average indebtedness upon graduation:* $40,160.

Applying *Options:* electronic application, early action, deferred entrance. *Application fee:* $60. *Required:* essay or personal statement, high school transcript. *Application deadlines:* 2/1 (freshmen), 3/1 (transfers), 11/15 (early

action). *Notification:* 3/15 (freshmen), continuous (transfers), 12/25 (early action).

Freshman Application Contact Office of Admissions, Saint Joseph's University, 5600 City Avenue, Philadelphia, PA 19131-1395. *Phone:* 610-660-1300. *Toll-free phone:* 888-BE-A-HAWK (in-state); 800-BE-A-HAWK (out-of-state). *Fax:* 610-660-1314. *E-mail:* admit@sju.edu. *Web site:* http://www.sju.edu/.

See page 1554 for the College Close-Up.

Saint Vincent College

Latrobe, Pennsylvania

- **Independent Roman Catholic** comprehensive, founded 1846
- **Suburban** 200-acre campus with easy access to Pittsburgh
- **Coed** 1,711 undergraduate students, 95% full-time, 45% women, 55% men
- **Moderately difficult** entrance level, 67% of applicants were admitted

Undergraduates 1,625 full-time, 86 part-time. 16% are from out of state; 6% Black or African American, non-Hispanic/Latino; 3% Hispanic/Latino; 1% Asian, non-Hispanic/Latino; 0.1% Native Hawaiian or other Pacific Islander, non-Hispanic/Latino; 0.2% American Indian or Alaska Native, non-Hispanic/Latino; 0.4% Two or more races, non-Hispanic/Latino; 2% Race/ethnicity unknown; 0.8% international; 4% transferred in; 70% live on campus. *Retention:* 84% of full-time freshmen returned.

Freshmen *Admission:* 1,863 applied, 1,249 admitted, 409 enrolled. *Average high school GPA:* 3.51. *Test scores:* SAT critical reading scores over 500: 64%; SAT math scores over 500: 75%; SAT writing scores over 500: 56%; SAT critical reading scores over 600: 21%; SAT math scores over 600: 25%; SAT writing scores over 600: 16%; SAT critical reading scores over 700: 3%; SAT math scores over 700: 3%; SAT writing scores over 700: 3%.

Faculty *Total:* 195, 52% full-time, 62% with terminal degrees. *Student/faculty ratio:* 12:1.

Academics *Calendar:* semesters. *Degrees:* certificates, bachelor's, master's, and postbachelor's certificates. *Special study options:* external degree program, part-time degree program. *ROTC:* Army (c), Air Force (c).

Computers on Campus Students can access the following: campus intranet, computer help desk, free student e-mail accounts, online (class) grades, online (class) registration, online (class) schedules. Campuswide network is available. 100% of college-owned or -operated housing units are wired for high-speed Internet access. Wireless service is available via entire campus.

Student Life *Housing:* on-campus residence required for freshman year. *Options:* coed. Campus housing is university owned. Freshman applicants given priority for college housing. *Campus security:* 24-hour emergency response devices and patrols, late-night transport/escort service, controlled dormitory access, limited access to residence halls on weekends.

Athletics Member NCAA. All Division III. *Intercollegiate sports:* baseball M, basketball M/W, cheerleading M(c)/W(c), cross-country running M/W, equestrian sports M(c)/W(c), fencing M(c)/W(c), field hockey W, golf M/W, ice hockey M(c), lacrosse M/W, soccer M/W, softball W, swimming and diving M/W, tennis M/W, track and field M, volleyball W. *Intramural sports:* football M/W, ultimate Frisbee M/W, volleyball M/W.

Standardized Tests *Required:* SAT or ACT (for admission).

Costs (2011–12) *One-time required fee:* $180. *Comprehensive fee:* $37,310 includes full-time tuition ($27,510), mandatory fees ($918), and room and board ($8882). *Part-time tuition:* $860 per credit. *College room only:* $4548. Room and board charges vary according to board plan and housing facility.

Financial Aid Of all full-time matriculated undergraduates who enrolled in 2009, 1,492 applied for aid, 1,282 were judged to have need, 315 had their need fully met. In 2009, 386 non-need-based awards were made. *Average percent of need met:* 81%. *Average financial aid package:* $21,705. *Average need-based loan:* $4662. *Average need-based gift aid:* $16,506. *Average non-need-based aid:* $12,349. *Financial aid deadline:* 5/1.

Applying *Options:* electronic application, early admission, deferred entrance. *Application fee:* $25. *Required:* essay or personal statement, high school transcript, minimum 2.5 GPA. *Required for some:* interview. *Recommended:* minimum 3.2 GPA, 3 letters of recommendation, interview. *Application deadlines:* 4/1 (freshmen), 7/1 (transfers). *Notification:* continuous (freshmen), continuous (transfers).

Freshman Application Contact Mr. David Collins, Assistant Vice President of Admission and Financial Aid, Saint Vincent College, 300 Fraser Purchase Road, Latrobe, PA 15650-2690. *Phone:* 800-782-5549. *Toll-free phone:* 800-782-5549. *Fax:* 724-532-5069. *E-mail:* admission@stvincent.edu. *Web site:* http://www.stvincent.edu/.

Seton Hill University

Greensburg, Pennsylvania

- **Independent Roman Catholic** comprehensive, founded 1883
- **Small-town** 200-acre campus with easy access to Pittsburgh
- **Endowment** $30.2 million
- **Coed** 1,700 undergraduate students, 88% full-time, 64% women, 36% men
- **Moderately difficult** entrance level, 44% of applicants were admitted

Undergraduates 1,501 full-time, 199 part-time. Students come from 33 states and territories; 14 other countries; 21% are from out of state; 9% Black or African American, non-Hispanic/Latino; 3% Hispanic/Latino; 0.6% Asian, non-Hispanic/Latino; 0.3% American Indian or Alaska Native, non-Hispanic/Latino; 4% Race/ethnicity unknown; 2% international; 5% transferred in; 55% live on campus. *Retention:* 75% of full-time freshmen returned.

Freshmen *Admission:* 2,975 applied, 1,322 admitted, 360 enrolled. *Average high school GPA:* 3.45. *Test scores:* SAT critical reading scores over 500: 53%; SAT math scores over 500: 52%; SAT writing scores over 500: 50%; ACT scores over 18: 90%; SAT critical reading scores over 600: 16%; SAT math scores over 600: 16%; SAT writing scores over 600: 14%; ACT scores over 24: 39%; SAT critical reading scores over 700: 2%; SAT math scores over 700: 2%; SAT writing scores over 700: 2%; ACT scores over 30: 3%.

Faculty *Total:* 192, 49% full-time, 58% with terminal degrees. *Student/faculty ratio:* 16:1.

Academics *Calendar:* semesters. *Degrees:* certificates, bachelor's, master's, post-master's, and postbachelor's certificates. *Special study options:* academic remediation for entering students, adult/continuing education programs, advanced placement credit, distance learning, double majors, English as a second language, honors programs, independent study, internships, off-campus study, part-time degree program, services for LD students, student-designed majors, study abroad, summer session for credit. *ROTC:* Army (b). *Unusual degree programs:* 3-2 engineering with University of Pittsburgh, Pennsylvania State University- University park Campus, Georgia Institute of Technology; physician assistant with Seton Hill University, BS/DO and BS/DPharm with lake Erie College of Osteopathic Medicine.

Computers on Campus 450 computers/terminals and 750 ports are available on campus for general student use. Students can access the following: campus intranet, computer help desk, free student e-mail accounts, online (class) grades, online (class) registration, online (class) schedules. Campuswide network is available. 100% of college-owned or -operated housing units are wired for high-speed Internet access. Wireless service is available via entire campus.

Student Life *Housing:* on-campus residence required for freshman year. *Options:* coed, men-only, women-only, disabled students. Campus housing is university owned. Freshman campus housing is guaranteed. *Activities and organizations:* drama/theater group, student-run newspaper, choral group, marching band, Student Body Activities Council, SHU-A-thon, Peer Ministry Council, Biology Club, SITA - Students in the Arts. *Campus security:* 24-hour emergency response devices and patrols, late-night transport/escort service, controlled dormitory access. *Student services:* health clinic, personal/psychological counseling.

Athletics Member NCAA. All Division II. *Intercollegiate sports:* baseball M(s), basketball M(s)/W(s), cross-country running M(s)/W(s), equestrian sports W(s); field hockey W(s), football M(s), golf W(s), lacrosse M(s)/W(s), soccer M(s)/W(s), softball W(s), tennis W(s), track and field M(s)/W(s), volleyball W(s), wrestling M(s).

Standardized Tests *Recommended:* SAT or ACT (for admission).

Costs (2012–13) *Comprehensive fee:* $39,390 includes full-time tuition ($28,346), mandatory fees ($1100), and room and board ($9944). Full-time tuition and fees vary according to course load and program. Part-time tuition: $760 per credit hour. Part-time tuition and fees vary according to course load and program. *Required fees:* $25 per credit hour part-time, $50 per term part-time. *Room and board:* Room and board charges vary according to board plan and housing facility. *Payment plan:* installment. *Waivers:* employees or children of employees.

Financial Aid Of all full-time matriculated undergraduates who enrolled in 2011, 1,263 applied for aid, 1,176 were judged to have need, 191 had their need fully met. 625 Federal Work-Study jobs (averaging $1674). 113 state and other part-time jobs (averaging $2036). In 2011, 150 non-need-based awards were made. *Average percent of need met:* 73%. *Average financial aid package:* $22,649. *Average need-based loan:* $5373. *Average need-based gift aid:* $17,520. *Average non-need-based aid:* $11,128. *Average indebtedness upon graduation:* $30,979.

Applying *Options:* electronic application, deferred entrance. *Application fee:* $35. *Required:* essay or personal statement, high school transcript, 1 letter of recommendation, portfolio for art, audition for music and theatre. *Recommended:* interview. *Application deadlines:* rolling (freshmen), rolling (out-of-state freshmen), rolling (transfers). *Notification:* continuous (freshmen), continuous (out-of-state freshmen), continuous (transfers).

Freshman Application Contact Ms. Ashley Josay, Assistant Director of Admissions, Seton Hill University, Seton Hill Drive, Greensburg, PA 15601. *Phone:* 724-838-4255. *Toll-free phone:* 800-826-6234. *Fax:* 724-830-1294. *E-mail:* admit@setonhill.edu. *Web site:* http://www.setonhill.edu/.

See below for display ad and page 1576 for the College Close-Up.

Shippensburg University of Pennsylvania

Shippensburg, Pennsylvania

- **State-supported** comprehensive, founded 1871, part of Pennsylvania State System of Higher Education
- **Rural** 200-acre campus
- **Endowment** $28.3 million
- **Coed** 7,132 undergraduate students, 96% full-time, 52% women, 48% men
- **Moderately difficult** entrance level, 80% of applicants were admitted

Undergraduates 6,812 full-time, 320 part-time. Students come from 17 states and territories; 14 other countries; 6% are from out of state; 6% Black or African American, non-Hispanic/Latino; 3% Hispanic/Latino; 1% Asian, non-Hispanic/Latino; 0.1% Native Hawaiian or other Pacific Islander, non-Hispanic/Latino; 0.2% American Indian or Alaska Native, non-Hispanic/Latino; 2% Two or more races, non-Hispanic/Latino; 4% Race/ethnicity unknown; 0.3% international; 6% transferred in; 37% live on campus. *Retention:* 70% of full-time freshmen returned.

Freshmen *Admission:* 6,883 applied, 5,504 admitted, 1,752 enrolled. *Average high school GPA:* 3.15. *Test scores:* SAT critical reading scores over 500: 42%; SAT math scores over 500: 45%; SAT writing scores over 500: 33%; ACT scores over 18: 73%; SAT critical reading scores over 600: 8%; SAT math scores over 600: 10%; SAT writing scores over 600: 4%; ACT scores over 24: 20%; SAT critical reading scores over 700: 1%; SAT math scores over 700: 1%.

Faculty *Total:* 419, 77% full-time, 77% with terminal degrees. *Student/faculty ratio:* 21:1.

Academics *Calendar:* semesters. *Degrees:* certificates, bachelor's, master's, post-master's, and postbachelor's certificates. *Special study options:* academic remediation for entering students, accelerated degree program, advanced placement credit, cooperative education, distance learning, double majors, honors programs, independent study, internships, off-campus study, part-time

degree program, services for LD students, study abroad, summer session for credit. *ROTC:* Army (b). *Unusual degree programs:* 3-2 engineering with Pennsylvania State University - University Park and Harrisburg Campus, University of Maryland College Park.

Computers on Campus 1,100 computers/terminals are available on campus for general student use. Students can access the following: campus intranet, computer help desk, free student e-mail accounts, online (class) grades, online (class) registration, online (class) schedules, personal Web pages. Campuswide network is available. 100% of college-owned or -operated housing units are wired for high-speed Internet access. Wireless service is available via classrooms, computer centers, computer labs, learning centers, libraries, student centers.

Student Life *Housing:* on-campus residence required for freshman year. *Options:* coed. Campus housing is university owned and leased by the school. Freshman campus housing is guaranteed. *Activities and organizations:* drama/theater group, student-run newspaper, radio and television station, choral group, marching band, national fraternities, national sororities. *Campus security:* 24-hour emergency response devices and patrols, late-night transport/escort service, controlled dormitory access, surveillance cameras in certain parking lots and buildings, foot, vehicular and bicycle patrols by security officers. *Student services:* health clinic, personal/psychological counseling, women's center.

Athletics Member NCAA. All Division II. *Intercollegiate sports:* baseball M(s), basketball M(s)/W(s), cross-country running M(s)/W(s), field hockey W(s), football M(s), lacrosse W(s), soccer M(s)/W(s), softball W(s), swimming and diving M(s)/W(s), tennis W(s), track and field M(s)/W(s), volleyball W(s), wrestling M(s). *Intramural sports:* basketball M/W, ice hockey M(c), lacrosse M(c), racquetball W, rugby M(c)/W(c), soccer M/W, softball M/W, tennis M(c)/W(c), ultimate Frisbee M/W, volleyball M/W.

Standardized Tests *Required:* SAT or ACT (for admission).

Costs (2011–12) *Tuition:* state resident $6240 full-time, $260 per credit hour part-time; nonresident $15,600 full-time, $650 per credit hour part-time. *Required fees:* $2616 full-time, $330 per course part-time. *Room and board:* $7620; room only: $3980. Room and board charges vary according to board plan and housing facility. *Payment plan:* installment. *Waivers:* senior citizens and employees or children of employees.

Financial Aid Of all full-time matriculated undergraduates who enrolled in 2011, 5,674 applied for aid, 4,448 were judged to have need, 541 had their need fully met. 93 Federal Work-Study jobs (averaging $1482). 641 state and other part-time jobs (averaging $1971). In 2011, 474 non-need-based awards were made. *Average percent of need met:* 60%. *Average financial aid pack-*

age: $8103. *Average need-based loan:* $3958. *Average need-based gift aid:* $5957. *Average non-need-based aid:* $4578. *Average indebtedness upon graduation:* $24,818.

Applying *Options:* electronic application, early admission, early action, deferred entrance. *Application fee:* $30. *Required:* high school transcript. *Required for some:* interview. *Recommended:* essay or personal statement, class rank, letters of recommendation optional. *Application deadlines:* rolling (freshmen), rolling (transfers). *Notification:* continuous (freshmen), continuous (transfers).

Freshman Application Contact Dr. Thomas Speakman, Dean of Enrollment Services, Shippensburg University of Pennsylvania, 1871 Old Main Drive, Shippensburg, PA 17257-2299. *Phone:* 717-477-1231. *Toll-free phone:* 800-822-8028. *Fax:* 717-477-4016. *E-mail:* admiss@ship.edu. *Web site:* http://www.ship.edu/.

See page 1578 for the College Close-Up.

Slippery Rock University of Pennsylvania
Slippery Rock, Pennsylvania

- **State-supported** comprehensive, founded 1889, part of Pennsylvania State System of Higher Education
- **Small-town** 650-acre campus with easy access to Pittsburgh
- **Endowment** $17.7 million
- **Coed** 7,961 undergraduate students, 94% full-time, 57% women, 43% men
- **Moderately difficult** entrance level, 61% of applicants were admitted

Undergraduates 7,461 full-time, 500 part-time. Students come from 38 states and territories; 28 other countries; 10% are from out of state; 5% Black or African American, non-Hispanic/Latino; 2% Hispanic/Latino; 0.6% Asian, non-Hispanic/Latino; 0.1% American Indian or Alaska Native, non-Hispanic/Latino; 1% Two or more races, non-Hispanic/Latino; 5% Race/ethnicity unknown; 0.7% international; 7% transferred in; 36% live on campus. *Retention:* 81% of full-time freshmen returned.

Freshmen *Admission:* 6,418 applied, 3,943 admitted, 1,536 enrolled. *Average high school GPA:* 3.41. *Test scores:* SAT critical reading scores over 500: 52%; SAT math scores over 500: 57%; SAT writing scores over 500: 44%; ACT scores over 18: 91%; SAT critical reading scores over 600: 10%; SAT math scores over 600: 12%; SAT writing scores over 600: 7%; ACT scores over 24: 25%.

Faculty *Total:* 399, 88% full-time, 82% with terminal degrees. *Student/faculty ratio:* 20:1.

Academics *Calendar:* semesters. *Degrees:* certificates, bachelor's, master's, doctoral, and postbachelor's certificates. *Special study options:* academic remediation for entering students, adult/continuing education programs, advanced placement credit, distance learning, double majors, honors programs, independent study, internships, off-campus study, part-time degree program, services for LD students, student-designed majors, study abroad, summer session for credit. *ROTC:* Army (b). *Unusual degree programs:* 3-2 engineering with Pennsylvania State University, University Park Campus; Youngstown State University.

Computers on Campus 1,323 computers/terminals and 75 ports are available on campus for general student use. Students can access the following: computer help desk, free student e-mail accounts, online (class) grades, online (class) registration, online (class) schedules. Campuswide network is available. 100% of college-owned or -operated housing units are wired for high-speed Internet access. Wireless service is available via classrooms, computer labs, dorm rooms, libraries, student centers.

Student Life *Housing:* on-campus residence required for freshman year. *Options:* coed, disabled students. Campus housing is university owned. Freshman campus housing is guaranteed. *Activities and organizations:* drama/theater group, student-run newspaper, radio and television station, choral group, marching band, Exercise Science Society, Hunting and Fishing Club, Campus Crusade for Christ, Interfraternity Council, Panhellenic Council, national fraternities, national sororities. *Campus security:* 24-hour emergency response devices and patrols, late-night transport/escort service, controlled dormitory access. *Student services:* health clinic, personal/psychological counseling, women's center, legal services.

Athletics Member NCAA. All Division II. *Intercollegiate sports:* baseball M(s), basketball M(s)/W(s), cheerleading M(c)/W(c), cross-country running M(s)/W(s), equestrian sports M(c)/W(c), field hockey W(s), football M(s), golf M(c)/W(c), gymnastics W(c), ice hockey M(c)/W(c), lacrosse M(c)/W(s), racquetball M(c)/W(c), rugby M(c)/W(c), skiing (downhill) M(c)/W(c), soccer M(s)/W(s), softball W(s), swimming and diving M(c)/W(c), tennis M(c)/W(s), track and field M(s)/W(s), ultimate Frisbee M(c)/W(c), volleyball M(c)/W(s), water polo M(c), wrestling M(c)/W(c). *Intramural sports:* badminton M/W, basketball M/W, bowling M/W, football M/W, lacrosse W(c), racquetball M/

W, soccer M/W, softball M/W, table tennis M/W, tennis M/W(c), volleyball M/W, water polo M/W.

Standardized Tests *Required:* SAT or ACT (for admission).

Costs (2011–12) *Tuition:* state resident $6240 full-time, $260 per credit hour part-time; nonresident $9360 full-time, $520 per credit hour part-time. Full-time tuition and fees vary according to course load and degree level. Part-time tuition and fees vary according to course load and degree level. *Required fees:* $2266 full-time, $95 per credit hour part-time. *Room and board:* $9150; room only: $6084. Room and board charges vary according to board plan and housing facility. *Payment plan:* installment. *Waivers:* minority students, senior citizens, and employees or children of employees.

Financial Aid Of all full-time matriculated undergraduates who enrolled in 2011, 6,497 applied for aid, 5,384 were judged to have need, 672 had their need fully met. In 2011, 341 non-need-based awards were made. *Average percent of need met:* 62%. *Average financial aid package:* $8717. *Average need-based loan:* $4246. *Average need-based gift aid:* $5493. *Average non-need-based aid:* $2641. *Average indebtedness upon graduation:* $28,810.

Applying *Options:* electronic application, deferred entrance. *Application fee:* $30. *Required:* high school transcript, minimum 2.0 GPA. *Notification:* 6/15 (freshmen), continuous (transfers).

Freshman Application Contact Slippery Rock University of Pennsylvania, 1 Morrow Way, Slippery Rock, PA 16057-1383. *Phone:* 724-738-2015. *Toll-free phone:* 800-SRU-9111. *Web site:* http://www.sru.edu/.

Strayer University - Allentown Campus

Center Valley, Pennsylvania

- **Proprietary** comprehensive
- **Coed**

Academics *Degrees:* certificates, diplomas, associate, bachelor's, master's, and postbachelor's certificates.

Freshman Application Contact Strayer University - Allentown Campus, 3800 Sierra Circle, Suite 300, Center Valley, PA 18034. *Web site:* http://www.strayer.edu/allentown/.

Strayer University - Center City Campus

Philadelphia, Pennsylvania

- **Proprietary** comprehensive
- **Coed**

Academics *Degrees:* certificates, diplomas, associate, bachelor's, master's, and postbachelor's certificates.

Freshman Application Contact Strayer University - Center City Campus, 1601 Cherry Street, Suite 100, Philadelphia, PA 19102. *Web site:* http://www.strayer.edu/center_city.

Strayer University - Cranberry Woods Campus

Cranberry Township, Pennsylvania

- **Proprietary** comprehensive
- **Coed**

Academics *Degrees:* certificates, diplomas, associate, bachelor's, master's, and postbachelor's certificates.

Freshman Application Contact Strayer University - Cranberry Woods Campus, Regional Learning Alliance, 850 Cranberry Woods Drive, Suite 2241, Cranberry Township, PA 16066. *Web site:* http://www.strayer.edu/cranberry_woods.

Strayer University - Delaware County Campus

Springfield, Pennsylvania

- **Proprietary** comprehensive
- **Coed**

Academics *Degrees:* certificates, diplomas, associate, bachelor's, master's, and postbachelor's certificates.

Freshman Application Contact Strayer University - Delaware County Campus, 760 West Sproul Road, Suite 200, Springfield, PA 19064-1215. *Web site:* http://www.strayer.edu/delaware_county.

Strayer University - King of Prussia Campus

King of Prussia, Pennsylvania

- **Proprietary** comprehensive
- **Coed**

Academics *Degrees:* certificates, diplomas, associate, bachelor's, master's, and postbachelor's certificates.

Freshman Application Contact Strayer University - King of Prussia Campus, 234 Mall Boulevard, Suite G-50, King of Prussia, PA 19406. *Web site:* http://www.strayer.edu/king_of_prussia.

Strayer University - Lower Bucks County Campus

Trevose, Pennsylvania

- **Proprietary** comprehensive
- **Coed**

Academics *Degrees:* certificates, diplomas, associate, bachelor's, master's, and postbachelor's certificates.

Freshman Application Contact Strayer University - Lower Bucks County Campus, 3600 Horizon Boulevard, Suite 100, Trevose, PA 19053. *Web site:* http://www.strayer.edu/lower_bucks_county/.

Strayer University - Penn Center West Campus

Pittsburgh, Pennsylvania

- **Proprietary** comprehensive
- **Coed**

Academics *Degrees:* certificates, diplomas, associate, bachelor's, master's, and postbachelor's certificates.

Freshman Application Contact Strayer University - Penn Center West Campus, One Penn Center West, Suite 320, Pittsburgh, PA 15276. *Web site:* http://www.strayer.edu/penn_center_west/.

Susquehanna University

Selinsgrove, Pennsylvania

- **Independent** 4-year, founded 1858, affiliated with Evangelical Lutheran Church in America
- **Small-town** 306-acre campus with easy access to Harrisburg
- **Endowment** $11.4 million
- **Coed** 2,261 undergraduate students, 97% full-time, 54% women, 46% men
- **Moderately difficult** entrance level, 73% of applicants were admitted

Undergraduates 2,194 full-time, 67 part-time. Students come from 32 states and territories; 15 other countries; 49% are from out of state; 3% Black or African American, non-Hispanic/Latino; 4% Hispanic/Latino; 1% Asian, non-Hispanic/Latino; 0.1% Native Hawaiian or other Pacific Islander, non-Hispanic/Latino; 0.2% American Indian or Alaska Native, non-Hispanic/Latino; 1% Two or more races, non-Hispanic/Latino; 0.8% international; 2% transferred in; 76% live on campus. *Retention:* 84% of full-time freshmen returned.

Freshmen *Admission:* 3,610 applied, 2,644 admitted, 599 enrolled. *Average high school GPA:* 3.34. *Test scores:* SAT critical reading scores over 500: 84%; SAT math scores over 500: 84%; SAT writing scores over 500: 76%; ACT scores over 18: 100%; SAT critical reading scores over 600: 33%; SAT math scores over 600: 30%; SAT writing scores over 600: 26%; ACT scores over 24: 65%; SAT critical reading scores over 700: 5%; SAT math scores over 700: 1%; SAT writing scores over 700: 3%; ACT scores over 30: 7%.

Faculty *Total:* 252, 56% full-time, 64% with terminal degrees. *Student/faculty ratio:* 12:1.

Academics *Calendar:* semesters. *Degrees:* bachelor's (also offers evening associate degree program limited to local adult students). *Special study options:* accelerated degree program, advanced placement credit, distance learning, double majors, honors programs, independent study, internships, off-campus study, part-time degree program, services for LD students, student-designed majors, study abroad, summer session for credit. *ROTC:* Army (c). *Unusual degree programs:* forestry with Duke University.

Computers on Campus 300 computers/terminals and 60 ports are available on campus for general student use. Students can access the following: campus intranet, computer help desk, free student e-mail accounts, online (class) grades, online (class) registration, online (class) schedules, class listings and assignments, online voting booth. Campuswide network is available. 100% of college-owned or -operated housing units are wired for high-speed Internet

access. Wireless service is available via classrooms, computer centers, computer labs, dorm rooms, learning centers, libraries, student centers.

Student Life *Housing:* on-campus residence required through junior year. *Options:* coed. Campus housing is university owned. Freshman campus housing is guaranteed. *Activities and organizations:* drama/theater group, student-run newspaper, radio and television station, choral group, Student Government Association, community service organizations, music performance groups, theater performance groups, intramurals and outdoor recreation, national fraternities, national sororities. *Campus security:* 24-hour emergency response devices and patrols, late-night transport/escort service, controlled dormitory access. *Student services:* health clinic, personal/psychological counseling.

Athletics Member NCAA. All Division III. *Intercollegiate sports:* baseball M, basketball M/W, cheerleading M(c)/W(c), crew M(c)/W(c), cross-country running M/W, equestrian sports M(c)/W(c), field hockey W, football M, golf M/W, lacrosse M/W, rugby M(c)/W(c), soccer M/W, softball W, swimming and diving M/W, tennis M/W, track and field M/W, volleyball M(c)/W. *Intramural sports:* basketball M/W, racquetball M/W, soccer M/W, softball M/W, tennis M/W, volleyball M/W.

Standardized Tests *Recommended:* SAT or ACT (for admission).

Costs (2011–12) *Comprehensive fee:* $45,460 includes full-time tuition ($35,400), mandatory fees ($460), and room and board ($9600). Part-time tuition: $1125 per semester hour. *College room only:* $5050. Room and board charges vary according to board plan and housing facility. *Payment plans:* tuition prepayment, installment. *Waivers:* employees or children of employees.

Financial Aid Of all full-time matriculated undergraduates who enrolled in 2009, 1,712 applied for aid, 1,496 were judged to have need, 248 had their need fully met. 1,124 Federal Work-Study jobs (averaging $2044). 84 state and other part-time jobs (averaging $4425). In 2009, 537 non-need-based awards were made. *Average percent of need met:* 79%. *Average financial aid package:* $23,880. *Average need-based loan:* $4390. *Average need-based gift aid:* $19,015. *Average non-need-based aid:* $10,081. *Average indebtedness upon graduation:* $20,915.

Applying *Options:* electronic application, early admission, early decision, deferred entrance. *Application fee:* $35. *Required:* essay or personal statement, high school transcript, minimum 2.5 GPA, 1 letter of recommendation. *Required for some:* writing portfolio, auditions for music programs. *Recommended:* minimum 3.0 GPA, interview. *Application deadlines:* 3/1 (freshmen), 7/1 (transfers). *Early decision deadline:* 12/1. *Notification:* continuous until 12/15 (freshmen), continuous until 8/1 (transfers), 12/15 (early decision).

Freshman Application Contact Mr. Chris Markle, Director of Admissions, Susquehanna University, 514 University Avenue, Selinsgrove, PA 17870. *Phone:* 570-372-4260. *Toll-free phone:* 800-326-9672. *Fax:* 570-372-2722. *E-mail:* suadmiss@susqu.edu. *Web site:* http://www.susqu.edu/.

See below for display ad and page 1630 for the College Close-Up.

Swarthmore College
Swarthmore, Pennsylvania

- **Independent** 4-year, founded 1864
- **Suburban** 425-acre campus with easy access to Philadelphia
- **Endowment** $1.5 billion
- **Coed** 1,545 undergraduate students, 99% full-time, 51% women, 49% men
- **Most difficult** entrance level, 15% of applicants were admitted

Undergraduates 1,536 full-time, 9 part-time. Students come from 54 states and territories; 49 other countries; 87% are from out of state; 7% Black or African American, non-Hispanic/Latino; 13% Hispanic/Latino; 14% Asian, non-Hispanic/Latino; 0.5% American Indian or Alaska Native, non-Hispanic/Latino; 7% Two or more races, non-Hispanic/Latino; 8% Race/ethnicity unknown; 8% international; 0.6% transferred in; 94% live on campus. *Retention:* 97% of full-time freshmen returned.

Freshmen *Admission:* 6,547 applied, 987 admitted, 386 enrolled. *Test scores:* SAT critical reading scores over 500: 100%; SAT math scores over 500: 100%; SAT writing scores over 500: 100%; ACT scores over 18: 100%; SAT critical reading scores over 600: 97%; SAT math scores over 600: 94%; SAT writing scores over 600: 98%; ACT scores over 24: 99%; SAT critical reading scores over 700: 71%; SAT math scores over 700: 62%; SAT writing scores over 700: 69%; ACT scores over 30: 82%.

Faculty *Total:* 208, 81% full-time, 92% with terminal degrees. *Student/faculty ratio:* 8:1.

Academics *Calendar:* semesters. *Degree:* bachelor's. *Special study options:* accelerated degree program, advanced placement credit, double majors, honors programs, independent study, internships, off-campus study, services for LD students, student-designed majors, study abroad. *ROTC:* Army (c), Navy (c), Air Force (c).

Computers on Campus 332 computers/terminals and 3,300 ports are available on campus for general student use. Students can access the following: campus intranet, computer help desk, free student e-mail accounts, online (class) grades, online (class) registration, online (class) schedules, Course

materials and academic software are available online for many courses. Campuswide network is available. 100% of college-owned or -operated housing units are wired for high-speed Internet access. Wireless service is available via entire campus.

Student Life *Housing:* on-campus residence required for freshman year. *Options:* coed, men-only, women-only. Campus housing is university owned. Freshman campus housing is guaranteed. *Activities and organizations:* drama/theater group, student-run newspaper, radio station, choral group, community service and activist groups, club sports and intramurals, social/cultural clubs, music/acappella groups, political and debate clubs, national fraternities. *Campus security:* 24-hour emergency response devices and patrols, late-night transport/escort service, controlled dormitory access. *Student services:* health clinic, personal/psychological counseling, women's center.

Athletics Member NCAA. All Division III. *Intercollegiate sports:* badminton M(c)/W, baseball M, basketball M/W, cross-country running M/W, fencing M(c)/W(c), field hockey W, golf M, ice hockey M(c)/W(c), lacrosse M/W, rugby M(c)/W(c), soccer M/W, softball W, squash M(c)/W(c), swimming and diving M/W, tennis M/W, track and field M/W, ultimate Frisbee M(c)/W(c), volleyball M(c)/W, water polo M(c)/W(c). *Intramural sports:* basketball M/W, football M/W, soccer M/W, softball M/W, table tennis M/W, tennis M/W, volleyball M/W.

Standardized Tests *Required:* SAT and SAT Subject Tests or ACT (for admission).

Costs (2011–12) *Comprehensive fee:* $53,250 includes full-time tuition ($40,816), mandatory fees ($334), and room and board ($12,100). *College room only:* $6200. Room and board charges vary according to board plan. *Payment plan:* installment. *Waivers:* employees or children of employees.

Financial Aid Of all full-time matriculated undergraduates who enrolled in 2011, 899 applied for aid, 806 were judged to have need, 806 had their need fully met. 733 Federal Work-Study jobs (averaging $1710). In 2011, 9 non-need-based awards were made. *Average percent of need met:* 100%. *Average financial aid package:* $37,964. *Average need-based gift aid:* $36,385. *Average non-need-based aid:* $38,548. *Average indebtedness upon graduation:* $16,975. *Financial aid deadline:* 2/15.

Applying *Options:* electronic application, early admission, early decision, deferred entrance. *Application fee:* $60. *Required:* essay or personal statement, high school transcript, 3 letters of recommendation. *Recommended:* interview. *Application deadlines:* 1/1 (freshmen), 4/1 (transfers). *Early decision deadline:* 11/15 (for plan 1), 1/1 (for plan 2). *Notification:* 4/1 (freshmen), 5/30 (transfers), 12/15 (early decision plan 1), 2/15 (early decision plan 2).

Freshman Application Contact Mr. James L. Bock, Dean of Admissions and Financial Aid, Swarthmore College, 500 College Avenue, Swarthmore, PA 19081. *Phone:* 610-328-8300. *Toll-free phone:* 800-667-3110. *Fax:* 610-328-8580. *E-mail:* admissions@swarthmore.edu. *Web site:* http://www.swarthmore.edu/.

Talmudical Yeshiva of Philadelphia
Philadelphia, Pennsylvania

Freshman Application Contact Rabbi Shmuel Kamenetsky, Co-Dean, Talmudical Yeshiva of Philadelphia, 6063 Drexel Road, Philadelphia, PA 19131-1296. *Phone:* 215-473-1212.

Temple University
Philadelphia, Pennsylvania

- **State-related** university, founded 1884
- **Urban** 115-acre campus with easy access to Philadelphia
- **Endowment** $252.0 million
- **Coed** 27,702 undergraduate students, 89% full-time, 51% women, 49% men
- **Moderately difficult** entrance level, 63% of applicants were admitted

Undergraduates 24,525 full-time, 3,177 part-time. Students come from 52 states and territories; 126 other countries; 19% are from out of state; 14% Black or African American, non-Hispanic/Latino; 4% Hispanic/Latino; 10% Asian, non-Hispanic/Latino; 0.1% Native Hawaiian or other Pacific Islander, non-Hispanic/Latino; 0.3% American Indian or Alaska Native, non-Hispanic/Latino; 1% Two or more races, non-Hispanic/Latino; 8% Race/ethnicity unknown; 3% international; 10% transferred in; 17% live on campus. *Retention:* 87% of full-time freshmen returned.

Freshmen *Admission:* 18,977 applied, 11,926 admitted, 4,276 enrolled. *Average high school GPA:* 3.41. *Test scores:* SAT critical reading scores over 500: 77%; SAT math scores over 500: 83%; SAT writing scores over 500: 76%; ACT scores over 18: 95%; SAT critical reading scores over 600: 27%; SAT math scores over 600: 33%; SAT writing scores over 600: 27%; ACT scores over 24: 52%; SAT critical reading scores over 700: 4%; SAT math scores over 700: 4%; SAT writing scores over 700: 3%; ACT scores over 30: 6%.

Faculty *Total:* 2,894, 50% full-time, 43% with terminal degrees. *Student/faculty ratio:* 15:1.

Academics *Calendar:* semesters. *Degrees:* certificates, diplomas, associate, bachelor's, master's, doctoral, post-master's, postbachelor's, and first professional certificates. *Special study options:* academic remediation for entering students, accelerated degree program, adult/continuing education programs, advanced placement credit, cooperative education, distance learning, double majors, English as a second language, external degree program, honors programs, independent study, internships, off-campus study, part-time degree program, services for LD students, student-designed majors, study abroad, summer session for credit. *ROTC:* Army (b), Navy (c), Air Force (c). *Unusual degree programs:* 3-2 physical therapy, pharmacy, chemistry, physics.

Computers on Campus 3,670 computers/terminals are available on campus for general student use. Students can access the following: computer help desk, free student e-mail accounts, online (class) grades, online (class) registration, online (class) schedules, student accounts, Web hosting. Campuswide network is available. 100% of college-owned or -operated housing units are wired for high-speed Internet access. Wireless service is available via entire campus.

Student Life *Housing options:* coed. Campus housing is university owned, leased by the school and is provided by a third party. Freshman campus housing is guaranteed. *Activities and organizations:* drama/theater group, student-run newspaper, radio station, choral group, marching band, American Society of Mechanical Engineers, Anthropology Association, Cherry Crusade, Habitat for Humanity, Student Peace Alliance, national fraternities, national sororities. *Campus security:* 24-hour emergency response devices and patrols, late-night transport/escort service, controlled dormitory access. *Student services:* health clinic, personal/psychological counseling, legal services.

Athletics Member NCAA. All Division I except football (Division I-A). *Intercollegiate sports:* baseball M(s), basketball M(s)/W(s), cheerleading M(s)/W(s), crew M(s)/W(s), cross-country running M(s)/W(s), fencing W(s), field hockey W(s), golf M(s), gymnastics M(s)/W(s), lacrosse W(s), soccer M(s)/W(s), softball M/W(s), tennis M(s)/W(s), track and field M(s)/W(s), volleyball W(s). *Intramural sports:* badminton M(c)/W(c), basketball M/W, bowling M(c)/W(c), equestrian sports M(c)/W(c), fencing M(c)/W(c), gymnastics M(c)/W(c), ice hockey M(c), lacrosse M(c)/W(c), racquetball M/W, rugby M(c)/W(c), soccer M/W, softball W, tennis M/W, ultimate Frisbee M(c)/W(c), volleyball M/W.

Standardized Tests *Required:* SAT or ACT (for admission).

Costs (2011–12) *Tuition:* state resident $13,006 full-time, $502 per credit hour part-time; nonresident $22,832 full-time, $813 per credit hour part-time. Full-time tuition and fees vary according to course load, program, reciprocity agreements, and student level. Part-time tuition and fees vary according to course load, program, reciprocity agreements, and student level. *Required fees:* $590 full-time, $30 per credit hour part-time. *Room and board:* $9886; room only: $6664. Room and board charges vary according to board plan and housing facility. *Payment plan:* installment. *Waivers:* employees or children of employees.

Financial Aid Of all full-time matriculated undergraduates who enrolled in 2011, 22,200 applied for aid, 17,727 were judged to have need, 5,192 had their need fully met. 1,259 Federal Work-Study jobs. In 2011, 2577 non-need-based awards were made. *Average percent of need met:* 83%. *Average financial aid package:* $15,355. *Average need-based loan:* $4084. *Average need-based gift aid:* $5491. *Average non-need-based aid:* $8095. *Average indebtedness upon graduation:* $32,766.

Applying *Options:* electronic application, deferred entrance. *Application fee:* $50. *Required:* essay or personal statement, high school transcript. *Recommended:* minimum 3.0 GPA. *Application deadlines:* 3/1 (freshmen), 6/1 (transfers). *Notification:* continuous (freshmen), continuous (transfers).

Freshman Application Contact Temple University, 1801 North Broad Street, Philadelphia, PA 19122-6096. *Phone:* 215-204-7200. *Toll-free phone:* 888-340-2222. *Web site:* http://www.temple.edu/.

See page 813 for display ad and page 1636 for the College Close-Up.

Thiel College
Greenville, Pennsylvania

- **Independent** 4-year, founded 1866, affiliated with Evangelical Lutheran Church in America
- **Rural** 135-acre campus with easy access to Cleveland, Pittsburgh
- **Endowment** $20.9 million
- **Coed** 1,109 undergraduate students, 96% full-time, 47% women, 53% men
- **Moderately difficult** entrance level, 65% of applicants were admitted

Undergraduates 1,065 full-time, 44 part-time. Students come from 20 states and territories; 6 other countries; 34% are from out of state; 8% Black or African American, non-Hispanic/Latino; 2% Hispanic/Latino; 0.1% Asian, non-Hispanic/Latino; 0.7% American Indian or Alaska Native, non-Hispanic/Latino; 2% Two or more races, non-Hispanic/Latino; 15% Race/ethnicity

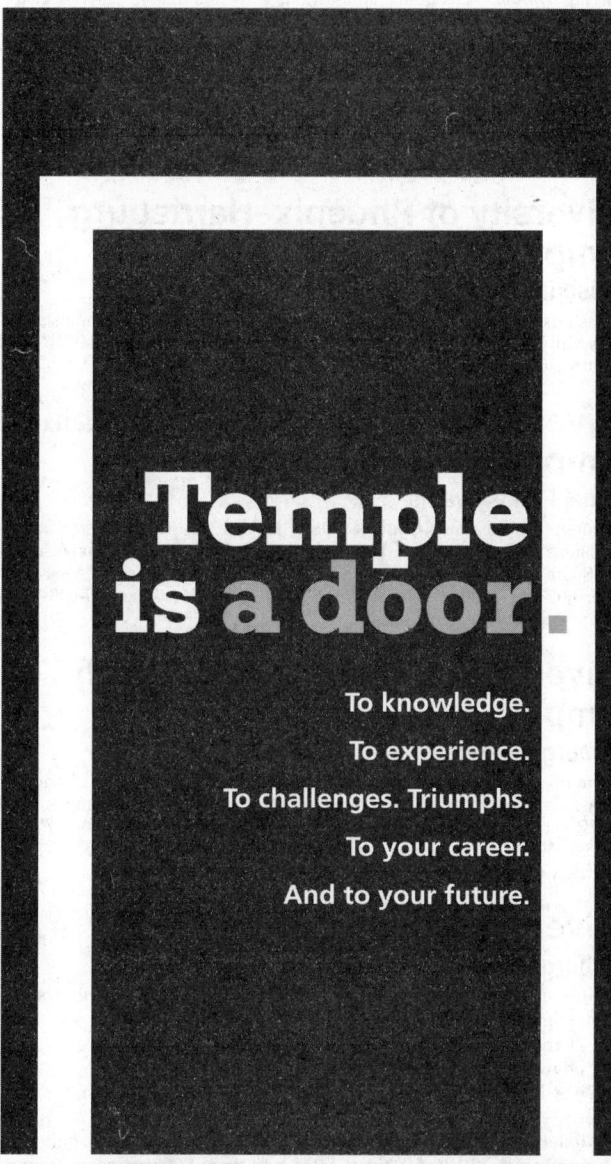

Temple is a door.

To knowledge.

To experience.

To challenges. Triumphs.

To your career.

And to your future.

➤ *Throw it open. Step through.*

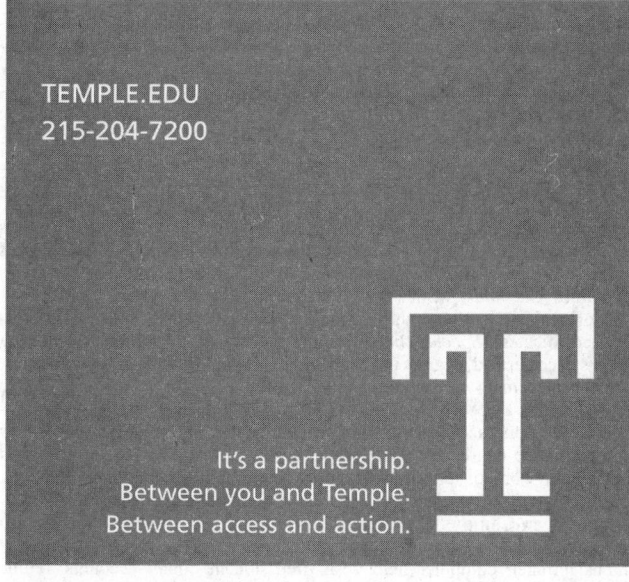

TEMPLE.EDU
215-204-7200

It's a partnership.
Between you and Temple.
Between access and action.

unknown; 1% international; 4% transferred in; 89% live on campus. *Retention:* 58% of full-time freshmen returned.

Freshmen *Admission:* 2,541 applied, 1,640 admitted, 371 enrolled. *Average high school GPA:* 3.07. *Test scores:* SAT critical reading scores over 500: 33%; SAT math scores over 500: 39%; SAT writing scores over 500: 26%; ACT scores over 18: 75%; SAT critical reading scores over 600: 9%; SAT math scores over 600: 8%; SAT writing scores over 600: 5%; ACT scores over 24: 20%; SAT critical reading scores over 700: 1%; SAT math scores over 700: 1%; ACT scores over 30: 1%.

Faculty *Total:* 105, 55% full-time, 49% with terminal degrees. *Student/faculty ratio:* 14:1.

Academics *Calendar:* semesters. *Degrees:* associate and bachelor's. *Special study options:* academic remediation for entering students, adult/continuing education programs, advanced placement credit, cooperative education, distance learning, double majors, honors programs, independent study, internships, off-campus study, part-time degree program, services for LD students, study abroad, summer session for credit. *Unusual degree programs:* 3-2 engineering with Case Western Reserve University, University of Pittsburgh; forestry with Duke University; physician assistant with Chatham University.

Computers on Campus 130 computers/terminals and 1,705 ports are available on campus for general student use. Students can access the following: campus intranet, computer help desk, free student e-mail accounts, online (class) grades, online (class) registration, online (class) schedules. Campus-wide network is available. 100% of college-owned or -operated housing units are wired for high-speed Internet access. Wireless service is available via classrooms, computer centers, computer labs, learning centers, libraries, student centers.

Student Life *Housing:* on-campus residence required through senior year. *Options:* coed. Campus housing is university owned and leased by the school. Freshman campus housing is guaranteed. *Activities and organizations:* drama/theater group, student-run newspaper, radio and television station, choral group, marching band, Thiel Players Theatre Group, student government, Thiel Choir, Ski Club, Thiel Christian Fellowship, national fraternities, national sororities. *Campus security:* 24-hour emergency response devices and patrols, late-night transport/escort service, controlled dormitory access. *Student services:* health clinic, personal/psychological counseling.

Athletics Member NCAA. All Division III. *Intercollegiate sports:* baseball M, basketball M/W, cheerleading M/W, cross-country running M/W, football M, golf M/W, lacrosse M/W, soccer M/W, softball W, tennis M/W, track and field M/W, volleyball M/W, wrestling M. *Intramural sports:* basketball M/W, football M/W, riflery M/W, rugby M, soccer M/W, softball M/W, volleyball M/W.

Standardized Tests *Required:* SAT or ACT (for admission).

Costs (2012–13) *One-time required fee:* $300. *Comprehensive fee:* $36,108 includes full-time tuition ($24,208), mandatory fees ($1780), and room and board ($10,120). Part-time tuition: $808 per credit. Part-time tuition and fees vary according to course load. *Required fees:* $890 per term part-time. *College room only:* $5060. Room and board charges vary according to board plan and housing facility. *Payment plan:* installment. *Waivers:* senior citizens and employees or children of employees.

Financial Aid Of all full-time matriculated undergraduates who enrolled in 2010, 1,001 applied for aid, 964 were judged to have need, 76 had their need fully met. 62 Federal Work-Study jobs, 277 state and other part-time jobs. In 2010, 112 non-need-based awards were made. *Average percent of need met:* 67%. *Average financial aid package:* $19,220. *Average need-based loan:* $4244. *Average need-based gift aid:* $15,076. *Average non-need-based aid:* $8565. *Average indebtedness upon graduation:* $34,606.

Applying *Options:* electronic application, deferred entrance. *Application fee:* $35. *Required:* essay or personal statement, high school transcript, minimum 2.0 GPA, 1 letter of recommendation. *Required for some:* interview. *Application deadlines:* rolling (freshmen), rolling (out-of-state freshmen), rolling (transfers). *Notification:* continuous (freshmen), continuous (out-of-state freshmen), continuous (transfers).

Freshman Application Contact Ms. Amy Becker, Chief Admissions Officer, Thiel College, 75 College Avenue, Greenville, PA 16125. *Phone:* 724-589-2182. *Toll-free phone:* 800-248-4435. *Fax:* 724-589-2013. *E-mail:* admissions@thiel.edu. *Web site:* http://www.thiel.edu/.

Thomas Jefferson University

Philadelphia, Pennsylvania

Freshman Application Contact Ms. Karen Jacobs, Director of Admissions, Thomas Jefferson University, Edison Building, 130 South Ninth Street, Philadelphia, PA 19107. *Phone:* 215-503-8890. *Toll-free phone:* 877-533-3247. *Fax:* 215-503-7241. *E-mail:* chpadmissions@mail.tju.edu. *Web site:* http://www.jefferson.edu/.

University of Pennsylvania
Philadelphia, Pennsylvania

- **Independent** university, founded 1740
- **Urban** 279-acre campus
- **Endowment** $6.6 billion
- **Coed** 9,779 undergraduate students, 97% full-time, 51% women, 49% men
- **Most difficult** entrance level, 12% of applicants were admitted

Undergraduates 9,516 full-time, 263 part-time. Students come from 54 states and territories; 123 other countries; 84% are from out of state; 7% Black or African American, non-Hispanic/Latino; 8% Hispanic/Latino; 19% Asian, non-Hispanic/Latino; 0.1% Native Hawaiian or other Pacific Islander, non-Hispanic/Latino; 0.3% American Indian or Alaska Native, non-Hispanic/Latino; 2% Two or more races, non-Hispanic/Latino; 6% Race/ethnicity unknown; 11% international; 1% transferred in; 56% live on campus. *Retention:* 97% of full-time freshmen returned.

Freshmen *Admission:* 31,663 applied, 3,935 admitted, 2,409 enrolled. *Average high school GPA:* 3.9. *Test scores:* SAT critical reading scores over 500: 99%; SAT math scores over 500: 100%; SAT writing scores over 500: 93%; ACT scores over 18: 100%; SAT critical reading scores over 600: 93%; SAT math scores over 600: 96%; SAT writing scores over 600: 88%; ACT scores over 24: 98%; SAT critical reading scores over 700: 60%; SAT math scores over 700: 71%; SAT writing scores over 700: 60%; ACT scores over 30: 77%.

Faculty *Total:* 2,196, 64% full-time, 100% with terminal degrees. *Student/faculty ratio:* 6:1.

Academics *Calendar:* semesters plus 2 5-week summer sessions. *Degrees:* certificates, associate, bachelor's, master's, doctoral, post-master's, postbachelor's, and first professional certificates (also offers evening program with significant enrollment not reflected in profile). *Special study options:* academic remediation for entering students, accelerated degree program, adult/continuing education programs, advanced placement credit, cooperative education, distance learning, double majors, English as a second language, honors programs, independent study, internships, off-campus study, part-time degree program, services for LD students, student-designed majors, study abroad, summer session for credit. *ROTC:* Army (c), Navy (b), Air Force (c).

Computers on Campus Students can access the following: campus intranet, computer help desk, free student e-mail accounts, online (class) grades, online (class) registration, online (class) schedules, billing information, financial aid application, status, academic records, student services. Campuswide network is available. 100% of college-owned or -operated housing units are wired for high-speed Internet access. Wireless service is available via entire campus.

Student Life *Housing options:* coed, disabled students. Campus housing is university owned. Freshman campus housing is guaranteed. *Activities and organizations:* drama/theater group, student-run newspaper, radio and television station, choral group, marching band, Kite and Key Society, Social Planning and Events Committee, Hillel at Penn, Sports Club Council, Interfraternity Council, national fraternities, national sororities. *Campus security:* 24-hour emergency response devices and patrols, late-night transport/escort service, controlled dormitory access. *Student services:* health clinic, personal/psychological counseling, women's center, legal services.

Athletics Member NCAA. All Division I except football (Division I-AA). *Intercollegiate sports:* baseball M, basketball M/W, crew M/W, cross-country running M/W, fencing M/W, field hockey W, golf M/W, gymnastics W, lacrosse M/W, soccer M/W, softball W, squash M/W, swimming and diving M/W, tennis M/W, track and field M/W, volleyball W, wrestling M. *Intramural sports:* badminton M(c)/W(c), baseball M(c)/W(c), basketball M(c)/W(c), cheerleading M/W, equestrian sports M(c)/W(c), field hockey M(c)/W(c), golf M(c)/W(c), gymnastics M(c)/W(c), ice hockey M(c)/W(c), lacrosse M/W, rugby M(c)/W(c), sailing M(c)/W(c), skiing (downhill) M(c)/W(c), soccer M/W, softball M/W, squash M/W, swimming and diving M/W, table tennis M/W, tennis M/W, ultimate Frisbee M(c)/W(c), volleyball M/W, water polo M(c)/W(c).

Standardized Tests *Required:* SAT and SAT Subject Tests or ACT (for admission).

Costs (2012–13) *Comprehensive fee:* $56,106 includes full-time tuition ($39,088), mandatory fees ($4650), and room and board ($12,368). Part-time tuition and fees vary according to course load. *Room and board:* Room and board charges vary according to board plan and housing facility. *Payment plans:* tuition prepayment, installment. *Waivers:* employees or children of employees.

Financial Aid Of all full-time matriculated undergraduates who enrolled in 2010, 5,858 applied for aid, 4,549 were judged to have need, 4,531 had their need fully met. 2,855 Federal Work-Study jobs (averaging $2884). 480 state and other part-time jobs (averaging $2905). *Average percent of need met:* 100%. *Average financial aid package:* $37,434. *Average need-based loan:* $386. *Average need-based gift aid:* $34,655. *Average indebtedness upon graduation:* $17,891.

Applying *Options:* electronic application, early admission, early decision, deferred entrance. *Application fee:* $75. *Required:* essay or personal statement, high school transcript, 2 letters of recommendation. *Application deadlines:* 1/1 (freshmen), 3/15 (transfers). *Early decision deadline:* 11/1. *Notification:* 4/1 (freshmen), 5/15 (transfers), 12/15 (early decision).

Freshman Application Contact The Office of Undergraduate Admissions, University of Pennsylvania, 1 College Hall, Room 1, Philadelphia, PA 19104. *Phone:* 215-898-7507. *Web site:* http://www.upenn.edu/.

University of Phoenix–Harrisburg Campus
Harrisburg, Pennsylvania

Admissions Office Contact University of Phoenix–Harrisburg Campus, 4050 Crums Mill Road, Harrisburg, PA 17112. *Toll-free phone:* 866-766-0766. *Web site:* http://www.phoenix.edu/.

University of Phoenix–Philadelphia Campus
Wayne, Pennsylvania

Freshman Application Contact Marc Booker, Sr. Director, Office of Admissions and Evaluation, University of Phoenix–Philadelphia Campus, 4035 South Riverpoint Parkway, Mail Stop CF-L101, Phoenix, AZ 85040. *Phone:* 602-557-4609. *Toll-free phone:* 866-766-0766. *Fax:* 480-643-1156. *Web site:* http://www.phoenix.edu/.

University of Phoenix–Pittsburgh Campus
Pittsburgh, Pennsylvania

Freshman Application Contact Marc Booker, Sr. Director, Office of Admissions and Evaluation, University of Phoenix–Pittsburgh Campus, 4035 South Riverpoint Parkway, Mail Stop CF-L101, Phoenix, AZ 85040. *Phone:* 602-557-4609. *Toll-free phone:* 866-766-0766. *Fax:* 480-643-1156. *Web site:* http://www.phoenix.edu/.

University of Pittsburgh
Pittsburgh, Pennsylvania

- **State-related** university, founded 1787, part of Commonwealth System of Higher Education
- **Urban** 132-acre campus with easy access to Pittsburgh
- **Endowment** $2.5 billion
- **Coed** 18,427 undergraduate students, 93% full-time, 50% women, 50% men
- **Moderately difficult** entrance level, 58% of applicants were admitted

Undergraduates 17,186 full-time, 1,241 part-time. Students come from 51 states and territories; 46 other countries; 24% are from out of state; 6% Black or African American, non-Hispanic/Latino; 2% Hispanic/Latino; 6% Asian, non-Hispanic/Latino; 0.1% Native Hawaiian or other Pacific Islander, non-Hispanic/Latino; 0.1% American Indian or Alaska Native, non-Hispanic/Latino; 2% Two or more races, non-Hispanic/Latino; 3% Race/ethnicity unknown; 3% international; 5% transferred in; 45% live on campus. *Retention:* 90% of full-time freshmen returned.

Freshmen *Admission:* 23,409 applied, 13,544 admitted, 3,718 enrolled. *Average high school GPA:* 3.94. *Test scores:* SAT critical reading scores over 500: 98%; SAT math scores over 500: 99%; SAT writing scores over 500: 96%; ACT scores over 18: 94%; SAT critical reading scores over 600: 66%; SAT math scores over 600: 78%; SAT writing scores over 600: 59%; ACT scores over 24: 86%; SAT critical reading scores over 700: 24%; SAT math scores over 700: 25%; SAT writing scores over 700: 14%; ACT scores over 30: 28%.

Academics *Calendar:* semesters plus summer term. *Degrees:* certificates, bachelor's, master's, doctoral, post-master's, postbachelor's, and first professional certificates. *Special study options:* academic remediation for entering students, accelerated degree program, adult/continuing education programs, advanced placement credit, cooperative education, distance learning, double majors, English as a second language, external degree program, freshman honors college, honors programs, independent study, internships, off-campus study, part-time degree program, services for LD students, student-designed majors, study abroad, summer session for credit. *ROTC:* Army (b), Navy (c), Air Force (b). *Unusual degree programs:* 3-2 engineering; statistics.

Computers on Campus 2,000 computers/terminals and 2,000 ports are available on campus for general student use. Students can access the following: campus intranet, computer help desk, free student e-mail accounts, online

(class) grades, online (class) registration, online (class) schedules, online class listings, online tuition payment. Campuswide network is available. 100% of college-owned or -operated housing units are wired for high-speed Internet access. Wireless service is available via entire campus.

Student Life *Housing options:* coed, women-only, disabled students. Campus housing is university owned. Freshman campus housing is guaranteed. *Activities and organizations:* drama/theater group, student-run newspaper, radio and television station, choral group, marching band, Resident Student Association, Black Action Society, Engineering Student Council, Interfraternity Council, Panhellenic Association, national fraternities, national sororities. *Campus security:* 24-hour emergency response devices and patrols, late-night transport/escort service, controlled dormitory access, on-call van transportation. *Student services:* health clinic, personal/psychological counseling.

Athletics Member NCAA. All Division I except football (Division I-A). *Intercollegiate sports:* baseball M(s), basketball M(s)/W(s), cross-country running M(s)/W(s), gymnastics W(s), soccer M(s)/W(s), softball W(s), swimming and diving M(s)/W(s), tennis W(s), track and field M(s)/W(s), volleyball W(s), wrestling M(s). *Intramural sports:* badminton M/W, basketball M/W, equestrian sports M(c)/W(c), fencing M(c)/W(c), football M, ice hockey M(c)/W(c), lacrosse M(c)/W(c), racquetball M(c)/W(c), rugby M(c)/W(c), skiing (downhill) M(c)/W(c), soccer M/W, squash M/W, tennis M(c)/W(c), ultimate Frisbee M/W, volleyball M/W, water polo M(c), wrestling M(c)/W(c).

Standardized Tests *Required:* SAT or ACT (for admission). *Required for some:* SAT and SAT Subject Tests or ACT (for admission), SAT Subject Tests (for admission).

Costs (2011–12) *Tuition:* state resident $15,272 full-time, $636 per credit part-time; nonresident $24,680 full-time, $1028 per credit part-time. Full-time tuition and fees vary according to program. Part-time tuition and fees vary according to program. *Required fees:* $860 full-time, $860 per term part-time. *Room and board:* $9430; room only: $5700. Room and board charges vary according to board plan and housing facility. *Payment plans:* installment, deferred payment. *Waivers:* employees or children of employees.

Financial Aid Of all full-time matriculated undergraduates who enrolled in 2010, 12,275 applied for aid, 9,845 were judged to have need, 873 had their need fully met. 3,100 Federal Work-Study jobs (averaging $2419). In 2010, 377 non-need-based awards were made. *Average percent of need met:* 56%. *Average financial aid package:* $11,381. *Average need-based loan:* $4806. *Average need-based gift aid:* $7363. *Average non-need-based aid:* $12,004. *Average indebtedness upon graduation:* $26,612.

Applying *Options:* electronic application. *Application fee:* $45. *Required:* high school transcript. *Recommended:* essay or personal statement, interview. *Application deadlines:* rolling (freshmen), rolling (transfers). *Notification:* continuous (freshmen), continuous (transfers).

Freshman Application Contact Dr. Betsy A. Porter, Director of Office of Admissions and Financial Aid, University of Pittsburgh, 4227 Fifth Avenue, First Floor, Alumni Hall, Pittsburgh, PA 15260. *Phone:* 412-624-7488. *Fax:* 412-648-8815. *E-mail:* oafa@pitt.edu. *Web site:* http://www.pitt.edu/.

University of Pittsburgh at Bradford
Bradford, Pennsylvania

- **State-related** 4-year, founded 1963, part of University of Pittsburgh System
- **Small-town** 317-acre campus with easy access to Buffalo
- **Endowment** $18.2 million
- **Coed** 1,565 undergraduate students, 92% full-time, 55% women, 45% men
- **Minimally difficult** entrance level, 42% of applicants were admitted

Undergraduates 1,435 full-time, 130 part-time. Students come from 24 states and territories; 12 other countries; 16% are from out of state; 8% Black or African American, non-Hispanic/Latino; 2% Hispanic/Latino; 3% Asian, non-Hispanic/Latino; 0.1% Native Hawaiian or other Pacific Islander, non-Hispanic/Latino; 0.4% American Indian or Alaska Native, non-Hispanic/Latino; 4% Race/ethnicity unknown; 2% international; 7% transferred in; 60% live on campus. *Retention:* 72% of full-time freshmen returned.

Freshmen *Admission:* 961 applied, 399 admitted, 369 enrolled. *Average high school GPA:* 3.24. *Test scores:* SAT critical reading scores over 500: 44%; SAT math scores over 500: 49%; SAT writing scores over 500: 33%; ACT scores over 18: 87%; SAT critical reading scores over 600: 9%; SAT math scores over 600: 11%; SAT writing scores over 600: 6%; ACT scores over 24: 23%; SAT critical reading scores over 700: 1%; SAT math scores over 700: 2%; ACT scores over 30: 2%.

Faculty *Total:* 157, 47% full-time, 39% with terminal degrees. *Student/faculty ratio:* 18:1.

Academics *Calendar:* semesters. *Degrees:* associate and bachelor's. *Special study options:* academic remediation for entering students, accelerated degree program, adult/continuing education programs, advanced placement credit, distance learning, double majors, independent study, internships, off-campus

study, part-time degree program, services for LD students, study abroad, summer session for credit. *ROTC:* Army (c).

Computers on Campus 120 computers/terminals and 1,056 ports are available on campus for general student use. Students can access the following: computer help desk, free student e-mail accounts, online (class) grades, online (class) registration, online (class) schedules, online bills. Campuswide network is available. 100% of college-owned or -operated housing units are wired for high-speed Internet access. Wireless service is available via entire campus.

Student Life *Housing:* on-campus residence required for freshman year. *Options:* coed, disabled students. Campus housing is university owned. Freshman campus housing is guaranteed. *Activities and organizations:* drama/theater group, student-run newspaper, radio station, choral group, Student Government Association, Student Activities Board, The Source (student newspaper), Alpha Phi Omega, WDRQ (student radio station), national fraternities. *Campus security:* 24-hour emergency response devices and patrols, late-night transport/escort service, controlled dormitory access. *Student services:* health clinic, personal/psychological counseling.

Athletics Member NCAA. All Division III. *Intercollegiate sports:* baseball M, basketball M/W, cross-country running M/W, golf M, soccer M/W, softball W, swimming and diving M/W, tennis M/W, volleyball W. *Intramural sports:* basketball M/W, cheerleading W(c), football M/W, golf M/W, ice hockey M/W, rock climbing M/W, skiing (cross-country) M/W, soccer M/W, softball M/W, swimming and diving M/W, table tennis M/W, ultimate Frisbee M/W, volleyball M/W, water polo M/W.

Standardized Tests *Required:* SAT or ACT (for admission).

Costs (2011–12) *One-time required fee:* $90. *Tuition:* state resident $11,736 full-time, $489 per credit hour part-time; nonresident $21,928 full-time, $913 per credit hour part-time. Full-time tuition and fees vary according to course load and program. Part-time tuition and fees vary according to course load and program. *Required fees:* $760 full-time, $130 per term part-time. *Room and board:* $8140; room only: $5192. Room and board charges vary according to board plan and housing facility. *Payment plan:* installment. *Waivers:* employees or children of employees.

Financial Aid Of all full-time matriculated undergraduates who enrolled in 2009, 1,449 applied for aid, 1,318 were judged to have need, 778 had their need fully met. 199 Federal Work-Study jobs (averaging $1740). 1 state and other part-time job (averaging $1740). In 2009, 267 non-need-based awards were made. *Average percent of need met:* 90%. *Average financial aid package:* $12,625. *Average need-based loan:* $4432. *Average need-based gift aid:* $5524. *Average non-need-based aid:* $5587. *Average indebtedness upon graduation:* $21,695.

Applying *Options:* electronic application, deferred entrance. *Application fee:* $45. *Required:* high school transcript, minimum 2.0 GPA. *Required for some:* minimum 3.0 GPA. *Recommended:* essay or personal statement, 2 letters of recommendation, interview. *Application deadlines:* rolling (freshmen), rolling (out-of-state freshmen), rolling (transfers). *Notification:* continuous (freshmen), continuous (out-of-state freshmen), continuous (transfers).

Freshman Application Contact Ms. Vicky Pingie, Associate Director of Admissions, University of Pittsburgh at Bradford, 300 Campus Drive, Bradford, PA 16701. *Phone:* 814-362-7552. *Toll-free phone:* 800-872-1787. *Fax:* 814-362-5150. *E-mail:* monti@pitt.edu. *Web site:* http://www.upb.pitt.edu/.

See page 816 for display ad and page 1698 for the College Close-Up.

University of Pittsburgh at Greensburg
Greensburg, Pennsylvania

- **State-related** 4-year, founded 1963, part of University of Pittsburgh System
- **Small-town** 219-acre campus with easy access to Pittsburgh
- **Coed** 1,846 undergraduate students, 92% full-time, 49% women, 51% men
- **Moderately difficult** entrance level, 86% of applicants were admitted

Undergraduates 1,692 full-time, 154 part-time. Students come from 13 states and territories; 4 other countries; 2% are from out of state; 5% Black or African American, non-Hispanic/Latino; 3% Hispanic/Latino; 2% Asian, non-Hispanic/Latino; 0.1% American Indian or Alaska Native, non-Hispanic/Latino; 2% Two or more races, non-Hispanic/Latino; 7% Race/ethnicity unknown; 1% international; 8% transferred in; 34% live on campus. *Retention:* 80% of full-time freshmen returned.

Freshmen *Admission:* 1,468 applied, 1,256 admitted, 450 enrolled. *Average high school GPA:* 3.46. *Test scores:* SAT critical reading scores over 500: 56%; SAT math scores over 500: 65%; SAT writing scores over 500: 53%; ACT scores over 18: 90%; SAT critical reading scores over 600: 11%; SAT math scores over 600: 18%; SAT writing scores over 600: 7%; ACT scores over 24: 28%; SAT math scores over 700: 2%; ACT scores over 30: 1%.

Faculty *Total:* 133, 55% full-time. *Student/faculty ratio:* 19:1.

Academics *Calendar:* semesters. *Degree:* certificates and bachelor's. *Special study options:* academic remediation for entering students, accelerated degree program, adult/continuing education programs, advanced placement credit, distance learning, double majors, independent study, internships, off-campus study, part-time degree program, services for LD students, student-designed majors, study abroad, summer session for credit. *ROTC:* Army (c), Air Force (c).

Computers on Campus 400 computers/terminals are available on campus for general student use. Students can access the following: campus intranet, computer help desk, free student e-mail accounts, online (class) grades, online (class) registration, online (class) schedules. Campuswide network is available. 100% of college-owned or -operated housing units are wired for high-speed Internet access. Wireless service is available via classrooms, computer centers, computer labs, learning centers, libraries, student centers.

Student Life *Housing options:* coed. Campus housing is university owned. *Activities and organizations:* drama/theater group, student-run newspaper, radio station, choral group, Student Government Association, Circle K, Freshmen Honor Society-Phi Eta Sigma, Senior Honor Society-Phi Kappa Phi, Student Activities Board. *Campus security:* 24-hour emergency response devices and patrols, late-night transport/escort service, controlled dormitory access. *Student services:* health clinic, personal/psychological counseling.

Athletics Member NCAA. All Division III. *Intercollegiate sports:* baseball M, basketball M/W, bowling W, cross-country running M/W, golf M/W, soccer M/W, softball W, tennis M, volleyball W. *Intramural sports:* baseball M, basketball M/W, bowling M/W, football M/W, golf M/W, racquetball M/W, skiing (cross-country) M/W, skiing (downhill) M/W, soccer M/W, softball M/W, table tennis M/W, tennis M/W, volleyball M/W, weight lifting M/W.

Standardized Tests *Required:* SAT or ACT (for admission).

Costs (2011–12) *Tuition:* state resident $11,736 full-time, $489 per credit hour part-time; nonresident $21,928 full-time, $913 per credit hour part-time. *Required fees:* $890 full-time. *Room and board:* $8410. Room and board charges vary according to board plan and housing facility. *Payment plan:* installment. *Waivers:* senior citizens and employees or children of employees.

Financial Aid Of all full-time matriculated undergraduates who enrolled in 2010, 1,457 applied for aid, 1,267 were judged to have need, 159 had their need fully met. In 2010, 34 non-need-based awards were made. *Average percent of need met:* 65%. *Average financial aid package:* $10,627. *Average need-based loan:* $4332. *Average need-based gift aid:* $5698. *Average non-need-based aid:* $3701. *Average indebtedness upon graduation:* $26,291.

Applying *Options:* electronic application, early admission, deferred entrance. *Application fee:* $45. *Required:* high school transcript, minimum 2.5 GPA. *Recommended:* essay or personal statement, interview. *Application deadlines:* 8/1 (freshmen), 8/1 (out-of-state freshmen), 8/1 (transfers). *Notification:* continuous (freshmen), continuous (transfers).

Freshman Application Contact Ms. Heather Kabala, Director of Admissions, University of Pittsburgh at Greensburg, 150 Finoli Drive, Greensburg, PA 15601. *Phone:* 724-836-9880. *Fax:* 724-836-7471. *E-mail:* upgadmit@pitt.edu. *Web site:* http://www.greensburg.pitt.edu/.

University of Pittsburgh at Johnstown
Johnstown, Pennsylvania

- **State-related** 4-year, founded 1927, part of University of Pittsburgh System
- **Suburban** 655-acre campus with easy access to Pittsburgh
- **Coed** 2,957 undergraduate students, 96% full-time, 46% women, 54% men
- **Moderately difficult** entrance level, 88% of applicants were admitted

Undergraduates 2,849 full-time, 108 part-time. Students come from 14 states and territories; 12 other countries; 2% are from out of state; 3% Black or African American, non-Hispanic/Latino; 2% Hispanic/Latino; 1% Asian, non-Hispanic/Latino; 0.1% Native Hawaiian or other Pacific Islander, non-Hispanic/Latino; 0.1% American Indian or Alaska Native, non-Hispanic/Latino; 1% Two or more races, non-Hispanic/Latino; 1% Race/ethnicity unknown; 1% international; 3% transferred in; 59% live on campus. *Retention:* 74% of full-time freshmen returned.

Freshmen *Admission:* 1,613 applied, 1,418 admitted, 738 enrolled. *Average high school GPA:* 3.38. *Test scores:* SAT critical reading scores over 500: 51%; SAT math scores over 500: 57%; SAT writing scores over 500: 41%; ACT scores over 18: 87%; SAT critical reading scores over 600: 10%; SAT math scores over 600: 16%; SAT writing scores over 600: 7%; ACT scores over 24: 31%; SAT critical reading scores over 700: 1%; SAT math scores over 700: 2%; ACT scores over 30: 3%.

Academics *Calendar:* semesters. *Degrees:* certificates, associate, and bachelor's. *Special study options:* accelerated degree program, adult/continuing education programs, advanced placement credit, cooperative education, distance learning, double majors, independent study, internships, off-campus

study, part-time degree program, services for LD students, student-designed majors, study abroad, summer session for credit.

Computers on Campus 222 computers/terminals and 100 ports are available on campus for general student use. Students can access the following: computer help desk, free student e-mail accounts, online (class) grades, online (class) registration, online (class) schedules. Campuswide network is available. 100% of college-owned or -operated housing units are wired for high-speed Internet access. Wireless service is available via entire campus.

Student Life *Housing options:* coed, disabled students. Campus housing is university owned. Freshman campus housing is guaranteed. *Activities and organizations:* drama/theater group, student-run newspaper, radio and television station, choral group, Dance Ensemble, Student Senate, Programming Board, academic clubs, national fraternities, national sororities. *Campus security:* 24-hour emergency response devices and patrols, late-night transport/escort service, controlled dormitory access. *Student services:* health clinic, personal/psychological counseling.

Athletics Member NCAA. All Division II. *Intercollegiate sports:* baseball M, basketball M(s)/W(s), cheerleading W, cross-country running W, golf M/W, soccer M/W, track and field W, volleyball W, wrestling M(s). *Intramural sports:* archery M(c)/W(c), basketball M/W, football M/W, ice hockey M(c), lacrosse M(c), rock climbing M(c)/W(c), rugby M(c)/W(c), sailing M(c)/W(c), skiing (downhill) M(c)/W(c), soccer M/W, softball M/W, ultimate Frisbee M(c)/W(c), volleyball M/W, water polo M/W.

Standardized Tests *Required:* SAT or ACT (for admission).

Costs (2011–12) *Tuition:* state resident $11,736 full-time, $489 per credit part-time; nonresident $21,928 full-time, $913 per credit part-time. Full-time tuition and fees vary according to program. Part-time tuition and fees vary according to program. *Required fees:* $792 full-time, $87 per term part-time. *Room and board:* $9132; room only: $5100. Room and board charges vary according to board plan and housing facility. *Payment plan:* installment. *Waivers:* employees or children of employees.

Financial Aid Of all full-time matriculated undergraduates who enrolled in 2010, 2,540 applied for aid, 2,198 were judged to have need, 217 had their need fully met. 138 Federal Work-Study jobs (averaging $2737). 270 state and other part-time jobs (averaging $2880). In 2010, 36 non-need-based awards were made. *Average percent of need met:* 55%. *Average financial aid package:* $10,364. *Average need-based loan:* $4329. *Average need-based gift aid:* $5041. *Average non-need-based aid:* $2765. *Average indebtedness upon graduation:* $27,905.

Applying *Options:* electronic application, early admission, deferred entrance. *Application fee:* $45. *Required:* high school transcript, minimum 2.0 GPA. *Required for some:* interview. *Recommended:* essay or personal statement, 3 letters of recommendation. *Application deadlines:* rolling (freshmen), rolling (out-of-state freshmen), rolling (transfers). *Notification:* continuous (freshmen), continuous (out-of-state freshmen), continuous (transfers).

Freshman Application Contact Office of Admissions, University of Pittsburgh at Johnstown, 157 Blackington Hall, Johnstown, PA 15904. *Phone:* 814-269-7050. *Toll-free phone:* 800-765-4875. *E-mail:* upjadmit@pitt.edu. *Web site:* http://www.upj.pitt.edu/.

See page 1700 for the College Close-Up.

University of Pittsburgh at Titusville
Titusville, Pennsylvania

- **State-related** primarily 2-year, founded 1963, part of University of Pittsburgh System
- **Small-town** 10-acre campus
- **Endowment** $850,000
- **Coed**
- **Minimally difficult** entrance level

Academics *Calendar:* semesters. *Degrees:* certificates, associate, and bachelor's.

Student Life *Campus security:* 24-hour emergency response devices and patrols, controlled dormitory access.

Athletics Member NJCAA.

Standardized Tests *Required:* SAT or ACT (for admission). *Recommended:* SAT (for admission).

Financial Aid *Of all full-time matriculated undergraduates who enrolled in 2009,* 429 applied for aid, 408 were judged to have need, 23 had their need fully met. *In 2009,* 10 non-need-based awards were made. *Average percent of need met:* 80. *Average financial aid package:* $15,305. *Average need-based loan:* $9451. *Average need-based gift aid:* $1992. *Average non-need-based aid:* $39,059.

Applying *Options:* electronic application, early admission, deferred entrance. *Application fee:* $45. *Required:* high school transcript, minimum 2.0 GPA. *Required for some:* essay or personal statement, 1 letter of recommendation. *Recommended:* interview.

Freshman Application Contact Mr. John R. Mumford, Executive Director of Enrollment Management, University of Pittsburgh at Titusville, PO Box 287, Titusville, PA 16354. *Phone:* 814-827-4409. *Toll-free phone:* 888-878-0462. *Fax:* 814-827-4519. *E-mail:* uptadm@pitt.edu. *Web site:* http://www.upt.pitt.edu/.

The University of Scranton
Scranton, Pennsylvania

- **Independent Roman Catholic (Jesuit)** comprehensive, founded 1888
- **Urban** 50-acre campus
- **Endowment** $131.9 million
- **Coed** 4,069 undergraduate students, 95% full-time, 55% women, 45% men
- **Moderately difficult** entrance level, 72% of applicants were admitted

Undergraduates 3,875 full-time, 194 part-time. Students come from 18 states and territories; 10 other countries; 56% are from out of state; 2% Black or African American, non-Hispanic/Latino; 7% Hispanic/Latino; 2% Asian, non-Hispanic/Latino; 0.7% Native Hawaiian or other Pacific Islander, non-Hispanic/Latino; 0.2% American Indian or Alaska Native, non-Hispanic/Latino; 1% Two or more races, non-Hispanic/Latino; 7% Race/ethnicity unknown; 0.3% international; 2% transferred in; 61% live on campus. *Retention:* 88% of full-time freshmen returned.

Freshmen *Admission:* 9,047 applied, 6,531 admitted, 1,050 enrolled. *Average high school GPA:* 3.35. *Test scores:* SAT critical reading scores over 500: 83%; SAT math scores over 500: 86%; ACT scores over 18: 97%; SAT critical reading scores over 600: 28%; SAT math scores over 600: 36%; ACT scores over 24: 56%; SAT critical reading scores over 700: 4%; SAT math scores over 700: 4%; ACT scores over 30: 7%.

Faculty *Total:* 494, 56% full-time, 49% with terminal degrees. *Student/faculty ratio:* 11:1.

Academics *Calendar:* 4-1-4. *Degrees:* certificates, associate, bachelor's, master's, doctoral, post-master's, and postbachelor's certificates. *Special study options:* academic remediation for entering students, accelerated degree program, adult/continuing education programs, advanced placement credit, distance learning, double majors, honors programs, independent study, internships, off-campus study, part-time degree program, services for LD students, student-designed majors, study abroad, summer session for credit. *ROTC:* Army (b), Air Force (c).

Computers on Campus 935 computers/terminals are available on campus for general student use. Students can access the following: computer help desk, free student e-mail accounts, online (class) grades, online (class) registration, online (class) schedules. Campuswide network is available. 100% of college-owned or -operated housing units are wired for high-speed Internet access. Wireless service is available via classrooms, computer centers, computer labs, dorm rooms, learning centers, libraries, student centers.

Student Life *Housing:* on-campus residence required through sophomore year. *Options:* coed, men-only, women-only, disabled students. Campus housing is university owned. Freshman campus housing is guaranteed. *Activities and organizations:* drama/theater group, student-run newspaper, radio and television station, choral group, Service-oriented student clubs, United Colors, retreat programs, Biology/Pre-Medicine clubs, Pre-Law Society. *Campus security:* 24-hour emergency response devices and patrols, student patrols, late-night transport/escort service, controlled dormitory access. *Student services:* health clinic, personal/psychological counseling, women's center.

Athletics Member NCAA. All Division III. *Intercollegiate sports:* baseball M, basketball M/W, crew M(c)/W(c), cross-country running M/W, equestrian sports M(c)/W(c), fencing M(c)/W(c), field hockey W, golf M, ice hockey M(c), lacrosse M/W, rugby M(c)/W(c), soccer M/W, softball W, swimming and diving M/W, tennis M/W, ultimate Frisbee M(c)/W(c), volleyball M(c)/W, wrestling M. *Intramural sports:* badminton M/W, basketball M/W, cheerleading M(c)/W(c), football M/W, racquetball M/W, rock climbing M(c)/W(c), skiing (downhill) M/W, soccer M/W, softball M/W, table tennis M/W, tennis M/W, ultimate Frisbee M/W, volleyball M/W.

Standardized Tests *Required:* SAT or ACT (for admission).

Costs (2012–13) *Comprehensive fee:* $50,260 includes full-time tuition ($37,106), mandatory fees ($350), and room and board ($12,804). Part-time tuition: $955 per credit. *College room only:* $7500. Room and board charges vary according to board plan and housing facility. *Payment plan:* installment. *Waivers:* senior citizens and employees or children of employees.

Financial Aid Of all full-time matriculated undergraduates who enrolled in 2010, 3,140 applied for aid, 2,738 were judged to have need, 270 had their need fully met. In 2010, 663 non-need-based awards were made. *Average percent of need met:* 70%. *Average financial aid package:* $22,597. *Average need-based loan:* $7833. *Average need-based gift aid:* $18,242. *Average non-need-based aid:* $11,107. *Average indebtedness upon graduation:* $32,582.

Applying *Options:* electronic application, early admission, early action, deferred entrance. *Required:* essay or personal statement, high school transcript, 1 letter of recommendation. *Required for some:* interview. *Application*

COLLEGES AT-A-GLANCE

deadlines: 3/1 (freshmen), rolling (transfers), 11/15 (early action). *Notification:* continuous until 1/15 (freshmen), continuous (transfers), 12/15 (early action).

Freshman Application Contact Mr. Joseph Roback, Associate Vice President, Admissions and Enrollment, The University of Scranton, The Estate Room 208, The University of Scranton, Scranton, PA 18510-4501. *Phone:* 570-941-7540. *Toll-free phone:* 888-SCRANTON. *Fax:* 570-941-5928. *E-mail:* admissions@scranton.edu. *Web site:* http://www.scranton.edu/.

The University of the Arts

Philadelphia, Pennsylvania

- **Independent** comprehensive, founded 1870
- **Urban** 21-acre campus
- **Coed** 2,002 undergraduate students, 98% full-time, 57% women, 43% men
- **Moderately difficult** entrance level, 46% of applicants were admitted

Undergraduates 1,953 full-time, 49 part-time. Students come from 39 states and territories; 22 other countries; 57% are from out of state; 12% Black or African American, non-Hispanic/Latino; 7% Hispanic/Latino; 3% Asian, non-Hispanic/Latino; 0.5% American Indian or Alaska Native, non-Hispanic/Latino; 2% Two or more races, non-Hispanic/Latino; 5% Race/ethnicity unknown; 6% international; 6% transferred in; 33% live on campus. *Retention:* 79% of full-time freshmen returned.

Freshmen *Admission:* 2,399 applied, 1,096 admitted, 432 enrolled. *Average high school GPA:* 2.8. *Test scores:* SAT critical reading scores over 500: 58%; SAT math scores over 500: 48%; SAT writing scores over 500: 52%; ACT scores over 18: 82%; SAT critical reading scores over 600: 20%; SAT math scores over 600: 15%; SAT writing scores over 600: 18%; ACT scores over 24: 37%; SAT critical reading scores over 700: 2%; SAT math scores over 700: 1%; SAT writing scores over 700: 3%; ACT scores over 30: 5%.

Faculty *Total:* 493, 26% full-time. *Student/faculty ratio:* 9:1.

Academics *Calendar:* semesters. *Degrees:* certificates, diplomas, bachelor's, master's, and postbachelor's certificates. *Special study options:* academic remediation for entering students, accelerated degree program, advanced placement credit, English as a second language, independent study, intern-ships, off-campus study, part-time degree program, services for LD students, study abroad.

Computers on Campus 400 computers/terminals are available on campus for general student use. Students can access the following: campus intranet, computer help desk, free student e-mail accounts, online (class) grades, online (class) registration, online (class) schedules. Campuswide network is available. 100% of college-owned or -operated housing units are wired for high-speed Internet access. Wireless service is available via entire campus.

Student Life *Housing options:* coed. Campus housing is university owned and leased by the school. Freshman applicants given priority for college housing. *Activities and organizations:* drama/theater group, choral group, Ladies of Service, Peer Support/Peer Education, Gallery One, African Diaspora Collection, The Fifth Circle (fencing). *Campus security:* 24-hour emergency response devices and patrols, late-night transport/escort service, crime prevention workshops and seminars. *Student services:* health clinic, personal/psychological counseling.

Athletics *Intramural sports:* fencing M/W.

Standardized Tests *Required for some:* SAT or ACT (for admission).

Costs (2011–12) *Comprehensive fee:* $45,800 includes full-time tuition ($33,500) and room and board ($12,300). Part-time tuition: $1396 per credit hour. *College room only:* $8100. Room and board charges vary according to board plan and housing facility. *Payment plan:* installment. *Waivers:* children of alumni and employees or children of employees.

Financial Aid In 2002, 561 non-need-based awards were made. *Average percent of need met:* 65%. *Average financial aid package:* $16,500. *Average indebtedness upon graduation:* $17,000.

Applying *Options:* electronic application, deferred entrance. *Application fee:* $60. *Required:* essay or personal statement, high school transcript, 1 letter of recommendation, portfolio or audition. *Required for some:* interview. *Recommended:* minimum 2.0 GPA, interview. *Application deadlines:* rolling (freshmen), rolling (out-of-state freshmen), rolling (transfers). *Notification:* continuous (freshmen), continuous (out-of-state freshmen), continuous (transfers).

Freshman Application Contact Ms. Susan Gandy, Dean of Admission, The University of the Arts, 320 South Broad Street, Philadelphia, PA 19102-4944. *Phone:* 215-717-6049. *Toll-free phone:* 800-616-ARTS. *Fax:* 215-717-6045. *E-mail:* admissions@uarts.edu. *Web site:* http://www.uarts.edu/.

See page 1714 for the College Close-Up.

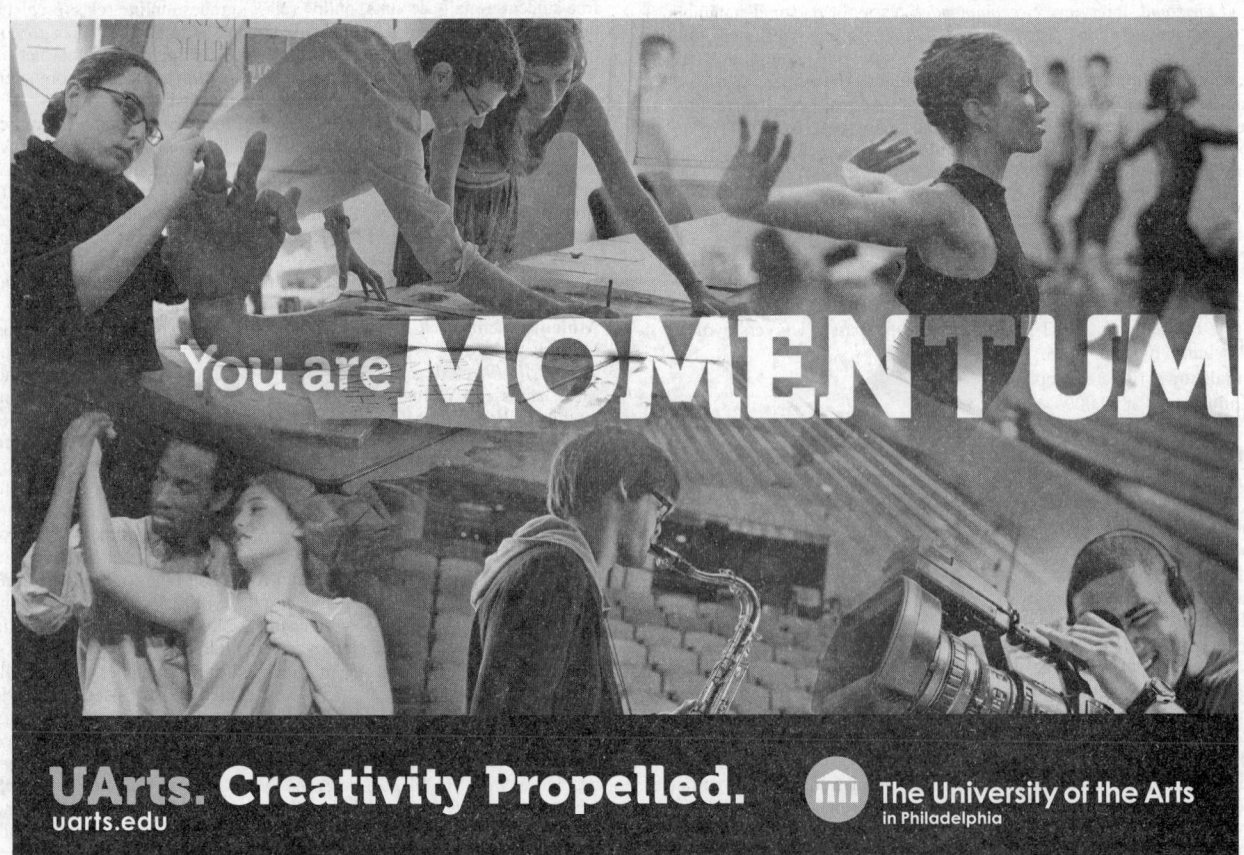

University of the Sciences in Philadelphia

Philadelphia, Pennsylvania

- **Independent** university, founded 1821
- **Urban** 35-acre campus
- **Endowment** $154.2 million
- **Coed** 2,487 undergraduate students, 99% full-time, 61% women, 39% men
- **Moderately difficult** entrance level, 63% of applicants were admitted

Undergraduates 2,457 full-time, 30 part-time. Students come from 30 states and territories; 14 other countries; 54% are from out of state; 5% Black or African American, non-Hispanic/Latino; 2% Hispanic/Latino; 38% Asian, non-Hispanic/Latino; 0.2% Native Hawaiian or other Pacific Islander, non-Hispanic/Latino; 0.1% American Indian or Alaska Native, non-Hispanic/Latino; 1% Two or more races, non-Hispanic/Latino; 5% Race/ethnicity unknown; 2% international; 2% transferred in; 32% live on campus. *Retention:* 83% of full-time freshmen returned.

Freshmen *Admission:* 3,723 applied, 2,358 admitted, 483 enrolled. *Average high school GPA:* 3.6. *Test scores:* SAT critical reading scores over 500: 82%; SAT math scores over 500: 94%; SAT writing scores over 500: 80%; ACT scores over 18: 100%; SAT critical reading scores over 600: 29%; SAT math scores over 600: 53%; SAT writing scores over 600: 33%; ACT scores over 24: 73%; SAT critical reading scores over 700: 4%; SAT math scores over 700: 11%; SAT writing scores over 700: 6%; ACT scores over 30: 8%.

Faculty *Total:* 267, 64% full-time. *Student/faculty ratio:* 11:1.

Academics *Calendar:* semesters. *Degrees:* bachelor's, master's, doctoral, postbachelor's, and first professional certificates. *Special study options:* academic remediation for entering students, adult/continuing education programs, advanced placement credit, cooperative education, distance learning, double majors, honors programs, internships, off-campus study, part-time degree program, services for LD students, study abroad, summer session for credit. *ROTC:* Army (c), Air Force (c).

Computers on Campus 350 computers/terminals are available on campus for general student use. Students can access the following: campus intranet, computer help desk, free student e-mail accounts, online (class) grades, online (class) registration, online (class) schedules. Campuswide network is available. 100% of college-owned or -operated housing units are wired for high-speed Internet access. Wireless service is available via classrooms, computer centers, computer labs, dorm rooms, learning centers, libraries, student centers.

Student Life *Housing:* on-campus residence required through sophomore year. *Options:* coed. Campus housing is university owned and leased by the school. Freshman campus housing is guaranteed. *Activities and organizations:* drama/theater group, student-run newspaper, choral group, student government, Bharat, Academy of Students of Pharmacy, Student Physical Therapy Association, Asian Student Association, national fraternities, national sororities. *Campus security:* 24-hour emergency response devices and patrols, late-night transport/escort service, controlled dormitory access. *Student services:* health clinic, personal/psychological counseling.

Athletics Member NCAA, NAIA. All NCAA Division II. *Intercollegiate sports:* baseball M(s), basketball M(s)/W(s), cross-country running M/W, golf M/W, riflery M/W, softball W(s), tennis M/W, volleyball W(s). *Intramural sports:* archery M/W, basketball M/W, bowling M/W, riflery M/W, softball M/W, table tennis M/W, volleyball M/W.

Standardized Tests *Required:* SAT or ACT (for admission). *Recommended:* SAT (for admission).

Costs (2011–12) *Comprehensive fee:* $44,712 includes full-time tuition ($30,580), mandatory fees ($1568), and room and board ($12,564). Full-time tuition and fees vary according to program. Part-time tuition: $1274 per credit hour. Part-time tuition and fees vary according to course load and program. *Room and board:* Room and board charges vary according to board plan. *Waivers:* employees or children of employees.

Financial Aid Of all full-time matriculated undergraduates who enrolled in 2009, 2,227 applied for aid, 2,075 were judged to have need, 928 had their need fully met. In 2009, 485 non-need-based awards were made. *Average percent of need met:* 88%. *Average financial aid package:* $32,647. *Average need-based loan:* $5576. *Average need-based gift aid:* $7155. *Average non-need-based aid:* $8328. *Average indebtedness upon graduation:* $12,005.

Applying *Options:* electronic application, deferred entrance. *Application fee:* $45. *Required:* high school transcript. *Recommended:* minimum 3.0 GPA. *Application deadline:* rolling (freshmen). *Notification:* continuous (freshmen), continuous (transfers).

Freshman Application Contact Ms. Dianna Collins, Executive Director of Admission and Enrollment Services, University of the Sciences in Philadelphia, 600 South 43rd Street, Philadelphia, PA 19104-4495. *Phone:* 215-596-8810. *Toll-free phone:* 888-996-8747. *Fax:* 215-596-8821. *E-mail:* admit@usp.edu. *Web site:* http://www.usciences.edu/.

See page 1718 for the College Close-Up.

Ursinus College

Collegeville, Pennsylvania

Freshman Application Contact Mr. Richard Floyd, Dean of Admission, Ursinus College, PO Box 1000, Main Street, Collegeville, PA 19426. *Phone:* 610-409-3200. *Fax:* 610-409-3197. *E-mail:* admissions@ursinus.edu. *Web site:* http://www.ursinus.edu/.

Valley Forge Christian College

Phoenixville, Pennsylvania

Freshman Application Contact Rev. William Chenco, Director of Admissions, Valley Forge Christian College, 1401 Charlestown Road, Phoenixville, PA 19460. *Phone:* 610-935-0450 Ext. 1430. *Toll-free phone:* 800-432-8322. *Fax:* 610-917-2069. *E-mail:* admissions@vfcc.edu. *Web site:* http://www.vfcc.edu/.

Villanova University

Villanova, Pennsylvania

- **Independent Roman Catholic** comprehensive, founded 1842
- **Suburban** 254-acre campus with easy access to Philadelphia
- **Endowment** $370.3 million
- **Coed** 7,111 undergraduate students, 93% full-time, 51% women, 49% men
- **Very difficult** entrance level, 44% of applicants were admitted

Undergraduates 6,603 full-time, 508 part-time. Students come from 51 states and territories; 50 other countries; 76% are from out of state; 5% Black or African American, non-Hispanic/Latino; 7% Hispanic/Latino; 6% Asian, non-Hispanic/Latino; 0.1% Native Hawaiian or other Pacific Islander, non-Hispanic/Latino; 2% Two or more races, non-Hispanic/Latino; 2% Race/ethnicity unknown; 3% international; 2% transferred in; 70% live on campus. *Retention:* 94% of full-time freshmen returned.

Freshmen *Admission:* 15,394 applied, 6,768 admitted, 1,644 enrolled. *Average high school GPA:* 3.86. *Test scores:* SAT critical reading scores over 500: 96%; SAT math scores over 500: 98%; ACT scores over 18: 100%; SAT critical reading scores over 600: 73%; SAT math scores over 600: 84%; ACT scores over 24: 97%; SAT critical reading scores over 700: 19%; SAT math scores over 700: 37%; ACT scores over 30: 64%.

Faculty *Total:* 951, 62% full-time, 68% with terminal degrees. *Student/faculty ratio:* 11:1.

Academics *Calendar:* semesters. *Degrees:* bachelor's, master's, doctoral, post-master's, postbachelor's, and first professional certificates. *Special study options:* accelerated degree program, adult/continuing education programs, advanced placement credit, cooperative education, distance learning, double majors, English as a second language, honors programs, independent study, internships, off-campus study, part-time degree program, services for LD students, study abroad, summer session for credit. *ROTC:* Army (b), Navy (b), Air Force (c). *Unusual degree programs:* 3-2 engineering with Civil Engineering, Chemical Engineering, Computer Engineering, Electrical Engineering, and Mechanical Engineering; arts/liberal studies; classical studies; communication; criminal justice; political science; psychology; Spanish; religious studies; computer science; biology; chemistry; mathematics; mathematics/applied statistics; human resources development; business information systems/software engineering.

Computers on Campus 6,609 computers/terminals and 20,000 ports are available on campus for general student use. Students can access the following: campus intranet, computer help desk, free student e-mail accounts, online (class) grades, online (class) registration, online (class) schedules, learning management system with anti-plagiarism software, testing software, online faculty hours, videoconferencing; electronic portfolios; data vaulting/backup service; emergency notification system; Citrix-based library of advanced software. Campuswide network is available. 100% of college-owned or -operated housing units are wired for high-speed Internet access. Wireless service is available via classrooms, computer centers, computer labs, dorm rooms, learning centers, libraries, student centers.

Student Life *Housing options:* coed, men-only, women-only, disabled students. Campus housing is university owned. Freshman campus housing is guaranteed. *Activities and organizations:* drama/theater group, student-run newspaper, radio and television station, choral group, marching band, Blue Key Society, New Student Orientation Counselor Program, Special Olympics, Campus Activities Team, Student Government Association, national fraternities, national sororities. *Campus security:* 24-hour emergency response devices and patrols, late-night transport/escort service, controlled dormitory access, Nova Alert - email, text messaging re: emergency situations. *Student services:* health clinic, personal/psychological counseling.

Athletics Member NCAA. All Division I except football (Division I-AA). *Intercollegiate sports:* baseball M(s), basketball M(s)/W(s), cheerleading M/W, crew M(c)/W, cross-country running M(s)/W(s), equestrian sports W(c), field hockey W(s), golf M, ice hockey M(c)/W(c), lacrosse M(s)/W(s), sailing

M(c)/W(c), skiing (downhill) M(c)/W(c), soccer M(s)/W(s), softball W(s), swimming and diving M/W(s), tennis M/W, track and field M(s)/W(s), volleyball M(c)/W(s), water polo M(c)/W. *Intramural sports:* badminton M(c)/W(c), baseball M(c), basketball M(c)/W(c), crew M(c), cross-country running M(c)/W(c), equestrian sports W(c), field hockey W(c), football M/W, golf M(c)/W(c), ice hockey M(c)/W(c), lacrosse M(c)/W(c), rugby M(c), sailing M(c)/W(c), skiing (downhill) M(c)/W(c), soccer M(c)/W(c), softball M/W, swimming and diving M(c)/W(c), tennis M(c)/W(c), ultimate Frisbee M(c)/W(c), volleyball M(c)/W(c), water polo M(c).

Standardized Tests *Required:* SAT or ACT (for admission).

Costs (2011–12) *Comprehensive fee:* $52,070 includes full-time tuition ($40,530), mandatory fees ($580), and room and board ($10,960). Part-time tuition: $1645 per course. Part-time tuition and fees vary according to class time and program. *Required fees:* $30 per year part-time. *College room only:* $5810. Room and board charges vary according to board plan and housing facility. *Payment plan:* installment. *Waivers:* senior citizens and employees or children of employees.

Financial Aid Of all full-time matriculated undergraduates who enrolled in 2011, 3,829 applied for aid, 3,100 were judged to have need, 471 had their need fully met. 2,542 Federal Work-Study jobs (averaging $2799). 41 state and other part-time jobs (averaging $2915). In 2011, 479 non-need-based awards were made. *Average percent of need met:* 81%. *Average financial aid package:* $29,762. *Average need-based loan:* $4460. *Average need-based gift aid:* $24,340. *Average non-need-based aid:* $11,076. *Average indebtedness upon graduation:* $38,055. *Financial aid deadline:* 2/7.

Applying *Options:* electronic application, early admission, early action, deferred entrance. *Application fee:* $80. *Required:* essay or personal statement, high school transcript, 1 letter of recommendation, Test Scores (SAT or ACT). *Application deadlines:* 1/7 (freshmen), 1/7 (out-of-state freshmen), 6/1 (transfers), 11/1 (early action). *Notification:* 4/1 (freshmen), 4/1 (out-of-state freshmen), continuous (transfers), 12/20 (early action).

Freshman Application Contact Mr. Michael Gaynor, Director of University Admission, Villanova University, 800 Lancaster Avenue, Villanova, PA 19085-1672. *Phone:* 610-519-4000. *Fax:* 610-519-6450. *E-mail:* gotovu@villanova.edu. *Web site:* http://www.villanova.edu/.

See page 1736 for the College Close-Up.

Washington & Jefferson College
Washington, Pennsylvania

- **Independent** 4-year, founded 1781
- **Suburban** 60-acre campus with easy access to Pittsburgh
- **Endowment** $105.4 million
- **Coed** 1,457 undergraduate students, 99% full-time, 50% women, 50% men
- **Very difficult** entrance level, 43% of applicants were admitted

Undergraduates 1,436 full-time, 21 part-time. Students come from 37 states and territories; 15 other countries; 28% are from out of state; 3% Black or African American, non-Hispanic/Latino; 2% Hispanic/Latino; 2% Asian, non-Hispanic/Latino; 0.1% Native Hawaiian or other Pacific Islander, non-Hispanic/Latino; 0.6% American Indian or Alaska Native, non-Hispanic/Latino; 2% Two or more races, non-Hispanic/Latino; 8% Race/ethnicity unknown; 3% international; 1% transferred in; 91% live on campus. *Retention:* 88% of full-time freshmen returned.

Freshmen *Admission:* 6,643 applied, 2,855 admitted, 387 enrolled. *Average high school GPA:* 3.33. *Test scores:* SAT critical reading scores over 500: 84%; SAT math scores over 500: 88%; ACT scores over 18: 99%; SAT critical reading scores over 600: 33%; SAT math scores over 600: 38%; ACT scores over 24: 71%; SAT critical reading scores over 700: 4%; SAT math scores over 700: 6%; ACT scores over 30: 14%.

Faculty *Total:* 160, 71% full-time, 74% with terminal degrees. *Student/faculty ratio:* 11:1.

Academics *Calendar:* 4-1-4. *Degree:* bachelor's. *Special study options:* academic remediation for entering students, accelerated degree program, advanced placement credit, double majors, honors programs, independent study, internships, off-campus study, part-time degree program, services for LD students, student-designed majors, study abroad, summer session for credit. *ROTC:* Army (b), Air Force (c). *Unusual degree programs:* 3-2 engineering with Columbia University in New York City; Case Western Reserve University in Ohio, Washington University in St. Louis; medicine program with Temple U; optometry program with PA College of Optometry at Salus U; physician assistant program with Saint Francis U & Chatham; podiatric medicine program with Temple & Ohio College; physical therapy program with Drexel & Chatham.

Computers on Campus 450 computers/terminals and 2,000 ports are available on campus for general student use. Students can access the following: campus intranet, computer help desk, free student e-mail accounts, online (class) grades, online (class) registration, online (class) schedules. Campus-wide network is available. 100% of college-owned or -operated housing units are wired for high-speed Internet access. Wireless service is available via entire campus.

Student Life *Housing:* on-campus residence required through senior year. *Options:* coed, men-only, women-only, disabled students. Campus housing is university owned. Freshman campus housing is guaranteed. *Activities and organizations:* drama/theater group, student-run newspaper, radio station, choral group, Student Government Association, Student Activities Board, Black Student Union, Pre-Legal Society, W&J American Mock Trial Association, national fraternities, national sororities. *Campus security:* 24-hour emergency response devices and patrols, late-night transport/escort service, controlled dormitory access, security cameras throughout campus, card access to buildings. *Student services:* health clinic, personal/psychological counseling, women's center.

Athletics Member NCAA. All Division III. *Intercollegiate sports:* baseball M, basketball M/W, cheerleading M(c)/W(c), cross-country running M/W, equestrian sports M(c)/W(c), fencing M(c)/W(c), field hockey W, football M, golf M/W, ice hockey M(c), lacrosse M/W, rugby M(c)/W(c), soccer M/W, softball W, swimming and diving M/W, tennis M/W, track and field M/W, ultimate Frisbee M(c)/W(c), volleyball M/W, water polo M/W, wrestling M. *Intramural sports:* basketball M/W, bowling M/W, racquetball M/W, soccer M/W, squash M/W, table tennis M/W, tennis M/W, ultimate Frisbee M/W, volleyball M/W.

Costs (2011–12) *Comprehensive fee:* $45,980 includes full-time tuition ($35,960), mandatory fees ($460), and room and board ($9560). Full-time tuition and fees vary according to reciprocity agreements. Part-time tuition: $903 per credit hour. Part-time tuition and fees vary according to course load. *College room only:* $5686. Room and board charges vary according to board plan and housing facility. *Payment plans:* installment, deferred payment. *Waivers:* employees or children of employees.

Financial Aid Of all full-time matriculated undergraduates who enrolled in 2011, 1,211 applied for aid, 1,106 were judged to have need, 200 had their need fully met. 609 Federal Work-Study jobs (averaging $1637). 200 state and other part-time jobs (averaging $800). In 2011, 277 non-need-based awards were made. *Average percent of need met:* 75%. *Average financial aid package:* $25,338. *Average need-based loan:* $4487. *Average need-based gift aid:* $10,845. *Average non-need-based aid:* $12,670.

Applying *Options:* electronic application, early admission, early decision, early action, deferred entrance. *Application fee:* $25. *Required:* essay or personal statement, high school transcript, 1 letter of recommendation. *Required for some:* interview. *Recommended:* interview. *Application deadlines:* 3/1 (freshmen), rolling (transfers), 1/15 (early action). *Early decision deadline:* 12/1. *Notification:* 3/15 (freshmen), 12/15 (early decision), 2/15 (early action).

Freshman Application Contact Mr. Alton E. Newell, Vice President for Enrollment, Washington & Jefferson College, 60 South Lincoln Street, Washington, PA 15301. *Phone:* 724-223-6025. *Toll-free phone:* 888-WANDJAY. *Fax:* 724-223-6534. *E-mail:* admission@washjeff.edu. *Web site:* http://www.washjeff.edu/.

Waynesburg University
Waynesburg, Pennsylvania

- **Independent** comprehensive, founded 1849, affiliated with Presbyterian Church (U.S.A.)
- **Small-town** 30-acre campus with easy access to Pittsburgh
- **Coed** 1,739 undergraduate students, 90% full-time, 61% women, 39% men
- **Moderately difficult** entrance level, 91% of applicants were admitted

Undergraduates 1,559 full-time, 180 part-time. Students come from 29 states and territories; 5 other countries; 17% are from out of state; 4% Black or African American, non-Hispanic/Latino; 2% Hispanic/Latino; 0.6% Asian, non-Hispanic/Latino; 0.1% Native Hawaiian or other Pacific Islander, non-Hispanic/Latino; 0.3% American Indian or Alaska Native, non-Hispanic/Latino; 0.6% Two or more races, non-Hispanic/Latino; 2% Race/ethnicity unknown; 2% transferred in; 59% live on campus. *Retention:* 78% of full-time freshmen returned.

Freshmen *Admission:* 1,888 applied, 1,719 admitted, 395 enrolled. *Average high school GPA:* 3.51.

Faculty *Total:* 259, 30% full-time, 31% with terminal degrees. *Student/faculty ratio:* 13:1.

Academics *Calendar:* semesters. *Degrees:* bachelor's, master's, and doctoral. *Special study options:* academic remediation for entering students, accelerated degree program, adult/continuing education programs, advanced placement credit, distance learning, double majors, honors programs, independent study, internships, part-time degree program, services for LD students, study abroad, summer session for credit. *ROTC:* Army (c). *Unusual degree programs:* 3-2 engineering with Washington University in St. Louis, Pennsylvania State University - University Park Campus.

Computers on Campus 150 computers/terminals are available on campus for general student use. Students can access the following: campus intranet, computer help desk, free student e-mail accounts, online (class) grades, online (class) registration, online (class) schedules. Campuswide network is available. 100% of college-owned or -operated housing units are wired for high-speed Internet access. Wireless service is available via classrooms, computer labs, libraries.

Student Life *Housing:* on-campus residence required through junior year. *Options:* men-only, women-only. Campus housing is university owned. Freshman campus housing is guaranteed. *Activities and organizations:* drama/theater group, student-run newspaper, radio and television station, choral group, marching band, Student Senate, Student Activities Board, Student Nurses Association, Christian Fellowship. *Campus security:* 24-hour emergency response devices and patrols, late-night transport/escort service, controlled dormitory access. *Student services:* health clinic, personal/psychological counseling.

Athletics Member NCAA. All Division III. *Intercollegiate sports:* baseball M, basketball M/W, cross-country running M/W, football M, golf M/W, lacrosse W, soccer M/W, softball W, tennis M/W, track and field M/W, volleyball W, wrestling M. *Intramural sports:* basketball M/W, bowling M/W, racquetball M/W, softball M/W, table tennis M/W, volleyball M/W.

Standardized Tests *Required:* SAT or ACT (for admission).

Costs (2011–12) *Comprehensive fee:* $27,020 includes full-time tuition ($18,730), mandatory fees ($360), and room and board ($7930). Full-time tuition and fees vary according to class time. Part-time tuition: $790 per credit hour. Part-time tuition and fees vary according to class time, course load, and location. *College room only:* $4010. Room and board charges vary according to board plan. *Payment plan:* installment. *Waivers:* employees or children of employees.

Financial Aid Of all full-time matriculated undergraduates who enrolled in 2011, 1,504 applied for aid, 1,342 were judged to have need, 337 had their need fully met. 300 Federal Work-Study jobs (averaging $1200). In 2011, 157 non-need-based awards were made. *Average percent of need met:* 75%. *Average financial aid package:* $13,880. *Average need-based loan:* $4188. *Average need-based gift aid:* $10,587. *Average non-need-based aid:* $8160. *Average indebtedness upon graduation:* $28,755.

Applying *Options:* electronic application, early admission. *Application fee:* $20. *Required:* high school transcript, minimum 2.8 GPA. *Required for some:* essay or personal statement, 2 letters of recommendation. *Recommended:* minimum 3.0 GPA, interview. *Application deadlines:* rolling (freshmen), rolling (transfers). *Notification:* continuous (freshmen), continuous (transfers).

Freshman Application Contact Ms. Robin L. King, Senior VP for Enrollment and Marketing, Waynesburg University, 51 West College Street, Waynesburg, PA 15370. *Phone:* 724-852-3333. *Toll-free phone:* 800-225-7393. *Fax:* 724-627-8124. *E-mail:* admissions@waynesburg.edu. *Web site:* http://www.waynesburg.edu/.

West Chester University of Pennsylvania
West Chester, Pennsylvania

- **State-supported** comprehensive, founded 1871, part of Pennsylvania State System of Higher Education
- **Suburban** 407-acre campus with easy access to Philadelphia
- **Endowment** $16.3 million
- **Coed** 12,834 undergraduate students, 91% full-time, 59% women, 41% men
- **Moderately difficult** entrance level, 47% of applicants were admitted

Undergraduates 11,635 full-time, 1,199 part-time. Students come from 25 states and territories; 56 other countries; 12% are from out of state; 9% Black or African American, non-Hispanic/Latino; 4% Hispanic/Latino; 2% Asian, non-Hispanic/Latino; 0.4% American Indian or Alaska Native, non-Hispanic/Latino; 0.0% Two or more races, non-Hispanic/Latino; 0.4% Race/ethnicity unknown; 0.3% international; 10% transferred in; 41% live on campus. *Retention:* 86% of full-time freshmen returned.

Freshmen *Admission:* 15,080 applied, 7,013 admitted, 2,292 enrolled. *Average high school GPA:* 3.21. *Test scores:* SAT critical reading scores over 500: 73%; SAT math scores over 500: 79%; SAT writing scores over 500: 67%; SAT critical reading scores over 600: 19%; SAT math scores over 600: 21%; SAT writing scores over 600: 16%; SAT critical reading scores over 700: 2%; SAT math scores over 700: 1%; SAT writing scores over 700: 1%.

Faculty *Total:* 878, 68% full-time, 64% with terminal degrees. *Student/faculty ratio:* 18:1.

Academics *Calendar:* semesters. *Degrees:* bachelor's, master's, post-master's, and postbachelor's certificates. *Special study options:* academic remediation for entering students, accelerated degree program, adult/continuing education programs, advanced placement credit, distance learning, double majors, freshman honors college, honors programs, independent study, internships, off-campus study, part-time degree program, services for LD students, student-designed majors, study abroad, summer session for credit. *ROTC:*

Army (b), Air Force (c). *Unusual degree programs:* 3-2 engineering with Pennsylvania State University, Philadelphia University.

Computers on Campus 1,900 computers/terminals are available on campus for general student use. Students can access the following: campus intranet, computer help desk, free student e-mail accounts, online (class) grades, online (class) registration, online (class) schedules. Campuswide network is available. 100% of college-owned or -operated housing units are wired for high-speed Internet access. Wireless service is available via classrooms, computer centers, computer labs, learning centers, libraries, student centers.

Student Life *Housing options:* coed, disabled students. Campus housing is university owned and is provided by a third party. Freshman applicants given priority for college housing. *Activities and organizations:* drama/theater group, student-run newspaper, radio and television station, choral group, marching band, Student Government Association, Residence Hall Association, Inter-Greek Council, Sports Club Council, Campus Crusade for Christ, national fraternities, national sororities. *Campus security:* 24-hour emergency response devices and patrols, late-night transport/escort service, controlled dormitory access. *Student services:* health clinic, personal/psychological counseling, women's center, legal services.

Athletics Member NCAA. All Division II. *Intercollegiate sports:* baseball M(s), basketball M(s)/W(s), bowling M(c)/W(c), cheerleading W, equestrian sports M(c)/W(c), fencing M(c)/W(c), field hockey W(s), football M(s), golf M(s)/W(s), gymnastics W(s), ice hockey M(c)/W(c), lacrosse M(c)/W(s), rugby M(c)/W(s), skiing (downhill) M(c)/W(c), soccer M(s)/W(s), softball W(s), swimming and diving M(s)/W(s), tennis M(s)/W(s), track and field M(s)/W(s), volleyball M(c)/W(s), water polo W(c), wrestling M(c). *Intramural sports:* basketball M/W, field hockey M/W, soccer M/W, softball M/W, tennis M/W, volleyball M/W.

Standardized Tests *Required:* SAT or ACT (for admission).

Costs (2011–12) *Tuition:* state resident $6240 full-time, $260 per credit hour part-time; nonresident $15,600 full-time, $650 per credit hour part-time. Full-time tuition and fees vary according to course load. Part-time tuition and fees vary according to course load. *Required fees:* $2034 full-time, $79 per credit hour part-time, $36 per term part-time. *Room and board:* $7784; room only: $4848. Room and board charges vary according to board plan and housing facility. *Payment plan:* installment. *Waivers:* senior citizens and employees or children of employees.

Financial Aid Of all full-time matriculated undergraduates who enrolled in 2010, 8,491 applied for aid, 6,519 were judged to have need, 743 had their need fully met. In 2010, 123 non-need-based awards were made. *Average percent of need met:* 54%. *Average financial aid package:* $7343. *Average need-based loan:* $4159. *Average need-based gift aid:* $5033. *Average non-need-based aid:* $3177. *Average indebtedness upon graduation:* $27,689.

Applying *Options:* electronic application, deferred entrance. *Application fee:* $45. *Required:* essay or personal statement, high school transcript, SAT or ACT. *Required for some:* interview. *Recommended:* minimum 3.0 GPA. *Application deadlines:* rolling (freshmen), rolling (transfers). *Notification:* continuous (freshmen), continuous (transfers).

Freshman Application Contact West Chester University of Pennsylvania, University Avenue and High Street, West Chester, PA 19383. *Phone:* 610-436-3414. *Toll-free phone:* 877-315-2165. *Web site:* http://www.wcupa.edu/.

See page 1752 for the College Close-Up.

Westminster College
New Wilmington, Pennsylvania

Freshman Application Contact Bradley Tokar, Director of Admissions, Westminster College, 319 South Market Street, New Wilmington, PA 16172-0001. *Phone:* 724-946-7100. *Toll-free phone:* 800-942-8033. *Fax:* 724-946-7171. *E-mail:* tokarbp@westminster.edu. *Web site:* http://www.westminster.edu/.

Widener University
Chester, Pennsylvania

- **Independent** comprehensive, founded 1821
- **Suburban** 110-acre campus with easy access to Philadelphia
- **Endowment** $78.7 million
- **Coed** 3,347 undergraduate students, 81% full-time, 56% women, 44% men
- **Moderately difficult** entrance level, 66% of applicants were admitted

Undergraduates 2,717 full-time, 630 part-time. Students come from 22 states and territories; 17 other countries; 40% are from out of state; 16% Black or African American, non-Hispanic/Latino; 4% Hispanic/Latino; 3% Asian, non-Hispanic/Latino; 0.2% Native Hawaiian or other Pacific Islander, non-Hispanic/Latino; 0.4% American Indian or Alaska Native, non-Hispanic/Latino; 2% Two or more races, non-Hispanic/Latino; 2% Race/ethnicity unknown; 2%

international; 4% transferred in; 50% live on campus. *Retention:* 72% of full-time freshmen returned.

Freshmen *Admission:* 5,336 applied, 3,538 admitted, 762 enrolled. *Average high school GPA:* 3.37. *Test scores:* SAT critical reading scores over 500: 40%; SAT math scores over 500: 52%; SAT math scores over 600: 8%; SAT critical reading scores over 600: 13%; SAT critical reading scores over 700: 1%; SAT math scores over 700: 2%.

Faculty *Total:* 681, 48% full-time, 64% with terminal degrees. *Student/faculty ratio:* 12:1.

Academics *Calendar:* semesters. *Degrees:* associate, bachelor's, master's, doctoral, and first professional. *Special study options:* academic remediation for entering students, accelerated degree program, adult/continuing education programs, advanced placement credit, cooperative education, distance learning, double majors, English as a second language, honors programs, independent study, internships, off-campus study, part-time degree program, services for LD students, student-designed majors, study abroad, summer session for credit. *ROTC:* Army (b), Navy (c), Air Force (c). *Unusual degree programs:* 3-2 business administration; engineering; social work; physical therapy, education.

Computers on Campus 710 computers/terminals are available on campus for general student use. Students can access the following: campus intranet, computer help desk, free student e-mail accounts, online (class) grades, online (class) registration, online (class) schedules. Campuswide network is available. 100% of college-owned or -operated housing units are wired for high-speed Internet access. Wireless service is available via classrooms, computer centers, computer labs, dorm rooms, learning centers, libraries, student centers.

Student Life *Housing:* on-campus residence required through sophomore year. *Options:* coed, men-only, women-only, cooperative. Campus housing is university owned. Freshman campus housing is guaranteed. *Activities and organizations:* drama/theater group, student-run newspaper, radio and television station, choral group, WDNR Radio, Black Student Union, volunteer services, rugby club, Theatre Widener, national fraternities, national sororities. *Campus security:* 24-hour emergency response devices and patrols, late-night transport/escort service, controlled dormitory access, blue light emergency phones located throughout campus. *Student services:* health clinic, personal/psychological counseling.

Athletics Member NCAA. All Division III. *Intercollegiate sports:* baseball M, basketball M/W, cheerleading W, cross-country running M/W, field hockey W, football M, golf M, lacrosse M/W, soccer M/W, softball W, swimming and diving M/W, track and field M/W, volleyball W. *Intramural sports:* crew M, ice hockey M(c), rock climbing M(c)/W(c), rugby M(c), skiing (downhill) M(c)/W(c), soccer M, volleyball M(c).

Standardized Tests *Required:* SAT or ACT (for admission).

Costs (2011–12) *Comprehensive fee:* $46,658 includes full-time tuition ($34,224), mandatory fees ($538), and room and board ($11,896). Full-time tuition and fees vary according to class time, course load, and program. Part-time tuition: $1138 per credit hour. *College room only:* $6172. Room and board charges vary according to board plan and housing facility. *Payment plan:* installment. *Waivers:* senior citizens and employees or children of employees.

Financial Aid Of all full-time matriculated undergraduates who enrolled in 2011, 2,382 applied for aid, 2,242 were judged to have need, 320 had their need fully met. 1,758 Federal Work-Study jobs (averaging $1100). In 2011, 305 non-need-based awards were made. *Average percent of need met:* 71%. *Average financial aid package:* $25,035. *Average need-based loan:* $4657. *Average need-based gift aid:* $8790. *Average non-need-based aid:* $13,528. *Average indebtedness upon graduation:* $44,430.

Applying *Options:* electronic application, deferred entrance. *Application fee:* $35. *Required:* essay or personal statement, high school transcript. *Required for some:* minimum 2.9 GPA. *Recommended:* interview. *Application deadlines:* rolling (freshmen), rolling (transfers). *Notification:* continuous (freshmen), continuous (transfers).

Freshman Application Contact Office of Admissions, Widener University, One University Place, Chester, PA 19013. *Phone:* 610-499-4126. *Toll-free phone:* 888-WIDENER. *Fax:* 610-499-4676. *E-mail:* admissions.office@widener.edu. *Web site:* http://www.widener.edu/.

Wilkes University
Wilkes-Barre, Pennsylvania

- **Independent** comprehensive, founded 1933
- **Urban** 25-acre campus
- **Endowment** $32.7 million
- **Coed** 2,211 undergraduate students, 91% full-time, 49% women, 51% men
- **Moderately difficult** entrance level, 76% of applicants were admitted

Undergraduates 2,023 full-time, 188 part-time. Students come from 19 states and territories; 11 other countries; 17% are from out of state; 3% Black or Afri-

can American, non-Hispanic/Latino; 3% Hispanic/Latino; 2% Asian, non-Hispanic/Latino; 0.1% American Indian or Alaska Native, non-Hispanic/Latino; 2% Two or more races, non-Hispanic/Latino; 11% Race/ethnicity unknown; 3% international; 7% transferred in; 36% live on campus. *Retention:* 82% of full-time freshmen returned.

Freshmen *Admission:* 2,811 applied, 2,146 admitted, 545 enrolled. *Test scores:* SAT critical reading scores over 500: 58%; SAT math scores over 500: 67%; SAT writing scores over 500: 57%; SAT critical reading scores over 600: 14%; SAT math scores over 600: 24%; SAT writing scores over 600: 12%; SAT critical reading scores over 700: 1%; SAT math scores over 700: 3%; SAT writing scores over 700: 1%.

Faculty *Total:* 416, 38% full-time. *Student/faculty ratio:* 14:1.

Academics *Calendar:* semesters. *Degrees:* bachelor's, master's, doctoral, and first professional. *Special study options:* academic remediation for entering students, accelerated degree program, adult/continuing education programs, advanced placement credit, cooperative education, distance learning, double majors, English as a second language, external degree program, honors programs, independent study, internships, off-campus study, part-time degree program, services for LD students, student-designed majors, study abroad, summer session for credit. *ROTC:* Army (c), Air Force (b).

Computers on Campus 709 computers/terminals are available on campus for general student use. Students can access the following: campus intranet, computer help desk, free student e-mail accounts, online (class) grades, online (class) registration, online (class) schedules. Campuswide network is available. Wireless service is available via libraries, student centers.

Student Life *Housing:* on-campus residence required through sophomore year. *Options:* coed, men-only, women-only. Campus housing is university owned. Freshman campus housing is guaranteed. *Activities and organizations:* drama/theater group, student-run newspaper, radio and television station, choral group. *Campus security:* 24-hour emergency response devices and patrols, late-night transport/escort service, controlled dormitory access. *Student services:* health clinic, personal/psychological counseling.

Athletics Member NCAA. All Division III. *Intercollegiate sports:* baseball M, basketball M/W, cross-country running M/W, field hockey W, football M, golf M, lacrosse W, soccer M/W, softball W, tennis M/W, volleyball W, wrestling M. *Intramural sports:* basketball M/W, football M, racquetball M/W, volleyball M/W, weight lifting M/W.

Standardized Tests *Required:* SAT or ACT (for admission).

Costs (2011–12) *Comprehensive fee:* $39,908 includes full-time tuition ($26,834), mandatory fees ($1376), and room and board ($11,698). Part-time tuition: $745 per credit hour. *Required fees:* $62 per credit hour part-time.

College room only: $7018. Room and board charges vary according to board plan and housing facility. *Payment plans:* installment, deferred payment. *Waivers:* employees or children of employees.

Financial Aid Of all full-time matriculated undergraduates who enrolled in 2011, 1,756 applied for aid, 1,663 were judged to have need, 202 had their need fully met. In 2011, 213 non-need-based awards were made. *Average percent of need met:* 71%. *Average financial aid package:* $20,619. *Average need-based loan:* $4302. *Average need-based gift aid:* $16,739. *Average non-need-based aid:* $10,378. *Average indebtedness upon graduation:* $35,684.

Applying *Options:* electronic application, early admission, deferred entrance. *Application fee:* $40. *Required:* high school transcript. *Required for some:* 2 letters of recommendation. *Recommended:* interview. *Application deadlines:* rolling (freshmen), rolling (transfers). *Notification:* 8/30 (freshmen), continuous until 8/30 (transfers).

Freshman Application Contact Ms. Melanie Mickelson, Vice President of Enrollment Services, Wilkes University, 84 West South Street, Wilkes-Barre, PA 18766. *Phone:* 570-408-4400. *Toll-free phone:* 800-945-5378 Ext. 4400. *Fax:* 570-408-4904. *E-mail:* admissions@wilkes.edu. *Web site:* http://www.wilkes.edu/.

See below for display ad and page 1764 for the College Close-Up.

Wilson College
Chambersburg, Pennsylvania

- **Independent** comprehensive, founded 1869, affiliated with Presbyterian Church (U.S.A.)
- **Small-town** 300-acre campus
- **Endowment** $60.5 million
- **Coed, primarily women** 698 undergraduate students
- **Moderately difficult** entrance level, 56% of applicants were admitted

Undergraduates 5% Black or African American, non-Hispanic/Latino; 3% Hispanic/Latino; 2% Two or more races, non-Hispanic/Latino; 10% Race/ethnicity unknown; 4% international; 74% live on campus. *Retention:* 76% of full-time freshmen returned.

Freshmen *Admission:* 407 applied, 226 admitted. *Average high school GPA:* 3.42.

Faculty *Total:* 85, 53% full-time, 52% with terminal degrees. *Student/faculty ratio:* 10:1.

Academics *Calendar:* 4-1-4. *Degrees:* associate, bachelor's, and master's. *Special study options:* academic remediation for entering students, adult/con-

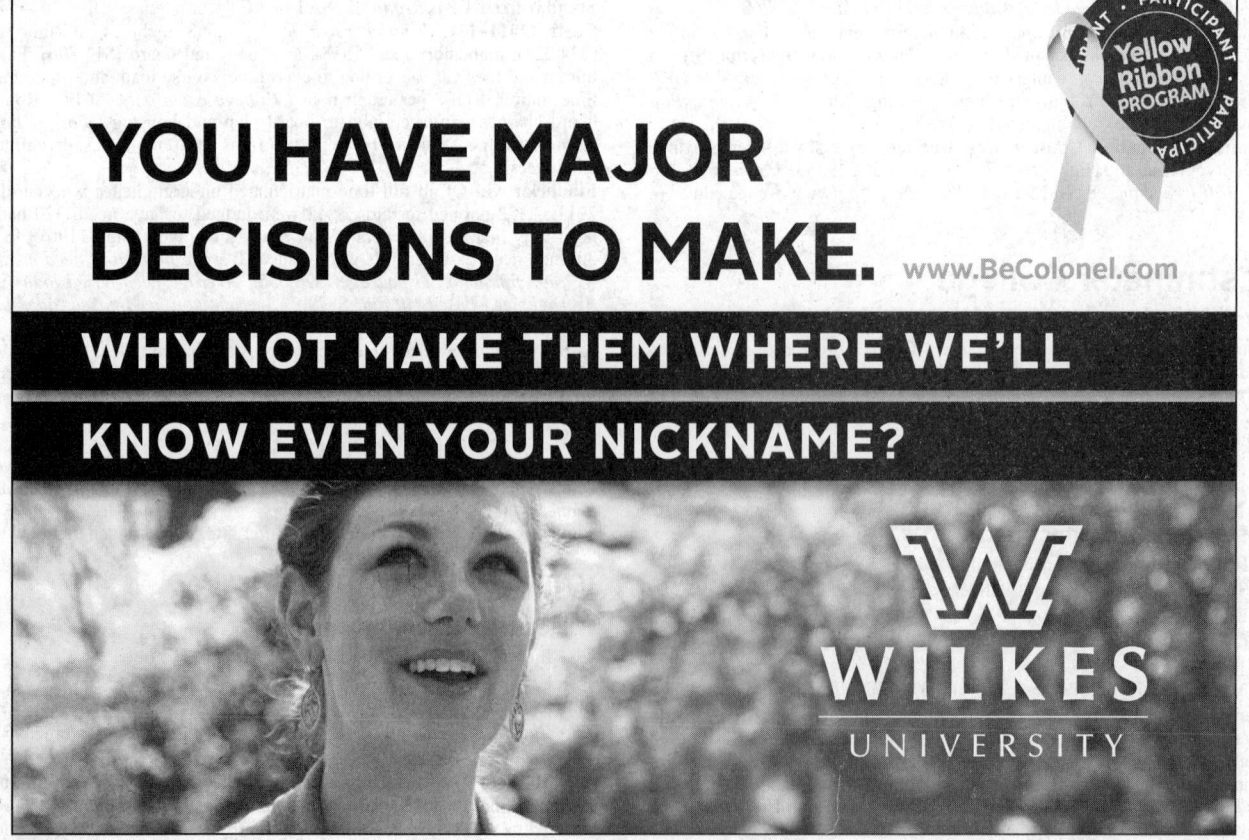

tinuing education programs, advanced placement credit, distance learning, double majors, honors programs, independent study, internships, off-campus study, part-time degree program, services for LD students, student-designed majors, study abroad, summer session for credit. *ROTC:* Army (c).

Computers on Campus 96 computers/terminals and 1,200 ports are available on campus for general student use. Students can access the following: campus intranet, free student e-mail accounts, online (class) grades, online (class) registration, online (class) schedules, online databases. Campuswide network is available. 100% of college-owned or -operated housing units are wired for high-speed Internet access. Wireless service is available via classrooms, learning centers, libraries, student centers.

Student Life *Housing:* on-campus residence required through junior year. *Options:* women-only. Campus housing is university owned. Freshman campus housing is guaranteed. *Activities and organizations:* drama/theater group, student-run newspaper, choral group, Muhibbah Club, Orchesis Club, student newspaper, student government, Campus Activity Board. *Campus security:* 24-hour emergency response devices and patrols, late-night transport/escort service, controlled dormitory access. *Student services:* health clinic, personal/psychological counseling, women's center.

Athletics Member NCAA. All Division III. *Intercollegiate sports:* basketball W, field hockey W, gymnastics W, lacrosse W, soccer W, softball W. *Intramural sports:* archery W, equestrian sports W, tennis W.

Standardized Tests *Required for some:* SAT or ACT (for admission), SAT/ACT optional for students with high school GPA of 3.0 and specified college prep curriculum from regionally accredited schools; TOEFL/IELTS/STEP for international students.

Costs (2011–12) *Comprehensive fee:* $39,051 includes full-time tuition ($28,745), mandatory fees ($595), and room and board ($9711). Part-time tuition: $2875 per course. Part-time tuition and fees vary according to course load. *Required fees:* $50 per course part-time, $50 per term part-time. *College room only:* $5055. Room and board charges vary according to board plan and housing facility. *Payment plan:* installment. *Waivers:* employees or children of employees.

Financial Aid Of all full-time matriculated undergraduates who enrolled in 2011, 316 applied for aid, 297 were judged to have need, 38 had their need fully met. 23 Federal Work-Study jobs (averaging $2000). 121 state and other part-time jobs (averaging $2000). In 2011, 39 non-need-based awards were made. *Average percent of need met:* 77%. *Average financial aid package:* $23,609. *Average need-based loan:* $4954. *Average need-based gift aid:* $19,235. *Average non-need-based aid:* $13,341. *Average indebtedness upon graduation:* $33,862.

Applying *Options:* electronic application, early admission, deferred entrance. *Required:* essay or personal statement, high school transcript, 1 letter of recommendation, college preparatory program that includes 4 units of English, 4 units of History/Civics, 3 units of Mathematics (preferably Algebra I, II or Geometry), 2 units of same Foreign Language, and 2 units of Natural Sciences with lab. *Recommended:* minimum 2.8 GPA, interview. *Application deadlines:* rolling (freshmen), rolling (out-of-state freshmen), rolling (transfers). *Notification:* continuous (freshmen), continuous (out-of-state freshmen), continuous (transfers).

Freshman Application Contact Ms. Nancy Myers, Admissions Administrator, Wilson College, 1015 Philadelphia Avenue, Chambersburg, PA 17201. *Phone:* 717-262-2002. *Toll-free phone:* 800-421-8402. *Fax:* 717-262-2546. *E-mail:* admissions@wilson.edu. *Web site:* http://www.wilson.edu/.

Yeshiva Beth Moshe
Scranton, Pennsylvania

Director of Admissions Dean, Yeshiva Beth Moshe, 930 Hickory Street, PO Box 1141, Scranton, PA 18505-2124. *Phone:* 717-346-1747.

York College of Pennsylvania
York, Pennsylvania

- **Independent** comprehensive, founded 1787
- **Suburban** 190-acre campus with easy access to Baltimore
- **Endowment** $64.0 million
- **Coed** 5,365 undergraduate students, 88% full-time, 56% women, 44% men
- **Moderately difficult** entrance level, 73% of applicants were admitted

Undergraduates 4,703 full-time, 662 part-time. Students come from 30 states and territories; 5 other countries; 42% are from out of state; 4% Black or African American, non-Hispanic/Latino; 4% Hispanic/Latino; 1% Asian, non-Hispanic/Latino; 0.1% Native Hawaiian or other Pacific Islander, non-Hispanic/Latino; 0.2% American Indian or Alaska Native, non-Hispanic/Latino; 1% Two or more races, non-Hispanic/Latino; 5% Race/ethnicity unknown; 0.3% international; 6% transferred in; 48% live on campus. *Retention:* 78% of full-time freshmen returned.

Freshmen *Admission:* 10,888 applied, 7,911 admitted, 1,176 enrolled. *Average high school GPA:* 3.43. *Test scores:* SAT critical reading scores over 500: 70%; SAT math scores over 500: 78%; SAT writing scores over 500: 58%; ACT scores over 18: 96%; SAT critical reading scores over 600: 17%; SAT math scores over 600: 23%; SAT writing scores over 600: 11%; ACT scores over 24: 42%; SAT critical reading scores over 700: 2%; SAT math scores over 700: 2%; SAT writing scores over 700: 1%; ACT scores over 30: 4%.

Faculty *Total:* 557, 32% full-time, 37% with terminal degrees. *Student/faculty ratio:* 16:1.

Academics *Calendar:* semesters. *Degrees:* associate, bachelor's, master's, and doctoral. *Special study options:* advanced placement credit, cooperative education, double majors, independent study, internships, part-time degree program, services for LD students, student-designed majors, study abroad, summer session for credit. *ROTC:* Army (c). *Unusual degree programs:* 3-2 business administration.

Computers on Campus 1,039 computers/terminals are available on campus for general student use. Students can access the following: campus intranet, computer help desk, free student e-mail accounts, online (class) grades, online (class) registration, online (class) schedules. Campuswide network is available. 100% of college-owned or -operated housing units are wired for high-speed Internet access. Wireless service is available via entire campus.

Student Life *Housing:* on-campus residence required through junior year. *Options:* coed, disabled students. Campus housing is university owned. Freshman campus housing is guaranteed. *Activities and organizations:* drama/theater group, student-run newspaper, radio station, choral group, Pre-Med Society, Ski and Outdoor Club, Habitat for Humanity, Students in Free Enterprise (SIFE), WVYC Radio Station, national fraternities, national sororities. *Campus security:* 24-hour emergency response devices and patrols, late-night transport/escort service. *Student services:* health clinic, personal/psychological counseling.

Athletics Member NCAA. All Division III. *Intercollegiate sports:* baseball M, basketball M/W, cheerleading M/W, cross-country running M/W, field hockey W, golf M, lacrosse M/W, soccer M/W, softball W, swimming and diving M/W, tennis M/W, track and field M/W, volleyball W, wrestling M. *Intramural sports:* badminton M/W, basketball M/W, equestrian sports M(c)/W(c), lacrosse M(c)/W(c), racquetball M/W, rugby M(c)/W(c), soccer M/W, softball M/W, table tennis M/W, tennis M/W, ultimate Frisbee M/W, volleyball M/W.

Standardized Tests *Required:* SAT or ACT (for admission).

Costs (2012–13) *Comprehensive fee:* $25,820 includes full-time tuition ($14,900), mandatory fees ($1620), and room and board ($9300). Full-time tuition and fees vary according to program. Part-time tuition: $460 per credit. *Required fees:* $350 per term part-time. *College room only:* $5220. Room and board charges vary according to board plan and housing facility. *Payment plan:* installment. *Waivers:* employees or children of employees.

Financial Aid Of all full-time matriculated undergraduates who enrolled in 2011, 3,953 applied for aid, 3,131 were judged to have need, 659 had their need fully met. 286 Federal Work-Study jobs (averaging $1985). 12 state and other part-time jobs (averaging $1854). In 2011, 822 non-need-based awards were made. *Average percent of need met:* 65%. *Average financial aid package:* $11,570. *Average need-based loan:* $6292. *Average need-based gift aid:* $5280. *Average non-need-based aid:* $3450. *Average indebtedness upon graduation:* $31,557.

Applying *Options:* electronic application, deferred entrance. *Required:* high school transcript, minimum 2.0 GPA. *Required for some:* interview. *Recommended:* essay or personal statement, 1 letter of recommendation. *Application deadlines:* 8/15 (freshmen), 8/15 (out-of-state freshmen), rolling (transfers). *Notification:* continuous (freshmen), continuous (out-of-state freshmen), continuous (transfers).

Freshman Application Contact York College of Pennsylvania, York, PA 17405-7199. *Phone:* 717-849-1600. *Toll-free phone:* 800-455-8018. *Web site:* http://www.ycp.edu/.

RHODE ISLAND

Brown University
Providence, Rhode Island

- **Independent** university, founded 1764
- **Urban** 140-acre campus with easy access to Boston
- **Endowment** $2.5 billion
- **Coed** 6,380 undergraduate students, 96% full-time, 52% women, 48% men
- **Most difficult** entrance level, 9% of applicants were admitted

Undergraduates 6,114 full-time, 266 part-time. Students come from 52 states and territories; 95% are from out of state; 6% Black or African American, non-Hispanic/Latino; 9% Hispanic/Latino; 14% Asian, non-Hispanic/Latino; 0.1%

Native Hawaiian or other Pacific Islander, non-Hispanic/Latino; 0.4% American Indian or Alaska Native, non-Hispanic/Latino; 4% Two or more races, non-Hispanic/Latino; 11% Race/ethnicity unknown; 11% international; 2% transferred in; 79% live on campus. *Retention:* 98% of full-time freshmen returned.

Freshmen *Admission:* 30,944 applied, 2,757 admitted, 1,507 enrolled. *Test scores:* SAT critical reading scores over 500: 100%; SAT math scores over 500: 100%; SAT writing scores over 500: 100%; ACT scores over 18: 100%; SAT critical reading scores over 600: 92%; SAT math scores over 600: 94%; SAT writing scores over 600: 94%; ACT scores over 24: 99%; SAT critical reading scores over 700: 62%; SAT math scores over 700: 67%; SAT writing scores over 700: 64%; ACT scores over 30: 72%.

Faculty *Total:* 977, 81% full-time, 88% with terminal degrees. *Student/faculty ratio:* 9:1.

Academics *Calendar:* semesters. *Degrees:* bachelor's, master's, doctoral, and first professional. *Special study options:* adult/continuing education programs, advanced placement credit, double majors, honors programs, independent study, internships, off-campus study, part-time degree program, services for LD students, student-designed majors, study abroad, summer session for credit. *ROTC:* Army (c).

Computers on Campus Students can access the following: campus intranet, computer help desk, free student e-mail accounts, online (class) grades, online (class) registration, online (class) schedules. Campuswide network is available. 100% of college-owned or -operated housing units are wired for high-speed Internet access. Wireless service is available via entire campus.

Student Life *Housing:* on-campus residence required through junior year. *Options:* coed, cooperative, disabled students. Campus housing is university owned. Freshman campus housing is guaranteed. *Activities and organizations:* drama/theater group, student-run newspaper, radio and television station, choral group, marching band, national fraternities, national sororities. *Campus security:* 24-hour emergency response devices and patrols, late-night transport/escort service, controlled dormitory access. *Student services:* health clinic, personal/psychological counseling, women's center.

Athletics Member NCAA. All Division I except football (Division I-AA). *Intercollegiate sports:* baseball M, basketball M/W, crew M/W, cross-country running M/W, equestrian sports W, fencing M/W, field hockey W, golf M/W, gymnastics W, ice hockey M/W, lacrosse M/W, rugby M(c)/W(c), sailing M(c)/W(c), skiing (downhill) M(c)/W(c), soccer M/W, softball W, squash M/W, swimming and diving M/W, tennis M/W, track and field M/W, volleyball M(c)/W, water polo M/W, wrestling M. *Intramural sports:* badminton M(c)/W(c), basketball M/W, cheerleading M/W, fencing M/W, field hockey W, football M, ice hockey M/W, lacrosse M/W, racquetball M(c)/W(c), rugby M/W, skiing (downhill) M/W, soccer M/W, softball M/W, squash M/W, swimming and diving M/W, table tennis M(c)/W(c), tennis M/W, ultimate Frisbee M(c)/W(c), volleyball M/W, water polo M/W.

Standardized Tests *Required:* SAT and SAT Subject Tests or ACT (for admission).

Costs (2011–12) *Comprehensive fee:* $53,136 includes full-time tuition ($41,328), mandatory fees ($902), and room and board ($10,906). *College room only:* $6748. Room and board charges vary according to board plan. *Payment plan:* installment. *Waivers:* employees or children of employees.

Financial Aid Of all full-time matriculated undergraduates who enrolled in 2011, 3,099 applied for aid, 2,693 were judged to have need, 2,693 had their need fully met. 1,451 Federal Work-Study jobs (averaging $2298). 332 state and other part-time jobs (averaging $2344). In 2011, 5 non-need-based awards were made. *Average percent of need met:* 100%. *Average financial aid package:* $38,490. *Average need-based loan:* $5772. *Average need-based gift aid:* $35,401. *Average non-need-based aid:* $10,946. *Average indebtedness upon graduation:* $20,455. *Financial aid deadline:* 2/1.

Applying *Options:* electronic application, early decision, deferred entrance. *Application fee:* $75. *Required:* essay or personal statement, high school transcript, 2 letters of recommendation, Common application; Brown University supplement. *Recommended:* interview. *Application deadlines:* 1/1 (freshmen), 3/1 (transfers). *Early decision deadline:* 11/1. *Notification:* 4/1 (freshmen), 5/15 (transfers), 12/15 (early decision).

Freshman Application Contact Mr. James Miller, Dean of Admission, Brown University, Box 1876, Providence, RI 02912. *Phone:* 401-863-2378. *Fax:* 401-863-9300. *E-mail:* admission_undergraduate@brown.edu. *Web site:* http://www.brown.edu/.

Bryant University
Smithfield, Rhode Island

- **Independent** comprehensive, founded 1863
- **Suburban** 420-acre campus with easy access to Boston, Providence
- **Endowment** $148.7 million
- **Coed** 3,337 undergraduate students, 96% full-time, 41% women, 59% men
- **Moderately difficult** entrance level, 77% of applicants were admitted

Undergraduates 3,211 full-time, 126 part-time. Students come from 31 states and territories; 55 other countries; 85% are from out of state; 4% Black or African American, non-Hispanic/Latino; 5% Hispanic/Latino; 3% Asian, non-Hispanic/Latino; 0.4% American Indian or Alaska Native, non-Hispanic/Latino; 0.1% Two or more races, non-Hispanic/Latino; 4% Race/ethnicity unknown; 6% international; 3% transferred in; 80% live on campus. *Retention:* 86% of full-time freshmen returned.

Freshmen *Admission:* 5,177 applied, 3,971 admitted, 814 enrolled. *Average high school GPA:* 3.3. *Test scores:* SAT critical reading scores over 500: 79%; SAT math scores over 500: 89%; SAT writing scores over 500: 79%; ACT scores over 18: 99%; SAT critical reading scores over 600: 22%; SAT math scores over 600: 40%; SAT writing scores over 600: 21%; ACT scores over 24: 58%; SAT critical reading scores over 700: 1%; SAT math scores over 700: 4%; SAT writing scores over 700: 1%; ACT scores over 30: 5%.

Faculty *Total:* 306, 54% full-time, 52% with terminal degrees. *Student/faculty ratio:* 15:1.

Academics *Calendar:* semesters. *Degrees:* bachelor's and master's. *Special study options:* adult/continuing education programs, advanced placement credit, double majors, English as a second language, honors programs, independent study, internships, part-time degree program, services for LD students, study abroad, summer session for credit. *ROTC:* Army (b).

Computers on Campus 478 computers/terminals and 9,000 ports are available on campus for general student use. Students can access the following: campus intranet, computer help desk, free student e-mail accounts, online (class) grades, online (class) registration, online (class) schedules, e-mail, online library, wireless network, student Web hosts. Campuswide network is available. 100% of college-owned or -operated housing units are wired for high-speed Internet access. Wireless service is available via entire campus.

Student Life *Housing options:* coed, women-only, disabled students. Campus housing is university owned. Freshman campus housing is guaranteed. *Activities and organizations:* drama/theater group, student-run newspaper, radio and television station, choral group, Bryant Outdoor Activities Club, Student Programming Board, Rhythm and Pride Dance Team, WJMF Radio, Bryant Players (drama club), national fraternities, national sororities. *Campus security:* 24-hour emergency response devices and patrols, late-night transport/escort service, controlled dormitory access, prevention/awareness programs; pamphlets/posters/films; monitored one point access to campus; bicycle patrols; video cameras. *Student services:* health clinic, personal/psychological counseling, women's center.

Athletics Member NCAA. All Division I except football (Division I-AA). *Intercollegiate sports:* badminton M(c)/W(c), baseball M(s), basketball M(s)/W(s), bowling M(c)/W(c), cheerleading W(c), crew W(c), cross-country running M(s)/W(s), field hockey W(s), golf M(s), ice hockey M(c), lacrosse M(s)/W(s), racquetball M(c)/W(c), rugby M(c)/W(c), soccer M(s)/W(s), softball W(s), squash M(c)/W(c), swimming and diving M(s)/W(s), table tennis M(c)/W(c), tennis M(s)/W(s), track and field M(s)/W(s), ultimate Frisbee M(c), volleyball M(c)/W(s), wrestling M(c). *Intramural sports:* basketball M/W, field hockey W, football M, soccer M/W, softball M/W, volleyball M/W.

Standardized Tests *Required:* SAT or ACT considered if submitted (for admission).

Costs (2012–13) *Comprehensive fee:* $49,180 includes full-time tuition ($35,591), mandatory fees ($349), and room and board ($13,240). Part-time tuition: $733 per credit. Part-time tuition and fees vary according to course load. *College room only:* $7771. Room and board charges vary according to board plan and housing facility. *Payment plan:* installment. *Waivers:* employees or children of employees.

Financial Aid Of all full-time matriculated undergraduates who enrolled in 2010, 2,465 applied for aid, 2,203 were judged to have need, 1,102 had their need fully met. In 2010, 397 non-need-based awards were made. *Average percent of need met:* 51%. *Average financial aid package:* $21,206. *Average need-based loan:* $4899. *Average need-based gift aid:* $11,553. *Average non-need-based aid:* $13,225. *Average indebtedness upon graduation:* $39,490.

Applying *Options:* electronic application, early decision, early action, deferred entrance. *Application fee:* $50. *Required:* essay or personal statement, high school transcript, 1 letter of recommendation, senior year first-quarter grades; SAT Reasoning Test or ACT results. *Recommended:* minimum 3.3 GPA, interview. *Application deadlines:* 2/1 (freshmen), 2/1 (out-of-state freshmen), rolling (transfers), 12/1 (early action). *Early decision deadline:* 11/15 (for plan 1), 1/14 (for plan 2). *Notification:* 3/20 (freshmen), 3/20 (out-of-state freshmen),

continuous (transfers), 12/15 (early decision plan 1), 2/14 (early decision plan 2), 1/20 (early action).
Freshman Application Contact Ms. Michelle Beauregard, Director of Admission, Bryant University, 1150 Douglas Pike, Smithfield, RI 02917. *Phone:* 401-232-6100. *Toll-free phone:* 800-622-7001. *Fax:* 401-232-6741. *E-mail:* admission@bryant.edu. *Web site:* http://www.bryant.edu/.

Johnson & Wales University
Providence, Rhode Island

- **Independent** comprehensive, founded 1914
- **Urban** 47-acre campus with easy access to Boston
- **Coed**
- **Moderately difficult** entrance level

Faculty *Student/faculty ratio:* 27:1.
Academics *Calendar:* quarters. *Degrees:* certificates, associate, bachelor's, master's, doctoral, and post-master's certificates (branch locations in Charlotte, NC; Denver, CO; North Miami, FL).
Student Life *Campus security:* 24-hour emergency response devices and patrols, student patrols, late-night transport/escort service.
Athletics Member NCAA. All Division III.
Standardized Tests *Required for some:* SAT or ACT (for admission).
Costs (2011–12) *One-time required fee:* $300. *Comprehensive fee:* $35,421 includes full-time tuition ($23,955), mandatory fees ($1152), and room and board ($10,314). *Room and board:* Room and board charges vary according to board plan, housing facility, and location.
Financial Aid *Of all full-time matriculated undergraduates who enrolled in 2010,* 6,987 applied for aid, 6,254 were judged to have need, 833 had their need fully met. *In 2010,* 1517 non-need-based awards were made. *Average percent of need met:* 69. *Average financial aid package:* $16,400. *Average need-based loan:* $5096. *Average need-based gift aid:* $7514. *Average non-need-based aid:* $4962.
Applying *Options:* electronic application, early admission, deferred entrance. *Required:* high school transcript. *Required for some:* essay or personal statement, minimum 2.8 GPA, interview. *Recommended:* minimum 2.0 GPA.
Freshman Application Contact Amy Podbelski, Dean of Undergraduate Admissions, Johnson & Wales University, 8 Abbott Park Place, Providence, RI 02903-3703. *Phone:* 401-598-2310. *Toll-free phone:* 800-342-5598. *Fax:* 401-598-2948. *E-mail:* pvd@admissions.jwu.edu. *Web site:* http://www.jwu.edu/.

See page 1386 for the College Close-Up.

Mater Ecclesiae College
Greenville, Rhode Island

Freshman Application Contact Admissions, Mater Ecclesiae College, 60 Austin Avenue, Greenville, RI 02828. *Phone:* 401-949-2820. *E-mail:* info@mecollege.org. *Web site:* http://www.mecollege.edu/.

New England Institute of Technology
Warwick, Rhode Island

- **Independent** comprehensive, founded 1940
- **Suburban** 225-acre campus with easy access to Boston
- **Coed** 2,894 undergraduate students, 87% full-time, 24% women, 76% men
- **Noncompetitive** entrance level

Undergraduates 2,523 full-time, 371 part-time. Students come from 8 states and territories; 13 other countries; 5% Black or African American, non-Hispanic/Latino; 7% Hispanic/Latino; 2% Asian, non-Hispanic/Latino; 0.1% Native Hawaiian or other Pacific Islander, non-Hispanic/Latino; 0.5% American Indian or Alaska Native, non-Hispanic/Latino; 0.9% Two or more races, non-Hispanic/Latino; 11% Race/ethnicity unknown; 3% international.
Freshmen *Admission:* 458 enrolled.
Faculty *Total:* 198, 60% full-time, 11% with terminal degrees.
Academics *Calendar:* quarters. *Degrees:* associate, bachelor's, and master's. *Special study options:* academic remediation for entering students, accelerated degree program, adult/continuing education programs, advanced placement credit, cooperative education, distance learning, double majors, internships, part-time degree program, services for LD students, student-designed majors, summer session for credit.
Computers on Campus 850 computers/terminals are available on campus for general student use. Students can access the following: computer help desk, free student e-mail accounts, online (class) grades, online (class) registration, online (class) schedules. Campuswide network is available. Wireless service is available via entire campus.
Student Life *Housing:* college housing not available. *Activities and organizations:* SkillsUSA, Game Developers Network, Vet Tech, Student Occupational Therapy Association, Phi Theta Kappa (International Honor Society). *Campus security:* security personnel during open hours. *Student services:* personal/psychological counseling.

Costs (2012–13) *Tuition:* $18,525 full-time. Full-time tuition and fees vary according to degree level and program. Part-time tuition and fees vary according to degree level and program. No tuition increase for student's term of enrollment. *Required fees:* $1455 full-time. *Payment plans:* tuition prepayment, installment. *Waivers:* employees or children of employees.

Financial Aid Of all full-time matriculated undergraduates who enrolled in 2010, 250 Federal Work-Study jobs (averaging $2290).

Applying *Options:* electronic application, early admission, deferred entrance. *Application fee:* $25. *Required:* high school transcript, interview, basic skills testing, Ronald P. Carver reading test used for placement. Portfolio recommended for drafting program. *Application deadlines:* rolling (freshmen), rolling (transfers).

Freshman Application Contact Mr. Mark Blondin, Director of Admissions, New England Institute of Technology, 2500 Post Road, Warwick, RI 02886-2244. *Phone:* 401-739-5000. *Toll-free phone:* 800-736-7744. *Fax:* 401-886-0868. *E-mail:* mblondin@neit.edu. *Web site:* http://www.neit.edu/.

Providence College

Providence, Rhode Island

- **Independent Roman Catholic** comprehensive, founded 1917
- **Suburban** 105-acre campus with easy access to Boston
- **Endowment** $166.5 million
- **Coed** 3,852 undergraduate students, 100% full-time, 58% women, 42% men
- **Very difficult** entrance level, 61% of applicants were admitted

Undergraduates 3,841 full-time, 11 part-time. Students come from 46 states and territories; 21 other countries; 87% are from out of state; 4% Black or African American, non-Hispanic/Latino; 4% Hispanic/Latino; 1% Asian, non-Hispanic/Latino; 0.2% Native Hawaiian or other Pacific Islander, non-Hispanic/Latino; 0.2% American Indian or Alaska Native, non-Hispanic/Latino; 1% Two or more races, non-Hispanic/Latino; 12% Race/ethnicity unknown; 2% international; 1% transferred in; 78% live on campus. *Retention:* 90% of full-time freshmen returned.

Freshmen *Admission:* 9,873 applied, 5,979 admitted, 982 enrolled. *Average high school GPA:* 3.39. *Test scores:* SAT critical reading scores over 500: 86%; SAT math scores over 500: 87%; SAT writing scores over 500: 88%; ACT scores over 18: 98%; SAT critical reading scores over 600: 39%; SAT math scores over 600: 43%; SAT writing scores over 600: 48%; ACT scores

over 24: 65%; SAT critical reading scores over 700: 7%; SAT math scores over 700: 7%; SAT writing scores over 700: 11%; ACT scores over 30: 13%.

Faculty *Total:* 401, 75% full-time, 80% with terminal degrees. *Student/faculty ratio:* 12:1.

Academics *Calendar:* semesters. *Degrees:* certificates, associate, bachelor's, and master's. *Special study options:* adult/continuing education programs, advanced placement credit, cooperative education, double majors, honors programs, independent study, internships, part-time degree program, services for LD students, student-designed majors, study abroad, summer session for credit. *ROTC:* Army (b). *Unusual degree programs:* 3-2 engineering with Columbia University, Washington University in St. Louis.

Computers on Campus 540 computers/terminals and 5,000 ports are available on campus for general student use. Students can access the following: campus intranet, computer help desk, free student e-mail accounts, online (class) grades, online (class) registration, online (class) schedules. Campus-wide network is available. 100% of college-owned or -operated housing units are wired for high-speed Internet access. Wireless service is available via classrooms, computer centers, computer labs, learning centers, libraries, student centers.

Student Life *Housing:* on-campus residence required through sophomore year. *Options:* coed, men-only, women-only, disabled students. Campus housing is university owned. Freshman campus housing is guaranteed. *Activities and organizations:* drama/theater group, student-run newspaper, radio and television station, choral group, Student Congress, Campus Ministry, Board of Multicultural Students Affairs, Future Friar Executives, Urban Action. *Campus security:* 24-hour emergency response devices and patrols, student patrols, late-night transport/escort service, controlled dormitory access. *Student services:* health clinic, personal/psychological counseling.

Athletics Member NCAA. All Division I. *Intercollegiate sports:* basketball M(s)/W(s), cheerleading W, cross-country running M(s)/W(s), field hockey W(s), golf M(c)/W(c), ice hockey M(s)/W(s), lacrosse M(s), racquetball M(c)/W(c), rugby M(c)/W(c), sailing M(c)/W(c), soccer M(s)/W(s), softball W(s), swimming and diving M(s)/W(s), tennis W(s), track and field M(s)/W(s), ultimate Frisbee M(c)/W(c), volleyball M(c)/W(s). *Intramural sports:* basketball M/W, field hockey W, football M/W, ice hockey M/W, lacrosse M/W, racquetball M/W, soccer M/W, softball M/W, tennis M/W, ultimate Frisbee M/W, volleyball M/W.

Standardized Tests *Recommended:* Test scores are considered if submitted.

Costs (2012–13) *Comprehensive fee:* $53,115 includes full-time tuition ($40,150), mandatory fees ($825), and room and board ($12,140). Full-time tuition and fees vary according to degree level and student level. Part-time

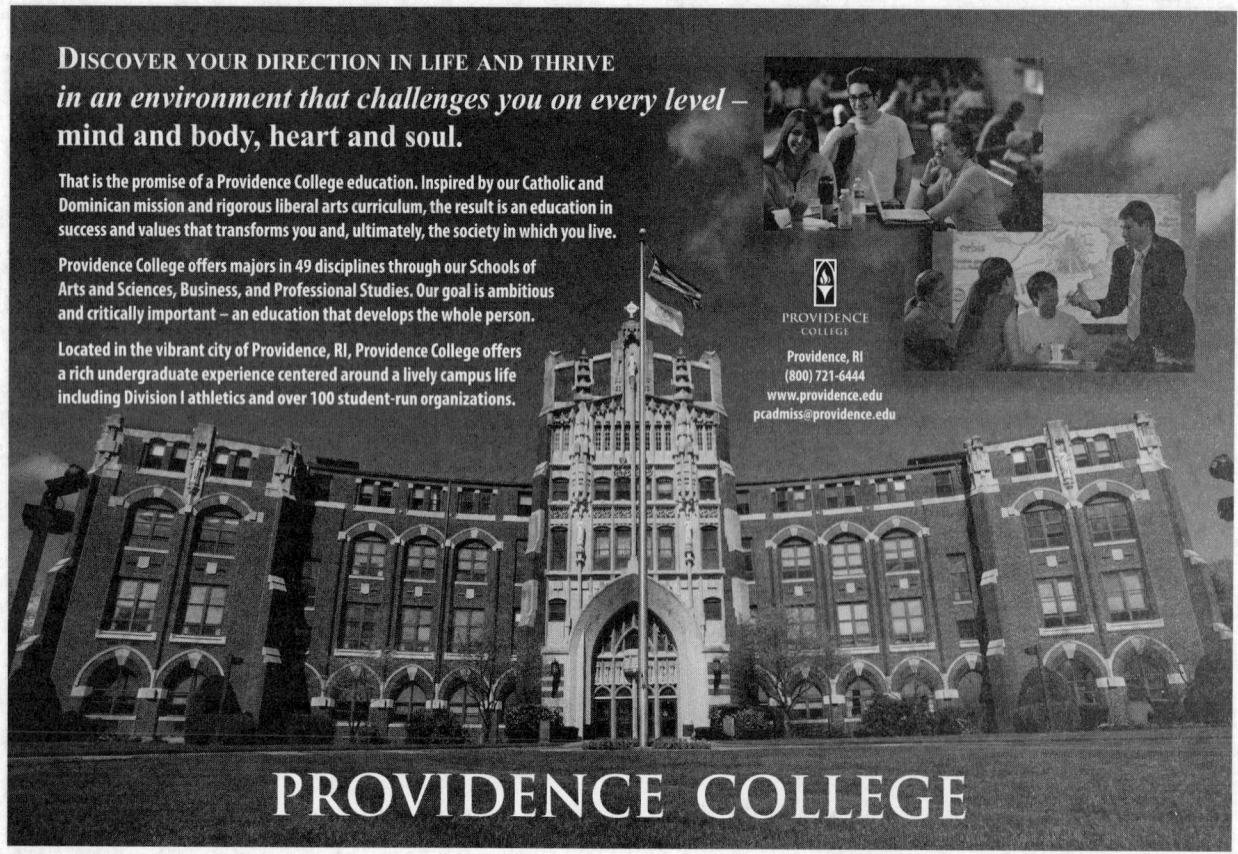

tuition: $1434 per credit. Part-time tuition and fees vary according to degree level. *College room only:* $7000. Room and board charges vary according to board plan and housing facility. *Payment plan:* installment. *Waivers:* senior citizens and employees or children of employees.

Financial Aid Of all full-time matriculated undergraduates who enrolled in 2010, 2,740 applied for aid, 2,242 were judged to have need, 902 had their need fully met. 700 Federal Work-Study jobs (averaging $1800). 700 state and other part-time jobs (averaging $1800). In 2010, 286 non-need-based awards were made. *Average percent of need met:* 83%. *Average financial aid package:* $24,085. *Average need-based loan:* $4946. *Average need-based gift aid:* $18,866. *Average non-need-based aid:* $26,763. *Average indebtedness upon graduation:* $32,850. *Financial aid deadline:* 2/1.

Applying *Options:* electronic application, early admission, early action, deferred entrance. *Application fee:* $55. *Required:* essay or personal statement, high school transcript, 2 letters of recommendation. *Application deadlines:* 1/15 (freshmen), 4/1 (transfers), 11/1 (early action). *Notification:* 4/1 (freshmen), 5/30 (transfers), 1/1 (early action).

Freshman Application Contact Providence College, 1 Cunningham Square, Providence, RI 02918. *Phone:* 401-865-2535. *Toll-free phone:* 800-721-6444. *Web site:* http://www.providence.edu/.

See page 1508 for the College Close-Up.

Rhode Island College
Providence, Rhode Island

- **State-supported** comprehensive, founded 1854
- **Suburban** 180-acre campus with easy access to Boston
- **Endowment** $15.3 million
- **Coed** 7,762 undergraduate students, 75% full-time, 65% women, 35% men
- **Moderately difficult** entrance level, 73% of applicants were admitted

Undergraduates 5,794 full-time, 1,968 part-time. Students come from 27 states and territories; 1 other country; 14% are from out of state; 7% Black or African American, non-Hispanic/Latino; 9% Hispanic/Latino; 2% Asian, non-Hispanic/Latino; 0.1% Native Hawaiian or other Pacific Islander, non-Hispanic/Latino; 0.3% American Indian or Alaska Native, non-Hispanic/Latino; 1% Two or more races, non-Hispanic/Latino; 13% Race/ethnicity unknown; 0.1% international; 10% transferred in; 15% live on campus. *Retention:* 76% of full-time freshmen returned.

Freshmen *Admission:* 3,349 applied, 2,445 admitted, 974 enrolled. *Test scores:* SAT critical reading scores over 500: 38%; SAT math scores over 500: 33%; SAT writing scores over 500: 37%; ACT scores over 18: 73%; SAT critical reading scores over 600: 9%; SAT math scores over 600: 6%; SAT writing scores over 600: 6%; ACT scores over 24: 17%; SAT critical reading scores over 700: 1%; SAT writing scores over 700: 1%; ACT scores over 30: 2%.

Faculty *Total:* 753, 43% full-time. *Student/faculty ratio:* 15:1.

Academics *Calendar:* semesters. *Degrees:* certificates, bachelor's, master's, doctoral, post-master's, postbachelor's, and first professional certificates. *Special study options:* academic remediation for entering students, adult/continuing education programs, advanced placement credit, double majors, English as a second language, honors programs, independent study, internships, off-campus study, part-time degree program, services for LD students, student-designed majors, study abroad, summer session for credit. *ROTC:* Army (c). *Unusual degree programs:* 3-2 public administration with University of Rhode Island.

Computers on Campus 220 computers/terminals are available on campus for general student use. Students can access the following: campus intranet, computer help desk, free student e-mail accounts, online (class) grades, online (class) registration, online (class) schedules. Campuswide network is available. 100% of college-owned or -operated housing units are wired for high-speed Internet access. Wireless service is available via classrooms, computer centers, computer labs, dorm rooms, learning centers, libraries, student centers.

Student Life *Housing options:* coed, women-only, disabled students. Campus housing is university owned. Freshman applicants given priority for college housing. *Activities and organizations:* drama/theater group, student-run newspaper, radio and television station, choral group, student government, newspaper (The Anchor), campus radio station (WXIN), Programming Board, Resident Student Association, national fraternities, national sororities. *Campus security:* 24-hour emergency response devices and patrols, late-night transport/escort service, controlled dormitory access. *Student services:* health clinic, personal/psychological counseling, women's center.

Athletics Member NCAA. All Division III. *Intercollegiate sports:* baseball M, basketball M/W, cross-country running M/W, golf M/W, gymnastics W, lacrosse W, soccer M/W, softball W, swimming and diving W, tennis M/W, track and field M/W, volleyball W, wrestling M. *Intramural sports:* badminton M/W, basketball M/W, football M, golf M/W, gymnastics W, sailing M/W, soccer M/W, softball M/W, swimming and diving M/W, tennis M/W, volleyball M/W, water polo M/W.

Standardized Tests *Required:* SAT or ACT (for admission).

Costs (2011–12) *Tuition:* state resident $6240 full-time, $260 per credit part-time; nonresident $16,526 full-time, $648 per credit part-time. Part-time tuition and fees vary according to course load. *Required fees:* $1028 full-time, $30 per credit part-time, $72 per term part-time. *Room and board:* $9256; room only: $5266. Room and board charges vary according to housing facility. *Payment plan:* installment. *Waivers:* employees or children of employees.

Financial Aid Of all full-time matriculated undergraduates who enrolled in 2011, 4,635 applied for aid, 3,773 were judged to have need, 877 had their need fully met. In 2011, 129 non-need-based awards were made. *Average percent of need met:* 72%. *Average financial aid package:* $8960. *Average need-based loan:* $4001. *Average need-based gift aid:* $5476. *Average non-need-based aid:* $2185. *Average indebtedness upon graduation:* $21,384.

Applying *Options:* electronic application, early admission. *Application fee:* $50. *Required:* essay or personal statement, high school transcript, 1 letter of recommendation, one letter from guidance counselor. *Required for some:* interview. *Recommended:* minimum 3.0 GPA. *Application deadlines:* 3/15 (freshmen), 3/15 (out-of-state freshmen), 6/1 (transfers). *Notification:* continuous (freshmen), continuous (out-of-state freshmen), continuous (transfers).

Freshman Application Contact Lucille Saunders, Interim Director of Admissions, Rhode Island College, 600 Mount Pleasant Avenue, Providence, RI 02908-1927. *Phone:* 401-456-8234. *Toll-free phone:* 800-669-5760. *Fax:* 401-456-8817. *E-mail:* admissions@ric.edu. *Web site:* http://www.ric.edu/.

Rhode Island School of Design
Providence, Rhode Island

Freshman Application Contact Mr. Edward Newhall, Director of Admissions, Rhode Island School of Design, 2 College Street, Providence, RI 02905-2791. *Phone:* 401-454-6307. *Toll-free phone:* 800-364-7473. *Fax:* 401-454-6309. *E-mail:* admissions@risd.edu. *Web site:* http://www.risd.edu/.

Roger Williams University
Bristol, Rhode Island

- **Independent** comprehensive, founded 1956
- **Small-town** 140-acre campus with easy access to Boston
- **Endowment** $58.6 million
- **Coed** 4,451 undergraduate students, 86% full-time, 49% women, 51% men
- **Moderately difficult** entrance level, 78% of applicants were admitted

Undergraduates 3,833 full-time, 618 part-time. Students come from 46 states and territories; 50 other countries; 84% are from out of state; 1% Black or African American, non-Hispanic/Latino; 3% Hispanic/Latino; 1% Asian, non-Hispanic/Latino; 0.1% American Indian or Alaska Native, non-Hispanic/Latino; 1% Two or more races, non-Hispanic/Latino; 29% Race/ethnicity unknown; 1% international; 4% transferred in. *Retention:* 80% of full-time freshmen returned.

Freshmen *Admission:* 8,853 applied, 6,876 admitted, 1,323 enrolled. *Average high school GPA:* 3.2. *Test scores:* SAT critical reading scores over 500: 77%; SAT math scores over 500: 73%; ACT scores over 18: 99%; SAT critical reading scores over 600: 22%; SAT math scores over 600: 21%; ACT scores over 24: 54%; SAT critical reading scores over 700: 2%; SAT math scores over 700: 1%; ACT scores over 30: 5%.

Faculty *Total:* 541, 37% full-time. *Student/faculty ratio:* 14:1.

Academics *Calendar:* semesters. *Degrees:* certificates, associate, bachelor's, master's, doctoral, and postbachelor's certificates. *Special study options:* adult/continuing education programs, advanced placement credit, cooperative education, distance learning, double majors, English as a second language, freshman honors college, honors programs, independent study, internships, part-time degree program, services for LD students, student-designed majors, study abroad, summer session for credit. *ROTC:* Army (c).

Computers on Campus Students can access the following: campus intranet, computer help desk, free student e-mail accounts, online (class) registration, online (class) schedules. Campuswide network is available. 100% of college-owned or -operated housing units are wired for high-speed Internet access. Wireless service is available via classrooms, computer centers, computer labs, dorm rooms, learning centers, libraries, student centers.

Student Life *Housing options:* coed, disabled students. Campus housing is university owned and leased by the school. Freshman campus housing is guaranteed. *Activities and organizations:* drama/theater group, student-run newspaper, radio station, choral group, Entertainment Network, Student Senate, American Institute of Architects, John Jay Society, residence hall councils. *Campus security:* 24-hour emergency response devices and patrols, student patrols, late-night transport/escort service, controlled dormitory access. *Student services:* health clinic, personal/psychological counseling, women's center.

Athletics Member NCAA. All Division III. *Intercollegiate sports:* baseball M, basketball M/W, cheerleading W(c), crew M(c)/W(c), cross-country running M/W, equestrian sports M/W, lacrosse M/W, rugby M(c), sailing M/W, soccer M/W, softball W, swimming and diving M/W, tennis M/W, track and field M(c)/W(c), volleyball M(c)/W, wrestling M. *Intramural sports:* badminton M/W, basketball M/W, field hockey M/W, football M/W, golf M/W, lacrosse M/W, racquetball M/W, soccer M/W, softball M/W, squash M/W, swimming and diving M/W, table tennis M/W, tennis M/W, ultimate Frisbee M/W, volleyball M/W.

Standardized Tests *Required:* SAT or ACT (for admission).

Costs (2012–13) *Comprehensive fee:* $45,308 includes full-time tuition ($29,976), mandatory fees ($1642), and room and board ($13,690). Full-time tuition and fees vary according to class time, course load, and program. Part-time tuition and fees vary according to class time. *College room only:* $7370. Room and board charges vary according to board plan and housing facility. *Payment plans:* installment, deferred payment. *Waivers:* employees or children of employees.

Financial Aid Of all full-time matriculated undergraduates who enrolled in 2011, 2,791 applied for aid, 2,246 were judged to have need, 167 had their need fully met. 405 Federal Work-Study jobs (averaging $1700). In 2011, 433 non-need-based awards were made. *Average percent of need met:* 88%. *Average financial aid package:* $19,970. *Average need-based loan:* $4638. *Average need-based gift aid:* $13,214. *Average non-need-based aid:* $9755. *Average indebtedness upon graduation:* $38,365. *Financial aid deadline:* 2/1.

Applying *Options:* electronic application, early action, deferred entrance. *Application fee:* $50. *Required:* essay or personal statement, high school transcript, letters of recommendation. *Required for some:* portfolio/audition. *Application deadlines:* 2/1 (freshmen), 2/1 (out-of-state freshmen), rolling (transfers), 11/7 (early action). *Notification:* 3/15 (freshmen), continuous (transfers), 12/5 (early action).

Freshman Application Contact Mr. Wesley Roy, Director of Admission and Recruitment, Roger Williams University, 1 Old Ferry Road, Bristol, RI 02809. *Phone:* 401-254-3500. *Toll-free phone:* 800-458-7144. *Fax:* 401-254-3557. *E-mail:* admit@rwu.edu. *Web site:* http://www.rwu.edu/.

See below for display ad and page 1532 for the College Close-Up.

Salve Regina University
Newport, Rhode Island

- **Independent Roman Catholic** comprehensive, founded 1934
- **Suburban** 75-acre campus with easy access to Boston, Providence
- **Endowment** $43.7 million
- **Coed** 2,028 undergraduate students, 96% full-time, 69% women, 31% men
- **Moderately difficult** entrance level, 70% of applicants were admitted

Undergraduates 1,944 full-time, 84 part-time. Students come from 36 states and territories; 20 other countries; 81% are from out of state; 2% Black or African American, non-Hispanic/Latino; 4% Hispanic/Latino; 1% Asian, non-Hispanic/Latino; 0.4% American Indian or Alaska Native, non-Hispanic/Latino; 2% Two or more races, non-Hispanic/Latino; 16% Race/ethnicity unknown; 0.8% international; 3% transferred in; 62% live on campus. *Retention:* 79% of full-time freshmen returned.

Freshmen *Admission:* 4,686 applied, 3,258 admitted, 545 enrolled. *Average high school GPA:* 3.2. *Test scores:* SAT critical reading scores over 500: 81%; SAT math scores over 500: 84%; SAT writing scores over 500: 87%; ACT scores over 18: 100%; SAT critical reading scores over 600: 26%; SAT math scores over 600: 28%; SAT writing scores over 600: 25%; ACT scores over 24: 60%; SAT critical reading scores over 700: 1%; SAT math scores over 700: 1%; SAT writing scores over 700: 2%; ACT scores over 30: 8%.

Faculty *Total:* 241, 48% full-time. *Student/faculty ratio:* 14:1.

Academics *Calendar:* semesters. *Degrees:* associate, bachelor's, master's, doctoral, post-master's, postbachelor's, and first professional certificates. *Special study options:* accelerated degree program, adult/continuing education programs, advanced placement credit, double majors, English as a second language, honors programs, independent study, internships, off-campus study, part-time degree program, services for LD students, study abroad, summer session for credit. *ROTC:* Army (c). *Unusual degree programs:* 3-2 business administration; administration of justice, holistic counseling, international relations, management, rehabilitation counseling.

Computers on Campus 163 computers/terminals are available on campus for general student use. Students can access the following: campus intranet, computer help desk, free student e-mail accounts, online (class) grades, online (class) registration, online (class) schedules. Campuswide network is available. 90% of college-owned or -operated housing units are wired for high-speed Internet access. Wireless service is available via entire campus.

Student Life *Housing:* on-campus residence required through sophomore year. *Options:* coed, men-only, women-only, disabled students. Campus housing is university owned and leased by the school. Freshman campus housing is guaranteed. *Activities and organizations:* drama/theater group, student-run newspaper, radio station, choral group, Orpheus Musical Society, Student Government Association, Student Outdoor Adventures, Student Nurse Organization, Stagefright Theatre Company. *Campus security:* 24-hour emergency response devices and patrols, late-night transport/escort service, controlled dormitory access. *Student services:* health clinic, personal/psychological counseling.

Athletics Member NCAA. All Division III. *Intercollegiate sports:* baseball M, basketball M/W, cross-country running M/W, field hockey W, football M, ice hockey M/W, lacrosse M/W, rugby M(c)/W(c), sailing M/W, soccer M/W, softball W, tennis M/W, track and field W, volleyball W. *Intramural sports:* baseball M, basketball M/W, cheerleading W(c), field hockey W, football M/W, soccer M/W, softball M/W, tennis M/W, track and field W, volleyball M/W, weight lifting M/W.

Standardized Tests *Required for some:* SAT or ACT (for admission).

Costs (2011–12) *Comprehensive fee:* $44,400 includes full-time tuition ($32,500), mandatory fees ($300), and room and board ($11,600). Full-time tuition and fees vary according to program. Part-time tuition: $1083 per credit. Part-time tuition and fees vary according to course load and program. *Required fees:* $40 per term part-time. *Room and board:* Room and board charges vary according to board plan and housing facility. *Payment plan:* installment. *Waivers:* employees or children of employees.

Financial Aid Of all full-time matriculated undergraduates who enrolled in 2011, 1,643 applied for aid, 1,463 were judged to have need, 122 had their need fully met. 410 Federal Work-Study jobs (averaging $764). 90 state and other part-time jobs (averaging $1333). In 2011, 290 non-need-based awards were made. *Average percent of need met:* 67%. *Average financial aid package:* $22,160. *Average need-based loan:* $4420. *Average need-based gift aid:* $17,648. *Average non-need-based aid:* $9119. *Average indebtedness upon graduation:* $43,237.

Applying *Options:* electronic application, early action, deferred entrance. *Application fee:* $50. *Required:* essay or personal statement, high school transcript, 2 letters of recommendation. *Recommended:* minimum 2.7 GPA. *Application deadlines:* 2/1 (freshmen), rolling (transfers), 11/1 (early action). *Notification:* 12/25 (freshmen), continuous (transfers), 12/25 (early action).

Freshman Application Contact Ms. Colleen Emerson, Dean of Undergraduate Admissions, Salve Regina University, 100 Ochre Point Avenue, Newport, RI 02840-4192. *Phone:* 401-341-2908. *Toll-free phone:* 888-GO

SALVE. *Fax:* 401-848-2823. *E-mail:* sruadmis@salve.edu. *Web site:* http://www.salve.edu/.

University of Rhode Island
Kingston, Rhode Island

- **State-supported** university, founded 1892, part of Rhode Island Board of Governors for Higher Education
- **Small-town** 1200-acre campus
- **Endowment** $84.9 million
- **Coed** 13,219 undergraduate students, 88% full-time, 55% women, 45% men
- **Moderately difficult** entrance level, 76% of applicants were admitted

Undergraduates 11,672 full-time, 1,547 part-time. Students come from 50 states and territories; 45 other countries; 38% are from out of state; 5% Black or African American, non-Hispanic/Latino; 7% Hispanic/Latino; 3% Asian, non-Hispanic/Latino; 0.1% Native Hawaiian or other Pacific Islander, non-Hispanic/Latino; 0.3% American Indian or Alaska Native, non-Hispanic/Latino; 1% Two or more races, non-Hispanic/Latino; 12% Race/ethnicity unknown; 0.4% international; 4% transferred in; 43% live on campus. *Retention:* 82% of full-time freshmen returned.

Freshmen *Admission:* 20,012 applied, 15,211 admitted, 2,987 enrolled. *Average high school GPA:* 3.4. *Test scores:* SAT critical reading scores over 500: 71%; SAT math scores over 500: 78%; SAT writing scores over 500: 74%; ACT scores over 18: 98%; SAT critical reading scores over 600: 21%; SAT math scores over 600: 30%; SAT writing scores over 600: 22%; ACT scores over 24: 50%; SAT critical reading scores over 700: 2%; SAT math scores over 700: 3%; SAT writing scores over 700: 2%; ACT scores over 30: 5%.

Faculty *Total:* 1,206, 57% full-time. *Student/faculty ratio:* 16:1.

Academics *Calendar:* semesters. *Degrees:* bachelor's, master's, doctoral, postbachelor's, and first professional certificates. *Special study options:* academic remediation for entering students, adult/continuing education programs, advanced placement credit, distance learning, double majors, honors programs, independent study, internships, off-campus study, part-time degree program, services for LD students, study abroad, summer session for credit. *ROTC:* Army (b). *Unusual degree programs:* 3-2 engineering; nursing; accounting, pharmacy, chemistry, education, psychology.

Computers on Campus 488 computers/terminals are available on campus for general student use. Students can access the following: campus intranet, computer help desk, free student e-mail accounts, online (class) grades, online

THE **UNIVERSITY** OF RHODE ISLAND

CHASE YOUR DREAMS. CHANGE THE WORLD.

uri.edu/admission

THINK BIG WE DO

(class) registration, online (class) schedules. Campuswide network is available. 100% of college-owned or -operated housing units are wired for high-speed Internet access. Wireless service is available via entire campus.

Student Life *Housing options:* coed, cooperative, disabled students. Campus housing is university owned and leased by the school. Freshman campus housing is guaranteed. *Activities and organizations:* drama/theater group, student-run newspaper, radio and television station, choral group, marching band, Student Entertainment Committee, Student radio station, Intramural sport clubs, Student Alumni Association, student newspaper, national fraternities, national sororities. *Campus security:* 24-hour emergency response devices and patrols, student patrols, late-night transport/escort service, controlled dormitory access. *Student services:* health clinic, personal/psychological counseling, women's center.

Athletics Member NCAA. All Division I. *Intercollegiate sports:* baseball M(s), basketball M(s)/W(s), crew W(s), cross-country running M(s)/W(s), football M(s), golf M(s), soccer M(s)/W(s), softball W(s), swimming and diving W(s), tennis W(s), track and field M(s)/W(s), volleyball W(s). *Intramural sports:* crew M(c), equestrian sports M(c)/W(c), field hockey W(c), football M, gymnastics W(c), ice hockey M(c)/W(c), lacrosse M(c)/W(c), rugby M(c)/W(c), sailing M(c)/W(c), skiing (downhill) M(c)/W(c), soccer M/W, swimming and diving M(c), ultimate Frisbee M(c)/W(c), volleyball M(c), wrestling M(c).

Standardized Tests *Required:* SAT or ACT (for admission).

Costs (2011–12) *Tuition:* state resident $9824 full-time, $409 per credit hour part-time; nonresident $25,912 full-time, $1080 per credit hour part-time. Full-time tuition and fees vary according to course load, location, and reciprocity agreements. Part-time tuition and fees vary according to course load, location, and reciprocity agreements. *Required fees:* $1542 full-time, $37 per credit hour part-time, $58 per term part-time. *Room and board:* $10,796; room only: $6798. Room and board charges vary according to board plan and housing facility. *Payment plan:* installment. *Waivers:* minority students, senior citizens, and employees or children of employees.

Financial Aid Of all full-time matriculated undergraduates who enrolled in 2011, 10,782 applied for aid, 9,320 were judged to have need, 6,386 had their need fully met. In 2011, 444 non-need-based awards were made. *Average percent of need met:* 59%. *Average financial aid package:* $14,464. *Average need-based loan:* $5357. *Average need-based gift aid:* $9120. *Average non-need-based aid:* $5506. *Average indebtedness upon graduation:* $25,973.

Applying *Options:* electronic application, early admission, early action, deferred entrance. *Application fee:* $65. *Required:* essay or personal statement, high school transcript, 1 letter of recommendation, minimum of 18 units of college preparatory work. *Application deadlines:* 2/1 (freshmen), 6/1 (transfers), 12/1 (early action). *Notification:* 3/31 (freshmen), continuous (transfers), 2/3 (early action).

Freshman Application Contact Ms. Joanne Lynch, Assistant Dean of Admissions, University of Rhode Island, Undergraduate Admission Office, Newman Hall, 14 Upper College Road, Kingston, RI 02881. *Phone:* 401-874-7110. *Fax:* 401-874-5523. *E-mail:* lynch@uri.edu. *Web site:* http://www.uri.edu/.

See page 831 for display ad and page 1706 for the College Close-Up.

SOUTH CAROLINA

Allen University
Columbia, South Carolina

Freshman Application Contact Terri Parker, Director of Admission, Allen University, 1530 Harden Street, Columbia, SC 29204. *Phone:* 803-376-5733. *Toll-free phone:* 877-625-5368. *E-mail:* tparker@allenuniversity.edu. *Web site:* http://www.allenuniversity.edu/.

Anderson University
Anderson, South Carolina

- **Independent Baptist** comprehensive, founded 1911
- **Suburban** 271-acre campus with easy access to Greenville
- **Endowment** $32.2 million
- **Coed** 2,465 undergraduate students, 79% full-time, 66% women, 34% men
- **Minimally difficult** entrance level, 75% of applicants were admitted

Undergraduates 1,957 full-time, 508 part-time. Students come from 35 states and territories; 17 other countries; 16% are from out of state; 12% Black or

African American, non-Hispanic/Latino; 2% Hispanic/Latino; 0.8% Asian, non-Hispanic/Latino; 0.8% Native Hawaiian or other Pacific Islander, non-Hispanic/Latino; 0.4% American Indian or Alaska Native, non-Hispanic/Latino; 1% Race/ethnicity unknown; 1% international; 4% transferred in; 53% live on campus. *Retention:* 72% of full-time freshmen returned.

Freshmen *Admission:* 2,118 applied, 1,586 admitted, 521 enrolled. *Average high school GPA:* 3.33. *Test scores:* SAT math scores over 500: 65%; SAT writing scores over 500: 61%; ACT scores over 18: 90%; SAT math scores over 600: 22%; SAT writing scores over 600: 17%; ACT scores over 24: 44%; SAT math scores over 700: 1%; SAT writing scores over 700: 3%; ACT scores over 30: 3%.

Faculty *Total:* 242, 36% full-time, 41% with terminal degrees. *Student/faculty ratio:* 17:1.

Academics *Calendar:* semesters. *Degrees:* bachelor's, master's, and doctoral. *Special study options:* academic remediation for entering students, accelerated degree program, adult/continuing education programs, advanced placement credit, cooperative education, distance learning, double majors, honors programs, independent study, internships, part-time degree program, services for LD students, study abroad, summer session for credit. *ROTC:* Army (c), Air Force (c).

Computers on Campus 192 computers/terminals are available on campus for general student use. Students can access the following: campus intranet, computer help desk, free student e-mail accounts, online (class) grades, online (class) registration, online (class) schedules. Campuswide network is available. 100% of college-owned or -operated housing units are wired for high-speed Internet access. Wireless service is available via entire campus.

Student Life *Housing:* on-campus residence required through sophomore year. *Options:* men-only, women-only. Campus housing is university owned. *Activities and organizations:* drama/theater group, student-run newspaper, choral group, Baptist Campus Ministries, Fellowship of Christian Athletes, Student Government Association, Gamma Beta Phi, Student Alumni Council. *Campus security:* 24-hour emergency response devices and patrols, late-night transport/escort service, controlled dormitory access. *Student services:* health clinic, personal/psychological counseling.

Athletics Member NCAA. All Division II. *Intercollegiate sports:* baseball M(s), basketball M(s)/W(s), cheerleading W(s), cross-country running M(s)/W(s), golf M(s)/W(s), soccer M(s)/W(s), softball W(s), tennis M(s)/W(s), track and field M(s)/W(s), volleyball W(s), wrestling M(s). *Intramural sports:* basketball M/W, football M/W, racquetball M/W, softball M/W, table tennis M/W, ultimate Frisbee M/W, volleyball M/W, weight lifting M.

Standardized Tests *Required:* SAT or ACT (for admission).

Costs (2011–12) *Comprehensive fee:* $28,635 includes full-time tuition ($19,250), mandatory fees ($1660), and room and board ($7725). Full-time tuition and fees vary according to course load and program. Part-time tuition: $480 per credit hour. Part-time tuition and fees vary according to program. *College room only:* $3950. Room and board charges vary according to board plan and housing facility. *Payment plan:* installment. *Waivers:* employees or children of employees.

Financial Aid *Financial aid deadline:* 7/30.

Applying *Options:* electronic application, deferred entrance. *Application fee:* $25. *Required:* high school transcript. *Required for some:* essay or personal statement, 2 letters of recommendation, interview. *Recommended:* minimum 2.5 GPA. *Application deadline:* 7/1 (freshmen). *Notification:* continuous (freshmen), continuous (transfers).

Freshman Application Contact Mrs. Pam Bryant-Ross, Anderson University, 316 Boulevard, Anderson, SC 29621-4035. *Phone:* 864-231-2030. *Toll-free phone:* 800-542-3594. *Web site:* http://www.andersonuniversity.edu/.

The Art Institute of Charleston
Charleston, South Carolina

- **Proprietary** 4-year, founded 2007, part of Education Management Corporation
- **Urban** campus
- **Coed**

Academics *Calendar:* quarters. *Degrees:* certificates, associate, and bachelor's.

Costs (2011–12) *Tuition:* Tuition cost varies by program. Prospective students should contact the school for current tuition costs. Other charges include a starting kit for all first-quarter students. Kits vary in price, depending on the program of study.

Freshman Application Contact The Art Institute of Charleston, 24 North Market Street, Charleston, SC 29401. *Phone:* 843-727-3500. *Toll-free phone:* 866-211-0107. *Web site:* http://www.artinstitutes.edu/charleston/.

See page 1088 for the College Close-Up.

Benedict College

Columbia, South Carolina

Freshman Application Contact Benedict College, 1600 Harden Street, Columbia, SC 29204. *Phone:* 803-705-4491. *Toll-free phone:* 800-868-6598. *Web site:* http://www.benedict.edu/.

Bob Jones University

Greenville, South Carolina

- **Independent Christian** university, founded 1927
- **Urban** 225-acre campus
- **Coed** 3,086 undergraduate students, 97% full-time, 57% women, 43% men
- **Minimally difficult** entrance level, 83% of applicants were admitted

Undergraduates 2,984 full-time, 102 part-time. Students come from 57 states and territories; 47 other countries; 69% are from out of state; 1% Black or African American, non-Hispanic/Latino; 5% Hispanic/Latino; 3% Asian, non-Hispanic/Latino; 0.2% Native Hawaiian or other Pacific Islander, non-Hispanic/Latino; 0.4% American Indian or Alaska Native, non-Hispanic/Latino; 2% Two or more races, non-Hispanic/Latino; 3% Race/ethnicity unknown; 4% international; 4% transferred in; 73% live on campus. *Retention:* 78% of full-time freshmen returned.

Freshmen *Admission:* 1,186 applied, 985 admitted, 701 enrolled. *Average high school GPA:* 3.42. *Test scores:* ACT scores over 18: 100%; ACT scores over 24: 46%; ACT scores over 30: 7%.

Faculty *Total:* 291, 79% full-time, 38% with terminal degrees. *Student/faculty ratio:* 12:1.

Academics *Calendar:* semesters. *Degrees:* associate, bachelor's, master's, doctoral, post-master's, and first professional certificates. *Special study options:* accelerated degree program, adult/continuing education programs, advanced placement credit, distance learning, English as a second language, internships, off-campus study, part-time degree program, services for LD students, summer session for credit.

Computers on Campus 450 computers/terminals and 500 ports are available on campus for general student use. Students can access the following: campus intranet, computer help desk, free student e-mail accounts, online (class) grades, online (class) registration, online (class) schedules. Campuswide network is available. 100% of college-owned or -operated housing units are wired for high-speed Internet access. Wireless service is available via classrooms, computer labs, dorm rooms, learning centers, libraries, student centers.

Student Life *Housing:* on-campus residence required through senior year. *Options:* men-only, women-only, disabled students. Campus housing is university owned. Freshman campus housing is guaranteed. *Activities and organizations:* drama/theater group, student-run newspaper, radio and television station, choral group, Community Relations Council, Extension Ministries, Societies, Mission Prayer Band, University Business Association. *Campus security:* 24-hour patrols, student patrols, late-night transport/escort service, controlled dormitory access, 24/7 emergency dispatcher. *Student services:* health clinic, personal/psychological counseling.

Athletics *Intramural sports:* badminton M/W, basketball M/W, cheerleading W, racquetball M, soccer M/W, softball M/W, table tennis M/W, tennis M/W, volleyball M/W, water polo W.

Standardized Tests *Required:* ACT (for admission).

Costs (2012–13) *One-time required fee:* $610. *Comprehensive fee:* $17,910 includes full-time tuition ($12,480) and room and board ($5430). Part-time tuition: $606 per credit hour. *Payment plan:* installment. *Waivers:* senior citizens and employees or children of employees.

Financial Aid Of all full-time matriculated undergraduates who enrolled in 2011, 2,478 applied for aid, 2,311 were judged to have need, 173 had their need fully met.

Applying *Options:* electronic application. *Required:* essay or personal statement, high school transcript, 3 letters of recommendation. *Application deadlines:* 8/1 (freshmen), 8/1 (transfers).

Freshman Application Contact Mr. Gary Deedrick, Director of Admissions, Bob Jones University, 1700 Wade Hampton Boulevard, Greenville, SC 29614. *Phone:* 864-242-5100. *Toll-free phone:* 800-BJANDME. *Fax:* 800-232-9258. *E-mail:* admission@bju.edu. *Web site:* http://www.bju.edu/.

Brown Mackie College–Greenville

Greenville, South Carolina

- **Proprietary** primarily 2-year, part of Education Management Corporation
- **Coed**

Academics *Degrees:* certificates, associate, and bachelor's.

Costs (2011–12) *Tuition:* Tuition varies by program. Students should contact Brown Mackie College for tuition information.

Freshman Application Contact Brown Mackie College–Greenville, Two Liberty Square, 75 Beattie Place, Suite 100, Greenville, SC 29601. *Phone:* 864-239-5300. *Toll-free phone:* 877-479-8465. *Web site:* http://www.brownmackie.edu/greenville/.

See page 1202 for the College Close-Up.

Charleston Southern University

Charleston, South Carolina

Freshman Application Contact Mr. Jim Rhoden, Director of Enrollment Management, Charleston Southern University, Charleston, SC 29423-8087. *Phone:* 843-863-7050. *Toll-free phone:* 800-947-7474. *E-mail:* enroll@csuniv.edu. *Web site:* http://www.charlestonsouthern.edu/.

The Citadel, The Military College of South Carolina

Charleston, South Carolina

- **State-supported** comprehensive, founded 1842
- **Suburban** 300-acre campus
- **Endowment** $58.7 million
- **Coed, primarily men** 2,477 undergraduate students, 93% full-time, 9% women, 91% men
- **Moderately difficult** entrance level, 77% of applicants were admitted

Undergraduates 2,307 full-time, 170 part-time. Students come from 45 states and territories; 12 other countries; 46% are from out of state; 8% Black or African American, non-Hispanic/Latino; 5% Hispanic/Latino; 2% Asian, non-Hispanic/Latino; 0.1% Native Hawaiian or other Pacific Islander, non-Hispanic/Latino; 0.7% American Indian or Alaska Native, non-Hispanic/Latino; 2% Two or more races, non-Hispanic/Latino; 0.1% Race/ethnicity unknown; 1% international; 4% transferred in; 100% live on campus. *Retention:* 82% of full-time freshmen returned.

Freshmen *Admission:* 2,523 applied, 1,940 admitted, 631 enrolled. *Average high school GPA:* 3.48. *Test scores:* SAT critical reading scores over 500: 67%; SAT math scores over 500: 78%; ACT scores over 18: 98%; SAT critical reading scores over 600: 19%; SAT math scores over 600: 25%; ACT scores over 24: 43%; SAT critical reading scores over 700: 5%; SAT math scores over 700: 4%; ACT scores over 30: 5%.

Faculty *Total:* 264, 67% full-time, 82% with terminal degrees. *Student/faculty ratio:* 13:1.

Academics *Calendar:* semesters. *Degrees:* bachelor's, master's, and post-master's certificates. *Special study options:* advanced placement credit, cooperative education, distance learning, double majors, English as a second language, honors programs, independent study, internships, off-campus study, part-time degree program, services for LD students, study abroad, summer session for credit. *ROTC:* Army (b), Navy (b), Air Force (b).

Computers on Campus 350 computers/terminals are available on campus for general student use. Students can access the following: campus intranet, computer help desk, free student e-mail accounts, online (class) grades, online (class) registration, online (class) schedules. Campuswide network is available. Wireless service is available via classrooms, dorm rooms, libraries, student centers.

Student Life *Housing:* on-campus residence required through senior year. *Options:* coed. Campus housing is university owned. Freshman campus housing is guaranteed. *Activities and organizations:* student-run newspaper, choral group, marching band, The Republican Society, Semper Fi Society, HESS Majors, Rod & Gun Club, Cordell Airborne Rangers. *Campus security:* 24-hour patrols. *Student services:* health clinic, personal/psychological counseling.

Athletics Member NCAA. All Division I except football (Division I-AA). *Intercollegiate sports:* baseball M(s), basketball M(s), cross-country running M(s)/W(s), golf W(s), ice hockey M(c), lacrosse M(c), riflery M(s)/W(s), rugby M(c)/W(c), soccer M(c)/W(s), tennis M(s), track and field M(s)/W(s), volleyball W(s), wrestling M(s). *Intramural sports:* badminton M/W, basketball M/W, football M, golf M/W, racquetball M/W, soccer M/W, softball M/W, swimming and diving M/W, table tennis M/W, tennis M/W, track and field M/W, ultimate Frisbee M/W, volleyball M/W, weight lifting M/W, wrestling M/W.

Standardized Tests *Required:* SAT or ACT (for admission).

Costs (2011–12) *Tuition:* state resident $10,216 full-time, $398 per credit part-time; nonresident $27,033 full-time, $698 per credit part-time. *Required fees:* $1249 full-time. *Room and board:* $5979. *Waivers:* senior citizens and employees or children of employees.

Financial Aid Of all full-time matriculated undergraduates who enrolled in 2011, 1,695 applied for aid, 1,340 were judged to have need, 333 had their need fully met. In 2011, 439 non-need-based awards were made. *Average percent of need met:* 62%. *Average financial aid package:* $14,307. *Average*

need-based loan: $4340. *Average need-based gift aid:* $13,858. *Average non-need-based aid:* $16,030. *Average indebtedness upon graduation:* $31,585.
Applying *Options:* electronic application. *Application fee:* $40. *Required:* high school transcript. *Recommended:* interview. *Application deadlines:* rolling (freshmen), rolling (transfers). *Notification:* continuous (freshmen), continuous (transfers).
Freshman Application Contact Lt. Col. John W. Powell Jr., Director of Admissions, The Citadel, The Military College of South Carolina, 171 Moultrie Street, Charleston, SC 29409. *Phone:* 843-953-5230. *Toll-free phone:* 800-868-1842. *Fax:* 843-953-7036. *E-mail:* john.powell@citadel.edu. *Web site:* http://www.citadel.edu/.

Claflin University
Orangeburg, South Carolina

- **Independent United Methodist** comprehensive, founded 1869
- **Small-town** 46-acre campus with easy access to Columbia
- **Endowment** $19.3 million
- **Coed** 1,893 undergraduate students, 95% full-time, 65% women, 35% men
- **Minimally difficult** entrance level, 39% of applicants were admitted

Undergraduates 1,796 full-time, 97 part-time. Students come from 27 states and territories; 12 other countries; 20% are from out of state; 93% Black or African American, non-Hispanic/Latino; 1% Hispanic/Latino; 0.2% Asian, non-Hispanic/Latino; 0.8% American Indian or Alaska Native, non-Hispanic/Latino; 0.6% Two or more races, non-Hispanic/Latino; 0.2% Race/ethnicity unknown; 2% international; 4% transferred in; 62% live on campus. *Retention:* 77% of full-time freshmen returned.
Freshmen *Admission:* 4,037 applied, 1,578 admitted, 408 enrolled. *Average high school GPA:* 3. *Test scores:* SAT critical reading scores over 500: 22%; SAT math scores over 500: 26%; ACT scores over 18: 46%; SAT critical reading scores over 600: 3%; SAT math scores over 600: 5%; ACT scores over 24: 9%.
Faculty *Total:* 158, 74% full-time, 66% with terminal degrees. *Student/faculty ratio:* 14:1.
Academics *Calendar:* semesters. *Degrees:* bachelor's and master's. *Special study options:* academic remediation for entering students, adult/continuing education programs, advanced placement credit, cooperative education, freshman honors college, honors programs, independent study, internships, off-campus study, part-time degree program, summer session for credit. *ROTC:* Army (c). *Unusual degree programs:* 3-2 engineering with Clemson University, South Carolina State University.
Computers on Campus 530 computers/terminals are available on campus for general student use. Students can access the following: computer help desk, free student e-mail accounts, online (class) grades, online (class) registration, online (class) schedules. Campuswide network is available. 100% of college-owned or -operated housing units are wired for high-speed Internet access. Wireless service is available via classrooms, computer centers, computer labs, learning centers, libraries, student centers.
Student Life *Housing options:* men-only, women-only. Campus housing is university owned. *Activities and organizations:* drama/theater group, student-run newspaper, radio and television station, choral group, national fraternities, national sororities. *Campus security:* 24-hour emergency response devices and patrols, student patrols, controlled dormitory access. *Student services:* health clinic, personal/psychological counseling.
Athletics Member NCAA. All Division II. *Intercollegiate sports:* baseball M(s)/W(s), basketball M(s)/W(s), cross-country running M(s)/W(s), softball W(s), track and field M(s)/W(s), volleyball W(s).
Standardized Tests *Required:* SAT or ACT (for admission). *Recommended:* SAT Subject Tests (for admission).
Costs (2012–13) *Comprehensive fee:* $17,848 includes full-time tuition ($13,974), mandatory fees ($450), and room and board ($3424). Full-time tuition and fees vary according to class time. Part-time tuition: $582 per credit hour. Part-time tuition and fees vary according to class time. *College room only:* $4622. Room and board charges vary according to housing facility. *Payment plans:* installment, deferred payment. *Waivers:* employees or children of employees.
Financial Aid Of all full-time matriculated undergraduates who enrolled in 2006, 1,517 applied for aid, 1,475 were judged to have need, 144 had their need fully met. In 2006, 300 non-need-based awards were made. *Average percent of need met:* 56%. *Average financial aid package:* $10,917. *Average need-based loan:* $3734. *Average need-based gift aid:* $8220. *Average non-need-based aid:* $17,712. *Average indebtedness upon graduation:* $19,993.
Applying *Options:* electronic application, deferred entrance. *Application fee:* $25. *Required:* essay or personal statement, high school transcript, minimum 2.0 GPA. *Application deadlines:* rolling (freshmen), rolling (transfers). *Notification:* continuous (freshmen), continuous (transfers).

Freshman Application Contact Claflin University, 400 Magnolia Street, Orangeburg, SC 29115. *Phone:* 803-5355340. *Toll-free phone:* 800-922-1276. *Web site:* http://www.claflin.edu/.

Clemson University
Clemson, South Carolina

- **State-supported** university, founded 1889
- **Small-town** 1400-acre campus
- **Endowment** $301.2 million
- **Coed** 15,836 undergraduate students, 94% full-time, 46% women, 54% men
- **Moderately difficult** entrance level, 60% of applicants were admitted

Undergraduates 14,834 full-time, 1,002 part-time. Students come from 53 states and territories; 84 other countries; 29% are from out of state; 6% Black or African American, non-Hispanic/Latino; 2% Hispanic/Latino; 2% Asian, non-Hispanic/Latino; 0.1% Native Hawaiian or other Pacific Islander, non-Hispanic/Latino; 0.2% American Indian or Alaska Native, non-Hispanic/Latino; 2% Two or more races, non-Hispanic/Latino; 2% Race/ethnicity unknown; 1% international; 7% transferred in; 37% live on campus. *Retention:* 90% of full-time freshmen returned.
Freshmen *Admission:* 17,016 applied, 10,215 admitted, 2,933 enrolled. *Average high school GPA:* 4.18. *Test scores:* SAT critical reading scores over 500: 92%; SAT math scores over 500: 96%; ACT scores over 18: 99%; SAT critical reading scores over 600: 53%; SAT math scores over 600: 72%; ACT scores over 24: 89%; SAT critical reading scores over 700: 10%; SAT math scores over 700: 17%; ACT scores over 30: 31%.
Faculty *Total:* 1,122, 90% full-time. *Student/faculty ratio:* 18:1.
Academics *Calendar:* semesters. *Degrees:* bachelor's, master's, doctoral, post-master's, and first professional certificates. *Special study options:* academic remediation for entering students, advanced placement credit, cooperative education, distance learning, double majors, freshman honors college, honors programs, independent study, internships, part-time degree program, services for LD students, study abroad, summer session for credit. *ROTC:* Army (b), Air Force (b).
Computers on Campus 1,250 computers/terminals are available on campus for general student use. Students can access the following: online (class) registration. Campuswide network is available. 100% of college-owned or -operated housing units are wired for high-speed Internet access. Wireless service is available via entire campus.
Student Life *Housing:* on-campus residence required for freshman year. *Options:* coed, men-only, women-only. Campus housing is university owned. Freshman campus housing is guaranteed. *Activities and organizations:* drama/theater group, student-run newspaper, radio and television station, choral group, marching band, student government, Fellowship of Christian Athletes, Tiger Band, national fraternities, national sororities. *Campus security:* 24-hour emergency response devices and patrols, late-night transport/escort service, controlled dormitory access. *Student services:* health clinic, personal/psychological counseling, legal services.
Athletics Member NCAA. All Division I except football (Division I-A). *Intercollegiate sports:* baseball M, basketball M(s)/W(s), bowling M(c)/W(c), cheerleading M/W, crew M(c)/W(s), cross-country running M(s)/W(s), equestrian sports M(c)/W(c), fencing M(c)/W(c), field hockey M(c)/W(c), golf M(s), ice hockey M(c)/W(c), lacrosse M(c)/W(c), riflery M(c)/W(c), rugby M(c)/W(c), sailing M(c)/W(c), soccer M(s)/W(s), softball W(c), tennis M(s)/W(s), track and field M(s)/W(s), ultimate Frisbee M(c)/W(c), volleyball M(c)/W(s), weight lifting M(c)/W(c), wrestling M(c). *Intramural sports:* basketball M/W, golf M/W, racquetball M/W, soccer M/W, softball M/W, swimming and diving M(c)/W(c), table tennis M/W, tennis M(c)/W(c), volleyball M/W, water polo M/W.
Standardized Tests *Required:* SAT or ACT (for admission).
Costs (2011–12) *Tuition:* state resident $12,668 full-time, $528 per credit hour part-time; nonresident $28,826 full-time, $1229 per credit hour part-time. Full-time tuition and fees vary according to course load, location, and program. Part-time tuition and fees vary according to program. *Room and board:* $7228. Room and board charges vary according to board plan, housing facility, and location. *Payment plan:* installment. *Waivers:* senior citizens.
Financial Aid Of all full-time matriculated undergraduates who enrolled in 2011, 8,689 applied for aid, 6,608 were judged to have need, 1,393 had their need fully met. 669 Federal Work-Study jobs (averaging $2322). 3,500 state and other part-time jobs (averaging $2000). In 2011, 2582 non-need-based awards were made. *Average percent of need met:* 55%. *Average financial aid package:* $11,198. *Average need-based loan:* $4515. *Average need-based gift aid:* $4421. *Average non-need-based aid:* $2280. *Average indebtedness upon graduation:* $25,826.
Applying *Options:* electronic application. *Application fee:* $60. *Required:* high school transcript. *Recommended:* essay or personal statement. *Applica-*

A Clemson Tiger
is among the best.

Ranked No. 23 among the nation's top public institutions, No. 12 among schools with a strong commitment to undergraduate instruction and No. 9 as an up-and-coming university, Clemson University is in good company.

But don't just look at our rankings — ask our students. In a recent survey, 92 percent of seniors said they would choose Clemson again. Plus, we hold the great honor of being No. 5 for Happiest Students and No. 1 for Town-Gown Relations are Great.

Put it all together, and Clemson is a well-rounded university that fosters an inclusive, student-centered community with high academic standards, a culture of collaboration, a competitive drive to excel and a determination to make a difference.

Find out more about becoming a Clemson Tiger at *clemson.edu/prospectivestudents.*

CLEMSON UNIVERSITY
1889

tion deadlines: 5/1 (freshmen), 7/1 (transfers). *Notification:* continuous (freshmen), continuous (transfers).

Freshman Application Contact Ms. Audrey R. Bodell, Associate Director of Admissions, Clemson University, PO Box 345124, 105 Sikes Hall, Clemson, SC 29634. *Phone:* 864-656-2287. *Fax:* 864-656-2464. *E-mail:* cuadmissions@clemson.edu. *Web site:* http://www.clemson.edu/.

See page 1266 for the College Close-Up.

Coastal Carolina University
Conway, South Carolina

- **State-supported** comprehensive, founded 1954
- **Suburban** 630-acre campus
- **Endowment** $31.2 million
- **Coed** 8,517 undergraduate students, 92% full-time, 53% women, 47% men
- **Moderately difficult** entrance level, 75% of applicants were admitted

Undergraduates 7,849 full-time, 668 part-time. Students come from 49 states and territories; 48 other countries; 48% are from out of state; 19% Black or African American, non-Hispanic/Latino; 3% Hispanic/Latino; 0.7% Asian, non-Hispanic/Latino; 0.2% Native Hawaiian or other Pacific Islander, non-Hispanic/Latino; 0.4% American Indian or Alaska Native, non-Hispanic/Latino; 2% Two or more races, non-Hispanic/Latino; 0.2% Race/ethnicity unknown; 1% international; 9% transferred in; 38% live on campus. *Retention:* 63% of full-time freshmen returned.

Freshmen *Admission:* 10,502 applied, 7,836 admitted, 2,137 enrolled. *Average high school GPA:* 3.34. *Test scores:* SAT critical reading scores over 500: 49%; SAT math scores over 500: 57%; ACT scores over 18: 90%; SAT critical reading scores over 600: 9%; SAT math scores over 600: 12%; ACT scores over 24: 13%; SAT critical reading scores over 700: 1%; SAT math scores over 700: 1%; ACT scores over 30: 1%.

Faculty *Total:* 619, 57% full-time, 56% with terminal degrees. *Student/faculty ratio:* 17:1.

Academics *Calendar:* semesters. *Degrees:* bachelor's, master's, and post-bachelor's certificates. *Special study options:* accelerated degree program, adult/continuing education programs, advanced placement credit, cooperative education, distance learning, double majors, honors programs, independent study, internships, part-time degree program, services for LD students, student-designed majors, study abroad, summer session for credit. *ROTC:* Army (b).

Computers on Campus 700 computers/terminals are available on campus for general student use. Students can access the following: computer help desk, free student e-mail accounts, online (class) grades, online (class) registration, online (class) schedules. Campuswide network is available. Wireless service is available via classrooms, computer centers, computer labs, dorm rooms, learning centers, libraries, student centers.

Student Life *Housing:* on-campus residence required through sophomore year. *Options:* coed, disabled students. Campus housing is university owned. Freshman campus housing is guaranteed. *Activities and organizations:* drama/theater group, student-run newspaper, radio station, choral group, marching band, Student Government Association, Campus Activities Board, STAR (Students Taking Active Responsibility), SCREAM (Student Spirit Organization), Leadership Challenge, national fraternities, national sororities. *Campus security:* 24-hour emergency response devices and patrols, late-night transport/escort service. *Student services:* health clinic, personal/psychological counseling, women's center.

Athletics Member NCAA. All Division I. *Intercollegiate sports:* baseball M(s), basketball M(s)/W(s), cheerleading M(c)/W(c), cross-country running M(s)/W(s), equestrian sports M(c)/W(c), field hockey W(c), football M(s), golf M(s)/W(s), lacrosse M(c)/W(c), rugby M(c)/W(c), soccer M(s)/W(s), softball W(s), swimming and diving M(c)/W(c), tennis M(s)/W(s), track and field M(s)/W(s), volleyball M(c)/W(c), wrestling M(c). *Intramural sports:* badminton M/W, basketball M/W, football M/W, golf M/W, soccer M/W, softball M/W, table tennis M/W, tennis M/W, volleyball M/W, water polo M/W.

Standardized Tests *Required:* SAT or ACT (for admission).

Costs (2011–12) *Tuition:* state resident $9680 full-time, $407 per credit hour part-time; nonresident $21,480 full-time, $898 per credit hour part-time. Full-time tuition and fees vary according to course load and degree level. Part-time tuition and fees vary according to course load and degree level. *Required fees:* $80 full-time. *Room and board:* $7700; room only: $5000. Room and board charges vary according to board plan and housing facility. *Payment plan:* installment. *Waivers:* senior citizens and employees or children of employees.

Financial Aid Of all full-time matriculated undergraduates who enrolled in 2010, 6,283 applied for aid, 5,269 were judged to have need, 492 had their need fully met. 178 Federal Work-Study jobs (averaging $1627). 1,012 state and other part-time jobs (averaging $2334). In 2010, 1128 non-need-based awards were made. *Average percent of need met:* 48%. *Average financial aid package:* $9365. *Average need-based loan:* $8199. *Average need-based gift*

aid: $5127. *Average non-need-based aid:* $11,973. *Average indebtedness upon graduation:* $31,629.

Applying *Options:* electronic application, deferred entrance. *Application fee:* $45. *Required:* high school transcript, minimum 2.0 GPA. *Recommended:* essay or personal statement, 1 letter of recommendation, interview. *Application deadlines:* 8/1 (freshmen), 8/1 (transfers). *Notification:* 9/1 (freshmen), continuous until 9/1 (transfers).

Freshman Application Contact Coastal Carolina University, PO Box 261954, Conway, SC 29528-6054. *Phone:* 843-349-2037. *Toll-free phone:* 800-277-7000. *Web site:* http://www.coastal.edu/.

Coker College
Hartsville, South Carolina

- **Independent** 4-year, founded 1908
- **Small-town** 30-acre campus with easy access to Charlotte
- **Coed**
- **Moderately difficult** entrance level

Faculty *Student/faculty ratio:* 12:1.

Academics *Calendar:* semesters. *Degrees:* bachelor's (also offers evening program with significant enrollment not reflected in profile).

Student Life *Campus security:* 24-hour patrols, late-night transport/escort service, controlled dormitory access.

Athletics Member NCAA. All Division II.

Standardized Tests *Required:* SAT or ACT (for admission).

Costs (2011–12) *Comprehensive fee:* $29,150 includes full-time tuition ($22,200) and room and board ($6950). *College room only:* $3400.

Financial Aid *Of all full-time matriculated undergraduates who enrolled in 2010,* 605 applied for aid, 564 were judged to have need, 165 had their need fully met. 98 Federal Work-Study jobs (averaging $974). *In 2010,* 50 non-need-based awards were made. *Average percent of need met:* 85. *Average financial aid package:* $20,486. *Average need-based loan:* $4527. *Average need-based gift aid:* $7456. *Average non-need-based aid:* $7196. *Average indebtedness upon graduation:* $25,593. *Financial aid deadline:* 6/1.

Applying *Options:* electronic application, deferred entrance. *Application fee:* $15.

Freshman Application Contact Director of Admissions, Coker College, 300 East College Avenue, Hartsville, SC 29550. *Phone:* 843-383-8050. *Toll-free phone:* 800-950-1908. *Fax:* 843-383-8056. *E-mail:* admissions@coker.edu. *Web site:* http://www.coker.edu/.

College of Charleston
Charleston, South Carolina

- **State-supported** comprehensive, founded 1770
- **Urban** 52-acre campus
- **Endowment** $55.2 million
- **Coed** 10,461 undergraduate students, 93% full-time, 62% women, 38% men
- **Moderately difficult** entrance level, 74% of applicants were admitted

Undergraduates 9,700 full-time, 761 part-time. Students come from 51 states and territories; 65 other countries; 37% are from out of state; 6% Black or African American, non-Hispanic/Latino; 3% Hispanic/Latino; 1% Asian, non-Hispanic/Latino; 0.2% Native Hawaiian or other Pacific Islander, non-Hispanic/Latino; 0.2% American Indian or Alaska Native, non-Hispanic/Latino; 3% Two or more races, non-Hispanic/Latino; 2% Race/ethnicity unknown; 1% international; 7% transferred in; 32% live on campus. *Retention:* 83% of full-time freshmen returned.

Freshmen *Admission:* 11,086 applied, 8,149 admitted, 2,334 enrolled. *Average high school GPA:* 3.84. *Test scores:* SAT critical reading scores over 500: 96%; SAT math scores over 500: 95%; ACT scores over 18: 100%; SAT critical reading scores over 600: 55%; SAT math scores over 600: 51%; ACT scores over 24: 67%; SAT critical reading scores over 700: 11%; SAT math scores over 700: 6%; ACT scores over 30: 7%.

Faculty *Total:* 937, 58% full-time, 65% with terminal degrees. *Student/faculty ratio:* 16:1.

Academics *Calendar:* semesters. *Degrees:* bachelor's, master's, post-master's, and postbachelor's certificates (also offers graduate degree programs through University of Charleston, South Carolina). *Special study options:* accelerated degree program, adult/continuing education programs, advanced placement credit, cooperative education, distance learning, double majors, English as a second language, honors programs, independent study, internships, off-campus study, part-time degree program, services for LD students, study abroad, summer session for credit. *ROTC:* Air Force (c).

Computers on Campus 750 computers/terminals and 1,200 ports are available on campus for general student use. Students can access the following: computer help desk, free student e-mail accounts, online (class) grades, online (class) registration, online (class) schedules. Campuswide network is available.

100% of college-owned or -operated housing units are wired for high-speed Internet access. Wireless service is available via entire campus.

Student Life *Housing options:* coed, men-only, women-only, disabled students. Campus housing is university owned. Freshman campus housing is guaranteed. *Activities and organizations:* drama/theater group, student-run newspaper, radio station, choral group, Student Government Association, Cougar Productions, intramural basketball, Black Student Union, national fraternities, national sororities. *Campus security:* 24-hour emergency response devices and patrols, student patrols, late-night transport/escort service, controlled dormitory access. *Student services:* health clinic, personal/psychological counseling, women's center, legal services.

Athletics Member NCAA. All Division I. *Intercollegiate sports:* baseball M(s), basketball M(s)/W(s), cross-country running M(s)/W(s), equestrian sports W, golf M(s)/W(s), sailing M/W, soccer M(s)/W(s), softball M/W(s), swimming and diving M(s)/W(s), tennis M(s)/W(s), track and field W(s), volleyball W(s). *Intramural sports:* badminton M(c)/W(c), basketball M/W, crew M(c)/W(c), golf M(c)/W(c), gymnastics M(c)/W(c), ice hockey M(c), lacrosse M(c)/W(c), racquetball M/W, rugby M(c)/W(c), soccer M/W, softball W, squash M(c)/W(c), swimming and diving M(c)/W(c), table tennis M/W, tennis M/W, ultimate Frisbee M/W, volleyball M/W(c), weight lifting M/W.

Standardized Tests *Required:* SAT or ACT (for admission).

Costs (2011–12) *Tuition:* state resident $9616 full-time, $401 per semester hour part-time; nonresident $24,330 full-time, $1014 per semester hour part-time. Full-time tuition and fees vary according to degree level. Part-time tuition and fees vary according to course load and degree level. *Room and board:* $10,179; room only: $6979. Room and board charges vary according to board plan and housing facility. *Payment plan:* installment. *Waivers:* senior citizens.

Financial Aid Of all full-time matriculated undergraduates who enrolled in 2011, 6,068 applied for aid, 4,751 were judged to have need, 823 had their need fully met. In 2011, 1684 non-need-based awards were made. *Average percent of need met:* 55%. *Average financial aid package:* $12,423. *Average need-based loan:* $3509. *Average need-based gift aid:* $3080. *Average non-need-based aid:* $10,412. *Average indebtedness upon graduation:* $26,024.

Applying *Options:* electronic application, early action, deferred entrance. *Application fee:* $50. *Required:* essay or personal statement, high school transcript, SAT or ACT. *Application deadlines:* 4/1 (freshmen), 5/1 (transfers), 11/1 (early action). *Notification:* 5/15 (freshmen), 6/1 (transfers), 12/15 (early action).

Freshman Application Contact Ms. Suzette Stille, Director of Undergraduate Admissions, College of Charleston, 66 George Street, Charleston, SC 29424-0001. *Phone:* 843-953-5670. *Fax:* 843-953-6322. *E-mail:* admissions@cofc.edu. *Web site:* http://www.cofc.edu/.

Columbia College
Columbia, South Carolina

- **Independent United Methodist** comprehensive, founded 1854
- **Suburban** 33-acre campus
- **Endowment** $19.0 million
- **Undergraduate: women only; graduate: coed** 1,121 undergraduate students, 78% full-time, 98% women, 2% men
- **Moderately difficult** entrance level, 69% of applicants were admitted

Undergraduates 876 full-time, 245 part-time. Students come from 23 states and territories; 11 other countries; 10% are from out of state; 41% Black or African American, non-Hispanic/Latino; 2% Hispanic/Latino; 2% Asian, non-Hispanic/Latino; 0.4% American Indian or Alaska Native, non-Hispanic/Latino; 4% Race/ethnicity unknown; 0.8% international; 6% transferred in; 44% live on campus. *Retention:* 69% of full-time freshmen returned.

Freshmen *Admission:* 893 applied, 617 admitted, 193 enrolled. *Average high school GPA:* 3.5. *Test scores:* SAT critical reading scores over 500: 51%; SAT writing scores over 500: 44%; ACT scores over 18: 88%; SAT critical reading scores over 600: 18%; SAT writing scores over 600: 8%; ACT scores over 24: 29%; SAT critical reading scores over 700: 5%; SAT writing scores over 700: 1%; ACT scores over 30: 4%.

Faculty *Total:* 135, 52% full-time, 57% with terminal degrees. *Student/faculty ratio:* 12:1.

Academics *Calendar:* semesters. *Degrees:* bachelor's, master's, and doctoral. *Special study options:* academic remediation for entering students, adult/continuing education programs, advanced placement credit, distance learning, double majors, honors programs, independent study, internships, off-campus study, part-time degree program, student-designed majors, study abroad, summer session for credit. *ROTC:* Army (c), Navy (c), Air Force (c).

Computers on Campus 165 computers/terminals are available on campus for general student use. Students can access the following: campus intranet, computer help desk, free student e-mail accounts, online (class) grades, online (class) registration, online (class) schedules. Campuswide network is available.

100% of college-owned or -operated housing units are wired for high-speed Internet access. Wireless service is available via student centers.

Student Life *Housing:* on-campus residence required through sophomore year. *Options:* women-only. Campus housing is university owned. Freshman campus housing is guaranteed. *Activities and organizations:* drama/theater group, student-run newspaper, choral group, Student Government Association, African-American Student Association, Columbia College Activities Board, Heavenly Creations Gospel Choir, Student Christian Association. *Campus security:* 24-hour emergency response devices and patrols, late-night transport/escort service, controlled dormitory access. *Student services:* health clinic, personal/psychological counseling, women's center.

Athletics Member NAIA. *Intercollegiate sports:* basketball W(s), soccer W(s), softball W(s), tennis W(s), volleyball W(s).

Standardized Tests *Required:* SAT or ACT (for admission).

Costs (2011–12) *Comprehensive fee:* $31,688 includes full-time tuition ($24,600), mandatory fees ($450), and room and board ($6638). Full-time tuition and fees vary according to class time. Part-time tuition: $660 per semester hour. Part-time tuition and fees vary according to course load. *Room and board:* Room and board charges vary according to board plan and housing facility. *Payment plan:* installment. *Waivers:* employees or children of employees.

Financial Aid Of all full-time matriculated undergraduates who enrolled in 2005, 794 applied for aid, 698 were judged to have need, 310 had their need fully met. 200 Federal Work-Study jobs (averaging $1000). In 2005, 152 non-need-based awards were made. *Average percent of need met:* 70%. *Average financial aid package:* $20,052. *Average need-based loan:* $3810. *Average need-based gift aid:* $8495. *Average non-need-based aid:* $7775. *Average indebtedness upon graduation:* $25,333.

Applying *Options:* electronic application. *Application fee:* $25. *Required:* high school transcript, minimum 2.0 GPA, 1 letter of recommendation. *Required for some:* interview. *Recommended:* essay or personal statement. *Application deadlines:* 8/1 (freshmen), 8/1 (transfers).

Freshman Application Contact Ms. Julie King, Director of Admissions, Columbia College, 1301 Columbia College Drive, Columbia, SC 29203. *Phone:* 803-786-3765. *Toll-free phone:* 800-277-1301. *Fax:* 803-786-3674. *E-mail:* admissions@colacoll.edu. *Web site:* http://www.columbiacollegesc.edu/.

Columbia International University

Columbia, South Carolina

Freshman Application Contact Columbia International University, PO Box 3122, Columbia, SC 29230-3122. *Phone:* 803-807-5024. *Toll-free phone:* 800-777-2227 Ext. 5024. *Fax:* 803-786-4041. *E-mail:* yesciu@ciu.edu. *Web site:* http://www.ciu.edu/.

Converse College

Spartanburg, South Carolina

- **Independent** comprehensive, founded 1889
- **Urban** 70-acre campus
- **Endowment** $71.4 million
- **Undergraduate: women only; graduate: coed** 699 undergraduate students, 90% full-time, 100% women
- **Moderately difficult** entrance level, 17% of applicants were admitted

Undergraduates 626 full-time, 73 part-time. Students come from 29 states and territories; 4 other countries; 23% are from out of state; 13% Black or African American, non-Hispanic/Latino; 4% Hispanic/Latino; 3% Native Hawaiian or other Pacific Islander, non-Hispanic/Latino; 0.7% American Indian or Alaska Native, non-Hispanic/Latino; 20% Race/ethnicity unknown; 1% international; 3% transferred in; 80% live on campus. *Retention:* 62% of full-time freshmen returned.

Freshmen *Admission:* 1,125 applied, 194 admitted, 194 enrolled. *Average high school GPA:* 3.41. *Test scores:* SAT critical reading scores over 500: 76%; SAT math scores over 500: 60%; ACT scores over 18: 98%; SAT critical reading scores over 600: 26%; SAT math scores over 600: 17%; ACT scores over 24: 54%; SAT critical reading scores over 700: 5%; ACT scores over 30: 3%.

Faculty *Total:* 88, 89% full-time, 89% with terminal degrees. *Student/faculty ratio:* 9:1.

Academics *Calendar:* 4-2-4. *Degrees:* bachelor's, master's, and post-master's certificates. *Special study options:* adult/continuing education programs, advanced placement credit, cooperative education, distance learning, double

majors, English as a second language, honors programs, independent study, internships, off-campus study, part-time degree program, services for LD students, student-designed majors, study abroad, summer session for credit. *ROTC:* Army (c). *Unusual degree programs:* engineering with Clemson University; nursing with Vanderbilt University.

Computers on Campus 140 computers/terminals are available on campus for general student use. Students can access the following: campus intranet, computer help desk, free student e-mail accounts, online (class) grades, online (class) registration, online (class) schedules. Campuswide network is available. 100% of college-owned or -operated housing units are wired for high-speed Internet access. Wireless service is available via classrooms, computer centers, learning centers, libraries, student centers.

Student Life *Housing:* on-campus residence required through senior year. *Options:* women-only. Campus housing is university owned. Freshman campus housing is guaranteed. *Activities and organizations:* drama/theater group, student-run newspaper, choral group, student government, student volunteer services, Student Christian Organization, Student Activities Committee, Athletic Association. *Campus security:* 24-hour emergency response devices and patrols, late-night transport/escort service, controlled dormitory access. *Student services:* health clinic, personal/psychological counseling, women's center.

Athletics Member NCAA. All Division II. *Intercollegiate sports:* basketball W(s), cross-country running W(s), equestrian sports W, golf W, lacrosse W(s), soccer W(s), swimming and diving W(s), tennis W(s), volleyball W(s). *Intramural sports:* archery W, baseball W, basketball W, bowling W, equestrian sports W, fencing W, field hockey W, soccer W, softball W, swimming and diving W, tennis W, volleyball W, weight lifting W.

Standardized Tests *Required:* SAT or ACT (for admission).

Costs (2012–13) *Comprehensive fee:* $37,130 includes full-time tuition ($28,276) and room and board ($8854). Full-time tuition and fees vary according to program and reciprocity agreements. Part-time tuition: $850 per credit hour. Part-time tuition and fees vary according to course load and program. *Room and board:* Room and board charges vary according to housing facility and student level. *Waivers:* employees or children of employees.

Financial Aid Of all full-time matriculated undergraduates who enrolled in 2011, 572 applied for aid, 535 were judged to have need, 127 had their need fully met. 88 Federal Work-Study jobs (averaging $1531). 60 state and other part-time jobs (averaging $1000). In 2011, 73 non-need-based awards were made. *Average percent of need met:* 77%. *Average financial aid package:* $23,425. *Average need-based loan:* $4850. *Average need-based gift aid:* $19,726. *Average non-need-based aid:* $15,127. *Average indebtedness upon graduation:* $26,866.

Applying *Options:* electronic application. *Required:* high school transcript, 1 letter of recommendation. *Required for some:* interview. *Recommended:* essay or personal statement, minimum 3.0 GPA. *Application deadlines:* rolling (freshmen), rolling (out-of-state freshmen), 7/1 (transfers). *Notification:* continuous until 5/1 (freshmen), continuous until 8/1 (transfers).

Freshman Application Contact Ms. April Lewis, Director of Admissions, Converse College, 580 East Main Street, Spartanburg, SC 29302. *Phone:* 864-596-9040 Ext. 9746. *Toll-free phone:* 800-766-1125. *Fax:* 864-596-9225. *E-mail:* admissions@converse.edu. *Web site:* http://www.converse.edu/.

ECPI College of Technology

Charleston, South Carolina

Admissions Office Contact ECPI College of Technology, 7410 Northside Drive, Suite 100, Charleston, SC 29420. *Toll-free phone:* 866-708-6166. *Web site:* http://www.ecpi.edu/.

ECPI College of Technology

Columbia, South Carolina

Admissions Office Contact ECPI College of Technology, 250 Berryhill Road, #300, Columbia, SC 29210. *Toll-free phone:* 866-708-6168. *Web site:* http://www.ecpi.edu/.

ECPI College of Technology

Greenville, South Carolina

Admissions Office Contact ECPI College of Technology, 1001 Keys Drive, #100, Greenville, SC 29615. *Toll-free phone:* 866-708-6171. *Web site:* http://www.ecpi.edu/.

Erskine College
Due West, South Carolina

- **Independent** comprehensive, founded 1839, affiliated with Associate Reformed Presbyterian Church
- **Rural** 90-acre campus
- **Endowment** $43.6 million
- **Coed**
- **Moderately difficult** entrance level

Faculty *Student/faculty ratio:* 11:1.
Academics *Calendar:* 4-1-4. *Degrees:* certificates, bachelor's, master's, doctoral, and first professional.
Student Life *Campus security:* 24-hour patrols, late-night transport/escort service, controlled dormitory access.
Athletics Member NCAA. All Division II.
Standardized Tests *Required:* SAT or ACT (for admission).
Costs (2011–12) *Comprehensive fee:* $37,360 includes full-time tuition ($26,350), mandatory fees ($1810), and room and board ($9200). Part-time tuition: $975 per semester hour.
Financial Aid *Of all full-time matriculated undergraduates who enrolled in 2009,* 498 applied for aid, 400 were judged to have need, 156 had their need fully met. *In 2009,* 121 non-need-based awards were made. *Average percent of need met:* 86. *Average financial aid package:* $21,093. *Average need-based loan:* $4750. *Average need-based gift aid:* $16,222. *Average non-need-based aid:* $10,725. *Average indebtedness upon graduation:* $24,450.
Applying *Options:* electronic application, early admission, early action, deferred entrance. *Application fee:* $25. *Required:* essay or personal statement, high school transcript, 1 letter of recommendation. *Recommended:* interview.
Freshman Application Contact Erskine College, 2 Washington Street, PO Box 338, Due West, SC 29639. *Phone:* 864-379-8838. *Toll-free phone:* 800-241-8721. *Web site:* http://www.erskine.edu/.

Francis Marion University
Florence, South Carolina

- **State-supported** comprehensive, founded 1970
- **Rural** 400-acre campus
- **Endowment** $24.6 million
- **Coed** 3,876 undergraduate students, 88% full-time, 67% women, 33% men
- **Moderately difficult** entrance level, 59% of applicants were admitted

Undergraduates 3,430 full-time, 446 part-time. Students come from 31 states and territories; 17 other countries; 4% are from out of state; 47% Black or African American, non-Hispanic/Latino; 0.9% Hispanic/Latino; 1% Asian, non-Hispanic/Latino; 0.1% Native Hawaiian or other Pacific Islander, non-Hispanic/Latino; 0.6% American Indian or Alaska Native, non-Hispanic/Latino; 0.2% Two or more races, non-Hispanic/Latino; 3% Race/ethnicity unknown; 1% international; 7% transferred in; 39% live on campus. *Retention:* 67% of full-time freshmen returned.
Freshmen *Admission:* 3,843 applied, 2,255 admitted, 743 enrolled. *Average high school GPA:* 3.51. *Test scores:* SAT critical reading scores over 500: 34%; SAT math scores over 500: 36%; SAT writing scores over 500: 26%; ACT scores over 18: 68%; SAT critical reading scores over 600: 10%; SAT math scores over 600: 7%; SAT writing scores over 600: 6%; ACT scores over 24: 18%; SAT critical reading scores over 700: 1%.
Faculty *Total:* 287, 68% full-time, 63% with terminal degrees. *Student/faculty ratio:* 16:1.
Academics *Calendar:* semesters. *Degrees:* bachelor's, master's, and post-master's certificates. *Special study options:* accelerated degree program, adult/continuing education programs, advanced placement credit, distance learning, double majors, honors programs, independent study, internships, off-campus study, part-time degree program, services for LD students, study abroad, summer session for credit. *ROTC:* Army (b). *Unusual degree programs:* 3-2 engineering with Clemson University; forestry with Clemson University.
Computers on Campus 624 computers/terminals are available on campus for general student use. Students can access the following: computer help desk, online (class) registration, Blackboard. Campuswide network is available. 100% of college-owned or -operated housing units are wired for high-speed Internet access. Wireless service is available via classrooms, computer labs, dorm rooms, libraries.
Student Life *Housing options:* men-only, women-only, disabled students. Campus housing is university owned and is provided by a third party. Freshman applicants given priority for college housing. *Activities and organizations:* drama/theater group, student-run newspaper, television station, choral group, Baptist Collegiate Ministries, University Programming Board, National Pan-Hellenic Association, Student Alumni Association, Student Government Association, national fraternities, national sororities. *Campus security:* 24-

hour emergency response devices and patrols, late-night transport/escort service, controlled dormitory access. *Student services:* health clinic, personal/psychological counseling.
Athletics Member NCAA. All Division II except golf (Division I), soccer (Division I). *Intercollegiate sports:* baseball M(s), basketball M(s)/W(s), cross-country running M(s)/W(s), golf M(s), soccer M(s)/W(s), softball W(s), tennis M(s)/W(s), track and field M/W, volleyball W(s). *Intramural sports:* basketball M/W, bowling M/W, cheerleading M(c)/W(c), football M/W, golf M/W, racquetball M/W, soccer M/W, softball M/W, table tennis M/W, tennis M/W, track and field M/W, ultimate Frisbee M/W, volleyball M/W.
Standardized Tests *Required:* SAT or ACT (for admission).
Costs (2011–12) *Tuition:* state resident $8467 full-time, $423 per credit hour part-time; nonresident $16,934 full-time, $847 per credit hour part-time. Part-time tuition and fees vary according to course load. *Required fees:* $335 full-time, $12 per credit hour part-time, $30 per term part-time. *Room and board:* $6620; room only: $3730. Room and board charges vary according to board plan and housing facility. *Payment plan:* installment. *Waivers:* senior citizens and employees or children of employees.
Financial Aid Of all full-time matriculated undergraduates who enrolled in 2011, 3,418 applied for aid, 3,187 were judged to have need. In 2011, 43 non-need-based awards were made. *Average financial aid package:* $9362. *Average need-based loan:* $3988. *Average need-based gift aid:* $4721. *Average non-need-based aid:* $1959. *Average indebtedness upon graduation:* $26,453. *Financial aid deadline:* 6/30.
Applying *Options:* electronic application, early admission, deferred entrance. *Application fee:* $31. *Required:* high school transcript, minimum 2.0 GPA. *Application deadlines:* 8/17 (freshmen), 8/17 (out-of-state freshmen), rolling (transfers). *Notification:* 9/1 (freshmen), 9/1 (out-of-state freshmen).
Freshman Application Contact Mrs. Perry Wilson, Director of Admissions, Francis Marion University, PO Box 100547, Florence, SC 29502-0547. *Phone:* 843-661-1231. *Toll-free phone:* 800-368-7551. *Fax:* 843-661-4635. *E-mail:* admission@fmarion.edu. *Web site:* http://www.fmarion.edu/.

Furman University
Greenville, South Carolina

- **Independent** comprehensive, founded 1826
- **Suburban** 800-acre campus
- **Endowment** $572.2 million
- **Coed** 2,825 undergraduate students, 95% full-time, 57% women, 43% men
- **Very difficult** entrance level, 83% of applicants were admitted

Undergraduates 2,694 full-time, 131 part-time. Students come from 46 states and territories; 49 other countries; 67% are from out of state; 5% Black or African American, non-Hispanic/Latino; 3% Hispanic/Latino; 2% Asian, non-Hispanic/Latino; 0.1% American Indian or Alaska Native, non-Hispanic/Latino; 1% Two or more races, non-Hispanic/Latino; 5% Race/ethnicity unknown; 2% international; 0.9% transferred in; 96% live on campus. *Retention:* 89% of full-time freshmen returned.
Freshmen *Admission:* 4,888 applied, 4,058 admitted, 785 enrolled. *Average high school GPA:* 3.5. *Test scores:* SAT critical reading scores over 500: 93%; SAT math scores over 500: 94%; SAT writing scores over 500: 93%; ACT scores over 18: 100%; SAT critical reading scores over 600: 61%; SAT math scores over 600: 65%; SAT writing scores over 600: 59%; ACT scores over 24: 88%; SAT critical reading scores over 700: 17%; SAT math scores over 700: 14%; SAT writing scores over 700: 16%; ACT scores over 30: 29%.
Faculty *Total:* 269, 88% full-time, 90% with terminal degrees. *Student/faculty ratio:* 11:1.
Academics *Calendar:* 3-2-3. *Degrees:* bachelor's and master's. *Special study options:* accelerated degree program, adult/continuing education programs, advanced placement credit, double majors, independent study, internships, part-time degree program, services for LD students, student-designed majors, study abroad, summer session for credit. *ROTC:* Army (b). *Unusual degree programs:* 3-2 engineering with Georgia Institute of Technology, Clemson University, Auburn University, North Carolina State University, Washington University in St. Louis; forestry with Duke University.
Computers on Campus 425 computers/terminals and 3,500 ports are available on campus for general student use. Students can access the following: campus intranet, computer help desk, free student e-mail accounts, online (class) grades, online (class) registration, online (class) schedules. Campuswide network is available. 100% of college-owned or -operated housing units are wired for high-speed Internet access. Wireless service is available via entire campus.
Student Life *Housing:* on-campus residence required through senior year. *Options:* coed, men-only, women-only. Campus housing is university owned. Freshman campus housing is guaranteed. *Activities and organizations:* drama/theater group, student-run newspaper, radio and television station, choral group, marching band, Collegiate Educational Service Corps, Fellowship of

Christian Athletes, Baptist Student Union, Student Activities Board, Furman Singers, national fraternities, national sororities. *Campus security:* 24-hour emergency response devices and patrols, student patrols, late-night transport/escort service, controlled dormitory access. *Student services:* health clinic, personal/psychological counseling, women's center.

Athletics Member NCAA. All Division I except football (Division I-AA). *Intercollegiate sports:* baseball M(s), basketball M(s)/W(s), cheerleading M/W, crew M(c)/W(c), cross-country running M(s)/W(s), equestrian sports W(c), fencing M(c)/W(c), golf M(s)/W(s), ice hockey M(c), lacrosse M(c)/W(c), rugby M(c)/W(c), soccer M(s)/W(s), softball W(s), swimming and diving M(c)/W(c), tennis M(s)/W(s), track and field M(s)/W(s), ultimate Frisbee M(c)/W(c), volleyball W(s), weight lifting M(c)/W(c), wrestling M(c). *Intramural sports:* basketball M/W, bowling M/W, cross-country running M/W, football M/W, golf M/W, racquetball M/W, soccer M/W, softball M/W, swimming and diving M/W, tennis M/W, track and field M/W, volleyball M/W.

Standardized Tests *Recommended:* SAT or ACT (for admission).

Costs (2011–12) *Comprehensive fee:* $49,752 includes full-time tuition ($39,200), mandatory fees ($360), and room and board ($10,192). Part-time tuition: $1225 per credit. Part-time tuition and fees vary according to course load. *College room only:* $5592. Room and board charges vary according to board plan and housing facility. *Payment plan:* installment. *Waivers:* employees or children of employees.

Financial Aid Of all full-time matriculated undergraduates who enrolled in 2011, 1,492 applied for aid, 1,241 were judged to have need, 452 had their need fully met. 681 Federal Work-Study jobs (averaging $1472). In 2011, 861 non-need-based awards were made. *Average percent of need met:* 80%. *Average financial aid package:* $30,613. *Average need-based loan:* $3972. *Average need-based gift aid:* $27,114. *Average non-need-based aid:* $16,796. *Average indebtedness upon graduation:* $26,600. *Financial aid deadline:* 1/15.

Applying *Options:* electronic application, early decision, early action. *Application fee:* $50. *Required:* essay or personal statement, high school transcript. *Recommended:* interview. *Application deadlines:* 1/15 (freshmen), 1/15 (transfers), 12/15 (early action). *Early decision deadline:* 11/1. *Notification:* 4/2 (freshmen), 4/2 (transfers), 12/1 (early decision), 2/1 (early action).

Freshman Application Contact Mr. Brad Pochard, Assistant Vice President of Admissions, Furman University, 3300 Poinsett Highway, Greenville, SC 29613. *Phone:* 864-294-2034. *Fax:* 864-294-2018. *E-mail:* admissions@furman.edu. *Web site:* http://www.furman.edu/.

ITT Technical Institute
Columbia, South Carolina

- **Proprietary** primarily 2-year, part of ITT Educational Services, Inc.
- **Coed**

Academics *Degrees:* associate and bachelor's.

Student Life *Housing:* college housing not available.

Freshman Application Contact Director of Recruitment, ITT Technical Institute, 1628 Browning Road, Suite 180, Columbia, SC 29210. *Phone:* 803-216-6000. *Toll-free phone:* 800-242-5158. *Web site:* http://www.itt-tech.edu/.

ITT Technical Institute
Greenville, South Carolina

- **Proprietary** primarily 2-year, founded 1992, part of ITT Educational Services, Inc.
- **Coed**
- **Minimally difficult** entrance level

Academics *Calendar:* quarters. *Degrees:* associate and bachelor's.

Student Life *Housing:* college housing not available.

Financial Aid Of all full-time matriculated undergraduates who enrolled in 2010, 3 Federal Work-Study jobs.

Freshman Application Contact Director of Recruitment, ITT Technical Institute, Independence Corporate Park, 6 Independence Pointe, Greenville, SC 29615. *Phone:* 864-288-0777. *Toll-free phone:* 800-932-4488. *Web site:* http://www.itt-tech.edu/.

ITT Technical Institute
Myrtle Beach, South Carolina

- **Proprietary** primarily 2-year, part of ITT Educational Services, Inc.
- **Coed**

Academics *Calendar:* quarters. *Degrees:* associate and bachelor's.

Freshman Application Contact Director of Recruitment, ITT Technical Institute, 9654 N. Kings Highway, Suite 101, Myrtle Beach, SC 29572. *Phone:* 843-497-7820. *Toll-free phone:* 877-316-7054. *Web site:* http://www.itt-tech.edu/.

ITT Technical Institute
North Charleston, South Carolina

- **Proprietary** primarily 2-year, part of ITT Educational Services, Inc.
- **Coed**

Academics *Calendar:* quarters. *Degrees:* associate and bachelor's.

Freshman Application Contact Director of Recruitment, ITT Technical Institute, 2431 W. Aviation Avenue, North Charleston, SC 29406. *Phone:* 843-745-5700. *Toll-free phone:* 877-291-0900. *Web site:* http://www.itt-tech.edu/.

Lander University
Greenwood, South Carolina

Freshman Application Contact Dr. Bettie R. Horne, Director of Admissions, Lander University, Greenwood, SC 29649. *Phone:* 864-388-8307. *Toll-free phone:* 888-452-6337. *Fax:* 864-388-8125. *E-mail:* admissions@lander.edu. *Web site:* http://www.lander.edu/.

Limestone College
Gaffney, South Carolina

- **Independent** 4-year, founded 1845
- **Suburban** 119-acre campus with easy access to Charlotte
- **Endowment** $12.4 million
- **Coed** 858 undergraduate students, 98% full-time, 41% women, 59% men
- **Minimally difficult** entrance level, 53% of applicants were admitted

Undergraduates 842 full-time, 16 part-time. Students come from 35 states and territories; 19 other countries; 46% are from out of state; 22% Black or African American, non-Hispanic/Latino; 3% Hispanic/Latino; 0.8% Asian, non-Hispanic/Latino; 0.5% American Indian or Alaska Native, non-Hispanic/Latino; 3% Race/ethnicity unknown; 7% international; 9% transferred in; 52% live on campus. *Retention:* 59% of full-time freshmen returned.

Freshmen *Admission:* 1,363 applied, 725 admitted, 223 enrolled. *Average high school GPA:* 3.18. *Test scores:* SAT critical reading scores over 500: 35%; SAT math scores over 500: 67%; SAT critical reading scores over 600: 10%; SAT math scores over 600: 15%; SAT critical reading scores over 700: 4%; SAT math scores over 700: 4%.

Faculty *Total:* 81, 80% full-time, 68% with terminal degrees. *Student/faculty ratio:* 12:1.

Academics *Calendar:* semesters. *Degrees:* associate and bachelor's. *Special study options:* academic remediation for entering students, accelerated degree program, adult/continuing education programs, advanced placement credit, distance learning, double majors, honors programs, independent study, internships, part-time degree program, services for LD students, student-designed majors, summer session for credit. *ROTC:* Army (b).

Computers on Campus 154 computers/terminals are available on campus for general student use. Students can access the following: computer help desk, free student e-mail accounts, online (class) grades, online registration for Internet classes only. Campuswide network is available. 100% of college-owned and -operated housing units are wired for high-speed Internet access. Wireless service is available via classrooms, learning centers, libraries, student centers.

Student Life *Housing:* on-campus residence required through junior year. *Options:* men-only, women-only. Campus housing is university owned. Freshman applicants given priority for college housing. *Activities and organizations:* drama/theater group, choral group, Fellowship of Christian Athletes, Student Government Association, Student Alumni Leadership Council, Students in Free Enterprise (SIFE), Limestone Activities Board. *Campus security:* 24-hour patrols, late-night transport/escort service, controlled dormitory access. *Student services:* health clinic, personal/psychological counseling.

Athletics Member NCAA. All Division II. *Intercollegiate sports:* baseball M(s), basketball M(s)/W(s), cross-country running M(s)/W(s), field hockey W(s), golf M(s)/W(s), lacrosse M(s)/W(s), soccer M(s)/W(s), softball W(s), swimming and diving M(s)/W(s), tennis M(s)/W(s), track and field M(s)/W(s), volleyball M(s)/W(s), wrestling M(s). *Intramural sports:* basketball M/W, bowling M/W, softball M/W, table tennis M/W, volleyball M/W.

Standardized Tests *Required:* SAT or ACT (for admission).

Costs (2012–13) *Comprehensive fee:* $28,500 includes full-time tuition ($21,000) and room and board ($7500). Full-time tuition and fees vary according to class time and location. Part-time tuition: $875 per semester hour. Part-time tuition and fees vary according to class time and location. *College room only:* $3750. *Payment plan:* installment. *Waivers:* employees or children of employees.

Financial Aid Of all full-time matriculated undergraduates who enrolled in 2011, 731 applied for aid, 676 were judged to have need, 83 had their need fully met. 103 Federal Work-Study jobs (averaging $1526). 83 state and other part-time jobs (averaging $803). In 2011, 57 non-need-based awards were made. *Average percent of need met:* 60%. *Average financial aid package:* $16,154. *Average need-based loan:* $4097. *Average need-based gift aid:*

$12,522. *Average non-need-based aid:* $5296. *Average indebtedness upon graduation:* $29,724.

Applying *Options:* electronic application. *Application fee:* $25. *Required:* high school transcript, minimum 2.0 GPA. *Recommended:* 2 letters of recommendation, interview. *Application deadlines:* rolling (freshmen), rolling (out-of-state freshmen), rolling (transfers). *Notification:* continuous (freshmen), continuous (out-of-state freshmen), continuous (transfers).

Freshman Application Contact Ms. Lisa Hobbs, Admissions Office Manager, Limestone College, 1115 College Drive, Gaffney, SC 29340-3799. *Phone:* 864-488-4554. *Toll-free phone:* 800-795-7151. *Fax:* 864-487-8706. *E-mail:* lhobbs@limestone.edu. *Web site:* http://www.limestone.edu/.

See below for display ad and page 1412 for the College Close-Up.

Medical University of South Carolina
Charleston, South Carolina

- **State-supported** upper-level, founded 1824
- **Urban** 82-acre campus
- **Endowment** $230.3 million
- **Coed** 200 undergraduate students, 99% full-time, 80% women, 21% men
- **Very difficult** entrance level

Undergraduates 197 full-time, 3 part-time. Students come from 23 states and territories; 10% are from out of state; 11% Black or African American, non-Hispanic/Latino; 6% Hispanic/Latino; 3% Asian, non-Hispanic/Latino; 0.5% American Indian or Alaska Native, non-Hispanic/Latino; 1% Two or more races, non-Hispanic/Latino; 5% Race/ethnicity unknown. **Faculty** *Total:* 223, 69% full-time, 84% with terminal degrees. *Student/faculty ratio:* 2:1.

Academics *Calendar:* semesters. *Degrees:* bachelor's, master's, doctoral, post-master's, postbachelor's, and first professional certificates. *Special study options:* accelerated degree program, distance learning, internships, off-campus study, services for LD students. *ROTC:* Air Force (c).

Computers on Campus 200 computers/terminals are available on campus for general student use. Students can access the following: campus intranet, computer help desk, free student e-mail accounts, online (class) grades, online (class) registration, online (class) schedules. Campuswide network is available. Wireless service is available via entire campus.

Student Life *Housing:* college housing not available. *Activities and organizations:* choral group, MUSC Student Government Association, Multicultural Group Advisory Board, Public Health Interest Group, International Association, Crisis Ministries. *Campus security:* 24-hour emergency response devices and patrols, late-night transport/escort service. *Student services:* health clinic, personal/psychological counseling, legal services.

Athletics *Intramural sports:* basketball M/W, softball M/W, volleyball M/W.

Costs (2011–12) *One-time required fee:* $485. *Tuition:* state resident $14,018 full-time, $634 per semester hour part-time; nonresident $23,824 full-time, $1102 per semester hour part-time. Full-time tuition and fees vary according to program. Part-time tuition and fees vary according to course load and program. *Required fees:* $1140 full-time, $996 per term part-time. *Payment plan:* installment. *Waivers:* minority students, adult students, senior citizens, and employees or children of employees.

Financial Aid Of all full-time matriculated undergraduates who enrolled in 2010, 162 applied for aid, 158 were judged to have need, 2 had their need fully met. *Average percent of need met:* 38%. *Average financial aid package:* $12,997. *Average need-based loan:* $9334. *Average need-based gift aid:* $4374.

Applying *Options:* electronic application, deferred entrance. *Application fee:* $95.

Application Contact Lyla E. Hudson, Director of Admissions, Medical University of South Carolina, 41 Bee Street MSC203, Charleston, SC 29425-2030. *Phone:* 843-792-7408. *E-mail:* hudsonly@musc.edu. *Web site:* http://www.musc.edu/.

Morris College
Sumter, South Carolina

- **Independent** 4-year, founded 1908, affiliated with Baptist Educational and Missionary Convention of South Carolina
- **Small-town** 34-acre campus
- **Endowment** $11.4 million
- **Coed** 979 undergraduate students, 98% full-time, 56% women, 44% men
- **Noncompetitive** entrance level, 88% of applicants were admitted

Undergraduates 958 full-time, 21 part-time. Students come from 22 states and territories; 16% are from out of state; 99% Black or African American, non-Hispanic/Latino; 0.2% Hispanic/Latino; 0.9% Two or more races, non-Hispanic/Latino; 5% transferred in; 72% live on campus. **Freshmen** *Admission:* 2,177 applied, 1,919 admitted, 284 enrolled. *Average high school GPA:* 2.49. **Faculty** *Total:* 68, 75% full-time, 57% with terminal degrees. *Student/faculty ratio:* 17:1.

Academics *Calendar:* semesters. *Degree:* bachelor's. *Special study options:* academic remediation for entering students, accelerated degree program, adult/continuing education programs, advanced placement credit, cooperative education, double majors, honors programs, internships, study abroad, summer session for credit. *ROTC:* Army (b). *Unusual degree programs:* 3-2 engineering with North Carolina Agricultural and Technical State University.

Computers on Campus 252 computers/terminals and 688 ports are available on campus for general student use. Students can access the following: campus intranet, free student e-mail accounts, online (class) grades, online (class) registration, online (class) schedules. Campuswide network is available. 100% of college-owned or -operated housing units are wired for high-speed Internet access. Wireless service is available via entire campus.

Student Life *Housing options:* men-only, women-only. Campus housing is university owned. Freshman applicants given priority for college housing. *Activities and organizations:* drama/theater group, student-run newspaper, radio station, choral group, Student Government Association, New Emphasis on Nontraditional Students (NEONS), Block M Club, Pre Alumni Council, Baptist Student Union, national fraternities, national sororities. *Campus security:* 24-hour patrols, controlled dormitory access, cameras in select locations. *Student services:* health clinic, personal/psychological counseling.

Athletics Member NAIA. *Intercollegiate sports:* baseball M(s), basketball M(s)/W(s), cheerleading M(s)/W(s), cross-country running M(s)/W(s), softball W(s), track and field M(s)/W(s), volleyball W(s). *Intramural sports:* basketball M/W, table tennis M/W.

Costs (2011–12) *Comprehensive fee:* $15,226 includes full-time tuition ($10,215), mandatory fees ($315), and room and board ($4696). Part-time tuition: $426 per credit hour. *Required fees:* $79 per term part-time. *College room only:* $2000. *Payment plan:* installment.

Financial Aid Of all full-time matriculated undergraduates who enrolled in 2010, 887 applied for aid, 859 were judged to have need, 10 had their need fully met. 300 Federal Work-Study jobs (averaging $818). *Average percent of need met:* 85%. *Average financial aid package:* $12,100. *Average need-based loan:* $3900. *Average need-based gift aid:* $7400. *Average indebtedness upon graduation:* $17,125.

Applying *Options:* electronic application, deferred entrance. *Application fee:* $20. *Required:* high school transcript, minimum 2.0 GPA, medical examination. *Required for some:* interview. *Application deadlines:* rolling (freshmen), rolling (out-of-state freshmen), rolling (transfers). *Notification:* continuous (freshmen), continuous (out-of-state freshmen), continuous (transfers).

Freshman Application Contact Ms. Deborah C. Calhoun, Director of Admissions and Records, Morris College, 100 West College Street, Sumter, SC 29150-3599. *Phone:* 803-934-3225. *Toll-free phone:* 866-853-1345. *Fax:* 803-773-8241. *E-mail:* dcalhoun@morris.edu. *Web site:* http://www.morris.edu/.

Newberry College
Newberry, South Carolina

- **Independent Evangelical Lutheran** 4-year, founded 1856
- **Small-town** 90-acre campus with easy access to Columbia, Greenville
- **Endowment** $20.8 million
- **Coed** 1,110 undergraduate students, 97% full-time, 45% women, 55% men
- **Moderately difficult** entrance level, 61% of applicants were admitted

Undergraduates 1,075 full-time, 35 part-time. Students come from 30 states and territories; 9 other countries; 12% are from out of state; 24% Black or African American, non-Hispanic/Latino; 4% Hispanic/Latino; 0.7% Asian, non-Hispanic/Latino; 0.4% American Indian or Alaska Native, non-Hispanic/Latino; 2% Two or more races, non-Hispanic/Latino; 2% Race/ethnicity unknown; 3% international; 5% transferred in; 75% live on campus. *Retention:* 64% of full-time freshmen returned.

Freshmen *Admission:* 1,400 applied, 852 admitted, 282 enrolled. *Average high school GPA:* 3.45. *Test scores:* SAT critical reading scores over 500: 40%; SAT math scores over 500: 56%; ACT scores over 18: 76%; SAT critical reading scores over 600: 7%; SAT math scores over 600: 7%; ACT scores over 24: 23%; ACT scores over 30: 1%.

Faculty *Total:* 99, 64% full-time, 39% with terminal degrees. *Student/faculty ratio:* 14:1.

Academics *Calendar:* semesters. *Degree:* bachelor's. *Special study options:* academic remediation for entering students, accelerated degree program, adult/continuing education programs, advanced placement credit, cooperative education, distance learning, double majors, honors programs, independent study, internships, off-campus study, part-time degree program, services for LD students, student-designed majors, study abroad, summer session for credit. *ROTC:* Army (b). *Unusual degree programs:* 3-2 medical technology with Palmetto Baptist Medical Center.

Computers on Campus 20 computers/terminals are available on campus for general student use. Students can access the following: campus intranet, com-

puter help desk, free student e-mail accounts, online (class) grades, online (class) registration, online (class) schedules. Campuswide network is available. 100% of college-owned or -operated housing units are wired for high-speed Internet access. Wireless service is available via entire campus.

Student Life *Housing:* on-campus residence required through senior year. *Options:* coed, men-only, women-only. Campus housing is university owned. Freshman applicants given priority for college housing. *Activities and organizations:* drama/theater group, student-run newspaper, radio and television station, choral group, marching band, Future Educators Association, Multi Cultural Student Association, American Chemistry Society, Blue key Honor Club, Baptist Collegiate Ministry, national fraternities, national sororities. *Campus security:* 24-hour emergency response devices and patrols, late-night transport/escort service, controlled dormitory access. *Student services:* health clinic, personal/psychological counseling.

Athletics Member NCAA. All Division II. *Intercollegiate sports:* baseball M(s), basketball M(s)/W(s), cheerleading W(s), cross-country running M(s)/W(s), football M(s), golf M(s)/W(s), soccer M(s)/W(s), softball W(s), tennis M(s)/W(s), volleyball W(s), wrestling M(s). *Intramural sports:* basketball M/W, football M, lacrosse W.

Standardized Tests *Required:* SAT or ACT (for admission).

Costs (2012–13) *Comprehensive fee:* $32,259 includes full-time tuition ($22,050), mandatory fees ($1525), and room and board ($8684). Full-time tuition and fees vary according to class time, course load, and student level. Part-time tuition: $525 per credit hour. Part-time tuition and fees vary according to class time, course load, and student level. *Required fees:* $125 per term part-time. *College room only:* $4200. Room and board charges vary according to board plan and housing facility. *Payment plan:* installment. *Waivers:* employees or children of employees.

Financial Aid Of all full-time matriculated undergraduates who enrolled in 2009, 977 applied for aid, 895 were judged to have need, 219 had their need fully met. In 2009, 147 non-need-based awards were made. *Average percent of need met:* 76%. *Average financial aid package:* $20,440. *Average need-based loan:* $4474. *Average need-based gift aid:* $16,969. *Average non-need-based aid:* $11,552. *Average indebtedness upon graduation:* $30,693.

Applying *Options:* electronic application, deferred entrance. *Application fee:* $30. *Required:* essay or personal statement, high school transcript, minimum 2.0 GPA. *Recommended:* 1 letter of recommendation, interview. *Application deadlines:* rolling (freshmen), rolling (transfers). *Notification:* continuous (freshmen), continuous (transfers).

Freshman Application Contact Mrs. Sheila Wendeln, Director of Admissions, Newberry College, 2100 College Street, Holland Hall, Newberry, SC 29108. *Phone:* 803-321-5131. *Toll-free phone:* 800-845-4955. *Fax:* 803-321-5138. *E-mail:* admissions@newberry.edu. *Web site:* http://www.newberry.edu/.

North Greenville University
Tigerville, South Carolina

- **Independent Southern Baptist** comprehensive, founded 1892
- **Rural** 330-acre campus with easy access to Greenville
- **Endowment** $16.9 million
- **Coed** 2,200 undergraduate students, 88% full-time, 52% women, 48% men
- **Minimally difficult** entrance level, 58% of applicants were admitted

Undergraduates 1,935 full-time, 265 part-time. Students come from 35 states and territories; 14 other countries; 22% are from out of state; 7% Black or African American, non-Hispanic/Latino; 1% Hispanic/Latino; 0.4% Asian, non-Hispanic/Latino; 0.1% American Indian or Alaska Native, non-Hispanic/Latino; 15% Race/ethnicity unknown; 0.5% international; 5% transferred in; 70% live on campus. *Retention:* 73% of full-time freshmen returned.

Freshmen *Admission:* 1,592 applied, 923 admitted, 540 enrolled. *Average high school GPA:* 3.6. *Test scores:* SAT critical reading scores over 500: 88%; SAT writing scores over 500: 86%; ACT scores over 18: 92%; SAT critical reading scores over 600: 44%; SAT writing scores over 600: 34%; ACT scores over 24: 43%; SAT critical reading scores over 700: 11%; SAT writing scores over 700: 10%; ACT scores over 30: 16%.

Faculty *Total:* 190, 66% full-time, 51% with terminal degrees. *Student/faculty ratio:* 14:1.

Academics *Calendar:* semesters. *Degrees:* bachelor's, master's, and doctoral. *Special study options:* academic remediation for entering students, accelerated degree program, advanced placement credit, cooperative education, distance learning, double majors, English as a second language, freshman honors college, honors programs, independent study, internships, part-time degree program, services for LD students, student-designed majors, study abroad, summer session for credit. *ROTC:* Army (c).

Computers on Campus 95 computers/terminals and 6 ports are available on campus for general student use. Students can access the following: campus intranet, computer help desk, free student e-mail accounts, online (class)

grades, online (class) registration, online (class) schedules. Campuswide network is available. 100% of college-owned or -operated housing units are wired for high-speed Internet access. Wireless service is available via libraries, student centers.

Student Life *Housing:* on-campus residence required through sophomore year. *Options:* men-only, women-only. Campus housing is university owned. Freshman campus housing is guaranteed. *Activities and organizations:* drama/theater group, student-run newspaper, radio station, choral group, marching band, Baptist Student Union, Fellowship of Christians in Service, Fellowship of Christian Athletes, Black Student Fellowship, Education Club. *Campus security:* 24-hour emergency response devices and patrols, late-night transport/escort service, controlled dormitory access. *Student services:* health clinic, personal/psychological counseling.

Athletics Member NCAA, NCCAA. All NCAA Division II. *Intercollegiate sports:* baseball M(s), basketball M(s)/W(s), cheerleading M(s)/W(s), cross-country running M(s)/W(s), football M(s), golf M(s)/W(s), soccer M(s)/W(s), softball W(s), tennis M(s)/W(s), track and field M(s)/W(s), volleyball W(s). *Intramural sports:* basketball M/W, bowling M/W, football M, golf M/W, softball M/W, table tennis M/W, tennis M/W, ultimate Frisbee M/W, volleyball W, weight lifting M/W.

Standardized Tests *Required:* SAT or ACT (for admission). *Required for some:* CPT. *Recommended:* CPT.

Costs (2012–13) *Comprehensive fee:* $22,100 includes full-time tuition ($13,936) and room and board ($8164). Full-time tuition and fees vary according to course load. Part-time tuition: $240 per unit. *Room and board:* Room and board charges vary according to housing facility. *Payment plan:* installment. *Waivers:* employees or children of employees.

Financial Aid Of all full-time matriculated undergraduates who enrolled in 2009, 1,800 applied for aid, 1,782 were judged to have need, 1,603 had their need fully met. *Average percent of need met:* 96%. *Average indebtedness upon graduation:* $18,200.

Applying *Options:* electronic application, early admission, deferred entrance. *Application fee:* $25. *Required:* high school transcript. *Required for some:* interview. *Recommended:* minimum 2.0 GPA. *Application deadlines:* 8/18 (freshmen), 8/21 (transfers). *Notification:* continuous (freshmen), continuous (transfers).

Freshman Application Contact North Greenville University, PO Box 1892, Tigerville, SC 29688-1892. *Phone:* 864-977-7052. *Toll-free phone:* 800-468-6642 Ext. 7001. *Web site:* http://www.ngu.edu/.

Presbyterian College

Clinton, South Carolina

- **Independent** comprehensive, founded 1880, affiliated with Presbyterian Church (U.S.A.)
- **Small-town** 240-acre campus with easy access to Greenville, Spartanburg
- **Endowment** $71.7 million
- **Coed** 1,202 undergraduate students, 97% full-time, 53% women, 47% men
- **Very difficult** entrance level, 67% of applicants were admitted

Undergraduates 1,165 full-time, 37 part-time. Students come from 34 states and territories; 15 other countries; 33% are from out of state; 10% Black or African American, non-Hispanic/Latino; 2% Hispanic/Latino; 1% Asian, non-Hispanic/Latino; 0.1% Native Hawaiian or other Pacific Islander, non-Hispanic/Latino; 0.5% American Indian or Alaska Native, non-Hispanic/Latino; 2% Two or more races, non-Hispanic/Latino; 0.1% Race/ethnicity unknown; 3% international; 1% transferred in; 97% live on campus. *Retention:* 76% of full-time freshmen returned.

Freshmen *Admission:* 1,484 applied, 1,000 admitted, 359 enrolled. *Average high school GPA:* 3.47. *Test scores:* SAT critical reading scores over 500: 76%; SAT math scores over 500: 83%; ACT scores over 18: 98%; SAT critical reading scores over 600: 28%; SAT math scores over 600: 36%; ACT scores over 24: 59%; SAT critical reading scores over 700: 4%; SAT math scores over 700: 6%; ACT scores over 30: 9%.

Faculty *Total:* 136, 72% full-time, 80% with terminal degrees. *Student/faculty ratio:* 13:1.

Academics *Calendar:* semesters. *Degrees:* bachelor's and doctoral. *Special study options:* advanced placement credit, double majors, honors programs, independent study, internships, off-campus study, services for LD students, study abroad, summer session for credit. *ROTC:* Army (b). *Unusual degree programs:* 3-2 engineering with Auburn University, Clemson University, Vanderbilt University, University of South Carolina.

Computers on Campus 100 computers/terminals and 275 ports are available on campus for general student use. Students can access the following: campus intranet, free student e-mail accounts, online (class) grades, online (class) registration, online (class) schedules. Campuswide network is available. 100% of

college-owned or -operated housing units are wired for high-speed Internet access. Wireless service is available via entire campus.

Student Life *Housing:* on-campus residence required through senior year. *Options:* coed, men-only, women-only, disabled students. Campus housing is university owned. Freshman campus housing is guaranteed. *Activities and organizations:* drama/theater group, student-run newspaper, radio station, choral group, Student Volunteer Services, Intramural sports, Student Union Board, Fellowship of Christian Athletes, Student Government Association, national fraternities, national sororities. *Campus security:* 24-hour emergency response devices and patrols, late-night transport/escort service, controlled dormitory access. *Student services:* health clinic, personal/psychological counseling.

Athletics Member NCAA. All Division I. *Intercollegiate sports:* baseball M(s), basketball M(s)/W(s), cheerleading M(s)/W(s), cross-country running M(s)/W(s), football M(s), golf M(s)/W(s), lacrosse W(s), soccer M(s)/W(s), softball W(s), tennis M(s)/W(s), volleyball W(s). *Intramural sports:* basketball M/W, football M/W, golf M/W, rock climbing M/W, skiing (cross-country) M/W, soccer M/W, softball M/W, table tennis M/W, tennis M/W, ultimate Frisbee M/W, volleyball M/W.

Standardized Tests *Required:* SAT or ACT (for admission).

Costs (2011–12) *Comprehensive fee:* $39,800 includes full-time tuition ($28,530), mandatory fees ($2600), and room and board ($8670). Full-time tuition and fees vary according to reciprocity agreements. Part-time tuition: $1200 per credit hour. Part-time tuition and fees vary according to course load and program. *Required fees:* $25 per credit hour part-time, $23 per term part-time. *Room and board:* Room and board charges vary according to board plan and housing facility. *Payment plan:* installment. *Waivers:* senior citizens and employees or children of employees.

Financial Aid Of all full-time matriculated undergraduates who enrolled in 2011, 954 applied for aid, 846 were judged to have need, 365 had their need fully met. In 2011, 222 non-need-based awards were made. *Average percent of need met:* 89%. *Average financial aid package:* $31,984. *Average need-based loan:* $3838. *Average need-based gift aid:* $28,146. *Average non-need-based aid:* $15,969. *Average indebtedness upon graduation:* $23,192. *Financial aid deadline:* 6/30.

Applying *Options:* electronic application, early admission, early decision, early action, deferred entrance. *Application fee:* $40. *Required:* essay or personal statement, high school transcript, 1 letter of recommendation. *Recommended:* interview. *Application deadlines:* 6/30 (freshmen), 6/30 (out-of-state freshmen), 7/1 (transfers), 11/15 (early action). *Early decision deadline:* 11/1. *Notification:* 3/15 (freshmen), 3/15 (out-of-state freshmen), 7/15 (transfers), 12/1 (early decision), 12/15 (early action).

Freshman Application Contact Mr. Brian J. Fortman, Dean of Admissions, Presbyterian College, 503 South Broad Street, Clinton, SC 29325. *Phone:* 864-833-8258. *Toll-free phone:* 800-960-7583 (in-state); 800-930-7583 (out-of-state). *Fax:* 864-833-8481. *E-mail:* bjfortman@presby.edu. *Web site:* http://www.presby.edu/.

South Carolina State University

Orangeburg, South Carolina

- **State-supported** comprehensive, founded 1896, part of South Carolina Commission on Higher Education
- **Small-town** 160-acre campus
- **Endowment** $766,537
- **Coed** 3,744 undergraduate students, 93% full-time, 54% women, 46% men
- **Minimally difficult** entrance level, 96% of applicants were admitted

Undergraduates 3,480 full-time, 264 part-time. Students come from 34 states and territories; 19 other countries; 16% are from out of state; 96% Black or African American, non-Hispanic/Latino; 0.6% Hispanic/Latino; 0.4% Asian, non-Hispanic/Latino; 0.1% American Indian or Alaska Native, non-Hispanic/Latino; 0.7% Race/ethnicity unknown; 6% transferred in; 60% live on campus. *Retention:* 65% of full-time freshmen returned.

Freshmen *Admission:* 3,267 applied, 3,130 admitted, 829 enrolled. *Average high school GPA:* 2.94. *Test scores:* SAT critical reading scores over 500: 18%; SAT math scores over 500: 19%; ACT scores over 18: 37%; SAT critical reading scores over 600: 3%; SAT math scores over 600: 7%; ACT scores over 24: 6%; SAT critical reading scores over 700: 1%; SAT math scores over 700: 2%.

Faculty *Total:* 279, 77% full-time, 65% with terminal degrees. *Student/faculty ratio:* 17:1.

Academics *Calendar:* semesters. *Degrees:* bachelor's, master's, doctoral, post-master's, postbachelor's, and first professional certificates. *Special study options:* adult/continuing education programs, advanced placement credit, cooperative education, distance learning, honors programs, independent study, internships, off-campus study, part-time degree program, study abroad, summer session for credit. *ROTC:* Army (b), Air Force (c).

Computers on Campus 600 computers/terminals are available on campus for general student use. Students can access the following: computer help desk, free student e-mail accounts, online (class) grades, online (class) registration, online (class) schedules. Campuswide network is available.

Student Life *Housing options:* coed, men-only, women-only, disabled students. Campus housing is university owned, leased by the school and is provided by a third party. Freshman applicants given priority for college housing. *Activities and organizations:* drama/theater group, student-run newspaper, choral group, marching band, student government, Campus Activity Board, NAACP, United Voices of Christ, student media, national fraternities, national sororities. *Campus security:* 24-hour emergency response devices and patrols, late-night transport/escort service, controlled dormitory access. *Student services:* health clinic, personal/psychological counseling.

Athletics Member NCAA. All Division I except football (Division I-AA). *Intercollegiate sports:* basketball M(s)/W(s), bowling W(s), cross-country running M(s)/W(s), golf M(s)/W(s), soccer W(s), softball W(s), tennis M(s)/W(s), track and field M(s)/W(s), volleyball W(s). *Intramural sports:* basketball M/W, softball M/W.

Standardized Tests *Required:* SAT or ACT (for admission). *Recommended:* SAT Subject Tests (for admission).

Costs (2011–12) *Tuition:* state resident $9258 full-time, $386 per credit hour part-time; nonresident $18,170 full-time, $757 per credit hour part-time. *Required fees:* $285 per term part-time. *Room and board:* $9286; room only: $6300. Room and board charges vary according to housing facility. *Payment plans:* installment, deferred payment. *Waivers:* senior citizens and employees or children of employees.

Financial Aid Of all full-time matriculated undergraduates who enrolled in 2007, 343 Federal Work-Study jobs (averaging $1048). 360 state and other part-time jobs (averaging $2050). *Average indebtedness upon graduation:* $26,678.

Applying *Options:* electronic application, deferred entrance. *Application fee:* $25. *Required:* high school transcript, minimum 2.0 GPA. *Application deadlines:* 7/31 (freshmen), 7/31 (transfers). *Notification:* continuous (freshmen), continuous (transfers).

Freshman Application Contact Mr. Antonio Boyle, Assistant Vice President of Enrollment Management, South Carolina State University, 300 College Street Northeast, Orangeburg, SC 29117-0001. *Phone:* 803-536-7186. *Toll-free phone:* 800-260-5956. *Fax:* 803-536-8990. *E-mail:* admissions@scsu.edu. *Web site:* http://www.scsu.edu/.

Southern Methodist College
Orangeburg, South Carolina

Freshman Application Contact Ms. Juanta Webb, Recruitment Officer, Southern Methodist College, PO Box 1027, Orangeburg, SC 29116-7827. *Phone:* 803-268-1322. *Fax:* 803-534-7827. *E-mail:* jwebb@smcollege.edu. *Web site:* http://www.smcollege.edu/.

Southern Wesleyan University
Central, South Carolina

- **Independent** comprehensive, founded 1906, affiliated with Wesleyan Church
- **Small-town** 350-acre campus
- **Endowment** $3.5 million
- **Coed**
- **Minimally difficult** entrance level

Faculty *Student/faculty ratio:* 18:1.

Academics *Calendar:* semesters. *Degrees:* associate, bachelor's, and master's.

Student Life *Campus security:* 24-hour emergency response devices, late night security patrols until 2:00 am, restricted access to campus after midnight.

Athletics Member NAIA, NCCAA.

Standardized Tests *Required:* SAT or ACT (for admission).

Costs (2011–12) *Comprehensive fee:* $28,100 includes full-time tuition ($19,950), mandatory fees ($600), and room and board ($7550). Full-time tuition and fees vary according to program. Part-time tuition: $825 per credit. Part-time tuition and fees vary according to program. *College room only:* $2750. Room and board charges vary according to board plan and housing facility.

Financial Aid *Of all full-time matriculated undergraduates who enrolled in 2006,* 437 applied for aid, 387 were judged to have need, 128 had their need fully met. 158 Federal Work-Study jobs (averaging $1150). 73 state and other part-time jobs (averaging $1150). *In 2006,* 90 non-need-based awards were made. *Average percent of need met:* 78. *Average financial aid package:*

$14,094. *Average need-based loan:* $4844. *Average need-based gift aid:* $9962. *Average non-need-based aid:* $9196. *Average indebtedness upon graduation:* $25,971.

Applying *Options:* electronic application, deferred entrance. *Application fee:* $25. *Required:* high school transcript, minimum 2.3 GPA. *Required for some:* interview.

Freshman Application Contact Mrs. Beth Roe, Director of First Year Experience, Southern Wesleyan University, PO Box 1020, 907 Wesleyan Drive, Central, SC 29630-1020. *Phone:* 864-644-5149. *Toll-free phone:* 800-CU-AT-SWU. *Fax:* 864-644-5901. *E-mail:* broe@swu.edu. *Web site:* http://www.swu.edu/.

South University
Columbia, South Carolina

- **Proprietary** comprehensive, founded 1935, part of Education Management Corporation
- **Coed**

Academics *Calendar:* quarters. *Degrees:* associate, bachelor's, and master's.

Costs (2011–12) *Tuition:* Information about tuition and fees can be obtained by contacting the South University Admissions Office.

Freshman Application Contact South University, 9 Science Court, Columbia, SC 29203. *Phone:* 803-799-9082. *Toll-free phone:* 866-629-3031. *Web site:* http://www.southuniversity.edu/columbia/.

See page 1608 for the College Close-Up.

Strayer University - Charleston Campus
North Charleston, South Carolina

- **Proprietary** comprehensive
- **Coed**

Academics *Degrees:* certificates, associate, bachelor's, master's, and post-bachelor's certificates.

Freshman Application Contact Strayer University - Charleston Campus, 5010 Wetland Crossing, North Charleston, SC 29418. *Web site:* http://www.strayer.edu/charleston/.

Strayer University - Columbia Campus
Columbia, South Carolina

- **Proprietary** comprehensive
- **Coed**

Academics *Degrees:* certificates, associate, bachelor's, master's, and post-bachelor's certificates.

Freshman Application Contact Strayer University - Columbia Campus, 200 Center Point Circle, Suite 300, Columbia, SC 29210. *Web site:* http://www.strayer.edu/columbia.

Strayer University - Greenville Campus
Greenville, South Carolina

- **Proprietary** comprehensive
- **Coed**

Academics *Degrees:* certificates, associate, bachelor's, master's, and post-bachelor's certificates.

Freshman Application Contact Strayer University - Greenville Campus, 555 North Pleasantburg Drive, Suite 300, Greenville, SC 29607. *Web site:* http://www.strayer.edu/greenville.

University of Phoenix–Columbia Campus
Columbia, South Carolina

Admissions Office Contact University of Phoenix–Columbia Campus, 1001 Pinnacle Point Drive, Suite 200, Columbia, SC 29223. *Toll-free phone:* 866-766-0766. *Web site:* http://www.phoenix.edu/.

University of South Carolina
Columbia, South Carolina

- **State-supported** university, founded 1801, part of University of South Carolina System
- **Urban** 438-acre campus
- **Endowment** $494.4 million
- **Coed** 22,556 undergraduate students, 92% full-time, 54% women, 46% men
- **Moderately difficult** entrance level, 63% of applicants were admitted

Undergraduates 20,700 full-time, 1,856 part-time. Students come from 53 states and territories; 112 other countries; 32% are from out of state; 11% Black or African American, non-Hispanic/Latino; 4% Hispanic/Latino; 3% Asian, non-Hispanic/Latino; 0.1% Native Hawaiian or other Pacific Islander, non-Hispanic/Latino; 0.3% American Indian or Alaska Native, non-Hispanic/Latino; 3% Two or more races, non-Hispanic/Latino; 0.4% Race/ethnicity unknown; 2% international; 9% transferred in; 36% live on campus. *Retention:* 87% of full-time freshmen returned.

Freshmen *Admission:* 21,311 applied, 13,451 admitted, 4,636 enrolled. *Average high school GPA:* 3.9. *Test scores:* SAT critical reading scores over 500: 91%; SAT math scores over 500: 96%; ACT scores over 18: 100%; SAT critical reading scores over 600: 46%; SAT math scores over 600: 58%; ACT scores over 24: 81%; SAT critical reading scores over 700: 8%; SAT math scores over 700: 11%; ACT scores over 30: 20%.

Faculty *Total:* 1,792, 69% full-time, 70% with terminal degrees. *Student/faculty ratio:* 17:1.

Academics *Calendar:* semesters. *Degrees:* bachelor's, master's, doctoral, post-master's, postbachelor's, and first professional certificates. *Special study options:* accelerated degree program, adult/continuing education programs, advanced placement credit, cooperative education, distance learning, double majors, English as a second language, freshman honors college, honors programs, independent study, internships, part-time degree program, services for LD students, student-designed majors, study abroad, summer session for credit. *ROTC:* Army (b), Navy (b), Air Force (b).

Computers on Campus 2,800 computers/terminals are available on campus for general student use. Students can access the following: computer help desk, free student e-mail accounts, online (class) grades, online (class) registration, online (class) schedules. Campuswide network is available. 100% of college-owned or -operated housing units are wired for high-speed Internet access. Wireless service is available via entire campus.

Student Life *Housing:* on-campus residence required for freshman year. *Options:* coed, men-only, women-only, disabled students. Campus housing is university owned. Freshman campus housing is guaranteed. *Activities and organizations:* drama/theater group, student-run newspaper, radio station, choral group, marching band, Social Work Student Association, Friendship Association of Chinese Students and Scholars, Alpha Lambda Delta, Residence Hall Association, Student Bar Association, national fraternities, national sororities. *Campus security:* 24-hour emergency response devices and patrols, student patrols, late-night transport/escort service, controlled dormitory access. *Student services:* health clinic, personal/psychological counseling.

Athletics Member NCAA. All Division I except football (Division I-A). *Intercollegiate sports:* baseball M(s), basketball M(s)/W(s), cross-country running W(s), equestrian sports W(s), golf M(s)/W(s), soccer M(s)/W(s), softball W(s), swimming and diving M(s)/W(s), tennis M(s)/W(s), track and field M(s)/W(s), volleyball W(s). *Intramural sports:* badminton M(c)/W(c), baseball M(c), basketball M/W, bowling M/W, equestrian sports M(c)/W(c), fencing M(c)/W(c), field hockey W(c), football M/W, golf M/W, ice hockey M(c), lacrosse M(c)/W(c), racquetball M/W, rock climbing M(c)/W(c), rugby M(c)/W(c), sailing M(c)/W(c), soccer M/W, softball M/W, swimming and diving M/W, table tennis M/W, tennis M/W, ultimate Frisbee M/W, volleyball M/W, water polo M(c)/W(c), weight lifting M/W, wrestling M(c).

Standardized Tests *Required:* SAT or ACT (for admission).

Costs (2011–12) *Tuition:* state resident $9768 full-time, $407 per credit hour part-time; nonresident $25,952 full-time, $1082 per credit hour part-time. Full-time tuition and fees vary according to program and reciprocity agreements. *Required fees:* $400 full-time. *Room and board:* $8026; room only: $5308. Room and board charges vary according to board plan, housing facility, and location. *Payment plan:* deferred payment. *Waivers:* senior citizens and employees or children of employees.

Financial Aid Of all full-time matriculated undergraduates who enrolled in 2011, 13,161 applied for aid, 9,832 were judged to have need, 2,821 had their need fully met. 702 Federal Work-Study jobs (averaging $1954). 2,772 state and other part-time jobs (averaging $1746). In 2011, 6473 non-need-based awards were made. *Average percent of need met:* 76%. *Average financial aid package:* $13,041. *Average need-based loan:* $3389. *Average need-based gift aid:* $5277. *Average non-need-based aid:* $6257. *Average indebtedness upon graduation:* $24,837.

Applying *Options:* electronic application, early action. *Application fee:* $50. *Required:* high school transcript, minimum 2.0 GPA. *Application deadlines:* 12/1 (freshmen), 6/1 (transfers), 10/15 (early action). *Notification:* continuous (transfers), 12/20 (early action).

Freshman Application Contact Dr. Mary Wagner, Senior Associate Director, Undergraduate Admissions, University of South Carolina, Columbia, SC 29208. *Phone:* 803-777-7700. *Toll-free phone:* 800-868-5872. *Fax:* 803-777-0101. *E-mail:* admissions-ugrad@sc.edu. *Web site:* http://www.sc.edu/.

University of South Carolina Aiken
Aiken, South Carolina

- **State-supported** comprehensive, founded 1961, part of University of South Carolina System
- **Suburban** 453-acre campus with easy access to Columbia
- **Endowment** $19.0 million
- **Coed** 3,194 undergraduate students, 78% full-time, 65% women, 35% men
- **Moderately difficult** entrance level, 36% of applicants were admitted

Undergraduates 2,487 full-time, 707 part-time. Students come from 31 states and territories; 19 other countries; 10% are from out of state; 29% Black or African American, non-Hispanic/Latino; 3% Hispanic/Latino; 0.8% Asian, non-Hispanic/Latino; 0.1% Native Hawaiian or other Pacific Islander, non-Hispanic/Latino; 0.5% American Indian or Alaska Native, non-Hispanic/Latino; 3% Two or more races, non-Hispanic/Latino; 0.8% Race/ethnicity unknown; 1% international; 8% transferred in; 29% live on campus. *Retention:* 70% of full-time freshmen returned.

Freshmen *Admission:* 2,747 applied, 1,000 admitted, 607 enrolled. *Average high school GPA:* 3.57. *Test scores:* SAT critical reading scores over 500: 43%; SAT math scores over 500: 47%; SAT writing scores over 500: 39%; ACT scores over 18: 81%; SAT critical reading scores over 600: 9%; SAT math scores over 600: 11%; SAT writing scores over 600: 8%; ACT scores over 24: 18%; SAT critical reading scores over 700: 1%; SAT math scores over 700: 1%; ACT scores over 30: 1%.

Faculty *Total:* 241, 60% full-time, 54% with terminal degrees. *Student/faculty ratio:* 16:1.

Academics *Calendar:* semesters. *Degrees:* bachelor's and master's. *Special study options:* adult/continuing education programs, advanced placement credit, cooperative education, distance learning, double majors, English as a second language, honors programs, independent study, internships, off-campus study, part-time degree program, services for LD students, student-designed majors, study abroad, summer session for credit.

Computers on Campus 550 computers/terminals and 796 ports are available on campus for general student use. Students can access the following: computer help desk, free student e-mail accounts, online (class) grades, online (class) registration, online (class) schedules. Campuswide network is available. 100% of college-owned or -operated housing units are wired for high-speed Internet access. Wireless service is available via entire campus.

Student Life *Housing options:* coed, disabled students. Campus housing is university owned. Freshman applicants given priority for college housing. *Activities and organizations:* drama/theater group, student-run newspaper, choral group, student government, Pacesetters, Student Alumni Ambassadors, African-American Student Alliance, Pacer Union Board, national fraternities, national sororities. *Campus security:* 24-hour emergency response devices and patrols, late-night transport/escort service, controlled dormitory access. *Student services:* health clinic, personal/psychological counseling.

Athletics Member NCAA. All Division II. *Intercollegiate sports:* baseball M(s), basketball M(s)/W(s), cross-country running W(s), golf M(s), soccer M(s)/W(s), softball W(s), tennis M(s)/W(s), volleyball W(s). *Intramural sports:* basketball M/W, cheerleading M(c)/W(c), equestrian sports M(c)/W(c), soccer M/W, ultimate Frisbee M/W, volleyball M/W.

Standardized Tests *Required:* SAT or ACT (for admission).

Costs (2011–12) *Tuition:* state resident $8460 full-time, $367 per credit hour part-time; nonresident $16,948 full-time, $734 per credit hour part-time. Full-time tuition and fees vary according to reciprocity agreements. Part-time tuition and fees vary according to course load and reciprocity agreements. *Required fees:* $290 full-time, $9 per credit hour part-time, $25 per term part-time. *Room and board:* $6630. Room and board charges vary according to board plan and housing facility. *Payment plan:* deferred payment. *Waivers:* senior citizens and employees or children of employees.

Financial Aid Of all full-time matriculated undergraduates who enrolled in 2010, 2,396 applied for aid, 1,733 were judged to have need, 505 had their need fully met. 147 Federal Work-Study jobs (averaging $2218). 468 state and other part-time jobs (averaging $1760). In 2010, 453 non-need-based awards were made. *Average percent of need met:* 79%. *Average financial aid package:* $11,643. *Average need-based loan:* $2435. *Average need-based gift aid:* $7791. *Average non-need-based aid:* $6378. *Average indebtedness upon graduation:* $18,995.

Applying *Options:* electronic application, early admission, deferred entrance. *Application fee:* $45. *Required:* high school transcript. *Application deadlines:* 8/1 (freshmen), 8/1 (out-of-state freshmen), 8/1 (transfers). *Notification:* continuous (freshmen), continuous (out-of-state freshmen), continuous (transfers).

Freshman Application Contact Mr. Andrew Hendrix, Director of Admissions, University of South Carolina Aiken, 471 University Parkway, Aiken, SC 29801-6309. *Phone:* 803-641-3366. *Toll-free phone:* 888-WOW-USCA. *Fax:* 803-641-3727. *E-mail:* admit@usca.edu. *Web site:* http://www.usca.edu/.

University of South Carolina Beaufort

Bluffton, South Carolina

- **State-supported** 4-year, founded 1959, part of University of South Carolina System
- **Suburban** 200-acre campus
- **Coed** 1,874 undergraduate students, 76% full-time, 62% women, 38% men
- **Minimally difficult** entrance level, 75% of applicants were admitted

Undergraduates 1,418 full-time, 456 part-time. Students come from 38 states and territories; 14 other countries; 22% are from out of state; 19% Black or African American, non-Hispanic/Latino; 6% Hispanic/Latino; 1% Asian, non-Hispanic/Latino; 0.2% Native Hawaiian or other Pacific Islander, non-Hispanic/Latino; 0.4% American Indian or Alaska Native, non-Hispanic/Latino; 3% Two or more races, non-Hispanic/Latino; 1% Race/ethnicity unknown; 0.5% international; 20% live on campus. *Retention:* 54% of full-time freshmen returned.

Freshmen *Admission:* 1,434 applied, 1,070 admitted.

Faculty *Total:* 141, 42% full-time. *Student/faculty ratio:* 18:1.

Academics *Calendar:* semesters. *Degree:* bachelor's. *Special study options:* adult/continuing education programs, advanced placement credit, distance learning, double majors, independent study, internships, part-time degree program, services for LD students, study abroad, summer session for credit.

Computers on Campus Students can access the following: free student e-mail accounts, online (class) grades, online (class) registration, online (class) schedules, Wireless computing. Campuswide network is available. 100% of college-owned or -operated housing units are wired for high-speed Internet access. Wireless service is available via entire campus.

Student Life *Housing:* on-campus residence required for freshman year. *Options:* Campus housing is university owned and leased by the school. *Activities and organizations:* drama/theater group, student-run newspaper, Student Government Association, Gamma Beta Phi, Black Student Organization, Business Club, Environmental Awareness Club. *Campus security:* 24-hour emergency response devices, evening security service. *Student services:* personal/psychological counseling.

Athletics Member NAIA. *Intercollegiate sports:* baseball M(s), cross-country running M(s)/W(s), golf M(s)/W(s), soccer W(s), softball W, track and field M(s)/W(s).

Standardized Tests *Required:* SAT or ACT (for admission).

Costs (2011–12) *Tuition:* state resident $7722 full-time, $323 per credit hour part-time; nonresident $16,834 full-time, $703 per credit hour part-time. Full-time tuition and fees vary according to course load and reciprocity agreements. Part-time tuition and fees vary according to course load and reciprocity agreements. *Required fees:* $436 full-time, $14 per credit hour part-time, $25 per term part-time. *Room and board:* $6530; room only: $4750. Room and board charges vary according to board plan and housing facility. *Payment plan:* deferred payment. *Waivers:* senior citizens and employees or children of employees.

Financial Aid Of all full-time matriculated undergraduates who enrolled in 2008, 30 Federal Work-Study jobs (averaging $2800).

Applying *Options:* electronic application, deferred entrance. *Application fee:* $40. *Required:* high school transcript, Specific college prep classes required from high school. *Recommended:* minimum 2.0 GPA. *Application deadlines:* rolling (freshmen), rolling (transfers). *Notification:* continuous (freshmen).

Freshman Application Contact Ms. Monica Williams, University of South Carolina Beaufort, 1 University Boulevard, Bluffton, SC 29909. *Phone:* 843-208-8112. *Fax:* 843-208-8015. *E-mail:* mrwilli5@uscb.edu. *Web site:* http://www.uscb.edu/.

University of South Carolina Upstate

Spartanburg, South Carolina

- **State-supported** comprehensive, founded 1967, part of University of South Carolina System
- **Urban** 300-acre campus with easy access to Charlotte
- **Endowment** $3.3 million
- **Coed** 5,418 undergraduate students, 77% full-time, 64% women, 36% men
- **Moderately difficult** entrance level, 59% of applicants were admitted

Undergraduates 4,174 full-time, 1,244 part-time. Students come from 35 states and territories; 36 other countries; 4% are from out of state; 26% Black or African American, non-Hispanic/Latino; 4% Hispanic/Latino; 2% Asian, non-Hispanic/Latino; 0.1% Native Hawaiian or other Pacific Islander, non-Hispanic/Latino; 0.2% American Indian or Alaska Native, non-Hispanic/Latino; 2% Two or more races, non-Hispanic/Latino; 2% Race/ethnicity unknown; 2% international; 1% transferred in; 18% live on campus. *Retention:* 67% of full-time freshmen returned.

Freshmen *Admission:* 3,096 applied, 1,816 admitted, 809 enrolled. *Average high school GPA:* 3.63. *Test scores:* SAT critical reading scores over 500: 35%; SAT math scores over 500: 46%; SAT writing scores over 500: 29%; ACT scores over 18: 85%; SAT critical reading scores over 600: 6%; SAT math scores over 600: 9%; SAT writing scores over 600: 5%; ACT scores over 24: 15%; SAT critical reading scores over 700: 1%; SAT math scores over 700: 1%; ACT scores over 30: 1%.

Faculty *Total:* 406, 51% full-time, 65% with terminal degrees. *Student/faculty ratio:* 17:1.

Academics *Calendar:* semesters. *Degrees:* bachelor's, master's, and post-bachelor's certificates. *Special study options:* academic remediation for entering students, accelerated degree program, adult/continuing education programs, advanced placement credit, cooperative education, distance learning, double majors, English as a second language, honors programs, independent study, internships, off-campus study, part-time degree program, services for LD students, student-designed majors, study abroad, summer session for credit. *ROTC:* Army (c).

Computers on Campus 430 computers/terminals are available on campus for general student use. Students can access the following: computer help desk, free student e-mail accounts, online (class) grades, online (class) registration. Campuswide network is available. Wireless service is available via classrooms, computer centers, computer labs, dorm rooms, libraries, student centers.

Student Life *Housing options:* coed, disabled students. Campus housing is university owned. Freshman applicants given priority for college housing. *Activities and organizations:* drama/theater group, student-run newspaper, choral group, African-American Association, Campus Activity Board, Student Nurses Association, Student Government Association, Impact, national fraternities, national sororities. *Campus security:* 24-hour emergency response devices and patrols, late-night transport/escort service, campus security cameras. *Student services:* health clinic, personal/psychological counseling, women's center.

Athletics Member NCAA. All Division I. *Intercollegiate sports:* baseball M(s), basketball M(s)/W(s), cheerleading M(s)/W(s), cross-country running M(s)/W(s), golf M(s)/W(s), soccer M(s)/W(s), softball W(s), tennis M(s)/W(s), track and field M(s)/W(s), volleyball W(s). *Intramural sports:* badminton M/W, baseball M, basketball M/W, bowling M/W, football M/W, golf M/W, racquetball M/W, soccer M/W, softball M/W, table tennis M/W, tennis M/W, track and field M/W, volleyball M/W.

Standardized Tests *Required:* SAT or ACT (for admission).

Costs (2011–12) *Tuition:* state resident $9146 full-time, $390 per semester hour part-time; nonresident $18,572 full-time, $789 per semester hour part-time. Full-time tuition and fees vary according to course load and program. Part-time tuition and fees vary according to course load and program. *Required fees:* $450 full-time. *Room and board:* $7122; room only: $4400. Room and board charges vary according to board plan and housing facility. *Payment plan:* deferred payment. *Waivers:* senior citizens.

Financial Aid Of all full-time matriculated undergraduates who enrolled in 2008, 3,328 applied for aid, 2,782 were judged to have need, 408 had their need fully met. 97 Federal Work-Study jobs (averaging $1730). 439 state and other part-time jobs (averaging $1244). In 2008, 94 non-need-based awards were made. *Average percent of need met:* 53%. *Average financial aid package:* $8944. *Average need-based loan:* $4011. *Average need-based gift aid:* $4214. *Average non-need-based aid:* $2048. *Average indebtedness upon graduation:* $18,762.

Applying *Options:* electronic application, deferred entrance. *Application fee:* $40. *Required:* high school transcript, minimum 2.0 GPA, college preparatory courses. *Notification:* continuous (freshmen), continuous (transfers).

Freshman Application Contact Ms. Donette Stewart, Assistant Vice Chancellor for Enrollment Services, University of South Carolina Upstate, 800 University Way, Spartanburg, SC 29303. *Phone:* 864-503-5280. *Toll-free phone:* 800-277-

8727. *Fax:* 864-503-5727. *E-mail:* dstewart@uscupstate.edu. *Web site:* http://www.uscupstate.edu/.

Voorhees College
Denmark, South Carolina

Freshman Application Contact Dr. Willie Jefferson, Dean of Enrollment Management, Voorhees College, PO Box 678, Denmark, SC 29042. *Phone:* 803-703-1049. *Toll-free phone:* 866-685-9904. *E-mail:* williej@voorhees.edu. *Web site:* http://www.voorhees.edu/.

Winthrop University
Rock Hill, South Carolina

- **State-supported** comprehensive, founded 1886, part of South Carolina Commission on Higher Education
- **Suburban** 445-acre campus with easy access to Charlotte
- **Endowment** $33.9 million
- **Coed** 4,859 undergraduate students, 88% full-time, 67% women, 33% men
- **Moderately difficult** entrance level, 68% of applicants were admitted

Undergraduates 4,258 full-time, 601 part-time. Students come from 41 states and territories; 40 other countries; 9% are from out of state; 28% Black or African American, non-Hispanic/Latino; 1% Hispanic/Latino; 1% Asian, non-Hispanic/Latino; 1% Native Hawaiian or other Pacific Islander, non-Hispanic/Latino; 0.5% American Indian or Alaska Native, non-Hispanic/Latino; 1% Two or more races, non-Hispanic/Latino; 3% international; 7% transferred in; 44% live on campus. *Retention:* 72% of full-time freshmen returned.
Freshmen *Admission:* 4,115 applied, 2,815 admitted, 983 enrolled. *Average high school GPA:* 3.8. *Test scores:* SAT critical reading scores over 500: 65%; SAT math scores over 500: 65%; ACT scores over 18: 97%; SAT critical reading scores over 600: 19%; SAT math scores over 600: 19%; ACT scores over 24: 38%; SAT critical reading scores over 700: 3%; SAT math scores over 700: 2%; ACT scores over 30: 5%.
Faculty *Total:* 508, 56% full-time, 62% with terminal degrees. *Student/faculty ratio:* 14:1.
Academics *Calendar:* semesters. *Degrees:* bachelor's, master's, post-master's, and postbachelor's certificates. *Special study options:* adult/continuing education programs, advanced placement credit, cooperative education, distance learning, double majors, honors programs, independent study, internships, off-campus study, part-time degree program, services for LD students, study abroad, summer session for credit. *ROTC:* Army (c), Air Force (c).
Computers on Campus 620 computers/terminals are available on campus for general student use. Students can access the following: campus intranet, computer help desk, free student e-mail accounts, online (class) grades, online (class) registration, online (class) schedules, vast majority of university services are available online. Campuswide network is available. 100% of college-owned or -operated housing units are wired for high-speed Internet access. Wireless service is available via entire campus.
Student Life *Housing:* on-campus residence required for freshman year. *Options:* coed, men-only, women-only, disabled students. Campus housing is university owned. Freshman campus housing is guaranteed. *Activities and organizations:* drama/theater group, student-run newspaper, radio station, choral group, Association of Ebonites, WU Crew, Greek Life, DiGiorgio Student Union, Campus Ministries, national fraternities, national sororities. *Campus security:* 24-hour emergency response devices and patrols, late-night transport/escort service, controlled dormitory access. *Student services:* health clinic, personal/psychological counseling.
Athletics Member NCAA. All Division I. *Intercollegiate sports:* baseball M(s), basketball M(s)/W(s), cheerleading M(c)/W(c), cross-country running M(s)/W(s), fencing M(c)/W(c), golf M(s)/W(s), lacrosse M(c)/W(c), rugby M(c), soccer M(s)/W(s), softball W(s), tennis M(s)/W(s), track and field M(s)/W(s), volleyball W(s). *Intramural sports:* badminton M/W, basketball M/W, cross-country running M/W, equestrian sports M(c)/W(c), football M/W, golf M/W, racquetball M/W, soccer M/W, softball M/W, swimming and diving M/W, table tennis M/W, tennis M/W, ultimate Frisbee M/W, volleyball M/W, water polo M/W, weight lifting M/W.
Standardized Tests *Required:* SAT or ACT (for admission).
Costs (2011–12) *Tuition:* state resident $12,656 full-time, $528 per credit hour part-time; nonresident $23,796 full-time, $992 per credit hour part-time. Full-time tuition and fees vary according to reciprocity agreements and student level. Part-time tuition and fees vary according to student level. *Room and board:* $7270; room only: $4697. Room and board charges vary according to board plan and housing facility. *Payment plan:* installment. *Waivers:* senior citizens and employees or children of employees.
Financial Aid Of all full-time matriculated undergraduates who enrolled in 2010, 3,576 applied for aid, 3,034 were judged to have need, 295 had their need fully met. In 2010, 415 non-need-based awards were made. *Average per-*

cent of need met: 63%. *Average financial aid package:* $11,287. *Average need-based loan:* $4374. *Average need-based gift aid:* $8181. *Average non-need-based aid:* $7735. *Average indebtedness upon graduation:* $26,066.
Applying *Options:* electronic application, deferred entrance. *Application fee:* $40. *Required:* high school transcript, minimum 3.0 GPA. *Required for some:* essay or personal statement. *Application deadlines:* 5/1 (freshmen), 5/1 (out-of-state freshmen), 5/1 (transfers). *Notification:* continuous (freshmen), continuous (transfers).
Freshman Application Contact Winthrop University, 701 Oakland Avenue, Rock Hill, SC 29733. *Phone:* 803-323-2191. *Toll-free phone:* 800-763-0230. *Web site:* http://www.winthrop.edu/.

Wofford College
Spartanburg, South Carolina

- **Independent** 4-year, founded 1854, affiliated with United Methodist Church
- **Urban** 170-acre campus with easy access to Charlotte
- **Endowment** $161.9 million
- **Coed** 1,536 undergraduate students, 97% full-time, 49% women, 51% men
- **Very difficult** entrance level, 65% of applicants were admitted

Undergraduates 1,497 full-time, 39 part-time. Students come from 35 states and territories; 15 other countries; 41% are from out of state; 8% Black or African American, non-Hispanic/Latino; 2% Hispanic/Latino; 2% Asian, non-Hispanic/Latino; 0.2% American Indian or Alaska Native, non-Hispanic/Latino; 2% Two or more races, non-Hispanic/Latino; 2% Race/ethnicity unknown; 1% international; 1% transferred in; 93% live on campus. *Retention:* 88% of full-time freshmen returned.
Freshmen *Admission:* 2,871 applied, 1,861 admitted, 446 enrolled. *Average high school GPA:* 3.56. *Test scores:* SAT critical reading scores over 500: 92%; SAT math scores over 500: 95%; SAT writing scores over 500: 92%; ACT scores over 18: 99%; SAT critical reading scores over 600: 68%; SAT math scores over 600: 70%; SAT writing scores over 600: 64%; ACT scores over 24: 74%; SAT critical reading scores over 700: 20%; SAT math scores over 700: 22%; SAT writing scores over 700: 17%; ACT scores over 30: 10%.
Faculty *Total:* 155, 81% full-time, 85% with terminal degrees. *Student/faculty ratio:* 11:1.
Academics *Calendar:* 4-1-4. *Degree:* bachelor's. *Special study options:* accelerated degree program, advanced placement credit, double majors, independent study, internships, off-campus study, part-time degree program, student-designed majors, study abroad, summer session for credit. *ROTC:* Army (b). *Unusual degree programs:* 3-2 engineering with Clemson University.
Computers on Campus 156 computers/terminals are available on campus for general student use. Students can access the following: campus intranet, computer help desk, free student e-mail accounts, online (class) grades, online (class) registration, online (class) schedules. Campuswide network is available. 100% of college-owned or -operated housing units are wired for high-speed Internet access. Wireless service is available via classrooms, computer centers, computer labs, libraries, student centers.
Student Life *Housing:* on-campus residence required through senior year. *Options:* coed. Campus housing is university owned. Freshman applicants given priority for college housing. *Activities and organizations:* drama/theater group, student-run newspaper, choral group, Ultimate Frisbee Club, W.A.C. (Wofford Activities Council), Psychology Kingdom, Beta Beta Beta (Biology), Twin Towers (Service), national fraternities, national sororities. *Campus security:* 24-hour emergency response devices and patrols, late-night transport/escort service, controlled dormitory access. *Student services:* health clinic, personal/psychological counseling.
Athletics Member NCAA. All Division I except football (Division I-AA). *Intercollegiate sports:* baseball M(s), basketball M(s)/W(s), cheerleading W, cross-country running M(s)/W(s), golf M(s)/W(s), riflery M/W, soccer M(s)/W(s), tennis M(s)/W(s), track and field M(s)/W(s), volleyball W(s). *Intramural sports:* basketball M/W, bowling M/W, football M/W, lacrosse M(c)/W(c), racquetball M/W, soccer M/W, softball M/W, tennis M/W, ultimate Frisbee M/W, volleyball M/W, weight lifting M/W.
Standardized Tests *Required:* SAT or ACT (for admission).
Costs (2011–12) *Comprehensive fee:* $42,565 includes full-time tuition ($33,190) and room and board ($9375). Part-time tuition: $1315 per credit hour. *Payment plan:* installment. *Waivers:* employees or children of employees.
Financial Aid Of all full-time matriculated undergraduates who enrolled in 2011, 1,093 applied for aid, 916 were judged to have need, 407 had their need fully met. In 2011, 393 non-need-based awards were made. *Average percent of need met:* 84%. *Average financial aid package:* $30,801. *Average need-based loan:* $4236. *Average need-based gift aid:* $27,668. *Average non-need-based aid:* $14,432. *Average indebtedness upon graduation:* $24,355.

Applying *Options:* electronic application, early admission, early decision, deferred entrance. *Application fee:* $35. *Required:* essay or personal statement, high school transcript. *Recommended:* 2 letters of recommendation, interview. *Application deadlines:* 2/1 (freshmen), rolling (transfers). *Early decision deadline:* 11/15. *Notification:* 3/15 (freshmen), continuous (transfers), 12/5 (early decision).

Freshman Application Contact Mr. S. Wells Shepard, Director of Admission, Wofford College, 429 North Church Street, Spartanburg, SC 29303-3663. *Phone:* 864-597-4130. *Fax:* 864-597-4147. *E-mail:* admission@wofford.edu. *Web site:* http://www.wofford.edu/.

SOUTH DAKOTA

Augustana College
Sioux Falls, South Dakota

- **Independent** comprehensive, founded 1860, affiliated with Evangelical Lutheran Church in America
- **Urban** 100-acre campus
- **Endowment** $56.7 million
- **Coed** 1,835 undergraduate students, 95% full-time, 62% women, 38% men
- **Moderately difficult** entrance level, 80% of applicants were admitted

Undergraduates 1,745 full-time, 90 part-time. Students come from 23 states and territories; 34 other countries; 54% are from out of state; 1% Black or African American, non-Hispanic/Latino; 1% Hispanic/Latino; 0.9% Asian, non-Hispanic/Latino; 0.2% American Indian or Alaska Native, non-Hispanic/Latino; 2% Two or more races, non-Hispanic/Latino; 0.7% Race/ethnicity unknown; 4% international; 4% transferred in; 72% live on campus. *Retention:* 83% of full-time freshmen returned.

Freshmen *Admission:* 1,261 applied, 1,005 admitted, 432 enrolled. *Average high school GPA:* 3.66. *Test scores:* ACT scores over 18: 99%; ACT scores over 24: 71%; ACT scores over 30: 13%.

Faculty *Total:* 204, 63% full-time, 56% with terminal degrees. *Student/faculty ratio:* 12:1.

Academics *Calendar:* 4-1-4. *Degrees:* bachelor's and master's. *Special study options:* academic remediation for entering students, advanced placement credit, cooperative education, distance learning, double majors, honors programs, independent study, internships, off-campus study, part-time degree program, services for LD students, student-designed majors, study abroad, summer session for credit. *ROTC:* Army (c), Air Force (c). *Unusual degree programs:* 3-2 engineering with Columbia University, University of Minnesota, Washington University (St. Louis); Medical Laboratory Scientist programs with Sanford Heath in Sioux Falls and St. Luke in Sioux City.

Computers on Campus 286 computers/terminals and 1,400 ports are available on campus for general student use. Students can access the following: campus intranet, computer help desk, free student e-mail accounts, online (class) grades, online (class) registration, online (class) schedules. Campuswide network is available. 100% of college-owned or -operated housing units are wired for high-speed Internet access. Wireless service is available via learning centers, libraries, student centers.

Student Life *Housing:* on-campus residence required through junior year. *Options:* coed, disabled students. Campus housing is university owned. Freshman campus housing is guaranteed. *Activities and organizations:* drama/theater group, student-run newspaper, choral group, Augieholics (student athletics support organization), Intramurals, Union Board of Governors (student union), Augie Green, Campus Ministries. *Campus security:* 24-hour emergency response devices and patrols, late-night transport/escort service, controlled dormitory access. *Student services:* health clinic, personal/psychological counseling.

Athletics Member NCAA. All Division II. *Intercollegiate sports:* baseball M(s), basketball M(s)/W(s), cheerleading W, cross-country running M(s)/W(s), football M(s), golf M(s)/W(s), rugby W(c), soccer M(c)/W(s), softball W(s), tennis M(s)/W(s), track and field M(s)/W(s), volleyball W(s), wrestling M(s). *Intramural sports:* basketball M/W, bowling M/W, cross-country running M/W, football M, golf M/W, racquetball M/W, rock climbing M/W, skiing (cross-country) M/W, soccer M/W, softball M/W, swimming and diving M/W, table tennis M/W, tennis M/W, ultimate Frisbee M/W, volleyball M/W, weight lifting M/W.

Standardized Tests *Required:* SAT or ACT (for admission), minimum ACT score of 20 (for admission).

Costs (2011–12) *Comprehensive fee:* $32,990 includes full-time tuition ($26,250), mandatory fees ($340), and room and board ($6400). Full-time tuition and fees vary according to course load and degree level. Part-time

tuition: $400 per credit hour. Part-time tuition and fees vary according to course load and degree level. *College room only:* $3120. Room and board charges vary according to board plan and housing facility. *Payment plan:* installment. *Waivers:* employees or children of employees.

Financial Aid Of all full-time matriculated undergraduates who enrolled in 2011, 1,381 applied for aid, 1,195 were judged to have need, 250 had their need fully met. 319 Federal Work-Study jobs (averaging $1578). 225 state and other part-time jobs (averaging $1177). In 2011, 532 non-need-based awards were made. *Average percent of need met:* 86%. *Average financial aid package:* $21,551. *Average need-based loan:* $5064. *Average need-based gift aid:* $17,027. *Average non-need-based aid:* $11,923. *Average indebtedness upon graduation:* $35,375.

Applying *Options:* electronic application, deferred entrance. *Required:* essay or personal statement, high school transcript, minimum 2.7 GPA, 1 letter of recommendation. *Recommended:* interview. *Application deadlines:* rolling (freshmen), rolling (out-of-state freshmen), rolling (transfers). *Notification:* continuous until 10/1 (freshmen), continuous until 10/1 (out-of-state freshmen), continuous (transfers).

Freshman Application Contact Nancy Davidson, Vice President for Enrollment, Augustana College, 2001 South Summit Avenue, Sioux Falls, SD 57197. *Phone:* 605-274-5516. *Toll-free phone:* 800-727-2844. *Fax:* 605-274-5518. *E-mail:* admission@augie.edu. *Web site:* http://www.augie.edu/.

Black Hills State University
Spearfish, South Dakota

- **State-supported** comprehensive, founded 1883, part of South Dakota State University System
- **Small-town** 123-acre campus
- **Coed** 4,009 undergraduate students, 65% full-time, 62% women, 38% men
- **Minimally difficult** entrance level, 94% of applicants were admitted

Undergraduates 2,623 full-time, 1,386 part-time. 22% are from out of state; 2% transferred in. *Retention:* 61% of full-time freshmen returned.

Freshmen *Admission:* 1,476 applied, 1,390 admitted, 606 enrolled. *Average high school GPA:* 3.13. *Test scores:* ACT scores over 18: 88%; ACT scores over 24: 24%; ACT scores over 30: 2%.

Academics *Calendar:* semesters. *Degrees:* associate, bachelor's, master's, post-master's, and postbachelor's certificates. *Special study options:* academic remediation for entering students, accelerated degree program, advanced placement credit, cooperative education, distance learning, double majors, honors programs, independent study, internships, off-campus study, part-time degree program, services for LD students, summer session for credit. *ROTC:* Army (b).

Computers on Campus 220 computers/terminals are available on campus for general student use. Students can access the following: campus intranet, computer help desk, free student e-mail accounts, online (class) grades, online (class) registration, online (class) schedules. Campuswide network is available. Wireless service is available via classrooms, computer centers, computer labs, dorm rooms, learning centers, libraries, student centers.

Student Life *Housing:* on-campus residence required through sophomore year. *Options:* coed, men-only, women-only, disabled students. Campus housing is university owned. Freshman applicants given priority for college housing. *Activities and organizations:* drama/theater group, student-run newspaper, radio and television station, choral group, Student Activities Committee, student government, national fraternities, national sororities. *Campus security:* 24-hour patrols, late-night transport/escort service, controlled dormitory access. *Student services:* health clinic, personal/psychological counseling.

Athletics Member NAIA. *Intercollegiate sports:* basketball M(s)/W(s), cross-country running M(s)/W(s), football M(s), golf W, track and field M(s)/W(s), volleyball W(s). *Intramural sports:* archery M/W, badminton M/W, basketball M/W, bowling M/W, football M, golf M/W, racquetball M/W, skiing (cross-country) M/W, skiing (downhill) M/W, soccer M/W, softball M/W, tennis M/W, volleyball M/W, weight lifting M/W.

Standardized Tests *Required:* SAT or ACT (for admission).

Financial Aid Of all full-time matriculated undergraduates who enrolled in 2010, 239 Federal Work-Study jobs (averaging $1714). 414 state and other part-time jobs (averaging $4217). *Average indebtedness upon graduation:* $25,628.

Applying *Options:* electronic application. *Application fee:* $20. *Required:* high school transcript, minimum 2.0 high school GPA in core curriculum. *Application deadlines:* 7/18 (freshmen), 7/18 (transfers).

Freshman Application Contact Black Hills State University, 1200 University Station, USB 9502, Spearfish, SD 57799-9502. *Phone:* 605-642-6343. *Toll-free phone:* 800-255-2478. *Fax:* 605-642-6254. *E-mail:* admissions@bhsu.edu. *Web site:* http://www.bhsu.edu/.

Colorado Technical University Sioux Falls

Sioux Falls, South Dakota

Freshman Application Contact Colorado Technical University Sioux Falls, 3901 West 59th Street, Sioux Falls, SD 57108. *Phone:* 605-361-0200. *Web site:* http://www.ctu-siouxfalls.com/.

Dakota State University

Madison, South Dakota

- **State-supported** comprehensive, founded 1881, part of South Dakota Board of Regents
- **Rural** 56-acre campus with easy access to Sioux Falls
- **Endowment** $6.4 million
- **Coed** 2,836 undergraduate students, 43% full-time, 53% women, 47% men
- **Minimally difficult** entrance level, 92% of applicants were admitted

Undergraduates 1,226 full-time, 1,610 part-time. Students come from 42 states and territories; 9 other countries; 24% are from out of state; 2% Black or African American, non-Hispanic/Latino; 2% Hispanic/Latino; 0.9% Asian, non-Hispanic/Latino; 0.4% Native Hawaiian or other Pacific Islander, non-Hispanic/Latino; 0.8% American Indian or Alaska Native, non-Hispanic/Latino; 2% Two or more races, non-Hispanic/Latino; 1% Race/ethnicity unknown; 2% international; 8% transferred in; 36% live on campus. *Retention:* 67% of full-time freshmen returned.

Freshmen *Admission:* 711 applied, 651 admitted, 319 enrolled. *Average high school GPA:* 3.09. *Test scores:* SAT critical reading scores over 500: 33%; SAT math scores over 500: 100%; ACT scores over 18: 85%; SAT critical reading scores over 600: 7%; SAT math scores over 600: 100%; ACT scores over 24: 33%; SAT math scores over 700: 7%; ACT scores over 30: 2%.

Faculty *Total:* 129, 74% full-time, 59% with terminal degrees. *Student/faculty ratio:* 17:1.

Academics *Calendar:* semesters. *Degrees:* certificates, associate, bachelor's, master's, doctoral, and first professional. *Special study options:* academic remediation for entering students, adult/continuing education programs, advanced placement credit, cooperative education, distance learning, double majors, English as a second language, honors programs, independent study, internships, off-campus study, part-time degree program, services for LD students, study abroad, summer session for credit. *ROTC:* Air Force (c).

Computers on Campus 165 computers/terminals and 356 ports are available on campus for general student use. Students can access the following: computer help desk, free student e-mail accounts, online (class) grades, online (class) registration, online (class) schedules, wireless computing initiative requires full-time students to have a tablet computer. Campuswide network is available. 100% of college-owned or -operated housing units are wired for high-speed Internet access. Wireless service is available via entire campus.

Student Life *Housing:* on-campus residence required through sophomore year. *Options:* coed, men-only, women-only. Campus housing is university owned and leased by the school. Freshman campus housing is guaranteed. *Activities and organizations:* drama/theater group, student-run newspaper, radio station, choral group, Gaming Club, Students in Free Enterprise (SIFE), Phi Beta Lambda Business Club, Student Senate, Student Activities Board. *Campus security:* late-night transport/escort service, controlled dormitory access, night watchman. *Student services:* health clinic, personal/psychological counseling.

Athletics Member NAIA. *Intercollegiate sports:* baseball M(s), basketball M(s)/W(s), cheerleading M/W, cross-country running M(s)/W(s), football M(s), softball W(s), track and field M(s)/W(s), volleyball W(s). *Intramural sports:* basketball M/W, softball M/W, volleyball M/W.

Standardized Tests *Required:* SAT or ACT (for admission).

Costs (2011–12) *Tuition:* state resident $3429 full-time, $114 per credit hour part-time; nonresident $5144 full-time, $171 per credit hour part-time. Full-time tuition and fees vary according to location and reciprocity agreements. Part-time tuition and fees vary according to location and reciprocity agreements. *Required fees:* $4192 full-time, $116 per credit hour part-time. *Room and board:* $5088; room only: $2703. Room and board charges vary according to board plan and housing facility. *Payment plans:* installment, deferred payment. *Waivers:* senior citizens and employees or children of employees.

Financial Aid Of all full-time matriculated undergraduates who enrolled in 2010, 1,039 applied for aid, 865 were judged to have need, 124 had their need fully met. 144 Federal Work-Study jobs (averaging $1912). 16 state and other part-time jobs (averaging $5939). In 2010, 89 non-need-based awards were made. *Average percent of need met:* 80%. *Average financial aid package:* $8005. *Average need-based loan:* $3908. *Average need-based gift aid:* $4787. *Average non-need-based aid:* $3661. *Average indebtedness upon graduation:* $27,937.

Applying *Options:* electronic application, deferred entrance. *Application fee:* $20. *Required:* high school transcript, minimum 2.6 GPA, rank in top 60% of high school class, 18 or higher ACT or 870 SAT (Combined Math and Critical Reading). *Application deadlines:* rolling (freshmen), rolling (out-of-state freshmen), rolling (transfers). *Notification:* continuous (freshmen), continuous (out-of-state freshmen), continuous (transfers).

Freshman Application Contact Ms. Tory Bickett, Admissions Secretary, Dakota State University, 820 North Washington, Madison, SD 57042-1799. *Phone:* 605-256-5139. *Toll-free phone:* 888-DSU-9988. *Fax:* 605-256-5020. *E-mail:* yourfuture@dsu.edu. *Web site:* http://www.dsu.edu/.

Dakota Wesleyan University

Mitchell, South Dakota

- **Independent United Methodist** comprehensive, founded 1885
- **Small-town** 50-acre campus
- **Endowment** $20.0 million
- **Coed**
- **Moderately difficult** entrance level

Faculty *Student/faculty ratio:* 12:1.

Academics *Calendar:* semesters. *Degrees:* associate, bachelor's, and master's.

Student Life *Campus security:* 24-hour emergency response devices, student patrols, late-night transport/escort service, controlled dormitory access, campus patrol from 2am to 6am by special request only.

Athletics Member NAIA.

Standardized Tests *Required:* SAT or ACT (for admission).

Costs (2011–12) *Comprehensive fee:* $27,110 includes full-time tuition ($20,810) and room and board ($6300). Part-time tuition: $450 per credit hour. *College room only:* $2800. Room and board charges vary according to board plan and housing facility.

Financial Aid *Of all full-time matriculated undergraduates who enrolled in 2010,* 613 applied for aid, 572 were judged to have need, 107 had their need fully met. 100 Federal Work-Study jobs (averaging $1400). 3 state and other part-time jobs (averaging $1200). *In 2010,* 87 non-need-based awards were made. *Average percent of need met:* 70. *Average financial aid package:* $17,000. *Average need-based loan:* $4400. *Average need-based gift aid:* $12,700. *Average non-need-based aid:* $8100. *Average indebtedness upon graduation:* $32,400.

Applying *Options:* electronic application. *Application fee:* $25. *Required:* high school transcript. *Recommended:* minimum 2.0 GPA.

Freshman Application Contact Mrs. Melissa Herr-Valburg, Director of Admissions, Dakota Wesleyan University, 1200 West University Avenue, Mitchell, SD 57301-4398. *Phone:* 605-995-2600 Ext. 2652. *Toll-free phone:* 800-333-8506. *Fax:* 605-995-2699. *E-mail:* admissions@dwu.edu. *Web site:* http://www.dwu.edu/.

Globe University–Sioux Falls

Sioux Falls, South Dakota

- **Proprietary** 4-year, part of Globe Education Network (GEN) which is composed of Globe University, Minnesota School of Business, Broadview University, The Institute of Production and Recording and Minnesota School of Cosmetology
- **Small-town** 3-acre campus
- **Coed** 368 undergraduate students, 42% full-time, 83% women, 17% men

Undergraduates 156 full-time, 212 part-time. Students come from 6 states and territories; 3% are from out of state; 2% Black or African American, non-Hispanic/Latino; 2% Hispanic/Latino; 0.8% Asian, non-Hispanic/Latino; 0.5% Native Hawaiian or other Pacific Islander, non-Hispanic/Latino; 1% American Indian or Alaska Native, non-Hispanic/Latino; 1% Two or more races, non-Hispanic/Latino; 10% Race/ethnicity unknown; 18% transferred in. *Retention:* 56% of full-time freshmen returned.

Freshmen *Admission:* 65 enrolled.

Faculty *Total:* 36, 33% full-time, 31% with terminal degrees. *Student/faculty ratio:* 14:1.

Academics *Degrees:* diplomas, associate, and bachelor's. *Special study options:* academic remediation for entering students, accelerated degree program, adult/continuing education programs, advanced placement credit, internships, part-time degree program, services for LD students, summer session for credit.

Computers on Campus 47 computers/terminals and 128 ports are available on campus for general student use. Students can access the following: computer help desk, free student e-mail accounts, online (class) grades, online (class) registration, online (class) schedules. Campuswide network is available. Wireless service is available via entire campus.

Student Life *Campus security:* 24-hour emergency response devices, late-night transport/escort service.

Standardized Tests *Required:* AccuPlacer is required of all applicants unless documentation of a minimum ACT composite score of 21 or documentation of a minimum composite score of 1485 on the SAT is presented (for admission). **Applying** *Options:* electronic application. *Application fee:* $50. *Required:* high school transcript, interview. *Required for some:* essay or personal statement, 2 letters of recommendation, GED certificate in lieu of high school transcript. *Application deadlines:* rolling (freshmen), rolling (out-of-state freshmen), rolling (transfers). *Notification:* continuous (freshmen), continuous (out-of-state freshmen), continuous (transfers).

Freshman Application Contact Globe University–Sioux Falls, 5101 South Broadband Lane, Sioux Falls, SD 57108-2208. *Toll-free phone:* 866-437-0705. *Web site:* http://www.globeuniversity.edu/.

Mount Marty College
Yankton, South Dakota

- **Independent Roman Catholic** comprehensive, founded 1936
- **Small-town** 80-acre campus
- **Endowment** $15.5 million
- **Coed** 1,113 undergraduate students, 54% full-time, 60% women, 40% men
- **Minimally difficult** entrance level, 69% of applicants were admitted

Undergraduates 599 full-time, 514 part-time. Students come from 9 states and territories; 35% are from out of state; 2% Black or African American, non-Hispanic/Latino; 6% Hispanic/Latino; 0.6% Asian, non-Hispanic/Latino; 0.6% Native Hawaiian or other Pacific Islander, non-Hispanic/Latino; 4% American Indian or Alaska Native, non-Hispanic/Latino; 0.4% Two or more races, non-Hispanic/Latino; 6% transferred in; 70% live on campus. *Retention:* 66% of full-time freshmen returned.

Freshmen *Admission:* 475 applied, 330 admitted, 148 enrolled. *Average high school GPA:* 3.28. *Test scores:* ACT scores over 18: 93%; ACT scores over 24: 43%; ACT scores over 30: 1%.

Faculty *Total:* 59, 75% full-time, 56% with terminal degrees. *Student/faculty ratio:* 11:1.

Academics *Calendar:* semesters. *Degrees:* certificates, associate, bachelor's, and master's. *Special study options:* academic remediation for entering students, accelerated degree program, adult/continuing education programs, advanced placement credit, cooperative education, distance learning, double majors, honors programs, independent study, internships, off-campus study, part-time degree program, services for LD students, student-designed majors, summer session for credit. *ROTC:* Army (c).

Computers on Campus 25 computers/terminals are available on campus for general student use. Students can access the following: campus intranet, computer help desk, free student e-mail accounts, online (class) grades, online (class) registration, online (class) schedules. Campuswide network is available. 100% of college-owned or -operated housing units are wired for high-speed Internet access. Wireless service is available via entire campus.

Student Life *Housing:* on-campus residence required through senior year. *Options:* men-only, women-only. Campus housing is university owned. Freshman campus housing is guaranteed. *Activities and organizations:* drama/theater group, student-run newspaper, choral group, Campus Ministry, Student Government Association, Nursing Club, Education Club, Theater Club. *Campus security:* 24-hour emergency response devices and patrols, controlled dormitory access. *Student services:* health clinic, personal/psychological counseling.

Athletics Member NAIA. *Intercollegiate sports:* archery M(c)/W(c), baseball M(s), basketball M(s)/W(s), cross-country running M(s)/W(s), golf M(s)/W(s), soccer M(s)/W(s), softball W(s), tennis M(s)/W(s), track and field M(s)/W(s), volleyball W(s). *Intramural sports:* archery M/W, basketball M/W, soccer M/W, softball W, volleyball M/W.

Standardized Tests *Required:* SAT or ACT (for admission).

Costs (2011–12) *Comprehensive fee:* $26,574 includes full-time tuition ($18,826), mandatory fees ($1830), and room and board ($5918). Full-time tuition and fees vary according to location. Part-time tuition: $250 per credit hour. Part-time tuition and fees vary according to course load and location. *Room and board:* Room and board charges vary according to board plan. *Payment plan:* installment. *Waivers:* employees or children of employees.

Financial Aid Of all full-time matriculated undergraduates who enrolled in 2011, 561 applied for aid, 488 were judged to have need, 230 had their need fully met. 203 Federal Work-Study jobs (averaging $1472). 36 state and other part-time jobs (averaging $1472). In 2011, 32 non-need-based awards were made. *Average percent of need met:* 99%. *Average financial aid package:* $21,894. *Average need-based loan:* $5942. *Average need-based gift aid:* $5638. *Average non-need-based aid:* $7483. *Average indebtedness upon graduation:* $25,844.

Applying *Options:* electronic application, early admission, deferred entrance. *Application fee:* $35. *Required:* high school transcript, minimum 2.0 GPA.

Recommended: interview. *Application deadlines:* rolling (freshmen), rolling (transfers). *Notification:* continuous (freshmen), continuous (transfers).

Freshman Application Contact Paula Tacke, Vice President for Marketing and Admissions, Mount Marty College, 1105 West 8th Street, Yankton, SD 57078. *Phone:* 605-668-1545. *Toll-free phone:* 800-658-4552. *E-mail:* paula.tacke@mtmc.edu. *Web site:* http://www.mtmc.edu/.

National American University
Rapid City, South Dakota

Freshman Application Contact Ms. Angela Beck, Director of Enrollment Management, National American University, 321 Kansas City Street, Rapid City, SD 57701. *Phone:* 605-394-4902. *Toll-free phone:* 800-209-0490 (in-state); 800-209-4090 (out-of-state). *Fax:* 605-394-4871. *E-mail:* abeck@national.edu. *Web site:* http://www.national.edu/.

National American University–Sioux Falls Branch
Sioux Falls, South Dakota

Freshman Application Contact Ms. Lisa Houtsma, Director of Admissions, National American University–Sioux Falls Branch, 2801 South Kiwanis Avenue, Suite 100, Sioux Falls, SD 57105-4293. *Phone:* 605-336-4600. *Toll-free phone:* 800-388-5430. *Fax:* 605-336-4605. *E-mail:* lhoutsma@national.edu. *Web site:* http://www.national.edu/.

Northern State University
Aberdeen, South Dakota

- **State-supported** comprehensive, founded 1901, part of South Dakota Board of Regents
- **Small-town** 72-acre campus
- **Endowment** $20.0 million
- **Coed** 2,880 undergraduate students, 58% full-time, 58% women, 42% men
- **Minimally difficult** entrance level, 94% of applicants were admitted

Undergraduates 1,672 full-time, 1,208 part-time. Students come from 44 states and territories; 14 other countries; 31% are from out of state; 1% Black or African American, non-Hispanic/Latino; 2% Hispanic/Latino; 0.4% Asian, non-Hispanic/Latino; 0.6% Native Hawaiian or other Pacific Islander, non-Hispanic/Latino; 2% American Indian or Alaska Native, non-Hispanic/Latino; 2% Two or more races, non-Hispanic/Latino; 0.8% Race/ethnicity unknown; 9% international; 6% transferred in; 81% live on campus.

Freshmen *Admission:* 1,134 applied, 1,063 admitted, 402 enrolled. *Average high school GPA:* 3.09. *Test scores:* SAT critical reading scores over 500: 53%; SAT math scores over 500: 58%; ACT scores over 18: 86%; SAT critical reading scores over 600: 5%; SAT math scores over 600: 5%; ACT scores over 24: 28%; ACT scores over 30: 2%.

Faculty *Total:* 90, 100% full-time. *Student/faculty ratio:* 20:1.

Academics *Calendar:* semesters. *Degrees:* certificates, associate, bachelor's, master's, and postbachelor's certificates. *Special study options:* academic remediation for entering students, accelerated degree program, adult/continuing education programs, advanced placement credit, cooperative education, distance learning, double majors, English as a second language, freshman honors college, honors programs, independent study, internships, off-campus study, part-time degree program, services for LD students, student-designed majors, study abroad, summer session for credit.

Computers on Campus 135 computers/terminals are available on campus for general student use. Students can access the following: campus intranet, computer help desk, free student e-mail accounts, online (class) grades, online (class) registration, online (class) schedules. Campuswide network is available. 100% of college-owned or -operated housing units are wired for high-speed Internet access. Wireless service is available via entire campus.

Student Life *Housing:* on-campus residence required through sophomore year. *Options:* coed. Campus housing is university owned. *Activities and organizations:* drama/theater group, student-run newspaper, television station, choral group, marching band, Student Ambassadors, Choices, honor society, Native American Student Association, International Student Association. *Campus security:* 24-hour emergency response devices, controlled dormitory access, evening patrols. *Student services:* health clinic, personal/psychological counseling, women's center, legal services.

Athletics Member NCAA. All Division II. *Intercollegiate sports:* baseball M(s), basketball M(s)/W(s), cheerleading W(s), cross-country running M(s)/W(s), football M(s), golf M(s)/W(s), soccer W(s), softball W(s), swimming and diving W(s), tennis W(s), track and field M(s)/W(s), volleyball W(s), wrestling M(s). *Intramural sports:* basketball M/W, football M/W, rugby M(c), soccer M(c), softball M/W, volleyball M/W.

Standardized Tests *Required:* SAT or ACT (for admission).

Costs (2012–13) *Tuition:* state resident $3429 full-time; nonresident $5143 full-time. Full-time tuition and fees vary according to course level, course load, and reciprocity agreements. Part-time tuition and fees vary according to course level, course load, and reciprocity agreements. *Required fees:* $3522 full-time. *Room and board:* $6059; room only: $2637. Room and board charges vary according to board plan. *Payment plan:* installment.

Financial Aid Of all full-time matriculated undergraduates who enrolled in 2011, 1,256 applied for aid, 1,003 were judged to have need, 198 had their need fully met. 300 Federal Work-Study jobs (averaging $2000). 335 state and other part-time jobs (averaging $1493). In 2011, 127 non-need-based awards were made. *Average percent of need met:* 69%. *Average financial aid package:* $7071. *Average need-based loan:* $4981. *Average need-based gift aid:* $3616. *Average non-need-based aid:* $1562.

Applying *Options:* electronic application, early admission, deferred entrance. *Application fee:* $20. *Required:* high school transcript, minimum 2.6 GPA. *Notification:* continuous (freshmen), continuous (transfers).

Freshman Application Contact Mr. Allan Vogel, Director of Admissions, Northern State University, 1200 South Jay Street, Aberdeen, SD 57401. *Phone:* 605-626-2544. *Toll-free phone:* 800-678-5330. *Fax:* 605-626-2587. *E-mail:* admission2@northern.edu. *Web site:* http://www.northern.edu/.

Oglala Lakota College
Kyle, South Dakota

Director of Admissions Director of Admissions, Oglala Lakota College, 490 Piya Wiconi Road, Kyle, SD 57752-0490. *Phone:* 605-455-2321 Ext. 236. *E-mail:* lmeseteth@olc.edu. *Web site:* http://www.olc.edu/.

Presentation College
Aberdeen, South Dakota

- **Independent Roman Catholic** 4-year, founded 1951
- **Small-town** 100-acre campus
- **Endowment** $7.5 million
- **Coed, primarily women** 718 undergraduate students, 62% full-time, 74% women, 26% men
- **Noncompetitive** entrance level, 75% of applicants were admitted

Undergraduates 444 full-time, 274 part-time. Students come from 25 states and territories; 2 other countries; 50% are from out of state; 7% Black or African American, non-Hispanic/Latino; 2% Hispanic/Latino; 1% Asian, non-Hispanic/Latino; 8% American Indian or Alaska Native, non-Hispanic/Latino; 12% Race/ethnicity unknown; 0.3% international; 18% transferred in; 19% live on campus. *Retention:* 67% of full-time freshmen returned.

Freshmen *Admission:* 288 applied, 216 admitted, 101 enrolled. *Average high school GPA:* 2.91. *Test scores:* ACT scores over 18: 72%; ACT scores over 24: 13%; ACT scores over 30: 1%.

Faculty *Total:* 70, 61% full-time, 23% with terminal degrees. *Student/faculty ratio:* 8:1.

Academics *Calendar:* semesters. *Degrees:* certificates, associate, and bachelor's. *Special study options:* academic remediation for entering students, accelerated degree program, adult/continuing education programs, advanced placement credit, cooperative education, distance learning, double majors, external degree program, internships, off-campus study, part-time degree program, summer session for credit.

Computers on Campus 45 computers/terminals are available on campus for general student use. Students can access the following: computer help desk, free student e-mail accounts, online (class) grades, online (class) registration, online (class) schedules, wireless network has 100% coverage for students. Campuswide network is available. 100% of college-owned or -operated housing units are wired for high-speed Internet access. Wireless service is available via entire campus.

Student Life *Housing:* on-campus residence required through sophomore year. *Options:* men-only, women-only, disabled students. Campus housing is university owned. Freshman applicants given priority for college housing. *Activities and organizations:* choral group, Wellness/athletics, National Student Nursing Association, Social Work Organization, Rad Tech Organization, Student Ambassadors. *Campus security:* 24-hour emergency response devices, late-night transport/escort service, controlled dormitory access. *Student services:* health clinic, personal/psychological counseling.

Athletics Member NCAA. All Division III. *Intercollegiate sports:* baseball M, basketball M/W, cross-country running W, football M, golf M/W, soccer M/W, softball W, track and field M, volleyball W.

Standardized Tests *Required:* SAT or ACT (for admission).

Costs (2012–13) *Comprehensive fee:* $21,370 includes full-time tuition ($15,870) and room and board ($5500). Full-time tuition and fees vary according to course load, location, and program. Part-time tuition: $588 per credit hour. Part-time tuition and fees vary according to course load, location, and

program. *College room only:* $4100. Room and board charges vary according to board plan. *Payment plan:* installment. *Waivers:* senior citizens and employees or children of employees.

Financial Aid Of all full-time matriculated undergraduates who enrolled in 2007, 494 applied for aid, 471 were judged to have need, 66 had their need fully met. 56 Federal Work-Study jobs (averaging $1874). 39 state and other part-time jobs (averaging $1950). In 2007, 23 non-need-based awards were made. *Average percent of need met:* 43%. *Average financial aid package:* $8737. *Average need-based loan:* $3741. *Average need-based gift aid:* $3769. *Average non-need-based aid:* $2814. *Average indebtedness upon graduation:* $27,430.

Applying *Options:* electronic application. *Application fee:* $25. *Required:* high school transcript. *Required for some:* 2 letters of recommendation, GED, if applicable; college transcripts. *Recommended:* minimum 2.0 GPA. *Application deadlines:* rolling (freshmen), rolling (transfers). *Notification:* continuous (freshmen), continuous (transfers).

Freshman Application Contact Ms. Jo Ellen Lindner, Vice President for Enrollment, Presentation College, 1500 North Main Street, Aberdeen, SD 57401. *Phone:* 605-229-8492. *Toll-free phone:* 800-437-6060. *Fax:* 605-229-8425. *E-mail:* admit@presentation.edu. *Web site:* http://www.presentation.edu/.

Sinte Gleska University
Mission, South Dakota

Director of Admissions Mr. Jack Herman, Registrar and Director of Admissions, Sinte Gleska University, 101 Antelope Lake Circle, PO Box 105, Mission, SD 57555. *Phone:* 605-856-8100 Ext. 8479. *Web site:* http://www.sintegleska.edu/.

South Dakota School of Mines and Technology
Rapid City, South Dakota

- **State-supported** university, founded 1885, part of South Dakota State Board of Regents University System
- **Suburban** 120-acre campus
- **Endowment** $42.5 million
- **Coed** 2,008 undergraduate students, 81% full-time, 26% women, 74% men
- **Moderately difficult** entrance level, 88% of applicants were admitted

Undergraduates 1,636 full-time, 372 part-time. Students come from 38 states and territories; 22 other countries; 41% are from out of state; 0.7% Black or African American, non-Hispanic/Latino; 2% Hispanic/Latino; 1% Asian, non-Hispanic/Latino; 0.2% Native Hawaiian or other Pacific Islander, non-Hispanic/Latino; 2% American Indian or Alaska Native, non-Hispanic/Latino; 3% Two or more races, non-Hispanic/Latino; 1% Race/ethnicity unknown; 3% international; 4% transferred in; 32% live on campus. *Retention:* 78% of full-time freshmen returned.

Freshmen *Admission:* 1,030 applied, 905 admitted, 419 enrolled. *Average high school GPA:* 3.5. *Test scores:* SAT critical reading scores over 500: 84%; SAT math scores over 500: 95%; SAT writing scores over 500: 79%; ACT scores over 18: 100%; SAT critical reading scores over 600: 52%; SAT math scores over 600: 58%; SAT writing scores over 600: 36%; ACT scores over 24: 80%; SAT critical reading scores over 700: 10%; SAT math scores over 700: 13%; ACT scores over 30: 18%.

Faculty *Total:* 153, 85% full-time, 81% with terminal degrees. *Student/faculty ratio:* 15:1.

Academics *Calendar:* semesters. *Degrees:* associate, bachelor's, master's, doctoral, postbachelor's, and first professional certificates. *Special study options:* academic remediation for entering students, adult/continuing education programs, advanced placement credit, cooperative education, distance learning, English as a second language, independent study, internships, off-campus study, part-time degree program, services for LD students, study abroad, summer session for credit. *ROTC:* Army (b).

Computers on Campus 105 computers/terminals and 662 ports are available on campus for general student use. Students can access the following: campus intranet, computer help desk, free student e-mail accounts, online (class) grades, online (class) registration, online (class) schedules, laptop rental, our whole campus has wireless connections. Campuswide network is available. 100% of college-owned or -operated housing units are wired for high-speed Internet access. Wireless service is available via entire campus.

Student Life *Housing:* on-campus residence required through sophomore year. *Options:* coed, men-only, women-only, disabled students. Campus housing is university owned and leased by the school. Freshman campus housing is guaranteed. *Activities and organizations:* drama/theater group, student-run newspaper, radio station, choral group, ASCE (American Society of Civil

Engineers), ASME (American Society of Mechanical Engineers), Drill and Crucible Club, Tau Beta Pi, Formula SAE (Mini Indy race car team), national fraternities, national sororities. *Campus security:* 24-hour emergency response devices and patrols, student patrols, late-night transport/escort service, controlled dormitory access. *Student services:* health clinic, personal/psychological counseling.

Athletics Member NCAA. All Division II. *Intercollegiate sports:* basketball M(s)/W(s), cross-country running M(s)/W(s), football M(s), golf M(s)/W(s), soccer M, track and field M(s)/W(s), volleyball W(s). *Intramural sports:* badminton M(c)/W(c), cheerleading M(c)/W(c), racquetball M/W, riflery M(c)/W(c), rock climbing M(c)/W(c), skiing (downhill) M(c)/W(c), soccer M(c)/W(c), squash M(c), tennis M(c)/W(c), ultimate Frisbee M(c)/W(c), volleyball M/W, water polo M/W.

Standardized Tests *Required:* SAT or ACT (for admission). *Required for some:* SAT or ACT (for admission). *Recommended:* SAT or ACT (for admission).

Costs (2011–12) *Tuition:* state resident $3430 full-time, $114 per credit hour part-time; nonresident $5140 full-time, $171 per credit hour part-time. Full-time tuition and fees vary according to course load, program, and reciprocity agreements. Part-time tuition and fees vary according to course load, program, and reciprocity agreements. *Required fees:* $5390 full-time. *Room and board:* $5700; room only: $3030. Room and board charges vary according to board plan and housing facility. *Payment plan:* installment. *Waivers:* senior citizens and employees or children of employees.

Financial Aid Of all full-time matriculated undergraduates who enrolled in 2011, 1,472 applied for aid, 952 were judged to have need, 314 had their need fully met. 130 Federal Work-Study jobs (averaging $1728). In 2011, 296 non-need-based awards were made. *Average percent of need met:* 75%. *Average financial aid package:* $12,549. *Average need-based loan:* $4201. *Average need-based gift aid:* $4118. *Average non-need-based aid:* $3018. *Average indebtedness upon graduation:* $31,169.

Applying *Options:* electronic application. *Application fee:* $20. *Required:* high school transcript. *Recommended:* minimum 2.8 GPA. *Application deadlines:* rolling (freshmen), rolling (out-of-state freshmen), rolling (transfers). *Notification:* continuous (freshmen), continuous (out-of-state freshmen), continuous (transfers).

Freshman Application Contact Genene Sigler, Applications Processor, South Dakota School of Mines and Technology, 501 East Saint Joseph Street, Rapid City, SD 57701-3995. *Phone:* 605-394-2414 Ext. 5209. *Toll-free phone:* 800-544-8162. *Fax:* 605-394-1979. *E-mail:* admissions@sdsmt.edu. *Web site:* http://www.sdsmt.edu/.

South Dakota State University

Brookings, South Dakota

- **State-supported** university, founded 1881, part of South Dakota Board of Regents
- **Small-town** 272-acre campus
- **Coed** 10,993 undergraduate students, 79% full-time, 52% women, 48% men
- **Minimally difficult** entrance level, 92% of applicants were admitted

Undergraduates 8,662 full-time, 2,331 part-time. Students come from 50 states and territories; 63 other countries; 33% are from out of state; 1% Black or African American, non-Hispanic/Latino; 1% Hispanic/Latino; 1% Asian, non-Hispanic/Latino; 0.1% Native Hawaiian or other Pacific Islander, non-Hispanic/Latino; 2% American Indian or Alaska Native, non-Hispanic/Latino; 1% Two or more races, non-Hispanic/Latino; 0.6% Race/ethnicity unknown; 1% international; 7% transferred in; 34% live on campus. *Retention:* 73% of full-time freshmen returned.

Freshmen *Admission:* 4,673 applied, 4,313 admitted, 2,241 enrolled. *Average high school GPA:* 3.34. *Test scores:* ACT scores over 18: 95%; ACT scores over 24: 47%; ACT scores over 30: 5%.

Faculty *Total:* 692, 67% full-time, 53% with terminal degrees. *Student/faculty ratio:* 19:1.

Academics *Calendar:* semesters. *Degrees:* certificates, associate, bachelor's, master's, doctoral, post-master's, postbachelor's, and first professional certificates. *Special study options:* academic remediation for entering students, accelerated degree program, adult/continuing education programs, advanced placement credit, cooperative education, distance learning, double majors, freshman honors college, honors programs, independent study, internships, off-campus study, part-time degree program, services for LD students, study abroad, summer session for credit. *ROTC:* Army (b), Air Force (b). *Unusual degree programs:* 3-2 economics.

Computers on Campus 437 computers/terminals and 750 ports are available on campus for general student use. Students can access the following: campus intranet, computer help desk, free student e-mail accounts, online (class) grades, online (class) registration, online (class) schedules. Campuswide net-

work is available. 100% of college-owned or -operated housing units are wired for high-speed Internet access. Wireless service is available via entire campus.

Student Life *Housing:* on-campus residence required through sophomore year. *Options:* coed, disabled students. Campus housing is university owned. Freshman campus housing is guaranteed. *Activities and organizations:* drama/theater group, student-run newspaper, radio station, choral group, marching band, Student Association, University Programming Council, Block and Bridle Club, national fraternities, national sororities. *Campus security:* 24-hour emergency response devices and patrols, student patrols, late-night transport/escort service, controlled dormitory access. *Student services:* health clinic, personal/psychological counseling, women's center, legal services.

Athletics Member NCAA. All Division I. *Intercollegiate sports:* baseball M(s), basketball M(s)/W(s), bowling M(c)/W(c), cheerleading M(c)/W(c), cross-country running M(s)/W(s), equestrian sports W, football M(s), golf M(s)/W(s), ice hockey M(c)/W(c), rugby M(c)/W(c), soccer M(c)/W(s), softball W(s), swimming and diving M(s)/W(s), tennis M(s)/W(s), track and field M(s)/W(s), volleyball W(s), wrestling M(s). *Intramural sports:* badminton M/W, basketball M/W, football M/W, golf M/W, racquetball M/W, soccer W, softball M/W, swimming and diving M/W, tennis M/W, track and field M/W, volleyball M/W, wrestling M.

Standardized Tests *Required:* SAT or ACT (for admission).

Costs (2011–12) *Tuition:* state resident $3429 full-time, $114 per credit hour part-time; nonresident $5144 full-time, $173 per credit hour part-time. Full-time tuition and fees vary according to course level, course load, degree level, location, program, and reciprocity agreements. Part-time tuition and fees vary according to course level, course load, degree level, location, program, and reciprocity agreements. *Required fees:* $3458 full-time. *Room and board:* $5778; room only: $3204. Room and board charges vary according to board plan and housing facility. *Payment plans:* installment, deferred payment. *Waivers:* children of alumni, senior citizens, and employees or children of employees.

Financial Aid Of all full-time matriculated undergraduates who enrolled in 2011, 7,486 applied for aid, 6,530 were judged to have need, 5,176 had their need fully met. 458 Federal Work-Study jobs (averaging $1628). 1,848 state and other part-time jobs (averaging $1785). In 2011, 1634 non-need-based awards were made. *Average percent of need met:* 89%. *Average financial aid package:* $9686. *Average need-based loan:* $5016. *Average need-based gift aid:* $4852. *Average non-need-based aid:* $1500. *Average indebtedness upon graduation:* $20,860.

Applying *Options:* electronic application, deferred entrance. *Application fee:* $20. *Required:* high school transcript, minimum 2.6 GPA. *Application deadlines:* rolling (freshmen), rolling (transfers). *Notification:* continuous (freshmen), continuous (transfers).

Freshman Application Contact Ms. Michelle Kuebler, Assistant Director of Admissions, South Dakota State University, PO Box 2201, Brookings, SD 57007. *Phone:* 605-688-4121. *Toll-free phone:* 800-952-3541. *Fax:* 605-688-6891. *E-mail:* sdsu.admissions@sdstate.edu. *Web site:* http://www.sdstate.edu/.

University of Sioux Falls

Sioux Falls, South Dakota

- **Independent American Baptist Churches in the USA** comprehensive, founded 1883
- **Suburban** 24-acre campus
- **Endowment** $17.2 million
- **Coed**
- **Moderately difficult** entrance level

Faculty *Student/faculty ratio:* 15:1.

Academics *Calendar:* 4-1-4. *Degrees:* associate, bachelor's, master's, and post-master's certificates.

Student Life *Campus security:* 24-hour emergency response devices and patrols, student patrols, late-night transport/escort service, controlled dormitory access.

Athletics Member NAIA.

Standardized Tests *Required:* SAT or ACT (for admission).

Costs (2011–12) *Comprehensive fee:* $29,420 includes full-time tuition ($22,090), mandatory fees ($760), and room and board ($6570). Full-time tuition and fees vary according to course load, degree level, and program. Part-time tuition: $310 per semester hour. Part-time tuition and fees vary according to course load, degree level, and program. *Required fees:* $150 per year part-time. *College room only:* $3070. Room and board charges vary according to board plan, housing facility, and student level.

Financial Aid *Of all full-time matriculated undergraduates who enrolled in 2004,* 130 Federal Work-Study jobs (averaging $1200).

Applying *Options:* electronic application. *Application fee:* $25. *Required:* high school transcript. *Required for some:* 2 letters of recommendation, interview. *Recommended:* essay or personal statement, minimum 2.8 GPA.

Freshman Application Contact Aimee Vander Feen, Director of Admissions, University of Sioux Falls, 1101 West 22nd Street, Sioux Falls, SD 57105. *Phone:* 605-331-6602. *Toll-free phone:* 800-888-1047. *Fax:* 605-331-6615. *E-mail:* admissions@usiouxfalls.edu. *Web site:* http://www.usiouxfalls.edu/.

The University of South Dakota
Vermillion, South Dakota

- **State-supported** university, founded 1862, part of South Dakota Board of Regents
- **Small-town** 275-acre campus
- **Endowment** $155.5 million
- **Coed** 7,473 undergraduate students, 60% full-time, 63% women, 37% men
- **Moderately difficult** entrance level, 89% of applicants were admitted

Undergraduates 4,513 full-time, 2,960 part-time. Students come from 46 states and territories; 41 other countries; 32% are from out of state; 2% Black or African American, non-Hispanic/Latino; 3% Hispanic/Latino; 1% Asian, non-Hispanic/Latino; 0.2% Native Hawaiian or other Pacific Islander, non-Hispanic/Latino; 2% American Indian or Alaska Native, non-Hispanic/Latino; 2% Two or more races, non-Hispanic/Latino; 2% Race/ethnicity unknown; 0.9% international; 11% transferred in; 26% live on campus. *Retention:* 76% of full-time freshmen returned.
Freshmen *Admission:* 3,287 applied, 2,923 admitted, 1,248 enrolled. *Average high school GPA:* 3.32. *Test scores:* SAT critical reading scores over 500: 61%; SAT math scores over 500: 65%; ACT scores over 18: 95%; SAT critical reading scores over 600: 16%; SAT math scores over 600: 26%; ACT scores over 24: 48%; SAT critical reading scores over 700: 4%; SAT math scores over 700: 4%; ACT scores over 30: 6%.
Faculty *Total:* 534, 69% full-time, 58% with terminal degrees. *Student/faculty ratio:* 18:1.
Academics *Calendar:* semesters. *Degrees:* certificates, associate, bachelor's, master's, doctoral, post-master's, postbachelor's, and first professional certificates. *Special study options:* academic remediation for entering students, accelerated degree program, adult/continuing education programs, advanced placement credit, cooperative education, distance learning, double majors, English as a second language, external degree program, honors programs, independent study, internships, off-campus study, part-time degree program, services for LD students, student-designed majors, study abroad, summer session for credit. *ROTC:* Army (b). *Unusual degree programs:* 3-2 business administration; social work; accounting, political science, public administration.
Computers on Campus 917 computers/terminals are available on campus for general student use. Students can access the following: campus intranet, computer help desk, free student e-mail accounts, online (class) registration. Campuswide network is available. Wireless service is available via computer centers, computer labs, learning centers, libraries, student centers.
Student Life *Housing:* on-campus residence required through sophomore year. *Options:* coed, men-only, women-only, disabled students. Campus housing is university owned. Freshman campus housing is guaranteed. *Activities and organizations:* drama/theater group, student-run newspaper, radio station, choral group, marching band, Program Council, Residence Hall Association, Student Ambassadors, Delta Sigma Pi, national fraternities, national sororities. *Campus security:* 24-hour emergency response devices and patrols, student patrols, late-night transport/escort service, controlled dormitory access. *Student services:* health clinic, personal/psychological counseling, legal services.
Athletics Member NCAA. All Division I. *Intercollegiate sports:* basketball M(s)/W(s), cross-country running M(s)/W(s), football M(s), golf M/W(s), soccer W(s), softball W(s), swimming and diving M(s)/W(s), tennis W(s), track and field M(s)/W(s), volleyball W(s). *Intramural sports:* baseball M(c), basketball M/W, bowling M/W, crew M(c)/W(c), fencing M(c)/W(c), football M, ice hockey M(c), lacrosse M(c)/W(c), rock climbing M(c)/W(c), rugby M(c)/W(c), soccer M(c)/W(c), softball M(c)/W(c), tennis M/W.
Standardized Tests *Required:* SAT or ACT (for admission).
Costs (2011–12) *Tuition:* state resident $3429 full-time, $114 per credit hour part-time; nonresident $5144 full-time, $171 per credit hour part-time. Full-time tuition and fees vary according to course load. Part-time tuition and fees vary according to course load. *Required fees:* $3780 full-time, $126 per credit hour part-time. *Room and board:* $6543; room only: $3349. Room and board charges vary according to board plan and housing facility. *Payment plan:* deferred payment. *Waivers:* children of alumni, senior citizens, and employees or children of employees.
Financial Aid Of all full-time matriculated undergraduates who enrolled in 2010, 4,243 applied for aid, 3,382 were judged to have need, 1,800 had their need fully met. In 2010, 853 non-need-based awards were made. *Average percent of need met:* 74%. *Average financial aid package:* $6709. *Average need-based loan:* $4123. *Average need-based gift aid:* $4500. *Average non-need-based aid:* $4250. *Average indebtedness upon graduation:* $23,338.

Applying *Options:* electronic application, early admission, deferred entrance. *Application fee:* $20. *Required:* high school transcript. *Recommended:* minimum 2.0 GPA. *Application deadlines:* rolling (freshmen), rolling (transfers). *Notification:* continuous (freshmen), continuous (transfers).
Freshman Application Contact Mr. Scott Pohlson, Director of Enrollment Services, The University of South Dakota, 414 East Clark Street, Vermillion, SD 57069-2390. *Phone:* 605-677-5434. *Toll-free phone:* 877-269-6837. *Fax:* 605-677-6753. *E-mail:* admiss@usd.edu. *Web site:* http://www.usd.edu/.

TENNESSEE

American Baptist College of American Baptist Theological Seminary
Nashville, Tennessee

- **Independent Baptist** comprehensive, founded 1924
- **Urban** 52-acre campus
- **Endowment** $875,540
- **Coed** 108 undergraduate students, 72% full-time, 15% women, 85% men
- **Noncompetitive** entrance level, 100% of applicants were admitted

Undergraduates 78 full-time, 30 part-time. Students come from 12 states and territories; 6% are from out of state; 21% transferred in; 20% live on campus. *Retention:* 85% of full-time freshmen returned.
Freshmen *Admission:* 13 applied, 13 admitted, 13 enrolled. *Average high school GPA:* 2.7.
Faculty *Total:* 13, 31% full-time, 38% with terminal degrees. *Student/faculty ratio:* 8:1.
Academics *Calendar:* semesters. *Degrees:* certificates, associate, bachelor's, and master's. *Special study options:* academic remediation for entering students, adult/continuing education programs, double majors, off-campus study, part-time degree program, summer session for credit.
Computers on Campus 10 computers/terminals and 1 port are available on campus for general student use. Students can access the following: campus intranet, free student e-mail accounts, online (class) grades, online (class) registration, online (class) schedules. Campuswide network is available.
Student Life *Housing options:* coed, men-only, women-only. Campus housing is university owned. *Activities and organizations:* choral group, Student Government Association, Vespers Service, Baptist Student Union, national fraternities. *Campus security:* student patrols, security patrols from 10 pm to 7 am.
Financial Aid Of all full-time matriculated undergraduates who enrolled in 2009, 60 applied for aid, 60 were judged to have need. 1 Federal Work-Study job (averaging $6741). *Average percent of need met:* 75%. *Average financial aid package:* $2675. *Average need-based gift aid:* $1161. *Financial aid deadline:* 7/23.
Applying *Options:* electronic application, deferred entrance. *Application fee:* $30. *Required:* essay or personal statement, high school transcript, minimum 2.0 GPA, 2 letters of recommendation, interview. *Application deadlines:* 8/5 (freshmen), 8/5 (out-of-state freshmen), 8/5 (transfers). *Notification:* 8/12 (freshmen), 8/12 (out-of-state freshmen), continuous until 8/12 (transfers).
Freshman Application Contact Ms. Pamela Tabor, Registrar, American Baptist College of American Baptist Theological Seminary, 1800 Baptist World Center Drive, Nashville, TN 37207. *Phone:* 615-687-6896. *Fax:* 615-226-7855. *E-mail:* admissions@abcnash.edu. *Web site:* http://www.abcnash.edu/.

Aquinas College
Nashville, Tennessee

- **Independent Roman Catholic** 4-year, founded 1961
- **Urban** 92-acre campus
- **Coed**
- **Minimally difficult** entrance level

Faculty *Student/faculty ratio:* 8:1.
Academics *Calendar:* semesters. *Degrees:* associate, bachelor's, and post-bachelor's certificates.
Student Life *Campus security:* 24-hour emergency response devices, patrols by security after class hours.
Standardized Tests *Required for some:* SAT or ACT (for admission).
Applying *Options:* electronic application, deferred entrance. *Application fee:* $25. *Required:* high school transcript, minimum 2.2 GPA. *Required for some:* essay or personal statement.
Freshman Application Contact Ms. Connie Hansom, Director of Admission, Aquinas College, 4210 Harding Road, Nashville, TN 37205-2005. *Phone:*

615-297-7545 Ext. 411. *Toll-free phone:* 800-649-9956. *Fax:* 615-279-3893. *E-mail:* hansomc@aquinascollege.edu. *Web site:* http://www.aquinascollege.edu/.

Argosy University, Nashville
Nashville, Tennessee

Freshman Application Contact Argosy University, Nashville, 100 Centerview Drive, Suite 225, Nashville, TN 37214. *Phone:* 615-525-2800. *Toll-free phone:* 866-833-6598. *Web site:* http://www.argosy.edu/nashville/.

See page 1062 for the College Close-Up.

The Art Institute of Tennessee–Nashville
Nashville, Tennessee

- **Proprietary** 4-year, founded 2006, part of Education Management Corporation
- **Urban** campus
- **Coed**

Academics *Degrees:* diplomas, associate, and bachelor's.
Costs (2011–12) *Tuition:* Tuition cost varies by program. Prospective students should contact the school for current tuition costs. Other charges include a starting kit for all first-quarter students. Kits vary in price, depending on the program of study.
Freshman Application Contact The Art Institute of Tennessee–Nashville, 100 Centerview Drive, Suite 250, Nashville, TN 37214. *Phone:* 615-874-1067. *Toll-free phone:* 866-747-5770. *Web site:* http://www.artinstitutes.edu/nashville/.

See page 1134 for the College Close-Up.

Austin Peay State University
Clarksville, Tennessee

- **State-supported** comprehensive, founded 1927, part of Tennessee Board of Regents
- **Suburban** 169-acre campus with easy access to Nashville
- **Endowment** $6.7 million
- **Coed** 10,020 undergraduate students, 71% full-time, 60% women, 40% men
- **Moderately difficult** entrance level, 88% of applicants were admitted

Undergraduates 7,164 full-time, 2,856 part-time. Students come from 43 states and territories; 22 other countries; 11% are from out of state; 19% Black or African American, non-Hispanic/Latino; 6% Hispanic/Latino; 2% Asian, non-Hispanic/Latino; 0.4% Native Hawaiian or other Pacific Islander, non-Hispanic/Latino; 0.6% American Indian or Alaska Native, non-Hispanic/Latino; 4% Two or more races, non-Hispanic/Latino; 3% Race/ethnicity unknown; 0.5% international; 10% transferred in; 14% live on campus. *Retention:* 69% of full-time freshmen returned.
Freshmen *Admission:* 3,290 applied, 2,897 admitted, 1,551 enrolled. *Average high school GPA:* 3.18. *Test scores:* SAT critical reading scores over 500: 41%; SAT math scores over 500: 48%; ACT scores over 18: 89%; SAT critical reading scores over 600: 20%; SAT math scores over 600: 16%; ACT scores over 24: 24%; SAT critical reading scores over 700: 7%; SAT math scores over 700: 3%; ACT scores over 30: 3%.
Faculty *Total:* 626, 55% full-time. *Student/faculty ratio:* 20:1.
Academics *Calendar:* semesters. *Degrees:* certificates, associate, bachelor's, master's, post-master's, and postbachelor's certificates. *Special study options:* academic remediation for entering students, accelerated degree program, adult/continuing education programs, advanced placement credit, cooperative education, distance learning, double majors, English as a second language, honors programs, independent study, internships, part-time degree program, services for LD students, study abroad, summer session for credit. *ROTC:* Army (b), Air Force (c).
Computers on Campus 850 computers/terminals are available on campus for general student use. Students can access the following: campus intranet, computer help desk, free student e-mail accounts, online (class) grades, online (class) registration, online (class) schedules. Campuswide network is available. Wireless service is available via entire campus.
Student Life *Housing:* on-campus residence required for freshman year. *Options:* coed, men-only, women-only, disabled students. Campus housing is university owned. Freshman campus housing is guaranteed. *Activities and organizations:* drama/theater group, student-run newspaper, radio and television station, choral group, marching band, national fraternities, national sorori-

ties. *Campus security:* 24-hour emergency response devices and patrols, student patrols, late-night transport/escort service, controlled dormitory access. *Student services:* health clinic, personal/psychological counseling.
Athletics Member NCAA. All Division I except football (Division I-AA). *Intercollegiate sports:* baseball M(s), basketball M(s)/W(s), cheerleading M(s)/W(s), cross-country running M(s)/W(s), golf M(s)/W(s), soccer W(s), softball W(s), tennis M(s)/W(s), track and field W(s), volleyball W(s). *Intramural sports:* badminton M/W, basketball M/W, football M/W, golf M/W, ice hockey M/W, racquetball M/W, soccer M/W, softball M/W, table tennis M/W, ultimate Frisbee M/W, volleyball M/W.
Standardized Tests *Required for some:* SAT or ACT (for admission).
Costs (2012–13) *One-time required fee:* $75. *Tuition:* state resident $5208 full-time, $350 per credit hour part-time; nonresident $18,768 full-time, $971 per credit hour part-time. Full-time tuition and fees vary according to location and program. Part-time tuition and fees vary according to location and program. *Required fees:* $1224 full-time. *Room and board:* $7014; room only: $4400. Room and board charges vary according to board plan and housing facility. *Waivers:* senior citizens and employees or children of employees.
Financial Aid Of all full-time matriculated undergraduates who enrolled in 2010, 7,151 applied for aid, 5,738 were judged to have need. 147 Federal Work-Study jobs (averaging $2068). 426 state and other part-time jobs (averaging $1638). In 2010, 583 non-need-based awards were made. *Average financial aid package:* $9103. *Average need-based loan:* $3759. *Average need-based gift aid:* $7005. *Average non-need-based aid:* $4453. *Average indebtedness upon graduation:* $20,335.
Applying *Options:* electronic application, early admission, deferred entrance. *Application fee:* $15. *Required:* high school transcript. *Required for some:* minimum 2.8 GPA. *Application deadlines:* 7/25 (freshmen), rolling (transfers). *Notification:* continuous (freshmen), continuous (transfers).
Freshman Application Contact Ms. Amy Deaton, Director of Admissions, Austin Peay State University, 601 College Street, Clarksville, TN 37044. *Phone:* 931-221-7661. *Toll-free phone:* 800-844-2778. *Fax:* 931-221-6168. *E-mail:* admissions@apsu.edu. *Web site:* http://www.apsu.edu/.

Baptist College of Health Sciences
Memphis, Tennessee

- **Independent Southern Baptist** 4-year, founded 1994
- **Urban** campus
- **Coed, primarily women** 975 undergraduate students, 42% full-time, 89% women, 11% men
- **Moderately difficult** entrance level, 16% of applicants were admitted

Undergraduates 407 full-time, 568 part-time. Students come from 11 states and territories; 31% are from out of state; 36% Black or African American, non-Hispanic/Latino; 0.7% Hispanic/Latino; 2% Asian, non-Hispanic/Latino; 0.2% American Indian or Alaska Native, non-Hispanic/Latino; 1% Two or more races, non-Hispanic/Latino; 3% Race/ethnicity unknown; 100% transferred in; 10% live on campus. *Retention:* 83% of full-time freshmen returned.
Freshmen *Admission:* 344 applied, 54 admitted, 35 enrolled.
Faculty *Total:* 62.
Academics *Calendar:* trimesters. *Degree:* bachelor's. *Special study options:* accelerated degree program, advanced placement credit, distance learning, part-time degree program, services for LD students, summer session for credit.
Computers on Campus 64 computers/terminals and 64 ports are available on campus for general student use. Students can access the following: campus intranet, computer help desk, free student e-mail accounts, online (class) grades, online (class) registration, online (class) schedules. Campuswide network is available. 100% of college-owned or -operated housing units are wired for high-speed Internet access. Wireless service is available via entire campus.
Student Life *Housing options:* coed. Campus housing is university owned. *Activities and organizations:* Student Government Association, Student Nursing Association, Allied Health Organization. *Campus security:* 24-hour emergency response devices, late-night transport/escort service, controlled dormitory access, trained security personnel. *Student services:* health clinic, personal/psychological counseling.
Standardized Tests *Required:* ACT (for admission), (for admission).
Costs (2011–12) *Tuition:* $9810 full-time, $327 per credit hour part-time. *Required fees:* $850 full-time, $25 per credit hour part-time, $50 per term part-time. *Room only:* $1100.
Applying *Options:* electronic application. *Application fee:* $25. *Required:* high school transcript, minimum 2.8 GPA, immunizations, health physical. *Required for some:* interview. *Application deadlines:* 5/1 (freshmen), 5/1 (transfers).
Freshman Application Contact Baptist College of Health Sciences, 1003 Monroe Avenue, Memphis, TN 38104. *Phone:* 901-572-2441. *Toll-free phone:* 866-575-2247. *Web site:* http://www.bchs.edu/.

Belhaven University

Memphis, Tennessee

Director of Admissions Don Jones, Director of Admission, Belhaven University, 5100 Poplar Avenue, Suite 200, Memphis, TN 38137. *Phone:* 901-888-3343. *Fax:* 901-888-0771. *E-mail:* memphisadmission@belhaven.edu. *Web site:* http://memphis.belhaven.edu/.

Belmont University

Nashville, Tennessee

- **Independent Christian** comprehensive, founded 1951
- **Urban** 77-acre campus
- **Endowment** $73.4 million
- **Coed** 4,974 undergraduate students, 93% full-time, 58% women, 42% men
- **Moderately difficult** entrance level, 82% of applicants were admitted

Undergraduates 4,619 full-time, 355 part-time. Students come from 48 states and territories; 21 other countries; 59% are from out of state; 4% Black or African American, non-Hispanic/Latino; 3% Hispanic/Latino; 2% Asian, non-Hispanic/Latino; 0.1% Native Hawaiian or other Pacific Islander, non-Hispanic/Latino; 0.2% American Indian or Alaska Native, non-Hispanic/Latino; 3% Two or more races, non-Hispanic/Latino; 2% Race/ethnicity unknown; 1% international; 12% transferred in; 52% live on campus. *Retention:* 80% of full-time freshmen returned.

Freshmen *Admission:* 3,878 applied, 3,161 admitted, 1,163 enrolled. *Average high school GPA:* 3.51. *Test scores:* SAT critical reading scores over 500: 90%; SAT math scores over 500: 89%; ACT scores over 18: 100%; SAT critical reading scores over 600: 46%; SAT math scores over 600: 43%; ACT scores over 24: 77%; SAT critical reading scores over 700: 7%; SAT math scores over 700: 6%; ACT scores over 30: 18%.

Faculty *Total:* 657, 48% full-time, 50% with terminal degrees. *Student/faculty ratio:* 14:1.

Academics *Calendar:* semesters. *Degrees:* bachelor's, master's, doctoral, and post-master's certificates. *Special study options:* accelerated degree program, adult/continuing education programs, advanced placement credit, cooperative education, distance learning, double majors, English as a second language, honors programs, independent study, internships, off-campus study, part-time degree program, student-designed majors, study abroad, summer session for credit. *ROTC:* Army (c), Navy (c), Air Force (c). *Unusual degree programs:* 3-2 engineering with Auburn University, Georgia Institute of Technology, University of Tennessee.

Computers on Campus 500 computers/terminals are available on campus for general student use. Students can access the following: campus intranet, free student e-mail accounts, online (class) grades, online (class) registration, online (class) schedules, individual student information via BANNER Web. Campuswide network is available. 100% of college-owned or -operated housing units are wired for high-speed Internet access. Wireless service is available via entire campus.

Student Life *Housing:* on-campus residence required through sophomore year. *Options:* men-only, women-only. Campus housing is university owned. Freshman applicants given priority for college housing. *Activities and organizations:* drama/theater group, student-run newspaper, radio and television station, choral group, marching band, Service Corp, Alpha Sigma Tau, Phi Mu, Phi Kappa Tau, MOB, national fraternities, national sororities. *Campus security:* 24-hour emergency response devices and patrols, late-night transport/escort service, controlled dormitory access, bicycle patrol. *Student services:* health clinic, personal/psychological counseling, women's center.

Athletics Member NCAA. All Division I. *Intercollegiate sports:* baseball M(s), basketball M(s)/W(s), cross-country running M(s)/W(s), golf M(s)/W(s), soccer M(s)/W(s), softball W(s), tennis M(s)/W(s), track and field M(s)/W(s), volleyball W(s). *Intramural sports:* baseball M, basketball M/W, bowling M/W, cheerleading M/W, football M, golf M, ice hockey M/W, racquetball M/W, soccer M/W, softball M/W, table tennis M/W, tennis M/W, volleyball M/W.

Standardized Tests *Required:* SAT or ACT (for admission).

Costs (2012–13) *Comprehensive fee:* $38,550 includes full-time tuition ($24,900), mandatory fees ($1230), and room and board ($12,420). Full-time tuition and fees vary according to class time, course load, and location. Part-time tuition: $950 per credit hour. Part-time tuition and fees vary according to course load. *Required fees:* $840 per year part-time. *College room only:* $8200. Room and board charges vary according to board plan, housing facility, and location. *Payment plans:* installment, deferred payment. *Waivers:* senior citizens and employees or children of employees.

Financial Aid Of all full-time matriculated undergraduates who enrolled in 2009, 4,001 applied for aid, 2,599 were judged to have need, 648 had their need fully met. 534 Federal Work-Study jobs (averaging $6297). In 2009, 522 non-need-based awards were made. *Average percent of need met:* 79%. *Average financial aid package:* $12,214. *Average need-based loan:* $4434. *Average need-based gift aid:* $6896. *Average non-need-based aid:* $4434. *Average indebtedness upon graduation:* $29,058.

Applying *Options:* electronic application, early admission, deferred entrance. *Application fee:* $50. *Required:* essay or personal statement, high school transcript, minimum 3.0 GPA, 2 letters of recommendation, resume of activities. *Required for some:* interview. *Application deadlines:* 8/1 (freshmen), 8/1 (transfers). *Notification:* continuous (freshmen), continuous (transfers).

Freshman Application Contact Mr. David Mee, Associate Provost and Dean of Enrollment, Belmont University, 1900 Belmont Boulevard, Nashville, TN 37212-3757. *Phone:* 615-460-5479. *Fax:* 615-460-5434. *E-mail:* david.mee@belmont.edu. *Web site:* http://www.belmont.edu/.

See page 1168 for the College Close-Up.

Bethel University

McKenzie, Tennessee

- **Independent Cumberland Presbyterian** comprehensive, founded 1842
- **Small-town** 100-acre campus
- **Endowment** $8.1 million
- **Coed** 2,724 undergraduate students, 69% full-time, 58% women, 42% men
- **Minimally difficult** entrance level, 54% of applicants were admitted

Undergraduates 1,876 full-time, 848 part-time. Students come from 25 states and territories; 19 other countries; 9% are from out of state; 2% transferred in; 29% live on campus. *Retention:* 64% of full-time freshmen returned.

Freshmen *Admission:* 1,057 applied, 566 admitted, 432 enrolled. *Average high school GPA:* 3.05.

Faculty *Total:* 291, 33% full-time. *Student/faculty ratio:* 19:1.

Academics *Calendar:* semesters. *Degrees:* bachelor's and master's. *Special study options:* academic remediation for entering students, accelerated degree program, adult/continuing education programs, advanced placement credit, cooperative education, distance learning, double majors, honors programs, independent study, internships, off-campus study, part-time degree program, services for LD students, student-designed majors, summer session for credit. *Unusual degree programs:* 3-2 engineering with Tennessee Technological University; pharmacy with University of Tennessee, Memphis.

Computers on Campus 12 computers/terminals and 30 ports are available on campus for general student use. Students can access the following: campus intranet, computer help desk, free student e-mail accounts, online (class) grades, online (class) registration, online (class) schedules. Campuswide network is available. 100% of college-owned or -operated housing units are wired for high-speed Internet access. Wireless service is available via classrooms, computer labs, dorm rooms, libraries, student centers.

Student Life *Housing:* on-campus residence required through junior year. *Options:* coed, men-only, women-only, disabled students. Campus housing is university owned and leased by the school. Freshman applicants given priority for college housing. *Activities and organizations:* drama/theater group, choral group, marching band, Campus Crusade for Christ, STEA (Education), Student Government Association, Students in Free Enterprise (SIFE), Arete. *Campus security:* night patrols by trained security personnel. *Student services:* personal/psychological counseling.

Athletics Member NAIA. *Intercollegiate sports:* baseball M(s), basketball M(s)/W(s), bowling M(s)/W(s), cheerleading M(s)/W(s), cross-country running M(s)/W(s), football M(s), golf M(s)/W(s), riflery M(s)/W(s), soccer M(s)/W(s), softball W(s), tennis M(s)/W(s), track and field M(s)/W(s), volleyball W(s). *Intramural sports:* basketball M/W, football M, golf M/W, soccer M/W, softball M/W, table tennis M/W, tennis M/W, volleyball M/W.

Standardized Tests *Recommended:* SAT or ACT (for admission).

Costs (2011–12) *Comprehensive fee:* $21,334 includes full-time tuition ($12,902), mandatory fees ($650), and room and board ($7782). Full-time tuition and fees vary according to program. Part-time tuition: $398 per credit hour. Part-time tuition and fees vary according to course load and program. *Payment plan:* installment. *Waivers:* employees or children of employees.

Applying *Options:* electronic application, early admission, deferred entrance. *Application fee:* $30. *Required:* high school transcript, minimum 2.0 GPA. *Required for some:* essay or personal statement, interview. *Application deadlines:* rolling (freshmen), rolling (transfers). *Notification:* continuous (freshmen), continuous (transfers).

Freshman Application Contact Tina Hodges, Enrollment Director of Admissions and Financial Aid, Bethel University, 325 Cherry Avenue, McKenzie, TN 38201. *Phone:* 731-352-4030. *Fax:* 731-352-4069. *E-mail:* hodgest@bethelu.edu. *Web site:* http://www.bethelu.edu/.

Bryan College

Dayton, Tennessee

- **Independent interdenominational** comprehensive, founded 1930
- **Small-town** 100-acre campus
- **Coed**
- **Moderately difficult** entrance level

Faculty *Student/faculty ratio:* 23:1.

Academics *Calendar:* semesters. *Degrees:* certificates, diplomas, associate, bachelor's, and master's.

Student Life *Campus security:* student patrols, late-night transport/escort service, controlled dormitory access, police patrols.

Athletics Member NAIA, NCCAA.

Standardized Tests *Required:* SAT or ACT (for admission).

Costs (2011–12) *Comprehensive fee:* $24,194 includes full-time tuition ($18,620), mandatory fees ($120), and room and board ($5454). Full-time tuition and fees vary according to course load. Part-time tuition: $775 per credit. Part-time tuition and fees vary according to course load. *Room and board:* Room and board charges vary according to board plan and housing facility.

Financial Aid *Of all full-time matriculated undergraduates who enrolled in 2010,* 918 applied for aid, 786 were judged to have need, 769 had their need fully met. *In 2010,* 105 non-need-based awards were made. *Average percent of need met:* 92. *Average financial aid package:* $31,573. *Average need-based loan:* $7073. *Average need-based gift aid:* $18,160. *Average non-need-based aid:* $8448. *Average indebtedness upon graduation:* $15,637.

Applying *Options:* electronic application, early action, deferred entrance. *Application fee:* $35. *Required:* essay or personal statement, high school transcript, minimum 2.0 GPA, 3 letters of recommendation. *Required for some:* interview.

Freshman Application Contact Michael Sapienza, Vice President for Enrollment Management, Bryan College, PO Box 7000, Dayton, TN 37321-7000. *Phone:* 423-775-2041. *Toll-free phone:* 800-277-9522. *Fax:* 423-775-7199. *E-mail:* admissions@bryan.edu. *Web site:* http://www.bryan.edu/.

Carson-Newman College

Jefferson City, Tennessee

- **Independent Southern Baptist** comprehensive, founded 1851
- **Small-town** 90-acre campus with easy access to Knoxville
- **Endowment** $45.8 million
- **Coed** 1,686 undergraduate students, 96% full-time, 54% women, 46% men
- **Moderately difficult** entrance level, 67% of applicants were admitted

Undergraduates 1,622 full-time, 64 part-time. Students come from 31 states and territories; 23 other countries; 31% are from out of state; 9% Black or African American, non-Hispanic/Latino; 2% Hispanic/Latino; 0.4% Asian, non-Hispanic/Latino; 0.1% Native Hawaiian or other Pacific Islander, non-Hispanic/Latino; 0.3% American Indian or Alaska Native, non-Hispanic/Latino; 2% Two or more races, non-Hispanic/Latino; 0.2% Race/ethnicity unknown; 4% international; 6% transferred in; 51% live on campus. *Retention:* 64% of full-time freshmen returned.

Freshmen *Admission:* 3,542 applied, 2,382 admitted, 446 enrolled. *Average high school GPA:* 3.4. *Test scores:* ACT scores over 18: 94%; ACT scores over 24: 41%; ACT scores over 30: 6%.

Faculty *Total:* 204, 60% full-time, 47% with terminal degrees. *Student/faculty ratio:* 12:1.

Academics *Calendar:* semesters. *Degrees:* associate, bachelor's, and master's. *Special study options:* academic remediation for entering students, accelerated degree program, adult/continuing education programs, advanced placement credit, English as a second language, honors programs, internships, off-campus study, part-time degree program, services for LD students, student-designed majors, study abroad, summer session for credit. *ROTC:* Army (b), Air Force (c). *Unusual degree programs:* 3-2 engineering with Georgia Institute of Technology, University of Tennessee, Tennessee Technological University; pharmacy with Campbell University, Mercer University, University of Georgia.

Computers on Campus 200 computers/terminals are available on campus for general student use. Campuswide network is available.

Student Life *Housing:* on-campus residence required through junior year. *Options:* men-only, women-only. Freshman campus housing is guaranteed. *Activities and organizations:* drama/theater group, student-run newspaper, choral group, marching band, Baptist Student Union, Fellowship of Christian Athletes, Student Government Association, Student Ambassadors Association, Columbians, national fraternities, national sororities. *Campus security:* 24-hour emergency response devices and patrols, late-night transport/escort service, controlled dormitory access. *Student services:* health clinic, personal/psychological counseling.

Athletics Member NCAA. All Division II. *Intercollegiate sports:* baseball M(s), basketball M(s)/W(s), cross-country running M(s)/W(s), football M(s), golf M(s), soccer M(s)/W(s), softball W(s), tennis M(s)/W(s), track and field M(s)/W(s), volleyball W(s), wrestling M(s). *Intramural sports:* badminton M/W, baseball M/W, basketball M/W, football M/W, golf M/W, racquetball M/W, skiing (downhill) M/W, soccer M/W, softball M/W, table tennis M/W, tennis M/W, volleyball M/W.

Standardized Tests *Required:* SAT or ACT (for admission).

Costs (2012–13) *Comprehensive fee:* $29,058 includes full-time tuition ($21,660), mandatory fees ($992), and room and board ($6406). Full-time tuition and fees vary according to class time and course load. Part-time tuition: $900 per credit hour. *Room and board:* Room and board charges vary according to board plan, gender, and housing facility. *Payment plans:* installment, deferred payment. *Waivers:* senior citizens and employees or children of employees.

Financial Aid Of all full-time matriculated undergraduates who enrolled in 2011, 1,576 applied for aid, 1,291 were judged to have need, 273 had their need fully met. 237 Federal Work-Study jobs (averaging $1497). 20 state and other part-time jobs (averaging $568). In 2011, 261 non-need-based awards were made. *Average percent of need met:* 73%. *Average financial aid package:* $17,820. *Average need-based loan:* $3714. *Average need-based gift aid:* $13,116. *Average non-need-based aid:* $8141. *Average indebtedness upon graduation:* $22,306.

Applying *Options:* electronic application, deferred entrance. *Application fee:* $25. *Required:* high school transcript, minimum 2.3 GPA, medical history. *Required for some:* essay or personal statement, interview. *Recommended:* interview. *Application deadlines:* 8/1 (freshmen), 8/1 (transfers). *Notification:* continuous (freshmen), continuous (transfers).

Freshman Application Contact Melanie Redding, Director of Admissions, Carson-Newman College, 1646 Russell Avenue, PO Box 557, Jefferson City, TN 37760. *Phone:* 865-471-3223. *Toll-free phone:* 800-678-9061. *Fax:* 865-471-3502. *E-mail:* cnadmiss@cn.edu. *Web site:* http://www.cn.edu/.

See below for display ad and page 1246 for the College Close-Up.

Christian Brothers University
Memphis, Tennessee

- **Independent Roman Catholic** comprehensive, founded 1871
- **Urban** 75-acre campus with easy access to Memphis
- **Endowment** $26.7 million
- **Coed** 1,330 undergraduate students, 90% full-time, 55% women, 45% men
- **Moderately difficult** entrance level, 46% of applicants were admitted

Undergraduates 1,200 full-time, 130 part-time. Students come from 28 states and territories; 21 other countries; 18% are from out of state; 35% Black or African American, non-Hispanic/Latino; 5% Hispanic/Latino; 5% Asian, non-Hispanic/Latino; 0.2% Native Hawaiian or other Pacific Islander, non-Hispanic/Latino; 0.3% American Indian or Alaska Native, non-Hispanic/Latino; 3% Two or more races, non-Hispanic/Latino; 1% Race/ethnicity unknown; 3% international; 6% transferred in; 40% live on campus. *Retention:* 78% of full-time freshmen returned.

Freshmen *Admission:* 2,124 applied, 986 admitted, 307 enrolled. *Average high school GPA:* 3.59. *Test scores:* ACT scores over 18: 99%; ACT scores over 24: 47%; ACT scores over 30: 6%.

Faculty *Total:* 194, 55% full-time, 58% with terminal degrees. *Student/faculty ratio:* 13:1.

Academics *Calendar:* semesters. *Degrees:* bachelor's, master's, and post-bachelor's certificates. *Special study options:* accelerated degree program, adult/continuing education programs, advanced placement credit, distance learning, double majors, honors programs, independent study, internships, off-campus study, part-time degree program, services for LD students, study abroad, summer session for credit. *ROTC:* Army (c), Navy (c), Air Force (c). *Unusual degree programs:* 3-2 engineering.

Computers on Campus 310 computers/terminals are available on campus for general student use. Students can access the following: campus intranet, computer help desk, free student e-mail accounts, online (class) grades, online (class) registration, online (class) schedules, online class listings, course assignments. Campuswide network is available. 100% of college-owned or -operated housing units are wired for high-speed Internet access. Wireless service is available via entire campus.

Student Life *Housing:* on-campus residence required through sophomore year. *Options:* coed, men-only, women-only. Campus housing is university owned. Freshman applicants given priority for college housing. *Activities and organizations:* drama/theater group, choral group, Black Student Association, BAC-

CHUS Alcohol Awareness Group, Intercultural Club, The Chosen Generation, Lasallian Collegians, national fraternities, national sororities. *Campus security:* 24-hour emergency response devices and patrols, student patrols, late-night transport/escort service, controlled dormitory access. *Student services:* health clinic, personal/psychological counseling.

Athletics Member NCAA. All Division II. *Intercollegiate sports:* baseball M(s), basketball M(s)/W(s), cross-country running M(s)/W(s), golf M(s)/W(s), soccer M(s)/W(s), softball W(s), tennis M(s)/W(s), volleyball W(s). *Intramural sports:* basketball M/W, bowling M/W, cross-country running M/W, football M/W, golf M, lacrosse M, racquetball M/W, soccer M/W, softball M/W, swimming and diving M/W, table tennis M/W, tennis M/W, ultimate Frisbee M/W, volleyball M/W, weight lifting M.

Standardized Tests *Required:* SAT or ACT (for admission).

Costs (2012–13) *Comprehensive fee:* $33,424 includes full-time tuition ($26,694), mandatory fees ($590), and room and board ($6140). Full-time tuition and fees vary according to class time. Part-time tuition: $936 per credit hour. Part-time tuition and fees vary according to class time. *Required fees:* $115 per term part-time. *Room and board:* Room and board charges vary according to board plan and housing facility.

Financial Aid Of all full-time matriculated undergraduates who enrolled in 2010, 1,080 applied for aid, 920 were judged to have need, 217 had their need fully met. 157 Federal Work-Study jobs (averaging $988). 186 state and other part-time jobs (averaging $978). In 2010, 198 non-need-based awards were made. *Average percent of need met:* 81%. *Average financial aid package:* $20,985. *Average need-based loan:* $4413. *Average need-based gift aid:* $6590. *Average non-need-based aid:* $9265. *Average indebtedness upon graduation:* $29,207.

Applying *Options:* electronic application, early admission, deferred entrance. *Application fee:* $25. *Required:* essay or personal statement, high school transcript, minimum 2.0 GPA. *Required for some:* 2 letters of recommendation. *Recommended:* interview. *Application deadlines:* 8/1 (freshmen), 8/23 (transfers). *Notification:* 12/1 (freshmen), continuous (transfers).

Freshman Application Contact Dr. Anne Kenworthy, Dean of Admissions, Christian Brothers University, 650 East Parkway South, Memphis, TN 38104. *Phone:* 901-321-3205. *Toll-free phone:* 877-321-4CBU. *Fax:* 901-321-3202. *E-mail:* admissions@cbu.edu. *Web site:* http://www.cbu.edu/.

Cumberland University

Lebanon, Tennessee

- **Independent** comprehensive, founded 1842
- **Small-town** 44-acre campus with easy access to Nashville
- **Endowment** $8.4 million
- **Coed**
- **Moderately difficult** entrance level

Faculty *Student/faculty ratio:* 15:1.

Academics *Calendar:* semesters. *Degrees:* associate, bachelor's, and master's.

Student Life *Campus security:* 24-hour emergency response devices and patrols, late-night transport/escort service.

Athletics Member NAIA.

Standardized Tests *Required:* SAT or ACT (for admission). *Recommended:* SAT (for admission).

Costs (2011–12) *One-time required fee:* $100. *Comprehensive fee:* $25,800 includes full-time tuition ($18,200), mandatory fees ($1000), and room and board ($6600). Full-time tuition and fees vary according to degree level. Part-time tuition: $758 per credit hour. Part-time tuition and fees vary according to course load and degree level.

Financial Aid *Of all full-time matriculated undergraduates who enrolled in 2007,* 837 applied for aid, 713 were judged to have need, 135 had their need fully met. 120 Federal Work-Study jobs (averaging $750). 16 state and other part-time jobs (averaging $750). In 2007, 125 non-need-based awards were made. *Average percent of need met:* 54. *Average financial aid package:* $12,176. *Average need-based loan:* $4073. *Average need-based gift aid:* $5669. *Average non-need-based aid:* $8069. *Average indebtedness upon graduation:* $21,562.

Applying *Options:* electronic application, deferred entrance. *Application fee:* $25. *Required:* high school transcript. *Required for some:* 3 letters of recommendation. *Recommended:* essay or personal statement, minimum 2.5 GPA.

Freshman Application Contact Ms. Beatrice LaChance, Director of Enrollment Services, Cumberland University, One Cumberland Square, Lebanon, TN 37087. *Phone:* 615-547-1244. *Toll-free phone:* 800-467-0562. *Fax:* 615-444-2569. *E-mail:* admissions@cumberland.edu. *Web site:* http://www.cumberland.edu/.

Daymar Institute

Clarksville, Tennessee

Freshman Application Contact Daymar Institute, 1860 Wilma Rudolph Boulevard, Clarksville, TN 37040. *Phone:* 931-552-7600 Ext. 204. *Web site:* http://www.daymarinstitute.edu/.

DeVry University

Memphis, Tennessee

Freshman Application Contact DeVry University, 6401 Poplar Avenue, Suite 600, Memphis, TN 38119. *Toll-free phone:* 866-338-7941. *Web site:* http://www.devry.edu/.

DeVry University

Nashville, Tennessee

Admissions Office Contact DeVry University, 3343 Perimeter Hill Drive, Suite 200, Nashville, TN 37211-4147. *Toll-free phone:* 866-338-7941. *Web site:* http://www.devry.edu/.

East Tennessee State University

Johnson City, Tennessee

- **State-supported** university, founded 1911, part of State University and Community College System of Tennessee; Tennessee Board of Regents
- **Small-town** 366-acre campus
- **Endowment** $96.8 million
- **Coed** 12,539 undergraduate students, 85% full-time, 56% women, 44% men
- **Moderately difficult** entrance level, 85% of applicants were admitted

Undergraduates 10,639 full-time, 1,900 part-time. Students come from 44 states and territories; 45 other countries; 11% are from out of state; 6% Black or African American, non-Hispanic/Latino; 2% Hispanic/Latino; 1% Asian, non-Hispanic/Latino; 0.1% Native Hawaiian or other Pacific Islander, non-Hispanic/Latino; 0.4% American Indian or Alaska Native, non-Hispanic/Latino; 2% Two or more races, non-Hispanic/Latino; 2% Race/ethnicity unknown; 1% international; 10% transferred in; 20% live on campus. *Retention:* 70% of full-time freshmen returned.

Freshmen *Admission:* 5,269 applied, 4,482 admitted, 2,140 enrolled. *Average high school GPA:* 3.29. *Test scores:* SAT critical reading scores over 500: 45%; SAT math scores over 500: 48%; ACT scores over 18: 84%; SAT critical reading scores over 600: 13%; SAT math scores over 600: 10%; ACT scores over 24: 31%; SAT critical reading scores over 700: 2%; ACT scores over 30: 3%.

Faculty *Total:* 828, 68% full-time, 57% with terminal degrees. *Student/faculty ratio:* 20:1.

Academics *Calendar:* semesters. *Degrees:* certificates, bachelor's, master's, doctoral, post-master's, postbachelor's, and first professional certificates. *Special study options:* adult/continuing education programs, advanced placement credit, cooperative education, distance learning, double majors, English as a second language, external degree program, freshman honors college, honors programs, independent study, internships, off-campus study, part-time degree program, services for LD students, student-designed majors, study abroad, summer session for credit. *ROTC:* Army (b).

Computers on Campus 1,400 computers/terminals are available on campus for general student use. Students can access the following: computer help desk, free student e-mail accounts, online (class) grades, online (class) registration, online (class) schedules. Campuswide network is available. Wireless service is available via entire campus.

Student Life *Housing options:* coed, men-only, women-only, disabled students. Campus housing is university owned. *Activities and organizations:* drama/theater group, student-run newspaper, radio and television station, choral group, honor societies, Volunteer ETSU, religious groups, residence hall councils, national fraternities, national sororities. *Campus security:* 24-hour emergency response devices and patrols, student patrols, late-night transport/escort service, controlled dormitory access. *Student services:* health clinic, personal/psychological counseling, women's center.

Athletics Member NCAA. All Division I. *Intercollegiate sports:* baseball M(s), basketball M(s)/W(s), cross-country running M(s)/W(s), golf M(s)/W(s), soccer M(s)/W(s), softball W(s), tennis M(s)/W(s), track and field M(s)/W(s), volleyball W(s). *Intramural sports:* basketball M/W, cross-country running M/W, football M/W, golf M/W, racquetball M/W, softball M/W, tennis M/W, volleyball W, weight lifting M.

Standardized Tests *Required:* SAT or ACT (for admission).

Costs (2011–12) *Tuition:* state resident $5208 full-time, $217 per credit hour part-time; nonresident $18,768 full-time, $782 per credit hour part-time. Full-

time tuition and fees vary according to course load and program. Part-time tuition and fees vary according to course load and program. *Required fees:* $1063 full-time, $65 per credit hour part-time. *Room and board:* $6000. Room and board charges vary according to board plan and housing facility.

Financial Aid Of all full-time matriculated undergraduates who enrolled in 2010, 8,339 applied for aid, 6,053 were judged to have need, 2,784 had their need fully met. 595 Federal Work-Study jobs (averaging $1117). In 2010, 1220 non-need-based awards were made. *Average percent of need met:* 81%. *Average financial aid package:* $5079. *Average need-based loan:* $3408. *Average need-based gift aid:* $3560. *Average non-need-based aid:* $3826. *Average indebtedness upon graduation:* $20,984.

Applying *Options:* electronic application, early admission. *Application fee:* $25. *Required:* high school transcript, minimum 2.3 GPA, 2.3 high school GPA or 19 ACT. *Application deadlines:* rolling (freshmen), rolling (out-of-state freshmen), rolling (transfers). *Notification:* continuous (freshmen), continuous (out-of-state freshmen), continuous (transfers).

Freshman Application Contact Mr. Mike Pitts, Director of Admissions, East Tennessee State University, PO Box 70731, Johnson City, TN 37614-0734. *Phone:* 423-439-4213. *Toll-free phone:* 800-462-3878. *Fax:* 423-439-4630. *E-mail:* go2etsu@etsu.edu. *Web site:* http://www.etsu.edu/.

Fisk University

Nashville, Tennessee

Freshman Application Contact Fisk University, 1000 17th Avenue North, Nashville, TN 37208-3051. *Phone:* 615-329-8665. *Toll-free phone:* 888-702-0022. *Fax:* 615-329-8774. *E-mail:* admit@fisk.edu. *Web site:* http://www.fisk.edu/.

Fountainhead College of Technology

Knoxville, Tennessee

- **Proprietary** primarily 2-year, founded 1947
- **Suburban** 6-acre campus
- **Coed** 219 undergraduate students
- **Noncompetitive** entrance level

Undergraduates *Retention:* 82% of full-time freshmen returned.

Faculty *Student/faculty ratio:* 9:1.

Academics *Calendar:* semesters. *Degrees:* associate and bachelor's. *Special study options:* accelerated degree program, distance learning, summer session for credit.

Computers on Campus Campuswide network is available. Wireless service is available via entire campus.

Student Life *Housing:* college housing not available. *Campus security:* 24-hour emergency response devices.

Standardized Tests *Required for some:* SAT or ACT (for admission).

Costs (2012–13) *Tuition:* $485 per credit hour part-time. No tuition increase for student's term of enrollment.

Applying *Required:* high school transcript, interview. *Application deadlines:* rolling (freshmen), rolling (transfers). *Notification:* continuous (freshmen), continuous (transfers).

Freshman Application Contact Mr. Todd Hill, Director of Admissions, Fountainhead College of Technology, 3203 Tazewell Pike, Knoxville, TN 37918-2530. *Phone:* 865-688-9422. *Toll-free phone:* 888-218-7335. *Fax:* 865-688-2419. *E-mail:* todd.hill@fountainheadcollege.edu. *Web site:* http://www.fountainheadcollege.edu/.

Freed-Hardeman University

Henderson, Tennessee

- **Independent** comprehensive, founded 1869, affiliated with Church of Christ
- **Small-town** 96-acre campus
- **Coed**
- 100% of applicants were admitted

Faculty *Student/faculty ratio:* 15:1.

Academics *Calendar:* semesters. *Degrees:* associate, bachelor's, master's, doctoral, post-master's, and postbachelor's certificates.

Student Life *Campus security:* 24-hour emergency response devices and patrols, late-night transport/escort service, controlled dormitory access.

Athletics Member NAIA.

Standardized Tests *Required:* SAT or ACT (for admission).

Costs (2011–12) *Comprehensive fee:* $24,500 includes full-time tuition ($13,590), mandatory fees ($3614), and room and board ($7296). Full-time tuition and fees vary according to course load and degree level. Part-time tuition: $453 per semester hour. Part-time tuition and fees vary according to course load and degree level. *College room only:* $3980. Room and board charges vary according to board plan and housing facility.

Financial Aid Of all full-time matriculated undergraduates who enrolled in 2010, 1,328 applied for aid, 1,170 were judged to have need, 231 had their need fully met. In 2010, 200 non-need-based awards were made. *Average percent of need met:* 65. *Average financial aid package:* $14,853. *Average need-based loan:* $3790. *Average need-based gift aid:* $11,230. *Average non-need-based aid:* $6437. *Average indebtedness upon graduation:* $34,533.

Applying *Options:* early admission, deferred entrance. *Required:* high school transcript, minimum 2.3 GPA. *Required for some:* interview. *Recommended:* essay or personal statement.

Freshman Application Contact Mr. Joseph Askew, Interim Director of Admissions, Freed-Hardeman University, 158 East Main Street, Henderson, TN 38340-2399. *Phone:* 731-989-6651. *Toll-free phone:* 800-FHU-FHU-1. *Fax:* 731-989-6047. *E-mail:* admissions@fhu.edu. *Web site:* http://www.fhu.edu/.

Free Will Baptist Bible College

Nashville, Tennessee

- **Independent Free Will Baptist** 4-year, founded 1942
- **Urban** 10-acre campus with easy access to Nashville
- **Endowment** $1.3 million
- **Coed** 291 undergraduate students, 69% full-time, 46% women, 54% men
- **Noncompetitive** entrance level, 49% of applicants were admitted

Undergraduates 201 full-time, 90 part-time. Students come from 20 states and territories; 5 other countries; 48% are from out of state; 9% Black or African American, non-Hispanic/Latino; 2% Hispanic/Latino; 0.3% Asian, non-Hispanic/Latino; 0.3% Two or more races, non-Hispanic/Latino; 15% international; 5% transferred in; 55% live on campus. *Retention:* 59% of full-time freshmen returned.

Freshmen *Admission:* 159 applied, 78 admitted, 58 enrolled. *Average high school GPA:* 3.16. *Test scores:* ACT scores over 18: 76%; ACT scores over 24: 39%; ACT scores over 30: 2%.

Faculty *Total:* 55, 38% full-time, 35% with terminal degrees. *Student/faculty ratio:* 9:1.

Academics *Calendar:* semesters. *Degrees:* associate and bachelor's. *Special study options:* academic remediation for entering students, advanced placement credit, distance learning, double majors, internships, part-time degree program, student-designed majors, summer session for credit. *ROTC:* Army (c), Air Force (c). *Unusual degree programs:* nursing.

Computers on Campus 41 computers/terminals are available on campus for general student use. Students can access the following: campus intranet, computer help desk, free student e-mail accounts, online (class) grades, online (class) schedules. Campuswide network is available. Wireless service is available via computer centers, computer labs, dorm rooms, libraries, student centers.

Student Life *Housing:* on-campus residence required through senior year. *Options:* men-only, women-only. Campus housing is university owned. Freshman campus housing is guaranteed. *Activities and organizations:* drama/theater group, choral group, GMF-Global Missions Fellowship, Four Women's Societies, Four Men's Societies. *Campus security:* 24-hour emergency response devices, student patrols, late-night transport/escort service, controlled dormitory access. *Student services:* personal/psychological counseling.

Athletics Member NCCAA. *Intercollegiate sports:* baseball M, basketball M/W, golf M/W, volleyball W. *Intramural sports:* basketball M/W, tennis M/W, volleyball M/W.

Standardized Tests *Required:* SAT or ACT (for admission).

Costs (2012–13) *Comprehensive fee:* $20,348 includes full-time tuition ($13,410), mandatory fees ($896), and room and board ($6042). *Room and board:* Room and board charges vary according to board plan. *Payment plans:* installment, deferred payment. *Waivers:* employees or children of employees.

Financial Aid Of all full-time matriculated undergraduates who enrolled in 2011, 178 applied for aid, 172 were judged to have need. 7 Federal Work-Study jobs (averaging $1871). 101 state and other part-time jobs (averaging $1960). *Average percent of need met:* 71%. *Average financial aid package:* $5331. *Average need-based loan:* $2195. *Average need-based gift aid:* $4214. *Average indebtedness upon graduation:* $19,688.

Applying *Options:* electronic application, early admission, deferred entrance. *Application fee:* $35. *Required:* essay or personal statement, high school transcript, 3 letters of recommendation, medical history. *Application deadlines:* rolling (freshmen), rolling (out-of-state freshmen), rolling (transfers). *Notification:* continuous (freshmen), continuous (out-of-state freshmen), continuous (transfers).

Freshman Application Contact Mr. Rusty Campbell, Director of Enrollment Services, Free Will Baptist Bible College, 3606 West End Avenue, Nashville, TN 37205. *Phone:* 615-844-5269. *Toll-free phone:* 800-763-9222. *Fax:* 615-269-6028. *E-mail:* rcampbell@fwbbc.edu. *Web site:* http://www.fwbbc.edu/.

Huntington College of Health Sciences

Knoxville, Tennessee

- **Proprietary** comprehensive, founded 1984
- **Suburban** campus
- **Coed**
- **Noncompetitive** entrance level

Faculty *Student/faculty ratio:* 29:1.

Academics *Calendar:* continuous. *Degrees:* certificates, diplomas, associate, bachelor's, master's, and postbachelor's certificates (offers only external degree programs conducted through home study).

Costs (2011–12) *Tuition:* $199 per semester hour part-time. Full-time tuition and fees vary according to course load and program. Part-time tuition and fees vary according to course load and program.

Applying *Options:* electronic application, deferred entrance. *Application fee:* $75. *Required for some:* high school transcript, interview. *Recommended:* minimum 2.0 GPA.

Freshman Application Contact Kim Galyon, Director of Admissions, Huntington College of Health Sciences, 1204 Kenesaw Avenue, Suite D, Knoxville, TN 37919. *Phone:* 800-290-4226. *Toll-free phone:* 800-290-4226. *Fax:* 865-524-8339. *E-mail:* studentservices@hchs.edu. *Web site:* http://www.hchs.edu/.

ITT Technical Institute

Chattanooga, Tennessee

- **Proprietary** primarily 2-year, part of ITT Educational Services, Inc.
- **Coed**
- **Minimally difficult** entrance level

Academics *Degrees:* associate and bachelor's.

Student Life *Housing:* college housing not available.

Freshman Application Contact Director of Recruitment, ITT Technical Institute, 5600 Brainerd Road, Suite G-1, Chattanooga, TN 37411. *Phone:* 423-510-6800. *Toll-free phone:* 877-474-8312. *Web site:* http://www.itt-tech.edu/.

ITT Technical Institute

Cordova, Tennessee

- **Proprietary** primarily 2-year, founded 1994, part of ITT Educational Services, Inc.
- **Suburban** campus
- **Coed**
- **Minimally difficult** entrance level

Academics *Calendar:* quarters. *Degrees:* associate and bachelor's.

Student Life *Housing:* college housing not available.

Freshman Application Contact Director of Recruitment, ITT Technical Institute, 7260 Goodlett Farms Parkway, Cordova, TN 38016. *Phone:* 901-381-0200. *Toll-free phone:* 866-444-5141. *Web site:* http://www.itt-tech.edu/.

ITT Technical Institute

Johnson City, Tennessee

- **Proprietary** primarily 2-year
- **Coed**
- **Minimally difficult** entrance level

Academics *Degrees:* associate and bachelor's.

Freshman Application Contact Director of Recruitment, ITT Technical Institute, 4721 Lake Park Drive, Suite 100, Johnson City, TN 37615. *Phone:* 423-952-4400. *Toll-free phone:* 877-301-9691. *Web site:* http://www.itt-tech.edu/.

ITT Technical Institute

Knoxville, Tennessee

- **Proprietary** primarily 2-year, founded 1988, part of ITT Educational Services, Inc.
- **Suburban** campus
- **Coed**
- **Minimally difficult** entrance level

Academics *Calendar:* quarters. *Degrees:* associate and bachelor's.

Student Life *Housing:* college housing not available.

Freshman Application Contact Director of Recruitment, ITT Technical Institute, 10208 Technology Drive, Knoxville, TN 37932. *Phone:* 865-671-2800. *Toll-free phone:* 800-671-2801. *Web site:* http://www.itt-tech.edu/.

ITT Technical Institute

Nashville, Tennessee

- **Proprietary** primarily 2-year, founded 1984, part of ITT Educational Services, Inc.
- **Urban** campus
- **Coed**
- **Minimally difficult** entrance level

Academics *Calendar:* quarters. *Degrees:* associate and bachelor's.

Student Life *Housing:* college housing not available.

Freshman Application Contact Director of Recruitment, ITT Technical Institute, 2845 Elm Hill Pike, Nashville, TN 37214. *Phone:* 615-889-8700. *Toll-free phone:* 800-331-8386. *Web site:* http://www.itt-tech.edu/.

Johnson University

Knoxville, Tennessee

- **Independent** comprehensive, founded 1893, affiliated with Christian Churches and Churches of Christ
- **Rural** 175-acre campus
- **Endowment** $99.9 million
- **Coed**
- **Moderately difficult** entrance level

Faculty *Student/faculty ratio:* 14:1.

Academics *Calendar:* semesters. *Degrees:* certificates, associate, bachelor's, master's, doctoral, and first professional.

Student Life *Campus security:* 24-hour emergency response devices, student patrols, controlled dormitory access.

Athletics Member NCCAA.

Standardized Tests *Required:* SAT or ACT (for admission). *Required for some:* ACT (for admission).

Costs (2011–12) *Comprehensive fee:* $14,880 includes full-time tuition ($8800), mandatory fees ($830), and room and board ($5250). Part-time tuition: $340 per credit hour. Part-time tuition and fees vary according to course load. *Required fees:* $35 per credit hour part-time. *College room only:* $2500. Room and board charges vary according to board plan and housing facility.

Financial Aid *Of all full-time matriculated undergraduates who enrolled in 2010,* 649 applied for aid, 543 were judged to have need, 51 had their need fully met. 64 Federal Work-Study jobs (averaging $1602). 335 state and other part-time jobs (averaging $1611). *Average percent of need met:* 63. *Average financial aid package:* $11,642. *Average need-based loan:* $3414. *Average need-based gift aid:* $6471. *Average indebtedness upon graduation:* $18,494.

Applying *Options:* electronic application, deferred entrance. *Application fee:* $35. *Required:* essay or personal statement, high school transcript, 3 letters of recommendation. *Required for some:* interview.

Freshman Application Contact Mr. Tim Wingfield, Director of Admissions, Johnson University, 7900 Johnson Drive, Knoxville, TN 37998-1001. *Phone:* 865-251-2346. *Toll-free phone:* 800-827-2122. *Fax:* 865-251-2336. *E-mail:* twingfield@jbc.edu. *Web site:* http://www.jbc.edu/.

King College

Bristol, Tennessee

- **Independent** comprehensive, founded 1867, affiliated with Presbyterian Church (U.S.A.)
- **Suburban** 135-acre campus
- **Endowment** $27.5 million
- **Coed** 1,802 undergraduate students, 91% full-time, 64% women, 36% men
- **Moderately difficult** entrance level, 66% of applicants were admitted

Undergraduates 1,644 full-time, 158 part-time. Students come from 32 states and territories; 28 other countries; 35% are from out of state; 4% Black or African American, non-Hispanic/Latino; 2% Hispanic/Latino; 0.4% Asian, non-Hispanic/Latino; 0.4% American Indian or Alaska Native, non-Hispanic/Latino; 0.6% Two or more races, non-Hispanic/Latino; 15% Race/ethnicity unknown; 3% international; 7% transferred in; 35% live on campus. *Retention:* 67% of full-time freshmen returned.

Freshmen *Admission:* 901 applied, 599 admitted, 174 enrolled. *Average high school GPA:* 3.4. *Test scores:* SAT critical reading scores over 500: 48%; SAT math scores over 500: 40%; SAT writing scores over 500: 38%; ACT scores over 18: 92%; SAT critical reading scores over 600: 13%; SAT math scores

over 600: 7%; SAT writing scores over 600: 7%; ACT scores over 24: 30%; SAT critical reading scores over 700: 1%; ACT scores over 30: 2%.
Faculty *Total:* 182, 47% full-time, 55% with terminal degrees. *Student/faculty ratio:* 16:1.
Academics *Calendar:* semesters. *Degrees:* bachelor's, master's, and post-master's certificates. *Special study options:* adult/continuing education programs, advanced placement credit, cooperative education, double majors, honors programs, independent study, internships, off-campus study, part-time degree program, services for LD students, student-designed majors, study abroad, summer session for credit. *ROTC:* Army (c). *Unusual degree programs:* 3-2 engineering with University of Tennessee, Vanderbilt University.
Computers on Campus 90 computers/terminals and 500 ports are available on campus for general student use. Students can access the following: campus intranet, computer help desk, free student e-mail accounts, online (class) grades, online (class) registration, online (class) schedules, student portal. Campuswide network is available. 100% of college-owned or -operated housing units are wired for high-speed Internet access. Wireless service is available via classrooms, computer centers, computer labs, learning centers, libraries, student centers.
Student Life *Housing:* on-campus residence required through junior year. *Options:* men-only, women-only, disabled students. Campus housing is university owned. Freshman campus housing is guaranteed. *Activities and organizations:* drama/theater group, student-run newspaper, choral group, Student Government Association, Campus Life Committee, World Christian Fellowship, Fellowship of Christian Athletes, Drama Club. *Campus security:* 24-hour patrols, late-night transport/escort service, controlled dormitory access. *Student services:* personal/psychological counseling.
Athletics Member NCAA. All Division II. *Intercollegiate sports:* baseball M(s), basketball M(s)/W(s), cheerleading M(s)/W(s), cross-country running M(s)/W(s), golf M(s)/W(s), soccer M(s)/W(s), softball W(s), swimming and diving M(s)/W(s), tennis M(s)/W(s), track and field M(s)/W(s), volleyball M(s)/W(s), wrestling M(s)/W(s). *Intramural sports:* badminton M/W, basketball M/W, soccer M/W, softball M/W, table tennis M/W, tennis M/W, ultimate Frisbee M/W, volleyball M/W, weight lifting M.
Standardized Tests *Required:* SAT or ACT (for admission).
Costs (2011–12) *Comprehensive fee:* $32,232 includes full-time tuition ($22,700), mandatory fees ($1352), and room and board ($8180). Full-time tuition and fees vary according to course load and program. Part-time tuition: $600 per credit hour. Part-time tuition and fees vary according to course load and program. *College room only:* $4108. Room and board charges vary according to board plan. *Payment plan:* installment. *Waivers:* senior citizens and employees or children of employees.
Financial Aid Of all full-time matriculated undergraduates who enrolled in 2011, 1,445 applied for aid, 1,329 were judged to have need, 190 had their need fully met. 43 Federal Work-Study jobs (averaging $1740). 146 state and other part-time jobs (averaging $1740). In 2011, 92 non-need-based awards were made. *Average percent of need met:* 69%. *Average financial aid package:* $16,176. *Average need-based loan:* $4693. *Average need-based gift aid:* $13,513. *Average non-need-based aid:* $8958. *Average indebtedness upon graduation:* $12,603.
Applying *Options:* electronic application, early admission, deferred entrance. *Application fee:* $20. *Required:* high school transcript, minimum 2.4 GPA. *Required for some:* essay or personal statement. *Recommended:* interview. *Application deadlines:* rolling (freshmen), rolling (out-of-state freshmen), rolling (transfers). *Notification:* continuous (freshmen), continuous (out-of-state freshmen), continuous (transfers).
Freshman Application Contact Mr. Greg King, Director of Recruitment, King College, 1350 King College Road, Bristol, TN 37620. *Phone:* 423-652-4861. *Toll-free phone:* 800-362-0014. *Fax:* 423-652-4727. *E-mail:* admissions@king.edu. *Web site:* http://www.king.edu/.

Lane College
Jackson, Tennessee

- **Independent** 4-year, founded 1882, affiliated with Christian Methodist Episcopal Church
- **Suburban** 25-acre campus with easy access to Memphis
- **Endowment** $3.8 million
- **Coed** 2,002 undergraduate students, 99% full-time, 52% women, 48% men
- **Minimally difficult** entrance level, 33% of applicants were admitted

Undergraduates 1,981 full-time, 21 part-time. Students come from 29 states and territories; 3 other countries; 36% are from out of state; 100% Black or African American, non-Hispanic/Latino; 0.1% international; 6% transferred in; 62% live on campus. *Retention:* 58% of full-time freshmen returned.
Freshmen *Admission:* 6,350 applied, 2,125 admitted, 601 enrolled. *Average high school GPA:* 2.8. *Test scores:* ACT scores over 18: 16%; ACT scores over 24: 1%.

Faculty *Total:* 102, 97% full-time, 78% with terminal degrees. *Student/faculty ratio:* 19:1.
Academics *Calendar:* semesters. *Degree:* bachelor's. *Special study options:* academic remediation for entering students, accelerated degree program, adult/continuing education programs, advanced placement credit, cooperative education, honors programs, independent study, internships, off-campus study, part-time degree program, study abroad, summer session for credit. *Unusual degree programs:* 3-2 engineering with Dual Degree Program with TSU.
Computers on Campus 258 computers/terminals and 258 ports are available on campus for general student use. Students can access the following: campus intranet, computer help desk, free student e-mail accounts, online admissions and advising. Campuswide network is available. 100% of college-owned or -operated housing units are wired for high-speed Internet access. Wireless service is available via classrooms, computer centers, computer labs, dorm rooms, learning centers, libraries, student centers.
Student Life *Housing:* on-campus residence required for freshman year. *Options:* men-only, women-only. Campus housing is university owned. Freshman applicants given priority for college housing. *Activities and organizations:* drama/theater group, choral group, marching band, Student Government Association, Pre-Law Club, Student Christian Association, Drama Club, Sociology Club, national fraternities, national sororities. *Campus security:* 24-hour emergency response devices and patrols, late-night transport/escort service, surveillance cameras, lighted parking areas. *Student services:* health clinic, personal/psychological counseling.
Athletics Member NCAA. All Division II. *Intercollegiate sports:* baseball M(s), basketball M(s)/W(s), cheerleading W, cross-country running M(s)/W(s), football M(s), softball W(s), tennis M(s)/W(s), track and field M(s)/W(s), volleyball W(s).
Standardized Tests *Required:* SAT or ACT (for admission).
Costs (2011–12) *Comprehensive fee:* $14,020 includes full-time tuition ($7550), mandatory fees ($670), and room and board ($5800). Full-time tuition and fees vary according to course load. Part-time tuition: $315 per credit hour. Part-time tuition and fees vary according to course load. *Required fees:* $670 per year part-time. *Payment plans:* installment, deferred payment. *Waivers:* adult students and employees or children of employees.
Financial Aid Of all full-time matriculated undergraduates who enrolled in 2010, 2,167 applied for aid, 2,161 were judged to have need, 901 had their need fully met. In 2010, 46 non-need-based awards were made. *Average percent of need met:* 45%. *Average financial aid package:* $3314. *Average need-based loan:* $1993. *Average need-based gift aid:* $1742. *Average non-need-based aid:* $2746. *Average indebtedness upon graduation:* $8754.
Applying *Options:* electronic application, deferred entrance. *Required:* high school transcript, 2 letters of recommendation. *Application deadlines:* rolling (freshmen), rolling (out-of-state freshmen), rolling (transfers). *Notification:* continuous (freshmen), continuous (transfers).
Freshman Application Contact Ms. Kelly Boyd, Director of Enrollment Management, Lane College, 545 Lane Avenue, Jackson, TN 38301. *Phone:* 731-426-7533. *Toll-free phone:* 800-960-7533. *Fax:* 731-426-7559. *E-mail:* kboyd@lanecollege.edu. *Web site:* http://www.lanecollege.edu/.

Lee University
Cleveland, Tennessee

- **Independent** comprehensive, founded 1918, affiliated with Church of God
- **Small-town** 120-acre campus with easy access to Chattanooga
- **Endowment** $8.5 million
- **Coed** 4,016 undergraduate students, 88% full-time, 58% women, 42% men
- **Minimally difficult** entrance level, 61% of applicants were admitted

Undergraduates 3,554 full-time, 462 part-time. Students come from 53 states and territories; 50 other countries; 55% are from out of state; 5% Black or African American, non-Hispanic/Latino; 4% Hispanic/Latino; 1% Asian, non-Hispanic/Latino; 0.1% Native Hawaiian or other Pacific Islander, non-Hispanic/Latino; 0.3% American Indian or Alaska Native, non-Hispanic/Latino; 0.7% Two or more races, non-Hispanic/Latino; 8% Race/ethnicity unknown; 5% international; 7% transferred in; 46% live on campus. *Retention:* 72% of full-time freshmen returned.
Freshmen *Admission:* 1,777 applied, 1,088 admitted, 875 enrolled. *Average high school GPA:* 3.5. *Test scores:* SAT critical reading scores over 500: 66%; SAT math scores over 500: 63%; ACT scores over 18: 89%; SAT critical reading scores over 600: 29%; SAT math scores over 600: 29%; ACT scores over 24: 57%; SAT critical reading scores over 700: 6%; SAT math scores over 700: 3%; ACT scores over 30: 13%.
Faculty *Total:* 380, 42% full-time, 47% with terminal degrees. *Student/faculty ratio:* 17:1.
Academics *Calendar:* semesters. *Degrees:* bachelor's, master's, and post-master's certificates. *Special study options:* academic remediation for entering

students, adult/continuing education programs, advanced placement credit, cooperative education, distance learning, double majors, English as a second language, external degree program, honors programs, independent study, internships, part-time degree program, services for LD students, study abroad, summer session for credit.

Computers on Campus 410 computers/terminals and 410 ports are available on campus for general student use. Students can access the following: campus intranet, computer help desk, free student e-mail accounts, online (class) grades, online (class) registration, online (class) schedules. Campuswide network is available. 95% of college-owned or -operated housing units are wired for high-speed Internet access. Wireless service is available via entire campus.

Student Life *Housing:* on-campus residence required through sophomore year. *Options:* men-only, women-only. Campus housing is university owned. Freshman campus housing is guaranteed. *Activities and organizations:* drama/theater group, student-run newspaper, choral group, Student Leadership Council, Pioneers for Christ, International Student Fellowship, Big Pal Little Pal, Back Yard Ministry. *Campus security:* 24-hour emergency response devices and patrols, late-night transport/escort service, controlled dormitory access. *Student services:* health clinic, personal/psychological counseling.

Athletics Member NAIA, NCCAA. *Intercollegiate sports:* baseball M(s), basketball M(s)/W(s), cheerleading M(c)/W(c), cross-country running M(s)/W(s), golf M(s), rugby M(c)/W(c), soccer M(s)/W(s), softball W(s), tennis M(s)/W(s), volleyball W(s). *Intramural sports:* badminton M/W, basketball M/W, bowling M/W, football M/W, racquetball M/W, soccer M/W, softball M/W, table tennis M/W, tennis M/W, ultimate Frisbee M/W, volleyball M/W, wrestling M.

Standardized Tests *Required:* SAT or ACT (for admission).

Costs (2011–12) *Comprehensive fee:* $18,690 includes full-time tuition ($12,120), mandatory fees ($560), and room and board ($6010). Full-time tuition and fees vary according to course load. Part-time tuition: $506 per credit hour. Part-time tuition and fees vary according to course load. *Required fees:* $506 per credit hour part-time. *College room only:* $2900. Room and board charges vary according to board plan and housing facility. *Payment plan:* deferred payment. *Waivers:* employees or children of employees.

Financial Aid Of all full-time matriculated undergraduates who enrolled in 2011, 2,960 applied for aid, 2,504 were judged to have need, 391 had their need fully met. 239 Federal Work-Study jobs (averaging $2142). In 2011, 528 non-need-based awards were made. *Average percent of need met:* 54%. *Average financial aid package:* $10,347. *Average need-based loan:* $4142. *Average need-based gift aid:* $8066. *Average non-need-based aid:* $6772. *Average indebtedness upon graduation:* $27,213.

Applying *Options:* electronic application, early admission, deferred entrance. *Application fee:* $25. *Required:* high school transcript, minimum 2.0 GPA, MMR immunization record. *Required for some:* 3 letters of recommendation. *Application deadlines:* 9/1 (freshmen), 9/1 (out-of-state freshmen), 9/1 (transfers). *Notification:* continuous (freshmen), continuous (out-of-state freshmen), continuous (transfers).

Freshman Application Contact Mr. Phillip Cook, Vice President for Enrollment, Lee University, PO Box 3450, Cleveland, TN 37320-3450. *Phone:* 423-614-8500. *Toll-free phone:* 800-533-9930. *Fax:* 423-614-8533. *E-mail:* admissions@leeuniversity.edu. *Web site:* http://www.leeuniversity.edu/.

LeMoyne-Owen College

Memphis, Tennessee

Freshman Application Contact LeMoyne-Owen College, 807 Walker Avenue, Memphis, TN 38126-6595. *Phone:* 901-435-1500. *Toll-free phone:* 800-737-7778. *Web site:* http://www.loc.edu/.

Lincoln Memorial University

Harrogate, Tennessee

- **Independent** comprehensive, founded 1897
- **Small-town** 1000-acre campus
- **Coed** 1,857 undergraduate students, 80% full-time, 71% women, 29% men
- **Moderately difficult** entrance level, 65% of applicants were admitted

Undergraduates 1,493 full-time, 364 part-time. Students come from 46 states and territories; 25 other countries; 36% are from out of state; 4% Black or African American, non-Hispanic/Latino; 1% Hispanic/Latino; 0.6% Asian, non-Hispanic/Latino; 0.1% Native Hawaiian or other Pacific Islander, non-Hispanic/Latino; 0.1% American Indian or Alaska Native, non-Hispanic/Latino; 0.1% Two or more races, non-Hispanic/Latino; 16% Race/ethnicity unknown; 2% international; 13% transferred in; 36% live on campus. *Retention:* 71% of full-time freshmen returned.

Freshmen *Admission:* 1,593 applied, 1,035 admitted, 318 enrolled. *Average high school GPA:* 3.44. *Test scores:* SAT critical reading scores over 500:

60%; SAT math scores over 500: 49%; ACT scores over 18: 90%; SAT critical reading scores over 600: 20%; SAT math scores over 600: 23%; ACT scores over 24: 33%; ACT scores over 30: 7%.

Faculty *Total:* 275, 69% full-time, 52% with terminal degrees. *Student/faculty ratio:* 13:1.

Academics *Calendar:* semesters. *Degrees:* associate, bachelor's, master's, doctoral, post-master's, and first professional certificates. *Special study options:* academic remediation for entering students, accelerated degree program, adult/continuing education programs, advanced placement credit, distance learning, double majors, English as a second language, honors programs, independent study, internships, part-time degree program, summer session for credit.

Computers on Campus Students can access the following: campus intranet, computer help desk, free student e-mail accounts, online (class) grades, online (class) registration, online (class) schedules. Campuswide network is available. 100% of college-owned or -operated housing units are wired for high-speed Internet access.

Student Life *Housing options:* coed, men-only, women-only, disabled students. Campus housing is university owned. *Activities and organizations:* drama/theater group, student-run radio and television station, choral group, Students in Free Enterprise (SIFE), Baptist Campus Ministries, Pre-Med Club, Fishing Club, Earth Club. *Campus security:* 24-hour emergency response devices and patrols. *Student services:* health clinic, personal/psychological counseling.

Athletics Member NCAA. All Division II. *Intercollegiate sports:* baseball M(s), basketball M(s)/W(s), cross-country running M(s)/W(s), golf M(s)/W(s), soccer M(s)/W(s), softball W(s), tennis M(s)/W(s), volleyball W(s). *Intramural sports:* basketball M/W, football M/W, soccer M/W, softball M/W, swimming and diving M/W, table tennis M/W, tennis M/W, ultimate Frisbee M/W, volleyball M/W.

Standardized Tests *Required:* SAT or ACT (for admission).

Costs (2011–12) *Comprehensive fee:* $23,940 includes full-time tuition ($17,520), mandatory fees ($200), and room and board ($6220). Part-time tuition: $730 per credit hour. Part-time tuition and fees vary according to course load. *Room and board:* Room and board charges vary according to board plan and housing facility. *Payment plan:* installment. *Waivers:* senior citizens and employees or children of employees.

Financial Aid Of all full-time matriculated undergraduates who enrolled in 2010, 1,426 applied for aid, 1,257 were judged to have need, 240 had their need fully met. In 2010, 155 non-need-based awards were made. *Average percent of need met:* 74%. *Average financial aid package:* $17,321. *Average need-based loan:* $3872. *Average need-based gift aid:* $13,112. *Average non-need-based aid:* $8412. *Average indebtedness upon graduation:* $21,749.

Applying *Options:* electronic application. *Application fee:* $25. *Required:* high school transcript, minimum 2.3 GPA, immunization records, financial aid application. *Application deadlines:* rolling (freshmen), rolling (transfers). *Notification:* continuous (freshmen), continuous (transfers).

Freshman Application Contact Lincoln Memorial University, 6965 Cumberland Gap Parkway, Harrogate, TN 37752-1901. *Phone:* 423-869-6280. *Toll-free phone:* 800-325-0900. *Web site:* http://www.lmunet.edu/.

Lipscomb University

Nashville, Tennessee

- **Independent** comprehensive, founded 1891, affiliated with Church of Christ
- **Suburban** 65-acre campus
- **Endowment** $59.6 million
- **Coed** 2,675 undergraduate students, 92% full-time, 58% women, 42% men
- **Moderately difficult** entrance level, 51% of applicants were admitted

Undergraduates 2,451 full-time, 224 part-time. Students come from 46 states and territories; 23 other countries; 32% are from out of state; 9% Black or African American, non-Hispanic/Latino; 4% Hispanic/Latino; 3% Asian, non-Hispanic/Latino; 0.1% Native Hawaiian or other Pacific Islander, non-Hispanic/Latino; 0.2% American Indian or Alaska Native, non-Hispanic/Latino; 0.6% Two or more races, non-Hispanic/Latino; 4% Race/ethnicity unknown; 2% international; 5% transferred in; 53% live on campus. *Retention:* 71% of full-time freshmen returned.

Freshmen *Admission:* 3,430 applied, 1,758 admitted, 629 enrolled. *Average high school GPA:* 3.5. *Test scores:* SAT critical reading scores over 500: 72%; SAT math scores over 500: 74%; ACT scores over 18: 98%; SAT critical reading scores over 600: 29%; SAT math scores over 600: 32%; ACT scores over 24: 61%; SAT critical reading scores over 700: 8%; SAT math scores over 700: 5%; ACT scores over 30: 18%.

Faculty *Total:* 417, 41% full-time, 60% with terminal degrees. *Student/faculty ratio:* 13:1.

Academics *Calendar:* semesters. *Degrees:* bachelor's, master's, doctoral, and postbachelor's certificates. *Special study options:* academic remediation for entering students, accelerated degree program, adult/continuing education programs, advanced placement credit, distance learning, double majors, freshman honors college, honors programs, independent study, internships, part-time degree program, services for LD students, study abroad, summer session for credit. *ROTC:* Army (c), Air Force (c).

Computers on Campus 175 computers/terminals are available on campus for general student use. Students can access the following: campus intranet, computer help desk, free student e-mail accounts, online (class) grades, online (class) registration, online (class) schedules. Campuswide network is available. 100% of college-owned or -operated housing units are wired for high-speed Internet access. Wireless service is available via entire campus.

Student Life *Housing:* on-campus residence required through junior year. *Options:* men-only, women-only. Campus housing is university owned. Freshman applicants given priority for college housing. *Activities and organizations:* drama/theater group, student-run newspaper, radio and television station, choral group, Sigma Pi Beta, business fraternities, Multicultural Association, Alpha Phi Chi men's service club, Pi Kappa Sigma women's service club. *Campus security:* 24-hour emergency response devices and patrols, late-night transport/escort service, controlled dormitory access. *Student services:* health clinic, personal/psychological counseling.

Athletics Member NCAA. All Division I. *Intercollegiate sports:* baseball M(s), basketball M(s)/W(s), cross-country running M(s)/W(s), golf M(s)/W(s), soccer M(s)/W(s), softball W(s), tennis M(s)/W(s), track and field M(s)/W(s), volleyball W(s). *Intramural sports:* badminton M/W, basketball M/W, football M/W, racquetball M/W, soccer M/W, softball M/W, table tennis M/W, ultimate Frisbee M/W, volleyball M/W.

Standardized Tests *Required:* SAT or ACT (for admission).

Costs (2012–13) *Comprehensive fee:* $33,878 includes full-time tuition ($22,978), mandatory fees ($1676), and room and board ($9224). Full-time tuition and fees vary according to course load. Part-time tuition: $550 per hour. Part-time tuition and fees vary according to course load. *Required fees:* $70 part-time. *College room only:* $5184. Room and board charges vary according to board plan and housing facility. *Payment plans:* installment, deferred payment. *Waivers:* employees or children of employees.

Financial Aid Of all full-time matriculated undergraduates who enrolled in 2010, 2,297 applied for aid, 1,616 were judged to have need, 414 had their need fully met. In 2010, 387 non-need-based awards were made. *Average percent of need met:* 62%. *Average financial aid package:* $18,174. *Average need-based loan:* $5366. *Average need-based gift aid:* $6804. *Average non-need-based aid:* $6992. *Average indebtedness upon graduation:* $21,034.

Applying *Options:* electronic application, early admission, deferred entrance. *Application fee:* $50. *Required:* high school transcript, minimum 2.3 GPA, 1 letter of recommendation, interview. *Recommended:* essay or personal statement. *Application deadlines:* rolling (freshmen), rolling (transfers). *Notification:* continuous (freshmen), continuous (transfers).

Freshman Application Contact Office of Admissions, Lipscomb University, One University Park Drive, Nashville, TN 37204-3951. *Phone:* 615-966-1776. *Toll-free phone:* 877-582-4766. *Fax:* 615-966-1804. *E-mail:* admissions@lipscomb.edu. *Web site:* http://www.lipscomb.edu/.

Martin Methodist College
Pulaski, Tennessee

Freshman Application Contact Lisa Smith, Director of Admissions, Martin Methodist College, 433 West Madison Street, Pulaski, TN 38478-2716. *Phone:* 931-363-9868. *Toll-free phone:* 800-467-1273. *Fax:* 931-363-9818. *E-mail:* admit@martinmethodist.edu. *Web site:* http://www.martinmethodist.edu/.

Maryville College
Maryville, Tennessee

- **Independent Presbyterian** 4-year, founded 1819
- **Suburban** 350-acre campus
- **Endowment** $57.6 million
- **Coed** 1,078 undergraduate students, 96% full-time, 54% women, 46% men
- **Moderately difficult** entrance level, 66% of applicants were admitted

Undergraduates 1,032 full-time, 46 part-time. Students come from 28 states and territories; 20 other countries; 19% are from out of state; 6% Black or African American, non-Hispanic/Latino; 3% Hispanic/Latino; 1% Asian, non-Hispanic/Latino; 0.1% Native Hawaiian or other Pacific Islander, non-Hispanic/Latino; 0.8% American Indian or Alaska Native, non-Hispanic/Latino; 0.8% Two or more races, non-Hispanic/Latino; 0.3% Race/ethnicity unknown; 4% international; 3% transferred in; 71% live on campus. *Retention:* 71% of full-time freshmen returned.

Freshmen *Admission:* 1,998 applied, 1,325 admitted, 293 enrolled. *Average high school GPA:* 3.5. *Test scores:* SAT critical reading scores over 500: 71%; SAT math scores over 500: 67%; ACT scores over 18: 100%; SAT critical reading scores over 600: 30%; SAT math scores over 600: 29%; ACT scores over 24: 59%; SAT critical reading scores over 700: 8%; ACT scores over 30: 13%.

Faculty *Total:* 107, 67% full-time, 78% with terminal degrees. *Student/faculty ratio:* 12:1.

Academics *Calendar:* 4-1-4. *Degree:* bachelor's. *Special study options:* academic remediation for entering students, advanced placement credit, double majors, English as a second language, honors programs, independent study, internships, off-campus study, part-time degree program, services for LD students, student-designed majors, study abroad, summer session for credit. *Unusual degree programs:* 3-2 engineering with Vanderbilt University, Washington University in St. Louis, Auburn University, Tennessee Technological University; nursing with Vanderbilt University.

Computers on Campus 290 computers/terminals are available on campus for general student use. Students can access the following: campus intranet, computer help desk, free student e-mail accounts, online (class) registration, online (class) schedules. Campuswide network is available. 100% of college-owned or -operated housing units are wired for high-speed Internet access. Wireless service is available via entire campus.

Student Life *Housing:* on-campus residence required through senior year. *Options:* coed, men-only, women-only, disabled students. Campus housing is university owned. Freshman campus housing is guaranteed. *Activities and organizations:* drama/theater group, student-run newspaper, choral group, Voices of Praise, student government, Student Programming Board, Global Citizenship, Peer Mentors. *Campus security:* 24-hour emergency response devices and patrols, late-night transport/escort service, controlled dormitory access, campus-wide emergency alert system via cell phones, home phones, and email. *Student services:* health clinic, personal/psychological counseling.

Athletics Member NCAA. All Division III. *Intercollegiate sports:* baseball M, basketball M/W, cheerleading M/W, cross-country running M/W, equestrian sports M(c)/W(c), football M, golf M/W, soccer M/W, softball W, swimming and diving M/W, tennis M/W, ultimate Frisbee M(c)/W(c), volleyball W. *Intramural sports:* archery M/W, badminton M/W, basketball M/W, bowling M/W, football M/W, racquetball M/W, rugby M/W, skiing (downhill) M/W, soccer M/W, softball M/W, table tennis M/W, tennis M/W, track and field M/W, ultimate Frisbee M/W, volleyball M/W, water polo M/W.

Standardized Tests *Required:* SAT or ACT (for admission).

Costs (2012–13) *Comprehensive fee:* $40,218 includes full-time tuition ($29,814), mandatory fees ($708), and room and board ($9696). Full-time tuition and fees vary according to course load. Part-time tuition and fees vary according to course load. *College room only:* $4812. Room and board charges vary according to board plan and housing facility. *Payment plan:* installment. *Waivers:* employees or children of employees.

Financial Aid Of all full-time matriculated undergraduates who enrolled in 2011, 1,032 applied for aid, 883 were judged to have need, 214 had their need fully met. 536 Federal Work-Study jobs (averaging $1702). 62 state and other part-time jobs (averaging $1770). In 2011, 123 non-need-based awards were made. *Average percent of need met:* 85%. *Average financial aid package:* $27,971. *Average need-based loan:* $4438. *Average need-based gift aid:* $24,295. *Average non-need-based aid:* $15,590. *Average indebtedness upon graduation:* $26,452.

Applying *Options:* electronic application, early admission, deferred entrance. *Required:* essay or personal statement, high school transcript, minimum 2.5 GPA. *Required for some:* interview. *Recommended:* minimum 3.0 GPA. *Application deadlines:* 3/1 (freshmen), rolling (transfers). *Notification:* continuous until 4/1 (freshmen).

Freshman Application Contact Ms. Linda L. Moore, Administrative Assistant of Admissions, Maryville College, 502 East Lamar Alexander Parkway, Maryville, TN 37804-5907. *Phone:* 865-981-8096. *Toll-free phone:* 800-597-2687. *Fax:* 865-981-8005. *E-mail:* admissions@maryvillecollege.edu. *Web site:* http://www.maryvillecollege.edu/.

Memphis College of Art
Memphis, Tennessee

- **Independent** comprehensive, founded 1936
- **Urban** 200-acre campus
- **Coed** 377 undergraduate students, 91% full-time, 64% women, 36% men
- **Moderately difficult** entrance level, 45% of applicants were admitted

Undergraduates 343 full-time, 34 part-time. Students come from 26 states and territories; 7 other countries; 55% are from out of state; 18% Black or African American, non-Hispanic/Latino; 6% Hispanic/Latino; 2% Asian, non-Hispanic/Latino; 5% Two or more races, non-Hispanic/Latino; 2% Race/ethnicity

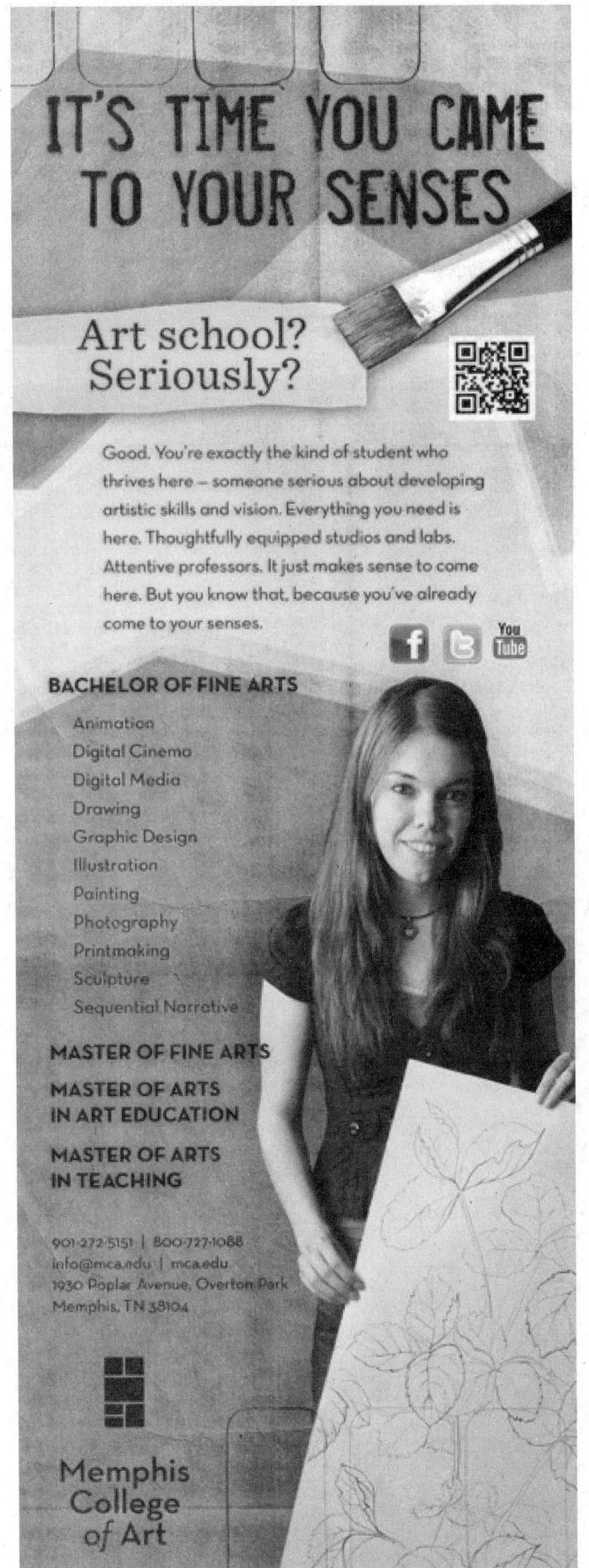

unknown; 2% international; 6% transferred in; 44% live on campus. *Retention:* 76% of full-time freshmen returned.

Freshmen *Admission:* 544 applied, 247 admitted, 94 enrolled. *Average high school GPA:* 3.14. *Test scores:* ACT scores over 18: 91%; ACT scores over 24: 26%; ACT scores over 30: 3%.

Faculty *Total:* 61, 43% full-time, 56% with terminal degrees. *Student/faculty ratio:* 10:1.

Academics *Calendar:* semesters. *Degrees:* bachelor's and master's. *Special study options:* academic remediation for entering students, adult/continuing education programs, advanced placement credit, independent study, internships, off-campus study, part-time degree program, services for LD students, study abroad, summer session for credit.

Computers on Campus 100 computers/terminals and 20 ports are available on campus for general student use. Students can access the following: free student e-mail accounts, online (class) schedules. Wireless service is available via entire campus.

Student Life *Housing:* on-campus residence required for freshman year. *Options:* coed. Campus housing is university owned. Freshman campus housing is guaranteed. *Activities and organizations:* student-run newspaper, Student Alliance, Photo Club, Design Club-AIGA, Clay Club. *Campus security:* 24-hour emergency response devices and patrols, late-night transport/escort service, controlled dormitory access. *Student services:* personal/psychological counseling.

Standardized Tests *Required:* SAT or ACT (for admission).

Costs (2012–13) *Comprehensive fee:* $34,250 includes full-time tuition ($25,600), mandatory fees ($650), and room and board ($8000). Full-time tuition and fees vary according to program. Part-time tuition: $1117 per credit. Part-time tuition and fees vary according to course load and program. *Required fees:* $650 per year part-time. *College room only:* $6000. Room and board charges vary according to housing facility. *Payment plan:* installment. *Waivers:* employees or children of employees.

Financial Aid Of all full-time matriculated undergraduates who enrolled in 2009, 302 applied for aid, 277 were judged to have need, 64 had their need fully met. 340 Federal Work-Study jobs (averaging $500). In 2009, 40 non-need-based awards were made. *Average percent of need met:* 80%. *Average financial aid package:* $10,862. *Average need-based loan:* $5500. *Average need-based gift aid:* $6252. *Average non-need-based aid:* $9000. *Average indebtedness upon graduation:* $34,360.

Applying *Options:* electronic application, deferred entrance. *Application fee:* $25. *Required:* high school transcript, minimum 2.0 GPA, portfolio. *Recommended:* essay or personal statement, interview. *Application deadlines:* rolling (freshmen), rolling (transfers). *Notification:* continuous (freshmen), continuous (transfers).

Freshman Application Contact Memphis College of Art, Overton Park, 1930 Poplar Avenue, Memphis, TN 38104-2764. *Phone:* 901-272-5153. *Toll-free phone:* 800-727-1088. *Web site:* http://www.mca.edu/.

See page 1438 for the College Close-Up.

Mid-America Baptist Theological Seminary
Cordova, Tennessee

Freshman Application Contact Mr. Duffy Guyton, Director of Admissions, Mid-America Baptist Theological Seminary, PO Box 2350, Cordova, TN 38016. *Phone:* 901-751-8453 Ext. 3066. *Toll-free phone:* 800-968-4508. *Fax:* 901-751-8454. *E-mail:* info@mabts.edu. *Web site:* http://www.mabts.edu/.

Middle Tennessee State University
Murfreesboro, Tennessee

- **State-supported** university, founded 1911, part of Tennessee Board of Regents
- **Urban** 500-acre campus with easy access to Nashville
- **Endowment** $64.6 million
- **Coed** 23,415 undergraduate students, 83% full-time, 52% women, 48% men
- **Moderately difficult** entrance level, 70% of applicants were admitted

Undergraduates 19,408 full-time, 4,007 part-time. 4% are from out of state; 18% Black or African American, non-Hispanic/Latino; 3% Hispanic/Latino; 3% Asian, non-Hispanic/Latino; 0.1% Native Hawaiian or other Pacific Islander, non-Hispanic/Latino; 0.3% American Indian or Alaska Native, non-Hispanic/Latino; 2% Two or more races, non-Hispanic/Latino; 2% Race/ethnicity unknown; 9% transferred in; 17% live on campus.

Freshmen *Admission:* 10,814 applied, 7,600 admitted, 3,439 enrolled. *Test scores:* SAT critical reading scores over 500: 62%; SAT math scores over 500: 57%; ACT scores over 18: 91%; SAT critical reading scores over 600: 25%;

SAT math scores over 600: 23%; ACT scores over 24: 32%; SAT critical reading scores over 700: 7%; SAT math scores over 700: 2%; ACT scores over 30: 4%.

Academics *Calendar:* semesters. *Degrees:* bachelor's, master's, doctoral, post-master's, postbachelor's, and first professional certificates. *Special study options:* adult/continuing education programs, part-time degree program. *ROTC:* Army (b), Air Force (c). *Unusual degree programs:* 3-2 engineering with University of Tennessee, Knoxville; Georgia Institute of Technology; Tennessee Technological University; The University of Memphis; Tennessee State University; Vanderbilt University.

Computers on Campus Students can access the following: online (class) registration. Campuswide network is available.

Student Life *Housing options:* coed, men-only, women-only. Campus housing is university owned. *Activities and organizations:* drama/theater group, student-run newspaper, radio and television station, choral group, marching band, national fraternities, national sororities. *Campus security:* 24-hour emergency response devices and patrols, student patrols, late-night transport/escort service, controlled dormitory access. *Student services:* health clinic, personal/psychological counseling, women's center, legal services.

Athletics Member NCAA. All Division I except football (Division I-A). *Intercollegiate sports:* baseball M(s), basketball M(s)/W(s), cheerleading M(s)/W(s), cross-country running M(s)/W(s), equestrian sports M/W, golf M(s), soccer W(s), softball W(s), tennis M(s)/W(s), track and field M(s)/W(s), volleyball W(s). *Intramural sports:* badminton M/W, basketball M/W, bowling M(c)/W(c), fencing M(c)/W(c), field hockey M(c)/W(c), football M, ice hockey M(c), lacrosse M(c)/W(c), racquetball M(c)/W(c), riflery M, rugby M(c)/W(c), soccer M(c)/W, softball M/W, swimming and diving M/W, tennis M/W, ultimate Frisbee M(c)/W(c), volleyball M(c)/W(c), wrestling M(c)/W(c).

Standardized Tests *Required:* SAT or ACT (for admission).

Costs (2011–12) *Tuition:* state resident $5520 full-time, $219 per credit hour part-time; nonresident $19,908 full-time, $790 per credit hour part-time. Full-time tuition and fees vary according to course load. Part-time tuition and fees vary according to course load. *Required fees:* $1498 full-time. *Room and board:* $8843; room only: $5528. Room and board charges vary according to board plan and housing facility.

Financial Aid Of all full-time matriculated undergraduates who enrolled in 2011, 17,332 applied for aid, 13,526 were judged to have need, 1,909 had their need fully met. 189 Federal Work-Study jobs (averaging $3750). In 2011, 915 non-need-based awards were made. *Average percent of need met:* 65%. *Average financial aid package:* $12,429. *Average need-based loan:* $3892. *Average need-based gift aid:* $5231. *Average non-need-based aid:* $2688. *Average indebtedness upon graduation:* $21,484.

Applying *Application fee:* $25. *Required:* high school transcript, minimum 3.0 GPA. *Required for some:* essay or personal statement. *Application deadlines:* rolling (freshmen), rolling (transfers). *Notification:* continuous (freshmen), continuous (transfers).

Freshman Application Contact Director of Admissions, Middle Tennessee State University, 1301 East Main Street, Murfreesboro, TN 37132. *Phone:* 615-898-2111. *Toll-free phone:* 800-331-MTSU. *Fax:* 615-898-5478. *E-mail:* admissions@mtsu.edu. *Web site:* http://www.mtsu.edu/.

Milligan College
Milligan College, Tennessee

- **Independent Christian** comprehensive, founded 1866
- **Suburban** 181-acre campus
- **Endowment** $17.3 million
- **Coed** 984 undergraduate students, 92% full-time, 60% women, 40% men
- **Moderately difficult** entrance level, 70% of applicants were admitted

Undergraduates 901 full-time, 83 part-time. Students come from 34 states and territories; 16 other countries; 35% are from out of state; 5% Black or African American, non-Hispanic/Latino; 3% Hispanic/Latino; 0.7% Asian, non-Hispanic/Latino; 0.4% American Indian or Alaska Native, non-Hispanic/Latino; 2% Two or more races, non-Hispanic/Latino; 1% Race/ethnicity unknown; 2% international; 9% transferred in; 74% live on campus. *Retention:* 80% of full-time freshmen returned.

Freshmen *Admission:* 603 applied, 424 admitted, 204 enrolled. *Average high school GPA:* 3.7. *Test scores:* SAT critical reading scores over 500: 71%; SAT math scores over 500: 72%; SAT writing scores over 500: 64%; ACT scores over 18: 97%; SAT critical reading scores over 600: 26%; SAT math scores over 600: 33%; SAT writing scores over 600: 19%; ACT scores over 24: 53%; SAT critical reading scores over 700: 1%; SAT math scores over 700: 3%; SAT writing scores over 700: 1%; ACT scores over 30: 10%.

Faculty *Total:* 134, 51% full-time, 54% with terminal degrees. *Student/faculty ratio:* 13:1.

Academics *Calendar:* semesters. *Degrees:* bachelor's and master's. *Special study options:* academic remediation for entering students, adult/continuing education programs, advanced placement credit, cooperative education, distance learning, double majors, independent study, internships, off-campus study, part-time degree program, study abroad, summer session for credit.

ROTC: Army (c). *Unusual degree programs:* 3-2 pharmacy with Gatton College of Pharmacy at East Tennessee State University.

Computers on Campus 97 computers/terminals are available on campus for general student use. Students can access the following: campus intranet, computer help desk, free student e-mail accounts, online (class) grades, online (class) registration, online (class) schedules. Campuswide network is available. 100% of college-owned or -operated housing units are wired for high-speed Internet access. Wireless service is available via classrooms, computer centers, computer labs, dorm rooms, libraries, student centers.

Student Life *Housing:* on-campus residence required through senior year. *Options:* men-only, women-only. Campus housing is university owned. Freshman campus housing is guaranteed. *Activities and organizations:* drama/theater group, student-run newspaper, radio station, choral group, Social Affairs Committee, Buffalo Ramblers, Concert Council, Volunteer Milligan, Students for Life. *Campus security:* 24-hour emergency response devices and patrols, late-night transport/escort service. *Student services:* health clinic, personal/psychological counseling.

Athletics Member NAIA. *Intercollegiate sports:* baseball M(s), basketball M(s)/W(s), cross-country running M(s)/W(s), golf M(s)/W(s), soccer M(s)/W(s), softball W(s), swimming and diving M(s)/W(s), tennis M(s)/W(s), volleyball W(s). *Intramural sports:* basketball M/W, cheerleading W, football M/W, softball M/W, swimming and diving M/W, table tennis M/W, tennis M/W, ultimate Frisbee M/W, volleyball M/W, weight lifting M/W.

Standardized Tests *Required:* SAT or ACT (for admission).

Costs (2011–12) *One-time required fee:* $75. *Comprehensive fee:* $30,910 includes full-time tuition ($24,360), mandatory fees ($900), and room and board ($5650). Full-time tuition and fees vary according to course load. Part-time tuition: $360 per credit hour. Part-time tuition and fees vary according to course load. *College room only:* $2650. Room and board charges vary according to housing facility. *Payment plan:* installment. *Waivers:* employees or children of employees.

Financial Aid Of all full-time matriculated undergraduates who enrolled in 2011, 822 applied for aid, 736 were judged to have need, 185 had their need fully met. 183 Federal Work-Study jobs (averaging $1200). 149 state and other part-time jobs (averaging $1552). In 2011, 103 non-need-based awards were made. *Average percent of need met:* 76%. *Average financial aid package:* $18,620. *Average need-based loan:* $4740. *Average need-based gift aid:* $15,380. *Average non-need-based aid:* $7606. *Average indebtedness upon graduation:* $18,394.

Applying *Options:* electronic application, deferred entrance. *Application fee:* $30. *Required:* essay or personal statement, high school transcript, minimum 2.0 GPA, 2 letters of recommendation. *Required for some:* interview. *Recommended:* minimum 3.0 GPA. *Application deadlines:* 8/1 (freshmen), rolling (transfers). *Notification:* continuous (freshmen), continuous (transfers).

Freshman Application Contact Ms. Tracy Brinn, Director of Enrollment Management, Milligan College, PO Box 210, Milligan College, TN 37682. *Phone:* 423-461-8730. *Toll-free phone:* 800-262-8337. *Fax:* 423-461-8982. *E-mail:* admissions@milligan.edu. *Web site:* http://www.milligan.edu/.

See page 1454 for the College Close-Up.

National College

Bristol, Tennessee

Freshman Application Contact National College, 1328 Highway 11 West, Bristol, TN 37620. *Phone:* 423-878-4440. *Toll-free phone:* 888-9-JOBREADY. *Web site:* http://www.national-college.edu/.

Nossi College of Art

Goodlettsville, Tennessee

- **Independent** primarily 2-year
- **Urban** 10-acre campus with easy access to Nashville
- **Coed**
- 63% of applicants were admitted

Faculty *Student/faculty ratio:* 10:1.

Academics *Calendar:* semesters. *Degrees:* associate and bachelor's.

Student Life *Campus security:* campus has a gated entrance, all doors are kept locked.

Costs (2011–12) *Tuition:* $14,100 full-time, $4700 per term part-time. Full-time tuition and fees vary according to course load, degree level, and program. Part-time tuition and fees vary according to course load, degree level, and program. No tuition increase for student's term of enrollment.

Applying *Options:* electronic application, early admission. *Application fee:* $100. *Required:* essay or personal statement, high school transcript, interview, portfolio of work is required for Associate or Bachelor of Graphic Art and Design program and the Bachelor of Illustration program.

Freshman Application Contact Ms. Mary Alexander, Admissions Director, Nossi College of Art, 590 Cheron Road, Madison, TN 37115. *Phone:* 615-

514-2787 (ARTS). *Toll-free phone:* 888-986-ARTS. *Fax:* 615-514-2788. *E-mail:* admissions@nossi.edu. *Web site:* http://www.nossi.edu/.

O'More College of Design

Franklin, Tennessee

- **Independent** 4-year, founded 1970
- **Small-town** 6-acre campus with easy access to Nashville
- **Coed, primarily women** 191 undergraduate students, 86% full-time, 87% women, 13% men
- **Moderately difficult** entrance level, 49% of applicants were admitted

Undergraduates 165 full-time, 26 part-time. Students come from 1 other state; 6 other countries; 4% Black or African American, non-Hispanic/Latino; 3% Hispanic/Latino; 1% Asian, non-Hispanic/Latino; 1% American Indian or Alaska Native, non-Hispanic/Latino; 2% Race/ethnicity unknown; 2% international; 13% transferred in. *Retention:* 82% of full-time freshmen returned.

Freshmen *Admission:* 61 applied, 30 admitted, 21 enrolled. *Average high school GPA:* 3.3. *Test scores:* ACT scores over 18: 100%; ACT scores over 24: 40%; ACT scores over 30: 3%.

Faculty *Total:* 40, 30% full-time, 20% with terminal degrees. *Student/faculty ratio:* 7:1.

Academics *Calendar:* semesters. *Degree:* bachelor's. *Special study options:* advanced placement credit, cooperative education, double majors, independent study, internships, off-campus study, part-time degree program, study abroad, summer session for credit.

Computers on Campus 20 computers/terminals and 16 ports are available on campus for general student use. Students can access the following: free student e-mail accounts, library card catalog. Campuswide network is available. Wireless service is available via entire campus.

Student Life *Housing:* college housing not available. *Options:* Campus housing is provided by a third party. *Activities and organizations:* American Society for Interior Design, Student Government Association, O'More Fashion Merchandising Association, Visual Communications Forum, International Interior Design Association. *Campus security:* 24-hour emergency response devices and patrols, security cards at The Factory campus (off-campus).

Standardized Tests *Required:* SAT or ACT (for admission).

Costs (2012–13) *Tuition:* $25,000 full-time, $1041 per hour part-time. Part-time tuition and fees vary according to course load. *Payment plan:* installment. *Waivers:* employees or children of employees.

Applying *Options:* electronic application, deferred entrance. *Application fee:* $50. *Required:* essay or personal statement, high school transcript, minimum 2.7 GPA, Departmental Requirement for Admissions. *Required for some:* interview. *Application deadlines:* 7/31 (freshmen), 7/31 (out-of-state freshmen), 7/31 (transfers). *Notification:* continuous (freshmen), continuous (out-of-state freshmen), continuous (transfers).

Freshman Application Contact Mrs. Melinda Dabbs, Assistant Director of Enrollment, O'More College of Design, 423 South Margin Street, Franklin, TN 37064-2816. *Phone:* 615-794-4254 Ext. 229. *Toll-free phone:* 888-662-1970. *Fax:* 615-790-1662. *E-mail:* meldabbs@omorecollege.edu. *Web site:* http://www.omorecollege.edu/.

Remington College–Memphis Campus

Memphis, Tennessee

Director of Admissions Randal Hayes, Director of Recruitment, Remington College–Memphis Campus, 2731 Nonconnah Boulevard, Memphis, TN 38132-2131. *Phone:* 901-345-1000. *Fax:* 901-396-8310. *E-mail:* randal.hayes@remingtoncollege.edu. *Web site:* http://www.remingtoncollege.edu/.

Rhodes College

Memphis, Tennessee

- **Independent** comprehensive, founded 1848
- **Suburban** 100-acre campus
- **Coed** 1,820 undergraduate students, 99% full-time, 60% women, 40% men
- **Very difficult** entrance level, 50% of applicants were admitted

Undergraduates 1,806 full-time, 14 part-time. 73% are from out of state; 7% Black or African American, non-Hispanic/Latino; 3% Hispanic/Latino; 5% Asian, non-Hispanic/Latino; 0.7% American Indian or Alaska Native, non-Hispanic/Latino; 2% Two or more races, non-Hispanic/Latino; 5% Race/ethnicity unknown; 3% international; 0.8% transferred in; 69% live on campus. *Retention:* 90% of full-time freshmen returned.

Freshmen *Admission:* 5,211 applied, 2,617 admitted, 554 enrolled. *Average high school GPA:* 3.83. *Test scores:* SAT critical reading scores over 500:

98%; SAT math scores over 500: 97%; ACT scores over 18: 100%; SAT critical reading scores over 600: 73%; SAT math scores over 600: 73%; ACT scores over 24: 98%; SAT critical reading scores over 700: 23%; SAT math scores over 700: 20%; ACT scores over 30: 37%.

Faculty *Total:* 205, 83% full-time, 87% with terminal degrees. *Student/faculty ratio:* 10:1.

Academics *Calendar:* semesters. *Degrees:* bachelor's and master's (master's degree in accounting only). *Special study options:* part-time degree program. *ROTC:* Army (c), Air Force (c). *Unusual degree programs:* 3-2 engineering with Washington University in St. Louis.

Computers on Campus Students can access the following: computer help desk, free student e-mail accounts, online (class) grades, online (class) registration, online (class) schedules. Campuswide network is available. Wireless service is available via entire campus.

Student Life *Housing:* on-campus residence required through sophomore year. *Options:* coed, men-only, women-only. Campus housing is university owned. Freshman campus housing is guaranteed. *Activities and organizations:* drama/theater group, student-run newspaper, radio and television station, choral group, national fraternities, national sororities. *Campus security:* 24-hour emergency response devices and patrols, student patrols, late-night transport/escort service, 24-hour monitored security cameras in parking areas, fenced campus with monitored access at night. *Student services:* health clinic, personal/psychological counseling, women's center.

Athletics Member NCAA. All Division III. *Intercollegiate sports:* baseball M, basketball M/W, cheerleading W(c), cross-country running M/W, field hockey W, football M, golf M/W, lacrosse M(c)/W(c), rugby M(c), soccer M/W, softball W, swimming and diving M/W, tennis M/W, track and field M/W, volleyball W. *Intramural sports:* basketball M/W, football M/W, racquetball M/W, soccer M/W, softball M/W, squash M, volleyball M/W.

Standardized Tests *Required:* SAT or ACT (for admission).

Costs (2011–12) *Comprehensive fee:* $43,060 includes full-time tuition ($34,270), mandatory fees ($310), and room and board ($8480). Part-time tuition: $1520 per credit hour. *Room and board:* Room and board charges vary according to board plan and housing facility. *Payment plan:* installment. *Waivers:* employees or children of employees.

Financial Aid Of all full-time matriculated undergraduates who enrolled in 2011, 1,182 applied for aid, 882 were judged to have need, 457 had their need fully met. In 2011, 758 non-need-based awards were made. *Average percent of need met:* 92%. *Average financial aid package:* $34,597. *Average need-based loan:* $5164. *Average need-based gift aid:* $25,727. *Average non-need-based aid:* $15,896. *Average indebtedness upon graduation:* $26,147. *Financial aid deadline:* 3/1.

Applying *Options:* electronic application, early admission, early decision, early action, deferred entrance. *Application fee:* $45. *Required:* essay or personal statement, high school transcript, 2 letters of recommendation. *Recommended:* interview. *Application deadlines:* 1/15 (freshmen), 1/15 (transfers), 11/15 (early action). *Early decision deadline:* 11/1 (for plan 1), 1/1 (for plan 2). *Notification:* 4/1 (freshmen), 4/1 (transfers), 12/1 (early decision plan 1), 2/1 (early decision plan 2), 1/15 (early action).

Freshman Application Contact Rhodes College, 2000 North Parkway, Memphis, TN 38112-1690. *Phone:* 901-843-3700. *Toll-free phone:* 800-844-5969. *Web site:* http://www.rhodes.edu/.

Sewanee: The University of the South

Sewanee, Tennessee

- **Independent Episcopal** comprehensive, founded 1857
- **Small-town** 13,000-acre campus
- **Endowment** $272.5 million
- **Coed** 1,477 undergraduate students, 99% full-time, 51% women, 49% men
- **Very difficult** entrance level, 61% of applicants were admitted

Undergraduates 1,459 full-time, 18 part-time. Students come from 41 states and territories; 23 other countries; 75% are from out of state; 4% Black or African American, non-Hispanic/Latino; 4% Hispanic/Latino; 2% Asian, non-Hispanic/Latino; 0.1% Native Hawaiian or other Pacific Islander, non-Hispanic/Latino; 0.1% American Indian or Alaska Native, non-Hispanic/Latino; 4% Two or more races, non-Hispanic/Latino; 0.6% Race/ethnicity unknown; 3% international; 0.7% transferred in; 96% live on campus. *Retention:* 90% of full-time freshmen returned.

Freshmen *Admission:* 2,920 applied, 1,793 admitted, 433 enrolled. *Average high school GPA:* 3.61. *Test scores:* SAT critical reading scores over 500: 97%; SAT math scores over 500: 97%; SAT writing scores over 500: 93%;

ACT scores over 18: 100%; SAT critical reading scores over 600: 68%; SAT math scores over 600: 56%; SAT writing scores over 600: 62%; ACT scores over 24: 95%; SAT critical reading scores over 700: 18%; SAT math scores over 700: 12%; SAT writing scores over 700: 14%; ACT scores over 30: 31%.

Faculty *Total:* 172, 80% full-time, 91% with terminal degrees. *Student/faculty ratio:* 10:1.

Academics *Calendar:* semesters. *Degrees:* bachelor's, master's, doctoral, post-master's, and postbachelor's certificates. *Special study options:* advanced placement credit, double majors, independent study, internships, services for LD students, student-designed majors, study abroad, summer session for credit. *Unusual degree programs:* 3-2 engineering with Washington University in St. Louis, Vanderbilt University, Rensselaer Polytechnic Institute, Columbia University; forestry with Duke University.

Computers on Campus 340 computers/terminals are available on campus for general student use. Students can access the following: campus intranet, computer help desk, free student e-mail accounts, online (class) grades, online (class) registration, online (class) schedules. Campuswide network is available. 100% of college-owned or -operated housing units are wired for high-speed Internet access. Wireless service is available via entire campus.

Student Life *Housing:* on-campus residence required through senior year. *Options:* coed, men-only, women-only, disabled students. Campus housing is university owned. Freshman campus housing is guaranteed. *Activities and organizations:* drama/theater group, student-run newspaper, radio station, choral group, Sewanee Outing Program, Community Service Council, Student Activities Programming Board, student radio station, BACCHUS (alcohol and drug education), national fraternities. *Campus security:* 24-hour emergency response devices and patrols, late-night transport/escort service, controlled dormitory access, security lighting. *Student services:* health clinic, personal/psychological counseling, women's center, legal services.

Athletics Member NCAA. All Division III. *Intercollegiate sports:* baseball M, basketball M/W, crew M(c)/W(c), cross-country running M/W, equestrian sports M(c)/W(c), fencing M(c)/W(c), field hockey W, football M, golf M/W, lacrosse M(c)/W(c), rugby M(c), soccer M/W, softball W(c), swimming and diving M/W, tennis M/W, track and field M/W, volleyball W. *Intramural sports:* basketball M/W, cross-country running M/W, football M, golf M/W, racquetball M/W, soccer M/W, softball M/W, swimming and diving M/W, table tennis M/W, tennis M/W, track and field M/W, volleyball M/W.

Standardized Tests *Required for some:* TEOFL for International Students. *Recommended:* SAT or ACT (for admission).

Costs (2012–13) *Comprehensive fee:* $44,630 includes full-time tuition ($34,442), mandatory fees ($272), and room and board ($9916). Full-time tuition and fees vary according to student level. Part-time tuition and fees vary according to student level. No tuition increase for student's term of enrollment. *College room only:* $5150. Room and board charges vary according to student level. *Payment plans:* installment, deferred payment. *Waivers:* employees or children of employees.

Financial Aid Of all full-time matriculated undergraduates who enrolled in 2011, 337 applied for aid, 330 were judged to have need, 268 had their need fully met. In 2011, 177 non-need-based awards were made. *Average percent of need met:* 97%. *Average financial aid package:* $28,550. *Average need-based loan:* $10,769. *Average need-based gift aid:* $19,915. *Average non-need-based aid:* $13,730. *Average indebtedness upon graduation:* $22,480. *Financial aid deadline:* 3/1.

Applying *Options:* electronic application, early admission, early decision, deferred entrance. *Application fee:* $45. *Required:* essay or personal statement, high school transcript, 2 letters of recommendation. *Recommended:* interview. *Application deadlines:* 2/1 (freshmen), 4/1 (transfers). *Early decision deadline:* 11/15 (for plan 1), 1/2 (for plan 2). *Notification:* 3/17 (freshmen), continuous (transfers), 12/17 (early decision plan 1), 2/8 (early decision plan 2).

Freshman Application Contact Ms. Lee Ann Afton, Dean of Admission and Financial Aid, Sewanee: The University of the South, 735 University Avenue, Sewanee, TN 37383-1000. *Phone:* 931-598-1238. *Toll-free phone:* 800-522-2234. *Fax:* 931-598-3248. *E-mail:* admiss@sewanee.edu. *Web site:* http://www.sewanee.edu/.

South College

Knoxville, Tennessee

Director of Admissions Mr. Walter Hosea, Director of Admissions, South College, 720 North Fifth Avenue, Knoxville, TN 37917. *Phone:* 865-524-3043 Ext. 1825. *E-mail:* whosea@southcollegetn.edu. *Web site:* http://www.southcollegetn.edu/.

Southern Adventist University

Collegedale, Tennessee

- **Independent Seventh-day Adventist** comprehensive, founded 1892
- **Small-town** 1000-acre campus with easy access to Chattanooga
- **Endowment** $21.1 million
- **Coed**
- **Moderately difficult** entrance level

Faculty *Student/faculty ratio:* 15:1.

Academics *Calendar:* semesters. *Degrees:* certificates, associate, bachelor's, master's, and post-master's certificates.

Student Life *Campus security:* 24-hour patrols, late-night transport/escort service, controlled dormitory access.

Standardized Tests *Required:* SAT or ACT (for admission).

Costs (2011–12) *Comprehensive fee:* $24,110 includes full-time tuition ($17,534), mandatory fees ($790), and room and board ($5786). Part-time tuition: $740 per semester hour. Part-time tuition and fees vary according to course load. *College room only:* $3286. Room and board charges vary according to housing facility. *Payment plans:* tuition prepayment, installment, deferred payment.

Financial Aid *Of all full-time matriculated undergraduates who enrolled in 2010,* 1,709 applied for aid, 1,217 were judged to have need, 1,062 had their need fully met. *In 2010,* 468 non-need-based awards were made. *Average percent of need met:* 85. *Average financial aid package:* $20,692. *Average need-based loan:* $4800. *Average need-based gift aid:* $9713. *Average non-need-based aid:* $5427. *Average indebtedness upon graduation:* $27,121.

Applying *Options:* deferred entrance. *Application fee:* $25. *Required:* high school transcript, minimum 2.3 GPA. *Required for some:* essay or personal statement.

Freshman Application Contact Mr. Marc Grundy, Associate Vice President, Marketing and Enrollment Services, Southern Adventist University, PO Box 370, Collegedale, TN 37315-0370. *Phone:* 423-236-2844. *Toll-free phone:* 800-768-8437. *Fax:* 423-236-1844. *E-mail:* admissions@southern.edu. *Web site:* http://www.southern.edu/.

Strayer University - Knoxville Campus

Knoxville, Tennessee

- **Proprietary** comprehensive
- **Coed**

Academics *Degrees:* certificates, diplomas, associate, bachelor's, master's, and postbachelor's certificates.

Freshman Application Contact Strayer University - Knoxville Campus, 10118 Parkside Drive, Suite 200, Knoxville, TN 37922. *Web site:* http://www.strayer.edu/knoxville/.

Strayer University - Nashville Campus

Nashville, Tennessee

- **Proprietary** comprehensive
- **Coed**

Academics *Degrees:* certificates, diplomas, associate, bachelor's, master's, and postbachelor's certificates.

Freshman Application Contact Strayer University - Nashville Campus, 1809 Dabbs Avenue, Nashville, TN 37210. *Web site:* http://www.strayer.edu/nashville.

Strayer University - Shelby Oaks Campus

Memphis, Tennessee

- **Proprietary** comprehensive
- **Coed**

Academics *Degrees:* certificates, diplomas, associate, bachelor's, master's, and postbachelor's certificates.

Freshman Application Contact Strayer University - Shelby Oaks Campus, 6211 Shelby Oaks Drive, Suite 100, Memphis, TN 38134. *Web site:* http://www.strayer.edu/shelby_oaks.

Strayer University - Thousand Oaks Campus

Memphis, Tennessee

- **Proprietary** comprehensive
- **Coed**

Academics *Degrees:* certificates, diplomas, associate, bachelor's, master's, and postbachelor's certificates.

Freshman Application Contact Strayer University - Thousand Oaks Campus, 2620 Thousand Oaks Boulevard, Suite 1100, Memphis, TN 38118. *Web site:* http://www.strayer.edu/thousand_oaks_campus.

Tennessee State University

Nashville, Tennessee

Freshman Application Contact Ms. Vernella Smith, Admissions Coordinator, Tennessee State University, 3500 John A Merritt Boulevard, Nashville, TN 37209-1561. *Phone:* 615-963-5104. *Fax:* 615-963-5108. *E-mail:* vsmith@tnstate.edu. *Web site:* http://www.tnstate.edu/.

Tennessee Technological University

Cookeville, Tennessee

- **State-supported** university, founded 1915, part of Tennessee Board of Regents
- **Small-town** 235-acre campus
- **Endowment** $50.0 million
- **Coed**
- **Moderately difficult** entrance level

Faculty *Student/faculty ratio:* 21:1.

Academics *Calendar:* semesters. *Degrees:* bachelor's, master's, doctoral, post-master's, postbachelor's, and first professional certificates.

Student Life *Campus security:* 24-hour emergency response devices and patrols, late-night transport/escort service, student safety organization, lighted pathways.

Athletics Member NCAA. All Division I except football (Division I-AA).

Standardized Tests *Required:* SAT or ACT (for admission). *Recommended:* ACT (for admission).

Costs (2011–12) *Tuition:* state resident $6406 full-time, $296 per credit hour part-time; nonresident $20,038 full-time, $864 per credit hour part-time. Full-time tuition and fees vary according to course load and program. Part-time tuition and fees vary according to course load and program. *Room and board:* $7384; room only: $3830. Room and board charges vary according to board plan and housing facility.

Financial Aid *Of all full-time matriculated undergraduates who enrolled in 2011,* 7,822 applied for aid, 6,039 were judged to have need, 1,347 had their need fully met. 1,393 Federal Work-Study jobs (averaging $1494). *In 2011,* 498 non-need-based awards were made. *Average percent of need met:* 59. *Average financial aid package:* $11,673. *Average need-based loan:* $3670. *Average need-based gift aid:* $4111. *Average non-need-based aid:* $1244. *Average indebtedness upon graduation:* $9952.

Applying *Options:* electronic application, early admission, deferred entrance. *Application fee:* $25. *Required:* high school transcript, minimum 2.5 GPA. *Recommended:* interview.

Freshman Application Contact Ms. Vanessa Palmer, Director of Admissions, Tennessee Technological University, PO Box 5006, Cookeville, TN 38505. *Phone:* 931-372-3888. *Toll-free phone:* 800-255-8881. *Fax:* 931-372-6250. *E-mail:* admissions@tntech.edu. *Web site:* http://www.tntech.edu/.

Tennessee Temple University

Chattanooga, Tennessee

Director of Admissions Eric Lovett, Director of Recruitment, Tennessee Temple University, 1815 Union Avenue, Chattanooga, TN 37404-3587. *Phone:* 423-493-4371. *Toll-free phone:* 800-553-4050. *E-mail:* eric.lovett@tntemple.edu. *Web site:* http://www.tntemple.edu/.

Tennessee Wesleyan College

Athens, Tennessee

- **Independent United Methodist** 4-year, founded 1857
- **Small-town** 40-acre campus with easy access to Knoxville, Chattanooga
- **Coed**
- **Minimally difficult** entrance level

Faculty *Student/faculty ratio:* 16:1.

Academics *Calendar:* semesters. *Degrees:* bachelor's (profile includes information for both the main and branch campuses).

Student Life *Campus security:* 24-hour patrols, late-night transport/escort service, controlled dormitory access, night patrols by trained security personnel.

Athletics Member NAIA.

Standardized Tests *Required:* SAT or ACT (for admission).

Costs (2011–12) *Comprehensive fee:* $26,180 includes full-time tuition ($19,000), mandatory fees ($700), and room and board ($6480). Full-time tuition and fees vary according to location. Part-time tuition: $520 per credit hour. Part-time tuition and fees vary according to class time and location. *Required fees:* $10 per credit hour part-time. *Room and board:* Room and board charges vary according to housing facility. *Payment plans:* installment, deferred payment.

Financial Aid *Of all full-time matriculated undergraduates who enrolled in 2010,* 1,008 applied for aid, 915 were judged to have need, 147 had their need fully met. *In 2010,* 75 non-need-based awards were made. *Average percent of need met:* 64. *Average financial aid package:* $16,120. *Average need-based loan:* $3885. *Average need-based gift aid:* $13,704. *Average non-need-based aid:* $7832. *Average indebtedness upon graduation:* $20,863.

Applying *Options:* electronic application, deferred entrance. *Application fee:* $25. *Required:* high school transcript, minimum 2.3 GPA, 1 letter of recommendation. *Required for some:* interview. *Recommended:* essay or personal statement.

Freshman Application Contact Stan Harrison, Vice President of Enrollment Services and Director of Athletics, Tennessee Wesleyan College, 204 East College Street, Athens, TN 37303. *Phone:* 423-746-5287. *Toll-free phone:* 800-PICK-TWC. *Fax:* 423-745-9335. *E-mail:* admissions@twcnet.edu. *Web site:* http://www.twcnet.edu/.

Trevecca Nazarene University

Nashville, Tennessee

- **Independent Nazarene** comprehensive, founded 1901
- **Urban** 65-acre campus
- **Endowment** $19.3 million
- **Coed** 1,419 undergraduate students, 84% full-time, 56% women, 44% men
- **Moderately difficult** entrance level, 77% of applicants were admitted

Undergraduates 1,198 full-time, 221 part-time. Students come from 37 states and territories; 13 other countries; 38% are from out of state; 8% Black or African American, non-Hispanic/Latino; 3% Hispanic/Latino; 0.8% Asian, non-Hispanic/Latino; 0.6% American Indian or Alaska Native, non-Hispanic/Latino; 0.8% Two or more races, non-Hispanic/Latino; 15% Race/ethnicity unknown; 1% international; 6% transferred in; 49% live on campus. *Retention:* 69% of full-time freshmen returned.

Freshmen *Admission:* 1,105 applied, 848 admitted, 262 enrolled. *Average high school GPA:* 3.31. *Test scores:* SAT critical reading scores over 500: 68%; SAT math scores over 500: 57%; ACT scores over 18: 87%; SAT critical reading scores over 600: 35%; SAT math scores over 600: 30%; ACT scores over 24: 44%; SAT critical reading scores over 700: 10%; SAT math scores over 700: 10%; ACT scores over 30: 5%.

Faculty *Total:* 230, 37% full-time, 60% with terminal degrees. *Student/faculty ratio:* 16:1.

Academics *Calendar:* semesters. *Degrees:* associate, bachelor's, master's, doctoral, and first professional. *Special study options:* academic remediation for entering students, adult/continuing education programs, advanced placement credit, distance learning, double majors, internships, services for LD students, study abroad, summer session for credit. *ROTC:* Army (c).

Computers on Campus 200 computers/terminals and 1,460 ports are available on campus for general student use. Students can access the following: campus intranet, computer help desk, free student e-mail accounts, online (class) grades, online (class) registration, online (class) schedules, Non-traditional and graduate student registered through Academic Records. Campuswide network is available. 100% of college-owned or -operated housing units are wired for high-speed Internet access. Wireless service is available via entire campus.

Student Life *Housing:* on-campus residence required through senior year. *Options:* men-only, women-only. Campus housing is university owned. *Activities and organizations:* drama/theater group, student-run newspaper, choral group, marching band. *Campus security:* 24-hour patrols, late-night transport/escort service, weather alert warning system (phone, email, siren). *Student services:* health clinic, personal/psychological counseling.

Athletics Member NAIA. *Intercollegiate sports:* baseball M(s), basketball M(s)/W(s), golf M(s)/W(s), soccer M(s)/W(s), softball W(s), track and field M(s)/W(s), volleyball W(s). *Intramural sports:* badminton M/W, basketball M/W, football M/W, golf M/W, racquetball M/W, softball M/W, table tennis M/W, track and field M/W, volleyball M/W.

Standardized Tests *Required:* SAT or ACT (for admission).

Costs (2011–12) *Comprehensive fee:* $28,078 includes full-time tuition ($19,990), mandatory fees ($600), and room and board ($7488). Full-time tuition and fees vary according to course load and program. Part-time tuition: $772 per credit hour. Part-time tuition and fees vary according to course load and program. *College room only:* $3744. Room and board charges vary according to board plan. *Payment plans:* tuition prepayment, installment. *Waivers:* senior citizens and employees or children of employees.

Financial Aid *Financial aid deadline:* 8/1.

Applying *Options:* electronic application, early admission, deferred entrance. *Application fee:* $25. *Required:* high school transcript, minimum 2.5 GPA, an ACT composite score of 18 or above, or SAT Critical Reading + Math score of 860 or above; enrollment fee; medical history and immunization records. *Application deadlines:* 8/1 (freshmen), rolling (transfers). *Notification:* continuous (freshmen), continuous (transfers).

Freshman Application Contact Ms. Holly Whitby, Director of Undergraduate Admissions, Trevecca Nazarene University, 333 Murfreesboro Road, Nashville, TN 37210-2834. *Phone:* 615-248-1320. *Toll-free phone:* 888-210-4TNU. *Fax:* 615-248-7406. *E-mail:* admissions_und@trevecca.edu. *Web site:* http://www.trevecca.edu/.

Tusculum College

Greeneville, Tennessee

- **Independent Presbyterian** comprehensive, founded 1794
- **Small-town** 140-acre campus
- **Endowment** $16.8 million
- **Coed** 2,129 undergraduate students, 97% full-time, 60% women, 40% men
- **Moderately difficult** entrance level, 69% of applicants were admitted

Undergraduates 2,064 full-time, 75 part-time. Students come from 30 states and territories; 15 other countries; 46% are from out of state; 13% Black or African American, non-Hispanic/Latino; 2% Hispanic/Latino; 0.6% Asian, non-Hispanic/Latino; 0.2% American Indian or Alaska Native, non-Hispanic/Latino; 2% Race/ethnicity unknown; 1% international; 3% transferred in; 65% live on campus. *Retention:* 59% of full-time freshmen returned.

Freshmen *Admission:* 3,081 applied, 2,137 admitted, 305 enrolled. *Average high school GPA:* 3.1. *Test scores:* SAT critical reading scores over 500: 38%; SAT math scores over 500: 48%; ACT scores over 18: 87%; SAT critical reading scores over 600: 9%; SAT math scores over 600: 14%; ACT scores over 24: 31%; SAT critical reading scores over 700: 1%; SAT math scores over 700: 1%; ACT scores over 30: 1%.

Faculty *Total:* 224, 34% full-time. *Student/faculty ratio:* 16:1.

Academics *Calendar:* semesters. *Degrees:* bachelor's and master's. *Special study options:* academic remediation for entering students, adult/continuing education programs, advanced placement credit, double majors, honors programs, independent study, internships, part-time degree program, services for LD students, student-designed majors, study abroad, summer session for credit.

Computers on Campus 200 computers/terminals are available on campus for general student use. Students can access the following: campus intranet, computer help desk, free student e-mail accounts, online (class) grades, online (class) registration, online (class) schedules. Campuswide network is available. 100% of college-owned or -operated housing units are wired for high-speed Internet access. Wireless service is available via classrooms, computer labs, learning centers, libraries, student centers.

Student Life *Housing:* on-campus residence required through junior year. *Options:* coed, men-only, women-only. Campus housing is university owned. Freshman campus housing is guaranteed. *Activities and organizations:* drama/theater group, student-run newspaper, radio and television station, choral group, marching band, Pioneer Newspaper, Bonwondi, Campus Activities Board, Fellowship of Christian Athletes, Tusculana (yearbook). *Campus security:* 24-hour emergency response devices and patrols, student patrols, late-night transport/escort service, controlled dormitory access, trained security personnel on duty. *Student services:* health clinic, personal/psychological counseling, women's center.

Athletics Member NCAA. All Division II. *Intercollegiate sports:* baseball M(s), basketball M(s)/W(s), cheerleading W(s), cross-country running M(s)/W(s), football M(s), golf M(s)/W(s), soccer M(s)/W(s), softball W(s), tennis M(s)/W(s), volleyball W(s). *Intramural sports:* baseball M, basketball M/W, football M, softball M, tennis M/W, volleyball M/W.

Standardized Tests *Required:* SAT or ACT (for admission).

Costs (2011–12) *Comprehensive fee:* $28,910 includes full-time tuition ($20,910) and room and board ($8000). Full-time tuition and fees vary according to degree level. Part-time tuition: $650 per semester hour. Part-time tuition and fees vary according to degree level. *Room and board:* Room and board charges vary according to board plan. *Payment plan:* installment. *Waivers:* employees or children of employees.

Financial Aid Of all full-time matriculated undergraduates who enrolled in 2008, 2,069 applied for aid, 1,470 were judged to have need. 264 Federal Work-Study jobs (averaging $2285). 16 state and other part-time jobs (averaging $2000). In 2008, 618 non-need-based awards were made. *Average financial aid package:* $17,651. *Average non-need-based aid:* $4088. *Average indebtedness upon graduation:* $8632.

Applying *Options:* electronic application, early admission, deferred entrance. *Required:* essay or personal statement, high school transcript, minimum 2.0 GPA. *Required for some:* 3 letters of recommendation. *Recommended:* interview. *Application deadlines:* rolling (freshmen), rolling (transfers).

Freshman Application Contact Ms. Melissa Ripley, Director of Operations, Tusculum College, PO Box 5047, Greeneville, TN 37743-9997. *Phone:* 423-636-7300 Ext. 5374. *Toll-free phone:* 800-729-0256. *Fax:* 423-798-1622. *E-mail:* admissions@tusculum.edu. *Web site:* http://www.tusculum.edu/.

Union University

Jackson, Tennessee

- **Independent Southern Baptist** comprehensive, founded 1823
- **Small-town** 360-acre campus with easy access to Memphis
- **Endowment** $31.4 million
- **Coed** 2,875 undergraduate students, 77% full-time, 58% women, 42% men
- **Moderately difficult** entrance level, 77% of applicants were admitted

Undergraduates 2,217 full-time, 658 part-time. Students come from 44 states and territories; 36 other countries; 25% are from out of state; 13% Black or African American, non-Hispanic/Latino; 2% Hispanic/Latino; 1% Asian, non-Hispanic/Latino; 0.2% Native Hawaiian or other Pacific Islander, non-Hispanic/Latino; 0.1% American Indian or Alaska Native, non-Hispanic/Latino; 0.7% Two or more races, non-Hispanic/Latino; 4% Race/ethnicity unknown; 0.8% international; 5% transferred in; 55% live on campus. *Retention:* 94% of full-time freshmen returned.

Freshmen *Admission:* 1,923 applied, 1,472 admitted, 482 enrolled. *Average high school GPA:* 3.65. *Test scores:* SAT critical reading scores over 500: 88%; SAT math scores over 500: 83%; ACT scores over 18: 97%; SAT critical reading scores over 600: 50%; SAT math scores over 600: 42%; ACT scores over 24: 67%; SAT critical reading scores over 700: 18%; SAT math scores over 700: 12%; ACT scores over 30: 21%.

Faculty *Total:* 242, 98% full-time, 77% with terminal degrees. *Student/faculty ratio:* 12:1.

Academics *Calendar:* 4-1-4. *Degrees:* certificates, diplomas, associate, bachelor's, master's, doctoral, post-master's, and first professional certificates. *Special study options:* academic remediation for entering students, accelerated degree program, adult/continuing education programs, advanced placement credit, cooperative education, distance learning, double majors, English as a second language, honors programs, independent study, internships, off-campus study, part-time degree program, services for LD students, study abroad, summer session for credit. *ROTC:* Army (c).

Computers on Campus 236 computers/terminals are available on campus for general student use. Students can access the following: campus intranet, computer help desk, free student e-mail accounts, online (class) grades, online (class) registration, online (class) schedules. Campuswide network is available. 100% of college-owned or -operated housing units are wired for high-speed Internet access. Wireless service is available via entire campus.

Student Life *Housing:* on-campus residence required through junior year. *Options:* men-only, women-only, disabled students. Campus housing is university owned. Freshman applicants given priority for college housing. *Activities and organizations:* drama/theater group, student-run newspaper, choral group, Campus Ministries, Student Government Association, Student Activities Council, Students in Free Enterprise (SIFE), national fraternities, national sororities. *Campus security:* 24-hour emergency response devices and patrols, student patrols, late-night transport/escort service. *Student services:* health clinic, personal/psychological counseling.

Athletics Member NCAA, NAIA, NCCAA. All NCAA Division II. *Intercollegiate sports:* baseball M(s), basketball M(s)/W(s), cheerleading W(s), cross-country running M/W(s), golf M(s), soccer M(s)/W(s), softball W(s), track and field M/W, volleyball W(s). *Intramural sports:* basketball M/W, bowling M/W, cross-country running M/W, football M/W, golf M/W, racquetball M/W, soccer W, softball M/W, swimming and diving M/W, table tennis M/W, track and field M/W, ultimate Frisbee M/W, volleyball M/W.

Standardized Tests *Required:* SAT or ACT (for admission). *Recommended:* SAT Subject Tests (for admission).

Costs (2011–12) *Comprehensive fee:* $32,140 includes full-time tuition ($23,330), mandatory fees ($700), and room and board ($8110). Full-time tuition and fees vary according to course load. Part-time tuition: $790 per credit hour. *Required fees:* $285 per term part-time. *Room and board:* Room and board charges vary according to board plan and housing facility. *Payment plans:* installment, deferred payment. *Waivers:* children of alumni and employees or children of employees.

Financial Aid Of all full-time matriculated undergraduates who enrolled in 2011, 1,577 applied for aid, 1,376 were judged to have need, 267 had their

need fully met. 108 Federal Work-Study jobs (averaging $1618). 240 state and other part-time jobs (averaging $1851). In 2011, 409 non-need-based awards were made. *Average percent of need met:* 68%. *Average financial aid package:* $20,001. *Average need-based loan:* $4558. *Average need-based gift aid:* $5961. *Average non-need-based aid:* $9971. *Average indebtedness upon graduation:* $23,070.

Applying *Options:* electronic application, early admission, early action, deferred entrance. *Application fee:* $35. *Required:* high school transcript, minimum 2.5 GPA. *Required for some:* 3 letters of recommendation. *Recommended:* essay or personal statement, interview. *Application deadlines:* rolling (freshmen), rolling (transfers), 12/1 (early action). *Notification:* 8/1 (freshmen), continuous until 8/15 (transfers), 12/15 (early action).

Freshman Application Contact Mr. Robbie Graves, Director of Enrollment Services, Union University, 1050 Union University Drive, Jackson, TN 38305-3697. *Phone:* 731-661-5590. *Toll-free phone:* 800-33-UNION. *Fax:* 731-661-5017. *E-mail:* rgraves@uu.edu. *Web site:* http://www.uu.edu/.

See page 869 for display ad and page 1650 for the College Close-Up.

University of Memphis

Memphis, Tennessee

- **State-supported** university, founded 1912, part of Tennessee Board of Regents
- **Urban** 1160-acre campus
- **Coed** 17,966 undergraduate students, 73% full-time, 62% women, 38% men
- **Moderately difficult** entrance level, 66% of applicants were admitted

Undergraduates 13,130 full-time, 4,836 part-time. 10% are from out of state; 42% Black or African American, non-Hispanic/Latino; 3% Hispanic/Latino; 2% Asian, non-Hispanic/Latino; 0.1% Native Hawaiian or other Pacific Islander, non-Hispanic/Latino; 0.3% American Indian or Alaska Native, non-Hispanic/Latino; 2% Two or more races, non-Hispanic/Latino; 1% Race/ethnicity unknown; 0.8% international; 9% transferred in; 18% live on campus. *Retention:* 78% of full-time freshmen returned.

Freshmen *Admission:* 6,710 applied, 4,452 admitted, 2,577 enrolled. *Average high school GPA:* 3.29. *Test scores:* ACT scores over 18: 87%; ACT scores over 24: 33%; ACT scores over 30: 5%.

Faculty *Total:* 1,497, 57% full-time, 59% with terminal degrees. *Student/faculty ratio:* 12:1.

Academics *Calendar:* semesters. *Degrees:* bachelor's, master's, doctoral, post-master's, postbachelor's, and first professional certificates. *Special study options:* academic remediation for entering students, accelerated degree program, adult/continuing education programs, advanced placement credit, cooperative education, distance learning, double majors, English as a second language, external degree program, honors programs, independent study, internships, off-campus study, part-time degree program, services for LD students, student-designed majors, study abroad, summer session for credit. *ROTC:* Army (b), Navy (b), Air Force (b).

Computers on Campus 1,600 computers/terminals and 35 ports are available on campus for general student use. Students can access the following: campus intranet, computer help desk, free student e-mail accounts, online (class) grades, online (class) registration, online (class) schedules. Campuswide network is available. Wireless service is available via entire campus.

Student Life *Housing options:* coed, men-only, women-only, disabled students. Campus housing is university owned. *Activities and organizations:* drama/theater group, student-run newspaper, radio station, choral group, marching band, Blue Crew, Up 'til Dawn, Black Student Association, national fraternities, national sororities. *Campus security:* 24-hour emergency response devices and patrols, student patrols, late-night transport/escort service, controlled dormitory access. *Student services:* health clinic, personal/psychological counseling, women's center.

Athletics Member NCAA. All Division I except football (Division I-A). *Intercollegiate sports:* baseball M(s), basketball M(s)/W(s), cheerleading M(s)/W(s), cross-country running M(s)/W(s), golf M(s)/W(s), racquetball M(c)/W(c), riflery M(s)/W(s), soccer M(s)/W(s), softball W, swimming and diving M(c)/W(c), tennis M(s)/W(s), track and field M(s)/W(s), volleyball W(s). *Intramural sports:* basketball M/W, bowling M/W, golf M/W, racquetball M/W, soccer M/W, softball M/W, table tennis M/W, tennis M/W, track and field M/W, ultimate Frisbee M/W, volleyball M/W, water polo M/W.

Standardized Tests *Required:* SAT or ACT (for admission).

Costs (2012–13) *Tuition:* state resident $6144 full-time; nonresident $20,856 full-time. Full-time tuition and fees vary according to course load, degree level, program, and reciprocity agreements. Part-time tuition and fees vary according to course load, degree level, and program. *Required fees:* $1246 full-time. *Room and board:* $8330; room only: $4998. Room and board charges vary according to board plan and housing facility.

Financial Aid Of all full-time matriculated undergraduates who enrolled in 2011, 12,128 applied for aid, 10,333 were judged to have need, 403 had their need fully met. 244 Federal Work-Study jobs (averaging $1909). In 2011, 1707 non-need-based awards were made. *Average percent of need met:* 71%.

Average financial aid package: $8926. *Average need-based loan:* $4279. *Average need-based gift aid:* $5831. *Average non-need-based aid:* $8122. *Average indebtedness upon graduation:* $25,629.

Applying *Options:* electronic application, early admission. *Application fee:* $25. *Required:* high school transcript. *Required for some:* minimum 2.0 GPA, 2 letters of recommendation, interview. *Application deadlines:* 7/1 (freshmen), 7/1 (transfers). *Notification:* continuous (freshmen), continuous (transfers).
Freshman Application Contact University of Memphis, Memphis, TN 38152. *Phone:* 901-678-2111. *Toll-free phone:* 800-669-2678. *Web site:* http://www.memphis.edu/.

See page 1686 for the College Close-Up.

University of Phoenix–Chattanooga Campus
Chattanooga, Tennessee

Admissions Office Contact University of Phoenix–Chattanooga Campus, 1208 Pointe Centre Drive, Chattanooga, TN 37421-3707. *Toll-free phone:* 866-766-0766. *Web site:* http://www.phoenix.edu/.

University of Phoenix–Memphis Campus
Cordova, Tennessee

Admissions Office Contact University of Phoenix–Memphis Campus, 65 Germantown Court, Cordova, TN 38018. *Toll-free phone:* 866-766-0766. *Web site:* http://www.phoenix.edu/.

University of Phoenix–Nashville Campus
Nashville, Tennessee

Freshman Application Contact Marc Booker, Sr. Director, Office of Admissions and Evaluation, University of Phoenix–Nashville Campus, 4035 South Riverpoint Parkway, Mail Stop CF-L101, Phoenix, AZ 85040. *Phone:* 602-557-4609. *Toll-free phone:* 866-766-0766. *Fax:* 480-643-1156. *Web site:* http://www.phoenix.edu/.

The University of Tennessee
Knoxville, Tennessee

- **State-supported** university, founded 1794, part of University of Tennessee System
- **Urban** 560-acre campus
- **Coed** 21,214 undergraduate students, 94% full-time, 49% women, 51% men
- **Moderately difficult** entrance level, 70% of applicants were admitted

Undergraduates 19,918 full-time, 1,296 part-time. Students come from 50 states and territories; 56 other countries; 7% Black or African American, non-Hispanic/Latino; 3% Hispanic/Latino; 3% Asian, non-Hispanic/Latino; 0.3% American Indian or Alaska Native, non-Hispanic/Latino; 2% Two or more races, non-Hispanic/Latino; 1% Race/ethnicity unknown; 1% international; 6% transferred in; 35% live on campus. *Retention:* 85% of full-time freshmen returned.
Freshmen *Admission:* 13,768 applied, 9,594 admitted, 4,188 enrolled. *Average high school GPA:* 3.87. *Test scores:* SAT critical reading scores over 500: 85%; SAT math scores over 500: 87%; ACT scores over 18: 100%; SAT critical reading scores over 600: 47%; SAT math scores over 600: 46%; ACT scores over 24: 83%; SAT critical reading scores over 700: 10%; SAT math scores over 700: 10%; ACT scores over 30: 22%.
Faculty *Total:* 1,919, 86% full-time. *Student/faculty ratio:* 15:1.
Academics *Calendar:* semesters. *Degrees:* bachelor's, master's, doctoral, post-master's, postbachelor's, and first professional certificates. *Special study options:* accelerated degree program, advanced placement credit, cooperative education, distance learning, double majors, English as a second language, freshman honors college, honors programs, independent study, internships, off-campus study, part-time degree program, services for LD students, student-designed majors, study abroad, summer session for credit. *ROTC:* Army (b), Air Force (b).
Computers on Campus 600 computers/terminals are available on campus for general student use. Students can access the following: campus intranet, computer help desk, free student e-mail accounts, online (class) grades, online (class) registration, online (class) schedules, Blackboard Course Management System. Campuswide network is available. 100% of college-owned or -oper-

ated housing units are wired for high-speed Internet access. Wireless service is available via entire campus.
Student Life *Housing:* on-campus residence required for freshman year. *Options:* coed, men-only, women-only, disabled students. Campus housing is university owned. Freshman campus housing is guaranteed. *Activities and organizations:* drama/theater group, student-run newspaper, radio and television station, choral group, marching band, Fraternities/Sororities, Religious organizations, Central Program Council, Black Cultural Programming Committee, Student Government Association, national fraternities, national sororities. *Campus security:* 24-hour emergency response devices and patrols, late-night transport/escort service, controlled dormitory access, security cameras on all building entrances; card entry into the living sections of residence hall buildings. *Student services:* health clinic, personal/psychological counseling, women's center.
Athletics Member NCAA. All Division I. *Intercollegiate sports:* baseball M(s), basketball M(s)/W(s), crew W(s), football M(s), golf M(s)/W(s), soccer W(s), softball W(s), swimming and diving M(s)/W(s), tennis M(s)/W(s), track and field M(s)/W(s), volleyball W(s). *Intramural sports:* badminton M/W, basketball M/W, bowling M/W, crew W, field hockey M/W, football M/W, golf M/W, racquetball M/W, soccer M/W, softball M/W, table tennis M/W, tennis M/W, ultimate Frisbee M/W, volleyball M/W, water polo M/W, weight lifting M/W.
Standardized Tests *Required:* SAT or ACT (for admission).
Costs (2011–12) *Tuition:* state resident $7224 full-time, $302 per hour part-time; nonresident $24,066 full-time, $1005 per hour part-time. Full-time tuition and fees vary according to course level, program, and reciprocity agreements. Part-time tuition and fees vary according to course level, program, and reciprocity agreements. *Required fees:* $1172 full-time, $56 per hour part-time. *Room and board:* $8480. Room and board charges vary according to board plan and housing facility. *Payment plan:* installment. *Waivers:* senior citizens and employees or children of employees.
Financial Aid Of all full-time matriculated undergraduates who enrolled in 2011, 16,799 applied for aid, 10,936 were judged to have need, 2,276 had their need fully met. 339 Federal Work-Study jobs (averaging $2352). In 2011, 2554 non-need-based awards were made. *Average percent of need met:* 69%. *Average financial aid package:* $11,525. *Average need-based loan:* $4592. *Average need-based gift aid:* $3233. *Average non-need-based aid:* $2293. *Average indebtedness upon graduation:* $20,926.
Applying *Options:* electronic application. *Application fee:* $30. *Required:* high school transcript, minimum 2.0 GPA, specific high school units. *Recommended:* essay or personal statement, 1 letter of recommendation. *Application deadlines:* 12/1 (freshmen), 7/1 (transfers). *Notification:* 3/31 (freshmen), continuous (transfers).
Freshman Application Contact Ms. Norma Harrington, Senior Associate Director, The University of Tennessee, 320 Student Services Building, Knoxville, TN 37996-0230. *Phone:* 865-974-2184. *Fax:* 865-974-4689. *E-mail:* admissions@utk.edu. *Web site:* http://www.utk.edu.

The University of Tennessee at Chattanooga
Chattanooga, Tennessee

- **State-supported** comprehensive, founded 1886, part of University of Tennessee System
- **Urban** 120-acre campus with easy access to Atlanta
- **Coed** 9,891 undergraduate students, 87% full-time, 55% women, 45% men
- **Moderately difficult** entrance level, 74% of applicants were admitted

Undergraduates 8,626 full-time, 1,265 part-time. 5% are from out of state; 12% Black or African American, non-Hispanic/Latino; 3% Hispanic/Latino; 2% Asian, non-Hispanic/Latino; 0.1% Native Hawaiian or other Pacific Islander, non-Hispanic/Latino; 0.2% American Indian or Alaska Native, non-Hispanic/Latino; 9% Two or more races, non-Hispanic/Latino; 2% Race/ethnicity unknown; 0.9% international; 8% transferred in; 31% live on campus. *Retention:* 69% of full-time freshmen returned.
Freshmen *Admission:* 6,703 applied, 4,938 admitted, 2,185 enrolled. *Average high school GPA:* 3.36. *Test scores:* SAT critical reading scores over 500: 69%; SAT math scores over 500: 61%; ACT scores over 18: 99%; SAT critical reading scores over 600: 25%; SAT math scores over 600: 21%; ACT scores over 24: 38%; SAT critical reading scores over 700: 4%; SAT math scores over 700: 2%; ACT scores over 30: 4%.
Faculty *Total:* 730, 59% full-time, 48% with terminal degrees. *Student/faculty ratio:* 18:1.
Academics *Calendar:* semesters. *Degrees:* certificates, bachelor's, master's, doctoral, post-master's, postbachelor's, and first professional certificates. *Special study options:* academic remediation for entering students, adult/continuing education programs, advanced placement credit, cooperative education, distance learning, double majors, English as a second language, honors pro-

grams, independent study, internships, off-campus study, part-time degree program, services for LD students, study abroad, summer session for credit. *ROTC:* Army (b). *Unusual degree programs:* 3-2 engineering.

Computers on Campus 965 computers/terminals are available on campus for general student use. Students can access the following: campus intranet, computer help desk, free student e-mail accounts, online (class) grades, online (class) registration, online (class) schedules, pay fees. Campuswide network is available. 100% of college-owned or -operated housing units are wired for high-speed Internet access. Wireless service is available via classrooms, computer labs, dorm rooms, libraries.

Student Life *Housing:* on-campus residence required for freshman year. *Options:* coed. Campus housing is university owned. Freshman applicants given priority for college housing. *Activities and organizations:* drama/theater group, student-run newspaper, radio station, choral group, marching band, Student Government Association, Black Student Association, Association for Campus Entertainment, International Student Association, Baptist Student Union, national fraternities, national sororities. *Campus security:* 24-hour emergency response devices and patrols, late-night transport/escort service, controlled dormitory access. *Student services:* health clinic, personal/psychological counseling.

Athletics Member NCAA. All Division I except football (Division I-AA). *Intercollegiate sports:* basketball M(s)/W(s), cross-country running M(s)/W(s), golf M(s)/W(s), soccer W(s), softball W(s), tennis M(s)/W(s), track and field M(s)/W(s), volleyball W(s), wrestling M(s). *Intramural sports:* badminton M/W, baseball M(c), basketball M/W, crew M(c)/W(c), cross-country running M/W, fencing M(c)/W(c), golf M/W, racquetball M/W, soccer M/W, swimming and diving M/W, tennis M/W, ultimate Frisbee M(c)/W(c), volleyball W, wrestling M.

Standardized Tests *Required:* SAT or ACT (for admission).

Costs (2011–12) *Tuition:* state resident $5398 full-time, $225 per credit hour part-time; nonresident $18,932 full-time, $789 per credit hour part-time. *Required fees:* $1320 full-time, $160 per credit hour part-time. *Room and board:* $8250; room only: $5300. Room and board charges vary according to board plan and housing facility. *Payment plan:* installment. *Waivers:* senior citizens and employees or children of employees.

Financial Aid Of all full-time matriculated undergraduates who enrolled in 2011, 7,720 applied for aid, 5,448 were judged to have need, 653 had their need fully met. In 2011, 70 non-need-based awards were made. *Average percent of need met:* 59%. *Average financial aid package:* $9085. *Average need-based loan:* $3789. *Average need-based gift aid:* $6771. *Average non-need-based aid:* $3281. *Average indebtedness upon graduation:* $13,845.

Applying *Options:* electronic application, deferred entrance. *Application fee:* $35. *Required:* high school transcript. *Recommended:* essay or personal statement. *Application deadlines:* 8/1 (freshmen), 8/1 (out-of-state freshmen), 8/1 (transfers). *Notification:* continuous (freshmen), continuous (out-of-state freshmen), continuous (transfers).

Freshman Application Contact Mr. Yancy Freeman, Director, Admissions and Recruitment, The University of Tennessee at Chattanooga, 715 Oak Street, Dept. 5105, Guerry Hall, Chattanooga, TN 37403. *Phone:* 423-425-4662. *Toll-free phone:* 800-UTC-MOCS (in-state); 800-UTC.MOCS (out-of-state). *Fax:* 423-425-4157. *E-mail:* yancy-freeman@utc.edu. *Web site:* http://www.utc.edu/.

The University of Tennessee at Martin
Martin, Tennessee

- **State-supported** comprehensive, founded 1900, part of University of Tennessee System
- **Small-town** 250-acre campus
- **Endowment** $26.7 million
- **Coed** 7,500 undergraduate students, 82% full-time, 58% women, 42% men
- **Moderately difficult** entrance level, 73% of applicants were admitted

Undergraduates 6,182 full-time, 1,318 part-time. Students come from 42 states and territories; 20 other countries; 4% are from out of state; 17% Black or African American, non-Hispanic/Latino; 2% Hispanic/Latino; 0.6% Asian, non-Hispanic/Latino; 0.2% American Indian or Alaska Native, non-Hispanic/Latino; 0.9% Two or more races, non-Hispanic/Latino; 2% international; 8% transferred in; 21% live on campus. *Retention:* 73% of full-time freshmen returned.

Freshmen *Admission:* 3,512 applied, 2,579 admitted, 1,304 enrolled. *Average high school GPA:* 3.41. *Test scores:* ACT scores over 18: 93%; ACT scores over 24: 34%; ACT scores over 30: 2%.

Faculty *Total:* 562, 50% full-time, 45% with terminal degrees. *Student/faculty ratio:* 18:1.

Academics *Calendar:* semesters. *Degrees:* bachelor's and master's. *Special study options:* accelerated degree program, adult/continuing education programs, advanced placement credit, cooperative education, distance learning,

double majors, English as a second language, honors programs, independent study, internships, off-campus study, part-time degree program, services for LD students, student-designed majors, study abroad, summer session for credit. *ROTC:* Army (b). *Unusual degree programs:* veterinary, medicine, dentistry, medicine, and pharmacy.

Computers on Campus 800 computers/terminals are available on campus for general student use. Students can access the following: campus intranet, computer help desk, free student e-mail accounts, online (class) grades, online (class) registration, online (class) schedules, online fee payments, degree progress, financial aid data, housing applications, transcripts. Campuswide network is available. 100% of college-owned or -operated housing units are wired for high-speed Internet access. Wireless service is available via entire campus.

Student Life *Housing:* on-campus residence required for freshman year. *Options:* men-only, women-only, disabled students. Campus housing is university owned. Freshman applicants given priority for college housing. *Activities and organizations:* drama/theater group, student-run newspaper, radio and television station, choral group, marching band, Student Government Association, Student Activities Council, Sigma Theta Tau, Gamma Beta Phi, Student Tennessee Education Association, national fraternities, national sororities. *Campus security:* 24-hour emergency response devices and patrols, student patrols, controlled dormitory access. *Student services:* health clinic, personal/psychological counseling, women's center.

Athletics Member NCAA. All Division I except football (Division I-AA). *Intercollegiate sports:* baseball M(s), basketball M(s)/W(s), cheerleading W(s), cross-country running M(s)/W(s), equestrian sports W(s), golf M(s), riflery M(s)/W(s), soccer W(s), softball W(s), tennis W(s), volleyball W(s). *Intramural sports:* basketball M/W, football M/W, golf M/W, racquetball M/W, soccer M/W, softball M/W, table tennis M/W, tennis M/W, ultimate Frisbee M/W, volleyball M/W, water polo M/W.

Standardized Tests *Required:* SAT or ACT (for admission).

Costs (2011–12) *Tuition:* state resident $5640 full-time, $235 per credit hour part-time; nonresident $18,050 full-time, $753 per credit hour part-time. Part-time tuition and fees vary according to course load. *Required fees:* $1078 full-time, $46 per credit hour part-time. *Room and board:* $5424; room only: $2650. Room and board charges vary according to board plan and housing facility. *Payment plan:* deferred payment. *Waivers:* senior citizens and employees or children of employees.

Financial Aid Of all full-time matriculated undergraduates who enrolled in 2011, 4,672 applied for aid, 3,526 were judged to have need, 1,180 had their need fully met. 250 Federal Work-Study jobs (averaging $2500). In 2011, 638 non-need-based awards were made. *Average percent of need met:* 83%. *Average financial aid package:* $12,290. *Average need-based loan:* $4137. *Average need-based gift aid:* $6278. *Average non-need-based aid:* $5969. *Average indebtedness upon graduation:* $23,328.

Applying *Options:* electronic application, early admission, deferred entrance. *Application fee:* $30. *Required:* high school transcript, minimum 2.5 GPA. *Application deadlines:* rolling (freshmen), rolling (transfers). *Notification:* 8/1 (freshmen), continuous until 8/1 (transfers).

Freshman Application Contact Ms. Judy Rayburn, Director of Admissions, The University of Tennessee at Martin, 200 Hall-Moody Administration Building, Martin, TN 38238. *Phone:* 731-881-7032. *Toll-free phone:* 800-829-8861. *Fax:* 731-881-7029. *E-mail:* jrayburn@utm.edu. *Web site:* http://www.utm.edu/.

Vanderbilt University
Nashville, Tennessee

- **Independent** university, founded 1873
- **Urban** 330-acre campus
- **Endowment** $3.4 billion
- **Coed** 6,817 undergraduate students, 99% full-time, 50% women, 50% men
- **Most difficult** entrance level, 16% of applicants were admitted

Undergraduates 6,747 full-time, 70 part-time. Students come from 52 states and territories; 36 other countries; 86% are from out of state; 8% Black or African American, non-Hispanic/Latino; 8% Hispanic/Latino; 7% Asian, non-Hispanic/Latino; 0.1% Native Hawaiian or other Pacific Islander, non-Hispanic/Latino; 0.3% American Indian or Alaska Native, non-Hispanic/Latino; 4% Two or more races, non-Hispanic/Latino; 5% Race/ethnicity unknown; 5% international; 3% transferred in; 86% live on campus. *Retention:* 96% of full-time freshmen returned.

Freshmen *Admission:* 24,837 applied, 4,078 admitted, 1,601 enrolled. *Average high school GPA:* 3.7. *Test scores:* SAT critical reading scores over 500: 99%; SAT math scores over 500: 99%; SAT writing scores over 500: 99%; ACT scores over 18: 100%; SAT critical reading scores over 600: 95%; SAT math scores over 600: 97%; SAT writing scores over 600: 94%; ACT scores over 24: 98%; SAT critical reading scores over 700: 70%; SAT math scores over 700: 77%; SAT writing scores over 700: 65%; ACT scores over 30: 89%.

Faculty *Total:* 1,128, 80% full-time. *Student/faculty ratio:* 8:1.

Academics *Calendar:* semesters. *Degrees:* bachelor's, master's, doctoral, and first professional. *Special study options:* accelerated degree program, advanced placement credit, cooperative education, double majors, English as a second language, honors programs, independent study, internships, off-campus study, services for LD students, student-designed majors, study abroad, summer session for credit. *ROTC:* Army (b), Navy (b), Air Force (c). *Unusual degree programs:* 3-2 business administration with Joint Five-Year Baccalaureate MBA Program. (one and one-half years of study in the Vanderbilt Owen Graduate School of Management, three and one-half years in Vanderbilt's College of Arts and Science); nursing with Students at Peabody College may complete the BS degree with a major in human and organizational development or child development and also earn the master of science in nursing (MSN) through a senior-in-absentia program in the School of Nursing.

Computers on Campus Students can access the following: campus intranet, computer help desk, free student e-mail accounts, online (class) grades, online (class) registration, online (class) schedules, productivity and educational software. Campuswide network is available. Wireless service is available via entire campus.

Student Life *Housing:* on-campus residence required for freshman year. *Options:* coed, men-only, women-only, disabled students. Campus housing is university owned. Freshman campus housing is guaranteed. *Activities and organizations:* drama/theater group, student-run newspaper, radio and television station, choral group, marching band, national fraternities, national sororities. *Campus security:* 24-hour emergency response devices and patrols, student patrols, late-night transport/escort service, controlled dormitory access. *Student services:* health clinic, personal/psychological counseling, women's center.

Athletics Member NCAA. All Division I except football (Division I-A). *Intercollegiate sports:* baseball M(s), basketball M(s)/W(s), bowling W(s), cross-country running M(s)/W(s), golf M(s)/W(s), lacrosse W(s), soccer W(s), swimming and diving W(s), tennis M(s)/W(s), track and field W(s). *Intramural sports:* badminton M(c)/W(c), baseball M(c), basketball M/W, bowling M(c)/W(c), crew M(c)/W(c), cross-country running M(c)/W(c), equestrian sports M(c)/W(c), fencing M(c)/W(c), field hockey M(c)/W(c), football M/W, golf M(c)/W(c), ice hockey M(c), lacrosse M(c)/W(c), racquetball M(c)/W(c), rugby M(c), sailing M(c)/W(c), soccer M(c)/W(c), softball M/W, squash M(c)/W(c), swimming and diving M(c)/W(c), table tennis M/W, tennis M(c)/W(c), track and field M(c), ultimate Frisbee M(c)/W(c), volleyball M(c)/W(c), water polo M(c)/W(c), weight lifting M/W, wrestling M(c).

Standardized Tests *Required:* SAT or ACT (for admission).

Costs (2011–12) *One-time required fee:* $664. *Comprehensive fee:* $54,892 includes full-time tuition ($40,320), mandatory fees ($1012), and room and board ($13,560). Part-time tuition: $1680 per credit hour. *College room only:* $8860. Room and board charges vary according to board plan. *Payment plans:* tuition prepayment, installment. *Waivers:* employees or children of employees.

Financial Aid Of all full-time matriculated undergraduates who enrolled in 2011, 3,586 applied for aid, 3,171 were judged to have need, 3,162 had their need fully met. 1,388 Federal Work-Study jobs (averaging $2104). In 2011, 650 non-need-based awards were made. *Average percent of need met:* 100%. *Average financial aid package:* $43,163. *Average need-based loan:* $3268. *Average need-based gift aid:* $37,478. *Average non-need-based aid:* $23,533. *Average indebtedness upon graduation:* $18,543.

Applying *Options:* electronic application, early decision. *Application fee:* $50. *Required:* essay or personal statement, high school transcript, 3 letters of recommendation, 3 letters of recommendation (two from teachers in core subject areas and one from counselor). *Application deadlines:* 1/3 (freshmen), 3/15 (transfers). *Early decision deadline:* 11/1 (for plan 1), 1/3 (for plan 2). *Notification:* 4/1 (freshmen), 4/1 (transfers), 12/15 (early decision plan 1), 2/15 (early decision plan 2).

Freshman Application Contact Mother Supr. John O. Gaines, Director of Undergraduate Admissions, Vanderbilt University, 2305 West End Avenue, Nashville, TN 37203. *Phone:* 615-936-2811. *Toll-free phone:* 800-288-0432. *Fax:* 615-343-8326. *E-mail:* admissions@vanderbilt.edu. *Web site:* http://www.vanderbilt.edu/.

See page 1730 for the College Close-Up.

Victory University

Memphis, Tennessee

- **Independent** comprehensive, founded 1941
- **Urban** 7-acre campus with easy access to Memphis
- **Coed**
- **Minimally difficult** entrance level

Faculty *Student/faculty ratio:* 12:1.

Academics *Calendar:* semesters. *Degrees:* certificates, associate, bachelor's, master's, and postbachelor's certificates.

Student Life *Campus security:* 24-hour patrols.

Athletics Member NCCAA.

Standardized Tests *Required for some:* SAT or ACT (for admission).

Financial Aid *Of all full-time matriculated undergraduates who enrolled in 2009,* 385 applied for aid, 358 were judged to have need, 29 had their need fully met. 50 Federal Work-Study jobs (averaging $2085). *Average percent of need met:* 76. *Average financial aid package:* $9029. *Average need-based loan:* $4376. *Average need-based gift aid:* $6488. *Average indebtedness upon graduation:* $27,625.

Applying *Options:* electronic application, deferred entrance. *Application fee:* $25. *Required:* minimum 2.0 GPA. *Required for some:* essay or personal statement, high school transcript, 3 letters of recommendation, transfer students must have a 2.0 college GPA. *Recommended:* interview.

Freshman Application Contact Ms. Shelley Dunn, Director of Admissions, Victory University, 255 North Highland, Memphis, TN 38111-1375. *Phone:* 901-320-9777. *Toll-free phone:* 800-960-9777. *Fax:* 901-320-9791. *E-mail:* admissions@victory.edu. *Web site:* http://www.victory.edu/.

Watkins College of Art, Design, & Film

Nashville, Tennessee

- **Independent** 4-year, founded 1885
- **Urban** 13-acre campus
- **Endowment** $1.3 million
- **Coed** 394 undergraduate students, 66% full-time, 52% women, 48% men
- **Moderately difficult** entrance level, 85% of applicants were admitted

Undergraduates 261 full-time, 133 part-time. Students come from 32 states and territories; 3 other countries; 33% are from out of state; 7% Black or African American, non-Hispanic/Latino; 3% Hispanic/Latino; 2% Asian, non-Hispanic/Latino; 0.3% Native Hawaiian or other Pacific Islander, non-Hispanic/Latino; 0.3% American Indian or Alaska Native, non-Hispanic/Latino; 4% Two or more races, non-Hispanic/Latino; 3% Race/ethnicity unknown; 0.8% international; 24% live on campus. *Retention:* 69% of full-time freshmen returned.

Freshmen *Admission:* 126 applied, 107 admitted. *Average high school GPA:* 3.01. *Test scores:* SAT critical reading scores over 500: 60%; ACT scores over 18: 89%; SAT critical reading scores over 600: 10%; ACT scores over 24: 38%; ACT scores over 30: 3%.

Faculty *Total:* 65, 31% full-time, 58% with terminal degrees. *Student/faculty ratio:* 7:1.

Academics *Calendar:* semesters. *Degree:* certificates and bachelor's. *Special study options:* advanced placement credit, cooperative education, independent study, internships, part-time degree program, services for LD students, summer session for credit.

Computers on Campus 200 computers/terminals and 175 ports are available on campus for general student use. Students can access the following: campus intranet, computer help desk, free student e-mail accounts, online (class) grades, online (class) schedules. Campuswide network is available. 100% of college-owned or -operated housing units are wired for high-speed Internet access. Wireless service is available via entire campus.

Student Life *Housing:* on-campus residence required for freshman year. *Options:* men-only, women-only, disabled students. Campus housing is university owned. Freshman applicants given priority for college housing. *Activities and organizations:* Company Q (art society), Film club, sports club, OWL (One Wise Life). *Campus security:* 24-hour emergency response devices and patrols, late-night transport/escort service, controlled dormitory access, monitored 24 hour camera security. *Student services:* health clinic, personal/psychological counseling.

Standardized Tests *Required:* SAT or ACT (for admission).

Costs (2012–13) *Tuition:* $19,650 full-time, $655 per credit part-time. *Required fees:* $1650 full-time, $55 per credit part-time. *Room only:* $6200. *Payment plan:* installment. *Waivers:* employees or children of employees.

Financial Aid Of all full-time matriculated undergraduates who enrolled in 2008, 174 applied for aid, 174 were judged to have need, 30 had their need fully met. 17 Federal Work-Study jobs (averaging $1300). 25 state and other part-time jobs (averaging $2000). In 2008, 30 non-need-based awards were made. *Average percent of need met:* 45%. *Average financial aid package:* $11,150. *Average need-based loan:* $4750. *Average need-based gift aid:* $4000. *Average non-need-based aid:* $4000. *Average indebtedness upon graduation:* $15,000.

Applying *Options:* electronic application, early admission, deferred entrance. *Application fee:* $50. *Required:* essay or personal statement, high school transcript, minimum 2.6 GPA, 1 letter of recommendation. *Required for some:* high school transcript, artistic exercises, optional portfolio. *Recommended:* interview. *Application deadlines:* 7/15 (freshmen), 7/15 (transfers). *Notification:* 8/1 (freshmen), 8/1 (transfers).

Freshman Application Contact Ms. Linda E. Schwab, Director of Admissions, Watkins College of Art, Design, & Film, 2298 Rosa L. Parks

Boulevard, Nashville, TN 37228. *Phone:* 615-383-4848 Ext. 7458. *Fax:* 615-383-4849. *E-mail:* admissions@watkins.edu. *Web site:* http://www.watkins.edu/.

Williamson Christian College
Franklin, Tennessee

Freshman Application Contact Ms. Mary Newby, Recruiter, Williamson Christian College, 200 Seaboard Lane, Franklin, TN 37067. *Phone:* 615-771-7821. *Fax:* 615-771-7810. *E-mail:* mary@williamsoncc.edu. *Web site:* http://www.williamsoncc.edu/.

TEXAS

Abilene Christian University
Abilene, Texas

- **Independent** comprehensive, founded 1906, affiliated with Church of Christ
- **Urban** 208-acre campus
- **Endowment** $302.2 million
- **Coed** 3,771 undergraduate students, 94% full-time, 54% women, 46% men
- **Moderately difficult** entrance level, 64% of applicants were admitted

Undergraduates 3,556 full-time, 215 part-time. Students come from 47 states and territories; 43 other countries; 16% are from out of state; 7% Black or African American, non-Hispanic/Latino; 9% Hispanic/Latino; 1% Asian, non-Hispanic/Latino; 0.1% Native Hawaiian or other Pacific Islander, non-Hispanic/Latino; 0.3% American Indian or Alaska Native, non-Hispanic/Latino; 2% Two or more races, non-Hispanic/Latino; 0.1% Race/ethnicity unknown; 5% international; 4% transferred in; 43% live on campus. *Retention:* 75% of full-time freshmen returned.

Freshmen *Admission:* 3,470 applied, 2,234 admitted, 864 enrolled. *Average high school GPA:* 3.56. *Test scores:* SAT critical reading scores over 500: 69%; SAT math scores over 500: 73%; ACT scores over 18: 99%; SAT critical reading scores over 600: 28%; SAT math scores over 600: 29%; ACT scores over 24: 64%; SAT critical reading scores over 700: 5%; SAT math scores over 700: 4%; ACT scores over 30: 15%.

Faculty *Total:* 354, 69% full-time, 67% with terminal degrees. *Student/faculty ratio:* 14:1.

Academics *Calendar:* semesters. *Degrees:* certificates, associate, bachelor's, master's, doctoral, post-master's, and postbachelor's certificates. *Special study options:* adult/continuing education programs, advanced placement credit, distance learning, double majors, English as a second language, honors programs, independent study, internships, off-campus study, part-time degree program, services for LD students, student-designed majors, study abroad, summer session for credit. *Unusual degree programs:* 3-2 engineering with The University of Texas at Arlington.

Computers on Campus 530 computers/terminals are available on campus for general student use. Students can access the following: campus intranet, computer help desk, free student e-mail accounts, online (class) grades, online (class) registration, online (class) schedules. Campuswide network is available. 100% of college-owned or -operated housing units are wired for high-speed Internet access. Wireless service is available via entire campus.

Student Life *Housing:* on-campus residence required through sophomore year. *Options:* men-only, women-only. Campus housing is university owned. Freshman campus housing is guaranteed. *Activities and organizations:* drama/theater group, student-run newspaper, radio and television station, choral group, marching band, Student Association, Graduate Students Association, Spring Break Campaigns, International Students Association, LYNAY. *Campus security:* 24-hour emergency response devices and patrols, student patrols, late-night transport/escort service, controlled dormitory access. *Student services:* health clinic, personal/psychological counseling.

Athletics Member NCAA. All Division II. *Intercollegiate sports:* baseball M(s), basketball M(s)/W(s), cross-country running M(s)/W(s), football M(s), golf M(s), soccer W(s), softball W(s), tennis M(s)/W(s), track and field M(s)/W(s), volleyball W(s). *Intramural sports:* basketball M/W, bowling M/W, football M/W, golf M/W, racquetball M/W, soccer M/W, softball M/W, tennis M/W, volleyball M/W, water polo M/W.

Standardized Tests *Required:* SAT or ACT (for admission).

Costs (2011–12) *Comprehensive fee:* $33,586 includes full-time tuition ($23,610), mandatory fees ($1660), and room and board ($8316). Full-time tuition and fees vary according to course load. Part-time tuition: $787 per credit hour. Part-time tuition and fees vary according to course load. *Required fees:* $82 per credit hour part-time, $10 per term part-time. *College room only:*

$3660. Room and board charges vary according to board plan and student level. *Payment plans:* tuition prepayment, installment. *Waivers:* employees or children of employees.

Financial Aid Of all full-time matriculated undergraduates who enrolled in 2011, 3,536 applied for aid, 2,330 were judged to have need, 492 had their need fully met. In 2011, 1127 non-need-based awards were made. *Average percent of need met:* 65%. *Average financial aid package:* $16,468. *Average need-based loan:* $4427. *Average need-based gift aid:* $12,357. *Average non-need-based aid:* $7174. *Average indebtedness upon graduation:* $39,508.

Applying *Options:* electronic application, early admission, early action. *Application fee:* $50. *Required:* essay or personal statement, high school transcript. *Application deadlines:* 2/15 (freshmen), rolling (transfers). *Notification:* 3/15 (freshmen), continuous until 9/1 (transfers).

Freshman Application Contact Admissions, Abilene Christian University, ACU Box 29000, Abilene, TX 79699-9000. *Phone:* 325-674-2650. *Fax:* 325-674-2130. *E-mail:* info@admissions.acu.edu. *Web site:* http://www.acu.edu/.

Amberton University
Garland, Texas

- **Independent nondenominational** upper-level, founded 1971
- **Suburban** 5-acre campus with easy access to Dallas-Fort Worth
- **Endowment** $10.0 million
- **Coed** 322 undergraduate students, 51% full-time, 60% women, 40% men
- **Minimally difficult** entrance level

Undergraduates 165 full-time, 157 part-time. Students come from 1 other state; 32% Black or African American, non-Hispanic/Latino; 8% Hispanic/Latino; 7% Asian, non-Hispanic/Latino; 7% Race/ethnicity unknown.

Faculty *Total:* 40, 38% full-time, 88% with terminal degrees. *Student/faculty ratio:* 25:1.

Academics *Calendar:* 4 10-week terms. *Degrees:* bachelor's and master's. *Special study options:* adult/continuing education programs, distance learning, external degree program, internships, part-time degree program, student-designed majors, summer session for credit.

Computers on Campus 30 computers/terminals are available on campus for general student use. Students can access the following: campus intranet, computer help desk, free student e-mail accounts, online (class) schedules.

Student Life *Housing:* college housing not available. *Campus security:* 24-hour emergency response devices and patrols.

Costs (2011–12) *Tuition:* $5600 full-time, $700 per course part-time. *Payment plan:* installment.

Applying *Options:* electronic application, deferred entrance. *Application deadline:* rolling (transfers). *Notification:* continuous (transfers).

Application Contact Dr. Don Hebbard, Academic Dean, Amberton University, 1700 Eastgate Drive, Garland, TX 75041-5595. *Phone:* 972-279-6511. *E-mail:* advisor@amberton.edu. *Web site:* http://www.amberton.edu/.

American InterContinental University Houston
Houston, Texas

Freshman Application Contact American InterContinental University Houston, 9999 Richmond Avenue, Houston, TX 77042. *Phone:* 877-564-6248. *Toll-free phone:* 888-607-9888. *Web site:* http://www.aiuniv.edu/.

Angelo State University
San Angelo, Texas

- **State-supported** comprehensive, founded 1928, part of Texas Tech University System
- **Urban** 268-acre campus
- **Endowment** $113.6 million
- **Coed** 6,267 undergraduate students, 83% full-time, 55% women, 45% men
- **Moderately difficult** entrance level, 93% of applicants were admitted

Undergraduates 5,218 full-time, 1,049 part-time. Students come from 44 states and territories; 24 other countries; 3% are from out of state; 7% Black or African American, non-Hispanic/Latino; 27% Hispanic/Latino; 1% Asian, non-Hispanic/Latino; 0.1% Native Hawaiian or other Pacific Islander, non-Hispanic/Latino; 0.6% American Indian or Alaska Native, non-Hispanic/Latino; 1% Two or more races, non-Hispanic/Latino; 0.4% Race/ethnicity unknown; 0.9% international; 7% transferred in; 35% live on campus. *Retention:* 61% of full-time freshmen returned.

Freshmen *Admission:* 4,527 applied, 4,202 admitted, 1,455 enrolled. *Test scores:* SAT critical reading scores over 500: 37%; SAT math scores over 500: 47%; ACT scores over 18: 77%; SAT critical reading scores over 600: 9%;

SAT math scores over 600: 13%; ACT scores over 24: 23%; SAT critical reading scores over 700: 1%; SAT math scores over 700: 1%; ACT scores over 30: 2%.

Faculty *Total:* 347, 78% full-time, 67% with terminal degrees. *Student/faculty ratio:* 21:1.

Academics *Calendar:* semesters. *Degrees:* associate, bachelor's, master's, and doctoral. *Special study options:* academic remediation for entering students, advanced placement credit, distance learning, double majors, English as a second language, honors programs, independent study, internships, part-time degree program, study abroad, summer session for credit. *ROTC:* Air Force (b). *Unusual degree programs:* 3-2 accounting.

Computers on Campus 553 computers/terminals and 3,600 ports are available on campus for general student use. Students can access the following: campus intranet, computer help desk, free student e-mail accounts, online (class) grades, online (class) registration, online (class) schedules, online courses, tuition payments, purchase books, purchase parking permits, university calendar, library card catalog and library resources. Discounted hardware and software programs for personally owned computers. Campuswide network is available. 100% of college-owned or -operated housing units are wired for high-speed Internet access. Wireless service is available via entire campus.

Student Life *Housing:* on-campus residence required through sophomore year. *Options:* coed, disabled students. Campus housing is university owned. *Activities and organizations:* drama/theater group, student-run newspaper, radio and television station, choral group, marching band, Association of Mexican-American Students, Block and Bridle Club, Air force ROTC, University Center Program Council, Baptist Student Union, national fraternities, national sororities. *Campus security:* 24-hour emergency response devices and patrols, student patrols, late-night transport/escort service, controlled dormitory access. *Student services:* health clinic, personal/psychological counseling.

Athletics Member NCAA. All Division II. *Intercollegiate sports:* baseball M(s), basketball M(s)/W(s), cross-country running M(s)/W(s), football M(s), golf W(s), soccer W(s), softball W(s), track and field M(s)/W(s), volleyball W(s). *Intramural sports:* badminton M/W, basketball M/W, bowling M/W, football M/W, golf M/W, racquetball M/W, soccer M/W, softball M/W, swimming and diving M/W, table tennis M/W, tennis M/W, ultimate Frisbee M/W, volleyball M/W, weight lifting M/W.

Standardized Tests *Required:* SAT or ACT (for admission).

Costs (2012–13) *Tuition:* state resident $4851 full-time, $259 per credit hour part-time; nonresident $14,240 full-time, $572 per credit hour part-time. *Required fees:* $2499 full-time, $28 per credit hour part-time, $580 per term part-time. *Room and board:* $6812; room only: $4814. Room and board charges vary according to board plan and housing facility. *Payment plan:* installment. *Waivers:* senior citizens and employees or children of employees.

Financial Aid Of all full-time matriculated undergraduates who enrolled in 2010, 4,374 applied for aid, 3,695 were judged to have need, 932 had their need fully met. In 2010, 540 non-need-based awards were made. *Average percent of need met:* 50%. *Average financial aid package:* $11,907. *Average need-based loan:* $3611. *Average need-based gift aid:* $3114. *Average non-need-based aid:* $3035. *Average indebtedness upon graduation:* $20,131.

Applying *Options:* electronic application, early admission, deferred entrance. *Application fee:* $35. *Required:* high school transcript, high school class rank. *Application deadlines:* rolling (freshmen), rolling (out-of-state freshmen), rolling (transfers). *Notification:* continuous (freshmen), continuous (out-of-state freshmen), continuous (transfers).

Freshman Application Contact Mr. Michael Loehring, Director of Recruitment Services and Admissions, Angelo State University, 2601 West Avenue N, San Angelo, TX 76909. *Phone:* 325-942-2185. *Toll-free phone:* 800-946-8627. *Fax:* 325-942-2078. *E-mail:* admissions@angelo.edu. *Web site:* http://www.angelo.edu/.

Argosy University, Dallas

Farmers Branch, Texas

Freshman Application Contact Argosy University, Dallas, 5001 Lyndon B. Johnson Freeway, Heritage Square, Farmers Branch, TX 75244. *Phone:* 214-890-9900. *Toll-free phone:* 866-954-9900. *Web site:* http://www.argosy.edu/dallas/.

See page 1062 for the College Close-Up.

Arlington Baptist College

Arlington, Texas

- **Independent Baptist** comprehensive, founded 1939
- **Urban** 32-acre campus with easy access to Dallas-Fort Worth
- **Endowment** $17,000
- **Coed** 220 undergraduate students, 90% full-time, 45% women, 55% men
- **Noncompetitive** entrance level, 100% of applicants were admitted

Undergraduates 198 full-time, 22 part-time. Students come from 15 states and territories; 6 other countries; 17% are from out of state; 18% Black or African American, non-Hispanic/Latino; 8% Hispanic/Latino; 2% American Indian or Alaska Native, non-Hispanic/Latino; 1% international; 18% transferred in; 46% live on campus. *Retention:* 51% of full-time freshmen returned.

Freshmen *Admission:* 86 applied, 86 admitted, 54 enrolled. *Average high school GPA:* 2.88.

Faculty *Total:* 17, 71% full-time, 12% with terminal degrees. *Student/faculty ratio:* 16:1.

Academics *Calendar:* semesters. *Degrees:* certificates, diplomas, bachelor's, and master's. *Special study options:* academic remediation for entering students, advanced placement credit, distance learning, double majors, independent study, internships, part-time degree program, summer session for credit.

Computers on Campus 25 computers/terminals are available on campus for general student use. Students can access the following: online (class) grades, online (class) registration, online (class) schedules. Campuswide network is available. Wireless service is available via classrooms, computer labs, dorm rooms, libraries, student centers.

Student Life *Housing:* on-campus residence required through senior year. *Options:* men-only, women-only. Campus housing is university owned. Freshman campus housing is guaranteed. *Activities and organizations:* drama/theater group, choral group, Student Missionary Association, 4-12 Group. *Campus security:* controlled dormitory access, night security guards. *Student services:* personal/psychological counseling.

Athletics Member NCCAA. *Intercollegiate sports:* baseball M, basketball M/W, cross-country running M/W, volleyball W.

Costs (2012–13) *Comprehensive fee:* $12,640 includes full-time tuition ($7100), mandatory fees ($740), and room and board ($4800). Full-time tuition and fees vary according to course load. Part-time tuition: $220 per credit hour. Part-time tuition and fees vary according to course load. *Required fees:* $740 per term part-time. *Payment plan:* installment. *Waivers:* employees or children of employees.

Financial Aid Of all full-time matriculated undergraduates who enrolled in 2006, 164 applied for aid, 118 were judged to have need, 93 had their need fully met. *Average financial aid package:* $6847. *Average indebtedness upon graduation:* $4838.

Applying *Options:* electronic application, early admission, deferred entrance. *Application fee:* $15. *Required:* essay or personal statement, high school transcript, 1 letter of recommendation, pastoral recommendation, medical examination. *Required for some:* interview. *Application deadlines:* rolling (freshmen), rolling (transfers). *Notification:* continuous (freshmen), continuous (transfers).

Freshman Application Contact Ms. Janie Taylor, Registrar/Admissions, Arlington Baptist College, 3001 West Division, Arlington, TX 76012-3425. *Phone:* 817-461-8741 Ext. 105. *Fax:* 817-274-1138. *E-mail:* jtaylor@arlingtonbaptistcollege.edu. *Web site:* http://www.abconline.org/.

The Art Institute of Austin

Austin, Texas

- **Proprietary** 4-year, part of Education Management Corporation
- **Coed**

Academics *Degrees:* associate and bachelor's.

Costs (2011–12) *Tuition:* Tuition cost varies by program. Prospective students should contact the school for current tuition costs. Other charges include a starting kit for all first-quarter students. Kits vary in price, depending on the program of study.

Freshman Application Contact The Art Institute of Austin, 101 W. Louis Henna Boulevard, Suite 100, Austin, TX 78728. *Phone:* 512-691-1707. *Toll-free phone:* 866-583-7952. *Web site:* http://www.artinstitutes.edu/austin.

See page 1070 for the College Close-Up.

The Art Institute of Dallas
Dallas, Texas

- **Proprietary** comprehensive, founded 1978, part of Education Management Corporation
- **Urban** 2-acre campus
- **Coed**

Academics *Calendar:* quarters. *Degrees:* certificates, associate, bachelor's, and master's.

Costs (2011–12) *Tuition:* Tuition cost varies by program. Prospective students should contact the school for current tuition costs. Other charges include a starting kit for all first-quarter students. Kits vary in price, depending on the program of study.

Freshman Application Contact The Art Institute of Dallas, 8080 Park Lane, Suite 100, Dallas, TX 75231-5993. *Phone:* 214-692-8080. *Toll-free phone:* 800-275-4243. *Web site:* http://www.artinstitutes.edu/dallas/.

See page 1094 for the College Close-Up.

The Art Institute of Fort Worth
Fort Worth, Texas

- **Proprietary** 4-year
- **Coed**

Academics *Degrees:* certificates, associate, and bachelor's.

Costs (2011–12) *Tuition:* Tuition cost varies by program. Prospective students should contact the school for current tuition costs. Other charges include a starting kit for all first-quarter students. Kits vary in price, depending on the program of study.

Freshman Application Contact The Art Institute of Fort Worth, 7000 Calmont Avenue, Suite 150, Fort Worth, TX 76116. *Phone:* 817-210-0808. *Toll-free phone:* 888-422-9686. *Web site:* http://www.artinstitutes.edu/fort-worth/.

See page 1098 for the College Close-Up.

The Art Institute of Houston
Houston, Texas

- **Proprietary** 4-year, founded 1978, part of Education Management Corporation
- **Urban** campus
- **Coed**

Academics *Calendar:* quarters. *Degrees:* diplomas, associate, and bachelor's.

Costs (2011–12) *Tuition:* Tuition cost varies by program. Prospective students should contact the school for current tuition costs. Other charges include a starting kit for all first-quarter students. Kits vary in price, depending on the program of study.

Freshman Application Contact The Art Institute of Houston, 1900 Yorktown Street, Houston, TX 77056. *Phone:* 713-623-2040. *Toll-free phone:* 800-275-4244. *Web site:* http://www.artinstitutes.edu/houston/.

See page 1100 for the College Close-Up.

The Art Institute of Houston - North
Houston, Texas

- **Proprietary** 4-year
- **Coed**

Academics *Degrees:* diplomas, associate, and bachelor's.

Costs (2011–12) *Tuition:* Tuition cost varies by program. Prospective students should contact the school for current tuition costs. Other charges include a starting kit for all first-quarter students. Kits vary in price, depending on the program of study.

Freshman Application Contact The Art Institute of Houston - North, 10740 North Gessner Drive, Suite 190, Houston, TX 77064. *Phone:* 281-671-3381. *Toll-free phone:* 866-830-4450. *Web site:* http://www.artinstitutes.edu/houston-north.

See page 1102 for the College Close-Up.

The Art Institute of San Antonio
San Antonio, Texas

- **Proprietary** 4-year
- **Coed**

Academics *Degrees:* diplomas, associate, and bachelor's.

Costs (2011–12) *Tuition:* Tuition cost varies by program. Prospective students should contact the school for current tuition costs. Other charges include a

starting kit for all first-quarter students. Kits vary in price, depending on the program of study.

Freshman Application Contact The Art Institute of San Antonio, 1000 IH-10 West, Suite 200, San Antonio, TX 78230. *Phone:* 210-338-7320. *Toll-free phone:* 888-222-0040. *Web site:* http://www.artinstitutes.edu/san-antonio/.

See page 1128 for the College Close-Up.

Austin College
Sherman, Texas

- **Independent Presbyterian** comprehensive, founded 1849
- **Small-town** 60-acre campus with easy access to Dallas-Fort Worth
- **Endowment** $124.9 million
- **Coed** 1,329 undergraduate students, 99% full-time, 53% women, 47% men
- **Very difficult** entrance level, 52% of applicants were admitted

Undergraduates 1,315 full-time, 14 part-time. Students come from 30 states and territories; 11 other countries; 12% are from out of state; 4% Black or African American, non-Hispanic/Latino; 14% Hispanic/Latino; 14% Asian, non-Hispanic/Latino; 0.5% American Indian or Alaska Native, non-Hispanic/Latino; 4% Two or more races, non-Hispanic/Latino; 1% Race/ethnicity unknown; 0.4% international; 2% transferred in; 75% live on campus. *Retention:* 84% of full-time freshmen returned.

Freshmen *Admission:* 3,309 applied, 1,736 admitted, 359 enrolled. *Average high school GPA:* 3.68. *Test scores:* SAT critical reading scores over 500: 94%; SAT math scores over 500: 92%; SAT writing scores over 500: 85%; ACT scores over 18: 100%; SAT critical reading scores over 600: 66%; SAT math scores over 600: 60%; SAT writing scores over 600: 48%; ACT scores over 24: 71%; SAT critical reading scores over 700: 14%; SAT math scores over 700: 14%; SAT writing scores over 700: 9%; ACT scores over 30: 18%.

Faculty *Total:* 146, 64% full-time, 71% with terminal degrees. *Student/faculty ratio:* 12:1.

Academics *Calendar:* 4-1-4. *Degrees:* bachelor's and master's. *Special study options:* adult/continuing education programs, advanced placement credit, double majors, honors programs, independent study, internships, off-campus study, part-time degree program, student-designed majors, study abroad, summer session for credit. *Unusual degree programs:* 3-2 engineering with University of Texas at Dallas, Texas A&M University, Washington University in St. Louis, Columbia University.

Computers on Campus 160 computers/terminals are available on campus for general student use. Students can access the following: campus intranet, computer help desk, free student e-mail accounts, online (class) grades, online (class) registration, online (class) schedules. Campuswide network is available. 100% of college-owned or -operated housing units are wired for high-speed Internet access. Wireless service is available via entire campus.

Student Life *Housing:* on-campus residence required through junior year. *Options:* coed, men-only, women-only, disabled students. Campus housing is university owned. Freshman campus housing is guaranteed. *Activities and organizations:* drama/theater group, student-run newspaper, choral group, Fellowship of Christian Athletes, Campus Activity Board, Indian Cultural Association, Student Development Board, International Relations Club. *Campus security:* 24-hour emergency response devices and patrols, late-night transport/escort service, controlled dormitory access. *Student services:* health clinic, personal/psychological counseling.

Athletics Member NCAA. All Division III. *Intercollegiate sports:* baseball M, basketball M/W, cheerleading M/W, football M, soccer M/W, softball W, swimming and diving M/W, tennis M/W, volleyball W. *Intramural sports:* basketball M/W, football M/W, soccer M/W, softball W, swimming and diving M/W, table tennis M/W, tennis M/W, ultimate Frisbee M/W, volleyball W.

Standardized Tests *Required:* SAT or ACT (for admission).

Costs (2012–13) *One-time required fee:* $25. *Comprehensive fee:* $42,979 includes full-time tuition ($32,665), mandatory fees ($160), and room and board ($10,154). Full-time tuition and fees vary according to student level. *Room and board:* Room and board charges vary according to board plan. *Payment plan:* installment. *Waivers:* employees or children of employees.

Financial Aid Of all full-time matriculated undergraduates who enrolled in 2011, 1,283 applied for aid, 897 were judged to have need, 897 had their need fully met. In 2011, 371 non-need-based awards were made. *Average percent of need met:* 100%. *Average financial aid package:* $32,280. *Average need-based loan:* $5126. *Average need-based gift aid:* $20,365. *Average non-need-based aid:* $15,057.

Applying *Options:* electronic application, early admission, deferred entrance. *Required:* essay or personal statement, high school transcript, 2 letters of recommendation. *Required for some:* interview. *Recommended:* minimum 3.0 GPA, interview. *Application deadlines:* 5/1 (freshmen), 5/1 (transfers).

Freshman Application Contact Ms. Nan Davis, Vice President for Institutional Enrollment, Austin College, 900 North Grand Avenue, Suite 6N, Sherman, TX 75090-4400. *Phone:* 903-813-3000. *Toll-free phone:* 800-596-

4276 (in-state); 800-526.4276 (out-of-state). *Fax:* 903-813-3198. *E-mail:* admission@austincollege.edu. *Web site:* http://www.austincollege.edu/.

Austin Graduate School of Theology
Austin, Texas

Application Contact Mrs. Celeste Scarbrough, Director of Admissions, Austin Graduate School of Theology, 7640 Guadalupe Street, Austin, TX 78752. *Phone:* 512-476-2772. *Toll-free phone:* 866-AUS-GRAD. *Fax:* 512-476-3919. *E-mail:* registrar@austingrad.edu. *Web site:* http://www.austingrad.edu/.

Baptist Missionary Association Theological Seminary
Jacksonville, Texas

Director of Admissions Dr. Philip Attebery, Dean and Registrar, Baptist Missionary Association Theological Seminary, 1530 East Pine Street, Jacksonville, TX 75766-5407. *Phone:* 903-586-2501 Ext. 229. *Toll-free phone:* 800-259-5673. *E-mail:* attebery@bmats.edu. *Web site:* http://www.bmats.edu/.

Baptist University of the Americas
San Antonio, Texas

- **Independent Baptist** 4-year, founded 1947
- **Urban** 90-acre campus with easy access to San Antonio
- **Coed** 175 undergraduate students

Undergraduates 5% are from out of state. *Retention:* 31% of full-time freshmen returned.
Faculty *Total:* 7, 100% full-time, 71% with terminal degrees. *Student/faculty ratio:* 12:1.
Academics *Calendar:* semesters. *Degrees:* certificates, diplomas, associate, bachelor's, and postbachelor's certificates (associate degree in Cross-Cultural Studies). *Special study options:* academic remediation for entering students, advanced placement credit, double majors, English as a second language, independent study, internships, part-time degree program, services for LD students.
Computers on Campus 22 computers/terminals are available on campus for general student use. Students can access the following: computer help desk, free student e-mail accounts. Campuswide network is available. Wireless service is available via classrooms, dorm rooms, libraries.
Student Life *Housing options:* coed, men-only, women-only, disabled students. Campus housing is university owned. *Activities and organizations:* choral group, Communities In Schools, Missions Society, Navigators. *Student services:* personal/psychological counseling.
Athletics *Intramural sports:* soccer M(c).
Standardized Tests *Required for some:* ACCUPLACER, THEA (Texas Higher Education Assessment).
Costs (2012–13) *Tuition:* $200 per hour part-time. *Waivers:* employees or children of employees.
Financial Aid Of all full-time matriculated undergraduates who enrolled in 2010, 3 Federal Work-Study jobs (averaging $4072). 81 state and other part-time jobs (averaging $216,657).
Applying *Application fee:* $25. *Required:* essay or personal statement, high school transcript, 3 letters of recommendation. *Required for some:* interview. *Application deadlines:* 2/15 (freshmen), 2/15 (out-of-state freshmen).
Freshman Application Contact Baptist University of the Americas, 8019 South Pan Am Expressway, San Antonio, TX 78224-2701. *Phone:* 210-924-4338 Ext. 202. *Toll-free phone:* 800-721-1396. *Web site:* http://www.bua.edu/.

Baylor University
Waco, Texas

- **Independent Baptist** university, founded 1845
- **Urban** 1000-acre campus with easy access to Dallas-Fort Worth
- **Endowment** $1.0 billion
- **Coed** 12,575 undergraduate students, 98% full-time, 58% women, 42% men
- **Moderately difficult** entrance level, 40% of applicants were admitted

Undergraduates 12,350 full-time, 225 part-time. Students come from 51 states and territories; 71 other countries; 20% are from out of state; 8% Black or African American, non-Hispanic/Latino; 13% Hispanic/Latino; 6% Asian, non-Hispanic/Latino; 0.1% Native Hawaiian or other Pacific Islander, non-Hispanic/Latino; 0.3% American Indian or Alaska Native, non-Hispanic/Latino; 4% Two or more races, non-Hispanic/Latino; 0.2% Race/ethnicity unknown; 2% international; 4% transferred in; 36% live on campus. *Retention:* 85% of full-time freshmen returned.
Freshmen *Admission:* 38,960 applied, 15,451 admitted, 3,033 enrolled. *Test scores:* SAT critical reading scores over 500: 95%; SAT math scores over 500: 97%; SAT writing scores over 500: 90%; ACT scores over 18: 100%; SAT critical reading scores over 600: 55%; SAT math scores over 600: 66%; SAT writing scores over 600: 48%; ACT scores over 24: 84%; SAT critical reading scores over 700: 15%; SAT math scores over 700: 17%; SAT writing scores over 700: 11%; ACT scores over 30: 24%.
Faculty *Total:* 1,211, 73% full-time. *Student/faculty ratio:* 14:1.
Academics *Calendar:* semesters. *Degrees:* certificates, bachelor's, master's, doctoral, post-master's, and first professional certificates. *Special study options:* accelerated degree program, advanced placement credit, double majors, honors programs, internships, part-time degree program, services for LD students, student-designed majors, study abroad, summer session for credit. *ROTC:* Army (b), Air Force (b). *Unusual degree programs:* 3-2 forestry with Duke University; clinical laboratory science, medicine, dentistry, optometry.
Computers on Campus 1,676 computers/terminals are available on campus for general student use. Students can access the following: campus intranet, computer help desk, free student e-mail accounts, online (class) grades, online (class) registration, online (class) schedules. Campuswide network is available. 99% of college-owned or -operated housing units are wired for high-speed Internet access. Wireless service is available via entire campus.
Student Life *Housing:* on-campus residence required for freshman year. *Options:* men-only, women-only, disabled students. Campus housing is university owned. Freshman campus housing is guaranteed. *Activities and organizations:* drama/theater group, student-run newspaper, radio and television station, choral group, marching band, The Bear Pit, Alpha Lambda Delta, Delta Epsilon Iota, National Society of Collegiate Scholars, American Medical Student Association, national fraternities, national sororities. *Campus security:* 24-hour emergency response devices and patrols, late-night transport/escort service, controlled dormitory access, bicycle patrols. *Student services:* health clinic, personal/psychological counseling, legal services.
Athletics Member NCAA. All Division I except football (Division I-A). *Intercollegiate sports:* baseball M(s), basketball M(s)/W(s), crew M(c)/W(c), cross-country running M(s)/W(s), equestrian sports W(s), fencing M(c)/W(c), golf M(s)/W(s), gymnastics M(c)/W(c), ice hockey M(c), lacrosse M(c)/W(c), rock climbing M(c)/W(c), rugby M(c), sailing M(c)/W(c), skiing (downhill) M(c)/W(c), soccer M(c)/W(s), softball W(s), tennis M(s)/W(s), track and field M(s)/W(s), ultimate Frisbee M(c), volleyball M(c)/W(s), water polo M(c)/W(c). *Intramural sports:* basketball M/W, cross-country running M/W, football M/W, racquetball M/W, soccer M/W, softball M/W, table tennis M/W, tennis M/W, ultimate Frisbee M/W, volleyball M/W.
Standardized Tests *Required:* SAT or ACT (for admission).
Costs (2012–13) *Comprehensive fee:* $43,138 includes full-time tuition ($30,586), mandatory fees ($3130), and room and board ($9422). Part-time tuition: $1274 per semester hour. *Required fees:* $131 per semester hour part-time. *College room only:* $5290. Room and board charges vary according to board plan and housing facility. *Payment plan:* installment. *Waivers:* employees or children of employees.
Financial Aid Of all full-time matriculated undergraduates who enrolled in 2011, 8,263 applied for aid, 7,126 were judged to have need, 1,172 had their need fully met. 4,913 Federal Work-Study jobs (averaging $2738). In 2011, 3861 non-need-based awards were made. *Average percent of need met:* 66%. *Average financial aid package:* $22,662. *Average need-based loan:* $3662. *Average need-based gift aid:* $16,935. *Average non-need-based aid:* $11,085.
Applying *Options:* electronic application, early admission, early action. *Application fee:* $50. *Required:* high school transcript. *Required for some:* essay or personal statement, minimum 2.5 GPA, 2 letters of recommendation. *Recommended:* interview. *Application deadlines:* 2/1 (freshmen), rolling (transfers), 11/1 (early action). *Notification:* 3/15 (freshmen), continuous (transfers), 1/15 (early action).
Freshman Application Contact Ms. Jessica King Gereghty, Director of Admissions, Baylor University, PO Box 97056, Waco, TX 76798. *Phone:* 254-710-3435. *Toll-free phone:* 800-BAYLORU. *Fax:* 254-710-3436. *E-mail:* admissions@baylor.edu. *Web site:* http://www.baylor.edu/.

Brazosport College
Lake Jackson, Texas

Freshman Application Contact Brazosport College, 500 College Drive, Lake Jackson, TX 77566-3199. *Phone:* 979-230-3020. *Web site:* http://www.brazosport.edu/.

Brown Mackie College–Dallas

Bedford, Texas

Admissions Office Contact Brown Mackie College–Dallas, 2200 North Highway 121, Suite 270, Bedford, TX 76021. *Web site:* http://www.brownmackie.edu/dallas/.

See page 1196 for the College Close-Up.

Brown Mackie College–San Antonio

San Antonio, Texas

- **Proprietary** 4-year, part of Education Management Corporation
- **Coed**

Academics *Degrees:* associate and bachelor's.

Costs (2011–12) *Tuition:* Tuition varies by program. Students should contact Brown Mackie College for tuition information.

Director of Admissions Director of Admissions, Brown Mackie College–San Antonio, 4715 Fredericksburg Road, Suite 100, San Antonio, TX 78229. *Phone:* 210-428-2210. *Toll-free phone:* 877-460-1714. *Web site:* http://www.brownmackie.edu/san-antonio.

See page 1222 for the College Close-Up.

Chamberlain College of Nursing

Houston, Texas

- **Proprietary** 4-year
- **Coed** 113 undergraduate students, 69% full-time, 90% women, 10% men
- **Moderately difficult** entrance level

Undergraduates 78 full-time, 35 part-time. 3% are from out of state; 46% Black or African American, non-Hispanic/Latino; 12% Hispanic/Latino; 6% Asian, non-Hispanic/Latino; 15% Race/ethnicity unknown; 91% transferred in.

Freshmen *Admission:* 4 enrolled.

Faculty *Total:* 6, 50% full-time. *Student/faculty ratio:* 22:1.

Academics *Degree:* bachelor's.

Student Life *Housing:* college housing not available.

Standardized Tests *Required:* SAT or ACT (for admission).

Applying *Application fee:* $95. *Application deadlines:* rolling (freshmen), rolling (transfers). *Notification:* continuous (freshmen), continuous (transfers).

Freshman Application Contact Director of Recruitment, Chamberlain College of Nursing, 10025 Equity Drive, Houston, TX 77041. *Phone:* 713-277-9800. *Web site:* http://www.chamberlain.edu/.

College of Biblical Studies–Houston

Houston, Texas

Freshman Application Contact Admissions, College of Biblical Studies–Houston, 7000 Regency Square Boulevard, Houston, TX 77036. *Phone:* 832-252-3377. *Fax:* 713-532-8150. *E-mail:* admissions@cbshouston.edu. *Web site:* http://www.cbshouston.edu/.

The College of Saints John Fisher & Thomas More

Fort Worth, Texas

Freshman Application Contact Dr. James A. Patrick, The College of Saints John Fisher & Thomas More, 3020 Lubbock Avenue, Fort Worth, TX 76109-2323. *Phone:* 817-928-8459. *Fax:* 817-924-3206. *E-mail:* more-info@cstm.edu. *Web site:* http://www.fishermore.edu/.

Concordia University Texas

Austin, Texas

- **Independent** comprehensive, founded 1926, affiliated with Lutheran Church–Missouri Synod, part of Concordia University System
- **Urban** 385-acre campus with easy access to Austin
- **Endowment** $12.1 million
- **Coed** 1,502 undergraduate students, 79% full-time, 63% women, 37% men
- **Moderately difficult** entrance level, 92% of applicants were admitted

Undergraduates 1,190 full-time, 312 part-time. Students come from 26 states and territories; 2 other countries; 4% are from out of state; 12% Black or African American, non-Hispanic/Latino; 19% Hispanic/Latino; 3% Asian, non-Hispanic/Latino; 0.6% American Indian or Alaska Native, non-Hispanic/Latino; 7% Race/ethnicity unknown; 12% transferred in; 15% live on campus. *Retention:* 54% of full-time freshmen returned.

Freshmen *Admission:* 813 applied, 752 admitted, 276 enrolled. *Average high school GPA:* 3.43. *Test scores:* SAT critical reading scores over 500: 46%; SAT math scores over 500: 60%; SAT writing scores over 500: 40%; ACT scores over 18: 87%; SAT critical reading scores over 600: 14%; SAT math scores over 600: 13%; SAT writing scores over 600: 10%; ACT scores over 24: 37%; SAT critical reading scores over 700: 2%; SAT math scores over 700: 1%; SAT writing scores over 700: 1%; ACT scores over 30: 4%.

Faculty *Total:* 270, 25% full-time, 64% with terminal degrees. *Student/faculty ratio:* 19:1.

Academics *Calendar:* semesters. *Degrees:* certificates, associate, bachelor's, master's, and postbachelor's certificates. *Special study options:* academic remediation for entering students, accelerated degree program, adult/continuing education programs, advanced placement credit, double majors, honors programs, independent study, internships, part-time degree program, services for LD students, study abroad, summer session for credit. *ROTC:* Army (c), Air Force (c).

Computers on Campus 25 computers/terminals and 50 ports are available on campus for general student use. Students can access the following: computer help desk, free student e-mail accounts, online (class) grades, online (class) registration, online (class) schedules. Campuswide network is available. 100% of college-owned or -operated housing units are wired for high-speed Internet access. Wireless service is available via entire campus.

Student Life *Housing:* on-campus residence required for freshman year. *Options:* coed. Campus housing is university owned. Freshman campus housing is guaranteed. *Activities and organizations:* drama/theater group, student-run newspaper, radio station, choral group, student government, Business Club (The Executives), Education Club, Student Nursing Association, Student Athlete Advisory Committee. *Campus security:* student patrols, late-night transport/escort service, controlled dormitory access. *Student services:* personal/psychological counseling.

Athletics Member NCAA. All Division III. *Intercollegiate sports:* baseball M, basketball M/W, cross-country running M/W, golf M/W, soccer M/W, softball W, track and field M/W, volleyball W. *Intramural sports:* badminton M/W, basketball M/W, football M/W, golf M/W, racquetball M/W, softball M/W, table tennis M/W, tennis M/W, volleyball M/W.

Standardized Tests *Required:* SAT or ACT (for admission).

Costs (2011–12) *Comprehensive fee:* $31,380 includes full-time tuition ($22,920) and room and board ($8460). Full-time tuition and fees vary according to course load, degree level, and program. Part-time tuition: $760 per hour. Part-time tuition and fees vary according to course load, degree level, and program. *College room only:* $4800. Room and board charges vary according to board plan. *Payment plan:* installment. *Waivers:* employees or children of employees.

Financial Aid Of all full-time matriculated undergraduates who enrolled in 2010, 811 applied for aid, 685 were judged to have need, 150 had their need fully met. In 2010, 159 non-need-based awards were made. *Average percent of need met:* 74%. *Average financial aid package:* $16,227. *Average need-based loan:* $4872. *Average need-based gift aid:* $11,786. *Average non-need-based aid:* $9437. *Average indebtedness upon graduation:* $24,472.

Applying *Options:* electronic application, early admission, deferred entrance. *Application fee:* $25. *Required:* high school transcript, minimum 2.5 GPA. *Required for some:* essay or personal statement, interview. *Application deadlines:* rolling (freshmen), rolling (transfers). *Notification:* continuous (freshmen), continuous (transfers).

Freshman Application Contact Ms. KC Pospisil, Assistant Director of Traditional Undergraduate Admissions, Concordia University Texas, 11400 Concordia University Drive, Austin, TX 78726. *Phone:* 512-313-3000. *Toll-free phone:* 800-865-4282. *Fax:* 512-459-8517. *E-mail:* admissions@concordia.edu. *Web site:* http://www.concordia.edu/.

The Criswell College

Dallas, Texas

- **Independent** comprehensive, founded 1970, affiliated with Southern Baptist Convention
- **Urban** 1-acre campus
- **Coed**
- **Minimally difficult** entrance level

Academics *Calendar:* semesters. *Degrees:* associate, bachelor's, and master's. *Special study options:* part-time degree program, summer session for credit.

Student Life *Housing:* college housing not available. *Campus security:* 24-hour emergency response devices and patrols, late-night transport/escort service.

Financial Aid Of all full-time matriculated undergraduates who enrolled in 2008, 173 applied for aid, 173 were judged to have need. 24 state and other

part-time jobs (averaging $2089). *Average financial aid package:* $1165. *Average non-need-based aid:* $1034.

Applying *Application fee:* $35.

Freshman Application Contact The Criswell College, 4010 Gaston Avenue, Dallas, TX 75246-1537. *Phone:* 214-821-5433. *Toll-free phone:* 800-899-0012. *Web site:* http://www.criswell.edu/.

Dallas Baptist University
Dallas, Texas

- **Independent** comprehensive, founded 1965, affiliated with Baptist General Convention of Texas
- **Urban** 293-acre campus
- **Endowment** $34.0 million
- **Coed** 3,485 undergraduate students, 67% full-time, 58% women, 42% men
- **Moderately difficult** entrance level, 44% of applicants were admitted

Undergraduates 2,347 full-time, 1,138 part-time. Students come from 44 states and territories; 46 other countries; 6% are from out of state; 17% Black or African American, non-Hispanic/Latino; 10% Hispanic/Latino; 2% Asian, non-Hispanic/Latino; 0.1% Native Hawaiian or other Pacific Islander, non-Hispanic/Latino; 1% American Indian or Alaska Native, non-Hispanic/Latino; 8% international; 8% transferred in; 49% live on campus. *Retention:* 73% of full-time freshmen returned.

Freshmen *Admission:* 2,126 applied, 930 admitted, 444 enrolled. *Average high school GPA:* 3.51. *Test scores:* SAT critical reading scores over 500: 79%; SAT math scores over 500: 81%; ACT scores over 18: 98%; SAT critical reading scores over 600: 31%; SAT math scores over 600: 34%; ACT scores over 24: 41%; SAT critical reading scores over 700: 5%; SAT math scores over 700: 3%; ACT scores over 30: 5%.

Faculty *Total:* 536, 24% full-time, 43% with terminal degrees. *Student/faculty ratio:* 15:1.

Academics *Calendar:* 4-1-4. *Degrees:* certificates, associate, bachelor's, master's, doctoral, post-master's, postbachelor's, and first professional certificates. *Special study options:* academic remediation for entering students, accelerated degree program, adult/continuing education programs, advanced placement credit, distance learning, double majors, English as a second language, honors programs, independent study, internships, off-campus study, part-time degree program, services for LD students, study abroad, summer session for credit. *ROTC:* Army (c), Air Force (c).

Computers on Campus 244 computers/terminals are available on campus for general student use. Students can access the following: computer help desk, free student e-mail accounts, online (class) grades, online (class) registration, online (class) schedules. Campuswide network is available. 100% of college-owned or -operated housing units are wired for high-speed Internet access. Wireless service is available via entire campus.

Student Life *Housing:* on-campus residence required through senior year. *Options:* men-only, women-only, disabled students. Campus housing is university owned and leased by the school. Freshman applicants given priority for college housing. *Activities and organizations:* drama/theater group, choral group, Ministry Fellowship, Baptist Student Ministry, Student Government Association, Student Education Association, International Student Organization. *Campus security:* 24-hour emergency response devices and patrols, late-night transport/escort service, controlled dormitory access. *Student services:* health clinic, personal/psychological counseling.

Athletics Member NCAA, NCCAA. All NCAA Division II. *Intercollegiate sports:* baseball M(s), basketball M(s), cheerleading W(c), cross-country running M/W(s), golf M/W(s), ice hockey M(c), soccer M/W(s), tennis M/W(s), track and field M/W(s), volleyball W(s). *Intramural sports:* basketball M/W, cross-country running M/W, football M/W, golf M/W, soccer M/W, softball M/W, table tennis M/W, tennis M/W, ultimate Frisbee M/W, volleyball M/W.

Standardized Tests *Required:* SAT or ACT (for admission).

Costs (2011–12) *Comprehensive fee:* $25,970 includes full-time tuition ($19,800), mandatory fees ($50), and room and board ($6120). Part-time tuition: $660 per unit. *College room only:* $2440. Room and board charges vary according to board plan and housing facility. *Payment plans:* installment, deferred payment. *Waivers:* employees or children of employees.

Financial Aid Of all full-time matriculated undergraduates who enrolled in 2011, 1,895 applied for aid, 1,538 were judged to have need, 680 had their need fully met. 179 Federal Work-Study jobs (averaging $2208). 46 state and other part-time jobs (averaging $781). In 2011, 412 non-need-based awards were made. *Average percent of need met:* 64%. *Average financial aid package:* $15,372. *Average need-based loan:* $4177. *Average need-based gift aid:* $3525. *Average non-need-based aid:* $7482. *Average indebtedness upon graduation:* $17,746.

Applying *Options:* electronic application, early admission, deferred entrance. *Application fee:* $25. *Required:* essay or personal statement, high school transcript, minimum 2.5 GPA, rank in upper 50% of high school class. *Recom-*

mended: interview. *Application deadlines:* rolling (freshmen), rolling (transfers). *Notification:* continuous (freshmen), continuous (transfers).

Freshman Application Contact Mr. Jason Williams, Assistant Vice President for Enrollment Services, Dallas Baptist University, 3000 Mountain Creek Parkway, Dallas, TX 75211-9299. *Phone:* 214-333-5360. *Toll-free phone:* 800-460-1328. *Fax:* 214-333-5447. *E-mail:* admiss@dbu.edu. *Web site:* http://www.dbu.edu/.

Dallas Christian College
Dallas, Texas

- **Independent** 4-year, founded 1950, affiliated with Christian Churches and Churches of Christ
- **Urban** 22-acre campus with easy access to Dallas-Fort Worth
- **Endowment** $169,907
- **Coed** 322 undergraduate students, 70% full-time, 43% women, 57% men
- **Minimally difficult** entrance level, 64% of applicants were admitted

Undergraduates 227 full-time, 95 part-time. Students come from 31 states and territories; 4 other countries; 20% are from out of state; 20% Black or African American, non-Hispanic/Latino; 18% Hispanic/Latino; 0.6% Asian, non-Hispanic/Latino; 2% American Indian or Alaska Native, non-Hispanic/Latino; 2% Two or more races, non-Hispanic/Latino; 4% Race/ethnicity unknown; 1% international; 18% transferred in; 41% live on campus. *Retention:* 67% of full-time freshmen returned.

Freshmen *Admission:* 107 applied, 68 admitted, 48 enrolled. *Average high school GPA:* 3.19.

Faculty *Total:* 56, 14% full-time, 29% with terminal degrees. *Student/faculty ratio:* 16:1.

Academics *Calendar:* semesters. *Degrees:* associate, bachelor's, and post-bachelor's certificates. *Special study options:* academic remediation for entering students, accelerated degree program, advanced placement credit, distance learning, double majors, independent study, internships, part-time degree program, summer session for credit.

Computers on Campus 16 computers/terminals are available on campus for general student use. Students can access the following: free student e-mail accounts, online (class) grades, online (class) registration, online (class) schedules. Campuswide network is available. Wireless service is available via entire campus.

Student Life *Housing:* on-campus residence required through sophomore year. *Options:* men-only, women-only. Campus housing is university owned. *Activities and organizations:* drama/theater group, student-run newspaper, choral group. *Campus security:* controlled dormitory access. *Student services:* personal/psychological counseling.

Athletics Member NCCAA. *Intercollegiate sports:* baseball M, basketball M/W, soccer M/W, volleyball W. *Intramural sports:* basketball M/W, volleyball M/W.

Standardized Tests *Required:* SAT or ACT (for admission).

Financial Aid Of all full-time matriculated undergraduates who enrolled in 2005, 189 applied for aid, 132 were judged to have need. 36 Federal Work-Study jobs (averaging $1404). In 2005, 26 non-need-based awards were made. *Average percent of need met:* 43%. *Average financial aid package:* $3940. *Average need-based loan:* $3589. *Average need-based gift aid:* $1282. *Average non-need-based aid:* $3664. *Average indebtedness upon graduation:* $15,000.

Applying *Options:* electronic application, deferred entrance. *Application fee:* $25. *Required:* essay or personal statement, high school transcript, minimum 2.0 GPA, 2 letters of recommendation. *Required for some:* interview. *Application deadlines:* rolling (freshmen), rolling (transfers).

Freshman Application Contact Mr. Brett Vance, Admissions Counselor, Dallas Christian College, 2700 Christian Parkway, Dallas, TX 75234-7299. *Phone:* 972-241-3371 Ext. 134. *Toll-free phone:* 800-688-1029. *Fax:* 972-241-8021. *E-mail:* bvance@dallas.edu. *Web site:* http://www.dallas.edu/.

DeVry University
Houston, Texas

- **Proprietary** comprehensive
- **Coed** 1,462 undergraduate students, 37% full-time, 51% women, 49% men
- **Minimally difficult** entrance level

Undergraduates 545 full-time, 917 part-time. 1% are from out of state; 37% Black or African American, non-Hispanic/Latino; 30% Hispanic/Latino; 3% Asian, non-Hispanic/Latino; 0.5% Native Hawaiian or other Pacific Islander, non-Hispanic/Latino; 0.3% American Indian or Alaska Native, non-Hispanic/Latino; 0.5% Two or more races, non-Hispanic/Latino; 9% Race/ethnicity unknown; 1% international; 22% transferred in.

Freshmen *Admission:* 196 enrolled.

Faculty *Total:* 184, 14% full-time. *Student/faculty ratio:* 13:1.

Academics *Calendar:* semesters. *Degrees:* associate, bachelor's, master's, and postbachelor's certificates.

Costs (2011–12) *Tuition:* $15,294 full-time, $597 per credit hour part-time. Full-time tuition and fees vary according to course load. Part-time tuition and fees vary according to course load. *Required fees:* $80 full-time, $40 per term part-time. *Payment plans:* installment, deferred payment. *Waivers:* employees or children of employees.

Financial Aid Of all full-time matriculated undergraduates who enrolled in 2007, 306 applied for aid, 299 were judged to have need, 3 had their need fully met. In 2007, 20 non-need-based awards were made. *Average percent of need met:* 39%. *Average financial aid package:* $12,662. *Average need-based loan:* $7855. *Average need-based gift aid:* $5374. *Average non-need-based aid:* $14,939. *Average indebtedness upon graduation:* $30,068.

Applying *Application fee:* $50. *Application deadlines:* rolling (freshmen), rolling (transfers). *Notification:* continuous (freshmen), continuous (transfers).

Freshman Application Contact DeVry University, 11125 Equity Drive, Houston, TX 77041. *Phone:* 713-973-3100. *Toll-free phone:* 866-338-7941. *Web site:* http://www.devry.edu/.

DeVry University
Irving, Texas

- **Proprietary** comprehensive, founded 1969, part of DeVry University
- **Suburban** campus
- **Coed** 1,369 undergraduate students, 43% full-time, 33% women, 67% men
- **Minimally difficult** entrance level

Undergraduates 588 full-time, 781 part-time. 3% are from out of state; 28% Black or African American, non-Hispanic/Latino; 23% Hispanic/Latino; 4% Asian, non-Hispanic/Latino; 0.2% Native Hawaiian or other Pacific Islander, non-Hispanic/Latino; 0.6% American Indian or Alaska Native, non-Hispanic/Latino; 1% Two or more races, non-Hispanic/Latino; 10% Race/ethnicity unknown; 0.4% international; 19% transferred in.

Freshmen *Admission:* 193 enrolled.

Faculty *Total:* 98, 42% full-time. *Student/faculty ratio:* 17:1.

Academics *Calendar:* semesters. *Degrees:* associate, bachelor's, master's, and postbachelor's certificates. *Special study options:* adult/continuing education programs, part-time degree program.

Student Life *Housing:* college housing not available.

Costs (2011–12) *Tuition:* $15,294 full-time, $597 per credit hour part-time. Full-time tuition and fees vary according to course load. Part-time tuition and fees vary according to course load. *Required fees:* $80 full-time, $40 per term part-time. *Payment plans:* installment, deferred payment. *Waivers:* employees or children of employees.

Financial Aid Of all full-time matriculated undergraduates who enrolled in 2007, 354 applied for aid, 343 were judged to have need, 9 had their need fully met. In 2007, 33 non-need-based awards were made. *Average percent of need met:* 40%. *Average financial aid package:* $12,581. *Average need-based loan:* $8675. *Average need-based gift aid:* $5995. *Average non-need-based aid:* $17,309. *Average indebtedness upon graduation:* $31,895.

Applying *Application fee:* $50. *Required:* high school transcript, interview. *Application deadlines:* rolling (freshmen), rolling (transfers). *Notification:* continuous (freshmen), continuous (transfers).

Freshman Application Contact DeVry University, 4800 Regent Boulevard, Irving, TX 75063-2439. *Phone:* 972-929-6777. *Toll-free phone:* 866-338-7941. *Web site:* http://www.devry.edu/.

DeVry University
Richardson, Texas

Admissions Office Contact DeVry University, Richardson Center, 2201 North Central Expressway, Richardson, TX 75080. *Toll-free phone:* 866-338-7941. *Web site:* http://www.devry.edu/.

East Texas Baptist University
Marshall, Texas

- **Independent Baptist** comprehensive, founded 1912
- **Small-town** 200-acre campus
- **Endowment** $61.1 million
- **Coed** 1,188 undergraduate students, 91% full-time, 53% women, 47% men
- **Moderately difficult** entrance level, 57% of applicants were admitted

Undergraduates 1,082 full-time, 106 part-time. Students come from 13 states and territories; 7 other countries; 10% are from out of state; 19% Black or African American, non-Hispanic/Latino; 9% Hispanic/Latino; 0.7% Asian, non-Hispanic/Latino; 0.7% American Indian or Alaska Native, non-Hispanic/

Latino; 2% Two or more races, non-Hispanic/Latino; 0.1% Race/ethnicity unknown; 2% international; 8% transferred in; 84% live on campus. *Retention:* 59% of full-time freshmen returned.

Freshmen *Admission:* 1,146 applied, 656 admitted, 330 enrolled. *Average high school GPA:* 3.35. *Test scores:* SAT critical reading scores over 500: 44%; SAT math scores over 500: 32%; ACT scores over 18: 86%; SAT critical reading scores over 600: 8%; SAT math scores over 600: 7%; ACT scores over 24: 13%; SAT math scores over 700: 1%; ACT scores over 30: 1%.

Faculty *Total:* 104, 63% full-time, 61% with terminal degrees. *Student/faculty ratio:* 14:1.

Academics *Calendar:* semesters 4-4-1. *Degrees:* certificates, bachelor's, and master's. *Special study options:* accelerated degree program, adult/continuing education programs, advanced placement credit, distance learning, double majors, honors programs, independent study, internships, off-campus study, part-time degree program, services for LD students, student-designed majors, study abroad, summer session for credit.

Computers on Campus 200 computers/terminals and 720 ports are available on campus for general student use. Students can access the following: campus intranet, computer help desk, free student e-mail accounts, online (class) grades, online (class) registration, online (class) schedules. Campuswide network is available. 100% of college-owned or -operated housing units are wired for high-speed Internet access. Wireless service is available via entire campus.

Student Life *Housing:* on-campus residence required through senior year. *Options:* men-only, women-only. Campus housing is university owned. Freshman campus housing is guaranteed. *Activities and organizations:* drama/theater group, student-run newspaper, radio station, choral group, marching band, Baptist Student Ministry, Student Activities Board, Blue Crew, Student Government Association, Fellowship of Christian Athletes. *Campus security:* 24-hour emergency response devices and patrols, controlled dormitory access. *Student services:* personal/psychological counseling.

Athletics Member NCAA. All Division III. *Intercollegiate sports:* baseball M, basketball M/W, cross-country running M/W, football M, soccer M/W, softball W, tennis M/W, volleyball W. *Intramural sports:* basketball M/W, football M/W, racquetball M/W, soccer M/W, softball M/W, table tennis M/W, ultimate Frisbee M/W, volleyball M/W.

Standardized Tests *Required:* SAT or ACT (for admission).

Costs (2012–13) *Comprehensive fee:* $27,675 includes full-time tuition ($20,670), mandatory fees ($860), and room and board ($6145). Part-time tuition: $689 per credit hour. *College room only:* $2540. Room and board charges vary according to board plan and housing facility. *Payment plan:* installment. *Waivers:* employees or children of employees.

Financial Aid Of all full-time matriculated undergraduates who enrolled in 2010, 997 applied for aid, 899 were judged to have need, 153 had their need fully met. 92 Federal Work-Study jobs (averaging $1412). 219 state and other part-time jobs (averaging $1465). In 2010, 152 non-need-based awards were made. *Average percent of need met:* 44%. *Average financial aid package:* $14,966. *Average need-based loan:* $3822. *Average need-based gift aid:* $6373. *Average non-need-based aid:* $8245. *Average indebtedness upon graduation:* $24,914.

Applying *Options:* electronic application. *Application fee:* $25. *Required:* high school transcript. *Required for some:* interview. *Application deadlines:* 8/16 (freshmen), 8/16 (out-of-state freshmen), 8/16 (transfers). *Notification:* continuous (freshmen), continuous (out-of-state freshmen), continuous (transfers).

Freshman Application Contact East Texas Baptist University, 1209 North Grove, Marshall, TX 75670-1498. *Phone:* 903-923-2000. *Toll-free phone:* 800-804-ETBU. *Web site:* http://www.etbu.edu/.

Hallmark College of Technology
San Antonio, Texas

- **Proprietary** primarily 2-year, founded 1969
- **Suburban** 3-acre campus
- **Coed**
- **Moderately difficult** entrance level

Faculty *Student/faculty ratio:* 8:1.

Academics *Calendar:* continuous. *Degrees:* certificates, associate, and bachelor's.

Student Life *Campus security:* 24-hour emergency response devices.

Standardized Tests *Required:* Wonderlic aptitude test (for admission).

Costs (2011–12) *Tuition:* Full-time tuition and fees vary according to degree level and program. Tuition varies by program: AAS degree in Computer Network Systems Technology tuition is $30,800. Bachelor of Science tuition is $55,000. AAS in Medical Assistant tuition is $19,850. AAS in Medical Assistant tuition is $19,850. Each program has a $110 registration fee except for nursing, the registration fee is $25. Books, supplies and equipment is included in the tuition for each program. *Payment plans:* tuition prepayment, installment, deferred payment.

Applying *Application fee:* $110. *Required:* high school transcript, interview, tour. *Required for some:* essay or personal statement.

Freshman Application Contact Hallmark College of Technology, 10401 IH 10 West, San Antonio, TX 78230. *Phone:* 210-690-9000 Ext. 212. *Web site:* http://www.hallmarkcollege.edu/.

Hardin-Simmons University
Abilene, Texas

- **Independent Baptist** comprehensive, founded 1891
- **Urban** 120-acre campus
- **Endowment** $105.7 million
- **Coed** 1,910 undergraduate students, 85% full-time, 54% women, 46% men
- **Moderately difficult** entrance level, 56% of applicants were admitted

Undergraduates 1,628 full-time, 282 part-time. Students come from 27 states and territories; 17 other countries; 4% are from out of state; 6% Black or African American, non-Hispanic/Latino; 13% Hispanic/Latino; 2% Asian, non-Hispanic/Latino; 0.2% Native Hawaiian or other Pacific Islander, non-Hispanic/Latino; 0.8% American Indian or Alaska Native, non-Hispanic/Latino; 1% Two or more races, non-Hispanic/Latino; 3% Race/ethnicity unknown; 1% international; 8% transferred in; 42% live on campus. *Retention:* 65% of full-time freshmen returned.

Freshmen *Admission:* 1,776 applied, 997 admitted, 397 enrolled. *Average high school GPA:* 3.56. *Test scores:* SAT critical reading scores over 500: 51%; SAT math scores over 500: 64%; SAT writing scores over 500: 48%; ACT scores over 18: 90%; SAT critical reading scores over 600: 16%; SAT math scores over 600: 22%; SAT writing scores over 600: 12%; ACT scores over 24: 44%; SAT critical reading scores over 700: 2%; SAT math scores over 700: 3%; SAT writing scores over 700: 1%; ACT scores over 30: 7%.

Faculty *Total:* 202, 68% full-time, 72% with terminal degrees. *Student/faculty ratio:* 13:1.

Academics *Calendar:* semesters. *Degrees:* bachelor's, master's, doctoral, post-master's, postbachelor's, and first professional certificates. *Special study options:* academic remediation for entering students, accelerated degree program, adult/continuing education programs, advanced placement credit, distance learning, double majors, honors programs, independent study, internships, off-campus study, part-time degree program, services for LD students, study abroad, summer session for credit.

Computers on Campus 245 computers/terminals and 1,100 ports are available on campus for general student use. Students can access the following: campus intranet, computer help desk, free student e-mail accounts, online (class) grades, online (class) registration, online (class) schedules. Campuswide network is available. 100% of college-owned or -operated housing units are wired for high-speed Internet access. Wireless service is available via entire campus.

Student Life *Housing:* on-campus residence required through sophomore year. *Options:* men-only, women-only, disabled students. Campus housing is university owned. Freshman campus housing is guaranteed. *Activities and organizations:* drama/theater group, student-run newspaper, choral group, marching band, Baptist Student Ministry, Student Foundation, Student Congress, Fellowship of Christian Athletes, Unity Group. *Campus security:* 24-hour emergency response devices and patrols, late-night transport/escort service, controlled dormitory access. *Student services:* health clinic, personal/psychological counseling.

Athletics Member NCAA. All Division III. *Intercollegiate sports:* baseball M, basketball M/W, cheerleading M(c)/W(c), cross-country running M/W, football M, golf M/W, soccer M/W, softball W, tennis M/W, track and field M/W, volleyball W. *Intramural sports:* badminton M/W, basketball M/W, bowling M/W, football M/W, golf M/W, gymnastics M(c)/W(c), racquetball M/W, rock climbing M(c)/W(c), soccer M/W, softball M/W, table tennis M(c)/W(c), tennis M(c)/W(c), ultimate Frisbee M/W, volleyball M/W.

Standardized Tests *Required:* SAT or ACT (for admission).

Costs (2012–13) *Comprehensive fee:* $29,190 includes full-time tuition ($21,450), mandatory fees ($1110), and room and board ($6630). Full-time tuition and fees vary according to program. Part-time tuition: $715 per credit hour. Part-time tuition and fees vary according to course load and program. No tuition increase for student's term of enrollment. *Required fees:* $200 per term part-time. *College room only:* $3400. Room and board charges vary according to board plan and housing facility. *Payment plan:* installment. *Waivers:* employees or children of employees.

Financial Aid Of all full-time matriculated undergraduates who enrolled in 2010, 1,682 applied for aid, 1,274 were judged to have need, 244 had their need fully met. 119 Federal Work-Study jobs (averaging $1900). 221 state and other part-time jobs (averaging $1900). In 2010, 356 non-need-based awards were made. *Average percent of need met:* 68%. *Average financial aid package:* $23,956. *Average need-based loan:* $4203. *Average need-based gift aid:*

$7520. *Average non-need-based aid:* $8214. *Average indebtedness upon graduation:* $37,383.

Applying *Options:* electronic application, deferred entrance. *Application fee:* $50. *Required:* high school transcript, minimum 2.0 GPA. *Required for some:* 3 letters of recommendation. *Application deadlines:* rolling (freshmen), rolling (transfers). *Notification:* continuous (freshmen), continuous (transfers).

Freshman Application Contact Ms. Brynn Reynolds, Visitor Coordinator, Hardin-Simmons University, Box 16050, Abilene, TX 79698-0001. *Phone:* 325-670-5890. *Toll-free phone:* 877-464-7889. *Fax:* 325-671-2115. *E-mail:* breynolds@hsutx.edu. *Web site:* http://www.hsutx.edu/.

Houston Baptist University
Houston, Texas

Freshman Application Contact Eduardo Borges, Director of Admissions, Houston Baptist University, 7502 Fondren Road, Houston, TX 77074-3298. *Phone:* 281-649-3299. *Toll-free phone:* 800-696-3210. *Fax:* 281-649-3217. *E-mail:* eborges@hbu.edu. *Web site:* http://www.hbu.edu/.

Howard Payne University
Brownwood, Texas

- **Independent** comprehensive, founded 1889, affiliated with Baptist General Convention of Texas
- **Small-town** 80-acre campus
- **Endowment** $45.3 million
- **Coed** 1,183 undergraduate students, 82% full-time, 50% women, 50% men
- **Moderately difficult** entrance level, 69% of applicants were admitted

Undergraduates 973 full-time, 210 part-time. Students come from 16 states and territories; 1 other country; 3% are from out of state; 7% Black or African American, non-Hispanic/Latino; 17% Hispanic/Latino; 0.3% Asian, non-Hispanic/Latino; 0.3% Native Hawaiian or other Pacific Islander, non-Hispanic/Latino; 1% American Indian or Alaska Native, non-Hispanic/Latino; 0.8% Two or more races, non-Hispanic/Latino; 5% Race/ethnicity unknown; 0.3% international; 6% transferred in; 47% live on campus. *Retention:* 57% of full-time freshmen returned.

Freshmen *Admission:* 971 applied, 674 admitted, 282 enrolled. *Average high school GPA:* 3.47. *Test scores:* SAT critical reading scores over 500: 44%; SAT math scores over 500: 55%; ACT scores over 18: 82%; SAT critical reading scores over 600: 8%; SAT math scores over 600: 15%; ACT scores over 24: 31%; SAT critical reading scores over 700: 1%; SAT math scores over 700: 1%; ACT scores over 30: 3%.

Faculty *Total:* 128, 66% full-time, 48% with terminal degrees. *Student/faculty ratio:* 11:1.

Academics *Calendar:* semesters. *Degrees:* certificates, associate, bachelor's, and master's. *Special study options:* academic remediation for entering students, advanced placement credit, distance learning, double majors, honors programs, independent study, internships, off-campus study, part-time degree program, services for LD students, study abroad, summer session for credit.

Computers on Campus 260 computers/terminals and 200 ports are available on campus for general student use. Students can access the following: campus intranet, computer help desk, free student e-mail accounts, online (class) grades, online (class) schedules. Campuswide network is available. 100% of college-owned or -operated housing units are wired for high-speed Internet access. Wireless service is available via entire campus.

Student Life *Housing:* on-campus residence required through sophomore year. *Options:* men-only, women-only. Campus housing is university owned. Freshman campus housing is guaranteed. *Activities and organizations:* drama/theater group, student-run newspaper, choral group, marching band, Baptist Student Ministry, Fellowship of Christian Athletes, Student Government Association, Student Foundation, Student Activities Council, national fraternities, national sororities. *Campus security:* 24-hour emergency response devices and patrols, late-night transport/escort service, controlled dormitory access. *Student services:* health clinic, personal/psychological counseling.

Athletics Member NCAA. All Division III. *Intercollegiate sports:* baseball M, basketball M/W, cheerleading M/W, cross-country running M/W, football M, soccer M/W, softball W, tennis M/W, volleyball W. *Intramural sports:* basketball M/W, football M/W, softball M/W, table tennis M/W, tennis M/W, volleyball M/W.

Standardized Tests *Required:* SAT or ACT (for admission). *Required for some:* ACCUPLACER.

Costs (2012–13) *Comprehensive fee:* $28,942 includes full-time tuition ($21,200), mandatory fees ($1360), and room and board ($6382). Full-time tuition and fees vary according to course load, location, and program. Part-time tuition: $675 per credit hour. Part-time tuition and fees vary according to location and program. *College room only:* $2820. Room and board charges vary

according to board plan and housing facility. *Payment plan:* installment. *Waivers:* employees or children of employees.

Financial Aid Of all full-time matriculated undergraduates who enrolled in 2010, 904 applied for aid, 827 were judged to have need, 230 had their need fully met. 103 Federal Work-Study jobs (averaging $1300). 9 state and other part-time jobs (averaging $9700). In 2010, 152 non-need-based awards were made. *Average percent of need met:* 82%. *Average financial aid package:* $16,145. *Average need-based loan:* $3937. *Average need-based gift aid:* $11,420. *Average non-need-based aid:* $6968. *Average indebtedness upon graduation:* $30,690.

Applying *Options:* electronic application, early admission. *Required:* high school transcript, minimum 3.0 GPA. *Required for some:* 3 letters of recommendation, interview. *Recommended:* essay or personal statement. *Application deadlines:* rolling (freshmen), rolling (out-of-state freshmen), rolling (transfers). *Notification:* continuous (freshmen), continuous (out-of-state freshmen), continuous (transfers).

Freshman Application Contact Ms. Cheryl Mangrum, Associate Director of Admission, Howard Payne University, 1000 Fisk Street, Brownwood, TX 76801. *Phone:* 325-649-8027. *Toll-free phone:* 800-880-4478. *Fax:* 325-649-8901. *E-mail:* enroll@hputx.edu. *Web site:* http://www.hputx.edu/.

Huston-Tillotson University

Austin, Texas

- **Independent interdenominational** 4-year, founded 1875
- **Urban** 23-acre campus
- **Endowment** $8.3 million
- **Coed** 889 undergraduate students, 86% full-time, 50% women, 50% men
- **Moderately difficult** entrance level, 76% of applicants were admitted

Undergraduates 766 full-time, 123 part-time. Students come from 24 states and territories; 13 other countries; 6% are from out of state; 69% Black or African American, non-Hispanic/Latino; 19% Hispanic/Latino; 1% Two or more races, non-Hispanic/Latino; 0.4% Race/ethnicity unknown; 4% international; 30% transferred in; 39% live on campus. *Retention:* 50% of full-time freshmen returned.

Freshmen *Admission:* 739 applied, 565 admitted, 216 enrolled. *Average high school GPA:* 3.

Faculty *Total:* 81, 60% full-time, 49% with terminal degrees. *Student/faculty ratio:* 14:1.

Academics *Calendar:* semesters. *Degrees:* bachelor's and postbachelor's certificates. *Special study options:* academic remediation for entering students, advanced placement credit, cooperative education, distance learning, double majors, honors programs, independent study, internships, services for LD students, study abroad, summer session for credit. *ROTC:* Army (c). *Unusual degree programs:* 3-2 engineering with Prairie View A&M University.

Computers on Campus 350 computers/terminals are available on campus for general student use. Students can access the following: campus intranet, computer help desk, free student e-mail accounts, online (class) grades, online (class) registration, online (class) schedules. Campuswide network is available. 100% of college-owned or -operated housing units are wired for high-speed Internet access. Wireless service is available via entire campus.

Student Life *Housing:* on-campus residence required for freshman year. *Options:* men-only, women-only. Campus housing is university owned. Freshman campus housing is guaranteed. *Activities and organizations:* drama/theater group, choral group, Campus Ministries, Zeta Phi Beta Sorority, Inc., Alpha Phi Alpha Fraternity, Inc., The Gentlemen's Club, Pre-Alumni Council, national fraternities, national sororities. *Campus security:* 24-hour emergency response devices and patrols, late-night transport/escort service, controlled dormitory access. *Student services:* health clinic, personal/psychological counseling.

Athletics Member NAIA. *Intercollegiate sports:* baseball M(s), basketball M(s)/W(s), cross-country running M(s), soccer M(s)/W(s), softball W(s), track and field M(s)/W(s), volleyball W(s). *Intramural sports:* cheerleading W.

Standardized Tests *Required:* SAT or ACT (for admission).

Costs (2012–13) *Comprehensive fee:* $26,946 includes full-time tuition ($11,020), mandatory fees ($2034), and room and board ($13,892). Full-time tuition and fees vary according to course load. Part-time tuition: $368 per credit hour. Part-time tuition and fees vary according to course load. *College room only:* $11,864. Room and board charges vary according to housing facility. *Payment plans:* installment, deferred payment. *Waivers:* employees or children of employees.

Financial Aid Of all full-time matriculated undergraduates who enrolled in 2009, 775 applied for aid, 768 were judged to have need, 158 had their need fully met. In 2009, 4 non-need-based awards were made. *Average percent of need met:* 78%. *Average financial aid package:* $14,885. *Average need-based loan:* $4875. *Average need-based gift aid:* $9772.

Applying *Options:* electronic application, deferred entrance. *Application fee:* $25. *Required:* high school transcript, minimum 2.3 GPA, university admis-

sion application. *Required for some:* essay or personal statement, interview. *Application deadlines:* 7/1 (freshmen), 7/1 (transfers).

Freshman Application Contact Ms. Shakitha Stinson, Director of Admission, Huston-Tillotson University, 900 Chicon Street, Austin, TX 78702. *Phone:* 512-505-3029. *Fax:* 512-505-3192. *E-mail:* slstinson@htu.edu. *Web site:* http://www.htu.edu/.

ITT Technical Institute

Arlington, Texas

- **Proprietary** primarily 2-year, founded 1982, part of ITT Educational Services, Inc.
- **Suburban** campus
- **Coed**
- **Minimally difficult** entrance level

Academics *Calendar:* quarters. *Degrees:* associate and bachelor's.

Student Life *Housing:* college housing not available.

Freshman Application Contact Director of Recruitment, ITT Technical Institute, 551 Ryan Plaza Drive, Arlington, TX 76011. *Phone:* 817-794-5100. *Toll-free phone:* 888-288-4950. *Fax:* 817-275-8446. *Web site:* http://www.itt-tech.edu/.

ITT Technical Institute

Austin, Texas

- **Proprietary** primarily 2-year, founded 1985, part of ITT Educational Services, Inc.
- **Urban** campus
- **Coed**
- **Minimally difficult** entrance level

Academics *Calendar:* quarters. *Degrees:* associate and bachelor's.

Student Life *Housing:* college housing not available.

Financial Aid Of all full-time matriculated undergraduates who enrolled in 2010, 1 Federal Work-Study job.

Freshman Application Contact Director of Recruitment, ITT Technical Institute, 6330 Highway 290 East, Austin, TX 78723. *Phone:* 512-467-6800. *Toll-free phone:* 800-431-0677. *Fax:* 512-467-6677. *Web site:* http://www.itt-tech.edu/.

ITT Technical Institute

DeSoto, Texas

- **Proprietary** primarily 2-year
- **Coed**
- **Minimally difficult** entrance level

Academics *Degrees:* associate and bachelor's.

Freshman Application Contact Director of Recruitment, ITT Technical Institute, 921 West Belt Line Road, Suite 181, DeSoto, TX 75115. *Phone:* 972-274-8600. *Toll-free phone:* 877-854-5728. *Web site:* http://www.itt-tech.edu/.

ITT Technical Institute

Houston, Texas

- **Proprietary** primarily 2-year, founded 1985, part of ITT Educational Services, Inc.
- **Suburban** campus
- **Coed**
- **Minimally difficult** entrance level

Academics *Calendar:* quarters. *Degrees:* associate and bachelor's.

Student Life *Housing:* college housing not available.

Freshman Application Contact Director of Recruitment, ITT Technical Institute, 15651 North Freeway, Houston, TX 77090. *Phone:* 281-873-0512. *Toll-free phone:* 800-879-6486. *Web site:* http://www.itt-tech.edu/.

ITT Technical Institute

Houston, Texas

- **Proprietary** primarily 2-year, founded 1983, part of ITT Educational Services, Inc.
- **Urban** campus
- **Coed**
- **Minimally difficult** entrance level

Academics *Calendar:* quarters. *Degrees:* associate and bachelor's.

Student Life *Housing:* college housing not available.

Freshman Application Contact Director of Recruitment, ITT Technical Institute, 2950 South Gessner, Houston, TX 77063-3751. *Phone:* 713-952-2294. *Toll-free phone:* 800-235-4787. *Web site:* http://www.itt-tech.edu/.

ITT Technical Institute
Richardson, Texas

- **Proprietary** primarily 2-year, founded 1989, part of ITT Educational Services, Inc.
- **Suburban** campus
- **Coed**
- **Minimally difficult** entrance level

Academics *Calendar:* quarters. *Degrees:* associate and bachelor's.
Student Life *Housing:* college housing not available.
Financial Aid Of all full-time matriculated undergraduates who enrolled in 2010, 5 Federal Work-Study jobs (averaging $5000).
Freshman Application Contact Director of Recruitment, ITT Technical Institute, 2101 Waterview Parkway, Richardson, TX 75080. *Phone:* 972-690-9100. *Toll-free phone:* 888-488-5761. *Web site:* http://www.itt-tech.edu/.

ITT Technical Institute
San Antonio, Texas

- **Proprietary** primarily 2-year, founded 1988, part of ITT Educational Services, Inc.
- **Urban** campus
- **Coed**
- **Minimally difficult** entrance level

Academics *Calendar:* quarters. *Degrees:* associate and bachelor's.
Student Life *Housing:* college housing not available.
Freshman Application Contact Director of Recruitment, ITT Technical Institute, 5700 Northwest Parkway, San Antonio, TX 78249-3303. *Phone:* 210-694-4612. *Toll-free phone:* 800-880-0570. *Web site:* http://www.itt-tech.edu/.

ITT Technical Institute
Waco, Texas

- **Proprietary** primarily 2-year, part of ITT Educational Services, Inc.
- **Coed**

Academics *Calendar:* quarters. *Degrees:* associate and bachelor's.
Freshman Application Contact Director of Recruitment, ITT Technical Institute, 3700 S. Jack Kultgen Expressway, Suite 100, Waco, TX 76706. *Phone:* 254-881-2200. *Toll-free phone:* 877-201-7143. *Web site:* http://www.itt-tech.edu/.

ITT Technical Institute
Webster, Texas

- **Proprietary** primarily 2-year, founded 1995, part of ITT Educational Services, Inc.
- **Coed**
- **Minimally difficult** entrance level

Academics *Calendar:* quarters. *Degrees:* associate and bachelor's.
Student Life *Housing:* college housing not available.
Freshman Application Contact Director of Recruitment, ITT Technical Institute, 1001 Magnolia Avenue, Webster, TX 77598. *Phone:* 281-316-4700. *Toll-free phone:* 888-488-9347. *Web site:* http://www.itt-tech.edu/.

Jarvis Christian College
Hawkins, Texas

- **Independent** 4-year, founded 1912, affiliated with Christian Church (Disciples of Christ)
- **Rural** 465-acre campus
- **Coed** 523 undergraduate students, 98% full-time, 49% women, 51% men
- **Minimally difficult** entrance level, 11% of applicants were admitted

Undergraduates 511 full-time, 12 part-time. Students come from 20 states and territories; 3 other countries; 10% are from out of state; 94% Black or African American, non-Hispanic/Latino; 1% Hispanic/Latino; 1% international; 8% transferred in; 76% live on campus. *Retention:* 39% of full-time freshmen returned.
Freshmen *Admission:* 1,149 applied, 129 admitted, 88 enrolled. *Average high school GPA:* 2.1.

Faculty *Total:* 59, 39% full-time, 29% with terminal degrees. *Student/faculty ratio:* 11:1.
Academics *Calendar:* semesters. *Degree:* bachelor's. *Special study options:* academic remediation for entering students, advanced placement credit, cooperative education, distance learning, double majors, honors programs, independent study, internships, off-campus study, student-designed majors, summer session for credit. *Unusual degree programs:* engineering; nursing.
Computers on Campus 100 computers/terminals and 500 ports are available on campus for general student use. Students can access the following: campus intranet, computer help desk, free student e-mail accounts, online (class) grades, online (class) registration, online (class) schedules. Campuswide network is available. 100% of college-owned or -operated housing units are wired for high-speed Internet access. Wireless service is available via classrooms, computer centers, computer labs, dorm rooms, learning centers, libraries, student centers.
Student Life *Housing options:* men-only, women-only, disabled students. Campus housing is university owned. *Activities and organizations:* drama/theater group, choral group, Student Government Association, Pre-Alumni Club, Student Ministers' Association, Women 2 Women, Pan-Hellenic Council, national fraternities, national sororities. *Campus security:* 24-hour emergency response devices and patrols.
Athletics Member NAIA. *Intercollegiate sports:* baseball M(s), basketball M(s)/W(s), cheerleading M/W, cross-country running M(s)/W(s). *Intramural sports:* baseball M, basketball M/W, football M/W, golf M, soccer M, softball M/W, swimming and diving M/W, table tennis M/W, tennis M/W, volleyball M/W, water polo M/W, weight lifting M/W.
Costs (2012–13) *One-time required fee:* $50. *Comprehensive fee:* $22,750 includes full-time tuition ($11,870), mandatory fees ($1504), and room and board ($9376). Part-time tuition: $495 per semester hour. *Required fees:* $1504 per year part-time. *College room only:* $5174. Room and board charges vary according to housing facility. *Payment plans:* installment, deferred payment.
Financial Aid Of all full-time matriculated undergraduates who enrolled in 2011, 476 applied for aid, 476 were judged to have need, 30 had their need fully met. 149 Federal Work-Study jobs (averaging $1538). 2 state and other part-time jobs (averaging $2315). In 2011, 5 non-need-based awards were made. *Average percent of need met:* 80%. *Average financial aid package:* $12,115. *Average need-based loan:* $5392. *Average need-based gift aid:* $8062. *Average non-need-based aid:* $17,192. *Average indebtedness upon graduation:* $29,296.
Applying *Application fee:* $50. *Required:* high school transcript. *Recommended:* minimum 2.0 GPA. *Application deadlines:* 8/1 (freshmen), rolling (transfers). *Notification:* 8/15 (freshmen).
Freshman Application Contact Dr. Robert Harper, Admissions Counselor, Jarvis Christian College, PO Box 1470, Hawkins, TX 75765-9989. *Phone:* 903-730-4890 Ext. 2201. *Fax:* 903-769-4842. *E-mail:* rharper@jarvis.edu. *Web site:* http://www.jarvis.edu/.

Lamar University
Beaumont, Texas

- **State-supported** university, founded 1923, part of Texas State University System
- **Suburban** 200-acre campus with easy access to Houston
- **Coed** 9,840 undergraduate students, 71% full-time, 59% women, 41% men
- **Minimally difficult** entrance level, 67% of applicants were admitted

Undergraduates 6,982 full-time, 2,858 part-time. Students come from 38 states and territories; 37 other countries; 2% are from out of state; 33% Black or African American, non-Hispanic/Latino; 8% Hispanic/Latino; 3% Asian, non-Hispanic/Latino; 0.7% American Indian or Alaska Native, non-Hispanic/Latino; 3% Race/ethnicity unknown; 0.8% international; 7% transferred in. *Retention:* 65% of full-time freshmen returned.
Freshmen *Admission:* 4,331 applied, 2,894 admitted, 1,564 enrolled. *Test scores:* SAT critical reading scores over 500: 39%; SAT math scores over 500: 46%; SAT writing scores over 500: 33%; ACT scores over 18: 77%; SAT critical reading scores over 600: 9%; SAT math scores over 600: 11%; SAT writing scores over 600: 6%; ACT scores over 24: 18%; SAT critical reading scores over 700: 1%; SAT math scores over 700: 1%; SAT writing scores over 700: 1%; ACT scores over 30: 3%.
Faculty *Total:* 592, 70% full-time, 55% with terminal degrees. *Student/faculty ratio:* 21:1.
Academics *Calendar:* semesters. *Degrees:* associate, bachelor's, master's, and doctoral. *Special study options:* academic remediation for entering students, accelerated degree program, advanced placement credit, cooperative education, English as a second language, honors programs, internships, off-campus study, part-time degree program, services for LD students, student-designed majors, summer session for credit.

Computers on Campus 120 computers/terminals are available on campus for general student use. Campuswide network is available. Wireless service is available via entire campus.

Student Life *Housing options:* coed. *Activities and organizations:* drama/theater group, student-run newspaper, television station, choral group, national fraternities, national sororities. *Campus security:* 24-hour emergency response devices and patrols, student patrols, late-night transport/escort service. *Student services:* health clinic, personal/psychological counseling.

Athletics Member NCAA. All Division I except football (Division I-AA). *Intercollegiate sports:* baseball M(s), basketball M(s)/W(s), cheerleading M/W, cross-country running M(s)/W(s), golf M(s)/W(s), soccer W(s), tennis M(s)/W(s), track and field M(s)/W(s), volleyball W(s). *Intramural sports:* basketball M/W, cross-country running M/W, football M, golf M/W, gymnastics W, racquetball M/W, rugby M/W, sailing M/W, soccer M/W, swimming and diving M/W, table tennis M, tennis M/W, track and field M/W, volleyball M/W, weight lifting M/W.

Standardized Tests *Required:* SAT or ACT (for admission). *Required for some:* SAT Subject Tests (for admission).

Costs (2012–13) *Tuition:* state resident $5940 full-time, $184 per credit hour part-time; nonresident $15,330 full-time, $490 per credit hour part-time. Full-time tuition and fees vary according to course load. Part-time tuition and fees vary according to course load. *Required fees:* $2556 full-time. *Room and board:* $7682; room only: $4950. Room and board charges vary according to board plan. *Payment plan:* installment. *Waivers:* senior citizens and employees or children of employees.

Financial Aid Of all full-time matriculated undergraduates who enrolled in 2010, 4,827 applied for aid, 3,321 were judged to have need. 182 Federal Work-Study jobs (averaging $3159). 62 state and other part-time jobs (averaging $1228). *Average percent of need met:* 64%. *Average financial aid package:* $4618. *Average need-based loan:* $2107. *Average need-based gift aid:* $2134. *Average indebtedness upon graduation:* $8234.

Applying *Options:* electronic application, early admission. *Required:* high school transcript. *Required for some:* essay or personal statement. *Application deadlines:* 8/1 (freshmen), 8/1 (transfers). *Notification:* continuous (freshmen).

Freshman Application Contact Ms. Melissa Chesser, Director of Recruitment, Lamar University, PO Box 10009, Beaumont, TX 77710. *Phone:* 409-880-8888. *Fax:* 409-880-8463. *E-mail:* admissions@lamar.edu. *Web site:* http://www.lamar.edu/.

LeTourneau University
Longview, Texas

- **Independent nondenominational** comprehensive, founded 1946
- **Suburban** 162-acre campus
- **Coed** 2,591 undergraduate students, 51% full-time, 52% women, 48% men
- **Moderately difficult** entrance level

Undergraduates 1,334 full-time, 1,257 part-time. 44% are from out of state; 18% Black or African American, non-Hispanic/Latino; 9% Hispanic/Latino; 0.7% Asian, non-Hispanic/Latino; 0.1% Native Hawaiian or other Pacific Islander, non-Hispanic/Latino; 0.5% American Indian or Alaska Native, non-Hispanic/Latino; 1% Two or more races, non-Hispanic/Latino; 4% Race/ethnicity unknown; 2% international; 3% transferred in; 74% live on campus. *Retention:* 74% of full-time freshmen returned.

Freshmen *Admission:* 307 enrolled. *Average high school GPA:* 3.59. *Test scores:* SAT critical reading scores over 500: 81%; SAT math scores over 500: 88%; SAT writing scores over 500: 72%; ACT scores over 18: 98%; SAT critical reading scores over 600: 47%; SAT math scores over 600: 53%; SAT writing scores over 600: 31%; ACT scores over 24: 62%; SAT critical reading scores over 700: 10%; SAT math scores over 700: 12%; SAT writing scores over 700: 6%; ACT scores over 30: 23%.

Faculty *Student/faculty ratio:* 13:1.

Academics *Calendar:* semesters. *Degrees:* associate, bachelor's, and master's. *Special study options:* adult/continuing education programs, part-time degree program.

Computers on Campus Students can access the following: campus intranet, computer help desk, free student e-mail accounts, online (class) grades, online (class) registration, online (class) schedules. Campuswide network is available. 100% of college-owned or -operated housing units are wired for high-speed Internet access. Wireless service is available via classrooms, computer centers, computer labs, dorm rooms, learning centers, libraries, student centers.

Student Life *Housing:* on-campus residence required through junior year. *Options:* men-only, women-only, disabled students. Campus housing is university owned. Freshman campus housing is guaranteed. *Campus security:* 24-hour emergency response devices and patrols, late-night transport/escort service, controlled dormitory access, University police department.

Athletics Member NCAA, NCCAA. All NCAA Division III. *Intercollegiate sports:* baseball M, basketball M/W, cross-country running M/W, golf M/W, soccer M/W, softball W, tennis M/W, volleyball W. *Intramural sports:* badminton M/W, basketball M/W, bowling M/W, cross-country running M/W, football M/W, golf M/W, racquetball M/W, soccer M/W, swimming and diving M/W, table tennis M/W, tennis M/W, volleyball M/W.

Standardized Tests *Required:* SAT or ACT (for admission).

Costs (2012–13) *Comprehensive fee:* $33,480 includes full-time tuition ($24,050), mandatory fees ($490), and room and board ($8940). Part-time tuition: $959 per credit hour. Part-time tuition and fees vary according to course load. *Room and board:* Room and board charges vary according to board plan. *Payment plan:* installment. *Waivers:* employees or children of employees.

Financial Aid Of all full-time matriculated undergraduates who enrolled in 2011, 1,143 applied for aid, 1,038 were judged to have need, 112 had their need fully met. In 2011, 23 non-need-based awards were made. *Average percent of need met:* 60%. *Average financial aid package:* $16,772. *Average need-based loan:* $3924. *Average need-based gift aid:* $12,235. *Average non-need-based aid:* $7575. *Average indebtedness upon graduation:* $30,295.

Applying *Options:* electronic application, deferred entrance. *Application fee:* $35. *Application deadlines:* rolling (freshmen), rolling (transfers). *Notification:* continuous (freshmen), continuous (transfers).

Freshman Application Contact Mr. James Townsend, Director of Admissions, LeTourneau University, PO Box 7001, Longview, TX 75607-7001. *Phone:* 903-233-3400. *Toll-free phone:* 800-759-8811. *Fax:* 903-233-3411. *E-mail:* admissions@letu.edu. *Web site:* http://www.letu.edu/.

Lubbock Christian University
Lubbock, Texas

- **Independent** comprehensive, founded 1957, affiliated with Church of Christ
- **Suburban** 120-acre campus
- **Endowment** $11.3 million
- **Coed** 1,596 undergraduate students, 85% full-time, 59% women, 41% men
- **Moderately difficult** entrance level, 61% of applicants were admitted

Undergraduates 1,362 full-time, 234 part-time. Students come from 35 states and territories; 23 other countries; 9% are from out of state; 6% Black or African American, non-Hispanic/Latino; 18% Hispanic/Latino; 0.5% Asian, non-Hispanic/Latino; 0.3% Native Hawaiian or other Pacific Islander, non-Hispanic/Latino; 0.8% American Indian or Alaska Native, non-Hispanic/Latino; 2% international; 16% transferred in; 36% live on campus. *Retention:* 61% of full-time freshmen returned.

Freshmen *Admission:* 1,485 applied, 909 admitted, 322 enrolled. *Average high school GPA:* 3.42. *Test scores:* SAT critical reading scores over 500: 41%; SAT math scores over 500: 50%; SAT writing scores over 500: 36%; ACT scores over 18: 84%; SAT critical reading scores over 600: 15%; SAT math scores over 600: 13%; SAT writing scores over 600: 13%; ACT scores over 24: 31%; SAT critical reading scores over 700: 4%; SAT math scores over 700: 3%; SAT writing scores over 700: 1%; ACT scores over 30: 3%.

Faculty *Total:* 179, 50% full-time, 54% with terminal degrees. *Student/faculty ratio:* 15:1.

Academics *Calendar:* semesters. *Degrees:* bachelor's and master's. *Special study options:* academic remediation for entering students, adult/continuing education programs, advanced placement credit, distance learning, double majors, English as a second language, honors programs, internships, part-time degree program, services for LD students, student-designed majors, study abroad, summer session for credit. *ROTC:* Army (c), Air Force (c). *Unusual degree programs:* 3-2 engineering with Texas Tech University.

Computers on Campus 169 computers/terminals are available on campus for general student use. Students can access the following: campus intranet, computer help desk, free student e-mail accounts, online (class) grades, online (class) registration, online (class) schedules. Campuswide network is available. 100% of college-owned or -operated housing units are wired for high-speed Internet access. Wireless service is available via entire campus.

Student Life *Housing:* on-campus residence required through sophomore year. *Options:* men-only, women-only, disabled students. Campus housing is university owned. Freshman campus housing is guaranteed. *Activities and organizations:* drama/theater group, student-run newspaper, choral group. *Campus security:* 24-hour patrols. *Student services:* health clinic, personal/psychological counseling.

Athletics Member NAIA. *Intercollegiate sports:* baseball M(s), basketball M(s)/W(s), cheerleading M/W, cross-country running M(s)/W(s), golf M(s)/W(s), soccer M(s)/W(s), softball W(s), track and field M/W, volleyball W(s). *Intramural sports:* badminton M/W, basketball M/W, bowling M/W, cross-country running M/W, football M/W, golf M/W, racquetball M/W, rock climb-

ing M/W, soccer M/W, softball M/W, table tennis M/W, tennis M/W, track and field M/W, volleyball M/W.

Standardized Tests *Required:* SAT or ACT (for admission).

Costs (2011–12) *Comprehensive fee:* $23,316 includes full-time tuition ($15,500), mandatory fees ($1370), and room and board ($6446). Full-time tuition and fees vary according to degree level and program. Part-time tuition: $500 per semester hour. Part-time tuition and fees vary according to course load, degree level, and program. *Required fees:* $500 per term part-time. *Room and board:* Room and board charges vary according to board plan and housing facility. *Payment plan:* installment. *Waivers:* employees or children of employees.

Financial Aid Of all full-time matriculated undergraduates who enrolled in 2010, 1,149 applied for aid, 1,013 were judged to have need, 65 had their need fully met. 849 Federal Work-Study jobs (averaging $1763). 89 state and other part-time jobs (averaging $257). In 2010, 169 non-need-based awards were made. *Average percent of need met:* 65%. *Average financial aid package:* $13,401. *Average need-based loan:* $4211. *Average need-based gift aid:* $9021. *Average non-need-based aid:* $4220. *Average indebtedness upon graduation:* $26,440.

Applying *Options:* electronic application. *Application fee:* $25. *Required:* high school transcript. *Application deadlines:* 8/1 (freshmen), rolling (transfers). *Notification:* continuous (freshmen), continuous (transfers).

Freshman Application Contact Mr. Charles Webb, Director of Admissions, Lubbock Christian University, 5601 19th Street, Lubbock, TX 79407. *Phone:* 806-720-7156. *Toll-free phone:* 800-933-7601. *Fax:* 806-720-7162. *E-mail:* admissions@lcu.edu. *Web site:* http://www.lcu.edu/.

McMurry University
Abilene, Texas

- **Independent United Methodist** 4-year, founded 1923
- **Suburban** 43-acre campus
- **Endowment** $62.2 million
- **Coed** 1,469 undergraduate students, 81% full-time, 48% women, 52% men
- **Moderately difficult** entrance level, 61% of applicants were admitted

Undergraduates 1,190 full-time, 279 part-time. Students come from 19 states and territories; 5 other countries; 5% are from out of state; 17% Black or African American, non-Hispanic/Latino; 20% Hispanic/Latino; 0.7% Asian, non-Hispanic/Latino; 0.2% Native Hawaiian or other Pacific Islander, non-Hispanic/Latino; 0.7% American Indian or Alaska Native, non-Hispanic/Latino; 3% Two or more races, non-Hispanic/Latino; 1% Race/ethnicity unknown; 0.4% international; 9% transferred in; 47% live on campus. *Retention:* 61% of full-time freshmen returned.

Freshmen *Admission:* 1,266 applied, 769 admitted, 330 enrolled. *Average high school GPA:* 3.31. *Test scores:* SAT critical reading scores over 500: 28%; SAT math scores over 500: 39%; ACT scores over 18: 72%; SAT critical reading scores over 600: 2%; SAT math scores over 600: 10%; ACT scores over 24: 19%; ACT scores over 30: 1%.

Faculty *Total:* 119, 66% full-time, 58% with terminal degrees. *Student/faculty ratio:* 14:1.

Academics *Calendar:* semesters plus May term. *Degree:* bachelor's. *Special study options:* academic remediation for entering students, accelerated degree program, adult/continuing education programs, advanced placement credit, double majors, honors programs, independent study, internships, part-time degree program, services for LD students, student-designed majors, study abroad, summer session for credit. *Unusual degree programs:* 3-2 dentistry at University of Texas Health Science Center at San Antonio-San Antonio School of Dentistry.

Computers on Campus 130 computers/terminals and 705 ports are available on campus for general student use. Students can access the following: campus intranet, computer help desk, free student e-mail accounts, online (class) grades, online (class) registration, online (class) schedules, Moodle. Campuswide network is available. 100% of college-owned or -operated housing units are wired for high-speed Internet access. Wireless service is available via entire campus.

Student Life *Housing:* on-campus residence required through junior year. *Options:* coed, men-only, women-only. Campus housing is university owned and is provided by a third party. Freshman campus housing is guaranteed. *Activities and organizations:* drama/theater group, student-run newspaper, choral group, marching band, Alpha Phi Omega, Religious Life Council, McMurry Student Government, Campus Activity Board, Servant Leadership. *Campus security:* 24-hour emergency response devices and patrols, late-night transport/escort service, controlled dormitory access. *Student services:* health clinic, personal/psychological counseling.

Athletics Member NCAA. All Division III. *Intercollegiate sports:* baseball M, basketball M/W, cross-country running M/W, football M, golf M/W, soccer M/W, swimming and diving M/W, tennis M/W, track and field M/W, volleyball

W. *Intramural sports:* basketball M/W, football M/W, golf M/W, racquetball M/W, soccer M/W, softball M/W, tennis M/W, ultimate Frisbee M/W, volleyball M/W.

Standardized Tests *Required:* SAT or ACT (for admission).

Costs (2011–12) *One-time required fee:* $175. *Comprehensive fee:* $29,084 includes full-time tuition ($21,010), mandatory fees ($860), and room and board ($7214). Full-time tuition and fees vary according to course load. Part-time tuition: $657 per credit hour. Part-time tuition and fees vary according to course load. *Required fees:* $35 per credit hour part-time. *College room only:* $3496. Room and board charges vary according to board plan and housing facility. *Payment plan:* installment. *Waivers:* employees or children of employees.

Financial Aid Of all full-time matriculated undergraduates who enrolled in 2011, 1,104 applied for aid, 1,015 were judged to have need, 84 had their need fully met. 293 Federal Work-Study jobs (averaging $2191). 58 state and other part-time jobs (averaging $2355). In 2011, 70 non-need-based awards were made. *Average percent of need met:* 77%. *Average financial aid package:* $17,530. *Average need-based loan:* $4350. *Average need-based gift aid:* $9520. *Average non-need-based aid:* $5545. *Average indebtedness upon graduation:* $34,311.

Applying *Options:* electronic application, deferred entrance. *Application fee:* $25. *Required:* essay or personal statement, high school transcript, minimum 2.0 GPA. *Required for some:* 3 letters of recommendation, interview. *Application deadlines:* 8/15 (freshmen), 8/5 (out-of-state freshmen), 8/15 (transfers). *Notification:* continuous (freshmen), continuous (out-of-state freshmen), continuous (transfers).

Freshman Application Contact Ms. Kim Poligala, Admission and Recruitment Coordinator, McMurry University, McMurry Station 278, Abilene, TX 79697. *Phone:* 325-793-4700. *Toll-free phone:* 800-460-2392. *Fax:* 325-793-4701. *E-mail:* admissions@mcm.edu. *Web site:* http://www.mcm.edu/.

Midland College
Midland, Texas

- **State and locally supported** 4-year, founded 1969
- **Suburban** 163-acre campus
- **Endowment** $34.7 million
- **Coed** 6,067 undergraduate students, 27% full-time, 58% women, 42% men
- **Noncompetitive** entrance level

Undergraduates 1,657 full-time, 4,410 part-time. Students come from 36 states and territories; 19 other countries; 12% are from out of state; 6% Black or African American, non-Hispanic/Latino; 31% Hispanic/Latino; 1% Native Hawaiian or other Pacific Islander, non-Hispanic/Latino; 0.3% American Indian or Alaska Native, non-Hispanic/Latino; 12% Two or more races, non-Hispanic/Latino; 9% Race/ethnicity unknown; 0.1% international; 5% transferred in.

Freshmen *Admission:* 884 enrolled.

Faculty *Total:* 276, 49% full-time, 14% with terminal degrees. *Student/faculty ratio:* 16:1.

Academics *Calendar:* semesters. *Degrees:* certificates, associate, and bachelor's. *Special study options:* academic remediation for entering students, adult/continuing education programs, advanced placement credit, distance learning, honors programs, services for LD students.

Computers on Campus 950 computers/terminals are available on campus for general student use. Students can access the following: free student e-mail accounts, online (class) grades, online (class) registration, online (class) schedules. Campuswide network is available. 100% of college-owned or -operated housing units are wired for high-speed Internet access. Wireless service is available via entire campus.

Student Life *Housing options:* coed, men-only, women-only. Campus housing is university owned. *Activities and organizations:* OIKOS, Midland College Latin American Student Society, Student Government Association, Student Nurses Association, Baptist Student Ministries. *Campus security:* 24-hour patrols. *Student services:* personal/psychological counseling.

Athletics Member NJCAA. *Intercollegiate sports:* baseball M(s), basketball M(s)/W(s), cheerleading W, golf M(s), softball W(s), volleyball W(s). *Intramural sports:* basketball M/W, cheerleading W, volleyball M/W.

Costs (2011–12) *Tuition:* area resident $2160 full-time; state resident $3180 full-time; nonresident $4350 full-time. Full-time tuition and fees vary according to course load, program, and reciprocity agreements. Part-time tuition and fees vary according to course load. *Room and board:* $4571. *Payment plans:* installment, deferred payment. *Waivers:* senior citizens and employees or children of employees.

Financial Aid Of all full-time matriculated undergraduates who enrolled in 2008, 75 Federal Work-Study jobs (averaging $2700). 5 state and other part-time jobs (averaging $2700).

Applying *Required:* high school transcript. *Application deadlines:* rolling (freshmen), rolling (transfers). *Notification:* continuous (freshmen), continuous (transfers).

Freshman Application Contact Mr. Jeremy Martinez, Director of Admissions, Midland College, 3600 North Garfield, Midland, TX 79705-6399. *Phone:* 432-685-5523. *Fax:* 432-685-6887. *E-mail:* jmartinez@midland.edu. *Web site:* http://www.midland.edu/.

Midwestern State University

Wichita Falls, Texas

- **State-supported** comprehensive, founded 1922
- **Urban** 255-acre campus
- **Coed** 5,464 undergraduate students, 74% full-time, 58% women, 42% men
- **Moderately difficult** entrance level, 52% of applicants were admitted

Undergraduates 4,053 full-time, 1,411 part-time. Students come from 26 states and territories; 51 other countries; 7% are from out of state; 12% Black or African American, non-Hispanic/Latino; 12% Hispanic/Latino; 3% Asian, non-Hispanic/Latino; 0.2% Native Hawaiian or other Pacific Islander, non-Hispanic/Latino; 0.9% American Indian or Alaska Native, non-Hispanic/Latino; 1% Two or more races, non-Hispanic/Latino; 0.8% Race/ethnicity unknown; 8% international; 10% transferred in; 23% live on campus. *Retention:* 68% of full-time freshmen returned.

Freshmen *Admission:* 2,751 applied, 1,436 admitted, 646 enrolled. *Average high school GPA:* 3.47. *Test scores:* SAT critical reading scores over 500: 51%; SAT math scores over 500: 62%; SAT writing scores over 500: 41%; ACT scores over 18: 94%; SAT critical reading scores over 600: 12%; SAT math scores over 600: 16%; SAT writing scores over 600: 10%; ACT scores over 24: 30%; SAT critical reading scores over 700: 1%; SAT math scores over 700: 2%; SAT writing scores over 700: 1%; ACT scores over 30: 2%.

Faculty *Total:* 337, 67% full-time, 59% with terminal degrees. *Student/faculty ratio:* 18:1.

Academics *Calendar:* semesters. *Degrees:* associate, bachelor's, master's, and postbachelor's certificates. *Special study options:* academic remediation for entering students, adult/continuing education programs, advanced placement credit, distance learning, double majors, English as a second language, honors programs, independent study, internships, part-time degree program, services for LD students, study abroad, summer session for credit. *ROTC:* Air Force (c). *Unusual degree programs:* 3-2 business administration.

Computers on Campus 405 computers/terminals are available on campus for general student use. Students can access the following: campus intranet, computer help desk, free student e-mail accounts, online (class) grades, online (class) registration, online (class) schedules. Campuswide network is available. 100% of college-owned or -operated housing units are wired for high-speed Internet access. Wireless service is available via entire campus.

Student Life *Housing:* on-campus residence required through sophomore year. *Options:* coed, men-only, women-only, disabled students. Campus housing is university owned. Freshman applicants given priority for college housing. *Activities and organizations:* drama/theater group, student-run newspaper, television station, choral group, marching band, Caribbean Students Organization, Baptist Student Ministry, Catholic Campus Ministry, African Students Organization, University Programming Board, national fraternities, national sororities. *Campus security:* 24-hour emergency response devices and patrols, controlled dormitory access. *Student services:* health clinic, personal/psychological counseling, legal services.

Athletics Member NCAA. All Division II. *Intercollegiate sports:* basketball M(s)/W(s), cheerleading M(s)(c)/W(s)(c), cross-country running W(s), fencing M(c)/W(c), football M(s), golf M(s)/W(s), soccer M(s)/W(s), softball W(s), tennis M(s)/W(s), volleyball W(s). *Intramural sports:* archery M/W, badminton M/W, basketball M/W, bowling M/W, football M/W, golf M/W, rugby M(c), soccer M/W, softball M/W, table tennis M/W, tennis M/W, ultimate Frisbee M/W, volleyball M/W, weight lifting M/W.

Standardized Tests *Required:* SAT or ACT (for admission).

Costs (2012–13) *Tuition:* state resident $4845 full-time, $162 per credit hour part-time; nonresident $6795 full-time, $227 per credit hour part-time. Full-time tuition and fees vary according to course load, location, and program. Part-time tuition and fees vary according to course load, location, and program. *Required fees:* $2393 full-time, $69 per credit hour part-time, $199 per credit hour part-time. *Room and board:* $6350; room only: $3350. Room and board charges vary according to board plan and housing facility. *Payment plan:* installment. *Waivers:* senior citizens and employees or children of employees.

Financial Aid Of all full-time matriculated undergraduates who enrolled in 2010, 2,994 applied for aid, 2,353 were judged to have need, 425 had their need fully met. 59 Federal Work-Study jobs (averaging $4055). In 2010, 513 non-need-based awards were made. *Average percent of need met:* 69%. *Average financial aid package:* $8992. *Average need-based loan:* $6967. *Average

need-based gift aid:* $6250. *Average non-need-based aid:* $1722. *Average indebtedness upon graduation:* $16,620.

Applying *Options:* electronic application, early action. *Application fee:* $25. *Required:* essay or personal statement, high school transcript. *Application deadlines:* 8/7 (freshmen), 8/7 (transfers). *Notification:* continuous (freshmen), continuous (transfers).

Freshman Application Contact Ms. Barbara Merkle, Director of Admissions, Midwestern State University, Wichita Falls, TX 76308. *Phone:* 940-397-4334. *Toll-free phone:* 800-842-1922. *Fax:* 940-397-4672. *E-mail:* admissions@mwsu.edu. *Web site:* http://www.mwsu.edu/.

Northwood University, Texas Campus

Cedar Hill, Texas

- **Independent** comprehensive, founded 1966
- **Small-town** 360-acre campus with easy access to Dallas-Fort Worth
- **Coed** 406 undergraduate students, 96% full-time, 42% women, 58% men
- **Moderately difficult** entrance level, 45% of applicants were admitted

Undergraduates 390 full-time, 16 part-time. Students come from 14 states and territories; 19 other countries; 6% are from out of state; 13% Black or African American, non-Hispanic/Latino; 34% Hispanic/Latino; 4% Asian, non-Hispanic/Latino; 0.5% American Indian or Alaska Native, non-Hispanic/Latino; 0.2% Two or more races, non-Hispanic/Latino; 5% Race/ethnicity unknown; 10% international; 18% transferred in; 36% live on campus. *Retention:* 59% of full-time freshmen returned.

Freshmen *Admission:* 509 applied, 227 admitted, 81 enrolled. *Average high school GPA:* 3.28. *Test scores:* SAT critical reading scores over 500: 21%; SAT math scores over 500: 35%; SAT writing scores over 500: 13%; ACT scores over 18: 63%; SAT critical reading scores over 600: 6%; SAT math scores over 600: 5%; SAT writing scores over 600: 2%; ACT scores over 24: 13%; SAT math scores over 700: 1%; ACT scores over 30: 3%.

Faculty *Total:* 31, 52% full-time, 39% with terminal degrees. *Student/faculty ratio:* 20:1.

Academics *Calendar:* quarters. *Degrees:* bachelor's and master's. *Special study options:* academic remediation for entering students, accelerated degree program, adult/continuing education programs, advanced placement credit, distance learning, double majors, external degree program, honors programs, independent study, internships, off-campus study, part-time degree program, summer session for credit.

Computers on Campus 73 computers/terminals are available on campus for general student use. Students can access the following: campus intranet, computer help desk, free student e-mail accounts, online (class) grades, online (class) registration, online (class) schedules. Campuswide network is available. 100% of college-owned or -operated housing units are wired for high-speed Internet access. Wireless service is available via entire campus.

Student Life *Housing:* on-campus residence required for freshman year. *Options:* men-only, women-only. Campus housing is university owned. Freshman campus housing is guaranteed. *Activities and organizations:* drama/theater group, student-run newspaper, choral group, Association of Entertainment and Sports Management, In-Line Hockey Club, Alpha Nu Omega, Alpha Omega, Delta Epsilon Chi. *Campus security:* 24-hour emergency response devices and patrols, student patrols, late-night transport/escort service, controlled dormitory access. *Student services:* health clinic, personal/psychological counseling.

Athletics Member NAIA. *Intercollegiate sports:* baseball M(s), cross-country running M(s)/W(s), golf M(s)/W(s), soccer M(s)/W(s), softball W(s), track and field M(s)/W(s). *Intramural sports:* basketball M/W, soccer M/W, volleyball M/W.

Standardized Tests *Required:* SAT or ACT (for admission).

Costs (2012–13) *Comprehensive fee:* $30,744 includes full-time tuition ($20,040), mandatory fees ($956), and room and board ($9748). Part-time tuition: $776 per semester hour. *College room only:* $5030. Room and board charges vary according to board plan.

Financial Aid Of all full-time matriculated undergraduates who enrolled in 2009, 384 applied for aid, 352 were judged to have need, 46 had their need fully met. In 2009, 62 non-need-based awards were made. *Average percent of need met:* 62%. *Average financial aid package:* $16,481. *Average need-based loan:* $4223. *Average need-based gift aid:* $5013. *Average indebtedness upon graduation:* $23,182.

Applying *Options:* electronic application, early admission, deferred entrance. *Application fee:* $25. *Required:* essay or personal statement, high school transcript, minimum 2.0 GPA. *Recommended:* 1 letter of recommendation, interview. *Application deadlines:* rolling (freshmen), rolling (transfers). *Notification:* continuous (freshmen), continuous (transfers).

Freshman Application Contact Dr. Terry Silva, Director of Admissions, Northwood University, Texas Campus, 1114 West FM 1382, Cedar Hill, TX 75104. *Phone:* 972-293-5400. *Toll-free phone:* 800-927-9663. *Fax:* 972-291-

3824. *E-mail:* txadmit@northwood.edu. *Web site:* http://www.northwood.edu/.

Our Lady of the Lake University of San Antonio

San Antonio, Texas

- **Independent Roman Catholic** comprehensive, founded 1895
- **Urban** 75-acre campus
- **Coed**
- **Moderately difficult** entrance level

Faculty *Student/faculty ratio:* 15:1.

Academics *Calendar:* semesters plus 2 summer sessions. *Degrees:* bachelor's, master's, doctoral, post-master's, postbachelor's, and first professional certificates.

Student Life *Campus security:* 24-hour emergency response devices and patrols, late-night transport/escort service, controlled dormitory access.

Athletics Member NAIA.

Standardized Tests *Required:* SAT or ACT (for admission).

Costs (2011–12) *Comprehensive fee:* $30,082 includes full-time tuition ($22,256), mandatory fees ($500), and room and board ($7326). Full-time tuition and fees vary according to degree level and location. Part-time tuition: $718 per credit hour. Part-time tuition and fees vary according to degree level and location. *Required fees:* $12 per credit hour part-time, $58 per term part-time. *Room and board:* Room and board charges vary according to board plan. *Payment plans:* installment, deferred payment.

Financial Aid *Of all full-time matriculated undergraduates who enrolled in 2010,* 1,169 applied for aid, 1,120 were judged to have need, 230 had their need fully met. *In 2010,* 4 non-need-based awards were made. *Average percent of need met:* 82. *Average financial aid package:* $24,580. *Average need-based loan:* $4382. *Average need-based gift aid:* $16,288. *Average non-need-based aid:* $11,762. *Average indebtedness upon graduation:* $32,356.

Applying *Options:* electronic application, deferred entrance. *Application fee:* $25. *Required:* high school transcript. *Required for some:* interview.

Freshman Application Contact Gilberto Becerra, Assistant Director of Undergraduate Admissions, Our Lady of the Lake University of San Antonio, 411 Southwest 24th Street, San Antonio, TX 78207-4689. *Phone:* 210-434-6711 Ext. 4129. *Toll-free phone:* 800-436-6558. *Fax:* 210-431-4036. *E-mail:* admission@lake.ollusa.edu. *Web site:* http://www.ollusa.edu/.

Paul Quinn College

Dallas, Texas

Director of Admissions Ms. Nena Taylor-Richey, Director of Admissions and Recruitment, Paul Quinn College, 3837 Simpson-Stuart Road, Dallas, TX 75241-4331. *Phone:* 214-302-3575. *Toll-free phone:* 877-346-1063. *Web site:* http://www.pqc.edu/.

Prairie View A&M University

Prairie View, Texas

- **State-supported** university, founded 1878, part of Texas A&M University System
- **Small-town** 1502-acre campus with easy access to Houston
- **Endowment** $54.1 million
- **Coed** 6,813 undergraduate students, 93% full-time, 60% women, 40% men
- **Moderately difficult** entrance level, 40% of applicants were admitted

Undergraduates 6,337 full-time, 476 part-time. Students come from 42 states and territories; 42 other countries; 7% are from out of state; 86% Black or African American, non-Hispanic/Latino; 5% Hispanic/Latino; 1% Asian, non-Hispanic/Latino; 0.1% Native Hawaiian or other Pacific Islander, non-Hispanic/Latino; 0.1% American Indian or Alaska Native, non-Hispanic/Latino; 1% Two or more races, non-Hispanic/Latino; 1% Race/ethnicity unknown; 2% international; 4% transferred in; 68% live on campus. *Retention:* 64% of full-time freshmen returned.

Freshmen *Admission:* 9,258 applied, 3,716 admitted, 1,689 enrolled. *Average high school GPA:* 2.94. *Test scores:* SAT critical reading scores over 500: 13%; SAT math scores over 500: 18%; SAT writing scores over 500: 11%; ACT scores over 18: 42%; SAT critical reading scores over 600: 1%; SAT math scores over 600: 3%; SAT writing scores over 600: 1%; ACT scores over 24: 6%.

Faculty *Total:* 457, 83% full-time, 61% with terminal degrees. *Student/faculty ratio:* 17:1.

Academics *Calendar:* semesters. *Degrees:* bachelor's, master's, doctoral, and first professional. *Special study options:* academic remediation for entering students, accelerated degree program, advanced placement credit, cooperative education, distance learning, double majors, honors programs, independent study, internships, off-campus study, part-time degree program, services for LD students, study abroad, summer session for credit. *ROTC:* Army (b), Navy (b).

Computers on Campus 4,400 computers/terminals and 4,400 ports are available on campus for general student use. Students can access the following: campus intranet, computer help desk, free student e-mail accounts, online (class) grades, online (class) registration, online (class) schedules. Campus-wide network is available. 100% of college-owned or -operated housing units are wired for high-speed Internet access. Wireless service is available via entire campus.

Student Life *Housing options:* men-only, women-only. Campus housing is provided by a third party. Freshman applicants given priority for college housing. *Activities and organizations:* drama/theater group, student-run newspaper, radio station, choral group, marching band, National Society of Black Engineers, National Association of Black Accountants, National Organization of Black Chemists and Chemical Engineers, Toastmasters International, Baptist Student Movement, national fraternities, national sororities. *Campus security:* 24-hour emergency response devices and patrols, late-night transport/escort service, controlled dormitory access. *Student services:* health clinic, personal/psychological counseling.

Athletics Member NCAA, NAIA. All NCAA Division I except football (Division I-AA). *Intercollegiate sports:* baseball M(s), basketball M(s)/W(s), cross-country running M(s)/W(s), golf M(s)/W(s), soccer W(s), softball W(s), tennis M(s)/W(s), track and field M(s)/W(s), volleyball W(s). *Intramural sports:* baseball M, basketball M/W, bowling W, cross-country running M/W, golf M/W, soccer W, softball W, tennis M/W, track and field M/W, volleyball M/W.

Standardized Tests *Required:* SAT or ACT (for admission).

Costs (2011–12) *Tuition:* state resident $5077 full-time, $169 per credit hour part-time; nonresident $14,377 full-time, $479 per credit hour part-time. Full-time tuition and fees vary according to course load, program, and reciprocity agreements. Part-time tuition and fees vary according to course load, program, and reciprocity agreements. *Required fees:* $2325 full-time, $57 per credit hour part-time, $365 per term part-time. *Room and board:* $7337. Room and board charges vary according to board plan, housing facility, and student level. *Payment plan:* installment. *Waivers:* senior citizens.

Financial Aid Of all full-time matriculated undergraduates who enrolled in 2010, 5,744 applied for aid, 5,429 were judged to have need, 3,943 had their need fully met. 486 Federal Work-Study jobs (averaging $1504). 35 state and other part-time jobs (averaging $1103). In 2010, 1139 non-need-based awards were made. *Average financial aid package:* $10,867. *Average need-based gift aid:* $6538. *Average non-need-based aid:* $4718.

Applying *Options:* electronic application, deferred entrance. *Application fee:* $25. *Required:* high school transcript, minimum 2.5 GPA. *Application deadlines:* 6/1 (freshmen), 6/1 (transfers). *Notification:* continuous (freshmen), continuous (transfers).

Freshman Application Contact Ms. Mary Gooch, Director of Admissions, Prairie View A&M University, PO Box 519, MS #1009, Prairie View, TX 77446-0188. *Phone:* 936-261-1066. *E-mail:* megooch@pvamu.edu. *Web site:* http://www.pvamu.edu/.

Rice University

Houston, Texas

- **Independent** university, founded 1912
- **Urban** 300-acre campus with easy access to Houston
- **Endowment** $4.5 billion
- **Coed** 3,755 undergraduate students, 99% full-time, 48% women, 52% men
- **Most difficult** entrance level, 19% of applicants were admitted

Undergraduates 3,705 full-time, 50 part-time. Students come from 51 states and territories; 41 other countries; 47% are from out of state; 7% Black or African American, non-Hispanic/Latino; 13% Hispanic/Latino; 20% Asian, non-Hispanic/Latino; 0.1% Native Hawaiian or other Pacific Islander, non-Hispanic/Latino; 0.3% American Indian or Alaska Native, non-Hispanic/Latino; 5% Two or more races, non-Hispanic/Latino; 1% Race/ethnicity unknown; 10% international; 2% transferred in; 75% live on campus. *Retention:* 97% of full-time freshmen returned.

Freshmen *Admission:* 13,816 applied, 2,600 admitted, 998 enrolled. *Test scores:* SAT critical reading scores over 500: 99%; SAT math scores over 500: 100%; SAT writing scores over 500: 98%; ACT scores over 18: 100%; SAT critical reading scores over 600: 90%; SAT math scores over 600: 94%; SAT writing scores over 600: 90%; ACT scores over 24: 98%; SAT critical reading scores over 700: 53%; SAT math scores over 700: 70%; SAT writing scores over 700: 56%; ACT scores over 30: 78%.

Faculty *Total:* 737, 88% full-time, 93% with terminal degrees. *Student/faculty ratio:* 6:1.

Academics *Calendar:* semesters. *Degrees:* bachelor's, master's, doctoral, and first professional. *Special study options:* accelerated degree program, advanced placement credit, double majors, English as a second language, honors programs, independent study, internships, off-campus study, services for LD students, student-designed majors, study abroad, summer session for credit. *ROTC:* Army (c), Navy (b), Air Force (c).

Computers on Campus 543 computers/terminals are available on campus for general student use. Students can access the following: campus intranet, computer help desk, free student e-mail accounts, online (class) grades, online (class) registration. Campuswide network is available. Wireless service is available via entire campus.

Student Life *Housing options:* coed. Campus housing is university owned. Freshman campus housing is guaranteed. *Activities and organizations:* drama/theater group, student-run newspaper, radio and television station, choral group, marching band, Drama Club, volunteer program, intramural sports, college government, Marching Owl Band. *Campus security:* 24-hour emergency response devices and patrols, late-night transport/escort service, controlled dormitory access. *Student services:* health clinic, personal/psychological counseling, women's center.

Athletics Member NCAA. All Division I except football (Division I-A). *Intercollegiate sports:* badminton M(c)/W(c), baseball M(s), basketball M(s)/W(s), cheerleading M(c)/W(c), crew M(c)/W(c), cross-country running M(s)/W(s), equestrian sports M(c)/W(c), fencing M(c)/W(c), field hockey W(c), golf M(s), lacrosse M(c)/W(c), riflery M(c)/W(c), rugby M(c)/W(c), sailing M(c)/W(c), soccer M(c)/W(s), softball W(s), swimming and diving W(s), tennis M(s)/W(s), track and field M(s)/W(s), ultimate Frisbee M(c)/W(c), volleyball M(c)/W(s), water polo M(c)/W(c). *Intramural sports:* badminton M/W, basketball M/W, cross-country running M/W, football M/W, racquetball M/W, soccer M/W, softball M/W, swimming and diving M/W, table tennis M/W, tennis M/W, track and field M/W, ultimate Frisbee M/W, volleyball M/W.

Standardized Tests *Required:* SAT and SAT Subject Tests or ACT (for admission).

Costs (2012–13) *One-time required fee:* $520. *Comprehensive fee:* $49,887 includes full-time tuition ($36,610), mandatory fees ($677), and room and board ($12,600). *College room only:* $8500. *Payment plan:* installment. *Waivers:* employees or children of employees.

Financial Aid Of all full-time matriculated undergraduates who enrolled in 2010, 2,343 applied for aid, 1,391 were judged to have need, 1,391 had their need fully met. In 2010, 701 non-need-based awards were made. *Average percent of need met:* 100%. *Average financial aid package:* $29,739. *Average need-based loan:* $1404. *Average need-based gift aid:* $27,671. *Average non-need-based aid:* $14,772. *Average indebtedness upon graduation:* $13,944.

Applying *Options:* electronic application, early decision, deferred entrance. *Application fee:* $70. *Required:* essay or personal statement, high school transcript, 2 letters of recommendation. *Required for some:* portfolio for architecture; audition for music. *Recommended:* interview. *Application deadlines:* 1/1 (freshmen), 3/15 (transfers). *Early decision deadline:* 11/1. *Notification:* 4/1 (freshmen), 5/15 (transfers), 12/15 (early decision).

Freshman Application Contact Office of Admission, Rice University, Office of Admission, PO Box 1892, MS 17, Houston, TX 77251-1892. *Phone:* 713-348-RICE. *Toll-free phone:* 800-527-OWLS. *E-mail:* admi@rice.edu. *Web site:* http://www.rice.edu/.

Rio Grande Bible Institute

Edinburg, Texas

Director of Admissions David Loyola, Director of Admissions, Rio Grande Bible Institute, 4300 S US Hwy 281, Edinburg, TX 78539. *Phone:* 956-380-8100. *Fax:* 956-380-8256. *E-mail:* admisiones@riogrande.edu. *Web site:* http://www.riogrande.edu/.

St. Edward's University

Austin, Texas

- **Independent Roman Catholic** comprehensive, founded 1885
- **Urban** 160-acre campus
- **Endowment** $54.8 million
- **Coed** 4,425 undergraduate students, 80% full-time, 61% women, 39% men
- **Moderately difficult** entrance level, 64% of applicants were admitted

Undergraduates 3,538 full-time, 887 part-time. Students come from 41 states and territories; 41 other countries; 7% are from out of state; 4% Black or African American, non-Hispanic/Latino; 33% Hispanic/Latino; 2% Asian, non-Hispanic/Latino; 0.3% Native Hawaiian or other Pacific Islander, non-Hispanic/Latino; 0.7% American Indian or Alaska Native, non-Hispanic/Latino; 3% Two or more races, non-Hispanic/Latino; 2% Race/ethnicity unknown; 5% international; 5% transferred in; 37% live on campus. *Retention:* 81% of full-time freshmen returned.

Freshmen *Admission:* 3,886 applied, 2,475 admitted, 786 enrolled. *Test scores:* SAT critical reading scores over 500: 82%; SAT math scores over 500: 81%; SAT writing scores over 500: 74%; ACT scores over 18: 100%; SAT critical reading scores over 600: 35%; SAT math scores over 600: 28%; SAT writing scores over 600: 30%; ACT scores over 24: 65%; SAT critical reading scores over 700: 6%; SAT math scores over 700: 3%; SAT writing scores over 700: 3%; ACT scores over 30: 11%.

Faculty *Total:* 519, 39% full-time, 63% with terminal degrees. *Student/faculty ratio:* 14:1.

Academics *Calendar:* semesters. *Degrees:* bachelor's, master's, and post-bachelor's certificates. *Special study options:* academic remediation for entering students, adult/continuing education programs, advanced placement credit, double majors, honors programs, independent study, internships, part-time degree program, services for LD students, study abroad, summer session for credit. *ROTC:* Army (c), Air Force (c).

Computers on Campus 790 computers/terminals and 7,200 ports are available on campus for general student use. Students can access the following: computer help desk, free student e-mail accounts, online (class) grades, online (class) registration, online (class) schedules, online library, ability to change address and biographical data, look at transcripts, pull up statements of account, grades, online progress reports and degree audit, campus job postings, student timesheets, financial aid information. Campuswide network is available. 100% of college-owned or -operated housing units are wired for high-speed Internet access. Wireless service is available via classrooms, computer centers, computer labs, dorm rooms, learning centers, libraries, student centers.

Student Life *Housing:* on-campus residence required for freshman year. *Options:* coed, women-only, disabled students. Campus housing is university owned. Freshman campus housing is guaranteed. *Activities and organizations:* drama/theater group, student-run newspaper, choral group, Promoting Respect, Inclusion, Diversity and Empowerment (PRIDE), Hispanic Student Association, HillRaisers, Academy of Science, Outdoor Adventure Club. *Campus security:* 24-hour emergency response devices and patrols, late-night transport/escort service, controlled dormitory access, self-defense education, informal discussions, pamphlets, posters, alcohol awareness meetings, lighted pathways and sidewalks. *Student services:* health clinic, personal/psychological counseling.

Athletics Member NCAA. All Division II. *Intercollegiate sports:* baseball M(s), basketball M(s)/W(s), golf M(s)/W(s), soccer M(s)/W(s), softball W(s), tennis M(s)/W(s), volleyball W(s). *Intramural sports:* basketball M/W, crew M(c)/W(c), cross-country running M(c)/W(c), lacrosse M(c)/W(c), racquetball M/W, rugby M(c), soccer M(c)/W(c), swimming and diving M(c)/W(c), tennis M/W, track and field M(c)/W(c), ultimate Frisbee M(c)/W(c), volleyball M/W.

Standardized Tests *Required:* SAT or ACT (for admission).

Costs (2012–13) *Comprehensive fee:* $41,154 includes full-time tuition ($30,710), mandatory fees ($400), and room and board ($10,044). Full-time tuition and fees vary according to course load and degree level. Part-time tuition: $1025 per credit hour. Part-time tuition and fees vary according to course load and degree level. *Required fees:* $50 per term part-time. *College room only:* $5844. Room and board charges vary according to board plan and housing facility. *Payment plans:* installment, deferred payment. *Waivers:* employees or children of employees.

Financial Aid Of all full-time matriculated undergraduates who enrolled in 2011, 2,633 applied for aid, 2,249 were judged to have need, 226 had their need fully met. 197 Federal Work-Study jobs (averaging $1909). 8 state and other part-time jobs (averaging $1913). In 2011, 177 non-need-based awards were made. *Average percent of need met:* 63%. *Average financial aid package:* $21,169. *Average need-based loan:* $4285. *Average need-based gift aid:* $13,101. *Average non-need-based aid:* $9073. *Average indebtedness upon graduation:* $32,828. *Financial aid deadline:* 5/1.

Applying *Options:* electronic application, deferred entrance. *Application fee:* $45. *Required:* essay or personal statement, high school transcript, 1 letter of recommendation. *Recommended:* interview. *Application deadlines:* 5/1 (freshmen), 5/1 (out-of-state freshmen), 7/1 (transfers). *Notification:* continuous (freshmen), continuous (out-of-state freshmen), continuous (transfers).

Freshman Application Contact Ms. Karen Gregg, Inquiry Coordinator, St. Edward's University, 3001 South Congress Avenue, Austin, TX 78704. *Phone:* 512-448-8580. *Toll-free phone:* 800-555-0164. *Fax:* 512-464-8877. *E-mail:* seu.admit@stedwards.edu. *Web site:* http://www.gotostedwards.com/.

St. Mary's University

San Antonio, Texas

- **Independent Roman Catholic** comprehensive, founded 1852
- **Urban** 135-acre campus
- **Endowment** $116.5 million
- **Coed** 2,508 undergraduate students, 93% full-time, 58% women, 42% men
- **Moderately difficult** entrance level, 61% of applicants were admitted

Undergraduates 2,330 full-time, 178 part-time. 3% Black or African American, non-Hispanic/Latino; 69% Hispanic/Latino; 3% Asian, non-Hispanic/Latino; 0.1% Native Hawaiian or other Pacific Islander, non-Hispanic/Latino; 0.3% American Indian or Alaska Native, non-Hispanic/Latino; 3% Race/ethnicity unknown; 6% international; 55% live on campus. *Retention:* 80% of full-time freshmen returned.

Freshmen *Admission:* 4,372 applied, 2,672 admitted, 641 enrolled. *Test scores:* SAT math scores over 500: 64%; SAT writing scores over 500: 48%; ACT scores over 18: 93%; SAT math scores over 600: 18%; SAT writing scores over 600: 10%; ACT scores over 24: 37%; SAT math scores over 700: 1%; SAT writing scores over 700: 1%; ACT scores over 30: 4%.

Faculty *Total:* 367, 54% full-time, 72% with terminal degrees. *Student/faculty ratio:* 12:1.

Academics *Calendar:* semesters. *Degrees:* bachelor's, master's, doctoral, and first professional. *Special study options:* academic remediation for entering students, adult/continuing education programs, advanced placement credit, cooperative education, distance learning, double majors, English as a second language, honors programs, independent study, internships, off-campus study, part-time degree program, services for LD students, study abroad, summer session for credit. *ROTC:* Army (b), Air Force (c).

Computers on Campus 100 computers/terminals are available on campus for general student use. Students can access the following: campus intranet, computer help desk, free student e-mail accounts, online (class) grades, online (class) registration, online (class) schedules. Campuswide network is available. 100% of college-owned or -operated housing units are wired for high-speed Internet access. Wireless service is available via entire campus.

Student Life *Housing:* on-campus residence required for freshman year. *Options:* coed, men-only, women-only, disabled students. Campus housing is university owned. Freshman applicants given priority for college housing. *Activities and organizations:* drama/theater group, student-run newspaper, choral group, Beta Beta Beta Biology Society, St. Mary's University Society of Honor Scholars, American Chemical Society of Students, Mexican Student Organization, Alpha Phi Omega, national fraternities, national sororities. *Campus security:* 24-hour emergency response devices and patrols, late-night transport/escort service, controlled dormitory access. *Student services:* health clinic, personal/psychological counseling.

Athletics Member NCAA. All Division II. *Intercollegiate sports:* baseball M(s), basketball M(s)/W(s), cheerleading M/W, cross-country running W, golf M(s)/W, rugby M(c), soccer M(s)/W(s), softball W, tennis M(s)/W(s), volleyball W(s). *Intramural sports:* basketball M/W, football M/W, racquetball M/W, soccer M/W, softball M/W, table tennis M/W, tennis M/W, volleyball M/W.

Standardized Tests *Required:* SAT or ACT (for admission).

Costs (2011–12) *Comprehensive fee:* $31,736 includes full-time tuition ($22,820), mandatory fees ($566), and room and board ($8350). Full-time tuition and fees vary according to course load. Part-time tuition: $685 per credit hour. Part-time tuition and fees vary according to course load. *Required fees:* $163 per term part-time. *Room and board:* Room and board charges vary according to board plan and housing facility.

Financial Aid Of all full-time matriculated undergraduates who enrolled in 2009, 1,747 applied for aid, 1,633 were judged to have need, 406 had their need fully met. In 2009, 509 non-need-based awards were made. *Average percent of need met:* 76%. *Average financial aid package:* $20,138. *Average need-based loan:* $6124. *Average need-based gift aid:* $14,206. *Average non-need-based aid:* $7292. *Average indebtedness upon graduation:* $22,592.

Applying *Options:* electronic application, deferred entrance. *Application fee:* $30. *Required:* high school transcript. *Recommended:* essay or personal statement, minimum 2.0 GPA, interview. *Application deadlines:* rolling (freshmen), rolling (transfers). *Notification:* continuous (freshmen), continuous (transfers).

Freshman Application Contact Mr. Chadd J. Bridwell, Director of Undergraduate Admission, St. Mary's University, One Camino Santa Maria, San Antonio, TX 78228. *Phone:* 210-436-3126. *Toll-free phone:* 800-FOR-STMU. *Fax:* 210-431-6742. *E-mail:* uadm@stmarytx.edu. *Web site:* http://www.stmarytx.edu/.

Sam Houston State University

Huntsville, Texas

- **State-supported** university, founded 1879, part of Texas State University System
- **Small-town** 1256-acre campus with easy access to Houston
- **Endowment** $44.9 million
- **Coed** 14,995 undergraduate students, 83% full-time, 57% women, 43% men
- **Moderately difficult** entrance level, 77% of applicants were admitted

Undergraduates 12,439 full-time, 2,556 part-time. Students come from 45 states and territories; 44 other countries; 1% are from out of state; 17% Black or African American, non-Hispanic/Latino; 16% Hispanic/Latino; 1% Asian, non-Hispanic/Latino; 0.1% Native Hawaiian or other Pacific Islander, non-Hispanic/Latino; 2% American Indian or Alaska Native, non-Hispanic/Latino; 0.5% Race/ethnicity unknown; 1% international; 14% transferred in; 22% live on campus. *Retention:* 71% of full-time freshmen returned.

Freshmen *Admission:* 7,070 applied, 5,473 admitted, 2,069 enrolled. *Test scores:* SAT critical reading scores over 500: 47%; SAT math scores over 500: 57%; ACT scores over 18: 87%; SAT critical reading scores over 600: 11%; SAT math scores over 600: 13%; ACT scores over 24: 21%; SAT critical reading scores over 700: 1%; SAT math scores over 700: 1%; ACT scores over 30: 2%.

Faculty *Total:* 843, 78% full-time, 55% with terminal degrees. *Student/faculty ratio:* 20:1.

Academics *Calendar:* semesters. *Degrees:* bachelor's, master's, doctoral, and first professional. *Special study options:* academic remediation for entering students, advanced placement credit, distance learning, double majors, English as a second language, external degree program, honors programs, independent study, internships, off-campus study, part-time degree program, services for LD students, summer session for credit. *ROTC:* Army (b).

Computers on Campus 607 computers/terminals are available on campus for general student use. Students can access the following: campus intranet, computer help desk, free student e-mail accounts, online (class) grades, online (class) registration, online (class) schedules. Campuswide network is available. Wireless service is available via entire campus.

Student Life *Housing:* on-campus residence required for freshman year. *Options:* coed, men-only, women-only, disabled students. Campus housing is university owned and is provided by a third party. Freshman campus housing is guaranteed. *Activities and organizations:* drama/theater group, student-run newspaper, radio and television station, choral group, marching band, Chi Alpha Christian Fellowship, Non-Traditional Student Organization, Sigma Alpha Pi Leadership Society, Baptist Student Ministry, Bearkats for Life, national fraternities, national sororities. *Campus security:* 24-hour emergency response devices and patrols, student patrols, late-night transport/escort service. *Student services:* health clinic, personal/psychological counseling, legal services.

Athletics Member NCAA. All Division I except football (Division I-AA). *Intercollegiate sports:* baseball M(s), basketball M(s)/W(s), bowling W(s), cross-country running M/W, golf M(s)/W(s), soccer W(s), softball W(s), tennis W(s), track and field M(s)/W(s), volleyball W(s). *Intramural sports:* basketball M/W, football M, lacrosse M, racquetball M/W, rugby M/W, soccer M/W, softball W, tennis M/W, volleyball M/W.

Standardized Tests *Required:* SAT or ACT (for admission).

Costs (2011–12) *Tuition:* state resident $5130 full-time, $171 per credit hour part-time; nonresident $14,520 full-time, $484 per credit hour part-time. Full-time tuition and fees vary according to course level, course load, location, and program. Part-time tuition and fees vary according to course level, course load, location, and program. *Required fees:* $2198 full-time. *Room and board:* $7644; room only: $4164. Room and board charges vary according to board plan and housing facility. *Payment plan:* installment. *Waivers:* employees or children of employees.

Financial Aid Of all full-time matriculated undergraduates who enrolled in 2008, 8,023 applied for aid, 3,703 were judged to have need, 4 had their need fully met. 291 Federal Work-Study jobs (averaging $1563). 90 state and other part-time jobs (averaging $1206). In 2008, 708 non-need-based awards were made. *Average percent of need met:* 31%. *Average financial aid package:* $4340. *Average need-based loan:* $189. *Average need-based gift aid:* $906. *Average non-need-based aid:* $322. *Average indebtedness upon graduation:* $6196.

Applying *Options:* electronic application. *Application fee:* $45. *Required:* high school transcript, minimum 2.0 GPA. *Application deadlines:* 8/1 (freshmen), 8/1 (out-of-state freshmen), 8/1 (transfers). *Notification:* continuous (freshmen), continuous (transfers).

Freshman Application Contact Mr. Trevor B. Thorn, Director of Admissions and Recruitment, Sam Houston State University, PO Box 2418, Huntsville, TX 77341. *Phone:* 936-294-1828. *Toll-free phone:* 866-232-7528 Ext. 1828.

Fax: 936-294-3758. *E-mail:* admissions@shsu.edu. *Web site:* http://www.shsu.edu/.

Schreiner University

Kerrville, Texas

- **Independent Presbyterian** comprehensive, founded 1923
- **Small-town** 175-acre campus with easy access to San Antonio, Austin
- **Endowment** $46.6 million
- **Coed** 1,026 undergraduate students, 96% full-time, 58% women, 42% men
- **Moderately difficult** entrance level, 61% of applicants were admitted

Undergraduates 984 full-time, 42 part-time. 3% are from out of state; 4% Black or African American, non-Hispanic/Latino; 26% Hispanic/Latino; 1% Asian, non-Hispanic/Latino; 0.1% Native Hawaiian or other Pacific Islander, non-Hispanic/Latino; 0.4% American Indian or Alaska Native, non-Hispanic/Latino; 3% Two or more races, non-Hispanic/Latino; 0.3% international; 6% transferred in; 68% live on campus. *Retention:* 64% of full-time freshmen returned.

Freshmen *Admission:* 1,109 applied, 677 admitted, 276 enrolled. *Average high school GPA:* 3.54. *Test scores:* SAT critical reading scores over 500: 50%; SAT math scores over 500: 61%; SAT writing scores over 500: 41%; SAT critical reading scores over 600: 17%; SAT math scores over 600: 15%; SAT writing scores over 600: 7%; SAT critical reading scores over 700: 2%; SAT math scores over 700: 1%; SAT writing scores over 700: 1%.

Faculty *Total:* 117, 46% full-time, 51% with terminal degrees. *Student/faculty ratio:* 14:1.

Academics *Calendar:* semesters. *Degrees:* certificates, associate, bachelor's, and master's. *Special study options:* academic remediation for entering students, accelerated degree program, advanced placement credit, cooperative education, double majors, honors programs, independent study, internships, part-time degree program, services for LD students, student-designed majors, study abroad, summer session for credit. *Unusual degree programs:* 3-2 engineering with University of Texas at Austin, Texas A&M University.

Computers on Campus 120 computers/terminals are available on campus for general student use. Students can access the following: computer help desk, free student e-mail accounts, online (class) grades, online (class) registration, online (class) schedules. Campuswide network is available. 100% of college-owned or -operated housing units are wired for high-speed Internet access. Wireless service is available via classrooms, computer centers, computer labs, dorm rooms, learning centers, libraries, student centers.

Student Life *Housing:* on-campus residence required through junior year. *Options:* coed, disabled students. Campus housing is university owned. Freshman campus housing is guaranteed. *Activities and organizations:* drama/theater group, student-run newspaper, choral group, Student Senate, Greek Life, Campus Ministry, honor societies, Hall Councils, national fraternities, national sororities. *Campus security:* 24-hour emergency response devices and patrols, late-night transport/escort service. *Student services:* health clinic, personal/psychological counseling.

Athletics Member NCAA. All Division III. *Intercollegiate sports:* baseball M, basketball M/W, cross-country running M/W, golf M/W, soccer M/W, softball W, tennis M/W, volleyball W. *Intramural sports:* cheerleading W.

Standardized Tests *Required:* SAT or ACT (for admission).

Costs (2012–13) *One-time required fee:* $25. *Comprehensive fee:* $31,702 includes full-time tuition ($21,040), mandatory fees ($600), and room and board ($10,062). *Room and board:* Room and board charges vary according to board plan and housing facility. *Payment plan:* installment. *Waivers:* employees or children of employees.

Financial Aid Of all full-time matriculated undergraduates who enrolled in 2010, 886 applied for aid, 791 were judged to have need, 110 had their need fully met. In 2010, 84 non-need-based awards were made. *Average percent of need met:* 71%. *Average financial aid package:* $15,592. *Average need-based loan:* $3696. *Average need-based gift aid:* $12,566. *Average non-need-based aid:* $7240. *Average indebtedness upon graduation:* $26,000.

Applying *Options:* electronic application, deferred entrance. *Application fee:* $25. *Required:* essay or personal statement, high school transcript. *Recommended:* interview. *Application deadlines:* 5/1 (freshmen), 5/1 (transfers). *Notification:* continuous (freshmen), continuous (transfers).

Freshman Application Contact Dean of Admission and Financial Aid, Schreiner University, 2100 Memorial Boulevard, Kerrville, TX 78028. *Phone:* 830-792-7217. *Toll-free phone:* 800-343-4919. *E-mail:* admissions@schreiner.edu. *Web site:* http://www.schreiner.edu/.

Southern Methodist University

Dallas, Texas

- **Independent** university, founded 1911, affiliated with United Methodist Church
- **Suburban** 231-acre campus
- **Endowment** $1.2 billion
- **Coed** 6,221 undergraduate students, 96% full-time, 52% women, 48% men
- **Moderately difficult** entrance level, 55% of applicants were admitted

Undergraduates 5,974 full-time, 247 part-time. Students come from 49 states and territories; 72 other countries; 49% are from out of state; 6% Black or African American, non-Hispanic/Latino; 11% Hispanic/Latino; 6% Asian, non-Hispanic/Latino; 0.4% Native Hawaiian or other Pacific Islander, non-Hispanic/Latino; 0.5% American Indian or Alaska Native, non-Hispanic/Latino; 2% Two or more races, non-Hispanic/Latino; 0.5% Race/ethnicity unknown; 7% international; 4% transferred in; 33% live on campus. *Retention:* 89% of full-time freshmen returned.

Freshmen *Admission:* 10,338 applied, 5,641 admitted, 1,382 enrolled. *Average high school GPA:* 3.64. *Test scores:* SAT critical reading scores over 500: 95%; SAT math scores over 500: 96%; SAT writing scores over 500: 94%; ACT scores over 18: 98%; SAT critical reading scores over 600: 67%; SAT math scores over 600: 78%; SAT writing scores over 600: 63%; ACT scores over 24: 91%; SAT critical reading scores over 700: 19%; SAT math scores over 700: 23%; SAT writing scores over 700: 18%; ACT scores over 30: 50%.

Faculty *Total:* 1,106, 64% full-time, 70% with terminal degrees. *Student/faculty ratio:* 11:1.

Academics *Calendar:* semesters. *Degrees:* bachelor's, master's, doctoral, postbachelor's, and first professional certificates. *Special study options:* academic remediation for entering students, accelerated degree program, adult/continuing education programs, advanced placement credit, cooperative education, distance learning, double majors, English as a second language, honors programs, independent study, internships, part-time degree program, services for LD students, student-designed majors, study abroad, summer session for credit. *ROTC:* Army (b), Air Force (c).

Computers on Campus 758 computers/terminals are available on campus for general student use. Students can access the following: campus intranet, computer help desk, free student e-mail accounts, online (class) grades, online (class) registration, online (class) schedules, online billing/payment processing. Campuswide network is available. Wireless service is available via classrooms, computer centers, computer labs, dorm rooms, learning centers, libraries, student centers.

Student Life *Housing:* on-campus residence required for freshman year. *Options:* coed, disabled students. Campus housing is university owned. Freshman campus housing is guaranteed. *Activities and organizations:* drama/theater group, student-run newspaper, radio and television station, choral group, marching band, Program Council, Student Senate, Student Foundation, Residence Hall Association, SPARC (Students Promoting Awareness, Responsibility, and Citizenship), national fraternities, national sororities. *Campus security:* 24-hour emergency response devices and patrols, late-night transport/escort service, controlled dormitory access. *Student services:* health clinic, personal/psychological counseling, women's center.

Athletics Member NCAA. All Division I except football (Division I-A). *Intercollegiate sports:* baseball M(c), basketball M(s)/W(s), cheerleading M(s)(c)/W(s)(c), crew W(s), cross-country running W(s), equestrian sports W(s), fencing M(c)/W(c), golf M(s)/W(s), ice hockey M(c), lacrosse M(c), rugby M(c)/W(c), soccer M(s)/W(s), swimming and diving M(s)/W(s), tennis M(s)/W(s), track and field W, volleyball W(s), wrestling M(c). *Intramural sports:* basketball M/W, bowling M/W, football M, golf M/W, racquetball M/W, rock climbing M(c)/W(c), soccer M/W, softball M/W, swimming and diving M/W, table tennis M(c)/W(c), tennis M/W, ultimate Frisbee M/W, volleyball M/W, water polo M/W, weight lifting M(c)/W(c).

Standardized Tests *Required:* SAT or ACT (for admission). *Required for some:* SAT Subject Tests (for admission).

Costs (2012–13) *Comprehensive fee:* $55,289 includes full-time tuition ($37,050), mandatory fees ($4700), and room and board ($13,539). Full-time tuition and fees vary according to class time. Part-time tuition and fees vary according to class time and course load. *Room and board:* Room and board charges vary according to board plan and housing facility. *Payment plans:* tuition prepayment, installment. *Waivers:* employees or children of employees.

Financial Aid Of all full-time matriculated undergraduates who enrolled in 2011, 2,846 applied for aid, 2,419 were judged to have need, 751 had their need fully met. 1,641 Federal Work-Study jobs (averaging $3468). 8 state and other part-time jobs (averaging $3503). In 2011, 1889 non-need-based awards were made. *Average percent of need met:* 85%. *Average financial aid package:* $33,903. *Average need-based loan:* $3747. *Average need-based gift aid:*

$17,794. *Average non-need-based aid:* $17,121. *Average indebtedness upon graduation:* $26,297.

Applying *Options:* electronic application, early admission, early action, deferred entrance. *Application fee:* $60. *Required:* high school transcript, minimum 2.0 GPA, 1 letter of recommendation, statement of good standing from prior institution(s). *Recommended:* essay or personal statement, minimum 2.7 GPA. *Application deadlines:* 3/15 (freshmen), 7/1 (transfers), 11/1 (early action). *Notification:* continuous (freshmen), continuous (transfers), 12/31 (early action).

Freshman Application Contact Mr. Wes Waggoner, Dean of Undergraduate Admission and Executive Director of Enrollment Services, Southern Methodist University, PO Box 750181, Dallas, TX 75275-0181. *Phone:* 214-768-3417. *Toll-free phone:* 800-323-0672. *Fax:* 214-768-1083. *E-mail:* ugadmission@smu.edu. *Web site:* http://www.smu.edu/.

South Texas College

McAllen, Texas

Freshman Application Contact Mr. Matthew Hebbard, Director of Enrollment Services and Registrar, South Texas College, 3201 West Pecan, McAllen, TX 78501. *Phone:* 956-872-2147. *Toll-free phone:* 800-742-7822. *E-mail:* mshebbar@southtexascollege.edu. *Web site:* http://www.southtexascollege.edu/.

South University

Austin, Texas

- **Proprietary** comprehensive
- **Coed**

Academics *Degrees:* associate, bachelor's, and master's.
Freshman Application Contact Director of Admissions, South University, 810 Hesters Crossing Road, Suite 220, Austin, TX 78681. *Phone:* 512-516-8800. *Fax:* 512-516-8680. *Web site:* http://www.southuniversity.edu/austin.aspx.

See page 1596 for the College Close-Up.

Southwestern Adventist University

Keene, Texas

- **Independent Seventh-day Adventist** comprehensive, founded 1894
- **Small-town** 150-acre campus with easy access to Dallas-Fort Worth
- **Endowment** $10.9 million
- **Coed** 803 undergraduate students, 82% full-time, 58% women, 42% men
- **Minimally difficult** entrance level, 56% of applicants were admitted

Undergraduates 659 full-time, 144 part-time. Students come from 36 states and territories; 32 other countries; 29% are from out of state; 14% Black or African American, non-Hispanic/Latino; 31% Hispanic/Latino; 3% Asian, non-Hispanic/Latino; 1% Native Hawaiian or other Pacific Islander, non-Hispanic/Latino; 0.6% American Indian or Alaska Native, non-Hispanic/Latino; 14% Two or more races, non-Hispanic/Latino; 0.5% Race/ethnicity unknown; 19% international; 40% live on campus. *Retention:* 58% of full-time freshmen returned.

Freshmen *Admission:* 663 applied, 370 admitted, 127 enrolled. *Average high school GPA:* 2.23. *Test scores:* SAT critical reading scores over 500: 43%; SAT math scores over 500: 28%; ACT scores over 18: 79%; SAT critical reading scores over 600: 9%; SAT math scores over 600: 3%; ACT scores over 24: 18%; SAT critical reading scores over 700: 1%; ACT scores over 30: 2%.

Faculty *Total:* 78, 67% full-time, 44% with terminal degrees. *Student/faculty ratio:* 12:1.

Academics *Calendar:* semesters. *Degrees:* associate, bachelor's, and master's. *Special study options:* academic remediation for entering students, accelerated degree program, adult/continuing education programs, advanced placement credit, double majors, English as a second language, external degree program, honors programs, independent study, internships, off-campus study, part-time degree program, services for LD students, student-designed majors, study abroad, summer session for credit.

Computers on Campus 100 computers/terminals are available on campus for general student use. Students can access the following: campus intranet, computer help desk, free student e-mail accounts, online (class) grades, online (class) registration, online (class) schedules. Campuswide network is available. 100% of college-owned or -operated housing units are wired for high-speed Internet access. Wireless service is available via entire campus.

Student Life *Housing:* on-campus residence required through sophomore year. *Options:* men-only, women-only, cooperative. Campus housing is university owned. Freshman campus housing is guaranteed. *Activities and organizations:* drama/theater group, student-run newspaper, radio and television station, choral group, Student Association, Students in Free Enterprise (SIFE), Education/

Psychology Club, Theology Club, Nursing Club. *Campus security:* 24-hour emergency response devices, student patrols. *Student services:* health clinic, personal/psychological counseling.

Athletics *Intramural sports:* basketball M(c)/W(c), football M/W, racquetball M/W, soccer M(c)/W(c), softball M/W, table tennis M/W, tennis M/W, volleyball M/W(c).

Standardized Tests *Required:* SAT or ACT (for admission).

Costs (2012–13) *Comprehensive fee:* $24,432 includes full-time tuition ($17,400) and room and board ($7032). Full-time tuition and fees vary according to course load and program. Part-time tuition: $725 per credit. Part-time tuition and fees vary according to course load and program. *College room only:* $3420. Room and board charges vary according to board plan. *Payment plans:* installment, deferred payment. *Waivers:* employees or children of employees.

Applying *Options:* electronic application, deferred entrance. *Required:* high school transcript, minimum 2.0 GPA. *Required for some:* essay or personal statement, 1 letter of recommendation, interview. *Application deadlines:* 8/31 (freshmen), 8/31 (transfers). *Notification:* 9/1 (freshmen), 9/1 (transfers).

Freshman Application Contact Ms. Diem Dennis, Associate Director of Admissions and Records, Southwestern Adventist University, 100 West Hillcrest, Keene, TX 76059. *Phone:* 817-202-6252. *Toll-free phone:* 800-433-2240. *E-mail:* ddennis@swau.edu. *Web site:* http://www.swau.edu/.

Southwestern Assemblies of God University

Waxahachie, Texas

- **Independent** comprehensive, founded 1927, affiliated with Assemblies of God
- **Small-town** 70-acre campus with easy access to Dallas-Fort Worth
- **Endowment** $4.0 million
- **Coed** 1,742 undergraduate students, 84% full-time, 49% women, 51% men
- **Noncompetitive** entrance level

Undergraduates 1,458 full-time, 284 part-time. Students come from 49 states and territories; 11 other countries; 40% are from out of state; 15% transferred in; 85% live on campus. *Retention:* 67% of full-time freshmen returned.

Freshmen *Admission:* 296 enrolled.

Faculty *Total:* 142, 49% full-time, 33% with terminal degrees. *Student/faculty ratio:* 16:1.

Academics *Calendar:* semesters. *Degrees:* associate, bachelor's, and master's. *Special study options:* academic remediation for entering students, adult/continuing education programs, advanced placement credit, distance learning, double majors, external degree program, independent study, internships, part-time degree program, services for LD students, summer session for credit. *ROTC:* Air Force (c).

Computers on Campus 96 computers/terminals and 1,000 ports are available on campus for general student use. Students can access the following: computer help desk, free student e-mail accounts, online (class) grades, online (class) registration, online (class) schedules. Campuswide network is available. 95% of college-owned or -operated housing units are wired for high-speed Internet access. Wireless service is available via entire campus.

Student Life *Housing:* on-campus residence required through senior year. *Options:* coed. Campus housing is university owned. Freshman campus housing is guaranteed. *Activities and organizations:* drama/theater group, student-run newspaper, choral group, Student Congress, Southwestern Missions Association, Street Hope, Gold Jackets, Women in Ministry. *Campus security:* 24-hour patrols, late-night transport/escort service, controlled dormitory access, 2 dorms electronic access; 4 dorms key access to rooms, camera surveillance, 24 hour dispatch monitored fire alarm systems (offsite). *Student services:* health clinic, personal/psychological counseling.

Athletics Member NAIA, NCCAA. *Intercollegiate sports:* baseball M(s), basketball M(s)/W(s), football M(s), soccer M(s)/W(s), softball W(s), volleyball W(s). *Intramural sports:* basketball M/W, cheerleading W, football M/W, soccer M(c)/W, softball M/W, table tennis M/W, tennis M/W, ultimate Frisbee M/W, volleyball M/W.

Standardized Tests *Required:* SAT or ACT (for admission).

Costs (2011–12) *Comprehensive fee:* $22,156 includes full-time tuition ($14,850), mandatory fees ($880), and room and board ($6426). Part-time tuition: $495 per credit. *College room only:* $3390. Room and board charges vary according to housing facility. *Payment plan:* deferred payment. *Waivers:* employees or children of employees.

Financial Aid Of all full-time matriculated undergraduates who enrolled in 2000, 1,116 applied for aid, 1,002 were judged to have need, 110 had their need fully met. 178 Federal Work-Study jobs, 7 state and other part-time jobs (averaging $890). In 2000, 316 non-need-based awards were made. *Average percent of need met:* 64%. *Average financial aid package:* $6728. *Average*

need-based loan: $3177. *Average need-based gift aid:* $3511. *Average indebtedness upon graduation:* $13,938. *Financial aid deadline:* 7/1.

Applying *Options:* early admission, deferred entrance. *Application fee:* $35. *Required:* essay or personal statement, high school transcript, minimum 2.0 GPA, 1 letter of recommendation, medical history, evidence of approved Christian character. *Application deadlines:* rolling (freshmen), rolling (transfers).

Freshman Application Contact Mr. Bryan Brooks, Assistant Dean of Admissions, Southwestern Assemblies of God University, 1200 Sycamore Street, Waxahachie, TX 75165. *Phone:* 972-825-4821. *Toll-free phone:* 888-937-7248. *Fax:* 972-923-8131. *E-mail:* bbrooks@sagu.edu. *Web site:* http://www.sagu.edu/.

Southwestern Christian College

Terrell, Texas

Freshman Application Contact Admissions Department, Southwestern Christian College, Box 10, 200 Bowser Street, Terrell, TX 75160. *Phone:* 214-524-3341. *Web site:* http://www.swcc.edu/.

Southwestern University

Georgetown, Texas

- **Independent Methodist** 4-year, founded 1840
- **Suburban** 700-acre campus with easy access to Austin
- **Coed** 1,347 undergraduate students, 99% full-time, 60% women, 40% men
- **Very difficult** entrance level, 13% of applicants were admitted

Undergraduates 1,333 full-time, 14 part-time. Students come from 31 states and territories; 10 other countries; 10% are from out of state; 3% Black or African American, non-Hispanic/Latino; 17% Hispanic/Latino; 4% Asian, non-Hispanic/Latino; 1% American Indian or Alaska Native, non-Hispanic/Latino; 0.7% Two or more races, non-Hispanic/Latino; 0.7% Race/ethnicity unknown; 0.2% international; 3% transferred in; 82% live on campus. *Retention:* 85% of full-time freshmen returned.

Freshmen *Admission:* 2,613 applied, 344 admitted, 344 enrolled. *Test scores:* SAT critical reading scores over 500: 91%; SAT math scores over 500: 93%; ACT scores over 18: 99%; SAT critical reading scores over 600: 61%; SAT math scores over 600: 57%; ACT scores over 24: 83%; SAT critical reading scores over 700: 18%; SAT math scores over 700: 13%; ACT scores over 30: 33%.

Faculty *Total:* 164, 74% full-time, 89% with terminal degrees. *Student/faculty ratio:* 10:1.

Academics *Calendar:* semesters. *Degree:* bachelor's. *Special study options:* advanced placement credit, double majors, honors programs, independent study, internships, off-campus study, services for LD students, student-designed majors, study abroad, summer session for credit. *Unusual degree programs:* 3-2 engineering with Washington University in St. Louis, Arizona State University, Texas A&M University.

Computers on Campus 410 computers/terminals are available on campus for general student use. Students can access the following: computer help desk, free student e-mail accounts, online (class) registration, online (class) schedules, transcripts. Campuswide network is available. Wireless service is available via entire campus.

Student Life *Housing:* on-campus residence required through sophomore year. *Options:* coed, men-only, women-only, disabled students. Campus housing is university owned. Freshman campus housing is guaranteed. *Activities and organizations:* drama/theater group, student-run newspaper, radio station, choral group, Student Peace Alliance (SPA), Students for Environmental Activism & Knowledge (SEAK), Alpha Phi Omega, Men's IFC, Women's Panhellenic, national fraternities, national sororities. *Campus security:* 24-hour emergency response devices and patrols, student patrols, late-night transport/escort service, controlled dormitory access. *Student services:* health clinic, personal/psychological counseling.

Athletics Member NCAA. All Division III. *Intercollegiate sports:* baseball M, basketball M/W, cross-country running M/W, golf M/W, lacrosse M, soccer M/W, softball W, swimming and diving M/W, tennis M/W, volleyball W. *Intramural sports:* basketball M/W, bowling M/W, football M/W, golf M/W, racquetball M/W, soccer M/W, softball M/W, swimming and diving M/W, table tennis M/W, tennis M/W, ultimate Frisbee M/W, volleyball M/W.

Standardized Tests *Required:* SAT (for admission). *Required for some:* SAT and SAT Subject Tests or ACT (for admission).

Costs (2011–12) *Comprehensive fee:* $43,120 includes full-time tuition ($33,440) and room and board ($9680). Part-time tuition: $1395 per semester hour. Part-time tuition and fees vary according to course load. *Room and board:* Room and board charges vary according to board plan and housing facility.

Financial Aid Of all full-time matriculated undergraduates who enrolled in 2011, 925 applied for aid, 801 were judged to have need, 241 had their need fully met. 168 Federal Work-Study jobs (averaging $1986). 531 state and other part-time jobs (averaging $2316). In 2011, 443 non-need-based awards were made. *Average percent of need met:* 86%. *Average financial aid package:* $28,669. *Average need-based loan:* $5380. *Average need-based gift aid:* $22,652. *Average non-need-based aid:* $15,402. *Average indebtedness upon graduation:* $31,848. *Financial aid deadline:* 3/1.

Applying *Options:* electronic application, early decision, early action, deferred entrance. *Application fee:* $40. *Required:* essay or personal statement, high school transcript, 1 letter of recommendation. *Required for some:* interview. *Recommended:* interview. *Application deadlines:* rolling (freshmen), rolling (out-of-state freshmen), 4/1 (transfers), 12/1 (early action). *Early decision deadline:* 11/1. *Notification:* 4/1 (freshmen), 4/1 (out-of-state freshmen), 10/1 (transfers), 12/15 (early decision), 2/1 (early action).

Freshman Application Contact Mr. Dave Voskuil, Vice President for Enrollment Services, Southwestern University, 1001 East University Avenue, Georgetown, TX 78626. *Phone:* 512-863-1200. *Toll-free phone:* 800-252-3166. *Fax:* 512-863-9601. *E-mail:* admission@southwestern.edu. *Web site:* http://www.southwestern.edu/.

Stephen F. Austin State University

Nacogdoches, Texas

- **State-supported** comprehensive, founded 1923
- **Small-town** 412-acre campus
- **Coed** 11,368 undergraduate students, 84% full-time, 63% women, 37% men
- **Moderately difficult** entrance level, 63% of applicants were admitted

Undergraduates 9,593 full-time, 1,775 part-time. Students come from 42 states and territories; 36 other countries; 2% are from out of state; 25% Black or African American, non-Hispanic/Latino; 11% Hispanic/Latino; 1% Asian, non-Hispanic/Latino; 0.7% American Indian or Alaska Native, non-Hispanic/Latino; 0.7% Two or more races, non-Hispanic/Latino; 4% Race/ethnicity unknown; 0.8% international; 8% transferred in; 43% live on campus. *Retention:* 65% of full-time freshmen returned.

Freshmen *Admission:* 10,975 applied, 6,883 admitted, 2,615 enrolled. *Test scores:* SAT critical reading scores over 500: 37%; SAT math scores over 500: 44%; SAT writing scores over 500: 32%; ACT scores over 18: 78%; SAT critical reading scores over 600: 8%; SAT math scores over 600: 8%; SAT writing scores over 600: 5%; ACT scores over 24: 20%; SAT critical reading scores over 700: 1%; SAT math scores over 700: 1%; ACT scores over 30: 1%.

Faculty *Total:* 674, 68% full-time, 63% with terminal degrees. *Student/faculty ratio:* 22:1.

Academics *Calendar:* semesters. *Degrees:* bachelor's, master's, doctoral, and first professional. *Special study options:* academic remediation for entering students, accelerated degree program, adult/continuing education programs, advanced placement credit, distance learning, double majors, freshman honors college, honors programs, independent study, internships, off-campus study, part-time degree program, services for LD students, student-designed majors, study abroad, summer session for credit. *ROTC:* Army (b). *Unusual degree programs:* 3-2 professional accountancy.

Computers on Campus 1,000 computers/terminals are available on campus for general student use. Students can access the following: campus intranet, computer help desk, free student e-mail accounts, online (class) grades, online (class) registration, online (class) schedules. Campuswide network is available. 100% of college-owned or -operated housing units are wired for high-speed Internet access. Wireless service is available via classrooms, computer centers, computer labs, dorm rooms, libraries, student centers.

Student Life *Housing:* on-campus residence required through sophomore year. *Options:* coed, men-only, women-only, disabled students. Campus housing is university owned. Freshman campus housing is guaranteed. *Activities and organizations:* drama/theater group, student-run newspaper, radio and television station, choral group, marching band, Baptist Student Ministry, National Society of Collegiate Scholars, Residence Hall Association, Crosspoint (Christian fellowship), Biology Club, national fraternities, national sororities. *Campus security:* 24-hour emergency response devices and patrols, student patrols, late-night transport/escort service, controlled dormitory access. *Student services:* health clinic, personal/psychological counseling, legal services.

Athletics Member NCAA. All Division I except football (Division I-AA). *Intercollegiate sports:* baseball M(s), basketball M(s)/W(s), bowling W(s), cross-country running M(s)/W(s), equestrian sports W, golf M(s)/W(s), soccer W(s), softball W(s), tennis W(s), track and field M(s)/W(s), volleyball W(s). *Intramural sports:* badminton M/W, baseball M(c), basketball M/W, football M/W, golf M/W, lacrosse M(c)/W(c), racquetball M(c)/W(c), rock climbing M/W, soccer M/W, softball M/W, table tennis M/W, tennis M/W, ultimate Frisbee M/W, volleyball M/W.

Standardized Tests *Required:* SAT or ACT (for admission).

Costs (2011–12) *Tuition:* state resident $5232 full-time, $174 per credit hour part-time; nonresident $14,622 full-time, $487 per credit hour part-time. Full-time tuition and fees vary according to course load, degree level, and location. Part-time tuition and fees vary according to course load, degree level, and location. *Required fees:* $2112 full-time, $154 per credit hour part-time. *Room and board:* $8186. Room and board charges vary according to board plan and housing facility. *Payment plan:* installment. *Waivers:* senior citizens and employees or children of employees.

Financial Aid Of all full-time matriculated undergraduates who enrolled in 2010, 7,851 applied for aid, 6,677 were judged to have need, 231 had their need fully met. In 2010, 709 non-need-based awards were made. *Average percent of need met:* 48%. *Average financial aid package:* $9633. *Average need-based loan:* $4089. *Average need-based gift aid:* $5905. *Average non-need-based aid:* $3680. *Average indebtedness upon graduation:* $21,302.

Applying *Options:* electronic application. *Application fee:* $35. *Required:* high school transcript. *Application deadlines:* rolling (freshmen), rolling (out-of-state freshmen), rolling (transfers). *Notification:* continuous (freshmen), continuous (out-of-state freshmen), continuous (transfers).

Freshman Application Contact Ms. Kimberly Lower, Associate Director of Admissions, Stephen F. Austin State University, PO Box 13051, SFA Station, Nacogdoches, TX 75962. *Phone:* 936-468-2504. *Toll-free phone:* 800-731-2902. *Fax:* 936-468-3849. *E-mail:* admissions@sfasu.edu. *Web site:* http://www.sfasu.edu/.

Strayer University - Cedar Hill Campus

Cedar Hill, Texas

- **Proprietary** comprehensive
- **Coed**

Academics *Degrees:* certificates, diplomas, associate, bachelor's, master's, and postbachelor's certificates.

Freshman Application Contact Strayer University - Cedar Hill Campus, 610 Uptown Boulevard, Suite 3500, Cedar Hill, TX 75104. *Web site:* http://www.strayer.edu/cedarhill.

Strayer University - Irving Campus

Irving, Texas

- **Proprietary** comprehensive
- **Coed**

Academics *Degrees:* certificates, diplomas, associate, bachelor's, master's, and postbachelor's certificates.

Freshman Application Contact Strayer University - Irving Campus, 7701 Las Colinas Ridge, Suite 450, Irving, TX 75063. *Web site:* http://www.strayer.edu/irving.

Strayer University - Katy Campus

Houston, Texas

- **Proprietary** comprehensive
- **Coed**

Academics *Degrees:* certificates, diplomas, associate, bachelor's, master's, and postbachelor's certificates.

Freshman Application Contact Strayer University - Katy Campus, 14511 Old Katy Road, Suite 200, Houston, TX 77079. *Web site:* http://www.strayer.edu/katy.

Strayer University - North Austin Campus

Austin, Texas

- **Proprietary** comprehensive
- **Coed**

Academics *Degrees:* certificates, diplomas, associate, bachelor's, master's, and postbachelor's certificates.

Freshman Application Contact Strayer University - North Austin Campus, 8501 North Mopac Expressway, Suite 100, Austin, TX 78759. *Web site:* http://www.strayer.edu/north_austin.

Strayer University - Northwest Houston Campus

Houston, Texas

- **Proprietary** comprehensive
- **Coed**

Academics *Degrees:* certificates, diplomas, associate, bachelor's, master's, and postbachelor's certificates.

Freshman Application Contact Strayer University - Northwest Houston Campus, 10940 W. Sam Houston Parkway N., Suite 200, Houston, TX 77064. *Web site:* http://www.strayer.edu/northwest_houston.

Strayer University - Plano Campus

Plano, Texas

- **Proprietary** comprehensive
- **Coed**

Academics *Degrees:* certificates, diplomas, associate, bachelor's, master's, and postbachelor's certificates.

Freshman Application Contact Strayer University - Plano Campus, 2701 North Dallas Parkway, Suite 300, Plano, TX 75093. *Web site:* http://www.strayer.edu/plano.

Sul Ross State University

Alpine, Texas

- **State-supported** comprehensive, founded 1920, part of Texas State University System
- **Small-town** 640-acre campus
- **Coed** 2,171 undergraduate students, 68% full-time, 56% women, 44% men
- **Noncompetitive** entrance level, 97% of applicants were admitted

Undergraduates 1,485 full-time, 686 part-time. 2% are from out of state; 6% Black or African American, non-Hispanic/Latino; 63% Hispanic/Latino; 0.3% Asian, non-Hispanic/Latino; 0.1% Native Hawaiian or other Pacific Islander, non-Hispanic/Latino; 0.4% American Indian or Alaska Native, non-Hispanic/Latino; 2% Two or more races, non-Hispanic/Latino; 2% Race/ethnicity unknown; 0.4% international; 15% transferred in; 31% live on campus.

Freshmen *Admission:* 1,106 applied, 1,077 admitted, 347 enrolled. *Average high school GPA:* 3.05. *Test scores:* SAT critical reading scores over 500: 12%; SAT math scores over 500: 21%; SAT writing scores over 500: 10%; ACT scores over 18: 52%; SAT critical reading scores over 600: 3%; SAT math scores over 600: 2%; ACT scores over 24: 8%; ACT scores over 30: 1%.

Faculty *Total:* 175, 69% full-time. *Student/faculty ratio:* 14:1.

Academics *Calendar:* semesters. *Degrees:* certificates, diplomas, associate, bachelor's, master's, and postbachelor's certificates. *Special study options:* part-time degree program.

Computers on Campus Students can access the following: campus intranet, computer help desk, free student e-mail accounts, online (class) grades. Campuswide network is available.

Student Life *Housing:* on-campus residence required through sophomore year. *Options:* coed. Campus housing is university owned. Freshman campus housing is guaranteed. *Campus security:* 24-hour patrols, late-night transport/escort service.

Athletics Member NCAA. All Division III. *Intercollegiate sports:* baseball M, basketball M/W, cheerleading M/W, cross-country running W, football M, softball W, tennis M/W, track and field M/W, volleyball W. *Intramural sports:* basketball M/W, cheerleading M/W, equestrian sports M/W, football M/W, racquetball M/W, soccer M/W, softball M, tennis M/W, ultimate Frisbee M/W, volleyball M/W, water polo M/W, weight lifting M/W.

Standardized Tests *Required:* SAT or ACT (for admission).

Costs (2011–12) *Tuition:* state resident $4320 full-time, $144 per credit hour part-time; nonresident $13,710 full-time, $457 per credit hour part-time. *Required fees:* $1740 full-time, $59 per credit hour part-time, $102 per term part-time. *Room and board:* $6810. Room and board charges vary according to board plan and housing facility.

Financial Aid Of all full-time matriculated undergraduates who enrolled in 2009, 1,176 applied for aid, 1,114 were judged to have need, 851 had their need fully met. In 2009, 37 non-need-based awards were made. *Average percent of need met:* 76%. *Average financial aid package:* $10,348. *Average need-based loan:* $2646. *Average need-based gift aid:* $6213. *Average non-need-based aid:* $48,166. *Financial aid deadline:* 4/1.

Applying *Options:* early decision, deferred entrance. *Application fee:* $25. *Required:* high school transcript. *Recommended:* interview. *Application deadlines:* rolling (freshmen), rolling (transfers). *Notification:* continuous (freshmen), continuous (transfers).

Freshman Application Contact Sul Ross State University, PO Box C - 114, Alpine, TX 79832. *Phone:* 432-837-8050. *Toll-free phone:* 888-722-7778. *Web site:* http://www.sulross.edu/.

Tarleton State University
Stephenville, Texas

- **State-supported** comprehensive, founded 1899, part of Texas A&M University System
- **Small-town** 175-acre campus with easy access to Fort Worth
- **Endowment** $25.2 million
- **Coed** 8,476 undergraduate students, 78% full-time, 59% women, 41% men
- **Moderately difficult** entrance level, 86% of applicants were admitted

Undergraduates 6,612 full-time, 1,864 part-time. Students come from 41 states and territories; 14 other countries; 2% are from out of state; 6% Black or African American, non-Hispanic/Latino; 12% Hispanic/Latino; 0.8% Asian, non-Hispanic/Latino; 0.2% Native Hawaiian or other Pacific Islander, non-Hispanic/Latino; 0.7% American Indian or Alaska Native, non-Hispanic/Latino; 2% Two or more races, non-Hispanic/Latino; 0.5% Race/ethnicity unknown; 0.3% international; 16% transferred in; 30% live on campus. *Retention:* 66% of full-time freshmen returned.
Freshmen *Admission:* 3,917 applied, 3,354 admitted, 1,577 enrolled. *Test scores:* SAT critical reading scores over 500: 39%; SAT math scores over 500: 51%; SAT writing scores over 500: 32%; ACT scores over 18: 83%; SAT critical reading scores over 600: 9%; SAT math scores over 600: 9%; SAT writing scores over 600: 4%; ACT scores over 24: 20%; SAT critical reading scores over 700: 1%; ACT scores over 30: 1%.
Academics *Calendar:* semesters. *Degrees:* associate, bachelor's, master's, doctoral, and first professional. *Special study options:* academic remediation for entering students, accelerated degree program, adult/continuing education programs, advanced placement credit, cooperative education, distance learning, double majors, honors programs, independent study, internships, off-campus study, part-time degree program, services for LD students, study abroad, summer session for credit. *ROTC:* Army (b).
Computers on Campus 1,000 computers/terminals are available on campus for general student use. Students can access the following: campus intranet, computer help desk, free student e-mail accounts, online (class) grades, online (class) registration, online (class) schedules. Campuswide network is available. 100% of college-owned or -operated housing units are wired for high-speed Internet access. Wireless service is available via classrooms, computer centers, computer labs, learning centers, libraries, student centers.
Student Life *Housing:* on-campus residence required through sophomore year. *Options:* coed, men-only, women-only. Campus housing is university owned and leased by the school. Freshman campus housing is guaranteed. *Activities and organizations:* drama/theater group, student-run newspaper, radio station, choral group, marching band, Student Government Association, Student Programming Association, Kappa Delta Rho, Delta Zeta, Chi Alpha, national fraternities, national sororities. *Campus security:* 24-hour emergency response devices and patrols, student patrols, late-night transport/escort service, controlled dormitory access. *Student services:* health clinic, personal/psychological counseling, legal services.
Athletics Member NCAA. All Division II. *Intercollegiate sports:* baseball M(s), basketball M(s)/W(s), cheerleading M(s)/W(s), cross-country running M(s)/W(s), football M(s), golf W(s), softball W(s), tennis W(s), track and field M(s)/W(s), volleyball W(s). *Intramural sports:* archery M/W, basketball M/W, football M/W, golf M/W, racquetball M/W, soccer M/W, softball M/W, table tennis M/W, tennis M/W, volleyball M/W.
Standardized Tests *Required:* SAT or ACT (for admission).
Costs (2011–12) *Tuition:* state resident $4319 full-time, $144 per credit hour part-time; nonresident $13,709 full-time, $457 per credit hour part-time. Full-time tuition and fees vary according to course load and degree level. Part-time tuition and fees vary according to course load and degree level. *Required fees:* $2090 full-time. *Room and board:* $7474; room only: $3972. Room and board charges vary according to board plan and housing facility. *Payment plan:* installment.
Financial Aid Of all full-time matriculated undergraduates who enrolled in 2010, 11,951 applied for aid, 11,768 were judged to have need, 2,888 had their need fully met. In 2010, 1892 non-need-based awards were made. *Average percent of need met:* 42%. *Average financial aid package:* $6321. *Average need-based loan:* $2433. *Average need-based gift aid:* $2836. *Average non-need-based aid:* $3918. *Average indebtedness upon graduation:* $15,889. *Financial aid deadline:* 11/1.
Applying *Options:* electronic application, early action. *Application fee:* $30. *Required:* high school transcript. *Application deadlines:* 8/1 (freshmen), 7/1 (transfers), 11/30 (early action).
Freshman Application Contact Ms. Cindy Hess, Director of Undergraduate Admissions, Tarleton State University, Box T-0030, Tarleton Station,

Stephenville, TX 76402. *Phone:* 254-968-9123. *Toll-free phone:* 800-687-8236. *Fax:* 254-968-9951. *E-mail:* uadm@tarleton.edu. *Web site:* http://www.tarleton.edu/.

Texas A&M Health Science Center
College Station, Texas

Application Contact Dr. Jack L. Long, Associate Dean for Student Services, Texas A&M Health Science Center, PO Box 660677, 3302 Gaston Avenue, Dallas, TX 75266-0677. *Phone:* 214-828-8232. *Fax:* 214-874-4567. *Web site:* http://www.tamhsc.edu/.

Texas A&M International University
Laredo, Texas

- **State-supported** comprehensive, founded 1969, part of Texas A&M University System
- **Urban** 300-acre campus
- **Endowment** $32.4 million
- **Coed** 6,099 undergraduate students, 63% full-time, 59% women, 41% men
- **Moderately difficult** entrance level, 50% of applicants were admitted

Undergraduates 3,822 full-time, 2,277 part-time. Students come from 24 states and territories; 17 other countries; 0.4% are from out of state; 0.7% Black or African American, non-Hispanic/Latino; 94% Hispanic/Latino; 0.7% Asian, non-Hispanic/Latino; 0.1% American Indian or Alaska Native, non-Hispanic/Latino; 0.1% Two or more races, non-Hispanic/Latino; 0.6% Race/ethnicity unknown; 2% international; 8% transferred in; 13% live on campus. *Retention:* 69% of full-time freshmen returned.
Freshmen *Admission:* 4,389 applied, 2,184 admitted, 693 enrolled. *Average high school GPA:* 3.7. *Test scores:* SAT critical reading scores over 500: 22%; SAT math scores over 500: 33%; SAT writing scores over 500: 20%; ACT scores over 18: 54%; SAT critical reading scores over 600: 4%; SAT math scores over 600: 5%; SAT writing scores over 600: 3%; ACT scores over 24: 5%.
Faculty *Total:* 291, 70% full-time, 54% with terminal degrees. *Student/faculty ratio:* 23:1.
Academics *Calendar:* semesters. *Degrees:* bachelor's, master's, doctoral, and first professional. *Special study options:* academic remediation for entering students, advanced placement credit, distance learning, double majors, English as a second language, honors programs, independent study, internships, part-time degree program, services for LD students, study abroad, summer session for credit. *ROTC:* Army (b).
Computers on Campus 410 computers/terminals are available on campus for general student use. Students can access the following: campus intranet, computer help desk, free student e-mail accounts, online (class) grades, online (class) registration, online (class) schedules. Campuswide network is available. 100% of college-owned or -operated housing units are wired for high-speed Internet access. Wireless service is available via classrooms, computer centers, computer labs, learning centers, libraries, student centers.
Student Life *Housing options:* coed. Campus housing is university owned and is provided by a third party. *Activities and organizations:* drama/theater group, student-run newspaper, choral group, marching band, Fellowship of Christian Athletes (FCA), National Student Speech Language Hearing Association (NSSLHA), Association of International Students (AIS), Campus Activities Board (CAB), Student Government Association (SGA), national fraternities, national sororities. *Campus security:* 24-hour emergency response devices and patrols, late-night transport/escort service, controlled dormitory access, provide training to faculty, staff, a new students on active shooter. Interoperable communications with local, county, state, federal. *Student services:* health clinic, personal/psychological counseling, women's center.
Athletics Member NCAA. All Division II. *Intercollegiate sports:* baseball M(s), basketball M(s)/W(s), cross-country running M(s)/W(s), golf M(s)/W(s), soccer M(s)/W(s), softball W(s), volleyball W(s). *Intramural sports:* badminton M/W, basketball M/W, soccer M/W, softball M/W, table tennis M/W, ultimate Frisbee M/W, volleyball M/W.
Standardized Tests *Required:* SAT or ACT (for admission).
Costs (2011–12) *Tuition:* state resident $4215 full-time, $141 per credit hour part-time; nonresident $13,605 full-time, $454 per credit hour part-time. Full-time tuition and fees vary according to course load. Part-time tuition and fees vary according to course load and reciprocity agreements. *Required fees:* $2343 full-time, $77 per credit hour part-time, $157 per term part-time. *Room and board:* $6496. Room and board charges vary according to board plan and housing facility. *Payment plan:* installment. *Waivers:* senior citizens.
Financial Aid Of all full-time matriculated undergraduates who enrolled in 2010, 3,514 applied for aid, 3,236 were judged to have need, 355 had their need fully met. 104 Federal Work-Study jobs (averaging $2361). 16 state and other part-time jobs (averaging $2361). In 2010, 157 non-need-based awards

were made. *Average percent of need met:* 67%. *Average financial aid package:* $10,749. *Average need-based loan:* $4095. *Average need-based gift aid:* $6408. *Average non-need-based aid:* $3604. *Average indebtedness upon graduation:* $19,400. *Financial aid deadline:* 8/1.

Applying *Options:* electronic application, early admission, deferred entrance. *Required:* high school transcript. *Application deadlines:* 7/1 (freshmen), 7/1 (transfers). *Notification:* 7/15 (freshmen), 7/15 (transfers).

Freshman Application Contact Ms. Rosa Dickinson, Director of Admissions, Texas A&M International University, 5201 University Boulevard, Laredo, TX 78041-1900. *Phone:* 956-326-2200. *Toll-free phone:* 888-489-2648. *E-mail:* adms@tamiu.edu. *Web site:* http://www.tamiu.edu/.

Texas A&M University

College Station, Texas

- **State-supported** university, founded 1876, part of Texas A&M University System
- **Suburban** 5200-acre campus with easy access to Houston
- **Endowment** $7.0 billion
- **Coed** 39,867 undergraduate students, 92% full-time, 48% women, 52% men
- **Moderately difficult** entrance level, 64% of applicants were admitted

Undergraduates 36,507 full-time, 3,360 part-time. Students come from 52 states and territories; 128 other countries; 3% are from out of state; 3% Black or African American, non-Hispanic/Latino; 17% Hispanic/Latino; 0.1% Native Hawaiian or other Pacific Islander, non-Hispanic/Latino; 0.2% Two or more races, non-Hispanic/Latino; 0.2% Race/ethnicity unknown; 2% international; 4% transferred in; 25% live on campus. *Retention:* 92% of full-time freshmen returned.

Freshmen *Admission:* 25,949 applied, 16,489 admitted, 8,254 enrolled. *Test scores:* SAT critical reading scores over 500: 85%; SAT math scores over 500: 94%; SAT writing scores over 500: 80%; ACT scores over 18: 99%; SAT critical reading scores over 600: 48%; SAT math scores over 600: 66%; SAT writing scores over 600: 37%; ACT scores over 24: 81%; SAT critical reading scores over 700: 10%; SAT math scores over 700: 17%; SAT writing scores over 700: 6%; ACT scores over 30: 27%.

Faculty *Total:* 2,501, 84% full-time, 90% with terminal degrees. *Student/faculty ratio:* 21:1.

Academics *Calendar:* semesters. *Degrees:* bachelor's, master's, doctoral, postbachelor's, and first professional certificates. *Special study options:* academic remediation for entering students, accelerated degree program, advanced placement credit, cooperative education, distance learning, double majors, English as a second language, honors programs, independent study, internships, off-campus study, part-time degree program, services for LD students, study abroad, summer session for credit. *ROTC:* Army (b), Navy (b), Air Force (b).

Computers on Campus 1,840 computers/terminals and 5,000 ports are available on campus for general student use. Students can access the following: campus intranet, computer help desk, free student e-mail accounts, online (class) grades, online (class) registration, online (class) schedules. Campus-wide network is available. 100% of college-owned or -operated housing units are wired for high-speed Internet access. Wireless service is available via classrooms, computer labs, learning centers, libraries, student centers.

Student Life *Housing options:* coed, men-only, women-only, disabled students. Campus housing is university owned. *Activities and organizations:* drama/theater group, student-run newspaper, radio and television station, choral group, marching band, Memorial Student Center, Corps of Cadets, Fish Camp, student government, national fraternities, national sororities. *Campus security:* 24-hour emergency response devices and patrols, late-night transport/escort service, controlled dormitory access, student escorts. *Student services:* health clinic, personal/psychological counseling, women's center, legal services.

Athletics Member NCAA. All Division I except football (Division I-A). *Intercollegiate sports:* archery W(s), baseball M(s), basketball M(s)/W(s), cross-country running M(s)/W(s), equestrian sports W(s), golf M(s)/W(s), soccer W(s), softball W(s), swimming and diving M(s)/W(s), tennis M(s)/W(s), track and field M(s)/W(s), volleyball W(s). *Intramural sports:* archery M/W, badminton M/W, basketball M/W, bowling M/W, cross-country running M/W, fencing M(c)/W(c), field hockey M(c)/W(c), football M/W, golf M/W, gymnastics M(c)/W(c), lacrosse M(c)/W(c), racquetball M(c)/W(c), riflery M/W, rugby M(c)/W(c), sailing M(c)/W(c), soccer M/W, softball M/W, squash M/W, swimming and diving M/W, table tennis M/W, tennis M/W, track and field M/W, ultimate Frisbee M(c)/W(c), volleyball M/W, water polo M/W, weight lifting M(c)/W(c), wrestling M(c).

Standardized Tests *Required:* SAT or ACT (for admission).

Costs (2011–12) *Tuition:* state resident $5297 full-time, $177 per credit hour part-time; nonresident $20,687 full-time, $690 per credit hour part-time. Full-time tuition and fees vary according to program. Part-time tuition and fees vary

according to program. *Required fees:* $3124 full-time. *Room and board:* $8200. Room and board charges vary according to board plan, housing facility, and location. *Payment plan:* installment.

Financial Aid Of all full-time matriculated undergraduates who enrolled in 2011, 21,674 applied for aid, 15,310 were judged to have need, 5,938 had their need fully met. 791 Federal Work-Study jobs (averaging $2828). 137 state and other part-time jobs (averaging $2139). In 2011, 2094 non-need-based awards were made. *Average percent of need met:* 70%. *Average financial aid package:* $14,695. *Average need-based loan:* $6659. *Average need-based gift aid:* $8632. *Average non-need-based aid:* $3528. *Average indebtedness upon graduation:* $22,716.

Applying *Options:* electronic application. *Application fee:* $60. *Required:* essay or personal statement, high school transcript. *Application deadlines:* 1/15 (freshmen), 3/15 (transfers). *Notification:* continuous (freshmen), continuous (transfers).

Freshman Application Contact Mr. Scott McDonald, Director of Admissions, Texas A&M University, 217 John J. Koldus Building, College Station, TX 77843-1265. *Phone:* 979-845-3741. *Fax:* 979-845-8737. *E-mail:* admissions@tamu.edu. *Web site:* http://www.tamu.edu/.

Texas A&M University at Galveston

Galveston, Texas

Freshman Application Contact Ms. Sarah Trombley, Associate Director of Admissions and Records, Texas A&M University at Galveston, PO Box 1675, Galveston, TX 77553-1675. *Phone:* 409-740-4448. *Fax:* 409-740-4731. *E-mail:* seaaggie@tamug.edu. *Web site:* http://www.tamug.edu/.

Texas A&M University–Commerce

Commerce, Texas

Freshman Application Contact Hope Young, Director of Admissions, Texas A&M University–Commerce, PO Box 3011, Commerce, TX 75429. *Phone:* 903-886-5103. *Toll-free phone:* 888-868-2682. *Fax:* 903-886-5888. *E-mail:* admissions@tamu-commerce.edu. *Web site:* http://www.tamu-commerce.edu/.

Texas A&M University–Corpus Christi

Corpus Christi, Texas

- **State-supported** university, founded 1947, part of Texas A&M University System
- **Suburban** 240-acre campus
- **Endowment** $4.5 million
- **Coed** 8,275 undergraduate students, 79% full-time, 60% women, 40% men
- **Moderately difficult** entrance level, 85% of applicants were admitted

Undergraduates 6,512 full-time, 1,763 part-time. Students come from 45 states and territories; 42 other countries; 3% are from out of state; 5% Black or African American, non-Hispanic/Latino; 43% Hispanic/Latino; 5% Asian, non-Hispanic/Latino; 0.6% American Indian or Alaska Native, non-Hispanic/Latino; 0.7% Two or more races, non-Hispanic/Latino; 0.9% Race/ethnicity unknown; 4% international; 10% transferred in; 16% live on campus. *Retention:* 60% of full-time freshmen returned.

Freshmen *Admission:* 5,732 applied, 4,879 admitted, 1,422 enrolled. *Average high school GPA:* 3.3. *Test scores:* SAT critical reading scores over 500: 36%; SAT math scores over 500: 46%; SAT writing scores over 500: 28%; ACT scores over 18: 73%; SAT critical reading scores over 600: 7%; SAT math scores over 600: 9%; SAT writing scores over 600: 4%; ACT scores over 24: 19%; SAT critical reading scores over 700: 1%; SAT math scores over 700: 1%; ACT scores over 30: 1%.

Faculty *Total:* 547, 58% full-time, 78% with terminal degrees. *Student/faculty ratio:* 21:1.

Academics *Calendar:* semesters. *Degrees:* bachelor's, master's, doctoral, and first professional. *Special study options:* academic remediation for entering students, advanced placement credit, cooperative education, distance learning, double majors, English as a second language, honors programs, independent study, internships, off-campus study, part-time degree program, services for LD students, study abroad, summer session for credit. *ROTC:* Army (b). *Unusual degree programs:* engineering; nursing; accounting.

Computers on Campus 500 computers/terminals are available on campus for general student use. Students can access the following: campus intranet, computer help desk, free student e-mail accounts, online (class) grades, online (class) registration, online (class) schedules. Campuswide network is available. 100% of college-owned or -operated housing units are wired for high-speed Internet access. Wireless service is available via entire campus.

Student Life *Housing options:* coed, men-only, women-only. Campus housing is provided by a third party. *Activities and organizations:* drama/theater group,

student-run newspaper, choral group, marching band, Student Accounting Society, Student Art Association, Islander Cultural Alliance, Graduate Student Association, Student Nurses Association, national fraternities, national sororities. *Campus security:* 24-hour emergency response devices and patrols, late-night transport/escort service, controlled dormitory access. *Student services:* health clinic, personal/psychological counseling, women's center.

Athletics Member NCAA. All Division I. *Intercollegiate sports:* baseball M(s), basketball M(s)/W(s), cross-country running M(s)/W(s), golf W(s), softball W(s), tennis M(s)/W(s), track and field M/W, volleyball W(s). *Intramural sports:* baseball M, basketball M/W, cross-country running M/W, golf W, racquetball M/W, softball W, tennis M/W, track and field M/W, volleyball W.

Standardized Tests *Required:* SAT or ACT (for admission).

Costs (2011–12) *Tuition:* state resident $4494 full-time, $157 per credit part-time; nonresident $13,884 full-time, $470 per credit part-time. Full-time tuition and fees vary according to course level, course load, and degree level. Part-time tuition and fees vary according to course level, course load, and degree level. *Required fees:* $2474 full-time, $86 per credit hour part-time, $142 per term part-time. *Room and board:* $9528; room only: $6677. Room and board charges vary according to housing facility and location. *Payment plan:* installment. *Waivers:* senior citizens and employees or children of employees.

Financial Aid Of all full-time matriculated undergraduates who enrolled in 2010, 3,401 applied for aid, 2,812 were judged to have need, 308 had their need fully met. 132 Federal Work-Study jobs (averaging $3599). 124 state and other part-time jobs (averaging $3384). In 2010, 472 non-need-based awards were made. *Average percent of need met:* 65%. *Average financial aid package:* $9559. *Average need-based loan:* $4183. *Average need-based gift aid:* $6498. *Average non-need-based aid:* $1984. *Average indebtedness upon graduation:* $18,314.

Applying *Options:* electronic application. *Application fee:* $25. *Required:* high school transcript, minimum 2.0 GPA. *Application deadlines:* 7/1 (freshmen), 7/1 (out-of-state freshmen), 7/1 (transfers). *Notification:* continuous (freshmen), continuous (out-of-state freshmen), continuous (transfers).

Freshman Application Contact Mrs. Monica Martinez, Assistant Director of Admissions, Texas A&M University–Corpus Christi, SSC 107, 6300 Ocean Drive, Unit 5774, Corpus Christi, TX 78412-5774. *Phone:* 361-825-2624. *Toll-free phone:* 800-482-6822. *Fax:* 361-825-5887. *E-mail:* monica.martinez@tamucc.edu. *Web site:* http://www.tamucc.edu/.

Texas A&M University–Kingsville
Kingsville, Texas

- **State-supported** university, founded 1925, part of Texas A&M University System
- **Small-town** 255-acre campus
- **Endowment** $15.0 million
- **Coed** 5,637 undergraduate students, 82% full-time, 49% women, 51% men
- **Moderately difficult** entrance level, 96% of applicants were admitted

Undergraduates 4,620 full-time, 1,017 part-time. Students come from 32 states and territories; 63 other countries; 2% are from out of state; 6% Black or African American, non-Hispanic/Latino; 69% Hispanic/Latino; 0.4% Asian, non-Hispanic/Latino; 0.1% Native Hawaiian or other Pacific Islander, non-Hispanic/Latino; 0.3% American Indian or Alaska Native, non-Hispanic/Latino; 2% Two or more races, non-Hispanic/Latino; 1% Race/ethnicity unknown; 1% international; 9% transferred in.

Freshmen *Admission:* 4,127 applied, 3,947 admitted, 1,261 enrolled. *Average high school GPA:* 3.27. *Test scores:* SAT math scores over 500: 31%; SAT writing scores over 500: 15%; ACT scores over 18: 51%; SAT math scores over 600: 7%; SAT writing scores over 600: 2%; ACT scores over 24: 6%; SAT math scores over 700: 1%; ACT scores over 30: 1%.

Faculty *Total:* 389, 61% full-time. *Student/faculty ratio:* 19:1.

Academics *Calendar:* semesters. *Degrees:* bachelor's, master's, doctoral, postbachelor's, and first professional certificates. *Special study options:* academic remediation for entering students, advanced placement credit, cooperative education, distance learning, double majors, English as a second language, honors programs, internships, off-campus study, part-time degree program, services for LD students, study abroad, summer session for credit. *ROTC:* Army (b). *Unusual degree programs:* 3-2 business administration.

Computers on Campus Students can access the following: campus intranet, computer help desk, free student e-mail accounts, online (class) grades, online (class) registration, online (class) schedules, Blackboard. Campuswide network is available. Wireless service is available via classrooms, computer centers, computer labs, dorm rooms, learning centers, libraries.

Student Life *Housing:* on-campus residence required for freshman year. *Options:* coed, men-only, women-only. Campus housing is university owned. Freshman campus housing is guaranteed. *Activities and organizations:* drama/theater group, student-run newspaper, radio and television station, choral

group, marching band, national fraternities, national sororities. *Campus security:* 24-hour emergency response devices and patrols, late-night transport/escort service, controlled dormitory access. *Student services:* health clinic, personal/psychological counseling, women's center.

Athletics Member NCAA. All Division II. *Intercollegiate sports:* baseball M(s), basketball M(s)/W(s), cross-country running M(s)/W(s), equestrian sports M/W, football M(s), golf W(s), softball W(s), track and field M(s)/W(s), volleyball W(s). *Intramural sports:* badminton M/W, basketball M/W, bowling M/W, football M/W, racquetball M/W, soccer M/W, softball M/W, volleyball M/W, weight lifting M/W.

Standardized Tests *Required:* SAT or ACT (for admission).

Costs (2011–12) *Tuition:* state resident $6640 full-time; nonresident $16,030 full-time. Full-time tuition and fees vary according to course load and degree level. Part-time tuition and fees vary according to course load and degree level. *Room and board:* $6138; room only: $3180. Room and board charges vary according to board plan and housing facility. *Payment plans:* tuition prepayment, installment, deferred payment. *Waivers:* senior citizens and employees or children of employees.

Financial Aid Of all full-time matriculated undergraduates who enrolled in 2005, 4,449 applied for aid, 4,214 were judged to have need, 2,899 had their need fully met. *Average financial aid package:* $6500. *Average need-based loan:* $3875. *Average need-based gift aid:* $6500. *Average indebtedness upon graduation:* $2867.

Applying *Options:* electronic application, early admission, deferred entrance. *Application fee:* $15. *Required:* high school transcript. *Required for some:* interview. *Recommended:* minimum 2.0 GPA. *Application deadlines:* rolling (freshmen), rolling (transfers). *Notification:* continuous (freshmen), continuous (transfers).

Freshman Application Contact Laura Knippers, Associate Director of Admissions and Enrollment Management, Texas A&M University–Kingsville, MSC 116, 700 University Boulevard, Kingsville, TX 78363. *Phone:* 361-593-3907. *Toll-free phone:* 800-687-6000. *Fax:* 361-593-2991. *E-mail:* laura.knippers@tamuk.edu. *Web site:* http://www.tamuk.edu/.

Texas A&M University–San Antonio
San Antonio, Texas

Freshman Application Contact Jennifer Zamarripa, Director of Admissions and Registrar, Texas A&M University–San Antonio, 1450 Gillette Boulevard, San Antonio, TX 78224. *Phone:* 210-932-6201. *E-mail:* jennifer.zamarripa@tamusa.tamus.edu. *Web site:* http://www.tamuk.edu/sanantonio/.

Texas A&M University–Texarkana
Texarkana, Texas

Application Contact Mrs. Patricia Black, Director of Admissions and Registrar, Texas A&M University–Texarkana, PO Box 5518, Texarkana, TX 75505-5518. *Phone:* 903-223-3068. *Fax:* 903-223-3140. *E-mail:* admissions@tamut.edu. *Web site:* http://www.tamut.edu/.

Texas Christian University
Fort Worth, Texas

- **Independent** university, founded 1873, affiliated with Christian Church (Disciples of Christ)
- **Suburban** 275-acre campus with easy access to Dallas-Fort Worth
- **Endowment** $1.2 million
- **Coed** 8,229 undergraduate students, 96% full-time, 59% women, 41% men
- **Very difficult** entrance level, 38% of applicants were admitted

Undergraduates 7,878 full-time, 351 part-time. Students come from 51 states and territories; 73 other countries; 29% are from out of state; 5% Black or African American, non-Hispanic/Latino; 10% Hispanic/Latino; 3% Asian, non-Hispanic/Latino; 0.2% Native Hawaiian or other Pacific Islander, non-Hispanic/Latino; 0.9% American Indian or Alaska Native, non-Hispanic/Latino; 0.7% Two or more races, non-Hispanic/Latino; 1% Race/ethnicity unknown; 5% international; 6% transferred in; 49% live on campus. *Retention:* 87% of full-time freshmen returned.

Freshmen *Admission:* 19,168 applied, 7,217 admitted, 1,871 enrolled.

Faculty *Total:* 845, 64% full-time, 65% with terminal degrees. *Student/faculty ratio:* 14:1.

Academics *Calendar:* semesters. *Degrees:* certificates, diplomas, bachelor's, master's, doctoral, post-master's, postbachelor's, and first professional certificates. *Special study options:* accelerated degree program, advanced placement credit, distance learning, double majors, English as a second language, freshman honors college, honors programs, independent study, internships, part-

time degree program, services for LD students, study abroad, summer session for credit. *ROTC:* Army (b), Air Force (b).

Computers on Campus 1,400 computers/terminals and 10,000 ports are available on campus for general student use. Students can access the following: campus intranet, computer help desk, free student e-mail accounts, online (class) grades, online (class) registration, online (class) schedules. Campuswide network is available. 100% of college-owned or -operated housing units are wired for high-speed Internet access. Wireless service is available via entire campus.

Student Life *Housing:* on-campus residence required through sophomore year. *Options:* coed, men-only, women-only, disabled students. Campus housing is university owned. Freshman campus housing is guaranteed. *Activities and organizations:* drama/theater group, student-run newspaper, radio and television station, choral group, marching band, national fraternities, national sororities. *Campus security:* 24-hour emergency response devices and patrols, late-night transport/escort service, controlled dormitory access, emergency call boxes, video surveillance in parking lots, self-defense education, lighted sidewalks, emergency notification system. *Student services:* health clinic, personal/psychological counseling, women's center, legal services.

Athletics Member NCAA. All Division I. *Intercollegiate sports:* baseball M(s), basketball M(s)/W(s), cross-country running M(s)/W(s), equestrian sports W(s), football M(s), golf M(s)/W(s), riflery W(s), soccer W(s), swimming and diving M(s)/W(s), tennis M(s)/W(s), track and field M(s)/W(s), volleyball W(s). *Intramural sports:* baseball M(c), basketball M/W, bowling M/W, golf M/W, gymnastics M(c)/W(c), lacrosse M(c)/W(c), racquetball M/W, rugby M(c)/W(c), soccer M(c)/W(c), table tennis M/W, tennis M(c)/W(c), ultimate Frisbee M(c)/W(c), volleyball W(c).

Standardized Tests *Required:* SAT or ACT (for admission).

Costs (2012–13) *Tuition:* $34,500 full-time. Part-time tuition and fees vary according to course load. *Room only:* Room and board charges vary according to board plan and housing facility. *Payment plan:* installment. *Waivers:* employees or children of employees.

Financial Aid Of all full-time matriculated undergraduates who enrolled in 2011, 4,194 applied for aid, 3,475 were judged to have need, 883 had their need fully met. 1,460 Federal Work-Study jobs (averaging $1738). 21 state and other part-time jobs (averaging $1921). In 2011, 1812 non-need-based awards were made. *Average percent of need met:* 61%. *Average financial aid package:* $20,115. *Average need-based loan:* $4641. *Average need-based gift aid:* $16,963. *Average non-need-based aid:* $10,925. *Average indebtedness upon graduation:* $35,468. *Financial aid deadline:* 5/1.

Applying *Options:* electronic application, early action, deferred entrance. *Application fee:* $40. *Required:* essay or personal statement, high school transcript, 1 letter of recommendation. *Recommended:* 2 letters of recommendation, interview. *Application deadlines:* 2/15 (freshmen), 8/1 (transfers), 11/1 (early action). *Notification:* 4/1 (freshmen), continuous (transfers), 1/1 (early action).

Freshman Application Contact TCU Office of Admission, Texas Christian University, 2800 South University Drive, Fort Worth, TX 76129-0002. *Phone:* 817-257-7490. *Toll-free phone:* 800-828-3764. *Fax:* 817-257-7268. *E-mail:* frogmail@tcu.edu. *Web site:* http://www.tcu.edu/.

Texas College
Tyler, Texas

- **Independent** 4-year, founded 1894, affiliated with Christian Methodist Episcopal Church
- **Urban** 25-acre campus
- **Endowment** $1.3 million
- **Coed** 860 undergraduate students, 98% full-time, 41% women, 59% men
- **Noncompetitive** entrance level

Undergraduates 841 full-time, 19 part-time. Students come from 26 states and territories; 1 other country; 14% are from out of state; 87% Black or African American, non-Hispanic/Latino; 9% Hispanic/Latino; 0.1% Asian, non-Hispanic/Latino; 0.1% international; 21% transferred in; 31% live on campus. *Retention:* 46% of full-time freshmen returned.

Freshmen *Admission:* 218 enrolled. *Average high school GPA:* 2.9. *Test scores:* ACT scores over 18: 31%; ACT scores over 24: 1%.

Faculty *Total:* 35, 43% with terminal degrees. *Student/faculty ratio:* 25:1.

Academics *Calendar:* semesters. *Degrees:* associate, bachelor's, and post-bachelor's certificates. *Special study options:* academic remediation for entering students, accelerated degree program, adult/continuing education programs, advanced placement credit, distance learning, double majors, honors programs, independent study, part-time degree program, services for LD students, summer session for credit.

Computers on Campus 252 computers/terminals are available on campus for general student use. Students can access the following: campus intranet, computer help desk, free student e-mail accounts, online (class) grades, online (class) schedules. Campuswide network is available. 100% of college-owned

or -operated housing units are wired for high-speed Internet access. Wireless service is available via dorm rooms, libraries, student centers.

Student Life *Housing options:* men-only, women-only. Campus housing is university owned. *Activities and organizations:* choral group, marching band, Omega Psi Phi, Delta Sigma Theta, Pre-Alumni Council, national fraternities, national sororities. *Campus security:* 24-hour emergency response devices and patrols, late-night transport/escort service. *Student services:* health clinic, personal/psychological counseling.

Athletics Member NAIA. *Intercollegiate sports:* baseball M, basketball M/W, cheerleading M/W, football M, soccer M/W, softball W, track and field M/W, volleyball W. *Intramural sports:* basketball M/W, football M/W, soccer M/W, softball W, volleyball W.

Standardized Tests *Required:* SAT or ACT (for admission).

Costs (2012–13) *Comprehensive fee:* $16,686 includes full-time tuition ($7996), mandatory fees ($1690), and room and board ($7000). *College room only:* $3600. *Payment plan:* installment. *Waivers:* employees or children of employees.

Financial Aid Of all full-time matriculated undergraduates who enrolled in 2010, 897 applied for aid, 880 were judged to have need, 35 had their need fully met. 151 Federal Work-Study jobs (averaging $1527). 21 state and other part-time jobs (averaging $1220). In 2010, 17 non-need-based awards were made. *Average percent of need met:* 61%. *Average financial aid package:* $10,095. *Average need-based loan:* $3349. *Average need-based gift aid:* $7040. *Average non-need-based aid:* $3349. *Average indebtedness upon graduation:* $26,292.

Applying *Options:* electronic application, early admission. *Application fee:* $20. *Required:* high school transcript, minimum 2.0 GPA. *Application deadlines:* rolling (freshmen), rolling (out-of-state freshmen), rolling (transfers). *Notification:* continuous (freshmen), continuous (out-of-state freshmen), continuous (transfers).

Freshman Application Contact Mr. John Roberts, Interim Dean for Enrollment Services, Texas College, 2404 North Grand Avenue, Tyler, TX 75702. *Phone:* 903-593-8311 Ext. 2297. *Toll-free phone:* 800-306-6299. *Fax:* 903-363-1854. *E-mail:* jroberts@texascollege.edu. *Web site:* http://www.texascollege.edu/.

Texas Lutheran University
Seguin, Texas

- **Independent** 4-year, founded 1891, affiliated with Evangelical Lutheran Church
- **Suburban** 196-acre campus with easy access to San Antonio, Austin
- **Endowment** $80.5 million
- **Coed** 1,415 undergraduate students, 93% full-time, 50% women, 50% men
- **Moderately difficult** entrance level, 65% of applicants were admitted

Undergraduates 1,309 full-time, 106 part-time. Students come from 23 states and territories; 6 other countries; 4% are from out of state; 10% Black or African American, non-Hispanic/Latino; 27% Hispanic/Latino; 0.7% Asian, non-Hispanic/Latino; 0.1% Native Hawaiian or other Pacific Islander, non-Hispanic/Latino; 0.5% American Indian or Alaska Native, non-Hispanic/Latino; 0.5% Two or more races, non-Hispanic/Latino; 3% Race/ethnicity unknown; 0.9% international; 5% transferred in; 60% live on campus. *Retention:* 75% of full-time freshmen returned.

Freshmen *Admission:* 1,552 applied, 1,007 admitted, 398 enrolled. *Average high school GPA:* 3.57. *Test scores:* SAT critical reading scores over 500: 50%; SAT math scores over 500: 64%; ACT scores over 18: 87%; SAT critical reading scores over 600: 12%; SAT math scores over 600: 20%; ACT scores over 24: 33%; SAT math scores over 700: 1%; ACT scores over 30: 2%.

Faculty *Total:* 126, 54% full-time, 57% with terminal degrees. *Student/faculty ratio:* 16:1.

Academics *Calendar:* semesters. *Degree:* bachelor's. *Special study options:* advanced placement credit, double majors, honors programs, independent study, internships, part-time degree program, services for LD students, study abroad, summer session for credit. *ROTC:* Army (c), Air Force (c). *Unusual degree programs:* 3-2 engineering with Texas A&M University, Texas Tech University, Texas State University.

Computers on Campus 237 computers/terminals are available on campus for general student use. Students can access the following: campus intranet, computer help desk, free student e-mail accounts, online (class) grades, online (class) registration, online (class) schedules, free printing. Campuswide network is available. 100% of college-owned or -operated housing units are wired for high-speed Internet access. Wireless service is available via classrooms, computer centers, computer labs, learning centers, libraries, student centers.

Student Life *Housing:* on-campus residence required through senior year. *Options:* coed, men-only, women-only. Campus housing is university owned. Freshman campus housing is guaranteed. *Activities and organizations:* drama/theater group, student-run newspaper, choral group, Campus Ministry, Mexi-

can American Student Association, Student Government Association, Black Student Union. *Campus security:* 24-hour emergency response devices and patrols, late-night transport/escort service, controlled dormitory access. *Student services:* health clinic, personal/psychological counseling, women's center.

Athletics Member NCAA. All Division III. *Intercollegiate sports:* baseball M, basketball M/W, cross-country running W, football M, golf M/W, soccer M/W, softball W, tennis M/W, track and field W, volleyball W. *Intramural sports:* basketball M/W, bowling M/W, football M, racquetball M/W, softball M/W, tennis M/W, volleyball M/W.

Standardized Tests *Required:* SAT or ACT (for admission).

Costs (2011–12) *Comprehensive fee:* $30,870 includes full-time tuition ($23,800), mandatory fees ($130), and room and board ($6940). Part-time tuition: $790 per semester hour. *Required fees:* $65 per term part-time. *College room only:* $3500. Room and board charges vary according to board plan and housing facility. *Payment plan:* installment. *Waivers:* children of alumni and employees or children of employees.

Financial Aid Of all full-time matriculated undergraduates who enrolled in 2011, 1,187 applied for aid, 1,059 were judged to have need, 205 had their need fully met. 613 Federal Work-Study jobs (averaging $1966). 17 state and other part-time jobs (averaging $1933). In 2011, 218 non-need-based awards were made. *Average percent of need met:* 77%. *Average financial aid package:* $20,126. *Average need-based loan:* $4769. *Average need-based gift aid:* $14,893. *Average non-need-based aid:* $10,184. *Average indebtedness upon graduation:* $35,743.

Applying *Options:* electronic application, deferred entrance. *Application fee:* $40. *Required:* essay or personal statement, high school transcript, 2 letters of recommendation. *Required for some:* minimum 2.0 GPA. *Recommended:* interview. *Application deadlines:* rolling (freshmen), rolling (transfers). *Notification:* 8/1 (freshmen), continuous until 8/1 (transfers).

Freshman Application Contact Mr. Tom Oliver, Vice President for Enrollment Services, Texas Lutheran University, 1000 West Court Street, Seguin, TX 78155-5999. *Phone:* 830-372-8053. *Toll-free phone:* 800-771-8521. *Fax:* 830-372-8096. *E-mail:* toliver@tlu.edu. *Web site:* http://www.tlu.edu/.

Texas Southern University

Houston, Texas

- **State-supported** university, founded 1947, part of Texas Higher Education Coordinating Board
- **Urban** 147-acre campus
- **Endowment** $31.0 million
- **Coed** 6,881 undergraduate students, 81% full-time, 57% women, 43% men
- **Noncompetitive** entrance level, 26% of applicants were admitted

Undergraduates 5,579 full-time, 1,302 part-time. Students come from 44 states and territories; 26 other countries; 13% are from out of state; 87% Black or African American, non-Hispanic/Latino; 5% Hispanic/Latino; 2% Asian, non-Hispanic/Latino; 0.2% American Indian or Alaska Native, non-Hispanic/Latino; 0.7% Race/ethnicity unknown; 4% international; 9% transferred in; 21% live on campus. *Retention:* 61% of full-time freshmen returned.

Freshmen *Admission:* 8,670 applied, 2,269 admitted, 1,184 enrolled. *Average high school GPA:* 2.77. *Test scores:* SAT critical reading scores over 500: 10%; SAT math scores over 500: 16%; SAT writing scores over 500: 8%; ACT scores over 18: 39%; SAT critical reading scores over 600: 2%; SAT math scores over 600: 2%; ACT scores over 24: 3%; SAT critical reading scores over 700: 1%.

Faculty *Total:* 553, 61% full-time. *Student/faculty ratio:* 20:1.

Academics *Calendar:* semesters. *Degrees:* bachelor's, master's, doctoral, and first professional. *Special study options:* academic remediation for entering students, accelerated degree program, adult/continuing education programs, cooperative education, distance learning, English as a second language, external degree program, honors programs, independent study, internships, off-campus study, part-time degree program, services for LD students, study abroad, summer session for credit. *ROTC:* Army (b), Navy (c), Air Force (c).

Computers on Campus Students can access the following: computer help desk, free student e-mail accounts, online (class) grades, online (class) registration, online (class) schedules, Blackboard Learning and Community Portal System (E-education). Campuswide network is available. Wireless service is available via entire campus.

Student Life *Housing options:* coed, men-only, women-only. Campus housing is university owned, leased by the school and is provided by a third party. Freshman campus housing is guaranteed. *Activities and organizations:* drama/theater group, student-run newspaper, radio station, choral group, marching band, Debate Team, University Program Council, Student Government Association, Band, national fraternities, national sororities. *Campus security:* 24-hour emergency response devices and patrols, student patrols, late-night trans-

port/escort service. *Student services:* health clinic, personal/psychological counseling, legal services.

Athletics Member NCAA. All Division I except football (Division I-AA). *Intercollegiate sports:* baseball M(s), basketball M(s)/W(s), bowling W(s), cross-country running M(s)/W(s), golf M(s), soccer M/W(s), softball W(s), tennis M(s)/W(s), track and field M(s)/W(s), volleyball M/W(s). *Intramural sports:* softball M/W, swimming and diving M/W, tennis M/W, volleyball M/W.

Standardized Tests *Required for some:* SAT or ACT (for admission).

Costs (2012–13) *Comprehensive fee:* $8958. Full-time tuition and fees vary according to course level, course load, degree level, and program. Part-time tuition and fees vary according to course level, course load, degree level, and program. *Room and board:* Room and board charges vary according to board plan, housing facility, and location. *Payment plans:* installment, deferred payment. *Waivers:* minority students and senior citizens.

Financial Aid Of all full-time matriculated undergraduates who enrolled in 2011, 5,310 applied for aid, 4,866 were judged to have need, 3,162 had their need fully met. 154 Federal Work-Study jobs (averaging $4000). 17 state and other part-time jobs (averaging $4000). *Average percent of need met:* 65%. *Average financial aid package:* $24,081. *Average need-based loan:* $4153. *Average need-based gift aid:* $18,747. *Average indebtedness upon graduation:* $5001.

Applying *Options:* electronic application, early admission, early decision. *Application fee:* $42. *Required:* high school transcript, minimum 2.0 GPA. *Application deadlines:* 8/15 (freshmen), 8/13 (transfers). *Notification:* 8/28 (freshmen), continuous until 8/28 (transfers).

Freshman Application Contact Enrollment Services Customer Service Center, Texas Southern University, 3100 Cleburne Street, Houston, TX 77004-4598. *Phone:* 713-313-7071. *Fax:* 713-313-7851. *E-mail:* eservices@em.tsu.edu. *Web site:* http://www.tsu.edu/.

Texas State University–San Marcos

San Marcos, Texas

- **State-supported** university, founded 1899, part of Texas State University System
- **Suburban** 423-acre campus with easy access to San Antonio, Austin
- **Endowment** $86.9 million
- **Coed** 28,959 undergraduate students, 82% full-time, 55% women, 45% men
- **Moderately difficult** entrance level, 77% of applicants were admitted

Undergraduates 23,722 full-time, 5,237 part-time. Students come from 48 states and territories; 47 other countries; 1% are from out of state; 6% Black or African American, non-Hispanic/Latino; 28% Hispanic/Latino; 2% Asian, non-Hispanic/Latino; 0.1% Native Hawaiian or other Pacific Islander, non-Hispanic/Latino; 0.5% American Indian or Alaska Native, non-Hispanic/Latino; 2% Two or more races, non-Hispanic/Latino; 2% Race/ethnicity unknown; 0.5% international; 13% transferred in; 20% live on campus. *Retention:* 79% of full-time freshmen returned.

Freshmen *Admission:* 14,878 applied, 11,530 admitted, 4,459 enrolled. *Test scores:* SAT critical reading scores over 500: 59%; SAT math scores over 500: 70%; SAT writing scores over 500: 51%; ACT scores over 18: 92%; SAT critical reading scores over 600: 15%; SAT math scores over 600: 19%; SAT writing scores over 600: 10%; ACT scores over 24: 33%; SAT critical reading scores over 700: 1%; SAT math scores over 700: 1%; SAT writing scores over 700: 1%; ACT scores over 30: 2%.

Faculty *Total:* 1,588, 70% full-time, 64% with terminal degrees. *Student/faculty ratio:* 20:1.

Academics *Calendar:* semesters. *Degrees:* bachelor's, master's, doctoral, postbachelor's, and first professional certificates. *Special study options:* academic remediation for entering students, accelerated degree program, adult/continuing education programs, advanced placement credit, distance learning, double majors, English as a second language, freshman honors college, honors programs, independent study, internships, off-campus study, part-time degree program, services for LD students, study abroad, summer session for credit. *ROTC:* Army (b), Air Force (b). *Unusual degree programs:* 3-2 engineering with University of Texas at Austin, Texas A&M University, Texas Tech University, University of Texas at San Antonio.

Computers on Campus 1,792 computers/terminals are available on campus for general student use. Students can access the following: computer help desk, free student e-mail accounts, online (class) grades, online (class) registration, online (class) schedules. Campuswide network is available. 100% of college-owned or -operated housing units are wired for high-speed Internet access. Wireless service is available via entire campus.

Student Life *Housing:* on-campus residence required through sophomore year. *Options:* coed, men-only, women-only. Campus housing is university owned. Freshman campus housing is guaranteed. *Activities and organizations:* drama/theater group, student-run newspaper, radio station, choral group, marching

band, Non-traditional Students Association, Student Association for Campus Activities, Association Student Government, Annual Martin Luther King Jr. Commemoration, national fraternities, national sororities. *Campus security:* 24-hour emergency response devices and patrols, late-night transport/escort service, controlled dormitory access. *Student services:* health clinic, personal/psychological counseling, legal services.

Athletics Member NCAA. All Division I except football (Division I-AA). *Intercollegiate sports:* baseball M(s), basketball M(s)/W(s), cheerleading M/W, cross-country running M(s)/W(s), equestrian sports M(c)/W(c), fencing M(c)/W(c), golf M(s)/W(s), gymnastics M(c)/W(c), lacrosse M(c)/W(c), rugby M(c)/W(c), soccer M(c)/W(s), softball M(c)/W(s), tennis M(c)/W(s), track and field M(s)/W(s), ultimate Frisbee M(c)/W(c), volleyball W(s), water polo M(c)/W(c), weight lifting M(c)/W(c), wrestling M(c)/W(c). *Intramural sports:* basketball M/W, bowling M/W, cross-country running M/W, football M/W, golf M/W, racquetball M/W, soccer M/W, softball M/W, tennis M/W, ultimate Frisbee M, volleyball M/W.

Standardized Tests *Required:* SAT or ACT (for admission). *Recommended:* SAT (for admission), ACT (for admission).

Costs (2011–12) *Tuition:* state resident $6030 full-time, $201 per credit hour part-time; nonresident $15,420 full-time, $514 per credit hour part-time. Full-time tuition and fees vary according to course load and degree level. Part-time tuition and fees vary according to course load and degree level. *Required fees:* $2202 full-time, $50 per credit hour part-time, $396 per term part-time. *Room and board:* $6912; room only: $4512. Room and board charges vary according to board plan and housing facility. *Payment plan:* installment. *Waivers:* employees or children of employees.

Financial Aid Of all full-time matriculated undergraduates who enrolled in 2011, 21,019 applied for aid, 14,882 were judged to have need, 4,795 had their need fully met. 788 Federal Work-Study jobs (averaging $2946). 99 state and other part-time jobs (averaging $3044). In 2011, 268 non-need-based awards were made. *Average percent of need met:* 75%. *Average financial aid package:* $12,048. *Average need-based loan:* $6745. *Average need-based gift aid:* $6636. *Average non-need-based aid:* $2686. *Average indebtedness upon graduation:* $22,757.

Applying *Options:* electronic application, early admission, deferred entrance. *Application fee:* $60. *Required:* essay or personal statement, high school transcript. *Application deadlines:* 5/1 (freshmen), 5/1 (out-of-state freshmen), 7/1 (transfers). *Notification:* continuous (freshmen), continuous (transfers).

Freshman Application Contact Texas State University–San Marcos, 601 University Drive, San Marcos, TX 78666. *Phone:* 512-245-2364 Ext. 2803. *Web site:* http://www.txstate.edu/.

Texas Tech University
Lubbock, Texas

- **State-supported** university, founded 1923, part of Texas Tech University System
- **Urban** 1839-acre campus
- **Endowment** $491.6 million
- **Coed** 26,063 undergraduate students, 90% full-time, 45% women, 55% men
- **Moderately difficult** entrance level, 66% of applicants were admitted

Undergraduates 23,453 full-time, 2,610 part-time. Students come from 56 states and territories; 78 other countries; 5% are from out of state; 5% Black or African American, non-Hispanic/Latino; 18% Hispanic/Latino; 3% Asian, non-Hispanic/Latino; 0.1% Native Hawaiian or other Pacific Islander, non-Hispanic/Latino; 0.5% American Indian or Alaska Native, non-Hispanic/Latino; 1% Two or more races, non-Hispanic/Latino; 2% Race/ethnicity unknown; 3% international; 10% transferred in; 24% live on campus. *Retention:* 82% of full-time freshmen returned.

Freshmen *Admission:* 17,569 applied, 11,645 admitted, 4,464 enrolled. *Test scores:* SAT critical reading scores over 500: 71%; SAT math scores over 500: 82%; SAT writing scores over 500: 61%; ACT scores over 18: 97%; SAT critical reading scores over 600: 21%; SAT math scores over 600: 32%; SAT writing scores over 600: 15%; ACT scores over 24: 50%; SAT critical reading scores over 700: 2%; SAT math scores over 700: 4%; SAT writing scores over 700: 1%; ACT scores over 30: 7%.

Faculty *Total:* 1,348, 86% full-time, 84% with terminal degrees. *Student/faculty ratio:* 24:1.

Academics *Calendar:* semesters. *Degrees:* bachelor's, master's, doctoral, postbachelor's, and first professional certificates. *Special study options:* academic remediation for entering students, accelerated degree program, advanced placement credit, cooperative education, distance learning, double majors, English as a second language, external degree program, freshman honors college, honors programs, independent study, internships, off-campus study, part-time degree program, services for LD students, student-designed majors, study abroad, summer session for credit. *ROTC:* Army (b), Air Force (b). *Unusual degree programs:* 3-2 business administration; engineering;

architecture, agriculture and applied economics, mathematics, computer science, art, public administration, science.

Computers on Campus 3,000 computers/terminals are available on campus for general student use. Students can access the following: computer help desk, free student e-mail accounts, online (class) grades, online (class) registration, online (class) schedules, online degree plans, accounts, transcripts, schedules. Campuswide network is available. 100% of college-owned or -operated housing units are wired for high-speed Internet access. Wireless service is available via entire campus.

Student Life *Housing:* on-campus residence required for freshman year. *Options:* coed, men-only, women-only, disabled students. Campus housing is university owned. Freshman campus housing is guaranteed. *Activities and organizations:* drama/theater group, student-run newspaper, choral group, marching band, Red Raider Club, Alpha Lambda Delta, Phi Eta Sigma, Paradigm, Campus Crusade for Christ, national fraternities, national sororities. *Campus security:* 24-hour emergency response devices and patrols, late-night transport/escort service, controlled dormitory access. *Student services:* health clinic, personal/psychological counseling, legal services.

Athletics Member NCAA. All Division I except football (Division I-A). *Intercollegiate sports:* baseball M(s), basketball M(s)/W(s), cross-country running M(s)/W(s), golf M(s)/W(s), soccer W(s), softball W(s), tennis M(s)/W(s), track and field M(s)/W(s), volleyball W(s). *Intramural sports:* badminton M/W, baseball M(c), basketball M/W, bowling M(c)/W, cross-country running M(c)/W(c), equestrian sports M(c)/W(c), fencing M(c)/W(c), football M/W, golf M/W, gymnastics M(c)/W(c), lacrosse M(c)/W(c), racquetball M/W, rock climbing M(c)/W(c), rugby M(c)/W(c), soccer M(c)/W(c), softball M/W, swimming and diving M/W, table tennis M/W, tennis M(c)/W(c), ultimate Frisbee M(c)/W(c), volleyball M/W, water polo M(c)/W(c), weight lifting M/W, wrestling M(c)/W(c).

Standardized Tests *Required:* SAT or ACT (for admission).

Costs (2011–12) *Tuition:* state resident $5874 full-time, $196 per credit hour part-time; nonresident $15,264 full-time, $509 per credit hour part-time. Full-time tuition and fees vary according to course load, location, and reciprocity agreements. Part-time tuition and fees vary according to course load, location, and reciprocity agreements. *Required fees:* $2891 full-time, $35 per credit hour part-time, $921 per term part-time. *Room and board:* $8095; room only: $4290. Room and board charges vary according to board plan and housing facility. *Payment plan:* installment. *Waivers:* senior citizens and employees or children of employees.

Financial Aid Of all full-time matriculated undergraduates who enrolled in 2010, 14,707 applied for aid, 11,088 were judged to have need, 665 had their need fully met. In 2010, 2317 non-need-based awards were made. *Average percent of need met:* 56%. *Average financial aid package:* $9695. *Average need-based loan:* $4371. *Average need-based gift aid:* $7368. *Average non-need-based aid:* $3023. *Average indebtedness upon graduation:* $10,138.

Applying *Options:* electronic application, early admission. *Application fee:* $60. *Required:* high school transcript. *Recommended:* essay or personal statement. *Application deadlines:* 3/1 (freshmen), rolling (transfers). *Notification:* continuous (freshmen), continuous (transfers).

Freshman Application Contact Texas Tech University, Lubbock, TX 79409. *Phone:* 806-742-1480. *Web site:* http://www.ttu.edu/.

Texas Wesleyan University
Fort Worth, Texas

- **Independent United Methodist** comprehensive, founded 1890
- **Urban** 74-acre campus with easy access to Dallas-Fort Worth
- **Endowment** $47.9 million
- **Coed** 1,726 undergraduate students, 69% full-time, 62% women, 38% men
- **Moderately difficult** entrance level, 52% of applicants were admitted

Undergraduates 1,195 full-time, 531 part-time. Students come from 17 states and territories; 25 other countries; 4% are from out of state; 18% Black or African American, non-Hispanic/Latino; 22% Hispanic/Latino; 2% Asian, non-Hispanic/Latino; 0.1% Native Hawaiian or other Pacific Islander, non-Hispanic/Latino; 1% American Indian or Alaska Native, non-Hispanic/Latino; 0.6% Two or more races, non-Hispanic/Latino; 16% Race/ethnicity unknown; 2% international; 16% transferred in; 21% live on campus. *Retention:* 59% of full-time freshmen returned.

Freshmen *Admission:* 912 applied, 477 admitted, 168 enrolled. *Average high school GPA:* 3.3. *Test scores:* SAT critical reading scores over 500: 42%; SAT math scores over 500: 53%; SAT writing scores over 500: 33%; ACT scores over 18: 87%; SAT critical reading scores over 600: 10%; SAT math scores over 600: 16%; SAT writing scores over 600: 5%; ACT scores over 24: 18%; SAT critical reading scores over 700: 1%; SAT math scores over 700: 2%; ACT scores over 30: 3%.

Faculty *Total:* 283, 63% full-time, 57% with terminal degrees. *Student/faculty ratio:* 15:1.

Academics *Calendar:* semesters. *Degrees:* bachelor's, master's, and doctoral. *Special study options:* academic remediation for entering students, accelerated degree program, advanced placement credit, distance learning, double majors, external degree program, honors programs, independent study, internships, off-campus study, part-time degree program, services for LD students, study abroad, summer session for credit. *ROTC:* Army (b), Air Force (c).

Computers on Campus 418 computers/terminals are available on campus for general student use. Students can access the following: computer help desk, free student e-mail accounts, online (class) grades, online (class) registration, online (class) schedules. Campuswide network is available. 100% of college-owned or -operated housing units are wired for high-speed Internet access. Wireless service is available via computer labs, dorm rooms, libraries.

Student Life *Housing options:* coed, men-only, women-only. Campus housing is university owned. *Activities and organizations:* drama/theater group, student-run newspaper, radio and television station, choral group, Alpha Xi Delta, Lambda Kappa Kappa, Wesleyan Justice Project, Accounting Society, Kappa Alpha Order, national fraternities, national sororities. *Campus security:* 24-hour emergency response devices and patrols, student patrols, late-night transport/escort service, controlled dormitory access. *Student services:* health clinic, personal/psychological counseling.

Athletics Member NAIA. *Intercollegiate sports:* baseball M(s), basketball M(s)/W(s), cross-country running M(s)/W(s), golf M(s), soccer M(s)/W(s), softball W(s), table tennis M(s)/W(s), track and field M(s)/W(s), volleyball W(s). *Intramural sports:* basketball M/W, golf M/W, table tennis M/W.

Standardized Tests *Required:* SAT or ACT (for admission).

Costs (2011–12) *Comprehensive fee:* $26,940 includes full-time tuition ($17,830), mandatory fees ($1930), and room and board ($7180). Full-time tuition and fees vary according to degree level and program. Part-time tuition: $605 per credit hour. Part-time tuition and fees vary according to degree level and program. *Required fees:* $73 per credit hour part-time. *College room only:* $4210. Room and board charges vary according to housing facility. *Payment plans:* installment, deferred payment. *Waivers:* employees or children of employees.

Financial Aid Of all full-time matriculated undergraduates who enrolled in 2010, 1,159 applied for aid, 1,050 were judged to have need, 59 had their need fully met. In 2010, 111 non-need-based awards were made. *Average percent of need met:* 65%. *Average financial aid package:* $15,000. *Average need-based loan:* $4079. *Average need-based gift aid:* $11,844. *Average non-need-based aid:* $6533.

Applying *Options:* electronic application, deferred entrance. *Required:* minimum 2.0 GPA. *Required for some:* essay or personal statement, high school transcript. *Application deadlines:* rolling (freshmen), rolling (transfers). *Notification:* continuous (freshmen), continuous (transfers).

Freshman Application Contact Texas Wesleyan University, 1201 Wesleyan Street, Fort Worth, TX 76105-1536. *Phone:* 817-531-4422. *Toll-free phone:* 800-580-8980. *Fax:* 817-531-7515. *E-mail:* admissions@txwes.edu. *Web site:* http://www.txwes.edu/.

Texas Woman's University
Denton, Texas

- **State-supported** university, founded 1901
- **Suburban** 270-acre campus with easy access to Dallas-Fort Worth
- **Endowment** $10.7 million
- **Coed, primarily women** 9,010 undergraduate students, 70% full-time, 91% women, 9% men
- **Minimally difficult** entrance level, 88% of applicants were admitted

Undergraduates 6,269 full-time, 2,741 part-time. Students come from 47 states and territories; 61 other countries; 1% are from out of state; 21% Black or African American, non-Hispanic/Latino; 21% Hispanic/Latino; 7% Asian, non-Hispanic/Latino; 0.3% Native Hawaiian or other Pacific Islander, non-Hispanic/Latino; 0.6% American Indian or Alaska Native, non-Hispanic/Latino; 0.9% Race/ethnicity unknown; 1% international; 17% transferred in; 22% live on campus. *Retention:* 64% of full-time freshmen returned.

Freshmen *Admission:* 3,364 applied, 2,972 admitted, 1,080 enrolled. *Average high school GPA:* 3.25. *Test scores:* SAT critical reading scores over 500: 32%; SAT math scores over 500: 38%; ACT scores over 18: 25%; SAT critical reading scores over 600: 6%; SAT math scores over 600: 8%; SAT critical reading scores over 700: 1%; SAT math scores over 700: 1%.

Faculty *Total:* 391, 93% full-time. *Student/faculty ratio:* 25:1.

Academics *Calendar:* semesters. *Degrees:* certificates, bachelor's, master's, doctoral, post-master's, postbachelor's, and first professional certificates. *Special study options:* academic remediation for entering students, accelerated degree program, adult/continuing education programs, advanced placement credit, cooperative education, distance learning, double majors, honors programs, independent study, internships, off-campus study, part-time degree program, services for LD students, study abroad, summer session for credit. *ROTC:* Army (c), Air Force (c).

Computers on Campus 1,380 computers/terminals and 2,143 ports are available on campus for general student use. Students can access the following: campus intranet, computer help desk, free student e-mail accounts, online (class) grades, online (class) registration, online (class) schedules. Campus-wide network is available. 100% of college-owned or -operated housing units are wired for high-speed Internet access. Wireless service is available via classrooms, computer centers, computer labs, learning centers, libraries, student centers.

Student Life *Housing:* on-campus residence required through sophomore year. *Options:* coed, women-only, disabled students. Campus housing is university owned and leased by the school. Freshman campus housing is guaranteed. *Activities and organizations:* drama/theater group, student-run newspaper, choral group, Helping Hands, Athenian Honor Society, Campus Activities Board, Nursing Student Organization, Graduate Library and Information Studies Association, national fraternities, national sororities. *Campus security:* 24-hour emergency response devices and patrols, late-night transport/escort service, controlled dormitory access. *Student services:* health clinic, personal/psychological counseling.

Athletics Member NCAA. All Division II. *Intercollegiate sports:* basketball W(s), gymnastics W(s), soccer W(s), softball W(s), volleyball W(s). *Intramural sports:* badminton M/W, basketball M(c)/W(c), football M/W, golf M(c)/W(c), soccer M(c)/W(c), softball M(c)/W(c), tennis M/W, track and field M(c)/W(c), volleyball M/W, weight lifting M(c)/W(c), wrestling M(c)/W(c).

Standardized Tests *Required for some:* SAT or ACT (for admission).

Costs (2012–13) *Tuition:* state resident $5040 full-time, $168 per credit part-time; nonresident $14,430 full-time, $481 per credit part-time. Full-time tuition and fees vary according to course load and reciprocity agreements. Part-time tuition and fees vary according to course load and reciprocity agreements. *Required fees:* $1920 full-time. *Room and board:* $6170; room only: $3276. Room and board charges vary according to board plan and housing facility. *Payment plan:* installment. *Waivers:* senior citizens.

Financial Aid Of all full-time matriculated undergraduates who enrolled in 2010, 4,788 applied for aid, 4,014 were judged to have need, 662 had their need fully met. In 2010, 624 non-need-based awards were made. *Average percent of need met:* 61%. *Average financial aid package:* $10,867. *Average need-based loan:* $3833. *Average need-based gift aid:* $5756. *Average non-need-based aid:* $2685. *Average indebtedness upon graduation:* $21,194.

Applying *Options:* electronic application, early admission, deferred entrance. *Application fee:* $50. *Required:* high school transcript, minimum 2.0 GPA. *Application deadlines:* 7/15 (freshmen), 7/15 (transfers). *Notification:* 8/15 (freshmen), continuous until 8/15 (transfers).

Freshman Application Contact Ms. Erma Nieto-Brecht, Director of Admissions, Texas Woman's University, 304 Administration Drive, Denton, TX 76201. *Phone:* 940-898-3188. *Toll-free phone:* 866-809-6130. *Fax:* 940-898-3081. *E-mail:* admissions@twu.edu. *Web site:* http://www.twu.edu/.

See page 902 for display ad and page 1638 for the College Close-Up.

Trinity University
San Antonio, Texas

- **Independent** comprehensive, founded 1869, affiliated with Presbyterian Church
- **Urban** 113-acre campus
- **Endowment** $974.9 million
- **Coed** 2,431 undergraduate students, 98% full-time, 54% women, 46% men
- **Very difficult** entrance level, 61% of applicants were admitted

Undergraduates 2,388 full-time, 43 part-time. Students come from 47 states and territories; 64 other countries; 29% are from out of state; 3% Black or African American, non-Hispanic/Latino; 13% Hispanic/Latino; 7% Asian, non-Hispanic/Latino; 0.4% American Indian or Alaska Native, non-Hispanic/Latino; 3% Two or more races, non-Hispanic/Latino; 4% Race/ethnicity unknown; 7% international; 0.8% transferred in; 74% live on campus. *Retention:* 89% of full-time freshmen returned.

Freshmen *Admission:* 4,507 applied, 2,755 admitted, 620 enrolled. *Average high school GPA:* 3.5. *Test scores:* SAT critical reading scores over 500: 96%; SAT math scores over 500: 99%; SAT writing scores over 500: 96%; ACT scores over 18: 100%; SAT critical reading scores over 600: 68%; SAT math scores over 600: 74%; SAT writing scores over 600: 62%; ACT scores over 24: 93%; SAT critical reading scores over 700: 21%; SAT math scores over 700: 19%; SAT writing scores over 700: 17%; ACT scores over 30: 44%.

Faculty *Total:* 325, 78% full-time, 82% with terminal degrees. *Student/faculty ratio:* 9:1.

Academics *Calendar:* semesters. *Degrees:* bachelor's and master's. *Special study options:* accelerated degree program, advanced placement credit, double majors, honors programs, independent study, internships, part-time degree program, services for LD students, study abroad, summer session for credit. *ROTC:* Air Force (c).

Computers on Campus 450 computers/terminals are available on campus for general student use. Students can access the following: campus intranet, computer help desk, free student e-mail accounts, online (class) grades, online (class) registration, online (class) schedules. Campuswide network is available. 100% of college-owned or -operated housing units are wired for high-speed Internet access. Wireless service is available via entire campus.

Student Life *Housing:* on-campus residence required through junior year. *Options:* coed. Campus housing is university owned. Freshman campus housing is guaranteed. *Activities and organizations:* drama/theater group, student-run newspaper, radio and television station, choral group, Voluntary Action Center, Alpha Phi Omega, Association of Student Representatives, Activities Council, Multicultural Network. *Campus security:* 24-hour emergency response devices and patrols, late-night transport/escort service, controlled dormitory access. *Student services:* health clinic, personal/psychological counseling.

Athletics Member NCAA. All Division III. *Intercollegiate sports:* baseball M, basketball M/W, cross-country running M/W, fencing M(c)/W(c), football M, golf M/W, lacrosse M(c)/W(c), riflery M(c)/W(c), soccer M/W, softball W, swimming and diving M/W, tennis M/W, track and field M/W, volleyball M(c)/W, water polo M(c)/W(c). *Intramural sports:* basketball M/W, cross-country running M/W, equestrian sports M(c)/W(c), football M, racquetball M/W, soccer M/W, softball M/W, swimming and diving M/W, table tennis M/W, tennis M/W, ultimate Frisbee M/W, volleyball M/W, wrestling M/W.

Standardized Tests *Required:* SAT or ACT (for admission).

Costs (2012–13) *Comprehensive fee:* $43,290 includes full-time tuition ($32,568), mandatory fees ($525), and room and board ($10,197). Full-time tuition and fees vary according to course load. Part-time tuition: $1357 per credit hour. Part-time tuition and fees vary according to course load. *College room only:* $6520. Room and board charges vary according to board plan. *Payment plan:* installment. *Waivers:* employees or children of employees.

Financial Aid Of all full-time matriculated undergraduates who enrolled in 2011, 1,330 applied for aid, 1,077 were judged to have need, 427 had their need fully met. In 2011, 961 non-need-based awards were made. *Average percent of need met:* 88%. *Average financial aid package:* $26,841. *Average need-based loan:* $6137. *Average need-based gift aid:* $20,900. *Average non-need-based aid:* $13,597. *Average indebtedness upon graduation:* $37,261.

Applying *Options:* electronic application, early decision, early action, deferred entrance. *Application fee:* $50. *Required:* essay or personal statement, high school transcript, 2 letters of recommendation. *Recommended:* interview. *Application deadlines:* 2/1 (freshmen), 3/1 (transfers), 11/1 (early action).

Early decision deadline: 11/1. *Notification:* 4/1 (freshmen), 4/1 (transfers), 12/1 (early decision), 12/15 (early action).

Freshman Application Contact Mr. Christopher Ellertson, Dean of Admissions and Financial Aid, Trinity University, One Trinity Place, San Antonio, TX 78212-7200. *Phone:* 210-999-7207. *Toll-free phone:* 800-TRINITY. *Fax:* 210-999-8164. *E-mail:* admissions@trinity.edu. *Web site:* http://www.trinity.edu/.

University of Dallas
Irving, Texas

- **Independent Roman Catholic** university, founded 1955
- **Suburban** 215-acre campus with easy access to Dallas-Fort Worth
- **Endowment** $43.7 million
- **Coed** 1,356 undergraduate students, 98% full-time, 51% women, 49% men
- **Moderately difficult** entrance level, 88% of applicants were admitted

Undergraduates 1,332 full-time, 24 part-time. Students come from 49 states and territories; 12 other countries; 55% are from out of state; 1% Black or African American, non-Hispanic/Latino; 16% Hispanic/Latino; 4% Asian, non-Hispanic/Latino; 0.1% Native Hawaiian or other Pacific Islander, non-Hispanic/Latino; 0.4% American Indian or Alaska Native, non-Hispanic/Latino; 3% Two or more races, non-Hispanic/Latino; 3% Race/ethnicity unknown; 3% international; 3% transferred in; 63% live on campus. *Retention:* 80% of full-time freshmen returned.

Freshmen *Admission:* 1,082 applied, 947 admitted, 371 enrolled. *Average high school GPA:* 3.64. *Test scores:* SAT critical reading scores over 500: 89%; SAT math scores over 500: 87%; SAT writing scores over 500: 85%; ACT scores over 18: 100%; SAT critical reading scores over 600: 61%; SAT math scores over 600: 46%; SAT writing scores over 600: 54%; ACT scores over 24: 76%; SAT critical reading scores over 700: 25%; SAT math scores over 700: 11%; SAT writing scores over 700: 15%; ACT scores over 30: 29%.

Faculty *Total:* 235, 54% full-time. *Student/faculty ratio:* 12:1.

Academics *Calendar:* semesters. *Degrees:* bachelor's, master's, doctoral, post-master's, postbachelor's, and first professional certificates. *Special study options:* advanced placement credit, double majors, independent study, internships, off-campus study, part-time degree program, services for LD students, student-designed majors, study abroad, summer session for credit. *ROTC:* Army (c), Air Force (c). *Unusual degree programs:* 3-2 nursing with Texas Woman's University-College of Nursing.

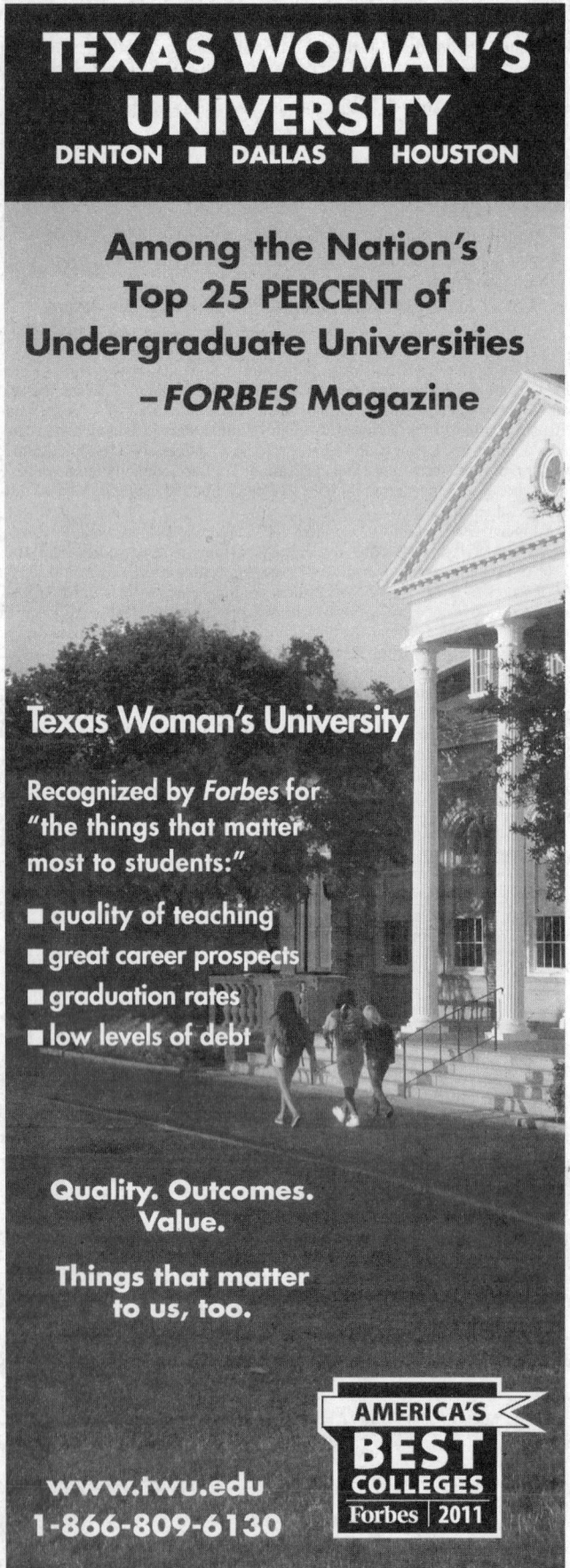

Computers on Campus 125 computers/terminals are available on campus for general student use. Students can access the following: campus intranet, computer help desk, free student e-mail accounts, online (class) grades, online (class) registration, online (class) schedules. Campuswide network is available. 100% of college-owned or -operated housing units are wired for high-speed Internet access. Wireless service is available via entire campus.

Student Life *Housing:* on-campus residence required through junior year. *Options:* men-only, women-only. Campus housing is university owned. Freshman campus housing is guaranteed. *Activities and organizations:* drama/theater group, student-run newspaper, choral group, SPUD (Programming Board), Residence Hall Association, student government, Best Buddies, Alpha Phi Omega. *Campus security:* 24-hour emergency response devices and patrols, late-night transport/escort service, controlled dormitory access. *Student services:* health clinic, personal/psychological counseling.

Athletics Member NCAA. All Division III. *Intercollegiate sports:* baseball M, basketball M/W, cross-country running M/W, golf M, lacrosse M/W, soccer M/W, softball W, track and field M/W, volleyball W. *Intramural sports:* basketball M, equestrian sports M(c)/W(c), football M/W, rugby M(c)/W(c), sailing M(c)/W(c), soccer M/W, softball M/W, tennis M(c)/W(c), ultimate Frisbee M(c)/W(c), volleyball M/W.

Standardized Tests *Required:* SAT or ACT (for admission).

Costs (2012–13) *Comprehensive fee:* $40,960 includes full-time tuition ($29,140), mandatory fees ($1930), and room and board ($9890). Part-time tuition: $1220 per credit. *Required fees:* $1930 per year part-time. *College room only:* $5690. Room and board charges vary according to board plan and housing facility. *Payment plan:* installment. *Waivers:* employees or children of employees.

Financial Aid Of all full-time matriculated undergraduates who enrolled in 2011, 925 applied for aid, 848 were judged to have need, 159 had their need fully met. 244 Federal Work-Study jobs (averaging $1242). 53 state and other part-time jobs (averaging $1567). In 2011, 437 non-need-based awards were made. *Average percent of need met:* 72%. *Average financial aid package:* $23,342. *Average need-based loan:* $5936. *Average need-based gift aid:* $18,234. *Average non-need-based aid:* $13,576. *Average indebtedness upon graduation:* $27,310.

Applying *Options:* electronic application, early action, deferred entrance. *Application fee:* $40. *Required:* essay or personal statement, high school transcript, 2 letters of recommendation. *Required for some:* interview. *Application deadlines:* 3/1 (freshmen), 3/1 (out-of-state freshmen), 8/1 (transfers), 12/1 (early action). *Notification:* continuous (freshmen), continuous (transfers), 1/15 (early action).

Freshman Application Contact Mr. Andrew Klein, Campus Visit Coordinator, University of Dallas, 1845 East Northgate Drive, Irving, TX 75062-4736. *Phone:* 800-628-6999. *Toll-free phone:* 800-628-6999. *Fax:* 972-721-5017. *E-mail:* ugadmis@udallas.edu. *Web site:* http://www.udallas.edu/.

See page 901 for display ad and page 1662 for the College Close-Up.

University of Houston
Houston, Texas

- **State-supported** university, founded 1927, part of University of Houston System
- **Urban** 594-acre campus
- **Endowment** $496.7 million
- **Coed** 31,764 undergraduate students, 73% full-time, 50% women, 50% men
- **Moderately difficult** entrance level, 64% of applicants were admitted

Undergraduates 23,213 full-time, 8,551 part-time. Students come from 52 states and territories; 125 other countries; 1% are from out of state; 13% Black or African American, non-Hispanic/Latino; 27% Hispanic/Latino; 21% Asian, non-Hispanic/Latino; 0.3% Native Hawaiian or other Pacific Islander, non-Hispanic/Latino; 0.2% American Indian or Alaska Native, non-Hispanic/Latino; 2% Two or more races, non-Hispanic/Latino; 0.7% Race/ethnicity unknown; 4% international; 13% transferred in; 15% live on campus. *Retention:* 81% of full-time freshmen returned.

Freshmen *Admission:* 14,725 applied, 9,359 admitted, 3,719 enrolled. *Test scores:* SAT critical reading scores over 500: 70%; SAT math scores over 500: 85%; ACT scores over 18: 94%; SAT critical reading scores over 600: 24%; SAT math scores over 600: 41%; ACT scores over 24: 51%; SAT critical reading scores over 700: 3%; SAT math scores over 700: 7%; ACT scores over 30: 8%.

Faculty *Total:* 1,813, 73% full-time, 76% with terminal degrees. *Student/faculty ratio:* 23:1.

Academics *Calendar:* semesters. *Degrees:* bachelor's, master's, doctoral, and first professional. *Special study options:* academic remediation for entering students, adult/continuing education programs, advanced placement credit, cooperative education, distance learning, double majors, English as a second

language, freshman honors college, honors programs, independent study, internships, off-campus study, part-time degree program, services for LD students, study abroad, summer session for credit. *ROTC:* Army (b), Navy (c), Air Force (b).

Computers on Campus 1,110 computers/terminals and 25,000 ports are available on campus for general student use. Students can access the following: computer help desk, free student e-mail accounts, online (class) grades, online (class) registration, online (class) schedules. Campuswide network is available. 100% of college-owned or -operated housing units are wired for high-speed Internet access. Wireless service is available via classrooms, computer centers, computer labs, dorm rooms, learning centers, libraries, student centers.

Student Life *Housing options:* coed, disabled students. Campus housing is university owned and is provided by a third party. *Activities and organizations:* drama/theater group, student-run newspaper, television station, choral group, marching band, Student Government Association, Residence Hall Association, Metropolitan Volunteer Program, Student Governing Board- Honors College, Student Alumni Connection, national fraternities, national sororities. *Campus security:* 24-hour emergency response devices and patrols, student patrols, late-night transport/escort service, controlled dormitory access, vehicle assistance. *Student services:* health clinic, personal/psychological counseling, women's center, legal services.

Athletics Member NCAA. All Division I except football (Division I-A). *Intercollegiate sports:* baseball M(s), basketball M(s)/W(s), cross-country running M(s)/W(s), golf M(s), soccer W(s), softball W(s), swimming and diving W(s), tennis W(s), track and field M(s)/W(s), volleyball W(s). *Intramural sports:* badminton M/W, basketball M/W, bowling M(c)/W, cross-country running M/W, fencing M(c)/W(c), golf M/W, racquetball M/W, rock climbing M/W, soccer M(c)/W(c), softball M/W, swimming and diving M/W, table tennis M/W, tennis M/W, track and field M/W, ultimate Frisbee M(c), volleyball M/W(c), water polo M.

Standardized Tests *Required:* SAT or ACT (for admission).

Costs (2011–12) *Tuition:* state resident $6466 full-time, $216 per credit hour part-time; nonresident $15,856 full-time, $529 per credit hour part-time. Full-time tuition and fees vary according to course level, course load, and program. Part-time tuition and fees vary according to course level, course load, and program. *Required fees:* $2745 full-time. *Room and board:* $8318; room only: $5098. Room and board charges vary according to board plan and housing facility. *Payment plans:* installment, deferred payment. *Waivers:* employees or children of employees.

Financial Aid Of all full-time matriculated undergraduates who enrolled in 2010, 15,241 applied for aid, 13,609 were judged to have need, 3,440 had their need fully met. 504 Federal Work-Study jobs (averaging $2832). 67 state and other part-time jobs (averaging $2723). In 2010, 353 non-need-based awards were made. *Average percent of need met:* 76%. *Average financial aid package:* $12,365. *Average need-based loan:* $7224. *Average need-based gift aid:* $6896. *Average non-need-based aid:* $4162. *Average indebtedness upon graduation:* $14,922.

Applying *Options:* electronic application. *Application fee:* $50. *Required:* high school transcript. *Application deadlines:* 4/1 (freshmen), 6/1 (transfers). *Notification:* continuous (freshmen), continuous (transfers).

Freshman Application Contact Jeff Fuller, Director, Student Recruitment, University of Houston, Welcome Center, 4400 University Boulevard, Houston, TX 77204-2023. *Phone:* 713-743-1010. *Fax:* 713-743-9633. *E-mail:* jdfuller@central.uh.edu. *Web site:* http://www.uh.edu/.

University of Houston–Clear Lake
Houston, Texas

- **State-supported** upper-level, founded 1971, part of University of Houston System
- **Suburban** 524-acre campus with easy access to Houston
- **Endowment** $18.6 million
- **Coed** 4,672 undergraduate students, 46% full-time, 67% women, 33% men
- **Minimally difficult** entrance level

Undergraduates 2,136 full-time, 2,536 part-time. Students come from 8 states and territories; 24 other countries; 9% Black or African American, non-Hispanic/Latino; 30% Hispanic/Latino; 6% Asian, non-Hispanic/Latino; 0.3% Native Hawaiian or other Pacific Islander, non-Hispanic/Latino; 0.4% American Indian or Alaska Native, non-Hispanic/Latino; 0.2% Two or more races, non-Hispanic/Latino; 1% Race/ethnicity unknown; 1% international; 24% transferred in.

Faculty *Total:* 458, 53% full-time, 60% with terminal degrees. *Student/faculty ratio:* 16:1.

Academics *Calendar:* semesters. *Degrees:* certificates, bachelor's, master's, and doctoral. *Special study options:* advanced placement credit, cooperative education, distance learning, double majors, English as a second language, independent study, internships, off-campus study, part-time degree program,

services for LD students, student-designed majors, study abroad, summer session for credit.

Computers on Campus 799 computers/terminals are available on campus for general student use. Students can access the following: campus intranet, computer help desk, free student e-mail accounts, online (class) grades, online (class) registration, online (class) schedules. Campuswide network is available. Wireless service is available via entire campus.

Student Life *Housing options:* coed. Campus housing is provided by a third party. *Activities and organizations:* student-run newspaper, Beta Alpha Psi, National Society of Leadership and Success, Applied Behavior Student Analysis Student Organization, Student Government Association, Accounting Association. *Campus security:* 24-hour emergency response devices and patrols, late-night transport/escort service. *Student services:* health clinic, personal/psychological counseling, women's center.

Costs (2011–12) *Tuition:* state resident $5326 full-time, $178 per credit hour part-time; nonresident $16,164 full-time, $539 per credit hour part-time. Full-time tuition and fees vary according to course load and program. Part-time tuition and fees vary according to course load and program. *Required fees:* $1182 full-time, $444 per term part-time. *Room only:* $8458. Room and board charges vary according to housing facility. *Payment plans:* installment, deferred payment. *Waivers:* senior citizens.

Financial Aid Of all full-time matriculated undergraduates who enrolled in 2011, 1,506 applied for aid, 1,407 were judged to have need, 355 had their need fully met. 37 Federal Work-Study jobs (averaging $1965). 25 state and other part-time jobs (averaging $2048). In 2011, 37 non-need-based awards were made. *Average percent of need met:* 41%. *Average financial aid package:* $7176. *Average need-based loan:* $4532. *Average need-based gift aid:* $3075. *Average non-need-based aid:* $785. *Average indebtedness upon graduation:* $6726.

Applying *Options:* electronic application, early admission, deferred entrance. *Application fee:* $35. *Application deadline:* rolling (transfers). *Notification:* continuous (transfers).

Application Contact Ms. Rauchelle Jones, Executive Director of Admissions, University of Houston–Clear Lake, Box 13, Houston, TX 77058-1098. *Phone:* 281-283-2518. *Fax:* 281-283-2530. *E-mail:* admissions@uhcl.edu. *Web site:* http://www.uhcl.edu/.

University of Houston–Downtown
Houston, Texas

- **State-supported** comprehensive, founded 1974, part of University of Houston System
- **Urban** 24-acre campus
- **Endowment** $34.7 million
- **Coed** 12,757 undergraduate students, 49% full-time, 61% women, 39% men
- **Noncompetitive** entrance level, 97% of applicants were admitted

Undergraduates 6,276 full-time, 6,481 part-time. Students come from 24 states and territories; 75 other countries; 28% Black or African American, non-Hispanic/Latino; 37% Hispanic/Latino; 9% Asian, non-Hispanic/Latino; 0.1% Native Hawaiian or other Pacific Islander, non-Hispanic/Latino; 0.3% American Indian or Alaska Native, non-Hispanic/Latino; 0.9% Two or more races, non-Hispanic/Latino; 0.6% Race/ethnicity unknown; 5% international; 15% transferred in. *Retention:* 60% of full-time freshmen returned.

Freshmen *Admission:* 2,883 applied, 2,794 admitted, 1,138 enrolled. *Average high school GPA:* 3.15. *Test scores:* SAT critical reading scores over 500: 16%; SAT math scores over 500: 24%; ACT scores over 18: 42%; SAT critical reading scores over 600: 2%; SAT math scores over 600: 3%; ACT scores over 24: 3%; ACT scores over 30: 1%.

Faculty *Total:* 642, 51% full-time, 61% with terminal degrees. *Student/faculty ratio:* 20:1.

Academics *Calendar:* semesters. *Degrees:* bachelor's and master's. *Special study options:* academic remediation for entering students, advanced placement credit, distance learning, double majors, English as a second language, honors programs, independent study, internships, off-campus study, part-time degree program, services for LD students, study abroad, summer session for credit. *ROTC:* Army (c), Air Force (c).

Computers on Campus 1,971 computers/terminals and 450 ports are available on campus for general student use. Students can access the following: computer help desk, free student e-mail accounts, online (class) grades, online (class) registration, online (class) schedules. Campuswide network is available. Wireless service is available via entire campus.

Student Life *Housing:* college housing not available. *Activities and organizations:* drama/theater group, student-run newspaper, Environmental Club, International Business Association, Photography Club, Professional Accounting Society, Student Government Association, national fraternities, national sororities. *Campus security:* 24-hour emergency response devices and patrols, late-

night transport/escort service. *Student services:* health clinic, personal/psychological counseling, legal services.

Athletics *Intramural sports:* badminton M/W, baseball M(c), basketball M(c)/W(c), bowling M/W, cheerleading M(c)/W(c), soccer M(c)/W(c), tennis M/W, volleyball M(c)/W(c), weight lifting M(c)/W(c).

Costs (2011–12) *Tuition:* state resident $4650 full-time, $155 per credit hour part-time; nonresident $14,040 full-time, $468 per credit hour part-time. Full-time tuition and fees vary according to course load and program. Part-time tuition and fees vary according to course load and program. *Required fees:* $1066 full-time, $155 per credit hour part-time. *Payment plan:* installment. *Waivers:* senior citizens.

Financial Aid Of all full-time matriculated undergraduates who enrolled in 2010, 3,946 applied for aid, 3,775 were judged to have need, 128 had their need fully met. 199 Federal Work-Study jobs (averaging $3312). 27 state and other part-time jobs (averaging $2893). In 2010, 128 non-need-based awards were made. *Average percent of need met:* 49%. *Average financial aid package:* $8441. *Average need-based loan:* $3686. *Average need-based gift aid:* $6222. *Average non-need-based aid:* $2668. *Average indebtedness upon graduation:* $15,484.

Applying *Options:* electronic application. *Application fee:* $35. *Required:* high school transcript. *Application deadlines:* 6/1 (freshmen), 7/15 (transfers). *Notification:* continuous (freshmen), continuous (transfers).

Freshman Application Contact Ms. Patricia Santos, Assistant Director of Admissions-Freshman Admissions, University of Houston–Downtown, One Main Street, Suite 350-S, Houston, TX 77002. *Phone:* 713-221-8522. *Fax:* 713-221-8157. *E-mail:* uhdadmit@uhd.edu. *Web site:* http://www.uhd.edu/.

University of Houston–Victoria
Victoria, Texas

- **State-supported** upper-level, founded 1973, part of University of Houston System
- **Small-town** 20-acre campus
- **Coed** 2,564 undergraduate students, 47% full-time, 67% women, 33% men
- **Minimally difficult** entrance level, 40% of applicants were admitted

Undergraduates 1,199 full-time, 1,365 part-time. 13% Black or African American, non-Hispanic/Latino; 27% Hispanic/Latino; 7% Asian, non-Hispanic/Latino; 0.2% Native Hawaiian or other Pacific Islander, non-Hispanic/Latino; 2% Two or more races, non-Hispanic/Latino; 0.7% Race/ethnicity unknown; 2% international; 19% transferred in.

Freshmen *Admission:* 1,960 applied, 787 admitted.

Faculty *Total:* 208, 60% full-time, 67% with terminal degrees. *Student/faculty ratio:* 18:1.

Academics *Calendar:* semesters. *Degrees:* bachelor's, master's, post-master's, and postbachelor's certificates. *Special study options:* adult/continuing education programs, part-time degree program. *ROTC:* Air Force (c).

Computers on Campus Students can access the following: campus intranet, computer help desk, free student e-mail accounts, online (class) grades, online (class) registration, online (class) schedules. Campuswide network is available. 100% of college-owned or -operated housing units are wired for high-speed Internet access. Wireless service is available via entire campus.

Student Life *Housing options:* coed. Campus housing is university owned. Freshman applicants given priority for college housing. *Campus security:* 24-hour emergency response devices and patrols, controlled dormitory access.

Athletics Member NAIA. *Intercollegiate sports:* baseball M, golf M/W, soccer M/W, softball W.

Costs (2011–12) *Tuition:* state resident $4694 full-time, $156 per credit hour part-time; nonresident $14,084 full-time, $469 per credit hour part-time. Full-time tuition and fees vary according to course level and course load. Part-time tuition and fees vary according to course level and course load. *Required fees:* $1134 full-time, $54 per credit hour part-time. *Room and board:* $6956. Room and board charges vary according to board plan. *Payment plan:* installment. *Waivers:* senior citizens and employees or children of employees.

Financial Aid Of all full-time matriculated undergraduates who enrolled in 2007, 201 applied for aid, 168 were judged to have need, 32 had their need fully met. 17 Federal Work-Study jobs (averaging $2755). 7 state and other part-time jobs (averaging $1272). In 2007, 4 non-need-based awards were made. *Average percent of need met:* 41%. *Average financial aid package:* $5311. *Average need-based loan:* $3676. *Average need-based gift aid:* $1376. *Average non-need-based aid:* $818. *Average indebtedness upon graduation:* $17,695.

Applying *Options:* electronic application, deferred entrance. *Application deadline:* rolling (transfers). *Notification:* continuous (transfers).

Application Contact Dr. Denee Thomas, Senior Director of LEAD and Student Recruitment, University of Houston–Victoria, 3007 North Ben Wilson, Victoria, TX 77901. *Phone:* 877-970-4848 Ext. 4184. *Toll-free phone:* 877-970-4848 Ext. 110. *E-mail:* recruitment@uhv.edu. *Web site:* http://www.uhv.edu/.

University of Mary Hardin-Baylor
Belton, Texas

- **Independent Southern Baptist** comprehensive, founded 1845
- **Small-town** 100-acre campus with easy access to Austin
- **Endowment** $63.1 million
- **Coed** 2,784 undergraduate students, 91% full-time, 63% women, 37% men
- **Moderately difficult** entrance level, 27% of applicants were admitted

Undergraduates 2,544 full-time, 240 part-time. Students come from 29 states and territories; 23 other countries; 3% are from out of state; 14% Black or African American, non-Hispanic/Latino; 14% Hispanic/Latino; 2% Asian, non-Hispanic/Latino; 0.5% Native Hawaiian or other Pacific Islander, non-Hispanic/Latino; 0.8% American Indian or Alaska Native, non-Hispanic/Latino; 0.4% Two or more races, non-Hispanic/Latino; 0.4% Race/ethnicity unknown; 1% international; 10% transferred in; 65% live on campus. *Retention:* 64% of full-time freshmen returned.

Freshmen *Admission:* 8,463 applied, 2,322 admitted, 630 enrolled. *Test scores:* SAT critical reading scores over 500: 54%; SAT math scores over 500: 64%; SAT writing scores over 500: 44%; ACT scores over 18: 97%; SAT critical reading scores over 600: 18%; SAT math scores over 600: 21%; SAT writing scores over 600: 14%; ACT scores over 24: 43%; SAT critical reading scores over 700: 2%; SAT math scores over 700: 2%; SAT writing scores over 700: 1%; ACT scores over 30: 8%.

Faculty *Total:* 261, 54% full-time, 51% with terminal degrees. *Student/faculty ratio:* 16:1.

Academics *Calendar:* semesters. *Degrees:* bachelor's, master's, doctoral, and first professional. *Special study options:* academic remediation for entering students, accelerated degree program, advanced placement credit, distance learning, double majors, English as a second language, honors programs, independent study, internships, part-time degree program, services for LD students, student-designed majors, study abroad, summer session for credit. *ROTC:* Army (b), Air Force (c). *Unusual degree programs:* 3-2 business administration.

Computers on Campus 275 computers/terminals are available on campus for general student use. Students can access the following: campus intranet, computer help desk, free student e-mail accounts, online (class) grades, online (class) registration, online (class) schedules. Campuswide network is available. Wireless service is available via entire campus.

Student Life *Housing:* on-campus residence required through sophomore year. *Options:* men-only, women-only, disabled students. Campus housing is university owned. Freshman applicants given priority for college housing. *Activities and organizations:* drama/theater group, student-run newspaper, choral group, marching band, Baptist Student Ministry, Student Government Association, Residence Hall Association, Campus Activities Board, Focus. *Campus security:* 24-hour emergency response devices and patrols, late-night transport/escort service, controlled dormitory access, campus police force, lighted pathways and sidewalks. *Student services:* health clinic, personal/psychological counseling.

Athletics Member NCAA. All Division III. *Intercollegiate sports:* baseball M, basketball M/W, football M, golf M/W, soccer M/W, softball W, tennis M/W, volleyball W. *Intramural sports:* basketball M/W, football M/W, golf M/W, soccer M/W, softball M/W, table tennis M/W, tennis M/W, ultimate Frisbee M/W, volleyball M/W.

Standardized Tests *Required:* SAT or ACT (for admission).

Costs (2011–12) *Comprehensive fee:* $29,271 includes full-time tuition ($20,700), mandatory fees ($2350), and room and board ($6221). Full-time tuition and fees vary according to course load and degree level. Part-time tuition: $690 per credit hour. Part-time tuition and fees vary according to course load and degree level. *Required fees:* $75 per credit hour part-time, $50 per term part-time. *Room and board:* Room and board charges vary according to board plan and housing facility. *Payment plan:* installment. *Waivers:* employees or children of employees.

Financial Aid Of all full-time matriculated undergraduates who enrolled in 2010, 2,279 applied for aid, 2,081 were judged to have need, 174 had their need fully met. 188 Federal Work-Study jobs (averaging $1969). 407 state and other part-time jobs (averaging $1606). In 2010, 321 non-need-based awards were made. *Average percent of need met:* 58%. *Average financial aid package:* $13,903. *Average need-based loan:* $4793. *Average need-based gift aid:* $9702. *Average non-need-based aid:* $5634. *Average indebtedness upon graduation:* $34,744.

Applying *Options:* electronic application, early admission, deferred entrance. *Application fee:* $35. *Required:* high school transcript. *Required for some:* essay or personal statement, interview. *Application deadlines:* rolling (freshmen), rolling (transfers). *Notification:* continuous (freshmen), continuous (transfers).

Freshman Application Contact Mr. Brent Burks, Director of Admissions, University of Mary Hardin-Baylor, UMHB Station Box 8004, 900 College

Street, Belton, TX 76513-2599. *Phone:* 254-295-4520. *Toll-free phone:* 800-727-8642. *Fax:* 254-295-5049. *E-mail:* admission@umhb.edu. *Web site:* http://www.umhb.edu/.

University of North Texas
Denton, Texas

- **State-supported** university, founded 1890, part of University of North Texas System
- **Suburban** 875-acre campus with easy access to Dallas-Fort Worth
- **Coed** 28,325 undergraduate students, 79% full-time, 52% women, 48% men
- 56% of applicants were admitted

Undergraduates 22,413 full-time, 5,912 part-time. 4% are from out of state; 13% Black or African American, non-Hispanic/Latino; 17% Hispanic/Latino; 6% Asian, non-Hispanic/Latino; 0.1% Native Hawaiian or other Pacific Islander, non-Hispanic/Latino; 0.7% American Indian or Alaska Native, non-Hispanic/Latino; 2% Two or more races, non-Hispanic/Latino; 1% Race/ethnicity unknown; 3% international; 13% transferred in; 19% live on campus. *Retention:* 80% of full-time freshmen returned.
Freshmen *Admission:* 14,563 applied, 8,113 admitted, 4,076 enrolled. *Test scores:* SAT critical reading scores over 500: 71%; SAT math scores over 500: 77%; SAT writing scores over 500: 60%; ACT scores over 18: 95%; SAT critical reading scores over 600: 27%; SAT math scores over 600: 32%; SAT writing scores over 600: 19%; ACT scores over 24: 45%; SAT critical reading scores over 700: 5%; SAT math scores over 700: 6%; SAT writing scores over 700: 3%; ACT scores over 30: 5%.
Faculty *Total:* 1,644, 64% full-time, 52% with terminal degrees. *Student/faculty ratio:* 23:1.
Academics *Calendar:* semesters. *Degrees:* bachelor's, master's, doctoral, postbachelor's, and first professional certificates. *Special study options:* academic remediation for entering students, accelerated degree program, advanced placement credit, cooperative education, distance learning, double majors, English as a second language, freshman honors college, honors programs, independent study, internships, off-campus study, part-time degree program, services for LD students, study abroad, summer session for credit. *ROTC:* Army (b), Air Force (b).
Computers on Campus Students can access the following: campus intranet, computer help desk, free student e-mail accounts, online (class) grades, online (class) registration, online (class) schedules. Campuswide network is available. 100% of college-owned or -operated housing units are wired for high-speed Internet access. Wireless service is available via entire campus.
Student Life *Housing:* on-campus residence required for freshman year. *Options:* coed, women-only, disabled students. Campus housing is university owned. Freshman applicants given priority for college housing. *Activities and organizations:* drama/theater group, student-run newspaper, radio and television station, choral group, marching band, Student Government Association, Residence Hall Association, Panhellenic Association, Interfraternity Council, College Life, national fraternities, national sororities. *Campus security:* 24-hour emergency response devices and patrols, late-night transport/escort service, controlled dormitory access. *Student services:* health clinic, personal/psychological counseling, women's center, legal services.
Athletics Member NCAA. All Division I except football (Division I-A). *Intercollegiate sports:* baseball M(c), basketball M(s)/W(s), bowling M(c)/W(c), cross-country running M(s)/W(s), fencing M(c)/W(c), golf M(s)/W(s), ice hockey M(c), lacrosse M(c)/W(c), racquetball M(c)/W(c), rock climbing M(c), sailing M(c)/W(c), soccer M(c)/W(s), softball M(s)/W, swimming and diving M(c)/W(s), tennis M(c)/W, track and field M(s)/W(s), ultimate Frisbee M(c)/W(c), volleyball W(s). *Intramural sports:* basketball M/W, bowling M/W, football M, golf M/W, racquetball M/W, soccer M/W, softball M/W, table tennis M/W, tennis M/W, volleyball M/W.
Standardized Tests *Required:* SAT or ACT (for admission).
Costs (2012–13) *Tuition:* state resident $6178 full-time, $206 per credit hour part-time; nonresident $15,568 full-time, $516 per credit hour part-time. *Required fees:* $2558 full-time. *Room and board:* $6892. Room and board charges vary according to board plan and housing facility. *Payment plan:* installment. *Waivers:* senior citizens and employees or children of employees.
Financial Aid Of all full-time matriculated undergraduates who enrolled in 2011, 16,413 applied for aid, 13,466 were judged to have need, 2,325 had their need fully met. In 2011, 2382 non-need-based awards were made. *Average percent of need met:* 63%. *Average financial aid package:* $10,412. *Average need-based loan:* $4539. *Average need-based gift aid:* $6617. *Average non-need-based aid:* $4403.
Applying *Options:* electronic application, early admission, deferred entrance. *Application fee:* $60. *Application deadlines:* 8/1 (freshmen), rolling (transfers). *Notification:* continuous (freshmen), continuous (transfers).
Freshman Application Contact Mr. Jasiel Perez, Associate Director of Admissions, University of North Texas, Denton, TX 76203. *Phone:* 940-369-7664. *Toll-free phone:* 800-868-8211. *E-mail:* jasiel.perez@unt.edu. *Web site:* http://www.unt.edu/.

University of Phoenix–Austin Campus
Austin, Texas

Admissions Office Contact University of Phoenix–Austin Campus, 10801 North Mopac, Austin, TX 78759. *Toll-free phone:* 866-766-0766. *Web site:* http://www.phoenix.edu/.

University of Phoenix–Dallas Campus
Dallas, Texas

Freshman Application Contact Marc Booker, Sr. Director, Office of Admissions and Evaluation, University of Phoenix–Dallas Campus, 4035 South Riverpoint Parkway, Mail Stop CF-L101, Phoenix, AZ 85040. *Phone:* 602-557-4609. *Toll-free phone:* 866-766-0766. *Fax:* 480-643-1156. *Web site:* http://www.phoenix.edu/.

University of Phoenix–Houston Campus
Houston, Texas

Freshman Application Contact Marc Booker, Sr. Director, Office of Admissions and Evaluation, University of Phoenix–Houston Campus, 4305 South Riverpoint Parkway, Mail Stop CF-L101, Phoenix, AZ 85040. *Phone:* 602-557-4609. *Toll-free phone:* 866-766-0766. *Fax:* 480-643-1156. *Web site:* http://www.phoenix.edu/.

University of Phoenix–San Antonio Campus
San Antonio, Texas

Admissions Office Contact University of Phoenix–San Antonio Campus, 8200 IH-10 West, Suite 900, San Antonio, TX 78230. *Toll-free phone:* 866-766-0766. *Web site:* http://www.phoenix.edu/.

University of St. Thomas
Houston, Texas

- **Independent Roman Catholic** comprehensive, founded 1947
- **Urban** 20-acre campus
- **Endowment** $59.9 million
- **Coed** 1,609 undergraduate students, 75% full-time, 62% women, 38% men
- **Moderately difficult** entrance level, 78% of applicants were admitted

Undergraduates 1,209 full-time, 400 part-time. Students come from 27 states and territories; 40 other countries; 4% are from out of state; 5% Black or African American, non-Hispanic/Latino; 38% Hispanic/Latino; 11% Asian, non-Hispanic/Latino; 0.1% Native Hawaiian or other Pacific Islander, non-Hispanic/Latino; 0.2% American Indian or Alaska Native, non-Hispanic/Latino; 2% Two or more races, non-Hispanic/Latino; 2% Race/ethnicity unknown; 7% international; 11% transferred in; 17% live on campus. *Retention:* 82% of full-time freshmen returned.
Freshmen *Admission:* 820 applied, 643 admitted, 238 enrolled. *Average high school GPA:* 3.59. *Test scores:* SAT critical reading scores over 500: 80%; SAT math scores over 500: 81%; SAT writing scores over 500: 77%; ACT scores over 18: 100%; SAT critical reading scores over 600: 30%; SAT math scores over 600: 34%; SAT writing scores over 600: 27%; ACT scores over 24: 81%; SAT critical reading scores over 700: 6%; SAT math scores over 700: 6%; SAT writing scores over 700: 5%; ACT scores over 30: 24%.
Faculty *Total:* 333, 45% full-time, 71% with terminal degrees. *Student/faculty ratio:* 11:1.
Academics *Calendar:* semesters. *Degrees:* diplomas, bachelor's, master's, doctoral, and first professional. *Special study options:* accelerated degree program, adult/continuing education programs, advanced placement credit, distance learning, double majors, honors programs, independent study, internships, off-campus study, part-time degree program, services for LD students, student-designed majors, study abroad, summer session for credit. *ROTC:* Army (c), Air Force (c). *Unusual degree programs:* 3-2 business administration; engineering with University of Notre Dame, University of Houston, Texas A&M University.
Computers on Campus 316 computers/terminals and 400 ports are available on campus for general student use. Students can access the following: campus intranet, computer help desk, free student e-mail accounts, online (class)

grades, online (class) registration, online (class) schedules. Campuswide network is available. 95% of college-owned or -operated housing units are wired for high-speed Internet access. Wireless service is available via entire campus. **Student Life** *Housing options:* coed. Campus housing is university owned. Freshman applicants given priority for college housing. *Activities and organizations:* drama/theater group, student-run newspaper, choral group, Health Occupations Students of America (HOSA), Pre Health Professions Society, Student Activities Board (SAB), American Chemical Society, tennis. *Campus security:* 24-hour emergency response devices and patrols, late-night transport/escort service, controlled dormitory access. *Student services:* personal/psychological counseling.
Athletics Member NAIA. *Intercollegiate sports:* baseball M(c), basketball M(s)/W(s), cheerleading M(c)/W(c), fencing M(c)/W(c), golf M(s)/W(s), rugby M(c), soccer M(s), table tennis M(c)/W(c), tennis M(c)/W(c), ultimate Frisbee M(c)/W(c), volleyball W(s). *Intramural sports:* basketball M/W, bowling M/W, racquetball M/W, soccer M(c)/W(c), table tennis M/W, tennis M/W, ultimate Frisbee M/W, volleyball M/W.
Standardized Tests *Required:* SAT or ACT (for admission).
Costs (2011–12) *Comprehensive fee:* $33,200 includes full-time tuition ($24,960), mandatory fees ($340), and room and board ($7900). Full-time tuition and fees vary according to course load. Part-time tuition: $832 per credit hour. Part-time tuition and fees vary according to course load. *College room only:* $4800. Room and board charges vary according to board plan and housing facility. *Payment plans:* installment, deferred payment. *Waivers:* senior citizens and employees or children of employees.
Financial Aid Of all full-time matriculated undergraduates who enrolled in 2011, 811 applied for aid, 739 were judged to have need, 118 had their need fully met. 33 Federal Work-Study jobs (averaging $3604). 4 state and other part-time jobs (averaging $3500). In 2011, 312 non-need-based awards were made. *Average percent of need met:* 67%. *Average financial aid package:* $17,028. *Average need-based loan:* $4972. *Average need-based gift aid:* $13,089. *Average non-need-based aid:* $8859. *Average indebtedness upon graduation:* $30,191.
Applying *Options:* electronic application, early action, deferred entrance. *Application fee:* $25. *Required:* essay or personal statement, high school transcript, minimum 2.8 GPA, 1070 SAT (Critical Reading and Math) or 23 ACT. *Application deadlines:* 5/1 (freshmen), 5/1 (out-of-state freshmen), rolling (transfers), 11/1 (early action). *Notification:* continuous until 11/15 (freshmen), continuous until 11/15 (out-of-state freshmen), continuous (transfers), 12/15 (early action).
Freshman Application Contact Mr. Arthur Ortiz, Director of Freshman Admissions, University of St. Thomas, 3800 Montrose Boulevard, Houston, TX 77006-4696. *Phone:* 713-525-3848. *Toll-free phone:* 800-856-8565. *Fax:* 713-525-3558. *E-mail:* admissions@stthom.edu. *Web site:* http://www.stthom.edu/.

The University of Texas at Arlington
Arlington, Texas

- **State-supported** university, founded 1895, part of University of Texas System
- **Urban** 420-acre campus with easy access to Dallas-Fort Worth
- **Endowment** $80.1 million
- **Coed** 25,419 undergraduate students, 63% full-time, 56% women, 44% men
- **Moderately difficult** entrance level, 69% of applicants were admitted

Undergraduates 15,909 full-time, 9,510 part-time. Students come from 50 states and territories; 101 other countries; 2% are from out of state; 15% Black or African American, non-Hispanic/Latino; 22% Hispanic/Latino; 11% Asian, non-Hispanic/Latino; 0.2% Native Hawaiian or other Pacific Islander, non-Hispanic/Latino; 0.4% American Indian or Alaska Native, non-Hispanic/Latino; 3% Two or more races, non-Hispanic/Latino; 1% Race/ethnicity unknown; 4% international; 17% transferred in; 13% live on campus. *Retention:* 74% of full-time freshmen returned.
Freshmen *Admission:* 9,559 applied, 6,593 admitted, 2,625 enrolled. *Test scores:* SAT critical reading scores over 500: 60%; SAT math scores over 500: 76%; ACT scores over 18: 90%; SAT critical reading scores over 600: 19%; SAT math scores over 600: 32%; ACT scores over 24: 41%; SAT critical reading scores over 700: 2%; SAT math scores over 700: 4%; ACT scores over 30: 4%.
Faculty *Total:* 1,316, 68% full-time. *Student/faculty ratio:* 23:1.
Academics *Calendar:* semesters. *Degrees:* bachelor's, master's, doctoral, post-master's, postbachelor's, and first professional certificates. *Special study options:* academic remediation for entering students, adult/continuing education programs, advanced placement credit, cooperative education, distance learning, double majors, English as a second language, freshman honors college, honors programs, independent study, internships, off-campus study, part-time degree program, services for LD students, student-designed majors, study

abroad, summer session for credit. *ROTC:* Army (b), Air Force (c). *Unusual degree programs:* 3-2 business administration; psychology, health care administration.
Computers on Campus 500 computers/terminals and 6,000 ports are available on campus for general student use. Students can access the following: campus intranet, computer help desk, free student e-mail accounts, online (class) grades, online (class) registration, online (class) schedules. Campus-wide network is available. 90% of college-owned or -operated housing units are wired for high-speed Internet access. Wireless service is available via classrooms, computer labs, learning centers, libraries, student centers.
Student Life *Housing options:* coed, men-only, women-only. Campus housing is university owned and leased by the school. *Activities and organizations:* drama/theater group, student-run newspaper, radio station, choral group, marching band, Honors College Council, Golden Key International Honor Society, National Society of Leadership & Success, National Society of Collegiate Scholars, Nursing Constituency Council, national fraternities, national sororities. *Campus security:* 24-hour emergency response devices and patrols, late-night transport/escort service, controlled dormitory access, remote emergency telephones, bicycle patrols, crime prevention program, student shuttle service. *Student services:* health clinic, personal/psychological counseling, legal services.
Athletics Member NCAA. All Division I. *Intercollegiate sports:* baseball M(s), basketball M(s)/W(s), golf M, softball W(s), tennis M(s)/W(s), track and field M(s)/W(s), volleyball W(s). *Intramural sports:* badminton M/W, basketball M/W, bowling M/W, golf M, racquetball M/W, soccer M/W, softball M/W, table tennis M/W, tennis M/W, volleyball M/W.
Standardized Tests *Required:* SAT or ACT (for admission).
Costs (2011–12) *Tuition:* state resident $8878 full-time; nonresident $18,268 full-time. Full-time tuition and fees vary according to course level, course load, and program. Part-time tuition and fees vary according to course level, course load, and program. *Room and board:* $7554; room only: $2950. Room and board charges vary according to board plan and housing facility. *Payment plan:* installment. *Waivers:* employees or children of employees.
Financial Aid Of all full-time matriculated undergraduates who enrolled in 2011, 11,982 applied for aid, 10,879 were judged to have need, 1,420 had their need fully met. 1,007 Federal Work-Study jobs (averaging $288,761). 261 state and other part-time jobs (averaging $273,277). In 2011, 200 non-need-based awards were made. *Average percent of need met:* 76%. *Average financial aid package:* $12,565. *Average need-based loan:* $4215. *Average need-based gift aid:* $6202. *Average non-need-based aid:* $5715. *Average indebtedness upon graduation:* $22,416.
Applying *Options:* electronic application, deferred entrance. *Application fee:* $50. *Required:* high school transcript, class rank. *Application deadlines:* 6/1 (freshmen), rolling (transfers). *Notification:* continuous (freshmen), continuous (transfers).
Freshman Application Contact Dr. Hans Gatterdam, Executive Director of Admissions and Records, The University of Texas at Arlington, UTA Box 19088, 701 South Nedderman Drive, Arlington, TX 76019-0088. *Phone:* 817-272-3275. *Fax:* 817-272-3435. *E-mail:* admissions@uta.edu. *Web site:* http://www.uta.edu/.

The University of Texas at Austin
Austin, Texas

- **State-supported** university, founded 1883, part of University of Texas System
- **Urban** 431-acre campus with easy access to San Antonio
- **Endowment** $2.8 billion
- **Coed** 38,437 undergraduate students, 93% full-time, 51% women, 49% men
- **Very difficult** entrance level, 47% of applicants were admitted

Undergraduates 35,608 full-time, 2,829 part-time. Students come from 49 states and territories; 91 other countries; 5% are from out of state; 5% Black or African American, non-Hispanic/Latino; 20% Hispanic/Latino; 18% Asian, non-Hispanic/Latino; 0.1% Native Hawaiian or other Pacific Islander, non-Hispanic/Latino; 0.3% American Indian or Alaska Native, non-Hispanic/Latino; 2% Two or more races, non-Hispanic/Latino; 0.4% Race/ethnicity unknown; 5% international; 6% transferred in; 19% live on campus. *Retention:* 92% of full-time freshmen returned.
Freshmen *Admission:* 32,589 applied, 15,172 admitted, 7,148 enrolled. *Test scores:* SAT critical reading scores over 500: 88%; SAT math scores over 500: 94%; SAT writing scores over 500: 88%; ACT scores over 18: 98%; SAT critical reading scores over 600: 57%; SAT math scores over 600: 72%; SAT writing scores over 600: 57%; ACT scores over 24: 84%; SAT critical reading scores over 700: 17%; SAT math scores over 700: 30%; SAT writing scores over 700: 19%; ACT scores over 30: 40%.
Faculty *Total:* 2,964, 91% full-time, 88% with terminal degrees. *Student/faculty ratio:* 18:1.

Academics *Calendar:* semesters. *Degrees:* certificates, bachelor's, master's, doctoral, and first professional. *Special study options:* academic remediation for entering students, accelerated degree program, advanced placement credit, cooperative education, distance learning, double majors, English as a second language, honors programs, independent study, internships, off-campus study, part-time degree program, services for LD students, student-designed majors, study abroad, summer session for credit. *ROTC:* Army (b), Navy (b), Air Force (b). *Unusual degree programs:* 3-2 business administration; engineering; computer science.

Computers on Campus 3,150 computers/terminals and 1,375 ports are available on campus for general student use. Students can access the following: campus intranet, computer help desk, free student e-mail accounts, online (class) grades, online (class) registration, online (class) schedules. Campus-wide network is available. 100% of college-owned or -operated housing units are wired for high-speed Internet access. Wireless service is available via entire campus.

Student Life *Housing options:* coed, men-only, women-only, disabled students. Campus housing is university owned. Freshman applicants given priority for college housing. *Activities and organizations:* drama/theater group, student-run newspaper, radio and television station, choral group, marching band, Alpha Phi Omega, Student Events Center, Texas Exes-Student Chapter, Longhorn Band Student Organization, Student Volunteer Board, national fraternities, national sororities. *Campus security:* 24-hour emergency response devices and patrols, late-night transport/escort service, controlled dormitory access. *Student services:* health clinic, personal/psychological counseling, women's center, legal services.

Athletics Member NCAA. All Division I except football (Division I-A). *Intercollegiate sports:* archery M(c)/W(c), badminton M(c)/W(c), baseball M(s)/W(c), basketball M(s)/W(s), crew M(c)/W(s), cross-country running M(s)/W(s), fencing M(c)/W(c), golf M(s)/W(s), gymnastics M(c)/W(c), ice hockey M(c)/W(c), lacrosse M(c)/W(c), racquetball M(c)/W(c), rugby M(c)/W(c), sailing M(c)/W(c), soccer M(c)/W(s), softball W(s), swimming and diving M(s)/W(s), table tennis M(c)/W(c), tennis M(s)/W(s), track and field M(s)/W(s), ultimate Frisbee M(c)/W(c), volleyball M(c)/W(s), water polo M(c)/W(c), weight lifting M(c)/W(c), wrestling M(c)/W(c). *Intramural sports:* badminton M/W, basketball M/W, football M/W, golf M/W, racquetball M/W, soccer M/W, softball M/W, swimming and diving M/W, table tennis M/W, tennis M/W, track and field M/W, ultimate Frisbee M/W, volleyball M/W.

Standardized Tests *Required:* SAT or ACT (for admission).

Costs (2011–12) *Tuition:* state resident $9794 full-time; nonresident $32,506 full-time. Full-time tuition and fees vary according to course load and program. Part-time tuition and fees vary according to course load and program. *Room and board:* $10,422. Room and board charges vary according to housing facility. *Payment plan:* installment. *Waivers:* senior citizens and employees or children of employees.

Financial Aid Of all full-time matriculated undergraduates who enrolled in 2011, 21,849 applied for aid, 16,345 were judged to have need, 2,969 had their need fully met. In 2011, 396 non-need-based awards were made. *Average percent of need met:* 67%. *Average financial aid package:* $12,045. *Average need-based loan:* $4959. *Average need-based gift aid:* $7959. *Average non-need-based aid:* $3151. *Average indebtedness upon graduation:* $25,227.

Applying *Options:* electronic application. *Application fee:* $75. *Required:* essay or personal statement, high school transcript. *Recommended:* letters of recommendation. *Application deadlines:* 12/1 (freshmen), 3/1 (transfers). *Notification:* continuous (freshmen), continuous (transfers).

Freshman Application Contact Dr. Kedra B. Ishop, Vice Provost and Director of Admissions, The University of Texas at Austin, Office of Admissions, Freshman Admissions Center, PO Box 8058, Austin, TX 78713-8058. *Phone:* 512-475-7440. *Fax:* 512-475-7475. *E-mail:* kedra.ishop@austin.utexas.edu. *Web site:* http://www.utexas.edu/.

The University of Texas at Brownsville

Brownsville, Texas

Freshman Application Contact Carlo Tamayo, New Student Relations Coordinator, The University of Texas at Brownsville, 80 Fort Brown, Brownsville, TX 78520-4991. *Phone:* 956-882-8860. *Toll-free phone:* 877-UTBTSC1. *Fax:* 956-882-8959. *E-mail:* admissions@utb.edu. *Web site:* http://www.utb.edu/.

The University of Texas at Dallas
Richardson, Texas

- **State-supported** university, founded 1969, part of University of Texas System
- **Suburban** 500-acre campus with easy access to Dallas-Fort Worth
- **Endowment** $244.4 million
- **Coed** 11,760 undergraduate students, 78% full-time, 44% women, 56% men
- **Very difficult** entrance level, 53% of applicants were admitted

Undergraduates 9,136 full-time, 2,624 part-time. Students come from 48 states and territories; 83 other countries; 4% are from out of state; 6% Black or African American, non-Hispanic/Latino; 15% Hispanic/Latino; 23% Asian, non-Hispanic/Latino; 0.1% Native Hawaiian or other Pacific Islander, non-Hispanic/Latino; 0.4% American Indian or Alaska Native, non-Hispanic/Latino; 3% Two or more races, non-Hispanic/Latino; 2% Race/ethnicity unknown; 5% international; 15% transferred in; 24% live on campus. *Retention:* 83% of full-time freshmen returned.

Freshmen *Admission:* 6,881 applied, 3,672 admitted, 1,789 enrolled. *Average high school GPA:* 3.82. *Test scores:* SAT critical reading scores over 500: 89%; SAT math scores over 500: 97%; SAT writing scores over 500: 85%; ACT scores over 18: 99%; SAT critical reading scores over 600: 54%; SAT math scores over 600: 76%; SAT writing scores over 600: 47%; ACT scores over 24: 83%; SAT critical reading scores over 700: 15%; SAT math scores over 700: 28%; SAT writing scores over 700: 11%; ACT scores over 30: 31%. **Faculty** *Total:* 877, 74% full-time, 82% with terminal degrees. *Student/faculty ratio:* 21:1.

Academics *Calendar:* semesters. *Degrees:* bachelor's, master's, doctoral, postbachelor's, and first professional certificates. *Special study options:* academic remediation for entering students, accelerated degree program, adult/continuing education programs, advanced placement credit, cooperative education, distance learning, double majors, freshman honors college, honors programs, independent study, internships, part-time degree program, services for LD students, student-designed majors, study abroad, summer session for credit. *ROTC:* Army (c), Air Force (c). *Unusual degree programs:* 3-2 engineering with Abilene Christian University, Austin College, Paul Quinn College, Texas Woman's University.

Computers on Campus 164 computers/terminals are available on campus for general student use. Students can access the following: computer help desk, free student e-mail accounts, online (class) grades, online (class) registration, online (class) schedules. Campuswide network is available. 100% of college-owned or -operated housing units are wired for high-speed Internet access. Wireless service is available via classrooms, computer centers, dorm rooms, libraries, student centers.

Student Life *Housing options:* coed. Campus housing is university owned and is provided by a third party. Freshman applicants given priority for college housing. *Activities and organizations:* drama/theater group, student-run newspaper, radio and television station, choral group, Student Government Association, Golden Key National Honor Society, Muslim Students Association, Indian Student Association, Friendship Association of Chinese Students and Scholars, national fraternities, national sororities. *Campus security:* 24-hour emergency response devices and patrols, student patrols, late-night transport/escort service, controlled dormitory access. *Student services:* health clinic, personal/psychological counseling, women's center, legal services.

Athletics Member NCAA. All Division III. *Intercollegiate sports:* baseball M, basketball M/W, cross-country running M/W, golf M/W, soccer M/W, softball W, tennis M/W, volleyball W. *Intramural sports:* badminton M(c)/W(c), basketball M(c)/W(c), bowling M(c)/W(c), cheerleading M/W, cross-country running M(c)/W(c), fencing M(c)/W(c), field hockey M(c)/W(c), football M(c)/W(c), gymnastics M(c)/W(c), rock climbing M(c)/W(c), rugby M(c)/W(c), soccer M(c)/W(c), squash M(c)/W(c), swimming and diving M(c)/W(c), table tennis M(c)/W(c), tennis M(c)/W(c), ultimate Frisbee M(c)/W(c), volleyball M(c)/W(c), water polo M(c)/W(c).

Standardized Tests *Required:* SAT or ACT (for admission). *Required for some:* THEA.

Costs (2011–12) *Tuition:* state resident $11,168 full-time, $372 per credit hour part-time; nonresident $28,194 full-time, $940 per credit hour part-time. Full-time tuition and fees vary according to course load and degree level. Part-time tuition and fees vary according to course load and degree level. No tuition increase for student's term of enrollment. *Room and board:* $8364. Room and board charges vary according to board plan and housing facility. *Payment plan:* installment. *Waivers:* senior citizens and employees or children of employees.

Financial Aid Of all full-time matriculated undergraduates who enrolled in 2010, 4,930 applied for aid, 4,244 were judged to have need, 815 had their need fully met. 248 Federal Work-Study jobs (averaging $3888). 36 state and other part-time jobs (averaging $2729). In 2010, 296 non-need-based awards were made. *Average percent of need met:* 64%. *Average financial aid pack-*

age: $11,160. *Average need-based loan:* $4498. *Average need-based gift aid:* $8026. *Average non-need-based aid:* $8595. *Average indebtedness upon graduation:* $16,813.

Applying *Options:* electronic application, deferred entrance. *Application fee:* $50. *Required:* essay or personal statement, high school transcript. *Required for some:* interview. *Recommended:* 3 letters of recommendation. *Application deadline:* 7/1 (freshmen). *Notification:* continuous (freshmen), continuous (transfers).

Freshman Application Contact Enrollment Services, The University of Texas at Dallas, 800 West Campbell Road, Mail Station ROC11, Richardson, TX 75083-0688. *Phone:* 972-883-2270. *Toll-free phone:* 800-889-2443. *Fax:* 972-883-2599. *E-mail:* interest@utdallas.edu. *Web site:* http://www.utdallas.edu/.

The University of Texas at El Paso

El Paso, Texas

- **State-supported** university, founded 1913, part of University of Texas System
- **Urban** 360-acre campus
- **Coed** 18,975 undergraduate students, 67% full-time, 54% women, 46% men
- **Minimally difficult** entrance level, 100% of applicants were admitted

Undergraduates 12,746 full-time, 6,229 part-time. Students come from 50 states and territories; 70 other countries; 3% are from out of state; 3% Black or African American, non-Hispanic/Latino; 81% Hispanic/Latino; 0.9% Asian, non-Hispanic/Latino; 0.1% Native Hawaiian or other Pacific Islander, non-Hispanic/Latino; 0.3% American Indian or Alaska Native, non-Hispanic/Latino; 0.3% Two or more races, non-Hispanic/Latino; 1% Race/ethnicity unknown; 6% international; 9% transferred in. *Retention:* 75% of full-time freshmen returned.

Freshmen *Admission:* 5,697 applied, 5,687 admitted, 2,798 enrolled. *Average high school GPA:* 3.16. *Test scores:* SAT critical reading scores over 500: 25%; SAT math scores over 500: 38%; ACT scores over 18: 67%; SAT critical reading scores over 600: 4%; SAT math scores over 600: 7%; ACT scores over 24: 15%; ACT scores over 30: 1%.

Faculty *Total:* 1,183, 60% full-time. *Student/faculty ratio:* 21:1.

Academics *Calendar:* semesters. *Degrees:* bachelor's, master's, doctoral, post-master's, and first professional certificates. *Special study options:* academic remediation for entering students, accelerated degree program, adult/continuing education programs, advanced placement credit, cooperative education, distance learning, double majors, English as a second language, honors programs, independent study, internships, off-campus study, part-time degree program, services for LD students, study abroad, summer session for credit. *ROTC:* Army (b), Air Force (b).

Computers on Campus Students can access the following: computer help desk, free student e-mail accounts, online (class) grades, online (class) registration, online (class) schedules. Campuswide network is available.

Student Life *Housing options:* coed, disabled students. Campus housing is university owned. *Activities and organizations:* drama/theater group, student-run newspaper, radio station, choral group, marching band, national fraternities, national sororities. *Campus security:* 24-hour emergency response devices and patrols, late-night transport/escort service. *Student services:* health clinic, personal/psychological counseling, women's center, legal services.

Athletics Member NCAA. All Division I except football (Division I-A). *Intercollegiate sports:* basketball M(s)/W(s), cross-country running M(s)/W(s), golf M(s), riflery M/W, tennis W(s), track and field M(s)/W(s), volleyball W(s). *Intramural sports:* archery M/W, badminton M/W, basketball M/W, bowling M/W, fencing M/W, field hockey M, golf M/W, gymnastics M/W, racquetball M/W, skiing (downhill) M, soccer M/W, squash M/W, swimming and diving M/W, tennis M/W, track and field M/W, volleyball M/W, water polo M/W, weight lifting M, wrestling M/W.

Standardized Tests *Required for some:* SAT or ACT (for admission).

Costs (2011–12) *Tuition:* state resident $5341 full-time, $178 per credit hour part-time; nonresident $14,731 full-time, $491 per credit hour part-time. Full-time tuition and fees vary according to course load. Part-time tuition and fees vary according to course load. *Required fees:* $1528 full-time, $46 per credit hour part-time, $126 per term part-time. *Room only:* $4725. Room and board charges vary according to housing facility.

Financial Aid Of all full-time matriculated undergraduates who enrolled in 2009, 8,696 applied for aid, 7,259 were judged to have need, 1,686 had their need fully met. In 2009, 741 non-need-based awards were made. *Average percent of need met:* 73%. *Average financial aid package:* $14,508. *Average need-based loan:* $6671. *Average need-based gift aid:* $9294. *Average non-need-based aid:* $2501. *Average indebtedness upon graduation:* $18,773.

Applying *Options:* deferred entrance. *Required:* high school transcript. *Application deadlines:* 7/31 (freshmen), 7/31 (transfers). *Notification:* continuous (transfers).

Freshman Application Contact Dr. Luisa S. Havens, Executive Director of Admissions, The University of Texas at El Paso, Academic Services Building, Room 102, El Paso, TX 779968. *Phone:* 915-747-5890. *Toll-free phone:* 877-74MINER. *Fax:* 915-747-5890. *E-mail:* futureminer@utep.edu. *Web site:* http://www.utep.edu/.

The University of Texas at San Antonio

San Antonio, Texas

- **State-supported** university, founded 1969, part of University of Texas System
- **Suburban** 600-acre campus
- **Endowment** $81.8 million
- **Coed** 26,268 undergraduate students, 81% full-time, 48% women, 52% men
- **79%** of applicants were admitted

Undergraduates 21,316 full-time, 4,952 part-time. 3% are from out of state; 9% Black or African American, non-Hispanic/Latino; 46% Hispanic/Latino; 5% Asian, non-Hispanic/Latino; 0.2% Native Hawaiian or other Pacific Islander, non-Hispanic/Latino; 0.2% American Indian or Alaska Native, non-Hispanic/Latino; 3% Two or more races, non-Hispanic/Latino; 2% Race/ethnicity unknown; 3% international; 10% transferred in; 12% live on campus. *Retention:* 62% of full-time freshmen returned.

Freshmen *Admission:* 14,438 applied, 11,450 admitted, 5,001 enrolled. *Test scores:* SAT critical reading scores over 500: 54%; SAT math scores over 500: 68%; SAT writing scores over 500: 45%; ACT scores over 18: 90%; SAT critical reading scores over 600: 14%; SAT math scores over 600: 22%; SAT writing scores over 600: 9%; ACT scores over 24: 33%; SAT critical reading scores over 700: 1%; SAT math scores over 700: 2%; SAT writing scores over 700: 1%; ACT scores over 30: 3%.

Faculty *Total:* 1,290, 73% full-time, 69% with terminal degrees. *Student/faculty ratio:* 24:1.

Academics *Calendar:* semesters. *Degrees:* bachelor's, master's, doctoral, postbachelor's, and first professional certificates. *Special study options:* academic remediation for entering students, adult/continuing education programs, advanced placement credit, cooperative education, distance learning, double majors, English as a second language, honors programs, independent study, internships, off-campus study, part-time degree program, services for LD students, study abroad, summer session for credit. *ROTC:* Army (b), Air Force (b).

Computers on Campus 542 computers/terminals are available on campus for general student use. Students can access the following: campus intranet, computer help desk, free student e-mail accounts, online (class) grades, online (class) registration, online (class) schedules. Campuswide network is available. 100% of college-owned or -operated housing units are wired for high-speed Internet access. Wireless service is available via entire campus.

Student Life *Housing options:* coed, women-only, disabled students. Campus housing is university owned and is provided by a third party. *Activities and organizations:* student-run newspaper, radio station, choral group, marching band, Student Government Association, Hispanic Student Association, Black Student Union, GLBTQ, Marching Band, national fraternities, national sororities. *Campus security:* 24-hour emergency response devices and patrols, late-night transport/escort service, controlled dormitory access, close to 1,000 security cameras, Reverse 911 emergency telephone notification system, and Giant Voice speaker arrays. *Student services:* health clinic, personal/psychological counseling, women's center.

Athletics Member NCAA. All Division I except football (Division I-AA). *Intercollegiate sports:* baseball M(s), basketball M(s)/W(s), cross-country running M(s)/W(s), golf M(s)/W(s), soccer W(s), softball W(s), tennis M(s)/W(s), track and field M(s)/W(s), volleyball W(s). *Intramural sports:* badminton M/W, baseball M(c), basketball M/W, cross-country running M/W, fencing M(c)/W(c), football M/W, golf M/W, ice hockey M(c), lacrosse M(c), racquetball M/W, rugby M(c), soccer M/W, softball M/W, table tennis M/W, tennis M/W, track and field M/W, ultimate Frisbee M/W, volleyball M/W, weight lifting M(c)/W(c), wrestling M(c)/W(c).

Standardized Tests *Required:* SAT or ACT (for admission).

Costs (2011–12) *Tuition:* state resident $5783 full-time, $193 per hour part-time; nonresident $15,683 full-time, $506 per hour part-time. Full-time tuition and fees vary according to course level, course load, and degree level. Part-time tuition and fees vary according to course level, course load, and degree level. *Required fees:* $2500 full-time. *Room and board:* $9271; room only: $5796. Room and board charges vary according to board plan and housing

facility. *Payment plans:* installment, deferred payment. *Waivers:* employees or children of employees.

Financial Aid Of all full-time matriculated undergraduates who enrolled in 2010, 15,617 applied for aid, 13,395 were judged to have need, 2,380 had their need fully met. 647 Federal Work-Study jobs (averaging $1545). 119 state and other part-time jobs (averaging $2467). In 2010, 770 non-need-based awards were made. *Average percent of need met:* 55%. *Average financial aid package:* $9868. *Average need-based loan:* $4097. *Average need-based gift aid:* $6793. *Average non-need-based aid:* $1592. *Average indebtedness upon graduation:* $24,677.

Applying *Options:* electronic application. *Application fee:* $40. *Required:* high school transcript. *Recommended:* essay or personal statement, letters of recommendation. *Application deadlines:* 6/1 (freshmen), 6/1 (out-of-state freshmen), 7/1 (transfers). *Notification:* continuous (freshmen), continuous (out-of-state freshmen), continuous (transfers).

Freshman Application Contact Ms. Jennifer Ehlers, Director of Admissions, The University of Texas at San Antonio, One UTSA Circle, San Antonio, TX 78249-0617. *Phone:* 210-458-4536. *Toll-free phone:* 800-669-0919. *Fax:* 210-458-2001. *E-mail:* prospects@utsa.edu. *Web site:* http://www.utsa.edu/.

The University of Texas at Tyler

Tyler, Texas

- **State-supported** comprehensive, founded 1971, part of University of Texas System
- **Urban** 200-acre campus
- **Coed** 5,116 undergraduate students, 76% full-time, 57% women, 43% men
- **Moderately difficult** entrance level, 69% of applicants were admitted

Undergraduates 3,900 full-time, 1,216 part-time. 2% are from out of state; 9% Black or African American, non-Hispanic/Latino; 12% Hispanic/Latino; 2% Asian, non-Hispanic/Latino; 0.2% Native Hawaiian or other Pacific Islander, non-Hispanic/Latino; 0.5% American Indian or Alaska Native, non-Hispanic/Latino; 7% Two or more races, non-Hispanic/Latino; 2% Race/ethnicity unknown; 0.6% international; 16% transferred in; 14% live on campus. *Retention:* 64% of full-time freshmen returned.

Freshmen *Admission:* 1,839 applied, 1,270 admitted, 651 enrolled. *Average high school GPA:* 3.4. *Test scores:* SAT critical reading scores over 500: 61%; SAT math scores over 500: 73%; ACT scores over 18: 96%; SAT critical reading scores over 600: 19%; SAT math scores over 600: 22%; ACT scores over 24: 41%; SAT critical reading scores over 700: 2%; SAT math scores over 700: 2%; ACT scores over 30: 4%.

Faculty *Total:* 380, 71% full-time, 60% with terminal degrees. *Student/faculty ratio:* 17:1.

Academics *Calendar:* semesters. *Degrees:* bachelor's, master's, doctoral, postbachelor's, and first professional certificates. *Special study options:* adult/continuing education programs, part-time degree program.

Computers on Campus Students can access the following: computer help desk, free student e-mail accounts, online (class) grades, online (class) registration, online (class) schedules. Campuswide network is available. 100% of college-owned or -operated housing units are wired for high-speed Internet access. Wireless service is available via classrooms, computer centers, computer labs, learning centers, libraries, student centers.

Student Life *Housing:* on-campus residence required for freshman year. *Options:* coed. Campus housing is university owned and is provided by a third party. Freshman applicants given priority for college housing. *Campus security:* 24-hour emergency response devices and patrols, late-night transport/escort service, controlled dormitory access.

Athletics Member NCAA. All Division III. *Intercollegiate sports:* baseball M, basketball M/W, cheerleading M/W, cross-country running M/W, golf M/W, soccer M/W, tennis M/W, track and field M/W, volleyball W. *Intramural sports:* baseball M, basketball M/W, bowling M/W, football M/W, golf M/W, racquetball M/W, soccer M/W, softball M/W, swimming and diving M/W, table tennis M/W, tennis M/W, ultimate Frisbee M/W, volleyball W, wrestling M.

Standardized Tests *Required:* SAT or ACT (for admission).

Costs (2011–12) *Tuition:* state resident $5190 full-time, $50 per semester hour part-time; nonresident $14,580 full-time, $363 per semester hour part-time. Full-time tuition and fees vary according to course load. Part-time tuition and fees vary according to course load. *Required fees:* $1402 full-time. *Room and board:* $8527; room only: $5345. Room and board charges vary according to board plan and housing facility. *Payment plan:* installment. *Waivers:* senior citizens and employees or children of employees.

Financial Aid Of all full-time matriculated undergraduates who enrolled in 2009, 2,674 applied for aid, 2,276 were judged to have need, 235 had their need fully met. In 2009, 255 non-need-based awards were made. *Average per-*

cent of need met: 57%. *Average financial aid package:* $8346. *Average need-based loan:* $6109. *Average need-based gift aid:* $6398. *Average non-need-based aid:* $2272. *Average indebtedness upon graduation:* $18,605.

Applying *Options:* electronic application, deferred entrance. *Application fee:* $40. *Required:* high school transcript. *Application deadlines:* 8/20 (freshmen), rolling (transfers). *Notification:* continuous (freshmen), continuous (transfers).

Freshman Application Contact Ms. Sarah Bowdin, Director of Admissions, The University of Texas at Tyler, 3900 University Boulevard, Tyler, TX 75799-0001. *Phone:* 903-566-7057. *Toll-free phone:* 800-UTTYLER. *Fax:* 903-566-7068. *E-mail:* admissions@uttyler.edu. *Web site:* http://www.uttyler.edu/.

The University of Texas Health Science Center at Houston

Houston, Texas

- **State-supported** upper-level, founded 1972, part of University of Texas System
- **Urban** campus with easy access to Houston
- **Coed** 594 undergraduate students, 86% full-time, 85% women, 15% men
- **Moderately difficult** entrance level

Undergraduates 511 full-time, 83 part-time. 10% Black or African American, non-Hispanic/Latino; 12% Hispanic/Latino; 14% Asian, non-Hispanic/Latino; 0.3% Native Hawaiian or other Pacific Islander, non-Hispanic/Latino; 0.2% American Indian or Alaska Native, non-Hispanic/Latino; 13% Race/ethnicity unknown.

Faculty *Total:* 103, 61% full-time, 100% with terminal degrees. *Student/faculty ratio:* 6:1.

Academics *Calendar:* semesters. *Degrees:* certificates, bachelor's, master's, doctoral, post-master's, postbachelor's, and first professional certificates. *Special study options:* accelerated degree program, distance learning, independent study, internships, part-time degree program, summer session for credit. *ROTC:* Army (c).

Computers on Campus Students can access the following: online (class) registration. Campuswide network is available.

Student Life *Housing:* college housing not available. *Activities and organizations:* student-run newspaper, Student Inter-council (SIC), School of Nursing Student Government Organization (School of Nursing), Student Council (Dental Branch), Student Senate (Medical School), SPH Student Association (School of Public Health). *Campus security:* 24-hour emergency response devices and patrols, late-night transport/escort service, controlled access to all buildings. *Student services:* health clinic, personal/psychological counseling.

Standardized Tests *Required:* HESI A2-Nursing Entrance Test for BSN programs (for admission).

Financial Aid Of all full-time matriculated undergraduates who enrolled in 2010, 284 applied for aid, 254 were judged to have need, 73 had their need fully met. In 2010, 9 non-need-based awards were made. *Average percent of need met:* 77%. *Average financial aid package:* $10,410. *Average need-based loan:* $6680. *Average need-based gift aid:* $5591. *Average non-need-based aid:* $6401.

Applying *Options:* electronic application. *Application fee:* $30. *Application deadline:* 9/1 (transfers). *Notification:* 12/1 (transfers).

Application Contact The University of Texas Health Science Center at Houston, PO Box 20036, Houston, TX 77225-0036. *Phone:* 713-500-3361. *Web site:* http://www.uthouston.edu/.

The University of Texas Health Science Center at San Antonio

San Antonio, Texas

Application Contact The University of Texas Health Science Center at San Antonio, 7703 Floyd Curl Drive, San Antonio, TX 78229-3900. *Phone:* 210-567-2659. *Web site:* http://www.uthscsa.edu/.

The University of Texas Medical Branch

Galveston, Texas

Freshman Application Contact The University of Texas Medical Branch, 301 University Boulevard, Galveston, TX 77555. *Phone:* 409-772-1215. *Web site:* http://www.utmb.edu/.

The University of Texas of the Permian Basin

Odessa, Texas

- **State-supported** comprehensive, founded 1969, part of University of Texas System
- **Urban** 600-acre campus
- **Endowment** $18.5 million
- **Coed** 3,094 undergraduate students, 66% full-time, 60% women, 40% men
- **Moderately difficult** entrance level, 82% of applicants were admitted

Undergraduates 2,027 full-time, 1,067 part-time. Students come from 27 states and territories; 11 other countries; 3% are from out of state; 5% Black or African American, non-Hispanic/Latino; 43% Hispanic/Latino; 2% Asian, non-Hispanic/Latino; 0.2% Native Hawaiian or other Pacific Islander, non-Hispanic/Latino; 0.9% American Indian or Alaska Native, non-Hispanic/Latino; 1% Two or more races, non-Hispanic/Latino; 0.4% Race/ethnicity unknown; 0.2% international; 16% transferred in; 15% live on campus. *Retention:* 59% of full-time freshmen returned.

Freshmen *Admission:* 954 applied, 781 admitted, 339 enrolled. *Test scores:* SAT math scores over 500: 58%; ACT scores over 18: 92%; SAT math scores over 600: 11%; ACT scores over 24: 20%; ACT scores over 30: 3%.

Faculty *Total:* 182, 65% full-time, 64% with terminal degrees. *Student/faculty ratio:* 19:1.

Academics *Calendar:* semesters. *Degrees:* bachelor's and master's. *Special study options:* academic remediation for entering students, accelerated degree program, advanced placement credit, distance learning, double majors, English as a second language, honors programs, independent study, internships, part-time degree program, services for LD students, study abroad, summer session for credit.

Computers on Campus 170 computers/terminals are available on campus for general student use. Students can access the following: campus intranet, computer help desk, free student e-mail accounts, online (class) grades, online (class) registration, online (class) schedules. Campuswide network is available. 100% of college-owned or -operated housing units are wired for high-speed Internet access. Wireless service is available via entire campus.

Student Life *Housing options:* coed. Campus housing is university owned. *Activities and organizations:* drama/theater group, student-run newspaper, choral group, Baptist Student ministries, Kappa Delta Rho, Catholic Student Association, National Society of Leadership and Success (NSLS), Coalition of Gamers (Formerly the Gamers club), national fraternities. *Campus security:* 24-hour patrols, late-night transport/escort service. *Student services:* health clinic, personal/psychological counseling.

Athletics Member NCAA. All Division II. *Intercollegiate sports:* baseball M(s), basketball M(s)/W(s), cheerleading M(s)/W(s), cross-country running M(s)/W(s), soccer M(s)/W(s), softball W(s), swimming and diving M(s)/W(s), tennis M/W, volleyball W(s). *Intramural sports:* basketball M/W, racquetball M/W, ultimate Frisbee M(c)/W(c), volleyball M/W, water polo M/W.

Standardized Tests *Required:* SAT or ACT (for admission).

Costs (2011–12) *Tuition:* state resident $4778 full-time, $159 per credit hour part-time; nonresident $14,168 full-time, $472 per credit hour part-time. Full-time tuition and fees vary according to course load and location. Part-time tuition and fees vary according to course load and location. *Required fees:* $1524 full-time, $51 per credit hour part-time. *Room and board:* $6970; room only: $3886. Room and board charges vary according to board plan and housing facility. *Payment plan:* installment. *Waivers:* senior citizens and employees or children of employees.

Financial Aid Of all full-time matriculated undergraduates who enrolled in 2010, 1,592 applied for aid, 1,411 were judged to have need, 75 had their need fully met. 44 Federal Work-Study jobs (averaging $1718). 30 state and other part-time jobs (averaging $7550). In 2010, 374 non-need-based awards were made. *Average percent of need met:* 47%. *Average financial aid package:* $8452. *Average need-based loan:* $3727. *Average need-based gift aid:* $5322. *Average non-need-based aid:* $2995. *Average indebtedness upon graduation:* $15,796.

Applying *Options:* electronic application, early admission, deferred entrance. *Required:* high school transcript. *Application deadlines:* 7/14 (freshmen), rolling (transfers). *Notification:* continuous (freshmen), continuous (transfers).

Freshman Application Contact The University of Texas of the Permian Basin, 4901 East University Boulevard, Odessa, TX 79762-0001. *Phone:* 432-552-2605. *Toll-free phone:* 866-552-UTPB. *Web site:* http://www.utpb.edu/.

The University of Texas–Pan American

Edinburg, Texas

- **State-supported** comprehensive, founded 1927, part of University of Texas System
- **Small-town** 329-acre campus with easy access to McAllen-Edinburg-Mission MSA
- **Endowment** $58.9 million
- **Coed** 16,630 undergraduate students, 73% full-time, 56% women, 44% men
- **Noncompetitive** entrance level, 68% of applicants were admitted

Undergraduates 12,091 full-time, 4,539 part-time. Students come from 35 states and territories; 52 other countries; 0.5% are from out of state; 0.6% Black or African American, non-Hispanic/Latino; 90% Hispanic/Latino; 0.8% Asian, non-Hispanic/Latino; 0.1% American Indian or Alaska Native, non-Hispanic/Latino; 0.3% Two or more races, non-Hispanic/Latino; 2% Race/ethnicity unknown; 2% international; 7% transferred in; 5% live on campus. *Retention:* 74% of full-time freshmen returned.

Freshmen *Admission:* 8,778 applied, 6,004 admitted, 3,146 enrolled. *Test scores:* SAT critical reading scores over 500: 34%; SAT math scores over 500: 49%; SAT writing scores over 500: 28%; ACT scores over 18: 78%; SAT critical reading scores over 600: 7%; SAT math scores over 600: 13%; SAT writing scores over 600: 5%; ACT scores over 24: 12%; SAT critical reading scores over 700: 1%; SAT math scores over 700: 1%; SAT writing scores over 700: 1%; ACT scores over 30: 1%.

Faculty *Total:* 761, 83% full-time, 76% with terminal degrees. *Student/faculty ratio:* 22:1.

Academics *Calendar:* semesters. *Degrees:* bachelor's, master's, doctoral, and first professional. *Special study options:* academic remediation for entering students, accelerated degree program, adult/continuing education programs, advanced placement credit, cooperative education, distance learning, double majors, English as a second language, honors programs, independent study, internships, part-time degree program, services for LD students, study abroad, summer session for credit. *ROTC:* Army (b). *Unusual degree programs:* accounting.

Computers on Campus Students can access the following: campus intranet, computer help desk, free student e-mail accounts, online (class) grades, online (class) registration, online (class) schedules. Campuswide network is available. Wireless service is available via entire campus.

Student Life *Housing options:* coed, men-only, women-only. Campus housing is university owned. *Activities and organizations:* drama/theater group, student-run newspaper, choral group, national fraternities, national sororities. *Campus security:* 24-hour emergency response devices and patrols, late-night transport/escort service. *Student services:* health clinic, personal/psychological counseling.

Athletics Member NCAA. All Division I. *Intercollegiate sports:* baseball M(s), basketball M(s)/W(s), cross-country running M(s)/W(s), golf M(s)/W(s), tennis M(s)/W(s), track and field M(s)/W(s), volleyball W(s). *Intramural sports:* badminton M/W, basketball M/W, bowling M/W, cheerleading M/W, football M/W, racquetball M/W, soccer M/W, softball M/W, tennis M/W, volleyball M/W.

Standardized Tests *Required:* SAT or ACT (for admission).

Costs (2011–12) *Tuition:* state resident $3969 full-time, $165 per credit hour part-time; nonresident $11,481 full-time, $478 per credit hour part-time. Full-time tuition and fees vary according to course load and degree level. Part-time tuition and fees vary according to course load and degree level. *Required fees:* $1065 full-time, $44 per credit hour part-time. *Room and board:* $5614; room only: $3400. Room and board charges vary according to board plan and housing facility. *Payment plan:* installment. *Waivers:* senior citizens.

Financial Aid Of all full-time matriculated undergraduates who enrolled in 2010, 10,168 applied for aid, 9,841 were judged to have need, 588 had their need fully met. 814 Federal Work-Study jobs (averaging $2259). 306 state and other part-time jobs (averaging $1751). In 2010, 281 non-need-based awards were made. *Average percent of need met:* 72%. *Average financial aid package:* $10,690. *Average need-based loan:* $4630. *Average need-based gift aid:* $11,454. *Average non-need-based aid:* $3533. *Average indebtedness upon graduation:* $14,748.

Applying *Options:* electronic application. *Required:* high school transcript, minimum 2.0 GPA. *Required for some:* interview. *Application deadlines:* 8/11 (freshmen), 8/11 (transfers). *Notification:* continuous (freshmen), continuous (transfers).

Freshman Application Contact Dr. Magdalena Hinojosa, Dean of Admissions and Enrollment Services, The University of Texas–Pan American, Office of Admissions and Records, 1201 West University Drive, Edinburg, TX 78539. *Phone:* 956-665-2999. *Fax:* 956-665-2212. *E-mail:* admissions@utpa.edu. *Web site:* http://www.utpa.edu/.

University of the Incarnate Word
San Antonio, Texas

- **Independent Roman Catholic** comprehensive, founded 1881
- **Urban** 200-acre campus with easy access to San Antonio
- **Endowment** $72.6 million
- **Coed** 5,971 undergraduate students, 69% full-time, 63% women, 37% men
- **Moderately difficult** entrance level, 95% of applicants were admitted

Undergraduates 4,099 full-time, 1,872 part-time. Students come from 45 states and territories; 41 other countries; 10% are from out of state; 7% Black or African American, non-Hispanic/Latino; 58% Hispanic/Latino; 2% Asian, non-Hispanic/Latino; 0.1% Native Hawaiian or other Pacific Islander, non-Hispanic/Latino; 0.5% American Indian or Alaska Native, non-Hispanic/Latino; 0.6% Two or more races, non-Hispanic/Latino; 8% Race/ethnicity unknown; 3% international; 11% transferred in; 21% live on campus. *Retention:* 78% of full-time freshmen returned.

Freshmen *Admission:* 3,595 applied, 3,401 admitted, 1,050 enrolled. *Average high school GPA:* 3.49. *Test scores:* SAT critical reading scores over 500: 40%; SAT math scores over 500: 49%; SAT writing scores over 500: 36%; ACT scores over 18: 74%; SAT critical reading scores over 600: 8%; SAT math scores over 600: 9%; SAT writing scores over 600: 5%; ACT scores over 24: 22%; ACT scores over 30: 1%.

Faculty *Total:* 499, 52% full-time, 57% with terminal degrees. *Student/faculty ratio:* 14:1.

Academics *Calendar:* semesters. *Degrees:* diplomas, associate, bachelor's, master's, doctoral, and first professional. *Special study options:* academic remediation for entering students, accelerated degree program, adult/continuing education programs, advanced placement credit, cooperative education, distance learning, double majors, English as a second language, freshman honors college, honors programs, independent study, internships, off-campus study, part-time degree program, services for LD students, study abroad, summer session for credit. *ROTC:* Army (c), Air Force (c). *Unusual degree programs:* 3-2 business administration; communications and accounting.

Computers on Campus 185 computers/terminals are available on campus for general student use. Students can access the following: computer help desk, free student e-mail accounts, online (class) grades, online (class) registration, online (class) schedules, Ports available in general use area and other locations. Also dedicated computers for graduate/doctoral students. Campuswide network is available. 100% of college-owned or -operated housing units are wired for high-speed Internet access. Wireless service is available via entire campus.

Student Life *Housing options:* coed, men-only, women-only, disabled students. Campus housing is university owned. Freshman campus housing is guaranteed. *Activities and organizations:* drama/theater group, student-run newspaper, radio and television station, choral group, marching band, Society of Leadership and Success, Pre-Pharmacy Association, Alpha Sigma Alpha, Lambda Chi Alpha, Student Government Association House, national fraternities, national sororities. *Campus security:* 24-hour emergency response devices and patrols, late-night transport/escort service, controlled dormitory access. *Student services:* health clinic, personal/psychological counseling.

Athletics Member NCAA. All Division II. *Intercollegiate sports:* baseball M(s), basketball M(s)/W(s), cross-country running M(s)/W(s), football M(s), golf M(s)/W(s), soccer M(s)/W(s), softball W(s), swimming and diving M(s)/W(s), tennis M(s)/W(s), track and field M(s)/W(s), volleyball W(s). *Intramural sports:* basketball M/W, cheerleading M/W, football M/W, racquetball M/W, soccer M/W, softball M/W, tennis M/W, ultimate Frisbee M/W, volleyball M/W, water polo M/W.

Standardized Tests *Required:* SAT or ACT (for admission).

Costs (2011–12) *Comprehensive fee:* $32,448 includes full-time tuition ($21,900), mandatory fees ($890), and room and board ($9658). Full-time tuition and fees vary according to course load, degree level, location, program, and reciprocity agreements. Part-time tuition: $725 per hour. Part-time tuition and fees vary according to course load, degree level, location, program, and reciprocity agreements. *College room only:* $5760. Room and board charges vary according to board plan and housing facility. *Payment plan:* installment. *Waivers:* senior citizens and employees or children of employees.

Financial Aid Of all full-time matriculated undergraduates who enrolled in 2010, 3,087 applied for aid, 2,892 were judged to have need, 902 had their need fully met. In 2010, 184 non-need-based awards were made. *Average percent of need met:* 66%. *Average financial aid package:* $17,425. *Average need-based loan:* $4311. *Average need-based gift aid:* $12,986. *Average non-need-based aid:* $7451.

Applying *Options:* electronic application, deferred entrance. *Application fee:* $20. *Required:* high school transcript. *Required for some:* essay or personal statement, interview. *Recommended:* minimum 2.0 GPA, letter(s) of recommendation recommended for all, required for some. *Application deadlines:* rolling (freshmen), rolling (out-of-state freshmen), rolling (transfers). *Notifi-*

cation: continuous (freshmen), continuous (out-of-state freshmen), continuous (transfers).

Freshman Application Contact Ms. Heather M. Rodriguez, Director of Undergraduate Admissions, University of the Incarnate Word, 4301 Broadway Avenue, University of the Incarnate Word, San Antonio, TN 78209. *Phone:* 210-829-6005. *Toll-free phone:* 800-749-WORD. *Fax:* 210-829-3921. *E-mail:* hrodrig1@uiwtx.edu. *Web site:* http://www.uiw.edu/.

Wade College
Dallas, Texas

- **Proprietary** primarily 2-year, founded 1965
- **Urban** 175-acre campus
- **Coed, primarily women**
- **Minimally difficult** entrance level

Faculty *Student/faculty ratio:* 15:1.

Academics *Calendar:* trimesters. *Degrees:* associate and bachelor's.

Student Life *Campus security:* 24-hour emergency response devices and patrols, late-night transport/escort service, controlled dormitory access.

Applying *Options:* electronic application. *Required:* high school transcript, interview.

Freshman Application Contact Wade College, INFOMart, 1950 Stemmons Freeway, Suite 4080, LB 562, Dallas, TX 75207. *Phone:* 214-637-3530. *Toll-free phone:* 800-624-4850. *Web site:* http://www.wadecollege.edu/.

Wayland Baptist University
Plainview, Texas

- **Independent Baptist** comprehensive, founded 1908
- **Small-town** 80-acre campus
- **Endowment** $58.4 million
- **Coed** 1,341 undergraduate students, 73% full-time, 46% women, 54% men
- **Minimally difficult** entrance level, 99% of applicants were admitted

Undergraduates 985 full-time, 356 part-time. Students come from 39 states and territories; 15 other countries; 16% are from out of state; 13% Black or African American, non-Hispanic/Latino; 28% Hispanic/Latino; 0.6% Asian, non-Hispanic/Latino; 0.2% Native Hawaiian or other Pacific Islander, non-Hispanic/Latino; 0.9% American Indian or Alaska Native, non-Hispanic/Latino; 2% Two or more races, non-Hispanic/Latino; 5% Race/ethnicity unknown; 3% international; 10% transferred in; 51% live on campus. *Retention:* 53% of full-time freshmen returned.

Freshmen *Admission:* 563 applied, 556 admitted, 357 enrolled. *Average high school GPA:* 3.3. *Test scores:* SAT critical reading scores over 500: 22%; SAT math scores over 500: 27%; SAT writing scores over 500: 18%; ACT scores over 18: 64%; SAT critical reading scores over 600: 4%; SAT math scores over 600: 7%; SAT writing scores over 600: 5%; ACT scores over 24: 16%; SAT critical reading scores over 700: 1%; SAT math scores over 700: 1%; SAT writing scores over 700: 1%; ACT scores over 30: 1%.

Faculty *Total:* 145, 62% full-time, 54% with terminal degrees. *Student/faculty ratio:* 10:1.

Academics *Calendar:* semesters. *Degrees:* associate, bachelor's, and master's (branch locations in Anchorage, AK; Amarillo, TX; Luke Air Force Base, AZ; Glorieta, NM; Aiea, HI; Lubbock, TX; San Antonio, TX; Wichita Falls, TX). *Special study options:* academic remediation for entering students, accelerated degree program, adult/continuing education programs, advanced placement credit, distance learning, double majors, external degree program, honors programs, part-time degree program, services for LD students, study abroad, summer session for credit. *ROTC:* Army (c), Air Force (c). *Unusual degree programs:* 3-2 engineering with Texas Tech University.

Computers on Campus 231 computers/terminals are available on campus for general student use. Students can access the following: computer help desk, free student e-mail accounts, online (class) grades, online (class) registration, online (class) schedules. Campuswide network is available. 100% of college-owned or -operated housing units are wired for high-speed Internet access. Wireless service is available via classrooms, computer labs, dorm rooms, libraries, student centers.

Student Life *Housing:* on-campus residence required through junior year. *Options:* men-only, women-only. Campus housing is university owned. Freshman campus housing is guaranteed. *Activities and organizations:* drama/theater group, student-run newspaper, radio and television station, choral group, marching band, student government, national fraternities, national sororities. *Campus security:* 24-hour emergency response devices and patrols, security lighting, campus police department. *Student services:* health clinic, personal/psychological counseling.

Athletics Member NAIA. *Intercollegiate sports:* baseball M(s), basketball M(s)/W(s), cheerleading M(s)/W(s), cross-country running M(s)/W(s), football M(s), golf M(s)/W(s), soccer M(s)/W(s), track and field M(s)/W(s), vol-

leyball W(s), wrestling M(s)/W(s). *Intramural sports:* basketball M/W, football M/W, soccer M/W, softball M/W, table tennis M/W, volleyball M/W.

Standardized Tests *Required:* SAT or ACT (for admission).

Costs (2012–13) *Tuition:* $13,650 full-time, $455 per credit hour part-time. Full-time tuition and fees vary according to course load and location. Part-time tuition and fees vary according to course load and location. *Required fees:* $980 full-time. *Room only:* Room and board charges vary according to board plan and housing facility. *Payment plan:* installment. *Waivers:* employees or children of employees.

Financial Aid Of all full-time matriculated undergraduates who enrolled in 2010, 719 applied for aid, 626 were judged to have need, 94 had their need fully met. 169 Federal Work-Study jobs (averaging $1582). 318 state and other part-time jobs (averaging $1969). In 2010, 143 non-need-based awards were made. *Average percent of need met:* 70%. *Average financial aid package:* $12,015. *Average need-based loan:* $3517. *Average need-based gift aid:* $9120. *Average non-need-based aid:* $8128. *Average indebtedness upon graduation:* $26,959.

Applying *Options:* electronic application. *Application fee:* $35. *Required:* high school transcript. *Required for some:* interview. *Application deadlines:* 8/1 (freshmen), rolling (transfers). *Notification:* continuous (freshmen), continuous (transfers).

Freshman Application Contact Ms. Debbie Stennett, Director of Student Admissions, Wayland Baptist University, 1900 West 7th Street, CMB 712, Plainview, TX 79072. *Phone:* 806-291-3500. *Toll-free phone:* 800-588-1928. *Fax:* 806-291-1973. *E-mail:* admityou@wbu.edu. *Web site:* http://www.wbu.edu/.

West Texas A&M University

Canyon, Texas

- **State-supported** comprehensive, founded 1909, part of Texas A&M University System
- **Small-town** 128-acre campus
- **Endowment** $45.7 million
- **Coed** 6,498 undergraduate students, 80% full-time, 54% women, 46% men
- **Moderately difficult** entrance level, 69% of applicants were admitted

Undergraduates 5,181 full-time, 1,317 part-time. Students come from 50 states and territories; 34 other countries; 9% are from out of state; 5% Black or African American, non-Hispanic/Latino; 22% Hispanic/Latino; 1% Asian, non-Hispanic/Latino; 0.1% Native Hawaiian or other Pacific Islander, non-Hispanic/Latino; 0.7% American Indian or Alaska Native, non-Hispanic/Latino; 1% Two or more races, non-Hispanic/Latino; 1% Race/ethnicity unknown; 1% international; 13% transferred in; 19% live on campus. *Retention:* 65% of full-time freshmen returned.

Freshmen *Admission:* 4,096 applied, 2,833 admitted, 1,214 enrolled. *Test scores:* SAT critical reading scores over 500: 41%; SAT math scores over 500: 47%; ACT scores over 18: 82%; SAT critical reading scores over 600: 9%; SAT math scores over 600: 11%; ACT scores over 24: 25%; SAT critical reading scores over 700: 1%; SAT math scores over 700: 1%; ACT scores over 30: 2%.

Faculty *Total:* 367, 69% full-time, 58% with terminal degrees. *Student/faculty ratio:* 22:1.

Academics *Calendar:* semesters. *Degrees:* bachelor's, master's, doctoral, and first professional. *Special study options:* academic remediation for entering students, adult/continuing education programs, advanced placement credit, cooperative education, distance learning, double majors, English as a second language, honors programs, independent study, internships, part-time degree program, services for LD students, study abroad, summer session for credit. *Unusual degree programs:* 3-2 engineering with Texas Tech University, Texas A&M University.

Computers on Campus 1,200 computers/terminals are available on campus for general student use. Students can access the following: free student e-mail accounts, online (class) registration. Campuswide network is available. Wireless service is available via entire campus.

Student Life *Housing:* on-campus residence required through sophomore year. *Options:* coed, men-only, women-only, disabled students. Campus housing is university owned. Freshman campus housing is guaranteed. *Activities and organizations:* drama/theater group, student-run newspaper, radio station, choral group, marching band, Residence Hall Association, Student Organizations' Roundtable, Student Government, Students in Free Enterprise (SIFE), national fraternities, national sororities. *Campus security:* 24-hour emergency response devices and patrols, late-night transport/escort service, controlled dormitory access. *Student services:* health clinic, personal/psychological counseling.

Athletics Member NCAA. All Division II. *Intercollegiate sports:* baseball M(s), basketball M(s)/W(s), bowling M(s)(c)/W(s)(c), cross-country running

M(s)/W(s), equestrian sports M(c)/W(s), football M(s), golf M(s)/W(s), soccer M(s)/W(s), softball W(s), volleyball W(s). *Intramural sports:* badminton M/W, basketball M/W, bowling M/W, football M/W, golf M/W, racquetball M/W, soccer M/W, softball M/W, swimming and diving M/W, table tennis M/W, tennis M/W, volleyball M/W, wrestling M.

Standardized Tests *Required:* SAT or ACT (for admission).

Costs (2012–13) *Tuition:* state resident $4730 full-time, $165 per credit hour part-time; nonresident $5630 full-time, $195 per credit hour part-time. Full-time tuition and fees vary according to course load. Part-time tuition and fees vary according to course load. *Required fees:* $2060 full-time, $66 per credit hour part-time, $182 per credit hour part-time. *Room and board:* $5000. Room and board charges vary according to board plan and housing facility. *Payment plan:* installment. *Waivers:* employees or children of employees.

Financial Aid Of all full-time matriculated undergraduates who enrolled in 2010, 3,848 applied for aid, 3,339 were judged to have need, 180 had their need fully met. 216 Federal Work-Study jobs (averaging $2291). 29 state and other part-time jobs (averaging $1584). In 2010, 220 non-need-based awards were made. *Average percent of need met:* 55%. *Average financial aid package:* $8535. *Average need-based loan:* $4231. *Average need-based gift aid:* $6418. *Average non-need-based aid:* $3178. *Average indebtedness upon graduation:* $19,490.

Applying *Options:* electronic application, deferred entrance. *Application fee:* $25. *Required:* high school transcript, class rank and Texas high school curriculum or equivalent. *Application deadlines:* rolling (freshmen), rolling (transfers). *Notification:* continuous (freshmen), continuous (transfers).

Freshman Application Contact Mr. Shawn Thomas, Director of Admissions, West Texas A&M University, WT Box 60907, Canyon, TX 79016-0001. *Phone:* 806-651-2020. *Toll-free phone:* 800-99-WTAMU. *Fax:* 806-651-5285. *E-mail:* sthomas@mail.wtamu.edu. *Web site:* http://www.wtamu.edu/.

Westwood College–Dallas

Dallas, Texas

Freshman Application Contact Westwood College–Dallas, 8390 LBJ Freeway, Executive Center 1, Suite 100, Dallas, TX 75243. *Phone:* 214-570-9100. *Toll-free phone:* 800-331-4879. *Web site:* http://www.westwood.edu/.

Westwood College–Fort Worth

Fort Worth, Texas

Freshman Application Contact Westwood College–Fort Worth, 4232 North Freeway, Fort Worth, TX 76137. *Phone:* 817-547-9601. *Toll-free phone:* 866-533-9997. *Web site:* http://www.westwood.edu/.

Westwood College–Houston South Campus

Houston, Texas

Freshman Application Contact Westwood College–Houston South Campus, 7322 Southwest Freeway #110, Houston, TX 77074. *Phone:* 713-777-4779. *Toll-free phone:* 866-340-3677. *Web site:* http://www.westwood.edu/.

Wiley College

Marshall, Texas

Director of Admissions Ms. Alvena Jones, Interim Director of Admissions/Recruitment, Wiley College, 711 Wiley Avenue, Marshall, TX 75670-5199. *Phone:* 903-927-3222. *Toll-free phone:* 800-658-6889. *Fax:* 903-923-8878. *E-mail:* ajones@wileyc.edu. *Web site:* http://www.wileyc.edu/.

UTAH

Argosy University, Salt Lake City

Draper, Utah

Freshman Application Contact Argosy University, Salt Lake City, 121 West Election Road, Suite 300, Draper, UT 84020. *Phone:* 801-601-5000. *Toll-free phone:* 888-639-4756. *Web site:* http://www.argosy.edu/locations/salt-lake-city/.

See page 1062 for the College Close-Up.

The Art Institute of Salt Lake City
Draper, Utah

- **Proprietary** 4-year, part of Education Management Corporation
- **Coed**

Academics *Degrees:* diplomas, associate, and bachelor's.

Costs (2011–12) *Tuition:* Tuition cost varies by program. Prospective students should contact the school for current tuition costs. Other charges include a starting kit for all first-quarter students. Kits vary in price, depending on the program of study.

Freshman Application Contact The Art Institute of Salt Lake City, 121 West Election Road, Suite 100, Draper, UT 84020-9492. *Phone:* 801-601-4700. *Toll-free phone:* 800-978-0096. *Web site:* http://www.artinstitutes.edu/SaltLakeCity/.

See page 1126 for the College Close-Up.

Brigham Young University
Provo, Utah

- **Independent** university, founded 1875, affiliated with The Church of Jesus Christ of Latter-day Saints, part of Church Education System (CES) of The Church of Jesus Christ of Latter-day Saints
- **Suburban** 557-acre campus with easy access to Salt Lake City
- **Coed** 30,684 undergraduate students, 91% full-time, 49% women, 51% men
- **Moderately difficult** entrance level, 63% of applicants were admitted

Undergraduates 28,005 full-time, 2,679 part-time. 65% are from out of state; 0.3% Black or African American, non-Hispanic/Latino; 5% Hispanic/Latino; 2% Asian, non-Hispanic/Latino; 0.6% Native Hawaiian or other Pacific Islander, non-Hispanic/Latino; 0.4% American Indian or Alaska Native, non-Hispanic/Latino; 3% Two or more races, non-Hispanic/Latino; 1% Race/ethnicity unknown; 5% international; 2% transferred in; 19% live on campus. *Retention:* 87% of full-time freshmen returned.

Freshmen *Admission:* 11,238 applied, 7,055 admitted, 5,631 enrolled. *Average high school GPA:* 3.78. *Test scores:* SAT math scores over 500: 95%; SAT writing scores over 500: 91%; ACT scores over 18: 100%; SAT math scores over 600: 69%; SAT writing scores over 600: 56%; ACT scores over 24: 93%; SAT math scores over 700: 21%; SAT writing scores over 700: 13%; ACT scores over 30: 33%.

Faculty *Total:* 1,699, 72% full-time, 78% with terminal degrees. *Student/faculty ratio:* 21:1.

Academics *Calendar:* semesters. *Degrees:* bachelor's, master's, doctoral, and first professional. *Special study options:* adult/continuing education programs, external degree program, off-campus study, part-time degree program. *ROTC:* Army (b), Air Force (b).

Computers on Campus Students can access the following: campus intranet, computer help desk, online (class) grades, online (class) registration, online (class) schedules. Campuswide network is available.

Student Life *Housing options:* men-only, women-only, disabled students. Campus housing is university owned. *Campus security:* 24-hour emergency response devices and patrols, late-night transport/escort service, controlled dormitory access.

Athletics Member NCAA. All Division I except football (Division I-A). *Intercollegiate sports:* baseball M(s), basketball M(s)/W(s), cheerleading M(s)/W(s), cross-country running M(s)/W(s), golf M(s)/W(s), gymnastics W(s), lacrosse M(c), racquetball M/W, rugby M(c), soccer M(c)/W(s), softball W(s), swimming and diving M(s)/W(s), tennis M(s)/W(s), track and field M(s)/W(s), volleyball M(s)/W(s). *Intramural sports:* badminton W, basketball M/W, field hockey M, football M/W, golf M/W, racquetball M/W, soccer M/W, softball M/W, table tennis M/W, tennis M/W, ultimate Frisbee M/W, volleyball M/W, water polo M/W, wrestling M.

Standardized Tests *Required:* SAT or ACT (for admission).

Costs (2012–13) *Comprehensive fee:* $11,938 includes full-time tuition ($4710) and room and board ($7228). Part-time tuition: $242 per credit hour. Part-time tuition and fees vary according to course load. Latter Day Saints full-time student $4,710 per year, non-LDS full-time student $9,420. *Room and board:* Room and board charges vary according to board plan, housing facility, and location. *Waivers:* employees or children of employees.

Financial Aid Of all full-time matriculated undergraduates who enrolled in 2010, 16,328 applied for aid, 14,397 were judged to have need, 480 had their need fully met. In 2010, 7111 non-need-based awards were made. *Average percent of need met:* 38%. *Average financial aid package:* $7450. *Average need-based loan:* $4222. *Average need-based gift aid:* $5333. *Average non-need-based aid:* $3398. *Average indebtedness upon graduation:* $14,320.

Applying *Options:* electronic application, early admission, deferred entrance. *Application fee:* $35. *Required:* essay or personal statement, high school transcript, 1 letter of recommendation, interview. *Application deadlines:* 2/1 (freshmen), 3/1 (transfers). *Notification:* continuous (freshmen), continuous (transfers).

Freshman Application Contact Mr. Tom Gourley, Dean of Admissions and Records, Brigham Young University, A-153 Abraham Smoot Building, Provo, UT 84602. *Phone:* 801-422-2507. *Fax:* 801-422-0005. *E-mail:* admissions@byu.edu. *Web site:* http://www.byu.edu/.

Broadview University
West Jordan, Utah

- **Proprietary** comprehensive, part of Globe Education Network (GEN) which is composed of Globe University, Minnesota School of Business, Broadview University, The Institute of Production and Recording and Minnesota School of Cosmetology
- **Urban** 4-acre campus
- **Coed** 701 undergraduate students, 19% full-time, 78% women, 22% men

Undergraduates 134 full-time, 567 part-time. Students come from 4 states and territories; 0.4% are from out of state; 2% Black or African American, non-Hispanic/Latino; 7% Hispanic/Latino; 1% Asian, non-Hispanic/Latino; 1% Native Hawaiian or other Pacific Islander, non-Hispanic/Latino; 2% American Indian or Alaska Native, non-Hispanic/Latino; 2% Two or more races, non-Hispanic/Latino; 13% Race/ethnicity unknown; 14% transferred in. *Retention:* 20% of full-time freshmen returned.

Freshmen *Admission:* 110 enrolled.

Faculty *Total:* 72, 36% full-time, 53% with terminal degrees. *Student/faculty ratio:* 15:1.

Academics *Calendar:* quarters. *Degrees:* diplomas, associate, bachelor's, and master's. *Special study options:* academic remediation for entering students, accelerated degree program, adult/continuing education programs, advanced placement credit, internships, part-time degree program, services for LD students, summer session for credit.

Computers on Campus 78 computers/terminals and 160 ports are available on campus for general student use. Students can access the following: computer help desk, free student e-mail accounts, online (class) grades, online (class) registration, online (class) schedules. Campuswide network is available. Wireless service is available via entire campus.

Student Life *Housing:* college housing not available. *Campus security:* 24-hour emergency response devices, late-night transport/escort service.

Standardized Tests *Required:* AccuPlacer is required of all applicants unless documentation of a minimum ACT composite score of 21 or documentation of a minimum composite score of 1485 on the SAT is presented (for admission).

Applying *Options:* electronic application. *Application fee:* $50. *Required:* high school transcript, interview, High school transcript or GED required of all applicants. Application fee for Nursing is $100. *Required for some:* essay or personal statement, 2 letters of recommendation. *Application deadlines:* rolling (freshmen), rolling (out-of-state freshmen), rolling (transfers). *Notification:* continuous (freshmen), continuous (out-of-state freshmen), continuous (transfers).

Freshman Application Contact Broadview University, 1902 West 7800 South, West Jordan, UT 84088. *Phone:* 801-304-4224. *Toll-free phone:* 866-304-4224. *E-mail:* kcooper@utahcollege.edu. *Web site:* http://www.broadviewuniversity.edu/.

Broadview University-Layton
Layton, Utah

- **Proprietary** 4-year, part of Globe Education Network (GEN) which is composed of Globe University, Minnesota School of Business, Broadview University, The Institute of Production and Recording and Minnesota School of Cosmetology
- **Suburban** campus
- **Coed** 434 undergraduate students, 17% full-time, 77% women, 23% men

Undergraduates 74 full-time, 360 part-time. Students come from 1 other state; 3% Black or African American, non-Hispanic/Latino; 7% Hispanic/Latino; 0.9% Asian, non-Hispanic/Latino; 0.7% Native Hawaiian or other Pacific Islander, non-Hispanic/Latino; 0.7% American Indian or Alaska Native, non-Hispanic/Latino; 3% Two or more races, non-Hispanic/Latino; 14% Race/ethnicity unknown; 71% transferred in. *Retention:* 75% of full-time freshmen returned.

Freshmen *Admission:* 58 enrolled.

Faculty *Total:* 30, 23% full-time, 33% with terminal degrees. *Student/faculty ratio:* 20:1.

Academics *Degrees:* diplomas, associate, and bachelor's. *Special study options:* academic remediation for entering students, accelerated degree program, adult/continuing education programs, advanced placement credit, internships, part-time degree program, services for LD students, summer session for credit.

Computers on Campus 66 computers/terminals and 128 ports are available on campus for general student use. Students can access the following: computer help desk, free student e-mail accounts, online (class) grades, online (class) registration, online (class) schedules. Campuswide network is available. Wireless service is available via entire campus.
Student Life *Housing:* college housing not available. *Campus security:* 24-hour emergency response devices, late-night transport/escort service.
Standardized Tests *Required:* AccuPlacer is required of all applicants unless documentation of a minimum ACT composite score of 21 or documentation of a minimum composite score of 1485 on the SAT is presented (for admission).
Applying *Options:* electronic application. *Application fee:* $50. *Required:* high school transcript, interview, High school transcript or GED required of all applicants. *Required for some:* essay or personal statement, 2 letters of recommendation. *Application deadlines:* rolling (freshmen), rolling (out-of-state freshmen), rolling (transfers). *Notification:* continuous (freshmen), continuous (out-of-state freshmen), continuous (transfers).
Freshman Application Contact Broadview University-Layton, 869 West Hill Field Road, Layton, UT 84041. *Phone:* 801-666-6000. *Toll-free phone:* 866-253-7744. *Web site:* http://www.broadviewuniversity.edu/.

Broadview University-Orem

Orem, Utah

- **Proprietary** 4-year, part of Globe Education Network (GEN) which is composed of Globe University, Minnesota School of Business, Broadview University, The Institute of Production and Recording and Minnesota School of Cosmetology
- **Small-town** 3-acre campus
- **Coed** 285 undergraduate students, 28% full-time, 72% women, 28% men

Undergraduates 81 full-time, 204 part-time. Students come from 2 states and territories; 0.4% are from out of state; 0.7% Black or African American, non-Hispanic/Latino; 8% Hispanic/Latino; 0.7% Asian, non-Hispanic/Latino; 0.4% Native Hawaiian or other Pacific Islander, non-Hispanic/Latino; 0.7% American Indian or Alaska Native, non-Hispanic/Latino; 2% Two or more races, non-Hispanic/Latino; 5% Race/ethnicity unknown; 19% transferred in. *Retention:* 25% of full-time freshmen returned.
Freshmen *Admission:* 59 enrolled.
Faculty *Total:* 25, 44% full-time, 16% with terminal degrees. *Student/faculty ratio:* 17:1.
Academics *Degrees:* diplomas, associate, and bachelor's. *Special study options:* academic remediation for entering students, accelerated degree program, adult/continuing education programs, advanced placement credit, internships, part-time degree program, services for LD students, summer session for credit.
Computers on Campus 47 computers/terminals and 96 ports are available on campus for general student use. Students can access the following: computer help desk, free student e-mail accounts, online (class) grades, online (class) registration, online (class) schedules. Campuswide network is available. Wireless service is available via entire campus.
Student Life *Housing:* college housing not available. *Campus security:* 24-hour emergency response devices, late-night transport/escort service.
Standardized Tests *Required:* AccuPlacer is required of all applicants unless documentation of a minimum ACT composite score of 21 or documentation of a minimum composite score of 1485 on the SAT is presented (for admission).
Applying *Options:* electronic application. *Application fee:* $50. *Required:* high school transcript, interview, High school transcript or GED required of all applicants. *Required for some:* essay or personal statement, 2 letters of recommendation. *Application deadlines:* rolling (freshmen), rolling (out-of-state freshmen), rolling (transfers). *Notification:* continuous (freshmen), continuous (out-of-state freshmen), continuous (transfers).
Freshman Application Contact Broadview University-Orem, 898 North 1200 West, Orem, UT 84057. *Toll-free phone:* 877-822-5838. *Web site:* http://www.broadviewuniversity.edu/.

Broadview University-Salt Lake City

Salt Lake City, Utah

- **Proprietary** 4-year, part of Globe Education Network (GEN) which is composed of Globe University, Minnesota School of Business, Broadview University, The Institute of Production and Recording and Minnesota School of Cosmetology
- **Urban** 3-acre campus
- **Coed** 34 undergraduate students, 35% full-time, 35% women, 65% men

Undergraduates 12 full-time, 22 part-time. Students come from 1 other state; 3% Black or African American, non-Hispanic/Latino; 21% Hispanic/Latino; 12% Asian, non-Hispanic/Latino; 9% Two or more races, non-Hispanic/Latino; 3% Race/ethnicity unknown; 29% transferred in.
Freshmen *Admission:* 16 enrolled.

Faculty *Total:* 8, 63% full-time, 25% with terminal degrees. *Student/faculty ratio:* 9:1.
Academics *Degrees:* associate and bachelor's. *Special study options:* academic remediation for entering students, accelerated degree program, adult/continuing education programs, advanced placement credit, internships, part-time degree program, services for LD students, summer session for credit.
Computers on Campus 43 computers/terminals and 251 ports are available on campus for general student use. Students can access the following: computer help desk, free student e-mail accounts, online (class) grades, online (class) registration, online (class) schedules. Campuswide network is available. Wireless service is available via entire campus.
Student Life *Housing:* college housing not available. *Campus security:* 24-hour emergency response devices, late-night transport/escort service.
Standardized Tests *Required:* AccuPlacer is required of all applicants unless documentation of a minimum ACT composite score of 21 or documentation of a minimum composite score of 1485 on the SAT is presented (for admission).
Applying *Options:* electronic application. *Application fee:* $50. *Required:* high school transcript, interview. *Required for some:* essay or personal statement, 2 letters of recommendation, GED certificate in lieu of high school transcript. *Application deadlines:* rolling (freshmen), rolling (out-of-state freshmen), rolling (transfers). *Notification:* continuous (freshmen), continuous (out-of-state freshmen), continuous (transfers).
Freshman Application Contact Broadview University-Salt Lake City, 240 East Morris Avenue, Salt Lake City, UT 84115. *Toll-free phone:* 877-801-8889. *Web site:* http://www.broadviewuniversity.edu/.

DeVry University

Sandy, Utah

Freshman Application Contact DeVry University, 9350 South 150 E, Suite 420, Sandy, UT 84070. *Toll-free phone:* 866-338-7941. *Web site:* http://www.devry.edu/.

Dixie State College of Utah

St. George, Utah

- **State-supported** 4-year, founded 1911, part of Utah System of Higher Education
- **Small-town** 117-acre campus
- **Endowment** $13.5 million
- **Coed** 9,044 undergraduate students, 61% full-time, 53% women, 47% men
- **Noncompetitive** entrance level, 63% of applicants were admitted

Undergraduates 5,473 full-time, 3,571 part-time. Students come from 51 states and territories; 19 other countries; 14% are from out of state; 2% Black or African American, non-Hispanic/Latino; 7% Hispanic/Latino; 0.7% Asian, non-Hispanic/Latino; 2% Native Hawaiian or other Pacific Islander, non-Hispanic/Latino; 1% American Indian or Alaska Native, non-Hispanic/Latino; 1% Two or more races, non-Hispanic/Latino; 2% Race/ethnicity unknown; 0.9% international; 6% transferred in; 3% live on campus. *Retention:* 57% of full-time freshmen returned.
Freshmen *Admission:* 4,894 applied, 3,088 admitted, 1,957 enrolled. *Average high school GPA:* 3.15. *Test scores:* SAT math scores over 500: 26%; ACT scores over 18: 77%; SAT math scores over 600: 6%; ACT scores over 24: 24%; SAT math scores over 700: 1%; ACT scores over 30: 1%.
Academics *Calendar:* semesters. *Degrees:* certificates, diplomas, associate, and bachelor's. *Special study options:* academic remediation for entering students, accelerated degree program, adult/continuing education programs, advanced placement credit, cooperative education, distance learning, double majors, English as a second language, honors programs, independent study, internships, off-campus study, part-time degree program, services for LD students, student-designed majors, study abroad, summer session for credit. *ROTC:* Army (b).
Computers on Campus 400 computers/terminals and 350 ports are available on campus for general student use. Students can access the following: computer help desk, free student e-mail accounts, online (class) grades, online (class) registration, online (class) schedules. Campuswide network is available. 100% of college-owned or -operated housing units are wired for high-speed Internet access. Wireless service is available via entire campus.
Student Life *Housing options:* coed, men-only. Campus housing is university owned. *Activities and organizations:* drama/theater group, student-run newspaper, radio and television station, choral group, marching band, Dixie Spirit, Outdoor Club, Association of Women Students, intramurals. *Campus security:* 24-hour emergency response devices and patrols. *Student services:* health clinic, personal/psychological counseling.
Athletics Member NCAA. except baseball (Division II), men's and women's basketball (Division II), men's and women's cross-country running (Division II), football (Division II), golf (Division II), men's and women's soccer (Divi-

sion II), softball (Division II), tennis (Division II), volleyball (Division II) *Intercollegiate sports:* baseball M(s), basketball M(s)/W(s), cross-country running M(s)/W(s), football M(s), golf M(s), soccer M(s)/W(s), softball W(s), tennis W(s), volleyball W(s). *Intramural sports:* basketball M/W, table tennis M/W, tennis M/W.

Standardized Tests *Recommended:* SAT or ACT (for admission).

Costs (2011–12) *Tuition:* state resident $3288 full-time, $137 per credit hour part-time; nonresident $12,936 full-time, $539 per credit hour part-time. Full-time tuition and fees vary according to course load and program. Part-time tuition and fees vary according to course load and program. *Required fees:* $600 full-time, $300 per term part-time. *Room and board:* $4348; room only: $1550. Room and board charges vary according to board plan and housing facility. *Payment plan:* installment. *Waivers:* children of alumni, senior citizens, and employees or children of employees.

Financial Aid Of all full-time matriculated undergraduates who enrolled in 2009, 3,221 applied for aid, 2,788 were judged to have need, 53 had their need fully met. In 2009, 919 non-need-based awards were made. *Average percent of need met:* 37%. *Average financial aid package:* $7614. *Average need-based loan:* $3826. *Average need-based gift aid:* $5917. *Average non-need-based aid:* $3241. *Average indebtedness upon graduation:* $15,564. *Financial aid deadline:* 5/1.

Applying *Options:* electronic application, early admission, deferred entrance. *Application fee:* $35. *Required:* high school transcript. *Application deadlines:* 8/15 (freshmen), 8/15 (out-of-state freshmen), 8/15 (transfers). *Notification:* continuous (freshmen), continuous (out-of-state freshmen), continuous (transfers).

Freshman Application Contact Dixie State College of Utah, 225 South 700 East, St. George, UT 84770-3876. *Phone:* 435-652-7698. *Web site:* http://www.dixie.edu/.

Independence University
Salt Lake City, Utah

Freshman Application Contact Ms. Deborah Hopkins, Enrollment Manager, Independence University, 5295 South Commerce Drive, Salt Lake City, UT 84107. *Toll-free phone:* 800-972-5149. *Web site:* http://www.independence.edu/.

ITT Technical Institute
Murray, Utah

- **Proprietary** primarily 2-year, founded 1984, part of ITT Educational Services, Inc.
- **Suburban** campus
- **Coed**
- **Minimally difficult** entrance level

Academics *Calendar:* quarters. *Degrees:* associate and bachelor's.

Student Life *Housing:* college housing not available.

Freshman Application Contact Director of Recruitment, ITT Technical Institute, 920 West Levoy Drive, Murray, UT 84123-2500. *Phone:* 801-263-3313. *Toll-free phone:* 800-365-2136. *Web site:* http://www.itt-tech.edu/.

Midwives College of Utah
Salt Lake City, Utah

Freshman Application Contact Kristi Ridd-Young, President, Midwives College of Utah, 1174 East 2700 South, Suite 2, Salt Lake City, UT 84106. *Phone:* 801-649-5230. *Toll-free phone:* 866-680-2756. *Fax:* 866-207-2024. *E-mail:* office@midwifery.edu. *Web site:* http://www.midwifery.edu/.

Neumont University
South Jordan, Utah

- **Proprietary** comprehensive, founded 2002
- **Suburban** campus with easy access to Salt Lake City
- **Coed, primarily men** 346 undergraduate students, 100% full-time, 9% women, 91% men
- **Moderately difficult** entrance level, 85% of applicants were admitted

Undergraduates 346 full-time. 60% live on campus. *Retention:* 83% of full-time freshmen returned.

Freshmen *Admission:* 530 applied, 452 admitted, 139 enrolled. *Average high school GPA:* 3.2. *Test scores:* ACT scores over 18: 92%; ACT scores over 24: 50%; ACT scores over 30: 12%.

Faculty *Total:* 33, 42% full-time. *Student/faculty ratio:* 17:1.

Academics *Calendar:* quarters. *Degrees:* bachelor's and master's. *Special study options:* accelerated degree program, services for LD students.

Computers on Campus Students can access the following: campus intranet, computer help desk, free student e-mail accounts, online (class) grades, online (class) registration, online (class) schedules. Campuswide network is available. Wireless service is available via entire campus.

Student Life *Housing options:* men-only, women-only, disabled students. Campus housing is leased by the school and is provided by a third party. Freshman campus housing is guaranteed. *Activities and organizations:* choral group, Neumont Tactical Federation, Epically Good Gamer's Group, Beyond The Screen Order, Rhythm Rockers Gaming Association, Unified Student Government. *Student services:* health clinic, personal/psychological counseling.

Athletics *Intramural sports:* basketball M(c), soccer M(c), table tennis M(c)/W(c).

Standardized Tests *Required:* SAT or ACT (for admission).

Costs (2012–13) *Tuition:* $21,600 full-time, $495 per unit part-time. No tuition increase for student's term of enrollment. *Required fees:* $1500 full-time. *Room only:* $4230. *Payment plans:* tuition prepayment, installment. *Waivers:* employees or children of employees.

Financial Aid *Financial aid deadline:* 7/1.

Applying *Options:* electronic application. *Application fee:* $35. *Required:* essay or personal statement, high school transcript. *Recommended:* 2 letters of recommendation, interview. *Application deadlines:* rolling (freshmen), rolling (transfers).

Freshman Application Contact Karick Heaton, Director of Admissions, Neumont University, 10701 South River Front Parkway, Suite 200, South Jordan, UT 84095. *Phone:* 801-302-2879. *Toll-free phone:* 888-NEUMONT. *Fax:* 801-302-2811. *E-mail:* karick.heaton@neumont.edu. *Web site:* http://www.neumont.edu/.

Southern Utah University
Cedar City, Utah

- **State-supported** comprehensive, founded 1897, part of Utah System of Higher Education
- **Small-town** 130-acre campus
- **Coed** 7,166 undergraduate students, 78% full-time, 56% women, 44% men
- **Moderately difficult** entrance level, 72% of applicants were admitted

Undergraduates 5,556 full-time, 1,610 part-time. 17% are from out of state; 2% Black or African American, non-Hispanic/Latino; 4% Hispanic/Latino; 0.9% Asian, non-Hispanic/Latino; 1% Native Hawaiian or other Pacific Islander, non-Hispanic/Latino; 2% American Indian or Alaska Native, non-Hispanic/Latino; 0.1% Two or more races, non-Hispanic/Latino; 1% Race/ethnicity unknown; 4% international; 5% transferred in; 13% live on campus. *Retention:* 66% of full-time freshmen returned.

Freshmen *Admission:* 4,249 applied, 3,071 admitted, 1,249 enrolled. *Average high school GPA:* 3.47. *Test scores:* SAT critical reading scores over 500: 58%; SAT math scores over 500: 49%; SAT writing scores over 500: 49%; ACT scores over 18: 85%; SAT critical reading scores over 600: 18%; SAT math scores over 600: 17%; SAT writing scores over 600: 8%; ACT scores over 24: 29%; SAT critical reading scores over 700: 5%; SAT math scores over 700: 4%; SAT writing scores over 700: 2%; ACT scores over 30: 2%.

Faculty *Total:* 419, 59% full-time, 49% with terminal degrees. *Student/faculty ratio:* 20:1.

Academics *Calendar:* semesters. *Degrees:* certificates, diplomas, associate, bachelor's, and master's. *Special study options:* academic remediation for entering students, adult/continuing education programs, advanced placement credit, cooperative education, distance learning, double majors, English as a second language, honors programs, independent study, internships, part-time degree program, services for LD students, study abroad, summer session for credit. *ROTC:* Army (b).

Computers on Campus 1,078 computers/terminals and 25 ports are available on campus for general student use. Students can access the following: campus intranet, computer help desk, free student e-mail accounts, online (class) grades, online (class) registration, online (class) schedules. Campuswide network is available. 100% of college-owned or -operated housing units are wired for high-speed Internet access.

Student Life *Housing options:* coed, disabled students. Campus housing is university owned. *Activities and organizations:* drama/theater group, student-run newspaper, radio and television station, choral group, national fraternities, national sororities. *Campus security:* 24-hour emergency response devices, student patrols, late-night transport/escort service, controlled dormitory access. *Student services:* health clinic, personal/psychological counseling, women's center.

Athletics Member NCAA. All Division I. *Intercollegiate sports:* basketball M(s)/W(s), golf M(s)/W, gymnastics W(s), soccer M/W, tennis W(s), track and field M(s)/W(s), volleyball M/W. *Intramural sports:* baseball M, basketball

M/W, cross-country running M/W, football M, golf M, gymnastics W, soccer W, softball W, tennis W, track and field M/W.

Standardized Tests *Required:* SAT or ACT (for admission).

Costs (2011–12) *Tuition:* state resident $4648 full-time, $220 per credit hour part-time; nonresident $15,370 full-time, $726 per credit hour part-time. Full-time tuition and fees vary according to program. *Required fees:* $540 full-time, $270 per term part-time. *Room only:* $2086. Room and board charges vary according to board plan and housing facility. *Payment plan:* installment. *Waivers:* children of alumni, senior citizens, and employees or children of employees.

Financial Aid Of all full-time matriculated undergraduates who enrolled in 2009, 4,069 applied for aid, 3,469 were judged to have need, 354 had their need fully met. In 2009, 2065 non-need-based awards were made. *Average percent of need met:* 62%. *Average financial aid package:* $7659. *Average need-based loan:* $3868. *Average need-based gift aid:* $5874. *Average non-need-based aid:* $7489. *Average indebtedness upon graduation:* $11,170.

Applying *Options:* electronic application, early admission, deferred entrance. *Application fee:* $45. *Required:* high school transcript, minimum 2.0 GPA. *Application deadline:* 5/1 (freshmen). *Notification:* continuous (freshmen).

Freshman Application Contact Southern Utah University, 351 West University Boulevard, Cedar City, UT 84720-2498. *Phone:* 435-586-7740. *Web site:* http://www.suu.edu/.

Stevens-Henager College
Ogden, Utah

Freshman Application Contact Admissions Office, Stevens-Henager College, 1890 South 1350 West, Ogden, UT 84401. *Phone:* 801-394-7791. *Toll-free phone:* 800-622-2640. *Web site:* http://www.stevenshenager.edu/.

Strayer University - Salt Lake Campus
Sandy, Utah

- **Proprietary** comprehensive
- **Coed**

Academics *Degrees:* certificates, diplomas, associate, bachelor's, master's, and postbachelor's certificates.

Freshman Application Contact Strayer University - Salt Lake Campus, 9815 South Monroe Street, Suite 200, Sandy, UT 84070. *Web site:* http://www.strayer.edu/salt_lake/.

University of Phoenix–Utah Campus
Salt Lake City, Utah

Freshman Application Contact Marc Booker, Sr. Director, Office of Admissions and Evaluation, University of Phoenix–Utah Campus, 4615 East Elwood Street, Mail Stop AA-K101, Phoenix, AZ 85040-1958. *Phone:* 602-557-4609. *Toll-free phone:* 866-766-0766. *Fax:* 480-643-1156. *Web site:* http://www.phoenix.edu/.

University of Utah
Salt Lake City, Utah

- **State-supported** university, founded 1850, part of Utah System of Higher Education
- **Urban** 1535-acre campus with easy access to Salt Lake City
- **Endowment** $531.6 million
- **Coed** 24,297 undergraduate students, 70% full-time, 45% women, 55% men
- **Moderately difficult** entrance level, 83% of applicants were admitted

Undergraduates 17,091 full-time, 7,206 part-time. Students come from 53 states and territories; 118 other countries; 17% are from out of state; 1% Black or African American, non-Hispanic/Latino; 7% Hispanic/Latino; 5% Asian, non-Hispanic/Latino; 0.7% Native Hawaiian or other Pacific Islander, non-Hispanic/Latino; 0.6% American Indian or Alaska Native, non-Hispanic/Latino; 2% Two or more races, non-Hispanic/Latino; 4% Race/ethnicity unknown; 5% international; 9% transferred in; 13% live on campus. *Retention:* 87% of full-time freshmen returned.

Freshmen *Admission:* 9,545 applied, 7,941 admitted, 3,268 enrolled. *Average high school GPA:* 3.53. *Test scores:* SAT critical reading scores over 500: 75%; SAT math scores over 500: 80%; SAT writing scores over 500: 72%; ACT scores over 18: 95%; SAT critical reading scores over 600: 39%; SAT math scores over 600: 44%; SAT writing scores over 600: 33%; ACT scores over 24: 55%; SAT critical reading scores over 700: 10%; SAT math scores over 700: 12%; SAT writing scores over 700: 9%; ACT scores over 30: 14%.

Faculty *Total:* 1,933, 67% full-time, 64% with terminal degrees. *Student/faculty ratio:* 14:1.

Academics *Calendar:* semesters. *Degrees:* bachelor's, master's, doctoral, post-master's, postbachelor's, and first professional certificates. *Special study options:* academic remediation for entering students, accelerated degree program, advanced placement credit, cooperative education, distance learning, double majors, English as a second language, freshman honors college, honors programs, independent study, internships, off-campus study, part-time degree program, services for LD students, student-designed majors, study abroad, summer session for credit. *ROTC:* Army (b), Navy (b), Air Force (b). *Unusual degree programs:* 3-2 physical therapy, occupational therapy.

Computers on Campus 3,000 computers/terminals are available on campus for general student use. Students can access the following: campus intranet, computer help desk, free student e-mail accounts, online (class) grades, online (class) registration, online (class) schedules, online classes. Campuswide network is available. 100% of college-owned or -operated housing units are wired for high-speed Internet access. Wireless service is available via entire campus.

Student Life *Housing options:* coed, men-only, women-only, disabled students. Campus housing is university owned. *Activities and organizations:* drama/theater group, student-run newspaper, radio and television station, choral group, marching band, Latter-Day Saints Student Association, Bennion Center, Newman Center, Center for Ethnic Student Affairs, national fraternities, national sororities. *Campus security:* 24-hour emergency response devices and patrols, student patrols, late-night transport/escort service, controlled dormitory access. *Student services:* health clinic, personal/psychological counseling, women's center, legal services.

Athletics Member NCAA. All Division I. *Intercollegiate sports:* baseball M(s), basketball M(s)/W(s), cheerleading M(s)/W(s), cross-country running W(s), football M(s), golf M(s), gymnastics W(s), rugby M(c), skiing (cross-country) M(s)/W(s), skiing (downhill) M(s)/W(s), soccer W(s), softball W(s), swimming and diving M(s)/W(s), table tennis M(c)/W(c), tennis M(s)/W(s), track and field W(s), volleyball W(s), water polo M(c)/W(c). *Intramural sports:* badminton M/W, basketball M/W, bowling M/W, fencing M/W, field hockey M/W, football M, ice hockey M, lacrosse M, racquetball M/W, riflery M/W, rugby M/W, soccer M/W, softball M/W, squash M/W, tennis M/W, ultimate Frisbee M/W, volleyball M/W.

Standardized Tests *Required:* ACT (for admission), SAT or ACT (for admission).

Costs (2011–12) *Tuition:* state resident $5850 full-time, $164 per credit hour part-time; nonresident $20,476 full-time, $565 per credit hour part-time. Full-time tuition and fees vary according to course level, course load, degree level, program, and student level. Part-time tuition and fees vary according to course level, course load, degree level, program, and student level. *Required fees:* $913 full-time. *Room and board:* $6699; room only: $3396. Room and board charges vary according to board plan and housing facility. *Payment plans:* installment, deferred payment. *Waivers:* children of alumni, senior citizens, and employees or children of employees.

Financial Aid Of all full-time matriculated undergraduates who enrolled in 2011, 9,520 applied for aid, 8,234 were judged to have need, 784 had their need fully met. 356 Federal Work-Study jobs (averaging $9560). In 2011, 575 non-need-based awards were made. *Average percent of need met:* 62%. *Average financial aid package:* $15,867. *Average need-based loan:* $4500. *Average need-based gift aid:* $5921. *Average non-need-based aid:* $5907. *Average indebtedness upon graduation:* $18,991.

Applying *Options:* electronic application, early admission. *Application fee:* $45. *Required:* high school transcript, minimum 2.6 GPA. *Required for some:* essay or personal statement. *Recommended:* minimum 3.0 GPA. *Application deadlines:* 4/1 (freshmen), 4/1 (out-of-state freshmen), 4/1 (transfers). *Notification:* continuous (freshmen), continuous (out-of-state freshmen), continuous (transfers).

Freshman Application Contact Mateo Remsburg, Director of High School Services, University of Utah, 200 Central Campus Drive, Room 280, Salt Lake City, UT 84112. *Phone:* 801-581-8761. *Toll-free phone:* 800-685-8856. *Fax:* 801-585-3257. *E-mail:* mremsburg@sa.utah.edu. *Web site:* http://www.utah.edu/.

Utah State University
Logan, Utah

- **State-supported** university, founded 1888, part of Utah System of Higher Education
- **Urban** 456-acre campus with easy access to Salt Lake City is 80 miles to the south
- **Endowment** $209.1 million
- **Coed** 23,279 undergraduate students, 62% full-time, 55% women, 45% men
- **Moderately difficult** entrance level, 97% of applicants were admitted

Undergraduates 14,435 full-time, 8,844 part-time. Students come from 52 states and territories; 49 other countries; 22% are from out of state; 1% Black or African American, non-Hispanic/Latino; 5% Hispanic/Latino; 1% Asian,

non-Hispanic/Latino; 0.3% Native Hawaiian or other Pacific Islander, non-Hispanic/Latino; 0.6% American Indian or Alaska Native, non-Hispanic/Latino; 1% Two or more races, non-Hispanic/Latino; 6% Race/ethnicity unknown; 2% international; 5% transferred in.

Freshmen *Admission:* 7,871 applied, 7,630 admitted, 3,491 enrolled. *Average high school GPA:* 3.47. *Test scores:* SAT critical reading scores over 500: 67%; SAT math scores over 500: 72%; ACT scores over 18: 94%; SAT critical reading scores over 600: 34%; SAT math scores over 600: 31%; ACT scores over 24: 49%; SAT critical reading scores over 700: 9%; SAT math scores over 700: 8%; ACT scores over 30: 10%.

Faculty *Total:* 961, 80% full-time. *Student/faculty ratio:* 23:1.

Academics *Calendar:* semesters. *Degrees:* certificates, associate, bachelor's, master's, doctoral, post-master's, postbachelor's, and first professional certificates. *Special study options:* academic remediation for entering students, accelerated degree program, adult/continuing education programs, advanced placement credit, cooperative education, distance learning, double majors, English as a second language, freshman honors college, honors programs, independent study, internships, off-campus study, part-time degree program, services for LD students, student-designed majors, study abroad, summer session for credit. *ROTC:* Army (b), Air Force (b).

Computers on Campus 1,000 computers/terminals are available on campus for general student use. Students can access the following: computer help desk, free student e-mail accounts, online (class) grades, online (class) registration, online (class) schedules. Campuswide network is available. 100% of college-owned or -operated housing units are wired for high-speed Internet access. Wireless service is available via classrooms, computer centers, computer labs, dorm rooms, learning centers, libraries, student centers.

Student Life *Housing options:* coed, men-only, women-only, disabled students. Campus housing is university owned. *Activities and organizations:* drama/theater group, student-run newspaper, radio station, choral group, marching band, Latter-Day Saints Student Association, multicultural clubs, volunteer groups, college councils, national fraternities, national sororities. *Campus security:* 24-hour emergency response devices and patrols, student patrols, late-night transport/escort service, video monitors in pedestrian tunnels. *Student services:* health clinic, personal/psychological counseling, women's center, legal services.

Athletics Member NCAA. All Division I except football (Division I-A). *Intercollegiate sports:* baseball M(c), basketball M(s)/W(s), cross-country running M(s)/W(s), equestrian sports M(c)/W(c), golf M(s), gymnastics W(s), ice hockey M(c), rugby M(c)/W(c), soccer M(c)/W(s), softball W(s), tennis M(s)/W(s), track and field M(s)/W(s), volleyball M(c)/W(s). *Intramural sports:* badminton M/W, basketball M/W, cross-country running M/W, fencing M(c)/W(c), football M/W, golf M/W, ice hockey W(c), lacrosse M(c), racquetball M(c)/W(c), skiing (cross-country) M(c)/W(c), skiing (downhill) M(c)/W(c), soccer M/W, softball M/W, squash M/W, swimming and diving M/W, table tennis M/W, tennis M/W, ultimate Frisbee M(c)/W(c), volleyball M/W, water polo M(c)/W(c).

Standardized Tests *Required:* SAT or ACT (for admission).

Costs (2011–12) *Tuition:* state resident $4737 full-time; nonresident $15,253 full-time. Full-time tuition and fees vary according to course load, location, program, and reciprocity agreements. Part-time tuition and fees vary according to course load, location, program, and reciprocity agreements. *Required fees:* $826 full-time. *Room and board:* $5280; room only: $1700. Room and board charges vary according to board plan and housing facility. *Payment plan:* deferred payment. *Waivers:* minority students, children of alumni, adult students, senior citizens, and employees or children of employees.

Financial Aid Of all full-time matriculated undergraduates who enrolled in 2011, 10,231 applied for aid, 9,024 were judged to have need, 1,345 had their need fully met. 191 Federal Work-Study jobs (averaging $3140). 290 state and other part-time jobs (averaging $3140). In 2011, 1445 non-need-based awards were made. *Average percent of need met:* 60%. *Average financial aid package:* $6970. *Average need-based loan:* $3900. *Average need-based gift aid:* $4300. *Average non-need-based aid:* $2132. *Average indebtedness upon graduation:* $17,200.

Applying *Options:* electronic application, deferred entrance. *Application fee:* $40. *Required:* high school transcript. *Recommended:* minimum 2.8 GPA. *Application deadlines:* rolling (freshmen), rolling (transfers). *Notification:* continuous (freshmen), continuous (transfers).

Freshman Application Contact Mr. Jeff Sorenson, Asst. Director, Admissions Office, Utah State University, 0160 Old Main Hill, Logan, UT 84322-0160. *Phone:* 435-797-1079. *Toll-free phone:* 800-488-8108. *Fax:* 435-797-3708. *E-mail:* admit@usu.edu. *Web site:* http://www.usu.edu/.

Utah Valley University
Orem, Utah

- **State-supported** comprehensive, founded 1941, affiliated with Advent Christian Church, part of Utah System of Higher Education
- **Suburban** 422-acre campus with easy access to Salt Lake City
- **Endowment** $11.0 million
- **Coed** 33,246 undergraduate students, 52% full-time, 44% women, 56% men
- **Noncompetitive** entrance level, 100% of applicants were admitted

Undergraduates 17,184 full-time, 16,062 part-time. Students come from 55 states and territories; 70 other countries; 14% are from out of state; 0.9% Black or African American, non-Hispanic/Latino; 9% Hispanic/Latino; 1% Asian, non-Hispanic/Latino; 0.9% Native Hawaiian or other Pacific Islander, non-Hispanic/Latino; 0.8% American Indian or Alaska Native, non-Hispanic/Latino; 2% Two or more races, non-Hispanic/Latino; 2% Race/ethnicity unknown; 1% international; 5% transferred in. *Retention:* 60% of full-time freshmen returned.

Freshmen *Admission:* 6,078 applied, 6,078 admitted, 4,265 enrolled. *Average high school GPA:* 3.24. *Test scores:* ACT scores over 18: 79%; ACT scores over 24: 27%; ACT scores over 30: 2%.

Faculty *Total:* 1,609, 34% full-time, 26% with terminal degrees. *Student/faculty ratio:* 25:1.

Academics *Calendar:* semesters. *Degrees:* certificates, diplomas, associate, bachelor's, and master's. *Special study options:* academic remediation for entering students, advanced placement credit, cooperative education, distance learning, double majors, English as a second language, honors programs, independent study, internships, off-campus study, part-time degree program, services for LD students, student-designed majors, study abroad, summer session for credit. *ROTC:* Army (b), Air Force (c).

Computers on Campus 1,000 computers/terminals are available on campus for general student use. Students can access the following: campus intranet, computer help desk, free student e-mail accounts, online (class) grades, online (class) registration, online (class) schedules. Campuswide network is available. Wireless service is available via entire campus.

Student Life *Housing:* college housing not available. *Activities and organizations:* drama/theater group, student-run newspaper, television station, choral group, LDSSA Orem Institute, Center for the Advancement of Leadership. *Campus security:* 24-hour patrols. *Student services:* health clinic, personal/psychological counseling, women's center, legal services.

Athletics Member NCAA. All Division I. *Intercollegiate sports:* baseball M(s), basketball M(s)/W(s), cross-country running M(s)/W(s), golf M(s)/W(s), soccer W(s), softball W(s), track and field M(s)/W(s), volleyball W(s), wrestling M(s).

Standardized Tests *Required:* SAT or ACT (for admission).

Costs (2011–12) *Tuition:* state resident $3944 full-time, $165 per credit part-time; nonresident $12,300 full-time, $516 per credit part-time. Full-time tuition and fees vary according to course load. Part-time tuition and fees vary according to course load. *Required fees:* $640 full-time, $640 per year part-time. *Payment plans:* installment, deferred payment. *Waivers:* employees or children of employees.

Financial Aid Of all full-time matriculated undergraduates who enrolled in 2010, 13,408 applied for aid, 11,327 were judged to have need, 603 had their need fully met. In 2010, 1289 non-need-based awards were made. *Average percent of need met:* 55%. *Average financial aid package:* $4964. *Average need-based loan:* $2576. *Average need-based gift aid:* $4878. *Average non-need-based aid:* $3780. *Average indebtedness upon graduation:* $13,407. *Financial aid deadline:* 5/1.

Applying *Options:* electronic application, deferred entrance. *Application fee:* $35. *Required:* ACT or SAT, or Accuplacer. *Required for some:* high school transcript. *Application deadlines:* 8/15 (freshmen), 8/15 (out-of-state freshmen), 8/15 (transfers). *Notification:* continuous (freshmen), continuous (transfers).

Freshman Application Contact Mrs. Liz Childs, Senior Director of Admissions, Utah Valley University, 800 West University Parkway, Orem, UT 84058-5999. *Phone:* 801-863-8460. *Fax:* 801-225-4677. *E-mail:* info@uvsc.edu. *Web site:* http://www.uvu.edu/.

Weber State University
Ogden, Utah

- **State-supported** comprehensive, founded 1889, part of Utah System of Higher Education
- **Urban** 526-acre campus with easy access to Salt Lake City
- **Endowment** $75.2 million
- **Coed** 24,617 undergraduate students, 47% full-time, 53% women, 47% men
- **Noncompetitive** entrance level, 100% of applicants were admitted

Undergraduates 11,450 full-time, 13,167 part-time. Students come from 55 states and territories; 44 other countries; 9% are from out of state; 1% Black or African American, non-Hispanic/Latino; 7% Hispanic/Latino; 1% Asian, non-Hispanic/Latino; 0.3% Native Hawaiian or other Pacific Islander, non-Hispanic/Latino; 0.4% American Indian or Alaska Native, non-Hispanic/Latino; 1% Two or more races, non-Hispanic/Latino; 27% Race/ethnicity unknown; 2% international; 3% transferred in; 1% live on campus. *Retention:* 71% of full-time freshmen returned.

Freshmen *Admission:* 5,346 applied, 5,346 admitted, 2,485 enrolled. *Average high school GPA:* 3.16. *Test scores:* ACT scores over 18: 81%; ACT scores over 24: 29%; ACT scores over 30: 2%.

Faculty *Total:* 940, 51% full-time, 35% with terminal degrees. *Student/faculty ratio:* 25:1.

Academics *Calendar:* semesters. *Degrees:* certificates, associate, bachelor's, master's, and postbachelor's certificates. *Special study options:* academic remediation for entering students, accelerated degree program, adult/continuing education programs, advanced placement credit, cooperative education, distance learning, double majors, English as a second language, external degree program, freshman honors college, honors programs, independent study, internships, off-campus study, part-time degree program, services for LD students, student-designed majors, study abroad, summer session for credit. *ROTC:* Army (b), Navy (b), Air Force (b).

Computers on Campus Students can access the following: campus intranet, computer help desk, free student e-mail accounts, online (class) grades, online (class) registration, online (class) schedules. Campuswide network is available. 100% of college-owned or -operated housing units are wired for high-speed Internet access. Wireless service is available via entire campus.

Student Life *Housing options:* men-only, women-only, cooperative, disabled students. Campus housing is university owned and is provided by a third party. *Activities and organizations:* drama/theater group, student-run newspaper, radio and television station, choral group, marching band, LDSSA, Mountaineering Club, Rodeo Club, Beta Alpha Psi, Student Nurses Organization, national fraternities, national sororities. *Campus security:* 24-hour emergency response devices and patrols, student patrols, late-night transport/escort service, controlled dormitory access. *Student services:* health clinic, personal/psychological counseling, women's center, legal services.

Athletics Member NCAA. All Division I. *Intercollegiate sports:* archery M(c)/W(c), baseball M(c), basketball M(s)/W(s), bowling M(c)/W(c), cheerleading M(s)/W(s), cross-country running M(s)/W(s), fencing M(c)/W(c), football M(s), golf M(s)/W(s), ice hockey M(c), lacrosse W(c), rock climbing M(c)/W(c), rugby M(c)/W(c), skiing (downhill) M(c)/W(c), soccer M(c)/W(c), softball W(s), tennis M(s)/W(s), track and field M(s)/W(s), volleyball M(c)/W(s), wrestling M(c). *Intramural sports:* basketball M/W, bowling M/W, football M/W, racquetball M/W, soccer M/W, tennis M/W, ultimate Frisbee M/W, volleyball M/W.

Standardized Tests *Required for some:* ACCUPLACER. *Recommended:* SAT or ACT (for admission).

Costs (2012–13) *Tuition:* state resident $3773 full-time, $157 per credit hour part-time; nonresident $11,485 full-time, $479 per credit hour part-time. Full-time tuition and fees vary according to course load. Part-time tuition and fees vary according to course load. *Required fees:* $775 full-time, $32 per credit hour part-time. *Room and board:* $4600. Room and board charges vary according to board plan and housing facility. *Payment plan:* installment. *Waivers:* children of alumni, senior citizens, and employees or children of employees.

Financial Aid Of all full-time matriculated undergraduates who enrolled in 2007, 4,981 applied for aid, 4,509 were judged to have need, 174 had their need fully met. In 2007, 1562 non-need-based awards were made. *Average percent of need met:* 50%. *Average financial aid package:* $5878. *Average need-based loan:* $4079. *Average need-based gift aid:* $3622. *Average non-need-based aid:* $2033.

Applying *Options:* electronic application, early admission, deferred entrance. *Application fee:* $30. *Required:* high school transcript. *Application deadlines:* 8/21 (freshmen), rolling (transfers). *Notification:* continuous (freshmen), continuous (transfers).

Freshman Application Contact Laura Albright, Student Recruitment, Weber State University, 1137 University Circle, Ogden, UT 84408-1137. *Phone:* 801-626-6050. *Toll-free phone:* 800-848-7700 (in-state); 800-848-7770 (out-of-state). *Fax:* 801-626-6744. *E-mail:* admissions@weber.edu. *Web site:* http://www.weber.edu/.

Western Governors University
Salt Lake City, Utah

Freshman Application Contact Western Governors University, 4001 South 700 East, Suite 700, Salt Lake City, UT 84107. *Phone:* 801-274-3280 Ext. 336. *Toll-free phone:* 866-225-5948. *Web site:* http://www.wgu.edu/.

Westminster College
Salt Lake City, Utah

- **Independent** comprehensive, founded 1875
- **Suburban** 27-acre campus
- **Endowment** $60.3 million
- **Coed** 2,549 undergraduate students, 90% full-time, 55% women, 45% men
- **Moderately difficult** entrance level, 68% of applicants were admitted

Undergraduates 2,296 full-time, 253 part-time. Students come from 47 states and territories; 37 other countries; 36% are from out of state; 0.9% Black or African American, non-Hispanic/Latino; 9% Hispanic/Latino; 3% Asian, non-Hispanic/Latino; 0.5% Native Hawaiian or other Pacific Islander, non-Hispanic/Latino; 0.8% American Indian or Alaska Native, non-Hispanic/Latino; 2% Two or more races, non-Hispanic/Latino; 8% Race/ethnicity unknown; 6% international; 8% transferred in; 26% live on campus. *Retention:* 80% of full-time freshmen returned.

Freshmen *Admission:* 3,414 applied, 2,321 admitted, 513 enrolled. *Average high school GPA:* 3.5. *Test scores:* SAT critical reading scores over 500: 72%; SAT math scores over 500: 80%; ACT scores over 18: 99%; SAT critical reading scores over 600: 34%; SAT math scores over 600: 32%; ACT scores over 24: 63%; SAT critical reading scores over 700: 12%; SAT math scores over 700: 8%; ACT scores over 30: 11%.

Faculty *Total:* 394, 37% full-time, 48% with terminal degrees. *Student/faculty ratio:* 10:1.

Academics *Calendar:* 4-4-1. *Degrees:* bachelor's, master's, and postbachelor's certificates. *Special study options:* academic remediation for entering students, accelerated degree program, advanced placement credit, cooperative education, distance learning, double majors, English as a second language, external degree program, freshman honors college, honors programs, independent study, internships, off-campus study, part-time degree program, services for LD students, student-designed majors, study abroad, summer session for credit. *ROTC:* Army (c), Navy (c), Air Force (c). *Unusual degree programs:* 3-2 engineering with University of Southern California, Washington University in St. Louis.

Computers on Campus 399 computers/terminals and 601 ports are available on campus for general student use. Students can access the following: campus intranet, computer help desk, free student e-mail accounts, online (class) grades, online (class) registration, online (class) schedules. Campuswide network is available. 100% of college-owned or -operated housing units are wired for high-speed Internet access. Wireless service is available via entire campus.

Student Life *Housing:* on-campus residence required for freshman year. *Options:* coed, cooperative, disabled students. Campus housing is university owned. Freshman applicants given priority for college housing. *Activities and organizations:* drama/theater group, student-run newspaper, choral group, Associated Students of Westminster College (Student Government), Associated Residents of Westminster College (Residential Government), Westminster Ski and Snowboard Club (WSSC), V-Day, Westminster Entrepreneurship Club. *Campus security:* 24-hour emergency response devices and patrols, student patrols, late-night transport/escort service, controlled dormitory access. *Student services:* health clinic, personal/psychological counseling.

Athletics Member NAIA. *Intercollegiate sports:* basketball M(s)/W(s), golf M(s)/W(s), lacrosse M(s)/W, skiing (cross-country) M(s)/W(s), skiing (downhill) M(s)/W(s), soccer M(s)/W(s), track and field M(s)/W(s), volleyball W(s). *Intramural sports:* basketball M/W, soccer M/W, volleyball M/W.

Standardized Tests *Required:* SAT or ACT (for admission).

Costs (2011–12) *Comprehensive fee:* $34,766 includes full-time tuition ($26,712), mandatory fees ($470), and room and board ($7584). Full-time tuition and fees vary according to course load and program. Part-time tuition: $1113 per credit hour. Part-time tuition and fees vary according to course load and program. *Room and board:* Room and board charges vary according to board plan. *Payment plans:* installment, deferred payment. *Waivers:* employees or children of employees.

Financial Aid Of all full-time matriculated undergraduates who enrolled in 2011, 1,519 applied for aid, 1,401 were judged to have need, 287 had their need fully met. 389 Federal Work-Study jobs (averaging $2472). 212 state and other part-time jobs (averaging $2420). In 2011, 697 non-need-based awards were made. *Average percent of need met:* 76%. *Average financial aid pack-*

age: $21,235. *Average need-based loan:* $4571. *Average need-based gift aid:* $16,556. *Average non-need-based aid:* $12,442. *Average indebtedness upon graduation:* $22,557.

Applying *Options:* electronic application, deferred entrance. *Application fee:* $50. *Required:* essay or personal statement, high school transcript, minimum 2.5 GPA, 1 letter of recommendation. *Recommended:* interview. *Application deadlines:* rolling (freshmen), rolling (out-of-state freshmen), rolling (transfers). *Notification:* continuous (freshmen), continuous (out-of-state freshmen), continuous (transfers).

Freshman Application Contact Elizabeth Key, Director of Admissions, Westminster College, 1840 South 1300 East, Salt Lake City, UT 84105-3697. *Phone:* 801-832-2200. *Toll-free phone:* 800-748-4753. *Fax:* 801-832-3101. *E-mail:* admission@westminstercollege.edu. *Web site:* http://www.westminstercollege.edu/.

VERMONT

Bennington College
Bennington, Vermont

- **Independent** comprehensive, founded 1932
- **Small-town** 440-acre campus with easy access to Albany, NY
- **Endowment** $15.1 million
- **Coed** 686 undergraduate students, 100% full-time, 66% women, 34% men
- **Very difficult** entrance level, 72% of applicants were admitted

Undergraduates 683 full-time, 3 part-time. Students come from 42 states and territories; 33 other countries; 90% are from out of state; 1% Black or African American, non-Hispanic/Latino; 4% Hispanic/Latino; 2% Asian, non-Hispanic/Latino; 0.9% American Indian or Alaska Native, non-Hispanic/Latino; 1% Two or more races, non-Hispanic/Latino; 3% Race/ethnicity unknown; 6% international; 2% transferred in; 93% live on campus. *Retention:* 85% of full-time freshmen returned.

Freshmen *Admission:* 1,145 applied, 829 admitted, 212 enrolled. *Average high school GPA:* 3.5. *Test scores:* SAT critical reading scores over 500: 98%; SAT math scores over 500: 88%; SAT writing scores over 500: 97%; ACT scores over 18: 100%; SAT critical reading scores over 600: 87%; SAT math scores over 600: 55%; SAT writing scores over 600: 74%; ACT scores over 24:

93%; SAT critical reading scores over 700: 33%; SAT math scores over 700: 9%; SAT writing scores over 700: 24%; ACT scores over 30: 34%.

Faculty *Total:* 82, 77% full-time, 66% with terminal degrees. *Student/faculty ratio:* 10:1.

Academics *Calendar:* semesters plus winter work term in January and February. *Degrees:* bachelor's, master's, and postbachelor's certificates. *Special study options:* accelerated degree program, double majors, independent study, internships, part-time degree program, services for LD students, student-designed majors, study abroad. *Unusual degree programs:* 3-2 teaching.

Computers on Campus 100 computers/terminals and 25 ports are available on campus for general student use. Students can access the following: campus intranet, computer help desk, free student e-mail accounts, online (class) schedules. Campuswide network is available. 100% of college-owned or -operated housing units are wired for high-speed Internet access. Wireless service is available via entire campus.

Student Life *Housing:* on-campus residence required through senior year. *Options:* coed, cooperative. Campus housing is university owned. Freshman campus housing is guaranteed. *Activities and organizations:* drama/theater group, student-run newspaper, choral group, Program Activity Council, Community Outreach and Action, Bennington Free Press, Student Endowment for the Arts, SILO: Student Journal of Arts and Letters. *Campus security:* 24-hour emergency response devices and patrols, late-night transport/escort service, prevention/awareness program. *Student services:* health clinic, personal/psychological counseling.

Athletics *Intercollegiate sports:* basketball M(c)/W(c), fencing M(c)/W(c), soccer M(c)/W(c). *Intramural sports:* archery M/W, badminton M/W, basketball M/W, bowling M/W, cross-country running M/W, equestrian sports M/W, fencing M/W, golf M/W, skiing (cross-country) M/W, skiing (downhill) M/W, soccer M/W, softball M/W, swimming and diving M/W, table tennis M/W, tennis M/W, ultimate Frisbee M/W, volleyball M/W, weight lifting M/W.

Costs (2011–12) *Comprehensive fee:* $54,960 includes full-time tuition ($41,690), mandatory fees ($1110), and room and board ($12,160). Part-time tuition: $1390 per credit hour. *College room only:* $6520. *Payment plan:* installment. *Waivers:* employees or children of employees.

Financial Aid Of all full-time matriculated undergraduates who enrolled in 2011, 527 applied for aid, 455 were judged to have need, 47 had their need fully met. 353 Federal Work-Study jobs (averaging $2300). 37 state and other part-time jobs (averaging $2300). In 2011, 141 non-need-based awards were made. *Average percent of need met:* 80%. *Average financial aid package:* $33,670. *Average need-based loan:* $3925. *Average need-based gift aid:*

$29,023. *Average non-need-based aid:* $17,932. *Average indebtedness upon graduation:* $23,002. *Financial aid deadline:* 2/15.

Applying *Options:* electronic application, early admission, early decision, early action, deferred entrance. *Application fee:* $60. *Required:* essay or personal statement, high school transcript, 2 letters of recommendation, graded analytic paper. *Recommended:* interview. *Application deadlines:* 1/3 (freshmen), 3/15 (transfers). *Early decision deadline:* 11/15 (for plan 1), 1/3 (for plan 2). *Notification:* 4/1 (freshmen), 5/1 (transfers), 12/20 (early decision plan 1), 2/1 (early decision plan 2).

Freshman Application Contact Mr. Ken Himmelman, Dean of Admissions and Financial Aid, Bennington College, One College Drive, Bennington, VT 05201-6003. *Phone:* 802-440-4312. *Toll-free phone:* 800-833-6845. *Fax:* 802-440-4320. *E-mail:* admissions@bennington.edu. *Web site:* http://www.bennington.edu/.

Burlington College
Burlington, Vermont

- **Independent** comprehensive, founded 1972
- **Urban** 32-acre campus with easy access to Montreal
- **Endowment** $100,784
- **Coed** 185 undergraduate students, 78% full-time, 48% women, 52% men
- **Moderately difficult** entrance level, 86% of applicants were admitted

Undergraduates 144 full-time, 41 part-time. Students come from 23 states and territories; 5 other countries; 46% are from out of state; 1% Black or African American, non-Hispanic/Latino; 2% Hispanic/Latino; 0.5% Asian, non-Hispanic/Latino; 0.5% American Indian or Alaska Native, non-Hispanic/Latino; 0.5% Two or more races, non-Hispanic/Latino; 13% Race/ethnicity unknown; 2% international; 16% transferred in; 17% live on campus. *Retention:* 40% of full-time freshmen returned.

Freshmen *Admission:* 180 applied, 154 admitted, 37 enrolled. *Average high school GPA:* 2.89.

Faculty *Total:* 76, 7% full-time, 36% with terminal degrees. *Student/faculty ratio:* 6:1.

Academics *Calendar:* semesters. *Degrees:* certificates, associate, bachelor's, and master's. *Special study options:* advanced placement credit, distance learning, double majors, external degree program, independent study, internships, off-campus study, part-time degree program, services for LD students, student-designed majors, study abroad, summer session for credit.

Computers on Campus 19 computers/terminals and 22 ports are available on campus for general student use. Students can access the following: campus intranet, computer help desk, free student e-mail accounts, online (class) schedules. Campuswide network is available. 100% of college-owned or -operated housing units are wired for high-speed Internet access. Wireless service is available via entire campus.

Student Life *Housing:* on-campus residence required for freshman year. *Options:* coed, men-only, women-only, cooperative. Campus housing is university owned. Freshman campus housing is guaranteed. *Activities and organizations:* Student Association. *Campus security:* student patrols. *Student services:* legal services.

Costs (2011–12) *Tuition:* $22,410 full-time, $740 per credit hour part-time. Full-time tuition and fees vary according to course load and program. Part-time tuition and fees vary according to course load and program. *Required fees:* $125 full-time. *Room only:* $6670. Room and board charges vary according to housing facility. *Payment plan:* installment. *Waivers:* employees or children of employees.

Financial Aid Of all full-time matriculated undergraduates who enrolled in 2011, 118 applied for aid, 111 were judged to have need, 1 had their need fully met. In 2011, 4 non-need-based awards were made. *Average percent of need met:* 48%. *Average financial aid package:* $14,453. *Average need-based loan:* $5421. *Average need-based gift aid:* $8672. *Average non-need-based aid:* $3750. *Average indebtedness upon graduation:* $55,240.

Applying *Options:* electronic application, deferred entrance. *Application fee:* $50. *Required:* essay or personal statement, high school transcript, minimum 2.0 GPA, 2 letters of recommendation. *Required for some:* art portfolio required for some. *Recommended:* interview. *Application deadlines:* 8/15 (freshmen), 8/15 (out-of-state freshmen), 8/15 (transfers). *Notification:* continuous (freshmen), continuous (out-of-state freshmen), continuous (transfers).

Freshman Application Contact Ms. Gillian Homsted, Admissions Director, Burlington College, 351 North Avenue, Burlington, VT 05401-2998. *Phone:* 802-862-9616 Ext. 104. *Toll-free phone:* 800-862-9616. *Fax:* 802-660-4331. *E-mail:* admissions@burlington.edu. *Web site:* http://www.burlington.edu/.

See page 919 for display ad and page 1234 for the College Close-Up.

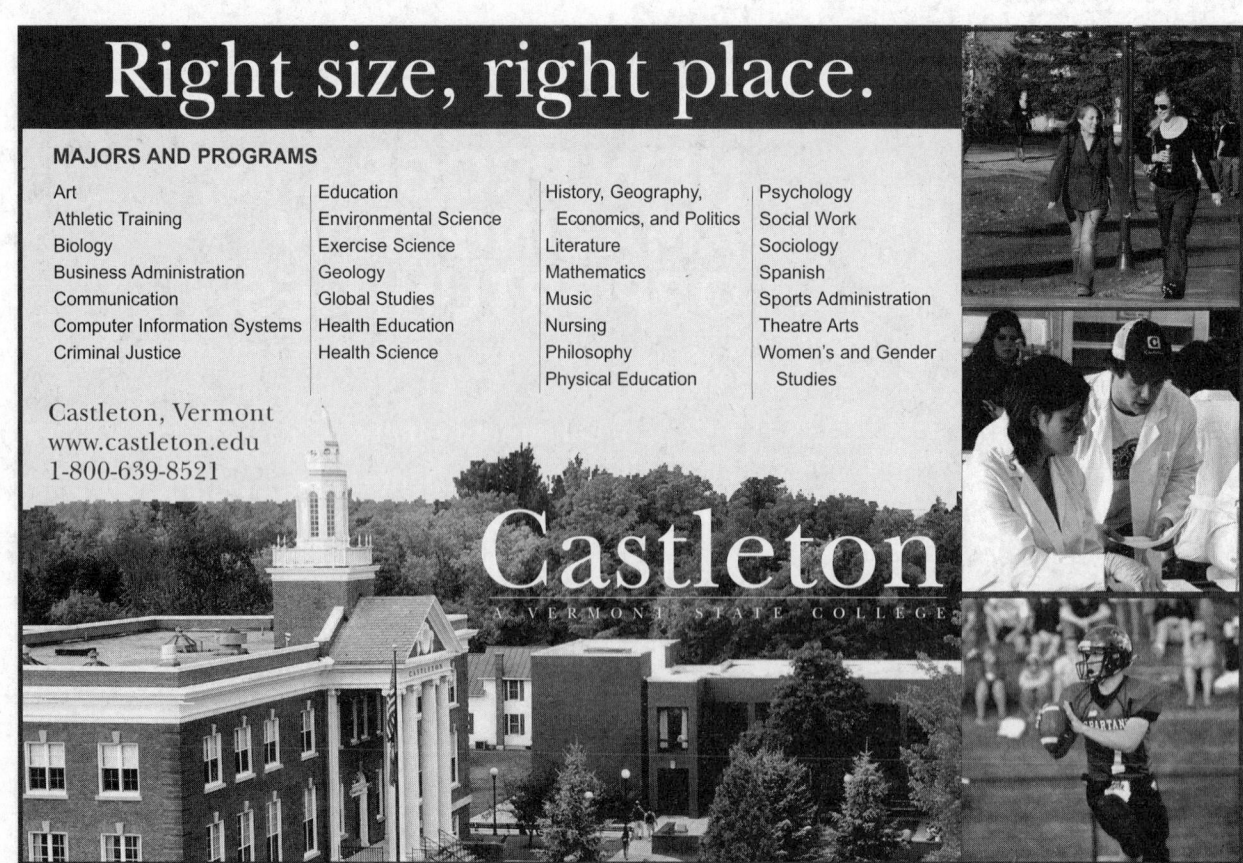

Castleton State College

Castleton, Vermont

- **State-supported** comprehensive, founded 1787, part of Vermont State Colleges System
- **Rural** 165-acre campus
- **Endowment** $4.9 million
- **Coed** 2,029 undergraduate students, 91% full-time, 53% women, 47% men
- **Moderately difficult** entrance level, 78% of applicants were admitted

Undergraduates 1,843 full-time, 186 part-time. Students come from 28 states and territories; 9 other countries; 31% are from out of state; 1% Black or African American, non-Hispanic/Latino; 2% Hispanic/Latino; 0.8% Asian, non-Hispanic/Latino; 0.8% American Indian or Alaska Native, non-Hispanic/Latino; 0.5% Two or more races, non-Hispanic/Latino; 3% Race/ethnicity unknown; 1% international; 8% transferred in; 56% live on campus. *Retention:* 69% of full-time freshmen returned.

Freshmen *Admission:* 2,094 applied, 1,623 admitted, 445 enrolled. *Average high school GPA:* 3. *Test scores:* SAT critical reading scores over 500: 39%; SAT math scores over 500: 43%; SAT writing scores over 500: 32%; ACT scores over 18: 77%; SAT critical reading scores over 600: 7%; SAT math scores over 600: 9%; SAT writing scores over 600: 6%; ACT scores over 24: 14%; SAT critical reading scores over 700: 1%; SAT math scores over 700: 1%; ACT scores over 30: 2%.

Faculty *Total:* 234, 39% full-time, 53% with terminal degrees. *Student/faculty ratio:* 14:1.

Academics *Calendar:* semesters. *Degrees:* associate, bachelor's, master's, post-master's, and postbachelor's certificates. *Special study options:* academic remediation for entering students, advanced placement credit, cooperative education, double majors, honors programs, independent study, internships, off-campus study, part-time degree program, services for LD students, student-designed majors, study abroad, summer session for credit. *ROTC:* Army (c).

Computers on Campus 225 computers/terminals are available on campus for general student use. Students can access the following: campus intranet, computer help desk, free student e-mail accounts, online (class) grades. Campuswide network is available. 100% of college-owned or -operated housing units are wired for high-speed Internet access. Wireless service is available via entire campus.

Student Life *Housing:* on-campus residence required for freshman year. *Options:* coed. Campus housing is university owned. Freshman campus housing is guaranteed. *Activities and organizations:* drama/theater group, student-run newspaper, radio station, choral group, marching band, community service, clubs in the academic majors, Women's issues organization, Spanish and International, Skiing/Snowboarding. *Campus security:* 24-hour emergency response devices and patrols, student patrols, late-night transport/escort service, controlled dormitory access. *Student services:* health clinic, personal/psychological counseling.

Athletics Member NCAA. All Division III. *Intercollegiate sports:* baseball M, basketball M/W, cheerleading M(c)/W(c), cross-country running M/W, equestrian sports W(c), field hockey W, football M, golf M, ice hockey M/W, lacrosse M/W, rugby M(c)/W(c), skiing (downhill) M/W, soccer M/W, softball W, tennis M/W, volleyball W. *Intramural sports:* basketball M/W, racquetball M/W, rock climbing M/W, soccer M/W, softball M/W, table tennis M/W, tennis M/W, volleyball M/W, water polo M/W.

Standardized Tests *Required:* SAT or ACT (for admission).

Costs (2012–13) *One-time required fee:* $200. *Tuition:* state resident $8928 full-time, $372 per credit part-time; nonresident $21,528 full-time, $897 per credit part-time. Part-time tuition and fees vary according to course load. *Required fees:* $936 full-time. *Room and board:* $8786; room only: $5232. Room and board charges vary according to board plan. *Payment plan:* installment. *Waivers:* senior citizens and employees or children of employees.

Financial Aid Of all full-time matriculated undergraduates who enrolled in 2006, 1,471 applied for aid, 1,174 were judged to have need, 371 had their need fully met. 360 Federal Work-Study jobs (averaging $1000). In 2006, 40 non-need-based awards were made. *Average percent of need met:* 72%. *Average financial aid package:* $9213. *Average need-based loan:* $3715. *Average need-based gift aid:* $4307. *Average non-need-based aid:* $3247. *Average indebtedness upon graduation:* $25,474.

Applying *Options:* electronic application, deferred entrance. *Application fee:* $40. *Required:* essay or personal statement, high school transcript, minimum 2.5 GPA, 2 letters of recommendation. *Recommended:* interview. *Application deadlines:* rolling (freshmen), rolling (transfers). *Notification:* continuous (freshmen), continuous (transfers).

Freshman Application Contact Mr. Maurice Ouimet, Admissions Director, Castleton State College, Castleton, VT 05735. *Phone:* 802-468-1213. *Toll-free phone:* 800-639-8521. *Fax:* 802-468-1476. *E-mail:* info@castleton.edu. *Web site:* http://www.castleton.edu/.

See page 920 for display ad and page 1250 for the College Close-Up.

Champlain College

Burlington, Vermont

- **Independent** comprehensive, founded 1878
- **Suburban** 21-acre campus with easy access to Montreal
- **Endowment** $7.6 million
- **Coed**
- **Moderately difficult** entrance level

Faculty *Student/faculty ratio:* 14:1.

Academics *Calendar:* semesters. *Degrees:* associate, bachelor's, and master's.

Student Life *Campus security:* 24-hour emergency response devices and patrols, late-night transport/escort service, controlled dormitory access.

Standardized Tests *Required:* SAT or ACT (for admission).

Costs (2011–12) *Comprehensive fee:* $40,920 includes full-time tuition ($28,350), mandatory fees ($50), and room and board ($12,520). Full-time tuition and fees vary according to course load. Part-time tuition: $1180 per credit. Part-time tuition and fees vary according to course load. *College room only:* $7620. Room and board charges vary according to housing facility.

Financial Aid Of all full-time matriculated undergraduates who enrolled in 2011, 1,852 applied for aid, 1,482 were judged to have need, 120 had their need fully met. 694 Federal Work-Study jobs (averaging $2555). In 2011, 263 non-need-based awards were made. *Average percent of need met:* 51. *Average financial aid package:* $15,953. *Average need-based loan:* $4681. *Average need-based gift aid:* $9479. *Average non-need-based aid:* $5117. *Average indebtedness upon graduation:* $32,102. *Financial aid deadline:* 3/1.

Applying *Options:* electronic application, early decision. *Application fee:* $50. *Required:* essay or personal statement, high school transcript. *Recommended:* 1 letter of recommendation, interview.

Freshman Application Contact Ian Mortimer, Director of Admissions, Champlain College, 163 South Willard Street, Burlington, VT 05401. *Phone:* 802-860-2727. *Toll-free phone:* 800-570-5858. *Fax:* 802-860-2767. *E-mail:* admission@champlain.edu. *Web site:* http://www.champlain.edu/.

See page 922 for display ad and page 1254 for the College Close-Up.

College of St. Joseph

Rutland, Vermont

- **Independent Roman Catholic** comprehensive, founded 1950
- **Small-town** 117-acre campus
- **Endowment** $4.5 million
- **Coed** 237 undergraduate students, 69% full-time, 61% women, 39% men
- **Minimally difficult** entrance level, 69% of applicants were admitted

Undergraduates 164 full-time, 73 part-time. Students come from 19 states and territories; 26% are from out of state; 10% Black or African American, non-Hispanic/Latino; 1% Hispanic/Latino; 1% American Indian or Alaska Native, non-Hispanic/Latino; 13% transferred in; 33% live on campus. *Retention:* 53% of full-time freshmen returned.

Freshmen *Admission:* 146 applied, 101 admitted, 44 enrolled. *Average high school GPA:* 2.8. *Test scores:* SAT critical reading scores over 500: 15%; SAT math scores over 500: 16%; SAT writing scores over 500: 15%; ACT scores over 18: 60%; SAT critical reading scores over 600: 1%; SAT math scores over 600: 1%; SAT writing scores over 600: 1%; ACT scores over 24: 20%.

Faculty *Total:* 58, 21% full-time, 28% with terminal degrees. *Student/faculty ratio:* 10:1.

Academics *Calendar:* semesters. *Degrees:* associate, bachelor's, master's, and postbachelor's certificates. *Special study options:* academic remediation for entering students, accelerated degree program, adult/continuing education programs, advanced placement credit, double majors, independent study, internships, part-time degree program, services for LD students, summer session for credit.

Computers on Campus 33 computers/terminals are available on campus for general student use. Students can access the following: campus intranet, computer help desk, free student e-mail accounts, online (class) grades, online (class) schedules, online statements/ability to pay tuition online. Campuswide network is available. 100% of college-owned or -operated housing units are wired for high-speed Internet access. Wireless service is available via entire campus.

Student Life *Housing:* on-campus residence required through sophomore year. *Options:* men-only, women-only. Campus housing is university owned. Freshman campus housing is guaranteed. *Activities and organizations:* choral group, Humans vs. Zombies Club, Business Club, Human Services Club, Student Government Association, Cooking Club. *Campus security:* 24-hour emergency response devices, trained security personnel from 8 pm to 6 am. *Student services:* personal/psychological counseling.

Athletics Member USCAA. *Intercollegiate sports:* basketball M/W, bowling M/W, cross-country running M/W, soccer M/W, softball W.

Standardized Tests *Required:* SAT or ACT (for admission).

Costs (2012–13) *Comprehensive fee:* $30,000 includes full-time tuition ($20,125), mandatory fees ($475), and room and board ($9400). Full-time tuition and fees vary according to course load, degree level, and program. Part-time tuition: $260 per credit. Part-time tuition and fees vary according to course load, degree level, and program. *Required fees:* $45 per credit part-time. *Room and board:* Room and board charges vary according to housing facility. *Payment plan:* installment. *Waivers:* senior citizens and employees or children of employees.

Financial Aid Of all full-time matriculated undergraduates who enrolled in 2009, 166 applied for aid, 158 were judged to have need, 13 had their need fully met. 32 Federal Work-Study jobs (averaging $886). 37 state and other part-time jobs (averaging $651). In 2009, 8 non-need-based awards were made. *Average percent of need met:* 87%. *Average financial aid package:* $19,062. *Average need-based loan:* $8905. *Average need-based gift aid:* $10,133. *Average non-need-based aid:* $2843. *Average indebtedness upon graduation:* $25,848.

Applying *Options:* electronic application, early admission, deferred entrance. *Application fee:* $25. *Required:* essay or personal statement, high school transcript, minimum 2.0 GPA, 2 letters of recommendation. *Recommended:* interview. *Application deadlines:* rolling (freshmen), rolling (out-of-state freshmen), rolling (transfers). *Notification:* continuous (freshmen), continuous (out-of-state freshmen), continuous (transfers).

Freshman Application Contact Mr. Alan Young, Dean of Admissions, College of St. Joseph, 71 Clement Road, Rutland, VT 05701-3899. *Phone:* 802-773-5227. *Toll-free phone:* 877-270-9998. *Fax:* 802-776-5310. *E-mail:* admissions@csj.edu. *Web site:* http://www.csj.edu/.

Goddard College
Plainfield, Vermont

- **Independent** comprehensive, founded 1938
- **Rural** 200-acre campus
- **Endowment** $932,377
- **Coed** 250 undergraduate students, 100% full-time, 68% women, 32% men
- **Moderately difficult** entrance level, 89% of applicants were admitted

Undergraduates 250 full-time. Students come from 40 states and territories; 4 other countries; 86% are from out of state; 26% transferred in. *Retention:* 67% of full-time freshmen returned.

Freshmen *Admission:* 9 applied, 8 admitted, 8 enrolled.

Faculty *Total:* 111, 13% full-time, 77% with terminal degrees.

Academics *Calendar:* semesters. *Degrees:* bachelor's, master's, and post-bachelor's certificates. *Special study options:* adult/continuing education programs, advanced placement credit, distance learning, double majors, external degree program, independent study, internships, off-campus study, services for LD students, student-designed majors.

Computers on Campus 55 computers/terminals are available on campus for general student use. Students can access the following: campus intranet, computer help desk, free student e-mail accounts, online (class) schedules, library services. Campuswide network is available. 80% of college-owned or -operated housing units are wired for high-speed Internet access. Wireless service is available via entire campus.

Student Life *Housing options:* coed, women-only, disabled students. Campus housing is university owned. *Activities and organizations:* student-run radio station. *Campus security:* 24-hour patrols, patrols by trained security personnel 9 pm to 6 am. *Student services:* personal/psychological counseling.

Costs (2011–12) *Comprehensive fee:* $14,982 includes full-time tuition ($13,496), mandatory fees ($174), and room and board ($1312). Full-time tuition and fees vary according to location and program. *Room and board:* Room and board charges vary according to location. *Payment plan:* installment. *Waivers:* employees or children of employees.

Financial Aid Of all full-time matriculated undergraduates who enrolled in 2010, 315 applied for aid, 273 were judged to have need, 6 had their need fully met. *Average percent of need met:* 41%. *Average financial aid package:* $7824. *Average need-based loan:* $4329. *Average need-based gift aid:* $4539. *Average indebtedness upon graduation:* $23,228.

Applying *Options:* electronic application, deferred entrance. *Application fee:* $40. *Required:* essay or personal statement, high school transcript, 2 letters of recommendation, interview. *Application deadlines:* rolling (freshmen), rolling (out-of-state freshmen), rolling (transfers). *Notification:* continuous (freshmen), continuous (out-of-state freshmen), continuous (transfers).

Freshman Application Contact Erin Johnson, Admissions Counselor, Goddard College, 123 Pitkin Road, Plainfield, VT 05667-9432. *Phone:* 800-906-8312 Ext. 262. *Toll-free phone:* 800-906-8312. *Fax:* 802-454-1029. *E-mail:* admissions@goddard.edu. *Web site:* http://www.goddard.edu/.

Green Mountain College

Poultney, Vermont

Freshman Application Contact Green Mountain College, One Brennan Circle, Poultney, VT 05764. *Phone:* 802-287-8207. *Toll-free phone:* 800-776-6675. *Web site:* http://www.greenmtn.edu/.

Johnson State College

Johnson, Vermont

- **State-supported** comprehensive, founded 1828, part of Vermont State Colleges System
- **Rural** 350-acre campus with easy access to Montreal
- **Endowment** $2.3 million
- **Coed** 1,662 undergraduate students, 68% full-time, 62% women, 38% men
- **Moderately difficult** entrance level, 86% of applicants were admitted

Undergraduates 1,137 full-time, 525 part-time. Students come from 18 states and territories; 20 other countries; 19% are from out of state; 3% Black or African American, non-Hispanic/Latino; 1% Hispanic/Latino; 1% Asian, non-Hispanic/Latino; 1% American Indian or Alaska Native, non-Hispanic/Latino; 8% Race/ethnicity unknown; 0.1% international; 9% transferred in; 60% live on campus. *Retention:* 64% of full-time freshmen returned.

Freshmen *Admission:* 1,291 applied, 1,107 admitted, 275 enrolled. *Average high school GPA:* 3.32. *Test scores:* SAT critical reading scores over 500: 45%; SAT math scores over 500: 36%; SAT critical reading scores over 600: 11%; SAT math scores over 600: 6%; SAT critical reading scores over 700: 1%.

Faculty *Total:* 137, 36% full-time, 52% with terminal degrees. *Student/faculty ratio:* 16:1.

Academics *Calendar:* semesters. *Degrees:* certificates, associate, bachelor's, master's, and post-master's certificates. *Special study options:* accelerated degree program, advanced placement credit, cooperative education, distance learning, double majors, English as a second language, external degree program, honors programs, independent study, internships, off-campus study, part-time degree program, services for LD students, study abroad, summer session for credit. *ROTC:* Army (c).

Computers on Campus 160 computers/terminals are available on campus for general student use. Students can access the following: campus intranet, computer help desk, free student e-mail accounts, online (class) grades, online (class) registration, online (class) schedules. Campuswide network is available. Wireless service is available via classrooms, libraries, student centers.

Student Life *Housing:* on-campus residence required through sophomore year. *Options:* coed. Campus housing is university owned. Freshman applicants given priority for college housing. *Activities and organizations:* drama/theater group, student-run newspaper, radio station, choral group, SERVE (Break Away), A Global partnership: Students for Children's Right, Ski/Snowboarding Club, Dance Club, Christian Fellowship Club. *Campus security:* 24-hour emergency response devices and patrols, student patrols, late-night transport/escort service, controlled dormitory access. *Student services:* health clinic, personal/psychological counseling, women's center.

Athletics Member NCAA. All Division III. *Intercollegiate sports:* basketball M/W, cross-country running M/W, golf M, lacrosse W, soccer M/W, softball W, tennis M/W, volleyball W. *Intramural sports:* badminton M/W, basketball M/W, cross-country running M/W, golf M(c)/W(c), ice hockey M(c)/W(c), lacrosse M(c)/W, racquetball M/W, rock climbing M(c)/W(c), soccer M/W, softball M/W, swimming and diving M(c)/W(c), table tennis M/W, tennis M/W, volleyball M/W, water polo M/W, weight lifting M/W.

Standardized Tests *Required:* SAT or ACT (for admission).

Costs (2012–13) *Tuition:* state resident $8568 full-time, $357 per credit part-time; nonresident $19,008 full-time, $792 per credit part-time. Full-time tuition and fees vary according to course load. Part-time tuition and fees vary according to course load. *Required fees:* $1104 full-time. *Room and board:* $8444; room only: $5029. Room and board charges vary according to board plan. *Payment plan:* installment. *Waivers:* employees or children of employees.

Financial Aid *Average percent of need met:* 80%. *Average financial aid package:* $7835. *Average indebtedness upon graduation:* $16,910.

Applying *Options:* electronic application, early action, deferred entrance. *Application fee:* $40. *Required:* essay or personal statement, high school transcript, minimum 2.0 GPA, 1 letter of recommendation. *Recommended:* minimum 2.5 GPA, interview. *Application deadlines:* rolling (freshmen), rolling (transfers). *Notification:* continuous (freshmen), continuous (transfers).

Freshman Application Contact Bethany Harrington, Admissions Specialist, Johnson State College, 337 College Hill, Johnson, VT 05656. *Phone:* 802-635-1219. *Toll-free phone:* 800-635-2356. *Fax:* 802-635-1230. *E-mail:* jscadmissions@jsc.edu. *Web site:* http://www.jsc.edu/.

Unique, hands-on professional programs in meteorology, mountain recreation, music business and industry, television studies, graphic and web design, exercise science, and more.

Turn your passion into a profession in a one-of-a-kind Vermont location.

A modern hill-top campus just 10 minutes from world-class mountain biking and winter sports fun— Lyndon is Vermont's adventure recreation campus.

LYNDONVILLE, VERMONT 1.800.225.1998

LyndonState.edu f Facebook.com/LyndonState

LYNDON
A *vermont* STATE COLLEGE

Lyndon State College

Lyndonville, Vermont

- **State-supported** comprehensive, founded 1911, part of Vermont State Colleges System
- **Rural** 175-acre campus
- **Endowment** $2.8 million
- **Coed**
- **Moderately difficult** entrance level

Faculty *Student/faculty ratio:* 15:1.

Academics *Calendar:* semesters. *Degrees:* associate, bachelor's, and master's.

Student Life *Campus security:* 24-hour emergency response devices, student patrols, late-night transport/escort service, controlled dormitory access.

Athletics Member NCAA. All Division III.

Standardized Tests *Required:* SAT or ACT (for admission).

Costs (2011–12) *Tuition:* state resident $8568 full-time, $357 per credit part-time; nonresident $18,456 full-time, $769 per credit part-time. Full-time tuition and fees vary according to course load. Part-time tuition and fees vary according to course load. *Required fees:* $1380 full-time, $75 per credit part-time. *Room and board:* $8446; room only: $5030. Room and board charges vary according to board plan and housing facility.

Applying *Options:* electronic application, early admission, deferred entrance. *Application fee:* $36. *Required:* high school transcript, minimum 2.0 GPA, 1 letter of recommendation. *Required for some:* essay or personal statement, minimum 3.0 GPA. *Recommended:* minimum 3.0 GPA, interview.

Freshman Application Contact Ms. Cheri Goldrick, Admissions Assistant, Lyndon State College, 1001 College Road, PO Box 919, Lyndonville, VT 05851. *Phone:* 802-626-6451. *Toll-free phone:* 800-225-1998. *Fax:* 802-626-6335. *E-mail:* admissions@lyndonstate.edu. *Web site:* http://www.lyndonstate.edu/.

See page 923 for display ad and page 1428 for the College Close-Up.

Marlboro College

Marlboro, Vermont

- **Independent** comprehensive, founded 1946
- **Rural** 350-acre campus
- **Endowment** $36.8 million
- **Coed** 267 undergraduate students, 97% full-time, 51% women, 49% men
- **Moderately difficult** entrance level, 75% of applicants were admitted

Undergraduates 260 full-time, 7 part-time. Students come from 34 states and territories; 3 other countries; 85% are from out of state; 0.7% Black or African American, non-Hispanic/Latino; 2% Hispanic/Latino; 3% Asian, non-Hispanic/Latino; 0.7% American Indian or Alaska Native, non-Hispanic/Latino; 4% Two or more races, non-Hispanic/Latino; 27% Race/ethnicity unknown; 6% transferred in; 80% live on campus. *Retention:* 77% of full-time freshmen returned.

Freshmen *Admission:* 279 applied, 209 admitted, 59 enrolled. *Average high school GPA:* 3.26. *Test scores:* SAT critical reading scores over 500: 99%; SAT math scores over 500: 83%; SAT writing scores over 500: 87%; SAT critical reading scores over 600: 76%; SAT math scores over 600: 38%; SAT writing scores over 600: 53%; SAT critical reading scores over 700: 20%; SAT math scores over 700: 6%; SAT writing scores over 700: 15%.

Faculty *Total:* 49, 82% full-time, 88% with terminal degrees. *Student/faculty ratio:* 6:1.

Academics *Calendar:* semesters. *Degrees:* bachelor's and master's. *Special study options:* accelerated degree program, advanced placement credit, double majors, independent study, internships, off-campus study, part-time degree program, services for LD students, student-designed majors, study abroad.

Computers on Campus 47 computers/terminals are available on campus for general student use. Students can access the following: campus intranet, computer help desk, free student e-mail accounts, online (class) grades, online (class) registration, online (class) schedules. Campuswide network is available. 100% of college-owned or -operated housing units are wired for high-speed Internet access. Wireless service is available via entire campus.

Student Life *Housing:* on-campus residence required for freshman year. *Options:* coed, women-only, cooperative. Campus housing is university owned. Freshman campus housing is guaranteed. *Activities and organizations:* drama/theater group, student-run newspaper, radio station, choral group, outdoor program, theater, farm program, Gay/Lesbian/Bisexual Alliance, madrigal and a cappella groups. *Campus security:* 24-hour emergency response

devices and patrols. *Student services:* health clinic, personal/psychological counseling, women's center.

Athletics *Intercollegiate sports:* soccer M/W. *Intramural sports:* basketball M/W, fencing M/W, rock climbing M/W, skiing (cross-country) M/W, skiing (downhill) M/W, soccer M/W, softball M/W, table tennis M/W, ultimate Frisbee M/W.

Costs (2012–13) *Comprehensive fee:* $47,570 includes full-time tuition ($36,300), mandatory fees ($1340), and room and board ($9930). Full-time tuition and fees vary according to program. Part-time tuition: $1210 per credit. Part-time tuition and fees vary according to course load and program. *Required fees:* $210 per year part-time. *College room only:* $5470. *Payment plan:* installment. *Waivers:* senior citizens and employees or children of employees.

Financial Aid Of all full-time matriculated undergraduates who enrolled in 2011, 221 applied for aid, 197 were judged to have need. In 2011, 44 non-need-based awards were made. *Average percent of need met:* 68%. *Average financial aid package:* $26,625. *Average need-based loan:* $4324. *Average need-based gift aid:* $20,433. *Average non-need-based aid:* $9403. *Average indebtedness upon graduation:* $20,886. *Financial aid deadline:* 3/1.

Applying *Options:* electronic application, early admission, early decision, early action, deferred entrance. *Application fee:* $50. *Required:* essay or personal statement, high school transcript, 2 letters of recommendation, analytical essay. *Required for some:* interview. *Recommended:* interview. *Application deadlines:* 3/1 (freshmen), 4/1 (transfers), 1/15 (early action). *Early decision deadline:* 11/15. *Notification:* continuous until 3/15 (freshmen), continuous until 4/15 (transfers), 12/1 (early decision), 2/1 (early action).

Freshman Application Contact Ms. Jessica Nelson, Assistant Director of Admissions, Marlboro College, PO Box A, 2582 South Road, Marlboro, VT 05344-0300. *Phone:* 800-343-0049. *Toll-free phone:* 800-343-0049. *Fax:* 802-451-7555. *E-mail:* admissions@marlboro.edu. *Web site:* http://www.marlboro.edu/.

See page 1432 for the College Close-Up.

Middlebury College
Middlebury, Vermont

- **Independent** comprehensive, founded 1800
- **Small-town** 350-acre campus
- **Endowment** $907.7 million
- **Coed** 2,507 undergraduate students, 99% full-time, 51% women, 49% men
- **Most difficult** entrance level, 18% of applicants were admitted

Undergraduates 2,480 full-time, 27 part-time. Students come from 52 states and territories; 67 other countries; 95% are from out of state; 2% Black or African American, non-Hispanic/Latino; 6% Hispanic/Latino; 6% Asian, non-Hispanic/Latino; 0.2% American Indian or Alaska Native, non-Hispanic/Latino; 4% Two or more races, non-Hispanic/Latino; 4% Race/ethnicity unknown; 11% international; 97% live on campus. *Retention:* 95% of full-time freshmen returned.

Freshmen *Admission:* 8,533 applied, 1,563 admitted, 602 enrolled. *Test scores:* SAT critical reading scores over 500: 99%; SAT math scores over 500: 99%; SAT writing scores over 500: 99%; ACT scores over 18: 100%; SAT critical reading scores over 600: 88%; SAT math scores over 600: 91%; SAT writing scores over 600: 91%; ACT scores over 24: 98%; SAT critical reading scores over 700: 50%; SAT math scores over 700: 51%; SAT writing scores over 700: 57%; ACT scores over 30: 77%.

Faculty *Total:* 323, 83% full-time, 89% with terminal degrees. *Student/faculty ratio:* 9:1.

Academics *Calendar:* 4-1-4. *Degrees:* bachelor's, master's, doctoral, and first professional. *Special study options:* accelerated degree program, advanced placement credit, double majors, honors programs, independent study, internships, off-campus study, services for LD students, student-designed majors, study abroad, summer session for credit. *ROTC:* Army (c). *Unusual degree programs:* 3-2 business administration with University of Chicago; New York University; Rutgers, The State University of New Jersey, Graduate School of Management; University of Rochester; Columbia University; Boston University; Dartmouth College; engineering with Columbia University, Rensselaer Polytechnic Institute, University of Rochester; forestry with Duke University; nursing with Columbia University.

Computers on Campus 494 computers/terminals are available on campus for general student use. Students can access the following: computer help desk, free student e-mail accounts, online (class) registration, online (class) schedules, help-line, personal Web pages, file servers. Campuswide network is available. Wireless service is available via entire campus.

Student Life *Housing:* on-campus residence required through junior year. *Options:* coed, disabled students. Campus housing is university owned. Freshman campus housing is guaranteed. *Activities and organizations:* drama/theater group, student-run newspaper, radio station, choral group, Volunteer

Service Organization, International Students Organization, Mountain Club, Activities Board, WRMC radio. *Campus security:* 24-hour patrols, student patrols, late-night transport/escort service, controlled dormitory access. *Student services:* health clinic, personal/psychological counseling, women's center.

Athletics Member NCAA. All Division III except men's and women's skiing (downhill) (Division I). *Intercollegiate sports:* baseball M, basketball M/W, cross-country running M/W, field hockey W, football M, golf M/W, ice hockey M/W, lacrosse M/W, skiing (cross-country) M/W, skiing (downhill) M/W, soccer M/W, softball W, squash W, swimming and diving M/W, tennis M/W, track and field M/W, volleyball W. *Intramural sports:* badminton M/W, basketball M/W, crew M(c)/W(c), cross-country running M/W, equestrian sports M(c)/W(c), football M/W, golf M/W, ice hockey M/W, rock climbing M(c)/W(c), rugby M(c)/W(c), sailing M(c)/W(c), skiing (cross-country) M/W, skiing (downhill) M/W, soccer M/W, softball M/W, squash M(c)/W(c), swimming and diving M/W, table tennis M/W, tennis M/W, ultimate Frisbee M(c)/W(c), volleyball M/W, water polo M(c)/W(c).

Standardized Tests *Required:* three tests to include: a writing test, a quantitative test, and an area of the applicant's choice (for admission).

Costs (2011–12) *Comprehensive fee:* $53,800. *Payment plan:* tuition prepayment. *Waivers:* employees or children of employees.

Financial Aid Of all full-time matriculated undergraduates who enrolled in 2010, 1,307 applied for aid, 1,041 were judged to have need, 1,039 had their need fully met. In 2010, 2 non-need-based awards were made. *Average percent of need met:* 100%. *Average financial aid package:* $35,517. *Average need-based loan:* $2552. *Average need-based gift aid:* $33,520. *Average non-need-based aid:* $2500. *Average indebtedness upon graduation:* $20,514. *Financial aid deadline:* 2/1.

Applying *Options:* electronic application, early admission, early decision, deferred entrance. *Application fee:* $65. *Required:* essay or personal statement, high school transcript, 3 letters of recommendation. *Recommended:* interview. *Application deadlines:* 1/1 (freshmen), 3/1 (transfers). *Early decision deadline:* 11/1 (for plan 1), 12/15 (for plan 2). *Notification:* 4/1 (freshmen), 4/10 (transfers), 12/15 (early decision plan 1), 2/15 (early decision plan 2).

Freshman Application Contact Mr. Greg Buckles, Dean of Admissions, Middlebury College, Emma Willard House, Middlebury, VT 05753-6002. *Phone:* 802-443-3000. *Fax:* 802-443-2056. *E-mail:* admissions@middlebury.edu. *Web site:* http://www.middlebury.edu/.

New England Culinary Institute
Montpelier, Vermont

Freshman Application Contact Jan Knutsen, Vice President of Enrollment, New England Culinary Institute, 56 College Street, Montpelier, VT 05602-3115. *Toll-free phone:* 877-223-6324. *Fax:* 802-225-3280. *E-mail:* janknutsen@neci.edu. *Web site:* http://www.neci.edu/.

Norwich University
Northfield, Vermont

- **Independent** comprehensive, founded 1819
- **Small-town** 1125-acre campus with easy access to Burlington
- **Endowment** $174.3 million
- **Coed, primarily men** 2,246 undergraduate students, 97% full-time, 26% women, 74% men
- **Moderately difficult** entrance level, 56% of applicants were admitted

Undergraduates 2,172 full-time, 74 part-time. Students come from 30 states and territories; 8 other countries; 85% are from out of state; 3% Black or African American, non-Hispanic/Latino; 4% Hispanic/Latino; 2% Asian, non-Hispanic/Latino; 0.1% Native Hawaiian or other Pacific Islander, non-Hispanic/Latino; 0.7% American Indian or Alaska Native, non-Hispanic/Latino; 2% Two or more races, non-Hispanic/Latino; 15% Race/ethnicity unknown; 2% international; 2% transferred in; 82% live on campus. *Retention:* 85% of full-time freshmen returned.

Freshmen *Admission:* 3,131 applied, 1,769 admitted, 605 enrolled. *Average high school GPA:* 3.12. *Test scores:* SAT critical reading scores over 500: 69%; SAT math scores over 500: 74%; SAT writing scores over 500: 58%; ACT scores over 18: 95%; SAT critical reading scores over 600: 20%; SAT math scores over 600: 24%; SAT writing scores over 600: 14%; ACT scores over 24: 53%; SAT critical reading scores over 700: 2%; SAT math scores over 700: 1%; SAT writing scores over 700: 1%; ACT scores over 30: 3%.

Faculty *Total:* 205, 68% full-time. *Student/faculty ratio:* 14:1.

Academics *Calendar:* semesters. *Degrees:* bachelor's, master's, and postbachelor's certificates. *Special study options:* academic remediation for entering students, adult/continuing education programs, advanced placement credit, cooperative education, distance learning, double majors, English as a second language, external degree program, honors programs, independent study,

internships, part-time degree program, services for LD students, study abroad, summer session for credit. *ROTC:* Army (b), Navy (b), Air Force (b).

Computers on Campus 200 computers/terminals are available on campus for general student use. Students can access the following: campus intranet, computer help desk, free student e-mail accounts, online (class) grades, online (class) schedules. Campuswide network is available. 100% of college-owned or -operated housing units are wired for high-speed Internet access. Wireless service is available via entire campus.

Student Life *Housing:* on-campus residence required through senior year. *Options:* coed. Campus housing is university owned. Freshman campus housing is guaranteed. *Activities and organizations:* drama/theater group, student-run newspaper, radio station, choral group, marching band, DREAM, NUEMS, IEEE, CJSA, Politeia/Model UN. *Campus security:* 24-hour emergency response devices and patrols, late-night transport/escort service. *Student services:* health clinic, personal/psychological counseling.

Athletics Member NCAA. All Division III. *Intercollegiate sports:* baseball M, basketball M/W, cross-country running M/W, fencing M(c)/W(c), football M, ice hockey M/W(c), lacrosse M, riflery M/W, rugby M(c)/W(c), sailing M(c)/W(c), skiing (cross-country) M(c)/W(c), skiing (downhill) M(c)/W(c), soccer M/W, softball W, swimming and diving M/W, tennis M/W(c), track and field M/W, volleyball M(c)/W(c), weight lifting M(c)/W(c), wrestling M. *Intramural sports:* basketball M/W, cross-country running M/W, football M, golf M/W, ice hockey M/W, lacrosse M/W, racquetball M/W, rugby M/W, soccer M/W, softball W, swimming and diving M/W, tennis M/W, track and field M/W, volleyball M/W, water polo M/W, weight lifting M/W, wrestling M.

Standardized Tests *Required:* SAT or ACT (for admission).

Costs (2012–13) *Comprehensive fee:* $42,758 includes full-time tuition ($30,048), mandatory fees ($1734), and room and board ($10,976). Part-time tuition and fees vary according to course load.

Applying *Options:* electronic application. *Application fee:* $35. *Required:* essay or personal statement, high school transcript. *Required for some:* portfolio. *Recommended:* minimum 2.0 GPA, 2 letters of recommendation, interview. *Application deadlines:* rolling (freshmen), rolling (transfers). *Notification:* continuous (freshmen), continuous (transfers).

Freshman Application Contact Norwich University, 158 Harmon Drive, Northfield, VT 05663. *Phone:* 802-485-2658. *Toll-free phone:* 800-468-6679. *Web site:* http://www.norwich.edu/.

See below for display ad and page 1488 for the College Close-Up.

Saint Michael's College
Colchester, Vermont

- **Independent Roman Catholic** comprehensive, founded 1904
- **Suburban** 440-acre campus with easy access to Montreal
- **Endowment** $70.9 million
- **Coed** 1,996 undergraduate students, 99% full-time, 52% women, 48% men
- **Moderately difficult** entrance level, 78% of applicants were admitted

Undergraduates 1,970 full-time, 26 part-time. Students come from 36 states and territories; 16 other countries; 81% are from out of state; 1% Black or African American, non-Hispanic/Latino; 3% Hispanic/Latino; 1% Asian, non-Hispanic/Latino; 0.2% American Indian or Alaska Native, non-Hispanic/Latino; 0.9% Two or more races, non-Hispanic/Latino; 0.7% Race/ethnicity unknown; 2% international; 2% transferred in; 97% live on campus. *Retention:* 87% of full-time freshmen returned.

Freshmen *Admission:* 4,474 applied, 3,493 admitted, 542 enrolled. *Average high school GPA:* 3.5. *Test scores:* SAT critical reading scores over 500: 89%; SAT math scores over 500: 88%; SAT writing scores over 500: 86%; ACT scores over 18: 98%; SAT critical reading scores over 600: 44%; SAT math scores over 600: 38%; SAT writing scores over 600: 37%; ACT scores over 24: 69%; SAT critical reading scores over 700: 10%; SAT math scores over 700: 6%; SAT writing scores over 700: 6%; ACT scores over 30: 11%.

Faculty *Total:* 208, 72% full-time, 75% with terminal degrees. *Student/faculty ratio:* 12:1.

Academics *Calendar:* semesters. *Degrees:* bachelor's, master's, post-master's, and postbachelor's certificates. *Special study options:* advanced placement credit, distance learning, double majors, English as a second language, honors programs, independent study, internships, off-campus study, part-time degree program, services for LD students, student-designed majors, study abroad, summer session for credit. *ROTC:* Army (c), Air Force (c). *Unusual degree programs:* 3-2 business administration with Clarkson University; engineering with University of Vermont, and Clarkson University; pre-pharmacy dual degree (BS/D.Pharm) with Albany College of Pharmacy and Health Sciences.

Computers on Campus 390 computers/terminals and 5,000 ports are available on campus for general student use. Students can access the following: computer help desk, free student e-mail accounts, online (class) grades, online (class) registration, online (class) schedules. Campuswide network is available. 100% of college-owned or -operated housing units are wired for high-speed

Internet access. Wireless service is available via classrooms, computer centers, computer labs, dorm rooms, libraries, student centers.

Student Life *Housing:* on-campus residence required through senior year. *Options:* coed, men-only, women-only, disabled students. Campus housing is university owned. Freshman campus housing is guaranteed. *Activities and organizations:* drama/theater group, student-run newspaper, radio station, choral group, Student Association (governing board), Mobilization of Volunteer Efforts (MOVE), WWPV-FM (student run radio station), Wilderness Program, student newspaper/online publication (The Defender). *Campus security:* 24-hour emergency response devices and patrols, student patrols, late-night transport/escort service, controlled dormitory access, bicycle patrols; Fire and Rescue Squad serving the surrounding community with professionally trained student volunteers. *Student services:* health clinic, personal/psychological counseling, women's center.

Athletics Member NCAA. All Division II. *Intercollegiate sports:* baseball M, basketball M(s)/W(s), cross-country running M/W, field hockey W, golf M, ice hockey M/W, lacrosse M/W, rugby M(c)/W(c), skiing (cross-country) M/W, skiing (downhill) M/W, soccer M/W, softball W, swimming and diving M/W, tennis M/W, volleyball W. *Intramural sports:* basketball M/W, cross-country running M/W, ice hockey M/W, racquetball M/W, rock climbing M/W, skiing (cross-country) M/W, skiing (downhill) M/W, soccer M/W, softball M/W, squash M/W, swimming and diving M/W, table tennis M/W, tennis M/W, track and field M(c)/W(c), ultimate Frisbee M(c)/W(c), volleyball M/W.

Standardized Tests *Recommended:* SAT or ACT (for admission), Saint Michael's is a test-optional institution. Therefore, you do not have to submit standardized test scores (SAT Reasoning Test or ACT with Writing) to be considered for admission. For more information please visit our website at: www.smcvt.edu/admission/newsat/default.asp.

Costs (2012–13) *Comprehensive fee:* $46,860 includes full-time tuition ($37,200), mandatory fees ($310), and room and board ($9350). Full-time tuition and fees vary according to course load. Part-time tuition: $1240 per credit. Part-time tuition and fees vary according to course load. *Room and board:* Room and board charges vary according to board plan and housing facility. *Payment plan:* installment. *Waivers:* employees or children of employees.

Financial Aid Of all full-time matriculated undergraduates who enrolled in 2011, 1,468 applied for aid, 1,270 were judged to have need, 343 had their need fully met. In 2011, 562 non-need-based awards were made. *Average percent of need met:* 76%. *Average financial aid package:* $23,073. *Average need-based loan:* $5212. *Average need-based gift aid:* $18,270. *Average non-need-based aid:* $10,546. *Average indebtedness upon graduation:* $31,736.

Applying *Options:* electronic application, early action, deferred entrance. *Application fee:* $50. *Required:* essay or personal statement, high school transcript. *Recommended:* minimum 3.0 GPA, 3 letters of recommendation, interview. *Application deadlines:* 2/1 (freshmen), 3/15 (transfers), 11/1 (early action). *Notification:* 4/1 (freshmen), 4/15 (transfers), 1/1 (early action).

Freshman Application Contact Ms. Jacqueline Murphy, Director of Admission, Saint Michael's College, One Winooski Park, Colchester, VT 05452. *Phone:* 802-654-3000. *Toll-free phone:* 800-762-8000. *Fax:* 802-654-2906. *E-mail:* admission@smcvt.edu. *Web site:* http://www.smcvt.edu/.

See below for display ad and page 1564 for the College Close-Up.

Southern Vermont College
Bennington, Vermont

- **Independent** 4-year, founded 1926
- **Small-town** 371-acre campus with easy access to Albany, NY
- **Endowment** $1.2 million
- **Coed** 530 undergraduate students, 89% full-time, 65% women, 35% men
- **Minimally difficult** entrance level, 75% of applicants were admitted

Undergraduates 470 full-time, 60 part-time. Students come from 13 states and territories; 4 other countries; 66% are from out of state; 8% Black or African American, non-Hispanic/Latino; 5% Hispanic/Latino; 2% Asian, non-Hispanic/Latino; 0.4% American Indian or Alaska Native, non-Hispanic/Latino; 4% Race/ethnicity unknown; 3% international; 12% transferred in; 55% live on campus. *Retention:* 53% of full-time freshmen returned.

Freshmen *Admission:* 463 applied, 349 admitted, 157 enrolled. *Average high school GPA:* 2.5. *Test scores:* SAT critical reading scores over 500: 24%; SAT math scores over 500: 27%; ACT scores over 18: 56%; SAT critical reading scores over 600: 7%; SAT math scores over 600: 3%; ACT scores over 24: 12%; SAT critical reading scores over 700: 1%.

Faculty *Total:* 54, 48% full-time, 28% with terminal degrees. *Student/faculty ratio:* 14:1.

Academics *Calendar:* semesters. *Degrees:* associate and bachelor's. *Special study options:* academic remediation for entering students, accelerated degree program, adult/continuing education programs, advanced placement credit, cooperative education, distance learning, double majors, external degree program, independent study, internships, off-campus study, part-time degree program, services for LD students, student-designed majors, study abroad, summer session for credit.

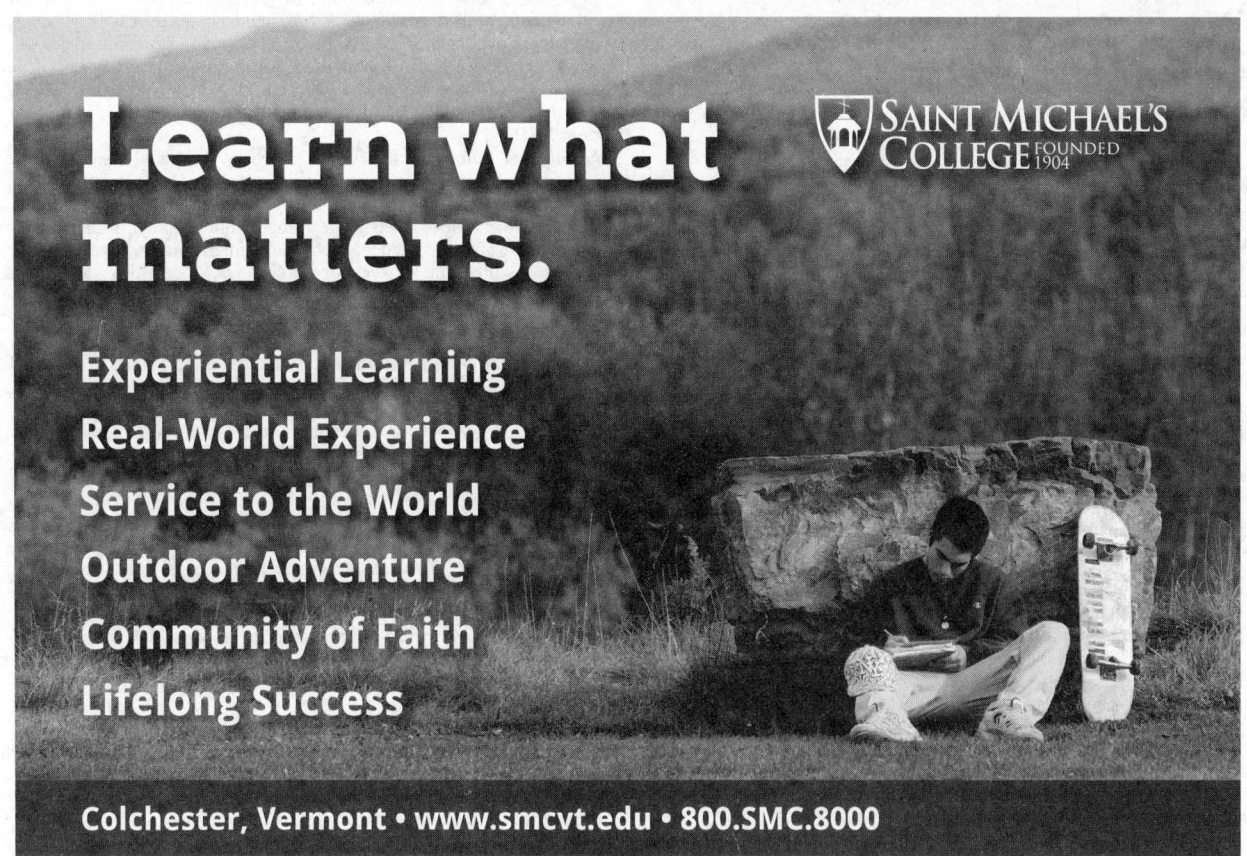

Computers on Campus 50 computers/terminals are available on campus for general student use. Students can access the following: campus intranet, computer help desk, free student e-mail accounts, online (class) grades, online (class) registration, online (class) schedules. Campuswide network is available. 100% of college-owned or -operated housing units are wired for high-speed Internet access. Wireless service is available via entire campus.

Student Life *Housing:* on-campus residence required through sophomore year. *Options:* coed. Campus housing is university owned. Freshman campus housing is guaranteed. *Activities and organizations:* drama/theater group, Student Government Association, Mountaineer Event Board, Japanese Culture and Anime Club, Big Brothers Big Sisters, Moosecorps. *Campus security:* 24-hour patrols, late-night transport/escort service, controlled dormitory access. *Student services:* health clinic, personal/psychological counseling.

Athletics Member NCAA. All Division III. *Intercollegiate sports:* baseball M, basketball M/W, cross-country running M/W, soccer M/W, softball W, volleyball M/W. *Intramural sports:* basketball M/W, cheerleading W(c), golf M/W, rugby M(c)/W(c), skiing (cross-country) M(c)/W(c), skiing (downhill) M(c)/W(c), soccer M/W, volleyball M/W.

Standardized Tests *Required:* SAT or ACT (for admission).

Costs (2012–13) *Comprehensive fee:* $30,010 includes full-time tuition ($20,200), mandatory fees ($250), and room and board ($9560). Full-time tuition and fees vary according to program. Part-time tuition: $690 per credit. Part-time tuition and fees vary according to course load and program. *College room only:* $4780. Room and board charges vary according to board plan and housing facility. *Payment plan:* installment. *Waivers:* employees or children of employees.

Financial Aid Of all full-time matriculated undergraduates who enrolled in 2006, 287 applied for aid, 262 were judged to have need, 32 had their need fully met. 71 Federal Work-Study jobs (averaging $1200). In 2006, 18 non-need-based awards were made. *Average percent of need met:* 65%. *Average financial aid package:* $12,689. *Average need-based loan:* $4231. *Average need-based gift aid:* $9088. *Average non-need-based aid:* $3461. *Average indebtedness upon graduation:* $20,244.

Applying *Options:* electronic application, early admission, deferred entrance. *Application fee:* $30. *Required:* essay or personal statement, high school transcript, 2 letters of recommendation. *Required for some:* interview, Deans report and college transcripts for transfer students. *Recommended:* minimum 2.0 GPA, interview. *Application deadlines:* rolling (freshmen), rolling (out-of-state freshmen), rolling (transfers). *Notification:* continuous (freshmen), continuous (out-of-state freshmen), continuous (transfers).

Freshman Application Contact Southern Vermont College, 982 Mansion Drive, Bennington, VT 05201. *Phone:* 802-447-6300. *Fax:* 802-681-2868. *E-mail:* admissions@svc.edu. *Web site:* http://www.svc.edu/.

Sterling College
Craftsbury Common, Vermont

- **Independent** 4-year, founded 1958
- **Rural** 430-acre campus
- **Endowment** $876,051
- **Coed** 98 undergraduate students, 96% full-time, 48% women, 52% men
- **Moderately difficult** entrance level, 89% of applicants were admitted

Undergraduates 94 full-time, 4 part-time. Students come from 24 states and territories; 1 other country; 80% are from out of state; 1% Black or African American, non-Hispanic/Latino; 3% Hispanic/Latino; 1% Asian, non-Hispanic/Latino; 2% Two or more races, non-Hispanic/Latino; 14% Race/ethnicity unknown; 13% transferred in; 80% live on campus. *Retention:* 75% of full-time freshmen returned.

Freshmen *Admission:* 53 applied, 47 admitted, 24 enrolled.

Faculty *Total:* 29, 34% full-time, 14% with terminal degrees. *Student/faculty ratio:* 6:1.

Academics *Calendar:* semesters. *Degree:* bachelor's. *Special study options:* advanced placement credit, double majors, independent study, internships, off-campus study, services for LD students, student-designed majors, study abroad, summer session for credit.

Computers on Campus 18 computers/terminals are available on campus for general student use. Students can access the following: campus intranet, computer help desk, free student e-mail accounts. Campuswide network is available. 100% of college-owned or -operated housing units are wired for high-speed Internet access. Wireless service is available via entire campus.

Student Life *Housing options:* coed. Campus housing is university owned. Freshman campus housing is guaranteed. *Activities and organizations:* drama/theater group, choral group, Outing Club, Timbersports Team, Student Union, Art Club, Musical Groups. *Campus security:* 24-hour pager. *Student services:* health clinic, personal/psychological counseling.

Costs (2012–13) *Comprehensive fee:* $37,092 includes full-time tuition ($28,410), mandatory fees ($350), and room and board ($8332). Full-time tuition and fees vary according to course load. Part-time tuition: $900 per

credit. Part-time tuition and fees vary according to course load. *Room and board:* Room and board charges vary according to board plan. *Payment plan:* installment. *Waivers:* employees or children of employees.

Financial Aid Of all full-time matriculated undergraduates who enrolled in 2010, 98 applied for aid, 91 were judged to have need, 4 had their need fully met. In 2010, 13 non-need-based awards were made. *Average percent of need met:* 80%. *Average financial aid package:* $24,457. *Average need-based loan:* $3778. *Average need-based gift aid:* $18,700. *Average non-need-based aid:* $4394. *Average indebtedness upon graduation:* $22,620.

Applying *Options:* electronic application, early admission, early action, deferred entrance. *Application fee:* $35. *Required:* essay or personal statement, high school transcript, 2 letters of recommendation. *Recommended:* minimum 2.0 GPA, interview. *Application deadlines:* rolling (freshmen), rolling (transfers), 12/15 (early action). *Notification:* continuous (freshmen), continuous (transfers), 1/15 (early action).

Freshman Application Contact Ms. Lynne A. Birdsall, Director of Admissions, Sterling College, PO Box 72, Craftsbury Common, VT 05827. *Phone:* 802-586-7711 Ext. 135. *Toll-free phone:* 800-648-3591 Ext. 100. *Fax:* 802-586-2596. *E-mail:* lbirdsall@sterlingcollege.edu. *Web site:* http://www.sterlingcollege.edu/.

University of Vermont
Burlington, Vermont

- **State-supported** university, founded 1791
- **Suburban** 459-acre campus
- **Endowment** $352.3 million
- **Coed** 11,504 undergraduate students, 89% full-time, 56% women, 44% men
- **Moderately difficult** entrance level, 35% of applicants were admitted

Undergraduates 10,258 full-time, 1,246 part-time. Students come from 49 states and territories; 30 other countries; 67% are from out of state; 1% Black or African American, non-Hispanic/Latino; 4% Hispanic/Latino; 2% Asian, non-Hispanic/Latino; 0.1% Native Hawaiian or other Pacific Islander, non-Hispanic/Latino; 0.3% American Indian or Alaska Native, non-Hispanic/Latino; 2% Two or more races, non-Hispanic/Latino; 3% Race/ethnicity unknown; 2% international; 4% transferred in; 51% live on campus. *Retention:* 85% of full-time freshmen returned.

Freshmen *Admission:* 22,341 applied, 7,841 admitted, 2,423 enrolled. *Test scores:* SAT critical reading scores over 500: 91%; SAT math scores over 500: 91%; SAT writing scores over 500: 90%; ACT scores over 18: 99%; SAT critical reading scores over 600: 47%; SAT math scores over 600: 51%; SAT writing scores over 600: 47%; ACT scores over 24: 79%; SAT critical reading scores over 700: 9%; SAT math scores over 700: 7%; SAT writing scores over 700: 8%; ACT scores over 30: 17%.

Faculty *Total:* 743, 80% full-time, 78% with terminal degrees. *Student/faculty ratio:* 17:1.

Academics *Calendar:* semesters. *Degrees:* bachelor's, master's, doctoral, post-master's, postbachelor's, and first professional certificates. *Special study options:* adult/continuing education programs, advanced placement credit, cooperative education, distance learning, double majors, freshman honors college, honors programs, independent study, internships, off-campus study, part-time degree program, services for LD students, student-designed majors, study abroad, summer session for credit. *ROTC:* Army (b). *Unusual degree programs:* 3-2 computer science.

Computers on Campus 850 computers/terminals and 299 ports are available on campus for general student use. Students can access the following: campus intranet, computer help desk, free student e-mail accounts, online (class) grades, online (class) registration, online (class) schedules, Web pages, online course support. Campuswide network is available. 100% of college-owned or -operated housing units are wired for high-speed Internet access. Wireless service is available via classrooms, computer centers, computer labs, learning centers, libraries, student centers.

Student Life *Housing:* on-campus residence required through sophomore year. *Options:* coed. Campus housing is university owned. Freshman campus housing is guaranteed. *Activities and organizations:* drama/theater group, student-run newspaper, radio and television station, choral group, Volunteers in Action, Outing Club, Ski and Snowboard Club, national fraternities, national sororities. *Campus security:* 24-hour emergency response devices and patrols, late-night transport/escort service, controlled dormitory access. *Student services:* health clinic, personal/psychological counseling, women's center, legal services.

Athletics Member NCAA. All Division I. *Intercollegiate sports:* basketball M(s)/W(s), cheerleading M(c)/W(c), crew M(c)/W(c), cross-country running M(s)/W(s), equestrian sports M(c)/W(c), fencing M(c)/W(c), field hockey W(s), gymnastics M(c)/W(c), ice hockey M(s)/W(s), lacrosse M(s)/W(s), rugby M(c)/W(c), sailing M(c)/W(c), skiing (cross-country) M(s)/W(s), skiing (downhill) M(s)/W(s), soccer M(s)/W(s), swimming and diving W(s), table

tennis M(c)/W(c), track and field M(s)/W(s), ultimate Frisbee M(c)/W(c), volleyball M(c)/W(c), water polo M(c)/W(c). *Intramural sports:* basketball M/W, bowling M/W, football M/W, ice hockey M/W, lacrosse M/W, racquetball M/W, soccer M/W, softball M/W, tennis M/W, volleyball M/W, water polo M/W.

Standardized Tests *Required:* SAT or ACT (for admission).

Costs (2011–12) *Tuition:* state resident $12,888 full-time, $537 per credit hour part-time; nonresident $32,528 full-time, $1355 per credit hour part-time. Part-time tuition and fees vary according to course load. *Required fees:* $1866 full-time. *Room and board:* $9738. Room and board charges vary according to board plan and housing facility. *Waivers:* employees or children of employees.

Financial Aid Of all full-time matriculated undergraduates who enrolled in 2010, 7,210 applied for aid, 6,189 were judged to have need, 801 had their need fully met. 1,271 Federal Work-Study jobs (averaging $1201). In 2010, 1770 non-need-based awards were made. *Average percent of need met:* 67%. *Average financial aid package:* $18,272. *Average need-based loan:* $4564. *Average need-based gift aid:* $14,589. *Average non-need-based aid:* $3559. *Average indebtedness upon graduation:* $27,725.

Applying *Options:* electronic application, early action, deferred entrance. *Application fee:* $55. *Required:* essay or personal statement, high school transcript, 1 letter of recommendation. *Application deadlines:* 1/15 (freshmen), 4/15 (transfers), 11/1 (early action). *Notification:* 3/31 (freshmen), continuous (transfers), 12/15 (early action).

Freshman Application Contact Beth A. Wiser PhD, Director of Admissions, University of Vermont, Office of Admissions, 194 South Prospect Street, Burlington, VT 05401-3596. *Phone:* 802-656-3370. *Fax:* 802-656-8611. *E-mail:* admissions@uvm.edu. *Web site:* http://www.uvm.edu/.

Vermont Technical College

Randolph Center, Vermont

- **State-supported** 4-year, founded 1866, part of Vermont State Colleges System
- **Rural** 544-acre campus
- **Coed** 1,607 undergraduate students, 77% full-time, 42% women, 58% men
- **Moderately difficult** entrance level, 63% of applicants were admitted

Undergraduates 1,234 full-time, 373 part-time. Students come from 15 states and territories; 14 other countries; 12% are from out of state; 2% Black or African American, non-Hispanic/Latino; 1% Hispanic/Latino; 1% Asian, non-His-

panic/Latino; 0.1% Native Hawaiian or other Pacific Islander, non-Hispanic/Latino; 1% American Indian or Alaska Native, non-Hispanic/Latino; 0.1% Race/ethnicity unknown; 0.3% international; 20% transferred in. *Retention:* 69% of full-time freshmen returned.

Freshmen *Admission:* 810 applied, 509 admitted, 254 enrolled. *Average high school GPA:* 3.01. *Test scores:* SAT critical reading scores over 500: 41%; SAT math scores over 500: 50%; SAT writing scores over 500: 28%; ACT scores over 18: 85%; SAT critical reading scores over 600: 10%; SAT math scores over 600: 12%; SAT writing scores over 600: 5%; ACT scores over 24: 26%; SAT critical reading scores over 700: 1%; SAT writing scores over 700: 1%.

Faculty *Total:* 182, 45% full-time, 14% with terminal degrees. *Student/faculty ratio:* 12:1.

Academics *Calendar:* semesters. *Degrees:* certificates, associate, and bachelor's. *Special study options:* academic remediation for entering students, accelerated degree program, advanced placement credit, cooperative education, distance learning, double majors, English as a second language, honors programs, independent study, internships, part-time degree program, services for LD students, summer session for credit. *ROTC:* Army (c).

Computers on Campus 480 computers/terminals and 600 ports are available on campus for general student use. Students can access the following: campus intranet, computer help desk, free student e-mail accounts, online (class) grades, online (class) registration, online (class) schedules, online (network) file storage, wireless network. Campuswide network is available. 98% of college-owned or -operated housing units are wired for high-speed Internet access. Wireless service is available via entire campus.

Student Life *Housing:* on-campus residence required through sophomore year. *Options:* coed. Campus housing is university owned. *Activities and organizations:* student-run radio and television station, choral group, Student Council (student government), Adventurer's Guild (board and video gaming), WVTC (student radio station), Outing Club, Veterinary Technology Club. *Campus security:* 24-hour emergency response devices and patrols, late-night transport/escort service, controlled dormitory access. *Student services:* health clinic.

Athletics Member USCAA. *Intercollegiate sports:* baseball M, basketball M/W, golf M/W, soccer M/W, softball W. *Intramural sports:* basketball M/W, bowling M(c)/W(c), cross-country running M/W, fencing M(c)/W(c), football M/W, golf M(c)/W(c), ice hockey M(c)/W(c), racquetball M/W, riflery M(c)/W(c), rock climbing M(c)/W(c), rugby M(c), skiing (cross-country) M(c)/W(c), skiing (downhill) M(c)/W(c), soccer M/W, softball M/W, swimming and diving M/W, table tennis M/W, tennis M/W, volleyball M/W, water polo M/W, weight lifting M(c)/W(c).

Standardized Tests *Required for some:* SAT or ACT (for admission).

Costs (2012–13) *Tuition:* state resident $11,088 full-time, $223 per credit hour part-time; nonresident $21,192 full-time, $446 per credit hour part-time. Full-time tuition and fees vary according to course load and program. Part-time tuition and fees vary according to program. *Required fees:* $700 full-time. *Room and board:* $8520; room only: $5232. Room and board charges vary according to board plan. *Payment plan:* installment. *Waivers:* employees and children of employees.

Financial Aid Of all full-time matriculated undergraduates who enrolled in 2011, 1,064 applied for aid, 951 were judged to have need, 102 had their need fully met. In 2011, 49 non-need-based awards were made. *Average percent of need met:* 56%. *Average financial aid package:* $10,978. *Average need-based loan:* $3987. *Average need-based gift aid:* $6393. *Average non-need-based aid:* $5200. *Average indebtedness upon graduation:* $21,373.

Applying *Options:* electronic application. *Application fee:* $40. *Required:* high school transcript. *Required for some:* essay or personal statement, 2 letters of recommendation, interview. *Recommended:* minimum 3.0 GPA, 2 letters of recommendation, interview. *Application deadlines:* rolling (freshmen), rolling (transfers). *Notification:* continuous (freshmen), continuous (transfers).

Freshman Application Contact Dwight A. Cross, Assistant Dean of Enrollment, Vermont Technical College, PO Box 500, Randolph Center, VT 05061. *Phone:* 802-728-1244. *Toll-free phone:* 800-442-VTC1. *Fax:* 802-728-1390. *E-mail:* admissions@vtc.edu. *Web site:* http://www.vtc.edu/.

See page 929 for display ad and page 1734 for the College Close-Up.

VIRGINIA

Argosy University, Washington DC

Arlington, Virginia

Freshman Application Contact Argosy University, Washington DC, 1550 Wilson Boulevard, Suite 600, Arlington, VA 22209. *Phone:* 703-526-5800. *Toll-free phone:* 866-703-2777. *Web site:* http://www.argosy.edu/washingtondc/.

See page 1062 for the College Close-Up.

The Art Institute of Virginia Beach

Virginia Beach, Virginia

- **Proprietary** 4-year
- **Coed**

Academics *Degrees:* diplomas, associate, and bachelor's.

Costs (2011–12) *Tuition:* Tuition cost varies by program. Prospective students should contact the school for current tuition costs. Other charges include a starting kit for all first-quarter students. Kits vary in price, depending on the program of study.

Freshman Application Contact The Art Institute of Virginia Beach, Two Columbus Center, 4500 Main Street, Suite 100, Virginia Beach, VA 23462. *Phone:* 757-493-6700. *Toll-free phone:* 877-437-4428. *Web site:* http://www.artinstitutes.edu/virginia-beach/.

See page 1138 for the College Close-Up.

The Art Institute of Washington

Arlington, Virginia

- **Proprietary** 4-year, founded 2000, part of Education Management Corporation
- **Urban** campus
- **Coed**

Academics *Calendar:* quarters. *Degrees:* diplomas, associate, and bachelor's.

Costs (2011–12) *Tuition:* Tuition cost varies by program. Prospective students should contact the school for current tuition costs. Other charges include a starting kit for all first-quarter students. Kits vary in price, depending on the program of study.

Freshman Application Contact The Art Institute of Washington, 1820 North Fort Meyer Drive, Arlington, VA 22209. *Phone:* 703-358-9550. *Toll-free phone:* 877-303-3771. *Web site:* http://www.artinstitutes.edu/arlington/.

See page 1140 for the College Close-Up.

The Art Institute of Washington–Dulles

Sterling, Virginia

- **Proprietary** 4-year
- **Coed**

Academics *Degrees:* diplomas, associate, and bachelor's.

Costs (2011–12) *Tuition:* Tuition cost varies by program. Prospective students should contact the school for current tuition costs. Other charges include a starting kit for all first-quarter students. Kits vary in price, depending on the program of study.

Freshman Application Contact The Art Institute of Washington–Dulles, The Corporate Office Park at Dulles Town Center, 21000 Atlantic Boulevard, Suite 100, Sterling, VA 20166. *Phone:* 571-449-4400. *Toll-free phone:* 888-627-5008. *Web site:* http://www.artinstitutes.edu/washington-dulles/.

See page 1142 for the College Close-Up.

Averett University

Danville, Virginia

- **Independent** comprehensive, founded 1859, affiliated with Baptist General Association of Virginia
- **Small-town** 252-acre campus with easy access to Greensboro, Raleigh
- **Endowment** $24.7 million
- **Coed** 877 undergraduate students, 95% full-time, 49% women, 51% men
- **Moderately difficult** entrance level, 54% of applicants were admitted

Undergraduates 834 full-time, 43 part-time. Students come from 26 states and territories; 20 other countries; 36% are from out of state; 25% Black or African American, non-Hispanic/Latino; 3% Hispanic/Latino; 1% Asian, non-Hispanic/Latino; 0.8% American Indian or Alaska Native, non-Hispanic/Latino; 0.5% Race/ethnicity unknown; 8% international; 9% transferred in; 54% live on campus. *Retention:* 58% of full-time freshmen returned.

Freshmen *Admission:* 2,315 applied, 1,254 admitted, 254 enrolled. *Average high school GPA:* 3.13. *Test scores:* SAT critical reading scores over 500: 34%; SAT math scores over 500: 38%; ACT scores over 18: 72%; SAT critical reading scores over 600: 8%; SAT math scores over 600: 10%; ACT scores over 24: 19%; SAT math scores over 700: 1%.

Faculty *Total:* 125, 47% full-time, 46% with terminal degrees. *Student/faculty ratio:* 10:1.

Academics *Calendar:* semesters. *Degrees:* associate, bachelor's, and master's. *Special study options:* accelerated degree program, advanced placement credit, cooperative education, distance learning, double majors, external degree program, honors programs, independent study, internships, off-campus study, part-time degree program, services for LD students, student-designed majors, study abroad, summer session for credit.

Computers on Campus 150 computers/terminals are available on campus for general student use. Students can access the following: computer help desk, free student e-mail accounts, online (class) grades, online (class) registration, online (class) schedules. Campuswide network is available. Wireless service is available via entire campus.

Student Life *Housing:* on-campus residence required through junior year. *Options:* coed, men-only, women-only. Campus housing is university owned. Freshman applicants given priority for college housing. *Activities and organizations:* drama/theater group, student-run newspaper, choral group, Student Government Association, Campus Activities Board, Christian Student Union, Averett Gospel Choir, Pi Kappa Phi, national fraternities. *Campus security:* 24-hour emergency response devices and patrols, late-night transport/escort service, controlled dormitory access. *Student services:* personal/psychological counseling.

Athletics Member NCAA. All Division III. *Intercollegiate sports:* baseball M, basketball M/W, cross-country running M/W, football M, golf M, soccer M/W, softball W, tennis M/W, volleyball W. *Intramural sports:* basketball M/W, cheerleading M/W, football M, soccer M/W, softball M/W, volleyball M/W.

Standardized Tests *Required:* SAT or ACT (for admission), TOEF for International students (for admission).

Costs (2012–13) *Comprehensive fee:* $34,320 includes full-time tuition ($25,950) and room and board ($8370). Full-time tuition and fees vary according to course load, degree level, location, and program. Part-time tuition: $1080 per credit hour. Part-time tuition and fees vary according to course load, degree level, location, and program. *College room only:* $5650. Room and board charges vary according to board plan and housing facility. *Payment plan:* installment. *Waivers:* senior citizens and employees or children of employees.

Financial Aid Of all full-time matriculated undergraduates who enrolled in 2011, 726 applied for aid, 674 were judged to have need, 123 had their need fully met. 139 Federal Work-Study jobs (averaging $1027). In 2011, 157 non-need-based awards were made. *Average percent of need met:* 76%. *Average*

financial aid package: $19,738. *Average need-based loan:* $4392. *Average need-based gift aid:* $15,894. *Average non-need-based aid:* $10,126. *Average indebtedness upon graduation:* $26,390.

Applying *Options:* electronic application. *Required:* high school transcript, minimum 2.5 GPA, High school diploma. *Recommended:* essay or personal statement, letters of recommendation. *Application deadlines:* 8/1 (freshmen), 8/15 (transfers). *Notification:* continuous (freshmen), continuous (transfers).

Freshman Application Contact Mr. Joel Nester, Director of Admissions and International, Averett University, 420 West Main Street, English Hall, Danville, VA 24541. *Phone:* 434-791-5663. *Toll-free phone:* 800-AVERETT. *E-mail:* joel.nester@averett.edu. *Web site:* http://www.averett.edu/.

Bluefield College
Bluefield, Virginia

- **Independent Southern Baptist** 4-year, founded 1922
- **Small-town** 82-acre campus
- **Endowment** $5.0 million
- **Coed** 701 undergraduate students, 85% full-time, 52% women, 48% men
- **Minimally difficult** entrance level, 49% of applicants were admitted

Undergraduates 597 full-time, 104 part-time. Students come from 25 states and territories; 4 other countries; 21% are from out of state; 23% Black or African American, non-Hispanic/Latino; 2% Hispanic/Latino; 0.9% Native Hawaiian or other Pacific Islander, non-Hispanic/Latino; 0.3% American Indian or Alaska Native, non-Hispanic/Latino; 1% Two or more races, non-Hispanic/Latino; 11% Race/ethnicity unknown; 0.9% international; 9% transferred in; 66% live on campus. *Retention:* 56% of full-time freshmen returned.

Freshmen *Admission:* 1,171 applied, 572 admitted, 148 enrolled. *Average high school GPA:* 3. *Test scores:* SAT critical reading scores over 500: 33%; SAT math scores over 500: 24%; ACT scores over 18: 53%; SAT critical reading scores over 600: 7%; SAT math scores over 600: 2%; ACT scores over 24: 10%; SAT critical reading scores over 700: 2%.

Faculty *Total:* 104, 37% full-time, 42% with terminal degrees. *Student/faculty ratio:* 10:1.

Academics *Calendar:* semesters. *Degree:* bachelor's. *Special study options:* academic remediation for entering students, accelerated degree program, adult/continuing education programs, advanced placement credit, cooperative education, distance learning, double majors, honors programs, internships, services for LD students, study abroad, summer session for credit.

Computers on Campus 110 computers/terminals are available on campus for general student use. Students can access the following: campus intranet, free student e-mail accounts, online (class) grades, online (class) registration, online (class) schedules, career assessment tests, library database. Campuswide network is available. 100% of college-owned or -operated housing units are wired for high-speed Internet access. Wireless service is available via entire campus.

Student Life *Housing:* on-campus residence required through junior year. *Options:* coed, men-only, women-only. Campus housing is university owned. Freshman applicants given priority for college housing. *Activities and organizations:* drama/theater group, student-run newspaper, choral group, Baptist Collegiate Ministries, Fellowship of Christian Athletes, Student Union Board, Student Government Association, Arts Club. *Campus security:* controlled dormitory access, night security patrols. *Student services:* personal/psychological counseling.

Athletics Member NAIA, NCCAA. *Intercollegiate sports:* baseball M(s), basketball M(s)/W(s), cross-country running M(s)/W(s), football M(s)(c), golf M(s), soccer M(s)/W(s), softball W(s), tennis M(s)/W(s), volleyball W(s). *Intramural sports:* badminton M/W, baseball M, basketball M/W, football M/W, softball M/W, table tennis M/W, tennis M/W, volleyball M/W.

Standardized Tests *Required:* SAT or ACT (for admission).

Costs (2012–13) *Comprehensive fee:* $28,700 includes full-time tuition ($21,060) and room and board ($7640). Full-time tuition and fees vary according to course load and program. Part-time tuition: $880 per credit. Part-time tuition and fees vary according to course load and program. *College room only:* $2990. Room and board charges vary according to housing facility. *Payment plan:* installment. *Waivers:* senior citizens and employees or children of employees.

Financial Aid Of all full-time matriculated undergraduates who enrolled in 2010, 545 applied for aid, 495 were judged to have need, 67 had their need fully met. 65 Federal Work-Study jobs (averaging $1125). In 2010, 69 non-need-based awards were made. *Average percent of need met:* 62%. *Average financial aid package:* $14,035. *Average need-based loan:* $4960. *Average need-based gift aid:* $9827. *Average non-need-based aid:* $5345. *Average indebtedness upon graduation:* $18,661.

Applying *Options:* electronic application, deferred entrance. *Application fee:* $30. *Required:* high school transcript, minimum 2.0 GPA. *Required for some:* essay or personal statement, interview. *Application deadlines:* rolling (fresh-

men), rolling (transfers). *Notification:* continuous (freshmen), continuous (transfers).

Freshman Application Contact Mr. Mark Hipes, Bluefield College, 3000 College Drive, Bluefield, VA 24605-1799. *Phone:* 276-326-4340. *Toll-free phone:* 800-872-0175. *Fax:* 276-326-4395. *E-mail:* mhipes@bluefield.edu. *Web site:* http://www.bluefield.edu/.

Bridgewater College
Bridgewater, Virginia

- **Independent** 4-year, founded 1880, affiliated with Church of the Brethren
- **Small-town** 300-acre campus
- **Endowment** $66.3 million
- **Coed** 1,648 undergraduate students, 99% full-time, 59% women, 41% men
- **Moderately difficult** entrance level, 52% of applicants were admitted

Undergraduates 1,637 full-time, 11 part-time. Students come from 26 states and territories; 5 other countries; 21% are from out of state; 8% Black or African American, non-Hispanic/Latino; 3% Hispanic/Latino; 0.8% Asian, non-Hispanic/Latino; 0.1% Native Hawaiian or other Pacific Islander, non-Hispanic/Latino; 0.2% American Indian or Alaska Native, non-Hispanic/Latino; 3% Two or more races, non-Hispanic/Latino; 4% Race/ethnicity unknown; 0.4% international; 2% transferred in; 85% live on campus. *Retention:* 76% of full-time freshmen returned.

Freshmen *Admission:* 6,459 applied, 3,327 admitted, 471 enrolled. *Average high school GPA:* 3.5. *Test scores:* SAT critical reading scores over 500: 55%; SAT math scores over 500: 60%; SAT writing scores over 500: 51%; ACT scores over 18: 87%; SAT critical reading scores over 600: 17%; SAT math scores over 600: 15%; SAT writing scores over 600: 13%; ACT scores over 24: 30%; SAT critical reading scores over 700: 1%; SAT math scores over 700: 1%; SAT writing scores over 700: 1%; ACT scores over 30: 5%.

Faculty *Total:* 141, 75% full-time, 70% with terminal degrees. *Student/faculty ratio:* 14:1.

Academics *Calendar:* 4-1-4. *Degree:* bachelor's. *Special study options:* adult/continuing education programs, advanced placement credit, double majors, honors programs, independent study, internships, off-campus study, part-time degree program, services for LD students, study abroad, summer session for credit. *Unusual degree programs:* 3-2 engineering with George Washington University; Virginia Tech; nursing with Vanderbilt University; physical therapy with Shenandoah University (3-4 program).

Computers on Campus 197 computers/terminals and 700 ports are available on campus for general student use. Students can access the following: campus intranet, computer help desk, free student e-mail accounts, online (class) grades, online (class) registration, online (class) schedules, Moodle (course management system), campus bulletin board system. Campuswide network is available. 100% of college-owned or -operated housing units are wired for high-speed Internet access. Wireless service is available via entire campus.

Student Life *Housing:* on-campus residence required through senior year. *Options:* coed, men-only, women-only, disabled students. Campus housing is university owned. Freshman campus housing is guaranteed. *Activities and organizations:* drama/theater group, student-run newspaper, radio station, choral group, Equestrian Club, Student Ambassadors, Campus Crusade for Christ (CRU), Eagle Productions (program board), Habitat for Humanity. *Campus security:* 24-hour emergency response devices and patrols, controlled dormitory access, emergency alert system. *Student services:* health clinic, personal/psychological counseling.

Athletics Member NCAA. All Division III. *Intercollegiate sports:* baseball M, basketball M/W, cheerleading M(c)/W(c), cross-country running M/W, equestrian sports M/W, field hockey W, football M, golf M/W, lacrosse M/W, soccer M/W, softball W, swimming and diving W, tennis M/W, track and field M/W, volleyball W. *Intramural sports:* badminton M/W, basketball M/W, bowling M/W, football M/W, golf M/W, racquetball M/W, soccer M/W, softball M/W, table tennis M/W, tennis M/W, ultimate Frisbee M/W, volleyball M/W.

Standardized Tests *Required:* SAT or ACT (for admission).

Costs (2011–12) *Comprehensive fee:* $37,100 includes full-time tuition ($26,200), mandatory fees ($550), and room and board ($10,350). Part-time tuition: $895 per credit hour. *Required fees:* $30 per term part-time. *College room only:* $5260. Room and board charges vary according to board plan and housing facility. *Payment plan:* installment. *Waivers:* minority students, senior citizens, and employees or children of employees.

Financial Aid Of all full-time matriculated undergraduates who enrolled in 2011, 1,464 applied for aid, 1,339 were judged to have need, 331 had their need fully met. 269 Federal Work-Study jobs (averaging $1184). 140 state and other part-time jobs (averaging $917). In 2011, 291 non-need-based awards were made. *Average percent of need met:* 77%. *Average financial aid package:* $22,155. *Average need-based loan:* $4615. *Average need-based gift aid:*

$18,707. *Average non-need-based aid:* $12,784. *Average indebtedness upon graduation:* $33,986.

Applying *Options:* electronic application, deferred entrance. *Application fee:* $30. *Required:* high school transcript, minimum 2.5 GPA, 1 letter of recommendation. *Required for some:* interview. *Recommended:* minimum 2.8 GPA, interview. *Application deadlines:* rolling (freshmen), rolling (transfers). *Notification:* continuous (freshmen), continuous (out-of-state freshmen), continuous (transfers).

Freshman Application Contact Mr. Jarret L. Smith, Director of Admissions, Bridgewater College, 402 East College Street, Bridgewater, VA 22812. *Phone:* 540-828-5469. *Toll-free phone:* 800-759-8328. *Fax:* 540-828-5481. *E-mail:* admissions@bridgewater.edu. *Web site:* http://www.bridgewater.edu/.

See below for display ad and page 1184 for the College Close-Up.

Bryant & Stratton College - Richmond Campus

Richmond, Virginia

Freshman Application Contact Mr. David K. Mayle, Director of Admissions, Bryant & Stratton College - Richmond Campus, 8141 Hull Street Road, Richmond, VA 23235-6411. *Phone:* 804-745-2444. *Fax:* 804-745-6884. *E-mail:* tlawson@bryanstratton.edu. *Web site:* http://www.bryantstratton.edu/.

Bryant & Stratton College - Virginia Beach

Virginia Beach, Virginia

Freshman Application Contact Bryant & Stratton College - Virginia Beach, 301 Centre Pointe Drive, Virginia Beach, VA 23462-4417. *Phone:* 757-499-7900 Ext. 173. *Web site:* http://www.bryantstratton.edu/.

Centura College

Virginia Beach, Virginia

Freshman Application Contact Admissions Office, Centura College, 2697 Dean Drive, Suite 100, Virginia Beach, VA 23452. *Phone:* 757-340-2121.

Toll-free phone: 877-575-5627. *Fax:* 757-340-9704. *Web site:* http://www.centuracollege.edu/.

Chamberlain College of Nursing

Arlington, Virginia

- **Proprietary** 4-year
- **Coed** 219 undergraduate students, 77% full-time, 87% women, 13% men

Undergraduates 169 full-time, 50 part-time. 46% are from out of state; 40% Black or African American, non-Hispanic/Latino; 14% Hispanic/Latino; 5% Asian, non-Hispanic/Latino; 0.9% Native Hawaiian or other Pacific Islander, non-Hispanic/Latino; 4% Two or more races, non-Hispanic/Latino; 3% Race/ethnicity unknown; 63% transferred in.

Freshmen *Admission:* 7 enrolled.

Faculty *Total:* 15, 47% full-time. *Student/faculty ratio:* 19:1.

Academics *Calendar:* semesters.

Standardized Tests *Required:* SAT or ACT (for admission).

Freshman Application Contact Admissions, Chamberlain College of Nursing, 2450 Crystal Drive, Arlington, VA 22202. *Phone:* 703-416-7300. *Toll-free phone:* 888-556-8CCN. *Web site:* http://www.chamberlain.edu/.

Christendom College

Front Royal, Virginia

- **Independent Roman Catholic** comprehensive, founded 1977
- **Rural** 100-acre campus with easy access to Washington, D.C.
- **Endowment** $3.1 million
- **Coed** 408 undergraduate students, 99% full-time, 55% women, 45% men
- **Moderately difficult** entrance level, 83% of applicants were admitted

Undergraduates 402 full-time, 6 part-time. Students come from 45 states and territories; 7 other countries; 75% are from out of state; 2% transferred in; 95% live on campus. *Retention:* 80% of full-time freshmen returned.

Freshmen *Admission:* 288 applied, 239 admitted, 112 enrolled. *Average high school GPA:* 3.6. *Test scores:* SAT critical reading scores over 500: 98%; SAT math scores over 500: 80%; SAT writing scores over 500: 99%; ACT scores over 18: 100%; SAT critical reading scores over 600: 66%; SAT math scores over 600: 38%; SAT writing scores over 600: 63%; ACT scores over 24: 75%; SAT critical reading scores over 700: 24%; SAT math scores over 700: 4%; SAT writing scores over 700: 20%; ACT scores over 30: 18%.

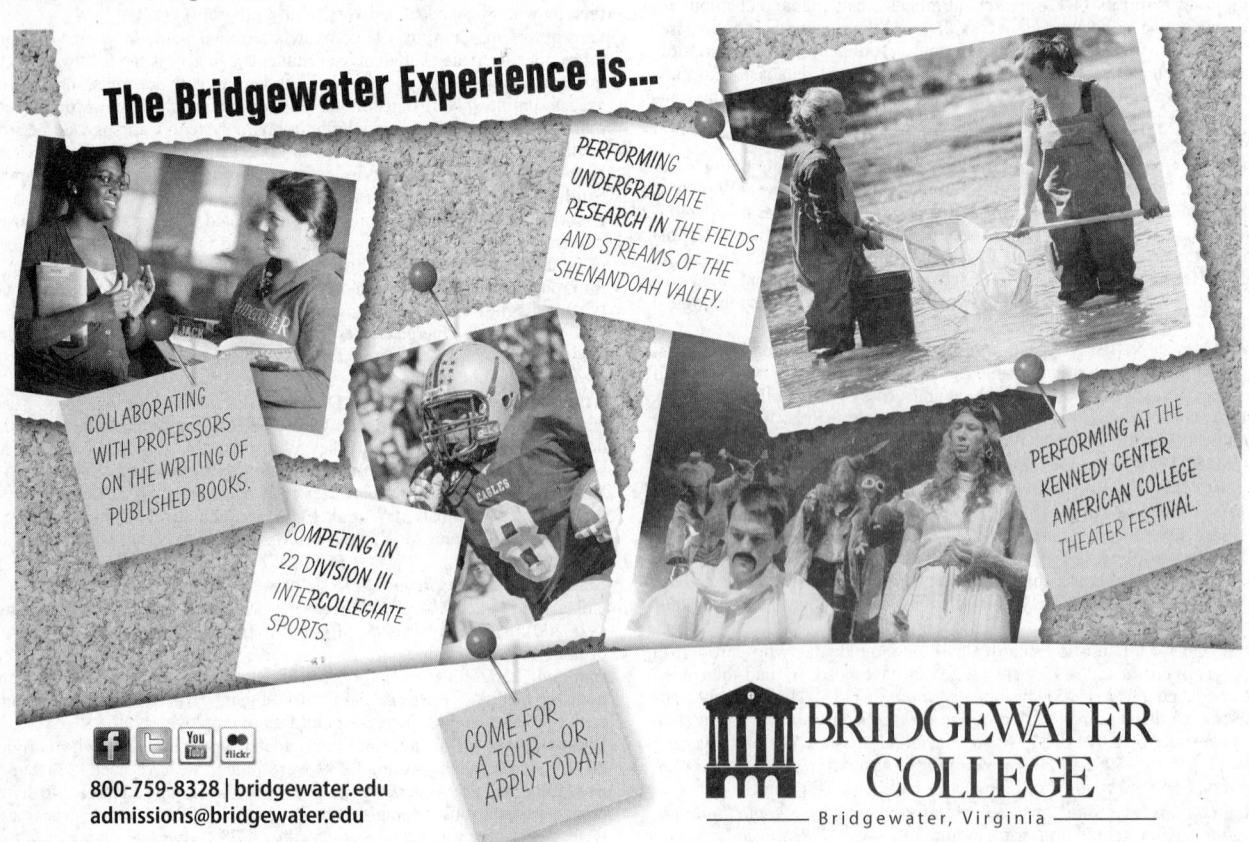

Faculty *Total:* 38, 47% full-time, 61% with terminal degrees. *Student/faculty ratio:* 15:1.

Academics *Calendar:* semesters. *Degrees:* associate, bachelor's, and master's. *Special study options:* academic remediation for entering students, accelerated degree program, advanced placement credit, cooperative education, double majors, independent study, internships, services for LD students, study abroad, summer session for credit.

Computers on Campus 60 computers/terminals are available on campus for general student use. Students can access the following: campus intranet, computer help desk, free student e-mail accounts. Wireless service is available via computer labs, libraries, student centers.

Student Life *Housing:* on-campus residence required through senior year. *Options:* men-only, women-only. Campus housing is university owned. Freshman campus housing is guaranteed. *Activities and organizations:* drama/theater group, student-run newspaper, choral group, drama, choir, Shield of Roses, Legion of Mary, debate team. *Campus security:* 24-hour emergency response devices, late-night transport/escort service, night patrols by trained security personnel. *Student services:* health clinic, personal/psychological counseling.

Athletics Member USCAA. *Intercollegiate sports:* baseball M, basketball M/W, rugby M, soccer M/W, volleyball W. *Intramural sports:* basketball M/W, equestrian sports M/W, fencing M/W, football M/W, racquetball M/W, soccer M/W, table tennis M/W, tennis M/W, volleyball M/W.

Standardized Tests *Required:* SAT or ACT (for admission).

Costs (2012–13) *Comprehensive fee:* $29,570 includes full-time tuition ($21,000), mandatory fees ($600), and room and board ($7970). *Payment plan:* installment. *Waivers:* employees or children of employees.

Financial Aid Of all full-time matriculated undergraduates who enrolled in 2011, 243 applied for aid, 216 were judged to have need, 216 had their need fully met. 145 state and other part-time jobs (averaging $1980). In 2011, 88 non-need-based awards were made. *Average percent of need met:* 90%. *Average financial aid package:* $14,678. *Average need-based loan:* $6150. *Average need-based gift aid:* $7020. *Average non-need-based aid:* $7065. *Average indebtedness upon graduation:* $24,060.

Applying *Options:* electronic application, early admission, early action. *Application fee:* $25. *Required:* essay or personal statement, high school transcript, 2 letters of recommendation. *Recommended:* minimum 3.0 GPA, interview. *Application deadlines:* 3/1 (freshmen), 3/1 (transfers), 12/1 (early action). *Notification:* 4/1 (freshmen), continuous until 4/1 (transfers), 12/15 (early action).

Freshman Application Contact Christendom College, 134 Christendom Drive, Front Royal, VA 22630-5103. *Phone:* 540-636-2900 Ext. 1290. *Toll-free phone:* 800-877-5456. *Web site:* http://www.christendom.edu/.

Christopher Newport University
Newport News, Virginia

- **State-supported** comprehensive, founded 1960
- **Suburban** 260-acre campus with easy access to Virginia Beach
- **Endowment** $16.6 million
- **Coed** 4,837 undergraduate students, 97% full-time, 57% women, 43% men
- 59% of applicants were admitted

Undergraduates 4,692 full-time, 145 part-time. Students come from 25 states and territories; 38 other countries; 7% are from out of state; 8% Black or African American, non-Hispanic/Latino; 5% Hispanic/Latino; 2% Asian, non-Hispanic/Latino; 0.3% Native Hawaiian or other Pacific Islander, non-Hispanic/Latino; 0.1% American Indian or Alaska Native, non-Hispanic/Latino; 5% Two or more races, non-Hispanic/Latino; 0.7% Race/ethnicity unknown; 0.4% international; 3% transferred in; 61% live on campus. *Retention:* 84% of full-time freshmen returned.

Freshmen *Admission:* 7,351 applied, 4,307 admitted, 1,243 enrolled. *Average high school GPA:* 3.67. *Test scores:* SAT critical reading scores over 500: 85%; SAT math scores over 500: 84%; ACT scores over 18: 98%; SAT critical reading scores over 600: 41%; SAT math scores over 600: 33%; ACT scores over 24: 50%; SAT critical reading scores over 700: 6%; SAT math scores over 700: 2%; ACT scores over 30: 6%.

Faculty *Total:* 388, 63% full-time, 67% with terminal degrees. *Student/faculty ratio:* 17:1.

Academics *Calendar:* semesters. *Degrees:* bachelor's and master's. *Special study options:* advanced placement credit, double majors, honors programs, independent study, internships, off-campus study, services for LD students, student-designed majors, study abroad, summer session for credit. *ROTC:* Army (b).

Computers on Campus 200 computers/terminals and 500 ports are available on campus for general student use. Students can access the following: computer help desk, free student e-mail accounts, online (class) grades, online (class) registration, online (class) schedules, online degree audit. Campuswide network is available. 100% of college-owned or -operated housing units are

wired for high-speed Internet access. Wireless service is available via classrooms, computer centers, computer labs, dorm rooms, learning centers, libraries, student centers.

Student Life *Housing:* on-campus residence required through junior year. *Options:* coed. Campus housing is university owned. Freshman campus housing is guaranteed. *Activities and organizations:* drama/theater group, student-run newspaper, radio and television station, choral group, marching band, national fraternities, national sororities. *Campus security:* 24-hour emergency response devices and patrols, student patrols, late-night transport/escort service, controlled dormitory access, campus-based University Police; Emergency Notification System; Crime Prevention Programs. *Student services:* health clinic, personal/psychological counseling.

Athletics Member NCAA. All Division III. *Intercollegiate sports:* baseball M, basketball M/W, cheerleading M/W, cross-country running M/W, field hockey W, football M, golf M, lacrosse M/W, sailing M/W, soccer M/W, softball W, tennis M/W, track and field M/W, volleyball W. *Intramural sports:* badminton M/W, basketball M/W, equestrian sports M(c)/W(c), football M/W, ice hockey M(c), lacrosse M(c), rock climbing M(c)/W(c), rugby M(c), soccer M/W, softball M/W, swimming and diving M(c)/W(c), table tennis M(c)/W(c), tennis M/W, ultimate Frisbee M(c)/W(c), volleyball M(c)/W(c).

Standardized Tests *Required for some:* SAT or ACT (for admission).

Costs (2011–12) *Tuition:* state resident $5914 full-time, $246 per credit hour part-time; nonresident $14,776 full-time, $616 per credit hour part-time. Full-time tuition and fees vary according to course load and degree level. Part-time tuition and fees vary according to course load and degree level. *Required fees:* $4170 full-time, $173 per credit hour part-time. *Room and board:* $9728; room only: $6558. Room and board charges vary according to board plan and housing facility. *Payment plan:* installment. *Waivers:* senior citizens and employees or children of employees.

Financial Aid Of all full-time matriculated undergraduates who enrolled in 2010, 3,047 applied for aid, 2,160 were judged to have need, 339 had their need fully met. 117 Federal Work-Study jobs (averaging $833). 1,762 state and other part-time jobs (averaging $1177). In 2010, 482 non-need-based awards were made. *Average percent of need met:* 69%. *Average financial aid package:* $8099. *Average need-based loan:* $4033. *Average need-based gift aid:* $5087. *Average non-need-based aid:* $1772. *Average indebtedness upon graduation:* $21,572.

Applying *Options:* electronic application, early admission, early decision, early action, deferred entrance. *Application fee:* $50. *Required:* high school transcript, minimum 3.0 GPA. *Required for some:* essay or personal statement, 3 letters of recommendation, interview. *Application deadlines:* 2/1 (freshmen), 3/1 (transfers), 12/1 (early action). *Early decision deadline:* 11/15. *Notification:* continuous (freshmen), 5/21 (transfers), 12/15 (early decision), 1/15 (early action).

Freshman Application Contact Mr. Rob Lange, Dean of Admissions, Christopher Newport University, Office of Admissions, 1 University Place, Newport News, VA 23606-2998. *Phone:* 757-594-7015. *Toll-free phone:* 800-333-4268. *Fax:* 757-594-7333. *E-mail:* admit@cnu.edu. *Web site:* http://www.cnu.edu/.

The College of William and Mary
Williamsburg, Virginia

- **State-supported** university, founded 1693
- **Small-town** 1200-acre campus with easy access to Richmond
- **Endowment** $624.7 million
- **Coed** 6,071 undergraduate students, 99% full-time, 55% women, 45% men
- **Most difficult** entrance level, 35% of applicants were admitted

Undergraduates 5,987 full-time, 84 part-time. Students come from 46 states and territories; 32 other countries; 32% are from out of state; 7% Black or African American, non-Hispanic/Latino; 8% Hispanic/Latino; 7% Asian, non-Hispanic/Latino; 0.0% Native Hawaiian or other Pacific Islander, non-Hispanic/Latino; 0.5% American Indian or Alaska Native, non-Hispanic/Latino; 3% Two or more races, non-Hispanic/Latino; 14% Race/ethnicity unknown; 3% international; 4% transferred in; 73% live on campus. *Retention:* 95% of full-time freshmen returned.

Freshmen *Admission:* 12,825 applied, 4,443 admitted, 1,485 enrolled. *Average high school GPA:* 4. *Test scores:* SAT critical reading scores over 500: 98%; SAT math scores over 500: 99%; SAT writing scores over 500: 98%; ACT scores over 18: 100%; SAT critical reading scores over 600: 83%; SAT math scores over 600: 84%; SAT writing scores over 600: 83%; ACT scores over 24: 95%; SAT critical reading scores over 700: 43%; SAT math scores over 700: 37%; SAT writing scores over 700: 40%; ACT scores over 30: 60%.

Academics *Calendar:* semesters. *Degrees:* bachelor's, master's, doctoral, post-master's, and first professional certificates. *Special study options:* accelerated degree program, advanced placement credit, double majors, honors programs, independent study, internships, off-campus study, part-time degree

program, services for LD students, student-designed majors, study abroad, summer session for credit. *ROTC:* Army (b). *Unusual degree programs:* 3-2 engineering with Columbia University, Rensselaer Polytechnic Institute.

Computers on Campus 300 computers/terminals and 6,500 ports are available on campus for general student use. Students can access the following: campus intranet, computer help desk, free student e-mail accounts, online (class) grades, online (class) registration, online (class) schedules. Campuswide network is available. 100% of college-owned or -operated housing units are wired for high-speed Internet access. Wireless service is available via entire campus.

Student Life *Housing:* on-campus residence required for freshman year. *Options:* coed, disabled students. Campus housing is university owned and leased by the school. Freshman campus housing is guaranteed. *Activities and organizations:* drama/theater group, student-run newspaper, radio and television station, choral group, Alma Mater Productions, College Partnership for Kids, Student Assembly, Flat Hat (student newspaper), Resident Hall Association, national fraternities, national sororities. *Campus security:* 24-hour emergency response devices and patrols, late-night transport/escort service, controlled dormitory access, certified police officers, accredited police department, foot, bicycle, and patrols provided by marked and unmarked police vehicles. *Student services:* health clinic, personal/psychological counseling, legal services.

Athletics Member NCAA. All Division I except football (Division I-AA). *Intercollegiate sports:* baseball M(s), basketball M(s)/W(s), cross-country running M(s)/W(s), field hockey W(s), golf M(s)/W(s), gymnastics M(s)/W(s), lacrosse W(s), soccer M(s)/W(s), swimming and diving M/W, tennis M(s)/W(s), track and field M(s)/W(s), volleyball W(s). *Intramural sports:* badminton M(c)/W(c), baseball M(c), basketball M/W, bowling M/W, crew M(c)/W(c), cross-country running M(c)/W(c), equestrian sports M(c)/W(c), fencing M(c)/W(c), field hockey W(c), football M/W, golf M(c)/W(c), gymnastics M(c)/W(c), ice hockey M(c), lacrosse M(c)/W(c), racquetball M(c)/W(c), rock climbing M(c)/W(c), rugby M(c)/W(c), sailing M(c)/W(c), soccer M/W, softball M/W, squash M(c)/W(c), swimming and diving M(c)/W(c), table tennis M(c)/W(c), tennis M(c)/W(c), ultimate Frisbee M(c)/W(c), volleyball M/W, water polo M(c)/W(c), weight lifting M/W, wrestling M(c).

Standardized Tests *Required:* SAT or ACT (for admission). *Recommended:* SAT Subject Tests (for admission).

Costs (2011–12) *One-time required fee:* $192. *Tuition:* state resident $8270 full-time, $286 per credit hour part-time; nonresident $30,547 full-time, $985 per credit hour part-time. *Required fees:* $4862 full-time. *Room and board:* $8772; room only: $5112. Room and board charges vary according to board plan and housing facility. *Payment plan:* installment. *Waivers:* senior citizens.

Financial Aid Of all full-time matriculated undergraduates who enrolled in 2010, 3,126 applied for aid, 2,122 were judged to have need, 577 had their need fully met. 193 Federal Work-Study jobs (averaging $776). In 2010, 268 non-need-based awards were made. *Average percent of need met:* 76%. *Average financial aid package:* $16,102. *Average need-based loan:* $4502. *Average need-based gift aid:* $12,109. *Average non-need-based aid:* $6428. *Average indebtedness upon graduation:* $21,267.

Applying *Options:* electronic application, early admission, early decision, deferred entrance. *Application fee:* $60. *Required:* essay or personal statement, high school transcript, 1 letter of recommendation. *Recommended:* 2 letters of recommendation. *Application deadlines:* 1/1 (freshmen), 3/1 (transfers). *Early decision deadline:* 11/1. *Notification:* 4/1 (freshmen), 5/1 (transfers), 12/1 (early decision).

Freshman Application Contact Timothy Wolfe, Dean of Admissions, The College of William and Mary, PO Box 8795, Williamsburg, VA 23187-8795. *Phone:* 757-221-4223. *Fax:* 757-221-1242. *E-mail:* admission@wm.edu. *Web site:* http://www.wm.edu/.

Culinary Institute of Virginia
Norfolk, Virginia

Freshman Application Contact Director of Admissions, Culinary Institute of Virginia, 2428 Almeda Avenue, Suite 316, Norfolk, VA 23513. *Phone:* 757-858-2433. *Toll-free phone:* 866-619-CHEF. *E-mail:* hsadmissions@chefva.com. *Web site:* http://www.chefva.com/.

DeVry University
Arlington, Virginia

- **Proprietary** comprehensive, founded 2001, part of DeVry University
- **Coed** 658 undergraduate students, 51% full-time, 31% women, 69% men
- **Minimally difficult** entrance level

Undergraduates 336 full-time, 322 part-time. 52% are from out of state; 50% Black or African American, non-Hispanic/Latino; 11% Hispanic/Latino; 4% Asian, non-Hispanic/Latino; 0.5% Native Hawaiian or other Pacific Islander, non-Hispanic/Latino; 0.8% American Indian or Alaska Native, non-Hispanic/

Latino; 2% Two or more races, non-Hispanic/Latino; 11% Race/ethnicity unknown; 2% international; 29% transferred in.

Freshmen *Admission:* 96 enrolled.

Faculty *Total:* 139, 12% full-time. *Student/faculty ratio:* 10:1.

Academics *Calendar:* semesters. *Degrees:* associate, bachelor's, master's, and postbachelor's certificates. *Special study options:* adult/continuing education programs, part-time degree program.

Computers on Campus Students can access the following: online (class) registration.

Student Life *Housing:* college housing not available.

Costs (2011–12) *Tuition:* $15,294 full-time, $597 per credit hour part-time. Full-time tuition and fees vary according to course load. Part-time tuition and fees vary according to course load. *Required fees:* $80 full-time, $40 per term part-time. *Payment plans:* installment, deferred payment. *Waivers:* employees or children of employees.

Financial Aid Of all full-time matriculated undergraduates who enrolled in 2007, 175 applied for aid, 164 were judged to have need, 9 had their need fully met. In 2007, 21 non-need-based awards were made. *Average percent of need met:* 38%. *Average financial aid package:* $11,581. *Average need-based loan:* $7979. *Average need-based gift aid:* $5610. *Average non-need-based aid:* $18,172. *Average indebtedness upon graduation:* $12,479.

Applying *Application fee:* $50. *Required:* high school transcript, interview. *Application deadlines:* rolling (freshmen), rolling (transfers). *Notification:* continuous (freshmen), continuous (transfers).

Freshman Application Contact DeVry University, 2450 Crystal Drive, Arlington, VA 22202. *Phone:* 703-414-4000. *Toll-free phone:* 866-338-7941. *Web site:* http://www.devry.edu/.

DeVry University
Chesapeake, Virginia

Admissions Office Contact DeVry University, 1317 Executive Boulevard, Suite 100, Chesapeake, VA 23320-3671. *Toll-free phone:* 866-338-7941. *Web site:* http://www.devry.edu/.

DeVry University
Manassas, Virginia

Admissions Office Contact DeVry University, 10432 Balls Ford Road, Suite 130, Manassas, VA 20109-3173. *Toll-free phone:* 866-338-7941. *Web site:* http://www.devry.edu/.

Eastern Mennonite University
Harrisonburg, Virginia

- **Independent Mennonite** comprehensive, founded 1917
- **Small-town** 93-acre campus
- **Coed** 1,062 undergraduate students, 94% full-time, 62% women, 38% men
- **Moderately difficult** entrance level, 68% of applicants were admitted

Undergraduates 1,002 full-time, 60 part-time. Students come from 35 states and territories; 17 other countries; 40% are from out of state; 6% Black or African American, non-Hispanic/Latino; 6% Hispanic/Latino; 2% Asian, non-Hispanic/Latino; 0.2% American Indian or Alaska Native, non-Hispanic/Latino; 0.9% Two or more races, non-Hispanic/Latino; 4% Race/ethnicity unknown; 3% international; 5% transferred in; 64% live on campus. *Retention:* 78% of full-time freshmen returned.

Freshmen *Admission:* 845 applied, 578 admitted, 234 enrolled. *Average high school GPA:* 3.5. *Test scores:* SAT critical reading scores over 500: 64%; SAT math scores over 500: 59%; SAT writing scores over 500: 58%; ACT scores over 18: 94%; SAT critical reading scores over 600: 28%; SAT math scores over 600: 25%; SAT writing scores over 600: 23%; ACT scores over 24: 57%; SAT critical reading scores over 700: 6%; SAT math scores over 700: 4%; SAT writing scores over 700: 2%; ACT scores over 30: 17%.

Faculty *Total:* 205, 51% full-time. *Student/faculty ratio:* 10:1.

Academics *Calendar:* semesters. *Degrees:* certificates, associate, bachelor's, master's, and postbachelor's certificates. *Special study options:* adult/continuing education programs, advanced placement credit, distance learning, double majors, English as a second language, honors programs, independent study, internships, off-campus study, part-time degree program, services for LD students, study abroad, summer session for credit.

Computers on Campus 154 computers/terminals are available on campus for general student use. Students can access the following: campus intranet, computer help desk, free student e-mail accounts, online (class) grades, online (class) registration, online (class) schedules. Campuswide network is available. 98% of college-owned or -operated housing units are wired for high-speed Internet access. Wireless service is available via classrooms, dorm rooms, learning centers, libraries, student centers.

Student Life *Housing:* on-campus residence required through junior year. *Options:* coed, men-only, women-only, disabled students. Campus housing is university owned. Freshman campus housing is guaranteed. *Activities and organizations:* drama/theater group, student-run newspaper, choral group, Young People's Christian Association, Student Government Association, Student Education Association, Creation Care Council, Black Student Union. *Campus security:* 24-hour emergency response devices, controlled dormitory access, night watchman. *Student services:* health clinic, personal/psychological counseling.

Athletics Member NCAA. All Division III. *Intercollegiate sports:* baseball M, basketball M/W, cross-country running M/W, field hockey W, soccer M/W, softball W, track and field M/W, volleyball M/W. *Intramural sports:* basketball M/W, football M/W, golf M/W, lacrosse M(c), rock climbing M/W, soccer M/W, softball M/W, table tennis M/W, tennis M/W, volleyball M/W.

Standardized Tests *Required:* SAT or ACT (for admission).

Costs (2011–12) *Comprehensive fee:* $34,920 includes full-time tuition ($26,260), mandatory fees ($140), and room and board ($8520). Part-time tuition: $1100 per credit hour. Part-time tuition and fees vary according to course load. *Room and board:* Room and board charges vary according to board plan and housing facility. *Payment plan:* installment. *Waivers:* employees or children of employees.

Financial Aid Of all full-time matriculated undergraduates who enrolled in 2003, 735 applied for aid, 652 were judged to have need, 246 had their need fully met. 326 Federal Work-Study jobs (averaging $1787). In 2003, 82 non-need-based awards were made. *Average percent of need met:* 87%. *Average financial aid package:* $15,530. *Average need-based loan:* $5665. *Average need-based gift aid:* $5520. *Average non-need-based aid:* $7765. *Average indebtedness upon graduation:* $18,208.

Applying *Options:* electronic application, deferred entrance. *Application fee:* $25. *Required:* high school transcript, minimum 2.2 GPA, Community Lifestyle Commitment. *Required for some:* 2 letters of recommendation. *Recommended:* interview. *Application deadlines:* rolling (freshmen), rolling (transfers). *Notification:* continuous (freshmen), continuous (transfers).

Freshman Application Contact Stephanie C. Shafer, Director of Admissions, Eastern Mennonite University, 1200 Park Road, Harrisonburg, VA 22802. *Phone:* 540-432-4118. *Toll-free phone:* 800-368-2665. *Fax:* 540-432-4444. *E-mail:* admiss@emu.edu. *Web site:* http://www.emu.edu/.

ECPI College of Technology

Glen Allen, Virginia

Freshman Application Contact Mr. Jacob Pope, Director, ECPI College of Technology, 4305 Cox Road, Glen Allen, VA 23060. *Phone:* 804-934-0100. *Toll-free phone:* 800-986-1200. *Fax:* 804-934-0054. *E-mail:* jpope@ecpi.edu. *Web site:* http://www.ecpi.edu/.

ECPI College of Technology

Manassas, Virginia

Admissions Office Contact ECPI College of Technology, 10021 Balls Ford Road, Manassas, VA 20109. *Toll-free phone:* 866-708-6172. *Web site:* http://www.ecpi.edu/.

ECPI College of Technology

Newport News, Virginia

Freshman Application Contact Ms. Cheryl Lokey, Provost, ECPI College of Technology, 1001 Omni Boulevard, #100, Newport News, VA 23606. *Phone:* 757-838-9191. *Toll-free phone:* 866-499-0335. *Fax:* 757-829-5351. *Web site:* http://www.ecpi.edu/.

ECPI College of Technology

Richmond, Virginia

Freshman Application Contact Director, ECPI College of Technology, 800 Moorefield Park Drive, Richmond, VA 23236. *Phone:* 804-330-5533. *Toll-free phone:* 800-986-1200. *Fax:* 804-330-5577. *E-mail:* agerard@ecpi.edu. *Web site:* http://www.ecpi.edu/.

ECPI College of Technology

Virginia Beach, Virginia

- **Proprietary** 4-year, founded 1966
- **Suburban** 8-acre campus
- **Coed**
- **Moderately difficult** entrance level

Faculty *Student/faculty ratio:* 17:1.

Academics *Calendar:* continuous. *Degrees:* certificates, diplomas, associate, and bachelor's.

Student Life *Campus security:* building and parking lot security.

Standardized Tests *Required:* ACT (for admission). *Recommended:* SAT (for admission), SAT or ACT (for admission), SAT Subject Tests (for admission).

Financial Aid *Of all full-time matriculated undergraduates who enrolled in 2010,* 8,500 applied for aid.

Applying *Options:* electronic application, deferred entrance. *Application fee:* $45. *Required:* high school transcript, interview.

Freshman Application Contact Mrs. Bernadette Rozman Bellas, Vice President, Accreditation and Regulatory Affairs, ECPI College of Technology, 5555 Greenwich Road, Suite 100, Virginia Beach, VA 23462. *Phone:* 757-671-7171. *Toll-free phone:* 866-499-0336. *Fax:* 757-671-8661. *E-mail:* rballance@ecpi.edu. *Web site:* http://www.ecpi.edu/.

Emory & Henry College

Emory, Virginia

- **Independent United Methodist** comprehensive, founded 1836
- **Rural** campus
- **Coed** 939 undergraduate students, 96% full-time, 48% women, 52% men
- **71%** of applicants were admitted

Undergraduates 901 full-time, 38 part-time. 9% Black or African American, non-Hispanic/Latino; 2% Hispanic/Latino; 0.4% Asian, non-Hispanic/Latino; 0.3% American Indian or Alaska Native, non-Hispanic/Latino; 2% Two or more races, non-Hispanic/Latino; 5% Race/ethnicity unknown; 0.5% international.

Freshmen *Admission:* 1,367 applied, 971 admitted, 277 enrolled. *Average high school GPA:* 3.45. *Test scores:* SAT critical reading scores over 500: 49%; SAT math scores over 500: 49%; SAT writing scores over 500: 45%; ACT scores over 18: 90%; SAT critical reading scores over 600: 14%; SAT math scores over 600: 10%; SAT writing scores over 600: 14%; ACT scores over 24: 41%; SAT critical reading scores over 700: 3%; SAT math scores over 700: 1%; SAT writing scores over 700: 1%; ACT scores over 30: 6%.

Faculty *Total:* 105, 66% full-time.

Academics *Calendar:* semesters. *Degrees:* diplomas, bachelor's, and master's. *Special study options:* advanced placement credit, cooperative education, distance learning, double majors, external degree program, honors programs, independent study, internships, off-campus study, services for LD students, student-designed majors, study abroad, summer session for credit.

Computers on Campus Students can access the following: campus intranet, computer help desk, free student e-mail accounts, online (class) grades, online (class) registration, online (class) schedules. Campuswide network is available. 100% of college-owned or -operated housing units are wired for high-speed Internet access. Wireless service is available via entire campus.

Student Life *Housing:* on-campus residence required through junior year. *Options:* coed, men-only, women-only. Campus housing is university owned. Freshman campus housing is guaranteed. *Activities and organizations:* drama/theater group, student-run newspaper, radio and television station, choral group. *Student services:* health clinic, personal/psychological counseling.

Athletics Member NCAA. All Division III. *Intercollegiate sports:* baseball M, basketball M/W, cross-country running M/W, football M, soccer M/W, softball W, swimming and diving W, tennis M/W, volleyball W. *Intramural sports:* basketball M/W, cheerleading M(c)/W(c), football M/W, soccer M/W, table tennis M/W, tennis M/W, ultimate Frisbee M/W, volleyball M/W.

Standardized Tests *Required:* SAT or ACT (for admission).

Costs (2012–13) *Comprehensive fee:* $37,548 includes full-time tuition ($28,122) and room and board ($9426). Full-time tuition and fees vary according to course load, degree level, and location. Part-time tuition and fees vary according to course load, degree level, and location. *College room only:* $4782. Room and board charges vary according to board plan and location. *Payment plans:* installment, deferred payment.

Financial Aid Of all full-time matriculated undergraduates who enrolled in 2011, 811 applied for aid, 747 were judged to have need, 259 had their need fully met. 72 Federal Work-Study jobs (averaging $1117). In 2011, 142 non-need-based awards were made. *Average percent of need met:* 88%. *Average financial aid package:* $24,642. *Average need-based loan:* $4445. *Average need-based gift aid:* $21,104. *Average non-need-based aid:* $13,552. *Average indebtedness upon graduation:* $26,682.

Applying *Options:* electronic application. *Required:* high school transcript. *Recommended:* essay or personal statement, interview. *Application deadlines:* rolling (freshmen), rolling (transfers). *Notification:* continuous (freshmen), continuous (transfers).

Freshman Application Contact Admissions Office, Emory & Henry College, PO Box 947, Emory, VA 24327-0947. *Phone:* 276-944-4121. *Toll-free phone:* 800-848-5493. *E-mail:* ehadmiss@ehc.edu. *Web site:* http://www.ehc.edu/.

Ferrum College

Ferrum, Virginia

- **Independent United Methodist** 4-year, founded 1913

- **Rural** 720-acre campus

- **Endowment** $35.8 million

- **Coed** 1,512 undergraduate students, 99% full-time, 47% women, 53% men

- **Minimally difficult** entrance level

Undergraduates 1,496 full-time, 16 part-time. Students come from 27 states and territories; 7 other countries; 15% are from out of state; 34% Black or African American, non-Hispanic/Latino; 4% Hispanic/Latino; 0.3% Asian, non-Hispanic/Latino; 0.1% Native Hawaiian or other Pacific Islander, non-Hispanic/Latino; 0.5% American Indian or Alaska Native, non-Hispanic/Latino; 4% Two or more races, non-Hispanic/Latino; 7% Race/ethnicity unknown; 0.8% international; 5% transferred in; 90% live on campus. *Retention:* 55% of full-time freshmen returned.

Freshmen *Admission:* 2,154 admitted, 578 enrolled. *Average high school GPA:* 2.8. *Test scores:* SAT critical reading scores over 500: 20%; SAT math scores over 500: 20%; SAT writing scores over 500: 16%; ACT scores over 18: 63%; SAT critical reading scores over 600: 2%; SAT math scores over 600: 4%; SAT writing scores over 600: 2%; ACT scores over 24: 12%.

Faculty *Total:* 123, 63% full-time, 57% with terminal degrees. *Student/faculty ratio:* 17:1.

Academics *Calendar:* semesters. *Degree:* bachelor's. *Special study options:* academic remediation for entering students, adult/continuing education programs, advanced placement credit, double majors, honors programs, internships, services for LD students, student-designed majors, study abroad, summer session for credit. *Unusual degree programs:* 3-2 Sherman College of Straight Chiropractic.

Computers on Campus 89 computers/terminals are available on campus for general student use. Students can access the following: campus intranet, computer help desk, free student e-mail accounts, online (class) grades, online (class) registration, online (class) schedules. Campuswide network is available. 100% of college-owned or -operated housing units are wired for high-speed Internet access. Wireless service is available via entire campus.

Student Life *Housing:* on-campus residence required through senior year. *Options:* coed, women-only, disabled students. Campus housing is university owned. Freshman campus housing is guaranteed. *Activities and organizations:* drama/theater group, student-run newspaper, radio station, choral group, Student Government Association, Agriculture Club, BACCHUS, Panther Productions, African American Student Association, Students in Free Enterprise (SIFE), national sororities. *Campus security:* 24-hour emergency response devices and patrols, student patrols, late-night transport/escort service, controlled dormitory access. *Student services:* health clinic, personal/psychological counseling.

Athletics Member NCAA. All Division III. *Intercollegiate sports:* baseball M, basketball M/W, cheerleading M/W, cross-country running M/W, football M, golf M, lacrosse M/W, soccer M/W, softball W, swimming and diving W, tennis M/W, volleyball W. *Intramural sports:* basketball M/W, football M/W, racquetball M/W, softball M/W, tennis M/W.

Standardized Tests *Required:* SAT or ACT (for admission).

Financial Aid Of all full-time matriculated undergraduates who enrolled in 2010, 1,037 applied for aid, 958 were judged to have need, 958 had their need fully met. 674 Federal Work-Study jobs (averaging $2093). In 2010, 1180 non-need-based awards were made. *Average percent of need met:* 54%. *Average financial aid package:* $29,147. *Average need-based loan:* $2070. *Average need-based gift aid:* $10,878. *Average non-need-based aid:* $9685. *Average indebtedness upon graduation:* $9313.

Applying *Options:* electronic application, early admission, deferred entrance. *Application fee:* $25. *Required:* high school transcript. *Required for some:* interview. *Recommended:* essay or personal statement, minimum 2.0 GPA, 2 letters of recommendation, interview. *Application deadline:* rolling (freshmen). *Notification:* continuous (freshmen).

Freshman Application Contact Ms. Gilda Q. Woods, Associate Vice President for Enrollment Management and Dean of Admissions, Ferrum College, Spilman-Daniel House, PO Box 1000, Ferrum, VA 24088-9001. *Phone:* 540-365-4290. *Toll-free phone:* 800-868-9797. *Fax:* 540-365-4266. *E-mail:* admissions@ferrum.edu. *Web site:* http://www.ferrum.edu/.

George Mason University

Fairfax, Virginia

- **State-supported** university, founded 1957
- **Suburban** 806-acre campus with easy access to Washington, D.C.
- **Endowment** $51.6 million
- **Coed** 20,782 undergraduate students, 78% full-time, 52% women, 48% men
- **Moderately difficult** entrance level, 53% of applicants were admitted

Undergraduates 16,304 full-time, 4,478 part-time. Students come from 51 states and territories; 134 other countries; 11% are from out of state; 9% Black or African American, non-Hispanic/Latino; 10% Hispanic/Latino; 17% Asian, non-Hispanic/Latino; 0.4% Native Hawaiian or other Pacific Islander, non-Hispanic/Latino; 0.2% American Indian or Alaska Native, non-Hispanic/Latino; 4% Two or more races, non-Hispanic/Latino; 9% Race/ethnicity unknown; 4% international; 12% transferred in; 27% live on campus. *Retention:* 87% of full-time freshmen returned.

Freshmen *Admission:* 17,548 applied, 9,263 admitted, 2,665 enrolled. *Average high school GPA:* 3.65. *Test scores:* SAT critical reading scores over 500: 85%; SAT math scores over 500: 89%; ACT scores over 18: 100%; SAT critical reading scores over 600: 37%; SAT math scores over 600: 41%; ACT scores over 24: 70%; SAT critical reading scores over 700: 6%; SAT math scores over 700: 7%; ACT scores over 30: 14%.

Faculty *Total:* 2,375, 49% full-time. *Student/faculty ratio:* 16:1.

Academics *Calendar:* semesters. *Degrees:* bachelor's, master's, doctoral, post-master's, postbachelor's, and first professional certificates. *Special study options:* accelerated degree program, adult/continuing education programs, advanced placement credit, cooperative education, distance learning, double majors, English as a second language, external degree program, freshman honors college, honors programs, independent study, internships, off-campus study, part-time degree program, services for LD students, student-designed majors, study abroad, summer session for credit. *ROTC:* Army (b), Air Force (c). *Unusual degree programs:* 3-2 engineering.

Computers on Campus 628 computers/terminals and 25,000 ports are available on campus for general student use. Students can access the following: campus intranet, computer help desk, free student e-mail accounts, online (class) grades, online (class) registration, online (class) schedules. Campuswide network is available. 100% of college-owned or -operated housing units are wired for high-speed Internet access. Wireless service is available via entire campus.

Student Life *Housing options:* coed. Campus housing is university owned and leased by the school. Freshman campus housing is guaranteed. *Activities and organizations:* drama/theater group, student-run newspaper, radio and television station, choral group, Special Interests Organizations, International and Multicultural Organizations, Religious Organizations, Academic Organizations, Athletic Organizations, national fraternities, national sororities. *Campus security:* 24-hour emergency response devices and patrols, student patrols, late-night transport/escort service, controlled dormitory access. *Student services:* health clinic, personal/psychological counseling, women's center.

Athletics Member NCAA. All Division I. *Intercollegiate sports:* baseball M(s), basketball M(s)/W(s), cheerleading M(s)/W(s), crew W(s), cross-country running M(s)/W(s), golf M(s), lacrosse W(s), soccer M(s)/W(s), softball W(s), swimming and diving M(s)/W(s), tennis M(s)/W(s), track and field M(s)/W(s), volleyball M(s)/W(s), wrestling M(s). *Intramural sports:* baseball M(c), basketball M/W, bowling M(c)/W(c), crew M(c), cross-country running M(c)/W(c), equestrian sports W(c), fencing M(c)/W(c), field hockey W(c), football M(c), golf M/W, ice hockey M(c), lacrosse M(c)/W(c), rugby M(c)/W(c), soccer M(c)/W(c), softball M/W, swimming and diving M/W, table tennis M/W, tennis M/W, track and field M/W, ultimate Frisbee M(c)/W(c), volleyball M/W.

Standardized Tests *Required for some:* SAT or ACT (for admission). *Recommended:* SAT and SAT Subject Tests or ACT (for admission).

Costs (2011–12) *Tuition:* state resident $9066 full-time; nonresident $26,544 full-time. Full-time tuition and fees vary according to course load. Part-time tuition and fees vary according to course load. *Room and board:* $8950; room only: $5350. Room and board charges vary according to board plan and housing facility. *Payment plan:* installment. *Waivers:* senior citizens and employees or children of employees.

Financial Aid Of all full-time matriculated undergraduates who enrolled in 2010, 10,070 applied for aid, 7,689 were judged to have need, 591 had their need fully met. 307 Federal Work-Study jobs (averaging $2393). In 2010, 500 non-need-based awards were made. *Average percent of need met:* 66%. *Average financial aid package:* $12,154. *Average need-based loan:* $4332. *Average need-based gift aid:* $6867. *Average non-need-based aid:* $5556. *Average indebtedness upon graduation:* $23,506.

Applying *Options:* electronic application, early admission, early action, deferred entrance. *Application fee:* $60. *Required:* essay or personal statement, high school transcript, minimum 2.0 GPA. *Required for some:* 3 letters

of recommendation, Audition required for Dance and Music applicants. Portfolio required for Art and Visual Technology BFA applicants and Computer Game Design applicants. Interview and audition or portfolio required for Theater applicants. *Recommended:* minimum 3.5 GPA. *Application deadlines:* 1/15 (freshmen), 1/15 (out-of-state freshmen), 3/1 (transfers), 11/1 (early action). *Notification:* 4/1 (freshmen), 4/1 (out-of-state freshmen), continuous until 4/1 (transfers), 12/19 (early action).

Freshman Application Contact Eddie Tallent, Assistant Dean, Executive Director of Undergraduate Admissions, George Mason University, 4400 University Drive, MSN 3A4, Fairfax, VA 22030-4444. *Phone:* 703-993-2398. *Fax:* 703-993-6330. *E-mail:* etallent@gmu.edu. *Web site:* http://www.gmu.edu/.

Hampden-Sydney College
Hampden-Sydney, Virginia

- **Independent** 4-year, founded 1776, affiliated with Presbyterian Church (U.S.A.)
- **Rural** 1340-acre campus with easy access to Richmond
- **Endowment** $131.3 million
- **Men only** 1,057 undergraduate students, 100% full-time
- **Moderately difficult** entrance level, 55% of applicants were admitted

Undergraduates 1,057 full-time. Students come from 28 states and territories; 20 other countries; 32% are from out of state; 8% Black or African American, non-Hispanic/Latino; 2% Hispanic/Latino; 1% Asian, non-Hispanic/Latino; 0.6% American Indian or Alaska Native, non-Hispanic/Latino; 2% Two or more races, non-Hispanic/Latino; 2% Race/ethnicity unknown; 1% international; 2% transferred in; 95% live on campus. *Retention:* 80% of full-time freshmen returned.

Freshmen *Admission:* 2,484 applied, 1,361 admitted, 320 enrolled. *Average high school GPA:* 3.4. *Test scores:* SAT critical reading scores over 500: 78%; SAT math scores over 500: 74%; SAT critical reading scores over 600: 30%; SAT math scores over 600: 29%; SAT critical reading scores over 700: 4%; SAT math scores over 700: 3%.

Faculty *Total:* 115, 88% full-time, 84% with terminal degrees. *Student/faculty ratio:* 10:1.

Academics *Calendar:* semesters. *Degree:* bachelor's. *Special study options:* academic remediation for entering students, advanced placement credit, double majors, honors programs, independent study, internships, off-campus study, study abroad, summer session for credit. *ROTC:* Army (c). *Unusual degree programs:* 3-2 engineering with University of Virginia.

Computers on Campus 200 computers/terminals are available on campus for general student use. Students can access the following: campus intranet, computer help desk, free student e-mail accounts, online (class) grades, online (class) registration, online (class) schedules. Campuswide network is available. 100% of college-owned or -operated housing units are wired for high-speed Internet access. Wireless service is available via classrooms, computer centers, computer labs, libraries, student centers.

Student Life *Housing:* on-campus residence required through senior year. *Options:* men-only. Campus housing is university owned. Freshman campus housing is guaranteed. *Activities and organizations:* drama/theater group, student-run newspaper, radio station, choral group, Republican Society, Pre-Health Society, Outsiders Club, Tiger Athletic Club, Pre-Law Society, national fraternities. *Campus security:* 24-hour emergency response devices and patrols. *Student services:* health clinic, personal/psychological counseling.

Athletics Member NCAA. All Division III. *Intercollegiate sports:* baseball M, basketball M, crew M(c), cross-country running M, fencing M(c), football M, golf M, lacrosse M(c), riflery M(c), rugby M(c), soccer M, swimming and diving M, tennis M, ultimate Frisbee M(c). *Intramural sports:* basketball M, football M, soccer M, softball M, volleyball M.

Standardized Tests *Required:* SAT or ACT (for admission). *Recommended:* SAT Subject Tests (for admission).

Costs (2011–12) *Comprehensive fee:* $44,506 includes full-time tuition ($32,854), mandatory fees ($1020), and room and board ($10,632). *Room and board:* Room and board charges vary according to board plan and housing facility. *Payment plan:* installment. *Waivers:* employees or children of employees.

Financial Aid Of all full-time matriculated undergraduates who enrolled in 2011, 723 applied for aid, 606 were judged to have need, 132 had their need fully met. 277 Federal Work-Study jobs (averaging $1647). In 2011, 430 non-need-based awards were made. *Average percent of need met:* 81%. *Average financial aid package:* $26,853. *Average need-based loan:* $5102. *Average need-based gift aid:* $21,967. *Average non-need-based aid:* $11,451. *Average indebtedness upon graduation:* $27,740.

Applying *Options:* electronic application, early admission, early decision, early action. *Application fee:* $30. *Required:* essay or personal statement, high school transcript, minimum 2.0 GPA, 2 letters of recommendation. *Recommended:* minimum 3.0 GPA, interview. *Application deadlines:* 3/1 (fresh-

men), 7/1 (transfers), 1/15 (early action). *Early decision deadline:* 11/15. *Notification:* 4/15 (freshmen), 7/31 (transfers), 12/15 (early decision), 2/15 (early action).

Freshman Application Contact Ms. Anita Garland, Dean of Admissions, Hampden-Sydney College, PO Box 667, Hampden-Sydney, VA 23943-0667. *Phone:* 434-223-6120. *Toll-free phone:* 800-755-0733. *Fax:* 434-223-6346. *E-mail:* hsapp@hsc.edu. *Web site:* http://www.hsc.edu/.

Hampton University
Hampton, Virginia

- **Independent** comprehensive, founded 1868
- **Urban** 334-acre campus with easy access to Norfolk
- **Endowment** $195.3 million
- **Coed** 4,265 undergraduate students, 91% full-time, 65% women, 35% men
- **Moderately difficult** entrance level, 37% of applicants were admitted

Undergraduates 3,886 full-time, 379 part-time. Students come from 47 states and territories; 28 other countries; 62% are from out of state; 91% Black or African American, non-Hispanic/Latino; 1% Hispanic/Latino; 9% Asian, non-Hispanic/Latino; 0.2% American Indian or Alaska Native, non-Hispanic/Latino; 1% international; 5% transferred in; 59% live on campus. *Retention:* 70% of full-time freshmen returned.

Freshmen *Admission:* 10,569 applied, 3,917 admitted, 938 enrolled. *Average high school GPA:* 3.3. *Test scores:* SAT critical reading scores over 500: 91%; SAT math scores over 500: 82%; ACT scores over 18: 77%; SAT critical reading scores over 600: 17%; SAT math scores over 600: 40%; ACT scores over 24: 22%; SAT critical reading scores over 700: 1%; SAT math scores over 700: 5%; ACT scores over 30: 2%.

Faculty *Total:* 779, 86% full-time, 40% with terminal degrees. *Student/faculty ratio:* 11:1.

Academics *Calendar:* semesters. *Degrees:* certificates, associate, bachelor's, master's, doctoral, post-master's, and first professional certificates. *Special study options:* academic remediation for entering students, accelerated degree program, adult/continuing education programs, advanced placement credit, cooperative education, distance learning, double majors, honors programs, independent study, internships, off-campus study, part-time degree program, services for LD students, study abroad, summer session for credit. *ROTC:* Army (b), Navy (b).

Computers on Campus 1,300 computers/terminals are available on campus for general student use. Students can access the following: online (class) registration, Banner Systems. Campuswide network is available.

Student Life *Housing options:* coed, men-only, women-only. Campus housing is university owned. Freshman applicants given priority for college housing. *Activities and organizations:* drama/theater group, student-run newspaper, radio station, choral group, marching band, student government, student leaders, Student Union Board, student recruitment team, resident assistants, national fraternities, national sororities. *Campus security:* 24-hour emergency response devices and patrols, controlled dormitory access, emergency call boxes. *Student services:* health clinic, personal/psychological counseling, women's center.

Athletics Member NCAA. All Division I. *Intercollegiate sports:* basketball M(s)/W(s), bowling W(s), cheerleading W, cross-country running M(s)/W(s), football M(s), golf M(s)/W(s), sailing M(s)/W(s), softball W(s), tennis M(s)/W(s), track and field M(s)/W(s), volleyball W(s). *Intramural sports:* badminton M/W, basketball M/W, bowling W, football M, lacrosse M, sailing M/W, soccer M/W, softball M/W, volleyball W.

Standardized Tests *Required:* SAT or ACT (for admission).

Costs (2012–13) *Comprehensive fee:* $27,168 includes full-time tuition ($16,888), mandatory fees ($1910), and room and board ($8370). Full-time tuition and fees vary according to course load, degree level, location, and program. *Part-time tuition:* $430 per credit. Part-time tuition and fees vary according to course load and location. *College room only:* $4354. Room and board charges vary according to board plan, housing facility, and location. *Payment plan:* deferred payment. *Waivers:* employees or children of employees.

Financial Aid Of all full-time matriculated undergraduates who enrolled in 2010, 2,176 applied for aid, 1,924 were judged to have need, 1,005 had their need fully met. 196 Federal Work-Study jobs (averaging $704). 14 state and other part-time jobs (averaging $1107). In 2010, 93 non-need-based awards were made. *Average percent of need met:* 54%. *Average financial aid package:* $4982. *Average need-based loan:* $4000. *Average need-based gift aid:* $4587. *Average non-need-based aid:* $12,737. *Average indebtedness upon graduation:* $10,119. *Financial aid deadline:* 4/15.

Applying *Options:* electronic application, early admission, early action, deferred entrance. *Application fee:* $35. *Required:* essay or personal statement, high school transcript, minimum 2.5 GPA, 3 letters of recommendation. *Application deadline:* 3/1 (freshmen). *Notification:* 7/31 (freshmen).

Freshman Application Contact Ms. Derrick Boone, Director, Freshman Studies, Hampton University, 200 Student Center, Hampton University, Hampton, VA 23668. *Phone:* 757-727-5901. *Toll-free phone:* 800-624-3328. *Fax:* 757-727-5095. *E-mail:* derrickboone@hamptonu.edu. *Web site:* http://www.hamptonu.edu/.

Hollins University

Roanoke, Virginia

- **Independent** comprehensive, founded 1842
- **Suburban** 475-acre campus
- **Endowment** $152.7 million
- **Undergraduate: women only; graduate: coed** 731 undergraduate students, 96% full-time, 100% women, 0% men
- **Moderately difficult** entrance level, 83% of applicants were admitted

Undergraduates 702 full-time, 29 part-time. Students come from 46 states and territories; 13 other countries; 45% are from out of state; 11% Black or African American, non-Hispanic/Latino; 5% Hispanic/Latino; 2% Asian, non-Hispanic/Latino; 0.3% Native Hawaiian or other Pacific Islander, non-Hispanic/Latino; 0.3% American Indian or Alaska Native, non-Hispanic/Latino; 3% Two or more races, non-Hispanic/Latino; 0.7% Race/ethnicity unknown; 5% international; 4% transferred in; 78% live on campus. *Retention:* 67% of full-time freshmen returned.

Freshmen *Admission:* 813 applied, 672 admitted, 182 enrolled. *Average high school GPA:* 3.5. *Test scores:* SAT critical reading scores over 500: 69%; SAT math scores over 500: 58%; SAT writing scores over 500: 66%; ACT scores over 18: 97%; SAT critical reading scores over 600: 36%; SAT math scores over 600: 22%; SAT writing scores over 600: 27%; ACT scores over 24: 72%; SAT critical reading scores over 700: 9%; SAT math scores over 700: 6%; SAT writing scores over 700: 7%; ACT scores over 30: 21%.

Faculty *Total:* 105, 65% full-time, 85% with terminal degrees. *Student/faculty ratio:* 10:1.

Academics *Calendar:* 4-1-4. *Degrees:* bachelor's, master's, post-master's, and postbachelor's certificates. *Special study options:* accelerated degree program, adult/continuing education programs, advanced placement credit, double majors, independent study, internships, off-campus study, part-time degree program, services for LD students, student-designed majors, study abroad.

Computers on Campus 100 computers/terminals and 3,000 ports are available on campus for general student use. Students can access the following: campus intranet, computer help desk, free student e-mail accounts, online (class) grades, online (class) registration, online (class) schedules, applications software. Campuswide network is available. 100% of college-owned or -operated housing units are wired for high-speed Internet access. Wireless service is available via entire campus.

Student Life *Housing:* on-campus residence required through senior year. *Options:* women-only, disabled students. Campus housing is university owned. Freshman campus housing is guaranteed. *Activities and organizations:* drama/theater group, student-run newspaper, television station, choral group, Student Government Association, SHARE (volunteer group), Hollins Activity Board, Student Athletic Association, Black Student Alliance. *Campus security:* 24-hour emergency response devices and patrols, late-night transport/escort service, controlled dormitory access, emergency call boxes. *Student services:* health clinic, personal/psychological counseling, women's center.

Athletics Member NCAA. All Division III. *Intercollegiate sports:* basketball W, cross-country running W(c), equestrian sports W, fencing W(c), golf W, lacrosse W, soccer W, softball W(c), swimming and diving W, tennis W, volleyball W.

Standardized Tests *Required:* SAT or ACT (for admission).

Costs (2011–12) *Comprehensive fee:* $41,465 includes full-time tuition ($30,220), mandatory fees ($575), and room and board ($10,670). Part-time tuition: $945 per credit hour. *Required fees:* $146 per term part-time. *College room only:* $6335. *Payment plans:* tuition prepayment, installment. *Waivers:* employees or children of employees.

Financial Aid Of all full-time matriculated undergraduates who enrolled in 2010, 662 applied for aid, 608 were judged to have need, 86 had their need fully met. 327 Federal Work-Study jobs (averaging $2347). 96 state and other part-time jobs (averaging $2421). In 2010, 121 non-need-based awards were made. *Average percent of need met:* 81%. *Average financial aid package:* $22,803. *Average need-based loan:* $5164. *Average need-based gift aid:* $17,890. *Average non-need-based aid:* $15,435. *Average indebtedness upon graduation:* $19,982. *Financial aid deadline:* 2/15.

Applying *Options:* electronic application, early admission, early decision, deferred entrance. *Application fee:* $40. *Required:* essay or personal statement, high school transcript, 2 letters of recommendation. *Recommended:* interview. *Application deadline:* rolling (freshmen). *Early decision deadline:* 12/1. *Notification:* continuous (freshmen), 12/15 (early decision).

Freshman Application Contact Ms. Nicole Johnson Williams, Associate Dean of Admissions, Hollins University, PO Box 9707, Roanoke, VA 24020-1707. *Phone:* 540-362-6401. *Toll-free phone:* 800-456-9595. *Fax:* 540-362-6218. *E-mail:* huadm@hollins.edu. *Web site:* http://www.hollins.edu/.

ITT Technical Institute

Chantilly, Virginia

- **Proprietary** primarily 2-year, founded 2002, part of ITT Educational Services, Inc.
- **Coed**
- **Minimally difficult** entrance level

Academics *Calendar:* quarters. *Degrees:* associate and bachelor's.

Student Life *Housing:* college housing not available.

Freshman Application Contact Director of Recruitment, ITT Technical Institute, 14420 Abermarle Point Place, Suite 100, Chantilly, VA 20151. *Phone:* 703-263-2541. *Toll-free phone:* 888-895-8324. *Web site:* http://www.itt-tech.edu/.

ITT Technical Institute

Norfolk, Virginia

- **Proprietary** primarily 2-year, founded 1988, part of ITT Educational Services, Inc.
- **Suburban** campus
- **Coed**
- **Minimally difficult** entrance level

Academics *Calendar:* quarters. *Degrees:* associate and bachelor's.

Student Life *Housing:* college housing not available.

Financial Aid Of all full-time matriculated undergraduates who enrolled in 2010, 3 Federal Work-Study jobs (averaging $5000).

Freshman Application Contact Director of Recruitment, ITT Technical Institute, 863 Glenrock Road, Suite 100, Norfolk, VA 23502-3701. *Phone:* 757-466-1260. *Toll-free phone:* 888-253-8324. *Web site:* http://www.itt-tech.edu/.

ITT Technical Institute

Richmond, Virginia

- **Proprietary** primarily 2-year, founded 1999, part of ITT Educational Services, Inc.
- **Coed**
- **Minimally difficult** entrance level

Academics *Calendar:* quarters. *Degrees:* associate and bachelor's.

Student Life *Housing:* college housing not available.

Freshman Application Contact Director of Recruitment, ITT Technical Institute, 300 Gateway Centre Parkway, Richmond, VA 23235. *Phone:* 804-330-4992. *Toll-free phone:* 888-330-4888. *Web site:* http://www.itt-tech.edu/.

ITT Technical Institute

Salem, Virginia

- **Proprietary** primarily 2-year
- **Coed**
- **Minimally difficult** entrance level

Academics *Degrees:* associate and bachelor's.

Freshman Application Contact Director of Recruitment, ITT Technical Institute, 2159 Apperson Drive, Salem, VA 24153. *Phone:* 540-989-2500. *Toll-free phone:* 877-208-6132. *Web site:* http://www.itt-tech.edu/.

ITT Technical Institute

Springfield, Virginia

- **Proprietary** primarily 2-year, founded 2002, part of ITT Educational Services, Inc.
- **Coed**
- **Minimally difficult** entrance level

Academics *Calendar:* quarters. *Degrees:* associate and bachelor's.

Student Life *Housing:* college housing not available.

Freshman Application Contact Director of Recruitment, ITT Technical Institute, 7300 Boston Boulevard, Springfield, VA 22153. *Phone:* 703-440-9535. *Toll-free phone:* 866-817-8324. *Web site:* http://www.itt-tech.edu/.

James Madison University
Harrisonburg, Virginia

- **State-supported** comprehensive, founded 1908
- **Small-town** 721-acre campus
- **Endowment** $58.1 million
- **Coed** 17,900 undergraduate students, 95% full-time, 59% women, 41% men
- **Very difficult** entrance level, 60% of applicants were admitted

Undergraduates 17,086 full-time, 814 part-time. Students come from 41 states and territories; 75 other countries; 27% are from out of state; 4% Black or African American, non-Hispanic/Latino; 4% Hispanic/Latino; 5% Asian, non-Hispanic/Latino; 0.4% Native Hawaiian or other Pacific Islander, non-Hispanic/Latino; 0.2% American Indian or Alaska Native, non-Hispanic/Latino; 2% Two or more races, non-Hispanic/Latino; 5% Race/ethnicity unknown; 1% international; 4% transferred in; 36% live on campus. *Retention:* 91% of full-time freshmen returned.
Freshmen *Admission:* 22,864 applied, 13,705 admitted, 4,029 enrolled. *Average high school GPA:* 3.8. *Test scores:* SAT critical reading scores over 500: 85%; SAT math scores over 500: 89%; ACT scores over 18: 99%; SAT critical reading scores over 600: 35%; SAT math scores over 600: 40%; ACT scores over 24: 65%; SAT critical reading scores over 700: 5%; SAT math scores over 700: 5%; ACT scores over 30: 6%.
Faculty *Total:* 1,400, 66% full-time, 61% with terminal degrees. *Student/faculty ratio:* 16:1.
Academics *Calendar:* semesters. *Degrees:* bachelor's, master's, doctoral, post-master's, and first professional certificates (also offers specialist in education degree). *Special study options:* accelerated degree program, adult/continuing education programs, advanced placement credit, distance learning, double majors, English as a second language, freshman honors college, honors programs, independent study, internships, off-campus study, part-time degree program, services for LD students, student-designed majors, study abroad, summer session for credit. *ROTC:* Army (b), Air Force (c). *Unusual degree programs:* 3-2 forestry with Virginia Polytechnic Institute and State University.
Computers on Campus 600 computers/terminals and 7,000 ports are available on campus for general student use. Students can access the following: campus intranet, computer help desk, free student e-mail accounts, online (class) grades, online (class) registration, online (class) schedules. Campuswide network is available. 100% of college-owned or -operated housing units are wired for high-speed Internet access. Wireless service is available via classrooms, dorm rooms, learning centers, libraries, student centers.
Student Life *Housing:* on-campus residence required for freshman year. *Options:* coed, disabled students. Campus housing is university owned and leased by the school. Freshman campus housing is guaranteed. *Activities and organizations:* drama/theater group, student-run newspaper, radio station, choral group, marching band, national fraternities, national sororities. *Campus security:* 24-hour emergency response devices and patrols, student patrols, late-night transport/escort service, controlled dormitory access, lighted pathways. *Student services:* health clinic, personal/psychological counseling, women's center.
Athletics Member NCAA. All Division I except football (Division I-AA). *Intercollegiate sports:* baseball M(s), basketball M(s)/W(s), cheerleading M/W, cross-country running W(s), field hockey W(s), golf M(s)/W(s), lacrosse W(s), soccer M(s)/W(s), softball W(s), swimming and diving W(s), tennis M(s)/W(s), track and field W(s), volleyball W(s). *Intramural sports:* archery M(c)/W(c), baseball M(c), basketball M/W, bowling M/W, cheerleading M/W, crew M(c)/W(c), cross-country running M(c)/W(c), equestrian sports M(c)/W(c), fencing M(c)/W(c), field hockey W(c), football M/W, golf M/W, gymnastics M(c)/W(c), ice hockey M(c)/W(c), lacrosse M(c)/W(c), racquetball M/W, rugby M(c)/W(c), skiing (downhill) M(c)/W(c), soccer M/W, softball M/W, squash M(c)/W(c), swimming and diving M(c)/W(c), table tennis M/W, tennis M/W, track and field M(c)/W(c), ultimate Frisbee M(c)/W(c), volleyball M/W, water polo M(c)/W(c), wrestling M(c).
Standardized Tests *Required:* SAT or ACT (for admission).
Costs (2011–12) *Tuition:* state resident $4642 full-time, $154 per credit hour part-time; nonresident $17,932 full-time, $580 per credit hour part-time. *Required fees:* $3806 full-time. *Room and board:* $8340; room only: $4184. Room and board charges vary according to board plan. *Payment plans:* tuition prepayment, installment. *Waivers:* employees or children of employees.
Financial Aid Of all full-time matriculated undergraduates who enrolled in 2011, 16,974 applied for aid, 7,767 were judged to have need, 724 had their need fully met. 235 Federal Work-Study jobs (averaging $1974). 2,555 state and other part-time jobs (averaging $2160). In 2011, 167 non-need-based awards were made. *Average percent of need met:* 47%. *Average financial aid package:* $8205. *Average need-based loan:* $4352. *Average need-based gift aid:* $6910. *Average non-need-based aid:* $2728. *Average indebtedness upon graduation:* $22,128.

Applying *Options:* electronic application, early action, deferred entrance. *Application fee:* $50. *Required:* high school transcript. *Recommended:* minimum 3.0 GPA. *Application deadlines:* 1/15 (freshmen), 3/15 (transfers), 11/1 (early action). *Notification:* 4/1 (freshmen), 5/1 (transfers), 1/1 (early action).
Freshman Application Contact James Madison University, 800 South Main Street, Harrisonburg, VA 22807. *Phone:* 540-568-5681. *Web site:* http://www.jmu.edu/.

Jefferson College of Health Sciences
Roanoke, Virginia

- **Independent** comprehensive, founded 1982
- **Urban** 1-acre campus
- **Endowment** $1.6 million
- **Coed**
- **Moderately difficult** entrance level

Faculty *Student/faculty ratio:* 10:1.
Academics *Calendar:* semesters. *Degrees:* certificates, associate, bachelor's, and master's.
Student Life *Campus security:* 24-hour emergency response devices and patrols, late-night transport/escort service, controlled dormitory access.
Standardized Tests *Required:* SAT or ACT (for admission). *Recommended:* SAT (for admission).
Financial Aid Of all full-time matriculated undergraduates who enrolled in 2010, 1,436 applied for aid, 1,230 were judged to have need, 47 had their need fully met. 91 Federal Work-Study jobs (averaging $952). 115 state and other part-time jobs (averaging $1513). In 2010, 47 non-need-based awards were made. *Average percent of need met:* 43. *Average financial aid package:* $11,113. *Average need-based loan:* $4931. *Average need-based gift aid:* $8103. *Average non-need-based aid:* $2909. *Average indebtedness upon graduation:* $18,133.
Applying *Options:* electronic application, deferred entrance. *Application fee:* $35. *Required:* high school transcript, minimum 2.0 GPA. *Required for some:* interview.
Freshman Application Contact Jefferson College of Health Sciences, PO Box 13186, Roanoke, VA 24031-3186. *Phone:* 540-985-9083. *Toll-free phone:* 888-985-8483. *Web site:* http://www.jchs.edu/.

Liberty University
Lynchburg, Virginia

- **Independent nondenominational** comprehensive, founded 1971
- **Suburban** 6500-acre campus
- **Coed** 11,553 undergraduate students, 97% full-time, 52% women, 48% men
- **Minimally difficult** entrance level, 25% of applicants were admitted

Undergraduates 11,229 full-time, 324 part-time. Students come from 95 other countries; 57% are from out of state; 7% Black or African American, non-Hispanic/Latino; 4% Hispanic/Latino; 1% Asian, non-Hispanic/Latino; 0.2% Native Hawaiian or other Pacific Islander, non-Hispanic/Latino; 0.4% American Indian or Alaska Native, non-Hispanic/Latino; 2% Two or more races, non-Hispanic/Latino; 9% Race/ethnicity unknown; 7% international; 6% transferred in; 61% live on campus. *Retention:* 78% of full-time freshmen returned.
Freshmen *Admission:* 22,415 applied, 5,507 admitted, 2,607 enrolled. *Average high school GPA:* 3.37. *Test scores:* SAT critical reading scores over 500: 61%; SAT math scores over 500: 55%; SAT writing scores over 500: 55%; ACT scores over 18: 89%; SAT critical reading scores over 600: 22%; SAT math scores over 600: 20%; SAT writing scores over 600: 18%; ACT scores over 24: 39%; SAT critical reading scores over 700: 3%; SAT math scores over 700: 2%; SAT writing scores over 700: 3%; ACT scores over 30: 7%.
Faculty *Student/faculty ratio:* 25:1.
Academics *Calendar:* semesters. *Degrees:* certificates, associate, bachelor's, master's, doctoral, post-master's, and first professional certificates (also offers external degree program with significant enrollment not reflected in profile). *Special study options:* academic remediation for entering students, accelerated degree program, advanced placement credit, cooperative education, distance learning, double majors, English as a second language, external degree program, honors programs, independent study, internships, off-campus study, part-time degree program, services for LD students, student-designed majors, study abroad, summer session for credit. *ROTC:* Army (b), Air Force (c).
Computers on Campus 800 computers/terminals are available on campus for general student use. Students can access the following: computer help desk, free student e-mail accounts, online (class) grades, online (class) registration, online (class) schedules. Campuswide network is available. 100% of college-owned or -operated housing units are wired for high-speed Internet access. Wireless service is available via entire campus.

Student Life *Housing:* on-campus residence required through senior year. *Options:* men-only, women-only, disabled students. Campus housing is university owned. Freshman campus housing is guaranteed. *Activities and organizations:* drama/theater group, student-run newspaper, radio station, choral group, marching band, Campus Serve. *Campus security:* 24-hour patrols, late-night transport/escort service, 24-hour emergency dispatch. *Student services:* health clinic, personal/psychological counseling.

Athletics Member NCAA. All Division I except football (Division I-AA). *Intercollegiate sports:* baseball M(s), basketball M(s)/W(s), cheerleading M(s)/W(s), crew M(c)/W(c), cross-country running M(s)/W(s), equestrian sports W(c), field hockey W(s), golf M(s), ice hockey M(c)/W(c), lacrosse W(s), soccer M(s)/W(s), softball W(s), swimming and diving W(s), tennis M(s)/W(s), track and field M(s)/W(s), volleyball W(s). *Intramural sports:* basketball M/W, football M/W, lacrosse M(c), soccer M/W, softball M/W, table tennis M/W, tennis M/W, ultimate Frisbee M/W, volleyball M/W, wrestling M(c).

Standardized Tests *Required:* SAT or ACT (for admission).

Costs (2012–13) *Comprehensive fee:* $27,018 includes full-time tuition ($18,562), mandatory fees ($1406), and room and board ($7050). Full-time tuition and fees vary according to course load. Part-time tuition: $619 per credit hour. Part-time tuition and fees vary according to course load. *Required fees:* $1406 per year part-time. *Room and board:* Room and board charges vary according to housing facility. *Payment plan:* installment. *Waivers:* employees or children of employees.

Financial Aid Of all full-time matriculated undergraduates who enrolled in 2011, 20,954 applied for aid, 18,807 were judged to have need, 1,066 had their need fully met. In 2011, 931 non-need-based awards were made. *Average percent of need met:* 38%. *Average financial aid package:* $8297. *Average need-based loan:* $2619. *Average need-based gift aid:* $6107. *Average non-need-based aid:* $6951. *Average indebtedness upon graduation:* $36,014. *Financial aid deadline:* 3/1.

Applying *Options:* electronic application. *Application fee:* $40. *Required:* essay or personal statement, high school transcript, minimum 2.0 GPA. *Recommended:* minimum 2.0 GPA. *Application deadlines:* rolling (freshmen), rolling (out-of-state freshmen), rolling (transfers). *Notification:* continuous (freshmen), continuous (out-of-state freshmen), continuous (transfers).

Freshman Application Contact Dr. Terry Elam, Director of Admissions, Liberty University, 1971 University Boulevard, Lynchburg, VA 24502.

Phone: 434-592-3966. *Toll-free phone:* 800-543-5317. *Fax:* 800-542-2311. *E-mail:* admissions@liberty.edu. *Web site:* http://www.liberty.edu/.

See below for display ad and page 1408 for the College Close-Up.

Longwood University
Farmville, Virginia

- **State-supported** comprehensive, founded 1839, part of The State Council of Higher Education for Virginia
- **Small-town** 160-acre campus with easy access to Richmond
- **Coed** 4,237 undergraduate students, 95% full-time, 66% women, 34% men
- **Moderately difficult** entrance level, 75% of applicants were admitted

Undergraduates 4,017 full-time, 220 part-time. Students come from 10 states and territories; 15 other countries; 3% are from out of state; 6% Black or African American, non-Hispanic/Latino; 3% Hispanic/Latino; 1% Asian, non-Hispanic/Latino; 0.2% Native Hawaiian or other Pacific Islander, non-Hispanic/Latino; 0.4% American Indian or Alaska Native, non-Hispanic/Latino; 3% Two or more races, non-Hispanic/Latino; 3% Race/ethnicity unknown; 0.8% international; 4% transferred in; 74% live on campus. *Retention:* 78% of full-time freshmen returned.

Freshmen *Admission:* 4,080 applied, 3,044 admitted, 1,034 enrolled. *Average high school GPA:* 3.41. *Test scores:* SAT critical reading scores over 500: 61%; SAT math scores over 500: 53%; ACT scores over 18: 92%; SAT critical reading scores over 600: 13%; SAT math scores over 600: 9%; ACT scores over 24: 21%; SAT critical reading scores over 700: 1%; ACT scores over 30: 2%.

Faculty *Total:* 300, 74% full-time, 68% with terminal degrees. *Student/faculty ratio:* 18:1.

Academics *Calendar:* semesters. *Degrees:* bachelor's, master's, post-master's, and postbachelor's certificates. *Special study options:* accelerated degree program, advanced placement credit, distance learning, double majors, English as a second language, honors programs, independent study, internships, off-campus study, part-time degree program, services for LD students, study abroad, summer session for credit. *ROTC:* Army (b). *Unusual degree programs:* 3-2 engineering with University of Virginia, Old Dominion University, University of Tennessee, Virginia Polytechnic Institute and University, Christopher Newport University.

Computers on Campus 265 computers/terminals and 650 ports are available on campus for general student use. Students can access the following: campus

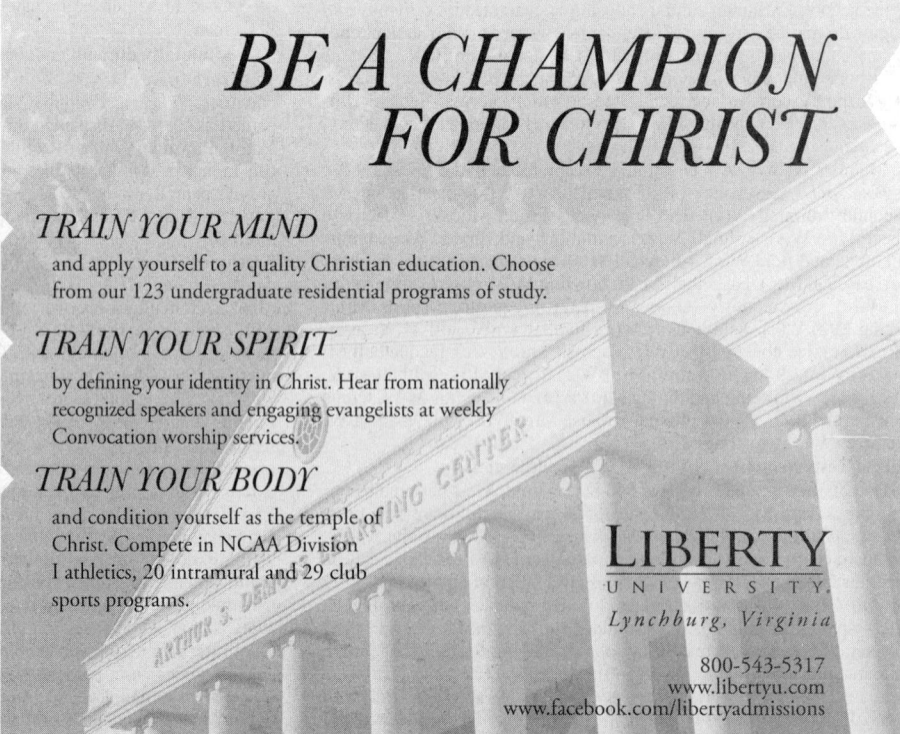

intranet, computer help desk, free student e-mail accounts, online (class) grades, online (class) registration, online (class) schedules. Campuswide network is available. 100% of college-owned or -operated housing units are wired for high-speed Internet access. Wireless service is available via classrooms, computer centers, computer labs, libraries, student centers.

Student Life *Housing:* on-campus residence required for freshman year. *Options:* coed, women-only, disabled students. Campus housing is university owned. Freshman campus housing is guaranteed. *Activities and organizations:* drama/theater group, student-run newspaper, radio and television station, choral group, Student Government Association, Alpha Phi Omega, Inter-Varsity Christian Fellowship, Longwood Ambassadors, Wellness Advocates, national fraternities, national sororities. *Campus security:* 24-hour emergency response devices and patrols, late-night transport/escort service, controlled dormitory access, security lighting. *Student services:* health clinic, personal/psychological counseling.

Athletics Member NCAA. All Division I. *Intercollegiate sports:* baseball M(s), basketball M(s)/W(s), cross-country running M(s)/W(s), equestrian sports M(c)/W(c), field hockey W(s), football M(c), golf M(s)/W(s), lacrosse M(c)/W(s), rugby M(c)/W(c), soccer M(s)/W(s), softball W(s), swimming and diving M(c)/W(c), tennis M(s)/W(s), volleyball M(c)/W(c), wrestling M(c). *Intramural sports:* badminton M/W, baseball M(c), basketball M(c)/W, bowling M/W, cheerleading M/W, field hockey W(c), football M/W, golf M/W, racquetball M/W, soccer M(c)/W(c), softball M/W, table tennis M/W, tennis M/W, ultimate Frisbee M/W, volleyball M/W.

Standardized Tests *Required:* SAT or ACT (for admission).

Costs (2011–12) *Tuition:* state resident $5880 full-time, $196 per credit hour part-time; nonresident $17,070 full-time, $569 per credit hour part-time. Full-time tuition and fees vary according to course load. Part-time tuition and fees vary according to course load. *Required fees:* $4650 full-time, $155 per credit hour part-time. *Room and board:* $8114; room only: $5260. Room and board charges vary according to board plan, housing facility, and location. *Payment plan:* installment. *Waivers:* senior citizens.

Financial Aid Of all full-time matriculated undergraduates who enrolled in 2010, 2,887 applied for aid, 2,166 were judged to have need, 1,056 had their need fully met. 292 Federal Work-Study jobs (averaging $1364). 428 state and other part-time jobs (averaging $1398). In 2010, 215 non-need-based awards were made. *Average percent of need met:* 82%. *Average financial aid package:* $11,961. *Average need-based loan:* $7248. *Average need-based gift aid:* $6010. *Average non-need-based aid:* $3509. *Average indebtedness upon graduation:* $23,672.

Applying *Options:* electronic application, early admission, early action, deferred entrance. *Application fee:* $50. *Required:* essay or personal statement, high school transcript. *Required for some:* interview. *Application deadlines:* 3/1 (freshmen), 3/1 (out-of-state freshmen), 3/1 (transfers), 12/1 (early action). *Notification:* 6/1 (freshmen), 6/1 (out-of-state freshmen), continuous until 6/1 (transfers), 1/15 (early action).

Freshman Application Contact Mrs. Sallie McMullin, Interim Dean of Admissions, Longwood University, 201 High Street, Farmville, VA 23909. *Phone:* 434-395-2060. *Toll-free phone:* 800-281-4677. *Fax:* 434-395-2332. *E-mail:* admissions@longwood.edu. *Web site:* http://www.longwood.edu/.

Lynchburg College

Lynchburg, Virginia

- **Independent** comprehensive, founded 1903, affiliated with Christian Church (Disciples of Christ)
- **Suburban** 214-acre campus
- **Endowment** $79.0 million
- **Coed** 2,279 undergraduate students, 94% full-time, 60% women, 40% men
- **Moderately difficult** entrance level, 68% of applicants were admitted

Undergraduates 2,142 full-time, 137 part-time. Students come from 37 states and territories; 9 other countries; 33% are from out of state; 10% Black or African American, non-Hispanic/Latino; 3% Hispanic/Latino; 1% Asian, non-Hispanic/Latino; 0.5% American Indian or Alaska Native, non-Hispanic/Latino; 2% Two or more races, non-Hispanic/Latino; 4% Race/ethnicity unknown; 0.4% international; 4% transferred in; 75% live on campus. *Retention:* 73% of full-time freshmen returned.

Freshmen *Admission:* 4,617 applied, 3,151 admitted, 609 enrolled. *Average high school GPA:* 3.21. *Test scores:* SAT critical reading scores over 500: 52%; SAT math scores over 500: 51%; SAT writing scores over 500: 47%; ACT scores over 18: 85%; SAT critical reading scores over 600: 15%; SAT math scores over 600: 12%; SAT writing scores over 600: 11%; ACT scores over 24: 28%; SAT critical reading scores over 700: 1%; SAT writing scores over 700: 1%; ACT scores over 30: 1%.

Faculty *Total:* 294, 60% full-time, 58% with terminal degrees. *Student/faculty ratio:* 12:1.

Academics *Calendar:* semesters. *Degrees:* bachelor's, master's, doctoral, post-master's, postbachelor's, and first professional certificates. *Special study options:* accelerated degree program, adult/continuing education programs, advanced placement credit, distance learning, double majors, honors programs, independent study, internships, off-campus study, part-time degree program, services for LD students, study abroad, summer session for credit. *Unusual degree programs:* 3-2 engineering with Old Dominion University, University of Virginia.

Computers on Campus 300 computers/terminals are available on campus for general student use. Students can access the following: campus intranet, computer help desk, free student e-mail accounts, online (class) grades, online (class) registration, online (class) schedules. Campuswide network is available. 100% of college-owned or -operated housing units are wired for high-speed Internet access. Wireless service is available via entire campus.

Student Life *Housing:* on-campus residence required through junior year. *Options:* coed, disabled students. Campus housing is university owned. Freshman campus housing is guaranteed. *Activities and organizations:* drama/theater group, student-run newspaper, choral group, Student Government Association, Student Activities Board, Enrollment Student Ambassadors, Emergency Services, Greek Life, national fraternities, national sororities. *Campus security:* 24-hour emergency response devices and patrols, late-night transport/escort service, controlled dormitory access. *Student services:* health clinic, personal/psychological counseling.

Athletics Member NCAA. All Division III. *Intercollegiate sports:* baseball M, basketball M/W, cheerleading M/W, cross-country running M/W, equestrian sports M/W, field hockey W, golf M, lacrosse M/W, soccer M/W, softball W, tennis M/W, track and field M/W, volleyball W. *Intramural sports:* basketball M(c)/W(c), equestrian sports M(c)/W(c), field hockey W(c), golf M(c)/W(c), ice hockey M(c), lacrosse M(c)/W(c), rugby M/W, soccer M(c)/W(c), softball W(c), tennis M(c)/W(c), volleyball M/W, wrestling M(c).

Standardized Tests *Required:* SAT or ACT (for admission).

Costs (2011–12) *Comprehensive fee:* $39,185 includes full-time tuition ($29,860), mandatory fees ($945), and room and board ($8380). Part-time tuition: $415 per credit hour. Part-time tuition and fees vary according to course load. *Required fees:* $5 per credit hour part-time. *College room only:* $4190. Room and board charges vary according to board plan and housing facility. *Payment plans:* tuition prepayment, installment. *Waivers:* adult students, senior citizens, and employees or children of employees.

Financial Aid Of all full-time matriculated undergraduates who enrolled in 2010, 1,740 applied for aid, 1,538 were judged to have need, 323 had their need fully met. In 2010, 495 non-need-based awards were made. *Average percent of need met:* 77%. *Average financial aid package:* $20,881. *Average need-based loan:* $3536. *Average need-based gift aid:* $17,342. *Average non-need-based aid:* $10,071. *Average indebtedness upon graduation:* $32,130.

Applying *Options:* electronic application, early admission, early decision, deferred entrance. *Application fee:* $30. *Required:* high school transcript. *Recommended:* essay or personal statement, 2 letters of recommendation, interview. *Application deadlines:* rolling (freshmen), rolling (transfers). *Early decision deadline:* 11/15. *Notification:* continuous (freshmen), continuous (transfers), 12/15 (early decision).

Freshman Application Contact Lynchburg College, 1501 Lakeside Drive, Lynchburg, VA 24501-3199. *Phone:* 434-544-8300. *Toll-free phone:* 800-426-8101. *Web site:* http://www.lynchburg.edu/.

See page 942 for display ad and page 1426 for the College Close-Up.

Mary Baldwin College

Staunton, Virginia

- **Independent** comprehensive, founded 1842
- **Small-town** 54-acre campus
- **Endowment** $32.2 million
- **Coed, primarily women** 1,528 undergraduate students, 71% full-time, 95% women, 5% men
- **Moderately difficult** entrance level, 52% of applicants were admitted

Undergraduates 1,091 full-time, 437 part-time. Students come from 35 states and territories; 8 other countries; 40% are from out of state; 24% Black or African American, non-Hispanic/Latino; 5% Hispanic/Latino; 3% Asian, non-Hispanic/Latino; 0.1% Native Hawaiian or other Pacific Islander, non-Hispanic/Latino; 0.7% American Indian or Alaska Native, non-Hispanic/Latino; 3% Two or more races, non-Hispanic/Latino; 3% Race/ethnicity unknown; 1% international; 2% transferred in; 62% live on campus. *Retention:* 67% of full-time freshmen returned.

Freshmen *Admission:* 3,129 applied, 1,638 admitted, 289 enrolled. *Average high school GPA:* 3.27. *Test scores:* SAT critical reading scores over 500: 51%; SAT math scores over 500: 40%; SAT writing scores over 500: 45%; ACT scores over 18: 74%; SAT critical reading scores over 600: 17%; SAT math scores over 600: 9%; SAT writing scores over 600: 14%; ACT scores

Lynchburg College

Where *Going Above and Beyond* is a way of life

Academics: Liberal arts curriculum: 39 majors, 49 minors, 13 pre-professional programs; doctoral studies in physical therapy and educational leadership; master's degrees including M.A., M.B.A., M.Ed., M.S.N.

Athletics: Outstanding Division III sports. Ranked in the top 50 in the country among Division III schools in the Learfield Sports Director's Cup.

National Recognition: *Colleges That Change Lives* by Loren Pope; *U. 5. News & World Report;* The Princeton Review; John Templeton Foundation's Honor Roll of Character-Building Colleges

Student Body: 2,800 undergraduate and graduate students from 35 states and 11 foreign countries

Location: Central Virginia metropolitan area of 240,000

Beyond The Classroom: 470-acre Claytor Nature Study Center for environmental study; faculty/student research; study abroad; honors program; performing and visual arts, service learning, Bonner Leaders program

Financial Aid: 97% of LC students benefit from some type of financial assistance.

Information: www.lynchburg.edu or 800.426.8101

over 24: 24%; SAT critical reading scores over 700: 4%; SAT math scores over 700: 1%; SAT writing scores over 700: 3%; ACT scores over 30: 4%.
Faculty *Total:* 136, 59% full-time, 113% with terminal degrees. *Student/faculty ratio:* 11:1.
Academics *Calendar:* 4-1-4. *Degrees:* certificates, bachelor's, and master's. *Special study options:* academic remediation for entering students, accelerated degree program, adult/continuing education programs, advanced placement credit, double majors, English as a second language, external degree program, freshman honors college, honors programs, independent study, internships, off-campus study, part-time degree program, services for LD students, student-designed majors, study abroad. *ROTC:* Army (b), Navy (c), Air Force (c). *Unusual degree programs:* 3-2 engineering with University of Virginia; nursing with Vanderbilt University.
Computers on Campus 244 computers/terminals are available on campus for general student use. Students can access the following: computer help desk, free student e-mail accounts, online (class) grades, online (class) registration, online (class) schedules, we are 100% wireless. Campuswide network is available. 100% of college-owned or -operated housing units are wired for high-speed Internet access. Wireless service is available via entire campus.
Student Life *Housing:* on-campus residence required through senior year. *Options:* women-only. Campus housing is university owned. Freshman campus housing is guaranteed. *Activities and organizations:* drama/theater group, student-run newspaper, radio station, choral group, marching band, International Club council, Minority Clubs United, Student Senate, Baldwin Program Board, Resident Hall Association. *Campus security:* 24-hour emergency response devices and patrols, late-night transport/escort service, controlled dormitory access. *Student services:* health clinic, personal/psychological counseling.
Athletics Member NCAA. All Division III. *Intercollegiate sports:* basketball W, cross-country running W, soccer W, softball W, swimming and diving W(c), tennis W, volleyball W. *Intramural sports:* basketball W, fencing W(c), racquetball W, swimming and diving W, volleyball W.
Standardized Tests *Required:* SAT or ACT (for admission).
Costs (2011–12) *Comprehensive fee:* $34,750 includes full-time tuition ($26,610), mandatory fees ($350), and room and board ($7790). Full-time tuition and fees vary according to degree level. Part-time tuition: $415 per semester hour. Part-time tuition and fees vary according to degree level. *Room and board:* Room and board charges vary according to housing facility. *Payment plan:* installment. *Waivers:* employees or children of employees.
Financial Aid Of all full-time matriculated undergraduates who enrolled in 2011, 1,106 applied for aid, 1,016 were judged to have need, 129 had their need fully met. 274 Federal Work-Study jobs (averaging $1328). 82 state and other part-time jobs (averaging $1513). In 2011, 106 non-need-based awards were made. *Average percent of need met:* 70%. *Average financial aid package:* $17,440. *Average need-based loan:* $4175. *Average need-based gift aid:* $13,773. *Average non-need-based aid:* $12,528. *Average indebtedness upon graduation:* $30,018.
Applying *Options:* electronic application, early admission, early decision, deferred entrance. *Application fee:* $35. *Required:* high school transcript, minimum 2.0 GPA, 1 letter of recommendation. *Recommended:* interview. *Application deadlines:* rolling (freshmen), rolling (transfers). *Early decision deadline:* 11/15. *Notification:* continuous (freshmen), continuous (transfers), 12/1 (early decision).
Freshman Application Contact Ms. Roberta Palmer, Director of Admissions, Mary Baldwin College, Frederick and New Streets, Staunton, VA 24401. *Phone:* 540-887-7260. *Toll-free phone:* 800-468-2262. *Fax:* 540-887-7229. *E-mail:* rpalmer@mbc.edu. *Web site:* http://www.mbc.edu/.

Marymount University
Arlington, Virginia

- **Independent** comprehensive, founded 1950, affiliated with Roman Catholic Church
- **Suburban** 21-acre campus with easy access to Washington, D.C.
- **Endowment** $25.2 million
- **Coed** 2,373 undergraduate students, 88% full-time, 70% women, 30% men
- **Moderately difficult** entrance level, 78% of applicants were admitted

Undergraduates 2,087 full-time, 286 part-time. Students come from 39 states and territories; 54 other countries; 38% are from out of state; 15% Black or African American, non-Hispanic/Latino; 13% Hispanic/Latino; 8% Asian, non-Hispanic/Latino; 0.4% Native Hawaiian or other Pacific Islander, non-Hispanic/Latino; 0.2% American Indian or Alaska Native, non-Hispanic/Latino; 2% Two or more races, non-Hispanic/Latino; 13% Race/ethnicity unknown; 10% international; 14% transferred in; 35% live on campus. *Retention:* 70% of full-time freshmen returned.
Freshmen *Admission:* 2,024 applied, 1,574 admitted, 409 enrolled. *Average high school GPA:* 3.09. *Test scores:* SAT critical reading scores over 500:

51%; SAT math scores over 500: 43%; SAT writing scores over 500: 48%; ACT scores over 18: 87%; SAT critical reading scores over 600: 14%; SAT math scores over 600: 11%; SAT writing scores over 600: 8%; ACT scores over 24: 21%; SAT critical reading scores over 700: 1%; SAT math scores over 700: 1%; SAT writing scores over 700: 1%.

Faculty *Total:* 346, 42% full-time, 64% with terminal degrees. *Student/faculty ratio:* 14:1.

Academics *Calendar:* semesters plus 2 summer terms. *Degrees:* certificates, bachelor's, master's, doctoral, post-master's, and postbachelor's certificates. *Special study options:* academic remediation for entering students, accelerated degree program, advanced placement credit, distance learning, double majors, English as a second language, honors programs, independent study, internships, off-campus study, part-time degree program, services for LD students, student-designed majors, study abroad, summer session for credit. *ROTC:* Army (c).

Computers on Campus 280 computers/terminals are available on campus for general student use. Students can access the following: campus intranet, computer help desk, free student e-mail accounts, online (class) grades, online (class) registration, online (class) schedules, online drive space. Campuswide network is available. 100% of college-owned or -operated housing units are wired for high-speed Internet access. Wireless service is available via computer centers, computer labs, dorm rooms, learning centers, libraries, student centers.

Student Life *Housing:* on-campus residence required through sophomore year. *Options:* coed, men-only, women-only. Campus housing is university owned and leased by the school. Freshman applicants given priority for college housing. *Activities and organizations:* drama/theater group, student-run newspaper, choral group, Interior Design Alliance, Student Nurses Association, Fashion Club, International Club, One 2 One (drama club). *Campus security:* 24-hour emergency response devices and patrols, late-night transport/escort service, controlled dormitory access. *Student services:* health clinic, personal/psychological counseling.

Athletics Member NCAA. All Division III. *Intercollegiate sports:* basketball M/W, cross-country running M/W, golf M, lacrosse M/W, soccer M/W, swimming and diving M/W, volleyball M/W. *Intramural sports:* basketball M/W, cheerleading W, football M/W, soccer M/W, volleyball M/W.

Standardized Tests *Required:* SAT or ACT (for admission).

Costs (2012–13) *One-time required fee:* $340. *Comprehensive fee:* $36,178 includes full-time tuition ($24,900), mandatory fees ($278), and room and board ($11,000). Part-time tuition: $810 per credit. *Room and board:* Room and board charges vary according to housing facility. *Payment plan:* installment. *Waivers:* senior citizens and employees or children of employees.

Financial Aid Of all full-time matriculated undergraduates who enrolled in 2010, 1,447 applied for aid, 1,259 were judged to have need, 180 had their need fully met. In 2010, 364 non-need-based awards were made. *Average percent of need met:* 65%. *Average financial aid package:* $15,824. *Average need-based loan:* $4399. *Average need-based gift aid:* $5840. *Average non-need-based aid:* $11,059. *Average indebtedness upon graduation:* $23,945.

Applying *Options:* electronic application, deferred entrance. *Application fee:* $40. *Required:* high school transcript, minimum 2.5 GPA, 1 letter of recommendation. *Recommended:* essay or personal statement, interview. *Application deadlines:* rolling (freshmen), rolling (transfers). *Notification:* continuous (freshmen), continuous (transfers).

Freshman Application Contact Mr. Mike Canfield, Director of Undergraduate Admissions, Marymount University, 2807 North Glebe Road, Arlington, VA 22207-4299. *Phone:* 703-284-1500. *Toll-free phone:* 800-548-7638. *Fax:* 703-522-0349. *E-mail:* admissions@marymount.edu. *Web site:* http://www.marymount.edu/.

National College
Danville, Virginia
Freshman Application Contact Admissions Office, National College, 734 Main Street, Danville, VA 24541-1819. *Phone:* 434-793-6822. *Toll-free phone:* 888-9-JOBREADY. *Web site:* http://www.national-college.edu/.

National College
Harrisonburg, Virginia
Director of Admissions Jack Evey, Campus Director, National College, 51 B Burgess Road, Harrisonburg, VA 22801-9709. *Phone:* 540-432-0943. *Toll-free phone:* 888-9-JOBREADY. *Web site:* http://www.national-college.edu/.

National College
Lynchburg, Virginia
Freshman Application Contact Admissions Representative, National College, 104 Candlewood Court, Lynchburg, VA 24502-2653. *Phone:* 804-

239-3500. *Toll-free phone:* 888-9-JOBREADY. *Web site:* http://www.national-college.edu/.

National College
Salem, Virginia
Freshman Application Contact Director of Admissions, National College, 1813 East Main Street, Salem, VA 24153. *Phone:* 540-986-1800. *Toll-free phone:* 888-9-JOBREADY. *Fax:* 540-444-4198. *Web site:* http://www.national-college.edu/.

Norfolk State University
Norfolk, Virginia
- **State-supported** comprehensive, founded 1935, part of State Council of Higher Education for Virginia
- **Urban** 134-acre campus
- **Coed** 6,264 undergraduate students, 80% full-time, 65% women, 35% men
- **Moderately difficult** entrance level, 65% of applicants were admitted

Undergraduates 5,005 full-time, 1,259 part-time. 16% are from out of state; 89% Black or African American, non-Hispanic/Latino; 0.7% Hispanic/Latino; 1% Asian, non-Hispanic/Latino; 0.1% Native Hawaiian or other Pacific Islander, non-Hispanic/Latino; 0.1% American Indian or Alaska Native, non-Hispanic/Latino; 2% Two or more races, non-Hispanic/Latino; 1% Race/ethnicity unknown; 0.4% international; 10% transferred in; 32% live on campus. *Retention:* 73% of full-time freshmen returned.

Freshmen *Admission:* 4,125 applied, 2,692 admitted, 923 enrolled. *Test scores:* SAT critical reading scores over 500: 18%; SAT math scores over 500: 17%; SAT critical reading scores over 600: 2%; SAT math scores over 600: 2%.

Faculty *Total:* 379, 71% full-time. *Student/faculty ratio:* 19:1.

Academics *Calendar:* semesters. *Degrees:* associate, bachelor's, master's, doctoral, and first professional. *ROTC:* Army (b), Navy (b).

Computers on Campus Students can access the following: online (class) registration. Campuswide network is available.

Student Life *Housing options:* men-only, women-only. Campus housing is university owned. *Campus security:* 24-hour emergency response devices and patrols, late-night transport/escort service.

Athletics Member NCAA. All Division I. *Intercollegiate sports:* baseball M(s), basketball M(s)/W(s), bowling W, football M(s), softball W, tennis M(s)/W(s), track and field M(s)/W(s), volleyball W(s).

Standardized Tests *Required:* SAT or ACT (for admission).

Costs (2011–12) *Tuition:* state resident $6700 full-time, $247 per credit hour part-time; nonresident $20,343 full-time, $702 per credit hour part-time. Full-time tuition and fees vary according to course load. Part-time tuition and fees vary according to course load. *Room and board:* $7927. Room and board charges vary according to board plan and housing facility.

Financial Aid *Financial aid deadline:* 5/31.

Applying *Options:* electronic application, deferred entrance. *Application fee:* $45. *Required:* high school transcript, minimum 2.3 GPA. *Application deadline:* rolling (transfers).

Freshman Application Contact Mr. Kevin M. Holmes, Director of Recruitment and Admissions, Norfolk State University, 700 Park Avenue, Norfolk, VA 23504. *Phone:* 757-823-9222. *Toll-free phone:* 800-274-1821. *Fax:* 757-823-2078. *E-mail:* admissions@nsu.edu. *Web site:* http://www.nsu.edu/.

Old Dominion University
Norfolk, Virginia
- **State-supported** university, founded 1930
- **Urban** 251-acre campus with easy access to Virginia Beach
- **Endowment** $170.2 million
- **Coed** 19,367 undergraduate students, 76% full-time, 53% women, 47% men
- **Moderately difficult** entrance level, 75% of applicants were admitted

Undergraduates 14,725 full-time, 4,642 part-time. Students come from 43 states and territories; 79 other countries; 6% are from out of state; 23% Black or African American, non-Hispanic/Latino; 5% Hispanic/Latino; 4% Asian, non-Hispanic/Latino; 0.6% Native Hawaiian or other Pacific Islander, non-Hispanic/Latino; 0.4% American Indian or Alaska Native, non-Hispanic/Latino; 4% Two or more races, non-Hispanic/Latino; 5% Race/ethnicity unknown; 1% international; 11% transferred in; 24% live on campus. *Retention:* 80% of full-time freshmen returned.

Freshmen *Admission:* 10,276 applied, 7,746 admitted, 2,738 enrolled. *Average high school GPA:* 3.24. *Test scores:* SAT critical reading scores over 500:

55%; SAT math scores over 500: 56%; SAT writing scores over 500: 46%; ACT scores over 18: 86%; SAT critical reading scores over 600: 14%; SAT math scores over 600: 16%; SAT writing scores over 600: 8%; ACT scores over 24: 26%; SAT critical reading scores over 700: 1%; SAT math scores over 700: 1%; SAT writing scores over 700: 1%; ACT scores over 30: 2%.

Faculty *Total:* 1,246, 60% full-time, 57% with terminal degrees. *Student/faculty ratio:* 21:1.

Academics *Calendar:* semesters. *Degrees:* bachelor's, master's, doctoral, post-master's, and first professional certificates. *Special study options:* accelerated degree program, adult/continuing education programs, advanced placement credit, cooperative education, distance learning, double majors, English as a second language, freshman honors college, honors programs, independent study, internships, off-campus study, part-time degree program, services for LD students, student-designed majors, study abroad, summer session for credit. *ROTC:* Army (b), Navy (b). *Unusual degree programs:* 3-2 business administration; engineering; nursing; international studies, dental hygiene, communications/humanities, English, English/applied linguistics, history, interdisciplinary studies/humanities, computer science, women's studies/humanities, philosophy/humanities, health science/public health, environmental health/public health.

Computers on Campus 1,130 computers/terminals and 10,000 ports are available on campus for general student use. Students can access the following: campus intranet, computer help desk, free student e-mail accounts, online (class) grades, online (class) registration, online (class) schedules, online courses. Campuswide network is available. 100% of college-owned or -operated housing units are wired for high-speed Internet access. Wireless service is available via classrooms, computer centers, computer labs, dorm rooms, learning centers, libraries, student centers.

Student Life *Housing options:* coed, disabled students. Campus housing is university owned and leased by the school. Freshman applicants given priority for college housing. *Activities and organizations:* drama/theater group, student-run newspaper, radio station, choral group, marching band, Student Activities Council, F.O.R.E.I.G.N.E.R.S, Monarch Maniacs, Anime Club, Ebony Impact Gospel Choir, national fraternities, national sororities. *Campus security:* 24-hour emergency response devices and patrols, student patrols, late-night transport/escort service, controlled dormitory access. *Student services:* health clinic, personal/psychological counseling, women's center.

Athletics Member NCAA. All Division I. *Intercollegiate sports:* baseball M(s), basketball M(s)/W(s), cheerleading M(c)/W(s)(c), crew M(c)/W(s), fencing M(c)/W(c), field hockey W(s), football M(s), golf M(s)/W(s), ice hockey M(c)/W(c), lacrosse M(c)/W(s), rock climbing M(c)/W(c), rugby M(c)/W(c), sailing M/W, soccer M(s)/W(s), softball W(c), swimming and diving M(s)/W(s), tennis M(s)/W(s), ultimate Frisbee M(c)/W(c), volleyball M(c)/W(c), wrestling M(s). *Intramural sports:* badminton M/W, basketball M/W, cross-country running M/W, golf M/W, racquetball M/W, rock climbing M/W, sailing M/W, soccer M/W, softball M/W, table tennis M/W, tennis M/W, ultimate Frisbee M/W, volleyball M/W.

Standardized Tests *Required:* SAT or ACT (for admission).

Costs (2011–12) *Tuition:* state resident $7890 full-time, $263 per credit hour part-time; nonresident $22,230 full-time, $741 per credit hour part-time. *Required fees:* $254 full-time, $59 per term part-time. *Room and board:* $8796; room only: $5058. Room and board charges vary according to board plan and housing facility. *Payment plans:* installment, deferred payment. *Waivers:* senior citizens and employees or children of employees.

Financial Aid Of all full-time matriculated undergraduates who enrolled in 2011, 11,121 applied for aid, 8,278 were judged to have need, 3,200 had their need fully met. 149 Federal Work-Study jobs (averaging $2234). In 2011, 351 non-need-based awards were made. *Average percent of need met:* 71%. *Average financial aid package:* $8595. *Average need-based loan:* $4346. *Average need-based gift aid:* $5139. *Average non-need-based aid:* $3439. *Average indebtedness upon graduation:* $16,500. *Financial aid deadline:* 3/15.

Applying *Options:* electronic application, early admission, early action, deferred entrance. *Application fee:* $50. *Required:* high school transcript, minimum 2.8 GPA, test scores. *Required for some:* interview. *Recommended:* essay or personal statement, 1 letter of recommendation. *Application deadlines:* 2/1 (freshmen), 2/1 (out-of-state freshmen), 5/1 (transfers), 12/1 (early action). *Notification:* continuous (freshmen), continuous (out-of-state freshmen), continuous (transfers), 1/15 (early action).

Freshman Application Contact Ms. Shereen Williams, Customer Service Manager, Admissions Office, Old Dominion University, 108 Rollins Hall, 5215 Hampton Boulevard, Norfolk, VA 23529. *Phone:* 757-683-3648. *Toll-free phone:* 800-348-7926. *Fax:* 757-683-3255. *E-mail:* admissions@odu.edu. *Web site:* http://www.odu.edu/.

Patrick Henry College

Purcellville, Virginia

- **Independent nondenominational** 4-year, founded 1999
- **Small-town** 106-acre campus with easy access to Washington, D.C.
- **Coed** 371 undergraduate students, 86% full-time, 46% women, 54% men
- **Very difficult** entrance level, 86% of applicants were admitted

Undergraduates 318 full-time, 53 part-time. Students come from 44 states and territories; 87% are from out of state; 0.6% Black or African American, non-Hispanic/Latino; 1% Hispanic/Latino; 3% Native Hawaiian or other Pacific Islander, non-Hispanic/Latino; 18% Race/ethnicity unknown; 4% transferred in; 90% live on campus. *Retention:* 93% of full-time freshmen returned.

Freshmen *Admission:* 213 applied, 184 admitted, 72 enrolled. *Average high school GPA:* 3.88. *Test scores:* SAT critical reading scores over 500: 98%; SAT math scores over 500: 97%; SAT writing scores over 500: 97%; ACT scores over 18: 100%; SAT critical reading scores over 600: 86%; SAT math scores over 600: 64%; SAT writing scores over 600: 79%; ACT scores over 24: 93%; SAT critical reading scores over 700: 44%; SAT math scores over 700: 15%; SAT writing scores over 700: 24%; ACT scores over 30: 52%.

Faculty *Total:* 50, 44% full-time, 66% with terminal degrees. *Student/faculty ratio:* 11:1.

Academics *Calendar:* semesters. *Degree:* bachelor's. *Special study options:* advanced placement credit, distance learning, independent study, internships, off-campus study, summer session for credit.

Computers on Campus 6 computers/terminals and 100 ports are available on campus for general student use. Students can access the following: campus intranet, computer help desk, free student e-mail accounts, online (class) grades, online (class) registration, online (class) schedules. Campuswide network is available. 100% of college-owned or -operated housing units are wired for high-speed Internet access. Wireless service is available via entire campus.

Student Life *Housing:* on-campus residence required through sophomore year. *Options:* men-only, women-only. Campus housing is university owned. Freshman applicants given priority for college housing. *Activities and organizations:* drama/theater group, student-run newspaper, choral group, Drama Club, Eden Troupe, student government, chorale, College Republicans, Debate/Moot Court. *Campus security:* 24-hour emergency response devices, student patrols, late-night transport/escort service, controlled dormitory access, after hours patrols by trained security personnel.

Athletics *Intercollegiate sports:* basketball M/W, soccer M/W. *Intramural sports:* baseball M, basketball M/W, fencing M(c)/W(c), football M(c), racquetball M(c)/W(c), rugby M(c), table tennis M(c)/W(c), tennis M/W, ultimate Frisbee M/W, volleyball M/W, weight lifting M.

Standardized Tests *Required:* SAT or ACT (for admission).

Costs (2011–12) *Comprehensive fee:* $32,136 includes full-time tuition ($22,758), mandatory fees ($250), and room and board ($9128). Full-time tuition and fees vary according to course load. Part-time tuition: $500 per credit hour. Part-time tuition and fees vary according to course level and course load. *Room and board:* Room and board charges vary according to board plan. *Payment plan:* installment. *Waivers:* employees or children of employees.

Financial Aid Of all full-time matriculated undergraduates who enrolled in 2011, 202 applied for aid, 183 were judged to have need. In 2011, 135 non-need-based awards were made. *Average percent of need met:* 50%. *Average financial aid package:* $14,000. *Average need-based gift aid:* $11,000. *Average non-need-based aid:* $8200. *Average indebtedness upon graduation:* $25,500. *Financial aid deadline:* 6/15.

Applying *Options:* electronic application, early action, deferred entrance. *Application fee:* $20. *Required:* essay or personal statement, high school transcript, 2 letters of recommendation, interview. *Application deadlines:* 6/15 (freshmen), 11/1 (early action). *Notification:* continuous (freshmen).

Freshman Application Contact Patrick Henry College, Ten Patrick Henry Circle, Purcellville, VA 20132. *Phone:* 540-338-1776. *E-mail:* admissions@phc.edu. *Web site:* http://www.phc.edu/.

Radford University

Radford, Virginia

- **State-supported** comprehensive, founded 1910
- **Small-town** 191-acre campus
- **Endowment** $42.3 million
- **Coed** 8,350 undergraduate students, 96% full-time, 56% women, 44% men
- **Moderately difficult** entrance level, 80% of applicants were admitted

Undergraduates 8,023 full-time, 327 part-time. Students come from 39 states and territories; 57 other countries; 6% are from out of state; 7% Black or African American, non-Hispanic/Latino; 3% Hispanic/Latino; 2% Asian, non-Hispanic/Latino; 0.3% Native Hawaiian or other Pacific Islander, non-Hispanic/Latino; 0.5% American Indian or Alaska Native, non-Hispanic/Latino; 2%

Two or more races, non-Hispanic/Latino; 2% Race/ethnicity unknown; 0.6% international; 10% transferred in; 37% live on campus. *Retention:* 76% of full-time freshmen returned.

Freshmen *Admission:* 7,596 applied, 6,095 admitted, 2,035 enrolled. *Average high school GPA:* 3.13. *Test scores:* SAT critical reading scores over 500: 57%; SAT math scores over 500: 51%; SAT writing scores over 500: 45%; ACT scores over 18: 69%; SAT critical reading scores over 600: 13%; SAT math scores over 600: 8%; SAT writing scores over 600: 7%; ACT scores over 24: 5%; SAT critical reading scores over 700: 1%.

Faculty *Total:* 623, 65% full-time, 64% with terminal degrees. *Student/faculty ratio:* 19:1.

Academics *Calendar:* semesters. *Degrees:* certificates, bachelor's, master's, doctoral, post-master's, and postbachelor's certificates. *Special study options:* accelerated degree program, advanced placement credit, distance learning, double majors, honors programs, independent study, internships, off-campus study, part-time degree program, services for LD students, student-designed majors, study abroad, summer session for credit. *ROTC:* Army (b).

Computers on Campus 772 computers/terminals are available on campus for general student use. Students can access the following: campus intranet, computer help desk, free student e-mail accounts, online (class) grades, online (class) registration, online (class) schedules, online financial aid status and student accounts payable. Campuswide network is available. 100% of college-owned or -operated housing units are wired for high-speed Internet access. Wireless service is available via entire campus.

Student Life *Housing:* on-campus residence required through sophomore year. *Options:* coed, disabled students. Campus housing is university owned and leased by the school. Freshman campus housing is guaranteed. *Activities and organizations:* drama/theater group, student-run newspaper, radio and television station, choral group, Think in Pink, National Society for Collegiate Scholars, Sigma Sigma Sigma (Greek sorority), Environmental Club, Gay-Straight Alliance, national fraternities, national sororities. *Campus security:* 24-hour emergency response devices and patrols, late-night transport/escort service, controlled dormitory access. *Student services:* health clinic, personal/psychological counseling.

Athletics Member NCAA. All Division I. *Intercollegiate sports:* baseball M(s), basketball M(s)/W(s), cross-country running M(s)/W(s), field hockey W(s), golf M(s)/W(s), soccer M(s)/W(s), softball W(s), swimming and diving W(s), tennis M(s)/W(s), track and field M(s)/W(s), volleyball W(s). *Intramural sports:* baseball M(c), basketball M/W, bowling M/W, cheerleading M(c)/W(c), cross-country running M/W, equestrian sports M(c)/W(c), field hockey W(c), football M/W, golf M(c)/W(c), gymnastics M(c)/W(c), ice hockey M(c), lacrosse M(c)/W(c), racquetball M/W, rock climbing M/W, rugby M(c), skiing (downhill) M(c)/W(c), soccer M/W, softball M/W, swimming and diving M(c)/W(c), table tennis M/W, tennis M/W, ultimate Frisbee M/W, volleyball M/W, weight lifting M/W, wrestling M(c)/W(c).

Standardized Tests *Required:* SAT or ACT (for admission).

Costs (2011–12) *Tuition:* state resident $5508 full-time, $230 per credit hour part-time; nonresident $16,256 full-time, $677 per credit hour part-time. Part-time tuition and fees vary according to course load. *Required fees:* $2812 full-time, $117 per credit hour part-time. *Room and board:* $7589; room only: $4117. Room and board charges vary according to board plan and housing facility. *Payment plan:* installment. *Waivers:* senior citizens and employees or children of employees.

Financial Aid Of all full-time matriculated undergraduates who enrolled in 2011, 5,658 applied for aid, 4,187 were judged to have need, 1,312 had their need fully met. 360 Federal Work-Study jobs (averaging $2229). 467 state and other part-time jobs (averaging $2090). In 2011, 286 non-need-based awards were made. *Average percent of need met:* 83%. *Average financial aid package:* $9297. *Average need-based loan:* $4076. *Average need-based gift aid:* $7530. *Average non-need-based aid:* $3744. *Average indebtedness upon graduation:* $21,484.

Applying *Options:* electronic application, early admission, early action, deferred entrance. *Application fee:* $50. *Required:* high school transcript. *Application deadlines:* 2/1 (freshmen), 6/1 (transfers), 12/1 (early action). *Notification:* 4/1 (freshmen), continuous (transfers), 1/15 (early action).

Freshman Application Contact Mr. James A. Pennix, Dean of Admissions/Interim Vice Provost for Enrollment Management, Radford University, PO Box 6903, Radford, VA 24142. *Phone:* 540-831-5371. *Fax:* 540-831-5038. *E-mail:* admissions@radford.edu. *Web site:* http://www.radford.edu/.

Randolph College
Lynchburg, Virginia

- **Independent Methodist** comprehensive, founded 1891
- **Suburban** 100-acre campus
- **Coed** 571 undergraduate students, 96% full-time, 66% women, 34% men
- **Moderately difficult** entrance level, 71% of applicants were admitted

Undergraduates 548 full-time, 23 part-time. 53% are from out of state; 9% Black or African American, non-Hispanic/Latino; 6% Hispanic/Latino; 2% Asian, non-Hispanic/Latino; 0.2% Native Hawaiian or other Pacific Islander, non-Hispanic/Latino; 0.2% American Indian or Alaska Native, non-Hispanic/

Latino; 3% Two or more races, non-Hispanic/Latino; 12% international; 5% transferred in; 91% live on campus. *Retention:* 75% of full-time freshmen returned.

Freshmen *Admission:* 979 applied, 696 admitted, 177 enrolled. *Average high school GPA:* 3.47. *Test scores:* SAT critical reading scores over 500: 75%; SAT math scores over 500: 67%; SAT writing scores over 500: 67%; ACT scores over 18: 90%; SAT critical reading scores over 600: 35%; SAT math scores over 600: 31%; SAT writing scores over 600: 32%; ACT scores over 24: 54%; SAT critical reading scores over 700: 8%; SAT math scores over 700: 11%; SAT writing scores over 700: 4%; ACT scores over 30: 8%.

Faculty *Total:* 74, 92% full-time, 91% with terminal degrees. *Student/faculty ratio:* 8:1.

Academics *Calendar:* semesters. *Degrees:* bachelor's and master's. *Special study options:* adult/continuing education programs, part-time degree program.

Computers on Campus Students can access the following: campus intranet, computer help desk, free student e-mail accounts, online (class) grades, online (class) registration, online (class) schedules. Campuswide network is available. 100% of college-owned or -operated housing units are wired for high-speed Internet access. Wireless service is available via entire campus.

Student Life *Housing:* on-campus residence required through senior year. *Options:* coed, women-only. Campus housing is university owned. Freshman campus housing is guaranteed. *Campus security:* 24-hour emergency response devices and patrols, late-night transport/escort service.

Athletics Member NCAA. All Division III. *Intercollegiate sports:* basketball M/W, cross-country running M/W, equestrian sports M/W, lacrosse M/W, soccer M/W, softball W, tennis M/W, volleyball W.

Standardized Tests *Required:* SAT or ACT (for admission).

Costs (2011–12) *Comprehensive fee:* $40,762 includes full-time tuition ($29,866), mandatory fees ($510), and room and board ($10,386). Part-time tuition: $1245 per credit hour. Part-time tuition and fees vary according to course load. *Required fees:* $53 per term part-time. *Payment plan:* installment. *Waivers:* adult students and employees or children of employees.

Financial Aid Of all full-time matriculated undergraduates who enrolled in 2010, 407 applied for aid, 369 were judged to have need, 73 had their need fully met. 180 Federal Work-Study jobs (averaging $1860). 119 state and other part-time jobs (averaging $1800). In 2010, 132 non-need-based awards were made. *Average percent of need met:* 75%. *Average financial aid package:* $24,013. *Average need-based loan:* $5370. *Average need-based gift aid:* $18,359. *Average non-need-based aid:* $16,268. *Average indebtedness upon graduation:* $22,000.

Applying *Options:* electronic application, early admission, early action, deferred entrance. *Application fee:* $35. *Required:* essay or personal statement, high school transcript, 2 letters of recommendation. *Recommended:* interview. *Application deadlines:* 3/1 (freshmen), 7/1 (transfers), 12/1 (early action). *Notification:* continuous (freshmen), continuous (transfers), 1/1 (early action).

Freshman Application Contact Ms. Margaret Blount, Director of Admissions, Randolph College, 2500 Rivermont Avenue, Lynchburg, VA 24503-1555. *Phone:* 434-947-8100. *Toll-free phone:* 800-745-7692. *Fax:* 434-947-8996. *E-mail:* admissions@randolphcollege.edu. *Web site:* http://www.randolphcollege.edu/.

See page 945 for display ad and page 1514 for the College Close-Up.

Randolph-Macon College

Ashland, Virginia

- **Independent United Methodist** 4-year, founded 1830
- **Suburban** 120-acre campus with easy access to Richmond
- **Endowment** $105.2 million
- **Coed** 1,257 undergraduate students, 98% full-time, 53% women, 47% men
- **Moderately difficult** entrance level, 56% of applicants were admitted

Undergraduates 1,234 full-time, 23 part-time. Students come from 29 states and territories; 14 other countries; 30% are from out of state; 13% Black or African American, non-Hispanic/Latino; 4% Hispanic/Latino; 2% Asian, non-Hispanic/Latino; 0.2% Native Hawaiian or other Pacific Islander, non-Hispanic/Latino; 0.5% American Indian or Alaska Native, non-Hispanic/Latino; 3% Two or more races, non-Hispanic/Latino; 0.6% Race/ethnicity unknown; 1% international; 2% transferred in; 79% live on campus. *Retention:* 80% of full-time freshmen returned.

Freshmen *Admission:* 4,249 applied, 2,369 admitted, 410 enrolled. *Average high school GPA:* 3.53. *Test scores:* SAT critical reading scores over 500: 76%; SAT math scores over 500: 70%; SAT writing scores over 500: 69%; ACT scores over 18: 97%; SAT critical reading scores over 600: 25%; SAT math scores over 600: 23%; SAT writing scores over 600: 19%; ACT scores over 24: 58%; SAT critical reading scores over 700: 3%; SAT math scores over 700: 2%; SAT writing scores over 700: 2%; ACT scores over 30: 7%.

Faculty *Total:* 151, 62% full-time, 68% with terminal degrees. *Student/faculty ratio:* 11:1.

Academics *Calendar:* 4-1-4. *Degree:* bachelor's. *Special study options:* academic remediation for entering students, accelerated degree program, advanced placement credit, double majors, honors programs, independent study, internships, off-campus study, part-time degree program, services for LD students, study abroad, summer session for credit. *ROTC:* Army (c). *Unusual degree programs:* 3-2 engineering with Columbia University, University of Virginia; forestry with Duke University; accounting with Virginia Commonwealth University.

Computers on Campus 356 computers/terminals and 1,500 ports are available on campus for general student use. Students can access the following: computer help desk, free student e-mail accounts, online (class) registration, online (class) schedules. Campuswide network is available. 100% of college-owned or -operated housing units are wired for high-speed Internet access. Wireless service is available via classrooms, computer labs, dorm rooms, libraries, student centers.

Student Life *Housing:* on-campus residence required through junior year. *Options:* coed, men-only, women-only, disabled students. Campus housing is university owned. Freshman campus housing is guaranteed. *Activities and organizations:* drama/theater group, student-run newspaper, radio and television station, choral group, Residence Hall Association, Campus Activities Board, Student Government Association, Drama Guild, Student Honors Association, national fraternities, national sororities. *Campus security:* 24-hour emergency response devices and patrols, late-night transport/escort service, controlled dormitory access. *Student services:* health clinic, personal/psychological counseling, women's center.

Athletics Member NCAA. All Division III. *Intercollegiate sports:* baseball M, basketball M/W, equestrian sports M(c)/W(c), field hockey W, football M, golf M, lacrosse M/W, soccer M/W, softball W, swimming and diving M/W, tennis M/W, volleyball W. *Intramural sports:* basketball M/W, cheerleading M/W, cross-country running M/W, football M/W, lacrosse M/W, racquetball M/W, rugby M/W, soccer M/W, softball M/W, swimming and diving M, table tennis M/W, tennis M/W, ultimate Frisbee M/W, volleyball M/W.

Standardized Tests *Required:* SAT or ACT (for admission). *Recommended:* SAT Subject Tests (for admission).

Costs (2011–12) *One-time required fee:* $100. *Comprehensive fee:* $41,235 includes full-time tuition ($30,400), mandatory fees ($865), and room and board ($9970). Full-time tuition and fees vary according to reciprocity agreements. Part-time tuition: $3450 per course. *Required fees:* $875 per year part-time. *College room only:* $5500. Room and board charges vary according to board plan and housing facility. *Payment plan:* installment. *Waivers:* employees or children of employees.

Financial Aid Of all full-time matriculated undergraduates who enrolled in 2010, 968 applied for aid, 842 were judged to have need, 193 had their need fully met. 235 Federal Work-Study jobs (averaging $2000). In 2010, 332 non-need-based awards were made. *Average percent of need met:* 79%. *Average financial aid package:* $23,140. *Average need-based loan:* $4560. *Average need-based gift aid:* $18,955. *Average non-need-based aid:* $12,029. *Average indebtedness upon graduation:* $31,603.

Applying *Options:* electronic application, early admission, early action, deferred entrance. *Application fee:* $30. *Required:* essay or personal statement, high school transcript, minimum 2.0 GPA, 1 letter of recommendation. *Recommended:* interview. *Application deadlines:* 3/1 (freshmen), 4/1 (transfers), 11/15 (early action). *Notification:* 4/1 (freshmen), 5/1 (transfers), 1/1 (early action).

Freshman Application Contact Anthony Ambrogi, Director of Admissions and Enrollment Research, Randolph-Macon College, PO Box 5005, Ashland, VA 23005-5505. *Phone:* 804-752-7305. *Toll-free phone:* 800-888-1762. *Fax:* 804-752-4707. *E-mail:* admissions@rmc.edu. *Web site:* http://www.rmc.edu/.

Regent University

Virginia Beach, Virginia

- **Independent Christian** comprehensive, founded 1977
- **Suburban** 70-acre campus
- **Endowment** $193.9 million
- **Coed** 2,333 undergraduate students, 58% full-time, 62% women, 38% men
- **Minimally difficult** entrance level, 84% of applicants were admitted

Undergraduates 1,349 full-time, 984 part-time. Students come from 50 states and territories; 34 other countries; 53% are from out of state; 22% Black or African American, non-Hispanic/Latino; 6% Hispanic/Latino; 2% Asian, non-Hispanic/Latino; 0.7% American Indian or Alaska Native, non-Hispanic/Latino; 14% Race/ethnicity unknown; 2% international; 19% transferred in; 16% live on campus. *Retention:* 72% of full-time freshmen returned.

Freshmen *Admission:* 1,450 applied, 1,216 admitted, 382 enrolled. *Average high school GPA:* 3.2. *Test scores:* SAT critical reading scores over 500: 71%;

SAT math scores over 500: 58%; SAT writing scores over 500: 61%; ACT scores over 18: 99%; SAT critical reading scores over 600: 27%; SAT math scores over 600: 20%; SAT writing scores over 600: 21%; ACT scores over 24: 31%; SAT critical reading scores over 700: 5%; SAT writing scores over 700: 2%; ACT scores over 30: 5%.

Faculty *Total:* 537, 36% full-time, 76% with terminal degrees. *Student/faculty ratio:* 17:1.

Academics *Calendar:* trimesters. *Degrees:* associate, bachelor's, master's, doctoral, post-master's, and first professional certificates. *Special study options:* academic remediation for entering students, adult/continuing education programs, advanced placement credit, distance learning, double majors, external degree program, internships, off-campus study, part-time degree program, services for LD students, study abroad, summer session for credit. *ROTC:* Army (c).

Computers on Campus 113 computers/terminals and 75 ports are available on campus for general student use. Students can access the following: campus intranet, computer help desk, free student e-mail accounts, online (class) grades, online (class) registration, online (class) schedules. Campuswide network is available. 100% of college-owned or -operated housing units are wired for high-speed Internet access. Wireless service is available via entire campus.

Student Life *Housing:* on-campus residence required for freshman year. *Options:* men-only, women-only, disabled students. Campus housing is university owned. Freshman applicants given priority for college housing. *Activities and organizations:* drama/theater group, student-run newspaper, choral group, Regent Undergraduate Council, Students in Free Enterprise (SIFE), Psychology Club, Student Alumni Ambassadors, Jabez Praise Dance Ministry, national fraternities, national sororities. *Campus security:* 24-hour emergency response devices and patrols, student patrols, late-night transport/escort service, controlled dormitory access. *Student services:* personal/psychological counseling.

Athletics *Intramural sports:* basketball M/W, soccer M/W, volleyball M/W.

Standardized Tests *Required for some:* SAT or ACT (for admission).

Costs (2011–12) *Tuition:* $14,850 full-time, $495 per credit hour part-time. Full-time tuition and fees vary according to course level, course load, program, and student level. Part-time tuition and fees vary according to course level, course load, program, and student level. *Required fees:* $458 full-time, $495 per credit hour part-time, $229 per term part-time. *Room only:* $5900. Room and board charges vary according to housing facility. *Payment plan:* installment. *Waivers:* employees or children of employees.

Financial Aid Of all full-time matriculated undergraduates who enrolled in 2011, 1,126 applied for aid, 1,075 were judged to have need, 28 had their need fully met. In 2011, 153 non-need-based awards were made. *Average percent of need met:* 60%. *Average financial aid package:* $12,287. *Average need-based loan:* $4145. *Average need-based gift aid:* $8539. *Average non-need-based aid:* $6024. *Average indebtedness upon graduation:* $26,355.

Applying *Options:* electronic application, deferred entrance. *Application fee:* $50. *Required:* essay or personal statement. *Required for some:* high school transcript, minimum 3.0 GPA. *Application deadlines:* 8/1 (freshmen), 8/1 (out-of-state freshmen), 8/1 (transfers). *Notification:* continuous (freshmen), continuous (out-of-state freshmen), continuous (transfers).

Freshman Application Contact Mr. Ken Baker, Director of Admissions, Regent University, 1000 Regent University Drive, SC 218, Virginia Beach, VA 23464. *Phone:* 757-352-4845. *Toll-free phone:* 800-373-5504. *Fax:* 757-352-4509. *E-mail:* kbaker@regent.edu. *Web site:* http://www.regent.edu/.

Roanoke College

Salem, Virginia

- **Independent** 4-year, founded 1842, affiliated with Evangelical Lutheran Church in America
- **Suburban** 80-acre campus
- **Endowment** $118.0 million
- **Coed** 2,057 undergraduate students, 96% full-time, 56% women, 44% men
- **Moderately difficult** entrance level, 70% of applicants were admitted

Undergraduates 1,972 full-time, 85 part-time. Students come from 41 states and territories; 23 other countries; 46% are from out of state; 4% Black or African American, non-Hispanic/Latino; 3% Hispanic/Latino; 0.8% Asian, non-Hispanic/Latino; 0.3% American Indian or Alaska Native, non-Hispanic/Latino; 2% Two or more races, non-Hispanic/Latino; 0.1% Race/ethnicity unknown; 2% international; 4% transferred in; 67% live on campus. *Retention:* 77% of full-time freshmen returned.

Freshmen *Admission:* 4,184 applied, 2,910 admitted, 533 enrolled. *Average high school GPA:* 3.4. *Test scores:* SAT critical reading scores over 500: 75%; SAT math scores over 500: 70%; SAT writing scores over 500: 72%; ACT scores over 18: 94%; SAT critical reading scores over 600: 24%; SAT math scores over 600: 22%; SAT writing scores over 600: 22%; ACT scores over 24: 40%; SAT critical reading scores over 700: 3%; SAT math scores over 700: 2%; SAT writing scores over 700: 3%; ACT scores over 30: 8%.

Faculty *Total:* 216, 77% full-time, 70% with terminal degrees. *Student/faculty ratio:* 11:1.

Academics *Calendar:* semesters. *Degree:* bachelor's. *Special study options:* accelerated degree program, adult/continuing education programs, advanced placement credit, double majors, English as a second language, honors programs, independent study, internships, off-campus study, part-time degree program, services for LD students, study abroad, summer session for credit. *Unusual degree programs:* 3-2 engineering with Virginia Polytechnic Institute and State University.

Computers on Campus 202 computers/terminals are available on campus for general student use. Students can access the following: campus intranet, computer help desk, free student e-mail accounts, online (class) grades, online (class) registration, online (class) schedules, discounts on computer hardware and software purchases, free Microsoft Office software, free security software. Campuswide network is available. 100% of college-owned or -operated housing units are wired for high-speed Internet access. Wireless service is available via entire campus.

Student Life *Housing:* on-campus residence required through senior year. *Options:* coed, women-only, disabled students. Campus housing is university owned. Freshman campus housing is guaranteed. *Activities and organizations:* drama/theater group, student-run newspaper, radio station, choral group, Outdoor Adventures, Habitat for Humanity, Honors Association, Campus Activities Board, Inter-Varsity Christian Fellowship, national fraternities, national sororities. *Campus security:* 24-hour emergency response devices and patrols, late-night transport/escort service, controlled dormitory access. *Student services:* health clinic, personal/psychological counseling.

Athletics Member NCAA. All Division III. *Intercollegiate sports:* baseball M, basketball M/W, cross-country running M/W, field hockey W, golf M, lacrosse M/W, soccer M/W, softball W, tennis M/W, track and field M/W, volleyball W. *Intramural sports:* badminton M/W, basketball M/W, cheerleading M/W, equestrian sports W(c), field hockey W, football M/W, ice hockey M(c), lacrosse M, racquetball M/W, rugby M(c), soccer M(c)/W(c), softball M/W, table tennis M/W, tennis M/W, ultimate Frisbee M(c)/W(c), volleyball M/W, water polo M/W.

Standardized Tests *Required:* SAT or ACT (for admission).

Costs (2012–13) *One-time required fee:* $125. *Comprehensive fee:* $45,988 includes full-time tuition ($33,516), mandatory fees ($1330), and room and board ($11,142). Full-time tuition and fees vary according to reciprocity agreements. Part-time tuition: $1604 per course. Part-time tuition and fees vary according to course load and reciprocity agreements. *College room only:* $5154. Room and board charges vary according to board plan and housing facility. *Payment plan:* installment. *Waivers:* senior citizens and employees or children of employees.

Financial Aid Of all full-time matriculated undergraduates who enrolled in 2010, 1,617 applied for aid, 1,412 were judged to have need, 323 had their need fully met. 1,016 Federal Work-Study jobs (averaging $1500). In 2010, 545 non-need-based awards were made. *Average percent of need met:* 79%. *Average financial aid package:* $24,218. *Average need-based loan:* $4644. *Average need-based gift aid:* $19,306. *Average non-need-based aid:* $11,717. *Average indebtedness upon graduation:* $27,984.

Applying *Options:* electronic application, early admission, early decision, early action, deferred entrance. *Application fee:* $30. *Required:* high school transcript. *Recommended:* essay or personal statement, 3 letters of recommendation, interview. *Application deadlines:* 3/15 (freshmen), 8/1 (transfers). *Early decision deadline:* 11/1. *Notification:* continuous until 4/1 (freshmen), continuous until 8/15 (transfers), 12/1 (early decision), 10/1 (early action).

Freshman Application Contact Admissions Office, Roanoke College, 221 College Lane, Salem, VA 24153. *Phone:* 540-375-2270. *Toll-free phone:* 800-388-2276. *Fax:* 540-375-2267. *E-mail:* admissions@roanoke.edu. *Web site:* http://www.roanoke.edu/.

Saint Paul's College

Lawrenceville, Virginia

Freshman Application Contact Saint Paul's College, 115 College Drive, Lawrenceville, VA 23868-1202. *Phone:* 434-848-6493. *Toll-free phone:* 800-678-7071. *Web site:* http://www.saintpauls.edu/.

Shenandoah University
Winchester, Virginia

- **Independent United Methodist** comprehensive, founded 1875
- **Small-town** 100-acre campus with easy access to Baltimore and Washington, D.C.
- **Endowment** $53.4 million
- **Coed** 2,292 undergraduate students, 77% full-time, 64% women, 36% men
- **Moderately difficult** entrance level, 77% of applicants were admitted

Undergraduates 1,759 full-time, 533 part-time. Students come from 35 states and territories; 43 other countries; 27% are from out of state; 10% Black or African American, non-Hispanic/Latino; 4% Hispanic/Latino; 3% Asian, non-Hispanic/Latino; 0.3% Native Hawaiian or other Pacific Islander, non-Hispanic/Latino; 1% American Indian or Alaska Native, non-Hispanic/Latino; 0.8% Two or more races, non-Hispanic/Latino; 16% Race/ethnicity unknown; 3% international; 9% transferred in; 42% live on campus. *Retention:* 76% of full-time freshmen returned.

Freshmen *Admission:* 1,397 applied, 1,070 admitted, 343 enrolled. *Average high school GPA:* 3.42. *Test scores:* SAT critical reading scores over 500: 54%; SAT math scores over 500: 58%; SAT writing scores over 500: 53%; ACT scores over 18: 86%; SAT critical reading scores over 600: 17%; SAT math scores over 600: 16%; SAT writing scores over 600: 13%; ACT scores over 24: 45%; SAT critical reading scores over 700: 3%; SAT math scores over 700: 2%; SAT writing scores over 700: 1%; ACT scores over 30: 10%.

Faculty *Total:* 428, 50% full-time, 58% with terminal degrees. *Student/faculty ratio:* 9:1.

Academics *Calendar:* semesters. *Degrees:* certificates, diplomas, bachelor's, master's, doctoral, post-master's, postbachelor's, and first professional certificates. *Special study options:* accelerated degree program, adult/continuing education programs, advanced placement credit, cooperative education, distance learning, double majors, English as a second language, independent study, internships, off-campus study, part-time degree program, services for LD students, student-designed majors, study abroad, summer session for credit. *Unusual degree programs:* 3-2 athletic training.

Computers on Campus 60 computers/terminals and 50 ports are available on campus for general student use. Students can access the following: campus intranet, computer help desk, free student e-mail accounts, online (class) grades, online (class) registration, online (class) schedules, online student account information. Campuswide network is available. 100% of college-owned or -operated housing units are wired for high-speed Internet access. Wireless service is available via entire campus.

Student Life *Housing options:* coed, disabled students. Campus housing is university owned and is provided by a third party. Freshman campus housing is guaranteed. *Activities and organizations:* drama/theater group, student-run newspaper, television station, choral group, Student Government Association, The Graduate Student Association, Campus Activities Network, American Pharmacists Association Academy of Student Pharmacists, Kappa Psi Pharmaceutical Fraternity, Inc. *Campus security:* 24-hour emergency response devices and patrols, late-night transport/escort service, controlled dormitory access, side door alarms. *Student services:* health clinic, personal/psychological counseling.

Athletics Member NCAA. All Division III. *Intercollegiate sports:* baseball M, basketball M/W, cross-country running M/W, field hockey W, football M, golf M, lacrosse M/W, soccer M/W, softball W, tennis M/W, track and field M/W, volleyball W. *Intramural sports:* basketball M/W, cheerleading M/W, football M/W, soccer M/W, softball M/W, tennis M/W, ultimate Frisbee M/W, volleyball M/W.

Standardized Tests *Required:* SAT or ACT (for admission).

Costs (2011–12) *Comprehensive fee:* $35,890 includes full-time tuition ($26,640), mandatory fees ($300), and room and board ($8950). Full-time tuition and fees vary according to course load, location, program, and student level. Part-time tuition: $775 per credit hour. Part-time tuition and fees vary according to course load, location, program, and student level. *Room and board:* Room and board charges vary according to board plan and housing facility. *Payment plan:* installment. *Waivers:* employees or children of employees.

Financial Aid Of all full-time matriculated undergraduates who enrolled in 2011, 1,141 applied for aid, 1,073 were judged to have need, 64 had their need fully met. 781 Federal Work-Study jobs (averaging $1941). 396 state and other part-time jobs (averaging $1937). In 2011, 146 non-need-based awards were made. *Average percent of need met:* 71%. *Average financial aid package:* $19,000. *Average need-based loan:* $4500. *Average need-based gift aid:* $8000. *Average non-need-based aid:* $5000. *Average indebtedness upon graduation:* $27,000.

Applying *Options:* electronic application, deferred entrance. *Application fee:* $30. *Required:* high school transcript, 1 letter of recommendation. *Required for some:* essay or personal statement, interview, audition and/or portfolio for Conservatory applicants. *Recommended:* minimum 2.4 GPA. *Application deadlines:* rolling (freshmen), rolling (transfers). *Notification:* continuous (freshmen), continuous (transfers).

Freshman Application Contact Mr. David Anthony, Dean of Admissions, Shenandoah University, 1460 University Drive, Winchester, VA 22601-5195. *Phone:* 540-665-4581. *Toll-free phone:* 800-432-2266. *Fax:* 540-665-4627. *E-mail:* admit@su.edu. *Web site:* http://www.su.edu/.

Skyline College
Roanoke, Virginia

- **Proprietary** 4-year, founded 1966
- **Suburban** 3-acre campus
- **Coed**
- **Moderately difficult** entrance level

Faculty *Student/faculty ratio:* 11:1.

Academics *Calendar:* semesters. *Degrees:* certificates, diplomas, associate, and bachelor's.

Student Life *Campus security:* building and parking lot security.

Standardized Tests *Required:* ACT (for admission). *Recommended:* SAT (for admission), SAT Subject Tests (for admission).

Financial Aid Of all full-time matriculated undergraduates who enrolled in 2010, 380 applied for aid, 380 were judged to have need.

Applying *Options:* electronic application, deferred entrance. *Application fee:* $45. *Required:* high school transcript, interview.

Freshman Application Contact Dr. Walter Merchant, Campus Provost (Interim), Skyline College, 5234 Airport Road, Roanoke, VA 24012. *Phone:* 540-563-8080. *Toll-free phone:* 866-708-6178. *Fax:* 540-362-5400. *E-mail:* wmerchant@ecpi.edu. *Web site:* http://www.skyline.edu/.

Southern Virginia University
Buena Vista, Virginia

Freshman Application Contact Mr. Tony Caputo, Dean of Admissions, Southern Virginia University, One University Hill Drive, Buena Vista, VA 24416. *Phone:* 540-261-2756. *Toll-free phone:* 800-229-8420. *Fax:* 540-261-8559. *E-mail:* admissions@southernvirginia.edu. *Web site:* http://www.svu.edu/.

South University
Glen Allen, Virginia

- **Proprietary** comprehensive
- **Coed**

Academics *Degrees:* associate, bachelor's, and master's.

Costs (2011–12) *Tuition:* Information about tuition and fees can be obtained by contacting the South University Admissions Office.

Freshman Application Contact South University, 2151 Old Brick Road, Glen Allen, VA 23060. *Phone:* 804-727-6800. *Toll-free phone:* 888-422-5076. *Web site:* http://www.southuniversity.edu/richmond.

See page 1596 for the College Close-Up.

South University
Virginia Beach, Virginia

- **Proprietary** comprehensive
- **Coed**

Academics *Degrees:* associate, bachelor's, and master's.

Costs (2011–12) *Tuition:* Information about tuition and fees can be obtained by contacting the South University Admissions Office.

Freshman Application Contact South University, 301 Bendix Road, Suite 100, Virginia Beach, VA 23452. *Phone:* 757-493-6900. *Toll-free phone:* 877-206-1845. *Web site:* http://www.southuniversity.edu/virginia-beach.

See page 1596 for the College Close-Up.

Stratford University
Falls Church, Virginia

- **Proprietary** comprehensive, founded 1976
- **Suburban** campus with easy access to Washington, D.C.
- **Coed**
- **Minimally difficult** entrance level

Faculty *Student/faculty ratio:* 13:1.

Academics *Calendar:* quarters. *Degrees:* diplomas, associate, bachelor's, and master's.

Student Life *Campus security:* 24-hour emergency response devices.

Costs (2011–12) *Comprehensive fee:* $22,330 includes full-time tuition ($14,985), mandatory fees ($345), and room and board ($7000). Full-time tuition and fees vary according to course load and program. Part-time tuition and fees vary according to course load and program. *Payment plans:* installment, deferred payment.

Applying *Options:* electronic application, deferred entrance. *Application fee:* $50. *Required:* minimum 2.0 GPA, interview, proof of high school graduation or equivalent is required for all students; personal statement, transcript, and letters of recommendation are only required for the Nursing program. *Required for some:* essay or personal statement, high school transcript, 2 letters of recommendation.

Freshman Application Contact James W. Ray, Director of Admissions, Stratford University, 7777 Leesburg Pike, Falls Church, VA 22043. *Phone:* 703-821-8570. *Toll-free phone:* 800-444-0804. *Fax:* 703-734-5339. *E-mail:* jray@stratford.edu. *Web site:* http://www.stratford.edu/.

Stratford University

Woodbridge, Virginia

Freshman Application Contact Director of Admissions, Stratford University, 14349 Gideon Drive, Woodbridge, VA 22192. *Phone:* 703-897-1982. *Toll-free phone:* 888-546-1250. *E-mail:* admissions@stratford.edu. *Web site:* http://www.stratford.edu/.

Strayer University - Alexandria Campus

Alexandria, Virginia

- **Proprietary** comprehensive
- **Coed**

Academics *Degrees:* certificates, diplomas, associate, bachelor's, master's, and postbachelor's certificates.

Freshman Application Contact Strayer University - Alexandria Campus, 2730 Eisenhower Avenue, Alexandria, VA 22314. *Web site:* http://www.strayer.edu/alexandria.

Strayer University - Arlington Campus

Arlington, Virginia

- **Proprietary** comprehensive
- **Coed**

Academics *Degrees:* certificates, diplomas, associate, bachelor's, master's, and postbachelor's certificates.

Freshman Application Contact Strayer University - Arlington Campus, 2121 15th Street North, Arlington, VA 22201. *Web site:* http://www.strayer.edu/arlington.

Strayer University - Chesapeake Campus

Chesapeake, Virginia

- **Proprietary** comprehensive
- **Coed**

Academics *Degrees:* certificates, diplomas, associate, bachelor's, master's, and postbachelor's certificates.

Freshman Application Contact Strayer University - Chesapeake Campus, 700 Independent Parkway, Suite 400, Chesapeake, VA 23320. *Web site:* http://www.strayer.edu/chesapeake/.

Strayer University - Chesterfield Campus

Midlothian, Virginia

- **Proprietary** comprehensive
- **Coed**

Academics *Degrees:* certificates, diplomas, associate, bachelor's, master's, and postbachelor's certificates.

Freshman Application Contact Strayer University - Chesterfield Campus, 2820 Waterford Lake Drive, Suite 100, Midlothian, VA 23112. *Web site:* http://www.strayer.edu/chesterfield/.

Strayer University - Fredericksburg Campus

Fredericksburg, Virginia

- **Proprietary** comprehensive
- **Coed**

Academics *Degrees:* certificates, diplomas, associate, bachelor's, master's, and postbachelor's certificates.

Freshman Application Contact Strayer University - Fredericksburg Campus, 150 Riverside Parkway, Suite 100, Fredericksburg, VA 22406. *Web site:* http://www.strayer.edu/fredericksburg.

Strayer University - Henrico Campus

Glen Allen, Virginia

- **Proprietary** comprehensive, founded 1892
- **Coed**

Academics *Degrees:* certificates, diplomas, associate, bachelor's, master's, and postbachelor's certificates.

Freshman Application Contact Strayer University - Henrico Campus, 11501 Nuckols Road, Glen Allen, VA 23059. *Web site:* http://www.strayer.edu/henrico.

Strayer University - Loudoun Campus

Ashburn, Virginia

- **Proprietary** comprehensive
- **Coed**

Academics *Degrees:* certificates, diplomas, associate, bachelor's, master's, and postbachelor's certificates.

Freshman Application Contact Strayer University - Loudoun Campus, 45150 Russell Branch Parkway, Suite 200, Ashburn, VA 20147. *Web site:* http://www.strayer.edu/loudoun.

Strayer University - Manassas Campus

Manassas, Virginia

- **Proprietary** comprehensive
- **Coed**

Academics *Degrees:* certificates, diplomas, associate, bachelor's, master's, and postbachelor's certificates.

Freshman Application Contact Strayer University - Manassas Campus, 9990 Battleview Parkway, Manassas, VA 20109. *Web site:* http://www.strayer.edu/manassas.

Strayer University - Newport News Campus

Newport News, Virginia

- **Proprietary** comprehensive
- **Coed**

Academics *Degrees:* certificates, diplomas, associate, bachelor's, master's, and postbachelor's certificates.

Freshman Application Contact Strayer University - Newport News Campus, 813 Diligence Drive, Suite 100, Newport News, VA 23606. *Web site:* http://www.strayer.edu/newport_news.

Strayer University - Virginia Beach Campus

Virginia Beach, Virginia

- **Proprietary** comprehensive
- **Coed**

Academics *Degrees:* certificates, diplomas, associate, bachelor's, master's, and postbachelor's certificates.

Freshman Application Contact Strayer University - Virginia Beach Campus, 249 Central Park Avenue, Suite 350, Virginia Beach, VA 23462. *Web site:* http://www.strayer.edu/virginia_beach.

Strayer University - Woodbridge Campus
Woodbridge, Virginia

- **Proprietary** comprehensive
- **Coed**

Academics *Degrees:* certificates, diplomas, associate, bachelor's, master's, and postbachelor's certificates.
Freshman Application Contact Strayer University - Woodbridge Campus, 13385 Minnieville Road, Woodbridge, VA 22192. *Web site:* http://www.strayer.edu/woodbridge.

Sweet Briar College
Sweet Briar, Virginia

- **Independent** comprehensive, founded 1901
- **Rural** 3250-acre campus
- **Endowment** $93.8 million
- **Women only** 745 undergraduate students, 97% full-time
- **Moderately difficult** entrance level, 80% of applicants were admitted

Undergraduates 719 full-time, 26 part-time. Students come from 41 states and territories; 7 other countries; 50% are from out of state; 7% Black or African American, non-Hispanic/Latino; 6% Hispanic/Latino; 2% Asian, non-Hispanic/Latino; 0.2% Native Hawaiian or other Pacific Islander, non-Hispanic/Latino; 1% American Indian or Alaska Native, non-Hispanic/Latino; 1% Two or more races, non-Hispanic/Latino; 0.7% Race/ethnicity unknown; 2% international; 2% transferred in; 95% live on campus. *Retention:* 78% of full-time freshmen returned.
Freshmen *Admission:* 688 applied, 547 admitted, 194 enrolled. *Average high school GPA:* 3.41. *Test scores:* SAT critical reading scores over 500: 71%; SAT math scores over 500: 51%; SAT writing scores over 500: 70%; ACT scores over 18: 93%; SAT critical reading scores over 600: 31%; SAT math scores over 600: 22%; SAT writing scores over 600: 27%; ACT scores over 24: 56%; SAT critical reading scores over 700: 8%; SAT math scores over 700: 1%; SAT writing scores over 700: 5%; ACT scores over 30: 8%.
Faculty *Total:* 126, 61% full-time, 60% with terminal degrees. *Student/faculty ratio:* 8:1.
Academics *Calendar:* semesters. *Degrees:* bachelor's and master's. *Special study options:* accelerated degree program, adult/continuing education pro-grams, advanced placement credit, double majors, honors programs, independent study, internships, off-campus study, part-time degree program, services for LD students, student-designed majors, study abroad, summer session for credit. *Unusual degree programs:* 3-2 engineering with Virginia Polytechnic Institute and State University, University of Virginia, Columbia University, Washington University in St. Louis.
Computers on Campus 128 computers/terminals and 3,000 ports are available on campus for general student use. Students can access the following: campus intranet, computer help desk, free student e-mail accounts, online (class) grades, online (class) registration, online (class) schedules. Campuswide network is available. 100% of college-owned or -operated housing units are wired for high-speed Internet access. Wireless service is available via entire campus.
Student Life *Housing:* on-campus residence required through senior year. *Options:* women-only. Campus housing is university owned. Freshman campus housing is guaranteed. *Activities and organizations:* drama/theater group, student-run newspaper, radio and television station, choral group, Student Government Association, Campus Events Organization, Interclub Council, PnP, Environmental Club. *Campus security:* 24-hour emergency response devices and patrols, late-night transport/escort service, controlled dormitory access, front gate security. *Student services:* health clinic, personal/psychological counseling.
Athletics Member NCAA. All Division III. *Intercollegiate sports:* equestrian sports W(c), fencing W(c), field hockey W, lacrosse W, soccer W, softball W(c), swimming and diving W, tennis W, volleyball W(c).
Standardized Tests *Required:* SAT or ACT (for admission).
Costs (2011–12) *Comprehensive fee:* $42,195 includes full-time tuition ($30,620), mandatory fees ($475), and room and board ($11,100). Full-time tuition and fees vary according to program. Part-time tuition: $760 per credit hour. Part-time tuition and fees vary according to program. *Room and board:* Room and board charges vary according to board plan. *Payment plan:* installment. *Waivers:* adult students, senior citizens, and employees or children of employees.
Financial Aid Of all full-time matriculated undergraduates who enrolled in 2010, 457 applied for aid, 457 were judged to have need, 138 had their need fully met. 106 Federal Work-Study jobs (averaging $939). 120 state and other part-time jobs (averaging $725). In 2010, 135 non-need-based awards were made. *Average percent of need met:* 72%. *Average financial aid package:* $20,647. *Average need-based loan:* $4253. *Average need-based gift aid:* $16,337. *Average non-need-based aid:* $10,585. *Average indebtedness upon graduation:* $24,689.

Applying *Options:* electronic application, early admission, deferred entrance. *Application fee:* $40. *Required:* essay or personal statement, high school transcript, 2 letters of recommendation. *Required for some:* portfolio with courses taken, list of texts covered, essay about homeschooling, campus visit, interview for homeschooled applicants. *Recommended:* interview. *Application deadlines:* 2/1 (freshmen), 5/1 (transfers). *Notification:* continuous (freshmen), 5/15 (transfers).
Freshman Application Contact Sweet Briar College, PO Box B, Sweet Briar, VA 24595. *Phone:* 434-381-6142. *Toll-free phone:* 800-381-6142. *E-mail:* admissions@sbc.edu. *Web site:* http://www.sbc.edu/.

See page 1632 for the College Close-Up.

University of Management and Technology
Arlington, Virginia

Freshman Application Contact Vice President, University of Management and Technology, Suite 700, 1901 North Fort Meyers Drive, Arlington, VA 22209. *Phone:* 703-516-0035. *Toll-free phone:* 800-924-4883. *Fax:* 703-516-0985. *E-mail:* admissions@umtweb.edu. *Web site:* http://www.umtweb.edu/.

University of Mary Washington
Fredericksburg, Virginia

- **State-supported** comprehensive, founded 1908
- **Small-town** 176-acre campus with easy access to Richmond and Washington, D.C.
- **Endowment** $36.8 million
- **Coed** 4,464 undergraduate students, 86% full-time, 64% women, 36% men
- **Very difficult** entrance level, 76% of applicants were admitted

Undergraduates 3,846 full-time, 618 part-time. Students come from 40 states and territories; 23 other countries; 15% are from out of state; 6% Black or African American, non-Hispanic/Latino; 6% Hispanic/Latino; 5% Asian, non-Hispanic/Latino; 0.3% American Indian or Alaska Native, non-Hispanic/Latino; 3% Two or more races, non-Hispanic/Latino; 18% Race/ethnicity unknown; 0.8% international; 5% transferred in; 61% live on campus. *Retention:* 84% of full-time freshmen returned.
Freshmen *Admission:* 4,807 applied, 3,638 admitted, 970 enrolled. *Average high school GPA:* 3.57. *Test scores:* SAT critical reading scores over 500: 89%; SAT math scores over 500: 80%; SAT writing scores over 500: 85%; ACT scores over 18: 100%; SAT critical reading scores over 600: 44%; SAT math scores over 600: 30%; SAT writing scores over 600: 35%; ACT scores over 24: 61%; SAT critical reading scores over 700: 9%; SAT math scores over 700: 2%; SAT writing scores over 700: 6%; ACT scores over 30: 9%.
Faculty *Total:* 377, 65% full-time. *Student/faculty ratio:* 15:1.
Academics *Calendar:* semesters. *Degrees:* certificates, bachelor's, master's, and postbachelor's certificates. *Special study options:* accelerated degree program, adult/continuing education programs, advanced placement credit, cooperative education, distance learning, double majors, honors programs, independent study, internships, part-time degree program, services for LD students, student-designed majors, study abroad, summer session for credit. *ROTC:* Army (c). *Unusual degree programs:* computer science, elementary education.
Computers on Campus 306 computers/terminals are available on campus for general student use. Students can access the following: campus intranet, computer help desk, free student e-mail accounts, online (class) grades, online (class) registration, online (class) schedules, Library resources, foreign languages resources, course management system. Campuswide network is available. 100% of college-owned or -operated housing units are wired for high-speed Internet access. Wireless service is available via entire campus.
Student Life *Housing:* on-campus residence required through sophomore year. *Options:* coed, men-only, women-only, disabled students. Campus housing is university owned and leased by the school. Freshman campus housing is guaranteed. *Activities and organizations:* drama/theater group, student-run newspaper, radio station, choral group, Students Helping Honduras, Black Student Association, Giant Productions (campus entertainment group), PRISM, Cheap Seats Cinema. *Campus security:* 24-hour emergency response devices and patrols, student patrols, late-night transport/escort service, controlled dormitory access, self-defense and safety classes. *Student services:* health clinic, personal/psychological counseling.
Athletics Member NCAA. All Division III. *Intercollegiate sports:* baseball M, basketball M/W, cheerleading M(c)/W(c), crew M/W, cross-country running M/W, equestrian sports M/W, field hockey W, lacrosse M/W, rugby M(c)/W(c), soccer M/W, softball W, swimming and diving M/W, tennis M/W, track and field M/W, volleyball M(c)/W. *Intramural sports:* badminton M/W, baseball M(c), basketball M/W, bowling M/W, cheerleading M(c)/W(c), fencing

M(c)/W(c), field hockey W(c), football M/W, golf M/W, lacrosse M/W(c), skiing (downhill) M(c)/W(c), soccer M/W, softball M/W, swimming and diving M(c)/W(c), tennis M(c)/W(c), ultimate Frisbee M(c)/W(c), volleyball M/W, water polo M/W.
Standardized Tests *Required:* SAT or ACT (for admission). *Recommended:* SAT Subject Tests (for admission).
Costs (2011–12) *One-time required fee:* $75. *Tuition:* state resident $4460 full-time, $195 per credit hour part-time; nonresident $16,190 full-time, $740 per credit hour part-time. Part-time tuition and fees vary according to course load and location. *Required fees:* $4340 full-time, $110 per credit hour part-time, $30 per term part-time. *Room and board:* $8900; room only: $5350. Room and board charges vary according to board plan and housing facility. *Payment plan:* installment. *Waivers:* senior citizens.
Financial Aid Of all full-time matriculated undergraduates who enrolled in 2010, 2,168 applied for aid, 1,368 were judged to have need, 177 had their need fully met. 31 Federal Work-Study jobs (averaging $1400). 700 state and other part-time jobs (averaging $2200). In 2010, 336 non-need-based awards were made. *Average percent of need met:* 53%. *Average financial aid package:* $8430. *Average need-based loan:* $4280. *Average need-based gift aid:* $6800. *Average non-need-based aid:* $2400. *Average indebtedness upon graduation:* $17,775. *Financial aid deadline:* 5/15.
Applying *Options:* electronic application, early admission, early action, deferred entrance. *Application fee:* $50. *Required:* essay or personal statement, high school transcript. *Application deadlines:* 2/1 (freshmen), 3/1 (transfers). *Notification:* 4/1 (freshmen), 5/15 (transfers).
Freshman Application Contact Ms. Kimberly Johnston, Dean of Admissions, University of Mary Washington, 1301 College Avenue, Fredericksburg, VA 22401-5358. *Phone:* 540-654-2000. *Toll-free phone:* 800-468-5614. *Fax:* 540-654-1857. *E-mail:* admit@umw.edu. *Web site:* http://www.umw.edu/.

University of Phoenix–Northern Virginia Campus
Reston, Virginia

Freshman Application Contact Marc Booker, Sr. Director, Office of Admissions and Evaluation, University of Phoenix–Northern Virginia Campus, 4035 South Riverpoint Parkway, Mail Stop CF-L101, Phoenix, AZ 85040. *Phone:* 602-557-4609. *Toll-free phone:* 866-766-0766. *Fax:* 480-643-1156. *Web site:* http://www.phoenix.edu/.

University of Phoenix–Richmond Campus
Richmond, Virginia

Freshman Application Contact Marc Booker, Sr. Director, Office of Admissions and Evaluation, University of Phoenix–Richmond Campus, 4035 South Riverpoint Parkway, Mail Stop CF-L101, Phoenix, AZ 85040. *Phone:* 602-557-4609. *Toll-free phone:* 866-766-0766. *Fax:* 480-643-1156. *Web site:* http://www.phoenix.edu/.

University of Richmond
Richmond, Virginia

- **Independent** comprehensive, founded 1830
- **Suburban** 350-acre campus
- **Endowment** $1.9 billion
- **Coed** 3,000 undergraduate students, 99% full-time, 54% women, 46% men
- **Very difficult** entrance level, 33% of applicants were admitted

Undergraduates 2,963 full-time, 37 part-time. Students come from 47 states and territories; 68 other countries; 78% are from out of state; 7% Black or African American, non-Hispanic/Latino; 6% Hispanic/Latino; 5% Asian, non-Hispanic/Latino; 0.2% American Indian or Alaska Native, non-Hispanic/Latino; 2% Two or more races, non-Hispanic/Latino; 11% Race/ethnicity unknown; 7% international; 2% transferred in; 91% live on campus. *Retention:* 94% of full-time freshmen returned.
Freshmen *Admission:* 9,431 applied, 3,085 admitted, 781 enrolled. *Test scores:* SAT critical reading scores over 500: 93%; SAT math scores over 500: 97%; SAT writing scores over 500: 96%; ACT scores over 18: 99%; SAT critical reading scores over 600: 71%; SAT math scores over 600: 81%; SAT writing scores over 600: 72%; ACT scores over 24: 93%; SAT critical reading scores over 700: 21%; SAT math scores over 700: 27%; SAT writing scores over 700: 24%; ACT scores over 30: 49%.
Faculty *Total:* 427, 76% full-time, 81% with terminal degrees. *Student/faculty ratio:* 8:1.

Academics *Calendar:* semesters. *Degrees:* bachelor's, master's, and doctoral. *Special study options:* adult/continuing education programs, advanced placement credit, double majors, English as a second language, honors programs, independent study, internships, off-campus study, part-time degree program, services for LD students, student-designed majors, study abroad, summer session for credit. *ROTC:* Army (b). *Unusual degree programs:* 3-2 engineering with Columbia University School of Engineering & Applied Science; George Washington University School of Engineering & Applied Science; UVA School of Engineering; VCU School of Engineering; Virginia Polytechnic Institute College of Engineering.

Computers on Campus 1,018 computers/terminals and 3,300 ports are available on campus for general student use. Students can access the following: campus intranet, computer help desk, free student e-mail accounts, online (class) grades, online (class) registration, online (class) schedules. Campus-wide network is available. 100% of college-owned or -operated housing units are wired for high-speed Internet access. Wireless service is available via entire campus.

Student Life *Housing options:* coed, men-only, women-only. Campus housing is university owned. Freshman campus housing is guaranteed. *Activities and organizations:* drama/theater group, student-run newspaper, radio station, choral group, Club Sports, Richmond Rowdies - Facilitates school spirit at athletic events, Alpha Phi Omega Service Fraternity, InterVarsity Christian Fellowship, Student Government Associations, national fraternities, national sororities. *Campus security:* 24-hour emergency response devices and patrols, late-night transport/escort service, controlled dormitory access, campus police. *Student services:* health clinic, personal/psychological counseling, women's center.

Athletics Member NCAA. All Division I except football (Division I-AA). *Intercollegiate sports:* badminton M(c)/W(c), baseball M(s), basketball M(s)/W(s), cheerleading W(c), crew M(c)/W(c), cross-country running M/W(s), equestrian sports M(c)/W(c), field hockey W(s), golf M(s)/W(s), gymnastics M(c)/W(c), ice hockey M(c), lacrosse M(c)/W(s), rugby M(c)/W(c), soccer M(s)/W(s), squash M(c)/W(c), swimming and diving M(c)/W(s), tennis M(s)/W(s), track and field M/W(s), ultimate Frisbee M(c)/W(c), volleyball M(c)/W(c), water polo M(c)/W(c). *Intramural sports:* baseball M(c), basketball M/W, field hockey W(c), football M, golf M/W, lacrosse W(c), soccer M(c)/W(c), softball M/W, squash M/W, swimming and diving M/W, tennis M/W, volleyball M/W.

Standardized Tests *Required:* SAT or ACT (for admission).

Costs (2012–13) *Comprehensive fee:* $53,970 includes full-time tuition ($44,210) and room and board ($9760). Full-time tuition and fees vary according to course load and student level. Part-time tuition: $7738 per unit. Part-time tuition and fees vary according to course load and student level. *College room only:* $4420. Room and board charges vary according to board plan and housing facility. *Payment plans:* installment, deferred payment. *Waivers:* employees or children of employees.

Financial Aid Of all full-time matriculated undergraduates who enrolled in 2011, 1,738 applied for aid, 1,449 were judged to have need, 1,348 had their need fully met. 483 Federal Work-Study jobs (averaging $1380). In 2011, 433 non-need-based awards were made. *Average percent of need met:* 100%. *Average financial aid package:* $40,191. *Average need-based loan:* $3293. *Average need-based gift aid:* $36,151. *Average non-need-based aid:* $23,075. *Average indebtedness upon graduation:* $22,915. *Financial aid deadline:* 2/15.

Applying *Options:* electronic application, early decision, deferred entrance. *Application fee:* $50. *Required:* essay or personal statement, high school transcript, 1 letter of recommendation, signed character statement. *Application deadlines:* 1/15 (freshmen), 2/15 (transfers). *Early decision deadline:* 11/15 (for plan 1), 1/15 (for plan 2). *Notification:* 4/1 (freshmen), 4/15 (transfers), 12/15 (early decision plan 1), 2/15 (early decision plan 2).

Freshman Application Contact Mr. Gil Villanueva, Dean of Admission, University of Richmond, Brunet Memorial Hall, 28 Westhampton Way, University of Richmond, VA 23173. *Phone:* 804-289-8640. *Toll-free phone:* 800-700-1662. *Fax:* 804-287-6003. *E-mail:* admissions@richmond.edu. *Web site:* http://www.richmond.edu/.

University of Virginia

Charlottesville, Virginia

- **State-supported** university, founded 1819
- **Suburban** 1167-acre campus with easy access to Richmond
- **Endowment** $4.7 billion
- **Coed** 15,762 undergraduate students, 94% full-time, 55% women, 45% men
- **Very difficult** entrance level, 33% of applicants were admitted

Undergraduates 14,842 full-time, 920 part-time. Students come from 49 states and territories; 118 other countries; 26% are from out of state; 7% Black or African American, non-Hispanic/Latino; 5% Hispanic/Latino; 12% Asian, non-Hispanic/Latino; 0.1% Native Hawaiian or other Pacific Islander, non-Hispanic/Latino; 0.2% American Indian or Alaska Native, non-Hispanic/Latino; 3% Two or more races, non-Hispanic/Latino; 7% Race/ethnicity unknown; 6% international; 4% transferred in; 42% live on campus. *Retention:* 97% of full-time freshmen returned.

Freshmen *Admission:* 23,587 applied, 7,851 admitted, 3,434 enrolled. *Average high school GPA:* 4.19. *Test scores:* SAT critical reading scores over 500: 97%; SAT math scores over 500: 98%; SAT writing scores over 500: 98%; ACT scores over 18: 99%; SAT critical reading scores over 600: 81%; SAT math scores over 600: 86%; SAT writing scores over 600: 83%; ACT scores over 24: 95%; SAT critical reading scores over 700: 35%; SAT math scores over 700: 43%; SAT writing scores over 700: 38%; ACT scores over 30: 58%.

Faculty *Total:* 1,296, 95% full-time, 91% with terminal degrees. *Student/faculty ratio:* 16:1.

Academics *Calendar:* semesters. *Degrees:* bachelor's, master's, doctoral, post-master's, and first professional certificates. *Special study options:* accelerated degree program, adult/continuing education programs, advanced placement credit, cooperative education, double majors, English as a second language, honors programs, independent study, internships, part-time degree program, services for LD students, student-designed majors, study abroad, summer session for credit. *ROTC:* Army (b), Navy (b), Air Force (b). *Unusual degree programs:* 3-2 joint BA in College of Arts and Sciences/MT in Education.

Computers on Campus 506 computers/terminals are available on campus for general student use. Students can access the following: campus intranet, computer help desk, free student e-mail accounts, online (class) grades, online (class) registration, online (class) schedules, online course management tool. Campuswide network is available. 100% of college-owned or -operated housing units are wired for high-speed Internet access. Wireless service is available via classrooms, computer centers, computer labs, dorm rooms, learning centers, libraries, student centers.

Student Life *Housing:* on-campus residence required for freshman year. *Options:* coed. Campus housing is university owned. Freshman campus housing is guaranteed. *Activities and organizations:* drama/theater group, student-run newspaper, radio and television station, choral group, marching band, Madison House, student government, university guides, University Union, The Cavalier Daily, national fraternities, national sororities. *Campus security:* 24-hour emergency response devices and patrols, late-night transport/escort service, controlled dormitory access. *Student services:* health clinic, personal/psychological counseling, women's center, legal services.

Athletics Member NCAA. All Division I except football (Division I-A). *Intercollegiate sports:* baseball M(s), basketball M(s)/W(s), crew W(s), cross-country running M(s)/W(s), field hockey W(s), golf M(s)/W(s), lacrosse M(s)/W(s), soccer M(s)/W(s), softball W(s), swimming and diving M(s)/W(s), tennis M(s)/W(s), track and field M(s)/W(s), volleyball W(s), wrestling M(s). *Intramural sports:* archery M(c)/W(c), badminton M(c)/W(c), baseball M(c), basketball M(c)/W(c), cheerleading M(c)/W(c), crew M(c)/W, cross-country running M(c)/W(c), equestrian sports M/W, fencing M(c)/W(c), field hockey W(c), football M, golf M(c)/W(c), gymnastics M(c)/W(c), ice hockey M(c)/W(c), lacrosse M(c)/W(c), racquetball M(c)/W(c), riflery M(c)/W(c), rugby M(c)/W(c), sailing M(c)/W(c), skiing (downhill) M(c)/W(c), soccer M(c)/W(c), softball M/W, squash W(c), swimming and diving M(c)/W(c), table tennis M(c)/W(c), tennis M(c)/W(c), track and field M(c)/W(c), ultimate Frisbee M(c)/W(c), volleyball M(c)/W(c), water polo M(c)/W(c), weight lifting M(c)/W(c).

Standardized Tests *Required:* SAT or ACT (for admission). *Recommended:* SAT Subject Tests (for admission), SAT or ACT plus optional ACT writing test (ACT alone does not satisfy requirement). At least two SAT subject tests (student's choice) are recommended.

Costs (2011–12) *Tuition:* state resident $9240 full-time, $308 per credit hour part-time; nonresident $33,562 full-time, $1119 per credit hour part-time. Full-time tuition and fees vary according to program. *Required fees:* $2336 full-time, $2336 per year part-time. *Room and board:* $8866; room only: $4946. Room and board charges vary according to board plan and housing facility. *Payment plan:* installment. *Waivers:* senior citizens and employees or children of employees.

Financial Aid Of all full-time matriculated undergraduates who enrolled in 2011, 8,196 applied for aid, 4,578 were judged to have need, 4,578 had their need fully met. In 2011, 1509 non-need-based awards were made. *Average percent of need met:* 100%. *Average financial aid package:* $22,201. *Average need-based loan:* $5851. *Average need-based gift aid:* $17,181. *Average non-need-based aid:* $9999. *Average indebtedness upon graduation:* $20,951.

Applying *Options:* electronic application, early action, deferred entrance. *Application fee:* $60. *Required:* essay or personal statement, high school transcript, 1 letter of recommendation. *Application deadlines:* 1/1 (freshmen), 3/1 (transfers), 11/1 (early action). *Notification:* 4/1 (freshmen), 5/1 (transfers), 1/31 (early action).

Freshman Application Contact Mr. Gregory W. Roberts, Dean of Admission, University of Virginia, PO Box 400160, Charlottesville, VA 22904-4727.

Phone: 434-982-3200. *Fax:* 434-924-3587. *E-mail:* undergrad-admission@virginia.edu. *Web site:* http://www.virginia.edu/.

The University of Virginia's College at Wise
Wise, Virginia

- **State-supported** 4-year, founded 1954, part of University of Virginia
- **Small-town** 396-acre campus
- **Endowment** $50.6 million
- **Coed** 2,067 undergraduate students, 73% full-time, 56% women, 44% men
- **Moderately difficult** entrance level, 77% of applicants were admitted

Undergraduates 1,518 full-time, 549 part-time. Students come from 11 other countries; 10% Black or African American, non-Hispanic/Latino; 2% Hispanic/Latino; 1% Asian, non-Hispanic/Latino; 0.2% American Indian or Alaska Native, non-Hispanic/Latino; 0.3% Two or more races, non-Hispanic/Latino; 4% Race/ethnicity unknown; 0.1% international; 6% transferred in; 33% live on campus. *Retention:* 62% of full-time freshmen returned.

Freshmen *Admission:* 1,121 applied, 865 admitted, 356 enrolled. *Average high school GPA:* 3.3. *Test scores:* SAT critical reading scores over 500: 44%; SAT math scores over 500: 40%; SAT writing scores over 500: 31%; ACT scores over 18: 67%; SAT critical reading scores over 600: 8%; SAT math scores over 600: 6%; SAT writing scores over 600: 4%; ACT scores over 24: 17%; SAT critical reading scores over 700: 1%; ACT scores over 30: 1%.

Faculty *Total:* 175, 50% full-time, 40% with terminal degrees. *Student/faculty ratio:* 15:1.

Academics *Calendar:* semesters. *Degrees:* bachelor's and postbachelor's certificates. *Special study options:* academic remediation for entering students, accelerated degree program, adult/continuing education programs, advanced placement credit, cooperative education, distance learning, double majors, honors programs, independent study, internships, part-time degree program, services for LD students, student-designed majors, summer session for credit. *ROTC:* Army (b).

Computers on Campus 300 computers/terminals are available on campus for general student use. Students can access the following: campus intranet, computer help desk, free student e-mail accounts, online (class) grades, online (class) registration, online (class) schedules. Campuswide network is available. 100% of college-owned or -operated housing units are wired for high-speed Internet access. Wireless service is available via learning centers, libraries, student centers.

Student Life *Housing:* on-campus residence required for freshman year. *Options:* coed, men-only, women-only. Campus housing is university owned. *Activities and organizations:* drama/theater group, student-run newspaper, radio and television station, choral group, marching band, Student Government, Student Activities Board, Multicultural Association, Residence Hall Association, Intramurals, national fraternities, national sororities. *Campus security:* 24-hour emergency response devices and patrols, student patrols, late-night transport/escort service, self-defense, informal discussions, pamphlets/posters/films, and crime prevention office. *Student services:* health clinic, personal/psychological counseling.

Athletics Member NAIA. *Intercollegiate sports:* baseball M(s), basketball M(s)/W(s), cross-country running M(s)/W(s), football M(s), golf M/W, softball W(s), tennis M(s)/W(s), track and field M/W, volleyball W(s). *Intramural sports:* badminton M/W, basketball M/W, football M/W, golf M/W, racquetball M/W, soccer M/W, softball M/W, table tennis M/W, tennis M/W, ultimate Frisbee M/W, volleyball M/W, water polo M/W.

Standardized Tests *Required:* SAT or ACT (for admission).

Costs (2011–12) *Tuition:* state resident $4242 full-time, $181 per credit hour part-time; nonresident $17,325 full-time, $734 per credit hour part-time. Part-time tuition and fees vary according to course load. *Required fees:* $3479 full-time, $118 per credit hour part-time, $1008 per term part-time. *Room and board:* $8362; room only: $4746. Room and board charges vary according to board plan and housing facility. *Payment plans:* installment, deferred payment. *Waivers:* senior citizens and employees or children of employees.

Financial Aid Of all full-time matriculated undergraduates who enrolled in 2010, 1,440 applied for aid, 1,231 were judged to have need, 961 had their need fully met. In 2010, 77 non-need-based awards were made. *Average percent of need met:* 97%. *Average financial aid package:* $9958. *Average need-based loan:* $3462. *Average need-based gift aid:* $5526. *Average non-need-based aid:* $5091. *Average indebtedness upon graduation:* $14,801.

Applying *Options:* early admission, early action. *Application fee:* $25. *Required:* high school transcript, minimum 2.3 GPA. *Recommended:* 2 letters of recommendation. *Application deadlines:* 8/1 (freshmen), 8/15 (transfers), 2/1 (early action). *Notification:* 8/20 (freshmen), continuous until 8/20 (transfers), 2/15 (early action).

Freshman Application Contact Mr. Russell D. Necessary, Vice Chancellor for Enrollment Management, The University of Virginia's College at Wise, 1

College Avenue, Wise, VA 24293. *Phone:* 276-328-0322. *Toll-free phone:* 888-282-9324. *Fax:* 276-328-0251. *E-mail:* admissions@uvawise.edu. *Web site:* http://www.uvawise.edu/.

Valley Forge Christian College Woodbridge Campus
Woodbridge, Virginia

- **Independent Assemblies of God** 4-year
- **Suburban** campus with easy access to Washington, D.C.
- **Coed** 131 undergraduate students, 45% full-time, 62% women, 38% men
- **Minimally difficult** entrance level, 81% of applicants were admitted

Undergraduates 59 full-time, 72 part-time. 32% Black or African American, non-Hispanic/Latino; 11% Hispanic/Latino; 2% Native Hawaiian or other Pacific Islander, non-Hispanic/Latino; 5% Two or more races, non-Hispanic/Latino; 3% international.

Freshmen *Admission:* 53 applied, 43 admitted, 19 enrolled.

Faculty *Total:* 36, 11% full-time, 33% with terminal degrees. *Student/faculty ratio:* 6:1.

Academics *Degrees:* certificates, associate, and bachelor's. *Special study options:* academic remediation for entering students, adult/continuing education programs, advanced placement credit, cooperative education, distance learning, double majors, independent study, internships, off-campus study, part-time degree program, services for LD students, summer session for credit.

Computers on Campus 40 computers/terminals are available on campus for general student use. Students can access the following: computer help desk, free student e-mail accounts, online (class) grades, online (class) registration, online (class) schedules. Wireless service is available via classrooms, student centers.

Student Life *Campus security:* 24-hour emergency response devices, We have a check in person at the front desk. Everyone has a badge. No one can enter the building unless they are let in by her.

Costs (2012–13) *Tuition:* $8398 full-time. *Required fees:* $500 full-time. *Payment plans:* installment, deferred payment. *Waivers:* senior citizens and employees or children of employees.

Applying *Application fee:* $75. *Required:* essay or personal statement, high school transcript, minimum 1.5 GPA, interview, Pastor's Recommendation. *Application deadlines:* rolling (freshmen), rolling (out-of-state freshmen), rolling (transfers). *Notification:* continuous (freshmen), continuous (out-of-state freshmen), continuous (transfers).

Freshman Application Contact Admissions Coordinator, Valley Forge Christian College Woodbridge Campus, 13909 Smoketown Road, Woodbridge, VA 22192. *Phone:* 703-580-4810 Ext. 210. *Toll-free phone:* 800-432-8322. *Web site:* http://www.vfcc.edu/woodbridge/.

Virginia Commonwealth University
Richmond, Virginia

- **State-supported** university, founded 1838
- **Urban** 143-acre campus
- **Coed** 23,754 undergraduate students, 84% full-time, 57% women, 43% men
- **66% of applicants were admitted**

Undergraduates 19,839 full-time, 3,915 part-time. Students come from 48 states and territories; 84 other countries; 7% are from out of state; 19% Black or African American, non-Hispanic/Latino; 6% Hispanic/Latino; 12% Asian, non-Hispanic/Latino; 0.3% Native Hawaiian or other Pacific Islander, non-Hispanic/Latino; 0.4% American Indian or Alaska Native, non-Hispanic/Latino; 4% Two or more races, non-Hispanic/Latino; 3% Race/ethnicity unknown; 3% international; 9% transferred in; 21% live on campus. *Retention:* 86% of full-time freshmen returned.

Freshmen *Admission:* 14,336 applied, 9,412 admitted, 3,803 enrolled. *Average high school GPA:* 3.51. *Test scores:* SAT critical reading scores over 500: 71%; SAT math scores over 500: 70%; ACT scores over 18: 92%; SAT critical reading scores over 600: 28%; SAT math scores over 600: 24%; ACT scores over 24: 44%; SAT critical reading scores over 700: 5%; SAT math scores over 700: 3%; ACT scores over 30: 7%.

Faculty *Total:* 3,164, 64% full-time. *Student/faculty ratio:* 19:1.

Academics *Calendar:* semesters. *Degrees:* certificates, bachelor's, master's, doctoral, post-master's, postbachelor's, and first professional certificates. *Special study options:* academic remediation for entering students, accelerated degree program, adult/continuing education programs, advanced placement credit, cooperative education, distance learning, double majors, English as a second language, freshman honors college, honors programs, independent study, internships, off-campus study, part-time degree program, services for LD students, student-designed majors, study abroad, summer session for credit. *ROTC:* Army (c).

Computers on Campus 1,500 computers/terminals and 75,125 ports are available on campus for general student use. Students can access the following: campus intranet, computer help desk, free student e-mail accounts, online (class) grades, online (class) registration, online (class) schedules. Campuswide network is available. 100% of college-owned or -operated housing units are wired for high-speed Internet access. Wireless service is available via classrooms, computer centers, computer labs, dorm rooms, learning centers, libraries, student centers.

Student Life *Housing options:* coed. Campus housing is university owned. *Activities and organizations:* drama/theater group, student-run newspaper, radio and television station, choral group, national fraternities, national sororities. *Campus security:* 24-hour emergency response devices and patrols, student patrols, late-night transport/escort service, controlled dormitory access, security personnel in residence halls. *Student services:* health clinic, personal/psychological counseling, women's center.

Athletics Member NCAA. All Division I. *Intercollegiate sports:* baseball M(s), basketball M(s)/W(s), cross-country running M(s)/W(s), field hockey W(s), golf M(s), soccer M(s)/W(s), tennis M(s)/W(s), track and field M(s)/W(s), volleyball W(s). *Intramural sports:* badminton M/W, baseball M(c), basketball M(c)/W, cross-country running M(c)/W(c), equestrian sports M(c)/W(c), field hockey W(c), football M, ice hockey M(c), lacrosse M(c)/W(c), racquetball M/W, rugby M(c)/W(c), skiing (downhill) M/W, soccer M(c)/W(c), softball M/W, swimming and diving M(c)/W(c), table tennis M(c)/W(c), tennis M(c)/W(c), ultimate Frisbee M(c)/W(c), volleyball M/W, weight lifting M(c)/W(c).

Standardized Tests *Required:* SAT or ACT (for admission).

Costs (2011–12) *Tuition:* state resident $7600 full-time, $318 per credit hour part-time; nonresident $20,456 full-time, $854 per credit hour part-time. *Required fees:* $1917 full-time. *Room and board:* $8646; room only: $5262. Room and board charges vary according to board plan. *Payment plan:* installment. *Waivers:* senior citizens and employees or children of employees.

Financial Aid Of all full-time matriculated undergraduates who enrolled in 2010, 13,401 applied for aid, 11,029 were judged to have need, 810 had their need fully met. 739 Federal Work-Study jobs (averaging $1519). In 2010, 1447 non-need-based awards were made. *Average percent of need met:* 54%. *Average financial aid package:* $9929. *Average need-based loan:* $4352. *Average need-based gift aid:* $3132. *Average non-need-based aid:* $7882. *Average indebtedness upon graduation:* $27,179.

Applying *Options:* electronic application, early admission. *Application fee:* $40. *Required:* high school transcript, letters of recommendation. *Application deadline:* 1/15 (freshmen). *Notification:* 11/1 (freshmen).

Freshman Application Contact Ms. Sybil Halloran, Director of Undergraduate Admissions, Virginia Commonwealth University, Box 842526, Richmond, VA 23284-2526. *Phone:* 804-828-6125. *Toll-free phone:* 800-841-3638. *Fax:* 804-828-1899. *E-mail:* schallor@vcu.edu. *Web site:* http://www.vcu.edu/.

Virginia Intermont College
Bristol, Virginia

- **Independent** 4-year, founded 1884, affiliated with Baptist Church
- **Small-town** 13-acre campus
- **Endowment** $4.1 million
- **Coed** 558 undergraduate students, 87% full-time, 71% women, 29% men
- **Moderately difficult** entrance level, 97% of applicants were admitted

Undergraduates 488 full-time, 70 part-time. Students come from 38 states and territories; 5 other countries; 45% are from out of state; 8% Black or African American, non-Hispanic/Latino; 2% Hispanic/Latino; 0.8% Asian, non-Hispanic/Latino; 0.8% American Indian or Alaska Native, non-Hispanic/Latino; 0.4% Two or more races, non-Hispanic/Latino; 5% Race/ethnicity unknown; 0.8% international; 11% transferred in; 53% live on campus. *Retention:* 59% of full-time freshmen returned.

Freshmen *Admission:* 370 applied, 359 admitted, 109 enrolled. *Average high school GPA:* 3.19. *Test scores:* SAT critical reading scores over 500: 41%; SAT math scores over 500: 39%; SAT writing scores over 500: 39%; ACT scores over 18: 86%; SAT critical reading scores over 600: 9%; SAT math scores over 600: 7%; SAT writing scores over 600: 5%; ACT scores over 24: 22%; SAT critical reading scores over 700: 3%; SAT math scores over 700: 3%; SAT writing scores over 700: 2%; ACT scores over 30: 2%.

Faculty *Total:* 139, 29% full-time, 53% with terminal degrees. *Student/faculty ratio:* 7:1.

Academics *Calendar:* semesters. *Degrees:* bachelor's and postbachelor's certificates. *Special study options:* academic remediation for entering students, accelerated degree program, adult/continuing education programs, advanced placement credit, double majors, honors programs, independent study, internships, off-campus study, part-time degree program, services for LD students, summer session for credit.

Computers on Campus 70 computers/terminals are available on campus for general student use. Students can access the following: campus intranet, computer help desk, free student e-mail accounts, online (class) grades, online (class) registration, online (class) schedules. Campuswide network is available. 100% of college-owned or -operated housing units are wired for high-speed Internet access. Wireless service is available via libraries, student centers.

Student Life *Housing:* on-campus residence required through junior year. *Options:* coed. Campus housing is university owned and leased by the school. Freshman campus housing is guaranteed. *Activities and organizations:* drama/theater group, student-run newspaper, choral group, Poetry Club, Gay-Straight Alliance, Student Government Association, equestrian club, International Issues Club. *Campus security:* 24-hour patrols, late-night transport/escort service. *Student services:* health clinic, personal/psychological counseling.

Athletics Member NAIA. *Intercollegiate sports:* baseball M(s), basketball M(s)/W(s), cheerleading W(s), equestrian sports M(s)/W(s), golf M(s), soccer M(s)/W(s), softball W(s), volleyball W(s). *Intramural sports:* basketball M/W, bowling M/W, football M/W, golf M/W, soccer M/W, ultimate Frisbee M/W, volleyball M/W.

Standardized Tests *Required:* SAT or ACT (for admission).

Costs (2012–13) *Comprehensive fee:* $32,411 includes full-time tuition ($24,542), mandatory fees ($100), and room and board ($7769). Full-time tuition and fees vary according to course level, course load, program, and reciprocity agreements. Part-time tuition: $491 per credit hour. Part-time tuition and fees vary according to course level, course load, program, and reciprocity agreements. *College room only:* $3760. Room and board charges vary according to board plan and housing facility. *Payment plan:* deferred payment. *Waivers:* senior citizens and employees or children of employees.

Financial Aid Of all full-time matriculated undergraduates who enrolled in 2010, 491 applied for aid, 467 were judged to have need, 34 had their need fully met. 135 Federal Work-Study jobs (averaging $1229). In 2010, 51 non-need-based awards were made. *Average percent of need met:* 61%. *Average financial aid package:* $16,190. *Average need-based loan:* $3946. *Average need-based gift aid:* $12,824. *Average non-need-based aid:* $11,997. *Average indebtedness upon graduation:* $19,746.

Applying *Options:* electronic application, early admission, deferred entrance. *Application fee:* $25. *Required:* high school transcript, minimum 2.5 GPA. *Required for some:* essay or personal statement, interview, 2 letters of recommendation for students applying to Honors Program. *Application deadlines:* rolling (freshmen), rolling (out-of-state freshmen), rolling (transfers). *Notification:* continuous (freshmen), continuous (out-of-state freshmen), continuous (transfers).

Freshman Application Contact Geneva Perkins, Virginia Intermont College, 1013 Moore Street, Campus Box D-460, Bristol, VA 24201. *Phone:* 276-466-7892. *Toll-free phone:* 800-451-1842. *Fax:* 276-466-7855. *E-mail:* genevaperkins@vic.edu. *Web site:* http://www.vic.edu/.

See next page for display ad and page 1738 for the College Close-Up.

Virginia International University
Fairfax, Virginia

Freshman Application Contact Admissions Department, Virginia International University, 11200 Waples Mill Road, Fairfax, VA 22030. *Phone:* 703-591-7042 Ext. 313. *Toll-free phone:* 800-514-6848. *Fax:* 703-591-7048. *E-mail:* admissions@viu.edu. *Web site:* http://www.viu.edu/.

Virginia Military Institute
Lexington, Virginia

- **State-supported** 4-year, founded 1839
- **Small-town** 134-acre campus
- **Coed, primarily men**
- **Moderately difficult** entrance level

Faculty *Student/faculty ratio:* 11:1.

Academics *Calendar:* semesters. *Degree:* bachelor's.

Student Life *Campus security:* 24-hour emergency response devices and patrols, student patrols.

Athletics Member NCAA. All Division I.

Standardized Tests *Required:* SAT or ACT (for admission).

Costs (2011–12) *Tuition:* state resident $6622 full-time; nonresident $25,602 full-time. *Required fees:* $6562 full-time. *Room and board:* $7446.

Financial Aid *Of all full-time matriculated undergraduates who enrolled in 2010,* 1,051 applied for aid, 796 were judged to have need, 422 had their need fully met. *In 2010,* 255 non-need-based awards were made. *Average percent of need met:* 91. *Average financial aid package:* $17,691. *Average need-based loan:* $3486. *Average need-based gift aid:* $11,469. *Average non-need-based aid:* $4039. *Average indebtedness upon graduation:* $20,332.

Applying *Options:* electronic application, early admission, early decision. *Application fee:* $40. *Required:* high school transcript. *Recommended:* essay or personal statement, 2 letters of recommendation, interview.

Freshman Application Contact Lt. Col. Tom Mortenson, Associate Director of Admissions, Virginia Military Institute, Admissions Office, Lexington, VA 24450. *Phone:* 540-464-7211. *Toll-free phone:* 800-767-4207. *Fax:* 540-464-7746. *E-mail:* admissions@vmi.edu. *Web site:* http://www.vmi.edu/.

Virginia Polytechnic Institute and State University

Blacksburg, Virginia

- **State-supported** university, founded 1872
- **Small-town** 2600-acre campus
- **Endowment** $600.6 million
- **Coed** 23,700 undergraduate students, 98% full-time, 42% women, 58% men
- **Moderately difficult** entrance level, 64% of applicants were admitted

Undergraduates 23,176 full-time, 524 part-time. Students come from 113 other countries; 4% Black or African American, non-Hispanic/Latino; 4% Hispanic/Latino; 8% Asian, non-Hispanic/Latino; 0.1% Native Hawaiian or other Pacific Islander, non-Hispanic/Latino; 0.2% American Indian or Alaska Native, non-Hispanic/Latino; 3% Two or more races, non-Hispanic/Latino; 3% Race/ethnicity unknown; 3% international; 4% transferred in; 36% live on campus. *Retention:* 91% of full-time freshmen returned.

Freshmen *Admission:* 20,993 applied, 13,532 admitted, 5,221 enrolled. *Average high school GPA:* 4. *Test scores:* SAT critical reading scores over 500: 77%; SAT math scores over 500: 84%; SAT writing scores over 500: 70%; SAT critical reading scores over 600: 30%; SAT math scores over 600: 46%; SAT writing scores over 600: 26%; SAT critical reading scores over 700: 7%; SAT math scores over 700: 9%; SAT writing scores over 700: 3%.

Faculty *Total:* 1,579, 83% full-time. *Student/faculty ratio:* 16:1.

Academics *Calendar:* semesters. *Degrees:* associate, bachelor's, master's, doctoral, post-master's, and first professional certificates. *Special study options:* accelerated degree program, adult/continuing education programs, advanced placement credit, cooperative education, distance learning, double majors, English as a second language, honors programs, independent study, internships, part-time degree program, services for LD students, study abroad, summer session for credit. *ROTC:* Army (b), Navy (b), Air Force (b).

Computers on Campus 8,000 computers/terminals are available on campus for general student use. Students can access the following: campus intranet, computer help desk, free student e-mail accounts, online (class) grades, online (class) registration, online (class) schedules. Campuswide network is available. Wireless service is available via entire campus.

Student Life *Housing:* on-campus residence required for freshman year. *Options:* coed, men-only, women-only. Campus housing is university owned. Freshman campus housing is guaranteed. *Activities and organizations:* drama/theater group, student-run newspaper, radio and television station, choral group, marching band, Virginia Tech Union, Student Government Association, international student organizations, national fraternities, national sororities. *Campus security:* 24-hour emergency response devices and patrols, student patrols, late-night transport/escort service, controlled dormitory access. *Student services:* health clinic, personal/psychological counseling, women's center, legal services.

Athletics Member NCAA. All Division I except football (Division I-A). *Intercollegiate sports:* baseball M, basketball M, cross-country running M/W, golf M(s), lacrosse W(s), soccer M(s)/W(s), swimming and diving M(s)/W(s), tennis M(s)/W(s), track and field M(s)/W(s), ultimate Frisbee M/W, volleyball W. *Intramural sports:* baseball M(c), basketball M, bowling M/W, crew M(c)/W(c), cross-country running M/W, equestrian sports M(c)/W(c), fencing M(c)/W(c), field hockey M(c)/W(c), football M/W, golf M/W, gymnastics M(c)/W(c), ice hockey M/W, lacrosse M(c)/W(c), racquetball M/W, riflery M(c)/W(c), rugby M(c)/W(c), soccer M/W, softball M/W, swimming and diving M/W, table tennis M/W, tennis M/W, volleyball M/W, water polo M/W.

Standardized Tests *Required:* SAT or ACT (for admission). *Required for some:* SAT and SAT Subject Tests or ACT (for admission).

Costs (2011–12) *Tuition:* state resident $8852 full-time; nonresident $22,254 full-time. *Required fees:* $2226 full-time. *Room and board:* $6856. Room and board charges vary according to board plan. *Payment plan:* installment. *Waivers:* senior citizens and employees or children of employees.

Financial Aid Of all full-time matriculated undergraduates who enrolled in 2010, 15,577 applied for aid, 10,402 were judged to have need, 1,738 had their need fully met. In 2010, 1896 non-need-based awards were made. *Average percent of need met:* 66%. *Average financial aid package:* $10,839. *Average need-based loan:* $4534. *Average need-based gift aid:* $6611. *Average non-need-based aid:* $4872. *Average indebtedness upon graduation:* $24,320.

Applying *Options:* electronic application, early admission, early decision, deferred entrance. *Application fee:* $60. *Required:* high school transcript.

COLLEGES AT-A-GLANCE

Recommended: minimum 3.0 GPA. *Application deadlines:* 1/15 (freshmen), 2/15 (transfers). *Early decision deadline:* 11/1. *Notification:* 4/1 (freshmen), 5/1 (transfers), 12/15 (early decision).

Freshman Application Contact Virginia Polytechnic Institute and State University, Blacksburg, VA 24061. *Phone:* 540-231-6267. *Web site:* http://www.vt.edu/.

Virginia State University
Petersburg, Virginia

- **State-supported** comprehensive, founded 1882, part of State Council of Higher Education for Virginia
- **Suburban** 236-acre campus with easy access to Richmond
- **Endowment** $22.6 million
- **Coed** 5,301 undergraduate students, 94% full-time, 60% women, 40% men
- **Minimally difficult** entrance level, 71% of applicants were admitted

Undergraduates 4,971 full-time, 330 part-time. Students come from 39 states and territories; 32% are from out of state; 85% Black or African American, non-Hispanic/Latino; 2% Hispanic/Latino; 0.1% Asian, non-Hispanic/Latino; 0.2% American Indian or Alaska Native, non-Hispanic/Latino; 11% Race/ethnicity unknown; 6% transferred in; 52% live on campus. *Retention:* 71% of full-time freshmen returned.

Freshmen *Admission:* 6,515 applied, 4,606 admitted, 1,234 enrolled. *Average high school GPA:* 2.8. *Test scores:* SAT critical reading scores over 500: 13%; SAT math scores over 500: 13%; SAT writing scores over 500: 9%; ACT scores over 18: 37%; SAT critical reading scores over 600: 2%; SAT math scores over 600: 1%; SAT writing scores over 600: 1%; ACT scores over 24: 4%.

Faculty *Total:* 499, 56% full-time. *Student/faculty ratio:* 16:1.

Academics *Calendar:* semesters. *Degrees:* associate, bachelor's, master's, doctoral, postbachelor's, and first professional certificates. *Special study options:* adult/continuing education programs, advanced placement credit, cooperative education, double majors, honors programs, independent study, internships, off-campus study, part-time degree program, services for LD students, student-designed majors, study abroad, summer session for credit. *ROTC:* Army (b).

Computers on Campus 1,501 computers/terminals are available on campus for general student use. Students can access the following: computer help desk, free student e-mail accounts, online (class) grades, online (class) registration, online (class) schedules. Campuswide network is available. Wireless service is available via classrooms, computer labs, libraries.

Student Life *Housing:* on-campus residence required for freshman year. *Options:* coed, men-only, women-only. Campus housing is university owned. Freshman applicants given priority for college housing. *Activities and organizations:* drama/theater group, student-run newspaper, choral group, marching band, Betterment of Brothers/Sisters, The VSU Gospel Chorale, Sankofa, Panic 2000, Hospitality Management Program Students Association, national fraternities, national sororities. *Campus security:* 24-hour emergency response devices and patrols, late-night transport/escort service, controlled dormitory access. *Student services:* health clinic, personal/psychological counseling.

Athletics Member NCAA. All Division II. *Intercollegiate sports:* baseball M(s), basketball M(s)/W(s), bowling W(s), cheerleading M/W, cross-country running M(s)/W(s), football M(s), golf M(s)/W(s), softball W(s), tennis M(s)/W(s), track and field M(s)/W(s), volleyball W(s). *Intramural sports:* basketball M/W, football M, tennis M/W, track and field M/W, volleyball W.

Standardized Tests *Required:* SAT or ACT (for admission).

Costs (2011–12) *Tuition:* state resident $4406 full-time, $298 per credit hour part-time; nonresident $12,774 full-time, $646 per credit hour part-time. Full-time tuition and fees vary according to course load and program. Part-time tuition and fees vary according to course load and program. *Required fees:* $2684 full-time, $10 per credit hour part-time. *Room and board:* $8880; room only: $5016. Room and board charges vary according to board plan and housing facility. *Payment plan:* installment. *Waivers:* senior citizens.

Financial Aid Of all full-time matriculated undergraduates who enrolled in 2010, 4,965 applied for aid, 4,965 were judged to have need, 745 had their need fully met. 300 Federal Work-Study jobs (averaging $2000). In 2010, 546 non-need-based awards were made. *Average percent of need met:* 65%. *Average financial aid package:* $11,401. *Average need-based loan:* $5500. *Average need-based gift aid:* $7196. *Average non-need-based aid:* $1000. *Average indebtedness upon graduation:* $28,250.

Applying *Options:* electronic application. *Application fee:* $25. *Required:* essay or personal statement, high school transcript, minimum 2.2 GPA, 2 letters of recommendation. *Application deadlines:* 5/1 (freshmen), 5/1 (transfers). *Notification:* continuous (freshmen), continuous (transfers).

Freshman Application Contact Mrs. Irene Logan, Director of Admissions, Virginia State University, Office of Admissions, Petersburg, VA 23806-2096.

Phone: 804-524-5902. *Toll-free phone:* 800-871-7611. *Fax:* 804-524-5055. *E-mail:* ilogan@vsu.edu. *Web site:* http://www.vsu.edu/.

Virginia Union University
Richmond, Virginia

- **Independent Baptist** comprehensive, founded 1865
- **Urban** 84-acre campus
- **Endowment** $23.2 million
- **Coed** 1,333 undergraduate students, 97% full-time, 53% women, 47% men
- **Moderately difficult** entrance level, 95% of applicants were admitted

Undergraduates 1,296 full-time, 37 part-time. Students come from 29 states and territories; 50% are from out of state; 97% Black or African American, non-Hispanic/Latino; 0.8% Hispanic/Latino; 0.1% Asian, non-Hispanic/Latino; 0.1% American Indian or Alaska Native, non-Hispanic/Latino; 1% Race/ethnicity unknown; 0.1% international; 4% transferred in. *Retention:* 55% of full-time freshmen returned.

Freshmen *Admission:* 6,910 applied, 6,579 admitted, 418 enrolled. *Average high school GPA:* 2.52.

Faculty *Total:* 114, 68% full-time, 47% with terminal degrees. *Student/faculty ratio:* 15:1.

Academics *Calendar:* semesters. *Degrees:* bachelor's, master's, doctoral, and first professional. *Special study options:* academic remediation for entering students, adult/continuing education programs, advanced placement credit, cooperative education, English as a second language, honors programs, internships, off-campus study, summer session for credit. *ROTC:* Army (c). *Unusual degree programs:* 3-2 engineering with Howard University, University of Michigan, University of Iowa, Virginia Commonwealth University.

Computers on Campus 200 computers/terminals are available on campus for general student use. Students can access the following: campus intranet, computer help desk, free student e-mail accounts, online (class) grades, online (class) registration, online (class) schedules, academic research databases. Campuswide network is available. 100% of college-owned or -operated housing units are wired for high-speed Internet access. Wireless service is available via entire campus.

Student Life *Housing options:* coed, men-only, women-only. Campus housing is university owned and leased by the school. Freshman applicants given priority for college housing. *Activities and organizations:* drama/theater group, student-run newspaper, choral group, marching band, Student Government Association, NAACP, NPHC-VUU Chapter (National Pan-Hellenic Council), Mr. and Miss Royal Court, national fraternities, national sororities. *Campus security:* 24-hour emergency response devices and patrols, controlled dormitory access. *Student services:* health clinic, personal/psychological counseling.

Athletics Member NCAA. All Division II. *Intercollegiate sports:* basketball M(s)/W(s), cross-country running M(s)/W(s), football M(s), golf M(s), softball W(s), tennis M(s), track and field M(s)/W(s), volleyball W(s). *Intramural sports:* basketball M, softball W.

Standardized Tests *Required:* SAT or ACT (for admission).

Costs (2011–12) *Comprehensive fee:* $21,804 includes full-time tuition ($13,314), mandatory fees ($1316), and room and board ($7174). Full-time tuition and fees vary according to course level and course load. Part-time tuition: $422 per credit hour. Part-time tuition and fees vary according to course level and course load. *Required fees:* $40 per credit hour part-time. *College room only:* $3240. Room and board charges vary according to housing facility. *Payment plans:* installment, deferred payment. *Waivers:* employees or children of employees.

Financial Aid Of all full-time matriculated undergraduates who enrolled in 2009, 1,163 applied for aid, 1,101 were judged to have need. *Average financial aid package:* $10,921. *Average need-based loan:* $3894. *Average need-based gift aid:* $5371.

Applying *Options:* electronic application, deferred entrance. *Application fee:* $25. *Required:* high school transcript, minimum 2.3 GPA. *Required for some:* interview. *Recommended:* essay or personal statement, minimum 2.5 GPA, 3 letters of recommendation. *Application deadlines:* rolling (freshmen), rolling (transfers). *Notification:* continuous (freshmen), continuous (transfers).

Freshman Application Contact Ms. Sanada Spellman, Assistant Director of Admissions, Virginia Union University, 1500 North Lombardy Street, Richmond, VA 23220-1170. *Phone:* 804-342-3572. *Toll-free phone:* 800-368-3227. *Fax:* 804-342-3511. *E-mail:* slspellman@vuu.edu. *Web site:* http://www.vuu.edu/.

Virginia University of Lynchburg
Lynchburg, Virginia

Freshman Application Contact Ms. Cheryl Glass, Director of Admissions, Virginia University of Lynchburg, 2058 Garfield Avenue, Lynchburg, VA

24501. *Phone:* 434-528-5276 Ext. 106. *Fax:* 434-528-4275. *E-mail:* cglass@vul.edu. *Web site:* http://www.vul.edu/.

Virginia Wesleyan College
Norfolk, Virginia

- **Independent United Methodist** 4-year, founded 1961
- **Urban** 300-acre campus with easy access to Norfolk, Virginia Beach
- **Endowment** $53.3 million
- **Coed** 1,405 undergraduate students, 89% full-time, 63% women, 37% men
- **Moderately difficult** entrance level, 86% of applicants were admitted

Undergraduates 1,253 full-time, 152 part-time. Students come from 31 states and territories; 5 other countries; 23% are from out of state; 23% Black or African American, non-Hispanic/Latino; 6% Hispanic/Latino; 1% Asian, non-Hispanic/Latino; 0.3% Native Hawaiian or other Pacific Islander, non-Hispanic/Latino; 0.2% American Indian or Alaska Native, non-Hispanic/Latino; 3% Two or more races, non-Hispanic/Latino; 4% Race/ethnicity unknown; 0.4% international; 7% transferred in; 60% live on campus. *Retention:* 64% of full-time freshmen returned.

Freshmen *Admission:* 3,174 applied, 2,730 admitted, 439 enrolled. *Average high school GPA:* 3.19. *Test scores:* SAT critical reading scores over 500: 47%; SAT math scores over 500: 47%; SAT writing scores over 500: 40%; ACT scores over 18: 86%; SAT critical reading scores over 600: 12%; SAT math scores over 600: 11%; SAT writing scores over 600: 9%; ACT scores over 24: 19%; SAT critical reading scores over 700: 2%; SAT math scores over 700: 2%; SAT writing scores over 700: 2%.

Faculty *Total:* 131, 66% full-time. *Student/faculty ratio:* 12:1.

Academics *Calendar:* 4-1-4. *Degree:* bachelor's. *Special study options:* academic remediation for entering students, adult/continuing education programs, advanced placement credit, double majors, freshman honors college, honors programs, independent study, internships, off-campus study, part-time degree program, services for LD students, student-designed majors, study abroad, summer session for credit. *ROTC:* Army (c).

Computers on Campus 105 computers/terminals are available on campus for general student use. Students can access the following: campus intranet, computer help desk, free student e-mail accounts, online (class) grades, online (class) registration, online (class) schedules. Campuswide network is available. 100% of college-owned or -operated housing units are wired for high-speed Internet access. Wireless service is available via classrooms, computer centers, computer labs, learning centers, libraries, student centers.

Student Life *Housing:* on-campus residence required through senior year. *Options:* coed, women-only, disabled students. Campus housing is university owned. Freshman campus housing is guaranteed. *Activities and organizations:* drama/theater group, student-run newspaper, radio station, choral group, Wesleyan Activities Council, Community service, Student Government Association, student newspaper, Black Student Union, national fraternities, national sororities. *Campus security:* 24-hour emergency response devices and patrols, late-night transport/escort service, controlled dormitory access, well-lit pathways. *Student services:* health clinic, personal/psychological counseling, women's center.

Athletics Member NCAA. All Division III. *Intercollegiate sports:* baseball M, basketball M/W, cheerleading W, cross-country running M/W, field hockey W, golf M, lacrosse M/W, soccer M/W, softball W, tennis M/W, track and field M/W, volleyball W. *Intramural sports:* basketball M/W, crew M(c)/W(c), fencing M(c)/W(c), field hockey W, football M/W, racquetball M/W, soccer M/W, table tennis M/W, ultimate Frisbee M/W, volleyball M/W.

Standardized Tests *Required for some:* SAT or ACT (for admission).

Costs (2011–12) *One-time required fee:* $250. *Comprehensive fee:* $37,668 includes full-time tuition ($29,180), mandatory fees ($500), and room and board ($7988). Full-time tuition and fees vary according to course load. Part-time tuition: $1216 per credit hour. Part-time tuition and fees vary according to course load. *Required fees:* $500 per year part-time. *Room and board:* Room and board charges vary according to board plan and housing facility. *Payment plans:* installment, deferred payment. *Waivers:* adult students, senior citizens, and employees or children of employees.

Financial Aid Of all full-time matriculated undergraduates who enrolled in 2010, 1,082 applied for aid, 895 were judged to have need, 96 had their need fully met. 183 Federal Work-Study jobs (averaging $998). In 2010, 170 non-need-based awards were made. *Average percent of need met:* 65%. *Average financial aid package:* $19,272. *Average need-based loan:* $7299. *Average need-based gift aid:* $15,380. *Average non-need-based aid:* $9962. *Average indebtedness upon graduation:* $32,536.

Applying *Options:* electronic application. *Application fee:* $40. *Required:* essay or personal statement, high school transcript, minimum 2.5 GPA. *Required for some:* interview. *Application deadlines:* rolling (freshmen), rolling (transfers). *Notification:* continuous (freshmen), continuous (transfers).

Freshman Application Contact Mrs. Sara Gastler, Director of Admissions, Virginia Wesleyan College, 1584 Wesleyan Drive, Norfolk, VA 23502-5599. *Phone:* 757-455-3208. *Toll-free phone:* 800-737-8684. *Fax:* 757-461-5238. *E-mail:* admissions@vwc.edu. *Web site:* http://www.vwc.edu/.

Washington and Lee University
Lexington, Virginia

- **Independent** comprehensive, founded 1749
- **Small-town** 430-acre campus
- **Endowment** $1.2 billion
- **Coed** 1,791 undergraduate students, 100% full-time, 49% women, 51% men
- **Most difficult** entrance level, 18% of applicants were admitted

Undergraduates 1,789 full-time, 2 part-time. Students come from 47 states and territories; 36 other countries; 86% are from out of state; 3% Black or African American, non-Hispanic/Latino; 3% Hispanic/Latino; 3% Asian, non-Hispanic/Latino; 0.1% American Indian or Alaska Native, non-Hispanic/Latino; 2% Two or more races, non-Hispanic/Latino; 1% Race/ethnicity unknown; 4% international; 0.2% transferred in; 60% live on campus. *Retention:* 93% of full-time freshmen returned.

Freshmen *Admission:* 6,487 applied, 1,182 admitted, 494 enrolled. *Test scores:* SAT critical reading scores over 500: 100%; SAT math scores over 500: 100%; SAT writing scores over 500: 100%; ACT scores over 18: 100%; SAT critical reading scores over 600: 91%; SAT math scores over 600: 95%; SAT writing scores over 600: 92%; ACT scores over 24: 100%; SAT critical reading scores over 700: 38%; SAT math scores over 700: 37%; SAT writing scores over 700: 38%; ACT scores over 30: 70%.

Faculty *Total:* 285, 76% full-time, 93% with terminal degrees. *Student/faculty ratio:* 9:1.

Academics *Calendar:* 4-4-2. *Degrees:* bachelor's, master's, and doctoral. *Special study options:* advanced placement credit, double majors, honors programs, independent study, internships, off-campus study, services for LD students, student-designed majors, study abroad. *ROTC:* Army (c).

Computers on Campus 190 computers/terminals and 1,500 ports are available on campus for general student use. Students can access the following: campus intranet, computer help desk, free student e-mail accounts, online (class) grades, online (class) registration, online (class) schedules. Campuswide network is available. 100% of college-owned or -operated housing units are wired for high-speed Internet access. Wireless service is available via entire campus.

Student Life *Housing:* on-campus residence required through sophomore year. *Options:* coed, men-only, women-only, disabled students. Campus housing is university owned. Freshman campus housing is guaranteed. *Activities and organizations:* drama/theater group, student-run newspaper, radio and television station, choral group, Mock Convention, General Activities Board, Nabors Service League, Outing Club, Sports Clubs, national fraternities, national sororities. *Campus security:* 24-hour emergency response devices and patrols, late-night transport/escort service, controlled dormitory access, Emergency Alert System. *Student services:* health clinic, personal/psychological counseling, women's center.

Athletics Member NCAA. All Division III. *Intercollegiate sports:* baseball M, basketball M/W, cheerleading M(c)/W(c), cross-country running M/W, equestrian sports W, fencing M(c)/W(c), field hockey W, football M, golf M/W, ice hockey M(c)/W(c), lacrosse M/W, rugby M(c), skiing (cross-country) M(c)/W(c), soccer M/W, softball W(c), swimming and diving M/W, tennis M/W, track and field M/W, ultimate Frisbee M(c)/W(c), volleyball M(c)/W, wrestling M. *Intramural sports:* badminton M/W, baseball M(c), basketball M/W, equestrian sports W(c), football M/W, golf M/W, lacrosse M(c)/W(c), racquetball M/W, rock climbing M(c), skiing (downhill) M(c)/W(c), soccer M/W, softball M/W, squash M(c)/W(c), swimming and diving M/W, table tennis M/W, tennis M/W, track and field M/W, ultimate Frisbee M/W, volleyball M/W, wrestling M.

Standardized Tests *Required:* SAT or ACT (for admission). *Recommended:* SAT Subject Tests (for admission), 2 unrelated SAT subject tests (recommended, not required).

Costs (2011–12) *Comprehensive fee:* $50,967 includes full-time tuition ($40,900), mandatory fees ($937), and room and board ($9130). *College room only:* $3710. Room and board charges vary according to board plan and housing facility. *Payment plan:* installment. *Waivers:* employees or children of employees.

Financial Aid Of all full-time matriculated undergraduates who enrolled in 2011, 813 applied for aid, 716 were judged to have need, 706 had their need fully met. 157 Federal Work-Study jobs (averaging $1974). 406 state and other part-time jobs (averaging $1957). In 2011, 164 non-need-based awards were made. *Average percent of need met:* 99%. *Average financial aid package:* $44,115. *Average need-based loan:* $4578. *Average need-based gift aid:*

$35,834. *Average non-need-based aid:* $31,378. *Average indebtedness upon graduation:* $24,716. *Financial aid deadline:* 2/15.

Applying *Options:* electronic application, early decision, deferred entrance. *Application fee:* $50. *Required:* high school transcript, 3 letters of recommendation. *Recommended:* essay or personal statement, interview. *Application deadlines:* 1/2 (freshmen), 4/1 (transfers). *Early decision deadline:* 11/15 (for plan 1), 1/2 (for plan 2). *Notification:* 4/1 (freshmen), continuous (transfers), 12/21 (early decision plan 1), 2/1 (early decision plan 2).

Freshman Application Contact Mr. William M. Hartog, Dean of Admissions and Financial Aid, Washington and Lee University, 204 West Washington Street, Lexington, VA 24450-2116. *Phone:* 540-458-8710. *Fax:* 540-458-8062. *E-mail:* admissions@wlu.edu. *Web site:* http://www.wlu.edu/.

Westwood College–Annandale Campus

Annandale, Virginia

Freshman Application Contact Westwood College–Annandale Campus, 7619 Little River Turnpike, 5th Floor, Annandale, VA 22003. *Phone:* 703-642-3633. *Toll-free phone:* 877-305-0049. *Web site:* http://www.westwood.edu/.

Westwood College–Arlington Ballston Campus

Arlington, Virginia

Freshman Application Contact Westwood College–Arlington Ballston Campus, 4300 Wilson Boulevard, Suite 200, Arlington, VA 22203. *Phone:* 703-243-1662. *Toll-free phone:* 877-268-5278. *Web site:* http://www.westwood.edu/.

World College

Virginia Beach, Virginia

- **Proprietary** 4-year, founded 1992
- **Suburban** campus
- **Coed**
- **Noncompetitive** entrance level

Academics *Calendar:* semesters. *Degrees:* bachelor's (offers only external degree programs).

Costs (2011–12) *Tuition:* $3770 full-time. No tuition increase for student's term of enrollment. *Payment plans:* tuition prepayment, installment.

Applying *Options:* electronic application, early admission. *Required:* high school transcript.

Freshman Application Contact Mrs. Audre Piratzky, Admissions Counselor, World College, 5193 Shore Drive, Suite 105, Virginia Beach, VA 23455. *Phone:* 757-464-4600. *Toll-free phone:* 800-243-6446. *Fax:* 757-464-3687. *E-mail:* instruct@cie-wc.edu. *Web site:* http://www.worldcollege.edu/.

WASHINGTON

Antioch University Seattle

Seattle, Washington

Freshman Application Contact Admissions Office, Antioch University Seattle, 2326 Sixth Avenue, Seattle, WA 98121-1814. *Phone:* 206-268-4202. *Toll-free phone:* 888-268-4477. *E-mail:* admissions@antiochseattle.edu. *Web site:* http://www.antiochsea.edu/.

Argosy University, Seattle

Seattle, Washington

Freshman Application Contact Argosy University, Seattle, 2601-A Elliott Avenue, Seattle, WA 98121. *Phone:* 206-283-4500. *Toll-free phone:* 866-283-2777. *Web site:* http://www.argosy.edu/seattle/.

See page 1062 for the College Close-Up.

The Art Institute of Seattle

Seattle, Washington

- **Proprietary** primarily 2-year, founded 1982, part of Education Management Corporation
- **Urban** campus
- **Coed**

Academics *Calendar:* quarters. *Degrees:* diplomas, associate, and bachelor's.

Costs (2011–12) *Tuition:* Tuition cost varies by program. Prospective students should contact the school for current tuition costs. Other charges include a starting kit for all first-quarter students. Kits vary in price, depending on the program of study.

Freshman Application Contact The Art Institute of Seattle, 2323 Elliott Avenue, Seattle, WA 98121-1642. *Phone:* 206-448-6600. *Toll-free phone:* 800-275-2471. *Web site:* http://www.artinstitutes.edu/seattle/.

See page 1130 for the College Close-Up.

Bastyr University

Kenmore, Washington

- **Independent** upper-level, founded 1978
- **Suburban** 51-acre campus with easy access to Seattle
- **Coed** 216 undergraduate students, 84% full-time, 83% women, 17% men

Undergraduates 181 full-time, 35 part-time. Students come from 24 states and territories; 7 other countries; 3% Black or African American, non-Hispanic/Latino; 4% Hispanic/Latino; 9% Asian, non-Hispanic/Latino; 1% Native Hawaiian or other Pacific Islander, non-Hispanic/Latino; 1% American Indian or Alaska Native, non-Hispanic/Latino; 6% Two or more races, non-Hispanic/Latino; 4% Race/ethnicity unknown; 3% international; 45% transferred in; 8% live on campus.

Faculty *Total:* 108, 36% full-time, 69% with terminal degrees.

Academics *Calendar:* quarters. *Degrees:* certificates, bachelor's, master's, doctoral, and postbachelor's certificates. *Special study options:* cooperative education, double majors, independent study, internships, part-time degree program, summer session for credit.

Computers on Campus 71 computers/terminals and 20 ports are available on campus for general student use. Students can access the following: campus intranet, computer help desk, free student e-mail accounts, online (class) grades, online (class) schedules. Campuswide network is available. 100% of college-owned or -operated housing units are wired for high-speed Internet access. Wireless service is available via entire campus.

Student Life *Housing options:* coed, disabled students. Campus housing is university owned. *Activities and organizations:* Naturopaths Without Borders, Nature Club, Multicultural Student Association of Natural Medicine, Environmental Action Team, Venture Grant. *Campus security:* student patrols, late-night transport/escort service, controlled dormitory access. *Student services:* health clinic, personal/psychological counseling.

Athletics *Intramural sports:* basketball M, soccer M/W, ultimate Frisbee M/W, volleyball M/W.

Costs (2011–12) *Tuition:* $20,100 full-time, $560 per credit hour part-time. Full-time tuition and fees vary according to course load and program. Part-time tuition and fees vary according to course load and program. *Required fees:* $900 full-time. *Room only:* $7050. Room and board charges vary according to housing facility. *Waivers:* employees or children of employees.

Financial Aid Of all full-time matriculated undergraduates who enrolled in 2010, 167 applied for aid, 162 were judged to have need. 44 Federal Work-Study jobs (averaging $1219). 15 state and other part-time jobs (averaging $558). *Average percent of need met:* 31%. *Average financial aid package:* $12,586. *Average need-based loan:* $6246. *Average need-based gift aid:* $8385.

Applying *Options:* electronic application, deferred entrance. *Application fee:* $60. *Application deadline:* 3/15 (transfers).

Application Contact Ms. Lauren Marani, Assistant Director of Admissions, Bastyr University, 14500 Juanita Drive NE, Kenmore, WA 98028-4966. *Phone:* 425-602-1300. *Fax:* 425-602-3090. *E-mail:* admissions@bastyr.edu. *Web site:* http://www.bastyr.edu/.

Bellevue College

Bellevue, Washington

Freshman Application Contact Morenika Jacobs, Associate Dean of Enrollment Services, Bellevue College, 3000 Landerholm Circle, SE, Bellevue, WA 98007-6484. *Phone:* 425-564-2205. *Fax:* 425-564-4065. *Web site:* http://www.bcc.ctc.edu/.

Central Washington University
Ellensburg, Washington

- **State-supported** comprehensive, founded 1891
- **Small-town** 380-acre campus
- **Coed** 10,770 undergraduate students, 88% full-time, 51% women, 49% men
- **Moderately difficult** entrance level, 78% of applicants were admitted

Undergraduates 9,435 full-time, 1,335 part-time. 7% are from out of state; 3% Black or African American, non-Hispanic/Latino; 9% Hispanic/Latino; 4% Asian, non-Hispanic/Latino; 0.4% Native Hawaiian or other Pacific Islander, non-Hispanic/Latino; 0.4% American Indian or Alaska Native, non-Hispanic/Latino; 6% Two or more races, non-Hispanic/Latino; 6% Race/ethnicity unknown; 2% international; 15% transferred in; 26% live on campus. *Retention:* 78% of full-time freshmen returned.
Freshmen *Admission:* 4,553 applied, 3,568 admitted, 1,383 enrolled. *Average high school GPA:* 3.1. *Test scores:* SAT critical reading scores over 500: 50%; SAT math scores over 500: 52%; ACT scores over 18: 80%; SAT critical reading scores over 600: 12%; SAT math scores over 600: 13%; ACT scores over 24: 28%; SAT critical reading scores over 700: 1%; SAT math scores over 700: 1%; ACT scores over 30: 2%.
Faculty *Total:* 589, 72% full-time. *Student/faculty ratio:* 21:1.
Academics *Calendar:* quarters. *Degrees:* bachelor's, master's, and postbachelor's certificates. *Special study options:* part-time degree program. *ROTC:* Army (b), Air Force (b).
Computers on Campus Students can access the following: campus intranet, computer help desk, free student e-mail accounts, online (class) grades, online (class) registration, online (class) schedules. Campuswide network is available. 100% of college-owned or -operated housing units are wired for high-speed Internet access. Wireless service is available via classrooms, computer centers, dorm rooms, libraries, student centers.
Student Life *Housing:* on-campus residence required for freshman year. *Options:* coed, women-only, disabled students. Campus housing is university owned. Freshman campus housing is guaranteed. *Campus security:* 24-hour emergency response devices and patrols, late-night transport/escort service, controlled dormitory access.
Athletics Member NCAA. All Division II. *Intercollegiate sports:* baseball M(s), basketball M(s)/W(s), bowling M(c)/W(c), cheerleading M/W, cross-country running M(s)/W(s), fencing M(c)/W(c), football M(s), golf M(c)/W(c), ice hockey M(c)/W(c), rugby M(c)/W(c), soccer M(c)/W(s), softball W(s), track and field M(s)/W(s), volleyball W(s), water polo M(c)/W(c). *Intramural sports:* badminton M/W, basketball M/W, football M/W, golf M/W, racquetball M/W, soccer M/W, softball M/W, tennis M/W, ultimate Frisbee M/W, volleyball M/W.
Standardized Tests *Required:* SAT or ACT (for admission).
Costs (2012–13) *Tuition:* state resident $7962 full-time, $242 per credit hour part-time; nonresident $18,607 full-time, $596 per credit hour part-time. Part-time tuition and fees vary according to course load. *Required fees:* $984 full-time. *Room and board:* $9240. Room and board charges vary according to board plan and housing facility.
Financial Aid Of all full-time matriculated undergraduates who enrolled in 2009, 5,997 applied for aid, 4,667 were judged to have need, 2,470 had their need fully met. In 2009, 18 non-need-based awards were made. *Average percent of need met:* 70%. *Average financial aid package:* $8993. *Average need-based loan:* $4052. *Average need-based gift aid:* $6201. *Average non-need-based aid:* $710. *Average indebtedness upon graduation:* $16,507.
Applying *Options:* electronic application. *Application fee:* $50. *Required:* high school transcript, minimum 2.0 GPA. *Required for some:* essay or personal statement, interview. *Application deadlines:* 4/1 (freshmen), 4/1 (transfers). *Notification:* continuous (freshmen), continuous (transfers).
Freshman Application Contact Ms. Lisa Garcia-Hanson, Director of Admissions, Central Washington University, 400 East University Way, Ellensburg, WA 98926-7463. *Phone:* 509-963-1211. *Toll-free phone:* 866-298-4968. *Fax:* 509-963-3022. *E-mail:* cwuadmis@cwu.edu. *Web site:* http://www.cwu.edu/.

City University of Seattle
Bellevue, Washington

- **Independent** comprehensive, founded 1973
- **Suburban** campus with easy access to Seattle
- **Coed** 1,061 undergraduate students, 57% full-time, 59% women, 41% men
- **Noncompetitive** entrance level, 100% of applicants were admitted

Undergraduates 607 full-time, 454 part-time. Students come from 47 states and territories; 33 other countries; 7% Black or African American, non-Hispanic/Latino; 3% Hispanic/Latino; 4% Asian, non-Hispanic/Latino; 0.8% Native Hawaiian or other Pacific Islander, non-Hispanic/Latino; 0.3% Ameri-

can Indian or Alaska Native, non-Hispanic/Latino; 0.9% Two or more races, non-Hispanic/Latino; 30% Race/ethnicity unknown; 8% international; 21% transferred in.
Freshmen *Admission:* 43 applied, 43 admitted, 43 enrolled.
Faculty *Total:* 617, 5% full-time, 20% with terminal degrees. *Student/faculty ratio:* 8:1.
Academics *Calendar:* quarters. *Degrees:* certificates, diplomas, associate, bachelor's, master's, doctoral, post-master's, and postbachelor's certificates. *Special study options:* accelerated degree program, adult/continuing education programs, advanced placement credit, distance learning, double majors, English as a second language, internships, part-time degree program, services for LD students, student-designed majors, summer session for credit.
Computers on Campus 175 computers/terminals are available on campus for general student use. Students can access the following: campus intranet, computer help desk, free student e-mail accounts, online (class) grades, online (class) registration, online (class) schedules. Campuswide network is available. Wireless service is available via classrooms, computer centers, computer labs, libraries.
Student Life *Housing:* college housing not available. *Campus security:* 24-hour emergency response devices. *Student services:* personal/psychological counseling.
Costs (2012–13) *Tuition:* $15,280 full-time, $382 per credit hour part-time. Full-time tuition and fees vary according to course level, degree level, location, program, and reciprocity agreements. Part-time tuition and fees vary according to course level, degree level, location, program, and reciprocity agreements. *Payment plan:* installment. *Waivers:* employees or children of employees.
Financial Aid Of all full-time matriculated undergraduates who enrolled in 2003, 824 applied for aid, 721 were judged to have need. 1 Federal Work-Study job (averaging $1300). In 2003, 18 non-need-based awards were made. *Average percent of need met:* 15%. *Average financial aid package:* $4943. *Average need-based loan:* $4353. *Average need-based gift aid:* $2344. *Average non-need-based aid:* $3738. *Average indebtedness upon graduation:* $16,369.
Applying *Options:* electronic application, deferred entrance. *Application fee:* $50. *Recommended:* high school transcript. *Application deadlines:* rolling (freshmen), rolling (transfers). *Notification:* continuous (freshmen).
Freshman Application Contact Student Services Center, City University of Seattle, 11900 NE First Street, Bellevue, WA 98005. *Phone:* 888-422-4898. *Toll-free phone:* 888-42-CITYU. *Fax:* 425-709-5361. *E-mail:* info@cityu.edu. *Web site:* http://www.cityu.edu/.

Cornish College of the Arts
Seattle, Washington

- **Independent** 4-year, founded 1914
- **Urban** 4-acre campus
- **Endowment** $6.6 million
- **Coed** 834 undergraduate students, 100% full-time, 67% women, 33% men
- **Moderately difficult** entrance level, 58% of applicants were admitted

Undergraduates 834 full-time. Students come from 37 states and territories; 11 other countries; 43% are from out of state; 3% Black or African American, non-Hispanic/Latino; 7% Hispanic/Latino; 6% Asian, non-Hispanic/Latino; 0.5% Native Hawaiian or other Pacific Islander, non-Hispanic/Latino; 1% American Indian or Alaska Native, non-Hispanic/Latino; 5% Two or more races, non-Hispanic/Latino; 7% Race/ethnicity unknown; 2% international; 11% transferred in. *Retention:* 64% of full-time freshmen returned.
Freshmen *Admission:* 1,406 applied, 822 admitted, 212 enrolled. *Average high school GPA:* 3.15.
Faculty *Total:* 165, 33% full-time, 33% with terminal degrees. *Student/faculty ratio:* 6:1.
Academics *Calendar:* semesters. *Degree:* bachelor's. *Special study options:* advanced placement credit, cooperative education, independent study, internships, services for LD students, study abroad, summer session for credit.
Computers on Campus 28 computers/terminals and 50 ports are available on campus for general student use. Students can access the following: campus intranet, computer help desk, free student e-mail accounts, online (class) grades, online (class) registration, online (class) schedules. Campuswide network is available. 100% of college-owned or -operated housing units are wired for high-speed Internet access. Wireless service is available via entire campus.
Student Life *Housing:* on-campus residence required for freshman year. *Options:* coed. Campus housing is university owned. Freshman campus housing is guaranteed. *Activities and organizations:* drama/theater group, choral group, Student Leadership Council, Black Student Alliance, Sigma Alpha Phi, AIGA, Cheese Tasting. *Campus security:* 24-hour emergency response devices and patrols, late-night transport/escort service, controlled dormitory access. *Student services:* personal/psychological counseling.
Standardized Tests *Recommended:* SAT or ACT (for admission).

Financial Aid Of all full-time matriculated undergraduates who enrolled in 2010, 736 applied for aid, 654 were judged to have need, 60 had their need fully met. In 2010, 111 non-need-based awards were made. *Average percent of need met:* 52%. *Average financial aid package:* $16,134. *Average need-based loan:* $4494. *Average need-based gift aid:* $10,296. *Average non-need-based aid:* $4736. *Average indebtedness upon graduation:* $36,567.

Applying *Options:* electronic application, deferred entrance. *Application fee:* $40. *Required:* essay or personal statement, high school transcript, minimum 2.5 GPA, portfolio or audition. *Required for some:* 2 letters of recommendation. *Recommended:* 2 letters of recommendation, interview. *Application deadlines:* 8/15 (freshmen), 8/15 (transfers). *Notification:* continuous (freshmen), continuous (transfers).

Freshman Application Contact Ms. Sharron Starling, Director of Admissions, Cornish College of the Arts, 1000 Lenora Street, Seattle, WA 98121. *Phone:* 206-726-5017. *Toll-free phone:* 800-726-ARTS. *Fax:* 206-720-1011. *E-mail:* admissions@cornish.edu. *Web site:* http://www.cornish.edu/.

DeVry University

Bellevue, Washington

Admissions Office Contact DeVry University, 600 108th Avenue NE, Suite 230, Bellevue, WA 98004-5110. *Toll-free phone:* 866-338-7941. *Web site:* http://www.devry.edu/.

DeVry University

Federal Way, Washington

- **Proprietary** comprehensive, founded 2001, part of DeVry University
- **Suburban** campus
- **Coed** 635 undergraduate students, 57% full-time, 32% women, 68% men
- **Minimally difficult** entrance level

Undergraduates 360 full-time, 275 part-time. 5% are from out of state; 15% Black or African American, non-Hispanic/Latino; 9% Hispanic/Latino; 6% Asian, non-Hispanic/Latino; 2% Native Hawaiian or other Pacific Islander, non-Hispanic/Latino; 2% American Indian or Alaska Native, non-Hispanic/Latino; 4% Two or more races, non-Hispanic/Latino; 2% Race/ethnicity unknown; 22% transferred in.

Freshmen *Admission:* 62 enrolled.

Faculty *Total:* 79, 23% full-time. *Student/faculty ratio:* 13:1.

Academics *Calendar:* semesters. *Degrees:* associate, bachelor's, master's, and postbachelor's certificates. *Special study options:* adult/continuing education programs, part-time degree program.

Student Life *Housing:* college housing not available.

Costs (2011–12) *Tuition:* $15,294 full-time, $597 per credit hour part-time. Full-time tuition and fees vary according to course load. Part-time tuition and fees vary according to course load. *Required fees:* $80 full-time, $40 per term part-time. *Payment plans:* installment, deferred payment. *Waivers:* employees or children of employees.

Financial Aid Of all full-time matriculated undergraduates who enrolled in 2007, 259 applied for aid, 250 were judged to have need, 8 had their need fully met. In 2007, 15 non-need-based awards were made. *Average percent of need met:* 34%. *Average financial aid package:* $10,833. *Average need-based loan:* $6622. *Average need-based gift aid:* $5975. *Average non-need-based aid:* $20,202. *Average indebtedness upon graduation:* $50,600.

Applying *Options:* electronic application. *Application fee:* $50. *Required:* high school transcript, interview. *Application deadlines:* rolling (freshmen), rolling (transfers). *Notification:* continuous (freshmen), continuous (transfers).

Freshman Application Contact DeVry University, 3600 South 344th Way, Federal Way, WA 98001. *Phone:* 253-943-2800. *Toll-free phone:* 866-338-7941. *Web site:* http://www.devry.edu/.

DigiPen Institute of Technology

Redmond, Washington

- **Proprietary** comprehensive, founded 1988
- **Suburban** 2-acre campus with easy access to Seattle
- **Coed** 853 undergraduate students, 84% full-time, 16% women, 73% men
- **Minimally difficult** entrance level, 34% of applicants were admitted

Undergraduates 717 full-time, 41 part-time. Students come from 46 states and territories; 22 other countries; 49% are from out of state; 0.6% Black or African American, non-Hispanic/Latino; 6% Hispanic/Latino; 7% Asian, non-Hispanic/Latino; 0.1% Native Hawaiian or other Pacific Islander, non-Hispanic/Latino; 0.1% American Indian or Alaska Native, non-Hispanic/Latino; 5% Two or more races, non-Hispanic/Latino; 15% Race/ethnicity unknown; 10% international. *Retention:* 65% of full-time freshmen returned.

Freshmen *Admission:* 376 applied, 129 admitted.

Faculty *Total:* 82, 57% full-time, 34% with terminal degrees. *Student/faculty ratio:* 11:1.

Academics *Calendar:* semesters. *Degrees:* bachelor's and master's. *Special study options:* academic remediation for entering students, accelerated degree program, advanced placement credit, double majors, independent study, internships, services for LD students, study abroad, summer session for credit.

Computers on Campus 1,200 computers/terminals and 500 ports are available on campus for general student use. Students can access the following: campus intranet, computer help desk, free student e-mail accounts, online (class) grades, online (class) registration, online (class) schedules. Campus-wide network is available. Wireless service is available via entire campus.

Student Life *Housing options:* coed. Campus housing is leased by the school and is provided by a third party. Freshman applicants given priority for college housing. *Activities and organizations:* Game Testing Club, Guilty Gear Club, Student Association, Audio Freaks, Game Design Club. *Campus security:* late-night transport/escort service, controlled dormitory access, on-site security during campus hours. *Student services:* personal/psychological counseling.

Standardized Tests *Required for some:* SAT or ACT (for admission).

Costs (2012–13) *One-time required fee:* $150. *Comprehensive fee:* $35,924 includes full-time tuition ($25,600), mandatory fees ($160), and room and board ($10,164). Full-time tuition and fees vary according to course load and program. Part-time tuition: $825 per credit. Part-time tuition and fees vary according to course load and program. *Required fees:* $160 per year part-time. *Room and board:* Room and board charges vary according to board plan and housing facility. *Payment plan:* installment. *Waivers:* employees or children of employees.

Financial Aid Of all full-time matriculated undergraduates who enrolled in 2010, 11 applied for aid, 10 were judged to have need. In 2010, 58 non-need-based awards were made. *Average financial aid package:* $7000. *Average need-based loan:* $3981. *Average need-based gift aid:* $3345. *Average non-need-based aid:* $2050. *Average indebtedness upon graduation:* $47,500.

Applying *Options:* electronic application, deferred entrance. *Application fee:* $35. *Required:* essay or personal statement, high school transcript, minimum 2.5 GPA. *Required for some:* art portfolio for BFA in Digital Art and Animation applicants; specific essay requirements for Game Design applicants. *Recommended:* 2 letters of recommendation. *Application deadlines:* rolling (freshmen), rolling (out-of-state freshmen), rolling (transfers). *Notification:* continuous (freshmen), continuous (out-of-state freshmen), continuous (transfers).

Freshman Application Contact Ms. Danial Powers, Admissions Application Manager, DigiPen Institute of Technology, 9931 Willows Road NE, Redmond, WA 98052. *Phone:* 425-558-0299. *Fax:* 425-558-0378. *E-mail:* admissions@digipen.edu. *Web site:* http://www.digipen.edu/.

See page 961 for display ad and page 1300 for the College Close-Up.

Eastern Washington University

Cheney, Washington

- **State-supported** comprehensive, founded 1882
- **Small-town** 335-acre campus with easy access to Spokane
- **Endowment** $17.9 million
- **Coed** 10,906 undergraduate students, 85% full-time, 55% women, 45% men
- **Moderately difficult** entrance level, 79% of applicants were admitted

Undergraduates 9,232 full-time, 1,674 part-time. Students come from 46 states and territories; 20 other countries; 6% are from out of state; 4% Black or African American, non-Hispanic/Latino; 10% Hispanic/Latino; 3% Asian, non-Hispanic/Latino; 0.3% Native Hawaiian or other Pacific Islander, non-Hispanic/Latino; 1% American Indian or Alaska Native, non-Hispanic/Latino; 3% Two or more races, non-Hispanic/Latino; 11% Race/ethnicity unknown; 2% international; 12% transferred in; 20% live on campus. *Retention:* 75% of full-time freshmen returned.

Freshmen *Admission:* 4,525 applied, 3,575 admitted, 1,519 enrolled. *Average high school GPA:* 3.25. *Test scores:* SAT critical reading scores over 500: 41%; SAT math scores over 500: 47%; SAT writing scores over 500: 36%; ACT scores over 18: 76%; SAT critical reading scores over 600: 10%; SAT math scores over 600: 11%; SAT writing scores over 600: 6%; ACT scores over 24: 22%; SAT critical reading scores over 700: 1%; SAT math scores over 700: 1%; SAT writing scores over 700: 1%; ACT scores over 30: 2%.

Faculty *Total:* 647, 64% full-time, 62% with terminal degrees. *Student/faculty ratio:* 22:1.

Academics *Calendar:* quarters. *Degrees:* certificates, bachelor's, master's, doctoral, and postbachelor's certificates. *Special study options:* academic remediation for entering students, accelerated degree program, advanced placement credit, distance learning, double majors, English as a second language, honors programs, independent study, internships, off-campus study, part-time degree program, services for LD students, student-designed majors, study abroad, summer session for credit. *ROTC:* Army (b). *Unusual degree*

programs: 3-2 Master of Occupational Therapy with undergraduate exercise science, therapeutic recreation or interdisciplinary studies.

Computers on Campus 1,012 computers/terminals and 250 ports are available on campus for general student use. Students can access the following: computer help desk, free student e-mail accounts, online (class) grades, online (class) registration, online (class) schedules, 15 gb network disk storage per student; discounted Microsoft and Adobe software; laptops, still and video cameras, projectors for checkout; print credit; black white laser, color laser, and color photo options, large format print service. Campuswide network is available. 100% of college-owned or -operated housing units are wired for high-speed Internet access. Wireless service is available via classrooms, computer centers, computer labs, dorm rooms, learning centers, libraries, student centers.

Student Life *Housing options:* coed, disabled students. Campus housing is university owned. *Activities and organizations:* drama/theater group, student-run newspaper, radio station, choral group, marching band, Panhellenic Council, Hui O'Hawaii, Interfraternity Council (IFC), Saudi club, International Students, national fraternities, national sororities. *Campus security:* 24-hour emergency response devices and patrols, student patrols, late-night transport/escort service, controlled dormitory access, emergency call boxes. *Student services:* health clinic, personal/psychological counseling, women's center.

Athletics Member NCAA. All Division I except football (Division I-AA). *Intercollegiate sports:* archery M(c)/W(c), baseball M(c), basketball M(s)/W(s), cheerleading W(c), cross-country running M(s)/W(s), equestrian sports M(c)/W(c), fencing M(c)/W(c), golf W(s), ice hockey M(c)/W(c), rugby M(c)/W(c), soccer M(c)/W(s), softball W(c), tennis M(s)/W(s), track and field M(s)/W(s), volleyball W(s). *Intramural sports:* baseball M/W, basketball M/W, bowling M/W, cross-country running M/W, football M, golf W, racquetball M/W, soccer M/W, softball M/W, tennis M/W, track and field M/W, ultimate Frisbee M(c)/W(c), volleyball M/W, wrestling M(c)/W(c).

Standardized Tests *Required:* SAT or ACT (for admission).

Costs (2011–12) *Tuition:* state resident $6063 full-time, $202 per credit part-time; nonresident $14,781 full-time, $493 per credit part-time. Full-time tuition and fees vary according to course load, program, and reciprocity agreements. Part-time tuition and fees vary according to course load, program, and reciprocity agreements. *Required fees:* $541 full-time, $541 per year part-time. *Room and board:* $7470; room only: $3960. Room and board charges vary according to board plan and housing facility. *Payment plan:* installment.

Financial Aid Of all full-time matriculated undergraduates who enrolled in 2010, 6,980 applied for aid, 5,773 were judged to have need, 1,470 had their need fully met. 176 Federal Work-Study jobs (averaging $2165). 402 state and other part-time jobs (averaging $2434). In 2010, 438 non-need-based awards were made. *Average percent of need met:* 67%. *Average financial aid package:* $12,765. *Average need-based loan:* $3992. *Average need-based gift aid:* $7311. *Average non-need-based aid:* $3331. *Average indebtedness upon graduation:* $20,395.

Applying *Options:* electronic application, deferred entrance. *Application fee:* $50. *Required:* high school transcript, minimum 2.0 GPA. *Required for some:* essay or personal statement. *Recommended:* minimum 3.0 GPA. *Application deadlines:* 5/15 (freshmen), 7/1 (transfers). *Notification:* continuous (freshmen), continuous (transfers).

Freshman Application Contact Ms. Shannon Carr, Director of Admissions, Eastern Washington University, Eastern Washington University, 101 Sutton Hall, Cheney, WA 99004-2447. *Phone:* 509-359-6582. *Fax:* 509-359-6692. *E-mail:* admissions@mail.ewu.edu. *Web site:* http://www.ewu.edu/.

The Evergreen State College

Olympia, Washington

- **State-supported** comprehensive, founded 1967, part of Washington State Public Baccalaureate Institution
- **Rural** 1000-acre campus with easy access to Seattle
- **Endowment** $6.6 million
- **Coed** 4,467 undergraduate students, 92% full-time, 54% women, 46% men
- **Moderately difficult** entrance level, 96% of applicants were admitted

Undergraduates 4,090 full-time, 377 part-time. Students come from 51 states and territories; 21 other countries; 26% are from out of state; 5% Black or African American, non-Hispanic/Latino; 6% Hispanic/Latino; 2% Asian, non-Hispanic/Latino; 0.3% Native Hawaiian or other Pacific Islander, non-Hispanic/Latino; 2% American Indian or Alaska Native, non-Hispanic/Latino; 5% Two or more races, non-Hispanic/Latino; 10% Race/ethnicity unknown; 0.6% international; 21% transferred in; 20% live on campus. *Retention:* 71% of full-time freshmen returned.

Freshmen *Admission:* 1,725 applied, 1,651 admitted, 542 enrolled. *Average high school GPA:* 3.08. *Test scores:* SAT critical reading scores over 500: 80%; SAT math scores over 500: 63%; SAT writing scores over 500: 66%; ACT scores over 18: 92%; SAT critical reading scores over 600: 43%; SAT

math scores over 600: 23%; SAT writing scores over 600: 28%; ACT scores over 24: 50%; SAT critical reading scores over 700: 8%; SAT math scores over 700: 2%; SAT writing scores over 700: 4%; ACT scores over 30: 10%.

Faculty *Total:* 247, 71% full-time, 75% with terminal degrees. *Student/faculty ratio:* 23:1.

Academics *Calendar:* quarters. *Degrees:* bachelor's and master's. *Special study options:* accelerated degree program, advanced placement credit, double majors, independent study, internships, off-campus study, part-time degree program, services for LD students, student-designed majors, study abroad, summer session for credit.

Computers on Campus 470 computers/terminals are available on campus for general student use. Students can access the following: campus intranet, computer help desk, free student e-mail accounts, online (class) grades, online (class) registration, online (class) schedules, Online payment, student accounts history, financial aid records, academic history, housing application. Campuswide network is available. 100% of college-owned or -operated housing units are wired for high-speed Internet access. Wireless service is available via entire campus.

Student Life *Housing options:* coed, disabled students. Campus housing is university owned. Freshman campus housing is guaranteed. *Activities and organizations:* drama/theater group, student-run newspaper, radio and television station, choral group, Bike Shop, Women's Resource Center, Evergreen Queer Alliance, Evergreen Dance Co-op, Common Bread. *Campus security:* 24-hour emergency response devices and patrols, student patrols, late-night transport/escort service, controlled dormitory access. *Student services:* health clinic, personal/psychological counseling, women's center.

Athletics Member NAIA. *Intercollegiate sports:* basketball M(s)/W(s), crew M(c)/W(c), cross-country running M(s)/W(s), rugby M(c)/W(c), soccer M(s)/W(s), track and field M(s)/W(s), volleyball W(s). *Intramural sports:* basketball M/W, bowling M(c)/W(c), fencing M(c)/W(c), soccer M(c)/W(c), ultimate Frisbee M(c)/W(c), volleyball M(c)/W(c), wrestling M(c)/W(c).

Standardized Tests *Required:* SAT or ACT (for admission).

Costs (2011–12) *Tuition:* state resident $6909 full-time, $230 per credit hour part-time; nonresident $18,090 full-time, $603 per credit hour part-time. Full-time tuition and fees vary according to course load and location. Part-time tuition and fees vary according to course load and location. *Required fees:* $577 full-time, $8 per credit hour part-time, $71 per term part-time. *Room and board:* $9000; room only: $5994. Room and board charges vary according to board plan, housing facility, location, and student level. *Waivers:* senior citizens and employees or children of employees.

Financial Aid Of all full-time matriculated undergraduates who enrolled in 2010, 2,936 applied for aid, 2,589 were judged to have need, 444 had their need fully met. 125 Federal Work-Study jobs (averaging $3357). 263 state and other part-time jobs (averaging $3300). In 2010, 302 non-need-based awards were made. *Average percent of need met:* 67%. *Average financial aid package:* $11,459. *Average need-based loan:* $4298. *Average need-based gift aid:* $8596. *Average non-need-based aid:* $2460. *Average indebtedness upon graduation:* $16,700.

Applying *Options:* electronic application, deferred entrance. *Application fee:* $50. *Required:* high school transcript, minimum 2.0 GPA. *Required for some:* essay or personal statement. *Recommended:* essay or personal statement. *Application deadlines:* 3/1 (freshmen), 3/1 (transfers). *Notification:* continuous until 11/1 (freshmen), continuous until 11/1 (transfers).

Freshman Application Contact The Evergreen State College, 2700 Evergreen Parkway, NW, Olympia, WA 98505. *Phone:* 360-867-6170. *Web site:* http://www.evergreen.edu/.

Gonzaga University

Spokane, Washington

- **Independent Roman Catholic** comprehensive, founded 1887
- **Urban** 130-acre campus
- **Endowment** $144.8 million
- **Coed** 4,865 undergraduate students, 98% full-time, 54% women, 46% men
- **Moderately difficult** entrance level, 62% of applicants were admitted

Undergraduates 4,765 full-time, 100 part-time. Students come from 46 states and territories; 19 other countries; 49% are from out of state; 1% Black or African American, non-Hispanic/Latino; 7% Hispanic/Latino; 4% Asian, non-Hispanic/Latino; 0.6% Native Hawaiian or other Pacific Islander, non-Hispanic/Latino; 0.6% American Indian or Alaska Native, non-Hispanic/Latino; 3% Two or more races, non-Hispanic/Latino; 8% Race/ethnicity unknown; 2% international; 3% transferred in; 58% live on campus. *Retention:* 91% of full-time freshmen returned.

Freshmen *Admission:* 6,851 applied, 4,217 admitted, 1,131 enrolled. *Average high school GPA:* 3.74. *Test scores:* SAT critical reading scores over 500: 95%; SAT math scores over 500: 97%; ACT scores over 18: 100%; SAT critical reading scores over 600: 49%; SAT math scores over 600: 57%; ACT scores over 24: 85%; SAT critical reading scores over 700: 9%; SAT math scores over 700: 7%; ACT scores over 30: 23%.

Faculty *Total:* 720, 56% full-time, 50% with terminal degrees. *Student/faculty ratio:* 11:1.

Academics *Calendar:* semesters. *Degrees:* bachelor's, master's, doctoral, post-master's, postbachelor's, and first professional certificates. *Special study options:* accelerated degree program, adult/continuing education programs, advanced placement credit, double majors, English as a second language, honors programs, independent study, internships, off-campus study, part-time degree program, services for LD students, study abroad, summer session for credit. *ROTC:* Army (b). *Unusual degree programs:* 3-2 nursing.

Computers on Campus 300 computers/terminals and 900 ports are available on campus for general student use. Students can access the following: computer help desk, free student e-mail accounts, online (class) grades, online (class) registration, online (class) schedules. Campuswide network is available. 100% of college-owned or -operated housing units are wired for high-speed Internet access. Wireless service is available via classrooms, computer centers, computer labs, dorm rooms, libraries, student centers.

Student Life *Housing:* on-campus residence required through sophomore year. *Options:* coed, men-only, women-only, disabled students. Campus housing is university owned and leased by the school. Freshman campus housing is guaranteed. *Activities and organizations:* drama/theater group, student-run newspaper, radio and television station, choral group, Student Body Association, Search, Circle K, Encore, Knights and Setons. *Campus security:* 24-hour emergency response devices and patrols, late-night transport/escort service, controlled dormitory access. *Student services:* health clinic, personal/psychological counseling.

Athletics Member NCAA. All Division I. *Intercollegiate sports:* baseball M(s), basketball M(s)/W(s), crew M/W(s), cross-country running M(s)/W(s), golf M/W, ice hockey M(c), lacrosse M(c)/W(c), rugby M(c)/W(c), skiing (downhill) M(c)/W(c), soccer M(s)/W(s), tennis M(s)/W(s), track and field M(s)/W(s), ultimate Frisbee M(c)/W(c), volleyball M(c)/W(s). *Intramural sports:* badminton M/W, basketball M/W, football M/W, racquetball M/W, soccer M(c)/W(c), softball M/W, swimming and diving M(c)/W(c), ultimate Frisbee M/W, volleyball M/W.

Standardized Tests *Required:* SAT or ACT (for admission).

Costs (2011–12) *Comprehensive fee:* $40,562 includes full-time tuition ($31,730), mandatory fees ($492), and room and board ($8340). Full-time tuition and fees vary according to course load, location, program, reciprocity agreements, and student level. Part-time tuition: $885 per credit hour. Part-time tuition and fees vary according to course load, location, program, reciprocity agreements, and student level. *College room only:* $4360. Room and board charges vary according to board plan and housing facility. *Payment plans:* installment, deferred payment. *Waivers:* employees or children of employees.

Financial Aid Of all full-time matriculated undergraduates who enrolled in 2011, 3,488 applied for aid, 2,740 were judged to have need, 684 had their need fully met. 411 Federal Work-Study jobs (averaging $1.2 million). 476 state and other part-time jobs (averaging $3807). In 2011, 1747 non-need-based awards were made. *Average percent of need met:* 79%. *Average financial aid package:* $23,564. *Average need-based loan:* $5313. *Average need-based gift aid:* $17,704. *Average non-need-based aid:* $11,412. *Average indebtedness upon graduation:* $23,522.

Applying *Options:* electronic application, early action, deferred entrance. *Application fee:* $50. *Required:* essay or personal statement, high school transcript, minimum 3.0 GPA, 1 letter of recommendation. *Recommended:* interview. *Application deadlines:* 2/1 (freshmen), 6/1 (transfers), 11/15 (early action). *Notification:* 3/15 (freshmen), continuous (transfers), 1/15 (early action).

Freshman Application Contact Ms. Julie McCulloh, Dean of Admission, Gonzaga University, 502 East Boone Avenue, Spokane, WA 99258-0102. *Phone:* 800-322-2584. *Toll-free phone:* 800-322-2584 Ext. 6572. *Fax:* 509-313-6572. *E-mail:* admissions@gonzaga.edu. *Web site:* http://www.gonzaga.edu/.

Heritage University

Toppenish, Washington

Freshman Application Contact Miguel Puente, Director of Admissions and Recruitment, Heritage University, 3240 Fort Road, Toppenish, WA 98948-9599. *Phone:* 509-865-8508. *Toll-free phone:* 888-272-6190. *Fax:* 509-865-4469. *E-mail:* admissions@heritage.edu. *Web site:* http://www.heritage.edu/.

ITT Technical Institute

Everett, Washington

- **Proprietary** primarily 2-year, part of ITT Educational Services, Inc.
- **Coed**
- **Minimally difficult** entrance level

Academics *Degrees:* associate and bachelor's.

Freshman Application Contact Director of Recruitment, ITT Technical Institute, 1615 75th Street SW, Everett, WA 98203. *Phone:* 425-583-0200. *Toll-free phone:* 800-272-3791. *Web site:* http://www.itt-tech.edu/.

ITT Technical Institute

Seattle, Washington

- **Proprietary** primarily 2-year, founded 1932, part of ITT Educational Services, Inc.
- **Urban** campus
- **Coed**
- **Minimally difficult** entrance level

Academics *Calendar:* quarters. *Degrees:* associate and bachelor's.

Student Life *Housing:* college housing not available.

Freshman Application Contact Director of Recruitment, ITT Technical Institute, 12720 Gateway Drive, Suite 100, Seattle, WA 98168-3333. *Phone:* 206-244-3300. *Toll-free phone:* 800-422-2029. *Web site:* http://www.itt-tech.edu/.

ITT Technical Institute

Spokane Valley, Washington

- **Proprietary** primarily 2-year, founded 1985, part of ITT Educational Services, Inc.
- **Suburban** campus
- **Coed**
- **Minimally difficult** entrance level

Academics *Calendar:* quarters. *Degrees:* associate and bachelor's.

Student Life *Housing:* college housing not available.

Freshman Application Contact Director of Recruitment, ITT Technical Institute, 13518 East Indiana Avenue, Spokane Valley, WA 99216. *Phone:* 509-926-2900. *Toll-free phone:* 800-777-8324. *Web site:* http://www.itt-tech.edu/.

Northwest College of Art & Design

Poulsbo, Washington

Freshman Application Contact Mr. Mark Stoddard, Admissions, Northwest College of Art & Design, 16301 Creative Drive, NE, Poulsbo, WA 98370. *Phone:* 360-779-9993. *Toll-free phone:* 800-769-ARTS. *E-mail:* mstoddard@nca.edu. *Web site:* http://www.ncad.edu/.

Northwest Indian College

Bellingham, Washington

Freshman Application Contact Office of Admissions, Northwest Indian College, 2522 Kwina Road, Bellingham, WA 98226. *Phone:* 360-676-2772. *Toll-free phone:* 866-676-2772. *Fax:* 360-392-4333. *E-mail:* admissions@nwic.edu. *Web site:* http://www.nwic.edu/.

Northwest University

Kirkland, Washington

- **Independent** comprehensive, founded 1934, affiliated with Assemblies of God
- **Suburban** 56-acre campus with easy access to Seattle
- **Endowment** $9.3 million
- **Coed** 1,294 undergraduate students, 85% full-time, 59% women, 41% men
- **Moderately difficult** entrance level, 62% of applicants were admitted

Undergraduates 1,098 full-time, 196 part-time. Students come from 24 states and territories; 15 other countries; 8% are from out of state; 6% Black or African American, non-Hispanic/Latino; 8% Hispanic/Latino; 5% Asian, non-Hispanic/Latino; 0.9% American Indian or Alaska Native, non-Hispanic/Latino; 3% Two or more races, non-Hispanic/Latino; 7% Race/ethnicity unknown; 2% international; 14% transferred in; 55% live on campus. *Retention:* 69% of full-time freshmen returned.

Freshmen *Admission:* 704 applied, 434 admitted, 184 enrolled. *Average high school GPA:* 3.34. *Test scores:* SAT critical reading scores over 500: 63%; SAT math scores over 500: 48%; SAT writing scores over 500: 52%; ACT scores over 18: 74%; SAT critical reading scores over 600: 20%; SAT math scores over 600: 14%; SAT writing scores over 600: 19%; ACT scores over 24: 29%; SAT critical reading scores over 700: 3%; SAT writing scores over 700: 2%.

Faculty *Total:* 108, 50% full-time, 36% with terminal degrees. *Student/faculty ratio:* 17:1.

Academics *Calendar:* semesters. *Degrees:* certificates, diplomas, associate, bachelor's, master's, and doctoral. *Special study options:* academic remediation for entering students, accelerated degree program, adult/continuing education programs, advanced placement credit, cooperative education, double majors, English as a second language, independent study, internships, part-time degree program, study abroad, summer session for credit. *ROTC:* Army (c), Air Force (c).

Computers on Campus 134 computers/terminals are available on campus for general student use. Students can access the following: campus intranet, computer help desk, free student e-mail accounts, online (class) grades, online (class) registration, online (class) schedules, online classes. Campuswide network is available. 100% of college-owned or -operated housing units are wired for high-speed Internet access. Wireless service is available via entire campus.

Student Life *Housing:* on-campus residence required through sophomore year. *Options:* men-only, women-only. Campus housing is university owned. Freshman campus housing is guaranteed. *Activities and organizations:* drama/theater group, student-run newspaper, radio station, choral group, Student Ministries, Pursuit (worship service), Northwest University Business Club, Environmental Stewardship Club. *Campus security:* 24-hour emergency response devices and patrols, late-night transport/escort service, controlled dormitory access. *Student services:* health clinic, personal/psychological counseling.

Athletics Member NAIA. *Intercollegiate sports:* basketball M(s)/W(s), cross-country running M(s)/W(s), soccer M(s)/W(s), track and field M(s)/W(s), volleyball W(s).

Standardized Tests *Required:* SAT or ACT (for admission).

Costs (2011–12) *Comprehensive fee:* $30,354 includes full-time tuition ($23,030), mandatory fees ($440), and room and board ($6884). Full-time tuition and fees vary according to class time, location, and program. Part-time tuition: $960 per credit hour. Part-time tuition and fees vary according to course load and location. *Room and board:* Room and board charges vary according to board plan, housing facility, and location. *Payment plan:* installment. *Waivers:* employees or children of employees.

Financial Aid Of all full-time matriculated undergraduates who enrolled in 2011, 1,066 applied for aid, 949 were judged to have need, 151 had their need fully met. 81 Federal Work-Study jobs (averaging $2885). 13 state and other part-time jobs (averaging $3684). In 2011, 164 non-need-based awards were made. *Average percent of need met:* 68%. *Average financial aid package:* $16,673. *Average need-based loan:* $4117. *Average need-based gift aid:* $12,548. *Average non-need-based aid:* $8226. *Average indebtedness upon graduation:* $33,453. *Financial aid deadline:* 8/1.

Applying *Options:* electronic application, early action, deferred entrance. *Application fee:* $30. *Required:* essay or personal statement, high school transcript, minimum 2.3 GPA, 2 letters of recommendation. *Required for some:* interview. *Application deadlines:* 8/1 (freshmen), 8/1 (transfers), 1/15 (early action). *Notification:* continuous (freshmen), continuous (transfers), 2/15 (early action).

Freshman Application Contact Mrs. Jessica Velasco, Director of Admissions, Northwest University, PO Box 579, Kirkland, WA 98083-0579. *Phone:* 425-889-5212. *Toll-free phone:* 800-669-3781. *Fax:* 425-889-5224. *E-mail:* admissions@northwestu.edu. *Web site:* http://www.northwestu.edu/.

Olympic College

Bremerton, Washington

- **State-supported** primarily 2-year, founded 1946, part of Washington State Board for Community and Technical Colleges
- **Suburban** 33-acre campus with easy access to Seattle (30 miles by ferry)
- **Coed** 8,503 undergraduate students
- **Noncompetitive** entrance level, 100% of applicants were admitted

Undergraduates 4% Black or African American, non-Hispanic/Latino; 6% Hispanic/Latino; 8% Asian, non-Hispanic/Latino; 2% American Indian or Alaska Native, non-Hispanic/Latino; 0.8% international.

Freshmen *Admission:* 3,145 applied, 3,145 admitted.

Faculty *Total:* 509, 24% full-time.

Academics *Calendar:* quarters. *Degrees:* certificates, diplomas, associate, and bachelor's. *Special study options:* academic remediation for entering students, adult/continuing education programs, advanced placement credit, cooperative education, distance learning, English as a second language, honors programs, independent study, internships, off-campus study, part-time degree program, services for LD students, summer session for credit.

Computers on Campus Students can access the following: campus intranet, computer help desk, free student e-mail accounts, online (class) grades, online (class) registration, online (class) schedules. Campuswide network is available. Wireless service is available via entire campus.

Student Life *Housing:* college housing not available. *Activities and organizations:* drama/theater group, student-run newspaper, choral group, Phi Theta Kappa, International Student Club, Oceans (Nursing), ASOC, ADN. *Campus security:* 24-hour emergency response devices and patrols, student patrols, late-night transport/escort service. *Student services:* personal/psychological counseling.

Athletics *Intercollegiate sports:* baseball M(s), basketball M(s)/W(s), cross-country running M/W, golf M/W, soccer M(s)/W(s), softball W(s), volleyball W(s). *Intramural sports:* basketball M/W, table tennis M/W, volleyball M/W, weight lifting M/W.

Costs (2011–12) *Tuition:* state resident $3542 full-time, $96 per quarter hour part-time; nonresident $4007 full-time, $109 per quarter hour part-time. *Required fees:* $215 full-time, $4 per credit hour part-time, $48 per term part-time.

Financial Aid Of all full-time matriculated undergraduates who enrolled in 2010, 105 Federal Work-Study jobs (averaging $2380). 31 state and other part-time jobs (averaging $2880).

Applying *Options:* electronic application. *Required for some:* high school transcript. *Application deadlines:* rolling (freshmen), rolling (out-of-state freshmen), rolling (transfers).

Freshman Application Contact Ms. Jennifer Fyllingness, Director of Admissions and Outreach, Olympic College, 1600 Chester Avenue, Bremerton, WA 98337-1699. *Phone:* 360-475-7128. *Toll-free phone:* 800-259-6718. *Fax:* 360-475-7202. *E-mail:* jfyllingness@olympic.edu. *Web site:* http://www.olympic.edu/.

Pacific Lutheran University

Tacoma, Washington

- **Independent** comprehensive, founded 1890, affiliated with Evangelical Lutheran Church in America
- **Suburban** 156-acre campus with easy access to Seattle
- **Endowment** $74.7 million
- **Coed** 3,195 undergraduate students, 95% full-time, 62% women, 38% men
- **Moderately difficult** entrance level, 77% of applicants were admitted

Undergraduates 3,049 full-time, 146 part-time. Students come from 44 states and territories; 24 other countries; 23% are from out of state; 3% Black or African American, non-Hispanic/Latino; 6% Hispanic/Latino; 6% Asian, non-Hispanic/Latino; 0.6% Native Hawaiian or other Pacific Islander, non-Hispanic/Latino; 0.8% American Indian or Alaska Native, non-Hispanic/Latino; 6% Two or more races, non-Hispanic/Latino; 1% Race/ethnicity unknown; 4% international; 7% transferred in; 49% live on campus. *Retention:* 82% of full-time freshmen returned.

Freshmen *Admission:* 3,289 applied, 2,520 admitted, 731 enrolled. *Average high school GPA:* 3.62. *Test scores:* SAT critical reading scores over 500: 73%; SAT math scores over 500: 74%; SAT writing scores over 500: 67%; ACT scores over 18: 96%; SAT critical reading scores over 600: 34%; SAT math scores over 600: 30%; SAT writing scores over 600: 26%; ACT scores over 24: 59%; SAT critical reading scores over 700: 5%; SAT math scores over 700: 4%; SAT writing scores over 700: 3%; ACT scores over 30: 11%.

Faculty *Total:* 251, 82% full-time, 78% with terminal degrees. *Student/faculty ratio:* 15:1.

Academics *Calendar:* 4-1-4. *Degrees:* bachelor's, master's, and postbachelor's certificates. *Special study options:* advanced placement credit, cooperative education, double majors, English as a second language, honors programs, independent study, internships, part-time degree program, services for LD students, student-designed majors, study abroad, summer session for credit. *ROTC:* Army (b). *Unusual degree programs:* 3-2 engineering with Columbia University in New York and Washington University in Missouri.

Computers on Campus 435 computers/terminals and 1,200 ports are available on campus for general student use. Students can access the following: campus intranet, computer help desk, free student e-mail accounts, online (class) grades, online (class) registration, online (class) schedules. Campuswide network is available. 100% of college-owned or -operated housing units are wired for high-speed Internet access. Wireless service is available via entire campus.

Student Life *Housing:* on-campus residence required through sophomore year. *Options:* coed, women-only. Campus housing is university owned. Freshman campus housing is guaranteed. *Activities and organizations:* drama/theater

group, student-run newspaper, radio and television station, choral group, Ignite, Circle K, Adult Students Club, Residence Hall Government, Inter-Varsity Fellowship. *Campus security:* 24-hour emergency response devices and patrols, student patrols, late-night transport/escort service, controlled dormitory access. *Student services:* health clinic, personal/psychological counseling, women's center.

Athletics Member NCAA. All Division III. *Intercollegiate sports:* baseball M, basketball M/W, crew M/W, cross-country running M/W, football M, golf M/W, lacrosse M(c)/W(c), soccer M/W, softball W, swimming and diving M/W, tennis M/W, track and field M/W, ultimate Frisbee M(c)/W(c), volleyball M(c)/W. *Intramural sports:* basketball M/W, football M/W, soccer M/W, softball M/W, volleyball M/W.

Standardized Tests *Required:* SAT or ACT (for admission).

Costs (2012–13) *Comprehensive fee:* $42,420 includes full-time tuition ($32,800) and room and board ($9620). Full-time tuition and fees vary according to course load. Part-time tuition: $1030 per semester hour. Part-time tuition and fees vary according to course load. *College room only:* $4640. Room and board charges vary according to board plan and housing facility. *Payment plan:* installment. *Waivers:* children of alumni and employees or children of employees.

Financial Aid Of all full-time matriculated undergraduates who enrolled in 2011, 2,576 applied for aid, 2,278 were judged to have need, 515 had their need fully met. 652 Federal Work-Study jobs (averaging $2874). 982 state and other part-time jobs (averaging $3015). In 2011, 670 non-need-based awards were made. *Average percent of need met:* 86%. *Average financial aid package:* $29,814. *Average need-based loan:* $8856. *Average need-based gift aid:* $17,506. *Average non-need-based aid:* $13,580. *Average indebtedness upon graduation:* $29,774.

Applying *Options:* electronic application, early admission, deferred entrance. *Application fee:* $40. *Required:* essay or personal statement, high school transcript, 1 letter of recommendation. *Required for some:* interview. *Recommended:* minimum 2.5 GPA. *Application deadlines:* rolling (freshmen), rolling (transfers). *Notification:* continuous (freshmen), continuous (transfers).

Freshman Application Contact Jennifer Olsen Krengel, Director of Admission, Pacific Lutheran University, Tacoma, WA 98447. *Phone:* 253-535-7151. *Toll-free phone:* 800-274-6758. *Fax:* 253-536-5136. *E-mail:* admission@plu.edu. *Web site:* http://www.plu.edu/.

Peninsula College

Port Angeles, Washington

- **State-supported** primarily 2-year, founded 1961, part of Washington State Community and Technical Colleges
- **Small-town** 75-acre campus
- **Coed** 3,321 undergraduate students, 51% full-time, 55% women, 45% men
- **Noncompetitive** entrance level

Undergraduates 1,705 full-time, 1,616 part-time.

Faculty *Total:* 156, 37% full-time. *Student/faculty ratio:* 21:1.

Academics *Calendar:* quarters. *Degrees:* certificates, associate, and bachelor's. *Special study options:* academic remediation for entering students, adult/continuing education programs, advanced placement credit, distance learning, English as a second language, honors programs, internships, part-time degree program, services for LD students, summer session for credit.

Computers on Campus Students can access the following: online (class) grades, online (class) registration, online (class) schedules. Campuswide network is available. Wireless service is available via entire campus.

Student Life *Housing:* college housing not available. *Activities and organizations:* student-run newspaper. *Campus security:* 8-hour patrols by trained security personnel. *Student services:* women's center.

Athletics *Intercollegiate sports:* basketball M/W, soccer M/W. *Intramural sports:* badminton M/W, basketball M/W, bowling M/W, football M, golf M, skiing (cross-country) M/W, soccer M/W, softball M/W, table tennis M/W, tennis M/W, volleyball M/W.

Financial Aid Of all full-time matriculated undergraduates who enrolled in 2010, 30 Federal Work-Study jobs (averaging $3600). 25 state and other part-time jobs (averaging $3600).

Applying *Required for some:* high school transcript. *Application deadlines:* rolling (freshmen), rolling (transfers). *Notification:* continuous (freshmen), continuous (transfers).

Freshman Application Contact Ms. Pauline Marvin, Peninsula College, 1502 East Lauridsen Boulevard, Port Angeles, WA 98362. *Phone:* 360-417-6596. *Toll-free phone:* 877-452-9277. *Fax:* 360-457-8100. *E-mail:* admissions@pencol.edu. *Web site:* http://www.pc.ctc.edu/.

Pima Medical Institute

Seattle, Washington

- **Proprietary** primarily 2-year, founded 1989, part of Vocational Training Institutes, Inc.
- **Urban** campus
- **Coed**
- **Minimally difficult** entrance level

Academics *Calendar:* modular. *Degrees:* certificates, associate, and bachelor's.

Standardized Tests *Required:* Wonderlic aptitude test (for admission).

Applying *Required:* interview. *Required for some:* high school transcript.

Freshman Application Contact Admissions Office, Pima Medical Institute, 9709 Third Avenue NE, Suite 400, Seattle, WA 98115. *Phone:* 206-322-6100. *Toll-free phone:* 800-477-PIMA (in-state); 888-477-PIMA (out-of-state). *Web site:* http://www.pmi.edu/.

Saint Martin's University

Lacey, Washington

- **Independent Roman Catholic** comprehensive, founded 1895
- **Suburban** 380-acre campus with easy access to Seattle
- **Endowment** $17.3 million
- **Coed** 1,426 undergraduate students, 80% full-time, 51% women, 49% men
- **Moderately difficult** entrance level, 75% of applicants were admitted

Undergraduates 1,137 full-time, 289 part-time. Students come from 29 states and territories; 7 other countries; 21% are from out of state; 8% Black or African American, non-Hispanic/Latino; 10% Hispanic/Latino; 5% Asian, non-Hispanic/Latino; 3% Native Hawaiian or other Pacific Islander, non-Hispanic/Latino; 0.8% American Indian or Alaska Native, non-Hispanic/Latino; 6% Two or more races, non-Hispanic/Latino; 14% Race/ethnicity unknown; 5% international; 16% transferred in; 33% live on campus. *Retention:* 73% of full-time freshmen returned.

Freshmen *Admission:* 728 applied, 543 admitted, 234 enrolled. *Average high school GPA:* 3.25. *Test scores:* SAT critical reading scores over 500: 53%; SAT math scores over 500: 52%; SAT writing scores over 500: 46%; ACT scores over 18: 82%; SAT critical reading scores over 600: 13%; SAT math scores over 600: 15%; SAT writing scores over 600: 8%; ACT scores over 24: 31%; SAT critical reading scores over 700: 1%; SAT math scores over 700: 1%; ACT scores over 30: 4%.

Faculty *Total:* 202, 38% full-time, 45% with terminal degrees. *Student/faculty ratio:* 13:1.

Academics *Calendar:* semesters. *Degrees:* bachelor's, master's, post-master's, and postbachelor's certificates. *Special study options:* academic remediation for entering students, accelerated degree program, adult/continuing education programs, advanced placement credit, cooperative education, distance learning, double majors, English as a second language, independent study, internships, off-campus study, part-time degree program, services for LD students, study abroad, summer session for credit. *ROTC:* Army (c), Air Force (c).

Computers on Campus 80 computers/terminals and 130 ports are available on campus for general student use. Students can access the following: campus intranet, computer help desk, free student e-mail accounts, online (class) grades, online (class) registration, online (class) schedules. Campuswide network is available. 100% of college-owned or -operated housing units are wired for high-speed Internet access. Wireless service is available via entire campus.

Student Life *Housing:* on-campus residence required through sophomore year. *Options:* coed. Campus housing is university owned. Freshman campus housing is guaranteed. *Activities and organizations:* drama/theater group, student-run newspaper, choral group, International Club, Minorities in Action, Hui O Hawaii, American Society of Civil Engineers, Chemistry. *Campus security:* 24-hour emergency response devices and patrols, late-night transport/escort service, controlled dormitory access. *Student services:* health clinic, personal/psychological counseling.

Athletics Member NCAA. All Division II. *Intercollegiate sports:* baseball M(s), basketball M(s)/W(s), cross-country running M(s)/W(s), golf M(s)/W(s), soccer M/W(s), softball W(s), track and field M(s)/W(s), volleyball W(s). *Intramural sports:* basketball M/W, bowling M/W, golf M/W, soccer M/W, softball M/W, table tennis M/W, tennis M/W, ultimate Frisbee M/W, volleyball M/W.

Standardized Tests *Required:* SAT or ACT (for admission).

Costs (2011–12) *Comprehensive fee:* $36,080 includes full-time tuition ($27,300), mandatory fees ($322), and room and board ($8458). Full-time tuition and fees vary according to degree level and location. Part-time tuition: $910 per credit hour. Part-time tuition and fees vary according to course load, degree level, and location. *College room only:* $4460. Room and board

charges vary according to board plan. *Payment plan:* installment. *Waivers:* children of alumni and employees or children of employees.

Financial Aid Of all full-time matriculated undergraduates who enrolled in 2010, 1,038 applied for aid, 950 were judged to have need, 195 had their need fully met. 275 Federal Work-Study jobs (averaging $1900). 123 state and other part-time jobs (averaging $4175). In 2010, 96 non-need-based awards were made. *Average percent of need met:* 74%. *Average financial aid package:* $19,366. *Average need-based loan:* $4233. *Average need-based gift aid:* $15,209. *Average non-need-based aid:* $9070. *Average indebtedness upon graduation:* $28,439.

Applying *Options:* electronic application. *Application fee:* $35. *Required:* essay or personal statement, high school transcript, minimum 2.5 GPA, 1 letter of recommendation. *Required for some:* interview. *Application deadline:* 8/1 (transfers). *Notification:* 8/15 (freshmen), continuous until 8/15 (transfers).

Freshman Application Contact Scott Andrew Schultz, Director of Admissions, Saint Martin's University, 5000 Abbey Way SE, Lacey, WA 98503-7500. *Phone:* 360-438-4596. *Toll-free phone:* 800-368-8803. *Fax:* 360-412-6189. *E-mail:* admissions@stmartin.edu. *Web site:* http://www.stmartin.edu/.

Seattle Pacific University

Seattle, Washington

- **Independent Free Methodist** comprehensive, founded 1891
- **Urban** 35-acre campus
- **Coed** 3,194 undergraduate students, 97% full-time, 67% women, 33% men
- **Moderately difficult** entrance level, 18% of applicants were admitted

Undergraduates 3,083 full-time, 111 part-time. Students come from 43 states and territories; 40 other countries; 39% are from out of state; 4% Black or African American, non-Hispanic/Latino; 7% Hispanic/Latino; 9% Asian, non-Hispanic/Latino; 0.1% Native Hawaiian or other Pacific Islander, non-Hispanic/Latino; 0.4% American Indian or Alaska Native, non-Hispanic/Latino; 7% Two or more races, non-Hispanic/Latino; 3% Race/ethnicity unknown; 1% international; 7% transferred in; 54% live on campus. *Retention:* 85% of full-time freshmen returned.

Freshmen *Admission:* 4,211 applied, 760 admitted, 760 enrolled. *Average high school GPA:* 3.6. *Test scores:* SAT critical reading scores over 500: 85%; SAT math scores over 500: 83%; SAT writing scores over 500: 81%; ACT scores over 18: 99%; SAT critical reading scores over 600: 40%; SAT math scores over 600: 38%; SAT writing scores over 600: 35%; ACT scores over 24: 65%; SAT critical reading scores over 700: 9%; SAT math scores over 700: 5%; SAT writing scores over 700: 5%; ACT scores over 30: 14%.

Faculty *Total:* 363, 56% full-time, 53% with terminal degrees. *Student/faculty ratio:* 14:1.

Academics *Calendar:* quarters. *Degrees:* bachelor's, master's, doctoral, post-master's, and first professional certificates. *Special study options:* academic remediation for entering students, adult/continuing education programs, advanced placement credit, distance learning, double majors, external degree program, honors programs, independent study, internships, off-campus study, part-time degree program, services for LD students, student-designed majors, study abroad, summer session for credit. *ROTC:* Army (c), Navy (c), Air Force (c).

Computers on Campus 150 computers/terminals are available on campus for general student use. Students can access the following: campus intranet, computer help desk, free student e-mail accounts, online (class) grades, online (class) registration, online (class) schedules. Campuswide network is available. Wireless service is available via entire campus.

Student Life *Housing:* on-campus residence required through sophomore year. *Options:* coed, disabled students. Campus housing is university owned. Freshman campus housing is guaranteed. *Activities and organizations:* drama/theater group, student-run newspaper, radio station, choral group, Centurions, Falconettes, forensics organization, Amnesty International, University Players. *Campus security:* 24-hour emergency response devices and patrols, student patrols, late-night transport/escort service, closed-circuit TV monitors. *Student services:* health clinic, personal/psychological counseling.

Athletics Member NCAA. All Division II. *Intercollegiate sports:* basketball M(s)/W(s), crew M/W(s), cross-country running M(s)/W(s), gymnastics W(s), soccer M(s)/W(s), track and field M(s)/W(s), volleyball W(s). *Intramural sports:* archery M/W, basketball M/W, bowling M/W, cross-country running M/W, football M/W, soccer M/W(c), softball M/W, tennis M/W, volleyball M(c)/W(c), weight lifting M/W.

Standardized Tests *Required:* SAT or ACT (for admission).

Costs (2012–13) *Comprehensive fee:* $41,559 includes full-time tuition ($31,701), mandatory fees ($366), and room and board ($9492). Part-time tuition and fees vary according to course load. *College room only:* $5190. Room and board charges vary according to board plan and housing facility.

Payment plans: installment, deferred payment. *Waivers:* senior citizens and employees or children of employees.

Financial Aid Of all full-time matriculated undergraduates who enrolled in 2011, 2,509 applied for aid, 2,178 were judged to have need, 141 had their need fully met. 378 Federal Work-Study jobs (averaging $1431). 181 state and other part-time jobs (averaging $1869). In 2011, 644 non-need-based awards were made. *Average percent of need met:* 78%. *Average financial aid package:* $26,221. *Average need-based loan:* $5103. *Average need-based gift aid:* $21,866. *Average non-need-based aid:* $15,559. *Average indebtedness upon graduation:* $26,829.

Applying *Options:* electronic application, early admission, early action. *Application fee:* $50. *Required:* essay or personal statement, high school transcript, minimum 2.5 GPA, 2 letters of recommendation. *Recommended:* interview. *Application deadlines:* 2/1 (freshmen), 8/1 (transfers), 11/15 (early action). *Notification:* 3/1 (freshmen), continuous (transfers), 1/5 (early action). **Freshman Application Contact** Mr. Jobe Korb-Nice, Director of Admissions, Seattle Pacific University, 3307 3rd Avenue, West, Seattle, WA 98119-1997. *Phone:* 206-281-2021. *Toll-free phone:* 800-366-3344. *Fax:* 206-281-2669. *E-mail:* admissions@spu.edu. *Web site:* http://www.spu.edu/.

Seattle University

Seattle, Washington

- **Independent Roman Catholic** comprehensive, founded 1891
- **Urban** 50-acre campus with easy access to Seattle
- **Coed** 4,631 undergraduate students, 95% full-time, 60% women, 40% men
- **Moderately difficult** entrance level, 71% of applicants were admitted

Undergraduates 4,416 full-time, 215 part-time. Students come from 48 states and territories; 49 other countries; 51% are from out of state; 4% Black or African American, non-Hispanic/Latino; 8% Hispanic/Latino; 16% Asian, non-Hispanic/Latino; 1% Native Hawaiian or other Pacific Islander, non-Hispanic/Latino; 0.9% American Indian or Alaska Native, non-Hispanic/Latino; 4% Two or more races, non-Hispanic/Latino; 6% Race/ethnicity unknown; 9% international; 10% transferred in; 44% live on campus. *Retention:* 86% of full-time freshmen returned.

Freshmen *Admission:* 6,317 applied, 4,456 admitted, 870 enrolled. *Average high school GPA:* 3.57. *Test scores:* SAT critical reading scores over 500: 85%; SAT math scores over 500: 87%; SAT writing scores over 500: 85%; ACT scores over 18: 99%; SAT critical reading scores over 600: 41%; SAT math scores over 600: 44%; SAT writing scores over 600: 40%; ACT scores over 24: 76%; SAT critical reading scores over 700: 8%; SAT math scores over 700: 8%; SAT writing scores over 700: 6%; ACT scores over 30: 18%.

Faculty *Total:* 719, 65% full-time, 57% with terminal degrees. *Student/faculty ratio:* 13:1.

Academics *Calendar:* quarters. *Degrees:* bachelor's, master's, doctoral, postmaster's, postbachelor's, and first professional certificates. *Special study options:* accelerated degree program, adult/continuing education programs, advanced placement credit, double majors, English as a second language, freshman honors college, honors programs, independent study, internships, off-campus study, part-time degree program, services for LD students, student-designed majors, study abroad, summer session for credit. *ROTC:* Army (b), Navy (c), Air Force (c).

Computers on Campus 467 computers/terminals are available on campus for general student use. Students can access the following: campus intranet, computer help desk, free student e-mail accounts, online (class) registration, online (class) schedules. Campuswide network is available. 100% of college-owned or -operated housing units are wired for high-speed Internet access. Wireless service is available via entire campus.

Student Life *Housing:* on-campus residence required through sophomore year. *Options:* coed, men-only, disabled students. Campus housing is university owned. Freshman campus housing is guaranteed. *Activities and organizations:* drama/theater group, student-run newspaper, radio station, choral group, student government, volunteer center, Hawaiian Club, International Student Club. *Campus security:* 24-hour emergency response devices and patrols, late-night transport/escort service, controlled dormitory access, bicycle patrols. *Student services:* health clinic, personal/psychological counseling, women's center.

Athletics Member NCAA, NAIA. All NCAA Division I. *Intercollegiate sports:* archery M(c)/W(c), baseball M(c)/W(c), basketball M(s)/W(s), cheerleading M(c)/W(c), crew M(c)/W(c), cross-country running M(s)/W(s), golf M(c)/W(c), riflery M(c)/W(c), skiing (downhill) M(c)/W(c), soccer M(s)/W(s), softball W(s), swimming and diving M(s)/W(s), track and field M(s)/W(s), volleyball M(c)/W, water polo M(c)/W(c). *Intramural sports:* basketball M/W, field hockey M/W, football M/W, soccer M/W, softball M/W, tennis M/W, ultimate Frisbee M/W, volleyball M/W.

Standardized Tests *Required:* SAT or ACT (for admission).

Costs (2011–12) *Comprehensive fee:* $42,555 includes full-time tuition ($32,400), mandatory fees ($300), and room and board ($9855). Full-time

tuition and fees vary according to course load. Part-time tuition: $720 per credit hour. Part-time tuition and fees vary according to course load. *Room and board:* Room and board charges vary according to board plan.

Financial Aid Of all full-time matriculated undergraduates who enrolled in 2011, 3,348 applied for aid, 2,792 were judged to have need, 264 had their need fully met. In 2011, 244 non-need-based awards were made. *Average percent of need met:* 65%. *Average financial aid package:* $27,519. *Average need-based loan:* $4847. *Average need-based gift aid:* $14,722. *Average non-need-based aid:* $9025. *Average indebtedness upon graduation:* $27,741.

Applying *Options:* electronic application, early action, deferred entrance. *Application fee:* $50. *Required:* essay or personal statement, high school transcript, minimum 2.5 GPA, 2 letters of recommendation. *Application deadlines:* rolling (freshmen), 3/1 (transfers), 11/15 (early action). *Notification:* continuous until 3/1 (freshmen), continuous (transfers), 12/23 (early action). **Freshman Application Contact** Melore Nielsen, Acting Dean of Admissions, Seattle University, 901 12th Avenue, PO Box 222000, Seattle, WA 98122-1090. *Phone:* 206-296-2000. *Toll-free phone:* 800-542-0833 (in-state); 800-426-7123 (out-of-state). *Fax:* 206-296-5656. *E-mail:* admissions@seattleu.edu. *Web site:* http://www.seattleu.edu/.

See page 968 for display ad and page 1574 for the College Close-Up.

Trinity Lutheran College

Issaquah, Washington

- **Independent Lutheran** 4-year, founded 1944
- **Urban** 1-acre campus with easy access to Seattle
- **Coed** 163 undergraduate students, 94% full-time, 53% women, 47% men
- **Minimally difficult** entrance level, 72% of applicants were admitted

Undergraduates 153 full-time, 10 part-time. Students come from 21 states and territories; 6 other countries; 22% are from out of state; 7% Black or African American, non-Hispanic/Latino; 18% Hispanic/Latino; 5% Asian, non-Hispanic/Latino; 2% Native Hawaiian or other Pacific Islander, non-Hispanic/Latino; 1% American Indian or Alaska Native, non-Hispanic/Latino; 7% Two or more races, non-Hispanic/Latino; 1% Race/ethnicity unknown.

Freshmen *Admission:* 231 applied, 166 admitted. *Average high school GPA:* 3.2.

Faculty *Total:* 23, 43% full-time. *Student/faculty ratio:* 7:1.

Academics *Calendar:* quarters. *Degrees:* certificates, associate, bachelor's, and postbachelor's certificates. *Special study options:* academic remediation for entering students, advanced placement credit, double majors, English as a second language, independent study, internships, off-campus study, part-time degree program, services for LD students, study abroad.

Computers on Campus 15 computers/terminals are available on campus for general student use. Students can access the following: free student e-mail accounts, online (class) grades, online (class) registration, online (class) schedules. Campuswide network is available. 100% of college-owned or -operated housing units are wired for high-speed Internet access. Wireless service is available via entire campus.

Student Life *Housing options:* coed, men-only, women-only. Campus housing is university owned. Freshman campus housing is guaranteed. *Activities and organizations:* drama/theater group, choral group, Environmental Commission, student government, Worship Commission, Global Concerns, Activities Commission. *Campus security:* 24-hour emergency response devices, student patrols, controlled dormitory access. *Student services:* health clinic, personal/psychological counseling.

Athletics Member NCCAA. *Intercollegiate sports:* cross-country running M/W, golf M/W, soccer M(s)/W(s). *Intramural sports:* basketball M/W, crew M/W, softball M/W, tennis M/W, volleyball M/W.

Standardized Tests *Required:* SAT or ACT (for admission).

Costs (2012–13) *Comprehensive fee:* $30,616 includes full-time tuition ($23,283), mandatory fees ($500), and room and board ($6833). Part-time tuition: $910 per credit hour. Part-time tuition and fees vary according to course load and program. *Required fees:* $910 per credit hour part-time, $150 per year part-time. *College room only:* $5833. Room and board charges vary according to board plan and housing facility. *Payment plan:* installment. *Waivers:* children of alumni, senior citizens, and employees or children of employees.

Financial Aid Of all full-time matriculated undergraduates who enrolled in 2007, 45 Federal Work-Study jobs (averaging $744).

Applying *Options:* electronic application, early admission, deferred entrance. *Application fee:* $30. *Required:* essay or personal statement, high school transcript, minimum 2.0 GPA, 1 letter of recommendation. *Required for some:* interview. *Application deadlines:* 9/14 (freshmen), 9/14 (transfers). **Freshman Application Contact** Ms. Tracy Sisk, Admissions Counselor, Trinity Lutheran College, 2802 Wetmore AVE, Everett, WA 98201. *Phone:* 425-249-4755. *Toll-free phone:* 800-843-5659. *Fax:* 425-249-4801. *E-mail:* tracy.sisk@tlc.edu. *Web site:* http://www.tlc.edu/.

University of Phoenix–Eastern Washington Campus

Spokane Valley, Washington

Freshman Application Contact Marc Booker, Sr. Director, Office of Admissions and Evaluation, University of Phoenix–Eastern Washington Campus, 4035 South Riverpoint Parkway, Mail Stop CF-L101, Phoenix, AZ 85040. *Phone:* 602-557-4609. *Toll-free phone:* 866-766-0766. *Fax:* 480-643-1156. *Web site:* http://www.phoenix.edu/.

University of Phoenix–Washington Campus

Seattle, Washington

Freshman Application Contact Marc Booker, Sr. Director, Office of Admissions and Evaluation, University of Phoenix–Washington Campus, 4615 East Elwood Street, Mail Stop AA-K101, Phoenix, AZ 85040-1958. *Phone:* 602-557-4609. *Toll-free phone:* 866-766-0766. *Fax:* 480-643-1156. *Web site:* http://www.phoenix.edu/.

University of Puget Sound

Tacoma, Washington

- **Independent** comprehensive, founded 1888
- **Suburban** 97-acre campus with easy access to Seattle
- **Endowment** $217.7 million
- **Coed** 2,651 undergraduate students, 99% full-time, 57% women, 43% men
- **Very difficult** entrance level, 52% of applicants were admitted

Undergraduates 2,620 full-time, 31 part-time. Students come from 51 states and territories; 13 other countries; 76% are from out of state; 2% Black or African American, non-Hispanic/Latino; 5% Hispanic/Latino; 7% Asian, non-Hispanic/Latino; 0.2% Native Hawaiian or other Pacific Islander, non-Hispanic/Latino; 0.8% American Indian or Alaska Native, non-Hispanic/Latino; 4% Two or more races, non-Hispanic/Latino; 5% Race/ethnicity unknown; 0.6% international; 2% transferred in; 58% live on campus. *Retention:* 88% of full-time freshmen returned.

Freshmen *Admission:* 7,194 applied, 3,729 admitted, 686 enrolled. *Average high school GPA:* 3.51. *Test scores:* SAT critical reading scores over 500: 95%; SAT math scores over 500: 92%; SAT writing scores over 500: 93%; ACT scores over 18: 100%; SAT critical reading scores over 600: 68%; SAT math scores over 600: 61%; SAT writing scores over 600: 62%; ACT scores over 24: 91%; SAT critical reading scores over 700: 20%; SAT math scores over 700: 13%; SAT writing scores over 700: 17%; ACT scores over 30: 31%.

Faculty *Total:* 283, 81% full-time, 78% with terminal degrees. *Student/faculty ratio:* 12:1.

Academics *Calendar:* semesters. *Degrees:* bachelor's, master's, doctoral, and post-master's certificates. *Special study options:* advanced placement credit, cooperative education, double majors, honors programs, independent study, internships, part-time degree program, services for LD students, student-designed majors, study abroad, summer session for credit. *ROTC:* Army (c). *Unusual degree programs:* 3-2 engineering with Washington University in St. Louis, Columbia University, Duke University, and University of Southern California.

Computers on Campus 320 computers/terminals and 6,500 ports are available on campus for general student use. Students can access the following: campus intranet, computer help desk, free student e-mail accounts, online (class) grades, online (class) registration, online (class) schedules, financial aid, admission, student employment. Campuswide network is available. 100% of college-owned or -operated housing units are wired for high-speed Internet access. Wireless service is available via entire campus.

Student Life *Housing:* on-campus residence required through sophomore year. *Options:* coed, disabled students. Campus housing is university owned. Freshman campus housing is guaranteed. *Activities and organizations:* drama/theater group, student-run newspaper, radio station, choral group, Puget Sound Outdoors, Repertory Dance Group, Hui-O-Hawaii, Student Theatre Productions, Relay for Life, national fraternities, national sororities. *Campus security:* 24-hour emergency response devices and patrols, student patrols, late-night transport/escort service, controlled dormitory access, 24-hour locked residence hall entrances. *Student services:* health clinic, personal/psychological counseling, legal services.

Athletics Member NCAA. All Division III. *Intercollegiate sports:* baseball M, basketball M/W, cheerleading M/W, crew M/W, cross-country running M/W, fencing M(c)/W(c), football M, golf M/W, ice hockey M(c)/W(c), lacrosse M(c)/W, rugby M(c), sailing M(c)/W(c), skiing (downhill) M(c)/W(c), soccer M/W, softball W, swimming and diving M/W, tennis M/W, track and field M/W, volleyball W. *Intramural sports:* basketball M/W, football M/W, racquet-

Achieve Excellence.

At Seattle University, you learn by doing with professors who are personally engaged in helping you grow in your field of study. Professional internships, real-world projects and career development are important aspects of SU's commitment to academic excellence. Public service is a big draw for graduates, who often compete for and receive prestigious fellowships such as the Truman Scholarship and the Fulbright. As a nationally-ranked university with prestigious programs in Law, Business, Nursing, Science, and Criminal Justice, Seattle University is the premier independent university of the Northwest.

www.seattleu.edu

---

ball M/W, soccer M/W, softball M/W, tennis M/W, ultimate Frisbee M/W, volleyball M/W, water polo M(c)/W(c).

Standardized Tests *Required:* SAT or ACT (for admission).

Costs (2011–12) *Comprehensive fee:* $48,740 includes full-time tuition ($38,510), mandatory fees ($210), and room and board ($10,020). Full-time tuition and fees vary according to course load. Part-time tuition: $4860 per unit. Part-time tuition and fees vary according to course load. *College room only:* $5550. Room and board charges vary according to board plan and housing facility. *Payment plans:* installment, deferred payment. *Waivers:* employees or children of employees.

Financial Aid Of all full-time matriculated undergraduates who enrolled in 2011, 1,902 applied for aid, 1,714 were judged to have need, 316 had their need fully met. 553 Federal Work-Study jobs (averaging $2562). 805 state and other part-time jobs (averaging $2773). In 2011, 660 non-need-based awards were made. *Average percent of need met:* 77%. *Average financial aid package:* $28,547. *Average need-based loan:* $5258. *Average need-based gift aid:* $23,565. *Average non-need-based aid:* $10,760. *Average indebtedness upon graduation:* $28,524.

Applying *Options:* electronic application, early admission, early decision, deferred entrance. *Application fee:* $50. *Required:* essay or personal statement, high school transcript, 2 letters of recommendation, school report, application supplement, 2 recommendations. *Recommended:* minimum 3.0 GPA, interview. *Application deadlines:* 1/15 (freshmen), 3/1 (transfers). *Early decision deadline:* 11/1 (for plan 1), 1/2 (for plan 2). *Notification:* 4/1 (freshmen), continuous (transfers), 12/15 (early decision plan 1), 2/15 (early decision plan 2).

Freshman Application Contact Dr. George Mills, Vice President for Enrollment, University of Puget Sound, 1500 North Warner Street, Tacoma, WA 98416. *Phone:* 253-879-3211. *Toll-free phone:* 800-396-7191. *Fax:* 253-879-3993. *E-mail:* admission@pugetsound.edu. *Web site:* http://www.pugetsound.edu.

See page 967 for display ad and page 1702 for the College Close-Up.

University of Washington
Seattle, Washington

- **State-supported** university, founded 1861
- **Urban** 703-acre campus
- **Coed** 29,017 undergraduate students, 89% full-time, 52% women, 48% men
- **Moderately difficult** entrance level, 58% of applicants were admitted

Undergraduates 25,863 full-time, 3,154 part-time. 14% are from out of state; 3% Black or African American, non-Hispanic/Latino; 6% Hispanic/Latino; 26% Asian, non-Hispanic/Latino; 0.7% Native Hawaiian or other Pacific Islander, non-Hispanic/Latino; 1% American Indian or Alaska Native, non-Hispanic/Latino; 0.6% Two or more races, non-Hispanic/Latino; 4% Race/ethnicity unknown; 7% international; 6% transferred in; 11% live on campus. *Retention:* 93% of full-time freshmen returned.

Freshmen *Admission:* 24,540 applied, 14,340 admitted, 5,788 enrolled. *Average high school GPA:* 3.75. *Test scores:* SAT critical reading scores over 500: 81%; SAT math scores over 500: 92%; SAT writing scores over 500: 83%; ACT scores over 18: 97%; SAT critical reading scores over 600: 46%; SAT math scores over 600: 68%; SAT writing scores over 600: 44%; ACT scores over 24: 81%; SAT critical reading scores over 700: 11%; SAT math scores over 700: 25%; SAT writing scores over 700: 9%; ACT scores over 30: 25%.

Faculty *Total:* 3,602, 78% full-time, 82% with terminal degrees. *Student/faculty ratio:* 13:1.

Academics *Calendar:* quarters. *Degrees:* bachelor's, master's, doctoral, post-master's, and first professional certificates. *Special study options:* adult/continuing education programs, part-time degree program. *ROTC:* Army (b), Navy (b), Air Force (b).

Computers on Campus Students can access the following: computer help desk, free student e-mail accounts, online (class) grades, online (class) registration, online (class) schedules. Campuswide network is available. 100% of college-owned or -operated housing units are wired for high-speed Internet access. Wireless service is available via entire campus.

Student Life *Housing options:* coed, disabled students. Campus housing is university owned, leased by the school and is provided by a third party. *Campus security:* 24-hour emergency response devices and patrols, late-night transport/escort service, controlled dormitory access.

Athletics Member NCAA. All Division I except football (Division I-A). *Intercollegiate sports:* baseball M(s), basketball M(s)/W(s), cheerleading M/W, crew M(s)/W(s), cross-country running M(s)/W(s), golf M(s)/W(s), gymnastics W(s), soccer M(s)/W(s), softball W(s), tennis M(s)/W(s), track and field M(s)/W(s), volleyball W(s). *Intramural sports:* archery M(c)/W(c), badminton M/W, basketball M/W, bowling M/W, crew M(c)/W(c), fencing M(c)/W(c), field hockey M(c)/W(c), football M/W, golf M/W, gymnastics M(c)/W(c), ice hockey M(c), lacrosse M(c)/W(c), racquetball M(c)/W(c), rock

climbing M/W, rugby M(c)/W(c), sailing M(c)/W(c), skiing (cross-country) M(c)/W(c), skiing (downhill) M(c)/W(c), soccer M(c)/W(c), squash M(c)/W(c), table tennis M/W, tennis M/W, track and field M/W, ultimate Frisbee M(c)/W(c), volleyball M/W, water polo M(c)/W(c).

Standardized Tests *Required:* SAT or ACT (for admission).

Costs (2011–12) *Tuition:* state resident $8701 full-time; nonresident $25,329 full-time. Full-time tuition and fees vary according to course load. Part-time tuition and fees vary according to course load. *Required fees:* $272 full-time. *Room and board:* $8169. Room and board charges vary according to board plan and housing facility. *Waivers:* senior citizens and employees or children of employees.

Financial Aid Of all full-time matriculated undergraduates who enrolled in 2008, 13,572 applied for aid, 9,824 were judged to have need, 3,250 had their need fully met. 478 Federal Work-Study jobs (averaging $2800). 327 state and other part-time jobs (averaging $3160). In 2008, 706 non-need-based awards were made. *Average percent of need met:* 79%. *Average financial aid package:* $11,560. *Average need-based loan:* $2860. *Average need-based gift aid:* $8720. *Average non-need-based aid:* $4430. *Average indebtedness upon graduation:* $16,800.

Applying *Options:* electronic application, early admission. *Application fee:* $60. *Required:* essay or personal statement, minimum 2.0 GPA. *Required for some:* high school transcript. *Application deadlines:* 12/1 (freshmen), 2/15 (transfers).

Freshman Application Contact Emily Leggio, Senior Associate Director of Admissions, University of Washington, Seattle, WA 98195. *Phone:* 206-543-9686. *Fax:* 206-685-3655. *Web site:* http://www.washington.edu/.

University of Washington, Bothell
Bothell, Washington

- **State-supported** comprehensive, founded 1990, part of University of Washington
- **Suburban** 128-acre campus with easy access to Seattle
- **Endowment** $3.0 million
- **Coed** 3,242 undergraduate students, 81% full-time, 52% women, 48% men
- **Moderately difficult** entrance level, 74% of applicants were admitted

Undergraduates 2,625 full-time, 617 part-time. Students come from 16 states and territories; 19 other countries; 2% are from out of state; 4% Black or African American, non-Hispanic/Latino; 6% Hispanic/Latino; 21% Asian, non-Hispanic/Latino; 0.5% Native Hawaiian or other Pacific Islander, non-His-panic/Latino; 0.8% American Indian or Alaska Native, non-Hispanic/Latino; 2% Two or more races, non-Hispanic/Latino; 5% Race/ethnicity unknown; 3% international; 19% transferred in; 6% live on campus. *Retention:* 85% of full-time freshmen returned.

Freshmen *Admission:* 2,075 applied, 1,529 admitted, 529 enrolled. *Average high school GPA:* 3.31. *Test scores:* SAT critical reading scores over 500: 53%; SAT math scores over 500: 63%; SAT writing scores over 500: 42%; ACT scores over 18: 81%; SAT critical reading scores over 600: 17%; SAT math scores over 600: 21%; SAT writing scores over 600: 8%; ACT scores over 24: 33%; SAT critical reading scores over 700: 2%; SAT math scores over 700: 3%; SAT writing scores over 700: 1%; ACT scores over 30: 5%.

Faculty *Total:* 221, 60% full-time, 70% with terminal degrees. *Student/faculty ratio:* 19:1.

Academics *Degrees:* bachelor's, master's, and postbachelor's certificates. *Special study options:* adult/continuing education programs, advanced placement credit, cooperative education, double majors, honors programs, independent study, internships, off-campus study, part-time degree program, services for LD students, student-designed majors, study abroad, summer session for credit. *ROTC:* Army (c), Navy (c), Air Force (c).

Computers on Campus 350 computers/terminals and 1,000 ports are available on campus for general student use. Students can access the following: computer help desk, free student e-mail accounts, online (class) grades, online (class) registration, online (class) schedules, online course management system. Campuswide network is available. 100% of college-owned or -operated housing units are wired for high-speed Internet access. Wireless service is available via entire campus.

Student Life *Housing options:* coed, disabled students. Campus housing is university owned. Freshman applicants given priority for college housing. *Activities and organizations:* student-run newspaper, Dodge Ball, Beta Alpha Psi, Collegiate DECA, Campus Events Board, basketball. *Campus security:* 24-hour emergency response devices and patrols, late-night transport/escort service. *Student services:* personal/psychological counseling.

Athletics *Intramural sports:* basketball M(c)/W(c), cheerleading M(c)/W(c), golf M(c)/W(c), soccer M(c)/W(c), softball M(c)/W(c), table tennis M(c)/W(c), ultimate Frisbee M(c)/W(c), volleyball M(c)/W(c).

Standardized Tests *Required:* SAT or ACT (for admission).

Costs (2011–12) *Tuition:* state resident $9746 full-time; nonresident $27,230 full-time. Full-time tuition and fees vary according to course load. Part-time tuition and fees vary according to course load. *Required fees:* $495 full-time. *Room only:* $8340. Room and board charges vary according to housing facility. *Payment plan:* installment. *Waivers:* employees or children of employees.

Applying *Options:* electronic application, early admission, deferred entrance. *Application fee:* $60. *Required:* essay or personal statement, high school transcript, minimum 2.0 GPA. *Application deadlines:* 1/15 (freshmen), 1/15 (transfers). *Notification:* continuous (freshmen).

Freshman Application Contact Lindsey Wille, Associate Director of Admissions, University of Washington, Bothell, 18115 Campus Way NE, Box 358500, Bothell, WA 98011-8246. *Phone:* 425-352-5000. *Fax:* 425-352-5455. *E-mail:* freshmen@uwb.edu. *Web site:* http://www.uwb.edu/.

See page 969 for display ad and page 1724 for the College Close-Up.

University of Washington, Tacoma
Tacoma, Washington

- **State-supported** comprehensive, founded 1990, part of University of Washington
- **Urban** 46-acre campus with easy access to Seattle
- **Endowment** $22.6 million
- **Coed**
- **Minimally difficult** entrance level

Faculty *Student/faculty ratio:* 18:1.

Academics *Calendar:* quarters. *Degrees:* bachelor's, master's, post-master's, and postbachelor's certificates.

Student Life *Campus security:* 24-hour emergency response devices and patrols, late-night transport/escort service, key card access to buildings after hours.

Standardized Tests *Required:* SAT or ACT (for admission).

Financial Aid *Of all full-time matriculated undergraduates who enrolled in 2009,* 1,486 applied for aid, 1,268 were judged to have need, 321 had their need fully met. *In 2009,* 27 non-need-based awards were made. *Average percent of need met:* 77. *Average financial aid package:* $13,800. *Average need-based loan:* $6900. *Average need-based gift aid:* $11,200. *Average non-need-based aid:* $63,000. *Average indebtedness upon graduation:* $17,900.

Applying *Options:* electronic application, early decision, deferred entrance. *Application fee:* $60. *Required:* essay or personal statement, minimum 2.0 GPA. *Required for some:* high school transcript.

Freshman Application Contact Ms. Fiona Johnson, Admissions Advising and Outreach, University of Washington, Tacoma, 1900 Commerce Street, Tacoma, WA 98402-3100. *Phone:* 253-692-4742. *Toll-free phone:* 800-736-7750. *Fax:* 253-692-4788. *E-mail:* fionaj@u.washington.edu. *Web site:* http://www.tacoma.washington.edu/.

Walla Walla University
College Place, Washington

- **Independent Seventh-day Adventist** comprehensive, founded 1892
- **Small-town** 77-acre campus
- **Coed**
- **Moderately difficult** entrance level

Faculty *Student/faculty ratio:* 12:1.

Academics *Calendar:* quarters. *Degrees:* diplomas, associate, bachelor's, and master's.

Student Life *Campus security:* 24-hour emergency response devices and patrols, student patrols, late-night transport/escort service, controlled dormitory access.

Athletics Member NAIA.

Standardized Tests *Required:* SAT or ACT (for admission). *Recommended:* ACT (for admission).

Costs (2011–12) *Comprehensive fee:* $29,811 includes full-time tuition ($23,670), mandatory fees ($300), and room and board ($5841). Full-time tuition and fees vary according to course load and degree level. Part-time tuition: $618 per quarter hour. Part-time tuition and fees vary according to degree level. *Required fees:* $100 per term part-time. *Room and board:* Room and board charges vary according to housing facility and location.

Financial Aid *Of all full-time matriculated undergraduates who enrolled in 2010,* 1,269 applied for aid, 972 were judged to have need, 361 had their need fully met. *In 2010,* 256 non-need-based awards were made. *Average percent of need met:* 90. *Average financial aid package:* $22,111. *Average need-based loan:* $7475. *Average need-based gift aid:* $8796. *Average non-need-based aid:* $4643. *Average indebtedness upon graduation:* $34,818.

Applying *Options:* electronic application, early decision, deferred entrance. *Application fee:* $40. *Required:* high school transcript, minimum 2.5 GPA.

Freshman Application Contact Walla Walla University, 204 South College Avenue, College Place, WA 99324-1198. *Phone:* 509-527-2327. *Toll-free phone:* 800-541-8900. *Web site:* http://www.wallawalla.edu/.

Washington State University
Pullman, Washington

- **State-supported** university, founded 1890
- **Small-town** 620-acre campus with easy access to Spokane
- **Endowment** $638.4 million
- **Coed** 22,763 undergraduate students, 87% full-time, 51% women, 49% men
- **Moderately difficult** entrance level, 82% of applicants were admitted

Undergraduates 19,800 full-time, 2,963 part-time. 8% are from out of state; 3% Black or African American, non-Hispanic/Latino; 8% Hispanic/Latino; 5% Asian, non-Hispanic/Latino; 0.4% Native Hawaiian or other Pacific Islander, non-Hispanic/Latino; 0.9% American Indian or Alaska Native, non-Hispanic/Latino; 5% Two or more races, non-Hispanic/Latino; 4% Race/ethnicity unknown; 4% international; 12% transferred in; 36% live on campus. *Retention:* 84% of full-time freshmen returned.

Freshmen *Admission:* 14,071 applied, 11,601 admitted, 4,473 enrolled. *Average high school GPA:* 3.35. *Test scores:* SAT critical reading scores over 500: 63%; SAT math scores over 500: 68%; SAT writing scores over 500: 57%; ACT scores over 18: 91%; SAT critical reading scores over 600: 20%; SAT math scores over 600: 25%; SAT writing scores over 600: 15%; ACT scores over 24: 47%; SAT critical reading scores over 700: 2%; SAT math scores over 700: 3%; SAT writing scores over 700: 1%; ACT scores over 30: 7%.

Faculty *Total:* 1,650, 71% full-time, 78% with terminal degrees. *Student/faculty ratio:* 16:1.

Academics *Calendar:* semesters. *Degrees:* certificates, bachelor's, master's, doctoral, post-master's, postbachelor's, and first professional certificates. *Special study options:* accelerated degree program, adult/continuing education programs, advanced placement credit, cooperative education, distance learning, double majors, English as a second language, external degree program, honors programs, independent study, internships, off-campus study, part-time degree program, services for LD students, student-designed majors, study abroad, summer session for credit. *ROTC:* Army (b), Navy (c), Air Force (b).

Computers on Campus 2,500 computers/terminals and 2,500 ports are available on campus for general student use. Students can access the following: campus intranet, computer help desk, free student e-mail accounts, online (class) grades, online (class) registration, online (class) schedules. Campus-wide network is available. 100% of college-owned or -operated housing units are wired for high-speed Internet access. Wireless service is available via classrooms, computer centers, computer labs, dorm rooms, learning centers, libraries, student centers.

Student Life *Housing:* on-campus residence required for freshman year. *Options:* coed, men-only, women-only, cooperative, disabled students. Campus housing is university owned. Freshman campus housing is guaranteed. *Activities and organizations:* drama/theater group, student-run newspaper, radio and television station, choral group, marching band, Panhellenic Association - Sororities, Interfraternity Council - Fraternities, Student Entertainment Board, International Students Council, ChiLaStAl (Chicana/o Latina/o Student Alliance, national fraternities, national sororities. *Campus security:* 24-hour emergency response devices and patrols, student patrols, late-night transport/escort service, controlled dormitory access. *Student services:* health clinic, personal/psychological counseling, women's center, legal services.

Athletics Member NCAA. All Division I except football (Division I-A). *Intercollegiate sports:* baseball M(s), basketball M(s)/W(s), bowling M(c)/W(c), cheerleading M/W, crew M(c)/W(s), cross-country running M(s)/W(s), fencing M/W(c), golf M(s)/W(s), ice hockey M(c), lacrosse M(c)/W(c), rugby M(c)/W(c), sailing M(c)/W(c), skiing (cross-country) M(c)/W(c), skiing (downhill) M(c)/W(c), soccer M(c)/W(s), softball W(c), swimming and diving W(s), tennis M(c)/W(s), track and field M(s)/W(s), ultimate Frisbee M(c)/W(c), volleyball M(c)/W(s), water polo M(c)/W(c). *Intramural sports:* badminton M/W, basketball M/W, football M/W, golf M/W, racquetball M/W, rock climbing M/W, soccer M/W, softball M/W, table tennis M/W, tennis M/W, ultimate Frisbee M/W, volleyball M/W.

Standardized Tests *Required:* SAT or ACT (for admission).

Costs (2011–12) *Tuition:* state resident $9374 full-time, $495 per credit hour part-time; nonresident $20,652 full-time, $1059 per credit hour part-time. Full-time tuition and fees vary according to location and reciprocity agreements. Part-time tuition and fees vary according to course load, location, and reciprocity agreements. *Required fees:* $1424 full-time. *Room and board:* $9662; room only: $5782. Room and board charges vary according to board plan, housing facility, and location. *Waivers:* senior citizens and employees or children of employees.

Financial Aid *Of all full-time matriculated undergraduates who enrolled in 2010,* 13,305 applied for aid, 10,543 were judged to have need, 7,470 had their need fully met. *In 2010,* 2356 non-need-based awards were made. *Average percent of need met:* 93%. *Average financial aid package:* $15,996. *Average need-based loan:* $4485. *Average need-based gift aid:* $9265. *Average non-need-based aid:* $4093. *Average indebtedness upon graduation:* $22,686.

Applying *Options:* electronic application. *Application fee:* $50. *Required:* high school transcript, minimum 2.0 GPA. *Recommended:* essay or personal statement. *Application deadlines:* 1/31 (freshmen), 1/7 (out-of-state freshmen), 1/31 (transfers). *Notification:* continuous until 11/1 (freshmen), continuous until 11/1 (out-of-state freshmen), continuous until 11/1 (transfers).

Freshman Application Contact Ms. Wendy Peterson, Director of Admissions, Washington State University, PO Box 641067, Pullman, WA 99164-1067. *Phone:* 888-468-6978. *Toll-free phone:* 888-468-6978. *Fax:* 509-335-4902. *E-mail:* admissions@wsu.edu. *Web site:* http://www.wsu.edu/.

Washington State University Vancouver

Vancouver, Washington

Admissions Office Contact Washington State University Vancouver, 14204 Northeast Salmon Creek Avenue, Vancouver, WA 98686. *Web site:* http://www.vancouver.wsu.edu/.

Western Washington University

Bellingham, Washington

- **State-supported** comprehensive, founded 1893
- **Small-town** 223-acre campus with easy access to Seattle, Vancouver
- **Endowment** $46.0 million
- **Coed** 13,783 undergraduate students, 93% full-time, 56% women, 44% men
- **Moderately difficult** entrance level, 78% of applicants were admitted

Undergraduates 12,803 full-time, 980 part-time. Students come from 48 states and territories; 36 other countries; 8% are from out of state; 2% Black or African American, non-Hispanic/Latino; 6% Hispanic/Latino; 6% Asian, non-Hispanic/Latino; 0.2% Native Hawaiian or other Pacific Islander, non-Hispanic/Latino; 1% American Indian or Alaska Native, non-Hispanic/Latino; 5% Two or more races, non-Hispanic/Latino; 2% Race/ethnicity unknown; 1% international; 6% transferred in; 32% live on campus. *Retention:* 84% of full-time freshmen returned.

Freshmen *Admission:* 9,083 applied, 7,113 admitted, 2,695 enrolled. *Average high school GPA:* 3.46. *Test scores:* SAT critical reading scores over 500: 78%; SAT math scores over 500: 78%; ACT scores over 18: 96%; SAT critical reading scores over 600: 37%; SAT math scores over 600: 34%; ACT scores over 24: 61%; SAT critical reading scores over 700: 7%; SAT math scores over 700: 3%; ACT scores over 30: 12%.

Faculty *Total:* 730, 68% full-time, 71% with terminal degrees. *Student/faculty ratio:* 21:1.

Academics *Calendar:* quarters. *Degrees:* certificates, bachelor's, master's, post-master's, and postbachelor's certificates. *Special study options:* accelerated degree program, advanced placement credit, cooperative education, distance learning, double majors, English as a second language, honors programs, independent study, internships, off-campus study, services for LD students, student-designed majors, study abroad, summer session for credit.

Computers on Campus 2,408 computers/terminals are available on campus for general student use. Students can access the following: online (class) registration. Campuswide network is available. 99% of college-owned or -operated housing units are wired for high-speed Internet access. Wireless service is available via classrooms, computer centers, computer labs, dorm rooms, learning centers, libraries, student centers.

Student Life *Housing options:* coed, disabled students. Campus housing is university owned and leased by the school. Freshman campus housing is guaranteed. *Activities and organizations:* drama/theater group, student-run newspaper, radio and television station, choral group, intramurals, Residence Hall Association, Associated Students, Outdoor Center, Ethnic Student Center. *Campus security:* 24-hour emergency response devices and patrols, student patrols, late-night transport/escort service, controlled dormitory access. *Student services:* health clinic, personal/psychological counseling, women's center, legal services.

Athletics Member NCAA. All Division II. *Intercollegiate sports:* basketball M(s)/W(s), cheerleading M/W, crew M(s)/W(s), cross-country running M(s)/W(s), golf M(s)/W(s), soccer M(s)/W(s), softball W(s), track and field M(s)/W(s), volleyball W(s). *Intramural sports:* badminton M/W, baseball M, basketball M/W, ice hockey M, lacrosse M/W, racquetball M/W, rock climbing M/W, sailing M/W, skiing (downhill) M/W, soccer M/W, softball M/W, swimming and diving M/W, table tennis M/W, tennis M/W, volleyball M/W, water polo M/W, wrestling M.

Standardized Tests *Required:* SAT or ACT (for admission).

Costs (2011–12) *Tuition:* state resident $6973 full-time, $233 per credit hour part-time; nonresident $17,320 full-time, $577 per credit hour part-time. Full-time tuition and fees vary according to course load, location, and reciprocity agreements. Part-time tuition and fees vary according to course load, location,

and reciprocity agreements. *Required fees:* $783 full-time, $26 per credit hour part-time. *Room and board:* $9100. Room and board charges vary according to board plan, housing facility, and location. *Payment plan:* installment. *Waivers:* minority students and employees or children of employees.

Financial Aid Of all full-time matriculated undergraduates who enrolled in 2011, 8,462 applied for aid, 6,181 were judged to have need, 1,085 had their need fully met. 176 Federal Work-Study jobs (averaging $3173). 445 state and other part-time jobs (averaging $3129). In 2011, 274 non-need-based awards were made. *Average percent of need met:* 85%. *Average financial aid package:* $12,469. *Average need-based loan:* $4512. *Average need-based gift aid:* $7932. *Average non-need-based aid:* $1891. *Average indebtedness upon graduation:* $18,969.

Applying *Options:* electronic application, deferred entrance. *Application fee:* $55. *Required:* high school transcript. *Recommended:* essay or personal statement. *Application deadlines:* 3/1 (freshmen), 4/1 (transfers). *Notification:* 4/15 (freshmen), continuous until 6/1 (transfers).

Freshman Application Contact Ms. Clara Capron, Acting Director of Admissions, Western Washington University, 516 High Street, Bellingham, WA 98225-9009. *Phone:* 360-650-2422. *Fax:* 360-650-7369. *E-mail:* admit@wwu.edu. *Web site:* http://www.wwu.edu/.

Whitman College

Walla Walla, Washington

- **Independent** 4-year, founded 1859
- **Small-town** 117-acre campus
- **Endowment** $395.6 million
- **Coed** 1,596 undergraduate students, 98% full-time, 58% women, 42% men
- **Very difficult** entrance level, 54% of applicants were admitted

Undergraduates 1,566 full-time, 30 part-time. Students come from 43 states and territories; 29 other countries; 63% are from out of state; 2% Black or African American, non-Hispanic/Latino; 6% Hispanic/Latino; 8% Asian, non-Hispanic/Latino; 0.3% Native Hawaiian or other Pacific Islander, non-Hispanic/Latino; 0.8% American Indian or Alaska Native, non-Hispanic/Latino; 3% Two or more races, non-Hispanic/Latino; 8% Race/ethnicity unknown; 2% international; 1% transferred in; 68% live on campus. *Retention:* 95% of full-time freshmen returned.

Freshmen *Admission:* 3,086 applied, 1,654 admitted, 399 enrolled. *Average high school GPA:* 3.81. *Test scores:* SAT critical reading scores over 500: 98%; SAT math scores over 500: 99%; SAT writing scores over 500: 98%; ACT scores over 18: 100%; SAT critical reading scores over 600: 87%; SAT math scores over 600: 88%; SAT writing scores over 600: 85%; ACT scores over 24: 99%; SAT critical reading scores over 700: 44%; SAT math scores over 700: 32%; SAT writing scores over 700: 32%; ACT scores over 30: 65%.

Faculty *Total:* 200, 67% full-time, 84% with terminal degrees. *Student/faculty ratio:* 10:1.

Academics *Calendar:* semesters. *Degree:* bachelor's. *Special study options:* accelerated degree program, advanced placement credit, cooperative education, double majors, honors programs, independent study, off-campus study, services for LD students, student-designed majors, study abroad. *Unusual degree programs:* 3-2 engineering with California Institute of Technology, Columbia University, Duke University, University of Washington, Washington University in St. Louis; forestry with Duke University; international studies with Monterey Institute of International Studies; oceanography with University of Washington; teacher education with Bank Street College of Education; law with Columbia University.

Computers on Campus 397 computers/terminals are available on campus for general student use. Students can access the following: computer help desk, free student e-mail accounts, online (class) grades, online (class) registration, online (class) schedules, course registration information. Campuswide network is available. 100% of college-owned or -operated housing units are wired for high-speed Internet access. Wireless service is available via classrooms, computer centers, computer labs, dorm rooms, learning centers, libraries, student centers.

Student Life *Housing:* on-campus residence required through sophomore year. *Options:* coed, women-only. Campus housing is university owned. Freshman campus housing is guaranteed. *Activities and organizations:* drama/theater group, student-run newspaper, radio station, choral group, Associated Students, Outdoor Program, Center for Community Service, national fraternities, national sororities. *Campus security:* 24-hour emergency response devices and patrols, student patrols, late-night transport/escort service, controlled dormitory access. *Student services:* health clinic, personal/psychological counseling, women's center.

Athletics Member NCAA. All Division III. *Intercollegiate sports:* baseball M, basketball M/W, cross-country running M/W, fencing M(c)/W(c), golf M/W, ice hockey M(c), lacrosse M(c)/W(c), rugby M(c)/W(c), skiing (cross-country) M(c)/W(c), skiing (downhill) M(c)/W(c), soccer M/W, softball W(c),

swimming and diving M/W, tennis M/W, track and field M(c)/W(c), ultimate Frisbee M(c)/W(c), volleyball M(c)/W. *Intramural sports:* basketball M/W, bowling M/W, football M/W, soccer M/W, softball M/W, tennis M/W, ultimate Frisbee M/W, volleyball M/W.

Standardized Tests *Required:* SAT or ACT (for admission).

Costs (2012–13) *Comprehensive fee:* $52,666 includes full-time tuition ($41,790), mandatory fees ($316), and room and board ($10,560). Part-time tuition: $1741 per credit. *College room only:* $4880. Room and board charges vary according to board plan and housing facility. *Payment plan:* deferred payment. *Waivers:* employees or children of employees.

Financial Aid Of all full-time matriculated undergraduates who enrolled in 2011, 924 applied for aid, 788 were judged to have need, 442 had their need fully met. 417 Federal Work-Study jobs (averaging $2200). 180 state and other part-time jobs (averaging $1800). In 2011, 437 non-need-based awards were made. *Average percent of need met:* 97%. *Average financial aid package:* $31,725. *Average need-based loan:* $4726. *Average need-based gift aid:* $25,938. *Average non-need-based aid:* $8513. *Average indebtedness upon graduation:* $17,711. *Financial aid deadline:* 2/1.

Applying *Options:* electronic application, early decision, deferred entrance. *Application fee:* $50. *Required:* essay or personal statement, high school transcript, 1 letter of recommendation. *Recommended:* interview. *Application deadlines:* 1/15 (freshmen), 3/1 (transfers). *Early decision deadline:* 11/15. *Notification:* 4/1 (freshmen), 4/15 (transfers), 12/19 (early decision).

Freshman Application Contact Mr. Tony Cabasco, Dean of Admission and Financial Aid, Whitman College, 515 Boyer Avenue, Walla Walla, WA 99362-2083. *Phone:* 509-527-5176. *Toll-free phone:* 877-462-9448. *Fax:* 509-527-4967. *E-mail:* admission@whitman.edu. *Web site:* http://www.whitman.edu/.

See below for display ad and page 1762 for the College Close-Up.

Whitworth University

Spokane, Washington

Freshman Application Contact Ms. Marianne Hansen, Director of Admission, Whitworth University, 300 West, Hawthorne Road, Spokane, WA 99251. *Phone:* 509-777-4348. *Toll-free phone:* 800-533-4668. *Fax:* 509-777-3758. *E-mail:* admission@whitworth.edu. *Web site:* http://www.whitworth.edu/.

WEST VIRGINIA

Alderson-Broaddus College

Philippi, West Virginia

- **Independent** comprehensive, founded 1871, affiliated with American Baptist Churches in the U.S.A.
- **Rural** 170-acre campus
- **Endowment** $16.0 million
- **Coed**
- **Moderately difficult** entrance level

Faculty *Student/faculty ratio:* 9:1.

Academics *Calendar:* semesters. *Degrees:* certificates, associate, bachelor's, and master's.

Student Life *Campus security:* 24-hour patrols, controlled dormitory access, emergency notification system, lighted pathways and sidewalks.

Athletics Member NCAA. All Division II.

Standardized Tests *Required:* SAT and SAT Subject Tests or ACT (for admission).

Costs (2011–12) *Comprehensive fee:* $29,976 includes full-time tuition ($22,530), mandatory fees ($210), and room and board ($7236). Full-time tuition and fees vary according to program and student level. Part-time tuition: $751 per credit hour. Part-time tuition and fees vary according to program and student level. *Required fees:* $53 per term part-time. *College room only:* $3560. Room and board charges vary according to housing facility.

Financial Aid *Of all full-time matriculated undergraduates who enrolled in 2010,* 520 applied for aid, 495 were judged to have need, 131 had their need fully met. 189 Federal Work-Study jobs (averaging $1390). 90 state and other part-time jobs (averaging $2198). In 2010, 33 non-need-based awards were made. *Average percent of need met:* 81. *Average financial aid package:* $21,596. *Average need-based loan:* $4838. *Average need-based gift aid:* $17,655. *Average non-need-based aid:* $8942. *Average indebtedness upon graduation:* $31,751.

Applying *Options:* electronic application, deferred entrance. *Application fee:* $25. *Required:* high school transcript, minimum 2.0 GPA. *Required for some:* 3 letters of recommendation, interview.

Freshman Application Contact Ms. Kimberly N. Klaus, Director of Admissions, Alderson-Broaddus College, 101 College Hill Drive, Campus Box 2003, Philippi, WV 26416. *Phone:* 304-457-1700. *Toll-free phone:* 800-

WHITMAN COLLEGE

For more information, contact:

Kevin Dyerly, Director of Admission

Admission Office

345 Boyer Avenue

Walla Walla, Washington 99362

Phone: 509-527-5176

877-462-9448 (toll-free)

E-mail: admission@whitman.edu

Web site: www.whitman.edu

263-1549. *Fax:* 304-457-6239. *E-mail:* admissions@ab.edu. *Web site:* http://www.ab.edu/.

American Public University System
Charles Town, West Virginia

- **Proprietary** comprehensive, founded 1991
- **Rural** campus with easy access to Washington, D.C.
- **Coed** 39,982 undergraduate students, 8% full-time, 39% women, 61% men
- **Noncompetitive** entrance level

Undergraduates 3,240 full-time, 36,742 part-time. Students come from 57 states and territories; 66 other countries; 9% Black or African American, non-Hispanic/Latino; 10% Hispanic/Latino; 16% Asian, non-Hispanic/Latino; 0.7% Native Hawaiian or other Pacific Islander, non-Hispanic/Latino; 1% American Indian or Alaska Native, non-Hispanic/Latino; 3% Two or more races, non-Hispanic/Latino; 5% Race/ethnicity unknown; 0.8% international; 13% transferred in.

Freshmen *Admission:* 6,888 enrolled.

Faculty *Total:* 1,805, 25% full-time. *Student/faculty ratio:* 22:1.

Academics *Calendar:* courses start on the first Monday of each month. *Degrees:* certificates, associate, bachelor's, master's, and postbachelor's certificates (profile includes American Public University, American Military University and American Community College). *Special study options:* adult/continuing education programs, advanced placement credit, distance learning, external degree program, independent study, internships, part-time degree program, services for LD students, summer session for credit.

Computers on Campus Students can access the following: free student e-mail accounts, online (class) grades, online (class) registration, online (class) schedules.

Student Life *Housing:* college housing not available.

Costs (2012–13) *Tuition:* $7500 full-time, $250 per credit hour part-time. *Payment plan:* installment. *Waivers:* employees or children of employees.

Applying *Options:* electronic application, deferred entrance. *Required:* high school transcript, orientation (no-fee). *Application deadlines:* rolling (freshmen), rolling (out-of-state freshmen), rolling (transfers).

Freshman Application Contact Ms. Terry Grant, Associate Vice President, Enrollment Management, American Public University System, 111 West Congress Street, Charles Town, WV 25414. *Phone:* 877-468-6268. *Toll-free phone:* 877-755-2787. *Fax:* 304-724-3788. *E-mail:* info@apus.edu. *Web site:* http://www.apus.edu/.

Appalachian Bible College
Bradley, West Virginia

- **Independent nondenominational** comprehensive, founded 1950
- **Small-town** 110-acre campus
- **Endowment** $316,677
- **Coed**
- **Noncompetitive** entrance level

Faculty *Student/faculty ratio:* 17:1.

Academics *Calendar:* semesters. *Degrees:* certificates, diplomas, associate, bachelor's, master's, and postbachelor's certificates.

Student Life *Campus security:* 24-hour emergency response devices, patrols by trained security personnel.

Athletics Member NCCAA.

Standardized Tests *Required:* SAT or ACT (for admission).

Costs (2011–12) *Comprehensive fee:* $17,922 includes full-time tuition ($10,032), mandatory fees ($1690), and room and board ($6200). Full-time tuition and fees vary according to course load and program. Part-time tuition: $418 per credit hour. Part-time tuition and fees vary according to program. *Required fees:* $44 per credit hour part-time, $345 per term part-time. *Room and board:* Room and board charges vary according to housing facility. *Payment plans:* tuition prepayment, installment.

Financial Aid *Of all full-time matriculated undergraduates who enrolled in 2010,* 211 applied for aid, 195 were judged to have need, 11 had their need fully met. 29 Federal Work-Study jobs (averaging $569). *In 2010,* 17 non-need-based awards were made. *Average percent of need met:* 53. *Average financial aid package:* $8477. *Average need-based loan:* $3079. *Average need-based gift aid:* $6867. *Average non-need-based aid:* $1982. *Average indebtedness upon graduation:* $10,585. *Financial aid deadline:* 6/15.

Applying *Options:* electronic application, early admission. *Application fee:* $20. *Required:* essay or personal statement, high school transcript, 3 letters of recommendation, interview. *Required for some:* interview. *Recommended:* minimum 2.5 GPA.

Freshman Application Contact Miss Rachel Delevan, Admissions Assistant, Appalachian Bible College, PO Box ABC, Bradley, WV 25818. *Phone:* 304-

877-6428 Ext. 3213. *Toll-free phone:* 800-678-9ABC. *Fax:* 304-877-5082. *E-mail:* admissions2@abc.edu. *Web site:* http://www.abc.edu/.

Bethany College
Bethany, West Virginia

- **Independent** comprehensive, founded 1840, affiliated with Christian Church (Disciples of Christ)
- **Rural** 1300-acre campus with easy access to Pittsburgh
- **Endowment** $44.0 million
- **Coed** 790 undergraduate students, 98% full-time, 45% women, 55% men
- **Moderately difficult** entrance level, 59% of applicants were admitted

Undergraduates 778 full-time, 12 part-time. Students come from 29 states and territories; 4 other countries; 78% are from out of state; 15% Black or African American, non-Hispanic/Latino; 0.1% Hispanic/Latino; 0.4% Asian, non-Hispanic/Latino; 0.5% American Indian or Alaska Native, non-Hispanic/Latino; 0.9% Two or more races, non-Hispanic/Latino; 12% Race/ethnicity unknown; 0.8% international; 5% transferred in; 90% live on campus. *Retention:* 59% of full-time freshmen returned.

Freshmen *Admission:* 1,463 applied, 865 admitted, 214 enrolled. *Average high school GPA:* 2.9. *Test scores:* SAT critical reading scores over 500: 30%; SAT math scores over 500: 28%; SAT writing scores over 500: 28%; ACT scores over 18: 73%; SAT critical reading scores over 600: 9%; SAT math scores over 600: 7%; SAT writing scores over 600: 8%; ACT scores over 24: 26%; SAT critical reading scores over 700: 1%; SAT math scores over 700: 2%; ACT scores over 30: 1%.

Faculty *Total:* 77, 61% full-time, 56% with terminal degrees. *Student/faculty ratio:* 14:1.

Academics *Calendar:* 4-1-4. *Degrees:* bachelor's and master's. *Special study options:* academic remediation for entering students, advanced placement credit, distance learning, double majors, independent study, internships, off-campus study, part-time degree program, services for LD students, student-designed majors, study abroad. *Unusual degree programs:* 3-2 engineering with Columbia University, Case Western Reserve University; Duquesne University, Carnegie Mellon University.

Computers on Campus 150 computers/terminals are available on campus for general student use. Students can access the following: computer help desk, free student e-mail accounts, online (class) grades, online (class) registration, online (class) schedules. Campuswide network is available. 100% of college-owned or -operated housing units are wired for high-speed Internet access. Wireless service is available via classrooms, computer centers, computer labs, learning centers, libraries, student centers.

Student Life *Housing:* on-campus residence required through senior year. *Options:* coed, men-only, women-only, disabled students. Campus housing is university owned. Freshman campus housing is guaranteed. *Activities and organizations:* drama/theater group, student-run newspaper, radio and television station, choral group, Student Board of Governors, Outdoor Club, Model United Nations, Public Relations Society, International Student Association, national fraternities, national sororities. *Campus security:* 24-hour emergency response devices and patrols, late-night transport/escort service, controlled dormitory access. *Student services:* health clinic, personal/psychological counseling.

Athletics Member NCAA. All Division III. *Intercollegiate sports:* baseball M, basketball M/W, cross-country running M/W, football M, golf M/W, lacrosse M, soccer M/W, softball W, swimming and diving M/W, tennis M/W, track and field M/W, volleyball W.

Standardized Tests *Required:* SAT or ACT (for admission).

Costs (2011–12) *Comprehensive fee:* $33,400 includes full-time tuition ($22,954), mandatory fees ($900), and room and board ($9546). Part-time tuition: $650 per credit hour. *Required fees:* $113 per term part-time. *College room only:* $5000. Room and board charges vary according to housing facility. *Payment plan:* installment. *Waivers:* children of alumni and employees or children of employees.

Financial Aid Of all full-time matriculated undergraduates who enrolled in 2009, 777 applied for aid, 699 were judged to have need. In 2009, 60 non-need-based awards were made. *Average percent of need met:* 49%. *Average need-based loan:* $7258. *Average need-based gift aid:* $9824. *Average non-need-based aid:* $7189.

Applying *Options:* electronic application, deferred entrance. *Required:* essay or personal statement, high school transcript, minimum 2.0 GPA, 1 letter of recommendation, documentation of student involvement. *Required for some:* interview. *Recommended:* interview. *Application deadlines:* rolling (freshmen), rolling (out-of-state freshmen), rolling (transfers). *Notification:* 8/15 (freshmen), 8/15 (out-of-state freshmen), continuous until 8/15 (transfers).

Freshman Application Contact R.J. Zitzelsberger, Director of Admission, Bethany College, Office of Admission, Bethany, WV 26032. *Phone:* 304-829-7611. *Toll-free phone:* 800-922-7611. *Fax:* 304-829-7142. *E-mail:* admission@bethanywv.edu. *Web site:* http://www.bethanywv.edu/.

Bluefield State College

Bluefield, West Virginia

- **State-supported** 4-year, founded 1895, part of West Virginia Higher Education Policy Commission
- **Small-town** 45-acre campus
- **Coed** 1,929 undergraduate students, 79% full-time, 64% women, 36% men
- **Noncompetitive** entrance level, 40% of applicants were admitted

Undergraduates 1,530 full-time, 399 part-time. 9% are from out of state; 11% Black or African American, non-Hispanic/Latino; 0.3% Hispanic/Latino; 0.1% Asian, non-Hispanic/Latino; 0.1% Native Hawaiian or other Pacific Islander, non-Hispanic/Latino; 0.2% Two or more races, non-Hispanic/Latino; 2% international; 12% transferred in. *Retention:* 56% of full-time freshmen returned.
Freshmen *Admission:* 980 applied, 388 admitted, 268 enrolled. *Test scores:* SAT critical reading scores over 500: 25%; SAT math scores over 500: 37%; ACT scores over 18: 68%; SAT critical reading scores over 600: 15%; SAT math scores over 600: 4%; ACT scores over 24: 11%; ACT scores over 30: 1%.
Faculty *Total:* 145, 52% full-time, 34% with terminal degrees. *Student/faculty ratio:* 17:1.
Academics *Calendar:* semesters. *Degrees:* associate and bachelor's. *Special study options:* adult/continuing education programs, part-time degree program.
Computers on Campus Students can access the following: computer help desk, free student e-mail accounts, online (class) grades, online (class) registration. Campuswide network is available. Wireless service is available via entire campus.
Student Life *Housing:* college housing not available. *Activities and organizations:* drama/theater group, student-run newspaper, radio station, choral group, national fraternities, national sororities. *Campus security:* 24-hour emergency response devices and patrols, student patrols. *Student services:* health clinic, personal/psychological counseling.
Athletics Member NCAA. All Division II. *Intercollegiate sports:* baseball M(s), basketball M(s)/W(s), cheerleading W, cross-country running M(s)/W(s), golf M(s), softball W(s), tennis M(s)/W(s). *Intramural sports:* badminton M/W, basketball M/W, football M, soccer M, swimming and diving M/W, table tennis M/W, volleyball M/W, water polo M/W.
Standardized Tests *Required:* SAT or ACT (for admission).
Costs (2011–12) *Tuition:* state resident $4908 full-time, $205 per credit hour part-time; nonresident $9456 full-time, $394 per credit hour part-time. *Payment plan:* installment. *Waivers:* adult students and senior citizens.
Financial Aid Of all full-time matriculated undergraduates who enrolled in 2010, 1,310 applied for aid, 1,120 were judged to have need, 440 had their need fully met. 50 Federal Work-Study jobs. In 2010, 400 non-need-based awards were made. *Average percent of need met:* 70%. *Average financial aid package:* $6800. *Average need-based loan:* $3600. *Average need-based gift aid:* $3500. *Average non-need-based aid:* $1500. *Average indebtedness upon graduation:* $22,000.
Applying *Options:* early admission, deferred entrance. *Required:* high school transcript, minimum 2.0 GPA. *Application deadlines:* rolling (freshmen), rolling (transfers). *Notification:* continuous (freshmen), continuous (transfers).
Freshman Application Contact Bluefield State College, 219 Rock Street, Bluefield, WV 24701-2198. *Phone:* 304-327-4067. *Toll-free phone:* 800-344-8892 Ext. 4065 (in-state); 800-654-7798 Ext. 4065 (out-of-state). *Web site:* http://www.bluefieldstate.edu/.

Concord University

Athens, West Virginia

- **State-supported** comprehensive, founded 1872, part of State College System of West Virginia
- **Rural** 100-acre campus
- **Endowment** $21.4 million
- **Coed**
- **Minimally difficult** entrance level

Faculty *Student/faculty ratio:* 17:1.
Academics *Calendar:* semesters. *Degrees:* associate, bachelor's, and master's.
Student Life *Campus security:* 24-hour emergency response devices and patrols, student patrols, late-night transport/escort service, controlled dormitory access.
Athletics Member NCAA. All Division II.
Standardized Tests *Required:* SAT or ACT (for admission).
Costs (2011–12) *Tuition:* state resident $5446 full-time, $227 per credit part-time; nonresident $12,100 full-time, $504 per credit part-time. Full-time tuition and fees vary according to course load. Part-time tuition and fees vary according to course load. *Room and board:* $7240; room only: $3688. Room and board charges vary according to housing facility.

Financial Aid Of all full-time matriculated undergraduates who enrolled in 2010, 2,092 applied for aid, 1,702 were judged to have need, 533 had their need fully met. 248 Federal Work-Study jobs (averaging $1205). 385 state and other part-time jobs (averaging $1191). In 2010, 175 non-need-based awards were made. *Average percent of need met:* 93. *Average financial aid package:* $11,726. *Average need-based loan:* $6642. *Average need-based gift aid:* $5292. *Average non-need-based aid:* $2760. *Average indebtedness upon graduation:* $14,700.
Applying *Options:* electronic application, early admission, early decision. *Required:* high school transcript, minimum 2.0 GPA. *Required for some:* essay or personal statement, interview. *Recommended:* interview.
Freshman Application Contact Mr. Kent Gamble, Director of Enrollment, Concord University, 1000 Vermillion Street, Athens, WV 24712. *Phone:* 304-384-5316. *Toll-free phone:* 888-384-5249. *Fax:* 304-384-9044. *E-mail:* admissions@concord.edu. *Web site:* http://www.concord.edu/.

Davis & Elkins College

Elkins, West Virginia

Freshman Application Contact Ms. Rene Heckel, Director of Enrollment Management, Davis & Elkins College, 100 Campus Drive, Elkins, WV 26241. *Phone:* 304-637-1974. *Toll-free phone:* 800-624-3157. *Fax:* 304-637-1800. *E-mail:* admiss@davisandelkins.edu. *Web site:* http://www.dewv.edu/.

Fairmont State University

Fairmont, West Virginia

- **State-supported** comprehensive, founded 1865, part of State College System of West Virginia
- **Small-town** 120-acre campus
- **Endowment** $14.8 million
- **Coed** 4,268 undergraduate students, 86% full-time, 56% women, 44% men
- **Minimally difficult** entrance level, 55% of applicants were admitted

Undergraduates 3,670 full-time, 598 part-time. 4% Black or African American, non-Hispanic/Latino; 2% Hispanic/Latino; 0.4% Asian, non-Hispanic/Latino; 0.1% Native Hawaiian or other Pacific Islander, non-Hispanic/Latino; 0.3% American Indian or Alaska Native, non-Hispanic/Latino; 2% Two or more races, non-Hispanic/Latino; 1% Race/ethnicity unknown; 2% international; 18% live on campus. *Retention:* 66% of full-time freshmen returned.
Freshmen *Admission:* 3,461 applied, 1,899 admitted, 751 enrolled. *Average high school GPA:* 3.16. *Test scores:* SAT critical reading scores over 500: 34%; SAT math scores over 500: 34%; ACT scores over 18: 84%; SAT critical reading scores over 600: 8%; SAT math scores over 600: 8%; ACT scores over 24: 23%; SAT critical reading scores over 700: 1%; ACT scores over 30: 1%.
Faculty *Total:* 317, 56% full-time, 54% with terminal degrees. *Student/faculty ratio:* 17:1.
Academics *Calendar:* semesters. *Degrees:* certificates, associate, bachelor's, and master's. *Special study options:* academic remediation for entering students, accelerated degree program, adult/continuing education programs, advanced placement credit, cooperative education, distance learning, double majors, English as a second language, honors programs, independent study, internships, off-campus study, part-time degree program, services for LD students, study abroad, summer session for credit. *ROTC:* Army (b), Air Force (c).
Computers on Campus 1,350 computers/terminals are available on campus for general student use. Students can access the following: campus intranet, computer help desk, free student e-mail accounts, online (class) grades, online (class) registration, online (class) schedules. Campuswide network is available. Wireless service is available via entire campus.
Student Life *Housing:* on-campus residence required through sophomore year. *Options:* coed, men-only, women-only. Campus housing is university owned. Freshman campus housing is guaranteed. *Activities and organizations:* drama/theater group, student-run newspaper, choral group, marching band, Alpha Phi Omega, Circle K, Society for Non-traditional Students, Criminal Justice Club, Honors Association, national fraternities, national sororities. *Campus security:* 24-hour emergency response devices and patrols, student patrols, controlled dormitory access. *Student services:* health clinic, personal/psychological counseling, legal services.
Athletics Member NCAA. All Division II. *Intercollegiate sports:* baseball M, basketball M(s)/W(s), cross-country running M/W, football M(s), golf M(s)/W, softball W, swimming and diving M(s)/W(s), tennis M(s)/W(s), volleyball W. *Intramural sports:* archery M/W, basketball M/W, bowling M/W, cross-country running M/W, football M/W, golf M/W, swimming and diving M/W, table tennis M/W, tennis M/W, volleyball M/W, wrestling M.
Standardized Tests *Required:* SAT or ACT (for admission).
Costs (2011–12) *Tuition:* state resident $5326 full-time; nonresident $11,230 full-time. Full-time tuition and fees vary according to degree level and loca-

tion. Part-time tuition and fees vary according to course load, degree level, and location. *Room and board:* $7132. Room and board charges vary according to board plan and housing facility. *Payment plan:* installment. *Waivers:* employees or children of employees.

Financial Aid Of all full-time matriculated undergraduates who enrolled in 2010, 3,376 applied for aid, 2,888 were judged to have need, 126 had their need fully met. In 2010, 250 non-need-based awards were made. *Average percent of need met:* 65%. *Average financial aid package:* $3041. *Average need-based loan:* $3858. *Average need-based gift aid:* $6047. *Average non-need-based aid:* $4878. *Average indebtedness upon graduation:* $23,307.

Applying *Options:* electronic application. *Required:* high school transcript. *Recommended:* minimum 2.0 GPA. *Application deadlines:* rolling (freshmen), rolling (transfers). *Notification:* continuous (freshmen), continuous (transfers).

Freshman Application Contact Mrs. Lori Schoonmaker, Director of Admissions and Recruiting (Interim Associate), Fairmont State University, 1201 Locust Avenue, Fairmont, WV 26554. *Phone:* 304-367-4892. *Toll-free phone:* 800-641-5678. *Fax:* 304-367-4938. *E-mail:* admit@fairmontstate.edu. *Web site:* http://www.fairmontstate.edu/.

Glenville State College
Glenville, West Virginia

- **State-supported** 4-year, founded 1872, part of West Virginia Higher Education Policy Commission
- **Rural** 331-acre campus
- **Endowment** $13.4 million
- **Coed** 1,857 undergraduate students, 64% full-time, 42% women, 58% men
- **Noncompetitive** entrance level, 82% of applicants were admitted

Undergraduates 1,188 full-time, 669 part-time. Students come from 23 states and territories; 4 other countries; 14% are from out of state; 16% Black or African American, non-Hispanic/Latino; 2% Hispanic/Latino; 0.7% Two or more races, non-Hispanic/Latino; 3% Race/ethnicity unknown; 4% transferred in; 33% live on campus. *Retention:* 70% of full-time freshmen returned.

Freshmen *Admission:* 1,246 applied, 1,023 admitted, 355 enrolled. *Average high school GPA:* 2.8. *Test scores:* SAT critical reading scores over 500: 8%; SAT math scores over 500: 7%; ACT scores over 18: 61%; SAT critical reading scores over 600: 5%; SAT math scores over 600: 2%; ACT scores over 24: 11%.

Faculty *Total:* 112, 61% full-time, 38% with terminal degrees. *Student/faculty ratio:* 19:1.

Academics *Calendar:* semesters. *Degrees:* associate and bachelor's. *Special study options:* academic remediation for entering students, accelerated degree program, adult/continuing education programs, advanced placement credit, cooperative education, distance learning, double majors, external degree program, honors programs, internships, off-campus study, part-time degree program, services for LD students, student-designed majors, study abroad, summer session for credit. *ROTC:* Army (b).

Computers on Campus 183 computers/terminals and 599 ports are available on campus for general student use. Students can access the following: campus intranet, computer help desk, free student e-mail accounts, online (class) grades, online (class) registration, online (class) schedules, WebVista, Wimba Classroom. Campuswide network is available. 100% of college-owned or -operated housing units are wired for high-speed Internet access. Wireless service is available via entire campus.

Student Life *Housing:* on-campus residence required through sophomore year. *Options:* coed, men-only, women-only, disabled students. Campus housing is university owned. Freshman campus housing is guaranteed. *Activities and organizations:* drama/theater group, student-run newspaper, choral group, marching band, Music Educators National Conference, Student Government Association, Student Support Services, Student Advisory Committee, Glenville Student Action, national fraternities. *Campus security:* 24-hour emergency response devices and patrols, student patrols, late-night transport/escort service, controlled dormitory access. *Student services:* health clinic, personal/psychological counseling.

Athletics Member NCAA. All Division II. *Intercollegiate sports:* basketball M(s)/W(s), cross-country running M(s)/W(s), football M(s), golf M(s)/W(s), softball W(s), track and field M(s)/W(s), volleyball W(s). *Intramural sports:* basketball M/W, fencing M/W, rock climbing M/W, softball M/W, swimming and diving M/W, table tennis M/W, tennis M/W, volleyball M/W.

Standardized Tests *Required:* SAT or ACT (for admission).

Costs (2011–12) *Tuition:* state resident $5352 full-time, $223 per credit hour part-time; nonresident $12,720 full-time, $530 per credit hour part-time. Full-time tuition and fees vary according to course load. *Required fees:* $223 per credit hour part-time. *Room and board:* $7900; room only: $4500. Room and board charges vary according to board plan and housing facility. *Payment plan:* installment. *Waivers:* senior citizens and employees or children of employees.

Financial Aid Of all full-time matriculated undergraduates who enrolled in 2011, 1,104 applied for aid, 999 were judged to have need, 203 had their need fully met. 139 Federal Work-Study jobs (averaging $1500). 294 state and other part-time jobs (averaging $1900). In 2011, 49 non-need-based awards were made. *Average percent of need met:* 73%. *Average financial aid package:* $12,445. *Average need-based loan:* $3801. *Average need-based gift aid:* $5419. *Average non-need-based aid:* $2077. *Average indebtedness upon graduation:* $25,957.

Applying *Options:* electronic application, deferred entrance. *Application fee:* $20. *Required:* high school transcript, minimum 3.0 GPA, college preparatory program. *Required for some:* interview. *Application deadlines:* rolling (freshmen), rolling (out-of-state freshmen), 8/24 (transfers). *Notification:* continuous (freshmen), continuous (out-of-state freshmen), 8/24 (transfers).

Freshman Application Contact Ms. Ashley Weir, Admission Counselor, Glenville State College, 200 High Street, Glenville, WV 26351-1200. *Phone:* 304-462-4128 Ext. 6133. *Toll-free phone:* 800-924-2010. *Fax:* 304-462-8619. *E-mail:* ashley.weir@glenville.edu. *Web site:* http://www.glenville.edu/.

Marshall University
Huntington, West Virginia

- **State-supported** university, founded 1837, part of University System of West Virginia
- **Urban** 100-acre campus
- **Coed** 10,053 undergraduate students, 86% full-time, 57% women, 43% men
- **Moderately difficult** entrance level, 81% of applicants were admitted

Undergraduates 8,612 full-time, 1,441 part-time. Students come from 44 states and territories; 34 other countries; 24% are from out of state; 6% Black or African American, non-Hispanic/Latino; 2% Hispanic/Latino; 0.8% Asian, non-Hispanic/Latino; 0.1% Native Hawaiian or other Pacific Islander, non-Hispanic/Latino; 0.4% American Indian or Alaska Native, non-Hispanic/Latino; 0.7% Two or more races, non-Hispanic/Latino; 3% Race/ethnicity unknown; 1% international; 8% transferred in; 24% live on campus. *Retention:* 70% of full-time freshmen returned.

Freshmen *Admission:* 2,912 applied, 2,368 admitted, 2,002 enrolled. *Average high school GPA:* 3.33. *Test scores:* SAT critical reading scores over 500: 59%; SAT math scores over 500: 48%; ACT scores over 18: 91%; SAT critical reading scores over 600: 17%; SAT math scores over 600: 16%; ACT scores over 24: 33%; SAT critical reading scores over 700: 2%; SAT math scores over 700: 3%; ACT scores over 30: 3%.

Faculty *Total:* 760, 67% full-time, 55% with terminal degrees. *Student/faculty ratio:* 19:1.

Academics *Calendar:* semesters. *Degrees:* associate, bachelor's, master's, doctoral, post-master's, postbachelor's, and first professional certificates. *Special study options:* academic remediation for entering students, accelerated degree program, adult/continuing education programs, advanced placement credit, cooperative education, distance learning, double majors, English as a second language, honors programs, independent study, internships, off-campus study, part-time degree program, services for LD students, study abroad, summer session for credit. *ROTC:* Army (b). *Unusual degree programs:* 3-2 forestry with Duke University.

Computers on Campus 1,461 computers/terminals and 2,900 ports are available on campus for general student use. Students can access the following: campus intranet, computer help desk, free student e-mail accounts, online (class) grades, online (class) registration, online (class) schedules, Virtual Computer Lab - MU Remote and Web Conferencing. Campuswide network is available. 100% of college-owned or -operated housing units are wired for high-speed Internet access. Wireless service is available via classrooms, computer centers, computer labs, dorm rooms, learning centers, libraries, student centers.

Student Life *Housing:* on-campus residence required through sophomore year. *Options:* coed, women-only, disabled students. Campus housing is university owned. Freshman campus housing is guaranteed. *Activities and organizations:* drama/theater group, student-run newspaper, radio and television station, choral group, marching band, Campus Crusade for Christ, Gamma Beta Phi, The International Students' Organization, Newman Association, Phi Alpha Theta, national fraternities, national sororities. *Campus security:* 24-hour emergency response devices and patrols, student patrols, late-night transport/escort service, controlled dormitory access. *Student services:* health clinic, personal/psychological counseling, women's center, legal services.

Athletics Member NCAA. All Division I except football (Division I-A). *Intercollegiate sports:* baseball M(s), basketball M(s)/W(s), cross-country running M(s)/W(s), golf M(s)/W(s), lacrosse M(c), rugby M(c)/W(c), soccer M(s)/W(s), softball W(s), swimming and diving W(s), tennis W(s), track and field M(s)/W(s), volleyball W(s). *Intramural sports:* basketball M/W, bowling M/W, football M/W, golf M/W, racquetball M/W, soccer M/W, softball M/

W, swimming and diving M/W, tennis M/W, track and field M/W, volleyball M/W.

Standardized Tests *Required:* SAT or ACT (for admission).

Costs (2011–12) *Tuition:* state resident $4582 full-time, $191 per credit hour part-time; nonresident $12,414 full-time, $518 per credit hour part-time. Full-time tuition and fees vary according to degree level, location, program, and reciprocity agreements. Part-time tuition and fees vary according to course load, degree level, location, program, and reciprocity agreements. *Required fees:* $1066 full-time. *Room and board:* $8710; room only: $5408. Room and board charges vary according to board plan and housing facility. *Payment plan:* installment. *Waivers:* senior citizens and employees or children of employees.

Financial Aid Of all full-time matriculated undergraduates who enrolled in 2011, 6,670 applied for aid, 5,335 were judged to have need, 1,802 had their need fully met. In 2011, 1269 non-need-based awards were made. *Average percent of need met:* 53%. *Average financial aid package:* $9579. *Average need-based loan:* $7043. *Average need-based gift aid:* $5642. *Average non-need-based aid:* $6018. *Average indebtedness upon graduation:* $24,376.

Applying *Options:* electronic application, deferred entrance. *Application fee:* $30. *Required for some:* high school transcript. *Application deadlines:* rolling (freshmen), rolling (transfers). *Notification:* continuous (freshmen), continuous (transfers).

Freshman Application Contact Dr. Tammy Johnson, Director of Admissions, Marshall University, 1 John Marshall Drive, Huntington, WV 25755. *Phone:* 800-642-3499. *Toll-free phone:* 800-642-3499. *Fax:* 304-696-3135. *E-mail:* admissions@marshall.edu. *Web site:* http://www.marshall.edu/.

Mountain State University
Beckley, West Virginia

- **Independent** comprehensive, founded 1933
- **Small-town** 35-acre campus
- **Endowment** $5.5 million
- **Coed** 4,209 undergraduate students, 62% full-time, 64% women, 36% men
- **Noncompetitive** entrance level, 100% of applicants were admitted

Undergraduates 2,624 full-time, 1,585 part-time. Students come from 50 states and territories; 29 other countries; 44% are from out of state; 20% Black or African American, non-Hispanic/Latino; 3% Hispanic/Latino; 0.9% Asian, non-Hispanic/Latino; 0.2% Native Hawaiian or other Pacific Islander, non-Hispanic/Latino; 0.6% American Indian or Alaska Native, non-Hispanic/Latino; 1% Two or more races, non-Hispanic/Latino; 4% Race/ethnicity unknown; 3% international; 16% transferred in; 37% live on campus. *Retention:* 45% of full-time freshmen returned.

Freshmen *Admission:* 1,611 applied, 1,611 admitted, 508 enrolled. *Average high school GPA:* 2.98. *Test scores:* SAT math scores over 500: 25%; ACT scores over 18: 55%; SAT math scores over 600: 13%; ACT scores over 24: 11%; ACT scores over 30: 1%.

Faculty *Total:* 457, 21% full-time, 14% with terminal degrees. *Student/faculty ratio:* 19:1.

Academics *Calendar:* semesters. *Degrees:* certificates, associate, bachelor's, master's, doctoral, post-master's, and postbachelor's certificates. *Special study options:* academic remediation for entering students, accelerated degree program, adult/continuing education programs, advanced placement credit, cooperative education, distance learning, double majors, English as a second language, external degree program, independent study, internships, part-time degree program, student-designed majors, summer session for credit.

Computers on Campus 230 computers/terminals are available on campus for general student use. Students can access the following: campus intranet, computer help desk, free student e-mail accounts, online (class) grades, online (class) registration, online (class) schedules. Campuswide network is available. 100% of college-owned or -operated housing units are wired for high-speed Internet access. Wireless service is available via entire campus.

Student Life *Housing:* on-campus residence required through sophomore year. *Options:* coed. Campus housing is university owned. Freshman campus housing is guaranteed. *Activities and organizations:* drama/theater group, choral group, FIA-Forensics Investigation Association, MSU Physician Assistant Society, Students in Free Enterprise (SIFE), MSU Christian Launch Organization, Student Social Work Organization, national sororities. *Campus security:* 24-hour emergency response devices and patrols, late-night transport/escort service, controlled dormitory access. *Student services:* personal/psychological counseling.

Athletics Member NAIA. *Intercollegiate sports:* basketball M(s), cheerleading M/W(s), cross-country running M(s)/W(s), soccer M(s)/W(s), track and field M(s)/W(s), volleyball W(s). *Intramural sports:* basketball M, soccer M/W, volleyball W.

Standardized Tests *Required for some:* SAT (for admission), ACT (for admission), SAT or ACT (for admission). *Recommended:* SAT Subject Tests (for admission).

Costs (2011–12) *Comprehensive fee:* $16,630 includes full-time tuition ($7350), mandatory fees ($2250), and room and board ($7030). Full-time tuition and fees vary according to course load, degree level, and program. Part-time tuition: $245 per credit hour. Part-time tuition and fees vary according to course load, degree level, and program. *Required fees:* $75 per credit hour part-time. *Room and board:* Room and board charges vary according to board plan and housing facility. *Payment plan:* installment. *Waivers:* senior citizens and employees or children of employees.

Financial Aid Of all full-time matriculated undergraduates who enrolled in 2010, 2,502 applied for aid, 2,502 were judged to have need, 2,260 had their need fully met. 58 Federal Work-Study jobs (averaging $1939). In 2010, 4 non-need-based awards were made. *Average percent of need met:* 85%. *Average financial aid package:* $13,287. *Average need-based loan:* $10,765. *Average need-based gift aid:* $5305. *Average non-need-based aid:* $2000. *Average indebtedness upon graduation:* $36,187.

Applying *Options:* electronic application, early admission, deferred entrance. *Application fee:* $25. *Required:* high school transcript. *Required for some:* essay or personal statement, interview, Statement of faith. *Application deadlines:* rolling (freshmen), rolling (transfers).

Freshman Application Contact Ms. Tammy Kyle, Mountain State University, 410 Neville Street, Beckley, WV 25801. *Phone:* 304-929-1563. *Toll-free phone:* 866-367-6781. *Fax:* 304-253-5072. *E-mail:* gomsu@mountainstate.edu. *Web site:* http://www.mountainstate.edu/.

Ohio Valley University
Vienna, West Virginia

- **Independent** comprehensive, founded 1960, affiliated with Church of Christ
- **Small-town** 299-acre campus
- **Coed** 488 undergraduate students, 90% full-time, 47% women, 53% men
- **Minimally difficult** entrance level, 46% of applicants were admitted

Undergraduates 438 full-time, 50 part-time. 6% Black or African American, non-Hispanic/Latino; 3% Hispanic/Latino; 0.4% Asian, non-Hispanic/Latino; 3% Two or more races, non-Hispanic/Latino; 3% Race/ethnicity unknown; 5% international; 8% transferred in; 53% live on campus. *Retention:* 67% of full-time freshmen returned.

Freshman *Admission:* 870 applied, 397 admitted, 147 enrolled. *Average high school GPA:* 2.97. *Test scores:* SAT critical reading scores over 500: 48%; SAT math scores over 500: 45%; SAT writing scores over 500: 43%; ACT scores over 18: 79%; SAT critical reading scores over 600: 20%; SAT math scores over 600: 13%; SAT writing scores over 600: 13%; ACT scores over 24: 26%; SAT critical reading scores over 700: 3%; ACT scores over 30: 2%.

Faculty *Total:* 89, 26% full-time, 33% with terminal degrees. *Student/faculty ratio:* 10:1.

Academics *Calendar:* semesters. *Degrees:* associate, bachelor's, and master's. *Special study options:* adult/continuing education programs, part-time degree program.

Computers on Campus Students can access the following: campus intranet, computer help desk, free student e-mail accounts, online (class) grades, online (class) registration, online (class) schedules. Campuswide network is available. 100% of college-owned or -operated housing units are wired for high-speed Internet access. Wireless service is available via entire campus.

Student Life *Housing:* on-campus residence required through sophomore year. *Options:* men-only, women-only. Campus housing is university owned. Freshman campus housing is guaranteed. *Campus security:* 24-hour emergency response devices and patrols, controlled dormitory access.

Athletics Member NCAA. All Division II. *Intercollegiate sports:* baseball M(s), basketball M(s)/W(s), cross-country running M(s)/W(s), golf M(s)/W(s), lacrosse M(s), soccer M(s)/W(s), softball W(s), volleyball W(s), wrestling M(s). *Intramural sports:* basketball M/W, bowling M/W, football M/W, golf M/W, soccer M/W, softball M/W, volleyball M/W.

Standardized Tests *Required:* SAT or ACT (for admission).

Costs (2011–12) *Comprehensive fee:* $24,496 includes full-time tuition ($16,338), mandatory fees ($1712), and room and board ($6446). Full-time tuition and fees vary according to course load. Part-time tuition: $525 per credit hour. Part-time tuition and fees vary according to course load. *Required fees:* $63 per credit hour part-time. *College room only:* $3269. Room and board charges vary according to board plan and housing facility. *Payment plan:* installment. *Waivers:* employees or children of employees.

Financial Aid Of all full-time matriculated undergraduates who enrolled in 2010, 373 applied for aid, 338 were judged to have need, 64 had their need fully met. 119 Federal Work-Study jobs (averaging $984). 8 state and other part-time jobs (averaging $1510). In 2010, 47 non-need-based awards were made. *Average percent of need met:* 69%. *Average financial aid package:*

$13,188. *Average need-based loan:* $3947. *Average need-based gift aid:* $9922. *Average non-need-based aid:* $6171. *Average indebtedness upon graduation:* $21,735.

Applying *Options:* electronic application, early admission, deferred entrance. *Required:* high school transcript. *Required for some:* essay or personal statement, interview. *Application deadlines:* 8/30 (freshmen), rolling (transfers). *Notification:* continuous (freshmen), continuous (transfers).

Freshman Application Contact Mrs. Valerie Wright, Admissions Office Manager, Ohio Valley University, 1 Campus View Drive, Vienna, WV 26105. *Phone:* 304-865-6200. *Toll-free phone:* 877-446-8668. *Fax:* 304-865-6001. *E-mail:* admissions@ovu.edu. *Web site:* http://www.ovu.edu/.

Potomac State College of West Virginia University

Keyser, West Virginia

- **State-supported** primarily 2-year, founded 1901, part of West Virginia Higher Education Policy Commission
- **Small-town** 18-acre campus
- **Coed**
- **Noncompetitive** entrance level

Faculty *Student/faculty ratio:* 25:1.

Academics *Calendar:* semesters. *Degrees:* certificates, associate, and bachelor's.

Student Life *Campus security:* 24-hour patrols, late-night transport/escort service, controlled dormitory access.

Athletics Member NJCAA.

Standardized Tests *Required for some:* SAT or ACT (for admission).

Costs (2011–12) *Tuition:* state resident $3058 full-time, $129 per credit hour part-time; nonresident $8990 full-time, $376 per credit hour part-time. Full-time tuition and fees vary according to degree level. Part-time tuition and fees vary according to course load and degree level. *Room and board:* $7290; room only: $3860. Room and board charges vary according to board plan and housing facility.

Financial Aid *Of all full-time matriculated undergraduates who enrolled in 2010,* 70 Federal Work-Study jobs (averaging $1300).

Applying *Options:* electronic application, early admission. *Required:* high school transcript.

Freshman Application Contact Ms. Beth Little, Director of Enrollment Services, Potomac State College of West Virginia University, 75 Arnold Street, Keyser, WV 26726. *Phone:* 304-788-6820. *Toll-free phone:* 800-262-7332 Ext. 6820. *Fax:* 304-788-6939. *E-mail:* go2psc@mail.wvu.edu. *Web site:* http://www.potomacstatecollege.edu/.

Salem International University

Salem, West Virginia

Freshman Application Contact Ms. Gina Cossey, Vice President, Recruiting and Admissions, Salem International University, PO Box 500, Salem, WV 26426-0500. *Phone:* 304-326-1359. *Toll-free phone:* 888-235-5024. *Fax:* 304-326-1592. *E-mail:* admissions@salemiu.edu. *Web site:* http://www.salemu.edu/.

Shepherd University

Shepherdstown, West Virginia

- **State-supported** comprehensive, founded 1871, part of West Virginia Higher Education Policy Commission
- **Small-town** 320-acre campus with easy access to Washington, D.C.
- **Endowment** $26.5 million
- **Coed** 4,240 undergraduate students, 82% full-time, 58% women, 42% men
- **Moderately difficult** entrance level, 87% of applicants were admitted

Undergraduates 3,477 full-time, 763 part-time. Students come from 51 states and territories; 10 other countries; 38% are from out of state; 7% Black or African American, non-Hispanic/Latino; 3% Hispanic/Latino; 2% Asian, non-Hispanic/Latino; 0.1% Native Hawaiian or other Pacific Islander, non-Hispanic/Latino; 0.8% American Indian or Alaska Native, non-Hispanic/Latino; 0.3% Two or more races, non-Hispanic/Latino; 6% Race/ethnicity unknown; 0.3% international; 10% transferred in; 34% live on campus. *Retention:* 68% of full-time freshmen returned.

Freshmen *Admission:* 2,056 applied, 1,798 admitted, 794 enrolled. *Average high school GPA:* 3.23. *Test scores:* SAT critical reading scores over 500: 57%; SAT math scores over 500: 48%; ACT scores over 18: 92%; SAT critical reading scores over 600: 15%; SAT math scores over 600: 13%; ACT scores over 24: 26%; SAT critical reading scores over 700: 2%; SAT math scores over 700: 2%; ACT scores over 30: 2%.

Faculty *Total:* 347, 39% full-time, 50% with terminal degrees. *Student/faculty ratio:* 19:1.

Academics *Calendar:* semesters. *Degrees:* bachelor's and master's. *Special study options:* academic remediation for entering students, adult/continuing education programs, advanced placement credit, cooperative education, distance learning, double majors, honors programs, independent study, internships, part-time degree program, services for LD students, study abroad, summer session for credit. *ROTC:* Air Force (c).

Computers on Campus 350 computers/terminals and 150 ports are available on campus for general student use. Students can access the following: campus intranet, computer help desk, free student e-mail accounts, online (class) grades, online (class) registration, online (class) schedules, personal Web pages. Campuswide network is available. 100% of college-owned or -operated housing units are wired for high-speed Internet access. Wireless service is available via classrooms, computer labs, libraries, student centers.

Student Life *Housing:* on-campus residence required through senior year. *Options:* coed. Campus housing is university owned. Freshman applicants given priority for college housing. *Activities and organizations:* drama/theater group, student-run newspaper, radio station, choral group, marching band, Student Government Association, Sigma Sigma Sigma, Delta Zeta, Relay for Life, marching band, national fraternities, national sororities. *Campus security:* 24-hour emergency response devices and patrols, late-night transport/escort service, controlled dormitory access, student security in academic buildings. *Student services:* health clinic, personal/psychological counseling.

Athletics Member NCAA. All Division II. *Intercollegiate sports:* baseball M(s), basketball M(s)/W(s), football M(s), golf M(s), lacrosse W(s), soccer M(s)/W(s), softball W(s), tennis M(s)/W(s), volleyball W(s). *Intramural sports:* basketball M/W, bowling M/W, football M/W, racquetball M/W, soccer M/W, softball M/W, swimming and diving M/W, table tennis M/W, tennis M/W, ultimate Frisbee M/W, volleyball M/W, water polo M/W, weight lifting M/W, wrestling M/W.

Standardized Tests *Required:* SAT or ACT (for admission).

Costs (2011–12) *Tuition:* state resident $5554 full-time, $226 per credit hour part-time; nonresident $14,418 full-time, $596 per credit hour part-time. Full-time tuition and fees vary according to program and reciprocity agreements. Part-time tuition and fees vary according to program. *Room and board:* $8190. Room and board charges vary according to board plan and housing facility. *Payment plan:* installment. *Waivers:* minority students, senior citizens, and employees or children of employees.

Financial Aid Of all full-time matriculated undergraduates who enrolled in 2011, 3,192 applied for aid, 2,169 were judged to have need, 549 had their need fully met. 140 Federal Work-Study jobs (averaging $1414). 482 state and other part-time jobs (averaging $2181). In 2011, 710 non-need-based awards were made. *Average percent of need met:* 76%. *Average financial aid package:* $11,406. *Average need-based loan:* $4001. *Average need-based gift aid:* $5267. *Average non-need-based aid:* $9826. *Average indebtedness upon graduation:* $22,060.

Applying *Options:* electronic application, early admission, early action, deferred entrance. *Application fee:* $45. *Required:* high school transcript, minimum 2.0 GPA. *Recommended:* essay or personal statement, minimum 3.0 GPA, 3 letters of recommendation. *Application deadlines:* rolling (freshmen), rolling (out-of-state freshmen), rolling (transfers), 11/15 (early action). *Notification:* continuous until 8/15 (freshmen), continuous until 8/15 (out-of-state freshmen), continuous until 8/15 (transfers), 12/15 (early action).

Freshman Application Contact Mr. Randall Friend, Director of Admissions, Shepherd University, PO Box 5000, Shepherdstown, WV 25443-5000. *Phone:* 304-876-5212. *Toll-free phone:* 800-344-5231. *Fax:* 304-876-5165. *E-mail:* admissions@shepherd.edu. *Web site:* http://www.shepherd.edu/.

Strayer University - Teays Valley Campus

Scott Depot, West Virginia

- **Proprietary** comprehensive
- **Coed**

Academics *Degrees:* certificates, diplomas, associate, bachelor's, master's, and postbachelor's certificates.

Freshman Application Contact Strayer University - Teays Valley Campus, 100 Corporate Center Drive, Scott Depot, WV 25560. *Web site:* http://www.strayer.edu/teays_valley.

University of Charleston
Charleston, West Virginia

- **Independent** comprehensive, founded 1888
- **Urban** 40-acre campus
- **Coed** 1,006 undergraduate students, 97% full-time, 60% women, 40% men
- **Moderately difficult** entrance level, 57% of applicants were admitted

Undergraduates 978 full-time, 28 part-time. Students come from 36 states and territories; 27 other countries; 42% are from out of state; 12% Black or African American, non-Hispanic/Latino; 2% Hispanic/Latino; 0.7% Asian, non-Hispanic/Latino; 0.3% American Indian or Alaska Native, non-Hispanic/Latino; 2% Two or more races, non-Hispanic/Latino; 15% Race/ethnicity unknown; 10% international; 9% transferred in; 61% live on campus. *Retention:* 61% of full-time freshmen returned.

Freshmen *Admission:* 1,701 applied, 967 admitted, 245 enrolled. *Average high school GPA:* 3.39. *Test scores:* SAT critical reading scores over 500: 49%; SAT math scores over 500: 49%; ACT scores over 18: 92%; SAT critical reading scores over 600: 6%; SAT math scores over 600: 11%; ACT scores over 24: 34%; SAT math scores over 700: 3%; ACT scores over 30: 4%.

Faculty *Student/faculty ratio:* 13:1.

Academics *Calendar:* semesters. *Degrees:* associate, bachelor's, master's, and doctoral. *Special study options:* academic remediation for entering students, accelerated degree program, adult/continuing education programs, advanced placement credit, cooperative education, double majors, English as a second language, independent study, internships, part-time degree program, services for LD students, student-designed majors, study abroad, summer session for credit. *ROTC:* Army (b). *Unusual degree programs:* 3-2 business administration.

Computers on Campus 200 computers/terminals are available on campus for general student use. Students can access the following: campus intranet, computer help desk, free student e-mail accounts, online (class) grades, online (class) registration, online (class) schedules. Campuswide network is available. 100% of college-owned or -operated housing units are wired for high-speed Internet access. Wireless service is available via entire campus.

Student Life *Housing:* on-campus residence required through sophomore year. *Options:* coed, disabled students. Campus housing is university owned. Freshman campus housing is guaranteed. *Activities and organizations:* drama/theater group, student-run newspaper, choral group, Student Activities Board, American Society of Interior Designers, Student Government Association, Capitol Association of Nursing Students, International Student Organization, national fraternities, national sororities. *Campus security:* 24-hour emergency response devices and patrols, student patrols, late-night transport/escort service, controlled dormitory access, radio connection to city police and ambulance. *Student services:* health clinic, personal/psychological counseling.

Athletics Member NCAA. All Division II. *Intercollegiate sports:* baseball M(s), basketball M(s)/W(s), cheerleading W(s), crew M(s)/W(s), cross-country running M(s)/W(s), football M(s), golf M(s), soccer M(s)/W(s), softball W(s), swimming and diving M(s)/W(s), tennis M(s)/W(s), track and field M(s)/W(s), volleyball W(s). *Intramural sports:* basketball M/W, bowling M/W, football M/W, tennis M/W, volleyball M/W, water polo M/W.

Standardized Tests *Required:* SAT or ACT (for admission).

Costs (2011–12) *Comprehensive fee:* $33,800 includes full-time tuition ($25,000) and room and board ($8800). Full-time tuition and fees vary according to student level. Part-time tuition: $410 per credit hour. Part-time tuition and fees vary according to course load and program. *College room only:* $4800. Room and board charges vary according to board plan and housing facility. *Payment plan:* installment. *Waivers:* children of alumni, senior citizens, and employees or children of employees.

Financial Aid Of all full-time matriculated undergraduates who enrolled in 2011, 971 applied for aid, 971 were judged to have need, 87 had their need fully met. 219 Federal Work-Study jobs (averaging $1200). *Average percent of need met:* 69%. *Average financial aid package:* $21,814. *Average need-based loan:* $4604. *Average need-based gift aid:* $12,787. *Financial aid deadline:* 8/15.

Applying *Options:* electronic application, early admission, deferred entrance. *Application fee:* $25. *Required:* high school transcript, minimum 2.3 GPA. *Required for some:* interview. *Recommended:* essay or personal statement, 3 letters of recommendation. *Application deadlines:* rolling (freshmen), rolling (out-of-state freshmen), rolling (transfers). *Notification:* continuous (freshmen), continuous (out-of-state freshmen), continuous (transfers).

Freshman Application Contact Sandy Dolin, Application Coordinator, University of Charleston, 2300 MacCorkle Avenue, SE, Charleston, WV 25304. *Phone:* 304-357-4752. *Toll-free phone:* 800-995-GOUC. *E-mail:* admissions@ucwv.edu. *Web site:* http://www.ucwv.edu/.

West Liberty University
West Liberty, West Virginia

- **State-supported** comprehensive, founded 1837, part of West Virginia Higher Education Policy Commission
- **Rural** campus
- **Coed** 2,730 undergraduate students, 86% full-time, 57% women, 43% men
- **Minimally difficult** entrance level

Undergraduates 2,349 full-time, 381 part-time. 30% are from out of state; 4% Black or African American, non-Hispanic/Latino; 0.9% Hispanic/Latino; 0.7% Asian, non-Hispanic/Latino; 0.2% American Indian or Alaska Native, non-Hispanic/Latino; 0.3% Two or more races, non-Hispanic/Latino; 0.8% Race/ethnicity unknown; 2% international; 10% transferred in; 47% live on campus. *Retention:* 67% of full-time freshmen returned.

Freshmen *Admission:* 556 enrolled. *Average high school GPA:* 3.28. *Test scores:* SAT critical reading scores over 500: 33%; SAT math scores over 500: 33%; SAT writing scores over 500: 27%; ACT scores over 18: 78%; SAT critical reading scores over 600: 11%; SAT math scores over 600: 10%; SAT writing scores over 600: 4%; ACT scores over 24: 20%; SAT critical reading scores over 700: 3%; ACT scores over 30: 1%.

Faculty *Total:* 224, 60% full-time, 44% with terminal degrees. *Student/faculty ratio:* 15:1.

Academics *Calendar:* semesters. *Degrees:* associate, bachelor's, and master's. *Special study options:* adult/continuing education programs, external degree program, part-time degree program.

Computers on Campus Students can access the following: campus intranet, computer help desk, free student e-mail accounts, online (class) grades, online (class) registration, online (class) schedules. Campuswide network is available. 100% of college-owned or -operated housing units are wired for high-speed Internet access. Wireless service is available via classrooms, computer labs, dorm rooms, learning centers, libraries, student centers.

Student Life *Housing options:* coed, men-only, women-only, disabled students. Campus housing is university owned. *Campus security:* 24-hour emergency response devices and patrols, controlled dormitory access.

Athletics Member NCAA. All Division II. *Intercollegiate sports:* baseball M(s), basketball M(s)/W(s), cross-country running M(s)/W(s), football M(s), golf M(s)/W(s), softball W(s), tennis M(s)/W(s), track and field M(s)/W(s), volleyball W(s), wrestling M(s). *Intramural sports:* basketball M/W, golf M/W, racquetball M/W, softball M/W, table tennis M/W, tennis M/W, volleyball M/W.

Standardized Tests *Required:* SAT or ACT (for admission).

Costs (2011–12) *Tuition:* state resident $5266 full-time; nonresident $13,140 full-time. Full-time tuition and fees vary according to course load, degree level, and program. Part-time tuition and fees vary according to course load, degree level, and program. *Room and board:* $7710; room only: $3360. Room and board charges vary according to board plan and housing facility. *Payment plans:* installment, deferred payment. *Waivers:* senior citizens and employees or children of employees.

Financial Aid Of all full-time matriculated undergraduates who enrolled in 2010, 2,138 applied for aid, 1,799 were judged to have need, 391 had their need fully met. In 2010, 43 non-need-based awards were made. *Average percent of need met:* 70%. *Average financial aid package:* $7990. *Average need-based loan:* $3974. *Average need-based gift aid:* $5196. *Average non-need-based aid:* $1507. *Average indebtedness upon graduation:* $25,000.

Applying *Options:* electronic application. *Required:* high school transcript, minimum 2.0 GPA. *Recommended:* interview. *Application deadlines:* rolling (freshmen), 8/1 (transfers). *Notification:* continuous (freshmen), continuous (transfers).

Freshman Application Contact Ms. Stephanie North, Admissions Counselor, West Liberty University, 208 University Drive, West Liberty, WV 26074. *Phone:* 304-336-8078. *Toll-free phone:* 800-732-6204 (in-state); 866-WESTLIB (out-of-state). *Fax:* 304-336-8403. *E-mail:* wladmsn1@westliberty.edu. *Web site:* http://www.westliberty.edu/.

West Virginia State University
Institute, West Virginia

- **State-supported** comprehensive, founded 1891, part of State College System of West Virginia
- **Suburban** 98-acre campus
- **Coed** 2,772 undergraduate students, 71% full-time, 58% women, 42% men
- **Minimally difficult** entrance level, 69% of applicants were admitted

Undergraduates 1,955 full-time, 817 part-time. Students come from 27 states and territories; 6 other countries; 8% are from out of state; 13% Black or African American, non-Hispanic/Latino; 0.8% Hispanic/Latino; 1% Asian, non-Hispanic/Latino; 0.5% American Indian or Alaska Native, non-Hispanic/

Latino; 24% Race/ethnicity unknown; 0.3% international; 7% live on campus. *Retention:* 58% of full-time freshmen returned.

Freshmen *Admission:* 913 applied, 630 admitted, 309 enrolled. *Average high school GPA:* 3.05.

Faculty *Total:* 202, 59% full-time. *Student/faculty ratio:* 15:1.

Academics *Calendar:* semesters. *Degrees:* bachelor's and master's. *Special study options:* academic remediation for entering students, accelerated degree program, adult/continuing education programs, advanced placement credit, cooperative education, external degree program, internships, part-time degree program, services for LD students, summer session for credit. *ROTC:* Army (b).

Computers on Campus Campuswide network is available.

Student Life *Housing:* on-campus residence required for freshman year. *Options:* men-only, women-only. Campus housing is university owned. *Activities and organizations:* student-run newspaper, choral group, marching band, national fraternities, national sororities. *Campus security:* 24-hour emergency response devices and patrols, late-night transport/escort service. *Student services:* health clinic, personal/psychological counseling.

Athletics Member NCAA. All Division II. *Intercollegiate sports:* baseball M, basketball M(s)/W(s), cross-country running M/W, football M(s), golf W, softball W(s), tennis M/W, track and field M/W, volleyball W. *Intramural sports:* baseball M, basketball M/W, bowling M/W, cheerleading W, cross-country running M/W, football M, golf W, softball W, tennis M/W, track and field M/W, volleyball W.

Standardized Tests *Required for some:* SAT or ACT (for admission). *Recommended:* SAT (for admission).

Costs (2011–12) *Tuition:* state resident $4918 full-time, $205 per credit hour part-time; nonresident $11,658 full-time, $486 per credit hour part-time. Full-time tuition and fees vary according to course load, degree level, and program. Part-time tuition and fees vary according to course load, degree level, and program. *Room and board:* $6602; room only: $3132. Room and board charges vary according to board plan and housing facility. *Payment plan:* installment.

Financial Aid *Financial aid deadline:* 6/15.

Applying *Options:* electronic application, early admission. *Required:* high school transcript. *Application deadlines:* 8/11 (freshmen), 8/11 (transfers). *Notification:* continuous (freshmen), continuous (transfers).

Freshman Application Contact Mr. Christopher D. Jackson, Interim Director of Recruiting, West Virginia State University, Campus Box 197, PO Box 1000, Ferrell Hall, Room 106, Institute, WV 25112-1000. *Phone:* 304-766-3033. *Toll-free phone:* 800-987-2112. *Fax:* 304-766-5182. *E-mail:* jacksoc@wvstateu.edu. *Web site:* http://www.wvstateu.edu/.

West Virginia University

Morgantown, West Virginia

- **State-supported** university, founded 1867, part of West Virginia Higher Education Policy Commission
- **Small-town** 1400-acre campus with easy access to Pittsburgh
- **Endowment** $363.5 million
- **Coed** 22,711 undergraduate students, 93% full-time, 45% women, 55% men
- **Moderately difficult** entrance level, 85% of applicants were admitted

Undergraduates 21,140 full-time, 1,571 part-time. Students come from 52 states and territories; 73 other countries; 47% are from out of state; 4% Black or African American, non-Hispanic/Latino; 3% Hispanic/Latino; 2% Asian, non-Hispanic/Latino; 0.1% Native Hawaiian or other Pacific Islander, non-Hispanic/Latino; 0.2% American Indian or Alaska Native, non-Hispanic/Latino; 2% Two or more races, non-Hispanic/Latino; 0.8% Race/ethnicity unknown; 3% international; 5% transferred in; 24% live on campus. *Retention:* 78% of full-time freshmen returned.

Freshmen *Admission:* 15,815 applied, 13,415 admitted, 5,022 enrolled. *Average high school GPA:* 3.36. *Test scores:* SAT critical reading scores over 500: 60%; SAT math scores over 500: 68%; ACT scores over 18: 96%; SAT critical reading scores over 600: 16%; SAT math scores over 600: 22%; ACT scores over 24: 47%; SAT critical reading scores over 700: 2%; SAT math scores over 700: 3%; ACT scores over 30: 7%.

Faculty *Total:* 1,324, 74% full-time, 75% with terminal degrees. *Student/faculty ratio:* 23:1.

Academics *Calendar:* semesters. *Degrees:* bachelor's, master's, doctoral, and first professional. *Special study options:* academic remediation for entering students, accelerated degree program, adult/continuing education programs, advanced placement credit, distance learning, double majors, English as a sec-

ond language, external degree program, honors programs, independent study, internships, off-campus study, part-time degree program, services for LD students, student-designed majors, study abroad, summer session for credit. *ROTC:* Army (b), Air Force (b). *Unusual degree programs:* 3-2 education, business/foreign language, occupational therapy, physical therapy, social work.

Computers on Campus 2,500 computers/terminals and 2,500 ports are available on campus for general student use. Students can access the following: campus intranet, computer help desk, free student e-mail accounts, online (class) grades, online (class) registration, online (class) schedules. Campus-wide network is available. 100% of college-owned or -operated housing units are wired for high-speed Internet access. Wireless service is available via entire campus.

Student Life *Housing:* on-campus residence required for freshman year. *Options:* coed, men-only, women-only, cooperative, disabled students. Campus housing is university owned and leased by the school. Freshman campus housing is guaranteed. *Activities and organizations:* drama/theater group, student-run newspaper, radio station, choral group, marching band, Residential Hall Association, Alpha Phi Omega, WVU Greek System, Mountaineer Maniacs, Campus Crusade for Christ, national fraternities, national sororities. *Campus security:* 24-hour emergency response devices and patrols, student patrols, late-night transport/escort service, controlled dormitory access, patrol officers just for housing. *Student services:* health clinic, personal/psychological counseling, women's center, legal services.

Athletics Member NCAA. All Division I except football (Division I-A). *Intercollegiate sports:* baseball M(s), basketball M(s)/W(s), crew W(s), cross-country running W(s), gymnastics W(s), riflery M(s)/W(s), soccer M(s)/W(s), swimming and diving M(s)/W(s), tennis W(s), track and field W(s), volleyball W(s), wrestling M(s). *Intramural sports:* archery M(c)/W(c), baseball M(c), basketball M(c)/W(c), bowling M(c)/W(c), cheerleading M(c)/W(c), crew M(c)/W(c), equestrian sports M(c)/W(c), fencing M(c)/W(c), field hockey M(c)/W(c), football M, golf M(c)/W(c), ice hockey M(c), lacrosse M(c)/W(c), racquetball M(c)/W(c), riflery M(c)/W(c), rock climbing M(c)/W(c), rugby M(c)/W(c), skiing (cross-country) M(c)/W(c), skiing (downhill) M(c)/W(c), soccer M(c)/W(c), softball W(c), swimming and diving M(c)/W(c), tennis M(c)/W(c), track and field M(c)/W(c), ultimate Frisbee M(c)/W(c), volleyball M(c)/W(c), wrestling M(c).

Standardized Tests *Required:* SAT or ACT (for admission).

Costs (2011–12) *Tuition:* state resident $5674 full-time, $236 per credit hour part-time; nonresident $17,844 full-time, $743 per credit hour part-time. Full-time tuition and fees vary according to location, program, and reciprocity agreements. Part-time tuition and fees vary according to course load, location, program, and reciprocity agreements. *Room and board:* $8404. Room and board charges vary according to board plan, housing facility, and location. *Payment plan:* installment. *Waivers:* senior citizens and employees or children of employees.

Financial Aid Of all full-time matriculated undergraduates who enrolled in 2011, 16,593 applied for aid, 14,104 were judged to have need, 4,057 had their need fully met. 1,700 Federal Work-Study jobs (averaging $1969). 1,200 state and other part-time jobs (averaging $1620). In 2011, 4288 non-need-based awards were made. *Average percent of need met:* 75%. *Average financial aid package:* $6306. *Average need-based loan:* $4294. *Average need-based gift aid:* $4913. *Average non-need-based aid:* $1982. *Average indebtedness upon graduation:* $27,003. *Financial aid deadline:* 3/1.

Applying *Application fee:* $45. *Required:* high school transcript, minimum 2.0 GPA. *Required for some:* essay or personal statement, minimum 2.3 GPA. *Application deadlines:* 8/1 (freshmen), 8/1 (transfers). *Notification:* continuous (transfers).

Freshman Application Contact Ms. Marilyn Potts, Director of Admissions, West Virginia University, PO Box 6009, Morgantown, WV 26506-6009. *Phone:* 304-293-2124. *Toll-free phone:* 800-344-9881. *Fax:* 304-293-3080. *E-mail:* marilyn.potts@mail.wvu.edu. *Web site:* http://www.wvu.edu/.

West Virginia University at Parkersburg

Parkersburg, West Virginia

Freshman Application Contact Christine Post, Associate Dean of Enrollment Management, West Virginia University at Parkersburg, 300 Campus Drive, Parkersburg, WV 26104. *Phone:* 304-424-8223 Ext. 223. *Toll-free phone:* 800-WVA-WVUP. *Fax:* 304-424-8332. *E-mail:* christine.post@mail.wvu.edu. *Web site:* http://www.wvup.edu/.

West Virginia University Institute of Technology

Montgomery, West Virginia

- **State-supported** comprehensive, founded 1895, part of University System of West Virginia
- **Small-town** 200-acre campus with easy access to Charleston
- **Endowment** $1.9 million
- **Coed** 1,316 undergraduate students, 78% full-time, 37% women, 63% men
- **Minimally difficult** entrance level, 30% of applicants were admitted

Undergraduates 1,024 full-time, 292 part-time. Students come from 21 states and territories; 2 other countries; 7% are from out of state; 9% Black or African American, non-Hispanic/Latino; 2% Hispanic/Latino; 2% Asian, non-Hispanic/Latino; 0.1% Native Hawaiian or other Pacific Islander, non-Hispanic/Latino; 0.5% American Indian or Alaska Native, non-Hispanic/Latino; 1% Two or more races, non-Hispanic/Latino; 4% Race/ethnicity unknown; 2% international; 8% transferred in; 25% live on campus. *Retention:* 51% of full-time freshmen returned.

Freshmen *Admission:* 626 applied, 185 admitted, 284 enrolled. *Average high school GPA:* 3.18.

Faculty *Student/faculty ratio:* 12:1.

Academics *Calendar:* semesters. *Degrees:* certificates, associate, bachelor's, and master's. *Special study options:* academic remediation for entering students, accelerated degree program, adult/continuing education programs, advanced placement credit, cooperative education, distance learning, double majors, external degree program, independent study, internships, part-time degree program, services for LD students, student-designed majors, study abroad, summer session for credit. *ROTC:* Army (b). *Unusual degree programs:* 3-2 education and sports management with West Virginia University.

Computers on Campus 100 computers/terminals and 2 ports are available on campus for general student use. Students can access the following: campus intranet, computer help desk, free student e-mail accounts, online (class) grades, online (class) registration, online (class) schedules. Campuswide network is available. 100% of college-owned or -operated housing units are wired for high-speed Internet access.

Student Life *Housing:* on-campus residence required through sophomore year. *Options:* coed. Campus housing is university owned. Freshman campus housing is guaranteed. *Activities and organizations:* drama/theater group, student-run newspaper, choral group, marching band, Christian Student Union, Student Activities Board, Alpha Phi Omega, Student Government Association, American Society of Mechanical Engineers, national fraternities, national sororities. *Campus security:* 24-hour emergency response devices and patrols, late-night transport/escort service. *Student services:* health clinic, personal/psychological counseling.

Athletics Member NAIA. *Intercollegiate sports:* baseball M(s), basketball M(s)/W(s), cheerleading M(s)/W(s), cross-country running M(s)/W(s), golf M(s), soccer M(s)/W, softball W(s), volleyball W(s), wrestling M(s). *Intramural sports:* basketball M/W, football M/W, soccer M/W, softball M/W.

Standardized Tests *Required:* SAT or ACT (for admission). *Required for some:* TOEFL or IELTS.

Costs (2011–12) *Tuition:* state resident $5344 full-time; nonresident $13,444 full-time. Full-time tuition and fees vary according to program. Part-time tuition and fees vary according to course load and program. *Room and board:* $8130; room only: $4800. Room and board charges vary according to board plan and housing facility. *Payment plan:* installment.

Financial Aid Of all full-time matriculated undergraduates who enrolled in 2011, 883 applied for aid, 751 were judged to have need, 305 had their need fully met. 28 Federal Work-Study jobs (averaging $4127). 60 state and other part-time jobs (averaging $13,564). *Average percent of need met:* 42%. *Average financial aid package:* $9125. *Average need-based loan:* $3407. *Average need-based gift aid:* $4974. *Average indebtedness upon graduation:* $19,024.

Applying *Options:* electronic application, early admission. *Required:* high school transcript, minimum 2.0 GPA. *Application deadlines:* rolling (freshmen), rolling (out-of-state freshmen), rolling (transfers). *Notification:* continuous until 8/15 (freshmen), continuous (out-of-state freshmen), continuous until 8/15 (transfers).

Freshman Application Contact West Virginia University Institute of Technology, 405 Fayette Pike, Montgomery, WV 25136. *Phone:* 304-981-6240. *Toll-free phone:* 888-554-8324. *Web site:* http://www.wvutech.edu/.

West Virginia Wesleyan College

Buckhannon, West Virginia

- **Independent** comprehensive, founded 1890, affiliated with United Methodist Church
- **Small-town** 100-acre campus
- **Endowment** $35.9 million
- **Coed** 1,360 undergraduate students, 98% full-time, 53% women, 47% men
- **Moderately difficult** entrance level, 78% of applicants were admitted

Undergraduates 1,335 full-time, 25 part-time. Students come from 25 states and territories; 25 other countries; 36% are from out of state; 10% Black or African American, non-Hispanic/Latino; 2% Hispanic/Latino; 0.6% Asian, non-Hispanic/Latino; 0.2% Native Hawaiian or other Pacific Islander, non-Hispanic/Latino; 0.4% American Indian or Alaska Native, non-Hispanic/Latino; 1% Two or more races, non-Hispanic/Latino; 3% Race/ethnicity unknown; 5% international; 4% transferred in; 78% live on campus. *Retention:* 67% of full-time freshmen returned.

Freshmen *Admission:* 1,743 applied, 1,361 admitted, 410 enrolled. *Average high school GPA:* 3.36. *Test scores:* SAT critical reading scores over 500: 38%; SAT math scores over 500: 46%; SAT writing scores over 500: 35%; ACT scores over 18: 89%; SAT critical reading scores over 600: 6%; SAT math scores over 600: 10%; SAT writing scores over 600: 9%; ACT scores over 24: 41%; SAT critical reading scores over 700: 2%; SAT math scores over 700: 2%; SAT writing scores over 700: 2%; ACT scores over 30: 5%.

Faculty *Total:* 171, 45% full-time. *Student/faculty ratio:* 13:1.

Academics *Calendar:* semesters. *Degrees:* bachelor's and master's. *Special study options:* academic remediation for entering students, advanced placement credit, double majors, English as a second language, honors programs, independent study, internships, off-campus study, part-time degree program, services for LD students, student-designed majors, study abroad, summer session for credit. *Unusual degree programs:* 3-2 engineering with University of Virginia, West Virginia University.

Computers on Campus Students can access the following: campus intranet, computer help desk, free student e-mail accounts, online (class) grades, online (class) registration, online (class) schedules. Campuswide network is available. 100% of college-owned or -operated housing units are wired for high-speed Internet access. Wireless service is available via learning centers, libraries, student centers.

Student Life *Housing:* on-campus residence required through senior year. *Options:* coed, men-only, women-only, disabled students. Campus housing is university owned. Freshman campus housing is guaranteed. *Activities and organizations:* drama/theater group, student-run newspaper, radio station, choral group, Campus Activities Board, Green Club, Students in Free Enterprise (SIFE), Wesleyan Ambassadors, national fraternities, national sororities. *Campus security:* 24-hour emergency response devices and patrols, student patrols, late-night transport/escort service, controlled dormitory access. *Student services:* health clinic, personal/psychological counseling.

Athletics Member NCAA. All Division II. *Intercollegiate sports:* baseball M(s), basketball M(s)/W(s), cheerleading M/W, cross-country running M(s)/W(s), football M(s), golf M(s)/W(s), lacrosse M(c)/W(s), skiing (downhill) M(c)/W(c), soccer M(s)/W(s), softball W(s), swimming and diving M(s)/W(s), tennis M(s)/W(s), track and field M(s)/W(s), volleyball W(s). *Intramural sports:* basketball M/W, bowling M/W, football M/W, golf M/W, racquetball M/W, soccer M/W, softball M/W, table tennis M/W, volleyball M/W, water polo M/W.

Standardized Tests *Required:* SAT or ACT (for admission). *Required for some:* SAT Subject Tests (for admission).

Costs (2012–13) *Comprehensive fee:* $33,318 includes full-time tuition ($24,780), mandatory fees ($1024), and room and board ($7514). Full-time tuition and fees vary according to course load. Part-time tuition and fees vary according to course load. *Room and board:* Room and board charges vary according to board plan and housing facility. *Payment plan:* installment. *Waivers:* employees or children of employees.

Financial Aid Of all full-time matriculated undergraduates who enrolled in 2010, 1,175 applied for aid, 1,077 were judged to have need, 316 had their need fully met. In 2010, 258 non-need-based awards were made. *Average percent of need met:* 83%. *Average financial aid package:* $23,631. *Average need-based loan:* $3084. *Average need-based gift aid:* $20,329. *Average non-need-based aid:* $10,754. *Average indebtedness upon graduation:* $25,240.

Applying *Options:* electronic application, deferred entrance. *Application fee:* $35. *Required:* high school transcript. *Recommended:* essay or personal statement, interview. *Notification:* continuous (freshmen), continuous (transfers).

Freshman Application Contact John Waltz, Director of Admission, West Virginia Wesleyan College, 59 College Avenue, Buckhannon, WV 26201. *Phone:* 304-473-8510. *Toll-free phone:* 800-722-9933. *Fax:* 304-473-8108. *E-mail:* admission@wvwc.edu. *Web site:* http://www.wvwc.edu/.

See page 981 for display ad and page 1758 for the College Close-Up.

What will the world will be like? What will you do for a living? What kind of person will you become? At **West Virginia Wesleyan**, not only will you meet professors that know you by name and friends that will last a lifetime, you will meet your dreams.

Academic distinction

99% placement rate into medical, law, and all graduate programs

Great faculty

14:1 student to faculty ratio means more face time with your professors

Prestigious outcomes

11 Fulbright Scholarships awarded to West Virginia Wesleyan students since 2007.

Your tomorrow begins today!
Call the Office of Admission at **800.722.9933** for an appointment, or go to **www.wvwc.edu** for information about upcoming campus visit days.

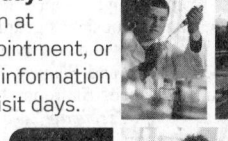

West Virginia Wesleyan
59 College Ave
Buckhannon, WV 26201
304.473.8510
www.wvwc.edu

Wheeling Jesuit University
Wheeling, West Virginia

- **Independent Roman Catholic (Jesuit)** comprehensive, founded 1954
- **Suburban** 65-acre campus with easy access to Pittsburgh
- **Endowment** $19.7 million
- **Coed** 1,063 undergraduate students, 79% full-time, 57% women, 43% men
- **Moderately difficult** entrance level, 66% of applicants were admitted

Undergraduates 844 full-time, 219 part-time. Students come from 23 states and territories; 12 other countries; 63% are from out of state; 3% Black or African American, non-Hispanic/Latino; 1% Hispanic/Latino; 1% Asian, non-Hispanic/Latino; 0.1% American Indian or Alaska Native, non-Hispanic/Latino; 9% Race/ethnicity unknown; 4% international; 3% transferred in; 67% live on campus. *Retention:* 71% of full-time freshmen returned.

Freshmen *Admission:* 1,237 applied, 819 admitted, 195 enrolled. *Average high school GPA:* 3.5. *Test scores:* SAT critical reading scores over 500: 59%; SAT math scores over 500: 59%; SAT writing scores over 500: 48%; ACT scores over 18: 96%; SAT critical reading scores over 600: 9%; SAT math scores over 600: 17%; SAT writing scores over 600: 5%; ACT scores over 24: 46%; SAT critical reading scores over 700: 1%; ACT scores over 30: 2%.

Faculty *Total:* 154, 56% full-time, 51% with terminal degrees. *Student/faculty ratio:* 11:1.

Academics *Calendar:* semesters. *Degrees:* bachelor's, master's, doctoral, and postbachelor's certificates. *Special study options:* academic remediation for entering students, accelerated degree program, adult/continuing education programs, advanced placement credit, distance learning, double majors, English as a second language, external degree program, honors programs, independent study, internships, off-campus study, part-time degree program, services for LD students, student-designed majors, study abroad, summer session for credit. *Unusual degree programs:* 3-2 engineering with Case Western Reserve University, West Virginia University.

Computers on Campus 274 computers/terminals are available on campus for general student use. Students can access the following: campus intranet, computer help desk, free student e-mail accounts, online (class) grades, online (class) registration, online (class) schedules. Campuswide network is available. 100% of college-owned or -operated housing units are wired for high-speed Internet access. Wireless service is available via entire campus.

Student Life *Housing:* on-campus residence required through senior year. *Options:* coed, men-only, women-only, cooperative, disabled students. Campus housing is university owned. Freshman campus housing is guaranteed. *Activities and organizations:* drama/theater group, student-run newspaper, television station, choral group, Campus Activity Board (CAB), Theater Guild, Student Senate, International Student Club, Campus Ministry. *Campus security:* 24-hour emergency response devices and patrols, student patrols, late-night transport/escort service, controlled dormitory access. *Student services:* health clinic, personal/psychological counseling.

Athletics Member NCAA. All Division II. *Intercollegiate sports:* baseball M(s), basketball M(s)/W(s), cheerleading M(c)/W(c), cross-country running M(s)/W(s), golf M(s)/W(s), lacrosse M(s)/W(s), rugby M(s)(c), soccer M(s)/W(s), softball W(s), swimming and diving M(s)/W(s), track and field M(s)/W(s), volleyball W(s). *Intramural sports:* basketball M/W, cross-country running M/W, football M, racquetball M/W, soccer M/W, softball M/W, tennis M/W, ultimate Frisbee M/W, volleyball M/W.

Standardized Tests *Required:* SAT or ACT (for admission).

Costs (2012–13) *Comprehensive fee:* $30,640 includes full-time tuition ($24,650), mandatory fees ($990), and room and board ($5000). Part-time tuition: $675 per credit hour. *Room and board:* Room and board charges vary according to board plan and housing facility. *Payment plan:* installment. *Waivers:* employees or children of employees.

Financial Aid Of all full-time matriculated undergraduates who enrolled in 2011, 748 applied for aid, 652 were judged to have need, 187 had their need fully met. 148 Federal Work-Study jobs (averaging $2200). 86 state and other part-time jobs (averaging $2200). In 2011, 160 non-need-based awards were made. *Average percent of need met:* 73%. *Average financial aid package:* $21,691. *Average need-based loan:* $4958. *Average need-based gift aid:* $6137. *Average non-need-based aid:* $12,344. *Average indebtedness upon graduation:* $35,047.

Applying *Options:* electronic application, deferred entrance. *Application fee:* $25. *Required:* high school transcript. *Required for some:* interview. *Recommended:* essay or personal statement, minimum 3.0 GPA, 2 letters of recommendation, interview. *Application deadlines:* rolling (freshmen), rolling (transfers). *Notification:* continuous (freshmen), continuous (transfers).

Freshman Application Contact Ms. Kimberly Klaus, Director of Undergraduate Enrollment, Wheeling Jesuit University, 316 Washington Avenue, Wheeling, WV 26003. *Phone:* 304-243-4376. *Toll-free phone:* 800-624-6992 Ext. 2359. *Fax:* 304-243-2397. *E-mail:* bloy@wju.edu. *Web site:* http://www.wju.edu/.

WISCONSIN

Alverno College

Milwaukee, Wisconsin

- **Independent Roman Catholic** comprehensive, founded 1887
- **Urban** 46-acre campus
- **Endowment** $20.9 million
- **Undergraduate: women only; graduate: coed** 2,094 undergraduate students, 71% full-time, 100% women, 0% men
- **Moderately difficult** entrance level, 82% of applicants were admitted

Undergraduates 1,490 full-time, 604 part-time. Students come from 14 states and territories; 12 other countries; 5% are from out of state; 18% Black or African American, non-Hispanic/Latino; 16% Hispanic/Latino; 5% Asian, non-Hispanic/Latino; 0.1% Native Hawaiian or other Pacific Islander, non-Hispanic/Latino; 1% American Indian or Alaska Native, non-Hispanic/Latino; 2% Two or more races, non-Hispanic/Latino; 0.6% international; 9% transferred in; 10% live on campus. *Retention:* 70% of full-time freshmen returned.

Freshmen *Admission:* 529 applied, 433 admitted, 199 enrolled. *Average high school GPA:* 2.87. *Test scores:* ACT scores over 18: 70%; ACT scores over 24: 17%; ACT scores over 30: 1%.

Faculty *Total:* 255, 47% full-time, 79% with terminal degrees. *Student/faculty ratio:* 11:1.

Academics *Calendar:* semesters. *Degrees:* associate, bachelor's, master's, post-master's, and postbachelor's certificates (also offers weekend program with significant enrollment not reflected in profile). *Special study options:* academic remediation for entering students, adult/continuing education programs, advanced placement credit, double majors, independent study, internships, part-time degree program, services for LD students, student-designed majors, study abroad, summer session for credit. *ROTC:* Army (c), Air Force (c).

Computers on Campus 610 computers/terminals are available on campus for general student use. Students can access the following: campus intranet, free student e-mail accounts, online (class) registration, online (class) schedules. Campuswide network is available. 100% of college-owned or -operated housing units are wired for high-speed Internet access. Wireless service is available via classrooms, computer centers, computer labs, dorm rooms, libraries.

Student Life *Housing options:* women-only. Campus housing is university owned. Freshman campus housing is guaranteed. *Activities and organizations:* drama/theater group, student-run newspaper, radio station, choral group, Student Nurses Association, Pre-Professional Women of Alverno, Women of Asian Ethnicity, Circle K, Gay-Straight Alliance. *Campus security:* 24-hour emergency response devices and patrols, late-night transport/escort service, controlled dormitory access, well-lit parking lots and pathways, emergency first-aid and CPR, crisis intervention team and plan in place. *Student services:* health clinic, personal/psychological counseling.

Athletics Member NCAA. All Division III. *Intercollegiate sports:* basketball W, cross-country running W, soccer W, softball W, tennis W, volleyball W.

Standardized Tests *Required:* SAT or ACT (for admission).

Costs (2011–12) *Comprehensive fee:* $28,029 includes full-time tuition ($20,538), mandatory fees ($525), and room and board ($6966). Full-time tuition and fees vary according to program. Part-time tuition: $856 per credit hour. Part-time tuition and fees vary according to program. *Room and board:* Room and board charges vary according to board plan and housing facility. *Payment plans:* installment, deferred payment. *Waivers:* employees or children of employees.

Financial Aid Of all full-time matriculated undergraduates who enrolled in 2011, 1,384 applied for aid, 1,327 were judged to have need. 97 Federal Work-Study jobs (averaging $2283). In 2011, 105 non-need-based awards were made. *Average financial aid package:* $15,473. *Average need-based loan:* $4176. *Average need-based gift aid:* $11,691. *Average non-need-based aid:* $6962. *Average indebtedness upon graduation:* $35,519.

Applying *Options:* electronic application, deferred entrance. *Application fee:* $20. *Required:* essay or personal statement, high school transcript, 2.0 on any college work, ACT or SAT. *Recommended:* minimum 2.0 GPA, interview. *Application deadlines:* rolling (freshmen), rolling (transfers). *Notification:* continuous (freshmen), continuous (transfers).

Freshman Application Contact Ms. Kate Lundeen, Director of Undergraduate Admissions, Alverno College, 3400 South 43 Street, PO Box 343922, Milwaukee, WI 53234-3922. *Phone:* 414-382-6103. *Toll-free phone:* 800-933-3401. *Fax:* 414-382-6055. *E-mail:* admissions@alverno.edu. *Web site:* http://www.alverno.edu/.

The Art Institute of Wisconsin

Milwaukee, Wisconsin

- **Proprietary** 4-year, part of Education Management Corporation
- **Coed**

Academics *Degrees:* associate and bachelor's.

Costs (2011–12) *Tuition:* Tuition cost varies by program. Prospective students should contact the school for current tuition costs. Other charges include a starting kit for all first-quarter students. Kits vary in price, depending on the program of study.

Freshman Application Contact The Art Institute of Wisconsin, 320 East Buffalo Street, Suite 600, Milwaukee, WI 53202. *Phone:* 414-978-5000. *Toll-free phone:* 877-285-4234. *Web site:* http://www.artinstitutes.edu/milwaukee.

See page 1144 for the College Close-Up.

Bellin College

Green Bay, Wisconsin

Freshman Application Contact Dr. Penny Croghan, Admissions Director, Bellin College, 3201 Eaton Road, Green Bay, WI 54305. *Phone:* 920-433-5803. *Toll-free phone:* 800-236-8707. *Fax:* 920-433-7416. *E-mail:* admissio@bcon.edu. *Web site:* http://www.bellincollege.edu/.

Beloit College

Beloit, Wisconsin

- **Independent** 4-year, founded 1846
- **Small-town** 65-acre campus with easy access to Chicago, Milwaukee
- **Endowment** $113.7 million
- **Coed** 1,385 undergraduate students, 95% full-time, 59% women, 41% men
- **Very difficult** entrance level, 71% of applicants were admitted

Undergraduates 1,319 full-time, 66 part-time. Students come from 51 states and territories; 36 other countries; 78% are from out of state; 3% Black or African American, non-Hispanic/Latino; 8% Hispanic/Latino; 2% Asian, non-Hispanic/Latino; 0.2% Native Hawaiian or other Pacific Islander, non-Hispanic/Latino; 0.5% American Indian or Alaska Native, non-Hispanic/Latino; 4% Two or more races, non-Hispanic/Latino; 2% Race/ethnicity unknown; 9% international; 94% live on campus. *Retention:* 86% of full-time freshmen returned.

Freshmen *Admission:* 2,107 applied, 1,487 admitted, 315 enrolled. *Average high school GPA:* 3.47. *Test scores:* SAT critical reading scores over 500: 84%; SAT math scores over 500: 87%; ACT scores over 18: 100%; SAT critical reading scores over 600: 62%; SAT math scores over 600: 56%; ACT scores over 24: 80%; SAT critical reading scores over 700: 22%; SAT math scores over 700: 19%; ACT scores over 30: 27%.

Faculty *Total:* 127, 90% full-time, 91% with terminal degrees. *Student/faculty ratio:* 12:1.

Academics *Calendar:* semesters. *Degree:* bachelor's. *Special study options:* adult/continuing education programs, advanced placement credit, double majors, English as a second language, independent study, internships, off-campus study, services for LD students, student-designed majors, study abroad, summer session for credit. *Unusual degree programs:* 3-2 engineering with University of Illinois at Urbana-Champaign, University of Michigan, Rensselaer Polytechnic Institute, Georgia Institute of Technology; forestry with Duke University; nursing with Rush University; medical technology with Rush University.

Computers on Campus Students can access the following: campus intranet, computer help desk, free student e-mail accounts, online (class) grades, online (class) schedules. Campuswide network is available. 100% of college-owned or -operated housing units are wired for high-speed Internet access. Wireless service is available via classrooms, computer centers, computer labs, dorm rooms, libraries, student centers.

Student Life *Housing:* on-campus residence required through junior year. *Options:* coed, women-only, cooperative. Campus housing is university owned. Freshman campus housing is guaranteed. *Activities and organizations:* drama/theater group, student-run newspaper, radio and television station, choral group, Science Fiction and Fantasy Association, Black Students Union, International Club, Alliance, Ballroom Dancing Club, national fraternities, national sororities. *Campus security:* 24-hour emergency response devices and patrols, late-night transport/escort service, controlled dormitory access. *Student services:* health clinic, personal/psychological counseling, women's center.

Athletics Member NCAA. All Division III. *Intercollegiate sports:* baseball M, basketball M/W, crew M(c)/W(c), cross-country running M/W, fencing M(c)/W(c), football M, golf M, ice hockey M(c)/W(c), lacrosse M(c)/W(c), soccer M/W, softball W, swimming and diving M/W, tennis M/W, track and

field M/W, volleyball W. *Intramural sports:* badminton M/W, basketball M/W, bowling M/W, football M, racquetball M/W, sailing M/W, soccer M/W, tennis M/W, ultimate Frisbee M/W, volleyball M/W, water polo M/W.

Standardized Tests *Required:* SAT or ACT (for admission).

Costs (2011–12) *Comprehensive fee:* $44,176 includes full-time tuition ($36,444), mandatory fees ($230), and room and board ($7502). Part-time tuition: $4555 per course. *College room only:* $3678. Room and board charges vary according to board plan. *Payment plan:* installment. *Waivers:* employees or children of employees.

Financial Aid Of all full-time matriculated undergraduates who enrolled in 2010, 1,004 applied for aid, 868 were judged to have need, 572 had their need fully met. 629 Federal Work-Study jobs (averaging $1741). 419 state and other part-time jobs (averaging $1253). In 2010, 331 non-need-based awards were made. *Average percent of need met:* 96%. *Average financial aid package:* $32,229. *Average need-based loan:* $7236. *Average need-based gift aid:* $22,612. *Average non-need-based aid:* $14,169. *Average indebtedness upon graduation:* $19,930.

Applying *Options:* electronic application, early admission, early action, deferred entrance. *Application fee:* $35. *Required:* essay or personal statement, high school transcript, 1 letter of recommendation. *Required for some:* interview. *Recommended:* interview. *Application deadlines:* 1/15 (freshmen), rolling (transfers), 11/1 (early action). *Notification:* continuous until 2/15 (freshmen), continuous (transfers), 12/15 (early action).

Freshman Application Contact Mr. James S. Zielinski, Director of Admissions, Beloit College, 700 College Street, Beloit, WI 53511-5596. *Phone:* 608-363-2500. *Toll-free phone:* 800-9-BELOIT. *Fax:* 608-363-2075. *E-mail:* admiss@beloit.edu. *Web site:* http://www.beloit.edu/.

See below for display ad and page 1170 for the College Close-Up.

Bryant & Stratton College - Milwaukee Campus

Milwaukee, Wisconsin

- **Proprietary** primarily 2-year, founded 1863, part of Bryant and Stratton College, Inc.
- **Urban** campus
- **Coed**
- **Minimally difficult** entrance level

Faculty *Student/faculty ratio:* 13:1.

Academics *Calendar:* semesters. *Degrees:* associate and bachelor's.

Student Life *Campus security:* 24-hour emergency response devices and patrols.

Standardized Tests *Required:* CPAt; ACCUPLACER (for admission). *Recommended:* SAT or ACT (for admission).

Costs (2011–12) *Tuition:* $15,570 full-time, $519 per credit hour part-time. Full-time tuition and fees vary according to class time and course load. Part-time tuition and fees vary according to course load. *Required fees:* $125 full-time.

Applying *Options:* electronic application. *Required:* high school transcript, interview, entrance and placement evaluations.

Freshman Application Contact Mr. Dan Basile, Director of Admissions, Bryant & Stratton College - Milwaukee Campus, 310 West Wisconsin Avenue, Suite 500 East, Milwaukee, WI 53203-2214. *Phone:* 414-276-5200. *Web site:* http://www.bryantstratton.edu/.

Bryant & Stratton College - Wauwatosa Campus

Wauwatosa, Wisconsin

- **Proprietary** 4-year
- **Suburban** campus with easy access to Milwaukee
- **Coed**

Faculty *Student/faculty ratio:* 10:1.

Academics *Calendar:* semesters. *Degrees:* associate and bachelor's.

Standardized Tests *Required:* TABE, CPAt (for admission). *Recommended:* SAT or ACT (for admission).

Costs (2011–12) *Tuition:* $15,570 full-time, $519 per credit hour part-time. Full-time tuition and fees vary according to class time and course load. Part-time tuition and fees vary according to course load. *Required fees:* $125 full-time.

Applying *Options:* electronic application. *Required:* high school transcript, interview, entrance and placement evaluation.

Freshman Application Contact Bryant & Stratton College - Wauwatosa Campus, 10950 W. Potter Road, Wauwatosa, WI 53226. *Phone:* 414-302-7000 Ext. 502. *Web site:* http://www.bryantstratton.edu/.

Cardinal Stritch University
Milwaukee, Wisconsin

- **Independent Roman Catholic** comprehensive, founded 1937
- **Suburban** 40-acre campus with easy access to Milwaukee
- **Endowment** $21.1 million
- **Coed** 2,795 undergraduate students, 94% full-time, 65% women, 35% men
- **Moderately difficult** entrance level, 48% of applicants were admitted

Undergraduates 2,631 full-time, 164 part-time. Students come from 30 states and territories; 1 other country; 25% Black or African American, non-Hispanic/Latino; 6% Hispanic/Latino; 2% Asian, non-Hispanic/Latino; 0.1% Native Hawaiian or other Pacific Islander, non-Hispanic/Latino; 0.3% American Indian or Alaska Native, non-Hispanic/Latino; 0.8% Two or more races, non-Hispanic/Latino; 4% Race/ethnicity unknown; 2% international; 5% transferred in; 5% live on campus.

Freshmen *Admission:* 955 applied, 455 admitted, 117 enrolled.

Faculty *Total:* 431, 24% full-time.

Academics *Calendar:* semesters. *Degrees:* certificates, associate, bachelor's, master's, doctoral, post-master's, postbachelor's, and first professional certificates. *Special study options:* academic remediation for entering students, accelerated degree program, adult/continuing education programs, advanced placement credit, cooperative education, distance learning, double majors, English as a second language, external degree program, honors programs, independent study, internships, off-campus study, part-time degree program, services for LD students, student-designed majors, summer session for credit.

Computers on Campus 549 computers/terminals and 1,251 ports are available on campus for general student use. Students can access the following: free student e-mail accounts, online (class) grades, online (class) registration, online (class) schedules. Campuswide network is available. Wireless service is available via entire campus.

Student Life *Housing options:* coed. Campus housing is university owned and leased by the school. *Activities and organizations:* drama/theater group, student-run newspaper, radio station, choral group, Residence Hall Association, Student Government Association, Student Activities Board. *Campus security:* 24-hour emergency response devices and patrols, late-night transport/escort service. *Student services:* health clinic, personal/psychological counseling.

Athletics Member NAIA. *Intercollegiate sports:* baseball M, basketball M/W, cross-country running M/W, soccer M/W, softball W, volleyball M/W. *Intramural sports:* basketball M/W, volleyball M/W.

Standardized Tests *Required:* SAT or ACT (for admission).

Costs (2011–12) *Comprehensive fee:* $30,180 includes full-time tuition ($22,720), mandatory fees ($610), and room and board ($6850). Full-time tuition and fees vary according to course load. Part-time tuition and fees vary according to course load. *College room only:* $2150. Room and board charges vary according to board plan. *Payment plans:* installment, deferred payment. *Waivers:* employees or children of employees.

Financial Aid Of all full-time matriculated undergraduates who enrolled in 2002, 2,176 applied for aid, 2,037 were judged to have need, 188 had their need fully met. In 2002, 234 non-need-based awards were made. *Average percent of need met:* 43%. *Average financial aid package:* $7843. *Average need-based loan:* $3575. *Average need-based gift aid:* $5634. *Average non-need-based aid:* $9402.

Applying *Options:* electronic application, deferred entrance. *Required:* essay or personal statement, high school transcript, minimum 2.0 GPA. *Recommended:* interview. *Application deadlines:* 8/1 (freshmen), rolling (transfers). *Notification:* continuous (freshmen).

Freshman Application Contact Ms. Sarah C. Blake, Associate Director of Admissions, Cardinal Stritch University, 6801 N. Yates Road, Milwaukee, WI 53217. *Phone:* 414-410-4052. *Toll-free phone:* 800-347-8822 Ext. 4040. *Fax:* 414-410-4058. *E-mail:* admityou@stritch.edu. *Web site:* http://www.stritch.edu/.

Carroll University
Waukesha, Wisconsin

- **Independent Presbyterian** comprehensive, founded 1846
- **Suburban** 52-acre campus with easy access to Milwaukee
- **Endowment** $32.7 million
- **Coed**
- **Moderately difficult** entrance level

Faculty *Student/faculty ratio:* 15:1.

Academics *Calendar:* semesters. *Degrees:* bachelor's, master's, and doctoral.

Student Life *Campus security:* 24-hour emergency response devices and patrols, student patrols, late-night transport/escort service, controlled dormitory access.

Athletics Member NCAA. All Division III.

Standardized Tests *Required:* SAT or ACT (for admission). *Recommended:* ACT (for admission).

Costs (2011–12) *Comprehensive fee:* $32,984 includes full-time tuition ($24,749), mandatory fees ($499), and room and board ($7736). Full-time tuition and fees vary according to program. Part-time tuition: $310 per credit. Part-time tuition and fees vary according to course load and program. *College room only:* $4222. Room and board charges vary according to board plan and housing facility.

Financial Aid Of all full-time matriculated undergraduates who enrolled in 2011, 2,596 applied for aid, 2,303 were judged to have need, 2,131 had their need fully met. 986 Federal Work-Study jobs (averaging $2223). 924 state and other part-time jobs (averaging $2167). In 2011, 505 non-need-based awards were made. *Average percent of need met:* 100. *Average financial aid package:* $19,824. *Average need-based loan:* $4337. *Average need-based gift aid:* $13,910. *Average non-need-based aid:* $10,974. *Average indebtedness upon graduation:* $33,513.

Applying *Options:* electronic application, deferred entrance. *Required:* high school transcript, minimum 2.0 GPA, 1 letter of recommendation. *Required for some:* essay or personal statement. *Recommended:* interview.

Freshman Application Contact Mr. James Wiseman, Vice President of Enrollment, Carroll University, 100 North East Avenue, Waukesha, WI 53186-5593. *Phone:* 262-524-7221. *Toll-free phone:* 800-CARROLL. *Fax:* 262-524-7139. *E-mail:* info@carrollu.edu. *Web site:* http://www.carrollu.edu/.

Carthage College
Kenosha, Wisconsin

Freshman Application Contact Carthage College, 2001 Alford Park Drive, Kenosha, WI 53140. *Phone:* 262-551-6000. *Toll-free phone:* 800-351-4058. *Web site:* http://www.carthage.edu/.

Columbia College of Nursing
Milwaukee, Wisconsin

- **Independent** 4-year, founded 1901
- **Urban** 1-acre campus with easy access to Milwaukee
- **Endowment** $700,000
- **Coed, primarily women**
- **Moderately difficult** entrance level

Faculty *Student/faculty ratio:* 9:1.

Academics *Calendar:* semesters. *Degrees:* bachelor's (nursing degree is awarded in conjunction with Mount Mary College).

Student Life *Campus security:* 24-hour emergency response devices and patrols, student patrols, late-night transport/escort service, security card entrances to academic areas.

Standardized Tests *Required:* SAT or ACT (for admission).

Costs (2011–12) *Tuition:* $22,318 full-time, $668 per credit part-time. Part-time tuition and fees vary according to program. *Required fees:* $1200 full-time, $55 per credit part-time.

Financial Aid Of all full-time matriculated undergraduates who enrolled in 2000, 1,782 applied for aid, 1,336 were judged to have need, 1,336 had their need fully met. In 2000, 426 non-need-based awards were made. *Average percent of need met:* 100. *Average financial aid package:* $13,219. *Average need-based loan:* $3186. *Average need-based gift aid:* $9050. *Average non-need-based aid:* $7051. *Average indebtedness upon graduation:* $16,000.

Applying *Options:* electronic application. *Application fee:* $25. *Required:* high school transcript, minimum 2.8 GPA, minimum 2.8 GPA in college level natural and social sciences. *Required for some:* essay or personal statement, interview. *Recommended:* essay or personal statement, 1 letter of recommendation.

Freshman Application Contact Columbia College of Nursing, 4425 N. Port Washington Road, Milwaukee, WI 53212. *Phone:* 414-326-2336. *Web site:* http://www.ccon.edu/.

Concordia University Wisconsin
Mequon, Wisconsin

- **Independent** comprehensive, founded 1881, affiliated with Lutheran Church–Missouri Synod, part of Concordia University System
- **Suburban** 192-acre campus with easy access to Milwaukee
- **Coed**
- **Moderately difficult** entrance level

Faculty *Student/faculty ratio:* 12:1.

Academics *Calendar:* 4-1-4. *Degrees:* certificates, associate, bachelor's, master's, doctoral, postbachelor's, and first professional certificates.

Student Life *Campus security:* 24-hour patrols, student patrols, late-night transport/escort service, controlled dormitory access.

Athletics Member NCAA. All Division III.

Standardized Tests *Required:* ACT (for admission).

Costs (2011–12) *Comprehensive fee:* $31,951 includes full-time tuition ($22,995) and room and board ($8956). Full-time tuition and fees vary according to program. Part-time tuition and fees vary according to program. *Room and board:* Room and board charges vary according to board plan.

Financial Aid *Of all full-time matriculated undergraduates who enrolled in 2011,* 2,096 applied for aid, 1,869 were judged to have need, 462 had their need fully met. 250 Federal Work-Study jobs (averaging $1621). *In 2011,* 299 non-need-based awards were made. *Average percent of need met:* 75. *Average financial aid package:* $18,530. *Average need-based loan:* $6264. *Average need-based gift aid:* $12,113. *Average non-need-based aid:* $9513. *Average indebtedness upon graduation:* $30,879.

Applying *Application fee:* $35. *Required:* high school transcript, minimum 2.0 GPA. *Required for some:* essay or personal statement, minimum 3.0 GPA, 3 letters of recommendation. *Recommended:* interview.

Freshman Application Contact Ms. Julie Schroeder, Concordia University Wisconsin, Admissions Office, 12800 North Lake Drive, Mequon, WI 53097. *Phone:* 262-243-4305 Ext. 4305. *Toll-free phone:* 888-628-9472. *E-mail:* admission@cuw.edu. *Web site:* http://www.cuw.edu/.

DeVry University
Milwaukee, Wisconsin

Freshman Application Contact DeVry University, 411 East Wisconsin Avenue, Suite 300, Milwaukee, WI 53202. *Toll-free phone:* 866-338-7941. *Web site:* http://www.devry.edu/.

DeVry University
Waukesha, Wisconsin

Admissions Office Contact DeVry University, N14 W23833 Stone Ridge Drive, Suite 450, Waukesha, WI 53188-1157. *Toll-free phone:* 866-338-7941. *Web site:* http://www.devry.edu/.

Edgewood College
Madison, Wisconsin

- **Independent Roman Catholic** comprehensive, founded 1927
- **Urban** 55-acre campus
- **Endowment** $18.2 million
- **Coed, primarily women** 1,951 undergraduate students, 82% full-time, 71% women, 29% men
- **Moderately difficult** entrance level, 72% of applicants were admitted

Undergraduates 1,591 full-time, 360 part-time. Students come from 18 states and territories; 29 other countries; 6% are from out of state; 3% Black or African American, non-Hispanic/Latino; 6% Hispanic/Latino; 2% Asian, non-Hispanic/Latino; 0.2% Native Hawaiian or other Pacific Islander, non-Hispanic/Latino; 0.4% American Indian or Alaska Native, non-Hispanic/Latino; 3% Two or more races, non-Hispanic/Latino; 1% Race/ethnicity unknown; 2% international; 9% transferred in; 30% live on campus. *Retention:* 80% of full-time freshmen returned.

Freshmen *Admission:* 1,292 applied, 929 admitted, 297 enrolled. *Average high school GPA:* 3.27. *Test scores:* ACT scores over 18: 95%; ACT scores over 24: 37%; ACT scores over 30: 5%.

Faculty *Total:* 304, 37% full-time, 41% with terminal degrees. *Student/faculty ratio:* 12:1.

Academics *Calendar:* semesters. *Degrees:* bachelor's, master's, doctoral, and first professional. *Special study options:* academic remediation for entering students, accelerated degree program, adult/continuing education programs, advanced placement credit, cooperative education, distance learning, double majors, honors programs, independent study, internships, off-campus study, part-time degree program, services for LD students, student-designed majors, study abroad, summer session for credit. *ROTC:* Army (c). *Unusual degree programs:* 3-2 business administration with Accountancy.

Computers on Campus 100 computers/terminals and 200 ports are available on campus for general student use. Students can access the following: campus intranet, computer help desk, free student e-mail accounts, online (class) grades, online (class) registration, online (class) schedules. Campuswide network is available. 100% of college-owned or -operated housing units are wired for high-speed Internet access. Wireless service is available via entire campus.

Student Life *Housing:* on-campus residence required through sophomore year. *Options:* coed, women-only, disabled students. Campus housing is university owned. Freshman applicants given priority for college housing. *Activities and organizations:* drama/theater group, student-run newspaper, choral group, Circle K, Student Education Association, Student Government Association, Campus Activities Board, Rotaract. *Campus security:* 24-hour emergency response devices and patrols, student patrols, late-night transport/escort service, con-

trolled dormitory access. *Student services:* health clinic, personal/psychological counseling.

Athletics Member NCAA. All Division III. *Intercollegiate sports:* baseball M, basketball M/W, cross-country running M/W, golf M/W, soccer M/W, softball W, tennis M/W, track and field M/W, volleyball W. *Intramural sports:* basketball M/W, soccer M/W, swimming and diving M/W, volleyball M/W.

Standardized Tests *Required:* SAT or ACT (for admission).

Costs (2011–12) *Comprehensive fee:* $30,963 includes full-time tuition ($22,850) and room and board ($8113). Full-time tuition and fees vary according to degree level. Part-time tuition: $719 per credit. Part-time tuition and fees vary according to course load and degree level. *College room only:* $4223. Room and board charges vary according to housing facility. *Payment plan:* installment. *Waivers:* employees or children of employees.

Financial Aid Of all full-time matriculated undergraduates who enrolled in 2010, 1,435 applied for aid, 1,313 were judged to have need, 139 had their need fully met. 263 Federal Work-Study jobs (averaging $546,848). 866 state and other part-time jobs (averaging $1.7 million). In 2010, 223 non-need-based awards were made. *Average percent of need met:* 69%. *Average financial aid package:* $14,237. *Average need-based loan:* $5283. *Average need-based gift aid:* $10,014. *Average non-need-based aid:* $4361. *Average indebtedness upon graduation:* $34,321.

Applying *Options:* electronic application, deferred entrance. *Application fee:* $25. *Required:* high school transcript, minimum 2.5 GPA. *Required for some:* essay or personal statement, 1 letter of recommendation, interview. *Application deadlines:* 8/14 (freshmen), 8/14 (transfers). *Notification:* continuous (freshmen), continuous (transfers).

Freshman Application Contact Ms. Christine Benedict, Director of Undergraduate Admissions, Edgewood College, 1000 Edgewood College Drive, Madison, WI 53711-1997. *Phone:* 608-663-2294. *Toll-free phone:* 800-444-4861 Ext. 2294. *Fax:* 608-663-2214. *E-mail:* admissions@edgewood.edu. *Web site:* http://www.edgewood.edu/.

Globe University–Appleton
Grand Chute, Wisconsin

- **Proprietary** 4-year, part of Globe Education Network (GEN) which is composed of Globe University, Minnesota School of Business, Broadview University, The Institute of Production and Recording and Minnesota School of Cosmetology
- **Small-town** 4-acre campus
- **Coed** 47 undergraduate students, 38% full-time, 83% women, 17% men

Undergraduates 18 full-time, 29 part-time. Students come from 2 states and territories; 2% Black or African American, non-Hispanic/Latino; 4% Hispanic/Latino; 2% American Indian or Alaska Native, non-Hispanic/Latino; 11% Race/ethnicity unknown; 30% transferred in.

Freshmen *Admission:* 24 enrolled.

Faculty *Total:* 27, 26% full-time, 37% with terminal degrees. *Student/faculty ratio:* 9:1.

Academics *Degrees:* diplomas, associate, and bachelor's. *Special study options:* academic remediation for entering students, accelerated degree program, adult/continuing education programs, advanced placement credit, internships, part-time degree program, services for LD students, summer session for credit.

Computers on Campus 52 computers/terminals and 128 ports are available on campus for general student use. Students can access the following: computer help desk, free student e-mail accounts, online (class) grades, online (class) registration, online (class) schedules. Campuswide network is available. Wireless service is available via entire campus.

Student Life *Housing:* college housing not available. *Campus security:* 24-hour emergency response devices, late-night transport/escort service.

Standardized Tests *Required:* AccuPlacer is required of all applicants unless documentation of a minimum ACT composite score of 21 or documentation of a minimum composite score of 1485 on the SAT is presented (for admission).

Applying *Options:* electronic application. *Application fee:* $50. *Required:* high school transcript, interview, High school transcript or GED required of all applicants. *Required for some:* essay or personal statement, 2 letters of recommendation. *Application deadlines:* rolling (freshmen), rolling (out-of-state freshmen), rolling (transfers). *Notification:* continuous (freshmen), continuous (out-of-state freshmen), continuous (transfers).

Freshman Application Contact Globe University–Appleton, 5045 West Grande Market Drive, Grand Chute, WI 54913. *Phone:* 920-364-1100. *Web site:* http://www.globeuniversity.edu/.

Globe University–Eau Claire
Eau Claire, Wisconsin

- **Proprietary** 4-year, part of Globe Education Network (GEN) which is composed of Globe University, Minnesota School of Business,

Broadview University, The Institute of Production and Recording and Minnesota School of Cosmetology
- **Small-town** 5-acre campus with easy access to Minneapolis-St. Paul
- **Coed** 719 undergraduate students, 38% full-time, 79% women, 21% men

Undergraduates 274 full-time, 445 part-time. Students come from 1 other state; 0.1% Black or African American, non-Hispanic/Latino; 1% Hispanic/Latino; 2% Asian, non-Hispanic/Latino; 0.8% American Indian or Alaska Native, non-Hispanic/Latino; 1% Two or more races, non-Hispanic/Latino; 7% Race/ethnicity unknown; 15% transferred in. *Retention:* 79% of full-time freshmen returned.

Freshmen *Admission:* 99 enrolled.

Faculty *Total:* 54, 17% full-time, 13% with terminal degrees. *Student/faculty ratio:* 19:1.

Academics *Degrees:* diplomas, associate, and bachelor's. *Special study options:* academic remediation for entering students, accelerated degree program, adult/continuing education programs, advanced placement credit, internships, part-time degree program, services for LD students, summer session for credit.

Computers on Campus 64 computers/terminals and 128 ports are available on campus for general student use. Students can access the following: computer help desk, free student e-mail accounts, online (class) grades, online (class) registration, online (class) schedules. Campuswide network is available. Wireless service is available via entire campus.

Student Life *Campus security:* 24-hour emergency response devices, late-night transport/escort service.

Standardized Tests *Required:* AccuPlacer is required of all applicants unless documentation of a minimum ACT composite score of 21 or documentation of a minimum composite score of 1485 on the SAT is presented (for admission).

Applying *Options:* electronic application. *Application fee:* $50. *Required:* high school transcript, interview. *Required for some:* essay or personal statement, 2 letters of recommendation, GED certificate in lieu of high school transcript. *Application deadlines:* rolling (freshmen), rolling (out-of-state freshmen), rolling (transfers). *Notification:* continuous (freshmen), continuous (out-of-state freshmen), continuous (transfers).

Freshman Application Contact Globe University–Eau Claire, 4955 Bullis Farm Road, Eau Claire, WI 54701-5168. *Phone:* 715-855-6600. *Toll-free phone:* 877-303-6060 (in-state); 377-303-6060 (out-of-state). *Web site:* http://www.globeuniversity.edu/.

Globe University–Green Bay

Bellevue, Wisconsin

- **Proprietary** 4-year, part of Globe Education Network (GEN) which is composed of Globe University, Minnesota School of Business, Broadview University, The Institute of Production and Recording and Minnesota School of Cosmetology
- **Urban** 5-acre campus
- **Coed** 215 undergraduate students, 54% full-time, 87% women, 13% men

Undergraduates 117 full-time, 98 part-time. Students come from 4 states and territories; 4% are from out of state; 2% Black or African American, non-Hispanic/Latino; 2% Hispanic/Latino; 1% Asian, non-Hispanic/Latino; 3% American Indian or Alaska Native, non-Hispanic/Latino; 2% Two or more races, non-Hispanic/Latino; 19% Race/ethnicity unknown; 53% transferred in.

Freshmen *Admission:* 91 enrolled.

Faculty *Total:* 40, 23% full-time, 30% with terminal degrees. *Student/faculty ratio:* 8:1.

Academics *Degrees:* diplomas, associate, and bachelor's. *Special study options:* academic remediation for entering students, accelerated degree program, adult/continuing education programs, advanced placement credit, internships, services for LD students, summer session for credit.

Computers on Campus 46 computers/terminals and 128 ports are available on campus for general student use. Students can access the following: computer help desk, free student e-mail accounts, online (class) grades, online (class) registration, online (class) schedules. Campuswide network is available. Wireless service is available via entire campus.

Student Life *Housing:* college housing not available. *Campus security:* 24-hour emergency response devices, late-night transport/escort service.

Applying *Options:* electronic application. *Application fee:* $50. *Required:* high school transcript, interview. *Required for some:* essay or personal statement, 2 letters of recommendation, GED certificate in lieu of high school transcript. *Application deadlines:* rolling (freshmen), rolling (out-of-state freshmen), rolling (transfers). *Notification:* continuous (freshmen), continuous (out-of-state freshmen), continuous (transfers).

Freshman Application Contact Globe University–Green Bay, 2620 Development Drive, Bellevue, WI 54311. *Phone:* 920-264-1600. *Web site:* http://www.globeuniversity.edu//.

Globe University–La Crosse

Onalaska, Wisconsin

- **Proprietary** 4-year, part of Globe Education Network (GEN) which is composed of Globe University, Minnesota School of Business, Broadview University, The Institute of Production and Recording and Minnesota School of Cosmetology
- **Small-town** campus
- **Coed** 534 undergraduate students, 77% full-time, 76% women, 24% men

Undergraduates 412 full-time, 122 part-time. Students come from 4 states and territories; 3% are from out of state; 2% Black or African American, non-Hispanic/Latino; 1% Asian, non-Hispanic/Latino; 0.9% American Indian or Alaska Native, non-Hispanic/Latino; 1% Two or more races, non-Hispanic/Latino; 11% Race/ethnicity unknown; 24% transferred in. *Retention:* 40% of full-time freshmen returned.

Freshmen *Admission:* 123 enrolled.

Faculty *Total:* 37, 27% full-time, 24% with terminal degrees. *Student/faculty ratio:* 9:1.

Academics *Degrees:* diplomas, associate, and bachelor's. *Special study options:* academic remediation for entering students, accelerated degree program, adult/continuing education programs, advanced placement credit, internships, part-time degree program, services for LD students, summer session for credit.

Computers on Campus 67 computers/terminals and 128 ports are available on campus for general student use. Students can access the following: computer help desk, free student e-mail accounts, online (class) grades, online (class) registration, online (class) schedules. Campuswide network is available. Wireless service is available via entire campus.

Student Life *Housing:* college housing not available. *Campus security:* 24-hour emergency response devices, late-night transport/escort service.

Standardized Tests *Required:* AccuPlacer is required of all applicants unless documentation of a minimum ACT composite score of 21 or documentation of a minimum composite score of 1485 on the SAT is presented (for admission).

Applying *Options:* electronic application. *Application fee:* $50. *Required:* high school transcript, interview. *Required for some:* essay or personal statement, 2 letters of recommendation, GED certificate in lieu of high school transcript. *Application deadlines:* rolling (freshmen), rolling (out-of-state freshmen), rolling (transfers). *Notification:* continuous (freshmen), continuous (out-of-state freshmen), continuous (transfers).

Freshman Application Contact Globe University–La Crosse, 2651 Midwest Drive, Onalaska, WI 54650. *Phone:* 608-779-2600. *Web site:* http://www.globeuniversity.edu/.

Globe University–Madison East

Madison, Wisconsin

- **Proprietary** 4-year, part of Globe Education Network (GEN) which is composed of Globe University, Minnesota School of Business, Broadview University, The Institute of Production and Recording and Minnesota School of Cosmetology
- **Urban** 7-acre campus
- **Coed** 290 undergraduate students, 34% full-time, 76% women, 24% men

Undergraduates 100 full-time, 190 part-time. Students come from 1 other state; 10% Black or African American, non-Hispanic/Latino; 3% Hispanic/Latino; 1% Asian, non-Hispanic/Latino; 0.3% Native Hawaiian or other Pacific Islander, non-Hispanic/Latino; 0.3% American Indian or Alaska Native, non-Hispanic/Latino; 0.7% Two or more races, non-Hispanic/Latino; 5% Race/ethnicity unknown; 37% transferred in.

Freshmen *Admission:* 81 enrolled.

Faculty *Total:* 47, 19% full-time, 43% with terminal degrees. *Student/faculty ratio:* 10:1.

Academics *Degrees:* diplomas, associate, and bachelor's. *Special study options:* academic remediation for entering students, accelerated degree program, adult/continuing education programs, advanced placement credit, internships, part-time degree program, services for LD students, summer session for credit.

Computers on Campus 62 computers/terminals and 128 ports are available on campus for general student use. Students can access the following: computer help desk, free student e-mail accounts, online (class) grades, online (class) registration, online (class) schedules. Campuswide network is available. Wireless service is available via entire campus.

Student Life *Housing:* college housing not available. *Campus security:* 24-hour emergency response devices, late-night transport/escort service.

Standardized Tests *Required:* AccuPlacer is required of all applicants unless documentation of a minimum ACT composite score of 21 or documentation of a minimum composite score of 1485 on the SAT is presented (for admission).

Applying *Options:* electronic application. *Application fee:* $50. *Required:* high school transcript, interview, High school transcript or GED required of all

applicants. *Required for some:* essay or personal statement, 2 letters of recommendation. *Application deadlines:* rolling (freshmen), rolling (out-of-state freshmen), rolling (transfers). *Notification:* continuous (freshmen), continuous (out-of-state freshmen), continuous (transfers).
Freshman Application Contact Globe University–Madison East, 4901 Eastpark Boulevard, Madison, WI 53718. *Phone:* 608-216-9400. *Web site:* http://www.globeuniversity.edu/.

Globe University–Madison West
Middleton, Wisconsin

- **Proprietary** 4-year, part of Globe Education Network (GEN) which is composed of Globe University, Minnesota School of Business, Broadview University, The Institute of Production and Recording and Minnesota School of Cosmetology
- **Small-town** campus
- **Coed** 338 undergraduate students, 29% full-time, 77% women, 23% men

Undergraduates 98 full-time, 240 part-time. Students come from 1 other state; 15% Black or African American, non-Hispanic/Latino; 3% Hispanic/Latino; 2% Asian, non-Hispanic/Latino; 0.3% American Indian or Alaska Native, non-Hispanic/Latino; 2% Two or more races, non-Hispanic/Latino; 8% Race/ethnicity unknown; 24% transferred in. *Retention:* 25% of full-time freshmen returned.
Freshmen *Admission:* 86 enrolled.
Faculty *Total:* 42, 7% full-time, 36% with terminal degrees. *Student/faculty ratio:* 12:1.
Academics *Degrees:* diplomas, associate, and bachelor's. *Special study options:* academic remediation for entering students, accelerated degree program, adult/continuing education programs, advanced placement credit, internships, part-time degree program, services for LD students, summer session for credit.
Computers on Campus 74 computers/terminals and 128 ports are available on campus for general student use. Students can access the following: computer help desk, free student e-mail accounts, online (class) grades, online (class) registration, online (class) schedules. Campuswide network is available. Wireless service is available via entire campus.
Student Life *Housing:* college housing not available. *Campus security:* 24-hour emergency response devices, late-night transport/escort service.
Standardized Tests *Required:* AccuPlacer is required of all applicants unless documentation of a minimum ACT composite score of 21 or documentation of a minimum composite score of 1485 on the SAT is presented (for admission).
Applying *Options:* electronic application. *Application fee:* $50. *Required:* high school transcript, interview. *Required for some:* essay or personal statement, 2 letters of recommendation, GED certificate in lieu of high school transcript. *Application deadlines:* rolling (freshmen), rolling (out-of-state freshmen), rolling (transfers). *Notification:* continuous (freshmen), continuous (out-of-state freshmen), continuous (transfers).
Freshman Application Contact Globe University–Madison West, 1345 Deming Way, Middleton, WI 53562. *Phone:* 608-830-6900. *Web site:* http://www.globeuniversity.edu/.

Globe University–Wausau
Rothschild, Wisconsin

- **Proprietary** 4-year, part of Globe Education Network (GEN) which is composed of Globe University, Minnesota School of Business, Broadview University, The Institute of Production and Recording and Minnesota School of Cosmetology
- **Small-town** 5-acre campus
- **Coed** 365 undergraduate students, 52% full-time, 83% women, 17% men

Undergraduates 190 full-time, 175 part-time. Students come from 1 other state; 1% Black or African American, non-Hispanic/Latino; 2% Hispanic/Latino; 2% Asian, non-Hispanic/Latino; 1% American Indian or Alaska Native, non-Hispanic/Latino; 0.5% Two or more races, non-Hispanic/Latino; 10% Race/ethnicity unknown; 39% transferred in.
Freshmen *Admission:* 114 enrolled.
Faculty *Total:* 50, 16% full-time, 30% with terminal degrees. *Student/faculty ratio:* 11:1.
Academics *Degrees:* diplomas, associate, and bachelor's. *Special study options:* academic remediation for entering students, accelerated degree program, adult/continuing education programs, advanced placement credit, internships, part-time degree program, services for LD students, summer session for credit.
Computers on Campus 66 computers/terminals and 128 ports are available on campus for general student use. Students can access the following: computer help desk, free student e-mail accounts, online (class) grades, online (class) registration, online (class) schedules. Campuswide network is available. Wireless service is available via entire campus.

Student Life *Housing:* college housing not available. *Campus security:* 24-hour emergency response devices, late-night transport/escort service.
Standardized Tests *Required:* AccuPlacer is required of all applicants unless documentation of a minimum ACT composite score of 21 or documentation of a minimum composite score of 1485 on the SAT is presented (for admission).
Applying *Options:* electronic application. *Application fee:* $50. *Required:* high school transcript, interview, High school transcript or GED required of all applicants. *Required for some:* essay or personal statement, 2 letters of recommendation. *Application deadlines:* rolling (freshmen), rolling (out-of-state freshmen), rolling (transfers). *Notification:* continuous (freshmen), continuous (out-of-state freshmen), continuous (transfers).
Freshman Application Contact Globe University–Wausau, 1480 Country Road XX, Rothschild, WI 54474. *Phone:* 715-301-1300. *Web site:* http://www.globeuniversity.edu/.

Herzing University
Brookfield, Wisconsin

Admissions Office Contact Herzing University, 555 South Executive Drive, Brookfield, WI 53005. *Toll-free phone:* 800-596-0724. *Web site:* http://www.herzing.edu/brookfield.

Herzing University
Kenosha, Wisconsin

Admissions Office Contact Herzing University, 4006 Washington Road, Kenosha, WI 53144. *Toll-free phone:* 800-596-0724. *Web site:* http://www.herzing.edu/kenosha.

Herzing University
Madison, Wisconsin

- **Proprietary** comprehensive, founded 1948, part of Herzing Institutes, Inc.
- **Suburban** campus with easy access to Madison, Milwaukee
- **Coed, primarily men** 857 undergraduate students

Faculty *Total:* 48, 58% full-time, 10% with terminal degrees.
Academics *Calendar:* semesters. *Degrees:* certificates, diplomas, associate, bachelor's, and master's. *Special study options:* academic remediation for entering students, accelerated degree program, adult/continuing education programs, advanced placement credit, cooperative education, distance learning, honors programs, independent study, internships, part-time degree program, services for LD students, study abroad, summer session for credit.
Computers on Campus 363 computers/terminals are available on campus for general student use. Campuswide network is available.
Student Life *Housing:* college housing not available. *Campus security:* 24-hour emergency response devices. *Student services:* personal/psychological counseling.
Costs (2012–13) *Tuition:* $18,315 full-time. Full-time tuition and fees vary according to course load, location, and program. Part-time tuition and fees vary according to course load, location, and program. *Payment plan:* installment. *Waivers:* employees or children of employees.
Financial Aid *Financial aid deadline:* 6/30.
Applying *Required:* high school transcript, interview. *Application deadline:* rolling (freshmen).
Freshman Application Contact Mr. Tom Beatty, Associate Director of Admissions, Herzing University, 5218 East Terrace Drive, Madison, WI 53718. *Phone:* 608-395-3441. *Toll-free phone:* 800-596-0724. *Fax:* 608-249-8593. *E-mail:* info@msn.herzing.edu. *Web site:* http://www.herzing.edu/madison/.

Herzing University Online
Milwaukee, Wisconsin

Admissions Office Contact Herzing University Online, 525 North 6th Street, Milwaukee, WI 53203. *Toll-free phone:* 866-508-0748. *Web site:* http://www.herzingonline.edu/.

ITT Technical Institute
Germantown, Wisconsin

- **Proprietary** 4-year
- **Coed**
- **Minimally difficult** entrance level

Academics *Degrees:* associate and bachelor's.
Freshman Application Contact Director of Recruiting, ITT Technical Institute, W177 N9886 Rivercrest Drive, Suite 200, Germantown, WI 53022.

Phone: 262-257-7100. *Toll-free phone:* 877-213-8538. *Web site:* http://www.itt-tech.edu/.

ITT Technical Institute
Green Bay, Wisconsin

- **Proprietary** primarily 2-year, founded 2000, part of ITT Educational Services, Inc.
- **Coed**
- **Minimally difficult** entrance level

Academics *Calendar:* quarters. *Degrees:* associate and bachelor's.
Student Life *Housing:* college housing not available.
Freshman Application Contact Director of Recruitment, ITT Technical Institute, 470 Security Boulevard, Green Bay, WI 54313. *Phone:* 920-662-9000. *Toll-free phone:* 888-884-3626. *Fax:* 920-662-9384. *Web site:* http://www.itt-tech.edu/.

ITT Technical Institute
Greenfield, Wisconsin

- **Proprietary** primarily 2-year, founded 1968, part of ITT Educational Services, Inc.
- **Suburban** campus
- **Coed**
- **Minimally difficult** entrance level

Academics *Calendar:* quarters. *Degrees:* associate and bachelor's.
Student Life *Housing:* college housing not available.
Freshman Application Contact Director of Recruitment, ITT Technical Institute, 6300 West Layton Avenue, Greenfield, WI 53220-4612. *Phone:* 414-282-9494. *Web site:* http://www.itt-tech.edu/.

ITT Technical Institute
Madison, Wisconsin

- **Proprietary** primarily 2-year, part of ITT Educational Services, Inc.
- **Coed**
- **Minimally difficult** entrance level

Academics *Degrees:* associate and bachelor's.
Freshman Application Contact Director of Recruitment, ITT Technical Institute, 2450 Rimrock Road, Suite 100, Madison, WI 53713. *Phone:* 608-288-6301. *Toll-free phone:* 877-628-5960. *Web site:* http://www.itt-tech.edu/.

Lakeland College
Sheboygan, Wisconsin

Freshman Application Contact Mr. Nick Spaeth, Director of Admissions, Lakeland College, PO Box 359, Nash Visitors Center, Sheboygan, WI 53082-0359. *Phone:* 920-565-1007. *Toll-free phone:* 800-569-2166. *Fax:* 920-565-1215. *E-mail:* admissions@lakeland.edu. *Web site:* http://www.lakeland.edu/.

Lawrence University
Appleton, Wisconsin

- **Independent** 4-year, founded 1847
- **Small-town** 84-acre campus
- **Endowment** $214.7 million
- **Coed** 1,496 undergraduate students, 96% full-time, 54% women, 46% men
- **Very difficult** entrance level, 53% of applicants were admitted

Undergraduates 1,443 full-time, 53 part-time. Students come from 45 states and territories; 35 other countries; 67% are from out of state; 3% Black or African American, non-Hispanic/Latino; 4% Hispanic/Latino; 3% Asian, non-Hispanic/Latino; 0.1% Native Hawaiian or other Pacific Islander, non-Hispanic/Latino; 0.5% American Indian or Alaska Native, non-Hispanic/Latino; 3% Two or more races, non-Hispanic/Latino; 1% Race/ethnicity unknown; 7% international; 2% transferred in; 98% live on campus. *Retention:* 89% of full-time freshmen returned.
Freshmen *Admission:* 2,666 applied, 1,405 admitted, 326 enrolled. *Average high school GPA:* 3.66. *Test scores:* SAT critical reading scores over 500: 99%; SAT math scores over 500: 98%; SAT writing scores over 500: 94%; ACT scores over 18: 100%; SAT critical reading scores over 600: 78%; SAT math scores over 600: 72%; SAT writing scores over 600: 63%; ACT scores over 24: 93%; SAT critical reading scores over 700: 30%; SAT math scores over 700: 24%; SAT writing scores over 700: 25%; ACT scores over 30: 46%.
Faculty *Total:* 201, 81% full-time, 82% with terminal degrees. *Student/faculty ratio:* 8:1.

Academics *Calendar:* trimesters. *Degree:* bachelor's. *Special study options:* advanced placement credit, double majors, independent study, internships, off-campus study, part-time degree program, services for LD students, student-designed majors, study abroad. *Unusual degree programs:* 3-2 engineering with Columbia University in New York, New York, Rensselaer Polytechnic Institute in Troy, New York, Washington University in St. Louis, Missouri; forestry with Duke University; occupational therapy with Washington University in St. Louis.
Computers on Campus 354 computers/terminals and 1,055 ports are available on campus for general student use. Students can access the following: campus intranet, computer help desk, free student e-mail accounts, online (class) grades, online (class) registration, online (class) schedules, online transcripts, financial aid, financial account information. Campuswide network is available. 100% of college-owned or -operated housing units are wired for high-speed Internet access. Wireless service is available via classrooms, computer centers, computer labs, dorm rooms, learning centers, libraries, student centers.
Student Life *Housing:* on-campus residence required through senior year. *Options:* coed, men-only, women-only, cooperative, disabled students. Campus housing is university owned. Freshman campus housing is guaranteed. *Activities and organizations:* drama/theater group, student-run newspaper, radio station, choral group, Lawrence Swing Dancers, Lawrence International, Outdoor Recreation Club, Sustainable Lawrence University Gardens (SLUG), Greenfire, national fraternities, national sororities. *Campus security:* 24-hour emergency response devices and patrols, student patrols, late-night transport/escort service, controlled dormitory access, evening patrols by trained security personnel. *Student services:* health clinic, personal/psychological counseling.
Athletics Member NCAA. All Division III. *Intercollegiate sports:* baseball M, basketball M/W, crew M(c)/W(c), cross-country running M/W, fencing M/W, football M, golf M, ice hockey M/W(c), soccer M/W, softball W, swimming and diving M/W, tennis M/W, track and field M/W, ultimate Frisbee M(c)/W(c), volleyball M(c)/W. *Intramural sports:* badminton M/W, basketball M/W, fencing M/W, racquetball M/W, skiing (downhill) M/W, soccer M/W, softball M/W, table tennis M/W, tennis M/W, volleyball M/W, water polo M/W.
Costs (2011–12) *Comprehensive fee:* $46,371 includes full-time tuition ($38,205), mandatory fees ($276), and room and board ($7890). *Room and board:* Room and board charges vary according to board plan. *Payment plans:* tuition prepayment, installment. *Waivers:* employees or children of employees.
Financial Aid Of all full-time matriculated undergraduates who enrolled in 2011, 1,027 applied for aid, 860 were judged to have need, 443 had their need fully met. 645 Federal Work-Study jobs (averaging $2325). 292 state and other part-time jobs (averaging $2157). In 2011, 467 non-need-based awards were made. *Average percent of need met:* 89%. *Average financial aid package:* $29,950. *Average need-based loan:* $5480. *Average need-based gift aid:* $23,207. *Average non-need-based aid:* $12,496. *Average indebtedness upon graduation:* $32,838.
Applying *Options:* electronic application, early admission, early decision, early action, deferred entrance. *Application fee:* $40. *Required:* essay or personal statement, high school transcript, 1 letter of recommendation, audition for music program. *Recommended:* minimum 3.0 GPA, interview. *Application deadlines:* 1/15 (freshmen), 4/1 (transfers), 12/1 (early action). *Early decision deadline:* 11/15. *Notification:* 4/1 (freshmen), 5/15 (transfers), 12/1 (early decision), 1/30 (early action).
Freshman Application Contact Mr. Ken Anselment, Dean of Admissions and Financial Aid, Lawrence University, 711 East Boldt Way SPC 29, Appleton, WI 54911-5699. *Phone:* 920-832-6500. *Toll-free phone:* 800-227-0982. *Fax:* 920-832-6782. *E-mail:* excel@lawrence.edu. *Web site:* http://www.lawrence.edu/.

Maranatha Baptist Bible College
Watertown, Wisconsin

- **Independent Baptist** comprehensive, founded 1968
- **Small-town** 60-acre campus with easy access to Milwaukee
- **Endowment** $218,513
- **Coed** 927 undergraduate students, 83% full-time, 54% women, 46% men
- **Noncompetitive** entrance level, 75% of applicants were admitted

Undergraduates 765 full-time, 162 part-time. Students come from 42 states and territories; 9 other countries; 73% are from out of state; 0.1% Black or African American, non-Hispanic/Latino; 1% Hispanic/Latino; 0.8% Asian, non-Hispanic/Latino; 0.4% American Indian or Alaska Native, non-Hispanic/Latino; 3% Two or more races, non-Hispanic/Latino; 23% Race/ethnicity unknown; 0.3% international; 4% transferred in; 71% live on campus. *Retention:* 76% of full-time freshmen returned.
Freshmen *Admission:* 426 applied, 321 admitted, 217 enrolled. *Test scores:* SAT critical reading scores over 500: 64%; SAT math scores over 500: 52%; SAT writing scores over 500: 51%; ACT scores over 18: 90%; SAT critical

reading scores over 600: 16%; SAT writing scores over 600: 29%; ACT scores over 24: 39%; SAT critical reading scores over 700: 8%; SAT writing scores over 700: 3%; ACT scores over 30: 5%.

Faculty *Total:* 76, 58% full-time, 24% with terminal degrees. *Student/faculty ratio:* 15:1.

Academics *Calendar:* semesters. *Degrees:* certificates, associate, bachelor's, and master's. *Special study options:* academic remediation for entering students, advanced placement credit, distance learning, double majors, independent study, internships, off-campus study, part-time degree program, study abroad, summer session for credit. *ROTC:* Army (b), Air Force (c).

Computers on Campus 120 computers/terminals are available on campus for general student use. Students can access the following: campus intranet, computer help desk, free student e-mail accounts, online (class) grades, online (class) registration, online (class) schedules. Campuswide network is available. 100% of college-owned or -operated housing units are wired for high-speed Internet access. Wireless service is available via classrooms, computer centers, computer labs, dorm rooms, libraries, student centers.

Student Life *Housing:* on-campus residence required through senior year. *Options:* men-only, women-only. Campus housing is university owned. Freshman campus housing is guaranteed. *Activities and organizations:* drama/theater group, choral group. *Campus security:* student patrols, late-night transport/escort service, controlled dormitory access. *Student services:* health clinic, personal/psychological counseling.

Athletics Member NCAA, NCCAA. All NCAA Division III. *Intercollegiate sports:* baseball M, basketball M/W, cross-country running M/W, football M, soccer M/W, softball W, volleyball W, wrestling M. *Intramural sports:* basketball M/W.

Standardized Tests *Required:* SAT or ACT (for admission).

Costs (2011–12) *Comprehensive fee:* $18,550 includes full-time tuition ($11,160), mandatory fees ($1100), and room and board ($6290). Full-time tuition and fees vary according to course load. Part-time tuition: $465 per credit hour. Part-time tuition and fees vary according to course load. *Payment plan:* installment. *Waivers:* employees or children of employees.

Financial Aid Of all full-time matriculated undergraduates who enrolled in 2009, 662 applied for aid, 602 were judged to have need, 33 had their need fully met. In 2009, 28 non-need-based awards were made. *Average percent of need met:* 53%. *Average financial aid package:* $8279. *Average need-based loan:* $4358. *Average need-based gift aid:* $4299. *Average non-need-based aid:* $1481. *Average indebtedness upon graduation:* $19,191.

Applying *Options:* electronic application. *Application fee:* $50. *Required:* essay or personal statement, high school transcript, 4 letters of recommendation. *Application deadlines:* rolling (freshmen), rolling (transfers). *Notification:* continuous (freshmen), continuous (transfers).

Freshman Application Contact Dr. James Harrison, Director of Admissions, Maranatha Baptist Bible College, 745 West Main Street, Watertown, WI 53094. *Phone:* 920-206-2327. *Toll-free phone:* 800-622-2947. *Fax:* 920-261-9109. *E-mail:* admissions@mbbc.edu. *Web site:* http://www.mbbc.edu/.

Marian University
Fond du Lac, Wisconsin

- **Independent Roman Catholic** comprehensive, founded 1936
- **Small-town** 104-acre campus with easy access to Milwaukee
- **Endowment** $7.2 million
- **Coed** 1,910 undergraduate students, 78% full-time, 73% women, 27% men
- **Moderately difficult** entrance level, 82% of applicants were admitted

Undergraduates 1,498 full-time, 412 part-time. Students come from 18 states and territories; 8 other countries; 6% are from out of state; 5% Black or African American, non-Hispanic/Latino; 5% Hispanic/Latino; 2% Asian, non-Hispanic/Latino; 0.2% Native Hawaiian or other Pacific Islander, non-Hispanic/Latino; 0.5% American Indian or Alaska Native, non-Hispanic/Latino; 0.7% Two or more races, non-Hispanic/Latino; 2% Race/ethnicity unknown; 1% international; 7% transferred in; 34% live on campus. *Retention:* 67% of full-time freshmen returned.

Freshmen *Admission:* 1,057 applied, 866 admitted, 321 enrolled. *Average high school GPA:* 3.05. *Test scores:* ACT scores over 18: 79%; ACT scores over 24: 20%; ACT scores over 30: 1%.

Faculty *Total:* 277, 32% full-time, 24% with terminal degrees. *Student/faculty ratio:* 13:1.

Academics *Calendar:* semesters. *Degrees:* certificates, bachelor's, master's, doctoral, postbachelor's, and first professional certificates. *Special study options:* academic remediation for entering students, accelerated degree program, advanced placement credit, cooperative education, distance learning, double majors, English as a second language, honors programs, independent study, internships, part-time degree program, services for LD students, student-designed majors, study abroad, summer session for credit.

Computers on Campus 500 computers/terminals are available on campus for general student use. Students can access the following: campus intranet, computer help desk, free student e-mail accounts, online (class) grades, online (class) registration, online (class) schedules. Campuswide network is available. 100% of college-owned or -operated housing units are wired for high-speed Internet access. Wireless service is available via entire campus.

Student Life *Housing:* on-campus residence required through sophomore year. *Options:* coed, disabled students. Campus housing is university owned. Freshman campus housing is guaranteed. *Activities and organizations:* student-run newspaper, choral group, Student Senate, Student Nurses Association, Student Education Association, Science and Math Association, African American Student Union, national fraternities, national sororities. *Campus security:* 24-hour emergency response devices and patrols, student patrols, late-night transport/escort service, controlled dormitory access. *Student services:* health clinic, personal/psychological counseling.

Athletics Member NCAA. All Division III. *Intercollegiate sports:* baseball M, basketball M/W, cross-country running M/W, golf M/W, ice hockey M/W, soccer M/W, softball W, tennis M/W, volleyball W. *Intramural sports:* badminton M/W, basketball M/W, bowling M/W, football M, skiing (downhill) M/W, softball M, tennis M/W, volleyball M/W.

Standardized Tests *Required:* SAT or ACT (for admission).

Costs (2011–12) *One-time required fee:* $100. *Comprehensive fee:* $28,340 includes full-time tuition ($22,090), mandatory fees ($350), and room and board ($5900). Full-time tuition and fees vary according to course load and program. Part-time tuition: $340 per credit hour. Part-time tuition and fees vary according to course load and program. *College room only:* $3550. Room and board charges vary according to board plan and housing facility. *Payment plan:* installment. *Waivers:* senior citizens and employees or children of employees.

Financial Aid Of all full-time matriculated undergraduates who enrolled in 2010, 1,341 applied for aid, 1,242 were judged to have need, 372 had their need fully met. 163 Federal Work-Study jobs (averaging $529). 419 state and other part-time jobs (averaging $1427). In 2010, 81 non-need-based awards were made. *Average percent of need met:* 83%. *Average financial aid package:* $20,715. *Average need-based loan:* $6562. *Average need-based gift aid:* $11,523. *Average non-need-based aid:* $4636. *Average indebtedness upon graduation:* $25,000.

Applying *Options:* electronic application, deferred entrance. *Application fee:* $20. *Required:* high school transcript. *Required for some:* interview. *Recommended:* minimum 2.0 GPA, interview. *Application deadlines:* rolling (freshmen), rolling (transfers). *Notification:* 8/15 (freshmen), continuous until 8/15 (transfers).

Freshman Application Contact Shannon LaLuzerne, Senior Director of Admissions, Marian University, 45 South National Avenue, Fond du Lac, WI 54935-4699. *Phone:* 800-262-7426. *Toll-free phone:* 800-2-MARIAN. *Fax:* 920-923-8755. *E-mail:* admit@marianuniversity.edu. *Web site:* http://www.marianuniversity.edu/.

Marquette University
Milwaukee, Wisconsin

- **Independent Roman Catholic (Jesuit)** university, founded 1881
- **Urban** 98-acre campus with easy access to Milwaukee
- **Endowment** $401.2 million
- **Coed** 8,387 undergraduate students, 95% full-time, 52% women, 48% men
- **Moderately difficult** entrance level, 57% of applicants were admitted

Undergraduates 7,999 full-time, 388 part-time. Students come from 51 states and territories; 44 other countries; 61% are from out of state; 5% Black or African American, non-Hispanic/Latino; 7% Hispanic/Latino; 4% Asian, non-Hispanic/Latino; 0.2% Native Hawaiian or other Pacific Islander, non-Hispanic/Latino; 0.3% American Indian or Alaska Native, non-Hispanic/Latino; 2% Two or more races, non-Hispanic/Latino; 4% Race/ethnicity unknown; 3% international; 2% transferred in; 54% live on campus. *Retention:* 90% of full-time freshmen returned.

Freshmen *Admission:* 22,354 applied, 12,707 admitted, 2,068 enrolled. *Test scores:* SAT critical reading scores over 500: 83%; SAT math scores over 500: 90%; SAT writing scores over 500: 82%; ACT scores over 18: 100%; SAT critical reading scores over 600: 42%; SAT math scores over 600: 49%; SAT writing scores over 600: 40%; ACT scores over 24: 84%; SAT critical reading scores over 700: 7%; SAT math scores over 700: 8%; SAT writing scores over 700: 8%; ACT scores over 30: 25%.

Faculty *Total:* 1,128, 56% full-time, 58% with terminal degrees. *Student/faculty ratio:* 15:1.

Academics *Calendar:* semesters. *Degrees:* bachelor's, master's, doctoral, post-master's, postbachelor's, and first professional certificates. *Special study options:* accelerated degree program, adult/continuing education programs, advanced placement credit, cooperative education, distance learning, double

majors, English as a second language, honors programs, independent study, internships, off-campus study, part-time degree program, services for LD students, student-designed majors, study abroad, summer session for credit. *ROTC:* Army (b), Navy (b), Air Force (b). *Unusual degree programs:* business administration; engineering with Biomedical Engineering, Civil Engineering, Electrical and Computer Engineering, Mechanical Engineering are administered through the Marquette University Graduate School; exercise science/clinical and translational rehabilitation health sciences, speech and language pathology, international affairs, and physical therapy programs are administered through the Graduate School; physical therapy is administered through the College of Health Sciences.

Computers on Campus 1,500 computers/terminals and 550 ports are available on campus for general student use. Students can access the following: campus intranet, computer help desk, free student e-mail accounts, online (class) grades, online (class) registration, online (class) schedules, AV Software, MATLAB. Campuswide network is available. 100% of college-owned or -operated housing units are wired for high-speed Internet access. Wireless service is available via classrooms, computer centers, computer labs, dorm rooms, learning centers, libraries, student centers.

Student Life *Housing:* on-campus residence required through sophomore year. *Options:* coed, men-only, women-only, disabled students. Campus housing is university owned. Freshman campus housing is guaranteed. *Activities and organizations:* drama/theater group, student-run newspaper, radio and television station, choral group, student government, club sports, community service organizations, band/jazz/orchestra, Residence Hall Association, national fraternities, national sororities. *Campus security:* 24-hour emergency response devices and patrols, student patrols, late-night transport/escort service, 24-hour desk attendants in residence halls. *Student services:* health clinic, personal/psychological counseling.

Athletics Member NCAA. All Division I. *Intercollegiate sports:* baseball M(c), basketball M(s)/W(s), cheerleading M/W, crew M(c)/W(c), cross-country running M(s)/W(s), football M(c), golf M(s), ice hockey M(c), lacrosse M(s)/W(s), rugby M(c)/W(c), sailing M(c)/W(c), skiing (downhill) M(c)/W(c), soccer M(s)/W(s), softball W(c), swimming and diving M(c)/W(c), tennis M(s)/W(s), track and field M(s)/W(s), ultimate Frisbee M(c)/W(c), volleyball M(c)/W(s). *Intramural sports:* badminton M/W, basketball M/W, bowling M(c)/W(c), fencing M(c)/W(c), football M/W, lacrosse M(c)/W(c), racquetball M/W, soccer M/W, softball M/W, tennis M/W, track and field M/W, ultimate Frisbee M/W, volleyball M/W, water polo M/W, weight lifting M/W, wrestling M(c).

Standardized Tests *Required:* SAT or ACT (for admission).

Costs (2012–13) *Comprehensive fee:* $43,664 includes full-time tuition ($32,810), mandatory fees ($434), and room and board ($10,420). Full-time tuition and fees vary according to course load and program. Part-time tuition: $955 per credit. Part-time tuition and fees vary according to program. *Required fees:* $955 per credit part-time. *College room only:* $6700. Room and board charges vary according to housing facility. *Payment plan:* installment. *Waivers:* adult students, senior citizens, and employees or children of employees.

Financial Aid Of all full-time matriculated undergraduates who enrolled in 2011, 5,946 applied for aid, 4,913 were judged to have need, 1,286 had their need fully met. In 2011, 2506 non-need-based awards were made. *Average percent of need met:* 76%. *Average financial aid package:* $22,399. *Average need-based loan:* $5263. *Average need-based gift aid:* $15,550. *Average non-need-based aid:* $8998. *Average indebtedness upon graduation:* $35,204.

Applying *Options:* electronic application, deferred entrance. *Application fee:* $30. *Required:* essay or personal statement, high school transcript, minimum 2.5 GPA. *Recommended:* minimum 3.4 GPA. *Application deadline:* 12/1 (freshmen). *Notification:* 1/31 (freshmen).

Freshman Application Contact Mr. Robert Blust, Dean of Undergraduate Admissions, Marquette University, PO Box 1881, Milwaukee, WI 53201-1881. *Phone:* 414-288-7004. *Toll-free phone:* 800-222-6544. *Fax:* 414-288-3764. *E-mail:* admissions@marquette.edu. *Web site:* http://www.marquette.edu/.

Milwaukee Institute of Art and Design

Milwaukee, Wisconsin

Freshman Application Contact Stacey Steinberg, Director of Admissions, Milwaukee Institute of Art and Design, 273 East Erie Street, Milwaukee, WI 53202. *Phone:* 414-847-3200. *Toll-free phone:* 888-749-MIAD. *Fax:* 414-291-8077. *E-mail:* admissions@miad.edu. *Web site:* http://www.miad.edu/.

Milwaukee School of Engineering

Milwaukee, Wisconsin

- **Independent** comprehensive, founded 1903
- **Urban** 15-acre campus
- **Endowment** $41.9 million
- **Coed, primarily men** 2,310 undergraduate students, 92% full-time, 21% women, 79% men
- **Moderately difficult** entrance level, 64% of applicants were admitted

Undergraduates 2,122 full-time, 188 part-time. Students come from 34 states and territories; 26 other countries; 29% are from out of state; 3% Black or African American, non-Hispanic/Latino; 4% Hispanic/Latino; 3% Asian, non-Hispanic/Latino; 0.2% Native Hawaiian or other Pacific Islander, non-Hispanic/Latino; 0.3% American Indian or Alaska Native, non-Hispanic/Latino; 1% Two or more races, non-Hispanic/Latino; 3% Race/ethnicity unknown; 5% international; 7% transferred in; 37% live on campus. *Retention:* 76% of full-time freshmen returned.

Freshmen *Admission:* 2,199 applied, 1,407 admitted, 448 enrolled. *Average high school GPA:* 3.6. *Test scores:* SAT critical reading scores over 500: 95%; SAT math scores over 500: 100%; ACT scores over 18: 100%; SAT critical reading scores over 600: 62%; SAT math scores over 600: 76%; ACT scores over 24: 85%; SAT critical reading scores over 700: 24%; SAT math scores over 700: 14%; ACT scores over 30: 24%.

Faculty *Total:* 243, 55% full-time, 53% with terminal degrees. *Student/faculty ratio:* 14:1.

Academics *Calendar:* quarters. *Degrees:* bachelor's and master's. *Special study options:* academic remediation for entering students, adult/continuing education programs, advanced placement credit, distance learning, double majors, English as a second language, honors programs, independent study, internships, part-time degree program, services for LD students, study abroad, summer session for credit. *ROTC:* Army (c), Navy (c), Air Force (c).

Computers on Campus 125 computers/terminals and 2,000 ports are available on campus for general student use. Students can access the following: campus intranet, computer help desk, free student e-mail accounts, online (class) grades, online (class) registration, online (class) schedules. Campuswide network is available. 100% of college-owned or -operated housing units are wired for high-speed Internet access. Wireless service is available via entire campus.

Student Life *Housing:* on-campus residence required through sophomore year. *Options:* coed, disabled students. Campus housing is university owned. Freshman campus housing is guaranteed. *Activities and organizations:* drama/theater group, student-run radio station, choral group, Architectural Engineering and Construction Management Societies, Student Athletic Advisory Committee, MAGE, Student Government Association, Student Union Board, national fraternities, national sororities. *Campus security:* 24-hour emergency response devices and patrols, late-night transport/escort service, controlled dormitory access. *Student services:* health clinic, personal/psychological counseling, women's center.

Athletics Member NCAA. All Division III. *Intercollegiate sports:* baseball M, basketball M/W, cheerleading M/W, crew M, cross-country running M/W, golf M/W, ice hockey M, lacrosse M, soccer M/W, softball W, tennis M/W, track and field M/W, volleyball M/W, wrestling M. *Intramural sports:* basketball M/W, bowling M(c)/W(c), fencing M(c)/W(c), football M/W, gymnastics M(c)/W(c), rugby M(c), soccer M/W, softball M/W, ultimate Frisbee M(c), volleyball M/W, weight lifting M(c)/W(c).

Standardized Tests *Required:* SAT or ACT (for admission).

Costs (2012–13) *Comprehensive fee:* $39,948 includes full-time tuition ($31,920) and room and board ($8028). Part-time tuition: $554 per quarter hour. Part-time tuition and fees vary according to course load. *College room only:* $5124. Room and board charges vary according to board plan and housing facility. *Payment plan:* installment. *Waivers:* employees or children of employees.

Financial Aid Of all full-time matriculated undergraduates who enrolled in 2009, 2,113 applied for aid, 1,936 were judged to have need, 286 had their need fully met. 284 Federal Work-Study jobs (averaging $1429). In 2009, 346 non-need-based awards were made. *Average percent of need met:* 68%. *Average financial aid package:* $19,411. *Average need-based loan:* $3547. *Average need-based gift aid:* $16,192. *Average non-need-based aid:* $10,136. *Average indebtedness upon graduation:* $35,236.

Applying *Options:* electronic application, deferred entrance. *Required:* high school transcript, minimum 2.5 GPA. *Required for some:* essay or personal statement, interview. *Application deadlines:* rolling (freshmen), rolling (transfers). *Notification:* continuous (freshmen), continuous (transfers).

Freshman Application Contact Dana-Marie Grennier, Director of Admissions, Milwaukee School of Engineering, 1025 North Broadway, Milwaukee, WI 53202-3109. *Phone:* 414-277-6761. *Toll-free phone:* 800-332-6763. *Fax:* 414-277-7475. *E-mail:* grennier@msoe.edu. *Web site:* http://www.msoe.edu/.

Mount Mary College

Milwaukee, Wisconsin

- **Independent Roman Catholic** comprehensive, founded 1913
- **Urban** 80-acre campus
- **Endowment** $9.9 million
- **Undergraduate: women only; graduate: coed** 1,209 undergraduate students, 67% full-time, 97% women, 3% men
- **Moderately difficult** entrance level, 53% of applicants were admitted

Undergraduates 806 full-time, 403 part-time. Students come from 15 states and territories; 13 other countries; 4% are from out of state; 23% Black or African American, non-Hispanic/Latino; 11% Hispanic/Latino; 5% Asian, non-Hispanic/Latino; 0.1% Native Hawaiian or other Pacific Islander, non-Hispanic/Latino; 0.5% American Indian or Alaska Native, non-Hispanic/Latino; 3% Two or more races, non-Hispanic/Latino; 3% Race/ethnicity unknown; 0.8% international; 9% transferred in; 15% live on campus. *Retention:* 66% of full-time freshmen returned.

Freshmen *Admission:* 423 applied, 226 admitted, 114 enrolled. *Average high school GPA:* 2.92. *Test scores:* ACT scores over 18: 77%; ACT scores over 24: 17%; ACT scores over 30: 1%.

Faculty *Total:* 213, 32% full-time, 37% with terminal degrees. *Student/faculty ratio:* 15:1.

Academics *Calendar:* semesters. *Degrees:* bachelor's, master's, doctoral, post-master's, and postbachelor's certificates. *Special study options:* academic remediation for entering students, accelerated degree program, adult/continuing education programs, advanced placement credit, distance learning, double majors, honors programs, independent study, internships, part-time degree program, services for LD students, student-designed majors, study abroad, summer session for credit. *ROTC:* Army (c), Air Force (c).

Computers on Campus 188 computers/terminals and 10 ports are available on campus for general student use. Students can access the following: campus intranet, computer help desk, free student e-mail accounts, online (class) grades, online (class) registration, online (class) schedules. Campuswide network is available. 100% of college-owned or -operated housing units are wired for high-speed Internet access. Wireless service is available via dorm rooms.

Student Life *Housing:* on-campus residence required for freshman year. *Options:* women-only. Campus housing is university owned. *Activities and organizations:* student-run newspaper, choral group, Department-affiliated clubs, Campus Ministry, International Club, Student government, Caroline Hall Council. *Campus security:* 24-hour patrols, late-night transport/escort service, controlled dormitory access. *Student services:* personal/psychological counseling.

Athletics Member NCAA. All Division III. *Intercollegiate sports:* basketball W, cross-country running W, soccer W, softball W, tennis W, volleyball W. *Intramural sports:* swimming and diving W.

Standardized Tests *Required:* SAT or ACT (for admission).

Costs (2011–12) *Comprehensive fee:* $30,498 includes full-time tuition ($22,540), mandatory fees ($460), and room and board ($7498). Full-time tuition and fees vary according to degree level and program. Part-time tuition: $675 per credit hour. Part-time tuition and fees vary according to course load, degree level, and program. *Required fees:* $125 per term part-time. *Room and board:* Room and board charges vary according to board plan.

Financial Aid Of all full-time matriculated undergraduates who enrolled in 2011, 910 applied for aid, 854 were judged to have need, 50 had their need fully met. 125 Federal Work-Study jobs (averaging $1247). 65 state and other part-time jobs (averaging $1388). In 2011, 86 non-need-based awards were made. *Average percent of need met:* 66%. *Average financial aid package:* $16,517. *Average need-based loan:* $4367. *Average need-based gift aid:* $12,132. *Average non-need-based aid:* $6275. *Average indebtedness upon graduation:* $27,145.

Applying *Options:* electronic application, deferred entrance. *Required:* high school transcript, minimum 2.5 GPA. *Required for some:* essay or personal statement, 2 letters of recommendation. *Recommended:* interview. *Application deadlines:* rolling (freshmen), rolling (transfers). *Notification:* continuous (freshmen), continuous (transfers).

Freshman Application Contact Mary Ellen Strieter, Admission Counselor Assistant/Receptionist, Mount Mary College, 2900 North Menomonee River Parkway, Milwaukee, WI 53222. *Phone:* 414-258-4810 Ext. 219. *Toll-free phone:* 800-321-6265. *Fax:* 414-256-0180. *E-mail:* admiss@mtmary.edu. *Web site:* http://www.mtmary.edu/.

Northland College

Ashland, Wisconsin

- **Independent** 4-year, founded 1892, affiliated with United Church of Christ
- **Small-town** 130-acre campus
- **Endowment** $19.5 million
- **Coed** 534 undergraduate students, 95% full-time, 53% women, 47% men
- **Moderately difficult** entrance level, 73% of applicants were admitted

Undergraduates 508 full-time, 26 part-time. Students come from 31 states and territories; 5 other countries; 51% are from out of state; 1% Black or African American, non-Hispanic/Latino; 5% Hispanic/Latino; 0.6% Asian, non-Hispanic/Latino; 0.2% Native Hawaiian or other Pacific Islander, non-Hispanic/Latino; 2% American Indian or Alaska Native, non-Hispanic/Latino; 1% Two or more races, non-Hispanic/Latino; 7% Race/ethnicity unknown; 4% international; 9% transferred in; 67% live on campus. *Retention:* 63% of full-time freshmen returned.

Freshmen *Admission:* 644 applied, 469 admitted, 146 enrolled. *Average high school GPA:* 3.3. *Test scores:* SAT critical reading scores over 500: 57%; SAT math scores over 500: 50%; SAT writing scores over 500: 50%; ACT scores over 18: 95%; SAT critical reading scores over 600: 21%; SAT math scores over 600: 7%; SAT writing scores over 600: 14%; ACT scores over 24: 49%; ACT scores over 30: 8%.

Faculty *Total:* 61, 75% full-time, 74% with terminal degrees. *Student/faculty ratio:* 10:1.

Academics *Calendar:* 4-4-1. *Degree:* bachelor's. *Special study options:* advanced placement credit, cooperative education, double majors, honors programs, independent study, internships, off-campus study, part-time degree program, services for LD students, student-designed majors, study abroad, summer session for credit. *Unusual degree programs:* 3-2 engineering with Michigan Technological University, Washington University in St. Louis.

Computers on Campus 125 computers/terminals are available on campus for general student use. Students can access the following: campus intranet, computer help desk, free student e-mail accounts, online (class) grades, online (class) registration, online (class) schedules. Campuswide network is available. 100% of college-owned or -operated housing units are wired for high-speed Internet access. Wireless service is available via classrooms, computer centers, computer labs, learning centers, libraries, student centers.

Student Life *Housing:* on-campus residence required through sophomore year. *Options:* coed, women-only, cooperative. Campus housing is university owned. Freshman campus housing is guaranteed. *Activities and organizations:* drama/theater group, student-run newspaper, radio station, choral group, Northland Volunteer Program, Northland College Student Association, Native American Student Association, Environmental Council, N Club. *Campus security:* 24-hour emergency response devices and patrols, late-night transport/escort service, controlled dormitory access. *Student services:* health clinic, personal/psychological counseling.

Athletics Member NCAA. All Division III. *Intercollegiate sports:* baseball M, basketball M/W, cross-country running M/W, ice hockey M, soccer M/W, softball W, volleyball W. *Intramural sports:* basketball M/W, football M/W, skiing (cross-country) M(c)/W(c), soccer M/W, softball M/W, table tennis M/W, ultimate Frisbee M/W, volleyball M/W.

Standardized Tests *Required:* SAT or ACT (for admission).

Costs (2011–12) *Comprehensive fee:* $33,776 includes full-time tuition ($25,725), mandatory fees ($841), and room and board ($7210). Full-time tuition and fees vary according to course load. Part-time tuition: $500 per credit hour. Part-time tuition and fees vary according to course load. *College room only:* $2990. Room and board charges vary according to board plan and housing facility. *Payment plan:* installment. *Waivers:* employees or children of employees.

Financial Aid Of all full-time matriculated undergraduates who enrolled in 2011, 464 applied for aid, 434 were judged to have need, 72 had their need fully met. 287 Federal Work-Study jobs (averaging $1721). 222 state and other part-time jobs (averaging $1618). In 2011, 68 non-need-based awards were made. *Average percent of need met:* 81%. *Average financial aid package:* $30,807. *Average need-based loan:* $4915. *Average need-based gift aid:* $17,705. *Average non-need-based aid:* $12,621. *Average indebtedness upon graduation:* $27,441.

Applying *Options:* electronic application, deferred entrance. *Required:* high school transcript. *Recommended:* minimum 2.0 GPA. *Application deadlines:* rolling (freshmen), rolling (transfers). *Notification:* continuous (freshmen), continuous (transfers).

Freshman Application Contact Max Metz, Associate Director of Admissions, Northland College, 1411 Ellis Avenue, Ashland, WI 54806. *Phone:* 715-682-1224. *Toll-free phone:* 800-753-1840 (in-state); 800-753-1040 (out-of-state). *Fax:* 715-682-1258. *E-mail:* admissions2@northland.edu. *Web site:* http://www.northland.edu/.

Rasmussen College Appleton

Appleton, Wisconsin

- **Proprietary** 4-year, part of Rasmussen College System
- **Suburban** campus
- **Coed** 213 undergraduate students
- **Minimally difficult** entrance level

Faculty *Student/faculty ratio:* 22:1.

Academics *Degrees:* certificates, diplomas, associate, and bachelor's. *Special study options:* academic remediation for entering students, accelerated degree program, adult/continuing education programs, distance learning, double majors, internships, part-time degree program, summer session for credit.

Computers on Campus 76 computers/terminals are available on campus for general student use. Students can access the following: computer help desk, free student e-mail accounts, online (class) grades, online (class) schedules. Campuswide network is available. Wireless service is available via entire campus.

Student Life *Housing:* college housing not available.

Standardized Tests *Required:* Internal Exam (for admission).

Costs (2012–13) *Tuition:* $12,600 full-time. Full-time tuition and fees vary according to course level, course load, degree level, location, and program. Part-time tuition and fees vary according to course level, course load, degree level, location, and program. *Required fees:* $40 full-time. *Payment plans:* installment, deferred payment. *Waivers:* employees or children of employees.

Applying *Options:* electronic application, early admission, deferred entrance. *Application fee:* $40. *Required:* high school transcript, minimum 2.0 GPA, interview. *Application deadlines:* rolling (freshmen), rolling (transfers).

Freshman Application Contact Susan Hammerstrom, Director of Admissions, Rasmussen College Appleton, 3500 E. Destination Drive, Appleton, WI 54915. *Phone:* 920-750-5900. *Toll-free phone:* 888-549-6755. *E-mail:* susan.hammerstrom@rasmussen.edu. *Web site:* http://www.rasmussen.edu/.

Rasmussen College Green Bay

Green Bay, Wisconsin

- **Proprietary** primarily 2-year, part of Rasmussen College System
- **Suburban** campus
- **Coed** 649 undergraduate students
- **Minimally difficult** entrance level

Faculty *Student/faculty ratio:* 22:1.

Academics *Degrees:* certificates, diplomas, associate, and bachelor's. *Special study options:* academic remediation for entering students, accelerated degree program, adult/continuing education programs, distance learning, double majors, internships, part-time degree program, summer session for credit.

Computers on Campus 137 computers/terminals are available on campus for general student use. Students can access the following: computer help desk, free student e-mail accounts, online (class) grades, online (class) schedules. Campuswide network is available. Wireless service is available via entire campus.

Student Life *Housing:* college housing not available.

Standardized Tests *Required:* Internal Exam (for admission).

Costs (2012–13) *Tuition:* $12,600 full-time. Full-time tuition and fees vary according to course level, course load, degree level, location, and program. Part-time tuition and fees vary according to course level, course load, degree level, location, and program. *Required fees:* $40 full-time. *Payment plans:* installment, deferred payment. *Waivers:* employees or children of employees.

Applying *Options:* electronic application, early admission, deferred entrance. *Application fee:* $40. *Required:* high school transcript, minimum 2.0 GPA, interview. *Application deadlines:* rolling (freshmen), rolling (transfers).

Freshman Application Contact Susan Hammerstrom, Director of Admissions, Rasmussen College Green Bay, 940 South Taylor Street, Suite 100, Green Bay, WI 54303. *Phone:* 920-593-8400. *Toll-free phone:* 888-549-6755. *E-mail:* susan.hammerstrom@rasmussen.edu. *Web site:* http://www.rasmussen.edu/.

Rasmussen College Wausau

Wausau, Wisconsin

- **Proprietary** 4-year, part of Rasmussen College System
- **Suburban** campus
- **Coed** 522 undergraduate students
- **Minimally difficult** entrance level

Faculty *Student/faculty ratio:* 22:1.

Academics *Degrees:* certificates, diplomas, associate, and bachelor's. *Special study options:* academic remediation for entering students, accelerated degree program, adult/continuing education programs, distance learning, double majors, internships, part-time degree program, summer session for credit.

Computers on Campus 74 computers/terminals are available on campus for general student use. Students can access the following: computer help desk, free student e-mail accounts, online (class) grades, online (class) schedules. Campuswide network is available. Wireless service is available via entire campus.

Student Life *Housing:* college housing not available.

Standardized Tests *Required:* Internal Exam (for admission).

Costs (2012–13) *Tuition:* $12,600 full-time. Full-time tuition and fees vary according to course level, course load, degree level, location, and program. Part-time tuition and fees vary according to course level, course load, degree level, location, and program. *Required fees:* $40 full-time. *Payment plans:* installment, deferred payment. *Waivers:* employees or children of employees.

Applying *Options:* electronic application, early admission, deferred entrance. *Application fee:* $40. *Required:* high school transcript, minimum 2.0 GPA, interview. *Application deadlines:* rolling (freshmen), rolling (transfers).

Freshman Application Contact Susan Hammerstrom, Director of Admissions, Rasmussen College Wausau, 1101 Westwood Drive, Wausau, WI 54401. *Phone:* 715-841-8000. *Toll-free phone:* 888-549-6755. *E-mail:* susan.hammerstrom@rasmussen.edu. *Web site:* http://www.rasmussen.edu/.

Ripon College

Ripon, Wisconsin

- **Independent** 4-year, founded 1851
- **Small-town** 250-acre campus with easy access to Milwaukee
- **Endowment** $62.4 million
- **Coed** 990 undergraduate students, 99% full-time, 50% women, 50% men
- **Moderately difficult** entrance level, 75% of applicants were admitted

Undergraduates 981 full-time, 9 part-time. Students come from 32 states and territories; 16 other countries; 25% are from out of state; 2% Black or African American, non-Hispanic/Latino; 4% Hispanic/Latino; 1% Asian, non-Hispanic/Latino; 0.6% American Indian or Alaska Native, non-Hispanic/Latino; 2% Two or more races, non-Hispanic/Latino; 1% Race/ethnicity unknown; 3% international; 2% transferred in; 91% live on campus. *Retention:* 81% of full-time freshmen returned.

Freshmen *Admission:* 1,115 applied, 837 admitted, 227 enrolled. *Average high school GPA:* 3.41. *Test scores:* SAT critical reading scores over 500: 75%; SAT math scores over 500: 67%; ACT scores over 18: 97%; SAT critical reading scores over 600: 42%; SAT math scores over 600: 17%; ACT scores over 24: 60%; SAT critical reading scores over 700: 17%; SAT math scores over 700: 13%; ACT scores over 30: 12%.

Faculty *Total:* 103, 65% full-time, 77% with terminal degrees. *Student/faculty ratio:* 13:1.

Academics *Calendar:* semesters. *Degree:* bachelor's. *Special study options:* accelerated degree program, advanced placement credit, double majors, internships, off-campus study, part-time degree program, services for LD students, student-designed majors, study abroad. *ROTC:* Army (b). *Unusual degree programs:* 3-2 engineering with Rensselaer Polytechnic Institute, Washington University in St. Louis, University of Wisconsin-Madison; forestry with Duke University; nursing with Rush University; environmental studies with Duke University.

Computers on Campus 150 computers/terminals are available on campus for general student use. Students can access the following: campus intranet, computer help desk, free student e-mail accounts, online (class) grades, online (class) schedules. Campuswide network is available. 100% of college-owned or -operated housing units are wired for high-speed Internet access. Wireless service is available via classrooms, libraries, student centers.

Student Life *Housing:* on-campus residence required through senior year. *Options:* coed, men-only, women-only. Campus housing is university owned. Freshman campus housing is guaranteed. *Activities and organizations:* drama/theater group, student-run newspaper, radio station, choral group, Environmental Group, Student Senate, Community Service Coalition, SMAC (Student Media and Activities Committee), national fraternities, national sororities. *Campus security:* 24-hour emergency response devices and patrols, student patrols, late-night transport/escort service, controlled dormitory access. *Student services:* health clinic, personal/psychological counseling.

Athletics Member NCAA. All Division III. *Intercollegiate sports:* baseball M, basketball M/W, cheerleading M(c)/W, cross-country running M/W, football M, golf M/W, rugby M(c)/W(c), soccer M/W, softball W, swimming and diving M/W, tennis M/W, track and field M/W, volleyball W. *Intramural sports:* basketball M/W, bowling M/W, equestrian sports M(c)/W(c), fencing M/W, football M/W, golf M/W, lacrosse M/W, racquetball M/W, soccer M/W, softball M/W, table tennis M/W, tennis M/W, ultimate Frisbee M/W, volleyball M/W.

Standardized Tests *Required:* SAT or ACT (for admission).

Costs (2012–13) *Comprehensive fee:* $38,655 includes full-time tuition ($29,835), mandatory fees ($275), and room and board ($8545). *College room only:* $4515. *Payment plan:* installment. *Waivers:* employees or children of employees.

Financial Aid Of all full-time matriculated undergraduates who enrolled in 2010, 941 applied for aid, 869 were judged to have need, 169 had their need fully met. 526 Federal Work-Study jobs (averaging $1556). 419 state and other part-time jobs (averaging $1556). In 2010, 138 non-need-based awards were made. *Average percent of need met:* 88%. *Average financial aid package:* $24,629. *Average need-based loan:* $4824. *Average need-based gift aid:* $19,509. *Average non-need-based aid:* $10,312. *Average indebtedness upon graduation:* $30,694.

Applying *Options:* electronic application, deferred entrance. *Application fee:* $30. *Required:* essay or personal statement, high school transcript, minimum 2.0 GPA, 1 letter of recommendation. *Required for some:* interview. *Recommended:* interview. *Application deadlines:* rolling (freshmen), rolling (transfers). *Notification:* continuous (freshmen), continuous (transfers).

Freshman Application Contact Office of Admission, Ripon College, 300 Seward Street, PO Box 248, Ripon, WI 54971. *Phone:* 920-748-8337. *Toll-free phone:* 800-947-4766. *Fax:* 920-748-8335. *E-mail:* adminfo@ripon.edu. *Web site:* http://www.ripon.edu/.

See below for display ad and page 1522 for the College Close-Up.

St. Norbert College

De Pere, Wisconsin

- **Independent Roman Catholic** comprehensive, founded 1898
- **Suburban** 93-acre campus
- **Endowment** $72.3 million
- **Coed** 2,174 undergraduate students, 97% full-time, 58% women, 42% men
- **Moderately difficult** entrance level, 80% of applicants were admitted

Undergraduates 2,112 full-time, 62 part-time. Students come from 26 states and territories; 35 other countries; 26% are from out of state; 0.9% Black or African American, non-Hispanic/Latino; 2% Hispanic/Latino; 0.8% Asian, non-Hispanic/Latino; 0.1% Native Hawaiian or other Pacific Islander, non-Hispanic/Latino; 0.6% American Indian or Alaska Native, non-Hispanic/Latino; 2% Two or more races, non-Hispanic/Latino; 5% international; 3% transferred in; 74% live on campus. *Retention:* 82% of full-time freshmen returned.

Freshmen *Admission:* 2,382 applied, 1,917 admitted, 594 enrolled. *Average high school GPA:* 3.46. *Test scores:* ACT scores over 18: 100%; ACT scores over 24: 62%; ACT scores over 30: 9%.

Faculty *Total:* 197, 71% full-time, 70% with terminal degrees. *Student/faculty ratio:* 14:1.

Academics *Calendar:* semesters. *Degrees:* bachelor's and master's. *Special study options:* academic remediation for entering students, advanced placement credit, distance learning, double majors, English as a second language, honors programs, independent study, internships, off-campus study, part-time degree program, services for LD students, student-designed majors, study abroad, summer session for credit. *ROTC:* Army (b).

Computers on Campus 247 computers/terminals are available on campus for general student use. Students can access the following: campus intranet, computer help desk, free student e-mail accounts, online (class) grades, online (class) registration, online (class) schedules. Campuswide network is available. 100% of college-owned or -operated housing units are wired for high-speed Internet access. Wireless service is available via classrooms, computer centers, computer labs, dorm rooms, learning centers, libraries, student centers.

Student Life *Housing:* on-campus residence required through senior year. *Options:* coed, women-only, disabled students. Campus housing is university owned. Freshman campus housing is guaranteed. *Activities and organizations:* drama/theater group, student-run newspaper, radio and television station, choral group, Student Education Association, SNC Radio, Circle K, Pre-Health Sciences, Spanish Club, national fraternities, national sororities. *Campus security:* 24-hour emergency response devices and patrols, student patrols, late-night transport/escort service, controlled dormitory access, crime prevention programs. *Student services:* health clinic, personal/psychological counseling, women's center.

Athletics Member NCAA. All Division III. *Intercollegiate sports:* baseball M, basketball M/W, cross-country running M/W, football M, golf M/W, ice hockey M/W, soccer M/W, softball W, tennis M/W, track and field M/W, volleyball W. *Intramural sports:* basketball M/W, cheerleading M(c)/W(c), crew M(c)/W(c), football M/W, lacrosse M, skiing (downhill) M(c)/W(c), softball M/W, volleyball M/W.

Standardized Tests *Required:* SAT or ACT (for admission).

Costs (2011–12) *Comprehensive fee:* $36,908 includes full-time tuition ($28,935), mandatory fees ($460), and room and board ($7513). Full-time tuition and fees vary according to course load. Part-time tuition: $904 per credit. Part-time tuition and fees vary according to course load. *College room only:* $4010. Room and board charges vary according to board plan, housing

facility, and student level. *Payment plans:* installment, deferred payment. *Waivers:* employees or children of employees.

Financial Aid Of all full-time matriculated undergraduates who enrolled in 2010, 1,678 applied for aid, 1,470 were judged to have need, 505 had their need fully met. 342 Federal Work-Study jobs (averaging $1223). 760 state and other part-time jobs (averaging $1138). In 2010, 545 non-need-based awards were made. *Average percent of need met:* 84%. *Average financial aid package:* $21,396. *Average need-based loan:* $4586. *Average need-based gift aid:* $16,414. *Average non-need-based aid:* $9762. *Average indebtedness upon graduation:* $25,714.

Applying *Options:* electronic application, deferred entrance. *Application fee:* $25. *Required:* high school transcript, 1 letter of recommendation. *Required for some:* interview. *Recommended:* essay or personal statement. *Application deadlines:* rolling (freshmen), rolling (out-of-state freshmen), rolling (transfers). *Notification:* continuous (freshmen), continuous (out-of-state freshmen), continuous (transfers).

Freshman Application Contact Mr. Edward Lamm, Associate Vice President of Graduate and Undergraduate Enrollment, St. Norbert College, 100 Grant Street, De Pere, WI 54115-2099. *Phone:* 920-403-3005. *Toll-free phone:* 800-236-4878. *Fax:* 920-403-4072. *E-mail:* admit@snc.edu. *Web site:* http://www.snc.edu/.

See below for display ad and page 1566 for the College Close-Up.

Silver Lake College

Manitowoc, Wisconsin

- **Independent Roman Catholic** comprehensive, founded 1869
- **Rural** 30-acre campus with easy access to Milwaukee
- **Endowment** $5.2 million
- **Coed**
- **Minimally difficult** entrance level

Faculty *Student/faculty ratio:* 7:1.

Academics *Calendar:* semesters. *Degrees:* certificates, associate, bachelor's, master's, and postbachelor's certificates.

Student Life *Campus security:* 24-hour emergency response devices, student patrols, late-night transport/escort service, controlled dormitory access.

Athletics Member USCAA.

Standardized Tests *Required:* SAT or ACT (for admission).

Costs (2011–12) *Comprehensive fee:* $30,320 includes full-time tuition ($21,580), mandatory fees ($240), and room and board ($8500). Full-time tuition and fees vary according to degree level, location, program, and reciprocity agreements. Part-time tuition: $720 per credit. Part-time tuition and fees vary according to course load, degree level, location, and program. *Required fees:* $65 per term part-time. *College room only:* $4900. Room and board charges vary according to board plan and housing facility. *Payment plans:* installment, deferred payment.

Financial Aid *Of all full-time matriculated undergraduates who enrolled in 2010,* 151 applied for aid, 145 were judged to have need, 17 had their need fully met. 88 Federal Work-Study jobs (averaging $1989). 3 state and other part-time jobs (averaging $2475). *In 2010,* 7 non-need-based awards were made. *Average percent of need met:* 67. *Average financial aid package:* $17,932. *Average need-based loan:* $4576. *Average need-based gift aid:* $9602. *Average non-need-based aid:* $9713. *Average indebtedness upon graduation:* $19,386.

Applying *Options:* electronic application, deferred entrance. *Required:* high school transcript, minimum 2.0 GPA. *Required for some:* interview.

Freshman Application Contact Dan Connolly, Admissions Counselor, Silver Lake College, 2406 South Alverno Road, Manitowoc, WI 54220. *Phone:* 920-686-6186. *Toll-free phone:* 800-236-4752 Ext. 175. *Fax:* 920-686-6322. *E-mail:* admslc@silver.sl.edu. *Web site:* http://www.sl.edu/.

Strayer University - Milwaukee Campus

Milwaukee, Wisconsin

- **Proprietary** comprehensive
- **Coed**

Academics *Degrees:* certificates, diplomas, associate, bachelor's, master's, and postbachelor's certificates.

Freshman Application Contact Strayer University - Milwaukee Campus, 9000 West Chester Street, Suite 300, Milwaukee, WI 53214. *Web site:* http://www.strayer.edu/milwaukee.

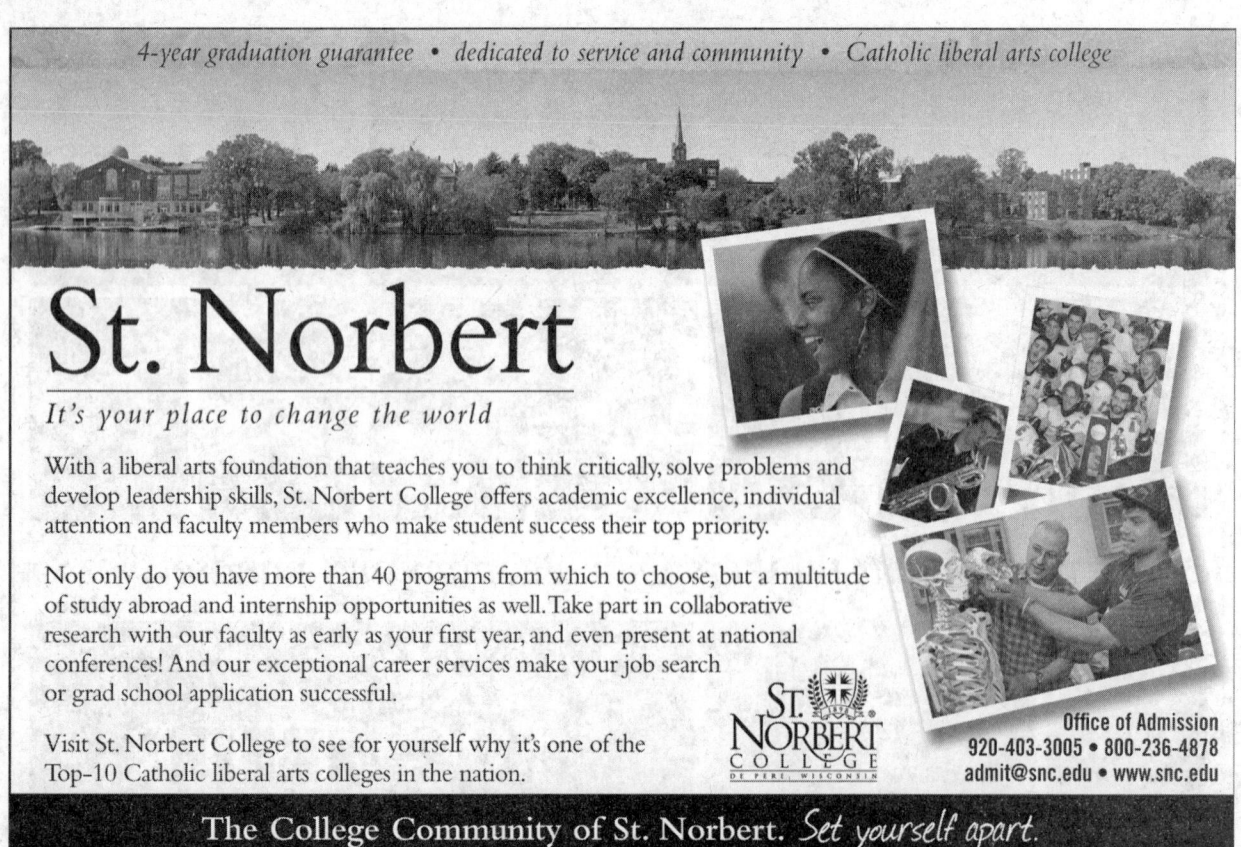

4-year graduation guarantee • dedicated to service and community • Catholic liberal arts college

St. Norbert

It's your place to change the world

With a liberal arts foundation that teaches you to think critically, solve problems and develop leadership skills, St. Norbert College offers academic excellence, individual attention and faculty members who make student success their top priority.

Not only do you have more than 40 programs from which to choose, but a multitude of study abroad and internship opportunities as well. Take part in collaborative research with our faculty as early as your first year, and even present at national conferences! And our exceptional career services make your job search or grad school application successful.

Visit St. Norbert College to see for yourself why it's one of the Top-10 Catholic liberal arts colleges in the nation.

ST. NORBERT COLLEGE DE PERE, WISCONSIN

Office of Admission
920-403-3005 • 800-236-4878
admit@snc.edu • www.snc.edu

The College Community of St. Norbert. *Set yourself apart.*

University of Phoenix–Madison Campus

Madison, Wisconsin

Admissions Office Contact University of Phoenix–Madison Campus, 2310 Crossroads Drive, Suite 3000, Madison, WI 53718-2416. *Toll-free phone:* 866-766-0766. *Web site:* http://www.phoenix.edu/.

University of Phoenix–Milwaukee Campus

Milwaukee, Wisconsin

Admissions Office Contact University of Phoenix–Milwaukee Campus, 20075 Watertower Boulevard, Milwaukee, WI 53045. *Toll-free phone:* 866-766-0766. *Web site:* http://www.phoenix.edu/.

University of Wisconsin–Eau Claire

Eau Claire, Wisconsin

- **State-supported** comprehensive, founded 1916, part of University of Wisconsin System
- **Small-town** 333-acre campus with easy access to Minneapolis-St. Paul
- **Endowment** $36.9 million
- **Coed** 10,578 undergraduate students, 92% full-time, 58% women, 42% men
- **Moderately difficult** entrance level, 77% of applicants were admitted

Undergraduates 9,742 full-time, 836 part-time. Students come from 37 states and territories; 38 other countries; 22% are from out of state; 0.6% Black or African American, non-Hispanic/Latino; 2% Hispanic/Latino; 3% Asian, non-Hispanic/Latino; 0.4% American Indian or Alaska Native, non-Hispanic/Latino; 1% Two or more races, non-Hispanic/Latino; 0.8% Race/ethnicity unknown; 2% international; 6% transferred in; 38% live on campus. *Retention:* 84% of full-time freshmen returned.

Freshmen *Admission:* 6,503 applied, 4,980 admitted, 1,948 enrolled. *Test scores:* SAT critical reading scores over 500: 87%; SAT math scores over 500: 84%; ACT scores over 18: 99%; SAT critical reading scores over 600: 50%; SAT math scores over 600: 50%; ACT scores over 24: 58%; SAT critical reading scores over 700: 24%; SAT math scores over 700: 13%; ACT scores over 30: 5%.

Faculty *Total:* 529, 80% full-time, 69% with terminal degrees. *Student/faculty ratio:* 22:1.

Academics *Calendar:* semesters. *Degrees:* certificates, associate, bachelor's, master's, doctoral, post-master's, and postbachelor's certificates. *Special study options:* academic remediation for entering students, accelerated degree program, adult/continuing education programs, advanced placement credit, cooperative education, distance learning, double majors, English as a second language, external degree program, honors programs, independent study, internships, off-campus study, part-time degree program, services for LD students, student-designed majors, study abroad, summer session for credit. *ROTC:* Army (b).

Computers on Campus 900 computers/terminals are available on campus for general student use. Students can access the following: campus intranet, computer help desk, free student e-mail accounts, online (class) grades, online (class) registration, online (class) schedules, course management system, library reference staff online chat, ability to check where there are open seats in the general access computer labs, laptop check out pool. Campuswide network is available. 100% of college-owned or -operated housing units are wired for high-speed Internet access. Wireless service is available via classrooms, computer centers, computer labs, learning centers, libraries, student centers.

Student Life *Housing:* on-campus residence required through sophomore year. *Options:* coed, men-only, women-only. Campus housing is university owned. Freshman campus housing is guaranteed. *Activities and organizations:* drama/theater group, student-run newspaper, radio and television station, choral group, marching band, American Marketing Association, Beta Upsilon Sigma, Blue Gold Marching Band, Singing Statesmen, Navigators, national fraternities, national sororities. *Campus security:* 24-hour emergency response devices and patrols, student patrols, late-night transport/escort service, controlled dormitory access. *Student services:* health clinic, personal/psychological counseling, women's center, legal services.

Athletics Member NCAA. All Division III. *Intercollegiate sports:* basketball M/W, cross-country running M/W, football M, golf M/W, gymnastics W, ice hockey M/W, soccer W, softball W, swimming and diving M/W, tennis M/W, track and field M/W, volleyball W, wrestling M. *Intramural sports:* baseball M(c), basketball M/W, bowling M(c)/W(c), cheerleading M(c)/W(c), equestrian sports M(c)/W(c), football M/W, ice hockey M, lacrosse M(c)/W(c), racquetball M/W, rock climbing M(c)/W(c), rugby M(c)/W(c), skiing (cross-country) M(c)/W(c), skiing (downhill) M(c)/W(c), soccer M/W, softball M/W, table tennis M(c)/W(c), tennis M/W, ultimate Frisbee M/W, volleyball M/W.

Standardized Tests *Required:* SAT or ACT (for admission).

Costs (2011–12) *Tuition:* state resident $6733 full-time, $281 per credit part-time; nonresident $14,306 full-time, $596 per credit part-time. Full-time tuition and fees vary according to reciprocity agreements. Part-time tuition and fees vary according to reciprocity agreements. *Required fees:* $1292 full-time, $54 per credit part-time, $3 per term part-time. *Room and board:* $5950; room only: $3038. Room and board charges vary according to board plan and housing facility. *Payment plan:* installment. *Waivers:* minority students.

Financial Aid Of all full-time matriculated undergraduates who enrolled in 2010, 7,207 applied for aid, 5,223 were judged to have need, 1,773 had their need fully met. 3,677 Federal Work-Study jobs (averaging $1666). In 2010, 472 non-need-based awards were made. *Average percent of need met:* 86%. *Average financial aid package:* $8854. *Average need-based loan:* $4245. *Average need-based gift aid:* $5514. *Average non-need-based aid:* $2118. *Average indebtedness upon graduation:* $22,391.

Applying *Options:* electronic application, early admission. *Application fee:* $44. *Required:* high school transcript. *Recommended:* essay or personal statement. *Application deadlines:* rolling (freshmen), rolling (transfers). *Notification:* continuous (freshmen), continuous (transfers).

Freshman Application Contact Ms. Kristina Anderson, Executive Director of Enrollment Management and Director of Admissions, University of Wisconsin–Eau Claire, PO Box 4004, Eau Claire, WI 54702-4004. *Phone:* 715-836-5415. *Fax:* 715-836-2409. *E-mail:* admissions@uwec.edu. *Web site:* http://www.uwec.edu/.

University of Wisconsin–Green Bay

Green Bay, Wisconsin

- **State-supported** comprehensive, founded 1968, part of University of Wisconsin System
- **Suburban** 700-acre campus with easy access to Milwaukee
- **Endowment** $16.8 million
- **Coed** 6,445 undergraduate students, 72% full-time, 63% women, 37% men
- **Moderately difficult** entrance level, 65% of applicants were admitted

Undergraduates 4,627 full-time, 1,818 part-time. Students come from 34 states and territories; 28 other countries; 6% are from out of state; 0.8% Black or African American, non-Hispanic/Latino; 2% Hispanic/Latino; 3% Asian, non-Hispanic/Latino; 0.0% Native Hawaiian or other Pacific Islander, non-Hispanic/Latino; 1% American Indian or Alaska Native, non-Hispanic/Latino; 1% Two or more races, non-Hispanic/Latino; 0.6% Race/ethnicity unknown; 0.9% international; 14% transferred in; 33% live on campus. *Retention:* 73% of full-time freshmen returned.

Freshmen *Admission:* 3,471 applied, 2,249 admitted, 910 enrolled. *Average high school GPA:* 3.33. *Test scores:* SAT critical reading scores over 500: 77%; SAT math scores over 500: 64%; SAT writing scores over 500: 65%; ACT scores over 18: 99%; SAT critical reading scores over 600: 24%; SAT math scores over 600: 24%; SAT writing scores over 600: 24%; ACT scores over 24: 41%; SAT critical reading scores over 700: 6%; SAT math scores over 700: 6%; SAT writing scores over 700: 6%; ACT scores over 30: 3%.

Faculty *Total:* 344, 53% full-time, 55% with terminal degrees. *Student/faculty ratio:* 23:1.

Academics *Calendar:* semesters. *Degrees:* associate, bachelor's, and master's. *Special study options:* academic remediation for entering students, adult/continuing education programs, advanced placement credit, distance learning, double majors, external degree program, independent study, internships, off-campus study, part-time degree program, services for LD students, student-designed majors, study abroad, summer session for credit. *ROTC:* Army (c). *Unusual degree programs:* 3-2 engineering with University of Wisconsin-Milwaukee.

Computers on Campus 550 computers/terminals are available on campus for general student use. Students can access the following: computer help desk, free student e-mail accounts, online (class) grades, online (class) registration, online (class) schedules, online degree progress, online financial records and bill paying. Campuswide network is available. 100% of college-owned or -operated housing units are wired for high-speed Internet access. Wireless service is available via entire campus.

Student Life *Housing options:* coed. Campus housing is university owned and is provided by a third party. Freshman applicants given priority for college housing. *Activities and organizations:* drama/theater group, student-run newspaper, radio station, choral group, Good Times, Psychology and Human Development Club, Student Ambassadors, Residence Hall Apartment Association, Student Government Association. *Campus security:* 24-hour emergency response devices and patrols, late-night transport/escort service, controlled dormitory access. *Student services:* health clinic, personal/psychological counseling.

Athletics Member NCAA. All Division I. *Intercollegiate sports:* basketball M(s)/W(s), cross-country running M(s)/W(s), golf M(s)/W(s), skiing (cross-country) M(s)/W(s), soccer M(s)/W(s), softball W(s), swimming and diving M(s)/W(s), tennis M(s)/W(s), volleyball W(s). *Intramural sports:* basketball M/W, bowling M/W, cheerleading M/W, football M/W, golf M/W, racquetball M/W, sailing M/W, skiing (cross-country) M/W, soccer M/W, softball M/W, swimming and diving M/W, tennis M/W, ultimate Frisbee M/W, volleyball M/W, weight lifting M/W.

Standardized Tests *Required:* SAT or ACT (for admission).

Costs (2011–12) *One-time required fee:* $200. *Tuition:* state resident $5970 full-time, $249 per credit hour part-time; nonresident $13,543 full-time, $564 per credit hour part-time. Full-time tuition and fees vary according to course load and reciprocity agreements. Part-time tuition and fees vary according to reciprocity agreements. *Required fees:* $1312 full-time, $55 per credit hour part-time. *Room and board:* $7210; room only: $3932. Room and board charges vary according to board plan and housing facility. *Payment plan:* installment. *Waivers:* senior citizens.

Financial Aid Of all full-time matriculated undergraduates who enrolled in 2011, 3,912 applied for aid, 3,212 were judged to have need, 1,412 had their need fully met. 225 Federal Work-Study jobs (averaging $1850). In 2011, 87 non-need-based awards were made. *Average percent of need met:* 84%. *Average financial aid package:* $11,060. *Average need-based loan:* $5355. *Average need-based gift aid:* $5555. *Average non-need-based aid:* $1359. *Average indebtedness upon graduation:* $23,530.

Applying *Options:* electronic application, deferred entrance. *Application fee:* $44. *Required:* essay or personal statement, high school transcript. *Required for some:* interview. *Application deadlines:* rolling (freshmen), rolling (out-of-state freshmen), rolling (transfers). *Notification:* continuous (freshmen), continuous (out-of-state freshmen), continuous (transfers).

Freshman Application Contact Ms. Pam Harvey-Jacobs, Director of Admissions, University of Wisconsin–Green Bay, 2420 Nicolet Drive, Green Bay, WI 54311-7001. *Phone:* 920-465-2111. *Fax:* 920-465-5754. *E-mail:* uwgb@uwgb.edu. *Web site:* http://www.uwgb.edu/.

University of Wisconsin–La Crosse
La Crosse, Wisconsin

- **State-supported** comprehensive, founded 1909, part of University of Wisconsin System
- **Suburban** 121-acre campus
- **Endowment** $16.6 million
- **Coed** 9,119 undergraduate students, 95% full-time, 58% women, 42% men
- **Moderately difficult** entrance level, 76% of applicants were admitted

Undergraduates 8,678 full-time, 441 part-time. Students come from 38 states and territories; 34 other countries; 16% are from out of state; 0.8% Black or African American, non-Hispanic/Latino; 2% Hispanic/Latino; 3% Asian, non-Hispanic/Latino; 0.1% Native Hawaiian or other Pacific Islander, non-Hispanic/Latino; 0.4% American Indian or Alaska Native, non-Hispanic/Latino; 2% Two or more races, non-Hispanic/Latino; 0.9% Race/ethnicity unknown; 3% international; 5% transferred in; 36% live on campus. *Retention:* 85% of full-time freshmen returned.

Freshmen *Admission:* 6,438 applied, 4,866 admitted, 1,978 enrolled. *Test scores:* ACT scores over 18: 99%; ACT scores over 24: 65%; ACT scores over 30: 6%.

Faculty *Total:* 551, 76% full-time, 60% with terminal degrees. *Student/faculty ratio:* 20:1.

Academics *Calendar:* semesters. *Degrees:* certificates, associate, bachelor's, master's, doctoral, and postbachelor's certificates. *Special study options:* academic remediation for entering students, adult/continuing education programs, advanced placement credit, cooperative education, distance learning, double majors, English as a second language, independent study, internships, off-campus study, part-time degree program, services for LD students, study abroad, summer session for credit. *ROTC:* Army (b). *Unusual degree programs:* 3-2 engineering with University of Wisconsin-Madison, University of Wisconsin-Milwaukee, University of Wisconsin- Platteville, University of Minnesota; physical therapy and physics, physical therapy and biology, occupational therapy and psychology.

Computers on Campus 689 computers/terminals and 125 ports are available on campus for general student use. Students can access the following: campus intranet, computer help desk, free student e-mail accounts, online (class) grades, online (class) registration, online (class) schedules. Campuswide network is available. 100% of college-owned or -operated housing units are wired for high-speed Internet access. Wireless service is available via classrooms, computer centers, computer labs, dorm rooms, learning centers, libraries, student centers.

Student Life *Housing:* on-campus residence required for freshman year. *Options:* coed, disabled students. Campus housing is university owned. Fresh-

man applicants given priority for college housing. *Activities and organizations:* drama/theater group, student-run newspaper, radio and television station, choral group, marching band, Sports and Activities Club, Residential Hall Council, religious/spiritual organizations, Human Diversity Organizations, departmental/professional, national fraternities, national sororities. *Campus security:* 24-hour emergency response devices and patrols, late-night transport/escort service, controlled dormitory access. *Student services:* health clinic, personal/psychological counseling, women's center, legal services.

Athletics Member NCAA. All Division III. *Intercollegiate sports:* baseball M, basketball M/W, cross-country running M/W, football M, gymnastics W, soccer W, softball W, swimming and diving M/W, tennis M/W, track and field M/W, volleyball W, wrestling M. *Intramural sports:* archery M(c)/W(c), badminton M/W, basketball M/W, cheerleading M/W, equestrian sports M(c)/W(c), football M/W, golf M/W, ice hockey W(c), lacrosse M(c)/W(c), racquetball M/W, rugby M(c)/W(c), skiing (downhill) M(c)/W(c), soccer M(c)/W, softball M/W, table tennis M/W, tennis M/W, ultimate Frisbee M(c)/W(c), volleyball M(c)/W(c), weight lifting M/W.

Standardized Tests *Required:* SAT or ACT (for admission).

Costs (2011–12) *Tuition:* state resident $7189 full-time, $300 per credit hour part-time; nonresident $14,762 full-time, $615 per credit hour part-time. Full-time tuition and fees vary according to program and reciprocity agreements. Part-time tuition and fees vary according to course load, program, and reciprocity agreements. *Required fees:* $1140 full-time. *Room and board:* $5930; room only: $3468. Room and board charges vary according to board plan and housing facility. *Payment plan:* installment. *Waivers:* minority students.

Financial Aid Of all full-time matriculated undergraduates who enrolled in 2010, 6,023 applied for aid, 4,240 were judged to have need, 829 had their need fully met. In 2010, 309 non-need-based awards were made. *Average percent of need met:* 72%. *Average financial aid package:* $7123. *Average need-based loan:* $3982. *Average need-based gift aid:* $5713. *Average non-need-based aid:* $1064. *Average indebtedness upon graduation:* $23,034.

Applying *Options:* electronic application. *Application fee:* $44. *Required:* essay or personal statement, high school transcript. *Required for some:* interview. *Application deadlines:* rolling (freshmen), rolling (out-of-state freshmen), rolling (transfers). *Notification:* continuous (freshmen), continuous (out-of-state freshmen), continuous (transfers).

Freshman Application Contact Ms. Kathryn Kiefer, Director of Admissions, University of Wisconsin–La Crosse, 1725 State Street, La Crosse, WI 54601. *Phone:* 608-785-8939. *Fax:* 608-785-8940. *E-mail:* admissions@uwlax.edu. *Web site:* http://www.uwlax.edu/.

University of Wisconsin–Madison
Madison, Wisconsin

- **State-supported** university, founded 1848, part of University of Wisconsin System
- **Urban** 936-acre campus with easy access to Milwaukee
- **Endowment** $1.8 billion
- **Coed** 30,367 undergraduate students, 91% full-time, 52% women, 48% men
- **Very difficult** entrance level, 50% of applicants were admitted

Undergraduates 27,750 full-time, 2,617 part-time. Students come from 52 states and territories; 92 other countries; 32% are from out of state; 2% Black or African American, non-Hispanic/Latino; 4% Hispanic/Latino; 5% Asian, non-Hispanic/Latino; 0.1% Native Hawaiian or other Pacific Islander, non-Hispanic/Latino; 0.3% American Indian or Alaska Native, non-Hispanic/Latino; 2% Two or more races, non-Hispanic/Latino; 1% Race/ethnicity unknown; 6% international; 4% transferred in; 24% live on campus. *Retention:* 94% of full-time freshmen returned.

Freshmen *Admission:* 28,983 applied, 14,627 admitted, 5,828 enrolled. *Average high school GPA:* 3.72. *Test scores:* SAT critical reading scores over 500: 91%; SAT math scores over 500: 97%; SAT writing scores over 500: 96%; ACT scores over 18: 100%; SAT critical reading scores over 600: 57%; SAT math scores over 600: 82%; SAT writing scores over 600: 72%; ACT scores over 24: 95%; SAT critical reading scores over 700: 16%; SAT math scores over 700: 40%; SAT writing scores over 700: 19%; ACT scores over 30: 35%.

Faculty *Total:* 2,856, 82% full-time, 87% with terminal degrees. *Student/faculty ratio:* 17:1.

Academics *Calendar:* semesters. *Degrees:* bachelor's, master's, doctoral, post-master's, and first professional certificates. *Special study options:* accelerated degree program, adult/continuing education programs, advanced placement credit, cooperative education, distance learning, double majors, English as a second language, honors programs, independent study, internships, part-time degree program, services for LD students, student-designed majors, study abroad, summer session for credit. *ROTC:* Army (b), Navy (b), Air Force (b). *Unusual degree programs:* 3-2 BS/MS, BBA/MACC.

Computers on Campus 1,000 computers/terminals are available on campus for general student use. Students can access the following: computer help desk,

free student e-mail accounts, online (class) grades, online (class) registration, online (class) schedules. Campuswide network is available. 100% of college-owned or -operated housing units are wired for high-speed Internet access. Wireless service is available via entire campus.

Student Life *Housing options:* coed, men-only, women-only, cooperative. Campus housing is university owned. Freshman applicants given priority for college housing. *Activities and organizations:* drama/theater group, student-run newspaper, radio station, choral group, marching band, national fraternities, national sororities. *Campus security:* 24-hour emergency response devices and patrols, late-night transport/escort service, controlled dormitory access. *Student services:* health clinic, personal/psychological counseling, women's center.

Athletics Member NCAA. All Division I except football (Division I-A). *Intercollegiate sports:* basketball M(s)/W(s), cheerleading M/W, crew M/W, cross-country running M(s)/W(s), fencing M(c)/W(c), golf M(s)/W(s), ice hockey M(s)/W(s), lacrosse M(c)/W(c), racquetball M(c)/W(c), rugby M(c)/W(c), sailing M(c)/W(c), soccer M(s)/W(s), softball W(s), swimming and diving M(s)/W(s), tennis M(s)/W(s), track and field M(s)/W(s), ultimate Frisbee M(c)/W(c), volleyball M(c)/W(s), water polo M(c)/W(c), wrestling M(s). *Intramural sports:* badminton M(c)/W(c), basketball M/W, fencing M(c)/W(c), racquetball M/W, softball M/W, tennis M/W, ultimate Frisbee M/W, volleyball M/W.

Standardized Tests *Required:* SAT or ACT (for admission).

Costs (2011–12) *Tuition:* state resident $8592 full-time, $358 per credit hour part-time; nonresident $24,342 full-time, $1014 per credit hour part-time. Full-time tuition and fees vary according to program and reciprocity agreements. Part-time tuition and fees vary according to course load, program, and reciprocity agreements. *Required fees:* $1079 full-time, $48 per credit hour part-time. *Room and board:* $7780. Room and board charges vary according to board plan and housing facility.

Financial Aid Of all full-time matriculated undergraduates who enrolled in 2010, 15,537 applied for aid, 11,489 were judged to have need, 2,722 had their need fully met. In 2010, 2336 non-need-based awards were made. *Average percent of need met:* 73%. *Average financial aid package:* $11,265. *Average need-based loan:* $4803. *Average need-based gift aid:* $6224. *Average non-need-based aid:* $3090. *Average indebtedness upon graduation:* $24,140.

Applying *Options:* electronic application, deferred entrance. *Application fee:* $44. *Required:* essay or personal statement, high school transcript. *Recommended:* 2 letters of recommendation. *Application deadlines:* 2/1 (freshmen), 2/1 (transfers). *Notification:* continuous (freshmen), continuous (transfers).

Freshman Application Contact Office of Admissions and Recruitment, University of Wisconsin–Madison, 702 West Johnson Street, Suite 101, Madison, WI 53706-1481. *Phone:* 608-262-3961. *Fax:* 608-262-7706. *E-mail:* onwisconsin@admissions.wisc.edu. *Web site:* http://www.wisc.edu/.

University of Wisconsin–Milwaukee
Milwaukee, Wisconsin

- **State-supported** university, founded 1956, part of University of Wisconsin System
- **Urban** 93-acre campus
- **Coed** 24,639 undergraduate students, 83% full-time, 51% women, 49% men
- **Moderately difficult** entrance level, 71% of applicants were admitted

Undergraduates 20,412 full-time, 4,227 part-time. Students come from 50 states and territories; 61 other countries; 3% are from out of state; 8% Black or African American, non-Hispanic/Latino; 6% Hispanic/Latino; 6% Asian, non-Hispanic/Latino; 0.1% Native Hawaiian or other Pacific Islander, non-Hispanic/Latino; 0.5% American Indian or Alaska Native, non-Hispanic/Latino; 2% Two or more races, non-Hispanic/Latino; 0.2% Race/ethnicity unknown; 2% international; 7% transferred in; 15% live on campus.

Freshmen *Admission:* 11,622 applied, 8,246 admitted, 3,746 enrolled. *Average high school GPA:* 3.06. *Test scores:* ACT scores over 18: 89%; ACT scores over 24: 33%; ACT scores over 30: 3%.

Academics *Calendar:* semesters. *Degrees:* certificates, bachelor's, master's, doctoral, post-master's, postbachelor's, and first professional certificates. *Special study options:* academic remediation for entering students, accelerated degree program, adult/continuing education programs, advanced placement credit, cooperative education, distance learning, double majors, English as a second language, honors programs, independent study, internships, off-campus study, part-time degree program, services for LD students, student-designed majors, study abroad, summer session for credit. *ROTC:* Army (c), Navy (c), Air Force (c).

Computers on Campus 582 computers/terminals and 3,200 ports are available on campus for general student use. Students can access the following: campus intranet, computer help desk, free student e-mail accounts, online (class) grades, online (class) registration, online (class) schedules. Campuswide network is available. 100% of college-owned or -operated housing units

are wired for high-speed Internet access. Wireless service is available via entire campus.

Student Life *Housing options:* coed, disabled students. Campus housing is university owned. *Activities and organizations:* drama/theater group, student-run newspaper, radio station, choral group, marching band, national fraternities, national sororities. *Campus security:* 24-hour emergency response devices, late-night transport/escort service, controlled dormitory access. *Student services:* health clinic, personal/psychological counseling, women's center, legal services.

Athletics Member NCAA. All Division I. *Intercollegiate sports:* baseball M, basketball M(s)/W(s), cross-country running M(s)/W(s), soccer M(s)/W(s), swimming and diving M(s)/W(s), tennis M(s)/W(s), track and field M(s)/W(s), volleyball M/W(s). *Intramural sports:* badminton M/W, baseball M(c), basketball M/W, bowling M(c)/W(c), equestrian sports M(c)/W(c), football M, lacrosse M(c)/W(c), racquetball M/W, rugby M(c)/W(c), sailing M(c)/W(c), skiing (downhill) M(c)/W(c), soccer M/W, softball M(c)/W(c), swimming and diving M/W, tennis M(c)/W(c), track and field M(c)/W(c), volleyball M/W, wrestling M.

Standardized Tests *Required:* SAT or ACT (for admission), ACT for state residents (for admission).

Costs (2011–12) *Tuition:* state resident $7669 full-time; nonresident $17,398 full-time. Full-time tuition and fees vary according to location, program, and reciprocity agreements. Part-time tuition and fees vary according to course load, location, program, and reciprocity agreements. *Required fees:* $1012 full-time. *Room and board:* $11,092; room only: $6990. Room and board charges vary according to board plan, housing facility, and location. *Payment plan:* installment. *Waivers:* senior citizens.

Financial Aid Of all full-time matriculated undergraduates who enrolled in 2011, 17,820 applied for aid, 15,836 were judged to have need, 2,694 had their need fully met. In 2011, 97 non-need-based awards were made. *Average percent of need met:* 46%. *Average financial aid package:* $7941. *Average need-based loan:* $4465. *Average need-based gift aid:* $6649. *Average non-need-based aid:* $3760. *Average indebtedness upon graduation:* $25,484.

Applying *Options:* electronic application, deferred entrance. *Application fee:* $44. *Required:* high school transcript. *Recommended:* essay or personal statement. *Application deadlines:* 7/1 (freshmen), 8/1 (transfers). *Notification:* continuous (freshmen).

Freshman Application Contact Ms. Jan Ford, Director, Recruitment and Outreach, University of Wisconsin–Milwaukee, PO Box 413, Milwaukee, WI 53201-0413. *Phone:* 414-229-4397. *Fax:* 414-229-6940. *E-mail:* uwmlook@uwm.edu. *Web site:* http://www.uwm.edu/.

University of Wisconsin–Oshkosh
Oshkosh, Wisconsin

Freshman Application Contact Mr. Richard Hillman, Associate Director of Admissions, University of Wisconsin–Oshkosh, 800 Algoma Boulevard, Oshkosh, WI 54901. *Phone:* 920-424-0202. *E-mail:* oshadmuw@uwosh.edu. *Web site:* http://www.uwosh.edu/.

University of Wisconsin–Parkside
Kenosha, Wisconsin

- **State-supported** comprehensive, founded 1968, part of University of Wisconsin System
- **Suburban** 700-acre campus with easy access to Chicago, Milwaukee
- **Endowment** $2.0 million
- **Coed**
- **Moderately difficult** entrance level

Faculty *Student/faculty ratio:* 19:1.

Academics *Calendar:* semesters. *Degrees:* certificates, bachelor's, and master's.

Student Life *Campus security:* 24-hour emergency response devices and patrols, late-night transport/escort service, controlled dormitory access.

Athletics Member NCAA. All Division II.

Standardized Tests *Required for some:* SAT or ACT (for admission).

Costs (2011–12) *Tuition:* state resident $6936 full-time, $236 per credit hour part-time; nonresident $14,509 full-time, $551 per credit hour part-time. Full-time tuition and fees vary according to course load and reciprocity agreements. Part-time tuition and fees vary according to course load. *Required fees:* $40 per credit hour part-time. *Room and board:* $6872; room only: $4432. Room and board charges vary according to board plan and housing facility.

Financial Aid Of all full-time matriculated undergraduates who enrolled in 2009, 2,149 applied for aid, 2,130 were judged to have need. *Average need-based gift aid:* $5959.

Applying *Options:* electronic application. *Application fee:* $44. *Required:* high school transcript, minimum of 17 high school units distribution.

Freshman Application Contact Mrs. DeAnn Possehl, Interim Director, Enrollment Management, University of Wisconsin–Parkside, PO Box 2000, 900 Wood Road, Kenosha, WI 53141-2000. *Phone:* 262-595-2454. *E-mail:* possehl@uwp.edu. *Web site:* http://www.uwp.edu/.

University of Wisconsin–Platteville

Platteville, Wisconsin

- **State-supported** comprehensive, founded 1866, part of University of Wisconsin System
- **Small-town** 820-acre campus
- **Coed** 7,397 undergraduate students, 90% full-time, 35% women, 65% men
- **Minimally difficult** entrance level, 80% of applicants were admitted

Undergraduates 6,657 full-time, 740 part-time. 21% are from out of state; 2% Black or African American, non-Hispanic/Latino; 2% Hispanic/Latino; 1% Asian, non-Hispanic/Latino; 0.1% Native Hawaiian or other Pacific Islander, non-Hispanic/Latino; 0.8% American Indian or Alaska Native, non-Hispanic/Latino; 1% Race/ethnicity unknown; 0.8% international; 5% transferred in; 36% live on campus. *Retention:* 74% of full-time freshmen returned.

Freshmen *Admission:* 4,007 applied, 3,195 admitted, 1,603 enrolled. *Test scores:* ACT scores over 18: 93%; ACT scores over 24: 42%; ACT scores over 30: 3%.

Faculty *Total:* 243, 98% full-time, 88% with terminal degrees. *Student/faculty ratio:* 24:1.

Academics *Calendar:* semesters. *Degrees:* certificates, associate, bachelor's, master's, and postbachelor's certificates. *Special study options:* adult/continuing education programs, external degree program, part-time degree program. *ROTC:* Army (c).

Computers on Campus Students can access the following: campus intranet, computer help desk, free student e-mail accounts, online (class) grades, online (class) registration, online (class) schedules. Campuswide network is available. 100% of college-owned or -operated housing units are wired for high-speed Internet access. Wireless service is available via classrooms, libraries, student centers.

Student Life *Housing:* on-campus residence required for freshman year. *Options:* coed, men-only, women-only, disabled students. Campus housing is university owned. Freshman campus housing is guaranteed. *Activities and organizations:* drama/theater group, student-run newspaper, radio and television station, choral group, marching band, national fraternities, national sororities. *Campus security:* 24-hour emergency response devices and patrols, student patrols, late-night transport/escort service. *Student services:* health clinic, personal/psychological counseling, women's center.

Athletics Member NCAA. All Division III. *Intercollegiate sports:* baseball M, basketball M/W, bowling M(c)/W(c), cheerleading M/W, cross-country running M/W, football M, golf W, ice hockey M(c)/W(c), lacrosse M(c)/W(c), rugby M(c)/W(c), soccer M/W, softball W, track and field M/W, ultimate Frisbee M(c)/W(c), volleyball M(c)/W, wrestling M. *Intramural sports:* badminton M/W, basketball M/W, bowling M/W, cheerleading M(c)/W(c), football M/W, racquetball M/W, soccer M/W, softball M/W, tennis M/W, ultimate Frisbee M/W, volleyball M/W, water polo M/W.

Standardized Tests *Required:* SAT or ACT (for admission).

Costs (2011–12) *Tuition:* state resident $6084 full-time; nonresident $13,656 full-time. Full-time tuition and fees vary according to course load, degree level, and reciprocity agreements. Part-time tuition and fees vary according to course load, degree level, and reciprocity agreements. *Required fees:* $1035 full-time. *Room and board:* $6064; room only: $3260. Room and board charges vary according to board plan, housing facility, and location.

Financial Aid Of all full-time matriculated undergraduates who enrolled in 2002, 3,289 applied for aid, 2,468 were judged to have need. 382 Federal Work-Study jobs (averaging $1392). In 2002, 652 non-need-based awards were made. *Average financial aid package:* $6161. *Average need-based loan:* $3499. *Average need-based gift aid:* $3599. *Average non-need-based aid:* $1427. *Average indebtedness upon graduation:* $15,785.

Applying *Options:* electronic application, deferred entrance. *Application fee:* $44. *Required:* high school transcript. *Recommended:* essay or personal statement. *Application deadlines:* rolling (freshmen), rolling (out-of-state freshmen), rolling (transfers). *Notification:* continuous (transfers).

Freshman Application Contact Mrs. Angela Udelhofen, Director of Admissions and Enrollment Management, University of Wisconsin–Platteville, 1 University Plaza, 120 Brigham Hall, Platteville, WI 53818-3099. *Phone:* 608-342-1125. *Toll-free phone:* 800-362-5515. *Fax:* 608-342-1122. *E-mail:* admit@uwplatt.edu. *Web site:* http://www.uwplatt.edu/.

University of Wisconsin–River Falls

River Falls, Wisconsin

- **State-supported** comprehensive, founded 1874, part of University of Wisconsin System
- **Suburban** 225-acre campus with easy access to Minneapolis-St. Paul
- **Coed** 6,324 undergraduate students, 91% full-time, 59% women, 41% men
- **Moderately difficult** entrance level, 79% of applicants were admitted

Undergraduates 5,785 full-time, 539 part-time. 52% are from out of state; 1% Black or African American, non-Hispanic/Latino; 2% Hispanic/Latino; 3% Asian, non-Hispanic/Latino; 0.1% Native Hawaiian or other Pacific Islander, non-Hispanic/Latino; 0.3% American Indian or Alaska Native, non-Hispanic/Latino; 1% Two or more races, non-Hispanic/Latino; 0.8% Race/ethnicity unknown; 1% international; 7% transferred in; 38% live on campus. *Retention:* 72% of full-time freshmen returned.

Freshmen *Admission:* 3,031 applied, 2,399 admitted, 1,205 enrolled. *Average high school GPA:* 3. *Test scores:* SAT critical reading scores over 500: 55%; SAT math scores over 500: 55%; SAT writing scores over 500: 36%; ACT scores over 18: 92%; SAT critical reading scores over 600: 9%; SAT math scores over 600: 9%; SAT writing scores over 600: 9%; ACT scores over 24: 33%; SAT critical reading scores over 700: 9%; SAT writing scores over 700: 9%; ACT scores over 30: 2%.

Faculty *Total:* 360, 77% full-time. *Student/faculty ratio:* 22:1.

Academics *Calendar:* semesters. *Degrees:* certificates, bachelor's, master's, post-master's, and postbachelor's certificates. *Special study options:* academic remediation for entering students, adult/continuing education programs, advanced placement credit, distance learning, double majors, English as a second language, external degree program, honors programs, independent study, internships, off-campus study, part-time degree program, services for LD students, study abroad, summer session for credit. *ROTC:* Army (b). *Unusual degree programs:* 3-2 engineering with University of Wisconsin-Madison and University of Minnesota-Twin Cities.

Computers on Campus Students can access the following: computer help desk, free student e-mail accounts, online (class) grades, online (class) registration, online (class) schedules. Campuswide network is available. Wireless service is available via classrooms, computer centers, computer labs, dorm rooms, learning centers, libraries, student centers.

Student Life *Housing:* on-campus residence required through sophomore year. *Options:* coed, women-only, disabled students. Campus housing is university owned. Freshman campus housing is guaranteed. *Activities and organizations:* drama/theater group, student-run newspaper, radio and television station, choral group, Falcon Programs, Badminton Club, Dairy Club, Agricultural Education Society, Intervarsity Christian Fellowship, national fraternities, national sororities. *Campus security:* 24-hour emergency response devices and patrols, student patrols, late-night transport/escort service, controlled dormitory access. *Student services:* health clinic, personal/psychological counseling.

Athletics Member NCAA. All Division III. *Intercollegiate sports:* badminton M(c)/W(c), baseball M(c), basketball M/W, cross-country running M/W, equestrian sports M(c)/W(c), football M, golf W, ice hockey M/W, lacrosse M(c)/W(c), racquetball M(c)/W(c), rock climbing M(c)/W(c), rugby M(c)/W(c), skiing (cross-country) M(c)/W(c), soccer W, softball W, swimming and diving M/W, tennis W, track and field M/W, volleyball M(c)/W, wrestling M(c). *Intramural sports:* basketball M/W, football M/W, soccer M/W, softball M/W, tennis W, ultimate Frisbee M/W, volleyball M/W.

Standardized Tests *Required:* SAT or ACT (for admission). *Recommended:* ACT (for admission).

Costs (2011–12) *Tuition:* state resident $6070 full-time, $253 per credit part-time; nonresident $13,643 full-time, $568 per credit part-time. Full-time tuition and fees vary according to course load, degree level, and reciprocity agreements. Part-time tuition and fees vary according to course load, degree level, and reciprocity agreements. *Required fees:* $1207 full-time. *Room and board:* $6574. Room and board charges vary according to board plan and housing facility.

Financial Aid Of all full-time matriculated undergraduates who enrolled in 2009, 5,116 applied for aid, 4,852 were judged to have need. *Average financial aid package:* $3157. *Average need-based gift aid:* $2317. *Average indebtedness upon graduation:* $14,800.

Applying *Options:* electronic application, deferred entrance. *Application fee:* $44. *Required:* essay or personal statement, high school transcript. *Recommended:* Rank in upper 40% of high school class. *Application deadlines:* rolling (freshmen), rolling (transfers). *Notification:* continuous (freshmen), continuous (transfers).

Freshman Application Contact University of Wisconsin–River Falls, 410 South Third Street, River Falls, WI 54022. *Phone:* 715-425-3500. *Web site:* http://www.uwrf.edu/.

University of Wisconsin–Stevens Point

Stevens Point, Wisconsin

- **State-supported** comprehensive, founded 1894, part of University of Wisconsin System
- **Small-town** 400-acre campus
- **Endowment** $13.9 million
- **Coed** 9,047 undergraduate students, 94% full-time, 53% women, 47% men
- **Moderately difficult** entrance level, 69% of applicants were admitted

Undergraduates 8,517 full-time, 530 part-time. Students come from 33 states and territories; 28 other countries; 7% are from out of state; 1% Black or African American, non-Hispanic/Latino; 2% Hispanic/Latino; 0.7% Asian, non-Hispanic/Latino; 2% Native Hawaiian or other Pacific Islander, non-Hispanic/Latino; 0.5% American Indian or Alaska Native, non-Hispanic/Latino; 1% Two or more races, non-Hispanic/Latino; 0.8% Race/ethnicity unknown; 2% international; 8% transferred in; 40% live on campus. *Retention:* 81% of full-time freshmen returned.

Freshmen *Admission:* 5,571 applied, 3,851 admitted, 1,606 enrolled. *Average high school GPA:* 3.45. *Test scores:* ACT scores over 18: 98%; ACT scores over 24: 44%; ACT scores over 30: 4%.

Faculty *Total:* 453, 91% full-time, 77% with terminal degrees. *Student/faculty ratio:* 20:1.

Academics *Calendar:* semesters. *Degrees:* associate, bachelor's, master's, and doctoral. *Special study options:* academic remediation for entering students, accelerated degree program, advanced placement credit, cooperative education, distance learning, double majors, English as a second language, independent study, internships, off-campus study, part-time degree program, services for LD students, student-designed majors, study abroad, summer session for credit. *ROTC:* Army (b).

Computers on Campus 1,233 computers/terminals and 3,963 ports are available on campus for general student use. Students can access the following: computer help desk, free student e-mail accounts, online (class) grades, online (class) registration, online (class) schedules. Campuswide network is available. 100% of college-owned or -operated housing units are wired for high-speed Internet access. Wireless service is available via entire campus.

Student Life *Housing:* on-campus residence required through sophomore year. *Options:* coed, men-only, women-only. Campus housing is university owned. Freshman applicants given priority for college housing. *Activities and organizations:* drama/theater group, student-run newspaper, radio and television station, choral group, The Wildlife Society, Student Impact, WWSP 90-FM radio station, Gender and Sexuality Alliance, Student Wisconsin Education Association, national fraternities, national sororities. *Campus security:* 24-hour emergency response devices and patrols, student patrols, late-night transport/escort service, controlled dormitory access. *Student services:* health clinic, personal/psychological counseling.

Athletics Member NCAA. All Division III. *Intercollegiate sports:* baseball M, basketball M/W, cross-country running M/W, football M, golf W, ice hockey M/W, soccer W, softball W, swimming and diving M/W, tennis W, track and field M/W, volleyball W, wrestling M. *Intramural sports:* archery M(c)/W(c), badminton M/W, basketball M/W, football M, golf M/W, ice hockey M/W, lacrosse M(c), racquetball M/W, rugby M(c)/W(c), skiing (downhill) M(c)/W(c), soccer M/W, softball M/W, table tennis M/W, tennis M/W, ultimate Frisbee M/W, volleyball M/W.

Standardized Tests *Required:* SAT or ACT (for admission).

Costs (2012–13) *Tuition:* state resident $5970 full-time; nonresident $13,543 full-time. Full-time tuition and fees vary according to course load, program, and reciprocity agreements. Part-time tuition and fees vary according to course load, program, and reciprocity agreements. *Required fees:* $1182 full-time. *Room and board:* $5893; room only: $3552. Room and board charges vary according to board plan and housing facility.

Financial Aid Of all full-time matriculated undergraduates who enrolled in 2010, 6,965 applied for aid, 5,408 were judged to have need, 3,711 had their need fully met. In 2010, 486 non-need-based awards were made. *Average percent of need met:* 72%. *Average financial aid package:* $8564. *Average need-based loan:* $5015. *Average need-based gift aid:* $6465. *Average non-need-based aid:* $2048. *Average indebtedness upon graduation:* $23,334. *Financial aid deadline:* 5/1.

Applying *Options:* electronic application, deferred entrance. *Application fee:* $44. *Required:* high school transcript. *Recommended:* essay or personal statement, 3 letters of recommendation. *Application deadlines:* rolling (freshmen), rolling (transfers). *Notification:* continuous (freshmen), continuous (transfers).

Freshman Application Contact Ms. Bill Jordan, Director of Admissions, University of Wisconsin–Stevens Point, 102 Student Services Center, University of Wisconsin–Stevens Point, Stevens Point, WI 54481. *Phone:* 715- 346-2441. *Fax:* 715-346-3296. *E-mail:* bjordan@uwsp.edu. *Web site:* http://www.uwsp.edu/.

University of Wisconsin–Stout

Menomonie, Wisconsin

- **State-supported** comprehensive, founded 1891, part of University of Wisconsin System
- **Small-town** 120-acre campus with easy access to Minneapolis-St. Paul
- **Coed** 8,353 undergraduate students, 83% full-time, 48% women, 52% men
- **Moderately difficult** entrance level, 78% of applicants were admitted

Undergraduates 6,944 full-time, 1,409 part-time. 30% are from out of state; 0.9% Black or African American, non-Hispanic/Latino; 0.6% Hispanic/Latino; 0.1% Asian, non-Hispanic/Latino; 90% Native Hawaiian or other Pacific Islander, non-Hispanic/Latino; 3% American Indian or Alaska Native, non-Hispanic/Latino; 2% Two or more races, non-Hispanic/Latino; 1% Race/ethnicity unknown; 0.9% international; 8% transferred in; 40% live on campus. *Retention:* 71% of full-time freshmen returned.

Freshmen *Admission:* 3,658 applied, 2,855 admitted, 1,476 enrolled. *Average high school GPA:* 3.2. *Test scores:* ACT scores over 18: 91%; ACT scores over 24: 28%; ACT scores over 30: 2%.

Faculty *Total:* 477, 81% full-time. *Student/faculty ratio:* 19:1.

Academics *Calendar:* 4-1-4. *Degrees:* certificates, bachelor's, master's, postmaster's, and postbachelor's certificates. *Special study options:* accelerated degree program, adult/continuing education programs, cooperative education, distance learning, double majors, external degree program, honors programs, independent study, internships, off-campus study, part-time degree program, services for LD students, study abroad, summer session for credit. *ROTC:* Army (b), Air Force (c).

Computers on Campus Students can access the following: computer help desk, free student e-mail accounts, online (class) grades, online (class) registration, online (class) schedules, all undergraduates receive a laptop computer and have unlimited access to Internet. Campuswide network is available. 100% of college-owned or -operated housing units are wired for high-speed Internet access. Wireless service is available via entire campus.

Student Life *Housing:* on-campus residence required through sophomore year. *Options:* coed, disabled students. Campus housing is university owned. Freshman campus housing is guaranteed. *Activities and organizations:* drama/theater group, student-run newspaper, radio and television station, choral group, marching band, national fraternities, national sororities. *Campus security:* 24-hour emergency response devices and patrols, student patrols, controlled dormitory access. *Student services:* health clinic, personal/psychological counseling, legal services.

Athletics Member NCAA. All Division III. *Intercollegiate sports:* baseball M, basketball M/W, cross-country running M/W, football M, gymnastics W, ice hockey M/W(c), soccer M(c)/W, softball W, tennis W, track and field M/W, volleyball M(c)/W. *Intramural sports:* baseball M/W, bowling M(c)/W(c), football M/W, golf M/W, ice hockey M/W, racquetball M/W, rugby M(c)/W(c), skiing (cross-country) M(c)/W(c), skiing (downhill) M(c)/W(c), softball M/W, ultimate Frisbee M/W, volleyball M/W.

Standardized Tests *Required:* SAT or ACT (for admission).

Costs (2011–12) *Tuition:* state resident $6649 full-time, $222 per credit hour part-time; nonresident $14,394 full-time, $480 per credit hour part-time. Full-time tuition and fees vary according to degree level and reciprocity agreements. Part-time tuition and fees vary according to degree level and reciprocity agreements. *Required fees:* $1893 full-time, $63 per credit hour part-time. *Room and board:* $5844. Room and board charges vary according to board plan and housing facility.

Financial Aid Of all full-time matriculated undergraduates who enrolled in 2011, 5,506 applied for aid, 4,191 were judged to have need, 1,837 had their need fully met. 1,402 Federal Work-Study jobs (averaging $1452). In 2011, 48 non-need-based awards were made. *Average percent of need met:* 84%. *Average financial aid package:* $10,181. *Average need-based loan:* $4380. *Average need-based gift aid:* $2471. *Average non-need-based aid:* $2372. *Average indebtedness upon graduation:* $28,576.

Applying *Options:* electronic application. *Application fee:* $44. *Required:* high school transcript. *Required for some:* minimum 2.8 GPA. *Recommended:* minimum 2.5 GPA. *Application deadlines:* rolling (freshmen), rolling (out-of-state freshmen), rolling (transfers). *Notification:* continuous (freshmen), continuous (out-of-state freshmen), continuous (transfers).

Freshman Application Contact Dr. Pamela Holsinger-Fuchs, Executive Director of Enrollment Services, University of Wisconsin–Stout, Admissions, Bowman Hall, Menomonie, WI 54751. *Phone:* 715-232-2639. *Toll-free phone:* 800-HI-STOUT. *Fax:* 715-232-1667. *E-mail:* admissions@uwstout.edu. *Web site:* http://www.uwstout.edu/.

University of Wisconsin–Superior
Superior, Wisconsin

- **State-supported** comprehensive, founded 1893, part of University of Wisconsin System
- **Suburban** 230-acre campus
- **Coed** 2,655 undergraduate students, 79% full-time, 56% women, 44% men
- **Moderately difficult** entrance level, 70% of applicants were admitted

Undergraduates 2,107 full-time, 548 part-time. Students come from 29 states and territories; 30 other countries; 46% are from out of state; 1% Black or African American, non-Hispanic/Latino; 1% Hispanic/Latino; 1% Asian, non-Hispanic/Latino; 0.1% Native Hawaiian or other Pacific Islander, non-Hispanic/Latino; 2% American Indian or Alaska Native, non-Hispanic/Latino; 2% Two or more races, non-Hispanic/Latino; 0.7% Race/ethnicity unknown; 6% international; 11% transferred in; 40% live on campus. *Retention:* 68% of full-time freshmen returned.

Freshmen *Admission:* 991 applied, 697 admitted, 352 enrolled. *Test scores:* ACT scores over 18: 94%; ACT scores over 24: 30%; ACT scores over 30: 2%.

Faculty *Total:* 223, 51% full-time, 50% with terminal degrees. *Student/faculty ratio:* 16:1.

Academics *Calendar:* semesters. *Degrees:* certificates, associate, bachelor's, master's, and post-master's certificates. *Special study options:* academic remediation for entering students, accelerated degree program, adult/continuing education programs, advanced placement credit, cooperative education, distance learning, double majors, English as a second language, external degree program, freshman honors college, independent study, internships, off-campus study, part-time degree program, services for LD students, student-designed majors, study abroad, summer session for credit. *ROTC:* Air Force (c). *Unusual degree programs:* 3-2 engineering with Michigan Technological University, University of Wisconsin-Madison; forestry with Michigan Technological University.

Computers on Campus 343 computers/terminals are available on campus for general student use. Students can access the following: campus intranet, computer help desk, free student e-mail accounts, online (class) grades, online (class) registration, online (class) schedules. Campuswide network is available. 100% of college-owned or -operated housing units are wired for high-speed Internet access. Wireless service is available via entire campus.

Student Life *Housing:* on-campus residence required through sophomore year. *Options:* coed, women-only, disabled students. Campus housing is university owned. Freshman campus housing is guaranteed. *Activities and organizations:* drama/theater group, student-run newspaper, radio station, choral group, Student Senate, Student Activities Board, Residence Hall Association, Inter-Varsity Christian Fellowship, World Student Association. *Campus security:* 24-hour emergency response devices and patrols, student patrols, late-night transport/escort service, controlled dormitory access. *Student services:* health clinic, personal/psychological counseling, women's center.

Athletics Member NCAA. All Division III. *Intercollegiate sports:* baseball M, basketball M/W, cheerleading M/W, cross-country running M/W, golf W, ice hockey M/W, soccer M/W, softball M/W, track and field M/W, volleyball W. *Intramural sports:* badminton M/W, baseball M/W, basketball M/W, bowling M/W, cross-country running M/W, football M/W, golf M/W, ice hockey M, racquetball M/W, riflery M/W, rock climbing M/W, rugby M, skiing (cross-country) M/W, skiing (downhill) M/W, soccer M/W, softball M/W, table tennis M/W, tennis M/W, volleyball M/W.

Standardized Tests *Required:* SAT or ACT (for admission).

Costs (2011–12) *Tuition:* state resident $6207 full-time, $349 per semester hour part-time; nonresident $13,780 full-time, $665 per semester hour part-time. Full-time tuition and fees vary according to course load, program, and reciprocity agreements. Part-time tuition and fees vary according to course load, program, and reciprocity agreements. *Required fees:* $1329 full-time. *Room and board:* $5730; room only: $3050. Room and board charges vary according to board plan, housing facility, and student level. *Payment plan:* installment.

Financial Aid Of all full-time matriculated undergraduates who enrolled in 2010, 1,697 applied for aid, 1,463 were judged to have need, 280 had their need fully met. In 2010, 31 non-need-based awards were made. *Average need-based loan:* $4220. *Average need-based gift aid:* $5570. *Average non-need-based aid:* $2288. *Average indebtedness upon graduation:* $23,466.

Applying *Options:* electronic application, early admission, deferred entrance. *Application fee:* $44. *Required:* high school transcript. *Required for some:* essay or personal statement, letters of recommendation. *Recommended:* interview. *Application deadlines:* rolling (freshmen), rolling (transfers). *Notification:* continuous (freshmen), continuous (out-of-state freshmen), continuous (transfers).

Freshman Application Contact Ms. Tonya Roth, Director of Admission, University of Wisconsin–Superior, Belknap and Catlin, PO Box 2000, Superior, WI 54880-4500. *Phone:* 715-394-8217. *Fax:* 715-394-8407. *E-mail:* admissions@uwsuper.edu. *Web site:* http://www.uwsuper.edu/.

University of Wisconsin–Whitewater
Whitewater, Wisconsin

- **State-supported** comprehensive, founded 1868, part of University of Wisconsin System
- **Small-town** 385-acre campus with easy access to Milwaukee
- **Endowment** $13.0 million
- **Coed** 10,214 undergraduate students, 93% full-time, 50% women, 50% men
- **Moderately difficult** entrance level, 71% of applicants were admitted

Undergraduates 9,535 full-time, 679 part-time. Students come from 32 states and territories; 37 other countries; 9% are from out of state; 5% Black or African American, non-Hispanic/Latino; 4% Hispanic/Latino; 1% Asian, non-Hispanic/Latino; 0.1% Native Hawaiian or other Pacific Islander, non-Hispanic/Latino; 0.2% American Indian or Alaska Native, non-Hispanic/Latino; 2% Two or more races, non-Hispanic/Latino; 0.5% Race/ethnicity unknown; 1% international; 7% transferred in. *Retention:* 79% of full-time freshmen returned.

Freshmen *Admission:* 6,309 applied, 4,477 admitted, 2,006 enrolled. *Average high school GPA:* 3.2. *Test scores:* SAT critical reading scores over 500: 49%; SAT math scores over 500: 49%; ACT scores over 18: 91%; SAT critical reading scores over 600: 12%; SAT math scores over 600: 22%; ACT scores over 24: 33%; SAT critical reading scores over 700: 2%; SAT math scores over 700: 2%; ACT scores over 30: 2%.

Faculty *Total:* 529, 77% full-time, 73% with terminal degrees. *Student/faculty ratio:* 23:1.

Academics *Calendar:* semesters. *Degrees:* associate, bachelor's, and master's. *Special study options:* academic remediation for entering students, accelerated degree program, adult/continuing education programs, advanced placement credit, cooperative education, distance learning, double majors, English as a second language, external degree program, honors programs, independent study, internships, part-time degree program, services for LD students, student-designed majors, study abroad, summer session for credit. *ROTC:* Army (b), Air Force (b).

Computers on Campus Students can access the following: campus intranet, computer help desk, free student e-mail accounts, online (class) grades, online (class) registration, online (class) schedules. Campuswide network is available. 100% of college-owned or -operated housing units are wired for high-speed Internet access. Wireless service is available via entire campus.

Student Life *Housing:* on-campus residence required through sophomore year. *Options:* coed, women-only. Campus housing is university owned. Freshman campus housing is guaranteed. *Activities and organizations:* drama/theater group, student-run newspaper, radio and television station, choral group, marching band, Finance Association, American Marketing Association, Black Student Union, Golden Key Honor Society, Wisconsin Education Association, national fraternities, national sororities. *Campus security:* 24-hour emergency response devices, late-night transport/escort service, controlled dormitory access. *Student services:* health clinic, personal/psychological counseling, women's center, legal services.

Athletics Member NCAA. All Division III. *Intercollegiate sports:* baseball M, basketball M/W, bowling M(c)/W, cheerleading M(c)/W(c), cross-country running M/W, football M, golf W, gymnastics W, ice hockey M(c)/W(c), lacrosse M(c), rugby M(c)/W(c), soccer M/W, softball W, swimming and diving M/W, tennis M/W, track and field M/W, volleyball M(c)/W, weight lifting M(c), wrestling M. *Intramural sports:* basketball M/W, bowling M/W, football M/W, golf M/W, racquetball M/W, rock climbing M(c)/W(c), skiing (downhill) M(c)/W(c), soccer M, softball M/W, table tennis M/W, tennis M/W, ultimate Frisbee M(c)/W(c), volleyball M/W, water polo M/W.

Standardized Tests *Required for some:* ACT (for admission). *Recommended:* SAT or ACT (for admission).

Costs (2011–12) *Tuition:* state resident $6179 full-time, $257 per credit part-time; nonresident $13,752 full-time, $573 per credit part-time. Full-time tuition and fees vary according to degree level and reciprocity agreements. *Required fees:* $1016 full-time. *Room and board:* $5500; room only: $3232. Room and board charges vary according to board plan. *Payment plan:* installment. *Waivers:* children of alumni and senior citizens.

Financial Aid Of all full-time matriculated undergraduates who enrolled in 2009, 7,074 applied for aid, 4,924 were judged to have need, 2,989 had their need fully met. 505 Federal Work-Study jobs (averaging $1261). 1,723 state and other part-time jobs (averaging $2031). In 2009, 396 non-need-based awards were made. *Average percent of need met:* 73%. *Average financial aid package:* $7957. *Average need-based loan:* $3984. *Average need-based gift aid:* $5220. *Average non-need-based aid:* $1424. *Average indebtedness upon graduation:* $20,715.

Applying *Options:* electronic application, deferred entrance. *Application fee:* $44. *Required:* high school transcript. *Application deadlines:* rolling (freshmen), rolling (transfers). *Notification:* 9/15 (freshmen), continuous (transfers).
Freshman Application Contact Mrs. Jodi Hare, Interim Director of Admissions, University of Wisconsin–Whitewater, 800 West Main Street, Whitewater, WI 53190-1790. *Phone:* 262-472-1440 Ext. 1512. *Fax:* 262-472-1515. *E-mail:* uwwadmit@uww.edu. *Web site:* http://www.uww.edu/.

Viterbo University

La Crosse, Wisconsin

- **Independent Roman Catholic** comprehensive, founded 1890
- **Suburban** 72-acre campus
- **Coed** 2,237 undergraduate students, 75% full-time, 72% women, 28% men
- **Moderately difficult** entrance level, 78% of applicants were admitted

Undergraduates 1,670 full-time, 567 part-time. 23% are from out of state; 2% Black or African American, non-Hispanic/Latino; 2% Hispanic/Latino; 2% Asian, non-Hispanic/Latino; 0.7% American Indian or Alaska Native, non-Hispanic/Latino; 4% Race/ethnicity unknown; 1% international; 12% transferred in; 28% live on campus. *Retention:* 71% of full-time freshmen returned.
Freshmen *Admission:* 1,610 applied, 1,254 admitted, 359 enrolled. *Average high school GPA:* 3.46. *Test scores:* ACT scores over 18: 97%; ACT scores over 24: 45%; ACT scores over 30: 7%.
Faculty *Total:* 378, 31% full-time, 30% with terminal degrees. *Student/faculty ratio:* 12:1.
Academics *Calendar:* semesters. *Degrees:* certificates, associate, bachelor's, master's, post-master's, and postbachelor's certificates. *Special study options:* adult/continuing education programs, part-time degree program. *ROTC:* Army (c).
Computers on Campus Students can access the following: campus intranet, computer help desk, free student e-mail accounts, online (class) grades, online (class) registration, online (class) schedules, Blackboard courses. Campuswide network is available. 100% of college-owned or -operated housing units are wired for high-speed Internet access. Wireless service is available via entire campus.
Student Life *Housing:* on-campus residence required through sophomore year. *Options:* men-only, women-only. Campus housing is university owned. Freshman campus housing is guaranteed. *Campus security:* 24-hour emergency response devices, late-night transport/escort service, controlled dormitory access, security officers on campus 5:00 pm to 7:00 am, lighted pathways, emergency evacuation plan, self-defense education programs.
Athletics Member NAIA. *Intercollegiate sports:* baseball M(s), basketball M(s)/W(s), bowling M(s)/W(s), cross-country running M(s)/W(s), golf M(s)/W(s), soccer M(s)/W(s), softball W(s), volleyball W(s). *Intramural sports:* badminton M/W, basketball M/W, bowling M/W, cross-country running M/W, golf M/W, racquetball M/W, rugby M/W, skiing (cross-country) M/W, skiing (downhill) M/W, soccer M/W, softball M/W, swimming and diving M/W, table tennis M/W, tennis M/W, ultimate Frisbee M/W, volleyball M/W.
Standardized Tests *Required:* ACT (for admission).
Costs (2011–12) *Comprehensive fee:* $29,050 includes full-time tuition ($21,280), mandatory fees ($590), and room and board ($7180). Part-time tuition: $625 per credit. *College room only:* $3210. Room and board charges vary according to board plan and housing facility.
Financial Aid Of all full-time matriculated undergraduates who enrolled in 2003, 1,311 applied for aid, 1,208 were judged to have need, 309 had their need fully met. 387 Federal Work-Study jobs (averaging $1680). 19 state and other part-time jobs (averaging $1615). In 2003, 223 non-need-based awards were made. *Average percent of need met:* 71%. *Average financial aid package:* $13,534. *Average need-based loan:* $4317. *Average need-based gift aid:* $8859. *Average non-need-based aid:* $5629. *Average indebtedness upon graduation:* $16,619.
Applying *Options:* electronic application, deferred entrance. *Application fee:* $25. *Required:* high school transcript, minimum 2.0 GPA. *Required for some:* essay or personal statement, interview, audition for theater and music, portfolio for art. *Application deadlines:* 8/15 (freshmen), 8/1 (transfers). *Notification:* continuous (freshmen), continuous (transfers).
Freshman Application Contact Mr. Wayne Wojciechowski, Assistant Academic Vice President, Viterbo University, 900 Viterbo Drive, LaCrosse, WI 54601. *Phone:* 608-796-3085. *Toll-free phone:* 800-VITERBO. *Fax:* 608-796-3020. *E-mail:* admission@viterbo.edu. *Web site:* http://www.viterbo.edu/.

Wisconsin Lutheran College

Milwaukee, Wisconsin

Freshman Application Contact Ms. Meghan Wieselmann, Admissions Office Manager, Wisconsin Lutheran College, 8800 West Bluemound Road, Milwaukee, WI 53226-9942. *Phone:* 414-443-8718. *Fax:* 414-443-8547. *E-mail:* meg.wieselmann@wlc.edu. *Web site:* http://www.wlc.edu/.

WYOMING

University of Phoenix–Cheyenne Campus
Cheyenne, Wyoming

Admissions Office Contact University of Phoenix–Cheyenne Campus, 6900 Yellowstone Road, Cheyenne, WY 82009. *Toll-free phone:* 866-766-0766. *Web site:* http://www.phoenix.edu/.

University of Wyoming
Laramie, Wyoming

- **State-supported** university, founded 1886
- **Small-town** 785-acre campus
- **Endowment** $314.8 million
- **Coed** 10,163 undergraduate students, 82% full-time, 52% women, 48% men
- **Moderately difficult** entrance level, 96% of applicants were admitted

Undergraduates 8,354 full-time, 1,809 part-time. Students come from 51 states and territories; 64 other countries; 29% are from out of state; 1% Black or African American, non-Hispanic/Latino; 5% Hispanic/Latino; 1% Asian, non-Hispanic/Latino; 0.2% Native Hawaiian or other Pacific Islander, non-Hispanic/Latino; 0.9% American Indian or Alaska Native, non-Hispanic/Latino; 2% Two or more races, non-Hispanic/Latino; 6% Race/ethnicity unknown; 3% international; 11% transferred in; 21% live on campus. *Retention:* 73% of full-time freshmen returned.

Freshmen *Admission:* 3,883 applied, 3,728 admitted, 1,536 enrolled. *Average high school GPA:* 3.46. *Test scores:* SAT critical reading scores over 500: 75%; SAT math scores over 500: 74%; ACT scores over 18: 97%; SAT critical reading scores over 600: 29%; SAT math scores over 600: 38%; ACT scores over 24: 58%; SAT critical reading scores over 700: 5%; SAT math scores over 700: 9%; ACT scores over 30: 11%.

Faculty *Total:* 811, 92% full-time, 82% with terminal degrees. *Student/faculty ratio:* 14:1.

Academics *Calendar:* semesters. *Degrees:* certificates, bachelor's, master's, doctoral, post-master's, postbachelor's, and first professional certificates. *Special study options:* accelerated degree program, advanced placement credit, distance learning, double majors, external degree program, honors programs, independent study, internships, off-campus study, part-time degree program, services for LD students, student-designed majors, study abroad, summer session for credit. *ROTC:* Army (b), Air Force (b).

Computers on Campus 1,413 computers/terminals are available on campus for general student use. Students can access the following: campus intranet, computer help desk, free student e-mail accounts, online (class) grades, online (class) registration, online (class) schedules. Campuswide network is available. 100% of college-owned or -operated housing units are wired for high-speed Internet access. Wireless service is available via classrooms, computer centers, computer labs, dorm rooms, learning centers, libraries, student centers.

Student Life *Housing:* on-campus residence required for freshman year. *Options:* coed, men-only, women-only, disabled students. Campus housing is university owned. Freshman campus housing is guaranteed. *Activities and organizations:* drama/theater group, student-run newspaper, television station, choral group, marching band, national fraternities, national sororities. *Campus security:* 24-hour emergency response devices and patrols, student patrols, late-night transport/escort service, controlled dormitory access, 24-hour front desk coverage at campus housing and at campus police. *Student services:* health clinic, personal/psychological counseling, women's center, legal services.

Athletics Member NCAA. All Division I except football (Division I-A). *Intercollegiate sports:* badminton M(c)/W(c), baseball M(c), basketball M(s)/W(s), cheerleading M(s)/W(s), cross-country running M(s)/W(s), equestrian sports M(c)/W(c), fencing M(c)/W(c), golf M(s)/W(s), ice hockey M(c)/W(c), lacrosse M(c)/W(c), racquetball M(c)/W(c), riflery M(c)/W(c), rugby M(c)/W(c), skiing (cross-country) M(c)/W(c), skiing (downhill) M(c)/W(c), soccer M(c)/W(s), softball W(c), swimming and diving M(s)/W(s), tennis M(c)/W(s), track and field M(s)/W(s), ultimate Frisbee M(c)/W(c), volleyball W(s), water polo M(c), wrestling M(s). *Intramural sports:* badminton M/W, basketball M/W, bowling M/W, football M/W, golf M/W, racquetball M/W, rock climbing M/W, soccer M/W, softball M/W, swimming and diving M/W, table tennis M/W, tennis M/W, track and field M/W, ultimate Frisbee M/W, volleyball M/W, water polo M/W, weight lifting M/W, wrestling M/W.

Standardized Tests *Required:* SAT or ACT (for admission).

Costs (2012–13) *One-time required fee:* $40. *Tuition:* state resident $3180 full-time, $106 per credit hour part-time; nonresident $12,330 full-time, $411 per credit hour part-time. Full-time tuition and fees vary according to course load, location, and reciprocity agreements. Part-time tuition and fees vary according to course load, location, and reciprocity agreements. *Required fees:* $1098 full-time. *Room and board:* $9084; room only: $4994. Room and board charges vary according to board plan and housing facility. *Payment plan:* installment. *Waivers:* children of alumni, senior citizens, and employees or children of employees.

Financial Aid Of all full-time matriculated undergraduates who enrolled in 2010, 5,385 applied for aid, 3,927 were judged to have need, 602 had their need fully met. In 2010, 1810 non-need-based awards were made. *Average percent of need met:* 47%. *Average financial aid package:* $2910. *Average need-based loan:* $2015. *Average need-based gift aid:* $1525. *Average non-need-based aid:* $1288. *Average indebtedness upon graduation:* $23,341.

Applying *Options:* electronic application, deferred entrance. *Application fee:* $40. *Required:* high school transcript, minimum 3.0 GPA, pre-college curriculum. *Application deadlines:* 8/10 (freshmen), 8/10 (out-of-state freshmen), 8/10 (transfers). *Notification:* continuous (freshmen), continuous (out-of-state freshmen), continuous (transfers).

Freshman Application Contact Mary Aguayo, Assistant Director of Admissions, University of Wyoming, 1000 E. University Avenue, Dept 3435, Laramie, WY 82071. *Phone:* 307-766-4075. *Toll-free phone:* 800-342-5996. *Fax:* 307-766-4042. *E-mail:* admissions@uwyo.edu. *Web site:* http://www.uwyo.edu/.

See page 1001 for display ad and page 1726 for the College Close-Up.

GUAM

Pacific Islands University
Mangilao, Guam

Freshman Application Contact Ethel Laco, Admissions Office, Pacific Islands University, 172 Kinney's Road, Mangilao, GU 96913. *Phone:* 671-734-1812. *Fax:* 671-734-1813. *E-mail:* guamcampus@pibc.edu. *Web site:* http://www.piu.edu/.

University of Guam
Mangilao, Guam

- **Territory-supported** comprehensive, founded 1952
- **Suburban** 100-acre campus
- **Endowment** $13.5 million
- **Coed** 3,373 undergraduate students, 75% full-time, 60% women, 40% men
- **Noncompetitive** entrance level, 85% of applicants were admitted

Undergraduates 2,529 full-time, 844 part-time. Students come from 36 states and territories; 24 other countries; 1% are from out of state; 0.6% Black or African American, non-Hispanic/Latino; 0.4% Hispanic/Latino; 42% Asian, non-Hispanic/Latino; 50% Native Hawaiian or other Pacific Islander, non-Hispanic/Latino; 0.1% American Indian or Alaska Native, non-Hispanic/Latino; 3% Race/ethnicity unknown; 0.6% international; 4% transferred in; 5% live on campus. *Retention:* 65% of full-time freshmen returned.

Freshmen *Admission:* 672 applied, 572 admitted, 553 enrolled. *Average high school GPA:* 3.1.

Faculty *Total:* 258, 71% full-time. *Student/faculty ratio:* 13:1.

Academics *Calendar:* semesters. *Degrees:* certificates, associate, bachelor's, master's, and postbachelor's certificates. *Special study options:* academic remediation for entering students, accelerated degree program, advanced placement credit, cooperative education, distance learning, double majors, English as a second language, honors programs, independent study, internships, off-campus study, part-time degree program, services for LD students, study abroad, summer session for credit. *ROTC:* Army (b).

Computers on Campus 545 computers/terminals and 600 ports are available on campus for general student use. Students can access the following: campus intranet, computer help desk, free student e-mail accounts, online (class) grades, online (class) registration, online (class) schedules, wireless internet access. Campuswide network is available. 100% of college-owned or -operated housing units are wired for high-speed Internet access. Wireless service is available via entire campus.

Student Life *Housing options:* coed. Campus housing is university owned. *Activities and organizations:* drama/theater group, student-run newspaper, choral group, American Marketing Association, Student Nurses Association of Guam, Social Work Student Alliance, GO CNMI, Association of Early Childhood Education International. *Campus security:* 24-hour emergency response devices and patrols, late-night transport/escort service. *Student services:* health clinic, personal/psychological counseling.

Athletics *Intramural sports:* basketball M/W, crew M(c)/W(c), football M, softball M/W, table tennis M/W, volleyball M/W.

Costs (2011–12) *Tuition:* territory resident $5320 full-time, $190 per credit hour part-time; nonresident $15,820 full-time, $565 per credit hour part-time. Part-time tuition and fees vary according to course load. *Required fees:* $498 full-time, $249 per term part-time. *Room only:* $2270. Room and board charges vary according to housing facility. *Payment plan:* installment. *Waivers:* senior citizens and employees or children of employees.

Applying *Options:* electronic application, deferred entrance. *Application fee:* $49. *Required:* high school transcript. *Application deadlines:* 6/1 (freshmen), 6/1 (out-of-state freshmen), 6/1 (transfers). *Notification:* continuous (freshmen), continuous (transfers).

Freshman Application Contact Ms. Angelica Anthonio, Admissions Supervisor, University of Guam, Admissions and Records Office, UOG Station, Mangilao, GU 96923. *Phone:* 671-735-2201. *Fax:* 671-735-2203. *E-mail:* admitme@uguam.uog.edu. *Web site:* http://www.uog.edu/.

NORTHERN MARIANA ISLANDS

Northern Marianas College
Saipan, Northern Mariana Islands

Freshman Application Contact Ms. Leilani M. Basa-Alam, Admission Specialist, Northern Marianas College, PO Box 501250, Saipan, MP 96950-1250. *Phone:* 670-234-3690 Ext. 1539. *Fax:* 670-235-4967. *E-mail:* leilanib@nmcnet.edu. *Web site:* http://www.nmcnet.edu/.

PUERTO RICO

American University of Puerto Rico
Bayamón, Puerto Rico

Freshman Application Contact Ms. Margarita Cruz Santiago, Director of Admissions, American University of Puerto Rico, PO Box 2037, Bayamón, PR 00960-2037. *Phone:* 787-740-6410. *Fax:* 787-785-7377. *Web site:* http://www.aupr.edu/.

Atlantic College
Guaynabo, Puerto Rico

Director of Admissions Ms. Zaida Perez, Admission's Officer, Atlantic College, PO Box 3918, Guaynabo, PR 00970. *Phone:* 787-720-1022 Ext. 13. *E-mail:* admisiones@atlanticcollege.edu. *Web site:* http://www.atlanticcollege.edu/.

Bayamón Central University
Bayamón, Puerto Rico

- **Independent Roman Catholic** comprehensive, founded 1970
- **Suburban** 55-acre campus with easy access to San Juan
- **Endowment** $1.4 million
- **Coed** 1,783 undergraduate students, 48% full-time, 35% women, 17% men
- **Moderately difficult** entrance level, 38% of applicants were admitted

Undergraduates 857 full-time, 81 part-time. 100% Hispanic/Latino.
Freshmen *Admission:* 1,068 applied, 406 admitted, 189 enrolled.
Faculty *Total:* 153, 25% full-time.
Academics *Calendar:* semesters for undergraduate programs, trimesters for graduate programs. *Degrees:* certificates, associate, bachelor's, and master's. *Special study options:* academic remediation for entering students, accelerated degree program, adult/continuing education programs, advanced placement credit, English as a second language, honors programs, independent study, internships, part-time degree program, services for LD students, student-designed majors, summer session for credit. *ROTC:* Army (c), Air Force (c).
Computers on Campus Campuswide network is available. Wireless service is available via classrooms, computer labs, libraries.
Student Life *Activities and organizations:* student-run newspaper, choral group. *Campus security:* 24-hour patrols. *Student services:* health clinic, personal/psychological counseling, legal services.
Athletics *Intercollegiate sports:* basketball M(s), bowling M/W, cross-country running M(s)/W(s), swimming and diving M(s)/W(s), track and field M(s)/W(s), volleyball M(s)/W(s), weight lifting M/W. *Intramural sports:* basket-

ball M/W, cross-country running M/W, softball M/W, swimming and diving M/W, table tennis M/W, track and field M/W, volleyball M/W, weight lifting M/W.
Standardized Tests *Required:* College Examination Entrance Board Test (for admission).
Costs (2012–13) *Tuition:* $7490 full-time, $165 per credit part-time. Full-time tuition and fees vary according to course level, degree level, and program. Part-time tuition and fees vary according to course level, degree level, and program. *Required fees:* $710 full-time, $165 per credit part-time, $350 per credit part-time. *Payment plan:* deferred payment. *Waivers:* employees or children of employees.
Applying *Application fee:* $25. *Required:* high school transcript, medical history. *Required for some:* interview. *Recommended:* minimum 2.0 GPA.
Freshman Application Contact Bayamón Central University, PO Box 1725, Bayamón, PR 00960-1725. *Phone:* 787-786-3030 Ext. 2102. *Web site:* http://www.ucb.edu.pr/.

Caribbean University
Bayamón, Puerto Rico

- **Independent** comprehensive, founded 1969
- **Urban** 16-acre campus with easy access to San Juan
- **Endowment** $321,559
- **Coed** 4,745 undergraduate students, 75% full-time, 59% women, 41% men
- **Minimally difficult** entrance level

Undergraduates 3,572 full-time, 1,173 part-time. Students come from 4 states and territories; 100% Hispanic/Latino.
Freshmen *Admission:* 1,369 enrolled.
Faculty *Total:* 424, 18% full-time, 20% with terminal degrees.
Academics *Calendar:* trimesters. *Degrees:* certificates, associate, bachelor's, and master's. *Special study options:* academic remediation for entering students, accelerated degree program, adult/continuing education programs, English as a second language, part-time degree program, services for LD students, summer session for credit. *ROTC:* Army (c).
Student Life *Activities and organizations:* drama/theater group, choral group, Engineering Student Association, Nursing, Social Work, Speech Therapy, Physical Education. *Campus security:* 24-hour patrols. *Student services:* health clinic, personal/psychological counseling.
Athletics *Intercollegiate sports:* baseball M, basketball M/W, bowling M/W, cheerleading M/W, cross-country running M/W, softball W, table tennis M/W, track and field M/W, volleyball M/W, weight lifting M/W, wrestling M/W. *Intramural sports:* basketball M, cross-country running M/W, gymnastics M/W, table tennis M/W, tennis M/W, track and field M/W, volleyball M/W, weight lifting M.
Standardized Tests *Required for some:* Only for the engineering applicants, we request test for verbal and math attitude offer by the College Board.
Costs (2012–13) *Comprehensive fee:* $12,465 includes full-time tuition ($4080), mandatory fees ($385), and room and board ($8000). Part-time tuition: $2040 per credit hour. *College room only:* $4500.
Applying *Options:* deferred entrance. *Application fee:* $30. *Required:* high school transcript. *Required for some:* 1 letter of recommendation, interview. *Application deadline:* rolling (freshmen).
Freshman Application Contact Caribbean University, Box 493, Bayamón, PR 00960-0493. *Phone:* 787-780-0070 Ext. 226. *Web site:* http://www.caribbean.edu/.

Carlos Albizu University
San Juan, Puerto Rico

- **Independent** university, founded 1966
- **Urban** campus
- **Endowment** $732,270
- **Coed, primarily women** 164 undergraduate students, 55% full-time, 89% women, 11% men
- **Noncompetitive** entrance level, 88% of applicants were admitted

Undergraduates 91 full-time, 73 part-time. 1% are from out of state; 99% Hispanic/Latino; 102% transferred in.
Freshmen *Admission:* 50 applied, 44 admitted.
Faculty *Total:* 28, 82% full-time, 100% with terminal degrees. *Student/faculty ratio:* 33:1.
Academics *Calendar:* semesters. *Degrees:* bachelor's, master's, doctoral, and first professional. *Special study options:* cooperative education, independent study, part-time degree program.
Computers on Campus 55 computers/terminals are available on campus for general student use. Students can access the following: free student e-mail accounts, online (class) grades, online (class) schedules. Campuswide network is available. Wireless service is available via entire campus.

Student Life *Housing:* college housing not available. *Activities and organizations:* Student Council, Community Services, Gender and Sexual Diversity Organization. *Campus security:* 24-hour emergency response devices, late-night transport/escort service, security cameras.

Standardized Tests *Required:* CEEB or SAT (for admission).

Costs (2012–13) *Tuition:* $5940 full-time, $165 per credit part-time. *Required fees:* $979 full-time, $333 per term part-time. *Payment plan:* deferred payment. *Waivers:* employees or children of employees.

Financial Aid Of all full-time matriculated undergraduates who enrolled in 2011, 66 applied for aid, 66 were judged to have need. 7 Federal Work-Study jobs (averaging $1235). *Average percent of need met:* 42%. *Average financial aid package:* $6495. *Average need-based loan:* $5550. *Average need-based gift aid:* $3751.

Applying *Options:* early admission, deferred entrance. *Required:* minimum 2.0 GPA, 1 letter of recommendation. *Required for some:* health certificate, Good Conduct Crete, official university transcript. *Application deadlines:* 7/16 (freshmen), 7/17 (transfers). *Notification:* continuous (freshmen), continuous (transfers).

Freshman Application Contact Carlos Albizu University, 151 Tanca Street, San Juan, PR 00901. *Phone:* 787-725-6500 Ext. 1521. *Web site:* http://www.albizu.edu/.

Colegio Universitario de San Juan
San Juan, Puerto Rico

Freshman Application Contact Colegio Universitario de San Juan, Jose R. Oliver Street, Hato Rey, PR 00918. *Phone:* 787-250-7111 Ext. 2227. *Web site:* http://www.cunisanjuan.edu/.

Columbia Centro Universitario
Caguas, Puerto Rico

- **Proprietary** comprehensive, founded 1966
- **Urban** 6-acre campus with easy access to San Juan
- **Coed** 1,329 undergraduate students, 51% full-time, 74% women, 26% men
- **Noncompetitive** entrance level

Undergraduates 674 full-time, 655 part-time. *Retention:* 54% of full-time freshmen returned.

Freshmen *Admission:* 644 applied, 205 enrolled. *Average high school GPA:* 2.

Faculty *Total:* 104, 16% full-time, 15% with terminal degrees. *Student/faculty ratio:* 14:1.

Academics *Calendar:* semesters. *Degrees:* certificates, associate, bachelor's, and master's. *Special study options:* accelerated degree program, part-time degree program.

Computers on Campus 136 computers/terminals are available on campus for general student use. Students can access the following: campus intranet, free student e-mail accounts. Campuswide network is available. Wireless service is available via entire campus.

Student Life *Housing:* college housing not available. *Campus security:* 24-hour patrols. *Student services:* personal/psychological counseling.

Costs (2011–12) *Tuition:* $9435 full-time. Full-time tuition and fees vary according to program. Part-time tuition and fees vary according to program. *Payment plan:* installment. *Waivers:* employees or children of employees.

Financial Aid Of all full-time matriculated undergraduates who enrolled in 2008, 974 applied for aid, 818 were judged to have need. 61 Federal Work-Study jobs (averaging $982). *Average percent of need met:* 11%. *Average financial aid package:* $4035.

Applying *Options:* electronic application. *Application fee:* $50. *Required:* high school transcript. *Required for some:* essay or personal statement, minimum 2.0 GPA, 3 letters of recommendation, interview. *Application deadline:* rolling (freshmen). *Notification:* continuous (freshmen).

Freshman Application Contact Mrs. Xiomara Sanchez, Admission Coordinator, Columbia Centro Universitario, PO Box 8517, Caguas, PR 00726. *Phone:* 787-743-4041 Ext. 239. *Fax:* 787-744-7031. *E-mail:* xsanchez@columbianco.edu. *Web site:* http://www.columbiaco.edu/.

Columbia Centro Universitario
Yauco, Puerto Rico

- **Proprietary** 4-year, founded 1976
- **Urban** campus
- **Coed** 430 undergraduate students, 50% full-time, 73% women, 27% men

Undergraduates 213 full-time, 217 part-time.

Freshmen *Admission:* 267 admitted, 71 enrolled. *Average high school GPA:* 2.

Faculty *Total:* 58, 17% full-time, 16% with terminal degrees. *Student/faculty ratio:* 14:1.

Academics *Calendar:* trimesters. *Degrees:* certificates, associate, and bachelor's. *Special study options:* cooperative education, honors programs.

Computers on Campus 83 computers/terminals are available on campus for general student use. Students can access the following: computer help desk. Wireless service is available via entire campus.

Student Life *Activities and organizations:* Nursing Group, Librarian Group. *Campus security:* late-night transport/escort service. *Student services:* personal/psychological counseling.

Costs (2011–12) *Tuition:* $9435 full-time. Full-time tuition and fees vary according to program. Part-time tuition and fees vary according to program. *Required fees:* $100 full-time. *Payment plan:* installment. *Waivers:* employees or children of employees.

Applying *Options:* electronic application. *Application fee:* $50. *Required:* high school transcript. *Required for some:* interview. *Application deadline:* rolling (freshmen). *Notification:* continuous (freshmen).

Freshman Application Contact Mrs. Rosario Padilla, Admissions, Columbia Centro Universitario, Calle Betances #3, Box 3062, Yauco, PR 00698. *Phone:* 787-856-0845 Ext. 11. *Fax:* 787-267-2335. *E-mail:* rpadilla@columbiaco.edu. *Web site:* http://www.columbiaco.edu/.

Conservatorio de Musica
San Juan, Puerto Rico

- **Public** comprehensive
- **Urban** 4-acre campus with easy access to Old San Juan
- **Endowment** $901,073
- **Coed** 421 undergraduate students, 71% full-time, 30% women, 70% men
- **Moderately difficult** entrance level, 58% of applicants were admitted

Undergraduates 300 full-time, 121 part-time. Students come from 4 states and territories; 7 other countries; 1% are from out of state; 91% Hispanic/Latino; 9% international; 8% transferred in. *Retention:* 70% of full-time freshmen returned.

Freshmen *Admission:* 141 applied, 82 admitted, 77 enrolled. *Average high school GPA:* 3.47.

Faculty *Total:* 91, 55% full-time, 14% with terminal degrees. *Student/faculty ratio:* 7:1.

Academics *Degrees:* bachelor's, master's, and postbachelor's certificates. *Special study options:* academic remediation for entering students, advanced placement credit, cooperative education, English as a second language, honors programs, off-campus study, part-time degree program, summer session for credit.

Computers on Campus 43 computers/terminals are available on campus for general student use. Students can access the following: campus intranet, free student e-mail accounts, online (class) registration. Campuswide network is available. Wireless service is available via classrooms, computer centers, computer labs, learning centers, libraries.

Student Life *Activities and organizations:* choral group. *Campus security:* 24-hour patrols.

Costs (2012–13) *Tuition:* commonwealth resident $1920 full-time, $80 per credit part-time; nonresident $1920 full-time, $80 per credit part-time. Full-time tuition and fees vary according to course load and degree level. Part-time tuition and fees vary according to course load and degree level. *Required fees:* $850 full-time, $425 per term part-time. *Room and board:* $10,000; room only: $4600. *Payment plan:* installment. *Waivers:* employees or children of employees.

Applying *Application fee:* $75. *Required:* high school transcript, minimum 2.0 GPA, instrument audition; ear training test. *Required for some:* essay or personal statement, minimum 2.5 GPA. *Recommended:* interview. *Application deadlines:* 12/15 (freshmen), 12/15 (out-of-state freshmen), 12/15 (transfers). *Notification:* 3/1 (freshmen), 3/1 (out-of-state freshmen), 3/1 (transfers).

Freshman Application Contact Mrs. Ilsamar Hernandez, Admission Director, Conservatorio de Musica, 951 Ponce de Leon Ave., San Juan, PR 00907-3373. *Phone:* 787-751-0160 Ext. 275. *Fax:* 787-764-3581. *E-mail:* ihernandez@cmpr.gobierno.pr. *Web site:* http://www.cmpr.edu/.

Conservatory of Music of Puerto Rico
San Juan, Puerto Rico

Freshman Application Contact Conservatory of Music of Puerto Rico, 350 Rafael Lamar St at FDR Ave, San Juan, PR 00918. *Phone:* 787-751-0160 Ext. 275. *Web site:* http://www.cmpr.edu/.

EDP College of Puerto Rico, Inc.

Hato Rey, Puerto Rico

- **Proprietary** comprehensive, founded 1968
- **Urban** 1-acre campus
- **Coed** 1,139 undergraduate students, 42% full-time, 62% women, 38% men
- **Minimally difficult** entrance level, 93% of applicants were admitted

Undergraduates 476 full-time, 663 part-time. Students come from 5 states and territories; 11% are from out of state; 23% transferred in. *Retention:* 94% of full-time freshmen returned.

Freshmen *Admission:* 300 applied, 279 admitted, 156 enrolled. *Average high school GPA:* 2.78.

Faculty *Total:* 96, 25% full-time, 11% with terminal degrees. *Student/faculty ratio:* 15:1.

Academics *Calendar:* semesters. *Degrees:* associate, bachelor's, master's, and postbachelor's certificates. *Special study options:* academic remediation for entering students, accelerated degree program, adult/continuing education programs, advanced placement credit, cooperative education, distance learning, English as a second language, independent study, internships, part-time degree program, services for LD students, summer session for credit.

Computers on Campus 199 computers/terminals and 4 ports are available on campus for general student use. Students can access the following: campus intranet, computer help desk, free student e-mail accounts, online (class) grades, online (class) registration, online (class) schedules. Campuswide network is available. Wireless service is available via entire campus.

Student Life *Housing:* college housing not available. *Activities and organizations:* Student Council, Graduate Student Association, JCI San Juan, Dynamic Dynasty, OEM EDP. *Campus security:* security and emergency telephones in working hours. *Student services:* personal/psychological counseling.

Standardized Tests *Required:* College Entrance Examination Board (CEEB) Test, Institution Admission Exam (for admission).

Costs (2012–13) *Tuition:* $5400 full-time, $156 per credit hour part-time. Full-time tuition and fees vary according to course load and program. Part-time tuition and fees vary according to course load and program. *Required fees:* $720 full-time, $156 per credit hour part-time, $360 per credit hour part-time. *Payment plan:* installment. *Waivers:* employees or children of employees.

Applying *Options:* early admission, early decision, early action, deferred entrance. *Application fee:* $15. *Required:* high school transcript, minimum 1.6 GPA, placement test or College Board test, vaccination certificate, social security number. *Required for some:* essay or personal statement, minimum 2.5 GPA, 2 letters of recommendation, interview, placement test or College Board test, vaccination certificate, social security number. *Recommended:* minimum 2.0 GPA. *Application deadlines:* rolling (freshmen), rolling (out-of-state freshmen), rolling (transfers).

Freshman Application Contact Ms. Enid Cartagena, Student Affairs Dean, EDP College of Puerto Rico, Inc., Avenue Ponce de Leon, #560, Hato Rey, PR 00918, Puerto Rico. *Phone:* 787-765-3560 Ext. 272. *Fax:* 787-777-0024. *E-mail:* ecartagena@edpcollege.edu. *Web site:* http://www.edpcollege.edu/.

EDP College of Puerto Rico–San Sebastian

San Sebastian, Puerto Rico

- **Proprietary** 4-year, founded 1976
- **Rural** campus
- **Coed** 881 undergraduate students, 69% full-time, 63% women, 37% men
- **Minimally difficult** entrance level, 94% of applicants were admitted

Undergraduates 605 full-time, 276 part-time. *Retention:* 44% of full-time freshmen returned.

Freshmen *Admission:* 67 applied, 63 admitted, 217 enrolled. *Average high school GPA:* 2.55.

Faculty *Total:* 82, 23% full-time, 9% with terminal degrees. *Student/faculty ratio:* 17:1.

Academics *Calendar:* semesters. *Degrees:* associate and bachelor's. *Special study options:* academic remediation for entering students, accelerated degree program, adult/continuing education programs, advanced placement credit, cooperative education, distance learning, English as a second language, independent study, internships, part-time degree program, services for LD students, summer session for credit.

Computers on Campus 125 computers/terminals and 60 ports are available on campus for general student use. Students can access the following: free student e-mail accounts, online (class) grades, online (class) registration, online (class) schedules. Campuswide network is available. Wireless service is available via entire campus.

Student Life *Activities and organizations:* drama/theater group. *Student services:* personal/psychological counseling.

Standardized Tests *Required:* College Board or institutional entrance test (for admission).

Costs (2012–13) *Tuition:* $5400 full-time, $156 per credit hour part-time. Full-time tuition and fees vary according to course load and program. Part-time tuition and fees vary according to course load and program. *Required fees:* $720 full-time, $156 per credit hour part-time, $360 per term part-time. *Payment plan:* installment. *Waivers:* employees or children of employees.

Financial Aid Of all full-time matriculated undergraduates who enrolled in 2010, 596 applied for aid, 558 were judged to have need. 95 Federal Work-Study jobs (averaging $1756). *Average percent of need met:* 88%. *Average financial aid package:* $5400. *Average need-based loan:* $3000. *Average need-based gift aid:* $5400. *Average indebtedness upon graduation:* $6700.

Applying *Application fee:* $15. *Required:* high school transcript, minimum 2.0 GPA. *Required for some:* minimum 2.5 GPA, interview. *Application deadlines:* rolling (freshmen), rolling (out-of-state freshmen), rolling (transfers).

Freshman Application Contact Ms. Pilar Cordero, Student Affairs Dean, EDP College of Puerto Rico–San Sebastian, Avenue Betances #49, San Sebastian, PR 00685. *Phone:* 787-896-2252 Ext. 303. *Fax:* 787-896-0066. *E-mail:* pcordero@edpcollege.edu. *Web site:* http://www.edpcollege.edu/.

Escuela de Artes Plasticas de Puerto Rico

San Juan, Puerto Rico

- **Commonwealth-supported** 4-year, founded 1966
- **Urban** campus
- **Endowment** $1.3 million
- **Coed** 527 undergraduate students, 61% full-time, 59% women, 41% men
- **Moderately difficult** entrance level, 72% of applicants were admitted

Undergraduates 324 full-time, 203 part-time. Students come from 1 other state; 1 other country; 100% Hispanic/Latino; 0.2% international; 8% transferred in. *Retention:* 86% of full-time freshmen returned.

Freshmen *Admission:* 119 applied, 86 admitted, 77 enrolled. *Average high school GPA:* 3.11.

Faculty *Total:* 60, 27% full-time, 58% with terminal degrees. *Student/faculty ratio:* 13:1.

Academics *Calendar:* 3 semesters each calendar year; participant in Year Round Pell. *Degree:* bachelor's. *Special study options:* accelerated degree program, adult/continuing education programs, advanced placement credit, internships, off-campus study, part-time degree program, services for LD students.

Computers on Campus 120 computers/terminals and 120 ports are available on campus for general student use. Students can access the following: computer help desk, library online catalog, wireless access. Wireless service is available via entire campus.

Student Life *Housing:* college housing not available. *Activities and organizations:* Student government, Literary magazine. *Campus security:* 24-hour emergency response devices and patrols, security cameras and institutional police of privacy. *Student services:* personal/psychological counseling.

Standardized Tests *Recommended:* SAT (for admission).

Costs (2011–12) *Tuition:* commonwealth resident $4404 full-time, $90 per credit part-time; nonresident $7644 full-time, $180 per credit part-time. Full-time tuition and fees vary according to course load and program. Part-time tuition and fees vary according to course load and program. *Required fees:* $375 full-time. *Payment plan:* deferred payment. *Waivers:* employees or children of employees.

Financial Aid Of all full-time matriculated undergraduates who enrolled in 2007, 276 applied for aid, 276 were judged to have need. 10 Federal Work-Study jobs (averaging $1850). *Average percent of need met:* 82%. *Financial aid deadline:* 5/25.

Applying *Application fee:* $25. *Required:* essay or personal statement, high school transcript, minimum 2.0 GPA, interview, The applicants must approve an evaluation regarding artistic skills through a portfolio or seminar and complete the security seminar. *Recommended:* 1 letter of recommendation. *Application deadlines:* 7/2 (freshmen), 6/10 (out-of-state freshmen), 7/2 (transfers). *Notification:* 7/30 (freshmen), 7/30 (out-of-state freshmen), 7/30 (transfers).

Freshman Application Contact Mrs. Nitza Mel??ndez, Officer of Admissions, Escuela de Artes Plasticas de Puerto Rico, PO Box 902112, San Juan, PR 00902-1112. *Phone:* 787-725-8120 Ext. 333. *Fax:* 787-721-3798. *E-mail:* nmelendez@eap.edu. *Web site:* http://www.eap.edu/.

Inter American University of Puerto Rico, Aguadilla Campus

Aguadilla, Puerto Rico

Freshman Application Contact Mrs. Doris Perez, Admissions Director, Inter American University of Puerto Rico, Aguadilla Campus, PO Box 20,000, Road 459 Intersection 463, Aguadilla, PR 00605. *Phone:* 787-891-0925 Ext. 2101. *Fax:* 787-882-3020. *Web site:* http://www.aguadilla.inter.edu/.

Inter American University of Puerto Rico, Arecibo Campus

Arecibo, Puerto Rico

Freshman Application Contact Ms. Provi Montalvo, Admission Director, Inter American University of Puerto Rico, Arecibo Campus, PO Box 4050, Arecibo, PR 00614-4050. *Phone:* 787-878-5475. *Fax:* 787-880-1624. *E-mail:* pmontalvo@arecibo.inter.edu. *Web site:* http://www.arecibo.inter.edu/.

Inter American University of Puerto Rico, Barranquitas Campus

Barranquitas, Puerto Rico

Freshman Application Contact Mrs. Aramilda Cartagena, Dean of Students, Inter American University of Puerto Rico, Barranquitas Campus, PO Box 517, Barranquitas, PR 00794. *Phone:* 787-857-3600 Ext. 2009. *Fax:* 787-857-2125. *E-mail:* acartagena@br.inter.edu. *Web site:* http://www.br.inter.edu/.

Inter American University of Puerto Rico, Bayamón Campus

Bayamón, Puerto Rico

- **Independent** comprehensive, founded 1912, part of Inter American University of Puerto Rico
- **Urban** 51-acre campus with easy access to San Juan
- **Endowment** $153.6 million
- **Coed** 5,110 undergraduate students, 86% full-time, 45% women, 55% men
- 36% of applicants were admitted

Undergraduates 4,374 full-time, 736 part-time. Students come from 1 other state; 4 other countries; 99% Hispanic/Latino; 1% Two or more races, non-Hispanic/Latino; 4% transferred in. *Retention:* 73% of full-time freshmen returned.
Freshmen *Admission:* 3,397 applied, 1,222 admitted, 1,081 enrolled. *Average high school GPA:* 3.
Faculty *Total:* 307, 33% full-time, 24% with terminal degrees. *Student/faculty ratio:* 28:1.
Academics *Calendar:* semesters. *Degrees:* certificates, associate, bachelor's, and master's. *Special study options:* accelerated degree program, adult/continuing education programs, advanced placement credit, cooperative education, distance learning, external degree program, honors programs, independent study, internships, part-time degree program, services for LD students, summer session for credit. *ROTC:* Army (c).
Computers on Campus 610 computers/terminals are available on campus for general student use. Students can access the following: computer help desk, free student e-mail accounts, online (class) grades, online (class) registration. Campuswide network is available.
Student Life *Housing options:* Campus housing is university owned. *Activities and organizations:* student-run newspaper, choral group, Asociacion de Estudiantes de Administracion de Empresas, Estudiantes Unidos por la Ciencia, Asociacion Estudiantes de Aviacion, Consejo de Estudiante, Asociacion Estudiantes de Ingenieria. *Campus security:* 24-hour patrols. *Student services:* health clinic, personal/psychological counseling.
Athletics *Intercollegiate sports:* baseball M(s), basketball M(s)/W(s), cross-country running M(s)/W(s), softball M(s)/W(s), swimming and diving M(s)/W(s), table tennis M(s)/W(s), track and field M(s)/W(s), volleyball M(s)/W(s), weight lifting M(s). *Intramural sports:* basketball M/W, cross-country running M/W, softball M/W, swimming and diving M/W, table tennis M/W, tennis M/W, track and field M/W, volleyball M/W, weight lifting M.
Standardized Tests *Required:* CEEB (for admission). *Required for some:* SAT (for admission).
Costs (2012–13) *Tuition:* $5100 full-time, $258 per semester hour part-time. Full-time tuition and fees vary according to course load and program. Part-time tuition and fees vary according to course load and program. *Required fees:* $516 full-time. *Payment plan:* deferred payment.

Financial Aid Of all full-time matriculated undergraduates who enrolled in 2011, 2,971 applied for aid, 2,945 were judged to have need, 4 had their need fully met. *Average percent of need met:* 6%. *Average financial aid package:* $996. *Average need-based loan:* $1589. *Average need-based gift aid:* $362.
Applying *Options:* electronic application. *Required:* high school transcript, minimum 2.0 GPA, 2.5 GPA for engineering programs. *Application deadline:* 7/30 (freshmen). *Notification:* continuous (freshmen), continuous (transfers).
Freshman Application Contact Inter American University of Puerto Rico, Bayamón Campus, 500 Road 830, Bayamón, PR 00957. *Phone:* 787-279-1912 Ext. 2017. *Web site:* http://www.bc.inter.edu/.

Inter American University of Puerto Rico, Fajardo Campus

Fajardo, Puerto Rico

- **Independent** comprehensive, founded 1965, part of Inter American University of Puerto Rico
- **Small-town** 11-acre campus with easy access to San Juan
- **Coed** 2,169 undergraduate students, 66% full-time, 66% women, 34% men
- **Moderately difficult** entrance level, 50% of applicants were admitted

Undergraduates 1,427 full-time, 742 part-time. *Retention:* 67% of full-time freshmen returned.
Freshmen *Admission:* 909 applied, 453 admitted, 459 enrolled. *Average high school GPA:* 2.
Faculty *Total:* 114, 35% full-time, 11% with terminal degrees. *Student/faculty ratio:* 11:1.
Academics *Calendar:* semesters. *Degrees:* associate, bachelor's, and master's. *Special study options:* academic remediation for entering students, adult/continuing education programs, advanced placement credit, cooperative education, distance learning, English as a second language, external degree program, honors programs, independent study, internships, off-campus study, part-time degree program, services for LD students, summer session for credit. *ROTC:* Army (c).
Computers on Campus 280 computers/terminals are available on campus for general student use. Students can access the following: free student e-mail accounts, online (class) grades, online (class) registration, online (class) schedules. Campuswide network is available. Wireless service is available via entire campus.
Student Life *Housing:* college housing not available. *Activities and organizations:* drama/theater group, Future Teachers Association, Criminal Justice Student Association, Honor Program Association, Practical Teaching Association, Social Work Association. *Campus security:* 24-hour patrols. *Student services:* personal/psychological counseling.
Athletics *Intercollegiate sports:* baseball M, basketball M(s)/W, bowling M, cheerleading W, softball W, table tennis M/W, tennis M/W, track and field M(s)/W(s), volleyball M/W.
Standardized Tests *Required:* College Board (for admission).
Costs (2012–13) *Tuition:* $4080 full-time, $170 per credit part-time. Full-time tuition and fees vary according to degree level. Part-time tuition and fees vary according to degree level. *Required fees:* $258 full-time. *Payment plans:* installment, deferred payment. *Waivers:* adult students and employees or children of employees.
Applying *Options:* electronic application, early admission, deferred entrance. *Required:* high school transcript. *Required for some:* interview. *Application deadlines:* 5/15 (freshmen), rolling (transfers).
Freshman Application Contact Ms. Ghisita M. Garcia, Administrative Assistant II, Inter American University of Puerto Rico, Fajardo Campus, Call Box 70003, Fajardo, PR 00738-7003. *Phone:* 787-863-2390 Ext. 2210. *Fax:* 787-860-3470. *E-mail:* ghisita.garcia@fajardo.inter.edu. *Web site:* http://www.fajardo.inter.edu/.

Inter American University of Puerto Rico, Guayama Campus

Guayama, Puerto Rico

- **Independent** comprehensive, founded 1958, part of Inter American University of Puerto Rico
- **Small-town** 50-acre campus
- **Endowment** $782,124
- **Coed**
- **Moderately difficult** entrance level

Faculty *Student/faculty ratio:* 23:1.
Academics *Calendar:* semesters. *Degrees:* certificates, associate, bachelor's, and master's.
Student Life *Campus security:* 24-hour emergency response devices.

Standardized Tests *Required:* SAT (for admission), PAA (for admission).
Costs (2011–12) *Tuition:* $4080 full-time. *Required fees:* $478 full-time.
Financial Aid *Of all full-time matriculated undergraduates who enrolled in 2011,* 1,883 applied for aid, 1,881 were judged to have need. *Average percent of need met:* 20. *Average financial aid package:* $3499. *Average need-based loan:* $3889. *Average need-based gift aid:* $716.
Applying *Options:* electronic application. *Required:* high school transcript, minimum 2.0 GPA. *Required for some:* essay or personal statement, interview.
Freshman Application Contact Inter American University of Puerto Rico, Guayama Campus, Call Box 10004, Guayama, PR 00785. *Phone:* 787-864-2222 Ext. 220. *Web site:* http://www.guayama.inter.edu/.

Inter American University of Puerto Rico, Metropolitan Campus

San Juan, Puerto Rico

- **Independent** comprehensive, founded 1960, part of Inter American University of Puerto Rico
- **Urban** campus
- **Endowment** $7.5 million
- **Coed**
- **Moderately difficult** entrance level

Academics *Calendar:* semesters. *Degrees:* certificates, associate, bachelor's, master's, doctoral, postbachelor's, and first professional certificates.
Student Life *Campus security:* 24-hour emergency response devices and patrols, video security system.
Standardized Tests *Required:* CEEB (for admission). *Required for some:* SAT (for admission).
Financial Aid *Of all full-time matriculated undergraduates who enrolled in 1999,* 4,328 applied for aid, 3,935 were judged to have need, 29 had their need fully met. *Average percent of need met:* 11. *Average financial aid package:* $2144. *Average need-based loan:* $1149. *Average need-based gift aid:* $1617. *Financial aid deadline:* 4/30.
Applying *Options:* electronic application. *Required:* high school transcript.
Freshman Application Contact Ms. Ida G. Betancourt, Official Admission, Inter American University of Puerto Rico, Metropolitan Campus, PO Box 191293, San Juan, PR 00919-1293. *Phone:* 787-250-1912 Ext. 2188. *Fax:* 787-250-1025. *E-mail:* jbetancourt@metro.inter.edu. *Web site:* http://metro.inter.edu/.

Inter American University of Puerto Rico, Ponce Campus

Mercedita, Puerto Rico

- **Independent** comprehensive, founded 1962, part of Inter American University of Puerto Rico
- **Urban** 50-acre campus with easy access to San Juan
- **Coed** 6,023 undergraduate students, 83% full-time, 61% women, 39% men
- **Moderately difficult** entrance level, 41% of applicants were admitted

Undergraduates 4,991 full-time, 1,032 part-time. Students come from 1 other state; 100% Hispanic/Latino; 4% transferred in. *Retention:* 72% of full-time freshmen returned.
Freshmen *Admission:* 4,399 applied, 1,808 admitted, 924 enrolled.
Faculty *Total:* 347, 29% full-time, 19% with terminal degrees. *Student/faculty ratio:* 31:1.
Academics *Calendar:* semesters. *Degrees:* associate, bachelor's, and master's. *Special study options:* academic remediation for entering students, adult/continuing education programs, cooperative education, distance learning, English as a second language, honors programs, independent study, internships, off-campus study, part-time degree program, services for LD students, study abroad, summer session for credit.
Computers on Campus 422 computers/terminals and 482 ports are available on campus for general student use. Students can access the following: online (class) registration. Campuswide network is available. 100% of college-owned or -operated housing units are wired for high-speed Internet access. Wireless service is available via entire campus.
Student Life *Housing:* college housing not available. *Activities and organizations:* drama/theater group, choral group, marching band, Association of Future Teachers of Special Education, Accounting Students Association, Hotel Management Association, Office Systems Administration Association, Criminal Justice Association. *Campus security:* 24-hour patrols. *Student services:* health clinic, personal/psychological counseling.
Athletics *Intercollegiate sports:* basketball M(s)/W(s), cross-country running M(s), softball M(s)/W(s), table tennis M(s)/W(s), track and field M(s)/W(s), weight lifting M(s), wrestling M(s). *Intramural sports:* basketball M/W,

cross-country running M/W, softball M/W, table tennis M/W, track and field M/W, volleyball M/W, weight lifting M/W.
Standardized Tests *Required:* CEEB (for admission). *Required for some:* SAT (for admission).
Costs (2011–12) *Tuition:* $4080 full-time, $170 per credit part-time. Full-time tuition and fees vary according to course load and program. Part-time tuition and fees vary according to course load and program. *Required fees:* $520 full-time, $473 per semester hour part-time. *Payment plan:* deferred payment.
Financial Aid *Of all full-time matriculated undergraduates who enrolled in 2008,* 3,209 applied for aid, 3,194 were judged to have need, 1 had their need fully met. *Average percent of need met:* 10%. *Average financial aid package:* $1702. *Average need-based loan:* $2248. *Average need-based gift aid:* $537.
Applying *Options:* deferred entrance. *Required:* high school transcript, minimum 2.0 GPA. *Application deadlines:* 5/15 (freshmen), 5/15 (transfers).
Freshman Application Contact Mr. Franco Diaz, Admissions Officer, Inter American University of Puerto Rico, Ponce Campus, 104 Turpo Industrial Park, Road #1, Mercedita, PR 00715-1602. *Phone:* 787-284-1912 Ext. 2025. *Fax:* 787-841-0103. *E-mail:* fidiaz@ponce.inter.edu. *Web site:* http://www.ponce.inter.edu/.

Inter American University of Puerto Rico, San Germán Campus

San Germán, Puerto Rico

- **Independent** university, founded 1912, part of Inter American University of Puerto Rico
- **Small-town** 260-acre campus with easy access to Ponce, Aguadilla, Mayaguez
- **Endowment** $153.6 million
- **Coed** 9,049 undergraduate students, 47% full-time, 28% women, 72% men
- **Moderately difficult** entrance level, 70% of applicants were admitted

Undergraduates 4,254 full-time, 4,795 part-time. Students come from 14 states and territories; 100% Hispanic/Latino; 1% transferred in; 10% live on campus. *Retention:* 75% of full-time freshmen returned.
Freshmen *Admission:* 1,584 applied, 1,107 admitted, 5,156 enrolled. *Average high school GPA:* 2.98.
Faculty *Total:* 326, 37% full-time, 33% with terminal degrees. *Student/faculty ratio:* 27:1.
Academics *Calendar:* semesters. *Degrees:* certificates, associate, bachelor's, master's, doctoral, postbachelor's, and first professional certificates. *Special study options:* academic remediation for entering students, accelerated degree program, adult/continuing education programs, advanced placement credit, cooperative education, distance learning, double majors, English as a second language, external degree program, honors programs, independent study, internships, off-campus study, part-time degree program, services for LD students, summer session for credit. *ROTC:* Army (c), Navy (c), Air Force (c).
Computers on Campus 1,250 computers/terminals are available on campus for general student use. Students can access the following: free student e-mail accounts, online (class) grades, online (class) registration, online (class) schedules. Campuswide network is available. Wireless service is available via computer centers, computer labs, dorm rooms, learning centers, libraries, student centers.
Student Life *Housing options:* men-only, women-only. Campus housing is university owned. *Activities and organizations:* drama/theater group, student-run newspaper, choral group, Asociacion de Pre-Medica-Caduceus, Futuros Maestros, Asociacion De Estudiantes De Psicologia (AEPSI), Asociacion de Estudiantes Inter Tecnicos (AEITEC), Asociacion de Estudiantes del Programa de Honor. *Campus security:* 24-hour emergency response devices and patrols. *Student services:* personal/psychological counseling.
Athletics *Intercollegiate sports:* baseball M(s), basketball M(s)/W(s), cross-country running M(s)/W(s), soccer M(s), softball M/W, swimming and diving M/W, table tennis M(s)/W(s), tennis M(s)/W(s), track and field M(s)/W(s), volleyball M(s)/W(s), weight lifting M(s). *Intramural sports:* badminton M/W, basketball M/W, cross-country running M/W, softball M/W, table tennis M/W, tennis M/W, track and field M/W, volleyball M/W.
Standardized Tests *Required:* CEEB (for admission). *Required for some:* SAT or ACT (for admission).
Costs (2012–13) *Comprehensive fee:* $8116 includes full-time tuition ($5100), mandatory fees ($516), and room and board ($2500). Part-time tuition: $170 per credit. *College room only:* $1000. Room and board charges vary according to board plan and housing facility. *Payment plan:* installment. *Waivers:* employees or children of employees.
Financial Aid *Of all full-time matriculated undergraduates who enrolled in 2009,* 2,797 applied for aid, 2,755 were judged to have need, 4 had their need fully met. *Average percent of need met:* 12%. *Average financial aid package:* $2009. *Average need-based loan:* $3080. *Average need-based gift aid:* $642.

Applying *Options:* electronic application, early admission. *Required:* high school transcript, medical history, vaccination. *Required for some:* 1 letter of recommendation, interview. *Recommended:* essay or personal statement, minimum 2.0 GPA. *Application deadlines:* 5/15 (freshmen), 5/15 (transfers). *Notification:* continuous (freshmen), continuous (transfers).

Freshman Application Contact Prof. Mildred Camacho, Director of Admissions, Inter American University of Puerto Rico, San Germán Campus, PO Box 5100, San German, PR 00683-5008. *Phone:* 787-264-1912 Ext. 7283. *Fax:* 787-892-7020. *E-mail:* milcama@sg.inter.edu. *Web site:* http://www.sg.inter.edu/.

National University College

Bayamón, Puerto Rico

Freshman Application Contact Admissions, National University College, PO Box 2036, National College Plaza Building, Bayamón, PR 00960. *Phone:* 787-780-5134. *Toll-free phone:* 800-780-5134. *Fax:* 787-779-4909. *E-mail:* infobayamon@nuc.edu. *Web site:* http://www.nuc.edu/.

Polytechnic University of Puerto Rico

Hato Rey, Puerto Rico

- **Independent** comprehensive, founded 1966
- **Urban** 10-acre campus with easy access to San Juan
- **Endowment** $10.8 million
- **Coed, primarily men** 4,317 undergraduate students, 53% full-time, 22% women, 78% men
- **Minimally difficult** entrance level, 95% of applicants were admitted

Undergraduates 2,272 full-time, 2,045 part-time. Students come from 2 states and territories; 12 other countries; 100% Hispanic/Latino. *Retention:* 74% of full-time freshmen returned.

Freshmen *Admission:* 737 applied, 697 admitted, 505 enrolled. *Average high school GPA:* 2.45.

Faculty *Total:* 265, 61% full-time, 28% with terminal degrees. *Student/faculty ratio:* 19:1.

Academics *Calendar:* trimesters. *Degrees:* bachelor's and master's. *Special study options:* academic remediation for entering students, distance learning, English as a second language, independent study, part-time degree program, student-designed majors, summer session for credit. *ROTC:* Army (c).

Computers on Campus 375 computers/terminals and 500 ports are available on campus for general student use. Students can access the following: campus intranet, free student e-mail accounts, online (class) grades, online (class) registration, online (class) schedules. Campuswide network is available. Wireless service is available via entire campus.

Student Life *Activities and organizations:* choral group, Society of Women Engineers, American Civil Engineering - Student Chapter, Society of Hispanic Professional Engineers, Society of Automotive Engineers, Capitulo Estudiantil Ingenieros Electricos. *Campus security:* 24-hour patrols. *Student services:* personal/psychological counseling.

Athletics *Intercollegiate sports:* basketball M(s), cross-country running M(s)/W(s), soccer M, table tennis M(s)/W(s), tennis M(s)/W(s), track and field M(s)/W(s), volleyball M(s)/W(s), wrestling M(s). *Intramural sports:* basketball M.

Standardized Tests *Required for some:* SAT (for admission).

Costs (2012–13) *Comprehensive fee:* $18,967 includes full-time tuition ($6588), mandatory fees ($675), and room and board ($11,704). Full-time tuition and fees vary according to course load, degree level, and program. Part-time tuition: $183 per credit hour. Part-time tuition and fees vary according to course load, degree level, and program. *Payment plan:* deferred payment. *Waivers:* employees or children of employees.

Financial Aid Of all full-time matriculated undergraduates who enrolled in 2008, 2,749 applied for aid, 2,679 were judged to have need, 25 had their need fully met. 121 Federal Work-Study jobs (averaging $1733). *Average percent of need met:* 63%. *Average financial aid package:* $5350. *Average need-based loan:* $4550. *Average need-based gift aid:* $4454. *Financial aid deadline:* 5/15.

Applying *Options:* electronic application, early admission, deferred entrance. *Application fee:* $30. *Required:* high school transcript. *Application deadline:* 8/15 (freshmen).

Freshman Application Contact Ms. Teresa Cardona, Director of Admissions, Polytechnic University of Puerto Rico, PO Box 192017, San Juan, PR 00919-2017. *Phone:* 787-754-8000 Ext. 240. *Fax:* 787-764-8712. *E-mail:* tcardona@pupr.edu. *Web site:* http://www.pupr.edu/.

Pontifical Catholic University of Puerto Rico

Ponce, Puerto Rico

Freshman Application Contact Sra. Ana O. Bonilla, Director of Admissions, Pontifical Catholic University of Puerto Rico, 2250 Avenida Las Americas Avenue, Suite 584, Ponce, PR 00717-9777. *Phone:* 787-841-2000 Ext. 1004. *Toll-free phone:* 800-961-7696. *Fax:* 787-840-4295. *E-mail:* admissions@email.pucpr.edu. *Web site:* http://www.pucpr.edu/.

Universidad Adventista de las Antillas

Mayagüez, Puerto Rico

Freshman Application Contact Ms. Evelyn del Valle, Director of Admissions, Universidad Adventista de las Antillas, Oficina de Admisiones, PO Box 118, Mayaguez, PR 00681-0118. *Phone:* 787-834-9595 Ext. 2208. *Fax:* 787-834-9597. *E-mail:* admissions@uaa.edu. *Web site:* http://www.uaa.edu/.

Universidad Central del Caribe

Bayamón, Puerto Rico

Director of Admissions Admissions Department, Universidad Central del Caribe, PO Box 60-327, Bayamón, PR 00960-6032. *Phone:* 787-740-1611. *Web site:* http://www.uccaribe.edu/.

Universidad del Este

Carolina, Puerto Rico

Freshman Application Contact Universidad del Este, PO Box 2010, Carolina, PR 00984. *Phone:* 787-257-7373 Ext. 3401. *Web site:* http://www.suagm.edu/une/.

Universidad del Turabo

Gurabo, Puerto Rico

- **Independent** university, founded 1972, part of Ana G. Méndez University System
- **Urban** 140-acre campus with easy access to San Juan
- **Coed** 13,817 undergraduate students, 77% full-time, 59% women, 41% men
- **Minimally difficult** entrance level, 46% of applicants were admitted

Undergraduates 10,644 full-time, 3,173 part-time. *Retention:* 74% of full-time freshmen returned.

Freshmen *Admission:* 9,581 applied, 4,406 admitted, 2,913 enrolled.

Faculty *Total:* 1,325, 15% full-time, 25% with terminal degrees. *Student/faculty ratio:* 38:1.

Academics *Calendar:* semesters. *Degrees:* certificates, associate, bachelor's, master's, doctoral, postbachelor's, and first professional certificates. *Special study options:* accelerated degree program, advanced placement credit, distance learning, double majors, honors programs, independent study, internships, off-campus study, part-time degree program, summer session for credit. *ROTC:* Army (c), Air Force (c).

Computers on Campus Campuswide network is available.

Student Life *Activities and organizations:* student-run newspaper, radio station. *Campus security:* 24-hour patrols. *Student services:* health clinic, personal/psychological counseling.

Standardized Tests *Recommended:* SAT (for admission).

Costs (2012–13) *Comprehensive fee:* $26,574 includes full-time tuition ($19,512) and room and board ($7062). Full-time tuition and fees vary according to course level, course load, and program.

Applying *Options:* electronic application. *Application fee:* $15. *Required:* high school transcript. *Application deadlines:* rolling (freshmen), rolling (transfers). *Notification:* continuous (freshmen), continuous (transfers).

Freshman Application Contact Universidad del Turabo, PO Box 3030, Gurabo, PR 00778-3030. *Phone:* 787-743-7979 Ext. 4453. *Web site:* http://www.suagm.edu/ut/.

Universidad Metropolitana

San Juan, Puerto Rico

Freshman Application Contact Mr. Julio Rodriguez Soiza, Director of Admissions, Universidad Metropolitana, Box 21150, San Juan, PR 00928-1150. *Phone:* 787-766-1717 Ext. 6587. *Toll-free phone:* 800-747-8362. *Fax:* 787-751-0992. *E-mail:* um_frivera@suagm1.suagm.edu. *Web site:* http://www.suagm.edu/umet/.

Universidad Pentecostal Mizpa
Río Piedras, Puerto Rico

Director of Admissions Omar Alicea, Recruitment, Universidad Pentecostal Mizpa, Bo Caimito Road 199, Apartado 20966, Río Piedras, PR 00928-0966. *Phone:* 787-720-4476. *Fax:* 787-720-2012. *Web site:* http://www.colmizpa.edu/.

Universidad Teológica del Caribe
St. Just, Puerto Rico

- **Independent Pentecostal** 4-year, founded 1956
- **Suburban** 4-acre campus with easy access to San Juan
- **Endowment** $1.0 million
- **Coed** 205 undergraduate students, 57% full-time, 42% women, 58% men

Undergraduates 116 full-time, 89 part-time. Students come from 1 other state; 3 other countries; 1% are from out of state; 98% Hispanic/Latino; 2% international; 15% transferred in. *Retention:* 64% of full-time freshmen returned.
Freshmen *Admission:* 40 admitted, 10 enrolled.
Faculty *Total:* 27, 26% full-time, 26% with terminal degrees. *Student/faculty ratio:* 9:1.
Academics *Calendar:* semesters. *Degree:* certificates, diplomas, and bachelor's. *Special study options:* honors programs, independent study, internships, off-campus study, part-time degree program, services for LD students, summer session for credit.
Computers on Campus 8 computers/terminals and 8 ports are available on campus for general student use. Students can access the following: computer help desk, free student e-mail accounts, online (class) grades, online (class) registration, online (class) schedules. 90% of college-owned or -operated housing units are wired for high-speed Internet access. Wireless service is available via classrooms, computer labs, dorm rooms, libraries, student centers.
Student Life *Housing options:* coed. Campus housing is university owned. *Activities and organizations:* Asociacion Pioneros por Cristo, Asociacion Misionera, Asociacion Ministerial, FESI. *Student services:* personal/psychological counseling.
Costs (2012–13) *One-time required fee:* $13. *Required fees:* $130 per credit hour part-time, $2720 per term part-time. *Room and board:* $2400; room only: $1200. Room and board charges vary according to board plan. *Payment plan:* deferred payment. *Waivers:* employees or children of employees.
Financial Aid Of all full-time matriculated undergraduates who enrolled in 2010, 88 applied for aid, 88 were judged to have need. *Financial aid deadline:* 6/30.
Applying *Options:* electronic application, early admission. *Application fee:* $25. *Required:* letters of recommendation, interview, medical certificate. *Required for some:* high school transcript.
Freshman Application Contact Ms. Abner Cotto, Admissions Officer, Universidad Teológica del Caribe, PO Box 901, Saint Just, PR 00978-901. *Phone:* 787-761-0640 Ext. 246. *Fax:* 787-748-9220. *E-mail:* reclutamiento.utc@gmail.com. *Web site:* http://www.utcpr.edu/.

University of Phoenix–Puerto Rico Campus
Guaynabo, Puerto Rico

Freshman Application Contact Marc Booker, Sr. Director, Office of Admissions and Evaluation, University of Phoenix–Puerto Rico Campus, 4035 South Riverpoint Parkway, Mail Stop CF-L101, Phoenix, AZ 85040. *Phone:* 602-557-4609. *Toll-free phone:* 866-766-0766. *Fax:* 480-643-1156. *Web site:* http://www.phoenix.edu/.

University of Puerto Rico, Aguadilla University College
Aguadilla, Puerto Rico

Director of Admissions Ms. Melba Serrano Lugo, Admissions Officer, University of Puerto Rico, Aguadilla University College, PO Box 6150, Aguadilla, PR 00604. *Phone:* 787-890-2681 Ext. 280. *Web site:* http://www.uprag.edu/.

University of Puerto Rico at Arecibo
Arecibo, Puerto Rico

Freshman Application Contact University of Puerto Rico at Arecibo, PO Box 4010, Arecibo, PR 00613. *Phone:* 787-878-2830 Ext. 4101. *Web site:* http://www.upra.edu/.

University of Puerto Rico at Bayamón
Bayamón, Puerto Rico

- **Commonwealth-supported** 4-year, founded 1971, part of University of Puerto Rico System
- **Urban** 78-acre campus with easy access to San Juan
- **Coed** 4,948 undergraduate students, 87% full-time, 52% women, 48% men
- **Very difficult** entrance level, 30% of applicants were admitted

Undergraduates 4,310 full-time, 638 part-time. 1% are from out of state; 100% Hispanic/Latino; 3% transferred in. *Retention:* 82% of full-time freshmen returned.
Freshmen *Admission:* 4,400 applied, 1,305 admitted, 1,145 enrolled. *Average high school GPA:* 3.51.
Faculty *Total:* 246, 67% full-time, 35% with terminal degrees. *Student/faculty ratio:* 22:1.
Academics *Calendar:* semesters. *Degrees:* associate and bachelor's. *Special study options:* academic remediation for entering students, adult/continuing education programs, advanced placement credit, cooperative education, honors programs, independent study, internships, part-time degree program, services for LD students, summer session for credit. *ROTC:* Army (b), Air Force (c).
Computers on Campus 700 computers/terminals are available on campus for general student use. Students can access the following: campus intranet, free student e-mail accounts, online (class) grades, online (class) schedules. Campuswide network is available. Wireless service is available via entire campus.
Student Life *Activities and organizations:* drama/theater group, choral group, American Marketing Association, Collegiate International Secretaries, Electronic Association, Materials Management Association, Society for Human Resources Management. *Campus security:* 24-hour patrols. *Student services:* health clinic, personal/psychological counseling.
Athletics Member NCAA. *Intercollegiate sports:* baseball M(s), basketball M(s)/W(s), cheerleading M(s)/W(s), cross-country running M(s)/W(s), softball W(s), table tennis M(s)/W(s), tennis M(s)/W(s), track and field M(s)/W(s), volleyball M(s)/W(s), weight lifting M(s)/W(s), wrestling M(s). *Intramural sports:* table tennis M/W, tennis M/W, volleyball M/W.
Standardized Tests *Required:* College Board (for admission).
Costs (2012–13) *Tuition:* commonwealth resident $1802 full-time, $55 per credit part-time; nonresident $3823 full-time, $112 per credit part-time. Full-time tuition and fees vary according to class time, course load, program, and student level. Part-time tuition and fees vary according to class time, course load, program, and student level. No tuition increase for student's term of enrollment. *Required fees:* $1142 full-time. *Payment plan:* deferred payment. *Waivers:* employees or children of employees.
Financial Aid Of all full-time matriculated undergraduates who enrolled in 2010, 213 Federal Work-Study jobs (averaging $1691).
Applying *Options:* electronic application. *Application fee:* $20. *Required:* high school transcript. *Application deadlines:* 12/15 (freshmen), 2/15 (transfers). *Notification:* 5/1 (freshmen), continuous until 7/1 (transfers).
Freshman Application Contact Ms. Carmen I. Montes, Admissions Director, University of Puerto Rico at Bayamón, OPEI Office, Street 174 #170 Minillas Industrial Park, Bayamon, PR 00959. *Phone:* 787-993-8952 Ext. 4015. *Fax:* 787-993-8929. *E-mail:* carmen.montes@upr.edu. *Web site:* http://www.uprb.edu/.

University of Puerto Rico at Carolina
Carolina, Puerto Rico

Director of Admissions Ms. Celia Mendez, Admissions Officer, University of Puerto Rico at Carolina, PO Box 4800, Carolina, PR 00984-4800. *Phone:* 787-757-1485. *Web site:* http://uprc.edu/.

University of Puerto Rico at Humacao
Humacao, Puerto Rico

- **Commonwealth-supported** 4-year, founded 1962, part of University of Puerto Rico System
- **Suburban** 62-acre campus with easy access to San Juan
- **Coed** 3,774 undergraduate students, 92% full-time, 66% women, 34% men
- **Moderately difficult** entrance level, 40% of applicants were admitted

Undergraduates 3,473 full-time, 301 part-time. 0.7% are from out of state; 0.2% Black or African American, non-Hispanic/Latino; 86% Hispanic/Latino; 0.1% Asian, non-Hispanic/Latino; 13% Race/ethnicity unknown; 0.1% international; 0.2% transferred in. *Retention:* 81% of full-time freshmen returned.
Freshmen *Admission:* 1,913 applied, 766 admitted, 658 enrolled. *Average high school GPA:* 3.69. *Test scores:* SAT critical reading scores over 500: 73%; SAT math scores over 500: 68%; SAT critical reading scores over 600:

27%; SAT math scores over 600: 28%; SAT critical reading scores over 700: 2%; SAT math scores over 700: 5%.

Faculty *Total:* 257, 85% full-time, 50% with terminal degrees. *Student/faculty ratio:* 16:1.

Academics *Calendar:* semesters. *Degrees:* associate and bachelor's. *Special study options:* academic remediation for entering students, advanced placement credit, English as a second language, honors programs, internships, part-time degree program, services for LD students, summer session for credit.

Computers on Campus 1,000 computers/terminals are available on campus for general student use. Students can access the following: free student e-mail accounts, online (class) grades, online (class) registration, online (class) schedules. Campuswide network is available. Wireless service is available via libraries, student centers.

Student Life *Activities and organizations:* drama/theater group, student-run radio station, choral group, marching band, Recreational Organization, Accounting Students Association, Management Students Association, Microbiology Students Association, Human Resources Students Association, national fraternities, national sororities. *Campus security:* 24-hour patrols, 24-hour gate security. *Student services:* personal/psychological counseling, women's center.

Athletics *Intercollegiate sports:* baseball M(s), basketball M(s)/W(s), cheerleading M(s)/W(s), cross-country running M(s)/W(s), softball W(s), swimming and diving M(s)/W(s), table tennis M(s)/W(s), tennis W(s), track and field M(s)/W(s), volleyball M(s)/W(s), weight lifting M(s)/W(s), wrestling M(s). *Intramural sports:* basketball M/W, softball W, volleyball M/W.

Standardized Tests *Required:* Pruebas de Evaluacion y Admision Universitaria (PEAU) (for admission). *Required for some:* SAT or ACT (for admission), SAT Subject Tests (for admission).

Costs (2011–12) *Tuition:* commonwealth resident $1802 full-time, $53 per credit hour part-time; nonresident $3824 full-time, $112 per credit hour part-time. Full-time tuition and fees vary according to class time, course load, and student level. Part-time tuition and fees vary according to class time, course load, and student level. No tuition increase for student's term of enrollment. *Required fees:* $1142 full-time. *Room and board:* $8280; room only: $3000. *Payment plan:* deferred payment. *Waivers:* employees or children of employees.

Financial Aid Of all full-time matriculated undergraduates who enrolled in 2001, 3,515 applied for aid, 2,883 were judged to have need, 7 had their need fully met. 278 Federal Work-Study jobs (averaging $1318). *Average percent of need met:* 50%. *Average financial aid package:* $3929. *Average need-based loan:* $3295. *Average need-based gift aid:* $3664. *Average indebtedness upon graduation:* $2749. *Financial aid deadline:* 6/30.

Applying *Options:* deferred entrance. *Application fee:* $20. *Required:* high school transcript. *Required for some:* interview. *Application deadlines:* 1/31 (freshmen), 3/8 (transfers). *Notification:* 4/15 (freshmen), continuous until 6/30 (transfers).

Freshman Application Contact Mrs. Elizabeth Gerena, Director of Admissions, University of Puerto Rico at Humacao, Call Box 860, Humacao, PR 00792. *Phone:* 787-850-9301. *Fax:* 787-850-9428. *E-mail:* elizabeth.gerena@upr.edu. *Web site:* http://www.uprh.edu/.

University of Puerto Rico at Ponce

Ponce, Puerto Rico

- **Commonwealth-supported** 4-year, founded 1970, part of University of Puerto Rico System
- **Urban** 86-acre campus with easy access to San Juan
- **Coed** 2,909 undergraduate students, 95% full-time, 59% women, 41% men
- **Moderately difficult** entrance level, 78% of applicants were admitted

Undergraduates 2,756 full-time, 153 part-time. Students come from 1 other state; 100% Hispanic/Latino; 11% transferred in. *Retention:* 77% of full-time freshmen returned.

Freshmen *Admission:* 1,042 applied, 812 admitted, 615 enrolled. *Average high school GPA:* 3.49.

Faculty *Total:* 178, 80% full-time, 30% with terminal degrees. *Student/faculty ratio:* 16:1.

Academics *Calendar:* semesters. *Degrees:* associate and bachelor's. *Special study options:* academic remediation for entering students, accelerated degree program, advanced placement credit, English as a second language, freshman honors college, honors programs, internships, part-time degree program, summer session for credit. *ROTC:* Army (b).

Computers on Campus 81 computers/terminals and 132 ports are available on campus for general student use. Students can access the following: campus intranet, free student e-mail accounts, online (class) registration, online (class) schedules. Campuswide network is available. Wireless service is available via computer centers, computer labs, learning centers, libraries, student centers.

Student Life *Activities and organizations:* drama/theater group, choral group. *Campus security:* 24-hour patrols. *Student services:* health clinic.

Athletics *Intercollegiate sports:* baseball M(s)/W(s), cross-country running M(s)/W(s), table tennis M/W, tennis M(s), track and field M(s)/W(s), volleyball M(s)/W(s), weight lifting M(s)/W(s). *Intramural sports:* basketball M/W, cross-country running M/W, racquetball M/W, softball M/W, table tennis M/W, tennis M/W, track and field M/W, volleyball M/W, weight lifting M/W.

Standardized Tests *Required:* SAT and SAT Subject Tests or ACT (for admission).

Costs (2012–13) *Tuition:* commonwealth resident $1870 full-time; nonresident $3824 full-time. Full-time tuition and fees vary according to student level. Part-time tuition and fees vary according to student level. No tuition increase for student's term of enrollment. *Required fees:* $949 full-time. *Room and board:* $8280. *Waivers:* employees or children of employees.

Financial Aid Of all full-time matriculated undergraduates who enrolled in 1998, 3,461 applied for aid, 3,133 were judged to have need. *Average percent of need met:* 40%. *Financial aid deadline:* 6/30.

Applying *Options:* early admission. *Application fee:* $20. *Required:* high school transcript. *Application deadlines:* 11/15 (freshmen), 2/23 (transfers). *Notification:* 3/4 (freshmen), continuous until 5/15 (transfers).

Freshman Application Contact University of Puerto Rico at Ponce, PO Box 7186, Ponce, PR 00732-7186. *Phone:* 787-844-8181 Ext. 2533. *Web site:* http://upr-ponce.upr.edu/.

University of Puerto Rico at Utuado

Utuado, Puerto Rico

Freshman Application Contact Mrs. Maria Robles Serrano, Admissions Officer, University of Puerto Rico at Utuado, PO Box 2500, Utuado, PR 00641-2500. *Phone:* 787-894-2828 Ext. 2240. *Web site:* http://www.uprutuado.edu/.

University of Puerto Rico, Cayey University College

Cayey, Puerto Rico

Freshman Application Contact University of Puerto Rico, Cayey University College, 205 Avenue Antonio R. Barcelo, Cayey, PR 00736. *Phone:* 787-738-2161 Ext. 2233. *Web site:* http://www.cayey.upr.edu/.

University of Puerto Rico, Mayagüez Campus

Mayagüez, Puerto Rico

Freshman Application Contact Ms. Sheila Marty-Rodriquez, Director, Admissions Office, University of Puerto Rico, Mayagüez Campus, PO Box 9000, Mayagüez, PR 00681-9000. *Phone:* 787-265-5465. *Fax:* 787-265-5465. *E-mail:* smarty@uprm.edu. *Web site:* http://www.uprm.edu/.

University of Puerto Rico, Medical Sciences Campus

San Juan, Puerto Rico

Freshman Application Contact University of Puerto Rico, Medical Sciences Campus, PO Box 365067, San Juan, PR 00936-5067. *Phone:* 787-758-2525 Ext. 5214. *Web site:* http://www.rcm.upr.edu/.

University of Puerto Rico, Río Piedras

San Juan, Puerto Rico

Freshman Application Contact University of Puerto Rico, Río Piedras, PO Box 23300, San Juan, PR 00931-3300. *Phone:* 787-764-0000 Ext. 85700. *Web site:* http://www.uprrp.edu/.

University of the Sacred Heart

San Juan, Puerto Rico

Director of Admissions Mr. Luis Heviquez, Director of Admissions, University of the Sacred Heart, PO Box 12383, San Juan, PR 00914-0383. *Phone:* 787-728-1515 Ext. 3237. *Web site:* http://www.sagrado.edu/.

VIRGIN ISLANDS

University of the Virgin Islands
Saint Thomas, Virgin Islands

- **Territory-supported** comprehensive, founded 1962
- **Small-town** 518-acre campus
- **Endowment** $26.4 million
- **Coed**
- **Minimally difficult** entrance level

Faculty *Student/faculty ratio:* 17:1.

Academics *Calendar:* semesters. *Degrees:* associate, bachelor's, master's, and post-master's certificates.

Student Life *Campus security:* 24-hour patrols.

Athletics Member NCAA.

Standardized Tests *Required:* SAT or ACT (for admission).

Costs (2011–12) *Tuition:* territory resident $3990 full-time, $133 per credit hour part-time; nonresident $11,970 full-time, $400 per credit hour part-time. Full-time tuition and fees vary according to reciprocity agreements. Part-time tuition and fees vary according to course load and reciprocity agreements. *Required fees:* $604 full-time. *Room and board:* $9386; room only: $3606. Room and board charges vary according to board plan and housing facility.

Financial Aid *Of all full-time matriculated undergraduates who enrolled in 2007,* 1,202 applied for aid, 1,118 were judged to have need, 10 had their need fully met. 39 Federal Work-Study jobs (averaging $2130). 28 state and other part-time jobs (averaging $1900). *In 2007,* 5 non-need-based awards were made. *Average financial aid package:* $4450. *Average need-based loan:* $3240. *Average need-based gift aid:* $3440. *Average non-need-based aid:* $8500. *Average indebtedness upon graduation:* $9480.

Applying *Options:* electronic application, early admission, deferred entrance. *Application fee:* $25. *Recommended:* high school transcript, minimum 2.0 GPA.

Freshman Application Contact Dr. Xuri Maurice Allen, Director of Admissions/Recruitment, University of the Virgin Islands, University of the Virgin Islands, #2 John Brewers Bay, St. Thomas, VI 00802. *Phone:* 340-693-1224. *Fax:* 340-693-1167. *E-mail:* xallen@uvi.edu. *Web site:* http://www.uvi.edu/.

CANADA

CANADA

Acadia University
Wolfville, Nova Scotia, Canada

- **Province-supported** comprehensive, founded 1838
- **Small-town** 250-acre campus
- **Coed** 3,294 undergraduate students, 95% full-time, 58% women, 42% men
- **Moderately difficult** entrance level, 30% of applicants were admitted

Undergraduates 3,136 full-time, 158 part-time. Students come from 13 provinces and territories; 43 other countries; 45% are from out of state; 5% transferred in; 50% live on campus. *Retention:* 81% of full-time freshmen returned.

Freshmen *Admission:* 3,898 applied, 1,153 admitted, 832 enrolled.

Faculty *Total:* 298, 62% full-time, 59% with terminal degrees. *Student/faculty ratio:* 11:1.

Academics *Calendar:* Canadian standard year. *Degrees:* bachelor's and master's. *Special study options:* academic remediation for entering students, advanced placement credit, cooperative education, distance learning, double majors, English as a second language, honors programs, internships, off-campus study, part-time degree program, study abroad, summer session for credit.

Computers on Campus 7,000 ports are available on campus for general student use. Students can access the following: campus intranet, computer help desk, free student e-mail accounts, online (class) grades, online (class) registration, online (class) schedules. Campuswide network is available. 100% of college-owned or -operated housing units are wired for high-speed Internet access. Wireless service is available via learning centers, libraries, student centers.

Student Life *Housing options:* coed, women-only. Campus housing is university owned. Freshman campus housing is guaranteed. *Activities and organizations:* drama/theater group, student-run newspaper, radio station, choral group, Dance Acadia, Power Cheerleading, Water Watch Canada, LINC, Biology. *Campus security:* 24-hour emergency response devices and patrols, student patrols, late-night transport/escort service, controlled dormitory access, video surveillance, emergency response, emergency notification, emergency management planning. *Student services:* health clinic, personal/psychological counseling, women's center, legal services.

Athletics Member CIS. *Intercollegiate sports:* basketball M(s)/W(s), cross-country running W, football M(s), ice hockey M(s), rugby W(s), soccer M(s)/W(s), swimming and diving M(s)/W(s), track and field W, volleyball W.

Costs (2011–12) *One-time required fee:* $477. *Tuition:* province resident $6384 full-time, $789 per course part-time; nonresident $7406 full-time, $891 per course part-time; International tuition $14,142 full-time. Full-time tuition and fees vary according to course level, course load, degree level, and program. Part-time tuition and fees vary according to course level, course load, degree level, and program. *Required fees:* $238 full-time, $10 per course part-time. *Room and board:* $8537; room only: $4750. Room and board charges vary according to board plan and housing facility. *Payment plan:* installment. *Waivers:* senior citizens and employees or children of employees.

Applying *Options:* electronic application, deferred entrance. *Application fee:* $25 Canadian dollars. *Required:* high school transcript, minimum 2.5 GPA. *Required for some:* essay or personal statement, 1 letter of recommendation, interview. *Application deadlines:* 7/1 (freshmen), 7/1 (out-of-state freshmen), 7/1 (transfers). *Notification:* continuous (freshmen), continuous (out-of-state freshmen), continuous (transfers).

Freshman Application Contact Ms. Anne Scott, Manager of Admissions, Acadia University, Wolfville, NS B4P 2R6, Canada. *Phone:* 902-585-1016. *Toll-free phone:* 877-585-1121. *Fax:* 902-585-1092. *E-mail:* admissions@acadiau.ca. *Web site:* http://www.acadiau.ca/.

Alberta Bible College
Calgary, Alberta, Canada

Director of Admissions Brad Olorenshaw, Recruitment Officer, Alberta Bible College, 635 Northmount Drive, NW, Calgary, AB T2K 3J6, Canada. *Phone:* 403-282-2994 Ext. 225. *Toll-free phone:* 877-542-9492. *E-mail:* admissions@abccampus.ca. *Web site:* http://www.abccampus.ca/.

Alberta College of Art & Design
Calgary, Alberta, Canada

- **Province-supported** 4-year, founded 1926
- **Urban** 1-acre campus
- **Endowment** $5.5 million
- **Coed** 1,206 undergraduate students, 90% full-time, 69% women, 31% men
- **Moderately difficult** entrance level, 55% of applicants were admitted

Undergraduates 1,091 full-time, 115 part-time. Students come from 10 provinces and territories; 20 other countries; 12% are from out of state; 96% Race/ethnicity unknown; 4% international; 3% transferred in; 9% live on campus. *Retention:* 72% of full-time freshmen returned.

Freshmen *Admission:* 584 applied, 323 admitted, 304 enrolled.

Faculty *Total:* 128, 36% full-time, 34% with terminal degrees. *Student/faculty ratio:* 17:1.

Academics *Calendar:* semesters. *Degree:* bachelor's. *Special study options:* academic remediation for entering students, adult/continuing education programs, advanced placement credit, independent study, internships, part-time degree program, services for LD students, study abroad, summer session for credit.

Computers on Campus 103 computers/terminals are available on campus for general student use. Students can access the following: campus intranet, computer help desk, free student e-mail accounts, online (class) grades, online (class) registration, online (class) schedules. Campuswide network is available. 100% of college-owned or -operated housing units are wired for high-speed Internet access. Wireless service is available via entire campus.

Student Life *Housing options:* coed, disabled students. Campus housing is provided by a third party. *Activities and organizations:* The Rendez-Vous Collective, Team NCECA, Arts Mob, Anime and Gaming Club, Feminist Book Club. *Campus security:* 24-hour emergency response devices and patrols, late-night transport/escort service, controlled dormitory access. *Student services:* health clinic, personal/psychological counseling.

Athletics *Intercollegiate sports:* basketball M/W, cross-country running M/W, ice hockey M/W, soccer M/W, volleyball M/W. *Intramural sports:* basketball M/W, bowling M/W, ice hockey M/W, soccer M/W, softball M/W, volleyball M/W.

Costs (2012–13) *Tuition:* province resident $4434 full-time, $148 per credit part-time; nonresident $468 per credit part-time; International tuition $14,044 full-time. Full-time tuition and fees vary according to course load, program, and student level. Part-time tuition and fees vary according to course load, program, and student level. *Required fees:* $830 full-time, $202 per term part-time. *Room only:* $5640. Room and board charges vary according to housing facility. *Waivers:* senior citizens.

Applying *Options:* electronic application, early decision. *Application fee:* $85 Canadian dollars. *Required:* essay or personal statement, high school transcript, minimum 2.0 GPA, portfolio of artwork. *Application deadlines:* 2/1 (freshmen), 2/1 (out-of-state freshmen), 3/1 (transfers). *Notification:* 3/15 (freshmen), 3/15 (out-of-state freshmen), 4/15 (transfers).

Freshman Application Contact Ms. Katie Potapoff, Admissions Officer, Alberta College of Art & Design, 1407-14 Avenue NW, Calgary, AB T2N 4R3, Canada. *Phone:* 403-284-7617. *Toll-free phone:* 800-251-8290. *Fax:* 403-284-7644. *E-mail:* admissions@acad.ca. *Web site:* http://www.acad.ca/.

Ambrose University College

Calgary, Alberta, Canada

Director of Admissions Admissions Officer, Ambrose University College, 630, 833 4th Avenue, SW, Calgary, AB T2P 3T5, Canada. *Toll-free phone:* 800-461-1222. *E-mail:* enrolment@ambrose.edu. *Web site:* http://www.ambrose.edu/.

Athabasca University

Athabasca, Alberta, Canada

- **Province-supported** comprehensive, founded 1970
- **Small-town** 480-acre campus
- **Endowment** $1.0 million
- **Coed** 35,071 undergraduate students, 68% women, 32% men
- **Noncompetitive** entrance level

Undergraduates 35,071 part-time. Students come from 33 provinces and territories; 87 other countries; 63% are from out of state.

Faculty *Total:* 384.

Academics *Calendar:* continuous. *Degrees:* certificates, diplomas, bachelor's, master's, doctoral, post-master's, and postbachelor's certificates (offers only external degree programs). *Special study options:* academic remediation for entering students, accelerated degree program, adult/continuing education programs, advanced placement credit, distance learning, double majors, English as a second language, external degree program, independent study, off-campus study, part-time degree program, services for LD students, student-designed majors, study abroad, summer session for credit.

Computers on Campus 28 computers/terminals are available on campus for general student use. Students can access the following: online (class) registration. Campuswide network is available.

Student Life *Housing:* college housing not available. *Activities and organizations:* student-run newspaper. *Campus security:* 24-hour emergency response devices.

Costs (2011–12) *Tuition:* province resident $646 Canadian dollars per course part-time; nonresident $751 Canadian dollars per course part-time. Full-time tuition and fees vary according to degree level. Part-time tuition and fees vary according to degree level. *Waivers:* senior citizens and employees or children of employees.

Applying *Options:* electronic application. *Application fee:* $60 Canadian dollars. *Application deadlines:* rolling (freshmen), rolling (transfers). *Notification:* continuous (freshmen), continuous (transfers).

Freshman Application Contact Information Centre, Athabasca University, 1 University Drive, Athabasca, AB T9S 3A3, Canada. *Phone:* 800-788-9041. *Toll-free phone:* 800-788-9041. *Fax:* 780-675-6437. *Web site:* http://www.athabascau.ca/.

Bishop's University

Sherbrooke, Quebec, Canada

- **Province-supported** comprehensive, founded 1843, part of Association of Universities and Colleges of Canada (AUCC)
- **Small-town** 500-acre campus
- **Coed**
- **Moderately difficult** entrance level

Undergraduates Students come from 20 provinces and territories; 40 other countries.

Faculty *Student/faculty ratio:* 15:1.

Academics *Calendar:* semesters most students study from September to late April. Spring semester is May-June. *Degrees:* certificates, bachelor's, and master's. *Special study options:* adult/continuing education programs, double majors, honors programs, part-time degree program, study abroad.

Computers on Campus 650 computers/terminals are available on campus for general student use. Students can access the following: campus intranet, computer help desk, free student e-mail accounts, online (class) registration, online (class) schedules, Web course management systems, individualized Web access. Campuswide network is available. Wireless service is available via entire campus.

Student Life *Housing options:* coed, women-only, disabled students. Campus housing is university owned. Freshman campus housing is guaranteed. *Campus security:* 24-hour emergency response devices and patrols, student patrols, late-night transport/escort service, controlled dormitory access.

Athletics Member CIS. *Intercollegiate sports:* basketball M/W, field hockey W(c), football M, golf M, ice hockey W(c), lacrosse M(c)/W(c), rock climbing M/W, skiing (downhill) M/W, soccer W, volleyball W(c). *Intramural sports:* badminton M/W, basketball M/W, cross-country running M/W, equestrian sports M(c)/W(c), football M, golf M/W, ice hockey M/W, riflery M(c)/W(c), soccer M/W, softball M/W, squash M/W, swimming and diving M/W, table tennis M/W, tennis M/W, ultimate Frisbee M/W, volleyball M/W, water polo M/W, weight lifting M/W.

Standardized Tests *Required:* SAT or ACT (for admission).

Applying *Options:* electronic application, early admission, deferred entrance. *Application fee:* $60 Canadian dollars. *Required:* high school transcript, minimum 3.0 GPA, birth certificate, copy of student visa. *Required for some:* essay or personal statement. *Recommended:* essay or personal statement. *Application deadlines:* 3/1 (freshmen), 3/1 (transfers). *Notification:* continuous (freshmen), continuous (transfers).

Freshman Application Contact Mrs. Jacqueline Belleau, Coordinator of Student Recruitment, Bishop's University, 2600 College Street, Sherbrooke, QC J1M 0C8, Canada. *Phone:* 819-822-9600 Ext. 2691. *Toll-free phone:* 877-822-8200. *Fax:* 819-822-9661. *E-mail:* recruitment@ubishops.ca. *Web site:* http://www.ubishops.ca/.

Booth University College

Winnipeg, Manitoba, Canada

Director of Admissions Chantel Burt, Director of Admission, Booth University College, 447 Webb Place, Winnipeg, MB R3B 2P2, Canada. *Phone:* 204-924-4867. *Toll-free phone:* 877-942-6684. *E-mail:* cburt@boothcollege.ca. *Web site:* http://www.boothuc.ca/.

Brandon University

Brandon, Manitoba, Canada

Freshman Application Contact Murray Kerr, Director of Admissions, Brandon University, 270 18th Street, Brandon, MB R7A 6A9, Canada. *Phone:* 204-727-7352. *Toll-free phone:* 800-644-7644. *Fax:* 204-728-3221. *E-mail:* kerr@brandonu.ca. *Web site:* http://www.brandonu.ca/.

Briercrest College

Caronport, Saskatchewan, Canada

- **Independent interdenominational** 4-year, founded 1935, part of Briercrest College and Seminary
- **Rural** 300-acre campus
- **Endowment** $1.4 million
- **Coed** 240 undergraduate students, 99% full-time, 53% women, 47% men
- **Noncompetitive** entrance level, 57% of applicants were admitted

Undergraduates 237 full-time, 3 part-time. Students come from 13 provinces and territories; 3 other countries; 0.1% are from out of state; 6% transferred in; 14% live on campus. *Retention:* 40% of full-time freshmen returned.

Freshmen *Admission:* 416 applied, 239 admitted, 196 enrolled.

Faculty *Total:* 52, 50% full-time, 62% with terminal degrees. *Student/faculty ratio:* 22:1.

Academics *Calendar:* semesters. *Degrees:* certificates, diplomas, associate, and bachelor's. *Special study options:* academic remediation for entering students, accelerated degree program, adult/continuing education programs, distance learning, double majors, English as a second language, external degree program, independent study, internships, off-campus study, part-time degree program, study abroad, summer session for credit. *Unusual degree programs:* 3-2 business administration; social work with Minot State University; education, addictions studies, and communication disorders with Minot State University.

Computers on Campus 21 computers/terminals are available on campus for general student use. Students can access the following: online (class) grades,

online (class) registration, online (class) schedules. Campuswide network is available. Wireless service is available via classrooms, computer centers, computer labs, dorm rooms, learning centers, libraries, student centers.

Student Life *Housing:* on-campus residence required through junior year. *Options:* men-only, women-only. Campus housing is university owned. Freshman campus housing is guaranteed. *Activities and organizations:* drama/theater group, choral group. *Campus security:* 24-hour patrols, controlled dormitory access. *Student services:* health clinic, personal/psychological counseling, legal services.

Athletics *Intercollegiate sports:* basketball M/W, ice hockey M, volleyball M/W. *Intramural sports:* basketball M/W, ice hockey M/W, soccer M/W, volleyball M/W.

Standardized Tests *Required for some:* SAT or ACT (for admission).

Costs (2012–13) *Comprehensive fee:* $14,064 Canadian dollars includes full-time tuition ($8310 Canadian dollars), mandatory fees ($150 Canadian dollars), and room and board ($5604 Canadian dollars). Full-time tuition and fees vary according to course load. Part-time tuition: $277 Canadian dollars per credit. Part-time tuition and fees vary according to course load. *Required fees:* $277 Canadian dollars per term part-time. *College room only:* $3488 Canadian dollars. Room and board charges vary according to board plan, housing facility, and location. *Payment plan:* installment.

Applying *Options:* electronic application, deferred entrance. *Application fee:* $50 Canadian dollars. *Required:* essay or personal statement, high school transcript, 1 letter of recommendation, statement of faith. *Required for some:* interview. *Application deadlines:* 8/15 (freshmen), 8/15 (transfers). *Notification:* continuous until 9/1 (freshmen), continuous until 9/1 (transfers).

Freshman Application Contact Mrs. Jennifer Johnson, Acting Manager, Admissions, Briercrest College, 510 College Drive, Caronport, SK S0H 0S0, Canada. *Phone:* 306-756-3200. *Toll-free phone:* 800-667-5199. *Fax:* 800-667.5199. *E-mail:* admissions@briercrest.ca. *Web site:* http://www.briercrest.ca/.

British Columbia Institute of Technology

Burnaby, British Columbia, Canada

Freshman Application Contact Ms. Anna Dosen, Supervisor of Admissions, British Columbia Institute of Technology, 3700 Willingdon Avenue, Burnaby, BC V5G 3H2, Canada. *Phone:* 604-432-8496. *Toll-free phone:* 866-434-1610. *Fax:* 604-431-6917. *Web site:* http://www.bcit.ca/.

Brock University

St. Catharines, Ontario, Canada

- **Province-supported** university, founded 1964
- **Urban** 540-acre campus with easy access to Toronto, ON and Buffalo, NY
- **Coed**

Faculty *Student/faculty ratio:* 30:1.

Academics *Calendar:* Canadian standard year. *Degrees:* certificates, bachelor's, master's, doctoral, and first professional.

Student Life *Campus security:* 24-hour emergency response devices and patrols, student patrols, late-night transport/escort service, controlled dormitory access.

Athletics Member CIS.

Standardized Tests *Required:* SAT or ACT (for admission).

Applying *Options:* electronic application. *Required:* high school transcript. *Required for some:* essay or personal statement, interview, audition for Dramatic Arts and Music programs, profile questionnaire for Concurrent Education programs. *Recommended:* minimum 3.0 GPA.

Freshman Application Contact Mrs. Lynn Thompson-Dovi, International Admissions Officer, Brock University, 500 Glenridge Avenue, L2S 3A1, Canada. *Phone:* 905-688-5550 Ext. 3431. *Fax:* 905-688-5488. *E-mail:* admissns@brocku.ca. *Web site:* http://www.brocku.ca/.

Canadian Mennonite University

Winnipeg, Manitoba, Canada

Freshman Application Contact Mr. Abe Bergen, Director of Enrollment Services, Canadian Mennonite University, 500 Shaftesbury Boulevard, Winnipeg, MB R3P 2N2, Canada. *Phone:* 204-487-3300 Ext. 652. *Toll-free phone:* 877-231-4570. *Fax:* 204-487-3858. *E-mail:* cu@cmu.ca. *Web site:* http://www.cmu.ca/.

Cape Breton University

Sydney, Nova Scotia, Canada

- **Province-supported** comprehensive, founded 1974
- **Urban** campus
- **Coed** 2,623 undergraduate students
- **Moderately difficult** entrance level

Undergraduates 24% live on campus. *Retention:* 74% of full-time freshmen returned.

Faculty *Total:* 129, 91% with terminal degrees.

Academics *Calendar:* semesters. *Degrees:* certificates, diplomas, bachelor's, and master's.

Computers on Campus Students can access the following: computer help desk, free student e-mail accounts, online (class) grades, online (class) registration, online (class) schedules. Campuswide network is available. 100% of college-owned or -operated housing units are wired for high-speed Internet access. Wireless service is available via entire campus.

Student Life *Housing options:* coed. Campus housing is university owned. *Campus security:* 24-hour emergency response devices and patrols, student patrols, late-night transport/escort service, controlled dormitory access.

Athletics Member CIS. *Intercollegiate sports:* basketball M/W, ice hockey W(c), rugby M(c), soccer M/W, volleyball W. *Intramural sports:* badminton M(c)/W(c), baseball M(c), basketball M/W, soccer M/W.

Costs (2011–12) *Tuition:* province resident $5107 full-time; nonresident $6129 full-time; International tuition $12,220 full-time. Full-time tuition and fees vary according to course load, degree level, and program. Part-time tuition and fees vary according to course load, degree level, and program. *Room and board:* $7300; room only: $3600. Room and board charges vary according to board plan and housing facility. *Payment plan:* installment. *Waivers:* senior citizens and employees or children of employees.

Applying *Options:* early admission, deferred entrance. *Application fee:* $35 Canadian dollars. *Required:* high school transcript. *Required for some:* essay or personal statement, 3 letters of recommendation, interview. *Application deadlines:* 8/1 (freshmen), rolling (transfers). *Notification:* continuous (freshmen), continuous (transfers).

Freshman Application Contact Cape Breton University, Box 5300, 1250 Grand Lake Road, Sydney, NS B1P 6L2, Canada. *Phone:* 902-563-1117. *Toll-free phone:* 888-959-9995. *Web site:* http://www.cbu.ca/.

Carleton University

Ottawa, Ontario, Canada

Freshman Application Contact Ms. Jean Mullan, Director, Undergraduate Recruitment Office, Carleton University, 1125 Colonel By Drive, Ottawa, ON K1S 5B6, Canada. *Phone:* 613-520-3663. *Toll-free phone:* 888-354-4414. *E-mail:* liaison@admissions.carleton.ca. *Web site:* http://www.carleton.ca/.

Centennial College

Scarborough, Ontario, Canada

- **Province-supported** 4-year, part of Ontario College Application System
- **Urban** campus with easy access to Greater Toronto Area
- **Coed**

Academics *Degree:* certificates, diplomas, and bachelor's.

Computers on Campus Campuswide network is available. Wireless service is available via entire campus.

Student Life *Housing options:* Campus housing is university owned. *Campus security:* 24-hour emergency response devices and patrols.

Applying *Options:* electronic application. *Application fee:* $95 Canadian dollars. *Required:* high school transcript.

Freshman Application Contact Enrolment Services, Centennial College, PO Box 631, Station 'A', Scarborough, ON M1K 5E9, Canada. *Phone:* 416-289-5325. *Toll-free phone:* 800-268-4419. *E-mail:* success@centennialcollege.ca. *Web site:* http://www.centennialcollege.ca/.

Collège Dominicain de Philosophie et de Théologie

Ottawa, Ontario, Canada

Freshman Application Contact Fr. Herve Tremblay OP, Registrar, Collège Dominicain de Philosophie et de Théologie, 96 Empress Avenue, Ottawa, ON K1R 7G3, Canada. *Phone:* 613-233-5696 Ext. 308. *Fax:* 613-233-6064. *E-mail:* registraire@collegedominicain.ca. *Web site:* http://www.collegedominicain.ca/.

Collège universitaire de Saint-Boniface
Saint-Boniface, Manitoba, Canada

Admissions Office Contact Collège universitaire de Saint-Boniface, 200 avenue de la Cathèdrale, Saint-Boniface, MB R2H 0H7, Canada. *Web site:* http://www.ustboniface.mb.ca/.

Columbia Bible College
Abbotsford, British Columbia, Canada

- **Independent Mennonite Brethren** 4-year, founded 1936
- **Urban** 9-acre campus with easy access to Vancouver
- **Endowment** $638,611
- **Coed** 478 undergraduate students
- **Noncompetitive** entrance level, 78% of applicants were admitted

Undergraduates Students come from 9 provinces and territories; 7 other countries; 19% are from out of state; 34% live on campus. *Retention:* 75% of full-time freshmen returned.
Freshmen *Admission:* 258 applied, 201 admitted.
Faculty *Total:* 47, 30% full-time, 13% with terminal degrees. *Student/faculty ratio:* 18:1.
Academics *Calendar:* semesters. *Degree:* certificates, diplomas, and bachelor's. *Special study options:* academic remediation for entering students, advanced placement credit, distance learning, independent study, internships, off-campus study, part-time degree program, services for LD students, study abroad.
Computers on Campus 30 computers/terminals are available on campus for general student use. Students can access the following: campus intranet, online (class) grades, online (class) schedules. Campuswide network is available. 85% of college-owned or -operated housing units are wired for high-speed Internet access. Wireless service is available via classrooms, computer labs, dorm rooms, libraries, student centers.
Student Life *Housing:* on-campus residence required through sophomore year. *Options:* men-only, women-only. Campus housing is university owned and leased by the school. Freshman applicants given priority for college housing. *Activities and organizations:* choral group. *Campus security:* late-night transport/escort service, controlled dormitory access, night watchman 11 pm to 6 am. *Student services:* personal/psychological counseling.
Athletics *Intercollegiate sports:* basketball M/W, soccer M/W, volleyball M/W.
Costs (2012–13) *Comprehensive fee:* $14,180 includes full-time tuition ($8970) and room and board ($5210). Full-time tuition and fees vary according to course load. Part-time tuition: $299 per credit. Part-time tuition and fees vary according to course load. *Room and board:* Room and board charges vary according to board plan. *Payment plans:* installment, deferred payment. *Waivers:* senior citizens and employees or children of employees.
Financial Aid *Financial aid deadline:* 5/15.
Applying *Options:* electronic application, early admission, early decision, deferred entrance. *Application fee:* $50. *Required:* essay or personal statement, high school transcript, minimum 2.0 GPA, 2 letters of recommendation, must be Christian. *Required for some:* interview. *Application deadlines:* 8/15 (freshmen), 8/15 (out-of-state freshmen), 8/15 (transfers). *Early decision deadline:* 5/1. *Notification:* continuous (freshmen), continuous (out-of-state freshmen), continuous (transfers).
Freshman Application Contact Candice Green, Director of Admissions, Columbia Bible College, 2940 Clearbrook Road, Abbotsford, BC V2T 2Z8, Canada. *Phone:* 604-853-3358 Ext. 309. *Toll-free phone:* 800-283-0881. *Fax:* 604-853-3063. *E-mail:* candice.green@columbiabc.edu. *Web site:* http://www.columbiabc.edu/.

Concordia University
Montréal, Quebec, Canada

- **Province-supported** university, founded 1974, part of Quebec University Network
- **Urban** 52-acre campus with easy access to Montreal
- **Endowment** $81.5 million
- **Coed** 30,049 undergraduate students, 66% full-time, 52% women, 48% men
- **Moderately difficult** entrance level, 68% of applicants were admitted

Undergraduates 19,756 full-time, 10,293 part-time. Students come from 13 provinces and territories; 145 other countries; 11% are from out of state; 2% live on campus. *Retention:* 84% of full-time freshmen returned.
Freshmen *Admission:* 14,373 applied, 9,725 admitted, 5,309 enrolled.
Faculty *Total:* 1,637, 59% full-time. *Student/faculty ratio:* 23:1.

Academics *Calendar:* semesters. *Degrees:* certificates, diplomas, bachelor's, master's, doctoral, postbachelor's, and first professional certificates. *Special study options:* academic remediation for entering students, accelerated degree program, adult/continuing education programs, advanced placement credit, cooperative education, distance learning, double majors, English as a second language, honors programs, independent study, internships, off-campus study, part-time degree program, services for LD students, student-designed majors, study abroad, summer session for credit.
Computers on Campus 350 computers/terminals and 3,000 ports are available on campus for general student use. Students can access the following: campus intranet, computer help desk, free student e-mail accounts, online (class) grades, online (class) registration, online (class) schedules, specialized software applications. Campuswide network is available. 67% of college-owned or -operated housing units are wired for high-speed Internet access. Wireless service is available via classrooms, computer centers, computer labs, learning centers, libraries, student centers.
Student Life *Housing options:* coed, men-only, women-only, disabled students. Campus housing is university owned. Freshman applicants given priority for college housing. *Activities and organizations:* drama/theater group, student-run newspaper, radio and television station, choral group, undergraduate student union, departmental clubs, religious clubs, ethnic clubs, social action groups, national fraternities, national sororities. *Campus security:* 24-hour emergency response devices and patrols, student patrols, late-night transport/escort service, controlled dormitory access. *Student services:* health clinic, personal/psychological counseling, women's center.
Athletics Member CIS. *Intercollegiate sports:* baseball M, basketball M(s)/W(s), cross-country running M(c)/W(c), football M(s), golf M(c)/W(c), ice hockey M(s)/W(s), rugby M(s)/W(s), skiing (downhill) M(c)/W(c), soccer M(s)/W(s), wrestling M(s)/W(s). *Intramural sports:* basketball M/W, cross-country running M/W, ice hockey M/W, soccer M/W, ultimate Frisbee M/W, volleyball M/W.
Costs (2011–12) *Tuition:* province resident $2168 Canadian dollars full-time, $72 Canadian dollars per credit part-time; nonresident $5858 Canadian dollars full-time, $195 Canadian dollars per credit part-time; International tuition $16,260 Canadian dollars full-time. Full-time tuition and fees vary according to course load. Part-time tuition and fees vary according to course load. *Required fees:* $1369 Canadian dollars full-time, $38 Canadian dollars per credit part-time, $28 Canadian dollars per term part-time. *Room and board:* $7066 Canadian dollars. Room and board charges vary according to board plan, housing facility, and location. *Payment plan:* installment. *Waivers:* senior citizens and employees or children of employees.
Financial Aid Of all full-time matriculated undergraduates who enrolled in 2010, 349 state and other part-time jobs (averaging $1286). *Financial aid deadline:* 3/31.
Applying *Options:* electronic application, deferred entrance. *Application fee:* $100 Canadian dollars. *Required:* high school transcript, minimum 2.5 GPA. *Required for some:* essay or personal statement, minimum 2.9 GPA, 2 letters of recommendation, interview, portfolio/auditions required for Performing and Visual Arts, Communications and Journalism require interview/essay/portfolio. *Application deadlines:* 3/1 (freshmen), 3/1 (out-of-state freshmen), 3/1 (transfers). *Notification:* continuous (freshmen), continuous (transfers).
Freshman Application Contact Ms. Ilze Kraulis, Associate Registrar, Concordia University, 1455 de Maisonneuve Boulevard West, Building LB-719-2, Montreal, QC H3G 1M8, Canada. *Phone:* 514-848-2424 Ext. 2628. *Fax:* 514-848-2621. *E-mail:* ijkrau@alcor.concordia.ca. *Web site:* http://www.concordia.ca/.

Concordia University College of Alberta
Edmonton, Alberta, Canada

Freshman Application Contact Student and Enrollment Services, Concordia University College of Alberta, 7128 Ada Boulevard, Edmonton, AB T5B 4E4, Canada. *Phone:* 780-479-9220. *Toll-free phone:* 866-479-5200. *Fax:* 780-378-8460. *E-mail:* admits@concordia.ab.ca. *Web site:* http://www.concordia.ab.ca/.

Crandall University
Moncton, New Brunswick, Canada

- **Independent Baptist** 4-year, founded 1949
- **Urban** 220-acre campus
- **Coed** 719 undergraduate students, 90% full-time, 66% women, 34% men
- **Minimally difficult** entrance level, 89% of applicants were admitted

Undergraduates 648 full-time, 71 part-time. Students come from 11 provinces and territories; 3 other countries; 15% are from out of state; 4% transferred in; 22% live on campus. *Retention:* 71% of full-time freshmen returned.

Freshmen *Admission:* 207 applied, 185 admitted, 99 enrolled. *Average high school GPA:* 2.67.

Faculty *Total:* 60. *Student/faculty ratio:* 17:1.

Academics *Calendar:* semesters. *Degrees:* certificates, bachelor's, post-master's, and postbachelor's certificates. *Special study options:* accelerated degree program, adult/continuing education programs, advanced placement credit, cooperative education, double majors, English as a second language, honors programs, internships, off-campus study, part-time degree program, summer session for credit.

Computers on Campus Students can access the following: campus intranet, computer help desk, free student e-mail accounts, online (class) schedules. Campuswide network is available. 100% of college-owned or -operated housing units are wired for high-speed Internet access. Wireless service is available via entire campus.

Student Life *Housing options:* men-only, women-only, disabled students. Campus housing is university owned. *Activities and organizations:* drama/theater group, student-run newspaper, choral group, Student Association, Business Society, intramurals, debate team, International Student Association. *Campus security:* 24-hour emergency response devices, student patrols, controlled dormitory access.

Athletics *Intercollegiate sports:* baseball M, basketball M/W, cross-country running M/W, soccer M/W. *Intramural sports:* badminton M/W, basketball M/W, football M/W, golf M/W, ice hockey M, skiing (downhill) M/W, soccer M/W, softball M/W, table tennis M/W, volleyball M/W, weight lifting M/W.

Costs *(2012–13)* *Comprehensive fee:* $14,296 includes full-time tuition ($7395), mandatory fees ($775), and room and board ($6126). *Part-time tuition:* $775 per course. *College room only:* $2686. Room and board charges vary according to board plan and housing facility. *Waivers:* employees or children of employees.

Financial Aid *Financial aid deadline:* 5/15.

Applying *Options:* electronic application, early admission, early decision, deferred entrance. *Application fee:* $35 Canadian dollars. *Required:* high school transcript, minimum 2.7 GPA, 3 letters of recommendation. *Required for some:* essay or personal statement, interview. *Application deadlines:* rolling (freshmen), rolling (transfers). *Early decision deadline:* 11/30. *Notification:* 9/15 (freshmen), continuous until 9/15 (transfers), 12/31 (early decision).

Freshman Application Contact Mrs. Laura Lutes, Administrative Officer-Admissions and Recruitment, Crandall University, Box 6004, Moncton, NB E1C 9L7, Canada. *Phone:* 506-858-8970 Ext. 6433. *Toll-free phone:* 888-YOU-N-ABU. *Fax:* 506-858-9694. *E-mail:* Laura.lutes@crandallu.ca. *Web site:* http://www.crandallu.ca/.

Dalhousie University

Halifax, Nova Scotia, Canada

- **Province-supported** university, founded 1818
- **Urban** 80-acre campus
- **Endowment** $335.9 million
- **Coed** 13,356 undergraduate students, 90% full-time, 55% women, 45% men
- **Moderately difficult** entrance level

Undergraduates 11,988 full-time, 1,368 part-time. Students come from 13 provinces and territories; 98 other countries.

Faculty *Student/faculty ratio:* 14:1.

Academics *Calendar:* semesters. *Degrees:* diplomas, bachelor's, master's, doctoral, postbachelor's, and first professional certificates. *Special study options:* academic remediation for entering students, accelerated degree program, advanced placement credit, cooperative education, distance learning, double majors, English as a second language, honors programs, internships, off-campus study, part-time degree program, services for LD students, study abroad, summer session for credit.

Computers on Campus 710 computers/terminals are available on campus for general student use. Students can access the following: campus intranet, computer help desk, free student e-mail accounts, online (class) grades, online (class) registration, online (class) schedules. Campuswide network is available. 100% of college-owned or -operated housing units are wired for high-speed Internet access. Wireless service is available via entire campus.

Student Life *Housing options:* coed, women-only, disabled students. Campus housing is university owned. Freshman applicants given priority for college housing. *Activities and organizations:* drama/theater group, student-run newspaper, radio station, choral group, International Students Association, Arts Society, Science Society, Commerce Society, Dalhousie Outdoors Club, national fraternities, national sororities. *Campus security:* 24-hour emergency response devices and patrols, student patrols, late-night transport/escort service, controlled dormitory access. *Student services:* health clinic, personal/psychological counseling, women's center, legal services.

Athletics Member CIS. *Intercollegiate sports:* basketball M/W, cross-country running M/W, field hockey W(c), ice hockey M/W, soccer M/W, swimming and diving M/W, track and field M/W, volleyball M/W. *Intramural sports:* badminton M(c)/W(c), baseball M(c), basketball M/W, crew M(c)/W(c), cross-country running M/W, fencing M(c)/W(c), field hockey W, football M/W, golf M/W, gymnastics M/W, ice hockey M, lacrosse M, racquetball M/W, rugby M(c)/W(c), sailing M(c)/W(c), skiing (cross-country) M/W, skiing (downhill) M/W, soccer M/W, softball M/W, squash M(c)/W(c), swimming and diving M(c)/W(c), tennis M/W, track and field M/W, ultimate Frisbee M/W, volleyball M/W, water polo M/W, weight lifting M/W, wrestling M(c)/W(c).

Standardized Tests *Required:* SAT or ACT (for admission).

Costs *(2012–13)* *Tuition:* province resident $7100 Canadian dollars full-time; nonresident $7100 Canadian dollars full-time; International tuition $15,090 Canadian dollars full-time. Full-time tuition and fees vary according to course load, degree level, and program. Part-time tuition and fees vary according to course load, degree level, and program. *Room and board:* $8900 Canadian dollars. Room and board charges vary according to board plan, housing facility, and location. *Waivers:* minority students, senior citizens, and employees or children of employees.

Applying *Options:* electronic application, early admission, early decision, deferred entrance. *Application fee:* $65 Canadian dollars. *Required:* high school transcript, minimum 3.0 GPA. *Required for some:* essay or personal statement, 1 letter of recommendation, interview. *Application deadlines:* 6/1 (freshmen), 6/1 (transfers). *Early decision deadline:* 3/15. *Notification:* continuous (freshmen), continuous (transfers), rolling (early decision).

Freshman Application Contact Mairead Barry, Associate Registrar and Director of Admissions, Dalhousie University, Office of the Registrar, Halifax, NS B3H 4H6, Canada. *Phone:* 902-494-2148. *Fax:* 902-494-1630. *E-mail:* admissions@dal.ca. *Web site:* http://www.dal.ca/.

École Polytechnique de Montréal

Montréal, Quebec, Canada

Admissions Office Contact École Polytechnique de Montréal, CP 6079, Succursale Centre-Ville, Montréal, QC H3C 3A7, Canada. *Web site:* http://www.polymtl.ca/.

Emily Carr University of Art + Design

Vancouver, British Columbia, Canada

- **Province-supported** comprehensive, founded 1925
- **Urban** campus
- **Coed** 1,558 undergraduate students
- **Moderately difficult** entrance level

Undergraduates *Retention:* 87% of full-time freshmen returned.

Faculty *Total:* 220, 25% full-time. *Student/faculty ratio:* 18:1.

Academics *Degrees:* bachelor's and master's. *Special study options:* advanced placement credit, cooperative education, part-time degree program, services for LD students, study abroad.

Computers on Campus Students can access the following: campus intranet, computer help desk, free student e-mail accounts, online (class) registration, online (class) schedules. Campuswide network is available. Wireless service is available via entire campus.

Student Life *Housing:* college housing not available. *Activities and organizations:* student-run newspaper. *Campus security:* 24-hour emergency response devices and patrols. *Student services:* personal/psychological counseling.

Costs *(2011–12)* *Tuition:* province resident $3570 full-time, $119 per credit part-time; International tuition $12,000 full-time. Full-time tuition and fees vary according to course load. Part-time tuition and fees vary according to course load. *Required fees:* $227 full-time. *Payment plan:* installment. *Waivers:* employees or children of employees.

Applying *Options:* electronic application. *Application fee:* $40 Canadian dollars. *Required:* essay or personal statement, high school transcript, minimum 2.5 GPA, portfolio and questionnaire. *Application deadlines:* 1/15 (freshmen), 1/15 (transfers). *Notification:* 3/1 (freshmen), 3/1 (transfers).

Freshman Application Contact Admissions, Emily Carr University of Art + Design, 1399 Johnston Street, Vancouver, BC V6H 3R9, Canada. *Phone:* 604-844-3800. *Toll-free phone:* 800-832-7788. *Fax:* 604-844-3801. *E-mail:* admissions@ecuad.ca. *Web site:* http://www.ecuad.ca/.

Emmanuel Bible College

Kitchener, Ontario, Canada

Freshman Application Contact Emmanuel Bible College, 100 Fergus Avenue, Kitchener, ON N2A 2H2, Canada. *Phone:* 519-894-8900 Ext. 224. *Web site:* http://www.ebcollege.on.ca/.

Eston College

Eston, Saskatchewan, Canada

Freshman Application Contact Admissions, Eston College, 730 1st Street E., Box 579, Eston, SK S0L 1A0, Canada. *Phone:* 306-962-3621. *Toll-free phone:* 888-440-3424. *Fax:* 306-962-3810. *E-mail:* admissions@estoncollege.ca. *Web site:* http://www.estoncollege.ca/.

HEC Montreal

Montréal, Quebec, Canada

- **Province-supported** comprehensive, founded 1910, part of Universite de Montreal
- **Urban** 9-acre campus
- **Coed** 9,160 undergraduate students, 49% full-time, 50% women, 50% men
- **Moderately difficult** entrance level, 60% of applicants were admitted

Undergraduates 4,444 full-time, 4,716 part-time. Students come from 3 provinces and territories; 36 other countries; 0.3% are from out of state. *Retention:* 89% of full-time freshmen returned.
Freshmen *Admission:* 2,654 applied, 1,582 admitted, 899 enrolled.
Faculty *Total:* 703, 40% full-time, 36% with terminal degrees. *Student/faculty ratio:* 20:1.
Academics *Calendar:* trimesters. *Degrees:* certificates, bachelor's, master's, doctoral, postbachelor's, and first professional certificates. *Special study options:* academic remediation for entering students, adult/continuing education programs, English as a second language, honors programs, independent study, off-campus study, student-designed majors, study abroad, summer session for credit.
Computers on Campus 260 computers/terminals and 10,000 ports are available on campus for general student use. Students can access the following: campus intranet, computer help desk, free student e-mail accounts, online (class) grades, online (class) registration, online (class) schedules, Complete Learning Management System, corporate calendar and web sites for all the resources available for classes. Campuswide network is available. Wireless service is available via entire campus.
Student Life *Housing options:* Campus housing is provided by a third party. *Activities and organizations:* student-run newspaper, radio station, choral group, AEMBA (MBA Students' Association), AEMD (MSc and PhD Students' Association), AEDES (Post-Bachelor's Certificate Students' Association), AEHEC (BBA Students' Association), AEPC (Certificate Students' Association). *Campus security:* 24-hour emergency response devices and patrols. *Student services:* health clinic, personal/psychological counseling.
Financial Aid Of all full-time matriculated undergraduates who enrolled in 2010, 2,900 applied for aid, 2,400 were judged to have need. *Average financial aid package:* $7700. *Average need-based loan:* $3300. *Average need-based gift aid:* $7000.
Applying *Options:* electronic application, deferred entrance. *Application fee:* $80 Canadian dollars. *Required:* high school transcript. *Required for some:* cote de rendement collegial. *Application deadlines:* 3/1 (freshmen), 2/1 (out-of-state freshmen). *Notification:* continuous (freshmen), continuous (out-of-state freshmen).
Freshman Application Contact Mrs. Yolaine Martineau, Head Admissions Officer, HEC Montreal, 3000 Chemin de la Cote-Sainte-Catherine, Montreal, QC H3T 2A7, Canada. *Phone:* 514-340-6151. *Fax:* 514-340-5640. *E-mail:* admission.info@hec.ca. *Web site:* http://www.hec.ca/.

Heritage Baptist College and Heritage Theological Seminary

Cambridge, Ontario, Canada

Freshman Application Contact Mr. Mark Walther, Assistant Dean of Students, Heritage Baptist College and Heritage Theological Seminary, New York, NY 10023-6588. *Phone:* 519-651-2869 Ext. 251. *Toll-free phone:* 800-465-1961. *Fax:* 519-651-2870. *E-mail:* mwalther@heritagecollege.net. *Web site:* http://www.heritage-theo.edu/.

Horizon College & Seminary

Saskatoon, Saskatchewan, Canada

Freshman Application Contact Mrs. Shannon Olson, Assistant Registrar, Horizon College & Seminary, 1303 Jackson Avenue, Saskatoon, SK S7H 2M9, Canada. *Phone:* 306-374-6655. *Toll-free phone:* 877-374-6655. *Fax:* 306-373-6968. *E-mail:* admissions@horizon.edu. *Web site:* http://www.horizon.edu/.

The King's University College

Edmonton, Alberta, Canada

- **Independent interdenominational** 4-year, founded 1979
- **Suburban** 20-acre campus
- **Endowment** $1.9 million
- **Coed** 607 undergraduate students, 94% full-time, 56% women, 44% men
- **Moderately difficult** entrance level, 75% of applicants were admitted

Undergraduates 568 full-time, 39 part-time. Students come from 7 provinces and territories; 15 other countries; 14% are from out of state; 18% transferred in; 29% live on campus. *Retention:* 67% of full-time freshmen returned.
Freshmen *Admission:* 314 applied, 235 admitted, 180 enrolled. *Average high school GPA:* 3.3.
Faculty *Total:* 108, 44% full-time, 86% with terminal degrees. *Student/faculty ratio:* 10:1.
Academics *Calendar:* Canadian standard year. *Degrees:* certificates, diplomas, bachelor's, and postbachelor's certificates. *Special study options:* adult/continuing education programs, advanced placement credit, double majors, English as a second language, independent study, internships, off-campus study, part-time degree program, services for LD students, study abroad, summer session for credit. *Unusual degree programs:* 3-2 elementary education, secondary education.
Computers on Campus 48 computers/terminals are available on campus for general student use. Students can access the following: campus intranet, computer help desk, free student e-mail accounts, online (class) grades, online (class) registration, online (class) schedules. Campuswide network is available. 100% of college-owned or -operated housing units are wired for high-speed Internet access. Wireless service is available via entire campus.
Student Life *Housing options:* coed, women-only. Campus housing is university owned. Freshman applicants given priority for college housing. *Activities and organizations:* drama/theater group, student-run newspaper, choral group, Micah Action and Awareness, The King's Players (drama club), Chamber and Concert Choirs, King's Science Society, The King's Commerce Association. *Campus security:* 24-hour emergency response devices, student patrols, controlled dormitory access. *Student services:* personal/psychological counseling.
Athletics *Intercollegiate sports:* basketball M(s)/W(s), soccer M(s)/W(s), volleyball M(s)/W(s). *Intramural sports:* basketball M/W, ice hockey M, soccer M/W, ultimate Frisbee M/W, volleyball M/W.
Costs (2012–13) *Comprehensive fee:* $16,340 includes full-time tuition ($9920), mandatory fees ($600), and room and board ($5820). Full-time tuition and fees vary according to course load. Part-time tuition: $320 per credit. Part-time tuition and fees vary according to course load. *Required fees:* $150 per term part-time. *College room only:* $3120. Room and board charges vary according to board plan and housing facility. *Waivers:* employees or children of employees.
Financial Aid Of all full-time matriculated undergraduates who enrolled in 2010, 247 applied for aid, 221 were judged to have need. *Financial aid deadline:* 3/31.
Applying *Options:* electronic application. *Application fee:* $70 Canadian dollars. *Required:* high school transcript, minimum 2.0 GPA, 1 letter of recommendation. *Required for some:* essay or personal statement, interview. *Application deadlines:* rolling (freshmen), rolling (transfers). *Notification:* 8/15 (freshmen), 8/15 (transfers).
Freshman Application Contact Mr. Glenn Keeler, Registrar/Director of Admissions, The King's University College, 9125-50 Street, Edmonton, AB T6B 2H3, Canada. *Phone:* 780-465-3500 Ext. 8035. *Toll-free phone:* 800-661-8582. *Fax:* 780-465-3534. *E-mail:* admissions@kingsu.ca. *Web site:* http://www.kingsu.ca/.

Kingswood University

Sussex, New Brunswick, Canada

- **Independent** 4-year, founded 1945, affiliated with Wesleyan Church
- **Small-town** 57-acre campus
- **Endowment** $249,921
- **Coed** 205 undergraduate students, 94% full-time, 49% women, 51% men
- **Moderately difficult** entrance level, 56% of applicants were admitted

Undergraduates 193 full-time, 12 part-time. Students come from 7 provinces and territories; 4 other countries; 69% are from out of state; 2% transferred in; 81% live on campus. *Retention:* 73% of full-time freshmen returned.
Freshmen *Admission:* 201 applied, 113 admitted, 55 enrolled. *Test scores:* SAT critical reading scores over 500: 83%; SAT writing scores over 500: 66%; SAT critical reading scores over 600: 33%; SAT writing scores over 600: 33%.
Faculty *Total:* 29, 38% full-time, 31% with terminal degrees. *Student/faculty ratio:* 14:1.
Academics *Calendar:* semesters. *Degrees:* certificates, associate, and bachelor's. *Special study options:* academic remediation for entering students,

advanced placement credit, double majors, internships, part-time degree program, summer session for credit.

Computers on Campus 20 computers/terminals are available on campus for general student use. Students can access the following: campus intranet, free student e-mail accounts, online (class) grades, online (class) schedules. 100% of college-owned or -operated housing units are wired for high-speed Internet access. Wireless service is available via entire campus.

Student Life *Housing:* on-campus residence required through junior year. *Options:* men-only, women-only. Campus housing is university owned. Freshman campus housing is guaranteed. *Activities and organizations:* drama/theater group, choral group, Outreach Association, Athletic Association, Student Global Impact, Social Committee, Chorale. *Campus security:* student patrols, controlled dormitory access. *Student services:* personal/psychological counseling.

Athletics *Intercollegiate sports:* basketball M/W, volleyball M/W. *Intramural sports:* basketball M/W, ice hockey M/W, soccer M/W, softball M/W, table tennis M/W, volleyball M/W.

Standardized Tests *Required for some:* SAT or ACT (for admission).

Costs (2012–13) *Comprehensive fee:* $14,600 Canadian dollars includes full-time tuition ($9100 Canadian dollars) and room and board ($5500 Canadian dollars). Part-time tuition: $305 Canadian dollars per credit hour. *College room only:* $2350 Canadian dollars. Room and board charges vary according to board plan and housing facility. *Payment plan:* installment. *Waivers:* senior citizens and employees or children of employees.

Financial Aid *Financial aid deadline:* 7/15.

Applying *Options:* electronic application, early admission. *Application fee:* $20 Canadian dollars. *Required:* high school transcript, 2 letters of recommendation. *Recommended:* interview. *Application deadlines:* rolling (freshmen), rolling (transfers).

Freshman Application Contact Mrs. Shelley Vail, Associate Director for Admissions and Financial Aid, Kingswood University, Kingswood University, PO Box 5125, Sussex, NB E4E 5L2, Canada. *Phone:* 506-432.4422. *Toll-free phone:* 888-432-4422. *Fax:* 506-432.4442. *E-mail:* vails@kingswood.edu. *Web site:* http://www.kingswood.edu/.

Kwantlen Polytechnic University
Surrey, British Columbia, Canada

Freshman Application Contact Admissions, Kwantlen Polytechnic University, 12666 - 72nd Avenue, Surrey, BC V3W 2M8, Canada. *Phone:* 604-599-2000. *Fax:* 604-599-2086. *E-mail:* admission@kwantlen.ca. *Web site:* http://www.kwantlen.ca/.

Lakehead University
Thunder Bay, Ontario, Canada

- **Province-supported** comprehensive, founded 1965
- **Suburban** 345-acre campus
- **Endowment** $37.0 million
- **Coed** 7,975 undergraduate students, 80% full-time, 59% women, 41% men
- **Moderately difficult** entrance level, 84% of applicants were admitted

Undergraduates 6,364 full-time, 1,611 part-time. Students come from 13 provinces and territories; 28 other countries; 20% live on campus. *Retention:* 88% of full-time freshmen returned.

Freshmen *Admission:* 8,277 applied, 6,917 admitted, 1,485 enrolled. *Average high school GPA:* 4.

Faculty *Total:* 319.

Academics *Calendar:* Canadian standard year. *Degrees:* certificates, diplomas, bachelor's, master's, doctoral, postbachelor's, and first professional certificates. *Special study options:* accelerated degree program, advanced placement credit, cooperative education, distance learning, double majors, English as a second language, external degree program, honors programs, independent study, internships, off-campus study, part-time degree program, services for LD students, study abroad, summer session for credit. *Unusual degree programs:* 3-2 social work; Concurrent Education.

Computers on Campus 594 computers/terminals and 3,000 ports are available on campus for general student use. Students can access the following: campus intranet, computer help desk, free student e-mail accounts, online (class) grades, online (class) registration, online (class) schedules. Campuswide network is available. 100% of college-owned or -operated housing units are wired for high-speed Internet access. Wireless service is available via learning centers, libraries, student centers.

Student Life *Housing options:* coed, disabled students. Campus housing is university owned. Freshman campus housing is guaranteed. *Activities and organizations:* student-run newspaper, radio station, choral group, Outdoor Recreation Students Association, Engineering Students Society, Business Association, Educational Students Association, Native Students Association. *Campus security:* 24-hour emergency response devices and patrols, student patrols, late-night transport/escort service, controlled dormitory access. *Student services:* health clinic, personal/psychological counseling, women's center.

Athletics Member CIS. *Intercollegiate sports:* baseball M(c), basketball M/W, cross-country running M/W, equestrian sports M(c)/W(c), golf M(c), ice hockey M, skiing (cross-country) M/W, skiing (downhill) M(c)/W(c), soccer M(c)/W(c), track and field M/W, volleyball W, wrestling M/W. *Intramural sports:* badminton M/W, basketball M/W, cross-country running M(c)/W(c), ice hockey M/W, lacrosse M(c), rugby M(c)/W(c), skiing (cross-country) M/W, soccer M/W, ultimate Frisbee M/W, volleyball M(c)/W(c), wrestling M(c)/W(c).

Standardized Tests *Required:* SAT or ACT (for admission).

Costs (2011–12) *Tuition:* province nonresident $1066 per course part-time; nonresident $5329 full-time, $2900 per course part-time; International tuition $14,500 full-time. Full-time tuition and fees vary according to course level, degree level, location, program, and student level. Part-time tuition and fees vary according to course level, course load, degree level, location, program, and student level. Tuition rates vary depending upon program and year level. *Required fees:* $889 full-time, $96 per course part-time. *Room and board:* $7790; room only: $6010. Room and board charges vary according to board plan, housing facility, and location. *Payment plan:* installment. *Waivers:* senior citizens and employees or children of employees.

Financial Aid *Financial aid deadline:* 6/30.

Applying *Options:* electronic application, early admission, deferred entrance. *Application fee:* $125 Canadian dollars. *Required:* portfolio for visual arts program, audition for music program, portfolio for media studies. *Required for some:* essay or personal statement, high school transcript. *Recommended:* minimum 3.0 GPA. *Application deadlines:* 9/12 (freshmen), 9/9 (out-of-state freshmen), 9/9 (transfers). *Notification:* continuous (freshmen), continuous (out-of-state freshmen), continuous (transfers).

Freshman Application Contact Mr. Nicholas Chamut, Manager of Undergraduate Admissions, Lakehead University, 955 Oliver Road, Thunder Bay, ON P7B 5E1, Canada. *Phone:* 807-343-8676. *Toll-free phone:* 800-465-3959. *Fax:* 807-766-7209. *E-mail:* admissions@lakeheadu.ca. *Web site:* http://www.lakeheadu.ca/.

Lakehead University–Orillia
Orillia, Ontario, Canada

- **Public** comprehensive
- **Coed**

Academics *Degrees:* bachelor's and master's.

Admissions Office Contact Lakehead University–Orillia, 500 University Avenue, Orillia, ON L3V 0B9, Canada. *Web site:* http://orillia.lakeheadu.ca/.

Laurentian University
Sudbury, Ontario, Canada

- **Province-supported** comprehensive, founded 1960
- **Suburban** 700-acre campus
- **Coed**

Academics *Calendar:* Canadian standard year. *Degrees:* certificates, diplomas, bachelor's, master's, doctoral, postbachelor's, and first professional certificates.

Student Life *Campus security:* 24-hour emergency response devices and patrols, late-night transport/escort service, controlled dormitory access.

Athletics Member CIS.

Financial Aid *Of all full-time matriculated undergraduates who enrolled in 2010,* 241 state and other part-time jobs (averaging $1563).

Applying *Options:* electronic application, early admission. *Application fee:* $40 Canadian dollars. *Required:* high school transcript. *Required for some:* essay or personal statement, 2 letters of recommendation, interview.

Freshman Application Contact Laurentian University, Ramsey Lake Road, P3E 2C6, Canada. *Phone:* 705-675-1151. *Toll-free phone:* 800-263-4188. *Fax:* 705-675-4891. *E-mail:* admissions@laurentian.ca. *Web site:* http://www.laurentian.ca/.

Master's College and Seminary

Toronto, Ontario, Canada

- **Independent Pentecostal** 4-year, founded 1939
- **Suburban** campus with easy access to Toronto
- **Endowment** $718,092
- **Coed** 274 undergraduate students
- **Noncompetitive** entrance level, 98% of applicants were admitted

Undergraduates Students come from 6 provinces and territories; 2 other countries; 6% are from out of state; 60% live on campus. *Retention:* 83% of full-time freshmen returned.

Freshmen *Admission:* 95 applied, 93 admitted.

Faculty *Total:* 31, 16% full-time, 23% with terminal degrees. *Student/faculty ratio:* 8:1.

Academics *Calendar:* semesters. *Degree:* certificates, diplomas, and bachelor's. *Special study options:* academic remediation for entering students, distance learning, independent study, internships, off-campus study, part-time degree program, services for LD students, summer session for credit.

Computers on Campus 6 computers/terminals are available on campus for general student use. Students can access the following: computer help desk, free student e-mail accounts, online (class) registration, online (class) schedules. Campuswide network is available. Wireless service is available via entire campus.

Student Life *Housing:* on-campus residence required for freshman year. *Options:* men-only, women-only. Campus housing is leased by the school. Freshman campus housing is guaranteed. *Campus security:* 24-hour emergency response devices, student patrols, controlled dormitory access.

Costs (2011–12) *Comprehensive fee:* $11,668 Canadian dollars includes full-time tuition ($5792 Canadian dollars), mandatory fees ($576 Canadian dollars), and room and board ($5300 Canadian dollars). Full-time tuition and fees vary according to course load, location, and program. Part-time tuition: $181 Canadian dollars per credit hour. Part-time tuition and fees vary according to course load, location, and program. *Required fees:* $18 Canadian dollars per credit hour part-time. *Payment plan:* deferred payment. *Waivers:* adult students, senior citizens, and employees or children of employees.

Applying *Options:* deferred entrance. *Application fee:* $75 Canadian dollars. *Required:* essay or personal statement, high school transcript, 3 letters of recommendation, Christian commitment. *Required for some:* interview. *Recommended:* minimum 2.0 GPA. *Application deadlines:* 8/31 (freshmen), 8/31 (transfers).

Freshman Application Contact Ms. Flora Anthony, Admissions, Master's College and Seminary, 780 Argyle Street, Peterborough, ON K9H 5T2, Canada. *Phone:* 800-295-6368. *Toll-free phone:* 800-295-6368. *Fax:* 705-749-0417. *E-mail:* flora.anthony@mcs.edu. *Web site:* http://www.mcs.edu/.

McGill University

Montréal, Quebec, Canada

Freshman Application Contact Enrollment Services, McGill University, 845 Sherbrooke Street West, James Administration Building, Room 205, Montreal, QC H3A 2T5, Canada. *Phone:* 514-398-3910. *Fax:* 514-398-4193. *E-mail:* admissions@mcgill.ca. *Web site:* http://www.mcgill.ca/.

McMaster University

Hamilton, Ontario, Canada

Freshman Application Contact Olivia Demerling, Admissions Officer, McMaster University, 1280 Main Street West, Hamilton, ON L8S 4M2, Canada. *Phone:* 905-525-4600. *Fax:* 905-527-1105. *E-mail:* admitmac@mcmaster.ca. *Web site:* http://www.mcmaster.ca/.

Memorial University of Newfoundland

St. John's, Newfoundland and Labrador, Canada

Freshman Application Contact Ms. Marian Abbott, Admissions Office, Memorial University of Newfoundland, Elizabeth Avenue, St. John's, NL A1C 5S7, Canada. *Phone:* 709-737-3705. *E-mail:* sturecru@morgan.ucs.mun.ca. *Web site:* http://www.mun.ca/.

Mount Allison University

Sackville, New Brunswick, Canada

- **Province-supported** comprehensive, founded 1839
- **Small-town** 50-acre campus
- **Endowment** $65.0 million
- **Coed** 2,675 undergraduate students, 96% full-time, 60% women, 40% men
- **Moderately difficult** entrance level, 74% of applicants were admitted

Undergraduates 2,569 full-time, 106 part-time. Students come from 22 provinces and territories; 45 other countries; 60% are from out of state; 4% transferred in; 50% live on campus. *Retention:* 80% of full-time freshmen returned.

Freshmen *Admission:* 2,110 applied, 1,551 admitted, 717 enrolled. *Average high school GPA:* 3.31.

Faculty *Total:* 187, 71% full-time, 88% with terminal degrees. *Student/faculty ratio:* 16:1.

Academics *Calendar:* Canadian standard year. *Degrees:* certificates, bachelor's, and master's. *Special study options:* academic remediation for entering students, adult/continuing education programs, advanced placement credit, distance learning, double majors, honors programs, independent study, internships, off-campus study, part-time degree program, services for LD students, student-designed majors, study abroad, summer session for credit.

Computers on Campus 100 computers/terminals and 240 ports are available on campus for general student use. Students can access the following: computer help desk, free student e-mail accounts, online (class) grades, online (class) registration, online (class) schedules, online student account/Websis. Campuswide network is available. 100% of college-owned or -operated housing units are wired for high-speed Internet access. Wireless service is available via entire campus.

Student Life *Housing options:* coed, women-only, cooperative. Campus housing is university owned. Freshman campus housing is guaranteed. *Activities and organizations:* drama/theater group, student-run newspaper, radio station, choral group, Commerce Society, Windsor Theatre, President's Leadership Development Certificate, Leadership Mount Allison, Garnet and Gold Society. *Campus security:* 24-hour emergency response devices, late-night transport/escort service. *Student services:* health clinic, personal/psychological counseling.

Athletics Member CIS. *Intercollegiate sports:* basketball M/W, football M, ice hockey W, rugby M/W, soccer M/W, swimming and diving M/W. *Intramural sports:* badminton M/W, baseball M/W, basketball M/W, football M/W, golf M/W, ice hockey M/W, rugby M/W, skiing (cross-country) M/W, skiing (downhill) M/W, soccer M/W, softball M/W, tennis M/W, ultimate Frisbee M/W, volleyball M/W, weight lifting M/W.

Costs (2011–12) *Tuition:* province resident $6920 full-time, $692 per course part-time; nonresident $1453 per course part-time; International tuition $14,530 full-time. Full-time tuition and fees vary according to course load. Part-time tuition and fees vary according to course load. *Required fees:* $402 full-time, $38 per term part-time. *Room and board:* $7992; room only: $4591. Room and board charges vary according to board plan and housing facility.

Applying *Options:* electronic application, deferred entrance. *Application fee:* $50 Canadian dollars. *Required:* high school transcript, minimum 2.5 GPA. *Required for some:* essay or personal statement, interview. *Recommended:* 2 letters of recommendation. *Application deadlines:* rolling (freshmen), rolling (transfers). *Notification:* continuous (freshmen), continuous (transfers).

Freshman Application Contact Mr. Joceylyn Ollerhead, Manager of Admissions, Mount Allison University, 65 York Street, Sackville, NB E4L 1E4, Canada. *Phone:* 506-364-3294. *Fax:* 506-364-2272. *E-mail:* admissions@mta.ca. *Web site:* http://www.mta.ca/.

Mount Royal University

Calgary, Alberta, Canada

Freshman Application Contact Admissions Office, Mount Royal University, 4825 Mount Royal Gate SW, Calgary, AB T3E 6K6, Canada. *Phone:* 403-440-5000. *Toll-free phone:* 877-440-5001. *Web site:* http://www.mtroyal.ca/.

Mount Saint Vincent University

Halifax, Nova Scotia, Canada

Freshman Application Contact Ms. Heidi Tattrie, Assistant Registrar/Admissions, Mount Saint Vincent University, 166 Bedford Highway, Halifax, NS B3M2J6, Canada. *Phone:* 902-457-6117. *Toll-free phone:* 877-733-6788. *Fax:* 902-457-6498. *E-mail:* admissions@msvu.ca. *Web site:* http://www.msvu.ca/.

Ner Israel Yeshiva College of Toronto

Thornhill, Ontario, Canada

Director of Admissions Rabbi Y. Kravetz, Director of Admissions, Ner Israel Yeshiva College of Toronto, 8950 Bathurst Street, Thornhill, ON L4J 8A7, Canada. *Phone:* 905-731-1224.

Nipissing University

North Bay, Ontario, Canada

Freshman Application Contact Ms. Lori-Ann Beckford, Assistant Registrar, Liaison, Nipissing University, 100 College Drive, Box 5002, North Bay, ON P1B 8L7, Canada. *Phone:* 705-474-3461 Ext. 4518. *Fax:* 705-474-1947. *E-mail:* liaison@nipissingu.ca. *Web site:* http://www.nipissingu.ca/.

Nova Scotia Agricultural College

Truro, Nova Scotia, Canada

- **Province-supported** comprehensive, founded 1905
- **Small-town** 408-acre campus with easy access to Halifax
- **Coed** 823 undergraduate students
- **Minimally difficult** entrance level, 78% of applicants were admitted

Undergraduates Students come from 3 provinces and territories; 15 other countries; 13% are from out of state; 50% live on campus. *Retention:* 85% of full-time freshmen returned.

Freshmen *Admission:* 622 applied, 487 admitted.

Faculty *Total:* 80, 78% full-time, 76% with terminal degrees. *Student/faculty ratio:* 13:1.

Academics *Calendar:* semesters. *Degrees:* diplomas, bachelor's, and master's. *Special study options:* academic remediation for entering students, adult/continuing education programs, advanced placement credit, cooperative education, distance learning, double majors, independent study, internships, off-campus study, part-time degree program, services for LD students, study abroad, summer session for credit.

Computers on Campus 110 computers/terminals are available on campus for general student use. Students can access the following: campus intranet, computer help desk, free student e-mail accounts, online (class) grades, online (class) registration, online (class) schedules. Campuswide network is available. 100% of college-owned or -operated housing units are wired for high-speed Internet access. Wireless service is available via classrooms, computer centers, libraries, student centers.

Student Life *Housing options:* coed. Campus housing is university owned. Freshman campus housing is guaranteed. *Activities and organizations:* drama/theater group, student-run newspaper, choral group, Pre-Vet Club, Equestrian Club, International Student's Association, Theatre Society, Christian Students Club. *Campus security:* 24-hour patrols, student patrols. *Student services:* health clinic, personal/psychological counseling.

Athletics *Intercollegiate sports:* badminton M/W, basketball M/W, equestrian sports M/W, golf M/W, rugby M/W, soccer M/W, volleyball M/W. *Intramural sports:* badminton M/W, basketball M/W, cross-country running M/W, equestrian sports M/W, golf M/W, ice hockey M/W, racquetball M/W, skiing (cross-country) M/W, skiing (downhill) M/W, soccer M/W, softball M/W, squash M/W, swimming and diving M/W, table tennis M/W, ultimate Frisbee M/W, volleyball M/W, water polo M/W.

Applying *Options:* electronic application, early admission. *Application fee:* $25 Canadian dollars. *Required:* high school transcript, minimum 2.5 GPA. *Required for some:* essay or personal statement, 1 letter of recommendation, interview, competency form. *Application deadline:* 8/1 (freshmen).

Freshman Application Contact Ms. Elizabeth Johnson, Admissions Officer, Nova Scotia Agricultural College, PO Box 550, Truro, NS B2N 5E3, Canada. *Phone:* 902-893-8212. *Toll-free phone:* 888-700-6722. *Fax:* 902-895-5529. *E-mail:* recruit@nsac.ca. *Web site:* http://nsac.ca/.

NSCAD University

Halifax, Nova Scotia, Canada

Freshman Application Contact Mr. Terry Bailey, Director of Admissions and Enrollment Services, NSCAD University, 5163 Duke Street, Halifax, NS B3J 3J6, Canada. *Phone:* 902-494-8129. *Toll-free phone:* 888-444-5989. *Fax:* 902-425-2987. *E-mail:* admissions@nscad.ca. *Web site:* http://www.nscad.ca/.

Okanagan College

Kelowna, British Columbia, Canada

- **Province-supported** 4-year, founded 2005, part of Ministry of Advanced Education
- **Urban** 13-acre campus
- **Coed** 3,332 undergraduate students, 65% full-time, 55% women, 45% men
- **14% of applicants were admitted**

Undergraduates 2,167 full-time, 1,165 part-time. Students come from 3 provinces and territories; 14 other countries; 3% are from out of state; 2% transferred in. *Retention:* 52% of full-time freshmen returned.

Freshmen *Admission:* 971 applied, 134 admitted, 1,001 enrolled.

Faculty *Total:* 242, 74% full-time, 24% with terminal degrees. *Student/faculty ratio:* 14:1.

Academics *Degrees:* certificates, diplomas, associate, and bachelor's. *Special study options:* academic remediation for entering students, adult/continuing education programs, advanced placement credit, cooperative education, distance learning, English as a second language, external degree program, honors programs, internships, off-campus study, part-time degree program, services for LD students, study abroad, summer session for credit.

Computers on Campus 1,050 computers/terminals are available on campus for general student use. Students can access the following: campus intranet, computer help desk, free student e-mail accounts, online (class) grades, online (class) registration, online (class) schedules. Campuswide network is available. 100% of college-owned or -operated housing units are wired for high-speed Internet access. Wireless service is available via entire campus.

Student Life *Housing options:* coed. Campus housing is university owned. *Activities and organizations:* student-run newspaper, choral group. *Campus security:* 24-hour patrols, late-night transport/escort service, controlled dormitory access, 24-hour emergency phone. *Student services:* personal/psychological counseling.

Athletics *Intercollegiate sports:* baseball M, ice hockey M. *Intramural sports:* softball M/W, tennis M/W.

Costs (2012–13) *Tuition:* province resident $3078 Canadian dollars full-time, $99 Canadian dollars per credit part-time; nonresident $3078 Canadian dollars full-time, $99 Canadian dollars per credit part-time; International tuition $11,000 Canadian dollars full-time. Full-time tuition and fees vary according to course level, course load, and location. Part-time tuition and fees vary according to course level, course load, and location. *Required fees:* $694 Canadian dollars full-time, $9 Canadian dollars per credit part-time, $151 Canadian dollars per term part-time. *Room only:* $3800 Canadian dollars. *Waivers:* senior citizens and employees or children of employees.

Applying *Options:* electronic application, early admission. *Application fee:* $30 Canadian dollars. *Required for some:* essay or personal statement, high school transcript, minimum 2.0 GPA, interview.

Freshman Application Contact Mr. Paul Campo, Okanagan College, 1000 KLO Road, Kelowna, BC V1Y 4X8, Canada. *Phone:* 250-762-5445 Ext. 4332. *Toll-free phone:* 877-755-2266. *E-mail:* pgcampo@okanagan.bc.ca. *Web site:* http://www.okanagan.bc.ca/.

Prairie Bible Institute

Three Hills, Alberta, Canada

Director of Admissions Mr. Kevin Kirk, Vice President, Marketing and Enrollment Management, Prairie Bible Institute, 330 Sixth Avenue North, PO Box 4000, Three Hills, AB T0M 2N0, Canada. *Phone:* 403-443-5511 Ext. 3007. *Toll-free phone:* 800-661-2425. *E-mail:* admissions@prairie.edu. *Web site:* http://www.prairie.edu/.

Providence College and Theological Seminary

Otterburne, Manitoba, Canada

Freshman Application Contact Mr. Adrian Enns, Director of College Enrollment, Providence College and Theological Seminary, 10 College Crescent, Otterburne, MB R0A 1G0, Canada. *Phone:* 204-433-7488. *Toll-free phone:* 800-668-7768. *Fax:* 204-433-7158. *E-mail:* info@prov.ca. *Web site:* http://www.prov.ca/.

Queen's University at Kingston
Kingston, Ontario, Canada

- **Province-supported** university, founded 1841
- **Urban** 160-acre campus
- **Endowment** $601.9 million
- **Coed** 18,833 undergraduate students, 82% full-time, 62% women, 38% men
- **Most difficult** entrance level

Undergraduates 15,536 full-time, 3,297 part-time. Students come from 46 provinces and territories; 84 other countries; 20% are from out of state; 0.5% transferred in; 32% live on campus. *Retention:* 96% of full-time freshmen returned.

Freshmen *Admission:* 23,019 applied, 3,730 enrolled.

Faculty *Total:* 1,525, 71% full-time, 86% with terminal degrees. *Student/faculty ratio:* 15:1.

Academics *Calendar:* Canadian standard year. *Degrees:* certificates, bachelor's, master's, doctoral, and first professional. *Special study options:* accelerated degree program, adult/continuing education programs, advanced placement credit, cooperative education, distance learning, double majors, English as a second language, honors programs, internships, part-time degree program, services for LD students, student-designed majors, study abroad, summer session for credit.

Computers on Campus 455 computers/terminals are available on campus for general student use. Students can access the following: computer help desk, free student e-mail accounts, online (class) grades, online (class) registration, online (class) schedules. Campuswide network is available. 100% of college-owned or -operated housing units are wired for high-speed Internet access. Wireless service is available via classrooms, computer centers, computer labs, learning centers, libraries, student centers.

Student Life *Housing options:* coed, men-only, women-only, cooperative, disabled students. Campus housing is university owned. Freshman campus housing is guaranteed. *Activities and organizations:* drama/theater group, student-run newspaper, radio station, choral group, marching band, Arts and Sciences Undergraduate Society, Alma Mater Society, Engineering Society, Commerce Society, dance club. *Campus security:* 24-hour emergency response devices and patrols, student patrols, late-night transport/escort service, controlled dormitory access. *Student services:* health clinic, personal/psychological counseling, women's center, legal services.

Athletics Member CIS. *Intercollegiate sports:* baseball M(c), basketball M/W, cheerleading M(c)/W(c), crew M/W, cross-country running M/W, fencing M/W, field hockey W, football M, golf M(c), gymnastics M(c)/W(c), ice hockey M/W, lacrosse M(c)/W, rugby M/W, sailing M(c)/W(c), skiing (cross-country) M(c)/W(c), skiing (downhill) M(c)/W(c), soccer M/W, squash M/W, swimming and diving M/W, track and field M/W, ultimate Frisbee M, volleyball M/W, water polo M/W, wrestling M/W. *Intramural sports:* basketball M/W, equestrian sports M(c)/W(c), fencing M(c)/W(c), football M, golf W(c), ice hockey M/W, rock climbing M/W, soccer M/W, softball W(c), squash M/W, swimming and diving M/W, ultimate Frisbee M(c), volleyball M/W, water polo M/W.

Standardized Tests *Required:* SAT or ACT (for admission).

Costs (2011–12) *Tuition:* province resident $5461 full-time, $1092 per course part-time; nonresident $4116 per course part-time; International tuition $20,601 full-time. Full-time tuition and fees vary according to course load, degree level, and program. Part-time tuition and fees vary according to course load, degree level, and program. *Required fees:* $1090 full-time, $20 per credit part-time. *Room and board:* $10,686; room only: $5966. Room and board charges vary according to board plan and location. *Payment plans:* installment, deferred payment.

Financial Aid Of all full-time matriculated undergraduates who enrolled in 2010, 365 state and other part-time jobs (averaging $1190). *Average financial aid package:* $8950.

Applying *Options:* deferred entrance. *Application fee:* $180 Canadian dollars. *Required:* essay or personal statement, high school transcript, minimum 2.7 GPA. *Required for some:* 1 letter of recommendation. *Application deadlines:* 2/1 (freshmen), 5/15 (transfers). *Notification:* 5/28 (freshmen), 6/15 (transfers).

Freshman Application Contact Ms. Iveta Reinikovaite, Admission Coordinator, Queen's University at Kingston, Undergraduate Admissions, Gordon Hall, 74 Union Street, Kingston, ON K7L 3N6, Canada. *Phone:* 613-533-2218. *Fax:* 613-533-6810. *E-mail:* admission@queensu.ca. *Web site:* http://www.queensu.ca/.

Redeemer University College
Ancaster, Ontario, Canada

Freshman Application Contact Recruitment, Redeemer University College, 777 Garner Road East, Ancaster, ON L9K 1J4, Canada. *Phone:* 905-648-2139

Ext. 4280. *Toll-free phone:* 800-263-6467. *Fax:* 905-648-9545. *E-mail:* recruitment@redeemer.ca. *Web site:* http://www.redeemer.ca/.

Rocky Mountain College
Calgary, Alberta, Canada

Freshman Application Contact Rocky Mountain College, 4039 Brentwood Road, NW, Calgary, AB T2L 1L1, Canada. *Phone:* 403-284-5100. *Toll-free phone:* 877-YOUnRMC. *Web site:* http://www.rockymountaincollege.ca/.

Royal Military College of Canada
Kingston, Ontario, Canada

Freshman Application Contact Royal Military College of Canada, PO Box 17000, Station Forces, Kingston, ON K7K 7B4, Canada. *Phone:* 613-541-6000 Ext. 6579. *Web site:* http://www.rmc.ca/.

Royal Roads University
Victoria, British Columbia, Canada

Application Contact Royal Roads University, 2005 Sooke Road, Victoria, BC V9B 5Y2, Canada. *Phone:* 250-391-2511. *Toll-free phone:* 800-788-8028. *Web site:* http://www.royalroads.ca/.

Ryerson University
Toronto, Ontario, Canada

- **Province-supported** comprehensive, founded 1948
- **Urban** 20-acre campus
- **Coed** 23,542 undergraduate students
- **Moderately difficult** entrance level

Undergraduates 3% live on campus. *Retention:* 90% of full-time freshmen returned.

Freshmen *Average high school GPA:* 3.

Faculty *Total:* 955, 78% full-time.

Academics *Calendar:* Canadian standard year or semesters depending on program. *Degrees:* certificates, bachelor's, and master's. *Special study options:* academic remediation for entering students, adult/continuing education programs, advanced placement credit, cooperative education, distance learning, English as a second language, honors programs, internships, off-campus study, part-time degree program, services for LD students, study abroad, summer session for credit. *Unusual degree programs:* 3-2 social work; urban and regional planning, public (occupational) health and safety.

Computers on Campus 1,400 computers/terminals are available on campus for general student use. Campuswide network is available.

Student Life *Housing options:* coed. Campus housing is university owned. Freshman applicants given priority for college housing. *Activities and organizations:* drama/theater group, student-run newspaper, radio station, choral group. *Campus security:* 24-hour emergency response devices and patrols, late-night transport/escort service, controlled dormitory access, staffed access control is in place 24 hours a day, with ID checks of all persons attempting to enter. *Student services:* health clinic, personal/psychological counseling, women's center.

Athletics Member CIS. *Intercollegiate sports:* badminton M/W, basketball M/W, crew M/W, fencing M/W, ice hockey M/W, soccer M/W, volleyball M/W. *Intramural sports:* badminton M/W, basketball M/W, crew M/W, ice hockey M/W, soccer M/W, softball M/W, squash M/W, table tennis M/W, volleyball M/W, weight lifting M/W.

Financial Aid *Financial aid deadline:* 1/15.

Applying *Options:* electronic application. *Application fee:* $80 Canadian dollars. *Required:* high school transcript. *Required for some:* essay or personal statement, interview, portfolio, audition, entrance examination. *Application deadline:* 2/1 (freshmen). *Notification:* continuous (freshmen).

Freshman Application Contact Michelle Beaton, Manager of International Student Recruitment, Ryerson University, 350 Victoria Street, Toronto, ON M5B 2K3, Canada. *Phone:* 416-979-5080. *Fax:* 416-979-5067. *E-mail:* inquire@ryerson.ca. *Web site:* http://www.ryerson.ca/.

St. Francis Xavier University
Antigonish, Nova Scotia, Canada

- **Independent Roman Catholic** comprehensive, founded 1853
- **Small-town** 100-acre campus
- **Endowment** $67.4 million
- **Coed**
- **Moderately difficult** entrance level

Faculty *Student/faculty ratio:* 12:1.

Academics *Calendar:* Canadian standard year. *Degrees:* certificates, diplomas, bachelor's, and master's.

Student Life *Campus security:* 24-hour emergency response devices and patrols, student patrols, late-night transport/escort service, controlled dormitory access.

Athletics Member CIS.

Standardized Tests *Required for some:* SAT or ACT (for admission). *Recommended:* SAT or ACT (for admission), SAT Subject Tests (for admission).

Costs (2011–12) *Tuition:* province resident $5108 Canadian dollars full-time, $182 Canadian dollars per credit part-time; nonresident $6130 Canadian dollars full-time, $216 Canadian dollars per credit part-time; International tuition $12,782 Canadian dollars full-time. Full-time tuition and fees vary according to degree level and program. Part-time tuition and fees vary according to course load, degree level, and program. *Required fees:* $621 Canadian dollars full-time, $16 Canadian dollars per credit part-time. *Room and board:* $9005 Canadian dollars; room only: $4825 Canadian dollars. Room and board charges vary according to board plan and housing facility.

Applying *Options:* electronic application, early admission, early decision, deferred entrance. *Application fee:* $40 Canadian dollars. *Required:* essay or personal statement, high school transcript, 2 letters of recommendation.

Freshman Application Contact Ms. Sarah Murray, Admissions Officer, St. Francis Xavier University, PO Box 5000, Antigonish, NS B2G 2W5, Canada. *Phone:* 902-867-2219. *Toll-free phone:* 877-867-7839 (in-state); 877-867-STFX (out-of-state). *Fax:* 902-867-2329. *E-mail:* mbarry@stfx.ca. *Web site:* http://www.stfx.ca/.

Saint Mary's University
Halifax, Nova Scotia, Canada

Director of Admissions Mr. Greg Ferguson, Director of Admissions, Saint Mary's University, Halifax, NS B3H 3C3, Canada. *Phone:* 902-420-5415. *Fax:* 902-496-8100. *E-mail:* greg.ferguson@smu.ca. *Web site:* http://www.smu.ca/.

Saint Paul University
Ottawa, Ontario, Canada

Director of Admissions Admission and Recruitment Office, Saint Paul University, 223 Main Street, Ottawa, ON K1S 1C4, Canada. *Phone:* 613-236-1393 Ext. 8990. *Toll-free phone:* 800-637-6859. *Fax:* 613-782-3014. *E-mail:* admission@ustpaul.ca. *Web site:* http://www.ustpaul.ca/.

St. Thomas University
Fredericton, New Brunswick, Canada

- **Independent Roman Catholic** 4-year, founded 1910
- **Small-town** 16-acre campus
- **Endowment** $30.0 million
- **Coed** 2,454 undergraduate students, 92% full-time, 66% women, 34% men
- **Moderately difficult** entrance level, 86% of applicants were admitted

Undergraduates 2,262 full-time, 192 part-time. Students come from 10 provinces and territories; 29 other countries; 21% are from out of state; 97% Race/ethnicity unknown; 3% international; 5% transferred in; 33% live on campus. *Retention:* 69% of full-time freshmen returned.

Freshmen *Admission:* 1,317 applied, 1,133 admitted, 709 enrolled. *Average high school GPA:* 3.4.

Faculty *Total:* 204, 53% full-time, 66% with terminal degrees. *Student/faculty ratio:* 18:1.

Academics *Calendar:* semesters. *Degrees:* certificates, bachelor's, and post-bachelor's certificates. *Special study options:* academic remediation for entering students, accelerated degree program, advanced placement credit, double majors, English as a second language, honors programs, independent study, internships, off-campus study, part-time degree program, services for LD students, student-designed majors, study abroad, summer session for credit.

Computers on Campus 130 computers/terminals are available on campus for general student use. Students can access the following: computer help desk, free student e-mail accounts, online (class) grades, online (class) registration, online (class) schedules, Moodle. Campuswide network is available. 100% of college-owned or -operated housing units are wired for high-speed Internet access. Wireless service is available via entire campus.

Student Life *Housing options:* coed, women-only, disabled students. Campus housing is university owned. Freshman campus housing is guaranteed. *Activities and organizations:* drama/theater group, student-run newspaper, radio station, choral group, Theatre St. Thomas, St. Thomas Student Union, Criminology Society, Model UN, International Students' Association. *Campus security:* 24-hour emergency response devices and patrols, student patrols,

late-night transport/escort service, controlled dormitory access. *Student services:* health clinic, personal/psychological counseling, women's center.

Athletics Member CIS. *Intercollegiate sports:* basketball M/W, cross-country running M/W, golf M/W, ice hockey M(s)/W(s), soccer M/W, volleyball M/W. *Intramural sports:* badminton M/W, basketball M/W, cross-country running M/W, fencing M/W, ice hockey M/W, rock climbing M/W, soccer M/W, softball M/W, squash M/W, swimming and diving M/W, table tennis M/W, track and field M/W, ultimate Frisbee M/W, volleyball M/W, water polo M/W.

Standardized Tests *Recommended:* SAT (for admission).

Costs (2011–12) *Comprehensive fee:* $12,616 Canadian dollars includes full-time tuition ($4770 Canadian dollars), mandatory fees ($346 Canadian dollars), and room and board ($7500 Canadian dollars). Full-time tuition and fees vary according to course load, degree level, and program. Part-time tuition: $530 Canadian dollars per course. Part-time tuition and fees vary according to course load. International tuition: $12,680 Canadian dollars full-time. *Required fees:* $31 Canadian dollars per course part-time. *Room and board:* Room and board charges vary according to board plan, housing facility, and location. *Payment plans:* installment, deferred payment. *Waivers:* senior citizens and employees or children of employees.

Financial Aid *Financial aid deadline:* 3/1.

Applying *Options:* electronic application, early action. *Application fee:* $35 Canadian dollars. *Required:* high school transcript, minimum 3.0 GPA. *Required for some:* essay or personal statement, interview. *Application deadlines:* 8/31 (freshmen), 8/31 (transfers), 12/7 (early action). *Notification:* continuous (freshmen), continuous (transfers).

Freshman Application Contact Ms. Kathryn Monti, Director of Admissions, St. Thomas University, Admissions and Welcome Building, Fredericton, NB E3B 5G3, Canada. *Phone:* 506-452-0532. *Fax:* 506-452-0617. *E-mail:* admissions@stu.ca. *Web site:* http://www.stu.ca/.

Simon Fraser University
Burnaby, British Columbia, Canada

- **Province-supported** university, founded 1965
- **Suburban** campus with easy access to Vancouver
- **Endowment** $176.9 million
- **Coed** 25,108 undergraduate students, 54% full-time, 54% women, 46% men
- **Moderately difficult** entrance level, 69% of applicants were admitted

Undergraduates 13,463 full-time, 11,645 part-time. Students come from 11 provinces and territories; 84 other countries; 9% are from out of state; 5% transferred in; 9% live on campus. *Retention:* 85% of full-time freshmen returned.

Freshmen *Admission:* 10,654 applied, 7,392 admitted, 2,841 enrolled. *Average high school GPA:* 3.35.

Faculty *Total:* 945, 99% full-time, 89% with terminal degrees. *Student/faculty ratio:* 23:1.

Academics *Calendar:* trimesters. *Degrees:* certificates, diplomas, bachelor's, master's, doctoral, post-master's, postbachelor's, and first professional certificates. *Special study options:* academic remediation for entering students, adult/continuing education programs, advanced placement credit, cooperative education, distance learning, double majors, English as a second language, honors programs, independent study, internships, off-campus study, part-time degree program, services for LD students, study abroad, summer session for credit.

Computers on Campus 900 computers/terminals are available on campus for general student use. Students can access the following: free student e-mail accounts, online (class) grades, online (class) registration, online (class) schedules. Campuswide network is available. 100% of college-owned or -operated housing units are wired for high-speed Internet access. Wireless service is available via entire campus.

Student Life *Housing options:* coed, women-only, disabled students. Campus housing is university owned. Freshman applicants given priority for college housing. *Activities and organizations:* drama/theater group, student-run newspaper, radio station, The Peak Newspaper, orientation leaders, Crisis line, Women's Centre, Simon Fraser Public Interest Research Group. *Campus security:* 24-hour emergency response devices and patrols, student patrols, late-night transport/escort service, controlled dormitory access, safe-walk stations, 24-hour safe study area. *Student services:* health clinic, personal/psychological counseling, women's center.

Athletics Member NCAA. All Division II. *Intercollegiate sports:* basketball M(s)/W(s), cross-country running M(s)/W(s), football M(s), golf M(s)/W, gymnastics M, soccer M(s)/W(s), softball W(s), swimming and diving M(s)/W(s), track and field M(s)/W(s), volleyball W(s), wrestling M(s)/W(s). *Intramural sports:* archery M(c)/W(c), badminton M(c)/W(c), basketball M/W, cheerleading M(c)/W(c), crew M(c)/W(c), fencing M(c)/W(c), field hockey W(c), football M/W, golf W(c), gymnastics W(c), ice hockey M(c)/W(c),

lacrosse M(c), rugby M(c)/W(c), soccer M/W, softball M/W, squash M(c)/W(c), table tennis M(c)/W(c), tennis M/W, ultimate Frisbee M(c)/W(c), volleyball M(c)/W(c), water polo M(c)/W(c).

Standardized Tests *Required for some:* SAT or ACT (for admission).

Financial Aid Of all full-time matriculated undergraduates who enrolled in 2009, 420 state and other part-time jobs (averaging $1131). *Financial aid deadline:* 11/15.

Applying *Options:* electronic application, early admission, deferred entrance. *Application fee:* $100 Canadian dollars. *Required:* high school transcript, minimum 3.0 GPA. *Required for some:* essay or personal statement, interview. *Application deadlines:* 4/30 (freshmen), rolling (transfers). *Notification:* continuous until 6/30 (freshmen), continuous (transfers).

Freshman Application Contact Ms. Louise Legris, Director of Admissions, Simon Fraser University, 8888 University Drive, Burnaby, BC V5A 1S6, Canada. *Phone:* 778-782-3498. *Fax:* 778-782-4969. *E-mail:* undergraduate-admissions@sfu.ca. *Web site:* http://www.sfu.ca/.

Southern Alberta Institute of Technology

Calgary, Alberta, Canada

- **Province-supported** primarily 2-year, founded 1916
- **Urban** 96-acre campus
- **Coed**

Academics *Calendar:* trimesters. *Degrees:* certificates, diplomas, associate, and bachelor's.

Student Life *Campus security:* 24-hour emergency response devices and patrols, late-night transport/escort service.

Costs (2011–12) *Tuition:* Full-time tuition and fees vary according to class time, course load, and program. Part-time tuition and fees vary according to class time, course load, and program. Tuition varies according to program and course load. *Room and board:* Room and board charges vary according to housing facility.

Applying *Options:* electronic application, early admission, early decision. *Application fee:* $50 Canadian dollars. *Required:* high school transcript. *Required for some:* essay or personal statement, interview.

Freshman Application Contact Southern Alberta Institute of Technology, 1301 16th Avenue NW, Calgary, AB T2M 0L4, Canada. *Phone:* 403-284-8857. *Toll-free phone:* 877-284-SAIT. *Web site:* http://www.sait.ca/.

Steinbach Bible College

Steinbach, Manitoba, Canada

Freshman Application Contact Mrs. Kaylene Buhler, Admissions Counselor, Steinbach Bible College, 50 PTH 12 North, Steinbach, MB R5G 1T4, Canada. *Phone:* 204-326-6451 Ext. 232. *Toll-free phone:* 800-230-8478. *Fax:* 204-326-6908. *E-mail:* info@sbcollege.ca. *Web site:* http://www.sbcollege.ca/.

Summit Pacific College

Abbotsford, British Columbia, Canada

Director of Admissions Ms. Melody Deeley, Admissions and Registration, Summit Pacific College, Box 1700, Abbotsford, BC V2S 7E7, Canada. *Phone:* 604-851-7225. *Toll-free phone:* 800-976-8388. *E-mail:* registrar@summitpacific.ca. *Web site:* http://www.summitpacific.ca/.

Télé-université

Québec, Quebec, Canada

Freshman Application Contact Ms. Louise Bertrand, Registraire, Télé-université, 455, rue de l'Église, C.P. 4800, succ. Terminus, Québec, QC G1K 9H5, Canada. *Phone:* 418-657-2262 Ext. 5307. *Toll-free phone:* 888-843-4333. *Web site:* http://www.teluq.uquebec.ca/.

Thompson Rivers University

Kamloops, British Columbia, Canada

- **Province-supported** comprehensive, founded 1970, part of Ministry of Advanced Education, Province of British Columbia
- **Small-town** 100-acre campus
- **Endowment** $16.1 million
- **Coed** 7,456 undergraduate students, 67% full-time, 53% women, 47% men
- **81% of applicants were admitted**

Undergraduates 4,996 full-time, 2,460 part-time. Students come from 10 provinces and territories; 76 other countries; 6% are from out of state; 13% live on campus.

Freshmen *Admission:* 3,281 applied, 2,653 admitted.

Faculty *Total:* 631, 71% full-time. *Student/faculty ratio:* 17:1.

Academics *Calendar:* semesters. *Degrees:* certificates, diplomas, associate, bachelor's, master's, and postbachelor's certificates. *Special study options:* academic remediation for entering students, accelerated degree program, adult/continuing education programs, advanced placement credit, cooperative education, distance learning, double majors, English as a second language, external degree program, honors programs, independent study, internships, off-campus study, part-time degree program, services for LD students, study abroad, summer session for credit.

Computers on Campus 1,200 computers/terminals are available on campus for general student use. Students can access the following: campus intranet, computer help desk, free student e-mail accounts, online (class) grades, online (class) registration, online (class) schedules, Learning Management systems including Moodle and Blackboard, Network drive space (250mb), Wireless access, Remote access to their network drive, student elections, Online payments, financial forms/info, updating personal contact information. Campus-wide network is available. 100% of college-owned or -operated housing units are wired for high-speed Internet access. Wireless service is available via entire campus.

Student Life *Housing options:* coed. Campus housing is university owned and is provided by a third party. *Activities and organizations:* drama/theater group, student-run newspaper, radio station, choral group, national fraternities, national sororities. *Campus security:* 24-hour emergency response devices and patrols, student patrols, late-night transport/escort service, controlled dormitory access. *Student services:* health clinic, personal/psychological counseling.

Athletics Member CIS. *Intercollegiate sports:* badminton M(s)/W(s), baseball M, basketball M(s)/W(s), cross-country running M/W, golf M, ice hockey M, soccer M(s)/W(s), volleyball M(s)/W(s). *Intramural sports:* crew M/W, football M, ice hockey M, racquetball M/W, rugby M, skiing (cross-country) M/W, skiing (downhill) M/W, softball M/W, squash M/W, swimming and diving M/W, table tennis M/W, track and field M/W.

Financial Aid Of all full-time matriculated undergraduates who enrolled in 2009, 85 state and other part-time jobs (averaging $2400). *Financial aid deadline:* 3/1.

Applying *Options:* electronic application. *Application fee:* $26 Canadian dollars. *Required:* high school transcript. *Required for some:* essay or personal statement, interview. *Application deadlines:* 3/1 (freshmen), 3/1 (transfers). *Notification:* continuous until 3/1 (freshmen).

Freshman Application Contact Mr. Josh Keller, Director, Student Recruitment and Liaison, Thompson Rivers University, 900 McGill Road, Kamloops, BC V2C 0C8, Canada. *Phone:* 250-828-5008. *Fax:* 250-828-5159. *E-mail:* jkeller@tru.ca. *Web site:* http://www.tru.ca/.

Trent University

Peterborough, Ontario, Canada

- **Province-supported** university, founded 1963
- **Suburban** 1400-acre campus with easy access to Toronto
- **Coed** 7,458 undergraduate students, 85% full-time, 64% women, 36% men
- **Moderately difficult** entrance level, 19% of applicants were admitted

Undergraduates 6,334 full-time, 1,124 part-time. Students come from 22 provinces and territories; 93 other countries; 1% are from out of state; 7% transferred in; 17% live on campus. *Retention:* 84% of full-time freshmen returned.

Freshmen *Admission:* 9,069 applied, 1,719 admitted, 1,635 enrolled.

Faculty *Total:* 500, 60% full-time. *Student/faculty ratio:* 18:1.

Academics *Calendar:* Canadian standard year. *Degrees:* diplomas, bachelor's, master's, doctoral, and first professional. *Special study options:* academic remediation for entering students, accelerated degree program, advanced placement credit, cooperative education, distance learning, double majors, English as a second language, honors programs, independent study, internships, off-campus study, part-time degree program, services for LD students, student-designed majors, study abroad, summer session for credit.

Computers on Campus Students can access the following: campus intranet, computer help desk, free student e-mail accounts, online (class) grades, online (class) registration, online (class) schedules, online tuition payment. Campuswide network is available. 100% of college-owned or -operated housing units are wired for high-speed Internet access. Wireless service is available via entire campus.

Student Life *Housing options:* coed, women-only. Campus housing is university owned. Freshman applicants given priority for college housing. *Activities and organizations:* drama/theater group, student-run newspaper, radio station, choral group, Trent Radio, Trent International Program, Trent Central Student Association, Arthur (student newspaper), Excalibur (yearbook). *Campus security:* 24-hour emergency response devices and patrols, student patrols, late-night transport/escort service, controlled dormitory access. *Student services:* health clinic, personal/psychological counseling, women's center.

Athletics Member CIS. *Intercollegiate sports:* crew M/W, cross-country running M/W, fencing M/W, golf M, lacrosse M, rugby M/W, soccer M/W, swimming and diving M/W, track and field M/W, volleyball M/W. *Intramural sports:* badminton M/W, baseball M/W, basketball M/W, cross-country running M/W, football M/W, ice hockey M/W, soccer M/W, softball M/W, squash M/W, swimming and diving M/W, tennis M/W, track and field M/W, ultimate Frisbee M/W, volleyball M/W, water polo M/W.

Applying *Options:* electronic application, deferred entrance. *Application fee:* $135 Canadian dollars. *Required:* high school transcript, minimum 2.7 GPA. *Required for some:* essay or personal statement, interview. *Application deadlines:* 6/1 (freshmen), 6/1 (transfers). *Notification:* continuous (freshmen), continuous (transfers).

Freshman Application Contact Mr. Kevin Whitmore, Manager, Admissions, Trent University, 1600 West Bank Drive, Peterborough, ON K9J 7B8, Canada. *Phone:* 705-748-1011 Ext. 7748. *Fax:* 705-748-1629. *E-mail:* admissions@trentu.ca. *Web site:* http://www.trentu.ca/.

Trinity Western University
Langley, British Columbia, Canada

Director of Admissions Director of Admissions, Trinity Western University, 7600 Glover Road, Langley, BC V2Y 1Y1, Canada. *Phone:* 604-888-7511 Ext. 3005. *Toll-free phone:* 888-468-6898. *E-mail:* admissions@twu.ca. *Web site:* http://www.twu.ca/.

Tyndale University College & Seminary
Toronto, Ontario, Canada

Freshman Application Contact Tricia McKenley, Admissions Office Coordinator, Tyndale University College & Seminary, 25 Ballyconnor Court, Toronto, ON M2M 4B3, Canada. *Phone:* 416-218-6757 Ext. 6738. *Toll-free phone:* 877-896-3253. *E-mail:* admissions@tydale.ca. *Web site:* http://www.tyndale.ca/.

Université de Moncton
Moncton, New Brunswick, Canada

Freshman Application Contact Miss Nicole Savois, Chief Admission Officer, Université de Moncton, Moncton, NB E1A 3E9, Canada. *Phone:* 506-858-4115. *Toll-free phone:* 800-363-8336. *E-mail:* gallanrm@umoncton.ca. *Web site:* http://www.umoncton.ca/.

Université de Montréal
Montréal, Quebec, Canada

Freshman Application Contact Mr. Pierre Chenard, Registrar, Université de Montréal, CP 6128, Succursale Centre-ville, Montréal, QC H3C 3J7, Canada. *Phone:* 514-343-2214. *Fax:* 514-343-2097. *E-mail:* pierre.chenard@umontreal.ca. *Web site:* http://www.umontreal.ca/.

Université de Sherbrooke
Sherbrooke, Quebec, Canada

- **Independent** university, founded 1954
- **Urban** 800-acre campus with easy access to Montreal
- **Coed** 13,663 undergraduate students, 79% full-time, 56% women, 44% men
- **Moderately difficult** entrance level, 59% of applicants were admitted

Undergraduates 10,820 full-time, 2,843 part-time. Students come from 3 provinces and territories; 53 other countries; 3% are from out of state; 6% transferred in.

Freshmen *Admission:* 15,897 applied, 9,310 admitted, 3,042 enrolled.

Faculty *Total:* 2,349, 46% full-time.

Academics *Calendar:* Canadian standard year. *Degrees:* certificates, diplomas, bachelor's, master's, doctoral, and first professional. *Special study options:* accelerated degree program, adult/continuing education programs, cooperative education, English as a second language, internships, off-campus study, part-time degree program, services for LD students, student-designed majors, study abroad, summer session for credit.

Computers on Campus 300 computers/terminals are available on campus for general student use. Students can access the following: computer help desk, free student e-mail accounts, online (class) registration, online (class) schedules. Campuswide network is available. Wireless service is available via classrooms, computer centers, computer labs, learning centers, libraries.

Student Life *Housing options:* coed. Campus housing is university owned. *Activities and organizations:* drama/theater group, student-run newspaper, radio station. *Campus security:* 24-hour emergency response devices and patrols. *Student services:* health clinic, personal/psychological counseling, legal services.

Athletics Member CIS. *Intercollegiate sports:* badminton M/W, cheerleading M/W, golf M/W, rugby M/W. *Intramural sports:* badminton M/W, basketball M/W, field hockey M/W, ice hockey M, racquetball M/W, soccer M/W, squash M/W, track and field M/W, ultimate Frisbee M/W, volleyball M/W, water polo M/W.

Costs (2011–12) *Tuition:* province resident $2166 full-time, $72 per credit part-time; nonresident $5858 full-time, $195 per credit part-time; International tuition $16,258 full-time. *Required fees:* $533 full-time, $12 per credit part-time, $72 per term part-time. *Room only:* $2740. *Waivers:* employees or children of employees.

Financial Aid *Financial aid deadline:* 3/31.

Applying *Options:* electronic application, early admission. *Application fee:* $70 Canadian dollars. *Required:* high school transcript. *Required for some:* interview. *Application deadline:* 3/1 (freshmen). *Notification:* continuous until 5/15 (freshmen).

Freshman Application Contact Ms. Lisa Bedard, Admissions Officer, Université de Sherbrooke, 2500, Boulevard de l'Universite, Sherbrooke, QC J1K 2R1, Canada. *Phone:* 819-821-7687. *Toll-free phone:* 800-267-UDES. *Web site:* http://www.usherbrooke.ca/.

Université du Québec à Chicoutimi
Chicoutimi, Quebec, Canada

Freshman Application Contact Mr. Claudio Zoccastello, Admissions Officer, Université du Québec à Chicoutimi, 555, boulevard de L'Université, Chicoutimi, QC G7H 2B1, Canada. *Phone:* 418-545-5005. *E-mail:* czoccast@uqac.uquebec.ca. *Web site:* http://www.uqac.ca/.

Université du Québec à Montréal
Montréal, Quebec, Canada

Freshman Application Contact Ms. Lucille Boisselle-Roy, Admissions Officer, Université du Québec à Montréal, CP 8888, Succursale Centreville, Montréal, QC H2L 4S8, Canada. *Phone:* 514-987-3132. *E-mail:* admission@uqam.ca. *Web site:* http://www.uqam.ca/.

Université du Québec à Rimouski
Rimouski, Quebec, Canada

Freshman Application Contact Ms. Marie Saint-Laurent, Admissions Officer, Université du Québec à Rimouski, 300 Allee des Ursulines, CP3300, Rimouski QC G5L 3A1, Canada. *Phone:* 418-724-1433. *E-mail:* philippe_horth@uqar.uquebec.ca. *Web site:* http://www.uqar.ca/.

Université du Québec à Trois-Rivières
Trois-Rivières, Quebec, Canada

Freshman Application Contact Ms. Jean Bois, Admissions Officer, Université du Québec à Trois-Rivières, 3351 blvd des Forges, Case post 500, Trois-Rivières, QC G9A 5H7, Canada. *Phone:* 819-376-5011. *Toll-free phone:* 800-365-0922. *Fax:* 819-376-5232. *E-mail:* registraire@uqtr.ca. *Web site:* http://www.uqtr.ca/.

Université du Québec, École de technologie supérieure
Montréal, Quebec, Canada

Director of Admissions Mme. Francine Gamache, Registraire, Université du Québec, École de technologie supérieure, 1100, rue Notre Dame Ouest, Montréal, QC H3C 1K3, Canada. *Phone:* 514-396-8885. *E-mail:* admission@ets.mtl.ca. *Web site:* http://www.etsmtl.ca/.

Université du Québec en Abitibi-Témiscamingue
Rouyn-Noranda, Quebec, Canada

Freshman Application Contact Mrs. Monique Fay, Admissions Officer, Université du Québec en Abitibi-Témiscamingue, 445 boulevard de l'Université, Rouyn-Noranda, QC J9X 5E4, Canada. *Phone:* 819-762-0971. *E-mail:* micheline.chevalier@uqat.uquebec.ca. *Web site:* http://www.uqat.ca/.

Université du Québec en Outaouais
Gatineau, Quebec, Canada

- **Province-supported** university, founded 1981, part of Universite du Quebec
- **Small-town** campus with easy access to Ottawa
- **Coed**
- **Noncompetitive** entrance level

Academics *Calendar:* trimesters. *Degrees:* certificates, bachelor's, master's, doctoral, postbachelor's, and first professional certificates.
Student Life *Campus security:* 24-hour emergency response devices and patrols.
Costs (2011–12) *Tuition:* province resident $2755 full-time, $72 per credit part-time; nonresident $6445 full-time; International tuition $15,113 full-time. Full-time tuition and fees vary according to class time, course load, degree level, program, and reciprocity agreements. Part-time tuition and fees vary according to class time, course load, degree level, and program. *Room only:* $5400. Room and board charges vary according to housing facility.
Applying *Options:* electronic application. *Application fee:* $60 Canadian dollars. *Required:* high school transcript, birth certificate. *Required for some:* essay or personal statement, 3 letters of recommendation, interview.
Freshman Application Contact Registrar Office, Université du Québec en Outaouais, CP 1250, Succursale Hull, 101 St-Jean-Bosco, 101 rue Saint-Jean-Bosco, Gatineau, QC J8X 3X7, Canada. *Phone:* 819-595-3900. *Toll-free phone:* 800-567-1283. *Fax:* 819-773-1835. *E-mail:* registraire@uqo.ca. *Web site:* http://www.uqo.ca/.

Université Laval
Québec, Quebec, Canada

Freshman Application Contact Promotion and Recruitment Division, Université Laval, Quebec, QC G1K 7P4, Canada. *Phone:* 418-656-2764. *Toll-free phone:* 877-785-2825. *Fax:* 418-656-5216. *E-mail:* info@dap.ulaval.ca. *Web site:* http://www.ulaval.ca/.

Université Sainte-Anne
Church Point, Nova Scotia, Canada

Freshman Application Contact Mrs. Blanche Thériault, Admissions Officer, Université Sainte-Anne, Church Point, NS B0W 1M0, Canada. *Phone:* 902-769-2114 Ext. 116. *E-mail:* admission@ustanne.ednet.ns.ca. *Web site:* http://www.usainteanne.ca/.

University of Alberta
Edmonton, Alberta, Canada

- **Province-supported** university, founded 1906
- **Urban** 1200-acre campus
- **Endowment** $767.2 million
- **Coed** 31,001 undergraduate students, 94% full-time, 56% women, 44% men
- **Moderately difficult** entrance level

Undergraduates 29,100 full-time, 1,844 part-time. Students come from 13 provinces and territories; 110 other countries; 9% are from out of state.
Freshmen *Average high school GPA:* 3.6.
Faculty *Student/faculty ratio:* 20:1.

Academics *Calendar:* Canadian standard year. *Degrees:* certificates, diplomas, bachelor's, master's, doctoral, postbachelor's, and first professional certificates. *Special study options:* academic remediation for entering students, accelerated degree program, adult/continuing education programs, advanced placement credit, cooperative education, distance learning, double majors, English as a second language, external degree program, honors programs, independent study, internships, off-campus study, part-time degree program, services for LD students, student-designed majors, study abroad, summer session for credit. *Unusual degree programs:* 3-2 education.
Computers on Campus 721 computers/terminals are available on campus for general student use. Students can access the following: computer help desk, free student e-mail accounts, online (class) grades, online (class) registration, online (class) schedules. Campuswide network is available. Wireless service is available via entire campus.
Student Life *Housing options:* coed, disabled students. Campus housing is university owned. Freshman applicants given priority for college housing. *Activities and organizations:* drama/theater group, student-run newspaper, radio station, choral group, national fraternities, national sororities. *Campus security:* 24-hour emergency response devices and patrols, student patrols, late-night transport/escort service, controlled dormitory access. *Student services:* health clinic, personal/psychological counseling, women's center, legal services.
Athletics Member CIS. *Intercollegiate sports:* basketball M(s)/W(s), cross-country running M/W, field hockey M(s)/W(s), football M(s), golf M/W, gymnastics M(s)/W(s), ice hockey M(s)/W(s), rugby W, skiing (cross-country) M/W, soccer M(s)/W(s), swimming and diving M(s)/W(s), tennis M/W, track and field M/W, volleyball M(s)/W(s), wrestling M(s)/W. *Intramural sports:* archery M(c)/W(c), badminton M(c)/W(c), basketball M/W, bowling M(c)/W(c), cheerleading M/W, crew M(c)/W(c), cross-country running M/W, fencing M(c)/W(c), field hockey W, football M, golf M/W, gymnastics M/W, ice hockey M/W, lacrosse M(c)/W(c), racquetball M/W, rock climbing M/W, rugby M(c)/W(c), skiing (cross-country) M(c)/W(c), skiing (downhill) M(c)/W(c), soccer M/W, squash M/W, swimming and diving M/W, table tennis M/W, tennis M/W, track and field M(c)/W(c), volleyball M/W, water polo M/W, weight lifting M(c)/W(c), wrestling M/W.
Standardized Tests *Recommended:* SAT (for admission), ACT (for admission), SAT or ACT (for admission), SAT and SAT Subject Tests or ACT (for admission), SAT Subject Tests (for admission).
Applying *Options:* electronic application, early admission, early decision, early action. *Application fee:* $115 Canadian dollars. *Required for some:* essay or personal statement, high school transcript, interview, portfolios/ auditions required for some programs. *Recommended:* minimum 2.0 GPA. *Application deadlines:* 5/1 (freshmen), 5/1 (transfers). *Notification:* continuous until 9/1 (freshmen), continuous until 9/1 (transfers).
Freshman Application Contact Ms. Patricia Dalton, Associate Registrar/Director of Enrollment Management, University of Alberta, 105 Administration Building, Edmonton, AB T6G 2M7, Canada. *Phone:* 780-492-3113. *Fax:* 780-492-4380. *E-mail:* registrar@ualberta.ca. *Web site:* http://www.ualberta.ca/.

The University of British Columbia
Vancouver, British Columbia, Canada

- **Province-supported** university, founded 1915
- **Urban** 1000-acre campus with easy access to Vancouver
- **Endowment** $950.2 million
- **Coed** 32,486 undergraduate students, 69% full-time, 55% women, 45% men
- **Very difficult** entrance level, 46% of applicants were admitted

Undergraduates 22,360 full-time, 10,126 part-time. Students come from 38 provinces and territories; 145 other countries; 5% transferred in; 25% live on campus. *Retention:* 91% of full-time freshmen returned.
Freshmen *Admission:* 33,731 applied, 15,601 admitted, 5,250 enrolled.
Faculty *Total:* 2,779, 98% full-time. *Student/faculty ratio:* 15:1.
Academics *Calendar:* Canadian standard year. *Degrees:* certificates, diplomas, bachelor's, master's, doctoral, postbachelor's, and first professional certificates. *Special study options:* academic remediation for entering students, adult/continuing education programs, advanced placement credit, cooperative education, distance learning, double majors, English as a second language, freshman honors college, honors programs, internships, off-campus study, part-time degree program, services for LD students, student-designed majors, study abroad, summer session for credit.
Computers on Campus 1,500 computers/terminals are available on campus for general student use. Students can access the following: free student e-mail accounts, online (class) grades, online (class) registration, online (class) schedules. Campuswide network is available. 100% of college-owned or -operated housing units are wired for high-speed Internet access. Wireless service is available via entire campus.

Student Life *Housing options:* coed, men-only, women-only, disabled students. Campus housing is university owned. Freshman applicants given priority for college housing. *Activities and organizations:* drama/theater group, student-run newspaper, radio station, choral group, Ski and Board Club, Dance Club, AIESEC (international leadership organization), UBC Film Society, Varsity Outdoors Club, national fraternities, national sororities. *Campus security:* 24-hour emergency response devices and patrols, student patrols, late-night transport/escort service, 24-hour desk attendants in residence halls. *Student services:* health clinic, personal/psychological counseling, women's center, legal services.

Athletics Member NAIA, CIS. *Intercollegiate sports:* baseball M(s), basketball M(s)/W(s), cheerleading W(c), crew M(s)/W(s), cross-country running M(s)/W(s), equestrian sports M/W, field hockey M(s)/W(s), football M(s), golf M(s)/W(s), ice hockey M(s)/W(s), rugby M(s)/W(s), skiing (downhill) M/W, soccer M(s)/W(s), softball M/W, swimming and diving M(s)/W(s), track and field M(s)/W(s), volleyball M(s)/W(s). *Intramural sports:* badminton M/W, basketball M/W, cross-country running M/W, fencing M/W, football M/W, gymnastics M/W, ice hockey M/W, racquetball M/W, rock climbing M/W, rugby M/W, sailing M/W, skiing (cross-country) M/W, skiing (downhill) M/W, soccer M/W, softball M/W, squash M/W, swimming and diving M/W, table tennis M/W, tennis M/W, ultimate Frisbee M/W, volleyball M/W, water polo M/W, weight lifting M/W, wrestling M/W.

Standardized Tests *Required for some:* SAT or ACT plus Writing required of applicants following US curriculum.

Financial Aid Of all full-time matriculated undergraduates who enrolled in 2009, 12,299 were judged to have need. 1,992 state and other part-time jobs (averaging $1561). In 2009, 6848 non-need-based awards were made. *Average financial aid package:* $10,938. *Average need-based loan:* $9066. *Average need-based gift aid:* $3219. *Average non-need-based aid:* $2495. *Financial aid deadline:* 9/15.

Applying *Options:* electronic application, deferred entrance. *Application fee:* $102 Canadian dollars. *Required:* essay or personal statement, high school transcript, minimum 2.6 GPA, English Language Admission Standard. *Application deadlines:* 1/31 (freshmen), 1/31 (out-of-state freshmen), 1/31 (transfers). *Notification:* continuous (freshmen), continuous (out-of-state freshmen), continuous (transfers).

Freshman Application Contact The University of British Columbia, V6T 1Z1, Canada. *Phone:* 604-822-3014. *Web site:* http://www.ubc.ca/.

The University of British Columbia–Okanagan
Kelowna, British Columbia, Canada

- **Province-supported** university, founded 2005
- **Urban** 500-acre campus with easy access to Kelowna
- **Endowment** $1.1 billion
- **Coed** 7,067 undergraduate students, 79% full-time, 55% women, 45% men
- **Moderately difficult** entrance level, 28% of applicants were admitted

Undergraduates 5,606 full-time, 1,461 part-time. Students come from 18 provinces and territories; 73 other countries; 40% live on campus. *Retention:* 73% of full-time freshmen returned.

Freshmen *Admission:* 5,113 applied, 1,441 admitted, 1,792 enrolled.

Faculty *Total:* 395, 91% full-time. *Student/faculty ratio:* 17:1.

Academics *Degrees:* certificates, diplomas, bachelor's, master's, doctoral, postbachelor's, and first professional certificates. *Special study options:* academic remediation for entering students, advanced placement credit, cooperative education, distance learning, double majors, English as a second language, freshman honors college, honors programs, internships, off-campus study, part-time degree program, services for LD students, student-designed majors, study abroad, summer session for credit.

Computers on Campus Students can access the following: campus intranet, computer help desk, free student e-mail accounts, online (class) grades, online (class) registration, online (class) schedules. Campuswide network is available. 100% of college-owned or -operated housing units are wired for high-speed Internet access. Wireless service is available via entire campus.

Student Life *Housing options:* coed, men-only, women-only. Campus housing is university owned. Freshman campus housing is guaranteed. *Activities and organizations:* drama/theater group, student-run newspaper, radio station, choral group, Save the World, Student Leadership, UBCSUO Mountain Riders Ski and Snowboard Club, Model United Nations, UBCSUO Asian Students' Association, national fraternities, national sororities. *Campus security:* 24-hour emergency response devices and patrols, controlled dormitory access, 24-hour desk attendants in residence halls. *Student services:* health clinic, personal/psychological counseling, women's center, legal services.

Athletics Member CIS. *Intercollegiate sports:* basketball M(s)/W(s), cross-country running M/W, golf M(s)/W(s), rugby M(s)/W(s), soccer M(s)/W(s), volleyball M(s)/W(s). *Intramural sports:* badminton M/W, basketball M/W,

cross-country running M/W, field hockey M/W, golf M/W, gymnastics M/W, ice hockey M/W, soccer M/W, tennis M/W, volleyball M/W.

Standardized Tests *Required for some:* SAT or ACT (for admission).

Applying *Options:* electronic application, deferred entrance. *Application fee:* $102 Canadian dollars. *Required:* essay or personal statement, high school transcript, minimum 2.6 GPA. *Application deadlines:* 1/31 (freshmen), 1/31 (out-of-state freshmen), 1/31 (transfers). *Notification:* continuous (freshmen), continuous (out-of-state freshmen), continuous (transfers).

Freshman Application Contact International Student Recruitment, The University of British Columbia–Okanagan, UC222 University Centre, 3333 University Way, Kelowna, BC V1V 1V7, Canada. *Phone:* 604-822-3014. *Fax:* 604-822-3599. *Web site:* http://www.ubc.ca/okanagan/welcome.html.

University of Calgary
Calgary, Alberta, Canada

Freshman Application Contact Kim Vandam, Associate Director of Admissions, University of Calgary, 2500 University Drive NW, Calgary, AB T2N 1N4, Canada. *Phone:* 403-220-3825. *E-mail:* vandam@ucalgary.ca. *Web site:* http://www.ucalgary.ca/.

University of Guelph
Guelph, Ontario, Canada

- **Province-supported** university, founded 1964
- **Urban** 1017-acre campus with easy access to Toronto
- **Coed** 17,436 undergraduate students
- **Moderately difficult** entrance level, 71% of applicants were admitted

Undergraduates Students come from 100 other countries; 24% live on campus. *Retention:* 89% of full-time freshmen returned.

Freshmen *Admission:* 22,220 applied, 15,849 admitted. *Average high school GPA:* 3.5.

Faculty *Total:* 860. *Student/faculty ratio:* 22:1.

Academics *Calendar:* trimesters. *Degrees:* certificates, diplomas, associate, bachelor's, master's, doctoral, and first professional. *Special study options:* academic remediation for entering students, accelerated degree program, advanced placement credit, cooperative education, distance learning, double majors, English as a second language, freshman honors college, honors programs, independent study, internships, off-campus study, part-time degree program, services for LD students, student-designed majors, study abroad, summer session for credit.

Computers on Campus 1,500 computers/terminals and 16,000 ports are available on campus for general student use. Students can access the following: campus intranet, computer help desk, free student e-mail accounts, online (class) registration. Campuswide network is available. 100% of college-owned or -operated housing units are wired for high-speed Internet access. Wireless service is available via entire campus.

Student Life *Housing options:* coed, men-only, women-only, cooperative, disabled students. Campus housing is university owned and is provided by a third party. Freshman campus housing is guaranteed. *Activities and organizations:* drama/theater group, student-run newspaper, radio station, choral group, Guelph Gryphon Athletics, Habitat for Humanity, Curtain Call Productions, West Indian Students Association, OXFAM-Guelph Chapter. *Campus security:* 24-hour emergency response devices and patrols, student patrols, late-night transport/escort service, controlled dormitory access, video camera surveillance in parking lots, alarms in women's locker room. *Student services:* health clinic, personal/psychological counseling, women's center, legal services.

Athletics Member CIS. *Intercollegiate sports:* baseball M, basketball M/W, crew M/W, cross-country running M/W, field hockey W, football M, golf M/W, ice hockey M/W, lacrosse M/W, rugby M/W, skiing (cross-country) M/W, soccer M/W, swimming and diving M/W, track and field M/W, volleyball M/W, wrestling M/W. *Intramural sports:* archery M(c)/W(c), badminton M/W, basketball M/W, cheerleading M(c)/W(c), fencing M(c)/W(c), football M/W, ice hockey M/W, lacrosse M(c)/W(c), rock climbing M(c)/W(c), soccer M/W, softball M/W, squash M(c)/W(c), tennis M/W, ultimate Frisbee M/W, volleyball M/W, water polo M(c)/W(c).

Standardized Tests *Required:* SAT or ACT (for admission).

Costs (2011–12) *Tuition:* province resident $5446 full-time, $1088 per credit part-time; International tuition $16,922 full-time. Full-time tuition and fees vary according to course level, degree level, location, and program. Part-time tuition and fees vary according to course level, course load, degree level, location, and program. No tuition increase for student's term of enrollment. *Required fees:* $1360 full-time, $40 per credit part-time, $442 per term part-time. *Room and board:* $9478; room only: $5202. Room and board charges vary according to board plan and housing facility. *Payment plan:* installment. *Waivers:* senior citizens and employees or children of employees.

Applying *Options:* electronic application, early admission, deferred entrance. *Application fee:* $125 Canadian dollars. *Required:* high school transcript, minimum 3.0 GPA. *Required for some:* essay or personal statement. *Application deadlines:* 3/1 (freshmen), 5/1 (transfers). *Notification:* continuous (freshmen), continuous (transfers).

Freshman Application Contact Ms. Janette Hogan, Assistant Registrar, Admissions, University of Guelph, L-3 University Centre, Guelph, ON N1G 2W1, Canada. *Phone:* 519-824-4120 Ext. 58529. *Fax:* 519-766-9481. *E-mail:* jhogan@registrar.uoguelph.ca. *Web site:* http://www.uoguelph.ca/.

See below for display ad and page 1670 for the College Close-Up.

University of King's College
Halifax, Nova Scotia, Canada

Freshman Application Contact Ms. Jill MacBeath, Admissions and Recruitment Coordinator, University of King's College, Registrar's Office, Halifax, NS B3H 3A1, Canada. *Phone:* 902-422-1271. *Fax:* 902-425-8183. *E-mail:* admissions@ukings.ns.ca. *Web site:* http://www.ukings.ca/.

University of Lethbridge
Lethbridge, Alberta, Canada

- **Province-supported** university, founded 1967
- **Urban** 576-acre campus
- **Endowment** $37.5 million
- **Coed** 7,826 undergraduate students, 88% full-time, 57% women, 43% men
- **Moderately difficult** entrance level, 52% of applicants were admitted

Undergraduates 6,893 full-time, 933 part-time. Students come from 21 provinces and territories; 65 other countries; 11% are from out of state; 10% live on campus. *Retention:* 76% of full-time freshmen returned.

Freshmen *Admission:* 2,483 applied, 1,281 admitted.

Faculty *Total:* 645, 88% full-time, 51% with terminal degrees. *Student/faculty ratio:* 12:1.

Academics *Calendar:* semesters. *Degrees:* certificates, diplomas, bachelor's, master's, doctoral, post-master's, postbachelor's, and first professional certificates. *Special study options:* academic remediation for entering students, accelerated degree program, cooperative education, distance learning, double majors, English as a second language, independent study, internships, off-campus study, part-time degree program, services for LD students, student-designed majors, study abroad, summer session for credit. *Unusual degree programs:* 3-2 education.

Computers on Campus 613 computers/terminals are available on campus for general student use. Students can access the following: computer help desk, free student e-mail accounts, online (class) grades, online (class) registration, online (class) schedules. Campuswide network is available. 100% of college-owned or -operated housing units are wired for high-speed Internet access. Wireless service is available via entire campus.

Student Life *Housing options:* coed. Campus housing is university owned. *Activities and organizations:* drama/theater group, student-run newspaper, radio station, choral group, Management Students Society, Inter-Varsity Christian Fellowship, Organization of Residence Students, Agricultural Students Society, Education Undergraduate Society, national fraternities. *Campus security:* 24-hour emergency response devices and patrols, student patrols, late-night transport/escort service, controlled dormitory access, video camera monitored entrances, hallways. *Student services:* health clinic, personal/psychological counseling, women's center.

Athletics Member CIS. *Intercollegiate sports:* basketball M(s)/W(s), ice hockey M(s)/W(s), rugby W(s), soccer M(s)/W(s), swimming and diving M(s)/W(s), track and field M(s)/W(s). *Intramural sports:* badminton M/W, fencing M(c)/W(c), golf M/W, ice hockey M/W, rock climbing M/W, rugby M(c)/W(c), soccer M/W, softball W, tennis M(c)/W(c), volleyball M/W, water polo M/W.

Costs (2012–13) *Tuition:* province resident $4900 full-time, $486 per course part-time; nonresident $4900 full-time, $486 per course part-time; International tuition $11,100 full-time. Full-time tuition and fees vary according to course load. Part-time tuition and fees vary according to course load. *Required fees:* $676 full-time, $115 per term part-time. *Room and board:* $7830; room only: $4664. Room and board charges vary according to board plan and housing facility. *Waivers:* employees or children of employees.

Applying *Options:* electronic application, deferred entrance. *Application fee:* $75 Canadian dollars. *Required:* high school transcript, minimum 2.0 GPA. *Required for some:* minimum 3.0 GPA, interview. *Application deadlines:* 6/1 (freshmen), 6/1 (transfers). *Notification:* continuous (freshmen), continuous (transfers).

Freshman Application Contact Ms. Alice Miller, Assistant Registrar, University of Lethbridge, 4401 University Drive, Lethbridge, AB T1K 3M4, Canada. *Phone:* 403-320-5700. *Fax:* 403-329-5159. *E-mail:* inquiries@uleth.ca. *Web site:* http://www.uleth.ca/.

University of Manitoba

Winnipeg, Manitoba, Canada

- **Province-supported** university, founded 1877
- **Suburban** 685-acre campus
- **Coed**
- **Moderately difficult** entrance level

Academics *Calendar:* 8-month academic year plus 6-week summer session. *Degrees:* certificates, diplomas, bachelor's, master's, doctoral, post-master's, postbachelor's, and first professional certificates.

Student Life *Campus security:* 24-hour emergency response devices, student patrols, late-night transport/escort service.

Athletics Member CIS.

Costs (2011–12) *Tuition:* Tuition varies by major. Contact institution for tuition information.

Financial Aid *Of all full-time matriculated undergraduates who enrolled in 2009,* 50 state and other part-time jobs (averaging $900).

Applying *Options:* electronic application, early admission. *Application fee:* $65 Canadian dollars. *Required:* high school transcript.

Freshman Application Contact Mr. Peter Dueck, Director of Enrollment Services, University of Manitoba, Winnipeg, MB R3T 2N2, Canada. *Phone:* 204-474-6382. *Web site:* http://www.umanitoba.ca/.

University of New Brunswick Fredericton

Fredericton, New Brunswick, Canada

- **Province-supported** university, founded 1785
- **Urban** 7100-acre campus
- **Endowment** $116.0 million
- **Coed**
- **Moderately difficult** entrance level

Academics *Calendar:* Canadian standard year. *Degrees:* bachelor's, master's, doctoral, and first professional.

Student Life *Campus security:* 24-hour emergency response devices and patrols, student patrols, late-night transport/escort service, controlled dormitory access.

Athletics Member CIS.

Standardized Tests *Required for some:* SAT (for admission).

Financial Aid *Of all full-time matriculated undergraduates who enrolled in 2007,* 123 state and other part-time jobs (averaging $1264). *Financial aid deadline:* 5/15.

Applying *Options:* electronic application, early admission, deferred entrance. *Application fee:* $45 Canadian dollars. *Required:* high school transcript. *Required for some:* essay or personal statement, 1 letter of recommendation, interview.

Freshman Application Contact University of New Brunswick Fredericton, PO Box 4400, Fredericton, NB E3B 5A3, Canada. *Phone:* 506-453-4865. *Web site:* http://www.unb.ca/.

University of New Brunswick Saint John

Saint John, New Brunswick, Canada

- **Province-supported** comprehensive, founded 1964
- **Urban** 250-acre campus
- **Coed**
- **Moderately difficult** entrance level

Academics *Calendar:* Canadian standard year. *Degrees:* certificates, diplomas, bachelor's, master's, doctoral, and postbachelor's certificates.

Student Life *Campus security:* 24-hour emergency response devices and patrols, student patrols, late-night transport/escort service, controlled dormitory access.

Standardized Tests *Required:* SAT (for admission).

Financial Aid *Of all full-time matriculated undergraduates who enrolled in 2010,* 140 state and other part-time jobs (averaging $500).

Applying *Options:* electronic application, early admission, deferred entrance. *Application fee:* $45 Canadian dollars. *Required:* high school transcript.

Freshman Application Contact University of New Brunswick Saint John, PO Box 5050, Saint John, NB E2L 4L5, Canada. *Web site:* http://www.unb.ca/.

University of Northern British Columbia

Prince George, British Columbia, Canada

Freshman Application Contact Mr. Grant Kerr, Assistant Registrar, Admissions, University of Northern British Columbia, Office of the Registrar, 3333 University Way, Prince George, BC V2N 4Z9, Canada. *Phone:* 250-960-6347. *Fax:* 250-960-6330. *E-mail:* registrar-info@unbc.ca. *Web site:* http://www.unbc.ca/.

University of Ottawa

Ottawa, Ontario, Canada

- **Province-supported** university, founded 1848
- **Urban** 43-hectare campus with easy access to Ottawa-Gatineau
- **Endowment** $177.9 million
- **Coed** 34,708 undergraduate students, 82% full-time, 60% women, 40% men
- **Moderately difficult** entrance level, 61% of applicants were admitted

Undergraduates 28,626 full-time, 6,082 part-time. Students come from 13 provinces and territories; 152 other countries; 20% are from out of state; 9% live on campus. *Retention:* 86% of full-time freshmen returned.

Freshmen *Admission:* 37,060 applied, 22,550 admitted. *Average high school GPA:* 3.28.

Faculty *Total:* 2,177, 58% full-time. *Student/faculty ratio:* 24:1.

Academics *Calendar:* semesters. *Degrees:* certificates, diplomas, bachelor's, master's, doctoral, postbachelor's, and first professional certificates. *Special study options:* academic remediation for entering students, advanced placement credit, cooperative education, distance learning, double majors, English as a second language, honors programs, internships, off-campus study, part-time degree program, services for LD students, study abroad, summer session for credit. *Unusual degree programs:* 3-2 law, education.

Computers on Campus 1,540 computers/terminals are available on campus for general student use. Students can access the following: computer help desk, free student e-mail accounts, online (class) grades, online (class) registration, online (class) schedules, wireless connection available on campus. Campuswide network is available. 100% of college-owned or -operated housing units are wired for high-speed Internet access. Wireless service is available via entire campus.

Student Life *Housing options:* coed, disabled students. Campus housing is university owned. Freshman campus housing is guaranteed. *Activities and organizations:* drama/theater group, student-run newspaper, radio station, choral group, Student Federation of the University of Ottawa, Graduate Students Association, national fraternities, national sororities. *Campus security:* 24-hour emergency response devices and patrols, student patrols, late-night transport/escort service, controlled dormitory access. *Student services:* health clinic, personal/psychological counseling, women's center, legal services.

Athletics Member CIS. *Intercollegiate sports:* badminton M(c)/W(c), baseball M(c)/W(c), basketball M(s)/W(s), cheerleading M(c)/W(c), crew M(c)/W(c), cross-country running M(s)/W(s), equestrian sports M(c)/W(c), fencing M(c)/W(c), football M(s), golf M(c)/W(c), ice hockey M(s)/W(s), rugby W(s), soccer M(s)(c)/W(s), swimming and diving M(s)/W(s), track and field M(s)/W(s), ultimate Frisbee M(c)/W(c), volleyball M(c)/W(s), water polo M(c)/W(c). *Intramural sports:* basketball M/W, football M, ice hockey M/W, soccer M/W, ultimate Frisbee M/W, volleyball M/W.

Standardized Tests *Required for some:* SAT or ACT required for American citizens.

Costs (2011–12) *One-time required fee:* $290. *Tuition:* province resident $5421 full-time, $215 per credit part-time; nonresident $662 per credit part-time; International tuition $17,080 full-time. Full-time tuition and fees vary according to course load, degree level, program, and student level. Part-time tuition and fees vary according to course load, degree level, program, and student level. *Required fees:* $640 full-time, $111 per term part-time. *Room and board:* $6666; room only: $4466. Room and board charges vary according to board plan and housing facility. *Waivers:* employees or children of employees.

Financial Aid *Financial aid deadline:* 1/31.

Applying *Options:* electronic application, early admission, deferred entrance. *Application fee:* $165 Canadian dollars. *Required:* high school transcript, minimum 3.0 GPA. *Required for some:* interview. *Application deadline:* 6/1 (freshmen). *Notification:* continuous until 8/30 (freshmen).

Freshman Application Contact Ms. Emilie Bertrand, University of Ottawa, 550 Cumberland Street, PO Box 450, Station A, Ottawa, ON K1N 6N5, Canada. *Phone:* 613-562-5800 Ext. 1593. *Fax:* 613-562-5790. *E-mail:* cpharand@uottawa.ca. *Web site:* http://www.uottawa.ca/.

University of Phoenix–Vancouver Campus
Burnaby, British Columbia, Canada

Freshman Application Contact Marc Booker, Sr. Director, Office of Admissions and Evaluation, University of Phoenix–Vancouver Campus, 4035 South Riverpoint Parkway, Mail Stop CF-L101, Phoenix, AZ 85040. *Phone:* 602-557-4609. *Toll-free phone:* 866-766-0766. *Fax:* 480-643-1156. *Web site:* http://www.phoenix.edu/.

University of Prince Edward Island
Charlottetown, Prince Edward Island, Canada

Freshman Application Contact University of Prince Edward Island, 550 University Avenue, Charlottetown, PE C1A 4P3, Canada. *Phone:* 902-566-0634. *Web site:* http://www.upei.ca/.

University of Regina
Regina, Saskatchewan, Canada

- **Province-supported** university, founded 1974
- **Urban** 445-acre campus
- **Endowment** $28.6 million
- **Coed** 11,144 undergraduate students, 79% full-time, 62% women, 38% men
- **Minimally difficult** entrance level, 79% of applicants were admitted

Undergraduates 8,858 full-time, 2,286 part-time. Students come from 13 provinces and territories; 88 other countries; 6% are from out of state; 4% transferred in; 10% live on campus. *Retention:* 80% of full-time freshmen returned.
Freshmen *Admission:* 3,243 applied, 2,572 admitted, 1,859 enrolled. *Average high school GPA:* 3.5.
Faculty *Total:* 498, 100% full-time, 81% with terminal degrees. *Student/faculty ratio:* 21:1.
Academics *Calendar:* semesters. *Degrees:* certificates, diplomas, bachelor's, master's, doctoral, postbachelor's, and first professional certificates. *Special study options:* academic remediation for entering students, adult/continuing education programs, advanced placement credit, cooperative education, distance learning, double majors, English as a second language, honors programs, independent study, internships, off-campus study, part-time degree program, services for LD students, student-designed majors, study abroad, summer session for credit.
Computers on Campus 315 computers/terminals and 1,200 ports are available on campus for general student use. Students can access the following: campus intranet, computer help desk, free student e-mail accounts, online (class) grades, online (class) registration, online (class) schedules. Campuswide network is available. 100% of college-owned or -operated housing units are wired for high-speed Internet access. Wireless service is available via entire campus.
Student Life *Housing options:* disabled students. Campus housing is university owned. Freshman campus housing is guaranteed. *Activities and organizations:* drama/theater group, student-run newspaper, television station, choral group. *Campus security:* 24-hour emergency response devices and patrols, late-night transport/escort service, controlled dormitory access, crime prevention assistance, CCTV, card access and some alarm monitoring. *Student services:* health clinic, personal/psychological counseling, women's center.
Athletics Member CIS. *Intercollegiate sports:* basketball M(s)/W(s), cross-country running M(s)/W(s), football M(s), ice hockey M(s)/W(s), soccer W(s), swimming and diving M(s)/W(s), track and field M(s)/W(s), volleyball M(s)/W(s), wrestling M(s)/W(s). *Intramural sports:* badminton M/W, basketball M/W, cheerleading M(c)/W(c), football M, soccer M/W, softball M/W(c), tennis M/W, ultimate Frisbee M/W, volleyball M/W, water polo M/W.
Standardized Tests *Required for some:* SAT or ACT (for admission), SAT Subject Tests (for admission).
Costs (2011–12) *Tuition:* province resident $5212 full-time, $164 per credit hour part-time; nonresident $164 per credit hour part-time; International tuition $15,052 full-time. Full-time tuition and fees vary according to course load and program. Part-time tuition and fees vary according to course load and program. *Required fees:* $394 full-time, $136 per term part-time. *Room and board:* $8368; room only: $5868. Room and board charges vary according to board plan and housing facility. *Waivers:* senior citizens and employees or children of employees.
Applying *Options:* electronic application, early admission, early action, deferred entrance. *Application fee:* $100 Canadian dollars. *Required:* high school transcript, minimum 2.3 GPA. *Required for some:* essay or personal statement, 2 letters of recommendation, interview, portfolio, audition, some

programs require a higher than 2.3 minimum GPA for admission. *Application deadlines:* 8/1 (freshmen), 8/1 (transfers), 3/15 (early action).
Freshman Application Contact University of Regina, 3737 Wascana Parkway, Regina, SK S4S 0A2, Canada. *Phone:* 306-585-4942. *Toll-free phone:* 800-664-4756. *Web site:* http://www.uregina.ca/.

University of Saskatchewan
Saskatoon, Saskatchewan, Canada

- **Province-supported** university, founded 1907
- **Urban** 1865-acre campus
- **Coed**

Academics *Calendar:* Canadian standard year. *Degrees:* certificates, diplomas, bachelor's, master's, doctoral, postbachelor's, and first professional certificates.
Student Life *Campus security:* 24-hour emergency response devices and patrols, student patrols, late-night transport/escort service, controlled dormitory access.
Athletics Member CIS.
Standardized Tests *Recommended:* scores sometimes used for home-educated students.
Costs (2011–12) *Tuition:* province resident $6153 Canadian dollars full-time, $187 Canadian dollars per credit part-time; nonresident $187 Canadian dollars per credit part-time; International tuition $15,997 Canadian dollars full-time. Tuition varies by major. Contact institution for more information. *Required fees:* $731 Canadian dollars full-time. *Room and board:* $7031 Canadian dollars. Room and board charges vary according to board plan, housing facility, and location.
Financial Aid *Financial aid deadline:* 3/15.
Applying *Options:* electronic application, early admission. *Application fee:* $90 Canadian dollars. *Required:* high school transcript. *Required for some:* essay or personal statement, interview.
Freshman Application Contact University of Saskatchewan, 105 Administration Place, Saskatoon, SK S7N 5A2, Canada. *Phone:* 306-966-5788. *Web site:* http://www.usask.ca/.

University of the Fraser Valley
Abbotsford, British Columbia, Canada

Freshman Application Contact Ms. Robin Smith, Admissions Coordinator, University of the Fraser Valley, 33844 King Road, Abbotsford, BC V2S 7M8, Canada. *Phone:* 604-504-7441 Ext. 4540. *Toll-free phone:* 888-823-8734. *Fax:* 604-853-0138. *E-mail:* reginfo@ucfv.ca. *Web site:* http://www.ufv.ca/.

University of Toronto
Toronto, Ontario, Canada

- **Province-supported** university, founded 1827
- **Urban** 714-hectare campus
- **Endowment** $1.5 billion
- **Coed** 64,970 undergraduate students, 89% full-time, 56% women, 44% men
- **Very difficult** entrance level, 69% of applicants were admitted

Undergraduates 58,064 full-time, 6,898 part-time. Students come from 12 provinces and territories; 162 other countries; 6% are from out of state; 1% transferred in; 15% live on campus. *Retention:* 90% of full-time freshmen returned.
Freshmen *Admission:* 67,955 applied, 46,712 admitted, 18,037 enrolled.
Faculty *Total:* 3,135, 89% full-time. *Student/faculty ratio:* 24:1.
Academics *Calendar:* Canadian standard year. *Degrees:* certificates, diplomas, bachelor's, master's, doctoral, and first professional. *Special study options:* adult/continuing education programs, cooperative education, double majors, English as a second language, off-campus study, part-time degree program, services for LD students, study abroad, summer session for credit.
Computers on Campus 2,000 computers/terminals are available on campus for general student use. Students can access the following: campus intranet, computer help desk, free student e-mail accounts, online (class) registration, online (class) schedules. Campuswide network is available. Wireless service is available via classrooms, computer centers, computer labs, dorm rooms, learning centers, libraries, student centers.
Student Life *Housing options:* coed, women-only. Campus housing is university owned and leased by the school. Freshman campus housing is guaranteed. *Activities and organizations:* drama/theater group, student-run newspaper, radio station, choral group, national fraternities, national sororities. *Campus security:* 24-hour emergency response devices and patrols, student patrols, late-night transport/escort service. *Student services:* health clinic, personal/psychological counseling, women's center, legal services.

Athletics Member CIS. *Intercollegiate sports:* archery M/W, badminton M/W, basketball M/W, crew M, cross-country running M/W, fencing M/W, field hockey W, football M, golf M, gymnastics M/W, ice hockey M/W, rugby M, skiing (cross-country) M/W, skiing (downhill) M/W, soccer M/W, squash M/W, swimming and diving M/W, tennis M/W, track and field M/W, volleyball M/W, wrestling M. *Intramural sports:* archery M/W, badminton M/W, basketball M/W, crew M, fencing M/W, field hockey W, football M/W, gymnastics M/W, ice hockey M/W, lacrosse M/W, racquetball M, rugby M, skiing (downhill) M/W, soccer M/W, squash M/W, swimming and diving M/W, tennis M/W, track and field M/W, volleyball M/W, water polo M/W.

Standardized Tests *Required:* SAT and SAT Subject Tests or ACT (for admission).

Costs (2011–12) *Tuition:* province resident $5450 full-time; nonresident $5450 full-time; International tuition $25,826 full-time. Full-time tuition and fees vary according to course level, course load, and program. Part-time tuition and fees vary according to course load. *Required fees:* $1200 full-time. *Room and board:* $12,000; room only: $7000. Room and board charges vary according to board plan, housing facility, and location. *Payment plan:* installment. *Waivers:* senior citizens and employees or children of employees.

Applying *Options:* deferred entrance. *Application fee:* $115 Canadian dollars. *Required:* high school transcript. *Required for some:* interview. *Application deadlines:* 3/1 (freshmen), 7/1 (transfers). *Notification:* continuous (freshmen), continuous (transfers).

Freshman Application Contact University of Toronto, Toronto, ON M5S 1A1, Canada. *Phone:* 416-978-2190. *Fax:* 416-978-7022. *E-mail:* admissions.help@utoronto.ca. *Web site:* http://www.utoronto.ca/uoft.html.

University of Victoria
Victoria, British Columbia, Canada

Freshman Application Contact Mr. Bruno Rocca, Student Recruitment Director, University of Victoria, PO Box 1700, STN CSC, Victoria, BC V8W 2Y2, Canada. *Phone:* 250-721-8121 Ext. 8109. *Fax:* 250-721-6225. *E-mail:* admit@uvic.ca. *Web site:* http://www.uvic.ca/.

University of Waterloo
Waterloo, Ontario, Canada

- **Province-supported** university, founded 1957
- **Suburban** 1000-acre campus with easy access to Toronto
- **Coed**
- **Moderately difficult** entrance level

Academics *Calendar:* trimesters. *Degrees:* certificates, diplomas, bachelor's, master's, doctoral, and postbachelor's certificates.

Student Life *Campus security:* 24-hour emergency response devices and patrols, student patrols, late-night transport/escort service.

Athletics Member CIS.

Standardized Tests *Required for some:* SAT or ACT (for admission), SAT Subject Tests (for admission).

Applying *Options:* electronic application, early admission, deferred entrance. *Application fee:* $110 Canadian dollars. *Required:* high school transcript. *Required for some:* essay or personal statement, minimum 3.0 GPA, interview.

Freshman Application Contact University of Waterloo, 200 University Avenue West, Waterloo, ON N2L 3G1, Canada. *Phone:* 519-888-4567 Ext. 32265. *Web site:* http://www.uwaterloo.ca/.

The University of Western Ontario
London, Ontario, Canada

- **Province-supported** university, founded 1878
- **Suburban** 499-hectare campus
- **Coed** 31,436 undergraduate students, 90% full-time, 57% women, 43% men
- **Very difficult** entrance level, 55% of applicants were admitted

Undergraduates 28,369 full-time, 3,067 part-time. Students come from 13 provinces and territories; 118 other countries; 6% are from out of state; 19% live on campus. *Retention:* 93% of full-time freshmen returned.

Freshmen *Admission:* 32,616 applied, 17,801 admitted. *Average high school GPA:* 3.9.

Faculty *Total:* 1,372, 100% full-time. *Student/faculty ratio:* 20:1.

Academics *Calendar:* Canadian standard year. *Degrees:* certificates, diplomas, bachelor's, master's, doctoral, and first professional. *Special study options:* academic remediation for entering students, accelerated degree program, adult/continuing education programs, advanced placement credit, cooperative education, distance learning, double majors, English as a second language, honors programs, independent study, internships, off-campus study,

part-time degree program, services for LD students, student-designed majors, study abroad, summer session for credit.

Computers on Campus 414 computers/terminals are available on campus for general student use. Students can access the following: campus intranet, computer help desk, free student e-mail accounts, online (class) grades, online (class) registration, online (class) schedules. Campuswide network is available. 100% of college-owned or -operated housing units are wired for high-speed Internet access. Wireless service is available via classrooms, computer centers, computer labs, learning centers, libraries, student centers.

Student Life *Housing options:* coed, disabled students. Campus housing is university owned. Freshman campus housing is guaranteed. *Activities and organizations:* drama/theater group, student-run newspaper, radio and television station, choral group, marching band, Pre-Medical Society, Western Investment Club, Western Snowboard Federation, Purple Spur Society, Canadian Asian International Students' Association (CAISA), national fraternities, national sororities. *Campus security:* 24-hour emergency response devices and patrols, student patrols, late-night transport/escort service, controlled dormitory access, Campus Community Police, SERT: Student Emergency Response Team, Western Foot Patrol. *Student services:* health clinic, personal/psychological counseling, legal services.

Athletics Member CIS. *Intercollegiate sports:* badminton M/W, baseball M, basketball M/W, cheerleading M/W, crew M/W, cross-country running M/W, equestrian sports W, fencing M/W, field hockey W, football M, golf M/W, ice hockey M/W, lacrosse M/W, rugby M/W, soccer M/W, softball W, squash M/W, swimming and diving M/W, table tennis M/W, tennis M/W, track and field M/W, volleyball M/W, water polo M/W, wrestling M/W. *Intramural sports:* badminton M/W, basketball M/W, fencing M(c)/W(c), ice hockey M/W, soccer M/W, softball M/W, squash M(c)/W(c), swimming and diving M/W, table tennis M(c)/W(c), tennis M/W/(c), ultimate Frisbee M/W, volleyball M/W, water polo M/W.

Standardized Tests *Required:* SAT or ACT (for admission).

Costs (2011–12) *Tuition:* province resident $5391 Canadian dollars full-time, $1078 Canadian dollars per course part-time; nonresident $3354 Canadian dollars per course part-time; International tuition $16,771 Canadian dollars full-time. Full-time tuition and fees vary according to program and student level. Part-time tuition and fees vary according to course load, location, program, and student level. *Required fees:* $1045 Canadian dollars full-time, $150 Canadian dollars per course part-time. *Room and board:* $9545 Canadian dollars; room only: $6670 Canadian dollars. Room and board charges vary according to board plan, housing facility, and location. *Payment plans:* installment, deferred payment. *Waivers:* senior citizens and employees or children of employees.

Financial Aid Of all full-time matriculated undergraduates who enrolled in 2010, 1,457 state and other part-time jobs (averaging $1817).

Applying *Options:* electronic application, deferred entrance. *Application fee:* $130 Canadian dollars. *Required:* high school transcript, minimum 3.5 GPA. *Application deadlines:* 6/1 (freshmen), 5/15 (out-of-state freshmen), 6/1 (transfers). *Notification:* continuous (freshmen), continuous (out-of-state freshmen).

Freshman Application Contact Undergraduate Recruitment and Admissions, The University of Western Ontario, The University of Western Ontario, Western Student Services Building, Room 3140, London, ON N6A 3K7, Canada. *Phone:* 519-661-2100. *Fax:* 519-661-3710. *E-mail:* reg-admissions@uwo.ca. *Web site:* http://www.uwo.ca/.

University of Windsor
Windsor, Ontario, Canada

- **Province-supported** university, founded 1857
- **Urban** 125-acre campus with easy access to Detroit
- **Endowment** $56.0 million
- **Coed** 13,620 undergraduate students, 78% full-time, 55% women, 45% men
- **Moderately difficult** entrance level, 78% of applicants were admitted

Undergraduates 10,560 full-time, 3,060 part-time. Students come from 16 provinces and territories; 91 other countries; 5% transferred in; 13% live on campus. *Retention:* 82% of full-time freshmen returned.

Freshmen *Admission:* 12,180 applied, 9,469 admitted, 2,998 enrolled.

Faculty *Total:* 871, 60% full-time, 53% with terminal degrees. *Student/faculty ratio:* 21:1.

Academics *Calendar:* semesters. *Degrees:* certificates, bachelor's, master's, doctoral, postbachelor's, and first professional certificates. *Special study options:* academic remediation for entering students, accelerated degree program, adult/continuing education programs, advanced placement credit, cooperative education, distance learning, double majors, external degree program, honors programs, internships, off-campus study, part-time degree program, services for LD students, student-designed majors, study abroad, summer session for credit. *Unusual degree programs:* 3-2 business administration; engineering; social work; computer science.

Computers on Campus 1,225 computers/terminals are available on campus for general student use. Students can access the following: campus intranet, computer help desk, free student e-mail accounts, online (class) grades, online (class) registration, online transcripts, degree audits, grades, bursaries, grants, online applications for graduation. Campuswide network is available. 100% of college-owned or -operated housing units are wired for high-speed Internet access. Wireless service is available via entire campus.

Student Life *Housing options:* coed, men-only, women-only, disabled students. Campus housing is university owned. Freshman campus housing is guaranteed. *Activities and organizations:* drama/theater group, student-run newspaper, radio station, choral group, University of Windsor Student Alliance, Environmental Awareness Association, Social Science Society, Commerce Society, Science Society. *Campus security:* 24-hour emergency response devices and patrols, student patrols, late-night transport/escort service, controlled dormitory access. *Student services:* health clinic, personal/psychological counseling, women's center, legal services.

Athletics Member NAIA, CIS. *Intercollegiate sports:* basketball M/W, cheerleading M/W, cross-country running M/W, football M, golf M/W, ice hockey M/W, rugby M/W, soccer M/W, softball W, track and field M/W, volleyball M/W. *Intramural sports:* badminton M/W, basketball M/W, bowling M/W, football M/W, golf M/W, ice hockey M/W, rugby M/W, soccer M/W, softball M/W, swimming and diving M/W, table tennis M/W, ultimate Frisbee M/W, volleyball M/W, water polo M/W.

Standardized Tests *Required for some:* SAT or ACT (for admission), SAT and SAT Subject Tests or ACT (for admission), SAT Subject Tests (for admission).

Financial Aid Of all full-time matriculated undergraduates who enrolled in 2010, 450 state and other part-time jobs (averaging $1166). *Financial aid deadline:* 6/15.

Applying *Options:* electronic application, early admission. *Application fee:* $60 Canadian dollars. *Required:* high school transcript, minimum 3.0 GPA. *Required for some:* essay or personal statement, minimum 3.3 GPA, 1 letter of recommendation, interview. *Application deadlines:* rolling (freshmen), 7/1 (out-of-state freshmen), rolling (transfers). *Notification:* continuous until 8/30 (freshmen), continuous until 8/30 (transfers).

Freshman Application Contact Ms. Charlene Yates, Manager of Undergraduate Admissions, University of Windsor, Office of the Registrar, 401 Sunset Avenue, Windsor, ON N9B 3P4, Canada. *Phone:* 519-253-3000 Ext. 3315. *Toll-free phone:* 800-864-2860. *Fax:* 519-971-3653. *E-mail:* registr@uwindsor.ca. *Web site:* http://www.uwindsor.ca/.

The University of Winnipeg
Winnipeg, Manitoba, Canada

Director of Admissions Mr. Colin Russell, Registrar, The University of Winnipeg, 515 Portage Avenue, Winnipeg, MB R3B 2E9, Canada. *Phone:* 204-786-9776. *Fax:* 204-786-8656. *E-mail:* admissions@uwinnipeg.ca. *Web site:* http://www.uwinnipeg.ca/.

Vancouver Island University
Nanaimo, British Columbia, Canada

Freshman Application Contact Ms. Leslie Peterson, Admissions Manager, Vancouver Island University, 900 Fifth Street, Nanaimo, BC V9R 5S5, Canada. *Phone:* 250-740-6355. *Fax:* 250-740-6479. *Web site:* http://www.viu.ca/.

Vanguard College
Edmonton, Alberta, Canada

- **Independent** 4-year, founded 1946, affiliated with Pentecostal Assemblies of Canada
- **Urban** 1-hectare campus
- **Coed**

Undergraduates 6% live on campus.

Faculty *Student/faculty ratio:* 11:1.

Academics *Calendar:* semesters. *Degree:* certificates, diplomas, and bachelor's. *Special study options:* accelerated degree program, advanced placement credit, distance learning, double majors, independent study, internships, off-campus study, part-time degree program, services for LD students, summer session for credit.

Computers on Campus 8 computers/terminals are available on campus for general student use. Students can access the following: computer help desk, free student e-mail accounts, online (class) grades, online (class) registration, online (class) schedules. Campuswide network is available. Wireless service is available via entire campus.

Student Life *Housing options:* men-only, women-only. Campus housing is leased by the school. Freshman applicants given priority for college housing. *Activities and organizations:* choral group.

Athletics *Intramural sports:* soccer M, volleyball M/W.

Costs (2012–13) *Tuition:* $6435 Canadian dollars full-time, $195 Canadian dollars per credit hour part-time. Full-time tuition and fees vary according to course load and program. Part-time tuition and fees vary according to course load and program. *Required fees:* $1000 Canadian dollars full-time, $12 Canadian dollars per credit hour part-time, $55 Canadian dollars per term part-time. *Room only:* $3600 Canadian dollars. Room and board charges vary according to housing facility. *Payment plan:* installment. *Waivers:* senior citizens.

Applying *Options:* electronic application, early decision. *Application fee:* $75 Canadian dollars. *Required:* essay or personal statement, high school transcript, 2 letters of recommendation. *Application deadline:* 8/19 (freshmen). *Early decision deadline:* 4/15.

Freshman Application Contact Vanguard College, 11617 106 Avenue, NW, Edmonton, AB T5H 0S1, Canada. *Phone:* 780-452-0808 Ext. 231. *Toll-free phone:* 866-222-0808. *E-mail:* admissions@vanguardcollege.com. *Web site:* http://www.vanguardcollege.com/.

Western Christian College
Regina, Saskatchewan, Canada

- **Independent** 4-year, founded 1957, affiliated with Church of Christ
- **Urban** campus
- **Coed**

Academics *Calendar:* semesters. *Degree:* certificates and bachelor's.

Standardized Tests *Required for some:* SAT or ACT (for admission).

Costs (2011–12) *Tuition:* $235 per credit hour part-time. Full-time tuition and fees vary according to course load. Part-time tuition and fees vary according to course load.

Applying *Options:* electronic application. *Application fee:* $50 Canadian dollars. *Required:* essay or personal statement, high school transcript. *Required for some:* interview.

Freshman Application Contact Ms. Trish Thompson, Registrar, Western Christian College, 100-400 Fourth Avenue, Regina, SK S4T 0H8, Canada. *Phone:* 306-545-1515 Ext. 500. *Fax:* 306-352-2198. *E-mail:* registrar@westernchristian.ca. *Web site:* http://www.westernchristian.ca/.

Wilfrid Laurier University
Waterloo, Ontario, Canada

- **Province-supported** comprehensive, founded 1911
- **Urban** 40-acre campus with easy access to Toronto
- **Coed**
- **Minimally difficult** entrance level

Faculty *Student/faculty ratio:* 25:1.

Academics *Calendar:* semesters Canadian standard year. *Degrees:* certificates, diplomas, bachelor's, master's, doctoral, and first professional.

Student Life *Campus security:* 24-hour emergency response devices and patrols, student patrols, late-night transport/escort service, controlled dormitory access.

Athletics Member CIS.

Standardized Tests *Required for some:* SAT or ACT (for admission).

Costs (2011–12) *Tuition:* province resident $5214 Canadian dollars full-time; International tuition $18,869 Canadian dollars full-time. Full-time tuition and fees vary according to course load, degree level, location, program, and student level. Part-time tuition and fees vary according to course load, degree level, location, program, and student level. *Required fees:* $964 Canadian dollars full-time. *Room and board:* $8047 Canadian dollars; room only: $4641 Canadian dollars. Room and board charges vary according to board plan, housing facility, and location.

Financial Aid *Financial aid deadline:* 1/17.

Applying *Options:* electronic application, early admission, early decision, deferred entrance. *Application fee:* $120 Canadian dollars. *Required:* high school transcript. *Required for some:* essay or personal statement, interview, audition for music programs.

Freshman Application Contact Wilfrid Laurier University, 75 University Avenue West, Waterloo, ON N2L 3C5, Canada. *Phone:* 519-884-0710 Ext. 6099. *Web site:* http://www.wlu.ca/.

York University
Toronto, Ontario, Canada

Freshman Application Contact Ms. Amber Holliday, International Recruitment Officer, York University, N301 Bennett Centre for Student Services, 4700 Keele Street, Toronto, ON M3J 1P3, Canada. *Phone:* 416-736-2100 Ext. 60595. *Fax:* 416-736-5741. *E-mail:* aburkett@yorku.ca. *Web site:* http://www.yorku.ca/.

INTERNATIONAL

BULGARIA

American University in Bulgaria

Blagoevgrad, Bulgaria

- **Independent** comprehensive, founded 1991
- **Small-town** campus with easy access to Sofia
- **Endowment** $17.4 million
- **Coed** 1,051 undergraduate students, 100% full-time, 51% women, 49% men
- **Very difficult** entrance level, 57% of applicants were admitted

Undergraduates 1,051 full-time. Students come from 43 other countries; 96% live on campus. *Retention:* 96% of full-time freshmen returned.

Freshmen *Admission:* 794 applied, 452 admitted, 296 enrolled. *Average high school GPA:* 3.5. *Test scores:* SAT critical reading scores over 500: 60%; SAT math scores over 500: 100%; SAT critical reading scores over 600: 10%; SAT math scores over 600: 70%; SAT math scores over 700: 19%.

Faculty *Total:* 77, 71% full-time, 75% with terminal degrees. *Student/faculty ratio:* 17:1.

Academics *Calendar:* semesters. *Degrees:* bachelor's and master's. *Special study options:* advanced placement credit, double majors, honors programs, independent study, internships, services for LD students, study abroad.

Computers on Campus 304 computers/terminals are available on campus for general student use. Students can access the following: computer help desk, free student e-mail accounts, online (class) grades, online (class) registration, online (class) schedules. Campuswide network is available. 100% of college-owned or -operated housing units are wired for high-speed Internet access. Wireless service is available via entire campus.

Student Life *Housing:* on-campus residence required through senior year. *Options:* disabled students. Campus housing is university owned. Freshman campus housing is guaranteed. *Activities and organizations:* drama/theater group, student-run newspaper, radio station, choral group, Computer Science Student Union, Debate Club, Better Community Club, AUBG Broadway Performance Club, Business Club. *Campus security:* 24-hour patrols. *Student services:* health clinic, personal/psychological counseling.

Athletics *Intramural sports:* basketball M/W, cheerleading W(c), equestrian sports M(c)/W(c), football M(c), gymnastics W, soccer M(c), softball M/W, volleyball M/W.

Standardized Tests *Required:* SAT or ACT (for admission). *Required for some:* TOEFL, IELTS, or ESOL for students whose primary language is not English.

Costs (2012–13) *Comprehensive fee:* $12,590 includes full-time tuition ($9800), mandatory fees ($350), and room and board ($2440). Part-time tuition: $408 per credit hour. *College room only:* $1240. Room and board charges vary according to housing facility. *Waivers:* employees or children of employees.

Applying *Options:* electronic application, early admission, deferred entrance. *Application fee:* $25. *Required:* essay or personal statement, high school transcript, minimum 3.0 GPA, 3 letters of recommendation. *Application deadlines:* 6/1 (freshmen), 6/1 (transfers).

Freshman Application Contact Ms. Iordanka Melnikliyska, Director of Admissions, American University in Bulgaria, 1 Izmirliev Square 1st floor, Blagoevgrad 2700, Bulgaria. *Phone:* 359-73 888 235. *Fax:* 359-73 883 227. *E-mail:* admissions@aubg.bg. *Web site:* http://www.aubg.bg/.

CAYMAN ISLANDS

International College of the Cayman Islands

Newlands, Cayman Islands

Freshman Application Contact International College of the Cayman Islands, PO Box 136, Savannah Post Office, Newlands, Grand Cayman, Cayman Islands. *Phone:* 345-325-6454. *Web site:* http://www.icci.edu.ky/.

EGYPT

The American University in Cairo

Cairo, Egypt

- **Independent** comprehensive, founded 1919
- **Urban** campus
- **Coed** 5,507 undergraduate students, 90% full-time, 52% women, 48% men
- **Very difficult** entrance level, 56% of applicants were admitted

Undergraduates 4,983 full-time, 524 part-time. 54% are from out of state; 0.3% transferred in; 10% live on campus. *Retention:* 89% of full-time freshmen returned.

Freshmen *Admission:* 2,891 applied, 1,618 admitted, 1,240 enrolled. *Test scores:* SAT critical reading scores over 500: 32%; SAT math scores over 500: 86%; SAT writing scores over 500: 78%; SAT critical reading scores over 600: 7%; SAT math scores over 600: 43%; SAT writing scores over 600: 29%; SAT critical reading scores over 700: 1%; SAT math scores over 700: 10%; SAT writing scores over 700: 4%.

Faculty *Total:* 805, 56% full-time, 68% with terminal degrees. *Student/faculty ratio:* 11:1.

Academics *Calendar:* semesters. *Degrees:* diplomas, bachelor's, master's, doctoral, and first professional (majority of students are Egyptians; enrollment open to all nationalities). *Special study options:* adult/continuing education programs, part-time degree program.

Computers on Campus Students can access the following: online (class) registration. Campuswide network is available.

Student Life *Housing options:* men-only, women-only, disabled students. Campus housing is university owned and leased by the school. Freshman applicants given priority for college housing. *Campus security:* 24-hour emergency response devices and patrols, controlled dormitory access.

Athletics *Intercollegiate sports:* archery M, badminton M/W, basketball M/W, crew M/W, fencing M/W, gymnastics M/W, soccer M/W, squash M/W, swimming and diving M/W, table tennis M/W, tennis M/W, track and field M/W, volleyball M/W, water polo M. *Intramural sports:* basketball M/W, soccer M/W, squash M/W, table tennis M/W, tennis M/W, volleyball M/W, weight lifting M.

Standardized Tests *Required for some:* SAT or ACT (for admission), SAT Subject Tests (for admission).

Applying *Application fee:* $50. *Required:* essay or personal statement, high school transcript, minimum 2.0 GPA. *Application deadline:* 5/15 (freshmen).

Freshman Application Contact Ms. Randa Kamel, Director of Enrollment Services, The American University in Cairo, The Office of Student Affairs, 420 Fifth Avenue, 3rd Floor, New York, NY 10018-2728. *Phone:* 212-797-5551. *E-mail:* randa_k@aucnyo.edu. *Web site:* http://www.aucegypt.edu/.

FRANCE

The American University of Paris

Paris, France

- **Independent** comprehensive, founded 1962
- **Urban** campus
- **Endowment** $932,889
- **Coed** 750 undergraduate students, 93% full-time, 69% women, 31% men
- **Moderately difficult** entrance level, 80% of applicants were admitted

Undergraduates 694 full-time, 56 part-time. Students come from 42 states and territories; 91 other countries; 57% are from out of state; 7% transferred in. *Retention:* 72% of full-time freshmen returned.

Freshmen *Admission:* 453 applied, 362 admitted, 143 enrolled.

Faculty *Total:* 127, 55% full-time, 61% with terminal degrees. *Student/faculty ratio:* 12:1.

Academics *Calendar:* semesters. *Degrees:* bachelor's and master's. *Special study options:* advanced placement credit, cooperative education, double majors, English as a second language, honors programs, independent study, internships, off-campus study, part-time degree program, student-designed majors, study abroad, summer session for credit.

Computers on Campus 100 computers/terminals are available on campus for general student use. Students can access the following: campus intranet, com-

puter help desk, free student e-mail accounts, online (class) grades, online (class) registration, online (class) schedules. Campuswide network is available. Wireless service is available via entire campus.

Student Life *Housing:* college housing not available. *Options:* Campus housing is provided by a third party. *Activities and organizations:* drama/theater group, student-run newspaper, radio and television station, choral group, AUP Student Media (ASM) - Print, Video, Audio, White Mask (Theatre), Student Senate, Student Government Association, Sports Association. *Campus security:* 24-hour emergency response devices. *Student services:* personal/psychological counseling.

Athletics *Intramural sports:* basketball M/W, equestrian sports M/W, football M, golf M/W, racquetball M/W, soccer M/W, squash M/W, tennis M/W, volleyball M/W.

Standardized Tests *Required for some:* SAT or ACT (for admission), TOEFL, TOEIC or IELTS for students whose primary language is not English.

Costs (2012–13) *Comprehensive fee:* 36,110 euros includes full-time tuition (25,060 euros), mandatory fees (1450 euros), and room and board (9600 euros). Full-time tuition and fees vary according to course load. Part-time tuition: 784 euros per credit hour. Part-time tuition and fees vary according to course load. *Required fees:* 784 euros per credit hour part-time. *Payment plan:* installment. *Waivers:* children of alumni and employees or children of employees.

Financial Aid Of all full-time matriculated undergraduates who enrolled in 2011, 240 applied for aid, 232 were judged to have need. In 2011, 19 non-need-based awards were made. *Average percent of need met:* 42%. *Average financial aid package:* $14,100. *Average need-based loan:* $5100. *Average need-based gift aid:* $14,100. *Average non-need-based aid:* $2100.

Applying *Options:* electronic application, deferred entrance. *Application fee:* $65. *Required:* essay or personal statement, high school transcript, 2 letters of recommendation. *Recommended:* minimum 3.0 GPA, interview. *Application deadlines:* 3/15 (freshmen), 3/15 (transfers). *Notification:* continuous (freshmen), continuous (transfers).

Freshman Application Contact International Admissions Office, The American University of Paris, 6 rue du Colonel Combes, Paris 75007, France. *Phone:* -+33 1 40 62 07 20. *Fax:* +33 1 47 05 34 32. *E-mail:* admissions@aup.edu. *Web site:* http://www.aup.edu/.

Parsons Paris School of Art + Design

Paris, France

Freshman Application Contact Sara Krauskopf, Parsons Paris School of Art + Design, 14 rue Letellier, F-75015 Paris, France. *Phone:* -331 4577 40 17. *Fax:* 331 4577 44 12. *E-mail:* sara.krauskopf@parsons-paris.com. *Web site:* http://www.parsons-paris.com/.

Schiller International University

Paris, France

Freshman Application Contact Ms. Kamala Dontamsetti, Associate Director of Admissions, Schiller International University, 300 East Bay Drive, Largo, FL 33770. *Phone:* 727-736-5082 Ext. 234. *Toll-free phone:* 800-261-9571 (in-state); 800-261-9751 (out-of-state). *Fax:* 727-734-0347. *E-mail:* admissions@schiller.edu. *Web site:* http://www.schiller.edu/.

GERMANY

Schiller International University

Heidelberg, Germany

Freshman Application Contact Ms. Kamala Dontamsetti, Associate Director of Admissions, Schiller International University, 300 East Bay Drive, Largo, FL 33770. *Phone:* 727-736-5082 Ext. 234. *Toll-free phone:* 800-261-9571 (in-state); 800-261-9751 (out-of-state). *Fax:* 727-734-0359. *E-mail:* kamala_dontamsetti@schiller.edu. *Web site:* http://www.schiller.edu/.

GREECE

American College of Thessaloniki

Pylea, Greece

- **Independent** comprehensive, founded 1886
- **Suburban** 40-acre campus with easy access to Thessaloniki
- **Endowment** $4.3 million
- **Coed** 425 undergraduate students, 78% full-time, 52% women, 48% men
- **Minimally difficult** entrance level, 79% of applicants were admitted

Undergraduates 333 full-time, 92 part-time. Students come from 15 other countries; 0.7% transferred in; 40% live on campus. *Retention:* 78% of full-time freshmen returned.

Freshmen *Admission:* 106 applied, 84 admitted, 48 enrolled. *Average high school GPA:* 3.

Faculty *Total:* 46, 28% full-time, 46% with terminal degrees. *Student/faculty ratio:* 15:1.

Academics *Calendar:* semesters. *Degrees:* certificates, bachelor's, and master's. *Special study options:* academic remediation for entering students, accelerated degree program, advanced placement credit, double majors, English as a second language, independent study, internships, part-time degree program, services for LD students, study abroad, summer session for credit.

Computers on Campus 155 computers/terminals and 20 ports are available on campus for general student use. Students can access the following: campus intranet, computer help desk, free student e-mail accounts, online (class) grades, online (class) schedules, Remote access to library resources. Campuswide network is available. 100% of college-owned or -operated housing units are wired for high-speed Internet access. Wireless service is available via classrooms, computer centers, learning centers, libraries, student centers.

Student Life *Housing options:* coed. Campus housing is university owned and leased by the school. Freshman applicants given priority for college housing. *Activities and organizations:* student-run radio station, Community Service, Field Trip Club, InterACT, Scuba diving club, Art Attack. *Campus security:* 24-hour patrols. *Student services:* personal/psychological counseling.

Athletics *Intercollegiate sports:* basketball M(c)/W(c), soccer M/W, table tennis M(c)/W(c), tennis M(c)/W(c). *Intramural sports:* basketball M(c)/W(c), sailing M(c)/W(c), soccer M(c)/W(c), table tennis M(c)/W(c), tennis M(c)/W(c), volleyball M(c)/W(c), wrestling M(c)/W(c).

Standardized Tests *Recommended:* SAT (for admission).

Costs (2011–12) *Tuition:* 8250 euros full-time, 275 euros per credit hour part-time. Part-time tuition and fees vary according to course load. *Required fees:* 100 euros full-time, 50 euros per term part-time. *Room only:* 4700 euros. Room and board charges vary according to housing facility. *Waivers:* employees or children of employees.

Applying *Options:* electronic application, deferred entrance. *Application fee:* 95 euros. *Required:* high school transcript, proficiency in English, CV. *Required for some:* essay or personal statement, interview. *Recommended:* minimum 2.0 GPA. *Application deadlines:* rolling (freshmen), rolling (transfers). *Notification:* continuous (freshmen), continuous (transfers).

Freshman Application Contact Mrs. Roula Lebetli, Director of Admissions, American College of Thessaloniki, PO Box 21021, Pylea, Thessaloniki 55510, Greece. *Phone:* +30-2310-398239. *Fax:* +30- 2310-398389. *E-mail:* admissions@act.edu. *Web site:* http://www.act.edu/.

The American University of Athens

Athens, Greece

Director of Admissions Ms. Thalia Poulos, Director of Admissions, The American University of Athens, 4 Sohou Street and Kifissias Avenue, Neo Psychiko, GR-115 25 Athens, Greece. *Phone:* -30 210-725-9301. *E-mail:* admissions@aua.edu. *Web site:* http://www.aua.edu/.

DEREE - The American College of Greece

Athens, Greece

- **Independent** comprehensive, founded 1875
- **Suburban** 64-acre campus
- **Coed** 2,954 undergraduate students, 53% full-time, 51% women, 49% men
- **Moderately difficult** entrance level, 80% of applicants were admitted

Undergraduates 1,558 full-time, 1,396 part-time. Students come from 39 other countries; 1% live on campus. *Retention:* 80% of full-time freshmen returned.

Freshmen *Admission:* 1,003 applied, 805 admitted. *Average high school GPA:* 2.85. *Test scores:* SAT critical reading scores over 500: 61%; SAT math

scores over 500: 63%; SAT critical reading scores over 600: 6%; SAT math scores over 600: 8%.

Faculty *Total:* 192, 71% full-time, 47% with terminal degrees. *Student/faculty ratio:* 11:1.

Academics *Calendar:* 4-1-4. *Degrees:* bachelor's, master's, and postbachelor's certificates. *Special study options:* academic remediation for entering students, accelerated degree program, adult/continuing education programs, advanced placement credit, double majors, English as a second language, honors programs, independent study, internships, part-time degree program, services for LD students, student-designed majors, study abroad, summer session for credit.

Computers on Campus 280 computers/terminals are available on campus for general student use. Students can access the following: computer help desk, free student e-mail accounts, online (class) grades, online (class) registration, online (class) schedules. 100% of college-owned or -operated housing units are wired for high-speed Internet access. Wireless service is available via computer labs, dorm rooms, libraries.

Student Life *Housing options:* coed. Campus housing is university owned. *Activities and organizations:* drama/theater group, student-run newspaper, DEREE SAB (Students Activity Board), DEREE Orientation Leaders, DEREE Ambassadors, DEREE Anime Club, DEREE S.E.R.F.. *Campus security:* 24-hour emergency response devices and patrols. *Student services:* health clinic, personal/psychological counseling.

Athletics *Intercollegiate sports:* basketball M/W, soccer M/W, swimming and diving M/W, tennis M/W, volleyball M/W(s), water polo M. *Intramural sports:* basketball M/W, rock climbing M/W, skiing (downhill) M/W, soccer M, swimming and diving M/W, table tennis M/W, tennis M/W, track and field M/W, volleyball M/W, water polo M.

Standardized Tests *Recommended:* SAT or ACT (for admission), Not required, optional for US Students.

Costs (2011–12) *One-time required fee:* 135 euros. *Tuition:* 7620 euros full-time, 254 euros per credit hour part-time. Full-time tuition and fees vary according to course load. Part-time tuition and fees vary according to course load. *Required fees:* 1028 euros full-time, 514 euros per term part-time. *Room only:* Room and board charges vary according to housing facility. *Payment plan:* installment. *Waivers:* employees or children of employees.

Financial Aid *Financial aid deadline:* 9/1.

Applying *Options:* electronic application, deferred entrance. *Required:* essay or personal statement, high school transcript, minimum 2.0 GPA, 1 letter of recommendation, interview. *Application deadlines:* rolling (freshmen), rolling (transfers). *Notification:* 7/25 (freshmen), 7/25 (transfers).

Freshman Application Contact Ms. Nancy Parkes, Dean of Admissions, DEREE - The American College of Greece, 6 Gravias Street, Aghia Paraskevi, Athens 15342, Greece. *Phone:* -30 210-600-9800 Ext. 1472. *E-mail:* nparkes@acg.edu. *Web site:* http://www.acg.edu/.

IRELAND

Institute of Public Administration
Dublin, Ireland

Director of Admissions Dr. Denis O'Brien, Registrar, Institute of Public Administration, 57-61 Lansdowne Road, Dublin 4, Ireland. *Phone:* 353-1-240-3600. *Fax:* 353-1-668-9135. *E-mail:* undergrad@ipa.ie. *Web site:* http://www.ipa.ie/.

ITALY

The American University of Rome
Rome, Italy

- **Independent** 4-year, founded 1969
- **Urban** 1-acre campus
- **Endowment** $1.2 million
- **Coed** 390 undergraduate students, 100% full-time, 67% women, 33% men
- **Moderately difficult** entrance level, 54% of applicants were admitted

Undergraduates 390 full-time. Students come from 22 states and territories; 40 other countries; 4% transferred in; 65% live on campus. *Retention:* 79% of full-time freshmen returned.

Freshmen *Admission:* 427 applied, 230 admitted, 39 enrolled. *Average high school GPA:* 3. *Test scores:* SAT critical reading scores over 500: 71%; SAT math scores over 500: 60%; SAT writing scores over 500: 95%; ACT scores over 18: 100%; SAT critical reading scores over 600: 29%; SAT math scores

over 600: 17%; SAT writing scores over 600: 12%; ACT scores over 24: 100%; SAT math scores over 700: 12%.

Faculty *Total:* 62, 18% full-time, 52% with terminal degrees. *Student/faculty ratio:* 16:1.

Academics *Calendar:* semesters. *Degrees:* associate and bachelor's. *Special study options:* academic remediation for entering students, advanced placement credit, double majors, English as a second language, independent study, internships, off-campus study, part-time degree program, services for LD students, student-designed majors, study abroad, summer session for credit.

Computers on Campus 68 computers/terminals and 80 ports are available on campus for general student use. Students can access the following: campus intranet, computer help desk, free student e-mail accounts, online (class) grades, online (class) registration, online (class) schedules, Learning Management System. Campuswide network is available. 100% of college-owned or -operated housing units are wired for high-speed Internet access. Wireless service is available via computer labs, dorm rooms, libraries, student centers.

Student Life *Housing options:* men-only, women-only. Campus housing is provided by a third party. Freshman applicants given priority for college housing. *Activities and organizations:* drama/theater group, student-run newspaper. *Campus security:* 24-hour emergency response devices, security guards during opening hours and 24-hour surveillance cameras. *Student services:* health clinic, personal/psychological counseling.

Athletics *Intercollegiate sports:* soccer M/W. *Intramural sports:* cross-country running M/W, gymnastics M/W, volleyball M/W.

Standardized Tests *Required for some:* SAT or ACT (for admission).

Costs (2012–13) *One-time required fee:* 190 euros. *Comprehensive fee:* 23,644 euros includes full-time tuition (13,940 euros), mandatory fees (144 euros), and room and board (9560 euros). Full-time tuition and fees vary according to course load. Part-time tuition: 1745 euros per course. Part-time tuition and fees vary according to course load. *College room only:* 7600 euros. Room and board charges vary according to housing facility. *Payment plan:* installment. *Waivers:* employees or children of employees.

Applying *Options:* electronic application, deferred entrance. *Application fee:* $65. *Required:* essay or personal statement, high school transcript, minimum 2.5 GPA, 1 letter of recommendation, interview, TOEFL OR IELTS FOR NON-ENGLISH HIGH SCHOOL STUDENTS. *Application deadlines:* rolling (freshmen), rolling (transfers). *Notification:* continuous (freshmen), continuous (transfers).

Freshman Application Contact Miss Melissa Abraham, Admissions Counselor, The American University of Rome, Via Pietro Roselli 4, Rome 00153, Italy. *Phone:* +39 0658330919. *Toll-free phone:* 877-592-1287. *Fax:* +39 0658330992. *E-mail:* admissions@aur.edu. *Web site:* http://www.aur.edu/.

See page 1033 for display ad and page 1052 for the College Close-Up.

John Cabot University
Rome, Italy

Freshman Application Contact Luke Kasim, Director of Admissions, John Cabot University, Via della Lungara 233, Roma 00165, Italy. *Phone:* -39 06 681 9121. *Toll-free phone:* 866-457-6160. *Fax:* 39 06 589 7429. *E-mail:* admissions@johncabot.edu. *Web site:* http://www.johncabot.edu/.

KENYA

United States International University
Nairobi, Kenya

- **Independent** comprehensive, founded 1977, part of Alliant International University
- **Urban** 120-acre campus
- **Coed** 4,185 undergraduate students, 93% full-time, 54% women, 46% men
- **Moderately difficult** entrance level, 77% of applicants were admitted

Undergraduates 3,873 full-time, 312 part-time. 5% live on campus.

Freshmen *Admission:* 833 applied, 644 admitted, 518 enrolled. *Average high school GPA:* 2.79.

Faculty *Total:* 219, 39% full-time, 31% with terminal degrees. *Student/faculty ratio:* 30:1.

Academics *Calendar:* trimesters. *Degrees:* bachelor's and master's. *Special study options:* adult/continuing education programs, off-campus study, part-time degree program, summer session for credit.

Student Life *Housing options:* coed. Campus housing is university owned and is provided by a third party. *Activities and organizations:* drama/theater group, student-run newspaper, radio station, choral group, Business club, Aiesec, Bas-

ket Ball, Hockey, Drama club. *Campus security:* 24-hour emergency response devices and patrols, 24-hour Hostel reception security desk. *Student services:* health clinic, personal/psychological counseling.

Athletics *Intercollegiate sports:* basketball M(s)/W(s), field hockey M(s)/W(s), rugby M(s), soccer M(s), swimming and diving M(s)/W(s), tennis M/W, track and field M(s)/W(s). *Intramural sports:* basketball M/W, field hockey M/W, rugby M, soccer M, softball M/W, swimming and diving M/W, table tennis M/W, tennis M/W, track and field M/W, weight lifting M/W.

Standardized Tests *Required for some:* TOEFL for students whose high school language of instruction was not English.

Costs (2011–12) *One-time required fee:* $2000. *Comprehensive fee:* $424,694 includes full-time tuition ($244,800), mandatory fees ($21,150), and room and board ($158,744). Full-time tuition and fees vary according to course load and program. Part-time tuition: $6800 per unit. Part-time tuition and fees vary according to course load and program. *Required fees:* $7050 per term part-time. *College room only:* $66,624. Room and board charges vary according to board plan. *Payment plan:* installment. *Waivers:* children of alumni and employees or children of employees.

Applying *Options:* deferred entrance. *Application fee:* 50 Kenyan shillings. *Required:* high school transcript, minimum 2.5 GPA. *Required for some:* interview. *Application deadlines:* rolling (freshmen), rolling (transfers). *Notification:* continuous (freshmen), continuous (transfers).

Freshman Application Contact United States International University, PO Box 14634, Thika Road Kasarani, Nairobi 00800, Kenya. *Phone:* 254-02-3606563. *Web site:* http://www.usiu.ac.ke/.

LEBANON

American University of Beirut
Beirut, Lebanon

- **Independent** university, founded 1866
- **Urban** 61-acre campus with easy access to Beirut
- **Endowment** $415.9 million
- **Coed** 6,342 undergraduate students, 95% full-time, 48% women, 52% men
- **67% of applicants were admitted**

Undergraduates 6,055 full-time, 287 part-time. Students come from 75 other countries; 0.6% transferred in; 16% live on campus. *Retention:* 92% of full-time freshmen returned.

Freshmen *Admission:* 3,952 applied, 2,650 admitted, 1,443 enrolled. *Average high school GPA:* 2.93. *Test scores:* SAT critical reading scores over 500: 48%; SAT math scores over 500: 97%; SAT writing scores over 500: 64%; SAT critical reading scores over 600: 10%; SAT math scores over 600: 76%; SAT writing scores over 600: 17%; SAT critical reading scores over 700: 1%; SAT math scores over 700: 25%; SAT writing scores over 700: 2%.

Faculty *Total:* 817, 65% full-time, 60% with terminal degrees. *Student/faculty ratio:* 11:1.

Academics *Calendar:* semesters. *Degrees:* certificates, diplomas, bachelor's, master's, doctoral, and first professional. *Special study options:* academic remediation for entering students, advanced placement credit, double majors, English as a second language, honors programs, independent study, internships, services for LD students, study abroad, summer session for credit.

Computers on Campus 1,229 computers/terminals and 1,500 ports are available on campus for general student use. Students can access the following: campus intranet, computer help desk, free student e-mail accounts, online (class) grades, online (class) registration, online (class) schedules, The number of students subscribed to the wireless network at AUB campus is 7,049. It is worth mentioning that many of these students use multiple devices such as laptops, tablets, PDAs or smart phones. Campuswide network is available. 100% of college-owned or -operated housing units are wired for high-speed Internet access. Wireless service is available via entire campus.

Student Life *Housing:* on-campus residence required for freshman year. *Options:* men-only, women-only. Campus housing is university owned. Freshman campus housing is guaranteed. *Activities and organizations:* drama/theater group, student-run newspaper, choral group, Red Cross Club, Biology Society, Business Society, Music Club, Palestinian Cultural Club. *Campus security:* 24-hour emergency response devices and patrols, late-night transport/escort service, staff monitors entrance 24/7. *Student services:* health clinic, personal/psychological counseling, legal services.

Athletics *Intercollegiate sports:* basketball M/W, cross-country running M/W, football M, gymnastics M, rugby M, skiing (downhill) M/W, soccer M/W, squash M/W, swimming and diving M/W, table tennis M/W, tennis M/W, track and field M/W, volleyball M/W, water polo M. *Intramural sports:* basketball M/W, cross-country running M/W, gymnastics M, lacrosse M/W, racquetball

M/W, soccer M/W, squash M/W, swimming and diving M/W, table tennis M/W, tennis M/W, volleyball M/W, weight lifting M/W.

Standardized Tests *Required:* SAT (for admission). *Required for some:* SAT Subject Tests (for admission).

Costs (2011–12) *Tuition:* $17,010 full-time, $567 per credit part-time. Full-time tuition and fees vary according to course load, degree level, program, and student level. Part-time tuition and fees vary according to course load, degree level, program, and student level. *Required fees:* $528 full-time. *Room only:* $2476. Room and board charges vary according to housing facility and location. *Payment plan:* deferred payment. *Waivers:* employees or children of employees.

Financial Aid Of all full-time matriculated undergraduates who enrolled in 2010, 3,146 applied for aid, 2,380 were judged to have need. 60 state and other part-time jobs (averaging $1393). In 2010, 37 non-need-based awards were made. *Average financial aid package:* $5672. *Average need-based loan:* $4156. *Average need-based gift aid:* $5518. *Average non-need-based aid:* $15,531. *Financial aid deadline:* 2/2.

Applying *Options:* electronic application, early admission, early action, deferred entrance. *Application fee:* $50. *Required:* high school transcript. *Required for some:* interview, TOEFL for international applicants. *Recommended:* essay or personal statement. *Application deadlines:* 2/1 (freshmen), 4/30 (transfers), 11/30 (early action). *Notification:* 4/30 (freshmen), continuous until 6/30 (transfers), 1/31 (early action).

Freshman Application Contact Dr. Salim Kanaan, Director of Admissions Office, American University of Beirut, PO Box 11-0236, Riad El-Solh, 1107 2020, Lebanon. *Phone:* -961 1-374 374 Ext. 2592. *Fax:* 961 1-750 775. *E-mail:* admissions@aub.edu.lb. *Web site:* http://www.aub.edu.lb/.

Lebanese American University

Beirut, Lebanon

- **Private** comprehensive, founded 1835
- **Urban** 49-acre campus with easy access to Beirut Campus:Beirut/Byblos Campus:Byblos, Tripoli
- **Endowment** $296.2 million
- **Coed** 7,500 undergraduate students, 92% full-time, 48% women, 52% men
- **Moderately difficult** entrance level, 76% of applicants were admitted

Undergraduates 6,930 full-time, 570 part-time. Students come from 82 other countries; 22% are from out of state; 1% transferred in; 4% live on campus. *Retention:* 92% of full-time freshmen returned.

Freshmen *Admission:* 3,617 applied, 2,754 admitted, 1,664 enrolled. *Average high school GPA:* 2.75. *Test scores:* SAT critical reading scores over 500: 16%; SAT math scores over 500: 80%; SAT writing scores over 500: 28%; SAT critical reading scores over 600: 1%; SAT math scores over 600: 38%; SAT writing scores over 600: 5%; SAT math scores over 700: 7%.

Faculty *Total:* 711, 38% full-time, 42% with terminal degrees. *Student/faculty ratio:* 24:1.

Academics *Degrees:* diplomas, associate, bachelor's, master's, and doctoral. *Special study options:* academic remediation for entering students, part-time degree program, services for LD students, study abroad, summer session for credit.

Computers on Campus 825 computers/terminals and 500 ports are available on campus for general student use. Students can access the following: campus intranet, computer help desk, free student e-mail accounts, online (class) grades, online (class) registration, online (class) schedules, online library book reservation. Campuswide network is available. 100% of college-owned or -operated housing units are wired for high-speed Internet access. Wireless service is available via entire campus.

Student Life *Housing options:* men-only, women-only, disabled students. Campus housing is university owned. Freshman applicants given priority for college housing. *Activities and organizations:* drama/theater group, student-run newspaper, choral group, Model United Nations, Event Organization Club, Red Cross Club, Extreme club, Campus Life Club. *Campus security:* 24-hour patrols, 24/7 security at Residence Halls. *Student services:* health clinic, personal/psychological counseling, women's center.

Athletics *Intercollegiate sports:* badminton M/W, basketball M(s)/W(s), rugby M(s), soccer M(s)/W(s), swimming and diving M(s)/W(s), table tennis M(s)/W(s), tennis M/W(s), track and field M/W(s), volleyball M/W. *Intramural sports:* basketball M/W, skiing (downhill) M(c)/W(c), soccer M/W, swimming and diving M/W, table tennis M/W, tennis M/W, volleyball M/W.

Standardized Tests *Required:* SAT (for admission), Institutional English Test (English Entrance Exam EEE) or International TOFEL (for admission). *Required for some:* SAT Subject Tests (for admission).

Applying *Options:* electronic application, early admission, early action, deferred entrance. *Application fee:* $50. *Required:* high school transcript,

Official high school diploma, SAT I, Institutional English Test (English Entrance Exam EEE) or International TOFEL or SAT Writing. *Application deadlines:* 7/31 (freshmen), 7/31 (out-of-state freshmen), 7/31 (transfers), 1/31 (early action). *Notification:* 4/1 (freshmen), 4/1 (out-of-state freshmen), 4/1 (transfers), 3/1 (early action).

Freshman Application Contact Lebanese American University, PO Box 13-5053, Beirut, Lebanon. *Phone:* -961 1 786456 Ext. 1162. *Web site:* http://www.lau.edu.lb/.

MEXICO

Alliant International University–México City

Mexico City, Mexico

- **Independent** comprehensive, founded 1970, part of Alliant International University
- **Urban** campus with easy access to Mexico City
- **Coed** 109 undergraduate students, 18% full-time, 47% women, 53% men
- **Moderately difficult** entrance level

Undergraduates 20 full-time, 89 part-time. Students come from 4 states and territories; 5 other countries. *Retention:* 75% of full-time freshmen returned.

Faculty *Total:* 24, 33% full-time, 54% with terminal degrees. *Student/faculty ratio:* 12:1.

Academics *Calendar:* semesters. *Degrees:* bachelor's and master's. *Special study options:* accelerated degree program, advanced placement credit, English as a second language, internships, summer session for credit.

Computers on Campus 15 computers/terminals are available on campus for general student use. Students can access the following: free student e-mail accounts, online (class) grades, online (class) registration, online (class) schedules. Wireless service is available via entire campus.

Student Life *Housing:* college housing not available. *Activities and organizations:* student-run newspaper, International Business Club, German Club, Student Council.

Standardized Tests *Recommended:* SAT or ACT (for admission).

Applying *Options:* electronic application, deferred entrance. *Application fee:* 500 Mexican pesos. *Required:* essay or personal statement, high school transcript, minimum 2.0 GPA, 1 letter of recommendation. *Required for some:* interview. *Recommended:* minimum 3.0 GPA. *Application deadlines:* rolling (freshmen), rolling (transfers).

Freshman Application Contact Alliant International University–México City, Hamburgo #115, Col. Juarez, Mexico D.F. 06600, Mexico. *Phone:* -52 5555257651. *E-mail:* mexicoadmissions@alliant.edu. *Web site:* http://www.alliant.edu/wps/wcm/connect/website/Home/Campuses/Mexico+City+Campus/.

Instituto Tecnológico y de Estudios Superiores de Monterrey, Campus Central de Veracruz

Córdoba, Mexico

Director of Admissions Ing. Luis Pablo Villareal, Registrar, Instituto Tecnológico y de Estudios Superiores de Monterrey, Campus Central de Veracruz, Avenida Eugenio Garza Sada 1, Apartado Postal 314, 94500 Córdoba, Veracruz, Mexico. *Phone:* -27-13-23-40 Ext. 123. *Web site:* http://www.ver.itesm.mx/.

Instituto Tecnológico y de Estudios Superiores de Monterrey, Campus Chiapas

Tuxtla Gutiérrez, Mexico

Director of Admissions Lic. Luis Enrique Cancino, Registrar, Instituto Tecnológico y de Estudios Superiores de Monterrey, Campus Chiapas, Carretera a Tapanatepec Km 149&746, Apartado Postal 312, 29000 Tuxtla Gutiérrez, Chiapas, Mexico. *Phone:* -96-15-1723. *Web site:* http://www.chs.itesm.mx/.

Instituto Tecnológico y de Estudios Superiores de Monterrey, Campus Chihuahua

Chihuahua, Mexico

Director of Admissions Ing. Juan Manuel Fernandez, Registrar, Instituto Tecnológico y de Estudios Superiores de Monterrey, Campus Chihuahua, Colegio Militar 4700, Colonia Nombre de Dios, Apartado Postal 728, 31300 Chihuahua, Chihuahua, Mexico. *Phone:* -14-17-48-58 Ext. 117. *Web site:* http://www.chi.itesm.mx/.

Instituto Tecnológico y de Estudios Superiores de Monterrey, Campus Ciudad de México

Ciudad de Mexico, Mexico

Freshman Application Contact Admissions Office, Instituto Tecnológico y de Estudios Superiores de Monterrey, Campus Ciudad de México, Calle del Puente #222 esquina con Periférico, 14380 Colonia Huipulco, Tlalpan, MDF, Mexico. *Phone:* -5-673-6488. *Web site:* http://www.ccm.itesm.mx/.

Instituto Tecnológico y de Estudios Superiores de Monterrey, Campus Ciudad Juárez

Ciudad Juárez, Mexico

Director of Admissions Lic. Alberto Trejo, Registrar, Instituto Tecnológico y de Estudios Superiores de Monterrey, Campus Ciudad Juárez, Boulevard Tomas Fernandez y Avenida A J Bermudez, Apartado Postal 3105-J, 32320 Ciudad Juárez, Chihuahua, Mexico. *Phone:* -16-17-88-07 Ext. 113. *Web site:* http://www.cdj.itesm.mx/.

Instituto Tecnológico y de Estudios Superiores de Monterrey, Campus Ciudad Obregón

Ciudad Obregón, Mexico

Director of Admissions Lic. Judith Almeida, Registrar, Instituto Tecnológico y de Estudios Superiores de Monterrey, Campus Ciudad Obregón, Dr Norman E Borlaug Km 14, Apartado Postal 662, 85000 Ciudad Obregón, Sonora, Mexico. *Phone:* -64-15-03-12. *Web site:* http://www.cob.itesm.mx/.

Instituto Tecnológico y de Estudios Superiores de Monterrey, Campus Colima

Colima, Mexico

Director of Admissions Lic. Manuel Perez Rivera, Registrar, Instituto Tecnológico y de Estudios Superiores de Monterrey, Campus Colima, Prolongacion Ignacio Sandoval s/n, Fraccionamiento Jardines de Vista Hermosa, Apartado Postal 190, 28010 Colima, Colima, Mexico. *Phone:* -33-12-53-39. *Web site:* http://www.col.itesm.mx/.

Instituto Tecnológico y de Estudios Superiores de Monterrey, Campus Cuernavaca

Temixco, Mexico

Director of Admissions Lic. Miguel Angel Machua, Registrar, Instituto Tecnológico y de Estudios Superiores de Monterrey, Campus Cuernavaca, Paseo de la Reforma 182-A, Colonia Lomas de Cuernavaca, 62000 Temixco, Morelos, Mexico. *Phone:* -73 18-49-57. *Web site:* http://www.cva.itesm.mx/.

Instituto Tecnológico y de Estudios Superiores de Monterrey, Campus Estado de México

Estado de Mexico, Mexico

Director of Admissions Prof. Jose de Jesus Molina, Registrar, Instituto Tecnológico y de Estudios Superiores de Monterrey, Campus Estado de México, Carretera Lago de Guadalupe Km. 3.5, Atizapan de Zaragoza, Estado de Mexico 52926, Mexico. *Phone:* -5-873-3600. *Web site:* http://www.cem.itesm.mx/.

Instituto Tecnológico y de Estudios Superiores de Monterrey, Campus Guadalajara

Zapopan, Mexico

Director of Admissions Ms. Janet Martell Sotomayor, Registration Director, Instituto Tecnológico y de Estudios Superiores de Monterrey, Campus Guadalajara, Avenida General Ramón Corona 2514, Colonia Nuevo Mexico, 45140 Zapopan, Jalisco, Mexico. *Phone:* -3-669-3006. *Web site:* http://www.gda.itesm.mx/.

Instituto Tecnológico y de Estudios Superiores de Monterrey, Campus Hidalgo

Pachuca, Mexico

Director of Admissions Lic. Lizbet Melo, Registrar, Instituto Tecnológico y de Estudios Superiores de Monterrey, Campus Hidalgo, Boulevard Felipe Angeles s/n al lado de la Unidad Deportiva, Apartado Postal 337, 42090 Pachuca, Hidalgo, Mexico. *Phone:* -714-25-00 Ext. 128. *Web site:* http://www.hgo.itesm.mx/.

Instituto Tecnológico y de Estudios Superiores de Monterrey, Campus Irapuato

Irapuato, Mexico

Director of Admissions Ing. Marcela Beltrán, Registrar, Instituto Tecnológico y de Estudios Superiores de Monterrey, Campus Irapuato, Paseo Mirador del Valle No. 445, Col. Villas de Irapuato, Apartado Postal 568, 36660 Irapuato, Guanajuato, Mexico. *Phone:* -46-230342. *Web site:* http://www.ira.itesm.mx/.

Instituto Tecnológico y de Estudios Superiores de Monterrey, Campus Laguna

Torreón, Mexico

Director of Admissions Ing. Aroldo Camargo Soto, Registrar, Instituto Tecnológico y de Estudios Superiores de Monterrey, Campus Laguna, Paseo del Tecnologico s/n Ampliacion La Rosita, Apartado Postal 506, 27250 Torreón, Coahuila, Mexico. *Phone:* -17-20-66-61 Ext. 23. *Web site:* http://www.lag.itesm.mx/.

Instituto Tecnológico y de Estudios Superiores de Monterrey, Campus León

León, Mexico

Director of Admissions Lic. Eddie Villegas, Registrar, Instituto Tecnológico y de Estudios Superiores de Monterrey, Campus León, Avenida Eugenio Garza Sada s/n Colonia Cerro Gordo, Apartado Postal 872, 37120 León, Guanajuato, Mexico. *Phone:* -47-17-10-00 Ext. 131. *Web site:* http://www.leo.itesm.mx/.

Instituto Tecnológico y de Estudios Superiores de Monterrey, Campus Mazatlán

Mazatlán, Mexico

Director of Admissions Ing. Martin Ley Urias, Registrar, Instituto Tecnológico y de Estudios Superiores de Monterrey, Campus Mazatlán, Carretera Mazatlan-Higueras, Km 3, Camino al Conchi, Apartado Postal 799, 82000 Mazatlán, Sinaloa, Mexico. *Phone:* -69-80-1143. *Web site:* http://www.maz.itesm.mx/.

Instituto Tecnológico y de Estudios Superiores de Monterrey, Campus Monterrey

Monterrey, Mexico

Director of Admissions Lic. Carlos Ordo|fnez, International Student Advisor, Instituto Tecnológico y de Estudios Superiores de Monterrey, Campus Monterrey, Avenida Eugenio Garza Sada 2501 Sur Colonia Tecnnologico, Sucursal de Correos J, 64849 Monterrey, Nuevo León, Mexico. *Phone:* -52 81 8328 4065 Ext. 3942. *Web site:* http://www.mty.itesm.mx/.

Instituto Tecnológico y de Estudios Superiores de Monterrey, Campus Querétaro

Santiago de Querétaro, Mexico

Director of Admissions Lic. Marco Vinicio Lopez, Registrar, Instituto Tecnológico y de Estudios Superiores de Monterrey, Campus Querétaro, Avenida Epigmenio González #500, Apartado Postal 37, 76130 Querétaro, Querétaro, Mexico. *Phone:* -42-17-38-25 Ext. 156. *Web site:* http://www.qro.itesm.mx/.

Instituto Tecnológico y de Estudios Superiores de Monterrey, Campus Saltillo

Saltillo, Mexico

Director of Admissions Lic. Esteban Ramos, Registrar, Instituto Tecnológico y de Estudios Superiores de Monterrey, Campus Saltillo, Prolongacion Juan de la Barrera 1241 Ote, Apartado Postal 539, 25270 Saltillo, Coahuila, Mexico. *Phone:* -84-15-06-90 Ext. 12. *Web site:* http://www.sal.itesm.mx/.

Instituto Tecnológico y de Estudios Superiores de Monterrey, Campus San Luis Potosí

San Luis Potosí, Mexico

Director of Admissions Ing. Consuelo Gonzalez, Registrar, Instituto Tecnológico y de Estudios Superiores de Monterrey, Campus San Luis Potosí, Avenida Robles 600, Colonia Jacarandas, Apartado Postal 1473 Suc E, 78140 San Luis Potosí, SLP, Mexico. *Phone:* -48 13-3441 Ext. 14. *Web site:* http://www.slp.itesm.mx/.

Instituto Tecnológico y de Estudios Superiores de Monterrey, Campus Sinaloa

Culiacán, Mexico

Director of Admissions Lic. Hugo Guerrero, Registrar, Instituto Tecnológico y de Estudios Superiores de Monterrey, Campus Sinaloa, Boulevard Culiacán 3773, Apartado Postal 69-F, 80800 Culiacán, Sinaloa, Mexico. *Phone:* -67-14-03-69. *Web site:* http://www.sin.itesm.mx/.

Instituto Tecnológico y de Estudios Superiores de Monterrey, Campus Sonora Norte

Hermosillo, Mexico

Director of Admissions Ing. Victor Eduardo Perez Orozco, Library and Admissions/Registration Director, Instituto Tecnológico y de Estudios Superiores de Monterrey, Campus Sonora Norte, Carretera Hermosillo-Nogales Km 9, Apartado Postal 216, 83000 Hermosillo, Sonora, Mexico. *Phone:* -62-15-52-05 Ext. 131. *Web site:* http://www.her.itesm.mx/.

Instituto Tecnológico y de Estudios Superiores de Monterrey, Campus Tampico

Altimira, Mexico

Director of Admissions Ing. Javier Ponce, Registrar, Instituto Tecnológico y de Estudios Superiores de Monterrey, Campus Tampico, Boulevard Petrocel Km 1.3, Corredor Industrial, Carretera Tampico-Mante, 89120 Altimira, Tamaulipas, Mexico. *Phone:* -126-4-19-79. *Web site:* http://www.itesm.edu/wps/portal?WCM_GLOBAL_CONTEXT=/migration/TAM2/Tampico.

Instituto Tecnológico y de Estudios Superiores de Monterrey, Campus Toluca

Toluca, Mexico

Director of Admissions Ing. Victor M. Martinez Orta, Registrar, Instituto Tecnológico y de Estudios Superiores de Monterrey, Campus Toluca, Ex-hacienda La Pila, 100 metros al norte de San Antonio Buenavista, 50252 Toluca, Estado de Mexico, Mexico. *Phone:* -72-74-11-92. *Web site:* http://www.tol.itesm.mx/.

Instituto Tecnológico y de Estudios Superiores de Monterrey, Campus Zacatecas

Zacatecas, Mexico

Director of Admissions Lic. de Lourdes Zorrilla, Business Affairs Director and Registrar, Instituto Tecnológico y de Estudios Superiores de Monterrey, Campus Zacatecas, Calzada Pedro Coronel #16, Frente al Club Bernades, Municipio de Guadalupe, 98000 Zacatecas, Zacatecas, Mexico. *Phone:* -49 23-00-40. *Web site:* http://www.zac.itesm.mx/.

Universidad de las Americas, A.C.

Mexico City, Mexico

Admissions Office Contact Universidad de las Americas, A.C., Calle de Puebla 223, Col. Roma, 06700 Mexico City, Mexico. *Web site:* http://www.udla.mx/.

Universidad de las Américas–Puebla

Puebla, Mexico

Freshman Application Contact Miss Madet Ruisenor-Quintero, Director of Student Enrollment Office, Universidad de las Américas–Puebla, Ex-Hacienda Santa Catarina Martir S/N, Cholula, Puebla 72820, Mexico. *Phone:* -52 229-2024. *Web site:* http://www.udlap.mx/.

Universidad de Monterrey

San Pedro Garza Garcia, Mexico

Admissions Office Contact Universidad de Monterrey, Av. Ignacio Morones Prieto 4500 Pte, 66238 San Pedro Garza Garca, NL, Mexico. *Toll-free phone:* 800-801-UDEM. *Web site:* http://www.udem.edu.mx/.

MONACO

The International University of Monaco
Monte Carlo, Monaco

Freshman Application Contact Dr. Gisele Dudognon, Director of Admissions, The International University of Monaco, 2, Avenue Albert II, MC-98000 Principality of Monaco, Monaco. *Phone:* -377 97986 994. *Fax:* 377 92052 830. *E-mail:* gdudognon@monaco.edu. *Web site:* http://www.monaco.edu/.

NICARAGUA

Ave Maria University–Latin American Campus
San Marcos, Nicaragua

Director of Admissions Mr. Patrick Clark, Director of Admissions, Ave Maria University–Latin American Campus, San Marcos, Carazo, Nicaragua. *Phone:* -43 22314-138. *Toll-free phone:* 800-969-1685. *E-mail:* patrick.clark@avemaria.edu.ni. *Web site:* http://www.avemaria.edu.ni/.

NIGERIA

The Nigerian Baptist Theological Seminary
Ogbomoso, Nigeria

Director of Admissions Mr. Daniel F. Oroniran, Registrar, The Nigerian Baptist Theological Seminary, PO Box 30, Ogbomoso, Oyo, Nigeria. *Phone:* -038-710011. *Web site:* http://www.nbtsng.org/.

SOUTH AFRICA

University of South Africa
Pretoria, South Africa

Freshman Application Contact Contact Centre, University of South Africa, PO Box 392, Pretoria 0003, South Africa. *Phone:* 27-11 670-9000. *Fax:* 012 429 4150. *E-mail:* study-info@unisa.ac.za. *Web site:* http://www.unisa.ac.za/.

SPAIN

Saint Louis University–Madrid Campus
Madrid, Spain

- **Independent Roman Catholic (Jesuit)** comprehensive
- **Urban** 1-acre campus
- **Coed**
- **Moderately difficult** entrance level

Faculty *Student/faculty ratio:* 7:1.

Academics *Calendar:* semesters. *Degrees:* certificates, bachelor's, and master's.

Student Life *Campus security:* 24-hour emergency response devices and patrols.

Standardized Tests *Required for some:* SAT or ACT (for admission), IB, A-Levels, French Baccalaureate, Selectividad, Maturita.

Costs (2011–12) *One-time required fee:* 200 euros. *Tuition:* 16,280 euros full-time, 700 euros per contact hour part-time. Full-time tuition and fees vary according to course load. *Room only:* 6360 euros. Room and board charges vary according to housing facility.

Applying *Options:* electronic application, deferred entrance. *Required:* essay or personal statement, high school transcript. *Recommended:* 2 letters of recommendation.

Freshman Application Contact Ms. Maria-Jose Morell, Director of Enrollment Management, Saint Louis University–Madrid Campus, Avenida del Valle, 34, Madrid 28003, Spain. *Phone:* -34 91-554-5858. *Fax:* 34 91-554-6202. *E-mail:* mmorell@slu.edu. *Web site:* http://spain.slu.edu/.

Schiller International University
Madrid, Spain

Freshman Application Contact Ms. Kamala Dontamsetti, Associate Director of Admissions, Schiller International University, 300 East Bay Drive, Largo, FL 33700. *Phone:* 727-736-5082 Ext. 234. *Toll-free phone:* 800-261-9571 (in-state); 800-261-9751 (out-of-state). *Fax:* 727-734-0359. *E-mail:* admissions@schiller.edu. *Web site:* http://www.schillermadrid.edu/.

SWITZERLAND

Ecole Hôtelière de Lausanne
Lausanne, Switzerland

Freshman Application Contact Ecole Hôtelière de Lausanne, Le Chalet-a-Gobet, CH-1000 Lausanne 25, Switzerland. *Phone:* -41 21 785 1111. *Web site:* http://www.ehl.ch/.

Franklin College Switzerland
Sorengo, Switzerland

- **Independent** 4-year, founded 1969
- **Suburban** 7-acre campus with easy access to Milan, Italy
- **Endowment** $2.6 million
- **Coed** 436 undergraduate students, 99% full-time, 65% women, 35% men
- **Moderately difficult** entrance level, 63% of applicants were admitted

Undergraduates 432 full-time, 4 part-time. Students come from 32 states and territories; 63 other countries; 100% are from out of state; 2% transferred in; 85% live on campus. *Retention:* 80% of full-time freshmen returned.

Freshmen *Admission:* 616 applied, 390 admitted, 132 enrolled. *Average high school GPA:* 3.12. *Test scores:* SAT critical reading scores over 500: 97%; SAT math scores over 500: 83%; SAT writing scores over 500: 87%; ACT scores over 18: 100%; SAT critical reading scores over 600: 55%; SAT math scores over 600: 29%; SAT writing scores over 600: 49%; ACT scores over 24: 78%; SAT critical reading scores over 700: 13%; SAT math scores over 700: 5%; SAT writing scores over 700: 10%; ACT scores over 30: 9%.

Faculty *Total:* 54, 46% full-time, 67% with terminal degrees. *Student/faculty ratio:* 10:1.

Academics *Calendar:* semesters. *Degrees:* associate and bachelor's. *Special study options:* accelerated degree program, advanced placement credit, double majors, English as a second language, honors programs, independent study, internships, part-time degree program, study abroad, summer session for credit.

Computers on Campus 140 computers/terminals and 20 ports are available on campus for general student use. Students can access the following: campus intranet, computer help desk, free student e-mail accounts, online (class) grades, online (class) registration, online (class) schedules, Live@EDU skydrive, Moodle, office on-line collaboration tools, LAN Storage space, student access to academic/financial records and portal available in student lounge and libraries. Campuswide network is available. 100% of college-owned or -operated housing units are wired for high-speed Internet access. Wireless service is available via entire campus.

Student Life *Housing:* on-campus residence required through sophomore year. *Options:* coed, women-only. Campus housing is university owned and leased by the school. Freshman campus housing is guaranteed. *Activities and organizations:* drama/theater group, student-run newspaper, Student Government Association, newspaper, Literary Society, Drama Society, Peer Educators Program. *Campus security:* 24-hour emergency response devices, student patrols, late-night transport/escort service, controlled dormitory access, late night patrols by professional security service personnel. *Student services:* health clinic, personal/psychological counseling.

Athletics *Intramural sports:* basketball M(c)/W(c), ice hockey M(c), skiing (downhill) M(c)/W(c), soccer M(c)/W(c), swimming and diving M(c), tennis M(c)/W(c), volleyball M(c)/W(c), water polo M(c).

"An American Degree.
A Global Experience.
A European Life."

Franklin College Switzerland is located on a hillside overlooking Lugano, the principal city of Switzerland's southernmost Italian-speaking canton of Ticino.

The College awards the Bachelor of Arts degree in a number of academic areas, and is fully accredited in the United States by the Commission on Higher Education of the Middle States Association of Colleges and Schools and in Switzerland by the Swiss University Conference.

FRANKLIN
COLLEGE SWITZERLAND

www.fc.edu

Standardized Tests *Required:* SAT or ACT (for admission). *Recommended:* SAT Subject Tests (for admission).

Costs (2011–12) *Comprehensive fee:* $48,620 includes full-time tuition ($36,300), mandatory fees ($1120), and room and board ($11,200). Full-time tuition and fees vary according to program. Part-time tuition: $3230 per course. Part-time tuition and fees vary according to program. *Required fees:* $235 per term part-time. *College room only:* $8000. Room and board charges vary according to board plan and housing facility. *Payment plan:* deferred payment. *Waivers:* employees or children of employees.

Financial Aid Of all full-time matriculated undergraduates who enrolled in 2010, 227 applied for aid, 176 were judged to have need, 19 had their need fully met. In 2010, 90 non-need-based awards were made. *Average percent of need met:* 70%. *Average financial aid package:* $18,331. *Average need-based loan:* $2731. *Average need-based gift aid:* $15,574. *Average non-need-based aid:* $14,235. *Financial aid deadline:* 3/15.

Applying *Options:* electronic application, early action, deferred entrance. *Application fee:* $90. *Required:* essay or personal statement, high school transcript, minimum 2.0 GPA, 3 letters of recommendation. *Recommended:* interview. *Application deadlines:* 3/15 (freshmen), 6/15 (transfers), 12/1 (early action). *Notification:* continuous (freshmen), continuous (transfers), 1/15 (early action).

Freshman Application Contact Karen Ballard, Dean of Admissions, Franklin College Switzerland, Franklin College, US Office, The Graybar Building, Suite 2746, 420 Lexington Avenue, New York, NY 10170. *Phone:* 212-922-9650. *Fax:* 212-922-9870. *E-mail:* Info@fc.edu. *Web site:* http://www.fc.edu/.

See page 1340 for the College Close-Up.

Glion Institute of Higher Education
Glion-sur-Montreux, Switzerland

Freshman Application Contact Admissions, Glion Institute of Higher Education, Route de Glion 111, CH-1823 Glion-sur-Montreux, Switzerland. *Phone:* 41-0 21 989 26 77. *Fax:* 41-0 21 989 26 78. *E-mail:* info@glion.edu. *Web site:* http://www.glion.edu/.

Les Roches International School of Hotel Management
Bluche, Switzerland

Freshman Application Contact Enrollment Management Department, Les Roches International School of Hotel Management, CH-3975 Bluche, Switzerland. *Phone:* 41-021 989 26 44. *Fax:* 41-021 989 26 45. *E-mail:* info@lesroches.edu. *Web site:* http://www.lesroches.cc/.

TAIWAN

Christ's College
Taipei, Taiwan

Freshman Application Contact Lucy Li, Recruiter, Christ's College, No. 51, Ziqiang Road, Tamsui District, New Taipei City 251, Taiwan. *Phone:* -+886-2-2809-7661. *Fax:* +886-2-8809-1084. *E-mail:* lucyli@christs-college.org. *Web site:* http://www.christc.org.tw/.

UNITED ARAB EMIRATES

The American University in Dubai
Dubai, United Arab Emirates

- **Proprietary** comprehensive, founded 1995
- **Urban** campus
- **Coed**
- 88% of applicants were admitted

Academics *Calendar:* semesters. *Degrees:* certificates, bachelor's, and master's.

Student Life *Campus security:* 24-hour patrols.

Applying *Options:* early admission. *Application fee:* 55 United Arab Emirates dirhams. *Required:* high school transcript, minimum 2.0 GPA, 2 letters of recommendation. *Recommended:* essay or personal statement.

Freshman Application Contact Mrs. Zeina Tannir, Associate Director of Admissions, The American University in Dubai, PO Box 28282, Dubai, United Arab Emirates. *Phone:* -971 4 399 9000 Ext. 171. *Fax:* 971 4 399 8899. *E-mail:* admissions@aud.edu. *Web site:* http://www.aud.edu/.

American University of Sharjah
Sharjah, United Arab Emirates

Director of Admissions Ali Shuhaimy, Vice Chancellor of Enrollment Management, American University of Sharjah, PO Box 26666, Sharjah, United Arab Emirates. *Phone:* -971 6 515-5555. *E-mail:* ashuhaimy@aus.edu. *Web site:* http://www.aus.edu/.

UNITED KINGDOM

American InterContinental University London
London, United Kingdom

Freshman Application Contact American InterContinental University London, 110 Marylebone High Street, London W1U 4RY, United Kingdom. *Phone:* 877-564-6248. *Toll-free phone:* 888-567-5888. *Fax:* 877-564-6248. *Web site:* http://www.aiuniv.edu/.

Hult International Business School
London, United Kingdom

Freshman Application Contact Mrs. Anna Frolander, Executive Director of Undergraduate Admissions, Hult International Business School, 46-47 Russell Square, London WC1B 4JP, United Kingdom. *Phone:* -44 207 341 8555. *E-mail:* anna.frolander@hult.edu. *Web site:* http://www.hult.edu/.

Regent's American College London
London, United Kingdom

Director of Admissions Admissions Director, Regent's American College London, Regent's College, Inner Circle, Regent's Park, London NW1 4NS, United Kingdom. *Phone:* 44-0 207 487 7505. *Fax:* 44-0 207 487 7425. *E-mail:* bacl@regents.ac.uk. *Web site:* http://www.bacl.ac.uk/.

Richmond, The American International University in London
Richmond, United Kingdom

Freshman Application Contact Mr. Nick Atkinson, Director of United States Admissions, Richmond, The American International University in London, 343 Congress Street, Suite 3100, Boston, MA 02210-1214. *Phone:* 617-450-5617. *Fax:* 617-450-5601. *E-mail:* us_admissions@richmond.ac.uk. *Web site:* http://www.richmond.ac.uk/.

See page 1520 for the College Close-Up.

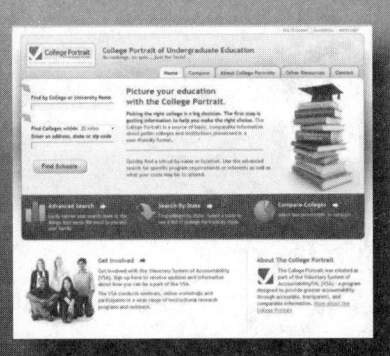

College Close-Ups

ACADEMY OF ART UNIVERSITY
SAN FRANCISCO, CALIFORNIA

The University

In 1929, Academy of Art University founder Richard S. Stephens, who was the advertising creative director of *Sunset* magazine, acted on his belief that "aspiring artists and designers, given proper instruction, hard work, and dedication, can learn the skills needed to become successful professionals." His new school of advertising art consisted of 46 students meeting in one room on San Francisco's Kearny Street.

The instructors, who are professional artists, bring real-world problems, situations, solutions, and practical experience to the students. Thus was born the school's philosophy by the founder: Hire today's best practicing professionals to teach the art and design professionals of tomorrow. At that time, advertising consisted primarily of illustrations, photos, and copy. Consequently, it became necessary to teach beginning students the fundamentals of drawing, painting, color, light, and photography as well as layout and typography.

When Richard A. Stephens succeeded his father as president in 1951, the Foundations Department was added, ensuring all students comprehended the basic principles of traditional art and design. Illustration soon expanded to include fine arts (drawing, painting, sculpture, and printmaking), and advertising design spawned the School of Graphic Design. Fashion (design, textiles, and merchandising) and Interior Design Schools were also added. In 1966, the Academy officially became a college, and in a decade, the Master of Fine Arts degree was offered. Five more buildings were purchased, and by 1992, there were more than 2,500 students.

The leadership of the Academy was then turned over to the third generation, Elisa Stephens, granddaughter of the school's founder. She quickly determined that the school's small School of Computer Arts: New Media had enormous potential to prepare students for multimedia careers when allied with such companies as Silicon Graphics, Pixar, Adobe, and Walt Disney Productions. It is now one of the largest departments at the Academy.

Today, Academy of Art University is the largest private accredited art and design school in the nation with an enrollment of more than 18,000. More than one fifth of the student body is made up of international students. The Academy has over thirty facilities that house classrooms, studios, galleries, and residence halls. The students, who are admitted through an open-enrollment policy, aspire to earn A.A., B.A., B.F.A., M.A., M.F.A., or M. Arch. degrees in eighteen majors. Students can study in San Francisco or through the Academy's flexible online programs.

The school maintains a fleet of buses to connect the different points of the campus, all of which are located within the city limits of San Francisco, one of the world's most vibrant and beautiful cities. The instructors, who are 80 percent part-time and made up of working art and design professionals, are recruited from all across the nation, and are drawn to the creative and intellectual center that is the Bay Area. Extensive senior-year internship programs allow students to gain valuable experience and develop strong portfolios in their chosen field before graduation.

The Academy is one of the few art and design schools that believe in nurturing the whole artist; this includes developing athletic talents along with artistic ones. Students can participate in intercollegiate, intramural and club sports.

Academy of Art University is an accredited member of the Western Association of Schools and Colleges (WASC), National Association of Schools of Art and Design (NASAD), Council for Interior Design (CIDA) for IAD BFA, and National Architectural Accrediting Board (NAAB) for M.Arch.

Location

The city of San Francisco is one of the great cultural centers of the world; a melting pot of diversity, ethnicity, and creativity that has spawned major museums and galleries, world-class opera and theaters, dance companies, film production and recording studios, technological innovation, performing artists ranging from classical to popular music, and numerous other cultural opportunities. The city's status as a tourist mecca located on the Pacific Rim ensures that one encounters people from all corners of the world.

The climate is moderate and offers kaleidoscopic blends of sunshine and fog nine months of the year. The Northpoint campus is located at world-famous Pier 39; one can view Alcatraz Island from classroom windows. Four other buildings are two blocks from historic Union Square in the commercial heart of the city. Three other buildings are located near the Financial District. The city offers myriad locations for field trips and studio visits. World-renowned artists display their creations in the Academy's three nonprofit art galleries, which are open to the public. The University is an urban institution that both draws upon and contributes to the cultural wealth of the community in which it resides.

Majors and Degrees

Academy of Art University offers A.A., B.A., B.F.A., M.A., M.F.A., and M.Arch. degrees and certificates in the following majors: acting (speech, improv, physical acting), advertising (account planning, art direction, copywriting, television commercials), animation/visual effects (background painting/layout design, character development, game design, storyboard art, VFX/compositing, visual development, 3-D modeling), architecture (residential, commercial, green architecture), art education (art studio and design, art history, art for educators, developmental psychology), fashion (fashion design, fashion illustration, knitwear, merchandising, textiles), fine art (ceramics, metal arts, painting/drawing, printmaking, sculpture), game design (prototyping, game art, level design, 3-D modeling) graphic design (corporate and brand identity, motion graphics, multimedia, package design, print and collateral, Web site design), illustration (cartooning, children's books, editorial, feature film animation, 2-D animation), industrial design (furniture, product, toy, transportation), interior architecture and design (commercial, furniture, residential), motion pictures and television (acting, advertising/director–camera, cinematography, directing, editing, producing, production design, screenwriting, special effects), multimedia communications (podcasting, broadcasting, multimedia journalism), music production and sound design for digital media (harmony, music production techniques, scoring for film, music for games), photography (advertising, digital photography, documentary, fine art, photo illustration, photojournalism), and Web design and new media (computer graphics, digital imaging, Web design, information architecture, interactive information graphics, interactive modeling). The Academy's newest program, landscape architecture, teaches students the latest techniques of plant design elements in landscape, grading and drainage, and urban open spaces.

Academic Programs

A total of 132 credit units are required to earn a Bachelor of Fine Arts degree, consisting of 18 units of foundations courses, 60 units in the major, 9 units of art electives, and 45 units of liberal arts courses. Fundamental courses are related specifically to students' majors to prepare them to begin intense focus courses in their field by the sophomore year. All major courses of study are structured so the student builds upon skills learned the previous semester and advances to the next level of technical or creative proficiency. Some related major courses may be taken concurrently. Each course is worth 3 credits.

Liberal arts courses teach practical applications for forging a professional career in art and design. International students who come from countries where English is not the primary language may take additional ESL classes, as determined by English language proficiency testing. Students are advised to meet with departmental directors at least once during the academic year to have their progress assessed. Portfolios are reviewed before the junior year to

determine whether or not a student has progressed sufficiently to continue study at the Academy.

Academic Facilities

The Academy's facilities reflect its commitment to training students for careers in art and design; not only do students have access to some of the most advanced facilities in the nation, but the Academy continually invests in new equipment to ensure that it remains on the cutting edge of technology. By learning on industry-standard equipment, students gain valuable professional skills that make them highly employable.

The School of Photography occupies two buildings, which house individual studios and a wide range of equipment, including full-length shooting studios; Hasselblad, Mamyia, Canon, and Sinar cameras; Broncolor, Norman, and Speedotron strobe systems; black-and-white darkrooms; a color lab facility with single-print stations; and the latest technology for digital imaging and output. In addition, the Academy's modern, professional studio is one of the largest of any photography school in the nation and is ideal for shooting automobiles, motorcycles, and large sets.

The Academy's Fine Art Sculpture Center houses state-of-the-art studios for figure, ceramic, neon/illumination, bronze, metal fabrication, and mold-making sculpture. Students also have use of an off-site bronze-casting facility and foundry. When students graduate from the Academy, they have the opportunity to exhibit in one of the three nonprofit galleries located in the heart of downtown San Francisco's premier gallery district. These street-level facilities are an excellent way for students to promote and sell their work and to gain networking experience.

Multimedia Communications and Graphic Design are housed in the Academy's main building in the heart of San Francisco. Multimedia Communications students have access to a professional studio on the building's first floor. At the School of Industrial Design, students draw inspiration from the Academy's Automotive Museum.

The Library houses more than 30,000 books and magazines, as well as 375 CD titles, 150,000 slides, and 2,000 videos. Computers with Internet access are available to students, as well as an online catalog, color scanners, and color and black-and-white copiers. Workshops and electronic study guides are also available. The Academy Resource Center offers all students free learning support services that include study hall, tutoring, mentoring, mid-point review and study-skills workshops, a writing lab, a state-of-the-art multimedia language lab, an English for Art Program, and a Conversation Partner Program.

Costs

Tuition is $765 per credit unit for undergraduates. Full-time students carry either 12 or 15 units per semester. There is a nonrefundable $120 registration fee—$100 is applicable toward tuition. Lab fees run from $25 to $400 per semester, depending on the class. Tuition and fees are subject to change at any time. Art supplies can run from $250 to $900 per semester, depending on the major. The Academy has most of the expensive technical equipment available for students to borrow or use in a lab.

Academy of Art University operates seventeen residence halls within the city. Several housing options are offered, and costs vary from $7200 to $14,180 per academic year (fall and spring semesters). For further information, students may contact the Academy Housing Office directly at housing@academyart.edu or 800-544-2787 (toll-free, U.S. only).

Financial Aid

The Academy offers financial aid packages consisting of grants, loans, and work-study to eligible students with a demonstrated need. Low-interest loans are available to all eligible students, regardless of need. As financial aid programs, procedures, and eligibility requirements change frequently, applicants should contact the Financial Aid Office at financialaid@academyart.edu or 800-544-2787 (toll-free, U.S. only).

Faculty

The Academy averages 950 instructors in fall/spring semester, most of whom are full-time art and design professionals and part-time teachers. The student-teacher ratio for undergraduate classes averages 18:1.

Student Government

Although there is no formal student government, each department has between 2 and 3 student representatives who meet with the president as needed throughout the semester to discuss any student issues.

Admission Requirements

Applicants for the A.A., B.A., and B.F.A. programs must have a high school diploma or GED equivalent. There is no portfolio requirement. M.A. and M.F.A. applicants must have a bachelor's degree and submit a portfolio and statement of intent. International students take written and speech tests to determine which ESL classes may have to be completed. Most ESL classes can be taken in conjunction with art and design classes. All foundations classes offer specialized ESL sections with instructors trained for language assistance. The application fee is $100 for undergraduates. A $500 tuition deposit applies to international applicants.

Application and Information

Students may apply to enter the Academy at the beginning of the spring, fall, or summer semesters. Information in this profile is subject to change. Students should contact Academy of Art University for current information or visit www.academyart.edu to learn about total costs, median student loan debt, potential occupations, and other information.

Academy of Art University
79 New Montgomery Street
San Francisco, California 94105
Phone: 415-274-2200
      800-544-2787 (U.S only)
Fax: 415-618-6287
E-mail: info@academyart.edu
Web site: http://academyart.edu

Academy of Art University's downtown campus.

ADELPHI UNIVERSITY
GARDEN CITY, NEW YORK

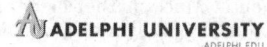

The University

Adelphi University, founded in 1896, is Long Island's first private coeducational institution of higher learning. A nonsectarian, independent university, Adelphi welcomes men and women of all backgrounds who display intellectual inquisitiveness, academic commitment, and a desire for achievement and purpose in life. The University enrolls 5,021 undergraduates and 2,901 graduate students. Forty-three states and forty-five countries are represented in its diverse student body. The campus is located on 75 landscaped acres in Garden City, New York, 20 miles east of New York City and easily accessible by public transportation. The University also has three off-campus centers: the Manhattan Center in New York City, the Hauppauge Center on Long Island, and the Hudson Valley Center in Poughkeepsie, New York.

Adelphi University's schools and programs include the College of Arts and Sciences; the Honors College; the Schools of Nursing and Social Work; the Robert B. Willumstad School of Business; the Ruth S. Ammon School of Education; the Gordon F. Derner Institute of Advanced Psychological Studies; and adult academic programs in University College.

The University's seven residence halls provide all the comforts of home and include a Green Community and honors housing. The residential life staff at Adelphi is committed to bringing education to the residence halls. A lecture and discussion series brings faculty members together with students to examine events of the day and issues related to the classroom. In addition, about 200 seminars, workshops, and events are offered each year. Faculty and guest lecturers lead discussions on such topics as American and global politics, ethnic diversity, legal affairs, job interviewing, sexual conduct, and AIDS.

Opportunities for enhancing life beyond the classroom abound at Adelphi. Students participate in intramural and intercollegiate athletics (including nationally ranked men's and women's soccer, softball, and baseball and men's basketball and lacrosse), drama productions, and more than 80 student clubs, community-service groups, and organizations. Students take advantage of thriving cultural arts programs, including plays, art exhibits, concerts, and lectures; the comprehensive sports and fitness services; and the breathtaking campus. Physical education facilities include a swimming pool; basketball courts; weight-training and exercise rooms; a large indoor running track; and fields for baseball, lacrosse, soccer, and softball. In addition, a vast array of activities such as movies, exhibits, cabarets, symposia, and field trips are scheduled every semester.

The Adelphi student newspaper *(The Delphian)* and the yearbook *(Oracle)* welcome writers and photographers.

In the Ruth S. Harley University Center (UC)—a central meeting place on campus—Adelphi students can browse the full-service bookstore, refresh themselves and relax in one of the center's lounges (commuter students have a special lounge equipped with lockers), eat in the UC Café, and enjoy a vast array of activities, including movies, comedy shows, lectures, dance parties, and musical events. Cultural trips are also offered. The UC also houses Adelphi's numerous student organizations.

Location

Adelphi's main campus is located in Garden City, New York, a village of stately homes, historic buildings, and parks. The cultural and commercial resources of New York City and the recreation and entertainment of Long Island are only a short distance away by public or private transit.

Majors and Degrees

Undergraduate studies leading to the degrees of Bachelor of Arts (B.A.), Bachelor of Business Administration (B.B.A.), Bachelor of Fine Arts (B.F.A.), Bachelor of Science (B.S.), and Bachelor of Social Work (B.S.W.) are offered at Adelphi. Programs of study at Adelphi include: accounting; African, Black, and Caribbean studies; anthropology/forensic anthropology; art, with specializations in art history, fine arts and studio art* (ceramics, painting, photography, printmaking, sculpture), and graphic design*; art education; biochemistry; biology; business; chemistry; communications (journalism, media studies, moving image production); communication sciences and disorders; computer and management information systems; computer science; criminal justice; dance; economics; education studies, with programs of study in childhood education (S.T.E.P.) and adolescent education (S.T.E.P.); English (literature, creative writing); environmental studies; exercise science; finance; French; history; interdisciplinary studies; languages and international studies (political science, environmental studies, business); Latin American studies; management; marketing; mathematics; music**; music education; nursing; philosophy; physical education; physical education/health education; physics; political science; psychology; social work; sociology; Spanish; sport management; theatre arts** (acting and design technology); undeclared arts and sciences; and undeclared business. (A * indicates that an art portfolio is required; ** indicates that an audition is required.)

Five-year bachelor's/master's programs are offered in social work and business, as well as the Scholars Teacher Education Program (S.T.E.P.) in childhood education and adolescence education.

Opportunities for preprofessional studies are available in pre-dental, pre-engineering, pre–environmental studies, pre-law, pre-medicine, pre-optometry, pre-pharmacy, pre–physical therapy/allied health, pre-podiatry, and pre–veterinary medicine.

Academic Programs

The goal of the academic programs at Adelphi is to provide higher education that cultivates the intellect and prepares students for the future. Consistent with the University's approach to liberal learning, students take part in the University's general education distribution requirements.

A minimum of 120 credits is required for a baccalaureate degree, with a specified number in the chosen major. Double majors and various minors may be elected. Seniors of superior academic ability may be admitted to graduate courses in their major field.

Off-Campus Programs

Adelphi University offers study-abroad programs that can last several weeks or span up to an academic year. Students can participate in Adelphi-run programs in such locations as Australia, Costa Rica, Florence, India, and Peru, or join programs run by other educational institutions. Adelphi offers students the opportunity to participate in internship programs that provide access to a variety of industries and locations—in the local Long Island community, the surrounding New York City area, and beyond. Students also have the opportunity to participate in the Community Fellows Program, which pairs

students with nonprofit organizations across Long Island and New York City, for 10-week, paid summer internships.

Academic Facilities

The University Libraries are composed of the Swirbul Library, the Archives and Special Collections, and the libraries at the Manhattan, Hauppauge, and Hudson Valley centers. These libraries contain 600,000 volumes and 806,000 items in microformat, plus 33,000 audiovisual materials and access to more than 61,000 electronic journal titles. The University Libraries are fully automated with holdings accessible through the Adelphi Libraries Catalog Online (ALICAT). As an enhancement of the traditional reference services, online access is provided to 221 research databases.

The Swirbul Library is also the center of information technology on campus. Its amenities include more than 100 computer workstations that are fully networked for student use, a faculty development lab, and a technology infrastructure that reaches into every classroom and every part of the curriculum to provide Web-based learning and other applications of communication and information media.

The 18,000-square-foot Adele and Herbert J. Klapper Center for Fine Arts has greatly expanded Adelphi's art studio and classroom space and offers greater opportunity for nonmajors to take art courses. This is in addition to the current state-of-the-art digital graphics design studio and faculty offices and the expansion of drawing studios in Blodgett Hall.

The Adelphi University Performing Arts Center (AUPAC) showcases prestigious programs in acting, design/technical theater, music, and dance together under one roof. The new center features a 500-seat music performance hall, dance and recital rooms, music practice rooms, temperature-controlled instrument storage rooms, and a black box theater.

The Center for Recreation and Sports is the home of Adelphi's successful athletics programs. The center's three-story, three-court gym, which converts into a 2,200-seat arena for basketball games and other events, accommodates recreational and intercollegiate athletes and health and physical education students, and can host NCAA tournaments and championships.

Costs

The 2011–12 tuition and fees for full-time undergraduates were $28,460. For students living on campus, additional costs included room ($8170 for a typical double room without air conditioning) and board ($3390 for a basic meal plan).

Financial Aid

The Office of Student Financial Services administers federal and New York State programs that provide funds to assist students in pursuing their academic goals. In addition to grants based on need, Adelphi annually offers almost 1,000 of its own scholarships based on merit, talent, and extracurricular excellence. Ninety-eight percent of Adelphi freshmen receive some form of financial aid each year. The average financial aid package award for a full-time undergraduate is approximately $20,475.

Faculty

At Adelphi, the quality of education is entrusted to its distinguished faculty members who are noted for their serious commitment to students, as well as for their research and professional contributions. Undergraduate courses are taught by professors, not graduate assistants, and students learn in small, intimate environments.

Student Government

The Student Government Association is the elected student group that represents the opinions of the full-time under-graduate body to the administration and other groups. The Student Government Association hosts speakers, sponsors awareness days, and serves as a voice for student concerns and interests.

Admission Requirements

Recommended admission qualifications include graduation from a four-year public or private high school or equivalent credentials, four years of English, three years of science, three years of mathematics, two to three years of a foreign language or languages, and 4 additional units chosen from the fields mentioned or from history and social studies. Official test results from the SAT or ACT with writing are required.

Personal interviews and campus tours are strongly recommended for all applicants. Arrangements can be made by contacting the Office of Admissions at 516-877-3050.

Application and Information

The following admission credentials should be submitted by applicants: a completed application for admission, the $40 nonrefundable application fee, an official secondary school transcript or GED certificate, official results of the SAT or ACT, and letters of recommendation. Transfer students must submit official transcripts from all colleges previously attended.

Adelphi accepts applications on a rolling basis, with admission twice each year for the semesters beginning in September and January. Freshmen filing dates are December 1 for early action, February 1 for priority consideration for joint-degree programs, March 1 for regular admission to the fall semester (applications received later are reviewed on a rolling basis), and November 1 for regular admission for the spring semester (applications received later are reviewed on a rolling basis). The nonbinding early-action plan is available only for the September term. An early-action decision means that applicants who submit their completed applications by December 1 receive an admissions decision by December 31 and that they are considered for scholarships and financial aid.

For more information, students should contact:

Office of University Admissions
Adelphi University
Garden City, New York 11530
Phone: 516-877-3050
    800-ADELPHI (toll-free)
E-mail: admissions@adelphi.edu
Web site: www.adelphi.edu

Adelphi University comprises students from 43 states and 45 countries.

ALLEGHENY COLLEGE
MEADVILLE, PENNSYLVANIA

The College

One of Loren Pope's forty "Colleges That Change Lives," Allegheny is cited as the premiere college in the country for students with "unusual combinations" of interests and talents. On its historic campus—where the liberal arts and sciences have been taught for almost 200 years—students develop combinations of majors and minors in areas that may, at first glance, seem unrelated: biology and economics, political science and music, history and psychology. Allegheny students share an abiding passion for learning and life, a spirit of camaraderie, and a respect for shared inquiry that spans all areas of study. Neuroscience majors play in the Civic Symphony and build houses during Alternative Spring Break. Students prepare for law school while playing basketball and interning in Washington, D.C. Computer science majors present work in philosophy at national conferences.

Building on a combination of academic disciplines and passions, every student completes the comprehensive Senior Project under the guidance of a faculty adviser in his or her major field. The project demonstrates the skills most prized by employers and graduate schools: the ability to complete a major assignment, work independently, analyze and synthesize information, and to write and speak persuasively.

Allegheny students are encouraged to explore all of their interests and to look at academic disciplines from multiple perspectives, which leads them to extraordinary outcomes. Biochemistry majors use the skills they learned in communication arts to start marketing careers with the Environmental Protection Agency. English majors collaborate with the College's pre-health advisers and enjoy acceptance rates to medical school between 80 and 100 percent—twice the national average. And over 90 percent of Allegheny's job-seeking graduates find employment within eight months.

Leaders in business, government, medicine, education, and community service frequently declare that the future belongs to individuals who are innovators, inventors, and big-picture thinkers, those who think both analytically and creatively. It is this preparation for the global marketplace, and for life, that Allegheny, with its emphasis on "unusual combinations," is nationally known for providing.

Location

Central campus looks like a traditional college with a rich liberal arts heritage and tradition, with its 79 acres of rolling lawns and brick walkways, historic buildings, and century-old oaks and elms. A 203-acre recreational complex and a 283-acre nature reserve complement state-of-the-art classrooms, labs, theaters, studios and other facilities.

The campus overlooks the town of Meadville, a county seat that features a courthouse, hospital, a variety of industries, and more. Allegheny students connect with the community in many ways, from running after-school programs to taking in the latest movies, from creating art installations to checking out live music.

Allegheny students live in a section of the country that most people get to see only on vacation. Northwest Pennsylvania is a nature-lover's paradise of verdant, undisturbed forests and streams and lakes that are gems of biodiversity. It's no wonder that the College has one of the oldest Outing Clubs in the country.

Allegheny is ideally situated within 2 hours of the social and transportation hubs of Pittsburgh, Cleveland, and Buffalo. Being just close enough to major cities allows for frequent excursions to major sporting events, concerts, and other attractions.

Majors and Degrees

Allegheny students can earn the Bachelor of Arts (B.A.) or the Bachelor of Science (B.S.) degree in the following programs of study: American studies; applied computing; applied economics; art and technology; art and the environment; art (studio); art history;

Asian studies; astronomy; biochemistry; biological and physical studies; biology; black studies; chemistry; Chinese studies; classical studies; communication arts; computer science; creative writing; dance and movement studies; economics; education; English; environmental geology; environmental science; environmental studies; environmental writing; French; French studies; geology; German; German studies; history; international studies; journalism; Latin; Latin American and Caribbean studies; lesbian and gay studies; managerial economics; mass communication/media studies; mathematics; medieval and Renaissance studies; music; music history; music performance; music theory; neuroscience; philosophy; physics; political science; pre-dental; pre-law; pre-medicine; pre-nursing; pre-pharmacy; pre-veterinary studies; psychology; religious studies; science, health, and society; Spanish; theatre; values, ethics, and social action (VESA); women's studies; writing; and self-designed majors.

Students may also take advantage of accelerated master's and doctoral degree programs, teacher certification programs, and engineering cooperative programs with other top institutions.

Academic Programs

Allegheny College believes so strongly in unusual combinations that they are built right into its curriculum; it is one of the few liberal arts colleges nationally that requires students to choose a minor as well as a major. In some ways, this may make school more difficult. But most students at Allegheny are individuals for whom the most difficult thing would be to give up some vital part of themselves. Some Allegheny students have majors and minors that complement each other in predictable ways—an international studies major with a minor in French, for example. But there are other students whose majors and minors represent very different aspects of themselves—an environmental studies major with a minor in creative writing or a chemistry major with a minor in history. Coupled with experiential learning and the distinctive Senior Project, seeing academic disciplines from multiple perspectives leads to extraordinary outcomes.

During the first two years, every Allegheny student participates in seminars that focus on written and oral communication as well as academic and career advising, and the faculty instructor serves as adviser for both years. This progressive course sequence, in addition to the Junior Seminar and Senior Project, helps students create a four-year experience to match all of their needs and goals.

Under the guidance of a faculty adviser in his or her major field, every student completes the Senior Project, a significant piece of original scholarly work with a creative, analytical, or experimental focus. The project mirrors a master's thesis and requires project management skills, independent work, writing and presentation skills, and the ability to analyze and synthesize information. Allegheny has required a senior capstone experience since the college's first commencement ceremony in 1821.

In the National Survey of Student Engagement, responses by college freshmen placed Allegheny within the top 10 percent in the United States for both a supportive campus environment and level of academic challenge.

Off-Campus Programs

Allegheny College recognizes the enormous academic, professional, and personal value of studying off-campus, nationally or internationally. Allegheny students can experience multiple off-campus adventures, learning with an eclectic group of students with diverse academic majors and interests. The Allegheny College Center for Experiential Learning (ACCEL) facilitates a variety of opportunities through study abroad, career services, community service, and more.

The College sponsors semester and year-long study-away programs, some of which require skills in languages other than English, and others with no language requirements. More than 190 Allegheny

students and faculty participate in forty Allegheny-sponsored study abroad programs in twenty countries.

In addition, faculty members lead students each year on intensive three-week experiential learning seminars. These for-credit, faculty-designed programs occur at the end of each spring semester. Recent excursions took students to Denmark and Germany, Greece, Italy, Turkey, and South Africa.

The Office of Career Services maintains a database of 2,500 internship and shadowing opportunities, including especially popular ones in Boston, New York City, Los Angeles, and Washington, D.C. Students at Allegheny can choose among several kinds of internships, including academic internships taken for credit that often take place during a spring or fall semester and noncredit internships throughout the summer.

Academic Facilities

Allegheny boasts the nationally acclaimed Steffee Hall of Life Sciences, which incorporates state-of-the-art labs located right next to classrooms and faculty offices. A new environmental science center features the best in sustainable practices with a living wall, aquaponics equipment, and solar panels. Students also benefit from the GIS learning lab, planetarium, and seismographic network station.

The multimillion-dollar Center for Communication Arts, which meets LEED certification standards and has a rooftop garden, features a learning theater, scene and costume shops, and video production facilities. Language students enjoy a multimedia learning lab, and dancers work in bright, functional studio and performance spaces. The Bowman, Penelec, and Megahan art galleries display student and faculty work as well as visiting exhibits.

Allegheny's Learning Commons provides academic support to all students through professional guidance, peer mentors, training, and effective learning tools. The center is housed in Pelletier Library, which offers more than 900,000 volumes, as well as extensive digital resources, research tools, and unique meeting spaces.

Costs

For 2012–13, tuition and fees are $37,610. Room and board is $9540.

Financial Aid

Through the generous support of its alumni, Allegheny is able to provide over $32 million in achievement-based scholarships and need-based grant assistance to supplement over $21 million in aid awarded to students from federal, state, and private sources. Allegheny's financial assistance allows many students the opportunity to make a college choice based on value and fit, rather than financial constraints.

Allegheny's Trustee Scholarships are awarded without regard to financial need to students who have balanced academic excellence with other distinctive activities while in high school. Awards range up to $80,000, distributed equally over four years of study at Allegheny (up to $20,000 per year), and renew automatically.

Faculty

Whether it's conducting research, teaching a First-Year Seminar, leading a three-week study tour, co-authoring an article or making an authentic French dinner, faculty work and learn alongside students every day. There's no graduate school buffer between undergraduates and faculty. Students don't have to wait behind graduate students for research positions on faculty-led projects or compete against hundreds of other students for the lead roles in plays or an editorship at the literary magazine.

Of the 157 full-time faculty members, 95 percent have earned the highest degree in their fields. The student to faculty ratio is 12:1, and introductory classes have an average of 21 students. Advanced classes have an average of 12 students, and some seminars have fewer than 10. Of all classes, 88 percent have fewer than 30 students.

Every student has a faculty adviser for the first two years and a faculty adviser in his/her major field for the final two years. Culminating with their work guiding students through the Senior Project, faculty members are not only supportive and engaging teachers but true leaders and mentors.

Student Government

The Allegheny Student Government is the official voice and administrative unit of the student body. This extremely active and influential organization concerns itself with the quality of the educational, cultural, and social aspects of the Allegheny community. Its members organize and coordinate programs of a cocurricular and extracurricular nature and sponsor over 100 student-run clubs and organizations.

Students serve on every major college committee, including faculty searches, sustainability efforts, and strategic planning. Their presence exemplifies the importance placed on student participation and represents the influence students have on the institution.

Admission Requirements

From the time a prospective student first contacts Allegheny, the college's approach is directed to addressing his or her unique character, needs, and aspirations. During the application process, primary attention is focused on those criteria that indicate academic promise, including difficulty of high school classes, GPA and rank, and board scores. Careful consideration is also given to those personal qualities that are important in the total success of the college experience: school and community activities, recommendation letters, and the personal essay. Students are encouraged to share additional information through the college's application supplement and an interview and visit.

The result is a highly personalized approach to the selection of students that remains consistent with the aims of the college, respects the individuality of each applicant, and ensures equal consideration of every candidate. The College encourages diversity and actively seeks students from all ethnic, religious, racial, political, geographic, and socioeconomic backgrounds.

Application and Information

Office of Admissions
Allegheny College
520 North Main Street
Meadville, Pennsylvania 16335
Phone: 814-332-4351
      800-521-5293 (toll-free)
Fax: 814-337-0431
E-mail: admissions@allegheny.edu
Web site: http://www.allegheny.edu/unusualcombinations
      http://www.allegheny.edu/distinctions
      http://www.allegheny.edu/visit
      http://www.allegheny.edu/apply

Allegheny College offers a traditional setting, but supports unusual combinations in its students' interests and talents.

ALVERNIA UNIVERSITY
READING, PENNSYLVANIA

The University

Located in Berks County, Pennsylvania, Alvernia University offers all the best features of an outstanding university—specialized professional programs, experiential learning, internships, and a variety of leadership opportunities—in the personal setting of a college environment. A private Franciscan institution rooted in the Catholic and liberal arts tradition, the core institutional values—service, humility, peacemaking, contemplation, and collegiality—are relevant today and have a universal ethical appeal. Students appreciate the small class sizes and breadth of academic programs offered, all taught by faculty who are experts in their fields and committed foremost to their students' success. Graduates are prepared to achieve their personal dreams and professional success, and to be engaged citizens and lifelong learners. Alvernia has been honored by the Templeton Foundation as one of the top 100 character-building colleges in the nation and a model of excellence in education. In addition, the University is regularly named to the President's Higher Education Community Service Honor Roll for its commitment to and achievement in community service.

The University's 3,000 total students (1,500 traditional undergraduates) can choose from over 600 courses and 50 majors and minors the College of Arts and Sciences and College of Professional Programs. Programs are geared toward real-world learning and preparing students for a rewarding career. Study abroad, internships, and international service trips make learning come alive and allow students to develop practical, valuable skills.

Master's degrees are awarded in occupational therapy, business administration, nursing, community counseling, education, and liberal studies. A Ph.D. program in leadership is also available.

Location

Situated on a scenic 121-acre suburban campus, Alvernia is bordered by a park that features hiking trails, a picnic grove, and a nine-hole disk-golf course. When students want to explore big city life, Philadelphia (60 miles), New York, Baltimore, and Washington, D.C. are all within an easy drive.

Majors and Degrees

Alvernia offers a breadth of academic programs with a boundary-free learning approach. Bachelor's degrees are awarded in the following majors: accounting, athletic training, behavioral health, biochemistry, biology medical technology, chemistry medical technology, communication, criminal justice administration, education (concentrations in early childhood, middle school, secondary, and special), English, forensic science, general science, history, human resource management, liberal studies, marketing, management, mathematics, nursing, occupational therapy, philosophy, political science, psychology, social work, sport management, theater, and theology. Pre-professional programs are available in dentistry, law, medicine, and veterinary studies. Alvernia also offers minors and certificate programs.

Since 1967, the Middle States Association of Colleges and Schools has granted Alvernia accreditation. The education program for elementary and secondary teachers is approved by the Pennsylvania Department of Education. The occupational therapy program is fully accredited by the American Occupational Therapy Association. The Bachelor of Science in Nursing has approval by the Pennsylvania State Board of Nursing and is accredited by the Commission on Collegiate Nursing Education. The athletic training program is accredited by the Commission on Accreditation of Allied Health Education Programs in cooperation with the Joint Review Committee on Educational Programs in Athletic Training. The social work program is accredited by the Council on Social Work Education. The behavioral health program is certified by the Pennsylvania

Certification Board. The business department is accredited by the Association of Collegiate Business Schools and Programs.

Academic Programs

Logical and critical thinking, accurate comprehension, and effective communication are at the heart of Alvernia's academic program. Students' personal development is also highly valued, and the University promotes integrity in academic pursuits, social responsibility, and moral values.

The Genesis Experience Program provides academic advisement for students who have not declared a major. It offers students the opportunity to dedicate the first few semesters of college to exploration, examination, and counseling to gain exposure to potential fields of study.

Qualified students may participate in the Honors Program, which assists students of outstanding intellectual promise and high motivation that seek a more challenging program and are interested in pursuing future graduate or professional studies. The program encourages students to achieve, often letting them work at their own pace. It facilitates a stimulating exchange of ideas and information between students' varied interests and different disciplines.

In order to earn a bachelor's degree from Alvernia, students must complete a minimum of 123 credits, with 54 credits in the liberal arts. Additional requirements vary by major.

Off-Campus Programs

The Washington Center experience is a popular way for students to expand their education beyond the classroom. Earning college credit while spending a semester in Washington D.C., students serve as interns in a congressional office, government agency, major corporation, newspaper, news network, or nonprofit groups, or an agency devoted to legal affairs, international relations, or business and economics.

Study abroad has become increasingly popular. In recent years, Alvernia students have studied in Great Britain, Germany, Italy, Spain, and in the Semester-at-Sea program.

Campus Facilities

Alvernia has recently invested in several additions to campus including a new laser laboratory to support science programs, state-of-the-art learning suites developed for the criminal justice program, an educational technology center that supports all majors, and a new recital hall and theater.

On-campus housing includes traditional residence halls, apartments, suites, and town houses. All residential facilities are clean, spacious and equipped with laundry, cable TV, and phones with voice mail.

Construction is under way on two new residence halls in Founders Village, scheduled to open in the fall 2012. A new student activities center, attached to one of the units, will house a fitness center, dance/aerobics studio, and a campus "living room," complete with a fireplace, for leisure activities, study, and programs.

Alvernia's campus is fully networked. Students have access to the academic information network and the Internet from their residence hall rooms as well as from other campus locations including classrooms, the library, and labs. All students may connect personal computers through the University's secure system. Network access and Alvernia email accounts are available to all students.

Costs

For the 2012–13 academic year tuition is $27,400, and room and board is $9850 (an approximate cost based on the highest priced residence hall and an all-you-can-eat meal plan).

Financial Aid

Ninety-nine percent of students receive some form of financial aid. Financial aid is offered to students whose personal and

family resources are insufficient to meet the full cost of an education. Aid usually comes in the form of scholarships, grants, loans, and work-study arrangements. Depending upon their academic record, incoming first-year students may be eligible for one of three merit-based scholarships: the Presidential Scholarship ($12,000), the Trustee's Scholarship ($10,000), and the Veronica Founder's Scholarship ($8000). Applicants interested in financial aid should submit the FAFSA as soon as possible after January 1.

Faculty

The dedicated faculty members are accomplished scholars who bring real-world experience into the classroom and are as diversified as the fields of interest that they represent. Faculty members publish in professional journals and other media; present papers and moderate conferences in the region and as far away as India, Italy, Mexico, and South Africa; and serve on boards and committees of professional associations and corporate and community boards.

Student Government and Activities

Alvernia encourages students to take advantage of learning opportunities outside the classroom by participating in any of the more than fifty-five student clubs, organizations, and service programs. Campus organizations offer opportunities to suit the interests of all students, to meet new people, to learn various skills, and to develop leadership abilities.

Athletics are a proud and integral part of the educational mission. Students may participate in intercollegiate, intramural, and club-level programs. Intercollegiate teams compete at the NCAA Division III level. Alvernia is part of the highly competitive Middle Atlantic States Athletic Conference (MAC), and is also a member of the Eastern Collegiate Athletic Conference.

The Office of Student Activities works with the many student organizations to provide a calendar of social, cultural, and other co-curricular activities. The Student Government Association provides an opportunity for leadership through the exercise of personal and group responsibility. All students complete approved community service hours as part of Alvernia's commitment to peace, justice, and the dignity of life. This helps foster devotion to service of others, especially the materially and spiritually disadvantaged of the local and global community.

Admission Requirements

Admission requirements normally include a high school diploma with 16 Carnegie units in the following subjects: English, 4 units; mathematics, 2 units; science, 2 units; social studies, 2 units; and modern languages, 2 units. The remaining units may be made up of academic electives. The University is willing to consider good students whose preparation does not include all of these subjects. Nursing students must fulfill the admission requirements established by the Pennsylvania State Board of Nurse Examiners. The State High School Equivalency Diploma is generally recognized as fulfilling the minimum entrance requirements. Applicants are required to take the SAT; the ACT is also acceptable. Outstanding candidates are considered for entrance to Alvernia at the end of their junior year of high school on the basis of requests made by the candidate and the school. With the approval of their school officials, students may also be admitted to certain courses during their senior year, simultaneously earning credit toward their high school diploma and a college degree.

Application and Information

Many factors are considered for admission, including academic performance, standardized test scores, class rank, extracurricular activities, and community involvement. Application and admission notification is on a rolling basis; however, applicants are encouraged to submit the admission application as early as possible. In addition to their transcripts and SAT or ACT scores, nursing applicants must also submit two letters of reference.

Alvernia accepts and/or offers special programs for accelerated high school students, nontraditional students (older than 24), transfer students, students with disabilities, and international students.

Applicants should submit an application for admission and enclose a nonrefundable $25 processing fee. The application form may be obtained from the Office of Admissions or the University's Web site at www.alvernia.edu/admissions/undergraduate/apply.html.

Applicants should have an official copy of their high school record sent to the Office of Admissions, along with the official results of the SAT or ACT.

Because Alvernia has a rolling admission policy, the Director of Admissions notifies an applicant of acceptance shortly after the necessary credentials are on file and have been reviewed, generally within one month. To reserve a place in the freshman class, all students must make a $300 deposit by May 1. This deposit is credited to the student's account for the first semester but is not refunded if the student fails to attend. Transfer students should have a grade point average of 2.0 or higher on a 4.0 scale and should be aware that only grades of C or better are eligible for credit transfer. Alvernia accepts a maximum of 75 transfer credits; at least 45 credits that are required for graduation must be earned at Alvernia and must satisfy all graduation requirements. A detailed analysis of credits to be transferred is done only after the University has accepted students.

The best way to get to know Alvernia is through a campus visit and tour. Applicants and those considering the school are strongly encouraged to come for an individual campus visit, which will be personalized to match each student's unique interests. Alvernia also hosts information sessions and open houses throughout the year that allow prospective freshmen or transfers to meet current students, talk to admissions and financial aid counselors, and meet faculty and coaches. Overnight and shadow visits are also available.

For more information or to schedule a visit, students should contact:

Director of Admissions
Alvernia University
Reading, Pennsylvania 19607
Phone: 888-ALVERNIA (258-3764, toll-free)
Fax: 610-790-2873
E-mail: admissions@alvernia.edu
Web site: http://www.alvernia.edu
      http://on.fb.me/Alvernia_University (Facebook)
      http://twitter.com/alverniauniv (Twitter)

With a 14:1 student-to-faculty ratio and an average class size of less than 20, the Alvernia experience is personal. The Student Center, shown here, is the hub for campus activity.

THE AMERICAN UNIVERSITY OF ROME
ROME, ITALY

The University

Preparing students from around the world to live and work across cultures, The American University of Rome (AUR) blends the best of two worlds, combining the academic attributes of higher education in the United States—American practical know-how, technological capability, and career preparation—with the European and Italian classical tradition education in the humanities and liberal arts. Students leave AUR trained in the fundamental portable skills of language, communication, and critical thinking that allow them to continue to learn and thrive in a complex and interconnected world. For many, the time spent in the uniquely energizing city of Rome is a life-transforming experience.

Founded in 1969, The American University of Rome is the oldest, private independent American institution of higher education in Rome, offering undergraduate degrees in eight disciplines to a student body of around 500 students each semester. It is also a destination for study-abroad students from American colleges and universities for year-long, semester, and summer programs.

AUR's robust academic program is complemented by a rich variety of extracurricular activities including clubs, performing groups, local events, and athletics. Highlights include competitive men's and women's soccer leagues, a coed running club, a yoga club, a men's basketball club, martial arts training, and even a rowing club that allows students to enjoy Rome from a unique and privileged perspective. Studying at AUR also gives students ample opportunities to travel across Italy and Europe.

AUR meets student health needs by offering services of a doctor on campus three to four days a week for primary care at no charge. In addition, a certified professional provides students with free, private psychological counseling.

Students may elect for AUR to arrange housing on their behalf or may choose to make their own housing arrangements. University-facilitated housing consists of furnished apartments in well-established neighborhoods surrounding the university campus. This housing is well suited for students looking for a full-immersion experience in Italian culture.

The American University of Rome is fully accredited by the Middle States Commission on Higher Education and is licensed by the State of Delaware Department of Education to award associate and bachelor's degrees. AUR is incorporated in the District of Columbia as a not-for-profit institution.

Location

Overlooking the historical center, the University is located in the prestigious area of the Janiculum, Rome's highest hill, just a few minutes' walk from the historic Trastevere district and the heart of Rome. With its own gardens of Roman pines, it offers a spectacular view of Rome. The campus is close to two city parks, Villa Sciarra and Villa Pamphili. The area also hosts diplomatic residences and international academies. The neighborhood offers a full range of amenities, including restaurants, shops, cafés, and outdoor markets.

Majors and Degrees

The American University of Rome offers a strong undergraduate curriculum with an international perspective. The Bachelor of Arts degree is awarded in Archeology and Classics, Art History, Communication, Film and Digital Media, Interdisciplinary Studies, International Relations and Global Politics, and Italian Studies. A Bachelor of Science degree is awarded in Business Administration. The Associate of Arts degree is offered in International Business and Liberal Studies. All courses (except for Italian, Latin, and Greek language courses) are taught in English.

Academic Program

Consistent with the mission of the University, the objectives of The American University of Rome's academic program are: to develop and strengthen basic skills that can prepare graduates for a modern working environment and that will be adaptable to a rapidly evolving economy; to cultivate an awareness of, and sensitivity to, cultural, ethnic, and social diversity and its importance in personal and professional decision making; and to enable students to discover the real-life application of their knowledge.

At a minimum, 1 semester credit hour equals 15 classroom-contact hours of lectures, 30 hours of laboratory or 45 hours of practicum; a total of 120 credits is required to earn a bachelor degree. At least 45 of the last 60 credit hours must be completed in residence at The American University of Rome, and the final semester must be completed in residence. The Associate of Arts and the Associate of Applied Arts degrees each require completion of at least 60 credit hours of coursework. All core courses in the major must be completed with a C grade (2.0) or better. A minimum cumulative or Career Total Grade Point Average (CGPA) of 2.0 is required for completion of all degrees. The majority of courses listed in AUR's catalog carry 3 semester credit hours. Intensive courses worth 4 to 6 credits and 1-credit courses are also available. Internships carry 3 semester credits and require 135 hours of work experience.

AUR follows a semester calendar (fall and spring) and also offers two short summer sessions (June and July).

Academic Facilities

AUR is an urban campus of around 30,000 square feet that provides study space, equipment, and an environment conductive to study and learning. Administrative and academic offices, computer labs, and a student lounge are housed in a four-story villa. Adjacent to the villa, a five-story building offers faculty offices, classrooms, a science lab, a computer classroom, art studios, and tutoring centers. Its terraces at the fourth and fifth floors feature breathtaking views of Rome. Other campus facilities include an auditorium and a multimedia lab, available to communication students enrolled in select film-related courses and equipped with Apple Pro computers and field software. Another two-story liberty villa, Evans' Hall, is AUR's library. It offers a book collection of 12,000 volumes and DVDs, as well as a wealth of electronic resources tailored to the requirements of the degree programs pursued at the University and carefully developed in collaboration with the faculty. The AUR library also participates in interlibrary loan programs throughout Italy.

All AUR classrooms are smart and wireless services are available from locations on and around the campus, such as the gardens and terraces of University buildings as well as a café and the park near the campus. The library and the main computer lab are open long hours and on weekends.

AUR recognizes the importance of supporting an efficient technological infrastructure; provision and enhancement of technology on campus is continuously and updated.

Costs

The estimated cost of attending The American University of Rome for the 2012–13 academic year for full-time undergraduates is €13,940. A nonrefundable tuition deposit of $500/€500 is required from all new students, payable by the deadline indicated on the acceptance letter. The tuition deposit is deducted from the final tuition payment. Some courses require travel or attendance at cultural events, as indicated by the course instructor. The cost of these events and travel is not included in the tuition and must be borne by the student.

The estimated cost of attendance for academic year 2012–13 includes the following: full-time tuition, €13,940; housing, €7600; food, €1600; transportation in Rome, personal expenses, and miscellaneous, €3650; books and supplies, €300; health insurance, €144; and new student fees, €380.

Financial Aid

The American University of Rome is committed to assisting students whose financial need and academic merit warrant support. The University aims to give every student the opportunity to take advantage of a high-quality education and, therefore, offers several scholarships. Funds awarded must be applied to tuition expenses. All scholarships offered by AUR are renewable annually, until degree requirements are met for a maximum of four years (depending which comes first).

The American University of Rome is authorized by the U.S. Department of Education to participate in Title IV student financial assistance programs. Eligible students may apply to participate in the Direct Loan Federal Family Education Loan (FFEL) program (subsidized and unsubsidized Federal Stafford Student Loans and Federal PLUS loans). The American University of Rome is considered a foreign school and is not authorized to award federal or state grants.

The American University of Rome offers degree programs that are listed as approved training for eligible U.S. citizens at the Department of Veterans Affairs Post 9/11 G.I. Bill, facility code 21100084.

Faculty

The American University of Rome has an international, culturally diverse faculty. Nearly 75 percent of the full-time faculty members have received doctoral degrees, and all professors either work professionally in their field or are active in scholarly research. The majority is bilingual, and all faculty members act as teachers as well as advisers. The University also invites visiting professors from other universities for short-term residencies.

Student Government

Students are encouraged to take an active role in the student government as a way of contributing to the continued growth and development of the University. Elected officers of the student government meet regularly with the University administration to discuss matters of administrative and academic relevance. They also take responsibility for directing a variety of student social activities, athletic tournaments, club activities, and cultural events. The student government maintains funds for these activities, and the student officers enjoy a wide degree of autonomy in managing these financial resources.

Admission Requirements

Admission to The American University of Rome is highly selective. Candidates for admission to the University are reviewed by the Admissions Committee. Students are selected without regard to age, race, sex, creed, national or ethnic origin, or handicap. Requests for financial aid do not affect decisions on admission.

Candidates for admission must show evidence that they have completed or anticipate completing a level of education equivalent to four years of high school. Applicants for admission from high school or a secondary school are required to submit a completed application form, accompanied by a nonrefundable application fee; an official transcript of high school work; one academic recommendation from a principal, guidance counselor, teacher, or professor; a 500-word personal statement indicating how a study experience in Rome could help further the student's career and life goals; and a 250-word essay of one of the three topics indicated on the application form. Results of the SAT or ACT are required for students graduating from a U.S. high school system, whether in the U.S. or abroad. Face-to-face or phone interviews are required of all applicants.

Each applicant is reviewed individually. Leadership, motivation, academic improvement, the level of difficulty of the high school program, involvement in activities, and potential for growth are important considerations in the application review process. Applicants whose native language is not English are required to submit scores from the TOEFL or another English language proficiency exam. The English language proficiency exam requirement may be waived for applicants who complete high school at English-speaking institutions. The American University of Rome TOEFL institutional code for reporting purposes is 0579. Students whose English language skills need development may apply for the AUREA program in order to benefit from the full academic curriculum at The American University of Rome. Through this program students will develop speaking, listening, reading, and writing skills in English while attending selected credit-based general education courses at AUR.

Advanced standing may be granted for academic credits earned at institutions outside the university system of the United States. Candidates who have credentials from European lyceums, such as the Italian maturità, the International Baccalaureate, the British GCSE A-levels, and other equivalent programs, are evaluated, and advanced credits may be granted on the basis of that evaluation. In most instances, the first year of college (equivalent to 30 semester hours) may be granted. Students applying for advanced standing must submit official records of the last year of lyceum and a copy of the diploma, if granted. If the records are not written in either English or Italian, the admissions office requires a certified translation into English.

The American University of Rome welcomes transfer students. Upon submission of complete official transcripts of all colleges and universities previously attended, the University evaluates the number of transfer credits to be accepted toward fulfilling the requirements for a degree at AUR. Credit is granted only for courses completed with a grade of C or above. Transfer credits may be applied to no more than 50 percent of a student's major degree requirements. Students must earn at least 30 credits at The American University of Rome for an associate degree and at least 45 credits at The American University of Rome for a bachelor's degree.

Application and Information

Applicants are notified of the admission decision two to four weeks after the application, supporting credentials, recommendation letter, and application fee are received.

Prospective students are encouraged to visit the campus. Further information may be obtained via the University's Web site at www.aur.edu and by contacting the University directly.

The American University of Rome
Via Pietro Roselli, 4
00153 Rome, Italy
Phone: +39-0658330919 (direct dial from U.S.)
    877-592-1287 (toll-free to Rome from U.S.)
    888-791-8327 (toll-free in the U.S.)
Fax: +39-0658330992 (direct fax from U.S.)
    866-287-2025 (toll-free in the U.S.)
Skype: AURomeadmissions or 415-992-5213
E-mail: admissions@aur.edu
Web site: http://www.aur.edu
    http://www.facebook.com/TheAmericanUniversityofRome
    http://twitter.com/#!/Life_at_AUR

The University is located in the prestigious area of the Janiculum, Rome's highest hill, just a short walk from the historic Trastevere district and the heart of Rome.

AMRIDGE UNIVERSITY
MONTGOMERY, ALABAMA

The University

Founded in 1967, Amridge University is an independent, coeducational institution dedicated to the spirit of its ideals and Christian heritage. All Amridge University programs are taught from a Christian perspective. Amridge University is one of the nation's leading universities offering distance learning programs and services to adults nationally since 1993. Adding to the prestige of the University is its selection in 1999 by the U.S. Department of Education as one of fifteen initial participants in the Distance Education Demonstration Program. Amridge University worked with the U.S. Department of Education to develop a national model to help chart the future of distance learning.

Accredited by the Southern Association of Colleges and Schools, Amridge University grants associate, bachelor's, master's, and doctoral degrees, all available via a distance learning format. Graduate degrees are awarded in counseling/family therapy, organizational leadership, and religious studies. These degrees foster leadership, counseling and family therapy skills, knowledge, and biblical and Christian ministry skills. The counseling degrees are designed to help prepare students for licensure. Doctoral degrees include Doctor of Ministry and Doctor of Philosophy degrees. These are advanced professional degrees for community organization and church-related vocations, with a concentration designed to prepare participants to counsel families and individuals.

The policy of Amridge University is to provide reasonable accommodation for persons who are handicapped or disabled as designated in Section 504 of the Rehabilitation Act of 1973 and the Americans with Disabilities Act of 1990. Although the Morgan W. Brown building is not equipped with an elevator, the needs of the physically challenged can be met from the first floor. These include registration, counseling, library facilities, classroom facilities, rest rooms, break room facilities, and others. Ample parking is provided.

Location

Amridge University is located in Montgomery, Alabama, the capital city of the state. Strategically located in the central part of the state between Huntsville and Mobile and Atlanta, Georgia, Montgomery is one of the fastest-growing cities in the state and the region. The city is clean and modern, with beautiful residential areas, parks and playgrounds, and fine schools and universities. Students and families can also enjoy its museums, zoo, and facilities of the capitol building.

Montgomery has two major U.S. Air Force installations: Maxwell Air Force Base and Gunter Annex. Maxwell is where the Air War College is located and is a strategic center for education.

The metropolitan area has a population of more than 350,000 citizens. There are many churches and educational institutions. The city has an abundance of good housing in addition to other advantages.

Majors and Degrees

Undergraduate degrees are awarded in Biblical studies, business, homeland security, human development, human resource management, liberal studies, management communication, and public safety and criminal justice. These degrees promote biblical and Christian ministry skills, human development skills, knowledge in the arts, and management communication skills. Amridge University students are fully matriculated students of Amridge University with full student privileges, rights, and responsibilities.

Academic Programs

Amridge University is primarily a distance learning institution, although there are many classes offered on campus. The academic year consists of three semesters: fall, spring, and summer.

A student must fulfill the required semester hours in a major as well as the basic requirements of the core curriculum. All core and major requirements can be received from the University. Amridge University programs have a traditional structure.

Distance education is approved by the Southern Association of Colleges and Schools and the U.S. Department of Education, ensuring that distance education students receive the same high-quality education as on-campus students. Faculty and student services for students on campus are available to distance learners. Amridge University ensures that students have regular contact with faculty and staff members via e-mail and telephone. No residency is required for undergraduates.

In addition to offering distance learning to a diverse array of individuals, Amridge University is a participating member of the GoArmyEd project. This is an online, streamlined process giving soldiers easy access to obtaining funding for their educations.

Academic Facilities

Amridge University sits stately on a 9-acre campus adjoining Interstate 85. A beautiful building houses the administration offices, classrooms, and Library Resource Center.

Costs

Undergraduate tuition per semester hour is $365. First-time full-time students receive a reduced rate of $250 per semester hour. This rate is guaranteed through summer 2015, as long as students maintain continuous full-time enrollment and are in good academic standing.

Financial Aid

Aid from institutionally generated funds is provided on the basis of academic merit, financial need, and other criteria. A limited number of scholarships are available. Priority is given to early applicants.

Federal funding available for undergraduates includes Federal Pell Grant, Federal Supplemental Educational Opportunity Grants (FSEOG), and direct subsidized and unsubsidized loans. Eighty percent of students receive financial aid.

Faculty

The instructional faculty members total approximately 100. Approximately 65 percent of the full-time faculty members hold doctoral degrees, 100 percent hold master's degrees, and 100 percent hold terminal degrees. Faculty members specialize in their areas and have exceptional training in distance learning delivery.

Student Government

Student volunteers serve as members of the Student Advisory Committee. Volunteers are appointed by the Student Services Team, with recommendations from the deans. The committee meets on a regular basis and is reorganized on an annual basis. Concerns, recommendations, and requests are presented directly from the committee to the appropriate University area.

Admission Requirements

Amridge University is open to all persons who are of good character and who are academically qualified. The University has a streamlined admissions process to help potential students complete the process in a timely manner so they can begin their studies. As new technologies and processes become available, Amridge University makes every effort to adopt and use the latest technologies to help the admissions process. Transfer students in good academic standing are invited to apply to Amridge University. Prospective students must submit a $50 nonrefundable fee along with the completed application for admission.

Application and Information

For further information, students may contact:
Carl Byrd
Amridge University
1200 Taylor Road
Montgomery, Alabama 36117
Phone: 334-387-7569
        800-351-4040 Ext. 7569 (toll-free)
Fax: 334-387-3878
E-mail: carlbyrd@amridgeuniversity.edu
Web site: http://www.amridgeuniversity.edu

ANNA MARIA COLLEGE
PAXTON, MASSACHUSETTS

The College

Anna Maria College (AMC), a private, four-year, coeducational Catholic college, was founded in 1946 by the Sisters of Saint Anne in Marlboro, Massachusetts. In 1952, AMC moved to its current 192-acre campus in Paxton, Massachusetts. Originally a women's college, AMC has been coeducational since 1973. The College has grown exponentially over the last sixty-five years with a total enrollment of 1,500.

Anna Maria College is a close-knit community. Small class sizes allow for mentor relationships to develop between faculty members and students. Freshman and sophomore classes generally have between 15 and 20 students; some upper-level classes have as few as 10 students. Faculty members teach and advise students based on their knowledge of each person as an individual; classes are never taught by graduate assistants.

A five-year strategic plan calls for the College to change and enhance its core curriculum and extracurricular activities to ensure that students have access to the programs and services that will help develop their mind, body, and spirit so they can become strong leaders in their communities. An honors program with unique study-abroad options has been added, as well as a B.S.N. and paramedic science program. AMC also launched a new business school in February 2012. In addition, the College has added new sports including lacrosse, tennis, and football, bringing the total to seventeen NCAA Division III men's and women's sports teams. As part of the master plan, AMC has already added an all-purpose athletic field and stadium; three new residence halls, one of which offers suite-style housing; a new fitness center; and a new athletic field facility. The College has also invested in new technologies and the entire campus is wireless.

Anna Maria College is accredited by the New England Association of Schools and Colleges, the Council on Social Work Education, and the National League for Nursing Accrediting Commission. AMC is approved by the Board of Registration in Nursing in Massachusetts and the Massachusetts Department of Education.

Approximately 70 percent of Anna Maria College's undergraduates reside on campus in the residence halls. Students enjoy a full social life both on campus and within the college-city atmosphere of nearby Worcester.

Anna Maria College's NCAA Division III athletic program offers intercollegiate competition for men (baseball, basketball, cross-country, football, golf, lacrosse, soccer, and tennis) and women (basketball, field hockey, golf, lacrosse, soccer, softball, tennis, and volleyball). Intramural athletics are also available to students who do not wish to participate on competitive sports teams.

Anna Maria College provides a wireless campus. More than 500 computer hookups link classrooms, offices, the Academic Computing Center, computer labs, the library, and all residence hall rooms. In addition to College-owned computers, students have the opportunity to access the College network to gain access to the Internet from any location on campus via the College wireless network and their own computers.

Location

Anna Maria College is located on a 192-acre campus in Paxton, Massachusetts, 8 miles from Worcester's vibrant downtown. The city offers numerous professional, cultural, and entertainment opportunities, and Boston, Providence, and Hartford are only an hour away.

Local attractions include big-name entertainment and minor league sports teams at the DCU Center; art, history, and science museums; classical music performances at Mechanics Hall; theater; and day and night skiing at Wachusett Mountain.

Majors and Degrees

Anna Maria College offers a four-year curriculum of undergraduate instruction leading to bachelor's degrees in the following areas: art, art and business, art therapy, business administration, business administration/MIS, criminal justice, early childhood education, elementary education, English, environmental science, fire science, graphic design, health science, history, human development/human services, humanities (interdisciplinary program), legal studies, liberal arts/general studies, media communications, modern languages, music, music education, music performance, music therapy, nursing, paralegal studies, paramedic science, political science, psychology, public policy, social science, social work, sociology, sport management, studio art, teacher preparation/licensure, teacher of visual art, and theology. Associate degrees are available in business administration and paralegal studies.

Art and music therapy, business, criminal justice, fire science, education, nursing, social work, and psychology are the most popular majors. The Fifth Year Option allows undergraduate students in good academic standing a unique opportunity to earn both their undergraduate and graduate degrees in five years. Fifth-year master's options are available in business administration, counseling psychology, criminal justice, education, emergency management, fire science, pastoral studies/counseling, and visual art.

Academic Programs

When the Sisters of St. Anne founded Anna Maria College in 1946, their mission was to increase access to high-quality education, educational innovation, and respect for service to others through the development of the total human being. That mission has not changed in more than fifty years. As a Catholic college, the relationship between faith and reason is looked at closely. An AMC education is distinct because of its integration of rich tradition, diversity of knowledge, and the understanding of human history, institutions, and societies with Catholic teachings and traditions. The cornerstone of AMC's academic programs is the core curriculum, which integrates the Catholic character with a commitment to liberal arts education.

Students are encouraged to travel beyond their immediate interests to disciplines that may be connected by similar methods, history, theory, or application. The end result is a strong liberal arts foundation with a focused knowledge and professional preparation in a chosen area of concentration. AMC also encourages students to explore their own areas of interest and design their own majors.

While at AMC, students can gain practical experience and explore career options through internship programs, fieldwork, academic seminars, and summer programs. They also learn through required practicums, part-time work, and community service.

Off-Campus Programs

Anna Maria College is a member of the Colleges of Worcester Consortium, a group of twelve area colleges (Anna Maria College, Assumption College, Becker College, Clark University, College of the Holy Cross, Massachusetts College of Pharmacy and Allied Health, Nichols College, Quinsigamond Community College, Tufts University School of Veterinary Medicine, University of Massachusetts Medical School, Worcester Polytechnic Institute, and Worcester State College). Students may enroll in nonmajor courses at any of the member institutions and have credits transferred at no additional cost.

AMC offers several off-campus opportunities for which academic credits are awarded. There are opportunities for study abroad, as well as an Urban Seminar course with travel to various locations worldwide. Students are also eligible to apply for Army and Air Force ROTC programs, available through the Colleges of Worcester Consortium. A Washington, D.C. internship is offered for students in all majors, and a Disney internship is also available.

Academic Facilities

The Mondor-Eagan Library houses Anna Maria College's volumes, stacks, periodicals, study rooms, computer center, resource centers, and language laboratory. The library also houses the main computer terminal, which links the combined material resources of central and western Massachusetts libraries, making more than 4 million books and periodicals accessible to students. Classrooms are located in Trinity Hall, Cardinal Cushing Hall, and Foundress Hall, which also houses the Zecco Performing Arts Center. Trinity Hall also houses the learning center. Other facilities include Madore Chapel, St. Joseph's Hall for sciences, and Miriam Hall for music, performance, and art. The College's master plan also calls for a new academic facility, which will allow AMC to expand both its academic offerings and student population while maintaining small class sizes.

Costs

Tuition and fees for the 20011–12 academic year included tuition, $27,144; fees; $2496; and room and board, $10,804. Tuition is slightly higher for music majors.

Financial Aid

Ninety-seven percent of the most recent freshman class received financial aid in the form of scholarships, grants, loans, and work-study program awards. Some available sources of funds are the Federal Pell Grant, Federal Supplemental Educational Opportunity Grant, and Federal Perkins Loan programs. To apply for aid, students should submit the Free Application for Federal Student Aid (FAFSA), which can be found at http://www.fafsa.ed.gov. Aid is awarded on the basis of need. Non-need-based scholarships are also available. For further information, students should call 508-849-3366.

Faculty

Anna Maria College has 150 full- and part-time faculty members. Faculty members have a deep respect for scholarship and research and are dedicated to teaching and to the success of the student. The Center for Teaching Excellence provides opportunities for faculty to hone new skills and pursue their research.

Student Government

The Student Government Association (SGA) is the official representative of the student body, serving as the link between students and the administration. There are more than twenty clubs and organizations under the SGA, offering many activities and opportunities to participate in the extracurricular life of AMC.

Admission Requirements

At Anna Maria College, every application is considered individually and weighed on its own merits. Emphasis is placed on the applicant's transcript and recommendations. SAT and ACT scores are optional. Extracurricular activities and leadership positions are also important. Successful completion of a four-year college-preparatory program is required. Application for admission to AMC is encouraged for all academically qualified candidates regardless of race, religion, age, gender, or creed.

Application and Information

To apply, students should submit a completed application form (AMC is a member of the Common Application). An official high school transcript should be sent to the Office of Admission along with an essay and letter of recommendation. Prospective students can schedule a campus visit via the AMC website (www.annamaria.edu) or by calling 508-849-3360. AMC is on rolling admissions, however, the application priority deadline for financial aid is March 1. Students who apply after March 1 do not receive priority for financial aid. Transfer students must submit official transcripts of all postsecondary courses.

Anna Maria College invites students to learn more about AMC's community by visiting the campus. Students should call the Undergraduate Office of Admission to schedule an appointment. For detailed information about Anna Maria College's distinctive programs and campus community, prospective students should contact:

Meghan McDonough
Director, Admissions
Anna Maria College
50 Sunset Lane
Paxton, Massachusetts 01612-1198
Phone: 508-849-3360
      800-344-4586 Ext. 360 (toll-free)
Fax: 508-849-3362
E-mail: admission@annamaria.edu
Web site: http://www.annamaria.edu

AMC students enjoy the beautiful New England Campus at Anna Maria College.

AQUINAS COLLEGE
GRAND RAPIDS, MICHIGAN

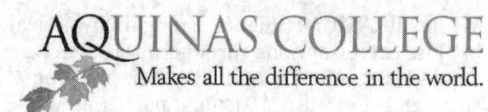

AQUINAS COLLEGE
Makes all the difference in the world.

The College

Located on the eastern edge of the city of Grand Rapids, Aquinas enjoys all of the advantages of Michigan's second-largest city and is just a 3-hour drive from Detroit or Chicago. The Aquinas College campus is an interesting blend of early-nineteenth century architecture coupled with modern-day structures. The campus abounds with natural beauty; it has been called the most beautiful small campus in Michigan. Its ninety species of trees, winding woodland paths, and inviting creeks and ponds create a peaceful 107-acre environment that students of all ages find welcoming.

Founded by the Dominican Sisters of Grand Rapids in 1886, Aquinas has a Catholic heritage and a Christian tradition. The Dominican charisms of prayer, study, service, and community remain alive at Aquinas. It is lived out by Aquinas students who volunteer their time and talents in the Grand Rapids community and by those who travel to places such as the Dominican Republic; Appalachia, Kentucky; or any of a dozen other service-learning project sites. An ability to see the world from different perspectives is the hallmark of an Aquinas-educated student. Aquinas, a coeducational liberal arts college, offers an approach to learning and living that teaches students unlimited ways of seeing the world. That is why every Aquinas student enrolls in the humanities program, a two-semester exploration of the best that has been thought, written, composed, and painted. As students find their way in the world of thought, the core curriculum in natural science ensures that they discover the workings of the physical world as well.

An Aquinas education makes graduates more employable. Each year, hundreds of Aquinas students find businesses, government agencies, and other organizations eager to offer field experience and internship opportunities. Students can write press releases, keep sports statistics, and travel around the country with such organizations as Major League Soccer; work on historic preservation projects with the Michigan Bureau of History in Lansing; or learn about politics from the inside as a congressional intern in Washington, D.C. Seven out of 10 applicants recommended by the Aquinas premedical advisory committee are admitted to medical school, and 19 of 20 are accepted into other graduate programs. In all, more than 90 percent of Aquinas seniors find jobs or enroll in graduate school soon after graduation.

Aquinas sees a liberal arts education as career preparation. The Aquinas general education plan exposes students to the necessary skills that enable them to become critical thinkers, articulate speakers, strong writers, and effective problem solvers. Aquinas faculty members insist that students carry values as well as skills into the workplace. The College's curriculum, with its more than sixty majors, is designed to provide students with both breadth and depth and to foster a thirst for knowledge and truth and a spirit of intellectual dialogue and inquiry. Coupled with nationally recognized internship programs, it prepares students to both live and work in the rapidly changing world of today and tomorrow.

Arriving from places as near as Grand Rapids, Chicago, and Detroit and as far as Japan and Russia, the 2,300 students include 1,600 full-time, 400 part-time, and 300 graduate students. The Insignis program at Aquinas encourages students of exceptional academic ability to participate in social and intellectual activities such as lectures and receptions for visiting scholars and trips to places of cultural interest. Aquinas offers more than sixty student organizations, ranging from intramural teams and departmental clubs to a wide variety of musical groups, student publications, and service organizations.

In addition to its undergraduate degrees, Aquinas also offers Master in the Art of Teaching, Master in Education, Master in Science Education, Master of Management, and Master of Sustainable Business degrees.

Location

Aquinas' location in Grand Rapids allows students to reap the benefits of west Michigan's economic, educational, and cultural center. The city is one of the fastest-growing areas in the Great Lakes region. Grand Rapids combines big-city excitement and small-town charm. There are cosmopolitan amenities ranging from four-star hotels and restaurants to top-notch cultural facilities and entertainment venues. Established attractions include ArtPrize, Laughfest, the Gerald R. Ford Presidential Museum, the Van Andel Public Museum, the 10,000-seat Fifth Third Park for Whitecaps minor-league baseball, the 70-acre Fredrik Meijer Gardens, and the 12,000-seat Van Andel Arena, home to the Grand Rapids Griffins AHL hockey team and a venue for nationally known music concerts and performances. These major facilities add to the list of popular points of interest, festivals, and special events. With nearly half a million residents, there are abundant recreation, arts, and cultural opportunities available.

Majors and Degrees

Aquinas College offers the following undergraduate degree programs: Bachelor of Arts, Bachelor of Fine Arts, Bachelor of Arts in general education, Bachelor of Music Education, Bachelor of Science, Bachelor of Science in Business Administration, Bachelor of Science in sustainable business, and Bachelor of Science in international business. A Bachelor of Science in Nursing degree program is offered in collaboration with the University of Detroit Mercy and St. Mary's Health Care. Majors and programs of study are offered in accounting, accounting/business administration, art, art/business administration, art history, biology, business administration, business administration/chemistry, business administration/communication, business administration/music, business administration/sport management, chemical physics, chemistry, communication, community leadership, computer information systems, conductive education, drawing, economics, education, English, environmental science, environmental studies, French, geography, German, health, history, international studies, Japanese, journalism/publications, learning disabilities, management information systems, mathematics, music, not-for-profit management, organizational communication, painting, philosophy, photography, physical education and recreation, physics, political science, pre-engineering, printmaking, psychology, sculpture, social science, sociology, Spanish, studio art, sustainable business, theater, theology, urban studies, visual arts administration, and women's studies. Pre-professional programs include dentistry, law, medicine, occupational therapy, physical therapy, and veterinary science.

Associate degrees are also available, including the Associate of Arts and the Associate of Science.

Academic Programs

In addition to their major and minor fields of study, students take an integrated skills course called Inquiry and Expression. This course spans the first semester of the freshman year and has an emphasis on writing integrated with reading critically, oral communication skills, critical thinking, library/electronic research methods, computer utilization, and basic quantitative

reasoning. The thematic content is American Pluralism: The Individual in a Diverse America. Sophomores take a yearlong course in the humanities. As juniors, they are required to take 3 hours in Theological Foundation. Students are also required to be proficient in a second language through the 102 level. There also is a distribution plan in the general education plan covering social science, history/philosophy, natural world, artistic and creative studies, technology, and health, physical education, and recreation. A career/professional development component begins in summer orientation and offers career planning courses and activities over four years; topics include assessment of students' strengths, skills, and interests; development of goals, a learning plan, and setting a direction; focus on the individual—wellness, personal finances, and leadership/team skills; awareness of careers, professions, and graduate study; information on making and maintaining a professional portfolio and resume; participating in a professional/career mentor program; career fairs and networking; and experiential learning (choices include internship, service learning, service trips, and study abroad). The College follows a two-semester calendar with a summer session. Aquinas also accepts credit through CLEP, Advanced Placement, and International Baccalaureate.

Off-Campus Programs

Students have the option of participating in the Dominican College Campus Interchange Program. Cooperating colleges are Barry University in Miami, Florida; Dominican College in San Rafael, California; and St. Thomas Aquinas College in Sparkill, New York. Students can increase their foreign language skills through cultural-immersion programs in Costa Rica, France, Italy, Japan, Spain, or Germany. Two Aquinas faculty members accompany 30 students to Aquinas' study center in Tully Cross, Ireland. Students have the opportunity to earn a full semester of credit, travel abroad, and live in a rural Irish community. The curriculum is centered on several aspects of Irish studies.

Academic Facilities

The newly opened Grace Hauenstein Library is a $6-million facility with resources that include a public access catalog, audiovisual materials, circulation and course reserve materials, reference services, and interlibrary loan services (free access to more than 60 million books and documents from libraries across the country). Albertus Magnus Hall of Science features the handicapped-accessible Baldwin Observatory and a greenhouse. Other facilities include the Cook Carriage House, a student center, and the Art and Music Center, featuring a darkroom, a 200-seat recital hall, an art gallery, and a sculpture studio. Four new apartment buildings have opened, providing more housing options. The Aquinas Performing Arts Center is a $7-million facility providing a state-of-the-art theater venue.

AQnet allows residents and commuters to wirelessly connect their personal computers or other devices to the Internet while on campus. Students will find centrally located kiosks and computer labs on campus in classrooms, residence halls, the Grace Hauenstein Library, and common areas. E-mail is powered by Google, and over 100 discipline-specific software applications are available as well as high-quality laser printing and access to multimedia technology.

Costs

For 2012–13, tuition is $25,070 and room and board are $7810 for a total of $32,880. Other expenses, including books, travel, and personal supplies, average $2000.

Financial Aid

Aquinas College awards both merit-based financial assistance and traditional need-based assistance to qualified students. The Spectrum Scholarship Program was developed to recognize students' achievements in academics, leadership, and service. More than 90 percent of entering freshmen receive some form of financial assistance. The College administers the traditional grant and loan programs, including Ford Federal Direct Loans

and Federal PLUS loans. Athletic grants are also available. The College participates in an automatic payment program. This plan assists students in paying costs over a period of time. To apply for financial assistance, students must complete the Free Application for Federal Student Aid (FAFSA).

Faculty

Aquinas faculty members are teachers first: while research plays an important part in the Aquinas faculty's development, teaching remains the number-one priority. In addition to teaching, faculty members serve as academic advisers, mentors, and advisers to various clubs and organizations on campus. With a student-professor ratio of 14:1, faculty members give individual attention and assistance to students. All classes and labs are taught by faculty members, not graduate assistants. Approximately 90 percent of Aquinas faculty members have doctoral or terminal degrees.

Student Government

The Student Senate is the governing body of Aquinas students. Senators are chosen by securing twenty-five signatures of students in support of their involvement. These students have both voice and vote on issues facing the College's Academic Assembly. The senate is responsible for many of the academic, social, recreational, and cultural activities on the campus.

Admission Requirements

Freshman and transfer applications are received on a rolling basis. A candidate for admission to Aquinas is considered on the basis of academic preparation, scholarship, and character. Admission depends on a number of factors, including high school academic record and ACT or SAT test scores. Transfer students must present a minimum 2.0 grade point average on a 4.0 scale. Paper and online applications do not require an application fee. The admissions office reserves the right to review applications on a case-by-case basis. Curriculum, extracurricular activities, and any extenuating circumstances are considered in the decision. Letters of recommendation are encouraged but not required.

Application and Information

Prospective students may submit a free online application for admission at www.aquinas.edu/undergraduate.

For further information, interested students should contact:

Tom Mikowski
Dean of Admissions
Aquinas College
1607 Robinson Road, SE
Grand Rapids, Michigan 49506
Phone: 616-632-2900
       800-678-9593 (toll-free)
E-mail: admissions@aquinas.edu
Web site: http://www.aquinas.edu

The Aquinas campus was once a private country estate.

ARCADIA UNIVERSITY
GLENSIDE, PENNSYLVANIA

The University

Arcadia is a top-ranked private university offering bachelor's, master's, and doctoral degrees. More than 4,000 students choose from among eighty fields of study. *U.S. News & World Report* ranks Arcadia University among the top 30 universities in the North and a top school for the percentage of undergraduate students studying abroad in the 2011 *Open Doors* report. Arcadia's diverse student population represents a cross section of cultural and socioeconomic backgrounds. Enrollment includes over 2,200 undergraduate and 1,800 graduate students. At present, Arcadia students come from forty-six states and twenty-one other countries, and 80 percent of the full-time undergraduate population resides on campus.

Campus life, which includes more than ninety clubs and organizations, athletics, and cultural and social events, is rich and varied. Community service is an integral part of the Arcadia University experience. Students volunteer on neighborhood improvement projects, work at literacy or gerontology centers, and assist disadvantaged or disabled children. NCAA Division III intercollegiate competition is offered in basketball, field hockey, lacrosse, soccer, softball, swimming, tennis, and volleyball for women and baseball, basketball, golf, lacrosse, soccer, swimming, and tennis for men. Cheerleading and equestrian are offered as club sports, while intramural sports provide other athletic opportunities.

Arcadia offers master's programs in business administration, counseling psychology, education, English, forensic science, genetic counseling, health education, humanities, international peace and conflict resolution, international relations and diplomacy, physician assistant studies, and public health. A Doctor of Physical Therapy (D.P.T.) and Doctor of Education (Ed.D.) programs in special education and educational leadership are also offered.

Location

Arcadia, located in metropolitan Philadelphia, features a beautiful rolling campus built around the historic landmark Grey Towers Castle. The University is 12 miles from Center City Philadelphia and only 90 minutes from the Jersey shore and Pennsylvania's Pocono Mountains. Students have access to dozens of museums, galleries, performing arts centers, and nightspots; and historic, government, and commercial sites in the metropolitan area.

Majors and Degrees

Arcadia offers Bachelor of Arts degrees in accounting, anthropology, art and design (B.A. or B.F.A.) (art education, art history, ceramics, graphic design, interior design, metals and jewelry, painting, photography, pre–art therapy, printmaking, studio art), biology (allied health, biological basis of behavior, biomedical, conservation, forensics, molecular), business (economics, international economics, international finance, international human resources, international marketing, marketing), chemistry (biochemistry, chemical professions, forensics, health professions), communications (cinema studies, corporate, international cinema, print, video), computer science, computing technology (design, technical), criminal justice, digital media/global media, education (art education, elementary and early childhood, middle level, secondary, special education), engineering, English (creative writing, professional writing), environmental studies, fashion studies, forensic science, French studies, global legal studies, global security and emergency management, health administration, history, interdisciplinary science, international business and culture, international peace and conflict resolution, international studies (global public health; globalization, development, and human rights; modern Mediterranean world), Italian studies, liberal studies (applied social science for the global citizen, individualized), management information systems, mathematics (actuarial science), media industries, modern languages, optometry, philosophy, physical therapy, physician assistant studies, political science (international politics, prelaw and political theory, U.S. politics and policy), predentistry, premedicine, prenursing, pre–veterinary medicine,

psychology (pre–art therapy, human resources), scientific illustration, sociology (human services), sound and music, Spanish, Spanish cultural studies, special education, sport psychology, sports management, and theater arts and English. A five-year program combines the B.A. in education with a Master of Education in special education.

Bachelor of Science degrees are offered in accounting, business administration, chemistry, chemistry and business, computer science, international finance, management information systems, marketing, and mathematics.

Bachelor of Fine Arts degrees are awarded to students majoring in acting or studio arts with concentrations in ceramics, graphic design, interior design, metals and jewelry, painting, photography, and printmaking. Preparation for certification in art education is offered in conjunction with the B.F.A. program, as is preparation for graduate study in art therapy.

Arcadia's physician assistant studies 4+2 program provides a four-year undergraduate degree in a related field, followed by two years of study in Arcadia's Master of Medical Science: Physician Assistant Program. Arcadia undergraduates who satisfy the prerequisites are assured admission to the program. Arcadia also offers a combined undergraduate and graduate (4+2.5) program leading to the Doctor of Physical Therapy, with assured admission for undergrads who meet established criteria. An accelerated 3+3 program also is offered, combining a bachelor's degree in biology with a doctorate in physical therapy. The International Peace and Conflict Resolution 4+2 Program is a four-year undergraduate degree followed by two years of study in the M.A. degree program; an accelerated 3+2 option is also offered. The forensic science program provides a four-year undergraduate program in a related field followed by two years in the Master of Science in Forensic Science (M.S.F.S.) program. A 3+2 Accelerated Forensic Science Program also is offered, allowing academically talented students to earn a B.A. or B.S. in biology/chemistry and an M.S. in forensic science.

Arcadia also offers accelerated three-year bachelor's degrees in business administration, communications, international business and culture, international studies, and psychology. The format includes one summer of service learning and one summer internship at an international or U.S. location.

Arcadia offers several five-year combined programs in education including master's degrees in special education, environmental education, literacy education/reading, literacy education/ESL, technology education, and library science.

A dual-degree (3+2) program in engineering is offered in conjunction with Columbia University. An accelerated (3+4) program with Salus University leads to B.A. and Doctor of Optometry degrees. The 3+2 Environmental Studies program leads to a B.A. in biology and an M.A. in education, with certification in environmental education.

Academic Programs

Arcadia's undergraduate curriculum provides a distinctively global, integrative, and personal learning experience that prepares students to contribute and prosper in a diverse and dynamic world. Students are encouraged to design their own path, explore the globe, make intellectual connections, and develop an area of expertise. There are opportunities to study around the world and make connections across disciplines and cultures. Every student pursues a major, participates in cultural experiences, explores areas of inquiry, and develops intellectual practices.

Highly qualified students may enhance their education through the Honors Program, which merges the best of Arcadia's academic traditions with innovative honors courses and features unique leadership and study-abroad opportunities.

Credit toward graduation is granted for scores of 3 or better on AP exams or earned through the College-Level Examination Program (CLEP) and locally administered examinations at the discretion of the department.

Arcadia's academic year is divided into two semesters. Three summer sessions are offered, beginning in May and continuing through early August. Most full-time students carry four academic courses in each regular semester; 128 semester hours are required for graduation.

Off-Campus Programs

Arcadia is top-ranked in the nation by *U.S. News & World Report* for international study. With over 100 programs around the world, the College of Global Studies supports and implements the University's commitment to international education. Students can spend a semester or full year abroad for approximately the same cost as remaining on campus. Many shorter-term options are also available.

Arcadia offers two distinct opportunities for students to study abroad during their first year. The University's Preview program enables first-year students in good academic standing to earn 2 credits while spending their spring break in England, Ireland, Mexico, Scotland, Spain, or other countries. The First Year Study Abroad Experience (FYSAE) gives select incoming students the chance to spend their first or second semester in London, England, or Stirling, Scotland. Arcadia's FYSAE and Preview programs have been recognized as among the most innovative international programs in the country by the American Council on Education, *U.S. News & World Report,* and the Princeton Review.

Arcadia also offers seven Majors Abroad Programs (MAPs). Students in these majors spend a year (two semesters) abroad, taking general courses as well as major-related courses at an overseas institution. Off-campus study in the Philadelphia area includes internships and fieldwork in most majors. The University requires students to partake in a global connections experience, which may occur overseas, through a domestic study-away program, or locally.

Academic Facilities

The campus includes historical buildings as well as extensive modern facilities. A prime academic resource on Arcadia's campus is Landman Library, which offers students increased technology and access to resources both on campus and around the globe.

Arcadia's newly renovated Kuch Athletic and Recreation Center features the Alumni Gymnasium, which seats 1,500, and the Lenox Pool, with adjacent Jacuzzi. The Kuch Center also includes an indoor track that overlooks the gym, an aerobics/dance studio, a fitness center, locker rooms, saunas, and first aid/training rooms. The Commons student center opened in spring 2012 and features a game room, fireplace lounge, dining area, flexible meeting rooms, an art exhibit space, and more.

Wireless Internet access is available everywhere on campus and extends to every room in the residence halls. Computer labs—including a Mac lab—are available for student use.

Costs

For 2011–12, undergraduate tuition was $34,150. Room and board charges were $11,640 per year and annual student fees were $580.

Financial Aid

On average, 98 percent of full-time undergraduates receive financial aid, and 96 percent receive grants and scholarships. Every effort is made to see that students requiring financial assistance are able to attend Arcadia. Aid is awarded on the basis of need, as determined by the Free Application for Federal Student Aid (FAFSA) and the Arcadia University Financial Aid Application, and is available in the form of grants, loans, and part-time campus employment or some combination of the three. Scholarships are presented annually to entering first-year and transfer students who have achieved academic distinction or have been recognized for outstanding extracurricular accomplishments. Distinguished Scholarships, ranging from $60,000 to $82,000 over four years, and Achievement Awards, ranging from $4000 to $58,000 over four years, recognize academic excellence, leadership, and extracurricular accomplishments. A limited number of full-tuition scholarships are available to the top entering first-year undergraduates. To receive full consideration, students should complete their applications and submit the FAFSA and Arcadia's Financial Aid Application by March 1.

Faculty

Arcadia University has a faculty with a primary commitment to teaching. The average class size is 16 students, and the student-faculty ratio is 13:1. This fosters an environment in which students and faculty members collaborate on research and writing and engage in informal discussions, field trips, and other activities outside the classroom. Eighty-nine percent of Arcadia faculty members hold doctorates or terminal degrees, and all courses are taught by faculty members, not graduate assistants.

Student Government

Student life is largely self-regulated by the Student Government Organization (SGO) through the Student Senate. Students serve on most major faculty committees, and student leaders attend Board of Trustees meetings.

Admission Requirements

Students are selected on the basis of educational preparation, intellectual promise, and potential. Emphasis is placed on the candidate's academic record, including the type of program followed and the grades and class rank earned. Standardized test scores also carry significant weight. Counselor and teacher recommendations, participation in school and community activities, and other supporting credentials also are strongly considered.

Freshman applicants must submit an official high school transcript, standardized test scores (SAT or ACT), and counselor and teacher recommendations. Students are encouraged to visit the campus for a student-guided tour and an information session or one-on-one meeting with an admissions counselor.

Transfer applicants may apply for the fall term or at midyear and must submit official college transcripts. In some cases, transfer applicants are required to submit high school transcripts and SAT or ACT scores.

Application and Information

Students are encouraged to submit their applications as early as possible in the senior year. Admission decisions are made on a rolling basis, and applicants are usually notified within four to six weeks of the date of submission of the completed application. For freshman applicants, the priority admissions application deadline for Distinguished Scholarship consideration—as well as consideration for the honors p,rogram, First Year Study Abroad Experience, and accelerated degree programs—is January 15. The priority admissions application deadline for Achievement Award consideration is March 1. The admissions application deadline is also March 1. The transfer student deadline for portfolio review, Honors Program, Distinguished Scholarship consideration, and priority admissions is June 15 for fall-term admission.

Requests for further information should be directed to:

Office of Enrollment Management
Arcadia University
450 South Easton Road
Glenside, Pennsylvania 19038-3295
Phone: 215-572-2910
      877-ARCADIA (877-272-2342, toll-free)
E-mail: admiss@arcadia.edu
Web site: http://www.arcadia.edu/pet.asp
         http://www.arcadia.edu/socialmedia

Arcadia University, Grey Towers Castle, Glenside, Pennsylvania.

ARGOSY UNIVERSITY

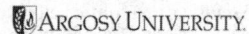

The University

Argosy University is a postsecondary institution of higher education offering a variety of degree programs that focus on the human side of success alongside professional competence. For students looking for a more personal approach to education, Argosy University may just be the answer. Drawing upon over thirty years of history, Argosy University has developed a curriculum that focuses on interpersonal skills and practical experience alongside academic learning. Argosy's programs are taught by practicing professionals who bring real-world experience into the classroom. Students graduate with both a solid foundation of knowledge and the power to put it to work. To accommodate busy working adults, many programs at Argosy University have a flexible structure, with both campus and online learning, and evening, weekend, and daytime classes. There are also financial aid options available for students who qualify.

Argosy University is a private institution of higher education dedicated to providing quality professional education programs at the doctoral, master's, bachelor's, and associate degree levels as well as continuing education to individuals who seek to enhance their professional and personal lives. The University emphasizes programs in the behavioral sciences (psychology and counseling), business, education, and the health-care professions. A limited number of preprofessional programs and general education offerings are provided to permit students to prepare for entry into these professional fields. The programs of Argosy University are designed to instill the knowledge, skills, and ethical values of professional practice and to foster values of social responsibility in a supportive, learning-centered environment of mutual respect and professional excellence.

With nineteen campuses nationwide, Argosy University provides students with a network of resources found at larger universities, including a career resources office, an academic resources center, and extensive information access for research. The University's innovative programs feature dynamic, relevant, and practical curricula delivered in flexible class formats. Students enjoy scheduling options that make it easier to fit school into their busy lives. They can choose from day and evening courses, on campus or online. Many students find a combination of both to be an ideal way of continuing their education while meeting family and professional demands.

Most students are full-time working professionals who live within driving distance of the campus. The University does not offer or operate student housing.

Argosy University is accredited by the Higher Learning Commission of the North Central Association and is a member of the North Central Association (230 South LaSalle Street, Suite 7-500, Chicago, Illinois 60604-1413; phone: 800-621-7440 (toll-free); Web site: http://ncahlc.org).

Location

Argosy University operates nineteen locations across the U.S. and offers a variety of degree programs online (http://www.argosy.edu). Campus locations include the following:

Atlanta, 980 Hammond Drive, Suite 100, Atlanta, Georgia 30328; phone: 770-671-1200 or 888-671-4777 (toll-free)

Chicago, 225 North Michigan Avenue, Suite 1300, Chicago, Illinois 60601; phone: 312-777-7600 or 800-626-4123 (toll-free)

Dallas, 5001 Lyndon B. Johnson Freeway, Heritage Square, Farmers Branch, Texas 75244; phone: 214-890-9900 or 866-954-9900 (toll-free)

Denver, 7600 E. Eastman Avenue, Denver, Colorado 80231; phone: 303-923-4110 or 866-431-5981 (toll-free)

Hawai'i, 400 ASB Tower, 1001 Bishop Street, Honolulu, Hawaii 96813; phone: 808-536-5555 or 888-323-2777 (toll-free)

Inland Empire, 3401 Centre Lake Drive, Suite 200, Ontario, California 91761; phone: 909-472-0800 or 866-217-9075 (toll-free)

Los Angeles, 5230 Pacific Concourse, Suite 200, Los Angeles, California 90045; phone: 310-866-4000 or 866-505-0332 (toll-free)

Nashville, 100 Centerview Drive, Suite 225, Nashville, Tennessee 37214; phone: 615-525-2800 or 866-833-6598 (toll-free)

Orange County, 601 South Lewis Street, Orange County, California 92868; phone: 714-620-3700 or 800-716-9598 (toll-free)

Phoenix, 2233 West Dunlap Avenue, Phoenix, Arizona 85021; phone: 602-216-2600 or 866-216-2777 (toll-free)

Salt Lake City, 121 Election Road, Suite 300, Draper, Utah 84020; phone: 801-601-5000 or 888-639-4756 (toll-free)

San Diego, 1615 Murray Canyon Road, Suite 100, San Diego, California 92108; phone: 619-321-3000 or 866-505-0333 (toll-free)

San Francisco Bay Area, 1005 Atlantic Avenue, Alameda, California 94501; phone: 510-217-4700 or 866-215-2777 (toll-free)

Sarasota, 5250 17th Street, Sarasota, Florida 34235; phone: 941-379-0404 or 800-331-5995 (toll-free)

Schaumburg, 999 North Plaza Drive, Suite 111, Schaumburg, Illinois 60173-5403; phone: 847-969-4900 or 866-290-2777 (toll-free)

Seattle, 2601-A Elliott Avenue, Seattle, Washington 98121; phone: 206-283-4500 or 888-283-2777 (toll-free)

Tampa, 1403 North Howard Avenue, Tampa, Florida 33607; phone: 813-393-5290 or 800-850-6488 (toll-free).

Twin Cities, 1515 Central Parkway, Eagan, Minnesota 55121; phone: 651-846-2882 or 888-844-2004 (toll-free)

Washington, D.C., 1550 Wilson Boulevard, Suite 600, Arlington, Virginia 22209; phone: 703-526-5800 or 866-703-2777 (toll-free)

Argosy University is certified by SCHEV to operate in Virginia.

Argosy University, Nashville is authorized for operation as a postsecondary educational institution by the Tennessee Higher Education Commission.

Majors and Degrees

Argosy University's College of Undergraduate Studies offers Bachelor of Arts (B.A.) programs in liberal arts and psychology as well as Bachelor of Science (B.S.) programs in business administration and criminal justice. Please note that not all degree programs are offered at all locations.

Academic Programs

The Bachelor of Arts (B.A.) in liberal arts program offers an integrative approach to learning which aims to develop competencies in the basic academic areas and disciplines in higher education. It extends the capacity for intellectual inquiry through the incorporation of courses that develop the individual, prepare them for the workplace, and for constructive participation in a global society. The B.A. in liberal arts gives students the opportunity to integrate real world experience with the critical acquisition of a variety of human knowledge and skills that not only encourages sensitivity to the diversity of human cultures, but also creates a desire to achieve personal and professional excellence.

The Bachelor of Arts (B.A.) in psychology program is designed to prepare students to begin a human services career as an entry-level counselor, case manager, or human resources administrator or in management and business services, as well as for graduate study in fields such as counseling, social work, and marriage and family therapy. The program is flexible enough to allow students to pursue opportunities offered by a number of states for credentialing or certification at the bachelor's level.

The Bachelor of Science (B.S.) in business administration degree program is designed to help students focus their academic and professional development consistent with their career objectives and experiences. In addition to the business core, students complete one of the following concentrations: accounting, finance, health-care management, human resources, international business, marketing, and organizational management. Students may choose one of five

optional concentrations: customized professional concentration, finance, health-care management, international business, or marketing.

The Bachelor of Science (B.S.) in criminal justice is a practitioner-oriented program that prepares students to become successful professionals in the fields of law enforcement, corrections, probation and parole, and security. The curriculum provides students with critical thinking, communication, research, and professional skills that contribute to career development. In addition to core course work, students will complete two of seven optional concentrations: corrections, forensic psychology, homeland security, management, police, security management, and substance abuse.

Argosy University's bachelor's degree programs are open to students and working professionals with no college experience and those who have attended a community college, junior college, or other university.

Program offerings vary by school.

Academic Facilities

Argosy University libraries provide curriculum support and educational resources including current text materials, diagnostic training documents, reference materials and databases, journals and dissertations, and major and current titles in program areas. There is an online public-access catalog of library resources available throughout the Argosy University system. Students enjoy full remote access to their campus library database, enabling them to study and conduct research at home. Academic databases offer dissertation abstracts, academic journals, and professional periodicals. All library computers are Internet accessible. Software applications include Word, Excel, PowerPoint, SPSS, and various test-scoring programs.

Costs

Tuition varies by program. Students should contact the Argosy University campus of their choice for tuition information.

Financial Aid

Financial aid options are available to students who qualify. Argosy University offers access to federal and state aid programs, merit-based awards, grants, loans, and a work-study program. As a first step, students should complete the Free Application for Federal Student Aid (FAFSA). Prospective students can apply electronically at http://www.fafsa.ed.gov or at the campus. To receive consideration for financial aid and ensure timely receipt of funds, it is best to submit an application promptly.

Faculty

The Argosy University faculty is composed of working professionals who have a passion to help students succeed. Members bring real-world experience and the latest practice innovations to the academic setting. The diverse faculty is widely recognized for contributions to the field. Most hold doctoral degrees. They provide a substantive education that combines comprehensive knowledge with critical skills and practical workplace relevance. Above all, faculty members are committed to their students' personal and professional development.

Student Government

Argosy University campuses offer unique opportunities for student involvement beyond individual programs of study. Most faculty committees include a student representative. In addition, a student group meets with faculty members and administrators regularly to discuss pertinent campus-related issues.

Admission Requirements

Admission requirements differ depending on the number of college credits completed prior to application.

Students who have earned 12 or fewer semester college credits must provide proof of high school graduation or GED and meet one of the following conditions for admission: ACT composite score of 18 or above, or a combined math and verbal SAT score of 870, or minimum ACCUPLACER scores of 86 in sentence skills and 53 in algebra. Applicants who do not meet any of the above conditions for admission will be admitted with academic support if they provide proof of high school graduation or GED and meet one of the following: ACT composite score of 14 to 17, or a combined math and verbal SAT score of 660 to 869, or minimum ACCUPLACER scores of 54 in sentence skills and 36 in arithmetic.

Applicants who have earned 13 or more semester college credits must provide proof of high school graduation or GED and meet one of the following conditions for admission: cumulative college GPA of 2.0 or above or minimum ACCUPLACER scores of 86 for sentence skills and 53 in algebra. Students who do not meet either of the above criteria will be admitted with academic support if they provide proof of high school graduation or GED and meet the following condition: minimum ACCUPLACER scores of 54 in reading and 36 in arithmetic.

Students admitted with academic support are limited to 12 credit hours of study during their first semester (6 credit hours per session). Students admitted with academic support will be required to complete developmental English and/or math courses unless they meet the following conditions: Writing Review (ENG099)— must meet one of the following: a minimum ACCUPLACER score of 86 in sentence skills, or a minimum ACT verbal score of 18, or a minimum SAT verbal score of 425, or completion of a college-level English composition course with a grade of C or above; Mathematics Review I (MAT096)—must meet one of the following: a minimum ACCUPLACER score of 53 in algebra, or a minimum ACT math score of 18, or a minimum SAT math score of 440, or completion of a college-level English composition course with a grade of C or above.

Other admission requirements may include credit hours of qualified transfer credit with a grade of C- or better from a regionally accredited institution or a nationally accredited institution approved and documented by the faculty and dean of the College of Business, or the College of Professional Psychology, at Argosy University or completion of an Associate of Arts or Associate of Science degree from a regionally accredited institution. A maximum of 78 lower-division or 90 total credit hours may be transferred. A minimum written TOEFL score of 500 (paper-based test), 173 (computer-based test), or 61 (Internet-based test) is required for all applicants whose native language is not English or who have not graduated from an institution in which English is the language of instruction.

Official transcripts from approved postsecondary institutions must include a minimum grade point average of 2.0 (on a scale of 4.0) for all academic work completed. Exceptions may be made for extenuating circumstances. All applications must include a completed application form, proof of high school graduation or successful completion of the GED test, official postsecondary transcripts, and a nonrefundable (except in California) application fee. Additional materials are required prior to matriculation. Some programs have additional application requirements or include exceptions to admission requirements. An admissions representative can provide further information.

Please refer to the University's catalog for additional information.

Application and Information

Argosy University accepts students on a rolling admissions basis year-round, depending on availability of required courses. Applications for admission are available online at http://www.argosy.edu or by contacting one of the campus locations.

Argosy University Administrative Office
Phone: 800-377-0617 (toll-free)
Web site: http://www.argosy.edu

ARGOSY UNIVERSITY, TWIN CITIES
EAGAN, MINNESOTA

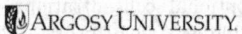

The University

Argosy University is an institution of higher education offering a variety of degree programs that focus on the human side of success alongside professional competence. For students looking for a more personal approach to education, Argosy University may just be the answer. Drawing upon over thirty years of history, Argosy University has developed a curriculum that focuses on interpersonal skills and practical experience alongside academic learning. Argosy's programs are taught by practicing professionals who bring real-world experience into the classroom. Students graduate with both a solid foundation of knowledge and the power to put it to work. To accommodate busy working adults, many programs at Argosy University have a flexible structure with both on-campus and online learning, and evening, weekend, and daytime classes. There are financial aid options available for students who qualify.

Argosy University is a private institution of higher education dedicated to providing quality professional education programs at the doctoral, master's, bachelor's, and associate degree levels as well as continuing education to individuals who seek to enhance their professional and personal lives. The University emphasizes programs in the behavioral sciences (psychology and counseling), business, education, and the health-care professions. A limited number of preprofessional programs and general education offerings are provided to permit students to prepare for entry into these professional fields. The programs of Argosy University are designed to instill the knowledge, skills, and ethical values of professional practice and to foster values of social responsibility in a supportive, learning-centered environment of mutual respect and professional excellence.

With nineteen campuses nationwide, Argosy University provides students with a network of resources found at larger universities, including a career resources office, an academic resources center, and extensive information access for research.

The University's innovative programs feature dynamic, relevant, and practical curricula delivered in flexible class formats. Students enjoy scheduling options that make it easier to fit school into their busy lives. They can choose from day and evening courses, on campus or online. Many students find a combination of both to be an ideal way of continuing their education while meeting family and professional demands.

Most students are full-time working professionals who live within driving distance of the campus. The University does not offer or operate student housing.

Argosy University is accredited by the Higher Learning Commission of the North Central Association and is a member of the North Central Association, 230 South LaSalle Street, Suite 7-500, Chicago, Illinois 60604-1413; phone: 800-621-7440 (toll-free); http://ncahlc.org.

Location

Argosy University's Twin Cities location offers academics in a supportive environment. The campus is nestled in a parklike suburban setting within 10 miles of the airport and the Mall of America. Students enjoy the convenience of nearby shops, restaurants, and housing, and easy freeway access. The neighboring Eagan Community Center offers many amenities, including walking paths, a fitness center, meeting rooms, and an outdoor amphitheater. The Twin Cities of Minneapolis and St. Paul have been rated by popular magazines as one of the most livable metropolitan areas in the country. With a population of 2.5 million, the area offers an abundance of recreational opportunities. Year-round outdoor activities; nationally acclaimed venues for theater, art, and music; and professional sports teams attract residents and visitors alike. The Minneapolis–St. Paul metropolitan area offers a diversified economic base fueled by a broad array of companies. Among the numerous publicly traded companies headquartered in the area are Target, UnitedHealth Group, 3M, General Mills, and U.S. Bancorp.

Majors and Degrees

The Bachelor of Arts (B.A.) in liberal arts program offers an integrative approach to learning which aims to develop competencies in the basic academic areas and disciplines in higher education. It extends the capacity for intellectual inquiry through the incorporation of courses that develop the individual, prepare them for the workplace, and for constructive participation in a global society. The B.A. in liberal arts gives students the opportunity to integrate real-world experience with the critical acquisition of a variety of human knowledge and skills that not only encourages sensitivity to the diversity of human cultures, but also creates a desire to achieve personal and professional excellence.

The Bachelor of Arts (B.A.) in psychology program is designed to prepare students to begin a human services career as an entry-level counselor, case manager, or human resources administrator; in management and business services; or for graduate study in fields such as counseling, social work, and marriage and family therapy. The program is flexible enough to allow students to pursue opportunities offered by a number of states for credentialing or certification at the bachelor's level.

The Bachelor of Science (B.S.) in business administration degree program is designed to help students focus their academic and professional development in ways consistent with their career objectives and experiences. In addition to the business core, students complete one of the following concentrations: accounting, finance, healthcare management, human resources, international business, marketing, and organizational management. Students may choose one of five optional concentrations: customized professional concentration, finance, healthcare management, international business, or marketing.

The Bachelor of Science (B.S.) in criminal justice is a practitioner-oriented program that prepares students to become successful professionals in the fields of law enforcement, corrections, probation and parole, and security. The curriculum provides students with critical thinking, communication, research, and professional skills that contribute to career development. In addition to core course work, students will complete two of seven optional concentrations: corrections, forensic psychology, homeland security, management, police, security management, and substance abuse.

The Bachelor of Science (B.S.) in medical technology degree program is designed for individuals who have completed an associate degree in medical laboratory technology. Medical technologists perform the more complex laboratory testing in the clinical lab which requires a higher level of judgment and expertise than that of a medical laboratory technician. Medical technologists write and implement new procedures, evaluate test results, and establish and monitor programs to ensure the accuracy of laboratory testing. Additionally, this program includes coursework designed to help students acquire the knowledge, skills, and competencies they need to seek entry-level management or leadership positions.

Argosy University Twin Cities also offers a variety of associate degree programs in the health sciences discipline.

Academic Programs

Argosy University's bachelor's degree programs are open to students and working professionals with no college experience and those who have attended a community college, junior college, or other university.

Academic Facilities

Argosy University libraries provide curriculum support and educational resources, including current text materials, diagnostic training documents, reference materials and databases, journals and dissertations, and major and current titles in program areas. The University provides an online public-access catalog of library resources throughout the Argosy University system. Students enjoy full remote access to their campus library database, enabling them to study and conduct research at home. Academic databases offer dissertation abstracts, academic journals, and professional periodicals. All library computers are Internet accessible. Software applications include Word, Excel, PowerPoint, SPSS, and various test-scoring programs.

Costs

Tuition varies by program. Students should contact Argosy University's Twin Cities location for tuition information.

Financial Aid

Financial aid options are available to students who qualify. Argosy University offers access to federal and state aid programs, merit-based awards, grants, loans, and a work-study program. As a first step, students should complete the Free Application for Federal Student Aid (FAFSA). Prospective students can apply online at http://www.fafsa.ed.gov or at the campus. To receive consideration for financial aid and ensure timely receipt of funds, it is best to submit an application promptly.

Faculty

The Argosy University faculty is composed of working professionals who are committed to student success. Members bring real-world experience and practice innovations to the academic setting. Argosy's diverse faculty is widely recognized for contributions to the field. Most hold doctoral degrees. They provide a substantive education that combines comprehensive knowledge with critical skills and practical workplace relevance. Above all, faculty members of the College of Health Sciences are committed to their students' personal and professional development.

Student Government

Argosy University campuses offer unique opportunities for student involvement beyond individual programs of study. Most faculty committees include a student representative. In addition, a student group meets with faculty members and administrators regularly to discuss pertinent campus-related issues.

Admission Requirements

Students who have successfully completed a program of secondary education or the equivalent (GED) are eligible for admission to Argosy University's programs. Entrance requirements include either an ACT composite score of 18 or above, a combined math and verbal SAT score of 960 or above, a passing score on the Argosy University Entrance Exam, or a minimum TOEFL score of 550 (paper version), 213 (computer version), or 79 (Internet version) for all applicants whose native language is not English or who have not graduated from an institution in which English is the language of instruction.

All applicants must include a completed application form; proof of high school graduation or successful completion of the GED test; official postsecondary transcripts; SAT, ACT, Argosy University exam, or TOEFL scores; and the nonrefundable application fee. Additional materials are required prior to matriculation. Some programs have additional application requirements. An admissions representative can provide further detailed information.

Application and Information

Argosy University, Twin Cities, accepts students on a rolling admissions basis year-round, depending on availability of required courses. Applications for admission are available online or by contacting the campus, using the information listed in this description.
Argosy University, Twin Cities
1515 Central Parkway
Eagan, Minnesota 55121
United States
Phone: 651-846-2882
800-377-0617 (toll-free)
E-mail: auadmissions@argosy.edu
Web site: http://www.argosy.edu/twincities

THE ART INSTITUTE OF ATLANTA
ATLANTA, GEORGIA

The Art Institute of Atlanta
CREATE TOMORROW

A focused education from The Art Institute of Atlanta can help students turn their creative energy into a powerful tool that can make a difference in the world. Students are part of a collaborative and supportive community, where experienced instructors provide the guidance and skills needed to pursue a career in the creative economy.

The school's programs in the areas of design, media arts, fashion, and culinary give students the opportunity to learn by using professional-grade technology and to build a portfolio of work to show potential employers after graduation.

The Art Institute of Atlanta, including its branch campuses—The Art Institute of Atlanta-Decatur, The Art Institute of Charleston, The Art Institute of Tennessee–Nashville, The Art Institute of Virginia Beach, The Art Institute of Washington and The Art Institute of Washington–Dulles—is accredited by the Commission on Colleges of the Southern Association of Colleges and Schools to award associate and baccalaureate degrees. Contact the Commission on Colleges at 1866 Southern Lane, Decatur, Georgia 30033-4097 or call 404-679-4500 for questions about the accreditation of The Art Institute of Atlanta.

The Associate in Arts degree in Culinary Arts and the Bachelor of Science degree in Culinary Arts Management programs are accredited by the Accrediting Commission of the American Culinary Federation Education Foundation.

The Interior Design program leading to the Bachelor of Science degree is accredited by the Council for Interior Design Accreditation, http://www.accredit-id.org, 206 Grandville Ave., Ste. 350, Grand Rapids, Michigan 49503.

The Art Institute of Atlanta is an accredited institutional member of the National Association of Schools of Art and Design (NASAD).

The Art Institute of Atlanta is licensed by the Georgia Nonpublic Postsecondary Education Commission, 2082 East Exchange Place, Suite 220, Tucker, Georgia 30084.

The Art Institute of Atlanta is licensed by the Alabama Department of Postsecondary Education, 401 Adams Avenue, Montgomery, Alabama, 36104-4340 and is approved for recruiting purposes only by the Alabama Commission on Higher Education, 100 North Union Street, Montgomery, Alabama 36104-3758.

Location

Located in bustling suburban Atlanta, the school is close to public transportation and within walking distance of a shopping center with movie theaters, several restaurants, and stores. One of the city's largest malls is less than a 10-minute drive—or one subway stop—from The Art Institute of Atlanta. There are at least thirty restaurants within a 15-minute drive. Students enjoy clubs and concerts, galleries and museums, baseball games, and rollerblading in Piedmont Park. The High Museum of Art, Michael C. Carlos Museum, Atlanta Contemporary Art Center, and dozens of art galleries throughout the city are wonderful resources for creative-minded students.

Programs of Study and Degrees

No matter which course of study a student may choose, the professionals at The Art Institute of Atlanta will guide, support, and help each student as their talents evolve on their journey of personal and professional transformation. Students studying design learn to fine-tune their visual thinking and problem-solving skills, as they create everything from logos to TV ads. Programs in the area of media arts focus on utilizing technology to deliver information and entertainment, while students studying fashion learn to design clothes for the runway or run a retail shop. Culinary programs focus on the fundamental techniques while exposing students to a full menu of international cuisines and management techniques.

Bachelor's degree programs are offered in the areas of advertising, audio production, culinary arts management, digital filmmaking and video production, fashion and retail management, food and beverage management, game art and design, graphic design, illustration, interior design, media arts and animation, photographic imaging, visual and game programming, visual effects and motion graphics, and Web design and interactive media.

Associate degree programs are offered in the areas of culinary arts, graphic design, photographic imaging, video production, Web design and interactive media, and wine, spirits, and beverage management*.

Diploma programs are offered in the areas of advertising design, baking and pastry, commercial photography, culinary arts, digital design, digital image management, fashion retailing, residential interiors, video skills, Web design and development, and Web design and interactive communications.

The Associate in Arts degree in culinary arts, Bachelor of Science degree in culinary arts management, Bachelor of Fine Arts degree in interior design, and Bachelor of Science degree in food and beverage management, as well as the programs in the areas of graphic design and Web design and interactive media programs, are available in an evening and weekend option format.

*Participation in the program for those under 21 years of age will be conducted in accord with state law regarding the possession and consumption of alcoholic beverages.

Academic Programs

The academic year of The Art Institute of Atlanta is divided into four quarters that begin in January, April, July, and October. Full-time students typically take 16 academic credits per quarter. An associate degree can be earned in as little as six to seven quarters (approximately two years), and a bachelor's degree can be earned in as little as twelve quarters (three to four years). Students may take online classes in order to earn a degree on a flexible schedule, or they may take online classes as a supplement to traditional classroom learning.

Academic Facilities

The Art Institute of Atlanta provides a learning environment with professional-grade technology applicable to each student's course of study. Students have the opportunity to build a portfolio of work that shows potential employers that they are trained to use the software, hardware, or equipment utilized within the industry. Depending upon the course of study, students are immersed in a creative environment—from classrooms to computer labs to studios—focused on relevant, hands-on education designed to prepare students for the real world.

Costs

Tuition cost varies by program. Prospective students should contact the school for current tuition costs. Other charges include a starting kit for all first-quarter students. Kits vary in price depending on the program of study.

Financial Aid

Financial aid is available for those who qualify. Students who require financial assistance should first complete and submit a Free Application for Federal Student Aid (FAFSA) and meet with a financial aid officer.

Faculty

Faculty members are experienced professionals who create a learning environment that is similar to the professional world students will face after graduation. Instructors are focused on helping students develop the skills they need to transform their creative potential into marketable skills.

Student Government

The Student Advisory Assembly, the representative body of students, meets regularly to discuss policy matters and to plan programs to enhance student life. The assembly offers a valuable opportunity for students to learn the principles of leadership as well as communication and human relations skills. Other organizations dedicated to student life include the Housing Council, International Student Association, Student Activities Board, and Student Ambassadors. Students may take part in several student organizations, such as professional organizations for creative artists, which provide networking and other career opportunities.

Admission Requirements

To apply to The Art Institute of Atlanta, students must submit an application for admission, a 150-word essay, a signed notice regarding transferability for credit earned, and high school transcripts or General Educational Development (GED) test scores. Official reports of SAT, ACT, ASSET, or COMPASS scores must also be given to the school. Finally, students are required to complete an interview with an assistant director of admissions and to present a portfolio of their work. There is a $50 application fee.

Admissions decisions are made by the Admissions Committee, which consists of school faculty and staff members. The committee determines whether an applicant has a reasonable chance to be successful at The Art Institute of Atlanta, based upon the applicant's academic record, essay, and the appropriateness of stated career goals as they relate to the chosen program of study.

For the most recent information regarding admission requirements, please refer to the current academic catalog.

Application and Information

To obtain an application, make arrangements for an interview, or tour the school, prospective students should contact:

The Art Institute of Atlanta
6600 Peachtree Dunwoody Road, N.E.
100 Embassy Row
Atlanta, Georgia 30328-1635
Phone: 770-394-8300
        800-275-4242 (toll-free)
Fax: 770-394-0008
Web site: http://www.artinstitutes.edu/atlanta

Over 50 schools: The Art Institute of Atlanta; The Art Institute of Atlanta—Decatur, A branch of The Art Institute of Atlanta; The Art Institute of Austin, A branch of The Art Institute of Houston; The Art Institute of California, a college of Argosy University, with locations in Hollywood, Inland Empire, Los Angeles, Orange County, Sacramento, San Diego, San Francisco, and Sunnyvale; The Art Institute of Charleston, A branch of The Art Institute of Atlanta; The Art Institute of Charlotte; The Art Institute of Colorado; The Art Institute of Dallas, A campus of South University; The Art Institute of Fort Lauderdale; The Art Institute of Fort Worth, A campus of South University; The Art Institute of Houston; The Art Institute of Houston—North, A branch of The Art Institute of Houston; The Art Institute of Indianapolis; The Art Institute of Jacksonville, A branch of Miami International University of Art & Design; The Art Institute of Las Vegas; The Art Institute of Michigan; The Art Institute of Michigan—Troy; The Art Institute of New York City; The Art Institute of Ohio—Cincinnati; The Art Institute of Philadelphia; The Art Institute of Phoenix; The Art Institute of Pittsburgh; The Art Institute of Portland; The Art Institute of Raleigh–Durham; The Art Institute of Salt Lake City; The Art Institute of San Antonio, A branch of The Art Institute of Houston; The Art Institute of Seattle; The Art Institute of Tampa, A branch of Miami International University of Art & Design; The Art Institute of Tennessee— Nashville, A branch of The Art Institute of Atlanta; The Art Institute of Tucson; The Art Institute of Vancouver; The Art Institute of Virginia Beach[1], A branch of The Art Institute of Atlanta; The Art Institute of Washington[1], A branch of The Art Institute of Atlanta; The Art Institute of Washington—Dulles[1], A branch of The Art Institute of Atlanta; The Art Institute of Wisconsin; The Art Institute of York—Pennsylvania; The Art Institutes International—Kansas City; The Art Institutes International Minnesota; The Illinois Institute of Art—Chicago; The Illinois Institute of Art—Schaumburg; The Illinois Institute of Art—Tinley Park; Miami International University of Art & Design; The New England Institute of Art

[1]Certified by SCHEV to operate in Virginia

See **aiprograms.info** for program duration, tuition, fees, and other costs, median debt, federal salary data, alumni success, and other important info. The Art Institutes is a system of over 50 schools throughout North America. Programs, credential levels, technology, and scheduling options vary by school, and employment opportunities are not guaranteed. Financial aid is available to those who qualify. Several institutions included in The Art Institutes system are campuses of South University or Argosy University. OH Registration # 04-01-1698B, AC0165, AC0080, Licensed by the Florida Commission for Independent Education, License No. 1287, 3427, 3110, 2581. Administrative office: 210 Sixth Avenue, 33rd Floor, Pittsburgh, PA 15222. ©2012 The Art Institutes International LLC.

THE ART INSTITUTE OF ATLANTA— DECATUR

DECATUR, GEORGIA

The Art Institute of Atlanta®–Decatur
A branch of The Art Institute of Atlanta

CREATE TOMORROW

A focused education from The Art Institute of Atlanta—Decatur, a branch of The Art Institute of Atlanta, can help students turn their creative energy into a powerful tool that can make a difference in the world. Students are part of a collaborative and supportive community, where experienced instructors provide the guidance and skills needed to pursue a career in the creative economy.

The school's programs in the areas of design, media arts, and fashion give students the opportunity to learn on professional-grade technology and to build a portfolio of work to show potential employers after graduation.

The Art Institute of Atlanta—Decatur is a branch campus of The Art Institute of Atlanta. The Art Institute of Atlanta is accredited by the Commission on Colleges of the Southern Association of Colleges and Schools to award associate and baccalaureate degrees. For questions about the accreditation of The Art Institute of Atlanta, contact the Commission on Colleges at 1866 Southern Lane, Decatur, Georgia 30033-4097; phone: 404-679-4500.

The Art Institute of Atlanta—Decatur is licensed by the Georgia Nonpublic Postsecondary Education Commission, 2082 East Exchange Place, Suite 220, Tucker, Georgia 30084.

The Art Institute of Atlanta—Decatur is approved for veteran's education benefits. This school is authorized under federal law to enroll nonimmigrant alien students.

Location

Decatur is a diverse, progressive community that retains a small-town feel, with quiet residential areas and historic districts. Decatur has easy access to the bustling city of Atlanta with its varied and plentiful arts, culture, entertainment, and sports venues.

Programs of Study and Degrees

No matter which course of study a student may choose, the professionals at The Art Institute of Atlanta—Decatur will guide, support, and help each student as their talents evolve on their journey of personal and professional transformation. Students studying design learn to fine-tune their visual thinking and problem-solving skills as they create everything from logos to TV ads. Programs in the area of media arts focus on utilizing technology to deliver information and entertainment, while students studying fashion learn to design clothes for the runway or run a retail shop.

Bachelor's degree programs are offered in the areas of advertising, fashion and retail management, game art and design, graphic design, interior design, media arts and animation, photographic imaging, and Web design and interactive media.

Associate degrees are offered in the areas of graphic design and Web design and interactive media.

Diploma programs are available in the areas of advertising design, digital design, digital image management, fashion retailing, residential interiors, Web design and development, and Web design and interactive communications.

Academic Programs

The Art Institute of Atlanta—Decatur operates on a year-round, four-quarter system.

Academic Facilities

The Art Institute of Atlanta—Decatur provides a learning environment with professional-grade technology applicable to each student's course of study. Students have the opportunity to build a portfolio of work that shows potential employers that they are trained to use the software, hardware, or equipment utilized within the industry. Depending upon the course of study, students are immersed in a creative environment—from classrooms to computer labs to studios—focused on relevant, hands-on education designed to prepare students for the real world.

Costs

Tuition cost varies by program. Prospective students should contact the school for current tuition costs. Other charges include a starting kit for all first-quarter students. Kits vary in price depending on the program of study.

Financial Aid

Financial aid is available for those who qualify. Students who require financial assistance should first complete and submit a Free Application for Federal Student Aid (FAFSA) and meet with a financial aid officer.

Faculty

Faculty members are experienced professionals who create a learning environment that is similar to the professional world students will face after graduation. Instructors are focused on helping students develop the skills they need to transform their creative potential into marketable skills.

Admission Requirements

Applicants must provide proof of high school graduation or achievement of a General Educational Development (GED) certificate as a prerequisite for admission. In lieu of documenting high school graduation or a GED certificate, applicants may provide proof of attaining an associate degree or higher from an accredited institution. An official transcript indicating date of high school graduation, GED certificate (including test scores), or date of college graduation (including degree granted) is required as proof.

All individuals seeking admission to The Art Institute of Atlanta—Decatur are interviewed in person or by phone by an assistant director of admissions, and each applicant must submit an original essay of at least 150 words stating how an education at The Art Institute of Atlanta—Decatur would help the student to achieve career goals. There is a $50 application fee.

For the most recent information regarding admission requirements, please refer to the current academic catalog.

Application and Information

To obtain an application, make arrangements for an interview, or tour the school, prospective students should contact:

The Art Institute of Atlanta—Decatur
A branch of The Art Institute of Atlanta
One West Court Square, Suite 110
Decatur, Georgia 30030
Phone: 404-942-1800
      866-856-6203 (toll-free)
Fax: 404-942-1818
Web site: http://www.artinstitutes.edu/decatur

COLLEGE CLOSE-UPS

Over 50 schools: The Art Institute of Atlanta; The Art Institute of Atlanta—Decatur, A branch of The Art Institute of Atlanta; The Art Institute of Austin, A branch of The Art Institute of Houston; The Art Institute of California, a college of Argosy University, with locations in Hollywood, Inland Empire, Los Angeles, Orange County, Sacramento, San Diego, San Francisco, and Sunnyvale; The Art Institute of Charleston, A branch of The Art Institute of Atlanta; The Art Institute of Charlotte; The Art Institute of Colorado; The Art Institute of Dallas, A campus of South University; The Art Institute of Fort Lauderdale; The Art Institute of Fort Worth, A campus of South University; The Art Institute of Houston; The Art Institute of Houston—North, A branch of The Art Institute of Houston; The Art Institute of Indianapolis; The Art Institute of Jacksonville, A branch of Miami International University of Art & Design; The Art Institute of Las Vegas; The Art Institute of Michigan; The Art Institute of Michigan—Troy; The Art Institute of New York City; The Art Institute of Ohio—Cincinnati; The Art Institute of Philadelphia; The Art Institute of Phoenix; The Art Institute of Pittsburgh; The Art Institute of Portland; The Art Institute of Raleigh—Durham; The Art Institute of Salt Lake City; The Art Institute of San Antonio, A branch of The Art Institute of Houston; The Art Institute of Seattle; The Art Institute of Tampa, A branch of Miami International University of Art & Design; The Art Institute of Tennessee—Nashville, A branch of The Art Institute of Atlanta; The Art Institute of Tucson; The Art Institute of Vancouver; The Art Institute of Virginia Beach[1], A branch of The Art Institute of Atlanta; The Art Institute of Washington[1], A branch of The Art Institute of Atlanta; The Art Institute of Washington—Dulles[1], A branch of The Art Institute of Atlanta; The Art Institute of Wisconsin; The Art Institute of York—Pennsylvania; The Art Institutes International—Kansas City; The Art Institutes International Minnesota; The Illinois Institute of Art—Chicago; The Illinois Institute of Art—Schaumburg; The Illinois Institute of Art—Tinley Park; Miami International University of Art & Design; The New England Institute of Art

[1]Certified by SCHEV to operate in Virginia

See **aiprograms.info** for program duration, tuition, fees, and other costs, median debt, federal salary data, alumni success, and other important info. The Art Institutes is a system of over 50 schools throughout North America. Programs, credential levels, technology, and scheduling options vary by school, and employment opportunities are not guaranteed. Financial aid is available to those who qualify. Several institutions included in The Art Institutes system are campuses of South University or Argosy University. OH Registration # 04-01-1698B, AC0165, AC0080, Licensed by the Florida Commission for Independent Education, License No. 1287, 3427, 3110, 2581. Administrative office: 210 Sixth Avenue, 33rd Floor, Pittsburgh, PA 15222. ©2012 The Art Institutes International LLC.

THE ART INSTITUTE OF AUSTIN
AUSTIN, TEXAS

The Art Institute of Austin
A branch of The Art Institute of Houston

CREATE TOMORROW

A focused education from The Art Institute of Austin, a branch of The Art Institute of Houston, can help students turn their creative energy into a powerful tool that can make a difference in the world. Students are part of a collaborative and supportive community, where experienced instructors provide the guidance and skills needed to pursue a career in the creative economy.

The school's programs in the areas of design, media arts, fashion, and culinary give students the opportunity to learn by using professional-grade technology and to build a portfolio of work to show potential employers after graduation.

The Art Institute of Austin is a branch campus of The Art Institute of Houston. The Art Institute of Houston is accredited by the Commission on Colleges of the Southern Association of Colleges and Schools to award associate and baccalaureate degrees. For questions about the accreditation of The Art Institute of Houston, contact the Commission on Colleges, 1866 Southern Lane, Decatur, Georgia 30033-4097; phone: 404-679-4500.

The Art Institute of Austin holds a certificate of authorization acknowledging exemption from Texas Higher Education Coordinating Board regulations.

Location

Located in bustling suburban Austin, the school is close to public transportation and within walking distance of a shopping center with movie theaters, several restaurants, and stores. There are at least thirty restaurants within a 15-minute drive. Students enjoy clubs and concerts, galleries and museums, baseball games, and rollerblading in Piedmont Park. The High Museum of Art, Michael C. Carlos Museum, Austin Contemporary Art Center, and dozens of art galleries throughout the city are wonderful resources for creative-minded students.

Programs of Study and Degrees

No matter which course of study a student may choose, the professionals at The Art Institute of Austin will guide, support, and help each student as their talents evolve on their journey of personal and professional transformation. Students studying design learn to fine-tune their visual thinking and problem-solving skills as they create everything from logos to TV ads. Programs in the area of media arts focus on utilizing technology to deliver information and entertainment, while students studying fashion learn to design clothes for the runway or run a retail shop. Culinary programs focus on the fundamental techniques while exposing students to a full menu of international cuisines and management techniques.

Bachelor's degree programs are offered in the areas of advertising design, audio production, culinary management, design and technical graphics, digital filmmaking and video production, fashion and retail management, food and beverage management, game art and design, graphic design, hospitality management, interior design, media arts and animation, photography, visual effects and motion graphics, and Web design and interactive media.

Associate degree programs are offered in the areas of baking and pastry, culinary arts, graphic design, restaurant and catering management, and Web design and interactive media.

Diploma programs are offered in the areas of baking and pastry, culinary arts, digital image management, fashion retailing, Web design and development, and Web design and interactive communications.

Academic Programs

The academic year of The Art Institute of Austin is divided into four quarters that begin in January, April, July, and October. Full-time students typically take 16 academic credits per quarter. An associate degree can be earned in as little as six to seven quarters (approximately two years), and a bachelor's degree can be earned in as little as twelve quarters (three to four years). Students may take online classes in order to earn a degree on a flexible schedule, or they may take online classes as a supplement to traditional classroom learning.

Academic Facilities

The Art Institute of Austin provides a learning environment with professional-grade technology applicable to each student's course of study. Students have the opportunity to build a portfolio of work that shows potential employers that they are trained to use the software, hardware, or equipment utilized within the industry. Depending upon the course of study, students are immersed in a creative environment—from classrooms to computer labs to studios—focused on relevant, hands-on education designed to prepare students for the real world.

Costs

Tuition cost varies by program. Prospective students should contact the school for current tuition costs. Other charges include a starting kit for all first-quarter students. Kits vary in price depending on the program of study.

Financial Aid

Financial aid is available for those who qualify. Students who require financial assistance should first complete and submit a Free Application for Federal Student Aid (FAFSA) and meet with a financial aid officer.

Faculty

Faculty members are experienced professionals who create a learning environment that is similar to the professional world students will face after graduation. Instructors are focused on helping students develop the skills they need to transform their creative potential into marketable skills.

Student Government

The Student Advisory Assembly, the representative body of students, meets regularly to discuss policy matters and to plan programs to enhance student life. The assembly offers a valuable opportunity for students to learn the principles of leadership as well as communication and human relations skills. Other organizations dedicated to student life include the Housing Council, International Student Association, Student Activities Board, and Student Ambassadors. Students may take part in several student organizations, such as professional organizations for creative artists, which provide networking and other career opportunities.

Admission Requirements

To apply to The Art Institute of Austin, students must submit an application for admission, a 150-word essay, a signed notice regarding transferability for credit earned, and high school transcripts or General Educational Development (GED) test scores. Official reports of SAT, ACT, ASSET, or COMPASS scores must also be given to the school. Finally, students are required to complete an interview with an assistant director of admissions and to present a portfolio of their work. There is a $50 application fee.

Admissions decisions are made by the Admissions Committee, which consists of school faculty and staff members. The committee determines whether an applicant has a reasonable chance to be successful at The Art Institute of Austin, based upon the applicant's academic record, essay, and the appropriateness of stated career goals as they relate to the chosen program of study.

For the most recent information regarding admission requirements, please refer to the current academic catalog.

Application and Information

To obtain an application, make arrangements for an interview, or tour the school, prospective students should contact:
The Art Institute of Austin
A branch of The Art Institute of Houston
101 West Louis Henna Boulevard, Suite 100
Austin, Texas 78728
Phone: 512-691-1707
          866-583-7952 (toll-free)
Fax: 512-691-1790
Web site: http://www.artinstitutes.edu/austin

THE ART INSTITUTE OF CALIFORNIA, A COLLEGE OF ARGOSY UNIVERISTY, HOLLYWOOD

NORTH HOLLYWOOD, CALIFORNIA

A focused education from The Art Institute of California, a college of Argosy University, Hollywood, can help students turn their creative energy into a powerful tool that can make a difference in the world. Students are part of a collaborative and supportive community, where experienced instructors provide the guidance and skills needed to pursue a career in the creative economy.

The school's programs in the areas of design, media arts, fashion, and culinary give students the opportunity to learn by using professional-grade technology and to build a portfolio of work to show potential employers after graduation.

The Art Institute of California, a college of Argosy University, Hollywood is a campus of Argosy University. Argosy University is accredited by the Accrediting Commission for Senior Colleges and Universities of the Western Association of Schools and Colleges (985 Atlantic Avenue, Suite 100, Alameda, California, 94501, http://www.wascsenior.org). The Art Institute of California, a college of Argosy University, Hollywood, is accredited by the Accrediting Council for Independent Colleges and Schools to award associate's degrees and bachelor's degrees. The Accrediting Council for Independent Colleges and Schools is listed as a nationally recognized accrediting agency by the United States Department of Education and is recognized by the Council for Higher Education Accreditation. ACICS can be contacted at 750 First Street NE, Suite 980, Washington, D.C. 20002. Telephone: 202-336-6780.

The Art Institute of California, a college of Argosy University, Hollywood has been granted approval to operate by the California Bureau for Private Post-secondary Education, California Department of Consumer Affairs, 2535 Capitol Oaks Drive, Suite 400, Sacramento, California, 95833; phone: 916-431-6959; www.bppe.ca.gov.

Location

The school is located at the crossroads of California's design, fashion, and entertainment industries. The Art Institute of California, Hollywood ("The Art Institute of Califorina") is designed with the creative student in mind.

Programs of Study and Degrees

No matter which course of study a student may choose, the professionals at The Art Institute of California will guide, support, and help each student as their talents evolve on their journey of personal and professional transformation. Students studying design learn to fine-tune their visual thinking and problem-solving skills as they create everything from logos to TV ads. Programs in the area of media arts focus on utilizing technology to deliver information and entertainment, while students studying fashion learn to design clothes for the runway or run a retail shop. Culinary programs focus on the fundamental techniques while exposing students to a full menu of international cuisines and management techniques.

Bachelor's degree programs are offered in the areas of culinary management, digital filmmaking and video production, digital photography, fashion design, fashion marketing and management, game art and design, graphic design, industrial design, interior design, media arts and animation, set and exhibit design, visual and game programming, visual effects and motion graphics, and Web design and interactive media.

Associate degree programs are offered in the areas of culinary arts, digital photography, fashion design, fashion marketing, graphic design, and Web design and interactive media.

Diploma programs are available in the areas of fashion retailing and Web design and interactive communications.

The graphic design and interior design programs are also available in an evening and weekend option format.

Academic Programs

The Art Institute of California operates on a year-round, four-quarter system.

Academic Facilities

The Art Institute of California provides a learning environment with professional-grade technology applicable to each student's course of study. Students have the opportunity to build a portfolio of work that shows potential employers that they are trained to use the software, hardware, or equipment utilized within the industry. Depending upon the course of study, students are immersed in a creative environment—from classrooms to computer labs to studios—focused on relevant, hands-on education designed to prepare students for the real world.

Costs

Tuition cost varies by program. Prospective students should contact the school for current tuition costs. Other charges include a starting kit for all first-quarter students. Kits vary in price depending on the program of study.

Financial Aid

Financial aid is available for those who qualify. Students who require financial assistance should first complete and submit a Free Application for Federal Student Aid (FAFSA) and meet with a financial aid officer.

Faculty

Faculty members are experienced professionals who create a learning environment that is similar to the professional world students will face after graduation. Instructors are focused on helping students develop the skills they need to transform their creative potential into marketable skills.

Admission Requirements

Applicants must provide proof of high school graduation or achievement of General Educational Development (GED) certificate as a prerequisite for admission. In lieu of documenting high school graduation or a GED certificate, applicants may provide proof of attaining an associate degree or higher from an accredited institution. An official transcript indicating date of high school graduation, GED certificate (including test scores), or date of college graduation (including degree granted) is required as proof.

All individuals seeking admission to The Art Institute of California are interviewed in person or by phone by an assistant director of admissions, and each applicant must create an original essay of at least 150 words stating how an education at The Art Institute of California would help the student to achieve career goals. There is a $50 application fee.

For the most recent information regarding admission requirements, please refer to the current academic catalog.

Application and Information

To obtain an application, make arrangements for an interview, or tour the school, prospective students should contact:

The Art Institute of California, a college of Argosy University
5250 Lankershim Boulevard
North Hollywood, California 91601
Phone: 818-299-5100
        877-468-6232 (toll-free)
Fax: 818-299-5150
Web site: http://www.artinstitutes.edu/hollywood

Over 50 schools: The Art Institute of Atlanta; The Art Institute of Atlanta—Decatur, A branch of The Art Institute of Atlanta; The Art Institute of Austin, A branch of The Art Institute of Houston; The Art Institute of California, a college of Argosy University, with locations in Hollywood, Inland Empire, Los Angeles, Orange County, Sacramento, San Diego, San Francisco, and Sunnyvale; The Art Institute of Charleston, A branch of The Art Institute of Atlanta; The Art Institute of Charlotte; The Art Institute of Colorado; The Art Institute of Dallas, A campus of South University; The Art Institute of Fort Lauderdale; The Art Institute of Fort Worth, A campus of South University; The Art Institute of Houston; The Art Institute of Houston—North, A branch of The Art Institute of Houston; The Art Institute of Indianapolis; The Art Institute of Jacksonville, A branch of Miami International University of Art & Design; The Art Institute of Las Vegas; The Art Institute of Michigan; The Art Institute of Michigan—Troy; The Art Institute of New York City; The Art Institute of Ohio—Cincinnati; The Art Institute of Philadelphia; The Art Institute of Phoenix; The Art Institute of Pittsburgh; The Art Institute of Portland; The Art Institute of Raleigh—Durham; The Art Institute of Salt Lake City; The Art Institute of San Antonio, A branch of The Art Institute of Houston; The Art Institute of Seattle; The Art Institute of Tampa, A branch of Miami International University of Art & Design; The Art Institute of Tennessee—Nashville, A branch of The Art Institute of Atlanta; The Art Institute of Tucson; The Art Institute of Vancouver; The Art Institute of Virginia Beach[1], A branch of The Art Institute of Atlanta; The Art Institute of Washington[1], A branch of The Art Institute of Atlanta; The Art Institute of Washington—Dulles[1], A branch of The Art Institute of Atlanta; The Art Institute of Wisconsin; The Art Institute of York—Pennsylvania; The Art Institutes International—Kansas City; The Art Institutes International Minnesota; The Illinois Institute of Art—Chicago; The Illinois Institute of Art—Schaumburg; The Illinois Institute of Art—Tinley Park; Miami International University of Art & Design; The New England Institute of Art

[1]Certified by SCHEV to operate in Virginia

See **aiprograms.info** for program duration, tuition, fees, and other costs, median debt, federal salary data, alumni success, and other important info. The Art Institutes is a system of over 50 schools throughout North America. Programs, credential levels, technology, and scheduling options vary by school, and employment opportunities are not guaranteed. Financial aid is available to those who qualify. Several institutions included in The Art Institutes system are campuses of South University or Argosy University. OH Registration # 04-01-1698B, AC0165, AC0080, Licensed by the Florida Commission for Independent Education, License No. 1287, 3427, 3110, 2581. Administrative office: 210 Sixth Avenue, 33rd Floor, Pittsburgh, PA 15222. ©2012 The Art Institutes International LLC.

THE ART INSTITUTE OF CALIFORNIA, A COLLEGE OF ARGOSY UNIVERSITY, INLAND EMPIRE

A focused education from The Art Institute of California, a college of Argosy University, Inland Empire, can help students turn their creative energy into a powerful tool that can make a difference in the world. Students are part of a collaborative and supportive community, where experienced instructors provide the guidance and skills needed to pursue a career in the creative economy.

The school's programs in the areas of design, media arts, fashion, and culinary give students the opportunity to learn by using professional-grade technology and to build a portfolio of work to show potential employers after graduation.

The Art Institute of California, a college of Argosy University, Inland Empire is a campus of Argosy University. Argosy University is accredited by the Accrediting Commission for Senior Colleges and Universities of the Western Association of Schools and Colleges (985 Atlantic Avenue, Suite 100, Alameda, California, 94501, http://www.wascsenior.org). Accredited Member, ACCSC.

The Art Institute of California, a college of Argosy University, Inland Empire has been granted approval to operate by the California Bureau for Private Post-secondary Education, California Department of Consumer Affairs, 2535 Capitol Oaks Drive, Suite 400, Sacramento, California, 95833; phone: 916-431-6959; www.bppe.ca.gov.

Location

The Art Institute of California, Inland Empire ("The Art Institute of California") is located in San Bernardino. Within a short drive from the school, students can enjoy mountains, deserts, Los Angeles, or Mexico. Surfing, water sports, tennis, golf, jogging, mountain biking, and many other outdoor activities are supported by the region's mild climate.

Programs of Study and Degrees

No matter which course of study a student may choose, the professionals at The Art Institute of California will guide, support, and help each student as their talents evolve on their journey of personal and professional transformation. Students studying design learn to fine-tune their visual thinking and problem-solving skills as they create everything from logos to TV ads. Programs in the area of media arts focus on utilizing technology to deliver information and entertainment, while students studying fashion learn to design clothes for the runway or run a retail shop. Culinary programs focus on the fundamental techniques while exposing students to a full menu of international cuisines and management techniques.

Bachelor's degree programs are offered in the areas of advertising, audio production, culinary management, fashion and retail management, fashion design, game art and design, graphic design, hospitality food and beverage management, interior design, media arts and animation, and Web design and interactive media.

Associate degree programs are offered in the areas of baking and pastry, culinary arts, and graphic design.

Diploma programs are offered in the areas of art of cooking, baking and pastry, fashion retailing, and Web design and interactive communications.

The culinary arts, graphic design, and interior design programs are available in an evening and weekend option format.

Academic Programs

The academic year is divided into four quarters, beginning in January, April, July, and October. Each program is offered on a year-round basis, allowing students to continue to work uninterrupted toward their degrees.

Academic Facilities

The Art Institute of California provides a learning environment with professional-grade technology applicable to each student's course of study. Students have the opportunity to build a portfolio of work that shows potential employers that they are trained to use the software, hardware, or equipment utilized within the industry. Depending upon the course of study, students are immersed in a creative environment—from classrooms to computer labs to studios—focused on relevant, hands-on education designed to prepare students for the real world.

Costs

Tuition cost varies by program. Prospective students should contact the school for current tuition costs. Other charges include a starting kit for all first-quarter students. Kits vary in price, depending on the program of study.

Financial Aid

Financial aid is available for those who qualify. Students who require financial assistance should first complete and submit a Free Application for Federal Student Aid (FAFSA) and meet with a financial aid officer.

Faculty

Faculty members are experienced professionals who create a learning environment that is similar to the professional world students will face after graduation. Instructors are focused on helping students develop the skills they need to transform their creative potential into marketable skills.

Student Government

The Student Federation is responsible for student government and acts as a liaison between the student body and faculty and staff members.

Admission Requirements

Applicants must provide proof of high school graduation or achievement of a General Educational Development (GED) certificate as a prerequisite for admission. In lieu of documenting high school graduation or a GED certificate, applicants may provide proof of attaining an associate degree or higher from an accredited institution. An official transcript indicating date of high school graduation, GED certificate (including test scores), or date of college graduation (including degree granted) is required as proof.

All individuals seeking admission to The Art Institute of California are interviewed in person or by phone by an assistant director of admissions, and each applicant must create an original essay of at least 150 words stating how an education at the school would help the student to achieve career goals. There is a $50 application fee.

For the most recent information regarding admission requirements, please refer to the current academic catalog.

Application and Information

To obtain an application, make arrangements for an interview, or tour the school, prospective students should contact:

The Art Institute of California, a college of Argosy University
674 East Brier Drive
San Bernardino, California 92408-2800
Phone: 909-915-2100
      800-353-0812 (toll-free)
Fax: 909-915-2130
Web site: http://www.artinstitutes.edu/inlandempire

THE ART INSTITUTE OF CALIFORNIA, A COLLEGE OF ARGOSY UNIVERSITY, LOS ANGELES

SANTA MONICA, CALIFORNIA

A focused education from The Art Institute of California, a college of Argosy University, Los Angeles, can help students turn their creative energy into a powerful tool that can make a difference in the world. Students are part of a collaborative and supportive community, where experienced instructors provide the guidance and skills needed to pursue a career in the creative economy.

The school's programs in the areas of design, media arts, fashion, and culinary give students the opportunity to learn by using professional-grade technology and to build a portfolio of work to show potential employers after graduation.

The Art Institute of California, a college of Argosy University, Los Angeles is a campus of Argosy University. Argosy University is accredited by the Accrediting Commission for Senior Colleges and Universities of the Western Association of Schools and Colleges (985 Atlantic Avenue, Suite 100, Alameda, California, 94501, http://www.wascsenior.org).

The Art Institute of California, a college of Argosy University, Los Angeles, is accredited by the Accrediting Council for Independent Colleges and Schools to award associate's degrees and bachelor's degrees. The Accrediting Council for Independent Colleges and Schools is listed as a nationally recognized accrediting agency by the United States Department of Education and is recognized by the Council for Higher Education Accreditation. ACICS can be contacted at 750 First Street NE, Suite 980, Washington, D.C. 20002. Telephone: 202-336-6780.

The Interior Design program leading to the Bachelor of Science Degree is accredited by the Council for Interior Design Accreditation, www.accredit-id.org, 206 Grandville Avenue, Suite 350, Grand Rapids, Michigan 49503. The Bachelor of Science degree in Culinary Arts, the Associate of Science degree in Culinary Arts, the Associate of Science degree in Baking & Pastry, and Diploma programs in Art of Cooking and Baking & Pastry at the Art Institute of California, a college of Argosy University, Los Angeles are accredited by the American Culinary Federation Foundation, Inc. Accrediting Commission, 180 Center Way, St. Augustine, Florida 32095; phone: 800-624-9458.

The Art Institute of California, a college of Argosy University, Los Angeles has been granted approval to operate by the California Bureau for Private Postsecondary Education, California Department of Consumer Affairs, 2535 Capitol Oaks Drive, Suite 400 Sacramento, California 95833; 916-431-6959; www.bppe.ca.gov.

Location

Located in Los Angeles, the arts and entertainment capital of the world, The Art Institute of California, Los Angeles ("The Art Institute of California") is within easy driving distance of the Pacific Coast Highway, Century City, and downtown. The city offers a rich diversity of food, fashion, architecture, entertainment, languages, world views, and religions that are showcased in numerous community and ethnic festivals throughout the year. Leisure activities include hiking on Santa Monica Mountain trails or visits to the Getty Museum, Los Angeles County Museum of Art, or Los Angeles Zoo. Students may also enjoy dining and shopping on Santa Monica's Third Street Promenade or in nearby Westwood Village. Music and theater venues include the Hollywood Bowl, the Greek Theatre, the Music Center, and the Dorothy Chandler Pavilion. Other popular destinations are Watts Towers, the La Brea Tar Pits, Hollywood Boulevard's Walk of Fame, and Mann's Chinese Theater.

Programs of Study and Degrees

No matter which course of study a student may choose, the professionals at The Art Institute of California will guide, support, and help each student as their talents evolve on their journey of personal and professional transformation. Students studying design learn to fine-tune their visual thinking and problem-solving skills as they create everything from logos to TV ads. Programs in the area of media arts focus on utilizing technology to deliver information and entertainment, while students studying fashion learn to design clothes for the runway or run a retail shop. Culinary programs focus on the fundamental techniques while exposing students to a full menu of international cuisines and management techniques.

Bachelor's degree programs are offered in the area of advertising, audio production, culinary management, digital filmmaking and video production, fashion design, fashion marketing and management, game art and design, game programming, graphic design, interior design, media arts and animation, visual effects and motion graphics, and Web design and interactive media.

Associate degree programs are offered in the areas of baking and pastry, culinary arts, digital photography, graphic design, video production, and Web design and interactive media.

Diploma programs are offered in the areas of art of cooking, baking and pastry, fashion retailing, and Web design and interactive communications.

The culinary arts, culinary management, graphic design, and interior design programs are available in an evening and weekend option format.

Academic Programs

The academic year is divided into four quarters that begin in January, April, July, and October. Associate degree candidates must complete 112 academic credits to graduate, including 28 general education credits. These are generally earned over seven quarters. Bachelor's degree candidates must complete 192 credits, including 56 general education credits. These are generally earned over eleven quarters. All students must complete their programs of study with a minimum 2.0 cumulative GPA to meet graduation requirements.

Academic Facilities

The Art Institute of California provides a learning environment with professional-grade technology applicable to each student's course of study. Students have the opportunity to build a portfolio of work that shows potential employers that they are trained to use the software, hardware, or equipment utilized within the industry. Depending upon the course of study, students are immersed in a creative environment—from classrooms to computer labs to studios—focused on relevant, hands-on education designed to prepare students for the real world.

Costs

Tuition cost varies by program. Prospective students should contact the school for current tuition costs. Other charges include a starting kit for all first-quarter students. Kits vary in price depending on the program of study.

Financial Aid

Financial aid is available for those who qualify. Students who require financial assistance should first complete and submit a Free Application for Federal Student Aid (FAFSA) and meet with a financial aid officer.

Faculty

Faculty members are experienced professionals who create a learning environment that is similar to the professional world students will face after graduation. Instructors are focused on helping students develop the skills they need to transform their creative potential into marketable skills.

Student Government

The Associated Student Council provides a forum to discuss student issues, facilitates the exchange of ideas and information among students, and acts as a liaison between students and members of the faculty and administration. It also organizes student activities at the school and provides student leadership opportunities. In addition, the Activities and Events Council consists of an elected board, representatives from each student organization, and other interested students.

Admission Requirements

The admission process at The Art Institute of California includes a student interview with the admissions office (either in person or by phone) and submission of a completed application form, a 150-word essay, high school transcripts or General Educational Development (GED) test scores, and official SAT or ACT scores. There is a $50 application fee.

For the most recent information regarding admission requirements, please refer to the current academic catalog.

Application and Information

To obtain an application, make arrangements for an interview, or tour the school, prospective students should contact:

The Art Institute of California, a college of Argosy University
2900 31st Street
Santa Monica, California 90405-3035
Phone: 310-752-4700
      888-646-4610 (toll-free)
Fax: 310-752-4708
Web site: http://www.artinstitutes.edu/losangeles

Over 50 schools: The Art Institute of Atlanta; The Art Institute of Atlanta—Decatur, A branch of The Art Institute of Atlanta; The Art Institute of Austin, A branch of The Art Institute of Houston; The Art Institute of California, a college of Argosy University, with locations in Hollywood, Inland Empire, Los Angeles, Orange County, Sacramento, San Diego, San Francisco, and Sunnyvale; The Art Institute of Charleston, A branch of The Art Institute of Atlanta; The Art Institute of Charlotte; The Art Institute of Colorado; The Art Institute of Dallas, A campus of South University; The Art Institute of Fort Lauderdale; The Art Institute of Fort Worth, A campus of South University; The Art Institute of Houston; The Art Institute of Houston—North, A branch of The Art Institute of Houston; The Art Institute of Indianapolis; The Art Institute of Jacksonville, A branch of Miami International University of Art & Design; The Art Institute of Las Vegas; The Art Institute of Michigan; The Art Institute of Michigan—Troy; The Art Institute of New York City; The Art Institute of Ohio—Cincinnati; The Art Institute of Philadelphia; The Art Institute of Phoenix; The Art Institute of Pittsburgh; The Art Institute of Portland; The Art Institute of Raleigh–Durham; The Art Institute of Salt Lake City; The Art Institute of San Antonio, A branch of The Art Institute of Houston; The Art Institute of Seattle; The Art Institute of Tampa, A branch of Miami International University of Art & Design; The Art Institute of Tennessee—Nashville, A branch of The Art Institute of Atlanta; The Art Institute of Tucson; The Art Institute of Vancouver; The Art Institute of Virginia Beach[1], A branch of The Art Institute of Atlanta; The Art Institute of Washington[1], A branch of The Art Institute of Atlanta; The Art Institute of Washington—Dulles[1], A branch of The Art Institute of Atlanta; The Art Institute of Wisconsin; The Art Institute of York—Pennsylvania; The Art Institutes International—Kansas City; The Art Institutes International Minnesota; The Illinois Institute of Art—Chicago; The Illinois Institute of Art—Schaumburg; The Illinois Institute of Art—Tinley Park; Miami International University of Art & Design; The New England Institute of Art

[1]Certified by SCHEV to operate in Virginia

See **aiprograms.info** for program duration, tuition, fees, and other costs, median debt, federal salary data, alumni success, and other important info. The Art Institutes is a system of over 50 schools throughout North America. Programs, credential levels, technology, and scheduling options vary by school, and employment opportunities are not guaranteed. Financial aid is available to those who qualify. Several institutions included in The Art Institutes system are campuses of South University or Argosy University. OH Registration # 04-01-1698B, AC0165, AC0080, Licensed by the Florida Commission for Independent Education, License No. 1287, 3427, 3110, 2581. Administrative office: 210 Sixth Avenue, 33rd Floor, Pittsburgh, PA 15222. ©2012 The Art Institutes International LLC.

THE ART INSTITUTE OF CALIFORNIA, A COLLEGE OF ARGOSY UNIVERSITY, ORANGE COUNTY

SANTA ANA, CALIFORNIA

The Art Institute of California
A College of Argosy University

Orange County

A focused education from The Art Institute of California, a college of Argosy University, Orange County, can help students turn their creative energy into a powerful tool that can make a difference in the world. Students are part of a collaborative and supportive community, where experienced instructors provide the guidance and skills needed to pursue a career in the creative economy.

The school's programs in the areas of design, media arts, fashion, and culinary give students the opportunity to learn by using professional-grade technology and to build a portfolio of work to show potential employers after graduation.

The Art Institute of California, a college of Argosy University, Orange County is a campus of Argosy University. Argosy University is accredited by the Accrediting Commission for Senior Colleges and Universities of the Western Association of Schools and Colleges (985 Atlantic Avenue, Suite 100, Alameda, California, 94501, http://www.wascsenior.org). The Art Institute of California, a college of Argosy University, Orange County, is accredited by the Accrediting Council for Independent Colleges and Schools to award associate's degrees and bachelor's degrees. The Accrediting Council for Independent Colleges and Schools is listed as a nationally recognized accrediting agency by the United States Department of Education and is recognized by the Council for Higher Education Accreditation. ACICS can be contacted at 750 First Street NE, Suite 980, Washington, D.C. 20002. Telephone: 202-336-6780.

The Art Institute of California, a college of Argosy University, Orange County has been granted approval to operate by the California Bureau for Private Post-secondary Education, California Department of Consumer Affairs, 2535 Capitol Oaks Drive, Suite 400, Sacramento, California, 95833; phone: 916-431-6959; www.bppe.ca.gov.

The Interior Design program leading to the Bachelor of Science degree is accredited by the Council for Interior Design Accreditation, 206 Grandville Ave., Suite 350, Grand Rapids, Michigan 49503; http://www.accredit-id.org.

Location

The Art Institute of California, Orange County ("The Art Institute of California") is strategically located in the heart of the booming Southern California region that includes the counties of Orange, Los Angeles, San Diego, and Ventura. Southern California is a central hub of the entertainment, advertising, design, aerospace, and culinary industries. Orange County offers 42 miles of beautiful, sandy Pacific Ocean coastline, and wilderness parks are minutes away for camping, hiking, and biking. The area has more than 250 sunny days a year and is home to Disneyland, Knott's Berry Farm, and world-renowned cultural events, including the annual Laguna Beach Festival of the Arts.

Programs of Study and Degrees

No matter which course of study a student may choose, the professionals at The Art Institute of California will guide, support, and help each student as their talents evolve on their journey of personal and professional transformation. Students studying design learn to fine-tune their visual thinking and problem-solving skills as they create everything from logos to TV ads. Programs in the area of media arts focus on utilizing technology to deliver information and entertainment, while students studying fashion learn to design clothes for the runway or run a retail shop. Culinary programs focus on the fundamental techniques while exposing students to a full menu of international cuisines and management techniques.

Bachelor's degree programs are offered in the areas of advertising, culinary management, digital filmmaking and video production, fashion design, fashion marketing and management, game art and design, graphic design, industrial design, interior design, media arts and animation, visual and game programming, visual effects and motion graphics, and Web design and interactive media.

Associate degree programs are offered in the areas of baking and pastry, culinary arts, digital photography, graphic design, and Web design and interactive media.

Diploma programs are offered in the areas of art of cooking, baking and pastry, fashion retailing, and Web design and interactive communications.

The culinary arts, culinary management, graphic design, and interior design programs are available in an evening and weekend option format.

Academic Programs

A bachelor's degree requires the completion of 192 credits, while an associate degree requires the completion of 112 academic credits. The academic year is divided into four quarters that begin in January, April, July, and October. Each program is offered on a year-round basis, allowing students to continue to work uninterrupted toward their degrees.

The school arranges study trips to local cultural and commercial sites. These visits offer an opportunity for valuable exposure to places and events relating to the student's field of study. In addition, out-of-town seminars and visits may be planned in individual programs.

The Student Tutoring Program is a peer-to-peer tutoring assistance program that is available to all current students. Each tutor has unique qualifications in his or her area of expertise.

Academic Facilities

The Art Institute of California provides a learning environment with professional-grade technology applicable to each student's course of study. Students have the opportunity to build a portfolio of work that shows potential employers that they are trained to use the software, hardware, or equipment utilized within the industry. Depending upon the course of study, students are immersed in a creative environment—from classrooms to computer labs to studios—focused on relevant, hands-on education designed to prepare students for the real world.

Costs

Tuition cost varies by program. Prospective students should contact the school for current tuition costs. Other charges include a starting kit for all first-quarter students. Kits vary in price depending on the program of study.

Financial Aid

Financial aid is available for those who qualify. Students who require financial assistance should first complete and submit a Free Application for Federal Student Aid (FAFSA) and meet with a financial aid officer.

Faculty

Faculty members are experienced professionals who create a learning environment that is similar to the professional world students will face after graduation. Instructors are focused on helping students develop the skills they need to transform their creative potential into marketable skills.

Student Government

The President's Club is a group of students who promote the philosophy of "students helping students." Members act as emissaries for the school and as liaisons between students and faculty and staff members. The club assists new students and helps in the organization and promotion of campus activities. Student members must be nominated for the organization by a member of the faculty or staff.

Admission Requirements

Prospective students must hold a high school diploma or General Educational Development (GED) certificate or have earned a bachelor's degree or higher from an accredited institution. High school seniors who have not yet graduated should submit a partial transcript that indicates their expected graduation date. All prospective students are required to submit two essays of approximately one page in length, describing what they expect from the school and how an education at The Art Institute of California may help them to reach their career goals. Applicants are interviewed either in person or by telephone by an assistant director of admissions. In addition, other standardized exams, such as the SAT or ACT, may be considered. Prospective students may apply at any time prior to the start of the upcoming quarter, and applications may be submitted online or mailed directly to the school. There is a $50 application fee.

For the most recent information regarding admission requirements, please refer to the current academic catalog.

Application and Information

To obtain an application, make arrangements for an interview, or tour the school, prospective students should contact:

The Art Institute of California, a college of Argosy University
3601 West Sunflower Avenue
Santa Ana, California 92704-7931
Phone: 714-830-0200
      888-549-3055 (toll-free)
Fax: 714-556-1923
Web site: http://www.artinstitutes.edu/orangecounty

THE ART INSTITUTE OF CALIFORNIA, A COLLEGE OF ARGOSY UNIVERSITY, SACRAMENTO

SACRAMENTO, CALIFORNIA

A focused education from The Art Institute of California, a college of Argosy University, Sacramento, can help students turn their creative energy into a powerful tool that can make a difference in the world. Students are part of a collaborative and supportive community, where experienced instructors provide the guidance and skills needed to pursue a career in the creative economy.

The school's programs in the areas of design, media arts, fashion, and culinary give students the opportunity to learn by using professional-grade technology and to build a portfolio of work to show potential employers after graduation.

The Art Institute of California, a college of Argosy University, Sacramento is a campus of Argosy University. Argosy University is accredited by the Accrediting Commission for Senior Colleges and Universities of the Western Association of Schools and Colleges (985 Atlantic Avenue, Suite 100, Alameda, California, 94501, http://www.wascsenior. org). The Art Institute of California, a college of Argosy University, Sacramento, is accredited by the Accrediting Council for Independent Colleges and Schools to award associate's degrees and bachelor's degrees. The Accrediting Council for Independent Colleges and Schools is listed as a nationally recognized accrediting agency by the United States Department of Education and is recognized by the Council for Higher Education Accreditation. ACICS can be contacted at 750 First Street NE, Suite 980, Washington, D.C. 20002. Telephone: 202-336-6780.

The Art Institute of California, a college of Argosy University, Sacramento has been granted approval to operate by the California Bureau for Private Postsecondary Education, California Department of Consumer Affairs, 2535 Capitol Oaks Drive, Suite 400, Sacramento, California 95833; 916-431-6959; www.bppe.ca.gov.

Location

Sacramento's metropolitan population of more than 2 million means that students have access to recreation and the arts. In addition to state government, the city is a major transportation and commerce hub linking the east with California's coastal cities.

Programs of Study and Degrees

No matter which course of study a student may choose, the professionals at The Art Institute of California, Sacramento ("The Art Institute of California") will guide, support, and help each student as their talents evolve on their journey of personal and professional transformation. Students studying design learn to fine-tune their visual thinking and problem-solving skills as they create everything from logos to TV ads. Programs in the area of media arts focus on utilizing technology to deliver information and entertainment, while students studying fashion learn to design clothes for the runway or run a retail shop. Culinary programs focus on the fundamental techniques while exposing students to a full menu of international cuisines and management techniques.

Bachelor's degree programs are available in the areas of culinary management, digital filmmaking and video production, game art and design, graphic design, interior design, media arts and animation, and Web design and interactive media.

Associate degrees are offered in the areas of baking and pastry, culinary arts, graphic design, and Web design and interactive media.

Diploma programs are offered in the areas of art of cooking, baking and pastry, fashion retailing, and Web design and interactive communications.

Academic Programs

The Art Institute of California operates on a year-round, four-quarter system.

Academic Facilities

The Art Institute of California provides a learning environment with professional-grade technology applicable to each student's course of study. Students have the opportunity to build a portfolio of work that shows potential employers that they are trained to use the software, hardware, or equipment utilized within the industry. Depending upon the course of study, students are immersed in a creative environment—from classrooms to computer labs to studios—focused on relevant, hands-on education designed to prepare students for the real world.

Costs

Tuition cost varies by program. Prospective students should contact the school for current tuition costs. Other charges include a starting kit for all first-quarter students. Kits vary in price depending on the program of study.

Financial Aid

Financial aid is available for those who qualify. Students who require financial assistance should first complete and submit a Free Application for Federal Student Aid (FAFSA) and meet with a financial aid officer.

Faculty

Faculty members are experienced professionals who create a learning environment that is similar to the professional world students will face after graduation. Instructors are focused on helping students develop the skills they need to transform their creative potential into marketable skills.

Admission Requirements

Applicants must provide proof of high school graduation or achievement of a General Educational Development (GED) certificate as a prerequisite for admission. In lieu of documenting high school graduation or a GED certificate, applicants may provide proof of attaining an associate degree or higher from an accredited institution. An official transcript indicating date of high school graduation, GED certificate (including test scores), or date of college graduation (including degree granted) is required as proof.

All individuals seeking admission to The Art Institute of California are interviewed in person or by phone by an assistant director of admissions, and each applicant must create an original essay of at least 150 words stating how an education at The Art Institute of California would help the student achieve career goals. There is a $50 application fee.

For the most recent information regarding admission requirements, please refer to the current academic catalog.

Application and Information

To obtain an application, make arrangements for an interview, or tour the school, prospective students should contact:

The Art Institute of California, a college of Argosy University
2850 Gateway Oaks Drive, Suite #100
Sacramento, California 95833
Phone: 916-830-6320
        800-477-1957 (toll-free)
Fax: 916-830-6344
Web site: http://www.artinstitutes.edu/sacramento

THE ART INSTITUTE OF CALIFORNIA, A COLLEGE OF ARGOSY UNIVERSITY, SAN DIEGO

SAN DIEGO, CALIFORNIA

A focused education from The Art Institute of California, a college of Argosy University, San Diego, can help students turn their creative energy into a powerful tool that can make a difference in the world. Students are part of a collaborative and supportive community, where experienced instructors provide the guidance and skills needed to pursue a career in the creative economy.

The school's programs in the areas of design, media arts, fashion, and culinary give students the opportunity to learn by using professional-grade technology and to build a portfolio of work to show potential employers after graduation.

The Art Institute of California, a college of Argosy University, San Diego is a campus of Argosy University. Argosy University is accredited by the Accrediting Commission for Senior Colleges and Universities of the Western Association of Schools and Colleges (985 Atlantic Avenue, Suite 100, Alameda, California, 94501; http://www.wascsenior.org). The Art Institute of California, a college of Argosy University, San Diego, is accredited by the Accrediting Commission of Career Schools and Colleges (ACCSC). ACCSC may be contacted at 2101 Wilson Boulevard., Suite 302, Arlington, Virginia 22201; Phone: 703-247-4212.

The Associate of Science degree in Culinary Arts is accredited by the Accrediting Commission of the American Culinary Federation Education Foundation.

The Art Institute of California, a college of Argosy University, San Diego of has been granted approval to operate by the California Bureau for Private Post-secondary Education, California Department of Consumer Affairs, 2535 Capitol Oaks Drive, Suite 400, Sacramento, California, 95833; phone: 916-431-6959; www.bppe.ca.gov.

Location

Within a 2-hour drive are mountains, deserts, Los Angeles, Mexico, surfing, water sports, tennis, golf, jogging, mountain biking, and beaches. San Diego offers many regional shopping centers as well as picturesque spots, including the San Diego Zoo, Wild Animal Park, Sea World, Seaport Village, Old Town, Horton Plaza, the Gaslamp District, and La Jolla. The opera, symphony, live theater district, professional and collegiate athletic events, and concerts are also nearby. San Diego's average daytime temperature is 70 degrees, and the city averages 267 sunny days each year.

Programs of Study and Degrees

No matter which course of study a student may choose, the professionals at The Art Institute of California, San Diego ("The Art Institute of California" will guide, support, and help each student as their talents evolve on their journey of personal and professional transformation. Students studying design learn to fine-tune their visual thinking and problem-solving skills as they create everything from logos to TV ads. Programs in the area of media arts focus on utilizing technology to deliver information and entertainment, while students studying fashion learn to design clothes for the runway or run a retail shop. Culinary programs focus on the fundamental techniques while exposing students to a full menu of international cuisines and management techniques.

Bachelor's degree programs are offered in the areas of advertising, audio production, culinary management, fashion design, fashion marketing and management, game art and design, graphic design, hospitality food and beverage management, interior design, media arts and animation, visual and game programming, and Web design and interactive media.

Associate degree programs are available in the areas of advertising, baking and pastry, culinary arts, and graphic design.

Diploma programs are offered in the areas of art of cooking, baking and pastry, fashion retailing, and Web design and interactive communications.

The Bachelor of Science degree programs in graphic design and interior design are also available in an evening and weekend option format.

Academic Programs

The Art Institute of California operates on a year-round, four-quarter system.

Academic Facilities

The Art Institute of California provides a learning environment with professional-grade technology applicable to each student's course of study. Students have the opportunity to build a portfolio of work that shows potential employers that they are trained to use the software, hardware, or equipment utilized within the industry. Depending upon the course of study, students are immersed in a creative environment—from classrooms to computer labs to studios—focused on relevant, hands-on education designed to prepare students for the real world.

Costs

Tuition cost varies by program. Prospective students should contact the school for current tuition costs. Other charges include a starting kit for all first-quarter students. Kits vary in price depending on the program of study.

Financial Aid

Financial aid is available for those who qualify. Students who require financial assistance should first complete and submit a Free Application for Federal Student Aid (FAFSA) and meet with a financial aid officer.

Faculty

Faculty members are experienced professionals who create a learning environment that is similar to the professional world students will face after graduation. Instructors are focused on helping students develop the skills they need to transform their creative potential into marketable skills.

Admission Requirements

Prospective students must be high school graduates or hold a General Educational Development (GED) certificate. High school seniors who have not yet graduated should submit a partial transcript that indicates their expected graduation date. All prospective students are required to write an essay of approximately 150 words describing how an education at The Art Institute of California will help them to attain their creative goals. An interview, either in person or by telephone, is required. SAT or ACT scores may also be considered. Applications may be submitted online or mailed to the school. There is a $50 application fee.

For the most recent information regarding admission requirements, please refer to the current academic catalog.

Application and Information

To obtain an application, make arrangements for an interview, or tour the school, prospective students should contact:

The Art Institute of California, a college of Argosy University
7650 Mission Valley Road
San Diego, California 92108-4423
Phone: 858-598-1200
        866-275-2422 (toll-free)
Fax: 619-291-3206
Web site: http://www.artinstitutes.edu/sandiego

Over 50 schools: The Art Institute of Atlanta; The Art Institute of Atlanta—Decatur, A branch of The Art Institute of Atlanta; The Art Institute of Austin, A branch of The Art Institute of Houston; The Art Institute of California, a college of Argosy University, with locations in Hollywood, Inland Empire, Los Angeles, Orange County, Sacramento, San Diego, San Francisco, and Sunnyvale; The Art Institute of Charleston, A branch of The Art Institute of Atlanta; The Art Institute of Charlotte; The Art Institute of Colorado; The Art Institute of Dallas, A campus of South University; The Art Institute of Fort Lauderdale; The Art Institute of Fort Worth, A campus of South University; The Art Institute of Houston; The Art Institute of Houston—North, A branch of The Art Institute of Houston; The Art Institute of Indianapolis; The Art Institute of Jacksonville, A branch of Miami International University of Art & Design; The Art Institute of Las Vegas; The Art Institute of Michigan; The Art Institute of Michigan—Troy; The Art Institute of New York City; The Art Institute of Ohio—Cincinnati; The Art Institute of Philadelphia; The Art Institute of Phoenix; The Art Institute of Pittsburgh; The Art Institute of Portland; The Art Institute of Raleigh–Durham; The Art Institute of Salt Lake City; The Art Institute of San Antonio, A branch of The Art Institute of Houston; The Art Institute of Seattle; The Art Institute of Tampa, A branch of Miami International University of Art & Design; The Art Institute of Tennessee—Nashville, A branch of The Art Institute of Atlanta; The Art Institute of Tucson; The Art Institute of Vancouver; The Art Institute of Virginia Beach[1], A branch of The Art Institute of Atlanta; The Art Institute of Washington[1], A branch of The Art Institute of Atlanta; The Art Institute of Washington—Dulles[1], A branch of The Art Institute of Atlanta; The Art Institute of Wisconsin; The Art Institute of York—Pennsylvania; The Art Institutes International—Kansas City; The Art Institutes International Minnesota; The Illinois Institute of Art—Chicago; The Illinois Institute of Art—Schaumburg; The Illinois Institute of Art—Tinley Park; Miami International University of Art & Design; The New England Institute of Art

[1]Certified by SCHEV to operate in Virginia

See **aiprograms.info** for program duration, tuition, fees, and other costs, median debt, federal salary data, alumni success, and other important info. The Art Institutes is a system of over 50 schools throughout North America. Programs, credential levels, technology, and scheduling options vary by school, and employment opportunities are not guaranteed. Financial aid is available to those who qualify. Several institutions included in The Art Institutes system are campuses of South University or Argosy University. OH Registration # 04-01-1698B, AC0165, AC0080, Licensed by the Florida Commission for Independent Education, License No. 1287, 3427, 3110, 2581. Administrative office: 210 Sixth Avenue, 33rd Floor, Pittsburgh, PA 15222. ©2012 The Art Institutes International LLC.

THE ART INSTITUTE OF CALIFORNIA, A COLLEGE OF ARGOSY UNIVERSITY, SAN FRANCISCO

SAN FRANCISCO, CALIFORNIA

A focused education from The Art Institute of California, a college of Argosy University, San Francisco, can help students turn their creative energy into a powerful tool that can make a difference in the world. Students are part of a collaborative and supportive community, where experienced instructors provide the guidance and skills needed to pursue a career in the creative economy.

The school's programs in the areas of design, media arts, fashion, and culinary give students the opportunity to learn by using professional-grade technology and to build a portfolio of work to show potential employers after graduation.

The Art Institute of California, a college of Argosy University, San Francisco is a campus of Argosy University. Argosy University is accredited by the Accrediting Commission for Senior Colleges and Universities of the Western Association of Schools and Colleges (985 Atlantic Avenue, Suite 100, Alameda, California, 94501, http://www.wascsenior.org). The Art Institute of California, a college of Argosy University, San Francisco, is accredited by the Accrediting Council for Independent Colleges and Schools to award associate's degrees and bachelor's degrees. The Accrediting Council for Independent Colleges and Schools is listed as a nationally recognized accrediting agency by the United States Department of Education and is recognized by the Council for Higher Education Accreditation. ACICS can be contacted at 750 First Street NE, Suite 980, Washington, D.C. 20002. Telephone: 202-336-6780.

The Art Institute of California, a college of Argosy University, San Francisco has been granted approval to operate by the California Bureau for Private Post-secondary Education, California Department of Consumer Affairs, 2535 Capitol Oaks Drive, Suite 400, Sacramento, California 95833; phone: 916-431-6959; http://www.bppe.ca.gov.

Location

The Art Institute of California, San Francisco ("The Art Institute of California") is located on Market Street, in the center of downtown San Francisco. San Francisco is home to the Golden Gate Bridge, Alcatraz Island, and the Haight-Ashbury district. With a population of more than 700,000, San Francisco has the highest concentration of arts organizations in the world. Students have access to public libraries, including the Center of Performing Arts Library with its specialized sections on fashion and costuming. Natural attractions include the rolling hills and mountains in nearby wine country and dramatic vistas overlooking the Pacific, which provide options for hiking, biking, and other outdoor activities. Asian, Hispanic, and Italian neighborhoods are within walking distance. Public transportation, including cable cars, is available. The Bay Area and nearby Silicon Valley are home to leading new-media companies.

Programs of Study and Degrees

No matter which course of study a student may choose, the professionals at The Art Institute of California will guide, support, and help each student as their talents evolve on their journey of personal and professional transformation. Students studying design learn to fine-tune their visual thinking and problem-solving skills as they create everything from logos to TV ads. Programs in the area of media arts focus on utilizing technology to deliver information and entertainment, while students studying fashion learn to design clothes for the runway or run a retail shop. Culinary programs focus on the fundamental techniques while exposing students to a full menu of international cuisines and management techniques.

Bachelor's degree programs are offered in the areas of advertising, audio production, culinary management, digital filmmaking and video production, fashion design, fashion marketing and management, game art and design, graphic design, interior design, media arts and animation, visual and game programming, visual effects and motion graphics, and Web design and interactive media.

Associate degree programs are available in the areas of baking and pastry, culinary arts, digital photography, fashion design, fashion marketing, graphic design, and Web design and interactive media.

Diploma programs are offered in the areas of art of cooking, baking and pastry, fashion retailing, and Web design and interactive communications.

A Master of Fine Arts degree in computer animation is offered.

Academic Programs

The academic year is divided into four quarters that begin in January, April, July, and October. A bachelor's degree requires completion of 192 credits. An associate degree requires completion of 112 academic credits.

Academic Facilities

The Art Institute of California provides a learning environment with professional-grade technology applicable to each student's course of study. Students have the opportunity to build a portfolio of work that shows potential employers that they are trained to use the software, hardware, or equipment utilized within the industry. Depending upon the course of study, students are immersed in a creative environment—from classrooms to computer labs to studios—focused on relevant, hands-on education designed to prepare students for the real world.

Costs

Tuition cost varies by program. Prospective students should contact the school for current tuition costs. Other charges

include a starting kit for all first-quarter students. Kits vary in price, depending on the program of study.

Financial Aid

Financial aid is available for those who qualify. Students who require financial assistance should first complete and submit a Free Application for Federal Student Aid (FAFSA) and meet with a financial aid officer.

Faculty

Faculty members are experienced professionals who create a learning environment that is similar to the professional world students will face after graduation. Instructors are focused on helping students develop the skills they need to transform their creative potential into marketable skills.

Student Government

The Student Federation is responsible for student government and acts as a liaison between the student body and faculty and staff members.

Admission Requirements

Prospective students must submit an application for admission, record of proof of high school graduation or a General Educational Development (GED) certificate, high school transcripts, and SAT or ACT scores, if available. High school seniors who have not yet graduated should submit a partial transcript that indicates their expected graduation date. Portfolios are welcomed but are not required. Applicants are evaluated on the basis of their previous education, background, and stated or demonstrated interest in the school's programs. Students must be interviewed either in person or via telephone by an assistant director of admissions. Prospective students may apply at any time prior to the start of the upcoming quarter. There is a $50 application fee.

For the most recent information regarding admission requirements, please refer to the current academic catalog.

Application and Information

To obtain an application, make arrangements for an interview, or tour the school, prospective students should contact:

The Art Institute of California, a college of Argosy University
1170 Market Street
San Francisco, California 94102-4928
Phone: 415-865-0198
        888-493-3261 (toll-free)
Fax: 415-863-6344
Web site: http://www.artinstitutes.edu/sanfrancisco

Over 50 schools: The Art Institute of Atlanta; The Art Institute of Atlanta—Decatur, A branch of The Art Institute of Atlanta; The Art Institute of Austin, A branch of The Art Institute of Houston; The Art Institute of California, a college of Argosy University, with locations in Hollywood, Inland Empire, Los Angeles, Orange County, Sacramento, San Diego, San Francisco, and Sunnyvale; The Art Institute of Charleston, A branch of The Art Institute of Atlanta; The Art Institute of Charlotte; The Art Institute of Colorado; The Art Institute of Dallas, A campus of South University; The Art Institute of Fort Lauderdale; The Art Institute of Fort Worth, A campus of South University; The Art Institute of Houston; The Art Institute of Houston—North, A branch of The Art Institute of Houston; The Art Institute of Indianapolis; The Art Institute of Jacksonville, A branch of Miami International University of Art & Design; The Art Institute of Las Vegas; The Art Institute of Michigan; The Art Institute of Michigan—Troy; The Art Institute of New York City; The Art Institute of Ohio—Cincinnati; The Art Institute of Philadelphia; The Art Institute of Phoenix; The Art Institute of Pittsburgh; The Art Institute of Portland; The Art Institute of Raleigh–Durham; The Art Institute of Salt Lake City; The Art Institute of San Antonio, A branch of The Art Institute of Houston; The Art Institute of Seattle; The Art Institute of Tampa, A branch of Miami International University of Art & Design; The Art Institute of Tennessee—Nashville, A branch of The Art Institute of Atlanta; The Art Institute of Tucson; The Art Institute of Vancouver; The Art Institute of Virginia Beach[1], A branch of The Art Institute of Atlanta; The Art Institute of Washington[1], A branch of The Art Institute of Atlanta; The Art Institute of Washington—Dulles[1], A branch of The Art Institute of Atlanta; The Art Institute of Wisconsin; The Art Institute of York—Pennsylvania; The Art Institutes International—Kansas City; The Art Institutes International Minnesota; The Illinois Institute of Art—Chicago; The Illinois Institute of Art—Schaumburg; The Illinois Institute of Art—Tinley Park; Miami International University of Art & Design; The New England Institute of Art

[1]Certified by SCHEV to operate in Virginia

See **aiprograms.info** for program duration, tuition, fees, and other costs, median debt, federal salary data, alumni success, and other important info. The Art Institutes is a system of over 50 schools throughout North America. Programs, credential levels, technology, and scheduling options vary by school, and employment opportunities are not guaranteed. Financial aid is available to those who qualify. Several institutions included in The Art Institutes system are campuses of South University or Argosy University. OH Registration # 04-01-1698B, AC0165, AC0080, Licensed by the Florida Commission for Independent Education, License No. 1287, 3427, 3110, 2581. Administrative office: 210 Sixth Avenue, 33rd Floor, Pittsburgh, PA 15222. ©2012 The Art Institutes International LLC.

THE ART INSTITUTE OF CALIFORNIA, A COLLEGE OF ARGOSY UNIVERSITY, SUNNYVALE

SUNNYVALE, CALIFORNIA

A focused education from The Art Institute of California, a college of Argosy University, Sunnyvale, can help students turn their creative energy into a powerful tool that can make a difference in the world. Students are part of a collaborative and supportive community, where experienced instructors provide the guidance and skills needed to pursue a career in the creative economy.

The school's programs in the areas of design, media arts, fashion, and culinary give students the opportunity to learn by using professional-grade technology and build a portfolio of work to show potential employers after graduation.

The Art Institute of California, a college of Argosy University, Sunnyvale is a campus of Argosy University. Argosy University is accredited by the Accrediting Commission for Senior Colleges and Universities of the Western Association of Schools and Colleges (985 Atlantic Avenue, Suite 100, Alameda, California, 94501, http://www.wascsenior.org). The Art Institute of California, a college of Argosy University, Sunnyvale, is accredited by the Accrediting Council for Independent Colleges and Schools to award associate's degrees and bachelor's degrees. The Accrediting Council for Independent Colleges and Schools is listed as a nationally recognized accrediting agency by the United States Department of Education and is recognized by the Council for Higher Education Accreditation. ACICS can be contacted at 750 First Street NE, Suite 980, Washington, D.C. 20002. Telephone: 202-336-6780.

The Art Institute of California, a college of Argosy University, Sunnyvale has been granted approval to operate by the California Bureau for Private Post-secondary Education, California Department of Consumer Affairs, 2535 Capitol Oaks Drive, Suite 400, Sacramento, California 95833; phone: 916-431-6959; www.bppe.ca.gov.

Location

Sunnyvale, a town of over 131,000 people, is one of the major cities that make up California's Silicon Valley. It's located between the San Francisco Bay and San Jose, providing easy access to cultural exhibitions, art museums, professional sports, and other entertainment options.

Programs of Study and Degrees

No matter which course of study a student may choose, the professionals at The Art Institute of California, Sunnyvale

("The Art Institute of California") will guide, support, and help each student as their talents evolve on their journey of personal and professional transformation. Students studying design learn to fine-tune their visual thinking and problem-solving skills as they create everything from logos to TV ads. Programs in the area of media arts focus on utilizing technology to deliver information and entertainment, while students studying fashion learn to design clothes for the runway or run a retail shop. Culinary programs focus on the fundamental techniques while exposing students to a full menu of international cuisines and management techniques.

Bachelor's degree programs are offered in the areas of culinary management, digital filmmaking and video production, digital photography, fashion marketing and management, game art and design, graphic design, interior design, media arts and animation, visual effects and motion graphics, and Web design and interactive media.

Associate degrees are offered in the areas of culinary arts, digital photography, graphic design, and Web design and interactive media.

Diploma programs are available in the areas of fashion retailing and Web design and interactive communications.

Academic Programs

The Art Institute of California operates on a year-round, four-quarter system.

Academic Facilities

The Art Institute of California provides a learning environment with professional-grade technology applicable to each student's course of study. Students have the opportunity to build a portfolio of work that shows potential employers that they are trained to use the software, hardware, or equipment utilized within the industry. Depending upon the course of study, students are immersed in a creative environment—from classrooms to computer labs to studios—focused on relevant, hands-on education designed to prepare students for the real world.

Costs

Tuition cost varies by program. Prospective students should contact the school for current tuition costs. Other charges

include a starting kit for all first-quarter students. Kits vary in price depending on the program of study.

Financial Aid

Financial aid is available for those who qualify. Students who require financial assistance should first complete and submit a Free Application for Federal Student Aid (FAFSA) and meet with a financial aid officer.

Faculty

Faculty members are experienced professionals who create a learning environment that is similar to the professional world students will face after graduation. Instructors are focused on helping students develop the skills they need to transform their creative potential into marketable skills.

Admission Requirements

Applicants must provide proof of high school graduation or achievement of a General Educational Development (GED) certificate as a prerequisite for admission. In lieu of documenting high school graduation or a GED certificate, applicants may provide proof of attaining an associate degree or higher from an accredited institution. An official transcript indicating date of high school graduation, GED certificate (including test scores), or date of college graduation (including degree granted) is required as proof.

All individuals seeking admission to The Art Institute of California are interviewed in person or by phone by an assistant director of admissions, and each applicant must create an original essay of at least 150 words stating how an education at The Art Institute of California would help the student to achieve career goals. There is a $50 application fee.

For the most recent information regarding admission requirements, please refer to the current academic catalog.

Application and Information

To obtain an application, make arrangements for an interview, or tour the school, prospective students should contact:

The Art Institute of California, a college of Argosy University
1120 Kifer Road
Sunnyvale, California 94086
Phone: 408-962-6400
        866-583-7961 (toll-free)
Fax: 408-962-6498
Web site: http://www.artinstitutes.edu/sunnyvale

Over 50 schools: The Art Institute of Atlanta; The Art Institute of Atlanta—Decatur, A branch of The Art Institute of Atlanta; The Art Institute of Austin, A branch of The Art Institute of Houston; The Art Institute of California, a college of Argosy University, with locations in Hollywood, Inland Empire, Los Angeles, Orange County, Sacramento, San Diego, San Francisco, and Sunnyvale; The Art Institute of Charleston, A branch of The Art Institute of Atlanta; The Art Institute of Charlotte; The Art Institute of Colorado; The Art Institute of Dallas, A campus of South University; The Art Institute of Fort Lauderdale; The Art Institute of Fort Worth, A campus of South University; The Art Institute of Houston; The Art Institute of Houston—North, A branch of The Art Institute of Houston; The Art Institute of Indianapolis; The Art Institute of Jacksonville, A branch of Miami International University of Art & Design; The Art Institute of Las Vegas; The Art Institute of Michigan; The Art Institute of Michigan—Troy; The Art Institute of New York City; The Art Institute of Ohio—Cincinnati; The Art Institute of Philadelphia; The Art Institute of Phoenix; The Art Institute of Pittsburgh; The Art Institute of Portland; The Art Institute of Raleigh–Durham; The Art Institute of Salt Lake City; The Art Institute of San Antonio, A branch of The Art Institute of Houston; The Art Institute of Seattle; The Art Institute of Tampa, A branch of Miami International University of Art & Design; The Art Institute of Tennessee—Nashville, A branch of The Art Institute of Atlanta; The Art Institute of Tucson; The Art Institute of Vancouver; The Art Institute of Virginia Beach[1], A branch of The Art Institute of Atlanta; The Art Institute of Washington[1], A branch of The Art Institute of Atlanta; The Art Institute of Washington—Dulles[1], A branch of The Art Institute of Atlanta; The Art Institute of Wisconsin; The Art Institute of York—Pennsylvania; The Art Institutes International—Kansas City; The Art Institutes International Minnesota; The Illinois Institute of Art—Chicago; The Illinois Institute of Art—Schaumburg; The Illinois Institute of Art—Tinley Park; Miami International University of Art & Design; The New England Institute of Art

[1]Certified by SCHEV to operate in Virginia

See **aiprograms.info** for program duration, tuition, fees, and other costs, median debt, federal salary data, alumni success, and other important info. The Art Institutes is a system of over 50 schools throughout North America. Programs, credential levels, technology, and scheduling options vary by school, and employment opportunities are not guaranteed. Financial aid is available to those who qualify. Several institutions included in The Art Institutes system are campuses of South University or Argosy University. OH Registration # 04-01-1698B, AC0165, AC0080, Licensed by the Florida Commission for Independent Education, License No. 1287, 3427, 3110, 2581. Administrative office: 210 Sixth Avenue, 33rd Floor, Pittsburgh, PA 15222. ©2012 The Art Institutes International LLC.

THE ART INSTITUTE OF CHARLESTON
CHARLESTON, SOUTH CAROLINA

The Art Institute of Charleston
A branch of The Art Institute of Atlanta
CREATE TOMORROW

A focused education from The Art Institute of Charleston, a branch of The Art Institute of Atlanta, can help students turn their creative energy into a powerful tool that can make a difference in the world. Students are part of a collaborative and supportive community, where experienced instructors provide the guidance and skills needed to pursue a career in the creative economy.

The school's programs in the areas of design, media arts, fashion, and culinary give students the opportunity to learn by using professional-grade technology and to build a portfolio of work to show potential employers after graduation.

The Art Institute of Charleston is a branch campus of The Art Institute of Atlanta. The Art Institute of Atlanta is accredited by the Commission on Colleges of the Southern Association of Colleges and Schools to award associate and baccalaureate degrees. For questions about the accreditation of The Art Institute of Atlanta, contact the Commission on Colleges at 1866 Southern Lane, Decatur, Georgia 30033-4097; phone: 404-679-4500.

The Art Institute of Charleston is licensed by the South Carolina Commission on Higher Education, 1122 Lady Street, Suite 300, Columbia, South Carolina 29201; phone: 803-737-2260. Licensure indicates only that minimum standards have been met; it is not equal to or synonymous with accreditation by an accrediting agency recognized by the U.S. Department of Education.

Location

Charleston, the second largest city in South Carolina, is located at the confluence of the Ashley and Cooper rivers. A city known for its history, Charleston is also known for its music, art, culinary, and fashion scene.

Programs of Study and Degrees

No matter which course of study a student may choose, the professionals at The Art Institute of Charleston will guide, support, and help each student as their talents evolve on their journey of personal and professional transformation. Students studying design learn to fine-tune their visual thinking and problem-solving skills as they create everything from logos to TV ads. Programs in the area of media arts focus on utilizing technology to deliver information and entertainment, while students studying fashion learn to design clothes for the runway or run a retail shop. Culinary programs focus on the fundamental techniques while

exposing students to a full menu of international cuisines and management techniques.

Bachelor's degree programs are offered in the areas of culinary arts management, digital filmmaking and video production, fashion and retail management, graphic design, interior design, photographic imaging, and Web design and interactive media.

Associate degree programs are offered in the areas of culinary arts, culinary arts with a concentration in baking and pastry, graphic design, Web design and interactive media, and wine, spirits, and beverage management.*

Certificate programs are available in the areas of baking and pastry, culinary arts, digital image management, fashion retailing, Web design and development, and Web design and interactive communications.

*Participation in the program for those under 21 years of age will be conducted in accord with state law regarding the possession and consumption of alcoholic beverages.

Academic Programs

The Art Institute of Charleston operates on a year-round, four-quarter system.

Academic Facilities

The Art Institute of Charleston provides a learning environment with professional-grade technology applicable to each student's course of study. Students have the opportunity to build a portfolio of work that shows potential employers that they are trained to use the software, hardware, or equipment utilized within the industry. Depending upon the course of study, students are immersed in a creative environment—from classrooms to computer labs to studios—focused on relevant, hands-on education designed to prepare students for the real world.

Costs

Tuition cost varies by program. Prospective students should contact the school for current tuition costs. Other charges include a starting kit for all first-quarter students. Kits vary in price depending on the program of study.

Financial Aid

Financial aid is available for those who qualify. Students who require financial assistance should first complete and submit a Free Application for Federal Student Aid (FAFSA) and meet with a financial aid officer.

Faculty

Faculty members are experienced professionals who create a learning environment that is similar to the professional world students will face after graduation. Instructors are focused on helping students develop the skills they need to transform their creative potential into marketable skills.

Admission Requirements

Applicants must provide proof of high school graduation or achievement of a General Educational Development (GED) certificate as a prerequisite for admission.

In lieu of documenting high school graduation or a GED certificate, applicants may provide proof of attaining an associate degree or higher from an accredited institution. An official transcript indicating date of high school graduation, GED certificate (including test scores), or date of college graduation (including degree granted) is required as proof.

All individuals seeking admission to The Art Institute of Charleston are interviewed in person or by phone by an assistant director of admissions, and each applicant must create an original essay of at least 150 words stating how an education at The Art Institute of Charleston would help the student to achieve career goals. There is a $50 application fee.

For the most recent information regarding admission requirements, please refer to the current academic catalog.

Application and Information

To obtain an application, make arrangements for an interview, or tour the school, prospective students should contact:

The Art Institute of Charleston
A branch of The Art Institute of Atlanta
24 North Market Street
Charleston, South Carolina 29401-2623
Phone: 843-727-3500
          866-211-0107 (toll-free)
Fax: 843-727-3440
Web site: http://www.artinstitutes.edu/charleston

Over 50 schools: The Art Institute of Atlanta; The Art Institute of Atlanta—Decatur, A branch of The Art Institute of Atlanta; The Art Institute of Austin, A branch of The Art Institute of Houston; The Art Institute of California, a college of Argosy University, with locations in Hollywood, Inland Empire, Los Angeles, Orange County, Sacramento, San Diego, San Francisco, and Sunnyvale; The Art Institute of Charleston, A branch of The Art Institute of Atlanta; The Art Institute of Charlotte; The Art Institute of Colorado; The Art Institute of Dallas, A campus of South University; The Art Institute of Fort Lauderdale; The Art Institute of Fort Worth, A campus of South University; The Art Institute of Houston; The Art Institute of Houston—North, A branch of The Art Institute of Houston; The Art Institute of Indianapolis; The Art Institute of Jacksonville, A branch of Miami International University of Art & Design; The Art Institute of Las Vegas; The Art Institute of Michigan; The Art Institute of Michigan—Troy; The Art Institute of New York City; The Art Institute of Ohio—Cincinnati; The Art Institute of Philadelphia; The Art Institute of Phoenix; The Art Institute of Pittsburgh; The Art Institute of Portland; The Art Institute of Raleigh–Durham; The Art Institute of Salt Lake City; The Art Institute of San Antonio, A branch of The Art Institute of Houston; The Art Institute of Seattle; The Art Institute of Tampa, A branch of Miami International University of Art & Design; The Art Institute of Tennessee—Nashville, A branch of The Art Institute of Atlanta; The Art Institute of Tucson; The Art Institute of Vancouver; The Art Institute of Virginia Beach[1], A branch of The Art Institute of Atlanta; The Art Institute of Washington[1], A branch of The Art Institute of Atlanta; The Art Institute of Washington—Dulles[1], A branch of The Art Institute of Atlanta; The Art Institute of Wisconsin; The Art Institute of York—Pennsylvania; The Art Institutes International—Kansas City; The Art Institutes International Minnesota; The Illinois Institute of Art—Chicago; The Illinois Institute of Art—Schaumburg; The Illinois Institute of Art—Tinley Park; Miami International University of Art & Design; The New England Institute of Art

[1]Certified by SCHEV to operate in Virginia

See **aiprograms.info** for program duration, tuition, fees, and other costs, median debt, federal salary data, alumni success, and other important info. The Art Institutes is a system of over 50 schools throughout North America. Programs, credential levels, technology, and scheduling options vary by school, and employment opportunities are not guaranteed. Financial aid is available to those who qualify. Several institutions included in The Art Institutes system are campuses of South University or Argosy University. OH Registration # 04-01-1698B, AC0165, AC0080, Licensed by the Florida Commission for Independent Education, License No. 1287, 3427, 3110, 2581. Administrative office: 210 Sixth Avenue, 33rd Floor, Pittsburgh, PA 15222. ©2012 The Art Institutes International LLC.

THE ART INSTITUTE OF CHARLOTTE
CHARLOTTE, NORTH CAROLINA

The Art Institute of Charlotte®

CREATE TOMORROW

A focused education from The Art Institute of Charlotte can help students turn their creative energy into a powerful tool that can make a difference in the world. Students are part of a collaborative and supportive community, where experienced instructors provide the guidance and skills needed to pursue a career in the creative economy.

The school's programs in the areas of design, media arts, fashion, and culinary give students the opportunity to learn by using professional-grade technology and to build a portfolio of work to show potential employers after graduation.

The Art Institute of Charlotte is accredited by the Accrediting Council for Independent Colleges and Schools to award certificates and associate and baccalaureate degrees. The Accrediting Council for Independent Colleges and Schools is listed as a nationally recognized accrediting agency by the United States Department of Education and is recognized by the Council for Higher Education Accreditation. ACICS can be contacted at 750 First Street NE, Suite 980, Washington, D.C. 20002; phone: 202-336-6780.

The Art Institute of Charlotte is licensed to award certificates by the North Carolina State Board of Community Colleges and is licensed to award associate and baccalaureate degrees by the Board of Governors of the University of North Carolina.

The Associate of Applied Science in Culinary Arts program is accredited by The Accrediting Commission of the American Culinary Federation Education Foundation.

Location

Charlotte mixes the characteristics of a large urban center with the charm of suburban life. With a mild climate and central location, Charlotte residents are only 2 hours from the Blue Ridge Mountains and 3 hours from the Atlantic coast. Charlotte is known for its arts community, sports, shopping, and restaurants. More than 300 Fortune 500 companies have offices in Charlotte, the nation's second-largest banking center and fifth-largest urban region, with 6.3 million people living within a 100-mile radius.

Programs of Study and Degrees

No matter which course of study a student may choose, the professionals at The Art Institute of Charlotte will guide, support, and help each student as their talents evolve on their journey of personal and professional transformation. Students studying design learn to fine-tune their visual thinking and problem-solving skills as they create everything from logos to TV ads. Programs in the area of media arts focus on utilizing technology to deliver information and entertainment, while students studying fashion learn to design clothes for the runway or run a retail shop. Culinary programs focus on the fundamental techniques while exposing students to a full menu of international cuisines and management techniques.

Bachelor's degree programs are available in the areas of culinary arts management, digital filmmaking and video production, fashion marketing and management, graphic design, interior design, photography, and Web design and interactive media.

Associate degree programs are offered in the areas of culinary arts, digital filmmaking and video production, fashion marketing, graphic design, interior design, photography, and Web design and interactive media.

Certificate programs are available in the areas of art of cooking, baking and pastry, digital image management, fashion retailing, Web design, Web design and development, and Web design and interactive communications.

Academic Programs

The Art Institute of Charlotte operates on a year-round, four-quarter system.

Academic Facilities

The Art Institute of Charlotte provides a learning environment with professional-grade technology applicable to each student's course of study. Students have the opportunity to build a portfolio of work that shows potential employers that they are trained to use the software, hardware, or equipment utilized within the industry. Depending upon the course of study, students are immersed in a creative environment—from classrooms to computer

labs to studios—focused on relevant, hands-on education designed to prepare students for the real world.

Costs

Tuition cost varies by program. Prospective students should contact the school for current tuition costs. Other charges include a starting kit for all first-quarter students. Kits vary in price depending on the program of study.

Financial Aid

Financial aid is available for those who qualify. Students who require financial assistance should first complete and submit a Free Application for Federal Student Aid (FAFSA) and meet with a financial aid officer.

Faculty

Faculty members are experienced professionals who create a learning environment that is similar to the professional world students will face after graduation. Instructors are focused on helping students develop the skills they need to transform their creative potential into marketable skills.

Admission Requirements

Applicants must be high school graduates or have a General Educational Development (GED) certificate. A 150-word written essay is required, as are high school transcripts and any records from other academic institutions attended. All interested students are interviewed in person or over the phone. Following this interview, prospective students complete an application for admission and submit the enrollment fee. Applicants who have taken the SAT or ACT are encouraged to submit their scores to the Admissions Office for evaluation. There is a $50 application fee.

For the most recent information regarding admission requirements, please refer to the current academic catalog.

Application and Information

To obtain an application, make arrangements for an interview, or tour the school, prospective students should contact:

The Art Institute of Charlotte
Three Lake Pointe Plaza
2110 Water Ridge Parkway
Charlotte, North Carolina 28217-4536
Phone: 704-357-8020
          800-872-4417 (toll-free)
Fax: 704-357-1133
Web site: http://www.artinstitutes.edu/charlotte

COLLEGE CLOSE-UPS

THE ART INSTITUTE OF COLORADO
DENVER, COLORADO

The Art Institute of Colorado®
CREATE TOMORROW

A focused education from The Art Institute of Colorado can help students turn their creative energy into a powerful tool that can make a difference in the world. Students are part of a collaborative and supportive community, where experienced instructors provide the guidance and skills needed to pursue a career in the creative economy.

The school's programs in the areas of design, media arts, fashion, and culinary give students the opportunity to learn by using professional-grade technology and build a portfolio of work to show potential employers after graduation.

The Art Institute of Colorado is accredited by the Higher Learning Commission and is a member of the North Central Association (NCA), located at 230 S. LaSalle Street, Suite 7-500, Chicago, Illinois, 60604-1413; phone: 800-621-7440; http://www.ncahlc.org.

The Art Institute of Colorado is authorized to award diplomas, Associate of Applied Science degrees, and Bachelor of Arts degrees by the Colorado Department of Higher Education, Commission on Higher Education, 1380 Lawrence Street, Suite 1200, Denver, Colorado 80202.

The Associate of Applied Science in Culinary Arts degree program is accredited by the Accrediting Commission of the American Culinary Federation Education Foundation.

The Interior Design program leading to the Bachelor of Science degree is accredited by the Council for Interior Design Accreditation, 206 Grandville Avenue, Suite 350, Grand Rapids, Michigan 49503; http://www.accredit-id.org.

The Associate of Applied Science in Kitchen and Bath Design degree program is accredited by the National Kitchen & Bath Association (NKBA). NKBA can be contacted at 687 Willow Grove Street, Hackettstown, New Jersey 07840; phone: 800-THE-NKBA; http://www.nkba.org.

Location

The Art Institute of Colorado is located in Denver, home to many major corporations and high-technology companies. Located near galleries, museums, and theaters, The Art Institute of Colorado provides easy access to music and dance performances at both the Performing Arts Complex and Red Rocks Amphitheater. Denver is a one-hour drive from world-class skiing and water sports, amid the Rocky Mountains' breathtaking scenery. The city itself offers ample opportunities for biking, hiking, in-line skating, and viewing professional sports.

Programs of Study and Degrees

No matter which course of study a student may choose, the professionals at The Art Institute of Colorado will guide, support, and help each student as their talents evolve on their journey of personal and professional transformation. Students studying design learn to fine-tune their visual thinking and problem-solving skills as they create everything from logos to TV ads. Programs in the area of media arts focus on utilizing technology to deliver information and entertainment, while students studying fashion learn to design clothes for the runway or run a retail shop. Culinary programs focus on the fundamental techniques while exposing students to a full menu of international cuisines and management techniques.

Bachelor's degrees are offered in the areas of audio production, culinary management, design and technical graphics, design management, digital filmmaking and video production, fashion design, fashion retail management, food and beverage management, game art and design, graphic design, hospitality management, interior design, media arts and animation, photography, visual effects and motion graphics, and Web design and interactive media.

Associate degree programs are available in the areas of baking and pastry, culinary arts, graphic design, kitchen and bath design, photography, video production, and Web design and interactive media.

Diploma programs are offered in the areas of baking and pastry, culinary arts, digital image management, fashion retailing, Web design and development, and Web design and interactive communications.

The fashion retail management and interior design programs, as well as the associate degree programs in culinary arts and photography, are available in an evening and weekend option format.

Academic Programs

The Art Institute of Colorado offers Bachelor of Arts degree programs that are designed to be thirty-six months in length. Associate's degree programs are designed to take twenty-one months to complete.

Academic Facilities

The Art Institute of Colorado provides a learning environment with professional-grade technology applicable to each student's course of study. Students have the opportunity to build a portfolio of work that shows potential employers that they are trained to use the software, hardware, or equipment utilized within the industry. Depending upon the course of study, students are immersed in a creative environment—from classrooms to computer labs to studios—focused on relevant, hands-on education designed to prepare students for the real world.

Costs

Tuition cost varies by program. Prospective students should contact the school for current tuition costs. Other charges include a starting kit for all first-quarter students. Kits vary in price, depending on the program of study.

Financial Aid

Financial aid is available for those who qualify. Students who require financial assistance should first complete and submit a Free Application for Federal Student Aid (FAFSA) and meet with a financial aid officer.

Faculty

Faculty members are experienced professionals who create a learning environment that is similar to the professional world students will face after graduation. Instructors are focused on helping students develop the skills they need to transform their creative potential into marketable skills.

Admission Requirements

All applicants are evaluated on the basis of previous education, background, and stated or demonstrated interest in a career program. Applicants must provide high school or college transcripts and an essay of approximately 150 words stating how an education at The Art Institute of Colorado will help them attain their creative goals. Portfolios are welcome but not required. Applicants who have taken the SAT or ACT are encouraged to submit scores for evaluation. There is a $50 application fee.

For the most recent information regarding admission requirements, please refer to the current academic catalog.

Application and Information

To obtain an application, make arrangements for an interview, or tour the school, prospective students should contact:

The Art Institute of Colorado
1200 Lincoln Street
Denver, Colorado 80203-2172
Phone: 303-837-0825
        800-275-2420 (toll-free)
Fax: 303-860-8520
Web site: http://www.artinstitutes.edu/denver

THE ART INSTITUTE OF DALLAS

DALLAS, TEXAS

The Art Institute of Dallas
A campus of South University

CREATE TOMORROW

A focused education from The Art Institute of Dallas, a campus of South University, can help students turn their creative energy into a powerful tool that can make a difference in the world. Students are part of a collaborative and supportive community, where experienced instructors provide the guidance and skills needed to pursue a career in the creative economy.

The school's programs in the areas of design, media arts, fashion, and culinary give students the opportunity to learn by using professional-grade technology and to build a portfolio of work to show potential employers after graduation.

The Art Institute of Dallas is a campus of South University. South University is accredited by the Commission on Colleges of the Southern Association of Colleges and Schools to award associate, baccalaureate, masters, and doctorate degrees. For questions about the accreditation of South University, contact the Commission on Colleges at 1866 Southern Lane, Decatur, Georgia 30033-4097; phone: 404-679-4500.

The Art Institute of Dallas holds a certificate of authorization acknowledging exemption from Texas Higher Education Coordinating Board regulations.

The Art Institute of Dallas is licensed by the Arkansas State Board of Private Career Education. The Art Institute of Dallas is licensed by the Oklahoma Board of Private Vocational Schools, which can be contacted at 3700 North Classen Boulevard, Suite 250, Oklahoma City, Oklahoma 73118; phone: 405-528-3370.

The Certificate in the Art of Cooking and the Associate of Applied Science in Culinary Arts degree programs are accredited by The Accrediting Commission of the American Culinary Federation Education Foundation.

The Interior Design program leading to the Bachelor of Science degree is accredited by the Council for Interior Design Accreditation, 206 Grandville Avenue, Suite 350, Grand Rapids, Michigan 49503; http://www.accredit-id.org.

Location

The school is located in the Dallas/Fort Worth area, which has one of the lowest cost-of-living indexes of any major metropolitan area. The Dallas/Fort Worth area offers a diverse range of cultural and recreational activities, including the Dallas Symphony, Mesquite Rodeo, Six Flags, Lone Star Park, concerts in the West End, and national sports teams. Many major employers have relocated to the Dallas/Fort Worth area due to its positive economic environment.

Programs of Study and Degrees

No matter which course of study a student may choose, the professionals at The Art Institute of Dallas will guide, support, and help each student as their talents evolve on their journey of personal and professional transformation. Students studying design learn to fine-tune their visual thinking and problem-solving skills as they create everything from logos to TV ads. Programs in the area of media arts focus on utilizing technology to deliver information and entertainment, while students studying fashion learn to design clothes for the runway or run a retail shop. Culinary programs focus on the fundamental techniques while exposing students to a full menu of international cuisines and management techniques.

The Art Institute of Dallas offers bachelor's degree programs in the areas of advertising design, culinary management, digital filmmaking and video production, fashion and retail management, fashion design, graphic design, interior design, media arts and animation, photography, and Web design and interactive media.

Associate degree programs include the areas of baking and pastry, culinary arts, fashion design, graphic design, kitchen and bath design, photography, restaurant and catering management, and video production.

Certificate programs are available in the areas of art of cooking, baking and pastry, culinary arts, digital image management, fashion retailing, Web design and development I, and Web design and development II.

The Associate of Applied Science in Culinary Arts, Bachelor of Fine Arts in Fashion Design, Bachelor of Fine Arts and Associate of Applied Arts in Graphic Design, and Bachelor of Fine Arts in Interior Design are available in an evening and weekend option format.

Students may also earn a Master of Arts in Design and Media Management.

Academic Programs

Associate degree programs can be completed in as little as twenty-one months. Bachelor's degree programs can be completed in as little as thirty-six months.

Academic Facilities

The Art Institute of Dallas provides a learning environment with professional-grade technology applicable to each student's course of study. Students have the opportunity to build a portfolio of work that shows potential employers that they are trained to use the software, hardware, or equipment utilized within the industry. Depending upon the course of study, students are immersed in a creative environment—from classrooms to computer labs to studios—focused on relevant, hands-on education designed to prepare students for the real world.

Costs

Tuition cost varies by program. Prospective students should contact the school for current tuition costs. Other charges include a starting kit for all first-quarter students. Kits vary in price depending on the program of study.

Financial Aid

Financial aid is available for those who qualify. Students who require financial assistance should first complete and submit a Free Application for Federal Student Aid (FAFSA) and meet with a financial aid officer.

Faculty

Faculty members are experienced professionals who create a learning environment that is similar to the professional world students will face after graduation. Instructors are focused on helping students develop the skills they need to transform their creative potential into marketable skills.

Student Government

The Student Ambassador Organization promotes high-quality representation of the student body. The group provides a channel of communication among students, the administration, and faculty members.

Admission Requirements

Applicants are required to write a paragraph of approximately 300 words stating how The Art Institute of Dallas may help them reach their creative goals. Applicants must present proof of high school graduation or a General Educational Development (GED) certificate as well as their accomplishments and core academic courses. Successful admission depends on QPA, accomplishments, SAT or ACT scores, and a personal interview with admission representatives. Applicants who do not submit a transcript of GED scores are required to take additional testing.

To enroll, students must submit an admission application and an enrollment agreement, along with a $50 application fee.

For the most recent information regarding admission requirements, please refer to the current academic catalog.

Application and Information

To obtain an application, make arrangements for an interview, or tour the school, prospective students should contact:

The Art Institute of Dallas
A Campus of South University
8080 Park Lane, Suite 100
Dallas, Texas 75231-5993
Phone: 214-692-8080
        800-275-4243 (toll-free)
Fax: 214-750-9460
Web site: http://www.artinstitutes.edu/dallas

THE ART INSTITUTE OF FORT LAUDERDALE

FORT LAUDERDALE, FLORIDA

The Art Institute of Fort Lauderdale®

CREATE TOMORROW

A focused education from The Art Institute of Fort Lauderdale can help students turn their creative energy into a powerful tool that can make a difference in the world. Students are part of a collaborative and supportive community, where experienced instructors provide the guidance and skills needed to pursue a career in the creative economy.

The school's programs in the areas of design, media arts, fashion, and culinary give students the opportunity to learn by using professional-grade technology and to build a portfolio of work to show potential employers after graduation.

The Art Institute of Fort Lauderdale is accredited by the Accrediting Council for Independent Colleges and Schools to award diplomas, associate's degrees, and bachelor's degrees. The Accrediting Council for Independent Colleges and Schools is listed as a nationally recognized accrediting agency by the United States Department of Education and is recognized by the Council for Higher Education Accreditation. ACICS can be contacted at 750 First Street NE, Suite 980, Washington, D.C. 20002; phone: 202-336-6780.

The Art Institute of Fort Lauderdale is licensed by the Commission for Independent Education, Florida Department of Education. Additional information regarding this institution may be obtained by contacting the commission at 325 W. Gaines Street, Suite 1414, Tallahassee, Florida 32399-0400; phone: 888-224-6684 (toll-free). License No. 1287.

The Associate of Science degree in Culinary Arts and the Bachelor of Science degree in Culinary Management are accredited by The Accrediting Commission of the American Culinary Federation Education Foundation.

The Interior Design program leading to the Bachelor of Science degree is accredited by the Council for Interior Design Accreditation, 206 Grandville Avenue, Suite. 350, Grand Rapids, Michigan 49503; http://www.accredit-id.org.

Location

Surrounded by waterways, Fort Lauderdale is known as "The Venice of America." The area has an average temperature of 70 degrees in the winter and offers many opportunities for fun in the sun. The Art Institute of Fort Lauderdale is close to 23 miles of beaches, shopping districts, museums, historical sites, restaurants, and nightclubs. Located between Miami and Palm Beach, Fort Lauderdale's many attractions include its world-famous beach, the picturesque Riverwalk, and Las Olas Boulevard—a centerpiece of fashion, fine dining, and entertainment. Tourists and residents alike enjoy the Broward Center for the Performing Arts, Museum of Discovery and Science, Museum of Art, and Old Fort Lauderdale Village and Museum. Fort Lauderdale also supports a diverse range of industries, including marine, manufacturing, finance, insurance, real estate, high technology, avionics/aerospace, and film and television production.

Programs of Study and Degrees

No matter which course of study a student may choose, the professionals at The Art Institute of Fort Lauderdale will guide, support, and help each student as their talents evolve on their journey of personal and professional transformation. Students studying design learn to fine-tune their visual thinking and problem-solving skills as they create everything from logos to TV ads. Programs in the area of media arts focus on utilizing technology to deliver information and entertainment, while students studying fashion learn to design clothes for the runway or run a retail shop. Culinary programs focus on the fundamental techniques while exposing students to a full menu of international cuisines and management techniques.

Bachelor's degree programs are offered in the areas of advertising, culinary management, digital filmmaking and video production, fashion design, fashion merchandising, game art and design, graphic design, illustration, industrial design, interior design, media arts and animation, photography, visual effects and motion graphics, and Web design and interactive media.

Associate degree programs are offered in the areas of baking and pastry, culinary arts, fashion design, graphic design, interior design, photography, video production, and Web design and interactive media.

Diploma programs are offered in the areas of art of cooking, baking and pastry, culinary arts, digital image management, fashion retailing, residential design, Web design and development, and Web design and interactive communications.

Academic Programs

The Art Institute of Fort Lauderdale offers Bachelor of Science degree programs, Associate of Science degree programs, and diploma programs.

Academic Facilities

The Art Institute of Fort Lauderdale provides a learning environment with professional-grade technology applicable to each student's course of study. Students have the opportunity to build a portfolio of work that shows potential employers that they are trained to use the software, hardware, or equipment utilized within the industry. Depending upon the course of study, students are immersed in a creative environment—from classrooms to computer labs to studios—focused on relevant, hands-on education designed to prepare students for the real world.

Costs

Tuition cost varies by program. Prospective students should contact the school for current tuition costs. Other charges include a starting kit for all first-quarter students. Kits vary in price depending on the program of study.

Financial Aid

Financial aid is available for those who qualify. Students who require financial assistance should first complete and submit a Free Application for Federal Student Aid (FAFSA) and meet with a financial aid officer.

Faculty

Faculty members are experienced professionals who create a learning environment that is similar to the professional world students will face after graduation. Instructors are focused on helping students develop the skills they need to transform their creative potential into marketable skills.

Student Government

All students have the right to participate and vote in Student Government elections and referenda. The Student Government works with faculty and staff members to provide numerous events, including student socials, community outreach programs, volunteer work, and student service events.

Admission Requirements

Admission to The Art Institute of Fort Lauderdale requires a completed application form, evidence of high school graduation or successful completion of the General Educational Development (GED) test, and an essay on how the school may assist in achieving the applicant's creative goals. Applicants are also required to schedule an interview with an admissions representative and, if financial aid is needed, to complete the FAFSA and PLUS loan forms found in the application packet. There is a $50 application fee.

For the most recent information regarding admission requirements, please refer to the current academic catalog.

Application and Information

To obtain an application, make arrangements for an interview, or tour the school, prospective students should contact:

The Art Institute of Fort Lauderdale
1799 S.E. 17th Street
Fort Lauderdale, Florida 33316-3013
Phone: 954-463-3000
          800-275-7603 (toll-free)
Fax: 954-728-8637
Web site: http://www.artinstitutes.edu/fortlauderdale

Over 50 schools: The Art Institute of Atlanta; The Art Institute of Atlanta—Decatur, A branch of The Art Institute of Atlanta; The Art Institute of Austin, A branch of The Art Institute of Houston; The Art Institute of California, a college of Argosy University, with locations in Hollywood, Inland Empire, Los Angeles, Orange County, Sacramento, San Diego, San Francisco, and Sunnyvale; The Art Institute of Charleston, A branch of The Art Institute of Atlanta; The Art Institute of Charlotte; The Art Institute of Colorado; The Art Institute of Dallas, A campus of South University; The Art Institute of Fort Lauderdale; The Art Institute of Fort Worth, A campus of South University; The Art Institute of Houston—North, A branch of The Art Institute of Houston; The Art Institute of Indianapolis; The Art Institute of Jacksonville, A branch of Miami International University of Art & Design; The Art Institute of Las Vegas; The Art Institute of Michigan; The Art Institute of Michigan—Troy; The Art Institute of New York City; The Art Institute of Ohio—Cincinnati; The Art Institute of Philadelphia; The Art Institute of Phoenix; The Art Institute of Pittsburgh; The Art Institute of Portland; The Art Institute of Raleigh–Durham; The Art Institute of Salt Lake City; The Art Institute of San Antonio, A branch of The Art Institute of Houston; The Art Institute of Seattle; The Art Institute of Tampa, A branch of Miami International University of Art & Design; The Art Institute of Tennessee—Nashville, A branch of The Art Institute of Atlanta; The Art Institute of Tucson; The Art Institute of Vancouver; The Art Institute of Virginia Beach[1], A branch of The Art Institute of Atlanta; The Art Institute of Washington[1], A branch of The Art Institute of Atlanta; The Art Institute of Washington—Dulles[1], A branch of The Art Institute of Atlanta; The Art Institute of Wisconsin; The Art Institute of York—Pennsylvania; The Art Institutes International—Kansas City; The Art Institutes International Minnesota; The Illinois Institute of Art—Chicago; The Illinois Institute of Art—Schaumburg; The Illinois Institute of Art—Tinley Park; Miami International University of Art & Design; The New England Institute of Art

[1]Certified by SCHEV to operate in Virginia

See **aiprograms.info** for program duration, tuition, fees, and other costs, median debt, federal salary data, alumni success, and other important info. The Art Institutes is a system of over 50 schools throughout North America. Programs, credential levels, technology, and scheduling options vary by school, and employment opportunities are not guaranteed. Financial aid is available to those who qualify. Several institutions included in The Art Institutes system are campuses of South University or Argosy University. OH Registration # 04-01-1698B, AC0165, AC0080, Licensed by the Florida Commission for Independent Education, License No. 1287, 3427, 3110, 2581. Administrative office: 210 Sixth Avenue, 33rd Floor, Pittsburgh, PA 15222. ©2012 The Art Institutes International LLC.

THE ART INSTITUTE OF FORT WORTH
FORT WORTH, TEXAS

A focused education from The Art Institute of Fort Worth, a campus of South University, can help students turn their creative energy into a powerful tool that can make a difference in the world. Students are part of a collaborative and supportive community, where experienced instructors provide the guidance and skills needed to pursue a career in the creative economy.

The school's programs in the areas of design, media arts, and fashion give students the opportunity to learn by using professional-grade technology and to build a portfolio of work to show potential employers after graduation.

The Art Institute of Fort Worth is a campus of South University. South University is accredited by the Commission on Colleges of the Southern Association of Colleges and Schools to award associate, baccalaureate, master's, and doctoral degrees. For questions about the accreditation of South University, contact the Commission on Colleges at 1866 Southern Lane, Decatur, Georgia 30033-4097; phone: 404-679-4500.

The Art Institute of Fort Worth holds a certificate of authorization acknowledging exemption from Texas Higher Education Coordinating Board regulations.

Location

Downtown Fort Worth is known for its art deco style buildings and culture, including theater, museums, and music. The city is also known for the popular Fort Worth Stockyards historic district.

Programs of Study and Degrees

No matter which course of study a student may choose, the professionals at The Art Institute of Fort Worth will guide, support, and help each student as their talents evolve on their journey of personal and professional transformation. Students studying design learn to fine-tune their visual thinking and problem-solving skills as they create everything from logos to TV ads. Programs in the area of media arts focus on utilizing technology to deliver information and entertainment, while students studying fashion learn to market clothing or run a retail shop.

Bachelor's degree programs are offered in the areas of advertising design, fashion and retail management, graphic design, interior design, media arts and animation, photography, and Web design and interactive media.

Associate degree programs are offered in the areas of graphic design, photography, and Web design and interactive media.

Certificate programs are available in digital image management, fashion retailing, Web design and development I, and Web design and development II.

Academic Programs

The Art Institute of Fort Worth operates on a year-round, four-quarter system.

Academic Facilities

The Art Institute of Fort Worth provides a learning environment with professional-grade technology applicable to each student's course of study. Students have the opportunity to build a portfolio of work that shows potential employers that they are trained to use the software, hardware, or equipment utilized within the industry. Depending upon the course of study, students are immersed in a creative environment—from classrooms to computer labs to studios—focused on relevant, hands-on education designed to prepare students for the real world.

Costs

Tuition cost varies by program. Prospective students should contact the school for current tuition costs. Other charges include a starting kit for all first-quarter students. Kits vary in price depending on the program of study.

Financial Aid

Financial aid is available for those who qualify. Students who require financial assistance should first complete and submit a Free Application for Federal Student Aid (FAFSA) and meet with a financial aid officer.

Faculty

Faculty members are experienced professionals who create a learning environment that is similar to the professional world students will face after graduation. Instructors are focused on helping students develop the skills they need to transform their creative potential into marketable skills.

Admission Requirements

Applicants must provide proof of high school graduation or achievement of a General Educational Development (GED) certificate as a prerequisite for admission. In lieu of documenting high school graduation or a GED certificate, applicants may provide proof of attaining an associate degree or higher from an accredited institution. An official transcript indicating date of high school graduation, GED certificate (including test scores), or date of college graduation (including degree granted) is required as proof.

All individuals seeking admission to The Art Institute of Fort Worth are interviewed in person or by phone by an assistant director of admissions, and each applicant must create an original essay of at least 150 words stating how an education at The Art Institute of Fort Worth would help the student to achieve career goals. There is a $50 application fee.

For the most recent information regarding admission requirements, please refer to the current academic catalog.

Application and Information

To obtain an application, make arrangements for an interview, or tour the school, prospective students should contact:

The Art Institute of Forth Worth
A campus of South University
7000 Calmont Avenue, Suite 150
Fort Worth, Texas 76116
Phone: 817-210-0808
        888-422-9686 (toll-free)
Fax: 817-210-0901
Web site: http://www.artinstitutes.edu/fort-worth

COLLEGE CLOSE-UPS

Over 50 schools: The Art Institute of Atlanta; The Art Institute of Atlanta—Decatur, A branch of The Art Institute of Atlanta; The Art Institute of Austin, A branch of The Art Institute of Houston; The Art Institute of California, a college of Argosy University, with locations in Hollywood, Inland Empire, Los Angeles, Orange County, Sacramento, San Diego, San Francisco, and Sunnyvale; The Art Institute of Charleston, A branch of The Art Institute of Atlanta; The Art Institute of Charlotte; The Art Institute of Colorado; The Art Institute of Dallas, A campus of South University; The Art Institute of Fort Lauderdale; The Art Institute of Fort Worth, A campus of South University; The Art Institute of Houston; The Art Institute of Houston—North, A branch of The Art Institute of Houston; The Art Institute of Indianapolis; The Art Institute of Jacksonville, A branch of Miami International University of Art & Design; The Art Institute of Las Vegas; The Art Institute of Michigan; The Art Institute of Michigan—Troy; The Art Institute of New York City; The Art Institute of Ohio—Cincinnati; The Art Institute of Philadelphia; The Art Institute of Phoenix; The Art Institute of Pittsburgh; The Art Institute of Portland; The Art Institute of Raleigh–Durham; The Art Institute of Salt Lake City; The Art Institute of San Antonio, A branch of The Art Institute of Houston; The Art Institute of Seattle; The Art Institute of Tampa, A branch of Miami International University of Art & Design; The Art Institute of Tennessee—Nashville, A branch of The Art Institute of Atlanta; The Art Institute of Tucson; The Art Institute of Vancouver; The Art Institute of Virginia Beach[1], A branch of The Art Institute of Atlanta; The Art Institute of Washington[1], A branch of The Art Institute of Atlanta; The Art Institute of Washington—Dulles[1], A branch of The Art Institute of Atlanta; The Art Institute of Wisconsin; The Art Institute of York—Pennsylvania; The Art Institutes International—Kansas City; The Art Institutes International Minnesota; The Illinois Institute of Art—Chicago; The Illinois Institute of Art—Schaumburg; The Illinois Institute of Art—Tinley Park; Miami International University of Art & Design; The New England Institute of Art

[1]Certified by SCHEV to operate in Virginia

See **aiprograms.info** for program duration, tuition, fees, and other costs, median debt, federal salary data, alumni success, and other important info. The Art Institutes is a system of over 50 schools throughout North America. Programs, credential levels, technology, and scheduling options vary by school, and employment opportunities are not guaranteed. Financial aid is available to those who qualify. Several institutions included in The Art Institutes system are campuses of South University or Argosy University. OH Registration # 04-01-1698B, AC0165, AC0080, Licensed by the Florida Commission for Independent Education, License No. 1287, 3427, 3110, 2581. Administrative office: 210 Sixth Avenue, 33rd Floor, Pittsburgh, PA 15222. ©2012 The Art Institutes International LLC.

THE ART INSTITUTE OF HOUSTON
HOUSTON, TEXAS

The Art Institute
of Houston®

CREATE TOMORROW

A focused education from The Art Institute of Houston can help students turn their creative energy into a powerful tool that can make a difference in the world. Students are part of a collaborative and supportive community, where experienced instructors provide the guidance and skills needed to pursue a career in the creative economy.

The school's programs in the areas of design, media arts, fashion, and culinary give students the opportunity to learn by using professional-grade technology and to build a portfolio of work to show potential employers after graduation.

The Art Institute of Houston, including its branch campuses—The Art Institute of Houston—North, The Art Institute of Austin, and The Art Institute of San Antonio—is accredited by the Commission on Colleges of the Southern Association of Colleges and Schools to award associate degrees and baccalaureate degrees. For questions about the accreditation of The Art Institute of Houston, contact the Commission on Colleges at 1866 Southern Lane, Decatur, Georgia 30033-4097; phone: 404-679-4500.

The Diploma in Culinary Arts, the Associate of Applied Science degree in Baking and Pastry, the Associate of Applied Science degree in Culinary Arts, and the Bachelor of Science degree in Culinary Management are accredited by The Accrediting Commission of the American Culinary Federation Education Foundation.

The Interior Design program leading to the Bachelor of Fine Arts degree is accredited by the Council for Interior Design Accreditation, 206 Grandville Avenue, Suite 350, Grand Rapids, Michigan 49503; http://www.accredit-id.org.

The Art Institute of Houston holds a Certificate of Authorization acknowledging exemption from Texas Higher Education Coordinating Board Regulations.

Location

The Art Institute of Houston is close to several major art museums, a premier opera, a ballet, a symphony, and live theater companies. Culturally diverse, Houston has several international ethnic communities, great restaurants, and an eclectic nightlife as well as national sports teams. The city features a mild, semitropical climate and sunny beaches in nearby Galveston and Mexico.

Programs of Study and Degrees

No matter which course of study a student may choose, the professionals at The Art Institute of Houston will guide, support, and help each student as their talents evolve on their journey of personal and professional transformation. Students studying design learn to fine-tune their visual thinking and problem-solving skills as they create everything from logos to TV ads. Programs in the area of media arts focus on utilizing technology to deliver information and entertainment, while students studying fashion learn to design clothes for the runway or run a retail shop. Culinary programs focus on the fundamental techniques while exposing students to a full menu of international cuisines and management techniques.

Bachelor's degree programs are offered in the areas of advertising design, audio production, culinary management, design and technical graphics, digital filmmaking and video production, fashion and retail management, fashion design, food and beverage management, game art and design, graphic design, hospitality management, interior design, media arts and animation, photography, visual effects and motion graphics, and Web design and interactive media.

Associate degree programs are available in the areas of baking and pastry, culinary arts, graphic design, restaurant and catering management, and Web design and interactive media.

Diploma programs are offered in the areas of baking and pastry, culinary arts, digital image management, fashion retailing, Web design and development, and Web design and interactive communications.

The bachelor's degree programs in the areas of culinary management, interior design, and Web design and interactive media, as well as the Associate of Applied Science degree program in Culinary Arts, are available in an evening and weekend option format.

Academic Programs

The academic year is divided into four quarters of approximately eleven weeks each. Students may start their program of study in any quarter. Bachelor's degrees can be earned upon completion of 180 academic credits over approximately twelve quarters. Associate's degrees are earned upon completion of 90 to 108 academic credits, depending on the program, and can take seven to eight quarters. Diploma programs require the completion of 61 academic credits. Online programs are offered in two sessions per academic quarter.

Academic Facilities

The Art Institute of Houston provides a learning environment with professional-grade technology applicable to each student's course of study. Students have the opportunity to build a portfolio of work that shows potential employers that they are trained to use the software, hardware, or equipment utilized within the industry. Depending upon the course of study, students are immersed in a creative environment—from classrooms to computer labs to studios—focused on relevant, hands-on education designed to prepare students for the real world.

Costs

Tuition cost varies by program. Prospective students should contact the school for current tuition costs. Other charges include a starting kit for all first-quarter students. Kits vary in price depending on the program of study.

Financial Aid

Financial aid is available for those who qualify. Students who require financial assistance should first complete and submit a Free Application for Federal Student Aid (FAFSA) and meet with a financial aid officer.

Faculty

Faculty members are experienced professionals who create a learning environment that is similar to the professional world students will face after graduation. Instructors are focused on helping students develop the skills they need to transform their creative potential into marketable skills.

Student Government

The Student Government is the primary vehicle for student participation in institutional decision making. The Student Government acts as a voice on behalf of the student body and sponsors speakers, workshops, seminars, and other activities. When students seek change or have a request that affects the student body as a whole, Student Government serves as a forum for discussion and decision making. All students are eligible to belong to Student Government.

Admission Requirements

Admission to The Art Institute of Houston begins with an interview with an assistant director of admissions, either in person or by phone. Upon approval, students submit an application for admission and an enrollment agreement. Prospective students must be high school graduates, hold a General Educational Development (GED) certificate, or have earned an associate's degree or higher from an accredited institution. The Art Institute of Houston considers alternative documentation from students who have completed high school or its equivalent but cannot provide the usual documentation. (The president of The Art Institute of Houston must approve all exceptions.) Evaluations are based on an applicant's previous education, background, and stated or demonstrated interest in a particular program. Portfolios are required for admission to the media arts and animation program; they are welcomed for other programs but not required. Applicants who have taken the SAT or ACT are encouraged to submit their scores for evaluation. There is a $50 application fee.

For the most recent information regarding admission requirements, please refer to the current academic catalog.

Application and Information

To obtain an application, make arrangements for an interview, or tour the school, prospective students should contact:

The Art Institute of Houston
River Oaks Plaza
4140 Southwest Freeway
Houston, Texas 77027
Phone: 713-623-2040
        800-275-4244 (toll-free)
Fax: 713-966-2797
Web site: http://www.artinstitutes.edu/houston

Over 50 schools: The Art Institute of Atlanta; The Art Institute of Atlanta—Decatur, A branch of The Art Institute of Atlanta; The Art Institute of Austin, A branch of The Art Institute of Houston; The Art Institute of California, a college of Argosy University, with locations in Hollywood, Inland Empire, Los Angeles, Orange County, Sacramento, San Diego, San Francisco, and Sunnyvale; The Art Institute of Charleston, A branch of The Art Institute of Atlanta; The Art Institute of Charlotte; The Art Institute of Colorado; The Art Institute of Dallas, A campus of South University; The Art Institute of Fort Lauderdale; The Art Institute of Fort Worth, A campus of South University; The Art Institute of Houston; The Art Institute of Houston—North, A branch of The Art Institute of Houston; The Art Institute of Indianapolis; The Art Institute of Jacksonville, A branch of Miami International University of Art & Design; The Art Institute of Las Vegas; The Art Institute of Michigan; The Art Institute of Michigan—Troy; The Art Institute of New York City; The Art Institute of Ohio—Cincinnati; The Art Institute of Philadelphia; The Art Institute of Phoenix; The Art Institute of Pittsburgh; The Art Institute of Portland; The Art Institute of Raleigh–Durham; The Art Institute of Salt Lake City; The Art Institute of San Antonio, A branch of The Art Institute of Houston; The Art Institute of Seattle; The Art Institute of Tampa, A branch of Miami International University of Art & Design; The Art Institute of Tennessee—Nashville, A branch of The Art Institute of Atlanta; The Art Institute of Tucson; The Art Institute of Vancouver; The Art Institute of Virginia Beach[1], A branch of The Art Institute of Atlanta; The Art Institute of Washington[1], A branch of The Art Institute of Atlanta; The Art Institute of Washington—Dulles[1], A branch of The Art Institute of Atlanta; The Art Institute of Wisconsin; The Art Institute of York—Pennsylvania; The Art Institutes International—Kansas City; The Art Institutes International Minnesota; The Illinois Institute of Art—Chicago; The Illinois Institute of Art—Schaumburg; The Illinois Institute of Art—Tinley Park; Miami International University of Art & Design; The New England Institute of Art

[1]Certified by SCHEV to operate in Virginia

See **aiprograms.info** for program duration, tuition, fees, and other costs, median debt, federal salary data, alumni success, and other important info. The Art Institutes is a system of over 50 schools throughout North America. Programs, credential levels, technology, and

THE ART INSTITUTE OF HOUSTON—NORTH

HOUSTON, TEXAS

The Art Institute of Houston®–North
A branch of The Art Institute of Houston
CREATE TOMORROW

A focused education from The Art Institute of Houston—North can help students turn their creative energy into a powerful tool that can make a difference in the world. Students are part of a collaborative and supportive community, where experienced instructors provide the guidance and skills needed to pursue a career in the creative economy.

The school's programs in the areas of design, media arts, and fashion give students the opportunity to learn by using professional-grade technology and to build a portfolio of work to show potential employers after graduation.

The Art Institute of Houston—North is a branch campus of The Art Institute of Houston. The Art Institute of Houston is accredited by the Commission on Colleges of the Southern Association of Colleges and Schools to award associate and baccalaureate degrees. For questions about the accreditation of The Art Institute of Houston, contact the Commission on Colleges at 1866 Southern Lane, Decatur, Georgia 30033-4097; phone: 404-679-4500.

The Art Institute of Houston—North holds a certificate of authorization acknowledging exemption from Texas Higher Education Coordinating Board regulations.

Location

A growing and exciting "edge city," northwest Houston is coming into its own as a center for the visual and performing arts, education, shopping, and recreation catering to the young—and the young at heart. Lakes and streams, forested parks, and safe neighborhoods can all be found just minutes from Houston's central business district.

Programs of Study and Degrees

No matter which course of study a student may choose, the professionals at The Art Institute of Houston—North will guide, support, and help each student as their talents evolve on their journey of personal and professional transformation. Students studying design learn to fine-tune their visual thinking and problem-solving skills as they create everything from logos to TV ads. Programs in the area of media arts focus on utilizing technology to deliver information and entertainment, while students studying fashion learn to market clothing or run a retail shop.

Bachelor's degree programs are offered in the areas of advertising design, design and technical graphics, fashion and retail management, game art and design, graphic design, interior design, media arts and animation, photography, visual effects and motion graphics, and Web design and interactive media.

Associate degree programs are offered in the areas of graphic design and Web design and interactive media.

Diploma programs are available in the areas of digital image management, fashion retailing, Web design and development, and Web design and interactive communications.

Academic Programs

The Art Institute of Houston—North operates on a year-round, four-quarter system.

Academic Facilities

The Art Institute of Houston—North provides a learning environment with professional-grade technology applicable to each student's course of study. Students have the opportunity to build a portfolio of work that shows potential employers that they are trained to use the software, hardware, or equipment utilized within the industry. Depending upon the course of study, students are immersed in a creative environment—from classrooms to computer labs to studios—focused on relevant, hands-on education designed to prepare students for the real world.

Costs

Tuition cost varies by program. Prospective students should contact the school for current tuition costs. Other charges include a starting kit for all first-quarter students. Kits vary in price depending on the program of study.

Financial Aid

Financial aid is available for those who qualify. Students who require financial assistance should first complete and submit a Free Application for Federal Student Aid (FAFSA) and meet with a financial aid officer.

Faculty

Faculty members are experienced professionals who create a learning environment that is similar to the professional world students will face after graduation. Instructors are focused on helping students develop the skills they need to transform their creative potential into marketable skills.

Admission Requirements

Applicants must provide proof of high school graduation or achievement of a General Educational Development (GED) certificate as a prerequisite for admission. In lieu of documenting high school graduation or a GED certificate, applicants may provide proof of attaining an associate degree or higher from an accredited institution. An official transcript indicating date of high school graduation, GED certificate (including test scores), or date of college graduation (including degree granted) is required as proof.

All individuals seeking admission to The Art Institute of Houston—North are interviewed in person or by phone by an assistant director of admissions, and each applicant must create an original essay of at least 150 words stating how an education at The Art Institute of Houston—North would help the student to achieve career goals. There is a $50 application fee.

For the most recent information regarding admission requirements, please refer to the current academic catalog.

Application and Information

To obtain an application, make arrangements for an interview, or tour the school, prospective students should contact:

The Art Institute of Houston—North
A branch of The Art Institute of Houston
10740 North Gessner Drive, Suite 190
Houston, Texas 77064
Phone: 281-671-3381
866-830-4450 (toll-free)
Fax: 281-671-3550
Web site: http://www.artinstitutes.edu/houston-north

COLLEGE CLOSE-UPS

THE ART INSTITUTE OF INDIANAPOLIS
INDIANAPOLIS, INDIANA

A focused education from The Art Institute of Indianapolis can help students turn their creative energy into a powerful tool that can make a difference in the world. Students are part of a collaborative and supportive community, where experienced instructors provide the guidance and skills needed to pursue a career in the creative economy.

The school's programs in the areas of design, media arts, fashion, and culinary give students the opportunity to learn by using professional-grade technology and to build a portfolio of work to show potential employers after graduation.

The Art Institute of Indianapolis is accredited by the Accrediting Council for Independent Colleges and Schools to award certificates, associate's degrees, and bachelor's degrees. The Accrediting Council for Independent Colleges and Schools is listed as a nationally recognized accrediting agency by the United States Department of Education and is recognized by the Council for Higher Education Accreditation. ACICS can be contacted at 750 First Street NE, Suite 980, Washington, D.C. 20002; phone: 202-336-6780. The Art Institute of Indianapolis is a branch of The Art Institute of Phoenix located in Phoenix, Arizona.

The Art Institute of Indianapolis is regulated by the Indiana Commission on Proprietary Education, 302 West Washington Street, Room E201, Indianapolis, Indiana 46204; phone: 800-227-5695 (toll-free) or 317-232-1320.

Location

Located in the northwest part of Indianapolis, at the Pyramids, the school is within minutes of a thriving metropolis. The Pyramids are situated on 45 acres, with a 25-acre lake. The Pyramids are adjacent to I-465 for convenient travel to all major thoroughfares.

Programs of Study and Degrees

No matter which course of study a student may choose, the professionals at The Art Institute of Indianapolis will guide, support, and help each student as their talents evolve on their journey of personal and professional transformation. Students studying design learn to fine-tune their visual thinking and problem-solving skills as they create everything from logos to TV ads. Programs in the area of media arts focus on utilizing technology to deliver information and entertainment, while students studying fashion learn to design clothes for the runway or run a retail shop. Culinary programs focus on the fundamental techniques while exposing students to a full menu of international cuisines and management techniques.

Bachelor's degree programs are offered in the areas of culinary management, digital photography, fashion and retail management, fashion design, graphic design, interior design, media arts and animation, and Web design and interactive media.

Associate degree programs are offered in the areas of baking and pastry, culinary arts, digital photography, and graphic design.

Certificate programs are available in the areas of baking and pastry, culinary arts, digital design, digital image management, fashion retailing, Web design and development, and Web design and interactive communications.

Academic Programs

The Art Institute of Indianapolis operates on a year-round, four-quarter system.

Academic Facilities

The Art Institute of Indianapolis provides a learning environment with professional-grade technology applicable to each student's course of study. Students have the opportunity to build a portfolio of work that shows potential employers that they are trained to use the software, hardware, or equipment utilized within the industry. Depending upon the course of study, students are immersed in a creative environment—from classrooms to computer labs to studios—focused on relevant, hands-on education designed to prepare students for the real world.

Costs

Tuition cost varies by program. Prospective students should contact the school for current tuition costs. Other charges include a starting kit for all first-quarter students. Kits vary in price depending on the program of study.

Financial Aid

Financial aid is available for those who qualify. Students who require financial assistance should first complete and submit a Free Application for Federal Student Aid (FAFSA) and meet with a financial aid officer.

Faculty

Faculty members are experienced professionals who create a learning environment that is similar to the professional world students will face after graduation. Instructors are focused on helping students develop the skills they need to transform their creative potential into marketable skills.

Admission Requirements

Applicants must provide proof of high school graduation or achievement of a General Educational Development (GED) certificate as a prerequisite for admission. In lieu of documenting high school graduation or a GED certificate, applicants may provide proof of attaining an associate degree or higher from an accredited institution. An official transcript indicating date of high school graduation, GED certificate (including test scores), or date of college graduation (including degree granted) is required as proof.

All individuals seeking admission to The Art Institute of Indianapolis are interviewed in person or by phone by an assistant director of admissions, and each applicant must create an original essay of at least 150 words stating how an education at The Art Institute of Indianapolis would help the student to achieve career goals. There is a $50 application fee.

For the most recent information regarding admission requirements, please refer to the current academic catalog.

Application and Information

To obtain an application, make arrangements for an interview, or tour the school, prospective students should contact:

The Art Institute of Indianapolis
A branch of The Art Institute of Phoenix
3500 Depauw Boulevard, Suite 1010
Indianapolis, Indiana 46268-6124
Phone: 317-613-4800
          866-441-9031 (toll-free)
Fax: 317-613-4808
Web site: http://www.artinstitutes.edu/indianapolis

Over 50 schools: The Art Institute of Atlanta; The Art Institute of Atlanta—Decatur, A branch of The Art Institute of Atlanta; The Art Institute of Austin, A branch of The Art Institute of Houston; The Art Institute of California, a college of Argosy University, with locations in Hollywood, Inland Empire, Los Angeles, Orange County, Sacramento, San Diego, San Francisco, and Sunnyvale; The Art Institute of Charleston, A branch of The Art Institute of Atlanta; The Art Institute of Charlotte; The Art Institute of Colorado; The Art Institute of Dallas, A campus of South University; The Art Institute of Fort Lauderdale; The Art Institute of Fort Worth, A campus of South University; The Art Institute of Houston; The Art Institute of Houston—North, A branch of The Art Institute of Houston; The Art Institute of Indianapolis; The Art Institute of Jacksonville, A branch of Miami International University of Art & Design; The Art Institute of Las Vegas; The Art Institute of Michigan; The Art Institute of Michigan—Troy; The Art Institute of New York City; The Art Institute of Ohio—Cincinnati; The Art Institute of Philadelphia; The Art Institute of Phoenix; The Art Institute of Pittsburgh; The Art Institute of Portland; The Art Institute of Raleigh–Durham; The Art Institute of Salt Lake City; The Art Institute of San Antonio, A branch of The Art Institute of Houston; The Art Institute of Seattle; The Art Institute of Tampa, A branch of Miami International University of Art & Design; The Art Institute of Tennessee—Nashville, A branch of The Art Institute of Atlanta; The Art Institute of Tucson; The Art Institute of Vancouver; The Art Institute of Virginia Beach[1], A branch of The Art Institute of Atlanta; The Art Institute of Washington[1], A branch of The Art Institute of Atlanta; The Art Institute of Washington—Dulles[1], A branch of The Art Institute of Atlanta; The Art Institute of Wisconsin; The Art Institute of York—Pennsylvania; The Art Institutes International—Kansas City; The Art Institutes International Minnesota; The Illinois Institute of Art—Chicago; The Illinois Institute of Art—Schaumburg; The Illinois Institute of Art—Tinley Park; Miami International University of Art & Design; The New England Institute of Art

[1]Certified by SCHEV to operate in Virginia

See **aiprograms.info** for program duration, tuition, fees, and other costs, median debt, federal salary data, alumni success, and other important info. The Art Institutes is a system of over 50 schools throughout North America. Programs, credential levels, technology, and scheduling options vary by school, and employment opportunities are not guaranteed. Financial aid is available to those who qualify. Several institutions included in The Art Institutes system are campuses of South University or Argosy University. OH Registration # 04-01-1698B, AC0165, AC0080, Licensed by the Florida Commission for Independent Education, License No. 1287, 3427, 3110, 2581. Administrative office: 210 Sixth Avenue, 33rd Floor, Pittsburgh, PA 15222. ©2012 The Art Institutes International LLC.

THE ART INSTITUTE OF JACKSONVILLE
JACKSONVILLE, FLORIDA

The Art Institute of Jacksonville™
A branch of Miami International University of Art & Design

CREATE TOMORROW

A focused education from The Art Institute of Jacksonville, a branch of Miami International University of Art & Design, can help students turn their creative energy into a powerful tool that can make a difference in the world. Students are part of a collaborative and supportive community, where experienced instructors provide the guidance and skills needed to pursue a career in the creative economy.

The school's programs in the areas of design, media arts, fashion, and culinary give students the opportunity to learn by using professional-grade technology and to build a portfolio of work to show potential employers after graduation.

The Art Institute of Jacksonville is a branch of Miami International University of Art & Design. Miami International University of Art & Design and its branch campuses are accredited by the Commission on Colleges of the Southern Association of Colleges and Schools to award diplomas, associate, baccalaureate, and master's degrees. For questions about the accreditation of Miami International University of Art & Design and its branches, contact the Commission on Colleges at 1866 Southern Lane, Decatur, Georgia 30033-4097; phone: 404-679-4500.

The Art Institute of Jacksonville is licensed by the Commission for Independent Education, Florida Department of Education. Additional information regarding this institution may be obtained by contacting the Commission at 325 West Gaines Street, Suite 1414, Tallahassee, Florida 32399-0400; phone: 888-224-6684 (toll-free). License No. 3427.

Location

The Art Institute of Jacksonville is located in Jacksonville, Florida's largest city. With mild winters and warm summers, Jacksonville is a popular tourist destination. The Jacksonville beaches, Florida Theater, and professional sports teams are exciting entertainment options within the region.

Programs of Study and Degrees

No matter which course of study a student may choose, the professionals at The Art Institute of Jacksonville will guide, support, and help each student as their talents evolve on their journey of personal and professional transformation. Students studying design learn to fine-tune their visual thinking and problem-solving skills as they create everything from logos to TV ads. Programs in the area of media arts focus on utilizing technology to deliver information and entertainment, while students studying fashion learn to design clothes for the runway or run a retail shop. Culinary programs focus on the fundamental techniques while exposing students to a full menu of international cuisines and management techniques.

Bachelor's degrees are offered in the areas of culinary management, digital filmmaking and video production, digital photography, fashion and retail management, graphic design, interior design, media arts and animation, and Web design and interactive media.

Associate degrees are offered in the areas of culinary arts, graphic design, and Web design and interactive media design.

Diploma programs are offered in the areas of baking and pastry, culinary arts, digital image management, fashion retailing, Web design and development I, and Web design and development II.

A Master of Arts in Design and Media Management is offered. The Design and Media Management degree program at Miami International University of Art & Design will be offered at its branch campuses, The Art Institute of Tampa and The Art Institute of Jacksonville, with both real-time and recorded online learning sessions.

Academic Programs

The academic year is divided into four quarters, beginning in January, April, July, and October. Each program is offered on a year-round basis, allowing students to continue to work uninterrupted toward their degrees.

Academic Facilities

The Art Institute of Jacksonville provides a learning environment with professional-grade technology applicable to each student's course of study. Students have the opportunity to build a portfolio of work that shows potential employers that they are trained to use the software, hardware, or equipment utilized within the industry. Depending upon the course of study, students are immersed in a creative environment—from classrooms to computer labs to studios—focused on relevant, hands-on education designed to prepare students for the real world.

Costs

Tuition cost varies by program. Prospective students should contact the school for current tuition costs. Other charges include a starting kit for all first-quarter students. Kits vary in price depending on the program of study.

Financial Aid

Financial aid is available for those who qualify. Students who require financial assistance should first complete and submit a Free Application for Federal Student Aid (FAFSA) and meet with a financial aid officer.

Faculty

Faculty members are experienced professionals who create a learning environment that is similar to the professional world students will face after graduation. Instructors are focused on helping students develop the skills they need to transform their creative potential into marketable skills.

Student Government

The Student Federation is responsible for student government and acts as a liaison between the student body and faculty and staff members.

Admission Requirements

Applicants must provide proof of high school graduation or achievement of a General Educational Development (GED) certificate as a prerequisite for admission. In lieu of documenting high school graduation or a GED certificate, applicants may provide proof of attaining an associate degree or higher from an accredited institution. An official transcript indicating date of high school graduation, GED certificate (including test scores), or date of college graduation (including degree granted) is required as proof.

All individuals seeking admission to The Art Institute of Jacksonville are interviewed in person or by phone by an assistant director of admissions, and each applicant must submit an original essay of at least 150 words stating how an education at the school would help the student to achieve career goals. There is a $50 application fee.

For the most recent information regarding admission requirements, please refer to the current academic catalog.

Application and Information

To obtain an application, make arrangements for an interview, or tour the school, prospective students should contact:

The Art Institute of Jacksonville
A branch of Miami International University of Art & Design
8775 Baypine Road
Jacksonville, Florida 32256-8528
Phone: 904-486-3000
        800-924-1589 (toll-free)
Fax: 904-732-9423
Web site: http://www.artinstitutes.edu/jacksonville

THE ART INSTITUTE OF LAS VEGAS
HENDERSON, NEVADA

The Art Institute
of Las Vegas®

CREATE TOMORROW

A focused education from The Art Institute of Las Vegas, a branch of The Art Institute of Phoenix, can help students turn their creative energy into a powerful tool that can make a difference in the world. Students are part of a collaborative and supportive community, where experienced instructors provide the guidance and skills needed to pursue a career in the creative economy.

The school's programs in the areas of design, media arts, fashion, and culinary give students the opportunity to learn by using professional-grade technology and to build a portfolio of work to show potential employers after graduation.

The Art Institute of Las Vegas is accredited by the Accrediting Council for Independent Colleges and Schools to award diplomas, associate's degrees, and bachelor's degrees. The Accrediting Council for Independent Colleges and Schools is listed as a nationally recognized accrediting agency by the United States Department of Education and is recognized by the Council for Higher Education Accreditation. ACICS can be contacted at 750 First Street NE, Suite 980, Washington, D.C. 20002; phone: 202-336-6780. The Art Institute of Las Vegas is a branch of The Art Institute of Phoenix located in Phoenix, Arizona.

The Art Institute of Las Vegas is licensed to operate by the Commission on Postsecondary Education, 3663 East Sunset Road, Suite 202, Las Vegas, Nevada 89120; phone: 702-486-7330.

The Bachelor of Arts in interior design degree program is accredited by the National Kitchen & Bath Association (NKBA). NKBA can be contacted at 687 Willow Grove Street, Hackettstown, New Jersey 07840; phone: 800-THE-NKBA; www.nkba.org.

The Interior Design program leading to the Bachelor of Arts degree is accredited by the Council for Interior Design Accreditation, 206 Grandville Avenue, Suite 350, Grand Rapids, Michigan 49503; www.accredit-id.org.

The Associate of Science in Baking & Pastry, Associate of Science in Culinary Arts, and Bachelor of Arts in Culinary Management programs are accredited by The Accrediting Commission of the American Culinary Federation Education Foundation.

Location

Las Vegas provides sunny days, museums, libraries, parks, gift shops, and historical sites. Just outside the city are some of the world's most beautiful natural wonders, including the Grand Canyon, Red Rock Canyon, Death Valley, Hoover Dam, and Valley of Fire State Park. Nearly 1.5 million residents live in the Las Vegas metro area.

Programs of Study and Degrees

No matter which course of study a student may choose, the professionals at The Art Institute of Las Vegas will guide, support, and help each student as their talents evolve on their journey of personal and professional transformation. Students studying design learn to fine-tune their visual thinking and problem-solving skills as they create everything from logos to TV ads. Programs in the area of media arts focus on utilizing technology to deliver information and entertainment, while students studying fashion learn to design clothes for the runway or run a retail shop. Culinary programs focus on the fundamental techniques while exposing students to a full menu of international cuisines and management techniques.

Bachelor's degree programs are offered in the areas of advertising, audio production, culinary management, digital filmmaking and video production, digital photography, fashion and retail management, food and beverage management, game art and design, graphic design, interior design, media arts and animation, visual effects and motion graphics, and Web design and interactive media.

Associate degree programs are available in the areas of baking and pastry, culinary arts, digital photography, and drafting technology and design.

Diploma programs are offered in the areas of baking and pastry, culinary arts, digital image management, fashion retailing, Web design and development, and Web design and interactive communications.

Academic Programs

To receive an associate degree, a student must complete a minimum of 112 quarter credits, with 28 quarter credits in general education courses and 84 quarter credits in a specialty area. To receive a bachelor's degree, a student must complete a minimum of 192 quarter credits, with 48 quarter credits in general education courses and 114 quarter credits in a specialty area. For both degrees, the student must achieve a cumulative GPA of 2.0 or higher, meet portfolio or other requirements, and satisfy all financial obligations to the school. A limited number of courses are available online for an additional fee per course.

Academic Facilities

The Art Institute of Las Vegas provides a learning environment with professional-grade technology applicable to each student's course of study. Students have the opportunity to build a portfolio of work that shows potential employers that they are trained to use the software, hardware, or equipment utilized within the industry. Depending upon the course of study, students are immersed in a creative environment—from classrooms to computer labs to studios—focused on relevant, hands-on education designed to prepare students for the real world.

Costs

Tuition cost varies by program. Prospective students should contact the school for current tuition costs. Other charges include a starting kit for all first-quarter students. Kits vary in price depending on the program of study.

Financial Aid

Financial aid is available for those who qualify. Students who require financial assistance should first complete and submit a Free Application for Federal Student Aid (FAFSA) and meet with a financial aid officer.

Faculty

Faculty members are experienced professionals who create a learning environment that is similar to the professional world students will face after graduation. Instructors are focused on helping students develop the skills they need to transform their creative potential into marketable skills.

Admission Requirements

As a prerequisite for admission, a prospective student must be a high school graduate, hold a General Educational Development (GED) certificate, or have earned a bachelor's degree or higher from an accredited institution of postsecondary education. Each prospective student is interviewed, either in person or by telephone, by an assistant director of admissions to determine whether the student and school are a good fit. Portfolios may qualify the student for advanced placement, and applications may be submitted any time prior to the start of the next quarter. There is a $50 application fee.

For the most recent information regarding admission requirements, please refer to the current academic catalog.

Application and Information

To obtain an application, make arrangements for an interview, or tour the school, prospective students should contact:

The Art Institute of Las Vegas
A branch of The Art Institute of Phoenix
2350 Corporate Circle
Henderson, Nevada 89074-7737
Phone: 702-369-9944
      800-833-2678 (toll-free)
Fax: 702-992-8458
Web site: http://www.artinstitutes.edu/lasvegas

THE ART INSTITUTE OF MICHIGAN

NOVI, MICHIGAN

The Art Institute of Michigan™

CREATE TOMORROW

A focused education from The Art Institute of Michigan, a branch of The Illinois Institute of Art—Chicago, can help students turn their creative energy into a powerful tool that can make a difference in the world. Students are part of a collaborative and supportive community, where experienced instructors provide the guidance and skills needed to pursue a career in the creative economy.

The school's programs in the areas of design, media arts, fashion, and culinary give students the opportunity to learn by using professional-grade technology and to build a portfolio of work to show potential employers after graduation.

The Art Institute of Michigan, as a branch of the Illinois Institute of Art—Chicago, is accredited by the Higher Learning Commission and a member of the North Central Association (NCA), located at 230 South LaSalle Street, Suite 7-500, Chicago, Illinois 60604-1413; http://www.ncahlc.org.

The Art Institute of Michigan is licensed under the laws of the Michigan Department of Labor and Economic Growth.

The Diploma in Baking & Pastry and Associate of Applied Science in Culinary Arts programs are accredited by The Accrediting Commission of the American Culinary Federation Education Foundation.

Location

Novi, a town of over 52,000, is a suburb of Detroit. One of the fastest-growing cities in Michigan, Novi is home to the Motorsports Hall of Fame of America and Twelve Oaks Mall and just a short drive from the cultural, entertainment, and sports facilities of Detroit.

Programs of Study and Degrees

No matter which course of study a student may choose, the professionals at The Art Institute of Michigan will guide, support, and help each student as their talents evolve on their journey of personal and professional transformation. Students studying design learn to fine-tune their visual thinking and problem-solving skills as they create everything from logos to TV ads. Programs in the area of media arts focus on utilizing technology to deliver information and entertainment, while students studying fashion learn to design clothes for the runway or run a retail shop. Culinary programs focus on the fundamental techniques while exposing students to a full menu of international cuisines and management techniques.

Bachelor's degree programs are offered in the areas of audio production, culinary management, digital photography, fashion marketing and management, graphic design, interior design, media arts and animation, and Web design and interactive media.

Associate degrees are offered in the areas of culinary arts, fashion merchandising, graphic design, interior design, and Web design and interactive media.

Diploma programs are offered in the areas of baking and pastry, culinary arts, digital image management, fashion retailing, Web design and development, and Web design and interactive communications.

Academic Programs

The Art Institute of Michigan operates on a year-round, four-quarter system.

Academic Facilities

The Art Institute of Michigan provides a learning environment with professional-grade technology applicable to each student's course of study. Students have the opportunity to build a portfolio of work that shows potential employers that they are trained to use the software, hardware, or equipment utilized within the industry. Depending upon the course of study, students are immersed in a creative environment—from classrooms to computer labs to studios—focused on relevant, hands-on education designed to prepare students for the real world.

Costs

Tuition cost varies by program. Prospective students should contact the school for current tuition costs. Other charges include a starting kit for all first-quarter students. Kits vary in price depending on the program of study.

Financial Aid

Financial aid is available for those who qualify. Students who require financial assistance should first complete and submit a Free Application for Federal Student Aid (FAFSA) and meet with a financial aid officer.

Faculty

Faculty members are experienced professionals who create a learning environment that is similar to the professional world students will face after graduation. Instructors are focused on helping students develop the skills they need to transform their creative potential into marketable skills.

Admission Requirements

Applicants must provide proof of high school graduation or achievement of a General Educational Development (GED) certificate as a prerequisite for admission. In lieu of documenting high school graduation or a GED certificate, applicants may provide proof of attaining an associate degree or higher from an accredited institution. An official transcript indicating date of high school graduation, GED certificate (including test scores), or date of college graduation (including degree granted) is required as proof.

All individuals seeking admission to The Art Institute of Michigan are interviewed in person or by phone by an assistant director of admissions, and each applicant must submit an original essay of at least 150 words stating how an education at The Art Institute of Michigan would help the student to achieve career goals.

There is a $50 application fee.

For the most recent information regarding admission requirements, please refer to the current academic catalog.

Application and Information

To obtain an application, make arrangements for an interview, or tour the school, students should contact:

The Art Institute of Michigan
A branch of The Illinois Institute of Art—Chicago
28125 Cabot Drive, Suite 120
Novi, Michigan 48377
Phone: 248-675-3800
      800-479-0087 (toll-free)
Fax: 248-675-3830
Web site: http://www.artinstitutes.edu/detroit

THE ART INSTITUTE OF MICHIGAN—TROY

TROY, MICHIGAN

Ai The Art Institute of Michigan™–Troy

CREATE TOMORROW

A focused education from The Art Institute of Michigan—Troy, an additional location of The Illinois Institute of Art—Chicago, can help students turn their creative energy into a powerful tool that can make a difference in the world. Students are part of a collaborative and supportive community, where experienced instructors provide the guidance and skills needed to pursue a career in the creative economy.

The school's programs in the areas of design, media arts, and fashion give students the opportunity to learn by using professional-grade technology and to build a portfolio of work to show potential employers after graduation.

The Art Institute of Michigan—Troy is an additional location of the Illinois Institute of Art—Chicago, which is accredited by the Higher Learning Commission and a member of the North Central Association (NCA), located at 230 South LaSalle Street, Suite 7-500, Chicago, Illinois 60604-1413; phone: 800-621-7440; www.ncahlc.org.

The Art Institute of Michigan—Troy is licensed under the laws of the Michigan Department of Labor and Economic Growth.

Location

Troy, a suburb of Detroit, was recently ranked by *CNN Money* as one of the "Best Places to Live" in the United States. Troy is also known for its community sports programs and is home to the Troy Sports Center, the training facility of the Detroit Red Wings.

Programs of Study and Degrees

No matter which course of study a student may choose, the professionals at The Art Institute of Michigan—Troy will guide, support, and help each student as their talents evolve on their journey of personal and professional transformation. Students studying design learn to fine-tune their visual thinking and problem-solving skills as they create everything from logos to TV ads. Programs in the area of media arts focus on utilizing technology to deliver information and entertainment, while students studying fashion learn to market and merchandise clothing.

Bachelor's degree programs are offered in the areas of digital photography, fashion marketing and management, graphic design, interior design, media arts and animation, and Web design and interactive media.

Associate degree programs are offered in the areas of fashion merchandising and graphic design.

Diploma programs are offered in the areas of digital image management, fashion retailing, Web design and development, and Web design and interactive communications.

Academic Programs

The Art Institute of Michigan—Troy operates on a year-round, four-quarter system.

Academic Facilities

The Art Institute of Michigan—Troy provides a learning environment with professional-grade technology applicable to each student's course of study. Students have the opportunity to build a portfolio of work that shows potential employers that they are trained to use the software, hardware, or equipment utilized within the industry. Depending upon the course of study, students are immersed in a creative environment—from classrooms to computer labs to studios—focused on relevant, hands-on education designed to prepare students for the real world.

Costs

Tuition cost varies by program. Prospective students should contact the school for current tuition costs. Other charges include a starting kit for all first-quarter students. Kits vary in price depending on the program of study.

Financial Aid

Financial aid is available for those who qualify. Students who require financial assistance should first complete and submit a Free Application for Federal Student Aid (FAFSA) and meet with a financial aid officer.

Faculty

Faculty members are experienced professionals who create a learning environment that is similar to the professional

world students will face after graduation. Instructors are focused on helping students develop the skills they need to transform their creative potential into marketable skills.

Admission Requirements

Applicants must provide proof of high school graduation or achievement of a General Educational Development (GED) certificate as a prerequisite for admission. In lieu of documenting high school graduation or a GED certificate, applicants may provide proof of attaining an associate degree or higher from an accredited institution. An official transcript indicating date of high school graduation, GED certificate (including test scores), or date of college graduation (including degree granted) is required as proof.

All individuals seeking admission to The Art Institute of Michigan—Troy are interviewed in person or by phone by an assistant director of admissions, and each applicant must create an original essay of at least 150 words stating how an education at The Art Institute of Michigan—Troy would help the student to achieve career goals. There is a $50 application fee.

For the most recent information regarding admission requirements, please refer to the current academic catalog.

Application and Information

To obtain an application, make arrangements for an interview, or tour the school, prospective students should contact:

The Art Institute of Michigan—Troy
A additional location of The Illinois Institute of Art—Chicago
1414 East Maple Road, Suite 150
Troy, Michigan 48083
Phone: 248-837-3200
        877-320-3275 (toll-free)
Fax: 248-837-3300
Web site: http://www.artinstitutes.edu/troy

THE ART INSTITUTE OF OHIO— CINCINNATI

CINCINNATI, OHIO

A focused education from The Art Institute of Ohio— Cincinnati, a branch of The Illinois Institute of Art—Chicago, can help students turn their creative energy into a powerful tool that can make a difference in the world. Students are part of a collaborative and supportive community, where experienced instructors provide the guidance and skills needed to pursue a career in the creative economy.

The school's programs in the areas of design, media arts, fashion, and culinary give students the opportunity to learn by using professional-grade technology and to build a portfolio of work to show potential employers after graduation.

The Art Institute of Ohio—Cincinnati, as a branch of the Illinois Institute of Art—Chicago, is accredited by the Higher Learning Commission and a member of the North Central Association (NCA), 230 South LaSalle Street, Suite 7-500, Chicago, Illinois 60604-1413; phone: 800-621-7440 (toll-free); http://www.ncahlc.org.

The Art Institute of Ohio—Cincinnati holds a provisional certificate of authorization for its academic programs by the Ohio Board of Regents, 30 East Broad Street, Columbus, Ohio 43215; phone: 614-466-6000. The provisional authorization expires on December 31, 2012.

The Art Institute of Ohio—Cincinnati is licensed by the Ohio State Board of Career Colleges and Schools, 30 East Broad Street, 24th Floor, Suite 2481, Columbus, Ohio 43215-3138; phone: 614-466-2752. OH Reg. # 04-01-1698B.

The Art Institute of Ohio—Cincinnati is regulated by the Indiana Commission on Proprietary Education, 302 West Washington Street, Room E201, Indianapolis, Indiana 46204-2767; phone: 317-232-1320 (in-state) or 800-227-5695 (toll-free). AC0165.

The Associate of Applied Science in Culinary Arts degree program is accredited by the Accrediting Commission of the American Culinary Federation Education Foundation.

Location

Cincinnati is home to major-league sporting events, concerts, a professional symphony, theater, Kings Island, award-winning restaurants, and downtown entertainment districts that offer exciting nightlife. The city is known for its great beauty, with steep hills, wooded suburbs, a picturesque downtown riverfront, and four distinct seasons.

Programs of Study and Degrees

No matter which course of study a student may choose, the professionals at The Art Institute of Ohio—Cincinnati will guide, support, and help each student as their talents evolve on their journey of personal and professional transformation. Students studying design learn to fine-tune their visual thinking and problem-solving skills as they create everything from logos to TV ads. Programs in the area of media arts focus on utilizing technology to deliver information and entertainment, while students studying fashion learn to design clothes for the runway or run a retail shop. Culinary programs focus on the fundamental techniques while exposing students to a full menu of international cuisines and management techniques.

Bachelor's degree programs are available in the areas of advertising, culinary management, digital filmmaking and video production, fashion marketing and management, graphic design, interior design, media arts and animation, and Web design and interactive media.

Associate degree programs include the areas of culinary arts, fashion merchandising, graphic design, interior design, video production, and Web design and interactive media.

Diploma programs are offered in the areas of baking and pastry, culinary arts, fashion retailing, Web design and development, and Web design and interactive communications.

Academic Programs

The Art Institute of Ohio—Cincinnati operates on a year-round, four-quarter system.

Academic Facilities

The Art Institute of Ohio—Cincinnati provides a learning environment with professional-grade technology applicable to each student's course of study. Students have the opportunity to build a portfolio of work that shows potential employers that they are trained to use the software, hardware, or equipment utilized within the industry. Depending upon the course of study, students are immersed

in a creative environment—from classrooms to computer labs to studios—focused on relevant, hands-on education designed to prepare students for the real world.

Costs

Tuition costs vary by program. Prospective students should contact the school for current tuition costs. Other charges include a starting kit for all first-quarter students. Kits vary in price, depending on the program of study.

Financial Aid

Financial aid is available for those who qualify.

Faculty

Faculty members are experienced professionals who create a learning environment that is similar to the professional world students will face after graduation. Instructors are focused on helping students develop the skills they need to transform their creative potential into marketable skills.

Admission Requirements

Applicants to The Art Institute of Ohio—Cincinnati must demonstrate proof of high school graduation or its equivalent. An official copy of the high school transcript or General Educational Development (GED) certificate is required. Candidates are interviewed and must write an essay on how an education at The Art Institute of Ohio—Cincinnati can help them reach their career goals.

Each applicant's academic transcript and completed essay are evaluated by the Admissions Acceptance Committee. A separate application and enrollment form must be completed and signed by the applicant and then submitted to The Art Institute of Ohio—Cincinnati. There is a $50 application fee.

For the most recent information regarding admission requirements, please refer to the current academic catalog.

Application and Information

To obtain an application, make arrangements for an interview, or tour the school, prospective students should contact:

The Art Institute of Ohio—Cincinnati
A branch of The Illinois Institute of Art—Chicago
8845 Governors Hill Drive
Cincinnati, Ohio 45249-3317
Phone: 513-833-2400
      866-613-5184 (toll-free)
Fax: 877-477-8486 (toll-free)
Web site: http://www.artinstitutes.edu/cincinnati

Over 50 schools: The Art Institute of Atlanta; The Art Institute of Atlanta—Decatur, A branch of The Art Institute of Atlanta; The Art Institute of Austin, A branch of The Art Institute of Houston; The Art Institute of California, a college of Argosy University, with locations in Hollywood, Inland Empire, Los Angeles, Orange County, Sacramento, San Diego, San Francisco, and Sunnyvale; The Art Institute of Charleston, A branch of The Art Institute of Atlanta; The Art Institute of Charlotte; The Art Institute of Colorado; The Art Institute of Dallas, A campus of South University; The Art Institute of Fort Lauderdale; The Art Institute of Fort Worth, A campus of South University; The Art Institute of Houston; The Art Institute of Houston—North, A branch of The Art Institute of Houston; The Art Institute of Indianapolis; The Art Institute of Jacksonville, A branch of Miami International University of Art & Design; The Art Institute of Las Vegas; The Art Institute of Michigan; The Art Institute of Michigan—Troy; The Art Institute of New York City; The Art Institute of Ohio—Cincinnati; The Art Institute of Philadelphia; The Art Institute of Phoenix; The Art Institute of Pittsburgh; The Art Institute of Portland; The Art Institute of Raleigh–Durham; The Art Institute of Salt Lake City; The Art Institute of San Antonio, A branch of The Art Institute of Houston; The Art Institute of Seattle; The Art Institute of Tampa, A branch of Miami International University of Art & Design; The Art Institute of Tennessee—Nashville, A branch of The Art Institute of Atlanta; The Art Institute of Tucson; The Art Institute of Vancouver; The Art Institute of Virginia Beach[1], A branch of The Art Institute of Atlanta; The Art Institute of Washington[1], A branch of The Art Institute of Atlanta; The Art Institute of Washington—Dulles[1], A branch of The Art Institute of Atlanta; The Art Institute of Wisconsin; The Art Institute of York—Pennsylvania; The Art Institutes International—Kansas City; The Art Institutes International Minnesota; The Illinois Institute of Art—Chicago; The Illinois Institute of Art—Schaumburg; The Illinois Institute of Art—Tinley Park; Miami International University of Art & Design; The New England Institute of Art

[1]Certified by SCHEV to operate in Virginia

See aiprograms.info for program duration, tuition, fees, and other costs, median debt, federal salary data, alumni success, and other important info. The Art Institutes is a system of over 50 schools throughout North America. Programs, credential levels, technology, and scheduling options vary by school, and employment opportunities are not guaranteed. Financial aid is available to those who qualify. Several institutions included in The Art Institutes system are campuses of South University or Argosy University. OH Registration # 04-01-1698B, AC0165, AC0080, Licensed by the Florida Commission for Independent Education, License No. 1287, 3427, 3110, 2581. Administrative office: 210 Sixth Avenue, 33rd Floor, Pittsburgh, PA 15222. ©2012 The Art Institutes International LLC.

THE ART INSTITUTE OF PHILADELPHIA
PHILADELPHIA, PENNSYLVANIA

A focused education from The Art Institute of Philadelphia can help students turn their creative energy into a powerful tool that can make a difference in the world. Students are part of a collaborative and supportive community, where experienced instructors provide the guidance and skills needed to pursue a career in the creative economy.

The school's programs in the areas of design, media arts, fashion, and culinary give students the opportunity to learn by using professional-grade technology and to build a portfolio of work to show potential employers after graduation.

The Art Institute of Philadelphia is accredited by the Accrediting Council for Independent Colleges and Schools (ACICS) to award diplomas, associate's degrees, and bachelor's degrees. The Accrediting Council for Independent Colleges and Schools is listed as a nationally recognized accrediting agency by the United States Department of Education and is recognized by the Council for Higher Education Accreditations. ACICS can be contacted at 750 First Street NE, Suite 980, Washington, D.C. 20002; phone: 202-336-6780.

The Art Institute of Philadelphia is authorized by the Pennsylvania Department of Education to confer Bachelor of Science degrees, Associate of Science degrees, and diplomas. The Department of Education can be contacted at Commonwealth of Pennsylvania, Department of Education Office of Postsecondary and Higher Education, 333 Market Street, Harrisburg, Pennsylvania 17126; phone: 717-783-6788.

The Associate of Science in Culinary Arts degree program is accredited by the Accrediting Commission of the American Culinary Federation Education Foundation.

The Bachelor of Science in Interior Design degree program is accredited by the National Kitchen and Bath Association (NKBA). NKBA can be contacted at 687 Willow Grove Street, Hackettstown, New Jersey 07840, phone: 800-THE-NKBA; www.nkba.org.

The Interior Design program leading to the Bachelor of Science degree is accredited by the Council for Interior Design Accreditation, 206 Grandville Avenue, Suite 350, Grand Rapids, Michigan 49503; http://www.accredit-id.org.

Location

Philadelphia is the birthplace of American democracy. The City of Brotherly Love surrounds the largest municipal landscaped park in the world, with tree-lined streets and an elegant blend of contemporary and historic architecture. Philadelphia has a renowned symphony orchestra, theater, films, jazz, and opera. With thirty-two major museums—including the expansive collections at the Museum of Art—the city is also home to fine shopping at locations such as the European-style Bourse, with its fifty international boutiques and restaurants, and to sports teams, such as baseball's Phillies, the NFL's Eagles, the NBA's 76ers, and the NHL's Flyers.

Programs of Study and Degrees

No matter which course of study a student may choose, the professionals at The Art Institute of Philadelphia will guide, support, and help each student as their talents evolve on their journey of personal and professional transformation. Students studying design learn to fine-tune their visual thinking and problem-solving skills as they create everything from logos to TV ads. Programs in the area of media arts focus on utilizing technology to deliver information and entertainment, while students studying fashion learn to design clothes for the runway or run a retail shop. Culinary programs focus on the fundamental techniques while exposing students to a full menu of international cuisines and management techniques.

The Art Institute of Philadelphia offers bachelor's degree programs in the areas of advertising, audio production, culinary management, digital filmmaking and video production, fashion design, fashion marketing, graphic design, industrial design technology, interior design, media arts and animation, photography, visual effects and motion graphics, and Web design and interactive media.

Associate degree programs are offered in the areas of culinary arts, digital filmmaking and video production, fashion design, fashion marketing, graphic design, interior design, photography, visual merchandising, and Web design and interactive media.

Diploma programs are offered in the areas of baking and pastry, culinary arts, digital image management, fashion retailing, Web design and development, and Web design and interactive communications.

The baking and pastry diploma program and the Associate of Science in Culinary Arts program are available in an evening and weekend option format.

Academic Programs

School quarters are eleven weeks long, and academic programs are between six and twelve quarters in length. Programs are offered on a year-round basis, allowing for strong continuity and the ability to work uninterrupted toward a degree.

The Art Institute of Philadelphia arranges student trips to local cultural and commercial sites. These visits can be an integral part of each student's learning experience. In addition to local student trips to support the curriculum, out-of-town seminars and visits are planned within individual programs.

Academic Facilities

The Art Institute of Philadelphia provides a learning environment with professional-grade technology applicable to each student's course of study. Students have the opportunity to build a portfolio of work that shows potential employers that they are trained to use the software, hardware, or equipment utilized within the industry. Depending upon the course of study, students are immersed in a creative environment—from classrooms to computer labs to studios—focused on relevant, hands-on education designed to prepare students for the real world.

Costs

Tuition cost varies by program. Prospective students should contact the school for current tuition costs. Other charges include a starting kit for all first-quarter students. Kits vary in price depending on the program of study.

Financial Aid

Financial aid is available for those who qualify. Students who require financial assistance should first complete and submit a Free Application for Federal Student Aid (FAFSA) and meet with a financial aid officer.

Faculty

Faculty members are experienced professionals who create a learning environment that is similar to the professional world students will face after graduation. Instructors are focused on helping students develop the skills they need to transform their creative potential into marketable skills.

Admission Requirements

High school graduation or a General Educational Development (GED) certificate is a prerequisite for admission. All applicants are evaluated on the basis of previous education and their background/interest in the program of interest. Portfolios are welcomed but not required.

The Art Institute of Philadelphia operates on a rolling admissions basis. High school and/or college transcripts must be submitted to The Art Institute of Philadelphia at least one month prior to starting classes. There is a $50 application fee.

For the most recent information regarding admission requirements, please refer to the current academic catalog.

Application and Information

To obtain an application, make arrangements for an interview, or tour the school, prospective students should contact:

The Art Institute of Philadelphia
1622 Chestnut Street
Philadelphia, Pennsylvania 19103-5119
Phone: 215-567-7080
      800-275-2474 (toll-free)
Fax: 215-405-6399
Web site: http://www.artinstitutes.edu/philadelphia

THE ART INSTITUTE OF PHOENIX
PHOENIX, ARIZONA

The Art Institute
of Phoenix®

CREATE TOMORROW

A focused education from The Art Institute of Phoenix can help students turn their creative energy into a powerful tool that can make a difference in the world. Students are part of a collaborative and supportive community, where experienced instructors provide the guidance and skills needed to pursue a career in the creative economy.

The school's programs in the areas of design, media arts, fashion, and culinary give students the opportunity to learn by using professional-grade technology and build a portfolio of work to show potential employers after graduation.

The Art Institute of Phoenix is accredited by the Accrediting Council for Independent Colleges and Schools to award diplomas, associate's degrees, and bachelor's degrees The Accrediting Council for Independent Colleges and Schools is listed as a nationally recognized accrediting agency by the United States Department of Education and is recognized by the Council for Higher Education Accreditation. ACICS can be contacted at 750 First Street NE, Suite 980, Washington, D.C. 20002; phone: 202-336-6780.

The Art Institute of Phoenix is authorized by the Arizona State Board for Private Postsecondary Education, located at 1400 West Washington Street, Room 2560, Phoenix, Arizona 85007; phone: 602-542-5709; http://azppse.state.az.us.

The Associate of Applied Science in Culinary Arts, the Associate of Applied Science in Baking & Pastry, and the Bachelor of Arts in Culinary Management degree programs are accredited by The Accrediting Commission of the American Culinary Federation Education Foundation.

The Interior Design program leading to the Bachelor of Arts degree is accredited by the Council for Interior Design Accreditation, 206 Grandville Avenue, Suite 350, Grand Rapids, Michigan 49503; www.accredit-id.org.

Location

Phoenix is one of the fastest-growing metropolitan areas in the country. Located in the heart of the beautiful Sonoran Desert, Phoenix is the gateway to cool pine forests, the red rock towers of Sedona, and the Grand Canyon. The city offers sun-filled days and a nightlife that ranges from top comedy and music clubs to the Phoenix Art Museum and Phoenix Symphony Orchestra. Professional sports teams include the Diamondbacks, Suns, Cardinals, and Coyotes.

Programs of Study and Degrees

No matter which course of study a student may choose, the professionals at The Art Institute of Phoenix will guide, support, and help each student as their talents evolve on their journey of personal and professional transformation. Students studying design learn to fine-tune their visual thinking and problem-solving skills as they create everything from logos to TV ads. Programs in the area of media arts focus on utilizing technology to deliver information and entertainment, while students studying fashion learn to design clothes for the runway or run a retail shop. Culinary programs focus on the fundamental techniques while exposing students to a full menu of international cuisines and management techniques.

Bachelor's degree programs are offered in the areas of advertising, culinary management, digital filmmaking and video production, digital photography, fashion marketing, game art and design, graphic design, interior design, media arts and animation, visual and game programming, visual effects and motion graphics, and Web design and interactive media.

Associate of Applied Science degree programs are offered in the areas of baking and pastry arts, culinary arts, and graphic design.

Diploma programs are offered in the areas of baking and pastry, culinary arts, digital image management, fashion retailing, Web design and development, and Web design and interactive communications.

The culinary management, graphic design, and Web design and interactive media programs, and the Associate of Applied Science in culinary arts program are also available in an evening and weekend option format.

Academic Programs

The Art Institute of Phoenix is in session year-round. Depending on the program, students can graduate in nine to thirty-six months with a diploma, an Associate of Applied Science degree, or a Bachelor of Arts degree in their chosen field.

Academic Facilities

The Art Institute of Phoenix provides a learning environment with professional-grade technology applicable to each student's course of study. Students have the opportunity to build a portfolio of work that shows potential employers that they are trained to use the software, hardware, or equipment utilized within the industry. Depending upon the course of study, students are immersed in a creative environment—from classrooms to computer labs to studios—focused on relevant, hands-on education designed to prepare students for the real world.

Costs

Tuition cost varies by program. Prospective students should contact the school for current tuition costs. Other charges include a starting kit for all first-quarter students. Kits vary in price depending on the program of study.

Financial Aid

Financial aid is available for those who qualify. Students who require financial assistance should first complete and submit a Free Application for Federal Student Aid (FAFSA) and meet with a financial aid officer.

Faculty

Faculty members are experienced professionals who create a learning environment that is similar to the professional world students will face after graduation. Instructors are focused on helping students develop the skills they need to transform their creative potential into marketable skills.

Student Government

The President's Club is a school organization that promotes the philosophy of students helping students. Those students selected to join the club assist new students with adjusting to life in Phoenix, studies at The Art Institute of Phoenix, and school activities. Criteria for selection into this club are a minimum GPA of 3.0 at The Art Institute of Phoenix, good attendance, completion of at least one full quarter of study, a desire to assist other students, and responsible behavior.

Admission Requirements

Many prospective students meet with an assistant director of admissions to discuss future goals and plan the admissions process. For admission to The Art Institute of Phoenix, students are evaluated on the basis of previous education, background, and a demonstrated interest in the selected program. Portfolio submission is encouraged but not required.

As part of the application process, students must write an essay stating how an education at The Art Institute of Phoenix will help them to attain their creative goals. Successful admission into The Art Institute of Phoenix and a satisfactory program start is dependent upon the essay; grade point average, as evidenced in transcript evaluation; an evaluation of General Educational Development (GED) test scores; a review of nationally based exams (preferred but not required), such as the SAT or ACT; and a personal interview with an assistant director of admissions. There is a $50 application fee.

For the most recent information regarding admission requirements, please refer to the current academic catalog.

Application and Information

To obtain an application, make arrangements for an interview, or tour the school, prospective students should contact:

The Art Institute of Phoenix
2233 West Dunlap Avenue
Phoenix, Arizona 85021-2859
Phone: 602-331-7500
       800-474-2479 (toll-free)
Fax: 602-331-5301
Web site: http://www.artinstitutes.edu/phoenix

Over 50 schools: The Art Institute of Atlanta; The Art Institute of Atlanta—Decatur, A branch of The Art Institute of Atlanta; The Art Institute of Austin, A branch of The Art Institute of Houston; The Art Institute of California, a college of Argosy University, with locations in Hollywood, Inland Empire, Los Angeles, Orange County, Sacramento, San Diego, San Francisco, and Sunnyvale; The Art Institute of Charleston, A branch of The Art Institute of Atlanta; The Art Institute of Charlotte; The Art Institute of Colorado; The Art Institute of Dallas, A campus of South University; The Art Institute of Fort Lauderdale; The Art Institute of Fort Worth, A campus of South University; The Art Institute of Houston; The Art Institute of Houston—North, A branch of The Art Institute of Houston; The Art Institute of Indianapolis; The Art Institute of Jacksonville, A branch of Miami International University of Art & Design; The Art Institute of Las Vegas; The Art Institute of Michigan; The Art Institute of Michigan—Troy; The Art Institute of New York City; The Art Institute of Ohio—Cincinnati; The Art Institute of Philadelphia; The Art Institute of Phoenix; The Art Institute of Pittsburgh; The Art Institute of Portland; The Art Institute of Raleigh–Durham; The Art Institute of Salt Lake City; The Art Institute of San Antonio, A branch of The Art Institute of Houston; The Art Institute of Seattle; The Art Institute of Tampa, A branch of Miami International University of Art & Design; The Art Institute of Tennessee—Nashville, A branch of The Art Institute of Atlanta; The Art Institute of Tucson; The Art Institute of Vancouver; The Art Institute of Virginia Beach[1], A branch of The Art Institute of Atlanta; The Art Institute of Washington[1], A branch of The Art Institute of Atlanta; The Art Institute of Washington—Dulles[1], A branch of The Art Institute of Atlanta; The Art Institute of Wisconsin; The Art Institute of York—Pennsylvania; The Art Institutes International—Kansas City; The Art Institutes International Minnesota; The Illinois Institute of Art—Chicago; The Illinois Institute of Art—Schaumburg; The Illinois Institute of Art—Tinley Park; Miami International University of Art & Design; The New England Institute of Art

[1]Certified by SCHEV to operate in Virginia

See **aiprograms.info** for program duration, tuition, fees, and other costs, median debt, federal salary data, alumni success, and other important info. The Art Institutes is a system of over 50 schools throughout North America. Programs, credential levels, technology, and scheduling options vary by school, and employment opportunities are not guaranteed. Financial aid is available to those who qualify. Several institutions included in The Art Institutes system are campuses of South University or Argosy University. OH Registration # 04-01-1698B, AC0165, AC0080, Licensed by the Florida Commission for Independent Education, License No. 1287, 3427, 3110, 2581. Administrative office: 210 Sixth Avenue, 33rd Floor, Pittsburgh, PA 15222. ©2012 The Art Institutes International LLC.

THE ART INSTITUTE OF PITTSBURGH
PITTSBURGH, PENNSYLVANIA

A focused education from The Art Institute of Pittsburgh can help students turn their creative energy into a powerful tool that can make a difference in the world. Students are part of a collaborative and supportive community, where experienced instructors provide the guidance and skills needed to pursue a career in the creative economy.

The school's programs in the areas of design, media arts, fashion, and culinary give students the opportunity to learn by using professional-grade technology and to build a portfolio of work to show potential employers after graduation.

The Art Institute of Pittsburgh is accredited by the Middle States Commission on Higher Education, 3624 Market Street, Philadelphia, Pennsylvania 19104; phone: 267-284-5000. The Middle States Commission on Higher Education is an institutional accrediting agency recognized by the U.S. Secretary of Education and the Council for Higher Education Accreditation.

The Art Institute of Pittsburgh is authorized by the Pennsylvania Department of Education to confer the Bachelor of Science degrees, Associate of Science degrees, and diplomas. The Department of Education can be contacted at Commonwealth of Pennsylvania, Department of Education Office of Postsecondary and Higher Education, 333 Market Street, Harrisburg, Pennsylvania 17126; phone: 717-783-6788.

The Art Institute of Pittsburgh is registered as a private institution with the Minnesota Office of Higher Education pursuant to Minnesota Statutes, sections 136A.61 to 136A.71. Registration is not an endorsement of the institution. Credits earned at the institution may not transfer to all other institutions.

The Associate of Science degree in culinary arts and the Bachelor of Science degree in culinary management are accredited by the Accrediting Commission of the American Culinary Federation Education Foundation.

The interior design program leading to the Bachelor of Science degree is accredited by the Council for Interior Design Accreditation, 206 Grandville Avenue, Suite. 350, Grand Rapids, Michigan 49503; http://www.accredit-id.org.

Location

The Art Institute of Pittsburgh is nestled in the heart of downtown Pittsburgh's Golden Triangle. Pittsburgh is a thriving metropolis, sprawling over 55 square miles. It is situated halfway between New York City and Chicago and is within a two-hour flight or a one-day drive of more than 70 percent of the U.S. population.

Pittsburgh is the international headquarters of many technology-driven businesses. Culture abounds, with summer concerts in the downtown's Market Square at no charge, new theaters, thriving nightlife districts, quaint coffee shops, and retail merchants on every corner. The Pittsburgh Steelers' stadium and the Pirates' waterfront PNC Park adorn the city's North Shore. Pittsburgh is serviced by Greater Pittsburgh International Airport, one of the largest and most retail-developed airports in the country.

Programs of Study and Degrees

No matter which course of study a student may choose, the professionals at The Art Institute of Pittsburgh will guide, support, and help each student as their talents evolve on their journey of personal and professional transformation. Students studying design learn to fine-tune their visual thinking and problem-solving skills as they create everything from logos to TV ads. Programs in the area of media arts focus on utilizing technology to deliver information and entertainment, while students studying fashion learn to design clothes for the runway or run a retail shop. Culinary programs focus on the fundamental techniques while exposing students to a full menu of international cuisines and management techniques.

The Art Institute of Pittsburgh offers bachelor's degree programs in the areas of advertising, culinary management, digital filmmaking and video production, entertainment design, fashion and retail management, fashion design, game art and design, graphic design, hotel and restaurant management, industrial design, interior design, media arts and animation, photography, visual effects and motion graphics, and web design and interactive media.

Associate of Science degree programs are offered in the areas of baking and pastry, culinary arts, digital filmmaking and video production, graphic design, industrial design technology, kitchen and bath design, photography, and Web design and interactive media.

Diploma programs are offered in the areas of art of cooking, baking and pastry digital design, residential planning, and Web design.

Certificate programs are available in the areas of in 2D animation, 3D animation, 3D modeling for games, character animation for games, digital workflow, event management, food and beverage operations, internet marketing, portrait photography, and studio photography.

Academic Facilities

The Art Institute of Pittsburgh provides a learning environment with professional-grade technology applicable to each student's course of study. Students have the opportunity to build a portfolio of work that shows potential employers that they are trained to use the software, hardware, or equipment utilized within the industry. Depending upon the course of study, students are immersed in a creative environment—from classrooms to computer labs to studios—focused on relevant, hands-on education designed to prepare students for the real world.

Costs

Tuition cost varies by program. Prospective students should contact the school for current tuition costs. Other charges include a starting kit for all first-quarter students. Kits vary in price depending on the program of study.

Financial Aid

Financial aid is available for those who qualify. Students who require financial assistance should first complete and submit a Free Application for Federal Student Aid (FAFSA) and meet with a financial aid officer.

Faculty

Faculty members are experienced professionals who create a learning environment that is similar to the professional world students will face after graduation. Instructors are focused on helping students develop the skills they need to transform their creative potential into marketable skills.

Admission Requirements

A prospective student must be a high school graduate with a high school QPA of 2.0 or higher (2.5 or higher QPA required for admission into game art and design), hold a General Educational Development (GED) certificate, or have a bachelor's degree or higher as a prerequisite for admission. Students who have completed high school or its equivalent but cannot provide the necessary documentation may provide alternate documentation to satisfy this requirement. The president of The Art Institute of Pittsburgh must approve all exceptions. A student who holds a bachelor's degree or higher may submit proof of the degree to satisfy the high school graduation or General Educational Development (GED) requirement. There is a portfolio requirement for media arts and animation and game art and design program candidates.

All applicants are evaluated on the basis of their previous education, background, and stated or demonstrated interest in their program of choice. Applicants who have taken the SAT or ACT are encouraged to submit scores to the Admissions Office for evaluation.

Applications are accepted on a rolling basis. An application for admission must be completed and signed by the applicant and be submitted along with an essay stating how The Art Institute of Pittsburgh can help the student to attain his or her creative goals. There is a $50 application fee.

For the most recent information regarding admission requirements, please refer to the current academic catalog.

Application and Information

To obtain an application, make arrangements for an interview, or tour the school, prospective students should contact:

The Art Institute of Pittsburgh
420 Boulevard of the Allies
Pittsburgh, Pennsylvania 15219-1301
Phone: 412-263-6600
　　　800-275-2470 (toll-free)
Fax: 412-263-6667
Web site: http://www.artinstitutes.edu/pittsburgh

Over 50 schools: The Art Institute of Atlanta; The Art Institute of Atlanta—Decatur, A branch of The Art Institute of Atlanta; The Art Institute of Austin, A branch of The Art Institute of Houston; The Art Institute of California, a college of Argosy University, with locations in Hollywood, Inland Empire, Los Angeles, Orange County, Sacramento, San Diego, San Francisco, and Sunnyvale; The Art Institute of Charleston, A branch of The Art Institute of Atlanta; The Art Institute of Charlotte; The Art Institute of Colorado; The Art Institute of Dallas, A campus of South University; The Art Institute of Fort Lauderdale; The Art Institute of Fort Worth, A campus of South University; The Art Institute of Houston; The Art Institute of Houston—North, A branch of The Art Institute of Houston; The Art Institute of Indianapolis; The Art Institute of Jacksonville, A branch of Miami International University of Art & Design; The Art Institute of Las Vegas; The Art Institute of Michigan; The Art Institute of Michigan—Troy; The Art Institute of New York City; The Art Institute of Ohio—Cincinnati; The Art Institute of Philadelphia; The Art Institute of Phoenix; The Art Institute of Pittsburgh; The Art Institute of Portland; The Art Institute of Raleigh–Durham; The Art Institute of Salt Lake City; The Art Institute of San Antonio, A branch of The Art Institute of Houston; The Art Institute of Seattle; The Art Institute of Tampa, A branch of Miami International University of Art & Design; The Art Institute of Tennessee—Nashville, A branch of The Art Institute of Atlanta; The Art Institute of Tucson; The Art Institute of Vancouver; The Art Institute of Virginia Beach[1], A branch of The Art Institute of Atlanta; The Art Institute of Washington[1], A branch of The Art Institute of Atlanta; The Art Institute of Washington—Dulles[1], A branch of The Art Institute of Atlanta; The Art Institute of Wisconsin; The Art Institute of York—Pennsylvania; The Art Institutes International—Kansas City; The Art Institutes International Minnesota; The Illinois Institute of Art—Chicago; The Illinois Institute of Art—Schaumburg; The Illinois Institute of Art—Tinley Park; Miami International University of Art & Design; The New England Institute of Art

[1]Certified by SCHEV to operate in Virginia

See **aiprograms.info** for program duration, tuition, fees, and other costs, median debt, federal salary data, alumni success, and other important info. The Art Institutes is a system of over 50 schools throughout North America. Programs, credential levels, technology, and scheduling options vary by school, and employment opportunities are not guaranteed. Financial aid is available to those who qualify. Several institutions included in The Art Institutes system are campuses of South University or Argosy University. OH Registration # 04-01-1698B, AC0165, AC0080, Licensed by the Florida Commission for Independent Education, License No. 1287, 3427, 3110, 2581. Administrative office: 210 Sixth Avenue, 33rd Floor, Pittsburgh, PA 15222. ©2012 The Art Institutes International LLC.

THE ART INSTITUTE OF PORTLAND
PORTLAND, OREGON

The Art Institute of Portland®

CREATE TOMORROW

A focused education from The Art Institute of Portland can help students turn their creative energy into a powerful tool that can make a difference in the world. Students are part of a collaborative and supportive community, where experienced instructors provide the guidance and skills needed to pursue a career in the creative economy.

The school's programs in the areas of design, media arts, fashion, and culinary give students the opportunity to learn by using professional-grade technology and to build a portfolio of work to show potential employers after graduation.

The Art Institute of Portland is accredited by the Northwest Commission on Colleges and Universities (NWCCU), an institutional accrediting body recognized by the United States Department of Education. NWCCU can be contacted at 8060 165th Avenue NE, Suite 100, Redmond, Washington 98052-3981.

The Interior Design program leading to the Bachelor of Fine Arts degree is accredited by the Council for Interior Design Accreditation, 206 Grandville Avenue, Suite 350, Grand Rapids, Michigan 49503; http://www.accredit-id.org.

Location

Portland is the largest city in Oregon, located on the Willamette River near its junction with the Columbia River. Since 1888, Portland has been known as the Rose City because of the thousands of flowers that bloom in Washington Park. Natural attractions include the Columbia River Gorge's 3,000-foot-high basaltic cliffs, Multnomah Falls, and Mount Hood—the site of America's longest ski season. Portland also has a wide array of coffee shops, Native American art galleries, bookstores, and brew pubs as well as the Oregon Symphony, Tygres Heart Shakespeare Company, Musical Theater Company, Portland Opera, Baroque Orchestra, Northwest Afrikan American Ballet, Oregon Ballet Theatre, and Mount Hood Festival of Jazz.

Portland is home to many large apparel companies— students in the apparel accessory design and the apparel design programs have the advantage of learning from talented professionals in the industry. In addition, The Art Institute of Portland has built valuable relationships with the Oregon Film and Video Office and the Oregon Media Production Association.

Programs of Study and Degrees

No matter which course of study a student may choose, the professionals at The Art Institute of Portland will guide, support, and help each student as their talents evolve on their journey of personal and professional transformation. Students studying design learn to fine-tune their visual thinking and problem-solving skills as they create everything from logos to TV ads. Programs in the area of media arts focus on utilizing technology to deliver information and entertainment, while students studying fashion learn to design clothes for the runway or run a retail shop. Culinary programs focus on the fundamental techniques while exposing students to a full menu of international cuisines and management techniques.

Bachelor's degrees are available in the areas of advertising, apparel accessory design, apparel design, culinary management, design management, design research, design visualization, digital film and video, fashion marketing, game art and design, graphic design, industrial design, interior design, media arts and animation, photography and design, visual and game programming, visual effects and motion graphics, and Web design and interactive media.

Associate degrees are offered in the areas of apparel accessory design, apparel design, culinary arts, and graphic design.

Diploma programs are offered in the areas of art of cooking, baking and pastry, and fashion retailing.

A minor in sustainability is offered with the bachelor's degree programs in the areas of apparel accessory design, apparel design, culinary management, design management, design research, fashion marketing, industrial design, and interior design.

Academic Programs

The academic year is divided into four quarters, beginning in January, April, July, and October. To earn a bachelor's degree, students must complete, at minimum, 180 academic credits. To earn an associate's degree, students must earn, at minimum, 105 academic credits.

Academic Facilities

The Art Institute of Portland provides a learning environment with professional-grade technology applicable to each

student's course of study. Students have the opportunity to build a portfolio of work that shows potential employers that they are trained to use the software, hardware, or equipment utilized within the industry. Depending upon the course of study, students are immersed in a creative environment—from classrooms to computer labs to studios—focused on relevant, hands-on education designed to prepare students for the real world.

Costs

Tuition varies by program. Prospective students should contact the school for current tuition costs. Other charges include a starting kit for all first-quarter students. Kits vary in price depending on the program of study.

Financial Aid

Financial aid is available for those who qualify. Students who require financial assistance should first complete and submit a Free Application for Federal Student Aid (FAFSA) and meet with a financial aid officer.

Faculty

Faculty members are experienced professionals who create a learning environment that is similar to the professional world students will face after graduation. Instructors are focused on helping students develop the skills they need to transform their creative potential into marketable skills.

Admission Requirements

Prospective students must submit an essay of approximately 150 words in which they describe the ways an education at The Art Institute of Portland may help to meet their creative objectives. Portfolios are encouraged but not required. An application for admission and enrollment agreement must be submitted to the school. Applicants who have taken the SAT or ACT should also submit these test scores. Each individual seeking admission is interviewed by an assistant director of admissions in order to explore the applicant's background, interests, and goals. There is a $50 application fee.

For the most recent information regarding admission requirements, please refer to the current academic catalog.

Application and Information

To obtain an application, make arrangements for an interview, or tour the school, prospective students should contact:

The Art Institute of Portland
1122 N.W. Davis Street
Portland, Oregon 97209-2911
Phone: 503-228-6528
     888-228-6528 (toll-free)
Fax: 503-227-1945
Web site: http://www.artinstitutes.edu/portland

Over 50 schools: The Art Institute of Atlanta; The Art Institute of Atlanta—Decatur, A branch of The Art Institute of Atlanta; The Art Institute of Austin, A branch of The Art Institute of Houston; The Art Institute of California, a college of Argosy University, with locations in Hollywood, Inland Empire, Los Angeles, Orange County, Sacramento, San Diego, San Francisco, and Sunnyvale; The Art Institute of Charleston, A branch of The Art Institute of Atlanta; The Art Institute of Charlotte; The Art Institute of Colorado; The Art Institute of Dallas, A campus of South University; The Art Institute of Fort Lauderdale; The Art Institute of Fort Worth, A campus of South University; The Art Institute of Houston; The Art Institute of Houston—North, A branch of The Art Institute of Houston; The Art Institute of Indianapolis; The Art Institute of Jacksonville, A branch of Miami International University of Art & Design; The Art Institute of Las Vegas; The Art Institute of Michigan; The Art Institute of Michigan—Troy; The Art Institute of New York City; The Art Institute of Ohio—Cincinnati; The Art Institute of Philadelphia; The Art Institute of Phoenix; The Art Institute of Pittsburgh; The Art Institute of Portland; The Art Institute of Raleigh–Durham; The Art Institute of Salt Lake City; The Art Institute of San Antonio, A branch of The Art Institute of Houston; The Art Institute of Seattle; The Art Institute of Tampa, A branch of Miami International University of Art & Design; The Art Institute of Tennessee—Nashville, A branch of The Art Institute of Atlanta; The Art Institute of Tucson; The Art Institute of Vancouver; The Art Institute of Virginia Beach[1], A branch of The Art Institute of Atlanta; The Art Institute of Washington[1], A branch of The Art Institute of Atlanta; The Art Institute of Washington—Dulles[1], A branch of The Art Institute of Atlanta; The Art Institute of Wisconsin; The Art Institute of York—Pennsylvania; The Art Institutes International—Kansas City; The Art Institutes International Minnesota; The Illinois Institute of Art—Chicago; The Illinois Institute of Art—Schaumburg; The Illinois Institute of Art—Tinley Park; Miami International University of Art & Design; The New England Institute of Art

[1]Certified by SCHEV to operate in Virginia

See **aiprograms.info** for program duration, tuition, fees, and other costs, median debt, federal salary data, alumni success, and other important info. The Art Institutes is a system of over 50 schools throughout North America. Programs, credential levels, technology, and scheduling options vary by school, and employment opportunities are not guaranteed. Financial aid is available to those who qualify. Several institutions included in The Art Institutes system are campuses of South University or Argosy University. OH Registration # 04-01-1698B, AC0165, AC0080, Licensed by the Florida Commission for Independent Education, License No. 1287, 3427, 3110, 2581. Administrative office: 210 Sixth Avenue, 33rd Floor, Pittsburgh, PA 15222. ©2012 The Art Institutes International LLC.

THE ART INSTITUTE OF RALEIGH-DURHAM
DURHAM, NORTH CAROLINA

The Art Institute of Raleigh–Durham®
CREATE TOMORROW

A focused education from The Art Institute of Raleigh-Durham, a branch of The Art Institute of Charlotte, can help students turn their creative energy into a powerful tool that can make a difference in the world. Students are part of a collaborative and supportive community, where experienced instructors provide the guidance and skills needed to pursue a career in the creative economy.

The school's programs in the areas of design, media arts, fashion, and culinary give students the opportunity to learn by using professional-grade technology and to build a portfolio of work to show potential employers after graduation.

The Art Institute of Raleigh-Durham, a branch of The Art Institute of Charlotte, is accredited by the Accrediting Council for Independent Colleges and Schools to award associate's degrees and bachelor's degrees. The Accrediting Council for Independent Colleges and Schools is listed as a nationally recognized accrediting agency by the United States Department of Education and is recognized by the Council for Higher Education Accreditation. ACICS can be contacted at 750 First Street NE, Suite 980, Washington, D.C. 20002; phone: 202-336-6780.

The Art Institute of Raleigh-Durham is licensed by the Board of Governors of the University of North Carolina to confer Associate of Applied Science and Bachelor of Art degrees.

Location

The Art Institute of Raleigh-Durham is located in the heart of the downtown Durham historical and entertainment district. The metropolitan area of North Carolina is known as the Research Triangle, with a population of over 1.6 million people.

Programs of Study and Degrees

No matter which course of study a student may choose, the professionals at The Art Institute of Raleigh-Durham will guide, support, and help each student as their talents evolve on their journey of personal and professional transformation. Students studying design learn to fine-tune their visual thinking and problem-solving skills as they create everything from logos to TV ads. Programs in the area of media arts focus on utilizing technology to deliver information and entertainment, while students studying fashion learn to design clothes for the runway or run a retail shop. Culinary programs focus on the fundamental techniques while exposing students to a full menu of international cuisines and management techniques.

Bachelor's degree programs are offered in the areas of culinary arts management, fashion marketing and management, game art and design, graphic design, interior design, photography, and Web design and interactive media.

Associate degree programs are offered in the areas of culinary arts, fashion marketing, graphic design, and Web design and interactive media.

Certificate programs are offered in the areas of art of cooking, baking and pastry, digital image management, fashion retailing, and Web design and development.

Academic Programs

The Art Institute of Raleigh-Durham operates on a year-round, four-quarter system.

Academic Facilities

The Art Institute of Raleigh-Durham provides a learning environment with professional-grade technology applicable to each student's course of study. Students have the opportunity to build a portfolio of work that shows potential employers that they are trained to use the software, hardware, or equipment utilized within the industry. Depending upon the course of study, students are immersed in a creative environment—from classrooms to computer labs to studios—focused on relevant, hands-on education designed to prepare students for the real world.

Costs

Tuition cost varies by program. Prospective students should contact the school for current tuition costs. Other charges include a starting kit for all first-quarter students. Kits vary in price depending on the program of study.

Financial Aid

Financial aid is available for those who qualify. Students who require financial assistance should first complete and submit a Free Application for Federal Student Aid (FAFSA) and meet with a financial aid officer.

Faculty

Faculty members are experienced professionals who create a learning environment that is similar to the professional world students will face after graduation. Instructors are focused on helping students develop the skills they need to transform their creative potential into marketable skills.

Admission Requirements

Applicants must provide proof of high school graduation or achievement of a General Educational Development (GED) certificate as a prerequisite for admission. In lieu of documenting high school graduation or a GED certificate, applicants may provide proof of attaining an associate degree or higher from an accredited institution. An official transcript indicating date of high school graduation, GED certificate (including test scores), or date of college graduation (including degree granted) is required as proof.

All individuals seeking admission to The Art Institute of Raleigh-Durham are interviewed in person or by phone by an assistant director of admissions, and each applicant must create an original essay of at least 150 words stating how an education at The Art Institute of Raleigh-Durham would help the student to achieve career goals. There is a $50 application fee.

For the most recent information regarding admission requirements, please refer to the current academic catalog.

Application and Information

To obtain an application, make arrangements for an interview, or tour the school, students should contact:

The Art Institute of Raleigh-Durham
A branch of The Art Institute of Charlotte
410 Blackwell Street, Suite 200
Durham, North Carolina 27701
Phone: 919-317-3050
    888-245-9593 (toll-free)
Fax: 919-317-3231/919-317-3230
Web site: http://www.artinstitutes.edu/raleigh-durham

Over 50 schools: The Art Institute of Atlanta; The Art Institute of Atlanta—Decatur, A branch of The Art Institute of Atlanta; The Art Institute of Austin, A branch of The Art Institute of Houston; The Art Institute of California, a college of Argosy University, with locations in Hollywood, Inland Empire, Los Angeles, Orange County, Sacramento, San Diego, San Francisco, and Sunnyvale; The Art Institute of Charleston, A branch of The Art Institute of Atlanta; The Art Institute of Charlotte; The Art Institute of Colorado; The Art Institute of Dallas, A campus of South University; The Art Institute of Fort Lauderdale; The Art Institute of Fort Worth, A campus of South University; The Art Institute of Houston; The Art Institute of Houston—North, A branch of The Art Institute of Houston; The Art Institute of Indianapolis; The Art Institute of Jacksonville, A branch of Miami International University of Art & Design; The Art Institute of Las Vegas; The Art Institute of Michigan; The Art Institute of Michigan—Troy; The Art Institute of New York City; The Art Institute of Ohio—Cincinnati; The Art Institute of Philadelphia; The Art Institute of Phoenix; The Art Institute of Pittsburgh; The Art Institute of Portland; The Art Institute of Raleigh–Durham; The Art Institute of Salt Lake City; The Art Institute of San Antonio, A branch of The Art Institute of Houston; The Art Institute of Seattle; The Art Institute of Tampa, A branch of Miami International University of Art & Design; The Art Institute of Tennessee—Nashville, A branch of The Art Institute of Atlanta; The Art Institute of Tucson; The Art Institute of Vancouver; The Art Institute of Virginia Beach[1], A branch of The Art Institute of Atlanta; The Art Institute of Washington[1], A branch of The Art Institute of Atlanta; The Art Institute of Washington—Dulles[1], A branch of The Art Institute of Atlanta; The Art Institute of Wisconsin; The Art Institute of York—Pennsylvania; The Art Institutes International—Kansas City; The Art Institutes International Minnesota; The Illinois Institute of Art—Chicago; The Illinois Institute of Art—Schaumburg; The Illinois Institute of Art—Tinley Park; Miami International University of Art & Design; The New England Institute of Art

[1]Certified by SCHEV to operate in Virginia

See **aiprograms.info** for program duration, tuition, fees, and other costs, median debt, federal salary data, alumni success, and other important info. The Art Institutes is a system of over 50 schools throughout North America. Programs, credential levels, technology, and scheduling options vary by school, and employment opportunities are not guaranteed. Financial aid is available to those who qualify. Several institutions included in The Art Institutes system are campuses of South University or Argosy University. OH Registration # 04-01-1698B, AC0165, AC0080, Licensed by the Florida Commission for Independent Education, License No. 1287, 3427, 3110, 2581. Administrative office: 210 Sixth Avenue, 33rd Floor, Pittsburgh, PA 15222. ©2012 The Art Institutes International LLC.

THE ART INSTITUTE OF SALT LAKE CITY
DRAPER, UTAH

The Art Institute of Salt Lake City™

CREATE TOMORROW

A focused education from The Art Institute of Salt Lake City, a branch of The Art Institute of Phoenix, can help students turn their creative energy into a powerful tool that can make a difference in the world. Students are part of a collaborative and supportive community, where experienced instructors provide the guidance and skills needed to pursue a career in the creative economy.

The school's programs in the areas of design, media arts, fashion, and culinary give students the opportunity to learn by using professional-grade technology and build a portfolio of work to show potential employers after graduation.

The Art Institute of Salt Lake City is accredited by the Accrediting Council for Independent Colleges and Schools to award diplomas, associate's degrees, and bachelor's degrees. The Accrediting Council for Independent Colleges and Schools is listed as a nationally recognized accrediting agency by the United States Department of Education and is recognized by the Council for Higher Education Accreditation. ACICS can be contacted at 750 First Street NE, Suite 980, Washington, D.C. 20002; phone: 202-336-6780. The Art Institute of Salt Lake City is a branch of The Art Institute of Phoenix located in Phoenix, Arizona.

The Art Institute of Salt Lake City is exempt from registration pursuant to the Utah Postsecondary Proprietary School Act. Any questions should be directed to the Utah Division of Consumer Protection (UDCP), 160 East 300 South, Second Floor, Salt Lake City, Utah 84114; phone: 801-530-6601.

Location

The Art Institute of Salt Lake City is located in Draper, which is in the Wasatch Mountains at the south end of the Salt Lake Valley. The city has long been known as a premier hang-gliding destination with breathtaking views. Draper is fast becoming a hub for new development in the Salt Lake and Utah Valleys.

Programs of Study and Degrees

No matter which course of study a student may choose, the professionals at The Art Institute of Salt Lake City will guide, support, and help each student as their talents evolve on their journey of personal and professional transformation. Students studying design learn to fine-tune their visual thinking and problem-solving skills as they create everything from logos to TV ads. Programs in the area of media arts focus on utilizing technology to deliver information and entertainment, while students studying fashion learn to design clothes for the runway or run a retail shop. Culinary programs focus on the fundamental techniques while exposing students to a full menu of international cuisines and management techniques.

Bachelor's degree programs are offered in the areas of culinary management, digital filmmaking and video production, digital photography, fashion and retail management, game art and design, graphic design, interior design, media arts and animation, and Web design and interactive media.

Associate degrees are offered in the areas of baking and pastry, culinary arts, and graphic design.

Diploma programs are offered in the areas of baking and pastry, culinary arts, digital image management, fashion retailing, Web design and development, and Web design and interactive communications.

Academic Programs

The Art Institute of Salt Lake City operates on a year-round, four-quarter system.

Academic Facilities

The Art Institute of Salt Lake City provides a learning environment with professional-grade technology applicable to each student's course of study. Students have the opportunity to build a portfolio of work that shows potential employers that they are trained to use the software, hardware, or equipment utilized within the industry. Depending upon the course of study, students are immersed in a creative environment—from classrooms to computer labs to studios—focused on relevant, hands-on education designed to prepare students for the real world.

Costs

Tuition cost varies by program. Prospective students should contact the school for current tuition costs. Other charges include a starting kit for all first-quarter students. Kits vary in price depending on the program of study.

Financial Aid

Financial aid is available for those who qualify. Students who require financial assistance should first complete and submit a Free Application for Federal Student Aid (FAFSA) and meet with a financial aid officer.

Faculty

Faculty members are experienced professionals who create a learning environment that is similar to the professional world students will face after graduation. Instructors are focused on helping students develop the skills they need to transform their creative potential into marketable skills.

Admission Requirements

Applicants must provide proof of high school graduation or achievement of a General Educational Development (GED) certificate as a prerequisite for admission. In lieu of documenting high school graduation or a GED certificate, applicants may provide proof of attaining an associate degree or higher from an accredited institution. An official transcript indicating date of high school graduation, receipt of a GED certificate (including test scores), or date of college graduation (including degree granted) is required as proof.

All individuals seeking admission to The Art Institute of Salt Lake City are interviewed in person or by phone by an assistant director of admissions, and each applicant must create an original essay of at least 150 words stating how an education at The Art Institute of Salt Lake City would help the student to achieve career goals. There is a $50 application fee.

For the most recent information regarding admission requirements, please refer to the current academic catalog.

Application and Information

To obtain an application, make arrangements for an interview, or tour the school, prospective students should contact:

The Art Institute of Salt Lake City
A branch of The Art Institute of Phoenix
121 West Election Road, Suite 100
Draper, Utah 84020-9492
Phone: 801-601-4700
      800-978-0096 (toll-free)
Fax: 801-601-4724
Web site: http://www.artinstitutes.edu/saltlakecity

Over 50 schools: The Art Institute of Atlanta; The Art Institute of Atlanta—Decatur, A branch of The Art Institute of Atlanta; The Art Institute of Austin, A branch of The Art Institute of Houston; The Art Institute of California, a college of Argosy University, with locations in Hollywood, Inland Empire, Los Angeles, Orange County, Sacramento, San Diego, San Francisco, and Sunnyvale; The Art Institute of Charleston, A branch of The Art Institute of Atlanta; The Art Institute of Charlotte; The Art Institute of Colorado; The Art Institute of Dallas, A campus of South University; The Art Institute of Fort Lauderdale; The Art Institute of Fort Worth, A campus of South University; The Art Institute of Houston; The Art Institute of Houston—North, A branch of The Art Institute of Houston; The Art Institute of Indianapolis; The Art Institute of Jacksonville, A branch of Miami International University of Art & Design; The Art Institute of Las Vegas; The Art Institute of Michigan; The Art Institute of Michigan—Troy; The Art Institute of New York City; The Art Institute of Ohio—Cincinnati; The Art Institute of Philadelphia; The Art Institute of Phoenix; The Art Institute of Pittsburgh; The Art Institute of Portland; The Art Institute of Raleigh–Durham; The Art Institute of Salt Lake City; The Art Institute of San Antonio, A branch of The Art Institute of Houston; The Art Institute of Seattle; The Art Institute of Tampa, A branch of Miami International University of Art & Design; The Art Institute of Tennessee—Nashville, A branch of The Art Institute of Atlanta; The Art Institute of Tucson; The Art Institute of Vancouver; The Art Institute of Virginia Beach[1], A branch of The Art Institute of Atlanta; The Art Institute of Washington[1], A branch of The Art Institute of Atlanta; The Art Institute of Washington—Dulles[1], A branch of The Art Institute of Atlanta; The Art Institute of Wisconsin; The Art Institute of York—Pennsylvania; The Art Institutes International—Kansas City; The Art Institutes International Minnesota; The Illinois Institute of Art—Chicago; The Illinois Institute of Art—Schaumburg; The Illinois Institute of Art—Tinley Park; Miami International University of Art & Design; The New England Institute of Art

[1]Certified by SCHEV to operate in Virginia

See **aiprograms.info** for program duration, tuition, fees, and other costs, median debt, federal salary data, alumni success, and other important info. The Art Institutes is a system of over 50 schools throughout North America. Programs, credential levels, technology, and scheduling options vary by school, and employment opportunities are not guaranteed. Financial aid is available to those who qualify. Several institutions included in The Art Institutes system are campuses of South University or Argosy University. OH Registration # 04-01-1698B, AC0165, AC0080, Licensed by the Florida Commission for Independent Education, License No. 1287, 3427, 3110, 2581. Administrative office: 210 Sixth Avenue, 33rd Floor, Pittsburgh, PA 15222. ©2012 The Art Institutes International LLC.

THE ART INSTITUTE OF SAN ANTONIO

SAN ANTONIO, TEXAS

The Art Institute of San Antonio™

A branch of The Art Institute of Houston

CREATE TOMORROW

A focused education from The Art Institute of San Antonio, a branch of The Art Institute of Houston, can help students turn their creative energy into a powerful tool that can make a difference in the world. Students are part of a collaborative and supportive community, where experienced instructors provide the guidance and skills needed to pursue a career in the creative economy.

The school's programs in the areas of design, media arts, fashion, and culinary give students the opportunity to learn by using professional-grade technology and to build a portfolio of work to show potential employers after graduation.

The Art Institute of San Antonio is a branch of The Art Institute of Houston. The Art Institute of Houston is accredited by the Commission on Colleges of the Southern Association of Colleges and Schools to award associate and baccalaureate degrees. For questions about the accreditation of The Art Institute of Houston, contact the Commission on Colleges at 1866 Southern Lane, Decatur, Georgia 30033-4097; phone: 404-679-4500.

The Art Institute of San Antonio holds a certificate of authorization acknowledging exemption from Texas Higher Education Coordinating Board regulations.

Location

San Antonio, the second-largest city in Texas, is one of the fastest-growing areas in the United States. There are five Fortune 500 companies in the area, and visitors and locals alike enjoy the River Walk, Majestic Theatre, Alamo complex, and Spanish Governor's Palace.

Programs of Study and Degrees

No matter which course of study a student may choose, the professionals at The Art Institute of San Antonio will guide, support, and help each student as their talents evolve on their journey of personal and professional transformation. Students studying design learn to fine-tune their visual thinking and problem-solving skills as they create everything from logos to TV ads. Programs in the area of media arts focus on utilizing technology to deliver information and entertainment, while students studying fashion learn to design clothes for the runway or run a retail shop. Culinary programs focus on the fundamental techniques while exposing students to a full menu of international cuisines and management techniques.

Bachelor's degree programs are offered in the areas of advertising design, culinary management, design and technical graphics, fashion and retail management, fashion design, food and beverage management, game art and design, graphic design, hospitality management, interior design, media arts and animation, photography, visual effects and motion graphics, and Web design and interactive media.

Associate degree programs are offered in the areas of baking and pastry, culinary arts, graphic design, restaurant and catering management, and Web design and interactive media.

Diploma programs are available in the areas of baking and pastry, culinary arts, digital image management, fashion retailing, Web design and development, and Web design and interactive communications.

Academic Programs

The Art Institute of San Antonio operates on a year-round, four-quarter system.

Academic Facilities

The Art Institute of San Antonio provides a learning environment with professional-grade technology applicable to each student's course of study. Students have the opportunity to build a portfolio of work that shows potential employers that they are trained to use the software, hardware, or equipment utilized within the industry. Depending upon the course of study, students are immersed in a creative environment—from classrooms to computer labs to studios—focused on relevant, hands-on education designed to prepare students for the real world.

Costs

Tuition cost varies by program. Prospective students should contact the school for current tuition costs. Other charges include a starting kit for all first-quarter students. Kits vary in price depending on the program of study.

Financial Aid

Financial aid is available for those who qualify. Students who require financial assistance should first complete and submit a Free Application for Federal Student Aid (FAFSA) and meet with a financial aid officer.

Faculty

Faculty members are experienced professionals who create a learning environment that is similar to the professional world students will face after graduation. Instructors are focused on helping students develop the skills they need to transform their creative potential into marketable skills.

Admission Requirements

Applicants must provide proof of high school graduation or achievement of a General Educational Development (GED) certificate as a prerequisite for admission.

In lieu of documenting high school graduation or a GED certificate, applicants may provide proof of attaining an associate degree or higher from an accredited institution. An official transcript indicating date of high school graduation, GED certificate (including test scores), or date of college graduation (including degree granted) is required as proof.

All individuals seeking admission to The Art Institute of San Antonio are interviewed in person or by phone by an assistant director of admissions, and each applicant must create an original essay of at least 150 words stating how an education at The Art Institute of San Antonio would help the student to achieve career goals. There is a $50 application fee.

For the most recent information regarding admission requirements, please refer to the current academic catalog.

Application and Information

To obtain an application, make arrangements for an interview, or tour the school, prospective students should contact:

The Art Institute of San Antonio
A branch of The Art Institute of Houston
10000 IH-10 West, Suite 200
San Antonio, Texas 78230
Phone: 210-338-7320
888-222-0040 (toll-free)
Fax: 210-338-7321
Web site: http://www.artinstitutes.edu/san-antonio

COLLEGE CLOSE-UPS

THE ART INSTITUTE OF SEATTLE

SEATTLE, WASHINGTON

The Art Institute of Seattle®

CREATE TOMORROW

A focused education from The Art Institute of Seattle can help students turn their creative energy into a powerful tool that can make a difference in the world. Students are part of a collaborative and supportive community, where experienced instructors provide the guidance and skills needed to pursue a career in the creative economy.

The school's programs in the areas of design, media arts, fashion, and culinary give students the opportunity to learn by using professional-grade technology and to build a portfolio of work to show potential employers after graduation.

The Art Institute of Seattle is accredited by the Northwest Commission on Colleges and Universities (NWCCU), an institutional accrediting body recognized by the United States Department of Education.

The Art Institute of Seattle is licensed under Chapter 28c.10RCW. Inquiries or complaints regarding this or any other private vocational school may be made to the Workforce Training and Education Coordinating Board, 128 10th Avenue SW, P.O. Box 43105, Olympia, Washington 98504-3105; phone: 360-753-5662.

The Associate of Applied Arts in Culinary Arts degree program is accredited by the Accrediting Commission of the American Culinary Federation Education Foundation.

The Interior Design program leading to the Bachelor of Fine Arts degree is accredited by the Council for Interior Design Accreditation, 206 Grandville Avenue, Suite 350, Grand Rapids, Michigan 49503; www.accredit-id.org.

Location

The Art Institute of Seattle is located in the city's Belltown district. Founded by Native Americans and traders, the city has retained respect for its different cultures and customs. People from all over the world come to study, work, and live in this city that is known for its friendly people and beautiful natural surroundings.

World-class companies, such as Microsoft, Boeing, Starbucks, Amazon.com, and Nordstrom, make their global headquarters in Seattle. As a gateway to the Pacific Rim, Seattle is a crossroads where creativity, technology, and business meet.

Programs of Study and Degrees

No matter which course of study a student may choose, the professionals at The Art Institute of Seattle will guide, support, and help each student as their talents evolve on their journey of personal and professional transformation. Students studying design learn to fine-tune their visual thinking and problem-solving skills as they create everything from logos to TV ads. Programs in the area of media arts focus on utilizing technology to deliver information and entertainment, while students studying fashion learn to design clothes for the runway or run a retail shop. Culinary programs focus on the fundamental techniques while exposing students to a full menu of international cuisines and management techniques.

Bachelor's degree programs are available in the areas of audio design technology, culinary arts management, digital filmmaking and video production, fashion design, fashion marketing, game art and design, graphic design, industrial design, interior design, media arts and animation, photography, and web design and interactive media.

Associate degrees are available in the areas of audio production, baking and pastry, culinary arts, fashion design, fashion marketing, graphic design, industrial design technology, interior design, photography, video production, and Web design and interactive media.

Diploma programs are offered in the areas of art of cooking, baking and pastry, digital design, digital image management, fashion retailing, residential design, Web design and development, and Web design and interactive communications.

Academic Programs

The Art Institute of Seattle operates on a year-round, quarterly basis. Each quarter totals eleven weeks. Bachelor's degree programs are twelve quarters in length.

Academic Facilities

The Art Institute of Seattle provides a learning environment with professional-grade technology applicable to each student's course of study. Students have the opportunity to build a portfolio of work that shows potential employers that they are trained to use the software, hardware, or equipment utilized within the industry. Depending upon the course of study, students

are immersed in a creative environment—from classrooms to computer labs to studios—focused on relevant, hands-on education designed to prepare students for the real world.

Costs

Tuition cost varies by program. Prospective students should contact the school for current tuition costs. Other charges include a starting kit for all first-quarter students. Kits vary in price depending on the program of study.

Financial Aid

Financial aid is available for those who qualify. Students who require financial assistance should first complete and submit a Free Application for Federal Student Aid (FAFSA) and meet with a financial aid officer.

Faculty

Faculty members are experienced professionals who create a learning environment that is similar to the professional world students will face after graduation. Instructors are focused on helping students develop the skills they need to transform their creative potential into marketable skills.

Admission Requirements

A student seeking admission to The Art Institute of Seattle is required to interview with an admissions representative (in person or over the phone). Applicants are required to have a high school diploma or a General Educational Development (GED) certificate and to submit an admissions application and an essay describing how an education at The Art Institute of Seattle may help the student to achieve career goals. For advanced placement, additional information, including college transcripts, letters of recommendation, or portfolio work, may be required. Students may apply for admission online.

The Art Institute of Seattle follows a rolling admissions schedule. Students are encouraged to apply for their chosen quarter early so that they may take advantage of orientation activities. Students may also apply until the actual start date for any given quarter, depending on space availability. There is a $50 application fee.

For the most recent information regarding admission requirements, please refer to the current academic catalog.

Application and Information

To obtain an application, make arrangements for an interview, or tour the school, prospective students should contact:

The Art Institute of Seattle
2323 Elliott Avenue
Seattle, Washington 98121-1642
Phone: 206-448-6600
        800-275-2471 (toll-free)
Fax: 206-269-0275
Web site: http://www.artinstitutes.edu/seattle

THE ART INSTITUTE OF TAMPA
TAMPA, FLORIDA

The Art Institute of Tampa
A branch of Miami International University of Art & Design
CREATE TOMORROW

A focused education from The Art Institute of Tampa, a branch of Miami International University of Art & Design, can help students turn their creative energy into a powerful tool that can make a difference in the world. Students are part of a collaborative and supportive community, where experienced instructors provide the guidance and skills needed to pursue a career in the creative economy.

The school's programs in the areas of design, media arts, fashion, and culinary give students the opportunity to learn by using professional-grade technology and to build a portfolio of work to show potential employers after graduation.

The Art Institute of Tampa is a branch of Miami International University of Art & Design. Miami International University of Art & Design is accredited by the Commission on Colleges of the Southern Association of Colleges and Schools to award associate, baccalaureate, and master's degrees. For questions about the accreditation of Miami International University of Art & Design and its branches, contact the Commission on Colleges at 1866 Southern Lane, Decatur, Georgia 30033-4097; phone: 404-679-4500.

The Art Institute of Tampa is licensed by the Commission for Independent Education, Florida Department of Education. Additional information regarding this institution may be obtained by contacting the commission at 325 West Gaines Street, Suite 1414, Tallahassee, Florida 32399-0400; phone: 888-224-6684 (toll-free).

The Associate of Arts in Baking & Pastry, Associate of Arts in Culinary Arts, and the Bachelor of Arts in Culinary Management programs are accredited by The Accrediting Commission of the American Culinary Federation Education Foundation.

Location

Located in Tampa's bustling business district, The Art Institute of Tampa is situated across from Raymond James Stadium and Al Lopez Park, comprising 126 acres of Florida's fauna and flora. Tampa's balmy climate makes the outdoors enjoyable year-round. Residents enjoy bicycling, jogging, sunbathing, walking, in-line skating, swimming, sport fishing, scuba diving, and snorkeling. Gyms and dance studios offer opportunities for aerobics, weight lifting, ballet, kickboxing, and the martial arts. Local attractions include Busch Gardens, the Florida Aquarium, Lowry Park Zoo, the Tampa Museum of Art, Shakespeare in the Park, the Clearwater Jazz Festival, and the world-renowned Salvador Dalí Museum. Sports fans follow the Tampa Bay Buccaneers, Rays, and Lightning, and popular nightlife spots include Channelside, Bay Street, and Ybor City—the center of the city's bustling music scene. Theater, symphony, and dance performances; museums; and a diverse range of art galleries showcase some of the world's greatest talent. Situated on the west coast of Florida, the Tampa Bay area has grown to become one of the most populous and affluent regions in Florida. With its unique blend of urban excitement and natural beauty, there really is something for everyone who lives in the beautiful, diverse communities connected by green spaces and waterways.

Programs of Study and Degrees

No matter which course of study a student may choose, the professionals at The Art Institute of Tampa will guide, support, and help each student as their talents evolve on their journey of personal and professional transformation. Students studying design learn to fine-tune their visual thinking and problem-solving skills as they create everything from logos to TV ads. Programs in the area of media arts focus on utilizing technology to deliver information and entertainment, while students studying fashion learn to design clothes for the runway or run a retail shop. Culinary programs focus on the fundamental techniques while exposing students to a full menu of international cuisines and management techniques.

Bachelor's degrees are offered in the areas of culinary management, digital filmmaking and video production, digital photography, fashion and retail management, game art and design, graphic design, interior design, media arts and animation, visual effects and motion graphics, and Web design and interactive media.

Associate degrees are available in the areas of baking and pastry, culinary arts, and graphic design.

A diploma is available in the areas of baking and pastry, digital image management, fashion retailing, Web design and development I, and Web design and development II.

A Master of Arts is offered in Design and Media Management.

Academic Programs

The academic year is divided into four quarters, beginning in January, April, July, and October. Bachelor's degrees require the completion of 192 credits, and associate's degrees require completion of 112 academic credits.

Academic Facilities

The Art Institute of Tampa provides a learning environment with professional-grade technology applicable to each student's course of study. Students have the opportunity to build a portfolio of work that shows potential employers that they are trained to use the software, hardware, or equipment utilized within the industry. Depending upon the course of study, students are immersed in a creative environment—from classrooms to computer labs to studios—focused on relevant, hands-on education designed to prepare students for the real world.

Costs

Tuition cost varies by program. Prospective students should contact the school for current tuition costs. Other charges include a starting kit for all first-quarter students. Kits vary in price, depending on the program of study.

Financial Aid

Financial aid is available for those who qualify. Students who require financial assistance should first complete and submit a Free Application for Federal Student Aid (FAFSA) and meet with a financial aid officer.

Faculty

Faculty members are experienced professionals who create a learning environment that is similar to the professional world students will face after graduation. Instructors are focused on helping students develop the skills they need to transform their creative potential into marketable skills.

Student Government

Student leadership is fundamental to academic success and is a way to network with and meet other students. Student leaders serve as role models for peers and act as student advocates for the school. Student leadership programs at The Art Institute of Tampa are designed to support the mission of the school, help students refine interpersonal skills, implement positive change for the student body, and promote school and community spirit. Students may become active members of The Art Institute of Tampa Student Government, start or join a university club, or attend school-sponsored seminars designed to improve leadership skills.

Admission Requirements

Applicants must demonstrate proof of high school graduation or its equivalent in order to receive final acceptance. An official copy of a high school transcript or General Educational Development (GED) transcript is required. Applicants are also required to interview with the school (either in person or by telephone) and write an essay of approximately 150 words in length describing how an education at The Art Institute of Tampa will help them attain creative goals. The Admissions Acceptance Committee determines the compatibility of the applicant with the school and reserves the right to request the results of the SAT or ACT exam and other additional information. A separate application and enrollment form must be completed and signed by the applicant. Prospective students may apply at any time of the year. Applications may be submitted online or mailed to the school. There is a $50 application fee.

For the most recent information regarding admission requirements, please refer to the current academic catalog.

Application and Information

To obtain an application, make arrangements for an interview, or tour the school, prospective students should contact:

The Art Institute of Tampa
A branch of Miami International University of Art & Design
Parkside at Tampa Bay Park
4401 North Himes Avenue, Suite 150
Tampa, Florida 33614-7086
Phone: 813-873-2112
          866-703-3277 (toll-free)
Fax: 813-873-2171
Web site: http://www.artinstitutes.edu/tampa

COLLEGE CLOSE-UPS

THE ART INSTITUTE OF TENNESSEE— NASHVILLE
NASHVILLE, TENNESSEE

The Art Institute
of Tennessee™–Nashville
A branch of The Art Institute of Atlanta

CREATE TOMORROW

A focused education from The Art Institute of Tennessee— Nashville, a branch of The Art Institute of Atlanta, Georgia, can help students turn their creative energy into a powerful tool that can make a difference in the world. Students are part of a collaborative and supportive community, where experienced instructors provide the guidance and skills needed to pursue a career in the creative economy.

The school's programs in the areas of design, media arts, fashion, and culinary give students the opportunity to learn by using professional-grade technology and to build a portfolio of work to show potential employers after graduation.

The Art Institute of Tennessee—Nashville is a branch campus of The Art Institute of Atlanta. The Art Institute of Atlanta is accredited by the Commission on Colleges of the Southern Association of Colleges and Schools to award associate and baccalaureate degrees. For questions about the accreditation of The Art Institute of Atlanta, contact the Commission on Colleges at 1866 Southern Lane, Decatur, Georgia 30033-4097; phone: 404-679-4500.

The Art Institute of Tennessee—Nashville is authorized for operation as a postsecondary educational institution by the Tennessee Higher Education Commission, located at Parkway Towers, Suite 1900, 404 James Robertson Parkway, Nashville, Tennessee 37243; phone: 615-741-6230; http://www.state.tn.us/thec.

Location

The Art Institute of Tennessee—Nashville is located close to downtown, providing students with ease of access, opportunities to volunteer for civic organizations, and the ability to enjoy all the culture and excitement that the city of Nashville has to offer.

Programs of Study and Degrees

No matter which course of study a student may choose, the professionals at The Art Institute of Tennessee— Nashville will guide, support, and help each student as their talents evolve on their journey of personal and professional transformation. Students studying design learn to fine-tune their visual thinking and problem-solving skills as they create everything from logos to TV ads. Programs in the area of media arts focus on utilizing technology to deliver information and entertainment, while students studying fashion learn to design clothes for the runway or run a retail shop. Culinary programs focus on the fundamental techniques while exposing students to a full menu of international cuisines and management techniques.

Bachelor's degrees are offered in the areas of advertising, audio production, culinary arts management, digital filmmaking and video production, fashion and retail management, graphic design, interior design, media arts and animation, photographic imaging, and Web design and interactive media.

Associate degrees are available in the areas of baking and pastry, culinary arts, graphic design, video production, and Web design and interactive media.

Diploma programs are offered in the areas of baking and pastry, culinary arts, digital image management, fashion retailing, Web design and development, and Web design and interactive communications.

The diploma in culinary arts–skills program is also available in an evening and weekend option format.

Academic Programs

The academic year is divided into four quarters, beginning in January, April, July, and October. Each program is offered on a year-round basis, allowing students to continue to work uninterrupted toward their degrees.

Academic Facilities

The Art Institute of Tennessee—Nashville provides a learning environment with professional-grade technology applicable to each student's course of study. Students have the opportunity to build a portfolio of work that shows potential employers that they are trained to use the software, hardware, or equipment utilized within the industry. Depending upon the course of study, students are immersed in a creative environment—from classrooms to computer labs to studios—focused on relevant, hands-on education designed to prepare students for the real world.

Costs

Tuition cost varies by program. Prospective students should contact the school for current tuition costs. Other charges

include a starting kit for all first-quarter students. Kits vary in price, depending on the program of study.

Financial Aid

Financial aid is available for those who qualify. Students who require financial assistance should first complete and submit a Free Application for Federal Student Aid (FAFSA) and meet with a financial aid officer.

Faculty

Faculty members are experienced professionals who create a learning environment that is similar to the professional world students will face after graduation. Instructors are focused on helping students develop the skills they need to transform their creative potential into marketable skills.

Student Government

The Student Federation is responsible for student government and acts as a liaison between the student body and faculty and staff members.

Admission Requirements

Applicants must provide proof of high school graduation or achievement of a General Educational Development (GED) certificate as a prerequisite for admission. In lieu of documenting high school graduation or a GED certificate, applicants may provide proof of receiving an associate degree or higher from an accredited institution. An official transcript indicating date of high school graduation, receipt of a GED certificate (including test scores), or date of college graduation (including degree granted) is required as proof.

All individuals seeking admission to The Art Institute of Tennessee—Nashville are interviewed in person or by phone by an assistant director of admissions, and each applicant must write an original essay of at least 150 words stating how an education at the school would help the student achieve career goals. There is a $50 application fee.

For the most recent information regarding admission requirements, please refer to the current academic catalog.

Application and Information

To obtain an application, make arrangements for an interview, or tour the school, prospective students should contact:

The Art Institute of Tennessee—Nashville
A branch of The Art Institute of Atlanta
100 Centerview Drive, Suite 250
Nashville, Tennessee 37214-3439
Phone: 615-874-1067
      866-747-5770 (toll-free)
Fax: 615-874-3530
Web site: http://www.artinstitutes.edu/nashville

Over 50 schools: The Art Institute of Atlanta; The Art Institute of Atlanta—Decatur, A branch of The Art Institute of Atlanta; The Art Institute of Austin, A branch of The Art Institute of Houston; The Art Institute of California, a college of Argosy University, with locations in Hollywood, Inland Empire, Los Angeles, Orange County, Sacramento, San Diego, San Francisco, and Sunnyvale; The Art Institute of Charleston, A branch of The Art Institute of Atlanta; The Art Institute of Charlotte; The Art Institute of Colorado; The Art Institute of Dallas, A campus of South University; The Art Institute of Fort Lauderdale; The Art Institute of Fort Worth, A campus of South University; The Art Institute of Houston; The Art Institute of Houston—North, A branch of The Art Institute of Houston; The Art Institute of Indianapolis; The Art Institute of Jacksonville, A branch of Miami International University of Art & Design; The Art Institute of Las Vegas; The Art Institute of Michigan; The Art Institute of Michigan—Troy; The Art Institute of New York City; The Art Institute of Ohio—Cincinnati; The Art Institute of Philadelphia; The Art Institute of Phoenix; The Art Institute of Pittsburgh; The Art Institute of Portland; The Art Institute of Raleigh–Durham; The Art Institute of Salt Lake City; The Art Institute of San Antonio, A branch of The Art Institute of Houston; The Art Institute of Seattle; The Art Institute of Tampa, A branch of Miami International University of Art & Design; The Art Institute of Tennessee—Nashville, A branch of The Art Institute of Atlanta; The Art Institute of Tucson; The Art Institute of Vancouver; The Art Institute of Virginia Beach[1], A branch of The Art Institute of Atlanta; The Art Institute of Washington[1], A branch of The Art Institute of Atlanta; The Art Institute of Washington—Dulles[1], A branch of The Art Institute of Atlanta; The Art Institute of Wisconsin; The Art Institute of York—Pennsylvania; The Art Institutes International—Kansas City; The Art Institutes International Minnesota; The Illinois Institute of Art—Chicago; The Illinois Institute of Art—Schaumburg; The Illinois Institute of Art—Tinley Park; Miami International University of Art & Design; The New England Institute of Art

[1]Certified by SCHEV to operate in Virginia

See **aiprograms.info** for program duration, tuition, fees, and other costs, median debt, federal salary data, alumni success, and other important info. The Art Institutes is a system of over 50 schools throughout North America. Programs, credential levels, technology, and scheduling options vary by school, and employment opportunities are not guaranteed. Financial aid is available to those who qualify. Several institutions included in The Art Institutes system are campuses of South University or Argosy University. OH Registration # 04-01-1698B, AC0165, AC0080, Licensed by the Florida Commission for Independent Education, License No. 1287, 3427, 3110, 2581. Administrative office: 210 Sixth Avenue, 33rd Floor, Pittsburgh, PA 15222. ©2012 The Art Institutes International LLC.

THE ART INSTITUTE OF TUCSON

TUCSON, ARIZONA

The Art Institute of Tucson™

CREATE TOMORROW

A focused education from The Art Institute of Tucson can help students turn their creative energy into a powerful tool that can make a difference in the world. Students are part of a collaborative and supportive community, where experienced instructors provide the guidance and skills needed to pursue a career in the creative economy.

The school's programs in the areas of design, media arts, fashion, and culinary give students the opportunity to learn by using professional-grade technology and to build a portfolio of work to show potential employers after graduation.

The Art Institute of Tucson is accredited by the Accrediting Council for Independent Colleges and Schools to award associate's degrees and bachelor's degrees. The Accrediting Council for Independent Colleges and Schools is listed as a nationally recognized accrediting agency by the United States Department of Education and is recognized by the Council for Higher Education Accreditation. ACICS can be contacted at 750 First Street NE, Suite 980, Washington, D.C. 20002; phone: 202-336-6780.

The Art Institute of Tucson is licensed, approved, and regulated by the Arizona State Board for Private Postsecondary Education.

Location

Tucson is a fast-growing, progressive metropolitan area with an incredibly rich cultural heritage. Arizona, also known as the Grand Canyon state, today combines the cultures of the United States and Mexico with continued influence from past settlement by Native Americans, Spanish explorers, and Anglo frontiersmen. The result is a diverse mix of people, architecture, food, and communities that can serve as a catalyst for inspiring our students' creativity.

Programs of Study and Degrees

No matter which course of study a student may choose, the professionals at The Art Institute of Tucson will guide, support, and help each student as their talents evolve on their journey of personal and professional transformation. Students studying design learn to fine-tune their visual thinking and problem-solving skills as they create everything from logos to TV ads. Programs in the area of media arts focus on utilizing technology to deliver information and entertainment, while students studying fashion learn to design clothes for the runway or run a retail shop. Culinary programs focus on the fundamental techniques while exposing students to a full menu of international cuisines and management techniques.

Bachelor's degree programs are offered in the areas of advertising, culinary arts, digital filmmaking and video production, digital photography, fashion design, fashion marketing, game art and design, graphic design, interior design, media arts and animation, visual effects and motion graphics, and Web design and interactive media.

Associate degree programs are offered in the areas of baking and pastry, culinary arts, and graphic design.

Diploma programs are offered in the areas of baking and pastry, digital image management, fashion retailing, Web design and development, and Web design and interactive communications.

Academic Programs

The Art Institute of Tucson operates on a year-round, four-quarter system.

Academic Facilities

The Art Institute of Tucson provides a learning environment with professional-grade technology applicable to each student's course of study. Students have the opportunity to build a portfolio of work that shows potential employers that they are trained to use the software, hardware, or equipment utilized within the industry. Depending upon the course of study, students are immersed in a creative environment— from classrooms to computer labs to studios—focused on relevant, hands-on education designed to prepare students for the real world.

Costs

Tuition cost varies by program. Prospective students should contact the school for current tuition costs. Other charges include a starting kit for all first-quarter students. Kits vary in price depending on the program of study.

Financial Aid

Financial aid is available for those who qualify. Students who require financial assistance should first complete and submit a Free Application for Federal Student Aid (FAFSA) and meet with a financial aid officer.

Faculty

Faculty members are experienced professionals who create a learning environment that is similar to the professional world students will face after graduation. Instructors are focused on helping students develop the skills they need to transform their creative potential into marketable skills.

Admission Requirements

Applicants must provide proof of high school graduation or achievement of a General Educational Development (GED) certificate as a prerequisite for admission.

In lieu of documenting high school graduation or a GED certificate, applicants may provide proof of attaining an associate degree or higher from an accredited institution. An official transcript indicating date of high school graduation, GED certificate (including test scores), or date of college graduation (including degree granted) is required as proof.

All individuals seeking admission to The Art Institute of Tucson are interviewed in person or by phone by an assistant director of admissions, and each applicant must create an original essay of at least 150 words stating how an education at The Art Institute of Tucson would help the student to achieve career goals. There is a $50 application fee.

For the most recent information regarding admission requirements, please refer to the current academic catalog.

Application and Information

To obtain an application, make arrangements for an interview, or tour the school, students should contact:

The Art Institute of Tucson
A branch of The Art Institute of Phoenix
5099 East Grant Road
Suite 100
Tucson, Arizona 85712
Phone: 520-318-2700
    866-690-8850 (toll-free)
Fax: 520-881-4794
Web site: http://www.artinstitutes.edu/tucson

THE ART INSTITUTE OF VIRGINIA BEACH

VIRGINIA BEACH, VIRGINIA

The Art Institute of Virginia Beach
A branch of The Art Institute of Atlanta

CREATE TOMORROW

A focused education from The Art Institute of Virginia Beach, a branch of The Art Institute of Atlanta, can help students turn their creative energy into a powerful tool that can make a difference in the world. Students are part of a collaborative and supportive community, where experienced instructors provide the guidance and skills needed to pursue a career in the creative economy.

The school's programs in the areas of design, media arts, fashion, and culinary give students the opportunity to learn by using professional-grade technology and to build a portfolio of work to show potential employers after graduation.

The Art Institute of Virginia Beach is a branch campus of The Art Institute of Atlanta. The Art Institute of Atlanta is accredited by the Commission on Colleges of the Southern Association of Colleges and Schools to award associate and baccalaureate degrees. For questions about the accreditation of The Art Institute of Atlanta, contact the Commission on Colleges at 1866 Southern Lane, Decatur, Georgia 30033-4097; phone: 404-679-4500.

The Art Institute of Virginia Beach, a branch of The Art Institute of Atlanta, is certified to operate in Virginia by the State Council of Higher Education for Virginia, located at James Monroe Building, 101 North Fourteenth Street, Richmond, Virginia 23219; phone: 804-225-2600.

Location

Virginia Beach gives students easy access to cultural and recreational opportunities. Located at the mouth of the Chesapeake Bay, Virginia Beach is home to nearly 450,000 people, miles of beach, and many historic sites.

Programs of Study and Degrees

No matter which course of study a student may choose, the professionals at The Art Institute of Virginia Beach will guide, support, and help each student as their talents evolve on their journey of personal and professional transformation. Students studying design learn to fine-tune their visual thinking and problem-solving skills as they create everything from logos to TV ads. Programs in the area of media arts focus on utilizing technology to deliver information and entertainment, while students studying fashion learn to design clothes for the runway or run a retail shop. Culinary programs focus on the fundamental techniques while exposing students to a full menu of international cuisines and management techniques.

Bachelor's degree programs are offered in the areas of advertising, culinary arts management, fashion and retail management, graphic design, interior design, media arts and animation, photographic imaging, and Web design and interactive media.

Associate degree programs are offered in the areas of culinary arts, graphic design, and Web design and interactive media.

Diploma programs are available in the areas of baking and pastry, culinary arts, digital image management, fashion retailing, Web design and development, and Web design and interactive communications.

Academic Programs

The Art Institute of Virginia Beach operates on a year-round, four-quarter system.

Academic Facilities

The Art Institute of Virginia Beach provides a learning environment with professional-grade technology applicable to each student's course of study. Students have the opportunity to build a portfolio of work that shows potential employers that they are trained to use the software, hardware, or equipment utilized within the industry. Depending upon the course of study, students are immersed in a creative environment—from classrooms to computer labs to studios—focused on relevant, hands-on education designed to prepare students for the real world.

Costs

Tuition cost varies by program. Prospective students should contact the school for current tuition costs. Other charges include a starting kit for all first-quarter students. Kits vary in price depending on the program of study.

Financial Aid

Financial aid is available for those who qualify. Students who require financial assistance should first complete and

submit a Free Application for Federal Student Aid (FAFSA) and meet with a financial aid officer.

Faculty

Faculty members are experienced professionals who create a learning environment that is similar to the professional world students will face after graduation. Instructors are focused on helping students develop the skills they need to transform their creative potential into marketable skills.

Admission Requirements

Applicants must provide proof of high school graduation or achievement of a General Educational Development (GED) certificate as a prerequisite for admission.

In lieu of documenting high school graduation or a GED certificate, applicants may provide proof of attaining an associate degree or higher from an accredited institution. An official transcript indicating date of high school graduation, GED certificate (including test scores), or date of college graduation (including degree granted) is required as proof.

All individuals seeking admission to The Art Institute of Virginia Beach are interviewed in person or by phone by an assistant director of admissions, and each applicant must create an original essay of at least 150 words stating how an education at The Art Institute of Virginia Beach would help the student to achieve career goals. There is a $50 application fee.

For the most recent information regarding admission requirements, please refer to the current academic catalog.

Application and Information

To obtain an application, make arrangements for an interview, or tour the school, prospective students should contact:

The Art Institute of Virginia Beach
A branch of The Art Institute of Atlanta
Two Columbus Center
4500 Main Street, Suite 100
Virginia Beach, Virginia 23462
Phone: 757-493-6700
      877-437-4428 (toll-free)
Fax: 757-493-6800
Web site: http://www.artinstitutes.edu/virginia-beach

Over 50 schools: The Art Institute of Atlanta; The Art Institute of Atlanta—Decatur, A branch of The Art Institute of Atlanta; The Art Institute of Austin, A branch of The Art Institute of Houston; The Art Institute of California, a college of Argosy University, with locations in Hollywood, Inland Empire, Los Angeles, Orange County, Sacramento, San Diego, San Francisco, and Sunnyvale; The Art Institute of Charleston, A branch of The Art Institute of Atlanta; The Art Institute of Charlotte; The Art Institute of Colorado; The Art Institute of Dallas, A campus of South University; The Art Institute of Fort Lauderdale; The Art Institute of Fort Worth, A campus of South University; The Art Institute of Houston; The Art Institute of Houston—North, A branch of The Art Institute of Houston; The Art Institute of Indianapolis; The Art Institute of Jacksonville, A branch of Miami International University of Art & Design; The Art Institute of Las Vegas; The Art Institute of Michigan; The Art Institute of Michigan—Troy; The Art Institute of New York City; The Art Institute of Ohio—Cincinnati; The Art Institute of Philadelphia; The Art Institute of Phoenix; The Art Institute of Pittsburgh; The Art Institute of Portland; The Art Institute of Raleigh–Durham; The Art Institute of Salt Lake City; The Art Institute of San Antonio, A branch of The Art Institute of Houston; The Art Institute of Seattle; The Art Institute of Tampa, A branch of Miami International University of Art & Design; The Art Institute of Tennessee—Nashville, A branch of The Art Institute of Atlanta; The Art Institute of Tucson; The Art Institute of Vancouver; The Art Institute of Virginia Beach[1], A branch of The Art Institute of Atlanta; The Art Institute of Washington[1], A branch of The Art Institute of Atlanta; The Art Institute of Washington—Dulles[1], A branch of The Art Institute of Atlanta; The Art Institute of Wisconsin; The Art Institute of York—Pennsylvania; The Art Institutes International—Kansas City; The Art Institutes International Minnesota; The Illinois Institute of Art—Chicago; The Illinois Institute of Art—Schaumburg; The Illinois Institute of Art—Tinley Park; Miami International University of Art & Design; The New England Institute of Art

[1]Certified by SCHEV to operate in Virginia

See **aiprograms.info** for program duration, tuition, fees, and other costs, median debt, federal salary data, alumni success, and other important info. The Art Institutes is a system of over 50 schools throughout North America. Programs, credential levels, technology, and scheduling options vary by school, and employment opportunities are not guaranteed. Financial aid is available to those who qualify. Several institutions included in The Art Institutes system are campuses of South University or Argosy University. OH Registration # 04-01-1698B, AC0165, AC0080, Licensed by the Florida Commission for Independent Education, License No. 1287, 3427, 3110, 2581. Administrative office: 210 Sixth Avenue, 33rd Floor, Pittsburgh, PA 15222. ©2012 The Art Institutes International LLC.

THE ART INSTITUTE OF WASHINGTON
ARLINGTON, VIRGINIA

Ai
The Art Institute of Washington
A branch of The Art Institute of Atlanta
CREATE TOMORROW

A focused education from The Art Institute of Washington, a branch of The Art Institute of Atlanta, can help students turn their creative energy into a powerful tool that can make a difference in the world. Students are part of a collaborative and supportive community, where experienced instructors provide the guidance and skills needed to pursue a career in the creative economy.

The school's programs in the areas of design, media arts, fashion, and culinary give students the opportunity to learn on professional-grade technology and to build a portfolio of work to show potential employers after graduation.

The Art Institute of Washington is a branch campus of The Art Institute of Atlanta. The Art Institute of Atlanta is accredited by the Commission on Colleges of the Southern Association of Colleges and Schools to award associate and baccalaureate degrees. For questions about the accreditation of The Art Institute of Atlanta, contact the Commission on Colleges at 1866 Southern Lane, Decatur, Georgia 30033-4097; phone: 404-679-4500.

The Associate in Arts in Culinary Arts and the Associate in Arts in Culinary Arts with a concentration in Baking & Pastry degree programs are accredited by The Accrediting Commission of the American Culinary Federation Education Foundation.

The Interior Design program leading to the Bachelor of Fine Arts degree is accredited by the Council for Interior Design Accreditation, 206 Grandville Avenue, Suite 350, Grand Rapids, Michigan 49503; www.accredit-id.org, .

Location

Located in Arlington, Virginia, directly across the Potomac River from Washington, D.C., The Art Institute of Washington occupies the ground floor and the ninth through twelfth floors of the Ames Center. The area is home to a variety of activities, including professional sports, first-rate theatrical and musical entertainment, beautiful parks, and cultural events. Some of the most popular places to visit are the Washington Monument, Lincoln Memorial, Vietnam and Korean War Memorials, Arlington National Cemetery, Smithsonian Institution and Museums, and Capitol Building. Arlington has more than 170 county parks and playgrounds, including over 80 miles of bicycle routes and jogging trails.

Programs of Study and Degrees

No matter which course of study a student may choose, the professionals at The Art Institute of Washington will guide, support, and help each student as their talents evolve on their journey of personal and professional transformation. Students studying design learn to fine-tune their visual thinking and problem-solving skills as they create everything from logos to TV ads. Programs in the area of media arts focus on utilizing technology to deliver information and entertainment, while students studying fashion learn to design clothes for the runway or run a retail shop. Culinary programs focus on the fundamental techniques while exposing students to a full menu of international cuisines and management techniques.

Bachelor's degrees are available in the areas of advertising, audio production, culinary arts management, digital filmmaking and video production, fashion and retail management, food and beverage management, game art and design, graphic design, interior design, media arts and animation, photographic imaging, visual and game programming, visual effects and motion graphics, and Web design and interactive media.

Associate degrees are offered in the areas of baking and pastry, culinary arts, graphic design, photographic imaging, video production, Web design and interactive media, and wine, spirits, and beverage management*.

Diploma programs are available in the areas of advertising design, baking and pastry, commercial photography, culinary arts, digital design, digital image management, fashion retailing, video skills, Web design and development, and Web design and interactive communications.

The Associate in Culinary Arts and Associate in Graphic Design degree programs are available in an evening and weekend option format.

*Participation in the program for those under 21 years of age will be conducted in accord with state law regarding the possession and consumption of alcoholic beverages.

Academic Programs

The academic year is divided into four quarters, beginning in January, April, July, and October. Students may begin their program of study during any quarter. Bachelor's degrees require the completion of 192 credit hours, and associate's degree programs require completion of 96 to 112 credit hours.

Academic Facilities

The Art Institute of Washington provides a learning environment with professional-grade technology applicable to each student's course of study. Students have the opportunity to build a portfolio of work that shows potential employers that they are trained to use the software, hardware, or equipment utilized within the industry. Depending upon the course of study, students are immersed in a creative environment—from classrooms to computer labs to studios—focused on relevant, hands-on education designed to prepare students for the real world.

Costs

Tuition cost varies by program. Prospective students should contact the school for current tuition costs. Other charges include a starting kit for all first-quarter students. Kits vary in price, depending on the program of study.

Financial Aid

Financial aid is available for those who qualify. Students who require financial assistance should first complete and submit a Free Application for Federal Student Aid (FAFSA) and meet with a financial aid officer.

Faculty

Faculty members are experienced professionals who create a learning environment that is similar to the professional world students will face after graduation. Instructors are focused on helping students develop the skills they need to transform their creative potential into marketable skills.

Admission Requirements

Prospective students must interview, either by telephone or in person, with a member of the admissions staff in order to explore the student's background and interests and how they relate to The Art Institute of Washington's programs. To apply, students must submit a completed application for admission, including an essay, high school transcripts or General Educational Development (GED) test scores, SAT or ACT scores, and a $50 nonrefundable application fee. Prospective students may apply at any time of the year. Applications may be submitted online or mailed to the school.

For the most recent information regarding admission requirements, please refer to the current academic catalog.

Application and Information

To obtain an application, make arrangements for an interview, or tour the school, prospective students should contact:

The Art Institute of Washington
A branch of The Art Institute of Atlanta
1820 North Fort Myer Drive
Arlington, Virginia 22209-1802
Phone: 703-358-9550
        877-303-3771 (toll-free)
Fax: 703-358-9759
Web site: http://www.artinstitutes.edu/arlington

COLLEGE CLOSE-UPS

THE ART INSTITUTE OF WASHINGTON—DULLES

DULLES, VIRGINIA

A focused education from The Art Institute of Washington—Dulles, a branch of The Art Institute of Atlanta, can help students turn their creative energy into a powerful tool that can make a difference in the world. Students are part of a collaborative and supportive community, where experienced instructors provide the guidance and skills needed to pursue a career in the creative economy.

The school's programs in the areas of design, media arts, and fashion give students the opportunity to learn by using professional-grade technology and to build a portfolio of work to show potential employers after graduation.

The Art Institute of Washington—Dulles is a branch campus of The Art Institute of Atlanta. The Art Institute of Atlanta is accredited by the Commission on Colleges of the Southern Association of Colleges and Schools to award associate and baccalaureate degrees. For questions about the accreditation of The Art Institute of Atlanta, contact the Commission on Colleges at 1866 Southern Lane, Decatur, Georgia 30033-4097; phone: 404-679-4500.

The Art Institute of Washington—Dulles, a branch of The Art Institute of Atlanta, is certified by the State Council for Higher Education in Virginia, located at James Monroe Building, 101 North Fourteenth Street, Richmond, Virginia 23219; phone: 804-225-2600, to operate in Virginia.

Location

Dulles is part of the Washington D.C. metropolitan area, with a regional population of 5.3 million people. Several large corporations, including MCI and AOL, are based here. The close proximity of Dulles to the nation's capital provides students the opportunity to experience the arts, museums, and national monuments. Students can enjoy performances by the National Symphony Orchestra, Washington National Opera, or the Washington Ballet at the John F. Kennedy Center for the Performing Arts. The area also offers five professional sports teams: the Wizards, Capitals, Nationals, D.C. United, and Redskins.

Programs of Study and Degrees

No matter which course of study a student may choose, the professionals at The Art Institute of Washington—Dulles will guide, support, and help each student as their talents evolve on their journey of personal and professional transformation. Students studying design learn to fine-tune their visual thinking and problem-solving skills as they create everything from logos to TV ads. Programs in the area of media arts focus on utilizing technology to deliver information and entertainment, while students studying fashion learn to market and merchandise clothing.

Bachelor's degree programs are offered in the areas of advertising, fashion and retail management, graphic design, interior design, media arts and animation, photographic imaging, and Web design and interactive media.

Associate degree programs are offered in the areas of graphic design and Web design and interactive media.

Diploma programs are available in the areas of digital image management, fashion retailing, Web design and development, and Web design and interactive communications.

Academic Programs

The Art Institute of Washington—Dulles operates on a year-round, four-quarter system.

Academic Facilities

The Art Institute of Washington—Dulles provides a learning environment with professional-grade technology applicable to each student's course of study. Students have the opportunity to build a portfolio of work that shows potential employers that they are trained to use the software, hardware, or equipment utilized within the industry. Depending upon the course of study, students are immersed in a creative environment—from classrooms to computer labs to studios—focused on relevant, hands-on education designed to prepare students for the real world.

Costs

Tuition cost varies by program. Prospective students should contact the school for current tuition costs. Other charges include a starting kit for all first-quarter students. Kits vary in price depending on the program of study.

Financial Aid

Financial aid is available for those who qualify. Students who require financial assistance should first complete and

submit a Free Application for Federal Student Aid (FAFSA) and meet with a financial aid officer.

Faculty

Faculty members are experienced professionals who create a learning environment that is similar to the professional world students will face after graduation. Instructors are focused on helping students develop the skills they need to transform their creative potential into marketable skills.

Admission Requirements

Applicants must provide proof of high school graduation or achievement of a General Educational Development (GED) certificate as a prerequisite for admission.

In lieu of documenting high school graduation or a GED certificate, applicants may provide proof of attaining an associate degree or higher from an accredited institution. An official transcript indicating date of high school graduation, GED certificate (including test scores), or date of college graduation (including degree granted) is required as proof.

All individuals seeking admission to The Art Institute of Washington—Dulles are interviewed in person or by phone by an assistant director of admissions, and each applicant must create an original essay of at least 150 words stating how an education at The Art Institute of Washington—Dulles would help the student to achieve career goals. There is a $50 application fee.

For the most recent information regarding admission requirements, please refer to the current academic catalog.

Application and Information

To obtain an application, make arrangements for an interview, or tour the school, prospective students should contact:

The Art Institute of Washington—Dulles
A branch of The Art Institute of Atlanta
The Corporate Office Park at Dulles Town Center
21000 Atlantic Blvd., Suite 100
Dulles, Virginia 20166
Phone: 571-449-4400
        888-627-5008 (toll-free)
Fax: 571-449-4500
Web site: http://www.artinstitutes.edu/dulles

THE ART INSTITUTE OF WISCONSIN
MILWAUKEE, WISCONSIN

The Art Institute of Wisconsin®
CREATE TOMORROW

A focused education from The Art Institute of Wisconsin, a branch of The Art Institute of Phoenix, can help students turn their creative energy into a powerful tool that can make a difference in the world. Students are part of a collaborative and supportive community, where experienced instructors provide the guidance and skills needed to pursue a career in the creative economy.

The school's programs in the areas of design, media arts, culinary, and fashion give students the opportunity to learn by using professional-grade technology and to build a portfolio of work to show potential employers after graduation.

The Art Institute of Wisconsin is accredited by the Accrediting Council for Independent Colleges and Schools to award bachelor's and associate's degrees. The Accrediting Council for Independent Colleges and Schools is listed as a nationally recognized accrediting agency by the United States Department of Education and is recognized by the Council for Higher Education Accreditation. ACICS can be contacted at 750 First Street NE, Suite 980, Washington, D.C. 20002; phone: 202-336-6780.

The Art Institute of Wisconsin is authorized by the Wisconsin Educational Approval Board, located at 201 W. Washington Avenue, 3rd Floor, P.O Box 8696, Madison, Wisconsin 53708-8696; http://eab.state.wi.us/default.asp.

Location

Milwaukee is the largest city in Wisconsin, located on the shores of Lake Michigan. The city is well known as a manufacturing center. Cultural amenities include the Milwaukee Art Museum, Grohmann Museum, Haggerty Museum of Art, and William F. Eisner Museum of Advertising & Design, as well as the Milwaukee Symphony Orchestra, Marcus Center for the Performing Arts, and Milwaukee Ballet.

Programs of Study and Degrees

No matter which course of study a student may choose, the professionals at The Art Institute of Wisconsin will guide, support, and help each student as their talents evolve on their journey of personal and professional transformation. Students studying design learn to fine-tune their visual thinking and problem-solving skills as they create everything from logos to TV ads. Programs in the area of media arts focus on utilizing technology to deliver information and entertainment, while students studying fashion learn to market and merchandise clothing. Culinary programs focus on the fundamental skills while exposing students to a full menu of international cuisines and management techniques.

Bachelor's degree programs are offered in the areas of advertising, culinary management, digital filmmaking and video production, fashion design, fashion marketing, game art and design, graphic design, interior design, media arts and animation, visual effects and motion graphics, and Web design and interactive media.

Associate degree programs are offered in the areas of baking and pastry, culinary arts, and graphic design.

Academic Programs

The Art Institute of Wisconsin operates on a year-round, four-quarter system.

Academic Facilities

The Art Institute of Wisconsin provides a learning environment with professional-grade technology applicable to each student's course of study. Students have the opportunity to build a portfolio of work that shows potential employers that they are trained to use the software, hardware, or equipment utilized within the industry. Depending upon the course of study, students are immersed in a creative environment—from classrooms to computer labs to studios—focused on relevant, hands-on education designed to prepare students for the real world.

Costs

Tuition cost varies by program. Prospective students should contact the school for current tuition costs. Other charges include a starting kit for all first-quarter students. Kits vary in price, depending on the program of study.

Financial Aid

Financial aid is available for those who qualify. Students who require financial assistance should first complete and submit a Free Application for Federal Student Aid (FAFSA) and meet with a financial aid officer.

Faculty

Faculty members are experienced professionals who create a learning environment that is similar to the professional world students will face after graduation. Instructors are focused on helping students develop the skills they need to transform their creative potential into marketable skills.

Admission Requirements

Applicants must provide proof of high school graduation or achievement of a General Educational Development (GED) certificate as a prerequisite for admission. In lieu of documenting high school graduation or a GED certificate, applicants may provide proof of attaining an associate degree or higher from an accredited institution. An official transcript indicating date of high school graduation, GED certificate (including test scores), or date of college graduation (including degree granted) is required as proof.

All individuals seeking admission to The Art Institute of Wisconsin are interviewed in person or by phone by an assistant director of admissions, and each applicant must create an original essay of at least 150 words stating how an education at The Art Institute of Wisconsin would help the student to achieve career goals. There is a $50 application fee.

For the most recent information regarding admission requirements, please refer to the current academic catalog.

Application and Information

To obtain an application, make arrangements for an interview, or tour the school, prospective students should contact:

The Art Institute of Wisconsin
A branch of The Art Institute of Phoenix
320 East Buffalo Street, Suite 100
Milwaukee, Wisconsin 53202
Phone: 414-978-5000
        877-285-4234 (toll-free)
Fax: 414-978-5182
Web site: http://www.artinstitutes.edu/milwaukee

THE ART INSTITUTE OF YORK— PENNSYLVANIA

YORK, PENNSYLVANIA

The Art Institute of York
Pennsylvania™
CREATE TOMORROW

A focused education from The Art Institute of York—Pennsylvania can help students turn their creative energy into a powerful tool that can make a difference in the world. Students are part of a collaborative and supportive community, where experienced instructors provide the guidance and skills needed to pursue a career in the creative economy.

The school's programs in the areas of design, media arts, and fashion give students the opportunity to learn by using professional-grade technology and to build a portfolio of work to show potential employers after graduation.

The Art Institute of York—Pennsylvania is accredited by the Accrediting Council for Independent Colleges and Schools to award associate's and bachelor's degrees. The Accrediting Council for Independent Colleges and Schools is listed as a nationally recognized accrediting agency by the United Stated Department of Education and is recognized by the Council for Higher Education Accreditation. ACICS can be contacted at 750 First Street NE, Suite 980, Washington, D.C. 20002; phone: 202-336-6780.

The Art Institute of York—Pennsylvania is authorized by the Pennsylvania Department of Education to confer the Bachelor of Science degrees and Associate of Science degrees. The Department of Education can be contacted at the Commonwealth of Pennsylvania, Department of Education, Office of Postsecondary and Higher Education, 333 Market Street, Harrisburg, Pennsylvania 17126; phone: 717-783-6788.

Location

The Art Institute of York—Pennsylvania is located in York, a suburban area in south-central Pennsylvania. Surrounded by sprawling hills and Amish farmlands, York offers visitors an abundance of shopping areas and museums and three centuries of American history, including battlefields from the Revolutionary and Civil wars. York is a 30-minute drive from Hershey and Harrisburg, Pennsylvania; approximately a 90-minute drive from Philadelphia; and a 1-hour drive from Baltimore, Maryland.

Programs of Study and Degrees

No matter which course of study a student may choose, the professionals at The Art Institute of York—Pennsylvania will guide, support, and help each student as their talents evolve on their journey of personal and professional transformation. Students studying design learn to fine-tune their visual thinking and problem-solving skills as they create everything from logos to TV ads. Programs in the area of media arts focus on utilizing technology to deliver information and entertainment, while students studying fashion learn to market and merchandise clothing.

Bachelor's degree programs are offered in the areas of fashion and retail management, graphic design, interior design, media arts and animation, and Web design and interactive media.

Associate degrees are offered in the areas of graphic design and kitchen and bath design.

Academic Programs

The Art Institute of York—Pennsylvania operates on a year-round, four-quarter system.

Academic Facilities

The Art Institute of York—Pennsylvania provides a learning environment with professional-grade technology applicable to each student's course of study. Students have the opportunity to build a portfolio of work that shows potential employers that they are trained to use the software, hardware, or equipment utilized within the industry. Depending upon the course of study, students are immersed in a creative environment—from classrooms to computer labs to studios—focused on relevant, hands-on education designed to prepare students for the real world.

Costs

Tuition cost varies by program. Prospective students should contact the school for current tuition costs. Other charges

include a starting kit for all first-quarter students. Kits vary in price depending on the program of study.

Financial Aid

Financial aid is available for those who qualify. Students who require financial assistance should first complete and submit a Free Application for Federal Student Aid (FAFSA) and meet with a financial aid officer.

Faculty

Faculty members are experienced professionals who create a learning environment that is similar to the professional world students will face after graduation. Instructors are focused on helping students develop the skills they need to transform their creative potential into marketable skills.

Admission Requirements

The Art Institute of York—Pennsylvania encourages interested students to apply early. To apply, students must possess a high school diploma or General Educational Development (GED) certificate and a minimum SAT score of 800 (at least 400 math and 400 verbal) or a minimum ACT score of 16. A portfolio review may be required. There is a $50 application fee.

For the most recent information regarding admission requirements, please refer to the current academic catalog.

Application and Information

To obtain an application, make arrangements for an interview, or tour the school, students should contact:

The Art Institute of York—Pennsylvania
1409 Williams Road
York, Pennsylvania 17402-9012
Phone: 717-755-2300
      800-864-7725 (toll-free)
Fax: 717-840-1951
Web site: http://www.artinstitutes.edu/york

COLLEGE CLOSE-UPS

THE ART INSTITUTES INTERNATIONAL—KANSAS CITY

LENEXA, KANSAS

A focused education from The Art Institutes International—Kansas City, a branch of The Art Institute of Phoenix, can help students turn their creative energy into a powerful tool that can make a difference in the world. Students are part of a collaborative and supportive community, where experienced instructors provide the guidance and skills needed to pursue a career in the creative economy.

The school's programs in the areas of design, media arts, fashion, and culinary give students the opportunity to learn by using professional-grade technology and to build a portfolio of work to show potential employers after graduation.

The Art Institutes International—Kansas City is accredited by the Accrediting Council for Independent Colleges and Schools to award associate's and bachelor's degrees. The Accrediting Council for Independent Colleges and Schools is listed as a nationally recognized accrediting agency by the United States Department of Education and is recognized by the Council for Higher Education Accreditation. ACICS can be contacted at 750 First Street NE, Suite 980, Washington, D.C. 20002; phone: 202-336-6780.

The Kansas Board of Regents has approved The Art Institutes International—Kansas City to operate in the state of Kansas. The Kansas Board of Regents may be contacted at Kansas Board of Regents, Private Postsecondary Education Division, 1000 SW Jackson Street, Suite 520, Topeka, Kansas 66612-1368; phone: 785-296-0911; fax: 785-296-4526.

Location

Lenexa is part of the Kansas City metropolitan area of nearly two million people. Kansas City's contributions to jazz and the blues are well known. The city is also home to over 200 fountains and more boulevards than any city besides Paris.

Programs of Study and Degrees

No matter which course of study a student may choose, the professionals at The Art Institutes International—Kansas City will guide, support, and help each student as their talents evolve on their journey of personal and professional transformation. Students studying design learn to fine-tune their visual thinking and problem-solving skills as they create everything from logos to TV ads. Programs in the area of media arts focus on utilizing technology to deliver information and entertainment, while students studying fashion learn to design clothes for the runway or run a retail shop. Culinary programs focus on the fundamental techniques while exposing students to a full menu of international cuisines and management techniques.

Bachelor's degree programs are offered in the areas of advertising, culinary arts, digital filmmaking and video production, fashion marketing, game art and design, graphic design, interior design, media arts and animation, photography, visual effects and motion graphics, and Web design and interactive media.

Associate degree programs are offered in the areas of baking and pastry arts, culinary arts, and graphic design.

Diploma programs are offered in the areas of baking and pastry, culinary arts, digital image management, fashion retailing, Web design and development, and Web design and interactive communications.

Academic Programs

The Art Institutes International—Kansas City operates on a year-round, four-quarter system.

Academic Facilities

The Art Institutes International—Kansas City provides a learning environment with professional-grade technology applicable to each student's course of study. Students have the opportunity to build a portfolio of work that shows potential employers that they are trained to use the software, hardware, or equipment utilized within the industry. Depending upon the course of study, students are immersed in a creative environment—from classrooms to computer labs to studios—focused on relevant, hands-on education designed to prepare students for the real world.

Costs

Tuition cost varies by program. Prospective students should contact the school for current tuition costs. Other charges include a starting kit for all first-quarter students. Kits vary in price depending on the program of study.

Financial Aid

Financial aid is available for those who qualify. Students who require financial assistance should first complete and submit a Free Application for Federal Student Aid (FAFSA) and meet with a financial aid officer.

Faculty

Faculty members are experienced professionals who create a learning environment that is similar to the professional world students will face after graduation. Instructors are focused on helping students develop the skills they need to transform their creative potential into marketable skills.

Admission Requirements

Applicants must provide proof of high school graduation or achievement of a General Educational Development (GED) certificate as a prerequisite for admission. In lieu of documenting high school graduation or a GED certificate, applicants may provide proof of attaining an associate degree or higher from an accredited institution. An official transcript indicating date of high school graduation, GED certificate (including test scores), or date of college graduation (including degree granted) is required as proof.

All individuals seeking admission to The Art Institutes International—Kansas City are interviewed in person or by phone by an assistant director of admissions, and each applicant must create an original essay of at least 150 words stating how an education at The Art Institutes International—Kansas City would help the student to achieve career goals. There is a $50 application fee.

For the most recent information regarding admission requirements, please refer to the current academic catalog.

Application and Information

To obtain an application, arrange for an interview, or tour the school, prospective students should contact:

The Art Institutes International—Kansas City
A branch of The Art Institute of Phoenix
8208 Melrose Drive
Lenexa, Kansas 66214
Phone: 913-217-4600
       866-530-8508 (toll-free)
Fax: 913-217-4690
Web site: http://www.artinstitutes.edu/kansascity

THE ART INSTITUTES INTERNATIONAL MINNESOTA

MINNEAPOLIS, MINNESOTA

The Art Institutes International Minnesota™

CREATE TOMORROW

A focused education from The Art Institutes International Minnesota can help students turn their creative energy into a powerful tool that can make a difference in the world. Students are part of a collaborative and supportive community, where experienced instructors provide the guidance and skills needed to pursue a career in the creative economy.

The school's programs in the areas of design, media arts, fashion, and culinary give students the opportunity to learn by using professional-grade technology and to build a portfolio of work to show potential employers after graduation.

The Art Institutes International Minnesota is accredited by the Accrediting Council for Independent Colleges and Schools (ACICS) to award certificates, associate's degrees, and bachelor's degrees. ACICS is listed as a nationally recognized accrediting agency by the United States Department of Education and is recognized by the Council for Higher Education Accreditation. ACICS can be contacted at 750 First Street NE, Suite 980, Washington, D.C. 20002; phone: 202-336-6780.

The Art Institutes International Minnesota is registered as a private institution with the Minnesota Office of Higher Education, located at 1450 Energy Park Drive, Suite 350, St. Paul, Minnesota 55108; phone: 651-642-0567; http://www.ohe.state.mn.us, pursuant to sections 136A.61 to 136A.71. Registration is not an endorsement of the institution. Credits earned at the institution may not transfer to all other institutions.

The Associate in Applied Science in Culinary Arts degree program is accredited by the Accrediting Commission of the American Culinary Federation Education Foundation.

Location

Minneapolis is a thriving environment for creative minds; home to culture, arts, and entertainment. The Twin Cities region has many Fortune 500 companies, including Target, Best Buy, 3M, and General Mills. The area is also home to a top design and advertising market and is a major U.S. business hub.

Programs of Study and Degrees

No matter which course of study a student may choose, the professionals at The Art Institutes International Minnesota will guide, support, and help each student as their talents evolve on their journey of personal and professional transformation. Students studying design learn to fine-tune their visual thinking and problem-solving skills as they create everything from logos to TV ads. Programs in the area of media arts focus on utilizing technology to deliver information and entertainment, while students studying fashion learn to design clothes for the runway or run a retail shop. Culinary programs focus on the fundamental techniques while exposing students to a full menu of international cuisines and management techniques.

Bachelor's degree programs are offered in the areas of advertising, audio production, culinary management, design management, digital film and video production, fashion and retail management, fashion design, graphic design, hospitality management, interior design, media arts and animation, photography, visual effects and motion graphics, and Web design and interactive media.

Associate degree programs are offered in the areas of baking and pastry, culinary arts, graphic design, interior design, interior planning with AutoCAD, and Web design and interactive media.

Diploma programs are offered in the areas of art of cooking, baking and pastry, digital image management, fashion retailing, Web design and development, and Web design and interactive communications.

The programs in culinary arts, culinary management, graphic design, and Web design and interactive media are available in an evening and weekend option format.

Academic Programs

The Art Institutes International Minnesota operates on a year-round, four-quarter system.

Academic Facilities

The Art Institutes International Minnesota provides a learning environment with professional-grade technology applicable to each student's course of study. Students have the opportunity to build a portfolio of work that shows potential employers that they are trained to use the software, hardware, or equipment utilized within the industry. Depending upon the course of study, students are immersed in a creative environment—from classrooms to computer labs to studios—focused on relevant, hands-on education designed to prepare students for the real world.

Costs

Tuition cost varies by program. Prospective students should contact the school for current tuition costs. Other charges include a starting kit for all first-quarter students. Kits vary in price depending on the program of study.

Financial Aid

Financial aid is available for those who qualify. Students who require financial assistance should first complete and submit a Free Application for Federal Student Aid (FAFSA) and meet with a financial aid officer.

Faculty

Faculty members are experienced professionals who create a learning environment that is similar to the professional world students will face after graduation. Instructors are focused on helping students develop the skills they need to transform their creative potential into marketable skills.

Admission Requirements

Applicants must provide proof of high school graduation or achievement of a General Educational Development (GED) certificate as a prerequisite for admission. In lieu of documenting high school graduation or a GED certificate, applicants may provide proof of attaining an associate degree or higher from an accredited institution. An official transcript indicating date of high school graduation, GED certificate (including test scores), or date of college graduation (including degree granted) is required as proof.

All individuals seeking admission to The Art Institutes International Minnesota are interviewed in person or by phone by an assistant director of admissions, and each applicant must create an original essay of at least 150 words stating how an education at The Art Institutes International Minnesota would help the student to achieve career goals. There is a $50 application fee.

For the most recent information regarding admission requirements, please refer to the current academic catalog.

Application and Information

To obtain an application, arrange for an interview, or tour the school, prospective students should contact:

The Art Institutes International Minnesota
15 South 9th Street
Minneapolis, Minnesota 55402-3105
Phone: 612-332-3361
      800-777-3643 (toll-free)
Fax: 612-332-3934
Web site: http://www.artinstitutes.edu/minneapolis

Over 50 schools: The Art Institute of Atlanta; The Art Institute of Atlanta—Decatur, A branch of The Art Institute of Atlanta; The Art Institute of Austin, A branch of The Art Institute of Houston; The Art Institute of California, a college of Argosy University, with locations in Hollywood, Inland Empire, Los Angeles, Orange County, Sacramento, San Diego, San Francisco, and Sunnyvale; The Art Institute of Charleston, A branch of The Art Institute of Atlanta; The Art Institute of Charlotte; The Art Institute of Colorado; The Art Institute of Dallas, A campus of South University; The Art Institute of Fort Lauderdale; The Art Institute of Fort Worth, A campus of South University; The Art Institute of Houston; The Art Institute of Houston—North, A branch of The Art Institute of Houston; The Art Institute of Indianapolis; The Art Institute of Jacksonville, A branch of Miami International University of Art & Design; The Art Institute of Las Vegas; The Art Institute of Michigan; The Art Institute of Michigan—Troy; The Art Institute of New York City; The Art Institute of Ohio—Cincinnati; The Art Institute of Philadelphia; The Art Institute of Phoenix; The Art Institute of Pittsburgh; The Art Institute of Portland; The Art Institute of Raleigh–Durham; The Art Institute of Salt Lake City; The Art Institute of San Antonio, A branch of The Art Institute of Houston; The Art Institute of Seattle; The Art Institute of Tampa, A branch of Miami International University of Art & Design; The Art Institute of Tennessee—Nashville, A branch of The Art Institute of Atlanta; The Art Institute of Tucson; The Art Institute of Vancouver; The Art Institute of Virginia Beach[1], A branch of The Art Institute of Atlanta; The Art Institute of Washington[1], A branch of The Art Institute of Atlanta; The Art Institute of Washington—Dulles[1], A branch of The Art Institute of Atlanta; The Art Institute of Wisconsin; The Art Institute of York—Pennsylvania; The Art Institutes International—Kansas City; The Art Institutes International Minnesota; The Illinois Institute of Art—Chicago; The Illinois Institute of Art—Schaumburg; The Illinois Institute of Art—Tinley Park; Miami International University of Art & Design; The New England Institute of Art

[1]Certified by SCHEV to operate in Virginia

See **aiprograms.info** for program duration, tuition, fees, and other costs, median debt, federal salary data, alumni success, and other important info. The Art Institutes is a system of over 50 schools throughout North America. Programs, credential levels, technology, and scheduling options vary by school, and employment opportunities are not guaranteed. Financial aid is available to those who qualify. Several institutions included in The Art Institutes system are campuses of South University or Argosy University. OH Registration # 04-01-1698B, AC0165, AC0080, Licensed by the Florida Commission for Independent Education, License No. 1287, 3427, 3110, 2581. Administrative office: 210 Sixth Avenue, 33rd Floor, Pittsburgh, PA 15222. ©2012 The Art Institutes International LLC.

ASSUMPTION COLLEGE
WORCESTER, MASSACHUSETTS

The College

Assumption College, established in 1904 by the Augustinians of the Assumption, is a coeducational institution known for its classic liberal arts curriculum and strong academic programs in business and professional studies. The College's 2,100 undergraduates choose among forty majors and forty-five minors, gaining a depth and breadth of knowledge that is the foundation of lifelong success. Their educational experience is grounded in the rich Catholic intellectual tradition, which cultivates both the intellect and personal values students need to meet the demands of a constantly changing world. Undergraduates and graduate students interact closely with faculty members and staff in a thriving community that develops graduates known for critical intelligence, thoughtful citizenship, and compassionate service.

The academic atmosphere is marked by individual attention and the quest for personal excellence. With a student-faculty ratio of just 11:1, Assumption's professors serve as mentors who challenge students to ask questions, find their own answers, and grow—intellectually, socially, and spiritually. Students are encouraged to gain hands-on experience at internships and to participate in individual research projects. The result is that 97 percent of the graduates who responded to a survey six months after graduation are either employed or in graduate school.

At Assumption, 90 percent of the undergraduates live on campus and housing is guaranteed for all four years. The campus is lively seven days a week with academic programming, activities sponsored by student clubs and organizations, community service opportunities, campus ministry programs, and intercollegiate, intramural, and club sports. The College's state-of-the-art recreation center supports the well-being of all students.

Location

The College's beautiful, 185-acre campus is situated in a residential neighborhood just minutes from downtown Worcester, Massachusetts. Worcester, the second-largest city in New England, is a vibrant college town, home to 30,000 students. The city offers extensive opportunities for internships in virtually every field, as well as numerous entertainment and community service options. Great restaurants, cultural venues and programs, retail shops, and professional sports teams provide students with many off-campus activities. Worcester is also centrally located, with Boston, Providence, Rhode Island, and Hartford, Connecticut, each an hour's drive away. There are numerous daily commuter trains to Boston.

Majors and Degrees

The College offers Bachelor of Arts degrees. The most popular majors include English (concentrations in literature or writing and mass communications), history, political science, psychology, the natural sciences (biology, biotechnology and molecular biology, chemistry, and environmental science),

education, human services and rehabilitation studies, and business disciplines such as accounting, international business, management, marketing, and organizational communication. Minors are offered in forty-five areas. Preprofessional programs are available for dentistry, medicine, and law.

The College has also developed partnerships with a number of highly regarded institutions to provide students with additional options. There is engineering with the University of Notre Dame, environment science with Duke University, and law (3+3 programs with Duquesne, Vermont, and Western New England Law Schools). There are agreements for numerous medical professions, and joint seven-year programs are also available for those interested in podiatry or optometry.

Assumption College offers graduate degrees in business, special education, school counseling, counseling psychology, and rehabilitation counseling.

Academic Programs

The College's classic liberal arts curriculum promotes the lively discussion of the books, ideas, people, and events that have shaped civilization. Faculty members and students explore the rich Catholic intellectual tradition as they seek truth and the nature of the world.

Assumption also offers academic programs and courses that help students achieve their full potential. The College's first-year program, the Tagaste Project, links courses from two disciplines and offers activities that complement classroom experiences. The same 20 students take courses in the fall and spring semesters, enabling them to make important intellectual connections, while getting to know other students. The honors program and the Fortin and Gonthier Foundations of Western Civilization Program encourage students to challenge themselves intellectually. Air Force and Army ROTC are also available.

Assumption College follows a traditional two-semester calendar, from late August to mid-May, as well as an optional January intersession. The Graduate Studies programs and the Center for Continuing and Career Education also offer two summer sessions for students.

Undergraduates complete a core curriculum that provides a strong foundation in the liberal arts. Students must complete 120 credit hours in all the academic programs to earn a degree.

Off-Campus Programs

The College and eleven other institutions of higher learning created the Colleges of Worcester Consortium to offer the 30,000 college students in the area even greater academic and social opportunities. Assumption students may cross-register for academic credit at any of the participating colleges and enjoy their social and cultural events. Free transportation to other participating institutions is available.

Eligible students may choose to spend a semester or a year abroad. Assumption is slated to open a campus in Rome in the spring of 2013, which will be open to sophomores. The College's students have studied abroad in Australia, Austria, Chile, China, Costa Rica, the Czech Republic, England, France, Germany, Greece, Ireland, Italy, Japan, the Netherlands, Spain, and other locations. There are also numerous one- and two-week international experiences led by Assumption faculty.

More than 50 percent of Assumption students have an internship. They explore their professional choices and broaden their workplace skills at local, regional, national, and international sites. In recent years, they have interned at PBS, the U.S. House of Representatives, Ralph Lauren, the Hungarian Embassy, Smith Barney, Fidelity, *The Daily Show with Jon Stewart*, ABC News, PricewaterhouseCoopers, AT&T, and Sony Japan.

Academic Facilities

The College has invested more than $80 million to enhance the campus facilities. The entire campus is wireless.

The Testa Science Center houses the Department of Natural Sciences and features multiuse classrooms with state-of-the-art technology, ten teaching laboratories, seven laboratories dedicated for faculty and student research, a working greenhouse, conference rooms, and student lounge areas.

The Information Technology Center houses computer labs, technology-rich classrooms, and experienced support staff. Students can learn Web authoring, graphics and animation, digital video, and multimedia production. The digital audio studio is available for all students and faculty members.

Assumption offers a variety of housing options to accommodate the 90 percent of students who live on campus. There are traditional residence halls, suites, a living and learning residence, and apartments. All resident students have individual hard-wired and wireless Internet access in their rooms. The outstanding stadium and athletic facilities support the College's 23 NCAA Division II intercollegiate teams, many recreational programs, and the physical well-being of the entire campus community.

Costs

For 2011–12, tuition was $33,390, room and board were $10,590, and student fees were $415. The board plan is required for all first-year students.

Financial Aid

The College offers financial aid based on demonstrated need and scholastic achievement. The College requires that students submit the Free Application for Federal Student Aid (FAFSA), which is available on January 1. This form should be filed by February 1, so that the College can consider the information as it makes financial aid awards.

All applicants for admission are considered for merit awards up to $20,000 per year. Funds awarded through this program reflect the College's commitment to academic excellence and student leadership.

Faculty

Approximately 90 percent of the Assumption College faculty members hold the doctoral or highest degree in their field.

They are active scholars presenting their ideas and research at professional conferences, writing books and articles, and publishing in journals. With a student-to-faculty ratio of 11:1, professors get to know the students—to mentor, encourage, and help students succeed. Professors work closely with students and challenge them to explore new paths of knowledge and make their own discoveries. All of Assumption's academic advisors are full-time faculty members.

Student Government

There are more than sixty clubs and organizations on campus, offering students opportunities in community service, sports, academics, leadership, and special interests. The Student Government Association (SGA), the elected representatives of the student body, coordinates official communication between the student community and the College administration and officially recognizes student clubs and activities.

Admission Requirements

All applicants must graduate from an accredited secondary school with a minimum of 18 academic units. These units should include 4 years of English, 3 years of mathematics, 2 years of a foreign language, 2 years of history, 2 years of science, and 5 additional academic units.

Admission to Assumption is test-score optional. When submitting an application an essay and recommendations are required. Interviews are recommended, but not required.

The number of solid academic courses, including the number of honors-level or Advanced Placement–level courses, is considered during the application review process.

The Admissions Committee understands that grading standards vary from school to school or from one course to another. Class rank provides some context within which to place the grades of students applying from a given school. Some schools also provide grade distribution charts. The Committee also considers whether the applicant's grade point average or rank in class is weighted or unweighted.

Application and Information

Campus visits are strongly recommended. Appointments can be scheduled Monday through Friday. Group Information Sessions are held most Saturdays in the fall.

Applicants must submit a completed application, a $50 application fee, official transcripts, a recommendation, and an essay. Applications for early action must be received by November 1. There is a second early action deadline of January 10. The deadline for regular admission is February 15. Students may complete the Common Application and Supplement at www.commonapp.org.

For more information, students should contact:

Office of Admissions
Assumption College
500 Salisbury Street
P.O. Box 15005
Worcester, Massachusetts 01609-1296
Phone: 508-767-7285
      866-477-7776 (toll-free)
E-mail: admiss@assumption.edu
Web site: http://www.assumption.edu

AVE MARIA UNIVERSITY
AVE MARIA, FLORIDA

The University

As the first new Catholic university in forty years, Ave Maria University exists to further teaching, research, and learning in the abiding tradition of Catholic thought in both national and international settings. The University sponsors a liberal arts education curriculum dedicated to the advancement of human culture, the promotion of dialogue between faith and reason, and the formation of men and women in the intellectual and moral virtues of the Catholic faith.

The University began as Thomas S. Monaghan's dream to build an institution that would be faithful to the Magisterium and produce exceptional educators, leaders, and mentors. Through his initial financial donation, the University opened its doors in August 2003 with 100 students; the enrollment as of fall 2011 was 745.

In addition to its undergraduate degree programs, the University's graduate department offers an M.T.S. in pastoral theology and a Master of Arts and Ph.D. in Theology.

The Office of Campus Ministry, in conjunction with Student Life, organizes retreats for students throughout the year. The University also encourages students to find opportunities to serve the poor, the infirm, and the elderly in the local community.

Ave Maria University recognizes the important role that athletics play in forming the whole person. To that end, club and intramural-level sports are offered in a variety of sports. In addition, the University was accepted into the National Association of Intercollegiate Athletics (NAIA) in February 2008. NAIA division sports slated for fall 2012 include men's baseball, football, and softball; men's and women's basketball, cross-country, golf, soccer, and tennis; and women's cheerleading and dance and volleyball.

Full-time students are required to live on campus, unless they are living at home with their parents. However, students who are 23 or older may only live on campus with permission of the Dean of Students. Each floor of a residence hall includes a live-in residence director and a student resident assistant, and access to common areas, kitchen and laundry facilities, meeting rooms, and a chapel is provided. Choice of housing on campus is granted each year primarily on the basis of academic seniority. The dining area is located in the Student Union. Breakfast, lunch, and dinner are served Monday through Friday. Brunch and an evening meal are served on Saturdays and Sundays.

Location

Ave Maria University's campus currently occupies 100 acres of land approximately 20 miles northeast of the city of Naples. The town center of Ave Maria, adjoining the University, is home to restaurants, a coffee shop, and the University Bookstore. Naples, nestled near the beaches of the Gulf of Mexico, is known for world-class shopping, dining, and more than thirty-five golf courses. Art lovers can spend an evening at the Philharmonic Center for the Arts or the popular Dinner Theater. The many nearby parks and nature preserves feature rare species of flora and fauna indigenous to the state.

Majors and Degrees

Ave Maria University offers a strong classical liberal arts core curriculum as well as an opportunity for students to choose one of the following majors: American Studies, Biochemistry, Biology, Business Administration, Catholic Studies, Classics, Economics, Global Affairs & International Business, Greek, History, Humanities & Liberal Studies, Literature, Mathematics, Managerial Economics & Strategic Analysis, Music, Philosophy, Physics, Political Economy & Government, Politics, Psychology, and Theology. The University also offers two pre-professional programs: Pre-Law and Pre-Med.

Academic Programs

The University's core curriculum requires students to take specific courses in the liberal arts, thus acquiring an indispensable foundation for a lifetime of learning. Of the 128 credits required to earn a bachelor's degree, the core curriculum comprises one-half, or 64 credits. The major of study comprises another 32 to 40 credits, and general electives comprise the final 24 to 32 credits. Students are required to take two noncredit practicums in the fine arts, the first being an introduction to Gregorian chant and the second in chorus, instrumental music, studio art, or theater. Other core courses include three courses each in theology and philosophy; two courses each in history, literature, and the natural sciences; and one course each in American civilization and mathematics. Some requirements may be met through CLEP, Advanced Placement (with an exam score of 4), and military service.

Off-Campus Programs

The University offers study-abroad programs at Ave Maria University–Latin America Campus, located in San Marcos, Nicaragua, and in Rome, Italy. Students may enroll in the program for one semester. Courses are taught in English and correspond to the requirements of the degree programs at the University. The cost for each program is the regular University cost of attendance, although students are expected to cover their travel expenses. Students must have at least sophomore status to enter one of the programs. Transfer students must have spent at least one full semester at the Ave Maria Florida campus before they are eligible to apply.

Academic Facilities

Ave Maria University's Canizaro Library has 4 librarians and a support staff of 10 members. With more than 200,000 volumes, the Canizaro Library has one of the largest permanent collections in the region. In addition to its impressive open-stack collection, the Canizaro Library has interlibrary loan privileges with university libraries throughout the United States and belongs to the Southwest Florida Library Network consortium. To supplement its print resources, the Canizaro Library provides students and faculty and staff members with access to several electronic databases for research purposes. These can be accessed from any network computer. Computer workstations located throughout the campus are connected to the campus network and include the most up-to-date software. All computer stations are equipped with printers and Internet access. Scanners for photos and graphics are also available. Facilities for viewing audiovisual materials are located throughout the campus. A writing lab program provides students with the opportunity to familiarize themselves with accepted standards for expository writing as well as the institutional style and research conventions.

Costs

For the 2011–12 academic year, undergraduate tuition and fees were $10,045 per semester or $20,090 for the year. Other costs per semester included $2397 for housing and $1812 for meals. The total cost of attendance was $14,255 per semester or $28,510 per academic year.

Financial Aid

Approximately 90 percent of students receive financial assistance. Ave Maria University is Title IV eligible, allowing students to participate in federal student financial aid programs. In addition to federal aid, institutional grants are offered. The Ave Maria University Grant is awarded to students who demonstrate considerable financial need. All financial aid decisions are based on the Free Application for Federal Student Aid (FAFSA). Ave Maria University also offers scholarships to students based on prior academic achievement, ACT or SAT scores, and leadership factors; those interested in a scholarship should apply early (early action deadline is November 15). On-campus employment opportunities are also available. The University offers the option of paying over a five- or ten-month period.

Faculty

The faculty consists of 59 professors, 98 percent of whom hold a terminal degree (Ph.D. or equivalent) in their fields of study. Faculty members are carefully chosen for a clear and strong commitment to Catholic education, and professors of philosophy and theology annually make the Profession of Faith and renew their Oath of Fidelity to the Magisterium of the Catholic Church.

Student Government

The student body is represented by a president, a vice president, a secretary, a treasurer, and two elected representatives from each class. The student representatives are responsible for hosting a number of student activities and programs and for setting the budget for other student organizations.

Application and Information

There is no fee to apply to Ave Maria University. Applications are evaluated on a rolling basis and may be submitted online or mailed to:

Office of Admissions
Ave Maria University
5050 Ave Maria Boulevard
Ave Maria, Florida 34142-9505
Phone: 239-280-2556
Fax: 239-280-2559
Web site: http://www.avemaria.edu

BABSON COLLEGE
WELLESLEY, MASSACHUSETTS

The College

Since its founding in 1919, Babson College has focused on educating business leaders capable of initiating and managing change, navigating ethical choices, understanding global perspectives, and motivating teams with a common purpose to create economic and social value everywhere. The 2011–12 undergraduate enrollment was 880 women and 1,127 men. An independent, coeducational institution, Babson is accredited by the International Association for Management Education, AACSB International–The Association to Advance Collegiate Schools of Business, the New England Association of Schools and Colleges, and the European Quality Improvement System (EQUIS).

Babson is a residential college and is a fast-paced community alive with intellectual, cultural, athletic, and social activities. Approximately 85 percent of the undergraduate student body lives on campus all four years in fourteen residence halls. Housing options include coed residence halls, fraternity and sorority housing, and substance-free, multicultural, entrepreneurial, and other specialty-themed housing.

Babson College is an NCAA Division III school. Most of the College's intercollegiate teams compete in the New England Women's and Men's Athletic Conference (NEWMAC). There are twenty-two men's and women's varsity sports teams, with additional club and intramural sports available to all students. More information is available at http://www.babsonathletics.com.

The Webster Center features an indoor, 200-meter, six-lane track; a field house; a gymnasium with three basketball courts; a racquetball court; a 25-yard, six-lane pool with 1- and 3-meter diving boards; a fitness center; squash courts; and a dance/aerobics studio. The Babson Skating Center features a 600-seat skating arena. Outdoor facilities include eight tennis courts, an AstroTurf field, a game field, a renovated softball diamond, a baseball field, two sand-based varsity fields, and a club rugby field.

Location

Babson's beautiful 370-acre campus is in Wellesley, Massachusetts, 14 miles west of Boston, a city renowned for its cultural and recreational opportunities. More than sixty colleges and universities bring more than 250,000 college students to the Boston area, making it one of the world's best college towns for cultural exchange and research.

Majors and Degrees

Babson offers a Bachelor of Science degree, a Master of Business Administration degree, three Master of Science degree programs, and executive education programs for business professionals.

Academic Programs

The curriculum breaks down the barriers between disciplines by emphasizing an integrated, holistic approach to learning. The curriculum integrates core competencies, key business disciplines, experiential learning, and the liberal arts into foundation, intermediate, and advanced programs. Babson's core competencies include rhetoric, quantitative analysis, entrepreneurial and creative thinking, global and multicultural perspectives, ethics and social responsibility, leadership and teamwork, and critical and integrative thinking.

These learning outcomes are introduced and reinforced as students progress through the undergraduate curriculum. The Foundation Program lays the groundwork by raising students' abilities to formulate, explore, and reflect critically. In the second year, students proceed to the Intermediate Program, which adds breadth and exposes them to more disciplinary and interdisciplinary analyses. The Advanced Program challenges students to think about issues with increased confidence, independence, and creativity.

Foundation Program courses may include quantitative methods with calculus, probability and statistics, financial accounting,

rhetoric, arts and humanities, history and society, business law, and science. The cornerstone of the Foundation Program is Foundations of Management and Entrepreneurship (FME), a yearlong immersion into the world of start-ups, where student teams actually create their own businesses, receiving grants of up to $3000 to cover costs. Babson is the only U.S. school to teach the management core curriculum as an integrated three-semester course where all aspects of business are covered, including accounting, marketing, finance, management operations, strategy, organizational behavior, IT sales, and economics.

In the Advanced and Intermediate Programs, students are free to expand and fine-tune core competencies as they reflect on their own career and life goals. During this time, students take courses in advanced management and liberal arts electives. Babson offers twenty-seven optional concentrations in both business and liberal arts disciplines; descriptions can be found at http://www.babson.edu/concentrations. This way, students may further plan their own course of study by focusing on certain areas of interest while continuing to benefit from Babson's interdisciplinary approach to learning. Students also have the opportunity to participate in experiential learning programs such as an internship or consulting experience. Special programs, such as the Weissman program, the honors program, the Women's Leadership Program, the Management Consulting Field Experience, the Babson College Fund (student-managed endowment), Master of Science in Accounting (M.S.A.), and independent research allow students to take advantage of customized learning opportunities at Babson.

Babson's flexible curriculum allows students to pursue courses that appeal to them and align with their goals. To aid in the decision-making process, students receive guidance from faculty mentors and professional staff throughout their four years.

To earn the Bachelor of Science degree, students are required to complete a minimum of 126 semester hours with a cumulative grade point average of at least 2.0, a minimum of 63 credits in the liberal arts, and a minimum of 40 credits in advanced courses. Transfer students must complete a minimum of 64 semester hours at Babson. Once a student has earned 96 credits, all remaining credits must be earned at Babson, at a Babson-approved cross-registration program, or at a Babson-affiliated study abroad program.

Entering students may be granted credit or advanced course placement for successful scores on Advanced Placement (AP) examinations administered by the College Board as well as some courses in the International Baccalaureate (I.B.) curriculum.

Babson operates on a two-semester academic calendar. Semesters run from September to December and from late January through May. An optional credit-bearing three-week winter session is offered in January, and two summer sessions are offered—one from late May to early July and one from mid-July to mid-August.

Off-Campus Programs

Babson has a partnership with Wellesley College and the Franklin W. Olin College of Engineering, an independent institution that opened in 2001, and is located on a 70-acre site adjacent to Babson. Babson, Olin, and Wellesley are collaborating inside and outside the classroom in order to provide extraordinary opportunities in all aspects of the student experience, including joint academic and research programming, student life programming, and lecture series.

Babson students can also take a course each semester at other area colleges, including Brandeis University and Regis College, for full academic credit. These off-campus programs offer greater access to liberal arts courses, including a wide range of foreign languages.

Babson's vibrant study abroad program enables students to spend either a summer or one or both semesters of their junior year overseas at a college or university. Currently, forty-seven programs are offered in twenty-six countries, and full academic credit is given for approved management and liberal arts courses.

Academic Facilities

Horn Library houses an extensive business collection of print, media, and computerized information resources. Students have campus-wide access to newspapers, journals, investment analyst reports, corporate records, directories, and international information. They also benefit from numerous electronic research and news services that supplement a selection of the best business and liberal arts books, newspapers, journals, CD-ROMs, audiocassettes, videocassettes, and videodiscs.

Horn Computer Center is equipped with a lab that remains open 24 hours a day. Wireless access is available throughout the campus. Every incoming Babson undergraduate student receives a leased laptop computer with integrated Wi-Fi wireless technology.

Other facilities are the Donald W. Reynolds Campus Center, the Richard W. Sorenson Family Visual Arts Center, the Stephen D. Cutler Center for Investments and Finance, the Glavin Family Chapel, and the Arthur M. Blank Center for Entrepreneurship.

Costs

For 2011–12, tuition and fees were $40,400. The total estimated cost for books was $1020 and other expenses (i.e. transportation and personal) were $1784.

Financial Aid

Babson is committed to educating students from diverse backgrounds. Applying for financial aid does not affect a student's chances of being admitted to Babson College. Financial assistance is awarded on merit and demonstrated financial need. Assistance for students begins with consideration for student loans and work-study. Those with need beyond the loan and work-study amounts are also considered for Babson grants.

In 2011–12, over 45 percent of all undergraduate students received need-based Babson scholarships or grants. Nearly half of Babson students receive some form of financial assistance. Students should note that need-based financial assistance is available to U.S. citizens and permanent residents of the United States. Babson's merit scholarships include Weissman Scholarships, Presidential Scholarships, the Women's Leadership Awards, and the Diversity Leadership Awards. Application for aid is made by submitting the Free Application for Federal Student Aid (FAFSA) and the Financial Aid PROFILE of the College Scholarship Service. The application deadline for first-year undergraduate students is January 15. For transfer students and September enrollment, the deadline is April 1, and November 1 for January enrollment.

Faculty

Because of Babson's close-knit community, students are able to form close relationships with the faculty. Of the 267 faculty members, 163 are full-time, and 87 percent of the full-time faculty members hold a doctoral degree or its equivalent. Faculty members are accomplished entrepreneurs, executives, scholars, authors, researchers, poets, and artists who bring an intellectual diversity that adds depth to Babson's educational programs and offers students a rich, challenging experience. Babson's student-faculty ratio is 14:1 and faculty members teach 100 percent of the courses. More information can be found at http://www.babson.edu/ugradfaculty.

Student Government

Students are encouraged to take an active role in campus activities and student government. The Student Government Association promotes students' interests; allocates funds to campus organizations for academic, social, and recreational activities; licenses student-run businesses; and helps formulate and maintain student regulations. There are over ninety student clubs and organizations currently on campus.

Admission Requirements

In selecting new students, the admission office considers each candidate based on academic factors such as high school record, recommendations, standardized test scores, and essays. Nonacademic factors are also considered, including extracurricular activities, demonstrated leadership abilities, character/personal qualities, volunteer work, work experience, creativity and enthusiasm, and a willingness to contribute to the Babson community in meaningful ways. Evaluation is based upon comparisons of the qualifications of those who apply. The degree of competition is set by the caliber of the applicants themselves. Consideration is given to the depth and rigor of each candidate's academic program, academic motivation and achievement, and progress from one year to the next. Prospective students are strongly encouraged to have completed or be currently enrolled in a pre-calculus math class.

The Admission Committee carefully reviews courses taken, math aptitude, and standardized test scores. Reading and writing skills as well as verbal expression are measured using English grades, essays, and standardized test scores. Intangible personal qualities are also important—leadership, creativity, enthusiasm, and an overall good fit with Babson that includes a willingness to contribute to the community in meaningful and positive ways. There is no standard format for submitting this information, so Babson relies on letters of recommendation, references, and personal statements. In addition, the College evaluates extracurricular activities and work experience, seeking candidates who have exceptional leadership qualities and have participated in activities that have potential carryover to college. Efforts are made to enroll students with diverse backgrounds and experiences.

Babson College offers three application plans: regular decision, early decision, and early action. For more information about these plans and their deadlines, prospective students should visit Babson's Web site at http://www.babson.edu/ugrad. Campus visits and group information sessions with an admission counselor are strongly recommended.

Application and Information

For further information or application forms, students should contact:

Lunder Undergraduate Admission Center
Babson College
Babson Park, Massachusetts 02457-0310
Phone: 781-239-5522
      800-488-3696 (toll-free)
Fax: 781-239-4006
E-mail: ugradadmission@babson.edu
Web site: http://www.babson.edu/ugrad
     http://www.facebook.com/babsoncollege
     http://twitter.com/babsoncollegeUG

Tomasso Hall.

BALDWIN-WALLACE COLLEGE
BEREA, OHIO

The College

Founded in 1845, Baldwin-Wallace College (B-W) in Berea, Ohio, is an accredited institution affiliated with the United Methodist Church that blends the hallmarks of a traditional liberal arts education with an emphasis on professional preparation. Baldwin-Wallace has a long history of diversity, as it was one of the first institutions of higher learning in Ohio to admit students without regard to race or gender. That spirit of inclusiveness has flourished and evolved into a personalized approach to education, one that stresses individual growth as students learn to learn, respond to new ideas, adapt to new situations, and prepare for the certainty of change.

With an enrollment of approximately 3,100 full-time undergraduate students, B-W offers unique opportunities for engaged, transformative learning. The student profile shows that 25 percent of incoming first-year students come from the top 10 percent of their high school classes, with more than 50 percent in the top quarter. In addition to the traditional-aged college student, Baldwin-Wallace has helped adult learners for more than fifty years to develop skills, redirect careers, and enhance lives. Today, 500 adult learners of all ages participate in evening and weekend classes in a variety of programs that are designed to accommodate the varying learning styles and schedules of busy adult learners. Another 700 students are enrolled in part-time graduate programs in education and business administration.

Experiential learning is the product of the Baldwin-Wallace education. An experienced and proven commitment to the liberal arts and sciences—characterized by excellence in teaching and learning—provides a strong foundation for internships, faculty-directed research, and service-learning programs. Students work closely with their faculty adviser to develop a personal action plan that combines these opportunities in a way that stresses the importance of lifelong learning and fully prepares graduates for success after college.

In a postgraduation alumni survey, more than 90 percent of respondents found rewarding jobs or entered the graduate or professional school of their choice within nine months after graduation. Some programs—including athletic training, communication disorders, and neuroscience—have close to 100 percent acceptance rates.

Baldwin-Wallace is also home to a world-renowned Conservatory of Music. The undergraduate-only nature of the conservatory offers collaborative mentoring opportunities with a faculty of accomplished artists and extraordinary opportunities for performance in a variety of ensembles. In addition to hosting the country's oldest collegiate Bach Festival, the conservatory serves over 2,000 community members each year through outreach initiatives.

B-W embraces practices and principles that demonstrate its commitment to the environment. An undergraduate major in sustainability—the first of its kind in Ohio—offers students the opportunity to lead in the twenty-first century. The campus community continues to reduce its environmental footprint through significant recycling efforts, the addition of a wind turbine and food composter, and the use of geothermal heating and cooling systems in three green campus complexes. In addition, B-W is slated to open a sustainable residence hall in fall 2012.

Location

B-W students enjoy the best of both worlds. Berea, Ohio, with its tree-lined streets, picturesque homes, and population of 19,000, is an ideal college town. At the same time, students are only 20 minutes from the heart of Cleveland, which is home to Fortune 500 companies as well as unique recreational and cultural opportunities. Cleveland offers outstanding museums and galleries, professional sporting events, a world-class orchestra, exciting nightlife, and an extensive park system.

Approximately 1,900 B-W students live on campus in a variety of settings, ranging from residence halls exclusively housing first-year students to the Carmel Living Learning Center, where students enroll in shared classes taken in the residence hall. Other opportunities include residential learning communities and College-owned apartments for upperclassmen. All full-time students are required to live on campus during their first and second years at Baldwin-Wallace, with residency exemptions available for commuting students who live with their families. Residence halls provide students with social and educational programming, a diverse living environment, and leadership opportunities.

Majors and Degrees

Baldwin-Wallace offers the Bachelor of Arts (B.A.), Bachelor of Science (B.S.), Bachelor of Science in Education (B.S.E.), Bachelor of Music (B.M.), and Bachelor of Music in Education (B.M.E.) degrees. Majors and programs include accounting, art history, art studio, arts management, athletic training, biology, broadcasting and mass communication, business, chemistry, communication disorders, communication studies, computer information systems, computer science, criminal justice, digital media and design, economics, education, English, exercise science, film studies, finance, French, German, health-care management, health promotion and education, history, human resource management, international business, international studies, management, marketing, mathematical economics, mathematics, medical technology, neuroscience, philosophy, physical education, physics, political science, pre-engineering, prepharmacy, pre–physical therapy, psychology, public health, public relations, religion, sociology, software engineering, Spanish, sport management, sustainability, and theater. The Conservatory of Music offers majors in music composition, music education, music history and literature, music in the liberal arts, music management, music performance, music theater, music theory, and music therapy.

Academic Programs

More than fifty majors and several 3-2 cooperative and preprofessional programs are available to traditional B-W undergraduates. Evening and weekend programs include thirteen majors and six certificate programs.

Off-Campus Programs

Baldwin-Wallace College has institutional partnerships with several other universities around the globe, some of which include Edge Hill College (England), University of the Sunshine Coast (Australia), Ewha University (Korea), Bohme Jesus (Brazil), University of Osnabrück (Germany), Kansai Gaidai University (Japan), Hong Kong Baptist University (China), University of Hull (England), Athlone Institute of Technology (Ireland), Galway Mayo Institute of Technology (Ireland), American Business School in Paris, York St. John University (England), Washington Center, New York Media Institute at Marist College, Christ College (India), and American University (Washington, D.C.).

In addition to traditional study-abroad programs, with students studying and living on a particular campus for the semester, B-W features a series of focused-study tours that are led by B-W faculty and staff members and examine specific topics or geographic regions. Some programs involve homestays, while others use hostels and hotels. Quite literally, students learn while on the road. Study tours are offered in alternating academic years.

B-W often sponsors faculty-led two- to three-week seminars for credit in May, which are perfect for students who seek an international experience but do not want to be away for extended periods. Destinations have included Vienna, Prague, and Budapest. Recent spring trips have included India and China, and there was a seminar in Europe as well as an environmental excursion to Ecuador. Most locations for study-abroad programs offered during the academic year—such as Australia, China, England, Korea, and

Peterson's Four-Year Colleges 2013

Spain—are also offered during the summer term. The Semester at Sea program sends students to ten different countries—such as Brazil, Egypt, India, Japan, and Vietnam—aboard a 23,000-ton ship with 600 other college undergraduates.

Academic Facilities

Baldwin-Wallace continues to invest in facilities for student learning. In August 2010, the College completed the $29-million renovation and expansion of the Thomas Family Center for Science and Innovation, a facility featuring a combined 100,000 square feet of comprehensive laboratory, research, and study space. This new complex includes the Center for Innovation and Growth, a facility that reflects the synergy of B-W's cross-curricular academic offerings through entrepreneurial study and innovation.

In addition, B-W opened renovated and expanded facilities for its Conservatory of Music in August 2011. This provides students with additional and improved rehearsal and performing spaces, while remaining home to the Jones Music Library and the Riemenschneider Bach Institute, where priceless Bach-related manuscripts and first editions are stored.

These new facilities complement the extensive offerings already available to students, including twenty campus computer labs; a 4,000-watt campus radio station; recently renovated recreation facilities; an on-campus gallery showcasing the work of student, faculty, and area artists; and the Burrell Memorial Observatory. A new campus master plan, already being implemented, will enhance facilities to support the College mission and create a pedestrian-friendly, environmentally responsible campus with inviting green spaces.

Costs

Baldwin-Wallace's tuition ranks among the lowest and most affordable of private colleges in Ohio. In 2012–13, full-time (12–18 credit hours) liberal arts students pay $35,940 per academic year in tuition, room, board, and fees. Conservatory students pay $38,190 per academic year. These amounts also include a fully refundable board plan, as well as the cost of a student's books.

Starting with the incoming first-year class in 2012, Baldwin-Wallace will offer its Four-Year Graduation Guarantee—a promise that academically prepared students who follow predetermined benchmarks during their study at B-W will earn their bachelor's degrees in four years or fewer. If a student who follows the agreement does not graduate in four years, B-W will pay up to one year's additional tuition for the additional course work needed to graduate.

Financial Aid

To help students and their families meet the cost of a high-quality education, B-W awards more than $50 million annually to students in the form of scholarships, grants, loans, and work-study opportunities. B-W is committed to working with students and their families to offer financial support. Nearly all Baldwin-Wallace students receive some sort of financial assistance.

Renewable merit scholarships ranging from $1000 to $13,000 are awarded to academically exceptional incoming freshmen. The College also offers special and competitive awards, ranging from $1000 to $4000, as well as scholarships for transfer students.

Faculty

Close relationships are at the heart of the B-W experience. Most classes average only 19 students, and the student-faculty ratio is 15:1. Professors share their wisdom and experience on a one-to-one basis, helping students choose classes or assisting students in their search for the perfect internship. Faculty members regularly give out their home phone numbers. From corporate executives and lifelong educators to environmentalists and practicing psychologists, B-W's more than 300 full-time and part-time faculty members bring impressive credentials from their fields. Nearly 80 percent have earned the highest degree in their field. They are dedicated and talented teachers who want to provide an educational experience that goes well beyond the textbook.

Student Government

Student Government consists of three branches—the legislative, the executive, and the judicial. The Student Senate is the official representative body of the students of Baldwin-Wallace College. All meetings are open, and all students are welcome to participate. The president and vice president of the student body lead the executive branch and work closely with the Senate to express student body views to the College faculty and administration. The judicial branch of Student Government consists of the supreme court of the student body, which hears cases pertaining to Student Government and the clubs it funds. Elections for student body government occur each February.

Admission Requirements

Applicants must submit the completed application (electronic or paper), a high school transcript, a teacher recommendation, the Secondary School Record Request Form, and the $25 application fee (waived if applying online). SAT and ACT results are optional. (In lieu of standardized test results, students must submit a graded writing sample.) Transfer applicants also must submit college or university transcripts. Candidates applying to the Conservatory of Music also must complete the Conservatory Audition Portfolio.

Application and Information

The deadline for undergraduate admission is May 1. The priority admission deadline is March 1. Applicants are notified, beginning November 1, on a rolling basis within four to six weeks of receipt of a completed application.

Office of Admission
Baldwin-Wallace College
275 Eastland Road
Berea, Ohio 44017-2088
Phone: 440-826-2222
        877-BW-APPLY (toll-free)
Fax: 440-826-3830
E-mail: admission@bw.edu
Web site: http://www.bw.edu/admission

Baldwin-Wallace College is located in suburban, tree-lined Berea, Ohio, but is just 20 minutes from the heart of Cleveland and its cultural, educational, and recreational resources.

BARD COLLEGE AT SIMON'S ROCK

GREAT BARRINGTON, MASSACHUSETTS

The College

Simon's Rock is the only four-year residential college of the liberal arts and sciences specifically designed to provide bright, highly motivated students with the opportunity to begin college after the tenth or eleventh grade. Students who successfully complete the requirements receive the Associate of Arts (A.A.) degree after two years of study and the Bachelor of Arts (B.A.) degree after four. Merit scholarships and need-based aid are available. The average age of entering students is 16.

Simon's Rock challenges the traditional assumption that students must be 18 before they can be asked to develop seriously their intelligence, imagination, and self-discipline. Students at Simon's Rock pursue an academic program that enables them to fulfill their potential at an age when their interest, energy, and curiosity are at a peak.

The College was founded in 1964 by Elizabeth Blodgett Hall and first admitted students in 1966. In 1979, Simon's Rock became a part of Bard College, located 50 miles away at Annandale-on-Hudson, New York.

Simon's Rock has been a model for a rapidly growing early college movement across the U.S. For forty-five years, Simon's Rock has proven that highly motivated students of high school age are fully capable of engaging in college work; that they are best able to develop in a small-college environment; that serving these students well requires a faculty committed to distinction in teaching and scholarship, as well as active participation in the students' social and personal development; and that a coherent general education in the liberal arts and sciences should be the foundation for early college students.

Location

The College is built on 275 rolling and wooded acres just outside of Great Barrington, a town of 8,500, in the Berkshire Hills of western Massachusetts. Boston and New York City are 2½ hours away; Albany and Springfield are 40 miles away. The Berkshires' natural beauty and wide variety of cultural attractions make the area an unusually attractive place in which to live. The countryside provides excellent terrain for hiking, bicycling, cross-country and Alpine skiing, canoeing, and climbing. The Tanglewood Music Festival, Jacob's Pillow Dance Festival, and numerous summer theaters are located in nearby towns. Great Barrington itself is a thriving business community with a variety of schools and service agencies in which Simon's Rock students work and volunteer.

Majors and Degrees

Simon's Rock offers programs leading to the A.A. and B.A. degrees in the liberal arts and sciences. Students may complete their B.A. studies with a concentration in most traditional disciplines, choose one of several interdisciplinary concentrations, and/or design their own second concentration. Most Simon's Rock B.A. students study more than one discipline.

Academic Programs

The academic program at Simon's Rock combines a core curriculum in the liberal arts and sciences with extensive opportunities for students to pursue their own interests through electives, and—at the more advanced levels—tutorials and independent studies.

Because Simon's Rock students begin college without completing high school, the College is particularly conscious of its responsibility to ensure that all students develop the skills and knowledge expected of an educated person. The core curriculum comprises approximately half of students' total academic load during their first two years. Requirements include a writing and thinking workshop, which new students attend during the week before the regular semester begins; first-year, sophomore, and cultural perspectives seminars; and courses in the arts, mathematics, natural science, and foreign language. The College also requires that students participate in the campus Active Community Engagement program, involving athletics, health and wellness programming, and community service opportunities on and off campus.

All new students are assigned a faculty adviser, who meets with them weekly during their first semester and regularly throughout the rest of their career at Simon's Rock. Classes are small, faculty members are accessible, and the opportunities for students to pursue diverse interests are extensive.

The curriculum of the first two years at Simon's Rock leads to the A.A. in liberal arts. Students who successfully complete the A.A. requirements may continue at Simon's Rock for the B.A. or transfer to another college or university to complete their baccalaureate degree. Close to half of each sophomore class remains to complete a B.A. at Simon's Rock in one of approximately forty concentrations; the remainder of the students transfer, often to highly competitive colleges and universities across the U.S. and abroad. Through the sophomore planning process, students receive individualized guidance from staff in the Win Student Resource Commons and their faculty as they explore options for their last two years of undergraduate study.

Students wishing to stay at Simon's Rock for a B.A. must apply for admission to a concentration through a process called Moderation. Each student meets with a group of faculty in his or her area(s) of interest to review the student's accomplishments and together plan the remainder of the student's education at Simon's Rock. Students suggest and are advised of junior- and senior-year opportunities. These traditionally include a semester or full year of study abroad, advanced seminars, independent study, involvement in faculty research projects, specialized tutorials, internships, and courses at Bard's Annandale campus.

The senior thesis is the focus of each B.A. student's final year. Drawing on the skills in analysis and synthesis acquired during the previous three years, students devote themselves wholeheartedly to the project, which is personally defined and developed under the guidance of 2 or more faculty members. Recent theses have taken many forms: critical studies in literature, psychological research, musical compositions, creative fiction, translations, scientific experiments, mathematical problem solving, artistic exhibitions and performances, and various combinations of these forms.

The regular academic program is supplemented by a number of signature programs. The Simon's Rock/Columbia University Engineering Program offers three years at Simon's Rock and two years in the engineering school at Columbia University in New York, at the end of which students receive both a B.A. from Simon's Rock and a B.S. from Columbia's School of Engineering and Applied Science. Simon's Rock also offers a similar arrangement with the engineering school at Dartmouth University.

Through Simon's Rock Scholars at Oxford, a select group of Simon's Rock students are admitted to spend their junior year at Lincoln College or St. Catherine's College of the University of Oxford in England each year.

Simon's Rock has a program in creative writing through which students are able to spend up to a full year at the Centre for New Writing at the University of Manchester in the UK. Launched in September 2007, the Centre was designed to develop and refine the creative and critical work of its students, explore and research collaboration between creative and critical writing, and broaden access to literature and writers in the region. The College also has a relationship with Qingdao University in China, where students have the opportunity for Chinese language immersion study. Students interested in theater can spend a year at London Dramatic Academy; those interested in photography can benefit from a connection, via Bard, to the International Center of Photography in New York City.

The proseminar in Social Scientific Inquiry, an in-house program first introduced in the 2008–09 academic year, provides students with an opportunity for immersion in social theory, social research, and social action through intensive interaction with scholars active

across the broad spectrum of the disciplines. The Arts Bridges Program offers a similar program of study with visiting artists.

Simon's Rock students also have the opportunity to study at Bard College at Annandale. Upper-college (B.A.) students can take classes at Bard's campus in Annandale-on-Hudson, New York, or spend a semester in residence at the Annandale campus. Students can also take advantage of Bard's study-abroad programs; its groundbreaking Manhattan-based Globalization and International Affairs Program; and the Bard Rockefeller Program, a collaborative venture with Rockefeller University offering advanced research opportunities in medicine and the sciences.

Off-Campus Programs

Students pursue a variety of study-abroad programs and options. The Simon's Rock Win Resource Commons works with students to find study-abroad opportunities suited to their goals and interests. They use established independent programs (the School for Field Studies, SEA Semester, Global Routes), programs through other schools (Oxford University, the Sorbonne), and special Simon's Rock programs (fieldwork in geography in China). The result is something very different from the standard tour of famous sites. Students have recently taken intensive math instruction at Central European University in Budapest, Hungary; helped build a school in a remote village in northern Thailand; and served as apprentices to dancers, drummers, mask carvers, and batik artists in Bali. Students can also take advantage of Bard's study-abroad and international programs, including special arrangements with universities in Germany, Russia, and South Africa and intensive language immersion programs in China, France, Germany, Italy, Japan, Morocco, Mexico, and Russia. Programs can last for a semester, a full academic year, or shorter periods during the breaks.

Academic Facilities

The Fisher Science and Academic Center houses the College's biology, chemistry, ecology, and physics laboratories; research labs for faculty members and students; classrooms and tutorial rooms; a sixty-seat lecture center; and faculty offices. The Daniel Arts Center, which opened in the fall of 2004, incorporates a 350-seat theater and concert hall, a black box theater, a dance studio, and rehearsal facilities; painting, drawing, photography, ceramics, metalworking, printmaking, 3-D, video production, and digital arts studios; exhibition areas; and spaces for large-scale art and set construction. A music hall, a recording studio, and music practice rooms are also available to students in the arts. The campus library houses 68,000 volumes and collections of recordings and periodicals, a listening room, and a language laboratory. Simon's Rock students also have access to the Bard College library. An interlibrary loan system provides access to other college and university collections. The Kilpatrick Athletic Center includes squash courts, a basketball court, an elevated track, a swimming pool, a rock-climbing wall, and a full-service fitness center.

The Liebowitz International Center, which opened in 2011, houses faculty and programs focused on global issues, as well as two state-of-the-art classrooms.

Costs

For 2011–12, tuition and fees were $43,850, and room and board were $11,960. There is also an orientation fee for first-year students.

Financial Aid

Simon's Rock is committed to making an early college education available to a diverse group of highly motivated, academically qualified students. U.S. citizens and permanent residents are eligible to apply for federal and state financial assistance programs as well as institutional scholarships and grants. International students are eligible to receive Simon's Rock scholarships and grants. Approximately 85 percent of students receive some form of financial aid.

Applicants wishing to be considered for a merit scholarship must submit their applications by February 1.

Faculty

The College has approximately 40 full-time faculty members, all of whom hold either a doctorate or an equivalent terminal degree in their field. Simon's Rock supplements this full-time faculty with visiting scholars, regular adjunct faculty members in music and studio arts, and part-time faculty members in other areas as needed. Faculty members are distinguished not only by their excellence in teaching and advising but also by their sensitivity to the particular developmental needs of the College's younger students.

Student Government

Students at Simon's Rock participate in the decision making and governance of the community through elected and appointed positions on College committees that oversee academic and social life. The campus is characterized by respect for individual rights and a strong sense of community.

Admission Requirements

Simon's Rock seeks students who are smart, independent-minded, self-directed, creative, and passionate about learning. The admission staff recognizes its special responsibility to work closely with prospective students and their parents to ensure that the decision to enter Simon's Rock is the right one. For this reason, a personal interview is required of each applicant. The application also requires an official high school transcript, three letters of recommendation, writing samples, and a parent's statement. Standardized test scores are optional for most applicants; however, international students for whom English is not a first language must submit TOEFL scores.

Application and Information

Candidates should submit their materials by May 31 for fall admission. Applications are reviewed on a rolling basis year-round, and early application is strongly encouraged. Applicants are generally notified as to the Admission Committee's decision within several weeks of the time they complete their applications. The application fee is $50.

Bard College at Simon's Rock is on Facebook (http://www.facebook.com/simonsrock) and Twitter (http://twitter.com/SimonsRock).

To schedule an interview or request further information, students should contact:

Office of Admission
Bard College at Simon's Rock
84 Alford Road
Great Barrington, Massachusetts 01230-2499
Phone: 800-235-7186 (toll-free)
Fax: 413-541-0081
E-mail: admit@simons-rock.edu
Web site: http://www.simons-rock.edu

"I have met so many different people from so many different places and different countries—everybody brings something different, says something different," student, Abdul Samad Sadri.

BARNARD COLLEGE
NEW YORK, NEW YORK

The College

Barnard College was among the pioneers in the late nineteenth-century crusade that sought to make higher education available to young women. Founded in 1889 and formally partnered with Columbia University since 1900, today Barnard serves 2,390 students from almost every state and nearly fifty countries. It remains a partner of Columbia, and students at both schools regularly cross-register for courses at either institution. Barnard students have access to the University's resources and graduates receive their degree from Columbia. Despite this close connection, Barnard College remains a small, independent liberal arts college, devoted solely to the undergraduate education of women. The College maintains its own Board of Trustees, faculty, and administrative staff; its own endowment; an independent admissions process; and sole ownership of its property and physical plant. It offers the intimacy of a small college with the added advantages of a university.

The self-contained Barnard campus occupies 4 acres of urban property along Broadway between 116th and 120th streets and serves as an oasis from the hustle and bustle of New York City. An amalgam of styles comprise Barnard's architectural influences, the result is a blending of classic and modern. Barnard Hall, home of the Ethel S. LeFrak '41 and Samuel J. LeFrak Gymnasium, the Barnard Center for Research on Women, the Athena Center for Leadership Studies, and the Julius S. Held Lecture Hall, stands opposite the main gates of the College. The south end of the campus, referred to as the Quad, contains the Brooks, Reid, Hewitt, and Sulzberger residence halls; first-year students are housed in three of the four buildings in the Quad. Additional housing provides those entering as first-years guaranteed housing for four years of continuous enrollment at Barnard. The latest campus addition, the Diana Center, a 70,000-square-foot student center, adds a new element of design. Its seven-story glass structure stretches across campus, linking the historic gates of the entrance, at the south end of campus, to one of the original campus buildings, Milbank Hall, to the north.

Location

Barnard is located on the upper west side of Manhattan, in the safe and student-friendly Morningside Heights neighborhood, directly across from Columbia University, with four other educational institutions as neighbors. Abounding with cultural, educational, internship, and professional opportunities and more than 500,000 college students, New York is Barnard's laboratory.

Majors and Degrees

Students can earn a Bachelor of Arts in the following subjects: Africana studies, American studies, ancient studies, anthropology, architecture, art history, Asian and Middle Eastern cultures, astronomy, biochemistry, biological sciences, chemistry, classics (Greek and Latin), comparative literature, computer science, dance, economics, education, English, environmental biology science or studies, European studies, film studies, French, German, history, human rights, Italian, Jewish studies, mathematics and applied mathematics, medieval and Renaissance studies, music, neuroscience, philosophy, physics, political science, psychology, religion, Russian and Slavic studies, sociology, Spanish and Latin American cultures, statistics, theater, urban studies, and women's studies. The College provides an excellent education program, leading to teaching certification, and prepares students for programs in health and medicine, law, and business.

Barnard College also offers double- and joint-degree programs in cooperation with other schools within the Columbia community. These include a five-year M.P.A./M.I.A. (3-2) program offered in conjunction with the School of International and Public Affairs. In cooperation with the School of Law, Barnard offers an accelerated program in interdisciplinary legal education, where select students can begin their legal studies after three years. Through the School of Engineering and Applied Science, Barnard students can pursue

a five-year (3-2) program in all branches of engineering, leading to both an A.B. and a B.S. degree. In cooperation with the School of Dentistry, a limited number of students may enter the Columbia School of Dental and Oral Surgery after three years of undergraduate work. Outside the university, a student can earn both an A.B. degree and a Master of Music (M.M.) in a five-year (3-2) program with the Juilliard School. Through an agreement with List College of the Jewish Theological Seminary, students can earn an A.B. degree from Barnard and a B.A. in Hebrew literature.

Academic Programs

Two required courses, First-Year Seminar and First-Year English, set the foundation for a Barnard education with small seminar classes, limited to 16 and 12 students, respectfully. General education requirements are organized around the Nine Ways of Knowing, reflecting the breadth and depth of a true liberal arts education. The Ways of Knowing offer a flexible structure and a wide array of courses in ethics and values, social analysis, cultures in comparison, language, laboratory science, quantitative and deductive reasoning, historical studies, literature, and visual and performing arts.

Advanced placement and I.B. credit are available. Barnard operates on a two-semester calendar, with classes beginning in early September. The fall semester ends in mid-December; classes resume for the spring semester in mid-January and end in mid-May.

Off-Campus Programs

As an independent partner of Columbia University, Barnard offers students open access to courses, libraries, and other facilities of the University. With special permission, students may also register for selected classes in Columbia's graduate and professional schools. In addition, two highly selective lesson exchange programs with the Juilliard School and the nearby Manhattan School of Music allow qualified Barnard students to take music lessons in a conservatory setting.

Barnard has a rich history and tradition of study abroad dating back to the 1930s. Today, qualified students are eligible to study in nearly 150 programs in more than fifty countries worldwide and nearly forty percent of Barnard students spend a semester or year abroad. Students are currently studying in Argentina, Australia, Austria, Bolivia, Brazil, British West Indies, Chile, China, Costa Rica, Czech Republic, Denmark, Ecuador, England, France, Germany, Greece, Hungary, Ireland, Israel, Italy, Japan, Jordan, Kenya, Madagascar, Netherlands, New Zealand, Panama, Peru, Russia, Scotland, Senegal, South Africa, Spain, Switzerland, and other locations. Students may also participate in a domestic exchange with Spelman College in Atlanta or Howard University in Washington, D.C.

Barnard's location offers its students a variety of work experiences through more than 2,500 internships. More than two thirds of Barnard students participate in internships throughout the academic year and summer.

Academic Facilities

Historic Milbank Hall anchors the north end of campus, topped by the 2,500-square-foot Arthur Ross Greenhouse, and housing administrative and faculty offices in addition to the Minor Latham Playhouse. Sulzberger Tower and the residential quadrangle secure the south end of campus where most Barnard students reside.

There are over 300,000 volumes in the library in Lehman Hall (and nearly 10 million in the University library system); dance studios and classrooms in Barnard Hall and its Annex; state-of-the-art science labs in the fourteen-story Altschul Hall; and architecture classrooms with a view in the multipurpose Diana Center, with its terra-cotta glass façade, black box theatre, and art gallery, among other remarkable features. At the heart of it all is the welcoming beauty of Barnard's beloved Lehman Lawn.

Costs

Tuition and fees for 2012–13 are $43,502. Room and board costs are an additional $13,810.

Financial Aid

Financial aid at Barnard is awarded based upon demonstrated need. Federal funds and institutional grants are administered as determined by federal and institutional methodology, assuming College aid is supplementary to family resources. Barnard gives no merit or athletic scholarships. Once need has been established, Barnard is covers 100 percent of demonstrated need with a combination of grants, loans, and work-study or student employment. Approximately 51 percent of the students at Barnard receive some form of financial aid.

Barnard College has a need-blind admission policy in which all applications from first-years who are U.S. citizens and permanent residents are judged solely on merit without reference to financial circumstances. International and transfer students are considered for need-based aid from a limited pool of funding.

Faculty

Barnard College employs more than 350 teaching faculty members with a student-faculty ratio is 7:1 (9:1 FTE). Barnard's faculty includes editors of leading scholarly journals, prize-winning novelists and translators, and frequent winners of awards from respected foundations, corporations, and government agencies. They are actively engaged in research and publication in their respective fields, but they regard teaching as their primary commitment. From the start of their time at the College, all students have faculty advisers who assist them in selecting courses and designing individual academic programs, in addition to a vast network of decanal, staff, and peer advising.

Student Government

Barnard women have access to more than eighty clubs and organizations on the College campus alone. Add to this list the hundreds of additional dually recognized clubs with members from both Barnard and Columbia provided for through Barnard's longstanding partnership with the University, and friendships develop among students on either side of Broadway. Student groups include performance groups, academic and pre-professional, ethnic and cultural, language, community service, and writing staffs. Social interaction and cooperation between Barnard and Columbia groups is virtually seamless, with Barnard women regularly joining and leading a variety of Columbia organizations. Students, faculty members, and administrators also serve on tripartite committees and share responsibility for policy on curriculum, housing, financial aid, orientation, and the library.

Admission Requirements

The Committee on Admissions selects young women of proven academic strength who exhibit the potential for further intellectual growth. Careful consideration is given to candidates' high school records, recommendations, writing skills, standardized test scores, special abilities and interests, and personal and educational context.

Admission to Barnard is highly selective and candidates for admission to the first-year class are expected to have taken a very rigorous college-preparatory program. Barnard also requires candidates to submit scores from the SAT Reasoning Test, along with two SAT Subject Tests. Alternatively, students may submit scores from the ACT with writing in place of the SAT and subject tests. Students educated in a non-English-speaking setting or who have studied in English for less than five years must also take the TOEFL or IELTS exam. An interview is recommended for first-year students, but is not required

Application and Information

Applicants for first-year admission should apply in the fall of their senior year of high school. Applications must be received by January 1 and must include the nonrefundable application fee. Students are notified in late March. Well-qualified high school seniors who have selected Barnard as their first-choice college may instead apply under the binding early decision plan. Early decision applications must be submitted by November 15. Barnard accepts sophomore and junior transfer students. Transfer applications must be submitted by March 15 for consideration for September and by November 1 for consideration for January.

For more information about Barnard College, students should contact:

Jennifer Fondille
Dean of Enrollment Management
Barnard College, Office of Admissions
3009 Broadway
New York, New York 10027
Phone: 212-854-2014
Fax: 212-854-6220
E-mail: admissions@barnard.edu
Web site: http://www.barnard.edu/admissions

A view of Milbank Hall from the Diana, Barnard's multipurpose student center..

BARRY UNIVERSITY
MIAMI SHORES, FLORIDA

The University

Barry University in Miami Shores, Florida, is the second-largest private, Catholic university in the southeastern United States. Founded in 1940 by the Dominican Sisters of Adrian, Michigan, the University provides a multicultural student body with a high-quality education; a caring environment; and a religious dimension, which encourages a commitment to social justice and community service. Classes are small, so students receive personal attention from distinguished faculty members and advisers. The student-faculty ratio is 14:1.

The palm-tree lined main campus is in Miami Shores, but the University also includes the Dwayne O. Andreas School of Law in Orlando; College of Health Sciences location in Hollywood, Florida; adult and continuing education programs at more than twenty additional locations from South Miami to Tallahassee; and sites in the Caribbean. Students come from all compass points, age groups, ethnicities, and faith perspectives, representing nearly all fifty states and close to 120 countries. Of the nearly 9,000 students enrolled, almost 3,000 are traditional undergraduate students and approximately 6,000 are graduate and continuing education students.

Barry offers more than 100 bachelor's, master's, and doctoral degree programs in the arts and sciences, business, education, health sciences, human performance and leisure sciences, law, podiatric medicine, and social work. Some are five-year bachelor's-to-master's programs. Students can also gain hands-on professional experience before graduation through internships and service-learning.

Resident students live in ten air-conditioned residence halls and three apartment buildings. Each room includes cable and high-speed Internet access. All students may keep cars on campus. The University's Office of Commuter Student Resources assists students who live off campus.

Barry holds membership in twenty honor societies and hosts more than sixty student organizations, including the dance club, gospel choir, Campus Activities Board, and WBRY student radio station, as well as fraternities and sororities. Barry also promotes community service through organizations including Best Buddies, Habitat for Humanity, Alternative Spring Break, and Pals-4-Paws animal rescue.

The 78,000-square-foot R. Kirk Landon Student Union houses the offices of student services and student organizations as well as a bookstore, dining room, snack bar, game room, and more. A fully equipped fitness center features weight and cardio equipment. Students can also participate in a variety of free fitness classes sponsored by the Department of Campus Recreation and Wellness. Intramural sports include basketball, flag football, soccer, softball, and table tennis.

The University fields twelve intercollegiate athletic teams that participate in the NCAA Division II and the Sunshine State Conference. Over the years, the Buccaneers have won nine NCAA championships; had 229 All-Americans; 245 Scholar All-Americans; and six NCAA Women of the Year finalists, the most of any Division II school and fourth overall.

The University is accredited by the Southern Association of Colleges and Schools to award bachelor's, master's, specialist, and doctoral degrees. Barry also holds a number of accreditations from professional organizations for specific programs.

Location

Barry University is located in sunny Miami Shores, Florida, just 5 miles from the ocean and minutes from the dynamic city of Miami. South Florida is a center for international business, tourism, and entertainment, providing a wide range of internship options and a vibrant cultural scene. Highlights include Urban Beach Week, the Calle Ocho street festival, the Miami International Book Fair, the Miami International Film Festival, and the world-famous Art Basel Miami Beach contemporary art festival. The New World Symphony and the Miami City Ballet provide a full season of performances. South Florida also hosts the Miami Dolphins football team, the Miami Heat basketball team, the Florida Marlins baseball team, and the Florida Panthers hockey team. The hospitable climate allows for swimming, sailing, scuba diving, golf, tennis, soccer, and other outdoor activities year-round, and the natural beauty of the Florida Keys, Everglades, and coral reefs are just a day trip away.

Majors and Degrees

Barry University offers the Bachelor of Arts degree in advertising, art (art history, ceramics, graphic design, and painting and/or drawing), broadcast and emerging media, communication studies, English (literature and professional writing), general studies, history, international studies, music, philosophy, photography (biomedical/forensic), prelaw, public relations, Spanish (language and literature and translation and interpretation), theater (acting, dance theater, technical theater, theater publicity), and theology.

The Bachelor of Science degree is offered in accounting, athletic training (five-year seamless B.S. to M.S.), biology (marine, preprofessional), cardiovascular perfusion, clinical biology (histotechnology, medical technology, nuclear medicine technology), chemistry (biochemistry, environmental chemistry, preprofessional), computer information sciences, computer science, criminology, education (B.S. to M.S. option, infancy through early-childhood education, early- and middle-childhood education, special education, ESOL, and reading endorsements), exercise physiology (five-year seamless B.S. to M.S.), finance, international business, management, marketing, mathematical sciences (computational, general, and statistics/actuarial science), physical education and coaching, political science, psychology (forensic, industrial/organizational), sociology, and sport management (diving industry, five-year seamless B.S. to M.S.).

The University also offers the Bachelor of Science in Nursing, the Bachelor of Fine Arts (art and photography), the Bachelor of Music (instrumental performance; sacred music; and voice, opera, and musical theater), and the Bachelor of Social Work.

Minor concentrations are available in specific subject areas as well as in the interdisciplinary areas of Africana studies, film studies, journalism, peace studies, social sciences, and women's studies. Certificates are also offered in Africana studies, photography, Spanish translation and interpretation, and women's studies.

Accelerated undergraduate degree programs are offered for working adults through Barry's evening and weekend programs.

Academic Programs

The University operates on a semester plan. The first semester extends from the end of August to mid-December, and the second semester extends from mid-January to early May.

Two 6-week sessions are offered during the summer. Students must maintain a minimum cumulative grade point average of 2.0 (or C) and earn a minimum of 120 credits for a degree. Of these 120 credits, 9 must be in philosophy and theology, 9 in communication—oral and written, 9 in humanities and arts, 9 in physical or natural sciences and mathematics, and 9 in social and behavioral sciences. The traditional full-time academic load is 12 to 18 credits each semester and 6 credits each summer term. Candidates for degree programs may elect a major and area of specialization and must satisfy all requirements of the program that they choose to follow, including all professional preparation requirements. Internships are required for many majors.

An ELS Language Centers program is available to international students who need to increase language proficiency. The Center for Advanced Learning offers a program designed to assist students with learning disabilities who have the intellectual potential and motivation to complete a four-year degree.

The Honors Program offers an active, interdisciplinary honors curriculum designed to add breadth and depth to the educational experience.

Off-Campus Programs

Barry University offers summer programs abroad in places such as Europe and China. Barry is also a member of the College Consortium for International Studies, enabling students to participate in programs offered by member colleges and universities in more than thirty countries. Barry University students may enroll in Air Force ROTC courses through cross-registration at a nearby university.

Academic Facilities

At Barry, students find the resources they need to support their education. Campus facilities include the Monsignor William Barry Memorial Library, an extensive library network, the Glenn Hubert Learning Center, photography and digital imaging labs, a human performance lab, an athletic training room, a biomechanics lab, a full-service digital television production studio, an academic computing center, multimedia business classrooms, art studios, a performing arts center, a nursing lab and resource center, and several other labs dedicated to Barry's health, science, and education programs.

Costs

For 2012–13, tuition for full-time undergraduate students for the academic year is $28,160. Student services fees are included in tuition. Room and board costs average $9440, based on a double-occupancy room. Expenses such as books, supplies, laboratory or other special fees, and transportation are not included in these costs.

Financial Aid

Nearly 90 percent of all undergraduate students at Barry University receive some form of financial aid. Barry participates in the full array of federal and state of Florida financial aid programs. Barry also offers an excellent scholarship program, awarding aid each year to students who have demonstrated academic success and promise. These scholarships may be renewed for up to four years as long as the student meets the renewal criteria. Athletic scholarships are also available.

To be considered for financial assistance, applicants must submit the Free Application for Federal Student Aid (FAFSA). Additional information may be obtained by calling the Office of Financial Aid at 305-899-3673 or 800-695-2279 (toll-free) or by e-mail at finaid@mail.barry.edu.

Faculty

Faculty members are easily accessible to students and are committed to providing personal attention. More than 80 percent of faculty members hold a Ph.D. or terminal degree in their field of study. The student-faculty ratio is 14:1.

Student Government

The Student Government Association serves as a liaison between the student body and the administration and faculty. All undergraduate students are members of the association, which is governed by an Executive Board comprising 4 members, and the Senate, which consists of 7 elected representatives. Unless otherwise specified, Senate meetings are open, and students are invited and encouraged to attend the weekly sessions.

Admission Requirements

In reviewing the credentials of students seeking admission, Barry University considers an applicant's composite efforts. Candidates must present the following materials: the completed application form, official high school or college transcripts, and the results of the SAT or ACT.

Application and Information

The University reviews applications as they are completed. Students are notified of their acceptance once the admissions staff has reviewed all required documents. Students may apply any time after completion of their junior year in high school. It is advisable to apply early. The student's completed application form and supporting credentials should be sent to the Office of Admissions. Students may also apply online at http://www.barry.edu/mybarry.

Ms. Magda Castineyra
Director of Undergraduate Admissions
Barry University
Division of Enrollment Services
11300 Northeast Second Avenue
Miami Shores, Florida 33161-6695
Phone: 305-899-3100
　　　　800-695-2279 (toll-free)
Fax: 305-899-2971
E-mail: admissions@mail.barry.edu
Web site: http://www.barry.edu
　　　　http://facebook.com/BarryUniversity (Facebook)
　　　　http://twitter.com/BarryUniversity (Twitter)

Barry's tropical, palm-tree lined main campus is in Miami Shores, just a few miles from the dynamic city of Miami.

BAY STATE COLLEGE
BOSTON, MASSACHUSETTS

The College

Founded in 1946, Bay State College is a private, independent coeducational institution located in Boston's historic Back Bay. Since its founding, Bay State College has been preparing graduates for outstanding careers and continued education.

The College primarily offers associate degrees and has expanded into bachelor's degree offerings. The educational experience offered through the variety of associate and bachelor's degree programs prepares students to excel in the career of their choice. Personalized attention is the cornerstone of a Bay State College education. Through the transformative power of its core values of quality, respect, and support, Bay State College has been able to assist students with setting and achieving goals that prepare them for careers and continued education. In fact, with its First-Year Experience, a 1-credit course all students must complete, Bay State College students are exposed to the concept of "action planning." The Bay State College action plan is designed to help students identify their goals and set about a course of action to achieve those goals. Students review their action plan each semester with their academic adviser and evaluate how they are progressing on their plan. This is just one method Bay State College graduates apply to their lives beyond college. The ability to identify, set, and achieve goals is a trait all people aspire to master.

Recognizing that one of the most important aspects of college is life outside the classroom, the Office of Student Affairs seeks to provide services to Bay State College students from orientation through graduation and beyond. There are many clubs and organizations on campus, such as the Criminal Justice Society, the Early Childhood Education Club, the Student Government Association, and the Entertainment Management Association. Bay State College students enjoy the opportunity to create clubs and organizations that meet their interests. Special events throughout the year include a fashion show and a host of events produced by the Entertainment Management Association. Students also enjoy professional sports teams such as the Boston Celtics and the Boston Red Sox.

One of the unique aspects of living at Bay State College is the residence halls. With their location in the historic Back Bay, the buildings are original Victorian town houses and brownstones. Each building has its own character and charm, making living on campus a distinctive experience. Each building has a computer lab with free Internet access, coin-operated laundry, vending machines, a house phone with free local calling, and a social lounge that includes cable television and a microwave oven. Each student room has basic cable service and wireless Internet access.

The Career Services office offers lifetime career assistance to both current students and alumni, continuing to provide assistance and support to them throughout their careers, with career-management counseling, workshops, career panels, guest speakers, resume and cover letter reviews, interview preparation, and job listings.

Bay State College is accredited by the New England Association of Schools and Colleges; is authorized to award the Associate in Science, Associate in Applied Science, and three Bachelor of Science degrees by the commonwealth of Massachusetts; and is a member of several professional educational associations. The College's medical assisting program is accredited by the Accrediting Bureau of Health Education Schools (ABHES). The College's nursing program is a candidate for accreditation by the National League for Nursing Accrediting Commission. The physical therapist assistant studies program is accredited by the Commission on Accreditation in Physical Therapy Education (CAPTE) of the American Physical Therapy Association (APTA).

Location

Located in the historic city of Boston, Massachusetts, and surrounded by dozens of colleges and universities, Bay State College is an ideal setting in which to pursue a college degree. Tree-lined streets around the school are mirrored in the skyscrapers of the Back Bay. The College is located within walking distance of several major-league sports franchises, concert halls, museums, the Freedom Trail, Boston Symphony Hall, the Boston Public Library, and the Boston Public Garden. World-class shopping and major cultural and sporting events help make college life an experience that students will always remember. The College is accessible by the MBTA, commuter rail, and bus and is near Boston Logan International Airport.

Majors and Degrees

Bay State College is continually reviewing, enhancing, and adding new programs to help graduates remain industry-current in their respective fields.

Bachelor's degrees are offered in criminal justice, entertainment management, fashion merchandising, and management.

Associate degrees are offered in business administration, criminal justice, early childhood education, entertainment management (with a concentration in audio production), fashion design, fashion merchandising, health studies, medical assisting, nursing, physical therapist assistant studies, retail business management, and hospitality management.

Academic Programs

Bay State College operates on a semester calendar. The fall semester runs from early September to late December. The spring semester runs from late January to mid-May. A satellite campus is located in Middleborough, Massachusetts.

Bay State College also offers courses on-ground and online to working adults in its Evening and Online Division. The courses, offered in eight-week sessions, allow more flexibility for students who must balance work and family commitments while pursuing their education.

Off-Campus Programs

The internship program, available in all major areas of study, provides students with practical field experience, enabling them to hone their skills and gain insight into the various technologies employed in their respective fields. Fieldwork is a requirement for many majors and is a great opportunity for students to build resumes, apply what they have learned in the classroom, and gain a competitive advantage in the job market.

Students from Bay State College are among the 250 students participating in the Walt Disney World College Program. During their stay at Walt Disney World, students receive on-the-job training and classroom experience. This is just one of the many internship possibilities for students each year at Bay State College.

Academic Facilities

The library has a combined book collection of approximately 5,300 books. In addition, Bay State College has 100 periodicals and 200 audiovisual titles. The College's sixty computers have access to the Internet and several databases for magazine and journal articles, including ProQuest Academic, LexisNexis Academic, JSTOR, Infotrac, Newsbank, EBSCO, the Internet Public Library, and the Library of Congress Research Tools. The library also participates in an interlibrary-loan program with the Boston Regional Library System.

Costs

Tuition for 2011–12 for full-time students was $21,930 per year. Room and board for 2011–12 were $11,800 per year; application fee, $40; student services fee, $375; and student activity fee, $50. The cost of books and additional fees varies by major. A residence hall security deposit of $300 and a technology fee of $250 are required of all resident students.

Financial Aid

Financial aid is available to those who qualify. The College's financial aid staff works one-on-one with every student to help them find what is best for their specific situation: scholarships, grants, loans, payment plans, or a combination of those. The College also offers numerous part-time employment and work-study opportunities during the academic year.

Faculty

There are 99 faculty members, with the majority holding advanced degrees. The student-faculty ratio is 15:1.

Student Government

The Student Association serves as the voice of the Bay State College student body. It consists of a group of elected student representatives from the various academic programs. Roles and responsibilities of Student Association members include providing input on College policies and procedures, assuming leadership roles on campus, acting as a voice of the student body, and planning activities and events.

Elections are held every fall, and all students are encouraged to vote. The group comprises representatives from each College department, club, and organization, and membership spans all four class years.

Admission Requirements

An applicant to Bay State College must be a high school graduate, a current high school student working toward graduation, or a recipient of a GED certificate. The Office of Admissions recommends that applicants to the associate degree programs have a minimum 2.0 GPA on a 4.0 scale; if available, applicants may submit SAT or ACT scores. Applicants must receive the recommendation of a Bay State College admissions officer. Applicants to the bachelor's degree programs must have a minimum 2.3 GPA on a 4.0 scale and must also submit SAT or ACT scores. A personal interview is highly recommended for all students, and parents are encouraged to attend. Students are responsible for arranging for their official high school transcripts, test scores, and letters of recommendation to be submitted to Bay State College. International applicants must also submit high school transcripts translated into English with an explanation of the grading system, a TOEFL score of at least 500 on the paper-based exam or 173 on the computer-based exam if English is not the native language, and financial documentation. The nursing, physical therapist assistant studies program, and Evening and Online Divisions have different or additional admission requirements. For more information about these programs, students should visit the Web site at http://www.baystate.edu.

The Bay State College Admissions Office notifies applicants of a decision within three weeks of receipt of the transcript and other required documents. When a student is accepted to Bay State College, there is a $100 nonrefundable tuition deposit required to ensure a place in the class, which is credited toward the tuition fee. Deposits are due within thirty days of acceptance. Once a student is accepted, a Bay State College representative creates a personalized financial plan that provides payment options for a Bay State College education.

Application and Information

Applications are accepted on a rolling basis. A $40 application fee is due with the application. The fall tuition payment due date is July 1; the spring tuition payment due date is December 1.

Applications should be submitted to:

Admissions Office
Bay State College
122 Commonwealth Avenue
Boston, Massachusetts 02116
Phone: 800-81-LEARN (toll-free)
Fax: 617-249-0400
E-mail: admissions@baystate.edu
Web site: http://www.baystate.edu
　　　　http://www.facebook.com/baystatecollege
　　　　http://twitter.com/baystatecollege

Located in Boston's Back Bay, Bay State College has built a reputation for offering a unique, high-quality curriculum for the serious student.

BELMONT UNIVERSITY
NASHVILLE, TENNESSEE

The University

Nationally recognized programs thrive on the Belmont University campus, which is located in the heart of the state capital, known both as Music City, U.S.A. and the Athens of the South (for its many educational institutions). Nashville offers big-city advantages with small-town charm.

Belmont's vision is to be a leader among teaching universities, bringing together the best of liberal arts and professional education in a Christian community of learning and service. Central to the fulfillment of that vision are faculty members who have a passion for teaching and the belief that premier teaching is interactive, technology-supported, motivational, creative, and exciting.

With an enrollment of approximately 6,400 students, Belmont is the second-largest of Tennessee's private colleges and universities.

In addition to the twenty-five countries represented in the student body, Belmont University attracts students from every state in the United States. The culturally diverse institution is committed to listening and learning from everyone. Students of today are helping shape the way students of tomorrow will be educated.

Belmont's beautiful, antebellum campus reflects a long, rich history that dates back to the nineteenth century, when the grounds were Adelicia Acklen's Belle Monte estate. University buildings that were erected over the past 110 years flank the Italianate mansion, which is still used by the campus. On the way to classes that prepare them for the twenty-first century, students enjoy Victorian gardens, statuary, and gazebos that recall a treasured past.

Two prestigious women's schools preceded the comprehensive liberal arts institution: the original Belmont College (1890–1913) and Ward-Belmont (1913–1951). In 1951, the Tennessee Baptist Convention founded the second Belmont College (1951–1991), with an initial coeducational enrollment of 136 students. Soon after celebrating 100 years of education on the same campus, the institution became a university in 1991, culminating a decade of dramatic growth and progress.

In addition to seven baccalaureate degrees, Belmont University offers fourteen graduate and doctoral degree programs: the Master of Accountancy, the Master of Arts in Teaching, the Master of Business Administration, the Master of Sport Administration, the Master of Arts in English, the Master of Music, the Master of Education, the Master of Science in Nursing, the Master of Science in Occupational Therapy, the Master of Arts in Special Education, the Doctor of Occupational Therapy, the Doctor of Pharmacy, the Doctor of Physical Therapy, and the Juris Doctor. In the fall of 2012, Belmont is scheduled to launch a Doctor of Nursing Practice program.

Location

Belmont University occupies a 75-acre campus in southeast Nashville. With a metropolitan area of roughly a million residents, Nashville is a cultural, educational, health-care, commercial, and financial center in the mid-South. Practical educational opportunities, offered through diverse curriculums, provide students with the hands-on experience they need in preparation for a meaningful career. The city's location halfway between the northern and southern boundaries of the United States, with three intersecting interstate highways and an international airport, makes it accessible to students from across the country.

Majors and Degrees

Belmont University is accredited by the Commission on Colleges of the Southern Association of Colleges and Schools to award baccalaureate, master's, and doctoral degrees. Belmont grants seven undergraduate degrees: the Bachelor of Arts, the Bachelor of Business Administration, the Bachelor of Fine Arts, the Bachelor of Music, the Bachelor of Science, the Bachelor of Science in Nursing, and the Bachelor of Social Work. Majors or concentrations are offered in accounting, applied discrete mathematics, art (art education,

art history, design communications, studio art), Asian studies, audio and video production, audio engineering technology, biblical languages, biblical studies, biochemistry and molecular biology, biology, business administration, chemistry, Christian ethics, Christian leadership, classics, communication studies, computer science, early childhood education, economics, engineering physics, English, entertainment industry studies, entrepreneurship, environmental science, European studies, exercise science, finance, French, German, health, history, information systems management, international business, international economics, international politics, journalism, management, marketing, mass communication, mathematics, medical imaging technology, medical physics, medical technology, middle school education, music (church music, commercial music, music composition, music education, music with an outside minor, musical theater, music performance, piano pedagogy, music theory), music business, neuroscience, nursing, organizational and corporate communications, pharmaceutical studies, philosophy, physical education and health, physics, politics and public law, political science, psychology, public relations, religion and the arts, religious studies, science and engineering management, social entrepreneurship, social work, sociology, songwriting, Spanish, theater and drama, video production, and Web programming and development.

Academic Programs

Uniquely positioned to provide the best of liberal arts and professional education, Belmont University offers celebrated professional programs structured to provide an academically well-rounded education. Belmont University operates on a two-semester schedule with classes beginning in late August and ending in early May. Two summer sessions are also offered. The academic program is arranged by school: the College of Arts and Sciences, the College of Business Administration, the Gordon E. Inman College of Health Sciences and Nursing, the College of Visual and Performing Arts, the Mike Curb College of Entertainment and Music Business, the College Of Pharmacy, and the School of Religion.

In addition to the degrees offered through the schools, Belmont University offers an honors program, which was created to provide an enrichment opportunity for students who have potential for superior academic performance and who seek added challenge and breadth to their studies. Students enrolled in the honors program are led in designing and working through a flexible, individual curriculum and interdisciplinary general education curriculum by a private tutor who is an honors faculty member.

The University's advancements in undergraduate research are credited to a faculty committed to helping students practice their disciplines. The annual Belmont Undergraduate Research Symposium puts Belmont at the forefront of this national movement by providing a public forum for in-depth research at the undergraduate level.

Off-Campus Programs

Belmont University has contracts for dual-degree programs with Auburn University and University of Tennessee, Knoxville. These programs require three years of study at Belmont University followed by approximately two years of study at one of the above institutions. The course of study at Belmont must be mathematics, physics, or chemistry. Following completion of the academic requirements at both institutions, a student is awarded a Bachelor of Science degree from Belmont University and the appropriate degree from the second institution.

Several programs at Belmont have agreements with area organizations to provide students practical training. Nursing students gain clinical experience at all fourteen local hospitals and other clinical agencies. Education students gain classroom experience in Metro-Davidson County Schools. Music business students gain real-world experience through internships in the Nashville music industry and in Los Angeles and New York City

through the Belmont West and East (respectively) programs of study and internships.

Through a wide variety of international study programs on the six populated continents, Belmont offers students the opportunity to broaden and deepen their education while earning credit hours toward their degrees. These programs, which range in duration from two weeks to a year, are available in Australia, the Bahamas, China, Costa Rica, England, France, Germany, Hong Kong, Ireland, Italy, Mexico, New Zealand, Russia, Scotland, South Africa, and Spain.

Academic Facilities

Belmont offers a quiet, secluded environment, and classes are held in nine buildings with the library and other facilities located in proximity to those classrooms.

The Lila D. Bunch Library includes a microcomputer center, multimedia room, and group study rooms. Adjacent to it is the 3,000-square-foot Leu Art Gallery. Located next to the library is the Leu Center for the Visual Arts, featuring state-of-the-art studios with natural lighting and spacious work areas.

The Sam A. Wilson School of Music Building houses classrooms, a resource room, seminar rooms, studio/offices, music practice rooms, a piano lab, and a music technology lab.

The Jack C. Massey Business Center provides classrooms, office space, study lounges, seminar and conference rooms, a copy center, a post office, and a convenience store. A state-of-the-art learning center includes five computer labs. In addition, Massey Business Center houses the 9,000-square-foot Center for Music Business, which provides classrooms, an academic resource center, two state-of-the-art recording studios and control rooms, four isolation booths, a MIDI pre–postproduction room, and an engineering repair shop.

The Gordon Inman Center for Health Sciences and Nursing houses Belmont's nursing, social work, and occupational therapy programs. The recently opened McWhorter Hall, a 90,000-square-foot, state-of-the-art academic building, houses the College of Pharmacy, Physical Therapy, and Psychological Science. Students train in state-of-the-art labs and classrooms that include lift equipment to teach student safety, simulated mannequins that respond to basic stimuli, and apartments to teach social work students how to work with clients with special needs.

In fall 2012, Belmont is scheduled to open both the Baskin Center, home to the College of Law, and Dickens Hall, its newest residential facility.

Costs

Belmont's tuition and fees were $24,960 per academic year in 2011–12. Room and board in campus residence halls were $9320.

Financial Aid

More than 75 percent of Belmont's students receive some type of financial assistance. The financial aid program at Belmont combines merit-based assistance with need-based assistance to make the University program affordable. Institutional merit awards range from full tuition Presidential Scholarships to performance scholarships. Also included are many levels of academic merit awards. Belmont University also administers traditional state and federal need-based programs, including the Federal Pell Grant, Federal Stafford Student Loan, Federal Perkins Loan, Federal PLUS loan, and Tennessee Student Assistance Grants and Scholarships. Campus employment is available. Parents may arrange monthly tuition payments through an outside vendor. To apply for assistance, the student must complete the Free Application for Federal Student Aid (FAFSA).

Faculty

A highly competent faculty is the paramount attribute of a strong institution of higher education. Belmont University has faculty members who are dedicated to their profession and to the University. Of the more than 300 full-time faculty members, 65 percent hold terminal degrees. Another 30 percent of faculty members have completed formal studies beyond the master's degree.

The influence of the Belmont University faculty is felt beyond the campus. Faculty members are active in church, civic, professional, and academic associations; frequently speak to various groups; and often write for denominational and secular publications. Most faculty members have traveled extensively and many have experienced life in other regions of the United States and abroad.

Student Government

A liaison between the University and student body, the Student Government Association seeks to address educational, social, and spiritual needs of students. As a service organization for the student body, it offers opportunity for campus involvement, acts as the coordinating body for all student organizations, serves as a resource for the campus community, and represents student interests to the faculty and administration.

Admission Requirements

Applicants are considered based on the total picture a student's credentials present. High school students are considered competitive for admission if they present a rigorous course of college-preparatory academic studies. Students should have an above-average academic and cumulative grade point average and rank in the top half of their graduating class. Any college-level work is also expected to be at the above-average level. A strong correlation between high school grades and entrance examination scores is expected. The personal supplement information, a resume of activities, and recommendations are also strongly considered as positive indicators of success at Belmont. Additional requirements, such as portfolios or auditions, are considered in conjunction with the academic credentials for those programs that require them. Each application is considered on an individual basis. No two applicants present the same credentials or the same degree of fit with the University. The University desires to work with each student to determine the likelihood for that student to enroll, graduate, and benefit from the Belmont educational experience.

Application and Information

Further information and application materials may be obtained by contacting:

Office of Admissions
Belmont University
1900 Belmont Boulevard
Nashville, Tennessee 37212
Phone: 615-460-6785
　　　　800-56ENROLL (toll-free)
Fax: 615-460-5434
E-mail: admissions@belmont.edu
Web site: http://www.belmont.edu
　　　　http://www.facebook.com/BelmontUniversity
　　　　http://www.twitter.com/BelmontUniv

Freeman Hall at Belmont University.

BELOIT COLLEGE
BELOIT, WISCONSIN

The College

Beloit College is a private, independent, residential college that engages its students' curiosity and intelligence by bringing the liberal arts to life. Beloit's focus is on teaching and on the close collaboration that takes place among students and faculty members in small classroom and lab settings. Undergraduates learn to approach problems ethically and thoughtfully in an academic community that places a high premium on international and interdisciplinary perspectives. Active learning is key to the college's educational experience; students are expected to think on their feet, learn outside of the classroom and put the liberal arts into practice.

Beloit is Wisconsin's first college, founded by New Englanders on the Midwestern frontier in 1846. Today, a geographically diverse population of 1,250 students is drawn to Beloit's residential campus from nearly all North American states and more than forty other countries. Ten percent come from countries outside the United States, 18 percent of U.S. students are non-Caucasian, and many religious orientations and socioeconomic backgrounds are represented on campus. Beloit students are equally diverse in their academic choices; no more than 10 percent of the seniors are represented in any one of more than fifty majors available.

Beloit students are informed about and active in political and social issues, and they value individual expression. Beloit students serve on College governance committees, create new clubs, manage an annual music festival, and host their own radio and cable TV shows. In a given week, students may have the choice of attending (or organizing) a lecture series, a movie, music performances, a poetry reading, or an environmental debate. Seventy percent of Beloit's students participate in some form of athletics—club, intramural, or varsity. Those who live on campus (most do) may choose to live on quiet or substance-free floors, in one of three fraternity houses or three sorority houses, or in one of the special-interest houses, such as those formed around particular languages, gay and lesbian issues, anthropology, the arts, black student issues, faith and spirituality, music, the environment, peace and justice issues, science fiction and fantasy, Latino student issues, and women's issues. Two town-house complexes have been constructed in the past ten years and offer roomy, apartment-style living for juniors and seniors. Meals, served in two locations on campus, include organic, vegetarian, and vegan meal options.

New students quickly become part of this active and diverse environment through the Beloit Initiatives Program, which places new students in interdisciplinary seminars taught by experienced professors and staff members. These seminars begin the day students arrive on campus and provide an academic grounding and a social network. They also begin two years of faculty advising, designed to help students transition to Beloit and focus on developing skills and perspectives that will help them put theory into practice through study abroad, community-based learning, internships, and more.

From Beloit College, students can see the world. Additional details are available on the College's YouTube channel at http://bit.ly/YouTube_Beloit.

Location

Beloit's 40-acre campus is located on the border between Wisconsin and Illinois, 90 miles northwest of Chicago, 50 miles south of Madison, and 70 miles southwest of Milwaukee, in a small, diverse city of 36,000 that Margaret Mead once called "American society in a microcosm." Students may take advantage of the resources of the three major metropolitan areas, and Beloit's businesses and civic and service organizations provide numerous internship, job shadowing, and community outreach opportunities. Beloit's academic buildings are clustered around lawns dotted with ancient North American Indian mounds, while residence halls on the other side of campus provide the base of the College's social scene. A 25-acre athletic field and Strong Memorial Stadium, featuring a new turf field and track, are located a few blocks east of campus.

Majors and Degrees

Beloit awards Bachelor of Arts and Bachelor of Science degrees in nineteen departments and more than fifty fields of study. In natural sciences and mathematics, students may choose majors from the departments of biology, biochemistry, chemistry, computer science, environmental studies, geology, mathematics, and physics. In social sciences, students may choose majors from the departments of anthropology, economics, education and youth studies, international relations, political science, psychology, and sociology. In arts and humanities, majors are offered in the departments of art and art history, classics, English, history, modern languages and literatures, music, philosophy and religious studies, theater/dance/media studies, and women's and gender studies. Students often create a unique interdisciplinary major or minor. The College offers departmental minors in anthropology, studio art and art history, biology, chemistry, computer science, English, environmental studies, geology, health and society, history, mathematics, modern languages and literatures, music, philosophy, physics, political science, and religious studies. Permanent interdisciplinary minors include African studies, American studies, ancient Mediterranean studies, Asian studies, computational visualization and modeling, environmental studies, European studies, health and society, interdisciplinary studies, journalism, Latin American and Caribbean studies, legal studies, medieval studies, museum studies, performing arts, Russian studies, and women's and gender studies.

Beloit offers 3-2 cooperative programs in engineering and environmental management and forestry, and preprofessional programs in dentistry, law, medicine, and nursing. These programs, which have strong advisory and internship components, complement a major in an appropriate discipline. Beloit students may also earn teaching certification.

Academic Programs

Beloit's academic calendar consists of two 14-week semesters with one-week midterm breaks. At the end of the sophomore year, students are required to declare a major and may add a second major, a minor, or teaching certification. The Advising Practicum, a full-day series of workshops and discussions held every semester before advising week, is designed to help students reflect on Beloit's educational opportunities and develop an academic plan tailored to individual interests and goals. Beloit requires completion of five breadth requirements, a senior-year capstone experience, an experience outside the classroom which puts the liberal arts into practice, three writing-intensive courses, and significant contact with a culture not one's own. Thirty-one units are required for graduation, each unit representing the equivalent of a course of study involving 4 hours of class time a week per semester.

Off-Campus Programs

Beloit has a century-old tradition of domestic and international off-campus study opportunities, and more than half of new Beloit graduates will have studied and/or conducted research in such a program. Domestic programs include an opportunity to study at the Marine Biological Laboratory at Woods Hole in Massachusetts; a science semester at the Oak Ridge National Laboratory in Knoxville, Tennessee; a semester in the arts, an urban studies program, and a Newberry Library semester in the humanities, all in Chicago; and a Washington Semester at American University in Washington, D.C. Internships, field terms in the humanities and sciences, and summer employment opportunities are arranged through the Liberal Arts in Practice Center.

At Beloit College, study abroad is more an expectation than a luxury. Whether through Beloit's own extensive programs or the Associated Colleges of the Midwest (ACM) and independent programs, Beloit students have studied in more than forty countries worldwide, from Australia to Zimbabwe.

Academic Facilities

Beloit's historic brick and stone buildings coexist with innovative contemporary structures such as the Center for the Sciences. Completed in 2008, the 117,000-square-foot center is LEED-certified Platinum and includes a vegetated roof, high recycled/reused content, water management systems, and other sustainable features. Platinum is the highest rating offered by the U.S. Green Building Council. The College's newest facility, the Hendricks Center for the Arts, opened in the fall of 2010 in downtown Beloit, in a building that formerly housed the city's public library. The 48,000-square-foot building provides a centralized home to the College's dance and music programs, and features four studio classrooms, a state-of-the-art film classroom, faculty offices, rehearsal rooms, and design and staging labs. The Logan Museum of Anthropology and the Wright Museum of Art are highly regarded teaching museums that offer students excellent resources for research and work experience. The Neese Performing Arts Theatre complex features a large thrust stage theater, a black-box theater, a scenic design studio, and a complete costume shop. The World Affairs Center is the hub of language and literature study. Nearly 250 student-accessible computer workstations are located throughout campus, with a combination of wireless and wired network Internet access in academic buildings. Residence halls have a wired Internet connection for every student. Beloit's library collection is in excess of half a million holdings and provides individual and group study areas, computer labs, and extensive listening and viewing areas for the use of audiovisual materials. A 6,000-square-foot center for entrepreneurship in downtown Beloit provides physical space, office resources, and a recording studio where students can put venture plans of their own design into action.

Costs

Tuition for the 2012–13 academic year is $38,194, fees are $280, a double room is $3854, and board (twenty-meal plan) is $4008, for a total comprehensive fee of $46,336. While the cost of books and incidental expenses varies, it averages about $1900.

Financial Aid

Beloit College is committed to making the Beloit experience affordable to all qualified students. The financial aid program recognizes two criteria—scholastic ability and financial need—that may qualify students for awards. During the 2011–12 academic year, more than 85 percent of first-year students received financial assistance through grants, loans, or work-study.

In 2011, new students from families with incomes below $50,000 received an average grant of $29,000; qualifying students from families with incomes above $100,000 received an average grant of $19,500. Beloit's attention to providing students high value has won the College recognition in the Princeton Review's guides, the *Fiske Guide to Colleges,* and *U.S. News & World Report* as among the nation's best buys in top colleges.

Faculty

The focus of Beloit's faculty is great teaching. Beloit professors are committed to an educational environment that emphasizes discussion and collaborative learning in small classes. Of the 114 full-time faculty members, 97 percent hold the highest academic degree in their field. All classes are taught by professors. In classrooms, it is easy for students and faculty members to become immersed in their work, since the student-faculty ratio is 10:1 and the average class size is 15 students. All Beloit professors are also academic advisers who are involved in students' academic concerns as well as their adjustment to life at the College. Discussions begun in the classroom are often continued in an informal setting, such as at a basketball game or over dinner at a professor's house.

Student Government

Students at Beloit are actively involved in the governance of the College. The Beloit Student Congress is the College's student government. Its committees (Governance Committee, Publicity Committee, Food Committee, Organization Task Force, and Programming Board) allow the congress to focus on representing the student body and meeting its goals. In addition to this entirely student-run governing body, students are elected to the College's Academic Senate and serve as voting members of major College committees. Students also sit on all academic search committees.

Admission Requirements

Admission to Beloit is selective. Beloit seeks applicants with special qualities and talents, as well as those from diverse ethnic, geographic, and economic backgrounds. When reviewing applications, the transcript is the most important element. Beloit has no absolute secondary school requirements but recommends a rigorous college-preparatory program. This includes 4 years of English, 4 years of college-preparatory mathematics, 4 years of laboratory science, 4 years of history or social science, and 4 years of a foreign language. Seventh-semester grades may be required. A counselor recommendation is a required part of the application. One teacher recommendation is also required. The essay component of Beloit's application is critical. There is no required topic, so students should write about a topic they believe will represent them well. Either SAT or ACT test scores are required, but they are the least important part of the application (TOEFL or IELTS scores are required for international students). Beloit does not consider the SAT or ACT writing exam for purposes of admission. Interviews are not required for admission but are encouraged. Off-campus alumni interviews can be arranged if a student would like to interview but cannot travel to the campus. Transfer applications are considered for August or January entrance. Applicants must hold at least a B average at an accredited college or university.

Application and Information

Beloit offers two nonbinding early action plans with deadlines of either November 1 or December 1; notification is December 15 and January 15, respectively. The regular decision priority application deadline is January 15, with notification beginning in March. Applications received after January 15 will be given full consideration as space remains available. Admitted students have until May 1 to reply to Beloit.

Students who wish to be considered for merit scholarships are strongly encouraged to apply under the Early Action plan. Review of transfer applications for the fall term begins March 15 and continues through the spring; the deadline for the spring term is November 1. Notification for transfer applications is rolling.

For more information, students should contact:

Admissions Office
Beloit College
700 College Street
Beloit, Wisconsin 53511
Phone: 608-363-2500
      800-9-BELOIT (toll-free)
Fax: 608-363-2075
E-mail: admiss@beloit.edu
Web site: http://www.beloit.edu
      http://www.facebook.com/BeloitCollege
      http://twitter.com/#!/beloit_college

Beloit College Spanish Professor Sylvia Lopez leads a class discussion in the World Affairs Center. At Beloit, professors engage students and encourage them to share their ideas.

BENTLEY UNIVERSITY
WALTHAM, MASSACHUSETTS

The University

Bentley University is a national leader in business education. Centered on education and research in business and related professions, Bentley blends the breadth and technological strength of a university with the values and student focus of a small college. A Bentley education is an unparalleled fusion of business and the arts and sciences that allows students to truly customize their learning; this includes a unique liberal studies double-major program. Bentley also stresses the benefits of hands-on learning through internships, service-learning, study abroad, and corporate partnerships.

In 2011, Bentley was ranked eighth in the nation by the Princeton Review for best career services. The Miller Center for Career Services (CSS) offers resources including an on-campus recruiting program involving 1,000 national and international companies, an online job and internship database, career fairs, and workshops on topics such as interviewing and networking.

In addition, students can develop a customized four-year development plan, which contributes to the university's outstanding placement rates. In 2011, more than 90 percent of students found employment or enrolled in graduate school within six months of graduation. Their median annual salary was $50,000.

Approximately 98 percent of freshmen live on campus. Twenty-three residence halls provide a range of housing options: dorms, suites, and apartments. Housing is provided for all four years. All residence halls are air-conditioned and typically include study lounges, exercise facilities, TV lounges, and game rooms. In 2010, the Princeton Review ranked Bentley eighteenth on its list of Dorms Like Palaces.

Students live and learn in a multicultural environment that prepares them to thrive in today's diverse world. International students representing nearly 100 countries are part of the Bentley community.

Supporting Bentley's commitment to diversity are offices such as the Multicultural Center, Spiritual Life Center, Center for International Students and Scholars, Center for Women in Business, and the Women's Center.

The Student Center is the hub of campus activity and is home to Seasons Dining Room and more than 100 student organizations. These groups represent academics, the arts, media, fraternity and sorority life, and cultural interests.

Athletic programs are a Bentley hallmark and include intramurals, recreational sports, and more than 20 varsity teams in NCAA Divisions I and II. The Dana Athletic Center houses a weight and fitness complex, food court, locker rooms, a gym, a basketball court, volleyball and racquetball courts, a competition-size pool with a diving tank, and saunas. Outdoor facilities include soccer and baseball fields, a track, and tennis courts.

Location

Bentley's location in Waltham, Massachusetts—just minutes west of Boston—puts the city within easy reach. As the country's ultimate university town, Boston's options range from theater to art exhibits, dance clubs to concerts, and championship sports to world-class shopping. Bentley's free shuttle makes regular trips to Harvard Square in Cambridge, just a subway ride from Boston. Boston also offers many opportunities for internships and jobs after graduation.

Majors and Degrees

Bentley's curriculum, focusing on business, technology, and the liberal arts, provides students with options for shaping an academic program that fits their skills, interests, and career goals.

Bachelor of Science (B.S.) degree programs enable students to gain in-depth knowledge and skills in specific business disciplines: accountancy, actuarial science, computer information systems, corporate finance and accounting, economics–finance, finance, information design and corporate communication, information systems audit and control, management, managerial economics, marketing, and mathematical sciences.

Bentley also offers Bachelor of Arts (B.A.) degree programs with majors in global studies, history, liberal arts, media and culture, philosophy, public policy, Spanish studies, and sustainable science. All Bachelor of Arts students gain business experience through either the business studies major or minor. All students can also choose from minors such as entrepreneurial studies, law, and sports management.

The Liberal Studies major (LSM), an optional double major, can be combined with any business program. It provides students with a competitive edge by building meaningful connections across and within disciplines. To complete the LSM, students do not need to take any extra courses beyond those normally required. It allows students to add another credential to their degree, helping them stand out to employers. LSM concentrations include American studies; earth, environment, and global sustainability; ethics and social responsibility; global perspectives; health and industry; media arts and society; and quantitative perspectives.

Academic Programs

The Bentley curriculum is an integration of business and the liberal arts. The university's 4,200 undergraduates benefit from a breadth of programs and the ability to combine subjects to best fit their interests.

A Bentley education also focuses on gaining hands-on experience in the classroom. Students benefit from classes where they partner with outside companies to solve current business problems and present their solutions directly to company executives. Bentley also offers top applicants a chance to enroll in the honors program. Participants select honors-level courses each semester that offer extra intellectual challenge in a seminar atmosphere.

The Five-Year Master's Candidate program enables students to earn a Bachelor of Business Administration degree and either an Emerging Leaders M.B.A. or Master of Science (M.S.) degree.

Off-Campus Programs

Hands-on experience is emphasized across the curriculum. Internships, study abroad, service-learning, and other opportunities allow students to apply classroom theory in the community.

Each year, more than 90 percent of students complete at least one internship, building valuable work experience and networking connections. Some of the top internship employers include Fidelity Investments, the TJX Companies, Liberty Mutual, Bain & Company, and all of the Big Four accounting firms.

Bentley students can gain insight into different cultures by studying abroad. Programs take place in more than twenty-five countries and vary in length from one week to a full academic year.

Through Bentley's Service-Learning Center, students build skills in business, communication, and teamwork while assisting nonprofit and community-based organizations both locally and internationally.

Academic Facilities

Concepts taught in the classroom are put to use in several high-tech learning laboratories.

Bentley's financial trading room combines state-of-the-art technology and real-time data to offer first-hand exposure to financial concepts in simulated trading sessions. Resources include Bloomberg, FactSet, Datastream, and Thomson One Analytics.

The Center for Marketing Technology plays an integral role in marketing programs. Students gain a full grasp of software options, familiarity with research tools and techniques, and knowledge of new digital marketing frameworks.

The Accounting Center for Electronic Learning and Business Management (ACELAB) introduces cutting-edge technologies that

are reshaping the accounting profession. Students have access to auditing and tax preparation software as well as other professional applications from industry leaders such as SAP and Oracle.

The Center for Languages and International Collaboration (CLIC) is a key resource for language courses, international studies majors, and students with an interest in global issues. The center promotes collaboration among Bentley students and their counterparts overseas.

The Media and Culture Labs and Studio feature resources for video production and editing as well as digital photography. The lab provides students with industry-standard software programs for screenwriting, sound mixing, graphic design, and DVD authoring.

The Design and Usability Center (DUC) features labs ideal for usability testing. Students use the applications employed by technical communicators, Web developers, user-interface designers, and usability specialists.

The brand-new CIS Learning and Technology Sandbox is a collaborative space for learning new technologies. Its resources include Google TVs, Xbox 360 with Kinect, study spaces, large-screen TVs, a smart board, specialized networking equipment, and tools such as Windows 8, Linux, and Android development software.

The Bentley Library is outfitted with computer workstations, group study rooms, and wireless network access. It also has an exceptional number of online database resources. In 2010, Bentley was ranked 14th on the Princeton Review's list of best college libraries.

Costs

Tuition for resident and nonresident students during the 2012–13 academic year is $38,130. Room and board (double room, meal plan) costs are $12,960. Additional expenses include books, supplies, laptop computer, and personal and travel expenses.

Financial Aid

Bentley's financial aid program includes both scholarships based on academic achievement, which are awarded through the admission process, as well as grants based on financial need. Bentley administered almost $75 million in aid to undergraduate students last year. Over two-thirds of that amount came in the form of grants and scholarships directly from Bentley. Significant institutional resources are committed each year so that all academically qualified students have access to a Bentley education regardless of their financial resources. Currently, more than 70 percent of undergraduates receive some type of financial assistance—either grants, scholarships, loans, and/or work study.

Faculty

Bentley faculty members are teacher-scholars known for their classroom skills and cutting-edge research. They bring practical, real-world experience to the classroom, based on years of professional involvement in their fields. Faculty research focuses on issues of prime importance to current business practice. Much of the research is conducted in partnership with leading organizations. A student-faculty ratio of 14:1 and average class size of 24 ensure a personal experience for students. All courses are taught by professors; there are no teaching assistants. Students often note that professors are accessible to them outside of the classroom.

Student Government

Bentley has a number of student governing associations, including the Student Government Association, Residence Hall Association, and the Graduate Student Association.

Admission Requirements

Applicants are encouraged to complete a competitive university preparatory program. Recommendations include 4 years of English, 4 years of mathematics (preferably algebra I and II, geometry, and precalculus or its equivalent), and 3 to 4 years each of history, laboratory science, and a foreign language.

Along with the application, students must submit a secondary school transcript, letters of recommendation from a teacher and a counselor, and official scores of either the SAT or ACT, including the ACT writing test. The University has special applications for international students and transfer students. Applicants who are nonnative speakers of English must also supply official scores of the Test of English as a Foreign Language (TOEFL).

Application and Information

Bentley University accepts the Common Application. The application deadline for students enrolling in September is January 15. For students planning to enroll in January, the deadline is November 1. Candidates for the fall semester are notified by April 1; spring semester candidates are notified on a rolling basis.

Please visit http://undergraduate.bentley.edu/applying for application information and deadlines.

For more information, students should contact:

Office of Undergraduate Admission
Bentley University
175 Forest Street
Waltham, Massachusetts 02452-4705
Phone: 781-891-2244
       800-523-2354 (toll-free)
Fax: 781-891-3414
E-mail: ugadmission@bentley.edu
Web site: http://www.bentley.edu
       https://www.facebook.com/bentleyadmission
       http://twitter.com/bentleyu

Bentley students have access to professional research tools, cutting-edge software, and other valuable resources in seven high-tech learning labs and state-of-the-art library.

BERKLEE COLLEGE OF MUSIC
BOSTON, MASSACHUSETTS

The College

Berklee College of Music was founded on the revolutionary principle that the best way to prepare students for careers in music is through the study and practice of contemporary music. For more than half a century, the college has evolved to reflect the state-of-the-art of music and the music business. With more than a dozen performance and non-performance majors, a diverse and talented student body of 4,000 students representing more than seventy countries, and a music industry "who's who" of alumni, Berklee is the world's premier learning lab for the music of today—and tomorrow.

Berklee has proven its commitment to this approach by wholeheartedly embracing change. The musical landscape looks nothing like it did when Berklee was founded in 1945, but the college has remained current by supplementing its core curriculum with studies in emerging musical genres and indispensable new technology. Berklee also has responded to important developments in music education and music therapy, making good on its promise to improve society through music.

At Berklee, students acquire a strong foundation of contemporary music theory and technique, then build upon that foundation by learning the practical, professional skills needed to sustain a career in music. Majors such as music production and engineering, film scoring, music business/management, electronic production and design, songwriting, and music therapy, as well as traditional mainstays of performance and composition, lead toward either a fully accredited four-year baccalaureate degree or a professional diploma. Perhaps more importantly, they prepare students for employment in the music industry.

Berklee attracts a diverse range of students who reflect the multiplicity of influences in today's music, be it jazz, rock, hip-hop, country, gospel, electronica, Latin, or funk. The college is a magnet for aspiring musicians from every corner of the earth, which gives the school a uniquely international flavor. Of all U.S. colleges and universities, Berklee has one of the largest percentages of undergraduates from outside the United States—25 percent. Reflecting the interplay between music and culture, Berklee creates an environment where aspiring music professionals learn how to integrate new ideas and showcase their distinctive skills in an evolving community.

The college's alumni form a wide network of industry professionals who use their openness, virtuosity, and versatility to take music in new directions. Notable alumni include Gary Burton, Terri Lyne Carrington, Bruce Cockburn, Juan Luis Guerra, Roy Hargrove, Quincy Jones, Diana Krall, Aimee Mann, Arif Mardin, Branford Marsalis, Danilo Pérez, John Scofield, Howard Shore, Alan Silvestri, Esperanza Spalding, Susan Tedeschi, and Gillian Welch.

Location

Berklee College of Music is located in Boston's Fenway Cultural District. An international hub of intellectual and creative exploration, the neighborhood includes treasure-filled museums and galleries and world-class performing arts centers such as Symphony Hall and the Wang Center. Great performers appear at the Berklee Performance Center; the college's all-ages venue Café 939 highlights up-and-coming international performers in all genres. Boston is also home to many of the world's other great colleges and universities. In addition to the music made at Berklee, there is a lively club and concert scene in the area with coffee houses featuring folk and bluegrass music; neighborhood clubs offering jazz, reggae, and world music; and clubs specializing in rock, blues, dance, urban, and country music.

Berklee students participate in intramural sports and fitness programs at nearby institutions; watch Boston's professional sports teams play in the TD Garden or at Fenway Park or other area sports venues; attend theater, club, and concert hall events year-round throughout the city; and walk, skate, or bike through the city's many scenic parks and public gardens. The college is on Boston's public transportation system, allowing students to take advantage of all that Boston has to offer.

Majors and Degrees

Berklee offers a Bachelor of Music (B.M.) degree program and a four-year program leading to a professional diploma. Students may choose to major in composition, contemporary writing and production, electronic production and design, film scoring, jazz composition, music business/management, music education, music production and engineering, music therapy, performance, professional music, and songwriting. In addition, students may choose from nine minors: acoustics, conducting, drama, English, Latin music performance, music and society, psychology, video game scoring, and visual culture/new media studies. The college also offers a five-year, dual-major option in which students graduate with an even more marketable education that expands their career options in the music industry.

Academic Programs

The Bachelor of Music program offers a complete music curriculum combined with liberal arts courses such as English, history, languages, mathematics, philosophy, and physical or social science. Intensive concentration in music subjects provides students with the necessary tools for developing their musical talents to the fullest and preparing for the multifaceted and ever-changing demands of today's professional music. The degree program is especially appropriate for students who wish to earn a formal degree; are interested in pursuing a career in music education, music therapy, or music business/management; or want to continue their studies at the graduate level.

The diploma is designed for students who want to focus exclusively on contemporary music studies and still get the benefits of a Berklee experience, as well as students who have already earned a bachelor's degree at another institution.

All students must complete the core music curriculum, which consists of harmony, arranging, ear training, and introduction to music technology; instrumental studies; ensembles and instrumental labs; and the concentrate courses designated for each major. All degree candidates must complete the general education curriculum and traditional music studies courses.

Off-Campus Programs

Through the Professional Arts Consortium (ProArts), an association of six area institutions dedicated to the performing and visual arts, Berklee students can take courses at leading Boston area arts institutions in communications, modern dance, visual arts, ballet, architectural and graphic design, theater arts, and liberal arts. The other members of the consortium are Boston Architectural Center, the Boston Conservatory, Emerson College, Massachusetts College of Art, and the School of the Museum of Fine Arts.

Students who major in music business/management may be eligible to receive credit for their Berklee course work toward an M.B.A. from Suffolk University.

The Berklee International Network is a shared endeavor designed to promote the effectiveness of contemporary music education among members and to advance the value of contemporary music education internationally. Berklee faculty and staff members visit network member schools annually to conduct workshops and clinics and to audition students for scholarships for full-time study at Berklee. There are currently thirteen members of the network: Fundacio L'Aula de Musica Moderna i Jazz in Barcelona, Spain; Rimon School of Jazz and Contemporary Music in Ramat Hasharon (Tel Aviv), Israel; Phillipos Nakas Conservatory in Athens, Greece; Music Academy International in Nancy, France; Instituto de Musica Contemporanea Universidad San Francisco de Quito, in Quito, Ecuador; Pop and Jazz Conservatory in Helsinki, Finland; Koyo Conservatory in Kobe, Japan; Jazz and Rock Schule in Freiburg, Germany; International College of Music in Kuala Lumpur, Malaysia; Conservatorio Souza Lima in São Paulo, Brazil; Seoul

COLLEGE CLOSE-UPS

Jazz Academy in Seoul, Korea; Metropolia University of Applied Sciences in Helsinki, Finland; and the Newpark Music Centre in Dublin, Ireland.

The college has a robust internship program, with students learning in music companies in Los Angeles, New York, Nashville, London, and beyond, as well as semester-long study-abroad programs at the Phillipos Nakas Conservatory in Athens, Greece and the Jazz and Rock Schule in Freiburg, Germany.

Academic Facilities

Berklee students have the opportunity to work in the college's state-of-the-art music technology facilities, using some of the most sophisticated recording and synthesis equipment currently available, in addition to facilities specifically designed for the areas of composition, arranging, and film scoring. The facilities at Berklee are furnished with the instruments and equipment that are being used in the world beyond the classroom. Berklee's performance facilities include the Berklee Performance Center, a 1,200-seat concert hall hosting more than 300 student, faculty, and other concerts each year; Cafe 939, a state-of-the-art, all-ages, student-run music venue and coffee house; four recital halls equipped with a variety of sound reinforcement systems; more than forty ensemble rooms; over eighty private instruction studios; about 300 private practice rooms; and an outdoor concert pavilion.

Technological facilities include the Recording Studio Complex, consisting of thirteen studio facilities that include 8-, 16-, and 24-track digital and analog recording capability; synthesis labs, featuring more than 250 MIDI-equipped synthesizers, drum machines, sequencers, and computers, including hard-disk recording; the Learning Center, with forty computer-based MIDI workstations; the Professional Writing Division MIDI Lab; and film scoring labs, providing professional training in the areas of film music composition, editing, sequencing, and computer applications.

Costs

Information on costs is available online at http://berklee.edu/cost.

Financial Aid

A very large percentage of the student body receives some form of financial aid, so no student should allow financial barriers to stop him or her from applying to the college. Funds are available from many different sources, including Berklee and federal and state programs. Students are eligible for merit-based scholarships and, in cases of demonstrated need, federal assistance is provided. Subsidized loans, a tuition-installment plan, and campus employment are also available. Financial aid counselors are available to students and their families to discuss the various options available to them. Students should be aware that there are specific deadlines for federal and state fund applications and for scholarships. Berklee awards over $30 million in scholarships each year to students from all over the world who demonstrate the potential to succeed in today's music industry.

Berklee's Office of Scholarships and Student Employment provides extensive opportunities for both domestic and international students to apply for merit-based scholarships via audition (entering students) or submission of an achievement portfolio (continuing and returning students who have successfully completed a minimum of two semesters).

Faculty

The personal attention students receive from teachers at Berklee guides them beyond the theoretical so that they can apply what they've learned in their next ensemble rehearsal, evening jam session, or gig. All instruction is administered by Berklee's more than 500 faculty members. Teachers are talented artists who demonstrate their commitment to music education in the classroom and beyond. Most faculty members also write and arrange music, perform in concert halls and clubs, make recordings, or perform on television and radio, and some do it all. All faculty members bring to the classroom knowledge of music and the wisdom that comes from professional music experience.

Student Government

Berklee's broad-based system of governance relies on participation from all areas of the college community. The Council of Students represents the voice and perspectives of students regarding all of the issues reviewed by the college. Students are also asked to serve on a wide variety of college committees that advise administrators on such topics as the college's master plan, honorary degree recipients,

Web site, and academic and student policies. And many of Berklee's student leaders have the opportunity to meet with the president, vice presidents, and trustees during the academic year to discuss current issues, concerns, and institutional activities.

Admission Requirements

Berklee's board of admissions seeks students who show high potential—who are creative, collaborative, and who have something extra that sets them apart. The college considers every aspect of an applicant's strengths and looks for candidates who reflect the rich diversity of Berklee's curriculum, with high musical aptitude as players or writers; or in business, production, music therapy, or music education.

The college takes academics into consideration as well as musical aptitude. Berklee does not have specific GPA or test score requirements, nor does it have specific class rank requirements. The audition and interview process, along with a comprehensive and holistic evaluation of each applicant, provides a wealth of information to assess students' ability to succeed at Berklee.

Application and Information

Berklee uses fixed application deadlines for each semester of entry. Applying to the college is a three-step process. All applicants must submit an online application, participate in a live audition and interview, and mail in the appropriate transcripts to be considered for full-time enrollment at the college.

The online application asks that students provide their personal contact information, including whether they are a vocalist or instrumentalist; their preferred audition location; and responses to fourteen questions that will be used in their interview. A live audition and interview is required as part of the application. A complete listing of audition dates, deadlines, and locations throughout the world is available on Berklee's Web site.

The college also asks that students provide information about their musical and academic background. All supporting materials must be postmarked by the posted deadline date. To learn more about how to apply to the college, and information about the audition and interview experience, students should take Berkelee's online tour at http://www.berklee.edu/campustour/index.html.

For further information, students should contact:

Office of Admissions
Berklee College of Music
1140 Boylston Street
Boston, Massachusetts 02215
Phone: 617-266-2222 (worldwide)
    800-BERKLEE (toll-free in the U.S. and Canada)
Fax: 617-747-2047
E-mail: admissions@berklee.edu
Web site: http://www.berklee.edu
    http://www.facebook.com/berkleecollege
    http://twitter.com/BerkleeCollege
    http://www.youtube.com/berkleecollege

Berklee College of Music students using state-of-the-art music technology.

BOSTON COLLEGE
CHESTNUT HILL, MASSACHUSETTS

The University

Boston College (BC) was founded in 1863 by the Jesuits to serve the sons of Boston's Irish immigrants. Today a coeducational university on more than 207 acres in Chestnut Hill, BC may seem a world apart from the small school in the crowded heart of Boston that was its first home. Through more than fourteen decades of growth and change, however, BC has held fast to the Jesuit ideals that inspired its founders. A Jesuit education today, as a century ago, is grounded in the liberal arts and in a commitment to the service of others.

Undergraduates may enroll in the College of Arts and Sciences, the Wallace E. Carroll School of Management, the Connell School of Nursing, or the Lynch School of Education.

BC's approximately 9,000 undergraduates come from many backgrounds. The university draws from nearly all fifty states and more than fifty countries. Students' religious and cultural backgrounds are similarly diverse. Today, the university's AHANA (African American, Hispanic, Asian, and Native American) and international students make up 27 percent of the undergraduate student body.

In today's complex and increasingly diverse world, the university believes that the best education is one that broadens a student's capacity to reason, think, and make critical judgments in a wide range of areas. Thus, each BC student fulfills a core of liberal arts courses from which he or she can pursue degrees in more than fifty areas of study and choose from more than 1,400 course offerings throughout the university.

According to several recent national publications, BC is in the top tier of the nation's colleges and universities. The foundation for that achievement is the university's scholars and researchers—737 full-time professionals who make up the faculty. The kinship between teachers and students is one of the hallmarks of a BC education; that relationship is nurtured by a student-teacher ratio of 14:1. The median class size at the university is 20 students.

At BC, learning continues beyond the classroom in more than 225 student-run organizations. These include student government, honor societies, language and cultural organizations, performance ensembles, political groups, preprofessional clubs, publications, and service organizations. BC also sponsors thirteen varsity teams for men and sixteen for women, all of which compete at the NCAA Division I level. The College also supports over sixty club and intramural sports.

Boston College's public affairs office maintains university profiles on two social networking sites. Prospective students can become a fan of BC on Facebook (http://www.facebook.com/BostonCollege) or follow BC on Twitter (http://twitter.com/BostonCollege).

Location

Located in the Chestnut Hill section of Newton, BC sits on the doorstep of one of America's great cities, a center of culture and education for more than three centuries. It is an energetic, cosmopolitan city that draws life and enthusiasm from the more than 200,000 college students in residence during the academic year. Located just 6 miles from downtown Boston and with easy access to the city via the trolley system that stops at the foot of the campus, BC offers the best of both worlds: a scenic suburban setting neighboring an exciting metropolitan center.

Majors and Degrees

The College of Arts and Sciences (A&S) is the oldest and largest of the four undergraduate schools at BC. A&S students must complete thirty-eight 1-semester courses, thirty-two of which are in A&S departments. The normal course load is five courses per semester for the first three years and four courses per semester during the senior year. The undergraduate curriculum includes the university core curriculum and ten to twelve courses in the major field, with the remainder of courses chosen as electives. A&S offers degrees in the following areas: art history, biochemistry, biology, chemistry, classical studies, communication, computer science, economics, English, environmental geosciences, film studies, French, geology, geological studies, geophysics, German studies, Hispanic studies, history, independent major, international studies, Islamic civilizations and societies, Italian, linguistics, mathematics, music, philosophy, physics, political science, psychology, Russian, Slavic studies, sociology, studio art, theater, and theology. Preprofessional advisement is also available in medical, dental, veterinary, and legal programs. Students can also select from twenty-one departmental minors, or seventeen interdisciplinary minors.

The Carroll School of Management educates students to be leaders in business and industry and in public agencies, educational institutions, and service organizations. The Carroll School offers concentrations in accounting, accounting information systems, computer science, corporate reporting and analysis, economics, finance, general management, human resource management, information systems, management and leadership, marketing, and operations and strategic management.

The Lynch School of Education prepares students for education and human services professions. Programs provide a general education, professional preparation, and specialized education in the major field. Fieldwork in area schools is closely linked to course work in each specialization. The Lynch School awards degrees upon completion of thirty-eight courses, including the university core curriculum, a major field of study in education, and a second major in a subject field or an interdisciplinary area in A&S that complements the student's program. Areas of specialization include early childhood education, elementary education, human development, and secondary education. The Lynch School also offers interdisciplinary majors in American heritages, general science, mathematics/computer science, and perspectives on Spanish America.

The Connell School of Nursing offers a four-year program of study leading to a Bachelor of Science degree. The three major components to the curriculum are nursing major courses, electives, and the required university core curriculum. In all courses, principles of wellness, illness, rehabilitation, and health maintenance serve as a theoretical basis in preparing students for professional nursing practice. Nursing courses include traditional classes, simulated and audiovisual laboratory activities on campus, and clinical learning activities in health-care settings.

Academic Programs

Every BC education is centered on a core curriculum—a set of required courses. BC offers a core curriculum because it believes in the unity of knowledge. While the core, which is continually reviewed by a committee of faculty members, varies somewhat by school, its common elements include literature, natural science, writing, philosophy, theology, social science, modern European history, mathematics, fine arts, and the study of a non-European culture.

There are a wide variety of extraordinary academic programs available to BC students to enhance their educational experience. They include, among others, honors programs within each of the university's four undergraduate schools, Undergraduate Faculty Research Fellows, the Scholar of the College, PULSE, and Perspectives on Western Culture.

Off-Campus Programs

BC encourages all students to take part in internship programs. More than half of BC undergraduates participate in at least one internship or prepracticum placement during their college years. Internships can be paid or unpaid and may take place during the academic year or the summer; some carry academic credit.

BC students may take on the challenge of international study in more than sixty programs administered by BC at universities in more than forty countries. BC students who study abroad typically do so in their junior year, but there is also a range of full-year and summer-abroad opportunities. The Office of International Programs helps students with program selection and applications and maintains a library of reference books and professional evaluations of international study programs.

Academic Facilities

BC's eight libraries contain more than 2.7 million printed volumes, over 4.2 million items in microform, 389,839 e-books, 215,443 government documents, 34,919 serial subscriptions, and a wide collection of films and archival items. The resources of the library system range from some of Europe's earliest printed books to hundreds of computerized databases. Students with personal computers have dorm-room access to these databases as well as to Quest and other library information sources through Agora, the campus information network. BC also offers a 24/7 "Ask a Librarian" e-mail service and the capability to text questions to a librarian. In addition, all of BC's libraries and classrooms offer a wireless network that provides access to these resources and the Internet.

Research laboratories in the state-of-the-art science facilities have been specially designed to accommodate the advanced instrumentation required for modern science and to provide flexibility for accommodating new equipment. The $85-million expansion to the Higgins Biology and Physics Center was carefully designed to place classrooms, laboratories, computer facilities, and office space in proximity and to facilitate interaction among faculty members, researchers, and students. In addition to the Center's seventeen new teaching laboratories, special working labs are designed and outfitted for research and teaching in the fields of biology and physics.

Costs

Tuition for the 2011–12 academic year was $41,480, which included a student activity fee and campus health fee. The total for room and board was $12,324, which included the board plan. Freshman mandatory fees include a one-time required charge of $450 for first-year orientation and student identification.

Financial Aid

BC maintains a financial aid program to assist deserving and qualified students who might otherwise not be able to attend the university. Boston College is committed to providing funds to meet the full demonstrated need of every admitted student who applies for financial aid. Overall, 69 percent of students receive some form of financial aid. Assistance for freshmen alone included more than $19 million in need-based grants. The university offers financial aid to students based on need as demonstrated by completion of the College Scholarship Service's Financial Aid PROFILE and the Free Application for Federal Student Aid (FAFSA). All requirements and deadlines and complete instructions are available in BC admission literature. An application for financial aid in no way affects a decision on admission.

Each year, BC chooses 15 incoming freshmen as Presidential Scholars to receive merit-based, full-tuition scholarships. Students are selected from all candidates who apply through the early action program.

Faculty

BC has 737 full-time faculty members. Of these faculty members, 98 percent hold doctoral degrees. Approximately 100 Jesuits live on BC property and make up one of the largest Apostolic Jesuit communities in the world. Nearly half of these members are active in the College's administration and teaching.

Student Government

The Undergraduate Government of Boston College (UGBC), formed in 1968, is led by the president and vice president, who are elected in the spring of each year by the entire student body. UGBC's goal is to serve the students by providing services and opportunities and by representing them in the best manner possible to the university community. To accomplish this goal, UGBC provides many educational, social, and cultural programs, such as concerts, lectures, roundtables, and more.

Admission Requirements

The undergraduate admission staff pays particular attention to students who have done well in a demanding college-preparatory curriculum, including Advanced Placement (AP) and honors courses when available. For the class of 2015, there were 32,974 applications for 2,113 places. The majority of incoming freshmen ranked comfortably in the top 10 percent of their high school class. The SAT scores of the middle half of admitted freshmen were 1890–2170 On the ACT, scores of the middle half were between 29 and 32.

Application and Information

Students applying to Boston College for a place in the freshman class must complete both the Common Application and the Boston College Supplemental Application. All applicants should submit the BC Supplemental Application as soon as they have decided to apply to Boston College. Students are encouraged to review the electronic application instructions on BC's Web site at http://www.bc.edu/applications and then apply at http://www.commonapp.org.

Students applying through the regular admission program must submit the Common Application and all other required forms, along with the $70 application fee, by January 1. Candidates are notified of action taken on their application in early April. Admitted students intending to matriculate are required to forward a confirmation fee to the Admission Office postmarked by May 1.

Students with superior academic credentials who view Boston College as a top choice may apply through the nonbinding early action program. These applicants must submit both application forms, along with the $70 application fee, by November 1. Candidates learn of their admission decision before December 25 but have the standard deadline (May 1) to reserve their places as freshmen. Boston College does permit students to apply under early action if they have applied to an early decision college.

BC accepts approximately 125 transfer students each year. Transfer candidates should request applications for transfer admission from the Office of Undergraduate Admission or via the Web site at http://www.bc.edu/transfer. In addition to high school records and standardized test results, transfer applicants must furnish transcripts from all postsecondary institutions they have attended.

For more information, students should contact:

Office of Undergraduate Admission
Devlin Hall 208
Boston College
Chestnut Hill, Massachusetts 02467
Phone: 617-552-3100
          800-360-2522 (toll-free)
Fax: 617-552-0798
Web site: http://www.bc.edu

BOSTON UNIVERSITY
·BOSTON, MASSACHUSETTS

The University

Boston University (BU) offers an extensive array of rigorous academic, research, extracurricular, and internship opportunities in the heart of the culturally diverse city of Boston.

With nine undergraduate schools and colleges, over 250 majors and minors, more than ninety study-abroad programs, and 2,022 labs in which to conduct research, the choices at BU are vast and varied. Students have until the end of their sophomore year to declare a major, giving them the opportunity to try out classes in subjects as diverse as biology, broadcast journalism, business, computer engineering, elementary education, film, international relations, physical therapy, psychology, theater, and more.

The BU faculty includes Pulitzer and Nobel Prize winners, Fulbright scholars, MacArthur Fellows, and a former poet laureate. The 13:1 student-faculty ratio and classes with an average size of 28 make it likely that instructors know students by name and are genuinely interested in what they have to say.

Students are guaranteed four years of housing on campus in a variety of residences, from historic brownstones to the modern, high-rise Student Village apartments.

BU welcomes students who are intellectually curious and who embrace academic challenges. But the University seeks to engage students beyond the classroom as well, with hundreds of extracurricular and social opportunities available.

Location

Boston provides an environment rich in intellectual and cultural stimuli; no other city in the world can compete with Boston's remarkable concentration of higher education facilities, world-renowned medical centers, and historic and cultural attractions. Students make up 20 percent of Boston's population during the academic year, enhancing the atmosphere of learning and excitement. The city provides many opportunities for impressive internship and research positions as well. Boston is also a world-class center for attractions including the Museum of Fine Arts, Fenway Park, the Boston Symphony Orchestra, and a thriving theater district.

Majors and Degrees

Boston University grants the B.A., B.S., B.S.B.A., B.L.S., Mus.B., and B.F.A. undergraduate degrees. Of the University's sixteen schools and colleges, nine offer opportunities for undergraduate study.

As BU's largest academic division, the College of Arts and Sciences (CAS) offers a diverse learning community with world-class research faculty. Students may major in American studies; ancient Greek; ancient Greek and Latin; anthropology; anthropology and religion; archaeology; architectural studies; astronomy; astronomy and physics; biochemistry and molecular biology; biology; biology with a specialization in behavioral biology; biology with a specialization in cell biology, molecular biology, and genetics; biology with a specialization in ecology and conservation biology; biology with a specialization in neurobiology; biology with a specialization in quantitative biology; chemistry; chemistry with specialization in biochemistry; chemistry with specialization in teaching; Chinese language and literature; classical civilization; classics and philosophy; classics and religion; comparative literature; computer science; earth sciences; East Asian studies; economics; economics and mathematics; English; environmental analysis and policy; environmental science; European studies; French studies; geography with a specialization in human geography; geography with a specialization in physical geography; geophysics and planetary sciences; German language and literature; Hispanic language and literatures; history; history of art and architecture; international relations; Italian studies; Japanese language and literature; Latin; Latin American studies; linguistics; linguistics and philosophy; marine science; mathematics (includes statistics); mathematics and computer science; mathematics and mathematics

education; mathematics and philosophy; music (nonperformance); neuroscience; philosophy; philosophy and physics; philosophy and political science; philosophy and psychology; philosophy and religion; physics; political science; pre-dentistry; pre-law; pre-medicine; pre–veterinary medicine; psychology; religion; Russian language and literature; and sociology. Special curricula include seven-year accelerated programs in liberal arts medicine or liberal arts dentistry; the Modular Medical Integrated Curriculum (MMEDIC); the BU dual-degree program; the CFA/CAS double-degree program; and various combined B.A./M.A. degree programs.

The College of Fine Arts (CFA) offers programs in the School of Music (composition, music education, music-nonperformance, musicology, and performance), the School of Theatre (acting, design, stage management, production, and theater arts/performing), and the School of Visual Arts (art education, graphic design, painting, and sculpture). There is also a double-degree program that allows students to earn two Bachelor's degrees simultaneously in the CFA and the CAS.

The College of General Studies (CGS) offers a demanding, two-year program in the liberal arts and sciences that features an integrated core curriculum. It stresses an interdisciplinary approach to teaching. After two years, students continue into one of BU's degree-granting schools or colleges to complete their studies.

Located in one of the largest media markets in the nation, the College of Communication (COM) offers majors in communication (advertising, public relations, communication); film and television (production, writing, management); and journalism (with specialization available in broadcast, magazine, news-editorial, online, and photojournalism).

Majors in the College of Engineering (ENG) include biomedical engineering (a program ranked eighth in the country by *U.S. News & World Report*), computer engineering, electrical engineering, mechanical engineering, mechanical engineering with specialization in aerospace, and mechanical engineering with specialization in manufacturing.

The College of Health and Rehabilitation Sciences: Sargent College (SAR) is one of the oldest and most prestigious health sciences schools in the country. It offers programs in athletic training; health science; human physiology; nutrition; and speech, language, and hearing sciences. Also offered are a rigorous five-year combined B.S./M.S. degree program in occupational therapy, ranked first in the country by *U.S. News & World Report;* a six-year B.S./D.P.T. program; and a six-year program resulting in a B.S. in athletic training/D.P.T.

Areas of concentration in the School of Education (SED) include bilingual education, deaf studies, early childhood education, elementary education, English education, Latin and classical studies education, mathematics education, modern foreign language education, science education, social studies education, and special education. SED is ranked in the top 3 percent of education schools in the country by *U.S. News & World Report.*

Located in one of the hospitality and tourism capitals of the world, the School of Hospitality Administration (SHA) offers a rigorous program in the management of hotels, restaurants, food and beverage service, travel and tourism, and entertainment.

With a unique global curriculum, the School of Management (SMG) offers majors in accounting, business law, entrepreneurship, finance, general management, international management, management information systems, marketing, operations and technology management, and organizational behavior. High-achieving students are invited to participate in specialized colloquia and seminars through the SMG honors program.

Academic Programs

A Boston University education combines the elements of a traditional liberal arts education with training for the professions. There are 250 programs of study to choose from, including BU's

top-ranked biomedical engineering, occupational therapy, deaf studies, international relations, management information systems, journalism, theatre, and archeology programs. Highly qualified freshmen may also be invited to participate in the prestigious Arvind and Chandan Nandlal Kilachand Honors College.

Boston University has more than ninety study-abroad opportunities that take students around the world for courses, internships, and fieldwork. Opportunities are offered on six continents, in over twenty-five countries, and in cities such as Auckland, Beijing, Dresden, London, Los Angeles, Madrid, Paris, Sydney, and Washington, D.C. Programs offered include studies in art/architecture, business/economics, engineering, health and human services, journalism/communications, visual/performing arts, and many more. Fieldwork programs may be found in locations that include Ecuador and Spain, with study-abroad options that include programs in Grenoble, Padova, Quito, and Venice. Summer study programs are available in Argentina, Australia, China, England, France, Ireland, Italy, Peru, Spain, and the United States.

BU's Center for Career Development works to provide students the resources they need to get internships or part-time jobs in any number of fields.

Boston University operates on a calendar of two semesters and two summer terms. Students generally take four courses each semester; thirty-two courses are required for graduation. Most degree programs are built around a core of humanities and social and natural sciences. Concentrations require eight to thirteen courses. Electives generally total 30–40 percent of the courses taken, allowing for interdisciplinary study.

Academic Facilities

The new 106,000-square-foot student center on Boston University's East Campus is set to open in fall 2012. This building will be home to BU's Center for Career Development, Educational Resource Center with pre-med and pre-law advising services, and several student dining and common areas. West campus now features the modern Student Village, including Agganis Arena; the Fitness and Recreation Center, complete with a 35-foot rock wall; and high-rise, apartment-style dorms. BU also has a life science and engineering facility with 187,000-square-feet of laboratory and research space for the biology, bioinformatics, chemistry, and bioengineering departments. The state-of-the-art Photonics Center features classroom and laboratory space for the College of Engineering as well as labs designed to support industry partners who seek to develop new photonics-based products. The School of Management building also offers technologically advanced educational facilities, with a dedicated career center and management library.

Through Boston University Information Services and Technology, students have access to public computing facilities equipped with workstations, terminals, and laser printers as well as a high-speed campus network. An 890-seat proscenium theater, studio space for visual arts students, practice rooms for music, and a 575-seat music performance center are indicative of BU's support for the arts. More than 2.8 million library volumes and more than 4.7 million microform units are contained in Mugar Memorial Library, where the Twentieth-Century Archives are held, including the papers of Dr. Martin Luther King, Jr., Theodore Roosevelt, Robert Frost, and Bette Davis.

Costs

Tuition for 2011–12 was $40,848, estimated room and board costs were $12,710, and University and college fees were $572. These costs are exclusive of books, supplies, transportation, and personal expenses.

Financial Assistance

Boston University helps students realize their dreams with several different kinds of financial aid: BU scholarships, federal and state grants, federal loans, federal work-study awards, and financing and payment plan options. Financial aid is offered on the basis of calculated financial eligibility, and two or more types of aid are often combined in award packages. Approximately 74 percent of students who apply for aid and enroll at BU receive assistance. Students must submit the FAFSA and the CSS/Financial Aid PROFILE by established deadlines to be considered. In addition, the Trustee Scholarship (full tuition) and the Presidential Scholarship ($20,000) are offered to the highest achieving students who apply for admission.

Boston University makes every effort to assist students with calculated financial eligibility, however funds are limited. All applicants who anticipate the need for financial aid are encouraged to apply.

Faculty

Seventy-eight percent of BU faculty members have a Ph.D. or equivalent and include Nobel Prize winners, Guggenheim scholars, Emmy Award winners, and Sloan Research Fellows. In addition to fulfilling their classroom responsibilities, faculty members are accessible as academic and career advisers who assist students in obtaining internships as well research opportunities.

Admission Requirements

The Board of Admissions considers each candidate individually. Primary emphasis is placed on the strength of the secondary school record, but required test scores, character, breadth of interest, school recommendations, and other personal qualifications are also carefully evaluated. Students are required to submit the SAT or the ACT (with writing). SAT Subject Tests are recommended, but not required, for students submitting the SAT. A full listing of the standardized testing requirements can be found in the requirements and standards chart at http://www.bu.edu/admissions/apply/freshman/program-requirements. Secondary school graduation or an equivalency diploma is required of all candidates; for the College of Fine Arts a prescreening, audition, or a portfolio may be required, depending on the program of interest. For certain programs, interviews and SAT Subject Test scores are required. Boston University offers programs of early decision (binding agreement), early admission, and deferred admission.

Transfer applicants are considered for September or January entrance. Transfer students are not eligible for admission to the accelerated liberal arts medical or dental programs. January admission to the College of Fine Arts School of Theatre is also not available to transfer students.

Boston University admits qualified students to all its programs and activities regardless of their race, color, national origin, religion, sex, age, or disability.

Application and Information

Boston University requires the Common Application and the Boston University Supplement. Information on applying is available online at http://www.bu.edu/admissions/apply. The deadline for regular decision applications is January 1. Applicants for early decision must apply by November 1. Accelerated medical and dental program applications are due November 15. The deadline for the Trustee Scholarship (full tuition) and the Presidential Scholarship ($20,000) is December 1. Students must submit the College Scholarship Service (CSS) Financial Aid PROFILE and the Free Application for Federal Student Aid (FAFSA) by February 15.

Transfer students applying for September admission should submit their applications, CSS/Financial Aid PROFILE forms, and Free Application for Federal Student Aid (FAFSA) forms by April 1 or by November 1 for January admission.

Boston University Admissions
121 Bay State Road
Boston, Massachusetts 02215
Phone: 617-353-2300
E-mail: admissions@bu.edu
Web site: http://www.bu.edu/admissions
        http://www.facebook.com/BUadmissions
        http://www.twitter@applytobu

BOWIE STATE UNIVERSITY
BOWIE, MARYLAND

The University

Bowie State University began as a normal school in the city of Baltimore in 1865, and it has evolved over the years into a four-year, coeducational, liberal arts institution. It is currently situated on a beautiful 500-acre campus in Prince Georges County, Maryland, and offers both graduate and undergraduate programs of study. Teacher education programs were established in 1925; in 1935, with state authorization, a four-year program for the training of elementary school teachers was begun and the school became the Maryland State Teachers College at Bowie. In 1951, with the approval of the State Board of Education, its governing body at the time, the college established a teacher-preparation curriculum for the training of teachers for the core program in the junior high schools. Ten years later, permission was granted to institute a teacher-training program for secondary education. A liberal arts program was established in 1963, and the institution's name was changed to Bowie State College. In 1988, Bowie State achieved university status and joined the University System of Maryland (USM).

Bowie State University's physical plant is valued at more than $225 million, and its current enrollment is 5,578 students, 1,217 of whom are in the Graduate School. The University has twenty-two buildings on campus with the addition of the $21-million state-of-the-art Center for Learning and Technology that opened in 2000, the $11.8-million Computer Science Center that opened in 2002, and the $19-million Center for Business and Graduate Studies opened in 2007. Two of the buildings, the Communication Arts Center and the physical education complex, were completed in 1973, and an administration building opened in 1977. Seven residence halls, including Goodloe Hall and Alex Haley Hall, a state-of-the-art residence hall that houses honors students, house approximately 850 students. In addition, a 460-bed apartment-style residence hall, Christa McAuliffe, was completed in 2004. The $2.6-million physical education complex houses a 3,000-seat basketball arena, an Olympic-size swimming pool with underwater viewing windows and facilities for 200 spectators, an apparatus gymnasium, a dance studio, a wrestling room, a weight-training room, eight handball/squash courts, a therapy room, and offices for instructors and coaches. The $5.5-million University Activities Center includes a cafeteria. Bowie State has broken ground for its new $79 million Fine and Performing Arts Center. The 123,000-square-foot building will include a 400-seat main theater, a 200-seat black box theater, a 200-seat recital hall, an art gallery, classrooms, labs, and offices.

Bowie State University considers the student activities program a vital part of the total educational program. Students have access to more than forty different activities. These include student government, the student union, intercollegiate athletics, eight fraternities and sororities, numerous departmental clubs and preprofessional organizations, and music and drama organizations.

The Graduate School grants the Master of Arts in counseling psychology, English, human resource development, mental health counseling, organizational communications, school psychology, and teaching (M.A.T.); the Master of Business Administration; the Master of Education in elementary education, reading education, school administration and supervision, school counseling, secondary education, and special education; the Master of Public Administration; and the Master of Science in applied computational mathematics, computer science, management information systems, and nursing. The Doctor of Education is granted in educational leadership and the Applied Doctor of Science is granted in computer science. The Adler-Dreikurs Institute of Human Relations at Bowie State University is the first fully accredited master's-degree-granting Adlerian institute in the United States.

Bowie State University admits students without regard to sex, religion, or nationality, and the University does not discriminate on the basis of race, creed, color, national or ethnic origin, age, sex, or handicap. The University is accredited by the Middle States Association of Colleges and Schools and approved by the Maryland State Department of Education. Its programs in teacher education, social work education, nursing, business, and computer science are accredited by the National Council for Accreditation of Teacher Education, the National Council on Social Work Education, the National League for Nursing Accrediting Commission, the Maryland Board of Nursing, the Association of Collegiate Business Schools and Programs, and the Computer Science Accreditation Commission of the Computing Sciences Accreditation Board, respectively.

Location

Bowie, Maryland, is in a triangle formed by Annapolis (20 miles east), Baltimore (25 miles north), and Washington, D.C. (17 miles southwest). The suburban setting provides an ideal, safe environment for students and scholars, with access to all of the important cultural, governmental, and business activities in any of the three metropolitan areas.

Majors and Degrees

Bowie State University offers the Bachelor of Arts or Bachelor of Science degree with majors in bioinformatics, biology, business administration, communications media, computer science, computer technology, early childhood education, elementary education, English, English education, fine art, government, history, mathematics, nursing, child and adolescent studies, psychology, science education, social work, sport management, sociology/criminal justice, and technology. A dual-degree program is offered in engineering.

Academic Programs

The University operates on a semester calendar. Academic offerings are housed under four schools (School of Arts and Sciences, School of Education, School of Professional Studies, and the new School of Business) and can be divided into four main areas: humanities, science and mathematics, social sciences, and education. To receive a bachelor's degree, a student must earn a minimum of 120 semester hours with a cumulative grade point average of 2.0 or better. Students are provided the opportunity to complete the General Education Program, acquire lifelong learning skills for a competitive world, and make a successful transition into their junior year. General studies requirements include communication skills, 9 hours; humanities, 9 hours; social sciences, 18 hours; science and mathematics, 9 hours; and physical education, 2 hours. The remaining credit hours can be electives or from major and minor areas of interest. Students must also pass the test of Proficiency in the English Language and must take the national standardized test in their major area.

The Honors Program is designed for students with outstanding academic records and potential and provides a special educational opportunity for young adults with exceptional talent. The program is comprehensive and multidisciplinary in structure and interdisciplinary in application. It has been designed to provide a creative approach to the teaching/learning process and to present activities that encourage the shaping of students' own experiences.

The Special Services Project is a federally funded program designed to retain and graduate first-generation, low-income, and disabled students who have been admitted to Bowie State

University. The purpose of the project is to help students overcome academic and nonacademic barriers to academic success, through participation in specially designed activities, including counseling, tutoring, and workshops on test taking and study skills.

Through the Cooperative Education Program, a student may choose either the alternate or parallel programs of study and work in business, industry, government, or a social-service agency. This program is open to Bowie State students who have completed at least one academic year with a minimum cumulative grade point average of 2.0.

The University participates in the College-Level Examination Program (CLEP), administered by the Educational Testing Service for the College Board, and in the Defense Activity for Non-Traditional Education Support (DANTES) program. The University also has a program for awarding students credit for learning acquired through life and work experience. Under this program, students document their backgrounds in a portfolio, which is reviewed by the faculty. Through all of these programs, qualified students may receive up to 30 credit hours toward their degree. In addition, the University offers an Army ROTC program. Two-year and three-year scholarships are available.

Academic Facilities

The Communication Arts Center, a $6.5-million building that houses the humanities division, contains classrooms, offices, conference rooms, and studio-laboratories and seats approximately 1,000 patrons. The $8.8-million, 345,514-volume Thurgood Marshall Library is centrally located on campus and provides excellent equipment and reference departments for the student body. The microfilm file contains 474,196 items; periodicals number 767. Campus research facilities include science laboratories, television and radio studios, language laboratories, and the Adler-Dreikurs Institute. Access to the library collection is provided through Victor Web, the electronic catalog that also links users to millions of USM volumes. The new Center for Learning and Technology, the main classroom building, features a new supercomputer (one of the fastest computers in the world), fourteen electronic classrooms, two interactive lecture halls, three computer labs, one speech lab, and a 300-seat auditorium and conference center. In addition, the new Computer Science Center has five classrooms and thirteen labs. Finally, the Center for Business and Graduate Studies, which opened in 2007, provides modern classrooms, labs, study space, offices, and administrative support space for the School of Business and the Division of Graduate Studies.

Costs

In 2011–12, the annual cost of tuition, fees, board, and room for a freshman who is a Maryland resident averaged $15,000; for a non-Maryland resident, the cost averaged $26,000. The annual cost for a commuting student who is a Maryland resident was about $7000; the cost for a commuting student who is not a Maryland resident was about $17,000.

Financial Aid

Federal Pell Grants, Supplemental Grants, Work-Study, Perkins Loans, and Direct Loans are available. University scholarships, tuition waivers, and diversity grants are awarded. Most awards are based on need. Academic scholarships could be offered to students with cumulative weighted grade point averages of at least 3.3 and minimum SAT (reading and math) scores of 1100. In addition, merit awards are given for athletics, music and fine arts, and ROTC. More than 77 percent of all undergraduate students receive some form of financial aid. Deadlines are March 1 for the fall semester and November 15 for the spring semester.

Faculty

More than 60 percent of the 160 full-time faculty members have earned doctoral degrees. The faculty-student ratio is 1:16.

Student Government

All students are members of the Student Government Association, which, in cooperation with the administration, sets the standards for student life. Students are encouraged to assume leadership roles and to participate in the various programs and activities of the University. The Residence Hall Council provides opportunities for students to participate in the administration of residence life and in the cultural growth of the campus community.

Admission Requirements

Maryland residents applying for admission should have a minimum cumulative grade point average in their core high school courses of 2.0 (on a 4.0 scale) and a minimum SAT (reading and math only) score of 900 (or a minimum ACT score of 19). A sliding scale is used for students who have higher grade point averages or SAT scores. Conditional admission may be offered to students with a minimum cumulative grade point average of 2.0 and minimum SAT (reading and math only) scores of 830 to 899 (or a minimum ACT score of 17). Applicants must have earned a high school diploma or a GED certificate. The following courses are required: English, 4 credits; social science/history, 3 credits; mathematics (algebra I, algebra II, and geometry), 3 credits; laboratory sciences, 2 credits; foreign language, 2 credits; and electives, 6 credits. A $40 application fee is charged, and a health certificate must be submitted before entering the University.

Transfer students must have a minimum 2.0 cumulative grade point average for a minimum of 24 transferable credits, or SAT scores are required. International students and mature adults are encouraged to apply.

Application and Information

The application deadline is April 1 for the fall semester and November 1 for spring. Students should apply online at http://www.bowiestate.edu/apply.

Admissions Office
Bowie State University
Bowie, Maryland 20715-9465
Phone: 301-860-3415
　　　　410-880-4100 Ext. 3415 (from the
　　　　　　Baltimore-Columbia area)
　　　　877-77-BOWIE (toll-free)
Fax: 301-860-3518
E-mail: undergradadmissions@bowiestate.edu
Web site: http://www.bowiestate.edu
　　　　http://www.facebook.com/bowiestate
　　　　http://twitter.com/bowiestate

Bowie State students often gather at the "Torch of Truth" near the center of campus.

BRIAR CLIFF UNIVERSITY
SIOUX CITY, IOWA

BRIAR•CLIFF
university
the catholic franciscan learning place

The University

Nurturing personal growth and professional promise—that's Briar Cliff University's goal. Perched on a hilltop in Northwest Iowa, Briar Cliff University (BCU) is a private institution rooted firmly in the liberal arts and sciences. This Catholic Franciscan institution welcomes students of all faiths. With academics that are second to none, the University believes the best education shapes more than a student's résumé but also their life and character.

Briar Cliff University's passion is an authentic interest in each person. Part of the University's mission as the Catholic Franciscan learning place is to provide a values-based experience that teaches students about personal integrity and social responsibility. BCU's core values are integrated in its culture and will make a huge difference in a student's life at Briar Cliff and beyond.

Briar Cliff is a vibrant campus where students succeed well beyond their expectations. BCU is where students become leaders and doers, where young men and women of diverse talents and interests share a commitment to serving those in need and caring for the environment.

Home to more than 1,150 students from 32 states and 11 countries, Briar Cliff provides a powerful sense of community, where the dignity of every individual is recognized. Students thrive in a supportive environment that fosters their personal growth and professional potential. The focus of the entire faculty and staff is on the students—even the University's president knows students by their names. Briar Cliff freshmen have access to Peer Advising Leaders, who are available to assist new students as they adjust to campus life. This exceptional student service sets Briar Cliff University apart.

BCU's Apple iPad program provides incoming Briar Cliff University freshmen with an Apple iPad tablet as part of the latest learning revolution. The ever-expanding library of books, textbooks, and educational iTunes U materials available through iPad technology fosters academic agility and provides cost savings. The iPad technology also makes studying more productive and enjoyable, allowing Briar Cliff students to be more efficient and attentive. For example, Briar Cliff theater students use a free application to construct potential theater sets and stage designs for productions. Science majors view internal structures of cells in 3-D with a free cell simulation app. With this technology, students have a wide variety of learning enhancement tools necessary for music, education, criminal justice, and other majors.

Briar Cliff professors are applying the new technology to develop multimedia curricula and to give students complete access to all course content. Some apps make textbooks interactive with peer learning experiences. If students have questions about passages, they can note or highlight the text for other students to see and respond.

Regardless of a student's personal or professional goals, a Briar Cliff University education prepares him or her well for the future. More than 93 percent of BCU students enter graduate school or begin working in their chosen fields.

Location

When students choose a college, they're choosing a second hometown. A dynamic metropolitan area of more than 140,000 residents, Sioux City is a great place to call home. Sioux City is a larger community that has a small-town feel. Students also appreciate the city's low crime rate, moderate cost of living, and the region's Midwestern hospitality.

Majors and Degrees

Briar Cliff University offers programs that lead to Bachelor of Arts and Bachelor of Science degrees.

The academic majors offered at BCU include accounting, art, biology, business administration, chemistry, computer science, criminal justice, education, elementary education, English, environmental science, graphic design, health, physical education and recreation, history, human resource management, journalism and mass communication, management information systems, marketing, mathematics, medical laboratory science, music, nursing, political science, professional studies, psychology, radiologic technology, secondary education, sociology, social work, Spanish, sports science, theater, theology, and writing.

Briar Cliff University offers pre-professional programs in chiropractic, church ministry, dentistry, engineering, law, medicine, occupational therapy, pharmacy, physical therapy, physician's assistant, and veterinary medicine.

Academic Programs

With more than 40 areas of study, Briar Cliff provides a challenging academic environment. Students receive a broad intellectual background with career development and a hands-on approach to career preparation. Internships, field studies, and research are all used in the curriculum.

Off-Campus Programs and Internships

Through internships, Briar Cliff students apply classroom learning to real-work situations. The region offers a wealth of internships and employment opportunities with nature centers, insurance companies, semi-pro sports teams, the court system, law enforcement, forensics, social service agencies, news media, and the YMCA. Many students also have internships in their hometowns.

Academic Facilities

Briar Cliff's main academic facility, Heelan Hall, is being expanded and renovated with the addition of a three-story, 16,650-square-foot wing. The completed project's design includes state-of-the-art science laboratories, lab prep rooms, classrooms, a business case room, and the project's signature piece—a four-story, 8,150-square-foot atrium with top-floor clerestory windows for natural light The expansion project will provide Briar Cliff biology and chemistry departments with several new labs, increasing opportunities for research projects and course offerings. Briar Cliff's cadaver lab will double in size, allowing many more students to take part in this valuable learning experience. The addition will allow generous space for nursing simulation labs and larger classrooms for enhanced learner experiences. The project also includes renovations to Heelan Hall, the historic jewel of the BCU campus, such as new heating, ventilation, and air conditioning systems along with the renovation of various classrooms and labs in the original structure.

The Bishop Mueller Library offers access to over 100,000 print and electronic resources. The library also has computer labs, study rooms, project collaboration spaces, and comfortable casual seating where students can work individually or collaboratively in small groups. Wireless network access is available throughout the facility. Notebook computers, iPad tablets, and digital media are available for check out at the library.

Costs

Briar Cliff University is ranked among the 2012 America's Best Regional Colleges by *U.S. News & World Report*. Offering high-quality, rigorous education, Briar Cliff's tuition for the 2012–13 academic year is $24,520.

Financial Aid

Briar Cliff is very affordable, with numerous scholarships and other forms of financial aid to help pay for your college tuition. On average, 98 percent of BCU students receive grants, scholarships, and/or other forms of financial assistance. The University understands the financial needs of families and works with them to provide generous scholarships to help with college tuition, including the following: Presidential Scholarships (full tuition); academic scholarships; art, music, and theater scholarships; athletic scholarships; transfer scholarships; Iowa Tuition Grants; Federal Pell Grants; Federal Perkins Loans; Federal SEOG Grants; Federal Direct Loans; Federal Work-study awards; Federal PLUS loans; and need-based grants.

Additional information regarding scholarship awards and other financial aid is available online at www.briarcliff.edu.

Faculty

Classes at Briar Cliff are small, averaging about 20 students. With a student-to-faculty ratio of 14:1, BCU students enjoy individualized attention from professors. Most Briar Cliff professors are full-time, and their first priority is teaching, not research. When Briar Cliff professors do research, they usually bring their findings right into their classes where students participate and classroom discussions flourish.

Student Activities

Campus life is rich with a wide variety of competitive sports, social activities, cultural events, international travel, spiritual growth, and service-learning and mission experiences.

At Briar Cliff, a majority of full-time students participate in at least one cocurricular activity. BCU has several nationally recognized intercollegiate athletic teams with a strong history of excellence in intercollegiate sports. Varsity student-athletes enjoy NAIA action in the highly competitive Great Plains Athletic Conference (GPAC).

The Briar Cliff University choirs have been lauded at performances in regional, national, and international venues, performing a wide variety of choral literature that embraces all genres. Briar Cliff students participate on the editorial staff for BCU's literary magazine, *The Briar Cliff Review,* widely acclaimed for its literary and artistic content, garnering multiple national awards. *The Briar Cliff Review* has published the works of 1,170 writers and artists from the United States and around the world.

Admission Requirements

Students applying to Briar Cliff University should have graduated from an accredited high school or home school with 16 units of high school work, including English, natural sciences, foreign language, social studies, mathematics, and 2 years (8 units) of high school foreign language, which fulfills the foreign language requirement. The requirement for total number of units and distribution of these units is flexible and can be found in the course catalog under Academics at www.briarcliff.edu. Exceptions may be made in certain cases in consultation with the Admissions Advisory Committee.

Applicants also should have satisfactory scores on the American College Test (ACT) or Scholastic Aptitude Test (SAT). This requirement is waived if the student has been out of high school five years or more. Students seeking full-time admission but whose test scores or GPA are below standard requirements may request their applications be reviewed by the Admissions Advisory Committee. These students will be asked to submit letters of recommendation.

Information for international students can be found online at www.briarcliff.edu under Prospective Students.

Application and Information

Briar Cliff University application information is available at www.briarcliff.edu; prospective students should click the Apply button. For BCU's Undergraduate Catalog, students should visit www.briarcliff.edu, select Academics, and then Undergraduate Catalog.

For additional information, students should contact:

Office of Admissions
Briar Cliff University
3303 Rebecca Street
Sioux City, Iowa 51104
Phone: 712-279-5200
        800-662-3303
Fax: 712-279-1632
E-mail: admissions@briarcliff.edu
Web site: http://www.briarcliff.edu

The Briar Cliff University campus in Sioux City, Iowa.

BRIDGEWATER COLLEGE
BRIDGEWATER, VIRGINIA

The College

Founded in 1880 as the first private, coeducational college in Virginia, Bridgewater College is committed to empowering every student to excel in their future lives and careers, embrace lifelong learning, understand personal and civic responsibility, develop ethical values, and become leaders in a global society.

Bridgewater offers Bachelor of Arts and Bachelor of Science degrees in more than sixty majors and minors. Through personalized advising programs, rigorous academics, and strong preprofessional programs, students are prepared to enter top graduate programs and pursue the careers they desire. Given its heritage of peace, justice, equality, service, and human dignity, the College has consistently promoted these values in an inclusive and caring community focused on developing the whole person—mind, body, and spirit.

Bridgewater College (BC) has a total enrollment of more than 1,650 students, with an average class size of 20, thus ensuring that the College provides a tightly knit academic community where faculty, staff, and students know each other on an individual basis. Students enjoy exceptional opportunities to work one-on-one with faculty mentors and engage in personalized independent study or directed research.

At Bridgewater, 85 percent of students live on campus in a variety of traditional residence halls, apartment buildings, and village-style community housing. The average age is 20, and 15 percent of students are from historically underrepresented races and ethnicities. Most Bridgewater students are residents of the Mid-Atlantic states, and six different countries are represented on campus.

With more than seventy social, cultural, religious, and academic clubs and organizations, there is an opportunity for everyone to be involved on campus. Theatrical and musical performances are integral to campus life, and nearly a third of the student body participates in intercollegiate athletics at the NCAA Division III level.

The Academic Support Center offers numerous services to Bridgewater students in need of special assistance, including disability services, an academic coach program, learning strategy workshops, and tutoring services. The Center for Cultural Engagement offers unique mentorship programs and support for students from all backgrounds, and the Center for International Education provides personal support for all international students.

Bridgewater College is accredited by the Commission on Colleges of the Southern Association of Colleges and Schools (1866 Southern Lane, Decatur, Georgia, 30033-4097; telephone: 404-679-4501) to award baccalaureate degrees.

Location

Bridgewater College is located in the heart of the Shenandoah Valley of Virginia, only two hours southwest of the Washington, D.C. metropolitan area. Situated in this beautiful and historic setting near the Blue Ridge Mountains, the Bridgewater campus is comprised of nearly 300 acres (including the BC Equestrian Center). The Valley area is rich in the history of the early United States and the Civil War. Air transportation is available through the Shenandoah Valley Regional Airport, 13 miles from the campus.

Majors and Degrees

Bridgewater College offers majors in applied physics (tracks in engineering physics, physical science, physics, technology), art, athletic training, biology, business administration, chemistry, communication studies, computer science, economics, English (tracks in language and literature, literary studies, writing), environmental science, family and consumer sciences, French, health and exercise science, health and physical education, history, history and political science, information systems management, international studies, liberal studies (available only to students in the elementary education program), mathematics, music, nutrition and wellness, philosophy and religion, physics, physics and mathematics, political science, psychology, sociology, and Spanish.

The College offers four-year curricula leading to the bachelor's degree and a program of teacher preparation at the PreK–6 (elementary) and 6–12 (secondary) levels approved by the state of Virginia.

Dual-degree programs are offered in engineering with George Washington University and Virginia Tech, nursing with Vanderbilt University, and physical therapy with Shenandoah University. Preprofessional programs are offered in dentistry, engineering, law, medicine, ministry, occupational therapy, pharmacy, physical therapy, and veterinary science.

Academic Programs

Bridgewater's emphasis on the liberal arts reflects a commitment to writing, public speaking, analytical and critical thinking, and global awareness and understanding.

To earn a Bachelor of Arts or Bachelor of Science degree, students must do the following:

- Complete a minimum of 123 credit hours with a minimum of 48 credit hours chosen from junior- and senior-level courses.

- Complete general education requirements for the respective degree.

- Complete course requirements for the major.

- Earn a minimum cumulative GPA of 2.0 and a minimum GPA of 2.0 in courses required for the major.

- Complete a minimum of 33 credit hours with 30 of the last 33 credit hours of academic work in residence at Bridgewater College or at a College-approved study-abroad or Washington Semester program.

Students may be exempted from certain course requirements by demonstrating proficiency in written expression, quantitative reasoning, or foreign languages. Credit and advanced placement are awarded to students on the basis of scores on Advanced Placement tests of the College Board. In order to be considered for unassigned credit, course credit, and/or exemption from certain requirements, students must earn scores of 3 or higher (varies by department) on Advanced Placement tests or a 5, 6, or 7 on the International Baccalaureate exams.

The academic calendar includes a fall semester, a three-week January interterm, and a spring semester, concluding with commencement exercises in mid-May.

The Dr. John S. Flory Fellowship of Scholars is an honors program consisting of stimulating and interesting opportunities both inside and outside the classroom. Students take a minimum

of six honors-designated courses plus a capstone seminar. First-year students begin the program with an honors section of PDP 150: Personal Development and the Liberal Arts, the College's freshman seminar.

Off-Campus Programs

The Center for International Education works to provide numerous international study experiences for BC students who wish to learn through immersion in another culture, whether for a few weeks, a semester, or even longer. Students have the option to study abroad for a semester through a College-approved study-abroad program at locations in Europe, Latin America, Africa, Asia, and Southeast Asia.

Additional study-abroad opportunities are available by participating in one or more interterm travel courses during the month of January. Bridgewater students have the opportunity to choose classes ranging from the study of marine ecology in the waters of the Atlantic to an exploration of the vast array of cultures in India. Interterm travel courses offer a study-abroad experience in a few short weeks, giving students expanded knowledge of another culture and inviting them to discover more about the world.

Academic Facilities

Bridgewater College has nine academic buildings on the main campus, including the McKinney Center for Science and Mathematics, which hosts all science laboratories and equips students with space to perform undergraduate research projects. The Alexander Mack Library gives students access to more than 174,000 books, electronic books, audio books, periodicals, and videos, as well as electronic access to more than 35,000 online journals in 80+ electronic databases and access to millions of online government documents through the library's membership in the government's electronic depository program.

Costs

In 2012–13, the comprehensive fee for residential students is $38,350; tuition and fees for a commuter student total $27,725. Accounts are payable by the semester or through a monthly payment plan arranged through an external agency.

Estimated miscellaneous costs range from $3380 for a residential student to $7400 for a nonresident.

Financial Aid

Scholarships, grants, loans, and on-campus jobs are available for qualified students through federal, state, institutional, and outside sources and are awarded in individualized financial aid packages. All applicants for need-based financial aid must submit the Free Application for Federal Student Aid (FAFSA) by March 1. A work-study program provides jobs for qualified students and early application is advised. Academic scholarships up to full tuition are awarded based on a student's GPA, SAT scores, and academic achievement. To be considered for an academic scholarship, a student must apply and be accepted. No additional application is necessary.

Faculty

Bridgewater College employs 106 full-time and 35 part-time instructional faculty members. Faculty members serve as faculty advisers, major professors, and sponsors of student organizations and activities. With a faculty-student ratio of 14:1, many professors at Bridgewater become mentors for their students, developing close working relationships as they take personal interest in each student's academic progress, oversee student research projects, and advise students in career preparations. Eighty-two percent of Bridgewater's full-time faculty members have terminal degrees.

Student Government

The student government acts as a representative of the student body by presenting student opinions and ideas to the faculty and administration and by interpreting the policies and standards of the College to the students. The student body president, vice president, and senators are elected by the students. The College Honor System is administered by the Honor Council, a judicial body composed of 9 students appointed by the student body president and with faculty members serving as advisers.

Active clubs include Eagle Productions, the student campus event-planning organization; faith-based organizations; pre-professional societies; clubs tailored to business, communications, and other majors; Student Senate; Habitat for Humanity; Pinion Players (theater), *Ripples* (the college yearbook), and *Veritas* (the college newspaper). A complete listing of the more than seventy clubs and organizations at BC can be found on the College Web site, www.bridgewater.edu.

Admission Requirements

Bridgewater College welcomes all applicants with a high school education or previous college experience, international students, and those looking to re-enter college for preparation for a new career.

Admissions decisions are made based on careful consideration of a student's academic achievement, including GPA, standardized test scores (SAT or ACT), curriculum, and letters of recommendation. Successful applicants are expected to have completed the following credits as part of their high school curriculum: 4 in English; 2 in one foreign language; 3 in college preparatory mathematics, to include algebra, geometry, and algebra II; 2 in social studies and history; 2 in sciences to include a lab unit(s); and 4 in suitable electives.

Application and Information

Application forms are available online at www.bridgewater.edu/admissions. Application deadlines are May 1 for fall semester and October 1 for spring semester. Under the College's rolling admissions policy, students can expect notification of the admission decision within thirty days of the College's receipt of all records and credentials.

For more information, students should contact:

Jarret L. Smith
Director of Admissions
Bridgewater College
402 East College Street
Bridgewater, Virginia 22812
Phone: 540-828-5375
    800-759-8328 (toll-free)
E-mail: admissions@bridgewater.edu
Web site: http://www.bridgewater.edu

Bridgewater College students on the campus mall.

BROWN MACKIE COLLEGE — AKRON

AKRON, OHIO

The College

Brown Mackie College — Akron (Brown Mackie College) is one of over twenty-five locations in the Brown Mackie College family of schools (www.brownmackie.edu), which is dedicated to providing educational programs that prepare students to pursue entry-level positions in a competitive, rapidly changing workplace. Brown Mackie College schools offer bachelor degree, associate degree, diploma, and certificate programs in health sciences, business, information technology, legal studies, and design to more than 20,000 students in the Midwest, Southeast, Southwest, and Western United States.

Brown Mackie College was founded in Cincinnati, Ohio, in February 1927, as a traditional business college. In March 1980, the college added a branch campus in Akron, Ohio. The college outgrew this space and relocated to its current address in January 2007.

Brown Mackie College — Akron is accredited by the Accrediting Council for Independent Colleges and Schools to award bachelor degrees, associate degrees, and diplomas. The Accrediting Council for Independent Colleges and Schools is listed as a nationally recognized accrediting agency by the United States Department of Education and is recognized by the Council for Higher Education Accreditation. ACICS can be contacted at 750 First Street NE, Suite 980, Washington, D.C. 20002; phone: 202-336-6780.

Brown Mackie College — Akron is licensed by the Ohio State Board of Career Colleges and Schools, 30 East Broad Street, 24th Floor, Suite 2481, Columbus, Ohio 43215-3138; phone: 614-466-2752. Ohio registration # 03-09-1685T.

The Associate of Applied Science in Medical Assisting program is accredited by the Commission of Accreditation of Allied Health Education Programs (www.caahep.org) upon the recommendation of the Curriculum Review Board of the Medical Assisting Education Review Board (MAERB). The Commission on Accreditation of Allied Health Education Programs is located at 1361 Park Street, Clearwater, Florida 33756; phone: 727-210-2350.

The Associate of Applied Science in Surgical Technology program is accredited by the Commission on Accreditation of Allied Health Education Programs (www.caahep.org) upon the recommendation of the Accreditation Review Council on Education in Surgical Technology and Surgical Assisting (ARC/STSA). The Commission on Accreditation of Allied Health Education Programs is located at 1361 Park Street, Clearwater, Florida 33756; phone: 727-210-2350; www.caahep.org.

The Associate of Applied Science in Occupational Therapy Assistant program is accredited by the Accreditation Council for Occupational Therapy Education (ACOTE) of the American Occupational Therapy Association (AOTA), located at 4720 Montgomery Lane, P.O. Box 31220, Bethesda, Maryland 20824-1220. ACOTE's phone number c/o AOTA is 301-652-AOTA.

The Associate of Applied Science in Veterinary Technology program has provisional programmatic accreditation granted by the American Veterinary Medical Association (AVMA) through the Committee on Veterinary Technician Education and Activities (CVTEA).

Location

Brown Mackie College — Akron is located at 755 White Pond Drive in Akron, Ohio.

Programs of Study and Degrees

Brown Mackie College — Akron provides higher education to traditional and nontraditional students through bachelor and associate degree and diploma programs that can assist them in enhancing their career opportunities, broadening their perspectives through appropriate general education courses, thinking independently and critically, and improving problem-solving abilities.

The Bachelor of Science degree is awarded in business administration, criminal justice, health care management, and legal studies.

The Associate of Applied Business degree is awarded in accounting technology, business management, criminal justice, and paralegal. The Associate of Applied Science degree is awarded in computer networking and applications, health care administration, information technology, medical assisting, occupational therapy assistant, pharmacy technology, surgical technology, and veterinary technology.

Brown Mackie College offers diploma programs in accounting, business, computer software applications, criminal justice, medical assistant, medical coding and billing, paralegal assistant, and practical nursing.

The American Medical Technologists (AMT), which offers the certification for Registered Medical Assistant (RMA), accepts the accreditation of Brown Mackie College — Akron. Students will qualify to take the Registered Medical Assistant certification examination upon graduating the Brown Mackie College — Akron Medical Assisting and Medical Assistant programs. Graduates of the 48-credit-hour Medical Assistant program are not qualified to take the AMT/RMA exam.

Brown Mackie College — Akron does not guarantee third-party certification. Outside agencies control the requirements for certifications and are subject to change without notice to Brown Mackie College.

Academic Programs

Each college quarter comprises twelve weeks. Bachelor degree programs require a minimum of fifteen quarters to complete. Associate degree programs require a minimum of eight quarters to complete. Programs are offered on a year-round basis, providing students with the ability to work uninterrupted toward their degree. Brown Mackie College offers all programs

in a unique One-Course-a-Month format. This schedule allows students to focus studies on only one course for four weeks and has proven convenient for students with multiple obligations, such as jobs and family.

Academic Facilities

Brown Mackie College provides media presentation rooms for special instructional needs, a library that provides instructional resources and academic support for both faculty members and students, and qualified and experienced faculty members who are committed to the academic and technical preparation of their students. Brown Mackie College is nonresidential; students who are unable to commute daily from their homes may request assistance from the Office of Admissions in locating off-campus housing. The college is accessible by public transportation and provides ample parking, available at no charge.

Costs

Tuition for the 2011–12 academic year was $294 per credit hour and $15 per credit hour for general fees. Tuition for the practical nursing program was $361 per credit hour and $25 per credit hour for general fees. Tuition for the surgical technology program was $340 per credit hour and $15 per credit hour for general fees. Tuition for the occupational therapy assistant program was $361 per credit hour and $15 per credit hour for general fees. The cost of textbooks and other instructional materials varies by program.

Financial Aid

Financial aid is available to those who qualify. The college maintains a full-time staff of Student Financial Services Advisors to assist qualified students in obtaining financial assistance. The college participates in several student aid programs. Forms of financial aid available through federal resources include the Federal Pell Grant Program, Federal Supplemental Educational Opportunity Grant (FSEOG) Program, Federal Work-Study Program, Federal Stafford Student Loan Program (subsidized and unsubsidized), and the Federal PLUS Loan Program. Eligible students may also apply for veterans' educational benefits. Students with physical or mental disabilities that are a handicap to employment may be eligible for training services through the state Agency for Vocational Rehabilitation. For further information, students should contact the Student Financial Services Office.

Each year, the college makes available President's Scholarships of $1000 each to qualifying seniors from area high schools. Up to three (3) scholarships may be awarded per high school. In order to qualify, a senior must be graduating from a participating high school, must have maintained a cumulative grade point average of at least 2.0, and must have submitted a brief essay. The student's extracurricular activities and community service are also considered. These scholarships are available only to students enrolling in one of the college's degree programs. Students awarded the scholarship must enroll at Brown Mackie College between June and September immediately following their high school graduation. Applications for these scholarships can be obtained from the guidance departments of participating high schools and must be completed and returned to Brown Mackie College by March 31.

Faculty

There are 20 full-time and 39 part-time faculty members. The student-faculty ratio is 17:1.

Admission Requirements

Each applicant for admission is assigned an Assistant Director of Admissions who directs the applicant through the steps of the admissions process, providing information on curriculum, policies, procedures, and services and assisting the applicant in setting up necessary appointments and interviews.

To qualify for admission, each applicant must provide documentation of graduation from an accredited high school or from a state-approved secondary education curriculum or official documentation of high school graduation equivalency. All transcripts become the property of Brown Mackie College. Admission to Brown Mackie College is based upon the applicant meeting the stated requirements, a review of the applicant's previous education records, and a review of the applicant's career interests. If previous academic records indicate that the Brown Mackie College education and training programs would not benefit the applicant, the college reserves the right to advise the applicant not to enroll. Special requirements for enrollment into certain programs are discussed in the descriptions of those programs.

For the most recent information regarding admission requirements, please refer to the current academic catalog.

Application and Information

Applicants must complete and submit an application form along with documentation of graduation from an accredited high school or state-approved secondary education curriculum or official documentation of high school graduation equivalency. For additional information, prospective students should contact:

See BMCprograms.info for program duration, tuition, fees and other costs, median debt, federal salary data, alumni success, programmatic accreditation, and other important info.

For additional information, prospective students should contact:

Senior Director of Admissions
Brown Mackie College — Akron
755 White Pond Drive
Akron, Ohio 44320
United States
Phone: 330-869-3600
Fax: 330-869-3650
E-mail: bmcakadm@brownmackie.edu
Web site: http://www.brownmackie.edu/Akron

BROWN MACKIE — ALBUQUERQUE
ALBUQUERQUE, NEW MEXICO

BROWN
MACKIE
COLLEGE
ALBUQUERQUE℠

The College

Brown Mackie College — Albuquerque (Brown Mackie College) is one of over twenty-five locations in the Brown Mackie College family of schools (www.brownmackie.edu), which is dedicated to providing educational programs that prepare students to pursue entry-level positions in a competitive, rapidly changing workplace. Brown Mackie College schools offer bachelor degree, associate degree, diploma, and certificate programs in health sciences, business, information technology, legal studies, and design to over 20,000 students in the Midwest, Southeast, Southwest, and Western United States.

Brown Mackie College was originally founded and approved by the Board of Trustees of Kansas Wesleyan College in Salina, Kansas on July 30, 1892. In 1938, the college was incorporated as the Brown Mackie School of Business under the ownership of Perry E. Brown and A.B. Mackie, former instructors at Kansas Wesleyan University in Salina, Kansas. Their last names formed the name of Brown Mackie. By January 1975, with improvements in curricula and higher degree-granting status, the Brown Mackie School of Business became Brown Mackie College.

Brown Mackie College — Albuquerque is accredited by the Accrediting Council for Independent Colleges and Schools to award bachelor degrees, associate degrees, and diplomas. The Accrediting Council for Independent Colleges and Schools is listed as a nationally recognized accrediting agency by the

United States Department of Education and is recognized by the Council for Higher Education Accreditation. ACICS can be contacted at 750 First Street NE, Suite 980, Washington, D.C. 20002; phone: 202-336-6780.

The Associate of Applied Science in occupational therapy assistant program is accredited by the Accreditation Council for Occupational Therapy Education (ACOTE) of the American Occupational Therapy Association (AOTA), located at 4720 Montgomery Lane, P.O. Box 31220, Bethesda, Maryland 20824; phone: 301-652-AOTA.

Location

Brown Mackie College — Albuquerque is conveniently located at 10500 Copper Avenue NE, in Albuquerque, New Mexico. The college has a generous parking area and is easily accessible by public transportation.

Programs of Study and Degrees

Brown Mackie College — Albuquerque provides higher education to traditional and nontraditional students through bachelor degree, associate degree, and diploma programs that assist in enhancing their career opportunities, broadening their perspectives through appropriate general education courses, thinking independently and critically, and improving problem-solving abilities. The college strives to develop within its students the desire for lifelong and continued education.

The Bachelor of Science degree is awarded in business administration, criminal justice, health care management, and legal studies.

The Associate of Applied Science degree is awarded in accounting technology, architectural design and drafting technology, business management, criminal justice, health care administration, information technology, medical assisting, occupational therapy assistant, paralegal, pharmacy technology, surgical technology, and veterinary technology.

Brown Mackie College — Albuquerque offers diploma programs in accounting, business, criminal justice, medical assistant, and paralegal assistant.

The American Medical Technologists (AMT), which offers the certification for Registered Medical Assistant (RMA), accepts the accreditation of Brown Mackie College — Albuquerque. Students will qualify to take the Registered Medical Assistant certification examination upon graduating the Brown Mackie College—Albuquerque Medical Assisting and Medical Assistant programs. Graduates of the 48-credit-hour Medical Assistant program are not qualified to take the AMT/RMA exam.

Brown Mackie College—Albuquerque does not guarantee third-party certification. Outside agencies control the requirements for certifications and are subject to change without notice to Brown Mackie College.

Academic Programs

Each college quarter comprises twelve weeks. Bachelor degree programs require a minimum of sixteen quarters to complete. Associate degree programs require a minimum of eight quarters to complete. Programs are offered on a year-round basis, providing students with the ability to work uninterrupted toward completion of their programs. The college offers all programs in a unique One-Course-a-Month format. This allows students to focus studies on only one course for four weeks. This schedule has proven convenient for students with multiple obligations such as jobs and family.

Academic Facilities

A modern facility, Brown Mackie College — Albuquerque comprises more than 35,000 square feet. The college is equipped with multiple computer labs, housing over 100 computers. High-speed access to the Internet and other online resources are available to students and faculty. Multimedia classrooms are outfitted with overhead projectors, VCR/DVD players, and computers.

In 2012, Brown Mackie College — Albuquerque began its transition to using eTextbooks and computer tablets in the classroom. Utilizing these tablets to access expanded course material, students will be able to increase their acumen for using this technology and further enhance their educational experience. Students have the ability to directly download their eTextbooks to their tablet, eliminating the need to carry heavy, physical textbooks and reducing the overall cost of supplies.

Brown Mackie College is nonresidential; public transportation and ample parking at no cost are available. The campus is a smoke-free facility.

Costs

Tuition in the 2011–12 academic year for all bachelor and associate degrees and certificates was $324 per credit hour; fees were $20 per credit hour. Tuition for the occupational therapy assistant program was $355 per credit hour; fees were $20 per credit hour. Tuition for the surgical technology program was $339 per credit hour; fees were $20 per credit hour. The cost of textbooks and other instructional materials varies by program.

Financial Aid

Financial aid is available for those who qualify. Brown Mackie College maintains a full-time staff of Student Financial Services Advisors to assist qualified students in obtaining the financial assistance they require to meet their educational expenses. Available resources include federal and state aid, student loans from private lenders, and Federal Work-Study opportunities, both on and off college premises.

Each year, the college makes available President's Scholarships of $1000 each to qualifying seniors from area high schools. Up to three (3) scholarships may be awarded per high school. In order to qualify, a senior must have graduated from a participating high school, must have maintained a cumulative grade point average of at least 2.0, and must have submitted a brief essay. The student's extracurricular activities and community service are also considered. These scholarships are available only to students enrolling in one of the college's degree programs. Students awarded the scholarship must enroll at Brown Mackie College — Albuquerque between June and September immediately following their high school graduation. Applications for these scholarships can be obtained from the guidance departments of participating high schools. These applications must be completed and returned to Brown Mackie College by March 31.

Faculty

Experienced faculty members provide academic support and are committed to the academic and technical preparation of their students. The college has both full-time and part-time instructors, with a student-faculty ratio of 15:1.

Admission Requirements

Each applicant for admission is assigned an Assistant Director of Admissions who directs the applicant through the steps of the admissions process. Assistant Directors provide information on curriculum, policies, procedures, and services and assist the applicant in setting up necessary appointments and interviews. To qualify for admission, each applicant must provide documentation of graduation from an accredited high school or from a state-approved secondary education curriculum or provide official documentation of high school graduation equivalency. All transcripts become the property of the college. Admission to the college is based on the applicant meeting the stated requirements, a review of the applicant's previous educational records, and a review of the applicant's career interests. If previous academic records indicate the college's education and training programs would not benefit the applicant, the college reserves the right to advise the applicant not to enroll. Special requirements for enrollment into certain programs are discussed in the descriptions of those programs.

For the most recent information regarding admission requirements, prospective students should refer to the current academic catalog.

Application and Information

Applicants must complete and submit an application form, along with documentation of graduation from an accredited high school or state-approved secondary education curriculum or official documentation of high school graduation equivalency.

See BMCprograms.info for program duration, tuition, fees and other costs, median debt, federal salary data, alumni success, programmatic accreditation and other important info.

For additional information, prospective students should contact:
Director of Admissions
Brown Mackie College — Albuquerque
10500 Copper Avenue
Albuquerque, New Mexico 87123
United States
Phone: 505-559-5200
     877-271-3488 (toll-free)
Fax: 505-559-5222
E-mail: bmcalbadm@brownmackie.edu
Web site: http://www.brownmackie.edu/Albuquerque

BROWN MACKIE COLLEGE — BIRMINGHAM
BIRMINGHAM, ALABAMA

The College

Brown Mackie College — Birmingham (Brown Mackie College) is one of over twenty-five locations in the Brown Mackie College family of schools (www.brownmackie.edu), which is dedicated to providing educational programs that prepare students to pursue entry-level positions in a competitive, rapidly changing workplace. Brown Mackie College schools offer bachelor degree, associate degree, diploma, and certificate programs in health sciences, business, information technology, legal studies, and design to over 20,000 students in the Midwest, Southeast, Southwest, and Western United States.

Brown Mackie College was originally founded and approved by the Board of Trustees of Kansas Wesleyan College in Salina, Kansas on July 30, 1892. In 1938, the College was incorporated as the Brown Mackie School of Business under the ownership of Perry E. Brown and A.B. Mackie, former instructors at Kansas Wesleyan University in Salina, Kansas. Their last names formed the name of Brown Mackie. By January 1975, with improvements in curricula and higher degree-granting status, the Brown Mackie School of Business became Brown Mackie College.

Brown Mackie College — Birmingham is accredited by the Accrediting Council for Independent Colleges and Schools to award bachelor degrees, associate degrees, and diplomas. The Accrediting Council for Independent Colleges and Schools is listed as a nationally recognized accrediting agency by the United States Department of Education and is recognized by the Council for Higher Education Accreditation. ACICS can be contacted at 750 First Street NE, Suite 980, Washington, D.C. 20002; phone: 202-336-6780.

The Associate of Applied Science in occupational therapy assistant program has applied for accreditation by the Accreditation Council for Occupational Therapy Education (ACOTE) of the American Occupational Therapy Association (AOTA), 4720 Montgomery Lane, P.O. Box 31220, Bethesda, MD 20824-1220; phone: (301) 652-AOTA.

Location

Brown Mackie College — Birmingham is conveniently located at 105 Vulcan Road, in Birmingham, Alabama. The college has a generous parking area and is easily accessible by public transportation.

Programs of Study and Degrees

Brown Mackie College — Birmingham provides higher education to traditional and nontraditional students through bachelor degree, associate degree, and diploma programs that assist in enhancing their career opportunities, broadening their perspectives through appropriate general education courses, thinking independently and critically, and improving problem-solving abilities. The college strives to develop within its students the desire for lifelong and continued education.

The Bachelor of Science degree is awarded in business administration, health care management, and legal studies.

The Associate of Science degree is awarded in accounting technology, architectural design and drafting technology, biomedical equipment technology, business management, graphic design, health care administration, information technology, medical assisting, paralegal, and surgical technology.

The Associate of Applied Science degree is awarded in occupational therapy assistant.

The college offers diploma programs in accounting, business, dental assistant, healthcare administrative specialist, medical assistant, and paralegal assistant.

The American Medical Technologists (AMT), which offers the certification for Registered Medical Assistant (RMA), accepts the ac-creditation of Brown Mackie College — Birmingham. Students will qualify to take the Registered Medical Assistant certification ex-amination upon graduating the Brown Mackie College–Birmingham Medical Assisting and Medical Assistant programs. Graduates of the 48-credit-hour Medical Assistant program are not qualified to take the AMT/RMA exam.

Brown Mackie College — Birmingham does not guarantee third-party certification. Outside agencies control the requirements for certifications and are subject to change without notice to Brown Mackie College.

Academic Programs

Each college quarter comprises twelve weeks. Bachelor degree programs require a minimum of sixteen quarters to complete. Associate degree programs require a minimum of eight quarters to complete. Programs are offered on a year-round basis, providing students with the ability to work uninterrupted toward completion of their programs. The college offers all programs in a unique One-Course-a-Month format. This allows students to focus studies on only one course for four weeks. This schedule has proven convenient for students with multiple obligations, such as jobs and family.

Academic Facilities

A modern facility, Brown Mackie College offers approximately 35,000 square feet of classroom, computer and allied health labs, library, and office space. The college is equipped with multiple computer labs, housing over 100 computers. High-speed access to the Internet and other online resources are available to students and faculty. Multimedia classrooms are outfitted with overhead projectors, VCR/DVD players, and computers.

In 2012, Brown Mackie College began its transition to using eTextbooks and computer tablets in the classroom. Utilizing these tablets to access expanded course material, students will be able to increase their acumen for using this technology and further enhance their educational experience. Students have the ability to directly download their eTextbooks to their tablet, eliminating the need to carry heavy, physical textbooks and reducing the overall cost of supplies.

Brown Mackie College is nonresidential; public transportation and ample parking at no cost are available. The campus is a smoke-free facility.

Costs

Tuition in the 2011–12 academic year for all bachelor and associate degrees and certificates was $315 per credit hour; fees were $15 per credit hour. Tuition for the surgical technology program was $350 per credit hour; fees were $15 per credit hour. Tuition for the occupational therapy assistant program was $381 per credit hour; fees were $15 per credit hour. The cost of textbooks and other instructional materials varies by program.

Financial Aid

Financial aid is available for those who qualify. Brown Mackie College maintains a full-time staff of Student Financial Services Advisors to assist qualified students in obtaining the financial assistance they require to meet their educational expenses. Available resources include federal and state aid, student loans from private lenders, and Federal Work-Study opportunities, both on and off college premises.

Each year, the college makes available President's Scholarships of $1000 each to qualifying seniors from area high schools. Up to three (3) scholarships may be awarded per high school. In order to qualify, a senior must have graduated from a participating high school, must have maintained a cumulative grade point average of at least 2.0, and must have submitted a brief essay. The student's extracurricular activities and community service are also considered. These scholarships are available only to students enrolling in one of the college's degree programs. Students awarded the scholarship must enroll at Brown Mackie College — Birmingham between June and September immediately following their high school graduation. Applications for these scholarships can be obtained from the guidance departments of participating high schools.

These applications must be completed and returned to Brown Mackie College by March 31.

Faculty

Experienced faculty members provide academic support and are committed to the academic and technical preparation of their students. The college has both full-time and part-time instructors, with a student-faculty ratio of 15:1.

Admission Requirements

Each applicant for admission is assigned an Assistant Director of Admissions who directs the applicant through the steps of the admissions process. Assistant Directors provide information on curriculum, policies, procedures, and services and assist the applicant in setting up necessary appointments and interviews. To qualify for admission, each applicant must provide documentation of graduation from an accredited high school or from a state-approved secondary education curriculum or provide official documentation of high school graduation equivalency. All transcripts become the property of the college. Admission to the college is based on the applicant meeting the stated requirements, a review of the applicant's previous educational records, and a review of the applicant's career interests. If previous academic records indicate the college's education and training programs would not benefit the applicant, the college reserves the right to advise the applicant not to enroll. Special requirements for enrollment into certain programs are discussed in the descriptions of those programs.

For the most recent information regarding admission requirements, prospective students should refer to the current academic catalog.

Application and Information

Applicants must complete and submit an application form, along with documentation of graduation from an accredited high school or state-approved secondary education curriculum or official documentation of high school graduation equivalency.

See BMCprograms.info for program duration, tuition, fees and other costs, median debt, federal salary data, alumni success, programmatic accreditation, and other important info.

For additional information, prospective students should contact:
Director of Admissions
Brown Mackie College — Birmingham
105 Vulcan Road
Suite 100
Birmingham, Alabama 35209
United States
Phone: 205-909-1500
        888-299-4699 (toll free)
Fax: 205-909-1588
E-mail: bmbirmadm@brownmackie.edu
Web site: http://www.brownmackie.edu/Birmingham

BROWN MACKIE COLLEGE — BOISE

BOISE, IDAHO

The College

Brown Mackie College — Boise (Brown Mackie College) is one of over twenty-five locations in the Brown Mackie College family of schools (www.brownmackie.edu), which is dedicated to providing educational programs that prepare students to pursue entry-level positions in a competitive, rapidly changing workplace. Brown Mackie College schools offer bachelor degree, associate degree, diploma, and certificate programs in health sciences, business, information technology, legal studies, and design to over 20,000 students in the Midwest, Southeast, Southwest, and Western United States.

Brown Mackie College — Boise is accredited by the Accrediting Council for Independent Colleges and Schools to award bachelor degrees, associate degrees, and diplomas. The Accrediting Council for Independent Colleges and Schools is listed as a nationally recognized accrediting agency by the United States Department of Education and is recognized by the Council for Higher Education Accreditation. ACICS can be contacted at 750 First Street NE, Suite 980, Washington, D.C. 20002; phone: 202-336-6780.

The Associate of Applied Science in occupational therapy assistant program is accredited by the Accreditation Council for Occupational Therapy Education (ACOTE) of the American Occupational Therapy Association (AOTA), 4720 Montgomery Lane, P.O. Box 31220, Bethesda, Maryland 20824-1220; phone: 301-652-AOTA.

Location

Brown Mackie College — Boise is conveniently located at 9050 West Overland Road in Boise, Idaho. The college has a generous parking area and is easily accessible by public transportation.

Programs of Study and Degrees

Brown Mackie College — Boise provides higher education to traditional and nontraditional students through bachelor degree, associate degree, and diploma programs that assist in enhancing their career opportunities, broadening their perspectives through appropriate general education courses, thinking independently and critically, and improving problem-solving abilities.

The Bachelor of Science degree is awarded in business administration, criminal justice, health care management, and legal studies.

The Associate of Science degree is awarded in accounting technology, architectural design and drafting technology, bioscience laboratory technology, business management, criminal justice, health care administration, information technology, medical assisting, paralegal, and veterinary technology.

The Associate of Applied Science degree is awarded in occupational therapy assistant.

Diploma programs are offered in accounting, business, criminal justice, medical assistant, and paralegal assistant.

The American Medical Technologists (AMT), which offers the certification for Registered Medical Assistant (RMA), accepts the accreditation of Brown Mackie College — Boise. Students will qualify to take the Registered Medical Assistant certification examination upon graduating the Brown Mackie College — Boise Medical Assisting and Medical Assistant programs. Graduates of the 48-credit-hour Medical Assistant program are not qualified to take the AMT/RMA exam.

Academic Programs

Each college quarter comprises twelve weeks. Bachelor degree programs require a minimum of sixteen quarters to complete. Associate degree programs require a minimum of eight quarters to complete. Programs are offered on a year-round basis, providing students with the opportunity to work uninterrupted toward completion of their programs. The college offers all programs in a unique One-Course-a-Month format. This allows students to focus studies on only one course for four weeks. This schedule has proven convenient for students with multiple obligations, such as jobs and family.

Academic Facilities

Opened in 2008, this modern facility offers more than 40,000 square feet of tastefully decorated classrooms, laboratories, and office space designed to specifications of the Brown Mackie College for its business, medical, and technical programs. Instructional equipment is comparable to current technology used in business and industry. Modern classrooms for special instructional needs offer multimedia capabilities with surround sound and overhead projectors accessible through computer or DVD. Internet access and instructional resources are available at the college's library. Experienced faculty members provide academic support and are committed to the academic and technical preparation of their students.

In 2012, Brown Mackie College — Boise began its transition to using eTextbooks and computer tablets in the classroom. Utilizing these tablets to access expanded course material, students will be able to increase their acumen for using this technology and further enhance their educational experience.

Students have the ability to directly download their eTextbooks to their tablet, eliminating the need to carry heavy, physical textbooks and reducing the overall cost of supplies.

The campus is nonresidential; public transportation and ample parking at no cost are available.

Costs

Tuition for programs in the 2011–12 academic year was $324 per credit hour, with a general fee of $15 per credit hour applied to instructional costs for activities and services. Textbooks and other instructional materials vary by program. Tuition for the occupational therapy assistant courses was $381 per credit hour with a $15 per credit fee applied to instructional costs for activities and services.

Financial Aid

Financial aid is available for those who qualify. The college maintains a full-time staff of Student Financial Services Advisors to assist qualified students in obtaining financial assistance. The college participates in several student aid programs. Forms of financial aid available through federal resources include the Federal Pell Grant Program, Federal Supplemental Educational Opportunity Grant (FSEOG) Program, Federal Work-Study Program, Federal Perkins Loan Program, Federal Stafford Student Loan Program (subsidized and unsubsidized), and the Federal PLUS Loan Program.

Each year, the college makes available President's Scholarships of $1000 each to qualifying seniors from area high schools. Up to three (3) scholarships may be awarded per high school. In order to qualify, a senior must be graduating from a participating high school, must be maintaining a cumulative grade point average of at least 2.0, and must submit a brief essay. The student's extracurricular activities and community service are also considered. The President's Scholarship is available only to students enrolling in one of the college's degree programs. Students awarded the scholarship must enroll at Brown Mackie College — Boise between June and September immediately following their high school graduation. Applications for these scholarships can be obtained from the guidance departments of participating high schools. These applications must be completed and returned to Brown Mackie College by March 31.

Faculty

There are 14 full-time and 34 part-time faculty members at the college. The average student-faculty ratio is 15:1. Each student is assigned a program department chair as an adviser.

Admission Requirements

Each applicant for admission is assigned an Assistant Director of Admissions who directs the applicant through the steps of the admissions process. Assistant Directors provide information on curriculum, policies, procedures, and services and assist the applicant in setting up necessary appointments and interviews. To qualify for admission, each applicant must provide documentation of graduation from an accredited high school or from a state-approved secondary education curriculum or provide official documentation of high school graduation equivalency. All transcripts become the property of the college.

As part of the admission process, students are given an assessment of academic skills. Although the results of this assessment do not determine eligibility for admission, they provide the college with a means of determining the need for academic support as well as a means by which the college can evaluate the effectiveness of its educational programs. All new students are required to complete this assessment, which is readministered at the end of the student's program, so results may be compared with those of the initial admiistration.

In addition to the college's general admission requirements, applicants enrolling in the occupational therapy assistant program must document one of the following: a high school cumulative grade point average of at least 2.5, a score on the GED examination of at least 57 (557 if taken on or after January 15, 2002), or completion of 12 quarter-credit hours or 8 semester-credit hours of collegiate course work with a grade point average of at least 2.5. Credit hours may not include Professional Development (CF 1100), the Brown Mackie College–Boise course. Students entering the program must also have completed a biology course with a grade of at least a C (or an average of at least 2.0 on a 4.0 scale).

For the most recent information regarding admission requirements, prospective students should refer to the current academic catalog.

Application and Information

Applicants must complete and submit an application form, along with documentation of graduation from an accredited high school or state-approved secondary education curriculum or official documentation of high school graduation equivalency.

See BMCprograms.info for program duration, tuition, fees and other costs, median debt, federal salary data, alumni success, programmatic accreditation, and other important info.

For additional information, prospective students should contact:

Director of Admissions
Brown Mackie College — Boise
9050 W. Overland Road, Suite 100
Boise, Idaho 83709
United States
Phone: 208-321-8800
        888-810-9286 (toll-free)
Fax: 208-375-3249
E-mail: bmcboiadm@brownmackie.edu
Web site: http://www.brownmackie.edu/Boise

BROWN MACKIE COLLEGE — CINCINNATI

CINCINNATI, OHIO

The College

Brown Mackie College — Cincinnati (Brown Mackie College) is one of over twenty-five locations in the Brown Mackie College family of schools (www.brownmackie.edu), which is dedicated to providing educational programs that prepare students to pursue entry-level positions in a competitive, rapidly changing workplace. Brown Mackie College schools offer bachelor degree, associate degree, diploma, and certificate programs in health sciences, business, information technology, legal studies, and design to more than 20,000 students in the Midwest, Southeast, Southwest, and Western United States.

Brown Mackie College — Cincinnati was founded in February 1927 as Southern Ohio Business College. In 1978, the college's main location was relocated from downtown Cincinnati to the Bond Hill–Roselawn area and in 1995 to its current location at 1011 Glendale-Milford Road in the community of Woodlawn.

Brown Mackie College — Cincinnati is accredited by the Accrediting Council for Independent Colleges and Schools to award bachelor degrees, associate degrees, diplomas, and certificates. The Accrediting Council for Independent Colleges and Schools is listed as a nationally recognized accrediting agency by the United States Department of Education and is recognized by the Council for Higher Education Accreditation. ACICS can be contacted at 750 First Street NE, Suite 980, Washington, D.C. 20002; phone: 202-336-6780.

The Brown Mackie College — Cincinnati Associate of Applied Science degree in surgical technology is accredited by the Commission on Accreditation of Allied Health Education Programs (www.caahep.org), upon the recommendation of the Accreditation Review Committee on Education in Surgical Technology. The Commission on Accreditation of Allied Health Education Programs is located at 1361 Park Street, Clearwater, Florida 33756; phone: 727-210-2350.

The Brown Mackie College — Cincinnati veterinary technology program has provisional programmatic accreditation granted by the American Veterinary Medical Association (AVMA) through the Committee on Veterinary Technician Education and Activities (CVTEA).

The Associate of Applied Science in Medical Assisting program is accredited by the Commission on Accreditation of Allied Health Education Programs (www.caahep.org) upon the recommendation of the Curriculum Review Board of the Medical Assisting Education Review Board (MAERB). The Commission on Accreditation of Allied Health Education Programs is located at 1361 Park Street, Clearwater, FL 33756; phone: 727-210-2350.

The Practical Nursing diploma program complies with the Ohio Board of Nursing guidelines as set forth in the Ohio Administrative Code, Chapter 4723-5. The program is administered at the following locations: Brown Mackie College — Cincinnati, Brown Mackie College — Findlay, Brown Mackie College — Akron, and Brown Mackie College — North Canton, and all operate under the same approval. The Ohio Board of Nursing is located at 17 South High Street, Suite 400, Columbus, OH 43215-3413; phone: 614-466-3947.

Brown Mackie College — Cincinnati is licensed by the Ohio State Board of Career Colleges and Schools, 30 East Broad Street, 24th Floor, Suite 2481, Columbus, OH 43215-3138; phone: 614-466-2752. Ohio registration #03-09-1686T.

Brown Mackie College — Cincinnati is regulated by the Indiana Commission on Proprietary Education, 302 West Washington Street, Room E201, Indianapolis, Indiana 46204; phone: 800-227-5695 (toll-free) or 317-232-1320. Indiana advertising code: AC0150.

Location

Brown Mackie College — Cincinnati is located in the Woodlawn section of Cincinnati, Ohio. The college is accessible by public transportation and provides parking at no cost. For added convenience, the college also holds classes at the Norwood Learning Site at 4805 Montgomery Road in Norwood, Ohio.

Programs of Study and Degrees

Brown Mackie College — Cincinnati provides higher education to traditional and nontraditional students through bachelor degrees, associate degrees, diploma, and certificate programs that can assist them in enhancing their career opportunities, broadening their perspectives through appropriate general education courses, thinking independently and critically, and improving problem-solving abilities. The college strives to develop within its students the desire for lifelong and continued education.

The Bachelor of Science degree is awarded in business administration, criminal justice, health care management, and legal studies.

The Associate of Applied Business degree is awarded in accounting technology, business management, computer networking and applications, criminal justice, information technology, office management, and paralegal. The Associate of Applied Science degree is awarded in architectural design and drafting technology, audio/video production, biomedical equipment technology, early childhood education, health care administration, medical assisting, pharmacy technology, surgical technology, and veterinary technology.

Diploma programs are offered in accounting, audio/video technician, business, criminal justice, medical assistant, paralegal assistant, and practical nursing.

The college offers a certificate program in computer networking.

The American Medical Technologists (AMT), which offers the certification for Registered Medical Assistant (RMA), accepts the accreditation of Brown Mackie College — Cincinnati. Students will qualify to take the Registered Medical Assistant certification examination upon graduating the Brown Mackie College — Cincinnati Medical Assisting and Medical Assistant programs. Graduates of the 48-credit-hour Medical Assistant program are not qualified to take the AMT/RMA exam.

Brown Mackie College — Cincinnati does not guarantee third-party certification. Outside agencies control the requirements for certifications and are subject to change without notice to Brown Mackie College.

Academic Programs

Each college quarter comprises twelve weeks. Bachelor degree programs require a minimum of sixteen quarters to complete. Associate degree programs require a minimum of eight quarters to complete. Programs are offered on a year-round basis, providing students with the ability to work uninterrupted toward their degrees. The college offers all programs in a unique One-Course-a-Month format. This schedule allows students to focus studies on only one course for four weeks and has proven convenient for students with multiple obligations, such as jobs and family.

Academic Facilities

Brown Mackie College — Cincinnati consists of more than 57,000 square feet of classroom, laboratory, and office space at the main campus and more than 28,000 square feet at the learning site. Both sites are designed to specifications of Brown Mackie College for its business, computer, medical, and creative programs.

Costs

Tuition for the 2011–12 academic year was $294 per credit hour and $15 per credit hour for general fees. Tuition for the practical nursing program was $361 per credit hour and $25 per credit hour for general fees. Tuition for the surgical technology program was $340 per credit hour and $15 per credit hour for general fees. The cost of textbooks and other instructional materials varies by program.

Financial Aid

Financial aid is available to those who qualify. Brown Mackie College maintains a full-time staff of Student Financial Services Advisors to assist qualified students in obtaining financial assistance. The college participates in several student aid programs. Forms of financial aid available to qualified students through federal resources include the Federal Pell Grant Program, Federal Supplemental Educational Opportunity Grant (FSEOG) Program, Federal Work-Study Program, Federal Perkins Loan Program, Federal Stafford Student Loan Program (subsidized and unsubsidized), and the Federal PLUS Loan Program. Eligible students may apply for state awards, such as veterans' educational benefits. Students with physical or mental disabilities that are a handicap to employment may be eligible for training services through the state Agency for Vocational Rehabilitation. For further information, students should contact the Student Financial Services Office.

Each year, the college makes available President's Scholarships of $1000 each to qualifying seniors from area high schools. Up to three (3) scholarships may be awarded per high school. In order to qualify, a senior must be graduating from a participating high school, must have maintained a cumulative grade point average of at least 2.0, and must have submitted a brief essay. The student's extracurricular activities and community service are also considered. The President's Scholarship is available only to students enrolling in one of the college's degree programs. Students awarded the scholarship must enroll at Brown Mackie College — Cincinnati between June and September immediately following their high school graduation. Applications for these scholarships can be obtained from the guidance departments of participating high schools. These applications must be completed and returned to Brown Mackie College by March 31.

The Education Foundation was established in 2000 to offer scholarship support to students interested in continuing their education at one of the postsecondary, career-focused schools in the EDMC system. The number and amount of the awards can vary, depending on the funds available. Scholarship applications are considered every quarter. At Brown Mackie College — Cincinnati, applicants must be currently enrolled in an associate degree program and in their fourth quarter or higher (but no further than their second-to-last quarter) at the time of application. Awards are made based on academic performance and potential, as well as financial need.

Faculty

There are 33 full-time and 90 part-time faculty members. The average student-faculty ratio is 20:1. Each student has a faculty and student adviser.

Admission Requirements

Each applicant for admission is assigned an Assistant Director of Admissions, who directs the applicant through the steps of the admissions process, providing information on curriculum, policies, procedures, and services and assisting the applicant in setting up necessary appointments and interviews.

To qualify for admission, each applicant must provide documentation of graduation from an accredited high school or from a state-approved secondary education curriculum or provide official documentation of high school graduation equivalency. All transcripts become the property of the college. Admission to the college is based on the applicant meeting the stated requirements, a review of the applicant's previous educational records, and a review of the applicant's career interests. If previous academic records indicate that the college's education and training programs would not benefit the applicant, the college reserves the right to advise the applicant not to enroll. Special requirements for enrollment into certain programs are discussed in the descriptions of those programs.

For the most recent information regarding admission requirements, please refer to the current academic catalog.

Application and Information

Applicants must complete and submit an application form, along with documentation of graduation from an accredited high school or state-approved secondary education curriculum or official documentation of high school graduation equivalency.

See BMCprograms.info for program duration, tuition, fees and other costs, median debt, federal salary data, alumni success, programmatic accreditation, and other important info.

For additional information, prospective students should contact:
Senior Director of Admissions
Brown Mackie College — Cincinnati i
1011 Glendale-Milford Road
Cincinnati, Ohio 45215
United States
Phone: 512-771-2424
        800-888-1445 (toll-free)
Fax: 513-771-3413
E-mail: bmcciadm@brownmackie.edu
Web site: http://www.brownmackie.edu/Cincinnati

BROWN MACKIE COLLEGE — DALLAS/FORT WORTH
BEDFORD, TEXAS

The College

Brown Mackie College — Dallas/Fort Worth (Brown Mackie College) is one of over twenty-five locations in the Brown Mackie College family of schools (www.brownmackie.edu), which is dedicated to providing educational programs that prepare students to pursue entry-level positions in a competitive, rapidly changing workplace. Brown Mackie College schools offer bachelor degree, associate degree, diploma, and certificate programs in health sciences, business, information technology, legal studies, and design to more than 20,000 students in the Midwest, Southeast, Southwest, and Western United States.

Brown Mackie College — Dallas/Fort Worth is accredited by the Accrediting Council for Independent Colleges and Schools to award bachelor degrees, associate degrees, and diplomas. The Accrediting Council for Independent Colleges and Schools is listed as a nationally recognized accrediting agency by the United States Department of Education and is recognized by the Council for Higher Education Accreditation. ACICS can be contacted at 750 First Street NE, Suite 980, Washington, D.C. 20002; phone: 202-336-6780.

Brown Mackie College — Dallas/Fort Worth is approved and regulated by the Texas Workforce Commission, Career Schools and Colleges, Austin, Texas.

Brown Mackie College — Dallas/Fort Worth holds a Certificate of Authorization acknowledging exemption from the Texas Higher Education Coordinating Board Regulations.

Location

Brown Mackie College — Dallas/Fort Worth is conveniently located at 2200 North Highway 121, Suite 270, Bedford, Texas 76021. A spacious parking lot provides ample parking at no additional charge.

Programs of Study and Degrees

Brown Mackie College — Dallas/Fort Worth provides higher education to traditional and nontraditional students through bachelor degree, associate degree, and diploma programs that assist them in enhancing their career opportunities, broadening their perspectives through appropriate general education courses, thinking independently and critically, and improving problem-solving abilities. The college strives to develop within its students the desire for lifelong and continued education.

The Bachelor of Science degree is awarded in accounting, business administration, criminal justice, health care management, and information technology.

The Associate of Science degree is awarded in accounting technology, architectural design and drafting technology, business management, biomedical equipment technology, computer networking, graphic design, health care administration, information technology, and surgical technology.

Brown Mackie College offers a medical assistant diploma program.

The American Medical Technologists (AMT), which offers the certification for Registered Medical Assistant (RMA), accepts the accreditation of Brown Mackie College — Dallas/Fort Worth. Students will qualify to take the Registered Medical Assistant certification examination upon graduating the Brown Mackie College — Dallas/Fort Worth Medical Assistant program. Graduates of the 48-credit-hour Medical Assistant program are not qualified to take the AMT/RMA exam.

Brown Mackie College — Dallas/Fort Worth does not guarantee third-party certification. Outside agencies control the requirements for certifications and are subject to change without notice to Brown Mackie College.

Academic Programs

Each college quarter comprises ten to twelve weeks. Bachelor degree programs require a minimum of sixteen quarters to complete. Associate degree programs require a minimum of eight quarters to complete. Programs are offered on a year-round basis, providing students with the ability to work uninterrupted toward their degrees. The college offers all programs in a unique One-Course-a-Month format. This allows students to focus studies on only one course for four weeks. This schedule has proven convenient for students with multiple obligations, such as jobs and family.

Academic Facilities

Brown Mackie College — Dallas/Fort Worth offers media presentation rooms for special instructional needs and a

library that provides instructional resources and academic support for both faculty members and students.

In 2012, Brown Mackie College — Dallas/Fort Worth began its transition to using eTextbooks and computer tablets in the classroom. Utilizing these tablets to access expanded course material, students will be able to increase their acumen for using this technology and further enhance their educational experience. Students have the ability to directly download their eTextbooks to their tablet, eliminating the need to carry heavy, physical textbooks and reducing the overall cost of supplies.

Brown Mackie College — Dallas/Fort Worth is nonresidential; public transportation and ample parking at no cost are available. The campus is a smoke-free facility.

Costs

Tuition for the 2012 academic year was $324 per credit hour and general fees were $15 per credit hour, with some exceptions. The surgical technology tuition was $371 per credit hour and general fees were $15 per credit hour. The cost of textbooks and other instructional materials varies by program.

Financial Aid

Financial aid is available to those who qualify. The college maintains a full-time staff of Student Financial Services Advisors to assist qualified students in obtaining financial assistance. The college participates in several student aid programs. Forms of financial aid available through federal resources include Federal Pell Grants, Federal Supplemental Educational Opportunity Grants (FSEOG), Federal Work-Study Program awards, Federal Perkins Loans, Federal Stafford Student Loans (subsidized and unsubsidized), and Federal PLUS loans. Eligible students may apply for veterans' educational benefits. Students with physical or mental disabilities that are a handicap to employment may be eligible for training services through the state Vocational Rehabilitation Agency. For further information, students should contact the college Student Financial Services Office.

Each year, the college makes available President's Scholarships of $1000 each to qualifying seniors from area high schools. Up to three (3) scholarships may be awarded per high school. In order to qualify, a senior must have graduated from a participating high school, must have maintained a cumulative grade point average of at least 2.0, and must have submitted a brief essay. The student's extracurricular activities and community service are also considered. The President's Scholarship is available only to students enrolling in one of the college's degree programs. Students who receive the scholarship must enroll at Brown Mackie College — Dallas/Fort Worth between June and September immediately following their high school graduation.

Applications for these scholarships can be obtained from the guidance departments of participating high schools. These applications must be completed and returned to Brown Mackie College by March 31.

Faculty

Classes at Brown Mackie College — Dallas/Fort Worth were scheduled to begin July 2, 2012. Faculty and student statistics were not available at time of publication.

Admission Requirements

Each applicant for admission is assigned an Assistant Director of Admissions, who directs the applicant through the steps of the admissions process, providing information on curriculum, policies, procedures, and services and assisting the applicant in setting up necessary appointments and interviews. To qualify for admission, each applicant must provide documentation of graduation from an accredited high school or from a state-approved secondary education curriculum or provide official documentation of high school graduation equivalency. All transcripts become the property of the college. Admission to the college is based upon the applicant meeting the stated requirements, a review of the applicant's previous education records, and a review of the applicant's career interests. If previous academic records indicate the college's education and training programs would not benefit the applicant, the college reserves the right to advise the applicant not to enroll. Special requirements for enrollment into certain programs are discussed in the descriptions of those programs.

For the most recent information regarding admission requirements, prospective students should refer to the current academic catalog.

Application and Information

Applicants must complete and submit an application form, along with documentation of graduation from an accredited high school or state-approved secondary education curriculum or official documentation of high school graduation equivalency.

See BMCprograms.info for program duration, tuition, fees and other costs, median debt, federal salary data, alumni success, programmatic accreditation, and other important info.

For additional information, prospective students should contact:
Director of Admissions
Brown Mackie College — Dallas/Fort Worth
2200 North Highway 121, Suite 270
Bedford, Texas 76021
United States
Phone: 888-299-4799 (toll-free)
Fax: Not available at time of publication
E-mail: bmcdaladm@brownmackie.edu
Web site: http://www.brownmackie.edu/Dallas

BROWN MACKIE COLLEGE — FINDLAY

FINDLAY, OHIO

BROWN
MACKIE
COLLEGE
FINDLAY™

The College

Brown Mackie — Findlay (Brown Mackie College) is one of over twenty-five locations in the Brown Mackie College family of schools (www.brownmackie.edu), which is dedicated to providing educational programs that prepare students to pursue entry-level positions in a competitive, rapidly changing workplace. Brown Mackie College schools offer bachelor degree, associate degree, diploma, and certificate programs in health sciences, business, information technology, legal studies, and design to more than 20,000 students in the Midwest, Southeast, Southwest, and Western United States.

Brown Mackie College — Findlay was founded in 1926 by William H. Stautzenberger to provide solid business education at a reasonable cost. In 1960, the College was acquired by George R. Hawes, who served as its president until 1969. The college changed its name from Southern Ohio College–Findlay in 2001 to AEC Southern Ohio College; it was changed again to Brown Mackie College — Findlay in November 2004.

Brown Mackie College — Findlay is accredited by the Accrediting Council for Independent Colleges and Schools to award bachelor degrees, associate degrees, and diplomas. The Accrediting Council for Independent Colleges and Schools is listed as a nationally recognized accrediting agency by the United States Department of Education and is recognized by the Council for Higher Education Accreditation. ACICS can be contacted at 750 First Street NE, Suite 980, Washington, D.C. 20002; phone: 202-336-6780.

The Associate of Applied Science in occupational therapy assistant program is accredited by the Accreditation Council for Occupational Therapy Education (ACOTE) of the American Occupational Therapy Association (AOTA), located at 4720 Montgomery Lane, P.O. Box 31220, Bethesda, Maryland 20824-1220; phone: 301-652-AOTA.

The Associate of Science in surgical technology program is accredited by the Commission on Accreditation of Allied Health Education Programs (www.caahep.org) upon the recommendation of the Accreditation Review Committee on Education in Surgical Technology.

The Associate of Applied Science in veterinary technology program has provisional programmatic accreditation granted by the American Veterinary Medical Association (AVMA) through the Committee on Veterinary Technician Education and Activities (CVTEA).

Brown Mackie College — Findlay is licensed by the Ohio State Board of Career Colleges and Schools, 30 East Broad Street, 24th Floor, Suite 2481, Columbus, Ohio 43215-3138; phone: 614-466-2752. Ohio registration # 03-09-1687T.

Location

Located at 1700 Fostoria Avenue, Suite 100, in Findlay, Ohio, the college is easily accessible from Interstate 75.

Programs of Study and Degrees

Brown Mackie College — Findlay provides higher education to traditional and nontraditional students through bachelor degree, associate degree, and diploma programs that can assist them in enhancing their career opportunities, broadening their perspectives through appropriate general education courses, thinking independently and critically, and improving problem-solving abilities. The college strives to develop within its students the desire for lifelong and continued education.

The Bachelor of Science degree is awarded in business administration, criminal justice, health care management, and legal studies.

The Associate of Applied Business degree is awarded in accounting technology, business management, criminal justice, and paralegal. The Associate of Applied Science degree is awarded in architectural design and drafting technology, health care administration, medical assistant, occupational therapy assistant, pharmacy technology, surgical technology, and veterinary technology.

In addition to the bachelor and associate degree programs, the college offers diploma programs in business, computer software applications, criminal justice, dental assisting, medical assistant, paralegal assistant, and practical nursing.

The American Medical Technologists (AMT), which offers the certification for Registered Medical Assistant (RMA), accepts the accreditation of Brown Mackie College — Findlay. Students will qualify to take the Registered Medical Assistant certification examination upon graduating the Brown Mackie College — Findlay Medical Assisting and Medical Assistant programs. Graduates of the 48-credit-hour Medical Assistant program are not qualified to take the AMT/RMA exam.

Brown Mackie College — Findlay does not guarantee third-party certification. Outside agencies control the requirements for certifications and are subject to change without notice to Brown Mackie College.

Academic Programs

Each college quarter comprises twelve weeks. Bachelor's degree programs require a minimum of sixteen quarters to complete. Associate degree programs require a minimum of eight quarters to complete. Programs are offered on a year-round basis, providing students with the ability to work uninterrupted toward completion of their programs. The college offers all programs in a unique One-Course-a-Month format. This

schedule allows students to focus studies on only one course for four weeks and has proven convenient for students with multiple obligations, such as jobs and family.

Academic Facilities

Brown Mackie College — Findlay is a nonresidential, smoke-free institution. Although the College does not offer residential housing, students who are unable to commute daily from their homes may request assistance from the Admissions Office in locating housing. Ample parking is available at no additional cost.

Costs

Tuition for programs in the 2011–12 academic year was $294 per credit hour, with a general fee of $15 per credit hour. Tuition for the practical nursing diploma program was $361 per credit hour, with a general fee of $25 per credit hour. Tuition for the occupational therapy assistant program was $361 per credit hour, with a general fee of $15 per credit hour. Tuition for the surgical technology program was $340 per credit hour, with a general fee of $15 per credit hour. The length of the program determines total cost. The cost of textbooks and other instructional materials varies by program.

Financial Aid

Financial aid is available to those who qualify. The college maintains a full-time staff of Student Financial Services Advisors to assist qualified students in obtaining financial assistance. The college participates in several student aid programs. Forms of financial aid available through federal resources include the Federal DIRECT Pell Grant Program, Federal Supplemental Educational Opportunity Grant (FSEOG) Program, Federal Work-Study Program, Federal DIRECT Stafford Student Loan Program (subsidized and unsubsidized), the Federal DIRECT PLUS Loan Program, the Ohio College Opportunity Grant (OHCOG), and the Smart Grant. Eligible students may apply for state awards, such as the veterans' educational benefits. Students with physical or mental disabilities that are a handicap to employment may be eligible for training services through the state Agency for Vocational Rehabilitation. For further information, students should contact the college's Student Financial Services Office.

Each year, the college makes available President's Scholarships of $1000 each to qualifying seniors from area high schools. Up to three (3) scholarships may be awarded per high school. In order to qualify, a senior must be graduating from a participating high school, must have maintained a cumulative grade point average of at least 2.0, and must have submitted a brief essay. The student's extracurricular activities and community service are also considered. The President's Scholarship is available only to students enrolling in one of the college's degree programs. Students awarded the scholarship must enroll at Brown Mackie College — Findlay between June and September immediately following their high school graduation. Applications for these scholarships can be obtained from the guidance departments of participating high schools. These applications must be completed and returned to Brown Mackie College by March 31.

Faculty

There are 27 full-time and 90 part-time adjunct instructors at the college. The average student-faculty ratio is 14:1. Each student is assigned a faculty adviser.

Admission Requirements

Each applicant for admission is assigned an Assistant Director of Admissions, who directs the applicant through the steps of the admissions process, providing information on curriculum, policies, procedures, and services and assisting the applicant in setting up necessary appointments and interviews.

To qualify for admission, each applicant must provide documentation of graduation from an accredited high school or from a state-approved secondary education curriculum or provide official documentation of high school graduation equivalency. All transcripts become the property of the college. Admission to the college is based upon the applicant meeting the stated requirements, a review of the applicant's previous educational records, and a review of the applicant's career interests. If previous academic records indicate that the college's education and training programs would not benefit the applicant, the college reserves the right to advise the applicant not to enroll. Special requirements for enrollment into certain programs are discussed in the descriptions of those programs.

For the most recent information regarding admission requirements, please refer to the current academic catalog.

Application and Information

Applicants must complete and submit an application form, along with documentation of graduation from an accredited high school or state-approved secondary education curriculum or official documentation of high school graduation equivalency.

See BMCprograms.info for program duration, tuition, fees and other costs, median debt, federal salary data, alumni success, programmatic accreditation, and other important info.

For additional information, prospective students should contact:

Director of Admissions
Brown Mackie College — Findlay
1700 Fostoria Avenue, Suite 100
Findlay, Ohio 45840
United States
Phone: 419-423-2211
        800-842-3687 (toll-free)
Fax: 419-423-0725
E-mail: bmcfiadm@brownmackie.edu
Web site: http://www.brownmackie.edu/Findlay

BROWN MACKIE COLLEGE — FORT WAYNE

FORT WAYNE, INDIANA

The College

Brown Mackie College — Fort Wayne (Brown Mackie College) is one of over twenty-five locations in the Brown Mackie College family of schools (www.brownmackie.edu), which is dedicated to providing educational programs that prepare students to pursue entry-level positions in a competitive, rapidly changing workplace. Brown Mackie College schools offer bachelor degree, associate degree, diploma, and certificate programs in health sciences, business, information technology, legal studies, and design to over 20,000 students in the Midwest, Southeast, Southwest, and Western United States.

Brown Mackie College — Fort Wayne is one of the oldest institutions of its kind in the country and the oldest in the state of Indiana. Established in 1882 as the South Bend Commercial College, the school later changed its name to Michiana College. In 1930, the college was incorporated under the laws of the state of Indiana and was authorized to confer associate degrees and certificates in business. In 1992, the College in South Bend added a branch location in Fort Wayne, Indiana. In 2004, Michiana College changed its name to Brown Mackie College — Fort Wayne.

Brown Mackie College — Fort Wayne is accredited by the Accrediting Council for Independent Colleges and Schools to award bachelor degrees, associate degrees, diplomas, and certificates. The Accrediting Council for Independent Colleges and Schools is listed as a nationally recognized accrediting agency by the United States Department of Education and is recognized by the Council for Higher Education Accreditation. ACICS can be contacted at 750 First Street NE, Suite 980, Washington, D.C. 20002; phone: 202-336-6780.

The Associate of Science in surgical technology program is accredited by the Accrediting Bureau of Health Education Schools and by the Commission on Accreditation of Allied Health Education Programs (www.caahep.org) upon the recommendation of the Accreditation Review Council on Education in Surgical Technology and Surgical Assisting (ARC/STSA). The Commission on Accreditation of Allied Health Education Programs is located at 1361 Park Street, Clearwater, Florida 33756; phone: 727-210-2350; www.caahep.org.

The Associate of Applied Science in occupational therapy assistant program is accredited by the Accreditation Council for Occupational Therapy Education (ACOTE) of the American Occupational Therapy Association (AOTA), located at 4720 Montgomery Lane, P.O. Box 31220, Bethesda, Maryland 20824-1220. ACOTE's phone number c/o AOTA is 301-652-AOTA.

The Associate of Applied Science in physical therapist assistant program at Brown Mackie College — Fort Wayne is accredited by the Commission on Accreditation in Physical Therapy Education (CAPTE), located at 1111 North Fairfax Street, Alexandria, Virginia 22314; phone: 703-706-3245; e-mail: accreditation@apta.org; www.capteonline.org.

The Associate of Science in medical assisting program is accredited by the Commission of Accreditation of Allied Health Education Programs (www.caahep.org) upon the recommendation of the Curriculum Review Board of the Medical Assisting Education Review Board (MAERB). The Commission on Accreditation of Allied Health Education Programs is located at 1361 Park Street, Clearwater, Florida 33756; phone: 727-210-2350.

The Associate of Applied Science in veterinary technology program has provisional programmatic accreditation granted by the American Veterinary Medical Association (AVMA) through the Committee on Veterinary Technician Education and Activities (CVTEA).

Brown Mackie College — Fort Wayne does not guarantee third-party certification. Outside agencies control the requirements for certifications and are subject to change without notice to Brown Mackie College.

Brown Mackie College — Fort Wayne is regulated by The Indiana Commission on Proprietary Education, 302 West Washington Street, Room E201, Indianapolis, Indiana 46204; phone: 800-227-5695 (toll-free) or 317-232-1320. Indiana advertising code: AC-0109.

Location

Brown Mackie College — Fort Wayne is located at 3000 East Coliseum Boulevard in Fort Wayne, Indiana. The college facility is accessible by public transportation. Ample parking is provided at no additional charge. For added convenience, the College also operates a learning site at 2135 South Hannah Drive in Fort Wayne.

Programs of Study and Degrees

Brown Mackie College — Fort Wayne provides higher education to traditional and nontraditional students through bachelor degree, associate degree, diploma, and certificate programs that assist them in enhancing their career opportunities, broadening their perspectives through appropriate general education courses, thinking independently and critically, and improving problem-solving abilities. The college strives to develop within its students the desire for lifelong and continued education.

The Bachelor of Science degree is awarded in business administration, criminal justice, and health care management.

The Associate of Science degree is awarded in accounting technology, business management, criminal justice, health care administration, medical assisting, office management, paralegal, and surgical technology.

The Associate of Applied Science degree is awarded in biomedical equipment technology, health and fitness training, nursing, occupational therapy assistant, physical therapist assistant, and veterinary technology.

A diploma is awarded in practical nursing.

Brown Mackie College — Fort Wayne offers certificate programs in accounting, business, criminal justice, fitness trainer, medical assistant, and paralegal assistant.

The American Medical Technologists (AMT), which offers the certification for Registered Medical Assistant (RMA), accepts the accreditation of Brown Mackie College — Fort Wayne. Students will qualify to take the Registered Medical Assistant certification examination upon graduating the Brown Mackie College — Fort Wayne Medical Assisting and Medical Assistant programs. Graduates of the 48-credit-hour Medical Assistant program are not qualified to take the AMT/RMA exam.

Academic Programs

Each college quarter comprises twelve weeks. Bachelor degree programs require a minimum of sixteen quarters to complete. Associate degree programs require a minimum of eight quarters to complete. Programs are offered on a year-round basis, providing students with the ability to work uninterrupted toward their degrees. The college offers all programs in a unique One-Course-a-Month format. This allows students to focus studies on only one course for four weeks. This schedule has proven convenient for students with multiple obligations, such as jobs and family.

Academic Facilities

In 2005, the campus relocated to a 75,000-square-foot facility at 3000 East Coliseum Boulevard. Record enrollment allowed the institution to triple in size in less than one year. The three-story building offers a modern, professional environment for study. Ten classrooms are outfitted as "classrooms of the future," with an instructor workstation, full multimedia capabilities, a surround sound system, and projection screen that can be accessed by computer, DVD, or VHS equipment. The Brown Mackie College — Fort Wayne facility includes a criminal justice lab, surgical technology labs, medical labs, computer labs, and occupational and physical therapy labs, as well as a library and bookstore. The labs provide students with hands-on opportunities to apply knowledge and skills learned in the classroom. Students are welcome to use the labs when those facilities are not in use for scheduled classes.

In 2012, Brown Mackie College — Fort Wayne began its transition to using eTextbooks and computer tablets in the classroom. Utilizing these tablets to access expanded course material, students will be able to increase their acumen for using this technology and further enhance their educational experience. Students have the ability to directly download their eTextbooks to their tablet, eliminating the need to carry heavy, physical textbooks and reducing the overall cost of supplies.

The college is nonresidential; public transportation and ample parking at no cost are available. The campus is a smoke-free facility.

Costs

Tuition in the 2011–12 academic year was $314 per credit hour with fees of $15 per credit hour for all programs except nursing, practical nursing, surgical technology, personal fitness training, occupational therapy assistant studies, and physical therapist assistant studies. Textbooks and other instructional materials vary by program. For the nursing program, tuition was $410 per credit hour; fees were $25 per credit hour. For the practical nursing program, tuition was $381 per credit hour; fees were $25 per credit hour. For the surgical technology program, tuition was $360 per credit hour; fees were $15. Tuition for the personal fitness training programs was $324 per credit hour; fees were $25 per credit hour. Textbook expenses are estimated at $400 for the first term, $600 for the second term, and $100 for the third, fourth, and fifth terms. For certain courses in the occupational therapy assistant studies and physical therapist assistant studies programs, tuition was $381 per credit hour; fees were $15 per credit hour. Textbook expenses are estimated at $370 per quarter for the first six terms and $460 for the seventh term.

Financial Aid

The college maintains a full-time staff of Student Financial Services Advisors to assist qualified students in obtaining financial assistance. The college participates in several student aid programs. Forms of financial aid available through federal resources include the Federal Pell Grant Program, Federal Supplemental Educational Opportunity Grant (FSEOG) Program, Federal Work-Study Program, Federal Perkins Loan Program, Federal Stafford Student Loan Program (subsidized and unsubsidized), and the Federal PLUS Loan Program. Eligible students may apply for Indiana state awards, such as the Frank O'Bannon Grant Program (formerly the Indiana State Grant Program), the Higher Education Award, and Twenty-First Century Scholarships for high school students; for the Core 40 awards; and for veterans' educational benefits. For further information, students should contact the Student Financial Services Office.

Each year, the college makes available President's Scholarships of $1000 each to qualifying seniors from area high schools. Up to three (3) scholarships may be awarded per high school. In order to qualify, a senior must have graduated from a participating high school, must have maintained a cumulative grade point average of at least 2.0, and must have submitted a brief essay. The student's extracurricular activities and community service are also considered. The President's Scholarship is available only to students enrolling in one of the college's degree programs. Students awarded the scholarship must enroll at Brown Mackie College — Fort Wayne between June and September immediately following their high school graduation. Applications for these scholarships can be obtained from the guidance departments of participating high schools. These applications must be completed and returned to Brown Mackie College by March 31.

Faculty

The college has 45 full-time and 80 part-time instructors, with a student-faculty ratio of 15:1. Each student is assigned a faculty adviser.

Admission Requirements

Each applicant for admission is assigned an Assistant Director of Admissions, who directs the applicant through the steps of the admissions process, providing information on curriculum, policies, procedures, and services and assisting the applicant in setting up necessary appointments and interviews. To qualify for admission, each applicant must provide documentation of graduation from an accredited high school or from a state-approved secondary education curriculum or provide official documentation of high school graduation equivalency. All transcripts become the property of the college. Admission to the college is based on the applicant meeting the stated requirements, a review of the applicant's previous educational records, and a review of the applicant's career interests. If previous academic records indicate the college's education and training programs would not benefit the applicant, the college reserves the right to advise the applicant not to enroll. Special requirements for enrollment into certain programs are discussed in the descriptions of those programs.

In addition to the college's general admission requirements, applicants enrolling in the practical nursing program must provide a number of documents, listed below. The paperwork must be completed, and a record of proof must appear in the student's file prior to the start of the nursing fundamentals course. No student will be admitted to a clinical agency unless all paperwork is completed. This paperwork is a requirement of all contracted agencies. This paperwork includes records of (1) a complete physical, current to within six months of admission; (2) a two-step Mantoux test that is kept current throughout schooling; (3) a hepatitis B vaccination or signed refusal; (4) up-to-date immunizations, including tetanus and rubella; (5) a record of current CPR certification that is maintained throughout the student's clinical experience; and (6) hospitalization insurance or a signed waiver.

Application and Information

Applicants must complete and submit an application form, along with documentation of graduation from an accredited high school or state-approved secondary education curriculum or official documentation of high school graduation equivalency.

See BMCprograms.info for program duration, tuition, fees and other costs, median debt, federal salary data, alumni success, programmatic accreditation, and other important info.

For additional information, prospective students should contact:

Director of Admissions
Brown Mackie College — Fort Wayne
3000 East Coliseum Boulevard
Fort Wayne, Indiana 46805
United States
Phone: 260-484-4400
        866-433-2289 (toll-free)
Fax: 260-484-2678
E-mail: bmcfwaadm@brownmackie.edu
Web site: http://www.brownmackie.edu/FortWayne

BROWN MACKIE COLLEGE — GREENVILLE
GREENVILLE, SOUTH CAROLINA

The College

Brown Mackie College — Greenville (Brown Mackie College) is one of over twenty-five locations in the Brown Mackie College family of schools (www.brownmackie.edu), which is dedicated to providing educational programs that prepare students to pursue entry-level positions in a competitive, rapidly changing workplace. Brown Mackie College schools offer bachelor degree, associate degree, diploma, and certificate programs in health sciences, business, information technology, and legal studies to over 20,000 students in the Midwest, Southeast, Southwest, and Western United States.

Brown Mackie College was originally founded and approved by the Board of Trustees of Kansas Wesleyan College in Salina, Kansas on July 30, 1892. In 1938, the College was incorporated as The Brown Mackie School of Business under the ownership of Perry E. Brown and A.B. Mackie, former instructors at Kansas Wesleyan University in Salina, Kansas. Their last names formed the name of Brown Mackie. By January 1975, with improvements in curricula and higher-degree-granting status, The Brown Mackie School of Business became Brown Mackie College.

Brown Mackie College — Greenville is accredited by the Accrediting Council for Independent Colleges and Schools to award bachelor degrees, associate degrees, and certificates. The Accrediting Council for Independent Colleges and Schools is listed as a nationally recognized accrediting agency by the United States Department of Education and is recognized by the Council for Higher Education Accreditation. ACICS can be contacted at 750 First Street NE, Suite 980, Washington, D.C. 20002; phone: 202-336-6780.

Brown Mackie College — Greenville is licensed by the South Carolina Commission on Higher Education, 1122 Lady Street, Suite 300, Columbia, South Carolina 29201; phone: 803-737-2260. Licensure indicates only that minimum standards have been met; it is not equal to or synonymous with accreditation by an accrediting agency recognized by the U.S. Department of Education.

The occupational therapy assistant program has applied for accreditation by the Accreditation Council for Occupational Therapy Education (ACOTE) of the American Occupational Therapy Association (AOTA), located at 4720 Montgomery Lane, P.O. Box 31220, Bethesda, Maryland 20824; phone: 301-652-AOTA.

The Brown Mackie College — Greenville Associate of Science in surgical technology program is accredited by the Accrediting Bureau of Health Education Schools.

Location

Brown Mackie College — Greenville is conveniently located at Two Liberty Square, 75 Beattie Place, Suite 100, in Greenville, South Carolina. The college has a generous parking area and is easily accessible by public transportation.

Programs of Study and Degrees

Brown Mackie College — Greenville provides higher education to traditional and nontraditional students through bachelor degree, associate degree, and certificate programs that assist in enhancing their career opportunities, broadening their perspectives through appropriate general education courses, thinking independently and critically, and improving problem-solving abilities. The college strives to develop within its students the desire for lifelong and continued education.

The Bachelor of Science degree is awarded in business administration, criminal justice, health care management, and legal studies.

The Associate of Applied Science degree is awarded in accounting technology, business management, criminal justice, health care administration, information technology, medical assisting, occupational therapy assistant, office management, paralegal, and surgical technology.

The certificate is awarded in accounting, business, criminal justice, medical assistant, and paralegal assistant.

The American Medical Technologists (AMT), which offers the certification for Registered Medical Assistant (RMA), accepts the accreditation of Brown Mackie College — Greenville. Students will qualify to take the Registered Medical Assistant certification examination upon graduating the Brown Mackie College — Greenville Medical Assisting and Medical Assistant programs. Graduates of the 48-credit-hour Medical Assistant program are not qualified to take the AMT/RMA exam.

Brown Mackie College — Greenville does not guarantee third-party certification. Outside agencies control the requirements for certifications and are subject to change without notice to Brown Mackie College.

Academic Programs

Each college quarter comprises twelve weeks. Bachelor degree programs require a minimum of sixteen quarters to complete. Associate degree programs require a minimum of eight quarters to complete. Programs are offered on a year-round basis, providing students with the ability to work uninterrupted

toward completion of their degrees. The college offers all programs in a unique One-Course-a-Month format. This allows students to focus their studies on only one course for four weeks. This schedule has proven convenient for students with multiple obligations, such as jobs and family.

Academic Facilities

A modern facility, Brown Mackie College — Greenville offers nearly 50,000 square feet. The college is equipped with multiple computer labs housing over one hundred computers. High-speed access to the Internet and other online resources are available for students and faculty. Multimedia classrooms are outfitted with overhead projectors, VCR/DVD players, and computers.

Brown Mackie College is nonresidential; public transportation and ample parking at no cost are available. The college is a smoke-free facility.

Costs

Tuition in the 2011–12 academic year for most bachelor and associate degrees and certificates was $294 per credit hour; fees were $15 per credit hour. Tuition for the occupational therapy assistant program was $361 per credit hour; fees were $15 per credit hour. Tuition for the surgical technology program was $340 per credit hour; fees were $15 per credit hour. The cost of textbooks and other instructional expenses vary by program.

Financial Aid

Financial aid is available for those who qualify. The college maintains a full-time staff of Student Financial Services Advisors to assist qualified students in obtaining the financial assistance they require to meet their educational expenses. Available resources include federal and state aid, student loans from private lenders, and Federal Work-Study opportunities, both on and off college premises.

Each year, the college makes available President's Scholarships of $1000 each to qualifying seniors from area high schools. Up to three (3) scholarships may be awarded per high school. In order to qualify, a senior must have graduated from a participating high school, must have maintained a cumulative grade point average of at least 2.0, and must have submitted a brief essay. The student's extracurricular activities and community service are also considered. The President's Scholarship is available only to students enrolling in one of Brown Mackie College's degree programs. Students awarded the scholarship must enroll at Brown Mackie College — Greenville between June and September immediately following their high school graduation. Applications for these scholarships can be obtained from the guidance departments of participating high schools. These applications must be completed and returned to Brown Mackie College by March 31.

Faculty

Experienced faculty members provide academic support and are committed to the academic and technical preparation of their students. The college has 9 full-time and 30 part-time instructors, with a student-faculty ratio of 24:1. Each student is assigned a faculty adviser.

Admission Requirements

Each applicant for admission is assigned an Assistant Director of Admissions who directs the applicant through the steps of the admissions process. Assistant Directors provide information on curriculum, policies, procedures, and services and assist the applicant in setting up necessary appointments and interviews. To qualify for admission, each applicant must provide documentation of graduation from an accredited high school or from a state-approved secondary education curriculum or provide official documentation of high school graduation equivalency. All transcripts become the property of the college. Admission to the college is based on the applicant meeting the stated requirements, a review of the applicant's previous educational records, and a review of the applicant's career interests. If previous academic records indicate the college's education and training programs would not benefit the applicant, the college reserves the right to advise the applicant not to enroll. Special requirements for enrollment into certain programs are discussed in the descriptions of those programs.

For the most recent information regarding admission requirements, prospective students should refer to the current academic catalog.

Application and Information

Applicants must complete and submit an application form along with documentation of graduation from an accredited high school or state-approved secondary education curriculum or official documentation of high school graduation equivalency.

See BMCprograms.info for program duration, tuition, fees and other costs, median debt, federal salary data, alumni success, programmatic accreditation, and other important info.

For additional information, prospective students should contact:

Director of Admissions
Brown Mackie College — Greenville
Two Liberty Square
75 Beattie Place, Suite 100
Greenville, South Carolina 29601
United States
Phone: 864-239-5300
        877-479-8465 (toll-free)
Fax: 864-232-4094
E-mail: bmcgrweb@brownmackie.edu
Web site: http://www.brownmackie.edu/greenville

BROWN MACKIE COLLEGE — INDIANAPOLIS
INDIANAPOLIS, INDIANA

BROWN
MACKIE
COLLEGE
INDIANAPOLIS℠

The College

Brown Mackie College — Indianapolis (Brown Mackie College) is one of over twenty-five locations in the Brown Mackie College family of schools (http://www.brownmackie.edu), which is dedicated to providing educational programs that prepare students to pursue entry-level positions in a competitive, rapidly changing workplace. Brown Mackie College schools offer bachelor degree, associate degree, diploma, and certificate programs in health sciences, business, information technology, legal studies, and design to more than 20,000 students in the Midwest, Southeast, Southwest, and Western United States.

Brown Mackie College — Indianapolis was founded in 2007 as a branch of Brown Mackie College — Findlay, Ohio.

Brown Mackie College — Indianapolis is accredited by the Accrediting Council for Independent Colleges and Schools to award bachelor degrees, associate degrees, diplomas, and certificates. The Accrediting Council for Independent Colleges and Schools is listed as a nationally recognized accrediting agency by the United States Department of Education and is recognized by the Council for Higher Education Accreditation. ACICS can be contacted at 750 First Street NE, Suite 980, Washington, D.C. 20002; phone: 202-336-6780.

The occupational therapy assistant program is accredited by the Accreditation Council for Occupational Therapy Education (ACOTE) of the American Occupational Therapy Association (AOTA), 4720 Montgomery Lane, P.O. Box 31220, Bethesda, Maryland 20824-1220; phone: 301-652-2682.

Brown Mackie College — Indianapolis is regulated by the Indiana Commission on Proprietary Education, 302 West Washington Street, Indianapolis, Indiana 46204; phone: 317-232-1320 or 800-227-5695 (toll-free). Indiana advertising code: AC0078.

The Brown Mackie College — Indianapolis Practical Nursing diploma program is approved by the Indiana State Board of Nursing, 402 West Washington Street, Room W066, Indianapolis, Indiana 46204; phone: 317-234-2043.

Location

Brown Mackie College — Indianapolis is conveniently located at 1200 North Meridian Street in Indianapolis, Indiana. The college has a generous parking area and is easily accessible by public transportation.

In November 2011, the college opened an innovative branch learning site on Level 4 of Circle Centre Mall located at 49 West Maryland Street in the heart of downtown Indianapolis. Daily shuttle service is provided to and from the main college.

Programs of Study and Degrees

Brown Mackie College — Indianapolis provides higher education to traditional and nontraditional students through bachelor degree, associate degree, diploma, and certificate programs that assist them in enhancing their career opportunities, broadening their perspectives through appropriate general education courses, thinking independently and critically, and improving problem-solving abilities. The college strives to develop within its students the desire for lifelong and continued education.

The Bachelor of Science degree is awarded in business administration, criminal justice, and legal studies.

The Associate of Science degree is awarded in business management, criminal justice, health care administration, medical assistant, and paralegal. The Associate of Applied Science degree is awarded in occupational therapy assistant.

A diploma program in practical nursing is offered.

Brown Mackie College — Indianapolis offers a medical assistant and business certificate programs.

The American Medical Technologists (AMT), which offers the certification for Registered Medical Assistant (RMA), accepts the accreditation of Brown Mackie College — Indianapolis. Students will qualify to take the Registered Medical Assistant certification examination upon graduating the Brown Mackie College — Indianapolis Medical Assisting and Medical Assistant programs. Graduates of the 48-credit-hour Medical Assistant program are not qualified to take the AMT/RMA exam.

Brown Mackie College — Indianapolis does not guarantee third-party certification. Outside agencies control the requirements for certifications and are subject to change without notice to Brown Mackie College.

Academic Programs

Each college quarter comprises twelve weeks. Bachelor degree programs require a minimum of sixteen quarters to complete. Associate degree programs require a minimum of eight quarters to complete. Programs are offered on a year-round basis, providing students with the ability to work uninterrupted toward their degrees. The college offers all programs in a unique One-Course-a-Month format. This allows students to focus studies on only one course for four weeks. This schedule has proven convenient for students with multiple obligations such as jobs and family.

Academic Facilities

Opened in January 2008, this modern facility offers more than 22,000 square feet of tastefully decorated classrooms, laboratories, and office space designed to the specifications of

the college for its business, healthcare, and technical programs. The Circle Centre Mall branch learning site boasts 25,000 square feet with 20 lecture rooms, computer labs, two medical labs, college store, and more. Instructional equipment is comparable to current technology used in business and industry today. Modern classrooms for special instructional needs offer multimedia capabilities with surround sound and overhead projectors accessible through computer, DVD, or VHS. Internet access and instructional resources are available at the college's library. Experienced faculty members provide academic support and are committed to the academic and technical preparation of their students.

Brown Mackie College — Indianapolis is nonresidential; public transportation and ample parking are available at no additional cost.

Costs

Tuition for most programs in the 2011–12 academic year was $312 per credit hour with a general fee of $15 per credit hour. Tuition for the practical nursing diploma program was $361 per credit hour with a general fee of $25 per credit hour applied to instructional costs for activities and services. For the occupational therapy assistant program, the tuition was $361 per credit hour with a general fee of $15 per credit hour.

Financial Aid

Financial aid is available to those who qualify. The college maintains a full-time staff of Student Financial Services Advisors to assist qualified students in obtaining the financial assistance they require to meet their educational expenses. Available resources include federal and state aid, student loans from private lenders, and federal work-study opportunities, both on and off college premises.

Each year, the college makes available President's Scholarships of $1000 each to qualifying seniors from area high schools. Up to three (3) scholarships may be awarded per high school. In order to qualify, a senior must be graduating from a participating high school, must be maintaining a cumulative grade point average of at least 2.0, and must submit a brief essay. The student's extracurricular activities and community service are also considered. These scholarships are available only to students enrolling in one of the college's degree programs. Students awarded the scholarship must enroll at Brown Mackie College — Indianapolis between June and September immediately following their high school graduation. Applications for these scholarships can be obtained from the guidance departments of participating high schools. These applications must be completed and returned to Brown Mackie College by March 31.

Faculty

The college has 24 full-time instructors, 77 adjunct instructors, and 16 lab assistants, with a student-faculty ratio of 12:1. Faculty members provide tutoring and additional academic services to students as needed.

Admission Requirements

Each applicant for admission is assigned an Assistant Director of Admissions, who directs the applicant through the steps of the admissions process, providing information on curriculum, policies, procedures, and services and assisting the applicant in setting up necessary appointments and interviews. To qualify for admission, each applicant must provide documentation of graduation from an accredited high school or from a state-approved secondary education curriculum or provide official documentation of high school graduation equivalency. All transcripts become the property of the college. Admission to the college is based on the applicant meeting the stated requirements, a review of the applicant's previous educational records, and a review of the applicant's career interests. If previous academic records indicate the college's education and training programs would not benefit the applicant, the college reserves the right to advise the applicant not to enroll. Special requirements for enrollment into certain programs are discussed in the descriptions of those programs.

In addition to the college's general admission requirements, applicants enrolling in the practical nursing program must document the following: fulfillment of Brown Mackie College — Indianapolis general requirements; complete physical (must be current to within six months of admission); two-step Mantoux TB skin test (must be current throughout schooling); hepatitis B vaccination or signed refusal; up-to-date immunizations, including tetanus and rubella; record of current CPR certification (certification must be current throughout the clinical experience through healthcare provider certification or the American Heart Association); and hospitalization insurance or a signed waiver.

For the most recent information regarding admission requirements, please refer to the current academic catalog.

Application and Information

Applicants must complete and submit an application form, along with documentation of graduation from an accredited high school or state-approved secondary education curriculum or official documentation of high school graduation equivalency.

See BMCprograms.info for program duration, tuition, fees and other costs, median debt, federal salary data, alumni success, programmatic accreditation, and other important info.

For additional information, prospective students should contact:

Senior Director of Admissions
Brown Mackie College — Indianapolis
1200 North Meridian Street, Suite 100
Indianapolis, Indiana 46204
United States
Phone: 317-554-8301
        866-255-0279 (toll-free)
Fax: 317-632-4557
E-mail: bmcindadm@brownmackie.edu
Web site: http://www.brownmackie.edu/Indianapolis

BROWN MACKIE COLLEGE — LOUISVILLE
LOUISVILLE, KENTUCKY

The College

Brown Mackie College — Louisville (Brown Mackie College) is one of over twenty-five locations in the Brown Mackie College family of schools (www.brownmackie.edu), which is dedicated to providing educational programs that prepare students to pursue entry-level positions in a competitive, rapidly changing workplace. Brown Mackie College schools offer bachelor degree, associate degree, diploma, and certificate programs in health sciences, business, information technology, legal studies, and design to over 20,000 students in the Midwest, Southeast, Southwest, and Western United States.

Brown Mackie College — Louisville opened in 1972 as RETS Institute of Technology. The first RETS school was founded in 1935 in Detroit in response to the rapid growth of radio broadcasting and the need for qualified radio technicians. The RETS Institute changed its name to Brown Mackie College — Louisville in 2004.

Brown Mackie College — Louisville is accredited by the Accrediting Council for Independent Colleges and Schools to award bachelor degrees, associate degrees, diplomas, and certificates. The Accrediting Council for Independent Colleges and Schools is listed as a nationally recognized accrediting agency by the United States Department of Education. Its accreditation of degree-granting institutions is recognized by the Council for Higher Education Accreditation. ACICS can be contacted at 750 First Street NE, Suite 980, Washington, D.C. 20002; phone: 202-336-6780.

Brown Mackie College — Louisville is licensed by the Kentucky Council on Postsecondary Education, located at 1024 Capital Center Drive, Suite 320, Frankfort, Kentucky 40601.

Brown Mackie College — Louisville is regulated by the Indiana Commission on Proprietary Education, located at 302 West Washington Street, Indianapolis, Indiana 46204; phone: 317-232-1320 or 800-227-5695 (toll-free). Indiana advertising code: AC-0045.

The Associate of Applied Science in veterinary technology program has provisional programmatic accreditation granted by the American Veterinary Medical Association (AVMA) through the Committee on Veterinary Technician Education and Activities (CVTEA).

The Associate of Applied Science in surgical technology program is accredited by the Accrediting Bureau of Health Education Schools.

The Associate of Applied Science in occupational therapy assistant program is accredited by the Accreditation Council for Occupational Therapy Education (ACOTE) of the American Occupational Therapy Association (AOTA), located at 4720 Montgomery Lane, P.O. Box 31220, Bethesda, Maryland 20824-1220. ACOTE's phone number is 301-652-AOTA.

The Associate of Applied Science in surgical technology program is accredited by the Commission on Accreditation of Allied Health Education Programs (www.caahep.org) upon the recommendation of the Accreditation Review Council on Education in Surgical Technology and Surgical Assisting (ARC/STSA). The Commission on Accreditation of Allied Health Education Programs is located at 1361 Park Street, Clearwater, Florida 33756; phone: 727-210-2350.

Location

Brown Mackie College — Louisville is conveniently located at 3605 Fern Valley Road in Louisville, Kentucky. The college has a generous parking area and is easily accessible by public transportation.

Programs of Study and Degrees

Brown Mackie College — Louisville provides higher education to traditional and nontraditional students through bachelor degree, associate degree, and diploma programs that assist in enhancing their career opportunities, broadening their perspectives through appropriate general education courses, thinking independently and critically, and improving problem-solving abilities.

The Bachelor of Science degree is awarded in business administration, criminal justice, health care management, and legal studies.

The Associate of Applied Business degree is awarded in accounting technology, business management, computer networking and applications, criminal justice, and paralegal.

The Associate of Applied Science degree is awarded in biomedical equipment technology, electronics, graphic design, health care administration, medical assisting, occupational therapy assistant, pharmacy technology, surgical technology, and veterinary technology.

The college offers a diploma program in practical nursing.

The college offers a certificate program in computer networking.

The American Medical Technologists (AMT), which offers the certification for Registered Medical Assistant (RMA), accepts the accreditation of Brown Mackie College — Louisville. Students will qualify to take the Registered Medical Assistant certification examination upon graduating the Brown Mackie College — Louisville Medical Assisting program.

Brown Mackie College — Louisville does not guarantee third-party certification. Outside agencies control the requirements for certifications and are subject to change without notice to Brown Mackie College.

Academic Programs

Each college quarter comprises twelve weeks. Bachelor degree programs require a minimum of sixteen quarters to complete. Associate degree programs require a minimum of eight quarters to complete. Programs are offered on a year-round basis, providing students with the ability to work uninterrupted toward completion of their programs. The college offers all programs in a unique One-Course-a-Month format. This allows students to focus studies on only one course for four weeks. This schedule has proven convenient for students with multiple obligations, such as jobs and family.

Academic Facilities

Brown Mackie College — Louisville has more than 69,000 square feet of multipurpose classrooms, including networked computer laboratories, electronics laboratories, veterinary technology labs, medical labs, nursing labs, a resource center, and offices for administrative personnel as well as for student services such

as admissions, student financial services, and career-services assistance. In 2009, 6,000 square feet were added to the Louisville location. Included in this build-out are an occupational therapy lab, a criminal justice lab, additional classrooms, and faculty space. In 2010, an additional 25,000 square feet opened at this location. This build-out included a biomedical equipment lab, additional classrooms, a career services center, and additional faculty/administration space.

Brown Mackie College — Louisville is nonresidential; ample parking at no cost is available. Brown Mackie College is a smoke-free facility.

Costs

Tuition for most programs in the 2011–12 academic year was $294 per credit hour, and the general fees were $15 per credit hour. The practical nursing diploma program was $361 per credit hour, and the general fees were $25 per credit hour. The surgical technology program was $340 per credit hour, and the general fees were $15 per credit hour. The occupational therapy program was $361 per credit hour, and the general fees were $15 per credit hour. The computer networking certificate program was $300 per credit hour, and the general fees were $25 per credit hour. The length of the program determines total cost. The cost of textbooks and other instructional materials varies by program.

Financial Aid

Financial aid is available for those who qualify. The college maintains a full-time staff of Student Financial Services Advisors to assist qualified students in obtaining financial assistance. The college participates in several student aid programs. Forms of financial aid available through federal resources include the Federal Pell Grant Program, Federal Supplemental Educational Opportunity Grant (FSEOG) Program, Federal Work-Study Program, Federal Perkins Loan Program, Federal Stafford Student Loan Program (subsidized and unsubsidized), and the Federal PLUS Loan Program.

Each year, the college makes available President's Scholarships of $1000 each to qualifying seniors from area high schools. Up to three (3) scholarships may be awarded per high school. In order to qualify, a senior must have graduated from a participating high school, must have maintained a cumulative grade point average of at least 2.0, and must have submitted a brief essay. The student's extracurricular activities and community service are also considered. The President's Scholarship is available only to students enrolling in one of the college's degree programs. Students awarded the scholarship must enroll at Brown Mackie College — Louisville between June and September immediately following their high school graduation. Applications for these scholarships can be obtained from the guidance departments of participating high schools and must be completed and returned to Brown Mackie College by March 31.

Faculty

There are 32 full-time and over 100 part-time faculty members at the college. The average student-faculty ratio is 20:1.

Admission Requirements

Each applicant for admission is assigned an Assistant Director of Admissions, who directs the applicant through the steps of the admissions process, providing information on curriculum, policies, procedures, and services and assisting the applicant in setting up necessary appointments and interviews.

To qualify for admission, each applicant must provide documentation of graduation from an accredited high school or from a state-approved secondary education curriculum or official documentation of high school graduation equivalency. All transcripts become the property of the college. Admission to the college is based on the applicant meeting the stated requirements, a review of the applicant's previous educational records, and a review of the applicant's career interests. If previous academic records indicate the college's education and training programs would not benefit the applicant, the college reserves the right to advise the applicant not to enroll. Special requirements for enrollment into certain programs are discussed in the descriptions of those programs.

In addition to the college's general admission requirements, applicants enrolling in either the occupational therapy assistant program or the surgical technology program must document one of the following: a high school cumulative grade point average of at least 2.5, a score on the GED examination of at least 57 (557 if taken on or after January 15, 2002), or completion of 12 quarter-credit hours or 8 semester-credit hours of collegiate course work with a grade point average of at least 2.5. Credit hours may not include Professional Development (CF 1100), the Brown Mackie College — Louisville course. Students entering the program must also have completed a biology course with a grade of at least a C (or an average of at least 2.0 on a 4.0 scale).

In addition to the college's general admission requirements, applicants enrolling in the practical nursing program must complete several documents, listed below. A record of proof must appear in the student's file prior to the start of the nursing fundamentals course. No student will be admitted to a clinical agency unless all paperwork is completed. The paperwork is a requirement of all contracted agencies. This paperwork includes records of (1) a complete physical, current to within six months of admission; (2) a two-step Mantoux test that is kept current throughout schooling; (3) a hepatitis B vaccination or signed refusal; (4) up-to-date immunizations, including tetanus and rubella; (5) a record of current CPR certification that is maintained throughout the student's clinical experience; and (6) hospitalization insurance or a signed waiver.

For the most recent information regarding admission requirements, prospective students should refer to the current academic catalog.

Application and Information

Applicants must complete and submit an application form along with documentation of graduation from an accredited high school or completion of state-approved secondary education curriculum or official documentation of high school graduation equivalency.

See BMCprograms.info for program duration, tuition, fees and other costs, median debt, federal salary data, alumni success, programmatic accreditation, and other important info.

For additional information, prospective students should contact:

Brown Mackie College — Louisville
3605 Fern Valley Road
Louisville, Kentucky 40219
United States
Phone: 502-968-7191
      800-999-7387 (toll-free)
Fax: 502-357-9956
E-mail: bmcloadm@brownmackie.edu
Web site: http://www.brownmackie.edu/Louisville

BROWN MACKIE COLLEGE — MERRILLVILLE
MERRILLVILLE, INDIANA

The College

Brown Mackie College — Merrillville (Brown Mackie College) is one of over twenty-five locations in the Brown Mackie College family of schools (www.brownmackie.edu), which is dedicated to providing educational programs that prepare students to pursue entry-level positions in a competitive, rapidly changing workplace. Brown Mackie College schools offer bachelor degree, associate degree, diploma, and certificate programs in health sciences, business, information technology, legal studies, and design to over 20,000 students in the Midwest, Southeast, Southwest, and Western United States.

Founded in 1890 by A. N. Hirons as LaPorte Business College in LaPorte, Indiana, the institution later became known as Commonwealth Business College. In 1919, ownership was transferred to Grace and J. J. Moore, who successfully operated the College under the name of Reese School of Business for several decades. In 1975, the College came under the ownership of Steven C. Smith as Commonwealth Business College. A second location, now known as Brown Mackie College — Merrillville, was opened in 1984 in Merrillville, Indiana.

Brown Mackie College — Merrillville is accredited by the Accrediting Council for Independent Colleges and Schools to award bachelor degrees, associate degrees, diplomas, and certificates. The Accrediting Council for Independent Colleges and Schools is listed as a nationally recognized accrediting agency by the United States Department of Education and is recognized by the Council for Higher Education Accreditation. ACICS can be contacted at 750 First Street NE, Suite 980, Washington, D.C. 20002; phone: 202-336-6780.

The college is regulated by the Indiana Commission on Proprietary Education, 302 West Washington Street, Indianapolis, Indiana 46204; phone: 800-227-5695 (toll-free) or 317-232-1320. Indiana advertising code: AC0138.

The Associate of Science in surgical technology is accredited by the Commission on Accreditation of Allied Health Education Programs (www.caahep.org) upon the recommendation of the Accreditation Review Committee on Education in Surgical Technology. The Commission on Accreditation of Allied Health Education Programs is located at 1361 Park Street, Clearwater, Florida 33756; phone: 727-210-2350.

The Associate of Applied Science in occupational therapy assistant program is accredited by the Accreditation Council for Occupational Therapy Education (ACOTE) of the American Occupational Therapy Association (AOTA), located at 4720 Montgomery Lane, P.O. Box 31220, Bethesda, Maryland 20824-1220. ACOTE's telephone number c/o AOTA is 301-652-AOTA.

The Associate of Science in medical assisting program is accredited by the Accrediting Bureau of Health Education Schools.

The college is a nonresidential, smoke-free institution.

Location

Brown Mackie College — Merrillville is conveniently located in northwest Indiana at 1000 East 80th Place, Merrillville, in the Twin Towers business complex just west of the intersection of U.S. Route 30 and Interstate 65. A spacious parking lot provides ample parking at no additional charge.

Programs of Study and Degrees

Brown Mackie College — Merrillville provides higher education to traditional and nontraditional students through bachelor degree, associate degree, diploma, and certificate programs that assist in enhancing their career opportunities, broadening their perspectives through appropriate general education courses, thinking independently and critically, and improving problem-solving abilities. The college strives to develop within its students the desire for lifelong and continued education.

The Bachelor of Science degree is awarded in business administration, criminal justice, health care management, and legal studies.

The Associate of Science degree is awarded in accounting technology, business management, criminal justice, medical assisting, medical office management, paralegal, and surgical technology.

The Associate of Applied Science degree is awarded in occupational therapy assistant.

The college offers certificate programs in accounting, business, criminal justice, medical assistant, and paralegal assistant.

The American Medical Technologists (AMT), which offers the certification for Registered Medical Assistant (RMA), accepts the accreditation of Brown Mackie College — Merrillville. Students will qualify to take the Registered Medical Assistant certification examination upon graduating the Brown Mackie College — Merrillville Medical Assisting and Medical Assistant programs. Graduates of the 48-credit-hour Medical Assistant program are not qualified to take the AMT/RMA exam.

Brown Mackie College — Merrillville does not guarantee third-party certification. Outside agencies control the requirements for certifications and are subject to change without notice to Brown Mackie College.

Academic Programs

Each college quarter comprises ten to twelve weeks. Bachelor degree programs require a minimum of sixteen quarters to complete. Associate degree programs require a minimum of eight quarters to complete. Programs are offered on a year-round basis, providing students with the ability to work uninterrupted toward completion of their programs. The college offers all programs in a unique One-Course-a-Month format. This allows students to focus on only one course for four weeks. This schedule has proven convenient for students with multiple obligations, such as jobs and family.

Academic Facilities

Occupying 26,000 square feet, Brown Mackie College — Merrillville was opened to students in October 1998 in the Twin Towers complex of Merrillville and comprises several instructional rooms, including five computer labs with networked computers and four medical laboratories. The administrative offices, college library, and student lounge are all easily accessible to students. The college bookstore stocks texts, courseware, and other educational supplies required for courses at the college. Students also find a variety of personal, recreational, and gift items, including apparel, supplies, and general merchandise incorporating the college logo. Hours are posted at the bookstore entrance.

Costs

Tuition for most programs in the 2011–12 academic year was $294 per credit hour and fees were $15 per credit hour, with some exceptions. For the surgical technology program, tuition was $340 per credit hour and fees were $15 per credit hour. For the occupational therapy assistant program, tuition was $361 per credit hour and fees were $15 per credit hour. The length of the program determines total cost. Textbook fees vary according to program.

Financial Aid

Financial aid is available to those who qualify. The college maintains a full-time staff of Student Financial Services Advisors to assist qualified students in obtaining financial assistance. The college participates in several student aid programs. Forms of financial aid available through federal resources include the Federal Pell Grant Program, Federal Supplemental Educational Opportunity Grant (FSEOG) Program, Federal Work-Study Program, Federal Perkins Loan Program, Federal Stafford Student Loan Program (subsidized and unsubsidized), and the Federal PLUS Loan Program. Eligible students may apply for Indiana state awards, such as the Higher Education Award and Twenty-First Century Scholarships for high school students, the Core 40 awards, and veterans' educational benefits. Students with physical or mental disabilities that are a handicap to employment may be eligible for training services through the state's Bureau of Vocational Rehabilitation. For further information, students should contact the college's Student Financial Services Office.

Each year, the college makes available President's Scholarships of $1000 each to qualifying seniors from area high schools. Up to three (3) scholarships may be awarded per high school. In order to qualify, a senior must be graduating from a participating high school, must be maintaining a cumulative grade point average of at least 2.0, and must submit a brief essay. The student's extracurricular activities and community service are also considered. These scholarships are available only to students enrolling in one of the college's degree programs. Students awarded the scholarship must enroll at Brown Mackie College — Merrillville between June and September immediately following their high school graduation. Applications for these scholarships can be obtained from the guidance departments of participating high schools and must be completed and returned to Brown Mackie College by March 31.

Faculty

There are approximately 60 full-time and 25 part-time faculty members at the college, practitioners in their fields of expertise. The average student-faculty ratio is 17:1.

Admission Requirements

Each applicant for admission is assigned an Assistant Director of Admissions who directs the applicant through the steps of the admissions process, providing information on curriculum, policies, procedures, and services and assisting the applicant in setting up necessary appointments and interviews. To qualify for admission, each applicant must provide documentation of graduation from an accredited high school or completion of a state-approved secondary education curriculum or official documentation of high school graduation equivalency. All transcripts become the property of the college.

As part of the admission process, students are given an assessment of academic skills. Although the results of this assessment do not determine eligibility for admission, they provide the college with a means of determining the need for academic support as well as a means by which the college can evaluate the effectiveness of its educational programs. All new students are required to complete this assessment, which is readministered at the end of the student's program, so results may be compared with those of the initial administration.

In addition to the college's general admission requirements, applicants enrolling in the practical nursing program must complete several documents, listed below. A record of proof must appear in the student's file prior to the start of the nursing fundamentals course. No student will be admitted to a clinical agency unless all paperwork is completed. The paperwork is a requirement of all contracted agencies. This paperwork includes records of (1) a complete physical, current to within six months of admission; (2) a two-step Mantoux test that is kept current throughout schooling; (3) a hepatitis B vaccination or signed refusal; (4) up-to-date immunizations, including tetanus and rubella; (5) a record of current CPR certification that is maintained throughout the student's clinical experience; and (6) hospitalization insurance or a signed waiver.

For the most recent information regarding admission requirements, please refer to the current academic catalog.

Application and Information

Applicants must complete and submit an application form along with documentation of graduation from an accredited high school or completion of state-approved secondary education curriculum or provide official documentation of high school graduation equivalency.

See BMCprograms.info for program duration, tuition, fees and other costs, median debt, federal salary data, alumni success, programmatic accreditation, and other important info.

For additional information, prospective students should contact:

Brown Mackie College — Merrillville
1000 East 80th Place, Suite 205M
Merrillville, Indiana 46410
United States
Phone: 219-769-3321
        800-258-3321 (toll-free)
Fax: 219-738-1076
E-mail: bmcmeadm@brownmackie.edu
Web site: http://www.brownmackie.edu/Merrillville

BROWN MACKIE COLLEGE — MIAMI
MIAMI, FLORIDA

The College

Brown Mackie College — Miami (Brown Mackie College) is one of over twenty-five locations in the Brown Mackie College family of schools (www.brownmackie.edu), which is dedicated to providing educational programs that prepare students to pursue entry-level positions in a competitive, rapidly changing workplace. Brown Mackie College schools offer bachelor degree, associate degree, diploma, and certificate programs in health sciences, business, information technology, legal studies, criminal justice, early childhood education, and design to over 20,000 students in the Midwest, Southeast, Southwest, and Western United States.

Brown Mackie College — Miami is accredited by the Accrediting Council for Independent Colleges and Schools to award bachelor degrees, associate degrees, and diplomas. The Accrediting Council for Independent Colleges and Schools is listed as a nationally recognized accrediting agency by the United States Department of Education and is recognized by the Council for Higher Education Accreditation. ACICS can be contacted at 750 First Street NE, Suite 980, Washington, D.C. 20002; phone: 202-336-6780.

Brown Mackie College — Miami is licensed by the Commission for Independent Education, Florida Department of Education. Additional information regarding this institution may be obtained by contacting the Commission at 325 West Gaines Street, Suite 1414; Tallahassee, Florida 32399-0400; phone: 888-224-6684 (toll-free).

The college is a nonresidential, smoke-free institution.

Location

Brown Mackie College — Miami occupies space within the newly renovated One Herald Plaza in Miami, Florida. It is conveniently located adjacent to the OMNI Metro Mover and bus stop, with access to Metro Rail and Florida's regional Tri-Rail system. Ample parking is also available.

Programs of Study and Degrees

Brown Mackie College — Miami provides higher education to traditional and nontraditional students through bachelor degree and associate degree programs that assist them in enhancing their career opportunities, broadening their perspectives through appropriate general education courses, thinking independently and critically, and improving problem-solving abilities. The college strives to develop within its students the desire for lifelong and continued education.

The Bachelor of Science degree is awarded in business administration, criminal justice, health care management, and information technology.

The Associate of Science degree is awarded in accounting technology, architectural design and drafting technology, biomedical equipment technology, business management, computer networking, criminal justice, early childhood education, graphic design, health care administration, information technology, medical assisting, nursing, and paralegal.

Brown Mackie College — Miami offers a medical assistant diploma program.

The American Medical Technologists (AMT), which offers the certification for Registered Medical Assistant (RMA), accepts the accreditation of Brown Mackie College–Miami. Students will qualify to take the Registered Medical Assistant certification examination upon graduating the Brown Mackie College — Miami Medical Assisting program.

Brown Mackie College — Miami does not guarantee third-party certification. Outside agencies control the requirements for certifications and are subject to change without notice to Brown Mackie College.

Academic Programs

Each college quarter comprises twelve weeks. Bachelor degree programs require a minimum of sixteen quarters to complete. Associate degree programs require a minimum of eight quarters to complete. Programs are offered on a year-round basis, providing students with the ability to work uninterrupted toward their degrees. The college offers all programs in a unique One-Course-a-Month format. This allows students to focus studies on only one course for four weeks. This schedule has proven convenient for students with multiple obligations, such as jobs and family.

Academic Facilities

Brown Mackie College — Miami is conveniently located at One Herald Plaza, Miami, Florida 33132. The college occupies 50,000 square feet on the top floor of the Miami Herald building, which sits on beautiful Biscayne Bay and offers a clear view of Miami and the Miami Beach skylines.

The computer networking lab as well as multiple computer classrooms offer students a modern and professional environment for study. Four medical labs are used to instruct clinical medical skills as well as biomedical equipment use and repair. Each student has access to the technology, tools, and facilities needed to complete projects in each subject area. Students are welcome to use the labs when they are not being used for scheduled classes.

The college features a comfortable student lounge as well as an on-site eatery available during all class shifts. The college bookstore offers retail items including textbooks, kits specific to programs of study, and college apparel. The on-site library offers multi-media resources including books, periodicals, and electronic resources specific to all academic programs offered. Course delivery at Brown Mackie College — Miami includes on-ground as well as blended courses.

In 2012, Brown Mackie College — Miami began its transition to using eTextbooks and computer tablets in the classroom. Utilizing these tablets to access expanded course material, students will be able to increase their acumen for using this technology and further enhance their educational experience. Students have the ability to directly download their eTextbooks to their tablet, eliminating the need to carry heavy, physical textbooks and reducing the overall cost of supplies.

Costs

Tuition in the 2011–12 academic year for all programs was $391 per credit hour; fees were $15 per credit hour. For the nursing program, tuition was $410 per credit hour; fees were $25 per credit hour. Textbooks and other instructional materials vary by program.

Financial Aid

Financial aid is available for those who qualify. The college maintains a full-time staff of Student Financial Services Advisors to assist qualified students in obtaining financial assistance. The college participates in several student aid programs. Forms of financial aid available to qualified students through federal resources include the Federal Pell Grant Program, Federal Supplemental Educational Opportunity Grant (FSEOG) Program, Federal Work-Study Program, Federal Perkins Loan Program, Federal Stafford Student Loan Program (subsidized and unsubsidized), Federal PLUS loan program, and Florida State grant program. Eligible students may apply for veterans' educational benefits. Students with physical or mental disabilities that are a handicap to employment may be eligible for training services through the state Agency for Vocational Rehabilitation. For further information, students should contact the Student Financial Services Office.

Each year, the college makes available President's Scholarships of $1000 each to qualifying seniors from area high schools. Up to three (3) scholarships may be awarded per high school. In order to qualify, a senior must be graduating from a participating high school, must be maintaining a cumulative grade point average of at least 2.0, and must submit a brief essay. The student's extracurricular activities and community service are also considered. The President's Scholarship is available only to students enrolling in one of the college's degree programs. Students awarded the scholarship must enroll at Brown Mackie College — Miami between June and September immediately following their high school graduation. Applications for these scholarships can be obtained from the guidance departments of participating high schools and must be completed and returned to Brown Mackie College by March 31. Those awarded scholarships will be notified by April 30. A list of participating high schools may be obtained from the campus Admissions Office.

Faculty

There are 15 full-time and more than 50 adjunct faculty members at the college. The average student-faculty ratio is 17:1.

Admission Requirements

Each applicant for admission is assigned an Assistant Director of Admissions who directs the applicant through the steps of the admissions process, providing information on curriculum, policies, procedures, and services, and assisting the applicant in setting up necessary appointments and interviews. To qualify for admission, applicants must be graduates of a public or private high school or a correspondence school or education center that is accredited by an agency that is recognized by the U.S. Department of Education or the State of Florida's Department of Education or any of its approved agents or must provide official documentation of high school graduation equivalency. As part of the admissions process, applicants must sign a document attesting to graduation or completion and containing the information to obtain verification of such. Official high school transcripts or official documentation of high school graduation equivalency must be obtained within the first term (90 days) or the student will be withdrawn from the institution following established guidelines for withdrawn students noted in the catalog. Title IV aid will not be dispersed until verification of graduation or completion has been received by the College.

Students seeking entry into the college with a high school diploma completed in a foreign country must provide an original U.S.-equivalency evaluation from an evaluating agency that is a member of the National Association of Credential Evaluation Services (NACES) (http://www.naces.org/) or the Association of International Credential Evaluators, Inc. (AICES) (http://www.aice-eval.org/). The cost of evaluating the foreign transcript is borne by the applicant.

Brown Mackie College — Miami is authorized under Federal law to enroll nonimmigrant students. Applicants seeking entry into the college with a high school diploma completed in a foreign country must provide an original U. S. equivalency evaluation from a recognized evaluating agency. The cost of evaluating the foreign transcript is borne by the applicant.

For the most recent information regarding admission requirements, please refer to the current academic catalog.

Application and Information

Applicants must complete and submit an application form, along with documentation of graduation from an accredited high school or state-approved secondary education curriculum or official documentation of high school graduation equivalency.

See BMCprograms.info for program duration, tuition, fees and other costs, median debt, federal salary data, alumni success, programmatic accreditation, and other important info.

For additional information, prospective students should contact:

Director of Admissions
Brown Mackie College — Miami
One Herald Plaza
Miami, Florida 33132-1418
United States
Phone: 305-341-6600
   866-505-0335 (toll-free)
Fax: 305-373-8814
E-mail: bmmiaadm@brownmackie.edu
Web site: http://www.brownmackie.edu/Miami

BROWN MACKIE COLLEGE — MICHIGAN CITY

MICHIGAN CITY, INDIANA

The College

Brown Mackie College — Michigan City (Brown Mackie College) is one of over twenty-five locations in the Brown Mackie College family of schools (www.brownmackie.edu), which is dedicated to providing educational programs that prepare students to pursue entry-level positions in a competitive, rapidly changing workplace. Brown Mackie College schools offer bachelor degree, associate degree, diploma, and certificate programs in health sciences, business, information technology, legal studies, and design to over 20,000 students in the Midwest, Southeast, Southwest, and Western United States.

Founded in 1890 by A. N. Hirons as LaPorte Business College in LaPorte, Indiana, the institution later became known as Commonwealth Business College. In 1919, ownership was transferred to Grace and J. J. Moore, who successfully operated the college under the name of Reese School of Business for several decades. In 1975, the college came under the ownership of Steven C. Smith as Commonwealth Business College. In 1997, the college relocated to its present site in Michigan City, Indiana. The College was acquired by Education Management Corporation (EDMC) on September 2, 2003, and changed its name to Brown Mackie College — Michigan City in November 2004.

Brown Mackie College — Michigan City is accredited by the Accrediting Council for Independent Colleges and Schools to award bachelor degrees, associate degrees, and certificates. The Accrediting Council for Independent Colleges and Schools is listed as a nationally recognized accrediting agency by the United States Department of Education and is recognized by the Council for Higher Education Accreditation. ACICS can be contacted at 750 First Street NE, Suite 980, Washington, D.C. 20002; phone: 202-336-6780.

Brown Mackie College — Michigan City is regulated by the Indiana Commission on Proprietary Education, 302 West Washington Street, Indianapolis, Indiana 46204; phone: 317-232-1320 or 800-227-5695 (toll-free). Indiana Advertising Code: AC0138.

The Associate of Science in medical assisting program is accredited by the Accrediting Bureau of Health Education Schools.

The Associate of Science in surgical technology is accredited by the Commission on Accreditation of Allied Health Education Programs (www.caahep.org) upon the recommendation of the Accreditation Review Committee on Education in Surgical Technology. Commission on Accreditation of Allied Health Education Programs 1361 Park Street, Clearwater, Florida 33756; phone: 727-210-2350.

The Associate of Science in veterinary technology program has provisional programmatic accreditation granted by the American Veterinary Medical Association (AVMA) through the Committee on Veterinary Technician Education and Activities (CVTEA).

The college is a nonresidential, smoke-free institution.

Location

Brown Mackie College — Michigan City is conveniently located in northwest Indiana, at 1001 East U.S. Highway 20, Michigan City, 1 mile north of Interstate 94, 1 mile east of the intersection of routes 20 and 421.

Programs of Study and Degrees

Brown Mackie College — Michigan City provides higher education to traditional and nontraditional students through bachelor degree, associate degree, and certificate programs that assist in enhancing their career opportunities, broadening their perspectives through appropriate general education courses, thinking independently and critically, and improving problem-solving abilities. Brown Mackie College strives to develop within its students the desire for lifelong and continued education.

The Bachelor of Science degree is awarded in business administration, criminal justice, and legal studies.

The Associate of Science degree is awarded in accounting technology, business management, criminal justice, health care administration, medical assisting, medical office management, paralegal, surgical technology, and veterinary technology.

The college offers certificate programs in accounting, business, criminal justice, medical assistant, medical coding and billing, and paralegal assistant.

The American Medical Technologists (AMT), which offers the certification for Registered Medical Assistant (RMA), accepts the accreditation of Brown Mackie College — Michigan City. Students will qualify to take the Registered Medical Assistant certification examination upon graduating the Brown Mackie College — Michigan City Medical Assisting and Medical Assistant programs. Graduates of the 48-credit-hour Medical Assistant program are not qualified to take the AMT/RMA exam.

Brown Mackie College — Michigan City does not guarantee third-party certification. Outside agencies control the requirements for certifications and are subject to change without notice to Brown Mackie College.

Academic Programs

Each college quarter comprises twelve weeks. Bachelor degree programs require a minimum of sixteen quarters to complete. Associate degree programs require a minimum of eight quarters

to complete. Programs are offered on a year-round basis, providing students with the ability to work uninterrupted toward their degrees. The college offers all programs in a unique One-Course-a-Month format. This allows students to focus studies on only one course for four weeks. This schedule has proven convenient for students with multiple obligations such as jobs and family.

Academic Facilities

In 2002, the college underwent a major renovation and added 3,360 square feet, for a total of 10,338 square feet of occupancy. An additional medical laboratory, a larger library, new classrooms, and a bookstore were added. All classrooms and the library are equipped with new technology, including multimedia projectors, surround-sound audio systems, VCRs, and DVD players. Five of the ten new classrooms are equipped with networked computer systems. The two medical laboratories contain newly acquired medical equipment and instructional tools and supplies. Administrative offices are easily accessible to students. In 2008, a learning site was opened at 1623 South Woodland Avenue, Michigan City, Indiana. Of approximately 6,500 square feet, this site is conveniently located within a mile of the main campus.

Costs

Tuition in the 2011–12 academic year was $294 per credit hour and fees were $15 per credit hour. For the surgical technology program, the tuition was $340 per credit hour and fees were $15 per credit hour. Textbook fees vary according to the program.

Financial Aid

The college maintains a full-time staff of Student Financial Services Advisors to assist qualified students in obtaining financial assistance. The college participates in several student aid programs. Forms of financial aid available to qualified students through federal resources include the Federal Pell Grant Program, Federal Supplemental Educational Opportunity Grant (FSEOG) Program, Federal Work-Study Program, Federal Stafford Student Loan Program (subsidized and unsubsidized), and Federal PLUS loan program.

Eligible students may apply for Indiana state awards, such as the Higher Education Award and Twenty-First Century Scholarships for high school students, the Core 40 awards, and veterans' educational benefits. Students with physical or mental disabilities that are a handicap to employment may be eligible for training services through the state's Bureau of Vocational Rehabilitation. For further information, students should contact the college's Student Financial Services Office.

Each year, the college makes available President's Scholarships of $1000 each to qualifying seniors from area high schools. Up to three (3) scholarships may be awarded per high school. In order to qualify, a senior must be graduating from a participating high school, must be maintaining a cumulative grade point average of at least 2.0, and must submit a brief essay. The student's extracurricular activities and community service are also considered. These scholarships are available only to students enrolling in one of the college's degree programs. Students awarded the scholarship must enroll at Brown Mackie College — Michigan City between June and

September immediately following their high school graduation. Applications for these scholarships can be obtained from the guidance departments of participating high schools. These applications must be completed and returned to Brown Mackie College by March 31.

Faculty

There are 9 full-time and 31 part-time faculty members at the college. The average student-faculty ratio is 13:1. Each student is assigned a department chair.

Admission Requirements

Each applicant for admission is assigned an Assistant Director of Admissions, who directs the applicant through the steps of the admissions process, providing information on curriculum, policies, procedures, and services and assisting the applicant in setting up necessary appointments and interviews. To qualify for admission, each applicant must provide documentation of graduation from an accredited high school or completion of a state-approved secondary education curriculum or official documentation of high school graduation equivalency. All transcripts become the property of Brown Mackie College.

As part of the admission process, students are given an assessment of academic skills. Although the results of this assessment do not determine eligibility for admission, they provide the college with a means of determining the need for academic support, as well as a means by which the college can evaluate the effectiveness of its educational programs. All new students are required to complete this assessment.

For the most recent information regarding admission requirements, please refer to the current academic catalog.

Application and Information

Applicants must complete and submit an application form along with documentation of graduation from an accredited high school or completion of a state-approved secondary education curriculum or provide official documentation of high school graduation equivalency.

See BMCprograms.info for program duration, tuition, fees and other costs, median debt, federal salary data, alumni success, programmatic accreditation, and other important info.

For additional information, prospective students should contact:

Director of Admissions
Brown Mackie College — Michigan City
1001 East U.S. Highway 20
Michigan City, Indiana 46360
United States
Phone: 219-877-3100
          800-519-2416 (toll-free)
Fax: 219-877-3110
E-mail: bmcmcadm@brownmackie.edu
Web site: http://www.brownmackie.edu/MichiganCity

BROWN MACKIE COLLEGE — NORTH CANTON

NORTH CANTON, OHIO

The College

Brown Mackie College — North Canton (Brown Mackie College) is one of over twenty-five locations in the Brown Mackie College family of schools (www.brownmackie.edu), which is dedicated to providing educational programs that prepare students to pursue entry-level positions in a competitive, rapidly changing workplace. Brown Mackie College schools offer bachelor degree, associate degree, diploma, and certificate programs in health sciences, business, information technology, legal studies, and design to more than 20,000 students in the Midwest, Southeast, Southwest, and Western United States.

The college opened in the 1980s as the National Electronics Institute. In 2002, the Southern Ohio College took ownership. The following year, it became part of the Brown Mackie College family of schools.

Brown Mackie College — North Canton is accredited by the Accrediting Council for Independent Colleges and Schools to award bachelor degrees, associate degrees, and diplomas. The Accrediting Council for Independent Colleges and Schools is listed as a nationally recognized accrediting agency by the United States Department of Education and is recognized by the Council for Higher Education Accreditation. ACICS can be contacted at 750 First Street NE, Suite 980, Washington, D.C. 20002; phone: 202-336-6780.

Brown Mackie College — North Canton is licensed by the Ohio State Board of Career Colleges and Schools, located at 30 East Broad Street, 24th Floor, Suite 2481, Columbus, Ohio 43215-3138; phone: 614-466-2752. Ohio registration # 03-09-1688T.

The Associate of Science in medical assisting program is accredited by the Accrediting Bureau of Health Education Schools.

The Associate of Science in surgical technology is accredited by the Commission on Accreditation of Allied Health Education Programs (www.caahep.org) upon the recommendation of the Accreditation Review Committee on Education in Surgical Technology. The Commission on Accreditation of Allied Health Education Programs is located at 1361 Park Street, Clearwater, Florida 33756; phone: 727-210-2350.

The Associate of Science in veterinary technology program has provisional programmatic accreditation granted by the American Veterinary Medical Association (AVMA) through the Committee on Veterinary Technician Education and Activities (CVTEA).

Location

Brown Mackie College — North Canton is located at 4300 Munson Street, NW in Canton, Ohio. The school is easily accessible from I-77 and Route 687 and by the SARTA bus line.

Programs of Study and Degrees

Brown Mackie College — North Canton provides higher education to traditional and nontraditional students through associate degree, bachelor degree, and diploma programs that can assist students in enhancing their career opportunities, broadening their perspectives through appropriate general education courses, thinking independently and critically, and improving problem-solving abilities. The college strives to develop within its students the desire for lifelong and continued education.

The Bachelor of Science degree is awarded in business administration, criminal justice, health care management, and legal studies.

The Associate of Applied Business degree is awarded in accounting technology, business management, computer networking and applications, criminal justice, and paralegal. The Associate of Applied Science degree is awarded in computer-aided design and drafting technology, health care administration, medical assisting, pharmacy technology, surgical technology, and veterinary technology.

The college also offers diploma programs in accounting, business, computer-aided design and drafting technician, criminal justice, medical assistant, paralegal assistant, and practical nursing.

The American Medical Technologists (AMT), which offers the certification for Registered Medical Assistant (RMA), accepts the accreditation of Brown Mackie College — North Canton. Students will qualify to take the Registered Medical Assistant certification examination upon graduating the Brown Mackie College — North Canton Medical Assisting and Medical Assistant programs. Graduates of the 48-credit-hour Medical Assistant program are not qualified to take the AMT/RMA exam.

Brown Mackie College — North Canton does not guarantee third-party certification. Outside agencies control the requirements for certifications and are subject to change without notice to Brown Mackie College.

Academic Programs

Each college quarter comprises twelve weeks. Bachelor degree programs require a minimum of sixteen quarters to complete.

Associate degree programs require a minimum of eight quarters to complete. Programs are offered on a year-round basis, providing students with the ability to work uninterrupted toward their degrees. The college offers all programs in a unique One-Course-a-Month format. This schedule allows students to focus studies on only one course for four weeks and has proven convenient for students with multiple obligations, such as jobs and family.

Academic Facilities

The college comprises administrative offices, faculty and student lounges, a reception area, and spacious classrooms and laboratories. Instructional equipment includes personal computers, LANs, printers, and LCD projectors. The library provides support for the academic programs through volumes covering a broad range of subjects, as well as through Internet access. Vehicle parking is provided for both students and staff members.

Costs

Tuition for the 2011–12 academic year was $294 per credit hour and $15 per credit hour for general fees. The tuition for the surgical technology program was $340 per credit hour and $15 per credit hour for general fees. The tuition for the practical nursing program was $361 per credit hour and $25 per credit hour for general fees. The cost of textbooks and other instructional materials varies by program.

Financial Aid

Financial aid is available to those who qualify. The college maintains a full-time staff of Student Financial Services Advisors to assist qualified students in obtaining financial assistance. The college participates in several student aid programs. Forms of financial aid available through federal resources include the Federal Pell Grant Program, Federal Supplemental Educational Opportunity Grant (FSEOG) Program, Federal Work-Study Program, Federal Perkins Loan Program, Federal Stafford Student Loan Program (subsidized and unsubsidized), and the Federal PLUS Loan Program. Eligible students may also apply for state awards and veterans' educational benefits. Students with physical or mental disabilities that are a handicap to employment may be eligible for training services through the state Agency for Vocational Rehabilitation. For further information, students should contact the college's Student Financial Services Office.

Each year, the college makes available President's Scholarships of $1000 each to qualifying seniors from area high schools. Up to three (3) scholarships may be awarded per high school. In order to qualify, a senior must be graduating from a participating high school, must be maintaining a cumulative grade point average of at least 2.0, and must submit a brief essay. The student's extracurricular activities and community service are also considered. The President's Scholarship is available only to students enrolling in one of the college's degree programs. Students awarded the scholarship must enroll at Brown Mackie College — North Canton between June and September immediately following their high school graduation. Applications for these scholarships can be obtained from the guidance departments of participating high schools. These applications must be completed and returned to Brown Mackie College by March 31.

Faculty

There are approximately 20 full-time and approximately 35 part-time faculty members. The average student-faculty ratio is approximately 19:1. Each student has a faculty and student adviser.

Admission Requirements

Each applicant for admission is assigned an Assistant Director of Admissions, who directs the applicant through the steps of the admissions process, providing information on curriculum, policies, procedures, and services and assisting the applicant in setting up necessary appointments and interviews. To qualify for admission, each applicant must provide documentation of graduation from an accredited high school or from a state-approved secondary education curriculum or official documentation of high school graduation equivalency. All transcripts become the property of the college. Admission to the college is based upon the applicant meeting the stated requirements, a review of the applicant's previous education records, and a review of the applicant's career interests. If previous academic records indicate that the college's education and training programs would not benefit the applicant, the college reserves the right to advise the applicant not to enroll. Special requirements for enrollment into certain programs are discussed in the descriptions of those programs.

For the most recent information regarding admission requirements, please refer to the current academic catalog.

Application and Information

Applicants must complete and submit an application form, along with documentation of graduation from an accredited high school or state-approved secondary education curriculum or official documentation of high school graduation equivalency.

See BMCprograms.info for program duration, tuition, fees and other costs, median debt, federal salary data, alumni success, programmatic accreditation, and other important info.

For additional information, prospective students should contact:

Director of Admissions
Brown Mackie College — North Canton
4300 Munson Street NW
Canton, Ohio 44718-3674
United States
Phone: 330-494-1214
Fax: 330-494-8112
E-mail: bmcncweb@brownmackie.edu
Web site: http://www.brownmackie.edu/North-Canton

BROWN MACKIE COLLEGE — NORTHERN KENTUCKY

FORT MITCHELL, KENTUCKY

The College

Brown Mackie College — Northern Kentucky (Brown Mackie College) is one of over twenty-five locations in the Brown Mackie College family of schools (www.brownmackie.edu), which is dedicated to providing educational programs that prepare students to pursue entry-level positions in a competitive, rapidly changing workplace. Brown Mackie College schools offer bachelor degree, associate degree, diploma, and certificate programs in health sciences, business, information technology, legal studies, and design to more than 20,000 students in the Midwest, Southeast, Southwest, and Western United States.

The college was founded in Cincinnati, Ohio, in February 1927 as a traditional business college. In May 1981, the college opened a branch location in northern Kentucky, which in 1986 moved to its current location in Fort Mitchell.

Brown Mackie College — Northern Kentucky is accredited by the Accrediting Council for Independent Colleges and Schools to award bachelor degrees, associate degrees, and diplomas. The Accrediting Council for Independent Colleges and Schools is listed as a nationally recognized accrediting agency by the United States Department of Education and is recognized by the Council for Higher Education Accreditation. ACICS can be contacted at 750 First Street NE, Suite 980, Washington, D.C. 20002; phone: 202-336-6780.

Brown Mackie College — Northern Kentucky is regulated by the Indiana Commission on Proprietary Education, located at 302 West Washington Street, Room E201, Indianapolis, Indiana 46204; phone: 317-232-1320 or 800-227-5695 (toll-free). Indiana Advertising Code: AC-0150.

Brown Mackie College — Northern Kentucky is licensed by the Ohio State Board of Career Colleges and Schools, located at 30 East Broad Street, 24th Floor, Suite 2481, Columbus, Ohio 43215-3138; phone: 614-466-2752. Ohio registration # 06-03-1781T.

Brown Mackie College — Northern Kentucky is licensed by the Kentucky Council on Postsecondary Education, located at 1024 Capital Center Drive, Suite 320, Frankfort, Kentucky 40601.

The Associate of Applied Science in occupational therapy assistant program is accredited by the Accreditation Council for Occupational Therapy Education (ACOTE) of the American Occupational Therapy Association (AOTA), located at 4720 Montgomery Lane, P.O. Box 31220, Bethesda, Maryland 20824; phone: 301-652-AOTA.

The Associate of Applied Science in surgical technology program is accredited by the Commission on Accreditation of Allied Health Education Programs (http://www.caahep.org) upon the recommendation of the Accreditation Review Council on Education in Surgical Technology and Surgical Assisting (ARC/STSA).

Location

Brown Mackie College — Northern Kentucky is conveniently located at 309 Buttermilk Pike in Fort Mitchell, Kentucky. A spacious parking lot provides ample parking at no additional charge.

Programs of Study and Degrees

Brown Mackie College — Northern Kentucky provides higher education to traditional and nontraditional students through bachelor degree, associate degree, and diploma programs that assist them in enhancing their career opportunities, broadening their perspectives through appropriate general education courses, thinking independently and critically, and improving problem-solving abilities. The college strives to develop within its students the desire for lifelong and continued education.

The Bachelor of Science degree is awarded in business administration, criminal justice, health care management, and legal studies.

The Associate of Applied Business degree is awarded in accounting technology, business management, criminal justice, health care administration, information technology, and paralegal.

The Associate of Applied Science degree is awarded in computer-aided design and drafting technology, medical assistant, occupational therapy assistant, and surgical technology.

Brown Mackie College — Northern Kentucky offers a diploma program in medical assistant and practical nursing.

The American Medical Technologists (AMT), which offers the certification for Registered Medical Assistant (RMA), accepts the accreditation of Brown Mackie College — Northern Kentucky. Students will qualify to take the Registered Medical Assistant certification examination upon graduating the Brown Mackie College — Northern Kentucky Medical Assisting and Medical Assistant programs. Graduates of the 48-credit-hour Medical Assistant program are not qualified to take the AMT/RMA exam.

Brown Mackie College — Northern Kentucky does not guarantee third-party certification. Outside agencies control the requirements for certifications and are subject to change without notice to Brown Mackie College.

Academic Programs

Each college quarter comprises ten to twelve weeks. Bachelor degree programs require a minimum of sixteen quarters to complete. Associate degree programs require a minimum of eight quarters to complete. Programs are offered on a year-round basis, providing students with the ability to work uninterrupted toward their degrees. The college offers all programs in a unique One-Course-a-Month format. This allows students to focus studies on only one course for four weeks.

This schedule has proven convenient for students with multiple obligations, such as jobs and family.

Academic Facilities

Brown Mackie College offers media presentation rooms for special instructional needs and a library that provides instructional resources and academic support for both faculty members and students.

The college is nonresidential; public transportation and ample parking at no cost are available. The school is a smoke-free facility.

Costs

Tuition for the 2011–12 academic year was $294 per credit hour and general fees were $15 per credit hour, with some exceptions. The practical nursing program tuition was $361 per credit hour and general fees were $25 per credit hour. The surgical technology tuition was $340 per credit hour. Tuition for the occupational therapy assistant program was $361 per credit hour and general fees were $15 per credit hour. The cost of textbooks and other instructional materials varies by program.

Financial Aid

Financial aid is available to those who qualify. The college maintains a full-time staff of Student Financial Services Advisors to assist qualified students in obtaining financial assistance. The college participates in several student aid programs. Forms of financial aid available through federal resources include Federal Pell Grants, Federal Supplemental Educational Opportunity Grants (FSEOG), Federal Work-Study Program awards, Federal Perkins Loans, Federal Stafford Student Loans (subsidized and unsubsidized), and Federal PLUS loans. Eligible students may apply for veterans' educational benefits. Students with physical or mental disabilities that are a handicap to employment may be eligible for training services through the state Vocational Rehabilitation Agency. For further information, students should contact the Student Financial Services Office.

Each year, the college makes available President's Scholarships of $1000 each to qualifying seniors from area high schools. Up to three (3) scholarships may be awarded per high school. In order to qualify, a senior must have graduated from a participating high school, must have maintained a cumulative grade point average of at least 2.0, and must have submitted a brief essay. The student's extracurricular activities and community service are also considered. The President's Scholarship is available only to students enrolling in one of the college's degree programs. Students who receive the scholarship must enroll at Brown Mackie College — Northern Kentucky between June and September immediately following their high school graduation. Applications for these scholarships can be obtained from the guidance departments of participating high schools. These applications must be completed and returned to Brown Mackie College by March 31.

Faculty

There are 11 full-time and 30 adjunct faculty members. The student-faculty ratio is 15:1.

Admission Requirements

Each applicant for admission is assigned an Assistant Director of Admissions, who directs the applicant through the steps of the admissions process, providing information on curriculum, policies, procedures, and services and assisting the applicant in setting up necessary appointments and interviews. To qualify for admission, each applicant must provide documentation of graduation from an accredited high school or from a state-approved secondary education curriculum or provide official documentation of high school graduation equivalency. All transcripts become the property of the college. Admission to the college is based upon the applicant meeting the stated requirements, a review of the applicant's previous education records, and a review of the applicant's career interests. If previous academic records indicate the college's education and training programs would not benefit the applicant, the college reserves the right to advise the applicant not to enroll. Special requirements for enrollment into certain programs are discussed in the descriptions of those programs.

In addition to the college's general admission requirements, applicants enrolling in the practical nursing program must complete several documents, listed below. A record of proof must appear in the student's file prior to the start of the nursing fundamentals course. No student will be admitted to a clinical agency unless all paperwork is completed. The paperwork is a requirement of all contracted agencies. This paperwork includes records of (1) a complete physical, current to within six months of admission; (2) a two-step Mantoux test that is kept current throughout schooling; (3) a hepatitis B vaccination or signed refusal; (4) up-to-date immunizations, including tetanus and rubella; (5) a record of current CPR certification that is maintained throughout the student's clinical experience; and (6) hospitalization insurance or a signed waiver.

For the most recent information regarding admission requirements, prospective students should refer to the current academic catalog.

Application and Information

Applicants must complete and submit an application form, along with documentation of graduation from an accredited high school or state-approved secondary education curriculum or official documentation of high school graduation equivalency.

See BMCprograms.info for program duration, tuition, fees and other costs, median debt, federal salary data, alumni success, programmatic accreditation, and other important info.

For additional information, prospective students should contact:

Director of Admissions
Brown Mackie College — Northern Kentucky
309 Buttermilk Pike
Fort Mitchell, Kentucky 41017
United States
Phone: 859-341-5627
Fax: 859-341-6483
E-mail: bmcnkadm@brownmackie.edu
Web site: http://www.brownmackie.edu/NorthernKentucky

BROWN MACKIE COLLEGE — PHOENIX
PHOENIX, ARIZONA

BROWN
MACKIE
COLLEGE
PHOENIX℠

The College

Brown Mackie College — Phoenix (Brown Mackie College) is one of over twenty-five locations in the Brown Mackie College family of schools (www.brownmackie.edu), which is dedicated to providing educational programs that prepare students to pursue entry-level positions in a competitive, rapidly changing workplace. Brown Mackie College schools offer bachelor degree, associate degree, diploma, and certificate programs in health sciences, business, information technology, legal studies, and design to over 20,000 students in the Midwest, Southeast, Southwest, and Western United States.

Brown Mackie College — Phoenix was founded in 2009 as a branch of Brown Mackie College — Tucson, Arizona.

Brown Mackie College — Phoenix is accredited by the Accrediting Council for Independent Colleges and Schools to award bachelor degrees, associate degrees, diplomas, and certificates. The Accrediting Council for Independent Colleges and Schools is listed as a nationally recognized accrediting agency by the United States Department of Education and is recognized by the Council for Higher Education Accreditation. ACICS can be contacted at 750 First Street NE, Suite 980, Washington, D.C. 20002; phone: 202-336-6780.

The Associate of Applied Science in occupational therapy assistant program is accredited by the Accreditation Council for Occupational Therapy Education (ACOTE) of the American Occupational Therapy Association (AOTA), located at 4720 Montgomery Lane, P.O. Box 31220, Bethesda, Maryland 20824-1220; phone: 301-652-2682.

The Associate of Science in surgical technology program is accredited by the Accrediting Bureau of Health Education Schools.

Brown Mackie College — Phoenix is authorized by the Arizona State Board for Private Postsecondary Education, located at 1400 West Washington Street, Room 2560, Phoenix, Arizona 85007; phone: 602-542-5709; http://azppse.state.az.us.

The college is a nonresidential, smoke-free institution.

Location

Brown Mackie College — Phoenix is conveniently located at 13430 North Black Canyon Highway, Suite 190, in Phoenix, Arizona. The college has a generous parking area and is easily accessible by public transportation.

Programs of Study and Degrees

Brown Mackie College provides higher education to traditional and nontraditional students through bachelor and associate degree programs that assist in enhancing their career opportunities, broadening their perspectives through appropriate general education courses, thinking independently and critically, and improving problem-solving abilities. The college strives to develop within its students the desire for lifelong and continued education.

The Bachelor of Science degree is awarded in business administration, criminal justice, health care management, and legal studies.

The Associate of Science degree is awarded in accounting technology, biomedical equipment technology, business management, criminal justice, health care administration, information technology, medical assisting, paralegal, and surgical technology.

The Associate of Applied Science degree is awarded in nursing and occupational therapy assistant.

Brown Mackie College — Phoenix offers a medical assistant diploma program.

The American Medical Technologists (AMT), which offers the certification for Registered Medical Assistant (RMA), accepts the accreditation of Brown Mackie College — Phoenix. Students will qualify to take the Registered Medical Assistant certification examination upon graduating the Brown Mackie College — Phoenix Medical Assisting and Medical Assistant programs. Graduates of the 48-credit-hour Medical Assistant program are not qualified to take the AMT/RMA exam.

Brown Mackie College — Phoenix does not guarantee third-party certification. Outside agencies control the requirements for certifications and are subject to change without notice to Brown Mackie College.

Academic Programs

Each college quarter comprises twelve weeks. Bachelor degree programs require a minimum of sixteen quarters to complete. Associate degree programs require a minimum of eight quarters to complete. Programs are offered on a year-round basis, providing students with the ability to work uninterrupted toward completion of their programs. The

college offers all programs in a unique One-Course-a-Month format. This allows students to focus studies on only one course for four weeks. This schedule has proven convenient for students with multiple obligations, such as jobs and family.

Academic Facilities

Brown Mackie College — Phoenix has a variety of classrooms, including computer labs housing the latest technology in the industry. High-speed access to the Internet and other online resources are available for students and faculty. Multimedia classrooms provide a learning environment equipped with overhead projectors, TVs, DVD/VCR players, computers, and sound systems.

Costs

Tuition for programs in the 2011–12 academic year was $294 per credit hour, with a general fee of $15 per credit hour applied to instructional costs for activities and services. For the surgical technology program, the tuition was $340 per credit hour, with a general fee of $15 per credit hour applied to instructional costs for activities. For the occupational therapy assistant program, the tuition was $361 per credit hour, with a general fee of $15 per credit hour applied to instructional costs for activities. For the nursing program, the tuition was $390 per credit hour, with a general fee of $25 per credit hour applied to instructional costs for activities. Textbooks and other instructional materials vary by program.

Financial Aid

Financial aid is available for those who qualify. The college maintains a full-time staff of Student Financial Services Advisors to assist qualified students in obtaining financial assistance. The college participates in several student aid programs. Forms of financial aid available to those who qualify through federal resources include the Federal Pell Grant Program, Federal Supplemental Educational Opportunity Grant (FSEOG) Program, Federal Work-Study Program, Federal Perkins Loan Program, Federal Stafford Student Loan Program (subsidized and unsubsidized), and the Federal PLUS Loan Program.

Each year, the college makes available President's Scholarships of $1000 each to qualifying seniors from area high schools. Up to three (3) scholarships may be awarded per high school. In order to qualify, a senior must be graduating from a participating high school, must be maintaining a cumulative grade point average of at least 2.0, and must submit a brief essay. The student's extracurricular activities and community service are also considered. The President's Scholarship is available only to students enrolling in one of the college's degree programs. Students awarded the scholarship must enroll at Brown Mackie College — Phoenix between June and September immediately following their high school graduation. Applications for these scholarships can be obtained from the guidance departments of participating high schools. These applications must be completed and returned to Brown Mackie College by March 31.

Faculty

Experienced faculty members provide academic support and are committed to the academic and technical preparation of their students. The college has both full- and part-time faculty members. The average student-faculty ratio is 14:1. Each student is assigned a program director as an adviser.

Admission Requirements

Each applicant for admission is assigned an Assistant Director of Admissions, who directs the applicant through the steps of the admissions process, providing information on curriculum, policies, procedures, and services and assisting the applicant in setting up necessary appointments and interviews. To qualify for admission, each applicant must provide documentation of graduation from an accredited high school or from a state-approved secondary education curriculum or official documentation of high school graduation equivalency. All transcripts become the property of the college.

For the most recent information regarding admission requirements, please refer to the current academic catalog.

Application and Information

Applicants must complete and submit an application form, along with documentation of graduation from an accredited high school or state-approved secondary education curriculum or official documentation of high school graduation equivalency.

See BMCprograms.info for program duration, tuition, fees and other costs, median debt, federal salary data, alumni success, programmatic accreditation, and other important info.

For additional information, prospective students should contact:

Director of Admissions
Brown Mackie College — Phoenix
13430 N. Black Canyon Highway, Suite 190
Phoenix, Arizona 85029
United States
Phone: 602-337-3044
        866-824-4793 (toll-free)
Fax: 480-375-2450
E-mail: bmcpxadmn@brownmackie.edu
Web site: http://www.brownmackie.edu/Phoenix

BROWN MACKIE COLLEGE — ST. LOUIS
FENTON, MISSOURI

The College

Brown Mackie College — St. Louis (Brown Mackie College) is one of over twenty-five locations in the Brown Mackie College family of schools (www.brownmackie.edu), which is dedicated to providing educational programs that prepare students to pursue entry-level positions in a competitive, rapidly changing workplace. Brown Mackie College schools offer bachelor degree, associate degree, diploma, and certificate programs in health sciences, business, information technology, legal studies, and design to over 20,000 students in the Midwest, Southeast, Southwest, and Western United States.

Brown Mackie College was originally founded and approved by the Board of Trustees of Kansas Wesleyan College in Salina, Kansas on July 30, 1892. In 1938, the College was incorporated as The Brown Mackie School of Business under the ownership of Perry E. Brown and A.B. Mackie, former instructors at Kansas Wesleyan University in Salina, Kansas. Their last names formed the name of Brown Mackie. By January 1975, with improvements in curricula and higher-degree-granting status, The Brown Mackie School of Business became Brown Mackie College.

Brown Mackie College — St. Louis is accredited by the Accrediting Council for Independent Colleges and Schools to award bachelor degrees, associate degrees, and certificates. The Accrediting Council for Independent Colleges and Schools is listed as a nationally recognized accrediting agency by the United States Department of Education and is recognized by the Council for Higher Education Accreditation. ACICS can be contacted at 750 First Street NE, Suite 980, Washington, D.C. 20002; phone: 202-336-6780.

The Associate of Applied Science in occupational therapy assistant program is accredited by the Accreditation Council for Occupational Therapy Education (ACOTE) of the American Occupational Therapy Association (AOTA), located at 4720 Montgomery Lane, P.O. Box 31220, Bethesda, Maryland 20824-1220; phone: 301-652-AOTA.

Location

Brown Mackie College — St. Louis is conveniently located at #2 Soccer Park Road in Fenton, Missouri. The college has a generous parking area and is easily accessible by public transportation.

Programs of Study and Degrees

Brown Mackie College — St. Louis provides higher education to traditional and nontraditional students through bachelor and associate degree programs that assist in enhancing their career opportunities, broadening their perspectives through appropriate general education courses, thinking independently and critically, and improving problem-solving abilities. The college strives to develop within its students the desire for lifelong and continued education.

The Bachelor of Science degree is awarded in business administration, criminal justice, health care management, and legal studies.

The Associate of Applied Science degree is awarded in accounting technology, architectural design and drafting technology, business management, criminal justice, health care administration, information technology, medical assisting, nursing, occupational therapy assistant, office management, paralegal, pharmacy technology, surgical technology, and veterinary technology.

The college offers certificate programs in accounting, business, criminal justice, medical assistant, and paralegal assistant.

The American Medical Technologists (AMT), which offers the certification for Registered Medical Assistant (RMA), accepts the accreditation of Brown Mackie College — St. Louis. Students will qualify to take the Registered Medical Assistant certification examination upon graduating the Brown Mackie College — St. Louis Medical Assisting and Medical Assistant programs. Graduates of the 48-credit-hour Medical Assistant program are not qualified to take the AMT/RMA exam.

Brown Mackie College — St. Louis does not guarantee third-party certification. Outside agencies control the requirements for certifications and are subject to change without notice to Brown Mackie College.

Academic Programs

Each college quarter comprises twelve weeks. Bachelor degree programs require a minimum of sixteen quarters to complete. Associate degree programs require a minimum of eight quarters to complete. Programs are offered on a year-round basis, providing students with the ability to work uninterrupted toward completion of their programs. The college offers all

programs in a unique One-Course-a-Month format. This allows students to focus studies on only one course for four weeks. This schedule has proven convenient for students with multiple obligations, such as jobs and family.

Academic Facilities

A modern facility, Brown Mackie College — St. Louis offers more than 30,000 square feet. The college is equipped with multiple computer labs, housing over 100 computers. High-speed access to the Internet and other online resources are available for students and faculty. Multimedia classrooms are outfitted with overhead projectors, VCR/DVD players, and computers.

Brown Mackie College — St. Louis is nonresidential; public transportation and parking at no cost are available. Brown Mackie College is a smoke-free facility.

Costs

Tuition in the 2011–12 academic year for all bachelor and associate degrees and diploma programs was $268 per credit hour; fees were $15 per credit hour. Tuition for the surgical technology program was $319 per credit hour; fees were $15 per credit hour. Tuition for the nursing program was $390 per credit hour; fees were $25 per credit hour. Tuition for the occupational therapy assistant program was $335 per credit hour; fees were $15 per credit hour. The cost of textbooks and other instructional materials varies by program.

Financial Aid

Financial aid is available for those who qualify. The college maintains a full-time staff of Student Financial Services Advisors to assist qualified students in obtaining the financial assistance they require to meet their educational expenses. Available resources include federal and state aid, student loans from private lenders, and Federal Work-Study opportunities, both on and off college premises.

Each year, the college makes available President's Scholarships of $1000 each to qualifying seniors from area high schools. Up to three (3) scholarships may be awarded per high school. In order to qualify, a senior must have graduated from a participating high school, must have maintained a cumulative grade point average of at least 2.0, and must have submitted a brief essay. The student's extracurricular activities and community service are also considered. These scholarships are available only to students enrolling in one of the college's degree programs. Students awarded the scholarship must enroll at Brown Mackie College — St. Louis between June and September immediately following their high school graduation. Applications for these scholarships can be obtained from the guidance departments of participating high schools. These applications must be completed and returned to Brown Mackie College by March 31.

Faculty

Experienced faculty members provide academic support and are committed to the academic and technical preparation of their students. The college has 12 full-time and 23 part-time instructors, with a student-faculty ratio of 20:1.

Admission Requirements

Each applicant for admission is assigned an Assistant Director of Admissions who directs the applicant through the steps of the admissions process. Assistant Directors provide information on curriculum, policies, procedures, and services and assist the applicant in setting up necessary appointments and interviews. To qualify for admission, each applicant must provide documentation of graduation from an accredited high school or from a state-approved secondary education curriculum or official documentation of high school graduation equivalency. All transcripts become the property of the college. Admission to the college is based on the applicant meeting the stated requirements, a review of the applicant's previous educational records, and a review of the applicant's career interests. If previous academic records indicate the college's education and training programs would not benefit the applicant, the college reserves the right to advise the applicant not to enroll. Special requirements for enrollment into certain programs are discussed in the descriptions of those programs.

For the most recent information regarding admission requirements, prospective students should refer to the current academic catalog.

Application and Information

Applicants must complete and submit an application form, along with documentation of graduation from an accredited high school or state-approved secondary education curriculum or official documentation of high school graduation equivalency.

See BMCprograms.info for program duration, tuition, fees and other costs, median debt, federal salary data, alumni success, programmatic accreditation, and other important info.

For additional information, prospective students should contact:

Director of Admissions
Brown Mackie College — St. Louis
#2 Soccer Park Road
Fenton, Missouri 63026
United States
Phone: 636-651-3290
    888-874-4375 (toll-free)
Fax: 636-651-3349
E-mail: bmcstladm@brownmackie.edu
Web site: http://www.brownmackie.edu/StLouis

BROWN MACKIE COLLEGE — SAN ANTONIO
SAN ANTONIO, TEXAS

The College

Brown Mackie College — San Antonio (Brown Mackie College) is one of over twenty-five locations in the Brown Mackie College family of schools (www.brownmackie.edu), which is dedicated to providing educational programs that prepare students to pursue entry-level positions in a competitive, rapidly changing workplace. Brown Mackie College schools offer bachelor degree, associate degree, diploma, and certificate programs in health sciences, business, information technology, legal studies, and design to over 20,000 students in the Midwest, Southeast, Southwest, and Western United States.

Brown Mackie College was originally founded and approved by the Board of Trustees of Kansas Wesleyan College in Salina, Kansas on July 30, 1892. In 1938, the College was incorporated as the Brown Mackie School of Business under the ownership of Perry E. Brown and A. B. Mackie, former instructors at Kansas Wesleyan University in Salina, Kansas. Their last names formed the name of Brown Mackie. By January 1975, with improvements in curricula and higher-degree-granting status, the Brown Mackie School of Business became Brown Mackie College.

Brown Mackie College — San Antonio is accredited by the Accrediting Council for Independent Colleges and Schools to award bachelor degrees and associate degrees. The Accrediting Council for Independent Colleges and Schools is listed as a nationally recognized accrediting agency by the United States Department of Education and is recognized by the Council for Higher Education Accreditation. ACICS can be contacted at 750 First Street NE, Suite 980, Washington, D.C. 20002; phone: 202-336-6780.

Brown Mackie College — San Antonio is approved and regulated by the Texas Workforce Commission, Career School and Colleges, Austin, Texas.

Brown Mackie College — San Antonio holds a Certificate of Authorization acknowledging exemption from Texas Higher Education Coordinating Board regulations.

Location

Brown Mackie College — San Antonio is conveniently located at 4715 Fredericksburg Road in San Antonio, Texas. The College has a generous parking area and is easily accessible by public transportation.

Programs of Study and Degrees

Brown Mackie College — San Antonio provides higher education to traditional and nontraditional students through bachelor degree and associate degree programs that assist in enhancing their career opportunities, broadening their perspectives through appropriate general education courses, thinking independently and critically, and improving problem-solving abilities. The college strives to develop within its students the desire for lifelong and continued education.

The Bachelor of Science degree is awarded in business administration, criminal justice, health care management, and legal studies.

The Associate of Science degree is awarded in accounting technology, architectural design and drafting technology, business management, criminal justice, health care administration, information technology, medical assisting, paralegal, pharmacy technology, and surgical technology.

The American Medical Technologists (AMT), which offers the certification for Registered Medical Assistant (RMA), accepts the accreditation of Brown Mackie College — San Antonio. Students will qualify to take the Registered Medical Assistant certification examination upon graduating the Brown Mackie College — San Antonio Medical Assisting program.

Brown Mackie College — San Antonio does not guarantee third-party certification. Outside agencies control the requirements for certifications and are subject to change without notice to Brown Mackie College.

Academic Programs

Each college quarter comprises twelve weeks. Bachelor degree programs require a minimum of sixteen quarters to complete. Associate degree programs require a minimum of eight quarters to complete. Programs are offered on a year-round basis, providing students with the ability to work uninterrupted toward completion of their programs. The college offers all programs in a unique One-Course-a-Month format. This allows students to focus studies on only one course for four weeks. This schedule has proven convenient for students with multiple obligations, such as jobs and family.

Academic Facilities

A modern facility, Brown Mackie College — San Antonio offers more than 35,000 square feet. The college is equipped with multiple computer labs, housing over 100 computers. High-speed access to the Internet and other online resources are

available to students and faculty. Multimedia classrooms are outfitted with overhead projectors, VCR/DVD players, and computers.

In 2012, Brown Mackie College — San Antonio began its transition to using eTextbooks and computer tablets in the classroom. Utilizing these tablets to access expanded course material, students will be able to increase their acumen for using this technology and further enhance their educational experience. Students have the ability to directly download their eTextbooks to their tablet, eliminating the need to carry heavy, physical textbooks and reducing the overall cost of supplies.

The college is nonresidential; public transportation and ample parking at no cost are available. The campus is a smoke-free facility.

Costs

Tuition in the 2011–12 academic year for all bachelor and associate degrees was $324 per credit hour; fees were $15 per credit hour. Tuition for the surgical technology program was $360 per credit hour; fees were $15 per credit hour. The cost of textbooks and other instructional materials varies by program.

Financial Aid

Financial aid is available for those who qualify. The college maintains a full-time staff of Student Financial Services Advisors to assist qualified students in obtaining the financial assistance they require to meet their educational expenses. Available resources include federal and state aid, student loans from private lenders, and Federal Work-Study opportunities, both on and off college premises.

Each year, the college makes available President's Scholarships of $1000 each to qualifying seniors from area high schools. Up to three (3) scholarships may be awarded per high school. In order to qualify, a senior must have graduated from a participating high school, must have maintained a cumulative grade point average of at least 2.0, and must have submitted a brief essay. The student's extracurricular activities and community service are also considered. These scholarships are available only to students enrolling in one of the college's degree programs. Students awarded the scholarship must enroll at Brown Mackie College — San Antonio between June and September immediately following their high school graduation. Applications for these scholarships can be obtained from the guidance departments of participating high schools. These applications must be completed and returned to Brown Mackie College by March 31.

Faculty

Experienced faculty members provide academic support and are committed to the academic and technical preparation of their students. The college has both full-time and part-time instructors, with a student-faculty ratio of 15:1.

Admission Requirements

Each applicant for admission is assigned an Assistant Director of Admissions who directs the applicant through the steps of the admissions process. Assistant Directors provide information on curriculum, policies, procedures, and services and assist the applicant in setting up necessary appointments and interviews. To qualify for admission, each applicant must provide documentation of graduation from an accredited high school or from a state-approved secondary education curriculum or official documentation of high school graduation equivalency. All transcripts become the property of the college. Admission to the college is based on the applicant meeting the stated requirements, a review of the applicant's previous educational records, and a review of the applicant's career interests. If previous academic records indicate the college's education and training programs would not benefit the applicant, the college reserves the right to advise the applicant not to enroll. Special requirements for enrollment into certain programs are discussed in the descriptions of those programs.

For the most recent information regarding admission requirements, prospective students should refer to the current academic catalog.

Application and Information

Applicants must complete and submit an application form, along with documentation of graduation from an accredited high school or state-approved secondary education curriculum or official documentation of high school graduation equivalency.

See BMCprograms.info for program duration, tuition, fees and other costs, median debt, federal salary data, alumni success, programmatic accreditation, and other important info.

For additional information, prospective students should contact:

Director of Admissions
Brown Mackie College — San Antonio
4715 Fredericksburg Road, Suite 100
San Antonio, Texas 78229
United States
Phone: 210-428-2210
      877-460-1714 (toll-free)
Fax: 210-428-2265
E-mail: bmsanadm@brownmackie.edu
Web site: http://www.brownmackie.edu/San Antonio

BROWN MACKIE COLLEGE — SOUTH BEND

SOUTH BEND, INDIANA

The College

Brown Mackie College — South Bend (Brown Mackie College) is one of over twenty-five locations in the Brown Mackie College family of schools (www.brownmackie.edu), which is dedicated to providing educational programs that prepare students to pursue entry-level positions in a competitive, rapidly changing workplace. Brown Mackie College schools offer bachelor degree, associate degree, diploma, and certificate programs in health sciences, business, information technology, legal studies, and design to over 20,000 students in the Midwest, Southeast, Southwest, and Western United States.

Brown Mackie College — South Bend is one of the oldest institutions of its kind in the country and the oldest in the state of Indiana. Established in 1882 as the South Bend Commercial College, the school later changed its name to Michiana College. In 1930, the school was incorporated under the laws of the state of Indiana and was authorized to confer associate degrees and certificates in business. The college relocated to East Jefferson Boulevard in 1987. In September 2009, Brown Mackie College — South Bend officially opened a new 46,000-square-foot facility at 3454 Douglas Road in South Bend, Indiana.

Brown Mackie College — South Bend is accredited by the Accrediting Council for Independent Colleges and Schools to award bachelor degrees, associate degrees, diplomas, and certificates. The Accrediting Council for Independent Colleges and Schools is listed as a nationally recognized accrediting agency by the United States Department of Education and is recognized by the Council for Higher Education Accreditation. ACICS can be contacted at 750 First Street NE, Suite 980, Washington, D.C. 20002; phone: 202-336-6780.

Brown Mackie College — South Bend is regulated by the Indiana Commission on Proprietary Education, 302 West Washington Street, Indianapolis, Indiana 46204; phone: 317-232-1320 or 800-227-5695 (toll-free). Indiana advertising code: AC-0110.

The practical nursing diploma program is accredited by the Indiana State Board of Nursing, located at 402 West Washington Street, Room W066, Indianapolis, IN 46204; phone: 317-234-2043.

The Associate of Science in medical assisting is accredited by the Commission on Accreditation of Allied Health Education Program (www.caahep.org) upon the recommendation of the Curriculum Review Board of the American Association of Medical Assistants Endowment (AAMAE). The Commission on Accreditation of Allied Health Education Programs is located at 1361 Park Street, Clearwater, FL 33756; phone: 727-210-2350

The Associate of Applied Science in occupational therapy assistant program is accredited by the Accreditation Council for Occupational Therapy Education (ACOTE) of the American Occupational Therapy Association (AOTA), located at 4720 Montgomery Lane, P.O. Box 31220, Bethesda, Maryland 20824-1220. ACOTE's phone number c/o AOTA is (301) 652-AOTA.

The Associate of Applied Science in physical therapist assistant program is accredited by the Commission on Accreditation in Physical Therapy Education (CAPTE) of the American Physical Therapy Association (APTA), 1111 North Fairfax Street, Alexandria, Virginia 22314; phone: 703-706-3241.

The Associate of Science in veterinary technology program has provisional programmatic accreditation granted by the American Veterinary Medical Association (AVMA) through the Committee on Veterinary Technician Education and Activities (CVTEA).

The college is a nonresidential, smoke-free institution.

Location

Brown Mackie College — South Bend is conveniently located at 3454 Douglas Road in South Bend, Indiana. The college has a generous parking area and is also easily accessible by public transportation.

Programs of Study and Degrees

Brown Mackie College — South Bend provides higher education to traditional and nontraditional students through bachelor degrees, associate degrees, diploma, and certificate programs that assist in enhancing their career opportunities, broadening their perspectives through appropriate general education courses, thinking independently and critically, and improving problem-solving abilities.

The Bachelor of Science degree is awarded in business administration, criminal justice, health care management, and legal studies.

The Associate of Science degree is awarded in accounting technology, business management, computer software technology, criminal justice, health care administration, information technology, medical assisting, paralegal, and veterinary technology.

The Associate of Applied Science degree is awarded in occupational therapy assistant and physical therapist assistant.

Brown Mackie College — South Bend offers a diploma program in practical nursing.

The college offers the following certificate programs: accounting, business, computer software applications, criminal justice, medical assistant, and paralegal assistant.

The American Medical Technologists (AMT), which offers the certification for Registered Medical Assistant (RMA), accepts the accreditation of Brown Mackie College — South Bend. Students will qualify to take the Registered Medical Assistant certification examination upon graduating the Brown Mackie College — South Bend Medical Assisting and Medical Assistant programs. Graduates of the 48-credit-hour Medical Assistant program are not qualified to take the AMT/RMA exam.

Brown Mackie College — South Bend does not guarantee third-party certification. Outside agencies control the requirements for certifications and are subject to change without notice to Brown Mackie College.

Academic Programs

Each college quarter comprises twelve weeks. Bachelor degree programs require a minimum of sixteen quarters to complete. Associate degree programs require a minimum of eight quarters to complete. Programs are offered on a year-round basis, providing students with the ability to work uninterrupted toward completion of their programs. The college offers all programs in a unique One-Course-a-Month format. This allows students to focus studies on only one course for four weeks. This schedule has proven convenient for students with multiple obligations, such as jobs and family.

Academic Facilities

Brown Mackie College — South Bend's new location has a generous parking area and is easily accessible by public transportation. The college's smoke-free, three-story 46,000-square-foot building offers a modern, professional environment for study. The facility offers "classrooms of the future," with instructor workstations and full multimedia capabilities that include surround sound and projection screens that can be accessed by computer, DVD, and VHS. The new facility includes medical, computer, and

occupational and physical therapy labs, as well as a library and bookstore. The labs provide students with hands-on opportunities to apply knowledge and skills learned in the classroom. The veterinary technology lab is 2,600 square feet and includes surgery areas, treatment areas, and kennels.

Costs

Tuition for programs in the 2011–12 academic year was $294 per credit hour, with a general fee of $15 per credit hour applied to instructional costs for activities and services. Textbooks and other instructional materials vary by program. Tuition for the practical nursing program was $361 per credit hour, with a general fee of $25 per credit hour applied to instructional costs for activities and services. Tuition for the physical therapist assistant program was $361 per credit hour with a general fee of $15 per credit hour. Tuition for the occupational therapy assistant program was $361 per credit hour with a general fee of $15 per credit hour.

Financial Aid

Financial aid is available for those who qualify. The college maintains a full-time staff of Student Financial Services Advisors to assist qualified students in obtaining financial assistance. The college participates in several student aid programs. Forms of financial aid available through federal resources include the Federal Pell Grant Program, Federal Supplemental Educational Opportunity Grant (FSEOG) Program, Federal Work-Study Program, Federal Perkins Loan Program, Federal Stafford Student Loan Program (subsidized and unsubsidized), and the Federal PLUS Loan Program.

Eligible students may apply for Indiana state awards, such as the Frank O'Bannon Grant Program (formerly the Indiana Higher Education Grant) and Twenty-First Century Scholars Program for high school students, for the Core 40 awards, and for veterans' educational benefits. Students with physical or mental disabilities that are a handicap may be eligible for training services through the state's Bureau of Vocational Rehabilitation. For further information, students should contact the Student Financial Services Office.

Each year, the college makes available President's Scholarships of $1000 each to qualifying seniors from area high schools. Up to three (3) scholarships may be awarded per high school. In order to qualify, a senior must be graduating from a participating high school, must be maintaining a cumulative grade point average of at least 2.0, and must submit a brief essay. The student's extracurricular activities and community service are also considered. The President's Scholarship is available only to students enrolling in one of the college's degree programs. Students awarded the scholarship must enroll at Brown Mackie College — South Bend between June and September immediately following their high school graduation. Applications for these scholarships can be obtained from the guidance departments of participating high schools. These applications must be completed and returned to Brown Mackie College by March 31.

Faculty

There are 29 full-time and 46 part-time faculty members at the college. The average student-faculty ratio is 12:1. Each student is assigned a program director as an adviser.

Admission Requirements

Each applicant for admission is assigned an Assistant Director of Admissions, who directs the applicant through the steps of the admissions process, providing information on curriculum, policies, procedures, and services and assisting the applicant in setting up necessary appointments and interviews. To qualify for admission, each applicant must provide documentation of graduation from an accredited high school or from a state-approved secondary education curriculum or official documentation of high school graduation equivalency. All transcripts become the property of the college.

Admission to the college is based on the applicant meeting the stated requirements, a review of the applicant's previous educational records, and a review of the applicant's career interests. If previous academic records indicate the college's education and training programs would not benefit the applicant, the college reserves the right to advise the applicant not to enroll. Special requirements for enrollment into certain programs are discussed in the descriptions of those programs.

In addition to the college's general admission requirements, applicants enrolling in the occupational therapy assistant (OTA) program must meet some additional requirements. They must complete the COMPASS assessment before the first course is scheduled to determine if transitional courses are needed (minimal scores: reading 75, writing 60, math 51). If minimum scores or better are attained on all three sections, the student is scheduled in CF1000–Professional Development. If the student's scores are below the minimum on any of the sections, the student is advised of placement in transitional course(s). After successful completion of all the required transitional courses, the student will have one opportunity to retake the COMPASS assessment and achieve the minimum score(s). If the student does not successfully obtain the minimum scores in all three sections on the second attempt, the student will not be allowed to continue in the OTA program, but can be considered for another program at Brown Mackie College.

In addition to the college's general admission requirements, applicants enrolling in the physical therapist assistant program must document the following: a minimum high school cumulative grade point average of 3.0 on a 4.0 scale or a minimum score of 600 on the GED examination (if taken on or after January 15, 2002) or 60 (if taken before January 15, 2002); a minimum of twelve quarter-credit hours or nine semester-credit hours of consecutive collegiate coursework with a minimum GPA of 3.0 on a 4.0 scale (may be completed at Brown Mackie College); a biology course in high school or college with a minimum grade of a B (3.0 on a 4.0 scale); and twenty hours (total) of documented observation, volunteer, or employment hours in at least two different physical therapy settings with no less than eight hours in one setting completed within the past three years.

In addition to the college's general admission requirements, applicants enrolling in the practical nursing program must document the following: fulfillment of Brown Mackie College — South Bend general requirements; complete physical (must be current to within six months of admission); two-step Mantoux TB skin test (must be current throughout schooling); hepatitis B vaccination or signed refusal; up-to-date immunizations, including tetanus and rubella; record of current CPR certification (certification must be current throughout the clinical experience through healthcare provider certification or the American Heart Association); and hospitalization insurance or a signed waiver.

For the most recent administration regarding admission requirements, please refer to the current academic catalog.

Application and Information

Applicants must complete and submit an application form, along with documentation of graduation from an accredited high school or state-approved secondary education curriculum or official documentation of high school graduation equivalency.

See BMCprograms.info for program duration, tuition, fees and other costs, median debt, federal salary data, alumni success, programmatic accreditation, and other important info.

For additional information, prospective students should contact:

Director of Admissions
Brown Mackie College — South Bend
3454 Douglas Road
South Bend, Indiana 46635
United States
Phone: 574-237-0774
        800-743-2447(toll-free)
Fax: 574-237-3585
E-mail: bmcsbadm@brownmackie.edu
Web site: http://www.brownmackie.edu/SouthBend

BROWN MACKIE COLLEGE — TUCSON
TUCSON, ARIZONA

The College

Brown Mackie College — Tucson (Brown Mackie College) is one of over twenty-five locations in the Brown Mackie College family of schools (www.brownmackie.edu), which is dedicated to providing educational programs that prepare students to pursue entry-level positions in a competitive, rapidly changing workplace. Brown Mackie College schools offer bachelor degree, associate degree, diploma, and certificate programs in health sciences, business, information technology, legal studies, and design to over 20,000 students in the Midwest, Southeast, Southwest, and Western United States.

Brown Mackie College was originally founded and approved by the Board of Trustees of Kansas Wesleyan College in Salina, Kansas on July 30, 1892. In 1938, the college was incorporated as The Brown Mackie School of Business under the ownership of Perry E. Brown and A. B. Mackie, former instructors at Kansas Wesleyan University in Salina, Kansas. Their last names formed the name of Brown Mackie. By January 1975, with improvements in curricula and higher-degree-granting status, The Brown Mackie School of Business became Brown Mackie College.

Brown Mackie College entered the Arizona market in 2007 when it purchased a school that had been previously established in the Tucson area. That school had an established history in the community and was converted into what is now known as Brown Mackie College — Tucson. The historical timeline of Brown Mackie College — Tucson started in 1972 when Rockland West Corporation first formed a partnership with Lamson Business College. At that time, the school was a career college that offered only short-term programs focusing on computer training and secretarial skills. In 1994, the college became accredited as a junior college and began offering associate degrees in academic subjects. The mission was then modified to include the goal of instilling in graduates an appreciation for lifelong learning through the general education courses that became a part of every program.

In 1996, the college applied for and received status as a senior college by the Accrediting Commission of Independent Colleges and Schools. This gave the school the ability to offer course work leading to a Bachelor of Science degree in business administration. Since then, the program offerings for bachelor and associate degrees have expanded.

In 1986, the college moved from 5001 East Speedway to the 4585 East Speedway location where it remains today. In 2008, two of the college's three buildings were remodeled, which resulted in updated classrooms; networked computer laboratories; new medical, surgical technology, and forensics laboratories; a larger library and offices for student services such as academics, admissions, and student financial services; and a full-service college store. In 2009, the third building was remodeled and now provides newer classrooms and a new career services department.

Brown Mackie College — Tucson is accredited by the Accrediting Council for Independent Colleges and Schools to award bachelor degrees, associate degrees, and certificates. The Accrediting Council for Independent Colleges and Schools is listed as a nationally recognized accrediting agency by the United States Department of Education and is recognized by the Council for Higher Education Accreditation. ACICS can be contacted at 750 First Street NE, Suite 980, Washington, D.C. 20002; phone: 202-336-6780.

Brown Mackie College — Tucson is authorized by the Arizona State Board for Private Post-secondary Education, located at 1400 West Washington Street, Room 2560, Phoenix, Arizona 85007; phone: 602-542-5709; http://azppse.state.az.us.

The Associate of Science in surgical technology program is accredited by the Accrediting Bureau of Health Education Schools.

The Associate of Applied Science in occupational therapy assistant program is accredited by the Accreditation Council for Occupational Therapy Education (ACOTE) of the American Occupational Therapy Association (AOTA), located at 4720 Montgomery Lane, P.O. Box 31220, Bethesda, Maryland 20824-1220. ACOTE's phone number c/o AOTA is 301-652-AOTA.

Location

Brown Mackie College–Tucson is conveniently located at 4585 East Speedway Boulevard in Tucson, Arizona. The College has a generous parking area and is also easily accessible by public transportation.

Programs of Study and Degrees

Brown Mackie College — Tucson provides higher education to traditional and nontraditional students through bachelor degree, associate degree, and diploma programs that assist in enhancing their career opportunities, broadening their perspectives through appropriate general education courses, thinking independently and critically, and improving problem-solving abilities. The college strives to develop within its students the desire for lifelong and continued education.

The Bachelor of Science degree is awarded in accounting, business administration, criminal justice, health care management, information technology, and legal studies.

The Associate of Science degree is awarded in accounting technology, business management, computer networking and security, criminal justice, graphic design, health care administration, information technology, medical assisting, paralegal, and surgical technology.

The Associate of Applied Science degree is awarded in biomedical equipment technology, health and fitness training, and occupational therapy assistant.

A diploma is awarded in fitness trainer, medical assistant, and practical nursing.

The American Medical Technologists (AMT), which offers the certification for Registered Medical Assistant (RMA), accepts the accreditation of Brown Mackie College — Tucson. Students will qualify to take the Registered Medical Assistant certification examination upon graduating the Brown Mackie College — Tucson Medical Assisting and Medical Assistant programs. Graduates of the 48-credit-hour Medical Assistant program are not qualified to take the AMT/RMA exam.

Brown Mackie College — Tucson does not guarantee third-party certification. Outside agencies control the requirements for certifications and are subject to change without notice to Brown Mackie College.

Academic Programs

Each college quarter comprises twelve weeks. Bachelor degree programs require a minimum of sixteen quarters to complete. Associate degree programs require a minimum of eight quarters to complete. Programs are offered on a year-round basis, providing students with the ability to work uninterrupted toward their degrees. The college offers all programs in a unique One-Course-a-Month format. This allows students to focus studies on only one course for four weeks. This schedule has proven convenient for students with multiple obligations, such as jobs and family.

Academic Facilities

A modern facility, Brown Mackie College — Tucson offers more than 31,000 square feet. The college is equipped with multiple computer labs housing over 200 computers. High-speed access to the Internet and other online resources are available for students and faculty. Multimedia classrooms are outfitted with overhead projectors, VCR/DVD players, and computers. The college is nonresidential; public transportation and parking at no cost are available.

Costs

Tuition in the 2011–12 academic year for most bachelor, associate, and diploma programs was $324 per credit hour; fees were $15 per credit hour. Tuition for the health and fitness training program was $324 per credit hour; fees were $25 per credit hour. Tuition for the surgical technology program was $340 per credit hour; fees were $15 per credit hour. Tuition for the occupational therapy assistant program was $361 per credit hour; fees were $15 per credit hour. Tuition for the practical nursing program was $361 per credit hour; fees were $25 per credit hour. Textbook and other instructional expenses vary by program.

Financial Aid

Financial aid is available for those who qualify. The college maintains a full-time staff of Student Financial Services Advisors to assist qualified students in obtaining the financial assistance they require to meet their educational expenses. Available resources include federal and state aid, student loans from private lenders, and Federal Work-Study opportunities, both on and off college premises.

Each year, the college makes available President's Scholarships of $1000 each to qualifying seniors from area high schools. Up to three (3) scholarships may be awarded per high school. In order to qualify, a senior must be graduating from a participating high school, must be maintaining a cumulative grade point average of at least 2.0, and must submit a brief essay. The student's extracurricular activities and community service are also considered. These scholarships are available only to students enrolling in one of the college's degree programs. Students awarded the scholarship must enroll at Brown Mackie College — Tucson between June and September immediately following their high school graduation. Applications for these scholarships can be obtained from the guidance departments of participating high schools. These applications must be completed and returned to Brown Mackie College by March 31.

Faculty

Experienced faculty members provide academic support and are committed to the academic and technical preparation of their students. The college has 15 full-time and 35 part-time instructors, with a student-faculty ratio of 12:1. Each student is assigned a faculty adviser.

Admission Requirements

Each applicant for admission is assigned an Assistant Director of Admissions who directs the applicant through the steps of the admissions process. Assistant Directors provide information on curriculum, policies, procedures, and services and assist the applicant in setting up necessary appointments and interviews. To qualify for admission, each applicant must provide documentation of graduation from an accredited high school or from a state-approved secondary education curriculum or official documentation of high school graduation equivalency. All transcripts become the property of the college. Admission to the college is based on the applicant meeting the stated requirements, a review of the applicant's previous educational records, and a review of the applicant's career interests. If previous academic records indicate the college's education and training programs would not benefit the applicant, the college reserves the right to advise the applicant not to enroll. Special requirements for enrollment into certain programs are discussed in the descriptions of those programs.

For the most recent information regarding admission requirements, please refer to the current academic catalog.

Application and Information

Applicants must complete and submit an application form, along with documentation of graduation from an accredited high school or state-approved secondary education curriculum or official documentation of high school graduation equivalency.

See BMCprograms.info for program duration, tuition, fees and other costs, median debt, federal salary data, alumni success, programmatic accreditation, and other important info.

For additional information, prospective students should contact:
Senior Director of Admissions
Brown Mackie College — Tucson
4585 East Speedway Boulevard, Suite 204
Tucson, Arizona 85712
United States
Phone: 520-319-3300
Fax: 520-319-3495
E-mail: bmctuadm@brownmackie.edu
Web site: http://www.brownmackie.edu/Tucson

BROWN MACKIE COLLEGE — TULSA
TULSA, OKLAHOMA

The College

Brown Mackie College — Tulsa (Brown Mackie College) is one of over twenty-five locations in the Brown Mackie College family of schools (www.brownmackie.edu), which is dedicated to providing educational programs that prepare students to pursue entry-level positions in a competitive, rapidly changing workplace. Brown Mackie College schools offer bachelor degree, associate degree, diploma, and certificate programs in health sciences, business, information technology, legal studies, and design to over 20,000 students in the Midwest, Southeast, Southwest, and Western United States.

Brown Mackie College — Tulsa was founded in 2008 as a branch of Brown Mackie College — South Bend, Indiana.

Brown Mackie College — Tulsa is accredited by the Accrediting Council for Independent Colleges and Schools to award bachelor degrees, associate degrees, and diplomas. The Accrediting Council for Independent Colleges and Schools is listed as a nationally recognized accrediting agency by the United States Department of Education and is recognized by the Council for Higher Education Accreditation. ACICS can be contacted at 750 First Street NE, Suite 980, Washington, D.C. 20002; phone: 202-336-6780.

This institution is licensed by the Oklahoma Board of Private Vocational Schools (OBPVS), 3700 North Classen Boulevard, Suite 250, Oklahoma City, Oklahoma 73118; phone: 405-528-3370.

This institution has been granted authority to operate in Oklahoma by the Oklahoma State Regents for Higher Education (OSRHE), 655 Research Parkway, Suite 200, Oklahoma City, Oklahoma 73101; phone: 405-225-9100; www.okhighered.org.

The occupational therapy assistant program is accredited by the Accreditation Council for Occupational Therapy Education (ACOTE) of the American Occupational Therapy Association (AOTA), located at 4720 Montgomery Lane, P.O. Box 31220, Bethesda, Maryland 20824; phone: 301-652-AOTA.

Location

Brown Mackie College — Tulsa is conveniently located at 4608 South Garnett Road, Suite 110 in Tulsa, Oklahoma.

The College has a generous parking area and is easily accessible by public transportation.

Programs of Study and Degrees

Brown Mackie College — Tulsa provides higher education to traditional and nontraditional students through bachelor degree, associate degree, and diploma programs that assist in enhancing their career opportunities, broadening their perspectives through appropriate general education courses, thinking independently and critically, and improving problem-solving abilities. The college strives to develop within its students the desire for lifelong and continued education.

The Bachelor of Science degree is awarded in business administration, criminal justice, health care management, and legal studies.

The Associate of Applied Science degree is awarded in accounting technology, business management, criminal justice, health care administration, information technology, medical assisting, nursing, occupational therapy assistant, paralegal, and surgical technology.

Diploma programs are offered in accounting, business, criminal justice, medical assistant, and paralegal assistant.

The American Medical Technologists (AMT), which offers the certification for Registered Medical Assistant (RMA), accepts the accreditation of Brown Mackie College — Tulsa. Students will qualify to take the Registered Medical Assistant certification examination upon graduating the Brown Mackie College — Tulsa Medical Assisting and Medical Assistant programs. Graduates of the 48-credit-hour Medical Assistant program are not qualified to take the AMT/RMA exam.

Brown Mackie College — Tulsa does not guarantee third-party certification. Outside agencies control the requirements for certifications and are subject to change without notice to Brown Mackie College.

Academic Programs

Each college quarter comprises twelve weeks. Bachelor degree programs require a minimum of fifteen quarters to complete. Associate degree programs require a minimum of eight quarters to complete. Programs are offered on a

year-round basis, providing students with the ability to work uninterrupted toward completion of their programs. The college offers all programs in a unique One-Course-a-Month format. This allows students to focus on only one course for four weeks. This schedule has proven convenient for students with multiple obligations, such as jobs and family.

Academic Facilities

Opened in 2008, this modern facility offers more than 25,000 square feet of tastefully decorated classrooms, laboratories, and office space designed to specifications of Brown Mackie College for its business, medical, and technical programs. Instructional equipment is comparable to current technology used in business and industry today. Modern classrooms for special instructional needs offer multimedia capabilities with surround sound and overhead projectors accessible through computer, DVD, or VHS. Internet access and instructional resources are available at the college's library. Experienced faculty members provide academic support and are committed to the academic and technical preparation of their students.

The college is nonresidential; public transportation and ample parking at no cost are available.

Costs

Tuition for programs in the 2011–12 academic year was $294 per credit hour, with a general fee of $15 per credit hour applied to instructional costs for activities and services. Tuition for the occupational therapy program was $361 per credit hour with a general fee of $15 per credit hour applied to instructional costs for activities. Tuition for the surgical technology program was $340 per credit hour with a general fee of $15 per credit hour applied to instructional costs for activities. Tuition for the nursing program was $390 per credit hour with a general fee of $25 per credit hour applied to instructional costs for activities. Textbooks and other instructional materials vary by program.

Financial Aid

Financial aid is available for those who qualify. The college maintains a full-time staff of Student Financial Services Advisors to assist qualified students in obtaining financial assistance. The college participates in several student aid programs. Forms of financial aid available through federal resources include the Federal Pell Grant Program, Federal Supplemental Educational Opportunity Grant (FSEOG) Program, Federal Work-Study Program, Federal Perkins Loan Program, Federal Stafford Student Loan Program (subsidized and unsubsidized), and the Federal PLUS Loan Program.

Admission Requirements

Each applicant for admission is assigned an Assistant Director of Admissions, who directs the applicant through the steps of the admissions process, providing information on curriculum, policies, procedures, and services and assisting the applicant in setting up necessary appointments and interviews. To qualify for admission, applicants must be a graduate of a public or private high school or a correspondence school or education center that is accredited by an agency that is recognized by the U.S. or State of Oklahoma Department of Education or any of its approved agents. As part of the admissions process, applicants must sign a document attesting to graduation or completion and containing the information to obtain verification of such. Verification must be obtained within the first term (90 days) or the student will be withdrawn from the institution following established guidelines for withdrawn students noted in the catalog. Title IV aid will not be dispersed until verification of graduation or completion has been received by the college. All transcripts become the property of the college.

Students are given an assessment of academic skills. Although the results of this assessment do not determine eligibility for admission, they provide the college with a means of determining the need for academic support.

For the most recent information regarding admission requirements, please refer to the current academic catalog.

Application and Information

Applicants must complete and submit an application form, along with documentation of graduation from an accredited high school or state-approved secondary education curriculum or official documentation of high school graduation equivalency.

See BMCprograms.info for program duration, tuition, fees and other costs, median debt, federal salary data, alumni success, programmatic accreditation, and other important info.

For additional information, prospective students should contact:

Senior Director of Admissions
Brown Mackie College–Tulsa
4608 South Garnett Road, Suite 110
Tulsa, Oklahoma 74146
United States
Phone: 918-628-3700
        888-794-8411 (toll-free)
Fax: 918-828-9083
E-mail: bmctuladm@brownmackie.edu
Web site: http://www.brownmackie.edu/Tulsa

BRYN MAWR COLLEGE
BRYN MAWR, PENNSYLVANIA

The College

Bryn Mawr women share an intense intellectual commitment, a purposeful vision of their lives, and a common desire to make a meaningful contribution to the world.

Every year 1,300 undergraduate women and 400 graduate students from around the world gather on the College's historic campus to study with leading scholars, conduct advanced research, and expand the boundaries of what's possible.

The undergraduate college is known as one of the most academically rigorous liberal-arts colleges in the nation and consistently ranks among the top feeder schools to the world's premier graduate programs and professional schools.

Bryn Mawr's Katherine Houghton Hepburn Center, Office of Civic Engagement, and the Praxis Program, which integrates fieldwork with theoretical study, provide students with extensive opportunities for internships in Philadelphia, where they may apply knowledge far beyond the classroom. Many students pursue independent and interdepartmental majors with faculty permission. Joint academic programs also exist with Haverford, Swarthmore, and the University of Pennsylvania.

Through advanced research projects, summer internships, and collaborative research with faculty members, students are involved in the local, national, and global communities.

Bryn Mawr offers a new and unique interdisciplinary experience, 360°, in which a cohort of students takes several courses together to engage multiple aspects of a topic or theme, giving students an opportunity to investigate thoroughly and thoughtfully a multitude of perspectives. Typical 360°s focus on the history, economic concerns, cultural intersections, and political impact of an era, decision, event, policy, or important scientific innovation. 360° participants hone their arguments and insights through writing and research, develop strategies for teamwork that push the limits of their talents and creativity, and work with professors and scholars to promote big-picture thinking.

Bryn Mawr's prestigious alumnae include the first woman to be president of Harvard University, one of the first women to receive the Nobel Peace Prize, the first woman neurosurgeon, and the first and only woman to receive four Academy Awards.

Diversity is central to Bryn Mawr's mission as an extraordinary liberal-arts college, improving the academic experience and enriching the campus community. Students of color and international students make up nearly 50 percent of the undergraduate enrollment. Bryn Mawr's student body is composed of women from forty-four states and sixty-one other countries.

Above all else, Bryn Mawr women share a tremendous respect for individual differences, not merely a passive tolerance of other lifestyles and points of view. The result is a community that resounds with the energy, healthy friction, and range of perspectives that can only come from true cultural and ideological diversity.

The diversity that Bryn Mawr students experience, in and out of the classroom, helps prepare them to be confident global citizens and leaders.

Bryn Mawr women share a commitment to a community that is based on inclusion and support, reinforced by the College's Honor Code, a set of principles stressing personal integrity and mutual respect. In the words of one graduating senior, "This is a place where being yourself makes you feel part of something larger than yourself. A strong sense of self is what we all have in common."

Bryn Mawr is a charter member of the Centennial Conference and is home to twelve NCAA varsity athletic teams. Students may compete in badminton, basketball, crew, cross-country, field hockey, lacrosse, soccer, swimming, tennis, indoor track and field, outdoor track and field, and volleyball. The newly-renovated Bern Schwartz Fitness and Athletic Center offers enhanced spaces for training, fitness, and aquatics.

The recently renovated Goodhart Hall serves as a hub for the College's performing arts scene and boasts a recently renovated theater for 500+, a teaching theater, scene shop, music rooms, and several performance spaces. Other performance spaces include the Pembroke Dance Studio and the Denbigh Studio.

Bryn Mawr students participate in more than 100 active student organizations. The tricollege community of Haverford, Swarthmore, and Bryn Mawr also sponsors many student groups and activities.

Location

Students at Bryn Mawr have the best of it all in terms of location. The campus itself is such a picture-perfect example of Collegiate Gothic that it has been used as the backdrop for many motion pictures. A quick 5-minute walk into the suburban town of Bryn Mawr finds an eclectic mix of funky independent and favorite franchise coffee shops, eateries, and retailers; an historic movie theater; and a commuter train that can take students to the heart of Philadelphia in less than 20 minutes.

Philadelphia has a bustling arts scene and nightlife and is home to more than 250,000 college students. Bryn Mawr women enjoy a rich academic and social life on their own campus and at neighboring tricollege partners, Haverford and Swarthmore Colleges, as well as the University of Pennsylvania.

Bryn Mawr's relationship with Haverford College is particularly close and students participate in many bicollege extracurricular activities, including the orchestra, the chorus, the drama program, and a bicollege newspaper. A 20-minute walk or a 5-minute ride on the bicollege Blue Bus brings students from one campus to the other.

Almost all students live on campus in one of thirteen main residence halls. Two of the buildings are listed on the National Register of Historic Places, and one is also a National Historic Landmark. Several residence halls house students with shared interests in topics including sustainability and foreign languages and cultures.

Majors and Degrees

Bryn Mawr College grants the Bachelor of Arts (A.B.) degree with majors, minors, and concentrations in more than forty areas: Africana studies, anthropology, astronomy, biology, chemistry, classical and Near Eastern archaeology, classical languages, classical studies, comparative literature, computational methods, computer science, creative writing, dance, East Asian studies, economics, education, English, environmental studies, film studies, fine arts, French and French studies, gender and sexuality, geology, German and German studies, Greek, growth and structure of cities, Hebrew and Judaic studies, history, history of art, international studies, Italian, Latin, Latin American, Latino and Iberian people and cultures, linguistics, mathematics, Middle East studies, music, neural and behavioral sciences, peace and conflict studies, philosophy, physics, political science, psychology, religion, Romance languages, Russian, sociology, Spanish, and theater and theater studies.

There are nearly 3,000 course exchanges between Bryn Mawr and Haverford each year, selected from a jointly published course list. Bryn Mawr students may major in any of Haverford's coordinate departments or in astronomy, classics, music, or religion while earning a Bachelor of Arts degree from Bryn Mawr. A new major in linguistics offered through Swarthmore College is also available. Haverford, Swarthmore, and Bryn Mawr have joined together to form the Middle East Studies program and to offer a degree in environmental studies.

Academic Programs

The Bryn Mawr curriculum is designed to encourage breadth of learning and training in the fundamentals of scholarship. At some point during their first three years at Bryn Mawr, students are required to complete Approaches to Inquiry, a curriculum designed to introduce possibilities and problems in scientific investigation, critical interpretation, cross-cultural analysis, and inquiry into the past. Many options are available to fulfill these requirements and students are encouraged to explore. Innovative curricular options

include the growth and structure of cities program; the Middle East Studies program; 360°; and Focus Courses, which are demanding, half-semester courses that may ignite a new intellectual passion. Mature, sophisticated, in-depth study in a major program during the last two years is designed to prepare students for the lifelong pleasure and responsibility of educating themselves and playing an active role in contemporary society. The curriculum encourages independence within a rigorous but flexible framework. Each student chooses and plans her major in consultation with her dean and faculty adviser. Some students take advantage of this freedom to design an independent major, while others fashion their own intellectual perspectives by enrolling in courses that span academic fields or assisting with a faculty member's research project.

With certain restrictions, full-time Bryn Mawr students may also take courses at Swarthmore College, the University of Pennsylvania, and Villanova University during the academic year without paying additional fees.

Off-Campus Programs

Bryn Mawr is only 20 minutes by car or seven short stops by train from the vast cultural and professional resources of Philadelphia, the nation's sixth-largest city. Philadelphia is an incredible resource for Bryn Mawr—a truly accessible city, rich with cultural and professional opportunities, including the Philadelphia Museum of Art, the Philadelphia Orchestra, the Pennsylvania Ballet, numerous theaters, professional sports teams, and some of the nation's most important historic sites. Students may also take advantage of internship opportunities in Center City law firms, art galleries, government agencies, hospitals, TV studios, banks, and schools. When Philadelphia seems too small, 1 in 3 Bryn Mawr students take advantage of one of Bryn Mawr's many study-abroad options.

Academic Facilities

Bryn Mawr ranks among the top 10 of all U.S. colleges and universities in the percentage of graduates going on to earn a Ph.D. Bryn Mawr students have unlimited access to libraries and laboratories equal to those of many graduate programs, allowing students to pursue independent research at a level unavailable at most undergraduate institutions. These resources include an extensive array of laboratory equipment for the study of science, such as a robotics lab, laser with rangefinder, DNA analyzers, and a geological subsurface profiling system. More than 1 million volumes in a network of open-stack libraries are available to Bryn Mawr students, as well as access to the libraries of both Haverford and Swarthmore Colleges via the Tripod Library System.

In addition, the College has recently enhanced several of its buildings to support student inquiry in all of the liberal arts, including a $19-million renovation of the Marjorie Goodhart Theater which consists of a new state-of-the-art theater, practice rooms, a teaching theater, and scene shop; the upgrade of Dalton Hall, home to Bryn Mawr's social science labs and classrooms; and Bettws-y-Coed, a center for the study of psychology complete with new labs, faculty offices, and meeting rooms. Four former faculty residences have also been renovated to house the student activities village, Cambrian Row.

Costs

In 2012–13, Bryn Mawr tuition, room and board, and fees total $55,586.

Financial Aid

To apply for financial aid, students must submit the Free Application for Federal Student Aid (FAFSA), the College Scholarship Service (CSS) PROFILE form, and if applicable, the CSS Noncustodial Parent PROFILE. The College also requires a signed copy of the custodial and noncustodial parents' and student's most recent federal income tax returns, including W-2 forms, and all schedules and attachments. Tax returns must be submitted to The College Board's Institutional Documentation Service (IDOC). Applicants who are not citizens of the U.S. may file the (CSS) PROFILE or may instead submit the International Student Financial Aid Application directly to the Financial Aid Office. Non–U.S. citizens must also submit letters (in English) from their parents' employers stating gross income and the value of any perquisites, subsidies, and benefits directly to the Financial Aid Office. Prospective freshmen are notified of admission and financial aid decisions simultaneously.

Faculty

The Bryn Mawr faculty has 157 full-time members, of whom 53 percent are women and 16 percent are professors of color. The College's student-faculty ratio is 8:1. Few colleges or universities can genuinely claim the intellectual curiosity, intensity, and passion found at Bryn Mawr. Classes are small (many have fewer than 15 students), and faculty members come to know their students as individuals. That means more than just being on a first-name basis. In fact, Bryn Mawr faculty members, world-renowned leaders in their fields, regard their students as junior colleagues, fully capable of working at a high level, developing their own ideas, and making important contributions. It is in this way that, perhaps more than at any other school, Bryn Mawr feels like a graduate school on an undergraduate level.

Student Government

Bryn Mawr's culture of innovative leadership dates back to 1892 and the founding of the Student Self-Government Association (SGA), the oldest undergraduate governing body in the country. SGA gives Bryn Mawr students the responsibility of running many campus organizations and activities and participating in discussions and resolutions of important issues, such as curriculum and faculty appointments.

Admission Requirements

Every year, Bryn Mawr receives many more outstanding applications for admission than can be admitted into the first-year class of about 360 students. As members of the Common Application, Bryn Mawr practices holistic review, with admission decisions based on a number of factors. Strength of the applicant's high school curriculum within the context of the high school and academic performance are of significant importance. Other factors considered are a student's writing, recommendations from the high school counselor and academic teachers, testing, involvement in school and community, and diverse or unique perspectives and talents a student might bring to the Bryn Mawr community.

Basic high school academic requirements include 4 years of English, 3 years of mathematics, at least 1 year each of a laboratory science and history, and a solid foundation in at least one foreign language. However, most applicants are well prepared for the academic rigor of Bryn Mawr and have taken at least three lab science courses as well as mathematics courses that include trigonometry.

Bryn Mawr has adopted a test-flexible admissions policy which allows students to submit a combination of the SAT, SAT Subject Tests, the ACT, and AP exam scores. Complete details on the test-flexible policy may be found on the Bryn Mawr Web site. For tests scores to be considered in the application process, tests must be taken by November of the senior year for early decision applicants and January for regular decision applicants.

An interview, either at the College or with a local alumnae representative, is also strongly recommended.

Bryn Mawr exclusively accepts the Common Application and waives the $50 application fee when students apply online. Application forms should be submitted by November 15 for fall early decision applicants, by January 1 for winter early decision applicants, and by January 15 for regular decision applicants.

Transfer students must complete a minimum of two years of work at Bryn Mawr to qualify for the A.B. degree.

Application and Information

The Admissions Office is open from 9 a.m. to 5 p.m. on weekdays and, some Saturdays throughout the year. Please visit the College Web site http://www.brynmawr.edu/admissions/ to plan a visit. Bryn Mawr accepts the Common Application, which can be found online (http://www.commonapplication.org). For further information, an application form, or the name of a local alumnae representative, prospective students should contact:

Bryn Mawr College Office of Admissions
101 North Merion Avenue
Bryn Mawr, Pennsylvania 19010-2899
Phone: 610-526-5152
Fax: 610-526-7471
E-mail: admissions@brynmawr.edu
Web site: http://www.brynmawr.edu
http://www.brynmawr.edu/admissions/
http://www.facebook.com/BrynMawrCollege
http://twitter.com/BrynMawrCollege

BUCKNELL UNIVERSITY
LEWISBURG, PENNSYLVANIA

The University

Bucknell University offers a personalized and comprehensive liberal arts education to exceptionally talented students from across the United States and around the world. With academic programs in the arts, engineering, humanities, management, and social and natural sciences, and broad opportunities outside of class, Bucknell is a place that prepares students for success in an increasingly complex and interconnected global society.

Bucknell's 3,500 undergraduates can choose from more than fifty majors and sixty-five minors. Opportunities abound—students build robots, write and perform in their own plays, or debate solutions to the crisis in Afghanistan; engineers make art; artists analyze DNA; and philosophers make music. Each student chooses his or her own pathway, but what unites everyone is a shared passion for learning and a desire to achieve deeper levels of understanding about life and the world.

Bucknell's faculty creates an environment of free-flowing ideas and stimulating discussions. Professors teach every class, getting to know students personally and challenging them to do their best. The professors are also dedicated scholars who frequently receive awards and grants for their work. Often, they engage students in research and creative projects outside of class. By doing so, they provide students with mentorship and guidance for the future.

Outside of class, students participate in myriad activities. Bucknell offers Division I athletics along with intramural and club sports, Greek life, and about 150 student-run clubs and organizations. These organizations focus on anything from social and environmental causes to cultural awareness, poetry slams, volunteering and service, or politics. Students can enrich their religious and spiritual lives through multiple University and student-led faith organizations.

The University is a residential campus, requiring nearly all of its undergraduates to live on campus. Living on campus does not, however, mean students are isolated from the "real" world—quite the opposite is true. Visiting scholars and speakers come to Bucknell nearly every week, and much of the curriculum focuses on cultures, societies, and economies around the globe. Learning happens off campus, too. Students frequently perform service work in places as close as the local nursing home and as far away as Nicaragua or Uganda. They secure summer internships with nonprofit organizations and corporations. They study abroad through one of University's own "in" programs or 130 other approved programs in Africa, Asia, Europe, and South America. And after they graduate, they live and work all over the world.

Alumni of Bucknell succeed in their careers because they offer a combination of skills, knowledge, and flexibility of mind that employers seek. To prepare students, the University offers career services including advising, networking, mock interviews, internship and externship support, and employer fairs to students throughout their four years at Bucknell. The placement rate is consistently high: 97 percent of the class of 2011 was employed, in graduate school, traveling, or volunteering within nine months of graduation. In 2011, PayScale Inc. included Bucknell on its list of colleges whose graduates earn the highest paychecks.

Location

With its green spaces, red brick buildings, and striking vistas, Bucknell's campus is a quintessential college environment in the heart of scenic central Pennsylvania. The shops of historic downtown Lewisburg, including the new Barnes & Noble at Bucknell University bookstore, lie within walking distance of campus. The University is located within a 3- to 4-hour drive of most of the major Eastern cities, including New York City; Washington, D.C.; Philadelphia; and Pittsburgh.

Majors and Degrees

Bucknell provides students with a choice of more than fifty majors in a variety of liberal arts and professional fields. Bachelor of Arts degrees are available in animal behavior, anthropology, art, art history, biology, chemistry, classics (Greek or Latin concentrations), comparative humanities, computer science, East Asian studies (China or Japan concentrations), economics, education, English (creative writing or film/media studies concentrations), environmental geology, environmental studies, French, geography, geology, German, history, international relations (Africa, Europe, East Asia, Latin America, Middle East, North America, or Russia concentrations), Italian studies, Latin American studies, linguistics, mathematics (general, pure mathematics, or statistics concentrations), music, philosophy, physics, political science, psychology, religion, Russian, sociology (general, human services, or legal studies concentrations), Spanish, theater, and women's and gender studies.

The music program offers a Bachelor of Music degree with majors in music composition, music education, music history, and performance.

Bachelor of Science degrees are available in animal behavior, biology, cell biology and biochemistry, chemistry, computer science, engineering (in the disciplines of biomedical, chemical, civil, computer, electrical, and mechanical engineering as well as a degree in computer science and engineering), environmental geology, environmental studies, geology, interdisciplinary studies in economics and mathematics, mathematics (general, pure mathematics, or statistics concentrations), neuroscience, and physics.

Bachelor of Science in Business Administration degrees are available in four majors: accounting and financial management; global management; managing for sustainability; and markets, innovation, and design.

Bachelor of Science in Education degrees are available in early childhood development and elementary education.

In consultation with an academic adviser, students also may design their own major based around their individualized educational goals. Select engineering students also have the option of completing one of two five-year interdisciplinary programs; these programs lead to a B.S. in an engineering field and either a B.A. in another discipline or a specially designed Bachelor of Management for Engineers degree.

Academic Programs

Requirements for each degree program vary, but all students are required to complete three writing courses. Special programs are offered to encourage each student's personal and intellectual development. Examples include the first-year foundation seminars, an introductory engineering course open to students in the College of Arts and Sciences, and Bucknell's Residential College living-learning community program. These living-learning communities are theme-based options for first-year students that combine classroom and out-of-class activities into a living and learning experience. The themes are the arts, environmental issues, global affairs, humanities, languages and cultures, social justice, and society and technology.

Off-Campus Programs

Bucknell University's Office of International Education offers one of the largest study-abroad programs available at an undergraduate liberal arts institution. More than 45 percent of Bucknell's students study abroad for a year, a semester, and/or a summer. Bucknell sponsors semester-long "Bucknell in" programs in London, France, and Spain. During the summer, the University offers programs in Denmark, Northern Ireland, Nicaragua, South Africa, and the Virgin Islands.

In addition to Bucknell-run programs, the University is affiliated with 130 other programs worldwide. Shorter-term service and learning programs are also available, along with internship programs in Philadelphia or Washington, D.C. Financial aid, grants, and scholarships apply toward study abroad.

Academic Facilities

Bucknell's 450-acre campus includes facilities for art, engineering, music, the sciences, theater, and dance and a 1,200-seat performance hall. Bertrand Library holds 833,000 volumes, provides access to more than 26,000 periodicals, and offers thousands of audiovisual materials. Computer labs are available across campus, and most of campus is wireless-accessible. Classrooms are equipped with projectors and computers, some with computers for each student. All student residences are connected to the residential network, featuring a high-speed data connection for each student. Science and engineering programs have sophisticated instrumentation available for student use.

Costs

The cost of tuition and fees for 2012–13 is $56,190, including $45,132 for tuition, $10,812 for room and board, and $246 for student fees.

Financial Aid

About 50 percent of students receive financial aid from the University, and 62 percent receive financial aid of some form, including need-based scholarships, loans, work-study, and a limited amount of merit scholarships. In 2011–12, Bucknell budgeted over $44 million toward scholarship aid for undergraduates. Another $17 million was awarded in student loans, $2.5 million in work-study, and $2.5 million in federal and state grants. The average total financial aid package in the fall of 2011 for first-year students with financial need was about $27,000. The average student loan debt upon graduation is about $20,000.

Arts merit scholarships are available in the areas of art and art history, creative writing, dance, music, and theater (design and technology, performance).

If prospective students and their families believe they will need financial aid, they must file the Financial Aid PROFILE with the College Scholarship Service before January 15.

Faculty

Bucknell has 358 full-time faculty members; 97 percent of them hold doctorates or appropriate terminal degrees. The student-faculty ratio is 10:1.

Bucknell's professors uphold the teacher-scholar ideal, through which they are committed to providing an excellent undergraduate education and also actively pursuing their scholarly work. Many students collaborate with faculty members in research, and projects regularly lead to joint publications or presentations at professional meetings.

Student Government

The Bucknell Student Government serves as the official voice of Bucknell's students. It dispenses funds for most student clubs and organizations, and its representatives serve on standing committees of the Board of Trustees and other University governance groups.

Admission Requirements

Admission decisions focus on intellectual ability; quality of preparation as demonstrated by achievement in rigorous high school courses and SAT or ACT scores; special talent; significant contribution to school or community; and evidence of strong character and integrity. Well-written essays weigh heavily in the admissions process. The University seeks qualified students from all backgrounds throughout the United States and abroad.

Application and Information

Regular decision applications should be filed before January 15 of the senior year in high school for notification by April 1. SAT and/or ACT results must be submitted before March 1. Early decision candidates may apply for early decision–round one consideration by November 15 or early decision–round two consideration by January 15. Applications for transfer students should be submitted by March 15 for studies beginning the following fall and by November 1 for the spring semester.

Robert G. Springall
Dean of Admissions
Bucknell University
Lewisburg, Pennsylvania 17837
United States
Phone: 570-577-1101
Fax: 570-577-3538
E-mail: admissions@bucknell.edu
Web site: http://www.bucknell.edu
    www.facebook.com/BucknellU
    www.facebook.com/LifeAtBucknell
    Twitter @BucknellU

The tower of Bertrand Library is both a landmark and a symbol of University life.

BURLINGTON COLLEGE

BURLINGTON, VERMONT

The College

Founded in 1972, Burlington College is a small, nontraditional private college in the heart of Burlington, Vermont. The 32-acre campus overlooks Lake Champlain and the Adirondack Mountains.

Burlington College is accredited by the New England Association of Schools and Colleges (NEASC) to offer undergraduate and graduate degrees. The following information applies to the College undergraduate program only.

A unique college experience—Burlington College invites students to be partners in planning their academic careers. Students are encouraged to take courses on a variety of subjects and develop their own vision. Working in small discussion-centered classes of between 6 and 15 members, students come to know each other and themselves well. Lead by knowledgeable and dedicated faculty, these stimulating classes can take on lives of their own as students make contributions to the discussions, and instructors, at times, become equal observer-learners in the process.

An integral part of Burlington College's progressive education is the collaboration between students and instructors, setting the goals and expectations for the semester. During evaluation week, both students and instructors provide written evaluations of progress made toward the agreed upon goals. Thus, the evaluation period becomes a time for reflection on what a student has learned and what they need to do moving forward to achieve their larger goals.

Location

Just a short walk from campus is Burlington's Church Street, a long pedestrian mall and the heart of Burlington's downtown, with numerous eateries, outdoor cafés, and coffee shops; a Ben & Jerry's Ice Cream scoop shop, and an indoor shopping mall.

Students can enjoy the things that earned Burlington the title of "Most Livable City in America." There is a wide array of festivals, the South End Art Hop, the Vermont International Film Festival, the Discover Jazz Festival, the Festival of Fools, and Winter Festival, to name just a few. The music scene is vibrant with many local performance venues: Higher Ground, Champlain Valley Expo, the Flynn Center for the Performing Arts, Red Square, and Nectar's—where the band Phish got its start.

The options are limitless when it comes to ways one can enjoy Vermont's extraordinary outdoors. Burlington College is just 45 minutes from the snowy slopes where the founder of Burton Snowboards, Jake Burton Carpenter, invented the snowboard and perfected his ride.

During the warmer months, students can stroll down to the College's sandy beach, swim in Lake Champlain, and walk or ride on the bike path that passes through the campus and runs along the shoreline. For adventurous spirits, the Green Mountain State offers an abundance of outdoor activities, such as hiking the Long Trail, scuba diving at shipwrecks, and some of the best wind-surfing in the northeast.

Burlington College is 2 hours south of Montreal, 4 hours northwest of Boston, and about 5½ hours from New York City.

Majors and Degrees

Burlington College provides a rare opportunity for students to self-design their major in the Individualized Studies program. This allows for interdisciplinary studies and enables students to explore their areas of interests more freely.

A Bachelor of Fine Arts degree is offered in cinema studies and film production, craftsmanship and design, graphic design, and photography.

A Bachelor of Arts is offered in cinema studies and film production, documentary studies, expressive arts, fine arts, hospitality and event planning, human services, inter-American studies, integral psychology, international relations and diplomacy, legal and justice studies, media activism, photography, and writing and literature. Students may also design their own majors.

An Associate of Arts degree is offered in craftsmanship and design, film studies, and liberal arts studies. The College has certificate programs in Cuban studies, with a semester of study in Cuba; documentary filmmaking; film production; paralegal studies; screenwriting; and woodworking and fine-furniture making, as well as an advanced certificate in fine-furniture making.

Other opportunities for course work are available through the three-college consortium with Champlain College and St. Michael's College, and the College's partnership with Vermont Law School.

Academic Programs

The founders of Burlington College created an undergraduate institution firmly rooted in a concern for, and interaction with, the greater Burlington community. In keeping with that philosophy, the College continues to offer rich and diverse opportunities for its students to participate in arts-related events, the natural environment, and civic and humanitarian projects. The College's mission gives direction to a program of education that addresses learners as individuals and helps them increase their awareness, knowledge, and competence. Students are actively engaged in the planning and implementation of their education in an atmosphere of open communication and shared responsibility.

Off-Campus Programs

Burlington College Distance Learning is a mode of instruction that meets the needs of students who want to earn their bachelor's degrees in courses outside the typical classroom environment. This personalized program offers flexibility for creative, self-directed, and mature individuals. Applicants must be experienced students who have already earned at least 30 college credits from one or more accredited college programs. Once accepted, students are assigned an academic adviser who assists with the planning and development of their major. In addition to online classes, individual instructors are selected to work with each student on a semester-to-semester basis.

Distance-learning students must attend at least one residency at the College per year. These residencies take place biannually over a long weekend at the start of the fall and spring semesters. During the residency, students meet with their adviser, faculty members, and College staff. Distance-learning students are encouraged and expected to connect with the on-campus community. They are invited to attend seminars, courses, workshops, and events.

Academic Facilities

Burlington College is committed to providing students with necessary resources throughout their educational journey and has many academic resources on campus. The city of Burlington has much to offer when it comes to the arts, museums, community organizations, and educational resources. Much like its classrooms, which break through conventional boundaries and extend into the community itself, Burlington College regularly reaches out to the community for resources for its students' individualized studies. On-campus resources include event spaces, a library, galleries, lounges, and a café. In addition, students have access to several local resources, such as the University of Vermont's lending library and the local YMCA.

Costs

For the 2011–12 academic year, full-time tuition (12–15 credits per semester) was $22,410 per year/$11,205 per semester. For more than 15 credits, $705 was charged per additional credit. Three-quarter-time tuition (9–11 credits per semester) cost $17,100 per year/$8550 per semester, and half-time tuition (6–8 credits per semester) cost $11,600 per year/$5800 per semester. The per-credit charge for less than half time (up to 5 credits) was $740 per credit.

Costs for housing were as follows: single-occupancy bedroom—$7450; double-occupancy bedroom—$6670; triple-occupancy bedroom—$6300; and premium bedroom—$7980.

Occasionally, courses and other learning activities may have additional charges. Students should see the course descriptions for any exceptions. All charges are subject to change without notice.

Financial Aid

The Financial Aid Office is available to assist students in navigating the variety of financial aid programs offered. Burlington College is a Yellow Ribbon School and works with veterans to maximize the benefits and minimize out-of-pocket expenses. Prospective students may contact the Financial Aid Office for more information at 800-862-9616 (toll-free).

Faculty

Burlington College students cite small class sizes, personal attention, and academic freedom as their reason for selecting the College. The student body is under 200 students and the faculty ratio is about 6 to 1 in this diverse, creative community.

Student Government

The student government meets with the College President to exchange ideas, share information, and address concerns. Members organize some of the student activities on campus.

The Student Judiciary Board is a panel made up of students, faculty members, and advisers. They determine sanctions when there is a serious infraction by a student of policies detailed in the student handbook.

Admission Requirements

Burlington College seeks students who are independent thinkers and share a commitment to collaborative learning. Burlington College's application process is highly personalized and holistic. Students must have a minimum of a high school diploma or GED in order to apply. The College selects students by reviewing their admission essay, academic track record, letters of recommendation, as well as through meaningful communication between the student and the Office of Admissions.

Application and Information

Burlington College accepts applications on a rolling basis. This means that an application is evaluated and a decision is made within two weeks of the application being received. Freshman and transfer applicants are considered for both the fall and spring semesters. In some cases, summer start dates may be an option. There is no official deadline for the submission of applications. However, scholarships, College financial aid, and spaces in each class are limited, so students are encouraged to apply by May 1 for the fall semester and December 15 for the spring semester. An application for admission is required of anyone who wishes to matriculate and enroll in a program of study leading to an academic degree or certificate.

Office of Admissions
Burlington College
351 North Avenue
Burlington, Vermont 05401
Phone: 800-862-9616 (toll-free)
E-mail: admissions@burlington.edu
Web site: http://www.burlington.edu/

Students enjoying campus life at Burlington College in Vermont.

CALIFORNIA COLLEGE OF THE ARTS
SAN FRANCISCO AND OAKLAND, CALIFORNIA

The College

California College of the Arts (CCA) (www.cca.edu), founded in 1907, offers studies in twenty-one undergraduate and seven graduate majors in the areas of fine art, architecture, design, and writing. It has two campuses, in San Francisco and Oakland, both of which provide an intimate, private-college environment. Students and faculty members create a supportive community of friends, colleagues, and mentors. Students discover their creative passions and develop their individual points of view, and they are particularly encouraged to experiment across disciplines. CCA welcomes students who want to make art that matters.

CCA offers cross-disciplinary opportunities, innovative courses with real-world applications, and outstanding faculty members who are professionally renowned in their respective fields. Whether a student's dream involves producing an experimental film, designing sustainable products or buildings, painting outside the lines, or working within their community, CCA offers an excellent environment to pursue those dreams. Students develop skills that will serve them well, both during their college years and after graduation.

CCA alumni have been successful in a vast range of creative endeavors. In the past year, two fashion design seniors received prestigious internships at Nicole Miller; alumni Jay Nelson and Rachel Kaye, with Nelson's experimental vehicle/camper/sculpture, were featured on the cover of *ReadyMade* magazine; and alumna Lia Tjandra received numerous awards and accolades for her graphic design of Rebecca Solnit's book *Infinite City*, a cartographic ode to San Francisco. In 2010, alumnus Alex Beckman was nominated for a primetime Emmy award in interactive media for his work on the TV show *Glee*. Fashion design alumna Amy Sarabi competed in season seven of the TV show *Project Runway*.

ENGAGE at CCA is a family of courses embedded throughout the college's curriculum in which students work with outside experts to find solutions to community issues. The IMPACT Social Entrepreneurship awards give multiple $10,000 awards each year to interdisciplinary teams of students, enabling them to undertake a major project over the summer, anywhere in the world.

BusinessWeek magazine named CCA one of the world's best design schools in 2009. The college is cited as one of the greenest colleges in the U.S. by the *Princeton Review*. CCA is accredited by the Western Association of Schools and Colleges, the National Association of Schools of Art and Design, the National Architectural Accrediting Board, and the Council for Interior Design Accreditation.

CCA has approximately 1,475 undergraduate and 500 graduate students. The average class size is 18. Among the undergraduates, 61 percent are women, 39 percent are men, 18 percent are from underrepresented populations, and 15 percent are international students. Of the entering class, 55 percent are first-time freshmen and 45 percent are transfer and second-degree students. About 28 percent come from out of state.

About 80 percent of first-year students live on campus. Throughout the year, the residential-life staff hosts social and educational programs ranging from movie nights to museum trips and lectures by outside professionals.

Students are encouraged to join existing clubs and organizations or to form new ones. They are active in preprofessional groups, including the American Institute of Architecture Students (AIAS), American Institute of Graphic Arts (AIGA), Industrial Designers Society of America (IDSA), and International Interior Design Association (IIDA).

Location

The San Francisco Bay Area is known for creative and technological innovation, environmental leadership, and thriving art and design communities. It is home to world-class museums and alternative galleries as well as active endeavors in theater, music, dance, film, and literature. Beaches, hiking and biking trails, the Napa Valley, Monterey, Lake Tahoe, the Sierra Nevada mountains, and Yosemite National Park are all nearby.

CCA's San Francisco campus spans a city block in the Potrero Hill neighborhood, near the design district. The Oakland campus occupies 4 acres in the Rockridge neighborhood, 3 miles from the University of California, Berkeley. A free shuttle connects the campuses and residence halls. Both campuses are easily accessible via public transportation.

Majors and Degrees

CCA offers the Bachelor of Fine Arts (B.F.A.) degree in animation, ceramics, community arts, fashion design, film, furniture, glass, graphic design, illustration, industrial design, interaction design, interior design, jewelry/metal arts, painting/drawing, photography, printmaking, sculpture, and textiles. The College offers the Bachelor of Arts (B.A.) degree in visual studies and writing and literature. CCA also offers a bachelor of architecture (B.Arch.) degree, a five-year program. More information is available at http://www.cca.edu/academics.

CCA offers the M.F.A. in design, fine arts, and writing; the M.A. in curatorial practice and visual and critical studies; the M.Arch. and M.A.AD. in architecture; and the M.B.A. in design strategy. Graduate fine arts concentrations include ceramics, film, furniture, glass, jewelry/metal arts, painting/drawing, photography, printmaking, sculpture, textiles, and social practice.

Academic Programs

The B.F.A. requires the completion of 126 semester units (75 in studio work and 51 in humanities and sciences). The B.A. requires 126 semester units (51 in humanities and sciences, 36 in the major, and 39 in studio work). The B.Arch. requires 165 semester units, including the core program and a 9-semester major program. For details, prospective students can visit http://www.cca.edu/academics.

Undergraduates begin with a core curriculum, which covers a variety of artistic media, principles, and processes as well as writing, literature, art history, and critical theory.

CCA operates on a two-semester academic calendar with a six-week summer session. Summer programs include the Pre-College Program for high school students (participants earn college credit). Continuing education programs are offered throughout the year.

Off-Campus Programs

Qualified upper-division students may spend a semester at one of thirty-two other U.S. art schools through the Association of Independent Colleges of Art and Design (AICAD). Students may cross-register at Mills College or Holy Names University, both in Oakland.

Through the International Exchange Program, students may spend a semester at one of more than thirty colleges around the world. CCA also offers summer study-abroad courses.

Academic Facilities

The Oakland campus is home to the First Year Program and the programs in animation, ceramics, community arts, glass, jewelry/metal arts, photography, printmaking, sculpture, textiles, visual studies, and writing and literature. Painting and drawing courses are held on both campuses. Animation students have dedicated studios and equipment for digital video, film, and sound production. The ceramics facilities include numerous gas and electric kilns. Sculpture facilities include a bronze foundry, a waxworking area, a plaster and mold-making room, a metal fabrication studio, and a woodshop. Textiles facilities include a computerized weaving lab, a digital Jacquard TC-1 loom, and a fiber sculpture studio. For printmaking there are lithography presses, a 40x60 American French Tool etching press, a silkscreening and papermaking complex, and a letterpress lab. The two-floor photography center was renovated in 2011.

The San Francisco campus houses the programs in architecture, fashion design, film, furniture, graphic design, illustration, industrial design, interaction design, and interior design as well as all of the graduate programs. There is a state-of-the-art digital production facility and stage. The studio and shop facilities include a furniture studio, a model-making studio, an alternative materials studio, a rapid-prototyping studio, a welding studio, a plaster room, a sanding room, and a spray booth. The MFA Program in writing has its own building.

CCA's fourteen dedicated computer labs are available to all students 16 to 24 hours daily, whenever they are not being used for classes. The labs have Intel-based Macintosh computers and a complete range of software. There is a rapid prototyping studio for 3-D printing.

CCA's libraries (one on each campus) specialize in art and design. On the San Francisco campus there is also a materials library (one of very few such libraries at an educational institution) that contains thousands of material samples.

The College has several dedicated on-campus spaces for the exhibition of student work, and individual departments and courses frequently present off-campus shows of student work. Many of these exhibitions are organized by the students, which gives them valuable hands-on gallery experience. Student exhibitions on both campuses change weekly.

Costs

Tuition for the 2011–12 year was $36,960 for full-time undergraduates and $1540 per unit for part-time students. Tuition is the same for California and out-of-state residents. Campus housing cost an additional $7400. Total costs for 2011–12 were $52,510, which included $37,310 in tuition and fees, $10,250 for room and board, $1500 for books and supplies, and $3450 for miscellaneous expenses.

Additional information is available at http://www.cca.edu/students/handbook/tuition_fees.

Financial Aid

In 2011–12, 87 percent of CCA students received financial aid from some source. Approximately 78 percent received CCA scholarships. The college offers financial aid in the form of scholarships, grants, loans, and work-study programs. There are both need- and merit-based awards. An estimate of potential scholarship and financial aid can be generated by the net cost calculator at http://www.cca.edu/financialaid.

Students seeking merit scholarships must submit their admissions application by February 1. Students applying for financial assistance should submit the FAFSA by March 1. CCA continues to award aid after March 1 as funding permits. Students can apply for grants and loans throughout the year. CCA is approved for veterans who wish to attend under the Veterans Administration Educational Benefits Program. CCA offers an interest-free payment plan.

Faculty

CCA's faculty includes 500 artists, architects, designers, writers, and scholars, most of whom combine teaching with professional work in their respective fields. Faculty members serve as advisers to first-year students. Additional details about CCA's faculty are available at http://www.cca.edu/academics/faculty.

Student Government

The Student Council includes students from all areas of CCA and sponsors extracurricular activities, including films, receptions, and gallery excursions.

Admission Requirements

Admitted undergraduates must have a high school diploma or equivalent. Applications are reviewed on an individualized basis, taking into account academic achievements, creative abilities, individual achievements and activities, a personal essay, recommendations, and a portfolio. Prospective students can find more information at http://www.cca.edu/admissions.

Application and Information

For undergraduates, there are two priority deadlines for fall admission: February 1 and March 1. Those interested in applying for merit scholarships should submit their applications by February 1. The priority deadline for spring undergraduate applicants is October 1. Students who meet the admissions priority deadlines receive first consideration for housing, financial aid, and course selection. Applications are reviewed in the order they are received. There is a nonrefundable application fee of $60. It is possible to register for courses as a nondegree student (on a space-available basis).

Students may schedule a campus visit, request information, and apply online at http://www.cca.edu/admissions. For additional information, please contact:

Office of Enrollment Services
California College of the Arts
1111 Eighth Street
San Francisco, California 94107-2247
Phone: 800-447-1ART (toll-free)
Fax: 415-703-9539
Web site: http://www.cca.edu
      http://www.facebook.com/CaliforniaCollegeoftheArts
      http://twitter.com/CACollegeofArts
      http://www.youtube.com/user/CCAart

A Fashion Design student at California College of the Arts puts the finishing touches on an experimental paper dress.

CALIFORNIA INSTITUTE OF THE ARTS   CaLARTS

VALENCIA, CALIFORNIA

The Institute

CalArts educates professional artists in a unique learning environment founded on the principles of art-making excellence, experimentation, critical reflection, and independent inquiry. Throughout its history, CalArts has sought to advance the practice of art and promote its understanding in a broad social, cultural, and historical context. CalArts offers students the knowledge and expertise of leading professional artists and scholars and a full complement of art-making tools. In return, it asks for the highest artistic and academic achievement. Reflecting its longstanding commitment to new forms and expressions in art, CalArts invites creative risk-taking and urges active collaboration and exchange among artists, artistic disciplines, and cultural traditions.

CalArts is the first higher educational institution in the United States to offer undergraduate and graduate degrees in both visual and performing arts. It was established in 1961 by Walt and Roy Disney through the merger of two professional schools, the Los Angeles Conservatory of Music and the Chouinard Art Institute.

Since its founding, CalArts has been recognized internationally as a leader in every discipline in which it provides instruction. Its artists and alumni have defined, and continue to extend, the very forefront of creative practice as we know it today.

At the graduate level, the Institute grants the Master of Fine Arts (M.F.A.) degree in art, dance, film/video, theater, and writing and the Master of Arts (M.A.) degree in aesthetics and politics, and a Doctor of Musical Arts (D.M.A.) degree in performer-composer. Graduate programs take one, two, or three years to complete, depending on the individual program. Certificates and advanced certificates are also offered.

The total enrollment of the Institute is approximately 1,454 men and women, of whom 895 are undergraduates. The student body is gender balanced and geographically diverse, with students hailing from fifty states and thirty-one different countries.

Location

Thirty miles north of downtown Los Angeles, CalArts occupies 60 acres on hills overlooking the incorporated city of Santa Clarita. Rapid development in this peaceful suburban area has resulted in new residential communities and an ever-increasing population of more than 150,000. Los Angeles, the second-largest city in the United States and an important international hub for the arts, offers a vast array of professional and cultural resources.

Majors and Degrees

California Institute of the Arts grants the Bachelor of Fine Arts (B.F.A.) degree in art, dance, film/video, music, and theater; the Master of Fine Arts (M.F.A.) degree in art, dance, film/video, theater, and writing; the Master of Arts (M.A.) degree in aesthetics and politics; and the Doctor of Musical Arts (D.M.A.) degree in performer-composer.

Academic Programs

Students must apply to and enroll in a specific program within a particular school. A modified, nontraditional grading system is utilized, with each school's curriculum being determined by the special demands of the discipline. Instruction proceeds according to the student's preparation and need, with the student receiving guidance from a faculty mentor.

Undergraduate programs take four years or eight semesters and a minimum of 120 semester units to complete. All undergraduate students must fulfill the Critical Studies Requirements (40 percent of the total curriculum), which include courses in the humanities, social sciences, cultural studies, and natural sciences. These courses are intended to inform and influence each student's artistic practice.

Academic Facilities

Open 24 hours a day, the campus houses classrooms, art studios, animation studios, rehearsal rooms, and dance studios; galleries; theaters for drama, dance, and film; a music performance hall; costume, scenery, and machine shops; photo labs; computer and media labs; editing suites for film and video; and digital recording studios.

CalArts students also take advantage of a variety of special initiatives designed to respond to the realities of the social and cultural world today. These range from the Community Arts Partnership (CAP), which offers students a chance to teach in community and public school settings to the Cotsen Center for Puppetry and the Arts, which allows students to explore the potential of puppetry in their art-making and from the groundbreaking Center for New Performance, the professional wing of CalArts' Schools of Performance where students and faculty members collaborate on professionally presented performances, to the Institute's contemporary art journal Afterall, copublished with London's Central Saint Martins College of Art and Design, and the literary magazine Black Clock, published in association with CalArts' M.F.A. Writing Program.

The most momentous of these initiatives is the Roy and Edna Disney/CalArts Theater, or REDCAT, part of the Walt Disney Concert Hall complex in downtown Los Angeles. Designed by Frank Gehry, REDCAT includes a state-of-the-art, flexible performance space, a 3,000-square-foot gallery, and a café. REDCAT plays host to the most interesting new experimental theater, dance, music, art, film and video, and literature from Southern California, the nation, and the world. In the process, CalArts brings new resources to its students' education through performances, master classes, and residencies by visiting artists and helps its students make a seamless transition into the local, national, and international arts communities.

The library contains a collection designed especially for the visual and performing arts. In addition to holding more than 95,000 volumes, the library includes musical scores, sound recordings, films, videotapes, and slides that enable students to progress on their own in obtaining knowledge relevant to their specific studies.

Costs

Tuition for 2012–13 is $38,438 for the academic year. Room charges range from $4100 to $7970 per year, and board costs between $3710 and $4265. The cost of books and supplies varies according to major.

Financial Aid

The Financial Aid Office at CalArts is dedicated to helping students meet the cost of attendance at the Institute. Funds made available through the Financial Aid Office are awarded on a combination of need and artistic merit. Need is determined by completing and submitting the FAFSA (Free Application for Federal Student Aid). CalArts offers a limited number of merit-only awards; however, to be considered for these awards, students must have completed the FAFSA.

CalArts offers the following financial aid programs: Institute scholarships and grants, Federal Pell Grants, Federal Supplemental Educational Opportunity Grants, Federal Work-Study Program awards, Federal Perkins Loans, Federal Stafford Loans, and Cal Grants. Details of these financial aid programs are available from the Financial Aid Office.

Faculty

The faculty numbers approximately 300, including both full- and part-time members. The student-faculty ratio is approximately 8:1. Faculty members maintain active, often prolific, careers in their respective disciplines. Their approach to teaching combines rigorous instruction with careful guidance and individualized attention, a process that empowers students to define their own artistic objectives. Every student works closely with an assigned faculty mentor.

Student Government

Student government is conducted through the Student Council, whose members are elected by the student body. In addition, students are active participants in a variety of Institute-wide standing committees, the composition of which also includes a Board of Trustees, faculty members, and staff members.

Admission Requirements

CalArts welcomes application for admission from any individual engaged in the visual and performing arts. The main criterion for admission is artistic merit, as assessed by the faculty of the individual programs. An artist statement, letters of recommendation, and school transcripts are also required.

Application and Information

For application forms and additional information, prospective students should visit http://calarts.edu/admissions/apply or contact:

Office of Admissions
California Institute of the Arts
24700 McBean Parkway
Valencia, California 91355
Phone: 661-255-1050
E-mail: admissions@calarts.edu
Web site: http://www.calarts.edu

The 60-acre campus of CalArts. 30 miles north of Los Angeles, overlooks the city of Santa Clarita.

CALIFORNIA LUTHERAN UNIVERSITY
THOUSAND OAKS, CALIFORNIA

The University

California Lutheran University (CLU) was founded in 1959, but its history goes back much farther than that. CLU is part of a 500-year-old tradition of Lutheran higher education—a tradition begun on a university campus as a teaching and reforming movement, a tradition of thoughtful investigation and bold discovery.

Following in this tradition, CLU insists on wide-ranging, critical inquiry into matters of both faith and reason. Students are encouraged to investigate personal beliefs that impact their educational and career choices and are asked to reflect on how their intellectual and spiritual convictions come together to define them as a whole person. Ultimately, the goal of CLU is to educate leaders for a global society who are strong in character and judgment, confident in their identity and vocation, and committed to service and justice. The individual exploration of truth is only a starting point for the whole educational experience by which students and professors work together to seek answers to the intellectual and professional questions that face world citizens.

CLU's 225-acre campus is home to 2,713 undergraduate and 1,390 graduate students that represent a diversity of faiths and cultures from across the nation and around the world. CLU provides access to a wide variety of organizations, sports, and other activities, providing ample opportunities for students to develop their leadership skills. KCLU-FM, a National Public Radio affiliate on the CLU campus, provides a valuable service to the community and a learning opportunity for students.

Master's degrees are awarded in business administration, computer science, education, marriage and family counseling, psychology, and public policy and administration. The NCATE-accredited School of Education offers an Ed.D. in educational leadership as well as a number of credential and certificate programs. International M.B.A. and post-M.B.A. programs are offered through the School of Business.

CLU is accredited by the Western Association of Schools and Colleges and is ranked in the top 20 by *U.S. News & World Report*.

Location

Poised at the intersection of the Americas on the Pacific Rim, CLU's location helps prepare students for careers in a global society. Thousand Oaks, which is located in one of America's significant technology corridors, the 101 Corridor, offers the conveniences of an urban area, but is situated in an area of scenic natural beauty with open spaces and rolling hills. Because of its location midway between downtown Los Angeles and Santa Barbara and 15 miles inland from the Pacific Ocean, CLU offers students numerous recreational and cultural opportunities as well as internship and career opportunities in government, entertainment, and social services.

Majors and Degrees

CLU offers thirty-seven majors within the College of Arts and Science, the School of Business, and the School of Education. In addition, undergraduate pre-professional preparation is available in law, medicine, and health-related fields. Undergraduate degrees are offered in accounting, art, biochemistry and molecular biology, bioengineering, biology, business administration, chemistry, communication, computer information systems, computer science, criminal justice, economics, English, environmental science, exercise science and sports medicine, French, geology, German, history, interdisciplinary studies, international studies, liberal studies (education), marketing communication, mathematics, multimedia, music, music production, philosophy, physics, political science, psychology, religion, social science, sociology, Spanish, and theater arts. Minors are offered in art, bioengineering, biology, business administration, chemistry, church music, communication, computer science, economics, English, environmental studies, ethnic studies, French, gender and women's studies, geography, geology, German, Greek, history, international business, international studies, legal studies, mathematics, multimedia, music, philosophy, physics, political science, psychology, religion, religion minor with church vocations, religion minor with youth ministry, sociology, Spanish, and theater arts.

Academic Programs

CLU's integrated curriculum helps students comprehend issues from a variety of perspectives. Students learn to ask the right questions and to think critically in order to analyze, process, transform, and communicate information. With thirty-six majors and thirty-one minors, students are encouraged to sample classes widely to build a broad base of knowledge. CLU feels that while planning for a career is important, the type of education that prepares students for a changing world is one of the greatest gifts a college education can provide.

At the heart of CLU's academic program is a general education curriculum called Core 21. Students' views of the world expand as they learn how disciplines connect in this interdisciplinary approach. Core 21 extends through all four years, beginning with Freshman Seminar. CLU realizes that students' interests may not fit neatly into an academic box. Whether a student enters college with a definite major in mind or an awareness of the areas he or she wants to explore, CLU's curriculum offers distinctive ways to combine academic interests and goals with practical career preparation.

Students who wish to delve deeper into the life of the mind in smaller, seminar-style classes may also have access to the Honors Program. Honors courses bring students and faculty members together to contemplate issues of enduring human concern as well as contemporary problems facing society. Students who successfully complete the requisite honors courses over four years are awarded University Honors at graduation. A second honors program, Departmental Honors, is open to junior and senior students who wish to participate in prolonged, mentored scholarship with a faculty member in their chosen major field.

Off-Campus Programs

Students may take courses abroad while maintaining their student status at CLU by enrolling in one of the more than forty study-abroad programs offered. The University offers ongoing study, internship, and exchange programs in Austria, Belgium, Germany, Hong Kong, India, Mexico, Sweden, Tanzania, and

Thailand. CLU also offers a Washington, D.C., semester for students in every field of study. This program allows students to live, study, and work in the nation's capital while earning a full semester of academic credit. While completing their professional internship and taking two academic courses, they also participate in orientation sessions, field trips, meetings with experts, and seminars on current events. Students are housed in furnished condominiums across the Potomac River in Arlington, Virginia.

Academic Facilities

The Swenson Center, CLU's first LEED-certified building, that houses nine classrooms, forty-three offices, two computer labs, a psychology lab, a conference room, and a faculty/staff lounge was added to the campus in 2010.

Several new athletic arenas have been added to the north side of the campus in recent years. William Rolland Stadium was completed in 2011 and is the new home for football and men's and women's soccer. The north side of campus also includes the 96,000-square-foot Gilbert Sports and Fitness Center, featuring two gymnasiums, an events center, fitness and strength conditioning centers, dance studios, and a Hall of Fame; the Samuelson Aquatics Center, the George "Sparky" Anderson baseball field at Ullman Stadium; and the Hutton softball field.

The campus is distinctive in its combination of mid-century modern and classic-contemporary architecture. The 600-seat Samuelson Chapel, with its towering wall of stained glass, mahogany carvings, and handcrafted Steiner-Reck organ, anchors the campus, which also includes the state-of-the-art Ahmanson Science Center, Pearson Library, and Soiland Humanities Center. The Preus-Brandt Forum is a 250-seat lecture/performance center equipped with modern sound and lighting equipment.

Costs

Tuition for the 2012–13 academic year is $33,910 (12–18 credits per semester). Room and board for the year is $11,190. Student fees are $250 per year.

Financial Aid

Available assistance includes need-based and non-need-based University scholarships; low-interest, long-term loans from external sources; Federal Supplemental Educational Opportunity Grants; Federal Pell Grants; and Federal Work-Study Program positions. Part-time jobs are available both on and off campus. Applicants for aid should submit the Free Application for Federal Student Aid (FAFSA). The parents' and/or student's most recent IRS 1040 form must also be submitted. The priority application deadline is March 1. CLU scholarships are awarded on the submission of a completed application.

Faculty

At CLU, professors care passionately about teaching and students. CLU's average class size of 22 students enables faculty members to know their students and enables students to develop relationships with mentors. Students have lively, in-depth discussions with the highly trained faculty members who teach their classes. Eighty-one percent of the full-time faculty members have earned their doctoral or terminal degree. They bring a depth of intellectual expertise and academic curiosity to the classroom. Among the faculty members are a former senior economist of the United Nations Development Programme (UNDP), as well as master scholars in everything from media law and Mexican narrative to artificial intelligence and classical and quantum chaos. The list of their areas of research and interests—the social psychology of moral development, molecular evolution, economic and business forecasting models, and politics in movies, to name a few—brings a broad and beneficial foundation to students' liberal arts experience.

Student Government

All undergraduate students carrying 9 or more units are automatically members of the Associated Students of California Lutheran University by virtue of their enrollment in the University. Student governance, including allocation of the student activity fee, is conducted by student body–elected officials.

Admission Requirements

Applicants for admission must complete the application form (the CLU application or the Common Application may be used) and submit a high school transcript, SAT or ACT scores, one recommendation, an essay/personal statement, and a $45 nonrefundable application fee ($25 for online applications). An interview is not required but is strongly recommended. International students whose native language is not English must also submit TOEFL or IELTS scores. All students are expected to have followed the most competitive college-prep curriculum available to them at their high school. Transfer students must also send a transcript of all completed college work (if more than 28 semester units of college work have been completed, SAT/ACT scores are not required).

Application and Information

The Early Action (EA) deadline is November 15. The Regular Decision deadline is February 1. For additional information, interested students should contact:

Office of Undergraduate Admission
California Lutheran University
60 West Olsen Road #1350
Thousand Oaks, California 91360-2700
Phone: 805-493-3135
    877-CLU-FOR-U (toll-free)
Fax: 805-493-3645
E-mail: admissions@callutheran.edu
Web site: www.callutheran.edu
    www.facebook.com/callutheran
    twitter.com/callutheran
    www.youtube.com/callutheran

The campus of California Lutheran University.

CALVIN COLLEGE
GRAND RAPIDS, MICHIGAN

The College

Calvin College is best known for the integration of intellect and Christian faith. In every aspect of college life—teaching and learning, athletics and the arts, campus life and community activities—the Calvin community aims to live *coram Deo*, before the face of God.

Calvin is one of the nation's largest and most respected Christian colleges, bringing together 3,967 students and 312 full-time faculty members in a collaborative learning process. Founded in 1876 and named for John Calvin, the sixteenth-century Protestant reformer, the College's commitment to students has not changed, teaching them to think courageously, connect globally, live faithfully, and become world-ready learners.

Calvin students come from nearly every state and forty-eight countries, and they study in more than 100 academic options. Most students are between 18 and 23 years old. Calvin maintains a strong affiliation with the Christian Reformed Church, yet students from more than fifty church denominations choose Calvin for its intentional blend of faith and learning.

A Calvin education helps students develop the faith, knowledge, and skills they need to walk confidently into life. In a survey of the class of 2010, 71 percent of the respondents were employed, and 29 percent were pursuing graduate study. The Career Development Office equips students for internships, job interviews, and the search for full-time employment after graduation. Calvin students also receive practical experience; more than 80 percent of recent graduates reported having at least one internship while at Calvin.

Calvin is an NCAA Division III school and participates in the Michigan Intercollegiate Athletic Association. Calvin ranks seventh among all NCAA schools in the number of Academic All-American student-athletes since 2000. Calvin's twenty-one teams regularly earn national rankings in Division III athletics. The women's volleyball team won the national championship in 2010; the men's basketball team won the national championship in 1992 and 2000; and the women's cross-country team captured the national championship in 1998 and 1999. In 2000, 2003, 2004, and 2006, the men's cross-country team won national championships. The men's ice-hockey club won the 2004 ACHA DIII national championship. Fourteen teams have finished as national runners-up. The most recent addition to Calvin athletics is lacrosse.

Designed by a student of Frank Lloyd Wright, Calvin's 400-acre wooded campus connects green spaces with modern architecture and remarkable resources. Fifteen residence halls, eleven apartment buildings, and two spacious dining halls accommodate 2,600 resident students. High-speed computing is available throughout the campus, and wireless service is offered in many locations. Calvin's athletic complex features a 5,000-seat arena, an indoor track and tennis center, a health center, and an Olympic-size pool. Calvin's outdoor athletic sites include baseball and softball diamonds, a premier soccer field with seating for 1,500 and two practice fields, an eight-lane track, a six-court tennis facility, a paved jogging path, and two sand volleyball courts.

Location

Calvin is located in Grand Rapids, Michigan, a metropolitan area of more than 600,000 people which offers every urban amenity. Hundreds of restaurants, dozens of theaters, seven shopping malls, and a fine selection of museums and parks are within a short drive. Premed and nursing students take advantage of the Medical Mile, a street running through the core of the city that is flanked with new medical and scientific research facilities. Lake Michigan beaches, ski areas, parks, and trails are within a 40-minute drive.

Majors and Degrees

The Bachelor of Arts and Bachelor of Science degrees are offered, with major concentrations in accounting, art, art history, Asian studies, biochemistry, biology, biotechnology, business, chemistry, Chinese, classical studies, communication arts and sciences, computer science, digital communications, Dutch, early childhood education, economics, elementary and secondary education, engineering, English, environmental science, environmental studies, exercise science, film studies, French, geography, geology, German, Greek, history, information systems, international development studies, international relations, Japanese, Latin, linguistics, literature, mathematics and statistics, media production, media studies, music, nursing, philosophy, physical education, physics/astronomy, political science, psychology, public health, recreation, religion, social work, sociology, Spanish, special education, speech pathology and audiology, sport management, theater, and writing.

Professional programs include engineering (chemical, civil/environmental, electrical/computer, mechanical); natural resources; architecture (minor); predentistry; prelaw; premedicine; prepharmacy; pre–physical therapy; pre–seminary studies; social work; and elementary, early childhood, secondary, and special education. Minor concentrations are available in African and African diaspora studies, archaeology, astronomy, coaching, congregational studies, dance, English as a second language, gender studies, health education, journalism, medieval studies, ministry studies, missions, urban studies, and youth ministry leadership. Calvin also offers a Master of Education (M.Ed.) degree and a Master of Speech-Language Pathology degree (MA-SP) program.

Academic Programs

Calvin's multifaceted liberal arts curriculum helps students connect the way they think with the way they live. Calvin's core curriculum begins with a first-year gateway course, *Developing a Christian Mind,* and ends with a capstone course in the senior year.

The College follows a 4-1-4 academic calendar, consisting of two 4-month semesters with a three-week January interim term.

Core curriculum requirements include foreign language, history, literature and arts, mathematics, natural sciences, philosophy, physical education, religion, social sciences, and written and spoken rhetoric. Some requirements can be satisfied by advanced high school work, by completing college-level work in high school, or by examination. Satisfactory scores on Advanced Placement (AP), International Baccalaureate (I.B.), and/or CLEP exams are also accepted. Incoming students with an ACT composite of at least 29 who are interested in nursing and meet other admissions requirements will receive automatic admission to Calvin's nursing program. The Calvin Honors Program offers highly motivated students a greater depth of learning and advanced course work. The Office of Student Academic Services provides academic counseling, tutoring, training in study skills, and review courses in key subjects for all students.

Off-Campus Programs

Calvin offers semester-long study-abroad programs in Britain, China, France, Ghana, Honduras, Hungary, the Netherlands, Peru, and Spain; there are U.S.-based programs in New Mexico

and Washington, D.C. Calvin offers many other programs in cooperation with other colleges, including programs of the Council for Christian Colleges and Universities in Central America, Hollywood, Egypt, and Moscow. Some students may fulfill their foreign language requirement through study-abroad programs. Many courses offered during the January interim are also taught abroad.

Academic Facilities

The four-floor Science Complex features extensive laboratories, an atom trapper, and an observatory. The Engineering Building provides space for engineering students to do research, design, and project construction. The DeVries Hall of Science includes medical research laboratories and classrooms. The Spoelhof College Center houses administrative offices, a social research center, six art studios, and a 340-seat auditorium. The Covenant Fine Arts Center features a 1,100-seat auditorium, the Center Art Gallery, a 240-seat recital hall, classrooms, and music suites.

The Hekman Library includes a five-level, computerized library containing more than 800,000 bound volumes, 2,750 periodicals, an extensive collection of microfiche, records and tapes, and government publications; more than 1,500 students can be comfortably seated at study carrels and tables. The complex also houses the Information Technology Center, the Calvin Center for Christian Scholarship, the Meeter Center for Calvinism Studies, a distance-learning classroom, a graphics production lab, and a curriculum center for teacher education students. The 55,000-square-foot DeVos Communications Center is home to a 150-seat video theater, a television studio, an audio studio, digital audio and video editing labs, and a speech pathology and audiology clinic. The Prince Conference Center houses seminars, meetings, retreats, and hotel rooms.

Costs

Tuition and fees for 2012–13 are $26,705. Room and board charges are $9110 for resident students with a twenty-one-meal-per-week plan (ten- and fifteen-meal-per-week plans are also available). About $1000 is needed for textbooks.

Financial Aid

Over 75 percent of first-year students are awarded an academic scholarship in amounts ranging from $15,000 to $1000. Sixty percent of Calvin students receive need-based financial aid; demonstrated need is the most important criterion in determining eligibility. Students wishing to be considered for financial aid must be admitted to the College and must submit the Free Application for Federal Student Aid (FAFSA) and Calvin's Supplemental Application for Financial Aid. February 15 is the filing deadline for maximum consideration. Financial awards to eligible applicants consist of state and federal grants, loans, Federal Work-Study Program funds, and institutional grants and scholarships. More than 1,800 jobs are available on campus, and placement preference is given to students with financial need. Calvin's Student Employment Office also helps students find off-campus employment.

Faculty

Calvin's outstanding faculty members have distinguished themselves through publication and research, yet each is available 10–15 hours per week outside of class. More than 82 percent have earned the highest academic degree in their field. Each faculty member is a professing Christian, committed to the integration of his or her personal faith and discipline. There are over 312 full-time and 72 part-time faculty members; the faculty-student ratio is 1:11.

Student Government

Calvin encourages student development and responsible action by clearly expressing its expectations and de-emphasizing regulations. Campus rules are designed to build a Christian academic community. The 27-member Student Senate oversees the budgets for student publications, homecoming, the film arts, and supervises most student activities. Student members serve on most faculty committees governing the College. Each residence hall has its own governing council and judiciary committee.

Admission Requirements

Applicants should be graduates of an accredited high school program and should have completed satisfactorily at least 15 units of college-preparatory work, including 3 in English and 3 in algebra and geometry. Applicants with high school averages of C+ (2.5) or higher who score above 20 on the ACT composite or above 470 on both the math and critical reading sections of the SAT are typically given regular admission. Applicants with lower grades and scores, or those with deficiencies in their high school preparation, may be admitted under special conditions. International students should refer to http://www.calvin.edu/international for application procedures. Students who come from a non-English-speaking culture must submit results of the TOEFL or IELTS or provide other documentation of English-language proficiency.

Application and Information

Applicants must submit a completed application form, a high school or college transcript, results of the ACT or SAT, and an educational recommendation completed by a teacher or counselor. Admission decisions are made on a rolling basis beginning in mid-October. Applicants for fall admission are urged to complete their file before February 1 in order to receive maximum consideration for scholarships; the deadline for admission is August 15 for U.S. and Canadian applicants and April 1 for international applicants, as long as space is available. Prospective students and parents are warmly invited to visit the campus to experience life at Calvin firsthand.

For more information, prospective students should contact:

Office of Admissions and Financial Aid

Calvin College

3201 Burton Street, SE

Grand Rapids, Michigan 49546

Phone: 616-526-6106 (admissions)

616-526-6134 (financial aid)

616-526-8480 (TTY)

800-688-0122 (toll-free in North America)

Fax: 616-526-6777

E-mail: admissions@calvin.edu

finaid@calvin.edu

Web site: http://www.calvin.edu

http://www.facebook.com/calvincollege

http://twitter.com/calvincollege

Recognized as one of the finest research libraries in western Michigan, the Hekman Library is a hub of student and faculty activity on the Calvin College campus.

CARROLL COLLEGE
HELENA, MONTANA

The College

Founded in 1909, Carroll College, in Montana's capital city of Helena, is a private Catholic four-year college, ranked by *U.S. News & World Report* as the number-one regional college in the West for 2012 and the top regional college Best Value School in the West. Students come to Carroll for its combination of top academic programs, affordable tuition with generous financial aid, and the deep sense of community the campus offers. The College's surroundings in the small capital city of Helena promise students a safe and welcoming environment with abundant employment opportunities; access to a healthy outdoor lifestyle; and plentiful entertainment, arts, and cultural offerings.

The typical Carroll student is interested in getting involved and serving others. At Carroll, service and involvement is a lifestyle; almost every student and employee at the College regularly performs some sort of volunteer work for worthy local, national, and global causes, and service is often incorporated into Carroll course work. Carroll professors take an active interest in their students' success, with an open-door policy and commitment to mentoring that result in student excellence academically, in the job market, and in graduate school admission. Students cherish these top professors as approachable role models. Carroll faculty members are not only student-centered but also distinguished as published authors, Fulbright Scholars, groundbreaking researchers, and recipients of National Endowment for the Arts and National Endowment for the Humanities grants and awards.

With 1,500 students, the College allows students to take the lead in campus life and make a difference. Carroll's registrar, financial aid, admission, and business office are particularly noted for the special care they take to address each student's needs, and Carroll is committed to seeing students graduate in four years with the major of their choice. This cuts costs while successfully launching students into their chosen career paths. Students also choose Carroll because it is a place where individual ideas and inspiration can become a student-directed customized major; a new student-run organization; student-designed, real-world scientific research and internships; or an entertainment program bringing national acts to campus.

The laid-back Rocky Mountain environs assures ease of access to almost any outdoor adventure possible, promoting fresh-air fun, physical health, and connection to the natural world. Forested wilderness, backcountry trails, and wild water are almost at the doorstep of Carroll's four on-campus residence halls where most students reside. Minutes from campus, students can hike and camp, ski and board, rock and ice climb, fly-fish and golf, mountain bike, and more. Student government, social and academic clubs, and intramural sports round out campus activities, with national touring entertainment, dances, concerts, and much more scheduled every week. For those inclined to be players or spectators, Carroll offers nationally ranked athletic teams. The history-making Fighting Saints football team is six-time NAIA national champions.

People of all beliefs feel welcome at Carroll, where the search for meaning and purpose in life is paramount. Students feel included in a healthy, energetic community where they get involved in many faith and service activities. Students say that these experiences were life-changers; service and inclusive faith activities at Carroll have often inspired students to enter service vocations after graduation.

Community at Carroll extends across the globe, with students studying, interning, and serving internationally. Students who choose to study abroad for a semester or a year have over fifty countries and over 125 institutions of higher education available to them. Students who opt to intern abroad can pick from over ten affiliate programs at overseas colleges. Short-term study abroad for a week or two is also open to all students, with faculty-guided visits to destinations in Europe, Asia, Africa, and South America. Service abroad is also encouraged, with Carroll's Engineers Without Borders and Carroll Outreach Team offering regular trips to Latin America, Europe, and Africa, where Carroll students and their professional

mentors improve public health and solve local problems. In addition to providing a wealth of opportunities for Carroll students to travel abroad, the College welcomes international students to campus, home to a small but vibrant student population hailing from Asia, Africa, Australia, South America, and Canada. While enriching campus life with their perspectives and religious diversity, these international students tend to be campus leaders, heading up initiatives, starring on the College's athletic squads, and headlining as champions on Carroll's forensics and mathematics teams.

Carroll College is accredited by the Northwest Association of Schools and Colleges. The College is a member of the National Association of Independent Colleges and Universities, the American Council on Education, the Council of Independent Colleges, the Association of Catholic Colleges and Universities, and the Western Independent College Fund.

Location

Helena, the state capital, is famous for its healthy outdoor lifestyle, Western hospitality, and enormous professional and preprofessional opportunities it offers college students. The city offers cultural, arts, and entertainment opportunities year-round, with world-renowned, award-winning artists, journalists and writers residing in Helena and congregating in places like the world-famous Archie Bray Foundation and the Myrna Loy Center. Students receive free or discounted rates to many of the art showings and dance, symphony, film, and theatrical productions in town and on campus year-round.

The local business community and state government prize Carroll students as interns and employees, with Carroll graduates often receiving outstanding job offers prior to earning their degrees. As the center of Montana's political life, Helena is a natural fit for students desiring civic involvement and a career in public service, law, or nonprofit advocacy. Helena has city amenities without the drawbacks; getting around is easy and quick, with no traffic congestion and a downtown within walking distance of campus.

Majors and Degrees

Carroll College offers four-year Bachelor of Arts and Bachelor of Science degree programs. Majors and areas of concentration include accounting; anthrozoology; biology; biochemistry-molecular biology; business administration (with concentrations in economics, finance, international business, management, and marketing); chemistry; civil engineering; civil engineering with a concentration in environmental engineering; classical studies; communication studies; community health; computer information systems (CIS); computer science; elementary education; engineering (3-2 and 4-2 programs); engineering science (mechanics, structural, aerospace, and environmental); English literature; English writing; environmental studies (with concentrations in biology, chemistry, community formation, culture integration, and public policy and management); ethics and values studies; finance; French; health and physical education (with concentrations in K–12 and sport management); health science; history; international relations; mathematics (with a cognate concentration); nursing; philosophy; physics; political science; psychology; public relations (with concentrations in marketing, print journalism, and TV production); secondary education (with concentrations in biology, chemistry, communication studies, English, history, mathematics, political science, and social studies); sociology; Spanish; Spanish education (K–12); theater; and theology (with concentrations in contextual and systematic).

Under the 3-2 engineering program, students attend Carroll for three years and then transfer to an affiliate school to complete their studies in a specialized engineering field (mechanical, electrical, chemical, etc). Upon completion, students receive two bachelor's degrees, one from Carroll in engineering mathematics, and one from the affiliate school in their chosen specialty field. Affiliate schools are Columbia University, Gonzaga University, Montana State University, Montana Tech, the University of Minnesota, Notre Dame, and the University of Southern California. Under

Carroll's 4-2 engineering program, upon graduation from Carroll, students attend graduate school for two years to earn a Master of Science degree in their chosen engineering discipline. Recent participants in Carroll's 4-2 program have attended Columbia University, University of Notre Dame, University of Washington, Massachusetts Institute of Technology, University of Colorado at Boulder, Montana State University, and Colorado State University. Carroll offers preprofessional programs in dentistry, law, medicine, optometry, pharmacy, physical therapy, physician's assistant studies, and veterinary medicine.

Off-Campus Programs

Nearly 90 percent of Carroll's academic disciplines offer professional internship opportunities to give students real-world experience in their future careers. While pursuing their undergraduate degrees, Carroll students are prized interns at a variety of businesses, including accounting, engineering, and law firms, and at several nonprofits. Students in nursing and premed receive hands-on medical experience in their clinicals and part-time work for local healthcare providers, including St. Peter's Hospital and the VA.

As the state capital, Helena provides students internships at the highest levels of state government focusing on all issues impacting Montana and the West, from the environment and economy to health and human rights. Every other year, Helena hosts the state legislature, where students actively participate at every level of lawmaking.

Academic Facilities

Carroll College offers comfortable learning facilities equipped with the latest technology. The Fortin Science Center provides outstanding chemistry, biology, and biochemistry–molecular biology laboratories where students perform real-world, published scientific research year-round. The nursing department's training facility is the regional leader, with a realistic ER triage unit and an extensive array of the most advanced patient-simulation equipment available to prepare future nurses for actual practice in every scenario. The Civil Engineering Laboratory houses professional-grade machinery and materials, including hydraulics-, machinery-, and structures-testing capabilities and a model water-treatment plant.

The College's Corette Library received a recent upgrade, making it a learning commons with the latest technology. Carroll's four coed residence halls provide classrooms, computer labs, chapels, a performing arts center, and art studios and galleries. Nelson Stadium and the Carroll PE Center are home to the six-time national football champions, the Fighting Saints, and to Carroll's other highly decorated athletic teams (soccer, volleyball, men's and women's basketball, cross-country, golf, and track and field), which regularly win conference championships and national acclaim.

Costs

For the 2012–13 academic year, Carroll's tuition and fees total $26,004; room and board fees, $8062; the technology and activities fee, $450; and the health center fee, $100. Other general personal expenses include books, supplies, and transportation. Generous financial aid provides substantial discounts to almost all students (see Financial Aid below), making a Carroll education competitive with, if not more economical than, other private education and even with public four-year colleges and universities in the West.

Financial Aid

Because of generous financial aid packages and the likelihood of graduating in four years, students matriculate with about the same debt as public-school alumni. In the 2010–11 academic year, Carroll awarded an average of $19,895 in financial aid packages to freshmen. Ninety-five percent of Carroll's full-time degree-seeking students receive College-sponsored, state, and federal financial aid. Merit scholarships range from $7000 to $13,000 annually.

Almost 80 percent of Carroll graduates earn their degrees in four years or fewer, which can lower debt and improve lifetime earning potential. This, combined with Carroll's overall affordability, generous financial aid, debt counseling for students, and its graduates' success in obtaining well-paying jobs, has made Carroll's student loan repayment default rate one of the lowest in the nation.

More information on Carroll scholarships is available at the Carroll College Web site at http://www.carroll.edu/finaid/. To receive priority consideration for scholarships, students must have a complete admission file by March 1. Carroll requires students interested in need-based financial assistance to submit the Free Application for Federal Student Aid (FAFSA) at http://www.fafsa.ed.gov, as early as possible after January

Faculty

Carroll's 87 full-time and 75 part-time professors are expert teachers and experts in their fields, with almost all holding doctorate or terminal degrees. Professors, not graduate students, instruct all Carroll courses, and small class sizes are the norm, with an average 14:1 student-professor ratio. Carroll professors play key roles in graduates' success stories by writing critical recommendations, guiding them to the right post-Carroll graduate programs, and connecting Carroll students with employers.

Admission Requirements

Degree candidates are those who have applied through the Office of Admission for a course of study leading to the bachelor's degree. They may be enrolled on a full- or part-time basis. Admission decisions are based upon a student's high school performance, personal essay, a secondary school report, letters of recommendation, demonstrated commitment to intellectual achievement, and performance on standardized college entrance exams.

When applying for admission, candidates must submit the application form, official transcripts from the high school and all colleges previously attended, a secondary school report and/or a letter of recommendation, ACT or SAT scores, and a $35 nonrefundable application fee. There is no fee for online applications at http://www.carroll.edu or through the Common Application at https://www.commonapp.org/. Transfer students who have successfully completed more than 24 college semester credits with at least a C (2.5) grade average are not required to submit high school transcripts or ACT or SAT scores.

Application and Information

Carroll College has a rolling admission policy. Deadlines for incoming freshmen are: early action, November 15; regular admission, February 15; and rolling admission, May 1. Transfer applicants have a regular admission deadline of March 15. Students should apply early to take advantage of financial aid opportunities. Applications received after May 1 are considered on a space-available basis. Students can apply online at the Carroll Web site or through the Common Application Web site.

For application forms or more information, students should contact:

Director of Admission
Carroll College
1601 North Benton Avenue
Helena, Montana 59625-0002
Phone: 406-447-4384
      800-992-3648 (toll-free)
E-mail: admission@carroll.edu
Web site: http://www.carroll.edu
      http://www.facebook.com/carrollcollege
      http://twitter.com/carrollcollege

Carroll College's St. Charles Hall.

CARSON-NEWMAN COLLEGE: A CHRISTIAN UNIVERSITY
JEFFERSON CITY, TENNESSEE

The University

Founded in 1851 by Tennessee Baptists, Carson-Newman (C-N) is a private, coeducational, Christian liberal arts university. C-N has an enrollment of approximately 2,000 students, of which some 290 are graduate students. The average class size is 16 students, and the student to faculty ratio is 12:1. Each fall, Carson-Newman enrolls approximately 450 new undergraduate students. While most states are represented, students come primarily from the Southeastern United States, with Tennessee accounting for 76 percent of C-N students.

In addition to its outstanding academics, the University also provides many opportunities for student involvement in various clubs and organizations, nationally recognized varsity athletics, intramural athletics, music and drama groups, an award-winning forensics team, and many other extracurricular activities. The majority of C-N students live on campus in one of the five residence halls or two apartment complexes.

Carson-Newman also offers twelve graduate programs including master's degrees in education and teaching (educational leadership, education/curriculum and instruction, teaching/curriculum and instruction, English as a second language), counseling (counseling, school counseling, spiritual guidance and care), business (business administration), nursing (RN to M.S.N., family nurse practitioner, nurse educator), and religion (applied theology).

Location

C-N is conveniently located in eastern Tennessee, just 30 miles from Knoxville, which has a population of 450,000, and 45 miles from Gatlinburg, the gateway to the Great Smoky Mountains. Students appreciate the diverse opportunities available in the city and in the outdoor areas. Shopping, dining, and entertainment opportunities are available near the campus.

Majors and Degrees

Carson-Newman is composed of nine schools: Business, Education, Family and Consumer Sciences, Fine Arts, Humanities, Natural Sciences and Mathematics, Nursing and Behavioral Health, Religion, and Social Sciences. The University awards Bachelor of Arts, Bachelor of Music, Bachelor of Science, and Bachelor of Science in Nursing degrees. In addition, an Associate of Arts in Christian ministries degree is also offered.

Majors are available in art (art, photography), business (accounting, business administration, international economics, management, marketing), church recreation, communication studies and theater (advertising/public relations, media studies, film, speech), education (athletic coaching, elementary education, physical education/health, secondary certification, special education), English (creative writing, literature), family and consumer sciences (child and family studies, consumer services, fashion design and merchandising, foods and nutrition, interior design, retail), early childhood education, foreign language (biblical languages, Spanish), general studies, history, human services, mathematics, music (church music, music composition, music education, music theory, music with an outside field, piano and organ performance, vocal performance), natural and physical science (biochemistry, biology, chemistry,

physics), nursing, philosophy (philosophy, philosophy/religion), political science, psychology (applied psychology, social entrepreneurship), religion, sociology, and sport science (exercise science).

Carson-Newman offers extremely strong curricula in preparation for professional and health professions. Preparatory programs are offered in dentistry, law, medicine, and physical therapy. In cooperation with several other institutions, C-N offers binary degrees (2-3 and 3-2 programs) in pharmacy.

Academic Programs

Carson-Newman operates on a traditional semester system. May term is a three-week intensive period of study giving students the opportunity to earn 3 credit hours. Summer terms are also offered.

All baccalaureate degrees require completion of 128 semester hours. Students must complete the C-N liberal arts core requirements and a total of 36 semester hours at the junior/senior level. Specific course requirements vary depending on major and degree program. Honors courses, independent study, and internships are available to students who qualify. Advanced credit is available for students who achieve required scores on AP exams, CLEP tests, and C-N departmental examinations.

New students are assigned a faculty adviser, who assists with course selection and student concerns. Career planning and tutoring services are also available through the Life Directions Center. Carson-Newman's exceptionally high placement rate in professional programs in medicine, law, business, and theological study is a testimony to the excellence of its rigorous academic program.

Off-Campus Programs

Students have the opportunity to spend an entire semester abroad by participating in the London Semester and other study-abroad opportunities. Carson-Newman, along with International Enrichment, Inc., provides all academic and nonacademic support services.

The Washington Semester is available as an internship program primarily for political science and prelaw majors. Through the program, students earn credit for work in the nation's capital. Art and foreign language majors may earn credit while studying and traveling throughout Europe during the three-week May term.

Academic Facilities

Carson-Newman offers the facilities and resources necessary for the enrichment of each student's education. Facilities include numerous computer labs; a campus-wide computer network; a media service center; two theaters for drama production; Thomas Recital Hall, two art galleries and twenty-three individual art studios; the Stephens-Burnette Library, with more than 500,000 volumes; and the award-winning Maddox Student Activities Center. Recent construction projects have added two academic buildings to campus. These include Blye-Poteat Hall, home to the School of Family and Consumer Sciences and Ted Russell Hall, which houses the School of Business.

Costs

The annual cost at Carson-Newman, including room, board, and tuition, is well below the national average for four-year private colleges. Tuition for 2011–12 was $20,786, room averaged $2566, board averaged $3680, the student activity fee was approximately $490, and the technology fee was approximately $490. Students should allow approximately $1000 for books per year.

Financial Aid

Carson-Newman allocates thousands of dollars each year to help supplement the resources of families. Financial aid awards are tailored to meet students' economic needs. Carson-Newman participates in all state and federal aid programs and awards aid based on demonstrated need as documented by a need analysis form, such as the Free Application for Federal Student Aid (FAFSA). Carson-Newman also awards merit academic scholarships based on achievement. The priority deadline for filing financial assistance forms is February 1. Additional information is available at http://www.cn.edu/administration/financial-assistance.

Faculty

Carson-Newman faculty members are known for their interaction with students both inside and outside of classes. The student-faculty ratio at C-N is 12:1, so students are sure to receive individual attention. Faculty members are involved in scholarly pursuits such as authoring books, leading national scholastic organizations, and research, but their primary focus is teaching.

Student Government

The Student Government Association (SGA) represents the entire student body by voicing student concerns in campus affairs. The purpose of SGA is to promote the welfare of every student through justice, to protect individual rights and freedoms, to encourage high standards of conduct, and to train students in the general principles of self-government.

Admission Requirements

Carson-Newman seeks applicants who demonstrate academic preparation and who possess an appreciation of and sensitivity to a Christian education and a liberal arts curriculum. Carson-Newman accepts applications for freshman and transfer admission for each term of enrollment (fall, spring, and summer). Prospective students can obtain additional admissions information at www.cn.edu/admissions.

Application and Information

Applicants must submit all required application materials (application, application fee, official transcripts, and test scores) in order to be considered for admission. Admission decisions are made on a rolling basis, and students are notified within two weeks of receipt of all required documents.

For more information, prospective students should contact the Office of Undergraduate Admissions at 865-471-3223, admitme@cn.edu or visit www.cn.edu.

Students may also follow C-N admissions on Facebook (www.facebook.com/Carson.Newman) or Twitter (twitter.com/cnadmissions).

For additional information, contact:

Office of Undergraduate Admissions
Carson-Newman College: A Christian University
Jefferson City, Tennessee 37760
Phone: 865-471-3223
      800-678-9061 (toll-free)
E-mail: admitme@cn.edu
Web site: http://www.cn.edu
      http://www.facebook.com/Carson.Newman
      http://twitter.com/cnadmissions

Located in the foothills of the Great Smoky Mountains, Carson-Newman's campus offers a great setting for students earning their degree.

CASE WESTERN RESERVE UNIVERSITY
CLEVELAND, OHIO

The University

Ranking consistently among the top private universities in the United States, Case Western Reserve University (CWRU) offers unlimited opportunities for motivated students. Its faculty members challenge and support students to help them flourish, and its partnerships with world-class cultural, educational, and scientific institutions ensure that undergraduate education extends beyond the classroom.

Challenging and innovative academic programs and experiential learning opportunities are at the core of the undergraduate experience. Currently, more than 4,200 undergraduates are enrolled in programs in engineering, natural sciences, management, nursing, the arts, the humanities, and the social and behavioral sciences. Students access CWRU's graduate and professional schools in applied social sciences, dental medicine, graduate studies, law, management, medicine, and nursing.

Nearly every type of student interest group, from political organizations to multiethnic student unions, is represented on campus. Campus Greek life consists of fifteen national fraternities and seven sororities, with approximately 30 percent of undergraduate students participating. Residence halls are coeducational, and over 80 percent of the students reside on campus.

A charter member of the University Athletic Association, an NCAA Division III conference, CWRU has won championships in cross-country, football, softball, track and field, and wrestling. Twenty percent of undergraduates wear the blue-and-white varsity uniform, and 70 percent join an intramural team. Club sports include fencing, golf, ice hockey, skiing, and Ultimate (Frisbee).

Location

CWRU is located in University Circle, a unique cultural district comprising 550 acres of parks, gardens, museums, schools, hospitals, churches, and human service institutions. The Cleveland Museum of Art, the Cleveland Museum of Natural History, and Severance Hall, home of the Cleveland Orchestra, are within walking distance; downtown Cleveland is 10 minutes away by car or public transportation. Partnerships in education and research among University Circle institutions enable students to make full use of resources beyond those of the University itself, and students receive free access to these and other local institutions, including the downtown Rock and Roll Hall of Fame and Museum and the Great Lakes Science Center.

Majors and Degrees

CWRU has a single-door admission policy—once students are admitted, they can pursue any major(s) they wish. Programs of study leading to the Bachelor of Arts degree include anthropology, art history (joint program with the Cleveland Museum of Art), Asian studies, astronomy, biochemistry, biology, chemistry, classics, cognitive science, communication sciences (collaborative program with the Cleveland Hearing and Speech Center), computer science, dance, economics, English, environmental geology, environmental studies, French, French and francophone studies, geological sciences, German, German studies, history, history and philosophy of science, international studies, Japanese studies, mathematics, music (joint program with the Cleveland Institute of Music), nutrition, nutritional biochemistry and metabolism, philosophy, physics, political science, psychology, religious studies, sociology, Spanish, statistics, theater, and world literature. The following B.A. programs are available as a second major only: American studies, evolutionary biology, gerontological studies, natural sciences, pre-architecture, teacher education, and women's and gender studies.

Bachelor of Science degrees are offered in the following fields: accountancy, aerospace engineering, applied mathematics, art education (joint program with the Cleveland Institute of Art), astronomy, biochemistry, biology, biomedical engineering, chemical engineering, chemistry, civil engineering, computer engineering, computer science, electrical engineering, engineering physics, geological sciences, management (business), materials science and engineering, mathematics, mathematics and physics (combined major), mechanical engineering, music education, nursing, nutrition, nutritional biochemistry and metabolism, physics, polymer science and engineering, statistics, systems and control engineering, systems biology, and an undesignated engineering major.

Minor areas of concentration are offered in many areas of major study, as well as American studies, art studio, artificial intelligence, Asian studies, banking and finance, childhood studies, Chinese, computer gaming, electronics (for B.A. only), entrepreneurial studies, ethnic studies, evolutionary biology, gerontological studies, health communication, Italian, Japanese, Judaic studies, management information and decision systems, marketing, mechanical design and manufacturing, natural sciences, pre-architecture, public policy, Russian, sports medicine, and world literature.

Students may work toward a combined B.A./B.S. degree or integrate undergraduate and graduate studies to complete both the bachelor's and master's degrees in five years or less. Students who are interested in both the liberal arts and engineering can benefit from the 3–2 engineering program. Students spend three years at one of forty participating liberal arts colleges and then spend two years at CWRU studying engineering or a related field. Graduates of this program receive both a B.A. and a B.S. degree.

Academic Programs

Students in all majors participate in SAGES, the Seminar Approach to General Education and Scholarship program. SAGES consists of four innovative and engaging seminars that emphasize written and verbal communication skills and concludes with a senior capstone project. As a result, all CWRU students benefit from building on these important skills throughout their undergraduate education. Through a combination of core curricula, major requirements, and minors or approved course sequences, all undergraduates receive a broad educational base as well as specialized knowledge in their chosen fields.

At Case Western Reserve University, hands-on learning comes in many forms. More than 75 percent of our graduates say they took advantage of at least one of the many hands-on learning opportunities available, including:

Co-op: CWRU has one of only eleven co-op programs in the U.S. recognized by the Accreditation Council for Cooperative Education (ACCE). Students studying engineering, science, management, and accounting are eligible.

Research: CWRU is among the country's leading independent research universities, ranking among the top 20 private universities receiving federal funding for research. The University operates nearly 100 designated research centers and laboratories. The SOURCE (Support of Undergraduate Research and Creative Endeavors) office allows students to engage in research relevant to their academic study as well as provide guidance on acquiring research funding.

Internships: Many students utilize the resources of the career center to help them find internships in their field of study. On-campus job fairs and employer visits also help students network and find opportunities.

Volunteer Work: CWRU offers numerous volunteer opportunities connected to a student's academic interests. The Center for Civic Engagement and Learning connects students with community partners.

Clinicals: A CWRU nursing student will get a clinical placement during his/her first semester on campus. Upon graduation, the student will leave with nearly double the national average of clinical hours (1,600+).

Study Abroad: CWRU offers many different types of study-abroad programs. Students have the opportunity to spend a full year or

a semester in a traditional immersion arrangement or can choose from shorter-term programs.

Off-Campus Programs

Selected students may enroll as juniors and seniors in the Washington Semester program, which is conducted each spring at American University. Students with a B average or higher may participate in the Junior Year Abroad program. Up to 36 hours of credit may be granted for study at an international university. Engineering students can participate in a Global Exchange with universities such as Waseda in Tokyo, Japan. Students may also cross-register at other Cleveland-area colleges and universities for one course per semester.

Academic Facilities

The $30-million Kelvin Smith Library is located in the heart of the campus. Through reciprocal borrowing arrangements, CWRU students have access to the holdings of the Cleveland Public Library as well as the libraries of five University Circle institutions; the members of OhioLINK, a network that includes state colleges and universities; the State Library of Ohio; and several private institutions. CWRU is classified by the Carnegie Foundation as a university with very high research activity (RU/VH), and its lab facilities are state of the art. The University operates two astronomical observatories, a biological field station, a $6-million undergraduate engineering lab, and nearly 100 other designated research centers and laboratories. The University's high-speed communications network links every residence hall room with computing centers, libraries, and databases on and off campus. CWRU's wireless network is one of the largest in the U.S. Other computer facilities on campus offer various models of computers and a wide variety of software programs, available free of charge to CWRU students.

The University Farm, located in nearby Hunting Valley, Ohio, offers educational opportunities in natural settings. Its 389 acres encompass a variety of deciduous forests, ravines, waterfalls, meadows, ponds, and a self-contained natural watershed.

Costs

For 2012–13, tuition totals $40,120. Room and board cost an average of $12,436. Other required fees total $835.

Financial Aid

Financial aid consisting of grants, loans, and work assistance is awarded on the basis of a student's need. Applicants are required to file the Free Application for Federal Student Aid (FAFSA) and the CSS/Financial Aid PROFILE, incurring a fee of $25 for the first college and $16 for subsequent college applications. Students are automatically considered for merit-based scholarships when they apply to the university; these awards typically range from $10,000 to $30,000.

Faculty

The undergraduate student-faculty ratio at CWRU is 9:1. Ninety-five percent of credit hours are taught by faculty members, not graduate students. Each college provides counselors who are available for both academic and personal advice. Once a major has been chosen, a member of the department in which the student is majoring acts as his or her academic adviser. Undergraduate students have several opportunities to partner with faculty members on research or special projects, allowing for valuable learning opportunities, mentoring, networking, and personal development.

Student Government

CWRU's Undergraduate Student Government represents all undergraduate students. The assembly acts as a liaison between undergraduate students and the faculty, administration, and other groups; grants recognition to undergraduate organizations; and has the responsibility and authority to allocate funds from student activity fees to student organizations. The Residence Hall Association is a governing body for on-campus living, the University Program Board plans special events, and the Interfraternity Congress and Panhellenic Council govern the Greek community.

Admission Requirements

Case Western Reserve University reviews each application for admission carefully, taking into consideration academic background, life experiences, and interests. There is no minimum test score or GPA range used to gauge a student's potential for admission. In terms of meeting academic requirements for admission, CWRU looks for students who have been successful in a variety of challenging classes. The admission staff understands that every school is different, so staff evaluates student transcripts specifically against their high school's curriculum.

Prior to high school graduation, it is recommended that students pursue 4 units of English, 3 units of math, 3 units of science (2 of which must be laboratory science), 3 units of social studies, and 2 units of foreign language. The University recommends that applicants interested in engineering and the sciences have an additional unit of math and laboratory science. For students interested in the liberal arts, it is recommended that students take an additional unit of social studies and foreign language.

The University requires an essay. The essay is a writing requirement with no word minimum or maximum and the content is chosen by the applicant. An interview is not a required part of the admission process, but it is strongly recommended. To receive full consideration for admission and scholarships, students must take the SAT or ACT prior to their selected application deadline.

Application and Information

The application deadline is January 15 for notification by March 20. Application deadlines for transfer students are May 1 for fall admission and October 1 for spring admission. The application deadline for the Pre-professional Scholars Program (medicine, dentistry, law, or social work) is December 1. Students can apply to CWRU via the online Common Application. The fall semester begins in late August.

Interviews with admission professionals, campus visits, group information sessions, and other resources are available to all prospective students.

For more information, students should contact:

Office of Undergraduate Admission
Case Western Reserve University
10900 Euclid Avenue
Cleveland, Ohio 44106-7055
Phone: 216-368-4450
E-mail: admission@case.edu
Web site: http://admission.case.edu
        http://facebook.com/cwruadmission
        http://twitter.com/cwruadmission

Case Western Reserve University campus.

CASTLETON STATE COLLEGE
CASTLETON, VERMONT

The College

Castleton State College was founded in 1787; it was the first institution of higher learning in Vermont and the eighteenth in the United States. The 165-acre campus is located in Castleton, a historic Vermont village. Sixty-five percent of the 1,900 full-time undergraduate students at the College are Vermonters; the balance of the student population comes from New England and the Middle Atlantic states.

Castleton is committed to providing an undergraduate education in which the liberal arts and career preparation complement each other. Through an innovative program called Soundings, freshmen earn academic credit by attending a series of special events that include theater, music, dance, film, debate, and opinion from influential people. New students also participate in the First-Year Seminar, giving them the opportunity to develop the skills of a successful college student. First-year students may apply for the College's honors program. Community service and internships play an important role in a Castleton education.

There are eleven major residence halls. Together, the residences accommodate nearly 1,100 students. Each residence hall room is equipped with at least two Internet hookups and wireless access, which give each student the opportunity to access the Web and e-mail using their own personal computer. There is no additional charge for this service. Each room is also equipped with cable TV connections. Off-campus housing is available in the Castleton, Fair Haven, and Rutland areas. Students who live on campus eat in Huden Dining Hall. All students are allowed to have automobiles on campus.

More than forty clubs and organizations provide a wide variety of student activities that include club sports, an FM radio station, the student newspaper, and an active outing club. Other clubs relate to college majors and future careers; still others serve the College or local community. Castleton is a member of the North Atlantic Conference of NCAA Division III. Castleton offers twenty intercollegiate sports. Men compete in baseball, basketball, cross-country running, football, golf, ice hockey, lacrosse, skiing, soccer, and tennis. Women compete in basketball, cross-country running, field hockey, ice hockey, lacrosse, skiing, soccer, softball, tennis, and volleyball. A majority of Castleton's students are involved in the intramural and recreational sports program.

Castleton recently completed a $25.7-million project that included renovation and expansion of the Campus Center and the gymnasium, construction of a stadium, and improvements to the athletic fields. In 2012, Castleton completed a new 162-bed residence hall overlooking the athletic fields.

Location

The campus is 12 miles west of Rutland, one of Vermont's largest cities. Montreal, Boston, Hartford, Albany, and New York City are all within easy driving distance. Amtrak passenger trains to and from New York City stop in the village of Castleton. Killington and Pico ski areas, Lake Bomoseen, and the Green Mountains provide excellent recreational opportunities and an exceptional living and learning environment.

Majors and Degrees

Castleton State College offers B.A. or B.S. degrees in more than thirty areas of study: accounting, American literature, art, athletic training, biology, children's literature, computer information systems, communication, criminal justice, digital media, elementary education, environmental science, exercise science, forensic psychology, geology, health education, health science, history, journalism, management, marketing, mass media, mathematics, music, music education, nursing, physical education, psychology, public relations, secondary education, social work, sociology, Spanish, special education, sports administration, theater arts, and world literature. Associate degrees can be earned in business, communication, computer programming, criminal justice, general studies, or nursing.

Academic Programs

The Castleton curriculum is designed to provide the student with a strong liberal arts background plus the opportunity for career preparation in a specific area. All four-year students are required to complete a core of general education requirements during the four-year degree program. The first year of study can be used by the undecided student to explore various areas of interest. The student with a specific career interest may begin study in the major field as a freshman, although four-year students are not required to formally declare their major until the end of the sophomore year.

Castleton students typically enroll in five courses each semester. The academic calendar consists of two 15-week semesters and three 4-week summer sessions. Grading is traditional, and a pass/no-pass option is available. Internships and field experiences complement many of the academic programs at Castleton and are required in the communication, criminal justice, social work, and education programs.

Students may transfer internally from two-year to four-year programs in business, communication, computer information systems, criminal justice, and general studies. Students who transfer to Castleton after graduating from an accredited two-year college are granted full transfer credit for all academic work up to 64 credits or the number required for the associate degree.

Freshman students achieving at least a 3.5 grade point average in their first year at Castleton are recognized by the Castleton Chapter of Phi Eta Sigma, a national honor society that recognizes freshman scholastic achievement in colleges throughout the country. Outstanding junior and senior scholars are recognized by the Castleton Chapter of Alpha Chi. Pinnacle, the honor society for nontraditional students, honors qualified candidates. There are honor societies in business administration, women's studies, history, science and mathematics, theater arts, education, psychology, and Spanish. Students who have achieved a 4.0 grade point average are named to the President's List of Outstanding Students and those with a 3.5 grade point average or better to the Dean's List.

Academic Facilities

The Calvin Coolidge Library houses a collection of more than 500,000 books, periodicals, microforms, and nonprint media. Access to Castleton's library resources and outside scholarly sources is made possible through numerous online and CD databases; a sophisticated, networked electronic library system; the Internet; and strong consortial relationships within the state of Vermont. An audiovisual media facility provides a wide range of audiovisual equipment, including digital video editing, digital cameras, and presentation equipment.

Castleton's Stafford Academic Center houses the Computing Center, a high-tech multimedia lecture hall, distance learning classrooms, and the departments of education, mathematics, and nursing.

The Spartan Athletic Complex houses Glenbrook Gymnasium, the athletic training rooms, a swimming pool, two racquetball courts, two fitness centers, and a large indoor activity area.

Spartan Arena, the home of the men's and women's ice hockey teams, is a short drive away.

The Fine Arts Center contains a 500-seat auditorium; facilities for art, drama, dance, and music. A new television studio opened in 2010 as part of an addition to Leavenworth Hall.

The Jeffords Center houses science classrooms and laboratories, a state-of-the-art auditorium, laboratories for faculty and student research projects, and a greenhouse. An astronomical observatory is a short walk away.

There are more than 225 personal computers designated for student use located in labs across the campus.

Costs

Costs for 2012–13 are as follows: tuition for Vermont residents, $8928, and for nonresidents, $21,528. Room and board expenses total $8786. Annual fees are $936. The orientation and registration for new students is $200.

Financial Aid

Eighty percent of Castleton's full-time undergraduate students receive financial assistance from federal, state, College, or other sources. Grants, loans, and work-study jobs are available for qualified students. Applicants for financial aid should file the Free Application for Federal Student Aid (FAFSA) form by April 1 of the senior year in high school. All financial aid awards are based on need.

Most Castleton scholarships are awarded as part of the College's honors scholarship program. Amounts range from $1000 to $10,000 per year. First-year students who have a combined critical reading and math SAT score of at least 1100 and have a GPA of at least 3.3 on a 4.0 scale are eligible for one of these scholarships. Additional scholarships are available to new students based on certain academic credentials, service to their community, and financial need. There are also special scholarships for students wishing to study music or Spanish.

Faculty

The full-time faculty at Castleton consists of 92 men and women, 96 percent of whom hold terminal degrees in their field.

Adjunct faculty members, many of them local businesspeople and members of the professions, complement the efforts of the full-time faculty. The student-faculty ratio is 14:1. Each student has a faculty member as an adviser.

Student Government

The Student Association is the chief vehicle of student government. All students who are registered for 8 or more credit hours are members. Elected representatives hold membership on most College committees, including the Curriculum and Cultural Affairs Committees. Students are also able to develop leadership qualities by participating in the various clubs and other organizations on campus.

Admission Requirements

Applicants are evaluated on the basis of their secondary school records, standardized test scores, and recommendations. Admission is granted to those applicants who have demonstrated their ability and potential to meet the challenges of a postsecondary learning experience.

Application and Information

Students may apply for admission through the Common Application. Under Castleton's rolling admission policy, applications are processed throughout the year, and candidates are notified of the admission decision as soon as their folders are complete. Students are admitted in the fall and spring semesters.

For more information about Castleton State College or to arrange a campus visit, students should contact:

Office of Admissions
Castleton State College
Castleton, Vermont 05735
Phone: 802-468-1213
      800-639-8521 (toll-free)
Fax: 802-468-1476
E-mail: info@castleton.edu
Web site: http://www.castleton.edu
      http://tiny.cc/nhamg (Facebook)

On the campus of Castleton State College.

CEDAR CREST COLLEGE
ALLENTOWN, PENNSYLVANIA

The College

Cedar Crest College was founded in 1867 and for more than 145 years has taken a bold approach to education by providing women with the competitive edge needed to succeed. A liberal arts college by design, Cedar Crest prepares women to lead in a global society. Approximately 1,600 students attend the College annually, representing twenty-seven states and twenty countries. Current students, alumnae, and future students maintain an active presence on the Cedar Crest Twitter and Facebook pages.

Cedar Crest College has more than thirty academic programs and faculty members who put a unique spin on traditional majors such as business and marketing, communication, English, and performing arts. In addition, Cedar Crest College has renowned programs in forensic science (one of fourteen accredited programs in the country and the only one affiliated with a women's college), social work (the only accredited program in the Lehigh Valley), and genetic engineering (one of the oldest programs in the country).

The College's health and wellness program has received a gold award for student health, wellness, and counseling from the National Association of Student Personnel Administrators. Their health and wellness initiative includes personal sports training; nutrition counseling; and a full schedule of dance, yoga, and aerobics classes. The Rodale Aquatic Center for Civic Health, a state-of-the-art, two-pool complex, offers health and fitness opportunities for the entire campus community. The campus also has tennis courts; regulation fields for field hockey, lacrosse, soccer, and softball; and a fitness center.

Cedar Crest students participate in eight NCAA Division III intercollegiate sports: basketball, cross-country, field hockey, lacrosse, soccer, softball, tennis, and volleyball. The College athletic department also supports club sports including equestrian, swimming, and cheerleading. The Falcons belong to the Colonial States Athletic Conference (CSAC) and compete against institutions in Pennsylvania, New Jersey, and Delaware. Cedar Crest student-athletes are held to high academic standards and have proven that it's possible to succeed both on the court and in the classroom. The CSAC recently awarded Cedar Crest student-athletes the first institutional achievement award for earning the highest grade point average in the Conference, and Cedar Crest teams have won several national academic awards. In 2011, basketball center Lizzy Sunderhause was recognized with the Jostens Trophy, awarded for excellence on the court and in the classroom and community.

Cedar Crest students hold leadership positions in more than forty clubs and organizations on campus. Student clubs range from the Student Government Association and Student Activities Board to the Literary Club and Biology Club. The College prepares women to lead in their future careers, community, and in life. Leadership retreats and community service opportunities are held throughout the year. The campus completes more than 20,000 hours in community service annually. Service opportunities are available throughout the Lehigh Valley at schools, hospitals, animal shelters, and Habitat for Humanity. At Cedar Crest, students serve early and often.

Cedar Crest upperclass students have the opportunity to live and learn together in the College's living-learning communities. These communities focus on a variety of relevant and timely topics such as global social justice, environmental ethics, entrepreneurship, and the arts. They bring together students who share a common interest, regardless of major or career focus. Sharing perspectives and lifestyles in this group setting enhances the students' educational journey as they gain intellectual appreciation and global awareness, apply and hone leadership skills, and make a difference locally and globally. These communities are the epitome of the seamless college experience as students live together, take a house class together, travel together, and develop close relationships with a faculty member affiliated with the community.

Through the Career Planning Office, students are placed in competitive internships near the campus and in major cities.

Cedar Crest's academic programs are fully accredited by the Middle States Association of Colleges and Schools and, where appropriate, by the American Academy of Forensic Science, American Medical Association, American Dietetic Association, American Bar Association, National League for Nursing Accrediting Commission, National Council on Social Work Education, and the Departments of Education of New York, New Jersey, and Pennsylvania. The College offers master's degrees in three fields: education, forensic science, and nursing.

Location

Students enjoy Cedar Crest's parklike campus, nestled in the heart of the Lehigh Valley in the West End of Allentown, Pennsylvania. The campus is a beautiful 84-acre nationally registered arboretum with more than 130 species of trees. The College is within easy distance of the extensive Allentown park system, high-end retail shopping, well-known restaurants, cultural activities, and the Pocono ski and outdoor resorts.

Cedar Crest is located in College Valley, home to more than 32,000 students at eight colleges within 20 minutes of campus. Students can participate in student- and faculty-led trips to nearby Philadelphia (less than 1 hour from campus) and New York City (less than 2 hours away). Students can explore the metropolitan areas of the East Coast, including Washington, D.C., Baltimore, and Boston, while enjoying the benefits of a small, suburban campus.

Majors and Degrees

Cedar Crest offers more than thirty fields of study in the arts, humanities, social sciences, business, and sciences. The combination of majors and course offerings provides students with a strong liberal arts background. The College also offers preprofessional programs in dentistry, law, medicine, and veterinary medicine. These well-respected academic programs provide individual support for students as they create an academic experience that is both personal and practical. Students are expected to be involved in planning their academic pathway from the very beginning.

Academic Programs

Self-designed majors, double majors, minors, and individual and group research projects are available and reflect the

academic emphasis at the undergraduate level. Students may begin conducting research as early as their first year on campus. Students can also begin writing for the campus newspaper or hosting their own radio shows early in their college career.

The honors program at Cedar Crest is cross-disciplinary and designed for women who have demonstrated a record of high academic achievement. The honors program offers students a unique opportunity for growth and enrichment. Honors courses are marked by their engaging classroom environment, diverse and challenging coursework, and graduate-level research experiences.

Through a consortium with the Lehigh Valley Association of Independent Colleges, Cedar Crest upperclass students may cross-register and take courses at Lehigh and DeSales Universities and Lafayette, Moravian, and Muhlenberg Colleges at no additional cost.

Off-Campus Programs

Cedar Crest students are encouraged to pursue internships in their area of study. Internships enable students to gain practical experience at major corporations, small businesses, national nonprofit organizations, and top health-care facilities. Cedar Crest students have served internships with CNN, as a foreign correspondent with the United Nations, and with the FBI, working on a database for DNA fingerprinting.

The College stresses the importance of global awareness and encourages students to take advantage of study-abroad opportunities. Cedar Crest also offers courses with a short trip-abroad component lasting one to two weeks.

Academic Facilities

Learning spaces include hospital simulation labs, a ceramic studio, a state-of-the art nutrition laboratory, music practice rooms, *The Crestiad* newsroom, dance and art studios and workshops, theaters, genetic engineering laboratories, forensic science laboratories, a papermaking studio, media convergence lab, and a greenhouse.

Cedar Crest students socialize and dine in the Tompkins College Center, the hub of student activity. The center is home to Samuels Theatre, club meeting rooms, the dining hall, and the Falcon's Nest café.

Costs

For 2011–12, tuition was $31,196; room and board were $9990.

Financial Aid

Student applications are reviewed for scholarship eligibility at the time of acceptance. The College's scholarships are awarded based on high school merit, leadership, and service. The College also holds an annual scholarship competition that awards one high-achieving student a full tuition scholarship for four years.

The financial aid program at Cedar Crest is based on financial need and includes grants, loans, and employment. Students applying for need-based financial aid should file the Free Application for Federal Student Aid (FAFSA).

Students are encouraged to use Cedar Crest's student aid calculator to receive a fast, accurate estimate of their financial aid package, including scholarships, grants, and loans. This calculator is available at http://www.cedarcrest.edu/calculator.

Faculty

Cedar Crest faculty members demand excellence, creating a challenging and supportive environment that allows students to grow and thrive. Faculty members are working artists, published writers, accomplished actors, international business professionals, and scientists making discoveries that will impact us all. They strive to ensure that student learning extends beyond the classroom.

Cedar Crest students meet one-on-one with a faculty mentor to build course schedules and discuss future plans. Students also work closely with faculty on groundbreaking research in all disciplines. This research can lead to national presentations and professional publications.

Admission Requirements

Cedar Crest welcomes applications from first-year students entering after high school and those seeking to transfer from another college or university. The admissions process looks at the entire student, from academic course work and standardized test scores to leadership potential, volunteer service, employment, and special talents.

Application and Information

Students are encouraged to visit the campus as they begin the application process, and can register for a visit at http://www.cedarcrest.edu/visit. Applications are reviewed on a rolling basis, so they are processed and evaluated as soon as all materials have been received. Applicants are notified of their admissions decision beginning September 15 for the following fall semester. The priority deadline to apply for scholarship review is February 15.

Students can apply online at http://www.cedarcrest.edu/apply or through the Common Application at https://www.commonapp.org.

Vice President for Enrollment Management
Cedar Crest College
100 College Drive
Allentown, Pennsylvania 18104-6196
Phone: 800-360-1222 (toll-free)
Fax: 610-606-4647
E-mail: admissions@cedarcrest.edu
Web site: http://www.cedarcrest.edu
      http://on.fb.me/CedarCrest (Facebook)
      http://twitter.com/cedarcrestcolle

Cedar Crest College is a great place to live and learn! The campus community comprises smart, creative women who will shape the world.

CHAMPLAIN COLLEGE
BURLINGTON, VERMONT

The College

Champlain College is a coeducational, private, nonprofit college founded in 1878. Career-minded students have been the focus of Champlain College since it was founded. Today, that long-standing tradition continues with outstanding undergraduate and online undergraduate courses, along with robust online certificate and degree programs, and nine master's degree programs.

Its 21-acre campus, home to 2,000 full-time students, is nestled among the stately maple trees of Burlington's historic Hill Section, overlooking Lake Champlain and the Adirondack Mountains of New York to the west. Many of the College's buildings, including most of its residence halls, are restored Victorian-era private homes, which give students a unique atmosphere in which to learn and live.

The spirit of innovation and relevance are highlighted in majors such as business, communications, creative media, education, social services, computer innovation and information technology. Traditional undergraduates find Champlain's unique Upside-Down Curriculum puts them into essential courses with award-winning professors from day one of their first semester, right through to graduation four years later.

During their time at Champlain, students participate in programs like Bring Your Own Business (BYOBiz), the Emergent Media Center, Center for Financial Literacy, Leahy Center for Digital Investigation, Champlain College Publishing Initiative and the Center for Service and Civic Engagement, gaining vital hands-on experience before they graduate. In addition, there are more than fifty student clubs and organizations offering a full range of activities and community service opportunities.

Champlain is striving to build a diverse community. Approximately 2,000 traditional undergraduates attend Champlain, representing forty-seven states and twenty-three countries. Classes are small (about 18 students), with the average overall student to faculty ratio at 15:1. Approximately 50 percent of Champlain students elect to study abroad at Champlain campuses in Montreal, Canada and Dublin, Ireland, or with Champlain-sponsored immersive programs in China or Morocco or other third-party programs. Professors and students are encouraged to bring their world travels and experience into the global discussions in the classroom.

Champlain College is accredited by the New England Association of Schools and Colleges, Inc. through its Commission on Institutions of Higher Education.

Location

Burlington is a small city of 46,000 people and a classic college town of nearly 15,000 students on the eastern shore of Lake Champlain. Covering 435 square miles, Lake Champlain is one of North America's largest lakes. The long ridgeline of the Green Mountains forms the eastern horizon and the Adirondack Mountains frame the western horizon. Montreal, Quebec, is only a 1½-hour drive to the north. Burlington is one of the nation's most progressive cities, and it is the cultural center of Vermont. Five colleges are located in the area, along with one of the leading medical centers on the East Coast. There is an international airport; an Amtrak passenger train route with connections to Montreal, New York City, and Washington, D.C.; and a long-distance bus service, Vermont Transit Lines. The Church Street Marketplace, located just a few blocks from the campus, attracts both locals and tourists to its numerous shops, coffee bars, and restaurants. Three television stations, fifteen radio stations, and daily newspapers serve the area. The Arts and Entertainment Channel (A&E) has ranked Burlington as the nation's Best Place to Live. Burlington consistently ranks as one of the best college towns in the country.

Majors and Degrees

Champlain College offers the Bachelor of Science, Fine Arts, Social Work, and Business Administration degrees, with majors in accounting, business administration, international business, management and innovation, management of creative media, marketing, broadcasting and streaming media, communication, creative media, digital filmmaking, game art and animation, game design, graphic design and digital media, professional writing, public relations, computer and digital forensics, computer information technology, computer networking and information security, computer science and innovation, game programming, criminal justice, education (certification for grades K–6, 5–9, and 7–12), environmental policy, legal studies, psychology, radiography, and social work. Champlain also allows a student to enter as an undeclared/undecided major.

Academic Programs

The Upside-Down Curriculum format offers a four-year bachelor's degree and allows students to concentrate on courses in their major in their first two years of college. Internships or on-the-job experiences are offered in many of the majors, often within the first two years of study, and a majority of students go directly into their chosen career field upon graduation. Recent statistics show that 86.8 percent of the graduated Class of 2010 secured employment relevant to their field of study. The mission of Champlain College is to provide motivated students with the opportunity, environment, and tools to achieve their goals for professional success and meaningful involvement in their community.

An Army ROTC program is provided in cooperation with the University of Vermont.

Off-Campus Programs

Students are encouraged to complete at least one internship experience, which may be done locally, nationally, or internationally. These internships give students practical job experience in a professional environment, often leading directly to positions after graduation. The criminal justice major offers two options for the second semester of the fourth year. Students may apply to spend the term at the Vermont Police Academy or at the Federal Law Enforcement Training Center in Georgia. Champlain College has campuses in Montreal, Canada and Dublin, Ireland, where students can spend a semester taking classes and participating in internships in their field of study. The College also has partnership programs in Shanghai and Morocco. Students are also able to participate in third-party study-abroad programs. Around 50 percent of Champlain College students study abroad at some point in their undergraduate career.

Academic Facilities

Champlain's commitment to hands-on learning is well evidenced by its outstanding teaching facilities and academic labs. The College's technical facilities are impressive and continue to expand and evolve every year to match the nature and requirements of cutting-edge majors and to incorporate the latest equipment and software.

Costs

Tuition for 2011–12 was $28,350; room and board were $12,520. Total tuition, fees, and room and board totalled $40,920.

Financial Aid

Champlain assists over 85 percent of its students with grants and scholarships directly from the College, and awards the funds based on both merit and financial need. The financial aid program at Champlain consists of grants and scholarships from the College, federal and state governments, and outside sources, federal work-study, and loans from the federal government and private lenders. Champlain College also participates in the Yellow Ribbon program for veterans.

Champlain continues to expand its capacity to provide financial and scholarship support for top students with a variety of backgrounds. Special effort is made to include opportunities for new Americans, U.S. veterans, single parents, and Vermont students first in their family to attend college.

Students interested in receiving financial aid must complete the Free Application for Federal Student Aid (FAFSA).

Faculty

Champlain's faculty members bring the requisite academic credentials to the classroom, but have also built their careers in the workplace, bringing practical professional experience to provide what students need to know in order to succeed professionally. In addition to the core of 101 full-time professors, the College seeks adjunct faculty who are actively employed in their profession and have an interest in teaching as well. Currently, there are 247 adjunct professors who bring their professional expertise and academic training to benefit Champlain's student body. The student-teacher ratio is 15:1. Champlain faculty members are noted for their accessibility and willingness to act as mentors for their students.

Admission Requirements

The College requires an official high school transcript, SAT or ACT scores, two letters of recommendation, and a completed application form in order to be considered for admission. Graduation from a recognized secondary school is required (or an equivalency certificate/GED) as a condition of acceptance. A personal interview is highly recommended for all candidates, and may be required of applicants to certain majors. Students applying to game design, game art and animation, graphic design and digital media, digital filmmaking, creative media, and professional writing must submit a portfolio to be considered for admission. Students may earn advanced standing by submitting appropriate scores on Advanced Placement and International Baccalaureate exams.

Students can apply to Champlain College through the early decision program or the regular decision program. Early decision is a binding agreement, and students are encouraged to apply through this program if Champlain College is their first choice. The deadline for early decision I is November 15 and students are notified of their decision around December 15. The deadline for early decision II is January 15 and students are notified of their decision around February 15. Regular decision applications are due on February 1 and admissions decisions are sent out around March 15.

All candidates for transfer admission are required to submit an official high school transcript with SAT or ACT scores, official college transcript(s), and a completed application form in order to be considered for admission with advanced standing. Transfer credit is given for academic courses from an accredited college completed with a grade of C or better.

Champlain College admits students without regard to race, creed, color, national and ethnic origin, religion, age, gender, sexual orientation, or qualified disability, and does not discriminate in the administration of its educational and admission policies, scholarships and loan programs, or other College-administered programs. Champlain College makes reasonable accommodations to the disabilities of otherwise-qualified students, applicants or employees.

Application Information

Champlain College uses the Common Application as well as its own Champlain College application. Links to both can be found at www.champlain.edu/apply.

Director of Admissions
Champlain College
163 South Willard Street
P.O. Box 670
Burlington, Vermont 05402-0670
Phone: 802-860-2727
      800-570-5858 (toll-free)
Fax: 802-860-2767
E-mail: admission@champlain.edu
Web site: http://www.champlain.edu

Students rate Champlain College's residential life experience and close-knit communit highly. The Princeton Review included Champlain in *The Best 376 Colleges: 2012 Edition.*

CHAPMAN UNIVERSITY
ORANGE, CALIFORNIA

The University

During its 151-year history, Chapman University has evolved from a small, traditional liberal arts college into a comprehensive university distinguished for its extraordinary blend of liberal arts, science, and professional programs. Film and television production, business and economics, theater, dance, music, education, and the natural and applied sciences—Chapman boasts a breadth of fields usually only found at larger institutions. Chapman University's mission: to develop global citizen-leaders who are distinctively prepared to improve their community and their world.

With beautiful grounds and stately buildings, Chapman is one of the oldest schools on the West Coast, yet its parklike campus is also one of the most modern. More than a dozen buildings have been built or renovated in just the last two decades, with four more on the drawing board. Architecturally impressive residence halls and apartment buildings offer students exciting lifestyle amenities within a vibrant Southern California setting.

Chapman University's academic structure includes the Wilkinson College of Humanities and Social Sciences; the Dodge College of Film and Media Arts; the AACSB International–accredited Argyros School of Business and Economics; the CTC-approved College of Educational Studies; the ABA-accredited School of Law; the Schmid College of Science; and the College of Performing Arts, which includes the NASM-accredited Conservatory of Music, the NAST-accredited Department of Theatre, and the NASD-accredited Department of Dance. Among other nationally accredited programs is the APTA-accredited Doctor of Physical Therapy program. Chapman has been further recognized by the Templeton Foundation as one of only 100 colleges nationally to be designated as a Templeton Foundation "Character-Building College" for its emphasis on global citizenry and for student involvement in community action and stewardship activities.

With its central Orange County, California, location and nearly 7,000 undergraduate, graduate, and professional school students, the University environment is alive with activity. In addition to the beautiful temperate climate, Chapman students enjoy a dynamic, eclectic, and outdoor-oriented lifestyle, both on campus and off. Students come from all walks of life; from across the country and from all over the world, each student brings his or her own unique view of what makes a true global citizen. Over the past five years, Chapman students have been named Truman Scholars, Coro Fellows, *USA Today* All-USA College Academic Team members, NCAA All-Americans, and NCAA Academic All-Americans.

Chapman's long and distinguished heritage in intercollegiate athletics includes five NCAA national championships in baseball, tennis, and softball. The Panthers compete in the NCAA Division III Southern California Intercollegiate Athletic Conference (SCIAC), and field teams in baseball, basketball, crew, cross-country, football, golf, lacrosse, soccer, softball, swimming, tennis, track and field, volleyball, and water polo. Approximately 20 percent of Chapman's student body participates in intercollegiate athletics.

More than ninety clubs and organizations are recognized on campus, many with commitments to a wide range of community service efforts. Chapman's Greek system includes seven nationally chartered fraternities for men and seven nationally chartered sororities for women. Intramural sports, on-campus intercollegiate athletic events, as well as music, art, and theater productions provide students with plenty to do outside of class. And that's just on campus—with San Diego to the south and Los Angeles to the north, the only hard thing is deciding what to do.

Prominent Chapman alumni include the Honorable Loretta Sanchez '88, member of Congress; the Honorable David Bonior '72, member of Congress; CNBC World anchorwoman, Bettina Chua '88; television and film producers John Copeland '73, Jon Garcia '93, and John David Currey '98; cinematographer Gene Jackson '70; Miss California 2011, Noelle Freeman '11; St. John's University basketball coach Steve Lavin '88; Major League Baseball executive, Gordon Blakely '76; Major League Baseball Cy Young Award winner Randy Jones '72; Tony Award nominee and star of Broadway's *Showboat*, Michel Bell '68; resident tenor at the Staatsoper-Vienna John Nuzzo '91; and former U.S. Ambassador to Spain and philanthropist George L. Argyros '65.

Location

Orange County, California, has been rated by *Places Rated Almanac* as the number-one place to live in North America, citing superior climate and cultural, recreational, educational, and career-entree opportunities. Orange County's central location between two major cities means there is never a lack of entertainment choices. Even Disneyland, known as the happiest place on Earth, is literally minutes from campus.

The Segerstrom Center for the Arts, Major League Baseball's Los Angeles Angels of Anaheim, and the National Hockey League's Anaheim Ducks are all nearby Chapman's campus in Old Towne Orange. Pristine West Coast beaches are less than 10 miles from the campus, and seasonal snow skiing is 90 minutes away. The average year-round temperature on campus is 71°F, and the daily sea breeze from the nearby Pacific Ocean keeps the air cool, clean, and smog free.

Majors and Degrees

Chapman awards the Bachelor of Arts degree in the fields of accounting, art, art history, athletic training, biochemistry, biological sciences, business administration, chemistry, communication studies, computer information systems, computer science, creative producing, creative writing, dance, dance performance, digital arts, economics, elementary education, English, environmental science and policy, film production, film studies, French, graphic design, health sciences, history, integrated educational studies, mathematics, mathematics and civil engineering, music, music composition, music education, music performance, peace studies, philosophy, physics and computational science, political science, psychology, public relations and advertising, religious studies, screen acting, screenwriting, sociology, Spanish, television and broadcast journalism, theater, and theater performance. Programs are offered in pre-law and pre-medicine, while graduate degrees are offered in business (M.B.A.); education (M.A., Ph.D.); English (M.A., M.F.A.); international studies, (M.A.); computational sciences (M.S., Ph.D.); food sciences (M.S., M.S./M.B.A.); film (M.A., M.F.A., M.F.A./M.B.A., M.F.A./J.D.); economic systems design (M.S.); health and strategic communication (M.S.); physical therapy (D.P.T.); and hazards, global, and environmental change (M.S.).

Academic Programs

For many, college is a time of uncertainty. The Academic Advising Center is a place students can come for information, resources, and referrals. Chapman's Academic Advising Center offers personalized services for all students, supporting and helping to shape their educational goals. Students are encouraged to develop individualized plans for realizing the goals they set. The Center is responsible for advising in all majors, and serves all undeclared students. General academic counseling is offered, plus placement testing services. Individual appointments are available, though students can stop by any time, or visit online. Advising workshops are regularly available. The Tutoring, Learning, and Testing Center, also offers students peer tutoring, study technique development, and advocacy services.

A wide variety of study and research opportunities are available through Chapman's academic and research centers. These include the A. Gary Anderson Center for Economic Research; the Albert Schweitzer Institute; the Rogers Center for Holocaust Education; the Center for Educational and Social Equity; the John Fowles Center for Creative Writing; the Leatherby Center for Entrepreneurship and Business Ethics; the Schmid Center for International Business; the Hoag Center for Real Estate and Finance; the Institute for the

Study of Media and the Public Interest; the Center for Global Law and Development; the Economic Science Institute; and the Center of Excellence in Applied, Computational, and Fundamental Sciences.

Requirements for graduation are commensurate with the philosophy of education fostered at Chapman. The program of studies is designed to ensure a breadth of selection in the liberal arts, as well as depth of preparation in the student's major field. The minimum graduation requirements include successful completion (C average) of 124 semester credits, of which 36 must be earned in the upper division. Competence in reading, written communication, oral communication, computation, and library usage is required of all students. Chapman's general education sequence provides a broad introduction to the humanities, social sciences, and natural sciences. Students select general education classes with the guidance of their faculty adviser. A maximum of 32 semester credits may be gained through Advanced Placement (AP), College-Level Examination Program (CLEP), and departmental examinations.

Chapman's academic year operates on a 4-1-4 modified semester system. January is reserved for an optional four-week Interterm during which students can take a traditional course in an accelerated time frame, or take more experiential courses such as travel-study or travel abroad opportunities. Ample opportunities are available for alternative learning experiences. Internships and cooperative education programs are recommended. Students may also undertake in-depth individual study or research in their major field in conjunction with a faculty member.

Academic Facilities

Chapman's stunning campus continues to grow by leaps and bounds. Major additions to the campus over the past few years include the 100,000-square-foot Leatherby Libraries complex, housing eight discipline-specific individual libraries, a cyber courtyard, and a 24-hour study commons and coffee bar. The Oliphant Hall addition to the Conservatory of Music is a 24,000-square-foot space featuring fourteen teaching studios, a 60-seat lecture hall, music therapy laboratory, and orchestra hall. In addition to the Conservatory of Music's Bertea and Oliphant Halls, the College of Performing Arts facilities include the Moulton Fine Arts Complex featuring the 250-seat repertory-style Waltmar Theatre, a black box theater, the Guggenheim Art Gallery, and the Partridge Dance Center. The Fish Interfaith Center features the 12,500-square-foot Wallace All-Faiths Chapel, recognized by *Architectural Digest* for innovation in design. The recently completed 200,000-square-foot Sandhu Residence and Conference center houses the primary on-campus dining facility for resident students, as well as a conference center and residence hall. The 90,000-square-foot Argyros Forum includes additional campus dining options, as well as conference and classroom facilities. The 800-seat Memorial Auditorium is the primary performance and assembly venue on campus and is listed on the National Register of Historic Places. Athletic facilities include the 2,500-seat Hutton Sports Center arena, and training and fitness facilities for the campus and surrounding community. The 2,000-seat Ernie Chapman Stadium for football, lacrosse, and soccer and the 500-seat Allred Aquatics Center swim stadium/Olympic pool complex round out recent additions to the athletic complex. Arnold Beckman Hall is the center for business and information technology, including the Argyros School of Business and Economics and the Hobbs Institute for Real Estate, Law, and Environmental Studies. The Hashinger Science Center features laboratories for nuclear science, radiation, crystallography, genetics, food science, physics, and computational sciences.

Costs

For the 2011–12 academic year, full-time tuition and fees (including accident and health services fee and associated student membership fee) were $40,234. Annual room and board costs averaged $13,000, while the estimated yearly cost for books was $1000.

Financial Aid

More than 85 percent of Chapman students benefit from some form of financial aid or scholarship assistance. Need-based financial awards include a combination of grants, scholarships, loans, and work-study jobs on campus. Awards are renewable, assuming that students complete the annual application process on time. By using a combination of Chapman's internal resources and federal and state funding, an individual financial aid package can be tailored in an effort to meet the student's financial need. Merit and talent scholarship awards, regardless of financial need, round out the impressive financial assistance that Chapman offers.

Faculty

The University's faculty is composed of some 430 individuals, more than 80 percent of whom hold doctoral or other terminal degrees. Their primary commitment is to undergraduate teaching, although most are also actively involved in scholarly research and publication. Many faculty members teach both undergraduate and graduate courses. Teaching assistants or graduate assistants are typically not used for the instruction of undergraduate classes, a fact upon which Chapman prides itself. Chapman's student-faculty ratio of 14:1 allows extensive interaction between the faculty members and students.

Student Government

Chapman has an annually elected associated student government that actively participates in the administration of the University. As well, a myriad of civic engagement opportunities exist via a student culture that fosters leadership, service, and sustainability.

Admission Requirements

Admission to Chapman is selective. In 2012, admission was granted to 41 percent of the applicant pool. The University is interested in admitting students whose prior records indicate that they will be successful in a competitive collegiate environment. Freshman applicants are considered for admission based primarily on the nature and sequence of their high school course work, grade point average achieved, their results on either the SAT or ACT examination, co-curricular involvements, and personal characteristics. Transfer candidates are considered for admission on the basis of their course work and cumulative grade point average earned at other regionally accredited postsecondary institutions, their co-curricular involvements, and personal characteristics.

Application and Information

Chapman University exclusively uses the Common Application (http://www.commonapp.org) as well as a Chapman-specific supplement to the Common Application, and departmental applications for those applying to the art, dance, film, music, or theater programs. Candidates are strongly encouraged to visit and tour the campus and participate in an information session led by an admission officer. Arrangements for a group information session and campus tour can be made through the Office of Admission.

Freshman applicants can choose either a nonbinding November 15 early action application deadline or the January 15 regular application deadline. Transfer applicants must apply before the March 15 transfer deadline. Freshman candidates who apply after January 15 and transfer candidates who apply after March 15 are considered on a space-available basis.

For further information, students should contact:

Office of Admission
Chapman University
One University Drive
Orange, California 92866
Phone: 714-997-6711
    888-CUAPPLY (toll-free)
Fax: 714-997-6713
E-mail: admit@chapman.edu
Web site: http://www.chapman.edu
    http://www.facebook.com/ChapmanUniversity

CHATHAM UNIVERSITY
PITTSBURGH, PENNSYLVANIA

The University

Founded in 1869, Chatham University is a coed university with a women's college at its historic heart. Chatham University provides students with a solid education built upon strong academics, public leadership, and global understanding. Chatham's Shadyside Campus is located on historic Woodland Road in Pittsburgh's Shadyside neighborhood, while its Eden Hall Campus is located 45 minutes north in Richland Township.

The University houses three distinctive colleges. Chatham College for Women provides academic and cocurricular programs for undergraduate women and embodies the traditions and rituals of one of the nation's oldest colleges for women. The College for Graduate Studies offers women and men both master's and doctoral programs. The College for Continuing and Professional Studies provides online and hybrid undergraduate and graduate degree programs for women and men, certificate programs, and community programming.

The University's total student body of almost 2,300 represents forty-four states and twenty-six other countries. Members of minority groups and international students compose 14 percent of the total student body. Resident and commuting students participate actively in the numerous professional, academic, social, and special-interest organizations at the University. Each year, Chatham students complete thousands of hours of community service with organizations throughout the region.

Chatham College for Women offers NCAA Division III intercollegiate competition in basketball, cross-country, ice hockey, soccer, softball, swimming and diving, tennis, volleyball, and water polo, as well as intramural and recreational competition in other sports. Chatham's Athletic and Fitness Center includes an eight-lane competition pool, a gymnasium, squash courts, cardio rooms, a climbing wall, a running track, and exercise and dance studios.

All incoming undergraduate students receive an Apple MacBook Pro that can access the University's wireless network and are incorporated into the curriculum for in-class note-taking, research, and online learning. Students are assessed a technology fee each year to lease the computers, which they own upon graduation.

All residence halls have computer labs and high-speed network printers as well as network ports in each room. Central computer equipment supports e-mail, computer-mediated courseware, personal Web pages, and file and print servers. Chatham participates in campuswide software license agreements that permit students to install select productivity software on their personal machines at no additional cost.

Location

Chatham's suburban, historic Shadyside Campus is located minutes from downtown Pittsburgh and features towering trees, wandering paths, and century-old mansions that serve as residence halls. The Shadyside Campus includes Chatham Eastside, a new LEED Silver facility that houses the University's interior architecture, landscape architecture, occupational therapy, physical therapy, and physician assistant studies programs. The University's new 388-acre Eden Hall Campus is located north of the city in Richland Township and is the home of Chatham's new School of Sustainability and the Environment.

Pittsburgh is one of the safest and most dynamic green cities in the country and is headquarters to major businesses and industries in finance, health care, and technology. Eclectic neighborhoods reflect Pittsburgh's historic qualities and appeal to a wide audience. Students may ride public transportation free within Allegheny County simply by presenting their Chatham ID. Arts and entertainment options range from the Pittsburgh Symphony to world-renowned opera, ballet, and theater companies and museums. For sports enthusiasts, Pittsburgh offers the Penguins, Pirates, and Steelers professional ice-hockey, baseball, and football teams. Pittsburgh has also been rated America's Most Livable City by *Places Rated Almanac* and

Most Livable City in the U.S. and twenty-ninth Most Livable City Worldwide by *The Economist*. Bus, rail, and air connections are available to and from most major cities. For more information, students should visit http://www.pittsburghregion.org.

Majors and Degrees

Chatham University offers the following majors leading to a Bachelor of Arts or Bachelor of Science degree: accounting, art history, arts management, biochemistry, biology, business, business economics, chemistry, creative writing, cultural studies, economics, education (elementary, early childhood, secondary, environmental science, visual arts), engineering (3-2 program), English, environmental science (B.A. or B.S.), environmental studies, exercise science, film and digital video-making, forensics, government, history, interior architecture, international business, international studies, landscape studies certificate, management, marketing, mathematics, music, nursing, physics, political science, policy studies (global or public), professional communication (broadcast journalism, print journalism, professional writing, public relations), psychology, social work, Spanish and Hispanic studies, visual arts (emerging media, photography or studio arts), and women's studies. Students may choose a traditional major, an interdisciplinary major, a double major, or a self-designed major.

Preprofessional programs are offered in education and law, medicine and health professions, physical therapy, teaching certification, and veterinary medicine. A joint-degree engineering program is offered with Carnegie Mellon University and the University of Pittsburgh. Teacher certification is available through the education program in early childhood, elementary, environmental, school counseling, secondary education, and special education.

The Accelerated Graduate Program enables qualified undergraduate students to become candidates for admission to one of the University's graduate programs during their junior year, enabling them to earn both a bachelor's and master's degree in as little as five years. The following degree programs are included: Master of Accounting, Master of Arts (M.A.) in food studies, M.A. in landscape studies, M.A. in Teaching, Master of Business Administration, Master of Fine Arts (M.F.A.) in film and digital technology, M.F.A. in creative writing, Master of Occupational Therapy, Master of Physician Assistant Studies, Master of Science (M.S.) in biology, and M.S. in counseling psychology. Chatham also offers its Accelerated Graduate Program with the prestigious H. John Heinz III School of Public Policy at Carnegie Mellon University. Students may apply during their junior year to one of the following Heinz School programs: Master of Arts Management, Master of Information Systems Management, M.S. in Healthcare Policy and Management, and M.S. in Public Policy and Management. Accepted students take courses at both Chatham and the Heinz School during their senior year and earn a bachelor's degree from Chatham and a master's degree from Carnegie Mellon. Beginning in 2011, students may apply during their junior year to one of the following Duquesne University programs: M.S. in biotechnology, M.S. in computational mathematics, or M.S. in forensic science and law.

Academic Program

Chatham's general education curriculum includes six required interdisciplinary courses, plus analytical reasoning, an international or intercultural experience, and wellness courses. Graduation requirements include the general education courses, a major, and the Senior Tutorial—an original research/capstone project. Students are mentored one-on-one by a faculty member throughout the tutorial process. The project provides an excellent bridge to graduate and professional schools and strong preparation for law and medical schools.

The University's 4-4-1 academic calendar consists of fall and spring terms plus a three-week "Maymester," which features study abroad, concentrated study, experimental projects, travel and field

experiences, internships, interdisciplinary study, and student exchanges with other institutions.

The First-Year Student Sequence introduces students to the faculty and the University community and its culture and provides opportunities to learn about the resources of the urban environment and study issues of concern to women. Interactive seminar courses provide students with the analytical and communication skills essential for successful academic performance.

Chatham's Programs for Academic Success, Career Development, and Educational Enrichment (PACE) offers students a comprehensive approach to academic and career planning as well as an academic support network designed to maximize each student's academic success. Career services include counseling for undecided students, student internships, placement, workshops, recruitment, and mentor programs.

The Rachel Carson Institute honors Chatham's 1929 alumna and her commitment to the environment. The Pennsylvania Center for Women, Politics, and Public Policy introduces students to the world of politics, public policy, and civic engagement. The Center for Women's Entrepreneurship provides support for women entrepreneurs in the Pittsburgh region.

Off-Campus Programs

Chatham students may register at no additional cost for classes at any of Pittsburgh's eight other colleges and universities, including Carnegie Mellon and the University of Pittsburgh, both of which are within walking distance of the campus and accessible via free shuttle service. Chatham Abroad is a three-week travel experience with faculty members during the sophomore year Maymester (for an additional fee); past trips featured Belize, Egypt, England, France, the Galapagos Islands, Ireland, Italy, Morocco, Russia, and Spain.

Chatham students may participate in up to six internships related to their major and career goal. Recent examples include American Cancer Society, Children's Institute, East End Cooperative Ministry, Greater Pittsburgh Community Food Bank, Pittsburgh Action Against Rape, Race for the Cure, Sojourner House, Womansplace, Women and Girls Foundation of Southwest Pennsylvania, YWCA, and various corporate, nonprofit, government, health-care, and communications sites.

Academic Facilities

The Jennie King Mellon (JKM) Library serves the Chatham community as a primary research, study, and resource center. Students may access the Library's books, current print journals, full-text electronic journals, and online databases through the library's Web page. Librarians are available for research assistance. Individual study rooms, special seminar rooms, and a 24/7 study room are also offered. Through consortium memberships, the library provides access to materials from hundreds of academic libraries nationwide.

The Science Laboratory Complex houses state-of-the-art laboratories and individual lab units. Psychology and language labs and audiovisual facilities are also available. The Broadcast Studio contains sophisticated audio- and video-editing technology, including Macintosh G5 computers, as well as a multifunctional studio. Chatham's Art and Design Center features fine and applied art studios, a computer lab, and classroom space as well as gallery and student exhibition space.

Costs

For 2010–11, full-time tuition was $28,088 per year, and room and board were approximately $8900. A one-time deposit of $150 for tuition and $150 for on-campus housing is paid by newly admitted students and is applied to first-semester charges. Regularly enrolled full-time students pay no additional costs for Maymester courses, except for special supplies or travel. Music lessons and art supplies are additional. Students must have health and accident insurance. A technology fee is assessed for the MacBook program.

Financial Aid

Financial aid is awarded on the basis of an individual's financial need, as determined through the Free Application for Federal Student Aid (FAFSA). The awards combine grants, loans, and employment. The priority financial aid deadline is March 15. Sources of financial aid include Chatham University grants and scholarships, state grants, Federal Pell Grants, Federal Supplemental Educational Opportunity Grants, Direct Loans, and employment under the Federal Work-Study

Program, as well as positions through the University. Chatham Merit scholarships for entering students are awarded without regard to need on the basis of high academic achievement and an on-campus interview. Scholarships begin at approximately $4000 and continue up to full tuition, room and board, and fees. Scholarships are awarded based on the student's match with Chatham's mission as well as the academic merits on her application for admission. Chatham also offers scholarships on the basis of music, art, leadership, interior architecture, Girl Scout participation, Rotary, and Phi Theta Kappa membership. Approximately 98 percent of undergraduate students receive aid administered by the University.

Faculty

The undergraduate student-teacher ratio of 9:1 ensures individual consideration and interaction between students and faculty members. Each student is assigned a faculty member who serves as her adviser through the completion of her degree program, including the Senior Tutorial capstone project. Ninety-eight percent of all undergraduate faculty members hold terminal degrees.

Admission Requirements

Evaluation is made on the basis of the prospective student's academic record, recommendations, essay, involvement in activities, and other submitted material. Chatham seeks to enroll students representing a variety of cultural, geographical, racial, religious, and socioeconomic backgrounds, with diverse talents in academic and creative areas. The admissions requirements now include a Standardized Test–Optional Policy. Applicants may choose to submit a graded writing sample and resume or a list of curricular and cocurricular activities as well as a portfolio or special project/activity in lieu of SAT or ACT scores. These materials are reviewed by Chatham faculty members and may be applied toward the scholarship review process.

Early action at Chatham University is a nonbinding admission option for first-year students who have completed their college search and know that Chatham is their first choice. Applicant deadline for early action is November 1 at midnight (Eastern time).

Admission decisions are provided within two weeks of receipt of a completed application. Applicants who apply early action will receive their merit scholarship award at the time of admission. They will also receive priority registration for housing and for the World Ready Women scholarship event in December. An estimated financial aid award is also provided in December for those who are admitted.

Applicants choosing to apply early action may apply for regular decision admission at any number of colleges and universities. Applicants who are admitted have until May 1 to respond to the admission offer.

It is strongly recommended that candidates arrange to visit the Chatham for a personal appointment, a student-guided campus tour, observation of one or more classes, and conversations with faculty and staff members and students. Early entrance is available for well-qualified and mature students who wish to begin at the end of their junior year in high school; candidates must have an on-campus interview. Chatham welcomes the opportunity to discuss future educational plans with transfer candidates in good academic standing, including junior college and community college graduates. Chatham grants college course credit for grades of 4 or 5 on Advanced Placement (AP) exams. Certain course prerequisites may be fulfilled by attaining scores of 3, 4, or 5.

Application and Information

Candidates for admission must file an application with the Admissions Office, together with a $35 nonrefundable processing fee. A free online application is available on the University's Web site. Applications are accepted on a rolling basis.

Vice President of Admissions and Financial Aid
Office of Admissions
Chatham University
Woodland Road
Pittsburgh, Pennsylvania 15232
Phone: 412-365-1290
      800-837-1290 (toll-free)
Fax: 412-365-1609
E-mail: admission@chatham.edu
Web site: http://www.chatham.edu
      http://www.facebook.com/chathamu

CHESTNUT HILL COLLEGE
PHILADELPHIA, PENNSYLVANIA

The College

Chestnut Hill College is a four-year, coeducational, Catholic liberal arts college. Founded in 1924 by the Sisters of St. Joseph, it is situated on a 75-acre campus overlooking the Wissahickon Creek. Enrolling more than 2,000 students, Chestnut Hill College is a diverse community of learners. Working adults are enrolled in the accelerated evening and weekend undergraduate program (School of Continuing and Professional Studies). In addition to its undergraduate degrees, Chestnut Hill awards the M.Ed., M.A., and M.S. (School of Graduate Studies) in administration of human services, clinical and counseling psychology, education, holistic spirituality, and instructional technology. The College also awards a doctoral degree in clinical psychology (Psy.D.).

When it comes to activities, students enthusiastically engage in the many clubs and organizations available and participate in everything from student government and horseback riding to golf and musical theater. The College is a member of NCAA Division II and competes in baseball (men), basketball (men and women), cross-country (men and women), golf (men and women), lacrosse (men and women), soccer (men and women), softball (women), tennis (men and women), and volleyball (women). A swimming pool, a gymnasium, a fitness room, and outdoor basketball and tennis courts provide excellent athletic facilities for Chestnut Hill's students.

Location

Chestnut Hill College is situated in a beautiful historical area at the northwestern edge of Philadelphia. The College is bounded by the wooded hills of Fairmount Park, yet it is only a 30-minute ride by train or car to downtown Philadelphia where students can enjoy a wide variety of dining, cultural, and sporting events. Among the many attractions are the museums that grace Philadelphia, from its landmark Art Museum to the Rodin Museum, the Living History Museum, the Franklin Institute, and numerous others. The city's history is reflected throughout but is most prominent in the areas surrounding Independence Hall, Society Hill, and Penn's Landing. In addition, more than seventy colleges, universities, and medical schools in the area offer opportunities for socialization and an extensive range of activities.

One mile beyond Chestnut Hill College on Germantown Avenue is the well-known area of Philadelphia also called Chestnut Hill. Reminiscent of a colonial village, this section of Philadelphia provides convenient opportunities for shopping, cultural experiences, and transportation to downtown Philadelphia. Chestnut Hill is a school in a suburban setting with all the advantages of a cosmopolitan experience—located where the northwest corner of the city meets the suburbs.

Majors and Degrees

The Bachelor of Arts, Bachelor of Science, and Bachelor of Music degrees are offered with majors in accounting; biochemistry; biology; chemistry; communications; communications and technology; computer and information science; computer and information technology; criminal justice; early childhood education: PreK –4 (with an option of Montessori certification); middle level education: 4–8; English literature; English literature and communications; environmental science; forensic biology; forensic chemistry; French; history; human services; international business, language, and culture; marketing; management; mathematics; mathematical and computer science; molecular biology; music; music education; political science; psychology; secondary education certification in various disciplines; sociology; and Spanish.

Dual degrees (B.S./M.S.) are offered in education, administration of human services, psychology, and instructional technology.

Academic Programs

The academic year consists of two 15-week semesters. There are also two 6-week summer sessions.

As a liberal arts college, Chestnut Hill offers courses of study that provide the student with a broad background in the fine arts and humanities, a knowledge of science, and a keen awareness of the social problems of the day, as well as intensive, in-depth study in a major field.

Chestnut Hill College confers a B.S., B.M., or B.A. degree to students who earn 120 semester hours of credit and satisfy specific requirements set by the faculty. Core seminars are interdisciplinary and provide opportunities for experiential learning. In addition, students must take 6 semester hours of religious studies, 6 hours beyond the elementary level in a classical or modern foreign language, and 3 hours in a writing course (unless exempted by the English department). Focused on six perspectives (historical, literary, artistic, scientific, behavior, and problem solving and analysis), the Ways of Knowing component of the core curriculum is designed to introduce students to different learning methodologies and strategies.

A student with the ability and proper motivation may be permitted to major in two departments. The student must consult with the chair of each department to determine the feasibility of the proposal and then submit it to the dean of the college for approval. It is understood that the student will satisfy the requirements of both departments.

Each year, selected first-year students and sophomores are invited into an interdisciplinary honors program that challenges intellectual initiative and provides the opportunity for independent study and seminar discussion. The completion of the four honors courses and an honors paper satisfies all distributional requirements. Students may apply for admission at the beginning of their first year or sophomore year.

Sophomores of high scholastic standing are invited by their major departments to engage in a program of independent study during their junior and senior years. This opportunity for independent study and original research culminates in an honors thesis, which is a prerequisite for the conferring of honors at graduation.

Off-Campus Programs

At Chestnut Hill College, a student may take advantage of the interim between semesters by coordinating travel and study. Students, with the assistance of one or more of their professors, can use their imagination and interests to develop

an off-campus program. Should the program be lengthier than the interim allows, students may schedule their travel and study for the summer. Past intersession programs have included studies of French culture in Paris, women in English literature in London, and marine biology in Florida.

Chestnut Hill College participates in a consortium arrangement with seven colleges throughout the nation, founded by the Sisters of St. Joseph. As participants, students can study at any other member institution for a semester or a year, while maintaining status as full-time Chestnut Hill students.

An average of B or above and approval of the academic dean allow an upperclass student to pursue organized study in another country. The major department must approve the course of study. In recent years, Chestnut Hill College students have enrolled in institutions in London, Madrid, Rome, Salzburg, Vienna, and other European centers. Chestnut Hill College maintains agreements with Regent's College London, the Sorbonne and the American Business School in Paris, the Centre d'Etudes Franco-Americain de Management in Lyons, and Seisen University in Japan for study abroad.

The growing interest of students in acquiring on-the-job experience while still in college has prompted the development of many departmental internship programs, which provide students with the opportunity to gain professional experience in their major while earning academic credit. Chestnut Hill has also an office of career development, through which Chestnut Hill College assists students in finding jobs that correspond to their career interests and academic pursuits.

Academic Facilities

Chestnut Hill College's Logue Library houses a collection of approximately 139,585 volumes and 544 current periodicals, a rare book room that contains first editions and special editions, the Gruber Theater, the fine Curriculum Library for elementary education, and an Irish literature collection. Well-equipped science laboratories, a math center, a multimedia technology center, a writing enrichment center, individual practice rooms for music students, a spacious art studio, a planetarium, and an observatory are among the many other outstanding facilities on campus. Martino Hall, which opened in 2000 and was designed to maintain the architectural history of the College, provides room for a performance center, gymnasium, or convocation center. The second and third floors house "smart" classrooms. Fitzsimmons Hall opened its doors in fall 2006 offering resident students suite-style living accommodations. The College recently acquired the neighboring 35-acre Sugerloaf Mansion estate and has renovated the existing buildings. This new facility offers additional resident housing, classrooms, a second student dining facility, office space, and conferencing capability.

Costs

General expenses for 2012–13 are tuition $29,100; and room and board approximately $9340.

Financial Aid

Financial aid is available in the form of academic scholarships, loans, work-study programs, federal grants, and Chestnut Hill College grants. Most of these are based on financial need and are awarded in financial aid packages that combine various forms of aid and are tailored to each student's need. More than 75 percent of Chestnut Hill College students receive financial aid to meet College costs. All applicants for aid should file a copy of the Free Application for Federal Student Aid (FAFSA). Merit-based scholarships and awards are granted for academic achievement.

Faculty

Evidence of Chestnut Hill's vitality can be seen in its faculty. While their primary interest is teaching, faculty members are also engaged in research, publication, travel, and other professional activities. More than 82 percent of the faculty members hold terminal degrees. The men and women who make up this group are deeply interested in both their subject and their students. Their qualifications include international degrees from Bangalore University (India), the University of London, and the University of Paris, and domestic degrees from Boston College, Bryn Mawr College, Catholic University of America, Columbia University, Creighton University, Duke University, Fordham University, Harvard University, Middlebury College, the New School for Social Research, New York University, Purdue University, Saint Louis University, Temple University, and the Universities of Arizona, Delaware, Massachusetts, Minnesota, Montana, New Mexico, North Carolina, Notre Dame, and Pennsylvania. Chestnut Hill College's faculty-student ratio is 1:11.

Student Government

A student at Chestnut Hill College has the opportunity to think independently and approach decisions creatively. Students, in conjunction with members of the faculty and administration, make judgments concerning all collegiate affairs. Several organizations provide structure for the decision-making process. Students join members of the faculty and administration on the Curriculum Committee and the College Council. The Academic, Social-Cultural, and Student Affairs Committees of the Student Organization identify, represent, and meet campus needs.

Admission Requirements

Chestnut Hill College welcomes students whose aptitudes and academic records show a desire to accept a challenge. Applications are judged by the Admissions Committee on the basis of intellectual ability, academic achievement (class rank and performance in high school, including completion of 16 academic units), and SAT or ACT results.

Students should submit a completed application, application fee, SAT or ACT scores, and a high school transcript. Letters of recommendation, a personal statement, and other supporting documentation are strongly encouraged. An interview is recommended and may be required. A student wishing to transfer to Chestnut Hill College is asked to submit a transcript from all colleges previously attended.

Application and Information

Applications are processed on a rolling admission system. To arrange an interview or to obtain more detailed information about the academic program, students should contact:

Office of Admissions
School of Undergraduate Studies
Chestnut Hill College
9601 Germantown Avenue
Philadelphia, Pennsylvania 19118
Phone: 215-248-7001
          800-248-0052 (toll-free)
E-mail: admissions@chc.edu
Web site: http://www.chc.edu

CHEYNEY UNIVERSITY OF PENNSYLVANIA
CHEYNEY, PENNSYLVANIA

The University

Founded in 1837, Cheyney University is America's oldest historically Black institution of higher education. Today it leverages that rich history of providing access to higher education for all students and producing visionary leaders and responsible citizens. Cheyney graduates are successful, talented individuals; some of the most well-known include 60 Minutes journalist, Ed Bradley, and NFL defensive back, Andre Waters. Cheyney University is in the business of developing human potential and talent and does so through an intellectually challenging environment and personal attention to every student—a hallmark of the Cheyney experience. Prospective students are encouraged to get to know the vibrant Cheyney University community. Cheney provides access to high-quality higher education, opportunities to help students realize their full potential, and academic excellence—all in a friendly, caring, and collegiate environment. Cheyney University's historic campus is located in one of the most scenic and developing suburban areas in Pennsylvania. Walk around the campus and feel the pride of the Cheyney University community—its faculty and staff members, its alumni, and its students.

The University sits on 275-acre campus of rolling hillsides in southeastern Pennsylvania. The heart of the campus is its historic quadrangle, with buildings dating back to the early 1900s. The campus offers five residence halls, including a 400-bed suite-style residence hall. The Center of Excellence in Communications Media, Fine Art and Entertainment Arts boasts of two theaters for the performing arts, Dudley Theatre and the recently renovated Marian Anderson Music Center, as well as a state-of-the art graphic design lab. Further, the University is complemented by a library, an Aquaponics Greenhouse, a dining hall, snack bar, fitness center, student union, and multiple athletic facilities.

Cheyney University also has a location in Philadelphia, which houses the University's graduate degree programs and undergraduate degree-completion programs. This location is also available for commuter students who wish to pursue their undergraduate degree.

Over 1,800 students choose from more than thirty undergraduate and graduate degree programs and participate in more than forty clubs, societies, and student organizations. The University is an NCAA Division II institution, with twelve intercollegiate sports teams. Cheyney's student-athletes are viewed as students first. Academics achievements in the classroom, together with the development of character, individual and team skills, the will to win, and a sense of fair play and sportsmanship in athletic competition create the distinction in the University's intercollegiate athletics programs.

Graduate degrees conferred are the Master of Education, Master of Science, Master of Arts in Teaching, and Master Public Administration.

Cheyney University is part of the Pennsylvania State System of Higher Education and is regionally accredited by the Middle States Commission on Higher Education.

Location

Cheyney University's main campus is 25 miles west of Philadelphia. SEPTA bus service is available between the campus, Center City Philadelphia, Chester, and several sites in Delaware County. Lancaster is 1½ hours away, and Harrisburg is 2 hours from Cheyney. Wilmington, Delaware, is 15 miles south of Cheyney; New York City and Washington, D.C. are 2 hours away. The campus is easily accessible via the Pennsylvania Turnpike and Interstate 95.

Cheyney University Center City (CUCC) is located at 701 Market Street in downtown Philadelphia.

Majors and Degrees

Undergraduate degrees conferred from the School of Education and Professional Studies and the School of Arts and Sciences are the Bachelor of Arts, Bachelor of Science, and Associate in Science. A complete list of academic majors is available on the University's Web site at www.cheyney.edu.

Academic Programs

The completion of 120 semester hours is required for a bachelor's degree. Of the 120 hours, 40 percent are in general education and 60 percent are in the humanities, social sciences, natural sciences, mathematics, health and physical education, and electives. In 2010 and 2011, the University's Hotel, Tourism and Restaurant Management program was recognized by Diverse Issues in Higher Education as a top degree producer. Further, Cheyney's faculty members continue to demonstrate their commitment to academic excellence in and out of the classroom.

Cheyney's Keystone Honors Academy is a learning community of high-achieving students. The Academy offers its members study-abroad opportunities, internship experiences, professional development, and graduate school preparation.

The University College Model is a unique program that helps freshmen and sophomore students mature academically and socially. The Model combines targeted advising, mentoring, counseling, and career services to help in the maturation and graduation process.

The Academic Success Center provides support services through tutors and counselors for students who seek academic support.

Academic Facilities

The Leslie Pinckney Hill Library houses approximately 200,000 books plus a periodical collection of more than 23,000 bound volumes and 1,100 current subscriptions. Audiovisual media and CD-ROM full-text/image databases as well as Internet access are also available. The library also houses the famed Schomburg Collection of African American History and Culture on microfilm.

The Center of Excellence in Communications Media, Fine Art and Entertainment Arts is complemented by the Marian Anderson Music Center, which recently underwent a $3.2 million restoration. The Center also features a state-of-the art graphic design lab, a newly refurbished radio broadcast studio, and the telecommunications center that offers a 240-seat

auditorium with state-of-the-art satellite television capabilities, a cable television control facility, a television studio, and the Distance Learning and Teleconferencing Center, offering twenty computers with teleconference network access.

The Vaux-Logan Auditorium supports academics and features newly enhanced lighting, sound and projection technology, upgraded seating, and new stage flooring.

The Aquaponics Greenhouse Center is a 12,000-foot-learning lab for biology, marketing, and business students. The Center also serves as a commercial production facility for wholesale basil production and tilapia fish sales, which benefit the University.

Coming soon, the new science center is a 40,000-square-foot, sustainable, LEED-certified facility, built with recycled and local building materials. It houses a planetarium; chemistry, biology, computer science, and physics labs; faculty offices; and seminar and lecture halls. Its design includes a demonstration green roof and a rain/gray water reuse and recycling system.

Costs

For the 2011–12 academic year, tuition for Pennsylvania residents was $8404 for full-time students (12–18 credits). For residents of Delaware, Maryland, New Jersey, and New York, tuition for 12–18 credits was $14,822. For students from other states and international students, full-time tuition was $17,942. For current tuition and fees information, prospective students should visit the Web site at www.cheyney.edu.

Financial Aid

The University makes every possible effort to enable interested and qualified students to take advantage of its educational opportunities. Financial assistance may be available in the form of academic scholarships, grants, loans, and the Federal Work-Study Program. Financial aid packages are developed for qualified students based on individual student need. Students wishing to apply for financial aid must complete the Free Application for Federal Student Aid (FAFSA). Students should pay strict attention to all state and federal application deadlines.

Faculty

Cheyney University has over 145 full-time and part-time faculty members. The student-to-faculty ratio is approximately 15:1, and each student has a faculty adviser.

Student Government

All students are members of the Student Government Cooperative Association (SGCA), which sponsors many cultural, educational, and social events and brings speakers and performers to the campus. SGCA and other student representatives sit on all University committees. A student representative is also selected to serve on the University's Council of Trustees.

Admission Requirements

Applicants to Cheyney University are evaluated on the following criteria: GPA, SAT or ACT scores, class rank, and academic curriculum. Letters of recommendation and an essay are encouraged. Admission requirements include graduation from an approved secondary school or a General Education Development (GED) certificate from an approved agency. Students are encouraged to visit the campus and have an admission interview. Transfer students in good standing, 12 credits and a 2.0 grade point average, are welcomed to apply for admission.

Application and Information

Students are admitted for the fall or spring semester and can apply online. Along with a completed application, the University must receive an official, final copy of the high school transcript, SAT or ACT scores, and a nonrefundable application fee. Transfer students are required to submit official transcripts from all colleges or universities previously attended..

For additional information contact:

Office of Admissions
Cheyney University of Pennsylvania
1837 University Circle
P.O. Box 149
Cheyney, Pennsylvania 19319-0149
Phone: 610-399-2275
        800-CHEYNEY (toll-free)
E-mail: admission@cheyney.edu
Web site: http://www.cheyney.edu

Cheyney University is located on a beautiful 275-acre campus, located in Southeastern Pennsylvania, 25 miles outside of Philadelphia, within a few hours of Baltimore and Washington, D.C.

CLARKSON UNIVERSITY
POTSDAM, NEW YORK

The University

Founded in 1896, Clarkson stands out among America's private, nationally ranked research institutions because of its dynamic collaborative learning environment, innovative degree and research programs, and unmatched record of accomplishment for producing leaders and innovators.

The University attracts 3,000 enterprising students from diverse backgrounds (including some 400 graduate students) who thrive in rigorous programs in engineering, arts, sciences, business, and health sciences and in the University's close-knit, residential learning/living community. Clarkson defies convention in the classroom, in its laboratories, and by the impact its graduates have in the world. The University is New York State's highest-ranked small research institution. However, size is Clarkson's advantage—fostering leadership and problem-solving skills and readily affording students and faculty members the flexibility to span the boundaries of traditional academic areas.

Clarkson students also enjoy extraordinary opportunities to pursue faculty-mentored research. They gain professional experience through internships and co-ops with corporations and government organizations and can broaden their perspectives through a wide range of study-abroad opportunities.

Top graduate schools welcome Clarkson graduates to study medicine, law, and other professions. Johns Hopkins, MIT, Princeton, Yale, Caltech, Rice, and Stanford are just some of the schools chosen by Clarkson students.

Clarkson's 98 percent placement rate is among the nation's highest, with the most recent starting salaries averaging nearly $51,000. Clarkson is a key recruitment source for many of America's industry leaders, including General Electric, Alcoa, Xerox, Accenture, IBM, and Procter & Gamble. In fact, 1 in 6 Clarkson alumni is already a CEO, president, vice president, or company owner.

Clarkson's active campus also offers a wide variety of extracurricular activities, including more than eighty clubs and interest groups. Students publish a lively campus newspaper and run campus radio and television stations. Active professional and honor societies enrich the campus experience.

There are Division I men's and women's hockey teams, as well as seventeen Division III intercollegiate athletic teams for women and men. Recreational facilities include a field house and gym with racquetball, basketball, and indoor tennis courts; a state-of-the-art fitness center; and a swimming pool.

Location

Clarkson is located in Potsdam, the quintessential college town, nestled in the foothills of the northern Adirondack region of New York. The beautiful Northeast corner of the state is the home of the 6-million-acre Adirondack Park. Lake Placid and the cosmopolitan Canadian cities of Montreal and Ottawa are less than 2 hours from the campus.

Majors and Degrees

Undergraduate degree programs offered are aeronautical engineering, American studies, applied mathematics and statistics, Areté (liberal arts/business), biology, biomolecular engineering, biomolecular science, chemical engineering, chemistry, civil engineering, communication, computer engineering, computer science, digital arts and sciences, electrical engineering, engineering and management, environmental engineering, environmental health science, environmental science and policy, financial information and analysis, global supply chain management, history, humanities, information systems and business processes, innovation and entrepreneurship, liberal studies, mathematics, mechanical engineering, physician assistant studies (pre–physician assistant studies leading to a master's degree), physical therapy (pre–physical therapy leading to a doctorate), physics, political science, psychology, social documentation, social sciences, and software engineering.

First-year students who are still deciding on a major may begin in a general program in business studies, engineering studies, science studies, or university studies.

Clarkson offers a University honors program, a three-year bachelor's degree option, a five-year B.S./M.S. in chemistry/biochemistry, a five-year B.S./M.B.A., and preprofessional programs in dentistry, law, medicine, physical therapy, and veterinary science.

Academic Programs

Clarkson's historic strengths in business, engineering, liberal arts, and science remain at the core of the curriculum. These programs have also been combined into cutting-edge, cross-disciplinary majors, including biomolecular science, digital arts and sciences, environmental science and policy, engineering and management, and software engineering.

A dynamic, hands-on approach to learning is one of the hallmarks of a Clarkson education. Clarkson students learn about business by actually starting a business. They conduct scientific research alongside distinguished faculty mentors in state-of-the-art laboratories. The University's undergraduate research program has produced 25 Goldwater Scholars since the highly competitive national scholarship program was launched in 1986.

Students can also take advantage of educational initiatives and research opportunities through the Institute for a Sustainable Environment, the Center for Sustainable Energy Systems, the Shipley Center for Innovation, the Center for Entrepreneurship, the Center for Rehabilitation Engineering and Science (CREST), and the Center for Air Resources Engineering and Sciences (CARES), among others.

In 2011, *Bloomberg Businessweek* placed Clarkson twentieth on its list of Fifty Affordable Colleges with the Best Return on Investment. Other national rankings and honors include the following: among the 125 Best National Universities–Doctoral, *U.S. News & World Report*, 2010; among the best undergraduate engineering programs, *U.S. News & World Report*, 2010; among the best undergraduate business programs in the nation, *Bloomberg Businessweek* 2011; and among The Best 373 Colleges, the Princeton Review, 2011.

The supply chain management program is ranked fourteenth in the nation by U.S. News & World Report, 2011; and in the top 20 in the nation for production/operations management by *U.S. News & World Report*, in America's Best Colleges, 2010.

The digital arts and sciences major at Clarkson was named the most innovative program in North America by the International Digital Media and Arts Association (iDMAa), November, 2010.

Clarkson was also ranked among the top 100 graduate schools in environmental engineering and civil engineering by *U.S. News & World Report's* Best Graduate Programs, 2009.

ROTC service at Clarkson ranked second in the nation by *Washington Monthly* magazine in 2010. Clarkson was rated among the nation's most environmentally focused colleges in the Princeton Review's *Guide to 311 Green Colleges*.

In addition, Clarkson's award-winning Student Projects for Engineering Experience and Design (SPEED) program promotes multidisciplinary, project-based extracurricular learning opportunities for more than 400 undergraduates annually. Some fifteen design teams compete in national and regional collegiate competitions that involve design and analysis, teamwork, and communication skills.

Off-Campus Programs

Students benefit from the resources of the Associated Colleges of the St. Lawrence Valley, which comprises Clarkson University, St. Lawrence University, SUNY Canton, and SUNY Potsdam. Benefits for students include opportunities to participate in activities ranging from clubs to concerts, interlibrary exchange, and cross-registration that allows students to pursue two courses per year at member colleges at no extra cost.

Academic Facilities

The University's 640-acre wooded campus is the site of forty-six buildings that comprise more than 1.2-million square feet of assignable space. Dedicated exclusively to instructional programs are more than 375,000 square feet, including some 54,000 square feet of traditional classrooms and more than 168,000 square feet assigned as laboratory areas. In the Center for Advanced Materials Processing (a New York State Center for Advanced Technology), there are seventy state-of-the-art research labs, including many related to nanotechnology and environmental research. Others include a multidisciplinary engineering and project laboratory for team-based projects, such as the mini-Baja and Formulae SAE racers, a robotics laboratory, a high-voltage lab, electron microscopy, a Class 10 clean room, a polymer fabrication lab, crystal growth labs, and a structural testing lab. School of Arts and Sciences facilities include a virtual-reality laboratory, the Clarkson Open Source Institute, a molecular design laboratory, a human brain electrophysiology laboratory, and other specialized facilities. In 2008, the 16,000-square-foot Technology Advancement Center was opened.

Bertrand H. Snell Hall houses the School of Business and the School of Arts and Sciences administrative offices as well as fully networked classrooms and study spaces and collaborative centers that feature wireless network access and videoconferencing capabilities. The facility includes three academic centers, which are available to all students: the Shipley Center for Innovation, the Center for Global Competitiveness, and the Eastman Kodak Center for Excellence in Communication. The Center for Health Sciences at Clarkson is a regional center of excellence for education, treatment, and research in physical rehabilitation and other health sciences.

Costs

Tuition is $37,770 for the 2012–13 year, room (2-person) was $6640, and the meal plan was $5894. Student fees totaled $840. In addition, students usually spend about $2000 annually on books, supplies, travel, and personal expenses.

Financial Aid

The University offers a variety of scholarships and loans, including state and federal student loans, state scholarships and awards, individual scholarships, federal grants, and federal work-study programs.

Faculty

Clarkson's 190 full-time faculty members teach undergraduate and graduate classes, with graduate students assisting only in undergraduate lab sciences. With an excellent student-faculty ratio of 15:1, undergraduates benefit from regular interaction with the school's faculty members and small class sizes (especially at the upper levels). The University attracts teacher/scholars who are also highly regarded scholars in their fields. 96 percent hold a doctorate.

Student Government

The Student Senate and the Interfraternity Council combine to form the student government at Clarkson University. The former supervises all extracurricular activities (except athletics) and has responsibility for the allocation of student activity funds and for other appropriate business. The latter prescribes standards and rules for fraternities. Students are involved in the formation of University policies through membership, with faculty and staff representatives, on all important committees.

Admission Requirements

Clarkson recommends that prospective students follow a challenging secondary school curriculum that includes mathematics, science, and English. Candidates for entrance to the Wallace H. Coulter School of Engineering or students pursuing a degree in the sciences or an engineering and management degree should have successfully completed secondary school courses in physics and chemistry. All candidates for admission are required to take the SAT or ACT. SAT Subject Tests are optional. The high school record is the most important factor in an admission decision. International students for whom English is a second language must submit a minimum TOEFL score of 550 (paper-based) or 212 (computer-based). All applicants must include a personal statement of 250 to 500 words.

Students achieving scores of 4 or better on the College Board's Advanced Placement examinations are considered for advanced placement and credit in virtually all academic areas.

An early decision plan is offered on a first-choice basis; this plan does not prohibit the student from making other applications, but it does commit the student to withdrawing other applications if accepted at Clarkson.

Although not required, a personal interview with a member of the Office of Admission is highly recommended, especially for early decision candidates. Interviews on campus should be arranged by letter or telephone at least one week prior to the intended visit. The Office of Admission is open Monday through Friday, from 8 a.m. to 4:30 p.m., and Saturday by appointment. The University welcomes visitors to the campus and makes arrangements, as requested, for families to tour and meet with academic and other departments on campus.

Application and Information

Office of Undergraduate Admission
Holcroft House
Clarkson University
P.O. Box 5605
Potsdam, New York 13699-5605
Phone: 315-268-6480
        800-527-6577 (toll-free)
Fax: 315-268-7647
E-mail: admission@clarkson.edu
Web site: http://www.clarkson.edu

CLEMSON UNIVERSITY
CLEMSON, SOUTH CAROLINA

The University

One of the country's most selective public research universities, Clemson was founded in 1889 with a mission to be a "high seminary of learning" dedicated to teaching, research, and service. Today, these three concepts remain at the heart of the University and provide the framework for an exceptional educational experience.

At Clemson University, professors take the time to get to know students and explore innovative ways of teaching. Exceptional teaching is one reason Clemson's retention and graduation rates rank among the highest in the country for public universities.

Exceptional teaching is also why Clemson continues to attract an increasingly talented student body. In 2011, over half of the entering freshmen were ranked in the top 10 percent of their high school classes, and the freshman class averaged 1230 on the critical reading and math sections of the SAT—one of the highest averages among the nation's public research universities.

Clemson is committed to world-class research. With roughly $200 million in sponsored research support annually, undergraduates have the opportunity to work closely with faculty members on exciting and challenging research projects.

The University also encourages faculty members to engage their classes through service learning. One example of this is the Clemson Elementary Outdoors project, in which more than 750 Clemson students from a broad range of disciplines researched and designed outdoor learning areas for the city's elementary school. Clemson has received national recognition for its innovative Communication-Across-the-Curriculum (CAC) program, in which professors focus on providing real-life challenges that require students to think and communicate effectively. At Clemson, CAC has become a standard teaching method used in nearly every department.

From cheering the Tigers at a football game to socializing at the Hendrix Student Center, Clemson students can participate in a wide variety of activities outside the classroom. The more than 325 campus clubs and organizations include fraternities and sororities, as well as honorary, international, military, performing arts, political, professional, religious, service, social interest, special interest, sports and fitness, student media, and union programs and activities.

With nineteen intercollegiate sports, Clemson offers exciting spectator sports year-round. Clemson is a charter member of the Atlantic Coast Conference and is an NCAA Division I school. Admission to regular-season home events is included in University fees for full-time students.

Clemson University is accredited by the Commission on Colleges of the Southern Association of Colleges and Schools to award bachelor's, master's, specialist, and doctoral degrees. Contact the Commission on Colleges at 1866 Southern Lane, Decatur, Georgia 30033-4097 or call 404-679-4500 for questions about the accreditation of Clemson University.

Location

Approximately midway between Charlotte, North Carolina, and Atlanta, Georgia, Clemson University is located on 1,400 acres in the foothills of the Blue Ridge Mountains and along the shores of Lake Hartwell. Great weather and proximity to natural wonders and large cities offer year-round recreational opportunities.

The University's enrollment of more than 19,000 undergraduate and graduate students makes it a defining presence in Clemson, South Carolina, a town of about 12,000. Students may live on campus in one of the twenty-one residence halls and four apartment complexes, most of which are within a 10-minute walk to class or downtown.

Majors and Degrees

Clemson offers approximately 80 undergraduate and 110 graduate degree programs through five academic colleges: Agriculture,

Forestry, and Life Sciences; Architecture, Arts, and Humanities; Business and Behavioral Science; Engineering and Science; and Health, Education, and Human Development. Undergraduate students can earn B.A., B.S., or preprofessional degrees in accounting; agricultural education; agricultural mechanization and business; animal and veterinary sciences; architecture; biochemistry; biological sciences; biosystems engineering; ceramic and materials engineering; chemical engineering; chemistry; civil engineering; communication studies; computer engineering; computer information systems; computer science; construction science and management; early childhood education; economics; electrical engineering; elementary education; English; environmental and natural resources; financial management; food science; forest resource management; genetics; geology; graphic communications; health science; history; horticulture; industrial engineering; landscape architecture; language and international health; language and international trade; management; marketing; mathematical sciences; mathematics teaching; mechanical engineering; microbiology; modern languages; nursing; packaging science; parks, recreation, and tourism management; philosophy; physics; political science; polymer and fiber chemistry; preprofessional health studies; prepharmacy; pre–rehabilitation sciences; pre–veterinary medicine; production studies in performing arts; psychology; science teaching; secondary education; sociology; soils and sustainable crop systems; special education; turfgrass; visual arts; and wildlife and fisheries biology.

Academic Programs

Clemson's academic year is divided into two semesters. The fall semester begins in mid-August and the spring semester starts in early January. Three summer sessions and four mini-semesters are also available. Students average 16 credit hours per semester, and Clemson requires all students to complete some general education classes specified by the University before graduation. The number of completed credit hours required for graduation varies, depending on the major.

Calhoun Honors College is a University-wide program that combines the strengths of a public, land-grant university with those of a highly selective small college. Calhoun Scholars may choose to pursue departmental honors within their specific academic discipline. In addition, EUREKA! (Experiences in Undergraduate Research, Exploration, and Knowledge Advancement) is a unique and exciting program that enables honors students to pursue research and scholarly activities with faculty members across all disciplines. The advantages of membership in the Honors College include priority registration, extended library loan privileges, honors research grants, and honors housing.

The National Scholars Program is a highly selective program for exceptional students who strive to meet their highest intellectual potential. One of its goals is to develop the interests and talents students need to compete for Rhodes, Marshall, and Truman scholarships; Fulbright Grants; National Science Foundation Graduate Fellowships; and other prestigious international fellowships.

Clemson's nationally recognized Programs for Educational Enrichment and Retention (PEER) is committed to improving the academic performance of underrepresented students in engineering and science. Today, thanks in large part to PEER, the six-year graduation rate for African American first-time freshmen is above the national average.

The Women in Science and Engineering (WISE) program focuses on recruiting women into science and engineering majors and helping them succeed in college and their careers. WISE offers support activities such as mentoring programs, career planning, and study groups.

Tutoring, supplemental instruction, academic skills workshops, and academic counseling are also available free to all Clemson students through the Academic Support Center.

Off-Campus Programs

Clemson's study-abroad and off-campus programs give students the opportunity to study almost anywhere in the world. The International Student Exchange Program and the Clemson Exchange Program allow students to enroll for a summer, semester or full academic year at one of more than 100 universities throughout the world. About 28 percent of the student body enriched their education through study abroad last year. Students in a variety of majors have opportunities at the Archbold Center in Dominica; the Daniel Center in Genoa, Italy; the Clemson University Brussels Center in Belgium; and other locations.

The Cooperative Education program provides an opportunity for students to alternate periods of academic study with semesters of paid, career-related, engaged-learning experiences to bridge the gap between academic study and its application in professional practice.

Academic Facilities

The Clemson campus is home to a blend of historic buildings and advanced research facilities surrounded by stately trees and lush greenery.

The libraries and the computing and information technology department are committed to providing students and faculty members with the latest ways to access information. Clemson's main library, the Robert M. Cooper Library, is located at the center of campus and provides a variety of services and up-to-date collections. The University's wireless networking capability lets students communicate with professors and classmates, read online course materials, check e-mail, and conduct research—all from their own laptops. Students are required to complete an electronic portfolio prior to graduation, allowing them the opportunity to present themselves through a creative venue to prospective employers and graduate schools.

The campus offers an array of facilities and programs designed to enhance a student's entire educational experience. These include the Pearce Center for Professional Communication, Class of 1941 Studio for Student Communication, Rutland Center for Ethics, and the Academic Support Center.

Clemson real estate holdings also include more than 32,000 acres of forestry and agricultural lands throughout the state, the majority of which are dedicated to the University's research and service missions.

Costs

For the 2011–12 academic year, undergraduate tuition and fees were $12,668 for South Carolina residents and $28,826 for out-of-state residents. Room and board costs were approximately $7228, and books and supplies were $1090. The one-time laptop computer cost was about $1600.

Financial Aid

Financial aid is usually awarded on the basis of need to supplement the amount students and their parents can contribute to college expenses. The University also awards some scholarships based entirely on academic merit. Clemson offers financial aid in the form of grants, scholarships, loans, and part-time employment.

Entering freshmen are evaluated on a competitive basis for scholarships using the admission application. There is no separate scholarship application. For academic recruiting scholarships, selection is based on test scores, high school rank-in-class, and other academic factors. This year, students offered one of these merit scholarships had a minimum SAT score of 1250 (combined score from critical reading and mathematics sections), or an ACT of at least 31, and were ranked no lower than the top 10 percent of their senior class. Stipends for in-state residents range from $500 per year to the full cost of attendance. Merit scholarships for out-of-state students range from $2500 per year to the full cost of attendance. Academic recruiting scholarships are available only to entering freshmen and are renewable for three additional years provided that the minimum standards are maintained. The application for admission is the first step for prospective freshmen to be considered for merit awards.

General scholarships are awarded to both entering freshmen and upperclassmen. These scholarships may have special criteria set up by the donor, such as a certain residency, major, or career interest. Because of the restrictions on many of these scholarships, it is impossible to predict the recipients. However, the scholarship selection process is very competitive. Stipends range from $250 to $7500.

Faculty

Clemson has more than 1,300 full-time faculty members, of whom 82 percent hold a Ph.D. or terminal degree in their fields. In addition, the University has more than 240 part-time faculty members. Faculty honors include the Fulbright Scholarship, Guggenheim Fellowship, National Science Foundation CAREER Award, National Institutes of Health Senior Scientist Award, and American Academy of Arts and Sciences membership. The average class size is 31, and the student-to-faculty ratio is 16:1.

Admission Requirements

Each year, the University receives about 18,000 applications for a fall freshman class of 3,000. Transfer applications are received from about 2,200 students, of whom Clemson enrolls 1,000. Undergraduate applications are available online at http://www.clemson.edu/admissions.

For freshman applicants, the following factors are considered: class standing, standardized test scores (SAT or ACT), high school curriculum, grades, and choice of major. All entering freshmen must have completed 4 credits of English, 3 credits of mathematics, 3 credits of laboratory science, 3 credits of a foreign language (in the same language), 3 credits of social sciences, 2 credits in other areas, and 1 credit of physical education.

To be considered for transfer admission, candidates must have completed a full year of college study (a minimum of 30 semester hours or 45 quarter hours of transferable work), earned a cumulative grade point average of at least 2.5 on a 4.0 scale (3.0 preferred), and completed freshman-level courses in English, science, and mathematics for their intended major at Clemson.

Application and Information

Application deadlines for freshman admissions are December 1 (priority date for fall semester), May 1 (fall semester), and December 15 (spring semester). For transfer admissions, the application deadlines are July 1 (fall semester) and December 15 (spring semester).

Office of Admissions
Clemson University
105 Sikes Hall, Box 345124
Clemson, South Carolina 29634-5124
Phone: 864-656-2287
Fax: 864-656-2464
E-mail: cuadmissions@clemson.edu
Web site: http://www.clemson.edu/admissions
　　　http://twitter.com/BeAClemsonTiger (Twitter)

Clemson's campus includes 1,400 acres, yet the residence halls and classroom buildings are an easy 10-minute walk from each other.

COLBY COLLEGE
WATERVILLE, MAINE

The College

Colby, founded in 1813 and one of America's best private liberal arts colleges, combines a challenging academic program, an emphasis on undergraduate research, and an active community life—all on one of the nation's most beautiful campuses. Colby's reach is global—in its recruitment of a diverse student body and faculty, in the scope of its curriculum, and in the number of undergraduates who study abroad.

The College is guided by the belief that the best preparation for life is a broad acquaintance with human knowledge. Liberal arts students graduate with the competence and flexibility to thrive in an increasingly complex world. Colby has a superior record of placing students who seek postgraduate study, and career opportunities for graduates are virtually unlimited.

Colby is a national leader at incorporating research into the curriculum in all disciplines. This approach to learning fosters strong critical-thinking skills, a lively imagination, and a capacity for independent work. It also contributes to faculty members' strong and supportive relationships with students. While many colleges lay claim to accessible faculty members, Colby ranks among the best in student-faculty interaction, both in and out of the classroom.

The College has been recognized by the EPA and Maine officials for its commitment to environmental stewardship, both in academic programs and in practices adopted on campus. Through student-led and institutional initiatives—including the construction of a biomass facility that will replace 90 percent of the heating oil used by the College each year—Colby is committed to becoming carbon neutral by 2015.

In 2005, Colby became one of the first ten colleges or universities in the U.S. to win a Senator Paul Simon Award for Campus Internationalization. The award recognized Colby's commitment to international content in the curriculum, a 70-percent participation rate in study abroad, and an internationally diverse student body.

The pace of life at Colby is brisk, with a host of clubs, activities, and teams as well as social and cultural events that keep students busy. Colby's 1,800 students, representing nearly every state and more than sixty countries, participate in more than 100 student-run organizations, thirty-two varsity teams, eleven club sports, and more than a half dozen intramural sports. Community service is also part of the fabric of the Colby experience. The student-run Colby Volunteer Center coordinates dozens of volunteer programs, and civic engagement is built into many courses.

Almost all students live on campus. A multiyear, $44-million project to add dorms and renovate all residence halls and dining facilities is completed. Notable facilities include the Pugh Center, a hub of multicultural organizations; one of the nation's finest college-based art museums; and the Alfond Athletic Center, one of the largest indoor athletic and fitness facilities in New England. The athletic center features an indoor track, swimming pool, ice arena, gymnasium, fitness center, aerobics studio, squash courts, tennis courts, and climbing wall. Outdoor facilities include two synthetic turf fields, 50 acres of playing fields, cross-country skiing and running trails, tennis courts, and an all-weather track.

Location

Located in Waterville, Maine, Colby is 20 minutes from the state capital and about an hour from Portland, Maine's largest city. Maine's western mountains, including the Sugarloaf/USA ski area, are just over an hour to the north, and the Atlantic Coast is less than an hour to the east. Acadia National Park and Mt. Katahdin are both accessible as day trips. The 714-acre campus includes Johnson Pond and a 128-acre arboretum and bird sanctuary.

Majors and Degrees

Colby awards the Bachelor of Arts degree, with majors in African-American studies; American studies; anthropology; art; art–art history; art–studio art; biology; biology–cell and molecular biology/biochemistry; biology–ecology and evolution; biology–interdisciplinary computation; biology–neuroscience; chemistry; chemistry–biochemistry; chemistry–cell and molecular biology/biochemistry; chemistry–environmental science; classical civilization; classical civilization–anthropology; classical civilization–English; classics; classics–English; computer science; East Asian studies; economics; economics–mathematics; economics–financial markets; English; English–creative writing; environmental studies–policy; environmental studies–science; environmental studies–interdisciplinary computation; French studies; geology; geoscience; German studies; global studies: government; history; Latin American studies; mathematics; mathematical sciences; mathematical sciences–statistics; music; philosophy; physics; psychology; psychology–neuroscience; religious studies; Russian language and culture; science, technology, and society; sociology; Spanish; theater and dance; theater and dance–interdisciplinary computation; and women's, gender, and sexuality studies.

Minors are available in thirty-one fields of study, including administrative science, African studies, Chinese, cinema studies, creative writing, education, environmental studies, German, human development, indigenous peoples of the Americas, Italian studies, Japanese, and Jewish studies.

Academic Programs

Colby's liberal arts program offers a broad educational foundation. In-depth study in a major provides a detailed understanding of at least one discipline's methods and perspectives. In addition to their major, students may complete one or two minors, a second major, a combined major, or an interdisciplinary major. A self-designed independent major may also be approved for students. Secondary school teacher certification may be obtained, and dual-degree engineering programs are offered with Dartmouth College and Columbia University. The 4-1-4 calendar includes a January term that offers opportunities on and off campus to explore special areas of interest and to pursue internships.

Distribution requirements include 4 credit hours of English composition, knowledge of one foreign language, 6 to 8 credit hours in the natural sciences, and 3 to 4 credit hours in each of the following areas: arts, historical studies, literature, quantitative reasoning, and the social sciences. Wellness, residence, and diversity requirements and the requirements of the major also must be filled. A minimum of 128 credit hours with a minimum cumulative 2.0 GPA is required for graduation. Three January terms, including one during the first year, are also required.

The Goldfarb Center for Public Affairs and Civic Engagement was formed in 2004 to connect teaching and research with contemporary political, economic, and social issues. The Goldfarb Center provides a venue in which students and faculty members can think and work across disciplinary boundaries to develop creative approaches to complex local, national, and global challenges.

Off-Campus Programs

More than two thirds of Colby students take advantage of international or off-campus domestic study opportunities. Many participate in Colby's own programs in France, Spain, and Russia. Other students select approved non-Colby programs in countries throughout the world. Domestic off-campus programs include the Washington Semester and Colby at Bigelow Laboratory in East Boothbay, Maine, as well as exchange programs with Howard University in Washington, D.C., and Clark Atlanta University in Georgia. Colby's financial aid may be applied to any approved off-campus study.

Academic Facilities

Colby is in the midst of an ambitious campus expansion. The recently completed Diamond Building houses social science departments, interdisciplinary programs, and the Goldfarb Center. A 26,000-square-foot-expansion to the Colby College Museum of Art, one of the nation's finest college-based art museums, is under way. In addition, Colby will soon break ground on a new natural science building, expected to be complete in 2014.

Colby has three libraries on campus with access to almost 1 million books, microtexts, and other items, most of which are found in open stacks. The library catalog is online, and many resources are available through the library's Web site.

The Bixler Art and Music Center, adjacent to the Colby College Museum of Art, includes an art and music library, music practice rooms, and a 300-seat auditorium. The Runnals Building contains the 274-seat Strider Theater, a dance studio, and the Cellar Theater for improvisational workshops and small productions.

Four interconnected buildings contain science facilities, including teaching and research laboratories, animal rooms, research greenhouses, exhibit space, and a science library. A wide range of sophisticated science equipment is accessible to students beginning in their first year. The Collins Observatory features a 14-inch telescope equipped with a high-quality CCD camera and other research-grade equipment.

Computers are available for student use in clusters and teaching labs throughout the campus. Every classroom, dorm room, office, and laboratory is connected to the Internet. All classrooms are served by data-video projectors. An extensive software library is available to students. The Information Technology Services staff runs a help desk for students and assists with applications appropriate to each discipline. There are no fees for any of these services.

Costs

For the 2012–13 academic year, the comprehensive fee is $55,700. Personal expenses, books, and supplies average $1600 annually.

Financial Aid

Colby's Office of Admissions and Financial Aid provides services to the families of all entering students regardless of their income levels. In addition to families' grants and special scholarships that are drawn from College funds, federal and state programs, and outside scholarship agencies, the Office of Admissions and Financial Aid offers information on several financing options as well as guidance on non-need-based student loans and campus jobs.

Faculty

Colby has 170 full-time faculty members. The student-faculty ratio is 10:1, and the median class size is 15. Ninety-five percent of faculty members hold doctorates or final degrees in their fields, and many have national or international reputations. A faculty-in-residence program provides housing for about a dozen faculty families in campus residence halls, and a faculty-associates program fosters further faculty involvement in campus life.

Student Government

Colby students govern many aspects of campus life through the Student Government Association (SGA). Students also serve on most College boards and committees, including the Board of Trustees. The SGA deals with academic, cultural, and residential affairs and supports more than 100 clubs and organizations. The Student Judiciary Board has jurisdiction over most incidents that call for possible disciplinary action.

Admission Requirements

Colby seeks applicants from diverse geographical, racial, and economic backgrounds who have special qualities or talents to contribute to the College. Admission is highly selective. Evaluations are made on the basis of academic achievement and ability, interest and excitement in learning, character, and maturity. The quality of a candidate's preparation is judged by his or her academic record, references from school authorities, and standardized test scores. A minimum of 16 academic preparatory credits is recommended, including 4 years of English, at least 3 years of a foreign language, 3 years of college-preparatory mathematics, 2 years of a laboratory science, 2 years of history or social science, and 2 academic electives.

Colby offers early entrance and early decision options. Advanced standing may be established by examination, taken either through the department or through the Advanced Placement Program, the International Baccalaureate, or other standard tests. Some transfer students are considered for admission each year.

Applicants are encouraged to visit the campus for interviews, tours, classes, and meals.

Application and Information

Applications for regular admission must be submitted by January 1. Those wishing to be considered for early decision may choose either the fall or winter option. Fall option applicants must complete the application process by November 15; winter option applicants, by January 1.

For applications and admission forms, students should contact:

Colby College
Office of Admissions and Financial Aid
Colby College
4800 Mayflower Hill
Waterville, Maine 04901-8848
Phone: 800-723-3032 (toll-free)
E-mail: admissions@colby.edu
Web site: http://www.colby.edu

Autumn beauty on the quad at Colby College.

THE COLLEGE OF NEW JERSEY
EWING TOWNSHIP, NEW JERSEY

The College

The College of New Jersey (TCNJ) welcomes students who have the talent and motivation to succeed in a highly rigorous academic environment. A public institution founded in 1855, the College enrolls about 6,500 full-time undergraduates, two thirds of whom reside on campus. Today it is heralded by *U.S. News & World Report* as well as *Barron's* as one of the most competitive schools in the nation, public or private. TCNJ serves a diverse student body, preparing graduates to be leaders in their chosen fields.

TCNJ has set the standard for public higher education. Students report they find TCNJ large enough to provide a full range of academic and extracurricular choices, yet small enough to be a genuine residential community of friends and fellow learners. With professors easily available in and out of class and facilities of enviable quality, TCNJ represents an exceptional value in higher education.

The College of New Jersey's academic approach combines those of both traditional liberal arts schools and professional schools. A liberal learning curriculum ensures that all students are grounded in the beliefs and values of civic responsibility and intellectual and scholarly growth and that they receive a well-rounded education in the liberal arts. Interdisciplinary studies, internships, research, and faculty mentoring all are part of an educational approach designed to produce successful leaders. While a very high percentage of graduates find immediate employment related to their fields of study, more than 20 percent go directly into graduate schools across the country.

All first- and second-year students are guaranteed on-campus housing, and most juniors and seniors continue to live on campus. Rooming arrangements are quite flexible, from doubles in freshman residence halls to suites and single rooms in campus town houses or apartments for upperclass students. A nationally recognized residence life program and more than 150 student organizations offer numerous opportunities for friendship, personal growth, and leadership. An exceptional 96 percent of first-year students return for their sophomore year.

The arts flourish in two theaters, a recital hall, an art gallery, and numerous other campus venues. Student performances, professional groups on tour, and a large variety of films, lectures, local bands, and solo entertainers fill the academic year with cultural options—many of them free, the rest at low cost.

Student wellness has a high priority, with many facilities for recreation and physical conditioning. In Packer Hall, the campus has access to a larger fitness center, a 25-meter swimming and diving pool, and a basketball court. The Student Recreation Center offers racquetball courts, four tennis courts that are convertible to basketball or volleyball use, a weight room, and an indoor track. Other facilities include a lighted Astroturf field, eight lighted outdoor tennis courts, an outdoor beach volleyball court, and numerous athletic fields.

As a Division III member of the National Collegiate Athletic Association, TCNJ offers twenty-one sports: eleven for men and ten for women. Since 1979, TCNJ student-athletes have amassed thirty-six national championships and twenty-nine runner-up awards, more than any other Division III institution in the country. In addition to its NCAA athletics, TCNJ offers a wide variety of recreation programs for intramural competition and self-governing sports clubs. More than 3,500 students play with these less demanding, but spirited and competitive teams, each year, some of which have intercollegiate schedules.

The College's undergraduate programs are accredited by the Middle States Association of Colleges and Schools and by professional associations in business, chemistry, computer science, education, education of the deaf, engineering, music, and nursing.

Location

The College of New Jersey is set on 289 acres in suburban Ewing Township, approximately 15 minutes from downtown Princeton; 10 minutes from Bucks County, Pennsylvania; and 5 miles from the state capital of Trenton. Woodlands and lakes surround the thirty-nine major academic and residential buildings. The campus is 30 miles from the theaters and museums of Philadelphia and 60 miles from those in New York City. In the summer of 2012, TCNJ will break ground on Campus Town, a series of residential and commercial establishments along the edge of the campus.

Majors and Degrees

The College of New Jersey offers programs leading to the Bachelor of Arts, Bachelor of Fine Arts, Bachelor of Music, Bachelor of Science, Bachelor of Science in Engineering, and Bachelor of Science in Nursing degrees.

The B.A. is awarded in art education; art history; communication studies; economics; English, including journalism and professional writing options; history; interactive multimedia; international studies; mathematics and statistics; philosophy; political science; psychology; sociology; Spanish; and women's and gender studies. The B.F.A. is awarded in digital arts, and fine art and graphic design. The B.M. is awarded in music (performance and education). The B.S. is granted in accountancy, biology, biomedical engineering, business administration (finance, general business, information systems management, international business, management, and marketing), chemistry, computer engineering, computer science, early childhood education, economics, electrical engineering, elementary education, engineering science, health and physical education, law and justice, mechanical engineering, physics, and technology education. Teacher preparation is available in many arts and science majors.

TCNJ offers three five-year combined Master of Arts in Teaching degrees with dual certification in elementary education, and either special education, urban education, or deaf and hard-of-hearing education. Students may also enroll in a seven-year B.S./M.D. degree program with UMDNJ—New Jersey Medical School (Newark) or a seven-year B.S./O.D. degree program with the State University of New York College of Optometry. The College also offers a Medical Careers Advisory Committee for premed students and a Pre-Law Advisement Committee for students planning a career in law.

Academic Programs

All academic courses contain a significant out-of-class requirement and provide for even more student-faculty interaction. All baccalaureate degrees require at least thirty-two courses, including a core curriculum in the traditional arts and sciences.

The thirty-week year is divided into fall and spring semesters; a summer session offers courses in two 5-week sessions and one 6-week session. The average class size for freshman-level lectures is 24 students and for upper-division lectures, 22 students.

All first-year students participate in a First Seminar Program that links residential learning with small classes taught by full-time faculty members. Seminars, independent studies, and capstone courses give many students the opportunity for challenging advanced study in close collaboration with faculty

members. TCNJ students publish the results of these endeavors or present them at national and regional conferences.

The honors program offers students the particularly challenging academic experiences that allow normal progress toward the degree. Whenever possible, honors courses have an interdisciplinary perspective and curriculum, concentrating on central themes within significant periods in the cultural development of civilization. Honors courses in the major consist of either specially designated sections or independent study. All honors classes are small, personal, and stimulating.

Off-Campus Programs

TCNJ offers students a variety of full-year and one-semester programs of study abroad as well as study at other state colleges and universities within the United States. Exchange programs are available in 80 cities in Australia, Austria, Canada, Denmark, France, Germany, Greece, Israel, Japan, Mexico, the United Kingdom, and numerous other countries. National exchanges are available at more than 130 participating institutions in the United States, the U.S. Virgin Islands, Puerto Rico, and Guam. The College of New Jersey hosts the New Jersey State Consortium for International Studies.

Academic Facilities

TCNJ has been nationally recognized as one of the most beautiful campuses in the nation. Within the past several years, TCNJ has built and opened a Science Complex, Biology Building, Social Science Building, College Spiritual Center, Art and Interactive Media Building, Education Building, student apartments, and a state-of-the-art library, which serves as the intellectual and social hub of the campus. Campuswide networking provides full Internet accessibility from all residence hall rooms and more than twenty student computing laboratories.

Costs

For up-to-date information on in-state and out-of state tuition and fees costs, as well as room and board figures, prospective students should go online to http://www.tcnj.edu/~sfs/tuition/index.html.

Financial Aid

Over 77 percent of full-time undergraduates receive some form of financial aid, such as federal, state, and institutional grants; merit scholarships; student employment; and loan assistance. The Free Application for Federal Student Aid (FAFSA) or Renewal FAFSA is used to apply for all types of aid.

Scholarships and grants include The College of New Jersey Merit Scholars Program, Bonner Scholars, Chairman of the Board Merit Scholars, the New Jersey Tuition Aid Grant, Federal Pell Grants, Federal Supplemental Educational Opportunity Grants (FSEOG), Educational Opportunity Fund (EOF) Promise Award, and Army and Air Force ROTC Scholarships, as well as other institutional scholarships. Loans include the Federal Subsidized and Unsubsidized Stafford Loans, the Federal Perkins Loan, the Federal Parent Loan for Undergraduate Students (PLUS), the New Jersey CLASS Loan, private/alternative loans, nursing loans, and short-term emergency loan funds. Student employment options include the need-based Federal Work-Study Program (on- and off-campus positions) as well as institutionally supported campus jobs.

Faculty

The approximately 335 full-time members of the College of New Jersey faculty are teachers and scholars. While teaching is their primary commitment, they are also active researchers, authors, artists, performers, and regular contributors in their academic disciplines. No classes are taught by graduate assistants. The student-faculty ratio is 12:1. From their first day, students study with faculty members who may be researching new ways to use solar energy; writing a new text, play, or novel; or investigating the life cycle of desert ferns. Members of the faculty have attracted many significant grants, fellowships, and awards, including the Bancroft Prize in history, Fulbright Scholarships, and grants from the National Science Foundation, the National Institute for Advanced Study, the Guggenheim Foundation, and the National Endowment for the Humanities. Faculty members mentor their students, preparing them for careers, graduate and professional schools, and prestigious fellowships such as the Fulbright, Truman, and Marshall Fellowships recently awarded to TCNJ students.

Student Government

The Student Government Association, comprising all undergraduate students at the College, is governed by elected representatives. The Residence Hall Association provides the mechanism for student input into campus housing policies, and members of the Student Finance Board oversee and administer approximately $500,000 in student funds. The College Union Board sponsors a wide range of special events, including recent visits by Seth Meyer, Cornel West, and Joel McHale.

Admission Requirements

The College of New Jersey seeks students who can succeed in a highly selective academic program and who show intellectual curiosity, academic talent, and the potential to contribute to the life of the College. The College is committed to attracting students from diverse economic, racial, social, and geographic backgrounds. A high school record of at least 16 college-preparatory credits, high school class rank, SAT scores, and special interests, skills, and qualities of all kinds can be influential. Certain departments, such as art and music, use additional criteria to evaluate candidates seeking admission into their programs. The College of New Jersey reviews candidates holistically and takes into consideration the variations in high schools and communities in which the applicants reside.

Application and Information

The College of New Jersey is a member of the Common Application. The deadline for applications for Spring admission is November 15 and for Fall admission, January 15. There is a $75 application fee. Candidates who apply only to the College of New Jersey under the early decision plan may apply before November 15 and will be notified on or before December 15. Students applying in to the seven-year medical program must apply by December 15. For Fall admission, the College subscribes to the candidates' reply date of May 1 for payment of $600.

For more information, students should contact:

Director of Admissions
The College of New Jersey
P.O. Box 7718
Ewing, New Jersey 08628-0718
Phone: 609-771-2131
Web site: http://www.tcnj.edu

The campus of The College of New Jersey, recognized as one of the most beautiful campuses in the United States.

THE COLLEGE OF NEW ROCHELLE
NEW ROCHELLE, NEW YORK

The College of New Rochelle

The College

The College of New Rochelle (CNR), founded in 1904 by the Ursuline Order, is an independent college that is Catholic in origin and heritage. Its primary purpose is the intellectual development of students through the maintenance of high standards of academic excellence. The College is comprised of four separate schools. The School of Arts and Sciences (women only) enrolls approximately 500 young women between the ages of 18 and 22 and offers baccalaureate degree programs in the liberal arts and sciences and in a number of professionally oriented fields. The School of Nursing (coeducational), founded in 1976 and accredited by the Commission on Collegiate Nursing Education (CCNE), offers baccalaureate and graduate-level professional nursing programs that combine clinical experience with a liberal arts background. A Master of Science (M.S.) degree program in nursing is available. About 400 women and men are enrolled in the nursing programs. The School of New Resources, which maintains six campuses in New Rochelle and New York City, offers a nontraditional baccalaureate program designed specifically for adults. The Graduate School offers professional degree programs in education, art, community/school psychology, gerontology, communication studies, career development, and guidance and counseling. The main campus includes four residence halls that provide guaranteed housing for all undergraduates. Other students live in Westchester County, and some commute from the Greater New York metropolitan area. Students come to CNR from twenty states and eight countries.

Location

The College of New Rochelle is located on a 20-acre historic campus in New Rochelle, New York, a suburban community in southern Westchester County, just 16 miles from New York City and easily accessible by commuter trains. The area contains numerous parks and recreational areas, and the Long Island Sound, with its many beaches, is within walking distance of the campus. Four airports—Kennedy, LaGuardia, Newark, and Westchester—are all within an hour of the College, and Amtrak makes daily stops at New Rochelle. New York City provides countless opportunities, including shopping expeditions, museums, and Broadway plays. Manhattan and the four other boroughs of New York City also contribute immeasurably to the education of the College's students through various internship, honors, and cooperative education programs, which are conducted by CNR in New York City.

Majors and Degrees

The School of Arts and Sciences at The College of New Rochelle confers the Bachelor of Arts (B.A.) degree in art (studio), art history, biology, chemistry, classics, communication arts, economics, English, environmental studies, history, mathematics, modern and classical languages, philosophy, political science, psychology, religious studies, and sociology; the Bachelor of Science (B.S.) degree in art education, biology, business, chemistry, mathematics, and social work; the Bachelor of Fine Arts (B.F.A.) degree in art education, art therapy, and studio art; and a Bachelor of Arts in interdisciplinary studies, which offers the student the viewpoints of several disciplines, including American studies, comparative literature, international studies, and women's studies. A series of field experiences and competency-based learning activities lead to certification in childhood education (grades 1–6) and adolescence education (grades 7–12). Childhood education allows for dual certification in early childhood (birth–grade 2), middle childhood (grades 5–9), and students with disabilities (grades 1–6). Adolescence education allows for dual certification in middle childhood and students with disabilities (grades 7–12). Certification is also available in art education (K–12). The School of Nursing offers a Bachelor of Science in Nursing (B.S.N.) degree program. Preprofessional programs are available in art therapy, health professions, law, and medicine.

Academic Programs

The College emphasizes the importance of a liberal arts background. Each undergraduate in the Schools of Arts and Sciences and Nursing must complete a variety of courses focusing on philosophy and religious studies, social analysis, literature and the arts, foreign languages, and scientific inquiry. To earn a B.A., B.S., or B.F.A., students must complete 120 credits. Typically, a B.A. degree requires 90 credits in liberal arts and 30 credits in a major area; B.S. and B.F.A. degrees require 60 credits in liberal arts and 60 credits in major and elective courses. To earn a B.S.N. degree, students must complete 120 credits. Students who earn successful scores of 3 or higher on the College Board's Advanced Placement examinations may qualify for credit and course exemption.

Interdisciplinary studies and dual-degree programs are available. Independent study options and seminars play important roles in undergraduate programs as well. The honors program, which provides an alternative structure for the liberal arts curriculum, fosters the growth of intellectual independence and initiative, offers the opportunity for independent study and research, and encourages the pursuit of scholarly interests in a broad variety of disciplines. The Center for Academic Excellence staff offers tutoring programs, quiet study areas, professional tutors, and student-peer tutors to help students.

The academic calendar consists of two 15-week semesters; during each semester, students generally take five courses. The fall semester is in session from September through December; the spring semester runs from late January through May. Courses are offered during the January intersession but are not required. Two 5-week summer sessions are also offered.

Off-Campus Programs

The College of New Rochelle offers an extensive internship program. Art students have opportunities to gain hands-on experience in art galleries and museums around the New York metropolitan area, such as the Metropolitan Museum of Art and the Guggenheim Museum, while continuing to develop their artistic talents. Communication arts majors participate in internships at numerous radio stations, newspapers, film companies, advertising and public relations firms, and national and cable broadcasting networks. Social science majors are offered opportunities with government agencies in Washington, D.C.; Albany; New York City; and Westchester, New York. Social work majors complete their fieldwork at a variety of human services agencies, and education majors gain experience through fieldwork and student teaching in local school districts and institutions. Business majors put theory into practice at companies such as Merrill Lynch and IBM, as well as at the New York Stock Exchange.

Clinical experiences for School of Nursing students take place in some of the most modern and sophisticated health-care institutions in the world, including Blythdale Children's Hospital, Hospital for Special Surgery, and Montefiore Medical Center.

Students in all academic areas are encouraged to study and travel abroad. The College works with the American Institute for Foreign Study and the Institute for European Studies. Scholarships for study abroad are also available.

Academic Facilities

The New Rochelle campus contains twenty buildings, including classroom and laboratory facilities, student residences, and centers for academic support services. In addition, the newly expanded wireless network allows Internet access from almost anywhere on campus. Each full-time, matriculating freshman or transfer student in the School of Arts and Sciences and the School of Nursing receives a laptop computer. MacBooks are given to students in the art and communication arts programs.

Our state-of-the-art Wellness Center opened its doors in the summer of 2008. Housed within the 55,000-square-foot facility are a gymnasium with basketball and volleyball courts, an interior

running track, an NCAA competition-sized swimming pool, a dance and aerobics studio, and a fitness and weight room.

The Mother Irene Gill Memorial Library holds more than 200,000 volumes in open stacks. About 3,000 new volumes are purchased each year. Holdings in education, psychology, health sciences, gerontology, and art are extensive. Renovations to the library included the addition of approximately 200 data ports and forty computer stations offering a variety of computer capabilities, including access to Gill Library's extensive online databases as well as the Internet. Gill Library is a member of an international network of libraries.

The Mooney Center provides technology and programs to assist students in the development of academic, professional, and personal lifetime goals. Facilities include state-of-the-art computer laboratories and classrooms, a computer graphics studio and desktop publishing facilities, a photography laboratory, a television studio, the Romita Auditorium, art studios and gallery space, a model classroom for student teachers, and the H. W. Taylor Institute for Entrepreneurial Studies. More than a dozen laboratories are housed in Rogick Life Science Center and Science Hall. Facilities include a research microscope room, a radiation laboratory and counting room, a plant/animal tissue-culture room, a computer room, a darkroom, a greenhouse, and laboratories set aside entirely for student research.

The Learning Center for Nursing is composed of a nursing laboratory, which simulates a hospital setting, and a multimedia laboratory equipped with four mobile television centers and a media library. The computer room in the nursing center contains computers and printers and COMMES, an artificial intelligence system that simulates a professional nursing consultant. The system supports clinical decision making by students and professional nurses.

The Sweeny Student Center houses the food service operation, featuring a variety of hot and cold food choices and an attractive, comfortable seating area; a completely renovated bookstore; centralized mailboxes for all students on campus; student activity rooms; and meeting rooms and lounge areas designed to hold large groups of people for lectures and special events.

Costs

Full-time freshman tuition for the 2011–12 academic year was $29,330. Room and board costs were $12,330. Total estimated annual costs, including travel, books, fees, and personal expenses, were $42,710.

Financial Aid

Approximately 90 percent of all freshmen receive some kind of financial aid through Pell Grants, Supplemental Educational Opportunity Grants, Federal Work-Study Program awards, institutional awards, and student loans. New York State residents are encouraged to apply for Tuition Assistance Program (TAP) awards. The College of New Rochelle offers merit scholarships and grants based on need. Merit scholarships are all based on academic achievement, community service, and leadership qualities; amounts vary from $7000 per year to $17,000 per year. All students applying for financial aid are required to fill out a College of New Rochelle Financial Aid Application and to complete the Free Application for Federal Student Aid (FAFSA).

Faculty

In no small measure, the College owes its growth and success to a highly committed faculty and administration. The faculty consists of dedicated scholars and teachers who have been recognized for excellence in teaching. Ninety percent of the faculty members hold doctoral degrees or the highest degree available in their field. No graduate students or teaching assistants teach undergraduates. Faculty advisers are available to students for consultation and guidance in academic and career planning. To supplement and complement its faculty, the College invites adjunct professors, artists, business executives, and social workers to teach courses in their areas of expertise. The student-faculty ratio is 10:1.

Student Government

The Office of Student Development and Programs oversees undergraduate extracurricular activities. The Student Government Association is comprised of elected officials and club and organization leaders.

Admission Requirements

The College is selective in its admission process and evaluates each candidate's secondary school record, class rank, grade point average, extracurricular activities, SAT (critical reading and math sections only) or ACT scores, essay, and a counselor's recommendation. The secondary school curriculum should include 16 academic units in English, mathematics, foreign language, social science, and natural science. Applicants to the School of Nursing should complete biology and chemistry lab courses plus one other science course and three years of high school mathematics, including algebra I, algebra II, and geometry. While an admission interview is not required, it is recommended. First-time and transfer students may apply for either the September or January term. Students interested in transferring to the School of Arts and Sciences must have maintained at least a 2.0 GPA at their previous institution. Students interested in transferring to the School of Nursing must have maintained at least a 3.0 GPA and earned at least a C+ in all prerequisite courses. International students are welcome and must submit scores on the Test of English as a Foreign Language (TOEFL), when necessary. A minimum TOEFL score of 550 (paper-based test) is required for admission.

Application and Information

Interested students should begin the admission process early in their senior year. The College accepts applications and renders decisions on a rolling basis. School of Nursing students should apply by the priority deadline of March 1 for the fall semester. Applications for admission are accepted until all class spaces are filled. On-campus housing is guaranteed. Enrollment deferrals are available.

For additional information about The College of New Rochelle, students should contact:

Office of Admission
The College of New Rochelle
New Rochelle, New York 10805
Phone: 800-933-5923 (toll-free)
E-mail: admission@cnr.edu
Web site: http://www.cnr.edu

New graduates of The College of New Rochelle enjoying commencement at Radio City Music Hall, New York City.

THE COLLEGE OF SAINT ROSE
ALBANY, NEW YORK

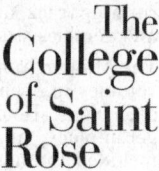

The College

The College of Saint Rose is an independent, residential, coeducational institution where academics and career preparation are top priorities. The College's progressive liberal education core prepares students to dive into one of the College's 68 undergraduate fields of study, most of which incorporate a field experience or internship component. The College offers small class sizes, with a student-faculty ratio of 14:1 and an experienced, mentoring faculty. *U.S. News & World Report* has ranked Saint Rose as one of the top colleges in the Northeast, based on such factors as affordability and high academic quality. With the capital of New York as its convenient location and a distinctly personal learning atmosphere on campus, The College of Saint Rose is a place dedicated to cultivating intellectual dynamic leaders appreciative of diversity and active citizenship.

Founded in 1920 by the Sisters of Saint Joseph of Carondelet with one house and $1000, the College today encompasses over 80 buildings, an outdoor sports complex, and an annual budget of $112 million.

Saint Rose students make up a community of leaders. Most of the 3,000 undergraduates at Saint Rose come from 16 states and 18 different countries. The College of Saint Rose actively seeks to enroll students of all backgrounds who can contribute to and benefit from the experience of shared learning and academic success.

Campus housing includes traditional, suite-style, and apartment-style residence halls and town houses as well as more than 30 Victorian homes, each with its own history and character—many with unique wraparound porches and stained-glass windows.

Students participate in organized social activities as well as 10 associations related to academic majors. The College of Saint Rose is a member of the National Collegiate Athletic Association (NCAA) Division II and the Northeast-10 Conference. Intercollegiate teams include men's baseball, lacrosse, and golf; men's and women's basketball, cross-country, soccer, swimming and diving, tennis, and track and field; and women's softball and volleyball.

Saint Rose students belong to more than 30 groups that include academic-related clubs as well as special-interest clubs. They also play in 10–15 intramural sports and produce three publications: *The Chronicle* weekly student newspaper, the *Sphere* literary magazine, and *Reflections,* the College's yearbook.

Location

Saint Rose is located in the historic Pine Hills neighborhood of Albany, New York. With more than 60,000 college students in the area, there are always things to do. A variety of restaurants, shops, museums, malls, and theaters are within walking distance or easily accessible by buses that stop at Saint Rose and are free for students to ride.

Majors and Degrees

The College of Saint Rose offers programs of study in the fields of accounting, American studies, art education (K–12), biochemistry, bioinformatics, biology, biology education (7–12), biology/cytotechnology, business administration, chemistry, chemistry education (7–12), childhood education, childhood education/special education, communication sciences and disorders, communications, computer information systems, computer science, criminal justice, early childhood education, early childhood/special education, earth science (7–12), economics, English, English education (7–12), forensic psychology, forensic science, geology, graphic design, history, history/political science, information technology, interdepartmental studies, mathematics, mathematics education (7–12), medical technology, music, music education (K–12), music industry, philosophy, political science, pre-law, pre-medicine, pre-veterinary studies, psychology, religious studies, social studies education (7–12), social work, sociology, Spanish, Spanish education (7–12), studio art, and women's studies.

Academic Programs

The College offers qualified students the opportunity to pursue accelerated bachelor's/master's degrees in approximately five years of study. The College offers these options in accounting (B.S./M.S.), business (B.S./M.B.A.), communications sciences and disorders/speech therapy (B.S./M.S.), computer science (B.S./M.S.), English (B.A./M.A.), and history (B.A./M.A.).

Qualified students may also participate in other special programs: a 3+3 option with Albany Law School, a 3+1 medical technology option with the School of Medical Technology at Rochester General Hospital, a 3+2 cytotechnology option with Albany College of Pharmacy and Health Sciences, and a 3+2 engineering option with Clarkson University and Rensselaer Polytechnic Institute. Students in these programs complete selected bachelor's degree programs at Saint Rose in three years and transfer to the cooperating institution to finish the professional program.

To earn a bachelor's degree, a student must complete a minimum of 122 credits, including, for most majors, the liberal education curriculum requirement of 41 credits, two courses in physical education, and the major requirements as specified. A minimum of 60 credits must be earned on the Saint Rose campus.

Off-Campus Programs

Saint Rose students can study in one of more than 30 countries, which is made possible by the school's affiliations with the College Consortium for International Studies, Regent's College in London, and the Center for Cross-Cultural Study. All study-abroad opportunities are offered at the same price as Saint Rose tuition (plus airfare and personal expenses), including the Saint Rose financial aid package. All credits count toward the student's degree.

Academic Facilities

The College is also known for bold investments in its facilities.

Scheduled for completion in fall 2012 is Centennial Hall, the new four-story student residence, which will house up to 224 juniors and seniors in two- and four-person furnished apartments, each with single bedrooms, a living area, and kitchen. Centennial Hall will also feature lounges, group study areas, laundry facilities, indoor bike storage, a small store, and a café.

Also slated to open in August 2012, the new Huether School of Business will dramatically enhance the academic experience of students and faculty alike providing the latest technology; additional classrooms; seminar rooms; and dedicated spaces for internship coordination, leadership, and entrepreneurship programming.

The William Randolph Hearst Center for Communications and Interactive Media features a television studio, Internet radio

station, newspaper production lab, music studio with recording lab, video projection room, and multimedia computer labs.

The Christian Plumeri Sports Complex, with a baseball field, softball field, and an artificial turf soccer/lacrosse field as well as a natural grass practice field, is home to the Saint Rose Golden Knights, who have regularly won bids to Northeast-10 conference and Division II national tournaments, as well as for the College's intramural and club sports.

The College's Massry Center for the Arts is a distinctive facility that provides musical and visual artists a prime environment to learn and showcase their work to the College community and the public. The 46,000-square-foot facility features a state-of-the-art performance hall, acoustically congruent and separate instrumental and choral rehearsal suites, applied teaching studios, piano keyboard laboratories, smart classrooms, and a bright, spacious art gallery.

The Picotte Center for Art and Design houses the student art gallery as well as extensive photography labs, graphic design computers, and one of the largest screen-printing facilities in the state of New York.

Science and mathematics majors have access to the latest equipment and research facilities in the College's 27,000-square-foot Science Center, including new geology and earth science labs, a neuroscience lab for psychology students, and dedicated space for undergraduate student/faculty research.

The 56,000-square-foot Thelma P. Lally School of Education features a multimedia education forum; classrooms; computer labs; offices; and a speech, hearing, and special education clinic that serves the public.

In the Events and Athletics Center (E&AC), the Nolan Gymnasium serves as a unique collegiate basketball venue in the Capital Region, large enough to accommodate the Golden Knights' loyal fan base. In addition, the E&AC has welcomed best-selling authors, Nobel Prize winners, and world-famous performers. The College's main dining hall, also in the E&AC, was recently renovated to resemble a hip restaurant and has a nationally award-winning chef to match.

Saint Joseph Hall, one of the College's original buildings, was renovated, making the building a student service hub centralized around the College's Student Solution Center.

Costs

Tuition for 2012–13 is $25,722. Room and board costs average $10,870 per year, depending on the meal plan chosen by the student. Estimated annual costs for books and personal expenses are $1000 and $1400, respectively.

Financial Aid

More than 98 percent of the students receive scholarships and financial assistance. The College of Saint Rose participates in the Federal Pell Grant, FSEOG, TAP, Federal Work-Study, and Federal Perkins Loan and Federal Stafford Loan programs. The College provides aid in the form of grants, service awards, and scholarships for need or academic achievement. Candidates for financial assistance must file the Free Application for Federal Student Aid. ISIR and SAR forms should be on file in the Financial Aid Office by March 1. Students interested in being considered for academic scholarships must apply to the College by February 1.

Faculty

Saint Rose has a full-time faculty of 220 members, with a student-faculty ratio of 14:1. The average class size is 20–25 students, with more than 55 percent of classes having less than 20 students.

Student Government

The Student Association (SA) consists of elected students that manage the student activity budgets, appoint representatives to College policymaking committees, and assist individual students and clubs in planning and carrying out projects. SA also oversees the College's 30 clubs and organizations.

Admission Requirements

The College wishes to admit students who show evidence of strong academic motivation and the ability to benefit from a challenging liberal arts and professional education. The average high school GPA of an incoming freshman is 88–93, and 90 percent of freshmen ranked in the top half of their high school class. Admission decisions are made after careful study of all the data available for each candidate. Interviews are strongly recommended but not required. Freshman applicants should submit a high school transcript, a letter of recommendation from a teacher or guidance counselor, an essay or graded paper, and scores on the SAT or ACT.

Transfer applicants must submit high school and college transcripts, a letter of recommendation from a college instructor, and a written statement of the reasons for transfer.

Application and Information

The College has an early action (nonbinding) application deadline of December 1. Students are accepted for admission for the fall and spring semesters on a rolling admissions basis. Interested students must apply by February 1 to be considered for academic scholarships ranging from $5000 to $14,000 for each undergraduate year. New students who are accepted for admission are asked to submit a $300 enrollment deposit to secure their place in the new class.

Information on all aspects of the campus and the academic programs can be obtained by contacting the Office of Admissions. This office also can arrange personal interviews, campus tours, classroom visits, and overnight accommodations.

Office of Undergraduate Admissions
The College of Saint Rose
432 Western Avenue
Albany, New York 12203
Phone: 518-454-5150
        800-637-8556 (toll-free)
Fax: 518-454-2013
E-mail: admit@strose.edu (admissions)
        finaid@strose.edu (financial aid)
Web site: http://www.strose.edu
        http://facebook.com/TheCollegeofSaintRose

Located in the historic Pine Hills neighborhood of Albany, New York, the Saint Rose campus features a mix of classic brick buildings and new stone and glass structures, with the Campus Green at its center.

COLLEGE OF STATEN ISLAND OF THE CITY UNIVERSITY OF NEW YORK
STATEN ISLAND, NEW YORK

CSI **CU NY**

The College and The University

Founded in 1976 from the merger of two existing colleges, the College of Staten Island (CSI) is a four-year senior college within the City University of New York (CUNY) and is Staten Island's only public institution of higher learning. CSI is dedicated to both access and excellence and currently serves over 14,100 students.

The College of Staten Island was established through the union of Staten Island Community College (CUNY's first community college, founded in 1955) and Richmond College (CUNY's first upper-division college, founded in 1965).

Offering over eighty programs and areas of study, the College ensures that students receive a thorough liberal arts education through core requirements that include classes in the arts and humanities, mathematics, science, and social sciences.

In addition to the exciting array of undergraduate degrees and majors available, CSI also awards the Master of Arts degree in cinema and media studies, English, environmental science, history, and liberal studies; the Master of Science degree in biology, computer science, neuroscience, mental retardation and developmental disabilities, and nursing: adult health and gerontological; and the Master of Science in Education degree in childhood education, adolescence, and special education in a selection of concentrations. Post-master's advanced certificates are offered in leadership in education, nursing: nursing education, and nursing: cultural competence.

The graduate teacher education program prepares students to teach at the early childhood, elementary, and secondary levels. The academic work and field experience meet the requirements for the certification and licensing examinations given by the state and city of New York.

Further, CSI offers doctoral programs jointly with the CUNY Graduate School in biochemistry, biology, polymer chemistry, computer science, physical therapy, and physics.

By fall 2013, CSI is slated to offer students an opportunity to live in luxury accommodations on campus. Currently under construction are two buildings with four and five stories that will contain 133 furnished apartments housing 454 residents. The buildings will offer both private and semi-private bedroom accommodations with semi-private bathrooms for residents. Housing will be filled on a first-come, first-served basis.

Location

CSI is located on a sprawling 204-acre campus located in the heart of Staten Island. The campus is the largest single site for a college, public or private, within New York City. With its scenic landscape, the grounds and facilities create a rural oasis in an urban setting. Classrooms and academic offices are located in fourteen neo-Georgian buildings that form two quadrangles connected by the campus walk, which extends between the library and the Campus Center. Five well-built and equipped buildings—the library, the Campus Center, the Biological Sciences/Chemical Sciences building, the Center for the Arts, and the Sports and Recreation Center—provide outstanding facilities for scholastic and community activities.

CSI's location offers students the best of two worlds, with Staten Island providing a suburban environment with some of the most interesting landscapes in the metropolitan area; and Manhattan, the center of cultural and social life of the city, being only 25 minutes from the island by ferry. The Verrazano-Narrows Bridge provides direct access between Staten Island and Brooklyn.

Majors and Degrees

CSI offers an Associate in Arts and an Associate in Science degree. The Associate in Applied Science degree is offered in business, computer technology, and nursing.

The Bachelor of Arts degree is conferred in African American studies; American studies; art, art with a studio art or art history concentration, cinema studies; economics; English; English

with a writing, linguistics, literature, and dramatic literature concentration; history; international studies; Italian studies (new); modern languages; music; philosophy; political science; psychology; science, letters, and society; sociology-anthropology; social work; Spanish; and women's, gender, and sexuality studies.

The Bachelor of Science degree is offered in accounting; art with a photography concentration; biochemistry; bioinformatics; biology; business with concentrations in finance, international business, management, or marketing; chemistry; communications with a journalism, media studies, design and digital media, or corporate communications concentration; computer science, computer science/mathematics; dramatic arts; economics; economics with a business or finance specialization; engineering science with a computer/electrical/mechanical specialization; mathematics; medical technology; music; music with an electronics concentration; nursing (upper-division program); pre-professional studies in dentistry, medicine, optometry, podiatry, and law; and physics.

Academic Programs

CSI offers two-year programs in career areas and in liberal arts and sciences and four-year programs with majors in the traditional fields of study. General education requirements have been established for all degrees. The associate degree programs require 60–64 credits, depending on the field; the bachelor's degree programs generally require 120 credits. Credit may be awarded for internships and independent study, and credit may also be earned by examination (CLEP) and for experiential learning. Minors are an additional 30 credits, and double majors are an additional 60 credits. Students may graduate with honors in most bachelor's degree majors.

The College follows a two-semester calendar, with classes scheduled both day and evening. The Office of Weekend and Evening Services offers a variety of course combinations leading to associate and bachelor's degrees, providing opportunities for nontraditional students with weekday career commitments to pursue a college education at more convenient times. Intensive summer and winter sessions are also offered to students who would like to accelerate their degrees.

Selective Programs: The College of Staten Island offers a number of selective academic programs, learning communities, and undergraduate research opportunities. Our programs include Macaulay Honors College at CSI (MHC): a full scholarship program that provides high achieving students with a special honors curriculum of innovative and challenging courses during the first and second years of study; the Verrazano School, a local honors program designed to offer students a unique undergraduate education through academically motivated learning communities; Teacher Education Honors Academy at CSI (TEHA), a scholarship program designed to highly train select students majoring in mathematics, biology, chemistry, or physics to teach in DOE middle and high schools; and the Science and Technology Expansion through Applied Mathematics program (STEAM), which supports undergraduate education and research in all areas of science, technology, engineering, and mathematics in the form of scholarships and grants.

Off-Campus Programs

The College gives a number of courses for credit at off-campus locations throughout the city through internships at major corporations and other fieldwork. Exceptional study-abroad opportunities are available through CSI's Center for International Service which offers students the option of earning academic credit for study in Belgium, China, Denmark, Ecuador, England, Greece, Italy, Japan, or Spain.

Academic Facilities

The academic buildings are designed to house approximately 300 state-of-the-art laboratories and classrooms, each with its own computer lab, study lounge for students, departmental program, and faculty offices. Academic and research programs are served by

a computer network that allows students and faculty full access to specialized software, the Internet, online library resources, and e-mail within a wireless environment.

The Campus Center incorporates cocurricular activities for a complete personal growth experience. The two-story rotunda at the heart of the structure contains the main dining facilities, the College's health services, a bookstore, offices for student organizations, study and sleep lounges, a small performance/café space, game rooms with the latest game consoles, and the state-of-the-art studios of WSIA, the student-operated FM radio station.

The Center for the Arts complex provides facilities for teaching in the instructional wing and areas of public assembly in the public wing. The complex of public facilities includes a 900-seat auditorium, a 450-seat fully equipped theater, a recital hall, an experimental theater, art galleries, and a conference center. Classrooms, lecture halls, studios, and offices for faculty members are located in the instructional wing.

The CSI Library is staffed with 12 full-time librarians and 10 adjunct librarians who also hold faculty status and rank. In addition, the library has 40 support staff members. The library's total collection consists of approximately 250,000 books, 150,000 eBooks, 215 print journal subscriptions, 53,000 electronic journals, 190 electronic resources, 3,500 films and videos, and more than 5,000 sound recordings. The library's online catalog, CUNY+Plus, provides complete access to the collections, including access to holdings of other CUNY libraries. Students also have electronic access to database and research tools 24 hours a day via the Internet. In addition, the library maintains a collection of current textbooks donated by the CSI Student Government. These and other course materials are available at the Reserve Desk. Wireless laptops are loaned to students for use throughout the library. The library building also houses the Office of Academic Support and the Cybercafé, which offers Starbucks® coffee.

The laboratory science building provides facilities for teaching and for two research centers: the Center for Environmental Science and the Center for Developmental Neuroscience and Developmental Disabilities. It consists of a research wing and an instructional wing. State-of-the-art laboratories serve students and faculty members in their teaching and research.

The CSI Astrophysical Observatory is a world-class resource that has been recognized by the International Astronomical Union as an official asteroid-tracking station.

The Sports and Recreation Center is a 77,000-square-foot multipurpose facility providing basketball, handball/paddleball, racquetball, and volleyball courts; locker rooms; a gym; instructional areas; an indoor eight-lane 25-meter swimming pool; and offices for faculty members. Recreational fields occupy the meadows in the northwest quadrant of the campus, providing a green and landscaped open area at the main approach to the campus that includes a running track, indoor and outdoor tennis courts, soccer field, handball/paddleball courts, softball fields, and semiprofessional baseball field (original home field to the Staten Island Yankees).

Costs

For 2012–13, undergraduate tuition for New York State residents (NYS) is $230 per credit for resident part-time matriculated students, $2715 per semester for resident full-time matriculated students, and $340 per credit for resident nondegree students. Nonresident full- and part-time students are charged $485 per credit, and nonresident nondegree students are charged $720 per credit. Graduate NYS resident tuition is $4345 per semester for students attending the College full-time and $365 per credit for resident part-time students. Nonresidents are charged $675 per credit for full- and part-time attendance.

Financial Aid

Financial aid is available through state and Federal programs and includes the New York State Tuition Assistance Program (TAP) awards, Federal Pell Grants, Federal Supplemental Educational Opportunity Grants (FSEOG), Search for Elevation and Education through Knowledge (SEEK) awards, Federal Work-Study Program awards, and student loan programs. Information about programs, application procedures, and deadlines is available from the Financial Aid Office.

CSI Presidential Scholarships are awarded annually to full-time students based on academic merit and service. In addition, endowments have been established for merit-based scholarships in a number of fields. Further information about scholarships is available from the Career and Scholarship Center.

Faculty

The College has a full-time faculty of 319, of whom approximately 92 percent hold a doctoral degree or the equivalent. These faculty members have made significant contributions in many areas of scholarship, creativity, and public service. Numerous faculty members have received prestigious grants and awards, and more than 30 serve as members of CUNY's doctoral faculty.

Student Government

A single body (Senate) comprised of 25 elected students represents the interests of the College's students, serving as liaison to faculty and administrators. The Senate derives funding from the Student Activity Fee, and through its various commissions and committees, it sponsors many academic and nonacademic programs.

Admission Requirements

A freshman applicant for admission to a bachelor degree program must pass the CUNY Assessment Tests (CATs) in reading, writing, and mathematics unless he or she qualifies for exemption based on the SAT, ACT, or Regents Examination scores. Admission to a bachelor's degree program is determined by a profile based on the applicant's high school courses, academic average, and the combined verbal and mathematics SAT scores. An applicant whose score reaches or exceeds the College's minimum index number is admitted to a bachelor's degree program. A faculty admissions committee may consider the admission of applicants whose scores approach the College's minimum index number. Students transferring to baccalaureate programs who have fewer than 25 credits must have a GPA of at least 2.00 and must meet freshman entrance criteria. Students must pass the CATs prior to enrolling in a bachelor degree program or if they are transferring from another college in CUNY.

Entering first-year students may be admitted to associate-level programs if they have graduated from an accredited high school or have earned an equivalency diploma (GED) with a satisfactory score.

As a general rule, the College requires a grade point average equivalent of 2.00 for transfer as a matriculated student into a two-year degree program.

Application and Information

Requests for further information and application materials should be directed to:

College of Staten Island
The City University of New York
Office of Recruitment and Admissions, Building 2A, Room 103
Staten Island, New York 10314
Phone: 718-982-2010
E-mail: admissions@csi.cuny.edu
Web site: www.csi.cuny.edu

The CSI Library offers electronic access to database and research tools 24 hours a day via the Internet, in addition to maintaining a collection of current textbooks donated by the CSI Student Government.

THE COLLEGE OF WOOSTER
WOOSTER, OHIO

The College

The College of Wooster is America's premier college for mentored undergraduate research. The academic program built around those research experiences helps every student develop abilities prized by employers and graduate schools alike: independent judgment, analytical ability, creativity, project- and time-management skills, self confidence, and strong written and oral communication skills.

Founded as a Presbyterian college in 1866, Wooster has been an independent, residential college of the liberal arts and sciences since 1969. With small classes (61 percent have fewer than 20 students) and an 11:1 student-faculty ratio, students receive close attention both in and out of the classroom. More information can be found at http://www.wooster.edu/About-Wooster.

Wooster's nearly 2,000 students come from forty-seven states and forty-one countries, from all backgrounds and life experiences. Wooster's distinctive sense of spirit is evident to visitors on campus.

Ninety-six percent of Wooster students live on campus. First-year students live together in various residence halls, and roommate matches are made using the Myers Briggs Personality test. After the first year, the options multiply. Wooster's program houses allow students to live with a group of 7 to 14 others and work on a service project in the community throughout the year (http://www.wooster.edu/Student-Life/Residence-Life).

Close to a third of Wooster students follow their passion for making music through three choirs, a symphony orchestra, symphonic and marching bands, a jazz ensemble, four a cappella groups, and other ensembles (http://www.wooster.edu/Music-and-the-Arts). Another third participate in intercollegiate athletics. Wooster has produced 45 All Americans in eleven sports in the past six years and won sixty-seven NCAC championships since 1985 (http://www.woosterathletics.com).

From the improv group Don't Throw Shoes, to the student-run investment club (managing a $2-million portfolio for the College's endowment), and the cricket team to the radio station, there is something for just about every interest.

Location

The College is located in Wooster, Ohio, a vibrant city of 26,000 with a strong, diversified economy; a downtown full of great restaurants and shops; national chains like Starbucks, Panera, and Kohl's; and easy access to outdoor recreation opportunities. Wooster's business community is strong and growing, and provides opportunities for Wooster students both before and after graduation. Wooster is 55 miles southwest of Cleveland and 30 miles southwest of Akron.

Majors and Degrees

The College of Wooster offers the degrees of Bachelor of Arts, Bachelor of Music, and Bachelor of Music Education (http://www.wooster.edu/Academics/Areas-of-Study). A student may choose from more than fifty-five majors and programs of study, including Africana studies; anthropology; ancient Mediterranean studies, archaeology; art history; art–studio; biochemistry and molecular biology; biology; business economics; chemical physics; chemistry; Chinese studies; classical studies (Greek, Latin, classical civilization); communication sciences and disorders; communication studies; comparative literature; computer science; East Asian Studies; economics; English; French; geology; German studies; history; international relations; mathematics; music; music education; music history and literature; music performance; music theory–composition; music therapy; neuroscience; philosophy; physics; political science; psychology; religious studies; Russian studies; sociology; Spanish; student-designed major (e.g., journalism, sports medicine); theater and dance; urban studies; and women's, gender, and sexuality studies. In addition, minors are available in most areas as well as education (with licensure in elementary or secondary teaching), environmental studies, film studies, international business, Latin American studies, physical education, and South Asian Studies.

Wooster offers dual-degree programs in cooperation with other institutions that lead to either two bachelor's degrees (one from each institution) or a bachelor's degree from Wooster and a master's from the cooperating institution. The dual-degree programs are in the areas of architecture, dentistry, engineering, forestry and environmental studies, nursing, polymer science, and social work.

The College's preprofessional advising programs provide students with advice on the development of an appropriate academic program, cocurricular and volunteer experiences, guidance on summer research opportunities, lectures by leaders in the various professions, and information about the process of selecting and applying to graduate and professional schools. Wooster's preprofessional programs are in the areas of architecture, business, engineering, forestry and environmental studies, heath professions, law, seminary studies, and social work.

Academic Programs

Students begin their academic journey with First-Year Seminar, a writing-intensive course that exercises their intellect and sharpens their critical faculties (http://www.wooster.edu/Academics). In a class of no more than 15, with a professor who is also their academic adviser, students approach a wide range of texts, questioning and analyzing them to tease out meaning and then formulating arguments through extensive writing and discussion.

To ensure that they are conversant with forms of inquiry and discourse in a range of disciplines, students select courses in each of three areas: arts and humanities, history and social sciences, and mathematical and natural sciences. They also gain insight into other cultures through a course in global and cultural perspectives and another in religious perspectives.

Once a major is selected, students engage with the scholarship of that field, master its particular methodologies, and have numerous opportunities to work with faculty members on research projects (as early as the second semester of the first year), participate in internships, or study abroad.

It all culminates in the senior Independent Study (I.S.) project. Working one-on-one with a faculty adviser over the course of a year, students conduct research, create art, or shape a performance that demonstrates their understanding of a discipline and their ability to communicate that knowledge to others. Although called Independent Study, it is a deeply collaborative journey that the student and the faculty adviser take together. In effect, students are guaranteed a 1:1 student-faculty ratio for one class each semester of their senior year. In weekly one-on-one meetings, the adviser helps refine and focus the topic, suggests areas for exploration, asks questions that provoke thought and creativity, and evaluates progress. Students, in turn, review and synthesize literature related to the subject, plan and conduct research in the lab, or work to realize a creative vision in the studio, recital hall, or theater. Students present drafts of their work to their advisers, who offer feedback as close collaborators.

If the I.S. project requires travel or special equipment or supplies, the College's Henry J. Copeland Fund for Independent Study can help. In a typical year, the fund disburses almost $100,000 to support a diverse array of student projects, from studying the lives of West African immigrants in Paris or producing a documentary on survivors of Hiroshima to researching ways to purify methane gas to permit its use as a renewable energy source. When the I.S. is complete, students may find themselves presenting the results at a national conference in their discipline or coauthoring papers with their advisers. (Geology professor Mark Wilson has published articles with more than 40 student coauthors.)

Throughout the I.S. project, students learn how to analyze a problem, gather and evaluate information, propose a solution, test its validity, and communicate the results clearly and persuasively. The completed I.S. gives employers tangible proof of resourcefulness, creativity, and communication skills. It also marks the student as an independent scholar who is ready to take on graduate-level research wherever his or her interests lead, which is why Wooster ranks

twenty-eighth overall among all liberal arts colleges for graduates who have gone on to earn a Ph.D., seventh in the physical sciences, twentieth in geology, thirty-seventh in math and computer science, and forty-first in life sciences.

To get a full sense of the range of possibilities, students can check out the I.S. database or listen to Wooster students talk about their projects at http://www.wooster.edu (click on Independent Study).

Off-Campus Programs

Students who wish to enrich their undergraduate experience by off-campus study may choose from a variety of fully accredited programs (http://www.wooster.edu/Academics/Off-Campus-Study). Wooster sponsors a number of its own off-campus programs in the United States and abroad, and through its membership in the Great Lakes Colleges Association and its affiliations, offers off-campus study opportunities in more than fifty countries spanning the globe.

A variety of off-campus opportunities within the United States provide both academic and internship experiences. The Washington Semester and the Semester at the United Nations offer extensive possibilities in national and international government. There is also a fine-arts semester in New York City. Other internship possibilities exist in business, the humanities, the natural sciences, and psychology.

Academic Facilities

The College libraries consist of the Andrews Library, the adjacent Flo K. Gault Library for Independent Study, and the nearby Timken Science Library in Frick Hall. Together, they contain more than 1 million books, periodicals, microforms, electronic journals, videotapes, and audio recordings. As a member of CONSORT and OhioLINK, the libraries can provide almost any book from Ohio's academic libraries within two to three days. The libraries subscribe to a wide variety of electronic databases and to some 5,000 periodicals in electronic form, all available campuswide via the computing network. The libraries house more than 300 study carrels, each of which is equipped with electrical and data connections.

The Collaborative Research Environment, or CoRE, is the latest addition to Andrews Library: a place for students to brainstorm ideas, work together on projects using digital and traditional media, or present their work to others.

All academic buildings and residence hall rooms are connected to the campus network, and secure wireless service is available throughout campus.

The College's science facilities contain the most up-to-date laboratory equipment, libraries, technology, and instrumentation, including ultraviolet, visible, fluorescence, and infrared spectrometers; a scanning electron microscope; an atomic force microscope; a nuclear magnetic resonance spectrometer; a mass spectrometer; an X-ray diffractometer; and various chromatographs.

Wooster's Learning Center provides academic support for students, and priority is given to students with identified learning disabilities. Professional staff work with individual students on time management, organization skills, and effective study strategies. The Writing Center provides writing assistance through one-to-one tutorial sessions and group workshops.

The Freedlander Theatre complex contains excellent technical equipment and a separate theater for students' experimental productions. The speech facility houses a radio station and a speech and hearing clinic that also serves the community.

The Scheide Music Center, a 35,000-square-foot complex, contains five classrooms, eleven teaching studios, twenty-three soundproof practice rooms, a music library, and a listening lab. The Timken Rehearsal Hall and the acoustically balanced Gault Recital Hall are "tunable" so that the halls can be rendered "live" to greater or lesser degrees.

The Ebert Art Center has space for studio art and art history. The building includes classrooms, individual studios for senior studio art majors, and the Sussel and Burton D. Morgan Art Galleries.

Costs

The comprehensive fee (room, board, tuition, and fees) for 2012–13 is $49,400. More information is available at http://www.wooster.edu/Admissions-and-Financial-Aid/Tuition-and-Fees.

Financial Aid

Financial assistance is awarded on merit and/or need (http://www.wooster.edu/Admissions-and-Financial-Aid/Financial-Aid).

Need-based aid is determined by the Free Application for Federal Student Aid (FAFSA). Applications for need-based aid should be submitted by February 15.

The College of Wooster believes in recognizing individual talent and hard work. Thus, Wooster offers merit-based scholarships ranging from $2000 to $20,000 in a number of academic, performance, and leadership areas. All scholarship awards are applicable only toward tuition and are renewable for four years (http://www.wooster.edu/Admissions/scholarships).

Faculty

Faculty members, 96 percent of whom hold a doctoral degree or terminal degree in their field, are dedicated to meeting the educational needs of individual students; they strive to help them realize their inherent potential.

Student Government

The Campus Council, which consists of representatives from the student body, faculty, and administration, is the main legislative body in the areas of student life and cocurricular affairs. The Student Government Association, the Black Students Association, and the International Student Association also contribute to policymaking at Wooster. Students may attend open meetings of the faculty and are represented on several faculty committees.

Admission Requirements

A list of admissions requirements and the steps in the application process can be found online at www.wooster.edu/admissions/apply.

The deadline for regular admission is February 15 with admissions notifications sent by April 1 and a reply deadline of May 1. Wooster offers two early decision deadlines; EDI deadline is November 1, notification is November 15 and reply deadline is December 1; EDII deadline is January 15, notification is February 1 and reply deadline is February 15. Early action candidates must apply by November 15 and are notified by December 31 (http://www.wooster.edu/Admissions/Apply). Students are encouraged to visit the campus and have a personal interview (http://www.wooster.edu/Admissions/visit).

The College of Wooster does not discriminate on the basis of age, sex, race, creed, national origin, handicap, sexual orientation, political affiliation, or veteran or military status in the admission of students or in their participation in College educational programs, activities, financial aid, or employment.

Application and Information

Office of Admissions
The College of Wooster
Wooster, Ohio 44691
Phone: 330-263-2000 Ext. 2270 or 2322
          800-877-9905 (toll-free)
Fax: 330-263-2621
E-mail: admissions@wooster.edu
Web site: http://www.wooster.edu
          http://www.facebook.com/#!/CollegeofWooster
          http://twitter.com/woosteredu

The campus at the College of Wooster.

COLUMBIA COLLEGE CHICAGO
CHICAGO, ILLINOIS

The College

Columbia College Chicago is the largest and most diverse private nonprofit arts and media college in the nation. The College offers a four-year liberal arts education specifically tailored for a community of highly motivated students who want to turn their creative talents into fulfilling, rewarding careers. The student body is comprised of approximately 12,000 students who come from all 50 states and 41 countries. When considering applicants, the College performs a holistic review of the whole student—not just test scores or class rank—and then provides the rigorous academics and unparalleled resources necessary to be successful in a highly competitive twenty-first century marketplace.

Columbia offers bachelor's degrees in more than 120 programs of study in the arts, media, and communications. The curriculum is designed to provide students with practical, real-world understanding of their chosen fields and to prepare them to meet professional expectations. Columbia's faculty members are industry insiders (artists, designers, writers, filmmakers, marketers, journalists, musicians, entrepreneurs, dancers) with national reputations. They are gifted, award-winning instructors who are able to share their first-hand experience with students both in and out of the classroom. This interaction with faculty members who are practicing professionals themselves provides students with access to valuable expertise, insight, viewpoints, and industry-current aesthetics.

The College hosts close to 700 on-campus events each year, including film screenings, student-produced television shows, dance concerts, readings, plays, radio broadcasts, music concerts, gallery openings, the annual Mary Blood Ball, and the 24-Hour Night celebration.

When students aren't showing at campus galleries, writing for the student magazine and award-winning newspaper, performing on stage, attending screenings, freestyling at poetry slams, producing shows for television and radio stations, or taking an active role in the College's 85+ social and academic clubs and organizations, they are interacting with the larger Chicago community around them. The presence of Columbia's students can be felt in theaters, bookstores, nightclubs, concert venues, museums, and media outlets throughout the city, and every spring Columbia returns the favor by inviting Chicago to its doorstep for Manifest, the city's largest student arts exhibition.

Location

Columbia is located in an eclectic, urban area of Chicago's historic South Loop neighborhood. Close by are several other colleges and universities, Navy Pier, the Adler Planetarium, the Art Institute, the Field Museum, the Chicago Symphony, the Museum of Contemporary Art, the Harold Washington Library, and the Goodman Theatre. Convenient public transportation allows Columbia's faculty and students to utilize the whole city as a social, cultural, educational, and professional resource, effectively turning the entire city into the campus. The central location and easy access to public transportation allows and encourages Columbia students to use the entire city as their campus.

Majors and Degrees

Columbia awards the Bachelor of Arts (B.A.), Bachelor of Fine Arts (B.F.A.), Bachelor of Science (B.S.), and Bachelor of Music (B.M.).

The School of Fine and Performing Arts offers majors in art and design (advertising art direction, art and design, art history, fine arts, graphic design, illustration, interior architecture, and product design); arts, entertainment, and media management (advanced management, live and performing arts management, media management, music business management, sports management, and visual arts management); dance (pedagogy, dancemaking); fashion studies (fashion design, fashion business); fiction writing (fiction writing, playwriting); music (composition; contemporary, urban, and popular music; instrumental performance; instrumental

jazz; vocal performance); photography; and theater (acting, directing, musical theater, theater, technical theater, and theater design).

The School of Media Arts offers majors in acoustics; audio arts and acoustics (audio for visual media, audio design and production, live sound reinforcement); film and video (animation, cinema studies, cinematography, directing, documentary, post-production, producing, screenwriting, sound for cinema,); interactive arts and media (game design, interactive arts and media); journalism (broadcast journalism, magazine writing/editing, news reporting and writing, and science reporting); marketing communication (advertising, marketing, and public relations); radio; television (internet and mobile media, post-production/effects, production/directing, writing/producing).

The School of Liberal Arts and Sciences offers majors in American Sign Language–English interpretation (ASL-English); humanities, history, and social sciences (cultural studies); education (early childhood education, teacher certification); English (creative writing–poetry, creative writing–nonfiction); and science and mathematics (art and materials conservation).

Academic Programs

Degree requirements are as follows: B.A. degree, 120 credits, 42 in the liberal arts and sciences (LAS) core curriculum; B.F.A. degree, 128 credits as designated by department, 36 in the LAS core; B.Mus. degree, 128 credits, 84 in music, 36 in LAS core; B.S. degree, 128 credits as designated by department, 36 in LAS core.

At the graduate level, Columbia College Chicago awards the Master of Arts (M.A.) in dance/movement therapy and counseling, interdisciplinary arts, and journalism; the Master of Fine Arts (M.F.A.) in creative writing–fiction (with the opportunity to earn a combined M.A. in the teaching of writing), creative writing–poetry, creative writing—nonfiction, film and video—creative producing, film and video—screen directing, interdisciplinary arts and media, interdisciplinary book and paper arts, music composition for the screen, and photography; the Master of Arts in Teaching (M.A.T.) in art education and elementary education; and the Master of Arts Management (M.A.M.) in arts, entertainment, and media management. Columbia also offers three certificate programs in the field of dance/movement therapy: the graduate Laban certificate in movement analysis, the alternate route certificate, and the movement pattern analysis consultant certificate.

Columbia also has an extensive internship program that offers its students access to some of the most renowned corporations and institutions in the world. The College believes that exposing students to real-world working environments is an invaluable element of their education and provides them with the necessary professional balance they will need upon graduation.

Columbia College Chicago's Portfolio Center is uniquely geared to assist students with professional-grade portfolio development. The Portfolio Center links industry professionals and alumni with current students through workshops, portfolio development sessions, and networking events. The Porfolio Center also maintains Talent Pool, a unique "3-D" portfolio tool that allows students to show off their work while simultaneously connecting with both their peers and industry professionals. Students are expected to graduate with a working portfolio suitable for professional presentation.

Open to all students, Columbia's Learning Studio is an academic support center designed to help students navigate Columbia's rigorous and creative curriculum by providing a comfortable space where students can find support for their individual learning needs and styles. Services include tutoring in math, science, and writing; peer study groups; and services for students with disabilities.

Off-Campus Programs

Columbia College offers several study-abroad opportunities through both student exchange and individual departmental programs. Among the countries in which students may have the opportunity

to study are Austria, the Czech Republic, England, France, Ireland, Italy, and Mexico.

Columbia also offers domestic off-campus training programs. Comedy studies is a full semester's worth of immersive study in comedic literature, history, writing, and performance under the experts in comedy at Chicago's Second City. Also, the semester in Los Angeles is a semester-long immersion program open to all students in which they gain invaluable real-world experience at Raleigh Studios in Hollywood, California.

Academic Facilities

Columbia College consists of 23 campus buildings in the historic South Loop neighborhood of downtown Chicago that house advanced facilities for radio, television, art, computer graphics, photography, interactive arts and media, fashion design, and film. These facilities are state-of-the-industry and include professionally equipped color and black-and-white darkrooms, digital imaging resources, photography and film stages, film and video editing suites, and studios for painting, drawing, and 3-D design. The campus also includes the Museum of Contemporary Photography (one of only two such facilities in the United States), and the Audio Technology Center (a recording production and research facility). In 2010 the College opened the state-of-the-art Media Production Center, a multimedia education and production complex that houses two soundstages, digital classrooms, labs, and a motion-capture studio. The dance, music, and theater departments have separate centers, and each is designed for their program's individual rehearsal and performance needs. In addition, Columbia has extensive computer facilities for use by students, as well as dedicated computer resources geared for specific departmental needs.

The College's library contains 258,000 volumes and provides open study spaces and group study rooms for collaborative research and study. The library houses the College Archives, Special Collections, and comprehensive collections in the visual, performing, media and communication arts. The library also subscribes to more than 1,000 journals and magazines and over 100 electronic databases. As a member of a statewide online computer catalog and resource-sharing network, the library provides students with access to the resources of 76 academic institutions and millions of books.

Costs

For the 2012–13 academic year, full tuition (12 to 16 credit hours) is $10,600 for each fifteen-week semester, or $21,200 per year. Part-time tuition (up to 11 credit hours) is $732 per credit hour. Summer school tuition is $586 per credit hour. Some courses require additional service or laboratory fees.

To enroll, applicants are required to confirm their decision by submitting a $250 tuition deposit (nonrefundable after May 1). Required nonrefundable fees that are charged each semester include the registration fee, $50; the student activity fee, $85 ($45 for part-time students); the U-Pass, $100 (for unlimited access to the public transportation system); and a health center fee, $40 ($25 for part-time students). There is also a one-time $30 library deposit that is refunded when the student leaves the College.

Financial Aid

Columbia makes every effort to help students obtain financial assistance, including grants, on-campus work, and loans. The Office of Student Financial Services administers federal and state grant and loan programs. The College also provides information for students seeking part-time employment both on and off campus. On-campus jobs are available in technical, clerical, secretarial, and food service areas.

Columbia College Chicago offers a variety of scholarships for incoming and continuing students. Scholarships offered are based on one or more of the following criteria: financial need, academic merit, creative accomplishments, and area of study. Information about scholarship opportunities, application forms, and general information about financial aid is available through the Office of Undergraduate Admissions.

Faculty

Many of the college's 1,540 full- and part-time faculty members are working professionals (artists, writers, filmmakers, marketers, journalists, etc.) with national reputations. They are gifted instructors and are able to share practical expertise with students in informal workshop settings and in the classroom. Interaction with faculty members who are practicing professionals provides students with invaluable access to the latest information in their fields. Students also begin developing their own professional network as faculty members share contacts and information on how to break into the market.

Admission Requirements

Columbia College invites applications from all students interested in studying the arts, media, and communication disciplines. Columbia does not require portfolios or previous experience in any discipline to be considered for admission. To apply for admission, all students must submit high school transcripts, a letter of recommendation, a personal essay, and a $35 application fee. ACT or SAT scores are not required but are strongly encouraged. Graduation from high school or an earned GED certificate is a requirement for admission consideration. Transfer students must submit transcripts from all other colleges and universities attended. Freshman applicants whose application materials suggest they are likely to be underprepared to meet the College's standards will be denied admission to the College. In some cases students may be required to successfully complete the Bridge Program before being admitted to the College.

Application and Information

Students are strongly advised to apply early. The priority date is May 1 for the fall semester, November 15 for the spring semester, and April 15 for the summer term. Applicants are notified of their admission decision within three to four weeks after the College receives all the required information and documents. Students who want to live in on-campus housing are strongly advised to apply early. Housing assignments are offered on a first-come, first-served basis until full occupancy is achieved.

All students are strongly encouraged to tour the College. To arrange for a tour, students should call the Office of Undergraduate Admissions or sign up online.

For more information, students should contact:

Office of Undergraduate Admissions
Columbia College Chicago
600 South Michigan Avenue
Chicago, Illinois 60605
Phone: 312-344-7130
Fax: 312-344-8024
E-mail: admissions@colum.edu
Web site: http://www.colum.ed

COLUMBIA UNIVERSITY
Columbia College/The Fu Foundation School of Engineering and Applied Science
NEW YORK, NEW YORK

The University

In 1754, King George II granted a charter to a group of New York citizens to found King's College, dedicated to instruction in "the Learned Languages and the Liberal Arts and Sciences." In its early days, King's College taught such students as Alexander Hamilton, John Jay, Robert Livingston, and Gouverneur Morris. After the Revolution, New York State issued the college a new charter with a more patriotic name—Columbia. In 1897, Columbia moved to a new site in Morningside Heights on the Upper West Side of Manhattan. The architectural firm of McKim, Mead and White, the preeminent architects of their day, designed an open central enclave six blocks long, with a majestic domed and colonnaded library at the center. To this day, it remains one of New York's most impressive settings.

Today, Columbia College and The Fu Foundation School of Engineering and Applied Science (Columbia Engineering) offer their students unique advantages; they are at the same time small, selective colleges and integral components of a major research university.

The Columbia College student body is approximately 4,400 students; the Columbia Engineering student body is roughly 1,400. Students come from all fifty states and over ninety countries. They represent a dazzling array of ethnic, social, economic, cultural, religious, and geographic backgrounds. The diversity of Columbia's student body reflects the diversity of New York City, the world's most international city.

Columbia guarantees four years of on-campus housing to all entering first-year students. Nearly all undergraduates remain in University residence halls for all four years.

Columbia students take part in extracurricular groups of all kinds: artistic (theater, musical, and dance), athletic (thirty-one Division I varsity sports and dozens of club and intramural sports), communications (the *Columbia Daily Spectator,* the *Columbia Journal of Literary Criticism,* WKCR-FM, a campus television station, and many others), community service (Amnesty International, Big Brother/Big Sister programs, after-hours tutoring programs, a volunteer ambulance squad, and partnerships with dozens of hospitals, soup kitchens, and homeless shelters), and preprofessional (the Charles Drew Pre-Medical Society and the National Society of Black Engineers). Other groups represent students' ethnic, religious, political, and gender identities. There are twenty-eight fraternities and sororities. Alfred Lerner Hall houses office and meeting space for student organizations, a black box theater, a cinema, the Center for Student Advising, and many dining options.

Location

Columbia shares its Morningside Heights neighborhood with a number of other famous institutions: Barnard College, the Cathedral of St. John the Divine, Union Theological Seminary, Jewish Theological Seminary, and the Manhattan School of Music, to name a few. Many of the faculty members from Columbia and the other surrounding schools make their homes in the neighborhood. Morningside Heights is an area known for bookstores, wonderfully varied restaurants, and merchants that cater to student tastes, student budgets, and student hours.

Students are encouraged and assisted in making full use of New York's breathtaking variety of cultural, recreational, and professional resources. Through the Columbia University Arts Initiative, students can receive discounted tickets to Broadway shows, film screenings, art galleries, and a multitude of cultural events in New York City. Passport to NYC offers students free access to thirty-four museums throughout the city. Columbia students can be found any day of the week exploring the Metropolitan Museum of Art, the Museum of Modern Art, the Guggenheim Museum, the Museum of African Art, the Museo del Barrio, the Asia Society, or any other of the city's hundreds of museums and galleries. Any evening, they might be discovering the theatrical offerings on, off, or "off-off" Broadway (or on campus); attending the opera, ballet, or symphony at Lincoln Center; taking in a movie on campus or in one of New York's 400-plus cinemas; enjoying jazz in Greenwich Village or blues at the Apollo; sampling *pai gwat* in Chinatown; or biking or boating in Central Park. Columbia's internship programs offer students opportunities to explore a career possibility in depth; nowhere else in the world does the concentration of industries allow such a range of possibilities. New York's public transportation system puts the entire city within easy reach of Columbia students; the campus is directly served by a subway line and five bus routes.

Majors and Degrees

Columbia College grants the B.A. degree in more than eighty programs of study in the humanities, social sciences, and pure sciences, including many interdisciplinary majors. Columbia Engineering grants the B.S. degree in sixteen engineering fields. A five-year program that begins in either school allows students to receive both a B.A. from Columbia College and a B.S. from Columbia Engineering.

Joint degree programs offer selected students the opportunity to combine their undergraduate work with study in Columbia University's schools of law and international affairs and with the Juilliard School.

Academic Programs

Columbia College is known for its Core Curriculum, a set of common courses required of all undergraduates and considered the necessary general education for students, irrespective of their choice in major. The communal learning—with all students encountering the same texts and issues at the same time—and the critical dialogue experienced in small seminars are the distinctive features of the core. Begun in the early part of the twentieth century, the Core Curriculum is one of the founding experiments in liberal higher education in the United States and it remains vibrant as it enters its tenth decade. One of the two oldest courses in the Core is Contemporary Civilization, a year-long historical survey of Western civilization's religious, political, and moral philosophies; the second is Literature Humanities, a year-long introduction to Western culture's most seminal and meaningful literary works. A second year of humanities offers a semester each of music and art appreciation, encouraging students to experience the cultural treasures of New York City. The Global Core requirement enlarges the scope of inquiry beyond the Western focus in order to promote learning and thought about the variety of cultures and the diversity of traditions that interact in the United States and the world today. The Frontiers of Science course outlines the approaches that scientists take to answer interesting problems in the natural world and introduces students to scientific research methods. The Core Curriculum exposes Columbia's multicultural student body to a variety of disciplines, preparing them for the complex questions and issues of modern society.

The strength of Columbia's Engineering's education is in its uniquely broad curriculum, preparing students not only to be world-class engineers, but also to be global leaders across industries. In addition to taking rigorous math and science courses typically offered at top undergraduate programs, Columbia Engineering students are also required to take courses in the liberal arts alongside their College counterparts, providing them with interdisciplinary tools for real-world problem solving. This type of broad academic exposure is what alumni often cite as the foundation of their later academic and professional success. Another hallmark of the Columbia Engineering education is The Art of Engineering, where students are introduced to the field through interactive lectures, group projects, and guest speakers. A key component of the course is a semester-long, hands-on group project. Past examples of projects include mathematically modeling the U.S. elections, designing vital signs monitors, and modifying a laser pointer by adding a microprocessor to enable it to transmit analog music to a wireless speaker and digital data over long distances. In addition to the technical issues discussed in the

course, other key issues of importance in professional engineering such as ethics, project management, and societal impact are addressed.

Off-Campus Programs

Columbia students, with the help of an adviser from the Office of Global Programs, may choose among nearly 200 study-abroad programs on nearly every continent, many of which are Columbia-specific programs and exchanges.

Columbia maintains a network of global centers, developing opportunities for research, scholarship, teaching, and service across borders. With seven locations ranging from Turkey to Chile and Kenya to China, undergraduate options include summer Arabic language programs in Amman, Jordan or a semester-long French literature program in Paris at Columbia's Reid Hall. Columbia also has direct enrollment agreements with many partner institutions abroad, as well as a growing number of exchange programs with universities abroad.

Columbia was the first U.S. college to offer an integrated year-abroad program with the Universities of Oxford and Cambridge. Other programs allow students to work at the University of Kyoto in Japan or at the Free University of Berlin in Germany.

Academic Facilities

Columbia has the fifth-largest research library system in the world, consisting of 10 million volumes and 26 million manuscripts within 3,000 collections. Included in the twenty-two libraries are collections of particular significance, such as those of the Avery Architectural and Fine Arts Library, the Starr East Asian Library, the Rare Book and Manuscript Library, and the Burke Library of Union Theological Seminary. All divisions are open to Columbia undergraduates. The majority of campus has wireless access including most residence halls. The new Northwest Corner Building houses cutting-edge labs that bring together researchers in biology, chemistry, physics, and engineering, as well as a science library, lecture hall, and café. Students may also make use of an electronic music lab, a cyclotron, an oral history collection, the facilities and programs of the Lamont-Doherty Earth Observatory, and oceanographic research ships.

Costs

Tuition for the 2011–12 academic year was $43,088. Room and board for all first-year students were $11,020. With typical fees, books, and supplies, the total cost of a year at Columbia was approximately $59,719.

Financial Aid

All first-year candidates who are U.S. citizens or have U.S. permanent resident or political refugee status, are considered for admission without regard to their financial need. International students who do not fit into the above categories should be aware that their admissions process is not need-blind; their financial need is taken into account at the time of admission. Regardless of citizenship, Columbia meets the full demonstrated need of every student admitted as a first-year for all four years of study. Columbia has eliminated loans for all students receiving financial aid and replaced them with University grant money. Parental contributions have also been significantly reduced for a large portion of students receiving financial aid. Prospective students should go to http://www.studentaffairs.columbia.edu/finaid/ for information on specific requirements and deadlines. All financial aid at Columbia is based on need; no aid is given in the form of academic, athletic, artistic, or other merit awards. The Office of Financial Aid and Educational Financing believes that cost should not be a barrier to students pursuing their educational dreams.

Faculty

The student-to-faculty ratio is 6:1. Core curriculum classes are capped at 22 students, and almost 80 percent of classes have 20 students or less. The Columbia faculty is committed to both teaching and research, and all faculty members teach undergraduates, even the president of the University. All faculty members maintain office hours, and each student receives a faculty adviser from the department that he or she chooses as a major.

Student Government

Each undergraduate division has its own student council and elects representatives to the Columbia University Senate.

Admission Requirements

The Columbia first-year class of 1,391 students is selected from a much larger pool of applicants through a holistic, committee-based review process. Candidates for admission are expected to demonstrate the necessary ability and interest to do successful college work in a variety of disciplines as required for the Columbia degree. The following secondary school preparation is recommended: 4 years of English, including meaningful work in literature and writing; 3 (preferably 4) years of mathematics, including precalculus and calculus where offered; 3 (preferably 4) years of history and social studies; 3 or more years of the same foreign language; and 3 (preferably 4) years of laboratory science (including chemistry and physics where available). The Admissions Committee recognizes that secondary schools vary in offerings and standards; consideration is given to applicants whose preparations differ from the recommended course of study but have taken advantage of what their schools offer.

Standardized tests are required for admission, according to the following guidelines. Students may take the SAT with Writing, and students who take the test more than once are evaluated on the highest score they receive in any individual section. Applicants may alternately take the ACT with Writing, which is graded on a 36-point scale. Students taking the test more than once are evaluated on the highest composite score they receive. The writing component of the ACT is mandatory for candidates for Columbia.

In addition to either the SAT or ACT, students must also take two SAT Subject Tests. For Columbia College, they may take any two tests; for The Fu Foundation School of Engineering and Applied Science, they must take any mathematics test and either the physics or the chemistry test.

Students who attend a school that does not give conventional grades or who are homeschooled must take two additional SAT Subject Tests in addition to all requirements outlined above for Columbia College or The Fu Foundation School of Engineering and Applied Science.

It is absolutely imperative that applicants have the testing service report their standardized test scores directly to either Columbia College (SAT code 2116, ACT code 2717) or The Fu Foundation School of Engineering and Applied Science (SAT code 2111, ACT code 2719), as appropriate.

Transfer students may enter Columbia in September only.

The College has a Visiting Students Program, which allows students to attend for one or both semesters of their sophomore, junior, or senior year.

Application and Information

Columbia utilizes the Common Application and requires the Columbia University Supplement. Candidates for whom Columbia is their definite first choice may apply under the early decision plan; the deadline is November 1 for all application material, and a decision is rendered by December 15. The deadline for regular decision applications is January 1. Candidates are notified of the Admissions Committee's decisions on or about April 1. Admitted candidates must respond to Columbia's offer of admission by May 1. Candidates admitted to Columbia under early decision are required to withdraw their applications to other colleges. The application fee is $80. The fee may be waived if a school official testifies that the fee would cause the candidate's family financial hardship. For further information, interested students should contact:

Office of Undergraduate Admissions
Columbia University
1130 Amsterdam Avenue, MC2807
New York, New York 10027
Phone: 212-854-2522
Fax: 212-854-1209
E-mail: ugrad-ask@columbia.edu
Web site: http://www.studentaffairs.columbia.edu/admissions
http://www.facebook.com/columbiaadmissions

COLUMBIA UNIVERSITY, SCHOOL OF GENERAL STUDIES

NEW YORK, NEW YORK

The University and The School

The School of General Studies (GS) of Columbia University is one of the finest liberal arts colleges in the United States created specifically for returning and nontraditional students seeking a rigorous, traditional, Ivy League undergraduate degree full- or part-time. Most students at GS have, for personal or professional reasons, interrupted their education, never attended college, or are only able to attend part-time. GS is unique among colleges of its type, because its students are fully integrated into the Columbia undergraduate curriculum: they take the same courses with the same faculty members and earn the same degree as all other Columbia undergraduates.

GS students come from varied backgrounds and all walks of life. Many students work full-time while pursuing a degree, and many have family responsibilities; others attend classes full-time and experience Columbia's more traditional college life. In the classroom, the diversity and varied personal experience of the student body promote discussion and debate, fostering an environment of academic rigor and intellectual development. GS has approximately 1,500 undergraduate degree candidates and more than 400 Postbac Premed students. The average age of a GS student is 29. More than 60 percent of GS students attend classes full-time.

In addition to its bachelor's degree program, GS offers combined undergraduate/graduate degree programs with Columbia's Schools of Social Work, International and Public Affairs, Law, Business, Dental Medicine, Teachers College, and the College of Physicians and Surgeons. More than 70 percent of the students go on to earn advanced degrees after graduation.

GS is home to the oldest and largest postbaccalaureate premedical program in the United States. In recent years, the acceptance rate for GS Postbaccalaureate Premedical Program students applying to U.S. medical schools is up to 90 percent.

Location

Columbia University is located in Morningside Heights, on the Upper West Side of Manhattan. The University's neighbors include the Union Theological Seminary, the Jewish Theological Seminary, the Manhattan School of Music, St. Luke's Hospital, Riverside Church, and the Cathedral of St. John the Divine. The diversity of intellectual and social activities offered by these institutions is one of Columbia's great assets as a university; another is New York City itself, which offers Columbia students a rich and almost boundless variety of social, cultural, and recreational opportunities that are themselves an education.

Majors and Degrees

The School of General Studies grants the B.A. and B.S. degrees and offers more than seventy majors and concentrations, which include: African studies; African American studies; American studies; ancient studies; anthropology; applied mathematics; archaeology; architecture; architecture, history and theory; art history; art history–visual arts; astronomy; astrophysics; biochemistry; biology; biophysics; chemical physics; chemistry; classical studies; classics; comparative literature and society; computer science; computer science–mathematics; creative writing; dance; drama and theater arts; earth science; East Asian studies; East Central European studies; economics; economics–mathematics; economics–operations research; economics–philosophy; economics–political science; economics–statistics; English and comparative literature; environmental biology; environmental chemistry; environmental science; ethnicity and race studies; evolutionary biology of the human species; film studies; financial economics; French; French and Francophone studies; German literature and cultural history; Hispanic studies; history; human rights; information science; Italian cultural studies; Italian language and literature; Latin American and Caribbean studies; mathematics; mathematics–statistics; Middle Eastern, South Asian, and African studies; music;

neuroscience and behavior; philosophy; physics; political science; political science–statistics; psychology; regional studies; religion; Russian language and culture; Russian literature and culture; Slavic studies; sociology; statistics; sustainable development; urban studies; visual arts; women's and gender studies; and Yiddish studies. Individually designed majors are also available.

In addition, Columbia University School of General Studies offers undergraduate dual-degree programs with the Columbia School of Engineering and Applied Science, the Jewish Theological Seminary, and the Dual BA Program between the French university Sciences Po and Columbia University.

The Dual BA Program is an intensive, transatlantic course of study in which undergraduate students earn bachelor's degrees from both Sciences Po and Columbia University in four years. Students will spend two years at one of three Sciences Po campuses, each of which is devoted to a particular region of the world and offers a heavy linguistic and cultural focus. After completing Sciences Po's interdisciplinary social-sciences curriculum, Dual BA students will matriculate at GS to complete the requirements for a major, as well as fulfill core distribution requirements in a variety of disciplines, including literature, art, music, science, and the humanities. Upon graduation, Dual BA. Program students are eligible for guaranteed admission to a graduate program at Sciences Po. Admission to the program is highly competitive, and high school seniors are eligible to apply.

Academic Programs

The School of General Studies offers a traditional liberal arts education designed to provide students with the broad knowledge and intellectual skills that foster continued education and growth in the years after college as well as providing a sound foundation for positions of responsibility in the professional world.

Requirements for the bachelor's degree comprise three elements: (1) core requirements, intended to develop in students the ability to write and communicate clearly; to understand the modes of thought that characterize the humanities, social sciences, and sciences; to gain familiarity with central cultural ideas through literature, fine arts, and music; and to acquire a working proficiency in a foreign language; (2) major requirements, designed to give students sustained and coherent exposure to a particular discipline in an area of strong intellectual interest; and (3) elective courses, in which students pursue particular interests and skills for their own personal growth or for their relationship to future professional or personal objectives. Students are required to complete a minimum of 124 credits for the bachelor's degree; 60 of these may be in transfer credit, but at least 64 credits (including the last 30 credits) must be completed at Columbia. In addition to the usual graduation honors (cum laude, magna cum laude, and summa cum laude), honors programs for superior students are available in a majority of the University's departments.

Off-Campus Programs

Columbia students may enhance their academic experiences through various study-abroad programs around the world. For example, students may spend a term at the Reid Hall Program in the Montparnasse district of Paris, the Berlin Consortium for German Studies, the Kyoto Consortium for Japanese Studies, or the Language Program in Beijing, China. In addition, students may apply to participate in one of the Columbia-approved study-abroad programs located in countries around the world.

Academic Facilities

The Columbia University Libraries constitute the nation's sixth-largest academic library system, with a collection of more than 10.4 million volumes, more than 6 million microform pieces, 26 million manuscript items, and 900,000 rare books. Of the twenty-two libraries in the system, five are designated Distinctive

Collections because of their unusual depth and nationally recognized excellence. All library divisions are available to GS students. The University's Computer Center is one of the largest and most powerful university installations in the world and has remote units and terminals in several parts of the campus to enhance its accessibility. The Fairchild Life Sciences Building houses research facilities, laboratories, electron microscopes, and a vast amount of biochemical equipment used for teaching and research. The University's physics building has been the scene of many important developments in the recent history of physics, including the invention of the laser and the first U.S. demonstration of nuclear fission.

Costs

For the 2011–12 academic year, tuition was $1392 per credit, and annual living (room and board) and personal expenses (books, local commuting costs, and miscellaneous expenses) were $23,664.

Financial Aid

The School of General Studies awards financial aid based upon need and academic ability. Approximately 70 percent of GS degree candidates receive some form of financial aid, including Federal Pell Grants, New York State TAP Grants, Federal Stafford and unsubsidized Stafford Loans, Federal Perkins Loans, General Studies Scholarships, and Federal Work-Study Program awards. Priority application deadlines for new students are June 1 for the fall semester and October 15 for the spring semester. The average scholarship award ranges from $6500 to $8000 for first-year students.

Faculty

Students in the School of General Studies take courses with professors who are members of the Columbia University Faculty of Arts and Sciences. These distinguished scholars in virtually every discipline also teach in Columbia College, the Graduate School of Arts and Sciences, and the School of International and Public Affairs. Full-time and part-time students have many opportunities to work closely with faculty members, both in small classes and in research projects. Faculty members also serve as advisers to students majoring in their area of study and maintain regular office hours to see students.

Student Government

One student of the School represents GS students in the University Senate, a decision-making body comprising students, faculty members, and administrative staff members from each division of the University. In addition, 2 GS students sit as voting members on the Committee on Instruction, which oversees the curriculum of the School. The General Studies Student Council elects officers each year and sponsors activities for students. *The Observer,* the School's student-run magazine, is published several times each year. The Premedical Association (PMA) sponsors events related to the medical school admissions process.

Admission Requirements

The GS admission policy is geared to the maturity and varied backgrounds of its students. Aptitude and motivation are considered along with past academic performance, standardized test scores, and employment history. The School's admission decisions are based on a careful review of each application and reflect the Admissions Committee's considered judgment of the applicant's maturity, academic potential, and present ability to undertake course work at Columbia.

Admission requirements include a completed application form; a 1,500- to 2,000-word autobiographical statement describing the applicant's past educational history and work experience, present situation, and future plans; two letters of recommendation from academic or professional evaluators; an official high school transcript; official transcripts from all colleges and universities attended; official SAT or ACT scores (applicants may take the General Studies Admissions Examination); and a nonrefundable application fee of $75.

Students from outside the United States may apply to the School of General Studies to start or complete a baccalaureate degree. In addition to the materials described above, international applicants must submit official TOEFL scores or take the Columbia University American Language Program Essay Exam.

Application and Information

Application deadlines are March 1 for early action (nonbinding), and June 1 for the fall semester, October 1 for early action (nonbinding), and November 1 for the spring semester, and April 1 for the summer semester. Applicants from countries outside the U.S. are urged to apply by August 15 for the spring semester and April 1 for the fall semester. Applications are reviewed as they are completed, and applicants are notified of decisions shortly thereafter.

For more information, students should contact:

Curtis M. Rodgers, Dean of Enrollment Management
Office of Admissions and Financial Aid
School of General Studies
408 Lewisohn Hall
2970 Broadway
Columbia University, Mail Code 4101
New York, New York 10027
Phone: 212-854-2772
E-mail: gsdegree@columbia.edu
Web site: http://www.gs.columbia.edu
    http://facebook.com/ColumbiaGS
    http://www.twitter.com/ColumbiaGS
    http://www.youtube.com/GSColumbia

Columbia University Low Memorial Library.

THE CULINARY INSTITUTE OF AMERICA
HYDE PARK, NEW YORK

THE WORLD'S PREMIER
CULINARY COLLEGE

The Institute

The Culinary Institute of America (CIA) is a private, not-for-profit college dedicated to providing the world's best undergraduate education in culinary arts and baking and pastry arts. Guided by its core values of excellence, leadership, professionalism, ethics, and respect for diversity, the CIA strives to foster an atmosphere where students can develop both professionally and personally. At the CIA, aspiring culinarians gain the general knowledge and specific skills they need to grow into positions of leadership in the foodservice and hospitality industry, the largest private employer in the United States.

Founded in 1946, The Culinary Institute of America today enrolls more than 2,800 students from virtually every state and thirty countries around the world, all united by their shared passion for food. The CIA student body has a balance of recent high school graduates and adults returning to higher education.

As the world's premier culinary college, the CIA is renowned for its degree programs, extraordinary faculty, and outstanding educational facilities. All CIA degree programs emphasize professional, hands-on learning in the college's kitchens, bakeshops, and restaurants. CIA classes span the culinary globe, exploring great cultures, cooking techniques, and cuisines to prepare students for the diversity and creativity of the foodservice industry. Classes are taken in a progressive sequence optimized to build skills, food knowledge, and production experience. These studies culminate in operations courses that give students both kitchen and front-of-the-house experiences in the college's famous restaurants. Bachelor's degree students also focus on foodservice management development, with a broad range of business management and liberal arts courses.

CIA students enjoy an active campus life, with a variety of year-round fitness programs, intercollegiate and intramural sports, student clubs, and extracurricular activities such as ski and camping trips, on-campus live entertainment events, presentations by leading chefs and industry executives, and cook-offs. The college's Student Recreation Center includes a six-lane pool, a gymnasium, racquetball courts, an aerobics studio, a fitness center and free-weight room, a game room, outdoor tennis courts, and the Courtside Café and Pub. Four coed residence halls, six lodges, and three townhouses provide on-campus housing for approximately 1,700 students. The college's dining plan provides students with two meals per instructional day.

The Culinary Institute of America is accredited by the Middle States Commission on Higher Education, 3624 Market Street, Philadelphia, Pennsylvania 19104 (telephone: 215-662-5000). The Middle States Commission on Higher Education is an institutional accrediting agency recognized by the U.S. Secretary of Education and the Council for Higher Education Accreditation.

Location

The CIA's scenic 170-acre campus is set along the east bank of the Hudson River in Hyde Park, New York, conveniently located 1½–2 hours from New York City and Albany.

The Mid-Hudson region's attractions and recreational opportunities offer something for everyone in both rural and urban settings. There are a number of state parks and historic sites throughout the area. Students can taste wines at local vineyards, visit farmer's markets, and pick apples at nearby orchards. To the west lie the Catskill and Shawangunk

Mountains, with many opportunities for hiking, skiing, rock climbing, mountain biking, and sightseeing. Concerts, plays, films, and other cultural and special events are offered regularly at the many colleges, theaters, and community facilities throughout the Hudson Valley and Catskill regions. In addition, students can take advantage of the campus's proximity to New York City to experience the culture, arts, and nightlife of this exciting city and food mecca.

Majors and Degrees

At its New York campus, The Culinary Institute of America awards the degree of Bachelor of Professional Studies (BPS) in baking and pastry arts management and in culinary arts management, as well as the degree of Associate in Occupational Studies (AOS) in baking and pastry arts and in culinary arts.

Academic Programs

At the core of The Culinary Institute of America's curriculum lies more than 1,300 hours of hands-on instruction in its kitchens and bakeshops as well as classes developing the managerial skills and creative thinking that today's culinary professional requires. Students learn about foods, cooking and baking techniques, cuisines, and business fundamentals while advancing through skills and production kitchens. They also gain invaluable experience in a paid externship program and by cooking and serving in the college's bakery café or in some of the four fine-dining public restaurants on campus. Bachelor's degree students also take courses in marketing, communications, psychology, foreign languages and cultures, accounting and the use of computers in the food business, and financial and human resources management.

Students must earn 132 total credits in culinary arts management or in baking and pastry arts management to graduate with a bachelor's degree. Students must earn 69 total credits in culinary arts or in baking and pastry arts to graduate with an associate degree. Students who earn their associate degrees at the CIA's California or Texas campuses can transfer to the New York campus to complete the bachelor's degree program.

Off-Campus Programs

All students work in externships for a minimum of 18 weeks (600 hours). These externships provide students with valuable on-the-job experience at one of more than 1,200 top food-service and hospitality properties—such as hotels, restaurants, and resorts—around the world. Bachelor's degree students also participate in a travel experience to one of a number of exciting destination choices—Northern and Southern California, the Pacific Northwest, Spain, Italy, China, and France—where they can learn from local purveyors and visit area restaurants, wineries, and vineyards.

Academic Facilities

CIA students learn the fundamentals of the culinary and baking and pastry arts in the college's forty-one professionally equipped production kitchens and bakeshops and five student-staffed public restaurants on campus—the American Bounty Restaurant, Escoffier Restaurant, Ristorante Caterina de' Medici, St. Andrew's Café, and Apple Pie Bakery Café. Classes are centered in the college's main building, Roth Hall, as well as in the Shunsuke Takaki School of Baking and Pastry, General Foods Nutrition Center, and Colavita Center for Italian Food and Wine. The CIA regularly hosts world-renowned chefs for lectures, cooking demonstrations, and discussions with

students in its Danny Kaye Theatre, Anheuser-Busch Theatre, and Ecolab Theatre.

Other valuable academic resources include the 86,000-volume Conrad N. Hilton Library, which contains the largest culinary collection of any culinary school; audiovisual programs to supplement course work; computer labs and workstations; and a wireless network that allows students to access online resources from almost anywhere on campus.

Costs

Freshman tuition for academic year 2012–13 is $25,900. Board is $1330 per semester, which includes two meals per instructional day. Housing costs range from $2630 to $3880 per semester, depending on the room to which the student is assigned.

Additional required fees for the freshman year include a confirmation fee of $100, equipment fees of $1840 for culinary supplies or $1735 for baking and pastry supplies, and a general fee of $615 per semester, which includes student activity and exam fees, as well as secondary student accident insurance. The CIA offers students a tuition installment plan. Details are available from the college's Bursar's Office.

Financial Aid

Approximately 90 percent of the CIA's students receive financial aid in the form of scholarships, grants, loans, and work-study. Federal programs offered at the college include the Federal Pell Grant, Federal Supplemental Educational Opportunity Grant (SEOG), Federal Direct Loans (Subsidized and Unsubsidized), Federal Perkins Loan, Federal Work-Study Program (which provides a variety of on-campus and community service jobs to eligible students), Federal PLUS, and veterans' benefits. Students should also investigate their own state's programs and apply if those grants or scholarships can be used in New York State.

Students who have applied for admission or who are currently enrolled at the CIA may apply for scholarships offered by various organizations in the foodservice industry. A list of these scholarships, which are administered by the college, is available from the Financial Aid Office.

Faculty

The college's faculty is composed of more than 150 chefs and instructors from sixteen countries whose credentials and industry experience are unmatched in culinary education. The 17:1 student-faculty ratio in hands-on classes provides student support and mentoring, while giving students the opportunity to work in an environment closely representative of the foodservice industry.

Student Government

All students in good standing are members of the Student Government Association (SGA). The association's Executive Board acts as a liaison between students and the administration. The SGA helps support student activities and funds all student clubs and committees.

Admission Requirements

The Admissions Committee seeks candidates who have demonstrated a commitment to a culinary career and who have the personal initiative, confidence, and motivation to succeed. The basic requirements are successful completion of a secondary school education or its equivalent and some experience in the foodservice and hospitality industry. The applicant's educational record is evaluated on the basis of overall performance and the type of program taken. Academics and leadership ability are key requirements for the bachelor's degree program. SATs or ACTs are strongly recommended but not required.

Preference is given to candidates who have worked in foodservice, particularly in a kitchen that offers a varied menu. Before entering the program, students should have had six months of hands-on food preparation experience in a professional kitchen or bakery working with fresh ingredients, for at least 10–15 hours a week. If students attend a high school or college culinary program, their experience there may fulfill this requirement. Candidates do not need this experience to apply for admission—the requirement must be met before they enter the CIA.

Applicants must submit a formal application for admission, a nonrefundable $50 application fee, an official secondary school transcript (not a student copy), a 500-word essay, and an official college transcript, if applicable. Students applying directly from high school may include an optional secondary school report. In addition, associate degree candidates must provide one recommendation, and bachelor's applicants must provide two.

Application and Information

Students may apply for admission to the CIA year-round, as the college offers multiple enrollment seasons from which to choose. Applicants should submit their materials according to the enrollment schedule (available at the Web site listed below) that corresponds to the season they are interested in beginning the degree program. Students are notified of an admission decision according to that schedule.

For information, to schedule a tour, or to participate in an Admissions Information Session, students should contact:

Admissions Office
The Culinary Institute of America
1946 Campus Drive
Hyde Park, New York 12538-1499
Phone: 1-800-CULINARY (toll-free)
E-mail: admissions@culinary.edu
Web site: http://www.ciachef.edu/admissions

Set along the banks of the Hudson River, The Culinary Institute of America's New York campus lies on 170 scenic acres in historic Hyde Park.

CURRY COLLEGE
MILTON, MASSACHUSETTS

The College

Curry College is a private institution that offers academic majors in liberal arts disciplines and in the professional fields. The College's curriculum and programs focus on the two hallmarks of a Curry education: a high respect for the individuality of every student and a developmental approach to learning that maximizes opportunities for achievement.

Students are attracted to Curry's friendly and caring academic community. One-on-one faculty-student relationships provide many opportunities for personalized instruction and close interaction. The average class size is 20 students, and the student-faculty ratio is 10:1. The student body consists of approximately 2,000 traditional undergraduate students. Approximately 1,450 students reside on the Curry campus.

Curry students have access to a wide range of cocurricular and extracurricular activities, including participation in the student newspaper and other campus media; performing arts programs, including theater and dance; and intramural sports or one of fourteen NCAA division III athletic teams. Varsity sports for men are baseball, basketball, football, ice hockey, lacrosse, soccer, and tennis; women's varsity sports are basketball, cross-country, lacrosse, soccer, softball, tennis, and volleyball.

Curry College is accredited by the New England Association of Schools and Colleges; its nursing programs are accredited by the Commission on Collegiate Nursing Education (CCNE).

The College was founded in Boston in 1879 and moved to its present campus in Milton in 1952. The internationally acclaimed Program for Advancement of Learning (PAL) was established in 1970 as the nation's first college-level program for students with language-based learning differences. In 1974, the College absorbed the Perry Normal School, which prepared teachers for careers, and in 1977 it entered into a collaborative relationship with Children's Hospital Medical Center, which resulted in the establishment of Curry's Division of Nursing Studies.

Curry offers four master's degree programs, including a Master of Education (M.Ed.) established in 1981; a Master of Arts (M.A.) in criminal justice established in 1998; a Master of Business Administration (M.B.A.) established in 2005; and a Master of Science in Nursing (M.S.N) established in 2008.

As at its founding, Curry remains a dynamic and forward-looking institution committed to providing a highly individualized educational experience.

Location

Curry is located in Milton, Massachusetts, a residential suburb near the exceptional resources of Boston. The greater Boston area provides students with a diversity of cultural, educational, recreational, and sports activities. A wide variety of corporations, hospitals, agencies, broadcasting stations, and schools provide excellent internship and job opportunities for Curry students. The College operates a shuttle bus to the MBTA trains that run into Boston. Curry students have the benefit of a traditional, 135-acre, wooded New England campus and access to the excitement of a large city.

Majors and Degrees

Curry College awards the following Bachelor of Arts (B.A.) degrees: biology; child, youth, and community education; communication (with concentrations in corporate communication, film, multimedia journalism, public relations, radio broadcasting/audio production, relational communication, television/digital video, and theater); criminal justice; early

childhood education; elementary education; English (with concentrations in American studies, creative writing, literary genre and movements, traditional literary heritage, journalism, professional writing, and women in literature); environmental science; graphic design; information technology; integrated liberal studies; management (with concentrations in accounting, entrepreneurship, finance, human resources, marketing, residential property management, and sports management); philosophy; politics and history; psychology (with concentrations in counseling, developmental psychology, gerontology, health, and substance-abuse counseling); sociology (with concentrations in ethnic and gender studies and service in the community); special education; and visual arts (with a concentration in studio arts).

Curry College awards the following Bachelor of Science (B.S.) degrees: community health and wellness, and nursing.

Special minors are available in numerous areas, including dance, music, religion, Spanish, women's studies, and writing. For students with design majors, provision is made in the areas in which they have a special interest.

Academic Programs

A central liberal arts curriculum, which is required for all students, incorporates a variety of academic disciplines into every student's plan of study. Curry's programs integrate theoretical classroom learning with a wide variety of field internships.

Curry College operates on a two-semester calendar with a summer session. To graduate, students must complete at least 120 credit hours for a B.A. or B.S. degree. In both cases, a minimum 2.0 cumulative average must be achieved.

Many academic programs enrich and facilitate a Curry education. The First-Year Seminar, the Honors Program, the Women's Studies Program, and the Internship Program are representative of that focus on special interests and diverse learning needs.

The Program for Advancement of Learning (PAL) is a credited program designed to help intelligent, motivated, language-based learning-disabled students to achieve at the college level. PAL provides individual or small-group instruction, textbooks on tape, and untimed examinations, as well as a variety of other applied technologies. Students must apply to the PAL program in order to take advantage of PAL's services. Students receive credit for enrollment in the program for the first year and are able to continue in the program as long as needed.

Off-Campus Programs

Curry students may earn up to 30 credit hours for field internships. In consultation with faculty members, students develop learning contracts that articulate their educational and personal goals and establish criteria for the evaluation of their field experience. Students may also arrange to study abroad or at another institution within the United States while enrolled at Curry.

Academic Facilities

The Levin Memorial Library houses more than 94,000 print volumes, 60,000 electronic books, 31,000 electronic journals, over 16,000 microforms, and 106 print/microform serial subscriptions. Levin Library is equipped with three computer labs containing PCs and Macintosh computers, laser printers, color printers, and state-of-the-art optical scanning equipment. The library houses the Academic Enrichment Center, where students may secure assistance in reading, writing, mathematics, and the development of study skills and is also home to the Educational

Technology Center full of resources and materials for education students.

The Science Building includes five laboratories. The Kennedy Academic Center houses a simulated hospital room for use as a nursing laboratory; the Nursing Resource Center, which is equipped with an interactive video lab; and a laboratory for experimental psychology equipped with biofeedback, computer control, and animal and human learning facilities. The Webb Learning Center, with its own computer lab, maintains a complete tape library of all textbooks used at the College. The Hafer Academic Center features the Hirsh Communication Center and its state-of-the-art television studio. Curry students operate WMLN-FM, the College's award-winning, 172-watt radio station.

The Academic and Performance Center features a 250-seat multipurpose auditorium, classrooms equipped with wireless laptop connectivity and SMART Board technology, breakout conference rooms, a stock-trading classroom, and a café-style food court.

The new Student Center is an 84,000-square-foot facility that includes state-of-the-art areas for studying, co-curricular and extracurricular activities, dining, and athletics.

Costs

Tuition for the 2012–13 academic year is $31,900. Room and board are $12,760 (based on a fourteen-meal plan). The cost of the Program for Advancement of Learning (PAL) is $6550. The cost of books, supplies, and personal expenses varies from $900 to $2000.

Financial Aid

Curry provides financial assistance for students who need funding in order to attend college. The financial aid program consists of federal, state, and Curry College scholarships, grants, work-study awards, student assistant jobs, and loans. Approximately 70 percent of the student body receives financial aid. All students applying for financial aid must submit the Free Application for Federal Student Aid (FAFSA) by March 1. Students applying for financial aid should contact the Financial Aid Office.

Faculty

There are 122 full-time faculty members at Curry, 73 percent of whom hold terminal degrees in their fields. In addition, each year the College hires highly qualified part-time faculty members and visiting lecturers to augment its teaching staff. Although primarily a teaching faculty, Curry's faculty members are also engaged in writing, research, and consulting.

Student Government

The purpose of the Student Government Association (SGA) is the advancement of the College community and the promotion of the general welfare of students. SGA seeks to increase student involvement in the formulation of College policies, communicate effectively with all constituencies of the College, and promote student participation within the institution. Members of SGA host an annual campus meeting with the College President and the senior management of the College.

Admission Requirements

Curry College accepts students who have the necessary preparation and educational background to meet the requirements of the College, regardless of race, religion, national or ethnic origin, age, sex, sexual orientation, or physical handicap. Freshman students are selected on the basis of a combination of the following: secondary school record, scores on the SAT or ACT, recommendation of the secondary school, and the candidate's readiness for college. To be considered for admission, students must generally present at least 16 units of high school work, preferably at the college-preparatory level, from an approved secondary school. A recommended program of studies includes

the following: 4 years of English, at least 3 years of mathematics, 2 years of a foreign language, 2 years of science (including at least 1 year of a laboratory science), and 2 years of social studies. Applicants should contact the Admission Office to discuss any possible exceptions to these requirements. A GED certificate is acceptable in lieu of a high school diploma. Curry College seeks well-rounded students who can contribute to the Curry community in athletic, artistic, and social endeavors, as well as in the academic sphere.

Application and Information

Curry's recommended application deadline is April 1; however, Curry operates on a rolling admission basis. Students may apply for September or January entrance. Applicants for the nursing program may only apply for the fall semester. Applicants must submit an application and fee, an official high school transcript, scores from the SAT or ACT, and a counselor's recommendation. Transfer students must also submit official college transcripts, along with a College Official's Report form. If English is not the primary language of the applicant, then results of the Test of English as a Foreign Language (TOEFL) must be submitted. An interview is optional but not required. The Admission Committee evaluates each application as soon as all required credentials are received, beginning in October. The College is a member of the Common Application.

Applicants to the Program for Advancement of Learning (PAL) must submit a completed application by March 1. PAL applicants must also submit the results of a recently administered Wechsler Adult Intelligence Scale (WAIS-R) test. Achievement testing in reading comprehension, written language, and math must also be submitted. The SAT or ACT requirement is waived for PAL applicants. Final decisions on admission to the program are made once all credentials are complete.

For more information about Curry College, students should contact:

Jane Patricia Fidler
Dean of Admission
Curry College
Milton, Massachusetts 02186
Phone: 617-333-2210
　　　800-669-0686 (toll-free)
Fax: 617-333-2114
E-mail: curryadm@curry.edu
Web site: http://www.curry.edu
　　　http://on.fb.me/CurryColl_adm
　　　http://twitter.com/CurryAdmission

The suburban campus of Curry College is only minutes from the city of Boston.

DAEMEN COLLEGE
AMHERST, NEW YORK

The College

Daemen College is a private college established by the Sisters of St. Francis of Penance and Christian Charity as Rosary Hill College in 1947 (a liberal arts college for women). The College became coeducational in 1971. In 1976, it became independent and nonsectarian, changing its name to Daemen College.

The goal at Daemen is to offer the best integrated learning experience possible. The College cultivates minds that embrace connections, welcome challenges, and celebrate innovation. It equips students with invaluable skills that will benefit them and their communities for the rest of their lives.

Daemen has approximately 2,000 undergraduate and 900 graduate students. Students come from all over New York and the United States, as well as from other countries. Small class sizes and a 15:1 student-faculty ratio ensure that students will have an engaging and interactive classroom experience.

Fifty student organizations, themed dinners, movie nights, internationally famous speakers, and more contribute to a dynamic campus life.

Location

Daemen's beautiful suburban 39-acre campus is located in Amherst, New York. Daemen is just minutes away from the city of Buffalo, which has been named a top collegiate destination by the American Institute for Economic Research. Buffalo is renowned for the arts, offering exceptional theater, music, art, restaurants, and major league sports; it is also very close to scenic Niagara Falls and Canada. The campus is easily accessible by the major rail, plane, and motor routes that serve Buffalo.

Majors and Degrees

Daemen's Division of Arts and Sciences is well-suited for students who are interested in becoming anything from a novelist to an occupational psychologist. In Daemen's Visual and Performing Arts program, students learn how to take their talents and skills to the professional level, in a myriad of creative outlets: animation, children's books, intensive studio experience, and more. Daemen's modern language students get personalized instruction and become fluent in French, Spanish, or Chinese. The history and government major examines everything from ancient history to the politics of globalization, leading to careers in paralegal work, public affairs, foreign correspondence, law, and more. English majors become acquainted with everything from syntax to Shakespeare, and may move on to careers such as a magazine journalist or high school teacher. A math degree can lead to careers in teaching, research, architecture, meteorology, and banking, among others. Those studying natural sciences will major in biochemistry, biology, or natural science; a chemistry minor is also available. Biology students can specialize in environmental studies, while other specializations include forensic science, health science, and individual studies. Students can explore Christianity, Buddhism, Judaism, and more in the philosophy and religious studies program. Students who choose psychology embrace everything from neuropsychology to human sexuality, in preparation for careers in family therapy, school counseling, law enforcement, or other challenging areas.

Daemen's Division of Health and Human Services is designed to provide students for many career paths with a common destination: a professional orientation toward dedication to others—from special education teachers to athletic trainers, tax accountants to parole officers. Accounting majors crunch numbers but also consider global issues, to become financial analysts, company comptrollers, tax accountants and more. A Master of Science in athletic training is a five-year B.S./M.S. program. The business administration majors focus on economics, accounting, marketing, diversity and global management, and more. Future teachers in the education program study childhood/early childhood, special education, and visual arts education with certification opportunities in several areas and the

potential for extensive service learning experiences. Health-care studies covers all aspects of practical health care delivery. Students may choose from concentrations in community health, health and fitness training, and complementary and alternative health-care practices. The nursing partner curriculum program allows future nurses to earn both their associate degree (from a partner school) and a bachelor's degree in just four years. Physical therapy at Daemen is nationally recognized, and the Doctorate in Physical Therapy is obtained after six years. Daemen was the first small liberal arts college in New York State accredited to offer the D.P.T. Studies span orthopedics, pediatrics, geriatrics, tissue mechanics, sports medicine, wound healing, and more. Daemen's physical therapy students have a first-time pass rate on the National Physical Therapy Examination at or above both New York State and national averages, with a current three-year weighted average ultimate pass rate of 100 percent. Daemen's physician assistant studies program prepares students to become licensed to practice medicine with physician supervision. Strong growth is projected in this profession. Physician assistants do everything from writing prescriptions to assisting in surgery. The program is one of only 156 in the country to be accredited. Extensive service-learning opportunities include an annual trip to the Dominican Republic. The rigor of the program is evident in the 97–100 percent first-attempt pass rate on the NCCPA Certification exam (the national average is 90–94 percent). Students interested in shaping communities will find Daemen's social work program ideal. Practical opportunities abound, including participation in the Seneca Babcock Community Initiative. Graduates enjoy careers as counselors, therapists, probation/parole officers, school social workers, and other human service professionals.

Interdisciplinary programs include global and local sustainability.

Majors at Daemen include: accounting (B.S./M.S.); animation; art, with an emphasis in applied design/printmaking, drawing/illustration, graphic design, illustration, painting/sculpture, or visual arts education K–12; arts administration, with an emphasis in comprehensive arts, fine arts, or theater; athletic training (B.S./M.S.); biology, with an emphasis available in adolescence education 7–12 or environmental studies; biochemistry, with several preprofessional programs available; business administration, with an emphasis available in human resource management, international business, marketing, or sports management; education, with an emphasis in childhood education 1–6, childhood education/special education 1–6, or early childhood education/special education B–2; English, with an emphasis available in adolescence education 7–12 or communication/public relations; French, with an emphasis available in adolescence education 7–12; health-care studies, with an emphasis available in community health, complementary and alternative health-care practices, or health and fitness training; history; history and government, with an emphasis available in adolescence education 7–12 or environmental studies; mathematics, with an emphasis available in adolescence education 7–12; natural sciences, with an emphasis available in environmental studies, forensic science, health science, or individualized studies; nursing; paralegal studies; physical therapy (B.S.N.S./D.P.T.); physician assistant studies (B.S./M.S.); political science; psychology; religious studies; social work; and Spanish, with an emphasis available in adolescence education 7–12; sustainability (global and local); Pre-professional programs are available in pre-dentistry, pre-law, pre-medicine, and pre–veterinary science.

Academic Programs

Daemen has been named a College of Distinction for its exemplary commitment to engaged students, great teaching, vibrant communities, and successful outcomes.

Daemen College recognizes that education needs to prepare students for professional, intellectual, and civic leadership. The key to fostering the development of these skills is the core curriculum—a common educational experience for all students, regardless of

major. The Daemen College core is designed to strengthen students' abilities to become intellectually curious, acquire professional rewards, become responsible citizens, and deal with change. The core experience consists of seven competencies identified as essential. These competencies are introduced at the freshman level, and are emphasized across the entire curriculum so that students develop a greater understanding of, appreciation for, and practice of these important life skills through their academic work. As students complete the core they acquire the ability to think, adapt, and act in a multicultural environment in which the pace and complexity of change are escalating.

Research is carried out on a host of different fronts, from an innovative student/faculty think tank, to a high-profile wound therapy initiative. General research projects that include an enormous diversity of interests are showcased annually in the College's increasingly popular Academic Festival, held each spring.

The honors program meets the intellectual needs of the best students, ensuring that the Daemen experience challenges their minds and fosters their potential to contribute both to the community and to society at large.

The Center for Veterans and Veteran Family Services at Daemen provides a comprehensive support system for postsecondary education.

Daemen has a close professional and collaborative association among all members of the College's community while maintaining a student-centered atmosphere.

Off-Campus Programs

Alongside the outstanding and innovative courses that provide the academic foundation at Daemen, there are many other opportunities to enhance a student's education, such as internships, global education programs, and service-learning projects.

Daemen's Career Services Office helps students to find an internship or co-op position so they can gain real-world experience in their area of interest. Daemen students say this chance to gain more insight into their fields prepares them better for employment after graduation. Internships are available in a wide range of fields, including business, the sports industry, the arts, industry, government, health-related entities, nonprofit organizations, educational institutions, and cultural organizations. These can be local, national, or international and include excellent opportunities with the Washington Internship Institute.

Daemen's Office of Global Programs coordinates distinctive international programs designed to facilitate students' professional aspirations. In today's global economy, it is vital that students learn about different cultures, political systems, and histories. International study is a staple of the Daemen experience and the College offers semesters abroad, summer programs, and accelerated January term trips.

Daemen believes strongly in learning through service. During their time at Daemen, all undergraduate students engage in various service learning activities. Students participate as individuals or groups in short- and long-term projects or assignments that benefit the local, national, or global communities. Daemen students work with environmental organizations; assist refugee groups; help with programs to benefit the needy; serve residents of nursing homes, hospitals, and clinics; mentor in city schools; and work on other service projects in various cities throughout the city and the world.

Daemen has been named to the President's Higher Education Community Service Honor Roll for the past four years. Daemen founded and operates the Center for Sustainable Communities and Civic Engagement and is founder and headquarters for the Western New York Service Learning Coalition.

Academic Facilities

Modern apartment-style residence halls provide separate housing for men and women, in addition to the existing five-story residence hall for freshmen. Full-service meals are served in the main dining hall in the WICK Student Center.

The Research and Information Commons, a green building, is a technological showcase—a hub of academic research, as well as the academic and social heart of the campus.

Costs

For the 2011–12 academic year, tuition and fees were $22,310, and room and board were $10,300.

Financial Aid

Daemen creates individualized financial aid packages. Generous scholarships make attending the College very affordable. Over 92 percent of full-time undergraduates received some kind of financial assistance. The average award made to full-time undergraduates is approximately $20,400.

Faculty

Daemen has approximately 297 faculty members (full- and part-time).

Student Government

All students are members of the Student Association. The controlling body, or Senate, is composed of an executive board of officers and representatives who are elected each year. A Programming Board works with the Student Activities Director to plan several special events. Students also serve on many institutional committees.

Admission Requirements

Daemen offers a rolling admissions policy. The average student enrolled has a 90 GPA and 1050 SAT. Daemen also has a test-optional policy which provides students with a choice regarding the submission of standardized test scores.

The admissions staff helps guide students through the process from start to finish. Students can create their own personalized Daemen Connection Web page at http://www.daemen.edu/admissions.

Application and Information

Prospective students can apply for free online at daemen.edu/apply or https://www.commonapp.org. They can also call Daemen with any questions at 716-839-8225 or 800-462-7652 (toll-free).

Daemen College
4380 Main Street
Amherst, New York 14226
Phone: 716-839-8225
       800-462-7652 (toll-free)
       716-218-8830 (text)
E-mail: admissions@daemen.edu
Web site: http://www.daemen.edu/admissions
       http://www.facebook.com/DaemenCollege
       http://twitter.com/#!/daemencollege
       http://www.youtube.com/daemencollege

Visit Daemen—that's the best way to really get a feel for what the College has to offer.

DEAN COLLEGE
FRANKLIN, MASSACHUSETTS

The College

Dean College, accredited by the New England Association of Schools and Colleges, is a private residential college located on 100 pristine acres in Franklin, Massachusetts. Dean College is committed to fostering the academic and personal success of students by offering a variety of associate degree programs, transfer preparation for four-year institutions, and baccalaureate degrees in dance and arts and entertainment management. Students further benefit from the high quality of teaching, personalized academic support, and leadership development opportunities that promote a lifetime of learning and achievement.

Dean's graduates are highly successful; 85 percent of baccalaureate graduates are employed by September, and 95 percent of 2011 graduates were employed or in graduate school by December. Ninety-eight percent of associate degree graduates are accepted for transfer at highly selective colleges and universities. In addition, many associate degree graduates choose to stay at Dean to complete their baccalaureate degree.

The College has 1,100 full- and 500 part-time students. Its diverse student body includes representation from twenty-eight states and sixteen countries. Dean College offers a variety of housing options, with approximately 90 percent of full-time students living in residence halls.

Students can choose from over twenty-five active clubs and activities, eleven athletic programs, a thriving theater arts scene, and a renowned dance school. The College also offers dances, concerts, comedy nights, and provocative speakers. Varsity league play and intramural sports are available, with 9 acres of playing fields, a 900-seat gym, a 1,500-seat football arena, and lots of screaming fans.

Location

Franklin, Massachusetts, is a quiet, charming New England town ideally situated between Boston, Massachusetts, and Providence, Rhode Island. As a result, Dean students enjoy the best of both worlds: a small-college atmosphere where there is ample solitude for learning, combined with access to a wealth of cultural and recreational opportunities located in the big city just a 40-mile car or train ride away—not to mention the joys of Cape Cod and New Hampshire, also within easy range.

Day trips from Dean include New England Patriots, Boston Red Sox, Bruins, and Celtics games; Cambridge and Harvard Square; Boston's theater district; the Museum of Fine Arts in Boston; the museum of the Rhode Island School of Design; Newbury Street in Boston's Back Bay; shopping at Wrentham Outlets; concerts at the Providence Dunkin' Donuts Center; Tweeter Center concerts at Great Woods; New York City; Vermont's Green Mountains; and the Maine seacoast.

Majors and Degrees

Dean College offers Bachelor of Arts degrees in business, dance, liberal arts and studies, and arts and entertainment management. The B.A. in dance provides specialized education in the four main dance disciplines—ballet, jazz, modern, and tap—within a broad liberal arts environment. The B.A. in arts management focuses on study related to the business side of the

arts and entertainment world. The business degree as well as the liberal arts and studies degree offers a variety of emphasis tracks to help students personalize their degree program.

Dean College also offers associate degree programs in fifteen majors, designed to prepare students for baccalaureate degree programs and for transfer to major four-year institutions. Associate degrees are offered in business (with concentrations in business administration and business technology), communications, criminal justice, dance, early childhood education, English, health sciences, history, liberal studies, math/science, philosophy, psychology, sociology, sport/fitness studies (with concentrations in athletic training, exercise science, physical education, and sports management), and theater arts (with concentrations in musical theater and theater).

Academic Programs

A full-time student is required to register for a minimum of 12 credits of academic work per semester. For graduation, candidates must maintain a 2.0 cumulative grade point average (GPA), and demonstrate competency in reading/writing, mathematics, and computers. Bachelor's degree candidates must complete a required internship or other approved experiential learning opportunity related to their major.

Transfer credit toward a Dean degree may be earned by successfully completing courses at another regionally accredited college or university. Students may also earn credits through Advanced Placement (AP) tests and the College Level Examination Program (CLEP). For an associate degree, a maximum of 30 credits may be transferred; however, 24 of a student's last 36 credits must be earned at Dean College. For a Bachelor of Arts degree a maximum of 70 credits may be transferred; however, 24 of a student's last 36 credits must be earned at Dean College. In addition, all courses must be approved by the department.

Dean Foundations, a course taken during the first semester, helps students make a successful transition to college by teaching the academic and personal strategies necessary for success at Dean and beyond. Students enroll jointly in a section of the course, which is paired with a liberal arts course. The course instructor, a learning specialist, attends the liberal arts course with the students and then directly models effective learning strategies for that course with the students. In addition, students participate in campus events that address critical issues facing college students.

The Honors Program offers academically talented students an opportunity to engage in stimulating and challenging courses, seminars, and colloquia during their tenure at Dean College. Open to students who meet the entrance criteria, honors scholars enroll in honors sections of specific courses and may enhance non-honors courses through additional intensive reading and analysis with instructors. Exciting academic and cultural activities outside the traditional class environment are also available.

Study-abroad and study-away opportunities are available to all students through cooperative arrangements facilitated by

the college. Students may study abroad anywhere across the globe and the college maintains a strong relationship with the Washington Center Program for study in Washington, D.C.

Academic Facilities

The newly renovated Library-Learning Commons at Dean serves as the hub of the College's academic support efforts. Here, academic coaches provide one-on-one professional tutoring through the Personalized Learning Services program. Students also have access to peer tutors and can participate in weekly faculty drop-in sessions where group tutoring takes place across various disciplines.

In addition, as part of this facility, the E. Ross Anderson Library has a comprehensive collection of print and online resources to support research needs. The library houses more than 44,000 books and 200 periodical subscriptions, including extensive reference and legal materials.

The A. W. Pierce Technology and Science Building houses academic computer labs, science labs, and classrooms. The Dean College Children's Center, a laboratory preschool, offers a developmental approach to learning, a wide variety of indoor and outdoor activities, and special annual events.

The Campus Center houses the newly constructed Main Stage Theatre (opened in 2011) and newly renovated classroom space featuring SmartBoard technology, allowing professors to better engage students by taking a multimedia approach to education.

Costs

In 2011–12, Dean College tuition and fees were $31,950. Room and board totaled $13,640.

Financial Aid

In 2010–11, Dean provided students with more than $15 million of merit-based aid, with the average Dean financial award ranging from $9000 to $19,000. These awards, which are based solely on the information students provide on their admission application, not on financial need, help to reduce their average cost of attendance by more than 30 percent.

Approximately 90 percent of all full-time students at Dean College receive a scholarship that is not based on demonstrated financial need. Since the mission of Dean College is to nurture the potential within its students, these scholarships focus on current performance as well as future potential. They are based on academic or athletic performance, performing arts talent, place of residence, and academic potential. In addition, most students apply for—and receive—federal and state financial aid, which is separate from (and can be added to) Dean's scholarship awards.

Student financial aid packages are generally a combination of grants, loans, and work-study, contingent upon demonstrated financial need and the availability of funds. Dean College participates in all federal Title IV aid programs and the Federal Family Education Loan Programs. Residents of Massachusetts and other reciprocal states may also be eligible for state scholarships, grants, or loans. In order to be considered for need-based financial aid, students must submit the Free Application for Federal Student Aid (FAFSA). After receipt of a valid FAFSA, full-time students are considered for all of the financial aid programs that Dean administers.

Faculty

Dean's dedicated faculty members, advisers, and educational specialists—some of the best in their respective fields—offer direct, personal involvement to help students obtain the full value of their college experience. The student-faculty ratio is 17:1.

Student Government

The Student Government Association (SGA) at Dean College is the voice of the students. The organization provides a liaison between the student body and the administration through which information regarding Dean policies is channeled, seeks out student opinion, speaks for the student body, allocates funds collected from the student activities fee to clubs and organizations through a budget request process, and coordinates College activities by planning and helping various College clubs and organizations to plan individual, group, and campuswide activities.

Admission Requirements

Every application to Dean College is carefully reviewed by the Admission Committee. In addition to the completed application, students must submit an official high school transcript, a letter of recommendation from a guidance counselor or teacher, a written statement or essay, and SAT or ACT scores. Interviews are not required for admission to the College, but they are strongly recommended. Students applying for the dance program or the B.A. in theater program must complete an audition process.

Application and Information

Dean College accepts applications on a rolling basis, though it is recommended that applications be submitted by March 15. Once a completed file is received, a decision is made within two weeks.

Office of Admission
Dean College
99 Main Street
Franklin, Massachusetts 02038
Phone: 508-541-1508
        877-TRY-DEAN (toll-free)
E-mail: admission@dean.edu
Web site: http://www.dean.edu

Dean Hall, built in 1865 when Dean College was established.

DELAWARE VALLEY COLLEGE
DOYLESTOWN, PENNSYLVANIA

The College

Founded in 1896, Delaware Valley College (DelVal) is a private, coeducational four-year college enrolling approximately 1,700 full-time undergraduate students. The College concentrates on producing graduates who can fill employers' needs. DelVal is known for its experiential learning philosophy which combines theory with practice. The College is growing and continuing to expand opportunities for experience-based, cross-disciplinary learning.

DelVal tends to attract pre–veterinary science students; some of its most popular majors are small animal science, equine science, and conservation and wildlife management. Other science offerings include chemistry, environmental design, food science, microbiology and biotechnology, and zoology. The College also offers strong programs in business, criminal justice, counseling psychology, and media and communications. DelVal offers master's programs and extensive course offerings in continuing education, including a curriculum that provides adult learners with teacher certification.

Students attend Delaware Valley College, first and foremost, to prepare to enter professional careers. DelVal has an excellent record when it comes to job placement, proving that the time-honored educational philosophy of "scholarship with applied experience" is successful. A high percentage of graduates find employment in their field of study or enter graduate school within six months of graduation.

In addition to its academic programs, the College offers a wide range of extracurricular activities and events. DelVal has more than seventy clubs and organizations, many of which are linked with a specific major. Student publications include the weekly *RamPages* (newspaper), the *Cornucopia* (yearbook), and the *The Gleaner* (literary magazine). The College band and chorale give students the chance to demonstrate their musical talents. There are active minority and international clubs on campus. DelVal students are connected to the community in a variety of ways that are relevant to their majors. A-Day, the student-run campuswide fair, annually attracts 50,000 visitors who enjoy the festival, the entertainment, and the academically oriented projects.

Approximately 60 percent of students live on campus in ten residence halls. A full range of intercollegiate and intramural athletics programs (NCAA Division III, ECAC, and MAC) for both women and men is offered. All elements of the College's educational and recreational programs are in place to develop students as open-minded professionals who are capable of expanding their horizons in a future of unlimited possibilities.

DelVal offers graduate programs in general business, educational leadership, food and agribusiness, and accounting. The College also offers an online master's program in global leadership.

DelVal is officially recognized by the Middle States Commission on Higher Education.

Location

The College is located in historic Bucks County, Pennsylvania, approximately 30 miles north of Philadelphia and 70 miles southwest of New York City. Bucks County is one of the fastest-growing areas in the United States, yet it maintains its rich historical and agricultural heritage. The Doylestown area, where DelVal's main campus is located is rich in educational and cultural resources, including museums, a county courthouse, and a library which further enhance the educational opportunities available to students.

The Pennsylvania and New Jersey Turnpikes provide quick access to the College. A commuter railway system links the College with Philadelphia, providing daily scheduled arrivals and departures, right on campus. The College enjoys a relationship with its surrounding community that is mutually beneficial. Many students find convenient employment opportunities with local businesses, and the community benefits from the many events and activities that are held on campus.

Majors and Degrees

Delaware Valley College offers a variety of strong programs and is particularly strong in the life sciences. The College offers more than twenty-seven majors and specializations including biology (with programs in botany, environmental biology, microbiology/biotechnology, pre-professional biology, and zoology); business administration (with programs in accounting, financial services, general business administration, entrepreneurship, management, marketing, and sports management); chemistry and biochemistry; counseling psychology; English; media and communication; secondary education (with programs in agriculture, biology, business, chemistry, English, general science, and social studies); agribusiness; animal biotechnology (with programs in conservation and wildlife management, small animal science, and zoo science); animal science (with programs in equine science and management, livestock science and management, and science); dairy science; equine studies (with programs in equibusiness and equine training); food science, nutrition, and management (with programs in food science, food technology, nutrition science and restaurant and food service management); agronomy and environmental science (with programs in crop science, environmental science, and turf management); horticulture (with programs in commercial crop production and marketing/plant health management, hydroponic crop science, and plant sciences and biotechnology); and ornamental horticulture (with programs in environmental design, floriculture and nursery production and marketing, and landscape contracting and management).

The College also offers pre-professional preparation in dentistry, law, medicine, optometry, and veterinary medicine.

For students interested in applying to veterinary school in their third year, Delaware Valley College offers the 3+1 Program, where a contract is completed prior to May of the sophomore year. The program allows the student to enter veterinary school after three years (96 credits). After acceptance and verified completion of the first full academic year at a nationally accredited professional school, DelVal will confer the Bachelor of Science degree to the student.

Academic Programs

All courses are taught from a liberal arts perspective, which broadens the students' appreciation of cultural heritage. The College is committed to producing graduates who are both highly competent in their areas of study and skilled in more general areas such as communication, mathematics, and technology. Academic programs at DelVal combine theory with practice and students leave with valuable work experience. The College stresses a practical, hands-on approach to learning. Delaware Valley College's Experiential Learning Program (ExLP) provides active, hands-on applied experiences tied to specific academic objectives and outcomes as a requirement for graduation. It provides students the opportunity to participate in real-world activities as a basis for learning and to develop specific career goals and aspirations.

The academic calendar consists of two 15-week semesters, with an optional January term, and two optional summer sessions.

Off-Campus Programs

Students can earn credit by studying abroad. DelVal has programs that take students to the Hartpury College in the United Kingdom and the University of Podlasie in Poland. The Polish exchange program is free for students and is funded by the Copernicus Society of America.

Academic Facilities

Many of the courses taught at Delaware Valley College are laboratory or field oriented. The 571-acre main campus includes classrooms, modern laboratories, greenhouses, an arboretum, a library, livestock and dairy farms, an equestrian center, 400 acres of agricultural land, and 60 acres of horticultural land. Approximately 225 acres are dedicated to field crops for dairy and livestock operations, which include beef and dairy cattle, sheep, swine and standard-bred horses. Approximately 60 acres are used for horticulture (including plantings of apples, peaches and various fruits, vegetables, and nuts). DelVal also maintains an apiary for beekeeping programs.

These facilities serve just one purpose: to support the education and experience students need to succeed. Two additional campuses provide extensive opportunities for students. The Roth Living Farm Museum, in Montgomery County, is dedicated to providing historical information on farming practices. The Gemmel Campus, located 8 miles from main campus in Jamison, Pennsylvania, is a pristine, 398-acre farm. It houses an 18-acre apple orchard and students enjoy soils and other environmental science classes there. The DelVal philosophy is that students learn best when classroom learning and hands-on experience are combined. The facilities are designed with that goal in mind, and the faculty and staff utilize every building on campus in pursuit of the mission of preparing students for careers and future studies.

DelVal students benefit from the low student-laboratory ratio. This enables ready access to equipment, which is imperative to learning. Specifically, the College utilizes biology, chemistry, physics, plant science, and animal science laboratories. Facilities include a tissue culture laboratory, a food processing plant, a greenhouse-laboratory complex, a dairy, a small-animal science center, equine breeding barns, and an indoor equestrian center. The campus is itself a recognized arboretum that is managed by students and faculty members. These facilities are all supported by the Krauskopf Memorial Library, which houses some 80,000 publications.

Costs

Estimated costs for the 2011–12 academic year were: tuition and fees $30,946, room $4916, residential meal plan $5926, and books and supplies $1000 (if purchasing new books). However, DelVal offers a textbook rental program which allows students to rent textbooks for one semester for 35 percent of the cost of a new book. To keep a book for two semesters students pay 54 percent of the cost of a new book. This program significantly reduces student costs. A student who would spend $1000 annually purchasing new books at another institution would spend just $350 annually if they rented all of their books at DelVal.

Financial Aid

The College is committed to providing financial assistance so that every student is able to meet the costs of obtaining a college education. Approximately 98 percent of full-time under-graduates receive some type of financial aid. The College offers merit scholarships and grants for students with exceptional academic promise and participates in federal government programs such as Federal Pell Grants, Federal Supplemental Educational Opportunity Grants, Federal Perkins Loans, FederalWork-Study, Federal Academic Competitiveness grants, Federal SMART grants, and Federal TEACH grants. Students can borrow under the Federal Direct Loan program, and parents can borrow under the Federal Parent Direct Loan program. Residents of Pennsylvania can also apply for state grants through PHEAA.

Faculty

All courses at DelVal are taught by faculty members, not graduate students. The College's faculty is made up of dedicated professors who combine professional experience with deep theoretical knowledge. The faculty includes 82 full-time members as well as additional part-time instructors, who are friendly and accessible and always ready to help individual students make the most of the educational opportunities offered by the College. Approximately 60 percent of DelVal professors hold the highest degree available in their fields. The student-faculty ratio is 15:1.

Student Government

Students are encouraged to make the most of extracurricular activities to ensure that their education includes as many different experiences as possible. The student government acts to coordinate the activities of all organizations on campus and sponsors a variety of mixers, movies, concerts, and speakers.

Admission Requirements

The College seeks to recruit a diverse population of talented, motivated, and promising students, and draws them from across the nation. Criteria for admission include the application, academic transcripts, class rank, SAT or ACT scores, letters of recommendation, and a personal interview (recommended). While DelVal has a rolling admission period, applications should be submitted as early as possible in the senior year of high school, preferably by the end of the first marking period.

Application and Information

For more information about Delaware Valley College and its academic, athletic, and financial aid programs, students should contact:

Office of Admissions
Delaware Valley College
700 East Butler Avenue
Doylestown, Pennsylvania 18901-2697
Phone: 215-489-2211
       800-2DELVAL (toll-free)
Fax: 215-230-2968
E-mail: admitme@delval.edu
Web site: http://www.delval.edu
       http://www.facebook.com/delval
       http://twitter.com/delvalcollege

Delaware Valley College is located in Doylestown, Pennsylvania, about 30 miles north of Philadelphia and 70 miles southwest of New York City.

DENISON UNIVERSITY
GRANVILLE, OHIO

The University

Denison University is a highly selective, four-year, independent residential college of liberal arts and sciences for men and women. Founded in 1831, it is steeped in tradition and focused on the success of its approximately 2,100 students, who are educated to be curious, resourceful, and reflective. The student body is geographically diverse, representing forty-eight states, the District of Columbia and thirty-four countries. The University welcomed 605 members to the class of 2015, 42 percent of whom were in the top 10 percent of their graduating class.

Denison has achieved a national reputation based on its lengthy cultural heritage, the vitality of its intellectual and ethical concerns, and the performance of its graduates. Denison has more than 34,664 alumni and, as of June 2011, an endowment of $654 million. The Denison Annual Fund received more than $5 million in gifts from alumni, parents, and friends during fiscal year 2010–11.

The Bryant Arts Center, renovated and reopened in 2009, was awarded the U.S. Green Building Council's LEED Gold certification. It houses both the studio art and art history departments and offers state-of-the-art facilities for ceramics, painting, printmaking, photography, and digital media.

Ebaugh Laboratories, home to the chemistry and biochemistry departments, was renovated and expanded by 19,000 feet, and reopened for classes in fall 2011. The $38.5-million renovation of the Mitchell Recreation and Athletics Center is also under way and includes a new natatorium with an Olympic-size pool scheduled to open in summer 2012. The renovation will provide outstanding training facilities for varsity athletes and modern recreational facilities for students, faculty, staff, and community members. Both projects are being built according to LEED standards.

Ninety percent of students take advantage of the career counseling available from the Office of Career Exploration and Development. Each year, approximately 300 Denison students take part in the University's summer internship programs. More than half of Denison's graduates enroll in graduate or professional schools within ten years of graduation.

As a residential college, Denison requires its students to live in University housing all four years and offers a variety of housing options in its thirty-five residence halls. A full slate of social and cultural events is scheduled each semester. Thirty-seven percent of the students join the twenty-one fraternities and sororities present on campus. The Denison International Student Association, the Black Student Union, the Asian-American Student Union, the Asian Culture Club, the Students of Caribbean Ancestry, and La Fuerza Latina help to enrich the campus community.

Twenty-three intercollegiate sports for men and women and a wide variety of club sports are available. More than 75 percent of students participate in athletics or recreational activities. Denison's varsity teams have won a record twelve North Coast Athletic Conference All-Sports titles and have captured 116 conference championships since 1984, the founding year of the conference.

Location

The 900-acre Denison campus is located on a ridge overlooking the village of Granville, in central Ohio. Founded in 1805 by settlers from Massachusetts, Granville bears a marked resemblance to a New England village. Columbus, the state capital and fifteenth-largest U.S. city, is 27 miles to the west and is served by numerous national airlines. Granville has several fine restaurants and some shopping facilities, but those seeking the larger department stores go to nearby Easton Town Center or downtown Columbus. More than 80 percent of the students contributed over 38,000 hours of community service during the 2010–11 school year. State parks, lakes, bike trails, and ski areas are nearby.

Majors and Degrees

Denison offers Bachelor of Arts, Bachelor of Science, and Bachelor of Fine Arts degrees. Departmental, interdivisional , and individually designed majors, as well as concentrations within departments, are available within the degree programs. The B.A. can be earned through departmental programs in art (history or studio), athletic training, biology, chemistry, cinema, classics, communication, computer science, dance, economics, English (literature or writing), environmental studies, geosciences, Greek, history, international studies (as a double major), Latin, mathematics, modern languages (French, German, and Spanish), music, philosophy, physics, political science, psychology, religion, sociology/anthropology, and theater. The B.A. can also be earned through interdepartmental programs in black studies; East Asian studies; educational studies; philosophy, politics, and economics (PPE); international studies and women's studies. The B.S. is offered in biochemistry, biology, chemistry, computer science, geosciences, mathematics, physics, and psychology. The B.F.A. major is art (studio).

Preprofessional preparation is available in business, dentistry, engineering, environmental management, forestry, law, medical technology, medicine, nursing, occupational therapy, and veterinary science. Denison offers 3–2 programs in engineering with Rensselaer Polytechnic Institute, Washington University in St. Louis, and Columbia University; in forestry and environmental management with Duke University; and in medical technology with Rochester General Hospital. Also available is a 3–4 program in dentistry with Case Western Reserve Dental School.

Academic Programs

Denison expects its students to benefit from exposure to a broad liberal arts education and to achieve proficiency in a major field. University degree requirements include successful completion of approximately thirty-five courses (127 semester hours) with a 2.0 or better average, both overall and in the major and minor fields; fulfillment of all general education requirements; passing comprehensive examinations if required in the major; and fulfillment of minimum residence requirements. Approximately one third of a student's course work (thirteen courses) must be chosen from core course offerings in the humanities, sciences, social sciences, and fine arts. Another third is in the major field of study, and the remainder is in electives. There are opportunities for directed and independent study. Students may receive advanced placement or credit through College Board Advanced Placement (AP) tests or International Baccalaureate higher-level examinations. Credit is given for an AP score of 4 or 5. Denison's academic calendar consists of two semesters and an optional summer internship program, which includes internships and travel seminars. The academic year begins in late August and ends in early May.

Off-Campus Programs

Off-campus study acts as a catalyst in a Denison education. Its purposeful combination of classroom and experiential learning gives students the opportunity to hone the analytical literacy and capacity for informed judgment and constructive social engagement that are associated with a liberal arts education.

More than half of Denison students participate in off-campus study during their undergraduate career. The Denison list of accepted off-campus study programs includes over 150 domestic and international opportunities to meet the diverse educational interests of the student body. Through extensive advising and support, the off-campus study program invites students to explore these program possibilities in depth and to imagine how they can seek to engage the world as part of their Denison education.

Academic Facilities

Denison's William Howard Doane Library offers a full range of traditional and online services and collections. Liaison librarians for fine arts, humanities, natural sciences, and social studies collaborate

with faculty and students in their respective divisions of the college. The online catalog CONSORT offers access to 4.17 million volumes. As a member of the OhioLINK institutions and the Five Colleges of Ohio, library users also have ready access to more than 48 million volumes. The library is one of thirteen academic and administrative buildings on the academic and science quadrangles.

More than 650 Macintosh and Dell personal computers are available for student use in forty-three public and departmental labs and student clusters. A network dataport is available to every student living in a residence hall and wireless networking covers most of the campus. Laptops may be used online almost anywhere on campus, indoors or outdoors. For more information, students should refer to the library or computing links on the home page of the Denison Web site, listed at the end of this description.

Samson Talbott Hall of Biological Science features flexible teaching labs and interactive lecture and seminar rooms crowned by a spectacular greenhouse. The Chemistry Center contains well-equipped laboratories and a 292-seat circular auditorium. Features of the $7.2-million F. W. Olin Science Hall include a forty-two-seat planetarium with a Zeiss Skymaster projector, a laser spectrometer, and computer-based learning centers for physics and astronomy, geology and geography, and mathematics and computer science. The fine arts quadrangle on the lower campus is made up of six buildings with classrooms and performance facilities for art, music, theater and cinema, and dance. Burke Hall features a recital hall, a theater workshop, and the Denison Museum. Other buildings are the Theatre Arts Building; the Doane Dance Building; Burton Hall, which houses the Department of Music; the newly dedicated Bryant Arts Center; and the Cinema Building, the center of Denison's nationally recognized cinematography program.

Costs

Charges for the 2012–13 academic year are: tuition, $41,380; room and board, $10,360; and student fees, $900, for a total of $52,640.

Financial Aid

In 2010–11, Denison students received more than $60 million in financial assistance. More than 68 percent was awarded from Denison funds. Financial aid packages based on need are comprised of grants, loans, and employment on campus. Applicants for both federal and Denison grant aid must complete a Free Application for Federal Student Aid (FAFSA) as early as possible after January 1 and request that the information be sent to Denison. In addition to the institutional need-based grants, Denison offers more than 1,000 merit-based scholarships to first-year students, which range from $10,000 to $40,000. Denison awards up to twenty Paschal Carter scholarships for selected first-year applicants who earn National Merit Finalist status as determined by the National Merit Scholarship Corporation. It approximates full tuition, and the amount of the award stays constant during a student's enrollment at Denison. Alumni awards in the amounts of $16,000 and $10,000, recognizing academic achievement, leadership, and talent, are also offered. The financial aid decision is entirely separate from the admission decision. For more information, students should request the financial aid brochure from Denison's Office of Financial Aid.

Faculty

Denison's 219 full-time faculty members are deeply committed to teaching and to students. Many have national reputations in their fields; each year faculty members win national awards for teaching excellence. One hundred percent of faculty members have an earned doctorate or terminal degree in their fields. The faculty-student ratio is 1:10. Small classes (average class size is 19) and unique opportunities for one-on-one research with a faculty member encourage active learning. In 2011, 127 summer scholars did research with their professors on campus. All incoming first-year students are assigned a faculty adviser to assist with course selection and to ease the transition to college life.

Student Government

Through the Denison Campus Governance Association, students budget and direct such campus organizations as the Student Senate, FM radio station, Denison Film Society, and campus newspaper. Students are strongly represented on the governance councils of the University.

Admission Requirements

Entering first-year students must have earned at least 16 academic credits in secondary school, including 4 years of college-preparatory English. Strongly recommended are 3 years each of mathematics, science, foreign language (at least two of which should be in the same language), and social studies. A candidate for admission must file a formal application and an essay. Submission of the results of the SAT or the ACT is optional. SAT Subject Tests are not required, although students may provide these scores as additional information in support of their application for admission. International applicants must submit the results of the Test of English as a Foreign Language (TOEFL) or the results of the SAT/ACT. The Admissions Committee is particularly interested in the rigor of the academic program and the grade point average. Other selection criteria are written references from a college adviser and an academic teacher, extracurricular and personal accomplishments, and the student's essay on the application. An interview is strongly encouraged. It is Denison's goal to enroll academically talented students. Denison University admits students of any race, color, religion, age, personal handicap, sex, sexual orientation, veteran status, and national or ethnic origin.

Application and Information

Denison University is an exclusive Common Application College (www.commonapp.org). First-choice early decision candidates should apply by November 15 or January 15, and will be notified of a decision on a rolling basis. All admitted early-decision candidates must send an enrollment deposit within two weeks of notification of acceptance. Students interested in applying for admission under regular application status and for merit-based scholarship consideration must apply by January 15. Those deferred under early decision and all regular applicants are given a final decision by mid-March. Admitted candidates must respond to the admission offer by May 1.

Director of Admissions
Denison University
Box 740
Granville, Ohio 43023-0740
Phone: 740-587-6276
    800-336-4766 (toll-free)
E-mail: admissions@denison.edu
Web site: http://www.denison.edu
    http://www.facebook.com/denisonuniversity
    http://twitter.com/denisonu

Denison delivers to its students a lifetime of personal and professional success, as well as the knowledge, ability, vision, and resolve to bring coherence to a complex world.

DeSALES UNIVERSITY
CENTER VALLEY, PENNSYLVANIA

DeSALES UNIVERSITY

The University

DeSales University is a private, four-year Catholic university for men and women that is administered by the Oblates of St. Francis de Sales. Its mission is to provide high-quality higher education according to the philosophy of Christian humanism. The University imparts knowledge about, and develops talents for, personal, familial, and societal living, enriching the human community and enhancing the dignity of the individual through its educational endeavors. The University is accredited by the Middle States Association of Colleges and Schools.

In 1961, Joseph McShea was appointed Bishop of the new Allentown Diocese. At the time, the Diocese did not include a Catholic college for men. At the request of Bishop McShea, the Oblates of St. Francis de Sales agreed to assume responsibility for establishing a liberal arts college to serve this need. Allentown College of St. Francis de Sales received a charter to grant bachelor's degrees in 1964, and the first classes began in 1965. The College became coeducational in 1970; throughout the 1980s and 1990s, it began to offer graduate and cooperative education programs. These changes led to the college attaining university status, and it was renamed DeSales University in 2001.

Today, DeSales is home to more than 3,000 undergraduate and graduate students. Life on campus best illustrates DeSales' identity as a Christian humanist institution. Approximately 70 percent of the University's 1,600 undergraduate students live on campus and take full advantage of the rich opportunities provided. Students participate in more than forty clubs and organizations that encompass art, politics, and intramural sports; sixteen athletic teams competing in the NCAA Division III, including basketball, soccer, field hockey, and lacrosse; social outreach; student activities; and a Campus Ministry that enables students to participate in retreats and social justice groups. Billera Hall houses facilities for intercollegiate and intramural sports and fitness activities. The McShea Student Union contains health services and counseling offices. The Labuda Center for the Performing Arts houses the largest department in the University and is proud of its forty-year history of success. The University Center includes the University bookstore and expanded meeting space in addition to the food court, student dining facility, and student lounge. Eight suite-style residence halls offer a range of living options, including living-learning communities, which allows students with common interests to live together. A building dedicated to the University's business and health-care programs is scheduled to open in 2013.

Location

The Lehigh Valley contains three cities, including Allentown, the third-largest city in Pennsylvania; Bethlehem; and Easton. The region offers a wide range of year-round recreational activities, from skiing and skating in the winter to golf and swimming in the summer, and theater, dance, fine dining, shopping, and music year-round.

The Lehigh Valley has a wide variety of museums, art galleries, and concert venues for every taste and age group, while farmers' markets are a common sight throughout the region.

Amusement parks like Dorney Park and Wildwater Kingdom and the Crayola Factory are nearby, as are Kutztown Festival and other annual celebrations. The Promenade Shops at Saucon Valley offer more than sixty-five stores and restaurants and a state-of-the-art movie theater. For those wanting to travel beyond the region, the Lehigh Valley is less than 2 hours from New York City and 1 hour from Philadelphia.

Majors and Degrees

The University offers undergraduate degrees in more than thirty programs, including accounting, biochemistry, biology, business, chemistry, communications, computer science, criminal justice, dance, digital art, elementary education, English, finance, history, international business, law and society, liberal studies, management, management of information technology, marketing, marriage and family studies, mathematics, media studies, nursing, pharmaceutical marketing, philosophy, physician assistant studies, political science, premedicine, psychology, Spanish, sport and exercise science, sport management, television and film, theater, and theology.

Academic Programs

Students must complete forty courses with a minimum GPA of 2.0 to earn a bachelor's degree. Each degree program has three components. The General Education Core requires completion of sixteen courses, including two courses in English; three physical education courses; two courses in a foreign language or world cultures; two courses in history or political science; one course in art or music; one course in literature; five courses in modes of thinking, concentrating on literature, mathematics, natural science, philosophy, and social science; and three courses in theology. The major provides a thorough and systematic study of one subject area. The major requires completion of sixteen courses. As an alternative, a student may choose to enroll in a special degree program, which may extend the number of required courses. Electives comprise the remaining eight course requirements. Electives provide opportunities for learning in areas of special interest outside the student's major. Some students may want to consider a dual major, in which case the student must complete the requirements of both fields of study. Students who wish to complete a minor must take six courses within that field of study.

Off-Campus Programs

DeSales encourages qualified students to study abroad during the summer and/or the academic year. Through an affiliation with the Lehigh Valley Association of Independent Colleges, the University offers qualified students in a number of disciplines the opportunity to spend a summer or semester in Germany, Italy, Mexico, Spain, or other countries. Shorter, more intensive trips are offered to all students through a variety of clubs, organizations, and academic programs. Recent trips have taken DeSales students to South Africa, India, Peru, Romania, and other countries.

Academic Facilities

The campus contains twenty-four buildings. A state-of-the-art 37,000-square-foot Science Center houses classrooms and

laboratories for the natural sciences. Trexler Library contains more than 550,000 items, including 132,000 volumes and 40,000 electronic books, more than 12,000 electronic journals and newspapers, and 400,000 microfiche items. The periodical collection includes 550 paper and microform subscriptions. Collections of the other five independent colleges of the Lehigh Valley, totaling more than 1 million volumes, are available through an interlibrary loan system.

The University maintains ten computing laboratories or classrooms. The Academic Computing Center contains approximately sixty PCs in its main area, while ACC Computing Classroom houses twenty-three systems. Dooling Hall has three dedicated computing classrooms, each containing approximately twenty-five workstations. Trexler Technology Center contains forty-nine PC systems for both public use and classroom support. Each computing area is supported by at least one high-volume laser printer. All systems have Internet access and contain a suite of both application and network software.

Costs

In 2011–12, full-time tuition was $28,000 per academic year. Other annual fees included a Student Center fee and a technology fee totaling $1200. For students living on campus, room and board cost $10,520 per year.

Financial Aid

Nearly 90 percent of incoming students receive some form of financial aid. Students must complete the Free Application for Federal Student Aid and mail it to the processing center indicated on the form with DeSales University's Title IV code number, which is 003986, after January 1 of the student's senior year. The Office of Financial Aid processes requests for assistance on both a date priority and a financial need basis. The types and amounts of assistance a student will receive are specified in an award letter. The package also provides students and parents with a payment options letter, which outlines the three ways a student can finance the remaining cost of education. Parents may apply for a Federal Parent Loan for Undergraduate Students, students may apply for an alternative loan, or they may take advantage of a monthly billing plan.

All applicants are automatically considered for merit scholarships, which are awarded to incoming first-year students based upon academic achievement. Priority consideration is given to students who apply by December 1 of their senior year. Scholarships include Presidential Scholarships, which can award up to full tuition to students who earn a combined SAT score (math and critical reasoning sections) of at least 1300 (29 ACT) and rank in the top 5 percent of their high school class; Trustee Scholarships of $7000 to $10,000 for students who achieve a combined SAT score (math and critical reasoning sections) of at least 1200 (27 ACT) and rank in the top 15 percent of their high school class; and DeSales Scholarships of $5000 for students who achieve a combined SAT score (math and critical reasoning sections) of at least 1100 (24 ACT) and rank in the top 25 percent of their high school class. Department scholarships are awarded to students who attend scholarship day and demonstrate excellence in their field of study.

Faculty

There are 103 full-time faculty members teaching at the University. Eighty-five percent of the professors have a doctorate or the highest degree in their specialty. The average class size is 18 students, and the student-faculty ratio is 15:1. Students are assigned a faculty member from their chosen field of study to serve as an academic adviser; undeclared students are assigned to a faculty member who assists them in planning courses, deciding upon a major, and moving toward declaring a major.

Student Government

The Student Government Association is the liaison between the students and the administration. The Executive Board and each of the four undergraduate classes elect a president, vice president, secretary, and treasurer, for a total of 20 officers.

Admission Requirements

Admission is based on past academic achievement, particularly within a college-preparatory course of study, as well as the student's potential for future growth. Preferably, this includes four years of English; three to four years of college-preparatory mathematics; two years of modern, foreign, or classical language; and at least two laboratory science courses. Quality of academic performance is the single most important factor in the decision-making process.

Application and Information

DeSales University is a Common Application school and it uses a rolling admissions process; the University notifies applicants of their admission status within four weeks of receiving all application materials. To apply, students must submit a completed application, official high school or home school transcripts, official SAT or ACT scores, two letters of recommendation, and the $30 application fee. An on-campus interview is recommended but not required. For maximum consideration for scholarships, students are encouraged to apply by December 1.

Prospective students may direct their applications or requests for additional information to:

Admissions Office
DeSales University
2755 Station Avenue
Center Valley, Pennsylvania 18034-9568
Phone: 610-282-1100
E-mail: admiss@desales.edu
Web site: http://www.desales.edu

Fr. Bernard O'Connor, O.S.F.S., president of DeSales University, teaches a philosophy class every fall semester. Here, he mingles with students.

DIGIPEN INSTITUTE OF TECHNOLOGY
REDMOND, WASHINGTON

The College

DigiPen Institute of Technology is a global leader in game development education. As the first school in the world to offer a bachelor's degree in game development, DigiPen has helped advance the game and simulation industries for more than two decades by empowering students to become world-class programmers, engineers, designers, and artists. Located in Redmond, Washington, with branch campuses in Singapore and Bilbao, Spain, DigiPen offers undergraduate and graduate degrees in fields related to video game development, 3-D animation, and computer simulation.

While DigiPen's programs often result in employment in the video game industry, that outcome is secondary to the academic experience DigiPen offers. Students at DigiPen learn more than the tools and processes needed to succeed in the game industry—they gain the foundational knowledge and team experience to create new tools and processes themselves. DigiPen's programs achieve this by combining extremely rigorous and highly academic courses in fundamental subjects like mathematics, physics, and the fine arts with applied project classes that challenge students to put their knowledge into practice in a collaborative, deadline-driven production environment.

Location

DigiPen is located in Redmond, Washington, about 10 miles east of Seattle. The area is a major hub for software and technology, with over 350 interactive media companies near DigiPen's campus, including Microsoft, Nintendo of America, and Valve Software. Redmond is situated near the foothills of the Cascade Mountains, and offers ample opportunities to play in the outdoors, including numerous parks, hiking trails, and bicycle paths. The climate is generally mild, with little to no snow during the cool, wet winters and months of warm temperatures and sunshine during the summers. Nearby Seattle, a short 15-minute drive from DigiPen, is the cultural center of the Pacific Northwest, featuring abundant restaurants, museums, theaters, and music venues.

Majors and Degrees

DigiPen currently offers six undergraduate degree programs. The B.S. in computer science in real-time interactive simulation focuses on the science and mathematics at the heart of graphical computer simulations, including video games. The B.F.A. in digital art and animation teaches the core visual principles and foundational art techniques necessary to create engaging characters and environments for video games and films. The B.S. in computer engineering combines elements of electrical engineering and computer science to prepare students to design computer hardware and software interfaces. The B.A. in game design explores the visual and narrative aspects of game design, while the B.S. in game design examines the technical side of game design through programming and scripting. The Bachelor of Arts in music and sound design focuses on the

creative principles of interactive sound design, and the B.S. in engineering and sound design focuses on software engineering with an emphasis on its applications in interactive audio production. DigiPen also offers two graduate degrees: the M.S. in computer science, and the M.F.A. in digital arts.

Academic Programs

DigiPen's degree programs each have different admission and graduation requirements, but they share a common approach: rigorous classroom instruction in the academic foundations of their field coupled with team-based projects under real-world conditions. This combination of theory and practice creates graduates with both a deep understanding of their field and a wealth of experience in their chosen profession. Some student projects have been so successful that companies have hired entire DigiPen teams, such as the DigiPen graduates who created Valve Software's Portal series.

Off-Campus Programs

DigiPen students have the opportunity to earn credit through internships during their junior and senior years. DigiPen's student internship program is a carefully monitored work experience in which students learn about their discipline in an actual workplace under the supervision of a seasoned professional. Internships may be part-time or full-time, paid or unpaid, and may vary in duration, though they general last for one semester. Many companies have gone on to hire their DigiPen interns after they prove themselves to be valuable members of their team.

Academic Facilities

In 2010, DigiPen relocated to a new campus. DigiPen designed it to be an environment that would stimulate collaboration and creativity among its students. The campus' facilities include a game production lab with more than 250 seats designed to replicate a professional game production environment, a dedicated game-testing lab, a computer engineering lab for electronics projects, a sound lab, and numerous PC labs for instruction and student use. Because of the school's relationships with Microsoft and Nintendo, DigiPen students have access to a variety of professional software development kits (SDKs) in DigiPen's computer labs, including those for the Nintendo Wii, the Nintendo DS, and the Microsoft Kinect. DigiPen's campus library offers a range of resources, including sound effects libraries, reference books, journals and periodicals, more than 2,500 books, and more than 120 console and computer games. DigiPen's on-site café provides students with fresh and healthy food options, and its on-site convenience store gives students a place to purchase snacks and supplies without leaving campus.

Costs

Tuition at DigiPen is based on the number of credits a student takes. For the 2012–13 academic year, tuition is $23,960

(assuming a typical course load of 20 credits per semester). It is estimated that an additional $1925 per semester for personal expenses enables students to enjoy a typical campus life.

Financial Aid

A number of financial aid options are available to DigiPen students who qualify, including loans, grants, and scholarships. DigiPen participates in federal and state financial aid programs and has private sources of scholarship monies to award to eligible students.

Faculty

DigiPen's student body of less than 1,000 and the student-to-faculty ratio of 12:1 means that students have greater access to instructors and other educational resources. The majority of DigiPen's faculty work full-time, and there is little turnover year to year, allowing students to develop lasting relationships with faculty. Many of DigiPen's faculty members have taught at DigiPen for years while continuing to work at local game companies like Microsoft Game Studios, Nintendo of America, and PopCap Games.

Student Government

Each year, DigiPen students elect representatives to its Student Association, which acts as the student body's voice in its interactions with DigiPen's faculty and administration. The Student Association also hosts a number of campus events throughout the year.

Admission Requirements

Admissions requirements vary by degree program. Students applying to DigiPen's B.S. programs should have completed at least pre-calculus with a grade of B or better. Applicants to the B.F.A. program must submit a portfolio for review, while those applying to either of the game design programs must submit a game design of their own creation. Students applying to the B.A. in music and sound design program must provide a recorded musical performance.

Application and Information

For application forms, a catalog, or further information, students should contact:

Office of Admission
DigiPen Institute of Technology
9931 Willows Road NE
Redmond, Washington 98052
Phone: 425-558-0299
     866-478-5236 (toll-free)
     Fax: 425-558-0378
E-mail: admissions@digipen.edu
Web site: http://www.digipen.edu

DigiPen's 100,000-square-foot campus offers plenty of space for students to meet and collaborate, including a 250-seat game production lab designed to simulate a professional studio environment.

DOMINICAN UNIVERSITY OF CALIFORNIA
SAN RAFAEL, CALIFORNIA

The University

Dominican University of California is an independent, international, learner-centered university of Dominican heritage. It offers a beautiful setting, a close-knit community of over 2,000 students, and an intimate social environment that is an important context for academic goals and personal development.

The University offers many services that support its educational programs. It provides tutoring, career, and personal counseling without charge to Dominican students; offers housing, health, and job placement services; and helps students make the most of their college experience by its readiness to assist them in resolving problems.

The University and the Associated Students of Dominican University sponsor a number of campus activities each year for both resident and nonresident students. Dominican supports twelve intercollegiate teams that compete in the NCAA's Pacific Western Conference: men's and women's basketball, golf, cross-country, and soccer; men's lacrosse; and women's softball, tennis, and volleyball. Students can participate in the chorus, drama group, literary magazine, campus newspaper, campus ministry activities, special interest clubs, dances, and other social events.

Campus Ministry responds to the spiritual needs of Catholic and non-Catholic members of the University community. Catholic liturgies, ecumenical activities for students of all faiths, and community service projects are scheduled throughout the year.

Graduate degrees (M.A., M.S., M.S.N., M.S.O.T., M.F.T., and M.B.A.) are granted in biological sciences, counseling psychology, education, global management, humanities, nursing, occupational therapy, strategic leadership, and sustainable enterprise (Green MBA®).

The University is approved by the California Commission on Teacher Credentialing to prepare and recommend candidates for credentials in elementary, secondary, and special education.

Four residence halls of varied architecture accommodate more than 600 students; there is a dining hall for resident students and others who wish to purchase meals on campus. Forest Meadows, which comprises approximately 25 acres, is the site of the Conlan Recreation Center, a new synthetic turf soccer and lacrosse field (scheduled to open in fall of 2012), tennis courts, and an outdoor amphitheater where commencement exercises are held. The Recreation Center features regulation basketball and volleyball courts, two cross-courts for volleyball and basketball, and 1,285 spectator seats. It also features a weight-training and fitness room, a multipurpose room, lockers, athletic department offices, and conference rooms. Outside are a six-lane, recreational swimming pool and grassy patio area.

Location

The University is located on 80 wooded acres in scenic Marin County, which is 12 miles north of San Francisco and within a half hour's drive of Pacific Ocean beaches.

Majors and Degrees

A broad range of degrees and certificate and credential programs are offered in letters, the arts and sciences, and professional and preprofessional disciplines.

Undergraduate degrees (B.A., B.S., B.S.N., and B.F.A.) are awarded in the academic areas of art, art history, biological sciences (with concentrations in ecology, environmental science, general biology, molecular cell biology, and premedical studies), business administration (with concentrations in accounting, finance, international business, management, management information systems, and marketing), chemistry, communications and media studies (with concentrations in broadcast media, cinema, journalism, and print), dance (LINES ballet), English, English with a writing emphasis, health science (pre–occupational therapy), history, humanities, interdisciplinary studies, international studies, liberal studies (elementary teacher education), music, music with a performance concentration, nursing, political science, psychology, religion, and women and gender studies.

Minors are offered in environmental studies, Latin American studies, leadership studies, mathematics, philosophy, prelaw, and sports management.

Academic Programs

The General Education Program offers more than a brief exposure to the major areas of knowledge in the humanities, arts, and natural and social sciences. It is designed to provide a sequence of courses with a thematic focus that integrates the wisdom and perspectives of several disciplines. The focus assists students in discovering relationships between areas of knowledge, beliefs, cultures, and peoples that differ globally and historically, as well as in acquiring an awareness of tradition, a love of discovery, a respect for the diversity of the human condition, and a realization of human interdependence. Courses within the General Education Program also expose students to a variety of learning experiences, including discussion, lectures, seminars, simulations, practicums, and quiet reflection.

A strong internship program offers students job experience in areas of their choice.

An evening bachelor's degree–completion program (Pathways) for nontraditional learners is also available.

The ELS Language Centers program provides intensive, high-quality English instruction to prepare international students to enter American colleges and universities. Completion of the ELS Language Centers Program level 112 satisfies Dominican's English requirement for admission for international students.

Off-Campus Programs

Dominican offers exchange programs with Aquinas College, Grand Rapids, Michigan; Barry University, Miami, Florida; the College of New Rochelle, New Rochelle, New York; and St. Thomas Aquinas College, Sparkill, New York. These programs enable students matriculated at any one of the five colleges to spend a semester on a campus in a different part of the country, taking advantage of its location and programs. Students pay tuition on their home campus and room and board on the host campus. Further information about the program, which is recommended for students in the sophomore or junior year, is available in the Academic Advising Office.

Individualized programs for study in other countries may be planned in consultation with the Office of International Studies, the student's academic adviser, and the transcript evaluator. Dominican grants credit for international study only after a student who obtained prior approval of the program of study has returned to the campus and enrolled for the following year.

Academic Facilities

Archbishop Alemany Library houses more than 100,000 volumes in open stacks; 3,200 reels of microfilm; 775 videocassettes, 225 audiocassettes, and compact discs; and subscriptions to 375 periodicals in print and another 19,000 periodical titles in full text online. Reference services, including access to a variety of computerized databases and indexes, and multimedia facilities

are provided to assist students with their studies and assignments. The library also houses the Fletcher Jones Computer Laboratory, an art gallery, a listening room, and a fireplace corner.

Guzman Hall, Albertus Magnus Hall, Bertrand Hall, and the San Marco Art Studios together house faculty offices, science laboratories, lecture halls, a computer center, art galleries and studios, and classrooms. Angelico Hall houses an 850-seat concert auditorium and theater, music studios and practice rooms, and faculty offices.

In 2005, ground was broken on a $20-million, 35,000-square-foot science and technology facility. The Science Center opened for the fall 2007 classes, featuring more than thirty teaching, research, and computer technology labs.

Costs

Undergraduate full-time tuition (12–17 units per semester) was $36,900 per year for 2011–12. Fees were $450; room and board (a fourteen-meal-per-week plan) cost approximately $12,000 for the year.

Financial Aid

Financial aid is awarded on the basis of need and merit. Merit awards are available for both freshmen and transfer students based on academic achievement. Dominican University of California participates in various federal and state need-based financial aid programs and also has its own financial aid funds, donated by generous alumni and friends, available to help meet University costs.

Need-based financial aid comes in the form of scholarships, grants, part-time employment, and loans. The federal and state financial aid programs are the Federal Supplemental Educational Opportunity Grant, Federal Pell Grant, Federal Work-Study Program, Federal Stafford Student Loan, CLAS/PLUS loan, and Cal Grants A and B. Eligibility for need-based aid is determined after the student, who must be a citizen or permanent resident of the United States, files the Free Application for Federal Student Aid (FAFSA). The need-based financial aid deadline for first-priority consideration is March 2, although late applications are accepted. Student assistantship positions are also available for graduate students.

Faculty

Students find themselves intellectually challenged by the faculty members, who hold degrees from colleges and universities throughout the world and who are committed to individualized teaching and careful supervision of students' development. Seventy-nine percent of Dominican University's full-time faculty members have terminal degrees (the highest obtainable degree in their field). The student-faculty ratio is 11:1.

Student Government

The primary vehicle through which students plan and provide activities, distribute activity funds, and represent themselves to the University's administration and broader community is ASDU—the Associated Students of Dominican University. ASDU is the student association and the student government body. Through elected and appointed representatives to various Dominican committees and governing groups, students may voice their opinions on institutional matters.

Admission Requirements

Dominican University of California welcomes applications from prospective students of all ages, religions, races, and national origins. The University believes that academic potential is measured by more than grades alone. Each candidate for admission is given individual consideration and is evaluated by the Admissions Office on the basis of the student's past scholastic record, present motivation, and potential intellectual development, as indicated by all of the admission materials submitted.

Recommended for undergraduate admission is graduation from an accredited high school with a total of at least 15 units in college-preparatory subjects, to include the following: 4 years of English, 2 years of the same foreign language, 2 years of college-preparatory mathematics (algebra, geometry, algebra 2/trigonometry), 2 years of laboratory sciences to be taken in grades 10–12, and 1 year of U.S. history (1 year of world history or Western civilization is an acceptable alternative for international students). The University encourages students to choose additional courses in at least two of the following areas: English, history, foreign language, social science, advanced mathematics, laboratory science, music, art, and computer science.

Dominican University of California admits highly qualified students after the completion of their junior year in high school if they have fulfilled all admission requirements for freshman standing or passed an equivalency exam and arranged a conference with a member of the admission staff prior to acceptance.

High school seniors wishing to take up to two Dominican courses per semester to meet high school graduation requirements may do so with the written permission of their high school principal or counselor. Arrangements must be made through Academic Advising and Support Services.

Application and Information

The Admissions Office makes its decision on each freshman candidate after receiving his or her completed application form with a $40 nonrefundable fee; an official high school transcript to date; one recommendation from a teacher, administrator, or counselor; scores from either the SAT or the ACT; and a personal essay, as described in the application. For information about the SAT, students should write to Educational Testing Service, 1947 Center Street, Berkeley, California 94704 or P.O. Box 592, Princeton, New Jersey 08541. For information about the ACT, students should write to American College Testing Program, Operations Division, P.O. Box 168, Iowa City, Iowa 52243.

Transfer students must also submit the application form, a $40 fee, and their high school transcript and official test scores if they have fewer than 24 transfer units. In addition, they must send official college transcripts to date; a personal essay, as described in the application; proof of high school graduation; and one academic letter of recommendation or one professional letter of reference.

International students should fulfill the admission requirements for native students; however, an SAT or ACT score is not required. Passing scores for the Test of English as a Foreign Language (TOEFL) of at least 550 (paper-based) or 80 (Internet-based) or official certification of achieving level 112 in the ELS program may be submitted in lieu of SAT or ACT scores. All transcripts must be translated into English and evaluated by an accredited evaluation agency. In addition, a notarized declaration of finances in U.S. dollars must be submitted.

An interview with a member of the admission staff is strongly recommended to enable the candidate and the University to become acquainted with one another.

Students may apply online at the University's Web site, or they may obtain application forms and information by contacting:

Office of Admissions
Dominican University of California
50 Acacia Avenue
San Rafael, California 94901-2298
Phone: 415-485-3204
          888-323-6763 (toll-free)
Fax: 415-485-3214
E-mail: enroll@dominican.edu
Web site: http://www.dominican.edu

DOWLING COLLEGE
OAKDALE, NEW YORK

The College

At Dowling College, students are not only the top priority, they are the mission. Dowling believes education leads to important discoveries—each student will make many discoveries about the world as well as about themselves. By working with Dowling's renowned faculty, students will discover talents and abilities that they may not yet know they have.

Dowling College's faculty and staff members seek to inspire students to reach beyond their expectations, to prepare them for the challenges and opportunities for today, for tomorrow, and for life. Students have access to an extensive array of career services support including career development workshops and internships as early as their sophomore year. Dowling is proud that within a year of graduation, 96 percent of its graduates are either employed or attending graduate school. And like all of Dowling's more than 35,000 alumni, today's students will also have lifetime access to Dowling's career services center.

The apartment-styles suites in the residence halls at the historic Rudolph-Oakdale campus and Brookhaven campus give students the opportunity to live on their own while learning how to manage their time between classes, working on or off campus, maintaining a comfortable living environment, and attending different school activities.

Location

Dowling College is located on the south shore of Long Island, just 50 miles from New York City and the Hamptons, and minutes from ocean beaches.

Majors and Degrees

Dowling recently launched several new degree programs, including a B.S. degree in TESOL (teaching English to speakers of other languages), an online B.B.A. degree in management and leadership, an online M.S. degree in educational technology leadership, and an Ed.D. degree in education administration with a concentration in health care. Also available are online advanced certificates in health care management, marketing, project management, and human resources management.

The School of Arts and Sciences has developed a core curriculum of arts and humanities, natural science, math, and social sciences that ensures career versatility in an ever-changing world. Dowling College is constantly evolving to prepare students for growing career sectors, as evidenced by newly revised programs in math and computer science, graphic design, and digital arts, and graduate studies in environmental microbiology. The School of Arts and Sciences prepares students for careers that can impact the world through art, poetry, and music or by exploring and preserving our natural environment.

Dowling College's School of Education is one of the largest teacher and administration preparation programs in New York. Approximately 5,000 teachers working on Long Island received their education degrees from Dowling College. Whether a student is interested in literacy education, early childhood education, or physical education, the School of Education can help prepare them to inspire the next generation.

Students enrolled in the Townsend School of Business learn the knowledge and skills that are in high demand by employers in today's economy. The School of Business readies students for the challenges and opportunities of today's marketplace and emerging world economy. As a result, graduates become motivated entrepreneurs and executives, taking full advantage of the growing business opportunities and trends that exist in today's business world.

The School of Aviation offers students the education they need to excel in careers like air traffic control, aviation management, and commercial piloting. Dowling graduates are intensely recruited by employers who know they receive a balanced liberal arts background as well as experience in with the industry's most advanced equipment. Situated at Brookhaven Airport, the School of Aviation offers extensive flying opportunities with close proximity to some of the world's most varied and demanding airspace.

Academic Programs

Dowling College is extremely proud of the more than 120 academic offerings available through our schools of Arts and Sciences, Aviation, Business, and Education. And *U.S. News and World Report* lists Dowling's online graduate business degree as one of the top online programs in the nation.

Academic Facilities

With over $50 million invested in the campus infrastructure since 2000, Dowling's facilities are designed to enhance every student's learning experience.

One thing students won't find on campus is a single lecture hall, which helps create a more personal learning environment. Smart classrooms bring the curriculum to life with Internet access, digital projectors, and the Blackboard Learning System, which enables students to access and share documents from anywhere in the world. A new science laboratory, flight and air traffic control simulators, new classrooms, a newly converted Music House, and a newly redesigned library are just some of the exciting improvements around the Dowling College campus.

On-campus amenities include the Lion's Den student lounge, convenient fitness centers, and two cafeterias—one newly redesigned, where students can dine overlooking the scenic Connetquot River.

Costs

For the 2011–12 academic year, full-time undergraduate tuition was $24,118 for 24–34 credits. Graduate tuition was $933 per credit hour. Tuition for the distance-learning M.B.A. was $796 per credit hour. Doctoral program tuition was $48,000 for the full program. Tuition for the Saturday M.B.A. was $37,500 for the full program.

Financial Aid

There are numerous sources of financial aid available to help students achieve their goal of earning a degree from Dowling College. More than 75 percent of Dowling students receive some sort of financial aid to cover all or part of their educational costs.

Dowling's goal is to bring its high-quality education within the financial reach of all its students.

Faculty

Dowling students have the advantage of small class sizes (15:1) that allow for one-on-one opportunities with professors. Over 95 percent of full-time faculty members have earned the highest degrees in their discipline, and are ready to share their knowledge and expertise. All classes at Dowling are taught by professors, not teaching assistants.

Student Government and Organizations

Through the elected Student Government Association (SGA), students stimulate interest, involvement, and cooperation in self-government. The SGA establishes and maintains conditions leading to high scholastic and creative achievements, develops a spirit of democratic student life in the student body, and fosters cooperation between all student organizations.

With more than forty clubs and organizations, fifteen NCAA Division II sports, special events, and more, Dowling offers a vibrant community for students. If a student sees an opportunity for a new club, they are welcome to create one. *The Lion's Voice* student paper, online event calendars, the Weekly Roar, and a ticker on campus keep students informed of upcoming events.

There's always something happening at Dowling. Students can paddle one of the campus kayaks in front of historic Fortunoff Hall, join other students working out on the Fit Trail, take part in an open mic night, feast at a club-sponsored cookout, take in a play at the Loft Theatre, or check out art exhibits at Dowling's Anthony Giordano Gallery.

Admission Requirements

Prospective students or applicants must provide evidence of a strong high school academic performance; SAT or ACT scores; and one or more letter(s) of recommendation from a high school or college guidance counselor, teacher, or school-based administrator. Letters from other sources, such as a volunteer coordinator, may also be considered. Applicants who do not meet the admissions requirements may be reviewed by the Admissions Academic Standards Committee and may be admitted under the Enhanced Right Start Program.

Dowling College will transfer up to 75 credits from a two-year college and up to 90 credits from a four-year college. Dowling accommodates transfer students by making the process easy, convenient, and personalized from start to finish—one of the many benefits available to students when they transfer to Dowling College.

Application and Information

Whether a student is looking to begin their college career, resume a degree program, or transfer from another institution, the best way to discover Dowling is to experience it first-hand.

Interested students can call 631-244-1390 for application information or to schedule a tour of the College's historic Vanderbilt mansion at the Rudolph-Oakdale campus or the airport runways and athletic fields at the 105-acre Brookhaven Campus. Prospective students are invited to visit the College's Web site at www.Dowling.edu and follow Dowling via Twitter or Facebook.

Office of Admission
Dowling College
150 Idle Hour Boulevard
Fortunoff Hall, Room 225
Oakdale, New York 11769
Phone: 631-244-3141
       800-369-5464 (toll-free)
Fax: 631-244-1078
E-mail: admissions@dowling.edu
Web site: http://www.dowling.edu

Dowling College's athletic fields are located at the 105-acre Brookhaven Campus.

DREXEL UNIVERSITY
PHILADELPHIA, PENNSYLVANIA

The University

Drexel University is a private, nonsectarian, coeducational university that has maintained a reputation for academic excellence since its founding in 1891. The University's technologically focused approach to learning prepares undergraduates for a variety of careers and graduate school. Full-time work experience through the cooperative education program is a vital part of a Drexel education. Students gain professional experience in jobs related to their career interests by alternating classroom study with periods of full-time employment. Last year's undergraduate enrollment numbered 12,004 full-time students representing forty-eight states and ninety-five other countries. International students comprise about 10 percent of the undergraduate population. Drexel University grants associate, bachelor's, master's, and doctoral degrees and certificates in a variety of programs.

Nine residential halls house almost 4,000 students on campus. Both the Campus Activities Board (CAB) and Drexel's nearly thirty active fraternities and sororities sponsor events such as dances, lectures, excursions, community service projects, and free movie screenings. Students can also take part in a variety of extracurricular activities and over 220 student organizations, including musical groups, MAD Dragon Records, a radio station, a filmmaking society, dance troupes, theatrical productions, a cable TV station, a student-run newspaper, and communities of faith. Drexel offers eighteen NCAA Division I varsity athletic programs and competes in the Colonial Athletic Association Conference. The University also sponsors intramural and club sports.

Drexel is committed to expanding its already vast educational opportunities. In 2006, Drexel opened the Earle Mack School of Law, which earned full accreditation from the American Bar Association in 2011. In January 2009, Drexel opened the Sacramento Center for Graduate Studies in California, which offers graduate degrees in both online and traditional classroom formats. In addition, through a partnership with Burlington County College (BCC) in Mount Laurel, New Jersey, Drexel at BCC offers a satellite campus where transfer students from southern New Jersey can earn a bachelor's degree in certain programs.

Location

Drexel is located in the heart of Philadelphia, the nation's fifth-largest metropolitan area and shares its University City neighborhood with the University of Pennsylvania and the University of the Sciences. With thousands of student residents, University City is a great place for students to spend their college years in an urban campus setting, surrounded by the experiences of the city and the diversity of their peers. Philadelphia is home to some of the nation's best historical and cultural attractions and offers all the amenities of a first-class city, including vibrant nightlife, choice restaurants, dynamic arts, and major league athletics. Drexel's location offers easy access to public transportation. The Drexel shuttle provides convenient, free transportation between campuses. Adjacent to Drexel's University City Main Campus, Amtrak's 30th Street Station is a hub for trains and buses to the Philadelphia suburbs, New York City, Washington, D.C., and beyond.

Majors and Degrees

Whatever their interests, students at Drexel are at the forefront of their fields. Drexel comprises thirteen colleges and schools that offer more than seventy undergraduate majors and over twenty accelerated degree programs. Academic majors and concentrations include accounting, animation and visual effects, anthropology, architectural engineering, architecture, behavioral health counseling, biological sciences, biomedical engineering, business administration, business and engineering, business for Still-Deciding Students®, chemical engineering, chemistry, civil engineering, communication, computer engineering, computer science, construction management, criminal justice, culinary arts, culinary science, custom-designed major, dance, design and merchandising, economics, electrical engineering, elementary education, engineering, engineering for Still-Deciding

Students®, engineering technology, English, entertainment and arts management, entrepreneurship, environmental engineering, environmental science, environmental studies, fashion design, film and video, finance, game art and production, general business, general humanities and social sciences for Still-Deciding Students®, graphic design, health services administration, history, hospitality management, information systems, information technology, interior design, international area studies, international business, invasive cardiovascular technology, legal studies, management information systems, marketing, materials science and engineering, mathematics, mechanical engineering, media arts and design for Still-Deciding Students®, music industry, nursing, nutrition and foods, operations management, pathway to health professions, philosophy, photography, physics, political science, product design, psychology, radiologic technology, science for Still-Deciding Students®, screenwriting and playwriting, sociology, software engineering, sport management, television, and Web development.

Drexel applicants can pursue an accelerated degree program, which allows students to earn more than one degree in a shortened period of time. Accelerated degree options include the B.A./B.S./J.D. in law; B.A./B.S./M.D. in medicine; B.S./D.P.T. in physical therapy; B.S./M.H.S. in physician assistant studies; B.S./M.P.H. in public health; B.S./M.B.A. programs in business, culinary arts, culinary science, design and merchandising, entertainment and arts management, hospitality management, and music industry; B.S./M.S. programs in accounting, biomedical engineering, communication, education, engineering, physics, psychology, and majors within the iSchool; B.S./Ph.D. in engineering; and B.A./B.S. in history/M.S. in library and information sciences.

Academic Programs

Qualified students can apply to the Pennoni Honors College, which is open to students in every academic discipline. The honors program offers special living communities designed for the exceptional student and opportunities for social activities, traveling, and independent projects. Specific classes for honors students and honors sections of general and required courses are available. Students who satisfy the program requirements qualify for Graduation with Distinction.

At Drexel, students have opportunities to conduct research. The STAR (Students Tackling Advanced Research) Scholars program invites qualified students to participate in faculty-mentored research projects in their chosen fields as early as the freshman year. Students who take part in these research opportunities may be eligible for stipends or academic credit.

Off-Campus Programs

Classroom study is essential, but experience makes all the difference. Through Drexel Co-op, students have the opportunity to test-drive their degree in a professional setting by alternating periods of full-time work experience with periods of classroom study. Students can earn up to eighteen months of workplace experience before graduation in paid full-time positions with employers such as Fortune 500 companies, major pharmaceutical companies, and top design firms, as well as nonprofit agencies and government organizations. More than 1,200 employers in forty-one states and forty-five international locations participate in the Drexel Co-op program. The average six-month co-op salary is $15,808.

Drexel has an active study-abroad program in thirty countries around the world that allows students from all majors to spend a term or several terms studying abroad, earning credit toward their degrees and gaining valuable international experience. With any Drexel-sponsored program, students pay Drexel tuition rates and receive financial aid while abroad.

Academic Facilities

Drexel has five campus locations: University City Main Campus, Hahnemann Center City Campus, Queen Lane Medical Campus, Sacramento Center for Graduate Studies, and Drexel at BCC. The University's library system comprises the W. W. Hagerty Library,

the Library Learning Terrace, the Legal Research Center, and three health sciences libraries. The W. W. Hagerty Library, the University's central library located on Main Campus, maintains subscriptions to nearly 12,000 electronic journals, which are accessed via the library website, along with academic journals and 200 databases. Students may borrow laptops for use in the library. The Library Learning Terrace, a 3,000-square-foot flexible learning space located in a residence hall and staffed by librarians, enables students to learn and research collaboratively through a variety of technologies. The Legal Research Center on the third floor of the law school shares University databases while continuing to acquire new material. The additional libraries on the health sciences campuses provide study space, 75,000 books, and network access to the same set of online journals and databases.

The University is expanding through the addition of several new, state-of-the-art buildings. The Papadakis Integrated Sciences Building, featuring North America's largest biowall, opened in 2011. This five-story, 130,000-square-foot building contains thirty-nine research and teaching laboratories used by the biological sciences. Millennium Hall is a seventeen-story, green-certified residence hall that opened in 2010 and serves as home to students in the Pennoni Honors College. Currently under construction are the URBN Center, designed to house the Westphal College of Media Arts & Design, and the twelve-story, 177,500-square-foot LeBow College of Business building.

Costs

Cost of attendance at Drexel is determined by the co-op plan. Depending on the academic course of study, students can select the Three Co-op Option or the One Co-op Option. The Three Co-op Option includes three six-month periods of full-time employment and takes five years to complete. The One Co-op Option includes just one six-month period of full-time employment and takes four years to complete. The full-time undergraduate tuition for the 2012–13 academic year is $33,800 for the Three Co-op Option and $41,500 for the One Co-op Option. Costs for on-campus housing and the campus meal plan average around $14,000 per year. Fees are approximately $2300 per year, depending on the degree program.

Financial Aid

Nearly 80 percent of freshmen applied for financial aid in the 2011–12 academic year. The average financial assistance package, including academic, athletic, or performing arts scholarships; grants; loans; part-time work-study employment; and federal programs, was $23,000. All incoming students are encouraged to submit the Free Application for Federal Student Aid (FAFSA) by February 15. Notification to students begins mid-March. Drexel offers an achievement-based award with an annual value of up to $27,000 to qualified incoming freshmen and transfer students. Criteria include a strong academic record and involvement in extracurricular and community service activities. The Drexel Liberty Scholarship also provides fifty full-tuition scholarships to low-income students who are Philadelphia residents and who attend Philadelphia high schools.

Faculty

Approximately 95 percent of Drexel's full-time faculty members hold a Ph.D. or the highest degree in their field. The University requires faculty members engaged in research and graduate-level teaching to also teach at the undergraduate level, allowing the undergraduate student to benefit from the research activities of the faculty. Specially selected faculty members serve as advisers for freshmen. The student-faculty ratio is 10:1.

Admission Requirements

All colleges within the University require completion of a college-preparatory program in high school that includes at least 3 years of mathematics and 1 year of laboratory science. Students applying to major in the sciences or business and engineering are required to take 4 years of mathematics (through trigonometry) and 2 years of laboratory science. Engineering requires 4 years of mathematics (through trigonometry and precalculus), chemistry, and physics. The quality of academic performance is more important than merely meeting minimum requirements. The strength of preparation is judged primarily by rank in class or relative grade point average, by the degree of improvement in the quality of the academic record, and by the comments and recommendations from principals, guidance counselors, or teachers. Freshman applicants are required to take the SAT or the ACT. Students who were accepted and enrolled in the fall of 2011 had an average unweighted GPA of 3.4 on a 4.0 scale and an average SAT of 1200 out of 1600, including the math and critical reading sections. An essay or personal statement is required, the subject of which is dependent on the major and program. Transfer applicants must have a minimum 2.5 cumulative average (2.75 for engineering, information systems, and information technology; 3.0 for nursing) for consideration and generally are expected to complete at least 24 credits at a regionally accredited four-year college or two-year community college in a program of study comparable to the one being sought at Drexel.

Application and Information

Applications to Drexel are available online (http://www.drexel.edu/apply) or from the address listed below. The Common Application is accepted as well. Applications must be accompanied by a nonrefundable application fee of $75; however, the fee is waived for online applications or applications submitted during a campus visit. Applications for the Westphal College of Media Arts & Design's early decision program are due November 15. Early decision is binding; students admitted through the early decision process are required to confirm their intention to enroll by February 1. Applications for the B.A./B.S./M.D. accelerated degree program are also due November 15. Applications for all other accelerated degree options are due December 1. Applications for regular full-time undergraduate status and regular decision applications for Westphal College are accepted throughout the senior year until February 1. Drexel subscribes to the College Board Candidates Reply Date of May 1. Transfer students should apply at least three months before the beginning of the term in which they wish to enroll.

Undergraduate Admissions
Drexel University
3141 Chestnut Street
Philadelphia, Pennsylvania 19104-2876
Phone: 215-895-2400
      800-2-DREXEL (toll-free)
Web site: http://www.drexel.edu/admissions (admissions)
      http://www.drexel.edu/undergrad/apply (application)
      http://www.facebook.com/drexeladmission (Facebook)
      http://twitter.com/DrexelAdmission (Twitter)

Ms. Joan McDonald
Senior Vice President of Enrollment Management
Drexel University
Phone: 800-2-DREXEL (toll-free)
Fax: 215-895-1285
E-mail: enroll@drexel.edu

Drexel University campus, Market Street, Philadelphia, Pennsylvania.

D'YOUVILLE COLLEGE
BUFFALO, NEW YORK

The College

D'Youville College is a leading institution of higher learning for traditional and nontraditional undergraduate, master's, and doctoral level students from around the world. A significant number of the students come from Western New York and Canada. Students receive a well-rounded general education and specific training and experiences to improve the quality of life across the globe. D'Youville is a nurturing community that seeks to ensure the success of each student in diverse fields such as health care, education, and business. D'Youville offers the diversity and academic excellence of a large school, and the attention and sincerity of a small one.

D'Youville is a private, coeducational, liberal arts and professional college that has offered students an education of high quality since 1908. The College was the first in western New York to offer baccalaureate degrees to women. Its current enrollment is 3,100 men and women. Students may choose from thirty undergraduate and graduate degree programs that are enhanced by a 14:1 student-faculty ratio. The College is committed to helping its students to grow not only in academics but also in the social and personal areas of their college experience.

Students residing in Marguerite Hall or the new student apartment complex have a scenic view of the Niagara River and Lake Erie, which separate the U.S. and Canadian shorelines. The Koessler Administration Building, which once housed the entire college, now contains administrative offices, the chapel, Kavinoky Theatre, and the Learning Center. The Student Center, the focal point of leisure and extracurricular activities, has a new gymnasium, a swimming pool, fitness and wellness area, a training room, a dance studio, a general recreation center, and the main dining facilities. Student organizations and regularly scheduled activities, including intramural sports, NCAA Division III intercollegiate sports (baseball, basketball, crew, volleyball, golf, cross-country, soccer, and softball), a club hockey team, a ski club, the College newspaper, the yearbook, and social organizations, as well as academic programs, all help to make up an active campus life.

Location

D'Youville is situated on Buffalo's residential west side. The College is within minutes of many local attractions, including the downtown shopping center, the Kleinhans Music Hall, the Albright-Knox Art Gallery, two museums, and several theaters that offer stage productions. Seasonal changes in the area offer a variety of recreational opportunities. Buffalo is only 90 miles from Toronto and 25 minutes from Niagara Falls, making it a gateway to recreation areas in western New York and Ontario. Holiday Valley, a skier's paradise, is an hour's drive away. The city is served by the New York State Thruway, Amtrak, Greyhound and Trailways bus lines, and most major airlines.

D'Youville enjoys a diversified interchange with the community due to its affiliations with schools, hospitals, and social agencies in the area. College students in the Buffalo area number more than 60,000.

Majors and Degrees

D'Youville offers the degrees of Bachelor of Arts (B.A.), Bachelor of Science (B.S.), and Bachelor of Science in Nursing (B.S.N.). Majors include accounting, biology, business management, chemistry, chiropractic, dietetics, education (elementary, secondary, and special), English, exercise and sports studies, global studies, health services management, history, information technology, international business, liberal studies for education, mathematics, nursing, occupational therapy, pharmacy, philosophy, physical therapy, physician assistant studies, preprofessional studies (dental, law, medicine, and veterinary studies), psychology, and sociology. Five-year combined bachelor's/master's (B.S./M.S.) programs are offered in accounting, dietetics, education, information technology (B.S.)/international business (M.S.), international business, nursing, occupational therapy, and physician assistant studies. A six-year B.S./D.P.T. program is offered in physical therapy. A seven-year B.S./D.C. program is offered in chiropractic studies. The Doctor of Pharmacy program began in 2010 with an early assurance program for prepharmacy students.

Academic Programs

The area of concentration recognizes individual differences and varying interests but still provides sufficient specialization in one discipline to form a foundation for graduate studies and professional careers. Students attending D'Youville are expected to complete the requirements of their chosen concentration while earning a minimum of 120 credit hours. Core requirements include humanities, 24 hours; social science, 12 hours; science, 7 hours; mathematics/computer science, 6 hours; and electives, 9 hours. A cumulative average of at least 2.0 must be maintained to meet graduation requirements. Sixteen credit hours, or five or six courses per semester, are considered a normal workload. Internships to meet specific career goals may be arranged in any major.

The College offers a Career Discovery Program that was purposely designed for the undecided student. This program, which can last for two years, offers credit courses and internships meeting two years of study in any major.

The academic year is composed of two semesters, each lasting approximately fifteen weeks. The first semester, including final examinations, ends before the Christmas holidays. During the eight-week summer sessions, programs of selected courses are given at all levels on a daily basis.

Off-Campus Programs

The baccalaureate program in nursing is affiliated with thirteen area hospitals and public health agencies. The education program is affiliated with local elementary, junior high, and secondary schools and with special education centers in the area for purposes of student teaching. The chiropractic, occupational therapy, physical therapy, and physician assistant programs are affiliated with appropriate clinical settings throughout the United States.

Academic Facilities

D'Youville's modern Montante Family Library offers state-of-the-art computer reference capabilities for both

in-house and off-site users, including access to over seventy online databases. The multimillion-dollar Alt Health Science Building houses laboratories, including those for anatomy, organic chemistry, and gross anatomy; activity and daily living labs for the health professions; and additional laboratories for physics, chemistry, quantitative analysis, and computer science. It also houses classrooms, faculty member offices, and development centers, including one for career development. This is augmented by the modern Bauer Family Academic Center, which provides state-of-the-art classrooms, laboratories, and faculty offices.

Costs

For 2012–13, tuition is $10,965 per semester, and room and board cost $5125 per semester. A general college fee is required and is based on credit hours taken; a Student Association fee of $40 per semester is applied toward concerts, yearbooks, activities, and guest lectures. A $100 deposit ($150 for dietetics, physician assistant studies, occupational therapy, and physical therapy programs), credited toward tuition, must be submitted by all candidates who accept an offer of admission.

Financial Aid

D'Youville attempts to provide financial aid for students who would not otherwise be able to attend. Determination of aid is based on the Free Application for Federal Student Aid. Aid is available in the form of grants, loans, and employment on campus. D'Youville automatically offers scholarships for academic achievement to all eligible incoming students.

All students may qualify for D'Youville's Academic Scholarship Program, which offers scholarships with total values up to $67,500. Students who apply, are accepted, and meet the criteria instantly qualify for one of these scholarships, all of which are renewable annually. These scholarships are not based on need. The three scholarship programs are the Honors Scholarship, the Academic Distinction Scholarship, and the Achievement Scholarship. The Honors Scholarship requires an 87 academic average, a minimum SAT score of 1100 (math and critical reading) or an ACT score of at least 24, and awards 50 percent of tuition and 25 percent of room and board costs. The Academic Distinction Scholarship requires SAT scores of at least 1000 (math and critical reading) or ACT scores of 21 to 23 and an academic average of at least 85. It awards 25 percent of tuition and 50 percent of room and board costs. The Achievement Scholarship criteria include SAT scores of 900 to 1090 (math and critical reading) or ACT scores of 19 to 23 and an academic average of 80 to 84. This scholarship awards $1000–$5000. The Transfer Honors Scholarship is based on a starting GPA of 2.75. This scholarship's award ranges from $1000 to $5000.

Faculty

The ratio of faculty members to students is 1:14. All members of the full-time instructional staff hold a doctorate or another advanced degree. Faculty members act as advisers and are available for consultation with students.

Student Government

The Student Association (SA), a representative form of student self-government, seeks to inspire in its members dedication to the intellectual, social, and moral ideals of the College and works closely with the administration and faculty. All students of D'Youville are considered members of the SA and may be elected to the executive council and the student senate. There are seventeen academic and social clubs affiliated with the SA.

Admission Requirements

An applicant must be a high school graduate or have a high school equivalency diploma before matriculating. The applicant should have a college-preparatory background, including required English and history courses and a sequence in either mathematics or science. Scores on the SAT or the ACT are also required for admission. High school advanced placement credit is acceptable and transferable. The admission decision is based on high school grade point average, rank in class, and scores on the SAT or ACT. Students who have difficulty meeting normal admission standards may be admitted with a reduced academic load.

The College Learning Center offers academic assistance to students whose education has been interrupted or has not prepared them adequately for college courses. The Tutor Bank, a system of peer tutoring, offers the assistance of qualified students to those who need help in specific academic disciplines.

Application and Information

D'Youville admits students on a rolling admission basis; therefore, applications are reviewed as they are received by the admissions office. Transfer students who have a quality point average of at least 2.0 are encouraged to apply by December 1 for the spring semester and by July 1 for the fall semester. A brochure listing course offerings and giving details about costs and room and board is available upon request.

Steve Smith
Director of Admissions
D'Youville College
One D'Youville Square
320 Porter Avenue
Buffalo, New York 14201-1084
Phone: 716-829-7600
      800-777-3921 (toll-free)
Fax: 716-829-7900
E-mail: admissions@dyc.edu
Web site: http://www.dyc.edu
      http://www.dyc.edu/facebook
      http://www.dyc.edu/twitter

EARLHAM COLLEGE
RICHMOND, INDIANA

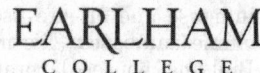

The College

Earlham College is a place where extraordinary lives begin. Earlham offers students a transformative educational experience that prepares graduates for lives of accomplishment and purpose. The College's 1,181 students—55 percent women and 45 percent men—represent forty-two states and seventy-seven other countries. Students of many races, religious backgrounds, economic levels, and ethnic traditions join together to share an experience rooted in the Quaker values of tolerance, equality, justice, respect, and collaboration. They explore an unending desire to see the world differently and to bring about change when necessary. Earlham's commitment to engaging students in a changing world is at the heart of its own mission.

Students at Earlham get involved in a wide variety of associations and organizations, including numerous extracurricular programs in music, theater, dance, social and political action, ethnic and international awareness, and intramural and varsity athletics. Students manage an FM public radio station, a food co-op, an equestrian program, a newspaper, and a literary magazine. Activities are coordinated by the Student Activities Board, the Earlham Events Committee, and various special interest groups, such as the Black Leadership Action Coalition, Women's Program Committee, International Club, and Earlham Service Learning Center. Students are active in community service and donate more than 50,000 hours of time to the Richmond community each year.

Earlham, an NCAA Division III affiliate, is a member of the Heartland Collegiate Athletic Conference. The College offers seven intercollegiate sports for men (baseball, basketball, cross-country, football, soccer, tennis, and track) and eight intercollegiate sports for women (basketball, cross-country, field hockey, soccer, tennis, track, and volleyball). Club sports include equestrian, swimming, Ultimate (Frisbee), and men's volleyball. Thirty percent of the students participate in intercollegiate athletics, and 50 percent participate in an extensive intramural program. Earlham athletic facilities include a recently renovated football and track facility and a $13-million athletics and wellness center.

Earlham is a residential college. Students live in the eight residence halls and thirty College-owned houses near the campus.

Earlham offers a Master of Arts in Teaching degree program. This eleven-month program for liberal arts and sciences graduates leads to certification in English/language arts, math, modern foreign languages, science, and social studies, all at the middle- and high-school levels. The College also offers a Master of Education degree program for licensed teachers.

Location

Earlham's 800-acre tree-shaded campus lies on the southwestern edge of Richmond, Indiana, a city of 36,000. Richmond is 65 miles from Cincinnati, Ohio, and Indianapolis, Indiana, and 40 miles from Dayton, Ohio. Many students find opportunities to join in local activities. The city's arboretum and parks system, symphony orchestra, theater company, and art museum all offer extra dimensions to student life.

Majors and Degrees

Earlham College awards the Bachelor of Arts (B.A.) degree in thirty-eight disciplinary and interdisciplinary programs. Among the most popular majors at Earlham are art, biology, history, and psychology. The College is also known for interdisciplinary programs such as environmental science, environmental studies, human development and social relations, Japanese studies, neuroscience, and peace and global studies. A complete list of academic programs is available online at www.earlham.edu/academics.

Academic Programs

Earlham aims to educate for depth and breadth, believing that one's success in the twenty-first century depends heavily on an ability to understand and make well-educated connections across different intellectual and experiential boundaries. Earlham's general education program encourages students to develop competencies in the arts, quantitative reasoning, scientific inquiry, wellness, and perspectives in diversity (including domestic multiculturalism, interculturalism, or global historical awareness and second language requirements). First- and second-year core courses emphasize ways of knowing and critical reading and writing skills.

Students gain an in-depth understanding of one or more disciplines in their major area of academic concentration. An academic major usually consists of eight to ten courses in one department, a senior research project or seminar, and a departmental comprehensive examination. Earlham grants credit for Advanced Placement examinations and higher-level International Baccalaureate subjects. Students may also receive credit for independent studies and academic internships.

The academic year consists of two semesters plus an optional May Term. During the summer, the College sponsors a two-week academic experience for high school students called Explore-A-College.

Off-Campus Programs

Earlham believes that classroom learning must go hand-in-hand with experience in the richness of the wider world. More than 65 percent of Earlham students participate in at least one off-campus study program, many led by Earlham faculty members. Academic credit is earned, and, except for transportation costs, no extra charge is incurred for off-campus study. Locations for recent off-campus programs led by Earlham faculty members have included Austria, the Bahamas, China, Curacao, East Africa, England, France, the Galapagos Islands, Germany, Ghana, Greece, Haiti, Japan, Martinique, Menorca, the Middle East, New Zealand, Nicaragua, Northern Ireland, Senegal, Sri Lanka, Spain, and Turkey. Earlhamites also participate in American programs along the U.S.-Mexico border (Border Studies) and in Philadelphia; New York; Chicago; Woods Hole, Massachusetts; and Oak Ridge, Tennessee. The academic focus of these programs varies, and students in all majors are encouraged to participate in at least one off-campus program. Earlham offers a three-week wilderness experience to incoming first-year students backpacking in the Uinta Mountains of Utah or canoeing in the boundary waters of Canada.

Academic Facilities

Long considered one of the nation's finest teaching libraries, Earlham's Lilly and Wildman Science Libraries received an Excellence in Academic Libraries Award from the Association of College and Research Libraries. In total, Earlham students and faculty members have ready access to some 3.5 million volumes. Locally, Earlham houses more than 400,000 volumes and currently subscribes to some 1,200 print periodicals and newspapers. Maps, music, and works of art are also available. Another 17,000 periodicals are available online. Special holdings include the Herbert Hoover Peace Studies Collection and the

Quaker Collection. Earlham is a Library of Congress selected depository for government documents.

The $13-million Landrum Bolling Center for Interdisciplinary Studies and Social Sciences opened in 2002, providing technologically equipped classrooms, offices, and common areas to enable pursuits in interdisciplinary programs, global outreach, experiential learning, collaborative projects, and networked information resources.

Major improvements to Earlham's science facilities are underway, with a complete renovation of Stanley Hall, followed by new construction of additional laboratory and classroom space for biology, chemistry, computer science, geology, mathematics, and physics. The facility is designed to encourage collaboration between faculty and students. The College will pursue LEED certification for this project.

There are eight computer labs on campus, and wireless Internet access is available throughout campus. All residence hall rooms are wired for Internet access and networked printing is available in several academic and residential buildings across campus. One computer lab is available to students and faculty and staff members 24 hours a day. All residence hall rooms are wired for Internet access, and wireless networking is available in all academic buildings and campus houses.

The College is also preparing to start construction on a new visual and performing arts center. The facility is designed to bring classrooms, studios, rehearsal areas, and a black box theater under one roof, and will also serve as a social hub for students and faculty from all academic areas. The College will also seek LEED certification on this building.

Costs

Tuition, fees, and room and board charges for 2012–13 will be $47,930. Students receive free admission to the Earlham Artist Series; athletic events; speaker series; and numerous lectures, concerts, and dances.

Financial Aid

Most financial aid is awarded on the basis of demonstrated need; more than 90 percent of Earlham's students receive College-based financial assistance. Earlham usually meets the full need of all accepted students with a combination of Earlham grants, endowed scholarships, loans, federal and state grants, and campus work. Students must file both the Free Application for Federal Student Aid (FAFSA).

Scholarships are awarded without regard to financial need and recognize academic achievement. Earlham also offers scholarships through the National Merit Scholarship Corporation. Special scholarships are available to members of the Religious Society of Friends (Quakers) and to students who are likely to enhance the diversity of the student body. Scholarships and limited financial aid are available for international students.

Faculty

Earlham's faculty members are dedicated professionals whose first priority is teaching. Ninety-six percent of the 101 teaching faculty members hold doctoral degrees or terminal degrees in their fields. Their teaching, creative endeavors, and scholarly research have been recognized by numerous grants and fellowships from the Ford Foundation; Danforth Foundation; IBM; Woodrow Wilson Foundation; Fulbright-Hays program; Kellogg Foundation; Japan Foundation; Lilly Endowment, Inc.; National Endowment for the Humanities; National Science Foundation; and Carnegie Mellon Foundation. The student-faculty ratio is 12:1.

Student Government

Earlham's distinctive approach to consensus governance is part of its Quaker character. The philosophical system is summarized in a code of principles and practices based on the ideals of respect for individuals and community, integrity, simplicity, peace and justice, and consensus governance. Campus organizations reach decisions by consensus rather than by parliamentary procedure or majority rule. The process emphasizes individual thought, group discussion, listening, and synthesizing.

Admission Requirements

Admission decisions are based on more than SAT and ACT scores or high school grades, as important as these criteria are. Earlham pays close attention to the quality of the academic program, teacher and counselor recommendations, application essays, and personal interviews. Applicants should have had an academic or college-preparatory high school program. The SAT or ACT is required. Interviews are strongly recommended although not required.

Application and Information

Earlham offers several admission options. The early decision deadline is December 1 (notification on December 15), the early action deadline is January 1 (notification on February 1), the regular decision deadline is February 15 (notification on March 15), and the transfer deadline is April 1. International students (non-U.S. citizens) should apply by February 1.

Students wishing additional information or materials on Earlham College should contact:

Office of Admissions
Earlham College
801 National Road West
Richmond, Indiana 47374-4095
Phone: 765-983-1600
800-EARLHAM (toll-free)
Fax: 765-983-1560
E-mail: admission@earlham.edu
Web site: http://www.earlham.edu

From Richmond, Indiana, Earlham College students engage a changing world and strive to make a difference.

EDINBORO UNIVERSITY
EDINBORO, PENNSYLVANIA

The University

Edinboro University, a part of the Pennsylvania State System of Higher Education, is located in the Borough of Edinboro, Erie County, Pennsylvania. It is the oldest teacher-training institution in Pennsylvania west of the Allegheny Mountains and the second-oldest in the state, but has grown into the region's largest and most comprehensive institution of higher education. The original Edinboro Academy was chartered in 1856. After the passage of the State Normal Act in 1857, the school opened as Edinboro Normal School for the preparation of teachers. Under its original charter, the school was privately administered until 1861, when the Commonwealth chartered it as a state normal school. The school was purchased by the Commonwealth of Pennsylvania in 1914. The state recognized Edinboro State Teachers College as a four-year college in 1926 and granted it the right to offer a Bachelor of Science in Education degree in the areas of elementary, secondary, and art education. The name of the institution was changed to Edinboro State College in 1960. In 1983, university status was given to each of the state colleges, and a comprehensive Commonwealth university system was established.

Edinboro's graduate school offers the Master of Arts, Master of Fine Arts, Master of Education, Master of Science, Master of Science in Nursing, Master of Social Work, and post-master's certifications.

The University is accredited by the Commission on Higher Education of the Middle States Association of Colleges and Schools (3624 Market Street, Philadelphia, Pennsylvania 19104; phone: 215-662-5606). The commission is an institutional accrediting agency that is recognized by the U.S. Secretary of Education and the Commission on Recognition of Postsecondary Accreditation. Other University accreditations and program approvals include the American Dietetic Association, the Council on Rehabilitation Education, the Council for Accreditation of Counseling and Related Educational Programs, the American Speech-Language-Hearing Association, the Council on Social Work Education, the National Association of Collegiate Business Schools and Programs, the Certified Financial Planner Board of Standards, Inc., the Commission on Collegiate Nursing Education, the National League for Nursing Accrediting Commission, and the National Council for Accreditation of Teacher Education.

Of the 8,000-plus students at Edinboro, some 6,000 are undergraduates. The University maintains on-campus residence. Each residence hall is wired for digital satellite cable television services, two high-speed data connections, and a telephone connection. Edinboro University recently undertook a $117-million housing project on campus—the Highlands at Edinboro University—that was completed in 2011, providing suite- and semi-suite–style housing units for students.

There are more than forty buildings situated on the spacious 585-acre campus, which includes open fields, a 5-acre lake, and many acres of woods.

Edinboro University in Erie–The Porreco Center and Edinboro University in Meadville offer classes and University services at convenient off-campus locations, all connected by Erie Metropolitan Transportation Authority bus service, free to all students.

Location

Located adjacent to the business district of Edinboro, Pennsylvania, the University is accessible by automobile from all sections of the state and is near the intersection of Interstates 90 and 79. Passenger service of all kinds operates on frequent schedules, connecting Edinboro with nearby cities and towns, including Erie, Pennsylvania's fourth-largest city. The Erie International Airport—Tom Ridge Field is approximately 15 miles to the north. Within walking distance of the campus, the community of Edinboro has eight churches of various denominations.

Majors and Degrees

The University awards the Associate of Arts, Associate of Engineering Technology, Associate of Science, Bachelor of Arts, Bachelor of Fine Arts, Bachelor of Science, Bachelor of Science in Education, and Bachelor of Science in Nursing degrees. These degrees permit majors in the following areas: anthropology, applied media arts (with concentrations in animation, cinema, graphic design, and photography), fine arts/crafts (with concentrations in ceramics, drawing, jewelry/metalry, painting, printmaking, sculpture, and wood/furniture design), art education, art history, biology, biology/premedical, broadcast journalism, business administration/accounting, business administration/administration, business administration/financial services, business administration/forensic accounting, business administration/marketing, business administration/management information systems, chemistry, chemistry/forensic sciences, chemistry/industrial biochemistry, communication studies (with concentrations in broadcasting, organizational communication, and public relations/advertising), computer science, criminal justice, earth sciences, economics, elementary education, elementary/early childhood education, elementary/special education, English/literature, English/writing, environmental science/biology, environmental studies/geography, environmental science/geology, foreign language, general business administration, general studies, geography, geology, German, health and physical education (with concentrations in health promotion, recreation administration, sport administration, and teacher education), history, humanities, human services/developmental disabilities, human services/social services, innovative nursing, liberal studies, manufacturing engineering technology, mathematics, medical technology, music, music education, natural science and math, natural science and math/wildlife, nuclear medicine technology, nursing, philosophy, physics 3-2 engineering, physics/liberal arts, physics/theoretical, political science, preschool education, print journalism, psychology, secondary education (biology, chemistry, earth and space science, English, general science, German, mathematics, physics, social studies, and Spanish), social science, social work, sociology, Spanish, special education, special education/elementary education, specialized studies, speech and hearing sciences, and women's studies. Pre-professional programs are offered in dentistry, law, medicine, pharmacy, and veterinary science. Minors also exist in fifty-seven specializations.

Academic Programs

Associate degrees require a minimum of 60 semester hours of credit, including a general education component.

Baccalaureate degrees require a minimum of 120 semester hours of credit. A general education requirement of 60 semester hours is distributed among the arts, humanities, and science and technology to ensure a basic liberal arts foundation. The remaining 60 semester hours are devoted to specialization and may include major and professional courses, a minor, and other concomitant courses.

Advanced Placement credit and honors courses are available.

The Office of Adult Student Information Services enables nontraditional students to enroll for academic programs at convenient times and locations on a full- or part-time basis.

An Army Reserve Officers' Training Corps (ROTC) (The Fighting Scots Battalion) program is available.

The Office for Students with Disabilities provides services that are essential for physically disabled, hearing-impaired, visually impaired, and learning-disabled individuals. Edinboro University has one of the finest programs in the nation for students with disabilities.

Academic Facilities

The seven-story Baron-Forness Library is the focal point of the University campus. The library houses more than 500,000 bound volumes and more than 1.4 million microform units. Technology and Communications supports and manages thirty-seven computer labs.

Costs

For fall 2011 and spring 2012, the tuition fee for a resident of Pennsylvania was $6240 per year; for nonresident students, the cost per year was $9360. Room rent per year was $5200 ($7400 in Highlands) and meals were $2868. Additional annual fees included a student activity fee of $403, a University Center fee of $520, a Health Center fee of $190, an instructional service fee of $659, and an instructional technology fee of $348. The cost of books and supplies varies with the academic major. Costs are subject to change.

Financial Aid

With more than $91 million in financial aid for eligible students, Edinboro offers student employment, loans, grants, and scholarships. In most cases, Pennsylvania State Grant and Free Application for Federal Student Aid forms are used to determine eligibility for these programs. Federal aid administered by the University is available for both the regular academic year and the summer sessions. The application priority date for upperclass students for these programs is normally March 15 for upcoming academic year. Freshmen may apply for aid upon acceptance by the University. Financial aid is also available through the University's ROTC program. For additional information, students should contact the Edinboro University Financial Aid Office at 888-611-2680 (toll-free) or access the information online at www.edinboro.edu.

Faculty

Edinboro's student-faculty ratio of 18:1 makes it possible to maintain close interaction between students and the highly qualified faculty members. A large percentage of the faculty has completed terminal degrees in their area of specialization.

Student Government

The Student Government Association is a vital and active organization on the campus and serves as the official student voice in all University matters. Student Government Association representatives serve on nearly all University committees and participate in the University governance system. This organization sponsors special events, activities, and student clubs and organizations to satisfy a variety of student interests. The Student Government Association participates in the annual budget recommendations regarding the budgeting of the student activity fund.

Admission Requirements

Edinboro University grants admission on the basis of general scholarship, character, interest, and motivation as they may be determined by graduation from an approved high school, home school, or institution of equivalent grade or equivalent preparation, as determined by the Credentials Division of the Department of Education; official scholastic records; aptitude tests; recommendations; and interviews. To fully prepare for a University program of study and increase the probability for academic success, students should pursue a college-preparatory curriculum at the secondary level and provide evidence of scholastic aptitude, as measured by scores on the SAT or ACT. Submission of aptitude scores can be waived for nontraditional adult learners. An audition is required for all applicants to any music curriculum; music students are invited to participate in the audition sometime after the application for admission is received by the Office of Undergraduate Admissions.

Application and Information

Students may apply for admission as early as July 1, after finishing the junior year of high school; the application can be found online at the University's Web site. Requests for application papers, viewbooks, financial aid forms, and further information should be addressed to:

Admissions Office
Academy Hall
200 East Normal Street
Edinboro University
Edinboro, Pennsylvania 16444
Phone: 814-732-2761
      888-8GO-BORO (toll-free)
Fax: 814-732-2420
E-mail: eup_admissions@edinboro.edu
Web site: http://www.edinboro.edu

Students gather around one of the newest additions to our ever-growing campus to show their Edinboro University pride!

ELIZABETHTOWN COLLEGE
ELIZABETHTOWN, PENNSYLVANIA

The College

Founded in 1899, Elizabethtown College is committed to an academic program of liberal arts and professional training, built upon a core curriculum that focuses on teaching students to think, analyze, and communicate. The more than 1,900 students at Elizabethtown come from thirty states and forty countries, providing a diversity of backgrounds that enhances the College as a whole.

Elizabethtown is a residential college, where 85 percent of students live on the 195-acre campus in eight residence halls and senior town houses. Student-run residence hall councils plan programs and provide service and leadership opportunities. A wide variety of campus cultural events and other activities keep 80 percent of the students on campus throughout the weekends. The College maintains an active intramural sports program and fields ten NCAA Division III teams for men (baseball, basketball, cross-country, golf, lacrosse, soccer, swimming, tennis, track and field, and wrestling) and ten for women (basketball, cross-country, field hockey, lacrosse, soccer, softball, swimming, tennis, track and field, and volleyball), several of which contend for national titles each year.

The College offers effective academic, personal, and career counseling services through the Center for Student Success, which encourages students to make use of its office as early as their first year. Ninety-five percent of students who graduate from Elizabethtown are employed or enrolled in graduate school within eight months after graduation.

In addition to its undergraduate degree programs, Elizabethtown also offers a Master of Science degree in occupational therapy.

Location

Elizabethtown is a community of 20,000 people located in southeastern Pennsylvania, within 20 minutes of Harrisburg (the state capital), Hershey, and Lancaster. Philadelphia and Baltimore are within 1½ hours of Elizabethtown; New York and Washington are within 4 hours. Elizabethtown is easily accessible by Amtrak train service from New York, Philadelphia, and Pittsburgh, and the Harrisburg International Airport is 15 minutes away.

Majors and Degrees

Bachelor of Arts degrees are awarded in communications, criminal justice, economics, engineering, English, fine art, French, German, history, international business, Japanese, music, philosophy, political philosophy and legal studies, political science, psychology, religious studies, secondary education, social work, sociology-anthropology, Spanish, and theater.

Bachelor of Science degrees are offered in accounting, actuarial science, biochemistry, biology, biotechnology, business administration, chemistry, citizenship education, computer engineering, computer science, elementary education, engineering, environmental science, forestry and environmental management, general science education, health and occupation, industrial engineering management, information systems, mathematics, physics, secondary education, social sciences, and social studies.

Bachelor of Music degrees are offered in music education and music therapy. More than eighty minors and concentrations as well as seven certification programs in secondary education are available.

The College offers joint 3-2 programs with Duke University, leading to a Master of Forestry or Master of Environmental Management. A 3-2 program in engineering with Pennsylvania State University is also offered, leading to a Bachelor of Arts in engineering from Elizabethtown and a Bachelor of Science in engineering from Penn State.

Elizabethtown offers cooperative programs in biology and allied health with Thomas Jefferson University and Widener University. These programs lead to a Bachelor of Science degree from Elizabethtown and a master's or doctoral degree from the cooperating university. The College also participates in a Cardiovascular Invasive Specialty Program with Lancaster General College of Nursing and Health Sciences. Through articulation agreements, qualified Elizabethtown students may be admitted to the Philadelphia College of Osteopathic Medicine's Doctor of Osteopathic Medicine Program or to Temple University's School of Dentistry.

Preprofessional majors are also offered in law, medicine, the ministry, and veterinary medicine.

The Primary Care Pre-Admissions Program through the Pennsylvania State University College of Medicine at the Milton S. Hershey Medical Center provides options for Elizabethtown students who are Pennsylvania residents and are pursuing careers in internal medicine, family practice, and pediatrics.

Academic Programs

Through Elizabethtown's core program of traditional and innovative liberal arts, students develop skills for critical analysis, effective communication, and habits of mind that ensure adaptability in the ever-changing global job market. Independent and directed studies and extensive internship and externship possibilities are available.

The Elizabethtown College Honors Program offers top academic students a highly selective program of study with the opportunity for a stipend to fund professional development, research, or travel-related study.

The College operates on a semester calendar. First-year students arrive in the last week of August, and examinations are given prior to the winter break. The spring semester begins in the middle of January and runs through early May. Intensive summer-session courses are available for students who wish to accelerate their academic program. Students may earn credit toward graduation through Advanced Placement examinations, College-Level Examination Program tests, or tests administered by the individual departments.

Off-Campus Programs

Elizabethtown College students may study abroad in twenty-six different locations on all six continents through one of five affiliate partners: AustraLearn (Australia and New Zealand); Brethren Colleges Abroad (fifteen locations worldwide); Queen's University International Study Centre at Herstmonceux Castle,

United Kingdom; Nihon University, Japan; and School for Field Studies (Costa Rica, Kenya, and Turks and Caicos Islands).

A number of short-term opportunities are available as well, including two- to three-week study tours at England's Oxford University and in Beijing, China; Costa Rica; Ecuador; and Prague. In addition, students majoring in programs including occupational therapy, music therapy, and social work are required to complete extensive fieldwork in on- and off-campus facilities.

Academic Facilities

Academic buildings include the High Library; Zug Memorial Hall, home of Hess Gallery and the Department of Fine and Performing Arts; Wenger Center for the Humanities; Steinman Center for the Communications and Art; Nicarry Hall; and the James B. Hoover Center for Business. The Masters Center for Science, Mathematics and Engineering includes the Lyet Wing for Biological Sciences as well as classroom and lab space for the ABET-accredited engineering program. In addition, the student center, Brossman Commons, is the location for the Tempest Theatre and a dance studio.

Costs

For 2012–13, tuition is $36,550 and room and board are $9060, for a total comprehensive fee of $45,600. Students should also plan on an additional cost of about $2000 for books, transportation, and personal expenses, for a total cost of $47,600. Financial aid is based on this figure.

Financial Aid

Financial aid packages are typically a combination of scholarships, grants, loans, and student employment; 90 percent of the students receive some form of aid. To apply for financial aid, students must file the Free Application for Federal Student Aid (FAFSA) and the Elizabethtown College Verification Form. Estimated data should not be filed. Signed copies of the parent's (and student's, if applicable) most recent federal income tax form, including all schedules, must also be submitted to the financial aid office.

More than half of Elizabethtown's first-year students with the strongest academic credentials receive merit-based scholarships, which are awarded on a competitive basis and without regard to need.

Elizabethtown's deadline for financial consideration is March 15.

Faculty

Elizabethtown has a teaching faculty of 131 full-time professors. The student-faculty ratio is 11:1. More than 90 percent of the full-time faculty members hold a Ph.D. or the highest earned degree in their field. In addition to being assigned a faculty adviser through the First-Year Seminar program, when students declare a major, they are assigned a new faculty adviser within that department.

Student Government

Students play an active role in campus governance through the Student Senate, the Campus Residence Association, and other organizations. Members of the Student Senate are elected from each class to advocate for students, coordinate special events, and allocate funds for student activities and more than ninety student-run clubs and organizations. Students Working to Entertain E-town (SWEET) allocates funding for weekend programs, campus social activities, and entertainment for the College community.

Admission Requirements

Decisions about admission to Elizabethtown are made without regard to sex, sexual orientation, race, religion, physical handicap, or place of residence. On average, 60 percent of all applicants are accepted. Students should have followed an academic curriculum, with the completion of at least 18 college-preparatory units recommended. The middle 50 percent of enrolled students scored between 1040 and 1240 on the critical reading and mathematics sections of the SAT, and 36 percent were in the top 10 percent of their high school class.

The College seeks diversity, and students who display leadership abilities or special talents are considered highly desirable. Campus interviews are highly recommended but not required for most students, although the College reserves the right to require interviews in special cases. Students applying to the Honors Program are required to interview, as are occupational therapy students. Auditions are required for music students.

Early admission is available for highly qualified high school juniors.

Application and Information

The College operates on a rolling admission basis—applications are processed as they are received—and the application deadline is March 1. Students can apply using the Common Application or online at the College's Web site. Applicants must submit a high school transcript, first-quarter grades, SAT or ACT scores, two letters of recommendation, and a personal statement, essay, or graded paper. Early application is strongly recommended. Accepted students should notify the College of their decision to attend by May 1; matriculation after that date is on a space-available basis. Students who are interested in the Elizabethtown College Honors Program must submit a completed application by January 15.

For more information, students should contact:

Debra Murray
Director of Admissions
Elizabethtown College
One Alpha Drive
Elizabethtown, Pennsylvania 17022-2298
Phone: 717-361-1400
Fax: 717-361-1365
E-mail: admissions@etown.edu
Web site: http://www.etown.edu

Elizabethtown offers more than 1,900 students liberal arts and professional programs through fifty-three majors and eighty minors and concentrations.

ELMIRA COLLEGE
ELMIRA, NEW YORK

The College

Elmira College is a small, private, coeducational college that is recognized for its emphasis on education of high quality in the liberal arts and preprofessional programs. One of the oldest colleges in the United States, Elmira was founded in 1855. The College has always produced graduates interested in both community service and successful careers. Friendliness, personal attention, strong college spirit, and support for learning beyond the classroom help to make Elmira a unique community. Elmira College is one of only 270 colleges in the nation to be granted a chapter of the prestigious Phi Beta Kappa honor society.

The full-time undergraduate enrollment is about 1,200 men and women. The students at Elmira represent more than thirty-five states, primarily those in the Northeast, with the highest representation coming from New York, New Jersey, Massachusetts, Connecticut, Maine, and Pennsylvania. International students from thirty-one countries were enrolled in 2010. Ninety-three percent of the full-time undergraduates live in College residence halls, and dormitory rooms are equipped to provide direct access to the Internet. Wireless access is also available in the library, Campus Center, and other hot spots campuswide.

The intercollegiate sports program includes men's and women's basketball, golf, ice hockey, lacrosse, soccer, and tennis and women's cheerleading, field hockey, softball, and volleyball. Intramural programs are also available. Emerson Hall houses the student fitness center, a pool, and a gym capable of seating 1,000, as well as the Gibson Theatre, which has a state-of-the-art sound and lighting system. Professional societies; clubs; music, dance, and drama groups; a student-operated FM radio station; and the student newspaper, yearbook, and literary magazine also provide numerous opportunities for extracurricular activity.

Location

Elmira College is located in the city of Elmira, which has a population of 35,000, in the Finger Lakes region of New York. The campus is a 10-minute walk from downtown Elmira. The relationship between the College and the local community is excellent, and numerous community activities and facilities are open to students, including the Elmira Symphony and Choral Society, the Elmira Little Theatre, clubs and civic groups, museums, movies, and a performing arts center. Excellent recreational areas are available in upstate New York and nearby Pennsylvania.

Majors and Degrees

Elmira College offers programs leading to the bachelor's degree in more than thirty-five majors, including accounting, American studies, art, art education, biology, biology-chemistry, business administration, chemistry, classical studies, clinical laboratory science, criminal justice, economics, childhood and adolescent education, English literature, environmental studies, French, history, human services, individualized studies, international business, international studies, mathematics, music, nursing, philosophy and religion, political science, psychology, public affairs, social studies, sociology and anthropology, Spanish, speech and hearing, and theater. Secondary teaching certification is offered in several areas. A 3-2 program in chemical engineering with Clarkson University is available, and 4-1 M.B.A. programs are available at Alfred University, Clarkson University, Rochester Institute of Technology, and Union College. Army and Air Force ROTC are available through respective units at Cornell University.

Preprofessional preparation is offered in education, medical technology, nursing, and speech pathology and audiology. Faculty advisers assist those who seek preparation for graduate study in dentistry, law, or medicine in choosing appropriate course work. Nearly 45 percent of Elmira graduates pursue graduate study.

Academic Programs

The College's calendar is comprised of two 12-week terms followed by a six-week term in the spring. Students enroll for four subjects during the twelve-week terms, completing the first term by mid-December and the second during the first week of April. Term III, the six-week term, running from mid-April through May, may be devoted to a particular project involving travel, internship, research, or independent study. Students are required to participate in internships in order to gain practical and meaningful experience related to their program of study. Credit is awarded for these experiences. Forty percent of Elmira College students study abroad at least once during their four years of study.

Special opportunities for outstanding students include participation in thirteen national honorary societies on campus and a chance to assist faculty members in research. The College also offers an accelerated three-year graduation option for outstanding students, and an Advanced Placement Program is available.

Army ROTC and Air Force ROTC are available.

Off-Campus Programs

Through the study-abroad programs, students may study in the United Kingdom, France, Spain, and Japan, as well as in other countries throughout Europe and Asia. Students from Elmira may spend Term III studying marine and island ecology or doing sociological research on the island of San Salvador in the Bahamas. The six-week Term III permits students in any major to study abroad, and students are able to participate in this program starting in their freshman year. Students have the opportunity to spend their junior year abroad studying for either one term or three years in any foreign country.

Academic Facilities

The Elmira campus offers exceptional academic facilities in a beautiful setting. The modern Gannett-Tripp Library houses more than 391,000 volumes, receives 2,500 periodicals, and includes a special Mark Twain collection room and photography and audiovisual facilities.

The College Computer Center offers four PC and Apple Macintosh microcomputer labs for student use.

A Center for Mark Twain Studies has been established at Quarry Farm, the author's summer home, which is located only a few miles from campus. The College also operates a Speech and Hearing Clinic on campus, which serves the public and provides valuable clinical experience for undergraduate students. Excellent facilities for drama and music are available.

Costs

Tuition for 2012–13 is $36,600, room is $6300, board is $5500, and fees are $1550.

Financial Aid

Financial aid is available for both freshmen and transfer students. Awards are based upon the Free Application for Federal Student Aid (FAFSA) as well as the student's past academic performance. Types of aid include grants, scholarships, loans, and work opportunities. Sources of aid include college, federal, state, and private dollars. In addition, superior students may qualify for non-need based Elmira College Honors Scholarships, which are available to both freshmen and transfer students and range from $10,000 to full tuition per year, renewable throughout four years. About 75 percent of the full-time undergraduates receive need-based financial aid. Twenty percent of students receive non-need merit aid.

Faculty

Members of the faculty are chosen for their ability in and dedication to teaching. All full-time faculty members serve as advisers. Currently, the full-time faculty consists of 10 full professors, 28 associate professors, 30 assistant professors, and 12 instructors. One hundred percent of the full-time faculty hold the Ph.D. or highest degree necessary to teach undergraduate students in their field.

Student Government

Student government, an important part of the educational system at Elmira College, prepares students for active and responsible citizenship in society. Student government organizations include the Student Senate, the Judicial Board, and the Student Activities Board.

Admission Requirements

The Office of Admissions at Elmira College uses a rolling admission system. Each applicant is evaluated individually on the basis of his or her total application, including academic record, rank in class, SAT or ACT scores, essay, activities, letters of recommendation, and goals. The College strongly advises a personal interview. The recommendations of teachers and guidance counselors are also important. Special consideration is given to applicants from distant states and other countries, applicants with special skills, and applicants who are prepared to become actively involved in the campus community.

Elmira has two early decision programs available to students.

Application and Information

For further information, applicants should contact:

Director of Admissions
Elmira College
Elmira, New York 14901
United States
Phone: 800-935-6472 (toll-free)
E-mail: admissions@elmira.edu
Web site: http://www.elmira.edu.

EMBRY-RIDDLE AERONAUTICAL UNIVERSITY

DAYTONA BEACH, FLORIDA

EMBRY-RIDDLE
Aeronautical University
DAYTONA BEACH, FLORIDA

The University

Embry-Riddle Aeronautical University's reputation as the leader in aviation and aerospace education is recognized worldwide. The University's history and legacy date back almost to the time of the Wright brothers, and in 2009 the University introduced the nation's first and only Ph.D. program in aviation. Embry-Riddle is an independent, nonsectarian, not-for-profit, coeducational university serving culturally diverse students seeking careers in aviation, aerospace, engineering, business, and related fields. Residential campuses in Daytona Beach, Florida, and Prescott, Arizona, provide education in a traditional setting, while the worldwide campus provides instruction through more than 150 centers in the United States, Europe, Canada, and the Middle East and through online learning.

Approximately 4,500 undergraduate students and 500 graduate students are currently enrolled at the 185-acre Daytona Beach residential campus. Students come from all fifty states, and nearly 100 countries are represented, making Embry-Riddle a truly international university.

More than twenty undergraduate degree programs, six graduate programs, and one doctoral program are offered at the Daytona Beach campus. Embry-Riddle's premier aeronautical science (professional pilot) program and award-winning aerospace engineering program are the largest on campus and among the largest of their type in the nation.

Embry-Riddle conducts applied research and is leading the development of the Next Generation Air Transportation System along with the Federal Aviation Administration, Lockheed Martin, Boeing, and other high-tech organizations. Student research projects include development of green technologies like Embry-Riddle's EcoCar and the world's first-of-its-kind hybrid aircraft. Alumni are leaders in every facet of the aviation and aerospace industries and serve as a strong network and resource for students.

Students at the Daytona Beach campus enjoy a wide array of activities and clubs, many focused on aviation and aerospace, as well as fraternities, sororities, and recreational opportunities. Forty-three percent of students live on campus.

Embry-Riddle's award-winning precision flight demonstration teams offer students the opportunity to compete nationally in air and ground events. Embry-Riddle also has the largest all-volunteer Air Force ROTC detachment in the country and among the fastest-growing Navy ROTC units and Army ROTC battalions. Embry-Riddle athletes compete in the NAIA Division as well as intramural sports, including baseball, basketball, crew, cross-country, golf, soccer, tennis, track, volleyball, and ice hockey.

The 68,000-square-foot ICI Center contains two full-size NCAA basketball courts, a fitness center, and a weight room. The ICI Center provides a place to host sporting events and assemblies. The University sports complex also includes a two soccer fields, the Sliwa Stadium ballpark, the Ambassador William Crotty Tennis Center, and the Track and Field Complex. The Tine Davis Fitness Center is adjacent to the pool and features comprehensive fitness services and wellness programs. Recent expansions to athletic facilities include a softball complex for the newest athletic offering in women's fast-pitch softball, as well as two artificial turf fields for intramural competition.

The 5,300-square-foot interfaith chapel accommodates the variety of faiths represented by the student body of Embry-Riddle. It consists of a 140-seat nondenominational worship area and four prayer rooms (Catholic, Jewish, Muslim, and Protestant).

Location

The year-round clear flying weather and the resort communities surrounding Embry-Riddle's residential campus in Daytona Beach, Florida, offer students an excellent environment in which to study, fly, and enjoy recreational activities. The campus, which is located adjacent to the Daytona Beach International Airport, is only 3 miles from what is called the world's most famous beach. The high-technology industries located in nearby Orlando provide the University with an outstanding support base. In addition, the Kennedy Space Center is less than a 2-hour drive away.

Majors and Degrees

The Daytona Beach campus of Embry-Riddle awards undergraduate degrees at the baccalaureate and associate level. Bachelor of Science degrees are offered in a variety of areas, each with a focus on the aviation and aerospace industries. The newest major in unmanned aircraft systems science combines Embry-Riddle's expertise in flight, air traffic management, safety and engineering. The College of Engineering offers majors in aerospace engineering, civil engineering, computer engineering, electrical engineering, mechanical engineering, and software engineering. All engineering programs, including Engineering Physics, are ABET accredited. Students who are interested in business administration may elect to major in management or air transportation. The College of Aviation awards degrees in aeronautical science (professional piloting), air traffic management, applied meteorology, aviation maintenance science, and safety science. Other majors include interdisciplinary studies (design your own major), communication, computational mathematics, homeland security, human factors psychology, and space physics. Students entering Embry-Riddle with an undecided major have the opportunity to explore a variety of academic pursuits before making a commitment to a specific track.

Academic Programs

Even a field as specialized as aviation requires a broad educational background. General education courses required of all students who are pursuing a baccalaureate program include communication skills, such as English composition, literature, and technical report writing; humanities; social sciences; mathematics; physical science; economics; and computer science. To ensure academic success, Embry-Riddle provides free tutorial services.

The academic year is divided into two semesters of fifteen weeks each, with the summer session divided into two terms. The average course load for each fall or spring semester is 15 credit hours.

Study abroad offers students the opportunity to better understand the global nature of the aviation and aerospace industries. Cooperative education adds value to the educational experience and allows students to gain real-world career skills.

Academic Facilities

The College of Aviation building at the Daytona Beach campus provides an unsurpassed environment for aviation education and research. The multimillion-dollar simulation laboratories duplicate the components and functions in the national airspace system, including capabilities to replicate actual weather reporting, airports, airways, air traffic control, flow control, and pilot and aircraft performance as found in the national air transportation system. Flight instruction is provided in the Embry-Riddle fleet of sixty-plus aircraft and a wide array of flight training devices. Aircraft are equipped with Automatic Dependent Surveillance-Broadcast (ADS-B) technology that decreases hazards associated with traffic, weather, and terrain. The High-Altitude Normobaric Lab allows students to experience the symptoms of high-altitude hypoxia to better enable them to recognize and recover from this threat. Embry-Riddle is the first university in the nation to acquire this technology.

The Advanced Flight Simulation Center gives Embry-Riddle students the opportunity to train in world-class simulators. The center, with more than 20,000 square feet of space and four high bays, currently houses two advanced aviation training devices (AATDs), eight Cessna 172S NAVIIIs (Skyhawk), two Diamond DA42 TAE Twin Stars, two Diamond DA42 L360s, and one Canadair Regional Jet (CRJ-200). These devices duplicate the actual cockpit, adverse weather conditions, a full range of emergency situations,

and virtually any flight pattern and complement flight training done in actual aircraft. Flight simulation enables students to learn aircraft performance, experience aerodynamic effects, and perform flight maneuvers immediately and without risk. Qualified to Level 6, the University's devices faithfully reproduce Embry-Riddle's fleet of single-engine and multiengine aircraft and are equipped with 220-degree panoramic visual theaters. In addition, the Aviation Building houses air traffic control and tower simulators, one motion-based disorientation trainer, and six basic aviation training devices (BATDs).

The James Hagedorn Aviation Complex, completed in the fall of 2011, includes 96,000 square feet in a three-building facility and is home to flight training operations, aircraft maintenance training, and a fleet maintenance hangar. The Emil Buehler Aviation Maintenance Science building's cutting-edge labs dedicated to aircraft systems, turbine engines, metallic and composite materials, avionics, and avionics electronics prepare students to become maintenance professionals. The facility includes classrooms, a licensed engine-repair station, a machine shop, offices, and a third-floor observation deck overlooking the flight line and Daytona Beach International Airport runways.

The facilities in the Lehman Engineering and Technology Center serve academic departments including Human Factors and Systems, Engineering Physics and Space Physics, Mathematics and Computer Science, and all the engineering disciplines. Labs include the atmospheric physics research lab, flight dynamics and simulation lab, materials testing lab, structures lab, aerospace composites lab, real time lab, aerospace engineering and design lab, wind tunnels, airport noise abatement lab, electronic communications and microwave lab, microcomputer and digital lab, circuits and power lab, electricity and magnetism thermo lab, human factors research lab, and many more. Students use the labs to work in teams to develop hands-on projects. Research is conducted by faculty members and graduate and undergraduate students.

The 18,500-square-foot Capt. Willie Miller Instructional Center, a lecture auditorium and classroom complex, provides space for large audience events, including presentations by distinguished lecturers and speakers.

The College of Business academic building features the aviation operations simulation lab, which is used to develop and evaluate aviation/airline operational strategies and processes. In addition, the College's Teaching Airport, a partnership between Embry-Riddle and Daytona Beach International Airport, is focused on teaching, research, and public outreach.

The Jack R. Hunt Memorial Library is a 49,000-square-foot facility with a seating capacity of 800. The library houses more than 230,000 volumes and book titles, and more than 340,000 items of microfiche, periodicals, documents, newspapers, and media programs. Among the library's resources is a historical aviation collection donated by the Manufacturers Aircraft Association (MAA) in 1976. This collection includes a continuous run of *Aviation Week & Space Technology* dating from 1916 to the present and a complete set of *Jane's All the World's Aircraft* dating from 1909 to the present. The library provides rapid interlibrary loan service and wireless access points as well as computer terminals for research.

Costs

For the 2011–12 academic year, tuition was $14,340 per semester. Flight fees are charged in addition to tuition. On-campus room and board costs were approximately $4500 per semester. Personal expenses, books, and fees are in addition to the above. Costs are subject to change.

Financial Aid

Applicants for financial aid are required to complete the Department of Education's Free Application for Federal Student Aid (FAFSA) and any other documents requested by the University. Students are encouraged to apply early if they wish to be considered for all types of programs. Florida residents may also apply for several additional programs that are available through the state. All applicants are automatically reviewed for merit scholarship eligibility.

Faculty

The faculty members provide an excellent balance of professional experience and academic achievement. There is also a healthy balance between maturity and youth among the faculty. Faculty members who teach in the specialized and major programs have had professional experience in their areas of instruction. The student-faculty ratio is 16:1, and the average class size is 25. The primary concern of each faculty member is personalized teaching in classrooms and laboratories, on the flight line, and in student advising.

Student Government

The University places great emphasis on student self-government. The Student Government Association supports publication of the weekly newspaper and oversees the Touch 'n Go Office that organizes campus entertainment and broadcast of the student radio station, Eagles FM. In addition, the president of the Student Government Association is a voting member of the University's Board of Trustees.

Admission Requirements

Admission is open to any qualified applicant, regardless of creed, sex, race, national origin, handicap, or geographical location. Admission decisions are based on high school grades and course load, college courses attempted, SAT or ACT scores, and letters of recommendation. Embry-Riddle encourages every student to visit the campus before making the decision to attend the University.

Transfer students are required to submit transcripts from all colleges and universities attended. High school transcripts are not required if the student has earned 30 college credits or more.

Application and Information

Embry-Riddle requires each applicant to submit an application form and fee, SAT or ACT scores, two letters of recommendation, and an official high school/college transcript. Flight students must provide an FAA Class I or Class II medical certificate. When a student is accepted for admission, tuition and housing deposits are required by May 1. Embry-Riddle operates on a rolling admissions basis and admission decisions are rendered throughout the year.

University Admissions
Embry-Riddle Aeronautical University
P.O. Box 11767
Daytona Beach, Florida 32120-1767
Phone: 386-226-6100
          800-862-2416 (toll-free nationwide)
E-mail: dbadmit@erau.edu
Web site: http://www.erau.edu/db
          http://twitter.com/ERAUniv
          http://www.youtube.com/EmbryRiddleUniv

Embry-Riddle Aeronautical University's Daytona Beach, Florida, campus.

EMERSON COLLEGE
BOSTON, MASSACHUSETTS

1880

The College

Founded in 1880, Emerson is one of the premier colleges in the United States for the study of communication and the arts. Students may choose from more than two dozen undergraduate and graduate programs supported by state-of-the-art facilities and a nationally renowned faculty. The campus is home to WERS-FM, the oldest noncommercial radio station in Boston; the historic 1,200-seat Cutler Majestic Theatre; and *Ploughshares,* the award-winning literary journal for new writing.

A pioneer in the fields of communication and performing arts, Emerson was one of the first colleges in the nation to establish a program in children's theater (1919), an undergraduate program in broadcasting (1937), professional-level training in speech pathology and audiology (1935), educational FM radio (1949), closed-circuit television (1955), and a B.F.A. degree program in film as early as 1972. In 1980, the College created the country's first graduate program in professional writing and publishing.

Today, Emerson's more than 3,400 undergraduate and 800 graduate students come from across the United States and more than forty countries. Approximately 1,900 students live on campus, some in special learning communities, such as the Writers' Block and Digital Culture Floor. All of the College's residence halls are air conditioned with cable television and Internet access. Wireless service is available in several campus locations. There is a fitness center, athletic field, and a brand-new facility that houses two theaters, multiple rehearsal spaces, a professional sound stage, and a fully functional scene shop.

Emerson College is fully accredited by the New England Association of Schools and Colleges.

In addition to its undergraduate programs, Emerson College offers ten master's degree programs for its graduate students.

Location

With dozens of institutions of higher learning, Boston is considered one of the country's best-known college towns. The city contains a wealth of diversions ranging from scenic harbor cruises and Boston Pops concerts to baseball's Fenway Park and the legendary Boston Marathon. Emerson's campus is located on Boston Common in the heart of the city's Theater District—within sight of the Massachusetts State House and walking distance from the historic Freedom Trail, Boston Public Garden, Chinatown, Financial District, and numerous restaurants and museums. Boston is also an international city with more than thirty foreign consulates, a busy international airport, and several multinational corporations.

Majors and Degrees

Emerson confers Bachelor of Arts, Bachelor of Fine Arts, and Bachelor of Science degrees. Students can major in acting; communication disorders; communication studies; marketing communications; media production (animation and motion media, digital postproduction, film, interactive media, sound design, studio television production, writing for film and television); media studies; musical theater; political communication: leadership, politics, and social advocacy; journalism; stage and production management; theater design/technology; theater education; theater studies; and writing, literature, and publishing. Popular minors include business studies and entrepreneurship. Interdisciplinary and self-designed majors,

as well as an honors program, are available through the College's Institute for Liberal Arts and Interdisciplinary Studies.

Academic Programs

Emerson's academic calendar consists of two fifteen-week semesters, plus two six-week sessions during the summer months. The requirements for graduation combine general education and liberal arts courses with advanced, specialized classes that are specific to individual departments and majors. Internships for academic credit are available in almost every major and the Institute for Liberal Arts and Interdisciplinary Studies offers exciting first-year seminars, independent study options, and innovative courses that cut across academic disciplines.

Off-Campus Programs

Internships are popular with Emerson students. Hundreds of placements exist throughout Boston and in major cities across the country, including the College's Los Angeles Center—a residential study and internship program in the heart of the world's entertainment capital.

Emerson also sponsors a semester-long study program in Washington, D.C., the Netherlands, and China. In addition, there is a summer film program in Prague and course cross-registration with the six-member Boston ProArts Consortium, whose members include the Berklee College of Music, the Boston Conservatory, Boston Architectural Center, Emerson, the School of the Museum of Fine Arts, and Massachusetts College of Art.

Academic Facilities

Emerson possesses the highest quality visual and media arts equipment, including sound-treated television studios, digital editing labs, audio postproduction suites with analog and digital peripherals, industry-standard software, and a professional marketing-research suite/focus room. In fact, more than half of Emerson's campus has been built new or completely refurbished since 2002. There are two radio stations, an on-campus clinic to observe speech and hearing therapy, and an integrated digital newsroom for aspiring journalists. The eleven-story Tufte Performance and Production Center houses expanded performance and rehearsal space, a theater design/technology center, makeup lab, and costume shop.

Emerson's Iwasaki Library houses more than 175,000 volumes and serial subscriptions, 11,000 microforms, 9,000 audio/visual materials, and 30,000 e-books. The library's Web pages are designed to serve as a gateway for research and can be accessed from the library's workstations, computers located throughout the campus, and dormitory rooms or off-campus apartments, using a student account. Emerson students can also access the resources of a dozen cooperating libraries through the College's membership in the Fenway Library Consortium.

Costs

The basic direct expenses related to attending Emerson College for the 2012–13 academic year are $34,198 for tuition and fees, and $13,958 for double room and board. Approximately $3700 should be allotted for books and supplies, health insurance, and personal expenses, including travel.

Financial Aid

Each year, more than two thirds of Emerson's student body receives some form of financial assistance, packaged in awards that typically combine grant and scholarship, loan, and College work-study. Academic scholarships ranging from $10,000 to half-tuition are awarded on a limited basis to students who meet high academic standards. Special performance-based scholarships are available up to $14,000 to exceptional students in the performing arts.

In order to apply for financial assistance, students must complete the Free Application for Federal Student Assistance (FAFSA) and CSS PROFILE form. Deadlines are March 1 for September admission or November 15 for January admission. More information about financial assistance at Emerson can be found online at http://www.emerson.edu/financial-aid or by contacting the Student Service Center at 617-824-8655 or finaid@emerson.edu.

Faculty

With a student-teacher ratio of 13:1, students at Emerson develop close relationships with remarkably talented and active instructors. Faculty members are nationally recognized and award-winning authors, directors, producers, consultants, playwrights, and editors. The vast majority of the faculty members have earned doctorates or the highest degree obtainable in their field.

Student Government

Emerson has more than eighty student organizations and performance groups, fourteen NCAA intercollegiate teams, and several student publications and honor societies. The Student Government Association, in cooperation with the Office of Student Affairs staff, plans and executes student activities, allocates and supervises funding for clubs, and serves as a liaison between the student body and the College administration.

Admission Requirements

Emerson accepts the Common Application and Application Supplement. Students whose interests and abilities are compatible with the College's specialty in communication and the arts are welcome to apply. Admission is competitive. Each year, more than 7,000 applications are received for a class of around 800. Selection is based on academic promise as indicated by secondary school performance, recommendations, writing competency, and SAT or ACT scores (or TOEFL if English is not the first language). The College also considers personal qualities as seen in extracurricular activities, community involvement, and demonstrated leadership.

The academic preparation for successful candidates should include 4 years of English and 3 years each of mathematics, science, social science, and a single foreign language. Candidates for programs offered by the Department of Performing Arts are asked to fulfill additional requirements (a theatrical resume and one of the following: audition, interview, portfolio, or essay) found on a dedicated Web site, http://stagedoor.emerson.edu. Applicants for the film program must submit a sample of creative work: either a five-to-ten page script or 5–7 minute video.

Application and Information

First-year candidates for September admission should file their application by January 5. Early action applications are due November 1. The regular admission deadline for January admission is November 1.

Transfer students should submit their applications and supporting credentials by March 15 for September admission or November 1 for January admission.

Office of Undergraduate Admission
Emerson College
120 Boylston Street
Boston, Massachusetts 02116-4624
Phone: 617-824-8600
Fax: 617-824-8609
E-mail: admission@emerson.edu
Web site: http://www.emerson.edu
　　　　http://www.facebook.com/emersoncollege
　　　　http://www.twitter.com/emersoncollege

Emerson College: Bringing innovation to communication and the arts.

FASHION INSTITUTE OF TECHNOLOGY
State University of New York
NEW YORK, NEW YORK

FIT Fashion Institute of Technology
State University of New York

The College

The Fashion Institute of Technology (FIT) is New York City's celebrated urban college for creative and business talent. A State University of New York (SUNY) college of art and design, business, and technology, FIT is a dynamic mix of innovative achievers, original thinkers, and industry pioneers, with nearly forty programs of study leading to the A.A.S., B.F.A., and B.S. degrees. The School of Graduate Studies offers seven programs leading to a Master of Arts (M.A.), Master of Fine Arts (M.F.A.), or Master of Professional Studies (M.P.S.) degree. FIT is accredited by the Middle States Association of Colleges and Schools, National Association of Schools of Art and Design, and Council for Interior Design Accreditation.

The college provides a singular approach to higher education—blending a real-world-based curriculum and hands-on instruction with a rigorous liberal arts foundation, marrying design and business, supporting individual creativity in a collaborative environment, and encouraging faculty members to match teaching expertise with professional experience. FIT's mission is to produce well-rounded graduates prepared for career success: doers and thinkers who become the next generation of business pacesetters and creative icons. It offers a complete college experience with a vibrant student and residential life.

FIT's four residence halls house 2,300 in fully furnished single-, double-, triple-, and quad-occupancy rooms and apartments. All students taking 12 or more credits are eligible for FIT housing, and students may apply for housing no matter where they live. Students have the option of either traditional dormitory-style (meal plan required) or apartment-style accommodations. Counselors and student staff members live in the residence halls, helping students adjust to college life and New York City.

The college is home to more than seventy student organizations, including merit societies, athletic teams, major-related organizations, and clubs based on areas of interest. Concerts, dances, field trips, films, flea markets, and other events are regularly scheduled. Student-run publications include a campus newspaper, a literary and art magazine, and the FIT yearbook.

FIT has intercollegiate teams in cross-country, half marathon, outdoor track, dance, table tennis, tennis, soccer, swimming and diving, and volleyball. Athletics and Recreation offers students group fitness classes at no extra cost. Open gym activities allow students to participate in team and individual sports.

The David Dubinsky Student Center houses lounges, a game room, a dining hall, a student radio station, a student-run boutique, student government and club offices, health services, gyms, a dance studio, a fitness center, a counseling center, studios, and laboratories.

FIT serves approximately 10,000 students from the greater metropolitan area, New York State, across the country, and around the world, offering full- and part-time study options, evening/weekend degree programs, and online studies. The School of Art and Design enrolls 37 percent of degree-seeking students. Another 40 percent are enrolled in the Jay and Patty Baker School of Business and Technology. Forty percent of FIT's students are New York City residents, 23 percent are New York State (non–New York City) residents, and 37 percent are out-of-state or international residents. The ethnic/racial makeup is approximately 0.1 percent American Indian or Alaskan, 18.7 percent Asian, 9.4 percent black, 11.6 percent Hispanic, 3.6 percent multiracial, 0.6 percent Native Hawaiian or Pacific Islander; and 55.9 percent white.

Location

Occupying an entire block in Manhattan's Chelsea neighborhood, FIT's campus places students at the heart of the fashion, advertising, visual arts, design, business, and communications industries. Students gain unparalleled exposure to their field through internships, field trips, and professional connections. A wide range of cultural and entertainment options—from dining to galleries to theater—are available within walking distance of the campus, which also offers convenient access to subway and bus lines and major rail and bus transportation hubs.

Majors and Degrees

FIT offers fifteen Associate in Applied Science (A.A.S.) and twenty-four baccalaureate programs. All students complete a two-year A.A.S. program in their major area of study and then typically continue in a related, two-year Bachelor of Fine Arts (B.F.A.) or Bachelor of Science (B.S.) program. Some students choose to begin their careers after earning the A.A.S., which qualifies them for entry-level positions in their chosen field. All programs include a required liberal arts component.

The School of Art and Design offers eleven A.A.S. and thirteen B.F.A. programs, the Jay and Patty Baker School of Business and Technology offers four A.A.S. and ten B.S. programs, and the School of Liberal Arts offers one B.S. program.

The fifteen A.A.S. programs, all of which provide the foundation for one or more corresponding baccalaureate-level programs, are accessories design*, advertising and marketing communications*, communication design foundation*, fashion design*, fashion merchandising management* (with an online option), fine arts, illustration, interior design, jewelry design*, menswear, photography, production management: fashion and related industries, textile development and marketing*, textile/surface design*, and visual presentation and exhibition design. Programs with an * are also available as a one-year option for students with acceptable transferable credits, and the one-year fashion merchandising management A.A.S. program is offered fully online.

The thirteen B.F.A. programs are accessories design, advertising design, computer animation and interactive media, fabric styling, fashion design (specializations in children's wear, intimate apparel, knitwear, special occasion, and sportswear), fine arts, graphic design, illustration, interior design, packaging design, photography and the digital image, textile/surface design, and toy design.

The eleven B.S. programs are advertising and marketing communications, art history and museum professions, cosmetics and fragrance marketing, direct and interactive marketing, entrepreneurship for the fashion and design industries, fashion merchandising management, home products development, international trade and marketing for the fashion industries, production management: fashion and related industries, technical design, and textile development and marketing.

For students looking to balance career or family with their education, FIT offers nine degree programs available through evening/weekend study that include advertising and marketing communications (A.A.S. and B.S.), communication design foundation (A.A.S.), fashion design (A.A.S.), fashion merchandising management (A.A.S. and B.S.), graphic design (B.F.A.), illustration (B.F.A.), and international trade and marketing for the fashion industries (B.S.).

Academic Programs

Each undergraduate program includes a core of traditional liberal arts courses. The School of Liberal Arts offers FIT students the opportunity to minor in a variety of liberal arts areas in two forms: traditional subject-based minors and interdisciplinary minors unique to the FIT liberal arts curriculum. Selected minors include film and media, economics, Latin American studies, and sustainability.

The Career and Internship Center offers lifetime placement services to graduates. Internships are a required element of most programs and are available to all students. Nearly one third of FIT student interns are offered employment on completion of their internships.

The Presidential Scholars honors program, available to academically exceptional students in all disciplines, offers special liberal arts courses, projects, colloquiums, extracurricular activities, and off-campus visits designed to broaden horizons and stimulate discourse. Presidential Scholars are also awarded priority course registration and an annual merit stipend.

Precollege programs (Saturday and Sunday/Summer Live) are available to middle and high school students during the fall, spring, and summer. More than sixty courses provide the chance to learn in an innovative environment, to develop art and design portfolios, to explore the business and technological sides of a wide range of creative careers, and to discover natural talents and abilities.

The School of Continuing Education and Professional Studies provides evening and weekend credit and noncredit classes to students and working professionals who want to pursue a degree or certificate or further their knowledge and in a particular area, as well as a wide range of classes for high school students on weekends and in the summer.

Off-Campus Programs

The study-abroad experience allows students to immerse themselves in diverse cultures and prepares them to live and work in a global community. Australia, China, England, France, and Mexico are some of the countries where FIT offers semester study-abroad courses. Students can also study abroad during the winter or summer sessions, or for a semester or a full academic year concentrating in fashion design or fashion merchandising management in Italy.

Academic Facilities

FIT provides its students with an urban campus of classrooms, laboratories, and studios that reflect the most advanced educational and professional practices. The Fred P. Pomerantz Art and Design Center houses studios, a printmaking room, display and exhibit design rooms, a model-making workshop, and a graphics printing service bureau. The Peter G. Scotese Computer-Aided Design and Communications Facility allows students to explore the latest advancements in technology and their integration in design, photography, and computer graphics and animation. The fragrance studio, a professionally equipped fragrance development laboratory, is the only one of its kind on a U.S. college campus. Cutting and sewing laboratories offer the most advanced design and cutting machinery among educational facilities in the United States. The lighting laboratory, an educational and professional development facility, features more than 400 commercially available lighting fixtures. Other college facilities include a broadcasting studio, knitting and weaving labs, a multimedia foreign language laboratory, twenty-three computer labs containing nearly 700 Mac and PC workstations, and several additional labs with computers reserved for students in specific programs.

The Museum at FIT is New York City's only museum dedicated to fashion. Students, designers, and historians use it for research and inspiration. The museum operates year-round, and its exhibitions are free and open to the public. The Gladys Marcus Library provides more than 300,000 volumes of print, nonprint, and electronic materials. The newspaper and periodicals collection includes 500 current subscriptions. Online resources include more than 90 searchable databases. The library also offers specialized resources, such as clipping files, fashion and trend forecasting services, and sketch collections.

Also on campus are three multimedia venues—the Katie Murphy Amphitheatre, the Morris W. and Fannie B. Haft Auditorium, and the John E. Reeves Great Hall—used for student presentations, industry panels, conferences, and special events.

Costs

For 2011–12, the associate-level tuition per semester was $1987 for in-state residents and $5961 for nonresidents. Baccalaureate-level tuition per semester was $2734 for in-state residents and $7245 for nonresidents. Housing costs ranged from $6119 to $6299 per semester for traditional residence hall accommodations with mandatory meal plan and from $5241 to $9521 for apartment-style accommodations. Meal plans varied from $1595 to $2045 per semester. Textbook costs and other nominal fees, such as locker rental or laboratory use, vary per program. Costs are subject to change.

Financial Aid

FIT attempts to remove financial barriers to college entrance by providing scholarships, grants, loans, and work-study employment for students in financial need. Nearly all full-time, matriculated students who complete the financial aid application process receive some type of assistance. The college directly administers its own institutional grants and scholarships, which are provided by the FIT Foundation.

College-administered federal funding includes Federal Pell Grants, Federal Perkins Loans, Federal Supplemental Educational Opportunity Grants, Federal Work-Study awards, and Federal Family Educational Loans, which include student and parent loans. New York State residents who meet state guidelines for eligibility may also receive Tuition Assistance Program (TAP) and/or Educational Opportunity Program (EOP) grants. Financial aid applicants must file the Free Application for Federal Student Aid (FAFSA), through which they apply for the Federal Pell Grant. They should also apply for all available outside sources of aid. Additional documentation may be requested by the Financial Aid Office. Applications for financial aid should be completed prior to February 15 for fall admission or prior to November 1 for spring admission.

Faculty

FIT's faculty is drawn from top professionals who bring their experience to the classroom and introduce students to the real-life opportunities and challenges of their disciplines through field trips, guest lectures, and sponsored competitions. Academic departments consult with industry advisory boards in their fields, ensuring that the curriculum and classroom technology reflect evolving industry practice. Student-instructor interaction is encouraged, with a maximum class size of 25, and courses are structured to foster participation, independent thinking, and self-expression.

Student Government

The Student Council, the governing body of the FIT Student Association, gives all students the privileges and responsibilities of citizens in a self-governing college community. Many faculty committees include student representatives, and the president of the student government sits on FIT's Board of Trustees.

Admission Requirements

Applicants for admission must be either candidates for or recipients of a high school diploma or a General Educational Development (GED) certificate. Admission is based on class rank, strength and performance in college-preparatory course work, and the student essay. A portfolio evaluation is required for art and design majors. Specific portfolio requirements are explained on FIT's Web site. SAT and ACT scores are required for placement in math and English classes and for students applying to the Presidential Scholars honors program. Letters of recommendation are not required.

Transfer students must submit official transcripts for credit evaluation. Students may qualify for the one-year A.A.S. option if they hold a baccalaureate degree from an accredited college or if they have a minimum of 30 transferable credits from an accredited college, including 24 credits that are equivalent to FIT's liberal arts requirements, and at least one semester of physical education.

Students seeking admission to a B.F.A. or B.S. program must hold an A.A.S. degree from FIT or an equivalent degree from an accredited and approved college. They must also meet the appropriate prerequisites for the specific major and must have completed FIT's liberal arts requirements. Further requirements may include an individual interview with a department committee, review of academic standing, and a portfolio review (for applicants to B.F.A. programs). Any student who applies for transfer to FIT from a four-year program must have completed a minimum of 60 credits, including the requisite art or technical courses and the liberal arts requirements.

Application and Information

Students wishing to visit FIT are encouraged to attend a group information session and take a tour of FIT's campus. The visit schedule is available online at www.fitnyc.edu/visitfit. A virtual tour of the campus can be found online at fitnyc.edu/virtualtour. Interested candidates may apply online at www.fitnyc.edu/admissions.

For more information, students should contact:

Admissions
Fashion Institute of Technology
227 West 27 Street, Room C139
New York, NY 10001-5992
Phone: 212-217-3760
        800-GO-TO-FIT (toll-free)
E-mail: fitinfo@fitnyc.edu
Web site: http://www.fitnyc.edu
        http://www.facebook.com/FashionInstituteofTechnology

COLLEGE CLOSE-UPS

FELICIAN COLLEGE
LODI, NEW JERSEY

The College

Felician College is a Catholic/Franciscan college serving more than 2,300 men and women. Its mission is to create a close-knit, nurturing community committed to putting students first and enabling every student's full potential. Felician provides a solid and supportive foundation within a liberal arts framework, which allows students to meet the challenges of the new century with informed minds and understanding hearts. The College is accredited by the Middle States Association of Colleges and Schools, and carries program accreditation from the Commission on Collegiate Nursing Education, Teacher Education Accreditation Council, and the International Assembly for Collegiate Business Education.

In addition to its undergraduate degree programs, Felician College offers the Master of Science in Nursing (M.S.N.), Master of Master of Business Administration (M.B.A.), Master of Science in Healthcare Administration (M.S.H.A.), Master of Arts in Religious Education, Master of Arts in education, and the Doctor of Nursing Practice (D.N.P.) degree.

Felician College competes in Division II of the National Collegiate Athletic Association (NCAA). The Felician teams, called the Golden Falcons, compete in men's baseball, men's and women's basketball, men's and women's soccer, men's and women's cross-country, men's golf, and women's softball and volleyball. The Athletic Department also sponsors numerous intramural sports activities, such as indoor soccer, faculty-student softball, and volleyball games on the quad.

Students may elect to reside in one of the spacious suites in Elliott Hall or Milton Court residence halls, both located on the Rutherford Campus, a 10-minute shuttle bus ride from the campus in Lodi. The campuses offer comfortable student lounge areas, student meeting rooms, dining halls, a gymnasium, a fitness center, and grassy areas for outdoor recreation.

Location

Felician College is located on two beautifully landscaped campuses in Lodi and Rutherford, in Bergen County, in northern New Jersey. Both campuses, nestled in suburban towns, are 12 miles from New York City and a few miles from the New Jersey Meadowlands sports complex.

Majors and Degrees

Felician College offers programs of study in the arts and sciences, business and management sciences, nursing and health management, and teacher education.

A liberal arts program leading to the Bachelor of Arts, Bachelor of Science, Bachelor of Science in Nursing, or Associate in Liberal Arts degree is designed to provide students with a broad general education and concentrated preparation in a major area. For the B.A. degree, a student may choose a departmental major in art, biology, communications, computer information systems, English, history, mathematics, music, philosophy, psychology, or religious studies. A student may choose an interdisciplinary major in one of three liberal arts areas: humanities, natural sciences and mathematics, or social and behavioral sciences. Concentrations are available in digital video production, fine arts, general science, global peace and justice, graphic design, international education and foreign languages, journalism, mathematical sciences, political science, sociology, and theater arts. Bachelor of Arts degree programs are available in elementary education (K–5), early childhood education (P–3 and K–5), elementary education with content area specializations (5–8), special education (K–5, dual certification), teacher of students with disabilities (K–12), and secondary education (art, English, history, math, and science).

The Bachelor of Science degree is offered in accounting, business administration, criminal justice, management, marketing, and nursing. A program leading to the Bachelor of Science degree in clinical laboratory science and eligibility for national certification is offered in collaboration with the University of Medicine and Dentistry of New Jersey's School of Health-Related Professions (UMDNJ–SHRP). For this degree, a student may concentrate in cytotechnology or medical technology. Also offered in conjunction with UMDNJ–SHRP is a Bachelor of Science program in allied-health technology. Students may study medical sonography, nuclear medicine technology, respiratory care, or vascular technology. Joint degree programs that lead to a master's or doctoral degree are offered for the following preprofessional programs: audiology, chiropractic studies, medicine, occupational therapy, optometry, physical therapy, physician assistant studies, and podiatry.

Academic Programs

A candidate for the B.A. in liberal arts is required to complete an organized program of study comprising a minimum of 120 semester hours distributed among prescribed and elective courses. Four interdisciplinary courses in the College's Core Curriculum are mandatory for all students. Each baccalaureate degree student in arts and sciences is required to prepare a written and oral senior research project. A minimum of 30 credit hours must be earned at the College. A student who pursues an A.A. degree is required to complete 64 to 66 credits in an approved program of study.

A candidate for the B.A. in elementary or special education is required to complete a program of 126 to 131 semester hours, including credits in general education, professional education, and a major in the arts and sciences. Field experience begins in the freshman year, students participate in a practicum in the junior year, and there is supervised teaching during the senior year in a public elementary school. The education programs are accredited by the Teacher Education Accreditation Council.

Accelerated evening classes provide adults with the opportunity to earn baccalaureate degrees at Felician College. Students choose from courses held on campus, online or at our off-campus locations at community colleges or hospitals.

The Honors Program, for students with strong academic records, provides an opportunity to conduct scholarly research and develop leadership skills through service learning. Upon successful completion of the program students graduate as Honors Scholars.

The Service Learning Program allows students to be of service to others while learning the value of citizenship and responsibility through action and reflection.

Academic Facilities

Seminar rooms, multimedia and learning resource centers, and laboratories in accounting, computers, psychology, science, and writing are updated annually with the latest instructional technology. Through the Internet laboratories, all students have access to e-mail and the World Wide Web. The College auditorium comfortably seats 1,500 people; its large stage with modern theatrical features hosts performing groups from all parts of the country. The College library has a selective collection of more than 110,000 volumes, as well as periodicals, cassettes, records, microfilms, and ultrafiche. A curriculum library serves as a resource center for the teacher education programs. The Nursing Skills Laboratory, located on the Lodi campus, furnishes convenient facilities for observation, application of learning, and field experiences.

Costs

Undergraduate tuition in 2012–13 is $27,800 per year for full-time students. The annual cost of room and board is $11,400 (double occupancy). There are additional student fees, commuter fees, and resident fees.

Financial Aid

Felician College participates in federal, state, and institutional programs of financial assistance. To determine the amount and type of aid needed, applicants must file a Free Application for Federal Student Aid (FAFSA) with the Department of Education. The College participates in the Federal Work-Study, Federal Pell Grant, Academic Competitiveness Grant, and Federal Supplemental Educational Opportunity Grant programs. Students from New Jersey may be considered for New Jersey tuition aid grants. Through a state-guaranteed loan program, students may also take out low-interest bank loans. A number of institutional scholarships are available for qualified students in need of financial assistance. The Office of Undergraduate Admission also awards merit-based scholarships to those who are eligible, regardless of need. To take advantage of federal financial aid programs exclusively for veterans, a certificate of eligibility should be submitted to the director of financial aid at Felician College. More than half of the students attending Felician receive some form of financial aid.

Faculty

All courses are taught by fully qualified faculty members with advanced degrees, who are dedicated primarily to teaching, advising, and continued involvement in their disciplines. The student-faculty ratio of 12:1 facilitates a close working relationship, as well as individualized programs of instruction. The faculty members are dedicated to supporting student growth and development in a supportive, learner-centered environment designed to help students reach their highest potential.

Student Government

All students participate in the Student Government Organization (SGO). The governing body of the SGO, comprised of elected representatives from various student groups, coordinates activities on and off campus, including community service, campus ministry, and social, cultural, civic, and athletic events. Student representatives also serve on College committees with faculty members and administrators.

Admission Requirements

Applicants must be graduates of an accredited high school or have the high school equivalency certificate and satisfactory SAT or ACT scores. A personal essay and interview are strongly recommended.

Students graduating with an associate degree from a recognized junior college are eligible for admission into the upper division of Felician College. Applications for transfer are considered for both fall and spring semesters. Admission requirements may be adjusted for adults on the basis of maturity and experience.

Felician College offers credit and advanced placement of up to 90 credits for coursework from accredited colleges as well as for acceptable scores on the College Board Advanced Placement tests and the College-Level Examination Program tests.

Application and Information

Applications, accompanied by a $30 fee, should be submitted during the fall of the senior year. The Office of Undergraduate Admission evaluates applicants' credentials on a rolling basis. However, applicants for the fall semester are strongly encouraged to apply before April 15.

Office of Undergraduate Admission
Felician College
262 South Main Street
Lodi, New Jersey 07644
Phone: 201-559-6131
Fax: 201-559-6138
Web site: http://www.felician.edu

Students find the on-campus library a convenient place to study.

FIDM/FASHION INSTITUTE OF DESIGN & MERCHANDISING
LOS ANGELES, CALIFORNIA

The Institute

FIDM/Fashion Institute of Design & Merchandising provides a dynamic and exciting community of learning in the fashion, interior design, digital arts, and entertainment industries. Students can launch into one of thousands of exciting careers in as little as two years. FIDM offers two-year and four-year degree programs—Bachelor of Science, Associate of Arts (A.A.), A.A. Professional Designation, and A.A. Advanced Study.

FIDM offers a highly focused education that prepares students for the professional world. Students can choose from twenty specialized creative business and design majors.

Established in 1969, FIDM is a private college that is proud to enroll more than 7,500 students a year and has graduated over 47,000 students. Graduates are automatically granted a free membership in the Alumni Association, which keeps them well connected while providing up-to-the-minute alumni news and information. FIDM alumni chapters can be found in thirty-five locations around the United States, Europe, and Asia.

Career planning and job placement are among the most important services offered by the college. Career assistance includes job search techniques, preparation for employment interviews, resume preparation, virtual portfolios, and job adjustment assistance. FIDM's full-time Career Center department and advisors partner one-on-one with current students and graduates to help them move forward on their career path, within their chosen major. Employers post over 19,000 jobs a year on FIDM's alumni job search site, which is available 24/7 exclusively to FIDM students and graduates. FIDM Career Advisors connect students to internships and directly to people in the industry. FIDM also offers Job Fairs, Open Portfolio Days, and networking days to allow students to meet alumni and industry leaders face-to-face. Because of the college's long-standing industry relationships, many firms come to FIDM first to recruit its students. Over 90 percent of FIDM Graduates in all majors are successfully employed in their field of study within six months of graduation. Some of FIDM's successful graduates include celebrity designers Nick Verreos, Monique Lhuillier, and the co-founder of Juicy Couture, as well as Hollywood costume designer Marlene Stewart.

FIDM's ethnically and culturally diverse student body is one of the factors that attracts students. The current population includes students from more than thirty different countries. The Student Activities Department plans and coordinates social activities, cultural events, and community projects. Student organizations include the ASID Student Chapter, Cross-Cultural Student Alliance, American Association of Textile Chemists and Colorists Phi Theta Kappa Honor Society, and the Alumni Association. The students also produce *MODE*, the student magazine that promotes awareness about the design industry, current events, and FIDM student life.

FIDM is accredited by the Accrediting Commission for Community and Junior and Senior Colleges of the Western Association of Schools and Colleges (WASC) and the National Association of Schools of Art and Design (NASAD).

Location

FIDM's main campus is in the heart of downtown Los Angeles near the famed California Mart and Fashion District. There are additional California campuses in San Francisco, San Diego, and Orange County. A virtual tour of the campuses and their locations is available at http://fidm.edu/visit-fidm/virtual-tour/.

FIDM Los Angeles is nestled at the center of an incredibly vibrant apparel and entertainment hub, surrounded by the fashion, entertainment, jewelry, and financial districts. It is situated next to beautiful Grand Hope Park, a tree-filled oasis amid the hustle and bustle of downtown Los Angeles. Newly renovated by acclaimed architect Clive Wilkinson, **FIDM San Francisco** stands in the heart of historic Union Square. The country's third-largest shopping

area and stimulating atmosphere combined with the industry-based staff and faculty make this campus as incredible as the city in which it is located. The **FIDM Orange County** campus is a dynamic visual experience with ultra-modern lofts, an indoor/outdoor student lounge, eye-popping colors, and a one-of-a-kind audio-visual igloo. Also designed by world-renowned architect Clive Wilkinson, this campus has received several prestigious architectural awards and has been featured in numerous national magazines. **FIDM San Diego's** gorgeous campus overlooks PETCO Park and is near the historic Gaslamp district and the San Diego harbor. FIDM's newest campus is sophisticated, stylish, and tech savvy, reflecting the importance of California's fastest-growing city and its appeal to the global industry.

Majors and Degrees

The Bachelor of Science (B.S.) in Business Management program offers students the opportunity to develop the additional necessary skills and knowledge to run a business or even launch their own. In the program, students learn business strategy, entrepreneurial creativity, and management skills for success in business. Graduates of this program are prepared to enter the global industries of fashion, interior design, and entertainment, and are ready to compete when entering the corporate world or undertaking an entrepreneurial venture.

Many FIDM A.A. graduates take their skills to the next level through FIDM's B.S. in Business Management program. Only FIDM Graduates from (A.A) majors are eligible to apply to the Bachelors program, which is offered at the Los Angeles and San Francisco campuses and available online. Students from all FIDM majors study and collaborate on business projects and take courses in accounting, human resource management, international finance, ethics, leadership, and more, giving them extensive knowledge of managing a business and the creative edge that is a growing necessity in the corporate world. FIDM's unique industry partnerships offer exciting opportunities for students through internships, events, and guest speakers, with companies such as Forever 21, JC Penney, Mattel, NBC Universal, Oakley, Smashbox, and Stila.

FIDM offers two-year Associate of Arts degree, Advanced Study programs that are available to students who have previously completed an A.A. degree from FIDM, and Professional Designation programs for students who want to enhance their previous education from another college or are interested in transferring to FIDM.

FIDM offers Associate of Arts degrees in Apparel Industry Management, Beauty Industry Merchandising & Marketing, Digital Media, Fashion Design, Fashion Knitwear Design, Graphic Design, Interior Design, Jewelry Design, Merchandise Marketing (Fashion Merchandising or Product Development), Textile Design, and Visual Communications. All of these programs offer the highly specialized curriculum of a specific major combined with a core general education/liberal arts foundation.

Students from other regionally accredited college programs have the opportunity to complement their previous college education by enrolling in FIDM's Professional Designation programs. Students can determine which credits will transfer and receive a personalized schedule toward completion of their Professional Designation program by consulting with FIDM Admissions Advisors. FIDM offers professional designation programs in apparel industry management, fashion design, beauty industry management, digital media, graphic design, interior design, jewelry design, merchandising and marketing (or product development), textile design, fashion knitwear design, and visual communications. For more information about FIDM transfer programs, students should visit http://fidm.edu/go/admissionstransfer.

Academic Programs

FIDM operates on a four-quarter academic calendar. Students can choose from twenty specialized creative business and design majors. New students may begin their studies at the start of any quarter throughout the year. Detailed information about FIDM majors is also available online at http://fidm.edu/en/Majors/Visual+Communications/.

Department chairs and other trained staff members assist students in selecting the correct sequence of courses to complete degree requirements. The counseling department provides personal guidance and referral to outside counseling services and matches peer tutors to specific students' needs. Individual Development and Education Assistance (IDEA) Centers at each campus provide students with additional educational assistance in the areas of writing, mathematics, computer competency, study skills, research skills, and reading comprehension.

FIDM's eLearning program, which includes the B.S. in Business Management and some classes in other majors, ensures that a student's educational experience can take place anywhere. The online courses are designed to replicate the experience of classes on campus. Students in the eLearning program are granted the same high-quality education as students on campus and have immediate access to valuable campus resources, including the FIDM Library, Career Advisors, and instructors.

Off-Campus Programs

Internships are available within each major. Paid and volunteer positions provide work experience for students to gain practical application of classroom skills.

FIDM provides the opportunity for students to participate in academic study tours in Europe, Asia, and New York. These tours are specifically designed to broaden and enhance the specialized education offered at FIDM. Participants may earn academic credit under faculty-supervised directed studies. Exchange programs are also available with Esmod, Paris; Instituto Artictico dell' Abbigliamento Marangoni, Milan; Accademia Internazionale d'Alta Mode e d'Arte del Costume Koefia, Rome; St. Martins School of Art, London; College of Distributive Trades, London; and Janette Klein Design School, Mexico City.

Academic Facilities

FIDM's award-winning campuses feature design studios with computer labs and innovative study spaces, spacious classrooms, imaginative common areas, and state-of-the-industry technology. Computer labs support and enhance the educational programs of the Institute. Specialized labs offer computerized cutting and marking; graphic, interior, and textile design; word processing; and database management.

The FIDM Library goes beyond traditional sources of information. It houses a print and electronic collection of over 2.5 million titles that encompass all subject areas, with an emphasis on fashion, interior design, retailing, and costume. The library subscribes to over 160 international and national periodicals, offering the latest information on art, design, graphics, fashion, beauty, business, and current trends. The FIDM Library also features an international video library, subscriptions to major predictive services, interior design workrooms, textile samples, a trimmings/findings collection, and access to the Internet. The FIDM Museum & Galleries Permanent and Study Collections contain more than 12,000 garments from the eighteenth century to present day, including film and theater costumes. One of the largest collections in the United States, it features top designer holdings including Chanel, Yves Saint Laurent, Dior, and Lacroix. The collection also includes items from the California Historical Society (First Families), the Hollywood Collection, and the Rudi Gernreich Collection.

Costs

For the 2011–12 academic year, tuition and fees started at $26,000, depending on the selected major. Textbooks and supplies started at $2100 per year, depending on the major. First-year application fees range from $225 for California residents to $525 for international students.

Financial Aid

There are several sources of financial funding available to the student, including federal financial aid and education loan programs, California state aid programs, institutional loan programs, and FIDM awards and scholarships. The FIDM Student Financial Services office and FIDM Admissions Advisors work one-on-one with students and parents to help them find funding for their FIDM education. More information on FIDM scholarships and financial aid can be found at http://fidm.edu/go/fidmscholarships.

Faculty

FIDM faculty members are selected as specialists in their fields, working professionals with impressive resumes and invaluable industry connections. They bring daily exposure from their industry into the classroom for the benefit of the students. In pursuit of the best faculty members, consideration is given to both academic excellence and practical experience.

Admission Requirements

Students are accepted into one of FIDM's specialized Associate of Arts degree programs packed with 16–25 challenging courses per major. Associate of Arts programs are designed for high school graduates or applicants with strong GED scores. They offer the highly specialized curriculum of a specific major, as well as a traditional liberal arts/general studies foundation. Official transcripts from high school/secondary schools and all colleges/universities attended are needed to apply. International students must send transcripts accompanied by official English translations. Three recommendations from teachers, counselors, or employers are also required for admission. FIDM provides a reference request form on its Web site on the Admissions section under "How To Apply." All references must be sealed and mailed to the school when applying. An admissions essay portion and portfolio entrance project requirement, which is specific to the student's selected major, are also available on the Web site's Admissions section under "How To Apply." For more information on the application process, prospective students can go to www.fidm.edu.

Application and Information

Applications are accepted on an ongoing basis. All prospective students should contact:

FIDM/Fashion Institute of Design & Merchandising
919 South Grand Avenue
Los Angeles, California 90015
Phone: 800-624-1200 (toll-free)
         213-624-1201 (outside the United States)
Fax: 213-624-4799
Web site: http://www.fidm.edu
         http://www.facebook.com/home.php#!/FIDMCollege
         http://twitter.com/#!/FIDM

FIDM Los Angeles Campus Exterior.

FITCHBURG STATE UNIVERSITY
FITCHBURG, MASSACHUSETTS

The University

Fitchburg State University is a public, liberal arts center of learning, dedicated to teaching, with thriving career-oriented and professional education programs. The University prepares its graduates for jobs in their fields and continues to place more than 70 percent of its graduates in their chosen professions within six months of graduation.

Fitchburg State's excellent academic reputation and graduate placement can be attributed to a nationally recognized faculty and a strong commitment to teaching. The University enrolls approximately 3,500 undergraduate students in its day and evening divisions and another 3,500 students in its graduate and continuing education programs. The average undergraduate class size is 21, and the overall student-teacher ratio remains low at 17:1. Each student is assigned to an academic adviser to assist with planning an individualized program of study. In addition, each department has access to state-of-the-art equipment and there is an extensive internship network that spreads throughout New England and across the country.

Student life at Fitchburg State is active and fun. There are numerous and varied opportunities for student leadership and involvement. More than sixty student-run clubs and organizations are on campus, including academic, cultural, and ethnic; profession-oriented; performance; sports and fitness; social and volunteer; fraternities and sororities; student government; and academic honor societies. Hundreds of popular and well-attended activities take place during the year, including films, lectures, concerts, seminars, coffeehouses, pub entertainment, recreational tournaments, a performing arts series, and visual arts exhibits, to name just a few. The University's students participate in exciting Division III athletics, offering sixteen intercollegiate varsity sports teams for both men and women, and there is a variety of intramural sports for all students. The beautiful, well-equipped Recreation Center has all the equipment and activities students need to stay healthy and have fun.

In addition to Bachelor of Arts and Bachelor of Science degrees, Fitchburg State confers the Master of Arts; the Master of Arts in Teaching (M.A.T.); the Master in Business Administration (M.B.A.); the Master of Education (M.Ed.) in several disciplines; and the Master of Science (M.S.) in applied communication, computer science, mental health and school counseling, and forensic nursing. Several Certificate of Advanced Graduate Studies (C.A.G.S.) and graduate-level certificate programs are available as well.

Location

The University is located in a residential area near the center of Fitchburg, a city with a population of 43,000, which serves as the hub of the commercial and industrial life of north-central Massachusetts. Fitchburg State owns the Wallace Civic Center which is home to the University's ice hockey team and provides many activities each year, such as exhibits, fairs, performances, free public ice skating, local hockey events, and lectures. The City of Fitchburg offers many opportunities for study and practical experience in the areas of sociology, psychology, health, computer technology, business, industry, political organization, and community service. Outdoor activities, including skiing, camping, hiking, canoeing, and fishing, are just minutes from the campus.

The historic and literary centers of Lexington and Concord and the city of Boston are only about an hour from the University. It's very easy to get to Boston—the commuter rail station is right on the edge of campus. The city of Worcester, the third largest in New England, is only one-half hour to the south. Fitchburg offers students the convenience of a residential campus with easy access to all the amenities that the surrounding area offers.

Majors and Degrees

Fitchburg State University offers the Bachelor of Arts, Bachelor of Science, and Bachelor of Science in Education degrees and offers the following undergraduate programs: accounting; architectural technology; biology; biotechnology; business administration; clinical exercise physiology; cognitive science; communications media studies; computer information systems; computer science; construction technology; criminal justice; developmental psychology; earth systems science; economics; education, with teacher education programs available in early childhood education, elementary education, middle school education, secondary education (with emphases in biology, English, history, and mathematics), special education with emphases in severe disabilities (all levels) and moderate disabilities (pre-K–8), and technology education; electronics engineering technology; English studies; environmental biology; exercise and sports science; energy management; film/video production; fitness management; geography; geo/physical sciences; graphic design; health sciences; history; human services; industrial and organizational psychology; interactive media; humanities–interdisciplinary studies; industrial technology; international business and economics; literature; management; manufacturing engineering technology; marketing; mathematics; nursing; photography; political science; professional communication; professional writing; psychology; sociology; technical theater arts; theater; undeclared/pre-major; and the following pre-professional programs: dentistry, law, medicine, and veterinary medicine.

Academic Programs

The University operates on a two-semester calendar. The first semester begins in early September and ends in mid-December, and the second semester begins in mid-January and ends in mid-May.

The curriculum has a strong liberal arts and sciences requirement, which provides a solid foundation for either further academic study or a career. Students obtain practical experience through numerous internships in social agencies, government offices, hospitals, and corporations related to their interests. Some major programs require an extensive supervised practicum to complete degree requirements. For education and nursing majors, a broad spectrum of student teaching and clinical experience is incorporated into their respective programs of study. The University's four-year honors program culminates in a senior thesis or project.

Off-Campus Programs

Fitchburg State is one of nine state universities under the jurisdiction of the Massachusetts Department of Higher Education. Through this affiliation, students may participate in the College Academic Program Sharing program, which allows study for a semester or a year at another university. For a rewarding cultural exchange experience, the Office of International Education provides undergraduate students the opportunity to study abroad at a variety of colleges and universities all over the world. Programs vary in length from a few weeks to as long as a semester or a year. Some of the locations in the exchange program include Australia, Canada, China, England, France, Ireland, Italy, Japan, New Zealand, Russia, Scotland, Spain, and Sweden.

Academic Facilities

The University has a number of special facilities. A well-equipped Academic Success Center includes offices for academic advising, career services, disability services, math and writing centers, multicultural student services, and peer tutoring. The McKay Campus School is a pre-K through fourth grade elementary school located on the campus, which gives education majors direct experience in a fully operational school. The Instructional Media Center has extensive, modern, well-equipped facilities which support the industrial education and industrial technology programs. The nursing program utilizes an on-campus clinical lab that simulates a hospital setting with several computerized training models: SimMan, SimBaby, and SimNewB. The communications media program possesses a full range of the latest equipment, such as media/film composers, digital audio work-

stations, a full-color dye-sublimation printer, CD recording and slide-scanning equipment, multiple editing rooms, a production studio, darkrooms, and graphic design computer labs. Communication students at Fitchburg State have access to many of the labs and facilities as early as their freshman year.

Costs

Fitchburg State University seeks to provide a very affordable education. Annual tuition for residents of Massachusetts was $970 per year in 2011–12; out-of-state tuition was $7050. Required annual fees in 2011–12 totaled $7330. The estimated annual total for a full-time, on-campus student from Massachusetts was $16,640 and for an out-of-state student, it was $22,720. Fees are subject to change.

Financial Aid

Many sources of financial aid are available to Fitchburg State students. The University participates in federal and state programs. Packages consisting of grants, loans, work-study awards, and scholarships are given to students demonstrating financial need and academic merit. All students who submit a completed application for admission by February 1 will automatically be considered for all available merit scholarships for the fall semester. Financial aid applications (including the FAFSA) for the fall semester must be completed by the preceding March 1 to be given priority consideration. Over $23 million in financial aid is granted annually to approximately 80 percent of Fitchburg State students making a quality education affordable for many deserving students.

Faculty

More than 92 percent of Fitchburg State's 192 full-time faculty members hold earned doctoral or other terminal degrees. Full professors teach freshman classes as well as advanced courses and serve as academic advisers to students majoring in their respective programs. Faculty members are accessible, engaging, and available to teach and advise students throughout their four years at the University.

Student Government

All full-time undergraduate students are members of the Student Government Association (SGA). The purpose of the SGA is to encourage responsibility and cooperation in democratic self-government; to form an official body for expressing the judgments of students and fostering activities and matters of general student interest; and to promote full understanding and cooperation among the students, the faculty members, and the administration in order to further the welfare of the University.

The governing body of the SGA consists of 6 SGA officers and a General Council, which includes these officers and 55 elected representatives of classes and residence halls, as well as the commuter student population. The SGA operates through a number of standing and ad hoc committees; membership is open to all students.

A 14-member All-University Committee, representing students, the faculty, and the administration, makes recommendations to the president of the University concerning matters of campus-wide policy.

Admission Requirements

As part of the Massachusetts State University system, Fitchburg State evaluates each applicant from any state, based on standards set by the Massachusetts Department of Higher Education and the University. The University considers high school curriculum, grade point average, SAT and/or ACT scores, school and community service, recommendations, application essay, life experience, special talents, and learning styles. The state admissions standards place significant attention on the student's high school record and SAT or ACT scores. The record of achievement in high school is the single most important item in the applicant's academic credentials. Freshman applicants should have completed a college-preparatory program that includes 16 college-preparatory units, with 4 units in English, 2 units in the same foreign language, 2 units in social studies, 3 units in mathematics (algebra I and II and geometry), 3 units in the natural sciences (2 of which must be laboratory courses), and 2 college-preparatory electives.

An essay is required; however, interviews are not required. Applicants who have questions about the programs and admission procedures at the University are encouraged to contact the Admissions Office to speak with a counselor.

The University encourages applications from transfer students and enrolls about 400 each year. An official transcript from each college previously attended must be submitted along with the application for admission.

International students are also encouraged to apply. Scores on the Test of English as a Foreign Language (TOEFL), evaluations of all international transcripts, and translations of international transcripts must be submitted in addition to the application for admission. Additional information for international students is available on the University's Web site.

Application and Information

Fitchburg State University reviews applications on a rolling basis, sending its first set of admission decisions for the fall semester by mid-December. The priority deadline for applications is March 1. Applicants to the communications media and nursing programs are reviewed against a higher set of admissions standards and are strongly encouraged to submit their applications by the January 1 priority deadline. In addition, applicants who wish to be considered for merit scholarships and the honors program must complete their admission and financial aid application process (i.e., submit all required materials) by February 1.

Transfer applicants are encouraged to apply by April 15 for the fall and by November 1 for the spring semester. International applicants applying for the fall semester must complete the application process by March 15 if they require on-campus housing and by July 15 if they are not in need of campus housing. Applicants for the spring semester must file their application for admission by December 1.

For further information, students should contact:

Admissions Office
Fitchburg State University
160 Pearl Street
Fitchburg, Massachusetts 01420
Phone: 800-705-9692 (toll-free)
Fax: 978-665-4540
E-mail: admissions@fitchburgstate.edu
Web site: http://www.fitchburgstate.edu
  http://on.fb.me/FitchburgState (Facebook)
  http://twitter.com/FITCHBURG_STATE

Built in 1910 as the Edgerly School, the current Edgerly Hall was one of the first junior high schools in the United States.

FIVE TOWNS COLLEGE
DIX HILLS, NEW YORK

The College

Located on Long Island's North Shore, Five Towns College offers students the opportunity to study in a suburban environment that is close to New York City. Founded in 1972, Five Towns College is an independent, nonsectarian, coeducational institution that places its emphasis on the student as an individual. Many students are drawn to the College because of its strong reputation in music, media, education, and the performing arts. The College offers associate and bachelor's degrees. The College also offers programs leading to the Master of Music (M.M.) degree in jazz/commercial music and in music education as well as a Master of Science in Education (M.S.Ed.) and a Doctor of Musical Arts (D.M.A.).

From as far away as England and South Korea and from as close as Long Island and New York City, the 1,100 undergraduate and graduate students reflect a rich cultural diversity. The College's enrollment is 55 percent men and 45 percent women, with a minority population of approximately 30 percent. The College's music programs are contemporary jazz in nature, although classical musicians are also part of this creative community. The most popular programs are audio recording technology, broadcasting, journalism, music performance, music business, music and elementary teacher education, theater, and film/video production.

Coeducational living accommodations are available on campus. The Five Towns College Living/Learning Center is a new complex containing four modern-life residence halls. Each residence hall contains single- and double-occupancy rooms equipped with private bathrooms, broadband Internet access, cable television, and other amenities.

Location

The College's beautiful 35-acre campus, located in the wooded countryside of Dix Hills, New York, provides students with a quiet college setting to pursue their studies. Just off campus is Long Island's bustling Route 110 corridor, home to numerous national and multinational corporations. New York City, with everything from Lincoln Center to Broadway, is just a train ride away and provides students with some of the best cultural advantages in the world.

Closer to the campus, the many communities of Long Island abound with cultural and recreational opportunities. The College is located within the historic town of Huntington, which is home to the Cinema Arts Center, Hecksher Museum, Vanderbilt Museum, and numerous restaurants, coffeehouses, and quaint shops. The nearby shores of Jones Beach State Park and the Fire Island National Seashore are world renowned for their white, sandy beaches.

Majors and Degrees

Five Towns College offers the Associate in Arts (A.A.) degree in liberal arts, the Associate in Science (A.S.) degree in business administration; and the Associate in Applied Science (A.A.S.) degree in business management and in jazz commercial music, with concentrations in audio recording technology and music business.

The College offers the Bachelor of Music (Mus.B.) degree in music education and in jazz/commercial music, with concentrations in audio recording technology, composition/songwriting, music business, musical theater, and performance; the Bachelor of Fine Arts (B.F.A.) degree in theater or film/video arts; the Bachelor of Professional Studies (B.P.S.) degree in business management, with concentrations in audio recording technology and music business; the Bachelor of Science (B.S.) degree in childhood education; and the B.S. in mass communication, which features broadcasting and journalism concentrations.

Academic Programs

The following describes some of the more popular programs at Five Towns College. For a complete description of the College's academic program, students should visit the Five Towns College Web site at http://www.ftc.edu.

The music education program is designed for students interested in a career as a teacher of music in a public or private school. The undergraduate program leads to New York State provisional certification. The course work provides professional training and includes a student-teaching experience. The audio recording technology concentration is designed to provide students with the tools needed to succeed as professional studio engineers and producers in the music industry. The music business concentration is designed for students interested in a career in entertainment-related business fields. The course work includes the technical, legal, production, management, and merchandising aspects of the music business. The composition/songwriting concentration provides intensive instruction in a core of technical studies in harmony, orchestration, counterpoint, MIDI, songwriting, form and analysis, arranging, and composition for those who intend to pursue careers as composers, arrangers, and songwriters. The performance concentration includes a common core of technical studies and a foundation of specialized courses, such as music history, harmony, counterpoint, improvisation, ensemble performance, and private instruction. The theater arts program is designed for students interested in careers as actors, entertainers, scenic designers, directors, stage managers, and lighting or sound directors. The film/video program includes extensive technical preparation in videography, filmmaking, linear and nonlinear editing, storyboarding, scriptwriting, producing, and directing for filmmakers and videographers. Elementary education students are prepared as teachers for grades 1–6, while those interested in journalism and broadcasting are prepared for careers in radio, television, newspaper, or editorial writing.

To earn a bachelor's degree, students must accumulate between 122 and 130 credits, depending on the program of study, with a proper distribution of courses and a GPA of a minimum of 2.0. To earn an associate degree, students must accumulate between 62 and 66 credits.

Off-Campus Programs

Off-campus internship opportunities are available to Five Towns College students who have fulfilled the necessary prerequisites, including a cumulative grade point average of at least 2.5, with a 3.0 in their major. In recent semesters, students have interned for major corporations such as MTV, Atlantic Records, Polygram Records, CBS, ABC, EMI Records, MCA Records, Sony Records, The Power Station, Universal Mastering Studios, Channel 12 News, and many others.

Academic Facilities

Five Towns College occupies a multiwinged facility that comprises approximately 120,000 square feet and includes a 500-seat auditorium, production studios, athletic and dining facilities, classrooms, PC and iMac computer labs with a student center. T-3 lines connect the College's completely fiber-optic computer network to the Internet. All students have access to this network and are provided with an e-mail account.

The Five Towns College Library has more than 50,000 print and nonprint materials. These include nearly 32,000 books and print items, 450 periodical titles, and approximately 5,000 records, 2,600 DVDs, and more than 4,300 CDs. Through its membership in the Long Island Library Resource Council (LILRC), students have access to other academic and public libraries.

The John Lennon Center for Music and Technology at Five Towns College houses state-of-the-art audio recording studios and a fully loaded electronic music/MIDI computer lab. The studios and lab feature industry-standard recording equipment and software programs that rival major recording facilities around the world, such as a 72-channel SSL 9000J and Neve Genesys mixing console; Telefunken, Neumann, AKG, Royer, Blue, and other microphones; outboard gear such as Manley, API, Chandler Limited, Lexicon, Universal Audio, and Apogee; and the latest versions of Pro Tools, Logic, Reason, and Sibelius. The film/video division uses Sony PMW-EX3 XD cameras with SxS cards, Canon 5D Mark II cameras, and Arriflex Super 16-mm film cameras. Editing suites offer Final Cut Pro and Adobe CS4 Creative Suite on iMac computers. Students utilize these facilities to develop their skills while creating professional-quality productions, both in the studio and on location under the supervision of industry professionals. Student productions include short films, music videos, documentaries, public service announcements, commercials, and live events, among many others.

The Dix Hills Center for Performing Arts at Five Towns College is an acoustically "perfect" venue, with digital lighting systems, digital sound reinforcement for concert production, and a Barco 6300 digital projection system for multimedia productions. The professional stage is 60 feet wide, with a proscenium opening of 16 feet and 32 feet of fly space. Students utilize this facility to produce live concerts, plays, musicals, and other performances or special presentations.

Costs

The tuition for 2012–13 is $19,800 per year. Miscellaneous fees total approximately $400, and books cost about $500. Private instruction fees for performing music students are $800 per semester.

Financial Aid

The annual tuition at Five Towns College is among the lowest of all the private colleges in the region. Nevertheless, approximately 82 percent of all students receive some form of financial assistance. Need-based and/or merit-based grants, scholarships, loans, and work-study programs are available to qualified recipients, including transfer students. Prospective students are urged to contact the Financial Aid Office as early as possible.

Faculty

The College's growing faculty consists of 120 full- and part-time members. The student-faculty ratio is 14:1. While the faculty is more strongly committed to teaching than to research, many members continue to be active in their respective areas of expertise.

Student Government

Student Government Association (SGA) serves as a voice of the students to the faculty and administration. Students can get involved through organizations and committees. All recognized organizations and committees fall under the jurisdiction of the SGA. The SGA is the elected representative student body of the campus and is responsible for creating many of the policy-making decisions that affect organizations and student life.

There are several media clubs and organizations for students. They include *Keynotes* (the College yearbook), *The Record* (the student newspaper), and WFTU (the College radio station).

Admission Requirements

The College encourages applications from students who will engage themselves in its creative community. Students applying to the College should have attained a minimum high school average grade of 78 percent. The SAT or ACT exam is required for all freshmen. Transfer students must also submit official transcripts of all college-level work as well as their high school transcripts. International students from non-English-speaking countries must submit a TOEFL Internet score of at least 80 or its equivalent. The College does not accept students on an early admissions basis, although early decision is available. Candidates for admission must submit a completed Application for Undergraduate Admission, official high school transcripts, at least two letters of recommendation, and a personal statement. International students must submit their TOEFL scores, financial documentation and sponsor information.

Application and Information

Admission into any music program is contingent upon passing an audition demonstrating skill in performance on a major instrument or vocally. Admission into any theater program is also contingent upon passing an audition. In some cases, the Admissions Committee may request an on-campus interview with an applicant. Music, theater, and film/video students are encouraged to submit an electronic portfolio or DVD, if available.

An online application is available on the College website at www.ftc.edu. Students can apply either electronically or by mail.

Except for applicants applying on an early decision basis, new students are accepted on a rolling basis, with decisions for the fall and spring semesters mailed starting February 15 and December 1, respectively. There is an application fee of $35.

For further information, students should contact the Admissions Office at 631-656-2110 or admissions@ftc.edu.

Director of Admissions
Five Towns College
305 North Service Road
Dix Hills, New York 11746-5871
Phone: 631-656-2110
Fax: 631-656-2172
E-mail: admissions@ftc.edu
Web site: http://www.ftc.edu

A student mixes on the SSL 9000J 72-channel console in one of the College's four state-of-the art recording studios.

FLORIDA ATLANTIC UNIVERSITY
BOCA RATON, FLORIDA

The University

Florida Atlantic University (FAU) is a midsize comprehensive university that serves more than 29,000 students on several campuses throughout South Florida. FAU was established in 1961, making it the fifth-oldest university in the state system. As an upper-division and graduate state university, FAU admitted its first students in September 1964. Enrollment has increased from 867 in the first year to more than 29,000 in the 2011–12 academic year.

Since the original Boca Raton campus was founded in 1964, the University has expanded to several other campuses in South Florida: Dania Beach, Davie, and Jupiter. Admission to incoming freshman students is limited to the Boca Raton campus and the Harriet L. Wilkes Honors College.

The Boca Raton campus provides an exciting and supportive learning environment for students. The Student Union hosts student activities and some of the meetings for over 200 clubs and organizations. In addition, its 2,400-seat auditorium enables students to enjoy a wide variety of musical performances.

The Boca Raton campus is also the home of FAU's Division I intercollegiate athletics program and facilities. A new 30,000-seat football stadium was opened in October 2011 and features many state-of-the-art amenities.

FAU's new recreation and fitness center includes an aquatic center, three indoor basketball/volleyball courts, treadmill and elliptical area, a free-weight area and personal trainers. The recreation and wellness complex includes tennis courts, a track, and a variety of fields for club and intramural sports competition. The five-story S. E. Wimberly Library houses a large collection of monographs, serials, and other academic resources. Computer labs, study lounges, a media center, and tutoring services also provide valuable academic support for students.

FAU's Davie campus is located on 38 acres in western Broward County and is FAU's second-largest campus. The Davie campus has served FAU students since 1990 with 2+2 programs in partnership with Broward College.

The John D. MacArthur campus presently enrolls more than 2,000 students and offers a wide range of upper division and graduate programs. It is home to the Harriet L. Wilkes Honors College, the Center for Environmental Studies, the Hibel Museum of Art, the new research facility for Scripps Florida, and the Max Planck Florida Institute.

In 2006, FAU opened the FAU/Harbor Branch Marine Sciences Building—a 40,000-square-foot, joint-use facility housing specially equipped marine science labs, classrooms and video-conferencing equipped meeting rooms—at the Harbor Branch Oceanographic Institution's 600-acre site in Fort Pierce. This state-of-the-art facility provides an ideal setting for marine science research and teaching.

Through its partnerships with other educational institutions, local businesses, industries, and civic and cultural organizations, FAU enhances the economic, human, and cultural development of the surrounding communities and beyond. Students at FAU may participate in a work-study program that combines their classroom learning with hands-on experience.

The University's Charles E. Schmidt College of Medicine enrolled its first medical school class in fall 2011. It also is partnering with FAU's Wilkes Honors College to offer select students early provisional admission to medical school, making it possible to receive both a bachelor's degree and an M.D. from FAU in only seven or eight years. Incoming freshmen who are accepted into the new Wilkes Medical Scholars Program will begin their undergraduate programs already assured of a spot in FAU's new medical school, provided they complete all program requirements and score at least 29 on the MCAT. Additional information is available online at www.fau.edu/divdept/honcol/admissions_med.

The University has developed a partnership with Broward College, Indian River State College, and Palm Beach State College called the LINK program. Through this program, students are prepared for guaranteed admission to FAU upon successful completion of their Associate in Arts degree. More information can be found at www.fau.edu/admissions/link.

Florida Atlantic University is accredited by the Commission on Colleges of the Southern Association of Colleges and Schools to award associate, bachelor's, master's, and doctoral degrees. In addition, it is accredited by fourteen professional agencies. FAU is also a member of the National Association of State Universities and Land-Grant Colleges and the Council of Graduate Schools in the United States.

Location

FAU's main campus in Boca Raton is on an 850-acre site located only 3 miles from the Atlantic Ocean. The campus is conveniently located halfway between Palm Beach and Fort Lauderdale and offers a broad range of academic programs, activities, and services.

South Florida's climate is subtropical, with an average year-round temperature of 75 degrees. FAU's campuses are within easy driving distance of some of the most beautiful beaches and recreational facilities to be found anywhere.

Majors and Degrees

FAU offers programs leading to the Bachelor of Arts (B.A.), Bachelor of Science (B.S.), and specialized bachelor's degrees. A minimum of 120 credit hours is required for a bachelor's degree.

The College for Design and Social Inquiry offers majors in architecture, criminal justice, public management, public safety administration, social work, and urban and regional planning.

The Dorothy F. Schmidt College of Arts and Letters offers majors in anthropology, arts and humanities, Caribbean and Latin American studies, communication and multimedia studies, English, history, Jewish studies, languages and linguistics (French, German, Italian, Japanese, and Spanish), music, philosophy, political science, social science, sociology, theater, and visual arts and art history.

The College of Business offers majors in accounting, economics, finance, health administration, hospitality management, international business and trade, management leadership and entrepreneurship, management information systems, and marketing.

The Harriet L. Wilkes Honors College in Jupiter offers a liberal arts and sciences education in a highly selective environment. Concentrations include American studies, anthropology, biological sciences/pre-med, chemistry, economics, English literature, environmental studies, history, international studies, Latin American studies, law and society, marine biology, math and science, mathematics, philosophy, physics, political science, psychology, Spanish, and women's studies.

The University Honors Program at the Boca Raton campus provides students with exceptional and rewarding learning opportunities through special honors seminars. The goal of the program is to give students a learning experience that will prepare them to continue their education throughout their lives.

The College of Education offers majors in early care and education, elementary education, exceptional student education, exercise science and health promotion, and secondary education.

The College of Engineering and Computer Science offers majors in computer science as well as civil, computer, electrical, environmental, geomatics, mechanical, ocean engineering, and information engineering technology. FAU established the nation's first ocean engineering degree program in 1965 and now conducts millions of dollars in research annually.

The Christine E. Lynn College of Nursing offers a B.S. in Nursing degree and is nationally and internationally known for developing

innovative approaches to nursing education within a caring philosophy.

The Charles E. Schmidt College of Science has majors in biological science (biotechnology, ecology and organismic biology, marine biology, microbiology, and molecular biology), chemistry, geography, geology, mathematics, neuroscience, physics, and psychology. The Charles E. Schmidt College of Science also offers a pre-health professions certificate for any students interested in pursuing careers in dentistry, general medicine, optometry, pharmacy, physical therapy, and veterinary medicine.

Academic Programs

Florida Atlantic University prepares its undergraduate students to be productive and thoughtful citizens by offering a broad liberal education coupled with the development of competency in fields of special interest. FAU encourages students to think creatively and critically and provides the tools needed for lifelong learning.

Off-Campus Programs

While there is no substitute for the dynamic synergy created in the classroom, FAU faculty and students seek out real-world experiences that enhance the classroom experience, such as internships, hands-on research, and study-abroad opportunities. FAU has exchange agreements with international schools in locations ranging from China to Germany. Arrangements can be made through the Office of International Programs (http://www.fau.edu/goabroad).

Academic Facilities

The Boca Raton campus resources feature the S. E. Wimberly Library, with more than 1 million holdings. The Dorothy F. Schmidt College of Arts and Letters features a 75,000-square-foot, three-building complex encompassing a performance arts center, an art gallery, an experimental theater, a visual arts center, lecture halls, classrooms, and offices. The College of Business occupies a four-story building including wireless classrooms with a simulated trading room floor. The College of Education's four-story, 90,000-square-foot facility houses its academic departments and offers a teaching gymnasium, an early childhood center, and the A. D. Henderson University School operated by the College of Education. There is also a marine sciences center, Gumbo Limbo, located between the Intracoastal Waterway and the Atlantic Ocean; it provides teaching and research facilities. The Christine E. Lynn College of Nursing is housed in a state-of-the-art building which is a LEED-certified Gold.

FAU continues to enhance the campus environment with the addition of many new facilities. Recently completed projects on the Boca Raton campus include the Marleen and Harold Forkas Alumni Center; the College of Engineering and Computer Science facility, which achieved LEED Platinum certification; and the new Culture and Society building that includes the Living Room Theaters, a 200-seat digital movie complex.

Costs

For the 2011–12 academic year, in-state tuition was $177.65 per credit hour and out-of-state tuition was $657.17 per credit hour. Average room and board costs are $10,940. Approximate expenses are $939 for books, $1678 for personal items, and $1993 for transportation for off-campus students. Fees are subject to change.

Financial Aid

Approximately $177 million in financial aid is awarded each year. A comprehensive program of student financial aid includes scholarships, grants, loans, and work-study that may provide assistance from initial enrollment through graduate study. As a member of the College Scholarship Service of the College Board, the University is guided by the principles and policies of that organization. Students who are interested in applying for need-based aid must complete the Free Application for Federal Student Aid (FAFSA), which is available online at http://www.fau.edu/finaid and at all U.S. high schools, colleges, and universities. Students are strongly encouraged to complete the FAFSA in January for fall admission. The process of applying for aid normally takes six to eight weeks. The priority deadline is March 1.

There are a variety of scholarships for academic, athletic, or artistic talent. Students should visit the Admissions Web site at http://www.fau.edu/admissions for more information on academic scholarships and should check with individual departments for information on athletic or artistic scholarships.

Faculty

Recognizing that the excellence of its faculty is the true measure of the worth of a university, FAU has brought together a distinguished group of scholars who hold a balanced dedication to both teaching and research. Faculty members come from more than thirty states and several countries. The majority hold a doctorate or professional degree. They all represent a high level of professional experience and academic attainment and are committed to the development of a vigorous educational program of high caliber. The FAU community has benefited from the presence of 17 Eminent Scholars, distributed over seven colleges. In addition, two Endowed Chairs have been fully funded and five others partially funded. The presence of these distinguished scholars and researchers has enhanced the academic climate of the University and has provided focal points for the development of new programs, particularly at the graduate level.

Student Government

FAU gives students an active role on virtually all University and faculty committees, including the Curriculum Committee. They serve on the Board of Trustees and college advisory councils and operate the Student Government Association and Residence Hall Councils as well as the interclub, interfraternity, and Panhellenic groups. Students also serve on the University Senate along with faculty and staff members.

Admission Requirements

Admission to the University is limited to applicants who have graduated from regionally accredited high schools or who hold a GED certificate. Evaluation is based on the academic course grade point average and rigor of curriculum combined with acceptable results on the SAT or ACT. Candidates for admission should have 18 academic high school units, including 4 units of English, 4 units of mathematics (algebra I and above), 3 units of natural science (2 with labs), 3 units of social science, 2 units of foreign language in sequence, and 2 academic electives. Applicants who have completed the GED test should request official high school transcripts (if applicable) and an official GED score report from the Department of Education.

Admission for freshman students requires an application for admission, a nonrefundable $30 application fee, official transcripts from an accredited high school, and the official results of the SAT or ACT. Admitted freshmen must confirm their intention to enroll and secure their place with the freshman class by submitting a nonrefundable $200 deposit, which is applied to the student's tuition and other expenses for the term in which they have been admitted to FAU.

Undergraduate students who wish to transfer to FAU must be in good academic standing at their previous college or university and have a minimum 2.5 GPA. Students with fewer than 60 transferable credits should submit an application for admission, a nonrefundable $30 application fee, official transcripts from high school and previously attended colleges or universities, and acceptable SAT or ACT scores. Students with 60 or more transferable credits must submit an application for admission, a nonrefundable $30 application fee, and official transcripts from each previously attended college or university.

Students who have completed all or part of their education abroad are required to have their foreign credentials evaluated by an independent evaluation service. International students must also furnish evidence of proficiency in English by submitting TOEFL scores. For additional requirements, students should visit http://www.fau.edu/admissions.

Application and Information

Office of Undergraduate Admissions
Florida Atlantic University
777 Glades Road
Boca Raton, Florida 33431
Phone: 561-297-3040
E-mail: admissions@fau.edu
Web site: http://www.fau.edu

FLORIDA SOUTHERN COLLEGE
LAKELAND, FLORIDA

The College

The oldest private college in the state, Florida Southern College (FSC) was chartered in 1885 and settled on the shores of spectacular Lake Hollingsworth in Lakeland in 1922.

Florida Southern today is a nationally ranked, residential, coeducational, and comprehensive college. Its 2,200 students represent forty-four states and more than forty countries. Students choose Florida Southern because of its national reputation for dynamic, hands-on learning that features guaranteed internships and study abroad. The atmosphere is friendly and personal, fostering a close-knit student body and faculty.

All members of the academic community take pride in the beautiful campus, a historic landmark and home to the world's largest single-site collection of buildings designed by renowned architect Frank Lloyd Wright.

Students, whether members of fraternities and sororities or as independents, live in a variety of contemporary on-campus accommodations, including the state-of-the-art Barnett Residential Life Center, which features stunning views of the lake, contemporary student lounges, modern kitchens and bathrooms, and wireless Internet access.

The George Jenkins Field House, which seats 3,000, includes a three-court gymnasium, a weight room, and an athletic training room. Facilities for tennis, racquetball, dance, swimming, and waterskiing are available at the popular Nina B. Hollis Wellness Center, which offers a fully equipped fitness center, an aerobics/dance studio, an intramural gymnasium, a competition-size swimming pool, and a wide-screen TV/lounge area.

There are branches of seven national Greek fraternities and seven national Greek sororities on campus. Popular student activities include intercollegiate and intramural sports, drama and music groups, publications, and more than seventy clubs and organizations related to academic, political, religious, and social interests. A high percentage of students are involved in volunteer programs and internships in the surrounding community, statewide, and internationally.

Location

Florida Southern's campus consists of approximately 100 acres on the shore of Lake Hollingsworth in Lakeland, Florida, a dynamic suburban community of about 120,000 residents in the heart of Florida's high-tech corridor. The campus is within walking or biking distance of Lakeland's historic downtown, and Lakeland is just 45 minutes from Tampa and an hour from Orlando. Within an hour's drive of the state's major recreational attractions, including Walt Disney World and award-winning beaches, the College is ideally situated for internships and job opportunities with leading corporations that tap into one of the largest markets in the United States. Students enjoy Festival of Fine Arts series performances in music, dance, and drama; distinguished speakers; and exciting College and business symposiums. The Lakeland Center also offers many cultural and entertainment opportunities.

Majors and Degrees

Florida Southern College offers Bachelor of Arts, Bachelor of Fine Arts, Bachelor of Music, Bachelor of Music Education, Bachelor of Science, and Bachelor of Science in Nursing degrees in more than fifty majors including accounting, art (art education, art history, graphic design, and studio art), athletic training, biochemistry and molecular biology, biology, business administration (career tracks in finance, international business, management, and marketing), chemistry, citrus, communication (advertising and public relations; broadcast, print, and online media; and interpersonal communication), criminology, economics, education (elementary education), English, history, horticultural science, mathematics, mathematics/computer science, music (music education and music performance), nursing, philosophy, physical education, political

science, psychology, religion, sociology, Spanish, theater arts (performance and technical), and youth ministry. Divisional majors are available in humanities and social science.

Preprofessional programs are offered in dentistry, engineering, law, medicine, pharmacy, physical therapy, theology, and veterinary medicine. Interdisciplinary professional programs include music management and sport management. Programs in environmental horticulture include recreational turfgrass management as well as landscape design. Students who wish to teach at the secondary level choose a major in a subject area and complete the requirements for secondary education certification by the state of Florida.

An honors program provides special opportunities for a select group of entering freshmen to explore topics of common interest in an integrated and interdisciplinary fashion.

Academic Programs

All degree programs require the satisfactory completion of a minimum of 128 semester hours with a minimum grade point average of 2.0. Students and professors work together in discussion-based classes featuring debate, collaborative projects, and other forms of engaged learning. The College operates on the semester system, with two 15-week semesters, a May term, and summer sessions. The average course load is 16 hours per semester. Students are required to complete a general education curriculum designed to help develop knowledge, skills, and attitudes for lifelong success, in addition to their major course work. Credit by examination is awarded on the basis of successful scores on Advanced Placement tests, the International Baccalaureate (I.B.), and College-Level Examination Program (CLEP) tests.

Florida Southern has a career center that assists students in clarifying their career and life goals and provides opportunities for them to explore these goals. Approximately 20 percent of Florida Southern graduates go immediately to graduate school, and some FSC signature programs, such as premedicine, have a 100 percent placement rate. Florida Southern guarantees every student an internship, and those real-world experiences help to place the vast majority of graduates in jobs in their chosen fields.

Off-campus Programs

The College sponsors a number of popular study-abroad opportunities, including May Option experiences in Harlaxton Manor (England), Cuernavaca (Mexico), and Salamanca and Alicante (Spain). Students are guaranteed a domestic or international travel experience in their junior or senior year.

Other study-abroad options include Angers (France) and semester or yearlong programs in England, Northern Ireland, Central America, and South America, or a vast array of additional options through one of the College's consortium programs.

Florida Southern College recently affiliated with The Washington Center (TWC), a highly regarded, nonpartisan internship provider with international scope. Florida Southern College is the only private institution of higher education in the state of Florida to affiliate with TWC. This affiliation allows FSC students to access prestigious and valuable field experiences as part of their undergraduate studies. Programs range from tailored internships that are academic and work-experience based for governmental, international, corporate, and nonprofit organizations, to intensive-learning academic seminars focused on timely topics.

Academic Facilities

The College recently opened the new Marshall and Vera Lea Rinker Technology Center, which is equipped with the latest technology and Wi-Fi, as are other computer labs on campus, such as the popular TúTû's CyberCafé in the library.

There are several new academic buildings on campus, including the state-of-the-art Joe K. and Alberta Blanton Nursing Building, home to the College's growing School of Nursing; and the Dr. Marcene H.

and Robert E. Christoverson Humanities Building, which features contemporary classrooms, a modern language lab, film studies center, and art gallery.

Florida Southern's Roux Library houses a collection of 175,213 volumes; more than 650 periodical subscriptions; access to more than 2,000 full-text electronic periodicals and more than 72,000 electronic books; a 5,700-item media collection that includes videocassettes, CDs, DVDs, and CD-ROMs; a substantial microforms collection; and seating for more than 350 students. The adjacent Sarah D. and L. Kirk McKay Jr. Archives Center houses records from the Florida Conference of the United Methodist Church; Frank Lloyd Wright drawings and documents; the Lawton M. Chiles Center for Florida History; and the Florida Citrus Archives.

In addition, the Branscomb Memorial Auditorium seats 1,800 and is nationally known for its perfect acoustics. The Ludd M. Spivey Fine Arts Center comprises the Marjorie M. McKinley Music Building, the Melvin Art Gallery, and the Loca Lee Buckner Theater, which seats 350. The Polk Science Building houses the College's state-of-the-art science laboratories and planetarium. The on-campus preschool provides an opportunity for students majoring in elementary education to observe and teach preschoolers.

Costs

The comprehensive cost for 2011–12 was $34,920 ($26,112 for tuition and standard fees and $8808 for room and board). There are additional fees for individual music instruction and the use of practice rooms. FSC estimates that another $1150 is adequate for books and supplies, and $1500 should cover personal expenses, exclusive of travel to and from home.

Financial Aid

The Student Financial Aid Office offers students its counsel and assistance in meeting their educational expenses. Aid is awarded on the basis of an applicant's need, academic performance, and promise. Ninety-six percent of the students at Florida Southern receive financial assistance. To demonstrate need, an applicant is required to file the Free Application for Federal Student Aid (FAFSA). Various forms of aid, such as scholarships, grants, loans, and campus employment, are used to help meet students' needs. Merit scholarships are available, and awards are based on academic promise; performance ability in music, theater, or art; or athletic ability in baseball, basketball, cross-country, golf, soccer, softball, swimming, tennis, volleyball, or lacrosse. Applicants for aid must reapply each year. Florida Southern participates in the Federal Perkins Loan, Federal Supplemental Educational Opportunity Grant, and Federal Work-Study college-based programs. All applicants are expected to apply for any entitlement grant for which they are eligible, such as a Federal Pell Grant and, for Florida residents, the Florida Student Assistance Grant. The Federal Stafford Direct Student Loan Program is also available. The completed FAFSA and the College's financial aid application must be filed with the Student Financial Aid Office by April 1. Early application is encouraged for students seeking academic scholarships.

Faculty

Ninety percent of Florida Southern's faculty members have doctoral or other terminal degrees in their fields. The faculty is devoted to teaching and the success of students; all faculty members have posted office hours and are available for consultation and advising. Faculty members are selected not only for their teaching ability but also for their ability to relate to the needs and concerns of college students. The student-faculty ratio is 14:1.

Student Government

The Student Government Association represents the student body in matters involving the College administration, faculty, and student body and is responsible for coordinating student government. Each full-time student is a member of the association and has a vote in its affairs. The subsidiaries of the association are the Association of Campus Entertainment (ACE), the House of Representatives, the Student Senate, and the four classes: freshman, sophomore, junior, and senior.

Admission Requirements

Florida Southern looks for two things in applicants: performance and promise. The majority of applicants who have been admitted as freshmen have had a grade of B or better in college-preparatory courses (including four courses in English, three in mathematics, and the balance divided among science, foreign language, and social science); and have earned minimum scores of 500 on each of the verbal and math portions of the SAT or a composite score of at least 23 on the ACT. The Admissions Office is committed to reviewing individual applicants on their own merits, based on the level of challenge attempted, patterns of grades over time, recommendations from references, and an applicant's own assessment of the learning environment best suited to his or her needs. Evidence of leadership and community service also are typical attributes of a successful applicant.

Applicants must graduate from an accredited high school with a minimum of 19 credits, 16 of which must be academic. Qualified high school juniors may apply for early admission if they have the recommendation of their secondary school and have had a personal interview with the Director of Admissions. Applications from transfers are welcome, as are those from students resuming their education and from older students who have delayed their entrance into college. Transfer applicants should have a minimum 2.5 grade point average and be graduates of or be eligible to return to their former institutions. Transfer students with fewer than 25 semester hours must submit high school transcripts and standardized test scores. Applicants who hold Associate of Arts degrees from regionally accredited two-year institutions are typically granted junior standing. All applicants are encouraged to interview; an interview may be required for some candidates.

Application and Information

An application is considered by the Admissions Committee when it has been received with required test scores and references, and transcripts from each school attended. Because all students are required to live on campus unless they are seniors, married, or living with their parents, early application is desirable to ensure that housing is available. The freshman application priority date is March 1. The deadline for early decision applicants is December 1.

For more information about Florida Southern College, prospective students should contact:

Office of Admissions
Florida Southern College
111 Lake Hollingsworth Drive
Lakeland, Florida 33801-5698
Phone: 800-274-4131 (toll-free)
E-mail: fscadm@flsouthern.edu
Web site: http://www.flsouthern.edu

Students walk alongside the Frank Lloyd Wright Water Dome.

FORDHAM UNIVERSITY
NEW YORK, NEW YORK

The University

Fordham, the Jesuit University of New York, offers a distinctive educational experience that is rooted in the nearly 500-year-old Jesuit tradition of intellectual rigor and personal respect for the individual. A Fordham education blends a challenging curriculum with the resources, culture, and energy of New York City—a unique combination by any measure.

The University enrolls approximately 15,158 students, of whom 8,220 are undergraduates. Fordham has four undergraduate colleges and six graduate and professional schools. In addition to its full-time undergraduate programs, the University offers part-time undergraduate study at Fordham School of Professional and Continuing Studies and through two summer sessions.

Fordham offers two residential campuses: Rose Hill, on 85 green, leafy acres adjacent to the New York Botanical Garden and the Bronx Zoo; and Lincoln Center, a cosmopolitan campus in the cultural heart of Manhattan, which features a 20-story complex that provides apartment-style living and great city views. Both campuses are easily accessible by public and private transportation. Enjoying the academic and student life of both is convenient with the University's Ram Van service, which operates between the two campuses.

The University has an extensive athletics program consisting of 23 varsity sports and numerous club and intramural sports. Murphy Field is the heart of intramural and recreational sports at Fordham, hosting softball, soccer, and flag football games. The Vincent T. Lombardi Memorial Center provides facilities for basketball, squash, swimming and diving, tennis, track, and water polo.

Location

As the Jesuit University of New York, Fordham offers its students the unparalleled academic, cultural, and recreational advantages of one of the world's great cities. Fordham draws students from across the country who want to live and learn while immersed in the diversity and opportunity of a global capital. More than 2,600 corporations and organizations—from the United Nations to Fortune 500 companies—offer valuable work experience to Fordham interns. New York City not only provides extraordinary internship possibilities and career advantages, but also a never-ending list of things to see and do—from Broadway theater, museums, and music to major league sports or a bike ride through Central Park.

Majors and Degrees

Fordham offers undergraduates more than 50 majors, minors, and certificates. Fordham College at Rose Hill provides programs of study in African and African American studies, American Catholic studies, American studies, anthropology, art history, biological sciences, chemistry, classical civilization, classical languages (Latin and Greek), communication and media studies, comparative literature, computer sciences, economics, engineering physics, English, environmental policy, environmental science, French language and literature, French studies, general science, German language and literature, German studies, history, information science, international political economy, Italian language and literature, Italian studies, Latin American and Latino studies, mathematics,

mathematics/economics, medieval studies, Middle East studies, music, Orthodox Christian studies, peace and justice studies, philosophy, physics, political science, psychology, religious studies, social work, sociology, Spanish language and literature, Spanish studies, theology, urban studies, visual arts, and women's studies.

Also located at the Rose Hill campus, the Gabelli School of Business offers programs leading to majors, minors, concentrations, or specializations in accounting, accounting information services, applied accounting and finance, business administration, business economics, business law and ethics, communication and media management, e-business, entrepreneurship, finance, human resource management, information systems, management of information and communication systems, management systems, marketing, and public accountancy. The G.L.O.B.E. Program (Global Learning Opportunities and Business Experiences) provides business students with an international study option that incorporates course offerings in language, culture, and history with business.

Special programs at Rose Hill include a cooperative engineering program, double majors or individualized majors, interdisciplinary studies, a B.S./M.B.A. program, numerous joint master's degree programs (dual degree), 3-3 law and honors programs. Preprofessional programs are offered in architecture, law, medicine, and health professions; a program for teacher certification is offered in elementary and secondary education.

At Fordham College at Lincoln Center students choose from African and African American studies, American Catholic studies, American studies, anthropology, art history, bioinformatics, business, classical civilization, classical languages (Latin and Greek), communication and media studies, comparative literature, computer science, dance, economics, English, environmental policy, environmental science, French language and literature, French studies, German language and literature, German studies, history, information science, international studies, Irish studies, Italian language and literature, Italian studies, Latin American and Latino studies, mathematics, mathematics/economics, medieval studies, Middle East studies, music, natural science, Orthodox Christian studies, peace and justice studies, philosophy, political science, psychology, religious studies, social work, sociology, Spanish language and literature, Spanish studies, theater, theology, urban studies, visual arts, and women's studies. Special programs at Fordham College at Lincoln Center include options in the performing arts (including a B.F.A. in dance with The Ailey School), creative writing, double majors or individualized majors, independent study, an honors program, and interdisciplinary studies. Preprofessional studies are offered in architecture, engineering, health professions, and law. A teacher certification program is offered in elementary and secondary education.

Academic Programs

Students in all undergraduate colleges pursue a common core curriculum designed to provide them with the breadth of knowledge that marks the educated person. The core involves foundational courses chosen from groups of academic disciplines: history, philosophy, theology, natural sciences, social sciences, languages, and literature. In every core course, students think, speak, write, and act in fundamentally new ways, with

a broadened appreciation of human values and a deepened commitment to the human community.

Off-Campus Programs

Reflecting the values-centered education that is a Fordham hallmark, more than 4,000 students engage in community service each year, locally and in distant corners of the world. The Global Outreach program is an ambitious international service program designed for students to live and work in communities of need. The University also provides access to yearlong, semester-long and summer study-abroad programs in more than fifty countries on six continents, including La Sorbonne in Paris and American University in Cairo.

Academic Facilities

The outstanding libraries on the two campuses have combined holdings of more than 2.28 million volumes and more than 40,476 electronic and print periodicals. On the Rose Hill campus, the William D. Walsh Family Library, which serves the entire Fordham community, has seating for more than 1,500 and a state-of-the-art Electronic Information Center, as well as media production laboratories, studios, and an auditorium. Students also have access to the vast library facilities of New York City, neighboring universities, and the various specialized collections maintained by numerous local museums and other institutions. Among laboratory facilities utilized by undergraduates are Mulcahy Hall (chemistry), Larkin Hall (biology), and Freeman Hall (physics and biology). The University has more than 40 buildings that provide ample space for smart classrooms, science laboratories, theaters, and athletic facilities.

Costs

At the Rose Hill and Lincoln Center campuses, undergraduate costs for the 2012–13 academic year are $42,057 for tuition and fees, and an average of $15,375 for room and board. Chemistry, physics, and biology fees were approximately $50 per laboratory course. Nominally priced meals are available in cafeterias on each campus. Such incidentals as transportation and laundry vary in cost. There is no difference in fees for out-of-state students.

Financial Aid

More than 90 percent of the entering students enroll with aid from Fordham as well as from outside sources. Among the major aid programs are Federal Pell Grants, Federal Supplemental Educational Opportunity Grants, Federal Perkins Loans, work grants sponsored by both the government and the University, and University grants-in-aid. Outside sources of aid include state scholarships, the New York State Tuition Assistance Program (TAP), privately sponsored scholarships, state government loan programs, and deferred-payment programs. The University also offers academic merit scholarships ranging from $10,000 to the full cost of tuition and room. Applicants for aid must submit the Free Application for Federal Student Aid (FAFSA) and the College Scholarship Service (CSS) PROFILE. Please direct inquiries to Fordham's Office of Undergraduate Admission or Office of Student Financial Services.

Faculty

The University has a full-time faculty of 699 and a student-faculty ratio of 13:1. Most members of the undergraduate faculty also teach at the graduate level, and 95 percent of the full-time faculty members hold doctoral or other terminal degrees.

Student Government

The traditional student governing body at Fordham has been the United Student Government, composed of undergraduates attending the University.

Admission Requirements

Admission is based on academic performance, class rank (if available), secondary school recommendations, and SAT or ACT scores. Extracurricular activities and essays are also factors in the evaluation process. Religious preference, physical handicap, race, or ethnic origin is not considered. Out-of-state students are encouraged to apply. More than 85 percent of the students accepted for the freshman class ranked in the top quarter of their secondary school class. The middle 50 percent combined SAT score for students accepted in fall 2011 was 1830–2050. Recommended are 22 high school units, including 4 in English, 3 in mathematics, 3 in science, 2 in social studies, 2 in foreign language, 2 in history, and 6 electives. For regular admission, the SAT or the ACT should be taken no later than the January preceding entrance. Candidates for early action should complete the examinations by October of their senior year. The University participates in the College Board's Advanced Placement Program. Personal interviews are not required.

Application and Information

Application may be made for either September or January enrollment. The regular decision application deadline is January 15 for fall admission. The completed application, the secondary school report, the results of the SAT or ACT, and an application fee of $50 (check or money order made payable to Fordham University) should be submitted by this date. All financial aid forms are due by February 1. Students are notified on or about April 1. Candidates for Early Action should apply by November 1 and receive notification by December 25. Transfer students must apply by December 1 for spring admission or by June 1 for fall admission.

For additional details and application forms, students should contact:

John Buckley
Associate Vice President of Undergraduate Enrollment
Fordham University
Duane Library
441 East Fordham Road
Bronx, New York 10458
Phone: 800-FORDHAM (367-3426)
E-mail: enroll@fordham.edu
Web site: http://www.fordham.edu

Members of a recent graduating class join Fordham's distinguished alumni family of more than 150,000.

FRANKLIN COLLEGE
FRANKLIN, INDIANA

The College

As an innovative scientist, diplomat, thinker, writer, and leader, Benjamin Franklin's remarkable life and accomplishments left a mark on not only a young nation, but also the world. Named in the spirit of this extraordinary American icon, Franklin College continues his legacy of exploration and knowledge.

Since its founding in 1834, Franklin College has a long history of preparing students for lives committed to excellence, leadership, and service. With a comprehensive liberal arts curriculum combined with a leading-edge professional development program, Franklin College provides an education that blends thinking with doing, reasoning with acting, and discovering with challenging.

Small classes and dedicated faculty members ensure that students get the attention needed to succeed, and Franklin's career and graduate school admission rates prove this.

Franklin combines liberal arts training with preprofessional development like no other college. Students can develop the competencies and resources necessary to be successful in their personal and professional lives through Franklin's innovative Professional Development Program (PDP). This exciting program gives them the opportunity to dine with corporate executives, network with national and community leaders, learn the finer points of corporate communication, and develop a level of polish and sophistication that sets them apart from other college graduates.

Location

Located in the heart of the Midwest, Franklin College offers students the best of both a small community and a big city's excitement.

Franklin, Indiana, is only 20 miles south of Indianapolis, which is the state's capital city and the thirteenth largest city in the U.S. It offers a wide variety of internship opportunities, as well as athletic, cultural, and entertainment events that appeal to all students.

Majors and Degrees

Flagship programs at Franklin College include athletic training, business, journalism, pre-med, and education. The Pulliam School of Journalism is one of a few comprehensive journalism schools housed at a small liberal arts institution. Student media opportunities include a student-run PR agency, a student newspaper, magazine, and radio show. Franklin's journalism students also have the opportunity to work at the Franklin College Statehouse Bureau in downtown Indianapolis. After graduation, education majors are placed at 97 percent or higher in the classroom, while business students repeatedly score in the top 5 percent on the National College Business Examination. One hundred percent of athletic training majors are employed six months after graduation. Preparation for graduate school is exceptional, with 85 percent of students gaining admission to medical school and 90 percent of applicants accepted to law school.

Franklin College confers more than thirty Bachelor of Arts degrees in the following areas: accounting, American studies, art (art history and studio art), biology, business (finance, international business, management/industrial relations, and marketing), Canadian studies, chemistry, computing/computer information systems, economics, education (elementary, middle school, and secondary), English, French, history, journalism (advertising/public relations, broadcasting, and news-editorial), mathematics, music (instrumental and vocal), philosophy, physical education, political science, psychology, religious studies, sociology (criminal justice and social work), Spanish, and theater. Franklin also offers thirty-six different minors, including areas like fine arts, leadership, and physics.

Engineering is offered as a 3+2 program. Students earn a Bachelor of Arts degree from Franklin College and a Bachelor of Science degree in one of the engineering disciplines from the Purdue School of Engineering and Technology (IUPUI).

Students considering a career in dentistry, forestry, medical technology, medicine, optometry, physical therapy, or veterinary medicine arrange their program with the advice of the preprofessional adviser of the science division. Students seeking a career in law plan their program in consultation with prelaw advisers. Students planning a career in secondary education may elect an academic area of concentration that will satisfy the state requirements for a teaching major. The education department is endorsed and approved by the Indiana Professional Standards Board and the National Council for Accreditation of Teacher Education (NCATE).

Academic Programs

The current academic program is the result of the faculty's plan to meet the express needs of students; the primary emphasis is on the unity of knowledge. Franklin believes in the importance of providing students with a liberal arts background while they develop talents for a particular professional career. Approximately one third of each student's total course work is composed of the prescribed and exploratory courses that make up the general education core curriculum.

All of Franklin's academic departments offer individualized study, allowing a student to pursue his or her field of interest in depth. Students interested in pursuing a major not offered at Franklin may submit a proposal for their individualized major.

As part of the 4-1-4 calendar, students complete up to 8 hours of credit in a special four-week winter-term program in January. The winter term is designed to allow students to study in areas of particular interest to them, either within or outside their major field of study. Some January classes offer students the opportunity to travel to locations such as Belize, England, France, Italy, and Mexico.

A large number of internships are available during the winter term and the summer, offering practical experience under the supervision of a professional. The fall semester ends before Christmas; the spring semester begins in February and ends in May. An eight-week summer session beginning in mid-June allows students to take up to 9 additional credit hours. Ninety-five percent of Franklin College students complete an internship prior to graduation.

Franklin gives credit in seventeen academic areas for successful scores on CLEP subject examinations; credit is also granted for successful scores on the Advanced Placement tests of the College Board. The Running Start Program enables talented high school students to get an early start on their college education.

Study-Abroad Programs

Franklin College students participate in a variety of international study opportunities, including a year or a semester of study through Acadia University of Nova Scotia, Telemark University of Norway, and Hong Kong Baptist University. Other off-campus

study programs include the American University Washington Semester; a junior year abroad; programs at Harlaxton College in England, Franklin College of Switzerland, and Brethren Colleges Abroad; and specific exchange programs in Japan and Taiwan. Students may also participate in a Semester at Sea program sponsored by the University of Pittsburgh.

Academic Facilities

Franklin College has two campus buildings listed on the National Historic Register. Old Main, the original home of the College, and Shirk Hall, home of the Pulliam School of Journalism, are footholds of the rich past and recent renovation of the Franklin College campus. Classrooms and administrative, business, and professorial offices, along with computer laboratories, occupy Old Main; Shirk Hall also houses classrooms and the radio station.

A. A. Barnes Science Building houses all physics, biology, and chemistry department classrooms and laboratories. The Spurlock Center gymnasium and fitness center provides workout and weight equipment to students in order to maintain a healthy lifestyle.

The Dietz Center for Professional Development is the home of the Professional Development Program. State-of-the-art conference rooms and computer facilities enhance Franklin's career programming commitment to its students.

The B. F. Hamilton Library, containing more than 117,000 volumes and collections of microfilm, slides, art reproductions, recordings, and periodicals, is a member of P.A.L.N.I. (Private Academic Library Network of Indiana). The library also houses the Academic Resource Center (ARC), where students can receive help with their individual studies. The Johnson Center for Fine Arts provides classrooms and practice and performance accommodations, and it houses the facilities and meeting rooms for the Leadership Program.

Costs

The direct cost for the 2012–13 academic year is $35,185. This amount is derived from tuition, which is $26,710; residence hall, which is $4720; student fees of $185; and Winter Term meal fees of $340 plus the meal plan, which is $3230.

Financial Aid

The Franklin College financial aid program assists students who might not otherwise be able to attend college and rewards applicants for excellent academic achievement in high school. Awards are based on scholarship, curricular and extracurricular activities, and financial need. Aid involving financial need includes Franklin College grants, loans, and employment. Franklin participates in the Federal Stafford Student Loan and Federal Work-Study programs. Merit-based scholarships ranging from $5500 to full tuition are awarded to students based on academic performance, activities, and standardized test scores. In addition, students identified by the state of Indiana as Twenty-first Century Scholars will be awarded full tuition scholarships, if they are eligible for the Pell Grant. Twenty-first Century Scholars who are not eligible for the Pell Grant will be awarded half-tuition scholarships. Scholarships are renewable for each of the recipient's four academic years at Franklin, provided students maintain specific GPA requirements and advance in class status each year. The Free Application for Federal Student Aid (FAFSA) is required.

Faculty

The 11:1 student-faculty ratio allows Franklin faculty members to provide excellent instruction in small classes that promote participatory learning. Nearly 90 percent of current faculty members have obtained the highest degree in their field. Faculty members serve as advisers and provide supplemental attention outside the classroom. While many faculty members carry on research and publish their work, their main emphasis is teaching. No classes are taught by graduate students or teaching assistants.

Student Organizations

Franklin College offers more than sixty clubs and organizations such as Student Congress, Black Student Union, Greek Life, and Student Entertainment Board. These organizations allow students to plan on-campus concerts/events, represent the student body to change campus policies, and volunteer their time with the College's Habitat for Humanity programs from the first year. In addition to the existing organizations, the College allows students to set up new groups of their interests.

Admission Requirements

Applications for admission to Franklin College are evaluated on an individual basis. A student's potential academic and personal contributions to the College, recommendations, school and community activities, academic record, and standardized test scores are taken into consideration by the Admissions Committee. A student should complete a strong college-preparatory program. Candidates for admission are urged to visit the campus in order to experience the College community. The College offers different visit opportunities—from personal visits to open houses, all provide opportunities to meet current students, professors, and coaches, and to take a campus tour.

Application and Information

To be considered for admission, an applicant must submit a completed application (paper or online), a transcript of all secondary school and college work attempted, and either SAT or ACT scores. A decision regarding acceptance is made after the College receives all necessary credentials. Notification is sent immediately after the Enrollment Committee has acted.

Office of Admission
Franklin College
101 Branigin Boulevard
Franklin, Indiana 46131
Phone: 317-738-8075
      888-852-6471 (toll-free)
Fax: 317-738-8274
E-mail: admissions@franklincollege.edu
Web site: http://admissions.franklincollege.edu
      http://www.facebook.com/fcadmissions

Old Main is the oldest academic building on the Franklin College campus.

FRANKLIN COLLEGE SWITZERLAND
LUGANO, SWITZERLAND

The College

Franklin College Switzerland, named for the United States' first and most illustrious ambassador to Europe, was founded in 1969 as a nonprofit, independent, postsecondary institution. It takes as its cornerstone Benjamin Franklin's vigorous support of intellectual interchange between nations. An American liberal arts institution in an international environment, Franklin is fully accredited in the United States by the Commission on Higher Education of the Middle States Association of Colleges and Schools and its programs are accredited in Switzerland by the Swiss University Conference.

Franklin College places a strong emphasis on cross-cultural perspectives, advocating that international studies should be an integral part of a college education, as a prelude to, and basis for, a student's commitment to a major field of study. Franklin defines higher education from its beginning as the experience of thinking internationally. Its emphasis, both academic and social, on global perspectives is designed to affect the direction and meaning of a student's college experience, life, and career.

The essence of a Franklin College education is the exposure of its students to cultures other than their own, providing them with a better understanding of others, the world, and their place in the world. The College's location in Lugano, a vibrant Swiss city that is part of the cultural milieu of northern Italy, ensures a constant commingling of cultures in a quadrilingual nation. Students and faculty members, many who have a cross-cultural background, come to Franklin College from every corner of the globe, further strengthening international study and international experiences.

Approximately 60 percent of the students come from the United States; 40 percent are from Europe, Asia, Africa, South America, and the Middle East. Bringing diverse experiences and perspectives to college life, they live in College residences both on and near the campus. These apartments all have kitchens available, and two campus dining facilities provide regular meal service and a diverse meal plan. Resident Assistants supervise all campus buildings.

Campus activities are varied. Franklin's Student Government Association (SGA) promotes a student newspaper; a literary magazine; a drama society; cultural, language, and sports clubs; and numerous social events that take advantage of southern Switzerland's extensive recreational resources. There are competitive College sports teams in men's and women's soccer, and intramural teams include basketball, soccer, and volleyball. In addition, the Athletic Director enrolls interested students in a considerable number of local Swiss clubs and teams that welcome newcomers: basketball, ice hockey, soccer, and volleyball teams, as well as crew, fencing, flying, golf, hang gliding, ice skating, judo, parachuting, riding, rock climbing, sailing, swimming, tennis, track, and windsurfing clubs. By joining these local groups, Franklin students become part of the region's local community; they are themselves essential to the cross-cultural learning the College promotes.

Location

Franklin College Switzerland's campus is in the community of Sorengo, a section of the city of Lugano, southern Switzerland's principal business, banking, medical, and cultural center. Easily accessible from the campus either by public transportation or on foot, downtown Lugano and its surrounding lakeside villages are renowned for their scenic beauty and Mediterranean climate. Palm trees line lakefront piazzas, and an outdoor lifestyle is typical of Ticino, the Italian-speaking canton of Switzerland that best exemplifies Swiss versatility in all three of the national languages—Italian, German, and French.

Throughout the year, Lugano features outstanding cultural activities at the world-famous Thyssen art collection, the Swiss-Italian radio station with its own permanent symphony orchestra, and the International Convention Center, which attracts guest performers from around the world. Nine public museums, many art galleries, several movie houses, and a multitude of restaurants and discotheques make for a range of recreational choices normally found only in a large city. A covered ice rink, swimming pools, and a wide range of other sports facilities are maintained by local sports clubs; Lugano and the southern part of Switzerland offer access to an extraordinary variety of sports activities. In the spring and fall, Ticino's most popular recreation is hiking. In winter, skiing is available in San Bernardino and Andermatt, about an hour from the campus, or in the fabled St. Moritz, Davos, Klosters, and Zermatt.

Majors and Degrees

The Bachelor of Arts program offers majors in art history and visual culture, communication and media studies, comparative literary and cultural studies, creative writing and literature, environmental studies, French studies, history, history and literature, international banking and finance, international economics, international management, international relations, Italian studies, literature, and visual and communication arts, with combined and double majors in a number of study areas. The Associate in Arts degree program provides a strong liberal arts foundation for students who usually continue their education in a baccalaureate degree program.

Academic Programs

Franklin's curricula promote international awareness and critical thinking, while being interdisciplinary in the highest tradition of a liberal arts education. The courses of study explore the diverse disciplines that enlighten an educated human being. Students must complete at least 125 credit hours to be eligible for the B.A. degree and 64 for the A.A. degree, while maintaining a minimum cumulative grade point average of 2.0 on a 4.0 scale.

As an integral credit-bearing part of the academic program, twice a year (in mid-October and mid-March) students participate in two-week, faculty-led Academic Travel programs to various destinations in Eastern and Western Europe, Africa, Asia, Latin America, and North America.

All degree candidates must demonstrate a foreign language proficiency in a language other than their mother tongue equivalent to three years of university-level instruction in one of the languages taught at Franklin. This requirement is met by successfully completing appropriate courses at Franklin or by passing an equivalency test administered by the language department.

In addition to their major field of study, students may minor in another course of study. The number of credit hours (12 to 15) and the program of courses are subject to departmental approval.

The College operates on a two-semester calendar, with classes starting in late August and mid-January; two 4-week intensive summer sessions are also available. A required orientation program for all new students is held in August and mid-January.

Off-Campus Programs

Franklin's renowned Academic Travel Program is a fully integrated part of the regular curriculum. Each semester, students participate in two weeks of faculty-led academic travel. More than any other program of study, it gives students an opportunity to learn through experience. Travel destinations for 2011–12 included Austria, the Baltic States, Brazil, Croatia, Cyprus, England, France, Germany, Greece, Hungary, Iceland, Italy, Malawi, Malaysia, Malta, Poland, Portugal, Romania and Moldova, Scotland, Serbia, Slovakia, Slovenia, South Korea, Spain, Thailand, Turkey, and the United States.

Internships are also available. Students with academic interest in any area may apply for an internship after two semesters of residence at Franklin, either by asking to be considered for one of the internships provided by the College or by arranging for an appointment themselves. The Assistant Dean of Student Life coordinates the internship program; a student may earn a maximum of 3 credit hours in an assignment.

Students in good standing who major in modern languages are eligible for study in a country where the target language is spoken; such study is limited to one semester at an approved institution.

Academic Facilities

The Franklin College Libraries contain over 38,000 volumes in English and six other languages, as well as over 100 print newspapers and journals. In addition to the print and multimedia collections, the libraries subscribe to many online indexes and full-text databases, including ProQuest resources, EBSCO resources, LexisNexis University, MarketLine, Columbia International Affairs Online (CIAO), and ARTstor. Public Internet-access computers are available in the libraries and computer lab for student research use.

Costs

The comprehensive fee for the 2011–12 academic year was $45,420. This figure includes the cost of tuition, room and board, academic travel, and student fees. The estimated cost of personal expenses and incidentals, including textbooks, is $6500 per year. The estimated cost range to fly round-trip from the United States is from $1100 to $1400.

Financial Aid

Franklin College Switzerland offers academic merit awards and need-based financial aid to qualified students. U.S. applicants for financial aid must submit the FAFSA for evaluation. Veterans' and Social Security benefits are also available to eligible students. Federal Stafford Student Loans and PLUS loans may be obtained through the Department of Education's Direct Loan Program. International students must submit the International Student Financial Aid Form. Campus internships are also available. Students interested in applying for one can do so by requesting information about available Life Long Learning Scholarships through the Office of Student Life at the beginning of each semester.

Faculty

Franklin College Switzerland has 58 full-time and part-time professors, approximately half of whom are American or British; others are of various nationalities. The majority have advanced degrees from prestigious American universities, the others from highly recognized British and Continental universities; most have lived, studied, and taught in a variety of countries. The teaching staff characterizes the cross-cultural essence of the College. Professors are committed to both the European and global arenas of study; are knowledgeable about particular countries enough to organize and lead rewarding academic travels; are competent in more than one language; and are dedicated to the personal, discursive style of teaching required by a small liberal arts college with small classes. The faculty members also advise the various student activities, lead local excursions, and regularly contribute to the College's cocurricular program of lectures. In addition, each faculty member acts as academic counselor to a number of students. The faculty-conducted Academic Travel Program promotes the intellectual friendship between teacher and student essential to a liberal arts education. Franklin's student-faculty ratio is approximately 10:1.

Student Government

The student body elects the members of the Student Government Association (SGA). The SGA sponsors several interest groups including an award-winning Model United Nations team, Investment Club, and AIESEC, as well as several social events. In addition, the SGA collaborates with the local community to host events, such as a biannual blood drive. The SGA is actively involved in campus governance by appointing members to participate in meetings of the Curriculum Committee, Faculty Assembly, and the Appeals Board.

Admission Requirements

Franklin College Switzerland seeks students who are eager to meet the challenge of studying and living in Europe, serious about undertaking college-level learning, and prepared to contribute positively to the intellectual life of the College. To identify such students, and also to ensure a diverse student population, the College Admissions Committee considers both academic and personal facts, including the student's academic record, evaluations by teachers and counselors, standardized test scores, extracurricular interests and talents, and academic distinctions. Admission to the College is limited and therefore competitive. To achieve the best match between the student and Franklin, a personal interview is strongly recommended; one can be arranged by contacting the Admissions Office in Lugano or New York. Applicants to the freshman class must submit a completed application form (using either the Franklin application or the Common Application) with a nonrefundable fee of $90; an essay and personal statement; an official transcript of their secondary school record; SAT or ACT scores, either included on transcripts or forwarded by the testing service to Franklin College (CEEB code number 0922; ACT code number 5223); and three letters of academic evaluation. Applicants whose first language is not English must submit their score on either the SAT or ACT, or Test of English as a Foreign Language (TOEFL)/International English Language Testing System (IELTS). TOEFL scores should be at least 79 (Internet-based test) or 550 (paper-based test). IELTS scores should be above 6.0. Transfer applicants and institute applicants are required to submit a completed application and a nonrefundable application fee of $90, an official transcript of their college record, a dean's report from the dean of students, and one letter of academic recommendation. The application fee is waived for all applicants who apply by January 15. In addition, applicants who submit their application by December 1 qualify for a free round trip ticket from New York to Zurich.

Application Deadlines and Information

The priority application deadline for fall entry is March 15 for applicants to the freshman class and June 15 for transfer and institute applicants. The application deadline for the spring semester is November 15. Admission decisions are made on a rolling basis. Applicants can usually expect a decision within three weeks from the time their application is completed. All inquiries and applications should be directed to the nearest Admissions Office.

Franklin College Switzerland
US Office, Suite 2746
420 Lexington Avenue
New York, NY 10170
Phone: 212-922-9650
Fax: 212-922-9870
E-mail: info@fc.edu

Karen Ballard
Dean of Admissions
Franklin College Switzerland
Via Ponte Tresa, 29
6924 Sorengo/Lugano
Switzerland
Phone: 41-91-986-3613
Fax: 41-91-993-3906
E-mail: info@fc.edu
Web site: http://www.fc.edu

Franklin students enjoying terrace dining at the Grotto, Franklin College Switzerland's casual dining area.

GANNON UNIVERSITY
ERIE, PENNSYLVANIA

Believe in the possibilities.

The University

Gannon University, which is consistently named one of America's Best Colleges by *U.S. News & World Report,* is dedicated to excellence in holistic education. The oldest part of the University is Villa Maria College, which was founded in 1925 by the Sisters of St. Joseph. In 1933, Archbishop John Mark Gannon established Cathedral College, a two-year institution, which by 1941 had evolved into a four-year college, the Gannon School of Arts and Sciences. The name Gannon College was adopted in 1944, and Gannon achieved university status in 1979. Villa Maria College subsequently merged with Gannon University in 1989.

Gannon's campus is located in the heart of downtown Erie, giving students the benefit of internships with businesses, law and law-enforcement agencies, health-care facilities, industries, and social service organizations. It is within walking distance of stores, shops, restaurants, and theaters. The campus consists of forty-six buildings located within six city blocks. Among these buildings is the Carneval Athletic Pavilion, which has a pool; three gyms; a running track; a weight room; courts for racquetball, handball, volleyball and basketball; and other facilities. Also on campus are three residence halls, nine apartment buildings, classroom and faculty office buildings, an administration building, and a multipurpose chapel building. The Waldron Campus Center is a focal point that gives students the opportunity to meet and socialize between classes with faculty members and other students.

Gannon offers students a broad intramural sports program that runs throughout the entire year. In Division II intercollegiate athletics, Gannon offers men's baseball, basketball, cross-country, football, golf, soccer, swimming and diving, water polo, and wrestling and women's basketball, cross-country, golf, lacrosse, soccer, softball, swimming and diving, volleyball, and water polo. Gannon's athletes utilize the Gannon University Field, a multipurpose athletic facility that is conveniently located on campus.

There are over 4,100 students at Gannon, more than 2,900 of whom are undergraduates. The ratio of commuters to resident students is approximately 1:4. To assist in internship placement, career development and employment, and tutoring services, students will find the Student Success Center a must to visit when on campus.

Location

Erie is Pennsylvania's fourth-largest city and is located in the northwestern corner of the state on the shore of Lake Erie. Erie is approximately 120 miles north of Pittsburgh, Pennsylvania; 90 miles east of Cleveland, Ohio; and 90 miles southwest of Buffalo, New York. The campus is within 5 miles of Interstates 79 and 90 and 5 miles from Erie International Airport. Erie is also serviced by rail and bus transportation.

Majors and Degrees

The College of Humanities, Education, and Social Sciences awards the Bachelor of Arts and Bachelor of Science degrees.

In the College of Humanities, Education and Social Sciences, the areas of study from which students may select a major are communication arts, criminal justice, English (with concentrations in applied communications, literature, and writing), foreign language and international studies, foreign language and literature, foreign language teaching (Spanish only), history, international studies, journalism communications, leadership studies, legal studies, liberal arts, mortuary science, philosophy, political science, prelaw, a 3+3 prelaw program that

includes early admission to Duquesne University, psychology, social work, theater, theater and communication arts, and theology.

In the School of Education, the areas of study from which students may select a major are early childhood education Pre-K–4, early childhood education PreK–4/special education PreK–8, middle level education 4–8, middle level education 4–8/special education Prek–8, secondary education (in biology, English, foreign language (Spanish only), mathematics, and social studies).

The Morosky College of Health Professions and Sciences offers degrees in the health professions and sciences. The degrees offered in the health professions include medical technology, nursing, nutrition and human performance, occupational therapy, physical therapy, physician assistant, radiologic sciences, respiratory care, sport and exercise science, and undecided health science.

The School of Sciences offers degrees in bioinformatics, biology, chemistry, environmental science, mathematics, and science. Also offered are preprofessional programs for students who wish to enter medical, dental, or veterinary school, as well as accelerated and cooperative medical programs in allopathy, osteopathy, optometry, podiatry, and pharmacy.

The Morosky College of Health Professions and Sciences is located in the Robert H. Morosky Academic Center. This 99,000-square-foot facility includes classrooms, labs, and faculty offices. It also includes a 5,800-square-foot state-of-the-art Patient Simulation Center.

The College of Engineering and Business offers degrees in a variety of areas. Students may choose from majors in biomedical engineering, chemical engineering (cooperative program), computer science, electrical engineering, electrical engineering (five-year co-op program), environmental engineering, information systems, mechanical engineering, mechanical engineering (five-year co-op program), and software engineering. Business majors include accounting, advertising communications, business administration, entrepreneurship, finance, international business, management, marketing, risk management and insurance, and sports management and marketing. All business students are required to participate in an internship before graduation.

The associate degree program offers Associate of Science and Associate of Arts degrees. Areas of study in which students may major are accounting, business administration, criminal justice, early childhood education, legal studies, radiologic sciences, and respiratory care.

Academic Programs

Each undergraduate program has its own sequence of requirements. Students in all programs must complete credits in liberal studies. A faculty adviser is assigned to each student to assist with academic planning. A department chairperson and faculty adviser also assist each student in selecting courses that fulfill requirements and best meet the student's desired career objectives. The basic graduation requirements for bachelor's degree candidates are 128 credit hours, including completion of requirements for their major and the liberal studies program. To earn an associate degree, students must usually complete 60 to 68 credit hours, depending on the program. Students may receive credit through the Advanced Placement program.

Gannon offers a program for students with learning disabilities (PSLD) and an Army ROTC program that is open to interested students.

Gannon's academic calendar consists of two full semesters, running from August to December and from January to May. There are also optional summer classes.

Academic Facilities

The Nash Library contains over 265,000 books, 4,000 audiovisual items, and 300 periodicals (along with online subscriptions to over 58,000 more). Special collections include University Archives, the curriculum library, and entertainment DVDs (over 1,000 and growing). Interlibrary loan is available for items not owned by Nash. In addition, reference service and information literacy instruction are integral components of the library's educational mission. The library is open 97 hours per week during fall and spring semesters and provides a variety of spaces for study including tables, lounge-type furniture, private study carrels, and group study rooms. There are several computer workstations with Internet and Microsoft Office access, and the entire building is covered by Gannon's wireless network. Laptop computers are available for in-library use.

The A. J. Palumbo Academic Center houses the College of Humanities, Education and Social Sciences. It offers some of the finest laboratories, technology, and classrooms available today. From education to criminal justice and foreign language programs, the faculty members and facilities in Palumbo provide high-quality education. The University's honors program also has a home in the Palumbo Center.

The Zurn Science Center has laboratories for research in biology, anatomy, physics, chemistry, and engineering. The building also houses an open engineering computer lab as well as additional computer labs for student use. There are numerous classrooms and two auditoriums in the building. Among other University facilities are additional classroom buildings, a radio station, and a theater. All academic buildings are wireless.

Costs

For 2011–12, full-time tuition was $12,990 per semester ($13,775 for engineering and health sciences), or $25,980 per academic year ($27,550 for engineering and health sciences). Tuition for part-time students was $625 per credit hour. Room and board were approximately $4750 per semester. The total cost for the academic year at Gannon was between $26,311 and $28,861 for commuting students and $35,811 and $38,361 for resident students, depending on the program of study.

Financial Aid

In order to bring a Gannon education to qualified students who could not otherwise afford it, the University offers an integrated financial aid program of scholarships, grants, loans, and employment. Gannon's financial aid program is open to all full-time students attending classes during the period from August to May. It is highly recommended that all students seeking financial aid should file the admissions and financial aid applications by the preferred deadline of March 15. Numerous scholarship opportunities are available to qualified students. Each year the University offers its top incoming freshmen the ability to compete for full tuition scholarships. Application deadline for this competition is December 15 with on-campus competition taking place in late January.

Faculty

Gannon's faculty consists of 200 lay and religious men and women, and 72 percent of the full-time faculty members have either doctoral or terminal degrees. The student-faculty ratio is about 14:1, and average class size is approximately 25 students in each class. Most faculty members assist in the faculty adviser program, giving each student individual attention and counseling on academic and personal matters.

Student Government

The Student Government Association (SGA) is composed of students elected by members of their class. Through the SGA, students can play a responsible role in the planning and working of the University. SGA has voting representatives on all of the standing committees of the University. Members of the SGA not only research existing policies and problems, they also look for new ways to improve the academic life of students. The SGA also plans social events for the student body.

Admission Requirements

Gannon University actively recruits students of all races, creeds, and ages from all geographic regions. Transfer and international students are encouraged to seek admission. Applicants are required to submit scores (including senior-year scores) on either the SAT or ACT; an up-to-date transcript of the high school record, showing rank in class (plus a college transcript for transfer applicants); a completed application form; and a nonrefundable $25 fee. Admission decisions are based upon numerous factors, central of which is the strength of the high school record, as demonstrated through grades and relative class standing and SAT and/or ACT scores and other test scores that may be available. Recommendations and personal statements also affect admission decisions. Transfer and international students should check with the admissions office for special application procedures.

Application and Information

Students applying for admission in the fall semester should start the application process at the beginning of their senior year in high school. Gannon operates on a rolling admissions basis, which means that there is no deadline for filing applications, with the exceptions of the LECOM (Lake Erie College of Osteopathic Medicine) and PCOM (Philadelphia College of Osteopathic Medicine) 4+4 Medical Programs and the accelerated pharmacy options, which have a deadline of January 15 for the fall semester. Due to the competitiveness of the program, students who are interested in the physician assistant studies or nursing programs are highly encouraged to file their applications in September. The physician assistant studies program has a November 1 application deadline. Early applications are recommended, as are enrollment deposits.

For further information, students should contact:

Office of Admissions
Gannon University
109 University Square
Erie, Pennsylvania 16541
Phone: 814-871-7240
        800-GANNON-U (426-6668, toll-free)
Fax: 814-871-5803
E-mail: admissions@gannon.edu
Web site: http://www.gannon.edu

Gannon University is a caring community of dynamic faculty and staff who educate motivated students in an environment focused on Catholic values.

THE GEORGE WASHINGTON UNIVERSITY
WASHINGTON, D.C.

THE GEORGE
WASHINGTON
UNIVERSITY
WASHINGTON DC

The University

Located just four blocks from the White House, The George Washington University (GW) is the largest institution of higher education in the nation's capital. Founded in 1821 by an Act of Congress, GW is a private nonsectarian coeducational institution accredited by the Middle States Association of Colleges and Universities. GW prides itself in being at the forefront of major research endeavors, while providing a stimulating intellectual environment for its diverse students and faculty members.

The student population at GW consists of approximately 10,400 undergraduates and 14,800 graduates. Undergraduates hail from all fifty states, the District of Columbia, Puerto Rico, the Virgin Islands, and 130 countries. The undergraduate student population is 9.6 percent Asian American, 7.2 percent African American, 7.3 percent Hispanic American, and 7.5 percent international.

GW is comprised of two fully integrated campuses, the Foggy Bottom campus and the Mount Vernon campus. Both campuses are located in historical and prestigious D.C. neighborhoods that offer vibrant and distinctive residential options to freshmen and continuing students. The Foggy Bottom campus is situated in the heart of downtown D.C., neighbored by the Kennedy Center, the Watergate complex, the State Department, and the White House. The 26-acre Mount Vernon campus is home to athletic facilities and is surrounded by embassy and diplomatic residences.

GW guarantees housing for entering freshmen and sophomores and houses more than 68 percent of undergraduates in thirty-two residence halls. GW offers a number of living arrangements, including apartment-style living for upperclassmen and residential town houses. GW's academic residential communities philosophy guarantees that residence hall life is a valuable extension of the undergraduate academic experience. With nearly 100 percent of the entering class living in University housing, the atmosphere proves to be academically as well as socially stimulating.

GW hosts a strong intercollegiate varsity athletic program with twenty-three teams participating in the NCAA Division I and Atlantic 10 Conference. They include men's baseball, basketball, crew, cross-country, golf, sailing, soccer, swimming, tennis, and water polo, and women's basketball, crew, cross-country, gymnastics, soccer, swimming and diving, tennis, volleyball, and water polo. Students interested in playing sports, but not quite up to the varsity level, may join a number of University-supported club and intramural sports.

There are more than 400 student-created and student-run organizations at GW. These organizations run the spectrum from academic to cultural, spiritual to recreational, and political to artistic. In addition to these special-interest organizations, GW is home to twenty-eight national sororities and fraternities, sixteen multicultural Greek chapters, the Student Association (details in the Student Government section), the Program Board, the *Hatchet* (GW's independent newspaper), and WRGW (the campus radio station). The Dean of Students Consortium plans hallmark program events for students on campus, ranging from Welcome Week to the Excellence in Student Life Awards.

Location

Many students at GW also choose to immerse themselves in the excitement of Washington, which has been called the most livable city on the East Coast and one of the best college towns in the United States. Washington, D.C., offers an infinite array of internships and cooperative education experiences, allowing GW students to explore their career aspirations outside of the four walls of the classroom. GW students have interned at the White House, the World Bank, IBM, the U.S. House of Representatives and Senate, NASA, the National Zoo, and CNN, among many other world famous organizations.

The 17 million tourists that flock to Washington, D.C., every year experience the vibrant college town and young professional social scene in the nation's capital. There are more than 50,000 college students in the D.C. metropolitan area.

Majors and Degrees

GW offers a wide range of undergraduate programs in six undergraduate schools: the Columbian College of Arts and Sciences, the Elliott School of International Affairs, the School of Business, the School of Engineering and Applied Science, the School of Media and Public Affairs, and the School of Public Health and Health Services.

GW offers more than 2,000 courses in over 70 majors, and yet, the average class size is only 28. Students may earn an undergraduate degree in a single field of study, or they may choose to double major, major in one field and minor in another, participate in an interdisciplinary program, or create their own individualized field of study.

The University awards an array of bachelor's degrees, including Bachelor of Arts (B.A.), Bachelor of Science (B.S.), Bachelor of Accountancy (B.Accy.), and Bachelor of Business Administration (B.B.A.).

A variety of joint-degree programs are available to undergraduates. In addition to a seven-year B.A./M.D. program, the University offers nearly fifty 5-year bachelors/masters combined programs, some of which students enter as freshmen.

Academic Programs

Most undergraduate students must complete 120 credit hours to be eligible for graduation, which means that the average student carries 15 credit hours (five courses) per semester. All students at GW are required to participate in the University's writing program. In addition, each school has general curriculum requirements, ranging from 17 to 45 credit hours.

GW is home to nineteen honor societies, including Phi Beta Kappa and Golden Key National Honor Society. GW offers a variety of specialized academic programs. The University Honors Program, which does not replace a regular program of study but rather enhances it with intellectually challenging analysis and discussion, consists of approximately 500 undergraduates.

The seven-year Integrated B.A./M.D. Program is designed for students who wish to obtain a strong foundation in the liberal arts prior to becoming physicians, enabling them to accomplish that goal in a shorter amount of time than a traditional program of study.

Off-Campus Programs

GW students are encouraged to study abroad in order to expand their worldview and their educational opportunities. GW offers study abroad centers in Madrid, Paris, England, and Latin America (Chile, Costa Rica, and Argentina), as well as

affiliated and exchange programs. Each year, more than 1,600 GW undergraduates study abroad in nearly sixty countries.

Many GW students also take advantage of cooperative education (co-op), which provides students with an opportunity to gain valuable paid work experiences directly related to their major. The Career Center manages the program, in partnership with area employers, to ensure that co-op experiences are substantive and well-supervised. Similarly, most GW students engage in internships, which serve as a means for students to gain practical, professional experience and to augment their academic knowledge. Internships can be paid or unpaid, offered for academic credit, and can last for as long (or short) as the student and employer choose. The Career Center also acts as a clearinghouse for internship positions.

Academic Facilities

The Gelman Library houses more than 2 million volumes and, as a member of the Washington Research Library Consortium (WRLC), offers GW students access to more than 6 million volumes at nine area universities. Gelman Library is open 168 hours per week, offering 24-hour study lounges, group discussion rooms, computer labs, walk-up reference consultation, and an interlibrary loan service. GW provides on-site and remote access to ALADIN, the shared online catalogue of WRLC libraries, plus databases indexing periodical articles and some full-text journals. GW is also home to the Eckles Library, the Jacob Burns Law Library, the Himmelfarb Health Sciences Library, and the Virginia Science and Technology Campus Library.

GW is infused with the latest, state-of-the-art facilities enhancing campus life. Completed and planned projects include the Elliott School of International Affairs classroom and residential complex, the School of Business, Potomac House, a 700-bed freshman residence hall, the Science and Engineering Hall, the School of Public Health and Health Sciences building, South Hall residence Hall, and West Hall, a 287-bed suite-style residence hall for first-year and upperclass students with multimedia studios, a black box theater, and a fitness center.

Costs

In response to family concerns about paying for college, GW has instituted a fixed tuition plan. Under this plan, the tuition remains the same each year for students who remain enrolled in full-time status during their undergraduate programs. Therefore, except for marginal increases in housing costs, cost of attendance will not rise. Students who entered in fall 2011 have tuition costs of $44,148 per year for four years. Room and board costs are approximately $10,325.

Financial Aid

The ability to finance a GW education is a priority, so the Office of Student Financial Assistance seeks to assist students and their families in meeting the costs to attend the University. The University budgets more than $150 million for undergraduate financial assistance, which includes scholarships and need-based assistance. In addition, GW offers families the opportunity to participate in a number of payment plans.

By applying for admission, students with outstanding academic credentials are automatically considered for Presidential Academic Scholarships. Approximately 20 percent of freshmen receive merit-based financial assistance. In addition, approximately 50 percent of GW's freshmen receive need-based assistance with an average package of over $39,578.

The Presidential Scholars in the Arts Program awards scholarships to, and encourages the work of, entering freshmen who have shown promise in the fine arts (ceramics, design, drawing, painting, photography, and sculpture), music, theater, technical theater, directing, dance, and choreography.

More information about financial aid at GW can be obtained online at http://www.gwu.edu. Both merit scholarships and a portion of need-based financial aid are guaranteed for all four years for students who remain enrolled in full-time status during their undergraduate program.

Faculty

There is 1 faculty member for every 14 students at GW. Ninety-three percent of GW's full-time faculty members hold a doctoral degree. Part-time and adjunct faculty members are often leaders in their fields of expertise. GW professors are engaging, eminently qualified, and well connected, which allows for a robust intellectual community.

Student Government

The Student Association (SA) is an organization chartered by GW's Board of Trustees to represent students and their concerns. Any person registered for any academic credit at GW is a member of the SA. The SA undertakes initiatives related to academics, community service, neighborhood relations, and student activities.

Admission Requirements

GW receives approximately 21,700 applications for freshman admission and aims to recruit a class of 2,350. Admitted students have strong academic records and the demonstrated ability to achieve success in their college endeavors. To be considered for admission, applicants must submit the following credentials: application and fee, high school transcripts, essay, letters of recommendation from a teacher and a guidance counselor, and either SAT or ACT scores. Details can be obtained online at http://www.gwu.edu. GW also accepts the Common Application, with the GW supplement to the Common Application. Freshman interviews are not required, but may be helpful.

Application and Information

GW has a number of application options: regular decision, early decision I, and early decision II. Prospective students should consult the Web site (http://www.gwu.edu) for the application and deadlines.

Office of Admissions
The George Washington University
2121 I Street, NW, Suite 201
Washington, D.C. 20052
Phone: 202-994-6040
E-mail: gwadm@gwu.edu
Web site: http://www.gwu.edu

Kogan Plaza on the GWU campus.

GRACE COLLEGE
WINONA LAKE, INDIANA

The College

Grace College is an evangelical Christian community of higher education that applies biblical values in strengthening character, sharpening competence, and preparing for service. The academic, residential, athletic, and social aspects of the College are designed to encourage intellectual and spiritual growth in a supportive campus community. At Grace, the students, administration, faculty, and staff aim together to make Christ preeminent in all things. Students learn this by living, studying, working, worshiping, and achieving academic success with other young people who share similar Christian ideals in a setting where the community lifestyle fosters devotion to serious academic inquiry, recreation and relaxation, and mature spiritual growth.

Grace Theological Seminary was founded in 1937, and Grace College was established eleven years later in 1948. Throughout the ensuing decades, the enrollment of Grace Theological Seminary and Grace College has grown exponentially and numerous buildings have been added to the campus. Throughout its history, the institution has remained committed to its heritage, emphasizing biblical authority, a deep experience of community, living under the sovereignty of God, and fostering experiential faith, even as it continues to offer an educational program that is rigorous and academically excellent, as well as practical. Grace offers quality undergraduate and graduate degree programs through six schools that constitute Grace College and Theological Seminary: the School of Arts and Sciences, the School of Behavioral Sciences, the School of Business, the School of Education, the School of Ministry Studies, and the School of Adult and Community Education.

Students choose Grace because of its Christian campus atmosphere, commitment to spiritual development, opportunities for Christian service, quality academic majors, dedicated faculty, excellence in career preparation and quality facilities. Grace is accredited by the Higher Learning Commission and is a member of the North Central Association. It has historically been among the top schools of its size and listed in *U.S. News & World Report* as one of America's best colleges. The Princeton Review has regularly awarded it the title of a Best Midwestern College.

With more than 1,200 undergraduate students representing thirty-four states/territories and six countries, Grace boasts fifteen primary student organizations and fifteen varsity men's and women's sports, plus intramurals and student clubs.

Location

Grace College is located on a 180-acre campus nestled in the historic lakeside village of Winona Lake—a unique pocket of artisanal culture that boasts restored residential areas, lakeside parks and recreation; miles of wooded walking and biking trails; quaint cafés; fine dining; a professional, summer-stock theater; and a dozen or more antique and handicraft shops. The area is also home to the world's three largest orthopaedic firms and many other excellent companies that fuel the thriving local economy. Grace is less than an hour from the Fort Wayne and South Bend airports and less than 3 hours from the Chicago and Indianapolis airports.

Majors and Degrees

Grace College offers Bachelor of Arts (B.A.) and Bachelor of Science (B.S.) degrees. Majors include Accounting/Business Administration, Applied Physics, Art, Art Education, Bible, Biblical Studies, Biology, Business Administration, Business Education, Communication, Counseling, Criminal Justice, Drawing and Painting, Educational Ministries, Elementary Education, English,

English Education, Environmental Biology, Environmental Science, Environmental Studies, Exercise Science, Facility and Event Management, Finance/Business Administration, Financial Planning/Business Administration, French, French Education, Engineering, Engineering Technology, General Business/Business Administration, General Science, Graphic Design, History, Illustration, Information Systems, Intercultural Studies, International Business/Business Administration, International Languages, Journalism, Journalism Education, Life Science Education, Management of Information Systems/Business Administration, Marketing/Business Administration, Math Education-Secondary, Mathematics, Political Science, Psychology, Secondary Education, Social Studies Education, Sociology, Spanish, Spanish Education, Sport Management, Sport Management/Business Administration, Sport Marketing, Sport Media, Sport Psychology, Teaching All Learners, Web Design and Development, and Youth Ministry.

Academic Programs

At the center of a Grace College education are academically challenging courses, specifically designed to foster a thirst for character, competence, and service within the hearts and minds of its students. Every student at Grace completes a series of liberal arts courses (called the Grace Core) and thus enjoys a common experience that stretches across all the disciplines. Explicitly taught from a liberal arts approach, these courses are driven by the mission and evangelical heritage of the college.

Undergraduate students must complete a minimum of 120 hours including all of the Grace Core, degree-specific, major, applied learning, and minor requirements (if required for that particular major).

In addition, Grace offers an accelerated degree option that allows students to earn a bachelor's degree in three years (and a master's degree in year four if they desire). The three-year bachelor's degree may be earned in any major or program offered at Grace and reduces the cost of college by more than 25 percent.

Grace's academic calendar operates on two-semester system with two eight-week sessions in the fall and spring semesters, as well as two eight-week online sessions during May/June and July/August. The compressed calendar gives students the option to graduate in three years regardless of major or program.

Off-Campus Programs

Throughout the year, Grace College students have the opportunity to take short-term missions trips to various countries on Go Encounter teams, led by experienced faculty and staff members. Go Encounter trips are one way to meet the cross-cultural field experience requirement for Global Perspectives, a class designed to develop a biblical lens for seeing the world in order to live meaningfully and biblically in increasingly multicultural societies. Previous Go Encounter trips have visited Turkey, Fiji, France, England, the British Virgin Islands, Germany, Mexico, Japan, South Korea, Cambodia, Uganda, Ireland, and many other countries.

The Grace College Study Abroad Office offers several types of programs to accommodate the goals and academic requirements of Grace students seeking an education experience in a foreign country. Study Abroad is required for several majors and minors, including international business, intercultural studies, and languages. However, students in other majors can also explore studying abroad to learn more about the world around them. Study Abroad is available in Argentina, Austria, France (Sorbonne-Paris and Dijon), Germany, and Spain.

Applied learning is another core aspect of the Grace experience. All Grace students must complete 12 credits of applied learning to graduate. These opportunities allow the student to step outside the classroom walls to experience what different careers are like. Grace has partnered with local organizations and companies to provide students with a wide range of applied learning opportunities. Some of the options available include Farmers State Bank, Lake City Radio, the Remnant Trust, Warsaw Police Department, and United Way.

Academic Facilities

Grace provides public computers and printers in all residence halls. There are also two larger public computer labs with printers. All academic and residential building spaces have Wi-Fi connectivity, including the campus green-space corridor, allowing study and connectivity while outside. Ninety-five percent of all classrooms are equipped with multimedia capabilities and several classrooms in the Orthopaedic Capital Center are outfitted with SMART podium technology.

The Morgan Library contains more than 150,000 volumes that are classified in the Library of Congress classification system. Special collections include the papers of American evangelist William A. "Billy" Sunday, as well as archives of the Winona Lake Bible Conference, Grace College and Seminary, and various Grace Brethren agencies.

The Gordon Recreation Center (GRC) is the primary student fitness center on campus. The GRC contains a fitness and weight room, exercise studio, and an indoor track. It also contains several courts for basketball, volleyball, and indoor soccer as well as an indoor practice driving net for golf.

Miller Field is the home turf for the Grace College Lancers. It hosts men's and women's soccer matches, men's and women's tennis matches, and baseball and softball games.

The Orthopaedic Capital Center (OCC) is a state-of-the-art facility that was finished in 2007 in conjunction with Biomet, DePuy, and Zimmer orthopaedic companies. It is the home for men's and women's basketball games and volleyball matches. It also houses the Bill and Ella Male Hospitality Suite.

Costs

For 2012–13, tuition is $23,290, and room and board is $7454. Miscellaneous expenses such as books, supplies, personal expenses, and transportation are estimated at $2800.

Financial Aid

In 2011, Grace College launched a three-year accelerated degree program in response to student and family financial concerns. By cutting a year of cost, and by entering their career a year early, students can significantly reduce the cost of college.

In addition to this innovative solution, Grace is aggressive with financial aid and scholarships. Grace's financial aid program offers 95 percent of undergraduate students financial aid to make Grace more affordable. Based on Grace's 2011 award history, students received an average of $18,200 per year in financial aid. This figure combines federal loans and grants, as well as institutional grants (academic or athletic scholarships). State aid and other outside independent scholarships are not included and are additional contributors that students should consider.

Faculty

With a 20:1 student-faculty ratio, class sizes are small and professors know their students by name. Over 70 percent of full-time faculty members hold doctoral or terminal degrees. All faculty members teach and work closely with undergraduates, particularly when advising junior and senior independent work.

Student Government and Organizations

Student Senate is comprised of elected student representatives from campus clubs, classes, and residence halls for the purpose of promoting campus unity, addressing relevant issues, and influencing change. Chaired by the student body president, Senate is the platform for communication between students and administration as they seek to constantly improve the student experience at Grace College.

The Student Activities Board (SAB) is an active group of event planners that facilitates activities to bring the campus together. Beyond simply having fun, these activities assist students in building and deepening relationships.

SERVE is a completely student-led ministry program providing opportunities for Grace students to come together in ministry teams to explore their dreams, talents, and passions to serve others. SERVE's mission is "Transforming God-given passions into a lifestyle of service." There are approximately twenty different teams that plan outreach events, help students, work with the elderly or disabled, and much more.

Admission Requirements

Regular admission is typically granted to students with a GPA of 2.3 or above and an ACT score of 20 or above or SAT of 950 or above. ACT and SAT writing scores are not used for merit scholarship awards, but are used for class placement. Students who receive a writing score at or above a 20 on the ACT or 420 on the SAT will be placed in the Effective Writing course. Students scoring below will be placed in Principles of Writing before taking Effective Writing.

Application and Information

Prospective students can apply online for free at www.grace.edu/apply. For more information about Grace College or to schedule a campus visit, students can visit www.grace.edu or call 866-974-7223.

For more information, contact:

Office of Admissions
Grace College
200 Seminary Drive
Winona Lake, Indiana 46590
Phone: 866-974-7223
Fax: 574-372-5120
E-mail: enroll@grace.edu
Web site: http://www.grace.edu
　　　　http://www.facebook.com/gracecollege
　　　　http://www.twitter.com/gracecollege

Students at Grace College experience intellectual and spiritual growth in a supportive campus community.

GRAND VIEW UNIVERSITY
DES MOINES, IOWA

The University

Grand View University is a liberal arts institution affiliated with the Evangelical Lutheran Church in America. Founded more than 100 years ago, Grand View offers a high-quality education to a diverse student body in a career-oriented, liberal arts–grounded curriculum at two campus locations in greater Des Moines. Grand View welcomes traditional students, adult learners, and graduate students representing a wide range of religious and cultural backgrounds.

At Grand View, students find a winning combination of high-quality programs, experienced professors, and caring individuals. With 2,300 students and an average class size of 16, students get to know their professors and other students well. They learn independence and seek responsibility in Grand View's educational environment. Learning is an interactive process at Grand View—students engage in lively discussions, work on real-world projects, and participate in career-related work experiences.

Grand View stands out from other universities because of its partnerships with leading businesses and organizations in Des Moines, which has led to challenging internships. Grand View is known for its ability to connect students with exciting and challenging career opportunities. For nearly a decade and a half, nearly 100 percent of students found jobs right after graduation or continued their education.

Students are encouraged to develop leadership and team skills through involvement in campus organizations, which include intercollegiate and intramural athletics, speech and theater groups, major department clubs, student government, and musical ensembles. Active honorary societies include Alpha Chi, Alpha Mu Gamma, Alpha Psi Omega, Alpha Sigma Lambda, Beta Beta Beta, Phi Eta Sigma, Sigma Theta Tau, and Theta Alpha Kappa among others. Grand View's student leadership program provides opportunities for students without leadership experience to seek and develop critical thinking, interpersonal, and networking skills.

Student athletes compete in men's baseball, basketball, bowling, cross-country, football, golf, soccer, tennis, track and field, volleyball, and wrestling, and women's basketball, bowling, competitive cheer, competitive dance, cross-country, golf, soccer, softball, tennis, track and field, and volleyball. Grand View participates in the Midwest Collegiate Conference of the National Association of Intercollegiate Athletics. Athletic scholarships are available.

Two locations offer Grand View students convenient scheduling options for their program of study. Weekend and evening classes are offered at the main campus in Des Moines and at Grand View's campus in Johnston, Iowa. For motivated students seeking to complete their degree quickly, accelerated schedules are offered for several of sixteen evening majors.

Location

Grand View is located in Des Moines, a metropolitan area of more than half a million people in central Iowa. Des Moines is the state capital and serves as the communications hub for Iowa. Nationally recognized organizations that have their corporate offices in Des Moines include Pioneer Hi-Bred International, Inc.; the Principal Financial Group; Meredith Corporation; and the *Des Moines Register*.

In essence, Grand View's campus is the entire city of Des Moines—as part of the Grand View community, students are not limited by the confines of a small school or small town. In a given day, students can catch an Iowa Cubs professional baseball doubleheader, head down to the Court Avenue district for great food and nightlife, or take in a concert at Wells Fargo Arena.

A thriving arts program in Des Moines features the Des Moines Metro Opera, Ballet Iowa, the Des Moines Symphony, the Des Moines Art Center, and the Des Moines Playhouse. The summer Des Moines Arts Festival is ranked third in the nation.

Des Moines features four distinct and beautiful seasons. Except for a month or so of bundle-up, see-your-breath weather, the climate is ideal for outdoor activities. Grand View students can take advantage of terrific recreational opportunities, including several golf courses, Saylorville Lake, and many city parks and state forests.

Easily accessible from Interstates 35 and 80, Grand View is 4 hours from Minneapolis, 6 hours from Chicago, and 3 hours from Kansas City.

Majors and Degrees

Grand View University grants the Bachelor of Arts degree and offers thirty-eight majors in areas such as accounting, applied mathematics, art education, biology, biotechnology, business administration (with concentrations in agricultural business, finance, human resource management, management, marketing, and real estate), computer science, criminal justice, digital media production, elementary education, English, general studies–liberal arts, graphic design, graphic journalism, health promotion, history, human services, individualized major, journalism, management information systems, mass communication, music, music education, organizational studies, paralegal studies, physical science, political studies (prelaw or public administration), psychology, religion, secondary education, service management, sociology–liberal arts, Spanish for careers and professionals, theater arts, and visual arts. Grand View also offers a Bachelor of Science degree in nursing, as well as an RN to B.S.N. program. In addition, the university offers certificate programs in art therapy, entrepreneurship, human resource management, in-house communication, real estate, Spanish essentials, and sport management, as well as postbaccalaureate certificates in accounting and management in accounting.

The Master of Science in innovative leadership program is an interdisciplinary advanced degree with tracks in business, education, and nursing. This cutting-edge, 40-credit-hour program qualifies graduates as organizational leaders, clinical nurse leaders, and teacher leaders.

Academic Programs

Grand View operates on a 4-4-1 academic calendar. The first semester runs from September to December. The second semester begins in early January and ends in late April. Three one-month summer sessions are offered in May, June, and July, as is a summer trimester evening program.

Grand View has adopted a competency-based general education core. Requirements for the core are defined in student learning goals. Completion of the educational core enables students to achieve a measurable level of competency in key skill and knowledge areas, such as writing, critical analysis, oral communication, and computer proficiency.

The Logos Honors Program provides an alternative to the general education core. By invitation, freshman and sophomore students enrolled in this program complete a series of courses designed to challenge exceptional students.

An active study-abroad program gives students opportunities to learn in an international setting, particularly through a partnership with the Danish Institute for Study Abroad.

The Grand View academic mission is to provide a diverse student body with an academically rigorous education. In order to meet this commitment, Grand View provides a variety of learning environments and teaching techniques. The university's academic support programs and services were lauded as a national model by the examining team from the North Central Association of Colleges and Schools during reaccreditation in 2005, when the University received complete ten-year accreditation with no follow-up required.

Costs

For 2011–12, the comprehensive cost for freshmen living on campus was approximately $28,244, which included tuition, an activity fee, a technology fee, a parking fee, and room and board. Students have several residential and meal plan options that affect cost. Health services and Internet access are also included in the comprehensive fee.

Financial Aid

Typically, most full-time Grand View students received financial assistance. The average freshman full-time award package is usually around $21,000 with about $13,000 in grants and scholarships, and the remainder in work-study and student loans. The amount of aid is determined through a combination of merit and analysis of need as determined through the Free Application for Federal Student Aid. The priority deadline for financial aid is March 1. Students receive notification of financial aid packages following acceptance of admission to the University and receipt of their financial aid analysis of need.

Faculty

There are approximately 90 full-time faculty members and 90 part-time faculty members. More than 50 percent hold terminal degrees. All classes are taught by professors; no graduate or teaching assistants instruct Grand View classes.

Student Government

Students participate in University governance. The Student Activities Council and Viking Council plan student activities that promote educational, social, cultural, and recreational aspects of student life. Students serve as representatives on faculty and staff search committees, programming committees, and student life committees.

Admission Requirements

Applicants' files are reviewed to determine their preparedness for a Grand View education. Official high school transcripts and submission of ACT or SAT scores are required for applicants with less than 24 semester hours of college credit. Applicants transferring from another college are required to submit official transcripts from all colleges previously attended.

Application and Information

For more information about Grand View, students should contact:
Admissions Office
Grand View University
1200 Grandview Avenue
Des Moines, Iowa 50316
Phone: 515-263-2810
       800-444-6083 (toll-free)
Fax: 515-263-2974
E-mail: admissions@grandview.edu
Website: http://www.admissions.grandview.edu
       http://on.fb.me/aGuPhF (Facebook)

Grand View students chat with a professor on their way to class.

GROVE CITY COLLEGE
GROVE CITY, PENNSYLVANIA

The College
Because Faith and Freedom Matter.

The beautifully landscaped campus of Grove City College (GCC) stretches more than 180 acres and includes twenty-eight neo-Gothic buildings valued at more than $100 million. The campus is considered one of the loveliest in the nation. While the College has changed to meet the needs of the society it serves, its basic philosophy has remained unchanged since its founding in 1876. It is a Christian liberal arts and sciences institution of ideal size and dedicated to the principle of providing the highest-quality education at the lowest possible cost. Wishing to remain truly independent and to retain its distinctive qualities as a private school governed by private citizens (trustees), it is one of the very few colleges in the country that does not accept any state or federal monies. It is informally affiliated with the Presbyterian Church (U.S.A.) but not narrowly denominational; the College believes that to be well educated a student should be exposed to the central ideas of the Christian faith. A 20-minute chapel program offered Tuesday and Thursday mornings, along with a Sunday evening worship service, challenges students in their faith. Sixteen chapel services per semester are required out of fifty opportunities. Christian organizations and activities exist to provide fellowship and spiritual growth.

Grove City attracts students from all over the United States. While most come from Pennsylvania, Ohio, New Jersey, Virginia, and New York, forty-four states and twelve other countries were represented in 2011–12. In the most recent freshman class, 77 percent of the women and 58 percent of the men ranked in the top fifth of their high school class. Their average SAT combined score was 1244 (combining only the critical reading and math scores); the average ACT composite score was 28.

Ninety-five percent of the 2,500 students live in separate men's and women's residence halls. All others are regular commuters or married students. A full program of cultural, professional, athletic, and social activities is offered. An arena, Crawford Auditorium, and the J. Howard Pew Fine Arts Center are used for athletics, concerts, movies, plays, and lectures. The Physical Learning Center is one of the finest among the nation's small colleges and includes an eight-lane bowling alley, two swimming pools, handball/racquetball courts, playing surfaces, fitness rooms with free weights, aerobic equipment and Cybex machines, an indoor three-lane running track, and the basketball arena. The Breen Student Union provides an eatery; mailroom; bookstore; commuters' lounge; and a commons area for dining, studying, and socializing. The Ketler and South Hall Recreation Lounges are also available for cooking, games, and socializing. There are more than 130 organizations and special interest groups, including local fraternities and sororities. No alcohol or drugs are permitted on campus. The athletic activities include extensive intramural, club, and varsity sports programs that provide nineteen intercollegiate teams that compete at the NCAA Division III level for men and women.

The College's well-established placement services, ranked recently by The Princeton Review among the top 20 in the nation, are used constantly by students who are interested in business and industrial employment and by those seeking educational positions in the teaching field. A complete file of personal data, scholastic records, and recommendations is prepared for each registrant. These files are available to the scores of prospective employers who visit the campus annually to interview the graduating seniors. One of Grove City's strengths is placing students in business, industrial, and teaching positions, as well as in professional institutions such as medical schools.

Prospective students can check out Grove City's Facebook page at http://on.fb.me/grovecity_coll.

Location

Grove City, a town of 8,000 people, is 60 miles north of Pittsburgh and is located 4 miles from restaurants, hotels, and a 140-store outlet mall. Convenient to I-79 and I-80, Grove City is only a day's drive from Chicago, New York City, Toronto, and Washington, D.C. The municipal airport has a 3,500-foot runway, and there is bus service to Pittsburgh.

Majors and Degrees

Grove City College offers undergraduate degrees in liberal arts, sciences, engineering, and music. The Bachelor of Arts (B.A.) is offered with majors in Biblical and religious studies, communication studies, economics, English, history, modern language (French and Spanish), philosophy, political science, psychology, secondary education, and sociology. Preprofessional students in law or theology usually earn the B.A. degree. Interdisciplinary major programs are also available for qualified students.

The Bachelor of Science is granted with majors in accounting, applied physics, applied physics/computer, biochemistry, biology, business management, chemistry, computer information systems, computer science, PreK–4 elementary education, PreK–8 special education, entrepreneurship, exercise science, financial management, industrial management, international business, marketing management, mathematics, middle level education, molecular biology, and psychology,. Pre-professional students often select one of these majors for dentistry, medicine, or other health fields.

The Bachelor of Science in Electrical and Computer Engineering degree is also offered. The Bachelor of Science in Mechanical Engineering major provides for mechanical systems design and/or thermal systems design. The electrical and computer and mechanical engineering programs are accredited by the Engineering Accreditation Commission of the Accreditation Board for Engineering and Technology, Inc. (ABET).

The Bachelor of Music degree is awarded to those who major in music. Programs may also include concentrations in business, education, performing arts, or religion.

Academic Programs

Grove City College's goal is to assist young men and women in developing as complete individuals—academically, spiritually, and physically. The general education requirements provide all students with a high level of cultural literacy and communication skills. They include 46 semester hours of courses with emphases in the humanities, social sciences, and natural sciences; in quantitative and logical reasoning; and in science, faith, and technology, as well as a language requirement for all majors except engineering and science. Degree candidates must also complete the requirements in their field of concentration, physical education, electives, and convocation. To graduate, a student must have completed 128 semester hours (130 hours for electrical engineering) plus 4 convocation credits. Seventy-eight percent of those entering as freshmen stay and receive a diploma in four years.

A distinctive liberal arts–engineering program includes engineering courses plus courses in the humanities to provide students with a well-grounded preparation for entering the engineering field, as well as the civic and cultural life of society. The Austrian economics program exposes students to all economic

philosophies, yet strongly advocates economic freedoms and free markets.

Grove City follows the early semester calendar plan. Academic credit may be granted to incoming freshmen on the basis of scores on appropriate Advanced Placement tests, International Baccalaureate tests, or College-Level Examination Program tests. Honors courses, independent study, seminars, and the opportunity for juniors to study abroad for credit are also offered.

Academic Facilities

The Hall of Arts and Letters opened in 2003. This state-of-the-art teaching facility features a 200-seat lecture hall, forty classrooms (including multimedia-equipped rooms and tiered "case study" rooms), eighty faculty offices, the Early Education Center, the Curriculum Library, and language, computer, and video production labs.

The College library houses 143,470 books and serial backfiles; 3,179 audio/video tapes, CDs, and DVDs; and 140 current serial subscriptions. In addition, the College has access to 58,885 journal titles through its collection of full-text journal databases. Modern, well-equipped laboratories for biology, chemistry, engineering, and physics are available, as are facilities for language and piano studies.

The College recently acquired an observatory and the remote structure will be utilized for astronomy classes as well as faculty and student research.

The Weir C. Ketler Technological Learning Center consists of fifty microcomputers and three big-screen projection systems and houses the help desk and repair center that support the student technology initiative. All freshmen receive their own tablet PC and color printer/scanner/copier.

The J. Howard Pew Fine Arts Center has art, photography, and music studios; a rehearsal hall; a little theater; a museum; an art gallery; music practice rooms; and an 800-seat, acoustically tunable auditorium and stage large enough to accommodate the most elaborate drama productions and concerts. An addition completed in 2002 contains additional classrooms, practice rooms, and a 200-seat recital hall.

Costs

As a relatively small, financially sound college, Grove City is able to charge an unusually low tuition in comparison to other independent institutions of similar quality. The 2011–12 annual tuition charge was $13,598 for all degrees. The cost of a tablet PC for all freshmen is included in the tuition fees. There is no comprehensive fee. Part-time tuition is $425 per credit. Room and board were $7410. Expenses for books, laundry, transportation, and personal needs vary considerably with the lifestyle of the individual.

Financial Aid

Because the College's tuition charges are low, every student, in effect, receives significant financial assistance. Forty-four percent of the freshmen receive additional aid from GCC. Students applying for financial assistance must complete Grove City College's financial aid form. Job opportunities are available both on and off campus.

Faculty

The focus of the Grove City faculty members is on teaching students, although many members are involved with research and writing. Ninety-five percent of the faculty members hold doctorates. Most of the administrative staff members also teach part-time in various departments. The student-faculty ratio is approximately 15:1. Faculty members emphasize teaching and attention to the students' individual needs; they also participate extensively in the College's extracurricular programs.

Student Government

The Student Government Association provides an opportunity for direct student interaction with the faculty members and administration in matters relating to campus activities. Students serve on regular College committees (library, publications, religious activities, and student activities) and also on the Men's and Women's Governing Board and the Discipline Committee.

Admission Requirements

The College seeks academically qualified students without regard to race, color, sex, religion, or national or ethnic origin. An applicant for admission should be a high school graduate with the following recommended units: English, 4; foreign language, 3; mathematics, 3; history, 2; and science, 2. Engineering, science, and mathematics majors should have 4 units each in both mathematics and science. Auditions are required for music majors. An interview is highly recommended, especially for those who live within a day's drive (400 miles).

Transfer students may receive advanced standing if they have been in good standing at their previous institutions and have maintained a minimum grade point average of 2.0 (on a 4.0 scale).

Application and Information

A regular admission applicant should take the SAT or ACT by October or November of the senior year in high school. The application should include scores on the SAT (preferred) or the ACT; a high school transcript; two letters of recommendation, one from the student's principal or counselor and the other from a pastor; and a nonrefundable application fee of $50. An application may be submitted after the eleventh grade. An early decision applicant should take the entrance test in the eleventh grade, visit the College for an interview, and submit the application by November 15; notification of the admission decision is mailed on December 15. Approved early decision applicants must accept by January 15 and submit a nonrefundable deposit of $250.

Applicants seeking regular decision must submit the completed application and supporting documents by February 1 of their senior year. Notification of the admission decision is mailed on March 15. Students who are offered admission should reply as soon as possible, but no later than May 1, and include a nonrefundable deposit of $250. Applications received after February 1 are considered as space permits. The College receives nearly three applications for every freshman vacancy.

Additional information may be obtained from:

Director of Admissions
Grove City College
100 Campus Drive
Grove City, Pennsylvania 16127-2104
Phone: 724-458-2100
Fax: 724-458-3395
E-mail: admissions@gcc.edu
Web site: http://www.gcc.edu
http://on.fb.me/grovecity_coll (Facebook)

Students leaving the Hall of Arts and Letters.

GUILFORD COLLEGE
GREENSBORO, NORTH CAROLINA

The College

Founded in 1837, Guilford College (www.guilford.edu) is located on 340 wooded acres in Greensboro, North Carolina. Guilford is among the oldest coeducational colleges in the nation and has a long-standing history of commitment to the individual student and to Quaker values. Drawing on its Quaker heritage, Guilford College is a community of open-minded learners who promote positive change in the world. The curriculum focuses on writing, reasoning, class discussions, and solving problems—preparing students for the world's future challenges.

Guilford's 2,800 students, aged 16 to 65, come from more than forty-five states and nineteen countries. The College's size ensures the academic community's commitment to personalized education (95 percent of classes have fewer than 30 students) while embracing academic diversity. Guilford students pursue variety with passion through the following opportunities: more than forty campus clubs and organizations; a thriving campus ministry program; an active multicultural education department; vibrant theater, music, and art programs; a campus radio station (WQFS-FM); an award-winning weekly student newspaper (The Guilfordian); and intercollegiate, intramural, and club athletics. The Campus Activities Board, a student organization, sponsors many of the social, recreational, and cultural programs offered at the College. Many students participate in a variety of community service projects and volunteer programs.

The Bryan Distinguished Visiting Professorship in the Arts, Humanities, and Public Affairs at Guilford College (www.guilford.edu/bryanseries) brings to campus individuals who are widely regarded as experts in their field. Past speakers include former President Bill Clinton, Tony Blair, Mikhail Gorbachev, Madeleine Albright, Twyla Tharp, Archbishop Desmond Tutu, David Gregory, Toni Morrison, and Sidney Poitier, among others. Guilford College students attend Bryan Series lectures free of charge.

Guilford's intercollegiate athletic teams (www.guilford.edu/athletics) compete at the NCAA Division III level and in the Old Dominion Athletic Conference (ODAC). The sports include women's basketball, cross-country, lacrosse, soccer, softball, swimming, tennis, indoor and outdoor track, and volleyball, as well as men's baseball, basketball, cross-country, football, golf, lacrosse, soccer, tennis, and indoor and outdoor track. Sports programs are coupled with special academic opportunities in sports medicine, sport management, and physical education. Guilford's athletic facilities include basketball courts, cardio and weight-training facilities, beach volleyball court, tennis courts, baseball batting center, and a multipurpose artificial turf stadium.

Guilford's commitment to sustaining the environment is campuswide and is reflected in a variety of initiatives, including solar panels on residence halls, dining hall composting, a student-led bioretention site project, occupancy sensors in the Frank Family Science Center, LEED-certified building standards, a bike shop to encourage alternative transportation opportunities, community vegetable gardens, and energy-efficient exercise equipment in the fitness area.

Location

A city of 245,000 people, Greensboro is located midway between Washington, D.C., and Atlanta, Georgia. The greater metropolitan area has a population of approximately 1.3 million. Greensboro is the home of six colleges and universities, with a total student enrollment of approximately 40,000. Guilford participates in an academic consortium with the other institutions. Two interstate highways serve the city, students enjoy close proximity to regional and national train and bus lines, and the Piedmont Triad International Airport is less than 5 miles from campus. Numerous historic sites as well as local, state, and national parks are within day-trip distance of the College. Greensboro's central location in the state allows easy access to the state's beautiful beaches and to several major ski areas in the mountains.

Majors and Degrees

Guilford College offers B.A. or B.S. degrees (www.guilford.edu/academics) in accounting, African-American studies, art, biology, business management, chemistry, community and justice studies, computing technology and information systems, criminal justice, economics, education studies, English, environmental studies, exercise and sports sciences, forensic biology, French, forensic accounting, geology, German, health sciences, history, integrative studies, international studies, mathematics, music, peace and conflict studies, philosophy, physics, political science, psychology, religious studies, sociology/anthropology, Spanish, sport management, theater studies, and women's gender and sexuality studies. The B.F.A. degree is offered in art. Also offered is a Bachelor of Music degree. Guilford offers fifty-four minors in a variety of disciplines; a full listing is available online at www.guilford.edu/academics/catalog/minors.

Most recently, Guilford College has entered into an agreement with University of North Carolina at Greensboro to offer an accelerated Master of Business Administration (M.B.A.) degree. Preprofessional programs are offered in dentistry, law, medicine, ministry, and veterinary science.

Academic Programs

Each student works closely with a faculty adviser to select courses that meet individual educational and career goals. Thirty-two semester courses are required for graduation, eight of which are generally in the major field of study. Required courses are few but represent a distribution over the principal fields of the arts and sciences. Flexible requirements allow for interdisciplinary and double majors.

Incoming first-year students and transfer students participate in an orientation program that includes computer training, learning skills, academic advising, self-awareness workshops, and outdoor experiences.

Independent studies, off-campus internships, and off-campus seminars are open to all students. An expanded honors program includes a variety of honors seminars and research opportunities for students with exceptional academic credentials and motivation. One pass/fail elective course may be taken each semester.

Entering students may waive courses through Advanced Placement (AP) examinations in English, history, laboratory science, mathematics, and foreign languages. Advanced placement requires an AP score of 3 or better or a general CLEP score of 500 or better; credit requires an AP score of 4 or better or a general CLEP score of 550 or better. Subject CLEP scores must be at least 50 for advanced placement and at least 55 for credit.

In addition to the fall and spring semesters, Guilford is slated to add a January Term in 2013. The January Term, an optional, special, three-week session, may offer opportunities for study abroad, study away, internships, independent study, and unique course offerings.

Off-Campus Programs

Semester-abroad programs (www.guilford.edu/studyabroad) enable students to study in China, England, France, Germany, Ghana, Greece, Ireland, Italy, Japan, Mexico, the Netherlands, Scotland, Spain, and Wales, as well as a variety of other locations. Students can choose Guilford-led programs or those managed by affiliated partners like the School for Field Studies, the Foundation for International Education, or the School for International Training. A full year of academic credit for study in Japan is available through a cooperative program with International Christian University in Tokyo. An on-campus program director assists students who wish to study abroad.

Guilford participates in two consortia that allow open registration in eight area colleges and universities without additional fees. Other member schools are Bennett College, Elon University, Greensboro College, Guilford Technical Community College, High

Point University, North Carolina A&T State University, and the University of North Carolina at Greensboro.

An internship director helps place students who wish to study elsewhere in the United States. Course credit is given for all approved off-campus study. The Washington Semester in Washington, D.C., supplements the academic program and helps students develop professional skills and career potential through internships with the federal government, lobbying organizations, or public agencies.

Internships may be done in any discipline. Locally, students may pursue internships as part of their academic and career development in business, education, government, health services, law, medicine, scientific research, and social services. In addition, the Guilford College Career Development Office is focused on assisting graduates as they pursue internships, jobs, and graduate school. Career Development services are a lifetime benefit for alums.

Academic Facilities

Guilford's stately Georgian-style buildings house classrooms, a spacious auditorium, the library, student center, administrative offices, and residence halls. The state-of-the-art 65,000-square-foot Frank Family Science Center features fourteen laboratories (with twenty-four workstations each), 1,600 computer connections, a rooftop observatory with a computer-driven telescope, and a 150-seat multipurpose auditorium/planetarium. Multiple studio spaces are available to students in the fine arts.

Guilford's Hege Library is one of the three largest private libraries in North Carolina. The library contains 250,000 volumes and includes an art gallery, a media center, and the only Friends Historical Collection in the Southeast. Hege Library is fully automated and is linked to buildings across the entire campus. Students also have library privileges at six colleges within 20 miles that have an additional 1.3 million volumes.

Bauman Telecommunications Center houses two computer-equipped classrooms, faculty offices, and three computer labs with ninety-one personal computers. In addition, there are 200 public terminals in the Center and other terminals in academic buildings around the campus. Guilford's campus is completely wireless. In addition, satellite connections make it possible to bring in foreign language programming from around the world. Guilford offers state-of-the-art computers in its multimedia learning center for cultures and languages. Most residential students have PCs in their rooms connected to the College network.

Costs

Basic expenses for the 2012–13 academic year are $31,490 for tuition and fees, and $8540 for room and board. Personal expenses, book costs, and transportation expenses vary according to individual need.

Financial Aid

Guilford College tries to meet the demonstrated financial need (www.guilford.edu/finaid) of all students, as determined by the Free Application for Federal Student Aid (FAFSA). More than $37.5 million in scholarships, loans, grants, and work-study opportunities was awarded to students last year. Academic scholarships are awarded on a competitive basis. Guilford offers several academic merit-based and special-interest scholarship programs. Approximately 90 percent of last year's student body received some form of merit-based or need-based assistance. The average need-based award was more than $23,000 a year per recipient. The average merit-based award was $6825.

Faculty

Guilford has 124 full-time faculty members. The College seeks faculty members who value the sense of community and concern for individuals that are part of Guilford's heritage. The student-faculty ratio is currently 16:1. The average class size is 19.

Student Government

Guilford entrusts its students with responsibility for governing their own actions and furthering the best interests of the entire College community. The student Community Senate is composed of representatives from residence halls and the day-student organization, a member of the administration, and 2 faculty members. Students serve on all faculty and administrative committees and on the College's Board of Trustees and Alumni Board.

Admission Requirements

As one of the oldest coeducational institutions in the nation, Guilford takes the commitment to academics and the liberal arts seriously. To that end, the Admission Committee (www.guilford.edu/admission) uses a holistic method of application evaluation. Each applicant is considered on an individual basis. Students are encouraged to challenge themselves within their high school environment, both in and out of the classroom. While the majority of applicants submit some form of standardized test scores (ACT or SAT), students have the option of submitting a portfolio of written work in lieu of standardized test scores. The College community is full of active and involved citizens. The evaluation process seeks to continue to admit students that bring a diverse variety of backgrounds and interests to the College. Interviews, although not required, are available so that the applicant can become better acquainted with Guilford and so that the admission staff can better evaluate the candidate. Guilford is competitive with respect to admission.

Application and Information

Admission plans (www.guilford.edu/apply) include early action and regular decision. Early action I applicants must apply by November 15 and are notified by December 15. Early action II applicants must apply by January 15 and are notified by February 15. The regular decision priority deadline is February 15, and applicants are notified by April 1. After February 15, applications are considered as space is available. Candidates admitted for both early action and regular decision must reply to their offers of admission by May 1.

Early entrance applicants are considered after their junior year of high school. They must have an outstanding academic record and must be sufficiently mature socially to adjust to college life.

Transfer candidates should apply for admission by December 1 for the spring semester and by June 1 for the fall semester.

The priority deadline for applying for financial aid is March 1.

The Admission Office is open for visits (www.guilford.edu/visit) Monday through Saturday during the academic year. During the summer, the Admission Office is open for visits Monday through Friday. Guilford College encourages students to visit for a campus tour. More than a classroom education, the Guilford experience is designed to stimulate the whole person and provide the critical thinking that will help today's students take their place as leaders who will guide tomorrow.

For further information and application forms for admission and financial aid, students should contact:

Admission Office
Guilford College
5800 West Friendly Avenue
Greensboro, North Carolina 27410
Phone: 336-316-2100
      800-992-7759 (toll-free)
E-mail: admission@guilford.edu
Web site: http://www.guilford.edu

The Quad at Guilford College.

GWYNEDD-MERCY COLLEGE
GWYNEDD VALLEY, PENNSYLVANIA

Gwynedd-Mercy College
BRINGING *FUTURES* INTO *FOCUS*

The College

Founded by the Sisters of Mercy, Gwynedd-Mercy College (GMC) is a Catholic college offering a strong foundation in the liberal arts. For more than sixty years, Gwynedd-Mercy College has been "Bringing Futures Into Focus" by preparing students to become top professionals in the fields of allied health professions, arts and sciences, business, education, and nursing. GMC offers more than forty associate, bachelor's, and master's degree programs on a full- and part-time basis. GMC's academic distinction lies in the intersection of excellent programs in health care, education, and business administration, which prepare students to become leaders in the region's powerful and growing life sciences industry.

Located just 30 minutes from Philadelphia and with an enrollment of nearly 2,700 students, Gwynedd-Mercy College is large enough to offer a vibrant campus life but small enough that professors can develop mentoring relationships with students. The College educates students in the Mercy tradition of service to society, preparing graduates who not only are recruited for jobs but also create lives and careers with deep meaning. In the 2012 edition of *U.S. News & World Report*'s "Best Colleges," Gwynedd-Mercy College ranked in the first tier of its category, in part because of its high graduation and retention rates.

Gwynedd-Mercy College has nineteen NCAA Division III athletic teams, including baseball, basketball, cheerleading, cross-country, field hockey, indoor/outdoor track and field, lacrosse, soccer, softball, tennis, and volleyball. The men's baseball and men's and women's basketball teams have won various championships. The College also offers a variety of intramural sports. The field hockey, soccer, lacrosse, and track and field teams compete at the College's new Outdoor Athletic Complex, which offers a turf field and Olympic-size track.

Students are encouraged to participate in activities and student government so that they can socialize with friends, develop talents, and build leadership skills. The College offers more than thirty clubs and organizations, including the drama club, campus ministry, a nationally renowned choir, the yearbook staff, and social committees. Students can write for the College newspaper, the *Gwynmercian,* which has received a first-place rating with special merit from the American Scholastic Press Association. Through the on-campus chapter of the Mercy Works Program, students can help the poor with fund-raising efforts and adopt-a-family programs at the Thanksgiving and Christmas holidays. Some students decide to give a year of service after graduation to Mercy Volunteer Corps' nationwide outreach program.

On campus, students can choose from four residence halls for rooming and dine at several eateries which offer full meals, sandwiches, pizza, salads, breakfast and coffee. The Late Night Lounge has events every weekend, including movie nights, dances, comedians, bingo, rock band competitions, and game parties.

At the graduate level, Gwynedd-Mercy College offers master's degree programs in business (management), education (educational administration, reading, school counseling, special education, and a Master Teacher program), and nursing (nurse educator, nurse practitioner, and clinical nurse specialist).

Location

Gwynedd-Mercy's idyllic 160-acre campus is located in Gwynedd Valley, Pennsylvania, a suburb 20 miles from downtown Philadelphia. Old City, South Street, and sports arenas are a 25- to 30-minute car or train ride from the campus. The College is situated just minutes from several major highways, including the Pennsylvania Turnpike. In addition to the vibrant city life of

Philadelphia, students can travel to the New Jersey beaches or the Pocono Mountains, which are only 2 hours from the campus.

Majors and Degrees

Gwynedd-Mercy offers baccalaureate degrees in accounting, behavioral/social gerontology, biology, business administration, business education, communication, computer information science, criminal justice, elementary education, English, history, human services, mathematics, nursing, psychology, and special education.

Associate in Science degrees are awarded in the allied health fields of cardiovascular technology, and respiratory care. Associate degrees are also granted in liberal studies, natural science, and nursing.

Academic Programs

The school year is divided into two semesters, and most baccalaureate degree programs require the completion of a minimum of 125 credit hours. GMC maintains a strong liberal arts component in all of its degree programs. Whether the student chooses to major in one of the liberal arts or to pursue a professionally oriented degree, courses are required in language, literature and the fine arts, humanities, and behavioral, social, and natural sciences. Students have access to the Academic Resource Center for free class tutoring and assistance with improving their writing skills.

Individualized internships and work-experience programs are available and recommended in all majors to give students firsthand experience in their chosen major. Nearby Fortune 500 companies offer a variety of experiences to students in business and accounting. TAP, the Teacher Assistant Program, places every education major in the classroom one day a week beginning in the freshman year. All allied health and nursing programs require clinical experience. The 2-2 programs—those with an associate degree to bachelor's degree progression—offer allied health and nursing students the opportunity to gain employment in their field while continuing toward the baccalaureate degree. The School of Business maintains a successful work-experience semester. Through this paid internship, students earn credit while gaining valuable experience in challenging positions.

Students are encouraged to develop a global perspective through various study-abroad opportunities. In 2010, the College launched a study-abroad program to Brescia, Italy. During the monthlong program, students took courses in Italian language, culture, and philosophy; rode bikes to get around town; and toured Italy on weekends.

Off-Campus Programs

The excellent on-campus laboratory facilities are extended by affiliations with more than 200 hospitals and health-care agencies in Pennsylvania, New Jersey, and Delaware, where students may complete their clinical experience. Merck provides a one-semester industrial laboratory experience for qualified biology majors. Gwynedd-Mercy College maintains a close relationship with nearby companies, including Johnson & Johnson, McNeil, and Sun Company, for work-experience programs.

Academic Facilities

Gwynedd-Mercy has expanded its physical facilities as its student enrollment has increased. The Sister Isabelle Keiss Center for Health and Science houses the Schools of Nursing and Allied Health Professions and the Division of Natural Sciences. The 50,000-square-foot state-of-the-art facility offers laboratories for areas such as nursing skills, respiratory care, cardiovascular technology, radiation therapy, health information technology,

organic chemistry, and microbiology. Plans are underway to construct a new academic facility to house both the School of Education and the School of Business. The College's Griffin Complex houses the College's Student Union—which is equipped with a game room, full gymnasium and track, racquetball court, and weight room. The College offers four residence halls that house 40 percent of the school population. Theaters include the Julia Ball Auditorium, a small in-the-round theater, and an upgraded TV production studio. The Student Technology Center is equipped with personal computers and printers and the latest software for student use. The Valie Genuardi Hobbit House, a private school for preschoolers where students in the School of Education are trained, is situated on campus.

Costs

The 2011–12 academic-year tuition (two semesters) for full-time students (12 to 18 credits per semester) was $26,670. The tuition for allied health and nursing students was $28,170. Room and board were, on average, $10,000. Professional liability fees for students enrolled in clinical components and lab fees are extra.

Financial Aid

Gwynedd-Mercy's financial aid program is designed to provide financial assistance to academically qualified students whose resources are inadequate to meet the costs of attending the College. The student Financial Aid Committee endeavors to assist as many students as possible, using Gwynedd-Mercy funds as well as federal, state, and other available funds. Aid is awarded on the basis of demonstrated financial need, academic proficiency, and responsible campus citizenship.

A financial aid packet is sent, with instructions, to those who request it on their application form. High school students should request the Free Application for Federal Student Aid (FAFSA) from their guidance office. In 2011–12, 91 percent of Gwynedd-Mercy College full-time students received some form of financial aid. March 15 is the deadline for freshmen entering in the fall semester. The deadline for Academic Scholarships is February 15.

Faculty

The student-faculty ratio is 13:1, allowing for personal contact, advising, and after-class instruction. This is a widely acknowledged strength of the GMC experience. For nursing students in the clinical setting, there are never more than 8 students to 1 clinical adviser; in the allied health programs, there often is one-to-one instruction. The quality of teaching is enhanced by the diversified interests of the faculty. The 181 faculty members teach both day and evening classes, allowing students the greatest flexibility in scheduling. Free tutoring is available in all disciplines.

Student Government

All students are encouraged to take part in the responsibilities of student government. This student participation and shared responsibility for the welfare of the College are promoted through a framework of committees. The student government president and 3 other students are members of the College Council, which is responsible for the continuing self-evaluation of the College and policy formation. In addition, students share membership in the Educational Planning Committee, Faculty/Student Committee, Financial Aid Committee, and Library Committee.

Admission Requirements

Admission to Gwynedd-Mercy College is based on a student's high school record, rank in class, SAT or ACT scores, counselor's recommendation, and choice of major. Entrance requirements vary with the program. The rolling admission policy allows the student to be informed of the admission decision within two to three weeks after submitting their application.

GMC awards College credit for satisfactory completion of Advanced Placement courses. The exam score must be 3 or above.

A minimum 2.0 grade point average (on a 4.0 scale) is generally required to transfer from another college. Gwynedd-Mercy College does, however, retain the right to require a higher GPA for admission to some programs.

GMC selects all students on the basis of academic achievement and does not discriminate on the basis of race, religion, gender, handicap, or sexual orientation.

Application and Information

All prospective applicants are urged to visit the campus to meet and talk with an admission counselor, a dean, or a program director. To apply for admission, applicants should complete an application form and submit it to the admissions office along with the required nonrefundable $25 application fee. The fee is waived for students who apply online at http://www.gmc.edu. First-time freshmen must also submit an official high school transcript or equivalency certificate; a written recommendation from a principal, teacher, guidance counselor, or employer; and results of the SAT or ACT (for recent high school graduates). All applicants should verify that they meet the specific requirements and have the necessary high school prerequisites for admission.

Students who wish to transfer to Gwynedd-Mercy College should complete the application form and submit it to the admissions office along with the required nonrefundable $25 application fee, high school and college transcripts, and a letter of recommendation.

For additional information or to schedule campus tours and visits, students are encouraged to contact the Campus Guest Program Office at campusguestprogram@gmc.edu or 215-641-5514.

For more information, contact:

Office of Admissions
Gwynedd-Mercy College
1325 Sumneytown Pike
P.O. Box 901
Gwynedd Valley, Pennsylvania 19437-0901
Phone: 800-DIAL-GMC (toll-free)
E-mail: admissions@gmc.edu
Web site: www.gmc.edu/admissions/
    http://twitter.com/gwyneddmercycol

Gwynedd-Mercy College students walking on campus during a beautiful spring day.

HARDING UNIVERSITY
SEARCY, ARKANSAS

The University

As an institution rooted in Christian principles and a liberal arts tradition since 1924, Harding University challenges its students to pursue scholarship, service, teamwork, excellence, and commitment. Harding is ranked by *U.S. News and World Report* and Princeton Review as one of the top liberal arts universities in the South and attracts exceptional high school students from every U.S. state and more than fifty-three countries.

The University is accredited by nine organizations, including the Higher Learning Commission of the North Central Association of Colleges and Schools. Housed within nine colleges, including the Honors College and newly created College of Allied Health, students can choose from a wide range of majors: from humanities and theology to business and education to natural and health sciences. In addition to undergraduate work, students may pursue graduate-, specialist-, and doctorate-level degrees in one of the fourteen programs offered. With a student-teacher ratio of 17 to 1, strong relationships are built in and out of the classroom.

Students can cultivate friendships and interests with 114 academic and professional organizations and twenty-nine social clubs. Ranging from the arts, music, politics, business, diversity, children, missions, service, and the environment, the clubs on campus offer a variety of interests to explore.

Provided with a Christian perspective through which to appreciate various disciplines, students excel as scholars and develop leadership skills. As a result, Harding alumni display character, conviction, and a competitive edge and are prepared for success at prestigious graduate schools and companies throughout the nation.

Location

Harding is located in Searcy, Arkansas, and offers students a hometown feeling with easy access to major cities. The University is about an hour away from Little Rock, Arkansas, and the Little Rock National Airport and is about 2 hours away from Memphis, Tennessee.

Majors and Degrees

The University offers more than 100 academic majors, including fourteen preprofessional programs, taught by top instructors.

Within the College of Allied Health, students may earn a bachelor of arts degree in communication sciences and disorders.

The College of Arts and Humanities offers a wide range of degrees in the humanities, arts, English language and literature, foreign language and international studies, history and social science, mass communication, music, oral communication, and theater.

In the College of Bible and Ministry, there are degrees in Bible and religion, biblical languages, Christian education, missions, preaching, and youth and family ministry.

Students in the Paul R. Carter College of Business Administration may receive degrees in accounting, economics, finance, global economic development, health care management, international business management, management information systems, marketing, and professional sales.

Those interested in teaching may earn degrees in early childhood P–4, middle childhood/early adolescence English/language arts/social science 4–8, middle childhood/early adolescence math/science 4–8, secondary education, and special education endorsement (P–3) in the Cannon-Clary College of Education.

The Carr College of Nursing offers a Bachelor of Science in Nursing.

Lastly, the College of Sciences allows students to study health sciences, behavioral sciences, biology, chemistry, computer science, engineering and physics, exercise and sport sciences, family and consumer sciences, kinesiology, and mathematics.

Academic Programs

For the basic requirements necessary for each degree, prospective students should visit the Harding University online catalog at www.harding.edu/catalog.

Students may apply and participate in the Honors College with acceptance based on acceptance to the University and an ACT score of 27 or higher or an SAT score of 1220 or higher. These students may take honors-level courses and graduate with honors.

In addition, various majors may allow students to receive their teaching licensure in the process.

Off-Campus Programs

Harding offers seven study abroad programs in Australia, Chile, England, France, Greece, Italy, and Zambia that will help expand cultural awareness and understanding. Nearly 50 percent of each graduating class takes advantage of one of these semester-long programs. At each location, students are accompanied and taught by University faculty. Costs are based on 16 tuition hours and include housing and meals.

Academic Facilities

Harding's campus consists of thirteen academic buildings, cafeteria, two auditoriums, a library, a performing arts center, a student center, student health services, fourteen residence halls, and six apartment complexes.

Costs

The basic undergraduate, on-campus cost for 2011–12 for 15 hours of enrollment per semester was $7080 for a semester and $14,160 for the year. Tuition was $472 per course hour. Students paid $450 a year for a required technology fee, $2988 for a standard dorm, and $3042 for a standard meal plan of 210 meals plus a $200 declining cash balance. The overall total came to $20,640.

Financial Aid

On average, 96 percent of Harding University undergraduate students receive financial assistance. In 2010–11, Harding awarded students more than $1 million in institutional need-based grants and more than $25 million in institutional scholarships. In addition, students received nearly $12 million in federal, state, and externally funded scholarships and grants.

Admission Requirements

Students wishing to apply to Harding must have a 19 ACT or 900 SAT and 3.0 high school GPA (on a 4.0 scale). In addition, high school graduates should have completed at least 15 units in academic subjects. Specifically, an applicant should have completed 4 units of English, 3 units of mathematics (taken from general math, geometry, algebra, trigonometry, precalculus, or calculus), 3 units of social studies (taken from civics, American history, world history, or geography), and 2 units of natural science (taken from physical science, biology, physics, or chemistry). Students planning to major in any area of health care are strongly encouraged to take one or more chemistry courses while in high school. Although not required for admission, two years of foreign language is recommended. The additional units may come from any academic area.

Application and Information

Prospective students may apply online at www.harding.edu/apply/.

Because Harding receives so many applications, it recommends that students apply before the fall of their senior year of high school—even if they haven't taken the ACT or SAT. Admissions advisers are glad to help students through this process.

For more information, prospective students should contact:

Harding University
Box 12234
Searcy, Arkansas 72143-2234
Phone: 501-279-4000
Web site: http://www.harding.edu
http://www.facebook.com/searcy
http://www.twitter.com/HardingU

Harding University offers students a wide range of academic choices to pursue, and helps them develop character, conviction, and a competitive edge.

HAVERFORD COLLEGE
HAVERFORD, PENNSYLVANIA

The College

Founded in 1833 as the first college established by members of the Society of Friends (Quakers), Haverford College has chosen to remain small, undergraduate, and residential in order to offer students remarkable classroom and research opportunities while maintaining a strong sense of community. Haverford's Honor Code, created and implemented by students, is an important part of the College's identity. The Code allows students to directly confront academic and social issues in a spirit of cooperation and mutual respect.

Haverford's 1,192 students represent forty-four states, Puerto Rico, the District of Columbia, and thirty-six countries. Thirty-two percent of the students are students of color and 7 percent are international students.

Haverford is a residential campus with 99 percent of the students and 50 percent of the faculty living on campus. Housing on Haverford's campus is single-sex or coed, and residence halls vary in accommodations from 4-person apartments to suites and singles. Other choices of residence facilities include the Ira De A. Reid House (Black Cultural Center), La Casa Hispanica, and an environmental house.

Haverford's athletic teams participate in Division III of the NCAA. Intercollegiate sports include baseball, basketball, cricket, cross-country, fencing, field hockey, lacrosse, soccer, softball, squash, tennis, track and field, and volleyball. Haverford also sponsors several club and intramural sports teams. Athletic facilities include the Douglas B. Gardner Integrated Athletic Center, the Alumni Field House, the John A. Lester Cricket Pavilion, and Swan Field—Haverford's turf field dedicated in 2008.

Location

The College is located 10 miles (16 kilometers) west of Center City Philadelphia on a wooded campus of 216 acres. Haverford's proximity to the fifth-largest city in the United States allows its students to take advantage of the many social, cultural, and educational resources that this historic area offers. Extensive public transportation allows students easy access to the city and environs.

Majors and Degrees

Majors leading to a B.A. or B.S. degree are offered in thirty departments: anthropology, archaeology, astronomy, biology, chemistry, classics, comparative literature, computer science, East Asian studies (including Chinese and Japanese), economics, English, fine arts, French, geology, German, growth and structure of cities, history, history of art, Italian, mathematics, music, philosophy, physics, political science, psychology, religion, Romance languages, Russian, sociology, and Spanish. Students may minor, arrange an interdepartmental or double major, or design an individual major. Approximately 30 percent of the students major in the sciences or mathematics, 40 percent in the social sciences, and 30 percent in the humanities. Ten percent have double, interdepartmental, or special majors. A 3-2 engineering program with Caltech is available to students who qualify.

Other programs that students may incorporate into their curricula include Africana studies, biochemistry and biophysics, creative writing, dance, education, environmental studies, gender and sexuality studies, Hebrew and Judaic studies, Hispanic and Hispanic American studies, international economic relations, Latin American and Iberian studies, linguistics, mathematical economics, neural and behavioral science, peace and conflict studies, pre-business, prelaw, pre-medicine, and theater.

Academic Programs

The academic experience at Haverford is centered around a deep commitment to the core values of a liberal arts education and its emphasis on the dual pursuit of a breadth of study and in-depth work. While the College mandates that all students take classes across the academic spectrum, there is no core curriculum of specific required courses. Instead, Haverford's system of distribution requirements ensures that students will take at least three classes in each of the divisions of the College (humanities, natural sciences, and social sciences) while allowing them the flexibility to choose courses they find truly interesting. In addition, students must fulfill requirements in foreign language, writing, and quantitative course work. Majors are selected at the end of the sophomore year.

Haverford's small size and exclusive focus on undergraduate education allow students to count on discussion-based classes and research opportunities that students at most colleges would not be able to experience until graduate school. It is common for Haverford students to pursue independent study and approximately half will study abroad, typically during the junior year.

Haverford's three academic centers—the John B. Hurford Humanities Center, the Marian E. Koshland Integrated Natural Sciences Center, and the Center for Peace and Global Citizenship—provide opportunities for integrated learning, bringing students and faculty in related fields together and promoting conversation and collaboration across disciplines. The centers also help to bring an outward view to students' education by sponsoring speaker series, artists in residence, and colloquia on campus.

One of Haverford's distinctive features is its extensive academic and social cooperation with Bryn Mawr College. Students may take courses or major at either school, live on either campus, and eat on either campus. There are more than 2,000 cross-registrations annually. Both colleges jointly operate a weekly newspaper, a drama club, a radio station, an orchestra, social action groups, and intramural sports. A free bus service between the two campuses, which are a mile apart, facilitates cooperative arrangements. Haverford and Bryn Mawr also share library resources with nearby Swarthmore College. All three college libraries are linked electronically, and students have instant access to library resources through the campus computer network. Combined holdings are in excess of 1.5 million volumes.

Off-Campus Programs

Haverford students may take advantage of course offerings at Swarthmore College and the University of Pennsylvania in

addition to courses at Bryn Mawr. Students may also enhance their college experiences by arranging study abroad at one of seventy-six programs overseas or study away at Claremont McKenna, Fisk, Spelman, or Pitzer colleges.

Academic Facilities

Major facilities include the James P. Magill Library (580,000 volumes); computer centers; the Koshland Integrated Natural Sciences Center for the physical sciences, biology, and psychology; the Strawbridge Observatory for astronomy; the Music Center; Gest Center for Cross-Cultural Study of Religion; the Fine Arts Center; Marshall Auditorium; and the Language Learning Center. Academic buildings and dormitories are linked by a campuswide computer network.

Costs

The total approximate costs for 2011–12 were $49,155 for new students and $55,050 for returning students. This consisted of $42,208 for tuition, $12,842 for room and board, and a student association fee of $378. New students have a one-time orientation fee of $200.

Financial Aid

Fifty-four percent of Haverford's students receive financial aid, which is awarded solely based on need. Candidates for Haverford College–funded aid must file the online College Board PROFILE application and the online Free Application for Federal Student Aid (FAFSA), along with other forms. Complete information on forms and deadlines to apply for financial aid at Haverford, including links to the PROFILE and FAFSA, are available at http://www.haverford.edu/financialaid. Early decision applicants must file for financial aid by November 15 and regular decision applicants by January 31. Further details are available on the Web site. Haverford's PROFILE code is 2289, and the FAFSA code is 003274.

Faculty

The student-faculty ratio is 8:1. The faculty devotes its full teaching time to undergraduates. There are no graduate assistants. The regular faculty is supplemented by 90 to 100 scholars, artists, and public figures who visit the College annually under the auspices of seven specially endowed funds.

Student Government

The Students' Association has responsibility for nearly all aspects of student life. The Haverford Honor Code, established and administered by students, has been in existence since 1897. The Honor Code makes possible a climate of trust, concern, and respect, which produces a campus atmosphere conducive to learning and personal growth. The code provides for students' academic and social freedom within the confines of agreed-upon community standards. Exams are not proctored, and the students schedule their own final exams. The code is administered by an elected Honor Council of 16 students, 4 from each class at the College. Each year, the students meet to discuss resolutions and changes in the Honor Code and to approve its adoption. The students also elect several members of the student body to serve on faculty committees and as nonvoting representatives to the Board of Managers (trustees).

Admission Requirements

Admission to Haverford is highly competitive. Admitted students have strong academic records and represent a diversity of backgrounds and interests. The primary criteria for admission are academic and personal qualities as shown by the school record, standardized test scores, extracurricular achievement, and personal recommendations. A combination of qualities that indicate academic and personal promise and potential for growth at Haverford is more significant than any single factor. Of the most recent first-year class, 94 percent rank in the top 10 percent of their high school class, and their SAT scores range from 500 to 800. The mean SAT ranges are 650–750 critical reasoning, 650–750 math, and 660–760 writing. All candidates are required to take the ACT with writing or the SAT Reasoning Test and two SAT Subject Tests. A visit to campus to meet students, observe classes, and have an interview is recommended. Students who live within 150 miles of the campus are strongly recommended to arrange an on-campus interview. A first-choice early decision plan and a deferred matriculation plan are offered.

Admission of transfer students to Haverford is also highly competitive. A limited number of transfer students are accepted each year. Candidates must have completed one full year of college, with a minimum grade point average of 3.0 (B). Campus visits are strongly recommended for those wishing to transfer. A transfer student must spend a minimum of two years at Haverford in order to receive a degree.

Application and Information

The application deadlines for admission are November 15 for early decision candidates, January 15 for regular decision candidates, and March 31 for transfer candidates. Haverford uses the Common Application, which is available in school guidance offices and online. The admission office is open from 9 a.m. to 5 p.m. on weekdays (8:30 a.m. to 4:30 p.m. from June through August) and, during the fall, from 10 a.m. to 1 p.m. on Saturday.

For more information or to arrange an interview or tour appointment, students should contact:

Office of Admission and Financial Aid
Haverford College
370 Lancaster Avenue
Haverford, Pennsylvania 19041-1392
Phone: 610-896-1350
　　　　610-896-1436 (TTY/TDD)
Fax: 610-896-1338
E-mail: admission@haverford.edu (Admission)
　　　　finaid@haverford.edu (Financial Aid)
Web site: http://www.haverford.edu

HAWAI'I PACIFIC UNIVERSITY
HONOLULU, HAWAI'I

The University

Hawai'i Pacific University (HPU) is a private, not-for-profit university with a student population of approximately 8,200. HPU is one of the most culturally diverse universities in America with students from all 50 U.S. states and more than 100 countries. Founded in 1965, HPU prides itself on maintaining strong academic programs, small class sizes, individual attention to students, and a diverse faculty and student population. HPU offers more than 50 acclaimed undergraduate programs and 14 distinguished graduate programs. HPU is recognized as a "Best in the West" college by *Princeton Review* and a "Best Buy" by *Barron's* business magazine. *Bloomberg Businessweek* also rates HPU as the "Best Undergraduate Return on Investment" among any Hawai'i College or University. HPU is accredited by the Western Association of Schools and Colleges, the National League for Nursing Accrediting Commission, and the Council on Social Work Education, and recognized by the Hawaii Commission on Postsecondary Education.

The diversity of the HPU student body stimulates learning about other cultures firsthand, both inside and outside of the classroom. There is no majority population at HPU. Students are encouraged to examine the values, customs, traditions, and principles of others to gain a clearer understanding of their own perspectives. HPU students develop friendships with students from throughout the world and form important connections for success in the global economy of the twenty-first century.

HPU has NCAA Division II intercollegiate sports. Men's athletic programs include baseball, basketball, cross-country, golf, soccer, and tennis. Women's athletics include basketball, cross-country, soccer, softball, tennis, and volleyball. HPU's women's softball team as well as its cheerleading squad and dance team have received national championship titles.

The housing office at HPU offers many services and living options for students. Residence halls with cafeteria service are available on the Hawai'i Loa campus, while off-campus apartments are available in the Honolulu and Waikiki areas for those seeking more independent living arrangements.

Location

Hawai'i Pacific University combines the excitement of an urban downtown campus with the serenity of a residential campus. The urban campus is located in downtown Honolulu, the business and financial center of the Pacific. This campus is composed of eight buildings in the center of Honolulu's business district, and is home to the College of Business Administration and the College of Humanities and Social Sciences. The campus location makes it easy for students to commute to and also find and maintain internship opportunities at neighboring businesses.

Eight miles away, on the windward side of the island, the 135-acre Hawai'i Loa campus is set in the lush foothills of the Ko'olau mountains and is home to the College of Nursing and Health Sciences and the College of Natural and Computational Sciences. The Hawai'i Loa campus has residence halls, dining commons, the Educational Technology Center, a student center, and outdoor recreational facilities, including a soccer field, tennis courts, a softball field, and an exercise room.

HPU is also affiliated with the Oceanic Institute, a 56-acre aquaculture research facility located at Makapu'u Point on the southeastern coast of O'ahu, Hawai'i. At the facility, undergraduate and graduate students are able to get hands-on experience in marine science. All three sites are conveniently linked by a free shuttle.

Majors and Degrees

Hawai'i Pacific University offers programs that lead to the undergraduate degrees of Bachelor of Arts (B.A.), Bachelor of Science (B.S.), Bachelor of Science in Business Administration (B.S.B.A.), Bachelor of Science in Nursing (B.S.N.), and Bachelor of Social Work (B.S.W.).

Undergraduate majors include accounting, advertising/public relations, anthropology, Asian studies, biochemistry, biology, business (general), business economics, chemistry, communication, computer information systems, computer science, diplomacy and military studies, economics, 4+1 secondary education, elementary education, English, entrepreneurial studies, environmental science, environmental studies, finance, health science, history, human resource development, human resource management, humanities, international business, international studies, journalism, justice administration, management, marine biology, marketing, mathematics (concentrations in applied math, engineering (3-2), mathematics education, and pure math), multimedia cinematic production, integrated multimedia, nursing, oceanography, political science, prechiropractic, premedical studies, pre–physical therapy, psychology, public administration, social science, social work, sociology, teaching English to speakers of other languages, and travel industry management.

In addition to the undergraduate programs, HPU offers fourteen graduate programs. The Master of Arts (M.A.) is offered in clinical mental health counseling, communications, diplomacy and military studies, global leadership and sustainable development, human resource management, organizational change, and teaching English as a second language. The Master of Business Administration (M.B.A.) is available in accounting, e-business, economics, finance, human resource management, information systems, international business, management, marketing, and travel industry management. Other graduate programs include Master of Education in Secondary Education and the Master of Education in Elementary Education (M.Ed.), Master of Science in Information Systems (M.S.I.S.), Master of Science in Marine Science (M.S.M.S.), Master of Science in Nursing (M.S.N.), and Master of Social Work (M.S.W.)

Academic Programs

The baccalaureate student must complete at least 124 semester hours of credit. Of these credits, 45 provide the student with a strong foundation in the liberal arts, while the remaining credits are composed of appropriate upper-division classes in the student's major and related areas. The academic year operates on a semester system, with regular fall and spring semesters as well as shorter sessions, including one winter and three summer sessions. By attending the supplemental summer and winter sessions, a student may complete the baccalaureate degree program in three years. A five-year B.S.B.A./M.B.A. program is also available.

Off-Campus Programs

As part of its emphasis on international education and global citizenship, Hawai'i Pacific University offers study-abroad opportunities that complement and enhance students' academic experience. Study-abroad opportunities are available in Australia, Austria, Brazil, China, France, Germany, Great Britain, Italy, Spain, Sweden, Taiwan, Thailand, and other locations. HPU undergraduates and graduates who have completed at least one semester of studies at HPU and intend to complete a degree at HPU are eligible to apply.

The Career Services Center offers a comprehensive education/internship program to further develop students' studies and elevate their career-related position through experience. HPU intertwines academic and cocurricular programs with the world of work so students gain academic credit, work experience, and a salary. HPU students have done co-ops and internships at some of the world's best-known companies and organizations, including American Express Financial Advisors; Deloitte & Touche, LLP; the FBI; Hilton Hotels; Microsoft; Oceanic Institute; Polo Ralph Lauren; and Walt Disney World. The staff at the Career Services Center continues to work with students before and after graduation, assisting with everything from resume writing to job interview preparation.

Academic Facilities

The downtown campus comprises eight buildings in the center of Honolulu's business district. One of these buildings is the HPU Frear Center, which houses state-of-the-art classrooms, a communication lab, and a high-tech information systems classroom. HPU's Meader Library provides a multitude of general and specialized resources, including a business reference collection, a National Endowment for the Humanities (NEH) collection, and many online databases and journals. The circulating book collections support communications, computer studies, education, literature, social sciences, and other curriculum areas. Also available are study areas, group study rooms, computer workstations, and wireless Internet. The Tutoring and Testing Center provides free tutoring in all core subjects. The expanded downtown computer lab includes more than 420 computers for student use.

On the suburban and residential Hawai'i Loa campus, academic life revolves around the Amos N. Starr and Juliette Montague Cooke Academic Center (AC). The AC houses classrooms; organic chemistry, nuclear magnetic resonance, and regular laboratories; faculty and staff offices; a theater; an art gallery; and the Atherton Library, which includes circulating and reference book collections in the areas of art, history, marine science, nursing, and Hawai'i and the Pacific. In addition, the library provides access to electronic books (e-books), databases, study rooms, IBM computers, and wireless Internet. Computers are also available for library research, e-mail, and word processing.

HPU is also affiliated with the Oceanic Institute, a major research center specializing in marine biology, marine aquaculture, biotechnology, and ocean resource management. It is located on a 56-acre site at Makapu'u Point on the windward coast of O'ahu, Hawai'i. Learning, internship, and research opportunities abound in this hands-on learning environment.

Costs

For the 2011–12 academic year, tuition was $16,510 for most majors, while books, health insurance, and other expenses cost approximately $3190. Tuition for marine science majors was $19,400, and tuition for junior- or senior-year nursing majors was $24,070. The cost to live in on-campus residence halls or off-campus apartments is comparable; room and board were $12,230 for a double occupancy room. There is an additional $500 refundable security deposit required for residence halls and off-campus apartments.

Financial Aid

HPU offers most forms of federal financial aid, including student grant and loan programs, as well as loans for parents of dependent students. Over 60 percent of the University's students benefit from federal financial aid programs or a wide range of institutional scholarships. Students should complete the Free Application for Federal Student Aid (FAFSA) to be considered for federal aid programs. While aid can be awarded throughout the academic year, students should complete the application prior to the March 1 priority deadline to be considered for all available funding. Current financial aid and scholarship information is available at http://www.hpu.edu/financialaid.

Faculty

HPU faculty members are renowned for the personal interest they take in each of their students. HPU is proud to offer more than 500 full- and part-time faculty members with outstanding academic and business credentials from around the world, giving HPU students access to a world's worth of knowledge and experiences. A vast majority of HPU faculty members hold the highest degrees in their fields. The student-faculty ratio is 15:1, and the average class size is less than 25.

Student Government

HPU students can join one of the more than 50 student clubs and organizations; run for office in the Associated Students of Hawai'i Pacific University (ASHPU), the University's governing body; participate in Army or Air Force ROTC; write for the student newspaper, *Kalamalama;* edit the school's literary journal, *Hawai'i Pacific Review;* or join HPU's stage and pep band or the International Choral and Vocal Ensemble.

A variety of on-campus activities and events are organized for students by the Student Life Office, including Movie on the Mall, Music on the Mall, intramural sports tournaments, and recreational activities. Annual events include Club Carnival, Welcome Week, Da Freakshow, Halloween Hoopla, and Pacific Bowl.

Admission Requirements

Hawai'i Pacific University seeks students who are motivated and show academic promise. The Admissions Office requires that applicants complete and forward the admission application and their high school transcripts. Transfer students should also submit college transcripts. SAT and/or ACT scores should be submitted if these scores are not posted in their transcripts. First-time freshmen are expected to have a minimum GPA of 2.5 (on a 4.0 scale) in college-preparatory courses. HPU recommends that students complete 4 years of English, 4 years of history or social science, 3 years of math, and 2 years of science. Transfer students with 24 or more postsecondary credits are required to have a GPA of 2.0 or above. For students with less than 24 credits, a combination of college and high school GPA is used.

The marine science and environmental science programs require a GPA of 3.0 or above and 3 years of science, including biology and chemistry (physics is recommended), as well as mathematics through trigonometry (calculus is recommended). Transfer students must demonstrate ability in science and math at the college level. Students not meeting the above criteria are encouraged to enroll at HPU without declaring a major to demonstrate the ability to do college-level work in science and math.

Application and Information

Candidates are notified of admission decisions on a rolling basis, usually within two weeks of receipt of application materials. Early entrance and deferred entrance are available.

For further information and for application materials, contact:

Office of Admissions
Hawai'i Pacific University
1164 Bishop Street, Suite 200
Honolulu, Hawai'i 96813
Phone: 808-544-0238
   866-CALL-HPU (toll-free in U.S. and Canada)
Fax: 808-544-1136
E-mail: admissions@hpu.edu
Web site: http://www.hpu.edu/petersons

HPU faculty are renowned for the personal interest they take in each and every one of their students. This happens naturally at HPU because of their student-centered approach, small class sizes, low student to faculty ratio, and emphasis on one-on-one guidance.

HICKEY COLLEGE
ST. LOUIS, MISSOURI

The College

Founded in 1933 by Dr. Margaret Hickey, Hickey College has grown from a business school to a college offering education and experience in the fields of accounting; administrative support; applied management; computer applications, networking, and programming; culinary arts; graphic design; legal administrative assistant; medical administrative assistant; paralegal studies; and veterinary studies.

In keeping with her feeling that "We must identify ourselves with public responsibility," Dr. Hickey developed a unique educational program based on thorough training and personality development combined with careful placement in positions best suited to the students' interests and abilities. While holding to Dr. Hickey's philosophy, the faculty and staff continuously strive to move toward the challenges of the future. The continuing success of Hickey College has been largely due to a highly motivated student population, a staff of dedicated teachers and personnel, and the respect and acceptance of the business community.

For the last reporting year (2011), Hickey College's graduation rate was 85 percent. This high rate reflects the College's committed faculty, hands-on curriculum, and accelerated programs.

Some students live in the College's student residence facilities, allowing them to make new friends and round out their Hickey College experience. The primary residence facility for students is West Pointe Apartments, located near the main campus. Students choosing to live in the residence facilities reside in furnished town houses. Each two-story town house offers two bedrooms, 1½ bathrooms, living area, kitchen, washer/dryer, and a patio. Students enjoy access to the clubhouse at West Pointe Apartments, which has the following amenities: Wi-Fi, two computer labs, a workout facility, three pools, and a spacious lounge for relaxing or watching television with friends.

Campus activities vary each year, but students may work together on fundraising initiatives, attend field trips related to their programs of study, and participate in holiday celebrations. An admissions representative can provide more specific information about recent activities.

Hickey College is accredited by the Accrediting Council for Independent Colleges and Schools to award diplomas, associate degrees, and bachelor's degrees. The Accrediting Council for Independent Colleges and Schools is listed as a nationally recognized accrediting agency by the United States Department of Education and is recognized by the Council for Higher Education Accreditation: 750 First Street NE, Suite 980, Washington, D.C. 20002; phone: 202-336-6780.

The Hickey College Veterinary Technician Program is accredited by the Committee on Veterinary Technician Education and Activities (CVTEA) of the American Veterinary Medical Association (AVMA).

Location

Hickey College is located at 940 West Port Plaza Drive, 15 minutes from downtown St. Louis, Missouri. The location offers convenient access to St. Louis' many cultural and recreational facilities. Among these are museums, botanical gardens, planetariums, theaters, cultural exhibitions, sporting events, parks, and public libraries.

Hickey College Veterinary Technician students attend classes at the Vet Tech Institute at Hickey College, 2780 North Lindbergh Boulevard, while the College's culinary arts students attend classes at the Culinary Institute of St. Louis at Hickey College, 2700 North Lindbergh Boulevard, both in St. Louis.

Academic Programs

Hickey College offers a wide choice of programs, each designed to prepare students for a particular career. Relatively short, yet remarkably comprehensive, these programs are carefully planned to provide the best education possible in the field of the student's choice. Hickey College offers seventeen specialized programs during the day. Students may select from nine major areas of study: accounting; administrative assistant; computer applications, programming, and network management; culinary arts; graphic design; legal administrative assistant; medical administrative assistant; paralegal studies; and veterinary technician studies.

Hickey College's evening education division offers a Bachelor of Applied Management. The program combines the technical and business-related courses completed in a Hickey College diploma or associate degree program.

Off-Campus Programs

Externships are available for students who choose to enroll into the culinary specialized associate degree, paralegal studies, or veterinary technician programs. The externship for these programs is part of the curriculum.

Academic Facilities

Hickey College provides a business atmosphere in an educational setting. The facilities are furnished with the latest instructional equipment. The school offers a professional learning and growing environment for today's career-minded students. Hickey College is equipped to accommodate the handicapped.

The general academic space contains a resource library and classrooms. Six of the classrooms are equipped with microcomputers, and the remainder is furnished as lecture rooms.

The Vet Tech Institute contains a learning resource center equipped with microcomputers as well as seven lecture/laboratory classrooms, which include space equipped with long tables and rolling chairs, a veterinary technician laboratory, a kennel, a radiography facility, a surgery suite, and a surgery preparation area.

The Culinary Institute of St. Louis at Hickey College building contains a learning resource center, five kitchens, five lecture classrooms, and one classroom equipped with microcomputers.

Costs

For calendar year 2012, all programs are $6780 per semester. The final half-semester of the 4½-semester veterinary technician program is $3390. Lab fees for culinary arts programs are $140 per semester. Residence facilities fees are $2920 per semester. Textbook and supplies will vary from semester to semester. These charges will range from $840 to $1300 per semester. The actual charges will be disclosed each academic year as the financial plan is completed.

Financial Aid

A variety of financial plans are available to assist qualified students in securing a business education, regardless of financial status or family income level. These plans include a combination of student loans, grants, scholarships, and payment plans. The variety of available plans affords flexibility in choosing the one best suited for a specific need. Hickey College offers individual financial planning sessions for each student and family beginning with the completion of the Free Application for Federal Student Aid. Information about these plans is available from the Admissions or Financial Aid Office.

Faculty

At Hickey College, the majority of classes are taught by faculty members teaching full-time. Having such a high proportion of full-time teachers is unusual and reflects the College's mission to provide a high-quality education. Hickey College's faculty members are committed to the students and the College. Students are the priority—faculty members take pride in encouraging and challenging students and make it a point to be available for help and direction. Although class size varies, it usually averages 30 students. This enables the faculty members to get to know the interests and goals of each student.

Admission Requirements

The basic requirement for admission to Hickey College is graduation from a valid high school, private school, or equivalent (GED). Applicants are admitted for enrollment on the basis of previous scholastic records as evidenced by a transcript of work completed in high school or college. Previous training in business subjects is generally not required.

Application and Information

Potential students should call or write the Admissions Department to request an application form. To apply for enrollment, the student should complete the application form and submit it with the $50 application fee to the Director of Admissions, Hickey College, 940 West Port Plaza, St. Louis, Missouri 63146. Potential students may also apply online at www.hickeycollege.edu.

For more information, contact:

Director of Admissions
Hickey College
940 West Port Plaza
St. Louis, Missouri 63146
Web site: www.hickeycollege.edu

Hickey College offers a unique educational program based on thorough training, personality development, and placement in areas best-suited to each student's interests and abilities.

HILLSDALE COLLEGE
HILLSDALE, MICHIGAN

The College

Hillsdale College is a private, independent, nonsectarian institution of higher learning founded in 1844 by men and women who described themselves as "grateful to God for the inestimable blessings" resulting from civil and religious liberty and as "believing that the diffusion of learning is essential to the perpetuity of those blessings." The College has maintained institutional independence since its founding by refusing to accept aid from or control by federal authorities. Far-reaching private support from a national constituency has enabled Hillsdale to continue its trusteeship of the intellectual and spiritual inheritance derived from the Judeo-Christian faith and Greco-Roman culture.

The undergraduate enrollment for fall 2011 was 1,400, of whom 48 percent were men. The College draws students from forty-seven states and eight other countries. Approximately 40 percent of students are from Michigan. The entering freshman class in 2011 had an average high school grade point average of 3.76 and mean ACT (29) and SAT (1980) scores well above national averages. Hillsdale students are housed in dormitories, fraternity and sorority houses, and various off-campus dwellings. Single and double rooms are available on campus; there are no coed dormitories. Each College-owned residence hall is supervised by a resident director and resident advisers. All freshmen (except commuters) are required to live on campus; upperclass students seeking to live off campus must apply to the dean of men or dean of women for this privilege.

Hillsdale's Charger athletes compete in 12 intercollegiate NCAA Division II varsity sports as part of the Great Lakes Intercollegiate Athletic Conference (GLIAC). In the past 20 years, the College has produced 196 athletic and academic All-Americans, 28 conference champions, and 18 teams that have finished tenth or better nationally. An active intramural program is also available. Four national fraternities, three national sororities, and more than 100 other social, academic, spiritual, and service organizations provide Hillsdale students with a diverse array of cocurricular opportunities. A resident drama troupe and dance company, a bagpipe and drum corps, a concert choir, and chamber chorale, a jazz program with big band and combos, instrumental chamber ensembles from string quartets to percussion ensemble, and a College-community orchestra and band constitute the College's performing arts organizations.

Special student services provided by the College include career planning and placement counseling, academic advising and tutoring, and a health service staffed by a physician and a resident nurse.

Location

Hillsdale College is located amidst the hills, dales, and lakes of south-central Michigan. The Indiana and Ohio turnpikes are each 30 minutes away, and the College is within close reach of such metropolitan areas as Detroit, Chicago, Cleveland, Toledo, Ft. Wayne, and Indianapolis. The town of Hillsdale is a county seat with a population of 10,000. Stores, churches, restaurants, and movie theaters are all within walking distance of the campus.

Majors and Degrees

Hillsdale awards Bachelor of Arts and Bachelor of Science degrees in accounting, art, biochemistry, biology, chemistry, classical studies, computational mathematics, economics, education, English, exercise science, financial management, French, German, Greek, history, Latin, marketing/management, mathematics, music, philosophy, physical education, physics, politics, psychology, religion, Spanish, speech, sport management, sport psychology, and theater. Interdisciplinary majors in American studies, Christian studies, comparative literature, European studies, international studies in business and foreign language, political economy, and sociology and social thought are also available. Preprofessional programs are offered in allied health services (including optometry, physical therapy, nursing, and medical technology), dentistry, engineering, environmental sciences, forestry, law, medicine, osteopathy, theology, and veterinary medicine.

Academic Programs

Hillsdale operates on a two-semester schedule, with the fall term beginning in late August and ending in mid-December and the spring term beginning in mid-January and ending in mid-May. Two 3-week summer sessions are also offered.

The College believes that a sound classical liberal arts education includes study in the humanities, natural sciences, and social sciences, and each student is required to complete a structured core of courses in these areas. All students declare a major by the end of the sophomore year. To graduate, students must complete a minimum 124 hours of course work and fulfill the requirements of at least one major field. The B.A. program includes a foreign language proficiency requirement. The B.S. program requires additional studies in mathematics and the natural sciences.

The honors program enables exceptionally talented students interested in an interdisciplinary community of learning to develop their intellectual potential through an accelerated college core and honors seminars in the junior and senior years. Discussions, guest lectures, and travel opportunities contribute to the social cohesiveness of the group. All honors students complete a senior thesis on an interdisciplinary topic of their choosing.

The Center for Constructive Alternatives conducts four weeklong symposia during the academic year and is one of the largest college lecture series in America. These programs, with themes ranging from historical to political, business, science, and the arts, bring to the campus distinguished scholars and public figures of national and international renown. All students are required to enroll in two full seminars for credit prior to graduation, one in the first two years and one in the final two years of the curriculum.

Off-Campus Programs

For over thirty-five years, the Washington Hillsdale Internship Program (WHIP) has provided students the opportunity to participate in full-time, academically intensive internships in the nation's capital. The program has been significantly bolstered with the 2008 establishment of the Hillsdale College Allan P. Kirby, Jr. Center for Constitutional Studies and Citizenship in Washington, D.C. Past interns and fellows have been placed in locations as challenging and rewarding as the U.S. House of Representatives, the U.S. Senate, the White House, various think tanks including the Heritage Foundation, news and media outlets, national security agencies, lobbying firms, international trade and relations organizations, and private sector companies.

Through the College's affiliations with the Center for Medieval and Renaissance Studies and the Oxford Study Abroad Program, Hillsdale students are able to study abroad for a summer or a year at one of the more than thirty colleges of Oxford University. Hillsdale offers a summer business program in cooperation with Regent's College in London, England, and the opportunity to study at the University of St. Andrews in St. Andrews, Scotland. Science students benefit from Hillsdale's 685-acre field research laboratory in northern Michigan, as well as from a marine biology program in the Florida Keys, internship opportunities with the Omaha Zoo, and a summer research program in South Africa. Foreign language students frequently study abroad in Argentina, France, Germany, and Spain. Qualified individual students who wish to study in another country for a semester or a year are assisted by their faculty adviser and the registrar in planning a program that enables them to gain academic credit as well as take full advantage of their experience.

Academic Facilities

The Hillsdale College Mossey Library is a three-floor facility with a collection of more than 642,000 volumes. In addition to the main study

and research collections, the Library also contains a number of rare and special holdings, including the Ludwig von Mises, Russell Kirk, Richardson Heritage, and Richard Weaver collections. Connected to other Michigan libraries through MelCat, and with college libraries nationwide via interlibrary loan, students have access to most any material necessary for on-campus research. Numerous individual study areas and group study rooms are available for students, as well as computer research terminals.

Lane and Kendall Halls at the front of campus serve as the primary academic facilities in the humanities and contain classroom space and faculty offices, as well as a special laboratory for experimental psychology. The Strosacker Science Center houses the departments of biology, chemistry, and physics. The Joseph H. Moss Family Laboratory Wing, completed in 2008, is a 17,000-square-foot addition that includes a microbiology/cell biology lab, anatomy/physiology lab with human cadaver access, conservation genetics lab, water lab, greenhouse, and organic/general chemistry labs. The 32,000-square-foot Herbert Henry Dow Science Building provides additional classrooms, research laboratories, animal rooms, and a computer lab. The Mary Randall Preschool is a circular laboratory school in which nursery school children are taught by students specializing in early childhood education and psychology. Experts in the field have called this building "a model for the nation." The Hillsdale Academy, a K–12 private model school, provides additional opportunities for classroom observation.

The Roche Sports Complex is a facility available to varsity athletes and the general student body alike. The building houses the 60,000-square-foot Jesse Philips Arena, which features a six-lane, 200-meter running track and basketball/volleyball court. The building also houses the John "Jack" McAvoy Natatorium for swimming and diving, an exercise physiology and sports medicine facility, three racquetball courts, extensive locker room space, and a weight/fitness room. Adjacent is the 7,000-seat capacity Frank "Muddy" Waters Stadium, which features an artificial surface football field; all-weather, Olympic-quality eight-lane running track; outdoor tennis courts; and fields for soccer, baseball, and women's softball.

The Sage Center for the Arts is home to the departments of art, theater, and speech. This 47,000-square-foot facility contains studios, classroom space, an exhibition gallery, a prop- and scene-construction shop, a sound studio, graphics lab, black box theatre, and the Markel Auditorium, a 353-seat performance hall (with orchestra pit). Completed in 2003, the 32,809-square-foot Howard Music Hall houses office, studio, classroom, rehearsal, and performance space for the John E. N. and Dede Howard Department of Music. Notable features include the McNamara Rehearsal Hall, Conrad Recital Hall, and studio space for percussion and jazz studies. Lower-level practice rooms are available to students during business hours without reservation.

Dedicated in January 2008, the 53,000-square-foot Grewcock Student Union is the center of student life. The two-story structure houses the cafeteria, bookstore, student mail center, offices for student activities and publications, a lounge with a 100-inch flat screen television, a formal lounge and conference room, AJ's Café, and a game area. The entire building is wireless, and any Hillsdale student can check out a laptop at the main desk.

Costs

Annual tuition for the 2012–13 academic year is $21,390, room is $4290, board is $4350, and mandatory fees are $540. Books, supplies, and personal expenses (including travel, recreation, and clothing) are estimated at $3000 per year.

Financial Aid

Financial aid at Hillsdale is available in many forms. Academic scholarships are awarded on a competitive basis, regardless of financial need, to students who rank in the top 10 percent of their high school class and have standardized test scores in the top 10 percent according to national test norms. The priority deadline for academic scholarship consideration is January 1. The application for admission also serves as the Hillsdale application for merit-based aid. Athletic scholarships are available on a competitive basis in men's baseball and football; men's and women's basketball, track, and cross-country; and women's swimming and volleyball. The departments of art and music also award a select number of scholarships based on strength of portfolio/audition.

To apply for aid on the basis of financial need, students are required to file Hillsdale's Confidential Family Financial Statement (CFFS) in January or February of the year of prospective enrollment at Hillsdale. Grants and loans are available from the College.

Faculty

The faculty consists of 124 full-time members. No classes are taught by graduate students. The size and closeness of the College community enable personal attention and faculty mentorship inside the classroom and during office visits after class. Each student has a faculty adviser for core and major coursework who directs the program of study and provides academic and career counseling. Hillsdale's faculty considers teaching their first priority. Many faculty members also engage in research and scholarly writing, supported by summer and sabbatical leaves funded by the College, and are often invited to comment on the national scene in lecture programs and media outlets.

Student Government

Hillsdale's student government and campus organizations offer students special opportunities to develop leadership skills that enrich both their collegiate experience and lives after graduation. The governing organization of the student body is the Student Federation, which is composed of 18 elected representatives. This group funds student organizations, sponsors all-College entertainment, and acts upon matters of concern to the student community.

Admission Requirements

Admission is a privilege extended to students who will benefit from, and contribute to, the academic, social, and spiritual environments of the College. Important determinants for admission are intellectual curiosity, ambition, leadership, and volunteerism. Accordingly, grade point average, test scores, class rank, strength of curriculum, extracurricular activities, interviews, self-evaluations, writing samples in the form of two essays, and recommendations are all reviewed carefully and are important in the evaluation process. An admissions interview is strongly encouraged. Although some factors are necessarily more important than others, seldom is any single criterion, however important, decisive.

Transfer students must submit the standard application, including the high school record, SAT or ACT scores, transcripts from all colleges previously attended, and a transfer form from the dean of students of the most recent college attended. Applications by transfers are evaluated similarly to nontransfers.

Candidates for admission from other countries follow the regular entrance procedures. Students who come from a non-English-speaking country must demonstrate proficiency in English by satisfactory performance on the Test of English as a Foreign Language (TOEFL) or the Michigan Test of English Proficiency or at an ESL Center.

Application and Information

Students may apply to Hillsdale College any time after the completion of the junior year of high school. A formal application includes a completed application form accompanied by a nonrefundable fee of $35 (free if submitted online) and all required credentials. Application plans include early decision (November 15), early action (December 15), and regular decision (February 15). Hillsdale College has been distinguished since its founding in 1844 by voluntarily adhering to a nondiscriminatory policy regarding race, religion, sex, and national or ethnic origin—long before the government began regulating such matters.

All records and forms should be mailed to:

Admissions Office
Hillsdale College
33 East College Street
Hillsdale, Michigan 49242-1298
Phone: 517-607-2327
Fax: 517-607-2223
E-mail: admissions@hillsdale.edu
Web site: http://www.hillsdale.edu

HOFSTRA UNIVERSITY
HEMPSTEAD, NEW YORK

The University

Hofstra University is the largest private college on Long Island, New York. Since its founding as a commuter college in 1935, Hofstra has evolved into a nationally and internationally renowned university that continues to achieve further recognition as an institution of academic excellence. That's why Hofstra is included in The Princeton Review's Best 373 Colleges (2011) and Best Northeastern Colleges, *U.S. News & World Report's* "America's Best Business Schools" (2010), and *Fiske Guide to Colleges* (2011) and is ranked by *Forbes* magazine.

Hofstra continually aspires to reach new heights and offer its students even more. The Hofstra North Shore-LIJ School of Medicine at Hofstra University welcomed its inaugural class in August 2011, and it strives to become a leader in medical education. The University recently established a School of Engineering and Applied Science with an innovative co-op and cross-disciplinary education program.

Hofstra's diverse and driven student body of more than 11,000 can choose from about 140 undergraduate and 150 graduate program options in liberal arts and sciences, business, engineering, communication, teacher education, law, health and human services, and honors studies. Hofstra offers more than 100 dual-degree programs, giving students the opportunity to earn both a graduate and undergraduate degree in less time than if each degree was pursued separately. More information about Hofstra's program options is available at hofstra.edu/academics or hofstra.edu/dualdegree.

Hofstra hosts more than 500 cultural events each year, drawing together scholars, business leaders, authors, celebrities, health-care professionals, politicians, and journalists from across the nation and around the world. These events help foster that connection between in-classroom work and extracurricular interests we know students are looking for. In addition, Hofstra offers 17 intercollegiate athletic programs that compete at the NCAA Division I level; and more than 200 academic, fraternal/sororal, media, multicultural, performance, pre-professional, religious, social, social/political, and sports clubs and organizations.

Each year, the University is visited by more than 400 employers who recognize how much Hofstra students have to offer. In addition to the plentiful networking opportunities on campus, students may choose to do an internship at a top company on Long Island or in New York City, thus gaining critical work experience that will give them an edge in a competitive job market.

At Hofstra, students join a network of almost 121,000 graduates. Outstanding alumni include Academy Award–winning film director and producer Francis Ford Coppola; best-selling author Nelson DeMille; vascular surgeon Dr. Donna Mendes; president of the New York Yankees Randy Levine; from *Everybody Loves Raymond*, creator, executive producer, and writer Philip Rosenthal and actress Monica Horan; president of H. J. Kalikow & Company and former MTA chairman Peter S. Kalikow; actresses Lainie Kazan and Susan Sullivan; and New York State Comptroller Thomas P. DiNapoli.

At Hofstra, it's all about choice. Students may choose to live and learn in one of the 37 residence halls, each with a unique flair, community, and life of its own. Hofstra also offers living/learning communities, which give students the opportunity to live with many of the same students they are in classes with, and well as students who share the same passion for political and civic issues, health sciences, and the arts. In addition, Hofstra students can choose from 20 on-campus dining facilities.

Location

Hofstra University, which blends longstanding traditions with twenty-first-century resources, is home to both ivy-covered classrooms buildings and modern, elegant facilities. On the vibrant campus, students will find exceptional and technologically advanced classrooms, six theaters, a state-of-the-art fitness center, an accredited museum, modern athletic facilities, and an impressive 10-floor library that offers 1.2 million print volumes and 24/7 electronic access to more than 95,000 journals and books.

In addition to the myriad opportunities available on Hofstra's campus, students have easy access to, and benefit from, the academic, cultural, media and career opportunities of nearby New York City. Students take advantage of theaters, museums, concerts and professional sports, as well as the many beneficial internship opportunities the city offers.

Majors and Degrees

The Bachelor of Arts (B.A.) is awarded in African studies, American studies, anthropology, art history, Asian studies, audio/video/film, biology, chemistry, Chinese, Chinese studies, classics, comparative literature and languages, computer science, criminology, dance, drama, early childhood and childhood education (with dual major in another discipline), early childhood education (with dual major in another discipline), economics, elementary education (with dual major in another discipline), engineering science, English, English education, film studies and production, fine arts, foreign language education (French, German, Italian, Russian, Spanish), French, geography, geology, German, global studies, Hebrew, history, Ibero-American studies, Italian, Jewish studies, journalism, labor studies, Latin, Latin American and Caribbean studies, liberal arts, linguistics, mass media studies, math education (with a dual major in another discipline), mathematical economics, mathematics, music, philosophy, physics, political science, pre-health, psychology, public relations, radio production, religion, Russian, science education (biology, chemistry, Earth science, physics), social studies education (with a dual major in another discipline), sociology, Spanish, speech communication and rhetorical studies, speech-language-hearing sciences, urban ecology, video/television, and women's studies.

The Bachelor of Business Administration (B.B.A.) is awarded in accounting, business, entrepreneurship, finance, information technology, international business, legal studies in business, management, marketing, and supply chain management.

The Bachelor of Science (B.S.) is offered in applied physics, athletic training, biochemistry, biology, business economics, chemistry, community health, computer engineering, computer science, computer science and mathematics (dual degree), electrical engineering, environmental resources, exercise specialist studies, fine arts, forensic science, geology, health education, health science, industrial engineering, mathematical business economics, mathematics, mechanical engineering, music, physics, pre-medical, urban ecology, video/television, video/television and business, and video/television and film.

The Bachelor of Science in Education (B.S.Ed.) is offered with specializations in dance, fine arts, music, and physical education.

The Bachelor of Engineering (B.E.) is offered in engineering science with specializations in biomedical engineering and civil engineering.

The Bachelor of Fine Arts (B.F.A.) is awarded in theater arts with specializations in performance and production.

Combined degrees offered include Bachelor of Arts/Juris Doctor (B.A./J.D.) in engineering science/law, B.S./M.S. in physician assistant studies, B.S./M.S. and B.A./M.S. in computer science, B.S./M.D. and B.A./M.D. through the Hofstra North Shore–LIJ School of Medicine at Hofstra University, and various B.B.A./M.S. programs through the Frank G. Zarb School of Business.

Academic Programs

Requirements for graduation vary among schools and majors. A liberal arts core curriculum is an integral part of all areas of concentration. The University calendar is organized on a traditional semester system, including one January session and three summer sessions.

Hofstra offers innovative programs designed to meet the needs of its diverse student body. These include Honors College, Legal

Education Accelerated Program (LEAP), Hofstra 4+4 Program, Living/Learning Communities, and First-Year Connections.

Hofstra University Honors College provides a rich academic and extracurricular experience for students who show both the potential and desire to excel. Honors students can elect to study in any of the University's undergraduate programs and are involved in all fields of advanced study, including premedicine, prelaw, engineering, business, communication and media arts, humanities, and social sciences.

The Legal Education Accelerated Program allows students to earn both a B.A. and a J.D. in just six years.

The Hofstra 4+4 Program allows students to earn both degrees (B.S.-B.A./M.D) in eight years through the Hofstra North Shore-LIJ School of Medicine at Hofstra University.

First-Year Connections, an integrated academic and social program, helps first-year students connect with one another as well as all the resources provided and opportunities offered at the University. The program, which offers seminars and clusters, features small classes taught by distinguished faculty in areas of interest ranging from architecture to writing. These courses introduce students to the intellectual and social life of the University and satisfy the general education requirements for all majors.

In the Living/Learning Communities, the learning experience is not limited to the four walls of the classroom, or even to the borders of the campus. Here, students are exposed to environments that are intellectually stimulating, supportive, and conducive to building lasting friendships and a memorable first-year college experience. These living/learning communities are associated with several first-year clusters and seminars, giving students the opportunity to live with many of the same students they are in class with, as well as students who share the same passion for political and civic issues, health science issues, or the arts.

Off-Campus Programs

Hofstra extends learning beyond the classroom through active internship programs and varied study-abroad opportunities. The internship program takes advantage of the proximity of New York City, allowing students to gain on-the-job experience in areas such as finance, business, media, advertising, and entertainment. Through study abroad programs in Europe, Asia, South America, and other locations, students can explore the world while earning college credits. More information is available at hofstra.edu/studyabroad.

Academic Facilities

Hofstra's students live and learn on a campus that is home to state-of-the-art facilities and resources. C. V. Starr Hall, home to the Frank G. Zarb School of Business, features the Martin B. Greenberg Trading Room, which has the largest number of Bloomberg Professional terminals among all academic trading rooms in the United States and around the world. The School of Communication's Dempster Hall contains one of the largest broadcast facilities in the northeastern United States as well as a converged newsroom and multimedia classroom. Plus, Hofstra students benefit from real-world experience at the on-campus radio station, WRHU 88.7 FM (Radio Hofstra University), which has a 35-mile broadcast range and is webcast at wrhu.org. Hagedorn Hall, where the School of Education, Health and Human Services is located, features a technologically robust learning environment complete with interactive whiteboards, computer-driven instructor stations and wireless communication.

The David S. Mack Sports and Exhibition Complex, a 93,000-square-foot facility, is home to the Hofstra Pride men's and women's basketball teams and wrestling, and is also the site for events such as commencements, exhibitions, trade shows, televised political events, and concerts. Other recreational and athletic facilities include an indoor, Olympic-sized swimming pool, and various athletic fields.

Costs

The annual cost of tuition and fees at Hofstra University for 2011–12 for a full-time undergraduate student was $34,150. The housing and dining plan was approximately $11,650. Books and supplies cost approximately $1000; personal expenses and transportation generally amount to $3056. For the full tuition and fees schedule, students should visit hofstra.edu/tuition.

Financial Aid

To help students achieve their educational goals, Hofstra University offers several financial-aid options. For 2011–12, Hofstra awarded more than $76 million in merit- and need-based financial aid. The average award for first-year students was $15,268. More than 1,400, or 86 percent, of first-year students received merit-based scholarships from Hofstra University. About 91 percent of all Hofstra students received some form of financial aid, including more than 94 percent of first-year students. For detailed information, students should visit hofstra.edu/FinancialAid.

Faculty

Hofstra's hardworking, ambitious students are taught by Guggenheim Fellows and Fulbright scholars; Emmy Award recipients; prize-winning scientists; leaders in business, education and the health sciences; and knowledgeable and insightful thinkers. The 1,114 faculty members, of whom 525 are full-time, are experts in their fields and are dedicated to and focused on providing the foundation and tools students need to succeed. Hofstra's faculty members affirm the value of education—92 percent of the full-time faculty members hold the highest degree attainable in their fields. Plus, students at Hofstra learn from faculty members—not graduate students. With an average undergraduate class size of 21 and a student-to-faculty ratio of 14-to-1, Hofstra students are challenged and encouraged to debate, question, research, discuss, and think critically in an open and broad-minded learning environment.

Student Government

The Student Government Association is a student-run governing body that supervises and coordinates all student activities and serves as a liaison with the faculty and administration. The Student Government Association sends representatives to the committees of the University Senate. A judicial board has responsibility for promoting justice in the conduct of student affairs.

Admission Requirements

Hofstra is a competitive institution that seeks to enroll students who demonstrate academic ability, intellectual curiosity, and the motivation to be successful and contribute to the campus community. Careful consideration is given to a student's high school record, types of courses taken, SAT or ACT scores, letters of recommendation, extracurricular involvement, and the personal essay. The most competitive applicants will have followed a rigorous college preparatory curriculum within their high school and will have taken advantage of honors and advanced placement level courses where appropriate. The Office of Admission prefers to see a high school curriculum, which includes 4 years of English, 3 to 4 years of social studies, 2 to 3 years of foreign language, 3 years of mathematics, and 3 years of science. Prospective engineering majors need at least 4 years of mathematics, 1 year of chemistry, and 1 year of physics. Campus visits are strongly recommended. Hofstra accepts applications from first-year, transfer, and international students.

The University offers an early action plan for students whose first choice is Hofstra. There are two early action periods: when submitted by November 15, notification is made to the student by December 15; when submitted by December 15, notification is made to the student by January 15. Students applying for regular decision are considered on a rolling basis.

First-year applicants must submit an application, $70 application fee, high school transcript, SAT or ACT scores, essay, and letter of recommendation. Hofstra accepts applications via mail or online and participates in the Common Application; the online application fee is $60.

For more information, students should contact:

Application and Information

Hofstra University
Office of Undergraduate Admission
100 Hofstra University
Hempstead, New York 11549-1000
Phone: 516-463-6700
      800-HOFSTRA (toll-free)
Fax: 516-463-5100
E-mail: admission@hofstra.edu
Web site: http://www.hofstra.edu/admission

HOLY FAMILY UNIVERSITY
PHILADELPHIA, PENNSYLVANIA

The University

Holy Family University is a fully accredited, Catholic, private, coeducational, four-year university located in Northeast Philadelphia's residential Torresdale neighborhood. Founded in 1954 by the Sisters of the Holy Family of Nazareth, Holy Family provides liberal arts and professional programs for more than 2,100 undergraduate students through day, evening, and summer sessions.

From the moment students arrive on campus, they are being prepared to make an impact. From classroom immersion and co-op experiences to service opportunities and Division II athletics, students learn and grow in an outcome-oriented environment that offers countless opportunities to get involved and engaged.

Holy Family University works to extend the learning experience beyond the classroom to create a holistic education that fosters a student's personal development. The University provides various residential housing experiences, including a traditional dormitory, apartment-style units, and the state-of-the-art Stevenson Lane Residence, which offers suite-style living with well thought-out design and amenities that reflect contemporary campus housing trends. All of these options are meant to help guide students through their own personal development within a supportive community.

Upon graduating, Holy Family students are ready for the next level of impact. They arrive with bold dreams, and they leave for careers in teaching, nursing, science, law, business, and more. The University offers a highly supportive learning environment that lifts and empowers students and values their aspirations. Holy Family is a place where dreams of every kind are honored, encouraged, and pursued with a passion.

Location

The University is based at its Northeast Philadelphia campus, which serves as home of the traditional undergraduate program. Located less than a mile from Bucks County, Holy Family offers the benefits of a big city in a quiet, park-like, suburban setting. The campus offers student housing for full-time undergraduates. With easy access to regional rail lines, city bus routes, and nearby expressways, students can experience all that Philadelphia has to offer.

Majors and Degrees

Holy Family offers undergraduate courses leading to the Bachelor of Arts (B.A.) and Bachelor of Science (B.S.) degrees. Majors include accounting, art (with tracks in graphic design, pre-art therapy, and studio art), biochemistry, biology, biology-medical technology, communications, computer management information systems, criminal justice, education (early childhood pre K–4; special education PK–8; middle level 4–8 with concentrations in language arts and reading, mathematics, science, and social studies; secondary education with certifications in art, biology, English, history/social studies, and mathematics), English/literature, finance, fire science and public safety administration (transfers only), history, interdisciplinary humanities, international business, management-marketing, mathematics, nursing, political science, psychobiology, psychology, psychology for business, radiologic science, religious studies, sociology, and sport marketing-management. Preprofessional programs are also available in art therapy, dentistry, law, medicine, optometry, pharmacy, physical therapy, podiatry, physician's assistant studies, and veterinary studies.

Academic Programs

Holy Family's curriculum stands within the mainstream of a 2,000-year-old Christian liberal arts tradition. The core curriculum of religious studies, philosophy, the humanities, and the social and natural sciences implements the objectives of the University in a general way. It also contributes to the formation of liberally educated students who find their education is functional in the twenty-first century. Students are encouraged to seek not merely information but also personal formation and enrichment.

In addition to the core curriculum, students take course work in their division concentrations within the School of Arts and Sciences, the School of Business Administration, the School of Education, the School of Nursing and Allied Health Professions, or the Division of Extended Learning. Interdisciplinary programs, specialized programs of study, and minors are also available.

Off-Campus Programs

Holy Family's cooperative education program is highly successful and nationally recognized. Co-ops and internships are designed to support classroom learning by enabling students to apply the concepts they've studied to actual job situations. These real-world lessons enhance students' skills and understanding and allow them to explore various work settings and careers, all while earning academic credit. Holy Family partners with more than 500 corporations, companies, government agencies, and nonprofit organizations throughout Greater Philadelphia, and the results are impressive. Students in the co-op program enjoy an 85 percent permanent placement rate, while the national average is just 76 percent.

Academic Facilities

The University Library houses 147,800 books, magazines, journals, DVDs, and videos to support the learning, teaching, and informational needs of the Holy Family community. The library offers print and online access to the full text of 10,800 journals and periodicals, and three dozen full-text databases

are available on and off campus. In addition, the library has over 14,500 electronic books available from home or campus via NetLibrary and other interfaces.

The library's curriculum section contains elementary and secondary school textbooks, curriculum guides, instruction kits, and hundreds of children's books, both fiction and nonfiction. It also has a special English as a second language (ESL) collection for those who teach non-native speakers.

Computer laboratories are located in several facilities, including Holy Family Hall, the Education and Technology Center, the Campus Center, and the University Library. Wireless network access is also available throughout the campus buildings and residence halls.

In addition to general classrooms and laboratories, Holy Family has special facilities to enable students in certain majors to learn in environments that mirror those they will encounter in their professional lives. The Education and Technology Center houses five classrooms specially designed to model primary and secondary classroom instruction for the University's education students. These model classrooms allow children with certain disabilities, such as vision or hearing impairment, to be integrated fully into a regular classroom and provide Holy Family's Education graduates with valuable experience using adaptive technology in a classroom environment. The Nurse Education Building includes a nursing simulation and practice laboratory.

Costs

For 2012–13, tuition and fees are $25,590, and room and board are $11,190.

Financial Aid

Holy Family is committed to helping students and their families achieve the goal of a private university education. Holy Family maintains one of the lowest tuition rates among private colleges and universities in the region, and more than 85 percent of its students receive some form of financial aid. The University is committed to providing education to qualified students regardless of means and views financial assistance as a cooperative investment in a student's education.

In addition to state and federal programs, students can take advantage of a variety of Holy Family need- and merit-based scholarships and grants.

Faculty

Classes at Holy Family are usually no larger than 20 students, and many have as few as 7–10 students. A student-to-faculty ratio of 12:1 provides a smaller, more personal learning environment. Students know their professors, and those professors know them as well. Personalized, individual treatment is the norm: students are called on by name, receive answers to their questions, and most importantly, get additional help if they need it. This is not a college where hundreds of students crowd into an auditorium and silently take notes from a distant, faceless instructor. A Holy Family education is designed to be

more—more personal, more welcoming, and more attuned to each student's success.

Student Government

Representatives to Holy Family's Student Government Association are elected by the student body for the following academic year and share responsibility for student life and activities. The Vice President for Student Services serves as an adviser to the Student Government Association and as the liaison between the students and the administration.

Admission Requirements

When it comes to potential students, Holy Family University is more interested in a student's quality of work and general promise and seriousness of purpose. While a student's academic record is considered, their interests, personal integrity, and desire to pursue a quality education are also important factors. Holy Family values diversity in all of its manifestations; neither religious affiliation nor ethnic characteristics influence the granting of admission.

Applicants are expected to have graduated from an accredited high school or equivalent; received acceptable scores on the SAT or ACT; and completed 4 units of English, 2 units of history, 3 units of mathematics, 2 units of modern foreign language, 2 units of science, and 3 electives.

Application and Information

For application forms, a catalog, or further information, students should contact:

Undergraduate Admissions Office
Holy Family University
9801 Frankford Avenue
Philadelphia, Pennsylvania 19114
Phone: 215-637-3050
Fax: 215-281-1022
E-mail: admissions@holyfamily.edu
Web site: http://www.holyfamily.edu
　　　　http://www.facebook.com/HolyFamilyUniversity
　　　　http://twitter.com/holyfamilyu

Holy Family's supportive scholarly community studies, works, and plays on a suburban-like campus just minutes from the vibrancy of Center City Philadelphia.

HOOD COLLEGE
FREDERICK, MARYLAND

The College

Founded in 1893, Hood College is an independent, coeducational liberal arts college.

Hood College prepares students to excel in meeting the personal, professional, and global challenges of the future. Hood is committed to the integration of the liberal arts, the professions and technology, the exploration of values, a sense of community, and to the preparation of students for lives of responsibility, leadership, and service.

Hood's notably small class sizes, extraordinary faculty, outstanding student-to-faculty ratio, and an attractive and friendly campus contribute to an exceptional learning experience. The College's total enrollment is more than 2,400 students: nearly 1,500 undergraduates and approximately 950 graduate students. The diverse student body hails from thirty-three states, the District of Columbia, Puerto Rico, and twenty-four countries; 21 percent are either members of racial or ethnic minorities or are from foreign countries.

There are numerous housing options: traditional residence halls, coed and women only; suite- and apartment-style living; language floors; and living-learning communities. There are more than sixty clubs and organizations, seventeen honor societies, and student-planned activities that offer a vibrant campus life, and opportunities to hone leadership skills and meet peers from diverse backgrounds. Hood's Blazer athletic teams face opponents in twenty men's and women's intercollegiate sports— men's basketball, cross-country, golf, lacrosse, soccer, swimming, tennis, and track and field; and women's basketball, cross-country, field hockey, lacrosse, soccer, softball, swimming, tennis, track and field, and volleyball. They compete in the highly competitive NCAA Division III Capital Athletic Conference. Cheerleading, equestrian, and women's golf are offered as club sports.

Hood prepares students for life after graduation by providing numerous opportunities for active, hands-on learning. These cocurricular experiences augment classroom learning and allow the application of skills in real-world environments. The Frederick-Baltimore-Washington, D.C., triangle abounds with internships at government agencies, laboratories, media firms, public and private schools, IT companies, and more. Recent research internships have been completed at prestigious sites such as National Institutes of Standards and Technology, U.S. Department of State, Pennsylvania Department of Environmental Protection, and the U.S. Army Medical Research Institute for Infectious Diseases, among others.

Hood College has a long history and tradition of faculty and student collaborative research that reaches across the disciplines. The Summer Science Research Institute—funded by Life Technologies—the Hodson Research Institute, and individual faculty research grants allows students to work side-by-side with faculty on topics of interest. For some students, the opportunity to engage in research sets the tone and the direction for their future academic work and their professional careers.

The graduate school offers fourteen programs of study: Master of Arts degrees in human sciences, humanities, and thanatology; Master of Business Administration; Master of Fine Arts in ceramic arts; and Master of Science degrees in computer science, curriculum and instruction, educational leadership, environmental biology, information technology, management of information technology, mathematics education, and reading specialization. Certificate programs are offered in ceramic arts, information security, regulatory compliance, secondary mathematics education, and thanatology.

Location

Hood's picturesque 50-acre campus is ideally situated in the middle of a residential neighborhood in charming, historic Frederick, Maryland. With a population of more than 65,000, it is the second-largest city in Maryland. Located about an hour's drive from Baltimore and Washington, D.C., the area abounds with cultural, social, and professional opportunities. Students head downtown to shop, sample fare at any number of eclectic restaurants and cafés, hear local bands, attend special events hosted by the City of Frederick, and visit the Weinberg Center for the Arts or the Delaplaine Visual Arts Center for performances and art exhibits. In this setting—among mountains, rolling farmlands, and rivers—students enjoy the outdoors in all seasons. Popular activities include camping, hiking, boating, swimming, biking, picnicking, playing tennis, and other sports. During the past decade, the Frederick community has been nationally recognized in a number of categories: named one of America's Dozen Distinct Destinations and Great American Main Street by the National Trust for Historic Preservation; designated a Preserve America Community, a White House initiative; named one of the Great Places in America in the neighborhood category by the American Planning Association; recognized as one of the ten most secure communities among the nation's largest metropolitan areas by Farmer's Insurance Group of Companies; and ranked number eight in the Top 25 Small Art Cities in the United States by AmericanStyle magazine.

Majors and Degrees

Thirty majors are offered at the bachelor's degree level: art and archaeology, biochemistry, biology, chemistry, communication arts, early childhood education, economics, elementary/special education, English, environmental science and policy, French, French/German, German, history, Latin American studies, law and society, management, mathematics, Middle Eastern studies, music, philosophy, political science, psychology, religion, social work, sociology, and Spanish. Bachelor of Science degrees are offered in computer science and computational science, and a Bachelor of Science in Nursing completion program is designed for students who are registered nurses. In addition, pre-professional programs in dentistry, law, and medicine are available. Within the majors there are twenty-two concentrations; forty-four minors are also offered.

Hood College is accredited by the Middle States Commission on Higher Education. The Hood social work program carries specialized accreditation by the Council of Social Work Education. The Hood Education Department's initial teacher certification and master's degree programs are accredited by the National Council for Accreditation of Teacher Education; and Hood's MBA Program and bachelor's degree in management program are accredited by the Accreditation Council for Business Schools and Programs.

Academic Programs

As a liberal arts–based institution of higher learning, Hood requires all students complete the 42- to 51-credit core curriculum, the purpose of which is to provide students with the basic skills needed to pursue a liberal arts education, to expose them to a variety of modes of inquiry in different disciplines, and to help them develop a better sense of historical perspectives in both Western and non-Western civilizations. The core curriculum comprises three parts: foundation, 14 to 19 credits; methods of inquiry, 22 to 23 credits; and civilization, 6 to 9 credits.

Off-Campus Programs

The Frederick-Washington, D.C.-Baltimore triangle not only features a vast and diverse array of world-famous social and cultural destinations, but also abounds with internships and volunteer opportunities. Students have secured internships at businesses, government organizations, nonprofit organizations, research sites, media firms, schools, and technology firms. Students interested in politics, justice foreign policy, or other related fields can enroll in Hood's Washington Semester in Washington, D.C. Hood's career center staff expertly guide students through résumé-building, offer mock interviews, and serve as a resource for all volunteer, internship, and career-related pursuits.

Hood students participate in semester-long study abroad programs in an array of countries, including Australia, Chile, Dominican Republic, France, Germany, Ireland, Japan, Korea, Peru, South Africa, Spain, and Egypt.

Students, faculty, and staff members participate in campus-organized alternative spring break programs, traveling to North Carolina, the Mississippi Gulf Coast, Florida, and New Windsor, Maryland, to pack disaster relief emergency kits for worldwide distribution, process handmade craft items created by emerging artists in developing countries, reconstruct homes destroyed by Hurricane Katrina, repair a retreat center that focuses on service and educating about racism and slavery, and help church members assist some of the poorest residents in local neighborhoods.

Academic Facilities

Academic and other facilities include a library and information center, advanced computing laboratories, a child development laboratory school, state-of-the-art science and language laboratories, a student center, a new fitness and athletic center, five stately residence halls, and three language residences.

Costs

The comprehensive cost of attendance for 2011–12, which includes tuition, room and board, living and travel expenses, and books is $43,210. Students who live on campus are required to purchase a meal plan.

Financial Aid

In *Kiplinger's Personal Finance* magazine, Hood College is one of only fifty private colleges and universities that qualify as best values. Hood is also ranked year after year by *U.S. News & World Report* as a Great School at a Great Price, noting Hood's academic quality and generous merit- and need-based financial support for students.

Hood's Office of Financial Aid helps students and their families develop a financial plan to make a Hood College education affordable. One Hood student in five receives an honors scholarship and more than 95 percent of undergraduates receive some form of financial aid.

Priority application deadline for financial aid is February 15. Students and families are highly encouraged to submit the Free Application for Federal Student Aid by that date to receive full consideration for grants.

Each year, Hood College awards more than $6 million in merit-based scholarships, including scholarships for first-year students entering from high school as well as for students transferring from other colleges. Students admitted to Hood are automatically considered for most merit scholarships (except for the Honors Program Scholarship, the Hodson-Gilliam Diversity Scholarship, and the Hood Heritage Scholarship, which require separate applications), the majority of which are renewable for up to four years (although some require a minimum GPA for their renewal). Overall academic performance, specific academic achievements, leadership, and participation in school and community activities are important factors in awarding scholarships to both first-year and transfer students. Some scholarships have application deadlines; priority for other scholarships is given to students who have completed their application by February 15.

Faculty

One hundred fifteen dedicated professors ensure a low student-to-teacher ratio, so students receive personal and high-quality attention; 97 percent of all full-time faculty hold the doctorate or terminal degree in their fields. Students enjoy a 12:1 student-to-faculty ratio at the undergraduate level and a 14:1 ratio at the graduate level. The average undergraduate class size is 17.

Admission Requirements

Admission to the undergraduate program at Hood College is selective; students are encouraged to pursue a strong college preparatory curriculum in high school. Applicants are admitted on the basis of academic achievements, personal qualities, and accomplishments, but there are no set admission standards regarding grade point average and standardized test scores. However, as a frame of reference, the first-year class of 2011 had an average GPA of 3.51 and average SAT score of 1081 (critical reading and math). Among first-year Hood College students, more than 80 percent graduated in the top 50 percent of their high school class.

Application and Information

The early decision deadline, which is binding, is November 15; early action I deadline is December 1; early action II deadline is January 15; and regular decision deadline is February 15. Hood accepts the Common Application as well as its own online or paper application. Application fees are waived for online applications.

Hood requires a high school transcript, counselor evaluation, and a minimum of one letter of recommendation from a teacher the student has had in an academic course; two or more letters are strongly encouraged. Official results of the SAT and/or ACT examination and an essay are also required.

Prospective students are encouraged to visit the campus and meet with admission counselors. There are numerous opportunities to visit throughout the year, including Discover Hood Days, Admitted Students Days, weekday and Saturday morning visits, and Transfer Advising Days. Visits can also be tailored to specific needs.

For additional information, contact:

Admission Office
Hood College
401 Rosemont Avenue
Frederick, Maryland 21701
Phone: 301-696-3400
      800-922-1599 (toll-free)
E-mail: admissions@hood.edu
Web site: http://www.hood.edu

Hood College integrates liberal arts, professions, and technology to prepare students for lives of responsibility, leadership, and service.

HOUGHTON COLLEGE

HOUGHTON, NEW YORK

The College

Founded in 1883, Houghton College is one of America's most highly regarded Christian liberal arts colleges. Founded by The Wesleyan Church, Houghton attracts students from more than forty denominations. Houghton has an enrollment of 1,100 full-time undergraduate students who represent forty states and twenty-five countries. Most students live in College housing within the distinctly residential environment, while many faculty members live within walking distance of the campus. Houghton's 1,300 acres in the scenic Genesee Valley of western New York offer students various recreational opportunities. The College operates a 386-acre equestrian center and both downhill and cross-country ski facilities.

Accredited by the Middle States Association of Colleges and Schools and the National Association of Schools of Music, Houghton's selective admission ensures an academically able student body. Most students represent the top 20 percent of their high school's graduating class, possess SAT or ACT scores commensurate with a competitive college, and are active in their churches and communities. Houghton offers more than forty majors and programs. Students benefit from the instruction and guidance of experienced professors beginning with their first year of study.

Extensive cocurricular opportunities at Houghton include a competitive NCAA Division III intercollegiate athletic program that fields eighteen teams for men and women, a wide array of intramural leagues, numerous Christian service organizations, student publications, music groups, and student government. Houghton's Artist Series brings well-known classical performers to the campus several times a year. The student-guided Campus Activities Board sponsors regular Christian contemporary concerts and other student activities. Student chapel services meet three times per week. *The Star,* the College's weekly student newspaper, offers practical journalism experience.

The residential experience is at the heart of a Houghton education. First-year students and sophomores are required to live in a College residential hall. Juniors and seniors may also choose from town houses and approved community houses for off-campus living.

All resident students are required to participate in the College's board plan. Most students enjoy Houghton's twenty-one-meal-per-week plan, while those living in a town house may opt for a reduced plan.

Year after year, Houghton is commended by numerous national publications. Of all member institutions of the Council for Christian Colleges and Universities, Houghton College is ranked fourth highest in the national liberal arts category by *U.S. News & World Report. Forbes* ranks Houghton in the top 3 percent of schools nationwide in terms of quality of teaching, career prospects for alumni, and graduation rates. The Princeton Review names Houghton a Best College in the Northeast and also lists Houghton in its Green College Guide.

In addition to its undergraduate programs, Houghton College also offers Master of Music and Master of Arts in Music degrees through the Greatbatch School of Music.

Location

Houghton students benefit from the College's location in the rolling hills of western New York. The College's vast property—among the nation's leaders in campus acreage—offers numerous recreational opportunities, while nearby Letchworth State Park is one of the state's natural treasures. The metropolitan cities of Rochester and Buffalo, an hour's drive from Houghton, offer cultural, entertainment, and shopping venues.

Majors and Degrees

Houghton grants Bachelor of Arts, Bachelor of Science, and Bachelor of Music degrees. Majors and programs are available in accounting, adolescence education (grades 7–12), art, art education (PreK–12), Bible, biology, business administration, chemistry, childhood education (grades 1–6), Christian formation, communication, computer science, English, environmental studies, general science, history, humanities, information technology management, intercultural studies, mathematics, medical technology, ministerial studies, music composition, music education, music performance, philosophy, physical education, physical/health education, physics, political science, pre-art therapy, pre-dentistry, pre-law, pre-medicine, pre-optometry, pre-pharmacy, pre–physical therapy, pre-seminary, pre–veterinary science, psychology, recreation, religion, sociology, Spanish, TESOL (grades K–12) and writing.

An adult degree-completion program (B.S. in management), designed for those with two years of college credit and who are at least 25 years old, is offered at locations throughout western New York, including West Seneca, Williamsville, Olean, Arcade, and Jamestown, New York.

Houghton provides accelerated graduate degree programs in conjunction with leading institutions across New York State. A 3-2 engineering program is available through cooperation with Clarkson University in Potsdam, New York. A 3+4 co-operative doctorate program in pharmacy (Pharm.D.) is offered in conjunction with the University of Buffalo. Accelerated 4+1 M.B.A. programs have been arranged through Alfred University, Clarkson University, Niagara University, and Rochester Institute of Technology.

Academic Programs

Most bachelor's degrees at Houghton consist of 124 credit hours. As a traditional liberal arts institution, Houghton requires all students to complete an extensive integrative studies curriculum in addition to courses in their major and minor fields of study. Integrative studies requirements include courses in writing, literature, communication, foreign language, social science, history, mathematics, natural science, Bible, religion/philosophy, and fine arts. Lecture and seminar courses with classes averaging 21 students create a positive learning environment and daily interaction between professors and students.

Houghton offers three interdisciplinary Honors Programs, giving talented first-year students a unique opportunity for enhanced study. Contemporary Contexts and East Meets West engage students in the study of significant questions and include a three-week study abroad trip to Europe. Science Honors allows students extensive opportunities for research and discovery within an integrative problem-driven program.

The College follows a 4-4-1 calendar. In addition to the fall and spring semesters, the College offers May Term, a two- to four-week term where students may enroll in one concentrated course. Both on- and off-campus courses are available during May Term.

Houghton accepts credit from the Advanced Placement Program of the College Board. Generally, students must achieve a final

exam score of 4 or higher to receive credit from Houghton. CLEP credit may also be accepted for subject exams only. Students may also earn credit through the International Baccalaureate program; credit is awarded for higher-level subjects passed with a 5 or above. Students wishing to challenge the College's foreign language requirement may take a College-administered placement test. A portion or all of the foreign language requirement may be waived, although no credit hours are granted.

Army ROTC is offered through cooperation with nearby St. Bonaventure University.

Off-Campus Programs

Over half of Houghton students study off-campus before they graduate. Houghton operates semester-long programs in Tanzania, the Balkans, and Australia/New Zealand. As a member of the Council for Christian Colleges and Universities, Houghton is able to offer many off-campus opportunities, including the American Studies Program in Washington, D.C.; the Contemporary Music Center in Nashville, Tennessee; the Latin American Studies Program in Costa Rica; the Film Studies Center in Los Angeles, California; the Middle East Studies Program in Cairo, Egypt; the Oxford Summer School Program; and programs in China, India, and Uganda.

Academic Facilities

The recently expanded Stephen Paine Science Center contains classrooms, teaching and research laboratories, offices, study areas, an instrument room, a greenhouse, and machine shop

A comprehensive academic building offers 49,000 square feet of classrooms, learning resource facilities, laboratories, faculty offices, digital media lab, a state-of-the-art business investment center, and the Center for Academic Success and Advisement. Other major facilities include a modern, well-equipped athletic complex; four major residence halls and thirty town houses accommodating more than 900 students; the 1,200-seat Wesley Chapel; the Campus Center; the Stevens Arts Studios; a 386-acre equestrian center; and several outdoor athletic and recreational areas. Houghton's Center for the Arts features an acoustically designed recital hall, a music library, numerous practice rooms, spacious teaching studios, an instrumental rehearsal hall, and a professional digital recording studio.

Costs

Houghton's tuition and fees were $26,924 for the 2012–13 academic year. Room and board (twenty-one meals per week) totaled $7778. Other indirect expenses, including books, supplies, and travel, averaged $1500.

Financial Aid

Houghton administers more than $27 million in aid annually, benefiting 97 percent of the student body. Traditional federal and New York State aid, including Federal Pell Grants, TAP, FSEOG, work-study, and Federal Perkins Loans, is available for students demonstrating need through the Free Application for Federal Student Aid (FAFSA). The priority application deadline for financial aid is March 1. Houghton also offers academic scholarships and Excellence Scholarships for students in various academic areas. The James S. Luckey Scholarship, named for the college's first president, covers 100 percent of tuition costs for 3 students each year.

Faculty

The College's faculty currently totals approximately 130 members, 80 of whom are full-time. More than 80 percent hold the terminal degree in their discipline. All courses are taught by qualified professors, not teaching assistants or graduate students. All full-time students work directly with a faculty adviser in their area of study. The College maintains a student-faculty ratio of 12:1, with classes averaging approximately 21 students.

Student Government

The Houghton Student Government Association (SGA) consists of elected student representatives. This College-sponsored organization allows students to have a direct impact on their college experience in areas ranging from academics to residence life to cocurricular activities. Most College committees include student representatives.

Admission Requirements

Houghton's competitive admission process seeks applicants who clearly possess the academic and spiritual qualities necessary for a successful experience at Houghton. Candidates for admission should submit a high school transcript indicating at least 16 units of college-preparatory course work. The academic evaluation of each applicant includes a review of the quality of the high school curriculum, grade point average, rank in class, and scores from the SAT or ACT. Other important application materials include the applicant's character recommendation and an essay regarding the student's desire to attend a Christian institution. Transfer students are evaluated on the basis of the above information in addition to the college-level course work completed to date.

The Office of Admission responds to applications for admission on a rolling basis. Students applying before December 1 will receive priority consideration for scholarships. The College subscribes to and supports the national Candidates Reply Date of May 1.

Application and Information

For application materials, students should contact:

Admission Office
Houghton College
1 Willard Avenue
Houghton, New York 14744
Phone: 585-567-9353
      800-777-2556 (toll-free)
E-mail: admission@houghton.edu
World Wide Web: http://www.houghton.edu

Looking across the quad at Houghton College.

HUNTER COLLEGE OF THE CITY UNIVERSITY OF NEW YORK

NEW YORK, NEW YORK

The College

In 1870, Thomas Hunter founded Hunter College to train young women to become school teachers. Their contributions helped make New York City's schools among the most highly regarded public school systems in the world. Today, Hunter College is a coeducational liberal arts college serving 21,000 undergraduate and graduate students of all racial, ethnic, and cultural backgrounds. Wide offerings in the liberal arts and sciences and three professional schools—education, health sciences, and social work—meet the highest academic standards. A distinguished faculty encourages intellectual and personal growth in each student.

Location

Hunter students study in the heart of Manhattan. Many of the world's finest museums, libraries, concert halls, cultural centers, and theaters are just a quick walk away.

Majors and Degrees

Hunter College offers bachelor's and master's degrees in the arts and sciences, education, health professions, nursing, and social work, along with several combined (B.A./M.A. or B.A./M.S.) degrees. The following programs of study are available: accounting, Africana and Puerto Rican/Latino studies, anthropology, archaeology, art history, biological sciences, chemistry, Chinese language and literature, classical studies, community health education, comparative literature, computer science, dance, economics, elementary education, environmental studies, English, English language arts, film, French, geography, German, Greek, Hebrew, history, honors curriculum, Italian, Jewish social studies, Latin, Latin American and Caribbean Studies, Latin and Greek, mathematics, media studies, medical laboratory sciences, music, nursing, nutrition and food science, philosophy, physics, political science, psychology, religion, Romance languages, Russian, secondary education, sociology, Spanish, statistics, studio art, theater, urban studies, and women's studies. Secondary education programs are for grades 7–12 unless otherwise noted and include biology, chemistry, Chinese, dance (pre-K–12), English, French, German, Hebrew, Italian, mathematics, music (pre-K–12, accelerated B.A./M.A. program only), physics, Russian, social studies, and Spanish.

Special programs in anthropology, biological sciences/environmental and occupational health sciences, biopharmacology, biotechnology, economics, English, history, mathematics, music, physics, sociology/social research, and statistics and applied mathematics lead to the combined bachelor's/master's degree, enabling highly qualified students to earn both degrees more quickly.

Hunter College also provides preprofessional advisement and preparation for advanced study in chiropractic, dentistry, engineering, law, medicine, optometry, osteopathy, pharmacy, podiatry, and veterinary medicine.

Academic Programs

Hunter instills a rich and informed sense of the possibilities of humanity in its students and expects them to carry their liberal arts education forward in their careers, their public responsibilities, and their personal lives.

The College trains its students in the sciences, the humanities, and a number of professional fields. As they strive to achieve their career goals, students are expected to perceive their chosen fields of study as only a part of a wider realm of knowledge. Undergraduate programs of study at Hunter consist of four parts, totaling 120 credits: a general education requirement, a pluralism and diversity requirement, a concentration of in-depth study (major), and elective courses.

Undergraduate students at Hunter who exhibit intellectual curiosity and exceptional ability may apply to the Thomas Hunter Scholars Program, an interdisciplinary program that individualizes study according to needs and interests and grants a Bachelor of Arts degree.

Students may earn sophomore standing (up to 30 credits) if they score well on the College-Level Examination Program (CLEP) subject tests, the Advanced Placement examinations of the College Board, and the Regents College Examination (RCE) Program of New York State.

Off-Campus Programs

Hunter College taps Manhattan to allow innumerable internships. Hosts have included Atlantic Records, CNN, the Council on Foreign Relations, DreamWorks SKG, Madison Square Garden, Metropolitan Museum of Art, New York City Council, Simon & Schuster, and many more. Interns perform curatorial and administrative work in museums, research and production work on TV news shows and newspapers, design work in commercial graphics, and booking, managing, and technical work in theaters.

Academic Facilities

The College is made up of five sites in Manhattan. The largest, a modern complex of buildings connected by skywalks at 68th Street and Lexington Avenue, sits above a convenient subway stop. This campus offers programs in the arts and sciences and in teacher education.

Downtown on East 25th Street, the Brookdale Campus houses the Division of the Schools of the Health Professions, which includes the Hunter-Bellevue School of Nursing, one of the nation's largest nursing programs, and the School of Health Sciences.

Uptown on East 119th Street is the Silberman School of Social Work at Hunter College, which was recently listed among the top ten schools of its kind in the nation by *U.S. News & World Report*.

On Manhattan's West Side, Hunter's Studio Art Building houses an 8,000-square-foot gallery and provides M.F.A. students with individual studios that are among the best in the city.

At East 94th Street, the Campus Schools house an elementary school and a high school for the intellectually gifted that are renowned, as is the College itself, for a long tradition of academic excellence.

All locations are minutes from Grand Central Terminal, Penn Station, and the New York/New Jersey Port Authority Bus

Terminal, making Hunter easily accessible from Connecticut, Westchester, New Jersey, and Long Island.

The collections of the Hunter College libraries are housed in the Jacqueline Grennan Wexler Library and the Art Slide Library (located at the main campus), as well as at the branch libraries at the Brookdale Campus and the School of Social Work. The libraries hold over 800,000 volumes, 3,000 periodicals, a nonprint collection of more than 1 million microforms, and 250,000 art slides in addition to records, tapes, scores, music CDs, and videos. Recently, Hunter installed new computer, multimedia, and Internet labs and its first CD-ROM network. The CD-ROM network provides access to indexes, abstracts, and complete texts and multimedia resources, and Internet labs make the World Wide Web accessible.

Costs

Hunter College is affordable. In 2012–13, New York State residents enrolled as full-time, matriculated students are slated to pay $2565 per semester ($215 per credit part-time). Nonresidents enrolled as full-time, matriculated students will pay $460 per credit. All students pay a student activity fee ($84.50 per semester for full-time students and $54.45 per semester for part-time students) and a $15-per-semester consolidated fee.

Financial Aid

Hunter College participates in all state and federal financial aid programs. Financial aid is available to matriculated students in the form of grants, loans, and work-study. Grants provide funds that do not have to be repaid. Loans must be repaid in regular installments over a prescribed period of time. Work-study consists of part-time employment, either on campus or in an outside agency. More information is available from the Office of Financial Aid at 212-772-4820.

Entering freshmen whose high school records indicate a high level of academic achievement may apply to the Macaulay Honors College at Hunter College. This prestigious program offers a generous financial aid package, including a full academic scholarship, as well as extensive benefits, including a free room at the Hunter College Residence Hall for two years. In addition, Hunter College offers a wide array of other scholarships.

Faculty

Thanks to its location in the heart of New York City, Hunter College attracts a special kind of faculty member. Some are well-known scholars and researchers in their fields, such as biologists involved in advanced research on genetic structure. Others are professionals with active careers in the city, including well-known painters, sculptors, architects, and urban design experts. Hunter's faculty also includes environmental health scientists who work on occupational health and safety issues, nursing administrators who work in the country's leading hospitals, and film directors, theater critics, and musicians who are engaged in New York City's cultural milieu. Many members of the faculty are nationally renowned; they maintain Hunter's reputation for academic excellence through outstanding teaching and cutting-edge publications and by securing millions of dollars in annual grants for research.

Student Government

Several governing assemblies involve students in Hunter's governance. The College Senate, the legislative body of the College, includes faculty members, students, and administrators. Two student governments (undergraduate and graduate) also play essential roles in the life of the College. Students with voting power sit on faculty and administrative committees.

Admission Requirements

Candidates for freshman admission are considered based on the overall strength of their academic preparation, cumulative high school averages, and SAT or ACT scores. Freshman students who entered in fall 2011 had a high school academic grade point average of 88.6 and an SAT score of 1197 (math and verbal only). The College recommends 4 years of English, 4 years of social studies, 3 years of mathematics, 2 years of a foreign language, 2 years of laboratory sciences, and 1 year of performing or visual arts as the minimum academic preparation for success in college.

Students are considered transfer applicants if they have previously attended any college, university, and/or proprietary school since graduating from high school or secondary school. This applies whether or not the student is seeking transfer credit. Transfer students in fall 2011 had a cumulative grade point average of 3.14 with an average of 75.6 credits attempted. For more information, applicants should visit Hunter College's Web site.

Application and Information

Applicants are considered for fall (September) and spring (February) admission. Applications for the fall must be filed no later than September 15 and for spring, no later than February 1. All applications must be filed on the CUNY Web site at http://www.cuny.edu.

Welcome Center
Hunter College
695 Park Avenue, Room 100N
New York, New York 10065
Phone: 212-772-4490
E-mail: WelcomeCenter@hunter.cuny.edu
Web site: http://www.hunter.cuny.edu/ugprospects
　　　http://www.facebook.com/groups/263613092099
　　　　(Welcome Center)
　　　http://www.flickr.com/photos/welcome_center

Students at Hunter College enjoy the convenience of skywalks that connect all four buildings at the 68th Street campus. Hunter's Upper East Side location provides easy access to some of New York's finest offerings; Central Park and the Metropolitan Museum of Art are just blocks away.

THE ILLINOIS INSTITUTE OF ART—CHICAGO

CHICAGO, ILLINOIS

The Illinois Institute of Art®
Chicago
CREATE TOMORROW

A focused education from The Illinois Institute of Art—Chicago can help students turn their creative energy into a powerful tool that can make a difference in the world. Students are part of a collaborative and supportive community, where experienced instructors provide the guidance and skills needed to pursue a career in the creative economy.

The school's programs in the areas of design, media arts, fashion, and culinary give students the opportunity to learn by using professional-grade technology and to build a portfolio of work to show potential employers after graduation.

The Illinois Institute of Art—Chicago is accredited by the Higher Learning Commission and is a member of the North Central Association (NCA), located at 230 S. LaSalle Street, Suite 7-500, Chicago, Illinois, 60604-1413; phone: 800-621-7440; http://www.ncahlc.org.

The Illinois Institute of Art—Chicago is authorized by the Illinois Board of Higher Education, 431 East Adams, Second Floor, Springfield, Illinois 62701; phone: 217-782-2551; http://www.ibhe.state.il.us/default.htm.

The Associate of Applied Science degree program in culinary arts is accredited by the Accrediting Commission of the American Culinary Federation Education Foundation.

The interior design program leading to the Bachelor of Science degree is accredited by the Council for Interior Design Accreditation, 206 Grandville Avenue, Suite 350, Grand Rapids, Michigan 49503; http://www.accredit-id.org.

Location

The city of Chicago provides a backdrop like no other. With two locations downtown, the school offers students the opportunity to learn both in the classroom and through the many events and experiences that come with being immersed in downtown Chicago.

Programs of Study and Degrees

No matter which course of study a student may choose, the professionals at The Illinois Institute of Art—Chicago will guide, support, and help each student as their talents evolve on their journey of personal and professional transformation. Students studying design learn to fine-tune their visual thinking and problem-solving skills as they create everything from logos to TV ads. Programs in the area of media arts focus on utilizing technology to deliver information and entertainment, while students studying fashion learn to design clothes for the runway or run a retail shop. Culinary programs focus on the fundamental techniques while exposing students to a full menu of international cuisines and management techniques.

Bachelor's degree programs are offered in the areas of advertising, audio production, culinary management, digital filmmaking and video production, digital photography, fashion design, fashion marketing and management, game art and design, graphic design, hospitality management, illustration and design, interior design, and media arts and animation.

Associate degree programs are offered in the areas of culinary arts, fashion merchandising, graphic design, and hospitality management.

A certificate program is offered in professional baking and pastry.

Diploma programs are offered in the areas of baking and pastry, culinary arts, digital image management, and fashion retailing.

The bachelor's degree programs in culinary management and interior design, as well as the associate's degree programs in culinary arts and graphic design are also available in an evening and weekend option format.

Academic Programs

The Illinois Institute of Art—Chicago operates on a year-round, four quarter system.

Academic Facilities

The Illinois Institute of Art—Chicago provides a learning environment with professional-grade technology applicable to each student's course of study. Students have the opportunity to build a portfolio of work that shows potential employers that they are trained to use the software, hardware, or equipment utilized within the industry. Depending upon the course of study, students are immersed in a creative environment—from classrooms to computer labs to studios—focused on relevant, hands-on education designed to prepare students for the real world.

Costs

Tuition cost varies by program. Prospective students should contact the school for current tuition costs. Other charges include a starting kit for all first-quarter students. Kits vary in price depending on the program of study.

Financial Aid

Financial aid is available for those who qualify. Students who require financial assistance should first complete and submit a Free Application for Federal Student Aid (FAFSA) and meet with a financial aid officer.

Faculty

Faculty members are experienced professionals who create a learning environment that is similar to the professional world students will face after graduation. Instructors are focused on helping students develop the skills they need to transform their creative potential into marketable skills.

Admission Requirements

Applicants must provide proof of high school graduation or achievement of a General Educational Development (GED) certificate as a prerequisite for admission. In lieu of documenting high school graduation or a GED certificate, applicants may provide proof of attaining an associate degree or higher from an accredited institution. An official transcript indicating date of high school graduation, GED certificate (including test scores), or date of college graduation (including degree granted) is required as proof.

All individuals seeking admission to The Illinois Institute of Art—Chicago are interviewed in person or by phone by an assistant director of admissions, and each applicant must create an original essay of at least 150 words stating how an education at The Illinois Institute of Art—Chicago would help the student to achieve career goals. There is a $50 application fee.

For the most recent information regarding admission requirements, please refer to the current academic catalog.

Application and Information

To obtain an application, make arrangements for an interview, or tour the school, students should contact:

The Illinois Institute of Art—Chicago
350 North Orleans Street
Chicago, Illinois 60654-1593
Phone: 312-280-3500
      800-351-3450 (toll-free)
Fax: 312-280-8562
Web site: http://www.artinstitutes.edu/chicago

Over 50 schools: The Art Institute of Atlanta; The Art Institute of Atlanta—Decatur, A branch of The Art Institute of Atlanta; The Art Institute of Austin, A branch of The Art Institute of Houston; The Art Institute of California, a college of Argosy University, with locations in Hollywood, Inland Empire, Los Angeles, Orange County, Sacramento, San Diego, San Francisco, and Sunnyvale; The Art Institute of Charleston, A branch of The Art Institute of Atlanta; The Art Institute of Charlotte; The Art Institute of Colorado; The Art Institute of Dallas, A campus of South University; The Art Institute of Fort Lauderdale; The Art Institute of Fort Worth, A campus of South University; The Art Institute of Houston; The Art Institute of Houston—North, A branch of The Art Institute of Houston; The Art Institute of Indianapolis; The Art Institute of Jacksonville, A branch of Miami International University of Art & Design; The Art Institute of Las Vegas; The Art Institute of Michigan; The Art Institute of Michigan—Troy; The Art Institute of New York City; The Art Institute of Ohio—Cincinnati; The Art Institute of Philadelphia; The Art Institute of Phoenix; The Art Institute of Pittsburgh; The Art Institute of Portland; The Art Institute of Raleigh–Durham; The Art Institute of Salt Lake City; The Art Institute of San Antonio, A branch of The Art Institute of Houston; The Art Institute of Seattle; The Art Institute of Tampa, A branch of Miami International University of Art & Design; The Art Institute of Tennessee—Nashville, A branch of The Art Institute of Atlanta; The Art Institute of Tucson; The Art Institute of Vancouver; The Art Institute of Virginia Beach[1], A branch of The Art Institute of Atlanta; The Art Institute of Washington[1], A branch of The Art Institute of Atlanta; The Art Institute of Washington—Dulles[1], A branch of The Art Institute of Atlanta; The Art Institute of Wisconsin; The Art Institute of York—Pennsylvania; The Art Institutes International—Kansas City; The Art Institutes International Minnesota; The Illinois Institute of Art—Chicago; The Illinois Institute of Art—Schaumburg; The Illinois Institute of Art—Tinley Park; Miami International University of Art & Design; The New England Institute of Art

[1]Certified by SCHEV to operate in Virginia

See **aiprograms.info** for program duration, tuition, fees, and other costs, median debt, federal salary data, alumni success, and other important info. The Art Institutes is a system of over 50 schools throughout North America. Programs, credential levels, technology, and scheduling options vary by school, and employment opportunities are not guaranteed. Financial aid is available to those who qualify. Several institutions included in The Art Institutes system are campuses of South University or Argosy University. OH Registration # 04-01-1698B, AC0165, AC0080, Licensed by the Florida Commission for Independent Education, License No. 1287, 3427, 3110, 2581. Administrative office: 210 Sixth Avenue, 33rd Floor, Pittsburgh, PA 15222. ©2012 The Art Institutes International LLC.

THE ILLINOIS INSTITUTE OF ART— SCHAUMBURG

SCHAUMBURG, ILLINOIS

A focused education from The Illinois Institute of Art— Schaumburg can help students turn their creative energy into a powerful tool that can make a difference in the world. Students are part of a collaborative and supportive community, where experienced instructors provide the guidance and skills needed to pursue a career in the creative economy.

The school's programs in the areas of design, media arts, fashion, and culinary give students the opportunity to learn by using professional-grade technology and to build a portfolio of work to show potential employers after graduation.

The Illinois Institute of Art—Schaumburg is accredited by the Higher Learning Commission and a member of the North Central Association (NCA), located at 230 S. LaSalle Street, Suite 7-500, Chicago, Illinois 60604-1413; phone: 800-621-7440; http://www.ncahlc.org.

The Illinois Institute of Art—Schaumburg is authorized by the Illinois Board of Higher Education, 431 East Adams, Second Floor, Springfield, Illinois 62701; phone: 217-782-2551; http://www.ibhe.state.il.us/default.htm.

The Interior Design program leading to the Bachelor of Fine Arts degree is accredited by the Council for Interior Design Accreditation, 206 Grandville Avenue, Suite 350, Grand Rapids, Michigan 49503; http://www.accredit-id.org.

Location

Located in suburban Chicago, in Schaumburg, the school provides easy access to the big city, while giving students a more suburban environment in which to live and learn.

Programs of Study and Degrees

No matter which course of study a student may choose, the professionals at The Illinois Institute of Art—Schaumburg will guide, support, and help each student as their talents evolve on their journey of personal and professional transformation. Students studying design learn to fine-tune their visual thinking and problem-solving skills as they create everything from logos to TV ads. Programs in the area of media arts focus on utilizing technology to deliver information and entertainment, while students studying fashion learn to design clothes for the runway or run a retail shop. Culinary programs focus on the fundamental skills while exposing students to a full menu of international cuisines and management techniques.

Bachelor's degree programs are offered in the areas of advertising, audio production, digital filmmaking and video production, digital photography, fashion design, fashion marketing and management, game art and design, graphic design, hospitality management, illustration and design, interior design, media arts and animation, visual effects and motion graphics, and Web design and interactive media.

Associate degree programs are offered in the areas of fashion merchandising, graphic design, hospitality management, and Web design and interactive media.

Diploma programs are offered in the areas of digital design, digital image management, fashion retailing, residential planning, Web design and development, and Web design and interactive communications.

The digital design, game art and design, graphic design, interior design, media arts and animation, residential planning, and Web design and interactive media programs are also available in an evening and weekend option format.

Academic Programs

The Illinois Institute of Art—Schaumburg operates on a year-round, four-quarter system.

Academic Facilities

The Illinois Institute of Art—Schaumburg provides a learning environment with professional-grade technology applicable to each student's course of study. Students have the opportunity to build a portfolio of work that shows potential employers that they are trained to use the software, hardware, or equipment utilized within the industry. Depending upon the course of study, students are immersed in a creative environment—from classrooms to computer labs to studios—focused on relevant, hands-on education designed to prepare students for the real world.

Costs

Tuition cost varies by program. Prospective students should contact the school for current tuition costs. Other charges include a starting kit for all first-quarter students. Kits vary in price depending on the program of study.

Financial Aid

Financial aid is available for those who qualify. Students who require financial assistance should first complete and submit a Free Application for Federal Student Aid (FAFSA) and meet with a financial aid officer.

Faculty

Faculty members are experienced professionals who create a learning environment that is similar to the professional world students will face after graduation. Instructors are focused on helping students develop the skills they need to transform their creative potential into marketable skills.

Admission Requirements

Applicants must provide proof of high school graduation or achievement of a General Educational Development (GED) certificate as a prerequisite for admission. In lieu of documenting high school graduation or a GED certificate, applicants may provide proof of attaining an associate degree or higher from an accredited institution. An official transcript indicating date of high school graduation, GED certificate (including test scores), or date of college graduation (including degree granted) is required as proof.

All individuals seeking admission to The Illinois Institute of Art—Schaumburg are interviewed in person or by phone by an assistant director of admissions, and each applicant must create an original essay of at least 150 words stating how an education at The Illinois Institute of Art—Schaumburg would help the student to achieve career goals. There is a $50 application fee.

For the most recent information regarding admission requirements, please refer to the current academic catalog.

Application and Information

To obtain an application, make arrangements for an interview, or tour the school, prospective students should contact:

The Illinois Institute of Art—Schaumburg
1000 North Plaza Drive, Suite 100
Schaumburg, Illinois 60173-4990
Phone: 847-619-3450
     800-314-3450 (toll-free)
Fax: 847-619-3064
Web site: http://www.artinstitutes.edu/schaumburg

Over 50 schools: The Art Institute of Atlanta; The Art Institute of Atlanta—Decatur, A branch of The Art Institute of Atlanta; The Art Institute of Austin, A branch of The Art Institute of Houston; The Art Institute of California, a college of Argosy University, with locations in Hollywood, Inland Empire, Los Angeles, Orange County, Sacramento, San Diego, San Francisco, and Sunnyvale; The Art Institute of Charleston, A branch of The Art Institute of Atlanta; The Art Institute of Charlotte; The Art Institute of Colorado; The Art Institute of Dallas, A campus of South University; The Art Institute of Fort Lauderdale; The Art Institute of Fort Worth, A campus of South University; The Art Institute of Houston; The Art Institute of Houston—North, A branch of The Art Institute of Houston; The Art Institute of Indianapolis; The Art Institute of Jacksonville, A branch of Miami International University of Art & Design; The Art Institute of Las Vegas; The Art Institute of Michigan; The Art Institute of Michigan—Troy; The Art Institute of New York City; The Art Institute of Ohio—Cincinnati; The Art Institute of Philadelphia; The Art Institute of Phoenix; The Art Institute of Pittsburgh; The Art Institute of Portland; The Art Institute of Raleigh–Durham; The Art Institute of Salt Lake City; The Art Institute of San Antonio, A branch of The Art Institute of Houston; The Art Institute of Seattle; The Art Institute of Tampa, A branch of Miami International University of Art & Design; The Art Institute of Tennessee—Nashville, A branch of The Art Institute of Atlanta; The Art Institute of Tucson; The Art Institute of Vancouver; The Art Institute of Virginia Beach[1], A branch of The Art Institute of Atlanta; The Art Institute of Washington[1], A branch of The Art Institute of Atlanta; The Art Institute of Washington—Dulles[1], A branch of The Art Institute of Atlanta; The Art Institute of Wisconsin; The Art Institute of York—Pennsylvania; The Art Institutes International—Kansas City; The Art Institutes International Minnesota; The Illinois Institute of Art—Chicago; The Illinois Institute of Art—Schaumburg; The Illinois Institute of Art—Tinley Park; Miami International University of Art & Design; The New England Institute of Art

[1]Certified by SCHEV to operate in Virginia

See **aiprograms.info** for program duration, tuition, fees, and other costs, median debt, federal salary data, alumni success, and other important info. The Art Institutes is a system of over 50 schools throughout North America. Programs, credential levels, technology, and scheduling options vary by school, and employment opportunities are not guaranteed. Financial aid is available to those who qualify. Several institutions included in The Art Institutes system are campuses of South University or Argosy University. OH Registration # 04-01-1698B, AC0165, AC0080, Licensed by the Florida Commission for Independent Education, License No. 1287, 3427, 3110, 2581. Administrative office: 210 Sixth Avenue, 33rd Floor, Pittsburgh, PA 15222. ©2012 The Art Institutes International LLC.

THE ILLINOIS INSTITUTE OF ART—TINLEY PARK

TINLEY PARK, ILLINOIS

The Illinois Institute of Art®
Tinley Park
CREATE TOMORROW

A focused education from The Illinois Institute of Art—Tinley Park, an additional location of The Illinois Institute of Art—Chicago, can help students turn their creative energy into a powerful tool that can make a difference in the world. Students are part of a collaborative and supportive community, where experienced instructors provide the guidance and skills needed to pursue a career in the creative economy.

The school's programs in the areas of design, media arts, and fashion give students the opportunity to learn by using professional-grade technology and to build a portfolio of work to show potential employers after graduation.

The Illinois Institute of Art—Tinley Park is an additional location of The Illinois Institute of Art—Chicago, which is accredited by the Higher Learning Commission and a member of the North Central Association (NCA), located at 230 South LaSalle Street, Suite 7-500, Chicago, Illinois 60604-1413; phone: 800-621-7440; www.ncahlc.org.

The Illinois Institute of Art—Tinley Park is authorized by the Illinois Board of Higher Education, 431 East Adams, Second Floor, Springfield, Illinois 62701; phone: 217-782-2551; www.ibhe.state.il.us/default.htm.

Location

Tinley Park is one of the fastest-growing Chicago suburbs and close to the city's vast cultural and sports experiences. In 2009, Business Week magazine listed Tinley Park as America's best place to raise children.

Programs of Study and Degrees

No matter which course of study a student may choose, the professionals at The Illinois Institute of Art—Tinley Park will guide, support, and help each student as their talents evolve on their journey of personal and professional transformation. Students studying design learn to fine-tune their visual thinking and problem-solving skills as they create everything from logos to TV ads. Programs in the area of media arts focus on utilizing technology to deliver information and entertainment, while students studying fashion learn to market and merchandise clothing.

Bachelor's degree programs are offered in the areas of advertising, digital photography, fashion marketing and management, graphic design, interior design, and media arts and animation.

Associate degree programs are offered in the areas of fashion merchandising and graphic design.

Diploma programs are offered in digital image management, fashion retailing, Web design and development, and Web design and interactive communications.

Academic Programs

The Illinois Institute operates on a year-round, four-quarter system.

Academic Facilities

The Illinois Institute of Art—Tinley Park provides a learning environment with professional-grade technology applicable to each student's course of study. Students have the opportunity to build a portfolio of work that shows potential employers that they are trained to use the software, hardware, or equipment utilized within the industry. Depending upon the course of study, students are immersed in a creative environment—from classrooms to computer labs to studios—focused on relevant, hands-on education designed to prepare students for the real world.

Costs

Tuition cost varies by program. Prospective students should contact the school for current tuition costs. Other charges include a starting kit for all first-quarter students. Kits vary in price depending on the program of study.

Financial Aid

Financial aid is available for those who qualify. Students who require financial assistance should first complete and submit a Free Application for Federal Student Aid (FAFSA) and meet with a financial aid officer.

Faculty

Faculty members are experienced professionals who create a learning environment that is similar to the professional

world students will face after graduation. Instructors are focused on helping students develop the skills they need to transform their creative potential into marketable skills.

Admission Requirements

Applicants must provide proof of high school graduation or achievement of a General Educational Development (GED) certificate as a prerequisite for admission. In lieu of documenting high school graduation or a GED certificate, applicants may provide proof of attaining an associate degree or higher from an accredited institution. An official transcript indicating date of high school graduation, GED certificate (including test scores), or date of college graduation (including degree granted) is required as proof.

All individuals seeking admission to The Illinois Institute of Art—Tinley Park are interviewed in person or by phone by an assistant director of admissions, and each applicant must create an original essay of at least 150 words stating how an education at The Illinois Institute of Art—Tinley Park would help the student to achieve career goals. There is a $50 application fee.

For the most recent information regarding admission requirements, please refer to the current academic catalog.

Application and Information

To obtain an application, make arrangements for an interview, or tour the school, prospective students should contact:

The Illinois Institute of Art—Tinley Park
An additional location of The Illinois Institute of Art—Chicago
18670 Graphic Drive
Tinley Park, Illinois 60477
Phone: 708-781-4200
      877-342-3298 (toll-free)
Fax: 708-781-4201
Web site: http://www.artinstitutes.edu/tinleypark

IMMACULATA UNIVERSITY
IMMACULATA, PENNSYLVANIA

The University

Immaculata University (IU), a comprehensive Catholic liberal arts university for students of all faiths, offers a high-quality education that is firmly grounded in values and tradition. Immaculata graduates are known for their skills and knowledge and for their desire to serve. The University was founded in 1920 and has since grown to enroll almost 4,000 students in bachelor's, master's, and doctoral degree programs and accelerated degree-completion programs.

Approximately 1,000 traditional-aged men and women attend the College of Undergraduate Studies, with 80 percent of first-year students living in University-sponsored housing. The College of Lifelong Learning includes undergraduate programs that are open to adult men and women. Students represent seventeen states and twenty-seven countries, giving the campus both ethnic and geographic diversity. Resident students live in four residence halls containing double rooms. Both resident and nonresident students participate in more than sixty student clubs and organizations that represent interests in athletics, student government, academic disciplines, community action, music, dance, theater, and student publications.

Intercollegiate sports include women's basketball, cross-country, field hockey, , lacrosse, soccer, softball, tennis, track and field, and volleyball and men's baseball, basketball, cross-country, golf, lacrosse, soccer, tennis, and track and field. Immaculata competes in Division III athletics as part of the Colonial States Athletic Conference. A turf field, stadium, indoor batting cages, gymnasia, fitness room, and pool are available for student use and provide numerous opportunities for physical activities and wellness programs. The Student Association of Immaculata University provides the unity, enthusiasm, and leadership that are integral parts of the traditional undergraduate experience.

Immaculata University celebrates unique traditions as a part of the overall collegiate experience, such as Sophomore pinning and Junior ring ceremonies. Carol Night, one of Immaculata's best-loved traditions, involves students, faculty members, alumni, and families singing around the Christmas tree in the rotunda of Villa Maria Hall.

The main building, Villa Maria Hall, is of neo-Renaissance architecture in gray stone with a red tile roof. The other thirteen major campus buildings are also of gray stone with red tile roofs, unifying the aesthetic appearance of the campus.

Graduate degrees offered in the College of Graduate Studies include the Master of Arts in counseling psychology, cultural and linguistic diversity, educational leadership and administration, music therapy, nursing, nutrition education, organization leadership, and public relations. Doctoral degrees are offered in educational administration, clinical psychology, and school psychology. ACCEL, the accelerated degree-completion program, offers bachelor's degrees in financial management, human performance management, health care management, organization dynamics, RN-B.S.N., and information technology.

Location

Immaculata's 375-acre campus is located in historic Chester County, 20 miles west of Philadelphia and 10 miles south of Valley Forge. The area is primarily suburban, with numerous colleges and universities offering a wide range of cultural and social activities. Many places of interest in Philadelphia and Lancaster are easily reached by car, train, or bus. The campus is 15 minutes from the King of Prussia Mall, the second largest mall in the U.S. Southern New Jersey shore resorts and New York City are within 1½ hours by car, with Pocono Mountain ski resorts and Washington, D.C., only 2½ hours away by car or train. The University provides numerous opportunities for internships in the business, educational, and scientific communities throughout the area.

Majors and Degrees

The College of Undergraduate Studies at Immaculata offers the Bachelor of Arts, Bachelor of Music, Bachelor of Science, Associate of Arts, and Associate of Science degrees. Undergraduate major fields of study include accounting, allied health, athletic training, biology, biology/psychology, business administration, chemistry, communication, criminology/sociology, education, English, exercise science, family and consumer sciences, fashion merchandising, finance, French, general science, history, information technology, international business/foreign language, marketing management, mathematics, mathematics/computer science, music, music education, music performance, music therapy, nursing, nutrition/dietetics, political science/international relations, prelaw, premedicine, pre–physical therapy, pre–veterinary medicine, psychology, sociology, sociology/social work, Spanish, Spanish/psychology, Spanish/social work, theology, and undecided. Allied health concentrations include: clinical laboratory science, diagnostic medical sonography, invasive cardiovascular technology, nuclear medicine technology, and surgical technology. IU also offers partnership programs with Thomas Jefferson University (TJU) in physical therapy, occupational therapy, bioscience technologies, and radiologic sciences. These programs allow students to seamlessly matriculate into TJU after three years of study at IU.

Academic Programs

Two factors are emphasized in the educational program at Immaculata: a comprehensive liberal arts background and a major field of concentration that prepares students to begin a career or to attend graduate school. The honors program offers an array of courses designed to give those who participate a special involvement in the learning process.

The Mary Bruder Center houses the offices for personal, career, and graduate study counseling and for educational and career testing. Workshops and seminars in resume writing, interviewing, career options, internship opportunities, and graduate fellowships are offered at regular intervals.

Off-Campus Programs

Both summer-abroad and junior-year-abroad programs combine travel with academic study to heighten the experience of students who seek these opportunities. Students can study in England and Ireland through IU and in other countries through the University's collaboration with Arcadia University.

Every undergraduate major department offers numerous internship opportunities for students in agencies, businesses, institutions, or corporations related to their study. Some majors, such as nutrition, fashion merchandising, and music therapy, require a multiweek internship for the degree to be granted.

Academic Facilities

The Gabriele Library houses 130,000 volumes and offers 714 periodical subscriptions. In addition to the computer center, students have access to networked computers in the library, an

interactive language lab with a video screen, and a multifaceted science lab with computer-simulated experiments; they also have Internet/Intranet access from their residence halls. Well-equipped laboratories, art studios, media centers, and a 1,150-seat theater give students a variety of settings in which to pursue their interests.

State-of-the-art computer labs include the Campus Learning and Language Laboratory, the Sister Maria Socorro Studio Laboratory for Mathematics and Science, a new Biology Laboratory, and the Loyola Executive Technology Center. Classrooms and the library utilize wireless technology in the smart classrooms.

Costs

For 2012–13, tuition and fees are $29,000 and room and board are $11,740. An additional $1000 is estimated to cover books and personal spending. Immaculata offers a fixed tuition program. This guarantees the same tuition cost for four years for all full-time students entering the College of Undergraduate Studies. Immaculata is the only college in the Commonwealth of Pennsylvania to offer this program.

Financial Aid

Financial aid is available in the form of scholarships, grants, loans, and part-time campus employment through the resources of Immaculata, federal and state governments, and private endowments. Scholarships are awarded for academic excellence. Approximately 90 percent of the students receive some form of aid, and all students who demonstrate need are offered financial aid packages. The University requires that students submit the Free Application for Federal Student Aid (FAFSA) to be considered for financial aid. The University sends financial aid packages to accepted students as their files are completed by the end of February. The FAFSA reporting code is 003276.

Faculty

The faculty has more than 90 full-time and 200 part-time members, more than half of whom hold doctorates. Several members of the Immaculata faculty conduct research and present papers in various disciplines, both nationally and internationally. High-quality teaching is of the greatest importance to Immaculata's academic program. Full-time faculty members serve as academic counselors and activity moderators. The student-faculty ratio is 11:1.

Student Government

The Student Government Association of Immaculata University (SGA) governs most aspects of student life for both resident and commuter students. The resident assistant program moderates residence life by holding open meetings to discuss safety issues and to set residence hall regulations. Students serve on the various University policymaking committees and handle all student activity funds.

Admission Requirements

In order to be considered for admission to the College of Undergraduate Studies, students must submit an official secondary school transcript indicating course selection for the senior year and SAT or ACT scores. The reporting code for the SAT is 2320, and the reporting code for the ACT is 3596. An essay and recommendations are required. The Admission Committee requires 14 or more course units, as follows: 4 units of English, 2 units of social science, 2 units of mathematics, 2 units of science (1 lab), and 2 consecutive years of the same foreign language. Most candidates exceed this curriculum. The mid-range GPA for the past two years was 3.2.

All admission credentials should be sent to the College of Undergraduate Studies. Students can apply online at the University's Web site, http://www.immaculata.edu/admissions.

The application fee of $35 is waived for students who apply online or who visit the campus and complete an application during their visit. Students also have the option to apply through the Common Application, http://www.commonapp.org, which is free as well.

Application and Information

Applications are accepted from prospective freshman and transfer students on a rolling admissions basis, and decisions are made three to four weeks after an applicant's file is complete. The only exceptions are those students applying for nursing and the Thomas Jefferson University programs. The application deadline for Thomas Jefferson is December 15. All of the credentials required for admission must be received and the file completed by that date.

For further information, students should contact:

Nicola DiFronzo-Heitzer, Ed.D., Director of Admissio
Immaculata University
P.O. Box 642
Immaculata, Pennsylvania 19345-0642
Phone: 610-647-4400 Ext. 3060
          877-42-TODAY (toll-free)
Fax: 610-640-0836
E-mail: admis@immaculata.edu
Web site: http://www.immaculata.edu

Immaculata's beautiful rotunda where students often gather to celebrate various IU traditions.

THE JOHNS HOPKINS UNIVERSITY
Krieger School of Arts and Sciences and Whiting School of Engineering
BALTIMORE, MARYLAND

JOHNS HOPKINS
UNIVERSITY

The University

Privately endowed, the Johns Hopkins University (JHU) was founded in 1876 as the first American university committed to the idea that knowledge should be discovered, rather than merely transmitted. Daniel Coit Gilman, the first president of Johns Hopkins, stated that the object of the University was "not so much to impart knowledge as to whet the appetite, exhibit methods, develop powers, strengthen judgment, and invigorate the intellectual and moral forces." Today, Johns Hopkins continues to stress creative scholarship by providing research-oriented education for undergraduates. Students in all disciplines are encouraged to explore intellectual questions and discover new ideas within a supportive environment.

Johns Hopkins seeks diversity in its students, who come from all fifty states and from seventy-one other countries. Of the total undergraduate enrollment of approximately 5,000 students, about 48 percent are women and 52 percent are men. All out-of-town freshmen and sophomores must live in campus residence halls. In addition, University-owned housing, located directly across from the University on North Charles Street, is available for juniors and seniors. Upperclassmen may also live in private housing or in Greek housing. Johns Hopkins has thirteen fraternities and nine sororities in the Inter-Fraternity Council and the Panhellenic Council.

The Homewood campus is active and lively, with many different events such as films, concerts, seminars, and athletic games being offered each week. The Student Council runs a number of activities, including a popular Spring Fair each year. Men's varsity teams compete in twelve sports. In the fall, men's teams compete in cross-country, football, soccer, and water polo. In the winter, basketball, fencing, swimming, and wrestling are offered. The big sports season at Johns Hopkins is spring, with baseball, lacrosse, tennis, and track and field. The men's and women's lacrosse teams compete at the Division I level, and the men have won forty-four national championships. Women's varsity sports also include basketball, cross-country, fencing, field hockey, soccer, swimming, tennis, track and field, and volleyball. An extensive and popular intramural program is also available. The O'Connor Recreation Center contains basketball and volleyball courts, a running track, racquetball courts, a rock-climbing wall, a weight room, and fitness and aerobic areas. In addition to the athletic programs, there are over 370 student-run clubs that hold events throughout the year. From the performing arts to hobby-centered clubs, there are many options for students of all interests.

Location

Johns Hopkins University's Homewood campus is on 140 acres of lush greenery, bounded on all sides by residential areas. Johns Hopkins offers the best of both worlds—the tranquil seclusion of the campus plus the adjacent urban environment. Two museums are owned by the University: Homewood Museum, on campus, and Evergreen Museum & Library, located nearby on North Charles Street, both of which provide academic opportunities for students. The Baltimore Museum of Art is on the southwest corner of the campus. The Walters Art Museum, a 10-minute drive away, has a collection that spans civilizations from Egypt to the 19th century, and many smaller museums, galleries, and outdoor showings feature local artists. The University is located just three miles from the heart of downtown Baltimore; the theater, symphony, and opera are 10 minutes away, as are Oriole Park at Camden Yards and M&T Bank Stadium. Weekend activities include visiting Baltimore's Inner Harbor, home to the National Aquarium and many other attractions; enjoying an ethnic festival by the water; sailing on the Chesapeake Bay; and hiking around the Maryland countryside. Washington, D.C. is a 50-minute drive by car or a 1-hour train ride. Opportunities abound for on- and off-campus entertainment.

Majors and Degrees

Bachelor of Arts degrees are awarded in Africana studies, anthropology, archaeology, behavioral biology, biology, biophysics, chemistry, classics, cognitive science, earth and planetary sciences, East Asian studies, economics, English, film and media studies, French, German, global environmental change and sustainability, history, history of art, history of science and technology, interdisciplinary studies, international studies, Italian, Latin American studies, mathematics, natural sciences, Near Eastern studies, neuroscience, philosophy, physics, political science, psychology, public health studies, Romance languages, sociology, Spanish, and the Writing Seminars. A Bachelor of Arts degree in engineering is available for students who seek preparation for professional careers (such as law or business) with a technological orientation. The B.A. in engineering is awarded in applied mathematics and statistics, biomedical engineering, computer science, electrical engineering, general engineering, and geography. Bachelor of Science degrees are awarded in applied mathematics and statistics, biomedical engineering, chemical and biomolecular engineering, civil engineering, computer engineering, computer science, electrical engineering, environmental engineering, materials science and engineering, mechanical engineering, molecular and cellular biology, and physics.

Accelerated bachelor's/master's degree programs are offered in biology, biophysics, German, history, international studies, mathematics, neuroscience, policy studies, psychology, public health studies, and Spanish. Accelerated B.S./M.S.E. programs are offered in most engineering departments. A dual-degree program leading to a Bachelor of Arts or Bachelor of Science degree and a Bachelor of Music degree is available in cooperation with the University's Peabody Institute and Conservatory of Music.

Academic Programs

The departments in the Krieger School of Arts and Sciences and the Whiting School of Engineering comprise four general areas for undergraduate programs: engineering, humanities, natural sciences, and social sciences. If a student has special interests that fall outside the bounds of the departmental majors, an individual program can be devised, or a student may study independently with the guidance of a faculty member. Qualified students may complete their degree requirements in fewer than four years.

Johns Hopkins has an extremely flexible program. There are no required freshman courses. All students must fulfill distribution requirements as well as the requirements for their major; the distribution requirements include a writing element. In most majors, 120 credits are required for graduation. Johns Hopkins has a 4-1-4 calendar.

The University offers the Army ROTC program on campus and the Air Force ROTC program in cooperation with the University of Maryland, College Park.

Off-Campus Programs

If qualified, a student may undertake a program for study abroad, normally during the junior year. Programs are offered at Johns Hopkins' international center in Bologna, Italy, as well as in Paris, France; Madrid, Spain; Berlin, Germany; and Latin America and through independent study-abroad programs with Johns Hopkins credit. Currently, there are more than 400 students studying abroad in over thirty countries. The University also participates in a cooperative program with other colleges in the Baltimore area. Undergraduates may take courses at the other divisions of Johns Hopkins University, including the Peabody Conservatory, the School of Nursing, the Bloomberg School of Public Health, the Nitze School of Advanced International Studies, the School of Education, the Carey Business School, and the School of Medicine.

Academic Facilities

The Milton S. Eisenhower Library on the Homewood campus is part of the University's Sheridan Libraries, which comprise the Milton S. Eisenhower Library, the John Work Garrett Library, the Albert D. Hutzler Undergraduate Reading Room, and the George

Peabody Library. Together, these libraries provide one of the most comprehensive learning resources in the world, containing more than 3.7 million books, more than 55,000 print and electronic journals, more than 700,000 electronic books, more than 10,000 videos and DVDs, more than 216,000 maps, and significant rare books, manuscripts, and archival resources.

The Mattin Student Arts Center contains the Swirnow Theater, a dance studio, music practice rooms, film and digital labs, darkrooms, a café, art studios, and spaces for students to gather. Hodson Hall includes classrooms, a meeting room for the Board of Trustees, the archives of the Hodson Trust, and a 500-seat auditorium, in which every seat is wired to the Internet. Clark Hall houses a state-of-the-art research and teaching facility for biomedical engineering. Charles Commons, a 618-person residential complex and dining facility, also houses the University's two-story Barnes and Noble bookstore.

Wireless network coverage is available throughout most areas of the campus with the use of a supported wireless LAN card. Those living off campus can remotely access University systems and library resources. The Homewood Academic Computing Lab is open 24 hours a day, has more than 115 computers, and provides student consultants who can assist with problems that arise. The Brown Foundation Digital Media Center offers an environment where students can bring artistic inspiration to life using digital tools. It features twelve high-end computers that enable digital and audio composition and editing, animation, virtual painting, and 3-D modeling. All campus buildings are networked with each other and the other Johns Hopkins campuses.

Costs

Costs for 2011–12 were $42,280 for tuition, $12,962 for room and board, and $2200 for books and personal expenses. Travel expenses vary.

Financial Aid

Financial aid is based on demonstrated eligibility, as determined by the Free Application for Federal Student Aid (FAFSA) at the time of acceptance. Approximately 46 percent of students receive financial assistance. Students must reapply for financial aid each year with the FAFSA and the College Scholarship Service (CSS) Financial Aid PROFILE. Johns Hopkins offers several merit-based scholarships, including the Hodson Trust Scholarship. Johns Hopkins also offers Army ROTC scholarships worth up to full tuition. The Baltimore Scholars Program provides full-tuition scholarships to eligible Baltimore City public high school graduates. In addition, several scholarships and grants allow undergraduates to pursue research opportunities, even as freshmen.

Faculty

The University's intellectual reputation is based on the strength of its faculty, of whom 87 percent hold a doctorate. The student-faculty ratio is 12:1. The well-known professors at Johns Hopkins teach both undergraduate and graduate students, which means that students receive a great deal of personal attention both in and out of the classroom. Johns Hopkins has a large number of notable professors, including 49 American Academy of Arts and Sciences fellows, 3 National Medal of Science winners, 2 Presidential Medal of Freedom winners, and 7 MacArthur Fellows. Faculty members are always accessible to advise and assist students and to work with them on research projects.

Student Government

Johns Hopkins students enjoy the benefits of a well-organized and far-reaching student government, which is led by a powerful Student Council. The council is composed of elected class representatives and officers, but it relies on the active participation of many students in its numerous committees, boards, and commissions. Through the Student Activities Commission, the University encourages initiative and independence by giving students full responsibility and control of funds for various clubs and organizations.

Admission Requirements

In choosing from a large number of applicants, the University selects those men and women who will benefit from a Johns Hopkins education, and who will add something to the campus community. A student's intellectual interests and accomplishments are of primary importance, and the Admissions Committee carefully examines each applicant's scholastic record, standardized test results, essays, and recommendations from secondary school officials and other sources about the student's character, intellectual curiosity, seriousness of purpose, and range of extracurricular involvement. The application essays are an important part of how the Admissions Committee learns more about students during the application review process. Two teacher recommendations are required. In addition, the SAT or the ACT with writing test is required. For students submitting SAT scores, Johns Hopkins recommends the submission of SAT Subject Tests, and if submitted, requests results from three tests. Students should consult the Web site for additional details on test requirements. Every year, the University enrolls a first-year class of approximately 1,250 men and women from all parts of the United States and a number of other countries. In addition, transfer students from other colleges and universities are admitted to the sophomore and junior classes. Advanced-standing credit is granted from college-level work completed at an accredited college or through the Advanced Placement and International Baccalaureate programs.

Application and Information

Johns Hopkins accepts the Common Application and the Universal College Application, both with a Johns Hopkins supplement. The application deadline is January 1. If applicants consider Johns Hopkins to be their first choice, they may apply under the early decision plan. This requires that the application be filed by November 1. Notification is given by April 1 for regular decision students and by December 15 for those applying under the early decision plan. Students wishing to enroll in the biomedical engineering (BME) program must indicate BME as their first choice of major on their application. Freshmen who are BME majors are admitted specifically as such.

Office of Undergraduate Admissions
The Johns Hopkins University
Mason Hall
3400 North Charles Street
Baltimore, Maryland 21218-2683
Phone: 410-516-8171
Fax: 410-516-6025
E-mail: gotojhu@jhu.edu
Web site: http://apply.jhu.edu

Johns Hopkins students enjoy class in front of Gilman Hall.

JOHNSON & WALES UNIVERSITY
PROVIDENCE, RHODE ISLAND

The University

Johnson & Wales University (JWU), founded in 1914, is a nonprofit, private institution. A recognized leader in career education, the University offers accredited degrees to more than 17,000 graduate and undergraduate students, representing all fifty states and ninety-seven countries. An innovative educational leader, JWU offers a broad range of undergraduate and graduate degree programs that inspire professional success and lifelong personal and intellectual growth by integrating arts and sciences and experiential education with leadership and personal development opportunities. The University has four campuses in Providence, Rhode Island; North Miami, Florida; Denver, Colorado; and Charlotte, North Carolina.

JWU is a career-oriented institution offering programs in a variety of areas. Most students are recent graduates of high school business, college-preparatory, and vocational/technical programs. The academic focus of the University is degree programs in business, culinary arts, education, hospitality, counseling psychology, and technology. JWU offers an M.B.A. program with concentrations in accounting, enhanced accounting, hospitality, and information technology. M.A. programs in teaching (with or without certification) include business, food service, and special education. The University also offers a doctoral program in educational leadership.

Students are involved in a variety of extracurricular activities. Nearly 20 percent of the students at the University are members of national student organizations such as Business Professionals of America; DECA (Collegiate DECA), Future Business Leaders of America (Phi Beta Lambda); Family, Career, Community Leaders of America (FCCLA); National FFA; Junior Achievement; SkillsUSA; and Technology Association of America. The Office of Student Activities (OSA) and fraternities and sororities are among the many groups that schedule social functions throughout the academic year. Sports and fitness programs include aerobics, baseball, basketball, golf, ice hockey, sailing, soccer, tennis, volleyball, and wrestling.

The University maintains twenty-six residence halls throughout its four campuses. In addition, City View Towers, which is independently owned and operated, offers housing near the Charlotte campus for upperclassmen. Student services include academic counseling and testing, a tutorial center, and health services. JWU's Experiential Education and Career Services office provides extensive career planning and placement services.

Johnson & Wales University is accredited by the New England Association of Schools and Colleges Inc. (NEASC), through its Commission on Institutions of Higher Education.

Location

The location of each of the University's campuses enables students to take advantage of internship and part-time work activities offered by many nearby businesses, community groups, and government agencies. All of Johnson & Wales' city campuses retain a small-town feel and easy accessibility to students. The urban setting of the Providence campus provides students proximity to the city's many cultural and recreational facilities. The North Miami campus is a short trip from the sun and fun of Fort Lauderdale and the culture and diversity of Miami. The Denver campus offers students great opportunities as the nation's sixth-leading tourist destination and *Fortune* magazine's "second best city in America to work and live." The Charlotte campus is located in a vibrant urban setting that combines commercial and residential life. More than 295 Fortune 500 companies have offices in Charlotte, which is known as the second-largest financial center in the U.S.

Majors and Degrees

The degree programs described in this section are for the 2012–13 academic year and are subject to change. Students may pursue concentrations related to their program of study to further tailor their degrees to their specific interests and career goals. They also have the opportunity to take concentrations through the School of Arts and Sciences.

The University's Providence campus offers degree programs in accounting; advertising and marketing communications; baking and pastry arts; baking and pastry arts and food service management; business administration; counseling psychology; criminal justice; culinary arts; culinary arts and food service management; culinary nutrition; electronics engineering; engineering design and configuration management; entrepreneurship; equine business management; equine business management/riding; fashion merchandising and retail marketing; finance; food service entrepreneurship; graphic design and digital media; hotel and lodging management; international business; international hotel and tourism management; management; management accounting; marketing; network engineering; restaurant, food, and beverage management; risk management; software engineering; sports/entertainment/event management; and travel, tourism, and hospitality management.

In its adult and continuing education division, Johnson & Wales' Providence campus offers associate and bachelor's degrees in business, culinary arts, hospitality, and technology.

The North Miami campus offers degree programs in baking and pastry arts; business administration; criminal justice; culinary arts; culinary arts and food service management; fashion merchandising and retail marketing; hotel and lodging management; management; marketing; pastry arts and food service management; restaurant, food, and beverage management; sports/entertainment/event management; and travel, tourism, and hospitality management.

The Denver campus offers degree programs in baking and pastry arts; baking and pastry arts and food service management; business administration; criminal justice; culinary arts; culinary arts and food service management; culinary nutrition; fashion merchandising and retail marketing; hotel and lodging management; restaurant, food, and beverage management; and sports/entertainment/event management. Students can also earn degrees in culinary arts and baking and pastry arts through the adult and continuing education division.

The Charlotte campus offers degree programs in baking and pastry arts; baking and pastry arts and food service management; business administration; culinary arts; culinary arts and food service management; fashion merchandising and retail marketing; hotel and lodging management; management; management accounting; marketing; restaurant, food, and beverage management; and sports/entertainment/event management.

Academic Programs

Johnson & Wales University offers programs in business, culinary arts, hospitality, counseling psychology, and technology within an academic structure of three 11-week terms.

Learning by doing is an important part of career training at JWU, and many programs include laboratory studies as well as formal internship requirements. Students get real-life work experience beginning their freshman year. Special advanced-placement programs are featured for high school seniors with exceptional skills in culinary arts or baking and pastry arts. In addition, JWU awards credit for certain courses based on the successful completion of Challenge, CLEP, or Portfolio Assessments. All degree candidates must successfully complete the required number of courses and/or quarter credit hours, as prescribed in the various curricula.

Off-Campus Programs

At Johnson & Wales, students get hands-on learning experiences from the start, inside and outside the classroom. Many of the majors offer internships at University-owned facilities. The hotel-restaurant management program features an internship at the Johnson & Wales Inn, Radisson Airport Hotel, or Doubletree Hotel; all are full-service hotel complexes that are owned and/or operated

by the University (the Radisson and Doubletree are corporate franchises). For all majors, optional selective career internships are available with cooperating businesses throughout the U.S. and worldwide, such as Marriott International, Compass Group NAD, Foxwoods Resort and Casino, and Putnam Investments. Most internships are one term in duration and carry 13.5 quarter hours of credit. International exchange and term-abroad programs are also offered.

Academic Facilities

The facilities of the Providence campus are located throughout the intimate state of Rhode Island and in nearby Massachusetts. The Downcity campus in Providence is home to the University's College of Business, The Hospitality College, the School of Arts and Sciences, and the School of Technology. A number of academic and residential facilities are located at this campus, as are several training facilities. The Harborside campus, also in Providence but located a short distance away from the Downcity campus, houses the University's College of Culinary Arts. This campus has five student residence halls as well as specialized classrooms and laboratories, production kitchens, bakeshops, dining rooms, a storeroom, and meat-cutting facilities. This campus is also home to the Alan Shawn Feinstein Graduate School, the School of Education, the University Recreation and Athletic Center, a student activities office, a bookstore, a gymnasium, a dining center, a snack bar, and an arcade.

JWU's North Miami campus is located in the heart of North Miami, between Miami and Fort Lauderdale. Facilities include academic classrooms, production/demonstration kitchens, a bakeshop, residence halls, and a specially designed conference center.

The Denver campus, located in the Park Hill neighborhood, combines old-world charm with the latest technological resources, including stately turn-of-the-century buildings and newer student centers in a quiet park landscape. The traditional residential campus is fully wired, with computers in every classroom and laboratory.

The Charlotte campus is located in the heart of Gateway Village in Uptown Charlotte. The academic center is home to a 200-seat auditorium, a production kitchen, state-of-the-art culinary laboratories, classrooms, seminar rooms, and computer labs.

Costs

Tuition at all campuses for 2012–13 is $26,112 ($24,913 tuition plus $1199 general fee). Room and board plans range from $8019 to $12,000. There is also an orientation fee of $300 for new students. Books and supplies are estimated at $800 to $900 per year, depending on the program.

Room and board fees vary at each campus. Students should consult the respective campus catalogs for further details.

Financial Aid

Johnson & Wales students are eligible to apply for a variety of financial aid programs, including the Federal Pell Grant, Federal Supplemental Educational Opportunity Grant, Federal Work-Study, and Federal Perkins Loan programs. They are also eligible for University-based student scholarship programs and state-supported grants and scholarships. In the past, approximately 90 percent of the University's entering students have received some sort of financial assistance. Students must submit the Free Application for Federal Student Aid (FAFSA) to the Federal Student Aid Processor to be considered for financial aid. Early application is strongly suggested for full consideration.

Faculty

The University's 517 full-time and 294 part-time faculty members (all campuses) are oriented toward instruction rather than research. Many are chosen for their professional experience in business, culinary arts, hospitality services, or technology. The student-faculty ratio is 27:1.

Student Government

Student Government Association (SGA) is the voice of students on campus and serves as the governing student organization on campus.

Students are elected to major leadership positions in the spring, and senator positions are available to any interested student in the fall. SGA is responsible for allocating student funds, recognizing new organizations, and addressing student concerns on campus.

Admission Requirements

Johnson & Wales seeks students who are career-focused and have a true desire to succeed. Academic qualifications are important, but an applicant's motivation and interest in doing well are given special consideration. Graduation from high school or the equivalent credentials are required for admission. It is recommended that students applying for admission into the culinary arts and baking and pastry arts programs have some prior education or experience in food service. Although tests are not required for most programs, all applicants are encouraged to submit scores from the SAT or ACT. Students who wish to apply for the honors program must have either a score of at least 500 math and 500 critical reading on the SAT or a score of at least 21 math and 21 verbal on the ACT. High school juniors may apply for early admission under the Early Enrollment Program (EEP). Transfer students are required to submit official high school and college transcripts and to have a minimum GPA of 2.0. Credits to be transferred from other institutions are evaluated on the basis of their equivalent at Johnson & Wales.

Application and Information

Johnson & Wales does not require an application fee. After submitting the application, the student is responsible for requesting that appropriate transcripts be forwarded to JWU's Admissions. While there is no deadline, students are advised to apply as early as possible before the intended date of enrollment to ensure full consideration of their application. Applications are accepted for terms beginning in September, December, and March and for the summer sessions (for most programs).

Inquiries and applications should be addressed to:

Kenneth DiSaia
Senior Vice President of Enrollment Management
Johnson & Wales University
8 Abbott Park Place
Providence, Rhode Island 02903
Phone: 401-598-1000
      800-DIAL-JWU (toll-free)
Fax: 401-598-4901
E-mail: jwu@admissions.jwu.edu
Web site: http://www.jwu.edu
      http://www.facebook.com/jwuadmissions

Johnson & Wales University offers degree programs in business, culinary arts, hospitality, counseling psychology, and technology.

KENDALL COLLEGE
CHICAGO, ILLINOIS

The College

For more than seventy-five years, Kendall College has offered engaging, specialized fields of study with a strong emphasis on immersive learning that is geared to a student's academic, personal, and professional success.

Whether choosing Kendall's acclaimed School of Culinary Arts, distinctive School of Hospitality Management, innovative School of Business, or well-established School of Education, students are encouraged to explore their talents, interests, and passions—and to discover a wealth of exciting opportunities.

Kendall's School of Culinary Arts has prepared outstanding culinary professionals for more than twenty-five years. Its bachelor's and associate degree programs are intensive, hands-on, and cutting-edge, utilizing twelve commercial-grade kitchens, an onsite fine-dining restaurant, and an equally well-regarded cafeteria. The programs are designed to help students successfully launch careers in the vast foodservice industry, equipped with superb culinary skills, and the equally critical business management and communication skills. Students intern locally, nationally, and internationally at top-notch hospitality and culinary venues. Kendall chef instructors possess formal culinary training and at least ten years of hands-on experience and expertise from all facets of the foodservice industry.

Kendall's School of Hospitality Management combines European customer-focused competencies with American management skills. The B.A. program offers a variety of concentrations: asset management, casino management, club management, meetings and events management, hotel and lodging management, restaurant and foodservice management, and sports and leisure management. Students intern locally, nationally, and internationally at leading hospitality and culinary venues.

Kendall's School of Business helps prepare graduates to succeed in today's global workforce by focusing on the service industries. The program offers a Bachelor of Arts in Business with four concentration options: food service management, management, psychology, and small business management. The curriculum is taught by an accomplished faculty of industry experts and uses situation-based challenges, actual case studies, management simulations, and integrative projects to produce employment-ready graduates.

The School of Education at Kendall offers a Bachelor of Arts degree in early childhood education, with optional Illinois Type 04 Teacher Certification preparation, as well as concentrations in childhood nutrition, English as a second language (ESL), infants and toddlers, and special education. Through continuing studies, additional licensure and licensure enhancement options are valuable to current teachers and those who already hold an undergraduate degree.

School of Education courses are offered in three convenient formats to support the needs of both full-time students and those choosing to work as they earn their degree. Formats include online, on campus, hybrid (a combination of online learning and campus instruction), or the option of mixing formats to suit a variety of schedules and learning preferences. All formats allow students to benefit from interaction with classmates and faculty in small class environments.

Kendall College is a member of the Laureate International Universities, a global network of more than fifty institutions of higher learning with more than 100 campuses in twenty-eight countries. Through this partnership, students have broad access to study-abroad programs, internships, and professional opportunities in Asia, Australia, Europe, and Latin America.

Kendall College is accredited by the Higher Learning Commission and is a member of the North Central Association of Colleges and Schools (NCA), http://www.ncahlc.org, phone: 312-263-0456. The American Culinary Federation Education Foundation (ACFEFAC) has accredited the culinary arts associate program since 1988 and the baking and pastry associate program since 2008. The early childhood education program in the School of Education is approved by the Illinois State Board of Education for Type 04 Illinois Teacher Certification preparation (birth through grade 3).

Location

Kendall College's campus, located near the heart of downtown Chicago, prepares its graduates for exciting opportunities in the culinary, hospitality, and business industries. The school is minutes from some of the country's best restaurants, hotels, and companies, providing students prime access to internships and work experiences. The facility offers sweeping views of the Chicago skyline, access to newly developed areas on the Chicago River, and all the cultural and social benefits of the third-largest city in the United States. Kendall College's residence hall is Presidential Towers, located at 555 West Madison Avenue, just steps away from renowned museums, shopping, and entertainment.

Majors and Degrees

Kendall College awards Bachelor of Arts (B.A.) degrees in business, culinary arts, early childhood education, and hospitality management. The College also awards the Associate of Applied Science (A.A.S.) degree in baking and pastry, and culinary arts.

Academic Programs

Kendall College operates on a quarter system. The first quarter term extends from October to mid-December, the second term extends from January to March, and the third term extends from April to June. Summer sessions are offered from July to September.

Academic Facilities

The Chicago Riverworks campus provides wireless Internet access, computer labs, and two distance-learning videoconference facilities. Classrooms and study environments are designed to give students an effective setting in which to learn. There are student lounges, twelve commercial grade kitchens, an academic success center, parking spaces, and a number of nearby health clubs.

Costs

In 2011–12, full-time (12–19 credit hours/term) tuition in the School of Culinary Arts was $22,095 for three quarters.

Full-time tuition for the School of Hospitality Management was $19,608 for three quarters.

Full-time tuition in the School of Business was $13,545 for three quarters.

Full-time tuition in the School of Education was $222 per credit hour for both classroom and online courses.

Housing is located at Presidential Towers, located at 555 West Madison Avenue in Chicago. Students may lease double-occupancy one-bedroom apartments for $13,356 per twelve-month lease. Single-occupancy one-bedroom apartments are leased to students for $26,712 per twelve-month lease. Quad-occupancy two-bedroom apartments are leased to students for $10,812 per twelve-month lease.

Financial Aid

Kendall College administers federal, state, and institutional aid for undergraduates. The College works with each student to help file required applications leading to the awarding of financial aid. The College's goal is to assist students to receive all funding for which they are eligible. The financial aid packaging process ensures effective use of available funds, providing fair and equitable treatment of all applicants.

Faculty

The student-faculty ratio is approximately 19:1, providing students the benefit of small classes and the ability to engage one-on-one with the faculty and the material. Faculty members at Kendall College believe students work best when they are actively involved in making choices about their own learning.

Student Government

Kendall College's Student Government Federation (SGF) is the students' organization. It provides students with a leadership role, a voice within Kendall College, and access to improving the campus community. SGF represents the student body to various committees and boards within the College such as the Board of Trustees' Student Affairs Committee and the Faculty Senate. SGF also oversees all student clubs and organizations, along with program activities for students. SGF is elected at the beginning of the fall quarter with the term of service extending for three academic quarters.

Admission Requirements

Students who apply to Kendall College are evaluated on individual merit. Each applicant is evaluated on the basis of probable success at Kendall College. Cumulative grade point average(s) (GPAs), standardized test scores, personal statements, and admissions interviews are among the methods of evaluation. Special consideration is given to adult students who are returning to school. To determine official GPAs, the College must receive an official institution transcript directly from the institution or the organization housing the institution's records. Admissions interviews are required either via a face-to-face tour of the campus or on the phone to help determine the admission decision. An official high school transcript with graduation date and unweighted final GPA of at least 2.0 (on a 4.0 scale) are required for acceptance. Kendall College requires all students who have graduated from high school within five years of their intended start date to submit ACT composite scores of 18 or greater or three-part SAT scores of 1350 or higher.

Students whose academic record does not meet Kendall admission standards in one or more admission categories (high school GPA, transfer GPA), but who demonstrate the potential for success at Kendall may be admitted with provisions.

Application and Information

Prospective students may obtain applications from the Office of Admissions or via the College's Web site at www.kendall.edu. Students may submit the admission application at any time. The Office of Admissions must be sent an official transcript.

For further information, students should contact:

Office of Admissions
Kendall College
900 N. North Branch Street
Chicago, Illinois 60642
Phone: 312-752-2020
      888-905-3632 (toll-free)
Fax: 312-752-2021
E-mail: info@kendall.edu
Web site: http://www.kendall.edu
    http://www.facebook.com/kendall.college
    http://twitter.com/kendallcollege

Kendall students share a passion for their fields of study: business, culinary arts, education, or hospitality management.

KENT STATE UNIVERSITY
KENT, OHIO

The University

Kent State University has experienced tremendous growth since its founding in 1910. Today, Kent State is a multicampus network serving more than 40,000 students at eight locations throughout northeastern Ohio. The eight-campus network is anchored by a classic residential campus in Kent, Ohio. Throughout the network, students can pursue certificate, bachelor's, master's, and doctoral degrees. The Kent Campus, serving more than 22,000 undergraduates and more than 5,400 graduates, offers more than 230 undergraduate study areas and numerous graduate degrees. Kent State's seven regional campuses are located in Ashtabula, Geauga (including the Twinsburg Center in Twinsburg, Ohio), Stark, Trumbull, and Tuscarawas counties, and the cities of Salem and East Liverpool.

As a residential campus, Kent State requires students to reside in one of the twenty-five residence halls until junior academic standing is achieved. Exceptions include commuting and nontraditional students. Students can easily walk to any of the more than 100 academic, residential, administrative, and recreational buildings. The University has an eighteen-hole golf course, a 291-acre airport, a two-rink indoor ice arena, three on-campus theaters, and a student recreation and wellness center. There are more than 200 student organizations, sixteen fraternities, six sororities, and eighteen varsity sports. The Career Services Center provides career counseling and job placement assistance for students and alumni.

Location

Kent, Ohio, a city with a population of 28,000, is within easy traveling distance of the major metropolitan areas of northeastern Ohio. Within a 40-mile radius are concerts, cultural events, museums, nature preserves, recreational areas, and year-round sports.

Majors and Degrees

The College of Architecture and Environmental Design offers the Bachelor of Science and Master of Architecture degrees. The School of Interior Design offers a Bachelor of Arts in interior design.

The College of the Arts offers the Bachelor of Arts, Bachelor of Fine Arts, Bachelor of Music, and Bachelor of Science degrees. The college also offers multiple-degree programs. The academic divisions are the Schools of Art, Fashion Design and Merchandising, Music, and Theatre and Dance.

The College of Arts and Sciences awards Bachelor of Arts, Bachelor of Science, and Bachelor of General Studies degrees. Major fields of concentration are American Sign Language; anthropology; applied conflict management; applied mathematics; biology; biochemistry; biotechnology; botany; chemistry; classics; computer science; criminology and justice studies; earth science; economics; English; environmental science and conservation; French literature, culture, and translation; geography; geology; German literature, culture, and translation; history; international relations; mathematics; medical technology; Pan-African studies; paralegal studies; philosophy; physics; political science; psychology; Russian literature, culture, and translation; sociology; Spanish literature, culture, and translation; and zoology. Numerous interdisciplinary and preprofessional programs are available, including general studies, integrated life sciences, pre-dentistry, pre-engineering, pre-law, pre-medicine, pre-osteopathy, pre-pharmacy, and pre–veterinary medicine.

The College of Business Administration awards the Bachelor of Business Administration degree. Major fields of concentration are accounting, business management, computer information systems, economics, entrepreneurship, finance, managerial marketing, and marketing. Students can choose a minor in any of these programs as well as in health-care systems management and international business.

The College of Communication and Information offers the Bachelor of Arts, Bachelor of Fine Arts, and the Bachelor of Science degrees. Major fields of concentration are advertising, communication studies, electronic media, news, photo illustration, public relations, radio-television, visual communication design, and visual journalism.

The College of Education, Health, and Human Services offers the Bachelor of Science in Education, Bachelor of Arts, Bachelor of Science degrees, and Master of Arts degrees, with licensure programs available in adolescence/young adult education, early childhood education, special education (majors include deaf education, educational interpreter studies, mild/moderate educational needs, and moderate/intensive educational needs), middle childhood education, multiage education, and trade and industrial education (vocational education). In addition, separate degree programs including majors in athletic training, hospitality management, human development and family studies, integrated health studies, nutrition, speech pathology and audiology, and sport administration are offered in the Schools of Health Sciences; Foundations, Leadership, and Administration; Lifespan Development and Educational Sciences; and Teaching, Learning, and Curriculum Studies.

The College of Nursing awards the Bachelor of Science in Nursing degree. The four-year program includes clinical practicums in the Cleveland-Akron-Warren-Youngstown areas.

The College of Public Health offers a baccalaureate program called the Bachelor of Science in Public Health degree. This academic degree addresses the health of populations and communities through instruction, service, and community-based research. A Master of Public Health degree is also offered.

The College of Applied Engineering, Sustainability and Technology offers bachelor's and master's degree programs throughout Kent State's eight-campus system. Students can select from a number of specialized academic programs in aeronautics, industrial, electrical, manufacturing, or educational technologies. Construction management and air traffic control are two new undergraduate programs.

The School of Digital Sciences offers the Bachelor of Arts and the Bachelor of Science degrees. Major fields of concentration include enterprise architecture, digital systems and analysis, cognition and communication, management and consulting, software development, and telecommunication networks.

Academic Programs

Kent State's colleges and schools all maintain separate academic programs; completion of about 36 credits of liberal education course work (known as the Kent Core) is a University requirement for all students. The number of credit hours required for graduation varies but is generally 121 semester hours. Credits can be transferred from previous college work satisfactorily completed or earned through courses taken at one of Kent State's regional campuses. Credit by examination is available. Generally, to earn a degree, students must earn 30 semester hours in residence.

The Honors College provides opportunities for students and faculty members to develop and implement special learning experiences. It offers four-year programs of undergraduate study with concurrent enrollment in one of the University's degree-granting programs. In addition, the Honors College awards Advanced Placement and International Baccalaureate credit and specialized academic advising. Its Experimental and Integrative Studies Division offers nontraditional learning experiences for students and faculty members of the entire University community.

Support services are available for students needing assistance to ensure a successful college experience. The Academic Success Center program offers tutoring, and Student Accessibility Services

assists students with various physical disabilities and specific learning disabilities. The Center for Adult and Veteran Services offers personal and career counseling and academic advising for nontraditional students and veterans of the U.S. Armed Forces. The Center also processes all G.I. Bill benefits, including the Post-9/11 G.I. Bill.

Army and Air Force ROTC programs are offered on campus.

Off-Campus Programs

Through the Office of Global Education, Kent State offers students a variety of overseas academic programs that provide a balance of academic, linguistic, and cross-cultural experiences and learning opportunities. Credit is granted toward degrees.

Academic Facilities

The collections of the University libraries total 2,950,165 bound volumes and 55,417 electronic and 2,224 print subscriptions. The Honors Center is a living-learning residential complex that houses undergraduate students as well as staff offices, a library-seminar room, a student computer facility, and an audiovisual center. The Center for Applied Conflict Management is an academic unit offering programs of study, research, and service activities that focus on the dynamics of change in human systems. The Instructional Television Service operates a closed-circuit, campuswide network and a production center for NETO, Inc., Channels 45 and 49, northeastern Ohio's public television stations. Audiovisual services support regularly scheduled classes with films and other educational materials. The Instructional Resources Center assists students in the production of educational media materials. The Language Laboratory provides tapes and other tools to assist students in foreign language studies. The Academic Testing Services Office offers test administration, test scoring, and research activities. The School of Fashion Design and Merchandising sponsors a working museum of fashion for students and the public. This school includes classrooms, labs, a library, and a collection of costumes donated from the Silverman-Rogers estate for hands-on study.

As a recognized leader in liquid crystal technology, Kent State's Glenn H. Brown Liquid Crystal Institute is the nation's only center devoted solely to liquid crystal research. With a recent grant from the National Science Foundation, Kent State became the home of Ohio's first Science and Technology Research Center for the Study of Advanced Liquid Crystalline Optical Materials.

Costs

Instructional and other fees for Ohio residents for 2012–13 are $9672 per year. For students residing outside Ohio, instructional and other fees are $17,632 per year. Although room rates vary, costs for board and a double room averaged $9176 per year. The average student spends $1420 per year for books and supplies and should budget extra money for personal needs and expenses. All fees and charges are subject to change.

Financial Aid

More than 80 percent of Kent State's freshmen receive assistance through scholarships, grants, loans, or employment opportunities. To be considered for financial aid awards, students must be admitted to the University and must submit the Free Application for Federal Student Aid (FAFSA) online. Ohio students should also check the Ohio College Opportunity Grant (OCOG) box on the FAFSA if they are interested in being considered. Students planning to attend the fall semester as freshmen should apply for financial aid online after January 1 and before March 1 of the same year. In order to meet the March 1 priority deadline, it is recommended that all financial aid forms be completed no later than February 1. Applications received after March 1 are considered, but sufficient funds to assist all late applicants may be lacking. Additional information is available from the Student Financial Aid Office at www.kent.edu/financialaid.

First-time freshmen and incoming transfer students from forty-nine states outside of Ohio are eligible for a $3980 University Award. For eligibility requirements, students should visit www.kent.edu/financialaid.

Kent State's Honors College awards merit scholarships to selected individuals who have the potential for superior scholarly and creative work at the University as determined by academic performance and creative artist competitions. For more information, visit the Honors College Web site at www.kent.edu/honors.

The Student Financial Aid Office also administers numerous scholarships, including the Founder's Scholarship, the Trustee Scholarship, the Oscar Ritchie Memorial Scholarship, the President's Scholarship for out-of-state students, the President's Grant for out-of-state students who are children of alumni, and various departmental scholarships.

To be considered for freshman scholarships at the Kent Campus, students must complete an application for admission by January 15 for priority consideration. Scholarships range from $1000 to full tuition and fees. Freshmen applying after this date are considered for scholarships if funds are available.

Faculty

The University's commitment to scholarship and teaching excellence is enhanced by a full-time faculty of approximately 1,590 members. Some of the faculty members are research oriented, and others publish widely.

Student Government

Students have leadership opportunities through residence hall and Greek organizations and the Undergraduate Student Senate. The senate is responsible for allocating student activity fees to registered undergraduate organizations, appointing undergraduates to all University committees and to other positions, conducting elections, and polling student opinion. Two students serve on Kent State's Board of Trustees.

Admission Requirements

Admission to the Kent Campus is selective. The academic profile of the fall 2011 incoming freshman class had an average 3.22 cumulative high school grade point average. The middle 50 percent had a composite ACT score of a 20–25 and a SAT combined math and verbal score of a 920–1140. The students most likely to be admitted and to succeed at the Kent campus are those who fit the academic profile and who have graduated with a full college-preparatory curriculum in high school.

For incoming freshmen and transfer students, some programs are selective. For freshmen, selective admission requirements apply to aeronautics flight technology, architecture, dance, education, fashion design and merchandising, interior design, music, nursing, sport administration, theater, and the six-year B.S./M.D. medical program with the Northeast Ohio Medical University (NEOMED). For transfer students, selective requirements apply to all of the preceding and to art and business. For more information, students should refer to www.kent.edu/admissions.

Application and Information

Students are strongly encouraged to apply for admission online at www.kent.edu/admissions/apply. A $40 nonrefundable application fee is required. Application early in the senior year helps ensure priority consideration for fall registration, residence hall preference, and financial aid. Applications are processed on a rolling basis.

Nancy J. DellaVecchia
Director, Admissions Office
Kent State University
P.O. Box 5190
Kent, Ohio 44242-0001
Phone: 330-672-2444
        800-988-KENT (toll-free)
E-mail: kentadm@kent.edu
Web site: http://www.kent.edu
        http://www.kent.edu/admissions
        http://www.facebook.com/kentstate
        http://twitter.com/kentstateuniv

KETTERING UNIVERSITY
FLINT, MICHIGAN

The University

Founded in 1919, Kettering University is a private university specializing in science, technology, engineering, math (STEM), and business degrees. The school enrolls about 1,800 undergraduate students and offers a 14:1 student-faculty ratio. Most classes have fewer than 20 students and are taught by Ph.D.-level professors, not teaching assistants. This combination of small class size and highly qualified teaching staff ensures students a much more personalized learning experience.

Kettering is a highly acclaimed university with the one of the country's most modern cooperative education and experiential learning programs. Whatever major is chosen, students alternate between study terms and full-time work terms. During study terms, students learn material in small, intense classes taught by University professors. During work terms, students work as paid professionals at corporations related to their studies and interests. Kettering students have done everything from testing ballistic systems for the U.S. government to reengineering crowd management at Disney World. Kettering has the only cooperative education and experiential learning program of its kind where students begin working as early as their freshman year. By graduation from Kettering, students have up to 2½ years of professional experience and impressive resumes. Traditionally, nearly all Kettering students graduate with job offers or grad school acceptances in hand.

Kettering University's cooperative education and experiential learning program pairs hands-on education with real-world experience—all undergraduate students alternate between on-campus study terms and full-time terms of employment with one of more than 500 corporate partners. This unique system of education prepares students to be technology innovators—professionals with cutting-edge skills who are ready to compete in tomorrow's business environment.

Kettering University is accredited by the North Central Association of Colleges and Schools, the Accreditation Board for Engineering and Technology (ABET), and the Association of Collegiate Business Schools and Programs (ACBSP). Kettering is also a member of the National Commission of Cooperative Education (NCCE) and the Association of Independent Technological Universities.

Besides being academically ahead of the game, Kettering students bring a wide range of skills and interests with them to campus. To make sure that students get a life along with an education, Kettering offers more than fifty student organizations, including thirteen fraternities and six sororities, an active student government, a state-of-the-art recreation and fitness facility, and very competitive intramural sports. Recreation facilities include athletic fields, tennis courts, and a recreation center with an Olympic-size, six-lane swimming pool; aerobic fitness rooms; a full line of Nautilus equipment; and basketball, tennis, and racquetball courts. A public golf course is adjacent to the campus.

Kettering also offers Master of Science degree programs in engineering, engineering management, information technology, manufacturing management, manufacturing operations, and operations management, and an M.B.A. program.

Professional counseling, support services, and health-care services are available. To learn more about Kettering, potential students may visit the University's site on Facebook at http://www.facebook.com/KetteringAdmissions or on Twitter at http://www.twitter.com/Ready4Kettering.

Location

Kettering University is located in Flint, Michigan, which is 60 miles west of Lake Huron and 60 miles north of Detroit. Flint has approximately 102,000 residents and a metropolitan area population of 420,000.

Flint is particularly proud of its Cultural Center, which is only 10 minutes from Kettering's campus. Built and endowed entirely by the gifts of private citizens, the Cultural Center includes the Alfred P. Sloan Museum, the Whiting Auditorium (home of the Flint Symphony and host to leading stage shows and entertainers), the Robert T. Longway Planetarium (Michigan's largest and best-equipped sky show facility), the Flint Institute of Arts, the F. A. Bower Theater, the Dort Institute of Music, Mott Community College, and the Flint Public Library. Nearby is the University of Michigan–Flint campus.

The area also offers numerous outdoor and indoor recreational opportunities. Within a few minutes' drive are downhill and cross-country skiing facilities, lakes for the entire range of water sports, a wide selection of good public golf courses, excellent indoor and outdoor skating rinks, and plentiful shopping facilities and restaurants

Majors and Degrees

Kettering University offers a 4½-year, professional cooperative education and experiential learning program with Bachelor of Science degrees in applied mathematics, applied physics, biochemistry, bioinformatics, business administration, chemical engineering, chemistry, computer engineering, computer science, electrical engineering, engineering physics, industrial engineering, and mechanical engineering. Kettering also offers a Bachelor of Business Administration degree.

Kettering also offers a variety of dual-degree programs and more than fifty minors, specialties, and concentrations, to ensure that students' degrees are custom-fit to their interests and career goals. Examples include computer gaming, fuel cells and hybrid technology, system and data security, premed, and prelaw.

Academic Programs

Although each program at Kettering University has its own requirements, 160 credit hours are generally required for graduation. The program involves nine academic terms and nine work terms, two of which are focused on the capstone thesis project, which is a major work project assigned by the employer. Students alternate between eleven-week periods of academic study on the campus in Flint and twelve-week periods of related work experience with their corporate employer. The academic year consists of two 3-month academic terms on campus and two 3-month terms of paid work experience.

Academic Facilities

Kettering University offers some of the best facilities, labs, and educational resources in the world, and students start using them as early as their freshman year. The Crash Safety Center, for example, is the only one of its kind in the nation used in an undergraduate program. The University also offers labs in areas such as fuel-cell research, polymer optimization, machining, acoustics, and more.

Kettering is fully networked and allows 24-hour access to computer resources and the Internet from dorms and labs. A 445-student residence hall and an apartment complex are located on the campus for student housing. The library offers more than 100,000 cataloged volumes and 540 periodicals. And through online resources like Kettering Connect and Blackboard, students can always be in touch with professors and University staff members.

Costs

For 2012–13, tuition costs are $33,946 and room and board cost $6660.

Starting in the 2012–13 academic year, Kettering is offering fixed-rate tuition, becoming the first STEM university in Michigan to do so. For students making normal progress towards their degrees, tuition rates will not change during their course of study, removing some of the guesswork associated with budgeting for college costs.

Financial Aid

Kettering University wants to invest in its students, so it does what it takes to help finance their education through scholarships, loans, and work-study opportunities. More than 92 percent of the students receive some sort of financial aid. Factor in co-op earnings—between $40,000 and $65,000 over the course of the college career—and the new fixed-rate tuition guarantee, and students are looking at one of the best values in education today. In addition, Kettering's Merit Scholarship program awards students with extremely generous scholarship packages.

Students should fill out the Free Application for Federal Student Aid (FAFSA) and request a copy of the analysis to be sent to Kettering University. The University works to create a financial aid package for based on those results.

Faculty

Kettering University's 124 full-time faculty members have teaching as their main responsibility. Most professors have industrial experience in addition to academic credentials and maintain contact with industry through consulting, sponsored research, and advising on student thesis projects. More than 90 percent of faculty members hold a doctorate. Because only half of the students are on campus at any one time, class sizes are small, and opportunities for enrichment and extra help are readily available.

Admission Requirements

Admission to Kettering University is competitive and based on scholastic achievement and extracurricular interests, activities, and achievements. Applicants are required to have earned the following: 3 years of English, 2 years algebra, 1 year of geometry, 1 semester of trigonometry, 2 years of lab science (1 must be physics or chemistry; both are recommended). Applicants must submit results of the SAT or ACT (Kettering's ACT code number is 1998 and the SAT code number is 1246).

Most Kettering University students are in the top 10 percent of their graduating class. Kettering University also welcomes students wishing to transfer from other colleges and universities. The transfer alternative is an excellent way to gain admission for students who do not enroll as freshmen.

Application and Information

There is more than one way to apply to Kettering. Students can apply online at http://www.kettering.edu/apply or print an application and send it by mail. Students should call 800-955-4464 ext. 7865 for assistance.

Kettering officials review applications and let students know if they have been accepted. Although Kettering accepts and processes applications throughout the year, it is best to apply as early as possible. Once accepted, students receive information on programs and the professional co-op program, which are only available to admitted students. Students should complete the co-op registration (resume) online and pay a $300 tuition deposit (to be credited to the first-semester tuition). The deposit shows that a student is as serious about Kettering as Kettering is about the student and ensures a place in the entering class and eligibility to begin the co-op employment search process.

Admissions Office
Kettering University
1700 University Avenue
Flint, Michigan 48504
United States
Phone: 810-762-7865
       800-955-4464 Ext. 7865 (toll-free in the United States and Canada)
E-mail: admissions@kettering.edu
Web site: http://www.kettering.edu/admissions
       http://www.facebook.com/KetteringAdmissions
       http:www.twitter.com/Ready4Kettering

Kettering prepares its students to go farther.

KEYSTONE COLLEGE
LA PLUME, PENNSYLVANIA

The College

Keystone College was founded in 1868 as Keystone Academy in La Plume, Pennsylvania. Initially opened as the only high school between Binghamton, New York, and Scranton, Pennsylvania, Keystone flourished as a secondary school for more than sixty-five years. Re-chartered as Scranton-Keystone Junior College in 1934 and then Keystone Junior College in 1944, the College served as one of the premier two-year institutions in the Northeast until 1995. In this year the school was again renamed, as Keystone College, and began its tenure as an "ideal" four-year degree-granting college. Today, Keystone is known as a private, co-ed, residential, and culturally diverse institution and for being one of the most popular colleges in the region. Keystone College currently enrolls over 1,700 students from fourteen states and twelve countries. Students can choose from over forty programs of study.

Keystone was recently ranked by *U.S. News and World Report* as one of the best regional baccalaureate colleges and also ranked in the top tier for highest proportion of classes under 20 students. Eighty percent of classes at Keystone College have fewer than 20 students, providing an individualized learning environment for all.

Location

Voted as the region's most beautiful campus, Keystone College is located at the foot of the Endless Mountains in northeastern Pennsylvania. The 270-acre campus is both scenic and historic, with buildings dating back to 1870, creating a unique, small rural community. Located 13 miles from Scranton, Pennsylvania, the campus offers easy access to major East Coast cities, including New York, Philadelphia, and Baltimore.

Majors and Degrees

The Bachelor of Arts degree is offered in communication arts and humanities and visual arts. The Bachelor of Science degree is offered in accounting; biology, with tracks in the medical professions; business (online or traditional); criminal justice, with a track in prelaw; early childhood education, with a special education certification option; wildlife biology; environmental biology; environmental resource management; forensic biology; information technology; organizational leadership; social sciences; psychology; sport and recreation management; teaching: art education; teaching: child and society (noncertification program); teaching: social studies education (4–8); teaching: language arts (4–8); teaching: math education (7–12); and teaching: social studies education (7–12).

Postbaccalaureate certification is available in teaching: art education (K–12), teaching: math education (7–12), and teaching: social studies education (7–12).

Associate of Applied Science degrees are offered in accounting, culinary arts, and information technology. The Associate in Fine Arts is offered in art. The Associate in Arts is offered in communications, environmental studies, forest/resource management, landscape architecture, liberal studies, liberal studies–education emphasis, and wildlife biology. The Associate in Science is offered in biology; business (online and traditional); criminal justice; early childhood education; health sciences with emphasis in medical technology, nursing/cytotechnology, occupational therapy/respiratory care, and radiotherapy/medical imaging/cardiac perfusion; and sport and recreation management.

Academic Programs

The College runs on a two-semester schedule (fall and spring) and has night, online, and weekend classes available. The number of credit hours required to earn a degree is dependent upon the field of study chosen, and students must have attained a minimum cumulative GPA of 2.0. Every student must complete a set of general core curriculum requirements in addition to the courses specific to his or her major course of study. Depending on their course of study, students may also be required to complete an internship or co-op before graduation.

Students have the opportunity to participate in both the Army and Air Force ROTC programs in conjunction with other local participating institutions. There are opportunities for double majors as well as minors in various fields of study.

Academic Facilities

Keystone's campus includes thirty-two academic and administrative buildings and six residence halls, as well as state-of-the-art athletic facilities. The Harry K. Miller Library is available on campus to all students. This facility offers standard print and online research opportunities. The Hibbard Campus Center is the setting for the campus bookstore, the student cafeteria, a full-service restaurant, The Chef's Table (a student-run restaurant), as well as a U.S. post office, a student-run radio station (WKCV), and reception halls. The campus also boasts an art gallery, a celestial observatory, early childhood center, career development center, student success center, theater, and the Poinsard Greenhouse. Keystone College also serves as the home for the Urban Forestry Center, Willary Water Resource Center, and the Countryside Conservancy.

There are more than 120 computers available on campus for general student use, and both the Internet and campus network can be accessed from all residence halls and most buildings on campus.

Costs

Tuition and fees for Keystone College for the 2012–13 academic year are $20,500, while room and board costs are $9500. Books and general supplies average $1500 annually and vary according to major.

Financial Aid

The Financial Aid Office provides adequate funds and resources to meet the financial needs of students from all income categories. In fact, 98 percent of incoming freshmen

receive financial aid. Scholarships are awarded based on merit, academic performance, and extracurricular involvement. Keystone College also participates in the following federally sponsored programs: Federal Perkins Loan, Federal Pell Grant, Federal Supplemental Educational Opportunity Grant (FSEOG), Federal PLUS Loan, and Federal Direct Student Loan. Keystone also offers College employment programs to students and alternative loans as well as state grants and Keystone grants. In order to be considered for financial aid, students must complete the Free Application for Federal Student Aid (FAFSA). Keystone's financial aid code is 003280.

Faculty

The student-faculty ratio is 11:1, and the average class size is 13 students. Keystone College is supported by strong interpersonal relationships among its students and faculty and staff members. All faculty members post regular office hours and are generally available outside of these hours for any student when necessary.

Student Government

Student Senate is the central governing body of all student government organizations on the campus. It serves as the liaison between the student body and the College administration. Members of Student Senate are chosen by their peers and are responsible for improving and maintaining student life both on and off campus. Students may choose from more than twenty-five different clubs and organizations, including those with academic, service-oriented, and social interests.

Admission Requirements

Keystone accepts qualified students regardless of race, religion, handicap, or national origin, and admissions are on a rolling basis. Admission is based on prior academic performance and the ability of the applicant to profit from and contribute to the academic, interpersonal, and extracurricular life of the College. Keystone considers applicants who meet the following criteria: graduation from an approved secondary school or the equivalent (with official transcripts), satisfactory scores on the SAT or ACT, one teacher evaluation, essay, and evidence of potential for successful college achievement. All students are strongly encouraged to visit the campus for a personal interview with the admissions staff and a member of the faculty from the student's area of interest. Students applying to the art and teaching–art education programs are required to participate in a portfolio interview.

Transfer students in good academic and financial standing at their current institution are also encouraged to apply to Keystone. Transfer students should contact the Office of Admissions and may be required to submit high school transcripts or transcripts from each college attended or both.

Admissions decisions are made within two weeks from the day all required materials are received in the Office of Admissions.

Application and Information

Students wishing to be considered for admission must submit an application and a $30 processing fee, along with official high school transcripts, college transcripts (if applicable), a teacher evaluation, essay, and scores from either the SAT or ACT (submitted directly to the Office of Admissions; Keystone's CEEB code numbers are 2351 for the SAT, 3602 for the ACT).

Applications and any additional information about Keystone College may be obtained by contacting:

Office of Admissions
Keystone College
One College Green
P.O. Box 50
La Plume, Pennsylvania 18440
United States
Phone: 570-945-8111
        800-824-2764 (toll-free), Option 1
E-mail: admissions@keystone.edu
Web site: http://www.keystone.edu

Students on the campus of Keystone College.

KING'S COLLEGE
WILKES-BARRE, PENNSYLVANIA

The College

King's College is an independent, coed, four-year Catholic college with 2,700 students. Founded in 1946 by the Holy Cross Fathers and Brothers from the University of Notre Dame, King's prepares students for a purposeful life, with an education that integrates the human values inherent in a broadly based liberal arts curriculum. The College encourages the religious, moral, personal, and social development of its students.

In addition to the undergraduate degrees, King's College offers a Master of Science (M.S.) degree in health-care administration, a Master of Education (M.Ed.) degree in reading or curriculum and development instruction, and a five-year physician assistant studies program leading to a master's degree.

Academic advising begins before students enroll and continues with an innovative program of career development across the curriculum. King's Academic Skills Center includes a nationally certified tutoring program and a faculty-staffed writing center. More than 70 percent of students who attend King's graduate from the College, which is well above the national average, and 99 percent are employed or attend graduate school within six months of graduation.

The quaint urban campus comprises eight city blocks and features many buildings and centers that house King's numerous academic programs, including the Charles E. and Mary Parente Life Sciences Center, the Mulligan Physical Sciences Center, and the William G. McGowan School of Business. The 15-acre campus also includes Monarch Court; the Sheehy-Farmer Campus Center, which offers an art gallery, an outdoor waterfall and patio, a student restaurant, and marketplace dining; the J. Carroll McCormick Campus Ministry Center; and the William S. Scandlon Physical Education Center, which features a 3,200-seat basketball arena, wrestling facilities, racquetball and handball courts, an Olympic-size swimming pool, a wellness center, and a state-of-the-art sports medicine facility. In addition, a gym expansion project will see a new facility attached to the Scandlon Center, including three multipurpose courts as well as new offices, meeting rooms, and additional sports medicine facilities. The student health center is located in Andre Hall, a newly renovated building which is almost twice the size of the former health center, with a consulting physician on call at all times. The six-story administration and science buildings form a unit that houses the College's newly renovated theater, the Susquehanna Room dining hall and coffee bar, administrative offices, science laboratories, and classrooms. Residence halls have cable television, Internet access, and 24-hour computer labs. Many of King's athletic teams train and compete just two miles from campus at the Robert L. Betzler Athletic Complex, a 33.5-acre athletic facility that includes McCarthy Stadium; a field house; and fields for baseball, softball, men's and women's soccer, football, and field hockey.

There are fifty student organizations that provide King's students with the opportunity to explore interests outside of the classroom. King's has 19 NCAA Division III teams including men's baseball, basketball, football, golf, lacrosse, soccer, swimming, tennis, and wrestling; women's basketball, field hockey, lacrosse, soccer, softball, swimming, tennis, and volleyball; and coed cross-country. The College offers cheerleading, ice hockey, and track and field as club sports. Intramural sports include basketball, flag football, indoor soccer, racquetball, dodge ball, and Zumba. Other cocurricular activities include: academic clubs in almost every department, the King's Players (theater), the nationally ranked debate team, Cantores Christi Regis (choir), Campus Ministry, the Experiencing the Arts Series, *The Crown* (student newspaper), the *Regis* (yearbook), and the *SCOP* (literary magazine).

Location

The King's campus is located in a residential area near downtown Wilkes-Barre, Pennsylvania, a city of approximately 50,000 on the banks of the Susquehanna River. A growing city, Wilkes-Barre has developed both economically and culturally, yet it has avoided many typical urban problems. The crime rate in the city is one of the lowest in the nation. Shopping malls, multiplex theaters, a brand new riverfront park, art galleries, and restaurants are nearby. Two blocks from King's is the F. M. Kirby Center, which has hosted national performances, music groups, traveling theater, and more. National recording acts regularly perform in nearby venues.

King's is a short drive from several ski resorts, state parks, and major lakes where students can participate in many seasonal outdoor activities. Students can also enjoy professional sports action including the New York Yankees' AAA baseball team, the Pocono International Raceway which hosts two NASCAR races each season, and the Pittsburgh Penguins' minor-league ice hockey team. The Mohegan Sun Arena is the host to many concerts and events, and is the site of the King's commencement. King's is close to major metropolitan areas including New York City and Philadelphia (each a 2½-hour drive); Washington, D.C. and the attractions of New England are within a 4-hour drive.

Majors and Degrees

King's awards the Master of Science, Master of Education, Bachelor of Arts, Bachelor of Science, Associate of Arts, and Associate of Science degrees. The College's thirty-five major programs are offered in the arts and sciences and the William G. McGowan School of Business, which is accredited by AACSB International—The Association to Advance Collegiate Schools of Business.

Arts and sciences include the humanities and social sciences division (computers and information systems, criminal justice, economics, English–literature, English–professional writing, French, history, mass communications, philosophy, political science, psychology, sociology, Spanish, theater, and theology); the education division, which is accredited by NCATE (preschool–grade 4, secondary certification, and special education); the science division (biology, chemistry, computer science, environmental science, environmental studies, general science, mathematics, and neuroscience); and the allied health division (clinical lab science, physician assistant studies, and athletics training education/sports medicine accredited by CAAHEP). Available majors in the William G. McGowan School of Business are accounting, finance, human resources management, international business, management, and marketing. King's offers preprofessional programs in chiropractic, dentistry, law, medicine, optometry, pharmacy, and veterinary science.

Academic Programs

The general education program at King's is recognized nationwide by its peers. King's is included in *Barron's Best Buys in College Education* and has been honored in seventeen consecutive issues of *U.S. News & World Report*'s *Best Colleges Guide*. The College was also recognized by the John Templeton Foundation Honor Roll for Character-Building Colleges, the Forbes/CCAP list of America's best colleges, and is one of sixteen institutions nationwide named to the Greater Expectations initiative.

The honors program offers highly motivated students the challenge of learning in discussion-centered courses that explore distinctive subject matter with exciting and innovative approaches. Sixteen honor societies encourage students to excel in their chosen fields and recognize students for their academic distinction; members are honored each year at the All-College Honors Convocation. Science students receive hands-on lab training much earlier than students at other institutions and work together with faculty members on real-world research projects.

Off-Campus Programs

Experiential learning (via internships) is available in conjunction with almost every major. King's students have interned at CNN, the New York Stock Exchange, PricewaterhouseCoopers, the U.S. House of Representatives, U.S. Senators' offices, the U.S. Department of Energy, Walt Disney World, and Xerox Corporation, among other

places. Every year, students are placed with local, regional, and national companies around the globe.

Through the study-abroad program many of King's students have studied on campuses throughout Europe, Thailand, China, and Australia.

Academic Facilities

King's facilities include the 51,000-square-foot, three-story D. Leonard Corgan Library, which contains several study rooms, a 100-seat auditorium, a 160,000-volume collection, and a computerized catalog, which students can access from their home or residence hall. The library provides full-text databases from every computer on campus, and access to college and research libraries throughout the United States. Students and faculty members also have direct access to more than 1 million volumes through the local library cooperative (NEPBC).

King's features computer labs with more than 440 PCs; 24-hour labs in residence halls; e-mail accounts for all students; computerized library databases; multimedia classrooms with a variety of instructional aids; course discussions on Moodle; a technology component in the core curriculum that requires all students to learn computer and information presentation skills; distance-learning facilities for teleconferencing; and cross-registration with area colleges that enables students to take courses complementary to their majors.

The $6.4-million Charles E. and Mary Parente Life Sciences Center, which contains a molecular biology laboratory and a genomics center, includes computer facilities, instrumentation rooms, a rooftop greenhouse, and environmental chambers. The $6-million Mulligan Physical Sciences Center includes modern research laboratories, computer facilities, and state-of-the-art instrumentation used for molecular identification.

Costs

For the 2011–12 academic year, tuition for full-time students was $27,680. Room and board totaled $10,670.

Financial Aid

King's assists all qualified students through its financial aid programs. Currently, more than 97 percent of King's students receive financial aid in the form of scholarships, grants, work-study, or loans. Aid is awarded on the basis of demonstrated financial need, the difference between the total cost of education and the expected family contribution.

In addition to financial aid programs, installment payment plans are available, offering students and/or their families the ability to make monthly payments throughout the academic year. Students who wish to be considered for financial aid must fill out the Free Application for Federal Student Aid (FAFSA) and the King's College Financial Aid Application. The preferred filing deadline for new freshmen is February 15. Forms are mailed to students accepted for admission but can be completed prior to acceptance.

Faculty

King's College has 132 full-time and 103 part-time faculty members. Eighty-one percent of the full-time faculty members have a Ph.D. or an equivalent terminal degree. Graduate assistants do not teach courses. The student-faculty ratio is 14:1.

Student Government

The student government coordinates and participates in numerous activities for both the student body and the surrounding community. It regularly holds open forums for students and senior administrators at the College, coordinates informal socials for the students with the College president, and makes presentations at each meeting of the Board of Directors. In addition, the student government sponsors events that foster awareness for social and justice issues and a celebration of cultural diversity. The Association for Campus Events, a student-operated organization, also sponsors comedians, movies, and performers throughout the year.

Admission Requirements

King's encourages applications from qualified high school students and those who wish to transfer from another institution. To be considered for admission, students must be prepared to successfully pursue a program of study at the College, as evidenced by the quality of previous academic and extracurricular performance, the recommendation of school officials and character references, and the student's display of personal promise, maturity, and motivation. King's admits students of any race, sex, color, creed, or national or ethnic origin.

Admission decisions are made for both high school students and transfer students with the understanding that all current courses and examinations will be completed satisfactorily. Candidates should complete 4 years of mathematics (through trigonometry or precalculus). One year each of high school chemistry, biology, and physics is also strongly recommended.

The Office of Admission offers two methods for candidates to apply for admission: the SAT/ACT Traditional Choice and the Standardized Test Option/Essay Choice. Applicants are required to state their preference prior to the application review, and the decision is nonreversible. Students who select the SAT/ACT Traditional Choice must submit a completed application, official high school transcripts, SAT or ACT scores, guidance counselor recommendation, an essay, and the $30 application fee, which is waived if students apply online. Students who choose the Standardized Test Option/Essay Choice must submit a completed application, official high school transcripts, an official graded writing sample from either their junior or senior year—submitted and notarized by the high school guidance office, guidance counselor recommendation, an essay, and the $30 application fee, which is waived if students apply online.

Application and Information

Applicants should forward a completed application and the $30 fee to the Office of Admission or apply online at www.kings.edu in order to waive the application fee. Secondary and postsecondary (if applicable) transcripts must be sent. Admission decisions are not made until all credentials are received. King's subscribes to a rolling admission policy. Decisions are announced within two weeks from the date of application. Upon notification of acceptance, a $200 nonrefundable deposit is requested to reserve a place in the class. The deposit deadline is May 1 but may be extended upon request. To schedule an interview, obtain an application form, or for more information, students should contact:

Office of Admission
King's College
133 North River Street
Wilkes-Barre, Pennsylvania 18711
Phone: 570-208-5858
      888-KINGS-PA (toll-free)
E-mail: admissions@kings.edu
Web site: http://www.kings.edu
      http://www.facebook.com/kingscollegepa
      http://twitter.com/KingsCollege_PA

On the campus of King's College, Wilkes-Barre, Pennsylvania.

LAFAYETTE COLLEGE
EASTON, PENNSYLVANIA

The College

Classified as one of the nation's most academically competitive colleges, Lafayette focuses exclusively on undergraduates, offering a wide variety of academic choices in the humanities, social sciences, natural sciences, and engineering. The College is committed to providing the best education for men and women who possess the ability to benefit from the Lafayette experience, and the capacity to contribute to a vibrant campus community with no graduate programs and no graduate students.

The breadth and depth of Lafayette's curriculum are unusual and unexpected in a college of its size. One of just a few undergraduate colleges with fully accredited programs in engineering, Lafayette enrolls 2,400 students from more than forty U.S. states and territories, and more than fifty other countries. The College draws strength from the diversity of its students, who represent a wide range of interests, special talents, and aspirations.

Lafayette is a residential college where learning continues outside the classroom. Living in college housing is guaranteed and required for all four years. About 95 percent of students live in College-owned residence halls, apartments, special-interest houses, fraternities, or sororities. An array of student organizations, cultural events, social opportunities, NCAA Division I varsity athletics, and intramural sports programs are available to all students.

Recent trends indicate that approximately two thirds of Lafayette graduates obtain a graduate or professional degree. A large and growing number obtain practical experience through employment, and then undertake full-time study for an advanced degree, often with an employer's financial support. Others continue academic pursuits on a part-time basis. Strong internship and externship programs with alumni and parent mentors help pave the way to fulfilling careers for Lafayette graduates.

Location

Lafayette is located in a picturesque setting atop a hill overlooking the Delaware and Lehigh rivers and the progressive city of Easton, population 30,000, located 70 miles from New York City, and 60 miles from Philadelphia.

Easton, Allentown, and Bethlehem are the principal cities of the Lehigh Valley, Pennsylvania's third-largest metropolitan area, which has a population of about 800,000.

Shops, restaurants, and other business establishments that serve the needs of Lafayette students are located adjacent to the campus, and in nearby downtown Easton. Beyond Easton to the west and north are great ski slopes, top fishing rivers, and challenging hiking trails.

Majors and Degrees

Lafayette awards the Bachelor of Science (B.S.) degree in biochemistry, biology, chemical engineering, chemistry, civil engineering, computer science, electrical and computer engineering, geology, mathematics, mechanical engineering, neuroscience, physics, and psychology.

The Bachelor of Arts (A.B.) degree is awarded with the following majors: Africana studies, American studies, anthropology and sociology, art, Asian studies, biochemistry, biology, chemistry, computer science, economics, engineering studies, English, film and media studies, French, geology, German; government and law, government and law and foreign language, history,

international affairs, mathematics, mathematics-economics, music, philosophy, physics, policy studies, psychology, religion and politics, religious studies, Russian and East European studies, Spanish, theater, and women's and gender studies. Minors are offered in many of these fields.

In addition, Lafayette offers a two-degree program leading to an A.B. in international studies and a B.S. in one of four engineering disciplines.

Academic Programs

High-level research, rigorous small-class discussion, field experiences, community-based learning projects, and global studies—these elements of a Lafayette education attract active and engaged learners. Students from different majors and faculty members work together to solve real-world problems. This results in the high-impact learning for which Lafayette is known, leading to a distinct career advantage where 94 percent or more of recent graduating classes are either employed or in graduate school or an internship within six months of graduation.

Interdisciplinary minor programs are offered in architectural studies; biotechnology/bioengineering; classical civilization; computational methods; environmental science; health and life sciences; health care and society; Jewish studies; Latin American and Caribbean studies; medieval, Renaissance, and early modern studies; Russian; and writing.

The Dean of the College's staff mentors students in their academic development, provides support for students interested in careers in law and the health professions, and works with students to pursue prestigious undergraduate and post-graduate fellowships and awards.

The academic year is divided into two semesters with a January interim session, where courses are offered on and off campus, including study overseas.

Off-Campus Programs

Lafayette recognizes that we live in an increasingly complex and interrelated global environment, and connecting the classroom to the world outside our walls is at the core of the College's mission. Off-campus study combines academic rigor with experiential learning through immersion in an international or culturally significant domestic setting.

Semester-long programs led by Lafayette professors are offered at Jacobs University Bremen; Saint Louis University in Madrid; Goldsmith's College at the University of London; and the University of Ghana. Lafayette students also choose from semester-long and yearlong programs, coordinated by affiliated institutions, in many countries.

During interim session, Lafayette faculty lead distinctive three-week courses around the world. Courses have been offered in Australia, China, East Africa, England, Guatemala, Italy, Japan, New Zealand, Russia, Scandinavia, Spain, South Africa, Thailand, Turkey, and the West Indies, among many other locations.

Academic Facilities

With an endowment per student that ranks among the top 8 percent of private colleges and universities nationally, the College has invested more than $200 million in new academic, residential, and recreational facilities recently, including a science center, a center for psychology and neuroscience, a center for the visual arts, and a center for intramural and

recreational sports. Improvements also include an expansion and transformation of the main library, a thorough modernization of the engineering complex, and new and renovated residence halls. An expansion of the downtown arts campus is under way to include new facilities for theater and for film and media studies. Funds have been secured to build a center for global studies that will enable the College to globalize the curriculum and add a global perspective to the educational experience of every student.

Costs

The tuition for 2012–13 is $41,920. Additional costs include a standard room fee of $7834, board fee of $4,874 (twenty meals/week), activity/technology fee of $360, matriculation fee of $700 (for new students only), and an estimated $2000 for books, travel, and miscellaneous expenses.

Financial Aid

An education that is personal—featuring faculty time with students on-task in the classroom and in student-faculty research—and emphasizes teams of students learning together across different majors will always be more costly to deliver than the traditional large, lecture-based classes taught by graduate students at large public or private research universities.

Lafayette is committed to providing need-based scholarships and grants to meet the full need of every admitted student. In addition, the College provides the Marquis Scholarship, worth $20,000 per year to applicants whose grades, high school curriculum, SAT scores, and activity leadership put them in the top 10 percent of the pool of accepted students. Students with financial need above $20,000, who are awarded a Marquis Scholarship, will have their full need (minus a small loan and work opportunity) met with a grant. In addition, each Marquis Scholar receives a scholarship of up to $4000 for one faculty-led, off-campus course during an interim session.

In 2011–12, Lafayette provided $35 million in scholarship and need-based grant assistance to 50 percent of enrolled students. Detailed information regarding financial assistance is available from the Office of Student Financial Aid, Lafayette College, Easton, Pennsylvania 18042-1777 (phone: 610-330-5055).

Faculty

Lafayette is committed to reducing the student-to-faculty ratio from the current 10.6:1 to below 10:1. Ninety-nine percent of the College's 213 full-time faculty members hold the doctorate or other terminal degree in their field. All faculty members—full professors and heads of departments as well as junior faculty members—teach courses and serve as academic advisers to students. Many have earned wide recognition for their research and scholarship and won awards for superior teaching.

Admission Requirements

Lafayette seeks to enroll students who can benefit from and contribute to the Lafayette experience. To maintain a student body that reflects society and to enhance every student's educational experience, the College seeks to enroll students from diverse backgrounds—from different cultures and ethnicities, from different parts of the country and the world, and from across the socioeconomic spectrum. The Admissions Office selects students with a wide variety of academic and extracurricular interests and talents, using a holistic evaluation process that employs no formulas. The most important aspect of the College's evaluation of applicants' ability to succeed academically at Lafayette is a review of the quality of the courses taken in high school, grades in academic courses, and, when available, class rank.

Applicants are required to submit scores from either the SAT reasoning test or ACT (with writing). SAT subject test results are recommended but not required. Prospective math, science, or engineering majors are encouraged to take subject tests in mathematics and science.

A campus interview or regional interview with an alumni representative is strongly encouraged, especially for applicants seeking merit scholarships.

Application and Information

The application deadline is January 15. Applicants are notified about admission decisions on or about April 1. May 1 is the National Candidate Reply Date, by which admitted students must reply to the College's offer of admission.

Students who have decided that Lafayette is their first choice may request consideration of their applications under early decision. The deadline for early decision I applications is November 15, with notification by December 15.

Applicants who decide that Lafayette is their first choice after November 15 may submit an early decision II application until January 15 or convert a regular decision application to early decision II until February 1. Notification will be made within thirty days of a completed application.

To be considered for early decision admission, students must sign and submit the early decision plan agreement. Applicants admitted under early decision must withdraw their applications to other institutions.

Office of Admissions
Lafayette College
Easton, Pennsylvania 18042-1770
Phone: 610-330-5100
Web site: http://www.lafayette.edu

A view of Lafayette College's campus.

LAWRENCE TECHNOLOGICAL UNIVERSITY

SOUTHFIELD, MICHIGAN

The University

Lawrence Technological University is a premier private university offering over 100 undergraduate and graduate degrees in architecture and design, arts and sciences, engineering, and management. The University's Leadership Program, integrated into all bachelor's degrees, helps students gain critical thinking, teamwork, and communication skills. An honors program is available to highly qualified students, as well as Quest, which encourages students to explore their interests on a deeper level. Lawrence Tech is known for cutting-edge technology, small class sizes, and a commitment to theory and practice. The 102-acre campus features state-of-the-art learning facilities and many housing, recreation, and meal service options.

The University, including its graduate programs, is accredited by the Higher Learning Commission and is a member of the North Central Association of Colleges and Schools. Appropriate national professional agencies provide additional accreditation to various programs in architecture, interior architecture/design, imaging, administration and management, chemistry, and engineering.

Most Lawrence Tech students are employed within one month of graduation and according to a Bloomberg Businessweek survey, the earning power of a Lawrence Tech bachelor's degree ranks in the top third of all U.S. university degrees.

Approximately 4,300 students attend Lawrence Tech; more than 500 live in on-campus housing. Women make up 24 percent of the student body, and 31 states and 42 countries are represented on campus.

Lawrence Tech offers an exciting student life. More than 60 student clubs and organizations, including fraternities, sororities, honor societies, and student chapters of professional groups, sponsor a variety of activities.

A member of the National Association of Intercollegiate Athletics, Lawrence Tech offers Blue Devil varsity sports in men's and women's basketball and soccer; men's cross-country, lacrosse, and bowling; and women's volleyball. The men's hockey team plays in the American Collegiate Hockey Association (ACHA Division III). Intramural sports leagues and tournaments in badminton, basketball, billiards, dodgeball, flag football, golf, racquetball, soccer, softball, table tennis, tennis, volleyball, and wallyball are active throughout the academic year. Club sports include lacrosse, mixed martial arts, and biking. The Don Ridler Field House is open to all students and features a fitness track, gymnasium, racquetball courts, game room, saunas, and weight and conditioning room.

Location

Southfield is a dynamic suburb in southeastern Michigan that provides a pleasant balance between big-city opportunities and a quiet residential atmosphere. Within a few miles of the campus, students can find many restaurants, parks, shopping areas, and cultural and recreational facilities. Research, manufacturing, scientific, and business enterprises are also nearby and convenient for students in co-op and internship programs as well as those who work full- or part-time while attending classes. More than 200 Fortune 500 companies have headquarters or business operations in the area.

Majors and Degrees

Most Lawrence Tech programs are available days or evenings; many are offered online and on weekends. Dual majors and customized degree programs are available. Preprofessional programs are offered in dentistry, law, and medicine. A postbaccalaureate certificate in premedical studies is also available.

The College of Architecture and Design offers bachelor's degrees in architecture, game art, graphic design, imaging–digital arts, industrial design, interior architecture, and transportation design. A certificate is available in building information modeling and computer visualization. Lawrence Tech enrolls more architectural students than any other school in Michigan, and is one of the ten largest architecture schools in the nation.

The College of Arts and Sciences awards bachelor's degrees in chemical biology, chemistry, computer science (business software development, game software development, network software development, and scientific software development), English and communication arts, environmental chemistry, humanities, mathematics, mathematics and computer science, media communication, molecular and cell biology, physics, physics and computer science, and psychology (clinical psychology, industrial/organizational psychology, and premedical/biobehavioral psychology). Associate degrees are offered in chemical technology, general studies, and radio and television broadcasting. Minors offered are biology, business management, chemistry, computer science, economics, English, general sciences, history, mathematics, media communication, philosophy, physics, psychology, Spanish, technical and professional communication, and television and video production. Certificates can be earned in computer science, entrepreneurial strategy, film and production techniques, industrial/organizational psychology, technical and professional communication, and television and video production.

The College of Engineering offers bachelor's degrees in architectural engineering (combining bachelor's and master's programs), audio engineering technology, biomedical engineering, biomedical engineering technology, civil engineering, civil engineering and architecture, computer engineering, construction management, electrical engineering (biomedical instrumentation, embedded systems, electronics engineering, and electrical energy systems), engineering technology, industrial operations engineering, mechanical engineering (alternative energy, automotive engineering, manufacturing engineering, mechanical system design, and thermal system design), and robotics engineering. The College offers evening associate programs in communications engineering technology, construction engineering technology, global engineering, manufacturing engineering technology, and mechanical engineering technology. Also available are minors in aeronautical engineering and energy engineering, and certificates in aeronautical engineering, alternative energy engineering technology, biochemical engineering, bioelectronics, biomechanics, electrical power systems, and embedded systems.

The College of Management awards bachelor's degrees in business management and information technology and a minor in business management, as well as undergraduate and graduate certificates in health information technology management.

Academic Programs

Graduation from Lawrence Tech's undergraduate programs requires completion with an overall GPA of at least 2.0. Most disciplines combine a strong concentration in the major with a core curriculum of natural science, social science, humanities, and mathematics requirements. Double majors are possible.

Off-Campus Programs

Lawrence Tech students have the opportunity to participate in co-op programs, alternating semesters of classes and work. Internships are also available.

The University also offers programs in Detroit, Lansing, Petoskey, and Traverse City, Michigan, and Toronto, Canada. Lawrence Tech partners with universities in China, Europe, India, Mexico, and the Middle East. Lawrence Tech's study-abroad program is open to all students.

Lawrence Tech's Detroit Studio and Innovation Center gives architecture students the opportunity to explore community-based architectural, urban design, and community development projects. Architecture students also regularly build homes for Habitat for Humanity.

The Global Engineering Program allows Lawrence Tech engineering students to work and study abroad and brings international engineering students to campus for further study.

Academic Facilities

Lawrence Tech is committed to providing students the tools they need to compete and succeed in a technology-driven world. The University supplies undergrads with high-end, personal computers customized with all the industry-standard software needed for their classes, a unique benefit valued up to $15,000.

The library houses a wide selection of print and electronic materials, including numerous online databases and full-text periodical titles accessible on or off campus.

Students use advanced facilities, including architectural and design studios; a structural testing center; a wind tunnel; wood, metal, and model shops; dedicated labs for constructing Baja- and Formula-style competition vehicles; and labs for alternative energy, robotics, biomedical research, graphics, and much more.

The Center for Innovative Materials Research is a state-of-the-art laboratory for the research, development, and testing of composite materials for defense and infrastructure applications. Students participate in related research projects as part of their academic programs.

The Automotive Engineering Institute provides students opportunities to conduct sponsored research on a unique four-wheel drive vehicle chassis dynamometer, which measures many areas of vehicle performance.

Lawrence Tech also owns a nearby Frank Lloyd Wright–designed home that is used as a study center.

The A. Alfred Taubman Student Services Center consolidates all student support services—from admissions through career services—into a convenient one-stop center. This innovative 42,000-square-foot building utilizes energy-efficient and environmentally friendly features and technologies, serving as a living laboratory for students to study.

Costs

Tuition for all undergrads includes a laptop or tablet computer. The 2011–12 tuition for students majoring in arts and sciences was $740 per credit hour for basic studies courses and $785 for other arts and sciences and management courses. Sophomores in arts and sciences and management paid $835 per credit hour, while the tuition for juniors and seniors in the two majors was $870 per credit hour. In architecture and design and engineering, tuition for freshmen and sophomores was $870 to $880 per credit hour; for juniors and seniors, it was $900 to $910 per credit hour.

A normal course load is 12–17 credit hours per semester. The undergraduate registration fee is $135 each semester. International students on temporary visas must have sufficient funds to pay for an entire year of tuition, room and board, and books at the time of first registration. Additional fees for specific labs and studio courses vary.

Financial Aid

Approximately 75 percent of full-time students receive financial assistance and the University awards over $43 million in scholarships, grants, loans, and work-study funds each academic year. Many privately funded scholarships are awarded to qualified students, based on need and/or scholastic performance. Part-time employment is available at the University for full-time students. Student loans are also available.

Faculty

Approximately 430 full- and part-time faculty members teach at Lawrence Tech. Many part-time faculty members hold full-time jobs in industry and bring their real-world perspective to the classroom. Nearly 80 percent of the full-time faculty members hold a doctoral or terminal degree in their field. Faculty involvement is extensive in student chapters of professional associations that meet on campus. Many faculty members are active and/or registered professionals in their fields. Lawrence Tech's student-faculty ratio is 11:1. Most classes average 19 or fewer students, and less than 1 percent of the classes have more than 50.

Student Government

The Student Government sponsors and supports a variety of campus activities. More than fifty student clubs and organizations, including fraternities, sororities, honor societies, and student chapters of professional groups, are also active on campus.

Admission Requirements

Admissions decisions are based on a student's recalculated GPA, ACT/SAT scores, essay, and letters of recommendation. Strong emphasis is placed on grade trends as well as the strength of the curriculum and rigor of a student's senior schedule. A portfolio is required for transportation design, industrial design, and game art majors.

Application and Information

Programs start in August and January. An optional summer semester begins in May. Students must submit transcripts from all schools attended, along with a nonrefundable $30 application fee. Applicants may have their application fee waived at www.ltu.edu/applyfree. To view a University catalog and learn more, potential students can visit www.ltu.edu or contact:

Office of Admissions
Lawrence Technological University
21000 West Ten Mile Road
Southfield, Michigan 48075-1058
Phone: 248-204-3160 or 800-225-5588 (toll-free)
Fax: 248-204-2228
E-mail: admissions@ltu.edu
Web site: http://www.ltu.edu
　　　　　http://www.facebook.com/lawrencetech
　　　　　http://twitter.com/LawrenceTechU

Below Lawrence Tech's campus quadrangle are 120 geothermal wells sunk 300 feet deep, which heat and cool the adjacent A. Alfred Taubman Student Services Center.

LEBANON VALLEY COLLEGE
ANNVILLE, PENNSYLVANIA

The College

Founded in 1866, Lebanon Valley College (LVC) was the first college east of the Alleghenies to offer higher education to both men and women. Now, 145 years later, the College remains a leader—enjoying the number three ranking on *U.S. News & World Report's* Great Schools, Great Prices list, and for the eighteenth consecutive year, ranking among the top baccalaureate colleges in its category. A remarkable student body, an exceptional faculty, academic programs that stress experience-based education, and a groundbreaking merit-based scholarship program distinguish this private liberal arts college. Students who graduate in the top 30 percent of their high school class can receive an automatic LVC scholarship equivalent to one-quarter to one-half of the cost of tuition.

Lebanon Valley aims to educate its 1,630 students to become people of broad vision, capable of making informed decisions and prepared for a life of service to others. To that end, the College provides an education that imparts the knowledge, skills, and values necessary to live and work in a changing, diverse, and fragile world. Students obtain a solid foundation in a major of their choosing as well as wide exposure to a variety of disciplines and intellectual tools. In the process, they develop the desire and ability to think deeply, ask critical questions, solve complex problems, and communicate effectively, preparing themselves to be competitive and flexible in whatever career they pursue or challenge they encounter.

Lebanon Valley College professors strive to continue the College's proud tradition of inspired teaching with the dedication and commitment to community service that has long been an LVC hallmark. A supportive intellectual community and a 13:1 student-faculty ratio ensure that students have direct access to the men and women who teach and guide them; relationships beyond the classroom are common.

One of the most significant aspects of teaching and learning at LVC is collaborative research in the sciences and humanities. Each summer, dozens of LVC students work alongside their professors as funded research assistants, contributing to important discoveries while gaining invaluable skills and experiences. Many LVC students coauthor articles in scientific or other academic journals or present their work at professional conferences while they are still in college. This experiential learning supports independent student research, internships, and student-faculty research/scholarly work across all disciplines, and provides opportunities seldom found at the undergraduate level.

LVC's strong advising, straightforward requirements, and outstanding student support services mean that the majority of students are able to graduate in four years. If a student is not able to earn the LVC bachelor's degree in four years because of a course scheduling problem, the College will cover the costs of any additional course work the student needs.

LVC's forty-nine buildings provide for every aspect of college life. The College's twenty-nine student residences include four apartment-style halls. Academic buildings feature enhanced classrooms with the latest technology for teaching and learning. Two student centers, one of which just benefitted from a $13.3-million renovation, support learning and development outside the traditional classroom, group study, and extracurricular interests. Students enjoy a recreational sports center; a varsity gymnasium; a soon-to-be-completed all-sports turf stadium; soccer, baseball, field hockey, and softball parks; and a state-of-the-art physical therapy facility. The baseball and soccer fields were each named National Collegiate Athletic Association (NCAA) field of the year in their respective categories, and the softball park has twice been recognized as regional field of the year.

LVC's Career Services staff helps students research careers and establish contacts with potential employers, and offers seminars on resume writing and interviewing skills. The Career Connections alumni database provides students direct access to successful alumni in their fields—men and women who have volunteered to mentor, advise, or otherwise assist LVC students or recent graduates. In an average year, approximately 76 percent of graduates who respond to an annual survey are employed, and approximately 30 percent are in graduate or professional school within six months of graduation.

Location

Annville is a small town of approximately 5,000 residents located near Pennsylvania Dutch country, just 10 minutes east of Hershey and within a 2- to 3-hour drive of Philadelphia, Baltimore, New York, and Washington, D.C. Nestled in a beautiful valley, the College is located on a 340-acre site. A wide variety of internship opportunities, potential employment options, cultural events, and other activities are available on campus and within the surrounding communities.

Majors and Degrees

The College confers five baccalaureate degrees. The Bachelor of Arts is available in art and art history, criminal justice, economics, English, French, German, historical communications, history, international studies, music, music business, philosophy, political science, religion, sociology, Spanish, and certain individualized majors.

The Bachelor of Science is available in accounting, actuarial science, biochemistry and molecular biology, biology, business administration, chemistry, computer science, cooperative engineering, cooperative forestry, digital communications, early childhood education, early childhood/special education, health-care management, health science, mathematics, music education, physics, psychobiology, psychology, and certain individualized majors.

The Bachelor of Science in Chemistry, Bachelor of Science in Medical Technology, and Bachelor of Music (with an emphasis in music recording technology) are also available.

Lebanon Valley offers master's degree programs in business, music education, and science education; a doctoral program in physical therapy; and preprofessional programs in dentistry, law, medicine, ministry, pharmacy, and veterinary medicine.

Academic Programs

Lebanon Valley has long been known for the strength of its academic programs and the achievement of its faculty members and alumni. The sciences are a particular strength, with well-equipped and up-to-date laboratories. The National Science Foundation has recognized LVC among the top 15 percent of the nation's private, predominantly undergraduate institutions for producing the most Ph.D. students in biology, biochemistry, and chemistry.

Other particularly well-known and respected LVC programs include actuarial science (nearly 100 percent of graduates land high-paying jobs), physical therapy (which offers a six-year doctoral program), music (the music recording technology major is especially popular), business (which provides the fundamentals of accounting and business administration within a strong liberal arts context), and education (alumni of which are in high demand throughout the region).

Each student's academic program is complemented by a wide range of extracurricular activities. The College's more than ninety clubs, organizations, and other student-run initiatives mean ample opportunities for leadership. Many students choose to participate in community outreach, often by volunteering with children from surrounding communities. More than 25 percent of students play on one or more of LVC's Division III athletics teams, and many more play club or intramural sports. All students benefit from extensive campus programming that includes guest lectures, concerts, conferences, symposia, and a variety of cultural activities.

Off-Campus Programs

Students are encouraged to take advantage of numerous off-campus study opportunities offered by the College. Options abroad include programs in Argentina, Australia, England, France, Germany, Greece, Italy, the Netherlands, New Zealand, Northern Ireland, Spain, and Sweden, or several short-term, faculty-led options. Internship-based programs in Washington, D.C., and Philadelphia are also popular options. A student's scholarship funding and financial aid can be transferred to any of the programs, making study abroad available to all students, regardless of their family's financial situation.

Internships are another important aspect of experience-based learning at LVC. With guidance from professors and help from professional counselors, students in every major find internship placements, gain professional experiences, and build confidence, all of which helps when it comes time to apply for a job.

Academic Facilities

While Lebanon Valley's tree-lined walkways and beautiful gardens recall campuses of yesteryear, the College teems with twenty-first-century technologies. The Bishop Library contains 160,000+ items, 100,000+ electronic books, 30,000+ electronic journals, and 100+ online databases. More than 7,000 popular DVDs/videos and 6,500 music CDs are available to be checked out. The library, residence halls, smart classrooms, and administrative offices are all linked to the campus wireless network, maximizing the effectiveness and mobility of learning. Well-equipped, up-to-date laboratories provide students with the tools and technologies they need to conduct cutting-edge research, independently or in partnership with faculty.

Costs

Annual tuition for the 2012–13 school year is $33,670. Room and board charges are $9180 and fees are $800.

Financial Aid

Committed to helping all families afford the first-rate education it offers, LVC has received national recognition for its generous and distinctive merit-based scholarship program, which rewards strong high school performance with automatic merit scholarships. Students who graduate in the top 30 percent of their high school class receive an automatic LVC scholarship equivalent to one-quarter to one-half the cost of tuition.

Merit- and need-based financial assistance is also available. In 2012–13, the College will commit more than $24 million in merit- and need-based aid. Overall, 95 percent of LVC students receive some form of financial assistance from the College. Students and their families should complete Free Application for Federal Student Aid (FAFSA) to determine eligibility. The priority deadline for filing for financial aid is March 1.

Faculty

The LVC faculty includes scientists, scholars, artists, and professionals in a wide range of fields, many of whom are respected contributors to their disciplines. LVC professors are dedicated to teaching and are drawn to the College for its close-knit community and for the opportunity to be actively involved in the students' educational growth. Most faculty members are involved in research, scholarship, and professional organizations and play an active role in helping students find internships and get started with their own research. Of LVC's 102 professors, 87 percent have earned a Ph.D. or equivalent terminal degree. The College is committed to maintaining a low student-teacher ratio of 13:1 (FTE). The average class size is 20, and all courses are taught by professors, not graduate students.

Student Government

Lebanon Valley students participate in the College's governing system through Student Government and the Student Programming Board. Student Government fosters understanding, communication, and cooperation among students, faculty, and administration. The Student Government president meets every other week with LVC president Stephen MacDonald, ensuring that there is a clear line of communication between the student body and the administration. The Student Programming Board organizes off-campus trips and schedules comedians, musicians, and other on-campus entertainment.

Admission Requirements

The LVC admission process is selective, and the applicant's academic record is the most important factor in admission decisions. The College seeks students from a variety of backgrounds as well as those who display leadership abilities, a commitment to community involvement, and special talents or interests that might benefit or enrich the LVC community. Competitive applicants will have pursued a challenging high school course of study that includes at least 4 courses in English, 2 in foreign language, 3 in mathematics, 2 in science, and 1 in social studies. Additional course work in math and science is strongly recommended. More than 70 percent of recent incoming LVC students rank among the top 30 percent of their high school class. Submission of SAT or ACT scores is optional. Advanced standing is offered through CLEP and AP examinations.

Application and Information

To apply, students should submit a completed application, a $30 application fee, and official copies of their high school transcript. Although Lebanon Valley has a rolling admission process, students are encouraged to apply during the fall of their senior year. Personal visits to campus are encouraged.

For more information, applicants should contact:

William J. Brown Jr.
Vice President of Enrollment
Lebanon Valley College
101 North College Avenue
Annville, Pennsylvania 17003-1400
Phone: 866-LVC-4ADM (866-582-4236, toll-free)
Fax: 717-867-6026
E-mail: admission@lvc.edu
Web site: http://www.lvc.edu

The Lebanon Valley College community is close-knit and welcoming.

LE MOYNE COLLEGE
SYRACUSE, NEW YORK

LE MOYNE
SPIRIT. INQUIRY. LEADERSHIP. *JESUIT.*

The College

Le Moyne College is a four-year, coeducational Jesuit college of approximately 2,500 undergraduate students that uniquely balances a comprehensive liberal arts education with preparation for specific career paths or graduate study. Founded by the Society of Jesus in 1946, Le Moyne is the second youngest of the twenty-eight Jesuit colleges and universities in the United States. Its emphasis is on the education of the whole person and on the search for meaning and value as integral parts of an intellectual life. Le Moyne's personal approach to education is reflected in the quality of contact between students and faculty members.

A wide range of student-directed activities, athletics, clubs, and service organizations complement the academic experience. Intramural sports are very popular with Le Moyne students; nearly 85 percent of the students participate. Le Moyne also has seventeen NCAA intercollegiate teams (eight for men and nine for women). Athletic facilities include a new soccer/lacrosse turf field, softball and baseball fields; basketball, and racquetball courts; a weight-training and fitness center; practice fields; and two gymnasiums. A recreation center houses an Olympic-size indoor swimming pool, jogging track, indoor tennis and volleyball courts, and additional basketball, racquetball, and fitness areas.

Nearly 80 percent of students live in residence halls, apartments, and town houses on campus. The Residence Hall Councils and the Le Moyne Student Programming Board organize a variety of campus activities, including concerts, dances, a weekly film series, student talent programs, and special lectures as well as off-campus trips and skiing excursions. The College recently opened a plaza, which houses its bookstore, a café, and a pizzeria. The new Dolphin Den, which features a food court and a convenience store, has quickly become a popular space for students to meet, have a bite to eat, or just spend a quiet moment relaxing.

Location

Le Moyne's 160-plus acre, tree-lined campus is located in a residential setting 10 minutes from downtown Syracuse, the heart of New York State, whose metropolitan population is about 700,000. Syracuse is convenient to most major cities throughout the Northeast, New England, and Canada and offers a wide array of shopping centers and restaurants, many near Le Moyne. Syracuse offers year-round entertainment in the form of rock concerts at the Landmark Theatre, professional baseball and hockey, Bristol Omnitheatre, Syracuse Stage, Everson Museum of Art, and the Armory Square district downtown, which offers one-of-a-kind eateries, pubs, and coffeehouses in addition to a wide variety of social and cultural events. All are easily accessible via the excellent public transportation service, which schedules regular stops on Le Moyne's campus. Just a few miles outside the city are the rolling hills, picturesque lakes, and miles of open country for which central New York is renowned. An extensive network of state and county parks, recreational areas, and other facilities offer an abundance of recreational opportunities, including swimming, boating, hiking, downhill and cross-country skiing, snowboarding, and golf.

Majors and Degrees

Le Moyne College awards the Bachelor of Arts degree in biological sciences, communication (advertising, filmmaking, journalism, media studies, music industry, music journalism, music and culture, public relations, television/radio), computer science, criminology (human services, international affairs, law enforcement, research), economics, English (creative writing, literature), French, history, mathematics (actuarial science, pure mathematics, statistics), peace and global studies, philosophy, physics, political science, psychology, religious studies, sociology (anthropology, criminology, human services, research and theory), Spanish, and theater arts. The Bachelor of Science degree is awarded in

biochemistry, biological sciences (health professions, molecular biology, neurobiology), chemistry, economics, environmental science systems, environmental studies, general science, physics, and psychology. The Bachelor of Science in business is awarded in accounting, applied management analysis, finance, information systems, management and leadership, and marketing. A Bachelor of Science in nursing is also offered.

Students may minor in business administration, Catholic studies, classical humanities, film, gender and women's studies, Irish literature, Italian, Latin, legal studies, human resource management, management information systems, music, urban and regional studies, or visual arts as well as most of the major fields of study offered. Preprofessional programs are offered in dentistry, law, medicine, optometry, physical therapy, physician assistant studies, podiatry, and veterinary science. Students may prepare for teaching careers through certification programs in adolescent education, dual adolescent/special education, dual childhood/special education, and TESOL.

Le Moyne College and the L. C. Smith College of Engineering and Computer Science at Syracuse University offer a dual-degree program in which students may earn a bachelor's degree from Le Moyne and a master's degree in engineering from Syracuse University in as few as five years. Concentrations include aerospace; chemical, electrical, and mechanical engineering; computer science; and other fields of engineering.

Formal accelerated 3-4 programs are offered in dentistry, optometry, and podiatry in cooperation with the State University of New York at Buffalo School of Dental Medicine, Pennsylvania College of Optometry at Salus University, and the New York College of Podiatric Medicine. Predental students may also participate in an early assurance program with the State University of New York at Buffalo School of Dental Medicine. Cooperative 3-2 dual-degree programs in engineering are available with Clarkson University, Manhattan College, and University of Detroit Mercy.

SUNY Upstate Medical University in Syracuse offers students pursuing careers in the health-related professions an accelerated 3-3 doctoral-level transfer program in physical therapy as well as two-year cooperative transfer programs in medical technology, and respiratory care. Premedical students at Le Moyne are also offered the opportunity to participate in a medical school early assurance program. An early assurance program for premedical students is also available through the State University of New York at Buffalo School of Medicine.

Academic Programs

While each major department has its own sequence requirements for the minimum 120 credit hours needed for the Le Moyne degree, the College is convinced that there is a fundamental intellectual discipline that should characterize the graduate of a superior liberal arts college. Le Moyne's core curriculum provides this foundation by including studies of English language and literature, philosophy, history, religious studies, natural sciences, and social sciences.

For exceptional students, Le Moyne offers an integral honors program that includes an interdisciplinary humanities sequence as well as departmental honors courses. Le Moyne also offers a part-time course of study during evening hours through its Center for Continuing Education.

Le Moyne students may enroll in Army and Air Force ROTC programs in conjunction with Syracuse University.

Off-Campus Programs

The study-abroad program allows qualified students to spend a semester or year in almost any country throughout the world. Le Moyne College has study-abroad programs or affiliations in the Czech Republic, Dominican Republic, England, Germany, Ireland,

Scotland, and Spain. Students can also use partner programs to study in locations such as Australia, Costa Rica, Egypt, France, Italy, Japan, and South Africa. Le Moyne is a participant in the sixty-member New York State Visiting Student Program. As part of the mission of preparing future leaders, Le Moyne College places a strong emphasis on career preparation through internships and other forms of experiential education. Academic departments and the Office of Career Services both provide programs and services for students interested in interning part-time and full-time, both locally and in major cities such as New York and Washington, D.C. The Offices of Service Learning and the Academic Deans are also involved in experiential education to promote learning outside the classroom. In the sciences, students take part in campus research with mentor faculty members. Others receive assistance in pursuing outstanding opportunities off campus in leading research laboratories and health-care settings. The College has maintained a long-standing relationship with the Washington Center internship programs, where students from all majors complete full-time semester-long internships in Washington, D.C., with government, business, or major nonprofit organizations. Faculty members in the Political Science Department assist students interested in opportunities in Albany, New York state's seat of government, with either the New York State Senate or Assembly. Finally, the education programs at Le Moyne put students into school classrooms starting immediately as freshmen and continuing each year until graduation.

Academic Facilities

Le Moyne students benefit from an ongoing commitment to technological excellence. The College's forty-two buildings are equipped with accounting, biology, chemistry, computer science, physics, psychology, and statistics laboratories. The W. Carroll Coyne Center for the Performing Arts houses generous production, performance, and classroom space; the latest light and sound technology; scene and costume shops; an aerobics and dance studio; and rehearsal rooms for instrumental and choral music. Academic facilities also include an extensively renovated color television studio; a radio/recording studio; a receiver-antenna satellite dish; transmission and scanning electron microscopes; a nuclear magnetic resonance spectrometer; a gas chromatograph/mass spectrophotometer; a 240,000-volume, open-stack library; and extensive on-site computer facilities. A fiber-optic network enables students to access the library system, the campus network, and the Internet from several computer labs around the campus or from their personal computers in their rooms. All classrooms are smart classrooms, with multimedia capabilities that expand and enrich the learning process. Le Moyne students have access to other libraries through the Central New York Library Resources Council, and the campus Academic Support Center is available to students for instructional support. In addition, Le Moyne recently opened a 48,000-square-foot addition to its existing science complex.

Costs

For 2012–13, Le Moyne's tuition is $28,470. Room and board charges are $11,320. Additional fees amount to approximately $990, and books and supplies cost approximately $700.

Financial Aid

Financial aid is offered to a large percentage of Le Moyne's students through scholarships, grants, loans, and work-study assignments. Le Moyne offers a generous program of merit-based academic and athletic scholarships as well as financial aid based on a student's need and academic promise. Federal funds are available through the Federal Pell Grant, Federal Work-Study, Federal Supplemental Educational Opportunity Grant, and Federal Perkins Loan programs. A student's eligibility for need-based financial aid is determined from both the Free Application for Federal Student Aid (FAFSA) and the Le Moyne Financial Aid Application Form. It is recommended that these forms be mailed by February 1.

Faculty

The Le Moyne full-time faculty numbers 158 men and women; 94 percent have earned the highest degree in their field. With an average class size of 20, a student-faculty ratio of 12:1, and private offices for all full-time faculty members, the College promotes a personal as well as an academic relationship between students and faculty members. All classroom instruction is done by faculty members, and they are happy to assist and encourage students who wish to pursue undergraduate research through tutorials or senior research projects. These projects are carried out in an atmosphere free of competition from graduate students for books, laboratories, or professors' time. Le Moyne emphasizes advising and academic counseling for students throughout their four years.

Student Government

The College encourages student leadership in all activities. Positions of leadership are open to students in all class years. Students are represented by a Student Senate and have formal representation through the senate on most College-wide committees involved in decision making and policy formation.

Admission Requirements

Le Moyne seeks qualified students who are well prepared for serious academic study. Secondary school preparation must have included at least 17 college-preparatory high school units, 4 of which must be in English, 4 in social studies, 3–4 in mathematics, 3–4 in foreign language, and 3–4 in science. It is also recommended that prospective science and mathematics majors complete 4 units of mathematics and science. The SAT or ACT is required and should be taken by December or January of the senior year in high school. Campus visits are strongly recommended, as the admission process is a personal one. As bases for selection, academic achievement and secondary school recommendations are of primary importance. SAT or ACT scores are important as they relate to the record of achievement and to recommendations. Out-of-state students are encouraged to apply.

Application and Information

The Admission Committee reviews applications and mails decisions on a rolling admission cycle beginning December 1. The priority deadline for applications is February 1; all students who wish to be considered for academic merit scholarships should have a completed application on file in the Office of Admission before this date. Transfer students are encouraged to apply before June 1 for the fall semester and December 1 for the spring semester. Orientation programs for incoming freshmen and transfer students take place in midsummer.

Dennis J. Nicholson
Dean of Admission
Le Moyne College
Syracuse, New York 13214-1399
Phone: 315-445-4300
        800-333-4733 (toll-free)
E-mail: admission@lemoyne.edu
Web site: http://www.lemoyne.edu

Grewen Hall, the College's oldest building, overlooks Le Moyne's beautiful 160-plus acre campus.

LEWIS & CLARK COLLEGE
PORTLAND, OREGON

Lewis & Clark College

The College

Founded in 1867 in a small town south of Portland, Lewis & Clark College moved to its present location in Portland's southwest hills in 1942. The 137-acre campus is situated in a wooded residential area 6 miles from the center of the city and overlooks the lush Willamette Valley and Mount Hood in the distance.

The student body is known for its geographic diversity. In fall 2011, of the 2141 undergraduates, 21 percent were from Oregon, and 79 percent came from forty-nine other states plus the District of Columbia and represented sixty-six countries. Approximately 62 percent live in housing on campus, most of which is coed (91 percent). There are no fraternities or sororities.

The College offers numerous cocurricular activities, including twelve music groups; nine media organizations; eight religious/spiritual life groups; seventeen international, cultural, and diversity groups; and more than fifty student organizations. Cultural events such as lectures, symposia, art exhibits, theater productions, concerts, recitals, and dance performances occur on a regular basis. Currently, there are nineteen NCAA Division III varsity athletic teams, eight club teams, and numerous intramural sports. Athletic facilities include three basketball courts, a competition-size swimming pool, a weight-training room, a stadium, a baseball/softball complex, and six tennis courts, four of which are covered by an airdome. The renowned College Outdoors Program offers adventures such as backpacking, rafting, skiing, snowshoeing, caving, winter camping, sea kayaking, and environmental service projects in Oregon's and Washington's nearby wilderness areas.

Location

Portland has long been known for its livability and its excellent transportation system. Public buses and a free College shuttle run from the Lewis & Clark campus to the center of Portland, 6 miles away. The metropolitan area (population 2 million) is bisected by the Willamette River. Mount Hood, offering skiing ten months per year, is 50 miles away, and Oregon's rugged coastline lies 90 miles to the west. The city has 10,447 acres of parks, thirty-three music associations, thirty-five theater and dance companies, more than ninety galleries and museums, and more than 1,000 restaurants. Professional sports teams compete in soccer, hockey, and NBA basketball. Students can take advantage of the many internship and service opportunities available in the Portland metro area.

Majors and Degrees

Lewis & Clark offers programs leading to the Bachelor of Arts degree. Academic majors include art (art history and studio art), biochemistry and molecular biology, biology, chemistry, computer science, computer science and mathematics, East Asian studies, economics (international, management, public policy, theory), English, environmental studies, foreign languages, French studies, German studies, Hispanic studies, history, international affairs, mathematics, music, philosophy, physics, political science, psychology, rhetoric and media studies, religious studies, sociology/anthropology, and theater. Students may also design a major or pursue a double major and numerous minors. Preprofessional preparation is available in the fields of law and medicine.

Dual-degree (3-2 and 4-2) programs in engineering are offered in cooperation with Columbia University, Washington University (St. Louis), the University of Southern California, and Oregon Health and Science University. A 4-2 B.A./M.B.A. program is offered in cooperation with the University of Rochester's Simon Graduate School of Business. A 4-1 B.A./M.A.T. program is offered through Lewis & Clark's Graduate School of Education and Counseling.

Academic Programs

The liberal arts curriculum offers sufficient structure to ensure depth and breadth of study, but it also incorporates a high degree of freedom in order to promote creative and critical thinking. In the four-year plan of study, approximately one third of a student's time is devoted to general education, one third to a major program, and one third to elective courses. Students are also encouraged to participate in departmental honors programs, undergraduate research, independent study, and internships.

The academic calendar consists of two 15-week semesters. A normal load is four 4-semester-hour academic courses, plus one or more activity courses. By graduation, a student is expected to have earned at least 128 semester hours—equivalent, roughly, to eight different classes a year. The fall semester begins early in September and ends before Christmas, and the spring semester begins in mid-January and ends in early May. There are also a limited number of courses offered during two summer sessions.

The community of scholars at Lewis & Clark College is dedicated to personal and academic excellence. Joining the Lewis & Clark community obligates each member to observe the principles of mutual respect, academic integrity, civil discourse, and responsible decision-making.

Off-Campus Programs

Lewis & Clark offers nationally recognized international and off-campus study opportunities that have been in existence for fifty years. Approximately thirty different overseas study programs and three domestic programs are available annually. Usually, 20 to 24 students plus a faculty leader participate in each program. More than half of the College's graduates have taken advantage of these outstanding programs, often satisfying General Education or major requirements at the same time.

Overseas study may have either a general-culture focus or a specialized academic focus. On general-culture programs, students become immersed in the everyday life of the host country by living with local families, traveling, studying in classes and seminars, and working on independent projects. Programs with a more specific academic focus may include studying German language and literature in Munich; perfecting language skills in France, Ecuador, Russia, Japan, or China; or studying literature in England. Sites for overseas study programs from 2012 through 2015 are Australia, Brazil, Chile, China, Cuba, Dominican Republic, Ecuador, England, France, Germany, Greece, India, Italy, Japan, Kenya/Tanzania, Morocco, New Zealand, Russia, Scotland, Senegal, and Spain. Domestic programs are available in the Arizona borderlands, New York, and Washington, D.C., for those interested in immigration, economics, political science, sociology, theater, or art. Students receive academic credit on all programs, both overseas and domestic.

Academic Facilities

The Aubrey R. Watzek Library (open 24 hours per day when school is in session) houses more than 740,000 items including books, documents, audiovisual materials, microforms, and periodicals. Its mission is to provide a solid core of materials designed to support the curriculum and the research needs of the Lewis & Clark community. The library offers individualized reference assistance in the use of both print and electronic resources. The library's Web site provides access to its catalog as well as to a full range of electronic databases and links to useful Internet resources. The library is a member of Summit, a consortium of thirty-six academic libraries that have a unified catalog that enables students to request and receive materials from member libraries within two days.

Music department facilities include Evans Auditorium, a 410-seat recital hall equipped with an orchestra pit and stage elevator; an extensive (more than 4,000) record, CD, and tape collection; twenty-two practice rooms; forty-three pianos, including several 6- and 7-foot concert grands and a 9-foot Steinway concert grand; two harpsichords; a Baroque organ; an electronic music studio with CD production capability; Zimbabwe marimbas; and an Indonesian gamelan orchestra. The 600-seat chapel houses an 85-rank Casavant organ.

The Fields Center for the Visual Arts is equipped with studio space for painting, drawing, ceramics, sculpture, design, and printmaking as well as a photography lab. The department also has a Visual Resources Collection of 50,000 slides and several thousand digital images representing artwork from a wide range of media, time periods, world regions, and cultures. The collection exists to support instruction in the art department as well as historical and cultural studies campuswide. The arts center contains gallery and classroom space as well. The humanities and social sciences also enjoy state-of-the-art classroom and lab facilities.

The natural sciences are housed in the Biology/Psychology, BoDine, and Olin Buildings, which are well equipped with modern instrumentation to support the College's emphasis on collaborative student-faculty research. These buildings contain numerous research laboratories used by students in classes or research projects, in addition to teaching labs and classrooms. Among the notable facilities are a laboratory for the study of human-computer interactions, a scanning electron microscope, a modern greenhouse, an astronomical observatory with Newtonian and solar telescopes, a molecular modeling laboratory, a laboratory for the study of parallel computing, a laboratory for studying the biomechanics of animal locomotion, and an astrophysics laboratory that is equipped to remotely operate and acquire data from a specialized telescope at Kitts Peak, Arizona. All labs are computerized for acquiring and analyzing data and are networked to allow sharing and acquisition of data remotely. Ecological investigations and studies of the environmental impacts of human activity can be conducted both on the College's heavily wooded campus and at the nearby Tryon Creek State Park.

Computer facilities include several public computer labs around campus available for student use. These labs house more than 130 Macintosh and Microsoft Windows computers, along with peripherals such as scanners, color and black and white laser printers, and digital video editing equipment. Other equipment, including digital still and video cameras, digital audio recorders, and more, are available for checkout. All residence halls have wireless networks. The institution has an 800 Mbps connection to the Internet.

Costs

Tuition and fees for 2011–12 were $38,500. The room and board charge is $9928 for fourteen (flex) meals per week; other meal plans are also available. The estimate for books and personal expenses is $2040.

Financial Aid

In 2010–11, 72 percent of the College's students received some form of financial assistance. Institutional, state, and federal resources, including Federal Pell Grants, Federal Supplemental Educational Opportunity Grants, Federal Perkins Loans, and Federal Work-Study awards, may be part of an aid award. Other options include low-interest Federal Stafford Student Loans and opportunities to work on and off campus. To receive priority consideration for need-based financial aid, students must meet appropriate deadlines for admission and should submit the Free Application for Federal Student Aid (FAFSA) and the CSS/Financial Aid PROFILE application by February 15.

Lewis & Clark offers renewable merit-based scholarships and participation awards to students who demonstrate the qualities of mind, self-discipline, and commitment to learning that characterize the best in Lewis & Clark students. These awards range from $1000 to full tuition. Many of these scholarships are awarded through the admissions process and don't require a separate application. Others require additional paper work. Full details on merit-based scholarship opportunities can be found at: www.go.lclark.edu/fao.

Faculty

The 142 full-time members of the faculty are committed to undergraduate teaching and advising and are also active in research, writing, and publishing. Involving students in the research process is of high priority. Ninety-seven percent of the full-time faculty members hold a Ph.D. or the highest advanced degree in their discipline. The student-faculty ratio is 12:1. The average class size is 19, with 85 percent of classes having 29 or fewer students.

Student Government

The Associated Students of Lewis & Clark (ASLC) has a decentralized structure that encourages co-curricular participation by students and places a high priority on participation with faculty and staff in the process of enriching the academic environment. ASLC consists of a Student Senate, governing boards, and appointed students who serve on faculty constitutional, standing, and special committees. The 30 members of the Student Academic Affairs Board (SAAB) are appointed on a departmental basis to support student academic initiatives ranging from student research and visiting speakers to conference attendance and fine arts exhibits. One quarter of the total ASLC budget of more than $400,000 is used by SAAB in support of fellow undergraduate students.

Admission Requirements

Lewis & Clark College seeks first-year and transfer applicants who are committed to academic excellence and personal growth. Admission is competitive. Applications are carefully reviewed and examined for degree of academic preparation, ability to express ideas in essay form, participation in activities, citizenship and community service, and support given by the school through recommendations. Campus visits are encouraged. Interviews are available but not required. Recommended high school preparation includes 4 years of English, 4 years of history or social science, 4 years of mathematics, 3 years of laboratory science, 2 to 3 years of foreign language, and 1 year of fine arts. The SAT or ACT is required, unless the student is applying via the test-optional Portfolio Path.

Application and Information

First-year applicants should submit the Common Application (online or paper); the required Common Application Supplement; a personal essay; an official academic transcript, including senior grades from the first marking period; one recommendation from a counselor; and at least one reference from an academic teacher. The application fee is waived if the applicant uses the online Common Application. Application deadlines for the fall semester are November 1 for nonbinding early action (notification by January 1) and January 15 for regular decision (notification by April 1).

Transfer applicants are evaluated on a rolling basis. To ensure full consideration, the College strongly recommends that transfer students submit all credentials before the end of March.

The application deadline for first-year and transfer students for the spring semester is November 1 (notification within three weeks of file completion). The test-optional Portfolio Path admissions program provides an opportunity for applicants who have shown exceptional academic initiative to demonstrate the full extent of their pursuits by presenting a portfolio of their academic work. Under this plan, SAT or ACT scores are optional. More details about the Portfolio Path can be found at http://www.lclark.edu/college/offices/admissions/apply.

For more information about Lewis & Clark College or to arrange a visit, students should contact:

Office of Admissions
Lewis & Clark College
0615 SW Palatine Hill Road
Portland, Oregon 97219-7899
Phone: 503-768-7040
    800-444-4111 (toll-free)
Fax: 503-768-7055
E-mail: admissions@lclark.edu
Web site: http://www.lclark.edu

LIBERTY UNIVERSITY
LYNCHBURG, VIRGINIA

The University

Founded in 1971 by Dr. Jerry Falwell, Sr., Liberty University provides a Christian, comprehensive, coeducational environment committed to serious education at the undergraduate, graduate, post-masters, and doctorate levels. The university is situated on a 6,700-acre campus complete with classroom, residence, study, leisure, and recreational facilities. Liberty is approved by the State Council of Higher Education for Virginia and is accredited by the Commission on Colleges of the Southern Association of Colleges and Schools (SACS) to award associate, bachelor's, master's, and doctoral degrees. There are more than 12,500 resident undergraduate and graduate students in the student body who represents all 50 states and more than 70 countries.

Liberty's facilities include A. L. Williams Stadium, the18,000-seat football stadium; the 10,000-seat Vines Convocation Center, home to Convocation, the largest weekly meeting of Christian young people, and men's and women's basketball and volleyball; the Matthews-Hopkins Track Complex, a superb outdoor-track facility; the Tolsma Indoor Track; the Worthington Stadium baseball field; the LaHaye Ice Center; the state-of-the-art, 83,968-square-foot LaHaye Student Center that includes a lounge, five full-length basketball courts, cardio and weight rooms, a cafe, multipurpose rooms, an aerobic room, a 25-yard swimming pool, and two spas; the Liberty University Equestrian Centre; the Williams Football Operations Center; and the Liberty Mountain Snowflex Centre—North America's only snowless ski slope. In addition, construction on the new Jerry Falwell Library will begin in 2012. The structure is projected to be the epicenter of the university.

Liberty's intercollegiate athletic competition is in NCAA Division I. Men compete in baseball, basketball, cross-country, football, golf, indoor track, soccer, tennis, and track and field. Women compete in basketball, cross-country, field hockey, lacrosse, soccer, softball, swimming, tennis, track and field, and volleyball. Other sports programs at the club level include ice hockey, lacrosse, and volleyball for men, and ice hockey and ice skating for women. Intramural competition is offered for both men and women in various sports, including ultimate frisbee and men's and women's flag football.

Residence halls include traditional-style hall housing, quad-living residences, and new apartment-style living within walking distance of main campus. These new apartments include full furnishings, a kitchen, laundry facilities, and the Campus East Clubhouse, which offers billiards, PlayStation, Xbox, satellite TV, a theater, a computer lounge, the Campus East Market, and an outdoor pool.

Liberty offers several majors in a wide variety of degrees on the graduate level, in addition to its undergraduate and associate degree programs. Teacher licensure is available at the graduate level in early childhood (K–3), elementary (K–6), and secondary (7–12) education; administration/supervision; gifted education; reading; school counseling; and special education.

Through the Liberty Baptist Theological Seminary, the university offers many online and resident graduate degrees, including a Master of Arts in Religion, Master of Religious Education, Master of Divinity, Master of Theology, and Doctor of Ministry.

Liberty University's School of Law opened in August 2004 and graduated its first class in May 2007. The American Bar Association (ABA) has fully accredited the School of Law, which is housed in the university's Green Hall. The school is equipped with multimedia technology and wireless Internet access, two seminar rooms, a mock trial courtroom, the Ehrhorn Law Library, a study center with 24-hour student access, law review offices, seven professional skills rooms, an administrative suite, a faculty suite, and an academic support suite.

For international students, Liberty offers the English Language Institute (ELI). English grammar, comprehension, and reading are taught for international students with little or no English skills. An ELI certification is awarded upon completion of these programs.

Location

The university is located in the heart of Virginia in Lynchburg (population 75,000), with the scenic Blue Ridge Mountains as a backdrop. The city is more than 200 years old and is noted for its culture, beauty, and educational advantages. Nearby are such sites as Thomas Jefferson's Poplar Forest; Appomattox Court House; Natural Bridge; historic Lexington; Washington, D.C.; and many other places of interest.

The city of Lynchburg offers a wide variety of activities for recreation and entertainment. Excellent sports facilities and programs, cultural events at the Lynchburg Fine Arts Center, beautiful lakes and streams, and many other local attractions enhance the lives of Lynchburg residents. Lynchburg also has more than 2,000 hotel rooms, numerous outlets and malls, and a number of restaurants that serve a wide variety of cuisines. Lynchburg is accessible by air, train, and bus.

Majors and Degrees

Liberty offers more than 200 programs of study—undergraduate and graduate courses, in residential and online formats. Visit www.liberty.edu/academics to view all of Liberty's programs.

A Teacher Licensure Option is available at the elementary (K–6), middle school (6–8), and secondary (7–12) levels in biology, business, computer science, English, history/social sciences, mathematics, and work and family studies and at the comprehensive (K–12) level in teaching English as a second language, health/physical education, music (choral or instrumental), and special education.

Academic Programs

In addition to all major requirements, students must complete general education courses in humanities, natural sciences and mathematics, social sciences, physical education, and religion.

Liberty is on a semester calendar. During the summer, there are several one- and two-week intensive courses offered. Winter courses are also offered between semesters.

The university offers higher education degrees for the adult learner online. As the world's largest, private, non-profit institution among online universities, Liberty University

Online is also accredited by the Commission on Colleges of the Southern Association of Colleges and Schools to award associate, bachelor's, master's, and doctoral degrees. For more information, students should call 877-298-9615 or visit the Web site at www.luonline.com.

Academic Facilities

Liberty has a strong commitment to first-class facilities and has taken the initiative to keep their campus up to date. The Arthur S. DeMoss Learning Center, Liberty's academic hub, is a 500,000-square-foot Jeffersonian-style building that encompasses many aspects of the university. All academic rooms are wired for Internet access, with large computer screens installed for interactive learning. This impressive facility is one of the largest academic buildings in central Virginia and houses the campus library, which currently contains 283,000 bound or microfilmed volumes. Construction on a new library began in spring 2012. The facility will carry the name of Liberty's founder and president, the late Dr. Jerry Falwell, Sr. The Jerry Falwell Library will have a new electronic robotic storage and retrieval system, allowing Liberty's collection of electronic and traditional print resources to grow to nearly a half-million items. Students may find employment or volunteer their services in the university's 50,000-watt FM radio station or student-run radio and TV stations.

The Theatre Arts department's Tower Theater features 640 seats and over 12,000-square-feet of backstage and support area. The Human Performance Laboratory functions to enhance student learning and research capabilities through the use of a Bodpod, Oxycon Mobile, Trackmaster treadmills, altitude chambers, and Concept2 Model E. Rowing Ergometers. Also, new aviation facilities are located near the Lynchburg Regional Airport.

Costs

Tuition, room, board, and fees were $27,218 for 12 to 18 credit hours in 2012–13. Additional fees, such as lab fees, are required for specific classes and are listed in the class registration book. Automobiles are permitted if they are registered with the university.

Financial Aid

Liberty offers a variety of grants, scholarships, and on-campus jobs. All major, federally funded student financial aid programs are available. Academic, athletic, merit, talent, National Merit, and other Liberty assistance grants are also available for qualified candidates. Students are required to submit a Free Application for Federal Student Aid (FAFSA) to the U.S. Department of Education and include Liberty University's school code (010392) on that application at http://www.fafsa.ed.gov. This form is the student's application for all financial aid, and it is recommended that all families use the IRS Data Retrieval Tool in the FAFSA, if available. Approximately 96 percent of the student body received some type of aid last year.

Faculty

The University employs more than 2,000 full- and part-time faculty members. More than 70 percent of Liberty's full-time faculty members hold terminal degrees in their field.

Student Government

Students elect representatives to serve on the Student Senate. This group provides leadership recommendations and suggestions to the student development staff. Student Senate members organize and direct activities and civic programs.

Admission Requirements

All applicants should be familiar with Liberty's philosophy and expectations before applying. Applicants to the A.A., B.A., and B.S. programs must be high school graduates and must submit an official copy of their high school transcript, indicating graduation date (or GED test scores, if applicable). An essay of 200 to 400 words must be submitted answering the question, 'How will your personal faith and beliefs contribute to Liberty's mission to develop Christ-centered leaders?' Applicants must also submit either ACT or SAT scores, which are used for academic counseling and placement. High school transcripts and SAT/ACT requirements are waived if the student transfers at least 60 hours or holds an associate degree. Test scores are also waived if the applicant is 22 years of age or older. The applicant must demonstrate the ability to do college work. Three personal references may be requested if needed. Although interviews are not required, prospective students are encouraged to visit the campus. Four "College For A Weekend" (CFAW) events are available each year, giving prospective students an opportunity to participate in classes, attend social and athletic events, experience residence hall life, and interact with students and faculty members.

Application and Information

Admissions decisions are made on a rolling basis; however January 31 is the priority deadline for fall enrollment. Applicants are encouraged to complete the application process by January 31 to be considered for maximum scholarship opportunities. Applicants for the spring term should complete the process by November 1, although early October is preferred. Late applicants are received on a space available basis.

To learn more about Liberty University, students should contact:

Resident Admissions Office
Liberty University
1971 University Boulevard
Lynchburg, Virginia 24502
Phone: 800-543-5317 (toll-free)
Fax: 800-542-2311 (toll-free)
E-mail: admissions@liberty.edu
Web site: http://www.libertyu.com
　　　　　http://www.liberty.edu

An aerial view of Liberty University, featuring the Arthur S. DeMoss Learning Center.

LIM COLLEGE
NEW YORK, NEW YORK

LIM COLLEGE

The College

With its flagship location situated in a lovely town house in the center of the fashion capital of the world, LIM College has been a major force in fashion and business education for over seven decades. Its graduates can be found throughout all aspects of the industry, and its high standards of education have earned LIM College accreditation from the Middle States Association of Colleges and Schools.

LIM College is a highly personal school where students learn about the business of fashion, with an emphasis on academic and professional study. Lifelong friends are made at LIM College, as well as lifelong careers. Although most students come to the College directly from high school or transfer from other colleges, there are also those of nontraditional college age who enroll. Students come to LIM College from many parts of the country and the world. The current enrollment is approximately 1,500 undergraduates.

LIM College prides itself on its employment rate. The Center for Career Development is one of LIM College's chief assets. Each student receives extensive career assistance throughout their time at the College, beginning in the first semester. This counseling helps direct students to positions within their field of study. Students seeking employment from the 2011 graduating class had a 90 percent employment rate within nine months of graduation.

The unique nature of LIM College's curriculum provides students with a foundation of core courses in liberal arts and business while offering diverse and intensive hands-on preparation in the fashion industry. This affords graduates the opportunity to accept executive training, merchandising, management, marketing, and communications positions in a wide variety of areas within the fashion and business worlds.

Support services are important at LIM College. In addition to academic and career advising, personal counseling is available. Because of the College's small size and the close relationships between students and staff members, any faculty member or administrator is readily accessible to help and advise all students. LIM College's Advisory Board members, all successful fashion industry executives, may also serve as mentors to students, offering additional guidance and advice.

LIM College has a very dynamic student life. Active clubs include the Fashion Club, Student Life Activities Board, Student Government Association, and many more. There are also student publications including the *LIMLIGHT* yearbook and *Fashion Sense* magazine.

LIM College proudly opened a new residence hall in 2008. Located at 1760 Third Avenue, this state-of-the-art facility boasts a plethora of modern amenities. All rooms have private bathrooms, complementary wireless Internet access, phone service, and 130 cable channels. Rooms are also equipped with full refrigerators and 25-inch flat-screen televisions. The facility also contains a private gym, game room, computer lab, and three full-service kitchens.

LIM College's Open House program offers students and their families the opportunity to tour the school's campus and learn not only of LIM College's unique academic programs, but also of the vast array of careers found in the fashion industry. The day also includes special presentations on financial aid, study abroad, clubs, and much more. Current LIM College students assist in hosting the event and are available to answer questions. LIM College also offers many other opportunities to visit including weekly information sessions, Transfer Nights, webinars, overnight visits for accepted students, and other periodically scheduled special events.

Location

LIM College is situated in four buildings—on East 53rd, East 54th, and East 45th Streets; and on Fifth Avenue, one of the most fashionable locales in the world. A whole world of fashion is at the College's doorstep and includes such famous stores as Saks Fifth Avenue, Henri Bendel, Armani, and Ralph Lauren. New York City is the headquarters for the garment, cosmetics, advertising,

publishing, and textile industries, all of which are essential to the fashion industry and are visited regularly by LIM College students. The College incorporates all of these resources into the curriculum. For example, the Fashion Magazines course may include trips to photography studios, modeling agencies, or tours of magazine offices and advertising firms. New York City offers LIM College students an unparalleled learning experience.

Majors and Degrees

LIM College offers four-year programs in fashion merchandising, management, marketing, and visual merchandising, leading to a Bachelor of Business Administration (B.B.A.) or a Bachelor of Professional Studies (B.P.S.) degree, and a two-year program in fashion merchandising leading to the Associate in Applied Sciences (A.A.S.) degree. LIM College also offers a Master of Business Administration (M.B.A.), which features two exciting courses of study in either entrepreneurship or fashion management. The College also offers a broad variety of concentrations that allow students to pursue a focused area of study that compliments their major.

Academic Programs

LIM College offers a combination of classroom education and supervised practical fieldwork that has been designed to prepare students for executive training programs and other entry-level executive positions in various areas of the fashion industry.

Experiential learning is an integral part of the LIM College curriculum. The internship program helps students become truly prepared for successful careers within fashion and fashion-related industries. All students are required to take three internships during their tenure at LIM College. Each internship has a prerequisite seminar attached to it that includes activities such as field trips, guest speakers, and portfolio-building that help students network with industry professionals and develop into dynamic business leaders. The Industry Exploration internship focuses on understanding the nature of the fashion industry through a retail experience, while the Career Pathing internship allows students to explore potential career fields, such as management, publishing, cosmetics, advertising, public relations, or fashion forecasting. Both of these internships dovetail with academic courses the students have taken during previous semesters. The third and final internship is the semester-long Senior Co-op, which is a required four-day-a-week placement in a field related to the student's chosen area of specialization. Co-ops may lead students to positions at fashion magazines, public relations firms, buying offices, or other essential areas of the fashion industry. The Senior Co-op serves as the ideal culmination of the academic experience and a perfect transition into the business world, preparing undergraduates for the challenge and excitement of their future careers.

To graduate, students must complete 127 credits for the bachelor's degree (130 for visual merchandising). Associate degree candidates must earn 68 credits. All students must maintain a grade point average of at least 2.0, and satisfactorily complete the cooperative work assignments.

LIM College accepts qualified students as transfers throughout the four years. The maximum number of credits that LIM will accept is 65. Transfer students must complete the last consecutive 46 credits at LIM College, including the Senior Co-op semester.

The College calendar runs on a traditional semester format, offering both fall and spring start dates. Also offered are summer and Saturday Fashion Lab programs for high school students. The specially selected courses, such as Fashion Buying and Fashion Magazines, blend academics with hands-on experience and are a great way to explore the fashion industry.

Off-Campus Programs

Study-abroad options are available, including study in locales such as Barcelona, Rome, Melbourne, Paris, London, and China.

Academic Facilities

The 5,000-square-foot Adrian G. Marcuse library contains 84,000 volumes and online books pertaining to fashion, management, marketing, and the liberal arts, as well as 225 professional and academic journals. The library has more than forty computer terminals that connect to the Internet and provide access to online databases through the library's subscriptions. DVDs and VHS cassettes useful for fashion-related studies are also available. Personal computers are available for use in the library, lounges, and classrooms. The student-to-computer ratio is 4:1. The Math Center and Writing Centers offer one-on-one tutoring for all students.

LIM College's facility on Fifth Avenue is equipped with two fashion merchandising studios. There are also two new 1,100-square-foot visual merchandising studios, as well as a state-of-the-art Color and Materials Laboratory at the new location.

Costs

Tuition for the 2012–13 school year is $22,420 with additional mandatory fees of $575. Housing charges for the 2012–13 year are $15,850. Students who commute spend from $1200 to $2000 for transportation, depending on distance. The estimated cost of books and supplies are $1100. The personal expense allowance is $2000.

Financial Aid

LIM College believes that lack of funds should not keep students from attaining a degree; thus, admissions decisions and financial aid are totally separate, and a request for aid has no effect on admissions. About 79 percent of LIM College's students received some form of financial aid during the 2010–11 school year. Institutional scholarships, Federal Pell Grants, Federal Supplemental Educational Opportunity Grants, and New York State TAP grants are all available for eligible students. In addition, the College participates in the Federal Stafford Loan program for students and Federal PLUS Loan program for parents. The College also works with several private lenders to offer alternative education loans for students to supplement their federal loans. International students are eligible to apply for alternative loans with a credit-worthy U.S.-based co-signer. The Free Application for Federal Student Aid (FAFSA) should be filed by all applicants by March 1 for priority consideration. Aid is granted on the basis of financial need and scholarships are merit based, although some awards take need into consideration. Details of the financial aid programs are available on the LIM College Web site or are available directly from the Office of Student Financial Services.

LIM College features a Merit Scholarship Program for incoming freshmen and transfer students. These scholarship monies are awarded for academic achievement in high school or college. Students can remain eligible for their scholarship throughout their stay at the College by maintaining a GPA of 3.0 or above. LIM College's nonprofit Fashion Education Foundation also administers a number of merit scholarships (both need and non-need based) other than direct institutional awards.

Faculty

LIM College prides itself on its faculty members. In the fall 2010 semester, 72 percent of the College's faculty had an advanced degree, including 100 percent of the faculty within the departments of Arts and Communications and Math, Finance, and Technology. All professional subject faculty members have wide business and professional experience and many, through their business contacts, bring guests to class to share in the lectures and discussions. The student-faculty ratio is 9:1, and the average class size is 17.

Each student is assigned an academic adviser. Work-study and career guidance is provided by the Center for Career Development, with conferences held before, during, and after the cooperative work assignments and prior to placement interviews. Students are always welcome to discuss career options at any other time as well.

Student Government

The Office of Student Life is the center of student activities and clubs at LIM College. This department supports student government, approves other student organizations, and establishes operating budgets. One of LIM College's more popular clubs is the Fashion Club, which plans an annual fashion show that recently hosted over 1,000 people. Another popular activity is the student-run *Fashion Sense* magazine. LIM College's Office of Student Life plans many other activities including diversity programming, philanthropic service, and new student orientation.

Admission Requirements

All undergraduate applicants are required to submit high school transcripts, SAT or ACT scores, two letters of recommendation, an essay, and the completed application with the application fee. Transfer students must also submit all college transcripts. Undergraduate Admissions will waive the standardized test requirement if the student has earned 30 credit hours. International students should have their transcripts evaluated by World Education Services and submit TOEFL, IETLS, or PTE test scores. It is also strongly suggested that all applicants create an activity sheet or resume highlighting their experience, with emphasis on business and fashion activities.

Application and Information

LIM College's Admissions Committee recognizes that many intangibles go into the making of a successful student, and it evaluates each applicant individually and holistically. The College uses a rolling admission policy. Applicants are informed of the admission decision within approximately four to six weeks after all admission requirements have been fulfilled. An application may be obtained from the LIM College Web site or by contacting the Admissions Office.

Kristina Ortiz
Assistant Dean of Admissions
LIM College
12 East 53rd Street
New York, New York 10022-5268
Phone: 212-752-1530
      800-677-1323 (toll-free outside New York City)
Fax: 212-750-3432
E-mail: admissions@limcollege.edu
Web site: http://www.limcollege.edu
      http://www.facebook.com/LIMCollege
      http://twitter.com/LIMcollege

LIM College's flagship location, The Townhouse, is located right off Fifth Avenue in Midtown Manhattan.

LIMESTONE COLLEGE
GAFFNEY, SOUTH CAROLINA

The College

Founded in 1845, Limestone is a fully accredited, private, coeducational liberal arts college. The College maintains a small student body and a well-qualified faculty in order to create an atmosphere in which each student develops intellectually, physically, and socially. The College endeavors to help students prepare for a satisfying, useful life through effective communication skills, responsible decision-making abilities, meaningful leisure-time activities, and lifelong aspirations.

In addition to its programs on campus, Limestone offers several of its academic majors in an accelerated format called the Block Program at several locations throughout South Carolina. These programs are intended primarily for working adults. The College also has an impressive Virtual Campus program on the Internet with many majors offered. Combined, these two programs form the Extended Campus.

Limestone is scheduled to launch a Master of Business Administration (M.B.A.) program in fall 2012. Leveraging its reputation as a pioneer of online-based degree programs (Limestone was among the first institutions to offer such programs in the mid-1990s), the M.B.A. program will primarily be an Internet-based offering, with courses offered in eight-week terms. In addition, three weekend seminars will be held on the Gaffney campus: one each at the beginning, middle, and end of the program. Initially the program will have only a single cohort of 25 students, with additional cohorts of 25 entering the program, up to an enrollment of approximately 150. New cohorts will usually begin the program in July, October, and March. Students will expand their skills in planning, staffing, organizing, directing, and controlling business activities. They will also continue the development of their decision-making, leadership, motivation, problem-solving, and teamwork skills.

Extracurricular activities play a vital part in the development of all students at Limestone College. Among these activities are intercollegiate athletics: men's baseball, basketball, cross-country, golf, lacrosse, soccer, swimming, tennis, track and field, volleyball, and wrestling; and women's basketball, cross-country, golf, field hockey, lacrosse, soccer, softball, swimming, tennis, track and field, and volleyball. Students who are interested in music have the opportunity to participate in several instrumental and choral ensembles. A theater program is also available.

The 115-plus-acre Limestone campus is well laid out for pleasant college living. The classrooms, library, laboratories, auditorium, bookstore, post office, and administrative offices are housed in buildings that border the central and circular drives, making each easily accessible to the others. The back campus has a plaza of five dormitories, and a dining hall is located nearby. The Timken LYFE Center and Timken East, a physical education complex, offer a 1,500-seat basketball arena, an AAU-size swimming pool, steam room, sauna, Jacuzzi, dance studio, and auxiliary gyms. The Walt Griffin Physical Education Center, named for the current Limestone College president, offers three classrooms, nine offices, locker rooms, athletic training and education facilities, a state-of-the-art fitness center, and a wrestling practice facility. The College also has eight lighted tennis courts, a baseball field, a softball field, a soccer/lacrosse field, field hockey field, and several practice fields.

Location

Gaffney, a small city with a population of 15,000, provides an ideal setting for a college campus. Whereas the distractions associated with a large city are absent from daily life, the cultural programs and services offered in Charlotte, North Carolina, and Spartanburg and Greenville, South Carolina, are all within a 50-mile radius of the campus. All are connected to Gaffney by Interstate 85.

The climate is free from extreme heat or cold. The well-known resort areas of the Blue Ridge Mountains, the Great Smoky Mountains, and the beaches of the Atlantic Coast are accessible for weekend visits. In the immediate area, facilities are available for all water sports, horseback riding, golf, tennis, and skiing.

Majors and Degrees

Limestone College offers the Bachelor of Arts, Bachelor of Science, and Bachelor of Social Work degrees with majors in art (concentrations in studio art and graphic design); athletic training; biology; business administration (concentrations in accounting, computer science, e-business, economics, general business, human resource management, health care administration, management, and marketing); chemistry; computer science (concentrations in Internet management, management information systems, and programming); criminal justice; English; history; liberal studies; mathematics; music; physical education (concentrations in athletic training and strength/conditioning); preprofessional programs in law, medicine, dentistry, chiropractic, veterinary medicine, nursing, pharmacy, and physical therapy; psychology; social work; sports management; and theater. Majors approved for South Carolina teacher certification are elementary education, English education, mathematics education, music education, physical education, and secondary education.

The Associate of Arts and Associate of Science degrees are offered with majors in business administration (concentrations in general business), computer science (majors in Internet management, management information systems, and programming), and liberal studies.

The M.B.A program is designed so that groups of 25 students (a cohort) proceed through the courses together. The online program will offer students the opportunity to expand skills in accounting, financial management, management, organizational development, and quality management.

Academic Programs

The course of study leading to the M.B.A., B.A., B.S., B.S.W., A.A., or A.S. degrees consists of four elements: requirements in communication and quantitative skills; a general liberal arts program, involving five different subject groups; courses in the major; and appropriate electives. The baccalaureate degree programs require the completion of a minimum of 123 semester hours. The associate degree programs require the completion of a minimum of 62 semester hours. The M.B.A. program consists of the completion of 36 semester hours of graduate-level course work, followed by a standardized comprehensive examination. A minimum cumulative grade point average of 3.0 on a 4.0 scale is required for graduation. The degree will be completed in approximately two calendar years.

Advanced placement and credit are given for scores of 3 or higher on the Advanced Placement examinations of the College Board.

An honors program involving special courses, seminars, and lectures is available for exceptional students. Admission to this program is contingent upon outstanding high school grades and scores on the SAT of the College Board, the completion of a special application, and an interview. Almost 10 percent of

all Limestone students are enrolled in this rigorous academic program.

A Program for Alternative Learning Styles (PALS) is available for qualified students with certified learning disabilities who might not otherwise succeed at the college level.

Academic Facilities

Limestone has outstanding computer facilities, including free e-mail accounts for all main campus students, residence hall high-speed Internet connections, and several well-equipped, state-of-the-art computer labs. There are also well-equipped science labs. The modern A. J. Eastwood Library houses approximately 112,976 volumes and is fully computerized, including student Internet access. Fullerton Auditorium, with a seating capacity of 975, is used for musical productions and is one of the finest such facilities in the state of South Carolina. The Limestone Center houses Limestone's theater department and the majority of the athletic offices. The intimate 150-seat theater has state-of-the-art lighting and sound, a self-contained workshop for set construction, and offices and classrooms. The athletic department portion of the building features a Hall of Fame room, a 75-person media room, and office suites for most team sports.

Costs

The direct cost for a student at Limestone College for the 2012–13 school year is $28,500; the tuition is $21,000, and room and board costs are $7500. In addition, the cost of books, supplies, laundry, travel, and personal expenses are estimated at $4000 per year.

Financial Aid

Limestone College, one of the least costly private colleges in South Carolina, endeavors to meet the financial need of any qualified student through scholarships, grants, loans, work-study opportunities, or a combination of these. Limestone offers merit scholarships to students with outstanding academic, leadership, or athletic abilities as well as to those who have exceptional talents in such areas as art, music, and theater.

More than 90 percent of Limestone College day students receive some type of financial aid. Because institutional financial aid is limited, students are urged to submit their applications for admission and financial aid as early as possible.

Faculty

Personal attention to students and high-quality instruction characterize the faculty at Limestone College. Nearly 82 percent of the faculty members hold Ph.D.'s or other terminal degrees in their fields. The student-faculty ratio is 12:1, and with 92 percent of classes being taught by full-time faculty and staff, students and instructors work closely together in both learning and counseling situations. Each student has an assigned faculty adviser for assistance in course selection and for personal counseling.

Student Government

The Student Government Association exemplifies the College's democratic tradition and the principles of honor and individual responsibility. It is every student's privilege to participate in the government of the learning community of which he or she is a member. The more highly organized activities, including student organizations and social events, are coordinated through the Student Government Association. The College also has a literary magazine and a yearbook.

Admission Requirements

Limestone College does not discriminate on the basis of race, color, creed, national origin, financial need, or physical handicap. Each candidate for admission is evaluated as an individual. The College recommends that applicants have the following high

school preparation: English, 4 units; social science, 3 units; mathematics, 3 units; and science, 2 units.

Applicants must submit an official transcript of the secondary school record, scores on the SAT, and a nonrefundable $25 application fee. The application fee is waived if the student applies online at the College's Web site. Transfer applications are encouraged.

Application and Information

Completed application forms for admission and for financial aid should be sent to the Office of Admissions at Limestone College. It is recommended that applications be submitted by May 1. Any admission applications received after that date are considered on a space-available basis. The College practices a rolling admissions policy. As soon as the application, high school transcript, and test scores have been received, the applicant is notified of his or her status. Upon acceptance, a student is required to submit a $100 tuition deposit.

Vice President of Enrollment Service
Limestone College
1115 College Drive
Gaffney, South Carolina 29340-3799
Phone: 864-488-4554
Fax: 864-488-8206
E-mail: admiss@limestone.edu
Web site: http://www.limestone.edu
  http://on.fb.me/limestone_coll (Facebook)
  http://twitter.com/at_LimestoneCo (Twitter)

The Winnie Davis Hall of History, named in honor of the daughter of Jefferson Davis, was completed about 1904 and is listed on the National Register of Historic Places.

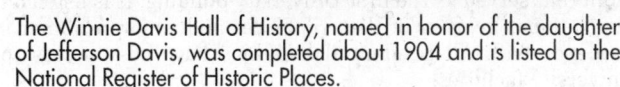

LINDENWOOD UNIVERSITY
ST. CHARLES, MISSOURI

The University

An independent teaching university founded in 1827, Lindenwood is the oldest university west of the Missouri River. Lindenwood is a dynamic four-year liberal arts institution dedicated to excellence, delivering a high-quality education that leads to the development of the whole person and preparation for life and work after graduation, through more than 120 undergraduate and graduate degree programs.

Lindenwood University is a member of and/or accredited by the Higher Learning Commission of the North Central Association of Colleges and Schools, the Accreditation Council for Business Schools and Programs, the Council on Social Work Education, the Commission on Accreditation of Athletic Training Education, and the Missouri Department of Elementary and Secondary Education, and it is fully endorsed by the Society for Human Resource Management. Lindenwood is a member of the Teacher Education Accreditation Council and the Council for Higher Education Accreditation.

Lindenwood University is authorized to grant associate, bachelor's, master's, Education Specialist, and Doctor of Education degrees. Lindenwood is an independent, public-serving, liberal arts university that has a historical relationship with the Presbyterian Church and is committed to the values inherent in the Judeo-Christian tradition. Lindenwood welcomes students from all religious denominations.

The University's athletic teams compete in the Heart of America Athletic Conference and the National Association of Intercollegiate Athletics (NAIA). Although Lindenwood was accepted into the NCAA Division II in July 2010, Lindenwood will compete in the NCAA's Mid-America Intercollegiate Athletics Association starting in the 2012–13 season. Lindenwood's men and women athletes participate in forty-six sports programs. Over the last ten years, Lindenwood athletic teams have won more than forty national championships. On-campus athletic facilities consist of the Robert F. Hyland Performance Arena, the Harlen C. Hunter Stadium, the Lou Brock Sports Complex for baseball and softball, and an eight-lane all-weather running track. Students also participate in an assortment of intramural sports at the University's Fitness Center.

More than seventy student organizations and clubs, including the Lindenwood Student Government Association and the Student Senate, provide avenues for extended personal growth, leadership, and community service. The University radio station, 50,000-watt KCLC-FM, and LUTV, Lindenwood's HD television station, are staffed by students, as is the *Lindenwood Legacy* student newspaper.

Students wishing to live on campus may choose from residence halls, houses, and apartment-style living. Eight new residence halls have opened since 2000, and in 2010, Lindenwood acquired the former Days Inn in St. Charles for student housing. Sibley Hall, named in honor of founders Mary Easton and Major George C. Sibley, was built in 1856 to replace the original log cabin that served as the first University building. It is listed on the National Register of Historic Places and is now a women's residence hall. All residential buildings have easy access to University facilities.

Location

The 500-acre campus is located in St. Charles, Missouri, a city of about 55,000 people, situated 20 miles from downtown St. Louis. Resting on the banks of the Missouri River, just south of the Mississippi, St. Charles is the site of Missouri's first state capital. The area offers a wide range of opportunities for all types of interests and is particularly rich in state heritage and attractions associated with the history of America's westward expansion. Lindenwood's proximity to a major city allows students to enjoy theme parks, a delightful zoo, professional sporting events, Broadway plays and theater, performances of a world-renowned symphony orchestra, state parks, and lakes. St. Louis–Lambert International Airport is located just 5 miles from Lindenwood University on Interstate 70.

Majors and Degrees

With a foundation as solid as the campus' century-old linden trees, the academic programs of Lindenwood University have a tradition of excellence and innovation. Lindenwood awards Bachelor of Arts, Bachelor of Fine Arts, and Bachelor of Science degrees with majors in sixty-five subject areas—from accounting to unified sciences.

Preprofessional courses are offered in chiropractic science, dentistry, engineering, health, law, medicine, optometry, nursing, and veterinary science. In addition, programs in engineering are available in conjunction with Washington University in St. Louis, the University of Missouri–Columbia, the University of Missouri—St. Louis, and the Missouri University of Science and Technology in Rolla.

Academic Programs

The emphasis at Lindenwood University is on an individualized liberal arts education with career-oriented preparation. Students fulfill general education requirements, participate in the University's Work and Learn Program when qualified, and acquire an in-depth knowledge of at least one area of study as a major. Lindenwood requires the completion of 128 credit hours to earn a bachelor's degree.

Academic Facilities

The Margaret Leggat Butler Library houses volumes, microfilm items, and a computer lab and subscribes to hundreds of periodicals. Roemer Hall serves as the main administration building and has classrooms and faculty offices on the upper floors. Young Science Hall houses an auditorium, laboratories, and classrooms for natural science, mathematics, and computer science, as well as a state-of-the-art television studio. Newly renovated and expanded Harmon Hall houses the School of Business and Entrepreneurship with classrooms, offices, and the Dunseth Auditorium. The Lindenwood University Cultural Center provides a 750-seat auditorium, classrooms, meeting rooms, and offices. It is the site of theatrical productions, concerts, convocations, and lectures. In addition, the Spellmann Center houses a state-of-the-art cafeteria, Macintosh and PC computer labs, classrooms, conference rooms, networking and campus life offices, and career planning and placement services. In August 2011, Lindenwood opened the 119,000-square-foot Evans Common, which houses a variety of amenities for

students, including basketball and multipurpose courts, an array of the latest fitness equipment, movie and music rooms, and a new dining hall with a food court configuration, among others. The 132,000-square-foot J. Scheidegger Center for the Arts, completed in 2008, is home to Lindenwood's Theatre, Dance, and Music Departments, as well as the 1,200-seat Bezemes Family Theater, the 250-seat Emerson Black Box Theater, the Boyle Family Gallery, and the Charter Communications LUTV HD Studio.

Costs

For the academic year 2012–13, tuition is $14,320. Students who choose to live on campus pay $7240 for room and board, plus $360 for communications service and $350 for a health and activity fee. There is a refundable $300 room deposit. Books and other supplies are extra.

Financial Aid

Financial aid is available to all qualified students. A student must submit the Free Application for Federal Student Aid (FAFSA). To qualify for the full amount of financial aid, students must submit their federal financial aid forms before April 1. As determined by the evaluation, a student's financial need may be met with a combination of federal, state, and institutional sources of aid. In addition, institutional awards are available in the areas of academics, leadership, athletics, drama, yearbook/newspaper, and music. Resident students may earn $2400 toward their expenses by working on campus.

Faculty

Lindenwood has 217 full-time faculty members, who serve as teachers, mentors, and advisers to their students. Faculty members advise students regarding majors and other matters to help them succeed academically.

Student Government

The Lindenwood Student Government Association (LSGA) is made up of representatives elected by the student body. LSGA has the responsibility of providing a balanced program of cultural, social, and recreational events and activities throughout the year.

Admission Requirements

To apply for admission, a student should submit a completed application form with a nonrefundable $30 application fee, a transcript of high school and/or college work, and ACT or SAT scores.

Applicants are evaluated on an individual basis, and admission is based on an analysis of the student's grade point average, ACT or SAT scores, extracurricular activities, recommendations, and personal qualifications. Students are admitted without regard to race, sex, or national origin.

Application and Information

Although admission to Lindenwood is on a rolling basis, students are encouraged to apply by April 15 for the fall semester and by December 1 for the spring semester. Notification of the admission decision is mailed soon after all required materials are received and evaluated by the Office of Undergraduate Day Admissions.

Applications for admission, financial aid, and scholarships and other information about Lindenwood University can be obtained by contacting:

Undergraduate Day Admissions
Lindenwood University
209 South Kingshighway
St. Charles, Missouri 63301-1695
Phone: 636-949-4949
Fax: 636-949-4989
Web site: http://www.lindenwood.edu
     http://www.facebook.com/LUDayAdmissions

Student life at Lindenwood University.

LINFIELD COLLEGE
McMINNVILLE, OREGON

The College

Linfield College (1858) is an independent, coeducational, residential, comprehensive liberal arts and sciences college dedicated to providing an educational environment conducive to learning and participation. There are 1,700 full-time students on the McMinnville campus. These students come primarily from the thirteen Western states (twenty states overall) but also from twenty-four other countries. Students of color make up 23 percent of the student body, and 7 percent of students are international. Most students are between 18 and 22. Linfield is primarily residential, with seventeen residence halls, each accommodating between 10 and 100 residents. Each hall establishes its own calendar of social, educational, and recreational events throughout the year. Students who reside on campus eat their meals in the College dining hall. Houses and apartments are available for upper-division students. Social clubs, professional organizations, four sororities and four fraternities, service clubs, and almost forty other organizations play an important role in the daily life of a Linfield student. Linfield's winning athletics tradition fosters participation at all levels of competition. Women compete in intercollegiate basketball, cross-country, golf, lacrosse, soccer, softball, swimming, tennis, track and field, and volleyball. Men compete in intercollegiate baseball, basketball, cross-country, football, golf, soccer, swimming, tennis, and track and field. Water polo, Ultimate (Frisbee), and men's lacrosse are club sports. Linfield also has an extensive and active year-round intramural program.

Linfield hosts the Oregon Nobel Laureate Symposium, one of five such symposiums worldwide. At each symposium, several Nobel laureates come to share their backgrounds and expertise within the context of a basic theme.

The Linfield–Good Samaritan School of Nursing, an academic unit of the College at its Portland campus, prepares students for careers in nursing. This campus, at the Good Samaritan Hospital and Medical Center, has residence facilities, food service options, and a residence life program. In 2006, the Portland campus programs became open only to transfer admission.

Location

Located in McMinnville, 40 miles southwest of Portland, Linfield College is a leader in the cultural, educational, and recreational events of the fast-growing community of 35,000. Linfield is situated on 193 acres with most classrooms no more than a 10-minute walk from any of the twenty-four on-campus apartment buildings and residence halls. With most students living on campus, Linfield offers a welcoming and lively community.

Coffeehouses, cinemas, boutiques, a community theater, the Evergreen Air and Space Museum (including an IMAX theater), bowling alleys, and a wide variety of restaurants are within walking distance for Linfield students. The central Oregon coast is an hour to the west, and the outdoor activity areas of the Oregon Cascade Range, including year-round skiing at Mount Hood, are two hours to the east. Salem, the state capital of Oregon, is 25 miles to the southeast, and Eugene is 80 miles south. Rainfall in western Oregon averages 42 inches annually and the winter temperature averages 41°F.

Majors and Degrees

Linfield offers the Bachelor of Arts degree in communication arts, creative writing, electronic arts, English, Francophone African Studies, French studies, German, German studies, history, intercultural communication, international relations, Japanese, mass communication, music, philosophy, political science, religious studies, sociology, Spanish, studio art, and theater arts.

The Bachelor of Arts or Bachelor of Science degree is offered in accounting, anthropology, applied physics, athletic training, biology, business, chemistry, computing science, economics, elementary education, environmental studies, exercise science, finance, general science, health education, international business, mathematics, physical education, physics, and psychology. A Bachelor of Science in Nursing (B.S.N.) is also available. The College has programs to prepare students for advanced study in any health profession, including medicine, as well as law. The education department offers a strong program of teacher certification at the secondary and elementary levels. A 3-2 engineering program is available in cooperation with Oregon State University, Washington State University, and the University of Southern California.

Academic Programs

The academic year is divided into two 15-week semesters (fall and spring) and an optional four-week winter term in January. The January Term offers regular departmental courses and off-campus and international study. Academic courses are assigned 1–5 semester credit hours each; 125 credits are required for a B.A. or a B.S. degree. Students divide their time equally among required general education courses, a major area of study, and elective subjects. The Linfield Curriculum courses, selected to provide a solid foundation in the liberal arts, require students to take 3 semester hours in each of the six Modes of Inquiry as well as one upper-division course in one of these areas. These Modes of Inquiry are as follows: Vital Past; Ultimate Questions; Individuals, Systems, and Societies; Natural World; Creative Studies; and Quantitative Reasoning. In addition, students are required to take a writing-intensive course, a course addressing global pluralisms, and a course dealing with United States pluralism. Individually designed majors are available with faculty approval. Students majoring in a foreign language spend an academic year in a country in which the language being studied is the native tongue.

The College offers courses in English through the English Language and Culture Program. These courses are designed to help international students whose native language is not English to achieve competence in academic and social English skills, so that they may work effectively in their undergraduate classes at Linfield.

Off-Campus Programs

Off-campus educational experiences include the Semester Abroad program, involving four months of study in Costa Rica, France, Austria, Japan, Norway, China, South Korea, Ireland, England, Ecuador, New Zealand, Senegal, Spain, and Australia. Transportation for the first round-trip is included in the cost of tuition, and most of these study programs cost the same as a semester on campus. January Term study-abroad programs for four weeks are also offered. Recent offerings included the Emergence of Modern Ghana (West Africa); Mainland Southeast Asia History (Cambodia, Vietnam, and China); American Expatriate Writers in Europe: The Lost Generation Tour (nine European cities); and Australia: From Colony to Asian Power.

Academic Facilities

Since 2000, the College has opened two residence halls, six apartment buildings, the James F. Miller Fine Arts Center, the Marshall Theatre and communication arts facility, the Vivian A. Bull Center for Music, and the Nicholson Library. The library covers 56,000 square feet and combines traditional collections of books and journals with the new and changing digital and electronic technology to provide access to the Web and Web-based

designs. The studio theater has an audience seating capacity of up to 140 and includes space for set construction and design.

In 2011, Linfield reopened the former library to provide new classroom and office space for the departments of business, economics, English, and philosophy. This state-of-the-art facility, T. J. Day Hall, includes the College's writing center and the Linfield Center for the Northwest (LCN). The LCN cultivates regionally relevant partnerships for training, research, service learning, and cultural or artistic exchanges. These opportunities promote student engagement in regional issues and produce real-world change. T. J. Day Hall is Linfield's first LEED-certified Silver building, underscoring the College's commitment to sustainability and conservation.

Murdock and Graf Halls house the biology, chemistry, and physics departments and up-to-date laboratories and equipment. Other facilities include art galleries and studios, a 250-watt FM radio station, an experimental psychology lab, dance and music studios, a preschool, and a 425-seat auditorium that houses a three-manual, 48-rank Casavant pipe organ.

Linfield students benefit from a communications and technology network that includes phone service, voice mail, e-mail, and wireless Internet connections in each residence hall room. In addition, there is wireless access in the library and other academic areas of the campus.

The Health and Physical Education/Recreation Complex houses three gymnasiums; weight rooms; fitness laboratories with a hydrostatic weighing tank, a metabolic and pulmonary measuring system, and an electrocardiovascular exercise ECG system; an eight-lane, 25-yard indoor pool; handball and racquetball courts; classrooms; offices; and a 28,000-square-foot field house.

Costs

For 2011–12, tuition and fees were $32,100 per two-semester year, board was $4020, and a double room was $4980. There was a $190 per-credit fee for on-campus January Term classes.

Financial Aid

Eligibility for most of Linfield's assistance programs is based on need as determined by a federally approved needs analysis processor. The only form required for need-based programs is the Free Application for Federal Student Aid (FAFSA). Linfield participates in the federal grant, loan, and work programs, and other forms of financial assistance on the basis of demonstrated need.

The College awards scholarships to full-time students based on scholastic achievement, independent of financial need. These academic scholarships vary from 20 to 75 percent of tuition. To be considered, students must have a minimum GPA of 3.4. A number of other criteria are used when determining scholarships. Linfield sponsors special scholarships for National Merit finalists. The College also sponsors an annual Competitive Scholarship Day in February. Participation is limited to high school seniors who meet particular academic requirements and apply by December 1. Each academic department offers prizes ranging from $10,000 to $16,000, divided over the student's four years at Linfield. Scholarships are also available to students from the departments of music, theater, and communication who demonstrate outstanding leadership and community service. Financial assistance for non-U.S. citizens is limited to partial-tuition scholarships and the opportunity to work part-time on campus.

Faculty

There are 124 faculty members, each of whom is committed to undergraduate teaching and scholarship. Ninety-three percent have doctoral or other terminal degrees within their field. The student-faculty ratio is 12:1, and faculty members serve as academic advisers. There are no teaching assistants.

Student Government

Students have a significant voice in establishing and changing College policies and regulations. The Student Senate, chosen through campus elections, is the focus of student opinion and debate. Students are represented on most College governing councils and committees with faculty members and trustees, and they are encouraged to express and implement their ideas on academic or extracurricular matters.

Admission Requirements

Admission to Linfield College is selective. Admission is granted to students who are likely to grow and succeed in a personal and challenging liberal arts environment. Each applicant is judged on individual merit, based on high school performance, a writing sample, recommendations from teachers and counselors, precollege standardized test results (ACT or SAT), and the depth and quality of an applicant's involvement in community and school activities. Linfield is a member of the Common Application Association.

International students whose education has been in a language other than English must submit certified English translations of their academic work. Proficiency in English is required, as demonstrated by an official TOEFL score report.

Application and Information

The early action deadline is November 15 (with notification by January 15) and the regular decision priority deadline is February 15 (with notification by April 1).

Interviews are not required, but students are encouraged to visit. Appointments should be made in advance and can be requested online at http://www.linfield.edu/stopby. The Linfield Web site provides students with information on academic programs, student life, and athletics.

Interested students are encouraged to contact:

Office of Admission
Linfield College
900 SE Baker Street
McMinnville, Oregon 97128
Phone: 503-883-2213
      800-640-2287 (toll-free)
Fax: 503-883-2472
E-mail: admission@linfield.edu
Web site: http://www.linfield.edu/admission
     http://www.facebook.com/linfieldadmit
     http://twitter.com/linfieldadmit

Linfield College is located 1 hour southwest of Portland, Oregon's largest city, on nearly 200 acres. Nearly sixty buildings, many built in Georgian colonial style, house forty academic departments among a grove of oak trees.

LOYOLA MARYMOUNT UNIVERSITY

LOS ANGELES, CALIFORNIA

The University

Loyola Marymount University (LMU), situated on a picturesque campus, offers competitive students an education of high quality in a dynamic and supportive atmosphere. As successor to the oldest institution of learning in southern California, St. Vincent's College, the University is steeped in a tradition and history of dedication to academic excellence and the total development of its students. Although the emphasis is within the undergraduate program (full-time enrollment is approximately 5,800 and part-time enrollment is approximately 250), approximately 1,950 students pursue master's degrees in the fields of arts, arts in teaching, business administration, education, and science (including engineering). The Doctor of Education in educational leadership for social justice is offered by the School of Education. The School of Law, situated at a separate campus, has both day and evening divisions and offers the Juris Doctor degree. Law school enrollment is 1,320.

Fifty-six percent of the undergraduate students (95 percent of freshmen) live on campus and are able to choose accommodations in one of eleven residential halls or six apartment complexes. Students have access to a sports pavilion, one swimming pool, baseball and soccer fields, tennis and volleyball courts, and four indoor racquetball courts. The Fritz B. Burns Recreation Center includes three additional courts and a fitness center. LMU fields teams in twelve intercollegiate sports (baseball, basketball, cheer, crew, cross-country, golf, soccer, softball, swimming, tennis, women's volleyball, and water polo) and has club teams in lacrosse, rugby, men's volleyball, and more. Over 2,000 undergraduate students participate in the active intramural program, which includes coed sports. Student organizations include seven service organizations, the AM/FM radio station (KXLU), Chemistry Society, Black Student Union, Han Tao Chinese Cultural Club, MEChA, Business Law Society, Student-Athlete Advisory Committee, University choruses, fraternities and sororities, and various honor and service groups. LMU's Debate Team and Air Force ROTC detachment have received national recognition in their respective areas.

Location

LMU is ideally located on a 142-acre bluff that overlooks the southwest section of Los Angeles and the Pacific Ocean from Malibu to Santa Monica. The campus is close to the beach, and the University community enjoys a cool, clean coastal climate. LMU is near the metropolitan complex, but it has the benefits of the slower pace of its residential community, Westchester. Los Angeles International Airport is 10 minutes away, and nearby freeways provide easy access to the city and its cultural and recreational activities.

Majors and Degrees

Loyola Marymount University offers the B.A. in the fields of African American studies, animation, art history, Asian Pacific studies, biology, Chicano studies, classical civilizations, classics, communication studies, dance, economics, English, European studies, film and television production, French, Greek, history, humanities, Latin, liberal studies (elementary education), mathematics, music, philosophy, political science, production (film and television), psychology, recording arts, screenwriting,

sociology, Spanish, studio arts, theater arts, theological studies, urban studies, and women's studies. The College of Business Administration offers the Bachelor of Science degree in accounting and applied information management systems and the Bachelor of Business Administration degree with majors in entrepreneurship, finance, management, and marketing. The College of Science and Engineering offers bachelor's degrees in applied mathematics, athletic training, biochemistry, biology, chemistry, computer science, engineering (civil, electrical, and mechanical), engineering physics, health and human sciences, mathematics, and physics. Areas of emphasis can include such fields as graphic arts and marine biology.

Academic Programs

While specific course requirements differ with each area of study, a common core with course work in the fields of American cultures, college writing, communication skills, creative and critical arts, history, literature, mathematics/science/technology, philosophy, social science, and theology provides the foundation for a well-rounded education for all LMU students. The interdepartmental honors program provides challenges for the exceptional student.

The academic calendar consists of two semesters and two 6-week optional summer sessions. The fall semester begins in late August and ends before Christmas. The spring semester usually begins in mid-January and ends in mid-May. Students may earn credit when receiving scores of 4 or 5 through Advanced Placement (AP) examinations.

Off-Campus Programs

Students who are interested in studying abroad can apply to LMU summer and semester programs, selected Association of Jesuit Colleges and Universities (AJCU) programs, reciprocal exchanges, and other approved programs in a variety of locations. LMU offers programs in Africa, Australia, China, England, France, Germany, Greece, Honduras, Ireland, Italy, Japan, Mexico, New Zealand, the Philippines, South Korea, Spain, and many others. Depending on the program, students may receive credits and/or grades for their participation. Financial aid eligibility for study abroad is determined by program and the type of aid the student receives. Courses may be conducted in English, the language of the host country, or both. In addition, LMU offers internship programs through which students can earn practical training and sometimes even course credit. The programs range from student involvement in political campaigns to the counseling of underrepresented youths to professional work at film/TV studios.

Academic Facilities

The William H. Hannon Library is the newest and most sophisticated library facility in Los Angeles. The new, state-of-the-art 88,000-square-foot library is the cultural and intellectual hub of the Loyola Marymount University campus. Its three above-ground stories and two basement levels have space for more than 1 million volumes, and the more than 100 computer workstations, four classrooms, and dozens of group study rooms will facilitate all forms of learning. The Law School Library, located within the School of Law in downtown Los Angeles, contains more than 560,000 volumes

and microforms and is a depository for government documents of the state of California and the United States. It also has complete holdings of all publications relating to California law. The communication arts complex houses the Louis B. Mayer Motion Picture Theatre, a full-size color-television studio, a motion-picture soundstage, and state-of-the-art industry equipment. Strub Theatre offers excellent theatrical facilities for the performing arts of drama and dance.

Costs

Tuition for the 2011–12 academic year was $37,605. The cost of room and board varies with options that students select—for example, a full- or partial-meal plan, an apartment on campus, or a residence hall. However, the average yearly cost is approximately $12,722. Students should expect to spend about $1656 for books and supplies and $2277 for additional miscellaneous expenses.

Financial Aid

Approximately 83 percent of the University's undergraduate students receive some type of financial assistance. The total amount of financial aid awarded to students for the 2010–11 academic year was $134.6 million. Students applying for aid must file the Free Application for Federal Student Aid (FAFSA). The CSS Financial Aid PROFILE is no longer required. All students are expected to apply for the Federal Pell Grant, and California residents must apply for the California grants. LMU offers both need-based aid and merit-based awards in amounts up to the full tuition Trustee Scholarship. The priority date for the financial aid application is February 1.

Faculty

LMU's faculty is dedicated to undergraduate teaching and is easily accessible to students. Ninety-nine percent of the faculty members hold a Ph.D. or terminal degree in their area of instruction; the average class size is 21.

Student Government

LMU believes that active student input is an essential part of the undergraduate years. Students sit on every University committee, including the Board of Trustees, with full voting rights. Students operate the campus recreation centers, manage the dormitories as resident advisers, and participate in over 160 clubs and organizations. Student actions have resulted in the development of such things as a campus farmer's market, outdoor concert series, club sports teams, social justice events, and community service programs.

Admission Requirements

Admission to LMU is selective, and a candidate is expected to present a strong record in college-preparatory courses. In determining an applicant's eligibility, the University gives careful consideration to the student's academic preparation, national test scores, letters of recommendation, extracurricular activities, and family relationships to the University. A personal interview is not required for admission. Prospective candidates are encouraged to visit the campus. LMU offers campus tours Monday through Saturday during the academic year and Monday through Friday during the summer.

Application and Information

Applicants must submit official transcripts from the last high school attended and from each college attended, arrange for SAT or ACT scores to be sent to the Office of Admission, submit a recommendation form from an official of the last school attended, and file the Common Application with the $60 nonrefundable fee. Applications are considered when all necessary documents have been received prior to the deadline of the semester for which application is made. The priority deadline for freshman applicants for the fall semester is November 1 for early action and January 15 for regular decision. Early action applicants receive a decision by December 20. The deadline for transfer applicants for the fall semester is March 15. Fall transfer applicants who apply by February 1 will receive early consideration for fall transfer. The priority deadline for spring semester admission is October 15 for both freshman and transfer applicants.

International students are welcome to apply to LMU and follow the same admission procedures as domestic students. International students must also demonstrate English proficiency by submitting TOEFL results with a minimum score of 80 or an IELTS exam of 6.5 overall bandwidth. LMU also offers conditional admission through ELS language centers. International students must also provide a statement of financial responsibility for all obligations covering the full period of time for which the student is making application. All records of previous academic training must be original or authentic copies with notarization and have notarized English translations.

For more information about Loyola Marymount University, prospective students should contact:

Matthew X. Fissinger
Director of Admission
Loyola Marymount University
1 LMU Drive, Suite 100
Los Angeles, California 90045
Phone: 310-338-2750
      800-LMU-INFO (toll-free)
Fax: 310-338-2797
E-mail: admissions@lmu.edu
Web site: http://www.lmu.edu/
      http://www.lmu.edu/mobile
      http://www.facebook.com/lmuadmission
      http://twitter.com/LMUAdmission
      http://www.youtube.com/user/LMUAdmission

Between classes at Loyola Marymount University.

LOYOLA UNIVERSITY MARYLAND
BALTIMORE, MARYLAND

The University

Loyola University Maryland is a private liberal arts school with the Catholic traditions of the Jesuits and the Sisters of Mercy. It is an educational community of students and faculty members cooperating for the intellectual, spiritual, and professional enrichment of all its members and for the improvement of the local community and society in general. The intellectual enterprise is a joint creation of the faculty members and the students. Loyola's current full-time undergraduate enrollment is 3,863; more than 80 percent of the student body lives on campus.

Loyola encourages co-curricular activities that contribute to the academic, social, and spiritual growth of the student. These include social and cultural organizations, Student Government activities, military science activities, national honor societies, and Division I athletic programs such as basketball, crew, cross-country, golf, lacrosse, soccer, swimming and diving, tennis, track, and volleyball. The majority of the student body participates in the wide variety of club and intramural sports offered.

In recent years, Loyola's campus has undergone significant expansion. Thirteen apartment complexes and four first-year residence halls provide Loyola students with on-campus housing. In 2011, the Donnelly Science Center was expanded, making it the largest academic building on the Evergreen Campus. The Andrew White Student Center offers several dining choices, and spacious meeting and recreational space. The Student Center also provides facilities for athletics, the Communication Department, and the fine arts, including the McManus Theatre and the 4,000-seat Reitz Arena. The Center also has an art gallery, classrooms, black box theater and music, photography, and studio art labs. Loyola's recreational sports facility is the Fitness and Aquatic Center. This 115,000-square-foot athletic facility provides an indoor pool, basketball courts, squash courts, a climbing wall, fitness equipment, tracks, and outdoor playing fields. The Ridley Athletic Complex, completed in spring 2010, is a 6,000-seat grandstand stadium with locker rooms, a weight-training suite, an expertly staffed first-aid suite, concession areas, and memorabilia for sale on-site.

Location

The Loyola campus is located in a residential area of north Baltimore, 5 miles from the Inner Harbor area. This location offers the student the advantages of quiet residential living with the attractions of city life. The metropolitan area has a wide variety of theaters, museums, professional and intercollegiate sports events, and historical points of interest. Other colleges and universities in the vicinity help to expand the social calendar and academic life.

Majors and Degrees

Loyola offers programs more than 35 majors. The Bachelor of Arts degree is awarded in art history, classical civilization, classics, communication, comparative cultures and literary studies, computer science, economics, elementary education, English, fine arts, French, German, global studies, history, philosophy, political science, psychology, sociology, Spanish, speech pathology/audiology, theology, and writing. The Bachelor of Business Administration degree is awarded in accounting, business economics, finance, general business, information systems, international business, management, and marketing. The Bachelor of Science degree is awarded in biology, chemistry, computer science, engineering science, mathematical science, statistics, and physics.

Academic Programs

The curriculum at Loyola is divided into three parts: the core, the major, and electives. The core contains those courses that Loyola considers essential to the liberal arts curriculum. These courses, which are required of all students regardless of major, are completed throughout the four years. The core consists of a classical or modern language, English literature, writing, mathematics and natural science, social science, fine arts, history, philosophy, ethics, and theology. The major enables students to pursue in depth their specialized area of study. Electives give students the opportunity to broaden their intellectual and cultural background in areas of special interest. To prepare for graduate study, students may enroll in one of the five pre-professional programs: dental, law, medical, nursing, or veterinary.

An honors program and honors housing are available to outstanding students. The honors program stresses independent work by specially grouped students in many of the core courses. Honors housing provides an environment that is conducive to study and close social interaction.

Off-Campus Programs

Loyola University Maryland participates in a cooperative program with Notre Dame of Maryland University, Johns Hopkins University, Goucher College, Morgan State University, Towson University, the Peabody Conservatory of Music, and the Maryland Institute College of Art. Loyola students may cross-register at any of these area colleges and universities.

Students in good academic standing may pursue studies abroad through Loyola's programs in Accra, Ghana; Copenhagen, Denmark; Glasgow, Scotland; Leuven, Belgium; Bangkok, Thailand; Alcalá, Spain; Melbourne, Australia; Newcastle, England; Auckland, New Zealand; Beijing, China; Cork, Ireland; Rome, Italy; Paris, France; and San Salvador, El Salvador. Loyola also participates in exchange programs with eight other countries and assists students in applying to a variety of non-Loyola affiliated international study programs each year.

Academic Facilities

Loyola celebrated the completion of the Donnelly Science Center expansion in September 2011. The 15,000-square-foot addition provides class laboratory spaces, research laboratories, offices, a conference room for the natural sciences, storage, a vivarium, a microscopy center, and a robotics laboratory. Spacious hallways connecting the building's wings on all levels include spaces for science displays and gathering areas for students and faculty in biology, chemistry, physics, computer science, and engineering.

The Sellinger School of Business and Management is Loyola's AACSB-accredited business school. Highlights of this school include experiential learning requirements, the Sellinger

Scholars program, many student associations, and a brand new Student Experiential Learning Lab which features such things as a six-screen video display for breaking news and real-time market updates, and a scrolling price ticker. In addition, 90 percent of Sellinger classes are taught in Internet-linked, multimedia classrooms.

Costs

For 2012–13, tuition for all undergraduate students is $41,026 per year. Room for first-year students is $9116. Student fees are estimated at $1400.

Financial Aid

It is the intent of Loyola to assist qualified students who might not otherwise be able to provide for themselves an opportunity for higher education. Financial aid is awarded on academic ability and financial need. Seventy-one percent of the student body receives financial assistance in the forms of Loyola University Maryland scholarships, state scholarships, Federal Pell Grants, Federal Supplemental Educational Opportunity Grants, Federal Perkins Loans, and Federal Work-Study Program opportunities. To apply for financial assistance, students must submit the Free Application for Federal Student Aid and the Financial Aid PROFILE through the College Scholarship Service in Princeton, New Jersey. The financial aid application deadline is February 15.

Faculty

Loyola intends to maintain its faculty-student ratio of approximately 1:13 and an average class size of 21 students to ensure interest in the individual student. Of the 410 faculty members, 83 percent are full-time and 76 percent are tenured or on the tenure track. No classes are taught by graduate students.

Student Government

The Student Government serves three chief functions, which make its existence not only valuable but also necessary. These functions are to represent the student body outside the University, to provide leadership within the student body, and to perform services, both social and academic, for the students. Responsibility for budgeting activities also rests with the Student Government. The president of the Student Government is a member of the College Academic Council.

Admission Requirements

The admission evaluation at Loyola combines an analysis of academic information submitted along with a review of recommendations, the record of extracurricular involvement and evidence of special talent, leadership, and service. The admission committee does not use a formula or have strict cutoffs. Instead, the admission office's goal is to conduct a balanced and individual review, taking a number of factors into account. Submission of SAT and ACT scores is optional for all first-year applicants, excluding home-school students. Students who choose not to choose to submit standardized test scores must submit an additional letter of recommendation or personal essay. The University welcomes applications from students of character, intelligence, and motivation, without discrimination on the grounds of race or religious belief.

Application and Information

Interested students seeking to enroll at Loyola may apply online using the Loyola Application or the Common Application. Each applicant must submit a school counselor letter of recommendation, a teacher letter of recommendation, and a personal statement. Applicants for all forms of financial aid must submit the Financial Aid PROFILE of the College Scholarship Service (CSS Profile) and the Free Application for Federal Student Aid (FAFSA). A $50 application fee must accompany the application for admission.

For additional information, students are encouraged to contact:

Undergraduate Admission Office
Loyola University Maryland
4501 North Charles Street
Baltimore, Maryland 21210-2699
Phone: 410-617-5012
      800-221-9107 (toll-free)
Web site: http://www.loyola.edu/admission
     http://www.facebook.com/
       LoyolaMarylandAdmission
     https://twitter.com/chooseloyola

Loyola University Maryland is located in residential Baltimore, six miles from the Inner Harbor and less than an hour from Washington, D.C., giving students access to an array of cultural events, restaurants, shops, and internship opportunities.

LOYOLA UNIVERSITY NEW ORLEANS
NEW ORLEANS, LOUISIANA

The University

Founded by the Jesuits in 1912, Loyola University's more than 35,000 graduates have excelled in innumerable professional fields for over ninety years. The 3,000 undergraduate students (5,000 students total) enjoy the individual attention of a caring faculty in a university dedicated to creating community and fostering individualism while educating the whole person, not only intellectually, but spiritually, socially, and athletically. Loyola students represent all fifty states and forty-eight countries. This diversity is found in a setting where the average class size is 17–24 students. Almost 70 percent of the students permanently reside outside Louisiana, and 37 percent belong to minority groups.

Loyola's 20-acre main campus and 4-acre Broadway campus are located in the historic uptown area of New Orleans and are hubs of student activity. The University's residence halls, equipped with computer labs, kitchen, laundry, and study facilities, are home to nearly 75 percent of the freshmen who reside on campus. The Joseph A. Danna Center, the student center, houses six food venues, including the Orleans Room, Flambeaux's, Fresh Market, Smoothie King, and Satchmo's, Loyola's own jazz hall. An art gallery and post office can also be found in the Danna Center. Nationally affiliated fraternities and sororities are among Loyola's more than 120 student organizations. During the fall's Organizational Fair, students can join the 2006 Pacemaker Award–winning newspaper, the Loyola University Community Action Program (a volunteer community service organization, the largest organization on campus), or one of the many special interest groups. Students can also take this opportunity to sign up for one of Loyola's club sports. Every year, approximately one third of the student body participates in club sports, such as cheerleading, crew, cycling, dance, golf, swimming, and volleyball, as well as in men's lacrosse, rugby, and soccer. Loyola participates in the National Association of Intercollegiate Athletics (NAIA) men's baseball, basketball, cross-country, tennis, and track (distance) and women's basketball, cross-country, golf, tennis, and volleyball. The University Sports Complex offers six multipurpose courts, an elevated running track, an Olympic-size swimming pool, weight rooms, and aerobics and combat-sports facilities.

The career services offered by the Career Development Center include career counseling and testing, assistance with choosing a course of study, recommendations about graduate and professional school, and assistance in securing internships and jobs.

Career development services include individualized consultation and counseling (with personality and career-interest testing), a career exploration course, career-related speakers, and a career information library. Publications include information on a wide range of career choices, graduate school directories, scholarship and financial aid directories, and field-specific directories of employers.

The Joseph A. Butt, S.J., College of Business is fully accredited at both the undergraduate and graduate levels by the Association to Advance Collegiate Schools of Business–AACSB International, and houses the Mildred Soule and Clarence A. Lengendre Chair in Business Ethics. The College of Music and Fine Arts offers students opportunities in music industry studies and music performance areas as well as visual and theater arts. Students in the College of Humanities and Natural Sciences might choose premed preparation, psychology, or areas in the humanities, such as history or modern foreign languages. The College of Social Sciences houses a School of Mass Communication that offers award winning programs in advertising, journalism, and public relations.

Location

Loyola's main campus fronts oak-lined St. Charles Avenue in uptown New Orleans. Its red-brick, Tudor-Gothic buildings overlook Audubon Park, home of the famous Audubon Zoo. The downtown area is a 20-minute streetcar ride away, allowing students to take advantage of the city's broad cultural and artistic environment. Considering that New Orleans enjoys an average temperature of 70 degrees, students can enjoy year-round outdoor activities in a city famous for its food, music, and cultural festivals. Lake Pontchartrain is within the city limits and provides facilities for water sports.

Majors and Degrees

Loyola University grants degrees in four-year undergraduate programs. The College of Humanities and Natural Sciences grants the B.A. degree in classical studies, English, English writing, environmental studies, French, history, philosophy, religious studies (Christianity and world religions), and Spanish. It grants the B.S. in biology (predentistry, premedicine, and pre–veterinary studies), chemistry (premedicine), chemistry–forensic science, environmental science, mathematics, physics, psychology, and psychology (premed). The College of Business awards the B.B.A. degree in economics, finance, international business, management, and marketing, as well as the Bachelor of Accountancy. The College of Music and Fine Arts grants the B.M. in composition, jazz studies, music education, music industry studies, music therapy and performance (instrumental and vocal), and grants the B.S. in music industry studies. The College also grants a B.A. in graphic arts, theater arts, theater arts–communications, theater arts (with a minor in business administration), and visual arts and a B.F.A. in visual arts. The College of Social Sciences offers the B.A. in criminal justice, political science, and sociology, and the School of Mass Communication offers the B.A. in advertising, journalism, and public relations.

Minors are available in all disciplines offered as majors. African and African-American, American, Asian, Catholic, computational science, environmental, film, Latin American, medieval, Middle East peace, New Orleans, and women's studies are offered as interdisciplinary minors addressing important areas of national and international concern.

Academic Programs

Once enrolled at Loyola, students are introduced to the Common Curriculum, designed to give them a well-rounded preparation in their major field of concentration, as well as the ability to understand and reflect on disciplines allied to or outside their major. The curriculum is divided into four categories: major, minor, Common Curriculum, and elective courses. Students must meet the requirements of their degree program as specified by their particular college; the minimum four-year program requires 120 hours. Common Curriculum courses include seven introductory courses in English composition, math, science, philosophy, religion, literature, and history and nine upper-division courses in humanities, social science, and natural science. The College of Business requires that all students with junior or senior standing complete a 3-credit-hour internship prior to graduation. Internships provide professional-level experience in area business firms and not-for-profit organizations, along with college credit for semester-long participation. The College of Humanities and Natural Sciences also requires a minimum of one year of study in a modern foreign language. The honors program and independent studies provide special opportunities for qualified students.

Off-Campus Programs

Through the Center for International Education, more than one third of the student body has an international experience each year. Loyola offers summer programs in Germany, Greece, Ireland, London, and Mexico, as well as opportunities to study in over forty different countries including Belgium, France, Japan, and Spain through various consortium programs. Through consortium arrangements in the city of New Orleans, students may cross-register for courses for credit at Xavier University, Tulane University, and Notre Dame Seminary and participate with these institutions in joint social-cultural events. In addition, the University offers a rigorous internship program in New Orleans at businesses, institutions, and schools to give students practical

experience in their fields, including business, communications, modern foreign languages, music, and writing. Loyola offers a 3-3 program with the Loyola College of Law for students interested in pursuing a prelaw track, an early acceptance program with Tulane University Medical School, and a five-year M.B.A. program through the College of Business.

Academic Facilities

A $13-million Communications/Music Complex includes classrooms, offices, specialized instructional facilities for the College of Music and Fine Arts and the School of Mass Communication, and a 600-seat performance facility for the College of Music and Fine Arts.

Computing is an integral part of campus life at Loyola. The University provides more than 450 computers in seventeen computer labs throughout the campus. These labs consist of Windows- and Macintosh-based computers with a wide variety of application software and access to the Internet. Loyola's high-speed Ethernet network can also be accessed from locations such as residence halls, the library, and other public areas. A noteworthy characteristic of Loyola's computing resources is its student-centered emphasis. For example, specialized computer labs exist in the Writing Across the Curriculum Center, English and Math Basic Skills Labs, Poverty Law Clinic, and Business Solutions Center.

The Broadway campus, two blocks down St. Charles Avenue, houses the Loyola College of Law, the visual arts department, the Division of Institutional Advancement, and a residence hall.

Other facilities on campus include the J. Edgar and Louise S. Monroe Library, the region's most technologically advanced facility and the 2003 recipient of the Association of College and Research Libraries' Excellence in Academic Libraries Award, which contains more than 367,000 volumes and provides access to over 27,000 electronic books and more than 23,000 electronic journals. The Monroe Library also offers more than 660,000 microform units and 2,500 media titles. There are also specialized libraries for music and law. The 150,000-square-foot Monroe Library contains 1,800 computer links, media/instructional technology services, a visual arts center, and the Lindy Boggs National Center for Community Literacy. The library also offers three 24-hour microcomputer labs, two multimedia classrooms, and sixteen group-study rooms.

Costs

For the full-time undergraduate student attending during 2012–13, tuition is $33,846 for the year. The cost of residence halls (double occupancy) and a complete meal plan is $11,346 for the year. This does not include a $1416 University fee.

Financial Aid

Loyola University's endowment provides money for financial aid in addition to that provided by federal funding. Assistance in the forms of merit- and talent-based scholarships, loans, work-study program awards, and grants is awarded on the basis of academic achievement and need. More than 450 scholarships are awarded annually to students with competitive grades and test scores. To apply for one of the scholarships, students must have a GPA of at least 3.2 and competitive standardized test scores. Offers of financial aid are not made until after admission. Notifications of awards are sent in early February. Awards of need-based financial aid packages are made on a first-come, first-served basis and are announced in mid-March. Eighty-four percent of Loyola students receive some form of financial aid.

Faculty

Behind every program at Loyola is a faculty of Jesuit and lay professors who are especially well qualified in their particular fields. The Jesuit Order, recognized throughout the world for its educational contributions over the centuries, administers the University's faculty of 258 full-time professors, of whom 91 percent hold the terminal degree in their field. Loyola also employs 148 part-time instructors. No graduate assistants teach classes. The student-faculty ratio of 12:1 emphasizes the University's special quality of personal involvement and concern for each student and his or her particular needs.

Student Government

Loyola's Student Government Association consists of representatives elected by the student body from each of the four colleges and the law school. The association conducts general meetings, elections, and student activities. Student representatives sit on nearly all University committees.

Admission Requirements

Prospective students must submit an application, resume, and essay; have a high school transcript or GED test results sent; submit ACT or SAT scores; and have their counselor or teacher send a recommendation. Individual attention is given to each application form. Final selection is based on high school grades, test scores, and counselor or teacher recommendations. Significant community involvement and demonstrated leadership abilities are recommended. Auditions are required for final acceptance to the College of Music and Fine Arts, which includes the Department of Theatre Arts and Dance. Portfolios are required for final acceptance to the Department of Visual Arts.

December 1 is the priority deadline for freshman admission and scholarship consideration. January 15 is the regular deadline for freshman scholarship consideration. February 15 is the regular deadline for freshman admission consideration.

Transfer students are required to submit an official transcript for each institution previously attended along with their transfer application. Transfer scholarships are available to spring applicants as well as fall. Transfer students interested in competing for a scholarship should apply by March 1 if possible, and no later than April 15. For nonscholarship admission consideration, transfer students should apply no later than May 15 for the fall semester and no later than December 1 for the spring semester.

Application and Information

Interested students are encouraged to contact:

Office of Admissions
Loyola University New Orleans
6363 St. Charles Avenue, Box 18
New Orleans, Louisiana 70118
Phone: 504-865-3240
       800-4-LOYOLA (toll-free)
Fax: 504-865-3383
E-mail: admit@loyno.edu
Web site: http://www.loyno.edu

Loyola is located on beautiful, oak-lined St. Charles Avenue adjacent to Audubon Park.

LUTHER COLLEGE
DECORAH, IOWA

The College

Luther College, founded in 1861 by Norwegian immigrants, is a four-year residential liberal arts college of the Lutheran church (ELCA). The College is an academic community of faith and learning where students of promise from all beliefs and backgrounds have the freedom to learn, to express themselves, to perform, to compete, and to grow. Located in Decorah, Iowa, the College is home to 2,500 students from thirty-seven states and forty-five countries. Thirty-two percent of the students are from Iowa; 86 percent come from the four-state area of Iowa, Minnesota, Wisconsin, and Illinois. Each year, over 115 international students choose to study at Luther.

In keeping with its liberal arts tradition, the College requires students to develop a depth of knowledge in their chosen major and a breadth of knowledge through exposure to a wide range of subjects and intellectual approaches (general requirements). Learning at Luther is about engagement: faculty members who are passionate in their teaching and scholarship, students who are active and involved, and a College community characterized by personal attention, hands-on experiences, academic challenge, and community support. At Luther, all students become immersed in the liberal arts through the College's common year-long course for first-year students called Paideia. The course, which is uncommon in its approach, helps train students' minds and develop their research and writing skills as they explore human cultures and history. In addition, Luther offers a Phi Beta Kappa chapter and departmental honor societies, evidence of the quality of teaching and learning on campus.

At Luther, students are encouraged to seek out connections between their lives in the classroom and their lives outside the classroom. The College provides a stimulating cultural and educational atmosphere by bringing distinguished public figures, theater groups, musicians, and educators to the campus. Cocurricular activities are an important part of college life. The College sponsors six choirs, three orchestras, three bands, two jazz bands, and a full theater and dance program. Numerous student organizations and societies provide ample opportunities for student involvement in meaningful activities. As a community of faith, students can participate in chapel, weekly Sunday worship, outreach teams, and midweek Eucharist.

Nineteen intercollegiate sports are offered. Men may participate in ten sports: baseball, basketball, cross-country, football, golf, soccer, swimming, tennis, track and field, and wrestling. Women compete in nine intercollegiate sports: basketball, cross-country, golf, soccer, softball, swimming, tennis, track and field, and volleyball. Club sports include Ultimate (Frisbee), rugby, and women's lacrosse. Seventy percent of the student body is involved in an extensive intramural and recreational sports program. Available for recreational use and for the physical education program are twelve outdoor tennis courts, an eight-lane polyurethane 400-meter track, numerous cross-country running and ski trails, and 15 acres of intramural fields. The well-equipped Regents Center houses a 25-yard indoor pool, three racquetball courts, four hardwood basketball courts, a wrestling complex, and a 3,000-seat gymnasium. A sports forum accommodates a six-lane, 200-meter indoor track; six indoor tennis courts; locker rooms; and athletic training facilities. The Legends Fitness for Life Center provides the latest fitness equipment and a 30-foot-high rock-climbing wall.

Location

The College is located in Decorah, a city of 8,100 people in the scenic bluff country of northeast Iowa. The Upper Iowa River, which runs through the campus, is designated as a National Scenic and Recreational River. Rich in Scandinavian heritage, Decorah is a popular recreation area, providing opportunities for canoeing, kayaking, fishing, hunting, cross-country skiing, camping, hiking, cycling, and spelunking. Three airports are located within a 75-mile radius of Decorah: in Rochester, Minnesota; Waterloo, Iowa; and La Crosse, Wisconsin.

Majors and Degrees

Luther College grants the Bachelor of Arts (B.A.) degree and offers majors in accounting, Africana studies, anthropology, art, athletic training, biblical languages, biology, business (management), chemistry, classics, communication studies, computer science, economics, elementary education, English, environmental studies, French, German, health, history, international studies, management, mathematics, mathematics/statistics, music, nursing, philosophy, physical education, physics, political science, psychology, religion, Russian studies, Scandinavian studies, secondary education, social work, sociology, Spanish, speech and theater, theater/dance, and women's and gender studies. Interdisciplinary programs are available in international management, museum studies, and music management. Preprofessional preparation is offered in dentistry, engineering, law, medicine, optometry, pharmacy, physical therapy, and veterinary medicine.

Academic Programs

Luther operates on a 4-1-4 academic calendar. The first semester runs from September to December, followed by a three-week January Term and the second semester, which runs from February to May. Two four-week summer sessions are offered in June and July. All students must complete at least thirty regular courses and two January-term courses in order to graduate from Luther. Other requirements for graduation include four common foundational courses: Paideia (two courses); foreign language (usually one or two courses); religion (two courses, one of which must be in biblical studies); and wellness (two 1-credit courses). In addition to a focused area of study (the major, which usually requires eight to ten courses), Luther requires all students to take courses in three general fields of inquiry: the natural world (two courses); human behavior (two courses); and human expression (two courses). Before graduating, students are required to bring together all they have learned in two culminating experiences: senior project (one course); and Paideia II (one course). Luther students also develop the perspectives and skills they will utilize in their lives as citizens and professionals equipped for distinguished service. Advanced placement and credit by examination are available. A qualified student may develop an interdisciplinary major with a faculty adviser.

Off-Campus Programs

Students may participate in off-campus programs during the fall and spring semesters, the January Term, and summer sessions. All of the programs carry academic credit. Luther participates in the Iowa General Assembly Legislative Intern Program during the spring semester of each year. Urban studies semesters may be arranged in conjunction with other colleges. The Washington Semester gives qualified juniors the opportunity to study at American University and work within one department of the federal government. Luther College also cosponsors a semester program in Washington, D.C., through the Lutheran College Washington Consortium. Students may elect to be exchange students at other colleges for one semester or a January Term.

Luther is an affiliate of the Institute of European Studies, which has centers in more than twenty European and Asian countries; students studying at one of these centers receive credit in accordance with the provisions for transfer credit for study abroad under the Junior Year Abroad programs. A community studies program in Nottingham, England, is staffed by a Luther professor each year. In alternate years, a Luther professor directs on-site programs in Münster, Germany; Lillehammer, Norway; and Sliema, Malta. In addition, opportunities for study are available in a variety of settings, such as the Bahamas, China, Russia, Tanzania, and Norway.

Academic Facilities

The 1,000-acre campus includes the Preus Library, housing 330,000 volumes, 800 print periodicals, 63,000 electronic books, and the College art collection. The library offers five online indexes and

ten commercial online services and provides access to more than 480 other libraries. Modern, well-equipped laboratories in Valders Hall of Science are supplemented by several other science-teaching facilities on campus: a planetarium, a greenhouse, a herbarium, a live-animal center, a human anatomy laboratory, a natural history museum, and a psychology sleep laboratory. Sampson Hoffland, a dynamic new 58,000-square-foot science and research center, was completed in fall 2008. The science facilities also include an extensive field study area and two electron microscopes. Within easy walking distance of the campus, the field study area offers an ideal setting for studies in aquatic biology, ecology, and field biology. Five ponds, two reestablished prairies, marshes, wooded areas, and agricultural lands are available for classwork and independent study. The College has fiber-based and wireless campus networks connecting a variety of PC and Macintosh computers (in several environments) to shared computing resources and to the Internet. More than 400 microcomputers and terminals are available for student use throughout the campus.

Luther College maintains radio station KWLC-AM, and the College's affiliate station, KLSE-FM, is part of the Minnesota Public Radio network. Luther also maintains the largest archaeological research center in Iowa. The Norwegian American Museum in Decorah, one of the finest ethnic museums in the country, provides an invaluable resource for museum and Scandinavian studies. The foreign language departments maintain a twenty-five-station electronic classroom, and the psychology department houses a twenty-station IBM interactive computer network.

The economics and business, mathematics, and computer science departments are located in the impressive F. W. Olin Building. Among the facility's technological wonders is the Luther Round Table Room, where students experience simultaneous decision making via a computer network.

The award-winning Jenson-Noble Hall of Music contains state-of-the-art computer facilities, a recording studio, and four pipe organs: 23-stop/34-rank and 42-stop/61-rank tracker organs for practice and performing and two Schlicker practice organs of 8 and 5 ranks, respectively. Jenson Hall of Music also contains 32,000 square feet of classrooms, studios, practice rooms, and rehearsal rooms for keyboard, vocal, and instrumental music. The Center for Faith and Life (CFL) houses a 42-stop/62-rank organ in the 1,600-seat auditorium for the performing arts. The CFL also houses the offices of the campus ministry, a 24-hour meditation chapel, a 200-seat recital hall, and one of four campus art galleries. The Center for the Arts serves as the home for theater, dance, and the arts.

Costs

For 2012–13, the comprehensive fee is $42,170, which includes tuition, facilities fees, room, board, subscription to student publications, and admission to College-supported concerts, lectures, and other events. A room telephone, cable TV, computer access from residence hall rooms, and a health-service program are also included. Private music lessons are $400 per semester. It is estimated that an additional $3000 is adequate for books, clothing, entertainment, and other personal expenses.

Financial Aid

More than 98 percent of all Luther students receive financial aid in the form of grants, such as the Federal Pell Grant; scholarships from Luther and other sources; loans; and jobs on campus. Luther awards Founders, President's, and Dean's Scholarships to those demonstrating superior academic achievement. The amount of aid given is determined by the College's analysis of the Free Application for Federal Student Aid (FAFSA). The priority deadline for a financial aid application is March 1.

Faculty

There are 178 full-time faculty members; 96 percent hold a Ph.D., first professional, or other terminal degree. The student-faculty ratio is 12:1.

Student Government

Students share in the governance of the College and participate in social and cultural programming. They have full membership on most College committees, majority representation in the Community Assembly, and nonvoting representation on the Board of Regents.

Admission Requirements

Admission is selective. An applicant must be a graduate of an accredited high school and have completed at least 4 units of English, 3 units of mathematics, 3 units of social science, and 2 units of natural science. It is strongly recommended that the applicant have at least two years of a foreign language. Sixty-four percent of entering students rank in the top quarter of their high school class. Transfer students may enroll at the beginning of the fall or spring semester or the January term.

Application and Information

An application, SAT or ACT scores, an educator's reference, and a transcript of previous academic work are required for admission. On-campus interviews are recommended but not required. For more information about Luther, students should contact:

Admissions Office
Luther College
700 College Drive
Decorah, Iowa 52101-1042
Phone: 563-387-1287
      800-458-8437 (toll-free)
Fax: 563-387-2159
E-mail: admissions@luther.edu (admissions)
      finaid@luther.edu (financial aid)
      intladmissions@luther.edu (international)
Web site: http://admissions.luther.edu
      http://www.facebook.com/luthercollege1861
      http://twitter.com/luthercollege

Luther College's wind turbine became operational in November of 2011 and generates one third of the college's electrical power.

LYNCHBURG COLLEGE
LYNCHBURG, VIRGINIA

The College

Lynchburg College is a fully accredited, coeducational, nonsectarian liberal arts college related to the Christian Church (Disciples of Christ). It offers undergraduate programs in the liberal arts, sciences, and professional disciplines (including business, communications, education, and nursing) and graduate programs in art, business, education, and nursing. A Doctorate of Physical Therapy program (www.lynchburg.edu/dpt) debuted in 2010 followed by a Doctorate in Educational Leadership in 2011. Lynchburg College (LC) is committed to the principle that every individual is of infinite worth, and it endeavors to provide a program of liberal education consistent with the needs of contemporary society. It draws its undergraduate student body of approximately 2,300 men and women from thirty-seven states and eleven countries. The College community is largely residential, with approximately 75 percent of the full-time undergraduate student body living on campus. Approximately 35 percent of the undergraduates are from out of state. The 214-acre campus has long been considered one of the most beautiful in the South. Thirty-seven buildings of mostly Georgian Colonial design have the majestic Blue Ridge Mountains as a backdrop.

A wide variety of activities are available in the Lynchburg College community: service and honor organizations, including the national Bonner Leader Program; more than 100 clubs and organizations; five fraternities; and six sororities as well as opportunities to participate in dramatic productions, student publications, religious activities, and musical performances. New Horizons provides adventure-based leadership and team-building opportunities for individuals and groups. Community service (www.lynchburg.edu/serve) is a distinguishing feature of the Lynchburg College students, staff, and faculty, who last year contributed more than 70,000 volunteer hours to the community through such projects as Habitat for Humanity, Camp Jaycees, Special Olympics, and other programs.

The varsity athletic program (http://athletics.lynchburg.edu) is diverse and includes twenty-one sports. The College participates in NCAA Division III and is a charter member of the Old Dominion Athletic Conference. In addition, the College supports several club sports for men and women. The Turner Athletic Facility includes state-of-the-art exercise and fitness areas, a dance studio, and one of the top exercise physiology labs in Virginia.

Shellenberger Field is a state-of-the-art athletic facility with a brand new artificial turf field and eight-lane track. With a 3,000-spectator capacity including chair and bleacher seating and night lighting, it is a formidable venue for opponents who compete with the home team in men's and women's soccer, lacrosse, track and field, and field hockey. Intramural and club sports take advantage of this facility. Also included are Moon Field upgrades—a permanent softball outfield fence and new areas for the track and field events of javelin, hammer, shot put, and discus. The baseball field, Fox Field, was updated recently to include seating for up to 1,000 fans, batting cages, and a press box.

Location

Lynchburg College (www.lynchburg.edu) is located in central Virginia, 100 miles from Richmond, 180 miles southwest of Washington, D.C., and 50 miles east of Roanoke. Greater Lynchburg is a growing business and industrial center with a population of more than 240,000. The city is noted for its climate, culture, and historic landmarks. It is within an easy drive of the Blue Ridge Mountains, where many popular lakes and resorts are located. Air, bus, and railroad transportation place Lynchburg within easy reach of any urban center.

Majors and Degrees

Lynchburg College offers the Bachelor of Arts degree in the following fields: accounting, art (graphic design or studio art), business administration, communication studies (journalism or speech communication), economics (financial or general), English (literature or writing), French, history, international relations, management, marketing, music, philosophy, political science, religious studies, sociology (criminology or general), Spanish, sports management, and theater. The Bachelor of Science degree is offered in the following fields: athletic training, biology, biomedical science, chemistry, computer science, environmental science, exercise physiology, health promotion, human development and learning (elementary education or special education), mathematics, nursing, physics, and psychology. For more information, prospective students should visit www.lynchburg.edu/majors.

Preprofessional and professional courses are available for students who want preparation for careers in art therapy, dentistry, engineering, forestry and wildlife management, law, library science, medicine, ministry and ministry-related occupations, occupational therapy, optometry, pharmacy, physical therapy, and veterinary medicine.

Academic Programs

To be eligible for a degree, a student must complete at least 124 semester hours of college-level academic work. In addition, a degree candidate must have a grade point average of at least 2.0 on all work undertaken, plus an average of at least 2.0 or higher depending on the program on all work undertaken in the major field.

The curriculum at Lynchburg College is divided into two general areas; some additional hours are available for students to explore course work in free elective areas of their choice. The first of the two areas of study consists of General Education Requirements (GERs) selected from the broad disciplines of world literature, fine arts, philosophy, religious studies, mathematics, history, social science, laboratory science, foreign languages, and health and movement science. All students are exposed to each of these academic areas. The second of the two general areas is the major. The College offers thirty-eight majors, ranging from education and business to the sciences and the humanities, forty-five minors, as well as thirteen preprofessional programs. This curriculum offers students breadth (GERs) as well as depth (the major). Students may devote their free elective hours to a minor to further enhance their education.

Outstanding students may be selected to participate in the College's Westover Honors Program (www.lynchburg.edu/westoverhonors), the purpose of which is to attract, stimulate, challenge, and fulfill academically gifted students. The program offers a challenging curriculum that promotes intellectual curiosity and independent thinking and places strong emphasis on creative problem solving.

The College operates on an early semester calendar. The first semester begins in late August and ends before Christmas, and the second semester runs from mid-January to early May. An optional winter term abroad is also offered.

Lynchburg offers twenty-three computer labs on campus, outfitted with both PCs and Macs. New students may bring a computer of their own or utilize one of the many available on campus. All students are assigned an e-mail account and have access to the Internet. All residence hall rooms are wired for network access and the Intranet, which serves the College community. Wireless Internet access is available in most areas of the campus.

Off-Campus Programs

Various agency and intercollegiate exchange programs are available. Students may engage in foreign-study programs and are encouraged to do so. In addition, any student who wishes to study abroad may do so as part of the College's study-abroad program (www.lynchburg.edu/studyabroad).

Internships, organized through the Academic and Career Services Office (www.lynchburg.edu/career), are available locally, nationally, and internationally. More than 1,000 internships are already established, and new sites are developed each year. In addition, Lynchburg College, Randolph College, and Sweet Briar College, as members of the Tri-College Consortium of Virginia, maintain cooperative relationships for sharing facilities and offerings.

Academic Facilities

The Hobbs Science Center provides an outstanding learning environment for students pursuing studies in biology, chemistry, physics, biomedical sciences, environmental science, psychology, mathematics, and computer science. In addition to state-of-the-art research labs, including a cadaver lab, students studying environmental science can utilize the online weather station, GIS and remote sensing software, and digitizer. This modern facility is also used during the summer by the Virginia Governor's School for Math and Science to provide programming for selected high school students. Extending over 470 acres, the Claytor Nature Study Center is a hands-on learning environment with natural woodlands, grasslands, two lakes, wetlands, and a mile-long stretch of the Big Otter River, and an 8,000-square-foot education/research facility.

Schewel Hall, Lynchburg College's newest $12-million classroom and laboratory facility, houses the School of Business and Economics, the Communication Studies program, foreign languages, performing arts, and multiple venues for students to congregate and study. This 67,000-square-foot facility includes technology-based classrooms, computer laboratories, and specialized teaching-learning settings, including a model stock exchange room, a digital darkroom, and a multimedia development center with television and recording studios, and Sydnor Performance Hall, which seats 250.

The Daura Art Gallery (www.lynchburg.edu/daura) is the major repository of more than 1,000 works of the Catalan-American artist, Pierre Daura. The expansion of this facility makes the Daura Gallery the largest visual art exhibit center in the city of Lynchburg. Each year, it is the site for the Senior Art Show in which chosen student works are exhibited.

Lynchburg College's Claytor Nature Study Center provides an outdoor classroom and laboratory for hands-on, field-based environmental study and research. Located at the foot of the Blue Ridge Mountains in Bedford County, the Claytor Center offers two small lakes; woodlands; wetlands; grasslands; rare plants; conference, meeting, and retreat facilities; gardens; a primitive campground; and 3 miles of hiking trails. The Center was run as a farm from the late 1700s until the mid-1990s, when it was given to the college by A. Boyd Claytor III. The land is now managed for environmental conservation and restoration through agreements with the Virginia Outdoors Foundation and the USDA's Natural Resources Conservation Service. The A. Boyd Claytor III Education and Research Facility, a 7,700-square-foot multipurpose building, offers LC students and regional K–12 students and teachers an ideal location for learning with seminar, laboratory, classroom, conference, and retreat space.

The Belk Astronomical Observatory is a 700-square-foot facility that boasts an RC Optical Systems 20-inch (0.51 meter) Truss Ritchey-Chrétien telescope. The facility also includes a 384-square-foot observation deck equipped with twelve piers for mounting smaller telescopes. An observatory control room is equipped with instrumentation that will allow LC to pursue astronomical research in conjunction with other regional colleges and universities.

Costs

For resident students who entered in the 2011–12 session, total charges were $38,385; this includes $29,860 for tuition, $7580 for room and board, and $945 for student fees (www.lynchburg.edu/tuition).

Financial Aid

Lynchburg College administers a financial aid program of more than $20 million. These resources are awarded to students for meritorious achievement and/or for demonstrated need. Lynchburg College offers academic scholarships (www.lynchburg.edu/scholarships) that range from $3000 to $14,000 and are based on performance and accomplishments at the high school or community college level. These awards are renewable each year until the student graduates, as long as the recipient maintains a qualifying minimum academic average each year. Students are identified to receive these scholarships through the admission application; no separate application is necessary. Free early aid estimates are available for students. More than 98 percent of last year's entering class received academic and/or need-based financial aid. The average amount of aid received was $22,000.

To determine eligibility for need-based financial aid, the student should complete the Free Application for Federal Student Aid (FAFSA), which may be obtained at most high schools and at the College. The FAFSA results determine the student's eligibility for federally funded grants and loans and other support such as work-study opportunities. In addition, students from Virginia are eligible to apply for the Virginia Tuition Assistance grant.

Faculty

The Lynchburg College faculty has 135 full-time members, 80 percent of whom hold the doctorate or terminal degree in their field. The student-faculty ratio is 12:1. While many faculty members are involved in research projects, it is a College policy that the faculty's top priorities must be in the classroom.

Admission Requirements

A candidate for admission (www.lynchburg.edu/admissions) to Lynchburg College should be a graduate of an approved secondary school with a minimum of 16 academic units or the equivalent, as shown by examination. It is required that the academic work include major emphases in the areas of English, foreign language, social science, natural sciences, and mathematics. An applicant must demonstrate above-average academic ability in all areas of study, as admission is competitive. In support of the record, a student must present satisfactory scores on the ACT or SAT (critical reading and math scores are used to determine admission decisions and merit scholarship awards). It is recommended that all students have a personal interview and visit the campus beginning the spring semester of their junior year or during their senior year. Enrollment Office hours during the academic year are 9 to 5 Monday through Friday and 10 to noon on Saturday during the academic year.

Application and Information

Early decision admission applications (www.lynchburg.edu/apply) must be received by November 15; notification of acceptance is made by December 15. All other applications are processed on a rolling admissions basis. Applicants are notified of the status of their application usually within two to four weeks of the date their application file is completed.

For information, students should contact:

Sharon Walters-Bower, Director of Admissions
Lynchburg College
1501 Lakeside Drive
Lynchburg, Virginia 24501
Phone: 434-544-8300
        800-426-8101 (toll-free)
Fax: 434-544-8653
E-mail: admissions@lynchburg.edu
Web site: http://www.lynchburg.edu
          http://www.facebook.com/lynchburgcollege
          http://twitter.com/lynchburg
          http://www.youtube.com/lynchburgcollege
          http://www.flickr.com/photos/lynchburgcollege

Students on the Lynchburg campus enjoy learning in a beautiful setting.

LYNDON STATE COLLEGE
LYNDONVILLE, VERMONT

The College

This small college shines a bright light. For the 1,400 students who come here from Vermont, New England, and around the world, Lyndon offers a hands-on, experiential education, nationally recognized professional programs, and an incredibly friendly atmosphere—all leading directly to rewarding careers or graduate study.

The hallmark of a Lyndon education is experience. New students participate in the First-Year Experience, a one- or two-day field trip that serves as an introduction to their major. This gives them confidence that they are pursuing the right field of study and provides an opportunity to rub shoulders with faculty members and other students in their department early in their academic career.

Lyndon graduates are recruited on campus for careers at top corporations and organizations. Employers seek out grads in part because they can apply classroom theory by participating in fieldwork as early as their sophomore year. There are 30 alumni (and counting) at ESPN. Lyndon grads are famously found everywhere there's weather, including Antarctica, the White House, the Olympics, and The Weather Channel. Graduates of Lyndon's Mountain Recreation Management program—the first program of its kind in the nation—are leaders in the winter resort industry. The College's Music Business and Industry students may be backstage, working on concert tours for world-famous musicians.

Lyndon students win prestigious national awards in their fields, such as Erica Kelleher, who was named *Ski Area Management* (SAM) magazine's Recruit of the Year. Lyndon's atmospheric sciences students regularly take first place in national weather forecasting competitions. The electronic journalism/television studies students routinely win national awards for their daily live news broadcasts—including a coveted Emmy award for the nation's best college newscast.

In academic disciplines such as mountain recreation management, Lyndon celebrates work and fun in equal measures. Alumni from the program designed and created Kingdom Trails, a 100-mile trail network consistently rated as the finest bike trail system in the eastern U.S., located just 10 minutes from campus.

Campus events range from the intellectual to the physical, with abundant opportunities for learning and fun. Recent activities include concerts with local resident Neko Case and her band; visits from U.N. ambassadors; a lecture and arts series featuring master classes with luminaries such as U.S. Poet Laureate Ted Kooser; plays and first-run films in the on-campus theater; ice climbing up the frozen fountain; canoeing in the campus ponds and kayaking in neighboring rivers; skiing and snowboarding on nearby Burke Mountain and Jay Peak; NCAA Division III athletics; and traditional Vermont events such as Sugar on Snow.

Lyndon was established in 1911 as a one-room teacher-training college and has grown to a comprehensive four-year college. It still offers a strong education major but remains progressive in its development of new professional programs, such as criminal justice; exercise science and sports management; animation and illustration (B.F.A.); music business and industry; a media major that integrates journalism with all media forms; and sustainability studies, the only undergraduate program of its kind in Vermont and one that reflects the Lyndon commitment to an evolving sustainable campus.

There are ten residence halls, including a new 132-unit, apartment-style hall for upperclassmen. Each residence hall room is equipped with Internet connections, cable TV connections, and telephone lines. Students who live on campus eat at the Stevens Dining Hall and the Hornet's Nest Snack Bar. All students are allowed to have vehicles on campus.

There are more than thirty active clubs and organizations including the campus radio station (91.5 FM The Impulse), the student newspaper *(The Critic),* sports clubs, and numerous social and academic clubs. Intercollegiate sports include baseball, basketball, cross-country, lacrosse, soccer, softball, tennis, and volleyball. Intercollege club sports include hockey and rugby. Lyndon's intramural program attracts the majority of the student body. Lyndon has a theater, which presents films and plays, and a 6,700-square-foot fitness center available to students, faculty, and staff members. World-class outdoor recreational activities and sports facilities are available within minutes of the campus.

Location

The modern 174-acre campus is located in Lyndonville, Vermont, high on a hillside overlooking Burke Mountain in the heart of Vermont's scenic Northeast Kingdom, a *National Geographic*–designated geotourism area. It is easily accessible from all points by Interstate 91. Lyndon is a 3-hour drive from Boston and Springfield, Massachusetts, and 2 hours from Montreal.

Majors and Degrees

Lyndon State College offers bachelor's degrees in the following majors: accounting, animation/illustration, atmospheric sciences/meteorology, business administration, computing, criminal justice, design for print and Web, elementary education, electronic journalism/television studies, English, environmental science, exercise science, human services, liberal studies, natural science, mathematics, mountain recreation management, music business and industry, philosophy, physical education (K–12), professional media communications, psychology, secondary education (English, mathematics, natural sciences, and social sciences), sports management, and sustainability studies.

Associate degrees are offered in business administration, computing, electronic journalism/television studies, general studies, human services, professional media communications, special education, visual arts, and visual communications. There are graduate programs in education.

Academic Programs

Lyndon operates on a two-semester calendar plus a six-week summer-session. To graduate with a bachelor's degree, students must complete 122 semester hours of credit and meet College and program requirements. Sixty-two semester hours are required for an associate degree. Each student is tested for competence in writing and mathematics at entry to Lyndon; deficiencies must be made up in noncredit classes during the first two semesters. Lyndon has a general education distribution requirement of 42 semester hours.

Academic departments advise and plan the student's core courses within the concentration. In bachelor's degree programs, most concentrations require at least 42 credits of junior- and senior-level course work. Lyndon requires that 30 of the last 39 hours toward any degree be spent in residence. Leaves of absence are granted to students in good academic standing.

The College offers fieldwork and practicums in most academic programs through the Cooperative Education Office.

Lyndon's Academic Support Center, Career Planning and Placement Office, Financial Aid Office, Student Life, and Health Services are just some of the entities that serve the needs and promote the well-being of students.

Off-Campus Programs

A key component of a Lyndon State education is the variety of opportunities for off-campus study for credit, on either a full-time or part-time basis. Students can apply professional theories and principles through practicums and internships in all majors.

Lyndon grants credit for study in other countries through an approved program such as the Experiment in International Living or the American Institute for Foreign Study. For students who prefer not to study abroad, but who would still enjoy experiencing another culture, Lyndon offers faculty- and staff-accompanied trips

each semester to places such as Greece, Russia, Ecuador, England, China, and many other countries of personal and academic interest.

Academic Facilities

Lyndon State College is a modern campus; the oldest building was completed in 1964. The new Academic Center features state-of-the-art academic and computer classrooms and laboratories, including a fully equipped computer laboratory that is linked to the College's expanding computer information network.

The library maintains a collection of more than 110,000 circulating volumes as well as periodicals, audio and video materials, and microfiche collections.

The state-of-the-art meteorology laboratory prepares weather and forecast information that is broadcast over Vermont radio and television stations. Atmospheric science students also operate a 24-hour weather-reporting telephone line.

Produced entirely by students, Lyndon's national-award-winning News 7 is a daily television broadcast that provides local news programming. Radio station WWLR 91.5 FM, The Impulse, is staffed by student DJs.

Costs

The 2012–13 tuition for Vermont residents is $8928 per year; for nonresidents, it is $19,200. Room and board (twenty-one-meal plan) for one academic year is $8786. Required College fees, not including health and accident insurance, total $936. Total expenses for a Vermont resident living on campus are $18,650; for a nonresident, $28,922. Miscellaneous expenses were estimated at $1100. Qualified students from New England and upstate New York can save up to 30 percent on regular out-of-state tuition.

Financial Aid

Financial aid is available in the form of loans, grants, and campus employment under the Federal Work-Study Program. Approximately 85 percent of the student population receives some type of financial aid from institutional and outside sources. Approximately 35 percent of students are employed by either the Federal Work-Study Program or the Lyndon dining hall.

Applicants for aid are required to complete the Free Application for Federal Student Aid (FAFSA). In addition to filing the FAFSA, transfer students are required to have a financial aid transcript completed by the financial aid officer of each college they attended. For a student to be considered an on-time applicant, the FAFSA should be filed in early February in order to reach the Lyndon's Financial Aid Office by the March 15 deadline.

Faculty

Lyndon's faculty consists of 155 members, 95 percent of whom hold the highest degree in their field from research institutions such as Harvard, Columbia, Yale, and USC. Many of Lyndon's professors have come to Lyndon to teach following prestigious careers at corporations and organizations such as CNN, National Public Radio, and Hewlett-Packard. Some are successful entrepreneurs, offering real world expertise to back up their classroom teaching.

Faculty members serve as academic advisers and mentors to students and student organizations. Student evaluation of teaching is a formal process and is used in personnel decisions.

Student Government

Students actively represent Lyndon on the Vermont State Colleges' Board of Trustees, in the Vermont State Colleges' Student Association, and on many campus committees. The Student Senate heads the student organizations.

Admission Requirements

Lyndon emphasizes academic success as reflected on high school or college transcripts, and social and academic potential as reflected in letters of recommendation. Lyndon seeks applicants whose academic record reveals maturity and motivation as well as a sense of responsibility and leadership.

Entrance requirements include 4 years of English and 2 to 3 years each of mathematics, science, and history. Foreign language is desired. International students seeking to attend Lyndon can find detailed information on the College's Web site. The SAT is required.

Students wishing to be considered for early action must apply by November 1. Admission decisions for first-year students are determined on the basis of the student's application, a copy of the secondary school transcript, one to three recommendations from secondary school guidance counselor(s) or teacher(s) that speak to the academic readiness and social preparedness of the applicant, and an interview either in person or by phone.

Applicants who have completed examinations taken through the College Board's Advanced Placement Program with a grade of 3 or higher are granted both advanced placement and course credit after evaluation by the Registrar's Office. Advanced standing is awarded for successful performance on the tests of the College-Level Examination Program. Lyndon grants up to 60 college credits for scores above the 40th percentile on the five general examinations in English composition, humanities, mathematics, natural science, and social science/history and for scores at or above the minimum score established by the College Board for a wide variety of subject examinations.

Admission requirements for transfer students are the same as those for freshman applicants, but an official transcript must also be obtained from each college-level institution that the applicant has attended. Transcripts are required even if no credit is being transferred from a particular institution. Transfer credit may be given at Lyndon for courses completed with the equivalent of a grade of C or better at accredited or officially approved institutions.

Application and Information

A nonrefundable $40 fee (paper) or $25 (online) must accompany each application. First-year applicants who are unable to afford the application fee should complete the paper application and ask their guidance counselor to sign a College Board fee waiver, or print a copy of the NACAC application fee waiver and ask their counselor to complete it. When these forms are ready, prospective students should mail them to Lyndon, along with their application, all transcripts of academic work completed, and their board scores.

For further information, students should contact:

Office of Admissions
Lyndon State College
P.O. Box 919
Lyndonville, Vermont 05851
Phone: 800-225-1998 (toll-free)
Fax: 802-626-6335
E-mail: admissions@lyndonstate.edu
Web site: http://www.lyndonstate.edu

Students on the set of Lyndon's award-winning News 7. Since 2004, the student-produced daily newscasts have garnered forty-four regional and national awards, including an Emmy for the nation's best college newscast.

MANHATTAN COLLEGE
RIVERDALE, NEW YORK

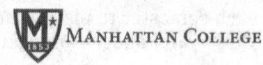

The College

With over 155 years of history as a Lasallian institution, Manhattan College maintains its fine reputation as an outstanding Catholic college, dedicated to educating students with a concern for the community and a love of independent and critical thinking. Since its inception in 1853, Manhattan College has never wavered from its principal goal—to ensure that its students fulfill their potential and are well prepared to take their places as contributing members of society.

The College has an enrollment of 3,657students, of whom 3,237 are undergraduates. Approximately 73 percent of Manhattan's students come from New York State; the remaining 27 percent represent thirty-six other states and thirty-eight other countries. Manhattan College offers a four-year guarantee of resident housing which includes on-campus residence halls and off-campus apartments. Nearly 61 percent of undergraduates choose to live on campus. Manhattan offers over eighty extracurricular organizations, five student publications and fields nineteen varsity and club sports teams. Of Manhattan's 40,000 active alumni, a large number are prominent leaders in business, government, education, the arts, the sciences, and engineering.

Location

Manhattan College's 22-acre campus is located 10 miles north of midtown Manhattan in the suburban Riverdale section of the Bronx, about a mile from Westchester County. The area offers the calm and quiet of a residential, suburban setting as well as easy access to the many cultural, business, and educational advantages of New York City. The College is easily accessible by subway, bus, or highway; three airports are also nearby.

Majors and Degrees

Manhattan College offers more than forty major fields of study within the arts, business, education, engineering, and science. Graduate degrees are also offered within business, education, and engineering, as well.

The liberal arts curriculum of the School of Arts provides programs that lead to a Bachelor of Arts or Bachelor of Science with majors in the humanities and the social sciences, including communication, economics, English, fine arts, French, government, history, labor studies, modern foreign languages, philosophy, psychology, religious studies, and sociology. Interdisciplinary majors include international studies, peace studies, and urban studies.

In the School of Science, programs lead to a Bachelor of Science or Bachelor of Arts with majors in biochemistry, biology, chemistry, computer science, mathematics, and physics. Premedical, predental, and pre–veterinary programs are also available.

The School of Engineering has a well-deserved reputation as one of the best small college engineering schools in the nation and offers programs leading to a Bachelor of Science in chemical, civil, computer, electrical, and mechanical engineering. The program is fully accredited by the Educational Accreditation Commission of ABET. Graduate programs are also available in chemical, civil, computer, electrical, environmental, and mechanical engineering.

The School of Business, accredited by AACSB International, has programs leading to a Bachelor of Science in Business Administration with majors in accounting, computer information systems, economics, finance, global business studies, management, and marketing. In addition, Manhattan College also offers the following graduate programs: the Bachelor of Science in Professional Accounting/Master of Business Administration and the Bachelor of Science in Business/Master of Business Administration, which offer students the opportunity to complete a five-year multiple award program.

The School of Education and Health offers a curriculum leading to a Bachelor of Arts in childhood education, childhood/special education (dual program), and adolescent education. The physical education curriculum leads to a Bachelor of Science in physical education and exercise science. The health curriculum leads to a Bachelor of Science in allied health, with a concentration in health-care administration, health counseling, or scientific foundations. Curricula in radiological and health sciences lead to a Bachelor of Science in radiation therapy or nuclear medicine technology. In addition, the School of Education and Health offers the five-year childhood/special education program, thereby allowing the student to receive a bachelor's and master's degree with eligibility to pursue certification for grades 1–6 in regular and special education. The School of Education and Health also offers master's degrees and professional diplomas in school counseling, mental health counseling, special education, and school building leadership. All programs are approved by the New York State Education Department and accredited by the Teacher Education Accreditation Council (TEAC).

Academic Programs

The core curriculum shared by the School of Arts and the School of Science studies some of the vital works of humankind, explores new ideas, examines the meaning of scientific experimentation, and encourages a student to develop his or her thinking and leadership abilities. The major programs offer advanced work in specific humanistic and scientific disciplines and opportunities to work on research projects in collaboration with faculty scholars.

In the School of Engineering, all engineering students follow a common core curriculum during the first two years and choose a major at the beginning of the junior year. Each curriculum includes a generous selection of courses in basic sciences, the engineering sciences, humanistic studies, and mathematics.

The School of Business prepares students for positions of executive responsibility in business, government, and nonprofit organizations. The business curriculum is based on a strong commitment to liberal education and is well balanced between professional business courses, humanities, sciences, and social sciences. This is a reflection of the school's belief that executives should be broadly educated and should involve themselves, as well as their organizations, in efforts to solve social problems.

The School of Education and Health prepares students for teaching, counseling, and health professions. Students complete the College's core curriculum in liberal arts and sciences and then complete a major in various programs in the school's three departments: education, physical education and exercise science, and radiological and health professions. All programs include internships/practicums in schools, hospitals, or other institutions. Graduates of the school's teacher-preparation programs receive New York State provisional teaching certification. The school also offers a five-year B.A./M.S. program in childhood/special education and special education.

Off-Campus Programs

Students in the liberal arts curricula who have demonstrated superior achievement in their first two years are encouraged to spend their junior year studying abroad. Manhattan College

also offers summer study-abroad programs in many countries; arrangements can be made to study in a country of choice. Students in the School of Business may participate in the International Field Studies Seminar. As participants, they spend time in another country studying the effect of that environment on international firms. Career services and co-op education integrate classroom theory with the practical experience of a job in industry, business, the social services, the arts, or government. Portions of the education courses are conducted in New York City schools, so that student teachers may gain experience in urban education at an early stage.

Academic Facilities

There are more than forty scientific and engineering laboratories at Manhattan, including the Research and Learning Center, as well as a modern language laboratory and a computer information systems laboratory. Manhattan's newly built O'Malley Library is a state-of-the-art facility featuring modern accommodations for study and research. It is connected to the renovated and updated Cardinal Hayes Pavilion (formerly the Cardinal Hayes Library).

Both commuters and residents can take advantage of the College's fitness center and newly renovated cafeterias. There are a variety of eating options, as well as spaces to relax and enjoy a snack while watching large screen televisions. The Commuter Lounge serves as a crossroads for students between classes while on campus.

Costs

For 2012–13, the tuition for Manhattan College is $30,100 per year plus program fee. The cost of room and board for the year is $12,220.

Financial Aid

Manhattan grants or administers financial assistance in the form of tuition awards to students on the basis of need and/or ability. Need is evaluated by submitting the FAFSA. In addition to a merit scholarship fund, Manhattan offers endowed scholarships, special category scholarships and grants, student athletic grants, Federal Pell Grants, Federal Supplemental Educational Opportunity Grants, student loans, Federal Work-Study Program awards, and New York State financial assistance are also available to students who qualify. A total of 2,013 students receive financial aid from Manhattan College, and approximately 70 percent receive financial aid from government or private agencies.

Faculty

Manhattan's faculty has 205 full-time and 169 part-time teachers. The faculty-student ratio is approximately 1:12. Nearly 93 percent of the faculty members hold doctorates. The maximum teaching load on the undergraduate level is 12 credit hours per semester. Faculty members serve on the college senate, the council for faculty affairs, and numerous faculty and campus committees. In addition, they are available to students for informal guidance and counseling and also serve as official moderators of many campus organizations.

Student Government

The Manhattan Student Government is composed of students elected annually by their peers to fill posts outlined in the Student Government Constitution. The Student Government allocates funds to all student organizations. Members are also full voting members of the College Senate.

Admission Requirements

Manhattan has a long-standing policy of nondiscrimination. No applicant is refused admission because of race, color, religion, age, national origin, sex, or disability. All applicants must present an academic diploma from an accredited high school and must offer a minimum of 16 credits in academic subjects.

Liberal arts candidates must be proficient in at least one foreign language. At the discretion of the Committee on Admissions, quantitative requirements may be modified for applicants with especially strong records who show promise of doing well in college. In the selection process, attention is given to scholastic ability, as indicated by grades and rank in class, as well as to standardized test scores and recommendations from teachers and counselors. All candidates must submit either SAT or ACT results. An interview with a member of the admission staff can be arranged but is not required. Applicants may submit scores on the General Educational Development test in lieu of a formal high school diploma; however, all such applicants must submit the results of the appropriate College Board tests. Manhattan College offers early acceptance for high school seniors, admission to advanced standing, advanced placement, and credit by examination. Junior college or other transfer students are welcome. Manhattan College requires applicants whose native language is not English to take the Test of English as a Foreign Language (TOEFL), the SAT, or ACT exam. The average SAT scores of entering freshmen in 2011 were 550 in mathematics and 528 in the verbal portion.

Application and Information

Application forms are furnished by the Admission Office on request and available on the Manhattan College Web site. The Common Application Form, which is available in many high school guidance offices and online, may also be used. After supplying the information required, students must send the application to the admission office at Manhattan College. The high school report, recommendation letters, and transcript must be submitted by the high school guidance counselor. This should be done after six terms of high school or right after the seventh term. There is a rolling admissions policy and a March 1 deadline for financial aid applications. A nonrefundable application fee of $60 is required.

For more information, contact:

William J. Bisset
Vice President for Enrollment Management
Manhattan College
Riverdale, New York 10471
United States
Phone: 718-862-7200
      800-MC2-XCEL (toll-free)
E-mail: admit@manhattan.edu
Web site: http://www.manhattan.edu

Manhattan College centers a great deal of its campus activity around the main quadrangle.

MARLBORO COLLEGE
MARLBORO, VERMONT

The College

Marlboro College, founded in 1946, is a small community of self-directed learners with a passion for intellectual engagement and a desire to create a course of study tailored to their own interests. Tucked away in the foothills of Vermont's Green Mountains, Marlboro offers a rigorous liberal arts curriculum through small classes and advanced one-to-one instruction, called tutorials. Marlboro's goal is to teach students to think clearly and learn independently, develop a command of concise and correct writing, and aspire to academic excellence, all while participating responsibly in a self-governing community. The College's 7:1 student-faculty ratio sparks dynamic exchanges between students and faculty members both in and out of the classroom and fosters a close-knit community in which asking questions is more important than knowing the right answers.

The fields and woodlands that make up its rural 300-acre campus include the original cluster of barns and other farm buildings that were converted by the first students and faculty members into classrooms and dormitories. The Outdoor Program offers instruction and equipment for backpacking, canoeing, cross-country skiing, kayaking, rock climbing, skating, and other sports that bring students in touch with the surrounding environment. The soccer team competes with other colleges, and more impromptu volleyball, basketball, softball, and Ultimate (Frisbee) compete as club teams. In addition, Marlboro's broomball (a game akin to hockey) tournament takes place each winter, with prizes for the winning teams and those with the best costumes. Campus committees organize many events both on and off campus, including concerts; lectures; poetry and fiction readings; art shows; and trips to Boston, Montreal, and New York for museum visits, shopping, and baseball games. Other activities that enrich campus life include parties, dances, plays, and weekly film screenings.

Marlboro is—and intends to remain—one of the nation's smallest liberal arts colleges, with some 300 students. Students come from nearly forty states and approximately six other countries. Transfer students—who make up one quarter of each incoming class—bring an important perspective to the campus community. More than 80 percent of all students live in campus housing, which consists of small dormitories (both single-sex and coed), several four-bedroom cottages, and a renovated country inn.

Location

The village of Marlboro with 1,200 residents, just 2 miles from the College, consists of a post office, a town clerk's office, and an inn. During the summer, the village swells to accommodate the famous Marlboro Music Festival. The town of Brattleboro, 12 miles away, is a lively cultural and commercial center with bookstores, restaurants, coffee shops, a community food cooperative, and a movie theater. The College is 2 hours by car from Boston and 4 hours from New York City and Montreal.

Areas of Study and Degrees

Marlboro confers the Bachelor of Arts and Bachelor of Science degrees in more than thirty areas of study, which can be combined in an endless number of ways. Students have the freedom to design their own majors, which allows them to make interdisciplinary connections and pursue individualized research. The College also offers Bachelor of Arts and Bachelor of Science degrees in international studies through its World Studies Program (WSP).

Areas of study offered at Marlboro include American studies, anthropology, art history, Asian studies, astronomy, biochemistry, biology, ceramics, chemistry, classics, computer science, cultural history, dance, development studies (in the WSP), economics, environmental studies, film/video studies, history, international studies, languages, literature, mathematics, music, painting, philosophy, photography, physics, political science, psychology, religion, sculpture, sociology, theater, visual arts, and writing.

Academic Programs

In the first two years, Marlboro students study broadly, discover new interests, and begin to see the connections that lead many to pursue interdisciplinary work. Each new student is paired with a faculty adviser and joins an advising group of sophomores, juniors, and seniors as well as freshmen. Students learn from each other at Marlboro in seminar-style classes.

Marlboro believes that clear writing both reflects and engenders clear thinking. The College, therefore, requires each new student to pass a Clear Writing Requirement within three semesters of enrolling at the College. Designated writing courses, faculty advisers, and student writing tutors all help new students meet the requirement.

Marlboro's Plan of Concentration, more than any other academic component, sets the College apart from other undergraduate programs. Undertaken by all Marlboro students in their junior and senior years, the plan is the collection of related projects and papers that form the final product of the student's academic work at Marlboro. It is an individualized program of classes, research, experiences, one-to-one study, and original thought, driven by the student's interests and academic goals and designed in close collaboration with faculty sponsors. Final evaluation of the student's plan is conducted by her or his faculty advisers and an outside examiner who is a recognized expert in the student's field.

Off-Campus Programs

The College sponsors multiple academic adventures and humanitarian trips each year, ranging from community service work in South Carolina and Costa Rica to interdisciplinary research in Cuba, China, Kenya, and Vietnam. Students working on their Plan of Concentration often travel abroad or attend other institutions for a period of time to augment their academic work. Marlboro faculty members may help plan these pursuits and frequently aid students in securing internships in academic fields.

The World Studies Program is a four-year program leading to a Bachelor of Arts or Bachelor of Science degree in international studies. The program involves intensive study on campus as well as a six- to eight-month internship abroad. In addition, WSP sponsors regular on-campus activities, which include a themed international dinner, music from around the world, and guest lectures and films related to current world issues.

Academic Facilities

Marlboro's academic facilities offer small classrooms and oversized faculty offices for students to meet in small groups and individually with their professors. Facilities are open 24 hours a day, supporting student research and creative explorations in a DNA lab, a state-of-the-art black-and-white/digital darkroom, a digital film-editing studio, two pottery studios, and an astronomical observatory. In the last five years, Marlboro's ongoing campus renewal project has doubled the size of the library and added a suite-style dorm. The new Rudolf and Irene Serkin Performing Arts Center has been added to offer more than 10,000 square feet for music, dance, and drama rehearsals and performances. In 2008, the campus added a Total Health Center to provide additional space for medical and psychological counseling services and a fitness room.

Costs

Tuition and fees at Marlboro are $36,300 for the 2012–13 academic year. Room and board costs are $9930.

Financial Aid

More than 80 percent of all Marlboro students receive financial help. The College is committed to helping any student who qualifies for admission assemble the financial resources necessary to attend, and need is not a factor in the admission decision. Merit scholarships and grants are also available.

Faculty

Marlboro's 40 full-time faculty members are committed first and foremost to teaching. The lively exchange of ideas between teachers and students is the cornerstone of the Marlboro curriculum.

Student Government

All students and faculty and staff members are equal members of the College Town Meeting. Since the opening of the College in 1946, the community has come together every month to debate and decide budget initiatives, College policies, and other issues that affect daily life. A board of Selectpersons, elected by the College community, serves the College's interests and is responsible for drafting Town Meeting rules and regulations. Students serve with faculty and staff members on more than thirty College committees, including those that make faculty-hiring decisions. Other important committees include the social committee and the Community Court, which is responsible for enforcing campus regulations.

Admission Requirements

The Admissions Committee seeks students with intellectual promise; a high degree of motivation, self-discipline, personal stability, and social concern; and the ability and desire to contribute to the College community. All applicants are considered without regard to race, creed, sex, sexual orientation, gender identity or its expression, national or ethnic origin, age, or disability. Homeschoolers, transfers, veterans, and older or returning students are encouraged to apply.

Like most colleges, Marlboro requires students to submit a variety of documentation, from high school transcripts to teacher recommendations. The Admissions Committee evaluates each applicant as a unique individual who possesses qualities that are not necessarily quantifiable.

A campus visit is strongly recommended for all applicants, and interviews are encouraged. Many campus interviews are conducted by faculty members in the applicant's area of interest. Marlboro does not use a formulaic approach in making admission decisions. Applicants are encouraged to demonstrate their particular strengths; the goal is a successful match between the student and the College.

Application and Information

New students and transfers are admitted for either the spring or the fall semester. Applicants for the fall semester have a choice of three admission plans. The early decision plan is for those students who have thoroughly researched Marlboro and for whom Marlboro is the first choice. Applicants should be aware that early decision is binding. The deadline for first-year students to submit application materials is November 15, and applicants are notified by December 15. Early action, a nonbinding plan, has a deadline of January 15. These applicants are notified of a decision on February 1. The regular admission deadline is March 1. The deadline for transfer students to submit applications materials for the fall semester is April 1, and for the spring semester it is November 15.

An application for admission must include a completed Common Application form and a Marlboro College Supplement Form with a "Why Marlboro" personal statement, a $50 fee, complete transcripts from all secondary schools and colleges, an analytical writing sample, and two letters of recommendation. SAT or ACT are not required, but will be taken into consideration if submitted by the prospective student. The Admissions Committee welcomes applications from homeschooled students. In lieu of a high school transcript, homeschooled students must submit a detailed description of their curriculum (including reading lists and academic study areas).

Office of Admissions
Marlboro College, 2582 South Road
Marlboro, Vermont 05344-0300
United States
Phone: 802-257-4333
      800-343-0049 (toll-free)
Fax: 802-451-7555
E-mail: admissions@marlboro.edu
Web site: http://www.marlboro.edu

Small classes and close working relationships with faculty members are at the center of a Marlboro education.

MARYMOUNT MANHATTAN COLLEGE

NEW YORK, NEW YORK

MarymountManhattan
a college of the liberal arts

The College

Marymount Manhattan College (MMC) is an urban, independent, coeducational, undergraduate liberal arts college. The mission of the College is to educate a socially and economically diverse population by fostering intellectual achievement and personal growth and by providing opportunities for career development. Inherent in this mission is the intent to develop an awareness of social, political, cultural, and ethical issues in the belief that this awareness will lead to concern for, participation in, and the improvement of society. To accomplish this mission, the College offers a strong program in the arts and sciences to students of all ages, as well as substantial preprofessional preparation. Central to these efforts is the particular attention given to the individual student. Marymount Manhattan College also seeks to be a resource and learning center for the metropolitan community.

The social and extracurricular life of the student body of approximately 2,000 students centers on more than forty clubs and organizations sponsored through the Office of Student Development and Activities, including the Global Citizens Society, Psychology Club, French Club, Philosophy Club, Science Society, Black and Latino Student Organization, the student newspaper and yearbook, WMMC Radio, Student Government Association, intramural sports, and other special interest organizations. Students attend musical events, and MMC's own off-Broadway theater, the only one on the Upper East Side of Manhattan, offers students an opportunity to participate in student productions.

The Office of Residence Life at Marymount Manhattan College is committed to providing residents with numerous opportunities and experiences that foster intellectual achievement and social and personal growth. Students are encouraged to become involved in the many activities that are sponsored by Residence Life and are assisted with assuming responsibility for their own lives and living environment. The College provides housing for approximately 750 students at the 55th Street Residence Hall and at 1760, located on Third Avenue and East 97th Street. The buildings offer suite-style, traditional dormitories, or apartment-style living, with classrooms, lounges, a laundry room, and rehearsal space. Additional off-campus facilities are obtained as needed.

The Office of Career Development and Internships serves the entire College community by providing an integrated program of academic and career counseling. The office helps students by offering internship opportunities and workshops in job placement, resume writing, and graduate school preparation. Other College services include personal and financial aid counseling and campus ministry.

Location

Marymount Manhattan College is centrally located on Manhattan's Upper East Side at 221 East 71st Street between Second and Third avenues. Within walking distance of the campus are the Frick, Metropolitan, Whitney, and Guggenheim museums; the Asian Society, French Institute, and National Audubon Society; Central Park; New York Hospital and Sloan-Kettering Research Center; and public libraries. All forms of public transportation are easily accessible. Within minutes of the College are shops, restaurants, and movie theaters. This location gives students the opportunity to take advantage of New York City's rich culture and to explore a variety of neighborhoods.

Majors and Degrees

Marymount Manhattan College offers programs leading to the Bachelor of Arts (B.A.), Bachelor of Science (B.S.), and Bachelor of Fine Arts (B.F.A.) degrees. Majors are offered in accounting, acting, art (concentrations in art history, graphic design, photography, and studio art), biology, business, business management, communication arts, dance, English and world literatures, history, interdisciplinary studies, international studies, philosophy and religious studies, political science, psychology, sociology, speech-language pathology and audiology, and theater arts. Minors offered are accounting, art history, arts management, art therapy, Asian studies, biology, business management, chemistry, creative writing, drama therapy, economics, English and world literatures, environmental studies, forensic psychology, French and Francophone studies, gender and sexuality studies, graphic design, Hispanic studies, history, industrial/organizational psychology, international studies, journalism, mathematics, media studies, music, musical theater, neuroscience, philosophy, photography, political economy, political science, promotional and professional communication, psychology, religious studies, sociology, social work, speech-language pathology and audiology, studio art, and theater.

Academic Programs

Marymount Manhattan College has designed its programs to enable students to meet the challenges of contemporary society. MMC is committed to the belief that a liberal arts education provides students with the ability and the flexibility to manage change and with broad understanding and the communication and problem-solving skills that are essential for success in any career and in life. To accomplish its goals, the College offers a liberal arts education, integrated with preprofessional training opportunities and individualized attention. The curricula are organized into five divisions: humanities, fine and performing arts, sciences, social sciences, and business management. Also offered are special-interest sequences that complement the student's major and minor, with added concentration in such areas as art history, creative writing, finance and investments, international business, marketing, photography, pre-dentistry, pre-law, pre-medicine, pre–veterinary science, and social work. The College's small size provides students with an individually planned academic career, reflects students' academic needs and interests, and supports their career goals.

Candidates for the B.A., B.S., and B.F.A. degrees must complete 120 credits. To qualify for a degree, a student must maintain an overall scholastic average of at least 2.0. Requirements for certificate programs vary.

The College recognizes various types of nontraditional credit, including credit for acceptable scores on the Advanced Placement (AP), International Baccalaureate (I.B.), College-Level Examination Program (CLEP), and New York State College Proficiency Examination (CPE) tests and credit for life experience.

MMC encourages its students to participate in internship programs in New York City at hospitals, financial institutions, magazines, publishing houses, media firms, art galleries, museums, and off-Broadway theaters.

Off-Campus Programs

The College's Academic Year Abroad offers an opportunity for students to broaden their educational experience and to gain cultural perspectives through study at other colleges in the Americas and overseas. Students may spend one or both semesters of their junior year in this program. MMC summer sessions and January inter-sessions also offer students opportunities in travel/study-abroad courses in Egypt, France, Great Britain, Greece, Eastern Europe, Ireland, Italy, Russia, Spain, and many others.

Academic Facilities

The Thomas J. Shanahan Library at MMC is a library/learning center. It contains more than 100,000 volumes in open stacks and maintains an extensive periodical collection. The media center, on the main library floor, houses nonprint materials, microfiche, microfilm, filmstrips, slides, tapes, videotapes, DVDs, and records. Through the library's affiliation with the New York Metropolitan Reference and Research Library Agency, MMC faculty members and students have access to the materials of the member libraries. The library also participates in the Online Computer Library Center (OCLC), a computerized database of the holdings of some

4,000 libraries that is currently being used for cataloging and reference purposes.

The modern 250-seat Theresa Lang Theatre is equipped with an orchestra pit capable of accommodating 40 musicians. The theater has a special acoustical design, a sprung dance floor, a full technical balcony with equipment for lighting and sound, thirty-five counterweighted-line sets in the fly system, dressing rooms with showers, and a scene shop. Students benefit from exposure to the numerous professional dance, opera, and theatrical groups that perform at the College.

Top-notch laboratory facilities strengthen education in two areas in which MMC has always excelled—science and communication arts.

MMC's science facilities in biology, chemistry, and physics underwent a total reconstruction valued at close to $1 million, thanks to the generosity of the Samuel Freeman Charitable Trust and the Ira De Camp Foundation. The Samuel Freeman Science Center opens many new doors of opportunity to students who are biology/pre-medicine majors or who are interested in pursuing careers in other science or health-related fields.

The College's Theresa Lang Center for Producing features the latest in digital computer technology and is one of the most advanced facilities of its kind in New York City. With digital multimedia capability, a decor inspired by top television postproduction houses, and access to the public library's B. Altman Advanced Learning Superblock, the center further enhances students' skills in traditional video and television production and allows them to develop, design, and evaluate cutting-edge multimedia projects. In conjunction with the Communication Arts Department, the College offers students a media library, where many videos, DVDs, and screening computers are available to students.

In fall 2009, the College opened the Commons, a two-tiered dining facility and student lounge. Students also have an outdoor dining option, since the Commons opens out onto the existing Lowerre Family Terrace, a 5,000-square-foot rooftop garden, complete with a stone water-wall, a deck, and Wi-Fi service, that connects the two main campus buildings.

Costs

For the 2011–12 academic year, full-time tuition and fees were $24,708. Room and board costs were $14,030 per year. For part-time students, tuition was $785 per credit. Additional fees are applicable for various laboratory and studio classes.

Financial Aid

The College administers a variety of financial aid programs, including scholarships sponsored by the College. Some of the awards are based on academic achievement; others are based on financial need. Students are also eligible for aid through a wide variety of state and federal programs. In addition, a number of jobs are available for students on campus, and the Offices of Financial Aid and Academic and Career Advisement can help students locate part-time off-campus jobs to help finance their education. More than 85 percent of MMC students receive some form of financial assistance. Therefore, limited finances alone need not prevent any student from attending the College. Priority consideration for merit- and need-based financial aid is November 15 for spring admission and March 15 for fall admission.

Faculty

Marymount Manhattan College's student-faculty ratio is 12:1. In addition to the staff of the advisement office, faculty members act as advisers to students. Full-time faculty members teach in all sessions and divisions (days, evenings, and some weekends). Part-time instructors, who are drawn from the wealth of experienced teaching professionals in New York City, supplement the full-time faculty.

Student Government

The Student Government Association responds to three areas of concern at MMC. The association primarily serves the needs of its constituents by managing the student government budget, planning and publicizing events, and establishing organizations that reflect the interests of the students. In addition, the association assists faculty and administrative groups and committees in their policy and procedural tasks and communicates the results of committee work to the student body. Finally, the Student Government Association provides special representatives for students' rights and freedoms through established and clearly defined channels of authority.

Admission Requirements

Marymount Manhattan College seeks candidates with qualities that indicate potential for success in higher education and the ability to contribute to the College community. Admission is based on a combination of factors: the student's academic program, including scholastic average; two recommendations (judicial form required for transfer students in lieu of one recommendation) from teachers, counselors, or employers; an essay; and SAT or ACT scores. TOEFL, IELTS, or PTE scores are required for international student applicants.

Each year the College enrolls an increasing number of transfer students. Transfer students may receive up to 90 credits for course work completed at a regionally accredited postsecondary institution with a grade of C- or better. Transcripts are evaluated on a course-by-course basis.

Application and Information

The admissions application must be received by March 15 (fall entry) and November 15 (spring entry) for priority consideration for MMC scholarships. Students may apply online. For application forms and for more information about Marymount Manhattan College, students should contact:

Office of Admission
Marymount Manhattan College
221 East 71st Street
New York, New York 10021
Phone: 212-517-0430
        800-MARYMOUNT (toll-free)
Fax: 212-517-0448
E-mail: admissions@mmm.edu
Web site: http://www.mmm.edu
        http://on.fb.me/MarymountManhattanColl (Facebook)
        http://twitter.com/NYCMarymount (Twitter)

Marymount Manhattan College, in the heart of Manhattan.

MARYWOOD UNIVERSITY
SCRANTON, PENNSYLVANIA

The University

Marywood University is coeducational, comprehensive, residential, and Catholic. Founded in 1915 by the Sisters, Servants of the Immaculate Heart of Mary, the University serves men and women from a variety of backgrounds and religions. The University enrolls more than 3,400 students in an array of undergraduate and graduate programs. Motivated by a pioneering, progressive spirit, Marywood provides a framework for educational excellence that enables students to develop fully as persons and to master professional and leadership skills that are necessary for meeting human needs.

Students at Marywood have the opportunity to build on their academic interests and proactively shape their educational experience. Students' energy and intellectual curiosity guides their work, growth, and success. Marywood believes in the power of the individual and in the premise that education is the most empowering tool.

Marywood is fully accredited by the Commission on Higher Education of the Middle States Association of Colleges and Schools. Accreditations/approvals have been granted by Accreditation Review Committee on Education for the Physician Assistant, American Psychological Association, American Art Therapy Association, American Music Therapy Association, Commission on Accreditation for Dietetics Education, American Dietetic Association, Council on Academic Accreditation, American Speech-Language-Hearing Association, Association of Collegiate Business Schools and Programs, Commission on Accreditation of Athletic Training Education, Council for Accreditation of Counseling and Related Educational Programs, Council on Social Work Education, National Association of Schools of Art and Design, National Association of Schools of Music, National Council for Accreditation of Teacher Education, and National League for Nursing Accrediting Commission.

The athletic program for women and men at Marywood provides students with opportunities to play on competitive intercollegiate, club, and intramural teams. Students compete on an intercollegiate basis in baseball, basketball, cross-country, field hockey, lacrosse, soccer, softball, swimming/diving, tennis, and volleyball. Marywood is a member of NCAA Division III, the Colonial States Athletic Conference (CSAC), and the Eastern College Athletic Conference. Marywood's teams have been successful, winning titles in basketball, field hockey, lacrosse, soccer, softball, tennis, and volleyball. In addition, Marywood teams and individuals have participated in tournaments at the national level.

Prospective students can connect with Marywood through social networks including Facebook (http://facebook.com/marywoodu), Twitter (http://twitter.com/marywoodu), and YouTube (http://youtube.com/marywoodu).

Location

Situated on a hilltop, Marywood's scenic 115-acre campus is part of an attractive residential area of the city of Scranton, in northeastern Pennsylvania. With a population of 78,000, Scranton is the fifth-largest city in Pennsylvania and is the county seat of Lackawanna County (the county population is approximately 213,000). Marywood is relatively close to many major cities of the Northeast; traveling by car, it is 1 hour to Binghamton; 2½ hours to New York and Philadelphia; 4 hours to Washington, D.C.; and 5½ hours to Boston. Several airlines serve the Wilkes-Barre/Scranton International Airport, which is 20 minutes from the campus. The Pocono Mountains, offering spectacular scenery and an abundance of outdoor recreational opportunities, including downhill skiing, are a short distance from the campus.

Majors and Degrees

Marywood University offers a variety of majors and minors at the undergraduate level. Individually designed majors, developed with faculty guidance, and double and interdisciplinary majors are also available. Several five-year bachelor's/master's degree programs are offered.

At the undergraduate level, Marywood University awards the Bachelor of Arts (B.A.), Bachelor of Architecture (B.Arch.), Bachelor of Business Administration (B.B.A.), Bachelor of Environmental Design in Architecture (B.E.D.A.), Bachelor of Fine Arts (B.F.A.), Bachelor of Music (B.M.), Bachelor of Science (B.S.), Bachelor of Science in Nursing (B.S.N.), and Bachelor of Social Work (B.S.W.).

Marywood offers majors and minors in the following areas of study: accounting, ad hoc (self-designed), advertising and public relations, architecture and interior architecture/design, art (studio: ceramics, painting, sculpture; design: graphic design, illustration, photography), art education, art therapy, arts administration (art, music, theater), aviation management, biology, biotechnology, communication sciences and disorders (speech-language pathology), comprehensive social sciences (general, history, sociology), computer information and telecommunications systems, computer science (minor), criminal justice, dance/movement (minor), digital media and broadcast production (broadcast, corporate), early childhood special education, education (elementary, secondary), English, environmental science, family and consumer sciences education, financial planning, French, general science education, health and physical education (athletic training, education, physical activity), health services administration, history/political science, hospitality management, industrial/organizational psychology, international business, journalism, management, marketing, mathematics, medical technology/clinical laboratory science, multimedia (minor), music, music education, music therapy, nursing (preservice, post-RN), nutrition and dietetics (coordinated program, didactic program), performance, performing arts, philosophy, physician assistant studies, psychology, psychology/clinical practice, public administration, religious studies, retail business management, science, social sciences secondary education, social work, Spanish, special education/elementary education (dual certification), theater, and women's studies (minor).

Preprofessional programs are offered in chiropractic, communication sciences and disorders, dentistry, law, medicine, physician assistant studies, and veterinary medicine. A joint seven-year bachelor's/doctoral program in chiropractic involves three years of study on the Marywood campus and additional work at New York Chiropractic College, which is located in Seneca Falls, New York.

Marywood offers five-year bachelor's to master's degree programs in architecture, biotechnology, communication arts, criminal justice, financial information services, health services administration, physician assistant studies, and speech language pathology.

Academic Programs

Undergraduate degrees are offered in approximately sixty academic programs, including the arts, sciences, music, fine arts, social work, and nursing. All students are required to complete a core curriculum in the liberal arts in addition to the courses in their major. Opportunities for undergraduates abound through double majors, honors and independent-study programs, practicums, internships, and study abroad. Army and Air Force ROTC programs are available.

Off-Campus Programs

Study-abroad opportunities are available in countries such as Australia, Canada, England, France, Mexico, and Spain. Through Studio Art Centers International (SACI), art students may study in Florence, Italy.

Academic Facilities

In recent years, the University has made $100 million in improvements to the campus, including new athletic, residence hall, and dining facilities, and one of the finest studio arts facilities in the northeast. The Insalaco Center for Studio Arts features

60,000 square feet of fully equipped studios, labs, and classroom spaces for a broad variety of artistic disciplines. The O'Neill Center for Healthy Families gives students an opportunity to study and perform research in a first-rate human performance laboratory.

Costs

Tuition for full-time students (12–18 credits per semester) for the 2012–13 academic year is a flat fee of $28,080. There is also a general fee of $1050 for full-time students. Costs for room and board for a full academic year are approximately $12,920, depending on which meal plan is selected and the desired room occupancy. Costs of books and supplies are estimated at $1000.

Financial Aid

Marywood offers a comprehensive program of financial aid to assist students in meeting educational costs. Eligibility for federal and state programs is based on demonstrated financial need, as determined by a federal eligibility formula that analyzes family income and assets. In addition, approximately $28 million in institutional aid is awarded annually to Marywood students. Applicants to Marywood are considered for all financial assistance programs for which they qualify. Candidates are required to submit the Free Application for Federal Student Aid (FAFSA) and the Marywood application form, preferably by February 15.

Faculty

Among faculty members at Marywood, 168 are full-time, and 91 percent of these hold the Ph.D. or the highest degree in their field. The student-faculty ratio is 13:1. Faculty members are evaluated on their teaching and on their scholarly and artistic activities.

Student Government

All matriculated students in the undergraduate school are members of the Student Government Association (SGA). The SGA operates with a number of committees, including the Student Council, the Resident Committee, and the Commuter Committee. The association plays a key role in establishing a positive campus environment.

Admission Requirements

Candidates for admission should demonstrate reasonable progress toward graduation in an accredited secondary school, have graduated from a secondary school, or offer evidence of an equivalent secondary education. Each candidate should show satisfactory academic preparation in 16 units of subject matter, including 4 units of English, 3 units of social studies, 2 units of mathematics, 1 unit of science with laboratory, and 6 additional units. Either SAT or ACT scores are required for those who wish to enter as freshmen.

In addition to fulfilling general admission requirements, candidates for admission to a degree program in architecture, art, education, music, nursing, pre–physician assistant studies, and speech language pathology must meet special standards established by the department. Prior to enrollment, music, theater, and art candidates are required to audition or to present an art portfolio.

For certain programs, candidates without the recommended distribution of units may be eligible for admission if their course work as a whole and the results of their tests offer evidence of a strong foundation for college work. Candidates who are deficient in required course work may complete the appropriate work during the summer or the first year in college.

A student who demonstrates satisfactory academic performance at another college may apply for admission as a transfer student. Academic courses presented for transfer should be equivalents of courses required by the programs of study at Marywood. Students should have earned a grade of C or higher in their course work; C– will not transfer. A student should expect to earn a minimum of 60 credits at Marywood University; ordinarily, at least one half of the credits required for a major must also be earned at Marywood.

International candidates are required to meet the academic standards for admission, demonstrate proficiency in the use of the English language, and submit documentation of having sufficient funds to cover educational and living expenses for the duration of study. To certify proficiency in the use of English, international applicants whose primary language is not English must submit scores from the Test of English as a Foreign Language (TOEFL) or the IELTS.

Application and Information

Applications for admission are considered on a rolling basis; however, candidates are strongly encouraged to submit applications by March 1. Applications received after March 1 are considered on the basis of available space in particular programs. To be considered for admission, freshman applicants must submit to the Office of Admissions a completed application (paper or online), a nonrefundable $35 application fee (waived if applying online), an official high school transcript with an indication of class rank, an official report of scores from the SAT or ACT, and at least one letter of recommendation. Students can apply online at http://www.mymarywood.com/home/apply.html.

Transfer students must submit a completed application, a nonrefundable $35 application fee (waived if applying online), an official high school transcript, official academic transcript(s) reflecting all college course work for which the candidate has enrolled, and at least one letter of recommendation.

All submitted credentials become the property of Marywood and are not returnable to the applicant. Admission standards and policies are free of discrimination on grounds of race, color, national origin, sex, age, or disability.

For further information, interested students should contact:

Christian DiGregorio, Director
University Admissions
Marywood University
2300 Adams Avenue
Scranton, Pennsylvania 18509
Phone: 570-348-6234
         TO-MARYWOOD (866-279-9663, toll-free)
Fax: 570-961-4763
E-mail: yourfuture@marywood.edu
Web site: http://www.mymarywood.com
         http://www.facebook.com/marywoodu
         http://www.twitter.com/marywoodu
         http://www.youtube.com/marywoodu

The Center for Architectural Studies in Marywood University's School of Architecture.

MEMPHIS COLLEGE OF ART
MEMPHIS, TENNESSEE

The College

Memphis College of Art (MCA) is a professional center of art and design education dedicated to preparing individuals for lives of creating, problem solving, and critical thinking. MCA is a cultural wellspring of creativity that has been nurturing and educating artists of all levels since 1936. MCA offers state-of-the-art facilities, excellent faculty members, interdisciplinary programs, and cutting-edge exhibitions to the public and those students pursuing B.F.A., M.F.A., or M.A. in Art Education and M.A.T. in Art Education degrees.

Rust Hall, the College's main building, is located within the 340-acre Overton Park in midtown Memphis. The Gibson Hall administration building, at the park's southwestern edge, houses faculty and staff offices including admissions, financial aid, business office, career services, and student affairs. Graduate programs, studios, classrooms, and labs are located in the new Nesin Graduate School in downtown Memphis. Daily shuttle service provides easy access to all three locations and to MCA's student housing. Student housing options include Fogelman and Metz Halls which offer apartment-style living spaces with full kitchen, private bedrooms, laundry, and shared studio space. Other campus houses offer a variety of choices and costs to fit any lifestyle.

Memphis College of Art is a private institution accredited by the Commission on Colleges of the Southern Association of Colleges and Schools and the National Association of Schools of Art and Design.

Location

The Memphis metropolitan area is home to over 1.1 million residents, and offers a rich history of blues, literature, the Mississippi River, and the National Civil Rights Museum. In this culture-soaked city, MCA has existed for seventy-five years as a veritable artist's colony where access to a professionally geared education is available to those whose passions burn brightest.

Majors and Degrees

Memphis College of Art offers concentrations and majors that lead to the Bachelor of Fine Arts (B.F.A.) degree along with programs of study that lead to a Master of Fine Arts (M.F.A.) degree and art education programs toward a Master of Art in Teaching (M.A.T.) in Art Education and a Master of Art in Art Education (M.A.). Undergraduate areas of study are available in animation, digital cinema, digital media, drawing, graphic design, illustration, painting, photography, printmaking, sculpture, and sequential narrative.

Academic Programs

As a professional school of art and design, MCA offers degrees in visual arts at the undergraduate level. Within these degrees, students choose from an array of majors and concentrations that provide a variety of avenues to suit individual interests and needs. Embedded throughout the curriculum is the teaching of the knowledge and skills, and providing the experiential opportunities of professional practice, ensuring MCA students are prepared to make the transition to the working world.

At the heart of the curriculum is a vigorous Foundations and Core program of studio practice and intellectual rigor. With an emphasis on ideas, students cultivate critical thinking skills and essential perspectives on art and culture through MCA's Liberal Studies courses. The research, writing, and presentation skills necessary for a professional approach to art and design further the development of well-rounded artists.

Two 15-week semesters begin in August and January and three summer sessions are held from mid-May to July. A minimum of 120 credit hours are required to complete the bachelor's degree

Off-Campus Programs

Beginning with orientation, MCA offers many educational opportunities to support the academic endeavor. Internships; a consortium exchange program with four local colleges and forty-three national and international art colleges; yearly museum seminar trips to places such as Paris, Mexico City, or San Francisco; the Horn Island Summer Workshop; and the New York Studio Program are just some of the out-of-classroom experiences available to students.

Academic Facilities

The Memphis College of Art campus is unlike any other. MCA is nestled in a 340-acre virgin woodland park next door to the Brooks Museum of Art and the Memphis Zoo. The striking architecture of the main building, Rust Hall, offers a glimpse of the wonders created within. In addition to classrooms, studio space, and lecture halls, there are two galleries which host up to a dozen exhibitions a year and an extensive library of valuable resources; not to mention MCA's delicious—and affordable—café that serves up three hot meals a day to "starving" artists.

The G. Pillow Lewis Library has more than 17,000 volumes, 120 fine arts periodical subscriptions, and 200 periodical titles. Full-text databases are accessible through the Tennessee Electronic Library InfoTrac. MCA's Main Gallery hosts visiting artists and juried exhibitions throughout the year, while the Lower Gallery is designated for student work. MCA's 4,400-square-foot shop has equipment for woodworking, metalworking, plastic molding, mat cutting, glass cutting, and stretcher and frame construction. MCA has large metal and clay sculpture studios, as well as separate foundry and welding

areas for castings and metalwork. The clay studios have five wheels, a space for hand-building and glazing, a spray booth, and a semi-enclosed firing room with electric and gas kilns.

Printmaking, papermaking, and book arts studios provide easy interaction between these related media. Printmaking has two presses for stone and plate lithography, three etching presses, serigraphy equipment, and equipment for photo printmaking processes as well. Book arts includes three letterpresses and a bindery. The wet room is equipped with beaters, a 36-square-foot vacuum table, a hydraulic press, and a pulper.

There are four fully equipped digital labs with digital cameras, slide and transparency scanners, flatbed scanners, and high-resolution printers. A separate large-format printing lab provides for large-scale archival printing on a variety of media. Two sound and animation studios are available for animations and video work. Projectors, video cameras, and other equipment are available for loan to students through the digital media faculty.

Photo lab facilities include ten workstations equipped with Omega large-format enlargers and twelve workstations equipped with Beseler medium-format enlargers. A lighting studio houses strobe equipment, backgrounds, and medium- and large-format cameras. Digital SLR cameras, portable strobe- and hot-light sets, and backdrop stands are available for checkout. Also available are facilities for nonsilver alternative photo processes including digital negative printers and a large UV exposure unit.

Costs

Undergraduate tuition and fees are $26,250 for the 2012–13 school year. In addition to that, there are other student costs such as room and board, transportation, clothing, and books/art supplies. The following one-year budget estimates are based on higher-end resident housing and other miscellaneous costs. Some students may spend less than these estimates. Estimated total costs for attending MCA and living in campus housing or in an apartment for one year are $39,400 (based on the cost of Metz/Fogelman Halls and estimated living expenses). Estimated total costs for attending MCA and living at home for one year are $32,900.

Financial Aid

While many families may not be able to afford the full cost of attending MCA, the College does everything possible to help everyone who wants to pursue a degree. Ninety-five percent of students receive some type of financial assistance, with the vast majority (74 percent) using loan programs to help them reach their educational goals. MCA will help students apply for any federal, state, and institutional aid for which they may be eligible.

Faculty

MCA has 62 full- and part-time faculty members, selected for their studio experience, professional accomplishments, and teaching skills. MCA has a 10:1 student-faculty ratio and an average class size of 17.

Student Government

The Student Alliance (SA) at MCA is the formal representative of the student body. The SA works closely with the Office of Student Life through elected representatives. Students plan entertainment events, film series, and exhibitions in the student gallery space. Meetings of the elected representatives are held biweekly throughout the semester and these meetings are open to all students.

Admission Requirements

Application requirements include a completed application (available online at http://www.mca.edu/admissions), $25 application fee, high school or college transcripts, ACT or SAT scores (for freshmen applicants), and a portfolio of 10 to 20 pieces of artwork (submit digital images to portfolio@mca.edu). International applicants should submit a TOEFL or IELTS score in lieu of the ACT or SAT.

Application and Information

Applications are accepted on a rolling basis. Responses are sent approximately three weeks after the application process is completed. Students are considered for admission and institutional scholarships through the application process.

Additional information can be obtained by contacting:

Office of Admissions
Memphis College of Art
1930 Poplar Avenue
Memphis, Tennessee 38104
Phone: 901-272-5151
 800-727-1088 (toll-free)
E-mail: info@mca.edu
Web site: http://www.mca.edu
 http://www.mca.edu/aboutmcablogs
 http://twitter.com/memphisart

Memphis College of Art—a professional center of art and design education.

MENLO COLLEGE
ATHERTON, CALIFORNIA

The College

Menlo College, an independent, coeducational, nonsectarian institution, stands out among institutions of higher education in five exciting ways: programs, location, small size, sports, and alumni. Rather than offer a traditional set of majors as many institutions do, Menlo concentrates on providing excellent programs in business management with a strong foundation in the liberal arts. Menlo's location in the heart of the Silicon Valley allows the College to train tomorrow's leaders in an intimate, student-centered, academically challenging environment. The College is small enough to be a real community but large enough to support a wide array of intercollegiate sports, student organizations, and internship opportunities, giving students the confidence and breadth of experience to flourish after graduation. The College's distinguished alumni provide a strong base of support for graduates, which helps students make the transition from college to career with great success.

A Menlo education is a process that trains and cultivates leaders. This process begins with a broad-based liberal arts foundation in the humanities, mathematics, sciences, and social sciences. At the same time, students are also challenged to enrich and develop their writing, critical-thinking, and decision-making skills. Next, students enter rich major programs staffed with outstanding faculty who are experts in their respective fields. The advantage is a cutting-edge curriculum that equips students to succeed. Menlo's superior business program is renowned throughout the world and has produced generations of dynamic and successful business, industrial, and civic leaders around the globe.

The learning process does not end in the classroom. Students in the management program are required to complete 6 units of internship as part of their degree program. All students are encouraged to participate in internships and study programs that bridge the gap between theory and practice. These opportunities range from Fortune 500 companies to innovative start-up enterprises, from San Francisco to South America, Asia, and Europe. Not only do participants gain hands-on experience, but also they grow personally as they encounter diverse peoples, cultures, and values.

As a whole, College-sponsored activities promote self-exploration and often lead to the discovery of hidden talents. Students can participate in a variety of clubs or organizations, ranging from the Alpha Chi National Honor Society and the Poetry, Art, and Music Society to the Menlo Oak Newspaper and the Outdoor Club. Leadership skills are cultivated through an activist student government and student life positions and special workshops that tackle pressing contemporary issues. In addition, Menlo's international exchange programs offer students opportunities to expand their horizons and bring global awareness to their futures.

This commitment to personal and intellectual growth, coupled with Menlo's ideal location in the heart of the Silicon Valley, draws students from all across the United States and around the world. The global village is a reality at Menlo, given the broad social, religious, cultural, and national makeup of the student body. The appreciation of different cultures that results becomes a tremendous advantage in the marketplace.

Menlo's warm, friendly atmosphere is enhanced by its residential status. Nearly two thirds of all students live in one of five residence halls. Nearby off-campus apartments (for students who are older than 21 or married) are also an option.

For those who enjoy the exhilaration of intercollegiate competition, Menlo offers men's baseball, basketball, cross-country, football, golf, soccer, and wrestling, and women's sports include basketball, cross-country, soccer, softball, volleyball, and wrestling. In addition, Menlo offers cheerleading as a coeducational sport. The College competes in the NAIA Pacific Conference. Intramural sports are also popular, and altogether almost 45 percent of students participate in sports.

To meet students' health needs, the College provides care via the Menlo Medical Clinic. Counseling services are offered by faculty and resident life staff members.

Whether in the classroom, in the laboratory, or on the playing field, Menlo College nurtures students by creating programs, activities, and services that foster individual success.

Location

Menlo College is located on the San Francisco peninsula in the town of Atherton, a residential community near the cities of Menlo Park and Palo Alto. The area ranks among the most attractive and exciting in the world, with numerous cultural resources and a temperate climate. San Francisco lies 30 miles to the north. Many other important educational centers are within an hour's drive of Menlo, making the area an exciting place in which to study and live. The campus is in the heart of Silicon Valley, where high-tech companies in the electronics, computer, aerospace, biotechnology, and pharmaceutical industries are literally transforming the world in which we live and work. Surrounding the San Francisco Bay Area is the great natural beauty of northern California, extending from the spectacular California coast to the majestic Sierra Nevada Mountains. Favorite spots such as Big Sur, Monterey Bay, Lake Tahoe, Napa Valley, and Yosemite National Park are just a few hours' drive from Menlo.

Majors and Degrees

Menlo College offers the following fields of study: accounting, entrepreneurship, finance, human resource management, international management, management, management information systems, marketing, marketing communication, psychology, sports management, real estate, pre-law, and an individually designed major where students can combine existing programs to create their own major.

Academic Programs

Menlo College operates on a semester calendar. To earn a bachelor's degree, students must complete 124 units of credit and maintain good academic standing.

Menlo's renowned Academic Success Center provides dynamic resources for increasing students' academic ability and morale. Included are innovative approaches to counseling and tutoring. The goal is to develop strong self-advocacy and to assist faculty members in meeting the needs of a varied student population using an assortment of individualized, small-group, and

computer-based instruction. This method facilitates study and discussion of course material, tutoring, and test preparation.

Off-Campus Programs

The difference between obtaining an exciting professional position with opportunity for advancement and growth and settling for second best often comes down to experience. Internships enable students to apply theory to practice—to take classroom knowledge and test its relevancy. Students spend one or more semesters working on- or off-campus in their fields of study obtaining academic credit and/or financial compensation and valuable insight. Menlo also has exchange agreements with Francisco de Vitoria University in Madrid, Spain; Peking University, in Beijing, China; Anáhuac University, in Mexico City; Universidad Adolfo Ibanez in Chile; Guangdong College of Business in Guangzhou, China; and with Kansai Gaidai University in Japan.

Academic Facilities

Bowman Library maintains a strong collection of books and periodicals, including electronic journals, books, and AV materials. The Bowman Library's Electronic Information Gateway provides access to general and specialized online research databases, including full-text periodicals and reference resources as well as high-speed access to the Internet and World Wide Web. The Bowman Library contains rooms for group study, viewing AV materials, and photocopying. In addition, wireless access to the campus network resources is available through the library's laptop computer checkout program.

The Resource for Online Services and Information Electronically (ROSIE) is Menlo College's electronic information gateway, providing access 24 hours a day, seven days a week through the Web from the library, dorms, and off-campus sites to the online catalog, electronic research databases, and reference assistance. For more information, students should visit http://www.menlo.edu/library. ROSIE also provides access to WOODIE, the online research-skills tutorial required of all students through the Menlo College General Education curriculum.

Menlo College's four computer labs provide students with access to state-of-the-art PC and Macintosh hardware, software, and networking capabilities. All computer-lab equipment is connected to the campus network as well as the Internet and World Wide Web. Classroom labs include both individual workstations and presentation facilities. The Open Access lab is open daily and is staffed by experienced monitors who are familiar with all lab equipment and applications and are able to provide students with the best possible technical and instructional services. With a 5:1 student-computer ratio, Menlo College offers students ample access to a wide range of computing resources for both classroom assignments and personal use.

Costs

Tuition and fees for 2012–13 are $35,510. Residence costs, including room and board, are $11,444.

Financial Aid

Menlo is noted for a strong program of merit and need-based aid. Approximately 86 percent of Menlo's students enroll with financial assistance, including Menlo scholarships, achievement awards, and on-campus employment as well as Federal Pell Grants, Federal Stafford Student Loans, State of California Grants, Federal PLUS loans, and others. Students transferring to Menlo are fully eligible to be considered for financial aid. Merit scholarships of up to $13,000 per year are available for both domestic and international students.

Faculty

Menlo's faculty members devote their full attention to teaching. The College faculty is composed of approximately 60 members, both full- and part-time. Guest lecturers from business, industry, and other professions add to the breadth of instruction. Faculty members are readily available to give students personal help and counseling. A student-teacher ratio of 14:1 allows for small classes and individual attention to students' progress.

Student Government

Students elect their own representatives to student government, which is responsible for legislative and executive decisions affecting student activities and the coordination of student affairs. At Menlo, students take the lead in shaping their education and the future of their College.

Admission Requirements

The Admission Committee considers each candidate individually, through the assessment of academic achievement and personal qualities, talents, and interests. There is an early action plan for entering freshmen, and transfer students are welcome. Applicants are evaluated on the basis of their academic record, course of study, personal recommendations, school activities, essay, and scores on either the SAT or ACT. A personal visit is strongly recommended but not required. The College looks for freshmen with both breadth and depth of academic background in college preparatory subjects. Transfer students are evaluated on the strength of their college programs. Applicants are considered without regard to age, race, color, creed, gender, sexual orientation, national origin, marital status, disability, or any other characteristic protected by law.

Application and Information

Students may enter Menlo College at the opening of the fall or spring semester. Application deadlines are: early action deadline, December 1; priority deadline for freshmen, February 1 for fall and November 1 for spring; and priority deadline for transfers, April 1.

For further information concerning admission, students should contact:

Office of Admission
Menlo College
1000 El Camino Real
Atherton, California 94027-4301
Phone: 650-543-3753
      800-55-MENLO (toll-free)
Fax: 650-543-4496
E-mail: admissions@menlo.edu
Web site: http://www.menlo.edu

MERCYHURST UNIVERSITY
ERIE, PENNSYLVANIA

The University

An outstanding educational experience, strong sense of tradition, and beautiful and safe campus are just a few of the many reasons why students from across the country and around the world come to Mercyhurst University. Located in Erie, Pennsylvania, and founded by the Sisters of Mercy in 1926, Mercyhurst is a fully accredited, four-year comprehensive Catholic institution. The 75-acre Erie campus offers more than 100 undergraduate majors, minors, and concentrations, as well as unique adult programs and seven graduate programs. In addition, Mercyhurst offers one- and two-year degree programs at three additional locations: a residential campus in scenic North East, Pennsylvania, just 20 minutes from Erie; in neighboring Girard, Pennsylvania; and in Corry, Pennsylvania.

Nearly 4,000 students, from more than forty states and thirty-five countries, attend classes at one of the four locations, with about 2,800 at the Erie campus. In 2012, the institution was granted university status by the Pennsylvania Department of Education.

The University serves students with a wide range of academic interests, from anthropology and archaeology, biology, business, and forensic sciences, to hospitality management, intelligence studies, and sports medicine. The University's internationally-renowned programs in applied forensic sciences and intelligence studies provide students with outstanding hands-on learning unique to Mercyhurst. Graduate programs in applied intelligence, exercise science, organizational leadership, administration of justice, anthropology, special education, and secondary education offer outstanding opportunities for those seeking advanced degrees. Mercyhurst also offers teaching certifications, advanced certificates, and graduate certificates.

Mercyhurst has consistently been ranked highly by *U.S. News & World Report* as a top-tier master's-level university. Alumni of Mercyhurst are found in every major profession and in every state in the nation as well as several countries around the world. A Mercyhurst education combines hands-on education with a progressive liberal arts approach to career preparation. Once enrolled, students work closely with academic advisers and academic support and career services personnel to ensure they reach their individual aspirations and objectives.

Mercyhurst's sense of tradition and excellence is reflected in its beautiful Tudor-Gothic collegiate setting. More than fifty buildings surround stately Old Main, the University's epicenter since 1926. Facilities abound for academics, the arts, athletics, student services, student recreation, and student housing.

The University's athletic facilities include the Mercyhurst Athletic Center, the Student Recreation Center, the Mercyhurst Ice Center, Tullio Field, and several additional playing fields. The Athletic Center houses a gymnasium complex, rowing tanks, and a fully equipped athletic training facility. The Ice Center includes a rink, four locker rooms, and capacity for 1,500 spectators. The Recreation Center is the home of most Mercyhurst intramural programs and contains a large physical fitness area and two all-purpose floors for basketball, volleyball, and other indoor uses.

Mercyhurst fields twenty-four NCAA athletic teams, including Division I men's and women's ice hockey. Division II sports include men's and women's basketball, cross-country, golf, lacrosse, rowing, soccer, tennis, and water polo. Other Division II sports fielded are baseball, field hockey, football, softball, women's volleyball, and wrestling. In 2011, the men's lacrosse team won the national championship.

At Mercyhurst, learning extends beyond the classroom. With more than 100 clubs and organizations, service learning opportunities, study-abroad programs, and on-campus housing, Mercyhurst graduates leave with more than just a diploma—they leave with the skills to succeed in employment, graduate and professional schools, community service, and most importantly, life.

Location

The Mercyhurst campus is situated on a beautiful site overlooking Lake Erie. One block from the Erie city limits, the University enjoys the advantages of a suburban pastoral setting only minutes from downtown's bustling shopping and entertainment district. These areas are accessible to Mercyhurst students via the "e" (the city's public transportation system).

Erie is a short drive from Cleveland, Pittsburgh, and Buffalo, and the campus is located just 10 miles from the Erie International Airport.

Majors and Degrees

Mercyhurst University awards the Bachelor of Arts degree in accounting, anthropology/archaeology (archaeology), art education, art therapy, biochemistry, biology (ecosystem conservation, neuroscience, predental, premedical, prepharmacy, and pre–veterinary medicine), business competitive intelligence, business marketing, chemistry, communication, computer systems (computer information systems, management information systems, and Web information systems), criminal justice (corrections, juvenile justice, law enforcement, and prelaw), dance, early childhood education, early childhood/special education, economics, English (creative writing, prelaw, and writing), French, French education, geology (environmental geology/hydrogeology and geoarchaeology), graphic design, history (public history), hospitality management (event management, food and beverage management, and hotel management), human resource management, intelligence studies, integrated marketing, interior design, international business, management, mathematics, middle childhood education, music, music therapy, philosophy, political science (applied politics, environmental studies and politics, international relations, and prelaw), psychology (applied behavior analysis, neuroscience), public health, religious studies, sociology (criminology), social work, Spanish, Spanish education, sport business management, studio art, and world languages and cultures.

The Bachelor of Science is conferred in anthropology/archaeology (archaeology and bioarchaeology), applied forensic science (criminalistics/forensic biology, forensic anthropology, and forensic chemistry and toxicology), athletic training, biochemistry, biology, chemistry, exercise science, fashion merchandising, geology, and sports medicine (premedical, pre–occupational therapy, pre–physical therapy, and pre–physician assistant studies).

The Bachelor of Music is awarded in music and music education.

Academic Programs

Core requirements, which include a select, limited number of courses from the liberal arts disciplines, furnish students with a broad base of skills and knowledge. In addition to completing the core program, students must complete a major. Graduation requirements for the Bachelor of Arts, Bachelor of Science, and Bachelor of Music degrees range from 120 to 140 credits, depending upon the chosen major.

Mercyhurst University offers an honors program, cooperative education, contract majors, independent/tutorial study, and off-campus study, including study abroad. Students may earn

credit or advanced placement through challenge examinations, life experience, Advanced Placement tests (scores of 4 or 5 are accepted), and CLEP tests.

The University operates on a three-term calendar (fall, winter, and spring), with an academic year that generally runs from the last week in August through the third week of May.

Off-Campus Programs

Mercyhurst has an increasingly active study-abroad program that is open to all students, irrespective of the (academic) program. Students have studied all over the globe, including Australia, Europe, Central America, and Russia. Students may also choose to pursue internships abroad. Mercyhurst University offers students the opportunity to take Mercyhurst classes in Dungarvan, Ireland or Taos, New Mexico.

Academic Facilities

Some of the nation's best science facilities are housed in Mercyhurst's Zurn Hall. The University has one of the finest archaeology/anthropology programs in the country and is the home of the Mercyhurst Archaeological Institute (MAI). Its state-of-the-art facilities include an artifact processing and curation laboratory, a lithics laboratory, a faunal analysis laboratory, and the R. L. Andrews Center for Perishables Analysis—the only laboratory in North America fully dedicated to the analysis of basketry, textiles, cordage, netting, sandals, and related perishable material. A customized DNA lab, the Donald and Judith Alstadt Laboratory for Molecular and Cellular Research, features a lab, a prep room, and DNA clean room.

In the DNA lab, students learn to use a geospatial information system (GIS) to plot sites for archaeological digs, a task formerly accomplished using ropes and stakes. Mercyhurst also has a museum-quality collection of prehistoric casts and fossils, including a cast of a *T. rex* skull, a set of 7-foot shark jaws, casts of several other skulls of large reptiles from the Jurassic period, a 2-ton section of petrified wood from Indonesia, a fossilized elephant specimen from Java, a dinosaur egg nest, and a stalactite from China. The collection was donated by Michael and Barbara Sincak, who have spent nearly twenty years traveling the globe to acquire specimens for their business and personal collections.

The Mary D'Angelo Performing Arts Center is a gorgeous facility built in 1996. The center seats 825 and has a performance stage of 3,400 square feet. As such, it is the only facility in the Erie-Cleveland-Pittsburgh-Buffalo area capable of handling the technical requirements of the most elaborate productions, including ballet and opera. Especially renowned for its acoustics, it was designed as a showcase for the performing arts. It is conducive not only to the cultural aspirations of the University and the Erie community, but also as a venue for students and faculty members to perform in a magnificent professional setting.

In 2003, Mercyhurst unveiled a newly built bookstore and coffee bar. Textbooks, trade books, periodicals, and a sizeable inventory of sundries, school needs, and clothing occupy a good part of the space, but the Starbucks coffee bar and the wireless environment make this cybercafé a popular place to relax.

The Audrey Hirt Academic Center, which opened in 2002, contains an atrium; technology-rich classroom and lecture halls; faculty offices; the Walker Recital Hall; special facilities for the graphic arts and communications; the comfortable Honors Lounge; and studios and working areas for Mercyhurst's newspaper, yearbook, and radio and television organizations.

The new Center for Academic Engagement, home to the departments of intelligence studies and hospitality management, and the Centers of Applied Politics and Ethics and Society, is scheduled to open in fall 2012.

Costs

Tuition for the 2011–12 academic year totaled $25,860 In addition to tuition, various fees totaled $1797. Room and board totaled $9738. The total for room, board, tuition, and fees was roughly $37,395. Students should budget an additional $2000 for books, supplies, and personal expenses.

Financial Aid

Mercyhurst is dedicated to assisting students with the cost of their education. Financial aid awards are both need- and merit-based (http://scholarships.mercyhurst.edu). In addition to federal and state programs, Mercyhurst awards nearly $30 million in institutional scholarships, grants, and loans annually. More than 90 percent of Mercyhurst's students receive financial aid in the form of grants, scholarships, on-campus employment, and/or student loans to be repaid after leaving the University. The typical student's financial aid award consists of aid from one or more of these sources.

Financing higher education is a challenging task and an important part of making a good enrollment decision. Mercyhurst's experienced admission and financial aid counselors look forward to assisting families in making Mercyhurst University affordable.

Faculty

There are 136 full-time faculty members who teach all undergraduate programs at Mercyhurst. More than 60 percent of the faculty members hold a Ph.D. in their fields of study. The primary faculty function is teaching, but faculty members are also active in research, publishing, and service to their community. The faculty-student ratio is 1:14.

Student Government

A student government organization is designed to help meet the academic, cultural, and social needs of the student body and is financed by an activity fee. Student government comprises an executive committee, a study activities committee, representatives from each major and club on campus, and 7 University senators.

Admission Requirements

Admission to Mercyhurst University is offered on a selective basis. In selecting a student for admission, the University looks for evidence in an applicant's academic record, extracurricular activities, and performance on standardized tests that demonstrate the student's potential for success at Mercyhurst. The entrance policy is free of discrimination on the grounds of race, creed, color, sex, or national origin.

Application and Information

The University operates on a rolling admission cycle. Beginning in November, notification is given as soon as possible after all credentials reach the Admissions Office.

Students applying to Mercyhurst may apply online via the Common Application or the University's own online application. Applicants must also submit an official copy of all high school transcripts, official copies of SAT and/or ACT scores, and a letter of recommendation or academic recommendation form. Applicants should also complete any required audition or portfolio review required by individual majors.

While interviews are not required, students in their junior or senior year of high school are strongly encouraged to schedule a campus visit and an interview. Campus tours are available by appointment Monday through Friday at 9, 10, 11, 1, and 2. Saturday tours (on selected Saturday) are scheduled at 9:30 and noon.

For additional information about Mercyhurst University, students should contact:

Mercyhurst University Admissions
501 East 38th Street
Erie, Pennsylvania 16546-0001
Phone: 814-824-2202
      800-825-1926 (toll-free)
E-mail: admissions@mercyhurst.edu
Web site: http://admissions.mercyhurst.edu

MESSIAH COLLEGE
MECHANICSBURG, PENNSYLVANIA

The College

Sharpening intellect, deepening faith, and inspiring action—since 1909, this has been Messiah College's goal for its students. The College is an independent, nationally ranked, private Christian college with a broadly evangelical faith base that includes students and employees from a variety of denominations and Christian faith traditions. The College is ranked by *U.S. News and World Report* as the fifth-best regional college in the northeastern U.S.

Messiah College has a student body of 2,976, of whom 2,800 are undergraduates from thirty-four U.S. states and thirty-two countries. More than 8 percent of students are from underrepresented racial, ethnic, and cultural populations and 2.1 percent are international students. Messiah has a distinctive residential atmosphere and a strong sense of community; 88 percent of undergraduate students live on campus.

The 2011–12 academic year marks 50 years of intercollegiate athletics at Messiah College, which competes in twenty-two intercollegiate sports and maintains one of the most successful NCAA Division III athletics programs in the nation (see www.gomessiah.com). Messiah athletic teams have garnered thirteen national championships and regularly achieve national rankings and conference titles. Messiah athletes have been recognized as all-Americans and have been featured in *Sports Illustrated, USA Today*, and on national network television. Several coaches have received national coaching awards. In 2010, Chris Heisey ('08) debuted with the Cincinnati Reds, becoming the first Messiah alumnus to play for a major league team.

Messiah students participate in more than sixty student groups and organizations, including theater and music groups, and a new student media hub called The Pulse, which encompasses Messiah's student newspaper, radio station, and yearbook. The Pulse provides opportunities for students to practice newswriting, photography, broadcasting, digital graphics, advertising, marketing, and communication in a real-world setting. The College's Student Government Association (SGA) represents the student body and develops students' leadership skills.

Messiah weaves opportunities for spiritual growth throughout students' college experience including chapel and worship services, discipleship groups, ministry outreach teams, community service, mission trips, and a variety of other special programs (www.messiah.edu/ministries/SpiritualFormation). In April 2008, Messiah College was selected to host *The Compassion Forum*, an unprecedented, nationally televised conversation with presidential candidates speaking on the integration of faith and public policy. The forum was viewed by millions on CNN and the Church Communication Network.

The College has been widely recognized for its commitment to service-learning and community engagement, and is committed to seeking increased understanding of the Christian faith and applying that faith to specific academic disciplines and world problems. In 2011, Messiah was ranked by *Washington Monthly* magazine as sixth in the nation among baccalaureate colleges for its commitment to community and public service. Messiah has also earned a spot on the national President's Higher Education Community Service Honor Roll, with distinction for exemplary service to disadvantaged youth. The College's service-learning program has been nationally recognized by *U.S. News & World Report* as a "Program to Look For" and the College has earned the Carnegie Foundation for the Advancement of Teaching's prestigious Community Engagement Classification for curricular engagement and outreach and partnership. Opportunities for community engagement at Messiah include the College's Agapé Center for Service and Learning, Collaboratory for Strategic Partnerships and Applied Research, Harrisburg Institute, Philadelphia campus, Ernest L. Boyer Center, Center for Public Humanities, School of the Arts, and Oakes Museum of Natural History.

Messiah College offers both traditional residence halls and apartment-style residences on campus (www.messiah.edu/offices/residence_life/index.html). Staffed by trained, full-time professional residence directors, student assistant residence directors, and student resident assistants, these facilities provide an environment that fosters personal growth and responsibility as students experience living in an intentional Christian community. All residence halls offer carpeting, air conditioning, cable television, Internet, and laundry facilities. Messiah does not have any fraternities or sororities at either the national or the local level.

The College operates a number of campus safety services for students (www.messiah.edu/offices/safety), such as an after-hours safety escort service; seventeen 24-hour emergency telephones on campus; a 24-hour, unarmed, professional security patrol; a staff of 15 full-time professionals, 3 part-time professionals, and 3 dispatchers; as well as student safety escorts and support personnel. Safety officers are well-trained in the appropriate areas of campus safety, including emergency medical response, CPR, first aid, crisis intervention and patrol, crime prevention, sexual assault response, and human relations skills. All entrances to the residence halls are electronically operated. A crisis management and response team, emergency text-messaging system, and emergency evacuation plan are also in place on the campus.

Location

Messiah College, named a 2008 Green College by the National Association of Independent Colleges and Universities, is situated on 471 scenic wooded suburban acres, just 12 miles from Harrisburg, Pennsylvania's capital. The College is approximately 2 hours from the major urban centers of Philadelphia, Baltimore, and Washington, D.C. There are many recreational and outdoor activities in the immediate vicinity, including the Yellow Breeches Creek, which flows through the campus, the nearby Susquehanna River, and the Appalachian Trail. The College also operates a satellite campus in downtown Harrisburg and another in Philadelphia in conjunction with Temple University.

Majors and Degrees

Messiah College awards Bachelor of Arts and Bachelor of Science degrees in more than fifty-five academic majors (www.messiah.edu/academics/majors/index.html). It also offers six preprofessional programs (pre–allied health, pre-dental, pre-law, pre-medical, pre–physical therapy, and pre–veterinary medicine) and six graduate programs (www.messiah.edu/academics/graduate_studies). Teacher certification is also available in many disciplines. Specialized programs include extensive off-campus study, individualized majors, independent study, service learning, internships, allied programs with other institutions (including pharmacy and occupational therapy), and a flourishing honors program. New majors introduced in the fall 2011 semester include: Chinese studies, Chinese business, dance, digital media, and ethnic and area studies.

Academic Programs

The College operates on a two-semester academic calendar, with a January term between the fall and spring terms. During January term, students take one intensive, three-week course of study with transcultural travel programs among the innovative courses offered during this term. A three-week May term immediately follows the spring term and is exclusively for cross-cultural studies.

Messiah's Internship Center (www.messiah.edu/external_programs/internship/index.html) is nationally recognized for excellence in training students for today's workforce. Messiah's Internship Center has been instrumental in the consistently high post-graduation placement rate of graduates.

Off-Campus Programs

Messiah offers study-abroad opportunities in more than 40 countries and is consistently ranked by the national Institute of International Education among institutions sending students to study abroad.

Academic Facilities

Messiah's outstanding academic facilities include Murray Library, a research library with more than 300,000 volumes, including more than 70,000 e-books (www.messiah.edu/murraylibrary); the Jordan Science Center, a state-of-the-art science facility providing technically advanced science laboratories and equipment as well as housing the College's Oakes Museum of Natural History that includes a unique treasury of large mammal, insect, seashell, and bird egg collections; Frey Hall, primarily an engineering, mathematics, and business building with engineering and physics labs, but also home to a variety of art studios; Climenhaga Fine Arts Center, complete with a 400-seat performance auditorium, a recital hall, and an art gallery; and Boyer Hall, a state-of-the-art academic facility that opened in 2003. The Calvin and Janet High Center for Worship and Performing Arts is currently under construction with completion scheduled for 2013. This 92,000-square-foot facility is designed to provide dedicated space for theater and musical arts programming. It also will include an expanded performing arts venue with seating for 825 and a choir loft seating 140–160, to be used for concerts, public lectures, and chapels. Students of the arts will have an acoustically-sound space in which to practice and perform. The Center will augment an already strong campus worship experience and expose students, faculty, and the greater community to an array of performances by gifted artists.

Students have access to hundreds of computers in general computer labs conveniently located across campus, as well as computers in department labs. All student rooms on campus are set up for both wired and wireless access to the campus network. In addition, wireless connections to the campus network are available in all major campus buildings and all academic halls.

Athletic and recreational facilities include the 90,000-square-foot Sollenberger Sports Center with an indoor track, wrestling and gymnastics areas, a natatorium including an eight-lane pool with separate diving well, racquetball and basketball courts, and exercise and fitness equipment; and the Starry Athletic Complex with a lighted artificial turf field for field hockey and lacrosse, lighted soccer stadium, eight-lane all-weather track, ten tennis courts, baseball and softball fields, and practice field space.

Costs

Messiah College is ranked in the top ten in its region in *U.S. News & World Report's* listing of "Great Schools at a Great Price." For the 2011–12 academic year, tuition was $27,536, room and board averaged $8510, and average basic fees were $820 (www.messiah. edu/admissions/financial_aid/cost.html).

Financial Aid

In 2006, the College announced an initiative to raise an additional $20 million in financial aid in five years. Currently all first-year students receive financial aid. The average first-year student aid package for fall 2011 was $24,725 (www.messiah.edu/admissions/financial_aid/big_difference.html).

Faculty

Messiah College selects its educators for their Christian commitment as well as their proven teaching ability. They are outstanding scholars, authors, artists, and experts in their chosen fields . Every Messiah professor signs a statement of faith as an indication of his or her commitment to the mission of the College.

Messiah College's 177 full-time faculty members hold degrees from nationally and internationally recognized graduate schools including Oxford University, Massachusetts Institute of Technology, Harvard University, and the University of Pennsylvania. Eighty-one percent have earned the terminal degree in their field.

Messiah professors are often sought after by local, regional, and national journalists for their commentary and expertise. They are not only experts in their fields, but also accomplished scholars, who contribute research, scholarly writing, and artistic works that inform their academic disciplines and the national conversation on faith in the academy and broader culture.

All classes at Messiah College are taught by professors rather than teaching assistants. The student-to-faculty ratio at the College is 13:1.

Admission Requirements

Messiah seeks students with demonstrated academic promise who wish to share in the College's multidenominational, multicultural Christian community. Messiah encourages transfer, home-schooled, international, and minority students to apply. The College provides two methods for candidates to apply for admission: Standard Choice and Write Choice (www.messiah.edu/admissions/policies/).

Selective in its admission policy, the College considers academic achievement, extracurricular involvement, leadership skills, and Christian service. The average SAT composite score for first-year students in fall 2011 was 1156 and their average ACT score was 25. Within the past 12 years, Messiah has produced graduates who have distinguished themselves as Rhodes, Fulbright, Carnegie, Truman, and Udall scholars.

Application and Information

Messiah College operates on a rolling admission basis. The Admissions Office is open weekdays from 8 a.m. to 5 p.m. Appointments can be made for Monday through Friday, and on some selected Saturdays, by calling 800-233-4220; via e-mail at admiss@messiah.edu; online at www.messiah.edu/admissions/visit/visit_calendar.php; or via mobile app at www.messiah.edu/mobile/iMessiah/index.html. A two-week notice is suggested.

Office of Admissions
Messiah College
One College Avenue
Mechanicsburg, Pennsylvania 17055
Phone: 717-691-6000
    800-233-4220 (toll-free)
Fax: 717-691-2307
E-mail: admiss@messiah.edu
Web site: http://www.messiah.edu
    http://www.facebook.com/MessiahCollege
    http://twitter.com/messiahcollege

Messiah professors challenge and mentor students through the many perspectives of the academic world, while inviting them to engage those ideas with their Christian faith.

MIAMI INTERNATIONAL UNIVERSITY OF ART & DESIGN

A focused education from Miami International University of Art & Design can help students turn their creative energy into a powerful tool that can make a difference in the world. Students are part of a collaborative and supportive community, where experienced instructors provide the guidance and skills needed to pursue a career in the creative economy.

The school's programs in the areas of design, media arts, and fashion give students the opportunity to learn by using professional-grade technology and to build a portfolio of work to show potential employers after graduation.

Miami International University of Art & Design, including its branches The Art Institute of Tampa and The Art Institute of Jacksonville, is accredited by the Commission on Colleges of the Southern Association of Colleges and Schools to award associate, baccalaureate, and masters degrees. For questions about the accreditation of Miami International University of Art & Design and its branches, contact the Commission on Colleges at 1866 Southern Lane, Decatur, Georgia 30033-4097; phone: 404-679-4500.

Miami International University of Art & Design is licensed by the Commission for Independent Education, Florida Department of Education. Additional information regarding this institution may be obtained by contacting the Commission at 325 W. Gaines Street, Suite 1414, Tallahassee, Florida 32399-0400; phone: 888-224-6684 (toll-free). License No. 2581.

The interior design program leading to the Bachelor of Fine Arts at Miami International University of Art & Design (Miami Campus) is accredited by the Council for Interior Design Accreditation, 206 Grandville Avenue, Suite 350, Grand Rapids, Michigan 49503; www.accredit-id.org.

The Design & Media Management degree program at Miami International University of Art & Design will be offered at its branch campuses, The Art Institute of Tampa and The Art Institute of Jacksonville, with both real-time and recorded online learning sessions.

Location

Miami is a culturally rich region that celebrates events year-round, including the African-American Heritage Festival, Haitian Heritage Week, the Viva Mexico Celebration, the Israel Independence Celebration, and Asian Cultural Week. The city is home to professional sports teams, and residents enjoy the sandy beaches, international cuisine, local clubs, the historic Art Deco District, Coral Gables, and Key Biscayne. The Florida Keys, Disney World, and the Bahamas are all just a short trip away.

Programs of Study and Degrees

No matter which course of study a student may choose, the professionals at Miami International University of Art & Design will guide, support, and help each student as their talents evolve on their journey of personal and professional transformation. Students studying design learn to fine-tune their visual thinking and problem-solving skills as they create everything from logos to TV ads. Programs in the area of media arts focus on utilizing technology to deliver information and entertainment, while students studying fashion learn to design clothes for the runway or run a retail shop.

Bachelor's degree programs are available in the areas of advertising, audio production, computer animation, digital filmmaking video production, fashion design, fashion merchandising, film and digital production, graphic design, interior design, photography, visual arts, visual effects and motion graphics, and Web design and interactive media.

Associate degrees are available in the areas of accessory design, fashion design, and fashion merchandising.

Diploma programs are offered in the areas of digital image management, fashion retailing, Web design development I, and Web design development II.

Master's degree programs are offered in design and media management, film, graphic design, interior design, and visual arts.

Academic Programs

Miami International University of Art & Design operates on a year-round, quarterly basis. Each quarter totals eleven weeks. Bachelor's degree programs are twelve quarters in length.

Academic Facilities

Miami International University of Art & Design provides a learning environment with professional-grade technology applicable to each student's course of study. Students have the opportunity to build a portfolio of work that shows potential employers that they are trained to use the software, hardware, or equipment utilized within the industry. Depending upon the course of study, students are immersed in a creative environment—from classrooms to computer labs to studios—focused on relevant, hands-on education designed to prepare students for the real world.

Costs

Tuition cost varies by program. Prospective students should contact the school for current tuition costs. Other charges include a starting kit for all first-quarter students. Kits vary in price, depending on the program of study.

COLLEGE CLOSE-UPS

Financial Aid

Financial aid is available for those who qualify. Students who require financial assistance should first complete and submit a Free Application for Federal Student Aid (FAFSA) and meet with a financial aid officer.

Faculty

Faculty members are experienced professionals who create a learning environment that is similar to the professional world students will face after graduation. Instructors are focused on helping students develop the skills they need to transform their creative potential into marketable skills.

Admission Requirements

Applicants must provide proof of high school graduation or achievement of a General Educational Development (GED) certificate as a prerequisite for admission. In lieu of documenting high school graduation or a GED certificate, applicants may provide proof of attaining an associate degree or higher from an accredited institution. An official transcript indicating date of high school graduation, GED certificate (including test scores), or date of college graduation (including degree granted) is required as proof.

All individuals seeking admission to the school are interviewed in person or by phone by an assistant director of admissions, and each applicant must create an original essay of at least 150 words stating how an education at Miami International University of Art & Design would help the student to achieve career goals. There is a $50 application fee.

For the most recent information regarding admission requirements, please refer to the current academic catalog.

Application and Information

To obtain an application, arrange for an interview, or tour the school, prospective students should contact:

Miami International University of Art & Design
1501 Biscayne Boulevard, Suite 100
Miami, Florida 33132-1418
Phone: 305-428-5700
800-225-9023 (toll-free)
Fax: 305-374-5933
Web site: http://www.artinstitutes.edu/miami

COLLEGE CLOSE-UPS

MICHIGAN TECHNOLOGICAL UNIVERSITY

HOUGHTON, MICHIGAN

MichiganTech
Create the Future

The University

Michigan Technological University is a leading public research university developing new technologies and preparing students to create the future for a prosperous and sustainable world. Michigan Tech offers more than 130 undergraduate and graduate degree programs in engineering; forest resources; computing; technology; business; economics; natural, physical, and environmental sciences; arts; humanities; and social sciences. More than 7,000 students from all fifty states and more than sixty nations enjoy beautiful Upper Michigan. Michigan Tech is rated a Best in the Midwest by the Princeton Review. Student comments in the Princeton Review included: "Michigan Tech provides an atmosphere that nurtures learning" and "puts students first by providing hands-on experience." The students also commented on "great computer and athletic facilities" and "great career services."

In addition, *U.S. News & World Report* has ranked Michigan Tech in the top tier of national universities, and fifty-seventh among national public universities. It also ranked the following graduate programs highly: environmental engineering ranked twenty-eighth; materials science and engineering and mechanical engineering–engineering mechanics each ranked forty-eighth; civil engineering ranked forty-ninth; and the M.B.A. Online was named to the honor roll of online graduate programs.

Students work together on real-world industry projects as part of the Enterprise program, from virtual reality to forest management and from satellites to hybrid SUVs. Michigan Tech has one of the nation's largest programs in scientific and technical communication and is in the top 10 nationally in degrees awarded in environmental, mechanical, and mining/geological engineering.

New to campus is the Great Lakes Research Center, an innovative, ecofriendly waterfront structure uniting Michigan Tech's strengths in freshwater and Great Lakes research and scholarship in interdisciplinary collaborations.

More than 58 percent of students are enrolled in the College of Engineering. The College of Sciences and Arts (CSA) accounts for 24 percent; Graduate School, 18.5 percent; the School of Business and Economics, 6.5 percent; the School of Technology, 5 percent; and the School of Forest Resources and Environmental Science, 3.9 percent. Michigan Tech's graduate programs continue to grow in stature. While students gain access to the latest theories, equipment, and scholarship, they work closely with faculty members who are acknowledged leaders in their fields. Enrollment of international students is at an all-time high of 14.5 percent.

Michigan Tech is accredited by the North Central Association of Colleges and Schools. Engineering programs are accredited by the Engineering Accreditation Commission of the Accreditation Board for Engineering and Technology (ABET), Inc.; technology programs are accredited by the Technology Accreditation Commission of ABET; and the surveying program is accredited by the Related Accreditation Commission of ABET. The forestry program is accredited by the Society of American Foresters, the chemistry program offers American Chemical Society–approved options, and the secondary teacher certification programs are approved by the Michigan Board of Education. The School of Business and Economics is accredited by AACSB International–The Association to Advance Collegiate Schools of Business, the premier business accrediting organization in the U.S. Only about 400 U.S. business programs have earned this distinction.

Residence halls are close to classrooms and well connected. They feature ultrafast Ethernet lines, and wireless zones abound all across the campus. Residence halls also feature Finnish saunas, their own cable TV system, lounges, and weight-lifting and laundry facilities. First-year students must live in the residence halls, and they can choose from meal plans and numerous food options. Some cafeterias are open later, especially during exam weeks, and students can also eat, relax, and study at the Memorial Union, the center of campus life and home to many student organization offices,

the bookstore, billiards, and a bowling alley. Guides to off-campus housing are available.

In athletics, the hockey Huskies have been national champions three times and compete in the NCAA Division I Western Collegiate Hockey Association. Football, men's and women's basketball, tennis, cross-country, track, and women's soccer and volleyball teams compete in the Division II Great Lakes Intercollegiate Athletic Conference against teams from Michigan, Wisconsin, Ohio, Pennsylvania, Indiana, and Illinois. The men's basketball team has been rated number one in NCAA Division II, the women's basketball team was national runner-up in 2011, and the football team has hosted an NCAA Division II playoff game. Most Michigan Tech students compete in intramural sports, from Ultimate Frisbee to wrestling and from water polo to floor hockey. Club sports include lacrosse, women's hockey, and paintball. The biggest game on campus, however, is broomball, where students slide around on ice and hit a rubber ball with a broom. The Student Development Complex includes a health center, swimming and diving pools, gyms (one with a running track), a rifle range, an ice arena, and a weight room. A community health center and child-care center are nearby.

Traditions include K-Day, which is an afternoon to enjoy McLain State Park on the shores of Lake Superior, the world's largest freshwater lake. The Parade of Nations is a celebration (including food) of the sixty nations of the world that have students and faculty and staff members at Michigan Tech. At Homecoming, students dress in their worst attire and parade through the campus in autos that barely run. During homecoming weekend, students enjoy a football game, a mixer, and various special events, including a cardboard boat race. The biggest event is Winter Carnival, when massive snow statues emerge on campus and in the towns. Skits, queen competitions, first-class entertainment, ice hockey, and tourists everywhere make this a great experience. Before finals, students take a break on the campus mall for Spring Fling and celebrate with games, food booths, music, and more. The student-run newspaper, the *Lode*, has won national and state awards, and the campus radio station, WMTU, allows students to be disc jockeys.

Location

Michigan Tech is situated on the Keweenaw Waterway in the hills of Houghton in a safe, friendly environment. The area offers abundant opportunities for outdoor recreation, including the University's own ski hill; cross-country skiing, running, and biking trails; and golf course. A waterfront jogging and biking trail cuts through the campus. Houghton is located about 4 hours' drive from Green Bay, 7 hours from Minneapolis, and 10 hours from Detroit. The Houghton County Memorial Airport has daily flights to Chicago that connect to other major cities; bus service to Houghton is also available.

Majors and Degrees

The School of Technology awards Bachelor of Science degrees in computer network and system administration, construction management, electrical engineering technology, industrial technology, mechanical engineering technology, and surveying engineering.

The College of Engineering offers Bachelor of Science degrees in applied geophysics, biomedical engineering, chemical engineering, civil engineering, computer engineering, electrical engineering, engineering (mechanical design or manufacturing), environmental engineering, geological engineering, geology, materials science and engineering, and mechanical engineering.

The School of Business and Economics awards Bachelor of Science degrees in in accounting, finance, management, management information systems, marketing, and operations and systems management, and economics.

The School of Forest Resources and Environmental Science awards Bachelor of Science degrees in applied ecology and environmental sciences, forestry, and wildlife ecology and management.

The College of Sciences and Arts awards Bachelor of Science degrees in anthropology; applied physics; audio production and technology; biochemistry and molecular biology; bioinformatics; biology, cheminformatics; chemistry; clinical laboratory science; communication, culture, and media; cultural studies; computer science; computer systems science; English; exercise science; mathematics; pharmaceutical chemistry; physics; preprofessional programs (medicine, dentistry, pharmacy, and law); psychology; scientific and technical communication; social sciences; software engineering; sports and fitness management; and theater and entertainment technology. The CSA awards the Bachelor of Arts degree in communication, culture, and media; liberal arts; physics; scientific and technical communication; sound design; theater and electronic media performance; and theater and entertainment technology. The College of Sciences and Arts also awards a two-year associate degree in humanities.

The secondary education program offers certification in biology, business education, chemistry, computer science, earth science, economics, English, mathematics, physics, social studies, and technology and design.

Michigan Tech offers certificate programs in actuarial science, advanced electric power engineering, advanced modern language (French, German, Spanish), coaching endorsement, electric power engineering, geographic information systems, global technological leadership, hybrid electric-drive vehicle engineering, industrial forestry, international sustainable development engineering, media, mine environmental engineering, modern language, nanotechnology, sustainability, sustainable water resources systems, teaching of English to speakers of other languages, and writing. An advanced certificate in modern language and area study and a graduate certificate in sustainability are also offered.

Academic Program

Michigan Tech operates on a fifteen-week fall and spring semester system, and there are three options available for summer: two 7-week tracks and one 14-week track. Typically, it takes 130 credits to graduate, but the amount varies by department. Students must also complete the general education requirements, which seek to develop in each student fundamental scholastic habits of careful reading, communication, critical reasoning, and balanced analysis and argument; the habit of applying multiple disciplinary perspectives in interpretation, analysis, and creative problem solving; respect for diversity and awareness of complex contexts of their study and their work; and knowledge of a broad range of topics and disciplines complementary to the major. Some graduate courses are open to undergraduates with faculty approval. The International Programs and Services Office helps international students adjust to life in Houghton. More than 1,000 students come from approximately sixty other nations to study at Michigan Tech. Students may also study abroad in one of thirty nations, improving their global perspective.

Off-Campus Programs

The Career Center works with more than 200 industries, businesses, and organizations to help students find cooperative, internship, and summer employment opportunities. Job fairs are held on campus and elsewhere in the region. Co-op assignments earn academic credits; internships do not. Michigan Tech students average five job interviews before they graduate.

Academic Facilities

The J. R. Van Pelt and John and Ruanne Opie Library contains more than 800,000 volumes and regularly receives approximately 10,000 serials and periodicals. The archives maintain a collection of original materials concerning the history of the Keweenaw region, including the records of various copper-mining companies. The Rozsa Center for the Performing Arts is within walking distance of all residence halls and features nationally known lecturers, musicians, comedians, and theatrical performers as well as Michigan Tech's own productions. The A. E. Seaman Mineral Museum, the official "Mineralogical Museum of Michigan," has moved to a beautiful new building and is the home of one of the nation's premier collections of crystals, minerals, and ores. The collection contains more than 30,000 specimens, including the world's finest display from Michigan's copper- and iron-mining districts.

Costs

Annual tuition is $12,615 for Michigan residents and $25,710 for out-of-state students; room and board is $8648. Required fees and computer fees total approximately $700, and books and supplies total approximately $1200.

Financial Aid

Currently, 89 percent of Michigan Tech's students receive financial aid, totaling nearly $97 million annually. Four kinds of assistance are available to Michigan Tech students, including scholarships, which are awarded on the basis of student potential and, in some cases, financial need; grants, which are provided by the federal or state government or by Michigan Tech and do not need to be repaid; student loans, in which the interest charged is below regular interest rates (payment of the interest and principal on need-based loans does not begin until after students leave Michigan Tech); and part-time employment, which consists of on-campus student employment opportunities. The financial aid process begins with filing an application for admission. Students should apply for admission by January 15 of the year in which they plan to enroll.

Faculty

Most of the 485 faculty members possess terminal degrees. Ninety-five percent of undergraduate classes are taught by faculty members; the student-faculty ratio is 12:1. Faculty members balance teaching and research and are known for their student guidance.

Student Government

Undergraduate Student Government and the Graduate Student Council are the two agencies of student involvement in University governance. Fraternities and sororities maintain a strong presence on campus, and there are more than 180 student organizations, including academic/professional, ethnic/cultural, service, religious, sporting, governmental, media, and honor societies.

Admission Requirements

Michigan Tech has a selective admissions policy. The University admits only those applicants who give definite evidence that they are qualified through education, academic capability, aptitudes, interests, and character to complete the University's requirements. Once students are accepted for admission, every effort is made by the faculty and staff members to help students realize their potential.

Application and Information

Applications received by January 15 are given priority consideration for admission and merit-based scholarships. Undergraduate and graduate applications are free. First-year applicants are required to submit official ACT or SAT test scores. A high school counselor information page must also be completed by a high school counselor or principal and sent to the admissions office with an official high school transcript. Transfer students must have official college transcripts sent directly to Michigan Tech. An official high school transcript and ACT/SAT scores may also be required. International students should contact the International Programs and Services office. Following acceptance by Michigan Tech, students receive a packet containing information regarding on-campus housing and various University deadlines.

Admissions Office
Michigan Technological University
1400 Townsend Drive
Houghton, Michigan 49931-1295
Phone: 888-688-1885 (toll-free)
Web site: http://admissions.mtu.edu

Overlooking the campus of Michigan Tech.

MIDAMERICA NAZARENE UNIVERSITY
OLATHE, KANSAS

The University

MidAmerica Nazarene University (MNU) is a comprehensive liberal arts university of approximately 1,350 undergraduate students and 500 graduate students. A faith-based university, MNU welcomes students of all religious backgrounds; approximately 40% of the student population is Nazarene.

MNU educates students for a life of purpose. With service-learning woven into course work and University-sponsored opportunities to minister in the local community, students prepare not only for a career, but to make the world a better place. The University's most popular areas of study include business, accounting, nursing, teacher education, forensic chemistry and biology, criminal justice, music, ministry, and multimedia. More information on MNU's academic programs is available online at http://www.mnu.edu/academic.

The average ACT score of incoming freshmen is 22.1; the average GPA is 3.32. Students hail from thirty-six states, five countries, and forty-plus denominations. The student to faculty ratio is 18:1.

MidAmerica Nazarene University offers NAIA Division I baseball, men's and women's basketball, cheerleading, football, men's and women's soccer, softball, and volleyball. Detailed information about MNU's athletic programs can be found at http://www.mnusports.com.

Each residence hall has a lobby or shared lobby where students can meet to study, watch television, or just hang out with friends. Each room is equipped for phone, satellite television, and Internet service. Several of MNU's residence halls offer suite-style living options for up to six students

Location

MidAmerica Nazarene University is located in Olathe, Kansas, a residential community of approximately 125,000 just 20 minutes from the heart of Kansas City, with all the cultural advantages of a major metropolitan area. Olathe offers a lifestyle of exceptional quality. The city's school district and health care system are routinely recognized among the best in the nation. Outdoor recreation offers a variety of activities, including running, jogging, bicycling, fishing, boating, team sports, and just relaxing. Olathe has two public lakes—Olathe Lake, with 172 acres of water surface, and Cedar Lake, with 45 acres. The proximity to downtown Kansas City provides internship opportunities in the areas of business, technology, the arts, creative services, and health care.

Majors and Degrees

Students can earn an Associate of Arts (A.A.) degree in general business, liberal arts, or music ministry.

The Bachelor of Arts (B.A.) degree is available in accounting, athletic training, the Bible and theology, biology, biology education, business administration, business education, business psychology, chemistry, corporate communication, criminal justice, elementary education, English, English language arts education, forensic biology, forensic chemistry, graphic design, history, history and government education, intercultural studies, kinesiology, marketing, mathematics, mathematics education, ministry, multimedia, music, organizational leadership, physical education, psychology, sociology, sports management, and youth and family ministry.

MNU also offers the Bachelor of Music Education (B.M.Ed.) degree and the Bachelor of Science in Nursing (B.S.N.) degree.

Academic Programs

MNU students receive direction from advisers in choosing a major, discovering their interests, finding a mentor, and preparation for interviews.

At MNU, hands-on learning and real-world experience are core components of each student's education. For example, criminal justice majors learn in the University's own forensics lab, then intern for local police departments or laboratories. Communications students build public relations skills by helping nonprofit organizations, and nursing majors train on the latest medical technology including state-of-the-art patient simulators.

Off-Campus Programs

MNU Europe is the University's international program. Students travel to, live, and study in Busingen, Germany, a quaint European village with a small college campus. Courses may last a few weeks to an entire semester. Courses are taught by MNU professors and adjuncts in a variety of subjects fulfilling both general education and elective requirements.

As a member of the Council for Christian Colleges and Universities (CCCU), a national association of more than 100 Christian colleges and universities, MNU makes a number of off-campus learning opportunities available. Domestic programs are available in Washington, D.C.; Los Angeles; and Martha's Vineyard, Massachusetts. Students have also studied abroad in China, Costa Rica, Egypt, Germany, Russia, and the United Kingdom through this cooperative program.

Academic Facilities

The 40,000-square-foot Bell Cultural Events Center features state-of-the-art practice, recital, and performance facilities for the fine arts division, as well as a black-box theater and 500-seat performance hall for music and drama productions. Osborne Hall houses the Department of Science and Mathematics, while Lunn Hall houses administrative offices. Dobson Hall

contains an art studio and a graphic-design computer lab. The largest facility on campus, the 70,000-square-foot Cook Center, houses Bell Family Arena, two practice gyms, and the Athletic Training and Athletics department offices. It is also home to MNU's School of Nursing and Health Science. Metz Hall houses the Department of Behavioral Sciences, School of Business Administration, and School of Education and Counseling. One of several on-campus computer labs is also located in this facility.

A virtual tour of the MNU campus is available online at http://www.mnu.edu/campus-virtual-tour.html.

Costs

While fees vary according to course load, costs for a full-time student total around $28,500, which includes tuition ($20,500), mandatory fees ($1000), and room and board ($7000). Part-time tuition and fees vary according to course load.

Financial Aid

The perception that a private university isn't affordable is false—the truth is, any higher education requires a significant investment. But about 92 percent of students at MNU receive some form of financial aid. MNU scholarships are available and range between $1000 and full tuition per year. For all full-time undergraduates who enrolled in 2009–10, the average financial aid package—including grants, loans, and scholarships—totaled $19,539. Information and applications may be obtained from Student Financial Services at 913-971-3298 or https://www.mnu.edu/financial-aid-scholarships.html.

Faculty

MNU students receive personal attention from their instructors. It is not uncommon to find faculty members in residence hall rooms talking with students or even inviting students into their homes for dinner. MNU faculty members have decades of real-world experience in many industries and fields.

Student Government

Associated Student Government (ASG) exists to discover God's agenda as students serve God and the campus community. ASG offers plenty of opportunities for students to get involved through many different campus activities and service-learning opportunities.

Admission Requirements

Prospective students should have graduated from an accredited high school and have completed the ACT or SAT exam. While the University does not require specific subjects for entrance, it does recommend that students complete 3 units of math, 4 units of English, 3 units of science, 3 units of social studies, and 1 unit of foreign language. Students over 18 who have not graduated from high school can submit GED scores.

Application and Information

Students must submit the completed application, the $25 nonrefundable application fee, official high school transcripts, ACT or SAT scores, a personal reference, and the housing, parent waiver, and health history forms provided by Admissions. International students must also submit TOEFL scores. The deadline for the fall semester is August 1; the spring semester deadline is December 15. For more information on how to apply to MNU, prospective students should visit www.mnu.edu/incoming-freshmen.html or contact:

MNU Admissions Team
MidAmerica Nazarene University
2030 East College Way
Olathe, Kansas 66062-1899
United States
Phone: 913-971-3380
        800-800-8887 (toll-free)
E-mail: admissions@mnu.edu
Web site: www.mnu.edu
        www.facebook.com/MNUPioneers
        twitter.com/MNU_Admissions
        www.vimeo.com/choosemnu

With majors in over 40 areas of study, MNU's academic programs prepare you for your future.

MILLERSVILLE UNIVERSITY OF PENNSYLVANIA

MILLERSVILLE, PENNSYLVANIA

The University

Millersville University is the highest ranked public university in its class in Pennsylvania according to the *U.S. News & World Report*. Millersville University offers a wide range of programs and a commitment to high-quality undergraduate instruction. Millersville's student body of approximately 8,700, including 7,600 undergraduates, is large enough for the University to offer a wide variety of programs. The University is small enough, however, to provide friendly service and individual attention. Students report that the relaxed, friendly campus atmosphere is one of the things they like best. The Millersville campus features a beautiful green and flowered landscape, a lake with resident swans, and clean, well-maintained facilities.

Millersville University was established more than 150 years ago, in 1855, as a normal school, the first one in Pennsylvania. It remained a teachers' college until 1962, when it was authorized to offer liberal arts degrees. It has been Millersville University of Pennsylvania since 1983.

The two reasons students most frequently cite for choosing Millersville are its excellent academic reputation and affordable tuition. The most popular majors are education, business administration, psychology, English, speech communications, and social work. Millersville's undergraduates are diverse; 1 in 9 students attends part-time, 17 percent are members of a racial/ethnic minority group, and 10 percent are more than 25 years old. Thirty-three percent of Millersville undergraduates are from Lancaster County, 63 percent from elsewhere in Pennsylvania, 4 percent from out of state, and 2 percent from other countries.

The University offers a wide range of intercollegiate varsity, intramural, and club sports; special interest clubs; fraternities and sororities; musical organizations; and publications. A broad program of cultural events is offered.

Thirty-one percent of undergraduates live in campus residence halls, with the rest commuting from home or living nearby. Coed dormitories and apartments are available for students. Freshmen and sophomores not commuting from home are required to live on campus. The possession, use, or sale of alcoholic beverages and illegal drugs is prohibited on the University campus. Smoking is prohibited in all academic and residential buildings on campus. Freshmen and sophomores living on campus are not permitted to have motor vehicles.

Special services provided for students include free tutoring, academic advisement, career planning and placement, personal counseling, health services, wellness activities, and special facilities for commuters.

Location

Millersville, in the heart of Pennsylvania Dutch country, is 3 miles from Lancaster city, a growing metropolitan area. Lancaster County is an exceptionally friendly and beautiful area with a large number of stores, restaurants, theaters, parks, and tourist attractions. The campus is served by the area bus system, and Lancaster has train and air service.

Lancaster County is one of the fastest-growing counties in Pennsylvania and has one of the lowest unemployment rates in the state. The local economy is unusually sound and diverse. Sixty percent of Millersville graduates settle within the county.

Majors and Degrees

Millersville offers the Bachelor of Arts degree in anthropology, art, biology, chemistry, earth sciences, economics, English, environmental geology, French, geography, German, government and political affairs, history, international studies, mathematics, music, philosophy, physics, psychology, social work, sociology, and Spanish.

The Bachelor of Science degree is offered in allied health technology, applied engineering, safety and technology; biology; business administration; chemistry; communications and theater; computer science; geology; mathematics; meteorology; occupational safety and environmental health; ocean sciences and coastal sciences; and physics.

The Bachelor of Science in Education degree with teaching certification is offered in art education, biology, chemistry, earth sciences, Pre-K–4 education, English, French, German, mathematics, middle level education, music education, physics, social studies, Spanish, special education, and technology education.

The University also offers the Bachelor of Fine Arts degree in art, the Bachelor of Science in Nursing degree for RNs only, the Associate of Science degree in chemistry, and the Associate of Technology degree in applied engineering, safety and technology.

Most majors offer several options that permit specialization, including accounting, finance, international business, management, and marketing in business. Students should refer to the Web site for a complete listing. More than sixty-five minors are offered along with 3-2 engineering programs for chemistry majors. Special advisement is available for students interested in premedicine and prelaw.

Academic Programs

Millersville University places a strong emphasis on the liberal arts. Nearly half of the courses required for all its undergraduate degrees, including those with technical or professional majors, are in the liberal arts. This prepares students for a lifetime of learning and gives them a background in writing, speaking, analysis, and critical thinking across a broad range of subjects.

Millersville's baccalaureate degree programs have four common curricular elements: proficiency requirements in English composition and speech; the general education program, which constitutes about half the curriculum; the major field of study; and elective courses, if needed, to meet the minimum of 120 credits required for graduation. Within this framework, students have many choices in developing programs of study.

The general education program has requirements in writing, speaking, humanities, natural sciences and mathematics, social sciences, and interdisciplinary and/or multicultural study. There is also a health and physical education requirement.

Millersville offers a University Honors College, departmental honors programs, independent study, a pass/fail option, remedial courses, and special advisement to students who are undecided about a major.

The University operates on a 4-1-4 academic calendar with summer sessions.

Off-Campus Programs

An exchange agreement with Franklin & Marshall College allows Millersville students to take Franklin & Marshall courses not offered at Millersville. Cooperative education internships are available to students in most majors, and some majors offer or require specialized internships. Millersville has study-abroad programs in Australia, Chile, China, England,

France, Germany, Ireland, Japan, Peru, Scotland, South Africa, and Spain. Qualified students who wish to study abroad elsewhere may do so through the University's cooperative arrangements with other colleges and universities.

Academic Facilities

Ganser Library houses more than 360,000 books and more than 138,000 other items and subscribes to more than 9,800 periodicals. Materials from other libraries are available through interlibrary loan. The library also houses computerized database-searching facilities, a curriculum center, a listening room, and archives.

The University's computing facilities support both PC and Macintosh platforms. There are over 400 terminals and computers available in multiple computer labs across campus. On-campus access to the Internet is available for all faculty members and students. Wireless access is available in all buildings, residence halls, classrooms, and offices.

Other University facilities include an extensive scientific instrumentation inventory, industry and technology laboratories, a variety of art studios and galleries, two visual and performing arts centers, three gymnasiums, two swimming pools, radio and television production facilities, soundproof music practice modules, and a language laboratory.

Costs

Annual tuition and fees in 2011–12 were $8361 for Pennsylvania residents and $17,899 for out-of-state students. Annual room and board charges for 2011–12 were $8732.

Financial Aid

Approximately 82 percent of Millersville undergraduates receive financial aid through grants, scholarships, employment, and loans. Scholarships are available on the basis of academic performance. Federal Pell and Federal Supplemental Educational Opportunity grants and Pennsylvania Higher Education Assistance Agency (PHEAA) grants are awarded on the basis of need. Students may also qualify for Federal Perkins Loans and Federal Stafford Student Loans. On-campus and off-campus job opportunities are plentiful.

Students applying for a federal or state grant, Federal Work-Study, or a Federal Perkins Loan must complete the Free Application for Federal Student Aid. The forms are available from high school guidance offices, from the Financial Aid Office, or online at http://www.fafsa.ed.gov. Deadlines are given in the forms' instructions.

Faculty

Millersville University faculty members are dedicated to teaching and to offering individual attention. They take a personal interest in their students' lives and careers and are solely responsible for providing academic advisement. The University keeps a relatively low student-faculty ratio of 22:1 and an average class size of approximately 25. No classes are taught by graduate assistants. Ninety-seven percent of the 279 full-time faculty members hold a doctorate or the terminal degree in their field.

Student Government

Millersville University students participate in University governance through the Student Senate, faculty-student committees, and representation on the Faculty Senate, the Council of Trustees, and the Millersville Borough Council. The Student Senate works with faculty members and the administration on major University policies.

Admission Requirements

Millersville University admits approximately half its applicants. More than 80 percent of its full-time freshmen rank in the top 40 percent of their high school class. Academic records are the most important factor in admission decisions. Applicants must have successfully completed at least 4 years of high school English, 3 years of social studies, 3 years of mathematics, and 3 years of science (1 unit must be a lab). In addition, 2 years of foreign language is strongly recommended.

Because an important part of the college experience is meeting people with backgrounds and interests different from one's own, Millersville University is committed to recruiting a diversified student body. SAT or ACT scores are required. Interviews, recommendations, and essays are not required. Out-of-state, international, and transfer applicants are welcome. Exceptional high school students may apply for early admission at the end of their junior year. Admitted applicants may request to defer their admission for one semester. Advanced standing is offered through CLEP and AP examinations.

Application and Information

To apply, students should submit a completed application along with a $50 processing fee and official copies of the high school record and SAT or ACT scores. The online application fee is $35. The University has a rolling admission policy, and students are encouraged to apply early (by mid-November) in their senior year for fall admission. Applicants are usually notified of a decision within a month after a completed application is received.

For application forms and additional information, students should contact:

Office of Admissions
Millersville University of Pennsylvania
P.O. Box 1002
Millersville, Pennsylvania 17551-0302
Phone: 717-872-3371
      800-MU-ADMIT (toll-free)
E-mail: admissions@millersville.edu
Web site: http://www.millersville.edu
      http://www.facebook.com/millersville.university
      http://twitter.com/#!/millersvilleu
      http://www.youtube.com/millersvilleu

The Millersville University of Pennsylvania campus.

MILLIGAN COLLEGE
MILLIGAN COLLEGE, TENNESSEE

The College

Milligan College is a four-year private Christian liberal arts college in northeast Tennessee. From its beginning in 1866, Milligan College has integrated academic excellence with a Christian worldview, and its mission is to educate men and women as Christian servant-leaders. A comprehensive humanities program and a core curriculum are complemented by specialized training in thirty majors and several master's degrees. Christian perspectives are integrated throughout the curriculum and student life activities as students are prepared intellectually and spiritually to change lives and shape culture.

Milligan's student body of 1,200 comes from more than thirty states and fourteen nations. Eighty percent of traditional students live on the campus in one of six residence halls. More than forty clubs and organizations provide opportunities to develop leadership skills. A wide variety of activities and campus events encourage social, cultural, and spiritual growth. Milligan College is affiliated with the Christian Churches/Churches of Christ, but the interdenominational student body is diverse.

All campus facilities are networked and most have wireless access. Every residence hall room and apartment features a high-speed data connection to the campus network and the Internet as well as telephone service, voice mail, and cable TV.

Milligan is well recognized as an NAIA athletic powerhouse with a highly competitive athletic program in twenty-three varsity sports. In the past ten years, Milligan has won more than fifty conference titles and made fifty-eight national tournament appearances. Men's varsity teams include baseball, basketball, cross-country, cycling, golf, soccer, swimming, tennis, and indoor and outdoor track and field. Women's varsity teams include basketball, cheerleading, cross-country, cycling, dance, golf, soccer, softball, swimming, tennis, indoor and outdoor track and field, and volleyball.

Milligan is accredited by the Commission on Colleges of the Southern Association of Colleges and Schools to award bachelor's and master's degrees. Questions about the accreditation of Milligan College can be directed to the Commission on Colleges, 1866 Southern Lane, Decatur, Georgia 30033-4097; phone: 404-679-4500.

In addition to thirty undergraduate majors, Milligan offers a Master of Science in Counseling degree, a Master of Education degree, a Master of Science in Occupational Therapy degree, and a Master of Business Administration degree. Milligan continues to be named among Southern colleges and universities in *U.S. News & World Report's* America's Best Colleges issue. More than 90 percent of its graduates are employed full-time, attending graduate school, or in voluntary service within six months after graduation, and more than 75 percent of premed students who take the MCAT are accepted to medical school

Location

Milligan's picturesque 195-acre campus, which comprises more than twenty buildings of Colonial architecture, is located in the beautiful mountains of northeast Tennessee, just minutes from Johnson City and the dynamic Tri-Cities region. Students enjoy historical locations, theaters, parks, restaurants, and shops; explore the breathtaking Appalachian Mountains by hiking or camping in state parks near the campus; visit local lakes and rivers for outdoor recreation; or ski the nearby North Carolina slopes. Because Milligan believes leadership is about service, students are encouraged to be active in the local community. Many are employed in internships or part-time work in area businesses.

Majors and Degrees

The Bachelor of Science, Bachelor of Arts, and Bachelor of Science in Nursing degrees are offered. Undergraduate majors include accounting, allied health science, applied finance and accounting, Bible (children's ministry, general studies, missions, pastoral ministry, youth ministry), biology, business administration (accounting, economics, general, health care administration, international business, legal studies, management, marketing, sports management), chemistry, child and youth development, child life, communications (digital media studies, film studies, interpersonal and public communication, multimedia journalism, public relations), computer information systems, education (professional teacher licensure), English, fine arts (art, film studies, music, photography, theater arts), history, human performance and exercise science (exercise science, fitness and wellness, physical education, sports management), humanities, interdisciplinary honors, language arts, mathematics, music (performance, jazz studies), music education (licensure in vocal, instrumental), nursing, psychology (general, preprofessional), public leadership and service, sociology, and worship leadership.

Professional teacher licensure areas include early childhood, elementary education, K–12, middle grades, secondary, and special education. Preprofessional programs are available in dentistry, law, medicine, occupational therapy, optometry, pharmacy, and physical therapy. An accelerated program for adults is available in business administration and early childhood education.

Academic Programs

Milligan College offers students a liberal arts education taught from a perspective of God's activity with humanity. The College's strong core curriculum educates students toward the world in an open and constructive way. The candidate for the bachelor's degree must have completed a major and electives to total a minimum of 128 semester hours of credit, with at least a 2.0 GPA. Core curriculum requirements include courses in humanities, the Bible, social sciences, ethnic studies, laboratory science, speech communication, mathematics, and health/fitness.

Realizing that not all college-level learning occurs in a college classroom, prior learning assessment programs provide a method by which other modes of learning can be evaluated for college credit. The Advanced Placement (AP) program, the College-Level Examination Program (CLEP), Defense Activity for Non-Traditional Educational Support (DANTES) programs, and the International Baccalaureate (I.B.) program are available to all students interested in receiving college credit for studies or work experience already completed.

Milligan College operates on a semester system (semesters begin in August and January) with two 4-week summer sessions in June and July or one 8-week term. Also available are short-term classes during January term (one week before the onset of the spring semester) and May term (the weeks between the spring semester and the summer sessions).

Rising juniors are required to take a test covering general knowledge, and graduating seniors are required to take a test to demonstrate knowledge in their major field of study.

Off-Campus Programs

Students can go beyond geographical and cultural boundaries and earn up to 16 hours of credit with Milligan's Study Abroad Program or with the many off-campus learning opportunities sponsored by the Council for Christian Colleges & Universities. These include an American Studies Program in Washington, D.C.; Australia Studies Centre; China Studies Program; Contemporary Music Center near Martha's Vineyard; India Studies Program; Latin American Studies Program in Costa Rica; Los Angeles Film Studies Center; Middle East Studies Program in Cairo; Oxford Summer Programme; Russian Studies Program; Scholars' Semester in Oxford; Summer Institute of Journalism in Washington, D.C.; and Uganda Studies Program.

Through an affiliation with the International Business Institute, business majors can earn college credit through an intensive ten-week summer program in Europe. Milligan also offers a three-week summer humanities tour in Europe, during which students explore the origins of Western civilization. In addition,

COLLEGE CLOSE-UPS

internship opportunities offer students college credit and work experience in their field of interest.

Academic Facilities

Milligan College's library has extensive holdings and online access to other major libraries and databases. Special collections within the library contain materials on the history of the College, the Restoration Movement, and the local area. The library also participates in resource-sharing agreements with Emmanuel School of Religion and East Tennessee State University. The Writing and Study Skills Center offers access to resources, instruction, and tutoring for academic success. Television and radio production studios and an FM radio station provide on-site training for communication students. A darkroom and art gallery feature works by fine arts students. Standardized laboratory facilities, including a gross anatomy lab, are available for general and advanced work in the sciences.

Recent on-campus projects include a new state-of-the-art theater and convocation facility; renovation of the College's main classroom building and several other lecture halls and labs; the addition of a new education center, a new tennis complex, and a new wellness center; and a 30-acre land acquisition.

Costs

Tuition for 2011–12 was $24,360. Room and board were $5650. Additional fees were approximately $900. Typical annual miscellaneous costs (books, supplies, etc.) were approximately $1000. As a private institution, Milligan supplements student fees with income from endowments and gifts from alumni, friends, and churches in order to keep tuition below the national average of similar four-year private institutions.

Financial Aid

Approximately 95 percent of all students at Milligan College receive federal, state, institutional, and/or outside (such as from a church or private foundation) aid, including both academic scholarships and need-based grants. Each year, Milligan budgets more than $5 million in institutional scholarships, grants, and work-study opportunities. Financial assistance is allocated on the basis of need demonstrated by information supplied on the Free Application for Federal Student Aid (FAFSA), which should be completed by January 1 for priority consideration. Returning students must complete and submit a Milligan College Financial Aid Scholarship/Renewal Application. The Milligan College Office of Financial Aid begins mailing award letters between March 1 and March 15.

Faculty

Eighty percent of Milligan's faculty members have earned the highest degree in their field from well-respected colleges and universities in the United States and abroad. Professors integrate biblical truths into their classes and are active leaders both on and off the campus. The low student-faculty ratio and small classes put the student at the center of attention and allow faculty members to cultivate special mentoring relationships with students. Professors serve as advisers to students from registration to graduation and are often instrumental in helping students find employment or gain admission to graduate school following graduation. Milligan's faculty members are mature and caring scholars who are committed to world-class scholarship, excellence in teaching, and their students.

Student Government

The Student Government Association (SGA) serves as the official representative voice of Milligan students and promotes academic, social, and spiritual activities for the campus community. SGA operates under a constitution approved and supported by the administration of the College, promotes well-ordered conduct among students, and enforces the regulations of the College. SGA leadership is provided by an executive council and representatives from throughout the campus. As a Christian college, Milligan adopts basic moral and social principles and expects students to serve Christ in an atmosphere of trust, encouragement, and respect for one another.

Admission Requirements

Character, ability, preparation, and seriousness of purpose are the qualities emphasized in considering applicants for acceptance to Milligan College. Overall excellence of performance in high school subjects, as well as evidence of Christian commitment and academic potential, provide the basis for admission to Milligan College. These qualities are evaluated by consideration of each applicant's academic record (based on transcripts), two personal references, ACT or SAT scores, and participation in extracurricular activities. Some majors, such as music and theater, may require auditions and interviews. All applicants should have a high school diploma or the equivalent and have completed a college-preparatory curriculum with course work in English, math, science, history and/or social sciences, foreign language, and some work in speech, music, or art in preparation for study in a liberal arts curriculum. Satisfactory scores on the ACT or SAT are required of all applicants to the freshman class. The average ACT score for the current first-year class is 24. Transfer students should have a grade point average of 2.5 or above and must follow the same application procedures as first-time students, with the addition of providing official transcripts of all previous college work. ACT or SAT scores and high school transcripts are not required for transfer students with at least 24 earned semester hours.

Application and Information

Applications are processed on a rolling basis, and early application is encouraged. Notification is also given on a rolling basis. An application packet, complete with detailed instructions and requirements, can be obtained from the Admissions Office.

For further information, students should contact:

Admissions Office
Milligan College
P.O. Box 210
Milligan College, Tennessee 37682
Phone: 423-461-8730
      800-262-8337 (toll-free)
Fax: 423-461-8982
E-mail: admissions@milligan.edu (general)
      visits@milligan.edu (visits)
Web site: http://www.milligan.edu

Milligan College is a Christian liberal arts college that unites humanities, sciences, and fine arts with a Christian worldview.

MILLS COLLEGE
OAKLAND, CALIFORNIA

MILLS

The College

For more than 150 years, Mills College has shaped women's lives. Offering a progressive liberal arts and sciences curriculum taught by nationally renowned faculty, Mills gives students the personal attention that leads to extraordinary learning. At Mills, students gain the ability to make their voices heard, the strength to risk bold visions, an eagerness to experiment, and a desire to change the world.

Nestled on 135 lush acres in the heart of the San Francisco Bay Area, Mills College is a hidden gem. The idyllic setting, combined with the College's community of forward-thinking individuals, makes Mills home to one of the most dynamic, creative liberal arts educations available to women today.

Historically a college for women only, Mills continues that proud tradition today at the undergraduate level. To provide enhanced professional opportunities for all students, Mills also offers renowned graduate programs that are open to both women and men. Ranked one of the top colleges in the West by *U.S. News & World Report,* Mills has also been named one of the greenest colleges in the nation by the Princeton Review.

Mills provides a collaborative, interactive learning environment that encourages intellectual exploration and self-discovery. The faculty of distinguished scholars and artists is dedicated to developing the strengths of every student, preparing them for lifelong intellectual, personal, and professional growth. With an impressive student-teacher ratio of 11:1, Mills women are assured of access to and support from these inspiring professors. The hallmark of a Mills education is the collaboration between students and faculty members that goes beyond the classroom and into innovative research.

Mills students also compete in six intercollegiate sports—cross-country, rowing, soccer, swimming, tennis, and volleyball—as members of the National Collegiate Athletic Association (NCAA) Division III. Students may also participate in recreational activity courses for credit or take advantage of the on-campus fitness facilities and off-campus excursions.

Location

Located in the foothills of Oakland, California, Mills offers students access to the diverse metropolitan centers that make up the greater San Francisco Bay Area. Amid the rolling hills and the century-old eucalyptus trees of the Mills campus, students find a welcoming place to live and learn, with new friends and new ideas at every turn. The campus is heavily accented with Mediterranean-style buildings, many designed by architectural innovator Julia Morgan. Paths and streams wind their way through groves and meadows that pervade the 135-acre wooded campus.

Outside the campus gates, students have access to the dynamic Bay Area, with Berkeley, San Francisco, Napa, and Silicon Valley nearby. The close proximity allows Mills students to connect with centers of learning, business, and technology; pursue research and internship opportunities; and explore the Bay Area's many sources of cultural, social, and recreational enrichment.

Majors and Degrees

With more than forty different majors to choose from at Mills, students find themselves active, engaged participants in their own learning. Students have the chance to work directly with nationally renowned faculty members and get involved in their innovative work and research.

Mills offers the Bachelor of Arts (B.A.) degree in American studies; anthropology and sociology; art (history and studio); biochemistry and molecular biology; biology; biopsychology; business economics; chemistry; child development; computer science; dance; economics; English (creative writing and literature); environmental science; environmental studies; ethnic studies; French and Francophone studies; government; history; intermedia arts; international relations; Latin American studies; literary and cultural studies;

mathematics; music; philosophy; political, legal, and economic analysis; psychology; public policy; sociology; Spanish and Spanish American studies; and women's, gender and sexuality studies. The major in child development meets the requirements for a state child development permit for teaching in preschool and day-care centers and provides a strong basis for graduate school and for many other careers. Special prelaw and premedical advising is available.

Mills offers the Bachelor of Science (B.S.) degree in biochemistry and molecular biology, biology, biopsychology, chemistry, environmental science, and mathematics. Mills also provides the first two years of courses leading to a Bachelor of Science in Nursing degree from Samuel Merritt University.

Students can also choose to create their own major, working with 3 faculty advisers to plan an individual program that draws courses from across the curriculum and creates an integrated and unique educational experience.

Mills offers six unique bachelor's-to-master's degree programs that enable undergraduates with clear career goals in certain fields to earn two academic degrees in five years. These degree programs are the 4+1 B.A./M.B.A. business administration program, the 4+1 B.A./M.A. infant mental health program, the 4+1 B.A./M.A. interdisciplinary computer science program, the 4+1 B.A./M.A. mathematics program, the 4+1 B.A./M.P.P. public policy program, and the 4+1 B.A./M.A./credential program in teacher education. Students must meet specific academic requirements to successfully complete these special programs.

Academic Programs

To earn a Mills bachelor's degree, students complete 34 semester course credits (usually four courses each semester). Grading is traditional, and a pass-fail option is available outside the major.

The innovative General Education Program is guided by a thoughtfully constructed set of learning outcomes, instead of a list of required courses. Each student designs her own program with the guidance of her faculty adviser, tailoring it to the student's specific needs and interests. The program places the work a student does in her major in a larger context and ensures that she explores and appreciates realms of knowledge beyond her field. The general education requirements fall into three outcome categories: skills (written communication, quantitative and computational reasoning, and information literacy/information technology skills), perspectives (women and gender, and multicultural), and disciplinary experiences (creation and criticism in the arts, historical perspectives, natural sciences, and human institutions and behavior).

Career Services offers a comprehensive career counseling and coaching program to assist students in clarifying their goals. Workshops, individual counseling sessions, an extensive internship program, a strong alumnae network, and special opportunities to meet Bay Area business leaders and top professional women all help students to focus their interests and plan career goals.

Off-Campus Programs

Mills has exchange or visiting programs with eleven American colleges and universities, including American, Barnard, Manhattanville, Mount Holyoke, Simmons, Spelman, Swarthmore, Wellesley, and Wheaton.

With programs in Europe, Africa, South America, Asia, and Australia—in nearly every country in the world—Mills encourages adventurous students with a minimum 3.0 GPA to study abroad. Mills also has exchange programs with universities in Hong Kong and South Korea.

Sophomores, juniors, and seniors may cross-register for one course per semester at the following schools: Berkeley City College; California College of the Arts; California State University, East Bay; Chabot College; City College of San Francisco; College of Alameda; College of Marin; Contra Costa College; Diablo Valley College; Graduate Theological Union; Holy Names University;

Laney College; Merritt College; Napa Valley College; St. Mary's College of California; Skyline College; Sonoma State University; and University of California, Berkeley.

Academic Facilities

Mills' commitment to providing students with exceptional academic resources is underscored by the two environmentally friendly buildings on campus. The home of the Lorry I. Lokey Graduate School of Business hosts both undergraduate and graduate classes and achieved Leadership in Energy and Environmental Design (LEED) Gold certification. Students enjoy smart classrooms and lecture halls with the latest educational technology and light-filled community areas that encourage student collaboration. The Betty Irene Moore Natural Sciences Building provides students with a state-of-the-art learning environment that is also a model of green construction. The LEED-certified Platinum facility features high-tech classrooms, multiple teaching laboratories, and a research lab.

Renovated in 2009, the Jeannik Méquet Littlefield Concert Hall features an expanded stage area for larger performances and enhanced acoustic features for improved performing and recording quality. Nearby Lisser Hall contains a flexible proscenium stage as well as a small experimental theater.

The open-stack, computerized F. W. Olin Library provides students with access to more than 240,000 volumes in addition to more than 22,000 rare books and manuscripts. A Web-based catalog and more than 60 databases, including Academic Search, LexisNexis, PsycINFO, and Britannica Online are available 24 hours a day via the library's Web site.

The Mills College Art Museum houses the largest permanent collection of any liberal arts college on the West Coast and presents a changing array of innovative exhibitions. The highly regarded Children's School at Mills College provides hands-on experience for students preparing for careers in early childhood education.

Costs

In 2011–12, tuition and fees were $39,264 and room and board were $12,052. Students should calculate the costs of travel, books, and personal expenses on an individual basis.

Financial Aid

Mills College is committed to ensuring that a Mills education is within reach for those who have the desire and the qualifications to attend. Financial aid options at Mills include grants and scholarships, loans, and student employment. Some are funded by Mills directly, and others are state and federal programs.

In fall 2011, more than 80 percent of undergraduates at the College received some type of financial assistance in the form of grants, scholarships, loans, or on-campus employment. Ninety-five percent of Mills students received some portion of their aid directly from Mills. Awards are based on need and academic merit. Mills makes a special effort to provide financial aid to all students who demonstrate need.

All first-year students and transfer candidates must file the Free Application for Federal Student Aid (FAFSA) and the Mills College Financial Aid Form to be considered for government aid and need-based Mills scholarship funds. The FAFSA is required for non-Mills aid, such as the Federal Pell Grant, and the Federal Supplemental Educational Opportunity Grant. California residents must also file the Cal Grant GPA Verification Form to be considered for a Cal Grant. More than 40 percent of Mills students have some of their determined need offset by such non-Mills awards.

Faculty

More than 65 percent of the Mills faculty members are women, enabling students to work with professional women mentors in every academic area. Faculty members are selected for their teaching ability and scholarly achievement; 89 percent of full-time faculty members hold the highest degrees in their fields. Nearly 30 percent of the full- and part-time faculty members are members of minority groups.

Student Government

An important goal of an education at Mills is to develop leadership skills, and participating in student government can be instrumental in furthering this goal. The Associated Students of Mills College (ASMC) is run by an executive board of 15 elected or appointed positions. Following a student-drafted Constitution, the board supports student organizations, student publications, campuswide events, and various student initiatives. From academic issues to social events to honor code concerns, the ASMC is the voice of the student body to the College administration.

Admission Requirements

Most first-year students admitted to Mills have a B+ average and have followed a full college-preparatory course in their secondary school, including 4 years of English, 3 to 4 years of mathematics, 2 to 4 years of foreign languages, 2 to 4 years of social sciences, and 2 to 4 years of a laboratory science. Additional course work in fine arts is given positive consideration, as is evidence of special talents or interests. Mills is interested in individuals, not statistical averages, so each application is carefully reviewed. Credit may be awarded for the College Board Advanced Placement tests and the International Baccalaureate program's higher level examinations.

Applications from transfers are welcome, as are those from students resuming their education or women who have delayed their entrance to college or who wish to continue work on their B.A. degrees. The SAT or ACT requirement is waived if 24 or more transferable semester hours are presented. For international applications, both the SAT and TOEFL are required. Applications should be accompanied by transcripts, letters of recommendation, SAT/ACT scores, and a writing sample. An interview, either on campus or with an alumna representative, is strongly recommended for all applicants.

Application and Information

For first-year students, fall admission application deadlines are November 15 for early action and February 1 for regular decision. All required materials are due by February 1.

For transfer students, fall admission application deadlines are March 1 for priority scholarship consideration and April 1 for regular decision.

The spring admission application deadline for both first-year and transfer students is November 1. Admission decisions are mailed on a rolling basis.

For more information, students should contact:

Office of Undergraduate Admission
Mills College
5000 MacArthur Boulevard
Oakland, California 94613
Phone: 510-430-2135
        800-87-MILLS (toll-free)
Fax: 510-430-3298
E-mail: admission@mills.edu
Web site: http://www.mills.edu
        http://www.facebook.com/millscollege (Facebook)
        http://twitter.com/millscollege (Twitter)
        http://youtube.com/millscollege (YouTube)

Mills women discover their best selves—and prepare to change the world.

MISERICORDIA UNIVERSITY
DALLAS, PENNSYLVANIA

The University

Misericordia University is a high-quality liberal arts and professional studies institution rooted in service to others and committed to challenging academics and the personal attention students deserve. Founded by the Religious Sisters of Mercy, Misericordia offers undergraduate and graduate programs to resident and commuter students, as well as adult students. Current enrollment is more than 2,800 men and women.

Misericordia provides an atmosphere designed to stimulate critical thinking, independent judgment, and creativity, as well as encourage the development of curiosity, good study habits, and personal values. The University also cultivates a spirit of community service and a lifelong love of learning in its students through extracurricular activities, experiential learning, and challenging academic programs. In the National Survey of Student Engagement, Misericordia students say they are more involved in learning and have better relationships with faculty members and peers than students at other similar institutions. Misericordia is also ranked in the top tier of U.S. News & World Report's America's Best Colleges 2011 in the Master's North category.

The University is fully accredited by the Middle States Association of Colleges and Schools. Its programs in nursing, social work, medical imaging, occupational therapy, physical therapy, and speech-language pathology are accredited by the National League for Nursing Accrediting Commission, the Council on Social Work Education, the Joint Review Committee on Education in Radiologic Technology, the American Occupational Therapy Association, the American Physical Therapy Association, and the American Speech-Language and Hearing Association, respectively. A new physician assistant studies program was granted Accreditation–Provisional by ARC-PA and is excited to accept new students.

Misericordia operates five residential facilities and eighteen townhouse units, with a total capacity for over 900 students. Two nearby homes are reserved for upper-level students. Residents have a number of options, including single rooms and wellness housing. Each residence hall offers study rooms, laundry facilities, and recreational lounges. The new Metz Dining Hall is located in the Banks Student Life Center, which also houses the Cougar's Den coffeehouse and the renovated Student Union, which features flat-screen televisions, pool, and foosball tables.

There are numerous campus activities. Besides Student Government, there are forty-one chartered student clubs and organizations. Cultural events, Campus Ministry, intramural and intercollegiate athletic programs, performing arts shows, art exhibits, and many other social activities complement the academic experience. In keeping with the University's tradition of mercy, service, justice, and hospitality, students have opportunities to develop leadership potential through service projects. MU earned a spot on the President's National Community Service Honor Roll for the past several years.

On spring break, students have served the needy in rural Appalachia, the Gulf Coast, Texas, California, and the South Bronx. Students have volunteered abroad in Jamaica and Romania.

Personalized attention is the key to the support available in the Student Success Center. A psychologist, counselors, therapists, and peer counselors conduct workshops each semester on a variety of topics, including test anxiety, stress management, time management, and goal setting. Many services are free of charge to students and contacts are confidential.

First-year students may join the Guaranteed Placement Program (GPP) through the Insalaco Center for Career Development. The GPP program includes academic standards; cocurricular activities, such as leadership and service projects; internships; resume development; and interviewing skills. If a student fulfills the program requirements and is not employed in his or her field or enrolled in graduate or professional school within six months of graduation, a paid internship is assured. The center also co-presents the Choice Program, offering special guidance for students who haven't chosen a major. Opportunities for career exploration, cooperative education, and internships help students to develop the skills they need to enter the working world.

Student Health Services staff members provide first aid, assessment and treatment of common illnesses, and referrals for more serious health conditions. Health center activities are directed by a registered nurse with a master's degree in nursing, under the guidance of a physician. A nurse practitioner is also available. A self-care room offers reference materials and up-to-date information on personal health concerns. All services are confidential.

A rapidly evolving world has increased the number of adults who seek higher education. Misericordia offers bachelor's, master's, and doctoral programs for adults, including Expressway, an accelerated bachelor's degree program; Women with Children, which provides housing and support services for single women with children; and evening, online, and weekend formats for people with families and full-time jobs.

A new field house and 118-bed residence hall with classrooms are set to open in fall 2012. A new artificial turf field was added to campus in early 2012, and another existing field will be resurfaced and prepared for football, which begins in 2012 as well.

At Misericordia University, students can earn master's and/or doctoral degrees by attending classes online, in the evening, and/or on weekends. The small-class format enhances critical thinking and decision-making skills and draws out a variety of viewpoints that help broaden the perspectives of the student. Master's degrees are available in education, nursing, occupational therapy, physician assistant, speech-language pathology, business administration, and organizational management. A doctoral program in physical therapy is available to students entering in a full-time and part-time format, and a doctoral program in occupational therapy is available for graduate students via part-time study, including online and in-class components.

Location

Located on a more than 124-acre campus in northeastern Pennsylvania, Misericordia University is the oldest institution of higher education in Luzerne County. Expansive lawns and thick stands of trees dominate the campus. It is 9 miles from the city of Wilkes-Barre. The area offers shopping centers, malls, cinemas, skiing, professional sporting events, and a variety of cultural activities. Pennsylvania's largest natural lake and two state parks are nearby, as are Pocono ski resorts. Metropolitan New York and Philadelphia are each within a 3-hour drive. Public and college-sponsored transportation serves the campus.

Majors and Degrees

Misericordia University awards the Bachelor of Arts (B.A.) degree in English, history, communications, government, liberal studies, and philosophy. The Bachelor of Science (B.S.) degree is awarded in accounting, biochemistry, biology, business administration, chemistry, clinical laboratory science, communications, computer science, diagnostic medical sonography, elementary education, health-care management, information technology, interdisciplinary studies, management, marketing, mathematics, math/computer science, medical imaging, medical science, professional studies, psychology, secondary education, special education, and sport management. After completing the medical science bachelor's degree, students can opt for seamless transition into the master's degree in physician assistant studies. A Bachelor of Science in Nursing (B.S.N.) is awarded to nursing majors, and a Bachelor of Science in Social Work (B.S.W.) is awarded to social work majors. Specializations in accounting, early childhood education, prelaw, special education, and preprofessional occupations are also available. Certification programs include addictions counseling, child welfare services, diagnostic medical sonography, geriatric

care management, gerontology, health-care informatics, nuclear medicine, and secondary education and may be taken in support of several degrees offered by Misericordia or as stand-alone programs.

The University offers five-year entry-level graduate majors in occupational therapy and speech-language pathology. Students graduate with a master's degree in speech-language pathology or occupational therapy and a bachelor's degree in health sciences. The physical therapy program is a 6½-year doctoral program. Students graduate with a bachelor's degree in one of several areas and a Doctor of Physical Therapy (D.P.T.) degree.

Academic Programs

Candidates for the B.A., B.S., B.S.N., or B.S.W. must fulfill a 48-credit liberal arts core curriculum in addition to the requirements of their chosen major to graduate. They must earn at least 36 credit hours in a chosen field. For regularly enrolled students, the average requirement for a baccalaureate degree is a total of 126 credits. Other options include minors, specializations, certifications, and electives.

Courses are offered on a semester basis, beginning in August and January and ending in December and May. Summer, weekend, and accelerated courses are also available.

Academic Facilities

The chemistry, physics, and biology departments all have fully equipped research laboratories available to students in these fields. State-of-the-art equipment includes high-performance liquid chromatography (HPLC), a rotary evaporator, an infrared spectrophotometer, and gas chromatography. The University also houses an energized radiation laboratory for the medical imaging program. The new Passan Hall–College of Health Sciences provides classrooms and high-tech laboratories for the occupational therapy, physical therapy, speech-language pathology, and nursing programs in a facility devoted to these majors.

In addition to the four main computer labs, most other campus buildings and common areas offer wireless Internet access. The University operates e-MU, a secure online portal where students can access e-mail, course schedules, class registration tools, and student account and registration information from a single sign-on.

Mercy Hall, the original administrative building, offers multipurpose academic classrooms and facilities. Many key student service departments, including the registrar, student accounts, and financial aid are centralized in one area in Mercy Hall. Insalaco Hall, a new state-of-the-art classroom and conference building, provides a modern art gallery, café, computer labs, an ensemble room, fine arts classroom, music teaching and practice areas, and the Assistive Technology Research Institute.

The three-story Bevevino Library covers 37,500 square feet and houses stacks for 90,000 volumes. Materials include information and communication technology and a reference section that offers books, serials, and a variety of periodicals as well as reference search tools.

Costs

Full-time undergraduate tuition for 2012–13 is $25,890 per year. The general fee is $1240. Housing options include traditional rooms, suites, town houses, and wellness housing. The median room cost is $6620. All resident students must participate in a ten-, fourteen-, or nineteen- meal plan. In addition, town-house residents are eligible to choose a five-meal plan. The median board cost is $4230.

Financial Aid

All students applying for financial aid must complete the Free Application for Federal Student Aid (FAFSA) by May 1. This is used for Federal Pell Grants, Federal Supplemental Educational Opportunity Grants (FSEOG), subsidized and unsubsidized Federal Direct Student Loans, Federal Perkins Loans, nursing loans, and the Federal Work-Study Program. This application is also the basis upon which state and institutional aid is awarded. The University also offers a no-interest monthly payment plan. Many scholarships are available including $11.4 million in presidential scholarships based on academic ability and $2.3 million in McAuley Awards for students who have experience in leadership roles and volunteer service.

Faculty

There are 109 full-time faculty members. A student-faculty ratio of 12:1 results in students receiving a great deal of individual attention from a highly qualified faculty; 87 percent of the faculty members hold doctorates or other terminal degrees. Besides student academic advising, the faculty members also serve as advisers to clubs.

Student Government

An active student government organization serves as a liaison between the students and the faculty and staff members. The administration enables students to become involved by serving as student representatives on various University committees.

Admission Requirements

Misericordia University admits applicants based on their secondary school record, high school recommendation, extracurricular activities, and personal promise. The University requires SAT or ACT scores. Although a personal interview is highly recommended, it is not necessary for all majors. Misericordia offers both early decision and early admissions programs.

Transfer students with a cumulative average of at least 2.0 (4.0 scale) may be considered for admission and may receive advanced standing. Some majors require a 2.5 or higher cumulative average. Transfer students must submit official high school transcripts and a transcript of work completed at other colleges and universities.

Application and Information

Applicants must submit an official application form (available upon request), transcripts, and SAT or ACT scores. Applicants may also apply through the University's Web site. There is a nonrefundable application fee of $35, which is waived for students who visit the campus.

The University considers applications on a rolling basis. Usually, candidates are notified of the admission decision within three weeks of receipt of all required materials.

Office of Admissions
Misericordia University
301 Lake Street
Dallas, Pennsylvania 18612-1090
Phone: 570-674-6461
       866-262-6363 (toll free)
Fax: 570-675-2441
E-mail: admiss@misericordia.edu
Web site: http://admissions.misericordia.edu
       www.twitter.com/misericordiau
       www.facebook.com/misericordiauniversity

Misericordia University introduced a minor in fine arts in 2011, supported by new studios in a reclaimed former auto dealership near the campus.

MITCHELL COLLEGE
NEW LONDON, CONNECTICUT

The College

All motivated students can realize their full potential at Mitchell College, a private, coeducational four-year residential college on the shores of Connecticut's Thames River. Noted for its student-centered learning environment, Mitchell is rich in the resources that promote success in college and in the future.

With a 12:1 student-to-faculty ratio and small classes, Mitchell's 900 students are assured of individual attention, advising, guidance, and support from professors. Mitchell College is proud to introduce its Ability Based Education (ABE) model. It seeks to answer the question, "What can students do with the information they have learned?" ABE takes the established benefits of a liberal arts education and partners them with the professional skills and personal development required to thrive at work, home, and in the community.

Not surprisingly, the College provides many opportunities for students to grow and learn outside of the classroom. Half of the student body hails from Connecticut and the remainder from twenty-nine states and twelve countries. The College's close-knit, residential campus community fosters close friendships among students of diverse backgrounds, cultures, interests, and talents. Eighty percent of students live on campus and can choose from traditional residence halls; smaller, restored historic homes on the banks of the Thames; themed, apartment-style housing; and a new suite-style residence hall.

Students also expand their learning through participation in Mitchell's campus clubs and organizations. These groups reflect the varied interests of the campus community and include academic honorary societies and academic-related clubs such as business, behavioral sciences, early childhood education, and pre-law. Other groups unite students who share interests in areas such as community service, multicultural affairs, the performing arts, communications and media, and recreation.

Mitchell's 68-acre, waterfront campus offers abundant options for students interested in athletics, personal fitness, and the great outdoors. Facilities include a fully equipped gymnasium, a new fitness center, athletic fields, private beaches, a sailing dock, and indoor recreation areas. The Mitchell College Woods include hiking trails, a freshwater pond, tennis courts, a sand volleyball court, and a picnic pavilion.

Scholar-athletes can build leadership and teamwork skills as members of one of Mitchell's thirteen men's and women's intercollegiate teams. A member of the NCAA Division III New England Collegiate Conference, the College has a history of athletic excellence, winning many national and New England championships. Men's teams include baseball, basketball, cross-country, golf, lacrosse, soccer, and tennis; women's teams include basketball, cross-country, golf, soccer, softball, tennis, and volleyball. Sailing is a coed intercollegiate sport. In addition, rugby is offered as a club sport. Participation in intramural sports is open to all students.

Location

The Mitchell campus is located in the most scenic residential section of New London, Connecticut, which is also home to the U.S. Coast Guard Academy and Connecticut College. The city has educational, cultural, historical, economic, social, and recreational assets that enhance the Mitchell experience and provide many opportunities for internships and service learning. New London's Historic Waterfront District is a center of arts and entertainment and the city is well-known for an active and eclectic music scene. Boston, Providence, and New York City are easily accessible by train and bus. Freshmen are allowed cars on campus.

The area is also home to major tourist attractions, such as Mystic Aquarium & Institute for Exploration, Mystic Seaport, Old Mystic Village, Foxwoods Resort, and the Mohegan Sun, all of which also offer internship opportunities to Mitchell students.

Majors and Degrees

The College awards baccalaureate degrees in business administration, communication, criminal justice, early childhood education, environmental studies, homeland security, hospitality and tourism, human development and family studies, liberal and professional studies, psychology, and sport management. Associate degrees are offered in early childhood education, graphic design, and liberal arts. Degree completion can be accelerated by taking courses during summer and winter breaks. Online and hybrid courses are offered.

Academic Programs

The academic calendar consists of two full semesters that run from September to December and from January to May. One week pre-enrollment programs and a three-week summer college academic skills transition program are offered for first year students prior to the start of the fall semester.

All first-year freshman students participate in the First Year College, a comprehensive program designed to ease the transition from high school to college and establish a firm foundation for academic success. Students participate in learning communities known as Freshman Interest Groups, which explore a common theme through project-based learning led by teams of instructors. The First Year College experience is also supported by one-on-one advising, tutoring, information literacy, and career exploration.

Students who are still considering which academic major might be best for them can take advantage of Mitchell's Discovery Program, which provides special courses, additional advising, and services that help students find the academic program which best matches their talents and their goals.

If a student is having difficulty, it can be recognized early through interim grade reports issued regularly throughout the semester. Faculty members team up with academic advisers to help students get back on course. Mitchell's Tutoring Center provides students with free, unlimited individualized tutoring by trained professionals (not peer tutors). The Center also offers assistance in improving writing, research, and computer skills as well as test and exam preparation and study skills development. Some of Mitchell's most successful students are also regular users of the Tutoring Center, and they attribute much of their success to its programs.

Students with diagnosed learning disabilities may enroll in the College's nationally recognized Learning Resource Center, which provides instruction and support to complement a student's regular academic program. Each student is assigned to learning specialists who work one-on-one with the student and in small-group settings. The program is designed to teach the learning strategies a student needs to gain independence.

Up to 39 seats are available in Thames Academy, a year-long pre-college transitional program for students who need extra preparation before college. Graduates earn 15–21 transferrable credits while living and learning in their own residence hall on the waterfront.

Off-Campus Programs

When not in class, Mitchell students gain the skills and experience they need to succeed in their careers and to make a difference in their communities. Nearly all academic programs require or encourage students to participate in volunteer opportunities, internships, or practical experiences as part of their curriculum.

Many of the opportunities involve Mitchell's partnerships with local schools, government agencies, businesses, historic and cultural sites, financial and legal firms, healthcare providers, and nonprofit agencies, providing students with hands-on experiences near at hand.

Academic Facilities and Technology

Mitchell's academic resources include a 73,590-volume library; classroom buildings; computer labs; and the Duquès Academic Success Center, which houses academic advising, the Career Center, the Learning Resource Center, and the Tutoring Center.

Graphic design classes take place in Mitchell's Mac Lab, equipped with state-of-the-art computers and other hardware, as well as the latest versions of professional design software. The campus waterfront is the site of the Mitchell Beach Restoration Project, an ongoing coastal habitat restoration that is used as a teaching tool and as a service-learning component in many courses.

The Mitchell College Library, dining hall, residence halls, and most classrooms are equipped with wireless network and high speed Internet access.

Tablets are used by over 30 percent of the student body for academic study. Instructional and curricular systems are used by over two thirds of the faculty to deliver and manage course content. Assistive technologies are readily available to serve students with documented disabilities.

Costs

Tuition, room and board, and fees for the 2011–12 academic year were $40,206. Additional annual miscellaneous expenses, including books, are estimated at $1500 per year. Students enrolled in the Learning Resource Center pay an additional $1700 to $6800 per year depending on the level of service received.

Financial Aid

Mitchell annually awards more than $8 million in financial aid, both in need-based and merit-based scholarships and in grant programs designed to recognize academic and leadership talent. About 90% of students receive aid. Accepted students may qualify for grants and scholarships that do not need to be repaid. Self-help aid in the form of loans is also available. On-campus job opportunities are plentiful for students regardless of their financial aid status.

Faculty

Thirty-four full-time and 58 part-time faculty members teach in Mitchell's classrooms. The student-faculty ratio is 12:1. Faculty members are well known for their extensive connections with business, industry, and education, using these relationships to establish internship opportunities for their students.

Student Government

The Student Government Association (SGA) carries out administrative responsibilities and sponsors campus and community events.

Admission Requirements

Mitchell's highly personalized approach to education is reflected in its admission process. Each student is evaluated individually as soon as the completed application, along with the official transcript, is received. Academic preparation, scholastic aptitude, personal character, and potential for academic success are all carefully considered. Other important factors include the student's motivation, initiative, maturity, seriousness of purpose, and leadership potential. Interviews are required and campus visits are strongly encouraged, evidence of Mitchell's interest in getting to know each applicant individually and personally.

Application and Information

Mitchell uses a rolling admission policy. Students can expect to be notified of decisions within weeks of the College's receipt of completed applications and official transcripts sent directly from the students' high schools.

For more information, students should contact:

Susan Bibeau
Vice President of Enrollment Management
Mitchell College
437 Pequot Avenue
New London, Connecticut 06320-4498
Phone: 800-443-2811 (toll-free)
Fax: 860-444-1209
E-mail: admissions@mitchell.edu
Web site: http://www.mitchell.edu

Mitchell is known for its sense of community and commitment to students' academic success.

MOLLOY COLLEGE
ROCKVILLE CENTRE, NEW YORK

The College

In 1955, 44 students became part of an exciting new tradition in higher education on Long Island. As the first freshman class of Molloy College, located in Rockville Centre, New York, these young students made a commitment to academic excellence. So did the College, which had a distinguished faculty of 15 and a library containing 5,000 books.

Today, Molloy offers students a rich and multidimensional education experience. The Long Island school encourages critical thinking and creative exploration in a personal community setting. Molloy combines the strengths of academic excellence and leadership with personal, compassionate mentoring to bring out the best in every student.

For over fifty years, Molloy College has evolved to become a dynamic learning institution with outstanding faculty, advanced technology, and a wide range of academic programs. In addition, Molloy has expanded its reach, offering graduate level courses at its Suffolk Center in East Farmingdale, New York, along with a number of on-site opportunities at area hospitals and school districts.

Molloy College students possess the confidence needed to live and work in this fast-paced, ever-changing world. The College has expanded its global learning program, where students travel from Rockville Centre and study abroad in Belgium, India, Italy, France, Spain, Thailand, and Australia. By traveling from Long Island and immersing themselves in cultures in other parts of the world, students gain knowledge while learning acceptance and understanding.

Closer to home, Molloy College students make a difference in Rockville Centre as well as other nearby local communities. For example, as part of Molloy's tradition of service, students become involved in a number of service projects that include BoxTown, a program to raise social consciousness about the issue of homelessness.

Athletics and academics go hand-in-hand at Molloy College, where students are known for both their athletic and scholastic success. The Long Island school has a winning tradition in a number of NCAA Division II athletic programs, and in 2010 the women's softball team became one of only eight teams in the country to qualify for the College World Series.

Campus life in Rockville Centre, New York, is alive and vibrant, with more than forty student clubs and honor societies. In 2011, Molloy opened its first residence hall, which can house more than 150 students. In addition, a new student center (which also opened in the fall of 2011) provides new opportunities for Molloy students to study, interact with their fellow students, or simply relax.

In recent years, Molloy College has become a focal point for civic discourse with key community forums. Top regional, national, and international leaders (including former Secretary of State Colin Powell and *Newsweek International* editor Fareed Zakaria) have come to Rockville Centre to visit the College and address critical and timely issues.

In recent years Molloy launched two new initiatives to enhance students' experience. The Sustainability Institute at Molloy College is Long Island's first-ever venture combining environmental advocacy and sustainability education within an academic institution, and the new sustainability minor provides students with a solid background in this critical subject. Molloy also started its new Irish Studies Institute recently with a presentation from Bertie Ahern, the former prime minister of Ireland.

Through Molloy College's divers programs, personal attention from faculty, and commitment to improving both Long Island and the world, students develop an "I will" attitude that prepares them to enter the professional world, ready and able to make a difference.

Location

Located on a 30-acre campus in Rockville Centre, Long Island, Molloy College is close to metropolitan New York and all its diverse and rich resources. The College is easily accessible from all parts of Nassau, Suffolk, and Queens counties.

Majors and Degrees

Molloy College offers the A.A. degree in liberal arts; the A.A.S. degree in nuclear medicine technology, respiratory therapy, and cardiovascular technology; and B.A., B.S., B.F.A., or B.S.W. degrees in accounting, art, biology, business management, communication arts, computer information systems, computer science, criminal justice, English, environmental studies, finance, history, interdisciplinary studies, international peace and justice studies, mathematics, modern languages, music, music therapy, nursing, philosophy, political science, psychology, social work, sociology, speech-language pathology/audiology, and theology. Teacher certification programs are available in childhood (1–6), adolescence (7–12), and special education. Dual certification is available for birth–grade 2/childhood 1–6.

Special advisement is offered for students interested in predental, prelaw, premedical, or pre–veterinary science programs.

On the graduate level, Molloy College offers a Master of Science degree as well as post-master's certification in nursing and education. M.B.A. programs are available in business, accounting, and personal financial planning. A Master of Social Work is offered through Molloy's partnership with Fordham University. Molloy also offers graduate degrees in criminal justice, music therapy, and speech pathology. In 2010, the College launched its first doctoral program, a Ph.D. in nursing.

The internship program at the College offers students the opportunity for on-the-job experience along with the classroom exposure so essential to the completely educated person. Internships are available in all areas of study.

Academic Programs

Advanced Placement credit is granted for a score of 3 or better on the AP exam. CLEP and CPE credit is also given. Molloy has a 4-1-4 academic calendar.

Academic Facilities

The Molloy campus has several new additions. The College's first residence hall opened in fall 2011, and there is also a new student center. In late 2011 Molloy also debuted a new 550-seat performing arts theater, which will serve the campus as well as the surrounding communities.

The James E. Tobin Library houses a collection of 110,000 volumes, along with hundreds of subscriptions to print journals and periodicals. Students and faculty members have access to the library's databases on campus and off campus as well as through the College's Web site. The library also houses a library instruction room, where librarians meet with professors and individual classes for instruction on the use of the databases and related research methods. The Tobin Library is a wireless

facility. In the Media Center, over 3,000 DVDs and VHS tapes support the curriculum.

Students may use more than 300 computers located in nineteen labs and open space areas. The College has 100 percent wireless coverage for portable devices.

The Wilbur Arts Center features numerous art studios, music studios, a cable television studio, and the Lucille B. Hays Theatre. Molloy's new performing arts center opened in the Public Square student center in fall 2011, providing additional rehearsal and performance space for students, while bringing world-class performers to the College's campus.

Kellenberg Hall houses six science labs, a language lab, and the education resource center. The Casey Center houses two nursing labs, and the behavioral sciences research facility is located in Siena Hall.

Costs

For 2011–12, tuition was $22,290 and required fees were approximately $1130. Students can expect to spend about $1400 on books and supplies and approximately $2400 in miscellaneous expenses.

Financial Aid

More than 85 percent of the student body of Molloy College is awarded financial aid in the form of scholarships, grants, loans, and Federal Work-Study Program employment. Financial aid awards are based on academic achievement and financial need. Completion of the Free Application for Federal Student Aid (FAFSA) is required. No-need scholarships and grants are also available.

Students who have attained a 95 percent or better high school average and a minimum combined score of 1280 on the SAT (composite math and verbal scores) are considered for the Molloy Scholars' Program, which awards full-tuition scholarships. Partial scholarships are available under Dominican, Community Service, and Fine Arts Scholarships. The Transfer Scholarship Program grants partial-tuition scholarships to students transferring into Molloy College with at least a 3.0 cumulative average. Athletic grants (Division II only) are awarded to full-time students based on athletic ability in a variety of sports. The Community Service Award is awarded to full-time freshmen demonstrating a commitment to their community and their school.

Faculty

The over 500 full-time and part-time faculty members at Molloy are dedicated as much to the students as to their respective fields. The 9:1 student-faculty ratio allows for small classes where students can receive the individual attention they deserve.

In addition to their teaching responsibilities, faculty members advise students in their fields to help them select courses that both satisfy major course requirements and lead to the attainment of career goals.

Student Government

Every member of the Molloy College student body belongs to the Molloy Student Association, whose elected leaders form the Molloy Student Government. This group of students provides the leadership necessary to keep extracurricular life at Molloy College alive, productive, and practical.

Admission Requirements

Recommended admission qualifications include graduation from a four-year public or private high school or equivalent (GED test) with a minimum of 18.5 units, including 4 in English, 4 in social studies, 3 in a foreign language, 3 in mathematics, and 3 in science. Nursing applicants must have taken courses in biology and chemistry. Mathematics applicants must have taken 4 units of math and 3 of science (including chemistry or physics). Biology applicants must have credits in biology, chemistry, and physics and 4 units of math. A portfolio is required of art applicants, and music students must audition. Social work applicants must file a special application with the director of the social work program.

The admissions committee bases its selection of candidates on the secondary school record, SAT or ACT scores, class rank, and the school's recommendation. A particular talent or ability can be important. Character and personality, extracurricular participation, and alumni relationships are all considered. On-campus interviews are recommended but not required.

The St. Thomas Aquinas Program, which houses both HEOP and the Albertus Magnus Program, may be an option for students not normally eligible for admission.

Molloy College also offers an honors program for a select group of academically gifted students. The program is open to entering freshmen in all majors.

Application and Information

To apply to Molloy College, students should submit the following credentials to the Admissions Office: a completed application for admission, a nonrefundable $30 application fee, an official high school transcript or GED score report, official results of the SAT or ACT, and official college transcripts (transfer students only).

The College uses a rolling admission system. Students are advised of an admission decision within a few weeks after the application filing process is complete.

For further information, prospective students should contact:

Director of Admissions
Molloy College
1000 Hempstead Avenue
P.O. Box 5002
Rockville Centre, New York 11571-5002
Phone: 888-4-MOLLOY (toll-free)
Web site: http://www.molloy.edu

Molloy College combines academic excellence and leadership with personal, compassionate mentoring to bring out the best in every student.

MONMOUTH UNIVERSITY
WEST LONG BRANCH, NEW JERSEY

The University

Monmouth University is a dynamic, first-tier, private university that empowers students to reach their full potential as leaders able to make significant contributions to their community and society. Through small classes, individual attention, and innovative faculty members, students are afforded a challenging learning environment on a campus that offers both the latest technology and classic beauty.

The University has a diverse student body of approximately 4,700 undergraduates and 1,800 graduate students. While many are from the Northeast, students also come from more than half of the continental United States and twenty-eight other nations. For those choosing University housing, Monmouth offers traditional residence halls and garden-style apartments. Some University-sponsored beachfront campus housing is also offered to students who meet certain requirements. Housing is guaranteed for first-year students.

There is a wide assortment of extracurricular activities available. Clubs and organizations include theater arts groups, the African American Student Union, Hillel, and sororities and fraternities that engage in service work on behalf of both the University and the community. There are also intramural and club sports including soccer, volleyball, lacrosse, and dance. Students can also get involved with the Student Government Association, the campus newspaper *(The Outlook)*, WMCX-FM, Hawk TV, the yearbook *(Shadows)*, or the literary magazine *(Monmouth Review)*. The University holds numerous events each year including art exhibits, concerts, lectures, and sightseeing trips offering students a shared experience outside the classroom.

The University is proud to host a successful NCAA Division I intercollegiate athletics program that includes nine men's teams (baseball, basketball, cross-country, football [FCS], golf, indoor track, outdoor track and field, soccer, and tennis) and eleven women's teams (basketball, bowling, cross-country, field hockey, golf, indoor track, lacrosse, outdoor track and field, soccer, softball, and tennis).

Being committed to an exceptional educational experience means having the facilities and services to provide state-of-the-art education and enrichment programs. The 153,200-square-foot Multipurpose Activity Center (MAC) features a 4,100-seat arena with premium suites; a 200-meter, six-lane indoor track; locker rooms; a fitness center; educational and conference space; the Hall of Champions; the University Store; and more. Also on campus are an outdoor tennis court; an all-weather track; and baseball, football, soccer, and softball fields.

Monmouth strives to ensure that incoming first-year students adapt well to their new environment. The Center for Student Success offers academic advising and individual personal and career counseling, while Academic Skills and Services provides personalized academic assistance including one-on-one tutoring.

The student newspaper, *The Outlook,* was named most outstanding newspaper by the American Scholastic Press Association. The Leon Hess Business School has been recognized by The Princeton Review as an outstanding business school in its 2012 edition of The Best 310 Business Schools. It was also recognized by *U.S. News & World Report* as having the best undergraduate business program. Undergraduate students in the sciences are involved in hands-on original research projects as part of student-faculty collaborative research teams. Undergraduate researchers have presented award-winning research at regional, national, and international conferences and earned co-authorship with faculty members on peer-reviewed publications. Monmouth students reach their goals by engaging their advisers early and often, and seniors describe faculty members as significantly more available, helpful, and sympathetic than do students at comparable institutions, according to the National Survey of Student Engagement.

Location

Part of a quality college experience is a location that is more than just a place—it is a destination. Monmouth is just such a destination in that it offers something for everyone. The University's secure 156-acre campus is in a residential area, a mile from the Atlantic Ocean and an hour from New York City and Philadelphia.

Monmouth is also close to many technology firms, financial institutions, and a business-industrial sector that provide both employment possibilities for graduates and opportunities for undergraduates to gain experience through internships and the cooperative education program.

Majors and Degrees

Monmouth University offers thirty-three baccalaureate degree programs in six academic schools that share the University's commitment to providing the highest level of education through innovative techniques and personal attention. The **Leon Hess Business School** awards bachelor's degrees in business administration with concentrations in accounting, economics, finance, management, marketing, and real estate. The **School of Education** awards bachelor's degrees that allow students to earn certification as elementary teachers, as P–3 with teacher of students with disabilities endorsement, as secondary teachers, or with K–12 endorsement. The **Wayne D. McMurray School of Humanities and Social Sciences** awards bachelor's degrees in anthropology, art, communication, criminal justice, English, fine arts, foreign language, graphic design, history, history/political science, music, political science, psychology, and theater. A Spanish and international business bachelor's degree is awarded jointly through the Leon Hess Business School and the School of Humanities and Social Sciences. The **School of Science** awards bachelor's degrees in biology, chemistry, clinical laboratory sciences, computer science, marine and environmental biology and policy, mathematics, medical technology, and software engineering. The **School of Social Work** awards the Bachelor of Social Work degree. The **Marjorie K. Unterberg School of Nursing and Health Studies** awards the Bachelor of Science in health studies and the Bachelor of Science in Nursing (available only to upper-division transfer students). A preprofessional advising program is available for students who intend to pursue careers in medicine, dentistry, or other health-care fields. Monmouth also offers the Five-Year Baccalaureate/Master's program, which enables qualified students to earn a bachelor's and a master's degree in five years in business, computer science, criminal justice, education (select programs), English, history, political science/public policy, psychology/school counseling, social work, or software engineering.

Academic Programs

The curriculum at Monmouth is focused on creating the next generation of leaders who are attuned to today's globally oriented, technological society and yet are grounded in the liberal arts. The University also emphasizes writing, speaking, and other interpersonal skills that are critical to personal growth and professional success. Monmouth equips every student with technological literacy and experiential education—real-world experience related to the student's academic major.

Beyond preparing students for successful careers in leadership roles, Monmouth strives to help students to develop values. These values include a sense of citizenship and a sense of social responsibility that enables graduates to contribute actively to the democratic society in which they live.

The Honors School at Monmouth University allows qualified students to participate in an educational environment that encourages and supports intellectual and personal excellence. First-year courses are clustered to enhance interactive learning, with professors who develop common themes and assignments. Honors classes are distinguished by in-depth coverage of material through discussion and writing, smaller class sizes, and a heightened student-faculty rapport. In their final year, each Honors School student researches, writes, and publicly presents an honors thesis, guided by a faculty member who serves as their academic mentor.

Experiential education is an invaluable part of the curriculum, enabling students to gain experience related to their majors while completing their studies. All education majors complete a semester of student teaching. The University also participates in the Washington Center, a partnership through which students may earn credit for experiential learning gained through internships and symposia in the nation's capital.

Genuine concern for the individual student characterizes the whole educational program. Professors, not teaching assistants, conduct all courses and supervise all laboratories.

Academic Facilities

Monmouth's fifty-four buildings provide a synthesis of historical architecture and modern aesthetics. The signature building is Woodrow Wilson Hall, a National Historic Landmark, which houses classrooms and administrative offices. The Jules L. Plangere Jr. Center for Communication provides state-of-the-art facilities, including an FM radio station and a TV studio.

The Monmouth University Library holds approximately 333,000 print and online monographs, 159 databases (e-journals, videos, and e-books), and over 43,000 electronic and print journal subscriptions.

Academic programs are amply supported by state-of-the-art computer hardware and software and classroom/laboratory facilities. The major components supporting Monmouth's academic programs include UNIX, Windows, and Apple systems connected by a campus wired and wireless network spanning twenty-three buildings and encompassing more than 2,400 workstations. Mobile devices are supported via a state-of-the-art wireless network available throughout the campus.

Monmouth University's new art building is under construction and is scheduled to be completed in fall 2012. Approximately 22,000 square feet, it includes a two-story gallery, a reception area, classrooms, faculty offices, and a student lounge.

The Lauren K. Woods Theatre lets students experience all phases of the theater arts, from acting to lighting. Students maintain control of all aspects of a theatrical performance.

Costs

For 2011–12, tuition and fees were approximately $28,000 per year. Annual room and board costs were approximately $10,459; actual costs are determined by the type of room and meal plan selected. Costs are subject to change for 2012–13.

Financial Aid

Monmouth believes that qualified students should not be denied an educational opportunity due to lack of financial resources. Financial aid staff members counsel students and their families and assist them in obtaining the maximum financial aid possible. In a cooperative effort, the University utilizes institutional, federal, and state resources and expects a reasonable family contribution toward the cost of attendance. In developing each student's award package, all resources available are utilized to address individual circumstances and provide equitable treatment for all applicants.

A wide range of University scholarships and grants are offered to all prospective full-time, first-year, and transfer students on the basis of academic performance and without regard to financial need. Eligibility for University scholarship and grant funding varies according to the quality of the student's previous academic record. Award amounts range from $3000 to $16,000. Scholarships and grants are renewed at the same amount for each year of the student's undergraduate career, provided the student maintains satisfactory levels of academic performance. Academic excellence scholarship recipients must maintain a minimum 3.0 cumulative GPA; academic excellence grant recipients must maintain a minimum 2.5 cumulative GPA; and incentive grant recipients must maintain a minimum 2.0 cumulative GPA. The University also participates in all federal and state grant and loan programs. To establish eligibility for these programs and capitalize on available assistance, students should complete the Free Application for Federal Student Aid (FAFSA) as soon after January 1 as possible. Students and their families may call 732-571-3463, e-mail finaid@monmouth.edu, or visit the Financial Aid Office for assistance.

Faculty

The University's professors are leaders in their fields and contribute through research, publishing, and consulting services to their respective academic areas. There are 259 full-time and 344 part-time faculty members. Approximately 85 percent of full-time faculty members have doctorates or terminal degrees in their fields. The average class size is 21, and the student-faculty ratio is 15:1.

Student Government

The Student Government Association (SGA) is an important and necessary voice in the University community; its views are recognized and respected. Monmouth students who wish to get involved with SGA can also do so as general members. This flexible form of involvement does not require a student to run for a position or participate in any one of the elections that are sponsored by SGA. More information is available at www.monmouth.edu/sga.

Admission Requirements

Many factors are considered in an admission application. For freshman applicants, a committee evaluates the required high school transcripts and SAT or ACT scores. Counselor recommendations, a resume of activities including leadership positions held, and other information supporting the application are welcome. Campus tours and information sessions with admission counselors are available. Transfer students must submit official transcripts from all colleges attended. If transfer students have earned fewer than 24 transferable credits, they must fulfill freshman admission requirements as well.

Application and Information

Early action is a nonbinding option for students with a strong desire to enroll at Monmouth. The early action application deadline is December 1, and the admission decision notification date is January 15. The application deadline for regular decision is March 1, with an admission decision notification date prior to April 1. Applications received after March 1 are considered on a space-available basis. Freshman housing is guaranteed for students who submit the required enrollment deposit, housing deposit, and housing contract by May 1. Students who submit their deposits and housing contract after May 1 may be placed on a wait list for admission and/or housing.

For further information, students should contact:

Office of Undergraduate Admission
Monmouth University
400 Cedar Avenue
West Long Branch, New Jersey 07764-1898
Phone: 732-571-3456
        800-543-9671 (toll-free)
Fax: 732-263-5166
E-mail: admission@monmouth.edu
Web site: http://www.monmouth.edu
          http://www.facebook.com/monmouthuniversity
          http://www.twitter.com/monmouthu

Monmouth students enjoy a challenging learning environment on a campus that offers classical beauty and the latest technology.

MORNINGSIDE COLLEGE
SIOUX CITY, IOWA

The College

The Morningside College experience cultivates a passion for lifelong learning and a dedication to ethical leadership and civic responsibility. For more than 115 years, the goal of Morningside College has been to provide students with an education of the highest quality. Morningside is rooted in a strong church-related, liberal arts tradition, and its challenge is to prepare students to be flexible in thought, open in attitude, and confident in themselves.

Founded in 1894, Morningside College is a private, four-year, coeducational, liberal arts institution affiliated with the United Methodist Church. The College seeks both students and faculty members representing diverse social, cultural, ethnic, racial, and national backgrounds.

At the graduate level, Morningside confers a Master of Arts in Teaching, with professional educator or special education tracks.

Morningside College's 1,200 full-time undergraduate students are encouraged to participate in a wide variety of activities, including departmental, professional, and religious organizations; honor societies; and sororities and fraternities. A newspaper, literary magazine, and campus radio station are all student directed. These activities provide students with many opportunities to develop leadership, interpersonal, and social skills. Since nearly all activities on campus are student initiated and student directed, ample opportunities for leadership development exist. Music recitals and concerts, theater productions, and a campus events series are held each semester. Intercollegiate athletics are available for men in baseball, basketball, cross-country, football, golf, soccer, swimming, tennis, track and field, and wrestling and for women in basketball, cross-country, golf, soccer, softball, swimming, tennis, track, and volleyball. Cheer and dance squads are also part of the athletic department. A variety of intramural activities are available.

The Hindman-Hobbs Center includes a pool, saunas, racquetball courts, a weight room, basketball courts, a wrestling room, and a jogging track as well as classroom facilities and offices.

Location

Morningside College is located on a 68-acre campus in Sioux City, the fourth-largest city in Iowa. The campus is based in a residential section of the community, adjacent to a city park, swimming pool, and tennis courts and within 5 minutes of a major regional shopping mall and a new shopping center. The Sioux City metropolitan area offers a blend of urban shopping, commerce, and recreation in a scenic setting. Students find Morningside's Sioux City location to be advantageous in seeking internship opportunities and full- or part-time employment.

Majors and Degrees

The five undergraduate degrees conferred by Morningside College are the Bachelor of Arts, Bachelor of Science, Bachelor of Science in Nursing, Bachelor of Music, and Bachelor of Music Education. Career programs consist of accounting, advertising, art, biology, business administration, chemistry, computer science, corporate communications, elementary education, engineering physics, English, graphic arts, history, interdisciplinary studies, marketing, mass communications, mathematics, music, nursing, philosophy, photography, political science, psychology, religious studies, Spanish, special

education, and theater. Students choosing to teach in secondary school may be certified in most academic majors.

In cooperation with other institutions, Morningside offers preprofessional programs in dentistry, engineering, law, medical technology, medicine, the ministry, optometry, pharmacy, physical therapy, physician assistant studies, and veterinary medicine.

Academic Programs

Morningside operates on a two-semester system; sessions are held from late August to December and from January to early May. Evening classes are offered each semester. A three-week May Term and a six-week summer session are also available.

The Morningside College experience provides an education that develops the whole person through an emphasis on critical thinking, effective communication, cultural understanding, practical wisdom, spiritual discernment, and ethical action. By working with talented faculty members in a large number of majors, caring college staff members who provide numerous opportunities for valuable cocurricular experiences, and other exceptional and interesting students with whom they will form lifelong connections, Morningside students gain the knowledge, skills, and personal dispositions that will ensure their success.

Special opportunities include a voluntary Interdepartmental Honors Program, in which students meet weekly to discuss ideas that have shaped history from the ancient world into the future. Friday Is Writing Day, offered in a weekly discussion format, allows students and faculty members to read aloud and react to one another's writing.

Every entering full-time student is provided with a notebook computer that is used in classroom work. Student technology services include high-speed Internet connection, ports in all residence halls and classrooms, Web-accessible personal e-mail accounts, a digital library accessible day and night, specialized computer labs to support academic programs, and wireless network access points across campus.

Off-Campus Programs

Morningside students who qualify have the opportunity to take advantage of special programs for off-campus study. Programs are available for a semester or the entire school year. The College has agreements with schools in Italy, England, Japan, and Northern Ireland.

Students participate in exchange programs with the Consortium Institute of Management and Business Analysis (CIMBA) in Italy; Kansai Gaidai University in Japan; Queen's University, the University of Ulster, Belfast Metropolitan College, Stranmillis University College, and St. Mary's University College in Northern Ireland; and Edge Hill University, the Centre for Medieval and Renaissance Studies, and Regent's American College London in England.

Starting with the spring 2013 semester, students can enroll in Morningside in Italy, a semester-long program for Morningside students and professors that combines classroom study and research with experiential learning opportunities.

A cooperative program with Central College in Pella, Iowa, allows Morningside students to study abroad in Australia,

China, England, France, Mexico, the Netherlands, Spain, and Wales.

In addition, Morningside has opportunities for students to enroll for a semester at American University in Washington, D.C., to study the U.S. government in action. Students may also be nominated for a semester at Drew University in New Jersey to study the United Nations. Students who participate in these programs maintain their enrollment at Morningside College.

Academic Facilities

The Hickman-Johnson-Furrow Learning Center is the home of the library and the Academic Support Services Center. The library has more than 99,000 volumes, nearly 3,000 audio recordings and video materials, and nearly 440 current print periodical subscriptions. Online accessibility includes student/faculty access to more than 18,000 full-text journals. The library's Web-based, integrated online system allows seamless access to numerous subscription databases as well as other online catalogs and Web sites. The library building also houses the Spoonholder Café, classrooms, the Mass Communication Department, and a computer lab.

Charles City College Hall is listed individually on the National Register of Historic Places and houses classrooms and offices for the History and Political Science, Philosophy, Religious Studies, and Theatre Departments.

The Eugene C. Eppley Fine Arts Building is one of the finest music and art facilities in the Midwest. The auditorium seats 1,400 and is noted for its acoustical qualities and the majestic Sanford Memorial Organ. The MacCollin Classroom Building, adjoining the auditorium, houses offices, art studios, practice rooms, and classrooms for music and art students.

The Helen Levitt Art Gallery adjoins the Eppley Auditorium and is home to the Levitt art collection, which includes work by internationally famous artists.

Lewis Hall, the second-oldest building on campus, is the site of the Education, English, Modern Languages, and Nursing Departments as well as administrative offices.

The Robert M. Lincoln Center houses the College's division of business administration and economics and contains a library, auditorium, a conference room, several classrooms, and the Center for Entrepreneurship Education.

The James and Sharon Walker Science Center, completely renovated in 2001, features up-to-date laboratories and classrooms and houses offices for the Natural Sciences and Mathematics Division.

Costs

Tuition and fees for 2011–12 were $24,050, and room and board were $7320. These figures do not include books and personal expenses.

Financial Aid

In 2010–11, more than $30 million was awarded in financial aid to Morningside students, with an average financial aid package of $23,726. The financial aid resources of federal, state, and College programs are available to Morningside students through a combination of scholarships, grants, loans, and work-study employment. Morningside values students who achieve both in and out of the classroom—people who are thinkers and doers. Morningside Celebration of Excellence Scholarships recognize academic excellence and outstanding service.

Students are encouraged to submit the Free Application for Federal Student Aid (FAFSA) as early as possible. The College's code number is 001879. The annual priority deadline for need-based financial aid is March 1.

Faculty

Seventy-one percent of Morningside College's 77 full-time faculty members have earned the terminal degree in their chosen field. The College also employs 62 part-time instructors and has a 13:1 student-faculty ratio.

Student Government

Student government is directly responsible for regulation, supervision, and coordination of student campus activities. The president of the student body is a voting member of the Board of Directors, allowing for student input in decisions facing the Board.

Admission Requirements

Morningside College selects students for admission whose scholastic achievement and personal abilities provide a foundation for success at the college level. While the College seeks students who rank in the upper half of their graduating class, each application is considered on an individual basis. The student's academic record, class rank, and test scores are considered. Transfer students must have earned 24 transferable semester hours of a 2.25 or better cumulative GPA on previous college work to qualify for automatic admission. It is the policy and practice of Morningside College to not discriminate against persons on the basis of age, sex, religion, creed, race, color, national or ethnic origin, sexual orientation, or physical or mental disability.

Application and Information

Rolling admission allows for flexibility; however, prospective students are encouraged to apply as early as possible before the semester in which they wish to enroll. Transfer and international students are welcome. Catalogs, application forms, and financial aid forms are available from the Office of Admissions.

For further information, students should contact:

Office of Admissions
Morningside College
1501 Morningside Avenue
Sioux City, Iowa 51106
Phone: 712-274-5111
        800-831-0806 (toll-free)
E-mail: mscadm@morningside.edu
Web site: http://www.morningside.edu
          http://www.facebook.com/msideadmissions

Morningside College students enjoy one of the most attractive campuses in the Midwest.

MOUNT ALOYSIUS COLLEGE
CRESSON, PENNSYLVANIA

The College

Mount Aloysius College is a private, accessible, and affordable Catholic liberal arts college sponsored by the Religious Sisters of Mercy. The College welcomes people of all faith traditions. Established in 1853, Mount Aloysius College offers both undergraduate and graduate education. Since the founding of the College, nearly 14,000 students have become proud Mount Aloysius alumni. The College is committed to providing a small class sizes, and students benefit from accessible faculty and staff. Mount Aloysius students come mostly from throughout Pennsylvania and the mid-Atlantic Region. There are over 2,500 students enrolled (unduplicated headcount).

Mount Aloysius College is one of 16 Mercy Colleges nationwide. Students are encouraged to synthesize faith with learning, to develop competence with compassion, to apply their talents and gifts to the service of others, and to assume leadership in their community.

Student activities play a distinctive role in personal growth. At Mount Aloysius College, there are approximately 100 organized clubs, groups, honor societies, and an intramural sports program. Activities include a student newspaper, residence hall associations, student government, cheerleading, dance team, scholarship-funded theater and choir programs, and a student activities planning board. Mount Aloysius fun includes social events, intramural sports, athletic events, comedians, live music, theater, educational events, campus forums, and awesome guest lectures.

Mount Aloysius College is a member of NCAA Division III. Athletic programs involve both women and men and include basketball, cross-country, golf, soccer, and tennis. Men's baseball and women's softball and volleyball are also offered. Athletes benefit from the Ray S. and Louise S. Walker Athletic Field Complex, which includes a softball field, one of the finest soccer fields in the area, and the Calandra-Smith baseball complex. Recently the Mountie Stables were opened to the College and to the community. The Stables add dugouts, lockers, showers, storage, and concession facilities to the school's athletic infrastructure. Ground has just been broken for a spectacular 90,000-square-foot Athletic Convocation and Wellness Center on the western edge of the beautiful and expansive campus. This facility is scheduled to open in early 2014 and will take Mount Aloysius College athletics to a new level. The facility will also add a welcomed special events venue to the Southern Allegheny Mountains.

The main campus building is a picturesque structure dating to 1897; it houses the admissions, financial aid, security, health, and academic offices, along with the Office of the President, classrooms, the Region's premiere nursing simulation center, and the Wolf-Kuhn Art Gallery. Cosgrave Center is the hub of campus life. The building contains the dining hall, snack bar, bookstore, child-care center (part of the elementary education/early childhood program at the College), lounges, recreational rooms, student affairs offices, and meeting rooms. The College's Health and Physical Fitness Center is currently the main athletic arena. It has seating capacity for 2,000 and serves as home to Mounties fans. The facility contains three basketball courts, three volleyball courts, a tennis court, a weight and exercise room equipped with a sauna, two locker rooms, office areas, changing rooms for sports officials, public restrooms, a lobby, and a vestibule. Ihmsen Halls are key housing facilities for residential students. Misciagna Residence is a state-of-the-art residence hall, providing 25 suites and private bathrooms. McAuley Hall features both double and single rooms and a large multipurpose room and study lounges on all three floors. Alumni Hall is a historic, multipurpose facility used for College drama, musicals, lectures, and performing arts events. The College operates 12 months per year and opens its facilities to the Southern Allegheny community.

The College is 100 percent wireless, and smart classrooms are located throughout the campus.

Mount Aloysius is fully accredited by the Middle States Association of Colleges and Schools and approved by the Pennsylvania Department of Education. All nursing and health studies programs are fully accredited by their professional accrediting bodies, including the National League for Nursing Accrediting Commission, the Commission on Accreditation for Programs of Diagnostic Medical Sonography, the Commission on Accreditation in Physical Therapy Education, the American Association of Medical Assistants, and the Joint Commission on Accreditation for Programs of Surgical Technology.

In addition to its undergraduate programs, Mount Aloysius offers master's degrees in business administration, community counseling, and psychology.

Location

Mount Aloysius College is located in the scenic Southern Allegheny Mountains of west-central Pennsylvania, in the town of Cresson. Convenient and accessible from U.S. Route 22, the College's setting is rural but mere minutes from State College, Altoona, and Johnstown, Pennsylvania. The area has warm, beautiful summers; brisk, breathtaking autumns; invigorating winters; and cool, blooming springs. Well maintained facilities are close and available for biking, golfing, swimming, horseback riding, waterskiing, boating, hiking, spelunking, cross-country and down-hill skiing, picnicking, and amusement and water parks. A well-kept system of State Parks is convenient to the College as are shopping malls, golf courses, and numerous historical sites.

Majors and Degrees

Mount Aloysius College awards bachelor's and associate degrees in the arts, sciences, and health studies fields in both career-oriented and traditional liberal arts programs. Baccalaureate degrees are available in accounting, behavioral and social science, biology and general science, business administration, which includes a fifth-year M.B.A. option, computer science, criminology, elementary/early childhood education and secondary education (with certifications), English, general science, history/political science, humanities, information technology, math/science, medical imaging, nursing (RN-B.S.N. program), nursing (2+2), occupational therapy (3-2), physical therapy (4-2), physician assistant studies (3-2), prelaw, psychology, sign language/interpreter education, and undecided/exploratory. Associate degrees are offered in applied technology, business administration, criminology, early childhood studies, general studies, legal studies, liberal arts, medical assistant studies, nursing, nursing (LPN to RN), physical therapist assistant studies, pre-nursing, radiography/medical imaging, sign language/deaf studies, and surgical technology.

Academic Programs

Whether preparing students for careers upon graduation or for graduate school, Mount Aloysius recognizes the importance of a broad and liberal education. Thus, in addition to receiving solid preparation for a chosen career, every student at the College receives a foundation in the arts, sciences, and humanities

through an outstanding core curriculum. Strong emphasis is placed on the specialized courses within each program of study, and many academic programs combine classroom experience with internships and related training at area clinical sites, agencies, and institutions. In addition to its regular academic programs, Mount Aloysius offers independent and directed study with a commitment to service, a central component to a Mercy education. The College has an excellent honors program and academic services area. The academic calendar has two traditional semesters and optional summer sessions.

Off-Campus Programs

An important feature of many academic programs is off-campus training. The majority of the College's programs of study require credit-yielding practicums at partnering hospitals, public and private schools, or health or human service agencies. Students in all health programs benefit from required clinical training during their time at the College.

Academic Facilities

In 1995, Mount Aloysius College opened both a new Library and a new era, signifying greater access to information for the College community. This state-of-the-art Library is the campus hub for technology and study. With a Buhl Electronic Classroom and more than 80,000 print and nonprint titles, the Library is an impressive, 31,000-square-foot facility with ample seating space, four group-study rooms, a reading lounge, a law library and classroom, an unparalleled 18,000-volume Ecumenical Collection donated by Pastor Gerald Myers, and ample room for expansion. This facility is completely automated, with an online catalog and access to remote libraries and the Internet through the more than 30 workstations. The Library also houses the Information Technology Center, home to 15 multimedia workstations and the latest educational software.

Pierce Hall serves as the campus science center. A state-of-the-art, 31,000-square-foot facility, it was completed in 1997. Pierce Hall houses all science labs, health science centers, and the offices of science faculty. Academic Hall is home to the College Honors Program. It houses classrooms, labs, seminar rooms, faculty offices, and electronic classrooms. The College is proud of its bridge to the past and its progress in providing twenty-first century learning facilities.

Costs

Annual tuition and fees for the 2012–13 academic year for full-time students are $18,640; room and board are $8080. Up-to-date cost information is available online at www.mtaloy.edu/tuition_and_aid/tuition_and_fees.

Financial Aid

Mount Aloysius prides itself on affordability. Many MAC students hail from proud families of modest means and many are first-generation students. The College understands the expense involved in acquiring a quality education and encourages all students to apply for all available aid. Through the Office of Financial Aid, the College assists students in applying for state and federal grants, loans, work-study awards, merit scholarships and more. The College awards academic monies based on GPA and SAT or ACT scores. These awards are renewable over a four-year period and range from $1000 to $10,000 per year. Mount Aloysius College participates in all federal and state programs; fully 94 percent of Mount Aloysius College students receive some form of financial aid. *U.S. News & World Report* has ranked Mount Aloysius College as one of the best-priced private liberal arts colleges in the United States.

Faculty

The Mount Aloysius faculty consists of approximately 175 members, whose primary responsibility is teaching and advising students. Many faculty members hold advanced or terminal degrees and are expected to maintain close instructional ties with students. Many professors hold national professional certificates in such disciplines as criminology, education, law, and nursing. The Mount Aloysius student-faculty ratio of 14:1 allows close contact between students and faculty members, providing personal attention in a highly structured environment—a key ingredient in the College's academic philosophy.

Student Government

The Student Government Association (SGA) represents students on all issues that concern the College. The SGA appoints student representatives to all student-oriented College committees. The College encourages active student participation in the general governance structure and in other matters concerning the development and implementation of policies on residential student life.

Admission Requirements

The College enrolls a freshman class of approximately 350 students. The total class of 550 includes transfer students. Admission is selective and based on academic promise, as indicated by a student's secondary school performance and activities, standardized test scores, and special experience and talents. Applicants are required to have, or expect to earn, a diploma from an approved secondary school or a GED diploma. Submission of official transcripts and SAT or ACT scores is required. In addition to the general admission requirements, specific admission requirements exist for the health programs.

For further information, students should visit the College's Web site at http://www.mtaloy.edu. Prospective students are encouraged to visit the scenic 193-acre campus. The College is open Monday to Friday from 8:30 to 5 and on select Saturdays.

Application and Information

To apply for admission to Mount Aloysius College, candidates are encouraged to submit their application and $30 application fee to the Office of Undergraduate and Graduate Admissions. In addition, students may apply online.

For further information, students should contact:

Office of Undergraduate and Graduate Admissions
Mount Aloysius College
7373 Admiral Peary Highway
Cresson, Pennsylvania 16630
Phone: 814-886-6383
      888-823-2220 (toll-free)
Fax: 814-886-6441
E-mail: admissions@mtaloy.edu
Web site: http://www.mtaloy.edu

MUHLENBERG COLLEGE
ALLENTOWN, PENNSYLVANIA

The College

Founded in 1848, Muhlenberg College aims to develop independent critical thinkers who are intellectually agile, characterized by a zeal for reasoned and civil debate, knowledgeable about the achievements and traditions of diverse civilizations and cultures, able to express ideas with clarity and grace, committed to lifelong learning, equipped with ethical values, and prepared for lives of leadership and service.

Muhlenberg students achieve the College's goals by assuming strong individual responsibility for intense involvement in vigorous academic work and for personal involvement within the College community. The more than 100 student organizations provide outlets for the diversified cultural, athletic, religious, social, leadership, and service interests of the students. The campus is primarily residential; more than 90 percent of the 2,200 students live on campus. A close sense of community develops naturally, one in which their diversified academic and personal interests enable students to contribute positively to the intellectual and personal growth of their peers.

Students are aided by an active Career Center in relating academic and personal knowledge and skills to appropriate career goals and in obtaining positions upon graduation. About one third of a typical graduating class proceeds immediately to graduate or professional school.

Location

Muhlenberg College is located on a campus of 86 acres in suburban west Allentown, an area made up primarily of attractive family homes and parks. The downtown area of Allentown, a city of approximately 104,000 people, is a 10-minute ride from the campus. The College is located 90 miles west of New York City and 60 miles north of Philadelphia.

Majors and Degrees

Muhlenberg offers the Bachelor of Arts (A.B.) degree in the following fields: accounting, American studies, anthropology, art, business, communication, dance, economics, English, film studies, finance, French, German, history, history/government, international studies, music, philosophy, philosophy/political thought, political economy, political science, psychology, religious studies, Russian studies, social science, sociology, Spanish, and theater arts. The Bachelor of Science (B.S.) degree is offered in the following fields: biochemistry, biology, chemistry, computer science, environmental science, mathematics, natural sciences, neuroscience, and physics. Students may also design their own major. Minors are offered in most of the major fields, as well as in Jewish studies, African American studies, women's studies, public health, and Asian traditions.

In addition, students may receive certification to teach at the elementary and secondary levels. Other opportunities include a 4-4 dual-admission program with Drexel University College of Medicine; a 3-4 dental program with the University of Pennsylvania; a 3-3 B.S./Ph.D. program in physical therapy with Thomas Jefferson University; a 3-2½ B.S./M.S. program in occupational therapy with Thomas Jefferson University; a 3-2/4-2 combined program in engineering, offered in cooperation with Columbia University; a 3-2 combined program in forestry, offered in cooperation with Duke University; and a 4-4 dual-admission program with SUNY College of Optometry.

Academic Programs

The A.B. and B.S. programs emphasize breadth of study in the liberal arts as well as in-depth study of a particular academic major. All students must fulfill requirements in foreign culture, the humanities, social sciences, and natural sciences. Strong achievement on Advanced Placement examinations may enable a student to receive advanced placement, possibly with credit. Scores of 4 or 5 earn automatic credit. Scores of 3 are evaluated by the appropriate department.

Students work closely with academic advisers to formulate programs well suited to their individual interests, abilities, needs, and goals. Generally, students are expected to declare their major at the end of the freshman year; however, many students later change their academic major with no difficulty. A double major is possible, and about a third of Muhlenberg students graduate with a double major. The College also enriches the freshman-year experience through more than thirty special-focus First-Year Seminars.

Off-Campus Programs

Study abroad is available through Muhlenberg's Semester-in-London Program, Netherlands semester, Dublin semester, or more than 160 affiliate agreements with international universities all over the world. In addition, the Lehigh Valley Association of Independent Colleges sponsors summer study-abroad options in England, France, Germany, Israel, and Spain. Credit for study-abroad programs sponsored by other institutions or by private agencies may also be transferred to Muhlenberg by special arrangement.

Students may participate in a variety of internships in local businesses, health-care facilities, schools, public agencies, theaters, broadcasting stations, and magazines. Government internships in Harrisburg, Pennsylvania, and Washington, D.C., and an Ethics and Public Affairs semester in Washington, D.C., as well as a New York City semester at Jewish Theological Seminary are also available.

Students may enroll in courses offered at any of the five other member institutions of the Lehigh Valley Association of Independent Colleges: Lafayette College, Lehigh University, Cedar Crest College, DeSales University, and Moravian College.

Academic Facilities

Muhlenberg's library collection contains more than 200,000 volumes as well as numerous government documents, periodicals, and electronic and online resources. The $12-million Harry C. Trexler Library, a state-of-the-art library facility, opened in 1988. Students may also use library materials owned by the other institutions participating in the Lehigh Valley Association of Independent Colleges.

The Baker Center for the Arts was designed for Muhlenberg by the well-known architect Philip Johnson. It houses a modern theater complex, a recital hall, classrooms, art studios, and a fine arts gallery. The Trexler Performing Arts Pavilion opened in 2000 and provides dance performance and studio space, a new theater, a Black Box, and additional arts spaces. The College augmented its arts facilities with the Rehearsal House in 2011.

Life science facilities include numerous laboratories, classrooms, two electron microscopes, a DNA sequencer, an isolation room used for growing and studying viruses, and a museum of natural history. Facilities supporting students in the physical sciences include equipment for optics, electronics, and atomic, nuclear, and solid-state physics. A new 40,000-square-foot addition to the science facilities opened in fall 2006. The College uses a UNIX/Windows computer system with Novell software.

Costs

The comprehensive tuition and fees for the 2011–12 academic year was $39,915. The room and board fee averaged $9040. The total cost for a resident student was approximately $48,955.

Financial Aid

Muhlenberg College endeavors to make its educational opportunities available to all qualified students regardless of their financial circumstances. While most financial aid at Muhlenberg is based on financial need as demonstrated by the College Scholarship Service Financial Aid PROFILE and FAFSA, there is also significant merit aid available. Typically, about 70 percent of Muhlenberg's students qualify for and receive financial aid.

Faculty

The Muhlenberg faculty consists of 171 full-time and 120 part-time members. Ninety percent of full-time faculty members hold doctoral or terminal degrees. While many faculty members are distinguished for their scholarly research, teaching is the main emphasis of their work. Professors at all levels work closely with students both inside and outside of the classroom. Most department heads teach introductory courses.

Student Government

Muhlenberg students are expected to demonstrate a high level of responsibility with regard to their own governance and to participate extensively in internal decision-making and communication processes throughout the campus. These responsibilities are coordinated by the United Student Government, which transacts all business pertaining to the student body. This organization is in charge of a student activities budget of more than $350,000. In addition, 2 students serve as representatives to the Board of Trustees, and students hold full voting privileges on many faculty committees.

Admission Requirements

The College selects students who give evidence of ability and scholastic achievement, seriousness of purpose, and the capacity to make constructive contributions to the College community. Approximately 70 percent of a typical freshman class ranked in the top fifth of their secondary school class. SAT scores for entering freshmen average approximately 610 verbal, 620 math, and 615 writing.

Submission of SAT or ACT scores is optional. An on-campus interview is strongly recommended for all applicants and required for students who choose not to submit standardized test scores.

Application and Information

Students who wish to be considered for admission should submit a completed application form as early as possible during their senior year of secondary school and no later than February 15. Regular decision candidates receive notice of admission decisions in late March. Early decision plans are available, and the College fills approximately half of its freshman class via early decision. Transfer admission is also possible.

For further information, interested students should contact:

Christopher Hooker-Haring
Dean of Admission and Financial Aid
Muhlenberg College
Allentown, Pennsylvania 18104-5586
Phone: 484-664-3200
E-mail: admissions@muhlenberg.edu
Web site: http://www.muhlenberg.edu

The Bell Tower of the Haas College Center stands as the focal point of the Muhlenberg College campus.

NEUMANN UNIVERSITY
ASTON, PENNSYLVANIA

The University

Neumann University (http://www.neumann.edu), a Catholic coeducational institution in the Franciscan tradition, recognizes the value of developing intellectual excellence, professional competence, and strong community life. As a university that balances the liberal arts with the professions, Neumann was founded to meet and expand the educational and professional horizons of men and women through instruction that is based on values, ethical behavior, and service to others. With the addition of the Living and Learning Center (multimedia-capable residences), Neumann University is able to serve a diverse geographic and demographic population.

Founded and sponsored by the Sisters of St. Francis of Philadelphia, the University is committed to a varied student body and welcomes students of all denominations. Current enrollment is 3,073.

The Life Center houses the Meagher Theatre, the Bruder Athletic Center, and the Crossroads Cafe dining facility. Intercollegiate sports include women's basketball, cross-country, field hockey, ice hockey, indoor track, lacrosse, soccer, softball, tennis, track, and volleyball; and men's baseball, basketball, cross-country, golf, ice hockey, indoor track, lacrosse, soccer, tennis, and track. Neumann University competes as a member of the National Collegiate Athletic Association (NCAA) Division III, the Colonial States Athletic Conference, and the Eastern Collegiate Athletic Conference (ECAC). Intramural sports are available to all members of the campus community.

The Living and Learning Center is designed to provide a state-of-the-art residential experience, with a focus on education within a real-world living environment. Technologically smart, the center connects students to both faculty members and friends via wireless Internet, which is available in every suite and apartment. The system provides full access to campus resources and activities, as well as activities and resources worldwide. The center also houses a separate computer lab, a fitness center, a reflection room, various study rooms with warming kitchens for group study or meetings, and a laundry.

The University provides a full range of services to students, including career placement, career and personal counseling, a tutoring program, and health services.

Neumann students are involved in a wide variety of campus and community activities. Major and special interest clubs are available for student participation. Clubs bring together students who share common interests and help foster new friendships.

At Neumann, the spiritual dimension of one's life is recognized as integral to total human development. The Ministry Team provides a pastoral presence on campus and promotes a sense of community. The entire University community is invited to serve the needs of the poor and neglected in society through various outreach programs, with special attention to the need for peace and justice in the world today.

Neumann is well positioned to respond to the academic and extracurricular needs of students who are of traditional or nontraditional age, commuters or residents, and full-time or part-time.

In addition to undergraduate programs, Neumann confers master's degrees in education, nursing, pastoral counseling, sport management, and strategic leadership as well as doctoral degrees in education (Ed.D.) and physical therapy (D.P.T.).

Location

Neumann, with a beautiful 68-acre suburban campus in Aston, Delaware County, Pennsylvania, is a short distance from Philadelphia; Wilmington, Delaware; southern New Jersey; and Maryland. It is easily accessible from major arteries such as I-95, Route 476, Route 1, and the Pennsylvania Turnpike.

Majors and Degrees

Neumann offers strong academic majors leading to a Bachelor of Arts degree or a Bachelor of Science degree in accounting, arts production and performance, athletic training, biology, business administration, communication and media arts, computer and information management, criminal justice, education, English, environmental studies, international business, liberal arts, marketing, nursing, political science, psychology, and sport and entertainment management. The education programs lead to teacher certification in early elementary (PK–4), special education (PK–8) or secondary education. Pre-professional programs in law and medicine are also available. An accelerated evening program for adults leads to an Associate of Arts, Bachelor of Arts, or Bachelor of Science degree in liberal studies or professional studies.

Academic Programs

The academic program at Neumann University is composed of a core curriculum (required of all students), a major area of study (chosen by each student), and a wide range of elective offerings. Students may also choose a minor area of study. The University's broad base of liberal arts offerings prepares students for the intellectual and social challenges they will face in the employment marketplace and throughout their lives. The core is intended to provide basic knowledge of the liberal arts and sciences; develop verbal, written, and symbolic communication skills; and stimulate interest in a broad range of topics for the purpose of enhancing the individual's contributions to society, thereby enabling the individual to realize full human potential.

Classroom instruction is supplemented by cooperative education and internships, through which students can earn credit and gain experience by working in a job related to their career interest. Fieldwork and student teaching are required of all education majors. Clinical practice for the nursing major occurs in a variety of health-care facilities in the tri-state area.

The honors program is an opportunity for academically talented students to explore imaginative and innovative perspectives on learning. It is also an opportunity to stimulate and motivate students to expand their knowledge and interest and to strive for greater excellence. Moreover, it is a reward for prior perseverance and dedication as well as an obligation to use skills and abilities in service to others. Admission to the honors program is by invitation.

Neumann University has transfer articulation agreements with numerous schools throughout the area.

Academic Facilities

The Child Development Center is a state-of-the-art, octagonal-shaped building, specifically designed to house an educational program for preschoolers. As a state-licensed day-care facility, it enrolls children of Neumann students, the faculty, and the community. The Child Development Center is part of the Division of Education and Human Services. Students enrolled in education courses use the center for observation, practical experience, and student teaching.

The Academic Computing Center is located on the ground floor of the University. The computers are viewed as tools to support all fields of study and all students and faculty members. Neumann University has installed a wireless Local Area Network (LAN) that connects various computers and provides shared services such as printing, e-mail, and support for the instructional use of computers by providing for the sharing of files. Computers are available to all students, as is software related to various academic disciplines. Access to the Web and the Internet is available.

The Academic Resource Center is a service that enables students to meet Neumann's academic standards and successfully attain their personal educational goals. Free tutoring is provided to students in all core courses.

The University library contains a balanced collection of more than 75,000 volumes, 95,000 microfilm units, 2,000 videos, and 400 periodical subscriptions. Private study rooms and conference rooms are available for both student and faculty use. In addition to traditional media services support, a full-color video studio and a graphics production area are available. Serving as a comprehensive resource for students, other holdings include Neumann's online catalog system, FRANCIS, which is accessible via the Web. The library is a member of the Tri-State College Library Cooperative, the Consortium for Health Information and Library Services, SEPCHE, and the Online Computer Library Center, which provide additional convenient resources for students. The library subscribes to various online research services.

Costs
Tuition for full-time students (12 to 19 credits per semester) in 2012–13 is $23,262. Room and board are $11,070 (full meal plan).

Financial Aid
Typically, about 95 percent of Neumann undergraduate students receive some form of financial aid (scholarships, grants, and student loans).

Neumann offers a variety of renewable scholarships each year to entering full-time freshmen and transfer students. Interested applicants should contact the Office of Admissions and Financial Aid as soon as possible to determine eligibility.

In addition to Neumann scholarships, funds are available through the Federal Pell Grant, Federal Supplemental Educational Opportunity Grant, and Federal Work-Study Programs. Many states provide grant money to attend Neumann (non-Pennsylvania residents should check with their state's higher education agency for details). Veterans Administration benefits can be received by qualified veterans or their dependents. Federal Stafford Student Loans and Federal PLUS Program loans are available and can be applied for through Neumann's preferred lender or any participating bank. Neumann also offers institutional need-based grants. All students requesting financial aid must complete the Free Application for Federal Student Aid (FAFSA) each year to determine eligibility. In order to expedite processing, the FAFSA should be submitted by March 15 for the following school year. Financial aid funds are renewable annually based on need, as determined by the FAFSA results.

Faculty
Neumann students describe faculty members as sincere, hard working, determined, and energetic. Faculty members view themselves, first, as teachers and are proud partners in their students' journeys toward professional careers. Each student has a faculty adviser, who assists in arranging a program designed to meet the student's educational goals. Many faculty members serve as moderators of student clubs. The student-faculty ratio is 13:1.

Student Government
The Student Government Association (SGA) is the representative body for all students. Its function is to implement the aims and purposes of the University, foster cooperation in student relationships, assist the University in being responsive to the needs of the student body, and encourage personal responsibility for an intelligent system of student self-government. Through the Student Activities Board, social functions are planned throughout the year. Students serve on various University committees, including the Student Affairs Committee of the Board, Academic Advising Committee, Honors Program Committee, Registration/Orientation Task Force, and Student Judicial Board. For full-time students, a Student Government Association fee of $80 per semester is required.

Admission Requirements
Neumann has a rolling admission policy and accepts applications throughout the year. Applicants are considered on the basis of high school record, SAT or ACT scores, recommendations, class rank, and other indicators of potential to succeed in university-level studies. Applications for admission are reviewed without regard to sex, race, creed, color, national origin, age, sexual orientation, pregnancy, military status, religion, or disability. Applicants should be graduates of an accredited high school (or present equivalent credentials) and have a recommended curriculum of 16 units of high school course work, distributed as follows: 4 in English, 2 to 3 in science, 2 in mathematics, 2 in social studies, 2 in foreign language, and 4 in electives. Students intending to pursue a major in biology or clinical laboratory science must have at least 1 year of high school biology and chemistry, and high school physics is highly recommended.

Neumann participates in the Advanced Placement (AP) Program and the College-Level Examination Program (CLEP).

An interview and tour of the campus are highly recommended for all prospective students and parents. Visits can be arranged by contacting the Office of Admissions.

Application and Information
Applicants for freshman admission are requested to have SAT or ACT scores and high school transcripts sent to the Office of Admissions. A nonrefundable $35 application fee should accompany the completed application. A free application is available online at http://www.neumann.edu.

Neumann University welcomes applications from students who have attended or are currently attending either two-year or four-year regionally accredited institutions of higher learning.

For further information, students should contact:

Office of Admissions
Neumann University
One Neumann Drive
Aston, Pennsylvania 19014-1298
Phone: 610-558-5616
      800-9NEUMANN (toll-free)
E-mail: neumann@neumann.edu
Web site: http://www.neumann.edu

Students love the newest building on campus, the Mirenda Center for Sport, Spirituality, and Character Development.

THE NEW ENGLAND INSTITUTE OF ART
BROOKLINE, MASSACHUSETTS

A focused education from The New England Institute of Art can help students turn their creative energy into a powerful tool that can make a difference in the world. Students are part of a collaborative and supportive community, where experienced instructors provide the guidance and skills needed to pursue a career in the creative economy.

The school's programs in the areas of design, media arts, and fashion give students the opportunity to learn by using professional-grade technology and build a portfolio of work to show potential employers after graduation.

The New England Institute of Art is accredited by the New England Association of Schools and Colleges (NEASC) through its Commission on Institutions of Higher Education (CIHE), 209 Burlington Rd, Suite 201, Bedford, Massachusetts 01730-1433; phone: 781-271-0022.

The New England Institute of Art is authorized to award Associate in Science and Bachelor of Science degrees by the Commonwealth of Massachusetts, Massachusetts Department of Higher Education, One Ashburton Place, Room 1401, Boston, Massachusetts 02108-1696; phone: 617-994-6950.

Location

The New England Institute of Art is located in the heart of the Boston area, the home to more colleges and universities than any other city in North America. Museums and sporting events, theater, and a top 10 media market, are all easily accessible from the school.

Programs of Study and Degrees

No matter which course of study a student may choose, the professionals at The New England Institute of Art will guide, support, and help each student as their talents evolve on their journey of personal and professional transformation. Students studying design learn to fine-tune their visual thinking and problem-solving skills as they create everything from logos to TV ads. Programs in the area of media arts focus on utilizing technology to deliver information and entertainment, while students studying fashion learn to market and merchandise clothing.

Bachelor's degree programs are offered in the areas of audio and media technology, digital filmmaking and video production, fashion and retail management, graphic design, interior design, media arts and animation, photography, sound and motion picture technical arts, and Web design and interactive media. A minor in game art is available with the media arts and animation program.

Associate degree programs are offered in the areas of audio production and photography.

Certificate programs are offered in the areas of audio production, multimedia and Web design I, multimedia and Web design II, and photography.

Academic Programs

The New England Institute of Art operates on a year-round, four-quarter system.

Academic Facilities

The New England Institute of Art provides a learning environment with professional-grade technology applicable to each student's course of study. Students have the opportunity to build a portfolio of work that shows potential employers that they are trained to use the software, hardware, or equipment utilized within the industry. Depending upon the course of study, students are immersed in a creative environment—from classrooms to computer labs to studios—focused on relevant, hands-on education designed to prepare students for the real world.

Costs

Tuition cost varies by program. Prospective students should contact the school for current tuition costs. Other charges include a starting kit for all first-quarter students. Kits vary in price, depending on the program of study.

Financial Aid

Financial aid is available for those who qualify. Students who require financial assistance should first complete and submit a Free Application for Federal Student Aid (FAFSA) and meet with a financial aid officer.

Faculty

Faculty members are experienced professionals who create a learning environment that is similar to the professional world students will face after graduation. Instructors are focused on helping students develop the skills they need to transform their creative potential into marketable skills.

Admission Requirements

Applicants must provide proof of high school graduation or achievement of a General Educational Development (GED) certificate as a prerequisite for admission. In lieu of documenting high school graduation or a GED certificate, applicants may provide proof of attaining an associate's degree or higher from an accredited institution. An official transcript indicating date of high school graduation, GED certificate (including test scores), or date of college graduation (including degree granted) is required as proof.

All individuals seeking admission to The New England Institute of Art are interviewed in person or by phone by an assistant director of admissions, and each applicant must create an original essay of at least 150 words stating how an education at The New England Institute of Art would help the student to achieve career goals. There is a $50 application fee.

For the most recent information regarding admission requirements, please refer to the current academic catalog.

Application and Information

To obtain an application, make arrangements for an interview, or tour the school, prospective students should contact:

The New England Institute of Art
10 Brookline Place West
Brookline, MA 02445-7295
Phone: 617-739-1700
        800-903-4425 (toll-free)
Fax: 617-582-4500
Web site: http://www.artinstitutes.edu/boston

Over 50 schools: The Art Institute of Atlanta; The Art Institute of Atlanta—Decatur, A branch of The Art Institute of Atlanta; The Art Institute of Austin, A branch of The Art Institute of Houston; The Art Institute of California, a college of Argosy University, with locations in Hollywood, Inland Empire, Los Angeles, Orange County, Sacramento, San Diego, San Francisco, and Sunnyvale; The Art Institute of Charleston, A branch of The Art Institute of Atlanta; The Art Institute of Charlotte; The Art Institute of Colorado; The Art Institute of Dallas, A campus of South University; The Art Institute of Fort Lauderdale; The Art Institute of Fort Worth, A campus of South University; The Art Institute of Houston; The Art Institute of Houston—North, A branch of The Art Institute of Houston; The Art Institute of Indianapolis; The Art Institute of Jacksonville, A branch of Miami International University of Art & Design; The Art Institute of Las Vegas; The Art Institute of Michigan; The Art Institute of Michigan—Troy; The Art Institute of New York City; The Art Institute of Ohio—Cincinnati; The Art Institute of Philadelphia; The Art Institute of Phoenix; The Art Institute of Pittsburgh; The Art Institute of Portland; The Art Institute of Raleigh—Durham; The Art Institute of Salt Lake City; The Art Institute of San Antonio, A branch of The Art Institute of Houston; The Art Institute of Seattle; The Art Institute of Tampa, A branch of Miami International University of Art & Design; The Art Institute of Tennessee—Nashville, A branch of The Art Institute of Atlanta; The Art Institute of Tucson; The Art Institute of Vancouver; The Art Institute of Virginia Beach[1], A branch of The Art Institute of Atlanta; The Art Institute of Washington[1], A branch of The Art Institute of Atlanta; The Art Institute of Washington—Dulles[1], A branch of The Art Institute of Atlanta; The Art Institute of Wisconsin; The Art Institute of York—Pennsylvania; The Art Institutes International—Kansas City; The Art Institutes International Minnesota; The Illinois Institute of Art—Chicago; The Illinois Institute of Art—Schaumburg; The Illinois Institute of Art—Tinley Park; Miami International University of Art & Design; The New England Institute of Art

[1]Certified by SCHEV to operate in Virginia

See **aiprograms.info** for program duration, tuition, fees, and other costs, median debt, federal salary data, alumni success, and other important info. The Art Institutes is a system of over 50 schools throughout North America. Programs, credential levels, technology, and scheduling options vary by school, and employment opportunities are not guaranteed. Financial aid is available to those who qualify. Several institutions included in The Art Institutes system are campuses of South University or Argosy University. OH Registration # 04-01-1698B, AC0165, AC0080, Licensed by the Florida Commission for Independent Education, License No. 1287, 3427, 3110, 2581. Administrative office: 210 Sixth Avenue, 33rd Floor, Pittsburgh, PA 15222. ©2012 The Art Institutes International LLC.

THE NEW SCHOOL
NEW YORK, NEW YORK

The University

An essential part of New York City's artistic and intellectual life since 1919, The New School is a leading university that offers some of the nation's most respected academic programs in art and design, liberal arts, management and policy, and the performing arts. These programs are closely connected with all that New York City has to offer—its history, its culture, its energy, and its opportunities.

Founded by a group of progressive educators, The New School aspired to be everything the old school was not—open to dissenting opinions and freedom of expression in art and scholarship. In 1933, The New School gave a home to the University in Exile, a refuge for German scholars fleeing persecution by the Nazis. An important intellectual tradition was born, forming the basis for contemporary scholarship in the social sciences. Today, New School students continue to create thoughtful and provocative art and collaborate across disciplines to address many of the world's most pressing problems.

For undergraduates, The New School offers four distinctive colleges in the arts and the humanities: Parsons The New School for Design, Eugene Lang College The New School for Liberal Arts, Mannes College The New School for Music, and The New School for Jazz and Contemporary Music. In addition, The New School for Public Engagement offers a liberal arts undergraduate program designed specifically for transfer students and working adults. Each of The New School's programs expose students to an exciting and challenging course of study headed by a faculty of artists, scholars, and professionals who practice what they teach.

Location

New York City offers virtually unlimited cultural, artistic, recreational, and intellectual resources that make it one of the world's great cities. New York's Greenwich Village is where most New School students attend class, and the streets themselves become a kind of classroom. While this famously artistic and intellectual neighborhood is well known for its performance spaces, music clubs, bookstores, theaters, and hundreds of restaurants and cafés, the neighborhood also has a relaxed side, including tree-lined streets, a riverfront park, and small shops, feeling much of the time not like a major metropolis, but a village.

Fashion students at Parsons The New School for Design take many of their classes in Midtown New York's Fashion District. Students of Mannes College The New School for Music attend school on Manhattan's Upper West Side, a short distance from Lincoln Center, Carnegie Hall, and other major music venues.

Majors and Degrees

Eugene Lang College The New School for Liberal Arts offers the B.A. in the arts (concentrations in arts in context, dance, music, theater, and visual arts), B.A. in culture and media, B.A. in economics, B.A./B.S. in environmental studies, B.A. in global studies, B.A. in history, B.A. in global studies, B.A. in interdisciplinary science (tracks in biology of health, science of the environment, and history and philosophy of science), and B.A. in liberal arts (self-designed program or concentration in social inquiry), B.A. in literary studies (concentrations in literature and writing), B.A. in philosophy, B.A. in politics, B.A. in psychology, B.A. in urban studies, and a B.A.-B.F.A. dual degree with Parsons The New School for Design and The New School for Jazz and Contemporary Music.

Parsons The New School for Design offers the B.F.A. in architectural design, B.F.A. in communication design, B.B.A. in design and management, B.F.A. in design and technology, B.A./B.S. in environmental studies, B.F.A. in fashion design, B.F.A. in fine arts, B.F.A. in illustration, B.F.A. in integrated design, B.F.A. in interior design, B.F.A. in photography, B.F.A. in product design, B.S. in urban design, and a B.A.-B.F.A. dual degree with Eugene Lang College.

Mannes College The New School for Music offers the Bachelor of Music, Bachelor of Science, and undergraduate diploma. Areas of study at Mannes are orchestral instruments, piano, harpsichord, orchestral conducting, choral conducting, voice, classical guitar, composition, and theory.

The New School for Jazz and Contemporary Music offers the Bachelor of Fine Arts and a B.A.-B.F.A. dual degree with Eugene Lang College.

Academic Programs

One of the nation's largest and most prestigious degree-granting colleges of art and design, **Parsons The New School for Design** has been a forerunner in the field since its founding in 1896. Its intensive programs and distinguished faculty embrace innovation, pioneer new uses of technology, and instill in students a global perspective in design. By focusing on the fundamentals of art and design as well as the liberal arts, Parsons leads designers to understand the social and economic implications of their work.

Eugene Lang College The New School for Liberal Arts provides the advantages of a small, intimate liberal arts college and the resources of a major university. Lang attracts smart, creative, and independent students who value the opportunity to be challenged in small, seminar-style classes. Committed leaders, scholars, and newsmakers teach these talented young people in an interdisciplinary context.

Lang enables students to accelerate their progress toward a master's degree by combining their undergraduate work with graduate study at one of The New School's graduate schools. Dual bachelor's-master's degree programs offered at Lang include anthropology, economics, international affairs, liberal studies, media studies, nonprofit management, organizational change management, philosophy, politics, psychology, teaching English to speakers of other languages, sociology, and urban policy analysis and management.

Mannes College The New School for Music is a preeminent conservatory of classical music for undergraduate students who are considering a career in music. Mannes College is a community of compassionate musicians who encourage collaboration rather than competition and professional development rather than personal pressure. Mannes College is small and selective, limiting degree enrollment to approximately 300 students, so these gifted musicians can receive more personal instruction from masters of their art. The comprehensive Techniques of Music curriculum sets Mannes apart, providing a broad foundation, including ear training, advanced music theory, and dictation.

The New School for Jazz and Contemporary Music was founded on the principle that working artists should play a role in jazz education. Jazz students' mentors are 75 of the city's leading musicians, and their companions are the most promising young players in the country. There are scores of student ensembles and literally hundreds of public performances every year.

The New School for Jazz and Contemporary Music awards the Bachelor of Fine Arts (B.F.A.) degree. It also offers students the opportunity to combine their B.F.A. studies with a certificate program in creative arts therapies in cooperation with The New School for Public Engagement.

The B.A.-B.F.A. program at The New School is a five-year, dual degree program through which students can earn a Bachelor of Arts degree from Eugene Lang College The New School for Liberal Arts and a Bachelor of Fine Arts degree from either Parsons The New School for Design or The New School for Jazz and Contemporary Music.

Off-Campus Programs

The New School believes that students learn both in and out of the classroom. With access to a wide array of internships, apprenticeships with top designers, and performance opportunities in venues from downtown clubs to Lincoln Center, students can shape their education and take advantage of all the university and the city has to offer.

Students can pursue internships in almost every field in New York City. Recently, New School students have landed internships at the ACLU, Apple, Beth Israel Hospital, *The Cobert Report*, Condé Nast, DKNY, GLAAD, Guggenheim, HBO, Marvel, MTV, NFL, Open Society Institute, Random House, Sesame Workshop, Sony Entertainment, the Village Voice, and WNYC, among many others.

Academic Facilities

In addition having access to the university's three libraries—devoted to social sciences, art and design, and European and American classical music—New School students can use the Research Library Consortium of South Manhattan, one of the largest university library consortiums in the United States. Students have access to state-of-the-art computing and media facilities, including an advanced production facility where portable production equipment is available for student use. The university also provides studios and practice rooms for students of art and design, music, and dance.

Costs

Tuition varies by division and by program. Tuition for full-time undergraduate programs in 2011–12 ranged from $35,940 to $38,510, plus fees. More specific information regarding tuition and fees is available online at www.newschool.edu/tuition. Room and board cost approximately $15,260, depending on the student's choice of meal plan and dormitory accommodations.

Financial Aid

Students are encouraged to apply for aid by filing the Free Application for Federal Student Aid (FAFSA) and requesting that a copy of the need analysis report be sent to The New School (FAFSA code number 002780). Qualified College students are eligible for all federal and state financial aid programs in addition to university gift aid. University aid is awarded on the basis of need and merit and is part of a package consisting of both gift aid (grants and/or scholarships) and a self-help component (loans and Federal Work-Study Program awards). Aid is renewable each year as long as need continues and students maintain satisfactory academic standing at the College. Special attention is given to continuing students who have done exceptionally well.

Faculty

The New School prides itself on its small student-faculty ratio and was ranked first in *U.S. News & Report*'s 2012 edition of Best Colleges for having the highest proportion of classes with fewer than 20 students.

Individual attention is one of the qualities that set New School programs apart. That means students will have the opportunity to work closely with legends of New York's music scene at The New School for Jazz and Contemporary Music, with leaders of

New York's art and design world at Parsons, with members of some of New York's most prestigious orchestras, chamber music groups, and opera companies at Mannes College, and with amazing scholars, artists, and professionals at Eugene Lang College and in The New School for Public Engagement's Undergraduate Programs for transfer students and working adults.

Student Government

The University Student Senate (USS) is the official student government of The New School. Elected from all divisions of the university, student senators present student concerns to administration, maintain a USS website, plan all-campus parties and events, and co-fund events thrown by other people.

Admission Requirements

The New School welcomes admission applications from students of diverse racial, ethnic, religious, and political backgrounds whose past performance and academic and personal promise make them likely to gain from and add to The New School community. The university seeks students who combine inquisitiveness and seriousness of purpose with the ability to engage in a distinctive, rigorous undergraduate program. Specific admission requirements vary by division. To learn about admission requirements for specific programs, prospective students may visit www.newschool.edu/admission.

Application and Information

Freshmen, transfers, and visiting students may apply for either the September (fall) or January (spring) semester. Application deadlines for freshman and transfer students vary by division. Details regarding fees, deadlines, and other application information can be found online at www.newschool.edu/admission.

For further information, students should contact:

The New School
Office of Admission
72 Fifth Avenue
New York, New York 10011
Phone: 212-229-5150
        800-292-3040 (toll-free)
E-mail: admission@newschool.edu
Web site: http://www.newschool.edu/admission

The New School offers fresh perspective, distinctive undergraduate programs, and freedom of expression in art and scholarship in New York City.

NEW YORK SCHOOL OF INTERIOR DESIGN
NEW YORK, NEW YORK

The School

The New York School of Interior Design (NYSID) is a nationally ranked, independent, nonprofit college accredited by National Association of Schools of Art and Design (NASAD). It was established in 1916 by architect Sherrill Whiton and chartered by the Board of Regents of the University of the State of New York in 1924. Throughout its history, the School has devoted all of its resources to a single field of study—interior design—and has played a significant role in the development of the interior design profession. Enrollment is approximately 800.

NYSID's curriculum is a reflection of the complex yet sophisticated profession of interior design. Courses stress the discipline's call to protect the health, safety, and welfare of the public while being functional and aesthetically pleasing. Today's students learn not only the colors and materials appropriate to residential interiors, but also how to design environmentally sound and accessible hospitals, offices, schools, restaurants, and more. Whether learning the importance of sustainability and historic preservation or the latest programs in computer-aided design, NYSID students obtain a wide range of skills and techniques taught by faculty members who work in the field. New York City is home to art and antique shops, museums, professional design studios, and showrooms that are all an exciting part of the college's "campus."

The atmosphere of the college is cosmopolitan, not only because of its excellent location but also because it attracts students from across the United States and abroad. International students make up approximately 13 percent of the student population. Many students also transfer from other colleges in order to obtain a more professional, career-directed education.

The School continues to maintain a close relationship with the interior design industry because of its select faculty and established reputation. This provides an excellent means for students to develop associations that offer opportunities to move into the profession after completing their degree program at NYSID.

In addition to the undergraduate programs in interior design listed below, NYSID also offers four graduate programs: a professional-level Master of Fine Arts (M.F.A.) degree in interior design, a post–professional-level M.F.A. degree in interior design, and Master of Professional Studies (M.P.S.) degrees in sustainable interior environments, interior lighting design, and healthcare design.

Location

The New York School of Interior Design is located on Manhattan's Upper East Side, where a number of the major interior design studios are located. Many of the world's most important galleries, museums, and showrooms are close by, most within walking distance. The city is world-renowned for its architecture, cosmopolitan urban experience, cultural activities, and historic districts. The college can be reached easily by bus, car, subway, and train.

Majors and Degrees

The New York School of Interior Design offers four undergraduate programs in interior design: a four-year Bachelor of Fine Arts

(B.F.A.) degree accredited by the Council for Interior Design Accreditation (CIDA), a two-year Associate in Applied Science (A.A.S.) degree, a 24-credit nondegree Basic Interior Design certificate, and a four-year Bachelor of Arts (B.A.) degree in the history of the interior and the decorative arts.

Academic Programs

The New York School of Interior Design is devoted exclusively to the design of the interior environment. The various academic programs make up an integrated curriculum covering interior design concepts; history of art, architecture, furniture, and interiors; technical and communication skills, materials and methods, and philosophy and theory; and professional design procedures and design problem solving.

The Basic Interior Design program consists of a 24-credit sequence of foundation courses in which all design students enroll. These courses provide a cultural, general, and professional introduction to the field of interior design. Although completion of the Basic Interior Design program may be the major goal for some, for most students it serves as the foundation for matriculation into the degree programs.

The A.A.S. degree program provides the minimum educational requirement to become a certified interior designer in New York State. The 66-credit program includes design, liberal arts, and professional courses.

The 132-credit Bachelor of Fine Arts degree program provides the education that, with practical experience, enables the graduate to take qualifying exams for interior design certification in many states and to join national and local professional associations. Studies focus on the development of a broad array of conceptual analysis, creative problem-solving, relevant cultural development, and technical skills. Students are required to take 32 credits of liberal arts courses in addition to 100 credits of professional design-related courses.

The 120-credit Bachelor of Arts in the history of the interior and the decorative arts program provides students with an undergraduate liberal arts degree in art history with a special focus on the interior environment and the objects it contains. Graduates of the program have the opportunity to apply to NYSID's professional-level graduate program with one year of advanced standing, allowing the student to complete the three-year program in just two years.

NYSID's curriculum is flexible and permits students to take courses on a full- or part-time basis during the day or evening and on weekends. The college maintains an active job placement service. Students may be placed in a wide variety of positions that reflect the full spectrum of job opportunities in the interior design profession.

Academic Facilities

The NYSID campus occupies two buildings on the Upper East Side as well as a new Graduate Center in the Gramercy Park area of Manhattan. The college has first-rate facilities with light-filled studios; a unique lighting laboratory; several computer facilities for computer-aided design (CAD); a large atelier for independent work furnished with drafting tables, computers, and a materials collection for use in projects; a lecture hall

and seminar rooms; a well-stocked bookstore; and a handsome auditorium. The library's collection includes more than 16,000 books on design, architecture, and allied disciplines; over 100 periodical subscriptions; a product literature collection; and an electronic image database for the study of the history of interior design and the decorative arts.

Costs

Tuition for B.I.D., A.A.S., and B.F.A. programs for 2012–13 is $828 per credit, plus a $335 registration/technology/activities fee each semester. Typical expenses for the first year are projected to be $27,324 for tuition and $670 in registration fees. For students entering the B.A. program in fall 2012, the cost is $12,438 per semester plus $335 in fees. NYSID housing costs are approximately $14,400 for nine months.

Financial Aid

Financial assistance is available to students who are matriculated and in good academic standing. Both need- and merit-based scholarships are offered, and there are financial aid programs for both full- and part-time study. An applicant is considered for financial assistance upon completion of the Free Application for Federal Student Aid (FAFSA). This single application will be reviewed to determine a student's eligibility for Federal Pell Grants, Federal Supplemental Educational Opportunity Grants, Federal Work-Study Program, NYSID scholarships, and New York State aid, if applicable.

Faculty

Since New York City is a world-class design center, many top designers, art historians, architects, and authorities on the decorative arts teach and lecture at the college. NYSID faculty work as practicing designers in addition to being educators, authors, and active members of professional design organizations, and as such, give NYSID students special insight into the practice of their chosen field. The student to faculty ratio at NYSID is 12:1.

Student Government

The Student Council of the New York School of Interior Design is the elected voice of the student body in academic, administrative, residential, and leisure matters at the college. It is the representative forum through which student concerns are brought to the attention of the administration. It also organizes and sponsors a number of social events throughout the academic year.

In addition, the college has an active student chapter of the American Society of Interior Designers (ASID). ASID organizes lectures, tours, workshops, and other events providing an inside view of the interior design industry. The Contract Club arranges visits to top commercial interior design firms providing the opportunity to see actual projects being designed, ask questions of senior designers, and tour professional working offices.

Admission Requirements

All applicants must submit an application, an application fee, an official secondary school transcript, SAT or ACT scores, and two letters of recommendation. Applicants to the A.A.S. and B.F.A. degree programs must meet the visual requirements by providing a portfolio as described in the catalog and Web site; transfer students must also submit college transcripts.

Additional application materials are required for international applicants. International applicants should contact the college's International Student Adviser for assistance in applying.

Application and Information

Admission decisions are made on a rolling basis. However, for processing purposes, it is recommended that the Admissions Office receive an application for fall admission by February 1. An application for spring admission should be received by October 1. Applicants are notified of the Admission Committee's decision by mail shortly after all required documents have been received and visual requirements fulfilled.

Inquiries and applications should be directed to:

The Office of Admissions
New York School of Interior Design
170 East 70th Street
New York, New York 10021-5110
Phone: 212-472-1500 Ext. 204
       800-33NYSID (toll-free)
Fax: 212-472-1867
E-mail: admissions@nysid.edu
Web site: http://www.nysid.edu
      http://www.facebook.com/nysidnyc
      http://twitter.com/NYSID

The campus of the New York School of Interior Design is centered on its building at 170 East 70th Street in the Upper East Side Historic District.

NIAGARA UNIVERSITY
NIAGARA UNIVERSITY, NEW YORK

NIAGARA UNIVERSITY
Education That Makes a Difference

The University

Niagara University (NU), founded in 1856, is a private, independent university rooted in a Catholic and Vincentian tradition. The suburban 160-acre campus combines the old and new; both ivy-covered buildings and modern architectural structures are among its thirty-three buildings. The University is easily accessible from every major city in the eastern and midwestern United States via the New York State Thruway, Buffalo International Airport, and rail and bus service.

There are approximately 3,300 undergraduate and 965 graduate students enrolled at Niagara. A large percentage of these students take advantage of the more than eighty extracurricular and cocurricular activities offered. Volunteer work in the community is popular among the students and enhances community relations. Students work with numerous organizations, including Habitat for Humanity, Big Brothers/Big Sisters, and the Skating Association for the Blind and Handicapped.

University teams compete on the Division I level and are members of the NCAA, the Metro Atlantic Athletic Conference, Atlantic Hockey Conference, and College Hockey America Conference. Intercollegiate sports for men include baseball, basketball, cross-country, golf, ice hockey, soccer, swimming and diving, and tennis. Intercollegiate sports for women include basketball, cross-country, golf, ice hockey, lacrosse, soccer, softball, swimming and diving, tennis, and volleyball. Club sports include cheerleading, danceline, hockey, martial arts, rugby, and skiing. The Kiernan Center offers a variety of sports and recreational facilities, including a multipurpose gymnasium, a swimming and diving pool, an indoor track, racquetball courts, free-weight and Nautilus rooms, and aerobics rooms. There are several outdoor athletic fields and basketball and tennis courts.

Additional student services include the Health Center, which provides inpatient and outpatient care during the day; the Learning Center, which provides free tutoring services; and the Career Development Office, which offers professional and career counseling. Other services include counseling, orientation, academic planning, career planning, and job placement.

Niagara University's housing accommodations include five residence halls, a grouping of five small cottages, and a student apartment complex. Both coed and single-gender accommodations are available.

The University offers graduate studies in business, counseling, criminal justice, education, and interdisciplinary studies.

Location

Niagara University's picturesque 160-acre campus is located in the town of Lewiston, New York, 2 minutes off I-190 on Route 104. The campus is situated on Monteagle Ridge overlooking the lower Niagara River, which connects the two Great Lakes of Erie and Ontario. The University's suburban campus setting is just a few miles from the world-famous Niagara Falls, 20 minutes from Buffalo, which offers a variety of cultural events, sports, and entertainment opportunities, and just 90 minutes from Toronto, Canada's largest metropolitan area. In addition, the University is minutes away from the quaint village of Lewiston, New York, and the city of Niagara Falls, New York.

Majors and Degrees

The College of Arts and Sciences offers the Bachelor of Arts degree in chemistry, communication studies, English, French, history, international studies, liberal arts, life sciences, mathematics, philosophy, political science, psychology, religious studies, social sciences, sociology, and Spanish. The Bachelor of Science degree is awarded in biochemistry (with a concentration in bioinformatics), biology (with concentrations in bioinformatics and biotechnology), chemistry (with a concentration in computational chemistry), computer and information sciences, criminal justice and criminology, mathematics, nursing, and social work. This division

also offers the Bachelor of Fine Arts degree in theater studies (with concentrations in design technology, general theater, and performance). Preprofessional programs are offered in dentistry, law, medicine, pharmacy, veterinary medicine, and Army ROTC. An Associate of Arts degree is available in general studies. In addition, Niagara offers an environmental studies concentration to supplement a degree in biology, chemistry, or political science. Enrichment courses in fine arts and languages are also available.

In addition to the programs listed above NU offers a number of preprofessional partnerships. These include a 3+4 partnership in pharmacy with the State University of New York at Buffalo (SUNY), a 2+3 partnership in pharmacy with Lake Erie College of Osteopathic Medicine (LECOM), a 3+4 partnership in medicine with LECOM, and a 3+4 partnership in dentistry with SUNY at Buffalo. Qualified premedical Niagara students are eligible to apply for the early assurance program sponsored by the SUNY at Buffalo.

Niagara University's College of Business Administration is accredited by AACSB International—The Association to Advance Collegiate Schools of Business and offers a B.B.A. and a combination B.B.A./M.B.A. degree (five-year program) in accounting. This division offers B.S. degrees in economics, finance, management (with concentrations in human resources, international business, and supply chain management), and marketing. In addition, an A.A.S. degree can be earned in business.

Real-world learning occurs through internships, study abroad, and cooperative education programs as well as research being conducted in several business-focused campus centers. These centers include the Family Business Center, the Center for Supply Chain Management, and the Center for International Accounting.

Holding the highest accreditations possible in both the United States and Canada—the United States National Council for Teacher Education (NCATE) and Canada's Ontario College of Teachers—Niagara University's College of Education provides students with an option of earning dual certification to teach in both countries. The College of Education offers bachelor's degree programs leading to New York State initial certification in early childhood (birth–grade 6), childhood (grades 1–6), childhood and middle childhood (grades 1–9), middle childhood and adolescence (grades 5–12), adolescence (grades 7–12), certification for teaching students with disabilities (grades 1–6 childhood and grades 7–12 adolescence), and in Teaching English to Speakers of Other Languages (TESOL). All education majors pursue an academic concentration to establish expertise in one of the following subject areas: biology, business, chemistry, English, French, liberal arts, mathematics, social studies, and Spanish. Business education is offered only at grades 5–12. The academic concentration in liberal arts can only be pursued in the early childhood and childhood (birth–grade 6), and special education and childhood (grades 1–6). Most other states, and Puerto Rico, have reciprocity agreements with New York, meaning that an NU education would qualify education majors to teach in those states as well. In addition, the Canadian province of Ontario recognizes Niagara graduates as qualified for the Letter of Eligibility to teach in that province.

The College of Hospitality and Tourism Management provides a career-oriented curriculum leading to a B.S. degree in three specific areas: hotel and restaurant management (with concentrations in food and beverage management; luxury hospitality operations; and hotel planning, development, and operations), sport management (with concentrations in sport operations and revenue management), and tourism and recreation management (with concentrations in event and meeting management and tourism destination management). The College of Hospitality and Tourism Management offered the world's first bachelor's degree in tourism. NU's hotel and restaurant program, the second oldest in New York State, has the distinction of being the seventh program nationally to be accredited by the Accreditation Commission for Programs in Hospitality Administration by the Council of Hotel, Restaurant, and Institutional

Education. The College introduces students to a comprehensive body of knowledge about the hotel, restaurant, tourism, and recreational areas and applies this knowledge to current industry challenges. The College requires that its students accumulate 800 hours of industry-related experience. These and other practical experiences offer NU students the knowledge necessary to advance in the field. Students work with industry leaders in classroom projects, join academic clubs and professional organizations, and participate in special trips to trade shows and conventions and specially designed study-abroad experiences, making NU a national leader in the area.

For students who are undecided about which major to choose, Niagara University offers an award-winning Academic Exploration Program (AEP). AEP provides a structured opportunity for students to participate in a thorough, organized process of selecting a major that meets their academic talents and career goals.

Academic Programs

Niagara University's curricula enable students to pursue their academic preferences and to complete courses that lead to proficiency in other academic areas. Courses that have been considered upper-division courses are available to all students. This provides students with the opportunity to avoid introductory and survey courses and permits motivated students to take advantage of more challenging courses early in their collegiate career. The honors program provides special academic opportunities that stimulate, encourage, and challenge participants. In addition, an accelerated three-year degree program is offered to qualified students.

Students pursuing a bachelor's degree must complete a total of 40 or 42 course units (120 or 126 hours) to meet graduation requirements. Niagara grants credit for successful scores on the Advanced Placement and College-Level Examination Program and the International Baccalaureate tests.

Internships, research, independent study, and cooperative education are available in many academic programs. An Army ROTC program is also offered.

The University operates on a two-semester plan (fall and spring). A comprehensive summer session offers a variety of courses.

NU is fully accredited by the Middle States Association of Colleges and Schools. The University's programs in the respective areas are accredited by the National Council for Accreditation of Teacher Education, AACSB International–The Association to Advance Collegiate Schools of Business, and the Council on Social Work Education. The chemistry department has the approval of the American Chemical Society. The travel, hotel, and restaurant administration program is accredited by the Commission for Programs in Hospitality Administration.

Off-Campus Programs

For those students who wish to study abroad, the University offers semester and summer programs in Chile, China, England, France, Ireland, Mexico, Spain, Thailand, and many other countries. Students may choose from 150 programs in more than thirty countries available through the University's membership in the American Institute for Foreign Studies, Center for Cross-Cultural Study, College Consortium for International Studies, Global Learning Semesters, and Semester at Sea.

Academic Facilities

The University's open-stack library exceeds 200,000 books and has more than 22,000 periodical titles as well as reference databases accessible through the Web. The library is housed in a modern facility that includes seating for 500 people, including individual study carrels. The library is affiliated with the Online Computer Library Center (OCLC) network.

The Academic Complex, the home to the College of Education and the College of Business Administration (Bisgrove Hall), is a state-of-the-art learning facility. Dunleavy Hall, outstanding both educationally and architecturally, includes a computerized lecture hall and TV production rooms. The University's facilities also include the Computer Center; DePaul Hall of Science; St. Vincent's Hall; the Kiernan Center, NU's athletic and recreation center; the Elizabeth Ann Clune Center for Theatre; the Castellani Art Museum; Bailo Hall, which houses the Office of Admissions; and the Dwyer Arena, a dual-rink ice hockey complex.

Costs

Tuition for 2011–12 was $25,300. Room and board (with a choice of meal plans) cost an additional $11,000 per year. Fees were estimated at $1100 per year. Niagara estimates that an additional $2500 to $3050 per year is adequate for books, laundry, and other essentials, such as travel to and from home.

Financial Aid

Ninety-nine percent of the entering freshmen received a financial aid package averaging more than $22,900 per year. They receive assistance in the form of merit scholarships, loans, grants, or campus employment. Students seeking financial aid should file the Free Application for Federal Student Aid (FAFSA). New York State residents should also file a Tuition Assistance Program (TAP) application.

Faculty

Niagara University has a dedicated, accessible faculty that genuinely cares about the academic and personal growth of their students. Their commitment to teaching is their primary concern. A student-faculty ratio of 12:1 and an average class size of approximately 24 allow personal attention and classroom interaction.

Student Government

The Student Government represents all parts of the student body equally. It coordinates and legislates all student activities, serving as both liaison to and a participating member of the University. In addition, students serve on all major departmental committees and on the University Senate, which is the major advisory committee to the president and Board of Trustees.

Admission Requirements

The University welcomes men and women who have demonstrated aptitude and academic achievement at the high school level. Either SAT or ACT test scores are required. International students are required to submit the results of their TOEFL examination. Interviews are recommended. Transfer students are accepted in any semester. (Transfer credit is evaluated individually by the dean of each division.) Students who complete high school in less than four years are eligible for early admission. Students may also apply under an early action program. Economically and educationally disadvantaged students from New York State are eligible to apply for admission through the Higher Educational Opportunity Program (HEOP).

Application and Information

Niagara operates on a rolling admission basis and adheres to the College Board Candidates Reply Date. A visit to the campus is encouraged, and overnight accommodations in a residence hall are available through the Niagara Nights program.

Information on all aspects of the University can be obtained by contacting the Office of Admissions or by visiting www.niagara.edu.

Harry Gong
Director of Admissions
Bailo Hall
Niagara University
Niagara University, New York 14109-2011
Phone: 716-286-8700
         800-462-2111 (toll-free)
Fax: 716-286-8710
E-mail: admissions@niagara.edu
Web site: http://www.niagara.edu
         http://www.facebook.com/niagarau
         http://twitter.com/niagarauniv

The main campus of Niagara University.

NORTHEASTERN UNIVERSITY
BOSTON, MASSACHUSETTS

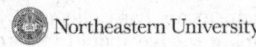

The University

There is a certain energy about Northeastern. It comes from bright, ambitious students with a sense of purpose. In the classroom, in the workplace, in campus activities, and in the city of Boston—the ultimate college town—Northeastern students stimulate their minds, investigate career options, participate in community affairs, and graduate personally and professionally prepared for their future careers or for graduate school.

Northeastern is a leader in interdisciplinary and translational research; urban engagement; and the integration of classroom learning with real-world experience. Classroom studies are integrated with experiential learning opportunities—anchored by the world's largest, most innovative cooperative education program—to prepare students for a lifetime of achievement. It is the Northeastern difference.

The current undergraduate enrollment of 16,385 is made up of students of all backgrounds, interests, and tastes, giving Northeastern its distinctive, urban style. This diversity shows in the range of available activities. Students can join a cultural club, participate in research, perform with the Silver Masque, go on a ski trip, play basketball, tutor local children, learn to ballroom dance, and much more. Students have many opportunities to make friends, try something new, become a leader, or simply have fun. Students can also find quiet corners of the campus that feel far from city streets where they can read or just relax, sprawled on a wooden bench under a shade tree; sip gourmet coffee from a nearby campus café; or listen to a midday jazz performance behind the Curry Student Center amid the art of Northeastern's sculpture park. The 73-acre campus is dynamic and welcoming, a beautiful stretch of leafy green in the heart of Boston. Its compact size lets students get to class on time or rush back for a forgotten book.

Location

Northeastern's residential campus lies in the heart of Boston, where the distinctive neighborhoods of the Back Bay, the South End, the Fenway, and Roxbury meet. In the past five years, Northeastern has built a host of new on-campus residence halls, more than doubling the amount of housing available to undergraduates. The newest residence halls offer apartment-style living with modern kitchens complete with dishwashers, disposals, and full-sized appliances; cable hookups; and data jacks. Many have amazing views of the Boston skyline.

The Back Bay area, known for its many cultural and educational institutions, is steps from Symphony Hall, the New England Conservatory of Music, the Museum of Fine Arts, and the Isabella Stewart Gardner Museum. The South End is home to elegant Victorian row houses, exciting arts, hidden gardens and some of the finest dining in Boston. The Fenway area, with its beautiful rose garden, bicycle and jogging paths, and Fenway Park (home of the Boston Red Sox), is just a few blocks away.

Majors and Degrees

Northeastern's academic programs are divided among eight colleges: the College of Arts, Media, and Design; the College of Business Administration; the College of Computer and Information Science; the College of Engineering; the Bouvé College of Health Sciences; the College of Professional Studies; the College of Science; and the College of Social Sciences and Humanities. Top-notch faculty members with a variety of research interests personally guide students through their studies.

The College of Arts, Media, and Design awards undergraduate degrees in architecture, art, cinema studies (combined major options only), communication studies, digital art, game design (combined major options only), graphic design, interactive media (combined major options only), landscape architecture, journalism, music (concentrations in music history and analysis, music industry, and music technology), studio art (in collaboration with the School of the Museum of Fine Arts, Boston), and theater (including concentrations in performance and production).

The College of Business Administration offers two tracks: the Bachelor of Science in Business Administration (B.S.B.A.) and the Bachelor of Science in International Business (B.S.I.B.). The B.S.I.B. program includes language instruction and international study and work. The College offers concentrations in accounting, entrepreneurship and innovation, finance and insurance, management, management information systems, marketing, and supply chain management.

The College of Computer and Information Science awards degrees in computer science and information science and also offers combined majors, combining computer science with business, cognitive psychology, game design, mathematics, physics, biology, multimedia arts, music technology, or digital art.

The College of Engineering offers degrees in chemical, civil, computer, electrical, industrial, and mechanical engineering.

The Bouvé College of Health Sciences awards degrees in health sciences, nursing, pharmacy, and speech-language pathology and audiology. The college also offers a six-year Doctor of Pharmacy degree and a six-year program leading to a Master of Science in Physical Therapy.

The College of Professional Studies offers undergraduate and graduate degree programs in a wide range of disciplines, with an emphasis on global options. The college is also home to the School of Education.

The College of Science awards undergraduate degrees in applied physics, behavioral neuroscience, biochemistry, biology, biomedical physics, chemistry, environmental science, environmental studies, linguistics, mathematics, physics, and psychology.

The College of Social Sciences and Humanities awards undergraduate degrees in African American studies, American Sign Language, Asian studies, criminal justice, cultural anthropology, economics, English, history, human services, international affairs, Jewish studies (combined major options only), philosophy, political science, religious studies, sociology, and Spanish.

Academic Programs

At the heart of a Northeastern education lies award-winning professors and faculty mentors, rigorous and innovative curriculum, undergraduate research and global experiences that challenge and transform. Innovative programs encompass a wide range of majors, concentrations, and interdisciplinary studies along with honors, preprofessional, and study-abroad programs.

Northeastern's approach integrates academics with a variety of experiential learning opportunities including research, global experience, service learning, and the University's signature cooperative education program (co-op), enabling students to discover their path before they leave college.

Through the internationally known co-op program, after completing their freshman year, students alternate classroom learning with periods of full-time (usually paid) work or other types of hands-on learning related to their major or interests, earning their bachelor's degree in either four or five years. Graduates accumulate as many as eighteen months of professional experience, professional contacts, and the social confidence that gives them a significant edge in the job market over new graduates without experience. By working in varied jobs and settings, students learn what they like—and do not like—before committing to a permanent position. In fact, some Northeastern graduates may even go to work for a co-op employer after graduation. Northeastern students graduate knowing what they only could have learned on the job: how to conduct themselves, what to wear, how to interpret a company's culture, how to get things done, and how to write a resume and interview successfully.

Co-op employers include some of the country's largest and most reputable companies, such as Pfizer, John Hancock, Fidelity Investments, General Electric, Massachusetts General Hospital, and the *Boston Globe*. Students also enjoy international placements

for a semester or a year abroad; co-op employers recruit from Australia, Scotland, Italy, and Spain, among many other countries.

Experiential learning opportunities—including U.S. and international co-op, service-learning, research, and study abroad—are currently available in 85 countries and 160 cities in the U.S. and around the world.

The University honors program gives students opportunities to participate in enriched educational experiences and offers opportunities that include honors sections of required academic courses, honors seminars, independent research, and study abroad. The University also offers Army, Naval Nursing, and Air Force ROTC. The Disability Resource Center provides many support services that enable students with disabilities to participate fully in the life of the University community.

Academic Facilities

Northeastern is home to thirty-seven research centers, including the Center for Labor Market Studies, the Barnett Institute of Chemical and Biological Analysis, the Center for High-rate Nanomanufacturing, the Institute on Race and Justice, and many others. Students have ample opportunities to work alongside their professors to aid and conduct research on a variety of topics as undergraduates.

The University libraries system comprises Snell Library, a 240,000-square-foot-central library on the Boston Campus, the School of Law Library (also on the Boston Campus) and a small supplemental collection at the Nahant Marine Science Center. Total non-law holdings as of June 30, 2011 include 932,999 print volumes, 206,507 e-books, 1,489,153 microfilms, and 70,225 current serials subscriptions, with access to 59,926 electronic journals. In addition, Snell Library houses 23,437 audio, video, and computer software items, and 5,712 linear feet of archival material. The library is a selective depository of federal government publications and currently holds 143,905 printed government documents.

Northeastern University provides a broad range of academic and administrative computer resources available to students and faculty and staff members. Many computing resources are available, including Internet connections for all offices and University-owned residence halls, technology-assisted classrooms, computer labs, and the myNEU portal, which allows student to access many administrative and academic functions online. There is also extensive wireless network access, found in the library, Student Center, and many dorms.

Costs

For 2011–12, tuition was $37,840, and room and board were $12,760. Whether students choose to earn their undergraduate degree in four or five years (including experiential educational periods), tuition is charged only for the academic experience, not for the experiential educational periods.

Financial Aid

The University operates a substantial aid program designed to make attendance at Northeastern feasible for all qualified students. By coordinating the resources of the University and various public and private scholarship programs, the Office of Student Financial Services was recently able to provide more than $170 million in grant and scholarship assistance. About 80 percent of the freshman class received some form of financial aid. Northeastern participates in all federal aid programs. Financial aid is based on need and academic merit and may consist of grants, loans, work-study employment, or any combination of the three. To apply, students must file a Free Application for Federal Student Aid (FAFSA) and a CSS PROFILE form with the College Scholarship Service by the priority filing date of February 15.

Faculty

The University has more than 1,500 full- and part-time faculty members with a wide variety of research and teaching interests and specialties and a staff of academic counselors in each college who work closely with students to assist them in developing programs suited to their interests and abilities. Each student is assigned both an academic and a co-op adviser. The co-op advisor aids in resume building and interview skills and tactics. In addition, the adviser aids in developing contacts with business and co-op employers as well as networking and eventual job searches.

Admission Requirements

Students may enter the University with advanced credit on the basis of test scores on Advanced Placement (AP) examinations, the College-Level Examination Program (CLEP), the International Baccalaureate (I.B.), or on successful completion of accredited college-level courses before enrollment at Northeastern. In addition to the application for admission, prospective freshmen must submit official high school transcript(s) (or official GED score reports), including their senior-year grades; official transcripts for any college-level course work taken while a secondary-school student; written recommendations from their secondary school guidance counselor and a teacher; and scores on the SAT (Northeastern's College Board code is 3667) or ACT, including the writing section. Please visit the University's Web site for additional admission details and transfer admissions requirements (www.northeastern.edu/admissions).

Application and Information

Admission to Northeastern is selective and competitive. For the freshman class entering in fall 2012, the University received more than 44,000 applications for 2,800 places in the freshman class. Students who thrive in a challenging academic environment—and outside the classroom in activities like Northeastern's dynamic global experiential learning options—are best suited for a Northeastern education. Experiential learning will expand the student's initiative, adaptability, confidence, poise, and ability to work collaboratively, which are the foundations of leadership.

November 1 is the deadline for the early action admission program. Students who have carefully explored their college options and have decided that Northeastern is where they want to enroll may choose to apply under the early action program. The deadline for the regular admission program is January 15. If accepted for fall admission either through the early action program or the regular admission program, freshmen are required to send a tuition deposit by May 1 to secure a place in the class. For transfer students, the priority deadline for the fall is May 1. Admission decisions for transfer applicants are made on a space-available, rolling basis. November 1 is the deadline for January transfer admission for both freshman and transfer applicants and for international applicants for January admission. Admission decisions for spring applicants are made on a space-available, rolling basis. Northeastern offers a variety of visit options including information sessions and campus tours. For more information, or to register, visit www.northeastern.edu/admissions/visitcampus.

For more information, students should contact:

Office of Undergraduate Admissions
240 West Village F
Northeastern University
360 Huntington Avenue
Boston, Massachusetts 02115
Phone: 617-373-2200
E-mail: admissions@neu.edu
Web site: http://www.northeastern.edu/admissions

Students in a West Village residence hall enjoy spectacular Boston vistas as well as interaction with the faculty-in-residence.

NORTHERN KENTUCKY UNIVERSITY
HIGHLAND HEIGHTS, KENTUCKY

The University

Northern Kentucky University (NKU) was founded in 1968 and is the newest of Kentucky's eight state universities. The atmosphere of the campus is futuristic, emphasizing a high-quality education by supporting the liberal arts. Major buildings are of modern, contemporary architectural design and are set on 300 acres of rolling countryside. NKU has an enrollment of approximately 16,000 students from forty-two states and ninety-two countries and is accredited by the Southern Association of Colleges and Schools. The Salmon P. Chase College of Law is accredited by both the American Bar Association and the Association of American Law Schools.

There are more than 200 student organizations. NKU competes in the NCAA Division I Atlantic Sun Conference. Intercollegiate sports are offered for men and women in basketball, cheerleading, cross-country, track, golf, soccer, and tennis; for men in baseball; and for women in fast-pitch softball and volleyball. Intramural activities vary by semester, but include basketball, dodgeball, field hockey, flag football, ice hockey, racquetball, soccer, softball, tae kwan do, volleyball, and many others. A complete listing is available on the University's Web site at http://www.nku.edu/~camprec/index.htm.

Location

NKU is located in the largest metropolitan area of any state university in Kentucky. It is located at the junction of U.S. Highway 27 and Interstates 275 and 471 in Highland Heights, Kentucky, 8 miles southeast of Cincinnati, Ohio. NKU is only 60 miles from Dayton, 79 miles from Lexington, 93 miles from Louisville, and 114 miles from Indianapolis. While the immediate surroundings are suburban, NKU is part of the metropolitan area of greater Cincinnati.

Majors and Degrees

Northern Kentucky University awards the Bachelor of Arts, Bachelor of Fine Arts, Bachelor of Music, Bachelor of Science, Bachelor of Science in Nursing, and Bachelor of Social Work degrees. NKU also offers preprofessional programs, secondary education teacher certification, certificates, and the Associate of Applied Science degree.

The B.A. and B.S. degrees are offered in accounting, anthropology, athletic training, art (teaching), biological sciences, business administration, business education, business informatics, chemistry, chemistry/biology, computer education technology, computer information technology, computer science, criminal justice, early childhood education, economics, electronic engineering technology, electronic media and broadcasting, elementary education, English, entrepreneurship, environmental science, finance, French, geography, geology, German, graphic design, health science, history, industrial education, human resources, construction management, international studies, journalism, liberal studies, management, mechanical and manufacturing engineering, marketing, mathematics, media informatics, mental health–human services, middle grades education, organizational leadership, organizational systems technology, organizational systems technology management, philosophy, photography, physical education, physical education recreation, physics,

political science, psychology, public relations, radio-TV, recreation-fitness, social studies (teaching), sociology, Spanish, special education, speech communication, sports business, and theater.

The B.F.A. degree is granted in art and in theater arts. The B.Mus. degree is offered in music. The B.S.N. degree is offered in the nursing major and the B.S.W. degree in the social work major.

Preprofessional programs are available in dentistry, engineering, forestry, human resources, law, medicine, optometry, pharmacy, physician assistant studies, physical therapy, veterinary medicine, and wildlife management. In addition, the University offers majors, minors, and areas of discipline for secondary education teacher certification.

The University also awards the A.A.S. degree in construction technology, criminal justice, human services, integrative studies, prebusiness studies, radiologic technology, and respiratory care.

Academic Programs

NKU operates on a semester calendar. To receive a bachelor's degree, students must complete a minimum of 120 credit hours. At least 60 credit hours are required for the associate degree.

The University offers a variety of career planning and placement, internship, independent study, work-study, and cooperative-education programs. There is also an advising, counseling, and testing Center available. Other programs include an honors program, a program that allows for the dual enrollment of high school students, a program where students can combine their career interests in the liberal arts and engineering fields, and University 101, an orientation program for freshmen and transfer students.

NKU recognizes credit earned through the Advanced Placement (AP) Program and the general, subject, and institutional tests of specific College-Level Examination Program (CLEP). A maximum of 45 credit hours may be applied toward the bachelor's degree from the AP and CLEP examinations. The International Baccalaureate program allows students to earn credit in science, mathematics, psychology, and languages.

Off-Campus Programs

A variety of study-abroad opportunities are available to NKU students through membership in several consortia, through NKU exchange agreements with international universities, and through independent NKU professor-led trips.

Study in Australia, Belize, England, Ghana, Hong Kong, India, Ireland, Jamaica, and Scotland is possible in a wide range of courses and programs available through NKU's membership in the Cooperative Center for Study Abroad (CCSA).

The Kentucky Institute for International Studies (KIIS) offers students academic language programs in Argentina, Austria, Brazil, China, Costa Rica, Czech Republic, Denmark, Ecuador, France, Germany, Greece, Italy, Japan, Mexico, Poland, Spain, Turkey, and Ukraine.

The NKU Office of International Programs has student and faculty exchanges with universities in Costa Rica, Denmark, France, Germany, Japan, Korea, Mexico, Russia, Scotland, and Spain.

Academic Facilities

Among the academic facilities at NKU are an anthropology museum, a biology museum, and an art gallery with rotating exhibits. NKU also has a new laser projection planetarium. NKU becomes only the seventh institution worldwide to boast such equipment, joining six major planetariums in cities such as Tokyo, Los Angeles, and London. In addition, the University has nursing, respiratory care, and radiologic technology laboratories. In spring of 2008, NKU opened a 9000-seat arena called the Bank of Kentucky Center. NKU's brand-new Student Union, a student-centered facility, and focal point for campus programs and student organizations, was also completed in 2008. In the fall of 2011, NKU's Griffin Hall opened. This building, the new home of the College of Informatics, is designed to help students interested in communication and media, computer science, information technology, or management information systems become the new generation of professionals who will build the region's information economy. The W. Frank Steely Library at NKU contains 311,155 book titles and maintains 1,729 paper periodical subscriptions (additional periodicals are available in electronic format). Computer laboratories offer students opportunities to learn and utilize a variety of software programs. The Computer Science Department and Criminal Justice Department have collaborated to offer students a computer forensics minor to teach students how to handle digital evidence and how to present such evidence in court.

Costs

Tuition and fees for 2011–12 were $7488 for Kentucky students, $12,168 for metro students and $14,976 for nonresidents. Other costs included $6500–$8000 for room and meals, about $850 for books and supplies, and $2773 for miscellaneous expenses.

Financial Aid

Last year, 80 percent of undergraduates received some form of financial assistance. To receive financial aid, applicants must complete the Free Application for Federal Student Aid (FAFSA). Academic, athletic, music-drama, and art scholarships and scholarships for members of minority groups are available at Northern Kentucky University.

The application deadline for all academic scholarships is January 15. There is no deadline for the University's financial aid application; however, students who wish to receive institutional aid must apply by February 1 for priority consideration. Applicants are notified of acceptance on a rolling basis.

Faculty

More than 82 percent of the faculty members at NKU hold a doctoral degree or the terminal degree in their field. Classes are small, with an average class size of 24 and a student-faculty ratio of 14:1. All classes are taught by faculty members; no classes are taught by graduate assistants.

Student Government

Student Government (SG) is the elected student assembly at Northern Kentucky University. It is the official student voice on campus and represents the student viewpoint on University committees. All SG meetings are open, and students are encouraged to attend.

Admission Requirements

Incoming freshmen must submit an application for admission; arrange for the official ACT, SAT, or COMPASS score report to be sent; and request that the high school send an official transcript. In order to be considered for regular admission, a student must meet precollege curriculum requirements for Kentucky and institutional admission standards. Out-of-state applicants must also meet the Kentucky precollege curriculum requirements.

Based on the review of official test results and the precollege curriculum, students are admitted into one of two categories: regular admission or admission with conditions. Students who have two or more deficiencies are encouraged to retake the ACT or SAT so an additional review can be completed. Students with two or more deficiencies may be asked to submit an essay, letters of recommendation, and an activities portfolio before an admission decision can be rendered. Some degree programs require that students meet additional criteria; more information is available in the current catalog (http://www.nku.edu).

Application and Information

The $40 paper application fee may be waived for applicants with demonstrated need. The fall semester early action and scholarship deadline is January 15, assured consideration deadline is May 1, and the final deadline is July 1. The priority application deadline for the nursing program is January 31. The priority application deadline for the respiratory care program is February 15.

For more information, students should contact:
Office of Admissions
Northern Kentucky University
Highland Heights, Kentucky 41099
Phone: 859-572-5220
   800-637-9948 (toll-free)
E-mail: admitnku@nku.edu
Web site: http://admissions.nku.edu
   http://www.facebook.com/nkuedu
   http://twitter.com.nkuedu

Northern Kentucky University's modern campus is set in Highland Heights, just minutes from downtown Cincinnati.

NORTHWOOD UNIVERSITY, FLORIDA
WEST PALM BEACH, FLORIDA

The University

Northwood University was founded in 1959 by Dr. Arthur E. Turner and Dr. R. Gary Stauffer in order to teach business and management infused with practical experience, based upon the concepts of freedom and free enterprise. Since the early days, the University has grown system-wide to include campuses in Michigan, Texas, and Florida as well as 28 satellite centers throughout the United States, with a system enrollment of more than 6,000 students. Northwood is a private, independent, coeducational institution and is accredited by the North Central Association of Schools and Colleges.

The Florida Campus, which opened in the mid-1980s, has grown to its current enrollment of more than 650 students. Attracting students from all over the globe, the campus is host to students who come to Northwood from thirty-seven different states and forty-seven different countries. Approximately 300 of the students reside on campus in attractive apartment-style residence halls.

The campus architecture is unique, with buildings directly influenced by the work of noted architect Alden B. Dow (a student of Frank Lloyd Wright). The low and rounded modern buildings create the feel of a corporate campus surrounded by lakes and dotted with palm trees. It has been described as a corporate campus in paradise.

Outside the classroom, Northwood offers its students a broad spectrum of activities and clubs in which to participate. Clubs include Collegiate DECA, Student Government, Campus Crusade for Christ, the CASH Club, the Drama Club, Blue Storm Dance Team, the Cycling Club, Circle K International, and organizations linked to major fields of study. Activities include cultural awareness programs, concerts, Big Brothers/Big Sisters, Northwood's Outstanding Business Leader Forum, intramural sports, and many others.

Athletics play an important role in student life. Northwood University, Florida competes in the National Association of Intercollegiate Athletics (NAIA). Men's intercollegiate sports include baseball, basketball, golf, soccer, and tennis. Women's sports include basketball, golf, soccer, softball, tennis, and volleyball. Several of the teams have been nationally ranked and are quite competitive within the Florida Sun Conference.

Facilities for tennis, racquetball, swimming, basketball, and fitness are in proximity to the student residence halls. The Countess de Hoernle Student Life Center includes a gym, fitness center, classrooms, bookstore, and snack bar.

Location

The beautiful 90-acre campus is located in West Palm Beach, Florida. West Palm Beach is a 1-hour drive from Fort Lauderdale, 30 minutes from Boca Raton, and within a 2½-hour drive from Orlando. The Palm Beach International Airport, 10 minutes from the campus, provides easy access to students and visitors.

West Palm Beach offers students a vast array of opportunities for both work and play. Great weather year-round and easy access to outdoor activities ranging from scuba and snorkeling to spring training major-league baseball and concerts at south Florida's premier outdoor concert venue supplement a very active on-campus activity program.

Majors and Degrees

Northwood University, Florida offers Bachelor of Business Administration (B.B.A.) and Master of Business Administration (M.B.A.) degrees. Degree programs are offered in accounting; advertising and marketing; after-market management; automotive marketing; entertainment, sport, and promotion management; entrepreneurship; finance; hotel, restaurant, and resort management; international business; management; and marketing.

Off-Campus Programs

Recognizing that the business world is truly global, the University offers several exciting study-abroad programs for its students. The Semester in Europe is a traveling study-abroad program that explores France, Germany, Greece, Hungary, and Italy. The Semester in Asia program is a residential study-abroad program in partnership with universities in Southeast Asia. The Semester in Australia includes visits to Sydney, Magnetic Islands, Cairns, Kuranda, and the Great Barrier Reef.

Academic Facilities

At the heart of Northwood's academic facilities is the DeVos-Cook Academic Center. This facility contains 23,000 square feet of space and houses state-of-the-art classrooms, faculty offices, and computer labs for both instructional and general student use.

Supplementing the DeVos-Cook Center is the Johann M. and Arthur E. Turner Education Center. This modern 38,000-square-foot facility houses the library, an art gallery, administrative offices, conference rooms, classrooms, and an auditorium.

Costs

The fee structure for the 2012–13 academic year is $20,996 for tuition and $9482 for room and board. Northwood estimates that annual books and supplies cost $500 to $600 per year. Since Northwood is a private university, the tuition and fee charge is the same for both in-state and out-of-state students.

Financial Aid

Over 70 percent of students at Northwood University, Florida receive some form of financial assistance. The University makes available academic merit scholarships, athletic scholarships, and general need-based aid.

Merit scholarships are based upon academic performance and standardized test results (ACT or SAT). Current academic scholarships range from $3000 to $15,000 per year with on-campus residency ($1000 to $13,000 per year without campus residency). Prospective students can check their scholarship eligibility by using the Scholarship and Grant Calculator located in the Financial Aid section of the University's Web site at www.northwood.edu. Scholarships are renewable if satisfactory academic progress is maintained.

Several other merit-based scholarships are available to those who qualify and are not need-based. Examples include grants

for students who have participated in organizations such as DECA, FBLA, BPA, FCCLA, competitive speech, mock trial, and Junior Achievement. These business club scholarships can be combined with merit scholarships.

In order to be considered for all need-based aid programs, students must file the Free Application for Federal Student Aid (FAFSA). Need-based aid is available in the form of federal, state, and Northwood grants, loans, and work-study programs to those who qualify.

Faculty

The student-faculty ratio at Northwood is currently 20:1. This affords the student not only small classes but also the opportunity to work closely with faculty members. The faculty is dedicated to bringing current business practices into the classroom. In addition to the fact that 90 percent of the faculty members hold advanced degrees, the vast majority has had prior experience in the business or management world. It is their practical experience in the real world, coupled with small classes, which creates a learning experience that combines both theory and practical skills.

Student Government

The Student Government Association (SGA) assists in the personal, social, and political development of Northwood students, both individually and collectively. The organization consists of 5 major officers, class presidents, and several subcommittees and/or appointed positions. SGA has representatives to confer with Student Services and campus administrative leaders throughout the academic year.

Admission Requirements

Northwood University, Florida seeks to enroll students who have an interest in pursuing business, management, or entrepreneurial ventures and who have demonstrated that desire through performance in the classroom. When reviewing a candidate for admission, the University takes into consideration the applicant's high school record, the results of the SAT or ACT, and a host of other factors, including extracurricular activity, recommendations, and involvement in business-related activities or clubs.

Northwood strongly encourages students who have followed an approved course of study at another college or university to apply for admission. The University's transfer program is designed to allow each student to transfer the maximum number of credit hours into their program of study. Transfer students with fewer than 24 credit hours must submit high school transcripts and standardized test scores. All students who apply should be in good academic and social standing at the college from which they are transferring.

All international students are required to take the TOEFL examination, unless they have taken the SAT or ACT. A minimum TOEFL score of 500 on the paper-based exam, or 61 Internet-based is required for regular admission. Official transcripts of all secondary (high school) and college work must be provided with the application. All transcripts must be translated into English.

Application and Information

The application fee is waived for online applications. A paper application is ready for consideration by the Admissions Committee when it has been received with the $25 application fee, required test scores, and transcripts from each school attended. Northwood encourages students to apply via the Web site.

For more information about Northwood University, Florida, prospective students should contact:

Office of Admissions
Northwood University, Florida
2600 North Military Trail
West Palm Beach, Florida 33409
United States
Phone: 561-478-5500
      800-622-9000 (toll-free)
E-mail: fladmit@northwood.edu
Web site: http://www.northwood.edu

Northwood University, Florida's campus has been described as a corporate campus in paradise.

NORWICH UNIVERSITY
NORTHFIELD, VERMONT

NORWICH
UNIVERSITY™
Expect Challenge. Achieve Distinction.

The University

Norwich University was established in 1819 as the first private military college in America. It was at Norwich that the idea of the citizen-soldier developed and eventually evolved into the Reserve Officer Training Corps (ROTC) program. Norwich was the first private college to offer civil engineering, and many University alumni were involved in the construction of the nation's continental railway system. In 1974, Norwich became one of the first military colleges to admit women into its Corps of Cadets, preceding the federal academies.

Norwich University offers a diverse blend of disciplines, teaching styles, and viewpoints. Students enrolled in the Corps of Cadets have a more disciplined, challenging, and structured path through college, while their civilian student classmates lead a more traditional collegiate lifestyle. However, both groups are coeducational and attend classes and participate in sports and other activities together.

In keeping with its mission, Norwich provides opportunities for all of its students to develop leadership skills with a strong commitment to community service. Both groups gain skills such as leadership, honor, and integrity, which are required to be successful in today's job market. These two diverse groups of students are very different and yet have much in common—they are Norwich.

Norwich University has an enrollment of 2,300 students from more than forty-five states and twenty countries. The University's minority enrollment is consistently higher (by percentage) than that of any other Vermont university or college.

The athletic facilities at Norwich are comparable to the best at any of New England's Division III universities. The main athletic complex, Andrews Hall, features a gymnasium, racquetball courts, a modernized athletic training room, an equipment room, and laundry facilities. Kreitzberg Arena is a multipurpose facility with a seating capacity of 1,500 and a fully equipped weight room. It was here that the University's men's hockey team won the Division III National Championship in 2003. The recently constructed 22,000-square-foot Doyle Hall facility connects the Kreitzberg Arena and Andrews Hall. Doyle Hall features a new Hall of Fame lobby at the main entrance into the athletic complex and includes a grand stairway, ticket booth, concessions area, and restroom facilities. The new facility also provides the athletic department with offices for coaches, team meeting rooms, and locker room facilities.

Plumley Armory has a huge gym as well as an indoor track, weight and aerobics rooms, a wrestling room, and an indoor swimming pool. Shapiro Field House has 50,000 square feet of floor space and includes a 200-meter indoor track, tennis courts, and a climbing wall. The newly developed Shaw Outdoor Center at the base of Paine Mountain offers students a variety of outdoor recreational activities including trails for jogging, cross-country running races, hiking, snowshoeing, cross-country skiing, sledding, and mountain biking. Equipment to participate in these activities is available to students free of charge. The 1,200-acre campus includes numerous playing fields for baseball, football, rugby, soccer, and softball. Norwich also has a paintball course, a rappel tower, and an obstacle and confidence course.

Norwich has the only professional five-year Master of Architecture program in northern New England. The University also offers online graduate degrees in business administration, diplomacy, information assurance, nursing, public administration, business continuity, organizational leadership, civil engineering, history and military history.

Location

Norwich University is located in the heart of the Green Mountains of Vermont, right in the middle of ski country. Some of the nation's most popular resorts, such as Stowe, Sugarbush, and Killington, are located within an hour's drive. Vermont is world renowned as one of America's most beautiful states. Nature's playground is just outside the dorm room—skiing, snowboarding, telemark skiing, cross-country skiing, snowshoeing, rock climbing, hiking, mountain biking, canoeing, kayaking, and more are available.

The University campus is located in the small town of Northfield, Vermont. Northfield is 10 miles south of the state capital of Montpelier and is 50 miles from Burlington, the largest city in Vermont. Both Montpelier and Burlington are cultural centers for the arts. Burlington International Airport is within an hour's drive. In addition, the cities of Boston and Montreal are only a 3-hour drive from the campus.

Majors and Degrees

Norwich offers students more than thirty academic majors from which to choose. The Bachelor of Arts degree is awarded in criminal justice, English, history, international studies, political science, studies in war and peace, psychology, and Spanish. The Bachelor of Science degree is awarded in accounting, architectural studies; biochemistry, biology, chemistry, civil engineering, communications, computer/electrical engineering, computer science, computer security and information assurance, engineering management, environmental science, geology, management, mathematics, mechanical engineering, nursing, physical education, physics, sports medicine, and strategic studies and defense analysis. Teacher licensure, prelaw, premedical, and predental programs are also available.

Academic Programs

Norwich University is dedicated to the discovery, preservation, and dissemination of knowledge and the search for truth. Norwich is distinctive in that it maintains a strong emphasis on the development of leadership in both military and civilian pursuits and in providing for the educational needs of students. The University's mission is to foster in each student the growth of self-discipline, personal integrity, social responsibility, physical fitness, respect for law, and intellectual ability essential for full and effective participation in a free society.

For students enrolling in the Corps of Cadets, six semesters of Reserve Officer Training Corps are required. Norwich is considered the birthplace of ROTC; therefore, all four service branches can be found on campus. Prior to their junior year, cadets may elect to contract with their ROTC program and be considered upon graduation for a commission as officers in the Army, Navy, Air Force, or Marine Corps. Cadets not on an ROTC scholarship are not required to join the military.

Students typically take an average of five classes per semester. Each semester is sixteen weeks long, with holiday breaks at Thanksgiving, Christmas, and New Year's and in March during

spring break. The academic year normally begins the last week in August and ends after the first week in May.

Academic Facilities

The academic facilities at Norwich are among the finest in New England. Completed in 1997, the math and science building was designed to keep classes small. Its labs hold no more than 16 students, and all of the classrooms are hardwired to allow for multimedia presentations. Students can find numerous computer labs across the campus, and the Kreitzberg Library offers students plenty of resources, space, and technology. Students may research Norwich's facilities on the University's Web site.

Costs

For 2012–13, tuition and fees are $15,891 per semester. The cost of room and board is $5488 per semester. Books and personal expenses average $1250 per semester. Cadets pay a uniform fee of $815 per semester in each of their first two years.

Financial Aid

Most families assume they cannot afford a private college education and fall victim to sticker shock, but a Norwich education can often be an affordable option for a family. Last year, 97 percent of Norwich students shared in more than $65 million of financial aid from all sources, including ROTC scholarships. This included an aggressive need-based financial aid program that enabled deserving students to secure a private education at Norwich.

Norwich awards many institutional scholarships based on academic merit. A student's high school GPA and ACT or SAT scores determine the level of scholarship. These scholarships may pay from $7000 to $18,000 of the student's tuition for four years. Students are required to maintain a specified GPA in order to renew the scholarship each year. Norwich also offers scholarships to students who attend the University's Future Leader Camp, participate in National Drill Team competitions, and who are in leadership positions in the Civil Air Patrol. Prospective students should contact an admissions counselor for more details about these scholarships.

Norwich also offers a large number of institutional grants based on financial need. A student must file the Free Application for Federal Student Aid (FAFSA) to be considered for these grants.

Students who bring a three- or four-year ROTC scholarship to Norwich are eligible for the General I. D. White Scholarship, which covers the cost of room and board. Students who are interested in applying for an ROTC scholarship should visit the individual ROTC detachment's Web page on the Norwich University Web site.

Faculty

The student-faculty ratio is 14:1. Faculty members are full-time instructors with advanced degrees; 72 percent hold a doctorate. Small classes help promote a close relationship between faculty members and students. Students are assigned faculty advisers within each academic division.

Student Government

The Norwich University Corps of Cadets is a military organization made up of and led by cadets under the supervision of the Commandant of Cadets. Members of the Corps and student body preside over the University Honor Council. The University's honor code binds all Norwich students. Members of the Corps and student body also participate on the Student Affairs Committee, whose members include the Dean of Students, members of the faculty, and the Senior Vice President and Commandant

of Cadets. This committee serves as the voice of the Norwich community and provides a channel of communication for change.

Admission Requirements

Admission to Norwich is based on a review of the applicant's academic record, personal essay, letters of recommendation, and extracurricular activities. Students at Norwich are heavily involved in community service and leadership development activities. Applicants should be able to demonstrate participation in activities both inside and outside of their high school.

Norwich is looking for students who want to become leaders, serve others, and give back to their communities. While the admissions office uses a rolling admissions system (meaning applications may be submitted at any time), there is a priority deadline of March 1. Students applying for admission or financial aid after March 1 are admitted on a space-available basis.

Application and Information

Students can visit the University's Web site or contact the University for more information.

Admissions Office
Norwich University
27 I. D. White Avenue
Northfield, Vermont 05663
Phone: 800-468-6679 (toll-free)
Fax: 802-485-2032
E-mail: nuadm@norwich.edu
Web site: http://www.norwich.edu
http://www.facebook.com/NorwichUniversity

A view of Norwich University's campus.

NOTRE DAME COLLEGE
SOUTH EUCLID, OHIO

The College

Notre Dame College, a Catholic institution in the tradition of the Sisters of Notre Dame, educates a diverse population in the liberal arts for personal, professional, and global responsibility. Notre Dame College offers stimulating academics, personalized attention, small class sizes, Division II intercollegiate athletics, and vibrant student life.

Founded in 1922 by the Sisters of Notre Dame, the College has grown strategically to keep pace with the rapidly changing needs of students and the dramatic changes in higher education. But it has never lost sight of its emphasis on teaching students not only how to make a good living but also how to live a good life. The College believes that truly progressive education selectively blends traditional values with new ideas that represent real growth. Within the scope of a career-oriented liberal arts education, students can grow to meet the challenges of the present and the future.

Under the leadership of President Dr. Andrew P. Roth since 2003, Notre Dame College (NDC) is rapidly becoming one of the finest small, Catholic, residential, liberal arts colleges in the Great Lakes region. Founded as an all-women's school, the College became coeducational in 2001, and total enrollment has since grown from 875 to 2,150, a remarkable 240 percent increase.

A snapshot of the fall 2011 traditional NDC student population shows the following: 45 percent female, 55 percent male; 55 percent Catholic; 28 percent minority; 55 percent student-athletes; and 53 percent live on campus. The mosaic of NDC students represents twenty states and twelve foreign countries.

A variety of clubs and activities enrich the overall experience of the 2,100-plus students. Campus Ministry promotes the spiritual growth of the College community and facilitates community service, and the award-winning FalconCorps service program provides students opportunities to serve at local charities and national programs such as Habitat for Humanity.

Most on-campus events are free, and students often may purchase tickets at reduced rates for off-campus programs such as performances of the world-famous Cleveland Orchestra, the Cleveland Opera, and road shows of Broadway productions at the Cleveland Play House, the Palace Theatre, the State Theatre, and the Ohio Theatre at Playhouse Square.

With twenty-two intercollegiate sports for men and women, Notre Dame is in the final year of transitioning from NAIA to NCAA Division II affiliation, which will be effective fall 2012. The College's newest programs include bowling, water polo, and a football team which had its its first season in fall 2010, complete with cheerleaders and marching band. Prospective students can learn more about NDC Falcon athletic programs at NotreDameFalcons.com/.

Notre Dame offers quality academic programs in over thirty disciplines including a nationally accredited education major, a business major, a Bachelor of Science in Nursing, intelligence analysis and research, and criminal justice. A Master of Education degree is offered with concentrations available in special education, reading, and critical and creative thinking. The College launched a Master of Arts in security policy studies in fall 2011.

The College is accredited by both the North Central Association of Colleges and Schools and NCATE and is registered for the awarding of state teachers' licenses by the State of Ohio Department of Education.

Location

Located in South Euclid, Ohio, the 48-acre campus is in a residential neighborhood just 25 minutes from downtown Cleveland and all the excitement and cultural wealth of the city, such as the Rock and Roll Hall of Fame and Museum; the Cleveland Metroparks; University Circle; several professional sports teams; and one of the richest cultural, theatrical, entertainment, health-care, and employment

regions in the nation. Only five minutes from Legacy Village and Beachwood Place, Cleveland's lifestyle retail centers, the area combines all the opportunities of a major urban and educational center with the relaxed atmosphere of a suburb.

The beautiful campus provides the perfect setting for the Clara Fritzsche Library; the historic Administration Building which houses classrooms, labs, and offices; Regina Hall and Regina Auditorium; Connelly Center, the dining hall and student center; Keller Center, the recreational and fitness facility; Falcon Café; and five residence halls, including two newer apartment-style facilities that house 288 upper-class students.

Majors and Degrees

The College awards the Bachelor of Arts degree in accounting (business administration); biology; chemistry; communication; education, including early childhood (pre-K–3), middle childhood (4–9), and young adult education and mild-moderate intervention specialist studies; English; graphic design; history/political science; information systems; international business; management; marketing; mathematics; psychology; public administration; sports management; studio art; and theology.

The Bachelor of Science is awarded in biology, chemistry, and mathematics. A student can also design his or her own major that leads to a Bachelor of Arts or Bachelor of Science degree by combining two or three academic areas, such as graphic design, human resource management, and public relations. Notre Dame College also offers a Bachelor of Science in Nursing program. An RN to B.S.N. completion program is also available.

Teacher licensure is available in early childhood education, middle childhood education, adolescent/young adult education, and multiage for mild/moderate intervention specialist studies.

The Associate in Arts degree is awarded at the completion of two-year programs in business management and pastoral ministry. The Center for Pastoral Theology and Ministry grants a two-year catechetical diploma and the College awards a Bachelor of Arts degree.

Academic Programs

For the bachelor's degree, students must earn 128 semester hours of credit, with a minimum cumulative grade point average of 2.0. From 36 to 68 semester hours of credit are required in the major field of study.

Through a cooperative education program, students can earn a maximum of 6 credit hours for paid or volunteer work experience related to their academic field of study. All students are required to complete a coop or internship experience.

Advanced Placement credit is awarded to students who have demonstrated the ability to pursue course work beyond the level of entering freshmen, as indicated by their scores on the Advanced Placement (AP) or College-Level Examination Program (CLEP) tests of the College Board. College credit is given on the basis of a decision made jointly by the academic dean and the department involved.

Academic Facilities

The Career Services Center coordinates co-op jobs and internships for students and interacts with faculty to create meaningful programs that link academics to the workplace. It further offers graduate school advising, résumé preparation assistance, interviewing and job search coaching, posting of positions available, and a resource library. On-campus recruiting opportunities attract scores of employers to the College to meet students firsthand.

The Clara Fritzsche Library houses a modern media center and has a capacity for 100,000 volumes. As a member of OhioLINK, the College also has online access to members throughout the state, with access to more than 31 million library items and more than 90 research databases.

The Dwyer Success Center consists of an electronic classroom, a student computer lab, a writing lab, a test proctoring room and a tutoring room. The writing lab is staffed by English faculty who provide professional writing assistance to students free of charge. The tutoring room is staffed with graduate assistants and upper-class peer tutors for one-on-one study skills and subject specific assistance.

The multimedia lab for graphic design majors offers PC and Macintosh technology for advanced multimedia production capabilities.

The Finn Center for Adult, Graduate, Online, and Professional Programs unifies all aspects of adult education at NDC, providing convenient, flexible programs for educational advancement on days, nights, weekends, and the Web. Housing the Office of Adult and Graduate Admissions and the Office of Professional Development, the Finn Center offers professional development classes, associate degrees, bachelor's degrees, postbaccalaureate programs, and master's degrees.

Students with documented learning differences, such as attention deficit disorder (ADD), attention deficit hyperactivity disorder (ADHD), dyslexia, Asperger's syndrome, and specific learning disabilities (SLD) can enroll in the College's Academic Support Center to receive comprehensive support services. These include tutoring, academic advising, and access to a large array of adaptive equipment. In order to be accepted into the Learning Differences Program, students must meet the admission requirements of Notre Dame College. To participate in the Academic Support Center, students must submit documentation of a learning disability.

Costs
For the 2011–12 academic year tuition and fee charges were $24,002. Room and board costs were $8054 for double occupancy.

Financial Aid
Notre Dame believes that all qualified students should have the opportunity to attend college, and provides need-, merit-, and athletic-based aid to its students. A comprehensive financial assistance program of more than $25 million assists nearly 93 percent of all full-time students. Students applying for aid must submit the Free Application for Federal Student Aid (FAFSA).

Faculty
The College has 62 full-time faculty members, augmented by highly qualified instructors. Faculty members hold advanced degrees from more than thirty universities in the United States, Canada, and Europe.

Student Government
The Undergraduate Student Government (USG) is the central coordinating group for all student organizations. In addition, students have representation on various College committees.

Admission Requirements
Notre Dame College admits students who demonstrate potential for success in rigorous academic work. In fulfilling its mission, the College seeks to attract students of diverse religious, racial, and economic backgrounds. Candidates for admission as first-time, full-time freshmen are reviewed on an individual basis, and decisions are based on a broad range of criteria. The most important consideration is the candidate's high school performance, as demonstrated by her/his overall grade average, class rank, grade trends, and level of courses completed. Aptitude for verbal and mathematical reasoning, as measured by performance on standardized tests, is also considered. In addition, counselor and teacher recommendations are reviewed.

Notre Dame College recommends that students complete at least 16 units of high school credit in academic subjects as a prerequisite for matriculation in the College. The distribution of these subject areas and the units are as follows: English, 4; mathematics, 3 (to include algebra I, geometry, and algebra II); science, 3 (with laboratory experience); social studies, 3; foreign language, 2 (from the same language); and fine arts, 1. Applicants should generally rank in the upper half of their high school graduating class and have a minimum average of C+. Either ACT or SAT scores are accepted.

The College has a fair and generous policy on the transfer of academic credit earned within the preceding five years at a regionally accredited college or university. Students wishing to transfer from other regionally accredited colleges and universities are admitted to advanced standing upon presentation of satisfactory evidence of scholarship and character.

Special consideration may be granted to an applicant whose academic preparation is not consistent with the requirements stated above.

Notre Dame College strongly recommends that prospective students schedule an appointment to visit the campus and talk with an admissions counselor.

Application and Information
A free application is available online at NotreDameCollege.edu. The College maintains a rolling admission policy. To apply, students should submit the completed application for undergraduate admission, an official transcript of their high school record and results of the ACT or SAT to:

Office of Admissions
Notre Dame College
4545 College Road
South Euclid, Ohio 44121
Phone: 216-373-5355
    877-NDC-OHIO Ext. 5355 (toll-free)
Fax: 216-373-5278
E-mail: admissions@ndc.edu
Web site: http://NotreDameCollege.edu
    http://www.facebook.com/NotreDameCollege
    http://twitter.com/NotreDameOhio
    http://www.youtube/naotredamecollege

Notre Dame College students in front of the iconic Administration Building, which is listed on the National Register of Historic Places.

OHIO NORTHERN UNIVERSITY
ADA, OHIO

The University
Founded in 1871, Ohio Northern University (ONU) is a private, comprehensive university, comprising five colleges (Arts & Sciences, Business Administration, Engineering, Law, and Pharmacy) that blend liberal and professional education. Talented, motivated students engage in abundant activities in and out of the classroom and graduate with an education that provides one of the highest returns on investment in the nation.

Ohio Northern is a student-centered, service-oriented, values-based institution affiliated with the United Methodist Church and committed to a rigorous pursuit of academic inquiry and achievement. Education is a collaborative process, and students work side-by-side with accomplished faculty in a constant pursuit of new knowledge. The result is serious research, real collaboration, and meaningful learning experiences.

Students can choose from a variety of campus activities including nearly 200 student organizations; four national sororities and six national fraternities; fine arts, music, and theatrical events; and intramural and club sports. Residence hall living is an integral part of the educational program, contributing to a student's personal development. There are ten residence halls on campus as well as seven campus apartment complexes and an Affinity Housing complex.

A member of the NCAA Division III Ohio Athletic Conference, ONU has eleven men's teams (baseball, basketball, cross-country, football, golf, soccer, swimming and diving, tennis, indoor and outdoor track, and wrestling) and ten women's teams (basketball, cross-country, fast-pitch softball, golf, soccer, swimming and diving, tennis, indoor and outdoor track, and volleyball).

Location
Ohio Northern University's campus is situated on 342 beautiful acres in the safe, friendly, rural village of Ada (population 5,500). Located in northwestern Ohio, ONU is easily accessible by major highways and conveniently located near major cities such as Columbus, Dayton, Toledo, and Fort Wayne, Indiana.

Majors and Degrees
Ohio Northern University offers the undergraduate degrees of Bachelor of Arts, Bachelor of Fine Arts, Bachelor of Music, Bachelor of Science, Bachelor of Science in Business Administration, Bachelor of Science in Civil Engineering, Bachelor of Science in Medical Laboratory Science, Bachelor of Science in Computer Engineering, Bachelor of Science in Electrical Engineering, Bachelor of Science in Engineering Education, Bachelor of Science in Mechanical Engineering, and Bachelor of Science in Nursing. In addition, to the undergraduate programs, ONU offers a Master of Professional Practice in Accountancy, Juris Doctor, and Doctor of Pharmacy (Pharm.D.), which is a 0-6, direct entry program.

Majors are offered in accounting, advertising design, applied mathematics, art education, athletic training, biochemistry, biology, chemistry, civil engineering, medical laboratory science, communication studies, computer engineering, computer science, construction management, creative writing, criminal justice, early childhood education, electrical engineering, electronic media and broadcasting, engineering education, environmental and field biology, exercise physiology, finance, forensic biology, French, German, graphic design, health education, history, international business and economics, international theatre production, journalism, language arts education, literature, management, manufacturing technology, marketing, mathematical statistics, mathematics, mechanical engineering, middle childhood education, molecular biology, music, music education, musical theatre, nursing, performance, pharmaceutical business, philosophy, physical education, physics, political science, professional writing, psychology, public relations, religion, social studies, sociology, Spanish, sport management, studio arts, technology education, theatre, and youth ministry.

Special preprofessional programs are available in art therapy, dentistry, law, medicine, occupational therapy, optometry, physical therapy, physician assisting, seminary, and veterinary medicine. Interdisciplinary degree programs are available in arts/engineering and arts–business/pharmacy. Teacher licensure programs are offered at the early childhood, middle childhood, adolescent/young adult, and multiage levels within eighteen programs and two endorsement areas.

Changes in programs of study are updated at www.onu.edu.

Academic Programs
The Getty College of Arts & Sciences creatively combines a traditional liberal arts education with cutting-edge preprofessional studies. The college offers more than fifty majors in sixteen academic departments, and students can earn a Bachelor of Arts, Bachelor of Fine Arts, Bachelor of Music, Bachelor of Science, Bachelor of Science in Clinical Laboratory Science, or Bachelor of Science in Nursing degree.

Students in the sciences have been honored by the Barry M. Goldwater Scholarship and Excellence in Education Foundation for eight consecutive years. The college has also been recognized as one of the top 200 programs in the nation for creative students in Creative Colleges: A Guide for Student Actors, Artists, Dancers, Musicians and Writers.

Working closely with dedicated faculty members, students complete the general education requirements, delve deeply into advanced courses, and engage in research, internships, practicum experiences, study abroad, and more.

The James F. Dicke College of Business Administration focuses on creating ethical, entrepreneurial, and engaged business and civic leaders. The college offers a rigorous academic curriculum with a signature program in pharmaceutical business. Internships are required by the college and are available year-round. There are international programs, including study abroad, work abroad, and study tours. An office of experiential learning supports students looking for these opportunities.

The course of study for the Bachelor of Science in Business Administration includes a four-year integrated general studies program and a four-year business core experience themed around business planning. To graduate, a student must satisfactorily complete a minimum of 122 semester hours of appropriate course work for the specific major(s) and maintain at least a 2.0 grade point average.

Personal attention and mentoring from faculty members, small intimate classes, and active student organizations combine with an emphasis on experiential learning, global awareness, and the entrepreneurial spirit. The college is accredited by the AACSB International—The Association to Advance Collegiate Schools of Business, making it one of the best business colleges in the world.

One of the top 50 undergraduate programs in the nation for the past five years (U.S. News & World Report), the T.J. Smull College of Engineering provides a premier undergraduate experience that inspires creativity and supports innovation. The college features five accredited, disciplinary majors in civil, computer, electrical, and mechanical engineering and computer science. Beginning in fall 2011, an additional engineering education degree supports the demand for high school math teachers with engineering degrees.

The courses for the first academic year are essentially the same for each degree program, offering students an easy track to move from one program to another if initially uncertain which disciplines they prefer to study. Students are required to maintain a minimum cumulative grade point average (GPA) of 2.0 as well as a minimum cumulative GPA of 2.0 for all engineering and computer science courses.

An optional five-year co-op program is available for students in each program, provided they maintain a minimum 2.5 GPA.

There is an emphasis on team projects, and students participate in various design competitions.

Many opportunities are available for valuable work experience through the co-op and internship programs, with a historically high job-placement rate for graduates.

For more than 125 years, the Raabe College of Pharmacy has offered distinctive, challenging, and comprehensive training for some of the nation's most talented pharmacists. This University signature program features a six-year Doctor of Pharmacy (Pharm.D.) degree accredited by the American Council on Pharmaceutical Education.

This program is direct-entry, admitting students immediately from high school into the college's professional program. This approach enables students to take pharmacy courses from the very first day. A rigorous curriculum utilizes an innovative modular format to organize learning around the human body systems and patient care implementation. Students complete a minimum of 216 semester hours and follow a prescribed curriculum and requirements, all while earning a grade of C or better in any course.

Cutting-edge clinical facilities include the Pharmacy Skills Center, where students access state-of-the-art compounding/counseling pods with portable OTC simulation stations. Students gain considerable experience through a strong undergraduate research program and may pursue minors or dual majors in other areas. Faculty members are teaching-focused but remain current in their research disciplines. Upon graduation, students are well schooled in every aspect of pharmacy and have a 100 percent placement rate.

Off-Campus Programs

Many majors may take part in study-abroad programs developed in consultation with faculty members. Field experiences and internships are available to most majors. Externships are required of all pharmacy majors and place students in retail and clinical experiences. Teacher licensure requires one semester of primary or secondary classroom teaching experience under the supervision of practicing teachers. Additional opportunities include computer science and mathematics co-op programs (professional practice), engineering co-op programs (professional practice, domestic and international), and an honors program. All off-campus learning experiences carry credit.

Academic Facilities

Among the nineteen modern academic buildings on campus, the newest is the Mathile Center for the Natural Sciences, which expands the science-learning environment. This 95,145-square-foot student-centered academic research and learning facility blends hands-on teaching excellence with advanced technology in a functional modern environment.

The College of Business Administration's Dicke Hall offers students a modern setting for high-tech classrooms, meeting rooms and a 150-seat lecture forum, as well as a real-time digital stock ticker.

ONU's Heterick Memorial Library and the Taggart Law Library provide information resources and services to support course offerings and foster independent study.

The Freed Center for the Performing Arts houses Communications and Theatre Arts classrooms and features a 550-seat theater/concert hall, a 120-seat studio theater, and television and radio production facilities. WONB-FM is the commercial-free voice of ONU.

Costs

Charges for the 2012–13 year are $45,898 for tuition, room, and board for the Colleges of Arts & Sciences and Business Administration, $48,310 for the College of Engineering, and $50,294 for the College of Pharmacy. These totals are based on tuition, double-occupancy air-conditioned room, a carte-blanche meal plan, and a technology fee of $240 per year.

Financial Aid

Even with one of the highest returns on investment in the nation, ONU invests more than $56 million toward merit-based scholarships and need-based resources and makes every effort to ensure that no qualified applicant is denied admission because of inability to pay the total cost. To be considered, the student should submit the FAFSA to the University along with the admission application.

Faculty

More than 200 full-time faculty members bring extensive academic, work, travel, and life experience to their classrooms. Ohio Northern

values excellence, innovation, technology, diversity, and its people. With a 12:1 student-faculty ratio, students get lots of personal attention from professors who are passionate about teaching and mentoring.

Student Government

The Student Senate provides self-government in many areas of student life and seeks to further ideals of character and service to the University. The Student Senate serves as the official representative group of the student body to the University administration and agencies in matters pertaining to the student body.

Admission Requirements

High school students applying for admission to the University should present an official transcript indicating at least 16 total units of study, including work in specific academic areas as indicated by each college. Applicants are also required to submit scores on the ACT and/or SAT. For scholarship purposes, the traditional sections of the ACT and the SAT are considered. An on-campus interview is also recommended.

Application and Information

A student's file is considered complete when it contains the application, $30 nonrefundable application fee (fee waived if student visits campus prior to application), official high school transcript, one letter of recommendation, personal statement, and ACT and/or SAT scores.

Early Action applications can be made to the Colleges of Arts & Sciences, Business Administration, and Engineering prior to December 1, while Regular Decision applications to these colleges can be made prior to February 1.

The College of Pharmacy's application deadline is December 1 for entering freshmen. A campus visit is strongly encouraged for consideration for admittance into this college.

Requests for catalogs, application forms, or additional information should be directed to:

Office of Admissions
Ohio Northern University
Ada, Ohio 45810
Phone: 888-408-4668 (toll-free)
Fax: 419-772-2821
E-mail: admissions-ug@onu.edu
Web site: www.onu.edu
    www.facebook.com/ohionorthern
    www.twitter.com/onuadmissions

Hill Memorial and its clock tower are mainstays of the front of campus.

OHIO WESLEYAN UNIVERSITY
DELAWARE, OHIO

The University

Founded by the United Methodist Church in 1842, Ohio Wesleyan is a national liberal arts university with a major international presence. It is remarkable for the depth of its academic and preprofessional programs, the international dimension of its curriculum, its focus on community through leadership and service, and its unwavering commitment to linking theory and practice in a global context and in every field of study.

A selective residential institution, Ohio Wesleyan is home to about 1,850 undergraduates, with a nearly equal number of men and women. Students come from more than forty states and more than fifty countries, lending a rich diversity to the campus community; most students live on the attractive 200-acre campus. Housing options include six large residence halls, one of which was fully renovated during the 2011–12 academic year; two newly remodeled residences primarily for seniors; a third remodeled living-learning residence for students in economics disciplines; a residential honors house; several small living units (SLUs); and seven fraternity houses. The five sorority houses are nonresidential.

One of the richest of OWU's cocurricular traditions is service. The University sends as many as ten service teams throughout the world each year. Nearly the entire student body participates in at least one community service or philanthropic project each year. From 2009 to 2012, the school has been found on the Presidential Honor Roll for Community Service, with distinction, and in 2009–10, the University earned the President's Award for Excellence in General Community Service, one of only three colleges and universities in the country to be so honored that year.

Students publish the nation's oldest independent student newspaper. They also participate in cultural- and ethnic-interest groups, College Republicans and College Democrats, and prelaw and premed clubs. Each year, students may enjoy more than 100 concerts, plays, dance programs, films, exhibits, and speakers. The Department of Theatre & Dance stages four major productions each year, while the Music Department sponsors four large performance groups and a variety of smaller ensembles.

OWU is home to twenty-three Division III varsity athletic teams. In 2011, the men's soccer team took the Division III National Championship for the second time, and with that win, OWU's coach, Dr. Jay Martin, became the all-time winningest coach in collegiate men's soccer across all NCAA divisions. The school also opened the Luttinger Tennis Center, with six new championship-caliber courts.

Intramural and club sports programs are extensive, and all students have access to racquet sports and weight-lifting facilities in the Branch Rickey Physical Education Center. Off-campus recreation opportunities are abundant.

Location

Delaware combines a small-town pace with easy access to the state capital, Columbus, the sixteenth-largest city in America. Twenty miles south of the campus, Columbus provides rich internship opportunities, fine dining and shopping, and cultural events that complement those on campus.

Majors and Degrees

Ohio Wesleyan offers the Bachelor of Arts in accounting; ancient, medieval, and Renaissance studies; astronomy; biological sciences (botany, genetics, microbiology, and zoology); chemistry; classics; computer science; economics (including accounting, international business, and management); education (elementary and secondary licensure in seventeen areas); English literature and writing; fine arts; French; geography; geology; German; history; humanities; journalism; mathematics; music (applied or history/literature); philosophy; physical education; physics; planetary science; politics and government; psychology; religion; sociology/anthropology; Spanish; and theater and dance. Interdisciplinary majors include Black world studies, East Asian studies, environmental studies, international studies, Latin American studies, neuroscience, urban studies, and women's and gender studies. Preprofessional studies include pre-law, pre-medicine, pre-engineering, pre-dentistry, pre-veterinary medicine, pre-optometry, pre-theology, and pre-physical therapy. Students also may design majors in topical, period, or regional studies.

Two professional degrees are awarded: the Bachelor of Fine Arts in art history, arts education, and studio art, and the Bachelor of Music in music education and performance. Combined-degree programs are offered in engineering, medical technology, optometry, and physical therapy. Ohio Wesleyan is one of only thirteen colleges in the United States that has a 3-2 engineering program with the California Institute of Technology.

Academic Programs

Ohio Wesleyan emphasizes theory-to-practice opportunities in a global context. Each year, travel-learning courses invite students to travel internationally with their classmates and professors as part of the course curriculum. Competitive theory-to-practice grants provide University-funded opportunities for students to design their own research projects, complete internships, participate in service, or experience cultural immersion throughout the world. Ohio Wesleyan also provides a robust offering of traditional study-abroad options; formal programs are offered in more than twenty countries. Ohio Wesleyan Course Connections networks provide opportunities for students to study a topic of interest in depth and over a protracted period of time by taking topical courses in a variety of disciplines and departments.

Ohio Wesleyan provides opportunities for students to acquire not only depth in a major area but also knowledge about their cultural past through the insight provided by a broad liberal arts curriculum. Students are required to demonstrate competence in English composition and a foreign language (often through placement testing) and to complete distributional study in the natural and social sciences, the humanities, and the arts; some of these requirements may be met in Course Connections classes. Many students double major and self-designed majors are not uncommon. Thirty-four courses are required for graduation.

Advanced placement is available with or without credit. In the four-year honors program, even first-year students have opportunities to work individually with faculty mentors on research, directed readings, or original creative work. Undergraduate students frequently present their research to prestigious societies and nationally recognized organizations. Upperclass students also are encouraged to participate in independent study. One of the twenty-six scholastic honorary societies with chapters on campus, Ohio Wesleyan's chapter of Phi Beta Kappa is 104 years old.

Ohio Wesleyan offers the Economics Management Fellows program for talented first-year students with an interest in economics, economics management, accounting, or international business. This program offers special classes and seminars, a generous book allowance, networking opportunities with alumni executives and others, and a spring study trip to meet with business leaders.

Off-Campus Programs

Full-semester internships and apprenticeships, as well as programs of advanced research, are available to students. Many are approved by the Great Lakes Colleges Association, Inc. (GLCA), a highly regarded academic consortium of thirteen independent institutions. Programs are available at the Philadelphia Center, the GLCA New York Arts Program, and the Oak Ridge Science Semester. Other cooperative arrangements include the Newberry Library Program, Wesleyan in Washington, and the Drew University United Nations Semester. Students also conduct research locally at the U.S. Department of Agriculture (USDA) Laboratories in Delaware, the nearby Columbus Zoo, The Wilds, and several other sites. The Summer Science Research Program offers selected students

the opportunity for an intensive, ten-week, one-to-one research experience with a faculty mentor. It concludes with a symposium at which research results are presented to the entire campus.

Academic Facilities

The Beeghly Library houses more than 550,000 holdings, one of the largest collections in the country for a private university of Ohio Wesleyan's size. The library's federal documents depository is among the nation's oldest and largest, providing an additional 200,000 reference publications. Beeghly Library also offers the Online Computer Library Center's most advanced cataloging system. The collection is enhanced by OhioLINK and CONSORT membership. An Internet Café within the Beeghly Library provides students with a 24-hour study area. The comprehensive academic computing system is accessible to students 24 hours per day, and all residence hall rooms are wired for campus network and global Internet access. The latest generation of wireless communication allows students to work online anywhere on the campus.

The Schimmel/Conrades Science Center includes a 145,000-square-foot, three-level building that houses state-of-the-art instrumentation, including a scanning transmission electron microscope, all for undergraduate use. The Hobson Science Library in the science center consolidates all of OWU's science holdings. The University has a state-of-the-art Geographic Information Systems Computer Laboratory. The R.W. Corns Building houses the Woltemade Center for Economics, Business, and Entrepreneurship; the Department of Economics; the Sagan Academic Resource Center, which includes the Writing Resource Center, the Academic Skills Center, and the Quantitative Skills Center; and Information Systems. Perkins Observatory features a 32-inch reflecting telescope and two smaller instruments; an on-campus student observatory includes a 9.5-inch refracting telescope. Two University wilderness preserves cover a total of 100 acres.

Other special facilities include the multistage Chappelear Drama Center; Sanborn Hall, home to the Music Department, Jemison Auditorium, and the Kinnison Music Library; and the 1,100-seat Gray Chapel, which houses the largest of only six Klais concert organs in the United States.

Costs

The general fee for 2012–13 is $49,460. This amount covers tuition and fees ($39,150) and room and board ($10,310). Books and personal expenses average $1100. Nominal fees are charged for some studio art courses, off-campus study, private music lessons for students who are not majoring in music, and student teaching.

Financial Aid

OWU awards financial assistance to almost every entering freshman who demonstrates need. Aid packages include a combination of grants, loans, and employment. Federal and state aid are often part of an aid package. Nearly 70 percent of all undergraduates receive need-based financial assistance; another 25 percent are granted merit-based aid. More than three quarters of all aid is awarded in the form of grants and scholarships.

The University awards several merit scholarship programs, ranging from $1000 to full tuition. The school awarded more than 2,000 scholarships to new and prospective students for 2010–11. Private loan programs and flexible payment plans are available to all students, regardless of demonstrated financial need.

Faculty

The full-time faculty numbers 137, providing a student-faculty ratio of approximately 11:1. One hundred percent of the full-time tenure-track faculty members hold the highest degree in their fields. Although committed first to teaching and advising, most faculty members maintain active research programs and publish important articles and books; others are practicing artists who create and exhibit original works of art and theater.

Student Government

Students have a significant voice in the government of campus life. The Wesleyan Council on Student Affairs formulates basic policy. Students also sit on judicial boards, individual department student boards, and nine faculty committees. They are represented at all meetings of the Board of Trustees.

Admission Requirements

The admission process is competitive. Each student's application is individually reviewed. Although the applicant's academic record and strength of academic program are the most important factors, followed closely by teacher and counselor evaluations and SAT or ACT scores, many other aspects are considered, such as evidence of creativity, community service, and leadership. A minimum sixteen-course preparatory program is required. Four units of English and 3 each of mathematics, social studies, science, and foreign language are recommended, but variations of this program are considered. SAT Subject Tests are not required but may qualify students for advanced placement. Candidates for the Bachelor of Music degree must audition (tapes are accepted). Early action and transfer admission are offered. Campus interviews are strongly recommended but not required. For the 2010–10 school year, approximately 4,200 applications were received; 65 percent of the applicants gained admission.

Application and Information

Students are urged to complete the application as early as possible in the senior year, especially if they are applying for merit- or need-based financial aid. Once complete credentials (application, transcript, recommendations, and SAT or ACT scores) are received, decisions are made on a rolling basis after January 1. The student's response is required by May 1. The deadline for Early Action I application is November 30; the deadline for Early Action II application is January 15. Notification is given within four weeks after application is complete. After April 1, students are admitted on a space-available, rolling admission basis.

For further information, students should contact:

Office of Admission
Ohio Wesleyan University
Delaware, Ohio 43015
Phone: 740-368-3020
800-922-8953 (toll-free)
Fax: 740-368-3314
E-mail: owuadmit@owu.edu
Web site: http://choose.owu.edu
http://www.facebook.com/OhioWesleyanUniversity
http://twitter.com/ohiowesleyan

Ohio Wesleyan's historic University Hall, which houses administrative offices and the 1,100-seat Gray Chapel.

OLIVET NAZARENE UNIVERSITY
BOURBONNAIS, ILLINOIS

The University

Olivet Nazarene University (ONU) is a private, Christian liberal arts university with a strong emphasis on both academic excellence and Christ-centered living. Olivet's campus offers world-class facilities for learning and entertainment—some of the finest in the Midwest. The educational atmosphere promotes academic rigor, fun, relationship building, and spiritual growth.

Olivet's high retention, graduation, and employment/placement rates demonstrate the University's commitment to student success. Faculty, staff, and administration are dedicated to teaching, encouraging, and mentoring each student as a whole person—academically, socially, and spiritually.

With 4,500 students (2,500 undergraduates), Olivet offers an ideal student population for a private institution, maintaining diversity without compromising the commitment to personalized attention. Among the student body, more than forty denominations, most U.S. states, and more than twenty countries are represented.

ONU offers a championship-caliber Tiger athletics program with twenty intercollegiate men's and women's sports in all, and more than half of the student body participates in a robust intramural sports program. Music and drama groups involve hundreds of students, and many clubs invite students to pursue a wide variety of interests. Olivet students also commit to serving in dozens of ministry groups and volunteer efforts, small-group Bible studies, and weekly student-led worship services.

The University recently completed several campus improvements. Construction of the Betty and Kenneth Hawkins Centennial Chapel added a 3,046-seat venue for worship, concerts, and events. Renovation of the lower level of Ludwig Center added a glass-enclosed gaming room featuring plasma TV screens, a convenience store, and new student leadership offices. The Department of Communication moved to a new, technologically advanced facility, which also houses some of the University's art programs, representing a partnership between the Departments of Communication and Art.

Construction of the new Student Life and Recreation Center is currently underway with the opening slated for December 2012. Once completed, the Center will include an eight-lane running track, two pools, a four-story rock climbing wall, four basketball courts, additional workout facilities, a game area, a spacious central lounge where students can gather for recreation or study, and several classrooms.

The University is home to the Chicago Bears' summer training camp. The camp draws thousands of fans to campus each year, as well as dozens of national sportscasters and media representatives from Chicago, the nation's second-largest media market.

Olivet is also home of the Shine.FM network, one of the top-rated contemporary Christian radio networks in the country. Shine.FM is a network of five stations impacting Chicagoland, Indianapolis, and Northwest Indiana, as well as the thousands of additional listeners who access Shine.FM online or through mobile apps. Olivet's broadcasting students work alongside seasoned professionals in operating the station. Students also benefit from the outstanding Christian recording artists Shine.FM brings to campus for concerts and appearances each year, such as Switchfoot, NeedtoBreathe, TobyMac, and Newsboys.

In addition to traditional undergraduate programs, Olivet offers eight degree completion and continuing studies programs, more than twenty master's degree programs, and a Doctor of Education in ethical leadership through the School of Graduate and Continuing Studies (SGCS). Striving to meet the needs of the ever-expanding number of adults returning to school, the SGCS helps working adults complete their degree requirements without interrupting their employment. Courses and programs also provide resources to help enhance their personal and professional lives in a constantly changing world.

The SGCS offers courses on the main campus in Bourbonnais and throughout the Chicago area. Numerous students gather with other working adults for classes in churches, schools, hospitals, and other locations convenient to their homes or workplaces.

Location

The main University campus is located just 50 miles south of Chicago's Loop in the historic village of Bourbonnais, Ill. The area includes malls, restaurants, entertainment, and outdoor recreation centered on the Kankakee River State Park system. Olivet students enjoy many activities nearby and often make the quick trip north for the limitless offerings of Chicago and its surroundings.

Students find numerous opportunities for employment and internships in the area and among the vast professional resources of Chicago. They also find themselves working side-by-side with faculty and staff members in local and regional ministry projects. Olivet students continue to make valuable contributions, both professionally and ministerially, to area businesses, churches, and parachurch and nonprofit organizations.

Majors and Degrees

Olivet confers Bachelor of Arts (B.A.) and/or Bachelor of Science (B.S.) degrees in more than 100 fields of study (majors, minors, and concentrations), including: accounting; actuarial science; art; art (education); athletic training; biblical languages; biblical studies; biochemistry; biology; broadcast journalism; business administration; business information systems; chemistry; child development; Christian education; children's ministry; coaching; commercial graphics/marketing; communication studies; computer science; corporate communication; criminal justice; dietetics; digital media: graphics; digital media: photography; drawing and illustration; early childhood education; earth and space science; economics and finance; elementary education; engineering (electrical, mechanical, computer, geological); English; English as a second language; English education; environmental science; exercise science; family and consumer sciences; family and consumer sciences education; family studies; fashion merchandising; film studies; finance; forensic chemistry; French; general studies; geography; geological sciences; geology; Greek; health education; Hebrew; history; housing and environmental design; hospitality; information systems; information technology; intercultural studies; international business; international marketing; literature; management; marketing; mass communication; mathematics; mathematics education; media production; military affairs; military science; missions/intercultural studies; multimedia studies; music; music composition; music education; music performance; musical theater; not-for-profit management; nursing; painting; pastoral ministry; philosophy; philosophy and religion; physical education/health; physical science; political science; pre-dental; pre-law; pre-medicine; pre-optometry; pre-pharmacy; pre–physician's assistant studies; pre–physical therapy; pre-seminary; pre–veterinary science; print/online journalism; psychology; public policy; public relations; radio broadcasting; recreation and leisure studies; religion; religious studies; science education; secondary education; social science; social science education; social work; sociology; Spanish; Spanish education; sport management; television/video production; theater; writing; youth ministry; and zoology.

Academic Programs

Olivet seeks to offer an "education with a Christian purpose." This commitment to Christ mandates nothing less than the highest-quality academic programs. Olivet's liberal arts curriculum requires that students complete 45 to 58 hours of general-education courses. With the addition of major and minor programs of study, students must complete a minimum of 128 credit hours to obtain a bachelor's degree. Credit may be earned through AP and CLEP tests. Students may also participate in ROTC.

Olivet operates on a two-semester schedule, from August to May. Two summer sessions are also available.

Off-Campus Programs

Olivet students are encouraged to participate in the various off-campus study programs offered each semester. Sponsored programs include: Nazarene International Language Institute; Focus Leadership Institute (Focus on the Family); and Council for Christian Colleges and Universities programs, such as American Studies Program in Washington, D.C., Australian Studies Center, China Studies Program, Contemporary Music Center in Martha's Vineyard, Los Angeles Film Studies Center, Middle East Studies Program, Russian Studies Program, Scholar's Semester in Oxford, Uganda Studies Program, and the Washington Journalism Center.

Other recognized programs include: AuSable Institute, International Business Institute, Romanian Studies Program, and Tokyo Christian University. Costs are usually comparable to a semester at Olivet, and credit is given for these programs. In addition, some sources of financial aid are applicable.

Many Olivet students participate in numerous educational and missions-oriented short-term trips that are available during the Christmas, spring, and summer breaks.

Academic Facilities

Olivet's 250-acre campus offers outstanding academic facilities. These include high-quality performance halls and athletic venues; natural science, engineering, and nursing laboratories with industry standard facilities and equipment; SMART classrooms; and an observatory. Each department uses the most current software in its field. More than a dozen campus computer labs are available for student use, and the campuswide wireless network gives students access to e-mail, the Internet, and classroom applications 24 hours a day.

Strickler Planetarium, one of the few all-digital planetaria located on a college campus, was completely renovated in 2008 with the same technology used in Chicago's Adler Planetarium.

Benner Library and Resource Center provides unlimited access to any material a student needs, either on site or through the interlibrary loan system. The library recently passed the 1 million mark in annual electronic resource searches. Links to electronic resources—such as eBooks and Web sites—in the library's online catalog are at 82,000. Full text downloads from Olivet's new Digital Commons, a virtual collection of scholarship by Olivet faculty and students, topped over 16,000 in just over a year. In 2010–11, library staff processed 36,500 circulation transactions, and gate count (human beings entering the library on campus) was 304,064.

Costs

Tuition, based on 12 to 18 credit hours, is $27,250 for 2012–13. Room and board, based on double occupancy and a meal plan, are estimated to cost $7900 for the year. Additional fees will be $840 per year.

Financial Aid

Approximately 99 percent of traditional undergraduates receive a total of $35.4 million in federal and state grants and institutional scholarships annually.

Olivet believes funding a student's education is a partnership between each family, Olivet, and the state and federal governments. Olivet's cost continues to be competitive for private colleges nationwide. The friendly staff is committed to making an Olivet education affordable for every young person.

The University participates in all federal and state financial aid programs. The priority deadline for filing the Free Application for Federal Student Aid (FAFSA) is March 1. To apply for aid, students must fill out the FAFSA as well as Olivet's application for financial aid. The student must be an accepted applicant before a financial aid package can be created.

Olivet offers a monthly installment plan in addition to the traditional three-payment plan.

Faculty

Teaching is a ministry for Olivet's more than 120 full-time faculty members. These dedicated Christians are the key to excellence in education, both inside and outside the classroom. Olivet's 17:1 student-faculty ratio gives them an opportunity to teach, mentor, and encourage students on a personal level. They are deeply committed and involved in campus life, whether sponsoring social organizations and clubs, participating in talent shows, tutoring students in their offices, or talking over lunch with students in the dining room.

Student Government

The Associated Student Council is the student government organization on campus. The executive council consists of a president, vice president of finance, vice president of spiritual life, vice president of social affairs, vice president of publicity, vice president of women's residential life, vice president of men's residential life, vice president of office management, the *GlimmerGlass* (student newspaper) editor, and the *Aurora* (yearbook) editor. They work alongside the University's administrative team to ensure the health and promotion of campus activities and organizations.

Admission Requirements

Admission to Olivet is moderately difficult. Students are considered for admission on the basis of their high school GPA and ACT or SAT scores. An ACT score is required for placement in courses. For international students, TOEFL results are an additional factor in the admission decision. Students with low test scores and GPAs may be admitted on a provisional basis. A campus visit and interview are strongly recommended for all prospective students.

Application and Information

Admission is on a rolling basis until the application deadline of May 1. An early decision is required for some scholarships. Students may apply online through Olivet's website or in print by mail. The application process includes the written (or electronic) application, high school transcripts, ACT or SAT scores, and a health form. An enrollment deposit is collected to prioritize both student housing and class registration.

For more information or to arrange a campus visit, contact:

Office of Admissions
Olivet Nazarene University
One University Avenue
Bourbonnais, Illinois 60914
Phone: 800-648-1463 (toll-free)
E-mail: admissions@olivet.edu
Web site: http://www.olivet.edu
  http://www.youtube.com/olivetnazareneu
  http://on.fb.me/OlivetNazareneUniversityClassof2016
    (Facebook)
  http://twitter.com/OlivetNazareneU
  http://www.flickr.com/photos/olivet/collections

Olivet's 250-acre, park-like campus is just 50 minutes south of Chicago's Loop, with additional locations in Rolling Meadows, Illinois; the Greater Chicago area; and Hong Kong.

PACE UNIVERSITY
NEW YORK CITY AND WESTCHESTER, NEW YORK

The University

Founded in 1906, Pace University is a leading private metropolitan university that offers an exceptional liberal arts education combined with superior career preparation, two strategic undergraduate New York locations, and robust scholarships and financial aid. The diverse student population of 7,900 undergraduates (5,000 in New York City and 3,100 in Westchester) is enrolled in more than 3,000 courses across 100-plus majors and combined degree programs. These are offered through five undergraduate schools and colleges: the Lubin School of Business, the Dyson College of Arts and Sciences, the Seidenberg School of Computer Science and Information Systems, the School of Education, and the College of Health Professions. Pace University offers career preparation through the largest internship programs in New York. Each year, over 1,200 students intern at more than 500 partner companies throughout metropolitan New York, Westchester County, and southern Connecticut.

Many student-led clubs and organizations are active on the campus, including the Pace Advertising Club, African Students Association, the Pace Press, the Student Government Association, and the Collegiate Italian American Organization. Pace also offers many campus activities, including student government associations, fraternities, sororities, two campus newspapers, two literary magazines, two yearbooks, and two campus broadcasting systems. Athletic facilities are available for students, and intercollegiate sports include baseball, basketball, cross-country, cheerleading, dance, equestrian, football, golf, lacrosse, women's soccer, women's softball, swimming and diving, tennis, and track and field.

The student body is diverse, representing forty-eight states, five U.S. territories, and more than 100 countries.

Location

Pace University is a multicampus institution with campuses in both New York City and Westchester, New York. Both locations are within reach of cultural, business, and social resources and opportunities. The New York City campus is located in the heart of the Financial District in lower Manhattan, and within a short walking distance of Wall Street and the South Street Seaport. Lincoln Center, Broadway theaters, museums, and many world-famous attractions are minutes away by public transportation. Located 35 miles north of New York City, the Westchester campus offers a traditional college experience: state-of-the-art science and video production labs, competitive athletics, fraternities and sororities, and access to internship opportunities at many Fortune 500 companies. Both campuses are accessible by car and public transportation.

Students can take courses at either campus, and housing is available in both New York City and Westchester. Residence halls are equipped with complimentary cable TV, telephone, and high-speed Internet access.

Majors and Degrees

The following programs are offered at both the New York City and Westchester campuses. The Bachelor of Business Administration (B.B.A.) is offered with majors in accounting–general, accounting–public, finance, information systems, international management, management (with concentrations in arts and entertainment, business, entrepreneurship, and human resources), and marketing (with concentrations in advertising and integrated marketing communications, e-business and interactive media, and global marketing management). In addition, a five-year combined B.B.A./M.B.A in public accounting is available for qualified students. The Bachelor of Arts (B.A.) degree is granted in American studies, applied psychology and human relations, economics, environmental studies, film and screen studies, history, liberal studies, mathematics, modern languages and cultures, philosophy and religious studies, political science, and psychology. The Bachelor of Science (B.S.) degree is offered in biochemistry, biology, biology–pre-professional (occupational therapy, optometry, physical therapy, and podiatry), business economics, chemistry, computer science, criminal justice, environmental science, information systems, information technology, mathematics, professional computer studies, professional studies, and professional technology studies.

Certain programs are available only on one campus. The B.S. program in forensic science; the B.B.A. programs in hospitality and tourism management, and quantitative business analysis/mathematics minor; the B.F.A. programs in acting, fine arts, and musical theater; and the B.A. programs in art history; communication science and disorders; communication studies; English language and literature; language, culture, and world trade; Latin American studies; sociology-anthropology; Spanish; teaching students with speech and language disabilities; theater arts (commercial dance); and women's and gender studies are offered only at the New York City campus. The B.A. programs in biological psychology, communication arts and journalism, communications, English, English and communications, education, and personality and social psychology, and the B.S. programs in art, education, and nursing are available at the Westchester campus only.

Pace University offers a five-year engineering programs in cooperation with Manhattan College and Rensselaer Polytechnic Institute. Students attend Pace for three years and either Manhattan College or Rensselaer for two years. Upon successful completion, students receive a B.S. degree in chemistry from Pace and either a Bachelor of Chemical Engineering (B.C.E.) in chemical engineering from Manhattan or a B.S. degree in engineering from Rensselaer.

Academic Programs

At Pace University, an innovative core curriculum allows students to develop critical thinking and communication skills by studying subject areas that are integrated around a theme. Students can choose from civic engagement and

public values, critical writing, world traditions and cultures, and public speaking. Students also participate in community-based learning where they are given opportunities to practice their skills in real-life settings. Selective academic programs in the University are preparatory for professional training in dentistry, law, medicine, and veterinary science.

The Pforzheimer Honors College is a highly esteemed opportunity at Pace—a community of talented undergraduate scholars studying under the distinguished faculty of the University's five undergraduate schools and colleges. It is a place to excel and realize potential.

Pace University's internship program is nationally recognized and offers qualified students the opportunity to gain experience in their field of study while earning a four-year degree. Students can choose full-time, part-time, or summer positions working in an area directly related to their major course of study. Pace is one of the top ten schools in the nation for internship placement and number one in New York, according to *U.S. News & World Report*.

Academic Facilities

The Pace University Library is a comprehensive teaching library and student learning center, a virtual library that combines strong core collections with ubiquitous access to global Internet resources to support broad and diversified curricula. Reciprocal borrowing and access accords, traditional interlibrary loan services, and commercial document delivery options supplement the aggregate library. Pace offers Instructional Services librarians, a state-of-the-art electronic classroom, digital reference services, and multimedia applications. Pace's computer resource centers are linked to high-speed data networks and feature sophisticated hardware and software to facilitate active learning. Pace supports high-speed Internet and Internet2 access on every campus— residence facilities are wired, and most public areas are enabled for wireless connectivity. Full-motion videoconference facilities enable remote delivery of instruction between campus sites for synchronous learning applications.

Costs

For the 2011–12 academic year, undergraduate tuition was $35,320 per year for full-time study. The cost for an on-campus double-occupancy room and board was $12,590–$14,800, with different housing options available.

Financial Aid

Pace University strives to provide opportunities to students of diverse backgrounds and varied circumstances and is committed to offering financial aid to students to the fullest extent of its resources. University-sponsored scholarships are awarded to students on the basis of academic merit, service to the community, and financial need. The goal is to offer every student as much financial assistance as possible, based upon availability and need. Last year, Pace students received more than $277 million in aid. Pace's comprehensive student financial aid assistance program includes scholarships, grants, on-campus employment, student loans (federal and alternative plans), and tuition payment plans. Pace participates in all federal financial aid programs and the New York State Tuition Assistance Program (TAP) and honors awards from other states' incentive grant programs.

Students should submit the Free Application for Federal Student Aid (FAFSA) by February 15 for priority consideration for the fall semester. Further information about any financial aid programs can be obtained by contacting the Office of Financial Aid at any campus location.

Faculty

First and foremost, Pace University professors are dedicated teachers. All Pace classes are taught by professors. Students will never take a course taught by a teaching assistant. Faculty members also bring real-world experience and scholarship into the classroom through their work with outside companies and organizations and by leading cutting-edge research projects. Faculty members come from the best graduate and doctoral programs in the country. Professors—75 percent of whom hold Ph.D.'s—have earned degrees from the University of Pennsylvania, Harvard, Brown, Columbia, and Yale. Pace professors work closely with students to not only broaden their academic horizons, but to show how their work in the classroom is applicable to their future careers.

Admission Requirements

A minimum of 16 units from an accredited secondary school, or equivalent, are required. Academic subjects in high school should be distributed as follows: 4 units of English, 3–4 units of college-preparatory mathematics, 2 units of foreign language, 4 units of history/social science, 2 units of laboratory science, and 4–5 units of academic electives. It is recommended that students applying to the Lubin School of Business complete 4 units of preparatory mathematics. Applicants to the Lienhard School of Nursing should complete 3–4 units of science (2 of which should be laboratory science) and 3–4 units of college-preparatory mathematics. All applicants are required to take either the SAT or ACT examination and have results forwarded to the University. International students are required to take the TOEFL.

Application and Information

The freshman application deadline is February 15. Transfer applications are reviewed on a rolling basis. Requests for application forms and information for both the New York City and Westchester campuses should be addressed to:

Enrollment Information Center
Pace University
One Pace Plaza
New York, New York 10038
Phone: 800-874-7223 (toll-free)
E-mail: infoctr@pace.edu
Web site: http://www.pace.edu

PEPPERDINE UNIVERSITY
Seaver College
MALIBU, CALIFORNIA

The University and The College

Pepperdine University is a private, faith-based university committed to the highest standards of academic excellence and Christian values, where students are strengthened for lives of purpose, service, and leadership.

Seaver College is the undergraduate liberal arts college of the University and is accredited by the Accrediting Commission for Senior Colleges and Universities of the Western Association of Schools and Colleges. Approximately 53 percent of Seaver's 3,246 students come from California, 39 percent from the other 49 states, and 8 percent from other countries. The 2011–12 freshman class had a median high school GPA of 3.65. On-campus housing is available to all students. However, first-year and second-year students are required to live on campus and receive priority housing. Students who live on campus may live in one of the 22 suite-style residence halls, Lovernich Residential Complex, Rockwell Tower Residence Hall, or the University apartments.

A wide range of student organizations and activities are available, including social, honor, service, spiritual, professional, divisional, and special interest clubs. Pepperdine also provides students with opportunities to be involved in the campus radio station, weekly student newspaper, and television broadcast.

Pepperdine participates in intercollegiate sports, including baseball, men's and women's basketball, men's and women's cross-country, men's and women's golf, men's and women's tennis, men's and women's track, men's and women's volleyball, men's water polo, and men's swimming and diving. The University is a member of the West Coast Conference, the National Collegiate Athletic Association, and the Southern California Women's Intercollegiate Athletic Conference. Both men's and women's teams compete in Division I and have been very successful in regional and national competitions. Sports facilities include a 3,500-seat gymnasium, an Olympic-size swimming pool, a tennis pavilion and sixteen additional tennis courts, an intramural field, a baseball diamond, and a 2,000-seat baseball stadium.

The Master of Arts degree is offered at Seaver College in American studies, communication, media production, and religion. The Master of Science degree is offered in the fields of communication and ministry. The Master of Divinity degree is also offered, as well as the Master of Fine Arts in writing for film and television.

The School of Law awards the J.D., Master of Dispute Resolution, and Master of Laws degrees, and the School of Public Policy offers the Master of Public Policy; both schools are located on the Malibu campus. The Graduate School of Education and Psychology and the George L. Graziadio School of Business and Management offer graduate degrees at four locations in the Los Angeles area.

Location

Nestled in the Santa Monica Mountains overlooking the Pacific Ocean but less than an hour from Los Angeles, Seaver's Malibu campus offers both the serenity of a tranquil setting and the advantages of proximity to a major metropolitan area. Malibu has a movie theater, excellent restaurants, and two small shopping centers complete with banking facilities and a variety of shops and services. The winding seashore, the rugged beauty of Malibu Canyon, and the clean air provide an environment conducive to study, while the moderate climate permits year-round outdoor recreation. In addition to making use of the physical education facilities on campus, students can enjoy swimming, surfing, horseback riding, fishing, hiking, boating, and other activities in the vicinity. As an international center for trade, recreation, culture, industry, and education, Los Angeles provides students with a wide range of opportunities.

Majors and Degrees

Seaver College awards the Bachelor of Arts in advertising, art, art history, biology, chemistry, communication, creative writing, economics, English, film studies, French, German, Hispanic studies, history, integrated marketing communication, international studies, Italian, journalism, liberal arts, math education, media production, music, natural science, philosophy, political science, psychology, public relations, religion, sociology, Spanish, sports medicine, theater and music, theater and television, and theater arts.

The Bachelor of Science is awarded in accounting, biology, business administration, chemistry, computer science/mathematics, international business, mathematics, nutritional science, physics, and sports medicine. A teacher education program offers credentials in single or multiple subjects.

Academic Programs

The academic programs at Seaver College provide students with a liberal arts education in a Christian atmosphere and relate it to the dynamic qualities of life in the twenty-first century. Students must complete 128 units for the B.A. or B.S. degree, including 64 units in general education requirements and 40 or more in upper-division studies. Major requirements may be fulfilled through three basic arrangements. Students who specialize in a discipline must complete at least 24 units of upper-division work in their chosen discipline. Students may choose an interdisciplinary major, entailing at least 40 units of upper-division work, with courses ranging broadly across disciplinary lines within a division and on occasion crossing divisional lines, in one of the following fields of study: Communication, English, humanities, international studies, liberal arts, or religion. Alternatively, students may initiate a contract major by presenting an application for specific upper-division courses to the Dean of Seaver College.

Seaver College functions on a semester plan; the regular academic year consists of two semesters from late August to April. In addition to the regular academic year, summer sessions run from late April to early August.

At Seaver, instruction and study are adapted both to students' abilities and to the nature of the course content, instead of utilizing only the traditional lecture method. Programs involve several types of learning experiences: Seminars, integrated lectures, individual study, fieldwork, and laboratories. The Dean's List of undergraduate students in the top 10 percent of the class with a grade point index not lower than 3.5 is published each semester. Other honors include cum laude for students graduating with a scholastic level of at least 3.5, magna cum laude for 3.7, and summa cum laude for 3.9.

Off-Campus Programs

Seaver offers students the opportunity to study abroad in Buenos Aires, Argentina; Florence, Italy; Heidelberg, Germany; Lausanne, Switzerland; London, England; and Shanghai, China. The academic programs emphasize European, Latin American, or Asian history and culture. Seaver also offers summer special interest programs in Fiji, Scotland, and East Africa. Classes are taught by Seaver faculty members. Serious study and the daily experiences of living in another country give students a special depth of understanding of other cultures and a broader world perspective.

The Buenos Aires program accommodates approximately 60 students who live in the homes of carefully selected host families. The Florence program houses approximately 55 students who live in a Florentine villa and residential complex with classrooms, a library, a computer facility, and recreational facilities. The Heidelberg program has space for approximately 50 students at the Moore Haus, located near the city's famous castle. Classes are held in modern facilities in downtown Heidelberg. The Lausanne program accommodates about 70 students. The Pepperdine facility is located in La Croisée near the center of Lausanne, which has a picturesque view of Lake Geneva and the French Alps. The London program has space for approximately 40 students in the Knightsbridge area.

In addition to living quarters, the facility includes classrooms, a library, a computer room, offices, and a student center. The Shanghai program accommodates approximately 40 students who live in the Pepperdine-owned jia, meaning "house," which is located in the French Concession area near the American Consulate. The majority of the international program facilities are University-owned.

Academic Facilities

The Malibu campus is home to academic complexes containing seminar and lecture rooms, art studios, communication facilities, science and computer laboratories, mini-theaters, a recital hall, and administrative offices. The Payson Library is the global gateway to knowledge and provides students access to thousands of online journals, articles, and periodicals through various databases. It houses a collection of approximately 461,000 volumes. Payson Library serves as a sanctuary for study, learning, and research by encouraging discovery, contemplation, social discourse, and creative expression. The 300-seat George Elkins Auditorium is used for public presentations and lectures. The Center for the Arts facility includes the renowned Frederick R. Weisman Museum of Art and the Smothers Theatre, which seats 450 people and is used for dance, music, and theater performances. The Center for Communication and Business building houses a state-of-the-art radio and television production center where students have the opportunity to work on Pepperdine's cable television and radio stations.

Costs

Costs for the 2011–12 academic year were $40,500 for tuition, $11,844 for room and board, and $252 for additional fees.

Financial Aid

Approximately 80 percent of Seaver's students receive some form of financial assistance through scholarships, loans, grants, work-study programs, or jobs within the University. To be eligible for financial assistance from institutional resources, an undergraduate student must be enrolled in at least 12 units. An applicant must be admitted to the University before being awarded assistance, but the financial assistance application may be submitted with an admission application. To ensure full consideration, the Pepperdine financial assistance application should be submitted by February 15 for the fall semester and October 15 for the spring semester. Students are also responsible for applying for the California State Scholarship (California residents only) and Federal Pell Grant by submitting the Free Application for Federal Student Aid (FAFSA) in addition to Pepperdine's one-page financial assistance form.

Faculty

Seaver College's faculty includes men and women of high academic distinction whose primary focus is instruction with a secondary focus on research. 56 percent of faculty members are full-time, and 91 percent of full-time faculty members hold a doctorate or terminal degree in their field. The student-faculty ratio of 13:1, with an average classroom size of 20 students, allows ample individual assistance through classroom instruction and counseling. Upon enrollment, each student is assigned an academic adviser from among the faculty members. A qualified counseling staff is also available to assist with personal, professional, and academic needs.

Student Government

The Student Government Association (SGA) is composed of student leaders dedicated to providing Pepperdine's students with quality representation through innovative advocacy programs. SGA serves as the voice of the students to the Seaver administration and works in coordination with the Campus Life Office in establishing activities and maintaining school policies. SGA coordinates over 150 on-campus events each year including movies, sightseeing trips, guest performances, dances, speakers, and more. Pepperdine has eight nationally recognized sororities and five fraternities and there are over sixty different student organizations on campus that focus on a range interests, including academic, language, art, music, dance, drama, sports, and politics.

Admission Requirements

Applicants are admitted on the basis of their academic record, SAT or ACT scores, and personal information and references. Students who have completed at least 30 transferable semester units with a minimum grade point average of 3.0 are considered for admission as transfer students. Students who apply with fewer than 30 units are classified as first-year students with transfer units. To ensure full consideration for the fall semester, students should apply by the January 5 deadline. October 15 is the regular deadline for the spring semester. Decision letter dates are announced in the current application form.

Seaver College seeks to enroll a diverse student body. As such, Pepperdine University does not unlawfully discriminate on the basis of any status or condition protected by applicable federal or state law in the administration of its educational policies, admission, financial assistance, employment, educational programs, or activities.

Application and Information

To request information, students should contact:

Laura Kalinkewicz, Director of Admission
Seaver College
Pepperdine University
Malibu, California 90263-4392
Phone: 310-506-4392
Fax: 310-506-4861
Web site: http://seaver.pepperdine.edu
Facebook: http://on.fb.me/Seaver_Admission
Twitter: http://twitter.com/#!/SeaverAdmission
YouTube: http://bit.ly/YouTube_Pepperdine
Flicker: http://www.flickr.com/photos/seaveradmission

The 830-acre Malibu campus of Pepperdine University, Seaver College, overlooks the Pacific Ocean, 35 miles west of Los Angeles, California.

PHILADELPHIA UNIVERSITY
PHILADELPHIA, PENNSYLVANIA

The University

Founded in 1884, Philadelphia University is a private institution of higher learning for students with high motivation and academic ability. Philadelphia University is professionally oriented and offers undergraduate and graduate degree programs in the areas of architecture, business, design, engineering, fashion, general sciences, health sciences, and textile materials technology. The University's enrollment of approximately 2,800 undergraduates represents a diverse and talented group of students from thirty-eight states and forty-two countries. With an average class size of 18 and a 14:1 student-faculty ratio, students receive the personal attention so important to social and professional growth.

Through a unique blend of liberal and specialized education with an interdisciplinary focus, the University prepares students for today's complex, global workplace. Recognized as a premier professional university, Philadelphia University has established a phenomenal record of career success for its graduates. The University is committed to a technologically advanced approach to career planning, and students have full access to the Career Services Center's CareerLink, an Internet-based resume and job-listing management system that electronically stores resumes, job listings, and employer information. Students have access to job-search resources, including ReferenceUSA, a database of 1.5 million companies nationwide. Prospective employers gain access to students through the various career fairs and industry spotlights hosted by the center annually. The University's innovative academic programs that meet emerging needs in the marketplace, extensive networking with prospective employers (connecting students with 150 employers on campus and 1,200 employers electronically in recent years), and extensive career and professional development opportunities for students all add up to a ten-year average of nearly 90 percent placement rate within just a few months of graduation.

Philadelphia University believes the college experience of every student should extend well beyond the classroom. The Student Life Programs at Philadelphia University build bridges between the classroom and out-of-class experiences to create a dynamic learning community for students. Fifteen varsity teams compose the intercollegiate athletics program. Men participate in baseball, basketball, cross-country/track, golf, rowing, soccer, and tennis. Women's teams include basketball, cross-country/track, lacrosse, rowing, soccer, softball, tennis, and volleyball. An extensive intramural sports program is available to all students. Students are actively engaged in campus life, whether through one of the nationally ranked athletic teams, events sponsored by Student Government, a wide array of community service opportunities, an extensive intramural program, or participation in the more than thirty student clubs and organizations.

The University provides on-campus housing for approximately 1,600 undergraduate students in traditional and apartment-style residence halls. Professional and student staff members live within each residential area to provide resources and services that enhance the student's residential and campus experience, as well as supports resident students in pursuing their academic endeavors.

The University holds accreditation from the Middle States Association of Colleges and Schools, the National Architectural Accrediting Board (NAAB), Council for Interior Design Accreditation (CIDA), the American Chemical Society (ACS), Accreditation Review Commission on Education for the Physician Assistant (ARC-PA), National Association of Schools of Art and Design (NASAD), the Landscape Architecture

Accreditation Board (LAAB), and the Engineering Accreditation Commission of the Accreditation Board for Engineering and Technology (ABET), Inc., as well as certification from the International College Reading and Learning Center Association.

Location

The University's sprawling, 100-acre campus is adjacent to Fairmount Park, the largest urban park system in the country. Students enjoy the best of both worlds—a beautiful campus with tree-lined walkways, spacious lawns, and classical architecture, and easy access to Philadelphia (just minutes away) for entertainment, cultural events, great night spots, and more than 300 years of American history.

Philadelphia also serves as a "living lab" where students frequently interact with area professionals for class projects, internships, and off-campus jobs.

Majors and Degrees

Philadelphia University offers the Bachelor of Science in more than thirty areas, including accounting, animation, architectural studies, architecture, biochemistry, biology, biopsychology, business (with concentrations in accounting, finance, international business, management, and marketing), chemistry, construction management, engineering (with minor tracks in architectural, composites, industrial, and textile), environmental and conservation biology, environmental design and technology (with concentrations in architectural design and technology, historic preservation, and photography and new media), environmental sustainability, fashion design, fashion merchandising and management (with concentrations in fashion merchandising and fashion industry management), graphic design communication, health sciences, health sciences/occupational therapy (B.S./M.S.), industrial design, interactive design and media, interior design, landscape architecture, law and society, mechanical engineering, physician assistant studies, premedical studies, professional communication, psychology, psychology/occupational therapy (B.S./M.S.), textile design, and textile materials technology.

The University also offers several five-year B.S./M.B.A. joint-degree programs and a five-year B.S./M.S. physician assistant studies program. The five-year architecture program leads to a Bachelor of Architecture (B.Arch.). For students wishing to keep their choices open, an undeclared option offers an introduction to college courses in preparation for entering a specific major in the sophomore year.

Academic Programs

Philadelphia University's commitment to quality professional education is realized in curricula that combine a solid foundation in liberal studies with career preparation. These curricula are designed to enhance students' ability and desire to learn; to ensure them an understanding of the ideas, traditions, and values of their own and other cultures; and to prepare them to apply the concepts and techniques of both general and specialized learning to their lives as citizens with productive careers. Degree requirements include successful completion of 121 to 138 credits (depending upon the major chosen), successful completion of both major and general education programs, and the satisfactory completion of at least 60 credits in residence at the University. All students have the option to participate in the University's internship program, through which they earn both academic credit and a salary.

As a rule, the University grants credit to students who obtain satisfactory grades in subject examinations developed by the Advanced Placement Program, the College-Level Examination

Program, and the Proficiency Examination Program. Students may, by invitation, participate in the honors program, which offers a number of courses expressly for honors students.

The University's academic calendar consists of two semesters and two summer sessions.

Off-Campus Programs

Academic Internships are facilitated through the Career Services Center. The University has affiliations with a wide variety of organizations, such as BCBG Max Azria, Isdaner & Company, Stantec Architecture, Target, the Philadelphia district attorney's office, PVH Corp, Urban Outfitters, and Nordstrom.

Study abroad at Philadelphia University prepares students for successful participation and competition in an increasingly interdependent world and to perform with distinction in the international and multicultural contexts that are increasingly shaping professional life. Students at Philadelphia University may study abroad and receive credit for courses that apply directly to their challenging, professions-oriented curricula. Opportunities are available for fall, spring, and summer semesters. The University has its own programs in Rome and Milan, Italy, and affiliations with more than twenty-five programs all over the world and in most majors.

Academic Facilities

In January 2013, the University is scheduled to open its newest building, home of the College of Design, Engineering and Commerce. This 38,500-square-foot building, built to LEED standards, boasts a large two-story forum space for design exhibits, presentations, large lectures, and social events. The building will reinforce the college's integrated curriculum that pushes students to think beyond the boundaries of existing disciplines and focus on market-driven innovation through teamwork, collaboration, and industry connections.

The Tuttleman Center at Philadelphia University, a 31,500-square-foot academic building, provides students and faculty members with access to the most sophisticated technologies for teaching and learning.

Many major labs and studios enable students to gain practical experience in engineering, design, textiles, apparel manufacturing, foreign languages, the sciences, computer technologies, and physician assistant studies. The University's Paul J. Gutman Library is a state-of-the-art information center. Through the contemporary information system, students can search the library's collections, as well as major indexes and full-text journals, from on or off campus. An international computer network links Philadelphia University to the resources of more than 14,000 libraries worldwide. With more than 400 study spaces and nine group study rooms, the library provides an ideal environment for reading and research. The Architecture and Design Center houses studio space, a photo lab, and computer-aided design labs.

General-purpose and departmental computing labs are updated using a multiyear migration strategy as changes in technology dictate. The labs are currently equipped with Pentium PCs and Macintoshes running at speeds from 1.0 to 1.8 MHz. The University operates a switched, 100-megabit network with building-to-building gigabit (1000-megabit) connections in high-traffic areas. The network provides students with access to the Internet, e-mail service, network storage (300 MB per student), digital library resources, online databases, and the Blackboard course management system.

Costs

The University's 2012–13 cost for regular tuition is $31,874. Room is $5032 and board is $5146.

Financial Aid

Philadelphia University's total financial aid program has amounted to more than $78 million annually. Approximately $32 million came from the University itself and the remainder from federal, state, and private sources. While 96 percent of the University's full-time day students receive direct institutional scholarship assistance, 97 percent receive some form of aid each year (e.g., other scholarships, loans, and job opportunities). Candidates for aid should complete the Free Application for Federal Student Aid by April 15. The University offers a wide range of institutional scholarships and grants to incoming students each year. Award amounts vary according to the quality of each student's academic record. The University's scholarship program is available to all prospective students (freshmen and transfer students). Scholarships are awarded regardless of financial need. Students and parents are strongly encouraged to call the admissions or financial aid offices for further information.

Faculty

Primarily a teaching institution, the University encourages close connections between the faculty and students. Classes are intentionally kept small, and faculty members make a practice of being available to students outside the classroom. Often, students can partner with faculty members to pursue joint research interests and gain career experience. The University's faculty is composed of a diverse group of professionals who not only hold strong academic credentials but also frequently possess impressive work experience. They are often sought out as consultants in their fields.

Student Government

The Student Government Association (SGA) is an independent, self-governing student group. In addition to the basic responsibility of protecting students' rights, SGA recommends students to University-wide committees, addresses student grievances, and sponsors campuswide events. The Campus Activities Board is the major programming organization on campus. Its primary responsibility is to provide a wide variety of cultural, scholastic, social, and educational programs.

Admission Requirements

The University evaluates applicants on the basis of their high school record (including GPA and quality of courses taken), scores on either the SAT or the ACT, essay, recommendation, and extracurricular activities. Normally, 15 units of secondary school preparation are required for admission. Three units of mathematics (including algebra II and geometry) are required for admission. Students who wish to enter a science curriculum are strongly encouraged to take 4 units of mathematics and 4 units of science. The University actively recruits qualified transfer students, who represent approximately one fifth of the incoming class each fall. The University also has a large international student population. These students must score at least 60 on the TOEFL in order to be considered for admission.

Application and Information

The University maintains a rolling admission plan. Applications are reviewed and decisions are made soon after an application, academic credentials, and standardized test scores are received. Students are encouraged to submit applications early in the senior year; applications received after March 1 are considered on a space-available basis. All applicants are encouraged to come to the campus for an interview with a member of the professional admission staff.

For more information, contact:

Greg Potts
Director of Admissions
Philadelphia University
4201 Henry Avenue
Philadelphia, Pennsylvania 19144
Phone: 215-951-2800
        800-951-7287 (toll-free)
Fax: 215-951-2907
E-mail: admissions@PhilaU.edu
Web site: http://www.PhilaU.edu

PITZER COLLEGE
CLAREMONT, CALIFORNIA

The College

Pitzer is a nationally recognized independent, residential liberal arts college. The College's emphasis on social responsibility, student engagement, environmental sustainability, interdisciplinary studies, and intercultural understanding sets it apart from other colleges in the country. Pitzer believes that students should take an active part in formulating their individualized plans of study, bringing a spirit of inquiry and adventure to the planning process. Because there are fewer required general education courses, Pitzer students have more freedom to choose the courses they want to take.

Pitzer offers the best of both worlds: membership in a small, close-knit academic community and access to the resources of a midsize university through the College's partnership with the Claremont Colleges. The Claremont Colleges are a consortium of five distinct undergraduate colleges (Pitzer, Claremont McKenna, Harvey Mudd, Pomona, and Scripps) and two graduate institutions (Claremont Graduate University and the Keck Institute for Applied Biological Sciences). Each college has its own personality, but all share major facilities such as the library, bookstore, campus security, health services, counseling center, ethnic study centers, and chaplains' offices. The total enrollment of all of the colleges is approximately 6,500 students. Students at Pitzer may enroll in courses offered by the other colleges and consult with professors on all of the adjoining campuses.

Pitzer was founded in 1963 and today offers forty majors in the arts, humanities, sciences, and social sciences. Majors with the largest enrollments currently include art, biology, English, environmental studies, intercultural and international studies, media studies, organizational studies, political studies, psychology, and sociology.

In 2011, the first-year class of 272 students represented twenty-eight different states and eight other countries. About 58 percent of the first-year students came from outside of California. Pitzer has had a deep commitment to welcoming members of underrepresented groups since its founding. In 2011, students of color made up approximately 28 percent of the entering class.

Residential life plays a significant role in a student's educational experience. Each of Pitzer's residence halls establishes its own Hall Council to serve as a forum for addressing and meeting the needs of the community. Pitzer students have a long tradition of arranging their living communities based on common interests. All rooms are wired for Internet access, television, and phone service. Three new LEED-certified Gold residence halls opened in 2007, and in the fall of 2012, the College is scheduled to open a LEED-certified Platinum residence hall for sophomores, juniors, and seniors.

Opportunities abound at Pitzer and the other Claremont Colleges. Students can participate in a wide variety of sports, clubs, community service programs, and social activities. Currently, more than 150 student organizations allow students to get involved in a wide variety of activities. Pitzer partners with Pomona College to field NCAA Division III teams in baseball, basketball, cross-country, football, golf, soccer, softball, swimming and diving, tennis, track and field, volleyball, and water polo. Club sports for men include crew, cycling, lacrosse, rugby, ultimate Frisbee, and volleyball. Club sports for women include crew, cycling, lacrosse, rugby, and Ultimate (Frisbee).

Location

Pitzer is located in the city of Claremont (population 35,000) at the base of the San Gabriel Mountains, about 35 miles east of Los Angeles and 78 miles west of Palm Springs. Pitzer is a short drive away from rock climbing at Joshua Tree National Park, ski resorts, the beaches of southern California, and the Getty, Norton Simon, and other Los Angeles County museums.

Majors and Degrees

Pitzer offers a Bachelor of Arts degree in Africana studies, American studies, anthropology, art, art history, Asian American studies, biochemistry, biology, chemistry, Chicano/Latino studies, classics, dance, economics, English/world literature, environmental analysis, gender and feminist studies, history, human biology, international and intercultural studies, international political economy, linguistics, management engineering, mathematical economics, mathematics, media studies, modern language, literature and cultures: Spanish, molecular biology, music, neuroscience, organismal biology, organizational studies, philosophy, physics, political studies, psychology, religious studies, science and management, science, technology and society, sociology, and theater.

Minors are available in Africana studies, anthropology, art, art history, Asian American studies, biology, classics, dance, economics, English/world literature, environmental analysis, gender and feminist studies, history, linguistics, mathematics, media studies, music, philosophy, science, technology and society, sociology, Spanish, and theater.

Academic Programs

To earn their Bachelor of Arts degree, students are required to complete thirty-two courses, approximately one third of which are in their major. Students work with faculty advisers to organize a curriculum that meets the educational objectives of the College: breadth of knowledge, understanding in depth, written expression, interdisciplinary and intercultural exploration, and social responsibility and the ethical implications of knowledge and action. Specific course requirements depend on the student's academic interests. Certain concentrations require a senior thesis.

The system of cross-registration at the Claremont Colleges provides Pitzer students with the opportunity to take advantage of the wide range of courses available at each of the other colleges. Advanced students may also enroll in certain courses at Claremont Graduate University with the instructor's approval.

The College observes a semester calendar; classes begin in early September and end in mid-May. There is a study break near the middle of each semester and another break between semesters from mid-December through mid-January.

Off-Campus Programs

Approximately 74 percent of students participate in study-abroad programs. Pitzer currently approves twelve exchanges with U.S. institutions and over fifty international study options in Argentina, Australia, Botswana, Brazil, Bulgaria, Canada, Chile, China, Costa Rica, Cuba, Denmark, Ecuador, England, France, Germany,

Ghana, Hong Kong, Hungary, Iceland, Israel, Italy, Japan, Korea, Mexico, Morocco, Netherlands, Nepal, New Zealand, Singapore, South Africa, Spain, Sweden, Thailand, and Turkey.

Academic Facilities

The central services of the Claremont Colleges include the Honnold-Mudd Library, which houses more than 2 million volumes and more than 6,000 serial subscriptions. Other shared facilities include theaters, music halls, music and dance studios, the W. M. Keck Science Center (shared with Claremont McKenna and Scripps Colleges), and a wellness center that includes counseling and health services.

Specialized facilities at Pitzer include a newly renovated auditorium, a television studio, film editing suites, art galleries, social science laboratories, an arboretum, a reading library, and several computing facilities, including a 24-hour computer center.

Costs

Expenses for 2011–12 were as follows: tuition and fees, $42,550; room and board, $12,438; and books and personal expenses, $2000. Travel expenses vary. Costs are subject to change for 2012–13.

Financial Aid

Approximately 42 percent of Pitzer's students receive aid in the forms of grants, loans, and work-study. To apply for aid, students must complete the Free Application for Federal Student Aid (FAFSA) and the CSS/Financial Aid PROFILE. California residents should also apply for California state grants. Students must reapply for aid each spring.

Faculty

One hundred percent of Pitzer's faculty members hold a Ph.D. or the terminal degree in their fields. All courses are taught by faculty members, and the student-faculty ratio is 11:1. Faculty members are readily available for academic advising. In keeping with Pitzer's commitment to interdisciplinary learning, most faculty members are conversant with at least one other field of study in addition to the area of their degrees and may teach in more than one area.

Student Government

Pitzer's governmental structure is distinctive among American colleges. Instead of the traditional college governance style which restricts student participation to limited areas, Pitzer students are represented on all standing committees of the College, including those that deal with the most vital and sensitive issues of the College community. Though this model demands a serious time commitment from those who choose to participate, it offers interested students an active educational experience and the opportunity to make a genuine impact on the life of the College and its students, faculty, and staff.

Admission Requirements

Pitzer has developed a highly personalized admission process. Each applicant is considered on the basis of his or her own strengths. In general, the College seeks students who have performed well in high school, have shown a significant amount of involvement in activities outside of the classroom, are motivated to learn, and are interested in the opportunity to take an active role in planning their education in a liberal arts framework. The selection process is designed to help achieve a diverse and energetic class. Selection is based on high school transcripts, rigor of curriculum, recommendations, essays, extracurricular activities and other special talents. Applicants are encouraged to visit campus and arrange for an interview.

Application and Information

Pitzer College offers both early decision and regular decision for prospective applicants. Students interested in applying early must submit a completed application by November 15 and are notified in late December. Interviews for early decision are required by December 1. Regular decision candidates must submit their applications for admission by January 1 and are notified by April 1. Interviews are not required for regular decision candidates but are highly recommended and should be completed by December 15. All applicants must supply an official transcript of grades, two teacher evaluations, one counselor or school official recommendation, and the application fee of $60 by the necessary deadline. Pitzer accepts the Common Application for first-year students. When submitting the Common Application, students must also complete a supplement, which is available on the Common Application Web site. Pitzer is test optional in the admission process, and students should contact the College for further details.

For additional information, students should contact:
Office of Admission
Pitzer College
1050 North Mills Avenue
Claremont, California 91711-6101
Phone: 909-621-8129
        800-PITZER1 (800-748-9371, toll-free)
Fax: 909-621-8770
E-mail: admission@pitzer.edu
Web site: http://www.pitzer.edu
        https://www.facebook.com/
            PitzerOfficeOfAdmission
        http://on.fb.me/Pitzer_Coll ("I'm Applying to
            Pitzer" Facebook page)
        http://twitter.com/pitzercollege

Residence halls at Pitzer College.

PRATT INSTITUTE
BROOKLYN, NEW YORK

The Institute

Industrialist and philanthropist Charles Pratt founded Pratt Institute in 1887 to educate students for various professions on a nondegree level. As the educational preparation necessary for various professions expanded, Pratt Institute moved to offer baccalaureate degrees with its first granted in 1938 and its first graduate degree granted in 1950. Now, with twenty-seven undergraduate majors and concentrations, Pratt offers students a wide variety of programs in which to major or take elective courses.

With all of its undergraduate ranked programs in art, design, and architecture ranked among the top ten in the country, Pratt has been ranked among the top design schools in the United States by *Business Week*. Pratt has continued to add programs at all educational levels, including undergraduate programs in creative writing and critical and visual studies; undergraduate and graduate programs in art history and art and design education (teacher certification); and graduate programs in arts and cultural management, historic preservation, and design management.

In addition to the four-year programs on its Brooklyn campus, Pratt offers students several additional locations to pursue their education: a two-year program in Utica, New York, at PrattMWP; an associate degree program and four-year degree in construction management in Manhattan; and an affiliated campus in Delaware, DCAD.

Although the characteristics and educational requirements of the professions for which Pratt prepares students have changed over the course of a century, the Institute has succeeded in pursuing its abiding purpose—to blend theoretical learning with professional and humanistic development—and has kept its curricula current by hiring practicing professionals to teach. Standards are high, modeled after the professional world. Faculty members connect students with internships and eventually jobs after graduation. Industry projects and internships provide students with real-world experience.

Pratt Institute offers four-year bachelor's, two-year associate, and master's degrees. In educating more than five generations of students to be creative, technically skilled, and adaptable professionals as well as responsible citizens, Pratt has gained a national and international reputation that attracts undergraduate and graduate students from forty-eight U.S. states and seventy countries. Most students who choose Pratt are committed to the study of art, design, architecture, or creative writing and to their career objectives.

A short subway or bus ride from the museums, galleries, and design centers of both Manhattan and Brooklyn, Pratt Institute's main campus in Brooklyn, New York features twenty-five buildings of differing architectural styles spread throughout a beautifully landscaped 25-acre campus. The campus was recently ranked by *Architectural Digest* as one of the top ten campuses nationwide with the best architecture. It includes a contemporary sculpture garden (ranked among the top ten campus art collections by *Public Art Review*), an athletic center, residence halls, dining halls, outstanding studio facilities, and historic buildings. Nineteen of the buildings house studios, classrooms, laboratories, administrative offices, auditoria, sports facilities, food services, and student centers. A new, green, LEED-certified Gold building houses student administrative services including admissions, undergraduate and graduate digital arts programs, and various administrative offices, including student financial services and the registrar's offices. Six buildings are student residences, including the Stabile Hall freshman residence,

which provides studio space on each floor. There are adequate parking facilities for residents and commuters. Student services include career planning and placement, health and counseling, and student development. More than sixty student organizations are available including fraternities and sororities, honorary societies, professional societies, and clubs.

Location

Pratt Institute, the country's premier college of art, design, writing, and architecture, has its main campus in the Clinton Hill section of Brooklyn, just minutes from downtown Manhattan. Eighty-eight percent of Pratt's freshmen and over half of its undergraduates live on the tree-lined Brooklyn campus. Minutes from the Brooklyn Museum and the Brooklyn Academy of Music, Pratt is ideally located, providing students with a green oasis just minutes from the art capital of the world, Manhattan. The Manhattan campus is located in Chelsea. The Utica campus, home to two-year programs in fine art, communications design, photography, and art and design education (teacher certification), is located in upstate New York. The affiliated Delaware campus, offering a two-year degree in fine art, communications design, photography, animation, and interior design, is located in Wilmington, Delaware.

Majors and Degrees

Pratt Institute offers the Bachelor of Architecture, Bachelor of Fine Arts, Bachelor of Art, Bachelor of Industrial Design, Bachelor of Professional Studies, Bachelor of Science, Associate of Occupational Studies, and Associate of Applied Science degrees.

The Bachelor of Architecture degree program is a five-year, accredited program. For the Bachelor of Fine Arts degree, a candidate may choose to major in art and design education (teacher certification), art history, communications design (advertising art direction, graphic design, illustration), digital arts (traditional and digital animation, interactive arts), fashion design, film/video, fine arts (ceramics, drawing, jewelry, painting, printmaking, sculpture), interior design, photography, or writing. The Bachelor of Arts is offered in critical and visual studies and art history. The Bachelor of Industrial Design is offered for students interested in car, product, and furniture design. In the Bachelor of Professional Studies degree program, the major is in construction management. Students seeking the Bachelor of Science degree can major in construction management.

The two-year Associate of Occupational Studies degree is offered in digital design and interactive media, graphic design, and illustration. The Associate of Applied Science is offered in painting/drawing and graphic design/illustration. The two-year Associate of Applied Science degree is transferable to a four-year program.

Students may also earn combined bachelor's/master's degrees. Programs include the B.F.A./M.S. in art and design education as well as art history.

Academic Programs

Educating artists and creative professionals to be responsible contributors to society has been the mission of Pratt Institute since it assembled its first group of students in 1887. Within the structure of that professional education, Pratt students are encouraged to acquire the diverse knowledge that is necessary for them to succeed in their chosen fields including sustainability. In addition to the professional studies, the curriculum in each of Pratt's schools includes a broad range of liberal arts courses. Students from all schools take these courses together and have

the opportunity to examine the interrelationships of art, science, technology, and human need.

At the time of graduation, students in the associate degree programs have completed 67 credit hours of course work. In the bachelor's programs, credit-hour requirements range from 132 to 135 credits, depending on the particular program. For the Bachelor of Architecture degree, 170 credits are required.

Pratt's academic calendar consists of two semesters plus optional summer terms that allow students to choose alternative courses or various options usually not offered during the fall or spring semester. Two summer sessions are offered.

Off-Campus Programs

Pratt Institute offers credit for a wide variety of off-campus study programs. The internship program offers qualified students challenging on-the-job experience related to their major fields of interest; this extension of the classroom and laboratory into the professional world adds a practical dimension to periods of on-campus study.

International programs, available during all academic sessions, have included art and design offerings in the cities of Copenhagen and Rome and in the countries of England, France, Italy, and South Africa. Architecture programs have been held in Italy, Finland, and Japan. New programs are developed regularly in these and other countries. A semester-long program is offered in Rome each year.

Academic Facilities

Founded as the first free library in Brooklyn, the Pratt Institute Library now has more than 176,674 bound volumes, 84,604 art books, 237 print and online art and art history journals, a rare book collection, and subscriptions to journals online through JSTOR, EBSCO, and others. The library also has serial backfiles and other material, including government documents; 251,603 audiovisual materials; and 3,996 microforms and subscribes to 925 periodicals—the largest collection of any independent art school. With their ID cards, Pratt students also have access to numerous college libraries in the metropolitan area. Multi-Media Services has been developed to facilitate and improve the educational communication process by providing materials in multimedia formats to support and enrich the Institute's curricula.

Extensive studio and state-of-the-art computer lab facilities are provided for all Pratt students. In the School of Art and Design, these include studio, shop, and technical facilities for work in all media, from the traditional to the most experimental. Gallery space, both on campus and at Pratt Manhattan, is extensive, showing the work of students, alumni, faculty members, staff members, and other well-known artists, architects, and designers. The Pratt Center for Community Development functions as a laboratory for the study of planning and advocacy issues in real-world situations including sustainable planning.

Costs

Tuition for the 2012–13 academic year is $39,282. Room charges are $6726 per academic year. A meal plan is available, and costs about $3780 for the year. The fees are approximately $1810. The estimated cost of books and supplies is $3000 per academic year. Students should allow an additional $1800 for transportation and personal expenses. For an updated list of tuition and fees, prospective students should visit www.pratt.edu/costs_and_budgeting.

Financial Aid

Pratt Institute offers a large number of merit-based scholarships, need-based grants, loans, and awards based on academic achievement, talent, financial need, or all three. More than 75 percent of Pratt students receive financial assistance through one or more of these kinds of aid. Through funds from the federal and state governments, contributions from Pratt alumni, and industry scholarships, Pratt is able to maintain generous financial aid program in a time of escalating costs.

Faculty

The faculty at Pratt Institute is exceptional in that a large number of practicing professionals augment the regular full-time faculty. There are 130 full-time and 875 part-time faculty members; there are no graduate teaching assistants. In small classes and studios, students have easy access to professors whose natural environment is the design studio, the architectural office, or the industrial research department. Faculty members often connect students with internships and eventually jobs.

Student Government

The Student Government Association (SGA) maintains primary responsibility for all student interests and involvement at Pratt. The SGA structure includes the Executive Committee, Senate, Finance Committee, Buildings and Grounds Committee, Academic and Administrative Affairs Committee, and Program Board. Student representatives serve on the Board of Trustees and on its various committees. All undergraduate students are encouraged to become involved in the SGA, whose main functions are allocating and administering funds collected through the student activities fee, scheduling student activities, and representing the student viewpoint to the rest of the Pratt community.

Admission Requirements

Pratt Institute attracts and enrolls highly motivated and talented students from diverse backgrounds. Applications are welcome from all qualified students, regardless of age, sex, race, color, religion, national origin, or handicap. Admission standards at Pratt are high. One of the major components for admission consideration in art, design, or architecture is the evaluation of a student's art or writing portfolio, which must be submitted along with the other required documents.

All applicants must submit official transcripts and one letter of recommendation from a guidance counselor or teacher. Additional professional requirements are specific to each school or major. Instructions can be found at www.pratt.edu/apply. Prospective students should select their level (freshman or transfer) and international students should also read the international requirements. Most disciplines at Pratt require a portfolio.

The admission committee bases its decisions on careful reviews of all credentials submitted by applicants in relation to the requirements of the program to which students seek admission. The SAT or ACT and a strong college-preparatory background are required of all applicants for four-year programs. International students must submit TOEFL or IELTS scores or SAT scores, but not both. In certain cases, an extraordinary talent may offset a low grade or a test score.

Application and Information

Pratt has two admissions deadlines: November 1 for early action and January 5 for regular admissions. To receive full consideration, students must submit their applications by January 5 for anticipated entrance in the fall semester and by October 1 for anticipated entrance in the spring semester.

For more information about Pratt Institute, students should contact:

Office of Admissions
Pratt Institute
200 Willoughby Avenue
Brooklyn, New York 11205
Phone: 718-636-3514
      800-331-0834 (toll-free)
E-mail: admissions@pratt.edu
Web site: http://www.pratt.edu
       http://on.fb.me/pratt_admissions (Facebook)
       http://www.pratt.edu/request (Catalog request)

PROVIDENCE COLLEGE
PROVIDENCE, RHODE ISLAND

The College

Providence College (PC), a Catholic, liberal arts college, was founded by the Order of Preachers of the Province of St. Joseph, commonly known as the Dominicans, in 1917. Originally a college for men, it became coeducational in 1971. The College's full-time undergraduate enrollment is 3,850 students. Approximately 1,800 students live in nine residential halls and a suite-style residence facility, and an additional 900 upperclass students are housed in one of the five College apartment complexes. The remainder of the students live in apartments directly off campus or commute from home. At the graduate level, the College offers M.A., M.S., M.Ed., and M.B.A. degree programs.

The newly renovated Slavin Center, as the nucleus of student, social, cultural, and recreational activity, provides space for programs, informal social gatherings, and numerous facilities. It offers lounges; McPhail's Entertainment Facility; a dining facility; an ATM machine; a bookstore/gift shop; the Student Activities, Involvement, and Leadership Office (SAIL); and student club offices and administrative offices.

The Concannon Fitness Center, a 23,000-square-foot, two-level, state-of-the-art facility, emphasizes the College's commitment to health and fitness. The center offers eight types of cardiovascular machines, including eighteen treadmills, twelve cross-trainers, twelve arc-trainers, six upright bikes, and six recumbent bikes; all but six are equipped with cable TV. The center also offers fitness options, from selectorized strength pieces and cable motion pieces to numerous workout benches and free weights.

The Peterson Recreation Center is the site of intramural athletic activities on campus, which have one of the highest participation rates in the country. The center has five convertible basketball, tennis, and volleyball courts; a 220-yard track; three racquetball courts; a 25-meter pool; and an aerobics room. Providence College has a fine tradition of competition in intercollegiate athletics, and it continues to play an active role through its membership in the NCAA, Hockey East Conference, and the Big East Conference. Additional on-campus sports facilities include Alumni Hall; Schneider Arena; three large fields and recreational areas; and a new artificial-turf field for varsity, club, and intramural sports.

Location

The College is situated on a 105-acre campus in the city of Providence, Rhode Island. It has the advantages of an atmosphere that is far removed from the traffic and commerce of the metropolitan area but is also conveniently located near the many cultural attractions of a vibrant city that is not only the capital of a historic state but also the center of a variety of institutions of higher learning. Providence College has an established relationship with the Tony Award–winning Trinity Square Repertory Company, in downtown Providence. Trinity provides special discount rates for students for the full spectrum of its programs. The Providence Performing Arts Center serves as the site of symphony concerts, opera, ballet, and road shows of Broadway musicals. In addition, the Dunkin' Donuts Center attracts well-known performers, trade shows, and sports events. The center is also the home court of the Friars, PC's basketball team. A Providence College ID enables students to travel free on any RIPTA bus route throughout Rhode Island.

Majors and Degrees

Providence College offers forty-nine bachelor's degrees in the School of Arts and Sciences, the School of Business, and the School of Professional Studies as detailed below.

School of Arts and Sciences: American studies, applied physics, art (studio), art history, biochemistry, biology, chemistry, computer science, economics, business economics, quantitative economics, English: literature, English: creative writing, French, global studies, history, humanities, Italian, mathematics, music, music education (K–12), philosophy, political science, pre-engineering (3+2 program),

psychology, public and community service studies, sociology, social science, Spanish, theater arts, theology, and women's studies.

School of Business: accountancy, finance, management, marketing, and a 4+1 M.B.A. program.

School of Professional Studies: health policy and management; social work; elementary/special education; and secondary education, with specializations in biology, chemistry, English, French, history, Italian, mathematics, physics, and Spanish.

Academic Programs

Providence College's motto consists of one word: "Veritas," the Latin word for truth. All teaching and learning at Providence begins with a belief in the truth—that faith and reason are compatible realities in the contemplation of truth, and that our greatest duty is to constantly seek it. All dimensions of the student experience are deeply rooted in the Dominican value of dynamic spirituality, with its concern for the whole person—mind and body, heart and soul—and respect for the gifts and uniqueness of every person. The College's programs are also designed to help students discover their particular aptitude and prepare them to undertake specialized studies leading to careers.

The rigorous core curriculum at Providence College, a values-centered examination of the traditional humanities curriculum, provides students of all majors with a well-balanced academic program. Through an in-depth immersion in the fundamental concepts and issues addressed by the social and natural sciences, literature, history, philosophy, mathematics, the fine arts, and theology, students learn to think critically, reason well, and communicate effectively. Demanding, exhilarating and memorable, the Development of Western Civilization program is the cornerstone of our core curriculum. It is one of the nation's most academically ambitious interdisciplinary programs which integrates the study of literature, history philosophy, theology, and the fine arts. Special academic programs are offered to enhance the educational experience and allow for a variety of interests, including double majors; individualized programs; non-departmental courses; liberal arts honors; preprofessional medical and health sciences, and legal programs; the Early Identification Program (offered to Rhode Island residents in cooperation with Brown University Medical School); and Army ROTC.

The College participates in the Advanced Placement (AP) Program, which is administered by the College Board. Students who demonstrate superior performance (a score of 4 or 5) on any of the Advanced Placement examinations are considered for advanced-placement credit.

Providence College recognizes credit earned through the International Baccalaureate (I.B.), an internationally recognized curriculum and examination program. The College recognizes the Higher Level examinations when a score of 5, 6, or 7 has been achieved. Each examination that is successfully passed in the Higher Level of the I.B. program earns 3 credits.

Students who are granted AP or I.B. credit are still required to complete the College's full-time, eight-semester requirement.

PC operates on a two-semester calendar. Fall-semester classes begin in early September, and spring-semester classes begin in mid-January.

Off-Campus Programs

Providence College recognizes that a liberal arts education can be enriched through diverse intellectual and social experiences and encourages all of its students to study abroad. With a new Center for International Studies, there is renewed energy in the opportunities available for students to gain an international academic experience. There are 197 year-long, semester-long, and short-term study-abroad programs offered across the Middle East, Africa, Asia, Australia and New Zealand, Central and South America, and Europe. The Providence College Center for Theology and Religious Studies is at

Villa Ferretti, in the heart of Rome. There, students learn Italian language, theology, and a wide variety of subjects such as art, history, business, and politics. The Washington Semester is also an option for students, allowing them to enrich their education by spending one semester of academic study and experiential learning at American University in Washington, D.C.

Academic Facilities

The Phillips Memorial Library, which has received two national architectural awards for its design, is the center of intellectual activity at the College. PC's library is an electronic resource complete with radio-frequency technology, a wireless network, electronic classrooms, and the second-largest electronic database access in the state. The library has current holdings of 366,000 volumes in open stacks and seating accommodations for 750 students. Phillips Library also houses various faculty offices, reading and rare book rooms, archives, the Department of English, and the Office of Academic Services. The library is a member of the Consortium of Rhode Island Academic and Research Libraries, which allows access to the resources of most of the libraries in the state. Located in Accinno Hall and Koffler Hall are the College's academic microcomputer laboratories, which serve computer instruction and research needs. The College's state-of-the-art science laboratories, computer workstations, and research facilities are located in the Albertus Magnus–Sowa–Hickey Science Complex. The Feinstein Academic Center is home to the Feinstein Institute for Public Service Program, the Liberal Arts Honors Program, and the Center for Teaching Excellence. The comprehensive new Smith Center for the Arts features a theater, a concert hall, an art gallery, a dance studio, a black-box theater, music practice rooms, and scenery and costume shops.

Costs

The total costs for the 2011–12 academic year were tuition, $40,150, and room and board, $12,140 (seven-day plan). Books, travel, and personal supplies were estimated to cost $800.

Financial Aid

Providence College's financial aid is distributed on the basis of demonstrated need and the student's ability to benefit from the educational opportunity the assistance offers. To apply for financial aid, candidates who are applying for early action must submit a College Scholarship Service PROFILE application by December 1 and the Free Application for Federal Student Aid (FAFSA) by February 1. Students applying for regular decision must submit both the College Scholarship Service PROFILE application and the FAFSA by February 1. Upon final determination of students' need, the Office of Financial Aid constructs aid packages consisting of work, loan, and grant assistance in accordance with federal regulations, the availability of funds, and institutional policy, as approved by the College's Financial Aid Advisory Committee. Sources of financial aid include Federal Work-Study Program awards, Federal Perkins Loans, Federal Pell Grants, Federal Supplemental Educational Opportunity Grants (FSEOG), Providence College grants-in-aid, Providence College Achievement Scholarships, and Merit Scholarships for highly qualified students. More information is available online at http://www.providence.edu/financial-aid.

Faculty

The faculty consists of 299 full-time professors; about 94 percent of them hold terminal degrees. The majority of PC instructors teach both undergraduate- and graduate-level courses; no graduate students or student assistants teach at either level. Professors engage in advanced research, and frequently publish books and articles, but they are focused primarily on teaching and advising undergraduates; all students are assigned a faculty adviser in their major area. The student-faculty ratio is 12:1.

Admission Requirements

The admission committee gives recognition to students with various talents, backgrounds, and geographic origins. Admission decisions are made without regard to race, color, sex, handicap, age, or national or ethnic origin. An estimate of the applicant's character and accomplishments by his or her college adviser in secondary school and an official transcript of the secondary school record should be sent to the College no later than November 1 for Early Action and January 15 for Regular Decision. The secondary school transcript should consist of courses of a substantially college-preparatory nature. Although individual cases may vary, the College highly recommends that a student complete 4 years of English; 4 of mathematics; 3 of one foreign language; 3 of science, with at least two laboratory courses; and 2 of social sciences. However, students who have been most competitive for admission in recent years have taken 4 years in all academic subject areas, taking advantage of honors or advanced-level courses that are available at their high school. Applicants are encouraged to submit letters of recommendation and evaluation from their secondary school teachers, especially from English teachers. Letters of recommendation from people who know the applicant personally and who have been involved in his or her scholastic development are most valuable.

Submission of standardized test scores is optional for students applying for admission. The academic review for admission at Providence College has always focused on each student's high school performance rather than standardized test results. This policy change allows each student to decide whether they wish to have their standardized test results considered as part of their application for admission. Students who choose not to submit SAT or ACT test scores are not penalized in the review for admission. Additional details about the test-optional policy can be found online at http://www.providence.edu/testoptionalpolicy.

Application and Information

As a member of the Common Application group, Providence College requires a completed Common Application as well as the Providence College Supplemental Form and an application fee of $55. The deadline for receiving freshman applications for the September term is November 1 for early action and January 15 for regular decision. The deadline for receiving freshman applications for the January term is December 1. The deadline for receiving transfer applications is April 1 for the fall term and December 1 for the spring term.

Further information may be obtained by contacting:

Providence College
1 Cunningham Square
Providence, Rhode Island 02918-0001
Phone: 401-865-2535
      800-721-6444 (toll-free)
Fax: 401-865-2826
E-mail: pcadmiss@providence.edu
Web site: http://www.providence.edu

Harkins Hall houses administrative offices and classrooms at Providence College.

QUEENS COLLEGE OF THE CITY UNIVERSITY OF NEW YORK

FLUSHING, NEW YORK

Q QUEENS COLLEGE

The College

Queens College (QC), with more than 12,500 undergraduates, is one of the largest of the four-year colleges in the City University of New York (CUNY) system. The College opened its doors in 1937 with the goal of offering a first-rate education to talented people of all backgrounds and financial means. It enjoys a national reputation for its liberal arts and sciences and preprofessional programs. Students come from more than 170 nations; the result is an unusually rich education that gives Queens College graduates a competitive edge in today's global society.

The 77-acre campus is lined with trees surrounding grassy open spaces and a traditional quad. Some of the original Spanish-style stucco-and-tile buildings from the early 1900s still stand, including Jefferson Hall, which houses the beautiful Welcome Center. Powdermaker Hall, the major classroom building, has state-of-the-art technology throughout, and the College's science labs recently underwent a $30-million renovation. The entire campus has Wi-Fi capability and students may relax and meet friends in the spacious Student Union and the College's many cafés, lounges, and recreation and dining areas.

With the opening of the College's first residence hall, The Summit, in August 2009, Queens College shed its commuter school identity. It now offers students the option of enjoying all the benefits of living on campus. The low-rise facility provides individually climate-controlled single- and double-room accommodations in suites with shared kitchen and lounge areas. It has its own exercise facility and was recently LEED-certified Gold for its green initiatives.

The administration remains dedicated to making its many commuter students feel that QC is their home away from home. The professionally staffed Child Development Center offers inexpensive child-care services to students with children. There are more than 100 clubs on campus, from the Accounting Honors Society and Alliance of Latin American Students to clubs for theater, fencing, environmental science, science fiction, and the fine arts. The only CUNY college that participates in Division II sports, Queens sponsors nineteen men's and women's teams and has some of the finest athletics facilities in the metro area. Ongoing cultural events include readings by renowned authors such as Margaret Atwood, E. L. Doctorow, and Jonathan Franzen; and concerts, theater, and dance performances by world-famous artists. QC is also home to the Godwin-Ternbach Museum, the only comprehensive museum in the borough of Queens, with art from antiquity to the present.

The College's centers and institutes serve students and the larger urban community by addressing society's most important challenges—such as cancer, pollution, and racism—and exploring the heritages of the borough's many ethnic communities, including Asians, Greeks, Italians, and Jews.

Queens College has had a chapter of Phi Beta Kappa since 1950 (less than 10 percent of U.S. liberal arts colleges are members of Phi Beta Kappa, the nation's oldest and most respected undergraduate honors organization). In 1968, Queens College became a member of Sigma Xi, the national science honor society. The American Association of University Women includes Queens College in its list of approved colleges for membership.

Location

Queens College, located off Exit 24 of the Long Island Expressway, is in a residential area of Flushing and is easily accessible by public transportation. It is only 20 minutes from Manhattan, whose magnificent skyline overlooks the campus quad.

Majors and Degrees

The Bachelor of Arts degree is awarded in accounting, Africana studies, American studies, anthropology, art, art history, biology, Byzantine and modern Greek studies, chemistry, Chinese, communication arts and media, communication sciences and disorders, comparative literature, computer science, drama and theater, East Asian studies, economics, education (early childhood and elementary), English, environmental sciences, environmental studies, film studies, French, geology, German, Greek, Hebrew, history, home economics, Italian, Jewish studies, labor studies, Latin, Latin American area studies, linguistics, mathematics, Middle Eastern studies, music, neuroscience, philosophy, physics, political science and government, psychology, religious studies, Russian, sociology, Spanish, studio art, theater-dance, urban studies, and women's studies.

The Bachelor of Arts program in secondary school teaching includes the following subject areas: Africana studies, anthropology, biology, chemistry, economics, English, French, geology, German, history, Italian, Latin American area studies, mathematics, physics, political science and government, sociology, Spanish, and urban studies.

The College also awards the Bachelor of Arts in interdisciplinary studies; an individualized Bachelor of Arts program; the Bachelor of Business Administration; the Bachelor of Fine Arts in studio art; the Bachelor of Music in instrumental or vocal performance studies; and the Bachelor of Science in applied social science, computer science, environmental sciences, geology, graphic design, nutrition and exercise sciences, physical education, and physics.

The Departments of Chemistry, Computer Science, Philosophy, Physics, and Political Science and the Aaron Copland School of Music offer qualified undergraduates the opportunity to take combined bachelor's and master's degree programs.

Pre-engineering students can take advantage of a 3-2 transfer program through the physics department that offers admission to Columbia University after three years at QC. Following two years at Columbia, students graduate with a B.A. in physics from Queens and an engineering B.A. from Columbia.

Special interdisciplinary programs include Africana studies, American studies, Asian-American community studies, business and liberal arts, business administration, Byzantine and modern Greek studies, Honors in Mathematics and Natural Sciences, Honors in the Humanities, Honors in the Social Sciences, Irish studies, Italian American studies, journalism, Latin American and Latino studies, and religious studies. Special programs and advisement are also available in accounting, pre-engineering, pre-law, and the pre–health professions.

Academic Programs

Queens College awards bachelor's and master's degrees in the arts and humanities, education, mathematics and the natural sciences, and social sciences. Certificate programs provide additional training in specialties in education, library science, and psychology. QC also participates in doctoral programs overseen by CUNY's graduate center; many of these programs involve lab work or clinical studies conducted on the Flushing campus.

Honors programs are central to the College's tradition of value and excellence, enhancing education by providing opportunities for faculty mentorship, advanced research, and other individualized projects. These programs create a community of learners in which students enjoy small classes, while still having access to QC's many resources and diverse student body. The emphasis is on discussion and projects rather than lectures.

Queens College is the only CUNY institution in the borough participating in the Macaulay Honors College, which supports gifted students with full tuition, a free laptop, a $7500 grant over four years, and other benefits. A flagship program of the University, it provides an enhanced undergraduate education to academically gifted students. Since its inauguration in 2001, the Honors College has grown rapidly, drawing on the unique resources of CUNY and New York's cultural, scientific, government, and business communities to provide its students with a broad-based and challenging liberal arts education.

In addition, QC has its own multidisciplinary Freshman Honors Program and divisional honors programs in the humanities, math and natural sciences, and social sciences. Outstanding high

school seniors may apply to become Queens College scholars. Prospective math teachers may qualify for scholarships and other incentives through QC's innovative math education program, TIME 2000. Business and Liberal Arts—designed for top-performing underclassmen regardless of their major—familiarizes students with basic business disciplines and offers internships sponsored by participating corporations.

The wide range of majors and interdisciplinary studies, combined with the award-winning Freshman Year Initiative program, encourages students to explore their interests and abilities to the fullest. Most degree programs require the completion of 120 credits.

The Bachelor of Business Administration (B.B.A.) degree provides a solid business education that responds to the demand of employers for specific quantitative and technological skills. Students may choose from three majors: finance, international business, and actuarial studies. The B.B.A. also has an investments/chartered financial analyst track to prepare students for the CFA examination, the only such undergraduate program in New York.

Study-abroad opportunities range from relatively short summer and winter intersession courses to programs that last a semester or two. Exchange programs allow Queens College students to study for up to a year in dozens of countries and other parts of the U.S.

The Adult Collegiate Education program, offered to students 25 and older, includes the option of obtaining college credit for life achievement. The Weekend College allows busy students to pursue their degrees by taking classes on Saturdays and Sundays.

Academic Facilities

Among the many centers where research and creativity are joined in the pursuit of knowledge is the Kupferberg Center for the Visual and Performing Arts, which brings together the College's academic departments in the arts (music, drama and dance, art, and media studies), and its museums (the Godwin-Ternbach, the Queens College Art Center, and the Louis Armstrong House Museum). The center's venues include the newly renovated 2,200-seat Colden Auditorium; the Goldstein Theatre, designed especially for the staging of experimental student productions; and the Aaron Copland School of Music facility, which includes thirty-five practice rooms and the 491-seat LeFrak Concert Hall. The College is also home to the Gertz Center, which investigates communication disabilities and provides clinical experience for students of speech and hearing therapy.

Queens College administers the historic Louis Armstrong House Museum in Corona with its vast personal collection of Armstrong photographs, papers, recordings, and memorabilia that draws scholars and jazz fans from around the world. The Benjamin Rosenthal Library, with its soaring, light-filled atrium and art center, has more than 1 million print and electronic volumes.

Costs

For New York State residents, undergraduate tuition is $2415 per semester. For out-of-state and international students, undergraduate tuition is $435 per credit. There are various expenses each semester, such as student activity and technology fees.

Financial Aid

More than 50 percent of Queens College students receive need-based financial aid, which may include state and federal loans and grants, Tuition Assistance Program awards, Regents Scholarships, Federal Direct Student Loans, Federal Pell Grants, State Aid for Native Americans, and Federal Work-Study awards.

The Queens College Scholars Program offers a variety of merit-based scholarships to full-time freshmen, with awards of $2400 per year. Selection is competitive, and scholarships are awarded on the basis of the high school record, test scores (SAT and SAT Subject Tests), writing ability, letters of recommendation, and extracurricular activities. Scholarships are renewable with continued high academic achievement. Applicants who rank in or near the top 10 percent of their class and have a rigorous academic program, excellent grades, and minimum combined SAT (critical reading and math) scores of 1250 are encouraged to apply. The deadline is December 1.

Faculty

The Queens College faculty consists of top scholars who are dedicated to teaching and research, and enjoy working in a diverse urban environment. Many are relatively new to campus; half were hired between 2002 and 2008. There are 636 full-time professors, almost 90 percent of whom have the terminal degree in their fields (not all fields offer doctorates); 65 percent have tenure. Many also teach in the doctoral programs at the CUNY Graduate Center. Faculty members have received numerous fellowships, awards, and research grants from such prestigious organizations as the National Science Foundation (including eight Early Career Development grants) and the National Institutes of Health. In recent years, faculty members received two Guggenheim awards and two Fulbright grants. CUNY has recognized the excellence of the faculty by honoring 11 members with the title of Distinguished Professor in fields as diverse as chemistry, economics, English, history, and physics. Among the more widely known faculty members are scientist Steven Markowitz; historian Morris Rossabi; sociologist Stephen Steinberg; and poets Jeffrey Renard Allen, Nicole Cooley, and Kimiko Hahn.

Student Government

Through the Student Association, students at Queens run many services and activities that influence the daily operations of the College. Its elected officers and senators poll students regularly about relevant topics and sponsor such services as free legal advice, apartment and tutor referral, and voter registration. In addition, students constitute one third of the College's Academic Senate.

Admission Requirements

Queens College seeks to admit freshmen who have completed a strong college-preparatory program in high school with at least a B+ average. Admission is based on a variety of factors, including the applicant's high school grades, academic program, and SAT or ACT scores. Successful candidates have chosen a well-rounded program of study that includes academic course work in English (4 years), foreign language (3 years), math (3 years), lab science (2 years), and social studies (4 years).

The Search for Education, Elevation & Knowledge Program (SEEK) offers academic support, counseling, and financial assistance to motivated students who would not otherwise qualify for admission. The SEEK Program has its own admissions criteria, including financial need.

For earliest consideration, students should apply by January 1 for fall admission and by September 15 for spring admission.

Application and Information

The staff of the Undergraduate Office of Admissions is available to answer questions and give more information. To make an appointment for a tour or to meet with a counselor, students should contact:

Office of Admissions
Jefferson Hall
Queens College of the City University of New York
65-30 Kissena Boulevard
Flushing, New York 11367-1597
Phone: 718-997-5600
E-mail: admissions@qc.edu
Web site: http://www.qc.cuny.edu
http://on.fb.me/QueensColl_CUNY (Facebook)
http://twitter.com/QC_News
http://bit.ly/YouTube_CUNY-QC (YouTube)
http://bit.ly/itunes_CUNY-QC (iTunes)

A view of the Queens College quad, part of a 77-acre campus in New York City, where students from more than 150 nations receive a solid education for today's global society.

QUINNIPIAC UNIVERSITY
HAMDEN, CONNECTICUT

The University

Quinnipiac offers four-year and graduate-level degree programs leading to careers in health sciences, nursing, business, communications, engineering, natural sciences, education, liberal arts, and law. A curriculum that combines a career focus with a globally oriented liberal arts background prepares graduates for the future, whether they start their careers right after commencement or opt to pursue advanced study. A School of Medicine is scheduled to open in fall 2013.

Quinnipiac is coeducational and nonsectarian and currently enrolls 5,988 full-time undergraduates, 1,185 full-time graduate and law students, and 1,179 part-time students in its undergraduate, graduate, and professional programs. Twenty-five percent of the students are residents of Connecticut; the rest represent primarily the northeast corridor, in all a total of twenty-eight states and several countries. Quinnipiac is big enough to sustain a wide variety of people and programs but small enough to keep students from getting lost in the shuffle. Life on campus emphasizes students' personal, as well as academic, growth. The approximately 100 student organizations and extracurricular activities, including intramural and intercollegiate (NCAA Division I) athletics, give students a chance to exercise their talents, muscles, and leadership skills. The University has a student newspaper, TV station, and an FM radio station (WQAQ) and twenty-one intercollegiate teams in men's baseball, basketball, cross-country, ice hockey, lacrosse, soccer, and tennis, and in women's acrobatics and tumbling, basketball, cross-country, field hockey, golf, ice hockey, lacrosse, rugby, soccer, softball, tennis, track (indoor and outdoor), and volleyball. Teams compete in the Northeast Conference (NEC); men's and women's ice hockey teams are members in the ECAC.

The University has three distinct campus settings. The 250-acre Mount Carmel campus has fifty buildings including the Arnold Bernhard Library, academic facilities, an athletic and recreation center, and twenty-five residence halls of different styles, mainly for freshmen and sophomores, with traditional double and quad (4-person) rooms, suites, and multilevel suites and apartments with kitchens. About 95 percent of all freshmen and 75 percent of the total undergraduate population live in Quinnipiac housing. The nearby 250-acre York Hill campus includes the TD Bank Sports Center with twin 3,500-seat arenas for ice hockey and basketball; a new suite-style 1,500-bed residence hall and townhouses for juniors and seniors; a lodge-like student center; spectacular views; and a multilevel parking garage for 2,000 vehicles. Seniors may also live in University-owned houses or apartments. A free shuttle takes students between the two campuses. Just 4 miles away is the 104-acre North Haven campus with state-of-the-art facilities for graduate and upper division offerings in several programs in the Schools of Health Sciences, Nursing, and Education. There are plans for phased expansion for additional graduate programs as well as a School of Medicine, slated to open in 2013–14.

The Athletic and Recreation Center includes a 24,000-square-foot recreation/fitness facility with a large free-weight room; an exercise machine center; aerobics studios; basketball, volleyball, and tennis courts; and a suspended indoor track. There are also lighted tennis courts, playing fields, and miles of scenic routes for running and biking.

Career planning takes place in each of the schools with assistance from the deans' offices. It begins with faculty advisement, along with career exploration, a strong focus on internships and clinical placements, exploration of various major and job fields, and exposure to prospective employers and job preparation. Approximately 30 percent of the undergraduate student population remains at Quinnipiac for their graduate degree in combined or direct entry majors, particularly in education, business, physical and occupational therapy, and physician assistant programs.

Graduate programs lead to the Master of Science (M.S.) degree in accounting, information technology, interactive media, journalism, molecular and cell biology, organizational leadership, public relations, and teacher leadership; the Master of Health Science in medical lab sciences, cardiovascular perfusion, pathologist assistant studies, and physician assistant studies; a Doctor of Nursing Practice in adult and family nursing; the Master of Business Administration; the Master of Business Administration in Health Care Management; the Master of Business Administration–Chartered Financial Analyst; and the Master of Arts in Teaching. The Quinnipiac University School of Law offers full-time and part-time programs leading to a J.D. degree or J.D./M.B.A. degree in combination with the School of Business. Several of the graduate degree programs are offered online or in a hybrid format.

Location

Situated at the foot of Sleeping Giant Mountain in Hamden, Connecticut, Quinnipiac provides the best of the suburbs and the city. The University is only 8 miles from New Haven, 30 minutes from Hartford (the state capital), and less than 2 hours from New York City and Boston. Bordering the campus is the 1,700-acre Sleeping Giant State Park, for walking and hiking. The free campus shuttle takes students to shopping and restaurants in nearby Hamden and North Haven, plus to New Haven, where they can visit the acclaimed Yale Center for British Art, attend a performance at the Shubert or Long Wharf Theater (which hosts productions by Quinnipiac's Theater Department), find great restaurants, and have easy access to Metro North and Amtrak at the New Haven train station.

Majors and Degrees

The Schools of Health Sciences and Nursing grant bachelor's degrees in athletic training/sports medicine, biomedical science, diagnostic imaging, health and science studies, microbiology/molecular biology, nursing, occupational therapy (5½-year entry-level master's), physical therapy (6- or 7-year entry-level doctorate), and physician assistant studies (6-year freshman entry-level master's). Students who wish to prepare for entry into medical, dental, chiropractic, veterinary, or other medical schools work with a premed adviser and take classes that prepare them to sit for the various entrance exams.

The School of Business and Engineering (accredited by AACSB International) offers bachelor's degree programs in accounting, advertising, biomedical marketing, entrepreneurship, finance, computer information systems, international business, management, and marketing. The school also offers a fast-track, five-year combined-degree program in which students may be awarded the B.S. degree in business and a graduate degree in accounting, business administration, or computer information systems (M.S. or M.B.A.). In cooperation with the School of Business, an engineering degree program is scheduled to begin in fall 2012, with majors in mechanical, industrial, civil, and software engineering.

The College of Arts and Sciences offers bachelor's degree programs in behavioral neuroscience, biochemistry, biology, chemistry, computer science, criminal justice, English, gerontology, history, interactive digital design, legal studies (paralegal), liberal studies, mathematics, philosophy, political science, psychology, social services, sociology, Spanish, and theater. Qualified students can go on to the Master of Science in molecular and cell biology program or pursue graduate programs in education, business, law, journalism, or interactive media.

The School of Communications offers undergraduate majors in communications/media studies; film, video, and interactive media; journalism; and public relations, plus a B.F.A. in film and graduate programs in journalism, public relations, and interactive media.

The School of Education's five-year program for undergraduates provides certification for teaching elementary and secondary grades through a B.A./Master of Arts in Teaching (M.A.T.) program (accredited by NCATE).

Academic Programs

All degree programs at Quinnipiac University are offered through one of the five academic schools. The academic year consists of two

15-week fall and spring semesters and two summer sessions. All baccalaureate candidates are required to complete the University Curriculum, which consists of up to 46 of the 120 semester hours of credit generally needed for graduation at the bachelor's degree level. The foundation of the University Curriculum is three university seminars, which focus on the broad theme of community: individual, national, and global in scope. The Writing Across the Curriculum initiative (WAC) stresses the improvement in writing skills in all subject areas. The University honors program addresses the needs and interests of the most academically talented and committed students. Advanced placement, credit, or both are given for appropriate scores on Advanced Placement tests and CLEP general and subject examinations as well as for scores of 4 or higher in the International Baccalaureate higher-level subjects.

Off-Campus Programs

Students can study abroad in a variety of countries. Most students choose a study-abroad option in their sophomore year. Students in any of the five undergraduate schools can also get hands-on experience in their field through off-campus internships. Academic credit is available for internships and affiliations, which are often part of degree requirements.

Academic Facilities

Academic life focuses on the Bernhard Library. This attractive facility provides individual carrels and small rooms for group study and is open 24/7 during the fall and spring semesters. A wireless network provides access to automated library systems and extensive Web-based resources.

Quinnipiac University was identified as one of the top ten most-wired campuses in the country by *PC Magazine* in January 2007. All incoming students must bring or purchase a laptop computer for use in classes and in the residence halls. An information technology desk offers tech support as needed.

The multimedia and video laboratories in the Ed McMahon Mass Communications Center each have the latest Mac workstations and software. The computer cluster in the Financial Technology Center at the School of Business is a high-tech, simulated trading floor providing students with the opportunity to access real-time financial data, conduct interactive trading simulations, and develop financial models in preparation for careers in finance.

The Lender School of Business has satellite capabilities and the Ed McMahon Mass Communications Center, and contains a state-of-the-art, fully digital, high-definition TV production studio; audio production, print journalism, and desktop publishing laboratories; and a news technology center.

The Graduate and Health Sciences Center on the North Haven campus provides state-of-the-art facilities for the health sciences programs in diagnostic imaging, nursing, occupational therapy, physical therapy, physician assistant, and radiologist assistant. In addition to a breathtaking location and expansive exterior and interior spaces, there are specialized facilities and equipment for the various health sciences disciplines, such as movement study/motion analysis and biomechanics labs; the ergonomics and assistive technology lab; a model adaptive apartment; an orthopedics lab; several rehabilitative sciences labs; CT scan, MRI, radiography, ultrasound, and mammography facilities; and the latest clinical skills simulation labs for adults and pediatric/neonatal patients including an intensive care unit, physical diagnosis lab, physical exam suite, and health assessment labs, which duplicate care in an outpatient primary care setting.

Costs

The 2012–13 cost is $51,800, of which tuition and fees (12–16 credits per semester) are $38,000. Room and board average $13,800. Other expenses, estimated at $2000 per year, include books, laboratory, and course fees associated with specific courses, and personal travel expenses.

Financial Aid

Quinnipiac designs financial aid packages to include need-based grants and merit-based scholarships that do not have to be repaid, plus self-help financial aid programs such as federal and University-based work study, and loans. Students and families seeking need-based aid will file the College Scholarship Service's Financial Aid PROFILE plus the Free Application for Federal Student Aid (FAFSA) to determine need. Transfer students are eligible for the same need-based financial aid consideration as first-time freshmen.

Faculty

The faculty is characterized by its teaching competence and outstanding academic qualifications. Of the 351 full-time faculty members, 85 percent have earned a Ph.D. or the appropriate terminal degree in their field. The faculty also includes a number of part-time teachers who are practicing professionals and experts in their fields. Classes are taught by these scholars and professionals and not by student instructors, and a low student-faculty ratio promotes close associations among faculty members and students.

Student Government

The Student Government is the student legislative body of Quinnipiac. It represents student opinion, promotes student welfare, supervises student organizations, appropriates funds for student groups, and provides voting student representation on the Board of Trustees.

Admission Requirements

Quinnipiac seeks students from a broad range of backgrounds. On average, freshman students have a 3.4 GPA or better average in college-preparatory courses (transfer students generally have a 2.5 GPA or better), rank in the top 25 percent of their high school class, and have an average combined score of 1120 on the SAT (critical reading plus math). Visits to the campus for an interview, open house, group information session, or a campus tour are strongly encouraged. Transfer students are welcome to make an appointment to discuss requirements and the transfer of credit from previous institutions. Quinnipiac sponsors four open house programs during the year and several Saturday morning information sessions followed by a campus tour.

Application and Information

Quinnipiac generally receives between 18,000 and 20,000 applications for admission and admits about 65 percent, to enroll an incoming class of 1,700 freshmen and 200 transfer students. Quinnipiac has a rolling admission policy for its undergraduate programs and therefore recommends that freshman applicants submit their application materials starting early in the fall of their senior year and well before the deadline of February 1. Students applying to the physical therapy, nursing, and physician assistant studies programs should submit their applications by November 15. An early decision (binding) option is available in all majors with an application deadline of November 1. Applications begin to be reviewed as soon as they are complete, and the University begins notifying students of decisions in December. Quinnipiac is a member of the Common Application and recommends that applications be submitted online. Students placed on a waiting list are notified of any openings by June 1. Quinnipiac subscribes to the May 1 Candidates Reply Date Agreement. For information about full-time undergraduate study, students should contact:

Office of Undergraduate Admissions
Quinnipiac University
Hamden, Connecticut 06518-1940
Phone: 203-582-8600
        800-462-1944 (toll-free)
Fax: 203-582-8906
E-mail: admissions@quinnipiac.edu
Web site: http://www.quinnipiac.edu
        http://www.facebook.com/QuinnipiacUniversity
        http://twitter.com/QU_Admissions
        http://quadmissions.blogspot.com/
        http://www.youtube.com/quinnipiacuniversity
        http://www.quinnipiac.edu/rss.xml

For information regarding transfer and part-time study:

Office of Transfer and Part-time Admissions
Quinnipiac University
Hamden, Connecticut 06518-1940
Phone: 203-582-8612
Fax: 203-582-8906
E-mail: transferadmissions@quinnipiac.edu

RANDOLPH COLLEGE
LYNCHBURG, VIRGINIA

The College

No two students are the same—each one is an original. That's the mindset at Randolph College. While DNA may be nature's starting point for individual development, what each student makes of themselves is subject to many different factors. And that's where Randolph College—a community of originals—can make a difference.

Academic excellence through the liberal arts and sciences and an emphasis on individual learning are Randolph's top priorities. Founded as Randolph-Macon Woman's College in 1891, it was the first women's college to be accredited by the Southern Association of Colleges and Schools and the first Southern women's college to be granted a Phi Beta Kappa charter. The College's enduring commitment to education has fostered strong programs in career development, experiential learning, and undergraduate research.

Randolph's current enrollment is about 575. Students come from more than forty states and thirty countries, choosing Randolph for its academic reputation, outstanding commitment to individual learning, and the warm, friendly community. There are six residence halls on the 100-acre campus, housing 90 percent of the students. The College's location near the Blue Ridge Mountains provides ample recreational opportunities, and proximity to neighboring colleges and major universities enhances the social and cocurricular life on and off campus. Most students are involved in at least one of the more than forty clubs or organizations and activities, which include campus publications; an organic garden; WRRM radio; vocal music groups Chorale, Voices, and Songshine; the Dance Group; political organizations; language clubs; theater; religious and volunteer organizations; and a nationally ranked riding program with its own world-class riding facility. The $6-million Student Center renovation, expected to be complete in 2012, will offer a two-level fitness center on the top floor; a 90-seat theater; the Skeller (a student grill); a wrap-around outside deck; an entertainment floor with pool tables, ping-pong, foosball, and other activities; a glass-enclosed studio for the student radio station, WWRM; and new student government and publications offices.

Intercollegiate sports for men include basketball, cross-country, lacrosse, riding, soccer, and tennis. Women's sports include basketball, cross-country, lacrosse, riding, soccer, softball, tennis, and volleyball. Courses are also offered in a variety of activities and sports, including aerobics, fencing, fitness walking, golf, kickboxing, weight training, and yoga.

The academic program is enhanced throughout the year by visiting speakers, performers, and artists. In recent years, these have included former Governor of Vermont and DNC Chairman Howard Dean; aquatic filmmaker and oceanographic explorer Fabien Cousteau; John Dau, a Lost Boy of Sudan known for his memoir and Sundance Film Festival award-winner *God Grew Tired of Us;* educator, poet, writer, and Civil Rights activist Nikki Giovanni; Frances Mayes, alumna of the College and author of several works including *Under the Tuscan Sun;* and political strategist Karl Rove. In addition, the College sponsors numerous plays, awards, and exhibitions.

Location

Randolph College is situated on 100 rolling acres in the historic district of Lynchburg, Virginia, a suburban college town with small-town charm near the Blue Ridge Mountains. Shopping areas, movie theaters, restaurants, and coffee shops are convenient to the campus, and public transportation is readily available. Lynchburg is within easy driving distance of Washington, D.C., and Richmond, Virginia.

Majors and Degrees

Randolph College offers more than fifty majors, concentrations (minors), and programs of study leading to a Bachelor of Arts (B.A.), Bachelor of Science (B.S.), or Bachelor of Fine Arts (B.F.A.) degree.

Majors are art (history, museum studies, and studio), biology, business, chemistry, classics, communication studies, curricular studies, dance, economics, engineering physics, English (creative writing and literature), environmental studies or science, French, global studies, health services, history, mathematics, music, philosophy, physical education and health with licensure, physics, physics education, political science, psychology, religious studies, sociology, Spanish, sport and exercise studies, and theater. The double major is a popular option, and there is also the opportunity to develop a self-designed major such as comparative literature or mathematical biology. In addition the education program offers courses that meet the requirements for primary and secondary education certification. Travel/study opportunities and visiting scholar programs augment the international curriculum.

Every student has the option of selecting up to two minors in addition to the major. Minors are offered in all of the major fields as well as the interdisciplinary areas of American culture, Asian studies, film studies, gender studies, global studies, human services, Renaissance studies, and sport and exercise studies. Students declare majors and concentrations in the spring of the sophomore year.

Randolph has 3-2 programs in engineering and nursing and preprofessional programs in law, medicine and veterinary studies, and teacher education.

Academic Programs

The academic program is structured to develop the student as a whole person. The curriculum is designed to ensure that students acquire a broad range of knowledge and depth in their chosen field while they are prepared for meaningful careers. Randolph College trains students to think critically and independently and speak and write effectively. The College's graduation requirement is 124 hours of credit with a quality point ratio of at least 2.0.

Students also use the Randolph Plan, an individualized, systematic plan that helps them define their personal, educational, and professional goals. Working with faculty and staff members, students move through a series of steps to identify the many courses, internships, study-abroad opportunities, and clubs and activities that constitute a coherent plan to meet their goals.

The College operates on a traditional semester system, with self-scheduled exams given before the December vacation and at the end of the second semester in May. Most classes meet either two or three times a week. Randolph College provides maximum opportunity for independent study and research.

The Writing Program includes formal evaluation of student writing skills in all courses at the end of every semester as well as writing-intensive sections across the curriculum. First-year students may be granted exemption from the English composition degree requirement on the basis of their entering record (usually Advanced Placement examination scores).

In a study conducted by the Higher Education Data Sharing (HEDS) Consortium, Randolph College ranks in the top 15 percent of institutions nationally in percentage of graduates who earned doctorates between 1997 and 2006. Over the same period, Randolph College ranked in the top 15 percent in biological sciences and the top 10 percent in humanities, notably English and foreign languages. Special advisers at the College counsel students who are preparing for medical, veterinary, or law school or other specialized graduate study. Research is encouraged in various areas of academic concentration, and in the senior year students may pursue honors work involving the presentation and defense of a thesis under the supervision of a faculty member. Class of 2010 graduates gained valuable experience through internships (46 percent), research (27 percent), volunteer service (50 percent), study abroad for a semester or academic year (26 percent), and employment during the summer (56 percent).

Off-Campus Programs

Internships provide an exciting opportunity for students to gain valuable work experience in area hospitals, veterinary clinics, schools, law firms, industries, courts, social service agencies, and radio and television stations. The College maintains a listing of nearly 1,000 internship opportunities through which students may earn up to 6 hours of credit toward their degree.

Many students choose to participate in study abroad, either through Randolph's flagship program, The World in Britain (affiliated with the University of Reading, England), or in other destinations around the globe on one of the College's affiliated programs or through another university sponsor. Recent study-abroad destinations include Australia, Belgium, Denmark, France, Ghana, Japan, Italy, Mexico, the Philippines, Russia, Scotland, and Spain.

Programs in this country include the Washington semester at American University and the Marine Biological Laboratory semester in environmental science. Randolph College participates in the Seven-College Exchange consortium in Virginia, along with Hampden-Sydney College, Hollins University, Mary Baldwin College, Randolph-Macon College, Sweet Briar College, and Washington and Lee University. The local Tri-College Consortium of Randolph College, Lynchburg College, and Sweet Briar College increases the number and diversity of courses open to students.

The College's spring semester American Culture Program offers an interdisciplinary immersion into the study of American culture both on campus and at key locations in Virginia and across the nation. The program capitalizes on the College's central location in historic Virginia as well as its own outstanding Maier Museum of Art's collection of American art. This one-semester program is open to students from Randolph College as well as to undergraduate students, both women and men, from other institutions.

The Susan F. Davenport Leadership Program is another unique opportunity at Randolph. It focuses on developing the skills and global perspectives students need to become leaders in the world today.

Academic Facilities

The recently renovated Lipscomb Library contains more than 200,000 volumes, as well as current magazine and journal titles with backfiles in microform and paper, extensive holdings in audiovisual formats, and domestic and foreign newspapers. Over 80,000 journal titles are available electronically. The Martin Science Building incorporates instrumentation, facilities for student-faculty research, and multimedia instructional centers. Equipment and resources readily available for hands-on student use include an FT-NMR, GC-MS, a seismograph, high-speed oscilloscopes and other instruments, exceptional herbarium and fossil collections, a greenhouse, and nature preserves. The Winfree Observatory houses a 14-inch pier-mounted telescope equipped with a computer-operated CCD camera for variable star research to support instruction in physics and astronomy. The Ethyl Science and Mathematics Resource Center in Martin offers a networked computer cluster with specific software for science and math applications and library, study, and lounge facilities.

The College's Maier Museum of Art houses an outstanding collection of nineteenth- and twentieth-century American paintings, while Presser Hall, the music building, has a concert auditorium, studios, and practice rooms. The Learning Resources Center and the Writing Lab offer academic support and tutorial services related to study skills, word processing, and the writing program.

Classroom equipment allows for appropriate technology integration into teaching and learning. The majority of classrooms on campus provide multimedia display capabilities, and several classrooms are equipped with student computer workstations for hands-on instruction in discipline-specific software and for general-purpose technology workshops. The campus also has a number of learning spaces equipped with special-purpose technology, including SMART Boards, computers-on-wheels for group collaboration, a small theater with computer/video display and surround sound, a media center/language lab where students can work on language drills and exercises as well as edit digital video, and a digital darkroom for high-end digital, still picture editing.

Macintosh and PC-compatible computers are provided in numerous labs on campus for student use 24 hours a day, seven days a week. Laser printers and scanners are also available in all computer labs. Web-based information resources allow students to view their student records, class schedules, and grades.

All computer labs and residence hall rooms have access to the Internet and to the College's extensive Web site. The Web site provides comprehensive information about the College and a variety of services to prospective students and their parents. Students enjoy the campus portal system and the College's 100 percent coverage for wireless connection to the network.

Costs

The 2011–12 comprehensive fee for room, board, and tuition was $40,222. The College recommends a budget of $2500 for books, supplies, fees, and personal expenses, excluding travel costs.

Financial Aid

Randolph College administers more than $15 million in aid each year through a comprehensive program of financial assistance, which includes academics-based scholarships, need-based grants, low-interest student loans, and campus employment. All students are encouraged to apply for financial aid, even those who assume that they are ineligible for assistance due to family income level. Academic scholarships, which range from $6000 per year to full tuition, are renewable for four years. The student's application for admission serves as the application for all academic scholarships. More than 95 percent of the College's students receive financial assistance of some kind. The average need-based financial aid package is $19,000. To apply for need-based aid, students are encouraged to submit the Free Application for Federal Student Aid (FAFSA) by February 1. International students are eligible for merit scholarships, which range from $6000 to $20,000 per year.

Admission Requirements

A minimum of 16 academic high school units is recommended and should be distributed as follows: 4 units of English, 3 units of mathematics, 3–4 units of a foreign language, 2 units of laboratory science, 2 units of social studies, and sufficient electives from these areas to make up the recommended total. Because of the flexible nature of the College's curriculum, favorable consideration may be given to students whose high school preparation departs from the recommendations outlined above. Each applicant must have maintained a strong academic record in college-preparatory courses and must submit scores on the SAT or ACT. Randolph College readily accepts the Common Application. An online application is available at http://www.randolphcollege.edu.

Application and Information

Each application for admission is evaluated when all necessary materials are received. Students are generally notified of a decision within three weeks of deadline dates or once all supporting credentials have been received. The application fee is $35. This fee may be waived in cases of hardship at the request of the student and the recommendation of their high school counselor. Randolph College also participates in the College Board test fee waiver program.

The deadline for submitting an application for early action is December 1 of a student's senior year. Students who apply by December 1 receive priority consideration for the Presidential Scholarship, a highly competitive full-tuition scholarship. The deadline for submitting an application for regular decision is March 1 of a student's senior year.

Accepted students must notify the College of their plans to enroll and submit the initial $300 enrollment deposit by May 1. The deposit is refundable if written notification is received by the Admissions Office prior to May 1.

For more information, students should contact:

Vice President for Enrollment Management
Randolph College
2500 Rivermont Avenue
Lynchburg, Virginia 24503
Phone: 434-947-8100
      800-745-7692 (toll-free)
E-mail: admissions@randolphcollege.edu
Web site: http://www.randolphcollege.edu
      http://www.facebook.com/randolphcollege
      http://twitter.com/randolphcollege

REED COLLEGE
PORTLAND, OREGON

The College

For its 1,447 students and 139 faculty members, Reed College is foremost an intellectual community. Since classes began in 1911, Reed has attracted students with a high degree of self-discipline and a genuine enthusiasm for academic work and intellectual challenge. Reed comprises a diverse student body; more than four fifths of Reed's students come from outside the Northwest, with 25 percent from the Northeast and 8 percent from outside the United States. A quarter of Reed's incoming students are members of historically underrepresented ethnic groups.

Campus social opportunities are open to all, with no closed clubs or organizations; there are no sororities or fraternities at Reed. Community life is full of activity and variety with more than seventy student organizations. Although there are competitive club sports at Reed, such as rugby, soccer, and Ultimate (Frisbee), there are no varsity athletic teams. Fitness and the development of lifelong skills take precedence over competition.

Location

Reed's 119-acre wooded campus is located in a quiet, residential section of southeast Portland. The nearby ocean and mountains of the Pacific Northwest provide a balance to the social and cultural offerings of the greater Portland metropolitan area.

Majors and Degrees

Reed awards the Bachelor of Arts degree in a wide variety of fields, based on work in traditional departments or in interdisciplinary combinations. Students may select from the following majors: American studies, anthropology, art, biochemistry and molecular biology, biology, chemistry, chemistry-physics, Chinese literature, Chinese studies, classics, classics-religion, dance-theater, economics, English literature, environmental studies, French literature, general literature, German literature, history, history-literature, international and comparative policy studies, linguistics, literature-theater, mathematics, mathematics-economics, mathematics-physics, music, philosophy, physics, political science, psychology, religion, Russian literature, sociology, Spanish literature, and theater.

Students may also design additional interdisciplinary majors. The approval of such special programs, which link two or more disciplines, is reviewed by the student's adviser and the departments concerned.

Reed offers several combined 3-2 programs, which allow the student to earn both a bachelor's degree from Reed and a professional degree from the cooperating institution. Science programs and institutions include engineering (California Institute of Technology, Columbia University, and Rensselaer Polytechnic Institute), computer science (University of Washington), and environmental sciences (Duke University). The College also has a combined program in fine arts (Pacific Northwest College of Art).

Academic Programs

Hallmarks of academic life at Reed include the small-group conference method of teaching and its reliance on active student participation, a de-emphasis of grades, a yearlong interdisciplinary humanities program, and an integrated academic program that balances the breadth of traditional course content and distribution requirements with flexibility in designing an in-depth senior thesis. The development of skills in preparation for a life of learning takes precedence over the mere memorization of facts. In addition to fulfilling the requirements for the major, taking the humanities course, and writing the senior thesis, students must satisfy a distributional requirement, consisting of two core classes from each of the following academic groups: literature, philosophy, and the arts; history, social sciences, and psychology; the natural sciences; and math, foreign language, logic, and linguistics. Students must also take two classes from one other department outside their major course of study.

Off-Campus Programs

Reed participates in domestic exchange programs with Howard University in Washington, D.C.; Sarah Lawrence College in New York; and Sea Education Association in Massachusetts. In addition, Reed provides study-abroad opportunities for students in Australia (Australian National University, University of Sydney, School for Field Studies), Argentina (University of Buenos Aires/FLASCO), China (East China Normal University in Shanghai, Capital Normal University in Beijing, Fujian Normal University in Fuzhou), Costa Rica (Organization for Tropical Studies, University of Costa Rica), Cuba (Sarah Lawrence College in Cuba), Ecuador (University of Quito), Egypt (American University in Cairo), France (Université de Rennes II Haute Bretagne, Université de Paris), Germany (University of Munich, Tübingen University, Freie University), Greece (College Year in Athens), Hungary (Budapest Semester in Mathematics), Ireland (Trinity College at the University of Dublin, University College Cork), Israel (Hebrew University), Morocco (Al Akhawayn University), Italy (Intercollegiate Centers for Classical Studies in Rome and Sicily, Florence Center of Syracuse University, Sarah Lawrence College Foreign Program in Florence), Kenya (School for Field Studies), Lebanon (American University of Beirut), Morocco (Al Akhawayn University), Russia (ACTR Russian Language, Middlebury School in Russia, National Theater Institute of Moscow, Smolny College at St. Petersburg University), South Africa (Organization for Tropical Studies), Spain (Hamilton College's Madrid Center, Middlebury School in Spain, University of Santiago de Compostela, University of Barcelona), Turks and Caicos (School for Field Studies), and the United Kingdom (Sarah Lawrence College Foreign Programs in London Theater and at Wadham College at Oxford University, University of East Anglia, Sussex University, University of Nottingham). Students may also arrange independent study plans in consultation with appropriate faculty members, the director for off-campus studies, and the registrar.

Academic Facilities

Students have access to Reed's substantial library collection (600,967 volumes, 2,700 periodicals, and 340,000 government documents) by searching the online catalog in the library or from any computer on the campus network. Through its participation in PORTALS (Portland Area Library System) and Summit, a union catalog of Oregon and Washington academic libraries, Reed provides online access to other library catalogs and databases. Students may borrow materials directly from academic libraries in the Portland area, and they have access to collections worldwide through interlibrary loan. In addition, the Reed library accommodates a first-rate art gallery, a language lab, and a music listening facility. The Reed library is open 18 hours most days and 24 hours a day during examinations.

Computer technology is highly developed at Reed and widely used for instruction, research, and communication by all members of the College community. A state-of-the-art campus network links all residence halls, classrooms, laboratories, offices, and the library to one another and to the global Internet. The Educational Technology Center houses more than 100 computers and a variety of other teaching and technology resources that are used by students and faculty and staff members. The science laboratories at Reed are among the best equipped of any undergraduate college in the United States. These include the A. A. Knowlton Laboratory of Physics, the Arthur F. Scott Laboratory of Chemistry, and the L. E. Griffin Memorial Biology Building, where a recent $10-million renovation includes improved student thesis space, a tiered-seating classroom, and new teaching labs. Reed's research nuclear reactor (the only such reactor in the country that is staffed primarily by undergraduates) and radiochemistry lab are actively used for student research, instruction, and training. For those interested in the arts, the campus houses studio art facilities that recently saw a $2-million expansion, performing arts facilities, twenty instrumental practice

rooms, a computer music laboratory, a recording system, and an 800-seat auditorium. Other popular facilities include a radio station and a modern sports center. In fall 2008, Reed opened five new residence halls, which enable 75 percent of students to live on campus.

Costs

Tuition for 2012–13 is $44,200, and room and board is $11,460. The student body fee is $260, bringing the yearly total cost to approximately $55,920. The cost of books and incidental expenses averages $2000.

Financial Aid

About half of the Reed student body receives financial assistance from the College. A full need-based financial aid program makes Reed accessible to students from a wide range of economic backgrounds. The College guarantees to meet the full demonstrated need of all continuing students in good academic standing who complete their financial aid applications on time. Reed's own funds are the primary source of grants to students. The College budgeted more than $22 million for this purpose in 2011–12. Reed also administers federal and state grants as well as federally subsidized loan programs. Campus employment and work-study programs are available. The size of a financial aid award is based solely upon analysis of the student's need. The average amount awarded to students receiving financial aid in 2011–12 was $35,990, which includes grants, loans, and work opportunities.

Faculty

All classes at Reed are taught by professors, about 90 percent of whom hold the highest degree in their field. The average class has 15 students. Reed students point to the opportunity to work closely with faculty members as one of the great benefits of a Reed education. Reed faculty members point to the opportunity to work with students who are serious scholars as one of the great benefits of teaching at Reed. Faculty members commit themselves primarily to teaching, with scholarly and scientific research furthering this primary goal; they view students as partners in learning, often serving as coauthors and coinvestigators on professional papers and research projects. This close association is due, in large part, to a 10:1 student-faculty ratio and the one-on-one relationship between thesis adviser (a professor) and student during the senior year.

Student Government

The Student Senate is the central body in student governance. The Senate consists of the student body president, vice president, and 8 student representatives, all elected by the students. Its two primary functions are to allocate student body funds and to represent student interests and concerns to the faculty, administration, and Board of Trustees. The Senate distributes approximately $40,000 each semester to the many student organizations on campus. As agreed under the community constitution, students participate fully in discussions and decisions on a wide variety of issues. The Student Committee on Academic Policy and Planning participates in debate about the curriculum at Reed; many other committees, from the Library Board to the Reactor Committee, have substantial student input. The Senate and student body president make all student appointments to such committees.

Admission Requirements

Reed welcomes applications from freshman and transfer candidates who are genuinely committed to the pursuit of a liberal arts education and a rigorous academic program. Those applicants are admitted who, in the view of the Admission Committee, are most likely to become successful members of and contribute significantly and honorably to the Reed community. The College is committed to maintaining a student body distinguished by its intellectual passion, yet diversified in its range of backgrounds, interests, and talents.

Admission decisions are based on many integrated factors, but academic accomplishments and talents are given the greatest weight in the selection process. A strong secondary school preparation, including honors and advanced courses where available, improves a student's chances for admission. Such a program usually includes 4 years of English and 3 to 4 years of mathematics (through precalculus), science, foreign language, and history or social studies. Given the wide variation in high school programs and quality, however, there are no fixed requirements for secondary school

courses. Applicants are expected to have obtained a secondary school diploma prior to enrollment, although exceptions are occasionally made. There are no cutoff points for high school or college grades or for test scores.

Reed recognizes the qualities of character—in particular, motivation, intellectual curiosity, individual responsibility, and community and social consciousness—as important considerations in the selection process, beyond a demonstrated commitment to academic excellence. Thus, the Admission Committee looks for students whose accomplishments and interests in various fields of endeavor will contribute to the overall liveliness of the Reed community. Personal interviews, either on or off campus, are not a requirement in the admission process but are strongly recommended whenever possible. Applications for early decision should be submitted by November 15 (Option I) or December 20 (Option II), regular freshman admission by January 15, and transfer candidates by March 1.

Application and Information

The Office of Admission is open Monday through Friday from 8:30 a.m. until 5 p.m. (Pacific time) all year, except for major holidays. Admission is also open on select Saturdays in the spring and fall. Students may apply online at http://www.reed.edu/apply/apply_reed.html.

For further information or to arrange a campus tour, overnight stay, information session, or interview, students should contact:

Office of Admission
Reed College
3203 Southeast Woodstock Boulevard
Portland, Oregon 97202-8199
Phone: 503-777-7511
        800-547-4750 (toll-free)
Fax: 503-777-7553
E-mail: admission@reed.edu
Web site: http://www.reed.edu

On a warm day at Reed College, it's not uncommon to see some classes meeting on the front lawn. Students have a great appreciation for passionate discussion, intellectual inquiry, and bright and sunny days.

THE RICHARD STOCKTON COLLEGE OF NEW JERSEY

GALLOWAY, NEW JERSEY

STOCKTON
NEW JERSEY'S
DISTINCTIVE
Public College
40 YEARS OF EXCELLENCE
1971–2011

The College

Thinking translates into doing at Stockton. Students can get hands-on experience in nursing, public health, or physical therapy at the two hospitals on campus; conduct computational science or IT research in the high-powered computer labs or at nearby technology centers; "live" a hospitality and tourism internship 24/7 at the Seaview, Stockton's world-class resort; study artistic techniques firsthand through a partnership with the nearby Noyes Museum of Art and at the Philadelphia Museum of Art, just an hour away; or bask in the beautiful, 2,000-acre campus in the Pinelands Natural Reserve just minutes from the ocean, natural labs perfect for Stockton's nationally recognized marine science and environmental studies programs.

Most Stockton students engage in independent study with a faculty mentor. Small classes allow for discussion, debate, and discovery—guided by Fulbright scholars, the most-published scientist in the world, and professors who care as much about teaching as research. Every major offers the personal attention and hands-on opportunities of a private college, yet at an affordable public price.

Rooted in a deep social and environmental consciousness, Stockton offers extensive service learning and human rights opportunities and has become an international leader in alternative energy research and conservation efforts.

Founded in 1969, the College was named for Richard Stockton, one of the New Jersey signers of the Declaration of Independence. A relatively young institution, Stockton already has a tradition of anticipating and leading changes that other universities and colleges follow. The College offers bachelor's, master's, and doctoral degree programs designed to challenge the brightest students. Stockton offers many of the academic, technological, and cultural advantages of a large university, but with the community spirit typical of smaller colleges.

Stockton enrolls over 8,000 students from New Jersey, the Mid-Atlantic states, and foreign countries, providing distinctive educational programs and experiences that extend learning beyond the classroom. The curriculum develops the students' analytic and creative capabilities and encourages individually planned courses of study.

Over 10,000 events, more than 130 clubs and organizations, Greek life, and academic and honor societies enhance the Stockton experience. Extensive intramural and club sports; NCAA Division III sports teams including men's baseball, basketball, lacrosse, and soccer, women's basketball, crew, field hockey, soccer, softball, tennis, and volleyball, and men's and women's cross-country and track and field; and a multipurpose Sports Center provide exercise for the body as well as the mind. Students who participate in cocurricular activities have their experiences documented through the ULTRA (Undergraduate Learning, Training, and Awareness) program, culminating in a co-curricular transcript.

A new 154,000-square-foot Campus Center provides a focal point for campus and hub for student, staff, and visitor activity. It is a one-stop-shop for conducting College business, bookstore purchases, student organization meetings, and larger all-College events, as well as performances and lectures in the 255-seat theater, a food court, coffee shop, game room, and plenty of space for students to meet and socialize.

The Residential Life Center offers yet another gathering space within two student housing areas. With large and small meeting rooms, convenience store, and computer lab, the center encourages activities for both organized and informal student groups.

Lakeside Lodge, in the apartment area, has a convenience store, snack bar, outdoor concert area, computer lab, multipurpose room for large programs, smaller meeting room, and a lakefront beach.

Stockton provides on-campus housing for almost 4,000 students in traditional residence halls, apartments, and for select students, at the Seaview, Stockton's four-star resort. All complexes are completely furnished and air conditioned, with cable TV, telephone service, and Internet access. Other students choose to live off campus in nearby townhouse and apartment complexes or winter rentals in one of the local seashore towns.

Stockton College is accredited by the Commission on Higher Education of the Middle States Association of Colleges and Schools. In addition, the social work program is accredited by the Council on Social Work Education; teacher education is approved by the New Jersey Department of Education, the National Association of State Directors of Teacher Education and Certification, and the Teacher Education Accreditation Council; nursing is accredited by the New Jersey Board of Nursing and the Commission on Collegiate Nursing Education; chemistry is accredited by the American Chemical Society; physical therapy is accredited by the Commission on Accreditation in Physical Therapy Education (CAPTE) of the American Physical Therapy Association; environmental health/public health is accredited by the National Environmental Health Sciences and Protection Accreditation Council; health administration is accredited by the Association of University Programs in Health Administration; occupational therapy is accredited by the Accreditation Council for Occupational Therapy Education (ACOTE) of the American Occupational Therapy Association (AOTA), and communication disorders (speech pathology/audiology) is accredited by the American Speech-Language-Hearing Association and Council on Academic Accreditation in Audiology and Speech-Language Pathology.

Location

Stockton is located on a stunning 2,000-acre campus in Galloway, New Jersey, nestled in the environmentally protected Pinelands National Reserve. The campus is just minutes west of Atlantic City and Jersey Shore beaches; an hour from Philadelphia and two hours from New York City. Courses are also offered online; at Stockton's Atlantic City campus (Carnegie Library Center); and at the College's educational centers in Hammonton and Manahawkin. Stockton owns the historic Seaview Resort and two championship golf courses in Absecon, New Jersey, allowing the College to expand its hospitality and tourism management program, enhance the college experience for students, and preserve an iconic landmark in the region. Collaboration with the Noyes Museum of Art in Oceanville provides enriching exhibitions and educational programs through the only fine art venue in southern New Jersey.

Concerts, art exhibitions, lectures, recreation, and sports on campus are complemented by nearby Jersey Shore resort destinations. Within a 15-minute drive, students find shopping, dining, and cultural attractions, as well as the entertainment of Atlantic City.

Majors and Degrees

The Bachelor of Arts, Bachelor of Fine Arts, and Bachelor of Science degrees are offered in studies in the arts (visual and performing), applied physics, biochemistry/molecular biology, biology, business (accounting, finance, management, marketing), chemistry, communication, computational science, computer science and information systems, criminal justice (forensic psychology/investigation, homeland security), economics, education, environmental science, geology, health science, historical studies, hospitality and tourism management, languages and culture studies, liberal studies, literature, marine science, mathematics, nursing, philosophy and religion, political science, psychology, public health, sociology and anthropology, social work, and sustainability.

Stockton's flexible curriculum allows students to prepare for professional careers, in dentistry, law, medicine, pharmacy, and veterinary medicine, while pursuing any major. The College also offers preprofessional preparation in communication disorders (speech therapy), occupational therapy, and physical therapy, with the master's in occupational therapy, master's in communication disorders, and the doctorate in physical therapy completed at Stockton.

Stockton has accelerated seven-year dual-degree articulation agreements with the University of Medicine and Dentistry of

New Jersey (Robert Wood Johnson Medical School, New Jersey Medical School, School of Osteopathic Medicine, New Jersey Dental School), the Pennsylvania College of Podiatric Medicine, the New York College of Podiatric Medicine, the New York State College of Optometry, and Rutgers School of Pharmacy. Stockton also has an articulation program with Cornell University for veterinary medicine and hospitality and tourism management, as well as five-year, dual-degree programs with New Jersey Institute of Technology and Rutgers University for students interested in engineering. A dual degree in pharmacy allows students to graduate from Stockton with a Bachelor of Science degree in biochemistry/molecular biology and finish their Doctor of Pharmacy degree at the Ernest Mario School of Pharmacy at Rutgers University.

Stockton offers the following graduate degrees: Doctor of Physical Therapy; Master of Arts in American studies, criminal justice, Holocaust and genocide studies, education, educational leadership, and instructional technology; Master of Business Administration; Master of Science in communication disorders, computational science, nursing, occupational therapy, and social work; and a Professional Science Master's in environmental science. Certificate and endorsement programs are offered in bilingual/bicultural education, ESL (English as a second language), family nurse practitioner, forensic psychology, health professions prep, homeland security, learning disabilities teacher consultant, middle school endorsement, New Jersey standard supervisor endorsement, preschool–grade 3 endorsement, reading specialist, special education, and student assistance coordinator.

Academic Programs

To earn a baccalaureate degree at Stockton, a student must satisfactorily complete a minimum of 128 semester credits. Degree programs include a combination of general studies and program (major field) studies. The Bachelor of Arts student must earn 64 credits in general studies; the Bachelor of Science student must earn 48. General studies courses are cross-disciplinary courses designed to introduce students to all major areas of the curriculum and to the intellectual skills necessary for success in college. Students must select courses from each major curricular area. The only required courses within general studies are the basic studies courses (up to three), but students may be exempt from these courses based on diagnostic testing. Bachelor of Arts students must earn 64 credits in major studies; Bachelor of Science students must earn 80. Requirements are carefully structured and emphasize sequences of specific courses.

Stockton students have the opportunity to influence what and how they learn by participating in the major decisions that shape their academic lives. The preceptorial system enables students to work on a personalized basis with an assigned faculty-staff preceptor in planning and evaluating individual courses of study and in exploring various career alternatives. Stockton's academic programs emphasize curricular organization and methods of instruction that promote independent learning and research, cross-disciplinary study, problem solving, and decision making through analysis and synthesis.

Off-Campus Programs

Off-campus experiences for credit are a key feature of most degree programs at Stockton. Internships, research projects, and field studies extend the principles and methods learned beyond the classroom. Study abroad, Semester at Sea, and an honors program are also available.

The Washington Internship Program gives students the opportunity to gain professional work experience. Stockton sends more students to the program than any other college or university outside the Washington, D.C., area.

Coordination of off-campus internship programs is provided by the academic offices as well as the Career Center; coordination of foreign study is provided by the coordinator of international education.

Academic Facilities

Stockton's academic complex serves as a living-learning center. Academic, recreational, and living spaces are mixed to promote interaction among students, faculty, and staff. The facilities, all constructed since 1971, include several large classroom/office buildings, library, lecture hall/auditorium, and a performing arts center.

The library contains more than 300,000 volumes, more than 2,600 periodical subscriptions, 280,000 government documents, more than 19,000 reels of microfilm, and about 68,000 other units of microtext. Media collections include films, slides, videotapes, audiotapes, CDs, and records. The library also houses a special New Jersey Pine Barrens collection; depository for federal, state, and Atlantic City documents; and the Sara and Sam Schoffer Holocaust Resource Center.

Costs

Costs for the 2011–12 academic year were $11,963 for in-state students and $18,170 for out-of-state students (flat-rate tuition up to 40 credits per year, fees); on-campus housing and board were $10,580 (double-occupancy residence room, Ultimate 19 meal plan). Books, supplies, transportation, and personal items are extra. Costs are subject to change.

Financial Aid

Financial aid is available as scholarships, grants, loans, and work-study. Need-based financial aid is awarded according to student and family need. Students seeking financial aid should file the Free Application for Federal Student Aid (FAFSA) by March 1. Merit-based aid is awarded to recognize academic excellence. Stockton offers aggressive and generous scholarship opportunities for academically talented freshmen and transfer students based on standardized test scores, grade point average, high school class rank, and college-level performance.

Faculty

Stockton's faculty members represent highly diverse academic, training, and social backgrounds, with 95 percent holding terminal degrees in their field. Faculty members work closely with students through small class sizes and individual research opportunities and share with students and staff members the initiative and responsibility for social, recreational, and cultural programs and activities. This arrangement supports the exceptional rapport and learning relationships among students and faculty members.

Student Government

The RSCNJ Student Senate consists of 25 student members. The advisory council is made up of 1 faculty member and 2 staff members. Student senators hold office for one year, with elections held every spring. Among other duties, the Student Senate reviews and makes recommendations on budgets of funded student organizations and acts as the official representative of the student body.

Admission Requirements

Stockton operates on a rolling admission basis. The deadline for fall admission is May 1 for most freshmen. Students should check the Web site for special program deadlines. Transfer student deadline for fall admission is June 1. Spring term (January) admission deadline for all students is December 1. Students may apply for admission to the fall or spring term and are notified of the admission decision as soon as their application file has been completed and reviewed. Freshman applicants must submit ACT and/or SAT scores. All students must submit official transcripts from all educational institutions attended. Admission is selective.

Early acceptance may be offered for highly qualified high school students in their junior year. Armed Services veterans and those who have been away from formal education for some time are also invited to apply for admission. Stockton makes no distinction between part- and full-time students in offering admission.

Stockton offers special admission to a limited number of New Jersey students from educationally and financially disadvantaged backgrounds. Students wishing to explore this opportunity should contact the Admissions Office.

Application and Information

For more information, prospective students should contact:

Dean of Enrollment Management
The Richard Stockton College of New Jersey
P.O. Box 195
Galloway, New Jersey 08205-9441
Phone: 609-652-4261
　　　 866-RSC-2885 (toll-free)
Fax: 609-626-5541
E-mail: admissions@stockton.edu
Web site: http://www.stockton.edu/admissions
　　　　 http://www.facebook.com/richardstocktoncollege
　　　　 http://twitter.com/#!/Stockton_edu

RICHMOND, THE AMERICAN INTERNATIONAL UNIVERSITY IN LONDON
LONDON, ENGLAND

The University

Richmond, The American International University in London, prepares men and women to serve with purpose and generosity in an interdependent and multicultural world. Richmond offers a strong academic program with many choices of fields of study, an exceptional faculty, superb campus life, and fellow students from all over the world. In the United States, Richmond is accredited by the Commission on Higher Education of the Middle States Association of Colleges and Schools, a regional accrediting body recognized by the U.S. Department of Education. Richmond is accredited in the United Kingdom by the Open University and holds related degree validation. The University's undergraduate and graduate degrees are designated by the United Kingdom's Department of Education and Employment. The University is a comprehensive American liberal arts and professional university. In addition to the undergraduate degree programs described below, Richmond offers Master of Arts degrees in art history and visual culture, and in international relations.

Freshmen and sophomores study and live at the Richmond campus, 7 miles from central London. Junior and senior years are spent at the Kensington campus in one of London's most beautiful residential and historic districts. As part of their four-year B.A. degree program, students may spend a semester or a year studying at one of the University's two international study centers in Florence and Rome, Italy. Richmond currently enrolls over 1,000 students from more than 100 countries. Approximately 38 percent of the degree students are from Europe and the United Kingdom, 4 percent are from Asia, 6 percent are from the Middle East, 6 percent of the student body represents the continent of Africa, and 1 percent is from South America. The remaining 45 percent of the degree students are from North America. About 350 study-abroad students from various universities are enrolled for a semester or a year at Richmond.

Small classes, averaging 17–20 students, enable students to receive personal attention from professors in a supportive environment. The curriculum and academic advising system are structured to enable students to choose courses that provide broad knowledge, relevant skills, and an understanding of the world's many cultures and nations.

Richmond students supplement academic programs with activities that complement and balance the classroom experience. Many extracurricular and cocurricular programs are available to students, including student government, the Green Project, Model United Nations, Amnesty International, RTV (Richmond Television), Top of the Hill music club, and sports and business clubs.

Location

The Richmond Hill campus in the London suburb of Richmond offers a variety of entertainment, shopping, cultural, and recreational opportunities. Only yards from the University campus is Richmond Park, more than 2,200 acres of rolling hills and lush woodland, where one can ride horses, play tennis, jog, or simply relax. The journey from Richmond into Central London takes approximately 30 minutes using public transportation.

The Kensington campus is located in the heart of London's Borough of Kensington, which has fine museums, libraries, theatres, concert halls, historic buildings, and well-known cultural and educational resources. The University takes full advantage of London's cultural and social resources through selected academic courses, work experience placements with multinational corporations, and special visits to museums, art galleries, theatres, and concert halls.

Majors and Degrees

Richmond operates its academic program on the American system. The University offers the four-year Bachelor of Arts (B.A.) degree in fifteen majors, with a further choice of seventeen minors. Majors offered by the University are art, design, and media; business administration (entrepreneurship, finance, international business, marketing); communications; development economics, development studies; economics; financial economics; history; international journalism and media; international relations; political science; and psychology.

Academic Programs

In order to graduate with the dual-validated U.S. and U.K. degree [B.A./B.A. (Honors)], students must earn a minimum of 120 credits. Usually, this means taking a full load for four years, or eight semesters. Within these 120 credits, students must complete all course requirements for their majors. Students must also meet the University's Language Proficiency and General Education requirements. In addition, valuable work experience for credit is offered through the International Internship program. Recent placements have been at the International Herald Tribune, General Electric, The House of Commons, CNN, the United Nations, Lloyds Bank, the Museum of London, and Sony Music Corporation.

Credit is also awarded for Advanced Placement tests (6 credits for each subject grade of 3, 4, or 5); a grade of A, B, or C on the A Level exams is awarded 9 credits (6 for D or E). Credit is also awarded for the International Baccalaureate, the Baccalauréat de l'Enseignement du Second Degré (France), the Abitur/Reifzuegnis (Germany), the Diploma di Maturità (Italy), and the School Leaving Diploma (Denmark, Finland, Norway, and Sweden).

The fall semester begins in late August and ends in mid-December. The spring semester begins in mid-January and runs through mid-May. Two sessions of summer school run from mid-May to mid-June and mid-June to mid-July.

Off-Campus Programs

Students may complement their studies in London with a semester, year, or summer at one of two international study centers. The centers are located in Florence and Rome, Italy, and each offer an intensive study of the language and culture of the country. The Florence Study Center emphasizes studio and fine arts. The Rome Study Center offers courses in Italian language and culture, art history, economics, and political science.

Academic Facilities

Information technology is integrated into the curriculum in ways that are natural to the discipline under study. Supporting this are eight student computer laboratories with more than 140 current-specification computers, which connect to the Internet and are networked for student, faculty, and administrative use. Wireless network access is also available on campus.

COLLEGE CLOSE-UPS

Richmond's libraries support the courses taught at each campus. Students may use either campus library. The libraries house over 95,000 items including books, DVDs, music CDs, company annual reports, and student theses. In addition, the libraries have subscriptions to a number of journal and magazine titles, along with a variety of national and international newspapers. Richmond students also have access to the many specialized libraries within the London area.

Costs

Tuition for the 2012–13 academic year is $27,000. Room and board is $13,740. Personal expenses, books and supplies, clothing, recreation, and travel costs also need to be factored in as these are not included in tuition and room and board fees.

Financial Aid

Merit-based scholarships are awarded annually to students of high academic ability. Financial aid for U.S. citizens includes Federal Direct Stafford Student Loans and Federal PLUS loans. All U.S. citizens must file the Free Application for Federal Student Aid (FAFSA) to qualify for federal loans. The FAFSA school code for Richmond is G10594. Students should contact the admissions office for details regarding application procedures for scholarships and financial aid.

Faculty

The student-faculty ratio of 11:1 enables optimum interaction and individualized instructional assistance. The 92 faculty members (44 full-time, 48 part-time) have professional degrees from top European and American universities such as Harvard, the University of California (Berkeley), the University of Michigan, Cambridge, Oxford, the London School of Economics, the Royal College of Art, and the University of Bonn.

Student Government

The Richmond Student Union acts as a resource for all students, student organizations, and clubs to voice their opinions and ideas. The Student Union functions as a network between the student body and the administration. Using student ideas, it holds events and seeks to feature student talent while enhancing the overall University experience. The Student Union is ongoing in its development and thus offers possibilities for students to shape and change it. It is an organization directed by students for students and is structured to provide flexibility as well as the opportunity for all students to become involved.

Admission Requirements

Applicants are admitted on the basis of academic performance, references, intended major, and career interests. The required autobiographical essay is of paramount importance. Applicants to Richmond have usually completed a total of twelve years of primary and secondary school with a minimum grade of C+ (2.5 out of 4.0) in the American high school grading system, or its equivalent. British system students should have attained a minimum of five GCSE passes (grades of A, B, or C) in acceptable academic subjects, one of which must be mathematics or science. Equivalent qualifications gained under other educational systems are also considered for the purpose of admission.

Students must submit a completed application form and application fee, an essay, transcripts of all secondary and postsecondary school work, and one confidential letter of academic recommendation. SAT or ACT scores are optional.

The ATP code for Richmond is 0823L. The ACT code is 5244. Evidence of proficiency in the English language is required from students whose first language is not English or who did not attend English-speaking schools. Standardized test scores, such as the TOEFL or the ALIGU, or completion of recognized examinations, such as GCSE, Pitman, RSA, or lower Cambridge, are considered in assessing students' language capability.

Richmond admits students on a rolling basis, and applicants are encouraged to submit their application at the earliest opportunity. All documents in languages other than English must be accompanied by official translations. Applicants are usually notified of a decision within two to three weeks.

Application and Information

An application for admission and further information may be obtained by contacting the appropriate admissions office.

Applicants residing in the United States should contact:
Director of U.S. Admissions
U.S. Office of Admissions
Richmond, The American International University in London
343 Congress Street, Suite 3100
Boston, Massachusetts 02210-1214
Phone: 617-450-5617
Fax: 617-450-5601
E-mail: usadmissions@richmond.ac.uk
Web site: http://www.richmond.ac.uk

Applicants residing in all other countries outside of the U.S. should contact:
Director of Admissions
UK Office of Admissions
Richmond, The American International University in London
Queens Road, Richmond
Surrey TW10 6JP
England
Phone: 44-20-8332-9000
Fax: 44-20-8332-1596
E-mail: enrol@richmond.ac.uk
Web site: http://www.richmond.ac.uk

Students can earn a dual-validated U.S. and UK degree at Richmond, The American International University in London.

RIPON COLLEGE
RIPON, WISCONSIN

The College

Together with the other members of its tightly knit learning community, Ripon students often feel as if they learn more deeply, live more fully, and achieve more success. There are more opportunities to be involved, lead, speak out, make a difference, and explore new interests than at many colleges many times its size. Through collaborative learning, group living, teamwork, and networking, students tap into the power of a community where all work together to ensure their success, at Ripon and beyond. The best residential liberal arts colleges strive to be true learning communities like Ripon. Ripon succeeds better than most, because the enrollment of just under 1,000 students is perfect for fostering connections inside and outside the classroom. Students flourish in this environment of mutual respect, where shared values are elevated and diverse ideas are valued. Students who are seeking academic challenge and want to benefit from an environment of personal attention and support should take a closer look at Ripon. In classes that average 20 students, professors are able to know the students and their strengths and capabilities extraordinarily well. They tailor course work to make sure students are always challenged to perform at the top of their game, yet they are always ready to provide extra support when needed. Faculty members collaborate with students on research projects, suggest independent-study topics, and connect them with internships and other active learning experiences.

A Ripon education can take graduates anywhere. A student could study psychology and play basketball and then become a seven-time Grammy winner like jazz singer Al Jarreau, '62; guide the space shuttle into orbit like Jeff Bantle, '80, a chief flight director with NASA; or become an international opera star like Gail Dobish, '76. A student could set records in medical science like neonatologist Dr. John Muraskas, '78, who is on record for saving the world's smallest premature baby, or a student might end up studying at Oxford University as a Rhodes Scholar like Zach Morris '02, who also found time to play touch football with former President Bill Clinton and spend an evening at Buckingham Palace with the Queen.

The list of student clubs and organizations is ever changing, reflecting students' ever-changing interests. A recent addition is FUERZA Alliance, designed to educate students about Latino cultures and to provide services to the Spanish-speaking community of Ripon.

Every day at Ripon is packed with a host of activities such as concerts (there are eight vocal and instrumental groups that perform regularly on campus, as well as many individual student and faculty recitals). The Caestecker Fine Arts Series and the Chamber Music at Ripon Series annually bring national performers to the campus. The Theatre Department sponsors two major productions annually, plus a series of student-directed one-act plays. The most recent Ripon Film Festival (an annual showcase for independent films from around the country) included the premiere of a feature-length horror film written, directed by, and starring a Ripon student.

Ripon's NCAA Division III intercollegiate teams compete in the Midwest Conference. Men's varsity sports include baseball, basketball, cross-country, cycling, football, golf, indoor and outdoor track and field, soccer, swimming and diving, and tennis. Women's varsity sports include basketball, cross-country, cycling, dance, golf, indoor and outdoor track and field, soccer, softball, swimming and diving, and tennis.

Location

Located on 250 tree-lined, rolling acres adjacent to downtown Ripon, the campus looks and feels like a college should. Ripon's twenty-six first-rate buildings are a striking combination of historic (ten campus structures listed on the National Register of Historic Places) and modern architecture.

Majors and Degrees

Majors include anthropology, art, art history, biology, business administration, chemistry, chemistry/biology, communication, computer science, economics, educational studies, English, environmental sciences, exercise science, foreign languages, French, German, global studies, history, Latin American area studies, mathematics, music, philosophy, physics, politics and government, psychobiology, psychology, religion, sociology/anthropology, Spanish, and theater. Programs are also available in leadership studies, sports medicine/athletic training, and women's studies.

Preprofessional programs include dentistry, journalism, law and government, library and information science, medicine, ministry, optometry, physical therapy, and veterinary medicine.

Dual-degree programs include allied health sciences/medical technology, engineering, forestry, and social welfare.

Certification programs include education certification, early childhood, elementary, elementary/middle school, secondary, secondary/middle, music K–12, and physical education K–12.

Academic Programs

Ripon's liberal arts curriculum is designed to introduce students to a wide variety of disciplines. About 40 percent of the students complete double or triple majors, whereas some create special self-designed majors. Excellent communications skills—written and oral—as well as critical-thinking and problem-solving skills are the hallmark of a Ripon education, regardless of major. In addition, the leadership studies program and the newly established ethical leadership program provide a strong foundation for leadership skills. An Army ROTC program is also available.

Off-Campus Programs

Ripon offers more than forty different off-campus programs of varying lengths to choose from, each one officially sanctioned by and affiliated with Ripon. Although most programs are connected with a major or minor program, all are open to every Ripon student, regardless of major.

U.S. programs include Chicago Urban Studies Semester, Fisk University–Ripon Exchange Program, Newberry Seminar in the Humanities, Oak Ridge Science Semester, Washington Semester, and Woods Hole Marine Biology.

International programs include Bonn, Germany, Program; Budapest Semester; Central European Studies Program in

the Czech Republic; Costa Rica; Cross-Cultural Study Center in Seville, Spain; Florence Program; France and Spain; Global Studies Program in Turkey; India Studies; Japan Study; London and Florence Program in the Arts; Madrid Program; Montpellier, France; Paris, France; Ripon and York St. John Exchange; Russia Program; Sea Education Association (marine biology abroad); Sea Semester at Woods Hole; Swansea Program; Tanzania; Toledo, Spain; and University of Wales in Bangor.

Academic Facilities

Constant additions and improvements, like a recent multimillion-dollar apartment-style residence hall, the renovation and classroom expansion of Todd Wehr Hall, and upgrades to upperclass residence halls, the library, the bookstore, dining facilities, and a coffee shop, maintain Ripon's ability to meet the needs of today and tomorrow. Technology services include high-speed Internet and e-mail, telephone, and video communication. Intranet and Internet services are accessible from systems located throughout the College. The campuswide network provides access from every room, and several wireless hot spots in key areas let students access the world without being tied down.

The library staff provides friendly, efficient circulation, reference, instruction, and interlibrary loan services that aid in research. The library also houses the College archives, a computer lab, and more than a dozen online databases. Library holdings include 164,000 volumes, 800 current periodicals, and microfilms.

The C. J. Rodman Center for the Arts is home to a theater with a state-of-the-art computerized lighting system, a recital hall with one of only fifty existing Bedient organs, an art gallery, and a sculpture garden.

The J. M. Storzer Center includes an Olympic-size pool, a first-class gymnasium, tennis and racquetball courts, a dance studio, training facilities, and a weight room. The outdoor playing fields and courts are among the best in their class. In addition, a large, modern exercise facility was recently added in the main student residence area.

Costs

Tuition is $29,835, room and board are $8545, and fees are $275, for a total cost of $38,655.

Financial Aid

Ripon has been consistently recognized as a best value by all of the national ranking organizations. More than 90 percent of Ripon students receive some form of merit-based scholarship and/or need-based grants and loans.

Ripon recognizes and rewards students' success in high school with its institutionally funded scholarships, based not only on academic merit but also on special achievements in other areas, such as the creative arts. The scholarships range from $1000 to full tuition. Ripon participates in all federal and state need-based financial aid programs. The financial aid counselors work individually with students and their families to investigate every possible financial resource for which they are eligible.

Faculty

Ripon has 57 full-time and 25 part-time faculty members. Ninety-seven percent of the full-time faculty members have Ph.D.'s.

Admission Requirements

Ripon enrolls students who are expected to contribute to and benefit from the academic and residential programs provided. Ripon does not discriminate on the basis of gender, sexual orientation, race, color, age, religion, national or ethnic origin, or disability in the administration of its educational policies, admission practices, scholarship and loan programs, and athletic and other College-administered programs.

Application and Information

The faculty committee on academic standards establishes the criteria for admission. The school considers a variety of factors, including secondary school record, standardized test scores (SAT or ACT), recommendations, a written essay, and extracurricular or community service activities. Ripon's admission process reflects the personal attention students can expect to receive during their college careers, and applicants are encouraged to provide any additional information they consider helpful.

For further information, students should contact:

Leigh D. Mlodzik
Dean of Admission
Ripon College
300 Seward Street
P.O. Box 248
Ripon, Wisconsin 54971-0248
Phone: 800-947-4766 (toll-free)
E-mail: adminfo@ripon.edu
Web site: http://www.ripon.edu

Ripon College students and their families celebrate commencement on the lawn of Harwood Memorial Union.

RIVIER COLLEGE
NASHUA, NEW HAMPSHIRE

The College

Rivier College, a private Catholic college founded in 1933, has gained a reputation for academic excellence in more than forty programs. The College has adapted to changing needs by developing liberal arts/career-oriented programs designed to prepare graduates in many fields.

Rivier's School of Undergraduate Studies enrolls approximately 1,500 students, including 900 full-time day students. With a 15:1 student-faculty ratio, day students have plenty of opportunities to connect with faculty and become active members of the academic community.

Most full-time undergraduate day students are of traditional age: between 18 and 22 years old. Though the majority comes from New England, Rivier attracts students from states around the country, including Florida, California, and Delaware. International students represent countries in Africa, Asia, Europe, the Middle East, and South America. Students who live on campus reside in four modern residence halls. Most rooms are doubles, with some triples, quads, and singles available. Rivier also provides substance-free housing in Presentation Hall. The newest hall offers suite-style living, with several double and triple rooms sharing a kitchenette and common area. The Dion Center houses the dining room, the commuter lounge, the mailroom, a campus store, student development offices, and meeting rooms. All students are permitted to have cars on the campus.

The Office of Student Development, the Student Government Association, and more than twenty-five student clubs and organizations provide a calendar of social, cultural, and recreational activities, including concerts, live entertainment, films, and sporting events. The College and student organizations frequently organize outings, including trips to Boston and New York. Students also enjoy a variety of performances by the Rivier Theater Company.

Rivier offers an orientation for new students to introduce them to the College's wide array of services. Academic advisers, staff at the Writing and Resource Center, and peer tutors help students meet their academic goals. The Health Services Center and Counseling Center ensure students' physical and emotional well-being. A full-time chaplain and Campus Ministry team coordinate spiritual activities and service opportunities, while a comprehensive career development service helps students prepare for employment after graduation.

Rivier offers a variety of team and individual sports, including NCAA Division III men's baseball, basketball, cross-country, lacrosse, soccer, and volleyball; and women's basketball, cross-country, field hockey, lacrosse, soccer, softball, and volleyball. The men's volleyball team has been nationally ranked every year since 2001. The Muldoon Health and Fitness Center is home to Rivier's varsity athletics and to many intramural sports and fitness activities, including volleyball, floor hockey, basketball, weight training, aerobics, self-defense, and more. The campus also has soccer and softball fields, as well as a beach volleyball court and cross-country trail. Student athletes and others can take advantage of an on-campus rehabilitation clinic offering free injury assessment, physical and occupational therapy, and athletic training.

Location

Nashua (population 87,000) is located in southern New Hampshire. The city of Boston lies within easy access 40 miles to the south. Local access to public transportation provides for easy travel to and from the campus. Recreational activities abound year-round at nearby lakes and ski areas, in the White Mountains to the north, and at the seacoast, just an hour's drive to the east.

Majors and Degrees

Rivier College awards Bachelor of Arts and Bachelor of Science degrees in the following areas of concentration: art (studio art, graphic design, and photography and digital media), biology (allied health and environmental science) and biology education, business, communications (advertising/public relations, journalism, photojournalism, scriptwriting, video production, and Web design/online publishing), criminal justice, education (early childhood/special education, elementary education/special education, and human development/interdisciplinary), English and English education, finance, history, human development, international studies, liberal studies, marketing, mathematics and mathematics education, modern languages (modern languages education and Spanish), nursing, political science, psychology, social studies education, and sociology. Five-year combined bachelor's/master's degree programs are available in business, English (teacher certification), and psychology. The College offers preprofessional programs in law, dentistry, medicine, and veterinary medicine. Associate degrees are offered in art, business management, early childhood education, liberal studies, and nursing.

Academic Programs

Rivier College takes special pride in its curriculum, which offers both professional studies and liberal arts to prepare students for a fast-changing, highly technological society. The broad-based curriculum focuses on preparing students for challenging and rewarding careers and furthering their personal growth. Core curriculum requirements vary slightly depending on the degree to be obtained, but generally include courses in English, mathematics and/or natural sciences, modern language and literature, philosophy, religious studies, social science, and Western civilization. No fewer than ten courses must be taken in the major field. Students may choose electives that suit their personal interests and professional goals. The bachelor's degree requires a minimum of 120 credits with a grade point average of at least 2.0. For the associate degree, the student must complete a minimum of 60 credits with a grade point average of at least 2.0.

All departments encourage qualified students to pursue internships in their field of study during their junior or senior year. Education specialists student teach in local schools. Nursing majors complete clinical rotations in health-care facilities throughout southern New Hampshire and northern Massachusetts. History, law, and political science majors may work in a law office, business, legal-assistance agency, or government agency. Sociology and psychology majors work with local social service agencies. English and communications majors work in public relations, broadcasting, or corporate communications positions. Art majors work in advertising or graphic design or at local galleries. Business majors work in marketing, management, and technology.

Honors awards include placement on the dean's list, membership in Kappa Gamma Pi, listing in *Who's Who Among Students in American Universities and Colleges*, listing in *The National Dean's List*, and degrees with honors. Academically talented students may also apply to the four-year honors program.

The college year is divided into two 15-week semesters, with first-semester examinations held before Christmas recess. Students usually take five courses each semester. Academic credit may be granted to incoming freshmen on the basis of scores on Advanced Placement tests and CLEP examinations. Students may also "challenge" courses and receive credit by special examination.

Off-Campus Programs

Through Rivier College's membership in the New Hampshire College and University Council, a sixteen-member consortium of senior and two-year colleges, Rivier students may register for courses at any of the member colleges and receive transfer credits.

Academic Facilities

Academic facilities include Memorial Hall, which houses fourteen classrooms, faculty offices, a lecture hall, a fully equipped digital imaging studio, a communications lab offering the most recent software and video/sound editing equipment, a behavioral science lab, the studio of community television station tv13 Nashua (WYCN), and art department facilities that include a gallery, a slide library, and studios. The Academic Computer Center features up to sixty-eight workstations with a full range of cutting-edge software and Internet/e-mail access. Regina Library houses more than 100,000 volumes and provides access to more than 3 million volumes in twelve area libraries, as well as online access to licensed databases in virtually every academic subject. The Writing and Resource Center offers assistance from professional writing consultants as well as student tutors. Other academic facilities include nursing and science laboratories; a physical assessment lab and nursing skills simulation lab, which provide nursing students with practical experience using blood pressure cuffs, ophthalmoscopes, IV pumps, patient simulators, and more; the McLean Center for Finance and Economics; the BAE Student Research Lab; a clinical psychology lab; electronic classrooms offering multimedia learning tools; and the Education Center, which houses an eight-classroom Early Childhood Center, observation rooms, and an educational resource center.

Costs

Tuition and fees for the academic year 2011–12 were $25,410; room and board, $9522; and books and supplies, approximately $700. Students should expect to pay a $100 activities fee and a $25 registration fee each semester.

Financial Aid

Financial aid is awarded on the basis of the financial need of the student and family. Approximately 98 percent of Rivier's full-time undergraduate students receive financial aid from the College or from government or private sources. Federal aid includes Federal Pell Grants, Federal Supplemental Educational Opportunity Grants, Federal Perkins Loans, Federal Stafford Student Loans, the Federal PLUS loan program, and the Federal Work-Study Program. To be considered for financial aid, a student must file the Free Application for Federal Student Aid (FAFSA) with the federal government as soon as possible after January 1 for the coming year. FAFSA results should be on file with the College Financial Aid Office prior to March 1 for the following academic year. Each applicant is assessed individually to determine the best combination of grant, work, scholarship, and loan amounts to meet the need of the student. The College awards more than $6 million in merit-based scholarships and grants annually, ranging in value from $1000 to full tuition. For more information, students should contact the Office of Financial Aid.

Faculty

The College employs 71 full-time faculty members. The full-time student–faculty ratio is 15:1. Part-time instructors in specialized areas are working professionals who bring current knowledge and expertise in their field to their classes. All classes are taught by faculty members, and department chairs serve as academic advisers to students in their major programs.

Student Government

Every full-time day student automatically becomes a member of the Student Government Association (SGA) upon registration and payment of the student activity fee. The main goals of the SGA are to stimulate active participation in all College functions, to establish and maintain effective channels of communication among members of the College community and the community at large, and to foster a mutual trust, encourage a spirit of cooperation, and initiate new endeavors. The SGA also supervises student clubs and organizations and oversees their finances. The SGA Executive Board serves as the channel of communication through which the views of the students on institutional policies reach the College administration.

Admission Requirements

Applicants for admission should ordinarily have completed, in an accredited high school, a minimum of 16 academic units, including 4 in English, 2 in a modern foreign language, 3 in mathematics, 2 in social science, 2 in science, and 3 in electives. The most successful candidates are in the upper half of their class, with at least a B average. Combined SAT scores average 1410–1500. A personal interview is strongly recommended but not required.

Rivier welcomes applications from qualified transfer candidates from accredited institutions, as well as applications from international students. Transfer students must forward transcripts of all previous college work and a high school transcript. International students must fulfill the requirements for general admission; they may also be required to submit Test of English as a Foreign Language (TOEFL) scores. Deferred admission may be granted to students who wish to postpone entrance for up to one year, provided they have not been enrolled full-time at another postsecondary institution.

Application and Information

Applications must be accompanied by a nonrefundable $25 application fee, SAT scores, one letter of recommendation, and a high school transcript. The School of Undergraduate Studies employs a system of rolling admission that allows qualified students to be admitted approximately one month after their application is completed. Transfers should apply by June 1 for fall admission and by December 1 for spring admission. Those applying for financial aid should observe the March 1 deadline. Interviews are arranged through the Admissions Office. Students may apply online at the College's Web site.

For an application or additional information, please contact:

Office of Undergraduate Admissions
Rivier College
420 South Main Street
Nashua, New Hampshire 03060
Phone: 603-897-8507
      800-44-RIVIER (toll-free)
Fax: 603-891-1799
E-mail: admissions@rivier.edu
Web site: http://www.rivier.edu

Students enjoy Rivier's great location in the heart of New England—approximately an hour's drive from Boston, the mountains, and the seacoast.

ROBERT MORRIS UNIVERSITY

CHICAGO, ARLINGTON HEIGHTS, BENSENVILLE, DUPAGE, ELGIN, LAKE COUNTY, ORLAND PARK, PEORIA, SCHAUMBURG, AND SPRINGFIELD, ILLINOIS

The Experience University.
ROBERT MORRIS UNIVERSITY
ILLINOIS

The University

As an accredited, private, not-for-profit institution, Robert Morris University (RMU) grants associate, bachelor's, and master's degrees to more than 3,000 students each year. Its mission is to offer professional, career-focused education in a collegiate setting to diverse communities. Besides associate degrees in twelve different fields of study, RMU awards the Bachelor of Business Administration degree with concentrations in accounting, economics, health/fitness management, hospitality management, information systems management, and management; the Bachelor of Applied Science degree in graphic design; the Bachelor of Applied Science degree in computer studies; and the Bachelor of Professional Studies degree with concentrations in architectural technology, advanced culinary arts, applied health science, law office administration, organizational writing, and Web development. Master's degrees offered by RMU include the Master of Business Administration with concentrations in accounting, finance, human resource management, and management; the Master of Information; and the Master of Management with specializations in higher education administration and health-care administration. RMU is accredited by the Higher Learning Commission and is a member of the North Central Association of Colleges and Schools (230 South LaSalle Street, Suite 7-500, Chicago, Illinois 60604-1413; 312-263-0456; http://www.ncahigherlearningcommission.org).

The history of Robert Morris University dates back to the founding of the Moser School, one of the outstanding independent business schools in Chicago, in 1913. Robert Morris University also has origins in Illinois at the site of the former Carthage College. Here, Robert Morris University was chartered and offered associate degrees in both liberal and vocational arts from 1965 to 1974. With the acquisition of the Moser School in 1975, RMU expanded to include business and allied health programs. The University now provides students with a choice of ten locations: Chicago, Arlington Heights, Bensenville, DuPage, Elgin, Orland Park, Lake County, Peoria, Schaumburg, and Springfield, Illinois.

RMU offers programs in the School of Business Administration, the College of Nursing & Health Studies, the Institute of Technology & Media, the Institute of Culinary Arts, the Institute of Art & Design, the Institute for Experiential Learning, the College of Liberal Arts, and the Morris Graduate School of Management. Each of these divisions uses the most modern computer technology. Acquisition of such technology is imperative to providing real-world educational experiences that are relevant to the evolving workplace.

RMU's unique five-quarter system is designed for continuous learning. It enables students to accelerate their education, completing a bachelor's degree in less than four years and an associate degree in eighteen months. In addition, Robert Morris University is the fifth-largest private undergraduate college in Illinois, and its tuition rate is among the lowest of Illinois' private colleges and universities.

The student body of approximately 7,120 is a cross-cultural mix representative of the communities served. Each student works with a team of advisers and instructors in an effort to achieve educational and career goals. The records of the University's students and graduates are the best indicators of what a prospective student can expect. More than 85 percent of RMU students graduate from the bachelor's degree program they begin, compared to significantly lower percentages at other private and public colleges and universities.

Robert Morris University is a member of the National Association of Intercollegiate Athletics (NAIA) and the Chicagoland Collegiate Athletic Conference (CCAC), Division II. RMU athletic teams compete in top-level facilities located near each campus. The University offers men's and women's basketball, club hockey, cross-country, golf, soccer, and swimming. It also offers men's baseball and women's bowling, dance, lacrosse, softball, tennis, and volleyball.

Housing options are available within a short distance of the main campus at Fornelli Hall and the University Center, which provide a wealth of amenities, shopping, entertainment, and events that bring the community together in apartment-style student living.

Location

Located in the heart of Chicago's bustling cultural and financial districts, the University's main campus is minutes from all that Chicago offers, including the Chicago Board of Trade, Art Institute, Field Museum, Merchandise Mart, lakefront, sports arenas, theaters, and all forms of public transportation. The Chicago campus is readily accessible from all parts of the city and suburbs by bus lines and trains. Parking is available in the immediate vicinity. Robert Morris University is across the street from the renowned Harold Washington Public Library.

The Bensenville campus opened to better serve the residents of western Cook and DuPage Counties and to meet the demands of employers in the area. The recently expanded Orland Park campus now includes a technology center with the latest computer facilities available to industry and education and is approximately 30 miles southwest of Chicago. It is accessible via public transportation and I-80 and I-55, which run parallel on the south and north ends of the campus, respectively. Orland Park is becoming a corporate center of the southwest Chicago suburbs, offering students opportunity for professional growth through internships and employment.

The DuPage campus opened on the border between Naperville and Aurora and serves students as well as employers along the East-West High Tech Corridor—the heart of rapid technological development and close to a wide range of employers. The RMU Institute of Culinary Arts started at the DuPage campus and grew so significantly and quickly, the program expanded to the main campus in downtown Chicago and Orland Park.

The Springfield campus represents the first step of the University's commitment to serve central Illinois. This campus has also expanded to a second building at the same location due to expansion of programs and increases in enrollment. The RMU presence in Illinois has further extended to a campus in Peoria, with a busy downtown location, and Waukegan, serving the northern region of Illinois. The most recent additions are the graduate studies center in Schaumburg and the undergraduate campus in Elgin.

All RMU campuses provide students with access to the unlimited variety of business services and enhance the students' understanding of the world of work, the employment process, and an appreciation for the attributes of each community.

Majors and Degrees

The Bachelor of Business Administration degree at Robert Morris University offers concentrations in accounting, economics, health/fitness management, hospitality management, information systems management, and management. The Bachelor of Applied Science degree in graphic design offers concentrations in graphic arts and digital video; the Bachelor of Professional Studies degree offers concentrations in architectural technology, advanced culinary arts, applied health sciences, Web development, organizational writing, and law office management; and the Bachelor of Applied Science degree in computer studies offers concentrations in systems integration and networking. The Associate of Applied Science degree is awarded in business administration, CADD (architectural/mechanical), computer networking, culinary arts, fitness and exercise, graphic design, interior space planning and design, medical assisting, nursing, paralegal studies, pharmacy technology, and surgical technology.

More than twenty-six transfer agreements have been established between RMU and community colleges, allowing students who have earned associate degrees at community colleges in the state of Illinois to complete their bachelor's degrees at RMU by transferring in as a junior.

Academic Programs

The University's academic calendar consists of five quarters, each of which is ten weeks long. The program of study is designed so that

students can complete their course work and enter their careers in the shortest time possible.

By concentrating on the specialized subjects related to the student's chosen career field, the University's curricula provide students with the skills and knowledge necessary to enter the job market. Each major consists of courses prescribed by the University to lead to this objective. An associate degree requires at least 92 quarter hours of credit, with a minimum of 36 hours of credit in general education in the areas of communications, humanities, math and science, and social and behavioral science. A minimum of 52 quarter hours of credit are required in career courses, and the remaining hours are electives split between general education and career courses. A bachelor's degree requires a minimum of 188 quarter hours of credit.

Robert Morris University offers students the opportunity to gain experience in their majors and improve their skills through internships and externships. Internships offer many educational and professional benefits and provide students with the opportunity to earn academic credit for participating in a career-specific work experience.

Off-Campus Programs

Robert Morris University offers students the opportunity to study abroad in Florence, Italy; Hamburg, Germany; London, England; and Paris, France.

Academic Facilities

General-purpose classrooms are Internet and multimedia ready. Students have ample study, practice, and leisure space on campus. The Student Center at RMU's Chicago Campus has been recognized by *American School & University* as an outstanding design. Specialized laboratories are available for the systems integration, surgical technology, interior space planning and design, and culinary arts programs. The technology-based library has online capabilities that connect the University's various campuses. Students have access via the Internet to advanced research tools, sizable collections of reference and resource volumes, and periodical subscriptions.

Costs

Robert Morris University has one of the lowest tuition rates of any baccalaureate degree–granting private college in the state. Tuition for 2011–12 was $7200 per quarter. Book and supply costs vary by major from $400 to $600 per quarter. Housing and program fees are also applicable.

Financial Aid

Robert Morris University participates in the following federal and state financial aid programs: the Federal Pell Grant, Illinois Monetary Award (SSIG/IMA), Federal Supplemental Educational Opportunity Grant (FSEOG), Federal Stafford Student Loan, Federal Perkins Loan, Federal PLUS loan, and Federal Work-Study (FWS) Program. In addition, the University awards institutional grants on the basis of athletic, need, leadership, academic major, or a combination of these factors. All students must complete a financial planning interview with their admissions counselor, and all are urged to complete the Free Application for Federal Student Aid (FAFSA). Approximately 85 percent of the student body receives some financial assistance. In the 2010–11 academic year, the University awarded more than $22 million in institutional aid.

Faculty

The faculty members at Robert Morris University are selected on the basis of their academic credentials, career experiences in their field, and dedication to giving individual attention to every student. All faculty members possess a master's degree in their chosen field, and many possess a Ph.D. in their area of specialization. In addition to teaching courses, faculty members promote the progress of their students through the individualized academic, employment, and personal development counseling they provide.

Student Government

Robert Morris University has no formal student government. Student representatives serve on committees that make recommendations about campus issues. Student organizations and activities are available.

Admission Requirements

All graduates of accredited high schools or the equivalent (GED) are eligible for admission to the University. All candidates are encouraged to have a personal interview with an admissions representative and take a tour of the campus.

A variety of materials are considered for various applicants. Freshman applicants just graduating from high school must submit their high school record or GED score and test results from the ACT, SAT, Applied Education Skills Assessment (AESA), Advanced Placement, and SAT Subject Area tests.

Those enrolling as an adult must submit their high school record or GED score; test results from the ACT, SAT, AESA, College-Level Examination Program (CLEP), and DANTES; and evidence of a successful employment experience.

Transfer students must present a minimum of 12 transferable credit hours from an accredited institution and their academic records from any high schools and colleges previously attended.

International students must forward their official education records, the results from either the TOEFL or AESA, and an affidavit of financial support.

Homeschooled students must submit a complete transcript of all classes they have taken, curriculum documentation and its state certification, and results from any standardized exams they have taken.

Application and Information

Applications can be obtained by contacting the Admissions Office at any of the University's campuses. The completed application and the $20 nonrefundable application fee ($100 nonrefundable application fee for international students) should be sent to the Admissions Office. The University operates on a rolling admissions basis, and students can enroll during any of the five times offered during the year. For further information, prospective students should visit the Web site or contact:

Robert Morris University
Chicago–Main Campus
401 South State Street
Chicago, Illinois 60605
Phone: 800-762-5960 (toll-free)
Web site: http://www.robertmorris.edu

Arlington Heights Campus
2123 South Goebbert Road
Arlington Heights, Illinois 60005

Bensenville Campus
1000 Tower Lane
Bensenville, Illinois 60106

DuPage Campus
905 Meridian Lake Drive
Aurora, Illinois 60504

Elgin Campus
1707 North Randall Road
Elgin, Illinois 60123

Orland Park Campus
82 Orland Square
Orland Park, Illinois 60462

Lake County Campus
1507 South Waukegan Road
Waukegan, Illinois 60085

Peoria Campus
211 Fulton Street
Peoria, Illinois 61602

Morris Graduate School of Management
A Division of Robert Morris University
Schaumburg Campus
1000 East Woodfield Road
Schaumburg, Illinois 60173

Springfield Campus
3101 Montvale Drive
Springfield, Illinois 62704

ROBERT MORRIS UNIVERSITY
MOON TOWNSHIP, PENNSYLVANIA

The University

A private university in Pittsburgh's suburban hills, Robert Morris University (RMU) is set on a 230-acre former estate that is a short drive from the cultural and commercial opportunities of a major city. Founded in 1921, RMU offers more than sixty undergraduate programs and twenty graduate programs, including many online options, providing its 5,000 students academic excellence with a professional focus.

The University built its reputation in the business fields of accounting, finance, marketing, and management. It has grown to include programs in communications, information systems, engineering, mathematics, science, education, social sciences, and nursing. RMU uses a student engagement transcript to document internships, service-learning activities, study abroad, leadership roles, and other learning outside the classroom. This focus on engaged learning contributes to the 95 percent placement rate of graduates in careers or graduate school within six months of graduation.

RMU is a teaching-centered institution featuring small classes taught by professors and a student-faculty ratio of 15:1. The campus is growing, with a new business school building added in 2011, a new communications and information systems complex set to open in fall 2012, and a new nursing simulation center in the design stage. RMU added two additional residence halls in 2011 to accommodate its growing student population. More than 80 percent of freshmen live in campus housing.

Visiting international scholars and a variety of opportunities to study abroad—for a semester or just a few weeks—enrich students' global perspectives. Students can participate in any of nearly 100 clubs and organizations. The Student Life Office organizes dances, parties, movie screenings, comedy acts, health and wellness fairs, educational programs, and day trips. Business organizations, professional clubs, and honor societies provide students with career preparation opportunities.

The University's competitive athletics program fields twenty-three NCAA Division I teams, and the Colonials have won numerous titles and championships. Both football and basketball draw large crowds to Joe Walton Stadium and the Charles Sewall Center, allowing students to show their school spirit. The region's only Division I men's and women's ice hockey teams play at the RMU Island Sports Center, a 32-acre sports and recreation complex with two ice rinks, two multipurpose rinks, an indoor golf driving range, a miniature golf course, a pro shop, and a restaurant and banquet facility. Students can also participate in a number of club and intramural sports on campus.

Location

The 230-acre main campus is located in Moon Township, Pennsylvania, just 15 minutes from Pittsburgh International Airport and 17 miles from downtown Pittsburgh. The RMU Island Sports Center is 15 minutes from campus on Neville Island.

Majors and Degrees

Robert Morris University offers more than sixty undergraduate programs of study: accounting, actuarial science, advertising, biology, biomedical engineering, business, communication, competitive intelligence systems, computer information systems, corporate communications, cyber forensics, economics, elementary education (early childhood, midlevel, and special education concentrations), engineering, English, environmental science, finance, graphic design, health services administration, history and government, hospitality and tourism management, industrial engineering, information sciences, intelligence systems, journalism, management, manufacturing engineering, marketing, mathematics, mechanical engineering, media arts, nuclear medicine technology, nursing, organizational leadership, photography, prelaw, premedicine, predentistry, pre–chiropractic medicine, pre–osteopathic medicine, pre–veterinary medicine, professional communications/information systems, public relations, psychology, secondary education (biology, business/computer/information technology, communication, English, mathematics, and social studies concentrations), social science, sociology, software development, software engineering, special education, sport management, sport psychology, theater, TV/video production, Web design, and Web development.

Fully online bachelor's degree programs are available in economics, health services administration, hospitality and tourism, organizational leadership, professional and technical writing, and psychology.

The University offers five-year integrated bachelor's/master's degree programs, medical school affiliation, cooperative education programs, and an honors program.

Academic Programs

Robert Morris operates on a two-semester schedule with various summer sessions. A total of 126 credits are required for the bachelor's degree. Internship or co-op credits of 3 to 12 hours may be used toward degree requirements. The University participates in a cross-registration program with nine local colleges through the Pittsburgh Council on Higher Education consortium.

Academic Facilities

Learning resources include a traditional library with more than 137,000 bound volumes, 80 reference databases, and 600 periodical subscriptions.

The Academic Media Center, with full production facilities, provides students with opportunities to collaborate on projects in all areas of media, including television/video production, audio production, and photography.

State-of-the-art laboratory facilities support the engineering, mathematics, science, and nursing programs. Graphic and Web design students benefit from a cutting-edge design studio.

The new business school facility features a simulated stock trading floor and videoconferencing center. The nursing school utilizes patient simulators.

Costs

Annual tuition for the 2011–12 year was a $22,406 flat rate, based on a 24- to 36-credit, two-semester schedule. Room and board fees were $11,030 based on double occupancy and a full meal plan.

Financial Aid

More than 90 percent of RMU undergraduates receive some sort of financial aid, including scholarships, grants, loans, and work-study programs. Both need-based and achievement-based awards are available. All applicants must complete the admissions application, the Free Application for Federal Student Aid, and the grant forms from their own state.

Faculty

The University has nearly 400 full- and part-time faculty members, 81 percent of whom hold terminal degrees. The student-faculty ratio is 15:1 and the average class size is 24. Students may take advantage of the expertise offered by the faculty in academic advisement and counseling, as well as counseling from the staff at the Center for Student Success.

Student Government

The Student Government Association represents all student organizations, including fraternities and sororities. Members participate in the planning of all social and cultural events on campus.

Admission Requirements

First-time freshmen must submit an application for admission with a $30 application fee (waived for online applicants), official high school transcripts or GED credential, and official SAT or ACT scores. Preference is given to applicants with a minimum 3.0 high school GPA and a combined SAT score of 1000 or a composite ACT score of 22.

Transfer students who have earned credits from another regionally accredited institution must submit transcripts from all postsecondary institutions attended and must have a minimum 2.0 GPA. Students with less than 30 college credits must also submit high school transcripts or GED credential.

Interviews are not required for admission except for students interested in the engineering, elementary education, and nursing programs. Students are encouraged to arrange for a campus visit with an enrollment manager.

Robert Morris University is committed to a policy of nondiscrimination on the basis of race, sex, color, religion, national origin, or handicap.

Application and Information

Students are encouraged to submit applications in the fall of their senior year of high school. Official transcripts and counselor recommendations should accompany the application; there is a $30 application processing fee that is waived for online applicants.

Robert Morris uses a rolling admission system; students are considered for acceptance as soon as all application materials have been received and evaluated.

For additional information and application materials, students should contact:

Kellie Laurenzi
Dean of Admissions
Robert Morris University
6001 University Boulevard
Moon Township, Pennsylvania 15108
Phone: 800-762-0097 (toll-free)
Web site: http://www.rmu.edu
http://www.facebook.com/rmunews
http://twitter.com/rmu
http://www.youtube.com/RMUNewsTube

The 240-acres campus in suburban Pittsburgh offers a scenic place to live, learn, and play.

ROCHESTER INSTITUTE OF TECHNOLOGY
ROCHESTER, NEW YORK

R·I·T

The Institute

Rochester Institute of Technology (RIT) is one of the world's leading career-oriented, technological universities. RIT offers more than ninety undergraduate programs in areas such as engineering, computing, information technology, engineering technology, business, hospitality, science, art, design, photography, biomedical sciences, game design and development, and the liberal arts including psychology, advertising and public relations, and public policy. Students may choose from more than ninety different minors to develop personal and professional interests that complement their academic program. RIT is a world leader in experiential education, which is integrated into many programs through cooperative education, internships, study abroad, and undergraduate research. As home to the National Technical Institute for the Deaf (NTID), RIT is a leader in providing access services for deaf and hard-of-hearing students. RIT enrolls students from every state and more than 100 countries.

Close to 70 percent of RIT's approximately 12,200 full-time undergraduate students live on the campus in residence halls or campus apartments.

Because RIT's student body is so diverse, there are many different activities, clubs, organizations, and sports in which students participate. There are seventeen fraternities and twelve sororities, which represent approximately 5 percent of the student population. A radio station and a biweekly student magazine allow those interested in media to gain experience on campus. A number of special interest clubs and career organizations are also available, and RIT offers twenty-three varsity sports, including Division I men's hockey. Recreational facilities are exceptional and include an ice rink, an aquatics center, a field house with an indoor track, and fitness facilities.

Location

The greater Rochester area has a population of about 800,000. Per-capita income is among the highest in the nation for metropolitan centers. The area's many internationally known industries employ a high proportion of scientists, technologists, and skilled workers. Rochester's industries have always been closely associated with RIT's programs and progress. Rochester is also a hub for higher education with twelve colleges and universities in the area.

Majors and Degrees

The College of Applied Science and Technology offers the Bachelor of Science (B.S.) degree in civil engineering technology, computer engineering technology, electrical engineering technology, electrical/mechanical engineering technology, manufacturing engineering technology, and mechanical engineering technology. It also grants the Bachelor of Science in environmental sustainability, health and safety, international hospitality and service management, and packaging science. An undeclared option allowing freshmen to delay selecting a major for up to a year is available in the School of Engineering Technology.

The E. Philip Saunders College of Business offers the B.S. in accounting, finance, graphic media marketing, international business, management, management information systems, and marketing. An accelerated B.S./M.B.A. option is available, as is a minor in entrepreneurship. An undeclared option allowing freshmen to delay the selection of their major for up to one year is available.

The B. Thomas Golisano College of Computing and Information Sciences offers the B.S. in computer science, game design and development, information technology, medical informatics, networking and systems administration, new media interactive development, and software engineering. The college also offers a computing exploration option and an informatics exploration option for undeclared freshman students.

The Kate Gleason College of Engineering grants the B.S. in biomedical engineering, chemical engineering, computer engineering, electrical engineering, industrial and systems engineering, mechanical engineering, and microelectronic engineering. Degree options in aerospace, automotive, bioengineering, biomedical, energy and environment, ergonomics, information systems, manufacturing, and software engineering are also offered within the college. Accelerated B.S./M.S. options are available. The Engineering Exploration Program, which allows freshmen to delay the selection of their major for up to one year, is available.

The College of Health Sciences and Technology offers B.S. programs in biomedical sciences, diagnostic medical sonography, nutrition management, and a five-year physician assistant B.S./M.S. program.

The College of Imaging Arts and Sciences offers the Bachelor of Fine Arts in advertising photography; ceramics and ceramic sculpture, digital cinema, film and animation, fine art photography, fine arts studio, glass, graphic design, illustration, industrial design, interior design, medical illustration, metals and jewelry design, new media design and imaging, photojournalism, 3D digital graphics, visual media, and woodworking and furniture design. The college also offers B.S. programs in biomedical photographic communications, digital media, graphic media, imaging and photographic technology, and new media/publishing. An undeclared option allowing freshmen to delay the selection of their major for up to one year is available in the School of Art, the School of Design, and the School for American Crafts.

The College of Liberal Arts offers B.S. programs in advertising and public relations, criminal justice, economics, journalism, international studies, museum studies, philosophy, professional and technical communication, psychology, public policy, and urban and community studies. The Liberal Arts Exploration Program is designed to help undecided students formulate education and career plans.

The College of Science offers B.S. programs in applied mathematics, applied statistics, biology, biochemistry, bioinformatics, biotechnology, chemistry, computational mathematics, environmental chemistry, environmental science, imaging science, physics, and polymer chemistry. Special options are available in premedical studies (medicine, dentistry, veterinary medicine). Minors are available in astronomy, exercise science, imaging science, mathematics, physics, and statistics. Accelerated B.S./M.S. and B.S./M.B.A. programs are available. General Science Exploration allows freshmen to delay the selection of their major for up to one year.

Home of the National Technical Institute for the Deaf, RIT is a leader in providing educational opportunities and access services for deaf and hard-of-hearing students. NTID awards associate degree programs and offers prebaccalaureate studies for deaf and hard-of-hearing students. The associate degree programs prepare students for immediate employment after graduation or transfer into one of RIT's bachelor's degree programs. The prebaccalaureate studies program prepares students, who may not qualify initially, for entry into RIT's bachelor's degree programs. Nearly 500 of the 1,300 deaf and hard-of-hearing students at RIT are enrolled in bachelor's degree programs in the other eight colleges.

Academic Programs

Most students entering as freshmen enroll directly in the college and academic program of their choice. Options for undeclared students are offered by most colleges. A University Studies program is available for entering freshmen who wish to explore programs in two or more colleges. Undergraduates may choose from more than ninety different minors. Double-majors and accelerated dual-degree (combined bachelor's/masters) options are available. The RIT honors program admits approximately 150 freshmen annually. Air Force and Army ROTC programs are available on the campus. A Naval ROTC program is offered jointly with the University of Rochester.

Every academic program at RIT offers some form of experiential education opportunity, including cooperative education, internships,

study abroad, undergraduate research, and industry-sponsored projects. Notable among these programs is RIT's world-renowned cooperative education program (co-op). The College of Applied Science and Technology, the E. Philip Saunders College of Business, the B. Thomas Golisano College of Computing and Information Sciences, and the Kate Gleason College of Engineering all require co-op for undergraduate students. It is available on an optional basis in other RIT colleges. Co-op students alternate periods of full-time study with periods of full-time paid work experience in business and industry directly related to their field of study and career interests. Last year more than 3,500 students completed co-op assignments with nearly 2,000 employers, earning collectively in excess of $33 million.

Off-Campus Programs

RIT has four international branch campuses. The American College of Management and Technology is located in Dubrovnik and Zagreb, Croatia and offers undergraduate degree programs in hospitality and service management, information technology, and international business. The American University of Kosovo in Pristina provides career-oriented programs that foster links between the university, industry, and government in support of workforce development. RIT Dubai offers graduate and undergraduate programs in business, engineering, service leadership, and information sciences. RIT offers a growing study-abroad program.

Academic Facilities

Excellent facilities add to the quality of academic life. Students have access to a laser-optics laboratory, an observatory, more than 100 color and black-and-white photography darkrooms, electronic prepress and publishing equipment, ceramic kilns, glass furnaces, a blacksmithing area, a student-operated restaurant, computer graphics and robotic labs, and some of the most up-to-date microelectronic, telecommunications, and computer engineering facilities in the U.S. RIT's Wallace Library is a true multimedia learning center. Its collections are exceptionally extensive in the areas of art and design, education for the deaf, photography, and printing.

RIT is a leader in academic computing, and students use state-of-the-art computer equipment regardless of their major. Central computer systems can be accessed via a high-speed data network connecting the library, academic facilities, residence hall rooms, and on-campus apartments. There are more than sixty locations campuswide, with wireless networking connectivity utilizing 802.11b technology. The RIT campus network is served by two OC3 connections, each operating at a data rate of 155 Mbps, and one T3 connection operating at 45 Mbps. RIT is among a select group of institutions with access to the Internet2 research network, a collaborative research and development effort led by more than 170 U.S. universities working in partnership with industry and government.

Costs

For 2011–12, undergraduate tuition for the academic year (three academic quarters) was $31,584. Fees, including the activities and health fees, are $453. Room and board (twenty meals per week) cost $10,413.

Financial Aid

Approximately 77 percent of RIT's full-time undergraduates receive some form of financial aid that includes RIT scholarships, alumni or industry-supported scholarships, and state and federal government grants. A variety of loans and part-time work positions are available. The FAFSA must be submitted by March 1. Giving full recognition to scholarship apart from financial need, RIT awards a number of academic scholarships based on grades, test scores, and activities. Freshmen applying by February 1 and transfers applying by April 1 are considered for these scholarships.

Faculty

There are 966 full-time faculty members, 509 part-time faculty members, and an administrative and supporting staff of more than 1,800. Approximately 70 percent of the faculty members have earned a Ph.D. or the terminal degree in their field.

Student Government

The Student Government is the representative body for students. It works with RIT administration, faculty, and staff members to communicate the needs and desires of the student body and to communicate decisions of the administration to students. Fraternity and sorority members, off-campus and hearing-impaired students, and students from minority groups elect special representative bodies. All full-time and part-time undergraduate and graduate students are represented in Student Government.

Admission Requirements

Admission to RIT is competitive and varies from selective to highly selective depending on the desired program of study. The major factors determining freshman admission are strength of academic program, high school performance, and ACT or SAT test results. College performance is the main factor for transfer candidates. Students applying for many programs in art and design must submit a portfolio as part of the application process.

RIT promotes and values diversity and admits qualified men and women of any race, color, national or ethnic origin, religion, sexual orientation, gender identity, gender expression, or marital status. RIT does not discriminate on the basis of handicap in the recruitment or admission of students or in the operation of any of its programs or activities, as specified by federal laws and regulations.

Application and Information

An application, a nonrefundable processing fee of $50, official transcripts of all secondary school or college records, and SAT or ACT scores (for prospective freshmen) should be forwarded to RIT. Freshman applicants who provide all required materials for fall entry by February 1 receive admission notification by March 15. Prospective freshmen who apply after February 1 are considered on a space-available basis; all transfer students are notified of the admission decision on a rolling basis four to six weeks after their applications are complete. A binding early decision plan is offered to prospective freshmen who have completed applications and credentials filed by December 1 to receive notification by January 15.

For application forms, students should contact:

Director of Undergraduate Admissions
Rochester Institute of Technology
60 Lomb Memorial Drive
Rochester, New York 14623-5604
Phone: 585-475-6631
Fax: 585-475-7424
E-mail: admissions@rit.edu
Web site: http://www.rit.edu
　　　　　http://www.facebook.com/RITfb
　　　　　http://twitter.com/RITAdmissions

A view of the campus.

ROGER WILLIAMS UNIVERSITY
BRISTOL, RHODE ISLAND

The University

Roger Williams University (RWU)(www.rwu.edu) located in Bristol, Rhode Island is a leading independent, coeducational university with programs in the liberal arts and the professions, where students become community- and globally-minded citizens.

With 42 academic majors, an array of cocurricular activities, and study-abroad opportunities on six continents, RWU is an open community dedicated to the success of students, commitment to a set of core values, and providing a world-class education above all else. In the last decade, the University has achieved unprecedented successes including recognition as one of the best colleges in the nation by *Forbes*, a College of Distinction by Student Horizons, Inc., and as both a best college in the Northeast and one of the nation's greenest universities by The Princeton Review.

A midsized university with 3,775 full-time undergraduate students, personal attention is guaranteed at RWU. Professors—not TAs or TFs—teach every course. The average class size at RWU is just 19 students, and the student-to-faculty ratio is 12:1. For students seeking additional academic support, the Center for Academic Development provides a multitude of tutoring, testing, and writing services. For students uncertain about which major to pursue, the professional staff at RWU's Advising Center is available to guide them through the registration and major declaration process.

In addition to academic support, entering freshmen receive support through Student Advocates. Every member of the freshman class is paired with a Student Advocate, an upperclassman who acts as a peer mentor and helps during the transition from high school to college, from living at home to living on campus. The Student Advocacy Office is another great resource, and is open to students daily.

Students at Roger Williams are committed to community service as well as their education. Students begin their RWU career with Community Connections, which sends over 1,500 freshmen and faculty and staff members throughout the region for the University's largest single day of service. Many students choose to continue volunteer service throughout their years at RWU, collaborating with the University's Feinstein Center for Service Learning and Community Outreach on projects with organizations around the state. The University's Community Partnership Center offers students the opportunity to provide service in their specifically chosen disciplines. Through collaborations with the city of Providence, the Rhode Island Economic Development Corporation, and many other organizations, students are refurbishing classic theaters, repurposing an elementary school as a community arts space, filing tax returns for the elderly, and providing public relations assistance to local businesses.

At RWU, students of diverse backgrounds from across the United States and fifty-two other countries come together for a community-oriented learning experience. Driven by a commitment to global citizenship, the University encourages all students to study abroad, whether it is for a year, semester, summer session or even a mini-mester.

On campus, students take part in programs at the Intercultural Center, home to international and multicultural student life, spiritual life, and LGBT initiatives. Global Heritage Hall, the academic center of campus, houses the Peggy and Marc Spiegel Center for Global and International Programs, as well as the Robert F. Stoico/FIRSTFED Global Languages Center and a series of heritage classrooms representing the myriad ethnic groups that both established and remain a strong presence in the local area.

Students can choose to live on or off campus in any of RWU's residence halls (shuttle service is available to students who live in an off-campus residence). Residences range from traditional dorms to apartment-style suites. RWU's newest residence hall for upperclassmen, North Campus Hall, combines living space, classroom and study space, a café, and a retail shop to create a modern living and learning community.

RWU students have access to more than seventy clubs and organizations and hundreds of events on campus every year. Students can join any of the University's intramural athletic teams, cheer on their twenty varsity athletic teams, debate current issues with professors and fellow students, listen to world-renowned speakers, attend concerts or plays at the Performing Arts Center, or run for Student Senate—the options go on and on.

The University is also committed to helping students maintain a healthy lifestyle. The Campus Recreation Center includes a swimming pool, basketball and squash courts, weight lifting and cardio rooms, a Jacuzzi, and a sauna, while RWU's waterfront is the perfect setting for sailing and kayaking. Students also enjoy locally grown, organic foods in the Upper Commons, which is consistently ranked in the top 5 percent nationwide.

RWU is committed to outcomes and the Career Center assists students in securing internships and job placement, as well as offering information sessions on resume writing and professional etiquette.

Roger Williams University is accredited by the following: New England Association of Schools and Colleges, National Architecture Accreditation Board, National Association of State Directors of Teacher Education and Certification, American Bar Association, American Chemical Society, and www.commonapp.org.

Location

Roger Williams University is located in Bristol, Rhode Island, a seaside town that is home to antique stores, gourmet restaurants, ice cream shops, and spas. Providence is just a 30-minute ride from campus and offers museums, coffee shops, the Providence Place Mall, live music, and more. By travelling 30 minutes in the other direction, students can visit Newport, home of famous beaches, shopping, festivals, and open markets. Boston is just an hour away, and New York City is less than 4 hours from campus.

Majors and Degrees

At the undergraduate level, RWU awards Bachelor of Science, Bachelor of Arts, and Bachelor of Fine Arts degrees. In addition, the University has several joint degree programs, including two 3+3 programs leading to bachelor's degrees paired with the Juris Doctor as well as several programs that pair bachelor's degrees with master's degrees in accelerated formats.

Professional programs are offered through the School of Architecture, Art and Historic Preservation, accredited by NAAB; the Gabelli School of Business, accredited by the prestigious AACSB International; the School of Engineering, Computing and Construction Management, accredited by ACCE, ABET, and EAC; and the School of Justice Studies.

Liberal arts majors are offered through the Feinstein College of Arts and Sciences and the School of Education. Continuing education opportunities are available through the School of Graduate and Continuing Studies, and RWU is also home to Rhode Island's only law school, accredited by the ABA.

Academic Programs

Roger Williams employs a shared general education curriculum for all undergraduate students. The interdisciplinary program guarantees that all students, regardless of a major, receive a well-rounded education that combines a liberal arts background with a major academic area of interest. With 42 different programs of study ranging from American studies and architecture to security assurance studies and theater, RWU offers a wide variety of choices for its students.

Off-Campus Programs

One of the University's core values is appreciation of global perspectives, and RWU encourages global exploration. All sophomores who maintain a 3.0 GPA receive a passport, free

of charge, to encourage travel. RWU's flagship programs are in Florence, Italy, and London, England, but RWU has affiliated programs in countries from Argentina to Vietnam and virtually everywhere in between.

The University also places an emphasis on internships, community service, and service learning. Career counselors work one-on-one with the students and alumni, providing career development guidance, assessment, employment-search skills, and placement assistance.

Academic Facilities

The University's 54,000-square-foot main library houses seating and quiet study and reading areas, computer databases, and an online catalog. The ground floor is also home to the Learning Commons, a dynamic space that encourages learning through collaboration by combining library resources and research assistance with the latest technology. And an online system allows students to take advantage of library resources and collections of four additional Rhode Island institutions.

The Marine and Natural Sciences Building houses the science and mathematics departments and features a wet lab with flowing seawater; research space; and modern physics, chemistry, and biology laboratories. RWU recently completed construction of a shellfish hatchery to further expand the University's work reseeding the oyster population in Mount Hope Bay.

The Engineering Building supports modern lab facilities equipped for computing, drafting, electronics, surveying, soil, fluid and materials mechanics, and digital and environmental systems.

The Performing Arts Center houses a dance studio, rehearsal rooms, and scene and costume shops as well as performance space, while the Fine Arts Building provides students with art and sculpting studios, an art gallery, and photography labs that support visual arts studies.

The award-winning School of Architecture, Art, and Historic Preservation Building includes design studios, review and seminar rooms, a library, a photography studio and darkroom, a model shop, computer labs, and an exhibition gallery.

The Gabelli School of Business (GSB) houses the Robert F. Stoico FIRSTFED Financial Services Center, a high-tech classroom/trading room featuring split computer screens for students. Also in GSB is the Center for Advanced Financial Education (CAFE), which provides hands-on training in securities analysis and portfolio management for students involved in the Student Investment Management Fund.

Global Heritage Hall completes the University's academic quad and houses a state-of-the-art language lab, several Mac labs, green screen technology, a news studio, heritage classrooms that honor local history, breakout rooms for meetings, and a café.

Costs

Tuition for the 2012–13 year is $29,976 for 12–17 credit hours ($33,792 for architecture students). Room and board average $13,690.

Financial Aid

Interested students are reminded to not just look at the price of a Roger Williams education. There are many resources available to help finance an RWU education, including need- and merit-based scholarships and educational loans. Because RWU is still growing, there are more opportunities to address each individual family's financial needs.

In the 2011–12 academic year, 95 percent of RWU's incoming students received financial aid through a combination of grants, scholarships, student loans, and on-campus jobs. The University's median freshman aid package is $20,819. The University awarded more than $35 million in financial assistance in the current year alone. As a private institution, RWU has greater ability than state schools to offer scholarships or tap endowment funds to help students.

The University requires the submission of the Free Application for Federal Student Aid (FAFSA) and the CSS/Financial Aid PROFILE. The Roger Williams University Title IV Federal Code Number is 003410. The FAFSA must be received at the federal processor no later than February 1 to be considered for maximum financial aid.

Prospective students can learn more about the true value of an RWU education at http://thedock.rwu.edu/scholarships-financial-aid/affordability.

Faculty

Renowned for their commitment to excellence in teaching, the Roger Williams University academic cadre features 625 faculty members, of whom 245 teach full time. Of the full-time faculty members, 38 percent have been with the University for more than ten years.

Student Government

The Student Government Association (SGA) represents the Roger Williams University student body. Elected by their peers, Student Senate members are responsible for the legislative and executive functions of the SGA and represent the entire student community to the faculty and administration.

Other leadership opportunities at Roger Williams include the Inter-Class Council, a group of peer-elected class representatives responsible for fostering school spirit, developing social programming opportunities for their respective classes, and representing their class to the Student Senate and University administration.

Admission Requirements

Roger Williams University seeks well-rounded, motivated students with a demonstrated capacity for academic achievement, and who also possess intellectual curiosity, strength of character, and a sense of social responsibility.

Applicants are evaluated based on a number of factors, including the rigor of the high school curriculum, scholastic record, standardized test scores (SAT or ACT are accepted), writing ability, interests, community involvement, and talents. Transfer students are evaluated based on the same criteria, along with academic performance on the college level.

All students must submit an official application, letter(s) of recommendation, and official transcripts from all secondary and postsecondary schools attended to be considered for admission.

Application and Information

The deadline for early action I is November 1, for early action II is November 15, and for regular decision is February 1. A nonrefundable fee of $50 must accompany the application. RWU utilizes the Common Application, available at www.commonapp.org. Additional information, application forms and admissions information may be obtained by contacting:

Office of Undergraduate Admission
Roger Williams University
One Old Ferry Road
Bristol, Rhode Island 02809-2921
Phone: 401-254-3500
      800-458-7144 Ext. 3500 (toll-free outside Rhode Island)
E-mail: admit@rwu.edu
Web site: http://www.rwu.edu
      http://www.facebook.com/rogerwilliamsuniversity
      http://twitter.com/myrwu

Roger Williams University is located on 143 scenic acres overlooking Mount Hope Bay.

ROWAN UNIVERSITY
GLASSBORO, NEW JERSEY

The University

A leading public institution, Rowan University combines a liberal arts education with professional preparation from the baccalaureate through the doctorate. Rowan provides a collaborative, learning-centered environment in which highly qualified and diverse faculty, staff, and students integrate teaching, research, scholarship, creative activity, and community service. Through intellectual, social, and cultural contributions, the University enriches the lives of those in the campus community and surrounding region.

The University is in the midst of a $530-million plan to expand the campus and further upgrade facilities, through newly purchased land. The anchor of the new tract is the South Jersey Technology Park at Rowan University, which will play a significant role in the economic development of the region. In 2008, the South Jersey Technology Park at Rowan University opened the doors of its first building, the Samuel H. Jones Innovation Center.

Rowan University and the Cooper Health System partnered in June 2009 to establish Cooper Medical School of Rowan University (CMSRU), the first new medical school in New Jersey in thirty years. Located in Camden, New Jersey, CMSRU will help address the physician shortage locally and nationally and improve health care throughout the region. Having already received preliminary accreditation from the Liaison Committee on Medical Education (LCME) in June 2011, its inaugural class is scheduled to begin in August 2012.

In addition, Rowan University and the town of Glassboro have partnered to create Rowan Boulevard, a roadway being constructed from the east end of campus to the historic downtown. Plans call for the construction of a mixed-use corridor lined with shops and restaurants on the street level, topped by apartments and offices. Key anchors to the project are an apartment complex for Rowan University students (opened in 2010); a Barnes & Noble college superstore (opened in 2010); the Whitney Center, a mixed-use building housing the Thomas N. Bantivoglio honors program (opened in 2011); and a Marriot Courtyard Hotel and Conference Center.

Students have access to the resources of a large university without sacrificing the personal attention and small class size of a college. All classes are taught by professors, not teaching assistants. The average class size is 21 students and the student/faculty ratio is 15:1.

U.S. News & World Report ranks Rowan twenty-first among Northern Regional Universities, and third among the publics in the category. Rowan's College of Engineering is ranked sixteenth nationally with two of its specializations ranked in the top ten. The Princeton Review included Rowan in the latest edition of its Best Northeastern Colleges, as did the Rohrer College of Business in its listing of the Best 300 Business Schools. *Forbes* recognized Rowan in its annual assessment of America's Best Colleges. Rowan's commitment to the environment was recognized when the United States Environmental Protection Agency named it a Top Green Power Purchaser in its athletic conference and the Princeton Review included it in its guide to 286 Green Colleges. The University has earned eleven awards for green initiatives since 2007.

Rowan's eighteen varsity athletic teams compete in NCAA Division III, the New Jersey Athletic Conference, and the Eastern College Athletic Conference. More than 130 clubs, pre-professional organizations, honor societies, and fraternities and sororities foster a sense of community life.

From its founding in 1923 as a school for teachers, to its current status as a top-rated regional institution, Rowan University has had a remarkable history. Such landmark events as the 1967 Summit Conference between President Lyndon Johnson and Soviet Premier Alexei Kosygin at Hollybush and the $100-million gift from Henry and Betty Rowan in 1992 truly put Rowan on the map as a place where current and future leaders and professionals thrive. Combining exceptional resources, great teaching, and engaged students, Rowan University seeks to set the standards for the future of higher education in New Jersey.

Location

The University maintains two New Jersey campuses: a 200-acre suburban residential setting in the historic town of Glassboro and a five-story urban facility in the University District of Camden.

The tree-lined Glassboro campus includes student residence halls, apartments, and townhouses; state-of-the-art classroom facilities; a student recreation center; theaters; galleries; and a planetarium. There are sixty-three computer labs and 120 TEC classrooms throughout the main campus and the Camden campus. Both campuses are within minutes from Philadelphia and major transportation hubs and an hour from the Jersey Shore points.

Majors and Degrees

Rowan University's programs of study include eighty-one majors, twenty-five minors, twenty master's degrees, eight certificates of advanced graduate studies, eleven certification programs, a Doctorate in Educational Leadership, and numerous interdisciplinary concentrations in six colleges (Business, Communication, Education, Engineering, Fine & Performing Arts, and Liberal Arts & Sciences). In addition, the College of Graduate and Continuing Education provides online and accelerated graduate programs as well as off-campus and Saturday degree-completion programs for individuals with busy schedules seeking to advance their professional careers.

Academic Programs

All degree programs include a general education requirement (approximately 60 semester hours) from the areas of communication, science and mathematics, social and behavioral sciences, humanities and languages, and fine arts. In addition, most academic majors have specific general education courses that students in that major must take. Each degree program includes individual major requirements and free electives. A minimum of 30 semester hours is required in a major program; many departments require more.

Students are encouraged to use free electives to establish a second major, minor, or concentration; strengthen their major program; pursue personal interests; or study abroad.

Internships are available in all majors, and some type of internship or academic field experience is required in most of them.

Students interested in applying to the College of Fine and Performing Arts must arrange a music audition, theater audition, or portfolio review.

The University calendar is based on the two-semester system with a summer session.

Off-Campus Programs

Rowan University offers the opportunity to spend a semester or a year living and learning in a new country and culture through study abroad, with destinations to more than 200 programs in fifty nations in Africa, Asia, Australia, Europe, and South and Central America. Students can also earn work-study dollars while exploring careers and building credentials and experience through the Off-Campus Work-Study program.

Academic Facilities

In just the past decade, Rowan has added a number of new buildings that are notable for their modern architecture, bright open spaces, and state-of-the-art equipment. They include the Student Recreation Center, a full-service health club for students, faculty members, and alumni; the Campbell Library, which combines spacious new study areas with a rich collection of print and electronic resources for research; and Henry M. Rowan Hall, a $28-million engineering building with a technology spine and modular classrooms and laboratories. The $45-million, state-of-the-art Science Hall, which opened in 2003, is home to the biological

sciences, chemistry, and physics departments and features a fully equipped laser laboratory, a rooftop greenhouse and telescope, a planetarium, twenty-two research laboratories, and twenty-seven teaching laboratories. Education Hall, opened in 2006, features state-of-the-art technology, learning centers, classrooms, and office space. Rowan is also expanding its campus to accommodate the South Jersey Technology Park, a facility that will be shared by students, faculty members, and private industry.

Construction of the $139-million dollar medical education building, which will house Cooper Medical School of Rowan University, is well under way and scheduled for completion in 2012. The six-story, 200,000-square-foot building will feature twenty-five active learning rooms, a 250-seat auditorium, 140-seat multipurpose room, common area, satellite medical library, clinical stimulation center, and research labs.

Costs

In 2011–12, tuition and fees were $12,018 for New Jersey residents and $19,598 for out-of-state students, based on flat-rate tuition for full-time undergraduates taking 24 to 36 semester hours per year. Room and board costs for the year were $10,652, based on a double-residence room rate and a primary meal plan. All freshmen are required to live in residence halls, with guaranteed housing. Apartment-style housing is available on the campus for upperclass students in any one of the University-owned apartment complexes and town houses.

Financial Aid

College costs can seem overwhelming, but Rowan University is committed to providing all of its students with a top-quality education within their means. Over 75 percent of Rowan students receive some form of financial aid, such as grants and loans, or scholarships from federal and state sources, alumni, friends of the University, and various other organizations.

Rowan University rewards academic success through an extensive scholarship program. Consideration is given to students in the top percentage of their class who have scored 1150 or better combined Critical Reading and Math on the SAT test. In addition to the traditional state and University scholarship awards, many academic departments and organizations at Rowan offer scholarships.

Faculty

Rowan University has 912 faculty members (402 full time). The faculty's regularly scheduled office hours, participation in virtually all areas of campus governance and operations, and individual guidance and support for every student who needs them, ensures a truly personal education. Part-time and adjunct faculty members, including business leaders, industry representatives, and practicing professionals, provide valuable links with the community and offer knowledge of practical experiences to Rowan University students.

Student Government

The Student Government Association (SGA) is composed entirely of students chosen through campuswide elections. All students paying student activity fees are members of the SGA. Free legal advice, personal property insurance, and a tenants' association are some of the SGA's projects. The SGA oversees more than 130 chartered clubs on campus and sponsors intercollegiate athletics, social events, and service activities. The University administration wholly supports the concept of student rights and student participation in all areas of campus governance.

Admission Requirements

Rowan University carefully considers each application it receives and selects candidates who will be academically successful, contribute to student life on campus, and benefit most from the Rowan experience. Rowan's admission standards are competitive.

Admission decisions are based on the strength and quality of the high school record, SAT or ACT scores, and class rank. Letters of recommendation, essay, and interviews are not required.

Applicants are expected to have completed a minimum of 16 college-preparatory units: 4 of English, 2 of laboratory science, 3 of college-preparatory mathematics (algebra I and II, geometry), 2 of social studies, and 5 of additional work in at least two of the following areas: English, social studies, languages, mathematics, and sciences. The College of Engineering seeks applicants with 3 units of laboratory science, including chemistry and physics, and 4 units of college-preparatory mathematics, including precalculus (calculus preferred).

Admission for transfer students is competitive and is based on college transcripts and available space in the desired major.

Application and Information

The University application, $65 application fee, high school and/or college transcript, and SAT or ACT scores should be forwarded to the Admissions Office. For September entrance, freshman and transfer applications are due March 1, with notification no later than April 15. The fall-enrollment deposit must be received by May 1. The application deadline for spring semester (January entrance) is November 1 for freshmen and transfers. Campus visits are highly recommended.

Prospective students should visit http://ru.rowan.edu. For additional information, students should contact:

Albert Betts
Director of Admissions
Rowan University
Glassboro, New Jersey 08028-1701
Phone: 856-256-4200
    877-RU-ROWAN (toll-free)
E-mail: admissions@rowan.edu
Web site: http://www.rowan.edu/petersons

Science Hall, Rowan's state-of-the-art science center, is one of the most advanced undergraduate research facilities at a public university on the East Coast.

SACRED HEART UNIVERSITY
FAIRFIELD, CONNECTICUT

SACRED HEART UNIVERSITY

The University

Characterized by the personal attention it provides its students, Sacred Heart University (SHU) in Fairfield, Connecticut is an independent, comprehensive liberal arts university. With more than forty-five academic programs for undergraduate, master's, and doctoral students in the arts, sciences, business, education, and health professions, Sacred Heart University is nationally recognized for its commitment to academic excellence, cutting-edge technology, championship Division I athletic teams, and award-winning community service programs.

Fully accredited by the New England Association of Schools and Colleges (NEASC), SHU is the second-largest Catholic university in New England, and the first in America to be led and staffed by lay people. A vibrant residential university with 3,500 full-time undergraduates and more than 6,000 total undergraduate and graduate students, the University's academic programs are housed in its five distinctive colleges: the College of Arts and Sciences, the AACSB-accredited John F. Welch College of Business, the NCATE-accredited Isabelle Farrington College of Education, the College of Health Professions, and University College.

Exemplified by its mission, Sacred Heart University is dedicated to the holistic development of its students through active, engaged learning that educates the whole person—mind, body, and spirit. Hands-on learning through research, internships, clinical placements, service learning, and study-abroad programs encourages students to apply their skills and knowledge outside the classroom, contributing to an exemplary 96 percent job and graduate school placement rate for graduating seniors.

With guaranteed housing for four years and over 90 percent of first-year students residing on campus, SHU provides a lively residential campus atmosphere with a rich student life program. There are over eighty student organizations, including popular performing arts groups (band and theater arts), media groups, spirit groups, national Greek letter organizations, intramural and club sports, community service organizations, ministry groups, leadership programs, student governance groups, multicultural organizations, and academic honor societies. Cultural events abound on campus, including live entertainment and poetry nights at the Holy Grounds Café; the Student Affairs Lecture Series which brings renowned guest speakers to campus; and professional-quality theatrical, musical, and dance performances at the Edgerton Center for the Performing Arts. SHU's robust school spirit is embodied by the University's successful Division I intercollegiate athletics program. Among the largest Division I programs in the country, the Pioneers compete in more than thirty varsity sports, and students also participate in various club sports teams.

Location

Sacred Heart University's campus location offers the best of both worlds: a safe, suburban campus located on 71 acres in beautiful Fairfield, Connecticut and a central location between the urban centers of New York City (55 miles) and Boston, Massachusetts (150 miles). SHU students enjoy a multitude of social, recreational, and professional opportunities in Fairfield County. The area is rich in New England history and features miles of stunning coastline, beaches, nature preserves, sports stadiums, restaurants, entertainment, shopping, and cultural exhibits, all complemented by dozens of local, national, and multinational corporations and easy access to New York City via Metro-North Railroad.

Drawing on the rich resources in New England and the New York metropolitan area, students are immersed in enriching activities throughout the year, including group events such as Broadway shows in New York City and trips to historical Philadelphia and Washington, D.C. The University's shuttle system provides free service to the local transportation centers; popular downtown Fairfield; the nearby shopping mall, movie theaters, and other shopping and recreational attractions; and favorite spots such as the culturally rich city of New Haven and the beach during late spring and early fall.

Majors and Degrees

The College of Arts and Sciences offers programs in art and design, biology (concentrations in ecology and conservation, molecular and cellular, neuroscience, and traditional biology), Catholic studies (minor), chemistry (concentrations in biochemistry and traditional chemistry), communication and technology studies, computer science/information technology (computer science track, information technology track, computer science gaming track, concentration in network security), criminal justice, English (concentrations in literature and writing), European studies (minor), fashion design (minor), French (minor), history, Irish studies (minor), Italian (minor), Latin American studies (minor), mathematics, media studies, Middle Eastern studies (minor), music (minor), philosophy, psychology, religious studies, social work, sociology, Spanish, and women's studies (minor), as well as pre-professional advising programs including pre-dental studies, pre-medical studies, pre-law, pre-optometry, pre-osteopathic studies, pre–physician's assistant studies, pre-pharmacy, and pre–veterinary studies. Several combined bachelor's and master's degree programs are offered in the college.

The AACSB-accredited John F. Welch College of Business offers programs in accounting, business administration (concentrations in business analysis, entrepreneurship and family business, human resource management, international business, management, and marketing), business economics, finance, marketing (concentration in fashion marketing and merchandising), and sport management. The Welch College of Business also offers a five-year B.S./M.B.A. option.

The NCATE-accredited Isabelle Farrington College of Education includes elementary and secondary education certification programs. Many education students choose the five-year program in which students work toward earning Connecticut teacher certification while completing a Master of Arts in Teaching (M.A.T.) degree and interning at a local school district during the fifth year.

The College of Health Professions offers degrees in the health sciences include athletic training, exercise science, health science (leadership track and pre-professional track), geriatric health and wellness (minor), nursing, and combined undergraduate/graduate programs in occupational therapy and physical therapy.

Academic Programs

Candidates for the bachelor's degree must complete a minimum of 120 credits. In addition to courses within the major field of study, the curriculum is made up of several components: the foundational core; the elective core; and SHU's innovative, nationally recognized Common Core, "The Human Journey." The Common Core emphasizes collaborative, team-taught classes, capstone experiences, and out-of-the-classroom experiential learning.

Special academic programs include the Thomas More Honors Program and the Major in Success program, a comprehensive, individualized program to help undeclared students make informed decisions about a major and career path. Students in the John F. Welch College of Business participate in the Welch Experience, an integrated professional and academic program which includes experiential learning opportunities such as internships and study abroad, special mentoring programs, undergraduate research opportunities, targeted career development activities, access to business leaders, and the development of a state-of-the-art online portfolio for all students.

Off-Campus Programs

Fairfield County boasts the third-highest concentration of Fortune 500 companies in the U.S., world-class hospitals, nationally ranked elementary and secondary schools, and countless additional sites

for students to intern and gain relevant work experience. SHU's PioneerLink internship and job database includes over 5,000 employers. Eighty percent of graduating seniors report participation in at least one internship, practicum, or field experience, which contributes to the University's 96 percent placement rate of graduating seniors in jobs and graduate school.

Study-abroad experiences are also a key component of the undergraduate experience. Students have the opportunity to study at SHU's own international campuses in Luxembourg and Ireland, and on programs led by University faculty in a number of countries each year. Other study-abroad opportunities are available through the University's membership in the College Consortium for International Studies.

Academic Facilities

Sacred Heart University is committed to anytime, anywhere learning, which is supported by the mobile computing program, a fully wireless campus, 24-hour computer labs with printing, a full program of group and one-on-one computer training, a help desk and IT call center, and easy digital equipment loans for students.

Other highlights of SHU's on-campus academic facilities are state-of-the-art laboratories dedicated to motion analysis, independent living, human performance, athletic training, acute care, ambulatory care, and clinical skills, which support SHU's health sciences programs; a model science classroom, educational technology laboratory, and the Book Ends literacy clinic, which offer education students exposure to stimulating teaching environments; and state-of-the art biology and chemistry laboratories in the newly-renovated science wing.

Cutting-edge studio and lab spaces for dedicated use by art and design students include an illustration studio, painting and drawing studio, graphic design studio, foundations studio, and fashion design studio.

The newly renovated Ryan-Matura Library contains over 140,000 holdings including online and print books, periodicals, microforms, audio and video resources, course reserves, and an interlibrary loan program that allows students to access works from libraries worldwide.

Other SHU facilities include the new Linda E. McMahon Commons, which offers a new bookstore, student dining hall, informal lounge spaces, outside seating, a presentation room, and a new career counseling center; the 776-seat Edgerton Center for the Performing Arts; WHRT, the student-run radio station; and the William H. Pitt Health and Recreation Center, which houses the Sacred Heart University Sports Medicine and Rehabilitation Center.

Costs

Full-time undergraduate tuition and fees for 2011–12 were $32,474; room and board were an additional $12,830–$13,070. Board only (for commuter students) ranged from $1100 to $3670, depending on the meal plan. The cost of books was estimated at $1200 per year.

Financial Aid

Financial aid is awarded on a first-come, first-served basis to admitted undergraduate students and may include loans and need-based aid (from University, federal, and state sources) and/or merit-based aid for academic and athletic achievement. Participation grants for select performing arts and community service programs are also awarded. Employment within the University is awarded under the terms of the Federal Work-Study Program. Completion of the College Scholarship Service PROFILE and the FAFSA are required in order to receive financial assistance.

Faculty

The University's student-faculty ratio is 14:1 and the average class size is 21 students. While research is important to the widely published faculty at SHU, the University's accessible, student-focused 645 professors are committed to their primary role, teaching, allowing students across disciplines to benefit from forming close relationships with faculty members. The University does not employ teaching assistants, thus 100 percent of undergraduate courses are taught by faculty members. The student-faculty connection begins immediately, as each first-year student is assigned a faculty member as their academic adviser for course selection and registration. This relationship is a seamless one, as the academic adviser also serves as the student's professor in a select Core Curriculum course, which meets weekly. Beyond their teaching, academic advising, and mentoring roles, faculty members serve as advisers to a variety of student clubs and organizations on campus; lead student service trips around the country and the world; serve as pre-fall program leaders for incoming first-year student groups; and participate in collaborative, cocurricular learning activities such as team-taught classes, capstone experiences, and cultural learning opportunities that extend beyond the customary classroom environment.

Student Government

Students play a major role in strategic planning and decision-making at SHU. Student government opportunities include the Executive Board, Student Government Senate, Class Boards, Council of Clubs and Organizations, and the Student Events Team.

Admission Requirements

Full-time students, both freshmen and transfer, may enroll in either the fall or spring semesters. Sacred Heart University believes in a personalized process in evaluating students for admission. The Admissions Office utilizes the Common Application and also requires high school transcripts (and college transcripts for transfer students) and a letter of recommendation. A campus visit is encouraged for applicants and is required for early decision candidates. Sacred Heart University will strongly consider SAT or ACT scores if students elect to submit them. Test scores must be submitted in order to be considered for merit scholarships. Additional documentation is required for students who choose not to submit standardized test scores. Additional documentation is also required for international applicants, and students who are not native English-speakers may be required to submit TOEFL scores.

Application and Information

The Common Application is available online beginning August 1, 2012. The deadline for early decision applications is November 15. Regular admission is rolling with a February 15 priority deadline. A campus visit is encouraged and can be scheduled by calling 203-371-7881 or visiting www.sacredheart.edu/visitplanner.cfm.

For further admissions information, please contact:
Jamie P. Romeo
Executive Director of Undergraduate Admissions
Sacred Heart University
5151 Park Avenue
Fairfield, Connecticut 06825
Phone: 203-371-7880
E-mail: enroll@sacredheart.edu
Web site: http://www.sacredheart.edu

Welcome to Sacred Heart University.

ST. ANDREWS UNIVERSITY
LAURINBURG, NORTH CAROLINA

The University

St. Andrews University, a branch of Webber International University (Babson Park, Florida), is a student and teaching-focused university located in Laurinburg, North Carolina. It offers a broad range of undergraduate liberal arts and sciences majors to both traditional residential students and adult learners, in a curriculum that is global in scope and practical in its application. The quality of the St. Andrews educational experience has been recognized by U.S. News and World Report, The Princeton Review, and GI Jobs among others. In addition to its many academic programs, St. Andrews has numerous men's and women's athletic teams, an acclaimed university press, a nationally competitive equestrian program, opportunities for international study, and an award-winning pipe band. St. Andrews is military-friendly.

Classes challenge the student to think critically and to express ideas clearly and effectively. Emphasis on interdisciplinary study and the acquisition and mastery of communication skills, analytical techniques, problem-solving strategies, leadership skills, and creative expression are focal points of the curriculum. Members of the faculty work cooperatively as teachers, mentors, and advisers while maintaining a commitment to scholarship and professional development. About 400 students are enrolled as undergraduates at St. Andrews.

The University offers intercollegiate sports for men in baseball, basketball, cross-country, golf, lacrosse, soccer, and wrestling; and women in basketball, cross-country, golf, lacrosse, softball, soccer, and volleyball. The University's physical education complex includes a main gym, a fitness room, a soccer field, an Olympic-size swimming pool, baseball field, and softball field.

Location

St. Andrews is located in the Sandhills of North Carolina in the city of Laurinburg. Laurinburg is the capital of Scotland County, a cultural crossroads.

Majors and Degrees

St. Andrews University offers bachelor's degrees in biology, business administration, elementary education, English, creative writing, forensic science, history, politics, interdisciplinary studies, philosophy, religious studies, physical education, psychology, sport and recreation studies, therapeutic horsemanship, and visual and performing arts.

Academic Programs

The school operates on the semester system with two 15-week semesters. The University requires the completion of 120 credit hours for the Bachelor of Arts, Bachelor of Science, and Bachelor of Fine Arts degrees with a minimum grade point average of 2.0. The average course load is 15 hours per semester. Students in the degree program are required to complete required hours in the major, 16 hours in the general education core, and 19–22 hours of tailored electives.

All students must complete the last 30 hours at St. Andrews University to receive a degree. Credit is awarded for successful scores on Advanced Placement (AP) and College-Level Examination Program (CLEP) general tests.

Off-Campus Programs

Academic internships are available in every program at St. Andrews for any student who meets eligibility requirements. Internships can occur during any semester or summer session and in almost any geographic location. Students have had internships with IBM, Southern Pines Equine Associates, Merrill Lynch, Scotland Memorial Hospital Rehabilitation, the EPA, NASA, law offices, social services agencies, radio and television stations, newspapers, and art museums.

International programs and residential programs abroad include fall semester in Brunnenburg Castle, Italy; spring semester in Beijing, China; summer session in Cuenca, Ecuador; and other short summer programs including trips to India, Vietnam, and England.

Academic Facilities

DeTamble Library is an 18,168-square-foot structure that houses the University Archives in addition to the University's book and journal collection.

The James L. Morgan Liberal Arts building houses administrative offices in addition to classrooms, art studios, a metal foundry, the Morris Morgan Theatre, the University computer center, computer labs, and four multimedia computer classrooms.

The Morgan-Jones Scince Center includes the 20,400-square-foot John Blue Laboratory, logistics center, classrooms, a computer-networking laboratory, the Suzanne Trezevant Little Instrument Center, a biology and chemistry computer graphics laboratory, woodworking and glassblowing shops, a greenhouse, a sterile culture laboratory, and a psychology laboratory.

The Vardell Building houses the Electronic Fine Arts Center, including a studio with digital mixing equipment as well as computer art and video recording facitilites. It also holds faculty offices, classrooms, the Hagan Choral Room, the Lindsay Warren Gallery, and music practice rooms.

Costs

In 2012–13, full-time residential student charges include $22,674 for tuition and $9376 for comprehensive fees. Comprehensive fees include food service, double room in a standard residence hall, fees, and vehicle registration fee. Additional fees such as lab and course fees or riding lessons, purchase of books, and miscellaneous expenses should also be anticipated. Additional expenses include health insurance and single room upgrades.

Financial Aid

The Student Financial Aid Department offers students its counsel and assistance in meeting their educational expenses. Aid is awarded on the basis of an applicant's need, academic performance, and promise. Approximately 98 percent of the students at St. Andrews University receive financial assistance. To demonstrate need, applicants are required to file the Free Application for Federal Student Aid (FAFSA). Various types of aid, such as scholarships, grants, loans, and Federal Work-Study awards, are used to meet student needs. A

limited number of no-need scholarships are available; these awards are based on academic performance, on community and college service, or on athletic ability as determined by the sport's coach. Applicants for aid must reapply each year. St. Andrews participates in the Federal Perkins Loan, Federal Supplemental Educational Opportunity Grant, and Federal Work-Study programs. All applicants are expected to apply for any entitlement grant for which they are eligible, such as the Federal Pell Grant. Federal Student Loans are also available. St. Andrews is nationally recognized as a military-friendly school and accepts the Post-9/11 GI Bill as well as a variety of other veteran's education benefits. Financial aid applicants should submit their requests and forms before April 1 in order to be eligible for certain financial aid programs.

Faculty

Of the full-time faculty members, 73 percent hold the earned terminal degree. Their first priority is to deliver quality teaching and effective advising. They are also accomplished scholars and actively contribute to the local community. A student-to-faculty ratio of 10:1 facilitates the highly interactive approach to teaching and learning that characterizes St. Andrews. A commitment by the faculty to interdisciplinary teamwork in the teaching of the general education program and in other academic programs enhances the vitality and appeal of the education experience at St. Andrews. Many of the faculty have lived, traveled, or studied in Europe, Africa, Asia, and Latin America. Others bring varied insights, applications, and connections from previous work and service experiences to the classroom.

Student Government

The Student Government Association, the chief governing body on St. Andrews campus, is composed of elected student representatives and a faculty adviser and deals with nonacademic areas of student life. The association serves as an advisory and coordinating body for student organizations and involves students in campus policy and actions. Representatives from various student organizations serve on the Student Government Association, as do members elected from the University community. Admission Requirements

Applicants must have graduated from high school with a recommended minimum of 4 years of English and 2 to 3 years of mathematics and preparation in seven other academic subjects. Most accepted candidates rank in the top 50 percent of their high school class. Scores on the SAT or ACT are required for admission. International applicants must submit scores on the Test of English as a Foreign Language (TOEFL).

Applications from transfer students are welcome, as are those from students resuming their education or adult students who have delayed their entrance to college. Transfer students must be in good standing at their former institution.

Applicants who fail to meet regular admission requirements may be considered on an individual basis for the Fresh Start program by the Fresh Start admissions committee. An interview is required for all Fresh Start applicants.

Application and Information

An application is ready for consideration by the Admissions Committee when it has been received with a $35 application fee for domestic students and $75 for international students, the required test scores and references, and transcripts from each school attended. The University uses a system of rolling admissions.

For application forms, catalogs, and additional information, students should contact:

St. Andrews University
1700 Dogwood Mile
Laurinburg, North Carolina 28352
Phone: 910-277-5555
      800-763-0198
E-mail: admissions@sapc.edu
Web site: http://www.sapc.edu

The Katherine McKay Belk Bell Tower at the center of campus.

SAINT ANSELM COLLEGE
MANCHESTER, NEW HAMPSHIRE

The College

Saint Anselm is a small liberal arts college of 2,000 undergraduates in the hills of southern New Hampshire, less than an hour north of Boston. Founded in 1889 by the Catholic Order of Saint Benedict, it maintains a strong sense of community that is characteristic of a Benedictine institution. The College has earned a national reputation for high academic standards. It prides itself on offering a challenging intellectual environment while encouraging the students' intellectual, social, spiritual, and physical development. Saint Anselm's extraordinary commitment to community engagement, evidenced by the involvement of students, faculty, and staff in projects that impact the local community and the world, has earned the College a new and special designation by the Carnegie Foundation for the Advancement of Teaching. Saint Anselm takes pride in being one of seventeen liberal arts colleges nationwide cited as an "institution of community engagement."

All Saint Anselm College students pursue specialized major courses of study in such areas as liberal arts, business, the sciences, nursing, and preprofessional preparation. A curriculum that emphasizes critical thinking, communication, research, and analysis skills leads to strong placement in graduate and professional schools. The College's primary goal, however, is to offer an educational experience that produces well-rounded graduates with a creative and open-minded spirit.

The beauty of Saint Anselm College's 400-acre campus changes with the seasons. Buildings surrounding the quad range from original ivy-covered brick to contemporary architecture, and the grounds include the New Hampshire Institute of Politics at Saint Anselm College and a church with an abbey. In addition to student housing, administration, and academic facilities, the campus includes a multipurpose activities facility with a new fitness center; Davison Hall dining commons; Stoutenburgh Gymnasium, home of Saint Anselm varsity athletics; the Thomas F. Sullivan hockey arena; and Cushing Student Center, which houses academic and career counseling offices, student organizations, health services, and an academic resource center. A short drive away is a 100-acre tract used for retreats and environmental study and research.

Saint Anselm College has students from thirty-one states and twelve countries, more than 88 percent of whom live on campus in traditional dormitories and modern apartments. The list of more than eighty clubs and organizations that match the students' diverse interests is constantly evolving and includes music, community service, theater, outdoor recreation, debating, prelaw and premedicine, and a local chapter of the Knights of Columbus. Intercollegiate sports are offered for men in baseball, basketball, cross-country, football, golf, hockey, lacrosse, skiing, soccer, and tennis. For women, teams are organized in basketball, cross-country, field hockey, lacrosse, skiing, soccer, softball, tennis, and volleyball. There are nearly twenty club sports, including field hockey, ice hockey, ice skating, lacrosse, rugby, soccer, and track.

Location

Less than an hour from Boston, Saint Anselm offers easy access to the cultural attractions of a large city, yet it is equally close to ski slopes, the Appalachian Trail, and the Atlantic coast. It has the feel of a rural campus, but is only minutes from downtown Manchester, the largest city in New Hampshire. In Manchester, students find excellent restaurants, galleries, shopping malls, and theaters as well as professional offices with internship and employment opportunities.

Majors and Degrees

Saint Anselm awards the Bachelor of Arts degree in the following academic programs and majors: accounting, biochemistry, biology, business, chemistry, classics, classical archaeology, communication, computer science, computer science with business, computer science with mathematics, criminal justice, education (secondary and elementary), economics, English, environmental science, environmental politics and sustainability, financial economics, fine arts, forensic science, French, history, international business, international relations, liberal studies in the great books, mathematics, mathematics with economics, natural science, nursing, peace and justice studies, philosophy, physics, politics, psychology, sociology, Spanish, and theology. It also offers a program leading to the Bachelor of Science in Nursing (B.S.N.) degree.

The College offers preprofessional programs in dentistry, law, medicine, and theology.

A 3-2 program in engineering is available in cooperation with the University of Notre Dame, Catholic University of America, Manhattan College, and the University of Massachusetts Lowell.

Academic Programs

Saint Anselm College provides students with a strong liberal arts background, including required courses in philosophy, theology, and foreign language. Students generally take ten to fifteen courses in their majors, while the liberal arts core courses and a wide range of electives make up the remainder of the forty courses required for graduation. Honors program participants distinguish themselves by taking additional courses in order to graduate with honors.

All Saint Anselm students participate in a nationally recognized humanities program, Portraits in Human Greatness, during their freshman and sophomore years. The program's nondisciplinary approach to Western culture integrates science, sociology, history, philosophy, and the arts. The heart of the program is its seminar component, which strengthens skills in reasoning, articulating ideas, and debating.

Saint Anselm College participates in the Advanced Placement Program of the College Board. Students who receive a score of 3 or better on the Advanced Placement examinations may obtain advanced placement and credit in the pertinent subject matter. Applicants who have completed examinations under the College-Level Examination Program may receive advanced placement and credit if the scores they receive are acceptable.

Off-Campus Programs

More than 50 percent of Saint Anselm students complete an internship related to their major field of study, usually during their junior or senior year. Internships help students apply theoretical knowledge, explore careers and graduate school choices, and improve employment prospects. Internships are arranged locally and in major cities such as Boston, New York, and Washington, D.C.

The College provides access to several approved semester-long study-abroad programs, and Saint Anselm faculty members often lead summer study trips abroad. The College has an archeological dig site in Umbria, Italy. Students of all academic majors can participate in fieldwork at the dig site. Service trips sponsored by the Office of Campus Ministry take place from Arizona to Maine as well as in Latin America.

Academic Facilities

Among the College's sixty buildings are facilities for classes, research, arts performances and exhibits, and campus events. Geisel Library holds 230,000 bound volumes and 68,000 microform titles and maintains a collection of 4,000 periodical titles and 1,700 video recordings, as well as CDs and audiotapes. Goulet Science Center has been expanded and renovated to meet the students' needs, and contains its own library. The 20,000-square-foot New Hampshire Institute of Politics is a center for civic education and engagement. It attracts diplomats, candidates, and political experts throughout the year and is in the national and international spotlight during presidential primary and election seasons. The Charles A. Dana Center houses a 700-seat theater and serves as the home of the humanities program. Poisson Computer Science Center contains more than 200 PCs and specially equipped classrooms and offices. Fine arts studios and a small theater are located in the Comiskey Center.

Costs

Tuition for the 2011–12 school year was $31,530, and room and board charges were $11,930. Books and other miscellaneous fees cost approximately $1850.

Financial Aid

Saint Anselm College offers financial aid through various federal and private programs. Assistance is awarded as a supplement to the reasonable financial sacrifice that the College expects will be made by the interested student and his or her parents. Eighty-eight percent of Saint Anselm's students receive some form of financial assistance to help defray the cost of their education. Financial aid packages consist of scholarships, grants, loans, and work opportunities. Merit awards (Presidential Scholarships) of up to $16,000 are awarded to outstanding students.

Two forms are required in applying for aid. The student must submit the CSS Financial Aid PROFILE and the Free Application for Federal Student Aid (FAFSA) to the College Scholarship Service by March 15.

Faculty

The College's faculty consists of full-time and part-time members. Ninety-six percent of the faculty members have earned doctorates or the appropriate terminal degrees in their fields. With a student-teacher ratio of 11:1, professors are extremely accessible. In addition to teaching, the faculty members serve as advisers to students in their departments. No classes are taught by graduate students or teaching assistants.

Student Government

Students participate in the affairs of the college in a variety of ways. Students are elected to positions as class officers and serve on the Student Senate and Campus Activities Board. They serve as student body representatives on the Board of Trustees and on administrative committees, including the college judiciary board, curriculum committee, and health committee. Saint Anselm encourages students to express their opinions and take active roles in shaping the life of their college and to be aware of their potential as active and engaged citizens to effect change in the world around them.

Admission Requirements

In selecting a freshman class, the admission committee considers each candidate personally and thoroughly, evaluating their high school record, SAT scores (if submitted for non-nursing majors), letters of recommendation, and essay (part of the application). Of greatest importance is the student's high school transcript, in terms of both the quality of courses taken and the grades earned.

Transfer and international students are welcome to apply. The same general admission procedures are required, along with at least a C average in all transferable courses and, for international students, a satisfactory score on the TOEFL.

Application and Information

The Office of Admission is open from 8:30 to 4:30 on weekdays and is open for Saturday Visit program in the fall. Please go to www.anselm.edu for a list of current visit programs and admission application deadlines. The College strongly recommends a campus visit and an interview in order to discover the many benefits of Saint Anselm.

For more information, students should contact:

Office of Admission
Saint Anselm College
100 Saint Anselm Drive
Manchester, New Hampshire 03102
Phone: 603-641-7500
      888-426-7356 (toll-free)
E-mail: admission@anselm.edu
Web site: http://www.anselm.edu

Alumni Hall on the campus of Saint Anselm College.

ST. BONAVENTURE UNIVERSITY
ST. BONAVENTURE, NEW YORK

The University

St. Bonaventure University provides a values-based education with individual attention from professors, a beautiful residential setting, and a friendly, close-knit atmosphere. Of the 2,500 students enrolled, 2,000 are undergraduates. More than 74 percent of the undergraduates are full-time residents. Complementing St. Bonaventure's traditions are innovative degree programs, computerized career placement aids, comprehensive student life activities, and modern academic facilities. Among major campus events during the academic year are concerts and coffeehouse acts, indoor and outdoor recreational programs, current and classic film offerings, and dramatic and musical plays. Aspiring writers and broadcasters from all academic majors—Bonaventure has produced 5 Pulitzer Prize winners—find challenging and plentiful opportunities working with one of the four University media: WSBU-88.3 FM-The Buzz, the nationally ranked campus radio station; *The Bona Venture*, the award-winning weekly newspaper; *The Bonadieu*, the yearbook; and *The Laurel*, the nation's oldest student literary publication, which marked its 113th anniversary in 2012. Other organizations on campus include academic fraternities, academic honor societies, a variety of club and intramural sports, and arts organizations that include choral, instrumental, dance, and drama ensembles. The Thomas Merton Ministry Center is open 24 hours a day and aims to foster a community of friendship and mutual service. Many students take the opportunity to serve as Bona Buddies to area children or senior citizens; help with the national award–winning soup kitchen The Warming House; or volunteer in one of many service organizations, including SIFE and BonaResponds, one of the most active collegiate disaster relief organizations in the nation. Volunteer opportunities include immersion experiences and service opportunities with the poor, both in the U.S. and abroad.

St. Bonaventure University students enjoy two athletic facilities: the new $6.2-million Richter Center, which is open 24 hours a day, features three basketball courts, a running/walking track, racquetball/squash/wallyball courts, an aerobics room, a recreational area for roller hockey, a weight room, a cardiovascular fitness room, locker rooms, an equipment check-out, a reception area, and a climbing wall; and the Reilly Center, housing a 5,500-seat sports arena, swimming pool, and weight room. Also available are outdoor tennis and basketball courts and a nine-hole golf course. NCAA Division I athletics for men are baseball, basketball, cross-country, golf, soccer, swimming, and tennis. Division I competition for women includes basketball, cross-country, lacrosse, soccer, softball, swimming, and tennis. St. Bonaventure is a member of the Atlantic 10 conference, and both basketball teams made their NCAA tournaments in 2012.

In addition to its undergraduate programs, St. Bonaventure offers the Master of Arts degree in English and in Franciscan studies (summers only). A Master of Science in Education program includes adolescence education, counselor education, differentiated instruction, educational leadership, literacy, school building leader, and school district leader. A Master of Business Administration program and a Master of Arts program in integrated marketing communications are also offered.

Location

St. Bonaventure is located on Route 417 between Olean, a city of approximately 17,000 residents, and Allegany, a village with about 2,000 residents. Shops, restaurants, and movie theaters are all within walking distance. The campus is spread over 500 acres in a valley surrounded by the Allegheny Mountains. The free Bona Bus connects the campus with Olean and Allegany,

carrying students to and from the area attractions. The region around St. Bonaventure provides a beautiful setting for many outdoor activities. Holiday Valley, a renowned ski resort, is just 20 miles away, and nearby Allegany State Park offers excellent facilities for swimming, boating, and hiking. St. Bonaventure is accessible by car, bus, and commercial air transportation, with Buffalo/Niagara International the nearest major airport.

Majors and Degrees

St. Bonaventure University grants the Bachelor of Arts degree with majors in art, art history, classical languages, English, gerontology, history, interdisciplinary studies, international studies, journalism and mass communication, strategic communication and digital media, modern languages (French and Spanish), music, philosophy, political science, psychology, sociology, theater, theology, and women's studies. The Bachelor of Science is granted with majors in biochemistry, bioinformatics, biology, chemistry, childhood studies, computer science, early childhood education, economics, elementary/special education (dual certification), environmental science, interdisciplinary studies, mathematics, physical education, physics, psychology, and sport studies. The Bachelor of Business Administration is granted with majors in accounting, finance, management sciences, and marketing. Popular five-year master's programs are also available in business, English, and integrated marketing communications, and dual-admission/combined-degree programs offer unique opportunities for students pursuing careers in medicine, dentistry, pharmacy, and physical therapy.

Academic Programs

Students in all majors begin their intellectual journey in Clare College, St. Bonaventure's nationally acclaimed core curriculum, which offers a values-based education grounded in the vision of St. Francis and St. Bonaventure.

A candidate for a bachelor's degree must complete at least 120 credit hours, with a cumulative index of 2.0 or better in the major field and the overall program. A pass/fail grade option, available to all upperclass students, may be elected for one course per semester, but not for courses in a student's major field.

Advanced credit is granted for grades of C or better on either the College Proficiency Examination or the College-Level Examination Program (CLEP) tests. Advanced placement is granted on the basis of scores obtained on the College Board's Advanced Placement (AP) examinations.

Men and women may also elect to participate in the University's Army ROTC program, MacArthur Award winner as best small unit in the nation in 1998.

Off-Campus Programs

Through St. Bonaventure's membership in the College Consortium for International Studies (CCIS), St. Bonaventure students have access to six continents. More than sixty semester-long international study programs, including St. Bonaventure–sponsored study in Italy, Spain, Ireland, and Australia, are available to students in good academic standing in their junior year. Faculty-directed, short-term opportunities include a three-week intersession in China, the Francis E. Kelly Oxford summer program, and a three-week travel study program to Mexico. For further information, students should contact the Office of International Studies. Fieldwork or internships are available in several major programs.

Academic Facilities

Friedsam Memorial Library houses more than 250,000 volumes and includes a trilevel resource center with a curriculum center, the University archives, and digital media and conferencing centers, as well as world-class special collections. An automated online card catalog greatly improves research capabilities.

The William F. Walsh Science Center opened in 2008 and doubled the space for science studies. It houses state-of-the-art computer science, laboratory and classroom space, biology labs, organic and general chemistry labs, a Natural World lab, a 150-seat indoor amphitheater, and faculty offices integrated with lab space for better student-teacher accessibility. It is attached to historic De La Roche Hall, which received a major face-lift in 2008.

The John J. Murphy Professional Building provides the most up-to-date equipment for the School of Business and the School of Journalism and Mass Communication. The Bob Koop Broadcast Journalism Laboratory features a television studio with an anchor desk, digital and videotape editing bays, while a remote TV production studio allows for live broadcasting of athletic events. A fiberoptic network connects microcomputers in academic and administrative areas. There are seven labs for student use with more than 100 Macintosh systems. St. Bonaventure students also have wireless Internet access across campus.

An annex to Plassmann Hall houses computer-adaptable education classrooms, seminar rooms, and offices for the education faculty. An observatory allows students access to three compact telescopes, two 8-inch Celestron telescopes, and one 11-inch Schmidt-Cassegrain telescope, and a heated classroom.

The Regina A. Quick Center for the Arts provides acoustically designed classroom space for music courses and painting and drawing studios. The center also includes a musical instrument digital interface lab, a 325-seat theater, and an atrium that is often used for receptions and impromptu musical performances. The F. Donald Kenney Museum and Art Study Wing includes four climate-controlled galleries offering nationally acclaimed traveling exhibits, works from the University's permanent collections, and student exhibits.

Historic Hickey Dining Hall received a spectacular makeover in 2006, and a 5,500-square-foot coffee café and gourmet deli opened in spring 2007. Some residence halls were overhauled in 2006, while the new science center and a $2.2-million library addition opened in 2008. A new building for the School of Business is scheduled to open in 2013.

Costs

For 2011–12, the annual costs were $26,925 for tuition and $965 for fees. Room and meal plans averaged $9852 per year.

Financial Aid

Students who qualify for financial aid normally receive a package consisting of a combination of scholarships, grants, loans, and work-study awards. An average financial aid package for an incoming freshman is more than $21,000. Athletic grants-in-aid are available for men in baseball, basketball, golf, soccer, swimming, and tennis; and for women in basketball, lacrosse, soccer, softball, swimming, and tennis. Music scholarships are also available. Students must file the Free Application for Federal Student Aid (FAFSA) to be considered for financial assistance. For more complete details, a student should contact the director of financial aid at the University.

Faculty

Like the student body, the 155 full-time and 67 part-time faculty members at St. Bonaventure come from a wide range of geographic, ethnic, and religious backgrounds. The student-faculty ratio of 14:1 allows faculty members the time to help each student to understand different modes of thinking, develop as a person, and lay a foundation for lifelong learning. Eighty-four percent of the faculty members hold the terminal degree in their field. Friars, many of whom teach and live on campus, add to the unique atmosphere of St. Bonaventure.

Student Government

Life at St. Bonaventure is centered on the residence halls, and the foundation of student government begins in the dormitories with the Residence Hall Councils. The elected council members determine the norms by which the residents are guided in their daily lives. The Student Government, whose members are elected from the student body, serves as the general student-governing unit, and its members serve on every major University board and committee.

Admission Requirements

St. Bonaventure University welcomes applications for admission from all serious candidates from a variety of backgrounds. St. Bonaventure University provides equal opportunity without regard to race, creed, color, gender, age, national or ethnic origin, marital status, veteran status, or disability in admission, employment, and in all of its educational programs and activities. Applicants, who are welcome to apply online, must show evidence of academic achievement to be selected for admission. The criteria used in making admission decisions, in order of importance, are quality of the high school curriculum, grade point average in college-preparatory courses, ACT (preferred) or SAT scores, class rank, recommendations from high school teachers and counselors, and extracurricular activities.

Application and Information

For more information about St. Bonaventure University, prospective students should contact:

Office of Admission
St. Bonaventure University
P.O. Box D
St. Bonaventure, New York 14778
Phone: 716-375-2400
        800-462-5050 (toll-free)
E-mail: admissions@sbu.edu
Web site: http://www.sbu.edu

Built in 1928 and renovated in 1999, Devereux Hall is an example of the beautiful Florentine architecture found at St. Bonaventure University.

ST. FRANCIS COLLEGE
BROOKLYN HEIGHTS, NEW YORK

The College

Minutes from Manhattan, St. Francis College is the small college of big dreams, offering a wealth of opportunities to put students on the path to success in both their personal and professional lives. An important part of the Franciscan tradition is to make sure every student reaches their individual goals. For more than 150 years, the mission of St. Francis College has been to provide an affordable, quality education to students of all racial, ethnic, and religious backgrounds. This is why St. Francis has consistently been ranked by *U.S. News and World Report* as one of the best regional colleges in the North (2012) as well as the fifth most diverse college in the North. In addition, Forbes.com has named the College to its America's Best Colleges List for the fourth year in a row.

The College offers more than seventy-two academic programs, majors, minors, and concentrations. Serving students from a wide range of interests, including a dual B.S./M.S. degree in accounting, biology, communication arts, criminal justice, education, management, pre-law, pre-health profession studies, and psychology, and an academically challenging honors program, which offers a series of small, intensive seminars, trips, and other activities that build toward your senior thesis. The B.S./M.S. degree in accounting and M.S. in accounting has positioned graduates to get jobs at both Big Four accounting firms and private companies and a graduate certificate program in project management has been developed and is growing in popularity.

As part of the NCAA Northeast Conference, students participate on nineteen Division I athletic teams, including men's basketball, cross-country, golf, soccer, swimming and diving, tennis, indoor/outdoor track, and the nationally ranked water polo team, which made the NCAA Final Four in 2010. Women compete in basketball, volleyball, bowling, cross-country, golf, tennis, indoor/outdoor track, swimming and diving, and water polo.

Students have a chance to get involved with extracurricular activities, as well as intramural sports. With more than thirty-five clubs and organizations, numerous active fraternities and sororities, honor societies including the Duns Scotus Honor Society, and a vast selection of national societies, students who participate are given the opportunity to grow socially and intellectually and further enhance their leadership skills.

Transfer students will find that St. Francis is the best place to complete their education and with up to 98 credits accepted, the College's personal approach will help ease the student's transition. A generous scholarship program is dedicated to transfers.

Location

Travel & Leisure magazine ranks Brooklyn Heights as one of America's most beautiful neighborhoods and also ranks nearby Brooklyn Bridge Park as one of the best spots, not just in the city, but in America, for it's iconic quality. Students consider Brooklyn Heights and Manhattan as their extended campus with access to museums, historical societies, cultural activities, theater, shopping, restaurants, and sports arenas offering abundant experiences for personal enrichment.

St. Francis College's off-campus housing is also located in the heart of Brooklyn Heights. The newly renovated rooms at the St. George Residence Hall offer full amenities and are within a few blocks of the College, Montague Street, and the Brooklyn Promenade where students can take a stroll or a run while taking in the view of Manhattan's skyline.

Majors and Degrees

Bachelor's degree programs are offered in accounting (B.S.), adolescence education 7–12 (B.A.,B.S.), childhood education 1–6 (B.A.,B.S.), communication arts (B.A.–advertising/public relations, English and communications, film and broadcasting, performance studies), criminal justice (B.S.), economics (B.A.–finance, international economics, public policy), English (B.A.), health promotion and science (B.S.), history (B.A.), information technology (B.S.), international cultural studies (B.A.–international business, Latin American/Caribbean studies, Western European studies), management (B.S.–e-commerce, finance, general business, human resources, management, international business, marketing, operations management, sports management), mathematics (B.S.), philosophy (B.A.), physical education K–12 (B.S.), physicians assistant studies (B.S.), political science (B.A.), professional studies (B.S.–organizational management and leadership, management of technology), psychology (B.A.), religious studies (B.A.), social studies (B.A.), sociology (B.A.–social work), and Spanish (B.A.).

Associate degrees programs are available in business administration (A.A.S.), criminal justice (A.A.S.), and liberal arts (A.A.).

Certificate programs are offered in American studies, information systems, instructional technology, and insurance.

Areas of special interest include pre-law, women's studies, and an honors program.

Bachelor's degree programs for pre-health professions (B.S.) are available in biomedical science/dentistry (NYU), biomedical science/podiatry (NY Podiatric),

diagnostic medical imaging (SUNY Downstate Medical Center), medical technology (NY Methodist Hospital), nursing (for transfer students only, restricted to those with RN certificates), and physician assistant studies (SUNY Downstate Medical Center and St. John's University); pre-medical (various majors), pre–veterinary science (various majors), and radiologic sciences.

Academic Programs

St. Francis College believes that there is big opportunity in a small community. The Office of Freshman Studies coordinates advisement and scheduling for all first-year students making sure that each student reaches their academic goals. During their first year, freshmen are enrolled in Freshman Seminar, which teaches time and stress management, success strategies, and how to search for a major and a career. Many go on to take a sophomore year life-lessons course that provides practical advice on how to search for a job or graduate school, prepare for an interview, and make and keep connections with successful graduates of St. Francis. Students must choose a major by the end of their sophomore year. If a student decides to obtain a minor designation, a minimum requirement of nine credits shall apply. All graduation requirements must be met for the completion of a degree program.

The Academic Enhancement Center provides tutoring, intensive reading and writing courses, and workshops to achieve academic success and independence at all levels of the student's college career.

The College calendar is organized on a traditional semester system, including one January Intersession, one May Intersession, and three summer sessions, all of which offer many courses to catch up, get ahead, or earn an elective.

Off-Campus Programs

Participating in an internship related to the student's career path offers hands-on experience. The College's Career Center provides services, tools, and an up-to-date listing of New York metropolitan area companies that offer internships, all designed to help students reach their goals, enhance learning outside the classroom, and prepare for a rewarding career. In addition, the Terrier Total Training program (T3) has been established for the College's Division I student-athletes to plan the next step beyond their sport. The program provides opportunities to explore career options, develop job search skills, and make informed career decisions.

Opportunities to go global are readily available at St. Francis College. As a member of the College Consortium for International Studies, students who wish to study abroad have great flexibility as to when, where, and how long they want to travel and study. Students can study in places as diverse as The Sorbonne in Paris, Madrid, Rome, Prague, Costa Rica, Australia, and even a Semester at Sea. They can

also explore the world of learning through the faculty-led program in Cortona, Italy experiencing the culture and history of the Tuscany region. Students also have the opportunity to experience a Franciscan pilgrimage to Assisi, Rome, and other places associated with Saint Francis and Saint Clare. This ten-day free pilgrimage is offered annually to two students so they can learn more about the Franciscan values and traditions associated with the College.

Academic Facilities

The Frank and Mary Macchiarola Academic Center is the newest building on the St. Francis campus. This 35,000-square-foot building houses the College's library, an HDTV studio and edit suite, black box theater, state-of-the-art classrooms, computer labs, and seminar rooms. The $20-million building emphasizes the College's commitment to small class size by limiting all new classrooms to no more than 35 students. The library provides 24/7 access from virtually anywhere to more than 200,000 in print and online books, 26,000 e-journals, and 40 subject-specific and multi-disciplinary databases. The collection has been developed specifically to support student research needs and departmental curricula. Much of it is downloadable to mobile devices. The library also offers than 50 computers in two labs, 40 netbooks that can be loaned out, dedicated study spaces, and reference help. Librarians provide one-on-one and group instruction for research projects using library resources. The library also includes a smart classroom and group study rooms with plasma screens for students to view films or practice multimedia presentations. As part of the Academic Center, the Maroney Forum for Arts, Culture and Education is a 90-seat theater for plays, musical performances, workshops, and lectures. The theater is equipped with an HDTV projector to play high-definition movies and videos created by students in the HDTV production studio. The theater has excellent acoustics, a catwalk to help adjust lighting, a control room, green room, and a sympodium that allows professors to include multimedia in their lectures. The College's HDTV studio is equipped with everything needed to produce a complete live program and features three Ikegami HD studio cameras, a lighting grid, professional switching and character generator equipment, and a chroma key curtain. Communication arts majors who are in production classes also have the opportunity to write, shoot, and edit their own video projects with the department's HD cameras and Final Cut Pro editing software loaded on to almost twenty Macs.

The state-of-the-art nursing lab is equipped with real-world medical simulators Sim Man and Sim Baby, which let nursing students diagnose and treat illnesses they would encounter on the job.

The Institute for International and Cross-Cultural Psychology promotes, develops, and implements workshops, symposia, lectures, and conferences at St. Francis College; involves students in cross-cultural research and programs; fosters a sense of involvement in the cultural richness; and creates network ties with other interested psychological institutions in the United States and abroad.

Division I men's and women's Terrier basketball teams take great pride as they play in the Generoso Pope Athletic Complex. Other recreational facilities include the fitness center, aquatics center, and Anthony J. Genovesi Center.

Costs

The annual tuition and fees for a full-time commuter student were $18,100 in 2011–12. Rates for off-campus housing room ranged from $11,950–14,300 (2011–12). A full tuition and fee schedule is available online at www.sfc.edu/studentlife/StudentFinancialServices/TuitionFees.

Financial Aid

St. Francis College prides itself on offering both academic excellence and value—it is one of the most affordable private colleges in the New York City area. Nearly 95 percent of SFC students receive some form of financial aid including federal and state grants, federal loans, and institutional scholarships. Merit-based scholarships that cover near-full tuition for graduating high school students with a 1200 on their SATs are the cornerstones of the College's financial aid program. During 2011–12, St. Francis College awarded $12 million in institutionally funded scholarships and grants with amounts that ranged from $5000 to 15,000. Additional partial scholarships, academic achievement grants, and transfer student scholarships are also part of the generous aid packages.

Faculty

St. Francis College professors have a strong commitment to developing each student's potential and helping them reach their goals. With a student-faculty ratio of 18:1, the small class setting allows for personalized attention and support, which increases personal achievement. Professors bring current theories and knowledge to the classroom and create opportunities for students to participate in active and ongoing learning. St. Francis College faculty members are also well-versed in the Franciscan tradition, which ensures an educational environment that supports students and helps develop the whole person.

Student Government

Student government serves as a sounding board for all student interests, while also providing efficient and productive leadership for the student body. Its goals are to facilitate student communication, coordinate and encourage student participation, provide means for responsible and effective student participation in appropriate decision-making processes of the College.

Admission Requirements

St. Francis College seeks to admit students who can successfully pursue courses leading to a degree. Students must submit evidence of successful high school completion, acceptable SAT or ACT scores, and an application for admission. While admission to St. Francis College is competitive, the admissions committee seeks a student body that is ethnically and socially diverse with the potential to succeed in college rather than meeting any prescribed pattern of entrance units. The office of admissions expects applicants to have pursued a challenging high school curriculum by taking advantage of honors and advanced placement classes where appropriate. Applicants seeking an associate or bachelor's degree must present a transcript from an approved secondary school. All applicants who are currently enrolled in secondary school are required to take the SAT or ACT and submit their test scores to the College.

Transfer students must submit official transcripts from the previously attended schools as well as a secondary school transcript or certificate of graduation. A catalogue from the colleges previously attended may be requested.

Application and Information

Students are encouraged to visit the campus and meet with an admissions counselor before applying. Applications are available on the College's Web site, www.sfc.edu, or from the Office of Admissions.

St. Francis College
Office of Admissions
180 Remsen Street
Brooklyn Heights, New York 11201-9864
Phone: 718-489-5200
Fax: 718-802-0453
E-mail: admissions@sfc.edu
Web site: http://www.sfc.edu

With a vibrant campus life and more than thirty-five clubs and organization, there's always something going on at St. Francis College.

SAINT FRANCIS UNIVERSITY
LORETTO, PENNSYLVANIA

SAINT FRANCIS
UNIVERSITY
FOUNDED 1847

The University

Saint Francis University is a small, coeducational, liberal arts university. The University was founded in 1847 and conducted under the tradition of the Franciscan Friars of the Third Order Regular. The University is concerned with the development of each student for the world of today. For more than 150 years, the University's philosophy of education and student life has continued to emphasize two values: instruction of high quality and respect for the student as an individual. The University believes that a liberal arts education, encompassing a major field of study, is the soundest kind of preparation a student can have for a productive life. In recent years, Saint Francis University has garnered recognition for advances in study abroad and outreach in health care. In addition, *U.S. News & World Report* has named Saint Francis as a Best Value institution. The University is accredited by the Middle States Association of Colleges and Schools. Departmental accreditations include the Accreditation Review Commission on Education for the Physician Assistant, Inc., Commission on Collegiate Nursing Education, Council on Social Work Education, and others. A complete list of accreditations may be found in the University catalog.

Students at Saint Francis University can find a number of outlets for their talents, interests, and abilities. Departmental clubs; volunteer organizations; social, business, and service fraternities; social sororities; and a service sorority are part of campus life. Athletics have played a major role in the University's history, and the athletics program offers twenty-two NCAA Division I sports for men and women as well as intramural sports. All athletic teams compete in the Northeast Conference. The Student Activities Organization sponsors an impressive program of lectures, films, and concerts. The Southern Alleghenies Museum of Art, separately chartered, is located on the campus as well.

The full-time undergraduate enrollment is 726 men and 916 women; the University as a whole enrolls 2,433 students. Saint Francis University offers Associate of Science degrees in business administration, and religious education. On the graduate level, Saint Francis grants a Master of Arts degree in human resource management and industrial relations. The University also offers the Master of Business Administration, Master of Education, Master of Health Science, Master of Medical Science, Master of Physician Assistant Science, and Master of Science in Occupational Therapy degrees. A doctoral degree in physical therapy is also available.

Location

Saint Francis University is situated on 600 acres in the heart of the Allegheny Mountains. The campus is located in the borough of Loretto, which has a population of approximately 1,400. The campus is 6 miles from the county seat of Ebensburg, which has a population of 4,000. The cities of Johnstown and Altoona are within 25 miles of Loretto and have populations of 35,000 and 55,000, respectively. The University is a 90-minute drive east of Pittsburgh.

Majors and Degrees

Saint Francis University grants the Bachelor of Arts degree and offers majors in American studies, biology, computer science, engineering (3-2 program), English, English/communications, history, mathematics, philosophy, political science, psychology, public administration/government service, religious studies, and sociology. The Bachelor of Science degree is also granted, with majors in accounting, biology, chemistry, computer science, economics and finance, elementary education/special education, environmental engineering, environmental management (3-2 program), environmental studies (interdisciplinary), exercise physiology, management information systems, marketing, mathematics, medical technology, nursing, occupational therapy (five-year master's), pharmacy (2+3 or 2+4), physical therapy (six-year doctoral degree), physician assistant science (five-year master's), podiatric science, psychology, public

administration/government service, public health, social work, and sociology.

Areas of pre-professional study include chiropractic studies, dentistry, engineering (3-2 program), law, medicine, optometry, pharmacy, podiatry, and veterinary medicine. Areas of concentration within majors include bioinformatics, computer science, criminal justice, environmental science, forensics, gaming/new media design and production, healthcare management, information technology and security, international studies, marine education, molecular biology, political communications, public management, and public relations. The University also grants secondary education certification in the areas of biology, chemistry, English, general science, history, mathematics, and social studies. A 3-2 cooperative program with Duke University in forestry and environmental management, a 3+4 accelerated program in primary care, a 2+3 accelerated program and a 3+3 program in pharmacy with Lake Erie College of Osteopathic Medicine, and a 3+4 accelerated program leading to the baccalaureate and Doctor of Dental Medicine degrees with Temple University are also offered.

It is possible for students to major in one area and minor in another or to have a double major. A self-designed major program is available as well. The University offers an honors program to challenge intellectually ambitious students from all disciplines. While pursuing their major field of study, students enroll in the full four-year curriculum, which allows in-depth, creative study in a variety of subject areas.

A continuing education program provides credit and noncredit courses on campus, online, and in the communities surrounding Loretto. The Office of Adult Degree and Continuing Studies offers a variety of academic programs ranging from certificate programs to bachelor's degree programs. Areas of study include business, computer systems management, health sciences, and religious studies.

Academic Programs

The program of study leading to a bachelor's degree is usually completed in eight semesters. To qualify for graduation, a student must follow a program of study approved by the Office of the Provost that totals at least 128 credits distributed among liberal arts courses, major requirements, collateral requirements, and general electives. All students, regardless of major, are required to complete the University's general education program of 58 credits.

The academic calendar is divided into two semesters and three summer sessions.

Electronic capabilities at Saint Francis University enable students to access library holdings and communicate with professors, fellow students, and the world through the use of personal computers via e-mail and the Internet. Every classroom and residence hall room is wired for Internet access or can be accessed through the wireless network. The University has several classrooms equipped with state-of-the-art equipment that allows videoconferencing. All students receive a laptop computer as part of their tuition.

Off-Campus Programs

Students at Saint Francis University may, with permission of the University's administration, spend their junior year of study abroad or may earn credit for participation in summer programs conducted in Canada, France, Germany, Spain, and other countries by accredited American colleges and universities.

Students are encouraged to take advantage of the University's study abroad facility in Ambialet, France. The Semester in France program offers study for students within any major for the same tuition costs as studying on campus.

A number of departments offer students the opportunity for off-campus study. For some majors, such as nursing, occupational therapy, physical therapy, physician assistant science, education, medical technology, and social work, off-campus study is required;

in all other majors, an internship is available as an elective. Such an internship can be a meaningful experience and can significantly enhance a student's career preparation.

Academic Facilities

Saint Francis University strives to address the needs of its student and support the vision of the institution. The recently completed DiSepio Institute for Rural Health & Wellness is the first phase of a three-phase plan to address the vision of the sciences and health sciences. The 30,000-square-foot education and research center opened its doors in April 2009. The facility includes a human performance laboratory, a state-of-the-art fitness facility, and rehabilitation services. Phase two is the new science center, currently under construction, which will serve as the campus' flagship facility for science and technology programs. The final phase of the project involves the renovation of Sullivan Hall to house modern classroom and lab space, tailored to meet the needs of health science students. An additional project centered on academic facilities includes the renovation of Schwab Hall in order to house the entire School of Business.

The six-story Pasquerilla Library contains more than 150,000 volumes. Other features of the library are general study areas, seminar rooms, reading rooms, reading rooms, several multimedia classrooms, and technologically equipped study rooms.

Costs

For 2011–12, tuition was $26,758, room and board were $9520, and the technology program was $1050, for a total of $37,328.

Financial Aid

Approximately 90 percent of the Saint Francis University student body receives financial aid. In addition to participating in federal and state need-based student aid programs, Saint Francis University offers its own substantial grant program and a generous scholarship program that is based on SAT or ACT scores, high school average, and class rank. Academic awards range from $1000 to $16,500.

Faculty

Faculty members are chosen for their knowledge of subject matter, as well as for their ability to communicate. Of the teaching faculty at Saint Francis University, 80 percent hold a doctorate or the highest degree attainable in their specific field of expertise. No teaching assistants or graduate students teach classes at Saint Francis University.

Student Government

The Student Government Association's Steering Committee involves students who are interested in self-government. Students also serve on a number of committees in the Faculty Senate. The Student Government offices are located in the John F. Kennedy Student Center, which also houses a 600-seat auditorium, a campus bookstore and post office, a study lounge, and a café.

Admission Requirements

The admission committee considers applicants and renders decisions on the basis of the secondary school record, the recommendation of the secondary school principal or counselor, and the results of the SAT or ACT. Applicants to the School of Health Science should be aware of specified application requirements and deadlines. Applicants should have a minimum of 16 academic units and are strongly encouraged to visit the University campus for an admission interview and tour. Interviews and campus tours are available Monday through Friday throughout the year and select Saturday mornings while classes are in session.

Transfer students must submit a formal transfer application and a college clearance form in addition to official transcripts from each high school and college previously attended. Transfer students receive an advanced standing evaluation after an offer of admission has been made.

Saint Francis University, an equal opportunity/affirmative action employer, complies with applicable federal and state laws regarding nondiscrimination and affirmative action, including Title IX of the Educational Amendments of 1972, Titles VI and VII of the Civil Rights Act of 1964, and Section 504 of the Rehabilitation Act of 1973. Saint Francis University is committed to a policy of nondiscrimination and equal opportunity in employment, education programs and activities, and admissions that includes all persons regardless of race, gender, color, religion, national origin or ancestry, age, marital status, disability, or Vietnam-era veteran status. Inquiries or complaints may be addressed to the University's Director of Human Resources/Affirmative Action/Title IX Coordinator, Saint Francis University, Loretto, Pennsylvania 15940; telephone: 814-472-3264. For other University information, students should call 814-472-3000.

Application and Information

The University operates under a rolling admission policy. The application deadline for the physical therapy, occupational therapy, and physician assistant programs is January 15. For more information about Saint Francis University, students should contact:

Vice President for Enrollment Management
Saint Francis University
P.O. Box 600
Loretto, Pennsylvania 15940
Phone: 814-472-3100
      866-342-5738 (toll-free)
E-mail: admissions@francis.edu
Web site: http://www.francis.edu
    http://www.facebook.com/SaintFrancisUniversity(Facebook)
    http://twitter.com/SaintFrancisPA (Twitter)

The Joseph and Marguerite DiSepio Institute for Rural Health & Wellness building is a state-of-the-art education and research facility.

ST. JOHN FISHER COLLEGE
ROCHESTER, NEW YORK

The College

Founded in 1948 by the Basilian fathers, St. John Fisher College is dedicated to serving the individual needs of its students. Originally a Catholic college for men, Fisher is now an independent, coeducational college with 58 percent women and 52 percent resident students. The College offers thirty-one undergraduate programs in business, the humanities, nursing, natural sciences, and social sciences, and is accredited by the Middle States Association of Colleges and Schools. The College also offers twelve master's programs and three doctoral programs leading to the Master of Business Administration, the Master of Science, the Master of Science in Education, the Doctor of Education, the Doctor of Nursing Practice, and the Doctor of Pharmacy.

Fisher's unique First-Year Program reaches beyond the transition to college to focus on developing responsible campus citizens with independent learning skills, who fully explore educational and career aspirations. The Learning Community Program gives first-year students the opportunity to take courses in clusters that focus on a central theme. Through this approach to learning, students and faculty members examine a complex topic from multiple perspectives and discover connections among various disciplines. Fisher's Learning Communities also enable students to learn cooperatively and develop close working relationships with other students and faculty members.

All of the residence halls have been renovated, giving all students access to the Internet and cable TV in their rooms. Keough Hall, the College's newest residence, opened in September 2005 and added more than 200 beds.

Fisher offers a full range of extracurricular activities designed to cater to the diverse interests of the 2,700 full-time and 200 part-time undergraduate students, over 700 master's students, and over 400 doctoral students. Such activities include a student newspaper, a student TV club, a complete intramural program, and more than seventy student clubs and organizations. In addition, the Student Activities Board sponsors appearances by on-campus lecturers and entertainers.

Fisher is a member of NCAA Division III, ECAC, and the Empire 8. Men's intercollegiate sports are baseball, basketball, cross-country, football, golf, indoor and outdoor track and field, lacrosse, rowing, soccer, and tennis. Women's intercollegiate sports are basketball, cross-country, field hockey, golf, indoor and outdoor track and field, lacrosse, rowing, soccer, softball, tennis, and volleyball. Club sports include ice hockey, volleyball, and men's and women's rugby. The Student Life Center, which is the hub of the athletic activities, includes courts for basketball, racquetball, squash, tennis, and volleyball; a sauna; a lounge; and a fitness area. Growney Stadium, complete with 2,100 bleacher seats and a press box, is equipped with an all-weather synthetic playing field to allow for all-season and nighttime play. Other on-campus athletics facilities include a nine-hole golf course, a softball field, a baseball complex, and two grass practice fields. In summer 2011, a new track and field complex opened in time for fall sports. Each summer, Fisher is proud to host the Buffalo Bills training camp on campus.

Location

Located on 154 park-like acres, Fisher offers a balance of city activity and suburban tranquility. Just 10 minutes from the Fisher campus, Rochester, New York, the "World's Image Centre," offers many cultural attractions, including the Eastman Theater, the Rochester Philharmonic Orchestra, the International Museum of Photography at George Eastman House, the Rochester Museum and Science Center, the Memorial Art Gallery, and the Strasenburgh Planetarium. Home to a number of Fortune 500 companies, such as Xerox Corporation and Bausch and Lomb, the city of Rochester offers Fisher students opportunities for internships and employment after graduation.

Majors and Degrees

St. John Fisher College offers courses leading to the Bachelor of Arts and Bachelor of Science degrees. Undergraduate majors are offered in accounting, American studies, anthropology, biology, chemistry, communication/journalism, computer science, economics, education (inclusive education in childhood and adolescence), English, finance, French, history, human resources management, interdisciplinary studies, international studies, legal studies, management, marketing, mathematics, nursing, philosophy, physics, political science, psychology, religious studies, sociology, Spanish, sport management, and statistics.

Fisher offers an online RN-to-B.S. in nursing degree-completion program and a fast-track B.S.-M.S. in advanced practice nursing. The College also offers a cooperative engineering program with the University of Detroit, Clarkson University, Manhattan College, Columbia University, and the University at Buffalo, the State University of New York.

Academic Programs

The bachelor's degree is conferred upon those who complete a minimum of 120 semester hours of credit with a cumulative GPA of at least 2.0. Thirty hours of credit and half of the requirements for the major must be earned at St. John Fisher College. Graduates of Fisher's undergraduate accounting program, or the M.B.A. with a concentration in accounting, who have 150 hours of credit and 33 hours of credit in accounting courses, are eligible to sit for the CPA exam in New York State.

Off-Campus Programs

Fisher offers a multitude of special programs that are designed to complement its academic programs. Students in many disciplines can take advantage of an internship program, Albany and Washington Semesters, and cross-registration with fourteen member colleges of the Rochester Area College Consortium. Study-abroad opportunities throughout the world are also available to students.

Academic Facilities

Over the last fourteen years, most of the academic and athletic facilities on campus have been upgraded and enhanced. Classrooms have been modernized and outfitted with state-of-the-art media facilities. Laboratory space has been upgraded with state-of-the-market educational technology. The Golisano Academic Gateway, complete with the Frontier Cyber Café and the learning resource center, opened in January 2001. The Ralph C. Wilson, Jr. Building opened in September 2003, expanding classroom capacity by 20 percent and providing additional faculty offices, seminar rooms, and meeting spaces.

The Campus Center opened in fall 2005 and serves as the hub and central gathering place of student activity on campus. This two-story facility supports general student gathering spaces, which include a performance space, recreational area, offices for student clubs and organizations, and the College Store (bookstore), all located on the first floor. The second floor of the Campus Center houses the Offices of the Dean of Students, Residential Life, Campus Life, and Campus Ministry, as well as additional student organization offices and meeting spaces.

The Charles J. Lavery Library meets the information needs of twenty-first-century students. A blend of traditional and electronic resources covering a broad range of subjects is available to the Fisher community. The library's print collection is supplemented by an extensive offering of online scholarly resources. Information resources include 200,000 volumes, 8,588 audiovisual items, and access to approximately 50,000 print and electronic periodical titles.

Professional librarians welcome students to the library reference desk during day and evening hours. There is also a 24/7 online-chat reference service. The librarians are information specialists committed to the academic success of all students. Individual

research guidance is available by appointment. Librarians also teach classes in information literacy and subject-specific research to all levels of students.

Lavery Library is a member of the Rochester Regional Library Council, representing a regional collection of more than 3,400,000 titles. Interlibrary loan staff can obtain resources not owned by Lavery Library from regional, national, and international libraries.

Costs

Tuition for 2012–13 is $26,810. Room and board costs are $10,643 with a meal plan and a room in one of Fisher's residence halls, and fees are $500.

Financial Aid

Committed to helping students meet the cost of their education, Fisher works to assess each individual's financial need. Financial aid is provided through scholarships, grants, loans, and work-study arrangements and is awarded by Fisher, the state, and the federal government. In 2011–12, the average financial aid package was $20,472 and 100 percent of incoming full-time freshmen receive a grant or scholarship.

St. John Fisher College offers a generous academic scholarship program that is based on high school average, strength of curriculum, and SAT or ACT scores. Students eligible for academic scholarships are automatically notified by the Office of Freshman Admissions. Scholarship award amounts are $10,000 to $12,500 per year. The College also offers an honors program and a science scholars program. The award in each of these programs is $3000 per year, in addition to any academic scholarships for which the student qualifies.

Sixteen years ago, the College introduced the Service Scholars Program. This program is designed to recognize and reward high school seniors who demonstrate an ongoing interest in serving the needs of others through a commitment to community service. Scholarship awards equal one third of the total yearly cost of tuition, and room and board for four years. St. John Fisher College was recently named, for the sixth time, to the President's Higher Education Community Service Honor Roll for exemplary service efforts and service to disadvantaged youth.

In 1998, the College announced the creation of the Fannie and Sam Constantino First Generation Scholarship Program, designed to provide financial and academic assistance to high school students whose parents did not graduate from a postsecondary institution—much like the pioneer classes of St. John Fisher College. Recipients receive annual scholarships ranging from $5000 to one half of the total cost of Fisher's tuition, room, and board.

Faculty

Fisher's 214 full-time faculty members are dedicated to helping students, both in and out of the classroom, as they strive to achieve their goals. Eighty-seven percent of full-time faculty members hold doctoral or terminal degrees. The student-teacher ratio of 13:1 offers a personal approach to education; 75 percent of all classes have fewer than 30 students. Fisher's Office of Academic Affairs and an outstanding faculty share responsibility for academic advising, helping students to explore the 31 majors that are available to them.

Student Government

Student leadership skills are developed through the Student Government Association, which is responsible for the social, cultural, and judicial areas of student life. Resident students elect a Resident Student Association, while commuting students elect a Commuter Council to represent them in planning special activities. The Student Activities Board is responsible for social activities and cultural events throughout the academic year.

Admission Requirements

Admission to St. John Fisher College is based primarily on the following: grade point average, strength of curriculum, scores on standardized tests (SAT/ACT); a personal statement, essay, or graded paper; extracurricular activities and/or work experience, and the counselor/teacher recommendation.

A candidate for admission to the freshman class must be a graduate of an approved secondary school and present a minimum of 16 units of college-preparatory course work in English, foreign languages, mathematics, and natural and social sciences. An applicant should present a secondary school average of 85 percent or above in these academic subjects.

Fisher welcomes qualified transfer students from two- and four-year colleges for both the fall and spring terms. To be considered for admission, transfer students must have a cumulative grade point average of 2.0 or better. If the student has obtained an A.A., A.S., or A.A.S. degree, 60 to 66 credit hours are transferred. All transfer applicants should consult the Undergraduate Catalog on the College's Web site for details.

The College has various special admission programs, including early decision, abbreviated procedures for veterans and other military personnel, and admission for part-time study.

The College offers the Arthur O. Eve Higher Education Opportunity Program (HEOP) for students who need special academic and financial assistance. The program provides academic support services, counseling, and financial aid for qualified students to help them achieve academic success.

Fisher grants college credit for satisfactory grades on the Advanced Placement test, the International Baccalaureate (I.B.) program exams, and the College-Level Examination Program (CLEP). Only students who receive a 3 or higher in all AP subjects and a 4 or higher on the AP science and language exams are granted Advanced Placement credit. CLEP and I.B. scoring guidelines are available through the Office of Freshman Admissions. Credit is only granted for subject-specific CLEP exams. In addition, recognizing the college-level course work being completed at the high school level, St. John Fisher College will consider granting credit for any college course work in which a student earns a grade of "C" or better.

Application and Information

Applications are accepted on a rolling basis. Early-decision applications are due December 1. The admissions application deadline for merit scholarship consideration is January 15.

Although a personal interview is not required for admission, all applicants are encouraged to visit the College. Interviews, information sessions, and campus tours are available during the week and on selected Saturdays throughout the year.

For additional information or an application, students should contact:

Office of Freshman Admissions
St. John Fisher College
3690 East Avenue
Rochester, New York 14618
Phone: 585-385-8064
      800-444-4640 (toll-free)
Fax: 585-385-8386
E-mail: admissions@sjfc.edu
Web site: http://www.sjfc.edu/admissions/freshman
      http://www.facebook.com/StJohnFisherCollege
      http://twitter.com/FisherNews
      http://www.youtube.com/user/StJohnFisherCollege

Kearney Hall, Fisher's main administration building.

ST. JOHN'S COLLEGE
ANNAPOLIS, MARYLAND, AND SANTA FE, NEW MEXICO

The College

St. John's College maintains two widely separated campuses, one in Annapolis, Maryland, and another in Santa Fe, New Mexico. Each has its own admissions and financial aid offices. A common curriculum, however, enables students and faculty members to move from one campus to the other. Both campuses are cohesive intellectual communities in which students are eagerly responsive to one another. Students also pursue interests in such activities as publications, dance, dramatics, photography, art, wilderness exploration, and sailing. The social climate is informal and lively, and students enjoy many celebrations each year. Facilities are available for almost any intramural sport; most students participate. There is a bookstore on each campus. In fall 2011, opening enrollment at the Annapolis campus was 213 women and 277 men, for a total of 490 students. The opening enrollment of 368 at the Santa Fe campus consisted of153 women and 215 men.

The students on both campuses are outstanding, yet they fit no pattern. Though their backgrounds are varied geographically, academically, and otherwise, they are, most typically, young people who habitually read books and value good conversation. Their commitment to ideas and their enthusiasm for the St. John's program are well illustrated by the fact that about one fifth of them on each campus have transferred to St. John's as freshmen after a year or more of college elsewhere.

Location

St. John's is the third-oldest college in the United States. It has been located since 1696 in the Colonial seaport city of Annapolis, the capital of Maryland, 30 miles from Washington, D.C. In 1964, a second campus was opened at the foot of the mountains surrounding Santa Fe, a cultural center and the capital of New Mexico. The campuses are alike in curriculum and methods, but their settings and moods are as different as sailing on the Chesapeake Bay and skiing in the Sangre de Cristo Mountains, as Georgian and Spanish Colonial architecture. St. John's students participate in a number of activities of benefit to their communities at large.

Majors and Degrees

St. John's College is committed to liberal education in the most traditional and yet radical way. It accomplishes this through direct engagement with the books in which the greatest minds of Western civilization have expressed themselves and through translation, mathematical demonstration, musical analysis, and laboratory experimentation. Whether in Annapolis or in Santa Fe, all St. John's students follow the same course of study leading to the B.A. degree. One of the purposes of this program is to emphasize the unity of knowledge; thus, the faculty is not divided into departments and there are no majors.

Academic Programs

The academic program is a unified, cohesive whole; instruction takes the form of annual sequences of related seminars, tutorials, and laboratories, in each of which the books that form the core of the curriculum are the basis of study and discussion. To ensure that the intellectual life of the College extends beyond the classroom and that students bring a common frame of reference to the continuing discussion, this academic program is required of everyone, but no two students are expected to approach any subject in the same way or to reach the same conclusions about it. A central purpose of the St. John's program is to give students both the opportunity and the obligation to think for themselves. The books at the heart of the program serve to foster that thinking. They not only illuminate the enduring questions of human existence but also have great relevance to contemporary problems. They can change minds, move hearts, and touch spirits. They help all students to arrive independently at rational opinions and conclusions of their own. From this common curriculum, about 70 percent of the students go on to graduate and professional study in a wide range of fields.

There are two semesters a year. All classes are small discussion groups and range in size from between 12 and 16 students in tutorials to between 18 and 20 in seminars and laboratories. Final examinations are oral and individual. Students are not routinely informed of their grades. Instead, a student's tutors, as members of the faculty are called, evaluate the student's intellectual performance twice a year in his or her presence and with his or her help. St. John's students are participants in their own education. Annual essays and shorter papers, prepared by students without recourse to secondary sources, are based directly on the books of the program.

Seminars are devoted to reading works of the greatest minds and engaging in thoughtful discussion about them. The first-year seminar focuses on Greek authors; the second on the works of the Roman, medieval, and early Renaissance periods; the third on books of the seventeenth and eighteenth centuries; and the fourth on writings from the nineteenth and twentieth centuries. The seminar consists almost exclusively of student conversation. The aim of the discussions is to ascertain not how things were but how things are. Everyone's opinion must be heard and must also be supported by argument and evidence. The role of the tutors is not to give information or to produce the "right" interpretation; it is to guide the discussion, to aid in defining the issues, and to help the students to understand the authors, the issues, and themselves. If tutors do take a definite stand and enter the argument, they are expected to defend their positions just as students do. Reason is the only recognized authority.

Preceptorials replace seminars for seven weeks of the junior and senior years. In the preceptorial, students and tutors gather in groups of 8 or 9 to discuss, with more leisure than the pace and discipline of the seminar permit, books or topics of particular interest to them.

In the language tutorial, Greek is studied in the first two years and French in the last two. By translating works written in Greek and French into English and comparing those languages with each other as well as with English, the student gains an appreciation of all three and learns something of the nature of language in general.

The language of number and figure does not require a special aptitude. Rather, mathematics is an integral and necessary part of comprehending the world. The mathematics tutorial seeks to affect an understanding of the fundamental nature

and intention of mathematics. Throughout the four years, the student is in contact not only with the pure science of mathematics but also with the foundations of mathematical physics and astronomy. The blackboard becomes an arena of logical struggle, which brings the imagination constantly into play.

The music tutorial aims at understanding music through study of musical theory and analysis of significant works. Students investigate rhythm, the diatonic system, ratios of musical intervals, melody, counterpoint, and harmony.

In the modern world, the liberal arts are practiced at their best and fullest in the laboratory. This practice puts into serious question the common distinction between the natural sciences and the humanities. The laboratory is a part of the program in all years but the second. It weaves together the main themes of physics, biology, and chemistry with careful scrutiny of the interplay of hypothesis, theory, and observed fact.

On Friday evenings, the College community assembles for a formal lecture or concert by a tutor or visitor. It is the only time the students are lectured to. Afterward, interested students and faculty members engage the speaker or performer in questions and discussion.

Academic Facilities

The library on each campus—about 100,000 volumes in Annapolis, nearly 60,000 in Santa Fe—emphasizes material appropriate to the nature of the academic program, supplemented by a more general collection and by a variety of special collections. Recordings and representative periodicals and newspapers are included. Academic facilities on each campus also include the resources and equipment necessary for study and experimentation in physics, chemistry, and biology (including a planetarium in Annapolis); for audition and performance of music; for display and studio work in art, photography, and other crafts; and for drama productions.

Costs

For 2012–13, annual tuition and fees total $44,554. Room and board are $10,644. Books and supplies range in cost from $450 to $600.

Financial Aid

The criterion for financial assistance is need. On both campuses the application for financial aid is the CSS PROFILE, supplemented by the Free Application for Federal Student Aid (FAFSA). More than half of all St. John's students receive aid, usually in a combination of grants, loans, and employment. Federal Perkins Loans, Federal Pell Grants, Federal Supplemental Educational Opportunity Grants, Federal Work-Study Program employment, and College grants and jobs are available.

Faculty

The faculty-student ratio is 1:8 on each campus. Faculty members all hold the same rank. Their intellectual range and vitality come from teaching throughout the curriculum. This breadth and tension and the fact that St. John's is an intellectual community in which all teach and all learn are distinctive characteristics of the St. John's faculty.

Student Government

Inside the classroom and out, the dignity of the students as adults is respected. On both campuses, student government is part of the general College pattern. A Delegate Council

and Student Committee on Instruction work with the faculty members and administrators on matters of mutual concern.

Admission Requirements

Criteria for admission to either campus are intellectual and academic, though any accomplishment showing initiative and drive may strengthen an application. The written application consists of a series of reflective essays. The academic record and recommendations are considered supplements to it. SAT or ACT scores are optional but may prove helpful. There are no minimums for grades or test scores; both may be made irrelevant by what the candidate writes. On each campus, applicants are judged on their own merits. Although interviews are not required except in special cases, interested students are urged to visit either campus for a day or overnight visit to sit in on seminars and tutorials.

Application and Information

Students may be admitted to either campus for the fall term or, if they are prepared to continue their studies through the following summer, in January on the Santa Fe campus. Application must be made to one campus or the other, not to both. Early application is advisable. Each campus seeks to complete its class by May 1. All applications for admission and financial aid are acted on as soon as they are complete, and the candidate is notified of the decision within two to three weeks.

St. John's is a member of the Common Application Group. For information about the academic program and the extracurricular life of the College, students should contact:

Sarah G. Morse
Director of Admissions
St. John's College
Annapolis, Maryland 21404
Phone: 800-727-9238 (toll-free)
E-mail: admissions@sjca.edu
Web site: http://www.stjohnscollege.edu

Larry Clendenin
Director of Admissions
St. John's College
Santa Fe, New Mexico 87501
Phone: 800-331-5232 (toll-free)
E-mail: admissions@sjcsf.edu
Web site: http://www.stjohnscollege.edu

St. John's College at Annapolis.

ST. JOSEPH'S COLLEGE
BROOKLYN AND PATCHOGUE, NEW YORK

The College

Since 1916, St. Joseph's College has been inspiring students to transform their lives. A private coeducational institution with campuses in Brooklyn and Patchogue, Long Island, the College enrolls nearly 6,000 undergraduates and over 500 graduate students in its School of Arts and Sciences and School of Professional and Graduate Studies. St. Joseph's consistently earns a place among top colleges in the Region, as ranked by *U.S. News & World Report*. In addition, St. Joseph's is the most affordable private college in the New York metropolitan area and Long Island.

St. Joseph's College helps students turn aspirations into accomplishments. In addition to offering a liberal arts education of the highest quality, St. Joseph's offers students an unrivaled degree of personal attention, encouraging them to lead lives characterized by integrity, a commitment to upholding intellectual and spiritual values, social responsibility, and service to others.

St. Joseph's students immerse themselves in learning in ways that go far beyond the classroom, through independent projects, team-building assignments, internships, community service opportunities, and study-abroad programs designed to suit every schedule. Moreover, with just 15 students for every professor on campus, St. Joseph's students easily find mentors to guide them in everything from academics to focusing on future career and life goals.

Although most of St. Joseph's students commute at both campuses, the Brooklyn campus offers student housing through Educational Housing Services at the nearby St. George Residence. Each of the campuses offers a lively atmosphere enriched by social events, athletic competitions, and a Common Hour to encourage students to explore new possibilities for fun, leadership, and connections. On any given day at St. Joseph's, students might come to campus to hear a Pulitzer Prize–winning author, enjoy a jazz concert, join a community service effort, view an art exhibit, attend an athletic event, or engage in a political debate over dinner with other students and professors. Each campus supports over thirty student clubs and activities, including intercollegiate basketball; women's softball, swimming, tennis, and volleyball; men's baseball, tennis, and volleyball; and coed cross-country. The Long Island campus also offers men's soccer, and a coed equestrian team.

For undergraduates, St. Joseph's offers fast tracks to advanced degrees through special affiliated programs in accounting, and podiatry. The School of Professional and Graduate Studies at St. Joseph's College offers a wide range of graduate programs in education, human services, management, and nursing, including the Executive M.B.A., an M.B.A. in accounting, an M.B.A. in health-care management, and the M.S. in nursing, to name a few.

Location

The Brooklyn campus is located in the Clinton Hill Historic District, a neighborhood where so many of New York's wealthiest citizens once lived that it was dubbed Brooklyn's "Gold Coast" in the 1920s. Today this area is home to several prestigious schools, including the Pratt Institute of Art and the Brooklyn Academy of Music, and serves as a hub of cultural and intellectual activity. This convenient location allows students to enjoy the freedom of a safe, well-landscaped campus easily accessible to New York City by car or public transportation.

St. Joseph's Long Island campus is located in the village of Patchogue on Great South Bay, about 50 miles from Manhattan and 60 miles from Montauk Point. Patchogue offers plenty to do, with fine harbors, shops, restaurants, athletic fields, and tennis courts right in the village. There are lovely parks nearby as well as museums, golf courses, hiking and ski trails, and beaches. Patchogue is easily accessible via Long Island Rail Road, bus service, or ferry. A major regional airport, MacArthur Airport, is just minutes away.

Majors and Degrees

Through individual attention, interactive teaching, and intensive advising, St. Joseph's meets students where they are academically, then guides them through the essential next steps to help them stretch intellectually, personally, and professionally. St. Joseph's offers four-year programs leading to B.A. and B.S. degrees at both the Brooklyn and Patchogue campuses, with majors in accounting, business administration, biology, chemistry, child study, computer information systems, criminal justice, English, history, human relations, marketing, mathematics, medical technology, recreation, psychology, social sciences: economics, sociology and political science, Spanish, and speech communication. Among these majors are a variety of minors and certificate programs from which students can choose.

No matter what major students choose, they can also earn additional certificates designed to help them delve deeper into specific interests and give them a head start when entering the workforce. Certificate programs include criminology/criminal justice; gerontology; information technology; leadership and supervision; management, marketing, advertising, and public relations; and religious studies.

For students interested in a fast track to an advanced degree after completing their undergraduate studies, St. Joseph's offers special affiliated programs. The Brooklyn campus also offers an accelerated biomedical program in cooperation with the New York College of Podiatric Medicine. This program allows students to receive a B.S. in biology and a doctorate in podiatric medicine within six years. Students at both the Brooklyn and Patchogue campuses can earn B.S./M.B.A. degrees in accounting within five years or can choose to pursue pre-professional programs in law, teaching, and numerous health fields, including dentistry, medicine, and optometry.

Those with nontraditional academic backgrounds or with professional training and experience can pursue degrees in community health, general studies, health administration, nursing, and organizational management through St. Joseph's School of Professional and Graduate Studies at either campus.

Academic Programs

The School of Arts and Sciences at each campus operates on the semester system, with additional courses offered in January and during the summer. St. Joseph's students take a core curriculum of 128 credits to graduate; a wide range of choices allows students to tailor their academic programs to their personal and professional needs. The College recognizes the Advanced Placement (AP) Program and offers credit and placement for

scores of 3 or above on AP tests. In each case, the score is reviewed by the registrar and/or department chairperson to determine credit and placement.

The School of Professional and Graduate Studies on each campus offers flexible schedules, summer programs, and online courses to meet the needs of working students. Courses may meet for a semester or for six- or twelve-week sessions.

Academic Facilities

The Brooklyn campus is composed of eight buildings, including historic landmark buildings. Students majoring in the widely recognized child-study program use the Dillon Child Study Center, which is a laboratory preschool enrolling approximately 100 hundred students and a teaching and observation resource right on campus. McEntegart Hall, a modern five-level structure, houses the library, audiovisual resource center, curriculum library, archives, and computer labs. Other academic facilities include top-notch biology, chemistry, computer, physics, and psychology research laboratories. A state-of-the-art athletic complex is under construction on school grounds, with a scheduled completion date of 2013.

At the Long Island campus, students enjoy 28 acres of well-landscaped grounds and athletic fields. The main building houses administrative and faculty offices; laboratories for biology, chemistry, physics, and psychology; the computer center; art and music studios; the Local History Center; and the Office of Counseling. The library building houses a curriculum library, seminar rooms, administrative offices, and classrooms. This campus also features the John A. Danzi Recreation/Fitness Center, which includes a competition-sized swimming pool, fitness rooms, and a full-sized gym with an elevated track. The 33,000-square-foot Business and Technology Center allows St. Joseph's students to integrate technology into their studies. The Clare Rose Playhouse serves as a cultural center where students and local communities can explore theater production and performance.

A high-speed fiber-optic network connects all offices, institutional facilities, computer laboratories, and libraries on both the Brooklyn and Long Island campuses. Direct Internet access is available to all students and faculty and staff members through the College's server. The integrated online library system enables students to locate and check out books at either campus and provides links to online databases and other electronic information sources.

Costs

The 2011–12 annual full-time tuition rate for undergraduates was $17,800, or $580 per-credit.

Financial Aid

St. Joseph's offers scholarships and grants-in-aid. Students who wish to apply for either form of assistance must file the Free Application for Federal Student Aid (FAFSA) and a state aid form. After a student has been accepted to the College and all financial aid forms are processed, the Financial Aid Office prepares aid packages that usually consist of federal, state, and College funds. St. Joseph's is fully approved for veterans. Campus work-study programs are also available.

Faculty

With nearly 500 faculty members who are widely respected scholars in their fields and a student-faculty ratio of 15:1, St. Joseph's students benefit from close professional and personal working relationships with their professors. Faculty members serve as academic advisers, are active on student affairs committees, and act as moderators in student organizations.

Admission Requirements

St. Joseph's College seeks a diverse student body and welcomes applications from high school students, transfer students, and those students who may have a nontraditional academic background. The College offers programs to serve all of these groups.

Students who wish to enter as freshmen are expected to have completed at least 18 units of college-preparatory work by the end of their senior year. This should include the following distribution: 4 years of English, 2 years of foreign language, 3 years of mathematics, 2 years of science, and 4 years of social studies. Applicants interested in accounting, allied health fields, biology, business administration, chemistry, or mathematics should have more extensive backgrounds in mathematics and science. In addition, the College requires the submission of official results from the critical reading and math sections of the SAT.

St. Joseph's College accepts a block transfer of credits from students holding an A.A. or A.S. degree in certain majors from an accredited junior or community college. All other transfers are considered on an individual basis.

Application and Information

Admission is offered on a rolling basis. Applications and supporting documents should be submitted online or to the appropriate school. The College reviews each application carefully and usually sends a decision one month after receiving all necessary credentials. For more information and an online application, students can access the Web site at http://www.sjcny.edu.

Brooklyn Campus:

Director of Admissions
St. Joseph's College
245 Clinton Avenue
Brooklyn, New York 11205
Phone: 718-940-5800

Long Island Campus:

Director of Admissions
St. Joseph's College
155 West Roe Boulevard
Patchogue, New York 11772
Phone: 631-687-4500
Web site: http://www.sjcny.edu
http://www.facebook.com/SJCNY
http://twitter.com/#!/SJCNY

Class sizes at St. Joseph's College are personal, with no more than 15 to 20 students..

SAINT JOSEPH'S UNIVERSITY
PHILADELPHIA, PENNSYLVANIA

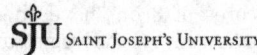

The University

Saint Joseph's University is a nationally recognized, Catholic, Jesuit university. For more than 150 years, Saint Joseph's has advanced the professional and personal ambitions of men and women by providing a rigorous Jesuit education—one that demands high achievement, expands knowledge, deepens understanding, stresses effective reasoning and communication, develops moral and spiritual character, and imparts enduring pride. One of only 152 schools with a Phi Beta Kappa chapter and business school accreditation by AACSB International–The Association to Advance Collegiate Schools of Business, Saint Joseph's is the home to 4,650 traditional undergraduate day students, 700 College of Professional and Liberal Studies adult undergraduate students, and 3,600 graduate and doctoral students.

As a Jesuit university, Saint Joseph's believes each student realizes his or her fullest potential through challenging classroom study, hands-on learning opportunities, and a commitment to excellence in all endeavors. The University also reinforces the individual's lifelong engagement with the wider world. Graduates of Saint Joseph's attain success in their careers with the help of an extensive network of alumni who have become leading figures in business, law, medicine, education, the arts, technology, government, and public service.

A Saint Joseph's education encompasses all aspects of personal growth and development, reflecting the Ignatian credo of *cura personalis*. Guided by a faculty that is committed to both teaching and scholarship, students develop intellectually through an intense Jesuit liberal arts curriculum and advanced study in a chosen discipline. Students mature socially by participating in Saint Joseph's campus life, noted for its rich variety of activities, infectious enthusiasm, and mutual respect. Students grow ethically and spiritually by living their own values in the larger society beyond the campus.

Steeped in the Jesuit, Catholic tradition, Saint Joseph's provides a rigorous, intensive education that both disciplines and expands the mind. Students develop a lifelong desire to learn and grow while also acquiring the skills and knowledge necessary for success in their professional lives. At the core of this education is a general education requirement, which exposes students to primary fields of inquiry and the cultural values that shape their world. A Jesuit emphasis on engaged teaching and mentoring permeates the university. Faculty members at Saint Joseph's, many of whom are leading scholars in their disciplines, expect students to perform at the highest level and set demanding standards in the classroom.

Saint Joseph's is at the forefront of utilizing innovative technologies to enhance and promote learning. These technologies are widely integrated into the educational process both in class and beyond, where they are also used for individual and collaborative research projects. By mastering these tools and achieving technological fluency, Saint Joseph's students gain a valuable edge in their careers.

Saint Joseph's students engage enthusiastically in all facets of campus life—academic, social, athletic, ethical, and spiritual. Their active participation creates a vibrant, dynamic campus community, one that embraces a "not for spectators" attitude. In all their activities, students emphasize personal integrity as well as a respect and concern for others. This produces a mutually supportive, humane, and tolerant environment for individual success and service to others.

Location

Located on the edge of metropolitan Philadelphia, Saint Joseph's provides ready access to the vast career opportunities and cultural resources of America's fifth-largest city, while affording students a cohesive and intimate campus experience.

Because of its location, Saint Joseph's has close ties to the people, professional opportunities, and cultural life of Philadelphia.

Students enjoy direct access to internships, cooperative education programs, and positions in virtually all careers, most of which have a major presence in the Philadelphia area. Saint Joseph's location also offers ample outlets for community involvement and service, and students can easily take advantage of Philadelphia's professional sports, entertainment, and cultural events.

Majors and Degrees

Saint Joseph's offers full-time baccalaureate degree programs in over forty-five major fields of study and numerous specialty programs, which are administered by two separate colleges.

The College of Arts and Sciences awards a bachelor's degree in actuarial science, ancient studies, art, art education, Asian studies, biology, chemical biology, chemistry, communication studies, computer science, criminal justice, economics, education (early childhood/elementary PreK–4; early childhood/elementary PreK–4 + special education K–8 (double major), elementary/middle years 4–8), English, environmental science, European studies, French, French studies, German, history, interdisciplinary health services, international relations, Italian, mathematics, music, philosophy, physics, political science, psychology, public administration, religious studies, sociology, Spanish, theater and film, and theology.

The Erivan K. Haub School of Business awards a bachelor's degree in accounting; business intelligence; business administration; family business and entrepreneurship; finance; financial planning; food marketing; international business; leadership, ethics, and organizational sustainability; managing human capital; marketing; pharmaceutical and healthcare marketing; risk management and insurance; and sports marketing. A co-op program is available for all business majors.

Five-year B.S./M.S. programs are offered in education, international marketing, psychology, and writing studies. The University also offers special academic programs in aerospace studies (Air Force ROTC), Africana studies, allied health (bioscience technologies, nursing, occupational therapy, physical therapy (D.P.T.), and radiologic sciences), American studies, autism studies, behavioral neuroscience, business ethics, environmental and sustainability studies, faith-justice studies, gender studies, interdisciplinary health care ethics, Latin American studies, linguistics, medieval and renaissance studies, music industry, and teacher certification at the elementary and secondary levels. Preprofessional study is available in most major fields.

Academic Programs

At Saint Joseph's University, the aim of providing the student with the qualities of a liberally educated individual is pursued through a threefold plan encompassing forty courses. The major concentration (ten to sixteen courses) is intended to provide students with depth in a given field in order to prepare them for effective work in that field or graduate study. The general education program (fifteen to eighteen courses) is intended to ensure that students have mastered basic skills necessary for further work, have been exposed to the main divisions of learning, have been introduced to several new fields of study, and have acquired an appreciation for diversity and an ethically-informed perspective. Art and literature, non-native languages, mathematics, natural sciences, history, social sciences, philosophy, and theology are among the areas of study included in the general education program. Free electives (six to fifteen courses) are intended to provide flexibility by encouraging students to pursue studies in areas they have found interesting, to test their interest in an unexplored area, or to deepen their knowledge in the major field.

A competitive honors program is available for qualified students, as are independent and interdisciplinary study options. Claver House provides a place for honors students to have meetings, take classes, study, and conduct research.

Off-Campus Programs

Saint Joseph's offers to an increasing number of students the opportunity to study abroad and directly sponsors programs each year in Europe, Africa, Asia, Australia, Latin America, and the United Kingdom. International study tours have been made to Africa, Australia, Brazil, Canada, Greece, Ireland, Italy, Japan, Scotland, and Spain.

Students may take advantage of an arrangement with the Washington Center for Internships and Academic Seminars, which allows for a one-semester internship in the nation's capital.

Fieldwork experiences are required in several majors, and the University's location provides for internship opportunities to support virtually all other disciplines. The Career Development Center offers a wide array of services and provides opportunities for on-campus interviews. The Alumni Mentor Alliance matches students with alumni in their fields of interest to gain real-world perspectives.

Academic Facilities

The facilities at Saint Joseph's are a blend of the old and the new. Barbelin/Lonergan Hall is a fine example of collegiate Gothic architecture. Its spire carillon tower rises above the campus and is easily the most recognizable landmark at Saint Joseph's. Mandeville Hall, a modern international academic center, opened in 1998. Home of the Erivan K. Haub School of Business, Mandeville offers distance learning technology and unique learning environments. The Francis A. Drexel Library and the Campbell Collection in Food Marketing house a collection of approximately 354,850 volumes, 1,450 print journals, 57,000 full-text electronic journals 4,700 online books, and 863,500 microforms. The University has completed construction of the Post Learning Commons and a new residence hall is scheduled to be completed in 2012.

Costs

Tuition for the 2011–12 academic year was $36,480. Room and board were $12,206. These costs do not include student fees associated with specific majors or residence halls.

Financial Aid

The majority of Saint Joseph's students receive merit and/or federal financial assistance. In the 2011–12 academic year, approximately 91 percent of the University's freshman class received assistance in the form of academic and athletic scholarships, grants, loans, and work-study funds, either singly or in combination.

Students are automatically considered for merit scholarships upon application to the University. Students who wish to be considered for federal financial assistance should submit the Free Application for Federal Student Aid (FAFSA). Residents from states other than Pennsylvania should file the FAFSA and the proper state grant application from the Education Assistance Agency of their resident state. The preferred deadline is February 15.

Faculty

Saint Joseph's possesses an esteemed research faculty that is committed to undergraduate teaching. A student-faculty ratio of 13:1 and an average class size of 24 offer excellent opportunities for student–faculty member exchange, both inside and outside the classroom. Approximately 99 percent of the full-time, tenure-track faculty members hold a doctorate or terminal degree in their field.

Student Government

The Office of Student Leadership and Activities is dedicated to enhancing the educational development of students by providing opportunities for involvement in cocurricular programs and services. These include leadership programs, student clubs and organizations, Greek life, event programming and planning, and the University Student Senate. Through innovative programming that complements academic and personal development, the University nurtures the mind, body, and spirit of each individual student while enhancing the Jesuit mission of the University.

The University Student Senate, the governing board for the student body, is dedicated to addressing student issues through advocacy and policy recommendations. The senate consists of an executive board that includes the president, executive vice president, speaker of the senate, vice president for financial affairs, vice president for student life, four elected representatives from each class, and five appointed at-large members. The senate has four standing committees: Academic Affairs, Student Budget Allocations, Campus Life, and Administrative Services. Elections for the senate take place in April. Freshman representatives are elected in September.

The Student Union Board, known as SUB, is a student-run organization that encourages the development of student leadership, responsibility, and social competency by planning and participating in campus programs. These activities are designed to enhance the educational, recreational, cultural, and social aspects of the collegiate experience. All registered undergraduate students are welcome to take part in the activities and to be a part of the standing committees that are responsible for the programming.

Admission Requirements

Candidates for admission to the freshman class must submit evidence of academic achievement in a college-preparatory program, which should emphasize study in English, mathematics, foreign languages (classical or modern), science, history, and social studies. Successful candidates have traditionally completed a secondary school background that included the following: 4 credits of English; 3 credits of mathematics; 3 credits of science; 3 credits of social science; 2 credits of second/foreign language; 1 credit fine or performing arts. Applicants are required to submit SAT or ACT scores.

Application and Information

A completed application form may be submitted with the $60 application fee at any time after the student's junior year. Students are accepted to the University and merit scholarships are awarded within the context of a deadline admissions policy with an early action application deadline of November 15 and a regular decision deadline of February 1. Students should visit the admissions Web site at http://www.sju.edu/admissions for current admission information.

Office of Undergraduate Admissions
Saint Joseph's University
5600 City Avenue
Philadelphia, Pennsylvania 19131-1395
Phone: 610-660-1300
      888-BE-A-HAWK (232-4295) (toll-free)
Fax: 610-660-1314
E-mail: admit@sju.edu
Web site: http://www.sju.edu/admissions/
      http://www.facebook.com/sjuadmissions

The Post Learning Commons Building at Saint Joseph's University, a new campus addition. Photo credit: Melissa Kelly

ST. LAWRENCE UNIVERSITY
CANTON, NEW YORK

The University

St. Lawrence University invites students to learn new ways of seeing the world, voicing ideas, and connecting with others. Graduates have the tools with which to think clearly, express themselves persuasively, and step into the world community with an understanding of their responsibility to all people and to the planet.

Founded in 1856, St. Lawrence is the oldest continuously coeducational degree-granting institution of higher learning in New York State. Initially established as a theology school for the Universalist Church, it quickly evolved into the liberal arts college that it is today. St. Lawrence is a private, nonsectarian university of approximately 2,300 undergraduate men and women, with a small graduate program in education. St. Lawrence is known for its residential/academic First-Year Program, its international study opportunities and area studies programs, its students' strong interest in the environment and the outdoors, and its friendliness.

St. Lawrence students are self-starters. The self-designed major is popular, intramural sports leagues are always full, and more than 100 student organizations serve broad interests, from communication to community service and creativity to social action. The University routinely hosts well-known speakers, and concerts, plays, and films are regulars on the weekly events calendar.

St. Lawrence students have historically placed high value on athletic activity, and a large number participate in varsity, intramural, or club sports. The thirty-two varsity men's and women's teams compete at the Division III level of the NCAA, with the exception of men's and women's ice hockey, which compete in Division I. Recreational facilities include cross-country ski and running trails, indoor and outdoor tennis courts, an athletic complex with a gymnasium, two field houses, a 133-station fitness center, a three-story climbing wall, a pool, an ice rink, an equestrian center, a boathouse, a golf course, a nine-lane all-weather track, an artificial-turf field for lacrosse and field hockey, ten squash courts, and performance fields for soccer, football, baseball, and softball.

Residential life is an important aspect of the St. Lawrence experience. The University's innovative and highly regarded First-Year Program creates communities where groups of approximately 30–35 first-year students live and learn together. In the upperclass years, students can choose from traditional dormitories, Greek chapter houses, and suites and theme cottages that focus on student interests such as low-impact living and community service. Seniors may also choose town houses. St. Lawrence sponsors a full range of student services, from counseling to career planning.

Location

St. Lawrence is situated on a 1,000-acre campus on the edge of the village of Canton, New York (population 6,400), the seat of St. Lawrence County. Canton, with its Victorian homes, tree-lined streets, village green, and small shops, is typical of college towns throughout the Northeast. Students and residents often mix in stores, at athletic events, and in community projects. Ottawa, Canada's capital, is 75 minutes to the north, while Lake Placid, one of America's hiking and skiing meccas, is 90 minutes to the southeast.

Majors and Degrees

St. Lawrence offers the Bachelor of Arts and Bachelor of Science degrees; students can choose from thirty-six majors and have the option of picking one of thirty-seven minors. Combined five-year programs with other institutions are in place in engineering and management, and specialized advising is offered in preparation for postgraduate work in dentistry, law, medicine, nursing, physical therapy, and veterinary medicine.

Academic Programs

St. Lawrence's foremost mission is to provide its students with a liberal arts education. Students complete requirements in six areas and concentrated work in a major field as well as demonstrating competence in writing. Close faculty-student interaction is a hallmark of a St. Lawrence education. Every semester, many students engage in independent or honors projects, often working with professors on joint research projects that lead to publication in leading scholarly journals. A senior project is required in most majors.

Off-Campus Programs

More than 50 percent of St. Lawrence students study in one of the University's international programs during their collegiate careers. St. Lawrence operates programs in Australia, Austria, Canada, China, Costa Rica, the Czech Republic, Denmark, England, France, India, Italy, Japan, Kenya, New Zealand, Spain, Thailand, and Trinidad and Tobago. In addition, the University's membership in the International Student Exchange Program permits students to directly enroll in universities in more than thirty-five additional countries. St. Lawrence also operates programs at two other campuses in the United States: Fisk University in Nashville, Tennessee, and American University in Washington, D.C. St. Lawrence also administers its own Adirondack Semester Program and a New York City Semester Program.

Academic Facilities

Owen D. Young Library and Launders Science Library contain more than half a million volumes as well as electronic resources and ample space for reading and research. Griffiths Arts Center is the home of the University's fine arts and performance and communication studies programs as well as two theaters and an art gallery in which selections from St. Lawrence's 7,000-piece collection are frequently shown. Facilities for the arts have undergone expansion into the building that was formerly the student center, and the Newell Center for Arts Technology opened in spring 2007. A unified science complex houses the Departments of Biology, Chemistry, Physics, Psychology, Geology, and Mathematics, Computer Science and Statistics and is connected via a covered hallway to the science library and computing center. The 120,000-square-foot Johnson Hall of Science, the first gold LEED science building in New York State, opened in fall 2007. Richardson Hall, St. Lawrence's oldest building and on the National Register of Historic Places, is home to the English and religious studies departments. Other departments can be found in academic buildings clustered on one part of the campus, so classrooms are not a long walk apart.

Costs

The comprehensive fee for 2011–12 was $53,740, including tuition, fees, and average room and board. Students should allow approximately $1650 for books and personal expenses.

Financial Aid

St. Lawrence awards both merit scholarships and need-based financial aid. More than 85 percent of the University's students receive some form of financial assistance, including scholarships, grants, student loans, and campus jobs. St. Lawrence is committed to assisting as many students as possible and recognizes academic and personal achievement in making financial aid decisions. To apply for need-based financial aid, students must file the Free Application for Federal Student Aid (FAFSA) and the CSS Profile form between January 1 and February 1 and request that the results be sent directly to St. Lawrence.

Faculty

The 192 members of St. Lawrence's faculty are teachers and scholars. While teaching and advising are their primary responsibilities, they are also active researchers, artists, performers, and regular contributors in their academic disciplines. Faculty members teach all courses at St. Lawrence; no undergraduate courses are taught by graduate students. Active teaching assistants and tutoring programs, involving qualified upperclass students, are closely supervised by faculty members. The student-faculty ratio is about 12:1. Faculty members hold regular office hours, serve as academic advisers to students, and frequently take part in extracurricular activities on campus.

Student Government

The Thelomathesian Society, comprising all students on campus, is governed by a senate of elected representatives. The senate distributes funds in support of student activities and provides 2 student delegates to the University's Board of Trustees.

Admission Requirements

St. Lawrence seeks students who can be successful in a demanding academic program and who can contribute to the quality of life of the community. The University is committed to enrolling students who represent the widest possible diversity of economic, social, ethnic, and geographic backgrounds. Academic preparation and ability are the most important criteria, but demonstrated ability in the creative arts, athletics, or social service is also a measure of a student's potential to benefit St. Lawrence. Candidates may choose whether or not they submit standardized test scores (SAT or ACT). A campus visit is strongly encouraged, and interviews may be scheduled on campus or off campus in certain areas.

Although there is no set distribution of required high school courses, successful applicants typically show strong preparation in the humanities, the social sciences, mathematics, and the natural sciences. Honors, Advanced Placement, and International Baccalaureate courses are opportunities for applicants to demonstrate intellectual maturity and curiosity, qualities highly valued in the admission process.

Application and Information

St. Lawrence uses the Common Application, with the St. Lawrence Supplement, as its sole application form. The application is available on the University's Web site. The application processing fee is $60. Regular decision applications should be submitted by February 1, with notification by late March. Students who decide that St. Lawrence is their first choice may apply Early Decision. The priority deadline for Early Decision is November 1, but students may commit to early decision up until February 1. Early Decision candidates will generally be notified within one month of receipt of a completed application.

Transfer candidates should submit applications no later than November 1 for the spring semester or March 1 for the fall semester.

To request an application or for more information, students should contact:

Office of Admissions and Financial Aid
St. Lawrence University
Canton, New York 13617
Phone: 315-229-5261
     800-285-1856 (toll-free)
E-mail: admissions@stlawu.edu
Web site: http://www.stlawu.edu
     http://www.facebook.com/SLU2017
     http://twitter.com/stlawu
     http://www.youtube.com/StLawrenceU

SAINT LEO UNIVERSITY
SAINT LEO, FLORIDA

The University

Founded in 1889, Saint Leo University is now recognized as one of the nation's leading Catholic teaching universities and a school of international consequence. The University Campus in Saint Leo, Florida, serves the education needs of more just under 2,000 traditional-age undergraduate students. The University also offers a variety of dynamic graduate programs, a weekend and evening program for working adults, and both undergraduate and graduate degree programs through seventeen education centers in seven states and through the Center for Online Learning, which houses the University's cutting-edge online degree programs.

The University College student body represents 39 states and territories, as well as 58 countries. International students make up 13 percent of the student population. Minority students represent 34 percent of the University College enrollment. Approximately 62 percent of traditional full-time students live in one of thirteen residence halls, with two more residence halls slated to come online for the 2012–13 academic year.

Students can participate in the nationally recognized honors program and the more than sixty different clubs and organizations on campus, including national fraternities and sororities. The Student Government Union and various campus organizations also sponsor movies, concerts, art exhibits, lectures, dances, and other special events throughout the academic year.

Saint Leo is a member of the Sunshine State Conference and competes in NCAA Division II intercollegiate athletics for men and women. Men's sports include baseball, basketball, cross-country, golf, lacrosse, soccer, swimming, and tennis. Women compete in basketball, cross-country, golf, lacrosse, soccer, softball, swimming, tennis, and volleyball. Students can also participate in a wide variety of intramurals. Campus recreational facilities include lighted racquetball and tennis courts; soccer, baseball, and softball fields; a weight room/fitness center; and a heated outdoor Olympic-size swimming pool. The campus is bordered by a 154-acre lake and an eighteen-hole golf course.

Saint Leo is committed to giving its students an education that prepares them for the future. The goal of the University is to develop the whole person, both academically and personally, by providing a values-based education in the Benedictine tradition. In a recent satisfaction survey, 93 percent of respondents said they would recommend Saint Leo to a friend.

Saint Leo University is accredited by the Commission on Colleges of the Southern Association of Colleges and Schools to award the associate, bachelor's, and master's degrees. Saint Leo University's degree program in social work is accredited by the Commission on Accreditation of the Council on Social Work Education (B.S.W. level). The School of Business is accredited by the International Assembly for Collegiate Business Education (IACBE). The University's undergraduate sport business program is nationally approved by the Sport Management Program Review Council (SMPRC). Saint Leo University also has Teacher Education Programs approval by the State of Florida Department of Education.

In addition to associate and bachelor's degrees, Saint Leo University offers a Master of Business Administration (M.B.A.) degree; a Master of Education (M.Ed.) degree; Master of Science (M.S.) degrees in criminal justice, criminal justice administration, critical incident management, and instructional design; a Master of Arts (M.A.) degree in theology; a Master of Social Work (M.S.W.); and an education specialist degree.

Location

Saint Leo is located 35 minutes north of Tampa and 90 minutes west of Orlando. The lakeside campus occupies 186 acres of rolling hills and wooded grounds. The rural setting is conducive to academic success, but the University is located near enough to metropolitan areas to give the students the advantage of a wide variety of social and professional opportunities.

Majors and Degrees

Saint Leo University offers 43 traditional majors, pre-professional studies, specializations, endorsements, and programs. Degrees offered are the Bachelor of Arts, Bachelor of Science, and Bachelor of Social Work.

The School of Business offers degrees in accounting, communication management, computer information systems, computer science, health care management, human resources management, international hospitality and tourism management, management, marketing, and sport business. The School of Arts and Sciences offers majors in biology, English, environmental science, history, international studies, mathematics, medical technology, political science, psychology, religion, and sociology. The School of Education and Social Services offers majors in criminal justice, elementary education, middle grades education, secondary education, and social work.

Pre-professional studies programs in chiropractic, dentistry, law, medicine, occupational therapy, physical therapy, and veterinary science are also offered, including 4+4 medical school and 3+4 dental and chiropractic school programs.

Academic Programs

Saint Leo's LINK (Learning Interdisciplinary Knowledge) general education program ensures that all graduates have a solid grounding in theories, issues, and knowledge to prepare them for successful careers and graduate work. The program develops the skills that are the foundation of a liberal arts education and that today's employers demand. Students learn to communicate effectively; function at a high level, both alone and as a part of a team; develop a general knowledge base in many different areas; and analyze and solve problems effectively.

Students complete foundation courses of core requirements (writing, computer literacy, math, and wellness), Perspectives courses (liberal arts, fine arts, humanities, and physical, social, and behavioral sciences), and a senior capstone course that connects all prior course work in the major and leads to research and independent projects demonstrating mastery of the field.

Saint Leo has an academic skills program to assist first-year students in their adjustment to university life. Included in this program are freshman studies, tutoring, and advising. All first-year students at Saint Leo are assigned faculty advisors, who act as mentors from the first day that the student arrives on campus through the time when the student selects a major.

Students who demonstrate course mastery for any course listed in the catalog have the opportunity to receive up to 40 hours of credit through examination. Detailed information about credit by examination is available through the Registrar's Office.

Most students at Saint Leo earn the credits needed for their bachelor's degree through a four-year program of study. All major programs require a 2.0 minimum grade point average for graduation.

Off-Campus Programs

Saint Leo University is committed to helping students expand their horizons through study-abroad programs. Saint Leo University students have the opportunity to spend a semester studying in London, Madrid, Paris, Rome, Singapore, Australia, Ecuador, Germany, Greece, Ireland, Scotland, and various cities within the United Kingdom. Articulation agreements also afford study opportunities throughout Asia and the Pacific Rim. The University continues to add new programs and partnerships in order to provide students with a wide variety of educational and cultural experiences.

Students are also able to work with their professors and academic advisor to identify and pursue a wide variety of internship options, further enhancing the real-world experience component of their education.

Academic Facilities

The Cannon Memorial Library contains 102,101 volumes, and provides access to 172,076 e-books (non-unique e-book titles), 611 print periodical subscriptions, 149,899 unique e-journal titles, and 76 online databases. Also located in the library are the Hugh Culverhouse Computer Instruction Center classrooms, a student computer lab, and two VTT-equipped instruction/conference rooms.

Lab facilities include three teaching labs and one research lab for biology; two teaching labs, one research lab, and an instrumentation room for chemistry; and one physics lab. The state-of-the-art Donald R. Tapia School of Business building opened in fall 2011. Most remaining classrooms are located in Crawford Hall and Lewis Hall with additional rooms in Saint Edward Hall, Saint Francis Hall, and the Marion Bowman Activities Center.

l students are encouraged to utilize the University's Learning Resource Center (LRC). The LRC is housed in the Student Activities Building and features study and meeting space for small groups as well as such technology as high-speed laser printers. Professional and peer tutoring services are available to students and may be scheduled through the LRC. Central to campus is the Student Community Center, which houses the dining hall, campus bookstore, student lounge, and Lion's Lair snack shop, as well as substantial meeting space for groups of various sizes.

The University's campus is a mostly wireless environment. All students who reside in campus housing receive a state-of-the-art laptop computer. For students living off campus, laptops are available for use through the library.

Costs

For the 2012–13 school year, tuition is $18,700; freshman room and board costs are $9394, and mandatory fees are $670. Miscellaneous indirect costs for the year (such as books, personal living expenses, insurance, and travel) are estimated at $4305.

Financial Aid

Financial aid, both federally funded and awarded by the University, is available in the form of scholarships, grants, and loans. Financial aid is allocated on the basis of academic performance and need, as determined by the federal government from the financial information provided on the Free Application for Federal Student Aid (FAFSA). On-campus jobs are available for students, with priority given to students with demonstrated financial need. Ninety-three percent of students receive some form of financial aid.

Faculty

At Saint Leo University, outstanding teaching and active learning go hand in hand. Caring and capable faculty members provide students with knowledge, guidance, academic support, and a broad range of learning opportunities both in and outside the classroom. Students enjoy small classes (average class size is 18) and develop close relationships with experienced, well-qualified professors. At Saint Leo, 83 percent of full-time instructional faculty members hold the terminal degree in their field.

Student Government

A significant contribution to the University comes from the activities initiated by the Student Government Union (SGU). The SGU is an annually elected body organized and conducted in accordance with democratic procedures. This organization strives to foster leadership and loyalty among the students, to formulate recommendations for student life, and to recognize all extracurricular activities.

Admission Requirements

All candidates for admission should be, or expect to be, graduates of secondary schools accredited by a regional or state accrediting agency. Applicants should show successful progress toward graduation with a minimum of 16 academic units of course work: 4 units of English, 3 units of mathematics (algebra I and II and geometry), 3 units of social studies, 2 units of science, and 4 units of electives, preferably to include 2 units of a foreign language. All domestic applicants are recommended to take the SAT or the ACT examination, although the University does offer a test-optional policy for admission. A letter of recommendation from the student's guidance counselor is also required. Preferred candidates are students with a GPA of 2.7 or better and an average SAT combined score (critical reading and math) of 970 or an average ACT score of 21. Students may request to be considered for admission under a test-optional policy that requires additional credentials in lieu of standardized test scores. The records of students who do not meet these criteria are also reviewed by the Admission Committee and considered for the Learning Enhancement for Academic Progress (LEAP) program, a preparatory program that has a summer attendance component.

Once the applicant has submitted the application with the $40 application fee (fee is waived if application is submitted online), high school transcripts, test scores (optional if utilizing test-optional policy), and letter of recommendation, the file is reviewed and a decision is rendered. Notification is on a rolling basis and generally takes less than two weeks. The priority application deadline is March 1, but all applicants are encouraged to apply early.

Transfer and international students are also encouraged to apply. The same general admission procedures are required, along with at least a 2.5 average for all college work (for transfer students) and a score of at least 550 (paper-based test) or 78 (Internet-based test) on the TOEFL (for international students for whom English is not the primary language of instruction).

Campus visits and interviews are recommended but not required. The Office of Admission is open from Monday through Friday from 8 a.m. to 5 p.m. and on select Saturdays during the academic year from 9 a.m. to noon. Appointments are preferred. Campus tours are available Monday through Friday at 10 a.m. and 2 p.m., as well as at 10 a.m. on select Saturdays during the academic year. Summer tours are available Monday through Friday at 10 a.m. and 2 p.m. as well. The Office of Admission is closed on Sunday.

Application and Information

Additional information and application forms can be obtained by contacting the Office of Admission. Candidates may apply online at www.saintleo.edu/apply.

Reggie Hill
Director of Admission
Office of Admission—MC2008
Saint Leo University
P.O. Box 6665
Saint Leo, Florida 33574-6665
Phone: 352-588-8283
    800-334-5532 (toll-free)
Fax: 352-588-8257
E-mail: admission@saintleo.edu
Web site: http://www.saintleo.edu

The Saint Leo University campus.

ST. LOUIS COLLEGE OF PHARMACY
ST. LOUIS, MISSOURI

The College

Founded in 1864, St. Louis College of Pharmacy is the fourth oldest and tenth largest college of pharmacy in the nation. Members of the first board of trustees included pharmacists, physicians, and business leaders, such as Henry Shaw, founder of the Missouri Botanical Garden, and John O'Fallon, nephew of explorer William Clark. Approximately 72 percent of St. Louis–area pharmacists are graduates of the College. Its 6,500 alumni practice in all fifty states and thirteen different countries.

Grounded in rich tradition and history, St. Louis College of Pharmacy faculty, students, alumni, and staff have collaborated to create a strategic plan, STLCOP 20/20, that will not only secure the College's legacy, but will enhance its impact on the practice of pharmacy locally, regionally, and nationally. Over the next decade, the College will strive to diversify academic offerings, advance a community-centered research and scholarship agenda, establish economically sustainable pharmacy practice models, ensure that personal and professional growth is a hallmark of the College community, and reach beyond campus to impact communities in innovative ways.

St. Louis College of Pharmacy is a small, private college that admits students directly from high school and integrates the liberal arts and sciences into a Doctor of Pharmacy program. Students in the most recent freshman class have an average ACT score of 27, an average class rank in the top 13 percent, and an average high school grade point average of 3.8. More than 1,260 students from twenty-five states are currently enrolled at the College.

The College offers a curriculum that is focused on math and science and integrates coursework in the liberal arts and professional studies. During the course of the program, students will apply their knowledge and explore pharmacy career options in diverse clinical settings through introductory and advanced pharmacy practice experiences. Students will have opportunities to conduct research, do original work, and present at professional conferences. A St. Louis College of Pharmacy education prepares students to practice in a variety of areas: community or hospital pharmacies, managed care, consultant pharmacies, the pharmaceutical industry, military, academia, or pharmacy associations.

With nearly 50 clubs and organizations on campus, St. Louis College of Pharmacy provides a full college experience, including professional and social fraternities, intramurals, club sports, pharmacy organizations, and special interest groups. The College participates in nine NAIA sports: men's and women's cross-country, men's and women's basketball, men's and women's track and field, men's and women's tennis, and women's volleyball. The College's small size offers its residents and commuters opportunities to become an integral part of the campus experience.

Residence Hall is in the center of the 5-acre campus and houses 290 students and 10 resident assistants. Students become part of a supportive community of friends and lively activities, including movie nights, ice cream socials, and trips to the City Museum. All students have use of the cafeteria space, attached to Residence Hall, for 3 meals a day and as a study space late into the night.

All first-year students are given priority for housing, regardless of where they live. First-year students are not allowed to have a vehicle on campus.

St. Louis College of Pharmacy also provides academic resources and support to help students succeed in class and manage college life. Assistance is offered in many ways, including individual counseling, disability accommodations, and student-to-student mentoring.

The St. Louis College of Pharmacy's Doctor of Pharmacy degree is accredited by the Accreditation Council for Pharmacy Education and the North Central Association of Colleges and Schools.

Location

Only a few miles from the Gateway Arch, St. Louis College of Pharmacy is located in one of America's most prestigious biomedical complexes, including Barnes-Jewish Hospital, Washington University School of Medicine, the Siteman Cancer Center, St. Louis Children's Hospital, and the Goldfarb School of Nursing at Barnes-Jewish College. The campus is one block from Forest Park, with its 1,300 acres of green space, tennis courts, ice-skating rink, golf course, and world-class museums, zoo, outdoor opera theater, and science center. Students at the College are near the cultural and entertainment scene of St. Louis on a safe, 5-acre campus within a block of public transportation.

Majors and Degrees

Students at St. Louis College of Pharmacy progress through a curriculum which integrates courses in liberal arts and sciences with a professional program leading to the Doctor of Pharmacy (Pharm.D.) degree.

Academic Programs

The Doctor of Pharmacy program includes intensive courses in biology, chemistry, mathematics, and physics, as well as electives in literature, humanities, and social and behavioral sciences. Introductory practice experiences throughout the curriculum give students the opportunity to apply their education and enable students to develop knowledge, communication skills, and professional values through interaction with other health-care practitioners and patients. During the sixth year of the curriculum, students participate in a series of eight 5-week pharmacy rotations.

Off-Campus Programs

Students have opportunities to participate in advanced practice experiences in twenty-six states at more than 600 community and hospital settings. The College's close proximity to Barnes-Jewish Hospital and Washington University School of Medicine also gives students access to nearby research, work-study, and volunteer opportunities.

Academic Facilities

Jones Hall contains the majority of College classrooms, lecture halls, laboratories, and faculty and administrative offices. The College's O. J. Cloughly Alumni Library, located on the first floor of Jones Hall, not only offers many educational resources, including subject databases, print and electronic books and journals, magazines, newspapers, and audiovisual materials but also provides a quiet, comfortable environment where students may read and study. In addition, the online portion of the library gives students, faculty, and staff of the College the opportunity to explore what the library has to offer, with access to databases, e-books, electronic journals, and interlibrary loan requests, all from the comfort of their home or office. Whelpley Hall features a 300-seat auditorium in addition to small- and medium-sized classrooms.

Costs

For the 2012–13 academic year tuition for students in year one is $24,517, in year two is $24,227, and in years three through six is $26,608. A notebook computer (issued to all new students) and lab fees are included in tuition costs. Room and board costs for the academic year are $8835 for shared units and $8437 for suites. Additional costs, including books, student activity fees, student health fees, professional program fees, and new student program fees vary each year but average $850 per semester.

Financial Aid

St. Louis College of Pharmacy offers need-based and merit-based financial assistance. The College participates in all applicable federal and state financial aid programs. Scholarships, grants, loans, and student employment are offered to help qualified students pay for college expenses. Financial aid may be funded by the federal or state government, the College, benefactors and friends of the College, or other sponsoring organizations or agencies. Merit-based scholarships are offered to qualified students regardless of need.

Students planning to attend the College in the fall semester should submit the Free Application for Federal Student Aid (FAFSA). The College begins awarding financial aid in February and continues until all funds are exhausted.

Student Government, Clubs, and Organizations

The Student Body Union (SBU) serves as the governing body of students at the College. SBU is responsible for student appointments to administrative and faculty committees. SBU oversees disbursement of student activity funds, which are used to support student publications, social activities, theater and musical productions, and provide support for student organizations.

Some campus organizations include the following: Campus Crusade for Christ (CRU), Catholic Students Organization, ConjuRings (literary magazine), Environmental Action Committee, EUTS Dance Team, Gay/Straight Alliance (GSA), GEARS (Gaming, Electronics, Anime, Rec, Sci-Fi), International Students Organization (ISO), Outdoor Club, Pharmakon (school newspaper), Prescripto (yearbook), Roller Hockey, Royal Chorale, Society of Apothecaries and Dreamers, STLCOP Book Club ("Booksies"), Student Ambassadors, Student Body Union (SBU), Student Organization for Drug and Alcohol Awareness (SODAA), and theater.

Admission Requirements

All students applying for admission to St. Louis College of Pharmacy must present evidence of the satisfactory completion of a four-year course of study in, and graduation from, a high school approved by a recognized accrediting body. The high school course of study should include 4 units of English; 4 units of math, including algebra 1 and 2 and geometry; and at least 3 units of science, including biology/lab and chemistry lab. First-year students must have a high GPA of at least 3.0 (on a 4.0 scale), rank in the upper 50 percent of their graduating class, and have a minimum composite score of 23 on the ACT and/or SAT combined score of 1110. Minimum subscore requirement for math is 24; minimum subscore requirements for English, science, and reading are 21.

Required application materials include the following: completed application and $50 nonrefundable application fee; high school transcripts including cumulative GPA and senior-year class rank; official ACT or SAT results; guidance counselor recommendation; science teacher recommendation; personal essay; declaration of finances form (international students only); English language test results, such as TOEFL (only U.S. and non-U.S. citizens whose native language is not English; a copy of U.S. Citizenship and Immigration Service status (international students only); and test results from the Pharmacy College Admission Test (transfer students only).

Early decision students who wish to accept an offer of admission must confirm their intention to enroll by submitting a $500 tuition deposit within 15 business days of acceptance notification. Regular decision students must submit a $300 deposit within 15 business days of acceptance of notification. The application deadline for transfer students is March 1. However, the PharmCAS deadline for submission of all admission materials is February 1. Transfer students are accepted into the third year of the program.

Application and Information

Application deadlines can be found online at www.stlcop.edu.

For additional information or to apply, students should contact:
Registrar/Director of Admissions
St. Louis College of Pharmacy
4588 Parkview Place
St. Louis, Missouri 63110
Phone: 314-367-8700 Ext. 8313
    800-278-5267 (toll-free)
E-mail: pbryant@stlcop.edu
Web site: http://www.stlcop.edu
    http://www.facebook.com/STLCOP
    http://twitter.com/#!/STLCOPEUT

SAINT MARY'S COLLEGE
NOTRE DAME, INDIANA

The College

Saint Mary's College, a pioneer in the education of women, is an academic community where women discover and develop their talents and prepare to make a difference in the world. A Saint Mary's education challenges students to reach beyond the ordinary. Every area of study emphasizes the exceptional writing and critical thinking skills needed to become a confident leader.

Saint Mary's offers more than thirty-five majors, including accounting, education, history, music, nursing, and communicative disorders. More than half of Saint Mary's students study abroad in locations such as Italy, Ireland, China, and Argentina, and each student completes the senior comprehensive, a capstone project in her major.

Founded by the Sisters of the Holy Cross in 1844, Saint Mary's is a nationally recognized Catholic college that empowers women by providing a strong liberal arts foundation, leadership development, and a focus on social responsibility.

With more than 1,500 students from forty-six states and fourteen countries, Saint Mary's brings together women from a wide range of backgrounds and experiences. International and diverse students compose 15 percent of the student body.

Saint Mary's has a unique relationship with the University of Notre Dame. Students at both schools can take courses at either institution. Saint Mary's students can audition for Notre Dame's legendary marching band (10 percent of its members attend Saint Mary's); work for the *Observer,* the daily newspaper published jointly by Notre Dame and Saint Mary's; or gain broadcast experience on WVFI, the Notre Dame/Saint Mary's radio station, or SMC-TV, Saint Mary's TV station. In addition, dances, concerts, lectures, and social organizations are open to students on both campuses.

One of the distinctive features of Saint Mary's is its campus life. Women lead and organize more than sixty clubs and organizations, eight varsity athletic teams, service opportunities through the Office for Civic and Social Engagement, and numerous other events and activities.

Saint Mary's is a residential campus with five residence halls, each with its own character. Seniors may choose to live in Opus Hall, which offers apartment-style living on campus. Residence halls offer events like dances, coffee nights with the College president, and intramural athletics. The College has a student center, a dining hall, and a clubhouse for extracurricular activities. All residence halls have chapels, and the Church of Loretto, the main worship space, offers daily Mass.

As an NCAA Division III school and a member of the Michigan Intercollegiate Athletic Association, Saint Mary's sponsors varsity teams in basketball, cross-country, golf, soccer, softball, swimming and diving, tennis, and volleyball. Club sports, cosponsored with Notre Dame, include gymnastics, lacrosse, and figure skating. In addition, Saint Mary's offers many intramural sports.

Angela Athletic Facility has multipurpose courts and a training and fitness center; the campus has tennis courts and fields for both soccer and softball.

Location

Saint Mary's beautiful 100-acre campus, set alongside the Saint Joseph River, is across the street from the University of Notre Dame, minutes north of the city of South Bend (population 101,000), and 90 miles from Chicago. South Bend provides opportunities for internships, practicums, and volunteer service. Eighty percent of Saint Mary's students engage in service by the time they graduate. The national average is approximately 55 percent.

Majors and Degrees

Saint Mary's College offers five degree programs: Bachelor of Arts, Bachelor of Science, Bachelor of Business Administration, Bachelor of Fine Arts, and Bachelor of Music.

The Bachelor of Arts degree program includes majors in art (concentrations in studio art and art history), biology, chemistry, communication studies, communicative disorders, economics, elementary education, English literature, English writing, French, history (including a concentration in women's history), humanistic studies, Italian, mathematics, music, philosophy, political science, psychology, religious studies, social work, sociology, Spanish, statistics and actuarial mathematics, and theater.

A Bachelor of Science degree may be obtained in biology (concentrations in ecology, evolution, and environmental biology, and cellular/molecular biology), chemistry (including a concentration in biochemistry), computational mathematics, mathematics, nursing, and statistics and actuarial mathematics.

The Bachelor of Business Administration degree program offers majors in accounting, business administration, and management information systems (concentrations include accounting, finance, international business, management, management information systems, and marketing).

Saint Mary's College offers a Bachelor of Fine Arts degree, with specialization in ceramics, fiber, new media art, painting, photo media, printmaking, and sculpture.

The Bachelor of Music degree program offers majors in music and music education. The College is a member of the National Association of Schools of Music.

Superior students who are candidates for either a B.A. or a B.S. degree may, with faculty approval, design a program of study outside the traditional department structure, called a student-designed major.

For students interested in engineering, a five-year, dual-degree program offered in cooperation with the University of Notre Dame leads to a bachelor's degree from Saint Mary's College and a Bachelor of Science in Engineering degree from Notre Dame in aerospace, chemical, civil, computer, electrical, environmental, or mechanical engineering.

Saint Mary's education department, accredited by the National Council for Accreditation of Teacher Education, offers an elementary education major (grades K–6) and a secondary education minor (grades 5–12). With an elementary education major, students can also receive mild intervention licensure (K–6) and an Indiana reading licensure (P–12). Minors in English as a second language and early childhood education are also offered. In addition, the department offers programs for those interested in teaching the visual arts or music. Secondary education requires a major in one of the following: business, English, modern languages (French, Spanish), mathematics, science (science majors must complete licensing requirements in chemistry or life science), history, or political science.

The College offers more than forty minors, including American history, anthropology, environmental studies, information science, justice studies, Latin American studies, and women's studies.

Academic Programs

In addition to completing the required credit hours in her major, every student must complete a senior comprehensive in her major, which may take the form of a thesis, a research or creative project, or a written or oral examination, depending on the discipline. All students must also complete a writing-intensive "W" course, usually in the first year, and an advanced portfolio of writing in the major discipline, usually in the senior year.

Off-Campus Programs

Saint Mary's offers study-abroad experiences in seventeen locations: Argentina, Australia, Austria, China, Ecuador, El Salvador, England, France, Greece, Honduras, Ireland, Italy, Morocco, South Africa, South Korea, Spain, and Uganda. Saint Mary's students may also study in other countries through a cooperative program with the University of Notre Dame. Students majoring

in political science may spend a semester at the American University in Washington, D.C.

Academic Facilities

Students have abundant access to technology systems, software, and services. Residence halls offer network access, and secure wireless network access is available in most public areas on campus. Several buildings have computer labs in addition to computer "collaboratories," where students and faculty members can conduct online research in classroom settings. Extensive support services are available to students, faculty, and staff members for instructional, administrative, and network systems.

The Cushwa-Leighton Library houses a collection of more than 228,000 volumes. Also located in the library are the Trumper Computer Center, the Instructional Technology Resource Center, and a rare book room.

Laboratory facilities are available for biology, chemistry, physics, psychology, and foreign language students. Art studios, music practice rooms, the O'Laughlin Auditorium, and Moreau's Little Theatre provide space for fine arts creation, practice, and performance. The Spes Unica academic building provides students with technology-equipped classrooms, group and individual study spaces, and presentation spaces.

The Early Childhood Development Center provides education and psychology majors with a unique opportunity to work with young children on campus. Other facilities include the Madeleva classroom building, Science Hall, Havican nursing facility, and Moreau Art Galleries.

Costs

Expenses for the 2011–12 academic year included tuition and fees, $32,000; room and board, $9750 (average); and miscellaneous expenses (books, transportation, and living costs), $2700.

Financial Aid

The College strives to make a Saint Mary's education available for every admitted student by offering financial aid packages that may include grants, scholarships, work-study, and loans. Last year more than 93 percent of Saint Mary's students received over $37 million in scholarships, grants, loans, and work opportunities. Of these funds, over $19 million were from Saint Mary's College in the form of grants and scholarships.

All applicants for financial aid must complete the College Board PROFILE and the Free Application for Federal Student Aid (FAFSA) each year that they desire assistance. Applications must be received at the processing center by March 1 to be given priority consideration. For non-early decision admission candidates, financial aid decisions are made in mid-March, as soon as possible after a student has been accepted and upon receipt of the required forms.

Faculty

Saint Mary's has 137 full-time and 61 part-time faculty members. Eighty-seven percent of full-time faculty members hold earned doctorates or other terminal degrees. All classes are taught by faculty members, not by teaching assistants.

Student Government

The Student Government Association sponsors many extracurricular and cocurricular activities. There are voting representatives on the president's two highest advisory boards, the Student Affairs Council and the Academic Affairs Council. A student is also a voting member of the College's Board of Trustees.

Admission Requirements

Applicants for admission to Saint Mary's College should be graduates of an accredited high school. Home-schooled students are encouraged to apply and should contact the Office of Admission for specific details. All applicants must complete a four-year, college-preparatory curriculum that consists of a minimum of 16 academic (Carnegie) units. One unit represents one full year of study. The minimum requirements are: 4 units of English literature and composition, 2 units of the same foreign language, 3 units of college-preparatory mathematics (beginning with algebra I), 2 units of laboratory science, and 2 units of history or social science. The remaining required units should consist of three additional units in the above listed subjects. The following subject areas are considered complementary to the college-preparatory courses and do not fulfill the minimum unit requirement: religion, business, home economics, physical education, health, American Sign Language, art, and music.

Applications must include an academic transcript showing current rank (if available) and senior-year courses, a counselor/administrator recommendation, SAT or ACT scores (at least one test should include the writing exam), and an essay. There is no application fee, and Saint Mary's is a member of the Common Application.

An interview with an admission officer is recommended. Saint Mary's encourages students to visit the campus. The Office of Admission can make arrangements for students who wish to attend classes or stay overnight.

Mature, well-qualified students who graduate from high school after three years and who wish to enter college immediately upon graduation may apply for early admission. Saint Mary's College also grants deferred admission upon request to candidates who are accepted in the normal application process.

Application and Information

Saint Mary's has two application and notification programs: early decision and modified rolling admission. Highly qualified students who have selected Saint Mary's as their first choice for admission may apply under the early decision program. The application deadline is November 15, and the notification date is December 15. Students who apply for modified rolling admission and whose application files are complete on or before December 1 are notified of the admission decision in mid-January. Applications received after December 1 are reviewed in the order in which they become complete. The priority application deadline for regular admission is February 15. Applications are accepted, however, as long as space is available.

Interested students are encouraged to contact:

Director of Admission
Saint Mary's College
Notre Dame, Indiana 46556-5001
Phone: 574-284-4587
        800-551-7621 (toll-free)
Fax: 574-284-4841
E-mail: admission@saintmarys.edu
Web site: www.saintmarys.edu

Saint Mary's College promises its students discovery.

The College

What matters?

Saint Michael's College believes that a college education should prepare students not only for a meaningful career, but also for a meaningful life.

That's why St. Michael's students start by building a strong liberal studies foundation, then they dive deep into their majors. By the time they graduate, students have developed essential skills and knowledge to help them be successful in any field. And in the meantime, they've also been engaged in service (through the College's popular MOVE program), in the great outdoors (with St. Michael's ground-breaking Wilderness Program and Smuggs' Ski Pass), and with the close campus community in meaningful ways that educate the body, mind, and spirit.

And happiness matters. At Saint Michael's, prospective students find bright, engaged, friendly, happy students and faculty members. The College's formula for happiness is its close campus community, its perspective-changing exploration of the liberal arts, its legacy of faith and service, and its stunning Vermont location.

All this happiness and engagement underscores Saint Michael's successes: The College is among only 280 colleges and universities nationwide to host a prestigious Phi Beta Kappa chapter on campus. Recent graduates are Rhodes Scholars, Pickering Fellows, medical students, law students, dental students, medical researchers, pharmacists, new media specialists, sports writers, nonprofit directors, and more. Alumni include a U.S. Senator, one of the founders of MTV, noted authors, scientists, investment bankers, doctors, social workers, teachers, professors, and scholars. No matter what career paths they choose, St. Michael's alumni take with them a solid liberal arts foundation, a strong sense of self, and a desire to give back to their communities.

Students at Saint Michael's are seriously involved with life on campus, taking on leadership roles, rallying support for worthy causes, and generally making things happen. Because everyone lives on campus (student housing is guaranteed for all four years), there's an incredible sense of community, and students always find someone ready for whatever adventures they have in mind—from taking on a research project to rock climbing. Nearly one third of St. Mike's students study abroad for a semester, an academic year, or a summer.

Location

Saint Michael's beautiful, safe 440-acre campus is just 3 miles from Burlington, which is Vermont's largest city. Burlington is a vibrant college town that is home to 14,000 students who attend five local colleges and universities. Downtown Burlington is a thriving city center of businesses that offer great opportunities for hands-on learning through internships. There are tons of shops, restaurants, and cafés, the Church Street Marketplace, and a lively local music scene as well as tons of places to ski, skate, kayak, and bike. The Smuggs' pass lets students to take advantage of some of the best skiing in the East, and the renowned Wilderness Program offers dozens of outdoor adventure opportunities. Saint Michael's Cultural Pass gives students deep discounts to fine arts performances at Burlington's famous Flynn Theater.

The Burlington International Airport, Amtrak station and Greyhound bus station are all only a 10-minute drive from the campus.

Majors and Degrees

Saint Michael's College offers bachelor's degrees with a liberal arts foundation. The College offers 34 majors in the following areas: accounting, American studies, art, art education, biochemistry, biology, business administration, chemistry, classics, computer science, economics, elementary and secondary education, engineering, English, environmental studies, French, gender/women's studies, history, information systems, mathematics, media studies/journalism/digital arts, modern languages and literature, music, philosophy, physics, political science, pre-pharmacy, psychology, religious studies, sociology, Spanish, and theater. In addition, advising programs for premedicine, prelaw, predentistry, and pre–veterinary studies are available in addition to 37 minors, including interdisciplinary areas.

Dual-degree programs are available in engineering through Clarkson University (Potsdam, New York) and the University of Vermont (Burlington, Vermont); pharmacy through Albany College of Pharmacy's Burlington campus; and physical therapy through the University of Vermont. A 4+1 M.B.A. program is offered in conjunction with Clarkson University.

Academic Programs

Saint Michael's prepares its students for life after college with a dynamic liberal arts curriculum designed to foster intellectual curiosity and exploration, including a highly competitive honors program and many opportunities for self-directed study. The College's curriculum emphasizes a solid understanding of building blocks of a meaningful life as a well-rounded, thoughtful person: humanities, social sciences, religious studies, philosophy, natural sciences, mathematics, and fine arts. Saint Michael's students develop excellent communication skills through writing intensive courses and foreign language requirements. And the curriculum pays serious attention to questions of ethics and responsible citizenship.

The Saint Michael's academic year consists of two semesters and an optional summer session. The College's focus is on undergraduate instruction, and its small classes support this primary emphasis. Saint Michael's has a strong faculty-student research tradition and provides competitive opportunities for research for academic credit and with faculty during the academic year and over the summer.

Nowhere is Saint Michael's mission more evident than in its service-learning opportunities. Service-learning at Saint Michael's is a credit-bearing, educational experience in which students in an academic course participate in a thoughtfully organized service activity that meets identified community needs. Students reflect on the service activities in ways that develop further understanding of course content, a broader appreciation of the discipline, and an enhanced sense of civic responsibility.

Off-Campus Programs

At Saint Michael's, students can gain hands-on experience with an internship related to their career goals and majors.

Internships are available both locally and in other selected areas around the United States and abroad. Sites include scientific research laboratories, brokerage houses, hospitals, schools, newspapers, and accounting firms.

More than a third of Saint Michael's students study abroad for a semester or an academic year. Unique Saint Michael's programs include study-abroad experiences at University of the Americas, Mexico; College of Ripon and York St. John, England; Kansai Gaidai University, Japan; and a Washington, D.C., semester program. In recent years, many students have studied abroad in locations such as Australia, Botswana, China, France, Ghana, Ireland, Italy, Nepal, Samoa, and Spain.

Academic Facilities

Saint Michael's has a Main Campus and a North Campus. Main Campus is home to almost all academic and administrative buildings. The Jeremiah Durick Library holds 227,000 volumes; 110 research databases; access to articles from more than 25,000 online journals; and 10,000 electronic books, maps, videos, and other items. Students have access to more than 120 computers connected to the College's campuswide information technology network. This network provides access to PC applications, including Microsoft Windows 7, the Internet, e-mail, and the College library. Most campus areas have wireless Internet access.

Cheray Science Center has recently renovated facilities for the study of biochemistry, biology, chemistry, environmental science, and physics.

Saint Edmund's Hall, an impressive academic complex, includes media labs, psychology labs, computer facilities, and language labs, in addition to traditional classroom and lecture hall space.

Costs

Tuition and residence fees for the 2012–13 academic year are $46,860. The residence fee includes housing and meals and is based on a standard double room and a standard meal plan. Housing options on campus include traditional residence halls, apartment-style housing, theme housing, and suite-style housing. Some science, journalism, language, and art courses require laboratory fees. Book, personal, and travel expenses vary according to course selection and individual needs.

Financial Aid

Approximately 90 percent of admitted students receive financial aid in the form of loans, grants, and work-study dollars. Students must file the FAFSA by February 15 for fall-semester enrollment.

Faculty

Saint Michael's faculty members are known not only for being experts in their fields but for sharing that expertise effectively with their students. Their doors are always open, too—it's not unusual to join professors for coffee or lunch, or to be invited to their homes for dinner. Students find faculty members at fundraisers and on the sidelines of athletic games. And chances are excellent that they'll know every student's name by the end of the first week of class. Saint Michael's remarkable faculty includes 150 full-time professors, 94 percent whom have the doctoral or terminal degree in their field. Many have been recipients of grants, awards, and honors in recent years. While undergraduate instruction is the focus of the College, faculty members remain active in their field through research and publication, often facilitated through sabbaticals.

Student Government

The Student Association (SA), an active and important part of campus life, is an elected body of students that authorizes and funds most other student activities and organizations. Representatives from the SA sit on many campuswide committees, including the Curriculum Committee and various committees of the Board of Trustees.

Admission Requirements

Successful applicants to Saint Michael's typically rank in the top 25 percent of their high school class and have a strong college-preparatory background. Students should have completed 16 units of courses in English, foreign language, mathematics, science, and social science. SAT or ACT scores are optional. For reference, of those who opted to submit them, the average SAT score last year ranged between 1600 and 1890, and the average ACT score ranged between 25 and 26. In addition, students should submit a counselor recommendation and any teacher recommendations they choose. Transfer applicants must submit transcripts of all college work in addition to their final high school transcript.

Application and Information

Saint Michael's offers an early action admission program deadline of either November 1 or December 1, as well as a regular action deadline of February 1. Students should consult the Web site for application deadlines and information. Candidates for the fall semester are notified of their admission decision on or before April 1. A limited number of students may be admitted to the spring semester and should have their applications in by November 1. The College adheres to the Candidates Reply Date of May 1 for the fall semester.

For further information, students should contact:
Office of Admission
Saint Michael's College
One Winooski Park, Box 7
Colchester, Vermont 05439
Phone: 800-762-8000 (toll-free)
Fax: 802-654-2906
E-mail: admission@smcvt.edu
Web site: http://www.smcvt.edu

A student takes a break to study in the Saint Michael's College one-of-a-kind 'Word Garden'.

ST. NORBERT COLLEGE
DE PERE, WISCONSIN

The College

A new state-of-the-art library, new apartment-style residence hall, new outdoor athletics complex, renovated student services center, new welcome center, new student commons, and plans to remodel science facilities—these are just a few of the exciting things happening at St. Norbert College. The riverfront campus is part of the thriving corporate, entertainment, educational, arts, and cultural environment of northeastern Wisconsin. Learning takes place in residence halls and classrooms, on campus, and, literally, around the world.

The St. Norbert learning community helps students become critical thinkers, strong writers, and able communicators, in a setting that encourages student-faculty collaborative research. The graduate-level work done by St. Norbert undergraduates, even as first-year students, is surprising and puts them ahead of their peers when heading to graduate school or the workforce.

St. Norbert seeks to challenge student viewpoints and encourage exploration of new or different ideas, in an environment where students from around the world come together in exploration of local and global perspectives.

Faculty members at St. Norbert are active researchers and creators who make ongoing contributions to their fields. They're also compassionate individuals who care not only about their students' grades, but also about their growth, making time for one-on-one conversations with students on a daily basis. Student success is their top priority, and they regularly give out their home phone numbers for easy student access.

St. Norbert College offers more than forty programs of study, including several pre-professional programs. Students can also design their own major, unique to their aspirations. Opportunities to study abroad abound, and there are numerous service opportunities for students locally, nationally, and internationally.

Each St. Norbert student is paired with an adviser who helps ensure that the student is on track with classes and will graduate in four years. St. Norbert's innovative career services office provides service throughout the college years and beyond; the alumni career network can help students find their first job as well as their last one. When St. Norbert students are surveyed nine months after graduation, 92 percent of them are typically employed or attending graduate school.

Student life offers a blend of learning and fun. Students flourish within the academically challenging environment, but with more than seventy clubs and organizations on campus, there's no shortage of ways to become involved outside the classroom. The twenty Division III athletic teams produce conference champions, national champions, and more Academic All-Americans than any school in the Midwest Conference.

Students frequently comment on the sense of community and worldwide opportunities available at St. Norbert. They talk about the challenges of the classroom and the heartfelt rewards of the service opportunities. Graduates value the friendships with peers and faculty members that started at St. Norbert and may last a lifetime. Some students love the campus so much they refer to St. Norbert as their home.

Location

The St. Norbert campus, approximately 93 acres, is located on the banks of the Fox River in De Pere, Wisconsin, just minutes south of Green Bay, a metropolitan area of about 230,000 people and home to the Green Bay Packers football team. Rich culture, arts, and entertainment are present in historic De Pere and the greater Green Bay area, recognized as one of the 100 best communities for young people by America's Promise Alliance. Located near the gateway to Door County, one of Wisconsin's favorite vacation spots, the campus is part of a vibrant eighteen-county region of 1.2 million people.

Majors and Degrees

St. Norbert offers programs leading to the Bachelor of Arts, Bachelor of Science, Bachelor of Music, and Bachelor of Business Administration degrees. Students also have the opportunity of applying their education at St. Norbert toward any of three master's degree programs: the Master of Science in Education, Master of Arts in Liberal Studies, and Master of Theological Studies.

St. Norbert College has partnered with other institutions to further extend its offerings. Students can earn a nursing degree through a partnership with Bellin College in Green Bay, or earn a master's degree in applied economics in just one additional year, rather than two, through a partnership with Marquette University.

Programs of study at St. Norbert include: accounting, American studies, anthropology, art–fine arts, art–graphic design, biology–biomedical, biology–organismal, business administration, chemistry, chemistry–biochemistry, classical studies, communication and media studies, computer science, computer science–business information systems, computer science–graphic design and implementation, economics, education, English, English–creative writing, environmental science, French, geography, geology, German, history, human services (social work), international business and language area studies, international studies, Japanese, leadership studies, mathematics, military science/ROTC, music, natural sciences, peace and justice, Philippine studies, philosophy, physics, political science, pre-dental, pre-engineering, pre-law, pre-medical, pre-pharmacy, pre-veterinary, psychology, religious studies, religious studies–youth ministry, sociology, Spanish, teacher education, theater studies, and women's and gender studies.

Academic Programs

Degrees are awarded upon the successful completion of thirty-two courses (128 semester hours) that include an approved major sequence, course work in general education, and either an academic minor or electives. Academic majors can be started as early as the first semester of the first year. Early selection of a major is encouraged but not required in most majors. Students are not required to officially declare a major until the end of the sophomore year. The college offers a four-year graduation guarantee and has one of the highest four-year graduation rates in the Midwest.

As a liberal arts institution, the college prepares students for a lifetime of challenges and opportunities by equipping them with exceptional communication abilities, as well as critical-thinking, problem-solving, and leadership skills. An honors program offers additional challenge in areas of general education to those of superior ability, and an honors degree is awarded to those who successfully complete the program.

Army ROTC is available and several St. Norbert students are recipients of full Army ROTC scholarships each year. Among the college's alumni are an impressive 12 Army generals who completed ROTC at St. Norbert.

Off-Campus Programs

St. Norbert students, regardless of major, can spend a summer, a semester, or a year abroad. In fact, 30 percent of St. Norbert students spend at least one semester abroad during their four years compared to just 1.4 percent nationally. The college has more than seventy-five study-abroad program sites in thirty-seven countries on six continents. An international study component is a part of majors in French, Spanish, and German, and both the international business program and the international studies major. All approved international study carries regular academic credit. St. Norbert scholarship assistance and other financial aid carry over to overseas study.

St. Norbert considers international experience vital to today's graduates and it is a key component of the college's educational mission. Study-abroad opportunities include a Third World science field trip; exchange programs in Australia, France, Japan,

Germany, the Philippines, Spain, and Ukraine; student teaching in Europe, Africa, Australia, and Latin America; and other study sites throughout Europe, South America, and Egypt. St. Norbert's international curriculum, taught by a faculty committed to global learning, prepares students to live in a global society. A Washington semester is also available through American University in Washington, D.C.

Additional service-learning opportunities are available throughout the year. Students can participate in the TRIPS (Turning Responsibility into Powerful Service) program in local, national, and international locations, or participate in a variety of other off-campus service opportunities.

Academic Facilities

A new $20-million state-of-the-art library opened in the fall of 2009. It houses more than 247,000 volumes, including books, journals and other serials, microforms, maps, and charts. More than 3,000 volumes are added to the collection each year. The 80,000-square-foot library features enhanced technology, flexible study and classroom spaces, and a welcome center with computers, media players, and a 24-hour computer study area.

The F. K. Bemis International Center provides students with opportunities to prepare for careers with greater international emphasis. Students from more than thirty countries attend St. Norbert College annually. The center also serves as a resource for K–12 schools and Wisconsin businesses for language instruction, translation, and interpretation.

The John Minahan Science Hall houses the science programs and thirty-eight laboratories. Planning is well underway for renovation and expansion of this building to facilitate current and future research and education in the natural sciences.

Thirteen residence halls provide the link between living and learning at St. Norbert. Some residence halls focus on community service or feature campus programs, such as the Women's Center or the honors program. A new apartment-style residence hall offers upperclassmen a transitional experience to living on their own. Many halls have chapels for students.

A new outdoor athletics complex provides the practice and competition venue for football, soccer, and track and field. New in 2012 is the remodeled Michels Commons, where students eat their meals and gather in Dale's Sports Lounge on evenings and weekends. Chefs prepare meals in front of the students and are able to get immediate feedback on favorite recipes.

Costs

For 2011–12, tuition and required fees for full-time students totaled $29,395. Room and board costs averaged $7513 per year.

Financial Aid

Students share in more than $50 million of financial aid each year, including scholarships and grants, campus jobs, and educational loans. More than 95 percent of St. Norbert students receive financial aid, with the average aid amount of $24,600 for first-year students. There are both need-based and merit-based awards.

Need-based awards are made on the basis of the Free Application for Federal Student Aid (FAFSA; St. Norbert College's code is 003892) and the St. Norbert College institutional application for financial aid. First-year applicants should submit these forms by March of their senior year of high school.

A multitude of work-study positions exists on campus, and students have paid internship opportunities on campus as well as in the community at Fortune 500 companies, hospitals, schools, or service organizations.

Faculty

The St. Norbert faculty is composed of 197 men and women, 139 of whom are full-time. At least 87 percent of the full-time faculty members hold the doctoral or other terminal degree in their field. The student-faculty ratio is 14:1, and student success is a top priority of the faculty. They work closely with students in their major area of study, help students prepare for graduate school, write letters of recommendation, and work with those who seek independent study

and research opportunities. Research fellowships and collaborations with faculty members are available to all students, who may ultimately have the opportunity to present their research findings collaboratively with faculty members at national conferences. Faculty members also work with Career Services in its professional practice program.

Student Government

The college's Student Government Association (SGA) is active on campus, with representation extending as far as the college's board of trustees. The president of the college and his cabinet respect the voice of the student body, and openly discuss issues that impact students and the college community. The SGA meets regularly and holds town-hall meetings for the campus community. Its goal is to serve as a representative governing body and to create an environment conducive to intellectual, spiritual, and personal growth throughout the campus community.

Admission Requirements

St. Norbert College welcomes enrollment from a diverse group of students who are prepared academically and who will make a contribution to the college's living and learning community. Every completed application is considered carefully, and students who are likely to succeed in this environment are accepted. In 2011, more than 86 percent of the first-year class ranked in the top half of their high school senior class, the average GPA was 3.5, and the average ACT composite score was 25. Students with superior scores and grades are invited to enroll in the honors program.

Application and Information

Because the college gives preference to students according to the date of admission and enrollment deposit, it benefits students to apply as early as possible in their senior year. Notification of the admission decision is made on a rolling basis beginning in late September. A $350 deposit is required to confirm enrollment. For more information about St. Norbert College, students should contact:

Edward Lamm
Associate Vice President of Undergraduate and Graduate Enrollment
St. Norbert College
100 Grant Street
De Pere, Wisconsin 54115
Phone: 920-403-3005
      800-236-4878 (toll-free)
E-mail: admit@snc.edu
Web site: http://www.snc.edu
      http://www.snc.edu/go/socialmedia

The quintessential college campus complete with crew team, St. Norbert College plays host to the Tail of the Fox Regatta each fall.

ST. THOMAS AQUINAS COLLEGE
SPARKILL, NEW YORK

The College

St. Thomas Aquinas College (STAC) was founded in 1952 as a three-year teacher-training college with 30 students. Today, the College offers more than 100 different majors, minors, specializations, and dual degree programs and has a total student body of 2,700 in all programs, on and off campus. Much growth and development has taken place over the College's history. The College offers a Master of Science in Education, with concentrations in literacy education, special education, and educational leadership as well as postgraduate certificate programs in literacy and special education. The College also offers a Master of Business Administration (M.B.A.) program with concentrations in finance, management, and marketing; and an online M.B.A. in general studies. St. Thomas offers a Master of Science in Teaching program for individuals without a background in teacher education who are seeking a career change. Certification is offered in childhood education, grades 1–6; childhood education and special education, grades 1–6; and adolescence education, grades 7–12. The College is home to New York University's Master in Social Work program.

The suburban campus includes two residential complexes: Aquinas Village, which consists of self-contained townhouse units that house 300 students, and the McNelis Commons, which consists of townhouse residential units that house 375 students and a common dining hall and laundry building. Approximately 40 percent of the College's full-time student population resides on campus.

Extracurricular activities are provided through forty different organizations, including the Spartan Volunteers, a community service program; a student-run radio station (WSTK); the Laetare Players dramatic and musical club; and the student-edited campus newspaper and yearbook. The College has excellent sports facilities, and several of its athletic teams have competed in national championships. The College fields NCAA Division II teams in men's and women's cross-country, golf, indoor track and field, and tennis; women's basketball, lacrosse, soccer, and softball; and men's baseball, basketball, and soccer. There are a number of club sports including equestrian, ice hockey, cheerleading and dance, bowling, and ski and snowboarding, as well as intramural athletics.

The College has a campus ministry office, a health office, and residence life, career placement, and counseling services.

Location

The College is located in Sparkill, a hamlet in southern Rockland County, New York, 16 miles north of New York City and adjacent to Bergen County, New Jersey.

Majors and Degrees

St. Thomas Aquinas College's School of Business offers accounting (and accounting as a dual degree with an M.B.A. degree), business administration, finance, marketing, and sports management. Minors are offered in business administration, marketing, economics, human resource management, international business, and management information systems. Specializations are in management relations/industrial and organizational psychology.

The School of Arts & Sciences offers degrees in the humanities, mathematics, natural sciences, and social sciences. Programs are available in art therapy, art and graphic design, communication arts, English, philosophy and religious studies, Romance languages, Spanish, mathematics, computer and information sciences, biology, forensic science, medical technology, natural sciences, criminal justice, psychology, therapeutic recreation, social science, and history. There are specializations in biology, chemistry, and physics. Minors include art therapy, biology, chemistry, communication arts, computer information science, criminal justice, English, fine arts, graphic design, history, journalism, mathematics, performing arts, physics, public relations, religious studies, Spanish, social media, sociology, therapeutic recreation, and writing. A full listing of all programs can be found online at www.stac.edu.

The School of Education offers programs in grades 1–6 childhood education, the same plus special education, and grades 7–12 adolescence education, the latter offering certification in biology, English, history, mathematics, science and technology, natural science with either biology or chemistry, social sciences, and Spanish. An art education program with certifications in grades K–12 is offered as well as a middle school extension that adds to either the elementary or secondary degree, enabling the student to certify for all middle school grades.

The College offers a five-year dual-degree program in mathematics/engineering with the George Washington University (GWU) or Manhattan College. Students study at St. Thomas for three years. After completion of their final two years at either GWU or Manhattan, they earn a B.S. in mathematics from STAC and a B.S. in engineering from one of the other two institutions. The College also offers several dual-degree options in biology: a dual degree in biology (B.S. from STAC) and biomedical engineering (M.S. from Polytechnic University), a dual degree in biology (B.S. from STAC) and physical therapy (D.P.T. from New York Medical College), a dual degree in biology (B.S. from STAC) and chiropractic (D.C. from New York Chiropractic College), and a dual degree in biology (B.S. from STAC) and podiatry (D.P.M. from New York College of Podiatric Medicine). There are several other strategic alliances, such as preferred admission to St. John's University School of Law in New York and a similar program with Barry University School of Law in Florida that includes scholarship funds. St. Thomas seeks out additional strategic opportunities for its undergraduate and graduate students on a regular basis; students should contact the College for information about new alliances.

Academic Programs

The College strives to develop students who are not only generally educated but also possess advanced knowledge in specialized areas, are prepared for further study, and have the background to undertake fulfilling careers. To earn a bachelor's degree, students must complete a total of 120 semester hours, including a minimum of 51 credits in a core curriculum; complete all requirements for the specific major; and complete the final 30 hours at St. Thomas. The College awards up to 30 credits for life experience and up to 30 credits for achievement on the College-Level Examination Program (CLEP). The College operates on a semester calendar (quarterly on the M.B.A. level). Students may enroll in classes in the fall, winter (a one-month session), spring, and summer (three separate sessions). Classes are scheduled during the day and evening, and students are permitted considerable academic flexibility in planning their programs.

Students can pursue independent study and internships, and many majors require a field practicum. The College maintains an active Center for Academic Excellence as a resource for enhancing academic performance, and students are encouraged to meet regularly with faculty advisers for academic guidance and career direction.

Several programs supplement the traditional academic areas. The College has a widely recognized program for college-age

learning-disabled students, called the Pathways Program (at an additional cost). The College also participates in the New York State Higher Education Opportunity Program and provides an honors program for exceptionally qualified students with a limited number of full-tuition-scholarships. The honors program includes summer study at Oxford University.

Off-Campus Programs

The College offers a campus interchange program involving three other fully accredited colleges (Barry University in Miami Shores, Florida; Dominican College of San Rafael in San Rafael, California; and Aquinas College in Grand Rapids, Michigan) through which a student may attend a semester at one of the participating colleges during the junior year. The College also offers a number of study-abroad opportunities for students throughout the entire year with as short a period as one week for a communication arts class in London.

The study-abroad program provides opportunities at colleges and universities in such places as Brazil, Canada, England, France, Hungary, Ireland, Italy, Morocco, and Spain. Several other locations are also available.

The College offers courses for an associate degree program at West Point for eligible students at the United States Military Academy.

Academic Facilities

Borelli Hall features new classrooms with interactive board technologies. Costello Hall houses the science laboratories, technology theaters, and Azarian-McCullough Art Gallery. Spellman Hall houses a multiroom technology corridor, with a state-of-the-art communication studio where students produce their own news show, and technology and language labs. Lougheed Library provides a variety of online research opportunities for students. Aquinas Hall houses athletic facilities and a fitness center. Maguire Hall is home to classrooms, art studios, and the Sullivan Theater. Additional meeting areas are provided in the Romano Student-Alumni Center and in the two residence complexes, McNelis Commons and Aquinas Village. There is an after-hours club in the McNelis Commons dining hall for student activities.

Costs

For 2012–13, the tuition for full-time study (12 to 16 credits per semester) is $24,610. Room and board at the College Commons are $11,000. Certain studio, laboratory, and computer courses carry fees.

Financial Aid

In 2011–12, 80 percent of the student body received financial aid. The College is committed to providing competent but needy students with the resources necessary to continue their education. Students must submit the Free Application for Federal Student Aid each year. The College awards academic and merit scholarships from $5000 up to full-tuition scholarships and provides need-based aid from the College as well as athletic grants and all federal and New York State aid programs.

St. Thomas strives to partner with the student to make college education affordable. The College has one of the lowest private college tuition rates in New York State, and scholarships make it even more affordable. The College is also a member of the Yellow Ribbon program for veterans enabling a qualified veteran to study with a full tuition scholarship.

Faculty

The faculty has 70 full-time and 55 part-time members; 80 percent have terminal degrees. The student-faculty ratio is 18:1. All faculty members participate in the academic advising of students and serve on College committees. Many serve as advisers to extracurricular activities.

Student Government

The Student Government consists of elected members who officially represent the student body, are responsible for planning and implementing student-originated programs, and coordinate and oversee all extracurricular organizations. Through its various offices, students play a vital part in offering consultation on new policies, planning social and cultural events, managing student funds, and operating the judicial system. In addition, the College Forum, which is composed of elected students, faculty members, alumni, administrators, and trustees, meets regularly to discuss policies, procedures, long-range plans, and any problems affecting the College.

Admission Requirements

All applicants must have successfully completed an approved secondary school program or the equivalent, including 4 years in English, 3 years in mathematics, 3 years in science, 3 years of foreign language, and 4 years of social studies. Applicants whose high school background varies from the recommended pattern are considered. Freshman applicants must submit the application for admission, including an essay, high school transcripts, SAT or ACT scores, and their guidance counselor's recommendation. Transfer students must submit the application and official transcripts of all previous college work. An academic evaluation is prepared for every matriculant.

Application and Information

Candidates should submit completed application forms to the Admissions and Financial Aid Office and must request that their official transcripts be sent to the Admissions Office from their school. Students are notified of the admission decision on a rolling basis upon receipt of all the necessary credentials. The College is a member of the Common Application and students can find the link to apply on its Web site, http://www.stac.edu.

The College does not discriminate against students, faculty and staff members, and other beneficiaries on the basis of race, color, national origin, gender, age, sexual orientation, disability, marital status, genetic predisposition, carrier status, veteran status, or religious affiliation in admission to or in the provision of its programs and services. The Section 504 Coordinator, the Title IX Coordinator, and the Age Act Coordinator is Marian Hall, Executive Director of Human Resources, 845-398-4038.

For more information or an application, students should contact:

Admissions and Financial Aid Office
St. Thomas Aquinas College
125 Route 340
Sparkill, New York 10976-1050
Phone: 800-999-STAC (toll-free)
Web site: http://www.stac.edu

A view of campus life at St. Thomas Aquinas College.

SALISBURY UNIVERSITY
SALISBURY, MARYLAND

The University

A Maryland University of National Distinction, Salisbury University (SU) consistently ranks in the top 10 percent of public and private institutions in national guidebooks and magazines. A member of the University System of Maryland (USM), SU emphasizes undergraduate research, study abroad, professional internships, and community engagement as pillars of its academic programs.

A midsize university of 7,892 undergraduates and 390 full-time faculty members on a 197-acre campus, SU provides a private college feel with the opportunities and affordability of a public institution. This distinct combination is why 98 percent of recent graduates say they would recommend SU. The foundation of SU's success is the relationship between students and professors. Full professors serve as undergraduate advisers, and routinely lead students on trips and retreats, from exploring the Chesapeake Bay to touring Europe. Their professional concern for educating the whole student has had measurable results. According to the latest figures, SU has the fastest time-to-degree average and the highest four-year graduation rate of all comprehensive institutions in the USM. This success has not gone unnoticed. For the fifteenth consecutive year, SU is among *U.S. News & World Report*'s Top Public Universities in the North, the highest-placing public master's-level university in Maryland. For the thirteenth consecutive year, SU is one of *The Princeton Review*'s Best Colleges. *Kiplinger's Personal Finance* magazine has named SU among the top 100 best value public colleges in the nation.

Salisbury students come from twenty-seven states, the District of Columbia, and sixty-five other countries. Some 60 percent are from Maryland's western shore (which contains the Metropolitan Baltimore-Washington corridor). Many of SU's 100-plus student organizations and clubs find a home in the Guerrieri University Center. An NCAA Division III member of intercollegiate athletics, SU has twenty-one varsity sports that compete in the Capital Athletic Conference and in the Empire Eight Athletic Football Conference. Women's sports are basketball, cross-country, field hockey, lacrosse, soccer, softball, swimming, tennis, indoor and outdoor track and field, and volleyball. Men's sports are baseball, basketball, cross-country, football, lacrosse, soccer, swimming, tennis, and indoor and outdoor track and field. The Sea Gulls have won fifteen national championships, nine in men's lacrosse, five in field hockey, and one in women's lacrosse. One of the leading Division III programs, Salisbury athletics are consistently ranked in the top 25 of the national Directors' Cup standings. Nearly half of the student body participates in twenty-two intramural programs and fourteen additional sports clubs.

The University has three art galleries; supports film and distinguished lecture series and artist-in-residence programs; maintains WSCL/WSDL-FM (national public radio affiliates) and WXSU-FM (a student-run radio station); offers performing arts disciplines in music, theater, and dance; and serves as the home of the Salisbury Symphony Orchestra. Beyond the campus are Maryland's scenic Eastern Shore, the pleasures of Ocean City, Maryland (a nearby popular beach resort), and the activities of an energetic Outdoor Club. Faculty members lead trips abroad during spring break, and winter and summer terms.

Location

With a population of roughly 94,000, Salisbury is the cultural and economic hub of Delmarva (containing portions of Delaware, Maryland, and Virginia), a historically and ecologically rich peninsula located between the Atlantic Ocean and Chesapeake Bay. The city is 30 minutes west of the beaches of Assateague and Ocean City, Maryland; about 2 hours from Baltimore, Wilmington, Norfolk, and Washington, D.C.; and 4½ hours from New York City.

Majors and Degrees

Three undergraduate degrees are offered in addition to the Bachelor of Arts and Bachelor of Science: the Bachelor of Arts in Social Work (B.A.S.W.), the Bachelor of Science in Nursing (B.S.N.), and the Bachelor of Fine Arts (B.F.A.) in art. B.A. degrees are awarded in art, communication arts, conflict analysis and dispute resolution, economics, English, English for speakers of other languages, environmental studies, fine arts, French, history, interdisciplinary studies, international studies, music, philosophy, political science, psychology, sociology, Spanish, social work, and theater. B.S. degrees are awarded in accounting, athletic training, biology, business administration, chemistry, clinical laboratory science/medical technology, computer science, early childhood education, elementary education, exercise science, finance, geography and geosciences, health education, interdisciplinary studies, management, management information systems, marketing, mathematics, nursing, physical education, physics, and respiratory therapy.

The University also offers fourteen graduate programs, and will offer courses in fall 2012 leading to a Doctorate of Nursing Practice.

Academic Programs

At Salisbury University, majors are designed to educate the whole student. No false distinctions are made between the liberal arts and the professions. While gaining a liberal education, for example, students in preprofessional programs prepare for careers in dentistry, law, medicine, optometry, pharmacy, physical therapy, podiatry, and veterinary science. Certification programs train educators for both elementary and secondary teaching. Dual-degree programs with the University of Maryland Eastern Shore (UMES) enable students to earn two bachelor's degrees in four years in biology/environmental marine science and social work/sociology. SU, Old Dominion University, Widener University, and the University of Maryland College Park also collaborate on an engineering degree. SU supports an Army Reserve Officers' Training Corps (ROTC) program on campus. Both the graduate and the undergraduate programs of SU's business school are accredited by The Association to Advance Collegiate Schools of Business and the Network of International Business Schools. Other national accreditations are in chemistry, education, allied health (respiratory therapy, exercise science, and athletic training programs), social work, clinical laboratory science (medical technology program), music, and nursing and through the Middle States Commission on Higher Education.

SU's fifty-six academic programs are administered through four schools: the Franklin P. Perdue School of Business, the Samuel W. and Marilyn C. Seidel School of Education and Professional Studies, the Charles R. and Martha N. Fulton School of Liberal Arts, and the Richard A. Henson School of Science and Technology. All four schools are endowed, a rarity among public institutions nationwide. These endowments have enriched the scholastic climate of the campus, providing expanded scholarships, resources, and opportunities.

University planning encourages interdisciplinary study. Students in all majors must take a minimum of nine courses in three disciplines: history, humanities and social sciences, and mathematical and natural sciences. Two courses are required in English composition and literature. One course is required in health fitness. All courses, from science to music to physical education, require written assignments in analysis/criticism, research, or creative writing.

SU's advising system has been praised by students in a Maryland Higher Education Commission survey as one of the best in the state. Orientation programs help freshmen make a successful transition to college. SU's New Student Seminars offer an orientation-in-the-wilderness experience, which won the Maryland Association for Higher Education Distinguished Program Award. Orientation options include cycling in Maine and canoeing in Canada.

Incoming students may earn credit through Advanced Placement and departmental challenge examinations and the College-Level Examination Program (CLEP) for nontraditional educational experiences. Internships have included work abroad, legislative service in Washington, D.C. and Annapolis, and media experience in fields from fine arts to television. Students who relish intellectual

challenge are invited to join the honors program housed in the Thomas E. Bellavance Honors Center. Others present research at national and international conferences. SU is also the only university in Maryland to twice host the National Conference on Undergraduate Research. Study-abroad programs are popular. Education students teach in New Zealand, nursing students provide aid in Africa, and all students may enroll in new Salisbury Abroad programs in Ecuador, Estonia, China, Spain, France, Scotland, and Italy for the same cost as tuition, room, and board in Maryland.

Academic Facilities

The SU campus is in the midst of an extensive transformation. Sea Gull Square, a new 600-bed residence hall and retail complex, opened in fall 2011, the same time as a new, state-of-the-art home for the Perdue School of Business. Also under way are multimillion-dollar renovations for older residence halls. The campus' first parking garage opened in fall 2009. SU is pursuing U.S. Green Building Council LEED Silver or Gold certifications for all current projects. New in 2008 was the University Fitness Center and SU's $65-million, 165,000-square-foot Teacher Education and Technology Center, lauded as a showcase facility for education in the mid-Atlantic region. The building, with its award-winning design, was the first new-construction project on Maryland's Eastern Shore to earn LEED Silver certification. With $5.3 million in new technology equipment, it features Smart classrooms and an Integrated Media Center with a 24-track audio recording studio, 15 editing suites, a cutting-edge digital exhibition gallery, a digital photography lab and one of the few campus-based high-definition digital video production studios in the nation.

Henson Science Hall, SU's $42-million science education and research building, is one of the largest in Maryland. Blackwell Library is the main research center on campus, with more than a quarter-million books and bound periodicals and computers with access to databases, such as FirstSearch. Fourteen computer labs are part of the campus network, providing students with various software applications, e-mail, and the Internet. Resident students have network connections in their rooms and all academic and administrative buildings offer wireless Internet access. Fulton Hall is home to the fine and performing arts, and the Center for Conflict Resolution engages students in mediation efforts at home and abroad. The only institution in the USM with an endowed theater program, SU boasts three theaters for performing arts, including the acoustically lauded Holloway Hall Auditorium. Off the main campus, the Edward H. Nabb Research Center for Delmarva History and Culture is a treasure trove of information for students and visitors. SU's Ward Museum of Wildfowl Art was named one of the "10 Great Places to See American Folk Art" by *USA Today*.

Costs

Maryland residents paid undergraduate tuition and fees of $7332 for the 2011–12 academic year. Tuition for out-of-state undergraduates was $15,678. Students living on campus paid about $8686 for room and board; the figure varies, depending on the residence hall and meal plan.

Financial Aid

Financial assistance is available to students through loans, grants, scholarships, and on- and off-campus employment. The University participates in the Federal Perkins Loan, Federal Pell Grant, Federal Supplemental Educational Opportunity Grant, and Federal Work-Study and Direct Loan Programs. Numerous other forms of financial aid on the state and local levels are based exclusively on demonstrated financial need. All students who wish to apply for financial assistance must complete the Free Application for Federal Student Aid (FAFSA) by February 15. Complete details are available through the University's Admissions and Financial Aid Offices.

The University's Work Experience Program provides on-campus jobs for students. They can work up to 20 hours a week and typically earn $1500 to $2000 per semester, in positions related to their academic interest or other areas. Non-need academic scholarships for incoming freshmen are awarded on the basis of high school performance and SAT scores, if provided. Applying for admission is the initial step in applying for these scholarships.

Faculty

Faculty members at Salisbury have won national teaching, research, and leadership awards. Ninety-five percent of the tenure-track faculty members, many of whom are National Endowment for the Humanities and Fulbright professors, have the Ph.D. or other highest degree in their field. Professors not only publish but also donate countless hours to community service, thus teaching by deed as well as word. The student-professor ratio is 17:1; smaller classes are not unusual.

Student Government

Shared governance is a hallmark of campus life, and students are actively involved in all its aspects. The Student Government Association (SGA) serves as a liaison to the faculty and administration. SGA officers serve on many University committees, both administrative and academic, including the President's Advisory Team. The all-student Appropriations Board budgets activity fees to clubs and organizations. Students are encouraged to participate in events, many sponsored by the Student Organization for Activity Planning.

Admission Requirements

The University seeks to admit outstanding students who bring diverse talents, experiences, and points of view to campus. Most successful candidates for admission have earned above-average high school grades in a strong academic program and a score above the national average on the SAT or ACT. The high school record, test scores, essay, and recommendations of the high school principal and guidance counselors are considered. Interviews are not required, but applicants are encouraged to discuss programs and procedures for housing and financial aid with the staff of the Admissions and Financial Aid Offices.

The University has an SAT/ACT optional admissions policy. Applicants who have earned a weighted GPA of 3.5 or higher on a 4.0 scale have the choice of submitting a standardized test score. The SAT or ACT is required for applicants with a weighted GPA below 3.5 or who wish to be considered for University scholarships.

Transfer students must have earned at least 24 semester hours at an accredited community college or four-year college or university and have a minimum 2.0 average (on a 4.0 scale). For transfer students who have attempted fewer than 24 hours at another institution, the University's admission policy for entering freshmen applies.

Application and Information

Applications are accepted beginning September 1 for the spring and fall semesters. Applications received by November 1 for the spring semester and by January 15 for the fall semester are given the fullest attention. The University reserves the right to close admissions when the projected enrollment is met. The application is available online at http://www.salisbury.edu/apply. For further information, students should contact:

Admissions Office
Salisbury University
1200 Camden Avenue
Salisbury, Maryland 21801-6862
Phone: 410-543-6161
      888-543-0148 (toll-free)
Fax: 410-546-6016
E-mail: admissions@salisbury.edu
Web site: http://www.salisbury.edu
      http://on.fb.me/SalisburyU (Facebook)
      http://twitter.com/salisburyu

Salisbury University's Perdue Hall, new home of the Franklin P. Perdue School of Business.

SCHOOL OF THE ART INSTITUTE OF CHICAGO
CHICAGO, ILLINOIS

The School

Founded in 1866, the School of the Art Institute of Chicago (SAIC) offers acclaimed liberal arts-based undergraduate degrees with studio practice at their core. The School of the Art Institute of Chicago fosters the conceptual and technical education of artists, designers, and scholars from across the nation and around the world in a highly professional, studio-oriented, and academically rigorous environment, encouraging excellence, critical inquiry, and experimentation. SAIC was recognized as "the most influential art school in the nation" by a poll conducted by Columbia University and a panel of national art critics. *U.S. News and World Report* ranked SAIC's Master of Fine Arts in Studio program as number two among 220 competing programs.

SAIC's 2,487 undergraduate and 734 graduate students and a faculty of artists, designers, and scholars work in an environment that facilitates the exchange of ideas, the sharing of resources, and the critiquing and refining of technical abilities and conceptual concerns. More than ever before, contemporary artists cross media and disciplinary practices and utilize a wide variety of materials and processes to create their work. Through SAIC's unique, interdisciplinary curriculum, emerging artists, designers, and visual scholars are prepared to work in this manner.

In order to prepare students for what is it like to be a creative professional, for whom the highest value is placed on the relationship between idea and execution, and to allow students to take creative risks, SAIC has a critique-based assessment tool and a credit/no-credit grading system. Students also take 6 credits of off-campus study—including study trips and internships—to allow them to make real-world connections and consider their work in the context of what is happening outside the classroom.

Students may live in one of two distinctive residence facilities, whose rooms are like loft-style apartments, each with their own bathroom and kitchenette. The residence halls have 24-hour security; controlled access; spacious, well-lit studios; TV lounges; computer labs; and laundry facilities. Students can immerse themselves in a community of fellow artists, live in the heart of Chicago's loop, and enjoy conveniences unavailable in most student apartments.

Students have access to a wide variety of unique resources, beginning with the premiere collection of SAIC's sister institution, the Art Institute of Chicago and the Ryerson & Burnham Libraries, the largest art and architecture research libraries in the country. The Gene Siskel Film Center presents significant programs of world cinema and presentations by an international array of film and video artists. SAIC's Video Data Bank houses more than 1,600 titles and is the leading resource in the United States for videotapes by and about contemporary artists.

The School of the Art Institute of Chicago also offers a broad spectrum of services to accommodate its diverse population, including an international student office, multicultural affairs office, health and counseling services, Disability and Learning Resource Center, an extensive program for academic advising, and a Career and Cooperative Internship Center.

The School of the Art Institute of Chicago is accredited by the Higher Learning Commission of the North Central Association of Colleges and Schools and by the National Association of Schools of Art and Design.

Location

The School of the Art Institute of Chicago is located in the heart of downtown Chicago, home to the nation's second-largest art scene that includes world-class museums, numerous galleries, alternative spaces, and organizations that support the arts. Chicago is a city of diverse neighborhoods, each with its own atmosphere, customs, and cuisine. Students have a wide variety of cultural and recreational resources from which to choose: ballet, opera, theater, orchestra halls, cinemas, libraries, architecture, blues and jazz clubs, parks,

ethnic restaurants, a variety of world-class sports venues, and street festivals.

Chicago itself is a vital part of the campus, as a source of social and cultural activities and the stimulus for ideas and attitudes ultimately expressed through art. Peter Frank, art critic and curator says, "Of all American cities, Chicago has contributed the most solid and distinctive artwork and art thinking. The School of the Art Institute of Chicago is at the nucleus of this longstanding distinction."

The School of the Art Institute of Chicago is located across the street from Millennium Park, a twenty-first-century marvel that SAIC faculty members and students played a key role in creating. One of the signature pieces of public art, the Crown Fountain by Spanish artist Jaume Plensa, was created with the assistance of SAIC students and faculty, who collaborated with Plensa in producing the 1,000 video portraits that are screened continuously on the fountain's twin video towers. The park, with its unique mix of art, architecture, and green space, has become SAIC's quad.

Majors and Degrees

SAIC students do not declare majors, and may work in multiple areas of interest or concentrate in a single discipline. Areas of study include: animation, architecture, art and technology, art education, art history, ceramics, designed objects, drawing, fashion design, fiber, filmmaking, interior architecture, new media, painting, performance, photography, print media, sculpture, sound, video, visual communication, visual and critical studies, and writing. Beginning in their first semester, students are assigned an academic adviser who helps mentor and guide them to ensure that they are making the most of the courses and opportunities available to them.

SAIC offers six undergraduate degrees. The Bachelor of Fine Arts (B.F.A.) degree in studio allows students to develop a particularized course of study in the visual arts. The openness of the curriculum allows for creative, idiosyncratic, and tailored programs, thereby emulating the very process of art making. Academic advising, provided by the Office of Student Affairs, helps students in determining their particular path of study. The School of the Art Institute of Chicago offers Illinois teacher certification (K–12) through its B.F.A. with an emphasis in art education, with a goal of graduating artists and teachers who are informed and engaged citizens, creators and critics of visual culture. The B.F.A. with an emphasis in art history, theory, and criticism emphasizes art history, theory, and criticism, while allowing students the ability to develop their own studio practice. The B.F.A. with an emphasis in writing offers a solid grounding in literary conventions, a practical exposure to form in fiction and poetry, and an enhanced ability to read and critique peers' work, while encouraging students to openly explore what "writing" is.

The Bachelor of Arts in visual and critical studies allows students to pursue in-depth academic study in the creative environment of an art school, sharing classes with students in the B.F.A. programs. Core courses provide students with diverse critical methods for exploring the cultural meanings of visual phenomena as they relate to social, economic, and material circumstances.

The Bachelor of Interior Architecture (B.I.A.) is intended for students interested in interdisciplinary study and a focus in contemporary, professional design practices, such as sustainability, embedded and emerging technologies, and designed objects.

Academic Program

Completion of 132 hours is required for the B.F.A. and B.A. degrees; approximately two thirds is in studio areas and one third is in academic course work. All entering students who have completed fewer than 15 credit hours of college-level studio art must enroll in the First Year Experience. Students take liberal arts courses in the humanities, natural sciences, mathematics, and social sciences and are required to complete an art history requirement.

Off-Campus Programs

The off-campus study requirement is an opportunity for students to gain practical experience at the same time as they gain a broader sense of society and the world.

Students can choose from a wide variety of off-campus programs. The Mobility program allows students to attend partner schools within the United States and Canada and includes the New York Studio semester. SAIC also maintains semester exchange agreements with more than twenty schools in Europe, Asia, and South America. The Off-Campus Programs Office works closely with students to help them develop their individual programs. SAIC faculty members lead study trips during each summer and winter interim session to such destinations as Cuba, New York, Puerto Rico, Venice, and Vietnam.

SAIC is home to the largest and most successful arts-related cooperative education program in the country, providing employment opportunities throughout Chicago and worldwide with individual artists; museums; galleries; multimedia firms; film, video, and animation production houses; interior architecture firms; fashion designers; and community service organizations.

Academic Facilities

SAIC's campus encompasses six buildings in downtown Chicago. There are fully equipped studios for each area of concentration, and SAIC's policy allows 24-hour access to facilities.

SAIC is committed to new technologies and the integration of computer-based resources throughout the curriculum. Currently, more than sixty digital technology courses are taught each semester in nearly all departmental areas. A laptop program coupled with state-of-the-art facilities and accessible resources provides cutting-edge creative capability to students. Facilities available to all students include general-access computer labs equipped with the latest-model Apple computers and high-end peripherals; a Service Bureau, providing professional digital output, including laser cutting and 3-D printing; a Media Center, offering a wide variety of equipment for student loan; wood and metal shops; and fabrication studios.

The John M. Flaxman Library's 120,000 items—books, magazines, movies, and special collections—support the entire SAIC curriculum in the arts, liberal arts, and sciences. Web-accessible resources include SAIC's own growing digital library, a traditional online library catalog, e-reserves, and a rich assortment of full-text licensed databases. The Joan Flasch Artists' Book Collection contains more than 3,000 artists' books along with a research collection of exhibition catalogs and other related material.

Exhibition spaces include the acclaimed Sullivan Galleries offering 32,000 square feet of exhibition space—the only single contemporary exhibition site of its size in the Chicago Loop, and the Betty Rymer Gallery, which highlights work from departments and presents special exhibitions. In addition, Gallery X and the Lounge Gallery, sponsored by the Student Union Galleries, provide exhibition space for currently enrolled students.

Costs

Tuition for the 2012–13 academic year is $38,340 for full-time undergraduate students or $1278 per credit hour. A double room in student housing is $10,400 and a meal plan costs $2000 meal plan for the academic year.

Financial Aid

The School of the Art Institute of Chicago makes every effort to assist students who need help in financing their education. Through an extensive financial aid program, a substantial amount of gift aid funding from private, institutional, state, and federal sources is distributed annually. In addition to scholarships and grants, SAIC grants merit scholarships and offers an extensive college work-study program. For the 2010–11 academic year, $27,000,000 in aid was awarded to undergraduate students, and 98 percent of the incoming class received some form of financial aid. To apply for financial aid, students should complete the FAFSA. To receive priority consideration, students should submit completed forms to the Financial Aid Office no later than March 1. All awards are made on a first-come, first-served basis to students in good standing who demonstrate need.

Faculty

Faculty members are selected for their skills, insight, and dedication as teachers and for their professional accomplishments as artists, designers, and scholars. There are currently more than 600 full- and part-time faculty members, among them NEA grant recipients, Louis Comfort Tiffany Foundation Fellowship recipients, and Rockefeller Foundation grant recipients. SAIC's faculty members have their work exhibited in museums, galleries, and festivals nationally and internationally. They publish books, plays, poetry, and criticism; organize and curate exhibitions; and design, build, and preserve buildings throughout the world. Each year, 100 or more well-known visiting artists, including poets, political activists, and visual artists, present workshops and provide individual student critiques through the Visiting Artists Program. Notable alumni include Claes Oldenburg, Ivan Albright, Georgia O'Keeffe, David Sedaris, Cynthia Rowley, and Vincente Minnelli.

Student Government

Student Government officers are elected each spring, and their mission is to promote student interests and concerns to the broader School community by serving on a variety of faculty and administrative staff committees. Student Government also provides funds for the more than forty student groups on campus. All students are encouraged to attend the weekly open Student Government meetings.

Admission Requirements

Applicants are required to submit SAIC's online application or the Common Application; a nonrefundable application fee of $65 for domestic students ($85 for international students); a portfolio consisting of ten to fifteen examples of recent work, a minimum of 5 minutes of time-based work; a statement of purpose; transcript(s) from high school(s) or an official copy of the high school equivalency certificate; transcripts from any college previously attended; and one letter of recommendation. Domestic applicants must submit either scores from the SAT or the ACT. Any transfer applicant who has successfully completed the School of the Art Institute of Chicago's English requirements and/or other liberal arts course work at another accredited college may be exempt from standardized test requirements for admission. All international undergraduate students who are not U.S. citizens or permanent residents or are nonnative English speakers are required to take either the TOEFL or the IELTS.

Application and Information

Prospective students are required to submit their applications electronically at http://www.saic.edu/ugapp. The applicant's portfolio and academic credentials are reviewed and evaluated by the Admissions Office. Students applying by the early application deadline of January 2 are eligible for priority housing and registration. Students who anticipate a need for financial assistance are urged to complete their applications for admission and financial aid by February 15 for the fall semester and November 15 for the spring semester in order to receive priority consideration. These dates are also priority deadlines for applicants who wish to be considered for the School of the Art Institute of Chicago's Merit Scholarship Program.

Admissions Office
School of the Art Institute of Chicago
36 South Wabash, Suite 1201
Chicago, Illinois 60603
Phone: 312-629-6100
        800-232-7242 (toll-free)
Fax: 312-629-6101
Email: ugadmiss@saic.edu
Web site: http://www.saic.edu/ug

SEATTLE UNIVERSITY
SEATTLE, WASHINGTON

The University

Seattle University (SU) provides an ideal environment for motivated students interested in self-reliance, awareness of different cultures, social justice, and the fulfillment that comes from making a difference in the world. Its location in the center of one of the nation's most diverse and progressive cities attracts a varied student body, faculty, and staff. Its urban setting promotes the development of leadership skills and independence and provides a variety of opportunities for students to apply what they learn through internships, clinical experiences, and volunteer work.

As a Jesuit institution, Seattle University is part of a network of twenty-eight colleges and universities and forty-six high schools across the United States noted for both academic strength and a commitment to social justice. Seattle U's core curriculum provides a rigorous liberal arts and sciences foundation designed to develop leadership skills, enhance global awareness, and enable graduates to serve others. In the Jesuit tradition, students are taught how to think, not what to think.

Seattle University is noted for its focus on the individual through small, faculty-taught classes and an engaging student life program. The result is graduates who enjoy successful and fulfilling lives. Seattle University is recognized as one of the leading institutions in the Pacific Northwest in producing Truman and Wilson scholars.

Fall quarter 2011 had a freshman class of 888, with 59 percent coming from outside Washington State. The ethnic breakdown for the class was 52 percent white, 20 percent Asian American, and 15 percent African American, Latino, and American Indian. The 4,631 undergraduate students represent fifty-two states and territories and ninety-four nations. International students make up approximately 9 percent of the student body.

Approximately 1,900 students in total and 92 percent of freshmen live on campus in four residence halls and an apartment complex. Students are required to live on campus for both their freshman and sophomore years unless they are able to commute from home.

Seattle University has more than 130 extracurricular clubs and organizations, including the Hui O Nani Hawaiian Club, Associated Students of African Descent, Outdoor Adventure and Recreation, Beta Alpha Psi (national accounting honorary), and other professional honoraries and clubs. SU Athletics (http://goseattleu.com/) is an NCAA Division I program and has eight varsity teams for men (baseball, basketball, cross-country, golf, soccer, swimming, tennis, and track) and ten for women (basketball, crew, cross-country, golf, soccer, softball, swimming, tennis, track, and volleyball).

The Connolly Athletic Center serves as the major facility for varsity and intramural athletics and recreation. The center features two swimming pools, two full-size gymnasiums, and locker room saunas. A 6-acre complex provides fields for outdoor sports. The William F. Eisiminger Fitness Center, which opened in fall 2011, provides 21,000 square feet of fitness and cardio equipment, weights, lockers, and studio and classroom spaces.

Seattle University receives the highest professional accreditation from the Accreditation Board for Engineering and Technology, AACSB International–The Association to Advance Collegiate Schools of Business, American Bar Association, American Chemical Society, Association of Theological Schools, Commission on Accreditation of Allied Health Education Programs, National Association of Schools of Public Affairs and Administration, National Council for Accreditation of Teacher Education, Commission on Collegiate Nursing Education, Council on Social Work Education, and Northwest Commission on Colleges and Universities.

Location

Nestled between two mountain ranges, containing three lakes, and situated along Puget Sound, Seattle is a magnificent setting for a university. The city pulses with music, art, and culture. Seattle is the Pacific Northwest's center for legal, medical, business, and high-tech industries, and Seattle University students supplement their studies through internships, research, volunteer projects, mentorships, and meeting alumni in their fields.

Seattle's residents love the outdoors, and areas for skiing, hiking, backpacking, and climbing are within an hour of campus. Biking, walking, and jogging are also popular, with paths and trails throughout the city.

Seattle's sights and sounds, rich ethnic diversity, celebrated restaurants, eclectic entertainment, major-league athletics, theater, opera, and ballet are within walking distance, and are a central part of the Seattle University experience.

Majors and Degrees

Seattle University offers programs in six major academic units. The Albers School of Business and Economics awards degrees in accounting, business administration, business economics, information systems, economics, finance, international business, international economic development, management, and marketing. The College of Arts and Sciences grants degrees in art history, Asian studies, communication studies, creative writing, criminal justice, cultural anthropology, digital design, environmental studies, English, film studies, fine arts, French, history, international studies, journalism, liberal studies, military science/ROTC, philosophy, photography, political science, psychology, public affairs, social work, sociology, Spanish, sport and exercise science, strategic communication, string performance, theater, theology/religious studies, visual art, and women and gender studies. The College of Nursing offers a Bachelor of Science in Nursing degree. The Matteo Ricci College awards degrees in humanities for leadership and humanities for teaching. The College of Science and Engineering offers degree programs in biochemistry, biology, cell and molecular biology, chemistry, civil engineering, clinical laboratory science, computer engineering, computer science, diagnostic ultrasound, electrical engineering, environmental engineering, environmental science, general science, marine and conservation biology, mathematics, mechanical engineering, and physics. Preprofessional programs include dentistry, law, medicine, optometry, and veterinary medicine.

Academic Programs

The Core Curriculum has several distinguishing characteristics in keeping with the Jesuit educational tradition: it provides an integrated freshman year; gives order and sequence to student learning; provides experience in the methods and content of the range of liberal arts, sciences, philosophy, and theology; calls for active learning in all classes, for practice in writing and thinking, and for an awareness of values; and it fosters a global perspective and a sense of social and personal responsibility.

Seattle University offers two honors program options for students seeking rigorous academic challenge. The University Honors Program is a small, humanities-focused learning community with a curriculum that examines the most significant texts and ideas of Western culture. The Core Honors Program involves seminar sections of nine required courses in English, history, philosophy, social science, and theology/religious studies; this option is particularly suited to students in professional degree programs, for whom participation in University Honors is less feasible due to specific major requirements and scheduling conflicts.

Seattle University operates on a quarter calendar. The fall quarter begins in mid-September; the winter quarter in early January; the spring quarter in late March; and the summer quarter in mid-June. Undergraduates typically take 15 credit hours per quarter for the fall, winter, and spring quarters.

Off-Campus Programs

Seattle University offers a diverse array of short- and long-term international study programs. Some are appropriate for any student

interested in study of a particular culture or language, while others are designed to complement specific majors. Short-term programs include opportunities in Brazil, Costa Rica, France, India, Ireland, Italy, Japan, Korea, Mexico, South Africa, and Sweden. Long-term programs, which last an entire academic quarter or more, are available for Austria, Belize, China, Denmark, Ecuador, France, Ghana, Japan, Mexico, and Spain. Students also have the opportunity to intern with non-governmental organizations in Asia, Africa, and Latin America through the unique International Development Internship Program (IDIP), which embodies the Jesuit emphasis on social justice and global awareness. Additional study-abroad programs in other nations, in conjunction with other colleges' overseas programs, are also offered. Arrangements are made through the Education Abroad Office.

Academic Facilities

The Seattle University campus has undergone more than $200 million in recent improvements. Twelve academic buildings house classrooms, thirty-four instructional laboratories, twenty-five specialized laboratories, computer facilities, and other instructional equipment to support state-of-the-art instruction.

The newly renovated Lemieux Library and McGoldrick Learning Commons has nearly 300,000 volumes and 2,700 current serial subscriptions, 1,300 online databases, and microforms periodicals. Study carrels provide quiet study space while lounges accommodate study groups. The library's Media Production Center houses a recording studio, control room, audio/video editing facilities, and a theater-style screening room.

The Albers School of Business and Economics features classrooms designed to enhance student interaction and access to high-tech teaching equipment.

The College of Nursing's 20,000-square-foot clinical performance laboratory is among the most technically advanced clinical laboratories in the country. It joins two clinical practice rooms and a suite of laboratories.

The Lee Center for the Arts is a showcase for theater and musical performances. This modern building seats 135 and includes a prop room, dressing room, costume shop, and professional lighting and sound booths that give students career-building technical skills.

The Chapel of St. Ignatius is Seattle University's spiritual center. This award-winning structure is recognized as a place of beauty, contemplation, and worship.

Costs

For academic year 2012–13, tuition is $34,200; room and meals were $10,296. The estimate for books, fees, and personal expenses is $6114. Costs are subject to change.

Financial Aid

Seattle University awarded $43.2 million in its own financial aid to fall 2011 freshmen, including merit scholarships ranging from $7000 to $44,500. The average financial aid package was $27,519. Students are required to apply for financial aid by February 1, as awards are made early each spring for the following fall quarter. Applications received after this deadline are evaluated in order received for any remaining aid. Students must submit the Free Application for Federal Student Aid (FAFSA) and be accepted for admission to be considered for financial assistance. Scholarships are awarded on the basis of academic achievement, extracurricular involvement, and community service.

Faculty

There are 464 full-time faculty members, 76 percent of whom possess doctoral or terminal degrees. All classes are taught by faculty. With an average class size of 20 and a faculty-to-student ratio of 1:13, the primary responsibility of Seattle University professors is the success of their students. Faculty members are available to provide assistance outside of class, to help students with research, and to assist in arranging internships. Faculty advisers provide guidance, direction, and encouragement throughout a student's academic career. New students are assigned faculty advisers prior to registration according to their major.

Student Government

All undergraduates belong to the Associated Students of Seattle University (ASSU), the central student organization on campus.

ASSU is organized around an elected president, an executive vice president, and an activities vice president. A 12-member representative council oversees every facet of the student body and is responsible for policymaking and providing a diverse activities program to meet the needs of Seattle University's student body. In addition, ASSU communicates student needs to the administration and faculty. ASSU oversees over 130 clubs and organizations.

Admission Requirements

Freshman applicants are required to have completed a college-preparatory program upon high school graduation, including 4 years of English, 3 years of social studies/history, 3 years of mathematics, 2 years of laboratory science, and 2 years of a foreign language. Applicants to the College of Science and Engineering must complete 4 units of college-preparatory mathematics for admission to any of its specific majors; laboratory chemistry and laboratory physics are prerequisites for engineering program consideration. Applicants to the nursing major must complete laboratory biology and chemistry to be considered for admission.

ACT or SAT scores, an official high school transcript, a counselor recommendation, a teacher recommendation, and an essay are also required for freshman admission consideration. The middle 50 percent of 2011 freshmen had GPAs between 3.3 and 3.9 on a 4.0 scale and ACT scores between 24 and 29 or SAT scores between 530 and 640 (critical reading), 520 and 630 (math), and 520 and 630 (writing). College credit is awarded to those who have successfully completed Advanced Placement or International Baccalaureate examinations. Qualifying scores can be obtained by contacting the Office of the Registrar.

Application and Information

Students can apply directly online at commonapp.org; the forms can also be downloaded from the Seattle University Web site at http://www.seattleu.edu.

High school students applying for early action consideration must apply by November 15 of their senior year. Those applying for regular admission consideration must apply by January 15. The priority application deadline for fall transfer applicants is March 1.

Campus visits can be scheduled Monday through Friday and many Saturdays. Prospective students should contact Admissions for availability. With two weeks' notice, visitors can be scheduled to attend a class, meet with a faculty adviser, participate in a campus tour, and speak individually with an Admissions representative.

For additional information students should contact:
Admissions Office
Seattle University
901 12th Avenue
Seattle, Washington 98122-1090
Phone: 206-296-2000
      800-426-7123 (toll-free)
E-mail: admissions@seattleu.edu
Web site: http://www.seattleu.edu
    http://www.facebook.com/seattleu
    http://twitter.com/seattleu

Seattle U's campus is in the heart of a vibrant, culturally rich city.

SETON HILL UNIVERSITY
GREENSBURG, PENNSYLVANIA

The University

A coeducational university located in Greensburg, Pennsylvania, Seton Hill offers more than thirty undergraduate majors and thirteen graduate programs in the natural and health sciences, performing and visual arts, humanities, education, business, and social sciences. Founded in 1885, Seton Hill offers students the benefit of a long history of educational excellence in the liberal arts and a tradition of preparing students "for that world in which you are destined to live."

Dedicated, expert faculty and University administrators work closely with students to ensure that they graduate with a clear understanding of where they are headed, and with the knowledge, skills, contacts, and resources to get them there. One example of this is Seton Hill's new mobile learning program that provides iPads and MacBook Pro laptops to all full-time students as they enter the university. This program, which helped Seton Hill become known as a national leader in using technology in education, allows all students to fully participate in the University's technologically advanced academic and campus life, and also prepares them for top careers.

A Catholic university founded by the Sisters of Charity, Seton Hill embraces students of all faiths, from across the country and around the world. The university maintains a 90 percent career placement rate after graduation, and 36 percent of its graduates also go on to graduate or professional schools.

Location

Located 35 miles from Pittsburgh, historic Greensburg lies in the middle of southwestern Pennsylvania's scenic Laurel Highlands. Seton Hill's main hilltop campus features 200 wooded acres and a mix of new and turn-of-the-century buildings, all equipped with modern technology. The University's Greensburg cultural district campus includes its new world-class Performing Arts Center, Visual Arts Center, and Center for Family Therapy.

Greensburg enjoys all the advantages of a large city while maintaining a small-town atmosphere. The seat of Westmoreland County, Greensburg is home to the Westmoreland Museum of Art, the Westmoreland Symphony Orchestra, and a thriving downtown cultural district featuring numerous shopping, dining, recreational, and entertainment opportunities.

Majors and Degrees

At the undergraduate level, the University grants the Bachelor of Arts, Bachelor of Fine Arts, Bachelor of Science, Bachelor of Music, and Bachelor of Social Work degrees. Students choose from the following programs: accounting; art, including art education, art history, art therapy, arts administration, fine arts studio–3-D or 2-D, graphic design, and studio art; biochemistry; biology; business, including entrepreneurial studies, human resources, information management, international organization, and marketing; chemistry; communication, including political communication; computer science; criminal justice; dance; elementary education (pre-K to grade 4) with special education; education certification (art; biology; business, computer, and information technology; chemistry; elementary education (pre-K to grade 4) with special education (pre-K to grade 8); English; family and consumer sciences; French; mathematics; music; social studies; and Spanish); engineering (3+2); English, including creative writing, journalism/new media, and literature; family and consumer sciences, including child care administration and education; forensic science; history; hospitality and tourism; international studies; mathematics, including actuary science; medical technology; music, including music education, music therapy, performance, and sacred music; nutrition/

dietetics; pharmacy; physician assistant studies; political science; pre-law; pre-med; pre–osteopathic medicine; pre-professional health; psychology; religious studies/theology; social work; sociology; Spanish; sports management; and theater, including theater arts, theater business, theater design and technology, theater performance, and music theater.

The University offers osteopathic medicine through a (3+3 or 3+4) program and pharmacy through a (3+3 or 3+4) cooperative program with the Lake Erie College of Osteopathic Medicine (LECOM). The Lake Erie College of Osteopathic Medicine has a medical school on Seton Hill's Greensburg campus, called the Lake Erie College of Osteopathic Medicine at Seton Hill. LECOM at Seton Hill reserves 25 medical school seats for qualifying Seton Hill pre–osteopathic medicine undergraduate students.

Academic Programs

Each of Seton Hill's undergraduate majors fall within one of the university's six academic divisions: the natural and health sciences, visual and performing arts, humanities, education, business, and social sciences. A minimum of 120 credits is required to earn a bachelor's degree; 39–48 credits must be taken from the University's required liberal arts curriculum (some courses required for degree completion in a specific major also satisfy liberal arts curriculum requirements).

Seton Hill's mobile learning program provides technology (currently an iPad and MacBook Pro laptop) to full-time students and faculty, and ongoing intensive training to faculty in the use of emerging technologies for teaching and learning.

Seton Hill offers accelerated/combined degree options that allow undergraduate students to move directly to graduate-level or medical school–level work in less time than with a traditional program. These offerings include a combined B.S./M.S. in physician assistant studies, a combined B.S./D.O. in pre–osteopathic medicine, and a combined B.S./D.Pharm in pharmacy.

Seton Hill also offers an honors program, academic support, academic honor societies, academic clubs, internship and career placement services, advanced placement credits, work-study and internship programs, distance and online courses, the opportunity to double-major or self-design a major, English as a second language, independent study, assistance with special learning needs, an ROTC program, and study-away and study-abroad programs.

Seton Hill students benefit from the resources of several centers housed at Seton Hill, including the E-Magnify Women's Business Center (which provides information and programs for both male and female students), the Wukich Center for Entrepreneurial Opportunities, the National Catholic Center for Holocaust Education, the Seton Hill University Center for Family Therapy, the Center for Innovative Teaching, and the Seton Hill University Center for Orthodontics.

The University offers an adult degree program that provides special course scheduling for busy adults who would like to earn an undergraduate degree in business (including specializations in human resources, marketing, entrepreneurial studies, and information management), accounting, human services, social work, and general studies. The adult degree program also offers a certificate in pastoral ministry.

Seton Hill's academic calendar includes fall and spring semesters. The University also offers optional intensive January and May terms (J-Term and M-Term, in which study-away and study-abroad courses are often offered) in addition to a summer session.

Off-Campus Programs

Seton Hill's comprehensive internship program and academic partnerships with local, regional, and national businesses, corporations, health care providers, and government agencies provide students with practical experience in their field of study and a competitive edge in the job market.

In addition, students may opt to spend a semester or a year studying abroad. Seton Hill offers many study-away (off-campus but within the U.S.) and study-abroad opportunities.

Academic Facilities

While all of Seton Hill's facilities feature interactive and assistive technology, the University continues to add new classrooms, academic buildings, and research/science facilities that represent the very best in adaptable learning spaces.

Seton Hill's new Technology Learning Commons includes the ultramodern MediaSphere and Inquiry Zone classrooms/labs, which include everything students need to create virtual worlds, teach online courses, or work on group projects with students or faculty members in other parts of the campus—or the globe.

The new Performing Arts Center incorporates the very best design and technology into its performance venues, classrooms, technical areas, and studios—from Steinway pianos to the latest in lighting, sound, video, and acoustics.

Seton Hill's twenty-one academic and residence facilities have been specifically designed to provide a seamless, supportive learning environment for students.

Costs

For full-time students, approximate costs for the 2012–13 academic year include tuition of $28,346; approximate room and board fees of $9944; and books, fees, and personal expenses amounting to approximately $1000 to $2000. Tuition and fees vary according to type and number of courses taken and academic program; room and board fees vary according to housing and meal plan choice.

Financial Aid

Seton Hill is dedicated to finding and keeping the students who will benefit most from a Seton Hill education, and will work with prospective students and their families to create a financial aid package tailored to their needs.

Traditional undergraduates at Seton Hill University are often eligible for both need-based and merit-based aid. Need-based aid is awarded based on the results of the Free Application for Federal Student Aid (FAFSA); merit-based aid (including a wide variety of scholarships, some of which are for full tuition) is awarded to students for achievements in academics, the arts, athletics, leadership projects, and community service.

Faculty

At Seton Hill, the emphasis is on teaching and advising. All courses are taught by faculty; no classes are taught by graduate assistants. In addition, Seton Hill faculty serve as academic advisors to the students in the majors in which they teach, and as academic and recreational student club advisors.

With a student-faculty ratio of 16:1, students can get to know their professors and classmates, and make new friends who will become professional mentors and colleagues in the years to come.

The Seton Hill faculty consists of 95 full-time professors, 84 percent of whom have doctoral or terminal degrees.

Student Government and Organizations

Seton Hill has more than sixty-six student clubs and organizations, including academic, recreational, and service organizations. Students also have the opportunity to participate in the government of the University through the Seton Hill Government Association, which provides students with voting representation on a number of faculty committees. In addition, the student government helps to sponsor numerous on-campus political, cultural, and social events.

Admission Requirements

Acceptance to the University is based on the successful completion of a college-preparatory curriculum in high school. Applicants should have completed at least 15 secondary school academic units. These units should include 4 units of English, 4 units of college-preparatory mathematics, 2 units of social science, 1 unit of laboratory science, 2 units of the same foreign language (if a foreign language was not taken, this requirement must be fulfilled while the student is enrolled at Seton Hill), and 4 academic electives.

Students who wish to transfer credits to Seton Hill from another college or university must present their transcripts for evaluation on a course-by-course basis. A transfer student will receive a credit evaluation upon admission to the University.

Application and Information

Seton Hill University has a rolling admissions policy. Decisions of the Admissions Committee are rendered shortly after all application materials have been submitted.

The first-time freshman applicant should submit a completed application form, a $35 nonrefundable application fee (or apply online for free), a minimum of one letter of recommendation from a teacher of guidance counselor, an official secondary school transcript or GED certificate, and official score reports from either the SAT or the ACT.

For more information, students should contact:

Office of Admissions
Seton Hill University
One Seton Hill Drive
Greensburg, Pennsylvania 15601
United States
Phone: 800-826-6234 (toll-free)
Fax: 724-830-1294
E-mail: admit@setonhill.edu
Web site: http://www.setonhill.edu

Every building on Seton Hill's historic campus has been renovated to support emerging technologies.

SHIPPENSBURG UNIVERSITY OF PENNSYLVANIA
SHIPPENSBURG, PENNSYLVANIA

The University

Shippensburg University, founded in 1871, is a comprehensive public institution in south-central Pennsylvania enrolling more than 7,200 undergraduate students and approximately 1,100 graduate students. Of the undergraduates, 52 percent are women and 48 percent are men. The University comprises the College of Arts and Sciences, the College of Education and Human Services, the John L. Grove College of Business, and the School of Graduate Studies. There is also a School of Academic Programs and Services, which includes the Office of Undeclared Students.

Shippensburg University is a member of the Pennsylvania State System of Higher Education and is accredited by the Middle States Association of Colleges and Schools. The University's programs are also accredited by AACSB International (business); ABET, Inc. (computer science); the American Chemical Society; the Council on Social Work Education; the Council for the Accreditation of Counseling and Related Educational Programs; the International Association of Counseling Services; the Council for Exceptional Children; and the National Council for the Accreditation of Teachers. Shippensburg University is a member of the Council of Graduate Schools.

Graduate degrees conferred are the Master of Arts, Master of Business Administration, Master of Education, Master of Science, Master of Social Work, and Master of Public Administration. Programs are as follows: Master of Arts in applied history; Master of Science in administration of justice, biology, communication studies, computer science, counseling (college, clinical mental health, student personnel), geoenvironmental studies, organizational development and leadership (business, communication, education, environmental management, higher education structure and policy, historical management, individual and organizational development, public organizations, social structure and organization), and psychological science; Master of Business Administration; Master of Public Administration; Master of Social Work; and Master of Education in counseling (Dual K–12 school), curriculum and instruction (biology, early childhood education, elementary education, geography/earth science, history, mathematics, middle school education, modern languages), reading, school administration, and special education (emotional/behavior disorders, comprehensive, learning disabilities, intellectual disabilities and autism). The School of Graduate Studies also offers post-master's degree curricula leading to various types of education certification, including supervisory certification, and is one of twenty-three national sites for a postgraduate academic training program in Reading Recovery.

More than 200 student clubs, organizations, and activity groups are available, resulting in nearly 600 leadership opportunities. Organizations include academic clubs, community service groups, special interest organizations, media organizations, musical groups, performing arts troupes, and national or local fraternities and sororities.

Student activities are complemented by programs that bring nationally and internationally known figures to campus. The University's Luhrs Performing Arts Center has recently hosted CNN anchor Soledad O'Brien, world-renowned brain surgeon Ben Carson, singer Willie Nelson, and comedian Bill Engvall.

Each of the eight residence halls is equipped with lounges, exercise rooms, music practice rooms, study rooms, and computer connections to the online library catalog system. Each residence hall room has one cable television and two direct computer network connections. Most residence hall rooms are double occupancy; some single rooms are available. Seavers Complex houses 6 students in each unit. Student safety is emphasized through controlled access to the residence halls, trained supervisory personnel, and a keycard entry system. There is also an apartment-style student housing facility with a living room, bathroom, full kitchen, and one, two, or four bedrooms.

The University offers a variety of athletic facilities for both intercollegiate and intramural sports. These include a 2,768-seat field house, an 8,000-seat stadium, a gymnasium, outdoor tennis courts, indoor and outdoor tracks, an indoor swimming pool, squash and handball courts, a rehabilitation center, and sand volleyball courts. The 62,000-square-foot student recreation center includes a cardio/strength area with thirty-nine cardiovascular machines with individual televisions, four multipurpose courts, a group fitness studio, and an elevated running track. The University is a member of the Pennsylvania State Athletic Conference and NCAA Division II. Men's intercollegiate sports include baseball, basketball, cross-country, football, soccer, swimming, track and field, and wrestling. Women's intercollegiate sports include basketball, cross-country, field hockey, lacrosse, soccer, softball, swimming, tennis, track and field, and volleyball. There are ten intramural sports, which include street hockey, and thirteen club sports, which include men's and women's rugby.

Etter Health Center is open from 7:30 a.m. to 11:30 p.m. and is equipped with modern examination, treatment, and emergency rooms. It has six beds for inpatient care and a self-care unit for minor health conditions. Chambersburg Hospital is only 20 minutes from campus.

Students have access to comprehensive counseling services on request in academic, career, psychological, social, personal growth, and religious areas. The Career Development Center offers career counseling, workshops in resume preparation, job interview techniques, and job search assistance.

Location

Shippensburg University is on 200 acres overlooking its namesake community, a borough of approximately 6,700 people in the Cumberland Valley. The University is about 40 minutes southwest of Harrisburg, 2 hours from both Baltimore and Washington, D.C., and 2½ hours from Philadelphia. The campus is within easy walking distance of the center of town.

Majors and Degrees

Undergraduate degrees conferred are the Bachelor of Arts (B.A.), Bachelor of Science (B.S.), Bachelor of Science in Business Administration (B.S.B.A.), Bachelor of Science in Education (B.S.Ed.), and Bachelor of Social Work (B.S.W.).

The College of Arts and Sciences awards the B.A. degree in art (computer graphics); communication/journalism (electronic media, print media, public relations); English (writing); French; history (public history); human communication studies; interdisciplinary arts; political science; psychology; secondary certification (art, English, French, and Spanish); sociology; and Spanish. The B.S. degree is awarded in applied physics (nanofabrication); biology (biotechnology/pre–forensic science, ecology and environment, health professions, medical technology); chemistry (biochemistry, business, computational, environmental, forensics, pre-pharmacy); computer engineering; computer science (computer graphics, embedded programming, related discipline, software engineering); economics (business, mathematics, political science, public administration, social studies); geoenvironmental studies; geography (geographic information systems, human-environmental, land use); healthcare administration; mathematics (applied, statistics); physics (nanofabrication); professional studies (technical leadership and administration); public administration; and secondary education (biology, biology/environmental education, chemistry, mathematics). The B.S.Ed. degree is awarded in earth and space science, physics, social studies/geography, and social studies/history.

The John L. Grove College of Business awards the B.S.B.A. degree in accounting, finance (personal financial planning), information technology for business education, management (entrepreneurship, human resource, international management), management

information systems, marketing, and supply chain management (logistics).

The College of Education and Human Services awards the B.S. degree in criminal justice and exercise science; the B.S.W. degree in social work; and the B.S.Ed. degree in early childhood/elementary education PK–4, and elementary/middle-level education 4–8, (language arts, math, science, social studies).

Preprofessional preparation is available for admission to schools of chiropractic, dentistry, engineering, forensic science, law, medicine, optometry, pharmacy, physical therapy, podiatry, and veterinary medicine.

Shippensburg University offers 2+2 transfer programs in the allied health fields of biotechnology, nursing, occupational therapy (2+3), P.A.C.E. Program (2+2, 3+3), and radiologic sciences.

Academic Programs

The University is on the semester system with a fall semester beginning in late August and a spring semester beginning in mid-January. Three terms, one of three weeks and two of five weeks, compose the summer program. Online courses are offered during a four-week winter term.

The general education program, which comprises one half of the credits required for graduation, is the core of the undergraduate curriculum. It includes courses to develop competence in writing, speaking, mathematics, and historical perspectives. The program ensures exposure to logic and numbers; linguistic, literary, artistic, and cultural traditions; biological and physical sciences; political, economic, and geographic sciences; and social and behavioral sciences. Ample elective opportunities are available.

The University requires students to take one approved diversity course for a total of 3 credit hours.

Academic options include an honors program, independent study and research, internships, field experience (mandatory in such areas as teacher education, social work, and medical technology), the Marine Science Consortium Program at Wallops Island, a 3+2 engineering program, and Army ROTC.

Academic Facilities

The library and multimedia services unit helps students develop skills in information gathering, critical evaluation, and creating media presentations of research findings. It provides assistance in locating and delivering books and articles in the Lehman Library, the Luhrs Library Media Center, online databases, and from other libraries through interlibrary loan services. Students can receive online reference and research support, guidance in citing resources and avoiding plagiarism, and technology support. Digital cameras, digital camcorders, LCD projectors, laptops, and other equipment are available and can be checked out for student use.

Student instruction is supported by multiple computer systems for student e-mail and computer network connections to the Internet. Every student has e-mail, file storage, and home page accounts on the University's servers. Several hundred terminals or personal computers for student use are available in residence halls, the library, academic buildings, microcomputer labs, and the Computing Technologies Center. Students with their own computers also have access to the systems. All students can use the systems 24 hours a day and have unlimited computer time at no additional expense. Most buildings have wireless network capabilities and several have satellite capability for distance education. The University also has its own campuswide information system available on and off campus.

Costs

For Pennsylvania residents, the cost per semester in 2011–12 included tuition of $3120; room and board, $3605; educational services fee, $329; technology fee, $174; student activities fee, $225; student union fee, $250; comprehensive health fee, $150; and student recreation fee, $180. Nonresidents paid tuition of $7800 per semester. Maryland residents paid tuition of $7020.

Financial Aid

The University's extensive financial aid program helps students who deserve a college education but who cannot afford to pay the full cost themselves. Shippensburg offers a wide range of aid in the form of grants, scholarships, loans, and campus employment. Most aid is awarded as a package consisting of all types for which the applicant is qualified. Nearly 80 percent of undergraduates receive some form of financial assistance.

Faculty

The University has 447 full- and part-time faculty members. The undergraduate student-faculty ratio is 20:1. Approximately 85 percent of the full-time instructional faculty members hold a doctorate or other terminal degree in their field. Each student has a faculty adviser.

Student Government

Shippensburg's strong student organization, built around a Student Senate, standing committees, and an Activities Program Board, provides a highly diversified program of student activities. Students sit on many policymaking administration-faculty committees and administer their own budget for the Student Services, Inc.

Admission Requirements

Shippensburg University, in compliance with federal and state laws and University policy, is committed to human understanding and provides equal educational, employment, and economic opportunities for all people without regard to race, color, sex, age, creed, national origin, religion, veteran status, or disability. A student's potential for success is judged by the high school average, rank in class, aptitude test scores (SAT or ACT), and recommendations. The high school record is generally considered the most important factor. A college-preparatory program, consisting of 4 units of English, at least 3 units of math, 3 units in the sciences, 2 units of social studies, and 2 units in the same foreign language, is strongly recommended. A campus interview and visit are encouraged. Transfer students in good standing are welcome.

Application and Information

To be considered for admission, a student should submit an application with a $40 application fee online at http://www.ship.edu/admissions/apply. The high school transcript, recommendations, and aptitude test results should be sent by the high school. Transfer students must submit college transcripts. The Admissions Office operates on a rolling basis.

For application materials and additional information, students should contact:

Dean of Enrollment Services
Shippensburg University of Pennsylvania
1871 Old Main Drive
Shippensburg, Pennsylvania 17257
Phone: 717-477-1231
      800-822-8028 (toll-free)
Fax: 717-477-4016
E-mail: admiss@ship.edu
Web site: http://www.ship.edu
      http://www.facebook.com/SHIPAdmissions

Located in southcentral Pennsylvania, Shippensburg University offers daily information sessions and tours for prospective students.

SHORTER UNIVERSITY

ROME, GEORGIA

The University

Since 1873, Shorter University has combined academic excellence with a caring Christian commitment. The University was established through the generosity of a Baptist layman, Alfred Shorter, and the vision of his pastor. They led a group of northwestern Georgia Baptists in founding the school, which was originally named Cherokee Baptist Female College. The name was changed to Shorter Female College in 1878 and to Shorter College in 1923. The College became coeducational in 1951. On June 1, 2010, the College changed its name to Shorter University.

Shorter's enrollment of 3,600 includes students in both traditional semester programs and innovative continuous programs for working adults. Approximately 1,500 of these students are located on the main campus in Rome, Georgia. Students come from all parts of the United States and from other countries around the world. Shorter University has an overall graduate school acceptance rate of 80 percent and an impressive 82 percent acceptance rate to medical colleges over the past twenty-one years.

Shorter University is committed to providing a high-quality education in an intentionally Christian atmosphere. Each year, the campus is visited by noted Christian leaders, scholars, and outstanding musical performers. The dean of the chapel and the campus minister work together to provide a wide range of opportunities for spiritual growth.

The largest religious organization on campus is the Baptist Collegiate Ministries (BCM), which includes Christians of many denominations. Student publications include a newspaper, a yearbook, and a literary magazine. Highly skilled music and drama groups include the Shorter Chorale, the Shorter Chorus, the Shorter Theater Company, the Opera Workshop, and the Shorter Marching Band. The Shorter Chorale was selected to represent the United States in choral festivals held in Yugoslavia, France, and Austria and represented the University in St. Petersburg, Russia. The Chorale was also selected in 2008 to perform mass at the Vatican during a tour of Italy. Shorter has also been the home of numerous National Metropolitan Opera Audition winners and finalists.

The University has three fraternities and three sororities as well as chapters of two national music fraternities and honor societies for majors in biology, communication, English, music, religion, and social sciences. Shorter University is a member of the Southern States Athletic Conference of the NAIA. The University also has a competitive cheerleading program and competes in the Mid-South Conference of the NAIA in football and track and field. Varsity teams compete in men's baseball, basketball, cross-country, football, golf, soccer, tennis, and track and field and in women's basketball, cheerleading, cross-country, fast-pitch softball, golf, soccer, tennis, track and field, and volleyball. Wrestling and men's and women's lacrosse were added in fall 2010.

Location

The University is situated on 150 acres atop Shorter Hill, in Rome, Georgia (area population 93,000). Rome is located just 65 miles northwest of Atlanta and 65 miles south of Chattanooga, Tennessee, and cultural opportunities abound. The city of Rome offers the Symphony Orchestra, Rome Little Theatre, Rome Area Council for the Arts events, popular concerts and attractions at The Forum, and the 334,859-volume modern city library. The University sponsors numerous events, including faculty, alumni, student, and guest musical recitals; four guest lecture series; recitals; drama and opera productions; art exhibits; and athletic events.

Majors and Degrees

Shorter University offers seven baccalaureate and five master's degrees: the Bachelor of Arts, the Bachelor of Science, the Bachelor of Science in Nursing, the Bachelor of Business Administration, the Bachelor of Science in Education, the Bachelor of Fine Arts, the Bachelor of Music, the Master of Education, the Master of Arts in Teaching, the Master of Arts, the Master of Accountancy, and the Master of Business Administration.

The Bachelor of Arts is offered in art, Christian studies, communication arts, English, English education, history and political science, international studies, liberal arts, music, psychology, sociology, and Spanish. The Bachelor of Science is offered in biology, chemistry, Christian studies, computer information systems, communication arts, criminal justice, ecology and field biology, general studies, history and political science, history education, mathematics, mathematics education, psychology, and sociology. The Bachelor of Business Administration is offered in accounting, accounting–M.Acc. bridge, business economics, management, marketing, management information systems, and sports management. The Bachelor of Science in Education is offered in early childhood education (K–4) and middle grades (4–8). Programs leading to certification in secondary school teaching are available in English, general science, history, and mathematics. Certification is also offered in music for grades K–12. The Bachelor of Fine Arts is offered in art, musical theater, and theater. The Bachelor of Music is offered in church music, music education, organ performance, piano pedagogy, piano performance, and voice performance. Preprofessional programs are available in allied health, dentistry, law, medicine, pharmacy, physical therapy, physician's assistant studies, and veterinary medicine. Courses are also available in French, German, health and physical education, and interdisciplinary studies.

Academic Programs

Shorter is accredited by the Southern Association of Colleges and Schools and the National Association of Schools of Music and strives to provide an academic environment of high quality. Teacher programs are approved by the Georgia Professional Standards Commission. Small classes (freshman lecture courses average 22 students) taught by dedicated and highly qualified professors (71 percent of freshman lecture courses are taught by full-time faculty members, 26 percent by full professors) ensure that each student receives an education that is both challenging and personally rewarding. For any degree, a candidate must have earned a minimum of 126 semester hours; some degrees require a greater number of hours.

As part of the orientation program at the beginning of the fall semester, each new student is assigned to one of several small orientation groups that assist the student in adjusting to University life; the student is also assigned to an academic adviser, who assists in the selection and scheduling of courses. Early registration sessions are available in the summer. Freshman advisers are specially trained faculty and staff members.

The academic calendar is divided into two semesters from September to May, with two mini sessions offered during the summer. On-campus evening classes are available in selected disciplines. Shorter offers an honors program that spans all four years and provides students with learning opportunities that are not generally available to undergraduates.

Off-Campus Programs

Shorter's School of Business and School of Education and Social Sciences offer the Professional Studies Programs, which are specifically designed for working adults, on campus and in Lawrenceville, Riverdale, and Marietta, Georgia. Majors are business, education, and human resources. Classes meet one evening or weekend per week, year-round, with a required weekly study group.

Shorter University offers several monthlong study-abroad programs immediately following the end of the second semester in May, including MAYTERM (in Europe), the Asia Program, and the Americas Program. Students earn 12 semester hours of credit through travel, study, and classroom experiences. Students are housed in student residences or college dormitories, and the cost of

most meals is usually included. Shorter University faculty members accompany the students and teach the courses that are offered. MAYTERM is usually based at British American College London and includes visits to England and to one other European country. The Asia Program is generally based at Zhengzhou University in China or at Mahidol University in Thailand. The Americas Program includes two weeks in Ecuador and the Galapagos Islands and two weeks in another Central or South American country. Studies in other countries can be arranged on an individual basis through the Office of International Programs.

Academic Facilities

Livingston Library, which was dedicated in 1976 as a memorial to Ray Livingston, houses more than 213,297 books, 582 periodical subscriptions, 8,099 microform materials, 12,134 audio/video items, 38,312 e-books, and 7,000 e-journals. The library also contains conference rooms (for both individual and group study), projection rooms, a graphics preparation room, computer terminals, typewriters, and music listening facilities for student use.

The Alice Allgood Cooper Fine Arts Building and the Randall H. Minor Fine Arts Building are connected to form an outstanding fine arts complex, providing up-to-date facilities for the departments of music, communication arts, and art. The Cooper Building contains classrooms, music faculty offices, the art department's drawing and painting studio, and Brookes Chapel, the meeting place for convocations, concerts, recitals, and lectures. A renovated home adjacent to the campus houses expanded art facilities. The Minor Building contains classrooms, twenty-five music practice rooms (with a baby grand piano in each), a choral rehearsal room, faculty offices, photography facilities, a theater, a desktop publishing lab, a radio studio, and an art gallery. Rome Hall was named in honor of the citizens of Rome in appreciation of their generous support of the University. It contains classrooms, science laboratories (including the Stergus Collection of Internal Organs, one of the most complete pathology collections in the United States), faculty offices, lounges, and the Robert T. Connor exhibit of some 150 African and North American animals and skins. Alumni Hall houses the educational materials center and faculty offices. The Winthrop-King Centre houses classrooms, offices for coaches, a basketball gym, a dance and aerobic studio, two racquetball courts, a fitness center, and an indoor jogging track. The Fitton Student Union contains the campus bookstore, a 24-hour study room, a 24-hour game room, and an indoor swimming pool. Two computer labs are available for general student use. Computer labs for business and communication arts are also available. Smaller computer labs are available for art, music, and recreation. All residence halls have computer and Internet access. The Robert H. Ledbetter College of Business is located adjacent to the main campus in a newly renovated facility that offers seven academic classrooms, three computer labs, faculty offices, and student lounges. The College of Nursing is located in the heart of Rome's medical community and provides state-of-the-art lab equipment, simulators, computer labs, and classroom facilities.

Costs

Tuition for the 2011–12 academic year was $17,500 and fees were $350. Room and board charges were $8600.

Financial Aid

Shorter University offers aid through each of the five federal programs: the Federal Pell Grant, Federal Supplemental Educational Opportunity Grant, Federal Work-Study Program, Federal Perkins Loan, and Federal Stafford Student Loan. Full-time students who are Georgia residents are eligible to receive the Georgia Tuition Equalization Grant and may be eligible to receive the HOPE Scholarship. Scholarships are offered for achievement in academics, music, art, theater, humanities, and athletics. Awards range from $500 to full tuition, room, and board. Academic scholarships are renewable each year, provided the student maintains at least the required grade point average. Special grants and scholarships are available to students who plan to enter church-related vocations or who are dependents of full-time employees of a Southern Baptist church, institution, or agency. Shorter University offers need-based aid to students with demonstrated financial need as determined by the Free Application for Federal Student Aid (FAFSA).

Faculty

The Shorter faculty is composed of 110 full-time, highly qualified professors, of whom 67 percent hold doctoral degrees. The University also employs 50 part-time faculty members. A favorable student-teacher ratio of 11:1 in traditional programs ensures that each student receives individual attention.

Student Government

One of Shorter's truly distinctive features is that students may participate in a wide variety of significant extracurricular activities, each of which affords a chance to develop social and leadership skills that prepare a student to win in a competitive world. The Student Government Association (SGA) is the official voice of the students. Through SGA's Executive Council, Senate, judicial boards, and special committees, students are directly involved in the life of the University.

Admission Requirements

Students are admitted into the freshman class based on their academic grade point average, SAT or ACT scores, and required essay. A review of the student's goals and their compatibility with the purpose of the University are also determining factors. The University requires 4 years of English, 4 years of mathematics (including 2 years of algebra), 3 years of history/social science, 3 years of science, and 2 units of foreign language. In addition to the general requirements for admission to the University, students majoring in music must meet the following requirements: each student must perform in an audition of approximately 10 minutes in his or her major medium, and each student must take a series of music placement tests. Students must successfully fulfill these requirements prior to the beginning of classes in August of their freshman year, since the music curriculum requires at least four years for completion. An audition is also required for students majoring in theater, and an art portfolio review is required for students majoring in art. High school students who have completed their junior year, have an outstanding academic record, and have completed the units outlined above may be considered for early admission. High school seniors entering in their senior year may be admitted on a joint-enrollment basis. Such students should have above-average grades and SAT or ACT scores. Transfer and international students are also welcome to apply.

For international students, a minimum paper-based TOEFL score of 500, Internet-based score of 61, or computer-based score of 173 is required. All international students must have their academic credentials evaluated by WES or another transcript evaluation service affiliated with the National Association of Credential Evaluation Services (NACES). For all transfer students, credit for college work below a C cannot be transferred. Homeschooled students should contact the Office of Admissions directly for requirements.

Application and Information

Shorter University accepts students on a rolling basis. Campus visits are highly recommended through a personal campus tour or one of three Open Houses.

Director of Admissions
Shorter University
315 Shorter Avenue
Rome, Georgia 30165-4298
Phone: 706-233-7319
        800-868-6980 Ext. 7319 (toll-free)
Fax: 706-233-7224
E-mail: admissions@shorter.edu
Web site: http://www.shorter.edu

SIMMONS COLLEGE
BOSTON, MASSACHUSETTS

The College

Steeped in a tradition of cultivating the intellectual and professional growth of women, Simmons College is a warm and engaging community with a national reputation of academic excellence. Founded in 1899, Simmons was the first college in the United States to offer women a liberal arts education integrated with career preparation. Today, Simmons embraces the opportunity to provide a transformative learning experience for students, fostering intellectual growth alongside their passion to build a path to a meaningful career. Located in the heart of Boston, Simmons is best known for its small classes, access to faculty, and internship and research opportunities. Students say that Simmons's location offers the best of both worlds—an intimate college experience in the heart of a vibrant and bustling city. Simmons's nearly 2,000 undergraduates appreciate the fact that they can easily access the city's rich social and cultural resources but also come home to a safe, friendly campus. The quintessential New England residential campus features nine brick residence halls and a private, landscaped quad, as well as Bartol Dining Hall, the state-of-the-art Holmes Sports Center, a student-run café, and the campus health center.

Location

Considered by many to be the best college town in the nation, Boston has more than fifty colleges and universities, and approximately 250,000 students. The historic, tree-lined Simmons campus is located in Boston's eclectic Fenway neighborhood, which is alive with music and fine arts, medical care and research, action and activism, and the resounding cheers of baseball fans at legendary Fenway Park. From campus, it's a safe, easy stroll to other colleges and universities as well as shops, cafés, clubs, museums, movie theaters, parks, and public transportation. Students can hop aboard the "T" (Boston's public transportation system) and head to destinations such as the Italian North End, Chinatown, Harvard Square, the boutiques of Newbury Street, the Harbor, and Boston's many other diverse neighborhoods.

Majors and Degrees

Simmons offers more than forty majors and programs. Popular majors include psychology, nursing, business, political science, and communications. Faculty advisors help each student create a plan that fulfills requirements and satisfies her personal and professional goals. A number of integrated degrees and accelerated programs allow students to go directly from undergraduate study to earning a graduate degree in less time than traditional programs. Students can accelerate to graduate degrees in areas such as business, education, health care, liberal arts, physical therapy, social work, and science information technology. Simmons also offers individually designed preprofessional programs for dentistry, law, medicine, and veterinary medicine. Simmons students typically declare a major by the end of their sophomore year, and nearly a third choose to double major.

Academic Program

Simmons offers a strong foundation in the liberal arts that helps transform intellectual curiosity into meaningful life's work. Each student explores a variety of subjects while gaining an in-depth theoretical and practical understanding of her major. First-year core courses emphasize critical thinking and writing skills, while integrating two or more subjects, ranging from sustainability and Buddhist studies to social justice and visual communication. To complement the theoretical knowledge learned in the classroom, Simmons offers many experiential opportunities, including an outstanding honors program, an award-winning service-learning center, and an abundance of study-abroad options, from short travel courses to a full year abroad.

The hallmark of a Simmons education is the independent learning requirement, which students fulfill through internships, fieldwork, and research projects. Science students co-publish research with faculty in nationally recognized academic journals as undergraduate students. Most students take advantage of the abundance of competitive internship opportunities available in Boston. In addition, Simmons's Longwood Medical Area partnerships provide outstanding clinical opportunities at Boston's world-renowned hospitals. On campus, students conduct research using state-of-the-art equipment in areas such as materials science, gene splicing, and computer modeling. Yet the most important aspect of Simmons's approach to hands-on learning is that professors frequently invite undergraduates to collaborate on professional research projects, articles, and presentations, as early as their freshman year.

Off-Campus Programs

Simmons is a member of the Colleges of the Fenway consortium, which allows students to participate in social events and cross-register with neighboring colleges, including Emmanuel College, Massachusetts College of Art, Massachusetts College of Pharmacy and Allied Health Sciences, Wentworth Institute of Technology, and Wheelock College.

Simmons encourages students to spend an entire semester or year abroad, and assists them in finding programs and scholarships for international study. For students who are unable to spend this length of time abroad, there are more than twelve short-term travel courses, which take students to another location abroad for three weeks. Short-term international courses provide unique opportunities to study topics such as chemistry in China, sustainability in Iceland, Spanish in Argentina, or history and civilization in Japan.

A domestic exchange program allows qualified juniors to spend a semester at Belmont University, Mills College, Spelman College, or Fisk University. In addition, students, usually junior political science or international relations majors, may also apply for the Washington Semester at American University in Washington, D.C.

Service learning, a teaching method that combines community service with academic instruction, is integral to a Simmons education. More than 400 Simmons students participate in service learning each semester, administered by the award-winning Scott/Ross Center for Community Service. These opportunities range from education initiatives to physical therapy clinics in needy areas of Boston.

Other opportunities include Success Connection, a mentoring program that matches select seniors with highly successful Simmons alumnae, and the Barbara Lee Internship Fellows program, which places students in Massachusetts legislators' offices and policy advocacy groups for one semester.

Academic Facilities

The beautiful Simmons campus offers an attractive, practical mix of historic and modern architecture, including state-of-the-art facilities and conveniences. Wireless Internet service is available throughout the campus, as well as many

strategically placed Web and print stations where students can check email, print a paper, or surf the Internet. Students can also go to the Pottruck Technology Center, a state-of-the-art computer-learning lab, where staff are available to assist them with new software and general computer skills. In addition, students have access to iMac centers, scanners, printers, digital cameras, video equipment, art studios, and music practice rooms.

Simmons's award-winning radio station streams live every day, and the Trustman Art Gallery hosts seasonal openings featuring student art, as well as community artists. Students can relax, eat, and study at the Fens dining hall; two coffee bars; one of the many quiet spaces located around campus; or at the Student Activities Center, which has vending machines, meeting rooms, print stations, a flat screen TV, and a comfortable lounge area.

The Park Science Center offers technologically advanced learning environments, including faculty and student research facilities, fully equipped science laboratories, state-of-the art nursing simulation labs, environmental rooms, observation rooms for psychological testing, and food science kitchens.

The newly renovated Beatley Library offers a number of student-centered services, including laptop loans, sophisticated online library service, technology-equipped group study rooms, and interlibrary loans with connections to dozens of libraries throughout Boston. In addition, students can schedule a research appointment with a librarian to help refine search techniques and choose the highest-quality information available.

Costs

Undergraduate tuition and fees for the 2011–12 academic year were $16,188 per semester; room and board charges were $6453 per semester. Total costs, not including books, supplies, and personal expenses, were $46,262 per year.

Financial Aid

More than 97 percent of Simmons' first-year students receive some form of financial aid. Scholarships, grants, loans, and federal work-study are determined by the Free Application for Federal Student Aid (FAFSA). Simmons also awards academic merit scholarships, ranging from $2000 to full tuition awards, renewable for four years.

Faculty

As a student-focused institution, Simmons offers a learning experience that is highly collaborative and personal. Professors include distinguished researchers, published authors, Fulbright scholars, health professionals, and community leaders. They advise numerous government, nonprofit, and corporate organizations in the United States and around the world, yet they passionately uphold their primary obligation to teach. Students say the small classes, intellectual focus, and welcoming environment contribute to their confidence and success. Of Simmons's 147 full-time undergraduate professors, two thirds are women. Nearly all of the liberal arts faculty members hold doctorates in their field. A 13:1 student-teacher ratio ensures that every student receives individual attention and reinforces the strong tie between students and professors.

Student Government

The Student Government Association (SGA) coordinates the policies and activities of various student organizations, allocates the student activities funds, and promotes the interests of the student body by working closely with the Simmons faculty and administration. Simmons fosters a student-centered environment and encourages each individual to actively participate in the College community in a way that is right for her. Simmons has more than fifty student organizations, clubs, and academic liaisons, including honor societies, cultural organizations, volunteer programs, a literary magazine, a campus newspaper, and ten NCAA Division III varsity teams. In addition, every academic department has a student liaison that participates in department evaluations and helps promote educational and social activities for students and faculty and staff members.

Admission Requirements

Admission to Simmons College is highly selective. The admission committee looks for students who have shown academic excellence both in and out of the classroom, and evaluates high school performance, SAT or ACT scores, recommendations, and the application essay. If English is not the applicant's first language, the TOEFL, IELTS, or a comparable exam score is required. Typical high school preparation for entrance includes 4 years of English, 4 years of math, 3-4 years of lab sciences, and 3-4 years of a foreign language. Although not required, an interview is strongly recommended.

Simmons welcomes applications from prospective freshmen, transfer students, international students, and students who are beyond the traditional college age.

Application and Information

Students may apply online, using the Common Application, or submit a print application, along with the $55 fee and all supporting credentials. The early action deadline (nonbinding) is December 1. The regular freshman application deadline is February 1. Transfer students are evaluated on a continual basis; the preferred filing date for applications for the fall semester is April 1. All students applying for the spring should submit their application by November 1.

Simmons encourages prospective students and their families to attend an admission event or request an individual visit.

For further information, interested students should contact:
Office of Undergraduate Admission
Simmons College
300 The Fenway
Boston, Massachusetts 02115
Phone: 800-345-8468 (toll-free)
Fax: 617-521-3190
E-mail: ugadm@simmons.edu
Web site: www.simmons.edu
    www.facebook.com/SimmonsCollege
    www.twitter.com/SimmonsCollege
    www.youtube.com/SimmonsCollege

Simmons offers a private oasis in the heart of Boston, America's best college town.

SIMPSON COLLEGE
INDIANOLA, IOWA

The College

Founded in 1860, Simpson College is a private liberal arts college affiliated with the United Methodist Church. Simpson produces successful students by combining the best of a liberal arts education with outstanding career preparation and extracurricular programs. With 1,500 full-time students and a student to faculty ratio of 13:1, students have the opportunity to work closely with their professors. Simpson's faculty members are as dedicated to their fields of study as they are to teaching—and it shows in the classroom. When this type of dedication and passion is combined with well-prepared and motivated students, the potential for success is unlimited.

Located just a few miles from downtown Des Moines, Iowa's capitol city recently ranked number one for business and careers, Simpson students take advantage of an abundance of internship opportunities. Whether working with Fortune 500 companies, spending time in an elementary school, or gaining resume-building experiences in a medical field, students learn to push their own boundaries. Beginning in fall 2012, students have access to Simpson's guaranteed internship program, giving them another advantage in today's competitive job market.

Simpson's beautiful, tree-lined campus in Indianola provides small-town friendliness and safety, while the campus facilities are continually enhanced and updated for academic and recreational opportunities. Recent multimillion-dollar projects include the renovation and expansion of Blank Performing Arts Center (2011), renovation of athletic facilities (2011), and the addition of a stunning new student center scheduled to open in October 2012.

Simpson's 4-4-1 academic calendar includes a May Term that provides students with unique learning opportunities in the classroom, internship settings, or while studying abroad. Throughout the year, students take advantage of Simpson's innovative Engaged Citizenship Curriculum. The curriculum allows students to gain skills and experiences valued most by employers while choosing classes that interest them. Simpson's "SC in 3" pathway allows high school students entering college with 24 or more college credits to finish a full, high-quality Simpson degree in three years, decreasing the cost of college and increasing their earning potential.

Extracurricular activities at Simpson are designed to supplement and reinforce the academic program and contribute toward a total learning experience. Activities range from an award-winning music program to nationally recognized NCAA Division III athletic teams. Students have the opportunity to participate in student government, campus publications, religious life, music, theater, departmental clubs, and various other organizations. Simpson has seven Greek chapters on campus, including three national fraternities, one local fraternity, and three national sororities; each with their own house. Simpson competes in nineteen intercollegiate sports and has an extensive intramural program.

Location

Simpson is located in Indianola, a residential community with a population of 14,400. Indianola is 12 miles south of Des Moines, with easy access to Interstates 35 and 80. The Des Moines International Airport is 20 minutes from campus. Indianola is host to nationally known events including the Des Moines Metropolitan Opera and the National Balloon Classic. The vibrant, small-town community has many choices for entertainment and recreation including Lake Ahquabi State Park, Summerset Trail, and unique restaurants and shops within walking distance of campus on the town square. Indianola's proximity to Des Moines gives students plenty of distinct advantages. Within minutes, students are right in the heart of some of the best entertainment and employment options Iowa and the Midwest have to offer.

Majors and Degrees

Simpson College grants Bachelor of Arts and Bachelor of Music degrees. Majors include accounting, actuarial science, applied philosophy, art, athletic training, biochemistry, biology, chemistry, communication and media studies, computer information systems, computer science, criminal justice, economics, education (elementary and secondary including art), English, environmental science, exercise science, forensic science/biochemistry, French, German, graphic design, history, integrated marketing communication, interdisciplinary studies, international management, international relations, management, marketing, mathematics, music, music education, music performance, philosophy, physical education, physics, political science, psychology, religion, sociology, Spanish, sports administration, studio art, and theater arts.

Simpson also offers pre-professional programs in dentistry, engineering, law, medicine, optometry, pharmacy, physical therapy, theology/ministry, and veterinary medicine. Concentration areas such as early childhood education and ethics are available, as well as many additional minors, including women's studies, social work, human resources management, Latin American studies, and coaching endorsements.

Academic Programs

Simpson College operates on a 4-4-1 academic calendar. The first semester starts in late August and ends in mid-December; the second semester starts in mid-January and ends in late April. A three-week session takes place during the month of May. During this period, students participate in a field experience/internship, study abroad, or take a course on campus with a hands-on focus.

The First Year Program is an extensive program of orientation, team building, mentoring, community service, advising, and course work structured to help new students adapt to their first year of college. The program begins with summer orientation and continues throughout the academic year. College and Character, a national initiative of the John Templeton Foundation, named Simpson College one of the sixty colleges in the nation that offer students an exemplary program in their first year to develop moral character.

The academic component of the First-Year Program is the Simpson Colloquium, a joint classroom and advising concept that is unique among first-year programs. These courses are small in size—no more than 18 first-year students each—and all are taught by each student's faculty adviser.

With Simpson's leading-edge Engaged Citizenship Curriculum, the courses students take delve deeper and focus more on projects that provide hands-on understanding of the subject matter. These courses allow students to work closely and build strong relationships with faculty members, one of the hallmarks of a Simpson education. The curriculum encourages students to take advantage of Simpson's community partnerships, hold internships, study abroad, or conduct independent research. It was developed in response to research that indicates future employers are looking for effective communicators, innovators, and problem solvers. Simpson is on the forefront of providing the kind of experiential, liberal arts education that college graduates need to succeed in their careers and achieve fulfillment in their lives.

Off-Campus Programs

Simpson provides many opportunities for studying abroad, with the choice of a semester-long program or a three-week May Term. Simpson's semester-long, faculty-led study-abroad programs include London, England; Schorndorf, Germany; Chiang Mai, Thailand; Tahiti, French Polynesia; Adelaide, Australia; and Rosario, Argentina. Students also have the opportunity for semester study-abroad programs in France, Spain, Italy, Australia, and more locations.

In addition, 10 to 15 travel courses are offered each May Term. Recent destinations include Africa, Central America, Great Britain, France, Greece, Ireland, New Zealand, the Galapagos Islands, Brazil, Argentina, and Scandinavia. May Term study abroad courses are led by Simpson faculty members and give students the opportunity to experience a different culture while gaining a stronger global perspective. Simpson has been recognized as one of the top 100 colleges in the nation for the highest percentage of students who study abroad—43 percent of Simpson students will travel abroad by the time they graduate.

The Capitol Hill Internship Program (CHIP) provides students with the opportunity to spend either the fall or spring semester in Washington, D.C. Past participants have had various experiences including interning for members of Congress, the Smithsonian Institution, the Republican National Committee, the Justice Department, CNN, the Australian Embassy, and FOX News.

Academic Facilities

Simpson has a wireless campus network with high-speed Internet access. There are numerous computer labs throughout campus where students can use standard office suite applications or specialized, discipline-specific applications.

The Carver Science Center, named after Simpson's most distinguished alumnus George Washington Carver, provides state-of-the-art research facilities, computer labs, a cadaver lab, and classrooms.

The Henry H. and Thomas H. McNeill Hall houses classrooms for management, accounting, economics, and communication studies. In addition, the hall houses a seminar room and the Pioneer Hi-Bred International Conference Center.

The Amy Robertson Music Center is home to Simpson's acclaimed music department and contains the Sven and Mildred Lekberg Recital Hall, ten studios, twenty-two practice rooms, a music computer lab, and the band rehearsal room. The Salsbury Wing includes a choral rehearsal room, a classroom, and studios.

Dunn Library, a modern academic learning resource center, contains over 175,000 items including books, periodicals, videos/DVDs, and CDs. Many resources (print and online) can be located from the library Web site. Additional materials for research can be obtained through a national interlibrary loan network. The Hawley Academic Resource Center, which provides free academic support services to all students, is located in Dunn Library.

The A. H. and Theo Blank Performing Arts Center underwent a multimillion-dollar expansion and renovation in 2011. The center accommodates Simpson's well-known programs in theater arts and opera. It includes the magnificent 500-seat Pote Theatre, with both proscenium and hydraulically controlled thrust stages, a studio theater, the Barborka Gallery, technical facilities, and shops and classrooms.

Wallace Hall, named to the National Register of Historic Places in 1991, contains facilities for education, sociology, and applied social science.

Mary Berry Hall, renovated during the summer of 2008, houses the psychology department as well as faculty offices, six new labs, a control room for observation and data processing, and an animal care space. In addition, the building is home to humanities classrooms, a language lab, and the Farnham Art Gallery.

Faculty

Simpson offers one professor for every 13 students, and 90 percent of full-time faculty members have earned the highest degree in their fields. Simpson's faculty members serve as academic advisers as well as teachers. Their commitment goes beyond the classroom as they often attend college plays, operas, and athletic events, reinforcing their sincere interest in the lives of the students and their ultimate success.

Costs

Tuition for 2012–13 is $28,974; room charges are $3860; and board is $4103. These figures do not include books, music fees, or personal expenses.

Financial Aid

Simpson College is dedicated to making it financially feasible for qualified students to experience the advantages of a Simpson education. In fact, 98% of Simpson students receive some form of financial aid. Generous gifts from alumni, trustees, and friends of the College—in addition to state and federal student aid programs—make this opportunity possible. Simpson offers financial aid on both a need and non-need basis. Need is determined by filing the Free Application for Federal Student Aid.

Financial aid granted on a non-need basis includes generous academic scholarships (awarded on the basis of prior academic records) and talent scholarships (available in theater, music, and art). The talent scholarships are determined by audition/portfolio.

Also, specific scholarships such as the United Methodist Service to Community Grant, the John C. Culver Fellowship, and the Wesley Service Scholarship can be obtained through application.

Admission Requirements

Admission to Simpson College is selective and competitive. A strong academic record is essential. Applications are acted upon by an admissions committee, which is elected by the faculty and represents the five academic divisions of the College. These faculty members consider the college-preparatory courses taken and the grades received in those courses, rank in class, and standardized test scores (ACT and/or SAT), including test sub scores, as well as a guidance counselor recommendation form and short essay.

Transfer applicants are accepted on the basis of successful completion of academic work at an accredited college or university. In addition, transfer applicants are required to submit official high school transcripts and ACT/SAT results.

Application and Information

Simpson's rolling admission policy allows flexibility; however early application is recommended. Applications can be found on the school Web site or through the Common Application.

For additional information or to obtain application materials, students should contact:

Office of Admissions
Simpson College
701 North C Street
Indianola, Iowa 50125
Phone: 515-961-1624
        800-362-2454 Ext. 1624 (toll-free)
E-mail: admiss@simpson.edu
Web site: http://www.simpson.edu
        http://on.fb.me/Simpson_College (Facebook)
        http://twitter.com/simpsonnews
        http://www.youtube.com/simpsonweb

Simpson College in the Spring.

SKIDMORE COLLEGE
SARATOGA SPRINGS, NEW YORK

The College

Skidmore College is an independent liberal arts college of 2,400 men and women from fifty states and forty countries that prides itself on its creative approaches to just about everything. Hence, the College's belief that creative thought matters. Founded by Lucy Skidmore Scribner as the Skidmore School of Arts in 1911, it became Skidmore College in 1922. In addition to being accredited by the Middle States Association of Colleges and Schools, the College has a chapter of Phi Beta Kappa and program accreditation with the Council on Social Work Education and the National Association of Schools of Art and Design. Throughout its history, Skidmore has displayed a spirit of innovation and imagination in response to need and opportunity. In the 1960s the College built an entirely new campus; in 1971 it became coeducational; in 1983 it completely revised its curriculum, creating a comprehensive liberal studies program focused on interdisciplinarity (revised again in 2005 with the creation of the First-Year Experience program); and in 1993, it installed the Master of Arts in Liberal Studies program, primarily for adult learners. Skidmore has embraced change, seeing in it the opportunity to serve the needs and aspirations of its students. By expanding and refining its programs, the College has broadened its educational mission to respond to the opportunities and challenges of a global society.

Students enjoy a full schedule of intellectual, cultural, and social activities, such as lectures, visiting scholars in residence, art exhibits, concerts, and dance and theater performances. There are approximately 100 student organizations, including a weekly newspaper, radio and TV stations, numerous ethnic and cultural associations, an art and literary journal, and a student-volunteer network. There are no fraternities or sororities, which helps ensure an inclusive environment. A strong NCAA Division III intercollegiate sports program for men and women—nineteen teams in all—includes baseball, basketball, field hockey, golf, ice hockey, lacrosse, riding, rowing, soccer, softball, swimming and diving, tennis, and volleyball. Skidmore competes in the Liberty League, which also includes Bard, Clarkson, Hobart and William Smith, Rensselaer Polytechnic Institute, Rochester Institute of Technology, St. Lawrence, Union, and Vassar. The College has vigorous intramural; club sport; and health, fitness, and wellness programming.

Skidmore's campus includes more than fifty buildings. The Williamson Sports and Recreation Complex has a pool and diving well, racquet-sport courts, basketball and volleyball courts, several intramural gyms, three dance studios, a weight room, a fitness center, and a human performance laboratory. Adjacent to the complex are Wachenheim Field, a small stadium with an artificial turf field for soccer, lacrosse, and intramurals, and a 400-meter all-weather track; dedicated softball and field hockey turf fields; and the lighted Wenger Tennis Courts. The Frances Young Tang Teaching Museum and Art Gallery, unique in its interdisciplinary approach to exhibits and programming, opened in 2000.

Two major additions were made to the campus in 2006. The green Northwoods Apartments opened with 380 single-room units in ten new buildings. A completely renovated dining hall, Murray-Aikins, also opened, offering extensive vegetarian, vegan, and international options, freshly made pasta, locally grown organic items, and a broad array of daily choices. The Arthur Zankel Music Center, an award-winning, state-of-the-art music building with a 600-seat auditorium, opened in 2010. Construction of new residence hall facilities, modeled on the Northwoods Apartments, are underway, with Phase I scheduled for completion in fall 2012.

Location

Saratoga Springs, 30 miles north of Albany, New York's state capital, is perennially short-listed as one of the most interesting and vibrant small cities in the U.S. Famed for health, history, and horses—its mineral waters, Revolutionary War battlefield, and the nation's oldest thoroughbred racetrack—Saratoga is equally renowned as an arts and cultural destination. The Saratoga Performing Arts Center is summer home to the New York City Ballet, Philadelphia Orchestra, and Lake George Opera, and is a performing venue for top rock and jazz musicians. The city's downtown is just a 10-minute walk from Skidmore and is brimming with galleries, clubs, shops, coffeehouses, and restaurants. The city's location near the foothills of the Adirondack Mountains puts an abundance of outdoor recreational opportunities—major ski areas, state parks, large lakes, and mountainous regions of eastern New York, Vermont, and western Massachusetts—within an hour's drive. Boston, New York City, and Montreal are each approximately 180 miles from the campus.

In terms of transportation, bus service is available from Saratoga Springs to New York City, Montreal, Boston, and other major cities. There are daily trains to and from New York City and Montreal. Rental cars are available at the Albany International Airport, which is served by major airlines. The College is located near Exit 15 of I-87 (the Northway).

Majors and Degrees

Skidmore College grants a Bachelor of Arts degree in the following liberal arts subjects: American studies, anthropology, Asian studies, biology, chemistry, classics, computer science, economics, English, environmental studies, foreign languages and literatures (French, German, and Spanish), French area studies, gender studies, geosciences, government, history, history of art, international affairs, mathematics, music, neuroscience, philosophy, physics, psychology, religious studies, and sociology. The Bachelor of Science degree is granted in areas of a more professional nature, including business, dance, education studies, exercise science, social work, studio art, and theater. There are more than twenty interdepartmental majors, economics-sociology and government-Spanish being just two examples. Self-determined majors, double majors, and minors are also available. In keeping with the College's creative spirit and the realities of the marketplace, more than half of Skidmore students choose a second major or minor.

Through partnerships with other institutions, Skidmore offers enhanced program/degree offerings in business, education, engineering, nursing, and physical and occupational therapy. These include 4+1 M.B.A. programs with Clarkson University and Union Graduate College; a 4+1 M.A.T. program with Union College; 3+2 programs in engineering with Dartmouth College and Clarkson; 4+1/4+2 programs in physical therapy and/or occupational therapy (Sage Graduate School), and a 4+1 nursing program (New York University School of Nursing). Skidmore also has certification programs in teaching and social work and pre-professional programs in law and medicine.

Academic Programs

The Skidmore journey begins with the First-Year Experience which introduces students to the rigorous interdisciplinary academic program and overall approach to learning and connects them with a faculty adviser/mentor. Talented but economically disadvantaged students who have been accepted into the Opportunity Program (Higher Education Opportunity Program or Academic Opportunity Program) participate in a month-long summer program. A small percentage of students opt to apply for entry into Skidmore's Honors Forum on the basis of academic achievement and aspirations, leadership qualities, and civic commitment.

Generally, students choose a major by the end of sophomore year. In the interest of breadth, they are also expected to take one to two courses in both quantitative reasoning and expository writing, and at least one course in each of the following: lab science, social science, arts, humanities, and culture. There is plenty of academic support through Student Academic Services. In addition there are specific programs for prelaw and premed students. In their junior and senior years, students often add value to their courses of study through faculty-student collaborative research, internships, volunteerism, service learning, and off-campus study.

Off-Campus Programs

About 60 percent of Skidmore's students spend a semester or year off campus. In addition to Skidmore programs in China, England, France, and Spain, students can access approximately 140 international programs through the College's Approved Programs structure, including programs in Africa, Asia, Europe, Latin America, and Australia. Students can also study at some 200 other U.S. campuses, thanks to Skidmore's affiliation with National Student Exchange. All academic majors and minors can be accommodated and transfer credits are guaranteed for students studying on an Approved Program. Financial aid is transferable to most off-campus study programs. The College also offers a Washington Semester (internship in conjunction with American University) and a semester at the Marine Biological Laboratory in Woods Hole, Massachusetts.

Arrangements for student internships (for academic credit) are made through Skidmore's academic departments or the Office of Career Services. More than 50 percent of students are involved in volunteer work, much of it local. There are also up to fifty courses each semester with service-learning components.

Academic Facilities

Skidmore's 890-acre campus offers more than fifty buildings, designed and arranged to blend with the natural surroundings and to foster intellectual and social interaction. The newest building, the Arthur Zankel Music Center, features a spectacular 600-seat recital hall and a state-of-the-art recording studio. Skidmore's visual and performing arts space includes the Saisselin Art Building, with studios and the Schick Art Gallery; the Janet Kinghorn Bernhard Theater, with a seating capacity of 350, and an experimental black box theater; and the Dance Center. The Tang Museum provides a focal point for cross-disciplinary study through the visual arts. The Dana Science Center offers state-of-the-art teaching and research space, including centers for microscopy imaging and geographic information systems. Dana links the College's science departments to the Department of Mathematics and Computer Science in neighboring Harder Hall, which features a Linux lab with more than 20 workstations for advanced computer science projects.

Costs

In 2012–13 tuition is $43,138, required fees $882, room $6944, and board $4800 for a total of $55,764.

Financial Aid

About half of Skidmore's students receive some form of financial assistance. Aid is awarded on the basis of demonstrated financial need and is provided in the form of a student-aid package that usually includes a grant, campus job, and loan. Students interested in applying for admission are encouraged to do so regardless of their intention to seek financial aid. The FAFSA, a copy of the federal income tax form, and the CSS PROFILE must be filed each year. The College hosts an annual Filene Music Scholarship Competition to award four $48,000 ($12,000 per year) scholarships on the basis of musical ability without regard to financial need. Five to seven $15,000 merit scholarships ($60,000 over four years) in math and science are also awarded annually. Information concerning scholarships, grants, loans, and/or work awards can be obtained through the Office of Financial Aid.

Faculty

Skidmore College has some 250 faculty members and 70 part-time members, 84 percent of whom hold the doctoral degree or the highest degree in their field. The student-to-faculty ratio is about 9:1 and the average class size is 16. Although actively engaged in research and publication in their individual fields, the Skidmore faculty members regard teaching as their primary commitment. All students have faculty advisers who assist them in selecting courses and in designing individual academic programs.

Student Government

Students at Skidmore play an active role in College governance. Through the Student Government Association (SGA) and membership on a number of major College committees, they participate in academic and social life. The SGA operates under the authority granted by the Board of Trustees and is dedicated to democratic self-government and responsible citizenship. Within the association, elected faculty members and student representatives serve on the All-College Council, the Academic Integrity Board, and the Social Integrity Board. Broad concerns of the SGA include educational policy, elections, social and student events, first-year orientation, student publications, and student clubs and organizations.

Admission Requirements

Those seeking admission to Skidmore's first-year class should complete a secondary school curriculum that includes at least 16 credits in college-preparatory courses. The Admissions Committee is also pleased to consider applications from qualified high school juniors who plan to accelerate and enter college early. Applicants typically have completed 4 years of English, 4 years of a foreign language, 4 years of mathematics, 4 years of social studies, and 3–4 years of laboratory science. Applicants must provide a secondary school transcript, standardized test scores (SAT I with writing or ACT with writing), letters of recommendation from two teachers of academic subjects, and a report from their guidance counselor. Skidmore recommends that applicants submit scores for three SAT II Subject Tests. A campus visit and interview is also recommended.

Through its participation in the Higher Education Opportunity Program (HEOP) Skidmore enrolls capable, energetic, and ambitious New York state residents who, because of their academic and financial situations, would not otherwise gain admission to the College under traditional requirements.

Application and Information

Applicants for admission must complete the Common Application—preferably online at www.commonapp.org—and submit it with a $65 fee or request a fee waiver from their adviser. All information should be postmarked by January 15. Applications from early decision candidates should be submitted by November 15 for the Round I early decision plan or by January 15 for the Round II early decision plan. Transfer candidates are urged to apply by April 1 for the next fall term and by November 15 for the next spring term. In addition to a high school transcript and standardized test scores, transfer candidates are required to submit, by the appropriate deadlines, an official transcript of all college-level work completed, recommendations from two professors, and a statement regarding personal and academic standing from the dean of students at the current college. International students are given special attention throughout the admissions process. Applicants whose first language is not English are encouraged to submit the results of the Test of English as a Foreign Language (TOEFL). There are a limited number of need-based financial aid awards available for outstanding international students.

Mary Lou W. Bates
Dean of Admissions and Financial Aid
Skidmore College
815 North Broadway
Saratoga Springs, New York 12866
Phone: 518-580-5570
      800-867-6007 (toll-free)
E-mail: admissions@skidmore.edu
Web site: http://www.skidmore.edu
      http://www.facebook.com/SkidmoreCollege
      http://twitter.com/skidmorecollege
      http://www.youtube.com/skidmorecollege

Autumn view of Skidmore's campus: Hapt Pond in the foreground, Case Center at left, and Scribner Library at right.

SMITH COLLEGE
NORTHAMPTON, MASSACHUSETTS

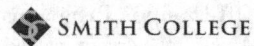

The College

Smith College was founded in 1871 as a liberal arts college for women and rapidly became one of the first such institutions to match the standards and facilities of the best colleges of the day. Today, with 2,500 undergraduates on campus and 250 studying elsewhere, Smith is the largest privately endowed college for women in the country. Graduate degrees (master's, Ph.D.) are offered in a number of departments and in the Smith College School for Social Work. Currently, fifty states and more than sixty countries are represented in the Smith student body. Approximately 60 percent of the students in each entering class were in the top 10 percent of their high school class; most chose Smith because of the excellence of its faculty and curriculum. Although most Smith students are between the ages of 18 and 22, Smith's Ada Comstock Scholars Program enables older women whose educations have been interrupted and who meet the College's admission standards to pursue an A.B. degree in part-time or full-time study.

Smith's house system is unusual and highly regarded. Each of the College's thirty-five houses is home to between 12 and 100 women. There are fifteen dining rooms that offer different menus, themes, and types of food. The house system stresses individual freedom, group autonomy, and mutual respect. Other residences, such as a cooperative house, and apartments, are also available. Smith offers a wide variety of extracurricular activities, ranging from service organizations to musical groups and from student publications to thirteen intercollegiate sports teams. The already varied cultural and social opportunities—lectures, workshops, dance and theatrical performances, art exhibits, concerts, and social events—are increased by participation in Five Colleges, Inc., a consortium that opens to Smith students classes and activities at Amherst, Hampshire, and Mount Holyoke colleges and at the University of Massachusetts. Smith's athletic facilities include two gymnasiums, five squash courts, a 75-foot six-lane swimming pool with 1- and 3-meter diving boards, a human performance laboratory, climbing wall, fitness center, and an indoor track and tennis facility, which houses four tennis courts and a 200-meter track. Outside are 30 acres of athletic fields, a 400-meter track, a 5,000-meter cross-country course, and twelve lighted tennis courts. Smith also has indoor and outdoor Olympic-size riding rings and a forty-two-unit stable.

Location

Northampton, a small cosmopolitan city with a population of more than 30,000, is in the Connecticut River valley of western Massachusetts. It is 93 miles west of Boston and 156 miles northeast of New York City. There are many shops and restaurants within walking distance of the campus and within the service area of a free Five College bus system. Buses run frequently to Boston and New York. Many students are involved in local organizations, and some intern in local city or county offices. Others participate on an extracurricular level in nonprofit agencies.

Majors and Degrees

Smith College awards the Bachelor of Arts (A.B.) degree. Areas of major concentration include Afro-American studies, American studies, anthropology, architecture, art (history and studio), astronomy, biochemistry, biological sciences, chemistry, classical studies, classics, comparative literature, computer science, dance, East Asian languages and cultures, East Asian studies, economics, education and child study, engineering, English language and literature, environmental science and policy, film studies, French studies, geosciences, German studies, government, Greek, history, Italian language and literature, Italian studies, Jewish studies, Latin, Latin American and Latino/Latina studies, mathematics, medieval studies, music, neuroscience, philosophy, physics, Portuguese-Brazilian studies, psychology, religion, Russian civilization, Russian literature, sociology, Spanish, theater, and women and gender studies. Interdepartmental majors and minors are offered in a variety of fields.

Academic Programs

The academic year is divided into two semesters, the first ending before winter recess. Noncredit Interterm courses are offered during January. Smith believes in the goals of a liberal arts education. With an open curriculum, students have flexibility to choose from more than 1,000 courses. The only requirement outside a student's field of concentration is one writing-intensive course. The normal course load consists of 16 credits in each of eight semesters, to total the 128 credits of academic work that are required. There are no specific distribution requirements, but 64 credits must be taken outside the major field of study. A student may also complete the requirements of two departmental majors or of one departmental major and another departmental minor. Concentrations in archives, biomathematical sciences, book studies, Buddhist studies, museum studies, poetry, and South Asia studies offer students a way to organize intellectual and practical experiences around a focused area of interest. The Smith Centers for Engagement, Learning, and Leadership—the Global Studies Center; the Center for the Environment, Ecological Design, and Sustainability; the Center for Work and Life; and the Center for Community Collaborations—respond to emerging student and scholarly interests, provide contexts for internships and independent projects, and address real-world challenges.

Through credit earned on Advanced Placement or International Baccalaureate examinations and by summer study, some students may be able to accelerate and complete degree requirements in six or seven semesters. The Departmental Honors Program enables a student with a strong academic background to study a particular topic in depth or undertake research in the field of her major.

Off-Campus Programs

Smith students may take academic courses and participate in social and cultural activities at any of the institutions participating in the Five College consortium, described above. Smith students may also spend a year at another member institution of the Twelve College Exchange Program (Amherst, Bowdoin, Connecticut, Dartmouth, Mount Holyoke, Trinity, Vassar, Wellesley, Wesleyan, and Wheaton) or spend a year at Spelman College or Pomona College. Some students participate in the Jean Picker Semester-in-Washington Program in public policy, a fall internship program in Washington, D.C., sponsored by the College's Department of Government. The American Studies Program offers an internship at the Smithsonian Institution.

Smith offers Junior Year Abroad programs in Florence, Geneva, Hamburg, and Paris. Students may apply to affiliated programs in more than thirty other countries. Students eligible for financial aid are able to take that aid with them to any approved program.

Academic Facilities

The Smith College Libraries comprise the largest undergraduate library system of any liberal arts college in the country. The 1.4 million holdings are housed in the centrally located William Allan Neilson Library and in the libraries of the fine arts, performing arts, and science centers. The Neilson Library also houses a rare book room, the Nonprint Resource Center, the

College archives, and the Sophia Smith Collection, a women's history archive. The Clark Science Center is a five-building complex that accommodates the nearly 30 percent of students who major in the sciences. The facilities include general laboratories, a molecular genetics facility, classrooms, a rooftop astronomy observatory, animal care facilities, scanning and transmission electron microscopes, an analytic ultracentrifuge, and a high-field nuclear magnetic resonance spectrometer. Ford Hall houses computer science, chemistry, biochemistry, molecular biology, and the Picker Engineering program. Academic computer facilities include networked Windows and Macintosh computers in public labs, classrooms, the libraries, and the foreign language center. All buildings and student residences are networked, and Internet access is available at no charge. There is wireless access in many buildings. Smith also has a digital design studio and several electronic classrooms. Bass Hall houses the psychology department, the scientific computing center, and Young Library, one of the largest undergraduate science libraries in the country. The Bass laboratories provide numerous facilities for research in neuroscience. The Mendenhall Center for the Performing Arts contains an experimental theater and a traditional theater, dance studios, and television and audio recording rooms. Sage Hall, the music building, includes an electronic music studio, a small recital hall, dozens of practice rooms, and a 750-seat concert hall. The Smith College Museum of Art houses one of the finest teaching collections in the country, and Hillyer Hall contains art studios as well as printmaking, darkroom, and sculpture facilities.

Costs

Tuition for 2012–13 is $41,190. The room and board charge for regular student residences is $13,860. The activity fee is $270.

Financial Aid

More than 70 percent of all Smith students receive some form of financial assistance from grants, loans, and/or campus jobs. Aid is awarded on the basis of need, as determined by the College. Each applicant must submit the Smith Aid Application (available on Smith's Web site), the Free Application for Federal Student Aid (FAFSA), the PROFILE form from the College Scholarship Service, and a copy of the current federal income tax return. Smith meets full demonstrated need for all admitted students who apply for aid by the published deadlines. The first portion of an aid award is an offer of a loan and campus employment; the remaining need is covered by grants from federal, state, and/or College funds. Merit-based aid is also available on a limited and highly competitive basis.

Faculty

The teaching of undergraduate women is the priority of the Smith faculty. There are approximately 290 faculty members; nearly all have earned doctoral degrees and are well-known in their professional fields. Close ties between undergraduates and their teachers are forged through small classes (70 percent have 20 or fewer students) and generous access to faculty members during and outside of regular office hours.

Student Government

Smith students assume much of the responsibility for their personal, social, and academic life at the College through the Student Government Association, which gives students representation on major college-policy committees.

Admission Requirements

Smith seeks students whose motivation, academic preparation, and diversity of interests will enable them to profit from and contribute to the varied possibilities of a liberal arts college. Smith is interested in the woman behind the numbers. As a highly competitive college, Smith gives primary consideration to the academic record of each candidate for admission. Strong high school programs have a basis of 4 years of English, at least 3 years in one foreign language or 2 years in each of two languages, 3 years of mathematics, 3 years of science, and 2 years of history. It is hoped that areas of special interest will have been pursued in depth. SAT or ACT scores are optional for U.S. citizens and U.S. permanent residents. Standardized tests (SAT, ACT, TOEFL or IELTS) are required for international citizens. SAT Subject Tests are optional for any applicant. An interview is strongly recommended. A first-choice early decision plan is available.

Applications are also welcomed from students who wish to transfer from other college-level institutions or who wish to enter the Visiting Students Program or the Ada Comstock Scholars Program.

Smith College is committed to maintaining a diverse community in an atmosphere of mutual respect and appreciation of differences. Smith College does not discriminate in its educational and employment policies on the bases of race, color, creed, religion, national/ethnic origin, sex, sexual orientation, or age or with regard to the bases outlined in the Veterans Readjustment Act and the Americans with Disabilities Act. Smith's admission policies and practices are guided by the same principle, concerning women applying to the undergraduate program and all applicants to the graduate programs.

Application and Information

A prospective first-year student interested in applying to Smith has three options: fall early decision, winter early decision, or regular decision. The fall early decision deadline is November 15, and applicants receive a decision by mid-December. The deadline for winter early decision is January 2, and students receive a decision in late January. Regular decision applicants must complete the Common Application by January 15; all other parts of the application are due by February 1. These candidates receive their admission decision by April 1. The deadline for January transfer admission is November 15; students receive an admission decision in mid-December. The preferred deadline for September transfer admission is February 1, with notification in late March. Transfer applications are accepted until May 15, and decisions are made by early June. Application deadlines for the Visiting Student Programs are July 1 (for September admission) and November 15 (for January admission). Deadlines for the Ada Comstock Scholars Program are November 15 (for January admission) and February 1 (for September admission).

For more information about Smith College, students should contact:

Dean of Admission
Smith College
Northampton, Massachusetts 01063
Phone: 413-585-2500
      800-383-3232 (toll-free)
Fax: 413-585-2527
E-mail: admission@smith.edu
Web site: http://www.smith.edu
      http://www.facebook.com/smithcollege
      http://twitter.com/smithcollege

Northampton combines small-town ambiance with big-city offerings.

SOMERSET CHRISTIAN COLLEGE
SOMERSET COUNTY AND NEWARK, NEW JERSEY

The College

Somerset Christian College (SCC) is a new college being built on an old foundation. For over a century, the College has offered biblically sound courses teaching men and women how to serve God, society, and the church in a wide variety of fields. Since 2001, SCC has been the only evangelical college chartered by the State of New Jersey, operating with educational sites in Newark and suburban areas of central New Jersey. SCC offers a unique blend of spiritual enrichment, academic excellence, and social fulfillment. The student body comprises a wide spectrum of ages, races, interests, and personalities, reflecting the diversity of the metropolitan corridor of the Northeast. Through Godly instructors, rich curricula in career-shaping majors, spiritually enthusiastic students, valuable enriching internships, and global learning experiences, SCC offers students all they need to be equipped for their best future.

Location

SCC is located in Newark and Somerset County, New Jersey. Its Newark Campus occupies over 13,000 square feet of classroom, administrative, and conference/community space on the seventh and twentieth floors of the Military Park Building in the heart of downtown Newark. Both locations enjoy easy access to public transportation, Route 21, and Interstate 78. SCC sites are a short drive from New York City, state parks, historical sites, hiking trails, professional and minor league sports, and New Jersey beaches.

Majors and Degrees

The Bachelor of Arts (B.A.) degree is a four-year, 120 credit-hour course of study. The B.A. is awarded upon successful completion of all requirements, which include a core curriculum consisting of Biblical studies, general education and major requirements. Majors include business administration/management, psychology/counseling, and Biblical studies. Areas of concentration include organizational leadership, family and marriage counseling, communications, and worship/music/media.

Academic Programs

Among its many course selections, the College offers a Life Enhancing Accelerated Degree (LEAD) for adult students to complete their baccalaureate degree so they can advance in their professional careers. These students form a small group, or cohort that creates a supportive relationship among its members to facilitate learning and collective completion of the program. To accommodate working students, SCC has scheduled sixteen modular courses one night a week/one course at a time, for the duration of the program.

SCC's Instructional Resource Center (IRC) is designed as a support service to assist all students to achieve their full academic potential.

Academic Facilities

The Newark Campus occupies two floors of the Military Park Building, 60 Park Place. Located one block south of the Performing Arts Center (PAC) and four blocks north of the Prudential Center, the Military Park Building is a prestigious high-rise building that hosts an interesting array of professional corporations. SCC's Newark Campus features beautiful views facing west and south from the five classrooms, which are state-of-the-art learning centers. The space also includes a reception area, admissions office, a student lounge with kitchenette, a media lab/classroom, a library, a large meeting room, and executive offices.

Costs

Somerset Christian College is committed to providing an excellent, cost-effective education for its students. Tuition and fee rates, payable each semester, are set annually according to economic conditions within the College and industry standards. For 2011–12, tuition was $15,000. Semester fees were $225. The estimated annual cost was $15,450.

Financial Aid

SCC operates a full student financial aid program, including grants, scholarships, loans, and employment, allowing any student a realistic opportunity to finance their college education. More than 95 percent of all SCC students who apply for financial assistance to further their education receive it. The College is aware that each family has a unique financial situation and the financial aid staff is available to work with students to find the resources to fund their education at SCC.

Student Government

The Student Government seeks to fairly represent the interests and concerns of each member of the student body. Its purpose is to address student needs efficiently and effectively, uphold the code of conduct of the community, and to initiate positive activities and programs for the benefit of SCC students. The Student Government, working in close cooperation with the College's Director of Student Life, brings the students as a community into a closer and more vital relationship with the rest of the College community.

Admission Requirements

Somerset Christian College admits all qualified students of any race, color, disability, national or ethnic origin to all the rights, privileges, programs, and activities available through the College. SCC does not discriminate on the basis of gender, race, color, disability, national or ethnic origin in administration of its educational policies, admission policies, financial aid, or other school-administered programs. In admission to enrolling at Somerset Christian College, students enter into a covenant of respect for the Faith Statement and agree to adhere to the Ethos Statement of SCC. Prospective students and other persons interested in learning more about Somerset Christian College are cordially invited to arrange for a campus visit. Admissions requirements include an application, two recommendations, a personal statement, and official transcripts from all previous institutions. Somerset Christian College, in compliance with the New Jersey Administrative Code (N.J.A.C. 8:57-6.5-6.9) and Health Department regulations, requires persons born January 1, 1957, or later to show proof of vaccinations for measles, mumps, rubella and Hepatitis-B prior to arrival at school.

Application and Information

For an application form, catalog, and all forms required for admissions, students can contact:

Somerset Christian College
60 Park Place, Suite 701
Newark, New Jersey 07102
Phone: (800) 234-9305
E-mail: info@somerset.edu
Web site: http://www.somerset.edu

Somerset Christian College offers students a unique blend of spiritual enrichment, academic excellence, and social fulfillment.

SOUTHERN CONNECTICUT STATE UNIVERSITY
NEW HAVEN, CONNECTICUT

The University

The rich academic and social environment at Southern Connecticut State University encourages students to discover who they are, who they want to be, and how to realize their dreams. A public coeducational university founded in 1893, Southern offers 114 undergraduate and graduate programs. Fascinating internships, unique research opportunities, a challenging faculty, and a dynamic campus enrich every program. Southern is located in New Haven, the heart of "academic Connecticut."

Southern has five academic schools: Arts and Sciences, Business, Education, Health and Human Services, and Graduate Studies. Southern offers several programs, including the Honors College, for high-achieving students. The Honors College is a four-year alternative program featuring team-taught interdisciplinary courses, symposia, and requires students to complete an honors thesis or project in their senior year. The Office of Student Supportive Services offers tutorial support and coordinates special programs for veterans, international students, and students with learning, physical, and emotional disabilities.

The student body represents diverse ethnic and socioeconomic groups. Although most students reside in Connecticut, students from more than twenty states and thirty countries also enroll at Southern. About 11,500 students attend Southern, including 8,700 undergraduates. More than a third of the full-time undergraduates live on campus in ten residence halls and townhouses. Other students commute or reside in off-campus housing in the Southern neighborhood.

Competitive athletes and eager amateurs enjoy intramural and intercollegiate sports programs at Southern. Intramural and club sports include coed three-on-three and five-on-five basketball, cheerleading, flag football, coed floor hockey, a golf tournament, ice hockey (men), karate, rugby (men and women), skiing and snowboarding, coed softball, Ultimate (Frisbee), coed soccer, a tennis tournament, Wiffle ball, and coed volleyball. A member of the National Collegiate Athletic Association (NCAA), the Eastern College Athletic Conference, and the Northeast-10 Conference, Southern offers student-athletes competitive opportunities in several intercollegiate sports. A university with a long tradition of athletic excellence, Southern is highly competitive among NCAA Division II colleges and universities, having earned ten NCAA team championships and seventy-one individual championships. Southern offers intercollegiate competition in men's baseball, basketball, cross-country, football, soccer, swimming, and track and field. Southern offers intercollegiate programs for women in basketball, cross-country, field hockey, gymnastics, lacrosse, soccer, softball, swimming, track and field, and volleyball. Outstanding facilities are available to all athletes in Moore Fieldhouse, Pelz Gymnasium, and the Jess Dow Field outdoor sports complex.

Location

New Haven, Connecticut, is a sophisticated city of 130,000 people that abuts picturesque Long Island Sound. Southern is located in the city's Westville section, near historic West Rock Park. Rich in tradition, New Haven is a classic college town; about 35,000 students attend its half-dozen fine universities and colleges. Only 75 miles from New York City and 3 hours from Boston, New Haven is an integral part of the economic, cultural, and social life of the Northeast. Students enjoy easy access to outstanding cultural opportunities, including movies, restaurants, clubs, concerts, seaside activities, sports, museums, and world-famous theater at the Yale Repertory, the Shubert, and Long Wharf.

Majors and Degrees

Southern offers the Bachelor of Arts (B.A.) and the Bachelor of Science (B.S.) degrees. The Bachelor of Arts degree is awarded in anthropology, art (art history and studio art), biology, chemistry (biochemistry), communication (communication disorders and media studies), earth science, economics, English, French, geography, German, history, Italian, journalism, liberal studies, mathematics, media studies, music, philosophy, physics, political science, psychology, sociology, Spanish, and theater.

The Bachelor of Science degree is awarded in anthropology (archeology, cultural, general, linguistics, and physical), art (ceramics, graphic design, jewelry making, painting, photography, printmaking, and sculpture), athletic training, biology, business (accounting, business economics, finance, international business, management, managing information systems, and marketing), chemistry and biochemistry, communication (creative message construction, interpersonal/relational, organizational communication, and video production), computer science (information systems), earth science (environmental, geology, and oceanography), exercise science (human performance and teacher education), geography, information and library science, journalism, mathematics, nursing, physics, political science, psychology (research), public health (environmental and health promotion), recreation and leisure (community, outdoor, and therapeutic), social work, and sociology.

The Bachelor of Science degree with teaching certification is offered in art education, early childhood education, and elementary education.

The Bachelor of Science degree with certification for secondary education is offered in biology, chemistry, earth science, English, exercise science, French, geography, German, history and social science, Italian, mathematics, physics, political science, Spanish, sociology, and special education.

Southern also offers preprofessional study in dentistry, engineering, law, medicine, and veterinary medicine.

Academic Programs

The University operates on a two-semester calendar. The fall semester usually begins the first week in September and ends in mid-December. The spring semester, which includes a one-week spring recess in March, typically begins in mid-January and ends in mid-May. Southern also offers several summer session programs and an intersession program in January.

Southern maintains a strong commitment to the liberal arts and sciences as fundamental elements of a high-quality education. To ensure all students acquire the best education possible, Southern offers a strong yet flexible program that underscores the basics while encouraging individual choice. All baccalaureate degree candidates must complete a minimum of 122 hours of credit. Majors consist of at least 30 prescribed hours of credit in one specific, approved field. Degree candidates also must fulfill the liberal education program requirements. In addition, all bachelor's degree candidates must meet a foreign language requirement. Some professional B.S. degree programs enable students to develop a minor or a concentration in addition to the major with 12 credits in electives.

Off-Campus Programs

Southern's location in the heart of a major urban area enables the University to cultivate a growing list of meaningful regional internships. Aspiring social workers enjoy learning opportunities that extend beyond the classroom into New Haven's dynamic urban environment. Students in the B.S. nursing degree program acquire clinical experience at Yale–New Haven Hospital, the Hospital of Saint Raphael, and other sites that are linked by distance learning programs. Internships also are available for journalism students in city newsrooms and local TV stations. The University also offers internships at Long Wharf Theatre; ESPN Broadcasting; the Circle in the Square Theatre in New York City; MTV; Shearson Lehman Brothers, Inc.; and others.

Academic Facilities

A $260-million building program has transformed Southern campus life. The four-level, 125,000-square-foot Michael J. Adanti Student Center is a hub of campus life and includes a ballroom, movie theater, fitness center, an expansive bookstore, a food court, a TV lounge, and many meeting and conference rooms. A new home for the School of Business opened in summer 2012. Engleman Hall, the University's main academic building, was renovated and expanded to include state-of-the-art classrooms, departmental libraries, and conference rooms. A new wing has been added to the Hilton C. Buley Library. When renovations to the library are completed in 2013, the facility's size will be doubled.

Southern supports more than 100 campus clubs and organizations, ranging from academic and career groups to religious, theatrical, and political clubs.

All on-campus housing includes high-speed Internet service via RESNET. Other campus facilities include a satellite-equipped journalism lab; a modern television studio in the Ralph Earl Hall of Fine Arts; the John Lyman Center for the Performing Arts, a 1,650-seat theater for major productions; the Robert Kendall Drama Lab for experimental theater; the Center for the Environment; the Multicultural Center; the Communication Disorders Center; the Adaptive Technology Lab; and the Disability Resources Center.

Costs

Annual tuition and fees for 2011–12 for Connecticut residents were $8248. Tuition and fees for out-of-state residents were $18,872. On-campus room and board fees for the year were $10,232. Student books, supplies, and personal expenses average about $2000 per year. All costs are subject to change. Prospective students should contact the Office of Financial Aid and Scholarships for current information.

Financial Aid

The Office of Financial Aid and Scholarships coordinates grants, scholarships, long-term low-interest loans, and part-time student employment for students and families who demonstrate financial need. The University offers the Federal Perkins Loan, the Federal Pell Grant, the Federal Supplemental Educational Opportunity Grant, the Federal Stafford Student Loan, the Federal PLUS loan, and the Federal Work-Study Program. Southern also provides alumni scholarships. Southern's tuition installment plan enables matriculated students to make monthly tuition payments throughout the academic year. More than 60 percent of Southern's undergraduates receive financial aid. Students who seek assistance must complete the Free Application for Federal Student Aid (FAFSA) and send it to the central processor for receipt by March 1. Prospective students can file the FAFSA form on paper or on the Web at http://www.fafsa.ed.gov.

Faculty

Like the University's student body, Southern's faculty members represent a broad spectrum of backgrounds, interests, and scholarly achievements. Southern's more than 700 faculty members share a deep commitment to teaching, writing, and research. Of the more than 400 full-time faculty members, about 85 percent hold a Ph.D. or terminal degree from major colleges and universities around the world. Many faculty members serve as academic advisers. In addition, the University offers counseling to help students with academic, personal, and career decisions.

Student Government

The Student Government Association is the voice of the undergraduate student body at Southern. The organization's 24 voting members meet regularly to discuss students' interests in a variety of areas, such as funding and academic policies. Student Government Association members also serve with administrators and faculty members on key University committees. Residential students govern themselves through their respective residence hall councils and the Inter-Residence Council.

Admission Requirements

Southern's selective admission policy considers each student as an individual, with particular consideration given to personal accomplishments and motivation. Southern seeks students with diverse cultural values and backgrounds; no applicant is accepted or rejected because of race, color, gender, sexual orientation, age, disability, religion, or national origin. Candidates must be high school graduates or hold an equivalency diploma. Their secondary school program should include at least 13 academic units of college-preparatory work, including 4 years of English, 3 years of mathematics (algebra 1, geometry, and algebra 2), 2 years of foreign language, 2 years of science (including 1 year of laboratory science), and 2 years of social sciences (including U.S. history). Other factors include the student's high school record, class rank (preferably in the upper 50 percent), and competitive SAT or ACT scores.

Application and Information

Candidates for admission should apply early in the fall of their high school senior year. The Admissions Office mails its first acceptance notice in early December. Early applicants have priority for housing and financial aid. Applicants must submit academic records, including a complete transcript of high school grades and class rank; an online admission application; a $50 nonrefundable fee; a written recommendation from a high school principal, teacher, or school guidance counselor; and a copy of the SAT or ACT score report. For additional information, students should contact the Admissions House, Southern Connecticut State University, 131 Farnham Avenue, New Haven, Connecticut 06515. Students are encouraged to apply online by visiting the University's Web site and clicking on Admissions. Students can find more information about the University on Facebook and Twitter.

Paula Kennedy
Associate Director of Admissions
Admissions House
Southern Connecticut State University
131 Farnham Avenue
New Haven, Connecticut 06515-1355
Phone: 203-392-SCSU
   888-500-SCSU (toll-free)
Web site: http://www.SouthernCT.edu

Students walking over the footbridge in front of the Michael J. Adanti Student Center.

SOUTHERN NEW HAMPSHIRE UNIVERSITY

MANCHESTER, NEW HAMPSHIRE

The University

The prevailing wisdom at Southern New Hampshire University (SNHU) has always been that there are no limits to what students can achieve. As an institution, there are seemingly no limits to what SNHU can achieve as well.

SNHU has been named the twelfth most innovative company in the world by Fast Company, trailing huge global brands like Apple, Facebook, and HBO, but ranking ahead of industry giants like the NFL, Starbucks, and LinkedIn. SNHU was the only educational institution on the list, an impressive achievement for a university that is committed to consistently reinventing the way that education is delivered and received.

Academic programs are created with the real world in mind, so students are prepared to launch successful careers when they graduate. Classes are taught by highly credentialed faculty who have professional experience and remain current in their fields. Academic and personal support is readily available, both inside and outside the classroom. If students need help, faculty and staff will rally around them quickly.

The University operates on the belief that college should change students' lives, not break the bank—a private university education should be affordable. That's why financial aid has been increased. Students with high school GPAs of 2.5 and higher may receive up to $18,000 in grants and scholarships. About 90 percent of the students at SNHU receive some kind of financial aid.

The University has just over 2,500 traditional, full-time undergraduate day students, with a total enrollment in all divisions (day, evening, weekend, and online undergraduate and graduate students) of about 9,400. Programs are offered on campus, on location at the University's centers in New Hampshire and Maine, and online. SNHU offers undergraduate programs in business, culinary arts, education, hospitality, and liberal arts and graduate programs in business, education, and hospitality.

SNHU is the first carbon-neutral school in New Hampshire. The wireless campus features a new academic center, a new dining hall, new dorms and apartment buildings, a simulated stock trading room, multimedia classrooms, an auditorium, the museum-quality McIninch Art Gallery, virtual science labs, technology-ready buildings, a library with resources that can be accessed via the Internet, a fitness center that rivals private commercial gyms, athletic fields, cooking labs, a bakery, and an award-winning student-run restaurant.

Students can participate in one of the University's more than fifty student clubs or start new ones. Intercollegiate teams compete in Division II of the NCAA, and the Northeast-10 Conference. Sports include baseball, men's and women's basketball, cheerleading, men's and women's cross-country, golf, ice hockey, men's and women's lacrosse, men's and women's soccer, softball, men's and women's tennis, and volleyball. Intramural sports, including basketball, flag football, indoor soccer, and volleyball are also extremely popular. SNHU's powerful athletic teams dominate on the field—and in the classroom. The University's student-athletes earned honors from the NCAA and *USA Today* for high grades and 100 percent graduation rates.

Athletic facilities include an indoor, 25-meter, competition-size swimming pool; a racquetball court; an aerobic studio; cardiovascular equipment; four outdoor lighted tennis courts; a soccer/lacrosse turf field; baseball and softball fields; and two indoor gymnasiums with four basketball courts and areas for indoor soccer, indoor tennis, volleyball, and other activities. The fitness center has 4,000 square feet of strength equipment and a 1,500-square-foot cardio deck.

The Wellness Center provides short-term health care, health education, and counseling services for students, and the buildings and facilities are accessible to people with disabilities. A well-qualified student-services staff provides personal, career, and academic counseling; counselors are available on campus. Lifetime career services and counseling are available to all current students and to alumni.

Location

The University is ideally located, with easy access to downtown Manchester, New Hampshire's largest city. Manchester has also been named one of the top college towns in the country. Public transportation is available, and students may keep cars on campus. The mountains, beaches, and Boston are only an hour away. CQ Press has repeatedly named New Hampshire one of the nation's most livable states.

Majors and Degrees

The University has three schools: the School of Arts and Sciences, the School of Business, and the School of Education. The University offers associate, bachelor's, master's, and doctoral degrees. Undergraduate programs provide students with a strong liberal arts foundation and the knowledge and skills they need to succeed in their careers.

The School of Arts and Sciences offers degrees in communication, community sociology, computer information technology (B.A. option), creative writing (three-year option available), English language and literature, environmental management, environmental science, game design and development (B.A. option), graphic design and media arts, history, justice studies (three-year option available), justice studies/crime & criminology, justice studies/law & legal process, justice studies/policing & law enforcement , justice studies/terrorism & homeland security, liberal arts, mathematics, political science, psychology, psychology/child and adolescent development, forensic psychology, and psychology/mental health.

The School of Business majors include accounting, accounting/finance, accounting/information systems, baking & pastry arts (A.S.), business administration, business studies, computer information technology (B.S. option), culinary arts (A.S.), culinary management, fashion merchandising, finance/economics, game design and development (B.S. option), hospitality business, international business, management advisory services, marketing, sport management, technical management, and the unique 3Year Honors Program in Business—the only three-year program of its kind in the country. Students save a full year of tuition by acquiring a bachelor's degree in just three years. Customized and outcomes-based, it is not a condensed four-year degree program and does not require night, weekend, or summer course work. The six-semester, 120-credit program features an interdisciplinary course of study and offers fifteen specializations. Students can start their careers earlier or use the fourth year to complete a master's degree.

The School of Education majors include child development leadership, early childhood education, elementary education, English education, middle school mathematics education, middle school science education, music education social studies education, and special education.

An honors program, a prelaw program, and a pre-M.B.A. program are also available for students seeking additional challenges.

Academic Programs

At Southern New Hampshire University, undergraduate students receive a broad education in the liberal arts and intense practice in oral and written communication, coupled with the specific knowledge and skills they need to succeed in their chosen fields.

Recognizing that successful leaders must be able to view problems from a variety of perspectives, the University mandates that all students complete courses in writing, the fine arts, the social sciences, mathematics, science, and public speaking. Students also have the opportunity to take elective courses in whatever areas capture their curiosity and may elect to concentrate their electives to earn a minor. The University curriculum offers both structure and flexibility.

Off-Campus Programs

Southern New Hampshire University is adept at mixing academic theory with practical experience inside and outside the classroom. Undergraduates participate in off-campus cooperative education experiences/internships, earning 3 to 12 academic credits. Such opportunities are based on a student's major and career goals and typically are taken during a student's junior or senior year. Students work with faculty members and the Career Development Office to find appropriate assignments. About 70 percent of those who complete co-ops/internships are offered positions by their employers.

The University has established relationships with a number of respected, high-profile employers who provide internship and job opportunities, including Fidelity Investments, Google, IBM, New York Life, Walt Disney World, LEGO Systems, the Boston Celtics, the Boston Red Sox, and Marriott International.

Students also work with real-world off-campus partners in their courses. For example, marketing students have created media campaigns for area businesses and education students assist local teachers in their classrooms. The University's graduates are in demand because businesses know they have been prepared to contribute both on the job and in their communities.

Opportunities for studying abroad are available at a number of partnering institutions in 32 countries around the world.

Academic Facilities

The Harry A. B. and Gertrude C. Shapiro Library features the Education Resource Center, networked computers, conference rooms, a career and placement resource center, and a growing collection of bound volumes, microfilm, microfiche, and ultrafiche; materials are available online as well. A recording studio, a listening room, and a closed-circuit television network that covers the entire campus are among the school's audiovisual assets. SNHU is slated to break ground on a new library and learning commons in 2013.

Costs

Undergraduate tuition and fees for the 2012–13 academic year are $28,050. Typical room and board charges are an additional $10,900. Students should plan to budget funds for books, supplies, travel, and personal expenses.

All students are required to bring wireless laptop computers. Culinary arts students need to purchase uniforms and knife sets.

Financial Aid

More than 90 percent of the University's students receive some form of financial aid, which may include need-based grants, academic and commuter scholarships, work-study funds, and loans. The average aid package has a value of more than $20,605 and includes a combination of scholarships, grants, loans, and employment sources.

The University participates in the Federal Work-Study Program, the Federal Perkins Loan Program, and the Federal Supplemental Educational Opportunity Grant Program. The school is also eligible under the Federal Stafford Student Loan Program and the Federal Pell Grant Program. Aid applicants must complete the Free Application for Federal Student Aid (FAFSA). The OneStop/ Financial Aid Office can provide the appropriate forms, or students can go online to http://www.fafsa.ed.gov. Academic, athletic, and leadership scholarships are available for students who qualify.

Faculty

The University has more than 128 full-time faculty members and more than 200 part-time instructors. The student-faculty ratio is 15:1. Nearly 75 percent of the full-time faculty members hold Ph.D.'s or the equivalent in their areas of expertise.

The instructional programs blend theory with practice to stimulate students' professional development and personal growth. Faculty members bring extensive academic, work, travel, and life experiences to their classrooms. Although their primary goal is teaching, faculty members remain current in their disciplines. Outside the classroom, faculty members are management consultants, CPAs, analysts, small-business owners, economists, accountants, marketing professionals, entrepreneurs, innkeepers, chefs, world travelers, artists, poets, novelists, and much more.

Student Government

The Student Government Association is led by 25 students, including 5 officers, who represent all the students at the University. Its primary function is to represent the student body in campus affairs and to dispense student activity funds. One student is appointed to represent the student body on the Board of Trustees. Students are also appointed to most other standing committees, including the Financial Aid Advisory Committee, the Curriculum Advisory Committee, the Library Committee, and judiciary committees.

Admission Requirements

Applicants for admission are evaluated individually on the basis of academic credentials and personal characteristics. When reviewing applicants, primary emphasis is placed on a student's academic record, as demonstrated by the quality and level of college-preparatory course work and achievement attained. Most successful candidates admitted to SNHU present a program of study consisting of 16 college-preparatory courses, including 4 years of English, 3 or more years of mathematics, 2 or more years of science, and 2 or more years of social science. Separate consideration is given to admission decisions for transfer, culinary arts, 3Year Honors Program, nontraditional, and international applicants. Students may apply online at www.snhu.edu or via the Common Application.

Application and Information

Applicants for undergraduate day programs must submit an application (Common Application or online at www.snhu.edu/apply), college essay, $40 application fee, and the following application materials: official high school transcript, one letter of recommendation from a school counselor or teacher, and SAT/ACT Scores (optional). In addition, creative writing majors must submit a 10-page writing sample, music education majors must complete an audition, and 3Year Honors Program in business applicants must submit SAT/ACT scores and complete an interview with the program director.

Freshman applicants can apply before November 15 to be considered for the early action deadline. The University operates on a rolling admission basis, however there is a priority application deadline of March 15. As applications are reviewed, the first consideration is academic background. The University seeks well-rounded students who have a variety of interests and have been involved in school and/or community activities. Admission decisions are made within 30 days of receiving the required admission materials.

For more information about Southern New Hampshire University, students should contact:

Office of Undergraduate Admission
Southern New Hampshire University
2500 North River Road
Manchester, New Hampshire 03106-1045
Phone: 603-645-9611
    800-642-4968 (toll-free)
Fax: 603-645-9693
Web site: http://www.snhu.edu
    http://www.facebook.com/snhuoncampus
    http://www.twitter.com/snhuoncampus

At SNHU, students can study over forty majors in the schools of arts and sciences, business, and education.

SOUTH UNIVERSITY
AUSTIN, TEXAS

South University
Austin

The University

Established in 1899, South University is a private academic institution dedicated to providing educational opportunities for the intellectual, social, and professional development of a diverse student population. To achieve this, the University offers focused and balanced curricula at the associate and bachelor's degree levels in the areas of accounting, business, criminal justice, healthcare management, information technology, and psychology. In addition, the University offers a Master of Business Administration (M.B.A.) degree program.

South University in Austin has a diverse student body enrolled in day, evening, weekend, and online classes. South University is designed to accommodate the range of needs of its student body. Students are primarily commuters who live within 50 miles of the city. They include men and women who have either enrolled directly after completing high school, transferred from another college or university, or have experience in the workforce and are pursuing an education that will prepare them to expand their current position or help them take a new professional direction.

The campus facility of South University in Austin includes faculty offices, lecture classrooms and a computer lab space to support the campus. Since most students live within driving distance of the campus, the campus does not currently offer or operate student housing. However, housing is planned in the near future. If housing is needed, prospective students should contact the Admissions Office.

South University is accredited by the Southern Association of Colleges and Schools Commission on Colleges to award associate, baccalaureate, masters, and doctorate degrees. Contact the Commission on Colleges at 1866 Southern Lane, Decatur, Georgia 30033-4097 or call 404-679-4500 for questions about the accreditation of South University.

South University–Austin holds a Certificate of Authorization acknowledging exemptions from Texas Higher Education Coordinating Board regulations.

Location

The campus is conveniently located just off of West Parmer Lane near Round Rock just north of Austin. Students attending the Austin campus will gain a well-rounded educational and cultural experience as a result of the free-spirited, eclectic culture of this musically focused community. The Austin-Round Rock area is also considered a major center for high-tech advancement while also emerging as a hub for pharmaceutical and biotechnology companies.

Majors and Degrees

South University in Austin awards the following two-year degrees: Associate of Science in business administration, Associate of Science in accounting and Associate of Science in information technology.

The following four-year bachelor's degrees are awarded: Bachelor of Business Administration, Bachelor of Science in Criminal Justice, Bachelor of Science in healthcare management, Bachelor of Science in information technology, and Bachelor of Arts in psychology.

Academic Programs

South University offers degree programs that are designed to meet the needs and objectives of students. Each curriculum combines didactic and practical educational experiences that provide students with the academic background needed to pursue the professions of their choice. In addition, faculty members strive to instill the value not only of education and professionalism but also of contribution and commitment to the advancement of community.

South University operates on a quarter academic calendar, and each University quarter comprises eleven weeks. Associate degree programs require a minimum of eight quarters to complete, and bachelor's degree programs require a minimum of twelve quarters for completion. Programs are offered on a year-round basis, providing students with the ability to work uninterrupted toward their degrees. More importantly, students have the opportunity to take classes on campus, online, or a combination of both through South University's unique Plus+ program. Combining campus and online classes provides students with maximum flexibility, allowing them to organize their college education around their work and/or family commitments.

Academic Facilities

The library has wireless technology throughout, comfortable seating, and quiet study space. The collection includes books, print and online periodicals, CDs, videos, and numerous online proprietary databases. Materials are housed in circulating, reference, and reserve collections and have

been selected to support the academic programs. An online library portal with access to more than 60 databases in all disciplines is available electronically 24/7 on and off campus to all authorized students and faculty. More than 50,000 e-books, video clips, images and full-text dissertations are also included in the library's offerings.

Costs

For information about tuition and fees, prospective students should contact the South University Admissions Office.

Financial Aid

South University's Student Financial Services Office helps qualified students secure financial assistance to complete their studies. The University participates in several student aid programs.

Faculty

The South University in Austin faculty includes individuals of high academic distinction. In addition to teaching, faculty members strive to help students develop the requisites to appreciate knowledge and understand how experiences in the classroom and laboratory relate to professional performance in the workplace. The average student-faculty ratio per class is 13:1. Each student is assigned a faculty adviser, who oversees the student's progress and can answer questions about academic and career concerns. Students are encouraged to discuss program-related issues with and seek academic and career advice from their faculty advisers.

Admission Requirements

To be admitted to South University, prospective undergraduate students must be high school graduates or hold a GED certificate and submit an SAT or ACT score or a satisfactory score on the University-administered admissions examination. Transfer students must meet University-established criteria for acceptance as a transfer student.

All applicants must demonstrate English as a first language through submission of a diploma from a secondary school (or above) in which English is the official language of instruction. Applicants whose first language is not English must submit a Test of English as a Foreign Language (TOEFL) score. Applicants should contact the Admissions Office to determine other examinations/scores that are acceptable as an alternative to the TOEFL.

Applicants not meeting the entrance testing standards for general admission may be accepted under academic support admission.

Application and Information

Applicants must complete and submit an application form along with transcripts from high school and all colleges attended. Applicants must also complete all tests administered by the University or submit their SAT or ACT scores to the Registrar's Office. Applications are accepted on a rolling basis and should be submitted as far in advance as possible. Admissions officers are available weekdays, Saturdays, and by appointment. An appointment for an admissions interview or tour of the campus should be made in advance.

All international (nonimmigrant) applicants to South University must meet the same admissions standards as all other students. In addition, international applicants must have official educational records prepared in English, verify sufficient funds to cover the cost of the educational program, and meet certain other immigration-mandated criteria. South University in Austin is authorized under federal law to admit nonimmigrant students.

For more information, prospective students should contact:

Suzanne Melton
Senior Director of Admissions
South University
7700 West Parmer Lane
Building A, Suite A100
Austin, Texas 78729
Phone: 512-516-8800
　　　877-659-5706 (toll-free)
Fax: 512-516-8680
E-mail: smelton@southuniversity.edu
Web site: http://www.southuniversity.edu

See suprograms.info for program duration; tuition, fees, and other costs; median debt; federal salary data; alumni success; and other important information.

South University in Austin, Texas, has a diverse student body enrolled in day, evening, weekend, and online classes.

SOUTH UNIVERSITY
CLEVELAND, OHIO

The University

Established in 1899, South University is a private academic institution dedicated to providing educational opportunities for the intellectual, social, and professional development of a diverse student population. To achieve this, the University offers focused and balanced curricula at the associate and bachelor's degree levels in the areas of business, criminal justice, healthcare management, information technology, legal studies, paralegal studies, and psychology. In addition, the University offers a Master of Business Administration (M.B.A.), and Master of Arts in clinical mental health counseling degree program.

South University in Cleveland has a diverse student body enrolled in day, evening, weekend, and online classes. South University is designed to accommodate the range of needs of its student body. Students are primarily commuters who live within 50 miles of the city. They include men and women who have either enrolled directly after completing high school, transferred from another college or university, or have experience in the workforce and are pursuing an education that will prepare them to expand their current position or help them take a new professional direction.

The campus facility of South University in Cleveland includes faculty offices, lecture classrooms and a computer lab space to support the campus. Since most students live within driving distance of the campus, the campus does not currently offer or operate student housing. If housing is needed, prospective students should contact the Admissions Office.

South University is accredited by the Southern Association of Colleges and Schools Commission on Colleges to award associate, baccalaureate, masters, and doctorate degrees. Contact the Commission on Colleges at 1866 Southern Lane, Decatur, Georgia 30033-4097 or call 404-679-4500 for questions about the accreditation of South University.

South University – Cleveland is licensed by the Ohio State Board of Career colleges and Schools, 30 Broad Street, 24th Floor, Suite 2481, Columbus, OH, 43215; phone: 614-466-2752, registration number 11-07-1971T. The Cleveland campus also holds a Certificate of Authorization for its academic programs from the Ohio Board of Regents, 30 East Broad Street, Columbus, Ohio 43215; phone: 614-466-6000.

Legal and Paralegal Studies programs offered at South University's Cleveland, Novi, Richmond, and Virginia Beach campuses will not be eligible to apply for ABA approval until they have graduates and have been operating for at least two years.

Location

The city of Cleveland is situated on the shores of Lake Erie and is home to a diverse population. With its museums, theaters, amusement parks, historical monuments, zoo and ample recreational opportunities, there is never a dull moment in Cleveland. Students of South University – Cleveland will study in the heart of this bustling city that is fast becoming a presences in the financial, insurance, legal and healthcare industries.

Majors and Degrees

South University in Cleveland awards the following two-year degrees: Associate of Science in business administration, Associate of Science in criminal justice, Associate of Science in information technology, and Associate of Science in paralegal studies.

The following four-year bachelor's degrees are awarded: Bachelor of Business Administration, Bachelor of Science in criminal justice, Bachelor of Science in healthcare management, Bachelor of Science in information technology, Bachelor of Science in legal studies, and Bachelor of Arts in psychology.

Academic Programs

South University offers degree programs that are designed to meet the needs and objectives of students. Each curriculum combines didactic and practical educational experiences that provide students with the academic background needed to pursue the professions of their choice. In addition, faculty members strive to instill the value not only of education and professionalism but also of contribution and commitment to the advancement of community.

South University operates on a quarter academic calendar, and each University quarter comprises eleven weeks. Associate degree programs require a minimum of eight quarters to complete, and bachelor's degree programs require a minimum of twelve quarters for completion. Programs are offered on a year-round basis, providing students with the ability to work uninterrupted toward their degrees. More importantly, students have the opportunity to take classes on campus, online, or a combination of both through South University's unique Plus+ program. Combining campus and online classes provides students with maximum flexibility,

allowing them to organize their college education around their work and/or family commitments.

Academic Facilities

The library has wireless technology throughout, comfortable seating, and quiet study space. The collection includes books, print and online periodicals, CDs, videos, and numerous online proprietary databases. Materials are housed in circulating, reference, and reserve collections and have been selected to support the academic programs.

Costs

For information about tuition and fees, prospective students should contact the South University Admissions Office.

Financial Aid

South University's Student Financial Services Office helps qualified students secure financial assistance to complete their studies. The University participates in several student aid programs.

Faculty

The South University in Cleveland faculty includes individuals of high academic distinction. In addition to teaching, faculty members strive to help students develop the requisites to appreciate knowledge and understand how experiences in the classroom and laboratory relate to professional performance in the workplace. The average student-faculty ratio per class is 13:1. Each student is assigned a faculty adviser, who oversees the student's progress and can answer questions about academic and career concerns. Students are encouraged to discuss program-related issues with and seek academic and career advice from their faculty advisers.

Admission Requirements

To be admitted to South University, prospective undergraduate students must be high school graduates or hold a GED certificate and submit an SAT or ACT score or a satisfactory score on the University-administered admissions examination. Transfer students must meet University-established criteria for acceptance as a transfer student.

All applicants must demonstrate English as a first language through submission of a diploma from a secondary school (or above) in which English is the official language of instruction. Applicants whose first language is not English must submit a Test of English as a Foreign Language (TOEFL) score. Applicants should contact the Admissions Office to determine other examinations/scores that are acceptable as an alternative to the TOEFL.

Applicants not meeting the entrance testing standards for general admission may be accepted under academic support admission.

Application and Information

Applicants must complete and submit an application form along with transcripts from high school and all colleges attended. Applicants must also complete all tests administered by the University or submit their SAT or ACT scores to the Registrar's Office. Applications are accepted on a rolling basis and should be submitted as far in advance as possible. Admissions officers are available weekdays, Saturdays, and by appointment. An appointment for an admissions interview or tour of the campus should be made in advance.

All international (nonimmigrant) applicants to South University must meet the same admissions standards as all other students. In addition, international applicants must have official educational records prepared in English, verify sufficient funds to cover the cost of the educational program, and meet certain other immigration-mandated criteria. South University in Cleveland is authorized under federal law to admit nonimmigrant students.

For additional information, students should contact:

Sarah Benko
Senior Director of Admissions
South University
4743 Richmond Road
Cleveland, Ohio 44128
Phone: 216-755-5000
     855-398-9280 (toll-free)
Fax: 216-755-5190
E-mail: sbenko@southuniversity.edu
Web site: http://www.southuniversity.edu

See suprograms.info for program duration; tuition, fees, and other costs; median debt; federal salary data; alumni success; and other important information.

South University in Cleveland, Ohio, has a diverse student body enrolled in day, evening, weekend, and online classes.

SOUTH UNIVERSITY
COLUMBIA, SOUTH CAROLINA

South University
Columbia

The University

Established in 1899, South University is a private academic institution dedicated to providing educational opportunities for the intellectual, social, and professional development of a diverse student population. The Columbia, South Carolina campus offers focused and balanced curricula at the associate and bachelor's degree levels in the areas of business, criminal justice, graphic design, healthcare management, health science, information technology, legal studies, nursing, R.N. to B.S.N. nursing degree completion, paralegal studies, and psychology. Other degree programs offered at South University in Columbia include a Master of Arts in Clinical Mental Health Counseling; a Master of Business Administration (M.B.A.); a Master of Science in criminal justice; and a Master of Business Administration in healthcare administration, both in traditional and twelve-month accelerated programs; and a Doctor of Pharmacy (Pharm.D.).

In addition, the Columbia campus offers students flexible scheduling with the choice of pursuing many of its courses on campus, online, or a combination of both through South University's unique Plus+ program. Combining campus and online classes provides students with maximum flexibility, allowing them to organize their college education around their work and/or family commitments. Most students live within driving distance of the campus, but the Admissions Office does maintain information on various housing options should students relocate to the Columbia area for their education.

South University has a diverse student body enrolled in day, evening, and weekend classes. A sizeable portion of students have experience in the workforce and are pursuing an education that will prepare them to expand on their current career or take them in a new professional direction.

South University is accredited by the Southern Association of Colleges and Schools Commission on Colleges to award associate, baccalaureate, masters, and doctorate degrees. Contact the Commission on Colleges at 1866 Southern Lane, Decatur, Georgia 30033-4097 or call 404-679-4500 for questions about the accreditation of South University.

South University in Columbia is licensed by the South Carolina Commission on Higher Education, 1122 Lady Street, Suite 300, Columbia, South Carolina 29201; phone: 803-737-8860. The Columbia campus is also chartered by the state of South Carolina and approved by the South Carolina Commission on Higher Education (Veterans' Education Section) for the training of veterans and other eligible persons.

Certain programs offered at South University in Columbia have earned programmatic accreditation. South University's Doctor of Pharmacy program is accredited by the Accreditation Council for Pharmacy Education, 20 North Clark Street, Suite 2500, Chicago, Illinois 60602-5109; phone: 312-664-3575; fax: 312-664-4652; Web site: http://www.acpeaccredit.org. The school is a member of the American Association of Colleges of Pharmacy (AACP). The South University Associate of Science degree in medical assisting is accredited by the Commission on Accreditation of Allied Health Education Programs (CAAHEP) (http://www.caahep.org) upon the recommendation of the Medical Assisting Education Review Board (MAERB) Commission on Accreditation of Allied Health Education Programs, 1361 Park

Street, Clearwater, Florida 33756; phone: 727-210-2350. The South Carolina State Board of Nursing has granted South University approval to accept qualified applicants for admission into the nursing program.

The nursing programs are also accredited by the Commission on Collegiate Nursing Education (CCNE), One DuPont Circle NW, Suite 530, Washington, D.C. 20036; phone: 202-887-6791; www.aacn.nche.edu.

The Bachelor of Science in legal studies and Associate of Science in paralegal studies are both approved by the American Bar Association, 321 North Clark Street, Chicago, Illinois 60654; phone: 312-988-5522.

Location

South University's Columbia campus relocated to the Carolina Research Park in northeast Columbia in fall 2006. The campus features spacious classrooms, multiple computer labs, a fully equipped medical lab, and a student lounge. The campus is located just minutes from downtown in the Carolina Research Park off I-77 at Farrow Road and Park Lane.

The campus surroundings are highlighted by a natural wooded landscape and vast green space featuring a tranquil campus courtyard. Convenient to malls, shopping, and the growing northeast side of Columbia, the new campus location provides easier access to students from throughout the greater Columbia area.

Majors and Degrees

South University in Columbia awards the following two-year degrees: Associate of Science in business administration, Associate of Science in graphic design, Associate of Science in information technology, Associate of Science in medical assisting, and Associate of Science in paralegal studies.

The following four-year bachelor's degrees are awarded: Bachelor of Business Administration, Bachelor of Science in criminal justice, Bachelor of Science in graphic design, Bachelor of Science in healthcare management, Bachelor of Science in health science, Bachelor of Science in information technology, Bachelor of Science in legal studies, Bachelor of Science in Nursing, Bachelor of Science in Nursing (R.N. to B.S.N. degree completion program), and Bachelor of Arts in psychology.

Academic Programs

South University in Columbia offers degree programs that are designed to meet the needs and objectives of students. Each curriculum combines didactic and practical educational experiences that provide students with the academic background needed to pursue the professions of their choice. In addition, faculty members strive to instill the value not only of education and professionalism but also of contribution and commitment to the advancement of community.

Each University quarter comprises eleven weeks. Associate degree programs require a minimum of eight quarters to complete, and bachelor's degree programs require a minimum of twelve quarters to complete. Programs are offered on a year-round basis, providing students with the ability to work uninterrupted toward their degrees.

Academic Facilities

South University's multimillion-dollar Columbia campus provides ample classroom and student service areas and features several smart classrooms with audiovisual technology. The campus also contains a tiered lecture hall with videoconferencing capability, a fully equipped medical lab, multiple computer labs featuring PC and Mac computers, and more.

The library houses a large collection that includes an extensive legal library. Students may retrieve periodicals in paper or electronic form. Students may also access several commercial online services, including Westlaw, the computerized legal research service; LIRN; SearchBank; Infotract; UMI ProQuest; and the Electronic Library. Internet access is available on all computers throughout the campus.

Costs

Information about tuition and fees can be obtained by contacting the South University Admissions Office.

Financial Aid

South University's Office of Student Financial Services helps qualified students secure financial assistance to complete their studies. The University participates in several student aid programs.

Faculty

The South University faculty includes individuals of high academic distinction. Of the nearly 60 instructors on the campus, 46 percent hold terminal degrees in their fields of expertise. In addition to teaching, faculty members strive to help students develop the requisites to appreciate knowledge and understand how experiences in the classroom and laboratory relate to professional performance in the workplace. The average student-faculty ratio per class is 14:1. Each student is assigned a faculty adviser, who oversees the student's progress and can answer questions about academic and career concerns. Students are encouraged to discuss program-related issues with and seek academic and career advice from their faculty adviser.

Admission Requirements

To be admitted to South University, prospective students must be high school graduates or hold a GED certificate and submit SAT or ACT scores or achieve a satisfactory score on the University-administered admissions examination. Students who wish to transfer must meet the criteria established for acceptance as a transfer student.

All applicants to South University in Columbia must demonstrate English as a first language through submission of a diploma from a secondary school (or above) in which English is the official language of instruction. Applicants whose first language is not English must submit a Test of English as a Foreign Language (TOEFL) score. Applicants should contact the Admissions Office to determine other examinations/scores that are acceptable as an alternative to the TOEFL.

General admission to the University does not guarantee admission to the nursing program. To obtain specific entrance requirements for the nursing program, prospective students should contact the campus Admissions Office or visit the South University Web site.

Application and Information

Applicants must complete and submit an application form, along with the general application fee, and official transcripts from all high schools and colleges attended. Applicants must also complete all tests administered by the University or submit their SAT or ACT scores to the Registrar's Office. Applications are accepted on a rolling basis and should be submitted as far in advance as possible.

All international (nonimmigrant) applicants to South University must meet the same admissions standards as all other students. In addition, international applicants must have official education records prepared in English, verify sufficient funds to cover the cost of the educational program, and meet certain other immigration-mandated criteria. South University in Columbia is authorized under federal law to admit nonimmigrant students.

Admissions officers are available weekdays, Saturdays, and by appointment. An appointment for an admissions interview or a tour of the campus should be made in advance.

For additional information, all prospective students should contact:

Trisha Wade
Director of Admissions
South University
9 Science Court
Columbia, South Carolina 29203-6443
Phone: 803-799-9082
        866-629-3031 (toll-free)
Fax: 803-935-4382
E-mail: twade@southuniversity.edu
Web site: http://www.southuniversity.edu

See suprograms.info for program duration; tuition, fees, and other costs; median debt; federal salary data; alumni success; and other important information.

South University is located on the fast-growing northeast side of Columbia, South Carolina.

SOUTH UNIVERSITY
MONTGOMERY, ALABAMA

The University

Established in 1899, South University is a private academic institution dedicated to providing educational opportunities for the intellectual, social, and professional development of a diverse student population. To achieve this, the University offers focused and balanced curricula at the associate, bachelor's, and master's degree levels in the areas of business, criminal justice, healthcare management, health science, information technology, legal studies, medical assisting, nursing, R.N. to B.S.N. nursing degree completion, paralegal studies, physical therapist assisting, and psychology. In addition, the University offers a Master of Science in Nursing, with a Family Nurse Practitioner specialization, a Master of Science in Criminal Justice, a Master of Arts degree in Clinical Mental Health Counseling, a Master of Business Administration, and a Master of Business Administration in healthcare administration.

South University in Montgomery became part of South University in 1997 and has been part of the postsecondary education community in Alabama since 1887.

South University in Montgomery has a diverse student body enrolled in day, evening, weekend, and online classes. South University is designed to accommodate the range of needs of its student body. Students are primarily commuters who live within 50 miles of the city. They include men and women who have either enrolled directly after completing high school or transferred from another college or university, or have experience in the workforce and are pursuing an education that will prepare them to expand their current position or help them take a new professional direction.

South University in Montgomery is located in two buildings on a 3.75-acre campus. The facilities house computer, health science, and nursing labs; classrooms; a library; a student lounge; a bookstore; and faculty and administrative offices. Since most students live within driving distance of the campus, the campus does not currently offer or operate student housing. However, housing is planned in the near future. If housing is needed, prospective students should contact the Admissions Office.

South University is accredited by the Southern Association of Colleges and Schools Commission on Colleges to award associate, baccalaureate, masters, and doctorate degrees. Contact the Commission on Colleges at 1866 Southern Lane, Decatur, Georgia 30033-4097 or call 404-679-4500 for questions about the accreditation of South University.

South University in Montgomery is authorized as an educational institution in the state of Alabama under Act No. 80-272, Regular Session, Alabama Legislature, 1980, to conduct programs within the state of Alabama. The institution is also authorized by the State Approving Agency for the training of veterans under chapters 31, 34, and 35.

Certain programs offered at South University in Montgomery have earned programmatic accreditation. The Alabama Board of Nursing has authorized the Bachelor of Science in Nursing degree program to operate by the Alabama Board of Nursing. The nursing program is also accredited by the commission on Collegiate Nursing Education (CCNE), One DuPont Circle

NW, Suite 530, Washington, D.C. 20036; phone: 202-887-6791; www.aacn.nche.edu. The Associate of Science degree program in medical assisting is accredited by the Commission on Accreditation of Allied Health Education Programs (CAAHEP, 1361 Park Street, Clearwater, Florida 33756; 727-210-2350) on recommendation of the Curriculum Review Board of the American Association of Medical Assistants Endowment (AAMAE). The Bachelor of Science in legal studies and Associate of Science in paralegal studies degree programs are approved by the American Bar Association (321 North Clark Street, Chicago, Illinois 60654; 312-988-5522). The Associate of Science in physical therapist assisting degree program is an expansion program accredited by the Commission on Accreditation in Physical Therapy Education of the American Physical Therapy Association (1111 North Fairfax Street, Alexandria, Virginia 22314; 703-684-2782).

Location

The campus is located on the rapidly growing east side of Alabama's capital city. As the state capital, Montgomery is a hub of government, banking, and law as well as a state center for culture and entertainment. Montgomery is situated in the middle of the southeastern U.S. and is less than a 3-hour drive from Atlanta and the Gulf of Mexico.

Majors and Degrees

South University in Montgomery awards the following two-year degrees: Associate of Science in business administration, Associate of Science in information technology, Associate of Science in medical assisting, Associate of Science in paralegal studies, and Associate of Science in physical therapist assisting.

The following four-year bachelor's degrees are awarded: Bachelor of Business Administration, Bachelor of Science in criminal justice, Bachelor of Science in healthcare management, Bachelor of Science in information technology, Bachelor of Science in legal studies, Bachelor of Science in health science, Bachelor of Science in Nursing, Bachelor of Science in nursing (R.N. to B.S.N. degree completion program), and Bachelor of Arts in psychology.

Academic Programs

South University offers degree programs that are designed to meet the needs and objectives of students. Each curriculum combines didactic and practical educational experiences that provide students with the academic background needed to pursue the professions of their choice. In addition, faculty members strive to instill the value not only of education and professionalism but also of contribution and commitment to the advancement of community.

South University operates on a quarter academic calendar, and each University quarter comprises eleven weeks. Associate degree programs require a minimum of eight quarters to complete, and bachelor's degree programs require a minimum of twelve quarters for completion. Programs are offered on a year-round basis, providing students with the ability to work uninterrupted toward their degrees. More importantly, students have the opportunity to take classes on campus, online, or a combination of both through South University's

unique Plus+ program. Combining campus and online classes provides students with maximum flexibility, allowing them to organize their college education around their work and/or family commitments.

Academic Facilities

The library has wireless technology throughout, comfortable seating, and quiet study space. The collection includes books, print and online periodicals, CDs, videos, and numerous online proprietary databases. Materials are housed in circulating, reference, and reserve collections and have been selected to support the academic programs. Also for student use, the library has a modern computer lab complete with Internet access, online database services, and an office suite.

Costs

For information about tuition and fees, prospective students should contact the South University Admissions Office.

Financial Aid

South University's Student Financial Services Office helps qualified students secure financial assistance to complete their studies. The University participates in several student aid programs.

Faculty

The South University in Montgomery faculty includes individuals of high academic distinction. Of the more than 40 instructors, 38 percent hold terminal degrees within their fields of expertise. In addition to teaching, faculty members strive to help students develop the requisites to appreciate knowledge and understand how experiences in the classroom and laboratory relate to professional performance in the workplace. The average student-faculty ratio per class is 13:1. Each student is assigned a faculty adviser, who oversees the student's progress and can answer questions about academic and career concerns. Students are encouraged to discuss program-related issues with and seek academic and career advice from their faculty advisers.

Admission Requirements

To be admitted to South University, prospective undergraduate students must be high school graduates or hold a GED certificate and submit an SAT or ACT score or a satisfactory score on the University-administered admissions examination. Transfer students must meet University-established criteria for acceptance as a transfer student.

All applicants must demonstrate English as a first language through submission of a diploma from a secondary school (or above) in which English is the official language of instruction. Applicants whose first language is not English must submit a Test of English as a Foreign Language (TOEFL) score. Applicants should contact the Admissions Office to determine other examinations/scores that are acceptable as an alternative to the TOEFL.

Applicants not meeting the entrance testing standards for general admission may be accepted under academic support admission. General admission to the University does not guarantee admission to the nursing program. To obtain specific entrance requirements for the nursing program, prospective students should contact the campus Admissions Office or visit the South University Web site.

Application and Information

Applicants must complete and submit an application form along with transcripts from high school and all colleges attended. Applicants must also complete all tests administered by the University or submit their SAT or ACT scores to the Registrar's Office. Applications are accepted on a rolling basis and should be submitted as far in advance as possible. Admissions officers are available weekdays, Saturdays, and by appointment. An appointment for an admissions interview or tour of the campus should be submitted in advance.

All international (nonimmigrant) applicants to South University must meet the same admissions standards as all other students. In addition, international applicants must have official educational records prepared in English, verify sufficient funds to cover the cost of the educational program, and meet certain other immigration-mandated criteria. South University in Montgomery is authorized under federal law to admit nonimmigrant students.

For additional information, prospective students should contact:

Anna Pearson
Director of Admissions
South University
5355 Vaughn Road
Montgomery, Alabama 36116-1120
Phone: 334-395-8800
      866-629-2962 (toll-free)
Fax: 334-395-8859
E-mail: apearson@southuniversity.edu
Web site: http://www.southuniversity.edu

See suprograms.info for program duration; tuition, fees, and other costs; median debt; federal salary data; alumni success; and other important information.

South University in Montgomery, Alabama, has a diverse student body enrolled in day, evening, weekend, and online classes.

SOUTH UNIVERSITY
NOVI, MICHIGAN

The University

Established in 1899, South University is a private academic institution dedicated to providing educational opportunities for the intellectual, social, and professional development of a diverse student population. The Novi, Michigan campus offers focused and balanced curricula at the associate's degree level in the areas of business administration and information technology and the bachelor's degree level in the areas of business administration, criminal justice, healthcare management, information technology, legal studies, an RN to BSN degree completion program, and psychology. Other degree programs offered at South University in Novi include a Master of Arts in Clinical Mental Health Counseling, Master of Science in Criminal Justice, Master of Science in Nursing with a specialization in Family Nurse Practitioner, and a Master of Business Administration.

In addition, the Novi campus offers students flexible scheduling with the choice of pursuing many of its courses on campus, online, or a combination of both, through South University's unique Plus+ program. Combining campus and online classes provides students with maximum flexibility, allowing them to organize their college education around their work and/or family commitments. Most students live within driving distance of the campus, but the Admissions Office does maintain information on various housing options should students relocate to the Novi area for their education.

South University has a diverse student body enrolled in day, evening, and weekend classes. A sizeable portion of students have experience in the workforce and are pursuing an education that will prepare them to expand on their current career or take them in a new professional direction.

South University is accredited by the Southern Association of Colleges and Schools Commission on Colleges to award associate, baccalaureate, masters, and doctorate degrees. Contact the Commission on Colleges at 1866 Southern Lane, Decatur, Georgia 30033-4097 or call 404-679-4500 for questions about the accreditation of South University.

South University in Novi is licensed under the laws of the Michigan Department of Energy, Labor, and Economic Growth to award bachelor's and master's degrees.

Location

South University's Novi campus occupies more than 30,000 square feet of a new building located at 41555 Twelve Mile Road in Novi, Michigan. The campus features spacious classrooms, a computer lab, nursing lab, health science lab, and physical therapy lab. The campus is located northwest of Detroit near the Ann Arbor area.

Majors and Degrees

South University in Novi awards the following two-year associate's degrees: Associate of Science in business administration and Associate of Science in information technology, and the following four-year bachelor's degrees: Bachelor of Business Administration, Bachelor of Science in criminal justice, Bachelor of Science in healthcare management, Bachelor of Science in information technology, Bachelor of Science in Nursing for the RN to BSN degree completion program, and Bachelor of Arts in psychology.

Academic Programs

South University in Novi offers degree programs that are designed to meet the needs and objectives of students. Each curriculum combines didactic and practical educational experiences that provide students with the academic background needed to pursue the professions of their choice. In addition, faculty members strive to instill the value not only of education and professionalism but also of contribution and commitment to the advancement of community.

Each University quarter comprises eleven weeks. Bachelor's degree programs require a minimum of twelve quarters to complete. Programs are offered on a year-round basis, providing students with the ability to work uninterrupted toward their degrees.

Academic Facilities

South University's Novi campus provides ample classroom and student service areas and features wireless technology, video conferencing equipment, smart classroom technology, and student computer labs.

The library at Novi is designed to provide comfortable seating and quiet study space. The library's collection includes print and online books, periodicals, journals, CDs, videos, newspapers and numerous databases.

Costs

Information about tuition and fees can be obtained by contacting the South University Admissions Office.

Financial Aid

South University's Office of Student Financial Services helps qualified students secure financial assistance to complete their studies. The University participates in several student aid programs.

Faculty

The South University faculty includes individuals of high academic distinction. In addition to teaching, faculty members strive to help students develop the requisites to appreciate knowledge and understand how experiences in the classroom and laboratory relate to professional performance in the workplace. The average student-faculty ratio is 14:1. Each student is assigned a faculty adviser who oversees the student's progress and can answer questions about academic and career concerns. Students are encouraged to discuss program-related issues with and seek academic and career advice from their faculty advisers.

Admission Requirements

To be admitted to South University, prospective students must be high school graduates or hold a GED certificate and submit SAT or ACT scores or a satisfactory score on the University-administered admissions examination. Students who wish to transfer must meet the criteria established for acceptance as a transfer student.

All applicants to South University in Novi must demonstrate English as a first language through submission of a diploma from a secondary school (or above) in which English is the official language of instruction. Applicants whose first language is not English must submit a Test of English as a Foreign Language (TOEFL) score. Applicants should contact the Admissions Office to determine other examinations/scores that are acceptable as an alternative to the TOEFL.

Applicants not meeting the testing standards for general admission may be accepted under academic support admission.

Application and Information

Applicants must complete and submit an application form, along with the general application fee, and official transcripts from all high schools and colleges attended. Faxed documents are not considered official. Applicants must also complete all tests administered by the University or submit their SAT or ACT scores to the Registrar's Office. Applications are accepted on a rolling basis and should be submitted as far in advance as possible.

All international (nonimmigrant) applicants to South University must meet the same admissions standards as all other students. In addition, international applicants must have official education records prepared in English, verify sufficient funds to cover the cost of the educational program, and meet certain other immigration-mandated criteria. South University in Novi is authorized under federal law to admit nonimmigrant students.

Admissions officers are available weekdays, Saturdays, and weekends. An appointment for an admissions interview or tour of the campus should be made in advance.

For additional information, prospective students should contact:

Gary Malisos
Director of Admissions
South University
41555 Twelve Mile Road
Novi, Michigan 48377
Phone: 248-675-0200
       877-693-2085(toll-free)
Fax: 248-675-0190
E-mail: gmalisos@southuniversity.edu
Web site: http://www.southuniversity.edu

See suprograms.info for program duration; tuition, fees, and other costs; median debt; federal salary data; alumni success; and other important information.

South University–Novi islocated in Novi, Michigan, a suburb of northwest Detroit, convenient to shopping, restaurants, and cultural and entertainment venues.

SOUTH UNIVERSITY
RICHMOND, VIRGINIA

The University

South University is a private academic institution dedicated to providing educational opportunities for the intellectual, social, and professional development of a diverse student population. To achieve this, the Richmond campus offers focused and balanced curricula at the associate and bachelor's degree levels in the areas of business, criminal justice, health science, healthcare management, paralegal studies, information technology and nursing, R.N. to B.S.N. nursing degree completion, legal studies, and psychology. In addition, the campus offers a Master of Arts in professional counseling, a Master of Arts in Clinical Mental Health Counseling, and a Master of Business Administration (M.B.A.) program.

South University traces its heritage back to 1899 and today has grown into a multicampus system with locations in Columbia, South Carolina; Montgomery, Alabama; Novi, Michigan; Savannah, Georgia; Richmond and Virginia Beach, Virginia; Cleveland, OH; Austin, Texas; and Tampa and West Palm Beach, Florida.

Students can also pursue degrees through a combination of on-campus and online classes as part of the University's unique Plus+ program, which provides maximum scheduling flexibility. This flexibility allows students to organize their college education around work and family commitments. For those who choose to take on-site courses, Richmond campus facilities and amenities include a bookstore, student lounge, wireless Internet access, and ample parking in addition to classrooms, labs, and offices.

The University strives to maintain small class sizes that permit students to receive individualized instruction and interaction with faculty and staff members.

The Richmond campus of South University has a diverse student body enrolled in day, evening, and weekend classes. Most students live within driving distance of the campus, but the Admissions Office does maintain information on various housing options should students relocate to the Richmond area for their education. The student body includes men and women who have either enrolled directly after completing high school or transferred from another college or university, or have experience in the workforce and are pursuing an education that will prepare them to grow in their current position or enable them to take a new professional direction.

South University is accredited by the Southern Association of Colleges and Schools Commission on Colleges to award associate, baccalaureate, masters, and doctorate degrees. Contact the Commission on Colleges at 1866 Southern Lane, Decatur, Georgia 30033-4097 or call 404-679-4500 for questions about the accreditation of South University. South University's Richmond campus is certified to operate in Virginia by the State Council for Higher Education in Virginia, James Monroe Building, 101 North Fourteenth Street, Richmond, Virginia 23219; phone: 804-225-2600.

The Bachelor of Science in nursing program is accredited by the Commission on Collegiate Nursing Education (CCNE), One DuPont Circle NW, Suite 530, Washington, D.C. 20036-1120; phone: 202-887-6791; www.aacn.nche.edu. Legal and Paralegal Studies programs offered at South University's Novi, Richmond, and Virginia Beach campuses will not be eligible to apply for ABA approval until they have graduates and have been operating for at least two years.

Location

South University Richmond is located in the West Broad Development in Glen Allen, Virginia, minutes from downtown Richmond and the area's cultural activities. The campus is situated in a vibrant and convenient community of mixed-use living space where shopping and restaurants are within a short walk.

Majors and Degrees

The Richmond campus of South University offers two-year Associate of Science degrees in the following areas of study: business administration, information technology, criminal justice, and paralegal studies.

Four-year degree programs include a Bachelor of Business Administration, Bachelor of Science in criminal justice, Bachelor of Science in healthcare management, Bachelor of Science in health science, Bachelor of Science in information technology, Bachelor of Science in legal studies, Bachelor of Science in nursing, Bachelor of Science in nursing (R.N. to B.S.N. degree completion for current registered nurses), and Bachelor of Arts in psychology.

Academic Programs

The Richmond campus of South University offers degree programs that are designed to meet the needs and objectives of students. Each curriculum combines classroom and practical educational experiences that provide students with the academic background needed to pursue the professions of their choice. In addition, faculty members strive to instill the value not only of education and professionalism but also of contribution and commitment to the advancement of community.

South University operates on a quarter system, with each quarter comprising eleven weeks. Associate degree programs require a minimum of eight quarters to complete, and bachelor's degree programs require a minimum of twelve quarters for completion. Undergraduate programs are offered on a year-round basis, providing students with the ability to work uninterrupted toward their degrees.

Academic Facilities

The Richmond campus library provides individual and group study areas, a computer lab, and a diversified collection of online, audiovisual, and printed materials. Professional librarians are available during all hours of operation to provide assistance in locating information and materials at South

University libraries and at other libraries. The collections include books, magazines, audiovisual, and digital sources that support class assignments, tutorial needs, current events, and recreational reading. The computer lab offers Internet access, online databases with indexing and full text access to thousands of journals, tutorial programs, and an office suite of software programs. Internet access is available on all computers throughout the campus and the University offers wireless Internet access through an on-campus Wi-Fi network.

Costs

Tuition information is available by contacting the South University Admissions Department.

Financial Aid

South University's Student Financial Services Office helps qualified students secure financial assistance to complete their studies. The University participates in several student aid programs.

Faculty

The South University faculty includes individuals of high academic distinction. In addition to teaching, faculty members strive to help students develop the requisites to appreciate knowledge and understand how experiences in the classroom and laboratory relate to professional performance in the workplace. The average student-faculty ratio is 14:1. Each student is assigned a faculty adviser who oversees the student's progress and can answer questions about academic and career concerns. Students are encouraged to discuss program-related issues with and seek academic and career advice from their faculty advisers.

Admission Requirements

To be admitted to South University, prospective students must be high school graduates or hold a GED certificate and submit an appropriate SAT or ACT score (students should contact the Admissions Office) or a satisfactory score on the University-administered placement examination. Students who wish to transfer must meet the criteria established for acceptance as a transfer student.

All applicants to South University must demonstrate English proficiency. Students may furnish proof of English-as-a-first-language competency through submission of a diploma from a secondary school (or higher level) in which English is the official language of instruction. Applicants whose first language is not English must submit Test of English as a Foreign Language (TOEFL) scores. Applicants should contact the Admissions Office to determine other examinations/scores that are acceptable as an alternative to the TOEFL.

Applicants not meeting the testing standards for general admission may be accepted under academic support admission. General admission to the University does not guarantee admission to the nursing program. To obtain specific entrance requirements for the nursing program, prospective students should contact the campus Admissions Office or visit the South University Web site.

Application and Information

Applicants must complete an application form and submit it along with the general application fee as well as official transcripts from all high schools and colleges attended. Faxed documents are not considered official. Applicants must also complete all tests administered by the University or submit their SAT or ACT scores to the Registrar's Office. Applications are accepted on a rolling basis and should be submitted as far in advance as possible.

All international (nonimmigrant) applicants to South University must meet the same admissions standards as all other students. In addition, international applicants must have official educational records prepared in English, verify sufficient funds to cover the cost of the educational program, and meet certain other immigration-mandated criteria. South University in Richmond is authorized under federal law to admit nonimmigrant students.

Admissions officers are available weekdays, Saturdays, and by appointment. An appointment for an admissions interview or tour of the campus should be made in advance.

For additional information, all prospective students should contact:

Susan Miller
Director of Admissions
South University
2151 Old Brick Road
Glen Allen, Virginia 23060
Phone: 804-727-6800
       888-422-5076 (toll-free)
Fax: 804-727-6790
E-mail: sumiller@southuniversity.edu
Web site: http://www.southuniversity.edu

See suprograms.info for program duration; tuition, fees, and other costs; median debt; federal salary data; alumni success; and other important information.

South University at Richmond is located in Glen Allen, Virginia, at West Broad Village, a mixed-use area of residents, shopping, and restaurants.

SOUTH UNIVERSITY
SAVANNAH, GEORGIA

The University

South University is a private academic institution dedicated to providing educational opportunities for the intellectual, social, and professional development of a diverse student population. To achieve this, the Savannah campus offers focused and balanced curricula at the associate and bachelor's degree level including, but not limited to, the areas of business, medical assisting, nursing, R.N. to B.S.N. and R.N. to M.S.N. nursing degree completion, criminal justice, information technology, paralegal studies, physical therapist assisting, and psychology. The University also offers master's degree programs in anesthesiology assistant studies, physician assistant studies, and healthcare administration. In addition, the campus offers a Master of Science in Nursing with Family Nurse Practitioner and Nurse Educator specializations; a Master of Arts in Clinical Mental Health Counseling and a Master of Arts in professional counseling; a Master of Business Administration (M.B.A.) and Master of Business Administration in healthcare administration, both in traditional and twelve-month accelerated programs; and a Doctor of Pharmacy degree through its School of Pharmacy—one of only three programs in the state of Georgia and the only one in the state that is currently available in an accelerated three-year format. South University is the first university or college in Savannah to offer a health professions doctoral degree program.

South University traces its heritage back to 1899 and today has grown into a multicampus system with locations in Columbia, South Carolina; Montgomery, Alabama; Novi, Michigan; Richmond and Virginia Beach, Virginia; Savannah, Georgia; Cleveland, Ohio; Austin, Texas; and Tampa and West Palm Beach, Florida.

Students can also pursue degrees through a combination of on-campus and online classes as part of the University's unique Plus+ program, which provides maximum scheduling flexibility. This flexibility allows students to organize their college education around work and family commitments. For those who choose to take on-site courses, Savannah campus facilities and amenities include a bookstore, student lounges, a career services center, wireless Internet access, and ample parking in addition to classrooms and offices.

The cornerstone of the Savannah campus is the School of Pharmacy building, which joins the College of Business and College of Health Professions buildings. The University strives to maintain small class sizes that permit students to receive individualized instruction and interaction with faculty and staff members.

The Savannah campus of South University has a diverse student body enrolled in day, evening, and weekend classes. Undergraduate students are primarily commuters who live within 60 miles of the city. Graduate students come from across the contiguous United States and as far away as Alaska. They include men and women who have either enrolled directly after completing high school or transferred from another college or university, or have experience in the workforce and are pursuing an education that will prepare them to grow in their current position or enable them to take a new professional direction. The University offers a school-sponsored housing option in conjunction with local apartment communities for students who are relocating to Savannah to pursue their degrees.

South University is accredited by the Southern Association of Colleges and Schools Commission on Colleges to award associate, baccalaureate, masters, and doctorate degrees. Contact the Commission on Colleges at 1866 Southern Lane, Decatur, Georgia 30033-4097 or call 404-679-4500 for questions about the accreditation of South University. The Savannah campus is also authorized under the Georgia Non-public Postsecondary Educational Institutions Act of 1990 to confer those degrees. In addition, the campus is approved for training military veterans and other individuals by the State of Georgia Department of Veterans' Services, State Approving Agency, in Atlanta, Georgia.

Certain programs offered at the Savannah campus have earned programmatic accreditation. The South University Associate of Science degree in medical assisting is accredited by the Commission on Accreditation of Allied Health Education Programs (CAAHEP) (http://www.caahep.org) on recommendation of the Curriculum Review Board of the American Association of Medical Assistants Endowment (AAMEA). The Associate of Science in physical therapist assisting program is accredited by the Commission on Accreditation in Physical Therapy Education of the American Physical Therapy Association (CAPTE), 1111 North Fairfax Street, Alexandria, Virginia 22314; phone: 703-684-2782; Web site: http://www.capteonline.org.

South University's Doctor of Pharmacy program is accredited by the Accreditation Council for Pharmacy Education, 20 North Clark Street, Suite 2500, Chicago, Illinois 60602-5109; phone: 312-664-3575; fax: 312-664-4652; Web site: http://www.acpeaccredit.org. The school is a member of the American Association of Colleges of Pharmacy (AACP).

The anesthesiologist assistant program has received accreditation from the Commission on Accreditation of Allied Health Education Programs (CAAHEP) through its Accreditation Review Committee for Anesthesiologist Assistant Programs (ARC-AA). Contact ARC-AA in care of Commission on Accreditation of Allied Health Education Programs, 1361 Park Street, Clearwater, Florida, 33756; 727-210-2350. The Master of Science in physician assistant studies program on the Savannah campus is accredited by the Accreditation Review Commission on Education for Physician Assistant Programs (ARC-PA), 1000 North Oak Avenue, Marshfield, Wisconsin 54449-5788; phone: 715-389-3785; or 12000 Findley Road, Suite 240, Johns Creek, Georgia 30097; phone: 770-476-1224; Web site: http://www.arc-pa.org. This accreditation status qualifies graduating students to take the national certifying examination administered by the National Commission on Certification of Physician Assistants (NCCPA). The physician assistant studies program is a member of the Association of Physician Assistants Programs, the national organization representing physician assistant education programs. The Bachelor of Science in legal studies and Associate of Science in paralegal studies programs are approved by the American Bar Association, 321 North Clark Street, Chicago, Illinois 60654; phone: 312-988-5522. The Master of Science in Nursing is accredited by the Commission on Collegiate Nursing Education (CCNE), One Dupont Circle NW, Suite 530, Washington, DC 20036-1120; www.aacn.nche.edu; telephone: 202.887.6791.

Location

This campus, the largest among South University's locations, is located in the midtown section of historic Savannah, Georgia, minutes from downtown, cultural activities, and the beach. The buildings are situated on nine acres of land and are easily accessible from any section of Savannah, the surrounding region, and coastal South Carolina.

Majors and Degrees

The Savannah campus of South University awards the following two-year degrees: Associate of Science in Accounting, Associate of Science in criminal justice, Associate of Science in business administration, Associate of Science in information technology, Associate of Science in medical assisting, Associate of Science in paralegal studies, and Associate of Science in physical therapist assisting.

Four-year degree programs include a Bachelor of Business Administration, Bachelor of Science in criminal justice, Bachelor of Science in healthcare management, Bachelor of Science in information technology, Bachelor of Science in legal studies, Bachelor of Science in nursing, and Bachelor of Arts in psychology.

Academic Programs

The Savannah campus of South University offers degree programs that are designed to meet the needs and objectives of students. Each curriculum combines classroom and practical educational experiences that provide students with the academic background needed to pursue the professions of their choice. In addition, faculty members strive to instill the value not only of education and professionalism but also of contribution and commitment to the advancement of community.

South University operates on a quarter system, with each quarter comprising eleven weeks. Associate degree programs require a minimum of eight quarters to complete, and bachelor's degree programs require a minimum of twelve quarters for completion. Undergraduate programs are offered on a year-round basis, providing students with the ability to work uninterrupted toward their degrees.

Academic Facilities

The Savannah campus library has a large collection that includes an extensive law and health professions library. Students may retrieve periodicals in paper or electronic form. Library-based computers provide access to several commercial online services, including Westlaw, the computerized legal research service; GALILEO, the Georgia network of databases; and MEDLINE, for health sciences students. CD-ROM resources include the Encyclopedia Britannica, the Official Code of Georgia Annotated, ADAM, and the EBSCO magazine full-text database. Internet access is available on all computers throughout the campus, and the University offers wireless Internet access through an on-campus Wi-Fi network.

Costs

Tuition information is available by contacting the South University Admissions Department.

Financial Aid

South University's Student Financial Services Office helps qualified students secure financial assistance to complete their studies. The University participates in several student aid programs.

Faculty

The South University faculty includes individuals of high academic distinction. Of the more than 80 instructors on the Savannah campus, 40 percent hold terminal degrees. In addition to teaching, faculty members strive to help students develop the requisites to appreciate knowledge and understand how experiences in the classroom and laboratory relate to professional performance in the workplace. The average student-faculty ratio is 14:1. Each student is assigned a faculty adviser who oversees the student's progress and can answer questions about academic and career concerns. Students are encouraged to discuss program-related issues with and seek academic and career advice from their faculty advisers.

Admission Requirements

To be admitted to South University, prospective students must be high school graduates or hold a GED certificate and submit an appropriate SAT or ACT score (students should contact the Admissions Office for detailed information) or a satisfactory score on the University-administered placement examination. Students who wish to transfer must meet the criteria established for acceptance as a transfer student.

All applicants to South University must demonstrate English proficiency. Students may furnish proof of English-as-a-first-language competency through submission of a diploma from a secondary school (or higher level) in which English is the official language of instruction. Applicants whose first language is not English must submit Test of English as a Foreign Language (TOEFL) scores. Applicants should contact the Admissions Office to determine other examinations/scores that are acceptable as an alternative to the TOEFL.

Applicants not meeting the testing standards for general admission may be accepted under academic support admission.

Application and Information

Applicants must complete an application form and submit it along with the general application fee as well as official transcripts from all high schools and colleges attended. Faxed documents are not considered official. Applicants must also complete all tests administered by the University or submit their SAT or ACT scores to the Registrar's Office. Applications are accepted on a rolling basis and should be submitted as far in advance as possible.

All international (nonimmigrant) applicants to South University must meet the same admissions standards as all other students. In addition, international applicants must have official educational records prepared in English, verify sufficient funds to cover the cost of the educational program, and meet certain other immigration-mandated criteria. South University in Savannah is authorized under federal law to admit nonimmigrant students.

Admissions officers are available weekdays, Saturdays, and by appointment. An appointment for an admissions interview or tour of the campus should be made in advance.

For additional information, all prospective students should contact:

Charlie Parker
Senior Director of Admissions
South University
709 Mall Boulevard
Savannah, Georgia 31406-4805
Phone: 912-201-8000
         866-629-2901 (toll-free)
Fax: 912-201-8070
E-mail: ceparker@southuniversity.edu
Web site: http://www.southuniversity.edu

See suprograms.info for program duration; tuition, fees, and other costs; median debt; federal salary data; alumni success; and other important information.

South University is located on the south side of historic Savannah, Georgia.

SOUTH UNIVERSITY
TAMPA, FLORIDA

The University

Established in 1899, South University is a private academic institution dedicated to providing educational opportunities for the intellectual, social, and professional development of a diverse student population.

The Tampa, Florida campus offers focused and balanced curricula at the associate and bachelor's degree levels in the areas of business administration, information technology, criminal justice, healthcare management, health science, nursing, RN to B.S.N. nursing degree completion, physical therapist assisting, and psychology. The University also offers a Master of Science in criminal justice, Master of Science in physician assistant studies, Master of Business Administration (M.B.A.), Master of Business Administration in healthcare administration, Master of Science in RN to MSN master's degree, Master of Science in Nursing with a Family Nurse Practitioner specialization.

In addition, the Tampa campus offers students flexible scheduling with the choice of pursuing many of its courses on campus, online, or a combination of both, through South University's unique Plus+ program. Combining campus and online classes provides students with maximum flexibility, allowing them to organize their college education around their work and/or family commitments.

The Tampa campus affords students the opportunity to learn in a modern facility based in a central location near Raymond James Stadium. Most students live within driving distance of the campus, but the Admissions Office does maintain information on various housing options should students relocate to the Tampa area for their education.

South University has a diverse student body enrolled in day, evening, and weekend classes. A sizeable portion of students have experience in the workforce and are pursuing an education that will prepare them to expand on their current career or take them in a new professional direction.

South University is accredited by the Southern Association of Colleges and Schools Commission on Colleges to award associate, baccalaureate, masters, and doctorate degrees. Contact the Commission on Colleges at 1866 Southern Lane, Decatur, Georgia 30033-4097 or call 404-679-4500 for questions about the accreditation of South University. South University's Tampa campus is licensed by the Commission for Independent Education, Florida Department of Education, license No. 2987, 325 West Gaines Street, Suite 1414, Tallahassee, Florida 32399; phone: 888-224-6684 (toll-free); Web site: http://www.fldoe.org/cie. The Tampa campus is approved for training veterans and other eligible individuals by the State of Florida Department of Veterans' Affairs, Division of Veterans' Benefits and Assistance, Bureau of State Approving for Veterans' Training.

Certain programs offered at South University in Tampa have earned programmatic accreditation. The physical therapist assisting program on the Tampa campus has been granted initial accreditation status by the Commission on Accreditation of Physical Therapy Education (CAPTE) of the American Physical Therapy Association, 1111 North Fairfax Street, Alexandria, Virginia 22314; phone: 703-684-2782. The Bachelor of Science in Nursing R.N. to B.S.N. Degree Completion offered at South University - Tampa is accredited by the Commission on Collegiate Nursing Education (CCNE), One DuPont Circle NW, Suite 530, Washington, D.C. 20036-1120; phone: 202-887-6791; Web site: http://www.aacn.nche.edu. The Bachelor of Science in Nursing program at South University is also authorized to operate by the Florida State Board of Nursing. The Physician Assistant Studies program offered at South University-Tampa is provisionally accredited by the Accreditation Review Commission on Education for the Physician Assistant, Inc. 12000 Findley Road, Suite 240, Johns Creek, Georgia; phone: 770-476-12224; Web site: www.arc-pa.org.

Location

Located on North Himes Avenue, South University's Tampa campus affords students the opportunity to enjoy all the culture and excitement a large city has to offer. Professional sporting events, major concerts, theater, world-renowned restaurants, and a cosmopolitan social scene are all within easy reach.

Majors and Degrees

South University in Tampa awards a two-year Associate of Science degree in information technology, criminal justice, and physical therapist assisting.

The following four-year bachelor's degrees are awarded: Bachelor of Business Administration, Bachelor of Science in information technology, Bachelor of Science in healthcare management, Bachelor of Science in health science, Bachelor of Science in Nursing, Bachelor of Science in nursing (R.N. to B.S.N. degree completion program), and Bachelor of Arts in psychology.

Academic Programs

South University in Tampa offers degree programs that are designed to meet the needs and objectives of students. Each curriculum combines didactic and practical educational experiences that provide students with the academic background needed to pursue the professions of their choice. In addition, faculty members strive to instill the value not only of education and professionalism but also of contribution and commitment to the advancement of community.

Each University quarter comprises eleven weeks. Associate degree programs require a minimum of eight quarters to complete, and bachelor's degree programs a minimum of twelve quarters to complete. Programs are offered on a year-round basis, providing students with the ability to work uninterrupted toward their degrees.

Academic Facilities

South University's Tampa campus provides ample classroom and student service areas and features several smart classrooms with audiovisual technology. The campus also contains a fully equipped medical lab, multiple computer labs featuring PC and Mac computers, and more. The library maintains a highly focused collection of resource materials, including current books, journals, and related materials. In addition, students have access to WebVoyager, an online catalog of holdings; the Internet; various bibliographic databases; and subject-specific software programs. Interlibrary loans are available through the Tampa Bay Library Consortium (TBLC), and OCLC, an organization serving 43,559 libraries in eighty-six countries and territories around the world.

Costs

Information about tuition and fees can be obtained by contacting the South University Admissions Office.

Financial Aid

South University's Office of Student Financial Services helps qualified students secure financial assistance to complete their studies. The University participates in several student aid programs.

Faculty

The South University faculty includes individuals of high academic distinction. Of the more than 50 instructors on the campus, 46 percent hold terminal degrees in their fields of expertise. In addition to teaching, faculty members strive to help students develop the requisites to appreciate knowledge and understand how experiences in the classroom and laboratory relate to professional performance in the workplace. The average student-faculty ratio per class is 14:1. Each student is assigned a faculty adviser, who oversees the student's progress and can answer questions about academic and career concerns. Students are encouraged to discuss program-related issues with and seek academic and career advice from their faculty adviser.

Admission Requirements

To be admitted to South University, prospective students must be high school graduates or hold a GED certificate and submit SAT or ACT scores or achieve a satisfactory score on the University-administered admissions examination. Students who wish to transfer must meet the criteria established for acceptance as a transfer student.

All applicants to South University in Tampa must demonstrate English as a first language through submission of a diploma from a secondary school (or above) in which English is the official language of instruction. Applicants whose first language is not English must submit a Test of English as a Foreign Language (TOEFL) score. Applicants should contact the Admissions Office to determine other examinations/scores that are acceptable as an alternative to the TOEFL. General admission to the University does not guarantee admission to the nursing program. To obtain specific entrance requirements for the nursing program, prospective students should contact the campus Admissions Office or visit the South University Web site.

Application and Information

Applicants must complete and submit an application form, along with the general application fee, and official transcripts from all high schools and colleges attended. Applicants must also complete all tests administered by the University or submit their SAT or ACT scores to the Registrar's Office. Applications are accepted on a rolling basis and should be submitted as far in advance as possible.

All international (nonimmigrant) applicants to South University must meet the same admissions standards as all other students. In addition, international applicants must have official education records prepared in English, verify sufficient funds to cover the cost of the educational program, and meet certain other immigration-mandated criteria. South University in Tampa is authorized under federal law to admit nonimmigrant students.

Admissions officers are available weekdays, Saturdays, and by appointment. An appointment for an admissions interview or a tour of the campus should be made in advance.

For additional information, all prospective students should contact:

Michele D'Alessio
Director of Admissions
South University
4401 North Himes Avenue, Suite 175
Tampa, Florida 33614-7095
Phone: 813-393-3800
        800-846-1472 (toll-free)
Fax: 813-393-3814
E-mail: mdalessio@southuniversity.edu
Web site: http://www.southuniversity.edu

See suprograms.info for program duration; tuition, fees, and other costs; median debt; federal salary data; alumni success; and other important information.

South University offers students a flexible education located in the heart of the excitement and activities of Tampa, Florida.

SOUTH UNIVERSITY
VIRGINIA BEACH, VIRGINIA

The University

South University is a private academic institution dedicated to providing educational opportunities for the intellectual, social, and professional development of a diverse student population. To achieve this, the Virginia Beach campus offers focused and balanced curricula at the associate and bachelor's degree levels in the areas of business, criminal justice, information technology, nursing, Allied Health Science, healthcare management, health science, R.N. to B.S.N. nursing degree completion, legal studies, paralegal studies, and psychology. In addition, the campus offers a Master of Arts in Clinical Mental Health Counseling, and a Master of Business Administration (M.B.A.) program.

South University traces its heritage back to 1899 and today has grown into a multicampus system with locations in Columbia, South Carolina; Montgomery, Alabama; Novi, Michigan; Savannah, Georgia; Richmond and Virginia Beach, Virginia; Cleveland, OH; Austin, TX; and Tampa and West Palm Beach, Florida.

Students can also pursue degrees through a combination of on-campus and online classes as part of the University's unique Plus+ program, which provides maximum scheduling flexibility. This flexibility allows students to organize their college education around work and family commitments. For those who choose to take on-site courses, Virginia Beach campus facilities and amenities include a bookstore, student lounge, wireless Internet access, and ample parking in addition to classrooms, labs and offices.

The University strives to maintain small class sizes that permit students to receive individualized instruction and interaction with faculty and staff members.

The Virginia Beach campus of South University has a diverse student body enrolled in day, evening, and weekend classes. Most students live within driving distance of the campus, but the Admissions Office does maintain information on various housing options should students relocate to the Virginia Beach area for their education. The student body includes men and women who have either enrolled directly after completing high school or have transferred from another college or university, or have experience in the workforce and are pursuing an education that will prepare them to grow in their current position or enable them to take a new professional direction.

South University is accredited by the Southern Association of Colleges and Schools Commission on Colleges to award associate, baccalaureate, masters, and doctorate degrees. Contact the Commission on Colleges at 1866 Southern Lane, Decatur, Georgia 30033-4097 or call 404-679-4500 for questions about the accreditation of South University.

South University's Virginia Beach campus is certified to operate in Virginia by the State Council for Higher Education in Virginia, James Monroe Building, 101 North Fourteenth Street, Richmond, Virginia 23219; phone: 804-225-2600.

The Bachelor of Science in Nursing and the R.N. to B.S.N. Degree Completion offered at South University-Virginia Beach is accredited by the Commission on Collegiate Nursing Education (CCNE), One Dupont Circle Nw Suite 530, Washington, DC 20036; www.aacn.nche.edu; phone 202-887-6791.

Location

The campus, located in the Convergence Center Business Park in Virginia Beach, is just minutes from shopping and outdoor and cultural activities.

Majors and Degrees

The Virginia Beach campus of South University awards two-year Associate of Science degrees in the following areas of study: business administration, information technology, criminal justice, and paralegal studies.

The following four-year bachelor's degrees are awarded: Bachelor of Business Administration, Bachelor of Science in criminal justice, Bachelor of Science in healthcare management, Bachelor of Science in health science, Bachelor of Science in information technology, Bachelor of Science in legal studies, Bachelor of Science in Nursing, Bachelor of Science in nursing (R.N. to B.S.N. degree completion program for current registered nurses), and Bachelor of Arts in psychology.

Academic Programs

The Virginia Beach campus of South University offers degree programs that are designed to meet the needs and objectives of students. Each curriculum combines classroom and practical educational experiences that provide students with the academic background needed to pursue the professions of their choice. In addition, faculty members strive to instill the value not only of education and professionalism but also of contribution and commitment to the advancement of community.

South University operates on a quarter system, with each quarter comprising eleven weeks. Associate degree programs require a minimum of eight quarters to complete, and bachelor's degree programs require a minimum of twelve quarters for completion. Undergraduate programs are offered on a year-round basis, providing students with the ability to work uninterrupted toward their degrees.

Academic Facilities

The Virginia Beach campus library provides individual and group study areas, a computer lab, and a diversified collection of online, audiovisual, and printed materials. Professional librarians are available during all hours of operation to provide assistance in locating information and materials at South University libraries and at other libraries. The collections include books, magazines, audiovisual, and digital sources that support class assignments, tutorial needs, current events, and recreational reading. The computer lab offers Internet access, online databases with indexing and full text access to thousands of journals, tutorial programs, and an office

suite of software programs. Internet access is available on all computers throughout the campus, and the University offers wireless Internet access through an on-campus Wi-Fi network.

Costs

Tuition information is available by contacting the South University Admissions Department.

Financial Aid

South University's Student Financial Services Office helps qualified students secure financial assistance to complete their studies. The University participates in several student aid programs.

Faculty

The South University faculty includes individuals of high academic distinction. In addition to teaching, faculty members strive to help students develop the requisites to appreciate knowledge and understand how experiences in the classroom and laboratory relate to professional performance in the workplace. The average student-faculty ratio is 14:1. Each student is assigned a faculty adviser who oversees the student's progress and can answer questions about academic and career concerns. Students are encouraged to discuss program-related issues with and seek academic and career advice from their faculty advisers.

Admission Requirements

To be admitted to South University, prospective students must be high school graduates or hold a GED certificate and submit an appropriate SAT or ACT score (students should contact the Admissions Office) or a satisfactory score on the University-administered placement examination. Students who wish to transfer must meet the criteria established for acceptance as a transfer student.

All applicants to South University must demonstrate English proficiency. Students may furnish proof of English-as-a-first-language competency through submission of a diploma from a secondary school (or higher level) in which English is the official language of instruction. Applicants whose first language is not English must submit Test of English as a Foreign Language (TOEFL) scores. Applicants should contact the Admissions Office to determine other examinations/scores that are acceptable as an alternative to the TOEFL.

Applicants not meeting the testing standards for general admission may be accepted under academic support admission. General admission to the

University does not guarantee admission to the nursing program. To obtain specific entrance requirements for the nursing program, prospective students should contact the campus Admissions Office or visit the South University Web site.

Application and Information

Applicants must complete an application form and submit it along with the general application fee as well as official transcripts from all high schools and colleges attended. Faxed documents are not considered official. Applicants must also complete all tests administered by the University or submit their SAT or ACT scores to the Registrar's Office. Applications are accepted on a rolling basis and should be submitted as far in advance as possible.

All international (nonimmigrant) applicants to South University must meet the same admissions standards as all other students. In addition, international applicants must have official educational records prepared in English, verify sufficient funds to cover the cost of the educational program, and meet certain other immigration-mandated criteria. South University in Virginia Beach is authorized under federal law to admit nonimmigrant students.

Admissions officers are available weekdays, Saturdays, and by appointment. An appointment for an admissions interview or tour of the campus should be made in advance.

For additional information, all prospective students should contact:

Richard Kriofsky
Director of Admissions
South University
301 Bendix Road
Virginia Beach, Virginia 23452
Phone: 757-493-6900
     877-206-1845 (toll-free)
Fax: 757-493-6990
E-mail rkriofsky@southuniversity.edu
Web site: http://www.southuniversity.edu

See suprograms.info for program duration; tuition, fees, and other costs; median debt; federal salary data; alumni success; and other important information.

South University in Virginia Beach, Virginia, is conveniently located and offers day, evening and weekend classes.

SOUTH UNIVERSITY
WEST PALM BEACH, FLORIDA

The University

Established in 1899, South University is a private academic institution dedicated to providing educational opportunities for the intellectual, social, and professional development of a diverse student population. To achieve this, South University in West Palm Beach offers focused and balanced curricula at the associate and bachelor's degree levels in the areas of business, criminal justice, healthcare management, health science, legal studies, paralegal studies, information technology, nursing, R.N. to B.S.N. nursing degree completion, occupational therapist assisting, physical therapy assisting, and psychology. Other degree programs offered by the University include a Master of Arts degree in Clinical Mental Health Counseling; a Master of Science in Criminal Justice; a Master of Business Administration (M.B.A.) and Master of Business Administration in healthcare administration, both in traditional and twelve-month accelerated programs; and a Master of Science in Nursing, with a Family Nurse Practitioner specialization.

The West Palm Beach location of South University, established in 1974, strives to maintain small class sizes that permit students to receive more individualized instruction and interaction with faculty and staff members.

South University in West Palm Beach has a diverse student body enrolled in both day and evening classes. Students are primarily commuters who live within 50 miles of Palm Beach County. They include men and women who have either enrolled directly after completing high school or transferred from another college or university, or have experience in the workforce and are pursuing an education that will prepare them to grow in their current role or take a new professional direction.

In addition to classrooms and administrative offices, the campus includes a bookstore, student lounge, career services center, and ample parking. Since most students live within driving distance of the campus, the campus does not offer or operate student housing. If housing is needed, students should contact the Admissions Department.

South University is accredited by the Southern Association of Colleges and Schools Commission on Colleges to award associate, baccalaureate, masters, and doctorate degrees. Contact the Commission on Colleges at 1866 Southern Lane, Decatur, Georgia 30033-4097 or call 404-679-4500 for questions about the accreditation of South University.

South University's West Palm Beach campus is licensed to confer associate, bachelor's, and master's degrees by the Commission for Independent Education, Florida Department of Education, 325 West Gaines Street, Suite 1414, Tallahassee, Florida 32399; phone 888-224-6684; Web site: http://www.fldoe.org/cie. The campus is approved for training veterans and other eligible individuals by the State of Florida Department of Veterans' Affairs, Division of Veterans' Benefits and Assistance, Bureau of State Approving for Veterans' Training.

Certain programs offered at the campus have earned programmatic accreditation. The Associate of Science in physical therapist assisting degree program is accredited by the Commission on Accreditation of Physical Therapy

Education of the American Physical Therapy Association, 1111 North Fairfax Street, Alexandria, Virginia 22314; phone: 703-684-2782. The Bachelor of Science in legal studies and Associate of Science in paralegal studies degree programs are approved by the American Bar Association, 321 North Clark Street Court, Chicago, Illinois 60654; phone: 312-988-5522. The Bachelor of Science in Nursing program is accredited by the Commission on Collegiate Nursing Education (CCNE), One DuPont Circle, NW, Suite 530, Washington, D.C. 20036-1120; phone: 202-887-6791; Web site: http://www.aacn.nche.edu. The Bachelor of Science in Nursing program at South University is also authorized to operate by the Florida State Board of Nursing.

Location

South University West Palm Beach is located at the University Centre complex in Royal Palm Beach.

Majors and Degrees

The West Palm Beach campus of South University awards the following two-year degrees: Associate of Science in paralegal studies, and Associate of Science in physical therapist assisting.

The following four-year bachelor's degrees are awarded: Bachelor of Business Administration, Bachelor of Science in criminal justice, Bachelor of Science in health science, bachelor of Science in healthcare management, Bachelor of Science in legal studies, Bachelor of Science in nursing, Bachelor of Science in Nursing (R.N. to B.S.N. degree completion program), and Bachelor of Arts in psychology.

Academic Programs

The West Palm Beach campus of South University offers degree programs that are designed to meet the needs and objectives of students. Each curriculum combines didactic and practical educational experiences that provide students with the academic background needed to pursue the professions of their choice. In addition, faculty members strive to instill the value not only of education and professionalism but also of contribution and commitment to the advancement of community.

Associate degree programs require a minimum of eight quarters to complete, and bachelor's degree programs require a minimum of twelve quarters for completion. Programs at the West Palm Beach campus are offered on a year-round basis, providing students with the ability to work uninterrupted toward their degrees.

Academic Facilities

South University West Palm Beach is located at University Centre in Royal Palm Beach, Florida, to better serve students and the broader Palm Beach County community. The facility features a hurricane-resistant infrastructure and includes several large labs, lecture halls, a library, and seminar rooms.

The West Palm Beach campus library houses a large collection that includes extensive law resources. Students may retrieve periodicals in paper or electronic form. Library-based computers provide access to several commercial online services, including Westlaw, the computerized legal research service; and the Southeastern Library Network (SOLINET). CD-ROM resources

include the Grolier's Multimedia Encyclopedia and the EBSCO magazine full-text database. Internet access is available in the library.

Costs

For information on South University's tuition and fees, prospective students should contact the campus Admissions Office.

Financial Aid

South University's Office of Student Financial Services helps qualified students secure financial assistance to complete their studies. The University participates in several student aid programs.

Faculty

The South University faculty includes individuals of high academic distinction. Of the more than 60 instructors on the West Palm Beach campus, 37 percent hold terminal degrees in their fields of expertise. In addition to teaching, faculty members strive to help students develop the requisites to appreciate knowledge and understand how experiences in the classroom and laboratory relate to professional performance in the workplace. The average student-faculty ratio is 16:1. Each student is assigned a faculty adviser, who oversees the student's progress and can answer questions about academic and career concerns. Students are encouraged to discuss program-related issues with and seek academic and career advice from their faculty advisers.

Admission Requirements

To be admitted to South University, prospective students must be high school graduates or hold a GED certificate and submit an SAT or ACT score or a satisfactory score on the University-administered admissions examination. Students who wish to transfer must meet the criteria established for acceptance as a transfer student.

All applicants to South University must demonstrate English as a first language through submission of a diploma from a secondary school (or above) in which English is the official language of instruction. Applicants whose first language is not English must submit a Test of English as a Foreign Language (TOEFL) score. Applicants should contact the Admissions Office to determine other examinations/scores that are acceptable as an alternative to the TOEFL.

Applicants not meeting the testing standards for general admission may be accepted under academic support admission. General admission to the University does not guarantee admission to the nursing program. To obtain specific entrance requirements for the nursing program, prospective students should contact the campus Admissions Office or visit the South University Web site.

Application and Information

Applicants must complete and submit an application form, along with the general application fee, and official transcripts from all high schools and colleges attended. Faxed documents are not considered official. Applicants must also complete all tests administered by the University or submit their SAT or ACT scores to the Registrar's Office. Applications are accepted on a rolling basis and should be submitted as far in advance as possible.

All international (nonimmigrant) applicants to South University's West Palm Beach campus must meet the same admissions standards as all other students. In addition, international applicants must have official education records prepared in English, verify sufficient funds to cover the cost of the educational program, and meet certain other immigration-mandated criteria. South University in West Palm Beach is authorized under federal law to admit nonimmigrant students.

Admissions officers are available weekdays, Saturdays, and weekends. An appointment for an admissions interview or tour of the campus should be made in advance.

For additional information, all prospective students should contact:

Gary Malisos
Senior Director of Admissions
South University
University Centre
9801 Belvedere Road
Royal Palm Beach, Florida 33411
Phone: 561-273-6500
        866-629-2902 (toll-free)
Fax: 561-273-6420
E-mail: gmalisos@southuniversity.edu
Web site: http://www.southuniversity.edu

See suprograms.info for program duration; tuition, fees, and other costs; median debt; federal salary data; alumni success; and other important information.

South University in West Palm Beach, Florida, has classroom and lab space for its arts and sciences, business, health professions, and nursing programs.

SPRINGFIELD COLLEGE
SPRINGFIELD, MASSACHUSETTS

The College

Springfield College graduates enter the workforce or advanced education with a competitive advantage: top quality academic preparation and real-world experience.

Founded in 1885, Springfield College has an international reputation for educating leaders in health sciences, human and social services, sports and movement studies, education, business, and the arts and sciences. Accredited by the New England Association of Schools and Colleges, it is a private, coeducational institution offering bachelor's, master's, and doctoral degree programs. It is designated by the YMCA of the USA as a premier leadership development center. Students perform field work, internships, or service learning as early as their first year, gaining real-world experience while serving the community. This learning advantage is based in the College's mission—education in spirit, mind, and body for leadership in service to others. The College has been named to the President's Higher Education Community Service Honor Roll, has received Carnegie Foundation Community Engagement Classification, and has won the Jostens/NADIIIAA Award of Merit for community service by student athletes. The Institute for International Sport named it one of the 15 most influential educators through sport in America.

An ethnically diverse student body of 3,400 undergraduate and graduate students at the main campus comes from many U.S. states and abroad, with the majority from the Northeast.

Springfield College is a vibrant living and learning environment. The picturesque, 150-acre lakeside campus is technologically up-to-date. Several new and newly renovated state-of-the-art facilities blend with traditional campus architecture.

Ten campus residence halls provide guaranteed on-campus housing. Options include traditional residence halls and suite-style accommodations with private rooms for two to four students and a shared lounge, kitchen, and bathrooms. There are single-sex and coeducational residences. Seniors may elect to live off campus. The main student dining facility features a range of fresh food options. There are snack and other light-fare services around the campus, including a food court with a two-story atrium.

Enriching the undergraduate experience is a wide array of cocurricular activities, health and wellness programs, arts and cultural events, an extensive campus recreation program, and one of the largest athletics programs in the nation for a mid-sized college. There are more than 100 organizations and opportunities for involvement. More than 80 percent of undergraduates participate in some form of athletics, including varsity teams, intramurals, or club sports. There are men's and women's teams in basketball, cross-country, gymnastics, lacrosse, soccer, swimming, diving, tennis, track, and volleyball. Women's teams also include field hockey and softball, and there are additional men's teams in baseball, football, golf, and wrestling.

Location

On Lake Massasoit in the Pioneer Valley, Springfield College is located in Springfield, the third-largest city in Massachusetts and fourth-largest in New England (Boston, Worcester, and Providence are larger). A wide range of social, cultural, and athletic activities enhance the valley, as well as 12 other colleges and universities. For example, Springfield Symphony Hall is the site of concerts, plays, musicals, and dance performances; the MassMutual Center in Springfield is home to the American Hockey League's Springfield Falcons; and the Naismith Memorial Basketball Hall of Fame is an international attraction.

Nearby cities and towns offer many additional attractions. Northampton bustles with trendy shops, coffee houses, galleries, theater productions, health food stores, nightclubs, and restaurants. The Berkshire Hills offer hiking, skiing, biking, and other outdoor activities. Boston lies 90 miles to the east, New York City is less than a 3-hour drive away, Vermont is 1 hour away, and Bradley International Airport is 20 miles south.

Majors and Degrees

Springfield College offers bachelor of science or bachelor of arts degrees in: American studies, applied exercise science, art, art therapy, athletic training, biology, business administration, communications/sports journalism, communication sciences and disorders, computer and information sciences, computer graphics/digital arts, criminal justice, dance, early childhood education, elementary education, emergency medical services management, English, exploratory studies, general studies, health science/general studies, health services administration, health education (health studies), history, mathematics, mathematics and computer technology, nutritional sciences, occupational therapy, physical education (movement and sport studies), physical therapy*, physician assistant**, psychology, recreation management, rehabilitation and disability studies, secondary education, sociology, sport management, sports biology, and youth development.

*Entry-level 6½-year program culminating in a Doctor of Physical Therapy degree.

**Entry-level five-year program culminating in a Master of Science degree.

Academic Program

Consistent with Springfield College's humanics philosophy, undergraduate education is designed to promote an understanding of how the spirit, mind, and body work together in preparing students for a life of leadership in service to others.

The College has a two-semester academic calendar. To graduate, students must complete 120 credits including required courses for the major field of study, electives, and required courses for all students (writing, computer applications, arts and humanities, analytical and natural sciences, social sciences, international/multicultural studies, social justice, and physical education). Students may also earn credit for successful completion of Advanced Placement (AP) high school courses, and through the DANTES subject standard test and the College-Level Examination Program (CLEP) administered by the College Board.

Springfield College has agreements with several medical schools, which guarantee acceptance of its qualified students. In addition, many Springfield College programs allow undergraduates to take graduate-level courses.

There are campus chapters of the following honor societies: Beta Beta Beta (biology), Kappa Delta Pi (education), Phi Alpha (social work), Phi Epsilon Kappa (health, physical education, recreation or safety), and Psi Chi (psychology).

Off-Campus Programs

For fieldwork, internships, and service learning, the College maintains relationships with businesses, not-for-profit organizations, public and private agencies, and schools. Sites have included the Naismith Memorial Basketball Hall of Fame, American Hockey League, *The Boston Globe*, YMCAs, American Heart Association, MassMutual, Children's Hospital, Hilton Head Crowne Plaza, Reebok Health and Fitness Center, Baystate Medical Center, parks and recreation departments, and many other venues.

Extensive study-abroad programs are available. Students may also enroll in courses at some of the other colleges in the Springfield area.

Academic Facilities

Technologically up-to-date, the campus has wireless zones, smart classrooms, computer labs, a videoconferencing facility, a conference center, a language laboratory, a television studio, a journalism lab, a radio station, and more.

Science facilities include the recently renovated Schoo-Bemis Science Center with state-of-the-art equipment; the new Athletic Training/Exercise Science Complex, cited as one of the most outstanding in

the nation; and the Allied Health Sciences Center, with a human anatomy laboratory and sophisticated equipment for physical testing, analysis, and treatment. Herbert P. Blake Hall contains labs, testing, and treatment facilities, including the medical simulation laboratory, or sim lab, that features high-fidelity 3G adult and baby patient-simulator mannequins that respond to treatment as human patients would, allowing students to experience realistic, hands-on training and complicated medical techniques. Locklin Hall contains a well-equipped rehabilitation assessment and counseling services center.

For arts studies and programs, the newly renovated Fuller Arts Center and Appleton Auditorium is the site of performances, and the Visual Arts Center contains studio work space and a public exhibition center.

The 52-acre East Campus comprises a forest ecosystem with camping facilities and lake shoreline. It is a training ground for students in several academic programs. The Springfield College Child Development Center is an exceptional fieldwork facility for students of education and psychology.

Babson Library, well known for its resources in physical education, psychology, education, and health and human services, contains a rich collection of full-text print and digital materials. Library staff members assist, and students have access to a full range of information sources.

Costs

For the 2012–13 academic year, tuition and fees are $31,690. Room and board costs $10,630.

Financial Aid

Students are encouraged to apply for grants, loans, and student employment. Springfield College financial aid is based on need and academic achievement. The College gives full consideration to students who submit the Free Application for Federal Student Aid and the Springfield College Financial Aid Application by March 15 for first-year students and May 1 for transfer students. Students not eligible for financial aid may be considered for campus employment.

Faculty

Most of the 342 faculty members hold doctorates or other terminal degrees. The student-teacher ratio is 13:1.

Student Government

The Student Government Association, managed by elected students, promotes students' interests and welfare. It guides and finances more than 30 student organizations, adopts policies affecting students, and is a liaison between students and the College administration.

Admission Requirements

Springfield College evaluates applicants on the basis of academic and personal factors. Applications for regular admission or early decision must be submitted to the Office of Undergraduate Admissions and include a completed application form, a high school transcript, one personal reference, and SAT I or ACT scores. Transfer students must also submit a transcript and a dean's report from each college attended.

Application due dates for the 2013–14 academic year are as follows: undergraduate applicants, April 1; transfer students, August 1; athletic training and physical therapy programs, December 1; and physician assistant and occupational therapy programs, January 15.

Springfield College is interested in meeting each applicant and encourages candidates to visit the College and experience campus life. The College offers personal interviews, campus tours, and open-house programs and also facilitates contact with alumni and current students.

Application and Information

Springfield College's Admissions Committee reviews applications upon receiving them.

Application forms and information may be obtained from:

Office of Admissions
Springfield College
263 Alden Street
Springfield, Massachusetts 01109
Phone: 413-748-3136
        800-343-1257 (toll-free)
E-mail: admissions@spfldcol.edu
Web site: www.springfieldcollege.edu

The Richard B. Flynn Campus Union at Springfield College.

STATE UNIVERSITY OF NEW YORK AT OSWEGO

OSWEGO, NEW YORK

The University

Founded in 1861, SUNY Oswego is well into its second century of meeting the needs of today's students. While proudly celebrating its sesquicentennial, Oswego is now a comprehensive college with an excellent academic reputation and commitment to teaching, learning, research, and service. Total enrollment, including part-time and graduate students, is approximately 8,100 students. Approximately 6,800 students are currently enrolled as full-time undergraduates. More than 110 liberal arts and career-oriented programs are offered through the College of Liberal Arts and Sciences, the School of Business, the School of Communication, Media, and the Arts, and through the School of Education. The School of Education is nationally accredited by the National Council for the Accreditation of Teacher Education (NCATE), and the School of Business is internationally accredited by AACSB–The Association to Advance Collegiate Schools of Business. Other individual programs within the College of Liberal Arts and Sciences and the School of Communication, Media, and the Arts are accredited by specific discipline-oriented accrediting organizations.

Located on 696 acres on the southern shore of Lake Ontario, the spacious tree-lined campus consists of fifty-six buildings. Eleven residence halls and The Village, a new townhouse complex, offer a variety of on-campus housing opportunities to all degree-seeking students. More than 170 extracurricular organizations cover a wide range of social, academic, cultural, and intellectual interests. Theater, art, film, music, dance, and discussion events fill the campus cultural calendar. There is a full slate of twenty-four NCAA Division III intercollegiate sports for men and women, along with a full complement of competitive club sports and intramural athletics.

Oswego, a selective college, receives over 13,000 applications for some 2,000 freshman and transfer openings each fall. Accredited by the Middle States Association of Colleges and Schools, it has been recognized by a number of authoritative guides for its outstanding academic opportunities and high academic standards. In recent years, SUNY Oswego has been cited for excellence and selectivity in *U.S. News & World Report's Best Colleges Guide, Colleges of Distinction,* and in both the Princeton Review's *Best Northeastern Colleges* and their *Best Value Colleges* for 2012.

Oswego is undergoing an $800 million comprehensive renewal project; recently completed projects include a $56-million campus and convocation center and a $35-million campus townhouse village for 350 students. Additional projects in progress are a $118-million science and engineering complex and the renovation of several other academic buildings including facilities for the School of Education.

Location

With a population of nearly 20,000, the city of Oswego is a modest-sized, friendly upstate New York community. It is the country's oldest freshwater port and one of the leading ports on the Great Lakes and St. Lawrence Seaway. The city and its surrounding area are known for summer and winter recreation, including camping, boating, sailing, fishing, tennis, golf, ice skating, alpine and cross-country skiing, snowboarding, and sledding. It is at the heart of the booming sports fishing industry, with a thriving tourism scene. The campus is conveniently located 35 miles northwest of Syracuse and 65 miles east of Rochester. Students traveling by rail or air may utilize bus service to Oswego through the Regional Transportation Center located adjacent to the Carousel Mall in Syracuse.

Majors and Degrees

SUNY Oswego awards the Bachelor of Arts (B.A.), Bachelor of Science (B.S.), and Bachelor of Fine Arts (B.F.A.) degrees.

Through the College of Liberal Arts and Sciences, students can earn a baccalaureate degree in American studies, anthropology, applied mathematics, applied mathematical economics, biochemistry, biology, chemistry, cinema and screen studies, cognitive science, computer science, creative writing, economics, English, French, geochemistry, geology, German, global and international studies, history, human development, information science, language and international trade, linguistics, mathematics, meteorology, philosophy, philosophy-psychology, physics, political science, psychology, public justice, sociology, software engineering, Spanish, women's studies, and zoology.

The School of Business offers B.S. degree programs in accounting, business administration, finance, human resource management, management accounting, marketing, operations management and information systems, and risk management and insurance.

The School of Communication, Media, and the Arts offers baccalaureate degree programs in art, broadcasting and mass communication, communication, graphic design, journalism, music, public relations, and theater.

The School of Education offers B.S. degree programs in adolescence education, childhood education, teaching English to speakers of other languages (TESOL), technology education, technology management, vocational-teacher preparation, and wellness management.

In addition, three innovative five-year combined bachelor's and master's programs are available: a bachelor's degree in accounting with a master's in business administration, a bachelor's in psychology with an M.B.A., and a bachelor's in psychology with a master's in human computer interaction.

Cooperative programs include a 3+2 engineering program leading to a bachelor's degree from Oswego in chemistry or physics and a B.S. in engineering from Case Western Reserve, Clarkson, or SUNY Binghamton; a 2+2 program leading to a B.S. in medical imaging sciences, as well as a 3+3 or 3+4 program leading to a B.S./D.P.T. in physical therapy from SUNY Upstate Medical University; and a 3+4 preoptometry program leading to a bachelor's in chemistry from Oswego and an O.D. in optometry from SUNY College of Optometry.

Academic Programs

Oswego offers students a broad range of courses in the liberal arts and in preprofessional and professional studies. In addition to core courses within a major, all students must satisfy general education requirements designed to strengthen basic writing and analytical proficiency, give students awareness of their cultural heritage, and provide a level of literacy in the social and behavioral sciences, natural sciences, and humanities. By completing these general education requirements during their first two years of study, students are able to select a major with a sense of confidence and purpose. Students who are certain of their academic interest may begin working on their major program in their first year.

Before arriving on campus, students are assigned an adviser from either their major area or the college's Student Advisement Center. Advisers assist students who have not declared a major; help with academic, personal, and career concerns; and collaborate in scheduling courses needed for graduation. In addition, most students are matched with a first-year peer adviser, an older student, to help them face the challenges of their first year. The college has more than 500 undeclared students; many drawn by Oswego's reputation for helping learners find their way in education and life.

Students may consider applying for the college's honors program, which provides a challenging academic experience for high achievers regardless of major. Students also have the option of receiving credit through proficiency CLEP and Advanced Placement examinations.

Off-Campus Programs

Opportunities exist for students to broaden their knowledge of other countries by participating in one of forty different summer or semester overseas academic programs offered. Programs are available throughout the world, and costs are held as close as possible to the cost of an average semester on the Oswego campus. A newer option is short study-abroad quarter courses offering an intensive curriculum followed by a one-to-two-week experience in a foreign country. Through cooperative arrangements, Oswego also participates in semester programs in Albany and Washington.

Internships and other field experiences are available for students from all disciplines through the Experience-Based Education Office. Each year, more than 1,000 Oswego students participate in internships and career-awareness activities on campus, in the local area, and throughout the Northeast, the country, and the world.

Academic Facilities

Penfield Library is a high-tech information center supporting the curriculum, teaching, and research of SUNY Oswego. The library houses a collection of over 450,000 bound volumes, including partial U.S. and New York State government documents depositories, and provides access to nearly 26,000 print and/or electronic journals, magazines, and newspapers. Through Interlibrary Loan, Penfield can provide additional materials from libraries all over the world. The library's listening area has more than 12,000 recordings, cassettes, and CDs. Additional facilities include the Lake Effect Café, an online catalog, a 24-hour study room with computers, study carrels, wireless Internet access, and computer labs with word processing.

Campuswide computer technology services support students in their classroom, residence, and Web activities. Students receive an account at the time of enrollment that can be activated online to access e-mail and other Internet services. High-speed Internet service is available from all residence hall rooms via Ethernet and wireless networks. Wireless access is also available in most locations throughout the campus, including academic buildings, the Campus Center complex, Hewitt Union, Penfield Library, and all resident dining centers. Other services include technology training workshops, Internet troubleshooting via an active helpdesk, Web support for student clubs and organizations, free antivirus software and campuswide Gmail. The campus maintains hundreds of Macintosh and Windows-based computers in ten public-access labs. Students also have access to more than 500 computers and numerous Sun workstations in forty specialized departmental labs.

Adjacent to the campus, the college maintains Rice Creek Field Station, including the 26-acre Rice Pond and 350 acres of natural habitat. The facility has two lab/classrooms, a lecture room, and exhibit areas with an indoor viewing gallery, providing a unique vista of the creek and pond. College classes and community education programs are regularly held at the field station, which ranks among the five most extensively used facilities of its kind in the country.

Tyler Hall, Oswego's fine arts center, has two art galleries that feature annual traveling exhibitions, locally produced theme exhibitions, and the best work of students and faculty members. Tyler Hall's Waterman Theatre hosts student plays, musical performances, and productions by internationally renowned traveling artists.

The WRVO Stations, the college's 50,000-watt public radio outlet, provides outstanding on-campus internship opportunities. Communication Department facilities also include two new all-digital television studios, a modern radio lab, and two new journalism labs in Lanigan Hall. Student-run TV and radio stations and the college newspaper are located in the new Campus Center facilities.

Costs

Tuition for 2011–12 was $2635 per semester for New York State residents and $7160 per semester for nonresidents. Room and board charges were approximately $6264 per semester for entering students, depending on the meal plan, and additional fees totaled approximately $1240 per semester. SUNY Oswego guarantees that a student's initial first-year costs for room and board will be frozen for up to four consecutive years. Although many activities on campus are free of charge, students need to budget for personal expenses.

Financial Aid

Need-based financial assistance consists of grants, loans, and part-time employment. Oswego offers approximately $80 million in aid to its students annually. Students interested in financial aid must file a Free Application for Federal Student Aid (FAFSA). New York State residents also need to file an application for the state's Tuition Assistance Program. Priority is given to applications on file by March 1 for the fall term and November 15 for the spring term.

Oswego offers a very generous merit scholarship program. Students receive over $2.7 million annually in merit scholarships and approximately 35 percent of the entering freshman class receives one. The average four-year renewable scholarship is more than $2300 per year. For scholarship qualifications and details, students should visit http://www.oswego.edu/admissions/scholarships.

Faculty

Consisting of more than 300 full-time members, Oswego's faculty is dedicated to undergraduate students. With approximately 88 percent of them holding doctoral or other terminal degrees from many of the finest institutions in the country, students can be assured of the opportunity for an outstanding undergraduate education. The student-faculty ratio is approximately 18:1. While dedicated to teaching first and foremost, Oswego's faculty members are also actively engaged in research—often in partnership with undergraduate students—as well as publications and public service.

Student Government

Students at SUNY Oswego are represented by the Student Association, which has as its aim the efficient and intelligent governance of a democratic student body. The functions of the Student Association are divided among various committees that allocate funds to student organizations, intercollegiate and intramural athletics, the student newspaper, literary magazine, TV studios, and radio station, as well as various social, cultural, and intellectual activities on campus.

Admission Requirements

Admission to Oswego is competitive, with high school average, academic program, and standardized test scores being the most important criteria for applicants. Special talents such as artistic, musical, athletic, and creative writing skills are also considered. The Committee on Admissions accepts results of either the ACT or the SAT. A campus admissions visit is encouraged.

Transfer students in good standing are encouraged to apply for admission. The average GPA for entering transfer students is 3.0.

Application and Information

Oswego accepts both The Common Application and the SUNY Application for admission. Both applications are available online at http://www.oswego.edu/apply or at high school guidance offices and college transfer offices. Oswego evaluates applications as they are completed and as space remains available. Applications completed by January 15 for the fall term or October 15 for the spring term are ensured equal consideration. Applications received after those dates are considered as space remains available.

Prospective students and their parents are encouraged to visit the campus to participate in a student-guided tour and speak with an admissions counselor. Visits can be scheduled online through the college's Web site (http://www.oswego.edu/visit). Interested candidates can also call the Office of Admissions in advance to schedule a visit.

For further information, students should contact:

Office of Admissions
229 Sheldon Hall
SUNY Oswego
Oswego, New York 13126
Phone: 315-312-2250
Fax: 315-312-3260
E-mail: admiss@oswego.edu
Web site: http://www.oswego.edu

SUNY Oswego is located on 696 acres on the southern shore of Lake Ontario.

STATE UNIVERSITY OF NEW YORK COLLEGE OF ENVIRONMENTAL SCIENCE AND FORESTRY

SYRACUSE, NEW YORK

The College

The SUNY College of Environmental Science and Forestry (ESF) is one of the nation's largest and most widely recognized environmental colleges. Founded in 1911, the College has grown beyond its original emphasis on forestry to include professional education in environmental science, landscape architecture, environmental studies, and engineering in addition to distinguished programs in the biological and physical sciences. Throughout its history, the College has focused on addressing the environmental issues of the time in its three mission areas—instruction, research, and public service. EFS graduates are well-prepared for environmental careers through specialized academic programs and a holistic approach to solving today's environmental and resource problems.

A leader in its field, ESF is one of the specialized doctoral degree–granting colleges within the State University of New York System. The College currently supports undergraduate and graduate degree programs in more than thirty environmentally-related disciplines. Graduate programs lead to the Master of Science (M.S.), Master of Landscape Architecture (M.L.A.), Master of Professional Studies (M.P.S.), and Doctor of Philosophy (Ph.D.) degrees. ESF's research program is conducted throughout the world and research funding totals more than $15 million per year.

ESF's main campus is located on 12 acres adjacent to Syracuse University and SUNY Upstate Medical University in an urban residential setting. There are 1,600 full-time and 500 part-time undergraduates enrolled (40 percent are women). The College's unique partnership with Syracuse University offers ESF students the opportunity to take additional classes there for academic diversity and depth, and to participate in cultural events, student clubs, fraternities and sororities, and professional organizations.

ESF celebrated its centennial anniversary in 2011 with special activities that included the opening of Centennial Hall, an environmentally friendly residence hall that houses 452 ESF students in a combination of double rooms and student apartments.

The new ESF Gateway Center is scheduled to open in 2012. It will provide a hub for campus events and serve as a showcase for the College's sustainability efforts. The center will feature a wood pellet–fueled heat-and-power plant designed to generate enough energy for five campus buildings.

Location

Syracuse, a metropolitan area of more than 730,000 people, is a leader in the health care and education industries and is recognized as one of the nation's emerging centers for the development of green technologies. It offers many cultural, recreational, and educational opportunities, including museums, live theater, college and professional sports, and historic points of interest. Syracuse is centrally located at the crossing point of two Northeast superhighways. The driving time to Syracuse from New York City, Philadelphia, Boston, Toronto, and Montreal is about 5 hours; from Buffalo and Albany, about 3 hours. The city is served by a modern international airport and major bus and rail lines.

Majors and Degrees

The SUNY College of Environmental Science and Forestry offers three undergraduate degrees: the Bachelor of Science (B.S.), the Bachelor of Landscape Architecture (B.L.A.), and the Associate in Applied Science (A.A.S.). The B.S. degree is awarded in aquatic and fisheries science, bioprocess engineering, biotechnology, chemistry, conservation biology, construction management, environmental biology, environmental resources engineering, environmental science, environmental studies, forest ecosystem science, forest health, forest resources management, natural history and interpretation, natural resources management, paper engineering, paper science, and wildlife science. A number of options and concentrations are offered within specific curricula. The B.L.A. degree, which requires a semester of off-campus study, is awarded

in landscape architecture. Two-year A.A.S. degrees are awarded in forest technology, land surveying technology, and environmental and natural resources conservation at ESF's Ranger School campus in Wanakena, New York.

Academic Programs

All students at ESF have opportunities for specialized study as well as research and field experience. The Department of Environmental and Forest Biology is the largest department on campus and encompasses seven different majors, including biotechnology, conservation biology, wildlife science, aquatic and fisheries science, forest health, and natural history and interpretation. Biology students are required to complete a four-week period of summer field study, usually at ESF's Cranberry Lake Biological Station, following their sophomore or junior year. Options for specialization within the chemistry program include biochemistry, environmental chemistry, and natural and synthetic polymer chemistry. Biology and chemistry students can also earn their secondary science teacher certification through Syracuse University.

The construction management program teaches management, analysis, and design skills used in today's green construction process, with an emphasis on environmental and engineering issues.

Environmental resources engineering students learn skills in such areas as biological, environmental, and water resources engineering; mapping science; and geographic information systems. The closely related environmental science program also deals with engineering science, along with areas of focus in watershed science, health and the environment, earth and atmospheric systems science, environmental analysis, and renewable energy.

Bioprocess engineering students focus on the engineering, biology, and chemistry of ecologically sound industrial technologies and processes, giving students career opportunities in areas such as chemical engineering and bioengineering, pharmaceuticals, and renewable energy. The forest resources management curriculum offers areas of focus in forest management, measurement, and policy, along with forest ecology and biology. The program includes a minor in management offered in conjunction with Syracuse University. Natural resources management students can concentrate in specialized areas such as recreation or water resources management. Forest and natural resources management students are required to complete a four-week period of summer field study at ESF's Wanakena campus prior to the junior year.

The environmental studies major offers specializations in environmental communication and writing; biological science applications; and environmental policy, planning, and law. The landscape architecture program is a five-year bachelor's degree that is accredited by the ASLA to provide preparation to enter this licensed profession. Students study site design, urban and regional planning, historic preservation, community and environmental design, and computer applications. During the first semester of the fifth year, the landscape architecture curriculum requires participation in off-campus independent study. Paper engineering students can study process and product design and environmental engineering applied to the pulp, paper, and related chemical industries, while paper science students focus on a variety of industry-specific research and management areas. In addition, ESF offers excellent preparation for graduate study in health professions, law, veterinary science, and medicine; the College has a joint admission agreement with the College of Medicine at nearby SUNY Upstate Medical University.

Academic Facilities

Specialized facilities and equipment include electron microscopes, plant-growth chambers, climate-controlled greenhouses, an animal environmental simulation chamber, a bioacoustical laboratory, a radioisotope laboratory, numerous computer labs, nuclear magnetic resonance spectrometers, gas chromatography apparatus, a mass spectrometer, ultracentrifuges, and X-ray and infrared

spectrophotometers. The photogrammetric and geodetic facilities of the environmental resources engineering department are among the most extensive available in the United States. The paper science and engineering laboratory has a semi-commercial paper mill with accessory equipment. The sustainable construction management and engineering department has a strength-of-materials laboratory, a pilot-scale plywood laboratory, and a machining laboratory. The landscape architecture faculty has a one-of-a-kind environmental simulation laboratory. The greenhouses and forest insectary in Illick Hall are used to produce plant and insect materials for the classroom and laboratory. Extensive collections are available, including wood samples from all over the world, botanical materials, insects, birds, mammals, and fishes. The Roosevelt Wild Life Collection contains more than 10,000 species of well-preserved vertebrate and invertebrate animals and also recognizes the environmental interests and contributions of U.S. president Theodore Roosevelt.

The F. Franklin Moon Library includes the Academic Success Center for tutorial support in mathematics, writing, and other courses. Moon Library contains more than 100,000 specialized catalog items, including more than 1,800 research journals. The library also provides comprehensive abstract and indexing services relevant to the College's programs. Library facilities and services are supplemented by the collections at Syracuse University and the SUNY Upstate Medical University, both within walking distance.

ESF's regional campuses in Tully, Warrensburg, Cranberry Lake, Newcomb, and Wanakena, New York, offer a great diversity of forest sites that are used as outdoor teaching laboratories and for intensive research. ESF operates numerous field stations and provides students and faculty with access to over 25,000 acres of College-owned forest properties to support its instruction, research, and public service programs. These special properties make ESF one of the largest college campuses in the world.

Costs

Estimated costs for the 2011–12 academic year included resident tuition and fees of $5941 and out-of-state tuition and fees of $14,351. Room and board expenses were $14,032. Books, personal expenses, and travel were estimated at $2450.

Financial Aid

A wide variety of financial aid is available for ESF students, and more than 85 percent of the students receive some type of support. The forms of financial aid include merit- and need-based scholarships, grants, low-interest student loans, and student employment programs. All students are encouraged to apply for financial aid by completing the Free Application for Federal Student Aid (FAFSA).

Faculty

Faculty members at ESF are highly trained and dedicated to the College's teaching, research, and public-service missions. There are close to 140 full-time and 46 adjunct faculty members. Many are nationally and internationally recognized for their expertise in specialized fields. Nearly all regular faculty members hold twelve-month appointments. Just over 80 percent are tenured, and more than half are full professors, of whom 93 percent have earned doctorates. There is no distinction between the undergraduate and graduate faculty. Faculty members teach at both levels, and no courses are taught by teaching assistants. Faculty members serve as advisers to students and student groups and encourage excellence in scholarship and research. The student-faculty ratio is about 12:1.

Student Government

The College has a representative Undergraduate Student Association, and student representatives also participate in a counterpart association at Syracuse University. The ESF student government organizes and presents student social activities, and its representatives attend College administrative meetings, communicate students' concerns and ideas to the administration, and serve as a conduit of information back to the student body. ESF students are obligated to abide by Syracuse University's rules and regulations when accessing classes or student services there.

Admission Requirements

Students who are interested in ESF have four enrollment options: early decision, regular freshman admission, guaranteed transfer admission, and regular transfer admission.

Outstanding high school seniors who have selected SUNY-ESF as their top choice may apply for early decision, a binding, first-choice application/early notification program for fall-entry freshmen. Students filing an application for early decision admission must meet the SUNY application filing deadline date of November 15 and provide supporting credentials to SUNY-ESF by December 1. Students applying for early decision are notified by February 1.

Regular freshman admission is a second option for applicants who want to enroll immediately following high school. These candidates should demonstrate strong academic performance in a college-preparatory program, with emphasis on mathematics and science preparation. Students applying for regular freshmen entry are notified by March 1. All freshman candidates apply for admission to their intended programs of study.

Guaranteed transfer admission (GTA) candidates apply to ESF as high school seniors but are offered admission for either their sophomore or junior year. Students who plan to attend another college prior to transferring to ESF select this option to ensure a place at ESF for their chosen entry date. This option may also be offered to students who do not meet the freshman admission criteria. Those who are accepted for guaranteed transfer admission receive a letter of acceptance, contingent upon the successful completion of all the prerequisite courses required for the curriculum they have selected. The prerequisite courses are outlined and described in an enclosure with the student's acceptance letter and can also be found on the College's Web site at http://www.esf.edu.

Students are considered for admission to ESF on the basis of their previous college course work, overall academic aptitude, and interest in the College's programs. Consideration is given to both the quality and the appropriateness of each student's prior academic experience. The College has developed cooperative transfer programs with two-year colleges in New York, Connecticut, Massachusetts, New Jersey, and Pennsylvania. All admission acceptances are conditional upon satisfactory completion of course work in progress.

Application and Information

Students may apply for fall or spring admission. Admission decisions are made on a rolling basis until the class is filled. ESF accepts either the State University of New York Application form or the Common Application. Links to both applications can be found online at http://www.esf.edu/admissions/freshman/apply.htm. Requests for more information should be directed to:

Office of Undergraduate Admissions
106 Bray Hall
State University of New York College of Environmental Science and Forestry
1 Forestry Drive
Syracuse, New York 13210-2779
Phone: 315-470-6600
Fax: 315-470-6933
E-mail: esfinfo@esf.edu
Web site: http://www.esf.edu
http://www.facebook.com/sunyesf
http://twitter.com/sunyesf/
http://www.youtube.com/user/SUNYESFVIDEO

The SUNY College of Environmental Science and Forestry is enhancing the student experience with the addition of a new residence hall, Centennial Hall, and the Gateway Center, which will house an event center and Admissions and Outreach offices.

STATE UNIVERSITY OF NEW YORK INSTITUTE OF TECHNOLOGY

UTICA, NEW YORK

The College

The State University of New York Institute of Technology (SUNYIT) offers undergraduate degree programs in technology and professional studies. SUNYIT's broad curriculum embraces the humanities, communications, math, and science. Students enjoy close contact with faculty members in small classes, many with fewer than 20 students.

Founded in 1966, SUNYIT offers twenty-one bachelor's degree programs for freshmen and undergraduate transfer students and eight graduate degrees, including the Master of Business Administration in technology management.

SUNYIT enrolled 2,300 undergraduate and 600 graduate students on both a full-time and part-time basis in fall 2011. The men-women ratio was approximately 1:1. International students comprise approximately 3 percent of the student body, representing over twenty nations, and 12.5 percent of students were members of minority groups.

SUNYIT students can receive services through the Campus Life, Career Services, Health and Wellness, and Counseling Center offices. Three residence halls provide on-campus housing for more than 800 students. In addition to providing a wide variety of intramural sports for students, SUNYIT has competitive intercollegiate teams in men's and women's basketball, cross-country, lacrosse, soccer, and volleyball; men's baseball; and women's softball.

Location

SUNYIT is located in Marcy, New York, part of the Utica-Rome metropolitan area. With a population of nearly 300,000, Utica-Rome is in the geographic center of New York State, approximately 220 miles from New York City and 190 miles from Buffalo on the New York State Thruway. Utica-Rome has a variety of recreational and educational opportunities; museums, theaters, restaurants, and professional sports events are minutes away from campus by car or bus. The Adirondack Mountains and a variety of recreational opportunities such as hiking, boating, and skiing are an important part of the region's quality of life. Served by bus, Amtrak, and major airlines (airports in Syracuse and Albany), the Utica-Rome area is easily reached from locations throughout the eastern United States.

Majors and Degrees

SUNYIT awards the following baccalaureate degrees: Bachelor of Professional Studies (B.P.S.), Bachelor of Science (B.S.), Bachelor of Arts (B.A.), and Bachelor of Business Administration (B.B.A.). At the graduate level, the Master of Science (M.S.) and Master of Business Administration (M.B.A.) degrees are awarded.

Academic majors available to undergraduate students include accounting, applied mathematics, applied computing, biology, business administration, civil engineering, civil engineering technology, community and behavioral health, communication and information design, computer and information science, computer engineering technology, computer information systems, electrical engineering, electrical engineering technology, health information management, mechanical engineering technology, network and computer security, nursing, psychology, and sociology.

A number of options and concentrations within specific curricula are also available, as are minors in accounting, anthropology, biology, computer and information science, communication and information design, computer information systems, computer science, entrepreneurship, finance, health information management, human resources management, marketing, mathematics, nanotechnology, network and computer security, physics, psychology, sociology, and technology and culture.

Academic Programs

SUNYIT's academic year is divided into two semesters and runs from September through May. Summer sessions are also available.

Baccalaureate degree requirements vary from program to program but usually consist of a combination of specific major courses and liberal arts studies. Specializations and other options exist within the departments of Business Management; Communication and Humanities; Computer Information Sciences; Engineering, Science, and Mathematics; Engineering Technologies; Nursing and Health Professions; and Social and Behavioral Sciences. Specializations are developed through the use of electives and individual advisement.

Off-Campus Programs

Internship and cooperative education experiences are integral to effective career planning and job search strategies. These experiences can influence career plans by providing an opportunity for occupational exploration, developing marketable career-related skills and characteristics, and establishing a network of contacts that can provide relevant and timely information critical to the career decision-making process. In addition, employers are increasingly using internships and cooperative education programs as training opportunities leading to full-time permanent employment. All students, regardless of major, are encouraged to consider gaining experience in their chosen field that complements classroom learning. For additional information, students should contact the academic department or the Office of Career Services.

Academic Facilities

SUNYIT's academic facilities are located on its large, scenic campus just north of the city of Utica, easily accessible by municipal bus service. The campus consists of six building complexes, a facilities building, and residence halls. Several new buildings have recently opened, including a $13.8-million student center, a $23-million first-year residence hall, and a $20-million field house that hosts athletic events and large campus functions. Construction is slated to begin in 2012 on a technology complex that will connect a sophisticated faculty- and student-learning environment with high-tech industry tenants.

The Cayan Library provides traditional and online library services and a learning commons, with individual help provided by learning center staff, as well as group and individual study rooms.

Kunsela Hall contains administrative offices, classrooms, the campus bookstore, and laboratories for many technology programs. Donovan Hall houses classrooms; faculty offices; and laboratory facilities for other programs, including business, mechanical engineering technology, communication and information design, nursing, and the arts and sciences. The Campus Center contains a newly renovated cafeteria for residential students, gymnasium, and recreational facilities.

Costs

Costs for the 2011–12 academic year included state resident tuition and fees of $6419. Out-of-state tuition and fees were $15,469. Room and board costs were $10,460; personal expenses, books, supplies, and travel cost approximately $3000. The

total expenses were $19,970 for New York State residents and $29,040 for out-of-state students. Costs may be subject to change. Graduate student costs will vary; more information is available on the SUNYIT Web site.

Financial Aid

A wide variety of financial aid is available to students at SUNYIT. Academic scholarships are awarded for the entering fall class, and are based on merit, personal achievement, and other factors. Additional financial aid is awarded on the basis of need, as determined by an assessment of the Free Application for Federal Student Aid. At present, approximately 85 percent of the students receive financial assistance. The forms of financial aid available include Tuition Assistance Program awards (for New York State residents only), Federal Supplemental Educational Opportunity Grants, Federal Pell Grants, Federal Work-Study Program employment, Federal Perkins Loans, federal Nursing Student Loans, Federal Direct Student Loans, a variety of state-sponsored loans, and a broad range of private scholarships and grants. Students with a cumulative transfer GPA of 3.25 or better or a high school average of 90 are automatically considered for merit scholarships at the time of their application.

Faculty

SUNYIT faculty members come from all over the world and are committed to teaching, research, and service to the community. Among the faculty members are a Distinguished Service Professor, a Fulbright Scholar, and numerous recipients of the Chancellor's Award for Excellence in Teaching. More than 80 percent of SUNYIT's full-time faculty members have doctoral or terminal degrees. The faculty members are fully engaged in academic orientation and advisement, individualized instruction, cooperative faculty-student efforts in research projects, and concern for students as individuals. In the classroom, the average student-faculty ratio is 19:1.

Student Government

All full-time undergraduates are members of the SUNYIT Student Association. Its primary functions are to develop and monitor the student-activity-fee budget, to approve and oversee all student organizations, to debate issues of concern to students and take action as needed, and to develop programs of interest to all students. Student government consists of a 7-person executive committee and 11 senators. Students are encouraged to take an active role in the governance process, and many opportunities for involvement, in addition to those listed above, are available for interested students.

Admission Requirements

Generally, freshman applicants should carry a B/B+ average in a college-preparatory program and have achieved an SAT score in the 1000–1100 range (or approximately 22–24 composite ACT score). Admission is based on high school average, SAT or ACT scores, strength of course work, and other relevant information.

For transfer students, most programs require a minimum GPA of 2.5 for guaranteed admission; some programs require a higher GPA or additional application materials. Transfer students below a 2.5 GPA but above a 2.0 GPA may be admitted under special circumstances. Transfer students are required to furnish an official transcript from all previous colleges they attended.

Students with a cumulative GPA of at least 3.25 are automatically considered for merit scholarships; no separate application is required.

Application and Information

The deadline for all applications is August 1 for fall entry and December 1 for spring entry. Prospective students are encouraged to apply early as programs may close prior to application deadlines.

All applications are reviewed on an individual basis. All EOP applicants are also required to complete a supplemental application and are encouraged to apply for fall semester by December 1. The recommended application deadline for EOP and regular admission is February 15. However, applications received after that date will be considered on a rolling basis. Notification of admissions decisions begins on December 15.

SUNYIT participates in the SUNY early action program. Early action students must submit their application by November 1 and complete their application by November 15; applications are reviewed and students are notified of admission by December 15. Students admitted under early action are required to submit a deposit by May 1.

Students who wish to apply should apply online through the SUNYIT Web site. A copy of the State University of New York application booklet can also be obtained from a two-year college, a local high school, or the Admissions Office. Application forms for international students may also be obtained through the SUNYIT Web site or the Admissions Office.

SUNYIT adheres to the principle that all persons should have equal opportunity and access to its educational facilities without regard to race, creed, sex, or national origin.

Official transcripts from all previously attended high schools and colleges should be sent to the Director of Admissions. All communications and requests for additional information should also be directed to:

Director of Admissions
SUNYIT
100 Seymour Road
Utica, New York 13502
Phone: 315-792-7500
        866-2SUNYIT (toll-free)
Fax: 315-792-7837
E-mail: admissions@sunyit.edu
Web site: http://www.sunyit.edu

SUNYIT students in front of new turf field near the Wildcat Field House.

STEVENSON UNIVERSITY
STEVENSON AND OWINGS MILLS, MARYLAND

The University

Stevenson University (SU), formerly Villa Julie College, is a coeducational, independent institution dedicated to providing its 3,400 undergraduate and graduate students with a career-focused liberal arts education. Individual attention from faculty members, extensive career preparation gained through real-world training, and two ideal locations just north of Baltimore, Maryland, in Stevenson and Owings Mills, make the University truly unique.

At SU, academic quality is viewed as a personalized education that fosters intellectual growth and prepares students to thrive in the working world after graduation. With a student-faculty ratio of 15:1, it is easy to understand why students often cite the congenial rapport with faculty members as one of the University's strong points.

Through Stevenson University's concept of Learning Beyond, students step outside of the classroom to take their learning to the next level. Experiential learning opportunities include study abroad, service learning, field placements, and independent research. In addition, through an approach known as Career Architecture^{SM}, each student develops a professional career plan based on their values, skills, and strengths.

Stevenson's graduates maintain a placement rate that tops 95 percent each year, with students acquiring jobs or going on to further their education within six months of graduation.

At SU, students enjoy more than forty-five clubs and organizations, multiple honor societies, and NCAA Division III athletics. The following sports are offered: men's and women's basketball, cross-country, golf, lacrosse, soccer, tennis, and volleyball; men's baseball and football; and women's field hockey, ice hockey, and softball. Cheerleading, dance, and intramural sports are also extremely popular.

In addition to its undergraduate programs, the University offers the following master's degree programs: business and technology management, forensic science, forensic studies, and nursing.

Location

Stevenson University has two beautiful campuses in the heart of Maryland, in Stevenson and Owings Mills. SU students truly appreciate the beauty of a rural campus as well as the convenience and appeal of a more urban setting.

The original 60-acre Greenspring Campus is nestled among the rolling hills in Stevenson, Maryland. The Owings Mills Campus is a thriving center of student activity and offers both academic and residential facilities. Classes are held on both campuses, and the University provides a free shuttle service that runs between these locations.

Majors and Degrees

Stevenson University offers the following bachelor's degree programs: accounting; applied mathematics; biology; biotechnology; business administration; business communication; business information systems; chemistry; computer information systems; criminal justice; early childhood education: liberal arts and technology; elementary education: liberal arts and technology; English language and literature; fashion design; fashion merchandising; film, video, and theater; human services; interdisciplinary studies; medical technology; middle school education; nursing; nursing: RN to B.S.; paralegal studies; psychology; public history; and visual communication design.

Stevenson's B.S. to M.S. degree programs give students the option of earning both a bachelor's and a master's degree in as few as five years. Graduate study begins in the spring semester of the junior year and runs concurrently with undergraduate work until the end of the spring semester of the senior year. All subsequent course work is at the graduate level.

Academic Programs

At SU, academic quality is regarded as a personalized curriculum that prepares students to enter the working world with the knowledge and skills that employers value. SU infuses the traditional liberal arts education with a distinct career focus. The University's goal is to prepare students for employment, graduate study, and productive involvement in today's world.

Academic Facilities

From recent enhancements to the Greenspring Campus to brand-new facilities at the Owings Mills Campus, the University provides modern facilities that serve the needs of all students.

The University's Greenspring Campus includes a 350-seat theater, multiple computer labs and classrooms, video and graphic studios, science laboratories, a student union, and athletic facilities. Each classroom and laboratory on the campus is capable of multimedia projection and computer-assisted learning.

Also at the Greenspring Campus is the Verizon Center for Excellence in Teaching and Learning. The center comprises classrooms equipped with technology that accommodates distance learning.

The Owings Mills Campus hosts the University's newest facilities, including an expansive student center and dining hall, a 10,000-square-foot community center, an expansive athletic complex with a new gymnasium, multiple classrooms and study spaces, a fitness center, and additional athletic fields. The state-of-the art Mustang Stadium opened in 2011.

The Howard S. Brown School of Business and Leadership offers twelve traditional classrooms and seven seminar halls. The facility also includes two distance-learning labs where students are able to interact with other learners worldwide, six computer labs utilizing the most up-to-date equipment, a student lounge, a law library, and a high-tech digital mock trial courtroom.

The University's library, located on the Greenspring Campus, has an extensive collection of more than 100,000 printed volumes, periodicals, videotapes and audiotapes, CDs, and microfilm and microfiche selections and an interlibrary loan consortium. In addition to the electronic databases it owns, the library has access to thousands of outside databases, such as LexisNexis Academic Universe, WESTLAW, Dialog, and Dow Jones News Retrieval.

Costs

Stevenson is among the most affordable universities in the state of Maryland. For the 2011–12 academic year, tuition and fees for full-time students were $23,636. Room and board for the 2010–11 year were $11,422.

Financial Aid

Stevenson University offers financial assistance to qualified students in the form of grants, scholarships, loans, student employment, and a special payment plan. On average, approximately 90 percent of the University's students receive some form of financial assistance. The University has a generous scholarship program that grants awards based on academic merit. SU participates in all major federal aid programs as well as all Maryland state programs. Applicants are required to file the Free Application for Federal Student Aid (FAFSA). The priority deadline for filing is February 15.

Faculty

The faculty at Stevenson University is primarily a teaching faculty. The University's 15:1 student-teacher ratio demonstrates the institution's dedication to personalized education. A majority of the full-time faculty members have the doctoral or terminal degree offered in their field, and a significant number are widely published. In addition, many are concurrently employed as professional specialists in their fields.

Student Government

The Student Government Association (SGA) facilitates an environment that encourages students to express their thoughts and opinions concerning Stevenson University, its policies, and sponsored activities. The SGA serves as the principal governing body of all campus clubs and activities. In conjunction with the Office of Student Affairs, the SGA organizes an array of campuswide events that promote the social aspects of college life. Each student at Stevenson is welcome and encouraged to participate in all SGA functions.

Admission Requirements

Applications for admission to Stevenson University are reviewed on a rolling basis. In evaluating each applicant, the University considers the applicant's high school academic record, SAT or ACT scores, recommendations, writing sample, and any other special talents or personal interests. Admission to the University is determined without regard for race, color, sex, religion, national or ethnic origin, or handicap. SU complies with all applicable laws and federal regulations regarding discrimination and accessibility on the condition of handicap, age, veteran status, or otherwise.

Application and Information

Applications for admission to undergraduate programs should be received by March 1 for fall-semester entry and October 15 for spring-semester entry. Scholarship consideration adheres to earlier deadlines. Applications received after these dates are reviewed on a space-available basis. Students applying to the University as freshmen must submit official high school transcripts, standardized test scores, the Counselor Recommendation Form, typed responses to the essay questions listed on the application, and a $40 nonrefundable application fee. The application fee is waived for all students who apply online at www.stevenson.edu. Transfer students must submit official transcripts from all colleges or universities they have attended and should contact the Transfer Admissions Counselor to discuss additional credential requirements.

For further information and application forms, students should contact:

Admissions Office
Garrison Hall, Suite 200
Stevenson University
100 Campus Circle
Owings Mills, Maryland 21117-7804
Phone: 410-486-7001
        877-468-6852 (toll-free)
Fax: 443-352-4440
E-mail: admissions@stevenson.edu
Web site: http://www.stevenson.edu

The residences at Stevenson University offer spacious apartments and suites with extensive amenities.

STONEHILL COLLEGE
EASTON, MASSACHUSETTS

STONEHILL
COLLEGE

The College

Stonehill College is a selective, coed Catholic college with a welcoming, academically challenging community of over 2,500 students on a beautiful, active campus located 22 miles south of Boston. Stonehill offers more than eighty diverse majors and minors in the liberal arts, sciences, and business to prepare students for a life of learning, leadership, and responsible citizenship. Nearly 80 percent of Stonehill students complete an internship, study abroad, practicum, or field experience by the time they graduate.

More than 80 percent of Stonehill students participate in at least one sport on campus. Stonehill competes in the Northeast-10 Conference, the largest NCAA Division II conference in the country, and offers twenty different varsity sports, including baseball, lacrosse, football, basketball, and soccer. The extensive intramural program offers two different levels of competition in basketball, dodgeball, field hockey, kickball, softball, and more. Club sports such as rugby and volleyball are yet another option, offering a spirited, fun experience without the demands of NCAA conference-sanctioned athletics.

Founded by the Congregation of Holy Cross in 1948, Stonehill's mission is "to educate the whole person so that each graduate thinks, acts, and leads with courage toward the creation of a more just and compassionate world." The idea of making the world a better place is part of the Catholic faith and an intrinsic element of the Stonehill experience. Each year, approximately 1,500 Stonehill students (more than 63 percent of the student body) participate in community service. Last year, Stonehill students provided more than 40,000 hours of service.

Stonehill consistently receives nationwide recognition as one of the country's top colleges. Recently, *U.S. News and World Report*'s "America's Best Colleges" guide singled out Stonehill as a top up-and-coming school. The Princeton Review recently chose Stonehill as one of the best in the nation for career services, most accessible professors, intramural sports, study abroad, and more.

Location

Stonehill is located in Easton, Massachusetts, a friendly residential community nestled between New England's largest capital cities. Just 22 miles from Boston and 37 miles from Providence, it is perfectly situated for internships, service opportunities, job prospects, museums, professional sports games, cultural events, and more.

Whether the countless trees are in full bloom in the spring or the leaves are bursting into reds and golds in the fall, Stonehill is beautiful every season of the year. Encompassing 384 acres, Stonehill's New England college campus features traditional landscaping, ponds, wooded trails, and Georgian-style architecture.

Majors and Degrees

Students may receive Bachelor of Arts degrees in American studies, art history, Catholic studies, chemistry, communication, computer science, criminology, economics, education (early childhood/elementary and secondary education minors), English, environmental studies, foreign languages, French, gender studies, graphic design, health-care administration, history, international studies, mathematics, multidisciplinary studies, philosophy, physics, political science, psychology, public administration, religious studies, sociology, Spanish, studio arts, and visual and performing arts (music and theater arts concentrations).

Bachelor of Science degrees are offered in biochemistry, biology, chemistry, computer science, mathematics, neuroscience, and physics. Bachelor of Science in Business Administration degrees are offered in accounting, finance, international business, management, and marketing. Stonehill's business department is accredited by the AACSB. In addition, Stonehill College partners with the University of Notre Dame to offer a combination 3+2 program in engineering with concentrations in aeronautical, chemical, civil, computer, electrical, environmental geosciences, and mechanical engineering.

Pre-professional advising programs are offered in dentistry, education, law, medicine, veterinary science, and medical technology. Students interested in the field of education can receive early childhood, elementary, middle, and secondary school teacher certification. Students may pursue a double major as well as design their own major by combining various departmental courses into a comprehensive multidisciplinary program.

Academic Programs

The core of Stonehill's liberal arts curriculum is the Cornerstone Program, which leads students to examine themselves, society, culture, and the natural world through courses in ethics, sciences, language, and more.

Stonehill's students and alumni succeed because the entire college community collaborates to help them develop the knowledge, skills, and character to meet their professional goals and to live lives of purpose and integrity. Its graduates can be found around the world enrolled in top graduate programs, enjoying meaningful careers, and working to improve their communities.

Within one year of graduation, 97 percent of Stonehill graduates over the last five years were employed, volunteering, or in graduate school. Last year, 38 percent of graduating seniors were employed at organizations such as Goldman Sachs, the New England Patriots, and Brigham and Women's Hospital. Others joined or applied for year-long volunteer service programs such as the Peace Corps, Teach for America, AmeriCorps, and World Teach.

On average, Stonehill students graduate at a higher rate and in less time than students at many other colleges and universities. About 84 percent of Stonehill students graduate within four years. Stonehill's four-year graduation rate is much higher than at public institutions where the national average is five years.

Off-Campus Programs

At Stonehill, students are given experiential learning opportunities that allow them in-depth exploration of what they learn in the classroom and the opportunity to apply it in the real world. The National Survey of Student Engagement ranks Stonehill in the top 10 percent of colleges nationwide for its enriching educational experiences such as competitive internships, nationally ranked study-abroad opportunities, and cocurricular programs.

Students take part in interdisciplinary Learning Communities (LCs), which combine two academic courses from different disciplines with a team-taught seminar that explores an interrelated topic. Some LCs even incorporate travel to places

like Ireland, Italy, the Florida Everglades, and the deserts of the Southwest.

In addition, Stonehill is ranked thirteenth in the nation among baccalaureate institutions for semester-long study abroad programs by the Institute of International Education. About 40 percent of Stonehill students study abroad before graduation in programs located in dozens of countries, including Argentina, Australia, China, Greece, Morocco, and South Africa.

Academic Facilities

Stonehill is dedicated to developing programs and projects that will continually improve quality of life for everyone on campus. Its multimillion dollar science center, opened in 2009, provides state-of-the-art facilities such as labs, observation rooms, research areas, and a café to faculty, staff, and students.

Kaplan's *Insiders Guide to the 320 Most Interesting Colleges* ranked Stonehill among the colleges with the Best Freshman Housing. It's no wonder that more than 90 percent of Stonehill's students live on campus and very few leave on the weekends. In addition, all resident students are guaranteed housing for all four years. Students can choose from a variety of living options, including suites, townhouses, and double- and triple-occupancy rooms, and take advantage of amenities such as communal TV lounges, kitchen and laundry facilities, recreation rooms, pool tables, basketball courts, beach volleyball courts, and outdoor grills for barbeques.

Costs

For the 2011–12 academic year, Stonehill's costs were $33,920 for tuition and $12,860 for room and board.

Financial Aid

Stonehill is committed to helping each qualified student find the resources to make the dream of a Stonehill education become reality. Stonehill offers loans, grants, scholarships, employment programs, and tuition payment plans to help students become a part of the community here. In the 2010–11 academic year, Stonehill distributed $47.5 million in financial aid to a student body of 2,558. This year, 92 percent of full-time students received some form of aid. On average, students received $20,150 each in scholarships, grants, loans, and work-study. A wide range of competitive merit-based scholarships is also available to outstanding students who do not demonstrate a financial need.

To file for Stonehill scholarship and/or financial aid consideration, students should complete the online CSS PROFILE form at https://profileonline.collegeboard.com. Stonehill's CSS PROFILE code is 3770. In addition, students must file the Free Application for Federal Student Aid (FAFSA) online at http://www.fafsa.ed.gov to be considered for government funds. Stonehill's FAFSA code is 002217.

Faculty

With a student-faculty ratio of 13:1 and an average class size of 20, Stonehill sees individual attention as a key component of our academic programs. Stonehill's accomplished faculty champions its students throughout all four years and is dedicated to teaching and conducting publishable research with students to help with their integrated learning process. Students benefit from graduate-level access to high-tech equipment, attend professional academic conferences, and coauthor in-depth papers, while guided by faculty mentors. Stonehill students take advantage of collaborating one-on-one with their professors on a regular basis and they will always be taught by a faculty member, not a teaching assistant or graduate student.

Student Government

From enjoying on-campus activities to just hanging out with friends, students have plenty of opportunities for fun at Stonehill. The Student Government Association (SGA) is one of the country's most active—its programming won an award

from the National Association of Campus Activities—so there's always something happening, from concerts and guest speakers to contests and game shows. More than seventy clubs and organizations are available, including the College's literary magazine *Rolling Stonehill,* the Ski/Snowboard Club, and the Neuroscience Society.

Stonehill also offers free transportation to Boston's public subway system, allowing easy access to the excitement of the city. And with Stonehill's unique Fun Fund, students can get up to $200 to pay for entertainment with friends, such as a show in New York City, a pottery class, or a Red Sox game.

Admission Requirements

Admission to Stonehill is selective. This year, more than 6,100 high school students applied for 675 first-year places to represent the Stonehill class of 2016. Stonehill actively seeks an academically strong and geographically, culturally, and ethnically diverse student body. In the admissions process, all information on each applicant is carefully considered, but academic performance and high school curriculum are given the greatest weight. The Admissions Committee evaluates the depth and strength of each applicant's course selection and the consistency of their grades. Competitive students should have completed a strong academic program from among their high school's most challenging offerings. Stonehill admission is test optional, but students may choose to submit scores from either the SAT or ACT. The Admissions Committee also evaluates extracurricular activities, work, volunteer and community activities, recommendations, and writing samples. Stonehill awards credit for strong scores on AP, CLEP, and higher-level International Baccalaureate exams.

Application and Information

Aspirants for Stonehill, as first-year, transfer, or international students may apply online at https://www.commonapp.org. The Common Application is also available in paper form at high school guidance offices.

Stonehill offers three admissions plans for first-year candidates: early decision (binding), early action (nonbinding), and regular decision. November 1 is the deadline for early acceptance and January 15 is the deadline for regular decision.

Dean of Admissions and Enrollment
Stonehill College
320 Washington Street
Easton, Massachusetts 02357-5610
United States
Phone: 508-565-1373
Fax: 508-565-1545
E-mail: admissions@stonehill.edu
Web site: http://www.stonehill.edu
      http://stonehillcollegeadmissions.org (Admissions)

Stonehill College campus.

STONY BROOK UNIVERSITY, STATE UNIVERSITY OF NEW YORK

STONY BROOK, LONG ISLAND, NEW YORK

The University

An educational and research institution of world renown, Stony Brook is included among the top 1 percent of universities worldwide by the *Times Higher Education World University Rankings* and among the top 100 public national universities by *U.S. News & World Report*. Stony Brook is one of just 61 research universities that belong to the elite Association of American Universities (AAU), based on the excellence of its research and education programs. Its tuition is one of the lowest among AAU institutions, making a Stony Brook education a smart choice.

Stony Brook offers more than 200 majors, minors, and combined-degree programs for undergraduates and has exceptional strength in the sciences, mathematics, humanities, fine arts, social sciences, engineering, and health professions. Major academic units of the University include the College of Arts and Sciences, College of Engineering and Applied Sciences, College of Business, School of Journalism, School of Marine and Atmospheric Sciences, and the five schools of the health sciences: Medicine, Health Technology and Management, Dental Medicine, Nursing, and Social Welfare.

The award-winning Undergraduate Research and Creative Activities (URECA) program involves undergraduates in research in nearly every discipline and has produced Beckman, Goldwater, and Marshall scholars.

Stony Brook enrolls 24,103 full- and part-time students—15,968 undergraduates and 8,135 graduate and professional students. Students hail from nearly all 50 states and more than 110 countries. Nearly 20,000 students are enrolled full time. Approximately 83 percent of Stony Brook's freshmen live in campus residence halls, which are organized as small residential colleges to foster social, intellectual, and cultural interaction.

The Stony Brook Seawolves' twenty varsity teams compete in NCAA Division I and include men's baseball and football; women's softball and volleyball; and men's and women's basketball, cross-country, lacrosse, soccer, swimming, tennis, and indoor and outdoor track and field. Athletic facilities include Kenneth P. LaValle Stadium, which seats up to 8,300 and Joe Nathan Field, dedicated to alumnus and Major League pitcher Joe Nathan ('97). The complex also features an 8,000-square-foot strength and conditioning center, basketball courts, tennis courts, bicycle and jogging paths, handball courts, and a track. A new 85,000-square-foot Campus Recreation Center is slated to open in 2012.

Location

Situated on 1,039 wooded acres, Stony Brook is located midway between New York City and the Hamptons on Long Island's East End, a setting rich in both natural and architectural beauty. Students enjoy large wooded areas on and around campus. Sandy beaches, a harbor, and a historic hamlet that was once home to George Washington's Revolutionary War spy ring are all close by, as well as a major indoor mall and multiplex movie theater. A train station on the University's perimeter offers students easy access to New York City.

Majors and Degrees

The University offers sixty-seven undergraduate majors leading to the Bachelor of Arts (B.A.), Bachelor of Science (B.S.), and Bachelor of Engineering (B.E.) degrees in the following: Africana studies; American studies; anthropology; applied mathematics and statistics; art history and criticism; Asian and Asian American studies; astronomy and planetary sciences; athletic training; atmospheric and oceanic sciences; biochemistry; biology; biomedical engineering; business management; chemical and molecular engineering; chemistry; cinema and cultural studies; civil engineering; clinical laboratory sciences; coastal environmental studies; comparative literature; computer engineering; computer science; earth and space sciences; economics; ecosystems and human impact; electrical engineering; engineering chemistry; engineering science; English;

environmental design, policy, and planning; environmental humanities; environmental studies; European studies; French; geology; German; health science; history; humanities; information systems; Italian; journalism; linguistics; marine sciences; marine vertebrate biology; mathematics; mechanical engineering; multidisciplinary studies; music; nursing; pharmacology; philosophy; physics; political science; psychology; religious studies; respiratory care; social work; sociology; Spanish; studio art; sustainability studies; technological systems management; theater arts; and women's and gender studies. The University also offers eighty-one minors.

Students may earn New York State provisional certification for secondary school teaching in biology, chemistry, earth science, English, French, German, Italian, mathematics, physics, Russian, social studies, Spanish, and K–12 in teaching English as a second language. A combined-degree program is available in which students earn an M.B.A. along with their choice of nearly any undergraduate major. Dual-bachelor's/master's-degree programs are also available in many other disciplines. Integrated eight-year bachelor's/M.D. and bachelor's/D.D.S. programs are offered to exceptional high school students, enabling them to participate in medical school and dental school classes and activities as undergraduates.

Academic Programs

All freshmen belong to one of six themed undergraduate colleges that offer a dynamic first-year experience designed to help students succeed. The undergraduate college program at Stony Brook is unique among SUNY schools and offers students academic and residential advising, one-credit classes in small-group settings, and informal gatherings with faculty members.

Innovative programs include a news literacy course, the first of its kind in the nation, offered through the School of Journalism, the only public undergraduate journalism school in New York. Other programs of note include sustainability studies, which offers eleven majors and minors leading to green careers, as well as the combined-degree, fast-track M.B.A. program, a major and minor in business management and a minor in accounting offered by the College of Business. Located on Long Island's East End, Stony Brook Southampton is the site of the School of Marine and Atmospheric Sciences Marine Station and graduate arts programs.

Stony Brook's Honors College has a special curriculum just for honors students. High-achieving students in the program enjoy small seminar courses and the opportunity to work closely with faculty members. A mentoring program, small study groups, and special classes are highlights of Stony Brook's Women in Science and Engineering (WISE) program, for women talented in math, science, or engineering. There also are Living-Learning Centers, which are designed to enable students with common interests to live and learn together.

Stony Brook may accept up to 30 credits by examination toward the bachelor's degree through such means as AP, CLEP, CPE, higher-level International Baccalaureate subjects, and Stony Brook's own Challenge Program. Students need a minimum of 120 credits for the B.A. or B.S. degree and 128 credits for the B.E. degree; 39 of these credits must be earned at the upper-division level. All students must satisfy general education requirements and maintain at least a 2.0 cumulative grade point average. Grading is traditional; a pass/no-credit option is available for some elective courses. Stony Brook's academic year starts in early September and ends in mid-May, with the exception of some health sciences programs that begin in June or July.

Off-Campus Programs

An international academic experience is now a necessity for students who wish to remain competitive for employment or for professional or graduate study. The Office of International Academic Programs

provides a variety of opportunities ranging in length from a winter or summer session, to a semester, to an academic year.

Opportunities also exist for students to earn academic credit and gain valuable experience while participating in internships and field research. Placements include government agencies and laboratories, hospitals and clinics, businesses and industries, and legal and social agencies on Long Island and in New York City, Albany, and Washington, D.C. Stony Brook also participates in the National Student Exchange Program.

Academic Facilities

Stony Brook's major academic facilities include the Frank Melville Jr. Memorial Library, Stony Brook University Hospital, and the five-theater Staller Center for the Arts. Stony Brook is also home to myriad centers, laboratories, and institutes. Some of these include the Simons Center for Geometry and Physics, Center of Excellence in Wireless and Information Technology, Advanced Energy Research and Technology Center, Institute for Theoretical Physics, Institute for Terrestrial and Planetary Atmospheres, Center for High-Pressure Research, Center for Biotechnology, Howard Hughes Medical Institute, and Center for Regional Policy Studies.

Costs

The University's high standards combined with its low tuition make a Stony Brook education an excellent value. For 2011–12, the annual tuition and fees for New York State residents were $6994. Nonresident tuition and fees were $16,444. Room and board cost $10,574. Books and supplies were estimated at $900.

Financial Aid

The Office of Financial Aid and Scholarship Services administers scholarships and three basic categories of aid: loans, employment opportunities, and grants. To apply for aid, a student must complete the Free Application for Federal Student Aid (FAFSA) as soon after January 1 as possible for the upcoming academic year. Stony Brook University's federal school code is 002838. Upon filing the FAFSA, New York State residents will receive the Express Tuition Assistance Program Application for New York State tuition assistance. The University's commitment to excellence shows in the number and value of merit scholarships offered to high-achieving students. Special scholarships are offered to those admitted to the Honors College and Women in Science and Engineering programs, as well as to Intel Science Talent Research and National Merit Scholarship Competition finalists and semifinalists, valedictorians, and salutatorians. To receive the fullest consideration for merit scholarships, freshman applicants should submit their application by January 15.

Faculty

Stony Brook's nearly 2,200 faculty members are tops in their fields and include scholars such as John Milnor, professor of mathematics and winner of the Abel Prize, and winners of four Nobel Prizes, two Pulitzer Prizes, five MacArthur Fellowships, and three Grammy Awards. They are also dedicated teachers and include more than 100 recipients of the Chancellor's Awards for Excellence in Teaching. Ninety-eight percent of full-time faculty members have doctorates or terminal degrees in their fields. Faculty members are credited with more than 1,500 inventions and more than 450 patents.

Student Government

Undergraduates are represented by the Undergraduate Student Government (USG), with members elected by the students. Student representatives help shape University policy and advise fellow students as members of the University Senate and other organizations. USG administers an annual budget of $3 million, which it uses to sponsor more than 300 student interest clubs and organizations. Varied student interests are represented by groups as diverse as Alternative Spring Break Outreach; the Belly Dancing Club; the Chess Club; the Commuter Student Association; the Pre-Med Society; the Science Fiction Forum; Stony Brook Pre-Law; and several cultural clubs that include the African Students Union, Asian Students Alliance, Caribbean Students Organization, Club India, and Latin American Student Organization.

Admission Requirements

Stony Brook is a selective institution and evaluates applicants on an individual basis. There is no automatic cutoff in the admission process, either in grade point average, rank, or test scores. The Admissions Committee seeks to enroll the strongest and most diverse class possible. Stony Brook welcomes applications from those with special talent or exceptional ability in a particular area. Freshman admission is based primarily upon the strength and breadth of the student's academic preparatory program, grade point average, and standardized test scores. Additional criteria include the essay, extracurricular activities, and letters of recommendation. Students who have attended college or university after graduating from high school are eligible to apply as transfers. Transfer applicants are expected to have performed well in a strong academic program. If fewer than 24 credits were earned, the student's high school record and standardized test scores are also required. Transfer students applying to the upper-division programs in the health sciences must have completed at least 57 credits in liberal arts and sciences and some specific course requirements.

Application and Information

Students are encouraged to submit applications for fall admission by December 1. Both the SUNY application and the Common Application are accepted. There is a $50 application fee. A supplemental application, which includes an essay and a letter of recommendation, is required for freshmen.

Information sessions with admissions counselors and campus tours with knowledgeable student guides also are available throughout the year; interested students should schedule their visit online.

For more information, contact:

Office of Undergraduate Admissions
Stony Brook University
Stony Brook, New York 11794-1901
Phone: 631-632-6868
   631-632-6859 (TDD)
Fax: 631-632-9898
E-mail: enroll@stonybrook.edu
Web site: http://www.stonybrook.edu/admissions

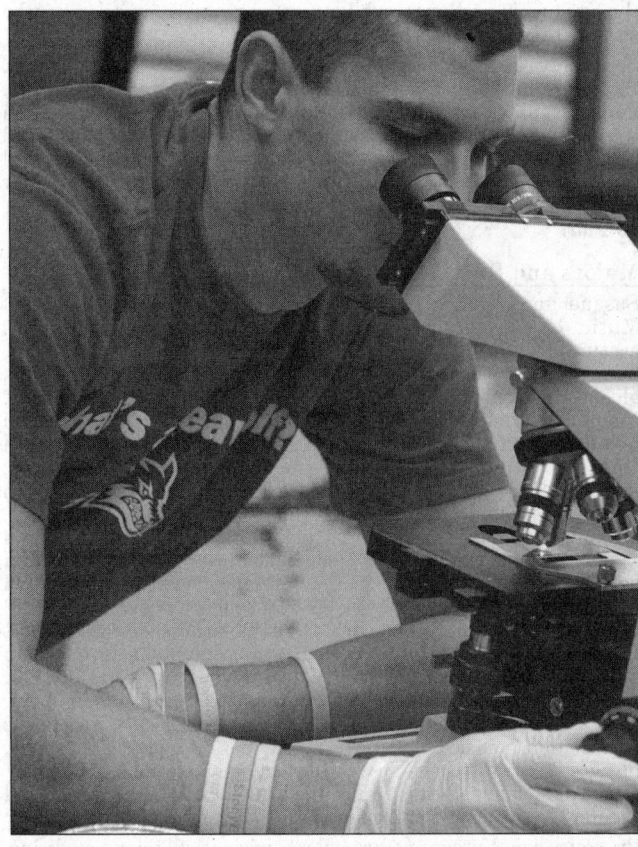

Stony Brook University combines a small-college environment with all the advantages of a major research university for a fraction of the cost of comparable institutions.

SUSQUEHANNA UNIVERSITY
SELINSGROVE, PENNSYLVANIA

The University

By nearly every indicator, Susquehanna University excels at preparing its graduates to achieve, lead, and serve in a diverse and interconnected world. Students benefit from more than fifty majors and minors encompassing a balance of liberal arts and professional studies programs, a highly qualified faculty, and state-of-the-art facilities that support intellectual and personal growth.

The value of experiential learning—study away, internships, and research—is supported by strong extracurriculars. With more than 100 student organizations, 23 NCAA Division III varsity sports, and nationally recognized volunteer programs, students find opportunities to learn and grow well beyond the classroom.

A Susquehanna education is a proven advantage. Graduates consistently say their Susquehanna experiences have given them a competitive edge over other recent graduates entering the workplace. A recent survey shows that 91 percent of graduates are employed full-time or enrolled in graduate or professional school within six months of graduation—an exceptionally high percentage compared with other institutions. Furthermore, 97 percent of graduates say they would recommend Susquehanna to a high school senior.

Location

Students find themselves at home in the eclectic town of Selinsgrove, Pennsylvania, nestled between the banks of the Susquehanna River and the foothills of the Appalachian Mountains. Favorite activities include checking out the shops on Market Street; enjoying the local flavor of downtown restaurants; kayaking, floating, or tubing down the Susquehanna River; or hiking, caving, and camping in nearby state parks and forests.

Selinsgrove is a 3-hour drive from New York City, Philadelphia, Baltimore, and Washington, D.C., and 4 hours from Pittsburgh. Pennsylvania's capital of Harrisburg is approximately 60 miles from the campus, and the Harrisburg International Airport is served by American, United, Delta, Northwest, and US Airways; several commuter airlines; and major rental-car agencies. The Penn Valley Airport in Selinsgrove provides facilities for private and charter aircraft.

Majors and Degrees

Susquehanna students pursue a Bachelor of Arts, Bachelor of Music, or Bachelor of Science degree in the following areas: accounting, anthropology, art history, biochemistry, biology, business administration (emphasis in entrepreneurship, finance, global management, information systems, or marketing), chemistry, communications (emphasis in digital media with tracks in broadcasting and journalism; emphasis in strategic communication with tracks in public relations and corporate communications; and emphasis in communication arts with tracks in speech communications, communications studies, and teacher certification), computer science, creative writing, earth and environmental sciences, ecology, economics (emphasis in financial economics, general economics, global economy, or financial markets), education (certification in early childhood, pre-K through 4, or secondary 7–12 in many areas), English, French, German, graphic design, history, information systems, international studies (emphasis in Asian studies, comparative cultural studies, developing world studies, diplomacy, European studies, international trade and development, or sustainable development), Italian, mathematics, music, music composition, music education, music performance, philosophy, physics, political science, psychology, religion, sociology, Spanish, studio art (emphasis in painting and drawing or photography), and theater (emphasis in performance or production and design).

Preprofessional programs are offered in dentistry, law, medicine, ministry, teaching and veterinary medicine and include one-on-one advising, related internships, and test preparation for the MCAT and LSAT. Cooperative programs in allied health are offered with Thomas Jefferson University in Philadelphia, in dentistry with Temple University School of Dental Medicine in Philadelphia, and in forestry and environmental management with Duke University in Durham, North Carolina.

Minors are available in almost every major area and in the following additional areas: actuarial science, advertising, anthropology, Asian studies, dance, diversity studies, film studies, health care studies, international business and foreign language, international relations, Italian, Jewish studies, legal studies, literature, music technology, music theory, publishing and editing, and women's studies.

Academic Programs

Susquehanna's Central Curriculum is a hybrid model of liberal arts and practical education that emphasizes critical-thinking skills and ethics, and teaches students to put those skills to work in today's world. Throughout their four years at Susquehanna, students develop intellectual skills through courses of their choosing that examine the richness of thought, human interaction, human connections, and the natural world.

Susquehanna's campus community explores a university theme each academic year. The theme is intended to focus classroom discussion, lectures, artistic performances, and student activities around a central idea for in-depth exploration. Past themes include Life on the Fringes, Water, Religion in the Public Square, Sustainability, and What Does It Mean to Be Educated? Reflecting the theme, the Common Reading Program asks Susquehanna faculty, staff, and incoming students to read a related common text every summer.

Susquehanna houses the Arlin M. Adams Center for Law and Society as a complementary program to the Central Curriculum. The Adams Center explores the rich intersections between law and various other disciplines. It provides a forum and research opportunities for examining issues affecting human rights and social responsibility, involving science and technology, and requiring constitutional interpretation. The Adams Center provides several venues for student learning, including internships and field experiences, networking, professional seminars, independent study, research projects, enhanced library resources, symposia, dialogue series, and the *Justice for All?* radio program. Guest speakers for the Adams Center have included nationally known experts and a Supreme Court justice.

Recently founded is the the Center for Adolescent Research and Education (CARE) at Susquehanna University which examines factors in teen decision-making. The center operates under the direction of Stephen Wallace, a 1981 graduate of the University who comes back to Susquehanna after 15 years as board chair and CEO of the national SADD (Students Against Destructive Decisions) organization, and with three decades of experience as a school psychologist, adolescent counselor, researcher, author, and motivational speaker. The center seeks to be the preeminent authoritative information source for parents, educators, mentors, coaches, and health professionals concerned with the attitudes and behaviors of adolescents and young adults.

Off-Campus Programs

Susquehanna's Global Opportunities (GO) program, the only one of its kind in the nation, requires every student to have a cross-cultural experience away from campus, either in the United States or abroad. It might include a traditional semester study-abroad program (GO Long), a short-term faculty or staff-led program (GO Short), a self-designed experience proposed and accepted in advance, or service in a cross-cultural setting.

GO is flexible and affordable. Susquehanna currently offers more than thirty GO Long programs that cost approximately the same as, or less than, a semester on campus. GO Short programs are even more affordable, because they involve a shorter stay away from campus. Most forms of financial aid, including scholarships, are available during GO Long or GO Short experiences

About two thirds of Susquehanna's students participate in nationally recognized community service projects, with an annual average of more than 25,000 hours of community service delivered to the Susquehanna Valley and beyond.

Academic Facilities

Susquehanna's facilities include a rich mix of historic and new buildings. Two buildings are on the National Register of Historic Places and others, completed in recent years, have won architectural and design awards.

In fall 2010 the Natural Sciences Center opened, which has transformed teaching and learning for all Susquehanna students. With a prominent spot on the 306-acre campus, the 81,000-square-foot science facility is the school's largest academic building. The facility houses Susquehanna's biology, chemistry, and earth and environmental sciences programs.

The new science building demonstrates Susquehanna's strong commitment to sustainability and environmental responsibility. The building earned the U.S. Green Building Council's LEED silver-level certification. The investment benefits all students, because science education is a part of the Central Curriculum. The initiative advances other programs at Susquehanna, with the former science building, Fisher Hall, renovated to accommodate anticipated enrollment gains.

Susquehanna's Natural Sciences Center complements the already outstanding academic facilities available to students. Apfelbaum Hall, completed in 1999, is home to the Sigmund Weis School of Business and the Department of Communications. Apfelbaum houses two television studios, multimedia classrooms, a presentation room, and numerous small-group study rooms. Bogar Hall, renovated in 2007, includes a language lab for students studying modern languages and the Writers Institute's Editing and Publishing Center. Cunningham Center for Music and Art, renovated and expanded in 2002, offers contemporary art and music teaching facilities and flexible practice and performance space, including Stretansky Concert Hall, a 320-seat venue designed to optimize choral and instrumental music. Weber Chapel Auditorium is home to a classic, 1,500-seat theater, with a revolving stage and recording studio for students studying music technology. Additional performance space for theater students is available in the Degenstein Center Theater, which houses a modern 450-seat proscenium teaching theater with a counterweight fly system and an intimate, black-box studio theater. Every student takes full advantage of the Blough-Weis Library. The attractive, technologically advanced library offers online access to thousands of journal articles; more than 330,000 books, DVDs and CDs; and comfortable spaces for group and quiet study. Students and faculty members have online access from any computer connected to the Internet. The library also houses Susquehanna's Media Center.

Costs

Tuition and fees for 2012–13 are $37,280. Room and board costs are $10,000. A student's personal expenses, including books, travel, and other costs, are estimated at $1600 to $1900 per year.

Financial Aid

More than 90 percent of Susquehanna students receive some form of financial aid. All students are encouraged to apply for need-based financial aid by filing both the Free Application for Federal Student Aid (FAFSA) and the CSS PROFILE forms. Every applicant for admission to Susquehanna also is considered for merit awards regardless of financial need. Renewable for four years, Susquehanna's merit scholarships are awarded based on academic achievement, talent in a particular area of University interest, or community involvement. Susquehanna is a participant in the Tuition Exchange program for children of employees at participating institutions. The University also participates in the Yellow Ribbon Program for veterans of the wars in Iraq and Afghanistan.

Faculty

Susquehanna's faculty members serve as advisers and creative mentors to their students both in the classroom and beyond. Whether meeting one-on-one with a student for more in-depth instruction after class or making their homes available for barbecues, faculty members make themselves accessible to students in a variety of formal and informal settings. Professors who seek employment at Susquehanna value the opportunity to live and learn alongside their students. By graduation, many Susquehanna students have shared a stage with faculty members, whether through a recital or a national conference presentation.

Of Susquehanna's 142 full-time professors, 92 percent hold a doctorate or terminal degree in their field. The student-faculty ratio is 13:1.

Student Government

Susquehanna's Student Government Association is a self-governing organization providing representation of the student body in University affairs. The main function of the legislative body is the allocation of student activities fees to recognized clubs, student groups, campus projects, and University activities. Senators are elected each year and serve as student representatives to various offices and groups on campus.

Admission Requirements

Susquehanna's average accepted student earns a GPA of 3.39 in a competitive college-prep curriculum. For those students who choose to submit test scores, the midrange SAT score is 1020–1220, and the midrange ACT score is 22–26. Students may choose to apply under the Write Option, which allows two graded, critical writing samples to serve as a substitute for SAT or ACT scores.

Susquehanna looks for exceptional students who are attracted by its academic challenges and extracurricular opportunities. Admission is competitive. The University considers what it can do for students and how students might contribute to Susquehanna. It assesses applications based on course selections, grades, and class rank as well as factors such as motivation, creativity, and leadership. Honors program students typically rank in the top 10 percent.

Susquehanna strongly encourages prospective students to visit the campus and interview with a member of the admissions staff. Counselors are happy to answer questions and explain programs firsthand. Students can see the facilities and meet with faculty members, coaches, and students. Susquehanna can arrange for class visits or overnight stays in residence halls during the academic year.

Application and Information

Susquehanna accepts the Susquehanna Application as well as the Common Application, with no preference given to one over the other. All applications are free to file online.

Students applying to the Bachelor of Music degree program are required to audition. Students applying to major in graphic design or creative writing are required to submit a portfolio of their work.

Office of Admissions
Susquehanna University
514 University Avenue
Selinsgrove, Pennsylvania 17870-1164
Phone: 570-372-4260
       800-326-9672 (toll-free)
Fax: 570-372-2722
E-mail: suadmiss@susqu.edu
Web site: http://www.susqu.edu

Historic Seibert Hall at Susquehanna University.

SWEET BRIAR COLLEGE
SWEET BRIAR, VIRGINIA

The College

Deeply committed to the education of women since its founding in 1901, Sweet Briar College is consistently ranked as one of the top national liberal arts and sciences colleges in the country. Its excellent academic reputation, beautiful campus, and attention to the individual attract ambitious, intellectually self-confident women who want to excel. Students can expect their Sweet Briar experience to allow them to fulfill their promise as scholars and leaders, while enjoying the close-knit friendships and camaraderie that come with a personal, residential community.

A Sweet Briar education sets in motion the conviction that any goal is achievable. Small classes (averaging 12 students per class) and a student-faculty ratio of 8:1 ensure personal attention and academic interaction. Students work one-on-one with faculty members who are committed to each student's academic success. The College has a wide geographic, ethnic, and socioeconomic representation. About 700 women from more than forty states and nineteen countries are enrolled at Sweet Briar's Virginia campus; another 120 students are enrolled in Sweet Briar's coed Junior Year in France and Junior Year in Spain programs. Any student may have a car.

Students who derive the most from the Sweet Briar experience are those who participate in and contribute to community life, striking a good balance between academic work and the rest of life. They recognize that one of the advantages of the College is the unlimited opportunities for women to participate and assume leadership roles in many types of organizations and activities. More than fifty campus organizations are available, including honor societies, a literary journal, community service groups, a multicultural club, political groups, a student newspaper, drama and dance clubs, a radio station, and singing groups. Students plan and participate in an extensive array of concerts, films, and dance and theater productions as well as workshops and master classes by visiting scholars and performers. Visitors have included the writer Rebecca Skloot, environmental attorney Robert F. Kennedy Jr., columnist Christine Brennan, and country music singer Stephanie Quayle.

Twenty-one campus buildings, the work of renowned American architect Ralph Adams Cram, are on the National Register of Historic Places. In 2006, Sweet Briar opened a beautiful new studio arts facility. Sweet Briar is the only college in the United States with a residential artists' colony on its campus. Known as the Virginia Center for the Creative Arts, the colony is a working retreat for international writers, visual artists, and composers. In 2009, the College opened a 53,000-square-foot fitness and athletic center addition to the existing gymnasium, and a sixty-bed apartment-style residence facility for upper class students. The on-campus equestrian center, one of the largest and best college facilities in the country, attracts both competitive and recreational riders. Sweet Briar's equestrian program, both competitive and instructional, has consistently garnered national recognition. The 100-acre Rogers Riding Center has a 120-foot by 300-foot indoor arena with Perma-Flex footing, well-appointed stables for approximately 90 horses, several outdoor rings, numerous paddocks, and miles of hacking trails—all within walking distance of the main campus.

In 2009, Sweet Briar upgraded its computer network to a state-of-the-art wireless platform that allows high-speed Internet access from all academic and administrative buildings, as well as residence hall rooms. Connection to the campus network is also possible from most outdoor, student-used spaces.

In 2004, Sweet Briar launched two graduate degree programs: the Master of Arts in Teaching and the Master of Education. These programs are rooted in the teaching philosophy of differentiated curriculum and instruction. Sweet Briar also established a new degree program in engineering, only the second such undergraduate program at a women's college. In 2011, the engineering program received ABET accreditation.

Varsity athletes compete in NCAA Division III field hockey, lacrosse, soccer, softball, swimming, and tennis. Club sports include cross-country, fencing, volleyball, and riding.

Location

Sweet Briar's 3,250-acre campus in the foothills of the Blue Ridge Mountains includes hiking, biking, and riding trails and two lakes that provide spectacular venues for outdoor recreational activities. The College is centrally located on the outskirts of Lynchburg, Virginia, southwest of Washington, D.C., and Charlottesville. Students also enjoy activities in nearby Roanoke and Richmond.

Majors and Degrees

Sweet Briar awards the Bachelor of Arts, Bachelor of Science, and Bachelor of Fine Arts degrees. The College offers thirty-four majors: anthropology, archaeology, art history, biochemistry and molecular biology, biology, business management, chemistry, classics, dance, economics, education, engineering and management, engineering science, English, English and creative writing, environmental science, environmental studies, French, German, German studies, government, history, international affairs, mathematics, modern languages and literatures, music, musical theater, philosophy, physics, psychology, religion, sociology, Spanish, studio art, and theater.

Additional area studies, minors, and certificate programs include arts management, equine studies, engineering (3-2 dual degree), journalism, new media, and communications, Latin American studies, law and society, medieval and Renaissance studies, pre-law, pre-medicine, pre–veterinary science, and statistics. Students may design an interdisciplinary major focused on a topic of special interest or may construct personalized majors.

Academic Programs

Sweet Briar's mission is to prepare women to be active, responsible members of a world community. Underscoring every one of the major fields of study is the idea that the best way to learn about the world is to experience it. The curriculum emphasizes hands-on learning, comprehensive understanding, analysis, reflection, creativity, and communication across disciplines. The academic programs are nationally celebrated. To add to this, the College recently adopted a strategic plan that includes emphasis on providing an education that is dynamic, sophisticated, connected, and entrepreneurial. Making the most effective use of Sweet Briar's unique campus as a "landscape for learning," the strategic plan aims at an educational experience that prepares students to engage with today's digital world, be ready to adapt to the dizzying rate of technological change, and encourage entrepreneurial thinking across disciplines.

The general education program has four components—English 104, skills requirements, experiences requirements, and knowledge areas requirements—that work together to ensure the development of strong communication and quantitative reasoning skills. Independent studies and seminars are included in most majors, with a culminating senior course or exercise required in most majors. Sweet Briar has a chapter of Phi Beta Kappa and was the first women's college to establish a chapter of the pre-law honorary society Phi Alpha Delta. It also has a four-year honors program that is nationally recognized for its innovative partnering of interdisciplinary academic and cocurricular programs. Honors students may take special tutorials and seminars as well as complete a yearlong research project culminating in an honors thesis on an original topic.

Sweet Briar's two-semester calendar allows students to participate in intensive courses, independent research projects, or internships on campus or throughout the world.

Off-Campus Programs

By the time they graduate, more than a third of Sweet Briar students have studied abroad. The Sweet Briar Junior Year in France, the first program in Paris for American students, is considered the most

academically rigorous program available today. Students from 258 colleges and universities have participated in the coed program. The successful Junior Year in Spain is recognized as the premier program in Seville. The College has special relationships with the University of St. Andrews in Scotland, Heidelberg University in Germany, Doshisha Women's College in Japan, and the University of Urbino in Italy. Sweet Briar students have also chosen the following destinations for study abroad: Australia, China, the Czech Republic, Denmark, Greece, Holland, Ireland, Jamaica, Korea, Mongolia, Morocco, New Zealand, and Thailand. Off-campus study may also include an Environmental Junior Year, the Washington Semester at American University, and summer programs at St. Anne's College in Oxford, England. In addition, summer programs are available in Australia; Central America, including Costa Rica; Münster, Germany; Rome and Urbino, Italy; Nepal; and Spain.

Sweet Briar participates in the Tri-College Consortium with Randolph College and Lynchburg College. In addition to taking courses at the other colleges, students can participate in combined social and cultural activities on those campuses.

Academic Facilities

Sweet Briar has the largest private undergraduate library collection in the state of Virginia, with resources of more than 240,000 volumes, 1,000 journal subscriptions, 430,000 microforms, 6,800 audiovisual materials, and special libraries in art, music, and the sciences. Some of the notable special holdings include Virginia Woolf, T. E. Lawrence, George Meredith, W. H. Auden, and a rare collection of twentieth-century Chinese works. Three computer labs with Macintosh and Windows/Intel Pentium computers are open free of charge 24 hours a day. The student-computer ratio is 6:1. A lab for Sweet Briar's new engineering department includes a 5-Kip-capacity Universal Test Machine; a United Tru-Blue Rockwell hardness tester; a set of gauged beams and test fixtures for mechanics experiments; eight new computers, each with NI ELVIS and Labview with Protoboards; and a well-equipped machine shop. Students studying science use state-of-the-art equipment that enhances faculty-student collaborative research. Biology equipment includes a scanning electron microscope with digital imaging system, equipment for plant and animal tissue culture, and DNA sequencing equipment. Chemistry students have access to two nuclear magnetic resonance spectrometers (NMR; 400 MHz and 60 MHz), an atomic absorption spectrometer (AAS), a diode array UV/Vis spectrometer, a Fourier-transform infrared spectrometer (FT-IR), a modular LASER laboratory, a gas chromatograph/mass spectrograph (GC/MS), a high-pressure liquid chromatograph (HPLC), and a differential scanning calorimeter (DSC). Physics equipment includes a scanning tunneling microscope, an X-ray crystallography system, a 10-inch-diameter reflecting telescope, and holographic instrumentation.

The environmental studies program occupies two sites. A renovated train station provides classroom and laboratory space equipped with a Rigaku Miniflex powder X-ray diffraction system for mineralogical analysis, a Rocklabs bench-top ring mill for grinding rock and soil samples, a drying oven and a high-temperature muffle furnace, and more. An adjacent caboose car provides office space for faculty members. A water treatment plant was also converted to an education/nature center and environmental lab; equipment includes water, soil, wastewater, and sediment sampling instrumentation, including N-Con composite samplers, macroinvertebrate samplers, and specialized water-collection devices.

The Babcock Fine Arts Center includes individual practice rooms, an electronic piano lab, dance studios, theaters, and Murchison Lane Auditorium for lectures and performing arts. Two former dairy barns were recently renovated for classroom and office space to house studio arts, including a ceramics and sculpture studio; four large studios for painting, drawing, and printmaking; and a photo studio and darkroom.

The Academic Resource Center (ARC) provides free of charge to all students academic support services that include assistance with papers and study strategies, a personalized time management system, stress management advice, tutoring information, and one-on-one peer mentoring. The ARC also provides support and learning strategies for students with diagnosed learning differences.

Costs

For 2011–12, tuition and fees were $31,095 and room and board totaled $11,100. Books and supplies were estimated at $1100 and personal expenses averaged $1150.

Financial Aid

A family's financial circumstance does not limit a student's choices at Sweet Briar because of the College's generous financial aid program. More than 90 percent of enrolling students receive financial assistance from the College, including merit scholarships, need-based grants, loans, and work-study awards. Scholarships for international students are also available on a competitive basis.

Faculty

Sweet Briar's faculty members have been commended by numerous regional and national educational groups for their excellence in teaching. Faculty members are actively engaged in teaching, research, publication, and other forms of creative activity. More than 95 percent of full-time faculty members have a doctorate or the highest professional degree in his or her field. All classes are taught by a faculty member. About half of the faculty members are women.

Student Government

The Student Government Association (SGA) is founded upon a highly developed concept of honor and student ownership and involvement. The Honor System applies to all phases of academic and social life. Each entering student becomes a full member of the Student Government Association upon taking the Honor Pledge, which states that Sweet Briar women do not lie, cheat, steal, or violate the rights of others. Students participate in the governance of the College through the many offices and committee positions of the Student Government Association. SGA and its committees are largely responsible for the self-governance of the student body.

Admission Requirements

Sweet Briar seeks talented women who are adventurous, are enthusiastic about learning, and want to take an active part in their education. The Admissions Committee looks for qualities such as independent thinking, ethical principles, assertiveness, and an appreciation of diversity. Sweet Briar welcomes students of all economic, ethnic, geographic, religious, and social backgrounds.

Requirements normally include a minimum of 4 units in English, 3 in mathematics, 3 in social studies, 2 sequential years in a foreign language, and 3 units in science, as well as additional units in these subjects to total 16. Most candidates have 20 such academic units. Special attention is given to the difficulty of the applicant's curriculum and her academic achievement in the classroom; scores on the SAT or ACT are required. An interview at the College is strongly encouraged but not required. Candidates who are unable to visit the campus are invited to meet with staff members or to talk with alumnae in their hometowns.

Application and Information

Sweet Briar has dropped its early decision application program in favor of being responsive to all applicants. An application deadline of February 1 is maintained, but students are invited to apply for admission as early as September of their senior year. Sweet Briar will notify each student of acceptance within one month of the date her application becomes complete. Transfer applications for the fall semester are due by July 1. A completed application includes a transcript of the candidate's academic work, scores on the required test, recommendations from the guidance counselor and a teacher, and an essay written by the candidate. There is a $40 application fee, which may be waived at the request of the student's guidance counselor if it is deemed to be a financial burden. Sweet Briar also accepts the Common Application (a supplement is required). All materials and requests for information should be sent to the admissions office at the address listed in this description.

Dean of Admissions
Sweet Briar College
P.O. Box 1052
Sweet Briar, Virginia 24595
Phone: 434-381-6142
        800-381-6142 (toll-free)
Fax: 434-381-6152
E-mail: admissions@sbc.edu
Web site: http://www.sbc.edu

SYRACUSE UNIVERSITY
SYRACUSE, NEW YORK

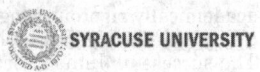

The University

Syracuse University (SU), which was founded in 1870, is an independent, privately endowed university with an international reputation. Students attend from all over the United States and from more than 100 other countries. There are about 17,300 students enrolled; 12,600 are undergraduates. Approximately 70 percent of the students live in University housing, which includes modern residence halls, apartments, and town houses. The 200-acre campus features a main grassy quadrangle surrounded by academic buildings, with residential facilities nearby. The campus is situated on a hill overlooking the downtown area of Syracuse. Social life is centered on the campus, and there are innumerable recreational, athletic, and academic activities. The 50,000-seat Carrier Dome is the site of concerts, sports events, and commencement. All of campus is connected to the University's wireless networks.

Location

The city of Syracuse (metropolitan-area population of over 650,000 is the business, educational, and cultural hub of central New York. The city offers professional theater and opera, as well as visiting artists and performers. Highlights of the downtown area include the Everson Museum of Art, the Milton J. Rubenstein Museum of Science and Technology (MOST), the impressive Civic Center, and the Armory Square shopping area. Central New York has many lakes, parks, mountains, and outstanding recreational opportunities.

Majors and Degrees

Syracuse University awards the Bachelor of Arts (B.A.), Bachelor of Science (B.S.), Bachelor of Architecture (B.Arch.), Bachelor of Industrial Design (B.I.D.), Bachelor of Music (B.Mus.), and Bachelor of Fine Arts (B.F.A.) degrees.

The School of Architecture offers a five-year baccalaureate program leading to the first professional degree of B.Arch.

Over 50 departmental and interdisciplinary majors are offered in the College of Arts and Sciences including African-American studies, American studies, anthropology, art, art history, biochemistry, biology, biophysical science, chemistry, classical civilization, classics (Greek and Latin), communication sciences and disorders, economics, English and textual studies, European literature, fine arts, French, geography, geology (Earth sciences), German, Greek, history, history of architecture, international relations, Italian, Latin, Latino–Latin American studies, linguistic studies, mathematics, Middle Eastern studies, modern foreign languages, music, music history and cultures, philosophy, physics, policy studies (public affairs), political philosophy, political science, psychology, religion, religion and society, Russian, Russian and Central European studies, sociology, Spanish, women's studies, and writing and rhetoric. Integrated Learning Majors are offered in ethics, forensic science, neuroscience, and energy and its impacts.

The David B. Falk College of Sport and Human Dynamics majors include child and family studies, nutrition/dietetics, nutrition science, public health, social work, and sport management.

The School of Education offers majors in art education, elementary education (inclusive with special education), health and exercise science (including pre–physical therapy and 3+3 D.P.T.), music education, physical education, health and physical education, secondary education, selected studies in education, and special education (inclusive with elementary education and with early childhood education).

The L. C. Smith College of Engineering and Computer Science majors include aerospace, chemical, civil, computer, electrical, environmental, and mechanical engineering; bioengineering; and computer science.

The School of Information Studies offers a four-year bachelor's degree program in information management and technology.

The Martin J. Whitman School of Management majors include accounting, entrepreneurship and emerging enterprises, finance, management, marketing management, real estate, retail management, and supply chain management.

The S. I. Newhouse School of Public Communications majors are in the following areas: advertising, broadcast and digital journalism, graphic design, magazine, newspaper and online journalism, photography, public relations, and television/radio/film.

The College of Visual and Performing Arts majors are in the following areas: art and design, communication and rhetorical studies, drama, music, and transmedia. Art and design majors offered are ceramics, communications design, (includes advertising design), fashion design, history of art, illustration, industrial and interaction design, environmental and interior design, jewelry and metalsmithing, painting, printmaking, and sculpture. Transmedia majors include art photography, art video, computer art and animation, and film. Drama majors include theater design and technology, acting, musical theater, and stage management. Music majors include the Bandier Program for Music and the Entertainment Industries, music composition, music industry, performance organ, performance percussion, performance piano, performance strings, performance voice, and performance wind instruments. The Department of Communication and Rhetorical Studies offers a Bachelor of Science degree.

Academic Programs

The University operates on a two-semester calendar with two 6-week summer sessions. Students generally take five 3-credit-hour courses each semester. A minimum of 120 credit hours is required for graduation. Special programs include dual and combined enrollment, selected studies, internships, an honors program, ROTC, and preprofessional advising for students going on to study dentistry, law, medicine, or veterinary science.

Off-Campus Programs

The Syracuse University Abroad program operates centers in London, Madrid, Hong Kong, Beijing, Florence, Santiago (Chile), Strasbourg, and Istanbul. SU Abroad also offers opportunities through world partners in over thirty other countries, including Australia, Costa Rica, Ecuador, Egypt, India, Ireland, Japan, Korea, Poland, and Russia.

Academic Facilities

The academic buildings at Syracuse University span the century, with fifteen listed in the National Register of Historic Places and others representative of some of the most modern and technologically sophisticated architecture in the country. The Ernest Stevenson Bird Library houses approximately 3.1 million printed volumes, more than 16,000 online and print journals, and extensive collections of microforms, maps, images, music scores, sound recordings, video, rare books, and manuscripts. The University has computer facilities with laboratories and a data communications network that links computers to hundreds of terminals. The $107-million, 230,000-square-foot Life Sciences Complex combines research and teaching wings for biology,

chemistry, and biochemistry. The Newhouse Communications Center has some of the finest facilities available for journalism and telecommunications. Slocum Hall, home to the School of Architecture, includes a new auditorium, gallery, and space for studio and research. The Center for Science and Technology is a state-of-the-art facility uniting research and academic programs in computer science and technology. It also houses the CASE Center for research in computer applications and software engineering. The new five-story addition to Link Hall, home of the L.C. Smith College of Engineering and Computer Science, features a three-story, high bay lab that houses a crane and space for civil engineering students to build and test structures. The high-tech Melvin A. Eggers Hall offers superior facilities for the University's social science programs. The multimillion-dollar Whitman School of Management building provides students with access to the latest educational technologies and plenty of space for team meetings and work.

Costs

Tuition for 2011–12 was $36,300. The costs for housing and meals averaged $13,254, and fees were $1367. Books and supplies averaged $1322; travel expenses, $600; and personal expenses, $940. Therefore, the total cost of attendance was approximately $53,790.

Financial Aid

About 80 percent of all entering first-year and transfer students receive some form of financial aid. By filing the Free Application for Federal Student Aid (FAFSA) and the CSS Financial Aid PROFILE, students are automatically considered for all financial aid programs administered by Syracuse University, including federal financial aid, Syracuse University Grants, and Federal Work-Study Program awards. Merit-based scholarships are available to both first-year and transfer students, based on the information provided in the application for admission. Syracuse University evaluates candidates for admission without respect to financial need. Information on financial aid policies, procedures, and deadlines can be obtained from the Office of Financial Aid and Scholarship Programs.

Faculty

The majority of faculty members hold the highest degree in their professional field. There are over 900 full-time faculty members, including recognized experts in their fields who teach at both the graduate and undergraduate levels.

Student Government

The Syracuse University Student Association works to protect students' rights and offers services through its three branches—the executive, the legislative, and the judicial.

Admission Requirements

Syracuse University seeks a diverse student body from all social, cultural, and educational backgrounds. Each candidate is evaluated individually, based on the requirements of the college of the University to which he or she has applied. Emphasis is placed on students' high school performance, standardized test scores (SAT or ACT), an essay, recommendations, extracurricular activities and community service, and portfolios or auditions, when required. Special admission requirements and deadlines for some programs are described on the University's Web site.

Syracuse University is an Equal Opportunity/Affirmative Action institution and does not discriminate on the basis of race, creed, color, gender, national origin, religion, marital status, age, disability, sexual orientation, or gender identity or expression.

Application and Information

Regular decision applicants for the fall semester should submit their completed application along with transcripts, standardized test scores, the essay, teacher recommendations, and the counselor evaluation by January 1 (submission deadline). Notification begins in mid-March. Completed applications for early decision applicants must be submitted by November 15. Notification begins in mid-December.

Detailed information may be obtained by contacting:

Office of Admissions
100 Crouse-Hinds Hall
900 South Crouse Avenue
Syracuse University
Syracuse, New York 13244-2130
Phone: 315-443-3611
E-mail: orange@syr.edu
Web site: http://admissions.syr.edu

The historic buildings that make up the SU campus stand in testimony to the many years of distinction that are at the foundation of Syracuse University.

TEMPLE UNIVERSITY
PHILADELPHIA, PENNSYLVANIA

The University

Students who visit Temple University's Main Campus find they are quite impressed. Cutting-edge facilities and great faculty members create a dynamic academic environment that draws students from around the world. But what can transform a student's life at Temple happens outside the classroom as well. Temple is located in Philadelphia, a dynamic, world-class city with a diverse ethnic mix, a robust economy, and a thriving music and art scene. It is the perfect place to live and study. Two spectacular new academic buildings opened on Main Campus in 2009—the Tyler School of Art and the Fox School of Business and Management's Alter Hall. Tyler's new architecture building opened in fall 2011. New academic and residential facilities are under construction and are slated to open in 2012 and 2013.

Students who prefer not to attend college in the city should take a look at the Ambler campus, Temple's 187-acre suburban home. Just about all undergraduate programs can be started there, and eighteen can be fully completed there. Ambler's $17-million Learning Center includes smart classrooms; fully integrated technology, including wireless access throughout the building; five computer lab/classrooms; a math, science, and writing center; a video editing lab; a café; and a 300-seat auditorium.

Temple's other local campus is the Health Sciences Center, where the College of Health Professions, Temple University Hospital, Temple University School of Medicine, and Temple Dental School are located.

Temple is in the city, but it has a large residential student population—about 12,000 students living on and around Main Campus. The calendar is crammed with theater, dance, and music performances. The Liacouras Center, Temple's 10,200-seat entertainment complex, hosts the University's NCAA Division I basketball games (free tickets for students!) as well as concerts. Great performers like Kanye West, Green Day, Maroon 5, John Mayer, Counting Crows, Rusted Root, Alicia Keys, and Bob Dylan have performed at the Liacouras Center. Temple has every type of student doing every type of activity. Beyond sports, students can join one of 100 or so clubs and organizations and take full advantage of the rich resources and recreation activities offered by Philadelphia and the surrounding area.

Location

Philadelphia has a lot more than juicy sandwiches and cream cheese. With more than 100 museums, 700 Zagat-rated restaurants, and the largest landscaped park in the country—Fairmount Park at 4,180 acres—Philly has a lot to offer. It is a walkable, manageable city that is just 1.5 miles from Temple's Main Campus. Just four stops on a quick subway ride and students are in Center City—or what most would call downtown. Shop, eat, play, or just chill. In addition, students can find a variety of internships in all fields in the Philadelphia area, and Temple has more than 100,000 alumni in the region who love to hire Temple students.

Majors and Degrees

The Tyler School of Art offers the Bachelor of Fine Arts with concentrations in ceramics/glass, fibers, graphic and interactive design, metals/jewelry/CAD-CAM, painting, photography, printmaking, and sculpture; the Bachelor of Arts in art history and visual studies; and the Bachelor of Science in art education. Tyler's Architecture Program confers the Bachelor of Science in architecture (preprofessional), architectural preservation, and facilities management.

The Fox School of Business and Management offers the Bachelor of Business Administration in accounting, actuarial science, business management, economics, entrepreneurship, finance, human resource management, international business administration, law and business, management information systems, marketing, real estate, and risk management and insurance.

The School of Communications and Theater offers the Bachelor of Arts in advertising; American culture and media arts; broadcasting, telecommunications, and mass media; communication studies; film and media arts; journalism; strategic communication; and theater.

The College of Education offers the Bachelor of Science in applied communications, career and technical education, elementary education, and secondary education.

The College of Engineering offers the Bachelor of Science in Engineering in engineering (general program), civil engineering, electrical engineering, and mechanical engineering. The Bachelor of Science is offered in construction management technology and general engineering technology.

The College of Health Professions offers the Bachelor of Science in communication sciences; health information management; linguistics; nursing; public health; speech, language, and hearing; therapeutic recreation, and kinesiology.

The College of Liberal Arts offers the Bachelor of Arts in African American studies, American studies, anthropology, Asian studies, classics, criminal justice, economics, English, French, geography and urban studies, German, Hebrew, history, Italian, neuroscience (systems, behavior, and plasticity), philosophy, political science, psychology, religion, Russian, sociology, Spanish, and women's studies.

The Boyer College of Music and Dance offers the Bachelor of Music in composition, dance, jazz studies, music education, music history, music therapy, performance (specific instrument or voice), and theory; the Bachelor of Fine Arts is offered in dance.

The College of Science and Technology offers the Bachelor of Science in biochemistry, biology, biophysics, chemistry, computer science, environmental studies, geology, mathematical economics, mathematics, physics, neuroscience (cell and molecular), and prepharmacy.

The School of Social Administration offers the Bachelor of Social Work degree.

The School of Tourism and Hospitality Management offers the Bachelor of Science in sport and recreation management and in tourism and hospitality management.

In addition, Ambler College offers Bachelor of Science degree programs in horticulture and landscape architecture and in community and regional planning.

Academic Programs

Temple provides an excellent and affordable education, which not only prepares the student for the specific demands of a career, but also enhances an understanding of the world and the ability to continue learning throughout life.

All students are required to complete the General Education curriculum, a cross-section of courses that form the intellectual foundation of a Temple education, which includes a Philadelphia Experience theme. Many first-year students take advantage of Learning Communities—groups of 20 to 30 participants who pursue common studies under the direction of a faculty team. They spend a semester together, taking a few common courses, participating in faculty-led discussion groups, studying together, and taking field trips related to their studies.

University Studies is a home for the many students who have not declared a major and for students interested in graduate or professional programs in health fields. Academically qualified students may seek extra intellectual challenge through the honors program, taking about a quarter of their course work in the program's smaller, more demanding classes.

After graduation, students are well prepared for the job world. Temple's Career Center arranges cooperative education assignments, schedules on-campus interviews with employers and graduate schools, offers employment skills workshops, provides career and graduate school advisement, and maintains a network of thousands of successful Temple alumni.

Academic Facilities

With more than fifty computer labs and a 90 percent wireless campus, information is more accessible than ever. An exciting new addition to the Main Campus is the Teaching, Education, Collaboration, and Help (TECH) Center. With up to 700 computers (600 fixed workstations and up to 100 laptop loaners), the TECH Center is one of the largest of its kind in the nation; thirteen breakout rooms where students can work on group projects and practice presentations; six specialized labs within the primary center, including video editing, graphic design/CAD, music composition, language/interactive audio, quiet zone, and software development facility; a 24-hour computer help desk for students and faculty and staff members; a 4,260-square-foot Temple Welcome Center (run by the Admissions Office) to host visits to the University by prospective students and their families; and a Starbucks café.

Costs

Tuition and fees for the 2011–12 academic year were $13,596 for Pennsylvania residents and $23,422 for out-of-state residents (tuition rates can vary by major). Room and board for the academic year were about $9300.

Financial Aid

Scholarships, grants, loans, and work-study programs are available; 2 out of every 3 Temple students receive financial aid. Four-year academic merit scholarships for talented entering freshmen begin at $2500. Students need only apply for admission to be eligible for these scholarships. Applicants for need-based aid must file the Free Application for Federal Student Aid (FAFSA). Transfer students must file a financial aid transcript, even if they have received no aid from their previous school.

Faculty

At Temple, faculty members are valued not only for their ability to pursue knowledge, but also to share that knowledge with students. Full-time faculty members teach many introductory courses, and often act as academic advisers; from their first semester students can expect to have contact with the people at the forefront of their fields, winners of prestigious teaching and research awards such as the Lindback, the Golden Apple, the Sowell, the Fulbright, the Guggenheim, the Carnegie, and the National Endowment.

In 2007, Temple officially welcomed the largest group of new tenured and tenure-track faculty members in recent history. Faculty members were hired away from leading universities and research centers, including Princeton University, Brown University, the University of Wisconsin–Madison, the University of Maryland, Wellesley College, and the Cleveland Clinic. Nearly every college at Temple has been joined by at least one new presidential faculty recruit.

In addition to being superlative teachers and researchers, Temple faculty members are also known for their practical experience. For example, a marketing class may be led by a successful entrepreneur or music lessons given by a member of the Philadelphia Orchestra. Marine biologists, newspaper editors, published authors, practicing architects, and health care professionals all bring their expertise to the classroom to enhance students' education.

Admission Requirements

For freshman admissions, high school grades (quality of courses, grade trends), standardized test scores, and other factors (the required essay, recommendations, extracurricular activities, work or leadership experience, and other personal circumstances) are considered. Temple uses a sliding scale rather than absolute cut-offs for GPA and test scores. SAT subject tests and personal interviews are not required. The deadline for freshman admission is March 1; however, students should apply in the fall of their senior year. Official copies of high school transcripts and standardized test scores must be sent directly to the admissions office. Counselor forms are not required. The deadline for spring admission is November 1.

Temple has rolling admissions. Freshman decisions begin in early fall, and letters are sent four to six weeks after that point. Temple's admissions process is holistic; every aspect of the student's academic history is considered. Typically, students with a B+ average or better in a strong, college-prep curriculum in grades 9–12 and in the top 30 percent of their graduating classes are accepted. The SAT is required with all three sections considered—admitted students average 500–600 on each section. If students opt to take the ACT, they must also complete the writing section.

Freshman students who apply are automatically considered for merit-based scholarships and honors. Recommendations are not required but are accepted and considered. There is no recommendation form. The best way to apply is online. The application fee is $55—most students apply online.

Temple University welcomes transfer applicants from both two-year and four-year colleges and universities around the country and the world. Transfer students comprise more than half of each entering class and are a vital part of the vibrant campus community. Applicants are considered transfer students if they will have attempted 15 or more college-level credits by the time they apply. If this is not the case, they should apply as freshman students. In making admissions decisions, careful consideration is given to the quality of a student's program and the number of credits earned and the grade point average achieved. A cumulative GPA of at least 2.5 (on a 4.0 scale) and academic progress is required for consideration, but is not a guarantee of admission. The average GPA for new transfer students is a 3.1 (on a 4.0 scale). The following programs have higher minimum grade point average requirements: architecture, nursing, pharmacy, and film and media arts. For most programs, transfer students must complete the application process by June 1 for the fall semester or by November 1 for the spring semester. The fall semester transfer application deadline for music is March 1. The fall priority deadline for nursing is February 15. Transfer applicants must request that all high schools and colleges that they previously attended send official transcripts to the Office of Undergraduate Admissions at Temple University by these deadlines. SAT or ACT scores are not required if an applicant has earned at least 15 college-level credits.

Application and Information

A completed file should contain an application form accompanied by a nonrefundable application fee, a secondary school transcript (sent by the student's school), and SAT or ACT scores. The University has a rolling admission policy; applicants are notified of the admission decision as soon as possible after all credentials have been received and reviewed.

For additional information, students may contact:

Office of Undergraduate Admissions
Temple University (041-09)
Philadelphia, Pennsylvania 19122-6096
Phone: 215-204-7200
        888-340-2222 (toll-free)
E-mail: tuadm@temple.edu
Web site: http://www.temple.edu/undergrad
        http://www.facebook.com/TempleU

TEXAS WOMAN'S UNIVERSITY
DENTON, TEXAS

The University

Texas Woman's University (TWU) is a public university offering bachelor's, master's, and doctoral degree programs. A teaching and research institution, TWU emphasizes the health sciences, education, and the liberal arts. With an enrollment of more than 14,700 students in fall 2011, the University enrolls 10 percent men and welcomes all qualified students.

Established in 1901 by the Texas Legislature, Texas Woman's University is organized into three major academic divisions: the University General Divisions, the Institute of Health Sciences, and the Graduate School. Included in the University General Divisions are the College of Arts and Sciences, College of Professional Education, and School of Library and Information Studies. The Institute of Health Sciences includes the College of Health Sciences, College of Nursing, School of Occupational Therapy, and School of Physical Therapy. The Graduate School coordinates advanced degree programs across the University.

Old Main, the University's first building, still stands amid high-rise buildings and other modern facilities that distinguish the beautiful 270-acre wooded campus in Denton. Residence halls, recreational facilities, the library, and classroom buildings are conveniently located throughout the campus. Special campus landmarks include the statue of the Pioneer Woman and the historic Little Chapel-in-the-Woods.

Location

TWU's main campus is in Denton, Texas (population 100,000+), just 35 miles north of Dallas and Fort Worth—one of the nation's largest urban centers. Clinical centers offering upper-level and graduate studies in the health sciences are located in Dallas' Southwestern Medical District and in Houston in the Texas Medical Center.

Majors and Degrees

Undergraduate programs lead to the Bachelor of Arts, Bachelor of Business Administration, Bachelor of Fine Arts, Bachelor of Science, Bachelor of Applied Science, Bachelor of General Studies, and Bachelor of Social Work degrees. Baccalaureate degrees are offered in art (with concentrations in art history, clay, graphic design, painting, photography, and sculpture), biology (including concentrations in human biology and research), business administration (with concentrations in accounting, finance, human resources management, and marketing), biochemistry, chemistry, child development, communication science, computer science, criminal justice, culinary science and food service management, dance, dental hygiene, dietetics, drama, English, family studies, fashion design, fashion merchandising, general studies, government (with concentrations in politics and legal studies), health studies, history, kinesiology, mathematics, medical technology, music, music therapy, nursing, nutrition (with concentrations in dietetics, nutritional science, and wellness), pre–dental science, pre-law, pre-medicine, pre–occupational therapy, pre–physical therapy, psychology, social work, sociology, and teacher preparation for elementary, reading and bilingual, secondary, and special education.

Academic Programs

TWU is accredited by the Commission on Colleges of the Southern Association of Colleges and Schools to award bachelor's, master's, and doctoral degrees. Various programs are also accredited by appropriate state, regional, and national agencies. The University emphasizes the importance of a liberal arts education and specialized or professional study, especially in the health sciences.

The University's requirement for all bachelor's degrees includes the successful completion of a minimum of 120 credit hours, with at least 42 semester credit hours of core curriculum requirements plus additional hours specified for each degree. The University calendar consists of two semesters of approximately four months each, one minimester, two summer terms of five weeks each, and one summer session of ten weeks. Most degree programs are designed to allow students who carry a normal course load to complete degree requirements in eight semesters.

In accordance with the Texas Success Initiative, all undergraduate students must prove academic readiness prior to enrollment in a college or university by passing the Texas Higher Education Assessment (THEA). Students are exempt from taking the THEA if a qualifying score has been met on the TAKS, the SAT, or the ACT; there are other exemptions as well. More information about the THEA and the Texas Success Initiative can be found at http://www.twu.edu/aac/tests.asp.

Off-Campus Programs

Programs in each of the University's colleges and schools include clinical and practicum experiences that give students access to outstanding facilities of major healthcare, business, and other institutions located in major metropolitan centers. Programs are offered annually to provide study-travel opportunities in the United States and abroad. A diverse cooperative education program integrates classroom study with planned and supervised work experience in educational activities outside the formal classroom.

Academic Facilities

The University library has holdings of 686,056 print and electronic titles, 46,164 current periodical and serial subscriptions, 15,382 microforms, and 6,307 audiovisual titles to support all major areas of study at TWU. In addition to the standard printed bibliographies, indexes, and abstracts, the library offers Web-based and local access to literature searches from 177 computer databases. Special resources include the Woman's Collection, the largest depository in the South and Southwest of research materials about women. Other materials include a rare book collection and a children's collection.

Students have access to Texas academic and public library collections through TexShare, and, through membership in Amigos Library Services (the OCLC regional network), the TWU Library has access to collections in libraries throughout the United States. The Dallas Center maintains a special collection for students in the health sciences. Through a consortia membership, the students at the Houston Center have access to printed and online database collections and full library services in the Houston Academy of Medicine–Texas Medical Center Library as well as to an in-house TWU librarian for assistance with accessing and using all TWU Library resources.

Numerous classroom and laboratory buildings, including an undergraduate science laboratory building, are conveniently located on the Denton campus to meet specific needs of the individual components of the University. Special facilities on the Denton campus include honors and international programs with special housing facilities, Margo Jones Performance Hall, Redbud Theater Complex, an auditorium, dance studios, a television studio, numerous art and music studios and practice rooms, science laboratories, a computer center and several computer laboratories, a writing laboratory, laboratory facilities for programs related to therapy, and the Institute for Women's Health. Clinics are provided for speech and hearing, dental hygiene, counseling and family therapy, and music therapy. Also included are tennis courts, a golf course, an indoor track, indoor and outdoor pools, a Wellness Center and fitness room, and other facilities that support programs in physical education and human movement. Residence hall rooms are linked to the campus computer network.

The TWU T. Boone Pickens Institute of Health Sciences–Dallas Center is located in the heart of Dallas's Southwestern Medical District. The Houston Center is located at the southern gateway to the Texas Medical Center. Both centers offer outstanding instructional facilities, including excellent library holdings, clinical learning resources, simulation and research laboratories, laboratories for occupational and physical therapy, and anatomy laboratories. The Dallas Center is home to the renowned TWU Stroke Center, and the Houston Center houses a nutrition research laboratory.

Costs

The average cost for in-state resident students in 2011–12 for one semester of 15 semester hours was $3293 plus course fees and $1020 for books and supplies. For out-of-state residents, the average cost of tuition for 15 semester hours was $7988. Residence hall rates, meals, and personal expenses vary. All rates are subject to change. Scholarship programs for honors students, class valedictorians from Texas, new freshmen, new transfer students, and international students are available.

Financial Aid

More than 70 percent of TWU's students receive financial aid in the form of scholarships, grants, loans, or on-campus employment. In addition to offering numerous scholarships and grants funded by the state and by friends of the University, TWU participates in many federally funded programs. Federal Pell Grants, Federal Supplemental Educational Opportunity Grants, Federal Perkins Loans, Federal Nursing Student Loans, Federal Stafford Loans, Federal Parent Loans, and Federal Work-Study Program awards are available. Suggested filing dates for financial aid and scholarship applicants are March 15 for the summer and fall terms and September 1 for spring sessions. Applications for scholarships and financial aid for both the fall and spring semesters should be made by March 15.

Faculty

A faculty of approximately 425 guides the academic program at TWU and gives careful attention to student needs. Faculty members hold the doctoral degree or another terminal or graduate degree in their field.

Student Government

All students are members of the United Student Association, which enables them to participate in a wide variety of activities. Students work with the faculty and administrators to develop University policies and programs of special interest and concern to the student body. Students also serve on various University committees. Leadership development is a special focus.

Admission Requirements

First-time freshman applicants are assured admission to Texas Woman's University if they have graduated from a regionally accredited high school in Texas within the last two years and have a class ranking that places them in the top 25 percent of their high school graduating class. Regular admission to the University is based on graduation from an accredited high school, a grade point average of at least 2.0 on a 4.0 scale, a score of at least 1000 (critical reading and math combined) on the SAT or a composite score of at least 21 on the ACT, and completion of at least 14 academic credits of the Recommended or Distinguished Texas High School Curriculum program. Transfer students must submit an official transcript from each college previously attended. They must have obtained a GPA of 2.0 or higher on a 4.0 scale when transferring to the University. Students holding an Associate of Arts or Associate of Science degree are assured admission.

Application and Information

Applicants should submit a completed application for admission and their official transcripts to the Office of Admissions. The fall and spring priority deadlines are March 1 and November 1, respectively. There is a $50 application fee for all new students ($75 for international students).

Additional information about the University and its programs is available from:

Office of Admissions
Texas Woman's University
P.O. Box 425589
Denton, Texas 76204-5589
Phone: 940-898-3188
　　　　866-809-6130 (toll-free)
E-mail: admissions@twu.edu
Web site: http://www.twu.edu

TWU welcomes women and men and traditional and nontraditional students to its campuses in Denton, Dallas, and Houston. TWU offers more than 100 degree programs and awards bachelor's, master's, and doctoral degrees.

THOMAS MORE COLLEGE
CRESTVIEW HILLS, KENTUCKY

The College

Thomas More College features a very strong academic reputation, small class sizes, and an ongoing dedication to scholarly pursuits based on the foundation of a Catholic liberal arts curriculum. Located in Northern Kentucky, just minutes from Cincinnati, Ohio, the College provides vibrant on-campus residential life in close proximity to a major metropolitan area. The result is an outstanding location offering all of the activities and resources of a major city with a suburban setting. With small class sizes and engaged faculty dedicated to teaching, the academic experience is one of personal attention and a hands-on approach to learning that forms the basis of a Thomas More education.

The student population includes 1,900 undergraduates and graduates. There are 960 traditional undergraduates attending classes full-time, of whom 350 are resident students. The student body is drawn primarily from the states of Kentucky, Ohio, and Indiana, but many other states and a number of countries are also represented. In addition to its undergraduate programs, Thomas More College offers graduate programs in business administration (M.B.A.) teaching (M.A.T.) and launched a Master of Education (M.Ed.) program in the fall of 2011. Students who choose to live on campus reside in either a suite-style residence hall or one of three town-house-style residence halls. All residence halls offer comfortable, air-conditioned rooms; Internet and cable TV access; academic tutoring; and free laundry facilities. The 27,000-square-foot Student Center contains a spacious bookstore, computer and study lounges, a game room, campus life offices, a café, and a dance rehearsal studio.

The college experience is enhanced through participation in many academic, social, and sports organizations. Intercollegiate athletics are part of the Presidents' Athletic Conference governed by NCAA Division III. Thomas More College competes in men's baseball, basketball, cross-country, football, golf, soccer, tennis, and track and field, and women's basketball, cross-country, fast-pitch softball, golf, soccer, tennis, track and field, and volleyball. Intramural sports offered include coed flag football, basketball, cornhole, dodgeball, softball, and volleyball. Thomas More College was proud to open a new on-campus athletic complex in fall 2008 for football, soccer, and track and field, in addition to the Connor Convocation Center which houses basketball and volleyball facilities, and the College's baseball and softball fields. Students can also enjoy beautiful facilities for swimming, tennis, racquetball, and basketball and a complete fitness area at the Five Seasons Sports Club, adjacent to the campus.

Location

Thomas More College is located in northern Kentucky, 10 minutes south of Cincinnati, Ohio. The campus is convenient to major highways, and the Greater Cincinnati/Northern Kentucky International Airport is just 10 minutes from the College. Thomas More's suburban setting provides a safe environment for students and numerous opportunities for employment and internships. All students are permitted to have cars on campus, with no charge for a parking pass.

The College's location offers a wide array of cultural and sporting events. Local attractions include the Broadway Series, the Cincinnati Pops, the Cincinnati Zoo, the Newport Aquarium, the Riverbend Music Center, and the Cincinnati Reds and Bengals. Numerous shopping areas and restaurants are also available, including the new Crestview Hills Town Center, located across the street from the College.

Majors and Degrees

Thomas More College offers bachelor's degrees in accounting, art, biology, business administration, chemistry, computer information systems, communications, criminal justice, economics, education, English, environmental science, forensic science, history, humanities, international studies, mathematics, medical laboratory science, nursing, philosophy, physics, political science, psychology, Spanish, sports and entertainment marketing, sociology, speech and theater, and theology. Associate degrees are available in each of these content areas as well as art history, French, gerontology, pre–legal studies, Spanish and Web design.

Preprofessional programs are available in dentistry, engineering, law, medicine, occupational therapy, optometry, pharmacy, physical therapy, and veterinary science.

TMC3: The Three-Year Degree Program at Thomas More College is an innovative three-year degree program that enables motivated undergraduate students in pursuit of a bachelor's degree a traditional college experience and an extra year of earning power. Qualified students can save both time and money by completing a traditional four-year bachelor's degree in just three years at a very competitive tuition rate. The three-year degree is completed during the course of eight semesters. While TMC3 compresses the time frame to attain a degree by an entire year, the classes themselves are not accelerated. The structure of TMC3 is year-round, with students generally taking 18 hours in the fall and spring semesters and 12 hours in two summer terms.

Academic Programs

To earn the Bachelor of Arts, Bachelor of Science, or Bachelor of Science in Nursing degree, a student must complete 128 credit hours, including 61 credit hours in liberal arts courses. The Associate of Arts degree requires the completion of 64 credit hours, including a liberal arts component. In addition to the traditional format, the College's TAP program offers associate, bachelor's, and master's degrees in business administration that are provided in an accelerated format for working adults.

The academic calendar for traditional students is composed of a fall and a spring semester and two summer sessions. The accelerated format includes classes year-round.

The Cooperative Education program enables students to gain hands-on professional experience in their field of interest. All students are eligible for this program after the completion of their freshman year. Cooperative Air Force and Army ROTC programs are available in conjunction with nearby universities. The nursing and sociology departments have excellent working relationships with nearby hospitals and social service agencies.

Off-Campus Programs

Nineteen area colleges, including Thomas More College, form the Greater Cincinnati Consortium of Colleges and Universities, through which all students at the local member colleges may take courses not available at their home institution. Thomas

More encourages full-time students to take advantage of this opportunity for curriculum enrichment through cross-registration. In addition, students who wish to study abroad as part of their undergraduate education have a number of possibilities open to them, including exchanges at Lingnan University in Hong Kong, Mary Immaculate College in Ireland, and Eichstaett University in Germany.

Academic Facilities

The recently renovated library has a collection of more than 129,000 volumes of books, periodicals, and audiovisual materials; as a selective depository, it houses more than 8,400 volumes of U.S. government documents. In addition, the library's membership in the Southwest Ohio and Neighboring Libraries gives Thomas More students access to more than 15 million books and more than 75,000 periodicals held by seventy-five other libraries in the region.

Thomas More's computer facilities include computer classrooms and six labs for student use. Student computers are also available in some academic departments and in the library. All PCs are connected to a campuswide Novell network, with wireless access to e-mail, the Internet, and an on-campus Intranet server.

Students in the science programs receive hands-on experience through the use of the newly remodeled classrooms and labs and Biology Field Station, located on the Ohio River. These facilities allow students to participate in undergraduate research programs in such areas as immunology, forestry, environmental studies, astronomy, trace analysis, and synthesis. Research projects have been funded by the National Science Foundation and the National Institutes of Health.

Costs

The 2011–12 annual cost for Thomas More College was $25,000 for tuition and $6480 for room (double occupancy) and board. There was a differential fee of $30 per semester hour for all nursing courses. The Student Government fee was $60 per semester and the computer fee was $360 per semester for full-time students. The cost of books was estimated at $800 per year.

Financial Aid

Thomas More College is an excellent educational value offering a wide range of financial aid opportunities, assisting more than 90 percent of its full-time students in meeting college costs. Awards are determined on a rolling basis, with priority consideration given to applications filed by February 1. Financial aid awards are based on economic need, merit, scholastic achievement, and extracurricular activities. The filing of the Free Application for Federal Student Aid (FAFSA) and the Thomas More College Application for Financial Aid and Scholarship is required before any awards are determined. Other Thomas More College awards may require additional applications.

An extensive Federal Work-Study Program is in place, and there are excellent opportunities for outside employment in the immediate area.

Faculty

The faculty is committed to the ideals of a Catholic liberal arts education, with the main focus on teaching. The faculty has 135 members, including 71 who are full-time; 66 percent hold tenure and 69 percent hold doctoral or other terminal degrees. Faculty members serve as academic advisers to students in their disciplines. The student-faculty ratio is 16:1.

Student Government

The purpose of the Student Government Association is to serve as the official representative organization of the Thomas More College student body; to serve as the liaison between the student body and the faculty, administration, and Board of Trustees; to promote student projects and activities and improve the quality of student life; to assist the Dean of Students in supervising student organizations and student activities on campus; to protect the rights of the individual; and to preserve the general welfare of the student body of Thomas More College.

Admission Requirements

The admission criteria are as follows: an applicant should have a high school grade point average (based on college-preparatory courses) of 85 percent or better (2.5 on 4.0 scale), and a minimum composite score of 20 on the ACT Assessment, with a minimum of 18 in English, or a minimum combined score of 980 on the SAT, with a minimum of 450 on the verbal portion. If the applicant does not meet all the admission criteria, the file is forwarded to the Admissions Committee for individual consideration.

Transfer students with 24 or more semester hours of transferable credit and an overall grade point average of at least 2.0 on a 4.0 scale are automatically accepted. Transfer students with fewer than 24 transferable hours must meet the general admission criteria outlined above.

The applicant must provide a completed application with a nonrefundable $25 fee (waived for online applicants), high school transcripts, college transcripts (if applicable), and ACT or SAT score reports.

Application and Information

Thomas More College operates under a rolling admission policy, with a final application deadline of August 15. Admission decisions are usually made within two weeks of receiving all application materials. Students can apply online at the College's Web site. The $25 application fee is waived for online applications.

For further information or to schedule a campus visit, students should contact:

Billy Sarge
Assistant Director of Admissions and Director of Recruitment
Thomas More College
333 Thomas More Parkway
Crestview Hills, Kentucky 41017-3495
Phone: 859-344-3332
      800-825-4557 (toll-free)
E-mail: admissions@thomasmore.edu
Web site: http://www.thomasmore.edu

Students on the Thomas More College campus.

TRINE UNIVERSITY
ANGOLA, INDIANA

The University

Trine University is a private, independent, coeducational institution offering associate, baccalaureate, and graduate degrees to students in more than thirty-five programs, including engineering, mathematics, forensic science, business, education, communication, golf management, exercise science, and criminal justice. Trine also offers a five-year combined Bachelor of Science and Master of Engineering program with majors in civil, mechanical, and biomedical engineering.

Since its founding in 1884, Trine has focused on providing an innovative, quality, career-oriented, project-based education. With a worldwide reputation for being job-ready, Trine graduates are in demand. In 2011, 91 percent of graduates were employed or enrolled in graduate school within six months of commencement.

Trine's current main campus undergraduate enrollment is more than 1,600. Over 1,000 students live on campus in one of sixteen residence halls, private villas, or fully furnished suite-style apartments—some of which overlook Trine's eighteen-hole championship golf course. Trine is one of very few small, private schools in the country to offer this amenity.

The University's 450-acre campus includes a unique University Center, which houses a dining hall, bookstore, fitness center, movie theater, post office, radio station and the LINK, a one-stop location that supports learning, and provides access to information, resources, and tools for knowledge discovery.

The University's inviting atmosphere complements the seriousness and determination with which Trine students pursue their academic goals. Students enjoy opportunities to develop friendships and to build leadership and teamwork skills through their participation in over sixty campus organizations.

Trine has a reputation for academic rigor and success. Chemical engineering seniors have won the American Institute of Chemical Engineers (AIChE) national individual design competition two of the last four years and have produced the safest design each of the past four years. Mechanical engineering students can study in one of the top cast-metals programs in North America, as determined by the Foundry Education Foundation. In 2009, the American Society of Civil Engineers (ASCE) named Trine graduate Ben Groeneweg a New Face of Civil Engineering, an award presented to only 10 civil engineers nationally each year. Trine's Tau Alpha Omicron chapter of the American Criminal Justice Association (ACJA) annually wins regional and national awards for marksmanship, crime scene investigation, and physical agility.

Trine is a member of National Collegiate Athletic Association Division III and the Michigan Intercollegiate Athletic Association (MIAA), the nation's oldest athletic conference. Men's sports include baseball, basketball, cross-country, football, golf, lacrosse, soccer, tennis, track, and wrestling. Women's sports include basketball, cross-country, golf, lacrosse, soccer, softball, tennis, track, and volleyball. Many students also play on intramural sports teams.

Trine's football team, the Thunder, is a three-time consecutive MIAA champion and advanced to round two of NCAA post-season play in both 2009 and 2010. Quarterback and 2010 graduate Eric Watt received the Gagliardi Trophy, the highest honor given to an NCAA Division III football player. Trine's softball, wrestling, and cross-country teams are also competitive at the national level.

The Keith Busse/Steel Dynamics Inc. Athletic and Recreation Center (ARC), which contains a 200-meter indoor track and training and practice facilities for other sports, opened in 2009 to develop Trine's track and field program year-round and to support tennis, additional sports, and intramurals.

The Fred Zollner Athletic Stadium opened in 2010 and serves the football, lacrosse, and other athletic programs.

Student organizations include the student senate, honor societies, professional organizations, campus newspaper, FM radio station, drama club, music ensembles, pep and marching bands, Habitat for Humanity, and more. In addition, thirteen social fraternities and sororities provide on-campus opportunities for service and camaraderie for upperclassmen.

Trine is accredited by the Higher Learning Commission and is a member of the North Central Association of Colleges and Schools (http://www.ncahigherlearningcommission.org; phone: 312-263-0456). Trine's programs in chemical, civil, computer, electrical, and mechanical engineering are accredited by ABET (111 Market Place, Suite 1050, Baltimore, Maryland 21202-4012; phone: 410-347-7700). All teacher preparation programs are accredited by the National Council for Accreditation of Teacher Education and the Indiana Department of Education/Office of Licensing and Development. All B.S.B.A. programs in the Ketner School of Business are accredited by the Accreditation Council for Business Schools and Programs.

Location

Trine is in Angola, Indiana, the heart of northeast Indiana's scenic lake resort region, halfway between the metropolitan areas of Chicago and Cleveland. Just a 45-minute drive from Fort Wayne, Indiana, Trine offers the safety and ease of a small-town environment, near some of the nation's most vital cities. Pokagon State Park provides year-round recreational opportunities for the community and is just 5 miles north of Trine's campus.

Majors and Degrees

The Allen School of Engineering and Technology awards Bachelor of Science degrees in chemical, civil, computer, electrical, computer, and mechanical engineering and design engineering technology. Minors are offered in aerospace, bioprocess, environmental, metallurgy, and robotics engineering.

Well-qualified high school graduates may be admitted directly into a five-year combined Bachelor of Science and Masters of Engineering program. Civil, mechanical, and biomedical engineers with the skills necessary to design complex systems are highly sought by industry professionals; therefore, the degree is practice-oriented with a heavy emphasis on design, as opposed to the research emphasis of a traditional Master of Science degree. Upon completion of this program, both the Bachelor of Science in civil, mechanical, or biomedical engineering and the Master of Engineering degree are awarded.

The Ketner School of Business awards Bachelor of Science in Business Administration degrees with majors in accounting, business administration, communication, entrepreneurship, finance, golf management, management, marketing, and sport management.

The Franks School of Education awards Bachelor of Science degrees in elementary, health and physical, mathematics, science, and social studies education.

The Jannen School of Arts and Sciences awards Bachelor of Arts degrees with majors in general studies (pre-legal, self-designated, and social studies), and psychology. The school also awards Bachelor of Science degrees with majors in biology, chemistry, criminal justice, forensic science, informatics, and mathematics. A premedical professional track is also available.

Academic Programs

Trine's engineering programs concentrate on providing a fundamental, application-oriented engineering education which includes extensive laboratory instruction. In addition to concentrated studies in a specialized area, students are required to complete courses in communication skills, socio-humanistic studies, and analysis and design.

The University's business programs include a broad range of practical experience to acquaint the student with the practices, procedures, and problems of the contemporary business professional. Guest

lecturers frequently visit campus and students are given many experiential learning opportunities.

Off-Campus Programs

Co-op and internship opportunities are available and encouraged. Semesters of classroom study are alternated with professional work experience, which can help students gain a competitive edge in the job market and offset college expenses. The length of a co-op program depends upon the student's class status when entering the program.

Academic Facilities

Fawick Hall of Engineering is home to the University's Chemical and Bioprocess, Civil and Environmental, Electrical and Computer, and Mechanical and Aerospace Engineering Departments, as well as the Engineering Technology Department. Trine students use sophisticated equipment such as a scanning electron microscope and rapid prototyping machines in their laboratories and design projects. Each computer lab has state-of-the-art software.

The Best Hall of Science contains classrooms, science laboratories; the Fairfield Lecture Room; the Department of Mathematics; the Department of Science; and the Department of Criminal Justice, Psychology, and Social Sciences.

Planned renovations to the Ketner School of Business and Franks School of Education include new infrastructure and technology, including a fiber-optic network, a wireless environment, and shared multimedia access to resources for teaching (SMART) classrooms. The new T. Furth Center for Performing Arts will preserve a landmark church while providing classrooms for choral and instrumental music and an auditorium for drama and music productions.

The University recently channeled over $2 million into campuswide technology upgrades. The LINK houses a digital classroom, a "my office" area with multiple computers, and a global workspace with videoconferencing stations to facilitate learning. In addition, iPads, Kindles, digital camcorders, and more are available for checkout from the Tech Bar in the LINK. More than 200 computers dedicated to student access are available in labs across campus. Every room in student residences is wired to the University network and the Internet, and residential common areas are fitted with wireless Internet access.

Costs

Tuition for the academic year (two semesters) in 2012–13 is $27,660 ($29,750 for engineering). Room and standard meal plan (nineteen meals per week) for the academic year costs $9200 (double occupancy).

Financial Aid

Financial aid may be awarded in the form of scholarships, grants, loans, or campus employment. Any of these aids or any combination may supplement family and student resources to meet basic educational expenses. Trine requires the Free Application for Federal Student Aid (FAFSA) and recommends its submission by March 1.

Faculty

Trine has a full-time faculty of 83 members. Most have doctoral degrees and professional experience. The student-faculty ratio is 15:1.

Student Government

The student senate is organized for the purpose of providing funding for campus organizations to host events. Representatives elected from campus organizations form the senate, which also aids in formulating policies for these organizations.

Admission Requirements

Graduation from an approved high school or equivalent preparation is required for admission. Selection is made without regard to race, religion, or gender. The University requires applicants to take the ACT or SAT prior to approval for admission (writing sections are optional).

Admission requirements for engineering include 4 years of English, 1 year of chemistry, 1 year of physics, 1 year of social studies, 2 years of algebra, 1 year of geometry, and ½ year of trigonometry. All other applicants must have the following high school credits: 4 years of English, 3 years of mathematics, 3 years of science, and 3 years of social studies.

Graduates of pre-professional or college-parallel programs at approved community or junior colleges are eligible for transfer into Trine's baccalaureate programs. Qualified graduates of these programs may be granted junior standing upon transfer. In general, credit may be allowed in subjects that parallel Trine programs, provided the student earned a grade of C or better in the course.

Application and Information

Trine University's online application is available at http://www.trine.edu; there is no application fee. The University admits applicants on the basis of scholastic achievement and academic potential. Admission decisions are made on a rolling basis. Applicants are notified of their status within two weeks after their application, high school record, and test scores have been received. Transfer students must also submit an official copy of their college transcript(s).

Interested students and their parents are encouraged to visit the campus. Arrangements can be made by writing or calling the Office of Admission.

For additional information, students should call or write:

Office of Admission
Trine University
One University Avenue
Angola, Indiana 46703-1764
United States
Phone: 260-665-4100
    800-347-4878 (toll-free within continental U.S.)
E-mail: admit@trine.edu
Web site: http://www.trine.edu
    http://www.facebook.com/trineadmissions
    http://www.youtube/trineuniversity
    http://www.trine.edu/blogs (student blogs)

Trine University

TRINITY COLLEGE
HARTFORD, CONNECTICUT

The College

Since its founding in 1823, Trinity has provided an undergraduate education of uncommon quality. Widely acknowledged as one of the top liberal arts colleges in the country, Trinity has been recognized by a panel of national education editors for its bold and innovative ideas to advance the cause of higher education and ensure greater access.

In its commitment to the rigorous pursuit of the liberal arts and to instruction that is personal and conversational, Trinity is an ideal college. At the same time, Trinity is in close touch with the world beyond its campus. In that respect and in terms of the outstanding opportunities Trinity's capital city location offers students, a Trinity education is indeed a real education.

While remaining faithful to the classic liberal arts tradition, Trinity offers a distinctive educational experience that prepares students for the challenges and opportunities of the twenty-first century. Building on its traditional strengths in the arts and humanities and exceptional offerings in science and engineering, Trinity engages students in a conversation with the world through its Center for Urban and Global Studies, study-abroad programs, interdisciplinary programs, and innovative, rigorous programs that draw on the rich cultural, educational, and professional assets of Hartford. State-of-the-art electronic facilities support Trinity's advanced use of information technology in classrooms. The heart of a Trinity education, however, remains the personal encounter between professor and student, the intellectual partnership that discovers a world of ideas and ignites a passion for learning.

Trinity's students come from forty-eight states and forty-nine countries. The College believes that a diverse community makes learning flourish. Trinity's undergraduate enrollment of more than 2,200 students is about equally comprised of men and women. More than 90 percent of undergraduates live on campus in College housing. Trinity is engaged in continuing campus revitalization programs that preserve its impressive Gothic buildings as it also develops a campus for the twenty-first century.

Trinity offers a rich array of extracurricular activities—films, plays, concerts, musical theater, sports, academic symposia, and visits by nationally and internationally known writers, speakers, and performers. Participation is an important word on campus, and Trinity students have abundant opportunities to lead and to be involved in numerous student clubs; special interest groups; theater, dance, and music groups; debate; academic programs; campus cinema; Trinity's radio station; and many student publications. With 19 acres of playing fields, Trinity also offers an extensive athletic program. About 40 percent of the student body participates on twenty-nine men's and women's varsity teams (Division III) and roster of intramural sports. The Ferris Athletic Center features a swimming pool, a fully equipped fitness center, crew tanks, eight international-size squash courts, basketball courts, and an indoor track.

Location

Situated on a beautiful 100-acre campus in the center of Hartford, the capital of Connecticut, Trinity offers the best of both worlds—a supportive and active campus community located in a city that provides students with myriad opportunities for internships, community service, and cultural exploration. Hartford's businesses, governmental agencies, cultural organizations, and nonprofit institutions offer Trinity students hundreds of opportunities to explore careers through the College's extensive internship program. Hartford has a number of cultural institutions, including the Wadsworth Atheneum (the oldest public art museum in the nation), Mark Twain House, Harriet Beecher Stowe Center, Hartford Symphony, Hartford Stage, and a number of smaller theaters and clubs that provide a cultural stew of dance, theater, and music. The shopping districts of Hartford and surrounding suburbs are nearby. The impressive Connecticut coast is easily accessible, and Boston and New York are each about 2 hours from campus. Off campus, Trinity students have access to a field station in Ashford, Connecticut, dedicated to research in the natural sciences and a wide range of environmental educational endeavors.

Majors and Degrees

On the undergraduate level, the College offers a Bachelor of Arts degree and a Bachelor of Science degree. Trinity offers thirty-eight majors, including American studies; anthropology; art history; biochemistry; biology; chemistry; classical civilization; classics; computer science; economics; educational studies; engineering; English; environmental science; French; German studies; Hispanic studies; history; interdisciplinary computing; international studies; Italian studies; Jewish studies; language and culture studies (Arabic, Chinese, Hebrew, Japanese); mathematics; music; neuroscience; philosophy; physics; political science; student-designed interdisciplinary major; psychology; public policy and law; religion; Russian; sociology; studio arts; theater and dance; and women, gender, and sexuality.

Academic Programs

Featuring approximately 900 courses, Trinity's curriculum provides a framework within which students may explore the many dimensions of an undergraduate education. At the same time, the curriculum offers each student flexibility to experiment, to deepen old interests and develop new ones, and to acquire specialized training in a major field. Students must demonstrate proficiency in writing, mathematics, and a second language, and fulfill a five-part distribution requirement that consists of at least one course in each of the following categories: arts, humanities, natural sciences, numerical and symbolic reasoning, and social sciences. They must complete a writing intensive requirement and also take a first-year seminar and at least one course that focuses on global engagement.

Off-Campus Programs

More than 50 percent of Trinity students study abroad for a semester or a year at Trinity's Rome Campus, at one of six Trinity global learning sites, or throughout the globe. Trinity-sponsored global learning sites operate in Argentina, Austria, France, Spain, South Africa (Cape Town), and Trinidad; and beginning in fall 2012, in Shanghai, China. Through the theater and dance department, Trinity offers the Trinity/La MaMa Performing Arts Program in New York City, an extraordinary program that provides intensive study in theater, dance, and performance.

Academic Facilities

The Raether Library and Information Technology Center is home to the Raether and Watkinson Libraries, as well as the Computing Center. It is a place where students and faculty members come together for the serious work of scholarship, where researchers can pore over a book or conduct investigations through a wide selection of online databases. The Raether Library houses nearly 1 million print volumes and approximately 700,000 nonprint materials, including slides, microforms, sound recordings, and other materials in audiovisual and electronic formats. In addition, an online catalog linked with Wesleyan University and Connecticut College provides access to more than 2 million

titles. The Watkinson Library, with its impressive collection of rare books, manuscripts, and other unique resources, supports a broad range of research interests.

The campus is fully wired, with every student room connected to the College network and the Web. Public access computers are also available 24 hours a day in select facilities.

Costs

Costs for the 2011–12 academic year were $41,980 for tuition, $11,380 for room and board, and $2115 for fees.

Financial Aid

Each student admitted to Trinity who qualifies for aid receives a package that fully meets his or her calculated need. Students must file the Free Application for Federal Student Aid (FAFSA) as well as the Financial Aid PROFILE of the College Scholarship Service. Admissions applications are due by January 1; FAFSA and PROFILE applications are due by February 1. Students are notified of admission and aid decisions by the first week of April. Normally, need is met with a financial aid package that includes grant assistance, work-study, and federal student loans. Federal funds for which accepted students are eligible include Pell Grants, Federal Supplemental Educational Opportunity Grants (FSEOG), Perkins Loans, Stafford Loans, and PLUS Loans. The College administers a large student employment program, and most students who demonstrate need are granted an on-campus job as part of their financial aid package. The ratio of grant assistance to loans and work-study aid is sometimes affected by the academic strength of the student's record. Trinity continues to expand its aid budget to keep pace with the College's goal to increase the socioeconomic and ethnic diversity on campus. Forty percent of the students receive financial aid.

Faculty

The distinctive strength of a Trinity education has always been the close interaction between students and a faculty of devoted teacher-scholars. A student-faculty ratio of 10:1 enables supportive yet challenging educational experiences that establish a foundation for lifetime learning and enables students to pursue academic interests with passion. Students have numerous opportunities to collaborate with faculty members in conducting research; many students have made joint presentations at international, national, or local symposia or have published jointly prepared papers. All courses are taught by Trinity faculty members and not by graduate assistants.

Although the first calling of Trinity's professors is teaching, they are also active publishing scholars of national and international distinction. History professor Joan Hedrick, for example, won the Pulitzer Prize for her biography of Harriet Beecher Stowe. Other notable professors include Henry DePhillips, distinguished chemist and researcher on art restoration; Dan Lloyd, acclaimed philosopher and author of Radiant Cool; Lesley Farlow, accomplished dancer and choreographer; Samuel Kassow, distinguished historian; and Joseph Bronzino, an authority on biomedical engineering. Trinity professors pride themselves on their accessibility and keen interest in helping students.

Student Government

Trinity fosters the growth of future leaders by providing students with many opportunities to exercise and test their leadership skills. The Student Government Association (SGA), for example, provides students a strong voice in social, cultural, and—through membership on faculty committees—academic matters. Composed of elected class representatives, the SGA constantly seeks the expertise and insights of all interested students, and its committees offer enterprising students many chances to participate and to develop leadership skills.

Admission Requirements

Trinity seeks an ethnically and geographically diverse group of highly motivated students who have completed a rigorous course of study in secondary school and have demonstrated energy, talent, and leadership in a variety of extracurricular activities. Trinity has no specific GPA minimums or test-score cutoffs. The College is highly selective, and its candidates typically have an A– high school average. At least 16 academic units of college-preparatory course work are recommended, including a minimum of 4 years of English, 3 years of foreign language, 2 years of laboratory science, 2 years of algebra, 1 year of geometry, and 2 years of history. Last year, over 6,000 men and women from all over the nation and world applied for admission to the College, which enrolls an entering class of approximately 585 students. Transfer students with a 3.0 GPA in a strong course of study at another accredited college or university are considered for admission to the sophomore or junior classes.

Admissions officers review each application individually; decisions are based on each candidate's academic record (course of study and GPA), recommendations from secondary school teachers and counselors, test scores, personal strengths, talents, activities, and application and supplemental essays.

Application and Information

Students must submit completed applications to the Admissions Office. Application deadlines are November 15 for early decision I applicants (with notification by mid-December), January 1 for early decision II applicants (with notification by mid-February), and January 1 for regular decision applicants (with notification by early April). Transfer applicants must submit applications by April 1 for admission in the following fall semester (with notification by mid-June) and by November 15 for admission in the following spring semester (with notification by early January). Prospective students may submit an electronic Common Application at http://www.commonapp.org.

Inquiries should be made to:

Larry Dow
Dean of Admissions and Financial Aid
Admissions Office
Trinity College
Hartford, Connecticut 06106-3100
Phone: 860-297-2180
Fax: 860-297-2287
E-mail: admissions.office@trincoll.edu
Web site: http://www.trincoll.edu/admissions
http://www.facebook.com/trincoll
http://www.youtube.com/trincoll#p/a/u/0/

The Long Walk at Trinity College. *(Photo by Bob Handelman)*

TRUMAN STATE UNIVERSITY
KIRKSVILLE, MISSOURI

The University

Truman has forged a national reputation for offering an exceptionally high-quality undergraduate education at a competitive price. For the fifteenth consecutive year, *U.S. News & World Report* has ranked Truman as the number one public institution in the Midwest offering bachelor's and master's degrees. In addition, Truman is ranked the number-one value in public colleges and universities by *Consumers Digest*.

A commitment to student achievement and learning is at the core of everything Truman does. This commitment is evidenced by faculty and staff members who recognize the importance of providing students with the opportunity to interact with their professors both in and out of the classroom. With class sizes averaging only 24 students and 93 percent of freshman-level academic courses being taught by instructional faculty members, students find ample opportunity to ask questions of professors as well as interact with their multitalented peers. Truman's academic environment is enhanced by a student body that achieves at remarkable levels. The 2011 freshman class had an ACT midrange of 25 to 30 and an average GPA of 3.76 on a 4.0 scale. In addition, numerous opportunities exist for students to engage in undergraduate research. Each year, approximately 1,200 students work alongside professors on University research projects, gaining confidence, knowledge, and skill in their chosen disciplines. The University offers these students the opportunity to present the results of their research at the annual Student Research Conference. In addition, selected students travel to the National Undergraduate Research Symposium to present their research findings. Undergraduate research stipends are also available.

Students wishing to attend Truman to become a teacher must first complete a bachelor's degree in an academic discipline and then apply for admission into professional study at the master's level to obtain a Master of Arts in Education (M.A.E). Through this program, certification can be achieved for elementary education, middle school education, secondary education, and special education.

With more than 240 University organizations available to students, encompassing service, Greek, honorary, professional, religious, social, political, and recreational influences, Truman students have tremendous opportunities to become involved while enrolled at the University. Truman's Student Activities Board provides special events such as Bill Nye, comic acts such as Demetri Martin and Daniel Tosh, and musical artists like Flogging Molly, Jack's Mannequin, and Regina Spektor. In addition, admission to all varsity athletic events, Truman theater productions, and Lyceum Series events is free to Truman students. Recent theater productions have included *Into the Woods*, *Dancing at Lughnasa*, and *Brighton Beach Memoirs*.

Location

Truman is located in Kirksville, a town of approximately 17,000 nestled in the northeast corner of Missouri. The town square, located within walking distance of the Truman campus, provides a connection to Kirksville's past. A multiplex movie theater is located on the town square; local merchants operate specialized gift, book, and clothing stores; and several restaurants offer a wide selection of American and international cuisine.

The Kirksville Aquatic Center is a great place to have fun and get fit. This indoor/outdoor pool complex offers a variety of activities, classes, and programs designed to appeal to people of all ages. The complex includes a six-lane indoor swimming pool, perfect for swimming, relaxing, or playing a game of water-basketball. The outdoor pool is designed with a zero-depth entry, a 1-meter diving board, and four 25-yard outdoor lap lanes as well as a 20-foot water slide.

The northeast region of Missouri is also home to Thousand Hills State Park. A 3,252-acre state park and 573-acre lake for camping, hiking, biking, fishing, swimming, boating, and waterskiing is located within 10 minutes of the Truman campus.

Majors and Degrees

Undergraduate degrees offered by Truman include the Bachelor of Arts (B.A.), Bachelor of Science (B.S.), Bachelor of Music: Performance (B.M.), Bachelor of Fine Arts (B.F.A.), and Bachelor of Science in Nursing (B.S.N.). Truman offers more than forty areas of study in the following disciplines: accounting, agricultural science, athletic training, art, art history, biology, business administration, chemistry, classics, communication, communication disorders, computer science, creative writing, economics, English, exercise science, French, German, health science, history, interdisciplinary studies, justice systems, linguistics, mathematics, music, music: performance, nursing, philosophy and religion, physics, political science, psychology, Romance languages, Russian, sociology/anthropology, Spanish, and theater.

Professional paths include but are not limited to dentistry, engineering, law, medicine, optometry, pharmacy, physical therapy, and veterinary medicine.

Academic Programs

Truman is Missouri's premier liberal arts and sciences university and the only highly selective public institution in the state. The Liberal Studies Program is the heart of Truman's curriculum and is intended to serve as a foundation for all major programs of study offered by the University. Truman's mission is to offer an exemplary undergraduate education, grounded in the liberal arts and sciences, in the context of a public institution of higher learning. Truman seeks to provide the kind of education in the liberal arts and sciences that has historically been offered only at private colleges. The program is a blend of two intellectual traditions in higher education, one that emphasizes the traditional thought and learning of the culture, as reflected in the classical works produced by it, and the other that emphasizes personal investigation and freedom of discovery. The philosophy behind the Liberal Studies Program is based on a commitment that Truman has made to provide students with essential skills needed for lifelong learning, breadth across the traditional liberal arts and sciences through exposure to various discipline-based modes of inquiry, and interconnecting perspectives that stress interdisciplinary thinking and integration as well as linkage to other cultures and experiences. All students graduating from Truman must complete 63 or more credit hours in liberal arts and sciences courses.

Truman also offers an especially challenging Honors Scholar Program. This program provides students with the opportunity to select the most rigorous honors courses to satisfy the liberal arts component of their respective programs. Students who successfully complete this program benefit from an even richer academic experience and also receive special recognition at graduation and distinction on their academic transcripts. Departmental honors are also available in several disciplines.

Off-Campus Programs

Each year, approximately 500 Truman students participate in enriching and life-changing study-abroad experiences. Truman's own study-abroad programs, combined with programs offered through Truman's membership in the College Consortium for International Studies, International Student Exchange Program, AustraLearn, and the Council on International Educational Exchange, provide students with study-abroad opportunities in more than sixty countries worldwide, including Australia, China, England, Finland, France, Italy, Russia, Spain, and Thailand.

In cooperation with the Washington Center for Internships and Academic Seminars, Truman offers a wide variety of experiential internships in Washington, D.C. Included are work-experience opportunities in such areas as public administration, the fine and performing arts, foreign affairs/diplomacy, government affairs, criminal justice, international relations, health and human services, environmental policy, business administration, and communications

as well as other areas. Placement sites include nonprofit groups, media organizations, the State Department, Congress, museums, and much more.

Truman requires internships in education, health science, and exercise science and annually offers internship opportunities with the Missouri State Legislature. In recent years, students have completed internships with United States senators, the governor of Missouri, business and industry managers, zoos, broadcast and print media professionals, accountants, advertising agencies, physical therapists, musicians, artists, and the United States Supreme Court.

Academic Facilities

The Truman campus is beautifully situated on an expanse of 140 acres near downtown Kirksville. Featured among the forty facilities on campus is Pickler Memorial Library. This 460,116-volume facility provides a state-of-the-art library resource for students and faculty members alike. Materials not available in Pickler Memorial Library can be obtained through the Interlibrary Loan Office and MOBIUS.

Recent improvements to campus facilities include the expansion of the Pershing Building with the new health sciences wing, which was completed for the fall 2011 semester. Facility improvements included the new Fontaine C. Piper Movement Analysis Lab, a human performance lab, an expanded clinic for communication disorders, athletic training rooms, and a brand-new nursing simulation center. The renovations to the Student Union Building were completed in 2008 with an expanded Center for Student Involvement, new technology, mural restoration, and a completely renovated university bookstore.

The West Campus Suites opened to students in 2006. Each suite is equipped with a living room, two bedrooms housing 2 students each, closet space, a large bathroom, and central air conditioning. Renovations have been completed on Missouri Hall. Improvements included a 2,500-square-foot addition, laundry facilities on every floor, and individually controlled heating and cooling in each room. Renovations are also complete on Blanton/Nason/Brewer, Dobson Hall, and Ryle Hall, which was finished in 2011.

Additional campus facilities include a student media center with a TV studio, a radio station, print media production facilities, a biofeedback laboratory, an organic chemistry lab, an analytical chemistry lab, an observatory, a greenhouse, a 5,000-seat football stadium, a soccer field, tennis courts, softball and baseball diamonds, a 3,000-seat arena with three basketball courts, an Olympic-size swimming pool, a multicultural affairs center, a writing center, a student success center, and a career center.

Costs

Tuition for Missouri residents for the 2011–12 academic year was $6772; out-of-state tuition was $12,316. Room and board totals for both Missouri residents and nonresidents start at $6790. Additional fees included a $305 freshman orientation fee, an annual $84 activities fee, a $52 Student Health Center fee, an annual $100 athletic fee, a $100 parking fee for those with a vehicle, and the costs of books and personal expenses.

Financial Aid

Truman offers automatic scholarships ranging from $500 to $3000. Competitive scholarship awards vary from $500 up to full tuition, room, and board plus a $4000 study-abroad stipend. The application for admission also serves as the application for the automatic and competitive scholarship programs.

Several scholarships are awarded to students for excellence in music, theatre, debate/forensics, or art. These scholarships are available for instrumental, strings, or vocal music; acting or dramatic production; speech or debate; and studio art or art history. Of special interest to piano students is the Truman Piano Fellowship Competition.

The National Collegiate Athletic Association and the University authorize a limited number of grants to outstanding athletes. The value of this aid may vary with each individual recipient.

Truman accepts the Free Application for Federal Student Aid (FAFSA) and participates in all Federal Title IV financial aid programs. Financial aid estimates are available upon request.

Faculty

Truman State University is committed to teaching the academically talented undergraduate student. The University has 318 full-time faculty members and 52 part-time faculty members. Of these, 98 percent teach undergraduates and 80 percent hold a doctoral degree or the highest terminal degree in their discipline. Most major graduate institutions are represented among the Truman faculty, including Harvard, Princeton, Yale, Brown, Cornell, Oxford, and the Sorbonne. The student-faculty ratio at Truman is 16:1.

Student Government

Student Senate is the official elected governing body of the Student Association, representing approximately 5,800 students. Its mission is to represent the views of the Student Association in the formulation of the University policy through legislation and membership on all University committees; to facilitate communication and mutual understanding among the Student Association, faculty and staff members, and administration; to maintain a cohesive vision for the future of the University; and to actively participate in the fulfillment of the University's mission as an exemplary public liberal arts and sciences university.

Admission Requirements

Admission to Truman is competitive. Each applicant is evaluated for admission based upon academic and cocurricular record, ACT or SAT results, and the admission essay. Truman requires the following high school core: 4 units of English, 3 units of mathematics (4 recommended), 3 units of social studies/history, 3 units of natural science, 1 unit of fine arts, and 2 units of the same foreign language.

Application and Information

The priority deadline for admission is December 1. Students who have applied by this date are considered for all applicable competitive scholarships. Applications are processed on a rolling basis. There is no application fee. Students may apply online at the University's Web site.

For further information or to schedule a campus visit, students should contact:

Admission Office
Ruth W. Towne Museum and Visitors Center
Truman State University
100 East Normal
Kirksville, Missouri 63501
Phone: 660-785-4114
　　　 800-892-7792
Fax: 660-785-7456
E-mail: admissions@truman.edu
Web site: http://admissions.truman.edu

View of Pickler Memorial Library from the Student Union Building.

UNION COLLEGE
SCHENECTADY, NEW YORK

The College

Chartered by the state of New York in 1795, Union College is one of the nation's oldest and most distinguished liberal arts colleges. A four-year, independent residential college serving approximately 2,200 undergraduate men and women, Union is known for its academic rigor, flexible programs, and close-knit community.

True to its 200-year tradition of innovation, the Union curriculum offers a multitude of academic and intellectual options. There is an increasing emphasis on interdepartmental and interdisciplinary programs that blend liberal arts with science and technology in a way that encourages students to think creatively, ethically, and entrepreneurially. Approximately 60 percent of Union students major in the arts, humanities, and social sciences, with 40 percent majoring in the sciences and engineering.

Originally all-male, the College became coeducational in 1970; today, half of Union's students are women. The 2011–12 freshman class is made up of 17 percent students of color and 5 percent international students. Students come from thirty-nine countries and thirty-eight states and U.S. territories.

The international experience is a hallmark of a Union education, with roughly 60 percent of students pursuing studies abroad. On campus, opportunities for leadership, discussion, and community abound in the Minerva system, offering residential, academic, and social programs. Every incoming student is assigned to one of seven Minerva Houses, which also involve faculty and staff.

There are about 100 student organizations, seventeen Greek organizations, and more than a dozen theme houses. Cultural events include concerts, theater, dance, film, and art exhibits at the Mandeville Gallery. About 87 percent of all students live in residence halls or college-owned houses, including traditional dorms, Minerva Houses, fraternity and sorority houses, townhouses, and College Park Hall, a renovated hotel. The Kenney Community Center connects students with Big Brothers Big Sisters, Habitat for Humanity, tutoring programs, and civic projects.

Union's comprehensive athletics program offers twenty-five varsity intercollegiate sports, organized intramurals, club sports, and recreational and fitness activities. Union is a member of the NCAA, Liberty League, and ECAC Hockey. Men's and women's ice hockey compete in NCAA Division I programs; other teams are Division III.

The Becker Career Center helps students with career planning, internships, and the graduate school and job search. Recent trends show that about a third of graduating seniors go directly to graduate or professional schools, and Union has earned an excellent reputation for placing graduates in medical, law, and business schools. Union's more than 22,000 alumni include U.S. President Chester A. Arthur (Class of 1848); Nobel Prize, National Book Award, and MacArthur genius award winners; Olympic medalists; and pioneers in business, engineering, entertainment, journalism, and medicine.

Location

Union is set on 100 acres in Schenectady, an historic city of 62,000 founded by the Dutch. Union became the first unified campus in America in 1813 with a distinctive design by noted French architect Joseph Jacques Ramée. Its centerpiece is the sixteen-sided Nott Memorial, a National Historic Landmark used for study, symposia, exhibits, and special events. Union is part of Upstate New York's picturesque Capital-Saratoga Region, with nearly 1 million residents. The region has a burgeoning high-tech industry and rich cultural heritage. A 15-minute drive from Albany International Airport, the College is 3 hours by car from New York City and Boston, 4 hours from Montreal, and close to East Coast ski slopes and the Adirondack Mountains.

Majors and Degrees

Union offers more than forty majors; double majors; combined majors and minors; interdepartmental and multidisciplinary concentrations; and area, ethnic, and cultural studies programs.

The self-designed organizing theme major is for the student with intellectual curiosity in a particular topic involving multiple disciplines. Most students take three courses in each of the three 10-week terms that comprise Union's trimester system. The average introductory class has 17 students; the average upper-level class, 14.

Most of Union's newest majors, such as bioengineering, neuroscience, and religious studies, and minors, such as computational methods and Judaic studies, encourage learning at the intersection of the liberal arts and sciences. Among the courses that cross traditional disciplinary boundaries are The Illustrated Organism, a class for artists and scientists, and "New Wall of China," offered through the departments of Modern Languages and Literatures, and Environmental Science, Policy and Engineering. Union's Internal Education Foundation provides funding for special, innovative projects.

Union offers Bachelor of Arts (B.A.) and Bachelor of Science (B.S.) degrees. Students may declare up to two minors. Union also offers a leadership in medicine program with Albany Medical College and Union Graduate College; the law and public policy program with Albany Law School; and five-year bachelor's/M.B.A. or bachelor's/M.A.T. programs with Union Graduate College. The fourteen academic honor societies include Phi Beta Kappa, the first chapter established in New York (1817).

Academic Programs

Nearly every academic department requires students to complete some form of research in their subject area, and students have opportunities to work one-on-one with their professors. They often coauthor publications and present at conferences, such as the National Conference on Undergraduate Research (NCUR). Many participate in internships at businesses, hospitals, and social service organizations. The Steinmetz Symposium showcases the work of hundreds of student researchers through oral, dance, music, art, and poster sessions each spring.

The Campus Wide Computation Initiative, part of a National Science Foundation grant, helps students integrate computation into various fields of study. Through the Michael Rapaport ('59) Ethics Across the Curriculum initiative, faculty members from different departments offer courses that provide extensive training in everyday ethics. Writing Across the Curriculum requires all students to take five designated courses from at least two divisions and one Senior Writing Experience. The First-Year Preceptorial (FYP), a mandatory interdisciplinary course for first-year students, emphasizes critical reading and thinking skills, writing, speaking, and gender and cultural diversity. The Sophomore Research Seminar (SRS), also required, promotes research and writing skills.

Off-Campus Programs

Roughly 60 percent of all Union students go abroad. Most programs are led by Union faculty. Many programs combine elements of entrepreneurship, research, or community service. There are also opportunities for extended terms, formal exchanges, research trips, and independent study. Three-week mini-terms, for 1 credit, are offered during winter and summer in various U.S. cities and countries. Many students get involved in continuing hurricane relief efforts in New Orleans. The Civil Rights Public History Mini-Term explores the American Civil Rights Movement in key cities and states. The newest mini-terms include Russia, Senegal and Uruguay. Union's innovative Minerva Fellows program sends graduating seniors to developing countries to work with welfare and anti-poverty initiatives. All programs are central to Union's mission of educating engaged, ethical contributors to a global society.

Academic Facilities

Union's nearly 100 buildings include the F. W. Olin Center, which features interactive computerization capabilities that make the building adaptable for use by nearly every academic department.

The Science and Engineering Center houses the Center for Bioengineering and Computational Biology. Here, students can use sophisticated research tools such as a nuclear magnetic resonance spectrometer, a Pelletron accelerator, a centrifuge, and a scanning electron microscope.

Schaffer Library has 610,000 volumes, 1,600 journals and 2 online databases that provide access to a quarter-million printed books, documents, and musical scores. Flanking the library are the Humanities and Social Sciences Buildings. The Arts Building, located in North Colonnade, includes the Burns Atrium, where work by students, faculty, and alumni is exhibited. The Taylor Music Center includes the Fred L. Emerson Auditorium, an all-Steinway performance and teaching space with state-of-the-art recording technology. The Yulman Theater is the College's major performance space.

The $22-million Peter Irving Wold Science and Engineering Center, opened in 2011, is a home for interdisciplinary studies across departments.

Costs

Union's tuition for the 2011–12 academic year was $43,131; room and board were $10,671 and mandatory fees were $471. The estimated cost for books and personal expense was $1777.

Financial Aid

Union is committed to admitting an economically diverse student body and to meeting the full demonstrated need of all admitted students. The College offers $35 million annually in aid. The average Union need-based scholarship is $29,000; the average merit award is $10,000. Those families that are unable to pay full tuition and fees are typically covered by a financial aid package consisting of a grant, loan, and work opportunity. About half of all applicants apply for financial aid; more than 60 percent of all students receive financial assistance from the College.

Candidates for aid should complete the Free Application for Federal Student Aid (FAFSA) and the College Scholarship Service's PROFILE form and mail them directly to the appropriate agencies by February 1. For more information, visit http://www.union.edu/Admissions/index.php.

Faculty

Close student-faculty interaction and small classes are a hallmark of the Union experience. The close relationship between students and faculty motivates students to learn through inquiry and discourse. Excluding library staff, 98 percent of the faculty members hold a doctorate or terminal degree. Class size is generally small, with a 10:1 student-faculty ratio. Many upper-level courses function as seminars.

Student Government

Students play an integral role in directing the present and future course of Union. With full voting rights on the two councils that recommend changes to educational policy and student life, students are engaged and active leaders on campus. Students also participate in groups that advise the President on matters like budgetary planning and long-range needs. Each year, two students are elected to membership on the College's Board of Trustees. Opportunities for leadership also abound with the Minerva houses, theme houses, Kenney Community Center, and other clubs.

Admission Requirements

Approximately 5,000 applicants seek freshman class positions on an annual basis; approximately 60 percent are in the top 10 percent of their secondary school class. In evaluating each application, admissions counselors look at the prospective student's grades, rigor of courses taken, class rank, teacher recommendations, and extracurricular involvement. Typically, 16 units of secondary school preparation are required for admission. These should include credits in certain fundamental subjects, such as English, a foreign language, mathematics, social studies, and science. It is strongly recommended that students visit Union for an admission interview and a student-guided tour. Alumni interviews may be requested online.

A student can choose not to submit his or her SAT or ACT scores for review, except for accelerated programs. Those interested in accelerated programs must submit the SAT and two SAT Subject Tests.

Application and Information

Early decision candidates have two options. The application deadline (including all supporting credentials) for Option I is November 15, with notification by December 15. Option II has a January 15 deadline (including all supporting credentials) and February 15 notification. Applications for regular decision admission must be filed by January 15, with decisions mailed by April 1.

Applications to the leadership in medicine program are due no later than December 15. Those for the law and public policy program must be filed no later than January 1. Those deferred under early decision and all regular applicants are given a final decision by April 1. Union adheres to the Candidates Reply Date of May 1.

Office of Admissions
Grant Hall
Union College
Schenectady, New York 12308
Phone: 518-388-6112
          888-843-6688 (toll-free)
Fax: 518-388-6986
E-mail: admissions@union.edu
Web site: http://www.union.edu

The sixteen-sided Nott Memorial is Union College's centerpiece.

UNION UNIVERSITY
JACKSON, TENNESSEE

The University

Union University is committed to renewing minds and reclaiming the great Christian intellectual tradition. Students benefit from more than 100 programs of study that are academically challenging as well as Christ-centered. This private, four-year, liberal arts–based university was founded in 1823 and is affiliated with the Tennessee Baptist Convention.

Union is committed to its four core values of being excellence-driven, Christ-centered, people-focused, and future-directed.

Union has consistently received national recognition for academic excellence, value, and community service. *U.S.News & World Report* again has ranked Union among the top 15 regional universities in the South. Union has been listed among the top-tier schools in the South every year since 1997. Union was listed among only fifty-six schools nationwide "where the faculty has an unusually strong commitment to undergraduate teaching." It was the third consecutive year Union appeared on that list. For the fourth straight year, the publication listed Union among forty-six up-and-coming schools in the nation that "have recently made the most promising and innovative changes in the areas of academics, faculty, student life, campus, or facilities." Also for the fourth straight year, Union was selected as one of nineteen "A-Plus Schools for B Students" in the South. Union's freshman retention rate of 88 percent was third highest among regional universities in the South.

America's 100 Best College Buys ranks Union among the nation's best for combining academic quality and affordable price.

Union has been named to the President's Higher Education Community Service Honor Roll every year since the award was established in 2006.

More than 4,200 undergraduate and graduate students from forty-four states and thirty-three countries are represented in the student body.

Union provides each resident student with a private bedroom within apartment-style complexes, most of which were built in 2008. The new units have four bedrooms with Internet connection, a kitchen, living room, washer/dryer unit, and two bathrooms.

A new student commons building features two fireplaces, TV and multipurpose rooms, piano and band practice rooms, two kitchens, a gymnasium, a walking track, and outdoor grills and patios. The University coffeehouse is another favorite student destination for concerts, conversation, and study.

Union offers more than fifty major student-produced music and theater events each year. The University has sixty campus clubs, societies, fraternities, sororities, and other organizations. Students enjoy varsity and intramural sports and community service activities. In addition, students and faculty set aside at least one day a year to serve the local community though more than fifty different volunteer projects.

Union graduates enjoy a high acceptance rate at top graduate and law schools. Nearly 100 percent of faculty-recommended health science students have been accepted to medical school or professional graduate study. More than 80 percent of all graduates are accepted by graduate schools or employed, some with Fortune 500 companies, within a month of receiving their degrees. Nearly 77 percent of Union seniors plan to complete postgraduate work.

The NCAA has approved Union's application to begin the transition to NCAA Division II affiliation. After successful completion of the three-year membership process, Union plans to join the Gulf South Conference, one of the premier conferences in Division II. Union will begin competing with GSC schools in 2012–2013.

Location

Union is located in Jackson, Tennessee, a growing community 80 miles east of Memphis and 120 miles west of Nashville along the I-40 corridor. The Jackson area has a population of about 100,000. Students find convenient access to entertainment, shopping, and other services. Jackson hosts many cultural, recreational, and sporting events. Daily commercial flights are available at airports in Memphis and Nashville; commuter air service to those cities is available from Jackson.

Majors and Degrees

Undergraduate students can choose majors from among the following programs of study: accounting, advertising, applied linguistics, art (ceramics, drawing, graphics design, painting, photography, sculpture), athletic training, biblical studies-languages, biochemistry, biology (general, zoology), broadcast journalism, business administration (economics, international business, management, marketing), cell and molecular biology, chemical physics, chemistry, Christian ministry and missions, Christian studies, Christian thought and tradition, church music (organ, piano, voice), computer science, conservation, digital media studies (art, communication arts, computer science), economics, elementary education (early childhood, elementary, middle grades), engineering (electrical, mechanical), engineering physics, English (creative writing, literature), family studies, French (language/culture, literature/culture), history, information technology, intercultural studies (global, regional), journalism, learning foundations, mathematics, media communications, medical technology, music (Christian studies, communication arts, management, marketing), music education (general/choral, instrumental/band), music performance (organ, piano, voice), music theory (instrumental, organ, piano, voice), nursing, philosophy, physical education, physical science, physics, political science (American, general, international relations, political theory), psychology, public relations, social work, sociology (general, social organization), Spanish (language/culture, literature/culture), special education (modified, comprehensive), speech, sport management (communication, marketing, ministry), sports medicine and wellness, teaching English as a second language, theater, and theater and speech.

Preprofessional programs include chiropractics, cytotechnology, dental hygiene, dentistry, health information management, medicine, occupational therapy, optometry, pharmacy, physical therapy, physician assistant studies, podiatry, and veterinary medicine.

Academic Programs

A Union University education is widely known for integrating faith and learning. Students are encouraged to move toward a mature reflection of what the truths of Christian faith mean in every field of study. Undergraduates are given research opportunities through the Scholarship Symposium and other programs.

The Honors Community is made up of serious-minded students who are eager to make the most of their college education, and faculty members who know them on a first-name basis. Honors courses are designed to stretch a student as a thinker, a reader,

and a writer with the support and guidance of faculty across the disciplines.

Union's acclaimed Keystone Program offers academic support for students who may fall short of some minimum admission requirements. The program provides these students with the necessary tools to progress academically, with many achieving a level of success they may not have thought possible.

Union's academic calendar is divided into fall (August to December) and spring (February to May) semesters, January term, and three summer terms. Evening accelerated courses are available each term.

Off-Campus Programs

Students from a variety of academic areas participate in internships with regional and national companies. Study abroad includes destinations such as Belgium, China, Costa Rica, France, Great Britain, Italy, Jordan, Mexico, Poland, and Spain. Union students also have the opportunity to go on short-term mission Global Outreach trips to locations in Africa, Asia, Central America, Europe, and the United States.

Academic Facilities

Union's wooded campus features about forty academic and residence buildings and excellent athletic facilities. More than $120 million in new campus construction has been completed during the past decade, including several new Georgian-Colonial classroom buildings that support top-level teaching and research facilities. Pharmacy, science, and nursing students benefit from state-of-the-art laboratories and simulation environments. Communication students produce a daily live news program in the University's HD television studio. Other academic amenities include top-quality lecture facilities; fine and performing arts practice rooms and recital halls; theaters; digital media labs; and biology, chemistry, physics, and engineering laboratories.

Plans for construction of a new library building are under way. Adjacent to classroom buildings and residence complexes, the new library is designed to meet the research and technology needs of the twenty-first century scholar. The current library houses open stacks as well as periodicals, microfilm and microfiche, archives, and electronic resources. Students also have easy access to the combined collections of more than 41,000 libraries worldwide. The Stephen Olford Center library and the R. C. Ryan Center for Biblical Studies library house several unique collections and are also available to students.

Union provides three large computer labs on the Jackson campus for student use. Each residential student has a port for the campus network and Internet access. Wireless access is available in many areas. Additional computer labs are specialized for use by various academic programs.

Costs

The annual cost for a full-time student for the 2011–12 academic year was $23,330 for tuition (up to 16 hours per semester) and $8110 for housing and meals (100 meals per semester). Prices for housing and meals may vary slightly according to a student's preferences.

Financial Aid

More than 90 percent of Union students receive some financial aid based on need or merit. Union awards competitive scholarships and grants to qualified students. The University helps connect students with other financial resources such as loans, student-work programs, privately funded scholarships, and a host of state and federal assistance programs.

Faculty

Union University invests in faculty members who are experts in their fields and committed to excellence in teaching, advising, and mentoring. These faculty members put a priority on classroom teaching, but also join students in the pursuit of significant research, especially at the undergraduate level. Eighty-four percent of the faculty members hold doctorates or the highest degree offered in their field of study. The student-faculty ratio is 11:1, and all classes are taught by faculty members.

Student Government

Union's Student Government Association functions through its executive, legislative, and judicial branches. Its elected officers and representatives serve as the official voice of the students in institutional matters.

Admission Requirements

Applicants must graduate from an accredited high school with at least 20 units in the areas of English, foreign language, mathematics, social and natural sciences, and approved electives. In addition, students who qualify for unconditional admission must meet or exceed two of the following three admissions criteria: a 2.5 core GPA, a composite score of 22 on the ACT or 1020 (math and critical reading combined) on the SAT, and a ranking in the top 50 percent of their high school class. A state high school equivalency diploma is accepted in lieu of a high school diploma. Union also actively seeks to admit home-schooled students.

Transfer students who have completed at least 24 semester hours of transferable credit at an accredited college may also apply. Transfer students with less than 24 semester hours must meet freshman and transfer admission requirements.

Application and Information

Applicants must complete and return the Union University application for undergraduate admission along with the $35 application fee. All official transcripts and results of either the ACT or SAT must be requested and mailed directly to the Office of Undergraduate Admissions. Applications are accepted and decisions rendered on a rolling basis.

For more information or to request an application, students should contact:

Office of Undergraduate Admissions
Union University
1050 Union University Drive
Jackson, Tennessee 38305-3697
Phone: 731-661-5100
      800-33-UNION (toll-free)
E-mail: info@uu.edu
Web site: www.uu.edu

More than 4,200 undergraduate and graduate students come to Union University from 44 states and 33 countries.

UNITED STATES AIR FORCE ACADEMY
COLORADO SPRINGS, COLORADO

U.S. AIR FORCE
ACADEMY

The Academy

Established in 1954, the Air Force Academy prepares and motivates cadets for careers as Air Force officers. The Academy stresses character development, military training, and physical fitness as well as academics, emphasizing leadership in all areas.

The total enrollment is approximately 4,000; nearly 1,000 fourth-class (freshman) students enter each year. The composition of the student body mirrors that of the Air Force officer corps: about 23 percent women and 30 percent minorities. Students come from all 50 states and several other countries. Their common bond is the desire to be military officers. All cadets must live in on-campus dormitories and wear uniforms.

The Academy is accredited by the North Central Association of Colleges and Schools. Its engineering programs are approved by the Engineering Accreditation Commission of the Accreditation Board for Engineering and Technology, and its computer courses are approved by the Computing Sciences Accreditation Board. The chemistry and biochemistry majors fulfill the requirements of the Commission on Professional Training of the American Chemical Society.

All cadets must participate in intramural, club, or intercollegiate athletics every semester. The intramural sports include basketball, boxing (men's), cross-country, flag football, flickerball, rugby (men's and women's), soccer, softball, team handball, tennis, Ultimate (Frisbee), volleyball, and wallyball. The intercollegiate teams compete in Division I of the NCAA regionally and nationally. The men's teams include baseball, basketball, boxing, cheerleading, cross-country, diving, fencing, football, golf, gymnastics, hockey, indoor and outdoor track, lacrosse, rifle, soccer, swimming, tennis, water polo, and wrestling. The women's teams include basketball, cheerleading, cross-country, diving, fencing, gymnastics, indoor and outdoor track, rifle, soccer, swimming, tennis, and volleyball. Cadets may also choose from more than 80 extracurricular activities, which include professional organizations, mission support, competitive and recreational clubs, sports groups, and hobby clubs.

Qualified Academy graduates may enter flight training upon graduation, and approximately 75 percent of the students in each graduating class pursue graduate education at other institutions within ten years of their graduation. Each year, numerous Academy graduates receive graduate scholarships and fellowships, such as the Marshall, Rhodes, National Science Foundation, National Collegiate Athletic Association, and Guggenheim awards.

Location

The Academy campus sits in the foothills of the Rampart Range of the Rocky Mountains in a setting of natural beauty. Built on a mesa at 7,000 feet, it is one of Colorado's top tourist attractions. The Cadet Chapel, with its 17 aluminum spires towering 150 feet into the air, highlights the contemporary architecture of the buildings in the cadet area. The space-age effect reflects the Academy's mission of preparing cadets to become officers and leaders in the Air Force of the future. The Academy borders the northern edge of Colorado Springs, which lies at the foot of the famous 14,100-foot Pikes Peak. Colorado Springs has a metropolitan population of more than 500,000. Denver, the state's capital, has a population of almost 2.5 million in its greater metropolitan area and is located 55 miles north of the Academy. In addition to the social, sports, and cultural activities available in these cities, cadets enjoy skiing, hunting, horseback riding, white-water rafting, and other activities in the Colorado Rocky Mountains and nearby resorts.

Majors and Degrees

Graduates of the four-year service academy receive the Bachelor of Science (B.S.) degree and a commission as second lieutenants in the Air Force. The B.S. is granted in aeronautical engineering, astronautical engineering, basic sciences, behavioral sciences, biology, chemistry, civil engineering, computer engineering, computer science, economics, electrical engineering, English, environmental engineering, foreign area studies, general engineering, geospatial science, history, humanities, legal studies, management, mathematical sciences, mechanical engineering, meteorology, military strategic studies, operations research, philosophy, physics, political science, social sciences, space operations, systems engineering, and systems engineering management. The Academy also offers minors in foreign languages and philosophy.

Academic Programs

A class enters the Academy during the last week in June or the first week in July. Incoming cadets undergo a strenuous 38-day summer training program that tests both their mental and physical abilities. Upperclass cadets conduct basic cadet training; commissioned officers serve as advisers. Basic cadets who complete this program are accepted into the Cadet Wing as fourth-class cadets. The academic year starts in early August and continues through May. During the first two years, cadets concentrate on core courses in engineering, humanities, science, and social science. During the last two years, they specialize in an academic major.

The required core courses prepare cadets for a broad scope of activity as Air Force officers. The core curriculum embraces courses in academic subjects, leadership and military training, and physical education and athletics. In addition, cadets complete the requirements for any of the academic majors. To be eligible for graduation, cadets must also demonstrate an aptitude for commissioned service and leadership, demonstrate character consistent with professional military service, maintain a minimum cumulative grade point average and core grade point average of 2.0, and complete a minimum of 141 credit hours. The curriculum includes many elective courses.

All students must begin as freshmen; however, cadets who have taken some of the core course material prior to entry into the Academy may receive transfer or validation credit for this work. They may then substitute other courses for those granted transfer credit. Cadets who maintain the required grade point average may take advanced study classes.

The Academy aviation program familiarizes all cadets with operational activities of the Air Force. Optional courses provide instruction in soaring, parachuting, navigation, and basic flying. Those who take these courses may fulfill the requirements for

Federal Aviation Administration pilot or glider certificates. Cadets who qualify and are selected for pilot or navigator training may enter Air Education and Training Command flight programs following graduation from the Academy. Diversified summer programs in aviation and military training prepare cadets for officer responsibilities in the Air Force. Cadets may select their programs from several optional assignments at the Air Force Academy and other military installations.

Off-Campus Programs

Selected cadets may exchange visits with cadets from the Military Academy, Naval Academy, Coast Guard Academy, or one of several international Air Force academies. The exchange program varies from one to two weeks for most of the international programs to a semester for the other U.S. service academies and the Canadian, Chilean, French, German, and Spanish Air Force academies, to name a few.

Academic Facilities

The Air Force Academy's excellent facilities support the academic, military, and athletics programs. Most classrooms accommodate small class sessions, averaging 17 students. Several classes and assemblies meet in larger lecture halls. Well-equipped laboratories supplement classroom instruction. Cadets conduct experiments using the aeronautics laboratory's wind tunnels, shock tubes, and rocket engines. A local network connects every dorm room, faculty and staff office, classroom, and laboratory at the Academy, and all entering cadets purchase notebook computers for academic and personal use. The Academy library, with more than 1.5 million volumes, supports all educational programs and maintains a collection of historical materials concerning aeronautics.

Costs

There are no tuition charges; the cost, including room, board, and medical and dental care, is borne entirely by the U.S. government. In addition, cadets receive a monthly salary to pay for supplies, clothing, and personal expenses. Careful management of the money covers obligations, with a small amount remaining for personal use.

Financial Aid

All cadets are on full scholarship at the Air Force Academy, as described above.

Faculty

The Academy's faculty is composed of Air Force officers and civilian professors. A few officers from other branches of the U.S. Armed Forces, those from allied nations, and distinguished civilian visiting professors supplement the faculty. There are no graduate student instructors. Faculty members must have a master's degree, and many have earned doctorates. Their educational backgrounds represent many outstanding colleges and universities in the United States, as well as some international institutions of higher education. Faculty members sponsor, coach, and referee extracurricular activities and athletics; adopt squadrons and attend their special events; and provide academic, career, and personal counseling.

Student Government

The Air Force Academy trains cadets for future leadership by allowing them to hold positions of responsibility in the Cadet Wing, the organization to which all cadets are assigned. The wing is under the operational supervision of first-class cadets (seniors). They hold cadet officer rank and command the wing and the subordinate units of groups, squadrons, flights, and

elements. Through this organization, upperclass cadets are responsible for military training of the underclasses, the honor education and honor system, character development, and ethics and human relations programs.

Admission Requirements

Each year, young men and women who are U.S. citizens may be appointed from all states and territories of the nation. Citizens of other countries are admitted in limited numbers. Applicants must be at least 17 and not yet 23 years of age on July 1 of the year in which they desire to be admitted, be unmarried, have no dependents, and be of high moral character. They must be in good physical health.

Applicants must receive an official nomination. Members of Congress make the majority of the nominations for residents of their states and districts. Senators and representatives nominate young men and women who have excelled academically in high school, have demonstrated leadership potential through school activities, are physically fit, are respected by associates, and want to pursue military careers. Applicants need not know their member of Congress personally. Students may be eligible in nomination categories other than congressional. Students should ask high school counselors or Air Force Admissions Liaison Officers about other categories and apply for nominations in all categories for which they are eligible.

To enter the Academy upon graduation from high school, students should apply as soon as possible after March 1 of their junior year. If successful in receiving a nomination, they must take a physical fitness test, a medical exam, and either the SAT or the ACT.

Application and Information

High school juniors may obtain the application online at http://www.academyadmissions.com. Applicants should study the instructions and follow the proper application procedures. Air Force Admissions Liaison Officers, located in all states, assist students and counselors with the application and testing requirements.

HQ USAFA/RRS
2304 Cadet Drive, Suite 2300
USAF Academy, Colorado 80840-5025
Phone: 800-443-9266 (toll-free)
Web site: http://www.academyadmissions.com

United States Air Force Academy Cadet Chapel.

UNITED STATES MERCHANT MARINE ACADEMY

KINGS POINT, NEW YORK

The Academy

The United States Merchant Marine Academy is a four-year, tuition-free federal service academy that was founded in 1943 to educate and train maritime shipping industry (merchant marine) officers, officers on active duty in the armed forces, and leaders in the maritime and intermodal transportation industry. It is an accredited, degree-granting college whose students are commissioned as ensigns in the Navy Reserve upon graduation. The Academy is one of the world's foremost institutions in the field of maritime education and is operated under the Maritime Administration (MARAD) of the U.S. Department of Transportation.

There are approximately 975 men and women enrolled as midshipmen at the Academy. Their daily routine at Kings Point is very demanding. The academic day begins at 7:30 a.m. and concludes at 4 p.m. After classes, midshipmen are free to participate in recreational activities until dinnertime. After dinner, they are required to devote their time to study and academic preparation.

The extracurricular program is broad and varied. In addition to varsity athletics in twenty-five intercollegiate sports, the Academy has an extensive intramural program that permits all students to enjoy physical activity and competition.

The nonathletic activities are also wide ranging and abundant, falling into as many categories as there are individual interests. Publications and the Drill Team, Glee Club, Regimental Band, Scuba-Diving Club, Eagle Scout Association, International Relations Club, and Fencing Club are but a few of the pursuits available to the midshipmen. Regimental and class dances and informal mixers provide the midshipmen with an interesting social program.

Midshipmen are granted liberty on weekends, leave at Thanksgiving, winter holidays (December), spring trimester break, and annual leave in June–July after graduation and before the next academic term begins. Perhaps the most unusual and exciting part of the Academy curriculum is the Shipboard Training Program (Sea Year). Each midshipman, during three trimesters of the sophomore and junior years, serves 300–360 days at sea aboard commercially operated American-flag merchant ships. This exceptional work-study program takes the midshipmen to many parts of the world and provides them with practical experience on several different types of vessels. It can be said that the world is their campus during their three trimesters of sea service.

Location

The Academy is located on 80.5 acres of land at Kings Point, on the North Shore of Long Island. Kings Point is a suburban residential community only 20 miles east of midtown New York City, close to various cultural and recreational facilities.

Majors and Degrees

A graduate of the U.S. Merchant Marine Academy receives a Bachelor of Science degree, a merchant marine license as a third mate or third assistant engineer, and a commission as an ensign in the U.S. Navy Reserve. Graduates may apply to the Army, Navy, Air Force, Marine Corps, Coast Guard, or National Oceanic and Atmospheric Administration (NOAA) to serve on active duty. Five major programs are offered: marine transportation for the preparation of deck officers; marine engineering for students interested in becoming engineering officers; marine engineering systems, which, in addition to leading to a license as a third

assistant engineer, is accredited by the Accreditation Board for Engineering and Technology (ABET) and includes a curriculum with greater depth in mathematics and a significant component of engineering design, as compared to the marine engineering curriculum; marine engineering and shipyard management, which is also accredited by ABET; and logistics and intermodal transportation, a marine transportation program focusing on logistics and intermodal systems management.

Academic Programs

During the first trimester of the plebe (or freshman) year, all students take a common program of mathematics, science, English, and professional courses. This background enables midshipmen to determine intelligently the area of their special interest. After the first trimester, midshipmen select their major and from then on concentrate on a program aligned with their career choice. The professional majors each consist of required core courses in technical and general education areas as well as selected electives. The option program consists of six courses for marine transportation and marine engineering majors, who have a choice of taking a series of related elective courses in a specific area of concentration or any individual elective course for which they qualify. These courses include such specialized fields as nuclear engineering, management science, computer science, chemistry, and naval architecture. By choosing to take the series of related courses, midshipmen can develop a proficiency in a subspecialty, supplementing their major field of study. Students in the marine engineering systems majors are not offered the choice of electives because of the required course load in their programs. General education courses make up about one third of each of the professional curriculums, and all midshipmen are required to take naval science courses prescribed by the Department of the Navy.

Thus, the Academy provides a balanced program of theoretical and practical study designed to provide the undergraduate with technical competence, leadership skills, and the well-rounded general education so essential for responsible citizenship in contemporary society.

Exemption credit may be awarded for college-level work completed at an accredited college if the course is equivalent to a course offered at the Academy.

Academic Facilities

With the exception of Wiley Hall, the former residence of Walter P. Chrysler and now an administration building, all the buildings of the Academy have been constructed since 1942. The interfaith chapel was dedicated in 1961, a three-story library was completed in 1968, and an indoor swimming pool and an engineering and science wing have been added since 1972. A modernization of all other academic buildings was completed in 1982. The Dean ('45) and Barbara White Admissions Center was dedicated in 2004. Upgrades to the dormitories and other facilities are currently under way.

Costs

Tuition, room and board, and medical and dental care are provided by the U.S. government. In addition, the government pays for books and the initial issue of uniforms. Each midshipman also receives $974.40 per month during periods when they are assigned aboard ship for training. Entering plebes are required to pay a little more than $2500 to cover the initial cost of a laptop computer as well as lab fees, equipment, and service,

license, and activity fees. Upperclass members are also charged for service, license, and activity fees for the trimesters they are on campus (when they are not at sea).

Financial Aid

In effect, each midshipman receives a four-year scholarship from the U.S. government. Financial assistance is also available through the Federal Pell Grant Program, the Federal Stafford Student Loan Program, the Federal PLUS (parent loan) Program, the Federal Academic Competitiveness Grant, and the National Science and Mathematics Access to Retain Talent (SMART) Grant. Students may use outside scholarships to defray their costs.

Faculty

The Academy has 84 full-time faculty members and a student-faculty ratio of approximately 11:1. One third of the faculty members are licensed deck or engineering officers. Most hold advanced degrees in an academic discipline: 90 percent of the total faculty members hold master's degrees or higher; 50 percent have earned doctorates.

Student Government

The student body at the Academy is organized along military lines as a regiment, consisting of two battalions. Regimental life at the Academy is a form of student government and is an important part of the midshipman's total educational and leadership learning experience. The first classmen, or seniors, under the direction of the Commandant of Midshipmen, are responsible for exercising military command of the regiment and for administering the daily routine of the midshipmen. The military program is designed to develop leadership ability, self-discipline, and a sense of responsibility—attributes that are essential for effective citizenship as well as for a successful career as an officer.

Admission Requirements

Candidates for admission must be American citizens, be at least 17 years of age, must not have passed their twenty-fifth birthday by July 1 of the year of entry into the Academy, and be of good moral character. Candidates must be nominated by a U.S. representative or senator and must compete for vacancies allocated to their state in proportion to its representation in Congress. Candidates must achieve qualifying scores on the standard administration (timed) SAT or ACT. Candidates must have successfully completed chemistry or physics (including lab), as well as mathematics up to and including one semester of trigonometry or precalculus. Candidates' competitive standing is determined by their College Board score, their high school academic record and extracurricular participation, and their overall leadership potential. All candidates must meet the physical requirements for appointment as a midshipman in the Navy Reserve. Although not required, all applicants are strongly encouraged to perform a day or overnight visit to learn firsthand about midshipman life and academics. Visits are arranged through the Admissions Office when classes are in session, which is from mid-August to May.

Application and Information

Prospective candidates should write to the Admissions Office. They are sent detailed information on the nomination process, required tests, application procedures, and specific requirements. It is advisable to apply for a nomination during the late spring of the junior year in high school. The deadline for applications is March 1 of the year of desired entry.

Further information may be obtained by contacting:

Director of Admissions
U.S. Merchant Marine Academy
300 Steamboat Road
Kings Point, New York 11024-1699
Phone: 516-773-5391
        866-546-4778 (toll-free)
Fax: 516-773-5390
E-mail: admissions@usmma.edu
Web site: http://www.usmma.edu

An aerial view of the 80.5 acre "sea campus" of the U.S. Merchant Marine Academy at Kings Point, Long Island, on the shores of Long Island Sound.

UNIVERSITY AT BUFFALO, THE STATE UNIVERSITY OF NEW YORK

BUFFALO, NEW YORK

The University

The University at Buffalo (UB) is one of the nation's premier public research universities. With about 100 bachelor's degree programs (including combined degrees), 205 master's programs, and eighty-four doctoral degree programs, UB offers more academic choices than any other public university in New York and New England. In addition to twenty-seven departments in the College of Arts and Sciences, the University includes the Schools of Architecture and Planning, Dental Medicine, Education, Engineering and Applied Sciences, Law, Management, Medicine and Biomedical Sciences, Nursing, Pharmacy and Pharmaceutical Sciences, Public Health and Health Professions, and Social Work, as well as the Roswell Park Cancer Institute Graduate Division.

Because the University at Buffalo is a research-intensive university, undergraduates study and work with faculty members who are leaders in their fields in academic and research facilities that support work at the most advanced levels of knowledge. Through initiatives like the Center for Undergraduate Research and Creative Activities and the Undergraduate Academies, UB undergraduates have the opportunity to collaborate with faculty members on groundbreaking research and creative projects.

As a large university with more than 29,000 students, including over 19,000 undergraduates, the University at Buffalo has a rich and varied student life. UB is home to a culturally diverse student body and ranks among the nation's leaders in international enrollment, with more than 5,000 students from 115 countries.

The University offers men's and women's sports programs at both the intramural and NCAA Division I levels; extensive recreational and entertainment facilities; more than 200 student organizations; the Distinguished Speaker Series, which has featured such guests as Al Gore, Stephen Colbert, and His Holiness the Fourteenth Dalai Lama; and a busy calendar of festivals, concerts, films, and more.

UB's North Campus, the seat of most of the undergraduate academic programs, occupies 2 square miles in suburban Amherst. Its residence hall options include apartment-style living space on or adjacent to campus.

The South Campus, 3 miles away in a residential corner of Buffalo, is largely devoted to the health sciences and architecture. Buffalo's rapid transit line connects the South Campus with the city center and the waterfront.

Recently, UB broadened its presence in Buffalo with a new Downtown Campus, home to the New York State Center for Excellence in Bioinformatics and Life Sciences, the Ross Eye Institute, and the Jacobs Executive Development Center. Additional expansion continues with the new UB-Kaleida Health building, housing the Clinical and Translational Research Center, and plans for a new medical school building.

Location

Buffalo is a Great Lakes city on an international border with a metropolitan area population of more than 1 million. It's a place of friendly neighborhoods, with big-city activity for all tastes: professional sports teams; the Buffalo Philharmonic Orchestra; the renowned Albright-Knox Art Gallery; and a vibrant theater, dining, and club scene, all in a dramatic setting on Lake Erie and the Niagara River. The natural wonder of Niagara Falls is just a 20-minute drive from the North Campus.

Majors and Degrees

The University is organized into one college and seven schools that serve undergraduates. The College of Arts and Sciences offers academic majors in African and African American studies, American studies, anthropology, art (studio art and fine arts), art history, Asian studies, bioinformatics and computational biology, biological sciences, chemistry, classics, communication, computational physics, dance, economics, English, environmental geosciences, film studies, geography, geological sciences, global gender studies, history, international trade, Jewish studies, linguistics, mathematical physics, mathematics, mathematics/economics, media study, medicinal chemistry, modern languages and literatures (French, German, Italian, and Spanish), music, music performance, music theatre, philosophy, physics, political science, psychology, sociology, speech and hearing science, and theatre. An interdisciplinary degree program in the social sciences is also offered, with concentrations in cognitive science, environmental studies, health and human services, international studies, legal studies, and urban and public policy studies.

The School of Architecture and Planning offers majors in architecture and environmental design.

The School of Engineering and Applied Sciences offers majors in computer science and engineering physics and in aerospace, biomedical, chemical, civil, computer, electrical, environmental, industrial, and mechanical engineering.

The School of Management offers a major in accounting and a major in business administration, with concentrations in financial analysis, human resources management, international business, management information systems, marketing, and operations and supply chain management.

The School of Medicine and Biomedical Sciences offers academic majors in biochemistry, biomedical sciences, biotechnology, medical technology, nuclear medicine technology, and pharmacology and toxicology. The School of Nursing offers an academic major in nursing.

The School of Pharmacy and Pharmaceutical Sciences offers an academic major in pharmaceutical sciences and a six-year Pharm.D. pharmacy program. The School of Public Health and Health Professions offers an academic major in exercise science. Physical therapy is offered as a six-year doctorate; undergraduates major in exercise science.

The University has twenty-six combined-degree programs (B.A./M.A. and B.S./M.B.A., for example). Students whose objectives cannot be met through existing programs can formulate their own degree programs.

Academic Programs

Candidates for a baccalaureate degree are required to complete a minimum of 120 semester hours, 30 of which must be completed in residence, and earn a minimum grade point average of 2.0.

Students have great flexibility in planning their academic programs. All students must fulfill a University general education requirement. They must also complete an academic major, which is usually selected by the end of the sophomore year. Students also have ample opportunity for independent study under departmental or faculty auspices. Placement and credit are granted on the basis of Advanced Placement or College-Level Examination Program scores. The academic year has two semesters: one beginning in late August and the other in mid-January. An extensive summer session is also offered.

Off-Campus Programs

Many students take advantage of study-abroad programs. The University has exchange programs with sixty-five universities around the world. Programs include the full academic year or fall, spring, or summer sessions. Students may also take advantage of nearly 300 programs offered by other colleges in the SUNY system.

Academic Facilities

The University at Buffalo's academic library collections are the largest in the SUNY system; in addition to more than 3.6 million bound volumes, they include more than 30,000 serials and periodicals, 5.4 million microforms, 10,000 full-text electronic journals, almost 1 million full-text electronic books, specialized holdings including the world's largest collection of James Joyce manuscripts, and a renowned collection of twentieth-century poetry

in manuscript. All library holdings are digitally cataloged and accessible from terminals and computers on and off campus. The University is among the first to have software that makes the entire SUNY library system—more than 18 million volumes—available to students. State-of-the-art computer workstations for student use are located at public sites in the University's libraries.

Costs

In 2011–12, tuition for New York state residents was $5270 and for out-of-state residents, $14,050. For all students, fees were $2212, and average room and board costs were $11,162. Students should expect additional expenses for books and supplies, transportation, and personal expenses. Costs are subject to change.

Financial Aid

The University participates in all New York state and federal financial aid programs, including the Tuition Assistance Program (available only to New York state residents) and the Federal Pell Grant, Federal Work-Study, Federal Direct Student Loan, and Federal Perkins Loan programs. The recommended deadline for completing the Free Application for Federal Student Aid is February 1 for fall semester entry. All inquiries concerning financial aid should be directed to the Office of Financial Aid in the Student Resource Center at 716-645-2450.

In fall 2011, UB awarded more than $4 million in merit scholarship support to incoming freshmen. UB's top incoming freshmen receive the Presidential Scholarship, which covers the full cost of attendance for all four years, and are invited to join the Honors College. Provost Scholarships range up to the full cost of tuition, depending on academic achievement, talent in the creative or performing arts, and the cost of attendance. The Daniel Acker Scholarship is for talented students from groups that are traditionally underrepresented in higher education. Acker Scholars receive aid up to the full cost of tuition and participate in a comprehensive program of support services and activities. Athletic grants-in-aid are awarded to students recruited to participate in the University's NCAA Division I athletics program.

Faculty

The University's nationally renowned faculty includes winners of the National Medal of Science, the Nobel Prize, the Pulitzer Prize, and other awards. A large number have published books or scholarly articles. Many have held major national or international fellowships; conducted research funded by government agencies or national foundations; served as consultants to business, education, and government; or otherwise demonstrated professional expertise. More than 100 have won the SUNY Chancellor's Award for Excellence in Teaching, the largest number of recipients of any SUNY campus.

Student Government

All daytime undergraduate students are members of the Student Association and are entitled to participate in its activities. The Student Association is involved at every level of student life, from freshman orientation to commencement. Through membership on many University-wide policy committees, representatives of the association are given a legitimate, permanent voice in the policies and direction of the University.

Admission Requirements

Applicants are required to submit their high school transcript, the results of the ACT or SAT critical reading and math sections, and at least one recommendation from a high school counselor or teacher. Applicants should plan to take the SAT or ACT no later than November of their senior year. Application review and notification begins in early February and continues until the freshman class is filled. Most freshmen admitted to the University apply to the major of their choice during the sophomore year. However, architecture, accounting and business management, engineering and applied sciences, exercise science, nuclear medicine technology, nursing, and occupational therapy may offer departmental admission to freshman applicants.

Admission to programs in dance, music, music theatre, and theatre requires an audition.

Admission is competitive. Most successful students at the University have come with a strong level of academic preparation in basic academic areas. Among accepted freshmen in fall 2011, the mean high school average grade was 92 percent, 34 percent were in the top 10 percent of their high school class, and 51 percent scored 1200 or higher on the SAT (critical reading and math).

The University enrolls and provides specialized advisement and support to a limited number of freshmen who demonstrate academic potential through means other than quantitative measures. Creative talent, athletics, special academic achievement, demonstrated leadership, community service, and personal circumstances are examples of areas that the University may consider.

Transfer applicants must have completed a minimum of 12 semester hours at a regionally accredited college prior to application. Students with fewer than 24 semester hours are evaluated on the basis of their college and high school credentials in combination with standardized test score results. Admission of transfer students is based on the quality of previous academic performance and space availability. In order to receive consideration for transfer admission to UB, it is recommended that students present a strong record of college study, earning a minimum cumulative grade point average of 2.5 on a 4.0 scale. It should be noted, however, that requirements may vary depending on the academic program.

Admission to an academic department may occur concurrently with University admission if the applicant has fulfilled prerequisite requirements. These requirements include completed courses, but may also comprise essay, portfolio, exam, or audition requirements. Some departments have significantly higher GPA standards and early deadlines for application.

Application and Information

Students can apply online at http://www.suny.edu/student/apply_online.cfm or http://www.commonapp.org. Or they can visit http://www.admissions.buffalo.edu/apply for more information on applying to UB.

For further information, please contact:

Office of Admissions
12 Capen Hall
University at Buffalo, the State University of New York
Buffalo, New York 14260-1660
Phone: 716-645-6900
      888-UB-ADMIT (toll-free)
E-mail: ubadmit@buffalo.edu
Web site: http://www.admissions.buffalo.edu
      http://www.facebook.com/UBAdmissions (Facebook)
      http://twitter.com/UBAdmissions (Twitter)

The University at Buffalo is one of the nation's premier public research universities and SUNY's largest and most comprehensive campus.

UNIVERSITY OF ALASKA FAIRBANKS

FAIRBANKS, ALASKA

The University

Founded in 1917, the University provides education, research, and service in the Last Frontier. The total University of Alaska Fairbanks (UAF) enrollment is close to 11,000 students. Eighty-five percent of the students are from Alaska. Fifteen percent are from the rest of the U.S. and fifty-two other countries.

The North is a theme found in many academic programs, including Alaska Native studies, anthropology, the arts, engineering, and the social sciences.

The University awards graduate degrees in many of the same areas as the undergraduate studies, often in conjunction with one of its research institutes.

The main campus contains a core of academic buildings and residences, as well as miles of trails, two lakes, and a boreal forest research and recreational area. Most of the University's research institutes, including the noted Geophysical Institute and the International Arctic Research Center, are clustered on the West Ridge, with incredible views of the Tanana Valley and Alaska Range. The University's Agricultural and Forestry Experiment Station is on campus, as are a Cooperative Fish and Wildlife Research Unit and various state and federal agencies and laboratories. The University is currently adding a new life sciences building with a scheduled completion date of fall 2013 (plans and progress can be viewed online at www.uaf.edu/lifescience/construction).

There are eight residence halls on the Fairbanks campus, capable of lodging 1,020 occupants.

The Student Recreation Complex houses a variety of sports and physical activities facilities, including multipurpose areas for basketball, volleyball, badminton, tennis, calisthenics, dance, gymnastics, judo, and karate; a rifle and pistol range; courts for handball, racquetball, and squash; an elevated 200-meter, three-lane jogging track; a swimming pool; weight-training and modern fitness equipment areas; an ice arena for recreational skating and hockey; a special aerobics area; and a three-story climbing wall. There is also an outdoor rock/ice climbing wall and plans for a snowboard terrain park.

The student union, the William Ransom Wood Center, is the focus of various out-of-class activities for students and faculty members. The center houses meeting and exhibit rooms, lounges and television areas, the student government offices, campus information, a pub, bowling alley, games room, cafeteria, snack bar, and an espresso bar.

Intercollegiate athletics include men's and women's basketball, cross-country running and skiing, intercollegiate ice hockey, and women's volleyball and swim teams. The University also has an outstanding rifle team which has produced several Olympic athletes and has earned ten national championships.

Location

The campus of the University of Alaska Fairbanks is situated on a ridge overlooking the valley of the Tanana River and the city of Fairbanks. Serving a population of more than 85,000, Fairbanks is a major trade center for outlying villages in Interior Alaska. The city is connected with the rest of the state and the lower forty-eight states by air and highway. Municipal bus service is available between downtown Fairbanks, the surrounding area, and campus. Shuttle bus service is available around the UAF campus.

Fairbanks offers the sophistication of larger cities while maintaining the atmosphere of smaller, more personal towns. Denali National Park and Preserve and other vast wilderness areas are close at hand, and Anchorage is 350 miles south via the Parks Highway. Members of the Fairbanks community and the University join together in the Fairbanks Symphony, Arctic Chamber Orchestra, and in many other musical and theatrical enterprises.

Majors and Degrees

The University of Alaska Fairbanks awards occupational endorsements, certificates, A.A., A.S., A.A.S., B.A., B.A.S., B.B.A., B.E.M., B.F.A., B.M., B.S., and B.T. degrees in accounting; administrative assistant; airframe studies; Alaska Native studies; anthropology; applied accounting; applied business; applied physics; apprenticeship technology; art; arts and sciences; aviation maintenance technology; automotive technology; aviation technology; biological sciences; bookkeeping technician; business administration; chemistry; child development and family services; civil engineering; communication; community health; computer science; culinary arts; diesel/heavy equipment; dental assisting; drafting technology; early childhood; earth science; economics; electrical engineering; elementary education; emergency services; English; entry-level welder; Eskimo (Inupiaq and Yup'ik); facility maintenance; film; financial services representative; fisheries; food science and nutrition; foreign languages; general science; geography; geological engineering; geology; health care reimbursement; health technology; high latitude range management; history; human services; information technology specialist; instrumentation technology; interdisciplinary studies; Japanese studies; journalism; justice; law enforcement academy; linguistics; mathematics; mechanical engineering; medical assistant; medical office technologies;; mining applications and technologies; mining engineering; music; Native language education; natural resources management (including forestry); Northern studies; nurse aide; paralegal studies; paramedic academy; paramedicine; petroleum engineering; philosophy; phlebotomy; physics; political science; powerplant; power generation; process technology; professional piloting; psychology; renewable resources; rural development; rural human services; rural utilities business management; Russian studies; safety; health; and environmental awareness technology; social work; sociology; sustainable energy; technology; theater; tribal management; veterinary science; welding and materials technology; and wildlife biology and conservation.

Pre-professional opportunities and advising are available in dentistry, law, library science, medicine, pharmacy, physical therapy, physician assistant studies, and veterinary medicine.

Academic Programs

The academic year is divided into two semesters; registration begins in early April for the fall semester and in November for the spring semester. Preregistration is available for returning students. In addition, there are three-week, six-week, and twelve-week summer sessions and two-week wintermesters and maymesters.

The University is organized into four colleges and four schools: the colleges of Liberal Arts, Natural Science and Mathematics, Engineering and Mines, Rural and Community Development, and the schools of Natural Resources and Agricultural Sciences, Education, Fisheries and Ocean Sciences, and Management. A minimum of 120 credits must be completed for the four-year baccalaureate degree programs.

Students who receive scores of 3 or higher on the College Board's Advanced Placement tests may be awarded credit by the University. Currently enrolled students may challenge courses for credit by successfully completing College-Level Examination Program (CLEP) examinations or by completing locally prepared examinations. Requests for advanced-placement credit and credit by examination are coordinated through the Office of Admissions and the Registrar.

The honors program is designed for highly motivated undergraduate students who wish to acquire a superior understanding of the natural and social sciences, the arts, and the humanities. Prospective honors students need a minimum ACT plus writing composite score of 27 or a minimum combined SAT score of 1820, with an emphasis placed on high scores in English and mathematics. UAF also has nationally recognized honors societies such as Golden Key and Phi Kappa Phi.

Off-Campus Programs

The University maintains active exchange programs with various universities around the world. Membership in the University of the Arctic's north2north exchange program provides UAF students an extensive array of placement opportunities throughout the circumpolar North. UAF also offers a variety of study-abroad programs, including the Northwest Council on Study Abroad (NCSA), which provides study opportunities with UAF and other U.S. faculty members worldwide. Additional study programs and internships are available through affiliates maintaining sites in numerous countries. UAF is also a member of the National Student Exchange, participating with more than 180 colleges and universities throughout the United States, in U.S. territories, and at nine locations in Canada.

Academic Facilities

The Fine Arts Complex features a 480-seat theater, a 1,072-seat concert hall, FM public radio (KUAC) and educational-television (PBS) studios, an art gallery, and the Elmer E. Rasmuson Library. The library collection contains more than 1.1 million volumes, including the prestigious Alaska and Polar Regions Collection. Electronic catalogs provide access to collections in 11,000 libraries nationwide.

Students have free use of the University's academic computing facilities, in labs, classrooms, dorm rooms, and other campus locations including wireless access.

The University of Alaska Museum of the North attracts nearly 100,000 visitors each year to Interior Alaska and is located on the Fairbanks campus. The museum collects, preserves, and exhibits materials from Alaska and the North.

Costs

In 2012–13, tuition and fees are $2954 per semester for full-time (15 credits) students. Nonresident students paid an additional $6349 for 15 credits of tuition each semester. Generally, to qualify as a resident, a student must show proof they have been living in Alaska for two years. Residents of Alaska, and cities having sister-city agreements with any Alaska city, are eligible for resident tuition rates.

The approximate cost per semester for books and supplies is $1400. A double-occupancy residence hall room on campus costs $1840 per semester. Meal plans cost $1740–$2040 per semester. All costs are subject to change.

If the student lives in a Western Undergraduate Exchange state (http://www.uaf.edu/admissions/other/wue), tuition is approximately 1.5 times that of an Alaska resident.

Financial Aid

A large portion of financial aid is derived from the Alaska Supplemental Education Loan Program, which is available to all students attending UAF, regardless of residency. Three kinds of aid are available: grants and scholarships (which need not be repaid), loans, and part-time employment. Inquiries should be addressed to the Financial Aid Office, University of Alaska Fairbanks, P.O. Box 756560, Fairbanks, Alaska 99775-6560, or by e-mail to financialaid@uaf.edu. Academic Merit and Human Achievement scholarships are one-year scholarships ranging from $2500–$15,000 that are awarded by the Office of Admissions and the Registrar. To apply, students should submit a scholarship application, an application for admission, a high school transcript, and test scores for review. Questions about this scholarship should be directed to the Office of Admissions and the Registrar. The deadline for University of Alaska and UAF-funded scholarships is February 15. Prospective students can check the financial aid Web site (www.uaf.edu/finaid) for information about grants, loans, and other aid and applicable due dates.

Faculty

Fifty-two percent of full-time faculty members and 32 percent of part-time faculty hold doctoral, professional, or terminal degrees, and many are actively engaged in research. In keeping with University policy, faculty members provide academic counseling for students. The combination of a student-faculty ratio of 11:1, and easy access to instructors for help outside of class produces a maximum educational benefit for students.

Student Government

The Associated Students of the University of Alaska Fairbanks (ASUAF) protects students' rights through its various governmental functions and also offers educational, social, recreational, and service activities. The school newspaper, the Sun Star, is published weekly with the sponsorship of ASUAF, which also supports KSUA, the campus radio station; the international cinema and weekly movie series; and dances, concerts, and other entertainment. ASUAF publishes the results of its faculty evaluations and sends several student lobbyists to the Alaska state legislature in Juneau each spring. There is a student member seat on the board of regents of the statewide university system.

Admission Requirements

For admission to a baccalaureate program, applicants must be high school graduates with a GPA of at least 2.5 in a high school core curriculum of 16 credits and a cumulative grade point average of at least 3.0, or 2.5 plus an ACT plus writing score of 18 or SAT score of 1290 (including writing skills section). Transfer students must also have a minimum grade point average of 2.0 in all previous college work.

Applicants for a major in a scientific or technical field may be required to present a higher grade point average and to have completed specific background courses before being accepted into the major department. All entering freshmen are required to submit scores from the ACT plus writing or SAT examination prior to registration for placement in English and math courses.

Application and Information

The application deadlines are May 1 for the summer semester, June 15 for the fall semester, and November 1 for the spring semester. An application fee is required when the application is submitted. Applicants are notified of the admission decision once all application materials have been received. Students who desire campus housing should apply as early as possible; a deposit is required.

For further information, applicants should contact:

Office of Admissions and the Registrar
University of Alaska Fairbanks
P.O. Box 757480
Fairbanks, Alaska 99775-7480
Phone: 907-474-7500
      800-478-1823 (toll-free)
E-mail: admissions@uaf.edu
Web site: http://www.uaf.edu/admissions
      http://www.uaf.edu/admissions/parents
      https://uaonline.alaska.edu (to apply)

Constitution Park, located between the Rasmuson Library, Gruening Building, Constitution Hall, and Fine Arts Complex, is just one of the popular hangouts between classes.

UNIVERSITY OF CENTRAL FLORIDA
ORLANDO, FLORIDA

UCF
Stands For Opportunity

The University

The University of Central Florida (UCF) is a comprehensive research university with approximately 58,000 students. As one of the nation's fastest-growing universities in the South and the second largest in the nation, UCF enrolls an academically talented and diverse student body representing all fifty states and more than 120 countries. The University offers educational and research programs that complement the regional economy, with strong components in aerospace engineering, business, education, film, health, hospitality management, medicine, nursing, and social sciences. UCF's programs in communication and the fine arts help to meet the cultural and recreational needs of a growing metropolitan area. The University also offers many graduate programs leading to master's and doctoral degrees, including a doctorate of physical therapy. The UCF College of Medicine offers the M.D. degree.

UCF is accredited by the Commission on Colleges of the Southern Association of Colleges and Schools. In addition, a number of scientific, professional, and academic bodies confer accreditation in specific disciplines and groups of disciplines.

UCF has established extensive partnerships with businesses and industries in the central Florida area that provide students with research and learning experiences. These partnerships bring practical learning environments to UCF students through co-op, internship programs, and joint curriculum development strategies.

The on-campus and campus-affiliated housing facilities include traditional residence halls, apartment-style options, and Greek housing that accommodate approximately 10,000 students. Several thousand students live in apartments located within walking distance of the campus. Approximately 400 students live in on-campus Greek housing.

Students participate in more than 400 student organizations, including special-interest clubs, multicultural organizations, fraternities and sororities, honor societies, and academic and preprofessional organizations. The Office of Student Involvement schedules a wide array of extracurricular programs, including concerts, movies, and guest speakers.

The University of Central Florida is a member of the NCAA and Conference USA. All teams compete on the NCAA Division I level. UCF's men's teams compete in intercollegiate baseball, basketball, football, golf, soccer, and tennis. Women's teams compete in basketball, cross-country, golf, rowing, soccer, softball, tennis, track and field, and volleyball. Intercollegiate coed club activities include championship cheerleading, crew, and waterskiing teams. The University intramural sports program offers many options including disc golf, flag football, floor hockey, racquetball, soccer, softball, tennis, and volleyball.

Location

The University of Central Florida is located on 1,415 acres approximately 13 miles east of downtown Orlando. In addition to the academic programs offered on the Orlando campus, upper-division students can work toward a degree at ten locations around the central Florida area. .

Majors and Degrees

The University offers the degrees of Bachelor of Applied Science, Bachelor of Arts, Bachelor of Arts in Business Administration, Bachelor of Engineering Technology, Bachelor of Fine Arts, Bachelor of Science, Bachelor of Science in Business Administration, Bachelor of Science in Education, Bachelor of Science Engineering, Bachelor of Science in Nursing, and Bachelor of Science in Social Sciences. These degrees are available in the colleges listed below, with majors or areas of specialization as indicated.

The College of Arts and Humanities offers degrees in art, architecture, digital media, English, film, French, history, humanities, Latin American studies, modern language combination, music, philosophy, photography, religious studies, Spanish, and theater.

The College of Business Administration offers degrees in accounting, business economics, economics, finance, general business administration, management, marketing, and real estate. The College also offers a minor in international business.

The College of Education offers degrees in art education, early childhood education, elementary education, English language arts education, foreign language education, mathematics education, science education, social science education, sports and exercise, and technical education and industry training.

The College of Engineering and Computer Science offers degrees in aerospace engineering, civil engineering, computer engineering, computer science, construction engineering, electrical engineering, engineering technology, environmental engineering, industrial engineering, information technology, and mechanical engineering.

The College of Health and Public Affairs offers degrees in athletic training, communication sciences and disorders, criminal justice, health informatics and information management, health services administration, health sciences, legal studies, public administration, physical therapy (master's program), and social work.

The College of Medicine and the Burnett School of Biomedical Sciences offers degrees in biomedical sciences, biotechnology, and medical laboratory sciences.

The College of Nursing offers degrees in nursing.

The College of Sciences offers degrees in advertising/public relations, anthropology, biology, chemistry, forensic science, interpersonal and organizational communications, international and global studies, journalism, mathematics, physics, political science, psychology, radio/television, sociology, social sciences, and statistics.

The Rosen College of Hospitality Management offers degrees in event management, hospitality management, and restaurant and foodservice management.

Preprofessional programs are offered in chiropractic, dentistry, medicine, optometry, pharmacy, physical assistant studies, physical therapy, podiatry, and veterinary medicine.

A degree in interdisciplinary studies is available through the Office of Undergraduate Studies.

Academic Programs

UCF provides a total education through a core curriculum of 36 hours of general education courses. In addition to fulfilling the general education requirement, each student must complete the necessary major and/or minor requirements to reach the minimum of 120 semester hours necessary for graduation.

Several special programs help students reach their academic and leadership potential. The Burnett Honors College at UCF encourages students to achieve academic excellence through small classes and interactive symposia. The innovative Leadership Enrichment and Academic Development (LEAD) Scholars Program fosters leadership and service commitment through a comprehensive student development program for freshmen. The Major Exploration Program (MEP) helps entering freshmen define their career goals and develop an academic strategy to reach those goals. The University also offers an increasing number of online courses and degree programs.

UCF offers Air Force and Army ROTC programs.

Off-Campus Programs

Career Services and Experiential Learning offers programs in which students alternate semesters of classroom study with equal periods of paid employment in government, industry, or business. The Department of Modern Languages offers summer study-abroad programs in Canada, Eastern Europe, France, Germany, Italy, Japan, Poland, Spain, Sweden, and Russia. Courses are available in the subject areas of language (all levels), art, and civilization. UCF is also a participant in the National Student Exchange Consortium.

Academic Facilities

In addition to the academic programs offered on the Orlando campus, upper division students can work toward a degree at ten campuses located throughout Central Florida. These regional campuses work cooperatively with local community colleges to provide all four years of course work in many academic areas. The library houses nearly 1.4 million volumes and subscribes to more than 10,000 periodicals and journals. In addition, students have access to an online computer catalog that provides information on the collections of the State University System libraries. An extensive online network of more than 500 computer terminals and a network of nearly 1,000 IBM PCs cover the campus. The Institute for Simulation and Training gives students the opportunity to pursue undergraduate research. The College of Optics and Photonics allows faculty members and students to work directly with industry personnel in conducting basic and applied research at the regional and national levels. The Central Florida Research Park, adjacent to the UCF campus, houses more than ninety important high-technology firms and agencies. This proximity fosters relationships between industry and the University, which strengthens the academic programs at UCF.

Costs

For Florida residents, the cost of tuition and fees in 2011–12, based on a full-time course load, was $5583 for the year; for out-of-state residents, the cost was $21,063. Room and board were approximately $8760 per year, books and supplies cost approximately $800.

Financial Aid

Financial aid is awarded according to each student's demonstrated financial need in relation to college costs and may include grants, loans, scholarships, and part-time employment. Programs based upon need include the Federal Perkins Loan, Federal Pell Grant, Florida Student Assistance Grant, Federal Work-Study, Florida College Career Work-Study Program, and Federal Stafford Student Loan. To qualify for these programs, students must complete the Free Application for Federal Student Aid (FAFSA). The priority application deadline is March 1. Sixty-seven percent of UCF students receive some form of financial assistance.

Faculty

The University's teaching faculty consists of 1,948 full-time members and adjunct members. Seventy-three percent of the full-time faculty members hold a doctoral degree. Undergraduate instruction is given primarily by the full-time and adjunct faculty members; graduate students play a very minor role in undergraduate instruction. Students are assigned to a faculty adviser in their area of specialization for assistance in academic matters. The student-faculty ratio is 30:1.

Student Government

UCF's Student Government Association provides an opportunity for students to become involved at UCF. Every UCF student is encouraged to voice his or her opinion through senate representatives. Student Government is divided into three branches—the student-elected executive branch, the student-elected legislative branch, and the appointed judicial branch. Student Government is responsible for the allocation of all activity and service fees paid by students as a part of their tuition. This money goes toward student services, including the online Macintosh lab, homecoming activities, campus activities board, legal services, and funding for clubs and organizations. Admission is free to all events directly sponsored by the Student Government.

Admission Requirements

A freshman applicant is a student with fewer than 12 hours of college course work after high school graduation. The most important criteria in the admission decision for these applicants are the high school academic record, quality and level of difficulty of courses, grade point average, grade trends, and SAT or ACT test scores. UCF operates on a rolling admission basis. Students are generally notified of their initial admission decision within two to three weeks after receipt of the application and all official supporting documents. If the number of qualified applicants exceeds the number that the University is permitted to enroll, a waiting list is established.

All applicants must have earned a minimum of 18 high school academic units (yearlong courses that are not remedial in nature).

These include 4 units of English (3 must include substantial writing), 4 units of mathematics at or above algebra I, 3 units of natural science (2 must include a laboratory), 3 units of social science, 2 units of one foreign language, and 2 units of academic electives. Grades in honors, International Baccalaureate, Advanced Placement, AICE, dual-enrollment, pre-AP, pre-IB, and pre-AICE courses are given additional weight in the GPA computation. Students must meet the Florida Department of Education minimum eligibility to be considered for admission. Applicants should understand that the satisfaction of minimum requirements does not guarantee admission to UCF.

Transfer applicants with fewer than 60 semester hours of college course work must submit official high school transcripts, SAT or ACT test scores, and all official college transcripts. Transfer students with more than 60 semester hours or who have earned an Associate in Arts degree or a statewide articulated Associate in Science degree from a Florida public community or state college need only submit all official college transcripts. A transfer credit summary evaluation is provided to students once they are offered admission to UCF.

Application and Information

Students are encouraged to apply several months in advance and can apply online at http://admissions.ucf.edu. It is recommended that freshman students apply early during the fall semester of their senior year. Applications are accepted up to one year prior to the start of the term for which enrollment is desired. Priority application deadlines are May 1 for the fall term (July 1 for transfers), November 1 for the spring term, and March 1 for the summer term.

The Campus Visit Experience, which includes an information session and a campus tour, is offered Monday through Friday at 10 and 2 (except holidays). Students can sign up for a campus visit online at http://admissions.ucf.edu.

Office of Undergraduate Admissions
University of Central Florida
P.O. Box 160111
Orlando, Florida 32816-0111
Phone: 407-823-3000
E-mail: admission@.ucf.edu
Web site: http://www.ucf.edu

The Charging Knight symbolizes UCF's excellence in academics, partnerships, and athletics.

The University

The University of Dallas is a private, Catholic coeducational liberal arts university dedicated to the pursuit of wisdom, truth, and virtue as the proper and primary goals of education. Approximately 1,350 undergraduate students from forty-nine states and fourteen countries make up the student body, and more than half of the undergraduate student body comes from outside the state of Texas. In addition, 82 percent of the current undergraduate student body is Catholic.

The University of Dallas (UD) is a center of learning, and the experience on campus is intensive and highly directed. Students choose to come to the University because they are serious students. While they engage in a full complement of extracurricular activities and independent study, it is the act of learning in association with professors that shapes their college years. Because the undergraduate college is small and largely residential, it forms a close-knit community.

Spiritual life on the University of Dallas campus is an important aspect of the undergraduate experience. The University's core values include embracing the Catholic intellection tradition and maintaining a dialogue between faith and reason; these values continually have an important role both inside and outside of the classroom. The main church on campus, Church of the Incarnation, offers daily Mass as well as reconciliation. Holy Trinity Seminary, Albert the Great Priory, and Cistercian Abbey are also available for students to participate in Mass and other spiritual growth activities, and Campus Ministry offers a wide variety of spiritual and service opportunities such as lectures and alternative spring break for students of all faiths and backgrounds.

Location

The University of Dallas' 744-acre main campus is located approximately 15 minutes from downtown Dallas in Irving, population 216,000. The Dallas-Fort Worth Metroplex, the fourth-largest metroplex in the country, offers a diverse mix of cultural and entertainment attractions including the Dallas Museum of Modern Art, the Nasher Sculpture Center, and the Kimball Museum in Fort Worth. Dallas is home to professional sports teams in hockey, soccer, and basketball. Nearby Arlington is home to the Texas Rangers and the Dallas Cowboys. The thriving Dallas-Fort Worth economy provides students the opportunity to connect with businesses and nonprofit organizations, including twenty Fortune 500 companies headquartered in the area.

The University of Dallas is conveniently located between two major airports, Dallas Love Field Airport and Dallas/Fort Worth International Airport. Additionally, the campus has its own stop on the Orange Line of the Dallas Area Rapid Transit (DART) light rail system, providing convenient access to Irving, the Trinity Railway Express, downtown Dallas, and major DFW attractions.

The University of Dallas' 12-acre Eugene Constantin campus is located just south of Rome, Italy, and includes amenities such as a working vineyard, swimming pool, tennis courts, classrooms, library, suite-style residence hall, and cappuccino bar. Students have the opportunity to spend an entire semester studying abroad on the Rome campus.

Majors and Degrees

Students are given the opportunity to further their curiosity in a particular area of study by choosing a specific major. The University of Dallas offers over twenty-nine majors, which can be combined in double majors to match each student's interest. Thirty concentrations (minors) are available to broaden academic expertise. Pre-professional programs in architecture, dentistry, engineering, law, medicine, ministerial programs, and physical therapy are also available to prepare students academically for rigorous graduate programs and demanding professions. The University of Dallas offers undergraduate and post-baccalaureate certification to students interested in teaching at the elementary, middle, or secondary school level.

Regardless of major, all University of Dallas students are required to complete a major-specific project to culminate their undergraduate career. Whether completing their own research, writing an extensive thesis, taking comprehensive exams covering all material studied over four years, or completing an intensive practicum, University of Dallas students find that they are well-prepared to succeed upon graduation.

Academic Programs

University of Dallas students thrive on a rigorous academic program distinguished by UD's nationally recognized Core curriculum. Based on the belief that truth and virtue exist and are the proper objects of search in an education, the Core curriculum is a two-year course of study through which every UD student directly encounters Western civilization's greatest authors, leaders, and artists by reading classic, original works. Every student becomes familiar with the same works of literature and the same great books and concepts, fostering a natural understanding and exchange of ideas. The Core curriculum is comprehensive, encompassing English, philosophy, mathematics, fine arts, science, classics, modern languages, American civilization, Western civilization, politics, economics, and theology.

Off-Campus Programs

The University of Dallas student's academic experience is heightened and enriched by spending a semester abroad on the Eugene Constantin campus in Italy. Because of the accessibility and affordability of the Rome program, all students are encouraged to participate and the majority chooses to, usually during their sophomore year. The Rome curriculum builds on the Core and is a coherent and integral part of the undergraduate education. The courses, such as Art and Architecture and Western Theological Tradition, are selected from the Core curriculum and deepen students' understanding and appreciation of Western civilization by allowing them to experience history and culture firsthand.

Students are also encouraged to become involved in the Irving community and to take advantage of the arts and entertainment offerings in the area. Community service opportunities such as spending time at local nursing homes, repairing homes for underprivileged families, and tutoring local students are available on a weekly basis. In addition, through a program called Dallas Year, students have access to highly-discounted tickets to area events such as the Texas State Fair or a Dallas Cowboys football game, and transportation is provided to and from the event.

Academic Facilities

The Science Center houses some of the most advanced tools for scientific research available, including a working observatory. The Haggerty Arts Village has established the University as

a leading center for ceramics and fine arts in the Southwest. Drama productions are staged in the Margaret Jonsson Theater. Blakely Library holds more than 300,000 volumes, including the personal library of the late political philosopher Wilmoore Kendall.

Costs

Annual tuition and fees for the 2012–13 academic year are $31,070. Room and board costs are approximately $9890. Costs are the same for both in-state and out-of-state students.

Financial Aid

Approximately 95 percent of University of Dallas students receive some type of merit- or need-based aid to help offset the cost of attendance. The application for admission serves as the application for institutional scholarships which range from $5000 to $18,000 per year and are based on GPA and test scores (ACT or SAT). Academic merit scholarships are renewable for four years, providing eligibility requirements set forth in the scholarship letter are met.

A limited number of other scholarships are available to students who excel in a particular area of study or have achieved superior academic achievement such as National Merit Finalists, National Achievement Scholars, National Hispanic Scholars, and Phi Theta Kappa members.

All students who submit a Free Application for Federal Student Aid (FAFSA) are considered for financial assistance based on their family's finances. These forms of assistance include federal, state, or institutional grants; low-interest student loans; and work-study programs. Priority is given to applicants whose FAFSA is received by the University of Dallas on or before March 1.

Faculty

The University of Dallas has 127 full-time faculty members, 85 percent of whom hold a doctorate or equivalent highest academic degree in their discipline. As top scholars in their field, professors value the academic freedom the University offers, allowing them to unreservedly explore intellectual inquires both within their disciplines and outside them. University of Dallas students benefit from a 12:1 student to faculty ratio and an average class size of 17 students, providing each and every student with the individual attention and mentoring they deserve.

Student Government, Clubs, and Organizations

Through the elected Student Governing Board, students are responsible for all nonacademic matters that affect their life at the University of Dallas. Guided by the mission of the University and in accordance with the teachings and principles of the Catholic Church, the representatives in student government are dedicated to enhancing the quality of student life by promoting both the academic and social traditions of the University.

The University of Dallas also offers over forty clubs and organizations that allow students to become involved in areas of extracurricular or academic interest, as well as develop vital leadership skills. From Best Buddies to the Pre-Health Society to Crusaders for Life, students can choose to get involved in many different ways. In addition, if several students have a shared interest that is not represented by current clubs and organizations, they are encouraged to come together to start a new club.

Furthermore, the University of Dallas competes in NCAA Division III athletics and is a member of the Southern Collegiate Athletic Conference. Sports include baseball (M), basketball (M, W), cross country (M, W), golf (M), lacrosse (M, W), soccer (M, W), softball (W), track and field (M, W), and volleyball (W). Intramural sports are also offered to all University students.

Admission Requirements

The University of Dallas performs a holistic review of applications, so no rigid cutoff for test scores or GPA is adhered to in the admission process. For the fall 2011 incoming freshman class, the average SAT score was approximately 1230 (on a 1600 scale), and the average ACT score was 27. The average GPA was 3.78 on a 4.0 scale.

The University seeks students who are not only academically well-prepared to succeed, but who will also contribute to the University of Dallas community. Letters of recommendation, the essay, and the supplement answers are all considered in determining a student's overall fit for the University. Interviews are not required, but students are highly encouraged to schedule a campus visit and meet with an admission counselor to discuss the admission process as well as any opportunities for scholarship or financial aid.

Application and Information

Applicants are required to submit the following items: application (Common Application or Apply Texas), UD supplement, the $40 application fee or fee waiver, essay, teacher recommendation, counselor recommendation, official high school transcript, and official test scores (ACT or SAT). The Early Action I deadline is November 1; the Early Action II deadline is December 1. The Freshman Priority Scholarship deadline is January 15, and the Regular Admission deadline is March 1. Rolling admission is March 2–August 1.

Students interested in transferring to the University of Dallas must submit transcripts from all colleges previously attended. Transfer students should apply by December 1 for spring entry or July 1 for fall entry.

For more information, students should contact:

Office of Undergraduate Admission and Financial Aid
University of Dallas
1845 East Northgate Drive
Irving, Texas 75062
Phone: 972-721-5266
        800-628-6999 (toll-free)
Web site: http://www.udallas.edu

University of Dallas students engaging in a discussion of assigned readings with their English professor.

UNIVERSITY OF DENVER
DENVER, COLORADO

UNIVERSITY OF
DENVER
START FROM A HIGHER PLACE

The University

Since its founding in 1864, the University of Denver (DU) has grown into one of the West's premier private universities, blending the friendliness and personal attention of a small college with the resources and intellectual diversity of an advanced research institution. As the oldest private university in the Rocky Mountain region, the University is home not only to a top-ranked undergraduate program but also to a number of world-renowned research centers and professional programs, including the Josef Korbel School of International Studies, the Sturm College of Law, and the Daniels College of Business.

The 125-acre campus brings together 5,087 traditional undergraduate students and 6,387 graduate students from fifty states and over eighty countries. In an environment that prizes innovation, cross-disciplinary exploration, and adventurous learning partnerships between students and faculty, students prepare to excel in their life's work and to confront the great issues of our day.

Whatever their backgrounds and majors, DU students are engaged and active, taking advantage of the region's many recreation and cultural opportunities—everything from world-class skiing and white-water rafting to award-winning professional theater and alternative music. On campus, students attend performances at the three-venue Newman Center for the Performing Arts and cheer for the 17 varsity teams that compete in NCAA Division I Athletics at the Ritchie Center for Sports & Wellness.

The University of Denver is accredited by the North Central Association of Colleges and Schools. The Carnegie Foundation classifies the University of Denver as a Doctoral/Research University–Extensive.

Location

Located just 8 miles from bustling downtown Denver and mere minutes from the Rocky Mountain foothills, the University of Denver's tree-shaded campus is surrounded by pleasant urban neighborhoods offering coffee shops, retail stores, and diverse restaurants. The institution is located along a light-rail line and major bus lines, providing access to the city's arts districts, shopping centers, sports arenas, and an extensive network of parks. DU students can ride all public transportation for free, using their University-supplied Eco-passes.

Majors and Degrees

The University of Denver offers twelve bachelor's degrees in over 100 programs of study, including the arts, business, computer science, engineering, humanities, international studies, mathematics, natural sciences, and social sciences. Students who are interested in pre-professional programs can choose from law, medical, dental, and veterinary programs that prepare them for professional study beyond their undergraduate degree.

In addition, the University offers 4+1 and 3+2 dual-degree programs that allow students to complete both a bachelor's and master's degree in five years or less. These dual-degree programs are offered in business, art history, international studies, public policy, and natural sciences, among others. Students in dual-degree programs maintain any financial aid and scholarships they have been awarded through their fifth year of study.

Academic Programs

Undergraduate programs at the University—which operates on the quarter system—emphasize experiential, active, and cross-disciplinary learning. All first-year undergraduate students are required to have laptop computers, which are used extensively in the classroom. DU students use their laptops as portable libraries and laboratories, extending their educational reach well beyond the classroom walls. The entire campus provides wireless Internet access through a secure connection. This includes classrooms, social areas, and even the campus greens.

First-year students enroll in a first-year seminar. Generally limited to 15 students, these seminars focus on a topic that reflects the professor's research interests. The professor, who serves as a mentor throughout the student's first year, introduces the class to university-level work and inquiry, while also advising students on everything from time management to University procedures. The seminar is complemented by a two-quarter writing sequence that trains students to conduct research, construct arguments, and write persuasively for the academic setting. The University's emphasis on writing continues throughout the next three years, with upper-division writing-intensive classes across the disciplines. By the time they graduate, DU students have developed the communication skills that are essential for career success.

Undergraduate students also complete foundations courses in mathematics and computer science, the arts and humanities, natural sciences, and social sciences. DU's common curriculum ensures that students have a wide base of knowledge upon graduation.

Because the University believes in the value of hands-on learning, students are encouraged to collaborate with faculty members and peers on research projects and creative endeavors. Through the Partners in Scholarship (PinS) program, the University sponsors student work through grants that fund field studies, research trips, and special materials. At year's end, students share their research and findings at a special symposium for their peers.

Thanks to opportunities like these, the University's academic programs earn high marks from students. In the 2008 National Survey of Student Engagement, a study of student satisfaction at 774 colleges and universities nationwide, first-year students and seniors at DU ranked it significantly higher than other participating doctoral-extensive schools in their appraisal of their level of academic challenge, their involvement in active and collaborative learning, their interaction with faculty members, and their enriching educational experiences.

Off-Campus Programs

To groom students for the challenges of global citizenship, the University of Denver sponsors Cherrington Global Scholars, a for-credit program that aims to send every eligible junior and senior abroad for at least a quarter of study. The University believes so strongly in this opportunity to expand understanding and foster connections that it ensures qualifying students pay no more for the experience than for a quarter spent on campus. The University budgets about $10 million each year in support of this outstanding program. Over 70 percent of all DU students participate in study-abroad programs, the third highest percentage in the nation.

Academic Facilities

In the last decade, the University has invested nearly $500 million in new buildings and learning centers to ensure that students can prepare for the challenges awaiting them after graduation. These include the Robert and Judi Newman Center for the Performing Arts, home to the University's celebrated Lamont School of Music and host to a performing arts series known for its adventurous offerings; the Daniels College of Business, which houses eleven case-style meeting rooms, nine seminar classrooms, and an Advanced Technology Center; the Knoebel School of Hospitality Management, home to a full-production kitchen, a beverage-management center, a 120-person dining hall, a student-run coffee shop, and a student-faculty-staff commons; F. W. Olin Hall, which houses ten teaching labs, a greenhouse, and a full complement of classrooms and group study rooms; and the Academic Commons, scheduled to open in winter 2012 as the new library and hub of the University.

Other new facilities support the University's commitment to community living and wellness, such as the Nelson Residence Hall which features suites, common kitchens on each floor, a central courtyard, a grand dining hall, and an outdoor dining patio. The Ritchie Center for Sports and Wellness brings students and members

of the Denver community together to work out, try new sports, and watch the Pioneer athletic teams. With a state-of-the-art fitness center, a natatorium, a field house, two ice arenas, a gymnastics venue, a lacrosse stadium, a newly remodeled soccer stadium, and a tennis pavilion, the Ritchie Center complex supports the active lifestyle that DU students value.

Nagel Residence Hall, which opened in August 2008, serves as a campus gathering place, welcoming students and faculty at its food court, providing numerous locations for group study sessions, and offering studio space for students wanting to explore their artistic side. In keeping with the University's far-reaching sustainability initiative, the green building is LEED certified, meaning it uses key resources more efficiently than conventional buildings.

The University recently completed construction on a spectacular new home for both the Morgridge College of Education and the Marsico Institute for Early Learning and Literacy. The influential institute serves as a regional and national hub for research and policy analysis on issues related to improving learning environments for young children.

Costs

For the 2011–12 academic year, tuition was $36,936, fees were estimated at $897, and on-campus room and board costs were $10,440—for a total cost of $48,273. Because the University of Denver is a private institution, costs are the same for in-state and out-of-state students.

Financial Aid

The University of Denver offers two types of financial assistance to students: need-based aid, which includes scholarships, grants, loans, and work-study based on financial need; and merit-based awards, which include scholarships based on merit or special talent. Each year, the Financial Aid office awards over $100 million in need- and merit-based assistance to undergraduate students. About 43 percent of full-time DU undergraduates demonstrate financial need and receive some form of need-based assistance.

To recognize achievement in the classroom, the sports arena, leadership, and in music, theater, and art, the University sponsors a number of merit-based scholarships. Although the requirements vary from scholarship to scholarship, most are renewable each year if the student maintains a specified minimum GPA. A complete listing of scholarships is posted at http://www.du.edu/finaid.

Need-based financial aid is computed using a number of factors, including family income, assets, size, and the number of family members attending college at the same time. DU utilizes both the CSS PROFILE and the Free Application for Federal Student Aid (FAFSA) to determine need-based aid. Need-based awards generally combine scholarships, grants, loans, and work-study opportunities from a variety of federal, state, and institutional sources. The financial aid offer may also include any competitive scholarships the student has been awarded at the point of admission.

The priority deadline for applying for financial aid is February 15. Because financial aid funds are limited, students who complete their financial aid applications in a timely manner are more likely to maximize financial aid resources. Funding for certain awards may not be available as time passes. The student's financial aid package cannot be determined until he or she is officially admitted to DU. More information on applying for financial aid at DU is available at http://www.du.edu/finaid.

Faculty

DU professors teach 95 percent of undergraduate courses, ensuring students work closely with faculty members and that the intensity of the learning environment is maximized. The average class size is 21 students; 63 percent of undergraduate classes have fewer than 20 students and 96 percent of classes have fewer than 50 students.

Committed teachers, innovative researchers, and prolific publishers, University of Denver professors often include undergraduate students in their research projects and fieldwork. It is not uncommon for an undergraduate student to share publication credit with a professor or to participate in groundbreaking research with tangible benefits for humankind.

Student Government

At the University of Denver, the student population is represented by the Undergraduate Student Government (USG), whose elected representatives participate in the University's legislative process and communicate student issues to the administration. In addition, the USG oversees the allocation of the student activities fee and the licensing of DU's 100-plus student organizations.

The USG includes senators from each major, each geographic area (on-campus, off-campus), and each class (senior, junior, etc.). The USG Executive Board includes an adviser, graduate adviser, president, vice president, and a cabinet of members.

Admission Requirements

Admission to the University of Denver is selective. Students are evaluated individually on the basis of their academic record, test scores, essay, and recommendations. In making its admission decisions, the University seeks to foster an academic community of geographically, ethnically, and economically diverse learners. The admission committee seeks students who are committed to integrity, innovation, inclusiveness, excellence, and community engagement.

Applicants are required to submit either the Common Application or the DU Pioneer Application, both of which are posted on the DU Web site. In addition, applicants are required to submit their high school transcripts, scores from either the SAT or ACT (DU uses the superscore system), an essay, and a high school counselor recommendation. Students may also submit a teacher recommendation, although it is not required.

Applicants are also strongly encouraged to participate in the Ammi Hyde Interview, a face-to-face 20-minute conversation with as many as three members of the University community. Interviews are conducted in over thirty major cities across the country in November and January and on campus throughout the year.

Application and Information

The University of Denver offers two application programs for first-year domestic students seeking fall-quarter admission. Early Action (postmarked by November 1) is a nonbinding program leading to an admission decision in early January. Hyde Interviews for Early Action applicants are conducted in November. Regular Decision (postmarked by January 15), also nonbinding, is the final admission deadline for fall-quarter consideration. Hyde Interviews for Regular Decision applicants are conducted in January, and admission decisions are mailed in mid-March.

To learn more about the University of Denver, students should contact:

University of Denver
Office of Undergraduate Admission
2197 South University Boulevard
Denver, Colorado, 80208-9401
United States
Phone: 303-871-2036
       800-525-9495 (toll-free)
E-mail: admission@du.edu
Web site: http://www.du.edu/admission
          http://www.du.edu/apply/admission/index.html
          http://du.ctpprojects.com (videos)
          http://www.facebook.com/uofdenveradmission
          http://twitter.com/uofdenver

The University of Denver

UNIVERSITY OF DUBUQUE
DUBUQUE, IOWA

UNIVERSITY *of*
DUBUQUE

The University

The University of Dubuque (UD) is a private, Presbyterian, professional university with a focus in the liberal arts, as well as a theological seminary located in Iowa's first city—Dubuque. The Key City is on the Mississippi River at the point where the borders of Wisconsin, Illinois, and Iowa meet. Founded in 1852, the University offers programs in the undergraduate and graduate college and in the graduate theological seminary. The University's mission of encouraging intellectual, moral, and spiritual development dates back to its founding.

Throughout its history, the University has been known as a place of educational opportunity. Even today, a large portion of its students are from first-generation or underrepresented populations. The University of Dubuque's welcoming interfaith community of approximately 2,000 students comes from across the country and around the globe.

Because students from many nations attend the University of Dubuque, UD offers students a cosmopolitan atmosphere. The school is convinced that students living in today's world are better prepared for life if they have a global perspective. American and international student interaction on campus, as well as the movement of faculty members and students across international boundaries, is essential for a meaningful education, human enrichment, and intercultural global awareness.

Location

The University of Dubuque's scenic 77-acre campus, located in eastern Iowa, is in the heart of the Midwest. Dubuque is a city for all seasons. From bluffs blazing with autumn oranges and reds to the river sparkling with summer's blues and greens, the area scenery is spectacular year-round. Dubuque, the oldest city in Iowa, is a dynamic community built along the majestic Mississippi River and surrounded by dramatic bluffs. The setting is ideal for outdoor enthusiasts, with four seasons of ample outlets for recreation, including hiking, biking, boating, skiing, camping, golfing, climbing, and caving.

Dubuque offers the amenities of a larger city with the security and comfort of a smaller town. A lively cultural scene includes the Grand Opera House, the Dubuque Symphony Orchestra, and the Dubuque Museum of Art. The National Mississippi River Museum and Aquarium and the National Farm Toy Museum provide glimpses of the area's past. The city's theater productions, boutiques, and restaurants are wonderful ways to take a study break.

Nearby are some of the Midwest's most interesting cities, an easy drive for a weekend road trip. Historic Galena offers quaint shops and period architecture, while vibrant Chicago is famous for its museums and night life. Madison, Milwaukee, and Minneapolis–St. Paul are only hours away.

Majors and Degrees

With twenty-four undergraduate majors, the University prepares students for careers in a variety of fields. From future teachers to corporate leaders to aspiring pilots, the University of Dubuque helps students achieve their career goals.

The University's business and education departments have the most majors. The education department's future teachers graduate with twice as many field-experience hours as required by the state of Iowa.

The University's nursing program was reinstated in the fall 2004 semester. The program offers a Bachelor of Science in Nursing (B.S.N.) degree. Nursing began at University of Dubuque in 1976 and, until 1997, the program offered fully accredited RN-to-B.S.N., B.S.N., and M.S.N. nursing preparation. The University is accredited by the American Association of Colleges of Nursing.

Academic departments encourage internships as an experiential component to complement classroom learning. For example, environmental science majors take advantage of the natural classroom of the Mississippi River, where students study the interaction between people and the environment. Aviation majors complete internships at the Dubuque Regional Airport or major airlines in addition to flying state-of-the-art equipment from UD's Garlick Flight Operations Center.

Academic Programs

The University of Dubuque education aims at helping students develop patterns of scholarship that make them effective learners throughout life. UD students are nurtured in the virtues of scholarship: the desire for understanding different peoples and cultures, an interest in learning, the skills to use multiple resources to explore ideas and find answers for life's questions, an understanding of conceptual connections, and the ability to reason and communicate effectively. Each graduate develops depth of knowledge in a particular field of study based on an integration of this field, the liberal arts, and his or her values.

University of Dubuque students begin to understand their chosen field of study by experiencing how it relates to other areas of knowledge. The process of exploring a variety of interests and possibilities in course work and in University activities results in the choice of a major. Current trends indicate that today's graduates change jobs and/or careers several times during their lifetimes. Therefore, professional preparation is more than a narrow, vocationally oriented process through which students prepare for one specific job. Rather, it is the development of transferable skills and attributes that allow students to succeed in a changing job market.

In the University of Dubuque community, the arts foster intellectual, emotional, and spiritual development. In literature, the visual arts, dance, drama, and music, students not only find aesthetic pleasure but also learn about other people's ideas, beliefs, and experiences and come to deeper understandings of their own.

Because of the University's location near the Mississippi—one of the world's great river systems—students have an appreciation of environmental issues. Through academic endeavors involving formal and experiential learning, students develop an understanding of the basic processes that underpin various ecological communities and of the complex interaction of human activities on the environment. The University of Dubuque encourages individuals to integrate their knowledge of the environment into personal, ethical, and spiritual guidelines, which can be used to improve their lives, their communities, and society.

The Lester G. and Michael Lester Wendt Character Initiative, supported by a substantial endowment, integrates virtues and values such as truthfulness, honesty, fairness, and the Golden Rule across the curriculum and throughout the University.

The University's Learning Institute for Fulfillment and Engagement (LIFE) offers an accelerated baccalaureate degree program for adult learners. Geared to adult learners age 23 and over, the UD LIFE program is designed to offer a flexible format, allowing students to earn a bachelor's degree in as few as three years and a master's degree in as few as eighteen months. Offering classes on weekday evenings as well as online, the program helps adults balance their studies, career, and family life.

Off-Campus Programs

As a member of the Dubuque Tri-College Cooperative Effort, the University of Dubuque offers its students the opportunity to attend and receive credit for courses at Clarke College and Loras College, also in the city, thus providing access to the many different faculty members, professional societies, educational opportunities, and social activities of combined campuses of more than 3,500 students.

The University of Dubuque affirms the value of an international/intercultural experience and considers it to be an important component of any student's education. Overseas travel, exchanges, and study programs are available to help increase the global perspective of the students and to promote cross-cultural education.

Academic Facilities

In May 2011, the University broke ground on an 80,000-square-foot performing arts and campus center. The new facility is expected to be central to the University of Dubuque campus, and will provide a multitude of venues to serve students, faculty, staff, and the public. "Art by osmosis" is the overarching theme of the new building, inviting people of all walks to happen upon art in its myriad forms, intentionally and accidentally, as they visit the new center for their work, study, recreation, and entertainment. The primary functions of the building can be categorized as a casual student campus center and formal public areas, with overlapping meant to encourage interaction and interest. The student areas are designed to provide educational spaces, group and individual study settings, student services, offices, and hospitality; the public areas provide performance venues, associated gathering spaces, gallery space, heritage display, offices, and hospitality. The center is slated to open in spring of 2013.

The Chlapaty Recreation and Wellness Center, which opened in October 2008, is an 87,000-square-foot facility enveloping the existing football stadium as well as additional construction to the west. Features include a 6,900-square-foot, two-level fitness center, including areas for cardiovascular workouts and free weights/machines, as well as a room for activities such as Pilates and yoga; a 200-meter, six-lane indoor track with synthetic flooring for fitness walking and performance; four multiuse courts nested in the center of the track for intramurals and indoor practices; a training room and examination rooms; home, visitor, officials, and faculty/staff locker rooms; a juice bar and lounge area; a 3,000-seat football stadium, including east side visitor seating for 1,000 and an expanded concessions area; and a lighted field, synthetic field turf surface, and new eight-lane outdoor track.

The expanded and renovated University Science Center opened for classes in January 2007. With an additional 21,000 square feet of space, the University can devote the proper resources to its growing science programs. The new facility accommodates efficient laboratories, including state-of-the-art equipment and safety measures, bringing the science programs to the forefront of current teaching methods. Laboratory spaces include geology, zoology, general biology, cell/microbiology, science education, nursing, general chemistry, organic chemistry, geographic information systems (GIS), and five research labs to accommodate student-faculty collaborative research projects.

Costs

Tuition costs for the 2012–13 academic year are $23,540. Average room and board costs are $7880. These costs do not include books, supplies, personal expenses, and travel.

Financial Aid

Ninety-six percent of the University of Dubuque's students receive financial assistance through scholarships, awards and grants, loans, or work-study programs. The average financial assistance package for 2011–12 was $18,851. All levels of household incomes receive financial assistance.

To apply for financial assistance, applicants must submit a completed application package for admission to the University of Dubuque, file a FAFSA after January 1 and before April 1 (the priority deadline), and send or fax a copy of the completed FAFSA to the University of Dubuque Office of Student Financial Planning. Institutional, federal, state, and alternative loan programs are all available as forms of financial assistance.

Faculty

Seventy percent of University of Dubuque faculty members have earned a Ph.D. or other terminal degree. The student-faculty ratio is 15:1.

Student Government

The Student Government Association (SGA) represents the student body through general election of individual student representatives. The SGA sponsors four campus organizations, the University Program Council (UPC), the Spartan Spirit Club, Under The Bell Tower (student newspaper), and The Key (student yearbook). SGA provides student representatives for a number of key administrative committees.

Admission Requirements

An applicant for admission to the University of Dubuque undergraduate program is a graduate of a high school or equivalent (GED) and presents a minimum of 15 high school units, of which 10 are from academic fields (English, social studies, natural science, mathematics, foreign language). Either ACT or SAT scores are required. The Admission Committee looks at the application and transcript for indications of school achievement as well as aspiration, creativity, and adventurousness. Applicants to the University are usually active in cocurricular activities and these, as well as leadership qualities and character, are considered. An on-campus visit is encouraged. Two recommendations and an essay are requested and read with care.

Application and Information

First-year students are admitted to the University on a rolling basis. When the application and all supporting materials (e.g., transcripts and teacher and counselor recommendations) have been received, admission decisions are made by the Admission Committee and students are advised of the University's decision.

Transfer students who are enrolled or who were previously enrolled at another college or university may apply for transfer to the University of Dubuque. The University considers transfer applications for fall and spring semesters.

In addition to completing the application materials required for first-year applicants, transfer applicants must submit a complete official transcript for all college courses taken and grades received and a complete official transcript for all secondary school courses taken and grades received.

For further information, students should contact:

Office of Admission
University of Dubuque
2000 University Avenue
Dubuque, Iowa 52001
Phone: 563-589-3000
      800-722-5583 (toll-free)
E-mail: admssns@dbq.edu
Web site: http://www.dbq.edu

Marking the entrance to South Campus is a colonnade reminiscent of the Steffens Colonnade that is a familiar Dubuque landmark along the North Campus entrance on University Avenue.

THE UNIVERSITY OF FINDLAY
FINDLAY, OHIO

FINDLAY
THE UNIVERSITY OF FINDLAY

The University

The University of Findlay (UF) is a private coeducational institution with more than 3,900 full- and part-time students. Founded in 1882 by the Churches of God, General Conference, and the citizens of Findlay, it emphasizes preparation for careers and professions in an educational program that blends liberal arts and career education. Service is a priority at Findlay, with new students spending a half-day volunteering in the community before they even begin classes. In 2010, the University was named to the President's Higher Education Community Service Honor Roll for exemplary service efforts to America's communities for the second consecutive year.

Bachelor's degree programs are available in nearly different majors. Master's degrees are offered in athletic training; business administration; education; health informatics, environmental, safety, and health management; occupational therapy; physician assistant studies; and teaching English to speakers of other languages (TESOL) and bilingual education. A Doctor of Pharmacy (Pharm.D.) degree program graduated its first class in 2010, and the first students in the Doctor of Physical Therapy program followed suit in 2011.

The largest programs at Findlay are animal science/pre–veterinary medicine, equestrian studies, pharmacy, business administration, and education. Majors in the sciences and health professions include athletic training, chemistry, computer science, equestrian studies (English, Western, and equine business management), nuclear medicine, occupational therapy, physical therapy, and animal science/pre–veterinary medicine. Business degrees are founded in a comprehensive core program with eleven different majors.

The University of Findlay's academic programs emphasize experiential learning, including opportunities for internships, undergraduate research, and work-related experiences.

Most of Findlay's students come from Ohio and the surrounding states of Michigan, Indiana, and Pennsylvania. More than thirty other states are also represented. UF also has a strong international student population, with more than 300 international students from twenty-seven countries and territories.

Resident students live in eight modern residence halls and several town-house-style apartments. Social life at Findlay centers on student organizations, fraternities, and sororities. Findlay has two officially recognized fraternities, Alpha Sigma Phi and Theta Chi, and two sororities, Phi Sigma Sigma and Sigma Kappa. Organizations include department and special interest clubs, the newspaper, musical groups, a radio and TV station, Circle K, and Aristos Eklektos (honors).

Athletic programs are affiliated with NCAA Division II and the Great Lakes Intercollegiate Athletic Conference, with the exception of the equestrian teams, which have won national championships in the Intercollegiate Horse Show Association. Findlay offers ten intercollegiate sports for men: baseball, basketball, cross-country, football, golf, indoor and outdoor track and field, soccer, swimming and diving, tennis, and wrestling. It has eleven varsity sports for women: basketball, cheerleading, cross-country, golf, indoor and outdoor track and field, lacrosse, soccer, softball, swimming and diving, tennis, and volleyball. UF also has two mixed sports, western and English equestrian riding. Athletic scholarships are available.

Croy Physical Education Center has a 25-meter swimming pool, a gymnasium, offices, and classrooms. The Gardner Fitness Center is a state-of-the-art facility. The 130,000-square-foot Koehler Recreation and Fitness Complex, opened in 1999, contains the Malcolm Athletic Center, with a six-lane, NCAA-regulation track; sand pits for long jump; state-of-the-art timing system; wrestling room; four multipurpose courts; locker rooms; and offices for the athletic department. Also under the same roof are a cardio center, which serves an average of 500 patrons a day during the winter months, and a new student recreation center with basketball, volleyball, and tennis courts, a rock-climbing wall, a game room, and more.

Student services include career and placement counseling, the Cosiano Health Center, the Oiler Success Center, academic tutoring and personal counseling, and study skills assistance through the Academic Support Center.

Location

Findlay was voted the most livable micropolitan city in Ohio and scored among the top twelve 12 in the United States. It is within easy driving distance of Toledo, Columbus, Detroit, and Fort Wayne. Interstate 75 and the Ohio Turnpike (Interstates 80 and 90) are major highways serving the area. Airports in Toledo, Columbus, and Detroit are convenient. The town of Findlay has nearly 39,000 residents and is home to Marathon Oil Corporation and Cooper Tire and Rubber Company. The Findlay campus consists of more than 388 acres on several sites. A 152-acre campus-owned farm houses the pre–veterinary medicine and Western equestrian studies programs, including a 31,000-square-foot animal science center dedicated in 2009 with two 50-seat classrooms, a laboratory, a pharmacy, a student lounge, locker rooms, offices, instructional demonstration areas, holding pens, and other animal servicing areas. A second 32-acre facility houses the English riding program. Approximately 450 horses are stabled and trained at the equestrian facilities, which offer barns and indoor and outdoor riding arenas.

Many opportunities exist for students who want business-related and social service agency experience. The University has established strong relationships with the community, which supports athletic and cultural events on the campus. Besides the full program of on-campus activities, off-campus trips to cultural and entertainment events are scheduled. The city of Findlay, which has an excellent business climate, offers part-time job opportunities, volunteer service organizations, and the chance to be involved with the larger civic community. Findlay's campus is attractive, safe, comfortable, and friendly.

Majors and Degrees

The Bachelor of Arts (B.A.) degree is awarded in the following majors: adolescent/young adult/integrated English/language arts, adolescent/young adult/integrated social studies, art, art management, children's book illustration, criminal justice, digital media, English, English as an international language, graphic design, health communication, history, Japanese, journalism, law and the liberal arts, middle childhood/language arts/social studies, multiage/drama/theater, multiage/Japanese, multiage/Spanish, multiage/visual arts, organizational communication, philosophy/applied philosophy, political science, psychology, public relations, religious studies, social work, sociology, Spanish, studio art, teaching English to speakers of other languages, and theater. Minors are offered in numerous areas.

The Bachelor of Science (B.S.) degree is granted in accounting; adolescent/young adult/earth science; adolescent/young adult/integrated mathematics; adolescent/young adult/life science; animal science; biology (recommended for those interested in physician assistant or medical studies); business administration; business management; chemistry (recommended for those interested in medical studies); computer science; early childhood; economics; entrepreneurship; environmental, safety, and occupational health management; equestrian studies (English and Western emphases); equine business management; finance; forensic science; health education; health science (in preparation for occupational therapy or physical therapy); health studies; hospitality management; human resource management; international business; intervention specialist/mild to moderate disabilities; marketing; mathematics; medical laboratory science; middle childhood/language arts/math; middle childhood/language arts/science; middle childhood/math/science; middle childhood/math/social studies; middle childhood/science/social studies; multiage/health education; multiage/physical education; nuclear medicine technology; operations and logistics; physical education; positron emission tomography/

computer technology; sport and event management and strength and conditioning.

The Associate of Arts degree is available in accounting, computer science, criminal justice administration (corrections or law enforcement emphases), English as an international language, equestrian studies (English and Western riding), financial management, general social studies, human resource management, humanities, management information systems, massage therapy, nuclear medicine technology, personal training, religious studies, sales/retail management, and small business/entrepreneurship. Certificate programs are available in a variety of areas.

Academic Programs

Findlay operates on the semester system. Students must complete at least 124 semester hours with a minimum overall grade point average of 2.0 to earn a bachelor's degree. General education requirements and competency requirements in English, computer literacy, and speech must be fulfilled. The Gateway Program offers students the chance to develop those skills in writing, reading, and thinking needed for their success as college students. Study skills, time management, and academic advising are included. Students are selected for this program at the time of admission. The honors program provides additional challenge to those students who qualify on the basis of academic credentials. Study- and travel-abroad programs are offered by various departments. Credit and/or placement can be earned through Advanced Placement (AP) exams.

The equestrian program is a well-recognized program of its kind and serves approximately 280 students from throughout the United States and abroad. Majors in equine business management and in English and western riding are offered. The instruction, both in the classroom and on horseback, makes use of the expertise of recognized national equestrian champions. The pre–veterinary medicine program, using the farm facilities, offers the advantages of hands-on experience with livestock and an internship program in a distinctive curriculum. Graduates of the pre–veterinary program have been accepted to all twenty-eight veterinary schools in the United States, and several internationally.

The Nuclear Medicine Institute provides the training necessary to qualify students for careers in nuclear medicine technology, a growing health-related career field.

Academic Facilities

The focal point of the Findlay campus is Old Main, which houses classrooms, faculty and administrative offices, the computer center, facilities for various student activities, the Oiler Success Center, and the Ritz Auditorium. Shafer Library is a member of a consortium that provides extensive resources to students. The Gardner Fine Arts Pavilion houses the Mazza Museum of International Art from Children's Books, the first and largest teaching museum in the world dedicated to literacy and children's book art. In 2006, the University acquired and renovated a building at 300 Davis St., with its 62,000 square feet comprising the largest addition of academic space since the construction of Old Main. Other academic buildings include the Frost Science Center and the Egner Center for the Performing Arts, which houses a 200-seat theater.

Costs

Tuition for the 2012–13 academic year is $28,080 for most programs. Room and board costs $9166. The estimated cost for transportation, books, fees, and supplies was $2496. There are additional tuition charges for equestrian studies and pre–veterinary medicine.

Financial Aid

Assistance is based on need as well as scholastic achievement. In 2011–12, 85 percent of UF students received institutional financial aid from the University. The average need-based financial aid package for freshmen was more than $20,000 in fall 2011. Merit scholarships at UF range from $9500 to $14,500 a year. Notification of aid awards is made on a rolling basis. Work-study jobs are available. Scholarships for high-achieving students and student athletes are offered.

Faculty

The 17:1 student-faculty ratio results in small classes, with an average class size of 20 students. Professors know their students, and every student has a faculty adviser.

Student Government

The Student Government Association (SGA) and the Campus Program Board are involved in planning and implementing student activities. SGA provides leadership experience for students and enhances cooperation among faculty members, the administration, and students. A representative from SGA sits on the Board of Trustees. The Campus Program Board plans activities for recreation and cultural enrichment.

Admission Requirements

The University of Findlay considers each applicant on an individualized basis. The University accepts applications on a rolling basis, but it encourages students to complete applications by January 15, as the class fills rapidly. Application deadlines are August 1 for the fall semester and December 15 for the spring semester. Major factors associated with rendering a decision include GPA, standardized test scores, and strength of curriculum. Although it is not required, a campus admission visit is encouraged. Applicants to Findlay should have a college-preparatory high school background, including 4 years of English, 3 to 4 years of mathematics, 2 to 3 years of social studies, and 2 years of science. A foreign language is recommended but not required. Results of the ACT or SAT should be submitted with the application for admission. Transfer students must be eligible to return to the institution last attended and must submit transcripts of all college work. For students not meeting regular minimum admission requirements, Findlay has a Gateway Program, which provides skill building and academic support during the first semester of the freshman year. Findlay is an equal opportunity institution in admission and employment.

Application and Information

For application forms and other information, students may contact:

Office of Undergraduate Admissions
The University of Findlay
1000 North Main Street
Findlay, Ohio 45840
Phone: 419-434-4732
　　　800-548-0932 (toll-free)
E-mail: admissions@findlay.edu
Web site: http://www.findlay.edu
　　　http://on.fb.me/UFindlay (Facebook)

The University of Findlay's Old Main is an original building on campus and houses the College of Business and many student support services.

UNIVERSITY OF GUELPH
GUELPH, ONTARIO, CANADA

The University

The University of Guelph is a high-quality, student-focused, residential university that is committed to innovative programs, dynamic student-faculty interaction, and an integration of learning and research. It offers a wide range of undergraduate and graduate programs in the arts, humanities, social sciences, engineering, and natural sciences. Building on these core disciplines, Guelph also has a strong commitment to interdisciplinary programs, to a selected range of professional and applied programs, and to agriculture and veterinary medicine as areas of special responsibility.

Established in 1964 when three century-old founding colleges joined with a new college of arts and science, the University of Guelph is a vital community of more than 21,000 students on a campus of historical and modern buildings and redbrick walkways. By Canadian standards, Guelph is of medium size, offering a wide range of academic programs while providing a safe, accommodating environment. On-campus living is available for more than 5,000 students, with new first-semester students guaranteed on-campus housing if they apply and submit a deposit before the deadline.

Guelph features state-of-the-art athletic facilities that include a double arena with an Olympic-size ice surface, two pools, a field house and indoor track, aerobic and weight-training gymnasiums, six squash courts, and a climbing wall. Guelph offers thirty varsity sports teams and in recent years has fielded national and provincial championship football, hockey, track and field, and rugby teams.

Guelph ensures a personal approach to learning with a 1:20 faculty-student ratio in 63 percent of its classes. The success of the Center for New Students, which assists students with the transition from secondary school to university, is reflected in Guelph's 89.3 percent student retention rate and a 96.8 percent graduate employment rate, both well above the Canadian national average.

The University of Guelph offers a Doctor of Veterinary Medicine degree as well as several diploma programs and more than eighty master's and doctoral degree programs. The graduate calendar is available on the Web at http://www.uoguelph.ca/GraduateStudies.

Location

The University of Guelph's main campus is located in the southwestern Ontario region the *New York Times* calls Canada's Technology Triangle, a locale known for its high-caliber educational institutions and innovative companies. This city of more than 118,000 features internationally recognized folk, jazz, and writers' festivals as well as a multipurpose performing arts center and a sports and entertainment center. Positioned within an hour's drive of Toronto, Canada's largest city, Guelph offers the comfort of small-community living with the excitement of an international metropolis at its doorstep. In addition to the main campus, the University of Guelph offers degrees in Toronto at the University of Guelph–Humber and regional campuses throughout Ontario in Alfred, Kemptville, and Ridgetown.

Majors and Degrees

The University of Guelph offers a number of undergraduate degree programs. Programs followed by an asterisk (*) indicate degrees that students can pursue in a traditional four-year or in a five-year co-op format. Co-ops offer students the opportunity to work in three to five different companies in paid work placements that result in one year of full-time work as a part of the degree experience.

The University of Guelph offers Bachelor of Arts degrees in anthropology; art history; classical studies; criminal justice and public policy; economics*; English; environmental governance; European studies; French studies; food, agriculture, and resource economics; geography; Hispanic studies; history; information systems and human behavior; international development; major to be determined; mathematical economics*; mathematics; music; philosophy; political science; psychology*; sociology; studio art; and theater studies. In addition, a Bachelor of Arts and Sciences degree is available to students who excel in both arts/social sciences and sciences.

Bachelor of Applied Science degrees are available in applied human nutrition; child, youth, and family*; and adult development*.

Bachelor of Commerce degrees are available in accounting, food and agricultural business*, hotel and food administration*, human resource management, management economics and finance*, marketing management*, public management*, real estate and housing*, tourism management, and undeclared (first year only).

Bachelor of Bio-Resource Management degrees are available in environmental management and equine management. Students in these programs begin their studies in the regional campuses and finish the final two years in Guelph.

The Bachelor of Computing degrees are available in computer science* and software engineering*.

Bachelor of Engineering degrees are available in biological engineering*, biomedical engineering*, computer engineering*, environmental engineering*, engineering systems and computing*, mechanical engineering*, water resources engineering*, and undeclared (first year only).

Bachelor of Science degrees are available in animal biology, applied mathematics and statistics* (co-op only), biological and pharmaceutical chemistry*, bio-medical science, biochemistry*, biodiversity, biological science, biological and medical physics, chemical physics*, chemistry*, environmental biology, environmental geoscience and geomatics, food science*, human kinetics, marine and freshwater biology, mathematics, microbiology*, molecular biology and genetics, nanoscience*, nutritional and nutraceutical sciences, physical science, physics*, plant science, psychology (brain and cognition), theoretical physics, toxicology*, wildlife biology and conservation, and zoology.

Bachelor of Science in Agriculture degrees are available in animal science; crop, horticulture, and turfgrass sciences; honors agriculture; and organic agriculture.

Bachelor of Science in Environmental Sciences degrees are available in ecology*, environmental economics and policy*, environment and resource management*, and environmental sciences*.

The University of Guelph also offers a Bachelor of Landscape Architecture degree, a Doctor of Veterinary Medicine degree, and associate diplomas.

University of Guelph–Humber programs include honors degrees in business administration (accounting, finance, international business, marketing, and small business management and entrepreneurship); applied science (early childhood services, family and community social services, justice studies, kinesiology, or psychology); and applied arts in media studies (journalism, public relations, digital communications, and image arts).

Academic Programs

The academic year is divided into three semesters: fall (September through December), winter (January through April), and summer (May through August), with the majority of students in attendance during the fall and winter semesters. Fall is the normal entry point for all semester one students. However, transfer students who apply by deadlines are considered for many programs at all entry points.

Four-year honors degrees require the completion of eight semesters. Three-year general degrees require the completion of six semesters. A typical full-time semester totals 2.5 credits.

Off-Campus Programs

An important part of Guelph's mission is to attract students from around the world and develop a global perspective in its students. The campus attracts more than 700 international students from over 100 countries, maintains fifty-six exchange programs with thirty countries, and offers six semester-abroad options. In addition,

approximately 500 Guelph students study, research, or work each year in Africa, Australia, Europe, and South and Central America.

Nearly 2,000 students participate in co-op work semesters, making the co-op program at the University of Guelph one of the highest in co-op student enrollments among Ontario universities. Guelph also offers more than 100 distance degree credit courses to nearly 8,000 Open Learning course registrants.

Academic Facilities

Guelph's two libraries are linked with libraries at two other universities in the region, providing students with access to 7.5 million items through a state-of-the-art automated library system. Guelph's library holdings include Canada's largest collection of theater archives, extensive Scottish study materials, and one of the best collections of postcolonial African literature in Canada.

A 30-acre research park adjacent to the campus is home to a growing number of research-intensive industries. Industry and government trust Guelph's faculty members to meet their research needs, offering approximately Can$157.9 million annually for research that ranges from workplace efficiency to developing better approaches to food packaging and marketing to ensuring the availability of clean water.

All students receive free central computing accounts, which allow access to the University's integrated electronic services from on or off campus. Services include e-mail, access to the Internet, computer-assisted instruction, conferencing, course selection, and high-quality laser printing. Student residences are directly connected to the Internet via the campus high-speed network. Off-campus students have access to chargeable high-speed Internet providers.

The campus also features two art galleries; a sculpture park; two performance stages; a covered field house; a Can$144-million Science Complex; a Can$44.6-million engineering facility expansion; the Guelph Institute for the Environment; the Biodiversity Institute of Ontario, which is the world's first center for high-volume DNA barcoding; and the Can$70-million pathobiology/animal health laboratory. The 408-acre arboretum on the west side of the campus has nearly 5 miles of jogging trails and nature paths.

Costs

Full-time tuition for the 2011–12 academic year ranged from Can$2723 to Can$4574 per semester for Canadian residents and from Can$8461 to Can$11,074 per semester for international students. Mandatory fees totaled approximately Can$500 per semester, with slight variations according to each college. International students must purchase health-care coverage through the University. The cost for international students to attend Guelph for two semesters, including tuition and academic fees, health coverage, housing, clothing, food, and books, totaled between Can$29,370 and Can$34,596.

Financial Aid

The University of Guelph is committed to ensuring that a university education remains an attainable goal. In total, Can$13.6 million in annual student financial aid is given in the form of scholarships, awards, bursaries, and work-study opportunities. There are scholarships (ranging from Can$500 to Can$6000) and bursaries specifically designed for international students who are allowed to work on and off campus.

Faculty

The percentage of Guelph's 794 full-time professors who hold the Ph.D. degree or its equivalent is 98.9 percent, and all strive to bring the excitement and process of research into the learning environment. More than 100 professors have been recognized for excellence in teaching by external agencies, their peers, and students. No comparably sized university in the country has more 3M awards, Canada's most prestigious university teaching honor. Guelph has 19 Fellows of the Royal Society of Canada among its researchers.

Student Government

Students are involved at all levels of University government, from the residence council to the Senate and the Board of Governors. The Central Student Association (CSA), which represents all undergraduate students, oversees more than fifty student clubs that range from political to recreational. In addition, there are more than fifty academic and other student-government organizations located on campus. Students also have access to a number of service groups on campus, which range from the Ontario Public Interest Research Group to a community radio station to Engineers without Borders and Habitat for Humanity.

Admission Requirements

Ontario applicants must present the Ontario Secondary School Diploma (OSSD), with a minimum of six 4U or 4M courses and specific subject requirements for the degree program desired. English 4U is required for all degree programs. For those outside Ontario, the secondary graduation certificate that would admit a student to a university in his or her home country is normally acceptable. Applicants must also satisfy the specific subject requirements for the program desired. Applicants who have completed the International Baccalaureate (I.B.) are granted credit for higher-level courses with grades of 5 or better to a maximum of 2.0 credits. Applicants who have completed Advanced Placement (AP) exams with a minimum grade of 4 are eligible to receive University credit to a maximum of 2.0 credits, which is subject to the discretion of the appropriate faculty. United States applicants are required to have a minimum unweighted grade point average of 3.0 and a combined SAT score of at least 1100 (critical reading and math components) or an ACT score of at least 24. Applicants should include specific subject requirements at the highest secondary school level offered.

Interested students should call Admission Services or refer to its Web site at http://admission.uoguelph.ca for application and deadline dates, detailed admission information, and downloadable application forms. Students interested in University of Guelph–Humber programs should contact Admission Services at http://www.guelphhumber.ca.

Application and Information

For additional information about admissions, academic programs, or University visits and tours, students should contact:

Admission Services
Office of Registrarial Services
Third Floor, University Centre
University of Guelph
Guelph, Ontario N1G 2W1
Canada
Phone: 519-821-2130 or 519-824-4120 Ext. 58721
Fax: 519-766-9481
E-mail: internat@registrar.uoguelph.ca (International inquiries)
usa@registrar.uoguelph.ca (U.S. inquiries)
admission@registrar.uoguelph.ca (Canadian inquiries)
Web site: http://admission.uoguelph.ca
http://www.guelphhumber.ca

Students on the campus of the University of Guelph.

UNIVERSITY OF HARTFORD
WEST HARTFORD, CONNECTICUT

The University

The University of Hartford is a fully accredited, independent, nonsectarian institution. The University is composed of seven degree-granting schools and colleges: the College of Arts and Sciences; College of Engineering, Technology, and Architecture; College of Education, Nursing, and Health Professions; Hillyer College; the Barney School of Business; the Hartford Art School; and The Hartt School.

The current full-time undergraduate enrollment is more than 4,700 men and women. A wide range of interests, goals, and backgrounds is found among the students, who represent forty-six states and fifty-three countries. There are about 100 organized student groups, including clubs devoted to special interests or to political, professional, religious, or civic activities as well as service learning and community service activities and groups. Intercollegiate (NCAA Division I) and intramural athletics, student publications, and AM and FM radio stations provide further opportunities for extracurricular involvement. In addition, The Hartt School, the Hartford Art School, and the University Players present a variety of concerts, exhibitions, and theatrical productions each year. Recreational and fitness needs of the University community as well as intramural and intercollegiate sports are served by a well-equipped 130,000-square-foot sports center and outdoor athletic facilities.

More than 66 percent of all full-time undergraduates reside on campus. The University offers a wide array of types of residence halls, from traditional dormitory-style to fully equipped town house–style apartments.

Location

The University is located in the residential suburb of West Hartford. The area provides an environment conducive to the development of the student's cultural and intellectual pursuits. There are many area facilities that students can take advantage of including libraries, museums, theaters, the XL Center and Convention Center, a symphony orchestra, several other colleges, modern shopping centers, fine restaurants, an international airport, surface transportation, and intercity highway systems.

Majors and Degrees

The College of Arts and Sciences offers majors in art history, biology, chemistry, chemistry-biology, cinema, communication, computer science, criminal justice, economics, English, foreign languages and cultures, history, international studies, Judaic studies, mathematics, philosophy, physics, political economy, politics and government, psychology, rhetoric and professional writing, and sociology.

Within the College of Education, Nursing, and Health Professions, there are majors in early childhood education, elementary education, integrated special education/elementary education, secondary education with a concentration in English or mathematics, health sciences, nursing (for registered nurses only), radiologic technology, respiratory therapy, a combined B.S. in health science, and doctorate in physical therapy (B.S./D.P.T.) program, as well as a combined B.S. in health science and a Master of Science in Prosthetics and Orthotics (B.S./M.S.P.O.) program.

The Hartford Art School offers Bachelor of Fine Arts degrees in ceramics, design, drawing, illustration, media arts, painting, photography, printmaking, sculpture, and visual communication.

At the Hartt School, students can major in actor training, applied music (guitar, orchestral instrument, organ, piano, pre–cantorial studies, and voice), composition, dance (ballet pedagogy or performance emphases), jazz studies, music, music education, music history, music management, music production and technology, music theater, music theory, and performing arts management (interdisciplinary program offered in conjunction with the Barney School of Business). There are also five-year double majors offered within the Hartt School.

Majors for the Bachelor of Science in Business Administration (B.S.B.A.) degree in the Barney School of Business are accounting, economics and finance, entrepreneurial studies, finance and insurance, management, and marketing.

Additional B.S. programs, offered by the College of Engineering, Technology, and Architecture include ABET-accredited programs in electrical, mechanical, civil, computer, and biomedical engineering as well as interdisciplinary B.S.E. options. The newest offering in the mechanical engineering department is a concentration in energy engineering and sustainable design. The most popular B.S.E. options are acoustical engineering and music (interdisciplinary program in conjunction with the Hartt School), biomedical engineering, and environmental engineering. Technology programs include the Bachelor of Science in architectural engineering technology, audio engineering technology, computer engineering technology, electronic engineering technology, and mechanical engineering technology as well as the Associate in Applied Science in electronic engineering technology (A.S.) and the Associate in Applied Science in computer engineering technology (A.S.).

Hillyer College offers the Associate of Arts and provides the general education course work required to complete most of the University's baccalaureate programs. Particular emphasis is placed on the development of academic skills through small classes and close faculty-student interaction.

University Studies offers the Bachelor of University Studies, a B.A. degree program created for the part-time adult student who typically has previous college experience and seeks to complete a baccalaureate degree. Also offered is a B.A. degree program in multimedia Web design and development for full-time undergraduates. Created for students who want to learn how to use and develop multimedia technologies that fit into today's wired world, this program combines courses across several disciplines where students create and use technology with user interaction in mind.

Academic Programs

The University of Hartford enjoys a national reputation for the breadth and depth of its academic programs. As highlighted above, eighty-four undergraduate majors are offered through seven schools and colleges. Students are encouraged to sample a variety of academic areas. Those who have special interests can develop interdisciplinary majors that combine courses from the different schools within the University. Academic advisers are assigned to all students to help guide them in curriculum choices, career exploration, and the transition to University life. In order to help students learn more about how different academic disciplines approach related problems, the All-University Curriculum was developed. Courses are often team taught from different fields of expertise, and topics are examined from the perspective of several academic disciplines. The University also has a special program to assist students who may be undecided about a major. A reading and writing center provides individual support to help students increase their proficiency in writing, research, reading comprehension, and speed as well as study and test-taking skills. Further help in math is given through the Math Tutoring Lab,

which is staffed by full-time faculty members and math majors. Career Services provides vocational counseling and information on occupations, employers, testing, and graduate schools; serves as a reference and credential source; and provides an on-campus recruiting program for graduating students. University College addresses the needs of the part-time adult learner through courses, programs, and educational counseling. A trained counseling staff is available to assist part-time students in planning their education and resolving their special concerns and needs. Selected students are encouraged to participate in the honors program. Honors students have the opportunity to graduate with an honors degree.

Off-Campus Programs

Intercampus registration through the Hartford Consortium for Higher Education permits University of Hartford students to take certain courses at the School of the Hartford Ballet, Saint Joseph College, and Trinity College. Teaching majors in the College of Education, Nursing, and Health Professions have opportunities for field and/or clinical experiences where applicable. A central internship and cooperative education office is available to custom-tailor work experiences within many of the University's programs.

Academic Facilities

Seven schools and colleges are housed on the main campus. The Harry Jack Gray Center houses the William H. Mortensen Library; the Mildred P. Allen Memorial Library; the Museum of American Political Life; the Harry J. Gray Conference Center; the Joseloff Gallery; the University Bookstore; studios for architecture, art, radio, and television; and the communication department. The library has approximately 583,000 items, including books, musical scores, recordings, periodicals, journals, and microfilm units as well as the latest in computer technology, including high-speed and wireless Internet access. Extensive resources are also available through the Hartford Consortium for Higher Education, the Hartford Library, and the Interlibrary Loan systems.

The new state-of-the-art Mort and Irma Handel Performing Arts Center, located 5 minutes from the main campus, is a 55,000-square-foot facility that houses five dance studios, four theater rehearsal studios, two black box theaters, a small dining facility, and faculty and staff offices. The Handel Performing Arts Center provides a rehearsal and performance environment for the Hartt School's dancers.

The Asylum Avenue campus is listed on the National Register of Historic Places. The 13-acre wooded campus contains beautiful examples of traditional ivy-covered Georgian architecture.

The University of Hartford Computer Center houses the central computer systems and operates a high-performance campus-wide network, which connects all student residential housing, all academic buildings on campus, and the University's remote locations. The University's network is connected via a high-speed telecommunication link to the Internet and the World Wide Web. The residential network gives each student resident his or her own high-speed Ethernet connection to the campus network and the Internet. The library is connected to the campus network and provides network access through computers in study carrels and study rooms and through wireless access. The online systems of the library include the online catalog for book, audio, and video collections; CD-ROM databases; and easy-to-use Web access for many of the library's online resources and electronic reserves. All of the University network resources may be accessed on campus in any University facility and off campus by using computers with network connectivity.

Public access computing labs, used by all students of the University, are provided at various locations around the campus. In addition, college-specific labs are available to students. All labs are equipped with microcomputers (both PCs and Macs) and are connected to the campus network and the Internet. Typical microcomputer software includes word processing, spreadsheet, database management, and graphics programs; programming languages; and Web browsers for accessing the Internet. Help is available from on-duty lab assistants. In addition to these computer labs, there are specialized computer facilities for instruction and learning. Wireless Internet access is available in all academic buildings, libraries, and dining facilities.

Costs

Tuition for incoming students was $29,440 for the 2011–12 academic year; student service fees, $1314; on-campus room costs, $7328; and board, $5150. A variety of on-campus housing accommodates 3,400 students.

Financial Aid

Financial aid for University of Hartford students totals approximately $98 million annually, including student loans. Scholarships, grants, loans, and work-study opportunities are provided through the federal government, private agencies, interested individuals, and University funds. University funds are disbursed based upon the college or school in which the student is enrolled, availability of funds, applicant pool, and competition for funds. More than 93 percent of new full-time undergraduate students receive some type of University assistance; the average out-of-pocket expense is $17,643 (estimate) per year. Partial-tuition scholarships are awarded to entering students who have demonstrated outstanding academic achievement or talent.

Faculty

There are 787 full-time and adjunct faculty members. The undergraduate and graduate faculties are essentially the same group, and 85 percent of the members hold the terminal degree in their field. Academic and personal advisory service is readily available. Each new student is assigned to a faculty adviser during summer orientation.

Student Government

The student governing body that represents all full-time students is the Student Government Association, through which students and faculty join in developing and coordinating the cocurricular activities of the University. Students are also represented on all major administrative committees, including the Board of Regents.

Admission Requirements

The Office of Admission considers the quality of the secondary school curriculum, academic performance in secondary school, ACT or SAT results, evidence of a desire to succeed, and leadership qualities shown by academic and extracurricular activities. Auditions, portfolios, and other tests are required of music and art applicants.

Application and Information

The University employs a rolling admission policy. For further information, students should visit the University on the Web at http://admission.hartford.edu or contact:
Office of Admission
University of Hartford
West Hartford, Connecticut 06117
Phone: 860-768-4296
      800-947-4303 (toll-free)
Fax: 860-768-4961
E-mail: admission@hartford.edu
Web site: http://admission.hartford.edu

UNIVERSITY OF INDIANAPOLIS
INDIANAPOLIS, INDIANA

The University

The University of Indianapolis (UIndy) seeks to inspire excellence with a personal approach to education and a commitment to academic quality. Outstanding faculty members inspire students in small classes that allow individual attention, and students are encouraged to apply their knowledge to real-world situations through internships, active learning in the classroom, and community service. A private, residential, comprehensive university founded in 1902 and affiliated with the United Methodist Church, the University of Indianapolis welcomes students of many nations and faiths from around the world. Every year, more than 5,000 full-time and part-time students, both undergraduate and graduate, benefit from the University's commitment to offering outstanding academic programs in more than eighty major fields of study. The University of Indianapolis accepts qualified applicants for admission without regard to race, color, sex, sexual orientation, age, religion, creed, marital status, and ethnic or national origin.

Students indicate that they chose UIndy because of its challenging yet supportive atmosphere, relatively small size, and the advantages of its location in the distinctive Southside area of a thriving state capital city. As a result, there is a great sense of community and pride on the campus. The University helps students to determine and achieve their individual academic goals. UIndy has experienced much growth and has instituted many enhancements recently, including Roberts Hall, the newest upperclassmen residence hall; the expansion of the Schwitzer Student Center; and the addition of the Athletics and Recreation Center.

More than 3,000 full-time undergraduate students are enrolled. There are students from more than sixty countries and thirty-five states. Approximately 85 percent of freshmen live in on-campus housing. The warmth and sensitivity of the faculty, staff members, and students alike enable those who are a part of the campus to feel a strong sense of community.

In addition to the undergraduate division, the University also offers a graduate division, including the nationally recognized Krannert School of Physical Therapy. The University of Indianapolis offers twenty-two graduate programs and four doctoral programs, including those in the College of Health Sciences, which rank among the finest in the nation. The most popular programs in the undergraduate division include pre–physical therapy, business, athletic training, communication, nursing, education, pre-medical studies, psychology, and music.

Social life is organized through the Campus Program Board, Indianapolis Student Government, and Residence Hall Association, which are student organizations that plan weekly activities for all students. There are numerous social clubs and common-interest groups available for students who wish to become involved in extracurricular activities. There are seven residence halls: six house both men and women, and one is only for women. Two-bedroom, one-bathroom apartments are also available to upperclassmen. Students must be admitted on a full-time basis in order to be assigned housing. NCAA Division II sports for men include baseball, basketball, cross-country, football, golf, soccer, swimming and diving, tennis, track and field (indoor and outdoor), and wrestling. NCAA Division II sports for women include basketball, cross-country, golf, soccer, softball, swimming and diving, tennis, track and field (indoor and outdoor), and volleyball. Intramural sports are offered for men and women in flag football, basketball, softball, soccer, volleyball, indoor soccer, Ultimate (Frisbee), and racquetball.

Location

The University is located in the University Heights neighborhood on the south side of Indianapolis, which is the nation's second-largest capital city. Indianapolis and the surrounding area constitute a metropolitan area of nearly 2-million people. The city offers numerous valuable internship and service-learning experiences as well as recreational and cultural opportunities for students. The campus is extremely accessible, just a few blocks from two major interstate highways (I-65 and I-465). Public transportation options in Indianapolis include IndyGo bus, Greyhound Lines, and Amtrak trains that arrive daily at historic Union Station, just 10 minutes from the campus. Indianapolis International Airport is about 15 minutes away.

Majors and Degrees

The undergraduate programs are offered through the College of Arts and Sciences, the School of Business, the School of Nursing, the School of Education, the College of Health Sciences, and the School of Psychological Sciences. The degrees awarded are the Associate in Arts, Associate in Science, Associate in Science in Nursing, Bachelor of Arts, Bachelor of Science, and Bachelor of Science in Nursing.

Baccalaureate and pre-professional fields of study include accounting (CMA/CPA), actuarial science, anthropology, archeology, art, athletic training, biology, business administration, chemistry, communication, community health education, computer engineering (dual degree), computer science, corporate communication, corrections, earth-space sciences, economics, electrical engineering (dual degree), electronic media, elementary education, English, entrepreneurship, environmental science, exercise science, (concentrations in applied anthropology, applied history, and applied theater), finance, French, German, global leadership, history, human biology, human communication, information systems, international business, international relations, journalism, law enforcement, management, marketing, mathematics, mechanical engineering (dual degree), medical technology, music, music performance, nursing, philosophy, physics, political science, pre–art therapy, pre-dental, pre-optometry, pre-pharmacy, pre-law, pre-medical studies, pre-medical illustration, pre-occupational therapy, pre-pharmacy, pre–physical therapy, pre-theology, pre–veterinary science, psychology, public relations, religion, respiratory therapy, secondary education, social work, sociology, Spanish, sports management, sports information, sports marketing, studio art, theater, youth ministry, and visual communication design.

Teaching majors are offered in business education (all grades), chemistry, earth-space science, English, French, life science, mathematics, music (all grades), physical education (all grades), physics, social studies, Spanish, speech communication, theater, and visual arts (grades 5–12).

Associate degrees are awarded in business administration, chemistry, corrections, information systems, law enforcement, liberal arts, nursing, and physical therapist assistant studies.

The University also offers the Healthy Diploma that provides students with the skills, knowledge, and motivation to achieve and/or maintain healthy a lifestyle as students and employees.

Academic Programs

The University of Indianapolis provides a top-notch education that combines a liberal arts and career-oriented curriculum that graduates describe as life changing. Students find a powerful combination of features designed to inspire them to excellence. Faculty and staff members take a personal interest in students and encourage them to explore their interests and apply what they learn, so they can excel when it comes time to make their place in the world.

Students can choose from more than eighty undergraduate academic programs. The goal of the liberal arts core classes is to provide learning above and beyond the student's major field, so students study topics and cultures that pique their interest in unexpected ways.

Students appreciate the curriculum because they don't have to wait to apply what they learn. University of Indianapolis students have time—before they graduate—to practice what they learn. Most majors offer practical experiences, which give students an edge in the

job market. The Indianapolis location is an excellent resource when it comes to finding internships, field experiences, service-learning opportunities, or part-time employment. Internships let students sample their future careers and gain some of the knowledge and experience they admire in their professors. The University offers a host of possibilities for virtually any major. The Office of Career Services helps students identify an appropriate major and arranges off-campus internships related to their field of study.

Off-Campus Programs

The University operates a fully owned branch campus in Athens, Greece, that offers students a unique exchange program. Located within walking distance of the storied Acropolis, the Plaka, Constitution Square, and other historic landmarks, the University of Indianapolis–Athens offers students the opportunity to explore and experience Greece both inside and outside the classroom. Currently, the Athens campus offers thirty-two undergraduate programs in the arts and sciences, business, and psychology. Short-term study trips, as well as full-semester study-abroad programs, are available to students through the Odyssey program. In addition, students at the main campus have many opportunities to travel to Athens on shorter trips during vacations or during the Spring Term in May. Other partnerships and extension sites for direct credit include Israel, Belize, and the People's Republic of China. Other off-campus study opportunities take place during the Spring Term, including assorted overseas travel options.

Academic Facilities

Krannert Memorial Library, which operates an online card catalog, houses more than 175,000 volumes, more than 1,000 periodicals, more than 19,000 microfilm/microform/microfiche records, and the Indianapolis Mayoral Archives. The library is home to a full media center. The communication department, with new state-of-the-art equipment for its radio station and television studio, is located in Esch Hall. Martin Hall contains outstanding resources for the Schools of Nursing, Physical Therapy, and Occupational Therapy and is connected to Lilly Science Hall, which recently underwent a major upgrade to all its science labs. Access to computers is available in all of the academic buildings and residence halls. Students have access to the campus-wide information system from their rooms in the residence halls, and the entire campus is wireless. Ransburg Auditorium, with seating for nearly 800, is the setting for concerts, recitals, and theatrical productions. The Christel DeHaan Fine Arts Center features state-of-the-art music and art facilities; an art gallery; and a 450-seat, Viennese-style concert hall.

Costs

Direct costs for the 2012–13 academic year are $23,590 for tuition and $8570 for room and board. Indirect costs are estimated at $800 for books and supplies, an average of $630 for transportation, and $1370 to $1830 for miscellaneous and personal expenses.

Financial Aid

All applicants for admission are eligible to apply for financial aid. Indiana residents should file the Free Application for Federal Student Aid (FAFSA) by March 10 to qualify for State of Indiana financial aid programs. All students should file the FAFSA along with the University of Indianapolis Application for Financial Aid by March 10 for priority consideration. For the 2010–11academic year, about 88 percent of the enrolled full-time students received financial aid with an average financial aid package of $15,132 for entering students.

Faculty

UIndy's student-faculty ratio is 15:1 and the average class size is 18. Graduate students do not teach any undergraduate classes.

Student Government

The Indianapolis Student Government (ISG) consists of students elected to leadership positions plus student representatives from each class, chosen for a one-year term in an annual student body election. ISG's main focus is to pass resolutions regarding student concerns.

Admission Requirements

Applicants for admission must be high school graduates or have a GED certificate and are expected to have taken a college-preparatory curriculum in high school. Applicants for regular admission should have completed a minimum of 4 years of English, 3 years of mathematics, 3 years of laboratory science, 2 years of social science (U.S. history, government, and economics), and 2 years of any foreign language. In addition, applicants for full-time admission without restrictions should rank in the upper half of their class and have average to above-average SAT or ACT scores. Essays are not required for admission. For immediate consideration, transfer applicants must have achieved a good overall record and have earned at least a C average in previous college or university work. An on-campus visit is recommended any time after the junior year of high school. To apply for admission, the Application for Admission, official high school transcript, official college transcript (if applicable), and official SAT or ACT scores should be forwarded to the Office of Admissions.

Application and Information

All applications are reviewed on a rolling basis—an admission decision is made as soon as all documents are received, and notifications are mailed immediately thereafter. There is no deadline for applications, but high school seniors are encouraged to apply during the fall semester of their senior year. Scholarships are also awarded on a rolling basis. Admitted students are notified of scholarships they have been awarded shortly after they have been accepted.

Requests for appointments and information about the University should be directed to:

University of Indianapolis
1400 East Hanna Avenue
Indianapolis, Indiana 46227-3697
United States
Phone: 317-STUDENT
      317-788-3216
      800-232-8634 (toll-free)
Fax: 317-788-3300
E-mail: admissions@uindy.edu
Web site: http://www.uindy.edu
      http://www.facebook.com/uindy
      http://twitter.com/uindy
      http://www.youtube.com/uindytv

Smith Mall, the centerpiece of the University of Indianapolis campus, features a beautifully landscaped water garden canal.

UNIVERSITY OF MAINE

ORONO, MAINE

The University

The University of Maine (UMaine) offers the extensive academic opportunities expected from a major research university, but with the close-knit feel of a small college. As Maine's flagship university, UMaine offers the state's most comprehensive academic experience, with more than 90 undergraduate majors and academic programs, 75 master's programs, and 30 doctoral programs. All majors benefit from a firm foundation in the liberal arts. Top students are invited to join UMaine's Honors College, one of the country's oldest honors programs.

The University of Maine is one of the National Science Foundation's top 100 research universities, and its facilities and faculty have an international reputation for excellence.

UMaine students have extraordinary opportunities to gain real-world experience through research and experiential learning. SPIFFY, the student investment club, manages a $1.6-million real-money portfolio. Wildlife ecology majors learn about bear behavior by going out and tagging cubs. Engineering majors take advantage of co-ops and internships that often lead to employment after graduation. Education majors take advantage of urban, rural, and international student-teaching opportunities.

Location

There's no place like Maine, and UMaine students take advantage of the great outdoors whenever they can. There are 15 miles of walking, biking, and cross-country skiing trails on campus. Some of the best skiing in the East is located within an easy driving distance of campus, as are Bar Harbor, Acadia National Park, and Baxter State Park, the northern terminus of the Appalachian Trail.

Orono is a classic college town, bounded by the Stillwater and Penobscot Rivers, located in the heart of Maine. The University of Maine is 10 minutes from the state's third-largest city, Bangor, and its international airport.

UMaine's 660-acre campus was designed by legendary landscape architect Frederick Law Olmsted, who also designed Central Park in New York City and the White House grounds in Washington, D.C. It is a traditional New England campus, with ivy-covered brick buildings, towering pines and incredible fall foliage.

Majors and Degrees

UMaine offers more than 90 majors and programs across five colleges—the College of Education and Human Development; the College of Engineering; the College of Liberal Arts and Sciences; the College of Natural Sciences, Forestry, and Agriculture; and the Honors College—and the Maine Business School. In addition, the Explorations program is designed to help undecided students identify a major from across UMaine's colleges while making progress toward their degree. The Division of Lifelong Learning offers online classes and distance-learning opportunities for students who need a flexible class schedule.

Academic Programs

UMaine provides a comprehensive academic and student experience, yielding graduates who are well-educated, well-adjusted, and well-prepared to assume leadership roles in society. The university seeks to foster excellence and innovation through inspired, dedicated teaching and the discovery of new knowledge.

Students at the University of Maine benefit from a solid liberal arts foundation. They develop and refine the qualities they need to more fully engage with the world around them—critical thinking, curiosity, a sense of discovery, and a broader perspective—no matter what discipline they choose.

UMaine's Honors College provides an in-depth, academically challenging curriculum for qualified students in any major.

Undergraduate research is a priority and a point of pride. UMaine is the state's largest research university and graduate degree-granting institution, providing rich and varied opportunities for undergraduates to participate in research. Students publish, travel, and work alongside UMaine's world-class scholars and scientists. The Center for Undergraduate Research was established in 2008 to connect students with faculty projects that suit their interests. For many, research provides an opportunity for a mentor-mentee relationship different from—and often richer than—that of teacher-student. Skills developed through research and scholarship make students more competitive in the workplace and in graduate school.

Off-Campus Programs

When UMaine students travel, they don't just go to Boston for the weekend. They go global, through study abroad, international volunteerism, and the worldwide research opportunities available to undergraduates. In recent semesters, UMaine students have traveled to China to learn more about the country's emerging financial markets, to Italy to explore Renaissance art history at the source, to Turkey to study film, and to Brazil to learn about a sensitive and diverse ecosystem from one of the world's leading conservation biologists (who also happens to be a UMaine professor and alumnus).

Academic Facilities

UMaine is home to state-of-the-art research facilities, classrooms, and teaching laboratories. Among the highlights are the Climate Change Institute, which has been featured on *60 Minutes*; the Laboratory for Surface Science and Technology, which is a hub for cutting-edge sensor and nanotechnology research; and the Advanced Structures & Composites Center, which is leading the nation in deepwater offshore wind energy development.

Fogler Library, the state's largest library, houses approximately 1 million volumes, subscribes to over 4,000 periodicals and serial titles, and serves as a depository for over 2.2 million government documents. In addition, Fogler provides 24-hour access to countless online documents.

The University of Maine is also a cultural hub, home to the region's premier performing arts center, the Collins Center for the Arts, as well as several museums and galleries.

Costs

The University of Maine System Board of Trustees adjusts costs annually. For the 2012–13 academic year, tuition is estimated at $279 per credit hour for undergraduate state residents and $841 per credit hour for nonresident students. The average credit load for full-time students is 15 credit hours per semester or 30 credit hours for the academic year. Canadian and nonresident students who qualify for the New England Regional Program will pay an estimated $419 per credit hour. Required university fees (about $2200 per year for a full-time student) include the Unified Fee, which provides a variety of health-care services and admission to cultural, recreational, and athletic events. Books and supplies average about $1000 for the academic year. Room and board charges for the academic year are about $9148. These costs are subject to change.

Financial Aid

UMaine requires all financial aid applicants to file the Free Application for Federal Student Aid (FAFSA) and encourages students to file online. The priority deadline to apply for aid is March 1. Awards usually consist of a combination of several types of aid, ranging from grants and scholarships to work-study jobs and student loans. In addition, students who apply through the early action admissions program (complete application submitted by December 15) will be considered for UMaine merit awards based on high school achievement as demonstrated by high school rank, grade point average, and standardized test results (SAT and ACT).

Faculty

There's a common misconception that if students choose a university rather than a small college, they'll get lost in the shuffle. They'll never see a professor—only teaching assistants—until they're in grad school. But at the University of Maine, the majority of undergraduate classes are taught by professors and many of those faculty members go on to become friends and mentors to their students. UMaine's professors are known for having an open-door policy. Students have opportunities to work alongside some of the most renowned scholars and scientists in the world, whether they're talking civil engineering over dinner at Pat's Pizza or traversing an Antarctic ice sheet with researchers from UMaine's Climate Change Institute.

Student Government

Student Government, Inc., is the independent, representative body for UMaine's undergraduate students. An elected president, vice president, and vice president of financial affairs direct and coordinate Student Government programs at the University of Maine. Student Government works closely with the Office of the Vice President for Student Affairs and appoints 200 student representatives to various university committees involved with the planning and implementation of residence hall programs, student discipline, athletics, and cultural activities on campus.

Admission Requirements

Admission to the University of Maine is a selective process. Successful applicants are those whose scholastic achievement, intellectual curiosity, and established study habits promise success in a comprehensive university environment. Strength of the high school curriculum, grades received, class rank, counselor recommendation, and either SAT or ACT scores are the primary criteria for admission. Essays and information regarding school and community activities provide additional information that may help the admissions committee evaluate potential for success.

UMaine recognizes advanced work completed in secondary schools by means of Advanced Placement tests. In addition, students who demonstrate advanced knowledge may be exempted from certain courses and requirements if they pass examinations specially developed by the university's academic departments.

Application and Information

Applicants may submit either electronic or paper versions of the Common Application or the University of Maine System application. UMaine requires a supplement for the Common Application. Additional required documents for all applicants include official high school transcripts and counselor recommendations. Traditional-age applicants are required to submit scores from either the SAT or ACT.

The University of Maine has an early action deadline of December 15. Students whose complete applications are postmarked by December 15 are reviewed by the end of January. Early action candidates are given first consideration for the Honors College and merit scholarships awarded by the Admissions Office.

Regular decision applicants are encouraged to submit their applications and all supporting documents by February 1 and are notified by rolling admission.

Students applying for the spring semester are encouraged to submit applications by December 1. Applications after these dates are processed on a space-available basis. Applications and all supporting documents should be sent to UMS Processing, P.O. Box 412, Bangor, Maine 04402-0412.

Office of Admissions
5713 Chadbourne Hall
University of Maine
Orono, Maine 04469-5713
Phone: 207-581-1561
          877-486-2364 (toll-free)
Fax: 207-581-1213
E-mail: um-admit@maine.edu
Web site: http://www.go.umaine.edu
          http://www.facebook.com/UMaineAdmissions
          http://twitter.com/GoUMaine

The Mall is the heart of the University of Maine campus.

UNIVERSITY OF MAINE AT MACHIAS
MACHIAS, MAINE

The University

Located on the spectacular Bold Coast of Maine, the University of Maine at Machias (UMM) is New England's only public environmental liberal arts college. The college was incorporated in 1909 and is a member of the University of Maine system. Small classes (the average is 17 students) and a faculty-student ratio of 1:13 contribute to an academic atmosphere that is intimate and intense and where independent thinking is encouraged.

Although many UMM students are from the state of Maine, the University's environmental emphasis, distinctive programs, and location attract many others from the New England, mid-Atlantic, and Midwest regions of the country.

Location

Machias, Maine, is a classic small New England town located on the tidal Machias River, with a town center that includes a number of retail stores, restaurants (including fast food), a supermarket, a natural foods store, and churches of various denominations. The greater Machias–area population is 5,000. The region is a popular outdoor recreation destination, with ocean beaches, inland lakes and streams, and miles of mountains, forests, and trails.

Downeast Maine has been a source of inspiration for generations of artists, outdoorsmen, mariners, and environmentalists. UMM's coastal location provides a unique learning environment, with excellent opportunities for fieldwork, hands-on learning, and cooperative education and internship experiences.

Majors and Degrees

The University of Maine at Machias awards Bachelor of Arts and Bachelor of Science degrees in biology (concentrations in fisheries biology, wildlife biology, and preprofessional preparation in dentistry, medicine, optometry, pharmacy, and veterinary medicine); business and entrepreneurial studies (concentrations in accounting, business sustainability, management, and sport and fitness management); college studies; elementary teacher education (concentrations in coaching, early childhood, history/social studies, humanities, outdoor environmental education, science/mathematics, special education, and teacher certification); English and book arts (concentrations in book arts, creative writing, and literary studies); environmental recreation and tourism management (concentrations in leisure programming, recreation and natural resources, and sport and fitness management); environmental studies; interdisciplinary fine arts (concentrations in book arts, creative writing, music, and visual arts); interdisciplinary studies; marine biology; psychology and community studies (disabilities in youth concentration); and secondary teacher education (concentrations in art, English, life science,

mathematics, physical science, social studies, and teacher certification).

Academic Programs

Bachelor's degree candidates must complete at least 120 credit hours with a minimum cumulative grade point average of 2.0 and must also complete the core requirements in business studies, fine arts, humanities, physical education, science/ mathematics, and social sciences.

Academic Facilities

All of the University's academic buildings are of modern construction and include a well-equipped science building with laboratories, a greenhouse, marine science aquariums, and a marine teaching and research laboratory. A Geographic Information Systems Laboratory and Service Center is located in Torrey Hall. Computer labs, some of which are open 24 hours a day, seven days a week for student use, house the latest in technology hardware and software. Located off-campus, UMM has an ongoing partnership with the Downeast Institute for Applied Marine Research and Education, where students conduct shellfish and finfish research.

Merrill Library provides a 24-hour study center with computer workstations for students, houses a collection of more than 100,000 volumes, and is linked to other libraries and educational resources throughout the state. A computer center with cross-campus networking and multiple computer labs enhances all of UMM's programs and provides access to the Internet and the Web. Individual computer access is also available in every residence hall room. The University of Maine at Machias Student Support Center provides faculty, peer, and professional assistance as well as computer and audiovisual aids for all students. A residence facility with contemporary suites and single rooms was completed in 2003.

The Reynolds Athletic Center includes a large gymnasium, an aquatics center with a competition-size pool, a state-of-the-art fitness center, racquetball/handball courts, and a recreational equipment center, in which students may check out canoes, kayaks, snowshoes, cross-country skis, bicycles, and camping equipment. The Flaherty Early Care and Education Center provides child-care facilities for the community and the University; it also provides an on-campus site for UMM elementary teacher education students to participate in field studies.

A wide variety of student activities, from meetings to coffeehouses and other social events, are accommodated in the Student Center. Located in the same building, the campus radio station, WUMM, is run entirely by students. The Performing Arts Center, a 358-seat amphitheater auditorium, is host to numerous campus and community meetings, seminars, festivals, and performing arts and theatrical presentations.

Costs

The basic expenses for the 2011–12 academic year (based on a 15-credit-hour load per semester) were $6660 per year for in-state tuition and $18,480 per year for out-of-state tuition. The University of Maine at Machias participates in the New England Board of Higher Education Regional Student program, which allows reduced tuition ($9990 per year) for students from the other New England states who are enrolled in specific academic programs.

Financial Aid

The University of Maine at Machias administers scholarships, loans, grants, and work-study awards. The Acada Scholarship in the amount of $7500 is awarded to first-year out-of-state students who have a 3.60 GPA, or a score of 1100 on the SAT (critical reading and math parts combined) or a 23 composite score on the ACT. The Sunrise Scholarship in the amount of $6500 is awarded to first-year out-of-state students who have a 3.0 GPA, or a score of 950 on the SAT (critical reading and math parts combined) or a 20 composite score on the ACT. The Bold Coast Award, in the amount of $1000 for in-state students and $2500 for out-of-state students, is awarded to first-year students with 2.40 GPA, or a score of 880 on the SAT (critical reading and math parts combined) or an 18 composite score on the ACT. The Presidential Scholarship in the amount of $2000 is awarded to first-year in-state students who have a 3.0 GPA, or a score of 1000 on the SAT (critical reading and math parts combined), or a 22 composite score on the ACT. Out-of-state transfer students receive a $5500 Presidential Scholarship if they have a 2.75 GPA. In-state transfer students receive a $2000 Presidential Scholarship if they have a 2.75 GPA. Financial aid awards are made on the basis of need, and students must submit the Free Application for Federal Student Aid (FAFSA) to the College Scholarship Service. March 15 is the University's financial aid priority deadline.

Faculty

Nearly all University of Maine at Machias faculty members hold the highest degree in their professional field. The faculty-student ratio is 1:13. All faculty members work as advisers and mentors to students within their areas of academic expertise. Usually on a first-name basis, faculty members develop a close relationship with students during their years of study at UMM and beyond.

Student Government

The University of Maine at Machias is a member of the University of Maine Organization of Student Governments and operates its own Student Senate. Students are encouraged to become involved and participate.

Admission Requirements

Graduation from secondary school or a high school equivalency diploma is the basic requirement for admission. Applicants to the University should have followed a college-preparatory high school program with 4 years of English, 3 years of math, 3 lab sciences, 2 social sciences, a foreign language, and computer utilization. If a student is entering one of the business programs, consideration is given to business courses taken in high school. However, college-preparatory English, math, science, and social science courses are still necessary. Scores from the SAT or ACT are also required. Applicants should rank in the top half of their high school class and have an overall grade average of B or better.

The University of Maine at Machias does not discriminate on the basis of race, creed, color, sex, or national origin and is an Equal Opportunity/Affirmative Action Employer.

Application and Information

The University of Maine at Machias operates on a rolling admission system. Candidates should complete their applications as early as possible. Students may apply for early admission, through which they may be admitted directly into the University after completing three years of secondary school. Candidates for this program must have recommendations of support from their guidance counselor, principal, superintendent, and/or school board. Their high school grades should place them in the top 15 percent of their class. UMM accepts applications from transfer students. Transfer applicants should complete their applications by June 1 for the fall term or by December 1 for the spring term.

Application materials and additional information may be obtained by contacting:

Director of Admissions
University of Maine at Machias
116 O'Brien Avenue
Machias, Maine 04654
Phone: 207-255-1318
       888-468-6866 (toll-free)
Fax: 207-255-1363
E-mail: ummadmissions@maine.edu
Web site: http://www.machias.edu

Students at the University of Maine at Machias engaged in experiential learning on the coast of Maine.

UNIVERSITY OF MASSACHUSETTS BOSTON
BOSTON, MASSACHUSETTS

The University

Since 1964 the University of Massachusetts Boston (UMass Boston) has provided access to superior public education at a modest cost, in the state's capital city of Boston. With nearly 16,000 commuting students in its undergraduate, graduate, and continuing education programs, UMass Boston is the second-largest campus in the University of Massachusetts system, comprised of scholars who take pride in academic excellence, diversity, research, and service. The school's academic research and scholarship are tightly woven into the public and community service needs of Boston and modern metropolitan life.

UMass Boston's students represent an extraordinary range of economic, political, spiritual, and ethnic backgrounds, talents, and interests. Many come straight from high school. Others transfer from two- and four-year colleges. And while most come from within the Commonwealth of Massachusetts, many grew up in other states and countries.

UMass Boston has a vibrant student life. No matter what a student's social and intellectual interests, he or she can find engaging activities. From student government to student literary endeavors; from a champion chess team to working with inner-city youth; from academically affiliated clubs and athletic opportunities to a unique course-credit-based leadership-development program, students are sure to find just the right activity to complement their own classroom experiences.

The University's student body shares a strong motivation to succeed academically and to relate their classroom pursuits to career aspirations. The University Advising Center helps by providing comprehensive academic support, planning, and career advising services. A team of professional counselors provides personalized assistance for students to design their course of study, utilize tutorial and mentoring services, choose a major and career path, and develop interviewing, resume-writing, and job-search skills.

Location

From its beautifully landscaped peninsula on Boston Harbor, just south of downtown Boston, the University overlooks Dorchester Bay and the harbor islands. Its neighbors are the John F. Kennedy Presidential Library and the Massachusetts State Archives and Commonwealth Museum, and soon it will also share the site with the Edward M. Kennedy Center for the United States Senate.

With its entrance along a bayside promenade drive just half a mile off Interstate Route 93, the campus is easily accessed by both public transportation and automobile. The Office of Undergraduate Admissions provides a number of free parking spaces for visitors in the campus's North Parking Lot. A free shuttle bus runs every few minutes between the Massachusetts Bay Transit Authority's (MBTA) JFK/UMass Red Line "T" stop and the front door of the school's Campus Center. Student MBTA discount passes are available for frequent users.

Many students commute from home, while others utilize the Office of Student Housing for help finding a rental property and/or roommates. The University wants all its students to be at home at UMass Boston.

Boston itself, with its worldwide standing as a cultural center and well-earned reputation as America's favorite college town, offers UMass Boston students a wealth of resources for exploration and entertainment. Everything, from Fenway Park and TD Garden to Symphony Hall and the Museum of Fine Arts, is easily accessible from UMass Boston.

Majors and Degrees

Five undergraduate colleges award bachelor's degrees: the College of Liberal Arts and the College of Science and Mathematics (with thirty-eight majors, twenty-six minors and programs of study, and seven certificate programs between them), the College of Management (with two majors and seven concentrations), the College of Nursing and Health Sciences (with a B.S.N., an online RN-to-B.S.N., and an accelerated B.S.N. program, as well as the B.S. program in exercise and health sciences), and the College of Public and Community Service (with four majors and two certificate programs). In addition, the College of Education and Human Development offers a non-licensure bachelor's degree in early education and care in inclusive settings (EECIS), as well as a program of study for those interested in teacher licensure at the undergraduate level. Also offered are premed and prelaw programs, and programs for honors study, credit by examination, and advanced placement.

A joint arts or science bachelor's/master's degree program in business is available for high academic achievers, as is a bachelor's degree in liberal arts or science with a minor in management.

Academic Programs

The academic calendar runs from early September through the end of May. There is also an optional, month-long winter session in January, and summer school sessions are available beginning in May, June, and July. Matriculating students may choose to attend full- or part-time and may adjust their schedules from semester to semester. A minimum of 30 credits must be earned at UMass Boston as a residency requirement for graduation.

The College of Liberal Arts and the College of Science and Mathematics require 120 credits to graduate. The general education curriculum comprises three elements: the distribution requirement, the core curriculum requirement, and the writing requirement. In addition, the requirements of the major must be fulfilled. The colleges offer both an honors program and an individual major option.

In the College of Management, the 120-credit undergraduate program leads to a B.S. degree in management or information technology. By fulfilling the general education, management, and elective course work requirements, students build a liberal arts foundation and receive the theoretical, technical, and functional training needed to succeed in the business world. An honors program is also offered.

The College of Nursing and Health Science's B.S. program in nursing requires 123 credits for graduation, including general education courses and 63 credits of intensive study in the principles and practices of nursing. The exercise and health sciences B.S. program prepares students for the technical aspects of a professional discipline and gives them a solid foundation in the liberal arts. Students may also elect to enter the honors program in nursing.

The College of Public and Community Service (CPCS) offers a curriculum with strong emphasis on social justice. Students may draw upon a variety of supplemental learning options in pursuit of their degree, including classroom study, self-directed study, and project-based learning. The University's honors program is also open to CPCS students.

Off-Campus Programs

The National Student Exchange Program offers UMass Boston students the opportunity to study at one of more than seventy participating colleges and universities in forty states at a cost comparable to the cost of attending UMass Boston. The study-abroad program is available for students with a 3.0 GPA or better, who seek international travel and academic experiences, and it offers summer and winter session programs in other countries as well. UMass Boston also participates in the New England Regional Student Program and the Boston Five-College Exchange Program.

Cooperative education and internship programs place students in work assignments related directly to their fields of study so that they may apply what they learn in the classroom to practical work settings. Under the co-op program, students are placed in full-time, paid positions for six-month work periods. Under the internship program, students are placed on a part-time basis, usually 15 to 20 hours per week, during a semester or over the summer months. Some are paid internships; others are volunteer opportunities. Both co-op and internship placements combine relevant practical learning, valuable work experience, career awareness, resume

enhancement, personal and professional growth, and, in many instances, opportunities for academic credit, good pay, and a permanent job after graduation.

Academic Facilities

The Joseph P. Healey Library holds a collection of more than 600,000 volumes, 85,000 electronic and print journals and newspapers, 60,000 electronic books, 100 databases, and 5,000 academic videos, DVDs, and films related to the campus's academic studies. The library's electronic resources are available on and off campus, 24/7 using a library barcode. UMass Boston is an active member of the Boston Library Consortium, and is also a partner in nationwide resource-sharing networks of scholarly and study resources. These offer access to a total of nearly 30 million volumes, via point-and-click. Students may obtain a library consortium card to check out books from any of the consortia libraries.

The Information Technology Services Division (ITSD) provides seven-day-a-week access to general-use computer labs, including the Adaptive Computing Lab, Graduate Research Center, media and language labs, and a media viewing center, all located within the Healey Library Information Commons, which also houses the IT Service Desk (ITSD). The campus has many technology-enhanced classrooms and auditoria equipped with state-of-the-art audiovisual equipment and network connections. ITSD provides wireless access in most public spaces, ensuring that a wide variety of information technology and data communications resources is available to students. The Kennedy Presidential Library is linked to the University by a variety of educational programs, enabling students to conduct research utilizing the extensive resources of the library's archives. Next door, the Archives of the Commonwealth of Massachusetts are also a rich informational depository, covering more than 5½ centuries of Massachusetts history. The new Edward M. Kennedy Institute for the United States Senate, scheduled to open in 2013, will provide further academic research opportunities.

The state-of-the-art Campus Center provides easy access to student services, dining services, and spectacular meeting spaces, along with computer terminals and wireless Internet access.

An integrated science complex, slated to open in 2013, is under construction. It is designed to provide enhanced academic opportunities for scientific study, research, and development for UMass Boston students and faculty.

Costs

Tuition and fees for the spring 2012 semester were $5714 for Massachusetts residents studying full-time (12 or more credits) or $12,474 for out-of-state students. Students enrolling part-time were charged tuition according to the number of credits taken, with Massachusetts residents paying tuition at $71.50 per credit and out-of-state residents paying $406.50 per credit. Annual mandatory fees for in-state residents ranged up to $9856 and up to $15,330 for out-of-state students.

Financial Aid

Financial aid is based on need and/or merit. Applicants must complete the Free Application for Federal Student Aid (FAFSA), keeping in mind a priority deadline of March 1 for fall semester and November 1 for spring semester. Need-based aid is awarded to students who demonstrate financial need, as determined by federal methodology. Aid consists of grants, waivers, and merit scholarships as well as self-help in the form of loans and work-study employment. An on-time applicant is automatically considered for all financial aid programs administered by the University's Office of Financial Aid Services.

Faculty

UMass Boston is proud of its 1,083 distinguished faculty members, some 93 percent of whom have terminal degrees in their field. UMass Boston has a student-faculty ratio of about 16:1 and a small class size that averages but 26 students. The faculty's top priority is teaching and advising students, although they also conduct research, publish materials, and participate in grant activities and professional organizations. Faculty members maintain office hours for students and make themselves accessible as mentors. Faculty and academic issues are governed by the Faculty Council.

Student Government

The undergraduate Student Senate consists of elected members from the undergraduate colleges and programs, and it participates fully in matters related to the quality of student life and the allocation of the student activities trust fund. Students are represented on numerous University- and college-based committees and councils that initiate major policy and procedural recommendations, forwarding those recommendations to governance bodies and the administration for enactment.

Admission Requirements

A freshman candidate for admission to the University should have earned a minimum of 16 academic units in high school that include 4 years of English, 3 years of mathematics, 3 years of science (including 2 with laboratory requirements), 2 years of social science (including 1 of U.S. history), 2 years of a single foreign language, and 2 years of electives in the arts or computer science (excluding vocational training). The student must also present satisfactory scores on either the SAT or ACT. The University looks for students with a strong academic background, as determined by a recalculated grade point average, and each candidate's academic program choices, motivation, achievement, and annual progress are closely scrutinized.

UMass Boston encourages qualified international students to apply for admission. Submission of a separate Declaration of Finances (DCF) form is required, along with supporting documents. Test of English as a Foreign Language (TOEFL) scores are required of all students educated in a non-English language educational system.

Transfer students are considered based on a review of all college academic credentials. Several academic majors and programs have specific higher requirements for transfer students, but, in general, a minimum 2.5 GPA is required.

Participation in a campus tour and group information session with an admissions counselor is strongly encouraged.

Application and Information

For information about the application process, deadlines, and informational materials, students should contact

Enrollment Information Services
University of Massachusetts Boston
100 Morrissey Boulevard
Boston, Massachusetts 02125-3393
Phone: 617-287-6000
      617-287-6010 (TTY/TDD)
Fax: 617-287-5999
E-mail: enrollment.info@umb.edu
Web site: http://www.umb.edu
    http://on.fb.me/UMassBoston (Facebook)
    http://twitter.com/umassboston (Twitter)

UMass Boston is situated on a scenic peninsula just south of downtown Boston.

UNIVERSITY OF MASSACHUSETTS DARTMOUTH

NORTH DARTMOUTH, MASSACHUSETTS

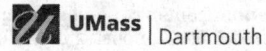

The University

The University of Massachusetts Dartmouth traces its roots to 1895 when the Massachusetts legislature chartered the New Bedford Textile School and the Bradford Durfee Textile School in Fall River. As the region's economic base shifted from textiles to more diverse manufacturing and service industries, the program of the colleges changed. Courses were developed to respond to the needs of new generations of students, stimulated by the clear economic and social advantages of a well-educated citizenry. In 1962, Southeastern Massachusetts Technological Institute (SMTI) was created, and in 1969, out of a need and a clear demand for a comprehensive public university, SMTI became Southeastern Massachusetts University. Then, in 1988, the Swain School of Design merged with the University's College of Visual and Performing Arts.

In 1991, a new University of Massachusetts system was created, which combined the Amherst and Boston campuses with the University of Lowell, Southeastern Massachusetts University, and the Medical Center in Worcester. Today, UMass Dartmouth provides educational programs, research, extension, and continuing education and cybereducation in the liberal and creative arts and sciences and in the professions. A broad range of bachelor's, master's, and doctoral degrees is offered. Graduate programs lead to the Master of Arts, Master of Business Administration, Master of Arts in Teaching, Master of Fine Arts, Master of Art Education, and Master of Science. A Ph.D. is offered in electrical engineering, chemical engineering, biomedical engineering, marine science, and physics.

UMass Dartmouth enrolls approximately 9,500 students; 90 percent are from Massachusetts, with a growing number from other states and countries outside the United States. A residential campus with a variety of student organizations, athletic programs, cultural opportunities, and interest groups, the University fosters personal development, diversity, and responsible citizenship.

Location

Located in historic and scenic southeastern Massachusetts, which includes the nearby cities of Fall River and New Bedford and the Cape Cod region to the east, the campus is situated on 710 acres. The dramatic campus is the work of architect Paul Rudolph, former dean of the Yale University School of Art and Architecture. Metropolitan areas, with libraries, museums, theaters, and numerous educational institutions, are within an hour's drive: Boston to the north and Providence, Rhode Island, to the west. Recreational sites are minutes away and include beaches, hiking, and cultural and nightlife opportunities. New York City is 4 hours by car; the mountains of New Hampshire and Vermont are 3 to 4 hours away. Students can walk to homes and shops in the immediate area of the campus, while public transportation is available to nearby communities.

Majors and Degrees

There are five colleges within the University: College of Arts and Sciences (nineteen majors); Charlton College of Business (seven majors); Engineering (eight majors); Nursing (one major); and Visual and Performing Arts (twelve majors). In addition, honors programs, interdisciplinary studies, prelaw, premedical advising, and a number of different minors and options are available within various departments. The University offers Bachelor of Arts, Bachelor of Fine Arts, Bachelor of Science, and Bachelor of Science in Nursing degrees at the undergraduate level. A complete list of majors is available online at www.umassd.edu/undergraduate/fieldsofstudy.

Academic Programs

The University operates on a two-semester calendar, with the fall semester beginning the first week of September and concluding in mid-December and the spring semester beginning in late January and concluding in late May. A three-week intersession is offered between semesters. Summer-term courses are offered in June, July, and early August. Undergraduate students usually enroll in four or five courses each semester, and a typical course earns 3 credits. An undergraduate degree requires a minimum of 120 credits (there are a few majors that require 135 credits); a student can complete degree requirements for a specified major within a department or an approved interdepartmental major (30 credits). Students must also complete requirements according to the degree being sought.

Other learning opportunities include independent study, contract learning, and directed study; study abroad; study at a nearby university through cross-registration; and credit by examination. UMass Dartmouth is a member of SACHEM (Southeastern Association for Cooperation in Higher Education in Massachusetts), allowing for cross-registration at Bridgewater State University, Bristol Community College, Cape Cod Community College, Dean College, Massachusetts Maritime Academy, Massasoit Community College, Stonehill College, and Wheaton College. Students can take advantage of exchange agreements with partner institutions in a number of countries including Australia, Belgium, China, Egypt, England, France, Germany, Ireland, Italy, Portugal, and Spain. Students may also take initiative in finding other programs in addition to the exchange-agreement institutions.

The College of Engineering provides students in any of the engineering fields an opportunity to gain work experience through cooperative education or internships.

Academic Facilities

Students will benefit from a campuswide $175-million building and renovation program to upgrade and improve academic facilities, including a $45-million renovation to the library, which will create a state-of-the-art, LEED-certified space to serve as both the intellectual and social heart of campus. Access to technology is an integral part of the curriculum. All academic buildings, including student residences, are connected to a campuswide network through both intranet and a WiMAX wireless network. UMass Dartmouth is only the second campus in the country to implement a WiMAX system. Computing clusters, located in the library and in most classroom buildings, support the classwork of students. Multiple computer labs (Apple and PC) are readily available throughout campus. The University library supports all programs of instruction and research with 460,000 volumes, 46,000 e-journals, and 2,800 periodicals. A large interlibrary loan network and delivery system makes millions of volumes available to the students.

Each of the five colleges within the University is housed in academic facilities designed for its purposes with classrooms, laboratories, study spaces, galleries, faculty offices, and lounges.

Costs

In-state tuition and fees for 2011–12 were $11,135; non-Massachusetts resident tuition and fees were $21,951. Room and board expenses were $10,178 (based on a nineteen-meal plan and a double room for a year). Books and supplies cost approximately $1200 a year depending on a student's courses. Specific fees may be assessed, depending on a student's course of study.

Financial Aid

Nearly all students are eligible for some type of financial aid. UMass Dartmouth awards financial aid based on federal, state, and institutional guidelines; students must submit the Free Application for Federal Student Aid (FAFSA). In determining need, the Financial Aid Services Office considers the total costs of attending the University (tuition, fees, books, room and board, the cost of commuting, and an allowance for living and personal expenses). The difference between total University cost and the estimate of expected family contribution is the amount that the financial aid staff considers to be financial need. Typically, UMass Dartmouth financial aid awards at least 90 percent of a student's demonstrated need. Students are encouraged to submit their FAFSA by March 1 for priority consideration in the awarding process. More information about UMass Dartmouth financial aid and scholarships is available online at www.umassd.edu/financialaid.

Faculty

The faculty, numbering 375 full-time members, is distributed over twenty-nine departments in the five colleges. Ninety-six percent of the faculty members hold the terminal degree in their chosen discipline (e.g., business, fine arts, education). A student-faculty ratio of 18:1 ensures that classes are reasonably sized, with an average class size of 25 students. Faculty members are actively engaged in advising students, providing guidance throughout a student's academic career.

Student Government

The Student Senate is the governing body offering a forum for debate on matters of importance to the student body. The Student Judiciary, a system of courts or judicial agencies, provides students and organizations with the protection of due process in all disciplinary matters. A student is also elected to the University of Massachusetts Board of Trustees. Students serve on the Board of Governors, policy makers for the Campus Center; the Resident Hall Congress; and the Student Activities Board. Students are active, voting participants on policymaking committees that regulate both academic and social aspects of the University.

Admission Requirements

Admission is selective. Applicants are evaluated both by the general standards of the University and by the special standards of the academic areas that they request. In addition, the Board of Higher Education sets guidelines governing admission standards for the University. Admission to some colleges or majors may be limited by spaces available. Students are admitted on a rolling basis with no set deadline. Qualified candidates are accepted until the capacity has been reached in the program of choice. Each applicant's record is assessed on the basis of the depth and rigor of the secondary school program, rank in class and grade point average, SAT or ACT results, college-level records for transfer applicants, and other appropriate measures.

The University realizes its commitment to equal access through standard, as well as alternative, admission programs. For College Now, the alternative program, applicants must meet at least one of three eligibility criteria: low-income status, limited English background, or first generation in the family to attend college.

All applicants for freshman admission to the University are required to submit an application form with the appropriate fee ($40 in state and $60 out of state/international), a transcript of the secondary school record, SAT or ACT results, and any other information that candidates consider important for the admissions committee to review. Transfer students, who compose approximately one quarter of the new student population every year, are required to submit records for all college-level work completed in addition to the application form. The admission process is virtually the same for transfer candidates, with primary emphasis on the student's previous college/university record. UMass Dartmouth participates in the Mass Transfer program for students from Massachusetts who are transferring from a public two-year institution, as well as several joint admission partnerships with regional two-year colleges. More information can be found online at www.umassd.edu/transferexperience.

Application and Information

Students are invited to visit the University for a campus tour and an information session with an admissions officer. Some majors, such as nursing, may close early due to enrollment capacity. Nursing applicants are encouraged to apply by February 1 for priority consideration. UMass Dartmouth practices rolling admission and decisions are made within three weeks of the completion of an application. Application forms and related information is available at www.umassd.edu/apply.

For more information, contact:

Office of Admissions
UMass Dartmouth
285 Old Westport Road
North Dartmouth, Massachusetts 02747-2300
Phone: 508-999-8605
Fax: 508-999-8755
E-mail: admissions@umassd.edu
Web site: www.umassd.edu/admissions/

UMass Dartmouth: World Class. Within Reach.

UNIVERSITY OF MASSACHUSETTS LOWELL

LOWELL, MASSACHUSETTS

The University

The University of Massachusetts (UMass) Lowell is a midsized, comprehensive research university that places a premium on high-caliber academics and student success. Throughout its 100-year history, the University has provided innovative programs that meet both the needs of its students for an education and the needs of the region for skilled leadership. Its graduates are ready to contribute meaningfully in the work place, to build lives around the principles and passions they develop at UMass, and to make a difference in communities anywhere in the world.

The University is part of the five-campus University of Massachusetts system and comprises six colleges: the College of Fine Arts, Humanities and Social Sciences; the College of Sciences; the Francis College of Engineering; the School of Health and Environment; the Manning School of Business; and the Graduate School of Education. Together, the colleges offer more than 120 programs to UMass Lowell's 8,600 undergraduate students. The Graduate School enrolls nearly 3,500 students in thirty-two master's degree and fifteen doctoral programs. The UMass Lowell education focuses on putting the lessons of the classroom into practice. Students have multiple opportunities for co-ops, internships, service-learning activities, and undergraduate research, all of which give them relevant hands-on experience in their fields. A real-world focus is reflected in the interdisciplinary nature of many academic initiatives. These include grant-funded projects such as Artbotics and Sound Thinking, which combine the arts and computer science, and interdisciplinary minors such as energy engineering; Asian studies; and technology, society, and human values.

UMass Lowell offers dozens of programs that allow students to stay as little as one extra year to earn both a bachelor's and a master's degree, giving them a competitive advantage as they enter the workplace. The undergraduate experience is enhanced by the diverse and international campus community and extensive opportunities for studying abroad. The University has developed partnerships with prestigious institutions in numerous countries that reflect the diversity its own community and contemporary geopolitics. UMass Lowell offers a robust honors program for those students who want to achieve at the highest level as well as programs and resources designed to help students succeed. Academic and residential learning communities help first-year students make the transition to college by fostering connections among small groups with similar academic interests. The Centers for Learning offers a range of tutoring and other support programs and the Center for Career Services and Cooperative Education helps students transition to the working world. The University maintains a student-faculty ratio of 14:1.

The University community is ethnically, culturally, and economically diverse. More than half of all students, and the majority of incoming freshmen, choose to live in University housing, which ranges from traditional residence halls to apartments and even a former hotel. Students are active in a wide variety of community service activities and in more than 120 campus organizations that range from academic and athletic to recreational and special interest groups. Examples include a marching band, a weekly student newspaper, an FM radio station, and the Off-Broadway Players. A vibrant campus life includes rallying for the nationally ranked Division I River Hawks men's ice hockey team and taking part in an active recreational sports program. Sixteen additional varsity teams for men and women compete in Division II.

Location

The University is located in Lowell, a city of 110,000 that has gained national attention by successfully leveraging its history, ethnic diversity, and entrepreneurial spirit to create a vital urban center. The site of a unique, urban National Historical Park that honors the city as the birthplace of the industrial revolution, Lowell is also home to an acclaimed professional theater company, literary and folk festivals, and museums that include the Museum of American Textile History and the Whistler House Museum. Located 25 miles from the cultural and educational riches of Boston and Cambridge, Lowell is situated within the region's major business corridors, which provide intership and co-op opportunities for students. It is also within an hour of ocean beaches and the lakes and mountains of New Hampshire via major highways and regional train and bus service.

Majors and Degrees

Dual majors are permitted. Dual B.A./B.S. and an array of bachelor's-to-master's degree programs are available in liberal arts, science, and engineering fields. Pre-dental and premedical programs are also available.

The College of Fine Arts, Humanities and Social Sciences offers baccalaureate programs in American studies, art, criminal justice, design, economics, English, environmental studies, history, liberal arts, modern languages, music business, music performance, music studies, peace and conflict studies, philosophy, political science, psychology, sociology, and sound recording technology.

The College of Sciences offers baccalaureate programs in biological sciences; chemistry with an option in forensics science; computer science; environmental, earth, and atmospheric sciences (meteorology); mathematics; and physics.

The James B. Francis College of Engineering offers baccalaureate day programs in chemical, civil and environmental, electrical and computer, mechanical, and plastics engineering. Engineering programs are accredited by the Accreditation Board for Engineering and Technology, Inc. (ABET).

The School of Health and Environment offers baccalaureate day programs in clinical sciences, which is accredited by the National Accrediting Agency for Clinical Laboratory Sciences (NAACLS); community health education; environmental health; exercise physiology; medical technology; nursing, which is accredited by the National League for Nursing Accrediting Commission (NLNAC); and nutritional science.

The Manning School of Business offers baccalaureate day programs, all of which are accredited by AACSB International—The Association to Advance Collegiate Schools of Business—in business administration (B.S.B.A.), with concentrations in accounting, entrepreneurship, finance, international business, management, management information systems, marketing, and supply chain and operations management.

The University's Graduate School of Education offers widely respected master's and doctoral programs, as well as a range of initial certification courses.

The University's Division of Continuing Studies and Corporate Education offers evening programs through all six colleges. Through the College of Fine Arts, Humanities and Social Sciences and the College of Sciences, baccalaureate programs in applied mathematics, criminal justice, information technology, and liberal arts are offered. Through the College of Engineering, associate and baccalaureate degrees are offered in civil engineering technology, electronic engineering technology, and mechanical engineering technology. Through the Manning School of Business, an associate degree program in accounting and a baccalaureate degree program in business administration are available. Certificate programs are offered in accounting, computer-assisted manufacturing, computer engineering technology, data/telecommunications, electro-optics, environmental technology, graphic design and digital imagery, hazardous-waste management, Internet technology, land surveying, manufacturing technology, multimedia applications, nutrition, paralegal studies, plastics engineering technology, quality assurance, Spanish, technical writing, UNIX, wastewater treatment, water treatment, and Web site design and development.

Academic Programs

The University operates on a calendar of two semesters, a three-week intersession in January, and a summer term with two sessions.

Full-time undergraduates generally take five courses each semester. A minimum of 120 credits is required for baccalaureate degrees; the minimum credits required for professional degree programs are generally higher. A University general education requirement is imposed for all baccalaureate programs. Majors require 30–60 credits. Elective course options vary widely according to the degree program and major area. Professional degree program options and requirements follow specific accreditation guidelines. Maximum curricular freedom is permitted in B.A. programs. The academic climate is serious and competitive and requires self-motivation.

Academic Facilities

The University campus comprises 100 acres on both sides of the Merrimack River and includes classroom and laboratory buildings, two libraries, a student center, two gymnasiums, three dining halls, a Center for the Performing Arts, two art galleries, and numerous residence halls. The Campus Recreation Center provides additional spaces for recreation and fitness instruction. Recent renovations to both libraries have created new learning commons equipped with learning technologies and areas for quiet and group study. State-of-the-art facilities include six sound recording technology studios, a nursing simulation lab, and a manufacturing lab where engineering and management students team up to produce microelectronic components. The ETIC, a $70-million research facility with labs, clean rooms, and high bays for nanomanufacturing is scheduled to open in the fall of 2012. A new building for programs in health and the humanities is under construction.

Costs

The annual costs for 2011–12 for full-time undergraduate residents of Massachusetts were $11,297 per year; for nonresidents of Massachusetts, they were $23,736 per year. Room and board charges were $9520 per year. Accident insurance is covered by fees; major medical insurance is optional. Books and supplies are estimated at $400 to $600, depending on the program. Quoted rates are subject to change.

Financial Aid

The University is committed to making higher education accessible to all qualified students. The University participates in federal and state programs, assisting students through grants-in-aid, loans, employment opportunities, and scholarships. The amount of a financial aid award is determined by need, as indicated by the Free Application for Federal Student Aid (FAFSA), which should be filed by March 1. The University awards a growing number of merit-based scholarships. In fiscal 2011, the campus awarded $119 million in financial aid and met approximately 90 percent of need.

Faculty

Faculty members are respected researchers who value their commitment to teaching and extend the learning experience beyond the classroom. The full-time resident faculty members number approximately 500. The part-time day faculty members number approximately 150. In addition, approximately 175 part-time faculty members are employed in continuing education programs. Most faculty members teach and conduct research in their disciplines. Graduate teaching assistants also hold part-time instructional positions, particularly as discussion section leaders and laboratory teaching assistants.

Student Government

The Student Government Association and the Residence Hall Association provide opportunities in student government at the all-campus level. Leadership opportunities are provided in residence halls and student organizations. Students also participate in the disciplinary system and in most University committees.

Admission Requirements

All undergraduate day applicants must have a high school diploma or a general equivalency diploma and satisfactory SAT scores. The incoming freshman class for fall 2011 had an average GPA of 3.26 and the average SAT score (combined reading and math) was 1114. Students whose high school average is below the required minimum may be considered for admission if they present SAT verbal and mathematics scores that are higher than those specified for the admission of degree candidates by the college or program to which they wish to apply.

Transfer students are considered for fall- or spring-semester admissions. Transcripts of completed work must be on file prior to acceptance. Depending on the number of transfer credits and college GPA, transfer students who seek admission as matriculating day students may be asked to provide a high school record and SAT scores.

Application and Information

For day programs, the University admits students through early action, regular admission, and transfer admission. Entering freshmen are admitted for the fall or spring semester. The early action deadline for freshman applications is December 1; the preferred deadline for regular admission is February 15. Applicants to the nursing program are encouraged to apply by the early action deadline. The preferred deadline for transfer applications is August 15 for the fall semester and January 7 for the spring semester.

For application forms and further information, students should contact:

Office of Undergraduate Admissions
University of Massachusetts Lowell
883 Broadway Street
Suite 110
Lowell, Massachusetts 01854-5104
Phone: 978-934-3931
Web site: http://www.uml.edu
 http://www.facebook.com/umlowell
 http://www.twitter.com/umasslowell
 http://www.youtube.com/user/umasslowell

UMass Lowell graduates are ready for work, life, and all that the world has to offer.

The University of Massachusetts Lowell is an Equal Opportunity/Affirmative Action, Title IX employer.

UNIVERSITY OF MEMPHIS
MEMPHIS, TENNESSEE

The University

Located on a beautifully landscaped campus in the heart of one of the South's largest and most progressive cities, the University of Memphis (U of M) is the flagship institution of the Tennessee Board of Regents System. Since its beginning in 1912, the University has matured into a major public, metropolitan university recognized regionally and nationally for its academic, research, and athletic programs. The U of M offers more than 254 areas of study from which to choose.

The University campus comprises 1,160 acres at eight sites. In addition to the main campus, the Park Avenue campus contains spacious living accommodations for married students, a research park, and outstanding varsity athletic training facilities. U of M also owns the Meeman Biological Field Station, a 623-acre tract used for biological and ecological studies.

The University of Memphis is an Equal Opportunity/Affirmative Action institution committed to the education of a diverse student body. It has a total enrollment of 22,725 students, including 17,966 undergraduates from almost every state and many other countries. Approximately 54 percent of University of Memphis students are between the ages of 18 and 22, and members of minority groups account for 35 percent of the enrollment.

Location

The greater Memphis area has a population of approximately 1.1 million, which makes the city the eighteenth largest in the country. Centrally located on the Mississippi River, Memphis is an active hub for business, agriculture, and the transportation industry. The city has the Mid-South's largest medical center and offers many cultural and entertainment opportunities. Major museum exhibits, sporting events, concerts, art shows, lectures, and even barbecue contests take place throughout the year. The AAA baseball team, the Redbirds, and the NBA team, the Grizzlies, both make their homes in Memphis. With its many businesses, industries, and schools, Memphis provides students with employment opportunities in a variety of fields during and after their college careers.

Majors and Degrees

The College of Arts and Sciences offers undergraduate majors organized into three concentration groups: the humanities, the natural and mathematical sciences, and the social sciences. Three degree programs are offered: the Bachelor of Arts, the Bachelor of Science, and the Bachelor of Science in Chemistry. Majors include African and African-American studies, anthropology, biology, chemistry, computer science, criminology and criminal justice, earth sciences, economics, English, foreign languages and literatures, history, international studies, mathematical sciences, philosophy, physics, political science, psychology, social work, and sociology. Minors are available in each of those areas, as well as interdisciplinary minors in aerospace studies, Asian studies, emergency management, environmental studies, Judaic studies, legal thought and liberal arts, military science, naval science, nonprofit management studies, public administration, religious studies, and women's studies.

The Fogelman College of Business and Economics offers programs of study leading to the Bachelor of Business Administration degree. Majors include accounting, business economics, finance, hospitality and resort management, international business, management, management information systems, marketing management, and supply chain management. The programs of the College of Business and Economics are fully accredited by AACSB International—The Association to Advance Collegiate Schools of Business.

The College of Communication and Fine Arts is made up of the Departments of Architecture, Art, Communication, Journalism, Theatre and Dance, and the Rudi E. Scheidt School of Music. Majors include architecture, art, art history, communication, interior design, journalism, music, music industry, and theater. The college offers three undergraduate degrees: the Bachelor of Arts, the Bachelor of Fine Arts, and the Bachelor of Music.

The College of Education, Health and Human Sciences (CEHHS) at the University of Memphis is among a select few institutions nationwide to meet, without a weakness, National Council for the Accreditation of Teacher Education standards. It is home to more nationally recognized educator programs than any other public university in Tennessee. In addition to teacher education, the college offers accredited degree programs in counseling, health and sport sciences, and leadership. CEHHS takes pride in being home to twenty-one research centers and/or institutes that are as diverse in their focus as the faculty and departments in the College, and in building partnerships with the dynamic communities that it serves.

The Herff College of Engineering offers undergraduate programs in biomedical, civil, computer, electrical, and mechanical engineering and engineering technology. High-ability students have the opportunity to work with faculty members on world-class research for global companies such as FedEx, for governmental organizations such as the U.S. Army Corps of Engineers, or for other premier organizations such as St. Jude Children's Research Hospital.

The University College offers two nontraditional degrees: the Bachelor of Liberal Studies and the Bachelor of Professional Studies, for students with experience, talents, and interests served through personally designed or multidisciplinary programs.

The University of Memphis also offers specialized degree programs. The Loewenberg School of Nursing offers a Bachelor of Science in Nursing degree. The program is accredited by the National League for Nursing Accrediting Commission and the Commission on Collegiate Education in Nursing. Students benefit from exceptional learning opportunities at healthcare agencies in the Memphis area, including ten major hospitals.

Preprofessional training is offered for students who intend to enter law school or a college of dentistry, medicine, nursing, optometry, pharmacy, physical therapy, or veterinary medicine. The University also offers Air Force, Army, and Navy ROTC programs.

The University of Memphis has joined forty-five Tennessee Board of Regents institutions in offering Regents Online Degree Programs. The U of M offers four degree programs: the Bachelor of Liberal Studies in interdisciplinary studies, the Bachelor of Professional Studies in information technology, the Bachelor of Professional Studies in organizational leadership, and the Bachelor of Professional Studies in international organizational leadership. These degree programs are entirely online and are transferable among the participating institutions.

Academic Programs

Freshmen who have not declared a major are advised through the Academic Counseling Center in preparation for formal enrollment in one of the degree-granting colleges. Those freshmen who have chosen a major are assigned to their degree-granting college immediately for academic advising. Each student initially selects courses from the General Education Program, which offers classes ensuring the acquisition of breadth as well as depth of knowledge in various fields. In addition to meeting the requirements of the General Education Program, all students must meet the requirements for their specific degree. The University-wide Helen Hardin Honors Program is available for academically talented students, and there is an active Emerging Leaders program.

The academic year begins in late August and is divided into two semesters and a summer session. The fall semester ends in mid-December, and the spring semester begins in mid-January. There are also courses offered during shorter sessions within the semesters.

Off-Campus Programs

Students at the University of Memphis have the opportunity to participate in study-abroad programs and the National Student Exchange program. These programs allow students to study in more than fifty other countries as well as in other locations within the continental United States. The University also offers credit and noncredit courses at various locations throughout west Tennessee.

Academic Facilities

The University Libraries of the University of Memphis comprises the Ned R. McWherter Library and three branch libraries: Communications Sciences, Mathematics, and Music. The University Libraries' collections include more than 1.2 million bound volumes, 9.7 million manuscripts, 3.56 million microfilms and fiches, 599,335 government documents, and 13,848 CDs. The library also serves the general public and maintains a strong user-instruction program. The learning commons extends throughout the McWherter Library, with a commons room on the first floor where the research and information services desk is located. The McWherter Library has wireless capabilities supporting the 168 public-use computers that give users access to all University-provided software applications. Laptop computers are available for loan to students. The University Libraries is the regional federal depository library for the State of Tennessee and receives all publications, maps, and electronic data distributed by the government printing office. The library's Preservation and Special Collections Department has holdings on the history and culture of the South, the lower Mississippi River valley, the Mid-South, Tennessee, the American Civil War, and African-American history, including the civil rights movement.

The Department of Theatre and Dance and the Rudi E. Scheidt School of Music, in their adjoining facilities, make an appreciable contribution to campus activities with live drama and concert series, films, and programming over WUMR, the student-staffed campus radio station. Included among the many research facilities at the University of Memphis are the Benjamin L. Hooks Institute for Social Change, the Integrated Microscopy Center, the FedEx Center for Supply Chain Management, the Institute for Artificial Intelligence, the Ground Water Institute, and the Barbara K. Lipman Early Childhood School and Research Institute.

The state of Tennessee has designated five Centers of Excellence at the University: the Center for Applied Psychological Research, the Center for Research Initiatives and Strategies for the Communicatively Impaired, the Center for Research in Educational Policy, the Institute of Egyptian Art and Archaeology, and the Center for Earthquake Research and Information.

Costs

In 2011–12, in-state students paid a maintenance fee of $256 per hour for part-time study until they reached 12 hours ($3072), when the maintenance fee was lowered to $51 per hour for additional hours over 12. Out-of-state students paid a maintenance fee of $869 per hour for part-time study until they reached 12 hours ($10,428), when the maintenance fee rate was reduced to $174 per hour for additional hours over 12. On-campus residence hall rates ranged from $2580 to $6580 for an academic year. All part-time students paid an additional program service fee of $80.50 per hour for part-time study until they reached six hours, when the program service fee was highest at $623.

Financial Aid

Financial assistance is provided through four basic sources: scholarships, grants, loans, and employment. Scholarships are offered through the Scholarship Office as well as through various academic, performance, and athletic departments. Residents of Tennessee may be eligible for the state's HOPE Scholarship. An application for admission is required to be considered for general and distinguished academic scholarship programs. Applicants for financial aid must submit the completed Free Application for Federal Student Aid (FAFSA) to the Financial Aid Office, which places the student under consideration for all financial aid programs. The priority deadline for filing the FAFSA is February 1. More than $200 million is awarded annually. The University operates two programs of student employment: the Federal Work-Study Program and a regular work program.

Faculty

The University of Memphis has 870 full-time faculty members. In addition, many adjunct professors are hired from the community to teach in their fields of expertise.

Student Government

The Student Government Association consists of officers, a senate, a cabinet, and a judiciary elected annually by the student body. Its goals are to present the opinions of the student body to the administration, to enact legislation beneficial to the students, and to promote a broad range of student activities.

Admission Requirements

The admission of entering freshmen is based on the transcript of a four-year course of study at an approved or accredited high school that includes prescribed units of English, mathematics, natural/physical sciences, U.S. history, social studies, foreign language, and visual/performing arts. The General Educational Development test and high school equivalency diploma are accepted when applicable. The admissions process is a competitive one and is based on a student's cumulative high school grade point average and ACT or SAT scores. The average ACT for the fall 2011 freshman class was 22, and the average GPA was 3.31. The admission of transfer students is based on the applicant's grade point average, academic standing at a former institution, and scores on the approved admission tests. Transfer students will often be required to provide a high school transcript.

Application and Information

Inquiries about admission and requests for information about any undergraduate college of the University should be addressed to the Office of Admissions. Applications and supporting credentials must be submitted to the Office of Admissions before the beginning of the intended term of entry. While the established application deadlines are July 1 for the fall semester, December 1 for the spring semester, and May 1 for the summer session, early application is strongly encouraged so applicants can be considered for scholarship opportunities and take advantage of early registration. A student must apply and be accepted by February 1 to be considered for academic merit scholarships. Additional scholarships may have earlier deadlines. Prospective students are encouraged to visit the University for a campus tour, which can be arranged by contacting the Office of Admissions.

For more information, contact:

Office of Admissions, Recruitment and Orientation Services
University of Memphis
101 John Wilder Tower
Memphis, Tennessee 38152-3520
Phone: 901-678-2169
      800-669-2678 (toll-free)
Web site: http://www.memphis.edu
      http://on.fb.me/UofMemphis (Facebook)
      http://www.twitter.com/uofmemphis

The beautiful University of Memphis campus.

UNIVERSITY OF NEVADA, LAS VEGAS

LAS VEGAS, NEVADA

The University

The University of Nevada, Las Vegas (UNLV), is recognized nationally as a comprehensive teaching and research university that provides students with an excellent education at a reasonable cost. UNLV has established an agenda for the next decade to become a premier metropolitan research university. All UNLV programs are accredited by the Northwest Association of Schools and Colleges. Individual programs have further accreditation from professional accrediting organizations.

Since its founding in 1957, UNLV has seen dramatic growth in both its academic programs and its facilities. There are 220 undergraduate, master's, and doctoral degree programs offered to more than 28,000 students. Of UNLV's students, 79 percent are undergraduates, 76 percent are Nevada residents, 31 percent are members of minority groups, and 4 percent are international students. The average class size is 30.

The University is located on a beautifully landscaped 350-acre campus. Classes are held in comfortable, well-equipped buildings that are showcases of modern architecture.

UNLV's residential life program provides students with a secure, convenient place to live on the University campus. The modern residence halls are organized into suites of two rooms joined by a bathroom. Four students share a suite, with 2 per room. UNLV's dining facilities are excellent, providing students with quality, quantity, and choice.

More than 300 groups offer students an active social life, including intramural sports, Greek organizations, ethnic and religious clubs, a student newspaper, and campus radio and television stations. UNLV's Division of Student Life provides an array of advising, tutorial, and counseling services. The Disability Resource Center provides textbooks on tape, interpreters for the deaf, lab assistants, and other services to students with disabilities.

Numerous concerts are performed throughout the year by UNLV's student music groups, choirs, dance companies, and ensembles. The Department of Theatre Arts also offers an excellent season of comedies, dramas, and musicals performed by students and community members, as well as performances by national professional touring companies. The student government sponsors lectures, films, concerts, and entertainment throughout the year.

Location

Las Vegas, touted by historian Hal Rothman as the First City of the Twenty-First Century, is located at the southern tip of Nevada in a desert valley surrounded by mountains. The Las Vegas metropolitan area is a rapidly growing community of more than 2 million residents with a strong sense of family and community pride. The surrounding area is one of the Southwest's most picturesque, offering residents outdoor recreation year-round. Within a 50-mile radius lie the shores of Lake Mead, Hoover Dam, and the Colorado River recreation area; the snow-skiing and hiking trails of 12,000-foot Mount Charleston; and a panoramic view of rugged rock mountains. Las Vegas has an average of 320 days of sunshine per year. The average daytime winter temperature is 60 degrees Fahrenheit. Summer daytime temperatures are usually more than 100 degrees Fahrenheit.

Majors and Degrees

Undergraduate programs are offered by the Colleges of Education, Fine Arts, Health Sciences, Honors, Liberal Arts, and Sciences; the School of Nursing, Health and Human Sciences, Lee School of Business, and the Greenspun College of Urban Affairs; the Howard R. Hughes College of Engineering; and the William F. Harrah College of Hotel Administration.

Majors include accounting, Afro-American studies, anthropology, applied physics, architecture, art, art history, Asian studies, athletic training, beverage management, biochemistry, biological sciences (including preprofessional), chemistry, civil and environmental engineering, clinical lab sciences, communications studies, comprehensive medical imaging, computational physics, computer engineering, computer science, construction management, criminal justice, culinary arts management, dance, early childhood education, earth science, economics, electrical engineering, elementary education, English, entertainment engineering and design, environmental studies, film, finance, fitness and sports management, French, geoscience, German, gerontology, health-care administration, health education, health physics, health sciences, history, hotel administration, human resources management, interior architecture and design, international business, jazz studies, journalism, kinesiological sciences, landscape architecture, Latin American studies, liberal studies, library science, linguistic studies, management, management information systems, marketing, mathematics, mechanical engineering, multidisciplinary studies, music, musical theater, nuclear medicine, nursing, nutritional sciences, philosophy, physical education, physics, political science, psychology, radiography, real estate, recreation, Romance languages, secondary education, senior adult theater, social science studies, social work, sociology, Spanish, special education, theater arts, urban and regional planning, women's studies, workforce education, and undeclared.

Academic Programs

The UNLV General Education Core requirement, which must be completed by all baccalaureate degree candidates, consists of courses in English composition and literature, international and multicultural studies, logic, mathematics, computer science or statistics, U.S. and Nevada constitutions, social sciences, natural sciences, fine arts, and humanities. The balance of baccalaureate degree programs consists of college and departmental requirements. The number of credit hours required for baccalaureate degrees varies between 124 and 136, depending on the program of study. Numerous special academic opportunities are available, such as dual majors, dual baccalaureates, approved minors, internships, international studies, interdisciplinary programs, honors programs, and nontraditional credit (military credits, Advanced Placement Program, College-Level Examination Program, and correspondence credits).

The UNLV academic calendar has two semesters (fall and spring), each lasting approximately sixteen weeks. Three summer sessions are held from mid-May through August.

Off-Campus Programs

International study-abroad programs are available throughout the year, with opportunities to spend one semester, one academic year, or a summer abroad. Academic credits earned in UNLV study-abroad programs are part of regular authorized course offerings. Students can make normal progress toward their UNLV degree while utilizing international resources and experiencing a different culture.

Academic Facilities

The campus has an excellent Curriculum Materials Library, which is used extensively by local school teachers and University students. The National Supercomputing Center for Energy and the Environment facilitates study of the engineering, socioeconomic, transportation, and social impacts of energy and hazardous waste management along with other appropriate studies. The center includes a Cray YMP 2/215 supercomputer and a Sun 4/490 front-end computer, ten color graphics workstations, and a Silicon Graphics workstation. There are many public computer labs on the UNLV campus with easy access for student use.

Costs

For the 2012–13 academic year, average room and board costs are under $10,000 per year. Nonresident tuition and fees are $18,740 per year (12 credits per semester), and in-state tuition and fees are $5144 per year (12 credits per semester). Residents of fourteen states (Alaska, Arizona, California, Colorado, Hawaii, Idaho, Montana, New Mexico, North Dakota, Oregon, South Dakota, Utah, Washington, and Wyoming) may also qualify for reduced tuition rates through the Western Undergraduate Exchange (WUE) Scholarship Program.

Financial Aid

UNLV provides a variety of financial assistance to qualified students. Loans, grants, scholarships, and employment are all awarded to help students meet their educational expenses while attending UNLV. All students should explore every possible resource. A student's eligibility may be determined by financial need, scholastic achievement, special skills, or service. Prospective students may complete a scholarship application prior to or at the same time as the application for admission. The deadline to apply for scholarships is February 1. It is recommended that the Free Application for Federal Student Aid (FAFSA) is submitted by the February 1 priority deadline. Additional information can be found at finaid.unlv.edu.

Faculty

More than 850 full-time instructional faculty members are involved in teaching, research, and community service. The scholars and scientists at UNLV are warm, caring people committed as much to excellence in teaching as they are to their research. Academic advising is available to every degree-seeking student at UNLV. Graduate assistants have limited teaching and laboratory assignments.

Student Government

All undergraduate students are automatically members of the Consolidated Students of the University of Nevada, Las Vegas (CSUN). CSUN is a self-governing body and is recognized by UNLV's faculty and the Nevada System of Higher Education. All officers are elected by the student body. CSUN has many boards and committees in which students are encouraged to get involved. CSUN provides students an opportunity to practice their communication skills and enrich their education both socially and academically.

Admission Requirements

Standard admission to UNLV is based on a student's academic record and placement examination scores. Incoming freshman students must earn a minimum 3.0 weighted grade point average (GPA) in the academic core in order to be considered for admission. The academic core consist of 4 years of English; 3 years of algebra or higher-level mathematics, such as algebra II, geometry, precalculus, or calculus; 3 years of natural science, with at least 2 years in a lab science; and 3 years of social studies. A minimum composite score of 22 on the ACT or a score of at least 1040 (critical reading and math) on the SAT can be used to waive the GPA requirement, however all students must meet the core course requirement. Official ACT or SAT test scores are also required for admission, scholarship consideration, and English and math placement.

Transfer students must earn a minimum of 24 transferable credits and earn a cumulative GPA of 2.5 or higher from a regionally accredited university or college to be considered for admission. The applicant must be in good standing and eligible to return to the educational institution last attended. Students with fewer than 24 transferable credits must apply as a freshman transfer and submit their college and high school transcripts for evaluation.

Students who do not meet the minimum requirements may be eligible to appeal through the Faculty Senate Admissions Committee.

Application and Information

Priority consideration is given to students who apply by February 1 for the fall and summer semester and October 1 for the spring semester. The nonrefundable application fee of $60 for domestic students and $95 for international students cannot be waived.

Prospective students may access the UNLV applications and catalog at unlv.edu.

For further assistance, students may contact:

Office of Admissions
University of Nevada, Las Vegas
Box 451021
4505 S Maryland Parkway
Las Vegas, Nevada 89154-1021
Phone: 702-774-UNLV (8658) or 702-774-TOUR (8687)
        702-895-3011 (main university number)
        702-895-3424 (financial aid)
Fax: 702-774-8008
Web site: http://www.unlv.edu

UNLV is located on a beautifully landscaped 350-acre campus.

UNIVERSITY OF NEW ENGLAND
BIDDEFORD AND PORTLAND, MAINE

The University

The University of New England (UNE) is a top-ranked, independent, coeducational, university committed to academic excellence and the enhancement of the quality of life for the people, organizations, and communities it serves. The University fosters critical inquiry through a student-centered academic environment rich in research, scholarship, creative activity, and service while providing opportunities for acquiring and applying knowledge in selected clinical, professional, and community settings.

UNE's student body of 5,587 includes 2,790 undergraduates, 967 doctor's degree–professional practice students, and 1,830 graduate students. Students are enrolled in a wide variety of academic programs in UNE's five colleges: the College of Arts and Sciences, the Westbrook College of Health Professions, the College of Pharmacy, the College of Osteopathic Medicine (housing Maine's only medical school), and the College of Dental Medicine, which will enroll its first entering class for fall 2013. At the undergraduate level students represent thirty-five different states and several other countries in over forty undergraduate degree programs.

UNE traces its history to 1831 with the founding of Westbrook College, one of Maine's oldest institutions of learning. Today's University represents a union of three unique higher education institutions through the combining of St. Francis College and the New England College of Osteopathic Medicine in 1978 and Westbrook College in 1996.

The University has chosen as its primary fields of education: business management, education, health sciences (both mental and physical), the humanities, the natural sciences, and social sciences. The University of New England's philosophy of education and student life places emphasis on the quality of instruction and the practical application of academic material.

Each program includes the opportunity for learning in a community-based setting. Internships, co-ops, clinicals, and student teaching add up to the practical experience that allows students at UNE to apply the skills learned in the classroom to real job situations.

The University of New England has two campuses. The oceanside Biddeford Campus is located on the southern coast of Maine, in Biddeford, 90 miles north of Boston and 20 miles south of Portland, Maine's largest city. UNE's Portland Campus is located in Portland, Maine.

The University encourages students to become involved in activities, clubs, and sports. Popular interests include scuba diving, skiing, hiking, biking, varsity and intramural sports, swimming, surfing, music, theater, community service programs, and photography. The University of New England offers a wide range of services on both campuses. Special features include a full health clinic, a dental hygiene clinic, career counseling, personal counseling, learning support services, and an extensive student leadership development program.

Student Support Services provides a wide-range of services to assist students with psychological and emotional health, academic support, educational and career planning, and equal opportunities during their academic experience. The Office of Career Services provides academic and career exploration assistance, assistance in applying to graduate schools, self-assessment and personal interest exploration, resume help, job listings, and job fairs.

Both campuses offer a variety of cultural and social events. The Campus Center at the Biddeford Campus and the Finley Recreation Center on the Portland Campus provide a setting for many recreational and sports activities. The University of New England Athletic Department operates an NCAA Division III varsity athletics program. Varsity sports for men are basketball, cross-country, golf, lacrosse, soccer, and ice hockey. Varsity sports for women are basketball, cross-country, field hockey, lacrosse, soccer, softball, swimming, and volleyball. Intramural teams in basketball, floor hockey, softball, skiing, and volleyball are popular.

The University also has a number of club sports teams. The new $20-million Harold Alfond Forum is a 106,000 square-foot facility featuring an ice hockey rink, a basketball court, classroom and lab space, a fitness center, and multipurpose indoor practice courts.

On the Biddeford Campus, Decary Hall houses a cafeteria, classrooms, meeting rooms, and faculty and administrative offices. The Campus Center contains a fitness center, bookstore, gym, pool, student union, racquetball courts, an indoor track, a variety of multipurpose rooms, and administrative offices. The University maintains ten residence halls on campus. Marcil Hall houses a variety of classrooms, and faculty offices. The George and Barbara Bush Center houses the offices of UNE's president and provost and the ground-floor Windward Café with outdoor terraces and flexible areas for students to study, meet, and socialize.

On the University of New England's Portland Campus, there are two residence halls and the Alexander Hall Student Union, which houses the dining hall, bookstore, the Wing Lounge, and a variety of meeting rooms. The Finley Recreation Center has a gym and fitness facilities. Ludcke Auditorium, whose main structure was built in 1887, is home to concerts, plays, and a number of workshops and meetings.

Location

The University of New England's two campuses are located in the picturesque southern coastal beach communities of Maine. The 540-acre Biddeford Campus, home to the College of Arts and Sciences and the College of Osteopathic Medicine, is situated on a beautiful coastal site where the Saco River flows into the Atlantic Ocean and includes more than 4,000 feet of water frontage. Located 20 miles to the north is the Portland Campus, home to the Westbrook College of Health Professions, the College of Pharmacy, and the College of Dental Medicine. It is set on 41 acres in a quiet residential setting in Portland. Students at both campuses can enjoy the vibrant social life offered in nearby metropolitan Boston (90 miles to the south) or Portland and the dynamic outdoor recreational activities that have made Maine a prime tourist destination. Southern Maine is conveniently serviced by a number of airlines at the Portland International Jetport and by bus and train service with stations in Biddeford/Saco and Portland, making the University's campuses very accessible to all areas of the Northeastern United States and beyond.

Majors and Degrees

UNE offers highly competitive undergraduate and graduate programs in a variety of areas. On the undergraduate level, the University confers Bachelor of Arts and Bachelor of Science degrees.

Bachelor's degrees are offered in animal behavior, applied exercise science, aquaculture and aquarium science, art education, athletic training, biochemistry, biological sciences, business, chemistry, communications, dental hygiene, elementary education, English, environmental science, environmental studies, health, wellness and occupational studies, history, liberal studies (including pre-law), marine sciences, mathematics, medical biology (health and medical sciences tracks for pre-dental, pre-medicine, and pre–veterinary studies), neuroscience, nursing, political science, psychology, psychology and social relations, sociology, secondary education, and sport management.

Various minors, a pre–physical therapy designation, an accelerated pre–physician assistant studies program, pre-pharmacy with a path to UNE's Pharm.D. program, and a secondary education certification (Teacher Certification Program) are also available at the undergraduate level.

Academic Programs

All undergraduate programs at UNE have a core curriculum as a common thread. Designed to provide a foundation in the liberal arts, the core reflects the values of the college and is designed to prepare

students for living informed, thoughtful, and active lives in a complex and changing society. It invites students to explore four college-wide themes: Environmental Awareness, Social and Global Awareness, Critical Thinking: Human Responses to Problems and Challenges, and Citizenship. Skills of communications, mathematics, and critical thinking are taught throughout the core.

Off-Campus Programs

UNE is committed to supplementing the traditional learning process with practical applications. All students are encouraged to participate in cooperative education programs, field placements, and practicums. These experiences provide valuable learning situations and increase a student's exposure to job-related opportunities, and they are required for graduation by most majors. Students also have the opportunity to arrange a study-abroad experience. For the same cost as a semester on campus in Maine, students can enroll in the UNE semester in Seville, Spain; take courses in Spanish and intercultural communication; and choose from a variety of courses in the sciences, humanities, social sciences, business, and the arts taught in English by the host university. Faculty-led short-term travel courses are another way to study abroad. Students and faculty meet throughout the term to prepare for travel academically and practically through readings, lectures, and coursework.

Academic Facilities

On the Biddeford Campus, Decary Hall houses classrooms, laboratories, and faculty and administrative offices. The Jack Ketchum Library has been expanded to provide more library and classroom space as well as a media center and special-event space. Marcil Hall houses classrooms and faculty offices. The Marine Science Education and Research Center is a $7.5-million facility featuring a marine mammal rehab center as well as classrooms, wet and dry laboratories, and research areas. The marine mammal rehabilitation center works primarily with seals, porpoise, and sea turtles. The Department of Creative and Fine Arts is housed in a dedicated building that provides faculty offices and studio space for drawing, painting, printmaking, sculpting, and photography. The Harold Alfond Center for Health Sciences houses biology and chemistry labs as well as lecture halls, classrooms, a gross anatomy lab, and UNE's medical school facilities. The Pickus Center for Biomedical Research is a state-of-the-art facility; the Peter and Cecile Morgane Hall is a science center providing additional classrooms and laboratories for biology, chemistry, and physics.

On the University's Portland Campus, Ludcke Auditorium is used for a variety of academic programs. Coleman Dental Hygiene Building houses classroom, clinic, and faculty space. The Blewett Science Center, home of UNE nursing programs, consists of science labs and classrooms. The University created a Performance Enhancement and Evaluation Center (PEEC) that is an entire center devoted to learning and assessment of patient evaluation skills. The equipment includes two METI Human Patient Simulators and two Laerdal SimMan simulators. Proctor Hall is also a classroom building and is home to the Proctor Learning and Career Center. Josephine S. Abplanalp Library houses study space and computer terminals, along with an outstanding collection of books and periodicals and the Maine Women Writers Collection. The College of Pharmacy and the College of Dental Medicine's renovated historical Goddard Hall are also located on this campus.

Costs

The costs per academic year for 2011–12 were tuition, $29,430; room and board, $12,020; and fees, $1070.

Financial Aid

In 2011–12, approximately 98 percent of all full-time students received some form of financial assistance. The average package was $26,000 including scholarships, grants, loans, and employment. The University of New England has an extensive scholarship program, ranging from $3000 to $18,000 that is based on academic performance.

Faculty

The teaching faculty at the University of New England is an experienced group of academics with more than 85 percent having earned the highest degree in their fields, and they bring to the University varied backgrounds as teachers and practitioners of their disciplines. They are highly competent, demanding, concerned, accessible, and willing to give individual attention to students.

Student Government

The Student Senate is a vital part of the student life at both campuses of the University of New England. The student government has its own operating budget, which is derived from the student fees. The organization covers student services and public relations.

Admission Requirements

Students applying for admission are expected to submit a completed application, a $40 nonrefundable application fee, transcripts of all academic work (high school and college), and scores on either the ACT or SAT. Students who do not use English as their primary language must submit TOEFL scores. Students applying for admission should have completed a curriculum that includes English, mathematics, science, and social sciences. International students must also complete the International Student Supplemental Application. All prospective students are strongly encouraged to visit the campuses of the University of New England for an information session and tour. Information sessions and tours are held weekdays from 10 a.m. to 4 p.m. Prospective students can register online at www.une.edu/admissions/undergrad/visits.

Application and Information

The undergraduate freshman admission application deadline is February 15; applications received after that date are reviewed on a space-available basis. There is a nonbinding December 1 early action application deadline with a December 31 notification date. Applications for the spring term are accepted through December 15.

For application information, students should contact:

Office of Undergraduate Admissions
University of New England
Hills Beach Road
Biddeford, Maine 04005
Phone: 207-283-0171
       800-477-4863 (toll-free)
Fax: 207-602-5900
E-mail: admissions@une.edu
Web site: http://www.une.edu

The 350-acre Biddeford Campus has more than 4,000 feet of ocean frontage at the mouth of the Saco River where it meets the Atlantic Ocean. UNE's own beach is very popular with students.

UNIVERSITY OF NEW HAMPSHIRE
DURHAM, NEW HAMPSHIRE

The University

The University of New Hampshire (UNH) is a rising star among American research universities, a community of exceptional faculty members and talented and energetic students from forty-four states and twenty-six countries. The University has a sizeable undergraduate population of approximately 12,500 but still feels cozy and intimate. This is due in part to a campus layout that is manageable and beautiful—with college greens, water, and a pleasing mix of classic and modern buildings that gradually give way to 2,600 acres of woods, fields, and farms. It is also due to the school's traditions of strong student-faculty interaction and active student culture. As one student put it, "It's easy to meet people and get involved in campus activities here. You need to have some initiative, but student leaders, residence hall staff, and others also seek you out."

The University offers students a variety of housing options, including halls of 100 to 600 students and two on-campus apartment complexes. Themed housing, such as honors, first-year experience, or international, is offered by dorm or floor. Holloway Commons, a spectacular dining and conference facility with seating for 850 and an after-hours café, opened in 2003, and Southeast Residential Community (SERC) Buildings A & B, 326- and 227-bed residence halls, opened in 2006. Parsons Hall, a chemistry teaching and research facility, underwent a $50-million renovation in 2009. Construction of the new Peter T. Paul College of Business and Economics building began in 2011.

The Memorial Union Building (MUB) is the University's community center. Housed in the MUB are two movie theaters, the UNH Copy Center, the UNH Bookstore, the Ticket Office, specific lounge/study space for both nontraditional and graduate students, and Granite Square Station, the undergraduate mail center. Computing and Information Services provides a computer cluster and a help desk with walk-in service. The MUB Food Court offers expanded dining options, and food service is also available in the Coffee Office. The Student Senate Office; Office of Multicultural Student Affairs; WUNH-radio; The New Hampshire, the student newspaper; and nearly 160 other student organizations originate in the MUB. Students at the University can participate in a rich cultural life. Numerous lectures, films, concerts, exhibitions, meet-the-artist receptions, master classes, dance performances, and theatrical productions are offered throughout the year. The UNH Celebrity Series, the Art Gallery, and the Departments of Music, Theater and Dance, and Art and Art History bring artists of international stature to campus. Most events are free for students.

Many opportunities for athletics and recreation, regardless of skill or ability, are offered through Campus Recreation. The Hamel Student Recreation Center is available to all full-time matriculating students. The center offers participants two multipurpose courts, a group exercise studio, a club/martial art studio, an 8,000-square-foot fitness center with more than 100 exercise stations, three basketball/volleyball courts, an indoor track, a lounge, several classrooms, locker rooms, towel and lock service at the equipment room, and saunas. Campus Recreation offers a variety of activities designed to make it easier to reach personal fitness goals and have fun. Participants may take part in one of the many group exercise classes, such as step aerobics, cycling, or cardio kickboxing. Other opportunities include Pilates, yoga, tai chi, a climbing wall, racquetball, personal training, or massage therapy. Noncredit courses are also offered, including CPR and first aid. The intramural sports program consists of more than twenty different sports and activities offered to men's, women's, and co-rec teams. Campus Recreation forms and assists special interest groups or sport club teams to reflect the varied recreation and cultural preferences of campus community members. Some clubs are intensely competitive, requiring a daily commitment to workouts and conditioning. They compete either on an intercollegiate basis with New England teams or sponsor University tournaments. Other clubs meet on a casual come-when-you-can basis. In addition, Campus Recreation offers ice skating, manages a large outdoor recreation facility with its own sailing and canoe center, runs a children's camp (Camp Wildcat) in the summer, and supports the men's and women's sport club crew boat house. UNH also has twenty different men's and women's Division I sports teams, including football, which is Division I-AA.

Location

Nestled in New Hampshire's seacoast region, the town of Durham is an outdoor-lover's dream, with ocean, ski and hiking mountains, and charming working-port cities nearby. Popular road trips for students include Boston (about an hour), Portsmouth (about 20 minutes), and the White Mountains (about an hour). With a nonstudent population of 8,000, Durham is a classic college town that caters to the student clientele. Durham's Main Street includes restaurants, coffeehouses, a bookstore, pizza shops, and other student hangouts.

Majors and Degrees

The University of New Hampshire comprises seven colleges and schools: College of Liberal Arts, College of Engineering and Physical Sciences, College of Health and Human Services, College of Life Sciences and Agriculture, Whittemore School of Business and Economics, Thompson School of Applied Science (which offers two-year associate degree programs), and the University of New Hampshire at Manchester, the University's urban campus. The University offers more than 100 majors through these fully accredited academic divisions. New Hampshire enjoys a strong reputation in a wide range of academic fields, with biology, business administration, English, communication, engineering, environmental studies, history, hospitality management, kinesiology, marine and animal sciences, performing arts, political science, and psychology among those topping the list. The business school offers several options under the business administration major that include accounting, entrepreneurial venture creation, information systems, international business and economics, management, and a student-designed track.

Academic Programs

The Discovery Program, which encompasses the University's general education requirements, provides students with a broad foundation in the liberal arts and an introduction to the methods of inquiry needed for academic success. All students must complete ten courses which include writing skills; quantitative reasoning; biological and physical sciences; historical perspectives; world cultures; fine and performing arts; social science; humanities; and environment, technology, and society. A senior year Capstone Experience as well as inquiry courses allow students to reflect on their education and synthesize knowledge and skills gained from the Discovery Program. Depending on their academic program, students may begin course work in their major as early as their first year.

A major research university, UNH prides itself on producing students who have had meaningful research experiences with a world-class faculty. Programs such as the Undergraduate Research Opportunities Program and International Research Opportunities Program provide research grants each year for undergraduates to work closely with faculty members, on campus or abroad, on original projects. Over 1,000 students participated in the Undergraduate Research Conference in 2011. Students majoring in a wide range of subjects can access a wealth of research centers and facilities, some on the campus itself, others in surrounding towns. As New Hampshire's major public institution, the University is involved in a wide range of outreach programs with state and industry groups. These partnerships provide abundant opportunities for students interested in internships.

Academic Facilities

The Dimond Library is the state's only public university research library. The library offers three grand reading rooms, seating for 1,200 students, and state-of-the-art technology, including wireless and Internet. The Parker Adaptive Technology Room provides an array of technological options for patrons who have learning, mobility, or vision disabilities. Through ResNet, students who live on-campus have high-speed Internet access to UNH library resources, class software and information, e-mail, and other services. The Environmental Technology Building is a multidisciplinary science and engineering research facility with a focus on environmental technology development. Most of the University's cultural events take place in the Paul Creative Arts Center, which houses two theaters, dressing rooms, a well-equipped scene shop, a costume shop, a green room, storage facilities, classrooms, and the faculty and staff offices. New Hampshire Hall contains the Newman Dance Studio and a smaller stage studio.

Costs

The 2011–12 tuition and fees for undergraduate in-state students were $15,250. For out-of-state students, tuition and fees were $28,570. Room (double) and board (unlimited meal plan) cost $9452.

Financial Aid

Approximately 60 percent of students receive some form of need-based financial assistance from UNH. University scholarships ranging from $1000 to $10,000 are awarded automatically to qualified first-year students who apply for admission. Amounts are subject to change. Other scholarships are awarded by individual academic departments. The average financial aid package, including gift, loan, and employment assistance, was $13,166 for New Hampshire residents and $17,874 for nonresidents. The University participates in the Federal Pell Grant program, the Federal Supplemental Educational Opportunity Grant program, the Federal Perkins Loan program, the Federal Work-Study Program, and the Federal Stafford Student Loan program. Students are required to submit the Free Application for Federal Student Aid (FAFSA) by March 1.

Faculty

The University of New Hampshire has 621 full-time and 406 part-time faculty members. The student-faculty ratio is 18:1. The UNH faculty includes winners of the Pulitzer Prize, Guggenheim awards, and many other prestigious awards and honors, while the University ranks among the top campuses in the nation in the percentage of faculty members who have won Fulbright scholarships. This research productivity has a powerful effect on students, who can share the experience of discovery.

Student Government

The Student Senate comprises a governing body of student officers and senators. They are the voice of the student body, representing student opinion to members of the faculty, staff, and administration as well as the University community and the state legislature. The Senate believes that all students have the right to participate in University decisions and policy making. Committees of the Senate include areas in academics, residential life, commuters, health and human services, judicial affairs, and community change. They also approve and monitor the rates and uses of all mandatory student fees.

Admission Requirements

Admission to a bachelor's degree program is based upon successful completion of a strong secondary school program of college-preparatory course work. Primary consideration is given to the academic record, as demonstrated by the quality of the candidate's secondary school course selection and achievement. Consideration is also given to the student's recommendation, personal essay, additional information, character, initiative, leadership, special talents, and SAT or ACT with writing component results. Most successful candidates present at least 4 years of English and mathematics and 3 or more years of laboratory science, social science, and foreign language. Recommended mathematics preparation includes the equivalent of algebra I, geometry, algebra II, and trigonometry or advanced math. Students who plan to specialize in health, physical sciences, life sciences, engineering, or mathematics should present at least 4 years of mathematics, including trigonometry as well as laboratory course work in chemistry and/or physics. Students pursuing business-related studies should also have completed 4 years of mathematics, including trigonometry.

All candidates for admission to bachelor's degree programs are required to submit SAT or ACT scores with writing component results. SAT Subject Tests are not required. A foreign language SAT Subject Test may satisfy the foreign language requirement of the Bachelor of Arts degree programs. Required scores vary by test. International students whose primary language is not English must submit TOEFL or IELTS results. The recommended minimum TOEFL score is 213 (computer-based) or 550 (paper-based) or 80 (Internet-based). The minimum IELTS score is 6.5.

Candidates applying for programs in the Department of Music must make arrangements with the department chairperson for an audition (603-862-2404).

Application and Information

High school students who seek fall-semester admission may apply anytime after the start of the senior year and before the February 1 regular decision deadline. Admission notifications are provided on a continuous basis through April 15. Admitted first-year students have until May 1 to confirm their intent to enroll at the University. The review of candidates begins with the receipt of all required application materials. The Early Action (EA) Program allows candidates to receive a response by mid-January of their senior year; EA candidates must submit admission applications by November 15. In some cases, the Admission Committee requests senior mid-year grade reports in order to make a final admission decision. All positive admission decisions made prior to the completion of a candidate's course work in progress are considered provisional and are subject to the verification of satisfactory senior-year achievement when final high school transcripts are reviewed.

Office of Admissions
University of New Hampshire
3 Garrison Avenue
Durham, New Hampshire 03824-3501
Phone: 603-862-1360
Fax: 603-862-0077
Web site: http://www.unh.edu/admissions
　　　　http://www.facebook.com/universityofnewhampshire

UNIVERSITY OF NEW HAVEN
WEST HAVEN, CONNECTICUT

The University

The University of New Haven's (UNH) mission is to prepare career-ready graduates for meaningful roles in today's global economy and to nurture the pursuit of lifelong learning. Founded in 1920, the University of New Haven is a private, independent institution focused on combining professional education with liberal arts and sciences. UNH is committed to educational innovation, continuous improvement in career and professional education, and support of scholarship and professional development. UNH became a four-year college in 1958. Moving to its present location in West Haven in 1960, UNH rapidly expanded its programs, facilities, and faculty, attracting a student body that now stands at over 6,300—including the current enrollment of 4,119 full-time day students among its undergraduates.

The University is fully accredited by the New England Association of Schools and Colleges (NEASC). Individual programs, departments, and schools hold various forms of national professional accreditation. Four of the University of New Haven's bachelor's degree programs—chemical, civil, electrical, and mechanical engineering—are fully accredited by the Engineering Accreditation Commission of the Accreditation Board for Engineering and Technology, Inc. (EAC/ABET). The computer science program is fully accredited by the Computing Accreditation Commission of the Accreditation Board for Engineering and Technology, Inc. (CAC/ABET).

Despite a broad academic program, UNH is small enough to accommodate individualized educational needs. Programs evolve and adapt to meet changing career interests as well as the requirements of business, industry, and professional fields. Small classes foster close student-faculty relationships. Accelerated weekend and evening programs in business and convenient evening hours provide access for part-time students in engineering, computers, public safety, and the arts and sciences.

The main campus is in West Haven, Connecticut, on a hillside close to Long Island Sound. UNH also operates a satellite branch, the Southeastern Center in New London, Connecticut. Main campus administrative and classroom buildings support the University's four academic colleges: the College of Arts and Sciences, the College of Business, the Tagliatela College of Engineering, and the Henry C. Lee College of Criminal Justice and Forensic Sciences. Following the addition of the Graduate School in 1969, New Haven College was designated a university. Thirty master's degree programs attract full- and part-time graduate students, while nearly 100 associate and bachelor's degree programs are available to entering freshmen and transfer students in a great variety of academic disciplines. In 2007, UNH established University College to oversee the graduate school admissions process as well as its evening, accelerated, cohort, and executive degree programs.

Other main campus buildings include the Marvin K. Peterson Library, Echlin Hall, the Bayer Hall admissions building, the Campus Bookstore, new residence halls and apartments, and Bartels Hall, the campus center, which houses dining facilities and student activities. The Charger Gymnasium and athletic fields are located on the North Campus, just two short blocks from Maxcy Hall, the main administration building. The David A. Beckerman Recreational Center, a state-of-the-art athletic facility for the benefit of all students, opened in fall 2007.

The University of New Haven has one of the most respected and successful NCAA Division II athletics programs in the country, with Charger teams combining to make over 120 post-season tournament appearances. UNH is a member of the Northeast-10 Conference, one of the most prestigious and celebrated conferences

in the nation. UNH and its student athletes have won numerous conference, regional, and national awards, both athletically and academically. The University offers sixteen varsity sports: men's baseball, basketball, cross-country, football, soccer, indoor and outdoor track and field; and women's basketball, cross-country, lacrosse, soccer, softball, tennis, indoor and outdoor track and field, and volleyball. In fall 2009, football made its highly anticipated return, playing its first varsity season since 2003.

Approximately two thirds of the full-time undergraduate day students live on campus in the fourteen residence halls. More than 150 clubs and organizations are open to students. Included are student chapters of professional societies, religious organizations, social groups, special-interest clubs, student councils, cultural groups, and fraternities and sororities.

Location

West Haven is contiguous to New Haven. There are theaters that attract star performers from the entertainment world, a deepwater harbor and beaches, fine restaurants, museums, and galleries in the area. Numerous social and cultural programs are presented by the many colleges and universities in the area. New Haven is served by a local airport and major railroads, and its location at the junction of two interstate highways places the University of New Haven within easy driving distance of New York, Boston, Cape Cod, and the ski areas of New England.

Majors and Degrees

The College of Arts and Sciences offers a Bachelor of Arts degree in art, chemistry, communication, English, global studies, graphic design, history, interior design, liberal studies, mathematics, music, music and sound recording, music industry, political science, and psychology; and a Bachelor of Science degree in biology, biotechnology, dental hygiene, environmental science, marine biology, mathematics, music and sound recording, and nutrition and dietetics.

The College of Business offers the Bachelor of Science degree in accounting, finance, hospitality and tourism management, management, management of sport industries, and marketing. In addition, the College of Business has launched a fast-track study program allowing academically strong students the opportunity to earn a Bachelor of Science degree in business and a Master of Business Administration (M.B.A.) in just four years.

The Tagliatela College of Engineering offers a Bachelor of Science degree in chemical engineering, chemistry, civil engineering, computer engineering, computer science, electrical engineering, general engineering, information technology, mechanical engineering, sustainability studies, and system engineering. The Tagliatela College of Engineering also offers a new certificate program in biomedical engineering.

The Henry C. Lee College of Criminal Justice and Forensic Sciences offers a Bachelor of Science degree in criminal justice, fire protection engineering, fire science, forensic science, and legal studies.

Academic Programs

The University of New Haven offers a broad range of programs in both liberal arts and professional areas. Experiential learning is emphasized, and there are diverse and numerous opportunities for career-oriented internships, cooperative education, independent study, and industrial projects. Certain types of professional experience are required in a number of degree programs. The Center for Learning Resources offers a tutoring service open to all students.

The undergraduate division operates on a 4-1-4 calendar. Credit is given for successful scores on the CLEP and Advanced Placement examinations. A University honors program provides outstanding study opportunities in most undergraduate disciplines. The residence requirement for all degrees is 30 credit hours.

UNH believes that all students pursuing a bachelor's degree should develop a common set of skills; the University's goal is to prepare all graduates for the complex lives they will lead in a changing world. This can best be done through the University Core Curriculum, which consists of a minimum of 40 credit hours in six basic competencies.

Academic Facilities

The Marvin K. Peterson Library contains more than 400,000 volumes in hard copy and provides access to about 20,000 electronic books and 20,000 e-journals from the library Web site and Voyager online catalog. Databases are available on a wide variety of subjects, with a focus on business, criminal justice/forensic science, engineering, and psychology, as well as general arts and sciences. Through interlibrary loan services, the University community has access to the holdings of more than 8,650 libraries.

Communication majors participate in workshops along with studying sound, film, and television production and radio broadcasting techniques in well-equipped radio/television studios and laboratories. The Tagliatela College of Engineering has modern laboratories and equipment to support its programs. The College of Arts and Sciences maintains art studios, state-of-the-art recording studios, music practice rooms, and science, psychology, and language labs. Hands-on instruction and demonstrations are available in kitchen facilities for students in the hospitality and tourism and the nutrition and dietetics programs. Dental hygiene students gain experience in the Dental Hygiene Clinic.

There are more than a dozen computer labs for student use and teaching on campus. One of these is devoted to forensic computing instruction for the Henry C. Lee College of Criminal Justice and Forensic Sciences.

Costs

Estimated full-time undergraduate tuition for the 2012–13 academic year, including all fees, is $31,500; room and board cost $13,230.

Financial Aid

UNH offers a comprehensive financial aid program that includes University resources as well as state, federal, and private-aid programs. More than 80 percent of full-time undergraduate students receive some form of assistance. Students receive federal aid through the Federal Pell Grant, Federal Supplemental Educational Opportunity Grant, Federal Work-Study, Federal Perkins Loan, Federal Direct Student Loan, and Federal Direct PLUS loan programs. The University also administers programs sponsored by the state of Connecticut for Connecticut residents attending the University. Some students also qualify for financial aid from other states and from private companies, organizations, and foundations.

Faculty

It is a long-standing University policy that the faculty members teach a mix of undergraduate and graduate courses in order to preserve academic quality at all levels. Faculty members are selected and promoted primarily on the basis of teaching effectiveness, professional qualifications and performance, and contributions to the academic community. No classes are taught by teaching assistants. Some faculty members hold administrative positions and continue to teach. There are 207 full-time and 400 part-time faculty members, making the student-faculty ratio 16:1. The majority of full-time faculty members (more than 90 percent) hold terminal degrees in their disciplines.

Student Government

The Undergraduate Student Government Association supervises annual expenditures by undergraduate clubs and organizations, directs liaison committees, supports student publications and the student-operated FM radio station, and schedules cultural and social events. Student representatives are elected annually to the University's Board of Governors.

Admission Requirements

To be eligible for admission, one must be a high school graduate or present evidence of equivalent preparation. Scores from the SAT or the ACT are required. The admission decision is based on the student's overall high school record, SAT or ACT results, letter(s) of recommendation, and a 250–300-word personal essay.

Prospective students are encouraged to visit the campus for an information session and tour. To arrange a campus visit, please go to: www.newhaven.edu/visitus. Out-of-state residents are considered for admission on the same basis as state residents.

Application and Information

To apply to the University of New Haven, a student must submit the completed application form, a nonrefundable $25 fee for electronic submission ($75 for paper submission), official records of all academic work completed, SAT or ACT results, a letter of recommendation, and a personal essay. International students are required to demonstrate proficiency in English as well as provide documentation of financial support. The University of New Haven does not discriminate on the basis of age, color, sex, religion, race, sexual orientation, national origin, or disability in admission or treatment of students, in administration or distribution of financial aid, or in recruitment or treatment of employees. The University is authorized under federal law to enroll nonimmigrant alien students who meet the University's academic and English proficiency standards. The admissions office employs a rolling admissions system with the opportunity to apply for early action.

Undergraduate Admissions
University of New Haven
300 Boston Post Road
West Haven, Connecticut 06516
Phone: 203-932-7319
        800-DIAL-UNH (342-5864) Ext. 7319 (toll-free)
E-mail: adminfo@newhaven.edu
Web site: http://www.newhaven.edu

Maxcy Hall on the main campus of the University of New Haven.

UNIVERSITY OF OREGON
EUGENE, OREGON

The University

At the University of Oregon (UO), students belong to a community dedicated to making a difference in the world. Whether changing a community, a law, or one person's mind, UO gives students the inspiration and resources needed to succeed. Potential students interested in exploring the UO online are invited to visit both the University's admissions Web site at http://admissions.uoregon.edu and Facebook page at http://www.facebook.com/UOAdmissions.

Many of UO's academic programs are internationally recognized for academic excellence. The architecture, business, economics, education, geography, journalism, neuroscience, psychology, and sports marketing programs all rank among the top 20 in the U.S.

With a student-teacher ratio of 19:1 and an average class size of 19, students connect easily with faculty members and peers. Students have access to all the resources of a major research university, with 269 comprehensive academic programs and more than 250 student organizations.

Set in a 295-acre arboretum, the University of Oregon is aesthetically and environmentally green. Academic programs and student activities bring students to the forests, mountains, and rivers of Oregon's wilderness areas. The world's first green chemistry teaching methods were developed by UO students and faculty. The Lillis Business Complex was the first certified-green business school facility in the United States. Students have access to nationally recognized programs in sustainable business, architecture, and technology.

Students learn to see the world differently at UO, attending classes alongside peers from all fifty states, two U.S. territories, and eighty-nine countries, and learning from faculty members of diverse religious, cultural, and ethnic heritages. The UO offers 165 study programs in ninety-five countries, giving students the opportunity to experience new cultures while earning credit toward their degree. More information can be found at http://studyabroad.uoregon.edu.

With seventeen NCAA Division I teams, as well as forty-one club sports, students have a variety of sports to play and teams to cheer for. Students root for the Ducks' football team at Autzen Stadium, the men's and women's basketball teams at the state-of-the-art Matthew Knight Arena, and track stars at the world-famous Hayward Field, often the site for U.S. Olympic team trials in track and field. Additional information regarding UO athletic programs is available at http://www.goducks.com.

Location

The UO is located in the center of Eugene (population 345,880), a classic college town that's small enough to bike across but large enough to offer diverse art, music, and social venues. The Hult Center for Performing Arts and the Grammy-winning Oregon Bach Festival lure a variety of acclaimed musical acts each year. Rolling Stone magazine included Eugene in its list of top 10 College Towns that Rock.

Eugene embraces the outdoors, with more than 100 city parks, 250 miles of bicycle trails, rock climbing areas, and beautiful public gardens, all within the city limits. Getting there is easy; the city is served by several major airlines and is on the main north-south Amtrak artery connecting Seattle and San Diego. More information is available at http://admissions.uoregon.edu/original.

Majors and Degrees

A complete list of undergraduate academic majors, minors, certificates, and preparatory programs is located at http://admissions.uoregon.edu/majors.

The School of Architecture and Allied Arts offers programs in architecture; art; art history; ceramics; community arts; digital arts; fibers; historic preservation; interior architecture; landscape architecture; material and product studies; metalsmithing and jewelry; multimedia; nonprofit administration; painting; photography; planning, public policy, and management; printmaking; product design; and sculpture.

The College of Arts and Sciences offers programs in African studies; anthropology; Asian studies; biochemistry; biology; chemistry; Chinese; cinema studies; classics; clinical laboratory science–medical technology*; comic and cartoon studies; comparative literature; computer and information science; computer information technology; dentistry*; East Asian studies; economics; engineering*; English; environmental science; environmental studies; ethnic studies; European studies; folklore; forensic science*; French; general science; general social science; geography; geological sciences; German; German studies; Greek; health sciences*; history; humanities; human physiology; international studies; Italian; Japanese; Judaic studies; Latin; Latin American studies; law*; linguistics; marine biology; mathematics; mathematics and computer science; medicine*; medieval studies; nursing*; occupational therapy*; optometry*; peace studies; pharmacy*; philosophy; physical therapy*; physician assistant studies*; physics; podiatry*; political science; psychology; queer studies; religious studies; Romance languages; Russian and East European studies; Scandinavian; second-language acquisition and teaching; social work*; sociology; Southeast Asian studies; Spanish; theater arts; veterinary medicine*; women's and gender studies; and writing, speaking, and critical reasoning.

The Charles H. Lundquist College of Business offers programs in accounting; business administration with concentrations in entrepreneurship, finance, information systems and operations management, marketing, and sports business.

The College of Education offers programs in communication disorders and sciences, educational foundations, family and human services, special education, and teacher education.*

The School of Journalism and Communication offers programs in communication studies, journalism, journalism: advertising, journalism: communication studies, and journalism: public relations.

The School of Music and Dance offers programs in dance, music, music composition, music education, music: jazz studies, and music performance.

An * denotes preparatory programs.

Academic Programs

The UO operates on a quarter system, and students spend about one third of their education on each of three areas: the general education requirements, major requirements, and elective credit. General education requirements include courses in the natural sciences, social sciences, humanities, and multicultural course work.

Freshman Interest Groups (FIGs) bring together a small group of first-year students interested in the same academic area in three related interdisciplinary courses. Freshman Seminars are small-group discussion courses taught by some of the UO's most outstanding faculty members. These academically rigorous programs provide a transition to college-level work. Details are available at http://firstyear.uoregon.edu. The Professional Distinctions Program gives students a competitive edge in the job market by complementing course work with a practical area of concentration. Skills are built through career workshops, internships, and other professional experiences. Learn more at http://uodistinctions.uoregon.edu.

The Robert D. Clark Honors College (CHC) offers the academic rigor of an outstanding small liberal arts college with the resources of a major research university. High-achieving students prepare for participation and leadership in society and come to understand the role of knowledge in their lives as global citizens. CHC classes are limited to 19 or fewer students and complement any UO major. The CHC application process is competitive, with an average of more

than 1,500 applications for the 200 openings each year. Additional information about CHC can be found at http://honors.uoregon.edu.

Upon acceptance, qualified students will be invited to join the College Scholars program, which provides access to specialized courses, internship opportunities, and special scholarships. Faculty members help students develop their plans to achieve department honors or professional distinctions upon graduation. More details are available at http://csch.uoregon.edu.

Off-Campus Programs

The Career Center offers off-campus internships in fields related to students' academic majors or extracurricular interests. The IE3 Global Internships Program provides academic credit while students gain career experience through overseas internships. Additional information can be found at http://career.uoregon.edu and http://ie3global.ous.edu.

The Oregon Institute of Marine Biology on the Pacific coast offers access to deep sea, coastal watershed, and estuary habitats. Pine Mountain Observatory, near Bend, Oregon, offers study options in physics and astronomy. Students can participate in the annual Archaeology Field School in central Oregon's Northern Great Basin. More details are available at http://admissions.uoregon.edu/beyondeugene.

Cooperatively run by students, the Outdoor Program takes students beyond campus to Oregon's great outdoors. Activities available include snowboarding, skiing, rock climbing, hiking, surfing, and white-water rafting. Interested students can visit http://outdoorprogram.uoregon.edu for more information.

Academic Facilities

The University of Oregon Libraries, an Association of Research Libraries member, houses the second-largest research collection in the Northwest, including 3 million volumes and 90,000 journal subscriptions, both print and electronic. More information can be found at http://libweb.uoregon.edu.

Campus museums are valuable resources in the sciences and visual arts. The Jordan Schnitzer Museum of Art offers exhibitions of classical and contemporary art. The Museum of Natural and Cultural History features Native American artifacts, archaeological finds, and historically and scientifically significant items. Students appear in music, dance, and theater performances in newly refurbished facilities, including proscenium and black box performance spaces. Films, lectures, and cultural events are an everyday part of campus life. Additional details regarding arts and culture at UO are available at http://www.uoregon.edu/arts-and-culture.

Science facilities are among the best in the nation. Cutting-edge equipment is housed in the underground Lokey Laboratories, designed to minimize vibrations and stray electric fields. The UO is a pioneer in integrative science, and the new Lewis Integrative Science Building encourages interdisciplinary research and studies in areas such as nanotechnology, neuroscience, and solar energy. More information can be found at http://isci.uoregon.edu. Wireless Internet access is available in all buildings, and computer labs are available in the library, residence halls, and academic facilities across campus.

Costs

Resident undergraduate tuition and fees for the 2011–12 academic year were $8883. Room and board in on-campus residence halls cost $9501 per academic year for double occupancy. Books and supplies were estimated at $1050 and personal expenses $2412. The total was $21,846.

Nonresident undergraduate tuition and fees for the 2011–12 academic year were $27,738. Room and board in on-campus residence halls cost $9501 per academic year for double occupancy. Books and supplies were estimated at $1050 and personal expenses $2412. The total cost for nonresidents was $40,701. Additional cost details are available at http://financialaid.uoregon.edu/cost_of_attendance.

Financial Aid

The UO makes a concerted effort to enable students to attend, regardless of family income. Financial aid in the form of grants, loans, and employment is available to qualifying students. The majority of students receive scholarships and financial aid that are awarded through the federal government, the University, and academic departments. To apply for financial aid, students must file the Free Application for Federal Student Aid (FAFSA) in early February. The UO's federal school code is 003223.

Incoming freshmen will be considered automatically for Dean's scholarships, Staton scholarships, Laurel scholarships, and general University scholarships by completing the UO admission application by January 15. Presidential scholarships and Diversity Excellence scholarships require separate applications due January 15.

Dean's scholarships are awarded to academically successful entering freshmen and range from $1000 to $7000 per year. Staton scholarships in the amount of approximately $5750 are awarded to incoming Oregon students with extraordinary financial need, and are renewable for up to four years. General University and Laurel scholarships range from $1500 to $2700 per year. Presidential scholarships, awarded each year to Oregon's brightest incoming freshmen, amount to approximately $8500 per year, and are renewable for up to four years. Diversity Excellence Scholarships (DES) are tuition-based, and awards range from partial- to full-tuition as well as fee waivers.

Western Undergraduate Exchange (WUE) offers selected freshmen from certain Western states to study at the University of Oregon for 150 percent of UO resident tuition.

More information regarding financial aid and scholarships can be found at http://financialaid.uoregon.edu.

Student Government

The Associated Students of the University of Oregon (ASUO) offers more than 250 student organizations, including cultural organizations, fraternities and sororities, student government, campus ministries, political groups, performing arts groups, international student clubs, and honor societies. The UO Student Vote Coalition led the nation in registering student voters in each of the past three presidential elections. The UO also ranks tenth in the nation for current Peace Corps volunteers. Additional details regarding the ASUO are available at http://asuo.uoregon.edu.

Admission Requirements

The early notification deadline for fall admission is November 1. The standard admission deadline for fall is January 15. To be eligible for freshman admission, an applicant must have a high school GPA of at least 3.0 on a 4.0 scale, be a graduate of a standard or accredited high school, submit SAT or ACT scores, and complete an application essay.

The UO requires the following college-preparatory courses: 4 years of English in preparatory composition and literature; 3 years of mathematics, including 1 year of algebra and 2 additional years of college-preparatory mathematics; 3 years of science in such areas as biology, chemistry, or physics; and 3 years of social science that could include 1 year of U.S. history, 1 year of global studies such as world history or geography, and one elective. Two years of the same second language in high school or two college terms of the same second language are also required.

Other factors considered for admission include the strength of high school course work, grade trend, class rank, essay, and senior-year course load. Academic potential and special talents also are considered. Additional admissions information is available at http://admissions.uoregon.edu/freshmen.

Application and Information

To apply, candidates should submit a completed application for admission, transcripts, SAT or ACT scores, essay, and a nonrefundable $50 application fee to the Office of Admissions.

For information and an application, students should contact:

Office of Admissions
1217 University of Oregon
Eugene, Oregon 97403-1217
Phone: 541-346-3201
      800-BE-A-DUCK (toll-free)
Web site: http://admissions.uoregon.edu
      http://admissions.uoregon.edu/virtualtour
      http://www.facebook.com/UOAdmissions
      http://twitter.com/BeAnOregonDuck

UNIVERSITY OF PITTSBURGH AT BRADFORD

BRADFORD, PENNSYLVANIA

University of Pittsburgh Bradford

The University

The University of Pittsburgh at Bradford (Pitt-Bradford) can take students beyond—beyond the classroom by offering internships and research opportunities; beyond the degree by providing a robust Career Services Office and an informal alumni network; beyond 9-to-5 by offering an active student life, a friendly residence-life environment, excellent athletic and cultural facilities, and a wide range of recreational opportunities; beyond place by exposing students to the world and offering many study-abroad opportunities; and beyond students' expectations by giving them a college experience that can transform them.

At Pitt-Bradford, students live and learn on a safe, intimate campus, where they receive individual and personalized attention from committed professors who work at their side. In addition, students earn a degree from the University of Pittsburgh, which commands respect around the world.

Students can work out in a state-of-the-art fitness center or swim in the six-lane swimming pool in the Sport and Fitness Center. The building also houses facilities for intercollegiate and intramural athletic events.

The Frame-Westerberg Commons offers a place to eat, gather, and participate in campus life. The building houses the dining hall, where students can help themselves to a wide assortment of meals; a bookstore, which features an after-hours convenience store; offices for many student clubs and organizations; and areas to read or relax.

There are more than fifty clubs and organizations, varying from the campus radio station and newspaper to academic clubs, honor societies, and fraternities and sororities. Pitt-Bradford competes in Division III of the NCAA and fields seven men's teams in baseball, basketball, cross-country, golf, soccer, swimming, and tennis and seven women's teams in basketball, cross-country, soccer, softball, swimming, tennis, and volleyball.

Location

Pitt-Bradford encompasses 317 acres in the foothills of the Allegheny Mountains, only steps from the Allegheny National Forest. Pitt-Bradford also is a short drive from larger cities such as Buffalo, New York (80 miles north); Pittsburgh (160 miles southeast); and Erie, Pennsylvania (90 miles west). Pitt-Bradford can also be reached easily by car and plane.

At Pitt-Bradford, students have many opportunities to participate in cocurricular opportunities in the region, including cross-country and downhill skiing, snowboarding, snowshoeing, ice skating, biking, fishing, hiking, and hunting.

Majors and Degrees

Students may pursue four-year degrees in accounting, applied mathematics, athletic training, biology, biology education 7–12, broadcast communications, business, computer and information technology K–12, business management, chemistry, chemistry education 7–12, computer information systems and technology, criminal justice, early level education preK–4, economics, English, English education 7–12, environmental studies, environmental education K–12, health and physical education K–12, history/political science, hospitality management, human relations, interdisciplinary arts, mathematics education 7–12, nursing, physical sciences, psychology, public relations, radiological science, social sciences, social studies education 7–12, sociology, sport and recreation management, sports medicine, and writing.

Pitt-Bradford also offers associate degrees in engineering science, information systems, liberal studies, nursing (RN), and petroleum technology.

Students may also study engineering for up to two years at Pitt-Bradford and then complete a program at the Oakland campus in bioengineering, chemical and petroleum engineering, civil and environmental engineering, electrical and computer engineering, industrial engineering, materials science and engineering, or mechanical engineering.

Pitt-Bradford also provides programs offered in conjunction with the University of Pittsburgh School of Dental Medicine and the Pennsylvania College of Optometry. Students begin their studies at Pitt-Bradford and, after three years, transfer to the appropriate graduate school to complete four more years of study.

Pitt-Bradford also offers the first two years of study leading to the doctorate in pharmacy. Students must complete the program at the Oakland campus, where admission is competitive. The Pittsburgh School of Pharmacy pre-admits some qualified high school seniors, pending completion of the first two years of the pre-professional program at Pitt-Bradford.

The University also has an agreement with Lake Erie College of Osteopathic Medicine (LECOM), which allows qualifying students to continue their education in medicine at LECOM after their third year at Pitt-Bradford. Students who have successfully completed their first year of medical school classes at LECOM will receive their bachelor's degree from Pitt-Bradford. They will then continue at LECOM to finish their medical studies.

Academic Programs

The academic programs stress critical-thinking and communication skills and encourage hands-on learning through field experience, internships, and faculty-student collaboration on research. A Pitt-Bradford bachelor's degree requires 120–128 credit hours (requirements differ slightly among programs). Students need to complete between 60 and 70 credit hours to earn an associate degree.

The accounting major prepares students for the workplace, which has a growing need for accountants. The major also prepares students to earn a master's degree in either professional accountancy or business administration.

The biology program prepares students for careers in health-related professions, education, and research; technical positions in governmental agencies; and careers with food, pharmaceutical, chemical, and biotechnology companies. Most students interested in medicine, dentistry, optometry, pharmacy, osteopathy, physical therapy, occupational therapy, podiatry, chiropractic medicine, veterinary medicine, preclinical dietetics and nutrition, and a variety of careers in health and rehabilitation sciences are biology majors.

Students who choose to major in broadcast communications, English, public relations, or writing are able to work on the award-winning student newspaper, The Source; broadcast over the college radio station, WDRQ; and publish original works in the award-winning student literary magazine, Baily's Beads. Students also have access to an all-digital television studio and two digital radio facilities.

The business management program places a strong emphasis on teaching practical applications; courses often focus on cases taken from real business situations. Students may concentrate in accounting, finance, international business, or management information systems.

In the criminal justice program, students are able to intern with local and regional police departments, county court and probation offices, and a federal prison. New, state-of-the-art crime-scene investigatory tools enable students to work a crime scene using many of the same tools as professional law enforcement agents. In 2008, the University opened a Crime Scene Investigation (CSI) House, which enables students to process simulated crime scenes and collect evidence just like the pros.

An education major prepares a student for a career as a teacher in a world of rapid political, economic, scientific, and cultural change. The Education Department seeks to graduate students who have general knowledge and specific content knowledge, as well as sound theory and practice.

Students who graduate from the hospitality management program are prepared to work in a large hotel or resort, in a convention bureau

or center, in the areas of event or banquet management, or on a cruise ship. As part of the program, students complete 800 hours of field work at such places as the ski resort in nearby Ellicottville, New York, and Glendorn, a luxurious mountain resort in Bradford.

The nursing program at Pitt-Bradford offers an Associate of Science degree that can be completed in two years and a Bachelor of Science in Nursing degree that requires two additional years. Students may commence this program upon completion of the associate degree.

In psychology, students gain knowledge in the scientific and theoretical aspects of psychology as well as the application of this knowledge. The major prepares students for graduate work in psychology and related disciplines and for employment in social service agencies, mental health centers, industries, and not-for-profit and governmental agencies.

Students may relocate to another University of Pittsburgh campus to complete academic programs not offered at Pitt-Bradford, but they may earn no more than 70 credits before transferring. All students in the arts and sciences may relocate, provided they are in good standing. Engineering students may relocate if they maintain a grade point average of at least 2.5.

Academic Facilities

In addition to the T. Edward and Tullah Hanley Library on campus, Pitt-Bradford students have online access to the entire University of Pittsburgh library system.

Blaisdell Hall, the fine arts and communication arts building, houses the art, communication arts, theater, and music programs and features state-of-the-art equipment. Students can find a computer graphics lab, two art studios, a music/theater rehearsal hall, and a radio and television studio. The building also houses a multipurpose theater and serves as the cultural center for the region by housing plays, concerts, lectures, and other arts-related events.

Fisher Hall houses the science programs, such as biology, chemistry, engineering, petroleum technology, and physics. The science labs, which were updated during the summer of 2010, are filled with up-to-date scientific equipment, enabling students to perform a variety of experiments. The building also has two computer-aided learning centers and, on the roof, a campus greenhouse.

In Swarts Hall, students take courses in business, education, sociology, anthropology, psychology, history/political science, languages, English, writing, and criminal justice. The building also houses a new nursing suite and multimedia classrooms that can turn a typical class into an audio and visual experience.

There is more to the Sport and Fitness Center than sports. The building also houses the athletic training, sports medicine, and sport and recreation management programs. The building houses a human performance lab and an athletic training room.

In the Ceramic Studio, students get their hands dirty—literally. Students have sixteen motorized pottery wheels, a manual kick wheel, a work table, and a kiln to help turn slabs of clay into art.

Costs

For 2011–12, tuition for full-time students was $5868 per fifteen-week term for Pennsylvania residents and $10,964 for nonresidents. Nursing tuition was $7517 per term for Pennsylvania residents and $13,982 for nonresidents. Room and board expenses were $3902 per term. Other costs include an activity fee of $85 per term, a health fee of $50 per term, and a computer fee of $175 per term. Books and supplies cost approximately $500 per term.

Financial Aid

Pitt-Bradford believes that the cost of a college education should not be a deterrent to any student regardless of family financial circumstances. A variety of grants, scholarships, loans, and work-study opportunities are administered through the Financial Aid Office. All aid applicants must submit the Free Application for Federal Student Aid (FAFSA) by March 1 to receive priority consideration. Pennsylvania residents who complete the FAFSA by March 1 are also eligible for Pennsylvania Higher Education Assistance Agency (PHEAA) grants. Students who live outside of Pennsylvania should contact their state agency to learn more about the prerequisites for grants.

The University awards merit-based scholarships to those who demonstrate exceptional academic achievement. The University ROTC program is another possible source of aid. The University encourages veterans to contact the VA about educational benefits.

To learn more about financial assistance, students should contact the Financial Aid Office or visit the financial aid Web site at http://www.upb.pitt.edu/financialaid.aspx.

Faculty

Pitt-Bradford's 78 full-time faculty members hold doctorates and master's degrees from some of the most prestigious universities in the nation, including Cornell, Harvard, Stanford, and the University of Pittsburgh. Teaching is the primary activity of the faculty, and personal attention is emphasized in the classroom. Faculty members welcome the chance to meet with their students and know them by name. The student-faculty ratio is 19:1.

Student Government

Because Pitt-Bradford is a personalized campus, opportunities for leadership abound. Many students become campus leaders as early as their sophomore year. Regardless of students' background or interests, most find many places to become involved at Pitt-Bradford.

The Student Activities Council schedules comedy performances, lectures, art exhibits, movies, and trips to such cities as Toronto, Niagara Falls, Cooperstown, and New York City.

Admission Requirements

The Admissions Committee considers three primary factors in evaluating an applicant's ability to succeed in college work: the high school record, the results of standardized tests (SAT or ACT), and the high school's recommendations. In addition, personal qualifications, extracurricular activities, and potential to contribute to the college community may be taken into consideration.

Application and Information

Pitt-Bradford has a rolling admissions program, and students may apply at any time. All candidates are notified as soon as action is taken on their application.

Candidates for admission should complete and return the application with a nonrefundable $45 fee. Students must also submit an official copy of their high school record and scores from either the SAT or ACT. In addition to fulfilling the above requirements, transfer applicants must submit all official college transcripts and must have a minimum cumulative grade point average of 2.0.

The Office of Admissions welcomes campus visits by students and their families; such visits help students arrive at a final decision about Pitt-Bradford. Interviews and tours are scheduled Monday through Friday, 9 a.m. to 3 p.m., and on selected Saturdays. Arrangements can be made by contacting the Office of Admissions or by going online to http://www.upb.pitt.edu/visit.aspx.

For application forms, catalogs, and further information, students should contact:

Office of Admissions
University of Pittsburgh at Bradford
300 Campus Drive
Bradford, Pennsylvania 16701-2898
Phone: 814-362-7555
　　　　800-872-1787 (toll-free)
Web site: http://www.upb.pitt.edu
　　　　http://www.facebook.com/PittBradford
　　　　https://twitter.com/#!/PittBradford

Students on the campus of the University of Pittsburgh at Bradford.

UNIVERSITY OF PITTSBURGH AT JOHNSTOWN

JOHNSTOWN, PENNSYLVANIA

University of Pittsburgh
Johnstown

The University

Founded in 1927 as one of the first regional campuses of a major university in the United States, the University of Pittsburgh at Johnstown (Pitt-Johnstown) is a four-year, degree-granting, fully accredited, coeducational, residential undergraduate college of the University of Pittsburgh. With 3,000 well-qualified students and a suburban campus of striking beauty, Pitt-Johnstown combines the strong academic reputation and outstanding resources of a major research university with the personal appeal of a smaller college.

There are thirty-six campus buildings, including a library, student union, sports center, performing arts center, and chapel, in addition to a 40-acre nature preserve and outdoor recreation areas. The college has six different styles of housing, including residence halls, small-group lodges, apartments, and the Living/Learning Center. A new state-of-the-art health and wellness center features workout equipment, an elevated track, climbing wall, courts, and an aquatic center.

In addition to the undergraduate degrees listed in the Majors and Degrees section, the University also offers postbaccalaureate nondegree teaching certificates.

Location

Located in a suburb of Johnstown, a metropolitan area of 100,000, only 70 miles east of Pittsburgh, the spacious 655-acre campus is the third largest in Pennsylvania and is recognized as one of the most attractive in the Eastern states. The University's facilities blend easily with the rustic wooded setting, creating a campus of distinctive natural beauty. Shops, entertainment, and cultural activities are conveniently available, and the city is in the heart of Pennsylvania ski country.

Majors and Degrees

Pitt-Johnstown offers the Bachelor of Arts (B.A.) degree in business (accounting, economics, finance, marketing, and management), communication, creative writing, economics, English literature, environmental studies, geography, history, humanities, journalism, professional writing, secondary education (several social science strands, communication, and English), social sciences, sociology, and theater arts. The Bachelor of Science (B.S.) degree is awarded in biology,

chemistry, civil engineering technology, computer engineering technology, computer science, electrical engineering technology, elementary education, energy and earth resources, geology, mathematics, mechanical engineering technology, natural sciences, nursing, psychology, and secondary education (biology, chemistry, earth and space science, general science, mathematics, and physics).

An Associate of Science (A.S.) degree is available in respiratory care and surgical technology.

Dual teaching certification and dual education degree programs are offered. A cooperative program with a local hospital allows students to combine a B.S. in biology with a certificate in medical technology. A certificate in international studies can be earned in conjunction with any major.

With the assistance of academic advisers, Pitt-Johnstown students can construct interdisciplinary majors, double majors, and self-designed majors. They can also develop their specific fields of study with preprofessional preparation for advanced study in such areas as dental medicine, law, medicine, optometry, physical therapy, and veterinary medicine.

Academic Programs

Pitt-Johnstown seeks to provide contemporary, innovative academic programs that combine the practical concerns of career orientation with the spirit of inquiry and the traditional goals of higher education. Practical experience of all types is encouraged, including campus activities, community service, media work, and research projects. A seminar series introduces freshmen to rigorous intellectual work through small-group elective seminars. Students who show extra potential receive special advising, registration privileges, and scholarships through the President's Scholars Program. Students may complete preliminary requirements for upper-division programs that require relocation to the Pittsburgh campus, including requirements for programs in pharmacy and other health-related areas. In some programs, guaranteed admission is offered to qualified students.

Off-Campus Programs

The University of Pittsburgh at Johnstown takes pride in offering international programming options to students. As part of the University Center for International Studies

(UCIS), the International Services Office promotes exposure to different cultures, languages, and more by having undergraduates earn credits at institutions throughout the world. Students may also consider pursuing one of several international studies certificates. These certificate programs enable students to become specialized in a particular area of the world or a global theme.

Academic Facilities

In addition to the numerous volumes housed in the Pitt-Johnstown library, students have online request and retrieval access to the extensive collections contained in the University Libraries system, including electronic journals and electronic books. The college maintains computer classrooms and laboratories equipped with more than 300 computers. All classrooms are wired for Internet access, and all computers at Pitt-Johnstown are connected to the Internet, allowing students access to information from around the world and to a large suite of software shared with the University's other campuses.

Costs

For full-time students in arts and sciences and education programs, 2011–12 tuition was $5868 per fifteen-week term for Pennsylvania residents and $10,964 for nonresidents. For full-time students in engineering programs, tuition was $6295 per fifteen-week term for Pennsylvania residents and $11,997 for nonresidents. Room and board expenses were approximately $4000 per term, depending on housing style and meal plan. Other costs included activities and facilities fees of $181 per term and a computing service fee of $175 per term. A $10 fee was charged for each physical education course. Books and supplies were estimated at $550 each term. All costs are subject to change.

Financial Aid

Nearly 88 percent of all Pitt-Johnstown students receive some form of financial assistance. In addition to the Pennsylvania Higher Education Assistance Agency (PHEAA) state grant, the Federal Pell Grant, and the Federal Stafford Student Loan, a variety of loans, grants, scholarships, and student-employment positions are awarded through the University. Applicants for all types of financial aid must submit the Free Application for Federal Student Aid (FAFSA) by April 1 prior to the academic year for which assistance is requested.

Faculty

Holding degrees from more than 100 distinguished American and international universities, the 133 full-time members of the Johnstown faculty represent a broad diversity in background and experience. Personally committed to undergraduate teaching, each faculty member is actively involved in a full range of intellectual activities as well as student advising, curriculum development, and the extracurricular and cultural life of the University community. Classes at Pitt-Johnstown are small, and opportunities for faculty-student interaction outside of the classroom are plentiful. Personalized instruction is emphasized. Full-time faculty members teach almost all courses. The student-faculty ratio is 20:1, and the typical class size is 25–30.

Student Government

The Student Senate plays a significant role in building cooperation among all members of the University community. It deals with matters affecting the entire student body and formally represents students in relations with the administration, faculty, and other nonstudent groups. The Programming Board, an administrative branch of the senate, schedules diversified entertainment.

Admission Requirements

All applicants for full-time study must have completed, or be in the process of completing, at least 15 units of work in an accredited secondary school. In addition, candidates must take either the SAT or the ACT. Writing sections of the entrance exams are considered for placement in freshman composition courses. Admission decisions are made after careful study of each applicant's high school record, performance on college entrance examinations, high school recommendations, and personal qualifications. Interviews are not required; however, applicants are encouraged to arrange a visit to the campus by phoning or writing the Office of Admissions.

Application requirements for transfer students include high school and college transcripts. Transfer students should have a minimum quality point average of 2.0.

High school graduates and transfer students must file an application, with a $45 fee, on forms provided by the school.

Application and Information

The candidate is notified as soon as action is taken on the application.

For more information about University of Pittsburgh at Johnstown, students should contact:

Office of Admissions
157 Blackington Hall
University of Pittsburgh at Johnstown
Johnstown, Pennsylvania 15904
Phone: 814-269-7050
   800-765-4875 (toll-free)
Web site: http://www.pitt-johnstown.pitt.edu

UNIVERSITY OF PUGET SOUND
TACOMA, WASHINGTON

The College

Founded in 1888, University of Puget Sound is an independent college committed to the liberal arts and sciences, superb teaching, and the recognition of each student as an individual. A nationally acclaimed teaching faculty, well-planned facilities, and a limited enrollment ensure excellence in education.

Puget Sound, the only national liberal arts college in western Washington, is one of only two independent colleges in Washington State to be granted a chapter by Phi Beta Kappa. It leads small colleges in Washington State (and ranks in the top 5 on the West Coast) in terms of alumni going on to earn a doctorate. Many graduates have received undergraduate and postgraduate honors, including Rhodes, National Science Foundation, Fulbright, Rotary, Watson, Phi Kappa Phi, Truman, Goldwater, Hertz, and National Endowment for the Humanities fellowships and scholarships. Equally impressive, among national colleges and universities with fewer than 5,000 undergraduate students, Puget Sound is consistently in the top five for number of alumni serving as Peace Corps volunteers worldwide.

Puget Sound enrolls 2,600 students, with more than 75 percent coming from outside Washington State. In addition, forty-seven states and fifteen countries are represented in the student body. Puget Sound is a 24-hour-a-day, seven-day-a-week residential community. Special theme houses and halls are available for students with common interests. The neighboring residential community provides many facilities for those who wish to live off campus. Athletic facilities include Memorial Fieldhouse and Pamplin Fitness Center, Wallace Pool, Peyton Field at Baker Stadium, an indoor climbing wall, and numerous varsity and intramural athletic fields.

Students find that participating in activities sponsored by the student government is an excellent way to learn outside the classroom and improve leadership abilities. Athletics include twenty-three varsity teams, various club teams, and numerous intramural teams. In addition, students are involved in a variety of clubs and associations, such as forensics, theater, music, radio station (Puget Sound's radio station received an award from MTV for best college radio station in the nation), art and literary magazine, weekly newspaper, yearbook, Student Senate, religious groups, a variety of faculty and trustee committees, Black Student Union, Hui-O-Hawaii, Earth Activists, B-GLAD (Bisexuals, Gays, Lesbians, and Allies for Diversity), Asian Pacific American Student Union, Community for Hispanic Awareness, and Habitat for Humanity. Seventy-five percent of students participate in community service activities.

Graduate degrees offered include the Master of Occupational Therapy, Doctor of Physical Therapy, Master of Arts in Teaching, and Master of Education.

Location

The campus is located in a residential neighborhood in the historic North End of Tacoma. Thirty-five miles south of Seattle and easily accessible from Interstate 5, Tacoma is a dynamic city of 200,000 people. It was ranked by *Money* magazine as one of the most livable medium-sized cities in the country. The college occupies thirty-nine buildings on a 97-acre campus. The architecture is Tudor Gothic, with its distinctive red-brick pattern arches and porticoes. Located close to the shores of Puget Sound and a short distance from ski slopes and the Pacific Ocean, the college is also a hub for much of Tacoma's cultural life. Tacoma also features Point Defiance Zoo and Aquarium, many parks, museums, a new convention center, and hospitals.

Majors and Degrees

Puget Sound offers more than forty-five majors leading to the Bachelor of Arts, Bachelor of Science, and Bachelor of Music degrees. Academic programs are art, Asian languages and culture (majors are offered in Chinese, Japanese, and East Asian languages), biochemistry, biology, business, chemistry, classics, communication, comparative sociology, computer science, computer science in business, economics, English, exercise science, foreign languages and literature (majors relating to language and literature and language and culture are available through the study of French, German, and Spanish), geology, history, international political economy, mathematics, molecular and cellular biology, music, natural science, philosophy, physics, politics and government, psychology, religion, and theatre arts. Minors are offered in Latin American studies, African-American studies, environmental policy and decision-making, gender studies, global development studies, neuroscience, and many other areas. The introduction of a special interdisciplinary major allows exceptional students the opportunity to pursue a degree in a recognized interdisciplinary or emergent field.

Puget Sound offers a dual-degree program in engineering, leading to a joint Bachelor of Arts/Bachelor of Science degree in engineering. Students in this program complete prerequisites in chemistry, mathematics/computer science, and physics, then transfer to an accredited engineering school for course work in chemical, civil, electrical, environmental, mechanical, or petroleum engineering, among others. Affiliated schools are Washington University in St. Louis, Columbia University, Duke University, and the University of Southern California.

Academic Programs

Academic rigor, freedom to take courses from across the curriculum, and opportunities for interdisciplinary study characterize the academic experience. At the heart of the academic program is the core curriculum—eight course groupings around which major and elective studies are arranged over a four-year period. The emphasis throughout a student's undergraduate education is on the acquisition of intellectual skills: the ability to express oneself clearly, both orally and in writing; the ability to reason quantitatively; and the ability to think logically, critically, and independently. By mastering the literature and techniques of a specific academic major, the student learns to cultivate the unique power of his or her own mind and to respond vigorously, but humanely, to important social, moral, and intellectual challenges.

A particularly well-designed curriculum for the freshman year and a model program of academic advising and career counseling enable each student to develop his or her own skills and interests in preparation for a lifetime of creative work and leisure. Puget Sound's highly successful and award-winning student orientation process—Prelude, Passages and Perspectives—is a nine-day program that allows new students to become involved in writing and thinking seminars, academic workshops, community service, and a three-day excursion to the nearby Olympic Peninsula.

The academic year is divided into two semesters, beginning in late August and mid-January, and a thirteen-week summer session (two condensed terms). A normal academic load is 4 units (typically four courses) per semester. Each unit of credit is equivalent to 6 quarter hours or 4 semester hours. Thirty-two units are required for graduation.

Off-Campus Programs

Puget Sound offers an outstanding selection of international opportunities for its students and offers about 100 programs in dozens of countries, including Australia, England, Scotland, Spain, France, Germany, Italy, Austria, China, Japan, Taiwan, Argentina, and Chile, among others. The Pacific Rim/Asia Study-Travel Program offers students an intense year of study and travel in six to eight Asian countries.

Puget Sound's location in one of the fastest-growing regions of the country places its internship program at the forefront of national liberal arts colleges. In fact, Tacoma was named the number one

midsized city in the nation for entrepreneurship by *Entrepreneur* magazine. Opportunities for student research abound, as students may apply for summer research grants in the sciences, social sciences, humanities, and the arts.

Academic Facilities

Collins Memorial Library contains more than 550,000 volumes of books and periodicals plus a sizable collection of federal and Washington State government publications, maps, microforms, videotapes, cassettes, compact discs, and other media materials. These resources are strengthened through participation in the Orbis Cascade Alliance, a consortium of twenty-seven public and private institutions of higher education in Oregon and Washington, with combined holdings of more than 22 million volumes. Other major academic facilities include Thompson Science Complex, Kittredge Art Gallery, Schneebeck Concert Hall, Norton Clapp Theatre, Gordon D. Alcorn Arboretum, Lowry Wyatt Hall, and Slater Museum of Natural History. The new Weyerhaeuser Center for Health Sciences opened in 2011.

Puget Sound provides students of environmental science and marine biology with a superb outdoor laboratory. A working relationship with Point Defiance Zoo and Aquarium, just minutes north of the campus, offers teaching and research opportunities in marine and biological sciences. Equipment and facilities in the Thompson Science Complex include a modern greenhouse; an observatory; an aquarium with a tidal cycle; a state-of-the-art genetics laboratory; a scanning electron microscope and a transmission electron microscope; ultraviolet, visible, fluorescence, infrared, and nuclear magnetic resonance spectrophotometric equipment; and a seismograph. Students also have access to human cadavers. Special facilities are available for students of occupational and physical therapy, education, counseling, foreign languages, and psychology. The music building has twenty-two individual practice rooms.

Wireless Internet access is available throughout campus. In addition, students have access to computer labs and state-of-the-art video editing facilities.

Costs

Tuition and student government fees are $40,040 and $210, respectively, for the 2012–13 academic year. Room and board cost $10,390. It is estimated that an additional $3300 per year is adequate for books, laundry, and other essentials, including travel to and from home.

Financial Aid

More than 90 percent of Puget Sound students receive financial aid in one or a combination of the following forms: scholarships, grants, low-interest loans, and part-time employment. Most financial aid is awarded on the basis of demonstrated financial need, as determined through analysis of the Free Application for Federal Student Aid (FAFSA). In addition, the college's Financial Aid Office administers scholarships based on academic merit that range from $7000 to $19,000 per year. Many other talent awards are available in the arts, selected academic areas, forensics, and leadership.

Faculty

Members of the faculty work closely with individual students both in the classroom and in student-originated research projects within and across the disciplines. Eighty-nine percent of the faculty members teach full-time; 98 percent of tenured faculty members hold a Ph.D. or an equivalent terminal degree. In agreement with Ted Taranovski, Professor Emeritus of History, faculty members feel that the University of Puget Sound is "an institution geared to human beings—small enough to give one a sense of community and yet large enough to provide an excellent academic curriculum; it is not an impersonal machine where people become cogs." In recent years, professors at Puget Sound have been recognized for their academic and teaching achievements through awards and distinctions, including the Graves Award in the Humanities and fellowships from various organizations, including the National Endowment for the Humanities, the American Council of Learned Societies, and the Danforth Foundation. In the last five years, three Puget Sound professors have been named Washington State Professor of the Year by the Carnegie Foundation for the Advancement of Teaching. Puget Sound has received more of these awards than any other college or university in the state.

Admission Requirements

Each applicant to the University of Puget Sound is considered individually and is admitted on the basis of his or her qualifications and achievements. In considering applicants for freshman admission, the Admission Committee evaluates the following: high school course selection, high school grade point average, rank in graduating class (if available), SAT or ACT scores, a counselor's and an academic teacher's recommendations, an essay, a recommended interview, and extracurricular activities. College credit is awarded to students who have earned scores of 4 or higher on Advanced Placement examinations. Credit for a score of 3 is available for selected examinations only. Credit is also available for a score of 5, 6, or 7 on the International Baccalaureate higher-level examinations.

Application and Information

Prospective freshmen may apply for admission anytime after the beginning of the senior year in high school using the Common Application for freshmen. Admission decisions are generally mailed on or before April 1. The application deadline is January 15. Students who have decided that Puget Sound is their first-choice college may choose one of two early decision plans. Early Decision I has a November 15 application deadline, with admission and tentative financial aid notification by December 15. Early Decision II has a January 2 application deadline, with admission and tentative financial aid notification by February 15. Transfer students are admitted in both semesters. Students applying for transfer admission should submit the Common Application for transfers.

For more information about Puget Sound or for application materials, students should contact:

Office of Admission
University of Puget Sound
1500 North Warner Street, #1062
Tacoma, Washington 98416-1062
Phone: 253-879-3211
          800-396-7191 (toll-free)
E-mail: admission@pugetsound.edu
Web site: http://www.pugetsound.edu

Jones Hall, built in 1924.

UNIVERSITY OF REDLANDS
REDLANDS, CALIFORNIA

The University

The University of Redlands has, for more than 100 years, offered its students a tradition of superior liberal arts education. While students may select from a variety of programs that prepare them for professional or graduate school, the heart and foundation of Redlands is in liberal studies. Its outstanding faculty, educated in the world's finest colleges and universities, provides students with extraordinary opportunities for learning and growth through excellent teaching and close, informal interaction. Intense intellectual activity is balanced by opportunities for quiet reflection, fun, and recreation.

The University College of Arts and Sciences enrolls more than 2,400 students. Sixty percent of the freshman class comes from California and the remainder from forty-two other states and ten countries. In addition to a strong academic program in the liberal arts, the sciences, pre-professional programs, and the arts, many extracurricular programs are available to the student, including music, drama, dance, and athletics. Internships are available for students in many academic programs. The School of Music and the Department of Theatre Arts provide a rich selection of cultural events throughout the year. Prominent speakers are invited to the campus each year to give major addresses and participate in classes and public discussion groups, and many social functions are organized by the Office of Student Life and individual residence halls. Additional social opportunities are provided for interested students by local nonresidential fraternities and sororities. The student services center provides assistance in the areas of career and personal counseling and academic support.

Seventy percent of the students live on campus in residence halls that offer a variety of accommodations, including single gender, coed by separate wings, and coed by alternate suites.

The University of Redlands is one of a select number of schools that have a chapter of Phi Beta Kappa, the nation's oldest and most prestigious academic honor society. In addition, 12 Redlands students have been awarded Fulbright awards within the past two years.

The University of Redlands offers master's programs in the fields of business, communicative disorders, education, geographic information systems, and music. The School of Education offers a Doctorate in Leadership for Educational Justice Ed.D. program.

Location

The University is located in the city of Redlands within the San Bernardino Valley. Overlooking the 160-acre campus are the two highest mountains in southern California, Mt. San Gorgonio and Mt. San Bernardino, each more than 10,000 feet high. Redlands has a population of 70,000 and is situated at an elevation of 1,500 feet. Metropolitan Los Angeles to the west and Palm Springs to the east are both about an hour's drive away by freeway.

Majors and Degrees

The B.A. degree is offered in the academic areas of Asian studies, biology, business administration, communicative disorders, creative writing, economics, English literature, environmental business, environmental studies, French, German, government, history, international relations, music, philosophy, psychology, race and ethnic studies, religion, sociology/anthropology, Spanish, studio art, theater arts, women's and gender studies, and visual and media studies. The B.S. degree is offered in accounting, biochemistry and molecular biology, biology, business administration, chemistry, economics, environmental policy and management, environmental science, mathematics, and physics. The professional degree of Bachelor of Music (B.M.) is offered by the School of Music. Primary and secondary credentials are granted by the School of Education. Strong interdisciplinary programs in Latin American studies, pre-law, and pre-medicine are also available.

Academic Programs

Academic majors are offered in the spirit of a liberal arts program, with emphasis on developing the whole student. In addition to the standard academic program, international-study programs, independent study, and an honors program are offered to provide greater diversity.

A liberal arts education, by definition, is an exposure to a wide variety of academic disciplines. Typically, such exposure carries no underlying theme but is distributed among broad categories such as the humanities, arts, social sciences, and natural sciences. The University of Redlands has never considered itself typical and, as a result, has developed an unusual approach to the implementation of its liberal arts philosophy by restructuring the general education requirements to provide a contemporary curriculum. This common experience emphasizes competence in writing, computing, problem solving, and creative skills, all of which are fundamental to a lifetime of learning and career development. In addition, the requirements include a first-year seminar that integrates the academic program and close personal relationships between students and faculty members. The overriding emphasis of this innovative curriculum is on a thorough investigation of human values as they affect the individual and society. An examination of the worth of the individual, respect for nature and life, free inquiry, and the understanding of other cultures are a few of the topics covered through various courses. The University hopes that this experience will broaden each student's understanding and better equip them to deal with today's dynamic society.

The Johnston Center for Integrative Studies provides a nontraditional approach for a select group of highly motivated students. Johnston Center students are exempted from most of the academic structure of Redlands and instead negotiate their entire course of study with a faculty/peer committee. Drawing from the Redlands curriculum as well as from courses created each semester by the Johnston community, each student proposes an individually designed general studies program and an area of concentration. Course performance is evaluated in a narrative format rather than with letter grades. These students live in the Johnston Center Complex, a living/learning community that includes student rooms, faculty offices, classrooms, and space for weekly community meetings.

Students who are enrolled in the Johnston Center are expected to contribute to the life of the center's community.

The academic calendar divides the school year into a 4-4-1 plan, providing a fall semester, a spring semester, and a May term. The four classes taken in the fall semester are completed prior to the third Friday in December. The spring semester begins in January and runs through April. The four-week May term offers students the chance to pursue one subject in depth. Extensive off-campus opportunities, including internships, international study, and on-campus independent study, are available.

Academic Facilities

The institution has facilities with a mix of Greek, Spanish, and modern California architecture. The newly renovated ground floor of the Armacost Library includes rooms for collaboration and learning, the Fletcher Jones Computing Center, a student study area, the Bulldog café, and an Internet lounge. Other facilities include the Stauffer Complex for Science, Mathematics, and Environmental Studies; and a brand-new Center for the Arts, featuring the Glen Wallichs Theatre, Frederick Loewe Performance Hall, and an art gallery. The library houses 400,000 publications and online databases such as Dialog, ABI/INFORM, PsychLIT, ERIC, Wilson Indexes, and the Music Index. These facilities and surrounding common spaces also have access to a wireless network.

Costs

Tuition for 2012–13 is $38,038, and room and board costs are $11,924.

Financial Aid

Recognizing that many worthy and capable students find it impossible to obtain a college education without financial assistance, the University has established a program of aid. Most aid is need-based, but no-need scholarships based on academic achievement in high school and/or college are available. Presidential Scholarships are also available, based on grades and test scores, as are Achievement Awards. Talent Awards, ranging from $500 to $10,000 each, are available in art, creative writing, music, and theater.

Students seeking financial assistance should inquire through the Office of Admissions when applying for admission. The Free Application for Federal Student Aid (FAFSA) should be submitted by March 2. FAFSA forms received after this date are evaluated subject to the availability of funding. Forms may be obtained online at http://www.fafsa.gov.

Faculty

The highly qualified full-time faculty numbers 167 men and women, 90 percent of whom hold doctorates or other terminal degrees in their field. The wide variety of academic backgrounds represented in the faculty provides students with an excellent opportunity to live and work in an atmosphere of intellectual inquiry. Academic advising is handled by faculty members, and all students are assigned an adviser in the area of their major interest.

Student Government

Authority and responsibility for student government is delegated to the Associated Students of the University by the president and the faculty to make possible genuine participation by students in the governance of the University. The organization is composed of all students in the college, and its officers are chosen by the student body. More than sixty positions of representation are open to students on faculty, administrative, trustee, and alumni committees. Among other activities and responsibilities, the student government finances and operates a student-union complex, on-campus shuttle, information center, vending program, convocation series, Internet radio station, and weekly newspaper.

Admission Requirements

Graduation from an accredited high school or the equivalent is necessary for admission. No set pattern of courses in high school is required, but applicants should have had 4 years of work in English and should have completed an academic program strongly emphasizing such studies as foreign language, science, mathematics (including algebra II), and social science. An average grade of at least B should have been maintained in the high school program. Applicants are requested to submit the results of the SAT or the ACT. The writing portion is used for placement in English classes but not admission. SAT Subject Tests are not required. Standardized test scores are not required of transfers who bring at least 24 transferable units to the University.

Transfer students should have maintained a minimum 2.8 grade point average and may transfer up to 66 units of credit from a community college and 96 units from a four-year institution.

Application and Information

Applications are processed on a rolling basis. Those wishing to be considered for an academic or merit scholarship should apply by November 15. Those applying for need-based financial aid should apply by January 15. Transfer applicants should apply by March 1. Applications made after this date are considered on a space-available basis.

Further inquiries should be addressed to:

Office of Admissions
University of Redlands
P.O. Box 3080
Redlands, California 92373-0999
Phone: 800-455-5064 (toll-free)
Fax: 909-335-4089
E-mail: admissions@redlands.edu
Web site: http://www.redlands.edu

The University of Redlands stands out brilliantly against the majestic San Bernardino Mountains.

UNIVERSITY OF RHODE ISLAND
KINGSTON, RHODE ISLAND

The University

As a land-grant college since its founding in 1892, the University of Rhode Island provides its students with an outstanding education and prepares them for responsible citizenship. The University also fosters significant research and takes its expertise to the community through a variety of extension and outreach programs. The current undergraduate enrollment is about 13,000 men and women. The center of the spacious country campus is a quadrangle of handsome, old granite buildings surrounded by other, newer academic buildings, student residence halls, and fraternity and sorority houses. On the plain below Kingston Hill are gymnasiums, athletic fields, tennis courts, a freshwater pond, agricultural fields, greenhouses, and a large event venue. There are twenty-two residence halls on campus, offering a variety of living accommodations, including several new residence halls and apartment buildings. A variety of dining centers and meal plans are offered to all students. There are approximately 1,000 fraternity and sorority members living in nationally affiliated houses that are privately owned by alumni corporations. Some students commute from home, and other students commute from houses or apartments in the local and surrounding beach communities. Approximately 45 percent of the undergraduate students come from outside Rhode Island.

Lectures, art programs, music and dance concerts, film programs, and theater presentations are available. An extensive program of intercollegiate and intramural athletics is offered and is sufficiently varied to provide an opportunity for every student to participate. The Mackal Field House, Tootell Physical Education Center, and the Keaney Gymnasium provide excellent facilities, including three pools, four gymnasiums, weight-training rooms, a dance studio, and a modern athletic training room. The Mackal Field House provides gymnasium space for a variety of recreational uses as well as an indoor track. In addition to a football stadium, there are twelve tennis courts, two softball diamonds, a baseball field, a lighted lacrosse/soccer field, a hockey field, and numerous practice fields for recreation and competition. The 8,000-seat Ryan Center houses the men's and women's basketball programs in addition to concerts and other large events. The Boss Ice Arena houses the club hockey teams and is also available for student skating. A sailing pavilion and rowing facility are located near campus. The Memorial Union Building houses a wide variety of educational, social, cultural, and recreational services, including lounges, study rooms, a radio station, the campus newspaper, a game room, dining facilities, a bookstore, a coffee shop, a restaurant, a ballroom, and a special events room.

Location

The University's 1,200-acre campus is located in the historic village of Kingston, 30 miles south of Providence. Bus transportation is available from the campus to most locations in the area, including Wakefield, where the nearest shopping facilities are located. The Kingston Amtrak train station is 1 mile from campus, and the T. F. Green International Airport in Warwick, Rhode Island, is only 25 miles from campus. The campus is 6 miles from the ocean, and weekend ski trips to the mountains are easily managed in the winter season.

Majors and Degrees

The College of Arts and Sciences offers the Bachelor of Arts in African and African American Studies, Anthropology, Art, Art History, Chemistry, Chinese, Classical Studies (with an option in classical civilization and culture), Communication Studies, Computer Science, Economics, English, Film Media, Music, French, German, History (minor in underwater archeology), Italian, Journalism, Mathematics, Military Science (Army ROTC), Music (options in jazz studies and music history and literature), Philosophy, Physics, Political Science, Psychology, Public Relations, Sociology, Spanish, Women's Studies, and Writing and Rhetoric. The College of Arts and Sciences also offers the Bachelor of Science in Chemistry, Chemistry and Forensic Chemistry, Computer Science (with options in 3-D graphics and digital forensics), Economics, International Computer Science Program (B.A. and B.S. 5-year program), Mathematics, Physics (5-year Medical Physics), Physics and Physical Oceanography, and Sociology (criminology and criminal justice). In addition, the College of Arts and Sciences offers the Bachelor of Fine Arts in Art and Theater (options in acting, design and theater technology, directing, and stage management), as well as the Bachelor of Music in Music Education, Music Composition, and Music Performance.

The College of Business Administration offers the Bachelor of Science in Accounting, Entrepreneurial Management, Finance, General Business Administration, Global Business Management, Marketing, and Supply Chain Management. The College of Business Administration also offers a dual-degree International Business Program: B.S. in one of seven business disciplines and a B.A. in French, German, Spanish, or a minor in Chinese.

The College of Engineering offers the Bachelor of Science in Biomedical Engineering, Chemical Engineering (with options in biology track and pharmaceutical track), Civil and Environmental Engineering, Computer Engineering, Electrical Engineering, Industrial and Systems Engineering, Mechanical Engineering, and Ocean Engineering. The College of Engineering also offers a dual-degree International Engineering Program: B.S. in one of the eight engineering disciplines and a B.A. in French, German, Spanish, or a minor in Chinese, as well as accelerated 5-year programs in Industrial Systems Engineering and Mechanical Engineering with both a Bachelor of Science and Master's in Business Administration.

The College of the Environment and Life Sciences offer the Bachelor of Arts in Biology and Marine Affairs; the Bachelor of Landscape Architecture in Landscape Architecture, and the Bachelor of Science in Animal Science and Technology (options in animal science, animal management, and pre–veterinary science), Aquaculture and Fishery Technology, Biological Sciences, Biology, Environmental and Natural Resources Economics, Environmental Horticulture and Turfgrass Management, Environmental Science and Management, Geosciences, Landscape Architecture, Marine Affairs, Marine Biology, Medical Laboratory Science and Biotechnology Manufacturing (with options in medical laboratory science and biotechnology), Microbiology (with a biotechnology option), Nutrition and Dietetics, and Wildlife and Conservation Biology.

The College of Human Science and Services offer the Bachelor of Science in Communicative Disorders, Education (with options in early childhood education, elementary education, music education, physical education, and secondary education), Health Studies, Human Development and Family Studies, Kinesiology (with options in exercise science, health studies, and early contingent physical therapy), Textiles, Fashion Merchandising and Design (with options in apparel studies, fashion merchandising, interior furnishings and design, and textile science), and Textile Marketing. The College of Human Science and Services also offers an accelerated Bachelor's-Master's Degree program in Speech-Language Pathology.

The College of Nursing offers the Bachelor of Science degree in Nursing, which is approved by the Commission on Collegiate Nursing Education and the Rhode Island Board of Nurse Registration and Nursing Education.

The College of Pharmacy offers a Bachelor of Science in Pharmaceutical Sciences. The College also offers a six-year Doctor of Pharmacy degree, which is accredited by the American Council on Pharmaceutical Education.

Pre-professional preparation is available in dentistry, law, medicine, physical therapy, and veterinary studies.

Academic Program

All programs of study aim for a balance of the natural and social sciences, the humanities, and professional subjects. All freshmen who enter the University to earn a bachelor's degree are first enrolled in University College; its advising program helps students choose a concentration and appropriate courses. A student must meet the curricular requirements of the college in which the degree is to be earned. As a general rule, 120 credits are required for a Bachelor of Arts degree and 130 for a Bachelor of Science degree, including the specified general education requirements. The University of Rhode Island operates on a two-semester calendar, with semesters beginning in September and January. Two 5-week summer sessions are also available. Credit is granted to students who have passed a College Board Advanced Placement examination with a grade of 3 or better in most subject areas. In addition, credit may be given for satisfactory scores on departmental proficiency examinations or College-Level Examination Program (CLEP) subject examinations and for the International Baccalaureate Program exam (IB Higher Level Tests). The University Honors Program offers academically talented students opportunities to broaden their intellectual development and to strengthen their preparation in their major fields of study.

Off-Campus Programs

The Office of Experiential Learning and Community Engagement offers internships for academic credit, including one-semester and one-year programs. The Office of International Education and National Student Exchange offers students the opportunity to study in more than 200 affiliated study-abroad programs, located in more than sixty different countries, including domestic exchange opportunities with other universities in the U.S. and its territories (National Student Exchange/NSE).

Academic Facilities

The University library has more than 1 million bound volumes and 1.5 million titles available electronically. Active research programs are carried on in all seven colleges. The Graduate School of Oceanography, located on the Narragansett Bay Campus, provides undergraduates with a living research lab for science-related courses. The University houses a large collection of American historic textiles, a center for robotics research, a planetarium, the Watson House Museum, a Confucius Institute, two animal science farms, and the state Crime Lab for forensic study.

Costs

The comprehensive cost for 2011–12 was estimated at $39,814 for out-of-state students and $23,726 for Rhode Islanders. This covers tuition, fees, and room and board. Books, travel, and personal expenses are not included in these figures. Laboratory fees are extra. The University participates in the cooperative plan of the New England Board of Higher Education, whereby students from other New England states are able to enroll in certain degree programs that are not offered in their own states and pay reduced tuition.

Financial Aid

To be considered for financial aid at the University, students must submit the Free Application for Federal Student Aid (FAFSA). Although there is no deadline for applying, priority is given to applications received by March 1. Most students receive notification of admission decisions by April 1. Merit scholarships are available to incoming freshmen with superior academic credentials. Consideration for these scholarships is given to freshmen who apply by the December 1 early action deadline. For 2011–12, 75 percent of new students who completed applications were awarded some form of aid. In addition, students have opportunities

for employment through work-study programs that use federal, state, and institutional funds.

Faculty

The faculty consists of 684 full-time equivalent members, or 1 professor for every 15.5 students. Approximately 86 percent of the full-time faculty members hold doctoral degrees. Faculty members serve both the graduate and undergraduate populations and have wide-ranging interests and responsibilities. In addition to teaching and research, they serve as student advisers.

Student Government

The Student Senate is a legislative body that represents the students to the administration and faculty and supervises extracurricular activities. It also distributes the activities funds among the various student organizations through its funding committee. Individual residence halls form their own governments. The Interfraternity Council supervises fraternity affairs, and the Panhellenic Association governs sorority life. The Commuter Association provides social activities and other assistance for commuter students.

Admission Requirements

Admission to the University is competitive. Applicants are given individual consideration, but it is expected that all candidates have completed at least 18 units of college-preparatory work; specific unit requirements vary for each of the seven colleges of the University. Academic achievement in a challenging high school program receives the strongest consideration in the review of an applicant's credentials. An audition is required for the Bachelor of Music degree. All freshman candidates must submit a high school transcript and scores on the SAT or the ACT examination, which should be taken no later than January 1 of the senior year. International students for whom English is not the primary language must take the Test of English as a Foreign Language (TOEFL). An English as a Second Language program is available on campus. Scores on equivalency examinations may be presented by applicants who have not been able to complete formal high school studies. Transfer students may enter in either semester (although some degree programs admit students only in the fall semester) and must submit transcripts of all previous work at both the high school and college levels. Early admission is available to high school juniors with superior records.

Students are selected primarily on the basis of academic competence and without regard to age, race, religion, color, sex, creed, national origin, disability, or sexual orientation.

Application and Information

Visits to the campus are encouraged. Information sessions and tours are scheduled daily during the week and on many Saturdays throughout the year. Students should visit the Admission Web site (http://www.uri.edu/admission) for details about these sessions as well as open house programs and directions to the campus. Admission representatives attend college fairs in Rhode Island and throughout the Northeast and beyond during the academic year.

Students are encouraged to submit applications early in their final year of high school. The early action deadline is December 1, and students receive notification by January 31. The regular deadline for fall term freshman applications is February 1, and the deadline for transfer applications is June 1. Regular decision freshman applicants will receive their decisions by March 31. The closing date for spring-term applications is November 1. The University of Rhode Island is a Common Application School. Requests for information should be directed to:

Office of Admission
University of Rhode Island
14 Upper College Road
Kingston, Rhode Island 02881
Phone: 401-874-7000
E-mail: admission@uri.edu
Web site: http://www.uri.edu/admission

UNIVERSITY OF SAINT JOSEPH
WEST HARTFORD, CONNECTICUT

The University

The University of Saint Joseph is focused on helping students fulfill their potential by combining excellence in liberal arts with a career-focused, professional education for women. Since the University's founding in 1932, the vision of the Sisters of Mercy has continued to shape the way the University of Saint Joseph (USJ) has grown. USJ offers students the opportunity to study in competitive undergraduate and graduate degree programs, including the University's first co-ed doctoral program—pharmacy—and a Doctor of Nursing Practice program set to begin in January 2013. With an emphasis on offering an academically rigorous education framed within a commitment to service in the community, the University of Saint Joseph is a place the student can quickly call home.

The core value of compassionate service, Catholic identity, commitment to women through academic excellence, and diversity is evident in the University's curriculum and daily life. Students from a multitude of faith traditions and backgrounds are empowered for success.

There are 870 undergraduates in the women's program. Faculty members and students emphasize leadership in academics, career, and community. Drawing on its Mercy heritage, the University is a community that promotes the growth of the whole person. This is accomplished in a caring environment that encourages strong ethical values, personal integrity, and a sense of responsibility to the needs of society. Women lead every organization on campus, from the Business Society and Student Government to honors societies. Students shine in artistic performances, as coordinators of community service projects, and on the athletic fields. Students also serve with faculty members and administrators on University-wide committees. In the field of athletics, the University's women compete in eight NCAA Division III sports: basketball, cross-country, lacrosse, softball, soccer, swimming/diving, tennis, and volleyball. The O'Connell Athletic Center features a six-lane pool, gymnasium, suspended jogging track, dance studio, fitness center, outdoor track, softball field, and tennis courts for all students' recreational purposes.

The University of Saint Joseph has a beautiful residential campus in the bustling town of West Hartford. Approximately 70 percent of the first-year students live on campus. Special student services include career planning, alumni mentoring, internship placement, counseling, health services, academic advisement, and campus ministry.

The University of Saint Joseph alumni have considerable impact on the welfare of their communities. They are leaders in many fields, including aerospace research, business, education, environmental science, law, medicine, and politics. Recent graduates enjoy successful careers in accounting, the arts, business, education, government, health care, human services, industry, the sciences, and nonprofit organizations.

The University of Saint Joseph is accredited by the New England Association of Schools and Colleges. Program accreditors include: Accreditation Council for Pharmacy Education, Commission on Accreditation of the American Dietetic Association, American Chemical Society, Commission on Collegiate Nursing Education, American Association for Marriage and Family Therapy, National Council for the Accreditation of Teacher Education, Council on Social Work Education, Council for Accreditation of Counseling and Related Educational Programs.

Location

The University of Saint Joseph is located in suburban West Hartford, 4 miles from the state capitol and the city of Hartford's arts and entertainment district. Among the nearby attractions are the XL Center and Coliseum; Bushnell Performing Arts Center, where the latest Broadway musicals are performed; and the Wadsworth Atheneum, the oldest public art gallery in the United States.

Hartford is a cosmopolitan city with diverse ethnic flavors. It is also the home of the Tony Award–winning Hartford Stage Company, the Hartford Symphony Orchestra, the Connecticut Opera Company, the Hartford Ballet, and the Dodge Music Center, which features indoor and outdoor concerts. West Hartford Center, just minutes from campus, offers an array of coffee bars, boutiques, restaurants, and a beautiful music theater in the newly completed Blue Back Square.

Majors and Degrees

The University of Saint Joseph has always enjoyed a strong academic reputation based on career-focused professional majors. The University awards the B.A. or B.S. in accounting, art history, biochemistry, biology, chemistry, child study, English, family studies, history, international studies, management, mathematics, nursing, nutrition and dietetics, philosophy, psychology, religious studies, social work, Spanish, special education, and women's studies. Pre-professional plans of study are offered in conjunction with an academic major and include pre-pharmacy, pre-dentistry, pre-law, pre-medicine, pre–physical therapy, and pre–veterinary studies.

Teaching certification is offered in elementary education, secondary education, and special education. Research, clinical, and work placements are important components of all academic programs.

Academic Programs

Each student must complete a minimum of 120 credits to obtain a baccalaureate degree, and 47 of those credits must be distributed among the general education/liberal arts courses at the University. Specifically, students must take courses in the humanities, social sciences, natural sciences, philosophy, religious studies, and physical education. An academic advisement counselor assists each student in planning her program of study.

Many unique facets to the academic programs offered increase students' propensity for success. An honors program and several dual degree programs are offered. The Center for Academic Excellence manages the University's award-winning Writing Portfolio Program, which enhances students' writing skills. The center also provides tutoring and other academic support services. An exciting component of most majors at the University of Saint Joseph is the internship. Students earn credit for internships at a variety of sites, including the state capitol, the Bushnell Performing Arts Center, Aetna, legislative offices, the Connecticut Department of Economic Development, WVIT-TV, Connecticut Children's Medical Center, the Science Center of Connecticut, and numerous other businesses.

Off-Campus Programs

Students at the University of Saint Joseph may take courses at cooperating institutions through the Hartford Consortium for Higher Education. This is a special arrangement among five Hartford-area colleges—the University of Saint Joseph, Trinity College, University of Connecticut Greater Hartford Branch, Central Connecticut State University, and the University of Hartford—through which students are able to cross-register for courses as part of their fulltime credit load. No additional tuition is charged, and all credits are transferable.

Students at the University of Saint Joseph have countless opportunities for global study experiences through many study-abroad programs. Students are assisted by the Director of International Studies and Programs in planning for an international-study experience during a semester, winter recess, or even over spring break. The University of Saint Joseph also offers specialized programs in Guyana, South America, and the Netherlands. In Guyana, students in the education and health science fields participate at the University's sister hospital to gain valuable work experience abroad during their junior or senior years. The University also

hosts an embedded course in the Netherlands, where students in psychology, social work, education, nutrition, and nursing travel to HAN University.

Students majoring in nursing, social work, and nutrition, and those in the graduate counseling program, may gain practical experience providing community-based, accessible health screenings and referrals; health and nutrition education; counseling services; and social work case management services at the Wellness Center on Church Street in Hartford. The University has also established a partnership with the Franciscan Center for Urban Ministry in order to reach out to its neighboring city and enhance the quality of life of its residents in need.

Academic Facilities

The Pope Pius XII Library has a collection of more than 134,000 volumes, including computer databases, periodicals, microforms, audiovisuals, a Sirsi online catalog, and OCLC interlibrary loans. A collection of materials used in elementary and secondary education is featured in the Curriculum Materials Center.

The University uses laboratory schools with several of its academic programs. The renowned School for Young Children, located one block from the campus, is an operating preschool that provides child study majors with training and experience. The Gengras Center, located on the campus, is a special education school serving children and young adults (ages 4–21) from approximately fifty-three area cities and towns in Connecticut and Massachusetts. It provides for special education needs and also helps to prepare special education teachers.

The University's primary technology centers are located in McDonough Hall; Internet/Wi-Fi access is available throughout campus. Additional facilities and services include a media center that provides production materials, expertise, and equipment for making and using a number of media instructional aids; science and nursing labs; and the Carol Autorino Center for the Arts and Humanities. The center includes Lynch Hall, which houses humanities, faculty offices, and classrooms; the Bruyette Athenaeum, featuring the 365-seat Hoffman Auditorium; the University of Saint Joseph Art Gallery; a print study room; large lecture hall; reception room; and music practice rooms. The building also houses the University's archives.

Costs

The tuition and fees for full-time freshmen entering in 2012 are $31,826. Room and board cost is $12,274. The cost per credit for part-time students is $670.

Financial Aid

The goal of the University of Saint Joseph financial aid program is to place a high-quality, private education within the reach of as many qualified students as possible. This goal is achieved by offering need- and merit-based financial aid that includes a combination of grants, loans, and on-campus employment opportunities. More than 90 percent of full-time undergraduate students receive some form of financial assistance. Merit-based scholarship awards are available to all eligible first-year, transfer, and international students.

Faculty

University of Saint Joseph faculty consists of 108 full-time faculty members and 4 librarians. Of the total faculty, 71 percent are women. Of the full-time faculty, 92 percent hold the highest possible degrees in their fields. Small classes benefit both students and professors. The student-faculty ratio is 12:1. The faculty and all members of the University community promote the welfare of students and help them attain the objectives set forth by the University's mission. Faculty members also serve as advisers for many extracurricular activities, including sports, campus ministry, and community service; direct students in independent study; involve students in scholarly research; and act as mentors before and after graduation.

Student Government

The Student Government Association works for effective communication among students, faculty members, and administrators. Students are encouraged to voice their opinions and concerns to the association for consideration and action. In addition, student representatives sit as voting members with faculty members and administrators on major University-wide committees. The Student Government Association encourages the development of leadership skills and provides funds annually for several of its members to attend leadership workshops and conferences.

Admission Requirements

The University of Saint Joseph seeks women who are anxious to accept the challenge of rigorous academic programs while pursuing the interests and careers that will help them achieve their goals. Applications are encouraged from interested students of every race, age, and religious affiliation. In accordance with Section 504 of the Rehabilitation Act of 1973, which prohibits discrimination on the basis of disability, and the Americans with Disabilities Act of 1990, the University of Saint Joseph is committed to the goal of achieving equal educational opportunities and full participation for people with disabilities in higher education.

Candidates for first-year admission should complete a four-year course of study in a regionally accredited secondary school or have equivalent homeschooling preparation. The program should include 16 academic units in college-preparatory courses distributed among the areas of English, mathematics, natural sciences, social studies, and foreign languages. Applicants are required to submit scores of the SAT or ACT tests. A personal interview is a highly recommended part of the admission procedure, since it offers a mutual opportunity for the student and Admissions Counselors to discuss educational and professional goals.

The Office of Admissions operates on the principle that a student's ability, motivation, and maturity should be determined by a careful individual review of all the applicant's credentials, including the academic record, standardized test scores, written personal statement, and letter(s) of recommendation. Special consideration may be given to some applicants whose preparation varies from the recommended pattern but whose record gives evidence of genuine intellectual ability and interest. International students should contact the Office of Admissions for further information. Additional information is available online at http://www.sjc.edu/admissions.

Application and Information

The University of Saint Joseph operates using a rolling admission, which means students can apply at any time during their senior year in high school. A nonrefundable $50 fee must be sent with paper applications; the application fee is waived for students who apply online. Students are encouraged to begin the financial aid process by completing the FAFSA form online at http://www.fafsa.ed.gov as soon as possible after January 1 of the year they are applying for admission. The priority deadline for completing the FAFSA is February 15. Students should complete the FAFSA using estimated income information if they or their families will not have completed their tax returns prior to February 15. Financial aid counselors are available to assist prospective students and families with the financial aid process.

For further information about admission to the University of Saint Joseph, students should contact:

Eileen Hocking
Director of Admissions
University of Saint Joseph
1678 Asylum Avenue
West Hartford, Connecticut 06117
United States
Phone: 860-231-5216
866-442-8752 (toll-free)
Fax: 860-231-5744
E-mail: admissions@usj.edu
Web site: http://www.usj.edu/admissions

UNIVERSITY OF SAN FRANCISCO
SAN FRANCISCO, CALIFORNIA

The University

From its beginnings as a one-room schoolhouse, founded in 1855 by the Jesuits, the University of San Francisco (USF) has developed into one of the premier Jesuit Catholic universities on the West Coast. Throughout its history, USF has been committed to preparing students to improve the world in which they live. With more than 9,500 undergraduate and graduate students, the University has remained faithful to the Jesuit tradition and has maintained its small class size and low student-faculty ratio. Its programs in the arts, the sciences, business, education, nursing, and law foster a love of learning grounded by the challenge to serve society. The University's foundation encompasses academic excellence; the Jesuit, Catholic learning tradition; a multicultural, diverse community; and a global perspective that begins in San Francisco, which offers unparalleled opportunities for internships, service, and connections.

USF is one of the most diverse university campuses in the United States. Living and learning with a student body that consists of students from forty-seven states and seventy-five other countries is a unique opportunity. All new incoming freshmen under the age of 21 are required to live on the campus, unless they live within 40 miles of the University. More than 90 percent of the incoming freshmen and 40 percent of all undergraduates live on-campus.

The University offers five on-campus residence halls, two on-campus apartment-style residences, and one off-campus traditional residence hall. Gillson, Hayes-Healy, and Phelan house freshmen, while Lone Mountain houses sophomores and upper-division students. Fromm Hall is the only all-female residence hall for first- and second-year students. Located just twelve blocks from the USF campus, Pedro Arrupe Hall is the off-campus traditional residence hall offered to upper-division students. Loyola Village is a residential community that features apartment-style living for third-year, fourth-year, and graduate students. Most rooms in residence halls are doubles, with some single rooms available for upper-division students. Each residence hall has laundry facilities, study rooms, community kitchens, television lounges, and 24-hour front desk staff.

On the campus, students have access to various University facilities. The Koret Health and Recreation Center is an exciting complex that provides facilities for exercise, racquetball, court games, weight training, massage, personal training, and various aquatic activities in an Olympic-size pool. Tai Chi, yoga, hip-hop, and spinning are just some of the classes offered at Koret. Outdoor adventures include horseback riding, camping, sailing, and sea kayaking. Intramural and club sports are offered in the fall and spring semesters and include basketball, boxing, flag football, fencing, karate, soccer, lacrosse, rugby, and co-ed volleyball. Special aquatic sports include a Masters swim team and a water polo club. NCAA Division I sports include baseball, basketball, cross-country, golf, soccer, tennis, track and field, and women's volleyball.

Dining facilities are located all over campus and are within walking distance of the residence halls and classrooms. Located on the main campus, The Market Café offers a food court experience with a variety of choices, including global, vegan, homestyle classics, and vegetarian options. Other dining options include Outtakes Café, Outtahere Café, Crossroads Café, Club Ed in the School of Education, and Kendrick Café at the Law School.

Undergraduates keep busy by participating in over 120 on-campus, student-run associations, fraternities and sororities, honor societies, and clubs, such as the USF Rugby Club and Los Locos, a club that supports USF athletics. Among these clubs are the oldest continuously performing theater group west of the Mississippi River, an award-winning weekly newspaper, and a literary magazine.

For students interested in giving back to the community, the Office of Service-Learning and Community Action forms a partnership between the local community and USF. Students may participate in community service activities that include preparing meals for the homeless, tutoring underprivileged children, habitat restoration, and annual events such as AIDS Walk San Francisco.

Location

The University of San Francisco is located on a stunning 58-acre campus in a residential neighborhood just minutes from downtown San Francisco, the Financial District, Fisherman's Wharf, and the Pacific Ocean. The hilltop campus, renowned for its beautiful landscaping, borders the 1,000-acre Golden Gate Park and offers spectacular panoramic views of the city. The dynamic city of San Francisco keeps students entertained with concerts, the ballet, opera, museum exhibits, theater, and sporting events. Because of the diversity and geographical compactness of San Francisco, students find research facilities, opportunities for community involvement, and employment experiences that cannot be matched by most cities.

Majors and Degrees

The College of Arts and Sciences offers both B.A. and B.S. degrees. Majors include advertising, architecture and community design, art history/arts management, biology, chemistry, communication studies, comparative literature and culture, computer science, design, economics, economics 4+1, education (dual-degree in teacher preparation), English, environmental science, environmental studies, exercise and sports science, fine arts, French studies, history, international and development economics 4+1, Japanese studies, Latin American studies, mathematics, media studies, performing arts and social justice, philosophy, physics, physics/engineering (dual-degree, 3+2 program), politics, psychology, sociology, Spanish, theology and religious studies, undeclared arts, and undeclared science. The School of Management offers Bachelor of Science degrees in accounting, advanced global entrepreneurship management, business administration, entrepreneurship, finance, hospitality industry management, international business, and marketing with a concentration in multicultural marketing. The School of Nursing and Health Professions offers a four-year Bachelor of Science in Nursing for qualified high school graduates and for second-baccalaureate candidates.

USF has seventy-two minors and offers unique programs that enhance the learning experience at USF. Special programs include astronomy; African and African-American studies; Asia Pacific studies; Catholic studies and social thought; ethnic studies; film studies; honors program in the humanities; journalism; Judaic studies; Latino/a and Chicano/a Studies; Middle Eastern studies; neuroscience; 4+3 dual degrees in law, military science, premedical, and other pre-professional health studies; public relations; Saint Ignatius Institute program; a five-year dual-degree teacher preparation program that results in teacher certification at the elementary or secondary level; and the School of Management honors cohort program.

Academic Programs

The University of San Francisco is committed to providing students with the essentials of a well-rounded education. A baccalaureate degree is issued upon the successful completion of a 128-unit curriculum. The curriculum consists of 44 units of core courses chosen from six specified categories in addition to 80–85 units that are divided among departmental major requirements and electives. An honors program is available for selected superior students seeking a strong academic challenge. The academic year is based on the two-semester system, with summer sessions and a winter intersession also available.

In an effort to encourage high school students to move rapidly into the study of subjects now customarily reserved for colleges, the University of San Francisco honors advanced placement credits, as certified by the College Board's Advanced Placement Program tests and the International Baccalaureate program. The University also cooperates with the College-Level Examination Program (CLEP). Students intending to earn such credit must take the

CLEP examinations prior to registering at the University for their freshman courses.

The USF Pre-Professional Health Committee serves to guide and recommend students to medical and dental professional health schools as well as to schools for pharmacy, optometry, veterinary medicine, and podiatry. A student may complete the premedical or other pre–health science requirements as part of, or in addition to, the requirements of an academic major. The Pre-Professional Health Committee assists students with the application process, develops a professional file for each student, collects and mails recommendations to professional schools, conducts interviews in preparation for application, and endorses approved candidates via a committee letter of recommendation sent to all professional schools selected by the student.

The St. Ignatius Institute has an integrated core curriculum based on the great books of Western civilization and an emphasis upon the great works of Christianity. Any undergraduate student at the University, regardless of major, may take courses through the Institute to meet general education requirements. The University also offers Army ROTC. ROTC scholarships are available for qualified applicants and continuing students.

Off-Campus Programs

The University of San Francisco's Center for Global Education has numerous study-abroad programs available to students with junior standing and a cumulative minimum GPA of 3.0. Exchanges with Jesuit universities include locations in Japan, Mexico, China, Spain, Philippines, El Salvador, and Chile. USF's St. Ignatius Institute program includes an exchange with Oxford University in England. Affiliations with other Jesuit universities make travel to other countries possible, e.g., Gonzaga University's study-abroad program in Florence, Italy, and Loyola University of Chicago's program in Rome. USF is also an associate member of the Institute of European and Asian Studies, which offers programs in Durham and London, England; Paris, Dijon, and Nantes, France; Berlin and Freiburg, Germany; Vienna, Austria; Madrid and Salamanca, Spain; Milan, Italy; Tokyo and Nagoya, Japan; Moscow, Russia; Adelaide and Canberra, Australia; Beijing, China; and Singapore. Numerous other study-abroad opportunities are also available. USF assists students in selecting a location, applying to programs, making financial arrangements, registering for academic credit, securing a passport and visa, and making travel plans.

Academic Facilities

University of San Francisco students have access to Gleeson Library's more than 1.8 million holdings and Harney Science Center, which houses the Computer Center, Applied Math Laboratory, the Institute of Chemical Biology, and the Physics Research Laboratories. Cowell Hall, the base for nursing classes and the Nursing Skills Laboratory, also includes the Instructional Media Center. Students also have access to Phelan Hall, the home of *The Foghorn,* the official campus newspaper. Malloy Hall, headquarters for the School of Management, houses an additional computer laboratory and special seminar rooms. Kalmanovitz Hall, the new home for humanities and social sciences, features state-of-the-art classrooms, a rooftop sculpture garden, and seventeen laboratories for language, writing, media, and psychology.

Costs

Tuition for the 2011–12 school year was $37,040. Room and board were $12,250 for the academic year. Books, travel, and other expenses are about $5100 per year.

Financial Aid

A variety of financial aid programs are available at the University, including scholarships, merit awards, grants, loans, and campus employment opportunities. Domestic students who wish to be considered for financial aid must file the Free Application for Federal Student Aid (FAFSA) by February 1. More than two thirds of all USF students receive some type of financial aid.

The University Scholars Program is available to new domestic freshmen applicants who have an exceptional cumulative GPA, SAT combined score, or ACT composite score. Scholars are awarded a non-need-based scholarship that pays a significant percentage of the cost of tuition for four years of undergraduate study. To remain eligible, University Scholars are expected to maintain a minimum

GPA of 3.25. Eligible students are identified during the admission process and must apply under early action by the November 15 deadline.

Faculty

The University has 962 full- and part-time faculty members; 91 percent of them hold doctoral or terminal degrees in the field they teach. The University of San Francisco fosters a close relationship between students and faculty members. This is reflected in the small size of classes, the low student-faculty ratio, and the faculty members' availability for advising. Classes are not taught by student teachers or teachers' assistants.

Student Government

All undergraduates are members of the Associated Students of the University of San Francisco (ASUSF). ASUSF is the official representative body of undergraduate students at USF. The ASUSF government has three functions: to represent the official student viewpoint, to recommend policies, and to fund activities and services. ASUSF consists of three branches: the executive branch, the Student Senate, and the Student Court. The Senate comprises an executive board and student senators.

Admission Requirements

The University seeks students who are sincerely interested in pursuing a well-rounded education. The admission process is selective, and each application is reviewed individually. To enhance the quality and diversity of its student body, the University of San Francisco encourages men and women of all races, nationalities, and religious beliefs to apply. Eligibility is based on high school course work and GPA, the application essay, an academic and personal recommendation, and satisfactory test scores. Domestic applicants are required to submit SAT or ACT test scores with writing. International applicants are required to submit TOEFL or IELTS test scores; however, if an international applicant submits sufficient SAT or ACT test scores, the TOEFL or IELTS may be waived.

Application and Information

A completed application includes the application form, the application fee, a personal essay, all academic transcripts, standardized test scores, and up to two letters of recommendation. For the fall semester, the application deadlines are November 15 for early action (freshmen only) and January 15 for regular action (freshmen and transfers).

Inquiries should be addressed to:

Office of Admission
University of San Francisco
2130 Fulton Street
San Francisco, California 94117-1080
Phone: 415-422-6563
      800-CALL-USF (toll-free outside California)
Fax: 415-422-2217
E-mail: admission@usfca.edu
Web site: http://www.usfca.edu
      http://www.facebook.com/University.of.San.Francisco
      http://twitter.com/USFCA
      http://www.youtube.com/usfcalifornia

The University of San Francisco—where students are invited to change the world.

UNIVERSITY OF SOUTH FLORIDA
TAMPA, FLORIDA

The University

The University of South Florida (USF) is among America's largest and most dynamic national research universities. Founded in 1956, USF opened in 1960 with an enrollment of nearly 2,000 and now has more than 47,000 students in more than 200 degree programs at all levels. As the principal university for the Tampa Bay region, USF serves the community and offers degrees on several campuses within the region.

USF's national stature as an academic institution was acknowledged by the Carnegie Foundation for the Advancement of Teaching, which ranked the University in the top tier of American colleges and universities as Research University (Very High Research Activity). USF is one of three universities in the state of Florida in the top tier. The University receives more than $394.1 million in external funding to support research and development projects. USF's libraries include more than 2.6 million titles and provide access to hundreds of databases worldwide.

USF's student body is as diverse as its academic program profile. African Americans, Hispanics, and students from other minority groups comprise 30 percent of the undergraduate student body. Approximately 60 percent of the students are women. Geographically, students come to the USF from all fifty states and more than 150 countries.

USF is accredited by the Commission on Colleges of the Southern Association of Colleges and Schools. In addition, a number of scientific, professional, and academic bodies confer accreditation in specific disciplines and groups of disciplines.

The Office of Career Services works with hundreds of companies to provide internships and cooperative education programs for students. The office also provides an online and on-campus referral service and interview program. Classes for students are available in resume writing, interviewing, and etiquette. The University hosts both full- and part-time career fairs each semester.

Traditional-style housing units, suites, apartments, fraternities and sororities, and married and family student housing units accommodate 16 percent of the students on the Tampa campus. Several thousand more students live in apartments located within walking distance of the campus. All residence halls are wired and furnished and include all utilities. Special-interest and honors housing is also available to students who qualify. Freshmen are required to live on campus their first year.

There are more than 400 student clubs and organizations at USF. The University also has over forty national fraternities and sororities. In addition, USF schedules a wide array of extracurricular programs, including concerts, movies, and a lecture series. USF is a member of the NCAA and the Big East Conference. All teams compete on the NCAA Division I level. USF's men's teams compete in intercollegiate baseball, basketball, cross-country, football, golf, soccer, tennis, and track. The USF women's teams compete in intercollegiate basketball, cross-country, golf, sailing, soccer, softball, tennis, track, and volleyball. Campus Recreation also offers club sports, intramural sports, and outdoor adventures. On the Tampa campus, there is an eighteen-hole championship golf course, four swimming pools, sand volleyball courts, tennis courts, a state-of-the-art recreation center, indoor and outdoor racquetball courts, and a private riverfront park.

Location

USF is located on 1,700 acres in north Tampa, across the street from the Busch Gardens Theme Park. Regional campuses are located in St. Petersburg and Sarasota/Manatee.

Majors and Degrees

The University awards the Bachelor of Arts and Bachelor of Sciences degrees and a variety of graduate and doctoral degrees through the Colleges of Arts and Sciences, Behavioral & Community Sciences, Business, Education, Engineering, Global Sustainability, Honors, Marine Science, Medicine, Nursing, Pharmacy, Public Health, The Arts, and University College.

At the undergraduate level, USF offers the following degree programs: accounting, advertising, Africana studies, American studies and humanities, anthropology, applied sciences, art studio and art history, athletic training, business administration, biology and microbiology, biomedical science, chemical engineering, chemistry, civil and environmental engineering, classics, communication, communication sciences and disorders, computer science and engineering, criminology, dance, dance studies, early childhood education, economics, electrical engineering, elementary education, English, environmental science and policy, finance, foreign languages, geography, geology, gerontology, government and international affairs, health professions (pre-health), health sciences, history, honors college research, hotel and restaurant management, industrial and management systems, engineering, information technology, interdisciplinary classical civilizations, interdisciplinary natural science, interdisciplinary social sciences, international business, international studies, management, management information systems, marketing, mass communications, mathematics, mechanical engineering, medical technology, music, music education, music studies, nursing, philosophy, physical education, physics, political science, pre-law, psychology, public health, religious studies, secondary education, social work, sociology, special education, theater, and women's studies.

Academic Programs

USF offers students a well-rounded education through a core curriculum of general education and liberal arts requirements. In addition to fulfilling the general education requirements, each student must complete the necessary major and/or minor requirements to reach the minimum of 120 hours for graduation. USF also requires students to complete 9 hours of exit requirements; these courses complement the overall curriculum of all degree programs.

The University Honors College and University Experience are programs that help students broaden their horizons and expand their critical thinking skills. The University also offers Army, Air Force, and Naval ROTC leadership courses and off-campus courses for those students who prefer to study independently.

Off-Campus Programs

A cooperative education program is offered through the Office of Career Services. Students may either alternate semesters between school and work experience or choose to do a parallel program. Education Abroad offers a variety of study abroad opportunities in more than 25 countries including USF faculty-led summer and short-term programs, semester exchanges, dual-degree programs, international internships, independent research, and service learning.

Costs

For 2011–12, tuition costs were as follows: $5800 for state residents attending full-time ($14,990 for nonresidents). Full- and part-time tuition and fees vary according to class time, course load, and location. Room and board costs were $9190 and vary according to board plan, housing facility, and location. Costs are subject to change each academic year.

Financial Aid

The University of South Florida awards $292 million in aid to help students reach their educational goals. Financial aid is awarded according to each student's need, academic standing, and/or talents in relation to college costs and may include grants, loans, scholarships, and/or part-time employment. The priority application deadline is January 2 for academic scholarships and March 1 for federal and institutional aid. Need-based programs include federal monetary awards such as Federal Pell Grants, Federal Work-Study Program awards, Federal Stafford Student Loans, and Federal Perkins Loans. State aid includes programs such as the Florida Student Assistance Grant program, Florida Work Experience Program, and the Florida Bright Futures Scholarship program. To qualify for federal and state aid, students should submit the Free Application for Federal Student Aid (FAFSA).

Faculty

The University has 1,820 instructional faculty members, including 53 endowed chairs. Approximately 92 percent are full-time and more than 81 percent of faculty members hold a terminal degree in their field. Each student is assigned an academic adviser and all faculty members are required to hold office hours to meet with students in groups or on an individual basis. The student-faculty ratio is 24:1.

Student Government

USF's Student Government is open to all students. Each college within the University and each regional campus elects its own Student Government representatives. The Student Government is divided into three branches: the executive, the legislative, and the judicial. Student Government is responsible for the allocation of all activity and service fees paid by student tuition. Student Government–sponsored events and services are free to students.

Admission Requirements

For admissions purposes, USF computes a high school GPA based on grades earned in all college-prep academic courses. In computing a GPA, USF assigns additional weight to grades earned in honors, dual enrollment, Advanced Placement (AP), Advanced Certificate of Education (AICE), and International Baccalaureate (IB) courses. The most important factors in determining admission to USF are the quality of the high school record, rigor of curriculum, and performance on either the SAT or ACT with writing.

To be considered for admission, freshman applicants must submit an application for admission, a nonrefundable $30 application fee, an official high school transcript, official SAT or ACT scores, and official GED or IETLS/TOEFL scores (if applicable).

Transfer applicants with fewer than 60 transferable semester credit hours are considered lower-level transfer students. These students must meet all freshman and transfer requirements and submit an application for admission, a nonrefundable $30 application fee, an official transcript from each college or university they have attended, an official high school transcript, SAT or ACT scores, and official GED or IETLS/TOEFL scores (if applicable). In addition, students with 12–23 transferrable credits are required to submit a personal statement that outlines the reasons why they wish to transfer to USF.

Upper-level transfer students are those with 60 or more transferable semester credit hours. These students must submit an application for admissions, a nonrefundable $30 application fee, an official transcript from each college or university they have

attended, and IELTS/TOEFL scores (if applicable). In addition, upper-level transfer applicants with 102 or more transferrable credits must submit a personal statement indicating the reasons why they wish to transfer to USF.

Some students who show potential, but who do not meet the criteria for admission, may be placed on a waiting list or may be considered for the Student Support Services/Freshman Summer Institute held during the summer.

USF accepts transfer credits from institutions that are accredited by one of the regional accrediting agencies/commissions recognized by USF at the time the credits are earned. To be considered for admission, transfer applicants must have at least a 2.50 GPA (2.00 for students from select public community colleges in Florida), a 67 percent course completion ratio, and be in good academic standing from the last college or university they attended.

Application and Information

Students are encouraged to visit USF and experience the campus for themselves. Campus visit programs are offered Monday through Friday at 10 a.m. and 2 p.m. Tours are also offered on most Saturdays at 10 a.m. during the academic year (September through April). Reservations are strongly encouraged, and students may make reservations online at http://www.usf.edu/campusvisit.

For more information, students should contact:

David Lee Henry, Director of Admissions
University of South Florida
4202 East Fowler Avenue, SVC 1036
Tampa, Florida 33620-9951
Phone: 813-974-3350
Fax: 813-974-9689
Web site: http://www.usf.edu/admissions

Here is where you want to be. Tampa not only has terrific weather, it has amazing cultural, recreational, internship, service-learning, and employment opportunities.

THE UNIVERSITY OF THE ARTS
Visual Arts, Design, Film, Music, Dance, Theater
PHILADELPHIA, PENNSYLVANIA

THE UNIVERSITY OF THE ARTS

The University

The University of the Arts (UArts) is located in the heart of Philadelphia's vibrant professional arts community. For over 135 years, UArts has been a leader in educating artists, performers, and creative individuals in a wide range of disciplines. More than 2,200 students from forty-four states and thirty-one countries are enrolled in the undergraduate and graduate programs in the visual and performing arts, film, and design. Comprising the College of Art, Media, and Design (CAMD) and the College of Performing Arts (CPA), the University offers intensive concentration within a major field as well as creative challenges in multidisciplinary exploration. CAMD is one of the country's leading art colleges, with nationally renowned design, fine arts, crafts, and film programs. CPA features outstanding programs in dance, music, and theater arts.

The University sponsors a variety of activities, including gallery and museum trips to New York City and Washington, D.C. One fourth of the students live in University housing, which provides coed apartment-style accommodations with bath facilities and laundry rooms on the premises. Resident advisers live on each floor, and there is 24-hour security. First-time students are guaranteed housing if their contracts are received by May 1. The University also assists students in finding off-campus residences. Dining services operates several locations on campus, which are available to residential and commuter students.

The graduate programs of the University of the Arts offer an impressive combination of strengths: accomplished faculty members, an individualized and interactive learning environment, access to outstanding facilities and resources, specialized studios, and programs of study that are highly focused and highly flexible. UArts offers graduate degrees in art education; book arts/printmaking; industrial design; jazz studies; museum communication; museum education; museum exhibition, planning, and design; music education; and studio art. A postbaccalaureate certificate in crafts is also offered.

Location

The University's campus spans the Avenue of the Arts from South Street to Walnut Street and is the cultural hub of Center City Philadelphia. Next door to the University's historic Hamilton Hall is the Kimmel Center for the Performing Arts; in adjacent blocks are the Academy of Music, Wilma Theater, Suzanne Roberts Theater, and the University's Merriam Theater. The area also has museums (Philadelphia Museum of Art and Barnes Museum), galleries, music and dance facilities, restaurants, and retail stores. Of historic importance, but also modern and sophisticated, Philadelphia is both a major metropolitan center and a series of small, close-knit neighborhoods. Fairmount Park, one of the country's largest public park systems, provides facilities for sports activities and picnicking. Statistics show that UArts is one of the safest campuses in the city.

Majors and Degrees

The College of Art, Media, and Design confers degrees in three areas: film (B.F.A. in animation, film/video, and writing for film and television); art (B.F.A. in crafts, illustration, multidisciplinary fine arts, painting/drawing, photography, printmaking, and sculpture) and design (B.F.A. in graphic design, and multimedia; B.S. in industrial design). The college also offers a certificate program in art education and a concentration in art therapy. The School of Music confers B.M. degrees in composition, instrumental performance (with a jazz/contemporary focus) and vocal performance, as well as a B.S. in music business, entrepreneurship, and technology. A four-year diploma in music is also available. The School of Dance offers a B.F.A. in dance. The School of Theater Arts offers B.F.A. degrees in acting; musical theater; theater design and technology; and directing, playwriting, and production. Two-year certificates are also available in dance and music.

Academic Programs

Students are attracted to the University of the Arts because of its dynamic, creative atmosphere. Regardless of major, students enjoy interacting and collaborating with their peers across all creative disciplines. Students are encouraged, to the extent that their schedules allow, to take elective courses outside their chosen major, and many participate in collaborative projects with students from other programs. All students take 42 credits in liberal arts, which provides them with the historical and theoretical framework of their major field.

Freshmen in the College of Art, Media, and Design have the option of entering directly into one of the three schools offered within the College, or coming in as undecided and sampling what the schools have to offer before selecting an area of study. In the schools of design and art, students spend their first year enrolling in Core Studies courses that expose them to the skills, concepts and techniques that provide the foundation for in-depth study of a specific area. Core Studies includes courses exploring concepts of time, object, image, and environment, as well as introductory courses to the various majors within the schools. While students can declare a major within their first two years, they are welcome to use that time to explore different disciplines and find the best avenue for expressing their creativity. Students in any discipline within the College of Art, Media, and Design can also add a concentration in art education and art therapy, in preparation for graduate programs in those areas.

In the film programs (animation, film and video, and writing for film and television), freshmen may choose to enter directly into a Core Studies program that focuses on the sensory bases of moving-image art, cinematic art, and storytelling. The film curriculum includes courses in film history, history of television, video production, documentary and narrative video, screenwriting, and cinema arts, with the goal of developing students' collaboration skills and learning to combine different application areas, and producing portfolio-quality work. Internships in professional settings provide students with real-life experience in the field. Writing for film and television students learn to create feature-length screenplays, episodic television series, and movies for television.

In the College of Performing Arts, the School of Music program stresses individualized training with a performance emphasis. Students undergo intensive training in theory and musicianship. Private lessons are supplemented by master classes and ensemble work. Students in the School of Dance begin with two years of intensive studio training in multiple forms before choosing an area of emphasis for their junior and senior years. In the Ira Brind School of Theater Arts, students can choose one of four majors. Acting majors focus on developing a strong rehearsal and performance process through a wide range of acting, speech, and movement techniques. Musical theater majors train in a similar foundation technique while strengthening their skills in music and dance. Directing, playwriting, and production majors study a range of disciplines, such as stage management, directing, playwriting, dramaturgy, production and arts administration, and mask and stage combat, preparing for careers or graduate study in these or related fields. The design and technology major explores the full spectrum of theatrical design and technical production.

For students interested in music education, the 17-credit MATPREP Program enables students to complete bachelor's and master's degrees in teaching music in five years. The University has close working relationships, including internships, with professional theater, dance, and music groups in Philadelphia and elsewhere. Students are also encouraged to seek professional roles.

Academic Facilities

The University facilities are comprised of numerous buildings along Philadelphia's Avenue of the Arts, with studios, classrooms, galleries, theaters, lounges, cafes, dormitories, performance spaces, and administrative offices. Terra Hall provides seventeen floors of

studios, computer labs, classrooms, state-of-the-art performing spaces, and TV and video production and recording studios. All design departments provide individual workstations for seniors and exhibition spaces that feature student and faculty work throughout the year. The University also maintains several public galleries, including the Rosenwald-Wolf Gallery, Arronson and Solmssen Court Galleries, and the Mednick Gallery, where students may exhibit their work along with curator-managed exhibitions of the work of distinguished guest artists. Student performances are held in the University's formal theaters, such as the 1,800-seat Merriam Theater, the 239-seat state-of-the-art Caplan Center for the Performing Arts recital hall and black box theater, the 200-seat dance theater, the Gershman Hall black box theater, the Arts Bank main theater and cabaret theater, as well as many informal spaces on campus.

UArts has a multifunctional telephone system and campuswide wired and wireless Internet access. Academic computing resources include over twenty labs on Macintosh and PC platforms that are used for special applications, as well as computers for word processing and general purposes. A number of smart classrooms enable faculty to use computer applications and Internet access in their presentations; smart studios allow students to function as they would in the professional world, with a computer in the studio or office.

Students work in a variety of specialized facilities throughout the campus that support the learning of their craft. Facilities include the typography lab, the Borowsky Center for Publication Arts, digital video editing suites, photo/film/animation labs and darkrooms, a scanner lab, an SGI lab, a bronze foundry and plaster workshop, and studios and workshops for ceramics, metals, wood, glassblowing, papermaking, and fibers. The performing arts facilities include a recording studio, music technology (MIDI) studios, editing suites, music studios and practice rooms, computer labs, dance and movement studios, and acting studios.

Library facilities include Albert M. Greenfield Library, which contains an extensive collection of books, journals, photographs, and videotapes; a picture resource file; special collections, with special strengths in book arts and textiles; a 140,000-image slide library; and a music library.

Costs

Tuition for the 2012–13 academic year is $34,840 plus an $800 technology fee for freshmen. Accommodations in 3- or 4-person apartment-style dormitory units start at $8200. The nineteen-meal-per-week board plan is $4500.

Financial Aid

Last year, UArts provided $9 million in scholarships and grants to new students. About one third went to those demonstrating financial need; the balance was awarded in talent- or merit-based scholarships. Overall, UArts students receive more than $50 million in scholarships, grants, loans, and part-time employment each year. Typically, more than 80 percent of the students enrolled on a full-time basis are eligible for some type of need-based aid. All students should apply using the FAFSA as early as possible after January 1. Where need exists, UArts assists in meeting costs within its available resources.

The University funds a number of scholarships based on artistic potential and academic achievement. Financial aid is also available on the applicant's demonstrated financial need. Applicants must submit the Free Application for Federal Student Aid (FAFSA). March 1 is the suggested filing date. The University administers a full range of Federal Aid programs. Applicants who wish to be considered for scholarships should complete applications for admission and financial aid prior to March 31. Families from many different income levels can qualify for some type of financial assistance. In addition, the University's location in a large, active city provides students with diverse opportunities for part-time employment.

Faculty

Faculty members are practicing professionals who are committed to the development of their students. As active participants in the arts, they have achieved recognition in their specific fields of study and real-world experience gives them the knowledge and understanding vital to the professional and personal growth of young, emerging artists. The faculty consists of 493 full- and part-time members; the majority hold advanced degrees. The faculty-student ratio is about 1:9.

Student Government

The student activities office sponsors a variety of activities to complement academic programs, including a Halloween event, open-mike nights, fall carnival, concerts, movie nights, ice skating parties, and trips to New York and Washington, D.C.

Student Council also supports a variety of organizations, including a community service organization and a student-run gallery.

Admission Requirements

In addition to submitting a portfolio or auditioning, applicants should submit their high school transcript, SAT or ACT scores, one letter of recommendation, and a personal essay.

The placement of transfer students is made after an evaluation of their portfolio or audition and a determination of their approved credits. Transfer students may be given advanced standing.

International applicants are required to submit scores on the Test of English as a Foreign Language (TOEFL) or the International English Language Testing System (IELTS). A minimum TOEFL score of 550 (paper test)/80 (Internet test) or an IELTS score of 6.0 is required for undergraduate programs. Early entrance and deferred entrance are possible.

The University of the Arts follows a system of rolling admission. Students are encouraged to submit applications by March 15 for fall admission and December 1 for spring admission. For additional information, students should contact:

Office of Admission
University of the Arts
320 South Broad Street
Philadelphia, Pennsylvania 19102
Phone: 215-717-6049
       800-616-ARTS (toll-free)
Fax: 215-717-6045
Web site: http://www.uarts.edu

Hamilton Hall, located on the Avenue of the Arts in Center City Philadelphia.

UNIVERSITY OF THE CUMBERLANDS
WILLIAMSBURG, KENTUCKY

The University

Founded in 1889, Cumberland College became University of the Cumberlands on July 1, 2005, reflecting the diversity and excellence of options offered in high-quality education. The University is committed to providing a superior education within an exceptional Christian atmosphere at an affordable cost. Recognition by *U.S. News & World Report* in its list of America's Best Colleges and by the John Templeton Foundation as a member of its Honor Roll of Character Building Colleges signals that a University of the Cumberlands (UC) education is an exceptional value. Emphasizing the growth of the individual student, the University strives to instill in students the desire to be agents of change in the world and to use knowledge for the benefit of others as well as themselves.

UC is one of the few institutions where all students complete a leadership program. All students participate in community service as a component of this program.

University of the Cumberlands is a four-year, coed, liberal arts institution for higher education that offers a broad curriculum with more than thirty-five programs of undergraduate study, including eight preprofessional programs for professional and health science careers. Graduates enjoy a high acceptance rate to graduate and professional schools, particularly in science, business, and education. In fact, within five years of graduation, 66 percent of UC's alumni have completed or are pursuing a graduate or professional degree.

Graduate studies at University of the Cumberlands offer individual graduate courses as well as a Master of Arts in Teaching and a Master of Arts in Education degree programs with certification or concentration in various areas. Other master's programs include business administration (M.B.A.), professional counseling (M.A.P.C.), physician assistant studies (M.P.A.S.), Christian studies (M.A.C.S.), justice administration, and information systems security. Doctoral programs include educational leadership and clinical psychology.

One of the largest private institutions in the state of Kentucky, UC serves a diverse body of more than 1,800 undergraduate students from forty states and thirty countries. Primarily a residential campus, UC provides on-campus housing for about 75 percent of its students in the University's ten residence halls. A director, assisted by student staff members, supervises each hall.

Extracurricular activities abound. More than forty clubs and organizations provide students with a wide variety of activities, including a debate team, theater, musical performance groups, academic societies, an FM radio station, a student newspaper, student government, Baptist Campus Ministries, Appalachian Ministries, Mountain Outreach, Patriot Adventure Club, departmental clubs, and intramural sports.

University of the Cumberlands participates in intercollegiate competition. UC is a member of the NAIA Division I Mid-South Conference and offers opportunities in women's basketball, cross-country, golf, soccer, softball, swimming, tennis, track and field, volleyball, and wrestling; men's baseball, basketball, cross-country, football, golf, soccer, swimming, tennis, track and field, and wrestling; and coed archery and cheerleading. The O. Wayne Rollins Convocation/Physical Education Center houses a 2,700-seat athletic arena, the Dinah Taylor Aquatic Center, an indoor batting cage, a weight room, an indoor walking/jogging track, locker rooms, an intramural gymnasium, athletic training facilities, athletic offices, and classrooms.

The James H. Taylor II Stadium complex, which seats 2,400, includes a football field; an eight-lane, 400-meter all-weather track and field; the Patriot Pavilion; and a football practice field.

The Doyle Buhl Stadium and James Keelty Field are the home of Patriot baseball, with dugouts and locker rooms.

UC also has separate golf, soccer, softball, tennis, and wrestling facilities.

Location

One of the state's oldest cities, Williamsburg is located in southern Kentucky, 185 miles south of Cincinnati, Ohio, and 70 miles north of Knoxville, Tennessee. Williamsburg is known for its beautiful homes and the hospitality of its people. The University of the Cumberlands campus is situated on three hills above the town and, about 1 mile from exit 11, is easily accessed from I-75. UC has a well-kept campus that blends stately old buildings with new ones and has a panoramic view of the surrounding mountains and the Cumberland River Valley, an area known throughout the country for its lovely waterfalls, forests, and lakes. Famed Cumberland Falls State Resort Park is just 20 minutes from campus.

Majors and Degrees

University of the Cumberlands is accredited by the Commission on Colleges of the Southern Association of Colleges and Schools to award baccalaureate, master's, and doctoral degrees. It is approved by the Kentucky State Department of Education for teacher education and certification. Inquiries concerning the accreditation status of the University may be directed to the Commission on Colleges at 1866 Southern Lane, Decatur, Georgia 30033-4097 or by calling 404-676-4500.

Major fields of study are accounting, art, biology, business administration, chemistry, church music, communication arts, criminal justice, education, English, exercise and sport science, fitness and sport management, health, history, human services, journalism and public relations, management information systems, mathematics, music, philosophy, physics, political science, psychology, religion, Spanish, special education, and theater arts.

Minor fields can be chosen from the major fields or in biblical languages or French.

Preprofessional and special curricula are offered in military science, pre-dentistry, pre-engineering, pre-law, pre-medicine, pre-optometry, pre-pharmacy, pre–physical therapy, pre–physician assistant studies, pre–veterinary medicine, and religious vocations.

Academic Programs

University of the Cumberlands seeks to provide academic specialization within a broad framework of a liberal arts education. To supplement the in-depth knowledge acquired within each major, 37 semester hours of general studies from the areas of Christian faith and values, cultural and aesthetic values, the English language, humanities, leadership and community service, natural and mathematical sciences, physical education, and social sciences are required. Students must earn at least 128 semester hours to graduate with a bachelor's degree.

The academic year begins in late August, with the first semester ending in mid-December. The second semester runs from early January to early May. Two 4-week undergraduate summer sessions and two 4-week graduate summer sessions are also

offered. Orientation, preregistration, and academic advising by faculty members begin in the summer preceding entrance.

Students may receive credit for successful scores on the Advanced Placement examinations of the College Board, the College-Level Examination Program (CLEP), and special departmental tests. Through the honors program, highly qualified students have the opportunity to undertake advanced independent study.

Students benefit from such special services as free tutorial assistance and those offered by the Career Services Center, the Center for Leadership Studies, and the Academic Resource Center.

Academic Facilities

The University of the Cumberlands campus contains thirty-five buildings reflecting antebellum architectural style. The new Correll Science Complex features state-of-the-art biology, chemistry, and physics labs providing graduate-level research opportunities.

The McGaw Music Building contains individual rehearsal and studio areas as well as a recital hall. The Norma Perkins Hagan Memorial Library houses thousands of book titles, periodical subscriptions, and microform titles. Sophisticated computer equipment provides access to millions of items from many of the nation's outstanding libraries. The instructional media center includes a children's library, a computerized language lab, and a listening library.

Other special academic features include a computer center, an art gallery, a word processing center for English composition, a theater, a 600-seat chapel, four large lecture halls, and the Distance Learning Laboratory.

Recent additions to the campus include the state-of-the-art Hutton School of Business, a 27,000-square-foot addition to the Science Building, and Harth Hall, a women's residence hall.

Costs

For 2012–13, the basic academic year expenses are $19,000 for tuition and fees and $7000 for room and board, for a total of $26,000. There are no additional fees for out-of-state students. The average cost for books and supplies is approximately $500 per semester.

Financial Aid

University of the Cumberlands sponsors a large financial aid program that coordinates monies from federal, state, private, and University sources. Ninety-five percent of UC students share more than $30 million in aid.

To apply for financial aid, it is necessary to complete the Free Application for Federal Student Aid (FAFSA). For further information about financial aid opportunities, students should contact the Director of Financial Planning at 800-343-1609 (toll free). Applications made by March 1 are given priority for the fall semester.

Numerous scholarships and grants are available.

Faculty

There are 101 full-time and 18 part-time faculty members who are respected scholars and whose primary responsibility is to teach. Graduate assistants do not teach courses. The student-faculty ratio is 13:1, enabling students to receive ample attention and assistance from professors. Faculty members also serve as advisers to help students in planning their academic programs.

Admission Requirements

In compliance with federal law, including provisions of Title IX of the Educational Amendments of 1972 and Section 504 of the Rehabilitation Act of 1973, University of the Cumberlands does not illegally discriminate on the basis of race, sex, color, national or ethnic origin, age, disability, or military service in its administration of education policies, programs, or activities; admissions policies; or employment. Under federal law, the University reserves the right to discriminate on the basis of sex in its undergraduate admissions programs. Further, the University reserves the right to deny admission to any applicant whose academic preparation, character, or personal conduct is determined to be inconsistent with the purpose and objectives of the University. Where possible, the University will seek to reasonably accommodate a student's disability. However, the University's obligation to reasonably accommodate a student's disability ends where the accommodation would pose an undue hardship on the University or where the accommodation in question would fundamentally alter the academic program. Inquiries or complaints should be directed to the Vice President for Academic Affairs.

The purpose of the admission process is to identify applicants who are likely to succeed academically at University of the Cumberlands and at the same time contribute positively to the campus community. The process considers such factors as high school records (including courses taken, grade trends, and rank in class), college records (if transferring from another institution), scores on the ACT or SAT, extracurricular activities and honors, and personal conduct.

Campus tours are available on weekdays by appointment and on selected Saturdays. Prospective students can take a tour of the beautiful campus; talk with students, professors, and coaches; spend the night in the residence halls; attend an athletic or extracurricular event; and get answers to questions during a session with an admissions counselor.

Application and Information

Applicants may apply online at http://www.ucumberlands.edu or may contact the Office of Admissions for an application form. Return the completed form to the University, along with the appropriate application fee, official transcripts of all high school and college work, and a copy of ACT or SAT scores. Each student is notified regarding official admission within ten working days after the application procedure has been completed.

Students accepted for admission must submit the required enrollment deposit.

Additional information can be obtained at:

Office of Admissions
University of the Cumberlands
Williamsburg, Kentucky 40769
Phone: 606-539-4241
        800-343-1609 (toll-free)
E-mail: admiss@ucumberlands.edu
Web site: http://www.ucumberlands.edu
        http://twitter.com/#!/UCumberlandsKy
        http://www.youtube.com/UCumberlandsMedia

University of the Cumberlands offers individualized learning and research opportunities.

UNIVERSITY OF THE SCIENCES
PHILADELPHIA, PENNSYLVANIA

The University

University of the Sciences (USciences) was founded in 1821 as Philadelphia College of Pharmacy, America's first college of pharmacy. University of the Sciences is located on a 35-acre campus in the University City section of Philadelphia, home to some of the nation's top universities, hospitals, and research facilities. Besides University of the Sciences, University of Pennsylvania and Drexel University also call University City home. The University currently enrolls approximately 2,500 undergraduate students in nineteen majors and over 300 students in twenty-one graduate programs. The campus consists of twenty-two buildings. The University offers a wide variety of cocurricular activities that include intercollegiate and intramural athletics; literary publications; social, professional, religious, and honors organizations; and musical and drama groups. University of the Sciences competes athletically at the NCAA Division II level and is a member of the Central Atlantic Collegiate Conference.

Location

The University's location in the University City section of Philadelphia offers considerable advantage and appeal. It not only offers a wide variety of educational opportunities, it also is a culturally, architecturally, and socially diverse community that caters to the local college student population. University of the Sciences is also actively involved with a number of local community organizations that are designed to foster improvement, development, and unity in the University City community. The Philadelphia metropolitan area is the home of more than forty other colleges and universities. University of the Sciences students realize that Philadelphia and its immediate region provide abundant off-campus clinical and scientific opportunities, which are required in a number of programs. Within a short 10-minute trolley ride to the Center City area are the vast cultural, historical, and shopping attractions of the fifth-largest city in the United States.

Majors and Degrees

University of the Sciences includes four undergraduate colleges: Philadelphia College of Pharmacy, which offers programs in pharmacy, pharmaceutical sciences, and pharmacology and toxicology; Samson College of Health Sciences, which offers programs in exercise science and wellness management, health science, medical laboratory science, occupational therapy, physical therapy, and physician assistant studies; Misher College of Arts and Sciences, which offers majors in biochemistry, biology, chemistry, environmental science, humanities and science, microbiology, pharmaceutical chemistry, physics, and psychology; and the newest college, Mayes College of Healthcare Business and Policy, which offers a number of graduate programs as well as a bachelor's degree in pharmaceutical and healthcare business. Students with strong academic interests in multiple areas may pursue double degrees, including two B.S. degrees or one B.S. degree and one entry-level professional degree.

Academic Programs

Three majors are offered in Philadelphia College of Pharmacy: a six-year Doctor of Pharmacy (Pharm.D.) program and four-year B.S. degree programs in pharmacology and toxicology and in pharmaceutical sciences. In the Doctor of Pharmacy program, students are guaranteed a seat in the professional phase (years 3–6) as long as the preprofessional phase (years 1–2) is successfully completed and an acceptable academic record is maintained. The pharmacy program at the University is recognized worldwide and prepares students for the increasingly clinical nature of pharmacy practice.

Pharmacology and toxicology, pharmaceutical sciences, and pharmaceutical and healthcare business are unique B.S. degree programs that provide excellent career opportunities and address specific manpower needs within the pharmaceutical and healthcare

industries. Many graduates pursue postgraduate study as well as enter careers in research, manufacturing, and business.

Six programs of study are available in Samson College of Health Sciences: exercise science and wellness management, health science, medical laboratory science, occupational therapy, physical therapy, and physician assistant studies. Both physical therapy and occupational therapy programs are direct-entry, integrated undergraduate/professional degree programs that lead to the Doctor of Physical Therapy (D.P.T.) and Doctor of Occupational Therapy (Dr.O.T.), respectively. The physical therapy program was one of America's first programs to receive approval to offer the six-year, direct-entry D.P.T. In both the physical therapy and occupational therapy programs, students are admitted as first-year students and are guaranteed a professional-phase seat, provided an acceptable academic record is maintained. In the newest major in Samson College of Health Sciences, the B.S. degree in exercise science and wellness management, students learn about healthy lifestyles and living as well as how sports and leisure activities improve community well-being.

The physician assistant studies program at University of the Sciences is a five-year program that leads to the Bachelor of Science in Health Science from USciences and Master of Science from the Philadelphia College of Osteopathic Medicine (PCOM). Students enrolled in the physician assistant studies program complete their preprofessional component (years 1–3) in the natural sciences, social sciences, and humanities at University of the Sciences. The professional component of the program (years 4–5) is completed at PCOM. The professional component of the program, resulting in the Master of Science degree, is expected to be offered at USciences by 2013, bringing the entire program in house.

A four-year B.S. degree in health science for students who want to focus on general health care and community service is also available.

Medical laboratory science students at University of the Sciences receive an excellent three-year academic foundation in preparation for their fourth year, which is spent in a clinical setting at an approved hospital school of medical laboratory science.

Nine different four-year Bachelor of Science degree programs are offered in the Misher College of Arts and Sciences. They include biochemistry, biology, chemistry, environmental science, humanities and science, microbiology, physics, pharmaceutical chemistry, and psychology. Psychology students may elect to remain at the University for an additional year and qualify for the M.S. in health psychology program. Misher College of Arts and Sciences combines the expertise of an outstanding group of scientists, researchers, and educators with academic facilities that are not often found at an institution the size of University of the Sciences. This combination creates an academic atmosphere of especially high quality. Misher College also offers a popular advisory track in forensic science, which can stand alone as a minor. A forensic science certificate can be earned when paired with a major in biology, biochemistry, chemistry, environmental science, medical laboratory science, microbiology, or pharmaceutical chemistry.

The newest major in Misher College of Arts and Sciences is the B.S. in humanities and science. This major provides a unique combination of scientific and humanistic study, which is particularly attractive to students who want to pursue medical, dental, or veterinary studies.

University of the Sciences' strong tradition of excellence prepares graduates to enter postbaccalaureate degrees in medicine, dentistry, veterinary medicine, and other health professions. Traditionally, pre-med students choose to major in chemistry, biochemistry, biology, microbiology, pharmacology and toxicology, or psychology. The curricula in these and most of the other programs include the basic courses required for admission to medical school. Beginning with the first year, pre-med students receive individualized counseling by the preprofessional advisor and their faculty advisor in selecting courses to meet their career goals. Pre-med students may also elect to take advantage of the University's agreements with

Philadelphia College of Osteopathic Medicine, the Commonwealth Medical College, Pennsylvania College of Optometry at Salus University, Korneg School of Dentistry at Temple University, or St. George University School of Veterinary Medicine, which reserve a number of seats each year for University of the Sciences students.

Students may enroll at University of the Sciences in the Misher pre-professional program, and through a special orientation program, be introduced to the various academic disciplines and career opportunities available to them. Misher pre-professional students formally declare a major during the spring semester of the first year and choose from pre-medical, pre-dental, pre-veterinarian, and pre-health professional specializations.

Academic Facilities

Classes and laboratory course work are conducted in ten academic buildings on the University of the Sciences campus, while the remaining buildings serve as residence halls or support-service facilities. University of the Sciences houses more than 100 scientific laboratories and many computer terminals for student use. The Joseph W. England Library contains more than 84,000 volumes and 8,400 periodicals in addition to numerous electronic information programs.

Costs

Tuition for the 2011–12 academic year was $30,580; room and board were $12,564. Costs are subject to change.

Financial Aid

Types and sources of aid include Federal Perkins Loans; Health Professions Student Loans; Federal Work-Study Program; USciences Merit Awards; Athletic Grants; University need-based grants, deferred tuition payment plans; federal student loans; and scholarships received from states, municipalities, and service clubs or other organizations. All applicants who seek financial assistance must complete the Free Application for Federal Student Aid (FAFSA). The University's merit scholarship and grant program provides awards for both first-year and transfer candidates.

Faculty

There are 161 full-time faculty members. Of these, more than 100 have doctoral degrees. All full-time faculty members teach undergraduates, and many also teach graduate students and conduct research. Graduate assistants do not teach but serve as laboratory aides.

Student Government

Student government is comprised of representatives from all undergraduate classes and class officers. It takes an active part in governance through participation in faculty and administrative committees and sponsors a number of campus activities and functions.

Admission Requirements

University of the Sciences seeks students whose aptitudes and achievements are in the areas of science, mathematics, and humanities. Sixteen total high school credits are required and must include English (4 credits), mathematics (3 credits, including algebra I and II and plane geometry), and science (3 credits of laboratory science, including at least two of the following: biology, chemistry, and physics). Physical science, IPS, general science, or similar courses without a laboratory component do not fulfill the laboratory science requirement. Class rank, if provided by the applicant's high school, and grade point average are also considered in the admission decision process. Candidates are required to submit the results of their SAT and/or ACT examinations. Supplemental testing or an interview may be requested to clarify a specific aspect of a candidate's record. For students whose first language is not English, the Test of English as a Foreign Language (TOEFL) is suggested. Applications for transfer are welcome, although the number of seats available each year is less than that for first-year students, since all students admitted to University of the Sciences are admitted for the entire program length. Advanced standing may be achieved through the College Board's Advanced Placement Program, the International Baccalaureate program, or earned college credit.

University of the Sciences does not discriminate in the administration of its educational policies, admission policies, scholarship and loan programs, or athletic and other University-administered programs on the basis of sex, age, handicap, race, creed, color, or national origin. All students are entitled to all of the rights, privileges, programs, and activities generally accorded or made available to students at the University. This institutional policy complies with the requirements of Title IX of the Education Amendments of 1972 (45 CRF 86), Section 504 of the Rehabilitation Act of 1973, and other applicable statutes and regulations.

Application and Information

An admission application may be obtained by calling the Admission Office. Applicants may submit an online application at http://www.usciences.edu/applying. Each paper application must be accompanied by a nonrefundable $45 application fee. However, there is no fee for an online application. University of the Sciences is also a member of the Common Application. First-year applications for admission are considered until the entering class roster has been completed. University of the Sciences follows a rolling admission policy, and applicants are notified of the admission decision after the University has received all required data. Students accepted into any of the programs have until May 1 to submit a nonrefundable enrollment reservation deposit of $300 for nonpharmacy candidates and $500 for pharmacy candidates to hold a place in the class. Applicants accepted after May 1 have two weeks to submit a tuition deposit.

Applicants for transfer to the professional programs should submit completed applications no later than the following dates: physical therapy (February 1), pharmacy (February 1), occupational therapy (March 1), and physician assistant studies (March 15). All transfer applications are reviewed on a rolling basis except for physical therapy and pharmacy, which are reviewed during the spring semester.

Executive Director of Admission and Enrollment Services
University of the Sciences
600 South 43rd Street
Philadelphia, Pennsylvania 19104-4495
Phone: 215-596-8810
      888-996-8747 (toll-free)
Fax: 215-596-8821
E-mail: admit@usciences.edu
Web site: http://www.usciences.edu

It all begins at University of the Sciences, where students embark on a challenging learning experience; where they get the education and training to be successful science and healthcare professionals; and where they go on to become pharmacists, occupational therapists, biologists, doctors, or health-policy specialists—just to name a few. USciences: where healthcare and science converge.

UNIVERSITY OF THE WEST
ROSEMEAD, CALIFORNIA

The University

University of the West (UWest) is a Buddhist-founded campus open to students of all backgrounds and faiths. UWest offers affordable, accredited programs that prepare students to work and live in a global society. UWest offers undergraduate and advanced education in religious studies, business administration, psychology, or languages. UWest is accredited by the Western Association of Schools and Colleges (WASC).

Founded in 1991 by Buddhist Venerable Master Hsing Yun, who is one of the earliest promoters of Humanistic Buddhism, University of the West's mission is to deliver an education informed by Buddhist wisdom and values as well as to serve as a bridge between the cultures of East and West.

Students and faculty members come together in small classes that average seven students per instructor. As a community of scholars, UWest students participate in an ongoing dialogue to advance knowledge, address societal and cultural issues, and promote education and understanding across cultures. At UWest, creativity, service, and leadership are fostered together with tolerance, ethical commitment, and social consciousness.

A range of activities and facilities that enhance learning and physical and mental well-being outside of the classroom are offered, such as yoga, basketball courts, a cardio fitness room, a weight-training room, swimming pool, martial arts program, music, meditation, clubs, and travel,

The Student Recreation Center is equipped with fitness and weight-training equipment, table tennis, billiards, and a student lounge with a kitchen. The two residential halls each have a 24-hour study room, a multipurpose student lounge on each floor, and a laundry facility. Each room is furnished and has its own air-conditioning unit, private bathroom, telephone, and high-speed Internet access.

UWest is a member of NAFSA: Association of International Educators and the American Association of Collegiate Registrars and Admissions Officers.

Location

UWest is located in the city of Rosemead in Los Angeles County. It occupies 13 acres of beautifully landscaped grounds and has modern, well-equipped facilities. The campus sits on a hillside overlooking the verdant Whittier Narrows nature preserve with an unobstructed view of the San Gabriel Mountain range and the Puente Hills range. UWest is about 10 minutes by car from downtown Los Angeles.

Majors and Degrees

Undergraduate programs at UWest include business administration with majors in accounting, computer information systems, international business, and marketing, as well as bachelor's degrees in psychology, general studies, and English.

Graduate programs offered at the University are the Executive Master of Business Administration (E.M.B.A.); Master of Business Administration with concentrations in computer information systems, finance, international business, or nonprofit management and organization; Master of Arts (M.A.) in psychology with concentrations in multicultural counseling (marriage and family therapist track) or Buddhist psychology (marriage and family therapist track); M.A. in religious studies with concentrations in Buddhist studies or comparative religious studies; and the Master of Divinity (M.Div.) in Buddhist chaplaincy.

UWest also offers an advanced degree program for the Doctor of Religious Studies (Ph.D.) with specializations in Buddhist studies or comparative religious studies.

Academic Programs

The business administration program offers deep perspectives on Eastern and Western business theory and practice.

The Department of Religious Studies' programs in Buddhist studies and comparative religious studies offer students the unique opportunity to study religion in a setting that is informed by Buddhist wisdom and values, and dedicated to furthering religious and cultural understanding between East and West, and among religions in general. All Buddhist traditions are covered, and students can choose to study any of the Buddhist canonical languages, i.e., Canonical Chinese, Pali, Sanskrit, or Tibetan. The library contains one of the best American collections of writing from all the major Buddhist traditions, including the largest set of Dunhuang Cave manuscript reproductions in the U.S.

UWest's undergraduate major in psychology prepares students as competitive graduate school candidates in the particular fields of research psychology, applied counseling psychology, clinical psychology, school psychology, Buddhist psychology, and social work. The M.A. in psychology with a concentration in multicultural counseling generalist (marriage and family therapist track) and the M.A. in psychology with a concentration in Buddhist psychology (marriage and family therapist track) prepares students to pass California's rigorous Marriage and Family Therapist licensure exam.

All of the bachelor's programs require the completion of a minimum of 120 semester units.

The ESL program provides a variety of instructional formats to improve students' command of the English language and familiarize them with American life and culture, including a residential English program and the Program in American Cultural Education (PACE), which provides short-term immersive experiences in the classroom, combined with travel and cultural experiences in the Los Angeles region.

Academic Facilities

The library provides access to the University's collection as well as Internet access to several major databases such as ProQuest and JSTOR.

Three research centers are located on campus. The Center for the Study of Minority and Small Business helps the Department of Business Administration reach out to minority-owned and small businesses and provides resources and support so students at UWest are exposed to and become familiar with business realities and the existing business environment.

The Institute of Chinese Buddhist Studies develops interdisciplinary research, teaching, and other scholarly activities relating to Chinese Buddhism.

The Digital Sanskrit Buddhist Canon is a joint research project by the University of the West and the Nagarjuna Institute of Exact Methods (NIEM) in Nepal for translating the vast corpus of Sanskrit Buddhist texts.

Costs

Undergraduate tuition for the 2012–13 academic year is $350 per unit for courses in the business administration and psychology programs. Graduate tuition is $380 per unit for the business administration program, $385 per unit for psychology, $375 per unit in the Buddhist chaplaincy program, and $370 for religious studies.

On a per-semester basis, room and board with meal plan are $4935 for single occupancy, $3035 for double occupancy, and $2555 for quadruple occupancy. Several meal plan options are available for purchase. Additional details regarding costs and fees are available at http://www.uwest.edu under Admissions/Admissions Procedures/Tuition and Fees.

Financial Aid

Financial aid is available in the form of federal and state aid, a work-study program, private scholarships, and grants (both need- and merit-based). UWest offers full- and half-tuition fellowships, scholarships for room and board, and the UWest Scholarship of $2000 per academic year. The International Buddhist Education Foundation scholarship provides more than 50 students in the religious studies program with scholarships of $2000 to $4000 depending on academic level. UWest also offers private scholarships ranging from $500 to $2000 per semester. For the fall 2012 semester, UWest awarded 50 merit-based scholarships of $10,000 and 100 merit-based scholarships of $5000.

Faculty

Among full-time faculty members, 82 percent have doctoral degrees. Adjunct faculty members are required to have a minimum of a master's degree and at least ten years of experience working in the fields relevant to the subjects they teach. UWest has 70 faculty members.

Student Government

The UWest Student Association acts as a liaison between the University and the students to provide services and programs that enhance the quality of education by extending the learning environment beyond the classroom into the extracurricular lives of UWest students. It also provides a forum for student expression and interests. All students who are enrolled at the University are included as members of the Student Association. In addition, UWSA provides Community Enrichment Grants to campus-based organizations to promote activities and events.

Admission Requirements

Applicants are required to supply accurate and complete information on the application for admission form and to submit official transcripts from each school or college attended. Other application requirements and documentation can be found on the University's Web site. Student selection is based on academic achievement and potential, irrespective of ethnicity, gender, disability, or religion. A minimum GPA of 2.0 is required of undergraduate applicants. Graduate applicants must have a minimum GPA of 2.5. Undergraduate applicants must submit two letters of recommendation with their application and answer a brief essay question. Graduate applicants must submit a 500-word essay and three letters of recommendation as part of their application. International students must meet the minimum TOEFL or IELTS requirement as published in the UWest catalog.

Application and Information

Application deadlines for domestic applicants are June 1 for fall, September 2 for spring, and April 2 for summer. There is a $50 nonrefundable application fee for domestic applicants and a $100 nonrefundable application fee for international applicants. Application-fee waivers are available to undergraduate students through the Enrollment Office.

Ms. Jason Kosareff
Enrollment Counselor
University of the West
1409 North Walnut Grove Avenue
Rosemead, California 91770
Phone: 855-GO-UWEST
Fax: 626-571-1413
E-mail: info@uwest.edu
Web site: http://www.uwest.edu

The University of the West seeks to deliver an education informed by Buddhist wisdom and values that also serves as a bridge between Eastern and Western cultures.

UNIVERSITY OF TULSA
TULSA, OKLAHOMA

The University

The University of Tulsa (TU) is a private, comprehensive degree-granting university that provides education of the highest quality in the arts, humanities, sciences, engineering, business, education, applied health sciences, and law. TU features three undergraduate colleges—the Henry Kendall College of Arts and Sciences, the Collins College of Business, and the College of Engineering and Natural Sciences—along with a College of Law and a Graduate School.

The University is fully accredited by the North Central Association of Colleges and Universities and is an NCAA Division IA participant in Conference USA. TU maintains a covenant relationship with the Presbyterian Church (U.S.A.).

TU's 11:1 student-faculty ratio, average class size of 19, and emphasis on individual attention anchor an educational culture where students receive both rigorous challenges and comprehensive support.

Extracurricular opportunities include intramural sports, special interest clubs, preprofessional organizations, national fraternities and sororities, community service organizations, student government, departmental honorary groups, and campus ministries.

Total fall 2011 enrollment was 4,187, with 3,084 undergraduates and 1,103 graduate and law students. The ratio of men to women is 54:46, and 18 percent of the students are multicultural. Over half the students are from out of state and international students make up 21 percent of the student population, with sixty-eight countries represented.

Based on academic reputation and other factors, *U.S. News & World Report* ranks TU seventy-fifth among doctoral/research universities in the United States.

Location

TU features a 216-acre residential campus in midtown Tulsa, Oklahoma. Tulsa's prominent industries include energy, telecommunications, technology, data processing, manufacturing, health care, aerospace, transportation, and education, all of which present TU students with opportunities for internships and employment after graduation. Tulsa has about 550,000 residents and has been named one of America's most livable cities by Forbes. Cultural assets include the Performing Arts Center, BOK Center (arena), acclaimed ballet and opera companies, a symphony, Philbrook Museum, Gilcrease Museum, and cultural festivals. Professional sports in Tulsa include minor league baseball, hockey, and arena football. The River Parks development has facilities for outdoor activities and extensive jogging and bicycling trails.

Majors and Degrees

The Henry Kendall College of Arts and Sciences grants the Bachelor of Arts, Bachelor of Fine Arts, Bachelor of Music, Bachelor of Music Education, and Bachelor of Science degrees in anthropology, art, art history, arts management, Chinese studies, communication, deaf education, economics, education, English, environmental policy, film studies, French, German, history, music, musical theater, organizational studies, philosophy, political science, psychology, religion, Russian studies, sociology, Spanish, speech/language pathology, theater, women's gender studies, and self-designed majors. Minors include most disciplines as well as advertising, classics, creative writing, dance, early childhood intervention, film scoring, Greek, Latin, and Russian. Secondary teacher certification is available in designated disciplines. Interdisciplinary certificate programs offer a way for students to focus their interests in advertising, African American studies, classics, creative writing, international studies, journalism studies, Judaic studies, legal thought, museum studies, and political philosophy.

The Collins College of Business awards the Bachelor of Science in Business Administration degree in accounting, economics, energy management, finance, management, management information systems, and marketing, and a Bachelor of Science in international business and language. Minors are available in most disciplines plus business administration (for nonmajors), coaching, health care informatics, and international business. Certificate programs are available in accounting, advertising, finance, management information systems, not-for-profit administration, and sports administration. Management majors may choose specializations in business law, entrepreneurship and family business management, or human resource management. The college is home to several specialized centers, including the Energy Management Program, Family Owned Business Institute, the Genave King Rogers Center for Business Law, and the Williams Risk Management Center. Within the college, the School of Nursing offers the Bachelor of Science degree in athletic training, exercise and sports science, and a Bachelor of Science in Nursing degree program.

The College of Engineering and Natural Sciences offers the Bachelor of Science degree in applied mathematics, biochemistry, biogeosciences, biological science (options in premedicine, predentristry, and preveterinary science), chemical engineering, chemistry, computer science, earth and environmental science, electrical engineering, engineering physics, geology, geophysics, information technology, mathematics, mechanical engineering, petroleum engineering, and physics. Minors are available in the science and computational science disciplines. The college features state-of-the-art research facilities, including the Center for Information Security and the Williams Communications Fiber Optic Networking Laboratory. Between 1995 and 2011, 48 TU engineering students were named recipients of the prestigious Barry M. Goldwater Scholarship, the nation's premier award for undergraduate students in engineering, math, or science.

Academic Programs

The Tulsa Curriculum links a broad, humanities-based core and writing-across-the-curriculum approach for all students with a highly flexible group of majors, minors, concentrations, and certificate programs. TU students can receive an education that is well-rounded, in-depth, and uniquely personalized. Candidates for graduation must complete at least 124 semester hours of course work, with more hours required of engineering and business administration majors.

The honors program engages students in a critical examination of the major epochs and ideas of Western thought and culture through careful study of primary texts. The acclaimed Tulsa Undergraduate Research Challenge (TURC) program combines advanced research in most disciplines, scholarship, and community service.

The TU Center for Information Security is developing defenses against cyber-terrorist attacks and information warfare. The center supports the University's National Security Agency (NSA)–accredited certificate program in information assurance, a curriculum that integrates information security with computer law and policy issues. TU has been designated a Center of Excellence in information assurance by the NSA and is one of six pioneer institutions selected by the National Science Foundation for the Federal Cyber Service Initiative (Cyber Corps).

Air Force ROTC is available through a satellite program.

Qualified students may receive credit through Advanced Placement testing. Students who complete the International Baccalaureate diploma can receive up to 30 college credit hours.

The University of Tulsa operates on a semester calendar. The fall term begins in late August and the spring term in early January.

Off-Campus Programs

The University is supportive of the study-abroad experience and the Office of Global Education helps students locate the perfect program, whether it is for TU credit or an intern/volunteer option. Students choose from hundreds of opportunities offered around the

world through a direct exchange with an international university, an affiliate-sponsored program, or as part of a faculty-led course.

Academic Facilities

The University of Tulsa's libraries, historic McFarlin Library and Mabee Legal Information Center, house more than 4 million items. McFarlin holdings include over 920,000 volumes, 620,000 titles, 120,000 e-books, 40,000 electronic periodicals, 7,500 videos, and 10,000 recordings. McFarlin's special collections rare book holdings number over 125,000 volumes and are internationally recognized, particularly for holdings of Native American history and law, along with nineteenth- and twentieth-century Irish, English, and American literature. McFarlin is home to the papers of 2001 Nobel Laureate V. S. Naipaul. The 12,000-square-foot Academic Technology Center annex was dedicated in 2009, adding computer labs, a coffee shop, and restored reading rooms.

In 2012 the College of Engineering and Natural Sciences added to its existing Keplinger Hall, J. Newton Rayzor Hall, a $14-million home for the computer science and electrical engineering departments with twenty-four integrated classrooms and state-of-the-art teaching/research laboratories and Stephenson Hall, the new 38,600-square-foot home for the mechanical engineering department and McDougall School of Petroleum Engineering. Additional research facilities are housed at Tulsa's North Campus where government- and industry-funded research consortia explore innovations and solve problems faced by the petroleum industry while fostering student learning.

The Mary K. Chapman Center for Communicative Disorders serves the community with its clinical facility and is the learning center for the Department of Communication Disorders. The department has the latest equipment and instrumentation available for use in research, diagnostic, and therapy activities.

Helmerich Hall houses the Collins College of Business and was recently renovated inside and out with architectural elements to blend with the rest of campus and innovative learning spaces such as the Williams Students Services Center and Studio Blue. The Williams Risk Management Center, an advanced learning environment located in the Collins College of Business, combines the latest in trading-floor technology and advanced study in risk management theories and techniques. The Genave King Rogers Center for Business Law supports the business law specialization within the management major.

The Roxana Rózsa and Robert Eugene Lorton Performance Center opened in 2011. Home to the School of Music and the film studies department, the 77,000-square-foot facility includes a 700-seat concert hall, specialized rehearsal and practice rooms, and a film production suite with postproduction editing and scoring capabilities.

Kendall Hall is home to the department of theater and musical theater and features two fully equipped theaters, a scene shop, costume shop, and computer-design lab.

The Donald W. Reynolds Center is the campus arena and convocation center. This $28-million facility is the home for the intercollegiate basketball and volleyball programs and has cutting-edge facilities for video editing and training.

The Allen Chapman Activity Center features the University bookstore, student organization offices, the Great Hall for lectures and entertainment, a sports bar, food court, and fast-food venues.

Dedicated in 2007, the 29,000-square-foot Case Athletic Complex is home to the Golden Hurricane football program and adjoins the renovated H. A. Chapman Stadium where players enjoy one of the nation's elite college football training and playing environments.

The University's 34-acre sports and recreation complex features a 64,000-square-foot student fitness center, competition-grade tennis complex, track, NCAA soccer and softball fields, and intramural fields.

TU manages the acclaimed Gilcrease Museum and the two entities have embarked on an expansion into Tulsa's Brady Arts District to open the Zarrow Center for Art and Education, providing classes and studio space.

Costs

For 2012–13, the typical cost for students living on campus is $43,079, including $32,410 for tuition, $9934 for room and board, and fees of $735. Expenses for books average about $1200 per year.

Financial Aid

In 2011 nearly 90 percent of entering students received some form of financial aid (including grants, scholarships, work-study, and loans). TU offers a limited number of highly competitive Presidential Scholarships which cover full tuition, room, and board. All applicants may be considered for a range of University scholarships based on academic merit. Performance scholarships are available in music and theater by audition. The University of Tulsa participates in National Merit and National Achievement Scholarship Corporation's Finalist program and the National Hispanic Scholar Program. Applicants for aid should submit the Free Application for Federal Student Aid (FAFSA) by February 1 for priority consideration.

Faculty

The University has 309 full-time faculty members, with 96 percent having earned the highest degree in their field of study. The faculty is primarily a teaching faculty, although most of its members are also involved in funded research or publishing activities

Admission Requirements

The University of Tulsa seeks students whose academic background indicates potential for success in the university's rigorous academic environment. Performance in high school college-preparatory subjects and scores on the SAT or ACT are key factors in the admission evaluation, but each applicant is reviewed holistically. Each applicant's counselor recommendation; extracurricular activities; and indicators of leadership, creativity, and focus are all taken into consideration. Campus visits and interviews are highly recommended but not required.

Application and Information

TU has a nonbinding, early action freshman admission plan with an application deadline of November 1. Decisions are mailed within three weeks. Applications received after November 1 are reviewed under a rolling admission process with notifications made on an ongoing basis after mid-December.

An application, high school transcript, ACT or SAT score results, and a guidance counselor recommendation are required of freshman applicants. TU accepts the Common Application or its own online or paper application form. TU adheres to the national Candidate's Reply Date of May 1.

Earl Johnson
Associate Vice President for Enrollment and Student Services and Dean of Admission
University of Tulsa
800 South Tucker Drive
Tulsa, Oklahoma 74104-3189
Phone: 918-631-2307 (in Tulsa)
    800-331-3050 (toll-free)
Fax: 918-631-5008
E-mail: admission@utulsa.edu
Web site: http://www.utulsa.edu/admission
    http://www.utulsa.edu/admissionblog

TU is among the top schools in *U.S. News & World Report's* 2011 *America's Best Colleges.*

UNIVERSITY OF WASHINGTON BOTHELL
BOTHELL, WASHINGTON

The University

The University of Washington Bothell (UW Bothell) opens the door to a nationally and internationally ranked university experience that inspires innovation and creativity. Faculty members are passionate about the knowledge they bring to the classroom and seek to provide a student-centered education in a collaborative learning environment. The University promotes a spirit of innovation and creativity where big ideas are born and tested. With 3,377 full-time students and approximately 200 faculty members, UW Bothell offers modest-sized classes, perfectly suited for meaningful interaction and critical thinking. Students take an active role in their educational experience, discover their own strengths and abilities, and ultimately learn how to fulfill their dreams, academic and otherwise.

The campus is located in the thriving, dynamic and globally-engaged greater Seattle area, home to some of the world's most iconic and entrepreneurial corporations, foundations, and arts organizations.

UW Bothell is one of three University of Washington campuses. Though providing distinctive offerings, its graduates earn a fully accredited UW degree.

The University offers both the benefits of modest class sizes with the resources of a world-renowned university. The curriculum emphasizes close student-faculty interactions, collaboration among students, and hands-on learning. Outstanding regional connections present students with unique opportunities for projects, internships, and research with leading businesses and organizations. At UW Bothell, students earn a University of Washington degree while building a solid foundation of relevant knowledge, practical skills, and professional preparation.

In additional to its undergraduate degree programs, UW Bothell offers several graduate programs in disciplines including business, computing and software systems, cultural studies, education, nursing, policy studies, and fine arts.

Location

UW Bothell is located in Bothell, Washington, approximately 30 minutes northeast of Seattle. The campus—which is shared with Cascadia Community College—sits atop a 128-acre plot of picturesque land overlooking protected wetlands and the Cascades beyond. The site was once home to the 500-acre, Boone-Truly purebred cattle ranch, which was sold in 1995 to the state of Washington.

Majors and Degrees

UW Bothell offers more than thirty degrees through a variety of programs as well as the UW Bothell School of Business and the UW Bothell School of Interdisciplinary Arts and Sciences. UW Bothell is proud of its reputation for innovative, specialized degree options.

Students can choose from an array of undergraduate in disciplines including: American studies; applied computing; biology; business; business administration; community psychology; computing and software systems; culture, literature, and the arts; electrical engineering; environmental science; environmental studies; global studies; interdisciplinary arts; interdisciplinary studies; nursing; science, technology and society; and society, ethics and human behavior.

Postbaccalaureate courses include K–8 teacher certification as well as professional certification.

Off-Campus Programs

Students attending UW Bothell are able to take part in a variety of exceptional educational and technical programs made possible through collaborative efforts with a broad range of community partners. These opportunities are helpful in addressing workforce needs, as well as local and global challenges. Closer community ties will foster a better understanding of the skills and programs students and employers need, while enriching the education of the University's students by providing real-world experiences to learn from and the opportunity to give back to local communities.

UW Bothell takes advantage of the region's extraordinary capacity for creativity and innovation by connecting students to career-building experiences. Committed to the greater good, UW Bothell builds regional partnerships, inspires change, creates knowledge, shares discoveries, and prepares students for leadership in the state of Washington and beyond.

Academic Facilities

Although thoroughly modern, UW Bothell buildings were designed to complement the land's natural beauty; they are environmentally friendly and are equipped with advanced technology for faculty and student use. The UW Bothell campus is well known for its eco-friendly award-winning architecture, state-of-the-art technology, and breathtaking views. Its stunning architecture and landscaping garnered the American Institute of Architects 2002 Honor Award for Washington architecture.

UW Bothell takes its reputation as a green campus very seriously. Sustainability efforts are more than a concept to be studied. Instead, practicing consistent environmental caretaking is the norm. Examples abound, and include everything from LEED-certified buildings and solar panels to worm-assisted composting and pesticide-free landscape maintenance.

UW Bothell offers outstanding student support services: an award-winning on-campus library with access to the full UW library system, a career center, writing center, personal counseling, computer support, and mentoring available for first-generation students and English language learners (ELL).

Work continues on two exciting campus projects, the Sarah Simonds Green Conservatory and the Sports Field and Recreation Complex. The conservatory is designed to include education and exhibit space for historical displays and interpretive materials, as well as a greenhouse to support plant propagation. The sports complex, a student-led and funded project scheduled to be completed in late 2012, will include a multipurpose synthetic turf sports field, tennis courts, basketball court, and a sand volleyball court.

UW Bothell is currently awaiting final approval on its long-anticipated third building, and expects to begin construction this summer. The 74,000-square-foot science and academic building, known as UW 3, will provide space for 11 science labs, several classrooms, gathering space and a 200-person lecture hall. The building will enable UW Bothell to increase enrollment by 1,000 students. UW 3 will be the first building constructed on the UW Bothell campus in ten years. For more information, including a building rendering, visit http://www.uwb.edu/about/neighbors/future/uw3.

Costs

Tuition rates for 2011–12 for full-time (10 to 18 credits) undergraduate studies were $3414 per quarter for Washington residents and $9242 per quarter nonresidents. Tuition rates for graduate and nondegree programs vary depending upon the individual program.

Financial Aid

As part of the University of Washington, UW Bothell participates in the Husky Promise Program, which is a vital part of the comprehensive financial aid program. The UW offers more than $160 million in financial aid each year, with nearly half of all undergraduates receiving aid. Each year, over 5,000 University of Washington students—both undergraduate and graduate—receive more than $20 million in scholarships alone through grants, gifts, or endowed funds.

Approximately one third of UW freshmen will be the first in their families to earn a bachelor's degree, and 30 percent of students come from families below the median income for the state of Washington. Beginning in fall quarter 2007, more than 5,000

UW students—nearly 20 percent of all undergraduates—are covered under the Husky Promise. Both the total number of students and the overall percentage covered by the Husky Promise are among the highest in the country when compared to similar programs at comparable institutions.

In addition to the Husky Promise Program, UW Bothell offers a variety of scholarship, fellowship, and financial aid opportunities. Detailed information about financial aid and scholarship opportunities are available in the Web version of the UW Bothell Financial Aid and Scholarships Guide at http://www.uwb.edu/financialaid.

Faculty

At UW Bothell the educational relationship between faculty members and their students is paramount. Modest class sizes provide ample opportunity for students to engage with their professors in an environment that is inspiring yet challenging. Faculty members are encouraged to be innovative and creative in the classroom, and are supported in their desire to pursue research and other endeavors as well. They represent a wide variety of disciplines, and are all given the freedom and respect they deserve.

Above all, UW Bothell faculty members pay attention to the changing needs and interests of their students. Students are not only allowed a voice in the classroom, but are strongly encouraged to share their ideas and help shape classroom dynamics.

In today's technologically advanced world, adaptability is the key to ultimate success. With this in mind, UW Bothell faculty members utilize innovative teaching methods and interdisciplinary approaches, thus providing hands-on preparation for real life and career.

Campus Student Housing

More than 220 students live in UW Bothell student housing and enjoy all the conveniences of apartment-style living along with with residence life programming, a vibrant community of learners, and a safe environment to student success.

This provides an opportunity for students to interact with diverse individuals, form study groups, and learn more about themselves. UW Bothell student residents socialize, thrive, and create lasting memories and friendships. On-campus student housing is located within a short distance from classrooms and services, as well as downtown Bothell shops, restaurants, and parks. Additional information is available online at http://www.uwb.edu/housingfacilitate.

Student Government

Located within the Office of Student Life, the Associated Students of UW Bothell (ASUWB) serve as a voice for all students. The goal is to empower the student body through promoting clear communication between faculty members, administration, and students. ASUWB is the sole governing body for students, and its officers are elected.

ASUWB members strive to create an open, friendly campus atmosphere where students can get involved, make a difference, and have fun. There is a diverse selection of clubs and groups focusing on academic and recreational interests. More information can be found online at http://www.uwb.edu/studentlife/asuwb/officers.

Admission Requirements

Admission requirements vary depending on specific program of interest. All freshman applicants must complete studies in the following minimum College Academic Distribution Requirements (advanced studies in each subject are encouraged): English, 4 years; mathematics, 3 years; social science, 3 years; lab science, 2 years; foreign language (includes American sign language), 2 years; fine, visual, or performing arts, ½ year; and academic electives ½ year.

The UW Bothell admissions Web site (http://www.uwb.edu/admissions) provides additional details about these and other requirements.

Application and Information

Application deadlines vary depending on specific program of interest. A detailed list of these dates can be found at http://www.uwb.edu/admissions/application-dates.

For additional information, contact:
UW Bothell Enrollment Management
P.O. Box 358500
18115 Campus Way, NE
Bothell, Washington 98011-8246
Phone: 425-352-5000
         425-352-5303 (TDD)
E-mail: info@uwb.edu
Web site: http://www.uwb.edu

University of Washington Bothell—inspiring innovation and creativity.

UNIVERSITY OF WYOMING
LARAMIE, WYOMING

The University

The University of Wyoming (UW) is a welcoming community of 13,000-plus students offering all the adventure, academic programs, research opportunities, advanced facilities, student life, and NCAA Division I athletics of a larger institution yet providing the individual attention, reasonable class sizes, and personalized instruction of a smaller school. The University offers the perfect environment for success complimented by endless outdoor activities. UW was founded in 1886 as a public land-grant institution and reflects the global community it serves, including hosting students from all fifty states and more than ninety countries.

Research done by UW professors and students pushes the boundaries of modern science and technology resulting in the University's classification as a Carnegie Doctoral/High Research institution. UW offers bachelor's degree programs through six undergraduate colleges and graduate and professional programs, including the Doctor of Pharmacy and the Juris Doctor. The average class size is 30 students, and the student-to-faculty ratio is 14:1.

Students can experience the camaraderie of 200-plus recognized student clubs and organizations, including fifteen national fraternities and sororities, honor and professional societies, political and faith-based organizations, and special interest groups. Students also have the opportunity to participate in more than sixty different intramural and club sports. UW is a NCAA Division I school with seventeen men's and women's sports competing in the Mountain West Conference.

UW has experienced tremendous growth in new academic, campus recreation, and student life facilities. UW's recently expanded $54-million College of Business building features behavioral and multimedia labs, and a state-of-the-art trading room where students manage a seven-figure portfolio. Students can engage their creative talents at UW's new visual arts center featuring 79,000 square feet of studio space for ceramics, drawing, painting, sculpting, and print making. Campus recreational facilities include the Wyoming Union, offering the UW bookstore, eating establishments, student computers, and study areas. Additional facilities on campus include Half Acre Gym, an indoor climbing wall, an eighteen-hole golf course, tennis and racquetball courts, weight rooms, and two swimming pools.

UW houses 2,400 students in six residence halls. First-year students are required to live on campus. While primarily coed, the residence halls offer unique living environments, including quiet/study floors, special-interest floors, honors floors, single-gender floors, and other academic living environments. UW also offers a variety of different Freshman Interest Groups (FIGS), which are living communities comprised of students who share common classes and academic interests. More information is available online at www.uwyo.edu/reslife-dining/.

Location

UW's 785-acre campus is located at the foot of the Rocky Mountains in Laramie, a scenic town of 30,000 people in southeastern Wyoming. No matter the time of year, UW students can be found outdoors. Many enjoy the easy access to skiing, boarding, snowmobiling, hiking, camping, hunting, fishing, rock climbing, and mountain biking. Laramie—with its blue skies, clean air, and 320 days of sunshine a year—is a friendly and supportive university town, located 45 miles west of Wyoming's capital, Cheyenne, and 130 miles northwest of Denver, Colorado.

Majors and Degrees

UW offers more than 190 areas of study within its six colleges, leading to B.A., B.S., B.F.A., and B.S.N. degrees.

The College of Agriculture and Natural Resources offers undergraduate majors in agricultural business (with options in agribusiness management, farm and ranch management, and international agriculture), agricultural communications, agroecology, animal and veterinary sciences (with options in animal biology, business, communication, meat science and food technology, pre–veterinary science, production, and range livestock), family and consumer science (with options in child development, dietetics, family and community services, human nutrition and food, premedicine, and textiles and merchandising), microbiology, molecular biology, and rangeland ecology and watershed management.

The College of Arts and Sciences offers undergraduate majors in American Indian studies, American studies, anthropology, art, astronomy/astrophysics, biology, botany, chemistry, communication, criminal justice, English, earth system science, French, geography, geology, geology and earth science, German, history, humanities/fine arts, international studies, journalism, management, mathematical sciences, mathematics, microbiology, music (with options in education, performance, and theory and composition), philosophy, physics, political science, psychology, Russian, social science, sociology, Spanish, statistics, theatre and dance, wildlife and fisheries biology and management, women's studies, and zoology and physiology as well as the option of a self-designed major.

The College of Business offers undergraduate majors in accounting, business administration, business economics, economics, finance, management, and marketing.

The College of Education offers undergraduate majors in elementary education (options in creative arts, international educational studies, American cultural diversity, environmental studies, interdisciplinary early childhood, or individual and society), and secondary education (options in agriculture education, art, English, industrial technology, mathematics, modern languages, sciences, and social studies).

The College of Engineering and Applied Science offers undergraduate majors in architectural engineering (with structural systems or mechanical systems options), chemical engineering (with biomaterials and polymers, biomedical engineering, biotechnology, chemistry, environmental engineering, international, or mathematics options), civil engineering (with environmental, geotechnical, international, structural, transportation, or water resources options), computer engineering (with an international option), computer science (with business or international options), electrical engineering (with bioengineering, computer, or international options), mechanical engineering (with aerodynamics, energy systems, international, manufacturing and design, or materials and solid mechanics options), and petroleum engineering (with an international option).

The College of Health Sciences offers majors in dental hygiene, kinesiology and health promotion (with an athletic coaching option), nursing, pharmacy, physical education teaching, social work, dental hygiene, and speech-language and hearing sciences.

UW offers preprofessional programs in dentistry, law, medicine, nursing, occupational therapy, optometry, pharmacy, physical therapy, and veterinary medicine.

The School of Environment and Natural Resources also offers interdisciplinary studies that can be combined with course work in seven other fields of study, including the humanities, physical sciences, and social sciences.

Two interdisciplinary degrees are offered at UW. Energy resource management and development offers a diverse curriculum that combines engineering, science, business, law, and natural resources content to build a fundamental understanding of interaction and trade-offs between energy, environment, policy, and the economy. Earth system science, on the other hand, provides an integrated approach to issues of global environmental change. Students must choose one of the options of anthropology, atmospheric science, biology, botany, geography, geology and geophysics, secondary education, or soil science.

Academic Programs

The UW academic calendar consists of two semesters and a complete summer session. Depending on the degree program, students are required to complete 120 to 164 credit hours for graduation. Undergraduate programs for most majors can be completed in four years. Students may choose to double major within the same college, or they may pursue majors in separate colleges. Minors are also available in many areas. All students are required to complete the University Studies Program, a core curriculum that assists students in developing their knowledge of oral and written communication, mathematics, science, diversity, global awareness, government, and culture.

The University Honors Program provides academically ambitious undergraduates innovative and intellectual learning opportunities. Award-winning faculty members, unique and challenging course work, and senior research projects are the hallmarks of this program.

Off-Campus Programs

UW has over 700 international students and close to 100 international researchers/scholars representing over 90 countries. The International Students and Scholars Office provide support to this population through an extensive orientation program, the Friendship Families program, and the International Student Association, which arranges International Education Week and the weekly International Coffee Hour, along with other activities.

UW partners with over 400 exchange sites or study-abroad programs, allowing students to go almost anywhere in the world and study in English or a foreign language. International Programs also coordinates the National Student Exchange (NSE), which is a domestic student exchange consortium of more than 180 colleges and universities throughout the U.S. NSE provides UW students with access to thousands of unique academic programs, classes, and faculty members on host campuses for either a semester or an academic year.

The UW Outreach School extends the university learning experience to Wyoming and the nation through credit and noncredit programs. Courses are delivered via Internet/Web-based instruction, compressed video, audio teleconferencing, flexible enrollment (correspondence study), and on-site instruction. Select programs are offered, and degree availability may be limited.

Academic Facilities

The University Libraries' collections number nearly 1.5 million volumes and offer links to a variety of library service collections. William Robertson Coe Library is the flagship library, housing the learning commons and materials from all academic disciplines outside of geology and law. Other library facilities include a geology library (Learning Resource Center), a plant research center (Rocky Mountain Herbarium Library), and a compact shelving facility (Library Annex) which houses the majority of UW Libraries' bound periodicals and government documents. Additional on-campus collections are housed in the American Heritage Center and the George W. Hopper Law Library.

Costs

UW annual tuition and fees for full-time undergraduates in the 2012–13 academic year are $4278 for Wyoming residents and $13,488 for nonresidents (based on an average class load of 15 credit hours). Room and board (double occupancy, unlimited meal plan) costs are $9084. Estimated expenses include $1200 for books and supplies, $890 for travel costs, and $2200 for personal expenses.

Financial Aid

Nearly 90 percent of all UW students receive financial assistance. More than $85 million is available in the form of scholarships, loans, grants, and work-study opportunities. The Free Application for Federal Student Aid (FAFSA) is required for need-based assistance (loans, grants, work-study) and for many scholarships. The priority deadline for FAFSA is March 1. Most scholarships at UW are based on academic merit. UW participates in the Western Undergraduate Exchange (WUE) program. The Rocky Mountain Scholars Award is available to nonresident students.

Faculty

More than 700 professors from the world's most respected colleges and universities have come to teach at UW. Recognized nationally and internationally as experts, 86 percent of faculty members hold the highest degree in their field. UW professors are deeply committed to the success of their students. Ninety-two percent of undergraduate courses are taught by professors or professional lecturers, and many of the most distinguished and accomplished professors at UW teach first-year courses.

Admission Requirements

For assured admission, high school graduates and new first-year students with fewer than 30 transferable college credit hours should have a cumulative high school GPA of 3.0 or above. Students should also have a composite ACT score of 21 or greater or an SAT critical reading/math score of 980 or greater. In addition, all students need to complete 4 years of English, 4 years of mathematics, 4 years of science (including a physical science), 3 years of a social science, 2 years of the same foreign language, and 2 years of additional coursework (behavioral or social sciences, visual arts, performing arts, or humanities). Students who are unable to qualify for assured admission may be admissible with support. Freshman students admitted with support will be required to take part in Synergy, a national award-winning mentoring and support program that assists in the transition to college and increases the academic success rate for participants. Additional details can be found online at www.uwyo.edu/admissions. Transfer students with 30 or more transferable semester credit hours must have a minimum cumulative college GPA of 2.0.

Application and Information

Students must submit a completed UW Application for Admission, official high school or college transcripts, ACT or SAT scores, and a $40 nonrefundable application fee. Students may apply and pay the application fee online at www.uwyo.edu/apply. UW strongly encourages all prospective students and their parents to visit the campus. Explore www.uwyo.edu/visit to check out UW's various visit options and programs.

Admissions Office
Department 3435
University of Wyoming
1000 East University Avenue
Laramie, Wyoming 82071-3435
United States
Phone: 307-766-5160
　　　　800-DIAL-WYO (342-5996; toll-free)
E-mail: admissions@uwyo.edu
Web site: http://www.uwyo.edu

UW Outdoor Program trip leader, Josh Fog, explains climbing-safety procedures to UW Honors students.

UTICA COLLEGE
UTICA, NEW YORK

The College

A private, independent college founded in 1946, Utica College (UC) is known for its excellent academic programs, outstanding faculty, personal attention, and diverse student population. The hallmarks of Utica College's academic programs are the integration of liberal and professional studies and a strong emphasis on internships, research, and other experiential learning opportunities, but UC is best known for the close, personal relationship students have with both faculty and staff members. Approximately 3,600 undergraduate and graduate students attend UC, including men and women from a wide variety of socioeconomic and cultural backgrounds as well as older students, veterans, and students with disabilities. While most students come from New York, New England, and the middle Atlantic states, students are drawn to UC from all parts of the United States, and there is a growing international student population.

Utica College offers thirty-seven majors, a broad selection of minors and special programs, and twenty-one graduate programs. UC also offers a robust selection of study-abroad opportunities as well as preprofessional programs and an honors program.

Utica College is located on a modern, 128-acre campus on the southwestern edge of Utica, New York. Its facilities include a recently completed science and technology complex comprised of state-of-the-art learning and research facilities for health professions and justice studies, the Frank E. Gannett Memorial Library, a fully equipped high-definition television studio and convergence media center, the Ralph F. Strebel Student Center, seven residence halls, an athletic center, a 1,200-seat stadium, and numerous athletic fields.

Half of UC's students live on campus in residence halls that feature a variety of housing options, modern amenities, and lounges for studying or relaxing with friends. Freshmen primarily live in North and South Halls, which offer mostly double-occupancy rooms. Campus dining services provide a wide variety of options, including American and international cuisines, vegetarian meals, a large salad bar, and lighter fare such as burgers and pizza. Students enjoy a range of dining venues, from the main dining commons in Strebel Student Center to a student-run coffeehouse, convenient cafés in the Library and academic buildings, and a Subway sandwich shop on campus.

Whether students live on or off campus, they can take advantage of more than eighty student organizations, focusing on community service, music, theater, and politics as well as fraternities, sororities, and major-related clubs that provide opportunities for students to organize career-related events. Students can write for the student newspaper, work at the College's radio station, submit entries for the literary magazine, or work on the yearbook. Students also have the opportunity to enjoy lectures, concerts, poetry readings, art exhibits, plays, and nationally recognized speakers.

Utica College offers twenty-five NCAA Division III varsity sports, including men's baseball, basketball, cross-country, football, ice hockey, lacrosse, soccer, swimming and diving, tennis, and track and field; women's basketball, cross-country, field hockey, ice hockey, lacrosse, soccer, softball, swimming and diving, tennis, track and field, volleyball, and water polo; and coed golf. UC also offers club sports and a wide variety of intramural opportunities. Utica College is a member of the Empire 8 Athletic Conference, the Eastern College Athletic Conference, and the New York State Women's Collegiate Athletic Association. Nearly a third of all UC students participate in at least one Division III intercollegiate sport, and more than 45 percent are active in intramural or nonvarsity club sports.

Athletic facilities include the 1,200-seat multisport Gaetano Stadium with a state-of-the-art field turf synthetic grass playing surface; the Clark Athletic Center, which contains a large gymnasium, racquetball courts, a swimming pool, saunas, a recently renovated 6,400-square-foot free-weight room and fully equipped fitness facility, and numerous outdoor fields and courts. Ice hockey games are played at the downtown Utica Memorial Auditorium, which features pro-style hockey locker rooms and training facilities.

Location

The city of Utica is located in the heart of the historic Mohawk Valley in the center of New York State. Just 90 miles west of Albany and 50 miles east of Syracuse, Utica has a thriving arts community, beautiful parks, and expanding shopping centers featuring national retailers. There are numerous recreational facilities, including a municipal ski slope and an excellent golf course less than a mile from the Utica College campus. Other nearby recreational opportunities include tennis, swimming, boating, fishing, hiking, and camping.

Majors and Degrees

Utica College offers undergraduate degree programs in accounting, biochemistry, biology, business economics, chemistry, communication arts, computer science, construction management, criminal justice, criminal justice–economic crime investigation, cybersecurity and information assurance, economics, English, foreign language, geoscience, gerontology, government and politics, health studies, health studies–human behavior, health studies–management, history, international studies, journalism studies, liberal studies, management, mathematics, nursing, occupational therapy, philosophy, physical therapy, physics, psychology, psychology–child life, public relations, public relations/journalism studies, risk management and insurance, sociology and anthropology, and therapeutic recreation.

Students interested in the occupational therapy or physical therapy major earn a bachelor's degree in health studies with direct entry into UC's graduate programs, as long as academic requirements are met. Utica College offers a master's degree in occupational therapy and a doctorate in physical therapy (D.P.T.).

Students may minor in anthropology, chemistry, communication arts, computer science, creative writing, economics, English language, film studies, French, gender studies, geoscience, gerontology, government, history, human rights advocacy, literature, management, mathematics, philosophy, psychology, recreation leadership, sociology, Spanish, theater, and writing.

Preprofessional programs include dentistry, law, medicine, optometry, podiatry, and veterinary medicine. Special programs are available in teacher education, gerontology, engineering, and joint health professions.

Academic Programs

In addition to majors and minors, Utica College also offers a rapidly growing education program; students wishing to pursue a career in teaching choose either a liberal arts major (to teach elementary education) or a major in their intended field (to teach at the secondary level).

For those students who are undecided, the Academic Support Services Center provides academic advising and career counseling, and Career Services offers students opportunities to explore career options.

To earn a bachelor's degree, students must complete a minimum of 120 to 128 credits, satisfy major and major-related requirements, and complete any special program requirements. In addition, all Utica College students, regardless of their major, must complete a liberal arts core program as part of the degree requirements.

First-year seminar offers freshmen and transfer students opportunities to earn academic credit while learning how to make the transition to college. Utica College offers the Higher Education Opportunity Program (HEOP), the Collegiate Science and Technology Entry Program (CSTEP), and a summer institute, which serves as an academic bridge between high school and college.

Off-Campus Programs

UC's study-abroad programs give students opportunities to widen their global perspectives through exchange programs with universities in Spain, Italy, Poland, Finland, Hungary, Peru, Scotland, and Wales, as well as American College in Dublin, Ireland, among other options. Special study-abroad opportunities include the College's annual forensic anthropology field school in Albania as well as learning experiences in London, Mexico, the Dominican Republic, and elsewhere.

Students are encouraged to complete internships and field placements to gain professional experience with businesses and organizations while they are earning college credit. Utica College's cooperative education program allows students to earn money while gaining professional experience.

Academic Facilities

The Frank E. Gannett Memorial Library includes a collection of some 200,000 volumes, 1,200 serial subscriptions, hundreds of online journals, and a microform collection of more than 60,000 journals, newspapers, and books. Located on the lower level of the library are the Media Center, computer labs, the Edith Langley Barrett Fine Art Gallery, and a large concourse—the site of special events, such as musical recitals, receptions, and guest lectures.

Classes, laboratories, and faculty offices are located in the main academic complex and within UC's new science and technology complex. F. Eugene Romano Hall, phase one of the new science and technology complex, opened in summer 2007 and provides state-of-the-art classroom, laboratory, and clinical space, as well as learning technology for students in the health sciences. The second phase, Utica College's innovative Economic Crime and Justice Studies building, opened in November 2008 and provides an appropriate platform for cutting-edge research and advanced learning at both the undergraduate and graduate levels.

Named in honor of one of UC's most celebrated faculty members, Professor Emeritus of Public Relations Raymond Simon, UC's state-of-the-art high-definition broadcast facility provides a hands-on learning environment for the next generation of media professionals.

Utica College maintains eight academic computer laboratories with both IBM-compatible and Macintosh computers, including two portable wireless laptop laboratories. Students have additional Internet access in the Pioneer Café and in all student residence hall rooms. Other resources include the Academic Support Services Center, the Math/Science Center, and the Writing Center.

Costs

For 2011–12, tuition was $29,476; room and board costs were $11,650. Student activity and technology fees totaled $520. Books and supplies average $1180 per year.

Financial Aid

The College has been recognized as a best buy in education and works to control costs and keep its education affordable. The average financial aid package for 2009–10 freshmen was $28,000. About two thirds of that aid came from grants and a third from loans and/or jobs. More than 90 percent of the freshmen received a financial aid package. At the same time, UC awarded numerous merit scholarships to students with outstanding grades and test scores.

Almost every federal and state financial aid program is available through Utica College. Students apply for institutional and governmental financial aid by filing the Free Application for Federal Student Aid (FAFSA) by February 15. UC offers three different deferred-payment programs that spread payments over the academic year.

Faculty

Utica College's faculty is diverse, energetic, accomplished, and devoted to their students. The vast majority of faculty members have earned their Ph.D. or other terminal degree, and while many are involved in research, the primary focus of faculty members is teaching. The typical class size is 20 students, the student-faculty ratio is 15:1, and all faculty members are involved in assisting students with their academic planning.

Student Government

One of Utica College's strongest traditions is student participation in the College's governance structure. Students may serve on a number of student governing bodies, and students also serve on all standing committees of the College.

Admission Requirements

Utica College admits students who can best benefit from the educational opportunities the College offers. The Admission Committee gives each application individual attention, and the potential for a student's success at UC is measured primarily by an evaluation of past academic performance, scholastic ability, and personal characteristics. Freshman applicants must have completed 16 academic units, including 4 years of English. Students should follow a college-preparatory program, including 3 units of mathematics, 3 units of science, 2 units of foreign language, and 3 units of social studies.

Application and Information

Students may apply for fall, spring, or summer admission. Materials required include a completed Utica College application form, official high school or college transcripts, and a $40 application fee. Utica College prefers, but does not require, SAT or ACT scores, with the exception of the programs listed below. A personal interview for all applications is strongly suggested.

Occupational therapy, physical therapy, nursing, and joint health professions program applicants must submit SAT or ACT scores, a preferred letter of clinical recommendation if applicable, and a personal statement. International students must complete the international student application form. The application fee is waived for students who apply to HEOP or CSTEP; however, SAT or ACT scores are required to be considered for either program.

The College conducts a rolling admissions program; however certain programs do have application deadlines. For students applying to the occupational therapy or physical therapy programs, the joint health professions program, or for academic achievement awards, the application deadline is January 15. For students applying to the nursing program, the preferred application deadline is February 1. The application deadline for the HEOP program is January 15. Students should note that a tuition deposit of $200 is required by April 1 to secure a place in the HEOP program.

Additional admissions information can be found online at http://www.utica.edu/admissions.

Inquiries should be sent to:

Director of Enrollment Management
Utica College
1600 Burrstone Road
Utica, New York 13502-4892
Phone: 315-792-3006
        800-782-8884 (toll-free)
E-mail: admiss@utica.edu
Web site: http://www.utica.edu
        http://www.facebook.com/UticaCollegeAdmissions
        http://twitter.com/uticacollege

F. Eugene Romano Hall on the Utica College campus.

VANDERBILT UNIVERSITY
NASHVILLE, TENNESSEE

VANDERBILT
UNIVERSITY

The University

In 1873, on the heels of the Civil War, Commodore Cornelius Vanderbilt gave $1 million to the university that now bears his name, with the hope that it would "contribute to strengthening the ties which should exist between all sections of our common country." Since then, Vanderbilt has consistently enrolled America's most talented students and challenged them to expand their intellectual horizons in an inclusive environment based on open inquiry and respect. Vanderbilt's comprehensive interdisciplinary approach to education allows students to pursue a wide array of academic and curricular interests outside of their main focus of study and the University's progressive financial aid policies assure that it is often cited among the country's best values in national universities.

Consistently ranked among the top 20 universities in the country by *U.S. News & World Report,* Vanderbilt is a private research university that features four undergraduate schools and six graduate and professional schools. Each year, 1,600 first-year students join the University, bringing the total undergraduate population to approximately 6,800 students, many of whom collaborate with professors on cutting-edge research projects and present their findings at professional conferences. The 8:1 student-faculty ratio gives each student access to faculty members of prominence in every area of academic study. Full-time faculty members share their perspectives as instructors and advisers united by one goal: providing a challenging, comprehensive education that encourages broad perspectives and critical thinking.

Known for the rolling splendor of its 330-acre campus, which is classified as a national arboretum, Vanderbilt also offers a top-ranked residential experience for its undergraduates, who live on campus all four years. First-year students live and learn in the Martha Rivers Ingram Commons, a collection of ten residence halls, or Houses, clustered along one side of campus (seven of the Houses are LEED-certified). The Commons incorporates more than just bricks and mortar. Faculty members, including the Dean of the Ingram Commons and his family, live there, facilitating easy and meaningful interactions between students and professors. Frequent educational and social programming at the Ingram Commons invites students and faculty to explore current events and social issues.

Vanderbilt students take full advantage of student life in over 350 student organizations, a full range of study-abroad programs, Division I Athletics, and a variety of internship opportunities.

Location

Vanderbilt University is located in Nashville, the capital of Tennessee. Described by *Rolling Stone* as having the best music scene in the country, Nashville boasts a rich mosaic of cultures, vibrant arts, business, health and education sectors, and an array of recreational opportunities. Nashville hosts thousands of live concerts each year in every conceivable genre and is recognized as a top college city in America and an excellent location for businesses. Nashville's many personalities and striking natural beauty attract people from around the world.

Majors and Degrees

College of Arts and Science: African American and Diaspora Studies; American Studies; Anthropology; Art; Asian Studies; Biological Sciences; Chemistry; Classical Civilizations; Classical Languages; Classics; Communication of Science and Technology; Communication Studies; Earth and Environmental Sciences; Ecology, Evolution, and Organismal Biology; Economics; Economics and History; English; English and History; Film Studies; French; French and European Studies; German; German and European Studies; History; History of Art; Italian and European Studies; Jewish Studies; Latin American Studies; Mathematics; Medicine, Health, and Society; Modern European Studies; Molecular and Cellular Biology; Neuroscience; Philosophy; Physics; Political Science; Psychology; Public Policy Studies; Religious Studies; Russian; Russian and European Studies; Sociology; Spanish;

Spanish and European Studies; Spanish and Portuguese; Spanish, Portuguese, and European Studies; Theater; Women's and Gender Studies; and individually designed majors.

Blair School of Music: Composition/Theory, Musical Arts, Musical Arts/Teacher Education, and Performance.

School of Engineering: Biomedical Engineering, Chemical Engineering, Civil Engineering, Computer Engineering, Computer Science, Electrical Engineering, Engineering Science, and Mechanical Engineering.

Peabody College of Education and Human Development: Child Development, Child Studies, Cognitive Studies, Early Childhood Education, Elementary Education, Human and Organizational Development, Secondary Education, and Special Education.

Graduate/Professional Schools: Divinity School, The Graduate School, Law School, Owen Graduate School of Management, School of Medicine, and School of Nursing.

Preprofessional advising is also available for students interested in pursuing graduate degrees in architecture, business, law, and medicine after undergraduate study.

Academic Programs

Students apply directly to one of the four schools that offer undergraduate programs: the College of Arts and Science, the School of Engineering, Peabody College of Education and Human Development, or the Blair School of Music. In all four schools, honors programs and opportunities for independent study and internships are available. Roughly 40 percent of undergraduate students pursue double majors within and across all four undergraduate schools. This leads to some diverse combinations, such as pre-med students who study Spanish, engineers who study violin, math majors who study songwriting, or chemistry majors who study art history.

Vanderbilt operates on a two-semester calendar, and classes begin in late August. First-semester exams take place prior to the winter holidays, and the second semester ends in early May. A variety of courses are offered during Maymester and two summer sessions.

The College of Arts and Science provides many opportunities to experience a wide range of academic disciplines and subjects. Within the requirements of the AXLE (Achieving eXcellence in Liberal Education) curriculum, students refine their skills in writing, mathematics, foreign language, the humanities, natural sciences, social sciences, history, and culture.

The Blair School of Music offers the Bachelor of Music degree in composition and theory, musical arts, musical arts/teacher education, and performance. Instruction is available in every instrument of the orchestra as well as piano, organ, euphonium, multiple woodwinds, saxophone, classical guitar, and voice. Unlike many schools of music, Blair has no graduate students. The curriculum combines intensive musical training with liberal arts studies. Approximately one third of a student's work is outside of music. The Blair School also offers a music minor and a wide variety of courses, private instruction, and performing organizations for nonmajors.

For more than 125 years, the School of Engineering has educated engineers for practice in industry, government, consulting, teaching, and research careers. In addition to technical courses, each student's program includes a rich complement of course work in the humanities and social sciences, resulting in a balanced foundation for future achievement and the assumption of leadership roles in their chosen fields. All programs leading to a Bachelor of Engineering degree are ABET-accredited, and students can earn the Bachelor of Science degree while majoring in Computer Science or Engineering Science.

The top-ranked graduate school of education (according to *U.S. News & World Report*) for four years running, Peabody College offers degree programs leading to teacher certification and to careers in other areas of education, including child development, child studies, cognitive studies, and human and organizational development. The

degree reflects a strong liberal arts foundation combined with a solid program of preprofessional courses and a multitude of internship and practicum opportunities. All undergraduates must complete requirements in communications, the humanities, mathematics, the natural sciences, and the social sciences. Moreover, students have an abundance of field experiences throughout their four years.

Off-Campus Programs

Study-abroad programs allow students to immerse themselves in languages and cultures around the world. More than 100 programs are offered in Argentina, Australia, Austria, Chile, China, Costa Rica, the Czech Republic, Denmark, the Dominican Republic, Egypt, England, France, Germany, Israel, Italy, Japan, Russia, Singapore, South Africa, and Spain, among others. Vanderbilt students receive direct credit for their courses, and the cost of tuition is usually the same as for study on campus in Nashville. In addition, any scholarships, grants, or loans a student has been awarded apply to Vanderbilt study-abroad programs. Students may also participate in programs sponsored by other universities by working with an adviser.

Academic Facilities

Students and faculty members take advantage of Vanderbilt's extensive library resources, obtaining easy access to books, periodicals, documents, microforms, and reference materials. The Jean and Alexander Heard Library is supported by nine major resource centers, which include special collections, University Archives, and more than 3.5 million volumes.

Costs

The estimated costs for 2012–13 include: tuition, $41,732; housing, $9170; books and supplies, $1370; student activities and recreation fee, $1042; personal expenses allowance, $2446; first-year experience fee, $688; new student transcript fee, $30; engineering lab fee*, $650; and engineering laptop allowance*, $1500. Travel allowances are variable. *The engineering laptop allowance and laboratory fee apply to engineering students only. First-year engineering students are required to either purchase a laptop from Vanderbilt or provide their own computer that meets published requirements.

Financial Aid

Three important commitments reflect the University's dedication to making a Vanderbilt education possible: Vanderbilt is need-blind for all U.S. citizens and eligible non-citizens, Vanderbilt meets 100 percent of demonstrated need for all admitted students, and Vanderbilt's financial aid packages do not include loans. These three commitments combined place Vanderbilt among a small number of universities to adopt such progressive policies.

More than 60 percent of the University's undergraduate students received some type of financial aid in the 2011–12 school year. Need-based aid is awarded according to the evaluation of the FAFSA and the CSS/Financial Aid PROFILE.

Vanderbilt also awards merit-based scholarships to selected first-year applicants who demonstrate exceptional accomplishment and intellectual promise. Three signature scholarship programs comprise the majority of these honor scholarships: the Ingram Scholarship Program (for students who plan to combine a professional or business career with an exceptional commitment to community service), the Cornelius Vanderbilt Scholarship Program (for students who combine outstanding academic achievements with strong leadership and contributions outside the classroom), and the Chancellor's Scholarship Program (for students who have worked to build strong high school communities by bridging gaps among economically, socially, and racially diverse groups).

Faculty

Excluding the Schools of Medicine and Nursing, Vanderbilt has 1,035 full-time faculty members. All undergraduate faculty members, many of whom hold awards for distinguished scholarship, are required to teach undergraduates. A low student-faculty ratio of 8:1 provides for an intimate academic experience between students and professors who are recognized nationally and worldwide for their research. 92 percent of classes have fewer than 50 students.

Student Government

The Vanderbilt Student Government provides students with an opportunity to participate actively in maintaining a high quality of life on campus. It works with many of the more than 350 student organizations to bring nationally prominent speakers to campus and provides an interesting and diverse array of programming throughout the year. A vital part of life at Vanderbilt is the honor system, which is governed entirely by students through representatives on the Honor Council. Each year, a senior is selected as a Young Alumni Trustee of the University's Board of Trust.

Admission Requirements

Vanderbilt seeks students with high standards of scholarship and character. Admission is based on a thorough and holistic review of academic and personal credentials.

The typical applicant will have completed 20 or more units in a challenging high school curriculum, including at least 2 years of foreign language study. Applicants to the School of Engineering must complete at least 4 units of mathematics; calculus and physics are strongly recommended. The Admissions Committee evaluates each student's secondary school academic record, extracurricular involvement, counselor and teacher recommendations, and personal essay. Students must also submit scores (including the writing subscore) from either the SAT Reasoning Test or the ACT. Applicants to the Blair School of Music are required to audition on their primary instrument. A personal audition is preferred, but applicants may audition by videotape with permission from the Blair School of Music.

Campus visits are highly recommended, though student interest is not used as a measure of admissibility. In addition to daily information sessions and campus tours, the Admissions Office offers various half-day and full-day visit programs for prospective students. All programs require reservations, so students are encouraged to call or visit http://admissions.vanderbilt.edu in advance of their visit for information about group information sessions, campus tours, and opportunities to attend classes.

Application and Information

Students whose first choice is Vanderbilt may apply under one of Vanderbilt's early decision plans. Applications and all supporting materials must be postmarked by November 1 for Early Decision I and by January 3 for Early Decision II; notification is made by December 15 for Early Decision I and by February 15 for Early Decision II. Regular Decision applications are due January 3. Students are informed of the admission decision by April 1. Personal auditions are scheduled in December, January, and February for students applying to the Blair School of Music. Students seeking transfer admission should submit an application and all supporting materials by March 15 for fall semester entry.

Office of Undergraduate Admissions
Vanderbilt University
2305 West End Avenue
Nashville, Tennessee 37203-1727
Phone: 615-322-2561
        800-288-0432 (toll-free)
E-mail: admissions@vanderbilt.edu
Web site: http://admissions.vanderbilt.edu
         http://facebook.com/Vanderbilt
         http://twitter.com/vanderbiltu

Kirkland Hall, Vanderbilt's oldest and most historic building.

VAUGHN COLLEGE OF AERONAUTICS AND TECHNOLOGY

FLUSHING, NEW YORK

VaughnCollege
of aeronautics and technology

The College

Vaughn College of Aeronautics and Technology is a private, four-year college committed to providing its students with the excellent education and skills needed to achieve professional success in engineering, technology, management and aviation. Founded in 1932, the College, adjacent to LaGuardia Airport, is a small, high-quality institution where students can experience personal attention as they progress through academic course work. The College fosters a culture of excellence in which rigorous degree, professional, technical, and certification programs are offered. These programs, built upon the College's aeronautical heritage, incorporate the latest technology and meet the universal needs of the industries they serve. The result is well-educated graduates who are successful in their fields. The College's student body of more than 1,600 and its low, 16:1 student-faculty ratio ensure a highly personalized learning environment. More than 95 percent of Vaughn College graduates are employed or continue their educations within one year of obtaining their degrees, and they work in twenty countries and all fifty states.

On September 1, 2004, the College of Aeronautics became Vaughn College of Aeronautics and Technology. The name reflects the College's aviation heritage as well as its future as a greatly expanded academic institution, with new programs that include a bachelor's degree in mechatronic engineering and a master's-level management offering. The name change is part of the College's strategic plan that also includes plans for a new library, additional degree programs, and other improvements to the campus.

Location

Located in New York City, the College offers numerous internship opportunities with an array of technology, manufacturing, and aviation companies. The cultural, spiritual, and physical needs of the students are met by the outstanding facilities of New York City. Restaurants are easily accessible, and hospitals and other medical facilities are among the best in the world. New York City's legendary museums focus on arts, natural history, science, and world civilization.

Majors and Degrees

The College awards the Associate of Applied Science (A.A.S.) degree in aeronautical engineering technology, airport management, aviation maintenance, animation and digital technologies, electronic engineering technology–avionics, and flight.

The Bachelor of Science (B.S.) degree is available in general management, airline management, airport management, aviation maintenance, aviation maintenance management, electronic engineering technology–avionics, electronic engineering technology–general electronics, flight, mechatronics engineering, mechanical engineering technology–aeronautical option, and mechanical engineering technology–computer-aided design option. A nondegree course of study in air traffic control, a Federal Aviation Administration Collegiate Training Initiative program (AT-CTI), is also available. The College is one of thirty-six institutions nationwide to offer this program. There is also an aircraft dispatch program offered.

Academic Programs

All students in associate and baccalaureate degree programs complete a core curriculum as part of their degree requirements. The core curriculum is derived from the mission of the College and reflects what the institution believes is important and fundamental to students' education and development. In general, the core instills in students critical-thinking skills, values appropriate to an educated person, and the ability to communicate, and the curriculum provides context for advanced learning. The baccalaureate core consists of three components: academic skills (13 credits, including a year of English composition, a course in oral communication, and precalculus), the liberal arts (12 credits, including a year of world and American literature), and math and science (15 credits).

Off-Campus Programs

Internships are an important part of a student's learning experience at Vaughn College, and they have led to job offers upon graduation. The department of career services and faculty chairs arrange for internships with top U.S. corporations. As a federally designated Hispanic-serving institution, the College participates with the Hispanic Association of Colleges and Universities (HACU) to place students in internships with various federal agencies year-round. Other active internships and cooperatives include the Boeing Company, Federal Aviation Administration (FAA), Federal Express, Global Air Dispatch, HACU, JetBlue, Lockheed Martin, the Metropolitan Transportation Authority (MTA), the National Broadcasting Company, the Northrop Grumman Corporation, Northwest Airlines, ORBIS, the Port Authority of New York and New Jersey, and Teterboro Airport.

Academic Facilities

Each laboratory provides the work/study environment suited to the requirements of each program. This practical, hands-on experience helps qualify students for immediate employment upon graduation. From the new mechatronics laboratory to the CATIA/NASTRAN computer center, the College is committed to providing students with the knowledge and tools they are likely to find in today's businesses. The College's $1-million flight simulator center features Frasca142 and 241 simulators, a Canadair regional jet trainer, and two Redbird simulators. In addition, a revolutionary educational partnership with Redbird Flight Simulations enables students to pursue FAA flight certifications and ratings at Redbird's innovative facility in San Marcos, Texas.

The College has substantially upgraded its technology environment over the past few years. Students have access to more than 200 computers in classrooms and labs, providing software applications for desktop publishing, word processing, spreadsheets, databases, and shared printing services. These computers also afford students the opportunity to interact with industry-leading applications used within their academic programs, including CATIA, SolidWorks, Nastran, Patran, and Mechanical Desktop. The College's recently created student portal provides online access to tools that enhance and support academic efforts. All of Vaughn's classrooms have updated instructional technologies, including projection, and Vaughn's T1 line provides Internet connectivity to classrooms and labs. Wireless access exists across campus, including

within the residential facilities, and each student is provided a vaughn.edu e-mail address. New identification cards are planned for fall 2012 that will provide students with access to secured facilities, laundry payment, dining services, library access, vending and purchasing options, and more.

The College's library offers extensive general, technical, resource, and periodical material totaling more than 125,000 volumes. The real and virtual resources include books, periodicals, videos, and research databases. The video collection consists of subject videos to support the College's curriculum, general-interest videos, and movies. The library houses VHS tapes and DVDs and its research databases contain more than 8,000 full-text periodicals and newspapers. Ten personal computers are available for student use in the reference area. Vaughn is also nearing the construction phase of a new library that will provide students and faculty with a one-stop location for research materials, academic support services, and technology support. This new library, scheduled to open in 2013, triples the size of the current facility and is part of a more than $30-million renovation of Vaughn's campus planned over the next several years.

Costs

In 2011–12, full-time tuition (12 to 18 credits per semester) was $9000. Students taking 11 credits or fewer paid $600 per credit. The semester fee, which covers the cost of orientation courses, Internet and computer usage, and student-support services, activities, and leadership programs, was $200.

For the 2011–12 academic year, rooms in Vaughn's four-year-old residence hall cost $4300 for a double room and $4950 for a single room, per semester. A $250 housing deposit is required. Residents live in either a two-person or a four-person suite with a semi-private bath. The residence hall has laundry, study, and kitchen facilities in a common area within the building. Residence hall rooms are supplied with a bed, dresser, closet, desk, chair, and wastebasket for each student. Each room is also equipped with phone and cable TV hookup and computer port.

Financial Aid

Vaughn College offers federal, state, and institutional funds to help students pay for their education. More than 85 percent of students are eligible for some type of financial aid. The first step is to file the Free Application for Federal Student Aid (FAFSA) and, if appropriate, the New York State Tuition Assistance Program (TAP) application. Applications for the fall semester should be filed by March 1. The College recognizes academic excellence by awarding scholarships to high-achieving students pursuing Bachelor of Science degree programs. Applicants must file the FAFSA to be eligible.

Awards for new students include Founders' Scholarships, which are merit-based and range from $500 to $6000 per year, and the need-based Vaughn College financial grants, which range from $250 to $2200.

Faculty

What separates Vaughn College from other institutions is its uniquely committed faculty, whose members come to the classroom with extensive experience in such fields as engineering, manufacturing, management, and communications. Working closely with industry, the College has developed rigorous curricula that incorporate the latest technology and the knowledge students need for that all-important first professional position. The student-faculty ratio of 16:1 enables students to work closely with faculty members in classroom and laboratory settings.

Student Government

The Student Government Association (SGA) is primarily concerned with the quality of student life on campus. SGA carries the concerns of its constituency, the student body, to the administration and is the voice of the student body. Serving students as the liaison to the administration, SGA coordinates social programming and provides a system for cocurricular involvement through many clubs and organizations. SGA meets on a regular basis and encourages all students to attend meetings and become involved.

Admission Requirements

High school graduates must submit a completed application (available online at www.vaughn.edu); the $40 application fee; SAT or ACT scores; an official copy of the high school transcript and any college transcripts (if applicable); a copy of the high school diploma (or GED), complete with scores; and immunization records. Some students may need to take a placement exam, while flight operations applicants must pass the FAA Class II physical examination. An interview with an admissions counselor and a financial aid counselor is required for all flight operations applicants and recommended for all others.

Students who have lived in the United States for less than three years and for whom English is a second language, or international applicants from countries where English is not an official language, can substitute results of the TOEFL exam. Students who have completed 24 or more college credits are exempt from the SAT/ACT requirement.

Application and Information

The admissions office reviews applications on a rolling basis. All applicants are encouraged to file by March 1 for the fall semester and November 15 for the spring semester to best take advantage of scholarship opportunities.

Vaughn College of Aeronautics and Technology
86-01 23rd Avenue
Flushing, New York 11369
Phone: 718-429-6600
         866-6VAUGHN (toll-free)
Fax: 718-779-2231
E-mail: admitme@vaughn.edu
Web site: http://www.vaughn.edu

Vaughn College is located in easy proximity of Manhattan.

VERMONT TECHNICAL COLLEGE
RANDOLPH CENTER AND WILLISTON, VERMONT

The College

Founded in 1866, Vermont Technical College's (VTC) main campus is situated on a hilltop in Randolph Center, Vermont, in the heart of the Green Mountains. The College also has campuses in Williston, Bennington, and Brattleboro, Vermont, plus a network of extended nursing campuses statewide. Vermont Technical College is the only technical college in the Vermont State Colleges system. Most of the 1,650 students enrolled come from Vermont and the other New England states.

Through its bachelor's, associate, and certificate programs, the College provides students with a broad-based, practical education. As a result, Vermont Tech graduates are prepared to work effectively in a variety of positions, such as engineers, technicians, managers, and nurses. Degrees offered in the allied health fields of nursing, dental hygiene, and respiratory therapy prepare students to assume medical positions operating on the frontline of patient care.

The Randolph Campus has more than 544-acres including a Student Health and Physical Education (SHAPE) facility with a double-court gymnasium; a six-lane indoor pool; two racquetball courts; a brand-new, state-of-the-art fitness center; and a wireless café/lounge. The four residence halls can house more than 600 students, and additional housing is available at the College's Williston campus, just minutes from Burlington, Vermont. Every student room has connections for direct access to the campuswide computer network, telephone service, and cable TV lines.

Campus life at Vermont Tech includes sports, recreation, social events, and community service-learning opportunities. The Student Life Office arranges weekly activities and social events and provides students with support and counseling. There are many student clubs, from the student-run radio station WVTC-FM to student chapters of professional organizations. There is also an on-campus ski hill, where students can snowboard and ski after classes conclude for the day.

Students enthusiastically participate in the College's varsity and intramural sports clubs. Fall varsity sports include men's baseball and men's and women's cross-country and soccer. In the winter, the men's and women's basketball teams take the court. In the spring, the women's softball and men's baseball teams swing into action for their "second season." Varsity athletic programs are well-supported at Vermont Tech.

Vermont Tech maintains a national affiliation with the United States Collegiate Athletic Association (USCAA) Vermont Tech athletes compete in the Yankee Small College Conference (YSCC). The College has a rich history of athletic success, with many conference championships in various sports to its credit.

The College is accredited by the New England Association of Schools and Colleges. In addition, the following degree programs are accredited by the Technology Accreditation Commission of the Accreditation Board for Engineering and Technology, Inc. (TAC of ABET): architectural and building engineering technology, architectural engineering technology, civil and environmental engineering technology, computer engineering technology, electrical engineering technology, electromechanical engineering technology, and mechanical engineering technology. The veterinary technology program is accredited by the American Veterinary Medical Association as a program for educating veterinary technicians. Practical nursing programs are approved by the Vermont Board of Nursing and accredited by the National League for Nursing Accrediting Commission (NLNAC). The associate degree program in nursing is approved by the Vermont Board of Nursing. The dental hygiene program is accredited by the American Dental Association Commission on Dental Accreditation (CODA), and the respiratory therapy program is accredited by the Committee on Accreditation of Respiratory Care Programs (CoARC).

Location

Vermont Tech has two residential campuses in Randolph Center and Williston, Vermont. Each campus offers a wide variety of majors and lifestyle choices ranging from suburban to rural. Vermont Tech's Randolph Center is rural but far from isolated—exit 4 of Interstate 89 is just 1 mile away. For day-to-day needs, the nearby village of Randolph offers a variety of shops and restaurants as well as a movie theater, a bowling alley, and the Chandler Music Hall. For special shopping and events, Burlington and Montpelier, Vermont, and Hanover, New Hampshire, are within an hour's drive. Boston and Montreal are just 3 hours away. There is convenient bus and train service in Randolph.

Vermont Tech's Williston campus is just minutes from downtown Burlington. More than 500 students take advantage of Williston's bachelor's, associate, and certificate programs. In addition to engineering and computer technology other majors offered on the Willison campus are dental hygiene, respiratory therapy, and professional pilot technology.

Students enjoy the variety of recreational activities available to them in Vermont. Some of the top ski resorts in the East are less than an hour from the campus. Students can also hike on the Appalachian Trail, canoe on numerous lakes and rivers, camp in the Green Mountain National Forest, and bike on the miles of country roads.

Majors and Degrees

Vermont Technical College offers a Bachelor of Science degree in architectural engineering technology, business technology and management, computer engineering technology, construction management, dental hygiene, diversified agriculture, electromechanical engineering technology, equine studies, fire and emergency services (proposed), information technology, software engineering, professional pilot technology, and sustainable design and technology.

Vermont Tech offers four programs leading to the Associate in Engineering degree: civil and environmental engineering technology, computer engineering technology, electrical engineering technology, and mechanical engineering technology.

Programs leading to the Associate in Applied Science degree include agribusiness management technology, architectural and building engineering technology, automotive technology, business technology and management, construction management, dairy farm management technology, diesel power technology, fire science, general engineering technology, landscape development and ornamental horticulture, and veterinary technology.

Programs leading to the Associate in Science degree include dental hygiene, information technology, nursing, respiratory therapy, and software engineering. The nursing programs (certificate and associate degree) offered by Vermont Tech are located several locations throughout Vermont, including Bennington, Brattleboro, and Williston, as well as on the College's main campus in Randolph Center.

Academic Programs

Whether preparing for an associate or a bachelor's degree, Vermont Tech students receive a rigorous broad-based education centered on a core curriculum that includes both technical and general education electives. The number of credits required for graduation ranges from 65 to 72 for the associate degree and from 130 to 139 for the bachelor's degree, depending on the program. Honors courses are offered in all engineering technology programs. Most degree programs also offer project courses, in which students work as teams on real-world applications in their fields of study.

Academic Facilities

Vermont Tech students learn in modern laboratories with state-of-the-art equipment. Hartness Library is the on-campus

library, serving about 3,000 on-campus, extended-campus, and distance education students of Vermont Tech and the Community College of Vermont. Open more than 80 hours per week during the academic year, Hartness houses an extensive collection of material and offers professional staff assistance with library research and information literacy skills. A library Web site (http://www.vctclib.org) gives access to thousands of full-text periodicals and reference databases. Students can request books 24 hours per day.

Facilities housed in the major academic buildings include four computer-aided drafting and design labs (one 13-station, one 19-station, and two 21-station); four 21-station general academic computing labs; an 8-station electrical/electronics lab; recently renovated mechanical labs that include computer numerically controlled equipment and computer-aided manufacturing software; state-of-the-art veterinary technology facilities, including a 12-station lab area, a radiography suite and darkroom, and a surgery suite; a biotechnology lab with instrumentation typical of the most modern research labs; a nursing lab with a dedicated computer room and nursing station; two civil engineering labs; architectural drafting studios; a campuswide microcomputer network with Internet access; four instrumented electronics labs; and a fully equipped automotive technology center with the latest in computerized diagnostics. Facilities at the College's Williston campus include an 8,400-square-foot dental hygiene clinic that features twenty-two dental operatories, four radiographic units, a dedicated classroom, faculty offices, and a patient reception area.

Agriculture students gain practical experience at the College's dairy facility, where a main free-stall barn houses a milking herd of 80 registered Holsteins. Students have the opportunity to participate in all aspects of the farm's management. Veterinary technology students work with several species of domestic animals in the livestock facility on the farm. Conant Hall houses most of the College's academic support services. Students visit the support services offices to sign up for tutoring, meet with counselors to discuss personal or academic issues, or visit the career/transfer center to update their resumes and explore career options and internship opportunities. Students with learning differences can find out about classroom accommodations and assistive technologies at the College's Center for Academic Success. The center offers drop-in and scheduled tutoring, supplemental instruction, study groups, and review sessions; the General Education Department's Writing and Communication Center is on the same floor and provides students with help in reading, writing, oral presentations, study skills, and assistive-technology training.

Costs

Tuition for 2011–12 was $10,656 per year for Vermont residents and $20,376 for out-of-state students. The yearly room rate was $5030, and the annual meal plan was $3416. Other required annual fees totaled $1120. An additional $1407 health insurance fee was required of students not covered by another medical plan. New students were assessed a $220 matriculation fee. Many of Vermont Tech's programs are available at reduced tuition to New England students through the New England Regional Student Program, sponsored by the New England Board of Higher Education.

Financial Aid

About 80 percent of Vermont Tech students receive financial aid from federal, state, and campus-based sources. There are a growing number of institutional scholarships available, including the Vermont Technical College Scholars Program, as well as work-study opportunities. Prospective students seeking aid must file the Free Application for Federal Student Aid (FAFSA). Some state agencies may require additional information. Students are urged to apply for financial aid by the March 1 priority deadline so awards can be announced by May. However, applications are reviewed on a rolling basis after March 1 until available funds are exhausted. The Vermont Tech Web site provides more financial aid information.

Faculty

The College's excellence in instruction is a direct result of the quality of the faculty at Vermont Tech. More than 140 full- and part-time faculty members bring a special blend of industrial experience and teaching expertise to the College. Almost all have advanced degrees. Students are assured of individual attention as a result of the 11:1 student-faculty ratio.

Admission Requirements

Each applicant receives individual consideration for admission based on receipt and review of the official secondary school transcript, letters of recommendation, proof of high school graduation or a high school equivalency diploma, and SAT scores. A personal interview is strongly recommended for all applicants. Because of the technical nature of the curriculum, applicants should have a strong math and science aptitude.

Application and Information

Vermont Technical College follows a rolling admission policy, but timely application is recommended. Applicants are notified of their status within two weeks of receipt of their completed application and supporting documents. For more information on Vermont Technical College, students should contact:

Office of Admissions
Vermont Technical College
P.O. Box 500
Randolph Center, Vermont 05061
Phone: 802-728-1000
      800-442-VTC-1 (admissions, toll-free)
Fax: 802-728-1321
E-mail: admissions@vtc.edu
Web site: http://www.vtc.edu

The high-tech campus of Vermont Technical College is situated in a scenic New England village in the heart of Vermont.

VILLANOVA UNIVERSITY
VILLANOVA, PENNSYLVANIA

The University

Since 1842, Villanova University's Augustinian Catholic intellectual tradition has been the cornerstone of an academic community in which students learn to think critically, act compassionately, and succeed while serving others. There are more than 10,000 undergraduate, graduate, and law students in the College of Liberal Arts and Sciences, the Villanova School of Business, the College of Engineering, the College of Nursing, and the Villanova University School of Law. As students grow intellectually, Villanova prepares them to become ethical leaders who create positive change everywhere life takes them.

Villanova offers more than 50 rigorous academic programs, and there are 265 student organizations and 36 national honor societies on campus. Undergraduate full-time enrollment is 6,352; total University enrollment is 10,467.

Located just 12 miles (20 kilometers) west of Philadelphia, Villanova's picturesque campus has 65 buildings, including 26 residence halls. Award-winning dining services are available in 3 residence dining halls and 16 à la carte eateries, all with many culinary options. Students have access to several athletic and fitness facilities on campus; the newest is the Davis Center for Athletics, with state-of-the-art cardio machines, weight equipment, and free weights. Group exercise classes, including yoga and Pilates, are also offered regularly. Nearly 20 percent of the student body participates in varsity or club athletics, and 13 intramural sports attract approximately 3,000 student participants annually.

To help facilitate the transition to college life, first-year students are encouraged to join a themed Learning Community. Community members live in the same residence halls, take their year-long Augustine and Culture Seminar together, and participate in co-curricular activities. These activities typically include lectures, plays, themed dinners, rich cultural events, and engaging trips. Through Learning Communities, students often form deeper, often lifelong, relationships with their classmates and professors, and become more fully engaged in their studies.

Location

Villanova students reap all the benefits of living within the beautiful and tranquil Philadelphia Main Line suburbs, while the University's convenient proximity to Philadelphia also provides endless opportunities to complement campus life with cultural, recreational, and social activities found only in a vibrant, major metropolitan area. Whether it's visiting world-class art and science museums, touring historic sites, sampling the impressive restaurant scene, browsing through countless stores and shops, or cheering on local professional sports teams, there is something for everyone to enjoy.

Majors and Degrees

Villanova's College of Liberal Arts and Sciences grants a Bachelor of Arts in Arab and Islamic Studies, Art History, Classical Studies, Communication, Criminal Justice, Cultural Studies, Economics, English, Environmental Studies, French and Francophone Studies, Gender and Women's Studies, Geography, Global Interdisciplinary Studies, History, Honors, Humanities, Italian, Latin American Studies, Philosophy, Political Science, Psychology, Secondary Education, Sociology, Spanish Studies, and Theology and Religious Studies. The college grants a Bachelor of Science in Astronomy and Astrophysics, Biochemistry, Biology, Chemistry, Comprehensive Science, Computer Science, Environmental Science, Honors, Mathematics, and Physics.

Villanova School of Business (VSB) offers a Bachelor of Science in Accountancy and a Bachelor of Business Administration in Economics, Finance, Management, Management Information Systems, and Marketing. VSB also offers co-majors in International Business and Real Estate.

Through the College of Engineering, Villanova grants a Bachelor of Science in Chemical Engineering, Civil Engineering, Computer Engineering, Electrical Engineering, and Mechanical Engineering.

Villanova offers a Bachelor of Science in Nursing through the College of Nursing and also offers the following Health Science Affiliation programs: Drexel University College of Medicine, Doctor of Medicine; University of Pennsylvania School of Dental Medicine, Doctor of Dental Medicine; Pennsylvania College of Optometry at Salus University, Doctor of Optometry; and Jefferson College of Health Professions of Thomas Jefferson University, Doctor of Physical Therapy, and a Master of Science in Occupational Therapy.

Accelerated bachelor's/master's degree programs are available in the following areas: Accountancy, Biology, Chemical Engineering, Chemistry, Civil Engineering, Classical Studies, Communication, Computer Engineering, Computer Science, Computer Science/ Software Engineering, Electrical Engineering, Finance, Hispanic Studies, Liberal Studies, Mathematics, Mathematics/ Applied Statistics, Mechanical Engineering, Nursing, Physics, Political Science, Psychology, Psychology and Human Resource Development, Secondary Education, Spanish Studies, and Theology and Religious Studies.

Academic Programs

Villanova, through the College of Liberal Arts and Sciences, is one of the few institutions in the country that offers an undergraduate program in Astronomy and Astrophysics, and one of only 18 Catholic colleges or universities in the nation to have a chapter of Phi Beta Kappa, the prestigious liberal arts and sciences honor society. It also is home to the Waterhouse Institute for the Study of Communication and Society—the only institute of its kind in the United States—which provides students with opportunities to explore the ethical dimensions of communication.

Highly ranked nationally, the Villanova School of Business is home to the Applied Finance Lab, which provides access to many of the real-time technologies available to Wall Street traders. The Clay Center at VSB assists students as they make important decisions regarding course selections, major and minors, and international experiences, and it helps coordinate internships and co-ops, which often lead to full-time job offers.

The College of Engineering, ranked among the best engineering programs in the nation, is home to three research units: the Center for Advanced Communications, the Center for Nonlinear Dynamics and Control, and the Center for the Advancement of Sustainability in Engineering. The Villanova Center for Engineering Education and Research houses state-of-the-art instructional and research labs, including the new Multidisciplinary Design Lab, and the 10,000-square-foot Structural Engineering Teaching and Research Laboratory offers additional engineering-related facilities.

The College of Nursing, designated a Center for Excellence in Nursing Education by the National League for Nursing, is housed in an advanced facility that features a 200-seat auditorium and a 200-seat lecture hall; future-oriented clinical simulation labs for health assessment, adult health, maternal/child health, anesthesia, and critical care; simulation labs for standardized patient observation and testing; a center for nursing research and scholarship; places for prayer and reflection; space for global health studies and international student activities; and areas for student, faculty, and alumni events and social interaction.

Naval and Marine Reserve Officers Training Corps (ROTC) programs are available on campus. Villanova has had an

NROTC program for more than 50 years, and it is structured to complement a normal college lifestyle. Midshipmen are encouraged to participate fully in their academic programs as well as in extracurricular activities.

Off-Campus Programs

Villanova has a rich study-abroad program. Each year, approximately 750 students take advantage of international study opportunities in nearly 40 nations, including Ireland, Switzerland, Peru, England, France, Germany, Italy, China, Chile, Russia, Poland, Thailand, Spain, Australia, Rwanda, the West Indies, Madagascar, and Samoa.

Academic Facilities

Villanova's state-of-the-art classrooms and labs are in keeping with the University's position as a leading institution of higher learning, and they are complemented with a vast array of learning and career resources. Falvey Memorial Library contains more than 1,000,000 items and offers access to a number of databases. The Office of Learning Support Services assists students with learning disabilities, neurologically based disorders, and chronic illnesses. The Villanova Career Center helps students set and reach their professional development goals. Ninety-six percent of the Villanova Class of 2011 was employed full-time or enrolled in graduate school within six months of degree completion. Approximately 4,000 jobs are posted on Villanova's job boards each year, and the average starting salary for recent graduates is $51,000.

Technology is widely available at Villanova. Each incoming student receives a new laptop computer (upgraded at the end of sophomore year), and all residence halls are connected to the campus network. Students can participate in learning experiences across campus; receive curricular advising services; and access tests, Webcasts, and library reserves online. Through Villanova's student portal, they can keep track of deadlines, class schedules, and financial aid information. Villanova's technology also provides easy access to meal plans, parking registration, laundry reservations, voting processes, ride sharing/carpooling, and basketball ticket lotteries. Students and parents can also sign up for NOVA Alert, the University's emergency notification system.

Costs

For the 2011–12 academic year, the average tuition was $40,530, and room and board were $10,940.

Financial Aid

For the 2011–12 freshman class, 74 percent of those who applied for need-based assistance were eligible to receive it, and 79 percent of those eligible for need-based assistance received Villanova Grants. More than $15 million in Villanova Grants were awarded, with an average award amount of $22,300. The average assistance package for students with demonstrated need (combining grants, scholarships, loans, and student employment) was $29,592.

Villanova offers a Presidential Scholarship program to attract academic, civic, and cultural leaders who represent diverse intellectual, social, racial, and economic backgrounds, including students from families in which few or no members have attended college. Successful candidates are awarded this renewable scholarship—which covers tuition, general fees, room and board, and books—for eight consecutive semesters.

Faculty

Villanova has 590 full-time faculty members; nearly 90 percent of them hold doctoral degrees. The student-to-faculty ratio is 11:1 and the average class size is 22.

Student Government

Empowering the Villanova student body since 1925, the Student Government Association (SGA) has three branches (administrative, community, and student relations) and twelve committees. The SGA provides opportunities for student leaders to serve the Villanova community as liaisons, representatives, and student senators.

Admission Requirements

Admission to Villanova is competitive. In addition to attracting academically talented, well-rounded students, Villanova seeks applicants who are compassionate and want to transform the world and make it a better place.

Villanova is a Common Application member institution. Prospective students are also required to complete the Villanova Supplement for Undergraduate Admission and submit an official high school transcript and Common Application School Report. Applicants must have their standardized test scores (SAT or ACT) reported directly by the College Board or ACT.

In the Villanova admissions process, high school performance is an extremely important selectivity factor. Each student's high school record, GPA, and class rank, along with each student's demonstration of character and personal abilities, are carefully considered. Extracurricular and volunteer activities are helpful to applicants in this regard. Another important factor is the personal essay. Since interviews are not part of the admission process, a well-crafted essay is essential for prospective students to explain who they are and why they should be selected to become Villanovans. (A recommendation from the secondary school counselor is also carefully considered.)

Prospective students who are not from the United States are encouraged to apply for admission to Villanova. Non-native English speakers must take the TOEFL or IELTS evaluations and have scores reported directly from the College Board. The International Student Services Office supports enrolled international students in areas including immigration rights and responsibilities; educational, social, and personal counseling; cultural adjustment issues; and campus and community activities.

Transferring to Villanova is possible, but selective. A completed transfer application, official transcripts from each postsecondary school attended, and a completed Dean of Students Transfer Evaluation form are required.

Application and Information

The deadline for early action and health affiliation program applications is November 1; regular decision deadline is January 7.

Villanova Office of University Admission
800 Lancaster Avenue
Villanova, Pennsylvania 19085-1672
Phone: 610-519-4000
Fax: 610-519-6450
E-mail: gotovu@villanova.edu
Web site: http://www.villanova.edu

St. Thomas of Villanova Church, Villanova University.

VIRGINIA INTERMONT COLLEGE
BRISTOL, VIRGINIA

Virginia **Intermont** *College*

The College

Founded in 1884, Virginia Intermont College (VI) is a private, coeducational college in Bristol, Virginia, with a longstanding commitment to a liberal arts education. Accredited by the Southern Association of Colleges and Schools Commission on Colleges, VI offers bachelor's degrees in more than forty academic concentrations including pre-professional studies and prestigious programs in photography and equine studies. The College offers an honors program, intercollegiate sports, and evening/weekend classes. Learning and leadership opportunities extend beyond the classroom with internships, travel/study programs, and undergraduate research, all of which provide a comprehensive educational experience for traditional students and working adults. Virginia Intermont currently enrolls approximately 600 students from more than thirty-five states and six other countries and welcomes applications from all students regardless of gender, faith, race, age, or national origin. The historic College campus, atop the highest hill in Bristol with views of the Blue Ridge Mountains, provides an ideal place for students to pursue their passion and find their voice.

Campus buildings are a blend of modern and historic structures. Residence halls provide high-speed Internet access, and most feature computer labs. Computer labs are also located in other strategic locations across campus. The main campus is Wi-Fi–enabled. Approximately 65 percent of traditional students live in campus housing, which consists of residence halls and apartment-style living. The Student Center is a popular leisure-time spot on campus and home to Café Intermont, VIBES bookstore, and a newly furnished student lounge with a big-screen television.

Intercollegiate sports are a big part of campus life, whether students are active participants or cheering spectators. In addition to equestrian sports, VI fields athletic teams which compete in the National Association of Intercollegiate Athletics (NAIA) and the Appalachian Athletic Conference (AAC). Men's teams compete in golf, basketball, baseball, and soccer; women's sports include softball, basketball, soccer, and volleyball, and the College recently added a coed cycling team. Students are also involved in a variety of intramural sports including flag football, bowling, and paintball.

With one of the largest equine studies programs in the United States, Virginia Intermont is a powerhouse in equestrian competition. The equestrian program fields the College's largest sports team, nearly 80 members strong, with competition for all levels of riders. Benefitting from a 120-acre riding center, VI equestrian teams have won fifteen national championship titles in intercollegiate riding since 2001. The equine program, in conjunction with the College, also hosts the VI Classic—an A-rated horse show drawing more than 400 horses and riders from the Southeast and Mid-Atlantic States to the show's venue in Lexington, Virginia.

Student life involves a wide array of campus clubs, organizations, and honor societies, including the Alpha Chi National Honor Society, Student Government Association, Fellowship of Christian Athletes, International Affairs Club, Social Work Action Group, Gay/Straight Alliance, Intermont Green, Jewish Student Union, and the Christian Student Union. The College offers student support services such as a tutoring lab and Career Services which work closely with students from all academic departments as well as undecided students, providing career-planning workshops, job postings, and individual counseling.

Location

The name Intermont, which means among the mountains, aptly describes the Bristol area along the Holston Mountain range. Bristol is considered one of the Tri-Cities along with Johnson City and Kingsport, Tennessee, with a regional population of 500,000. The region is serviced by Tri-Cities Regional Airport from which scheduled flights are operated by Delta, American, Allegiant, and U.S. Airways. Those traveling by car arrive via Interstate 81, just minutes from campus. The Tri-Cities offer urban amenities as well as an abundance of natural beauty. The Appalachian Trail passes within 25 miles of campus for those interested in hiking, and nearby recreational activities include biking or walking along the scenic Virginia Creeper Trail and water sports on South Holston Lake. Although best known for hosting NASCAR events at the famous Bristol Motor Speedway, the greater Bristol area also features a number of music, film, and theater venues, including the renowned Barter Theater in Abingdon.

Majors and Degrees

At VI, students may obtain Bachelor of Arts, Bachelor of Fine Arts, Bachelor of Science, and Bachelor of Social Work degrees. The College offers majors in art, biology, business administration, education, English, equine studies, history, legal studies, photography and digital imaging, physical education, political science, psychology, religious studies, social work, sport management, and theater arts. Students may choose to specialize within a major or a pre-professional program such as pre-medicine, pre-veterinary science, or pre-law. Minors are available in many of the concentrations listed above, as well as in chemistry, the classics, cultural heritage and public arts, Equine-Assisted Growth and Learning (EAGALA), mathematics, sociology, and sports medicine. VI is known for innovative curricular programs that offer exciting options for students, and the College has the distinction of being one of only two colleges in the nation to earn the EAGALA-endorsed equine therapy program. The cultural heritage program focuses on the culturally rich Southwest Virginia region with new courses that offer hands-on experience in cultural studies and public arts through coordinated training and internships.

Academic Programs

The liberal arts-based Comprehensive Core curriculum ensures that each Intermont graduate is equipped with a broad set of academic knowledge and includes specific course work in a first-year experience program to enhance foundational academic skills. Whether pursuing a B.S., B.A., B.S.W., or B.F.A. degree, VI students benefit from the Comprehensive Core, which includes courses in composition, speech communication, computer fundamentals, physical education, mathematics, history, literature, laboratory sciences, and the visual and performing arts. Students also may choose within the core requirements among courses in cultural studies, economics, political science, psychology, and sociology.

The academic year is divided into two semesters running from late August through December and from January through May. Four-week summer terms are offered for specialized study and for the Worrell Honors Study Abroad Program. Courses for adult students are offered evenings and weekends and utilize a cohort model.

Academic Facilities

The majority of academic buildings and residence halls surround the quad, with the J. F. Hicks Library, the Worrell Fine Arts Building, and campus auditorium nearby. In 2011, VI completed a major renovation and expansion to its largest academic building, Science Hall, which includes classrooms for science, math, business, and education. The Virginia Hutton Blevins Art Complex houses sculpture, drawing, and painting studios; classrooms and offices; and gallery and storage space. In addition to traditional labs and classrooms, the Trayer Theatre, the Fine Arts Gallery, art studios, and photography labs are all available for instruction and student use. Adjacent to the Student Center, the Smith-Canter Gymnasium, affectionately referred to as the Cobra Den, is home to sports events and the fitness center. Harrison-Jones Memorial Hall contains Kegley Auditorium (the largest facility of its kind in Bristol at 1,000-person capacity), dressing rooms, and reception areas for campus convocation and community events. Equine studies courses are taught at the Riding Center, located 10 minutes from the main campus. The 120-acre Riding Center has a classroom, two indoor rings, one outdoor ring, and stalls for 80 horses.

Costs

For 2011–12, tuition including room and board was $32,232; tuition for nonresidential students was $24,542. Tuition remains the same for the 2012–13 academic year.

Financial Aid

Virginia Intermont College offers academic, athletic, and performance-based scholarships as well as need-based grants to students. All students who apply to VI are automatically considered for institutional scholarships. The College awards approximately $4 million annually to students in institutional and need-based grants.

Students should complete the Free Application for Federal Student Aid (www.fafsa.ed.gov) to begin the financial aid process and find out if they are eligible for federal aid. Programs available to students through the federal government are the Federal Pell Grant, Federal Supplemental Educational Opportunity Grant, Federal Perkins Loan, and Federal Work-Study programs. All Virginia residents are eligible to receive a VTAG grant. Residents of Georgia, Rhode Island, Vermont, and Pennsylvania should also apply for state-based aid. Loans at low interest rates are available through the Federal Direct Lending program. Benefits are available for veterans and their dependents.

Faculty

Experts in their field with a calling to teach, 45 full-time and regular part-time faculty members eagerly impart their knowledge, experience, and passion for their work. In addition to classroom and workshop instruction, they play an active role in advising students regarding scheduling and campus activities. With a student-faculty ratio of 12:1, engaged learning is a hallmark of the VI experience, and a close-knit learning environment promotes personal and intellectual growth for each student.

Student Government

Along with the Dean of Student Life, the Student Government Association (SGA) is responsible for formulating regulations that govern student life. The SGA has as its stated purpose "to represent and to further the best interests of the student body, to secure cooperation between different organizations, and to promote responsibility, leadership, and community among the students."

Admission Requirements

Applications are evaluated individually with consideration given to ability, interests, preparation, character, and potential as indicated by school records, test results, and teacher or counselor recommendations. Students are encouraged to visit the campus to meet the faculty and to request an interview. Virginia Intermont does not discriminate—either in the admission of students or in any of its policies, programs or activities—on the basis of race, religion, color, gender, national or ethnic origin, disability, or age.

Applicants must have graduated from an accredited high school or an equivalent program of study with a minimum grade point average of 2.5 and course work in the following areas: 4 units of English, 3 units of college preparatory mathematics, 2 units laboratory science (biology, chemistry, or physics; it is strongly recommended that biology and pre-professional life science majors have 3-4 units), 2 units of social science, and 5 units of academic electives. Exceptions to this general policy may be made for applicants admitted under the Early Decision plan, those who have a GED diploma, those who have satisfactorily completed a certified home-schooling experience, or those who have satisfactorily completed 24 semester hours of college work. Candidates for admission must take the SAT or ACT and have test scores reported directly to Virginia Intermont College (code number 5857 for SAT and code number 4416 for ACT).

International students should be prepared to provide certified copies of all secondary transcripts, leaving certificates, and exam results. Students with documents in a language other than English must provide certified English translations. Students who speak English as a second language are required to provide proof of English language proficiency by submitting a TOEFL score or other approved language test score. Accepted international students are required to provide proof of financial support before immigration documentation can be issued.

Application and Information

Applicants should submit an application, a high school transcript, SAT or ACT scores, and transcripts of previous college work (if applicable). Students are encouraged to apply electronically at www.vic.edu.

For an application and financial aid or other information, students should contact:

Office of Admissions
Virginia Intermont College
1013 Moore Street
Bristol, Virginia 24201
Phone: 276-466-7867
800-451-1-VIC (toll-free)
Web site: http://www.vic.edu
http://www.facebook.com/VirginiaIntermont
http://twitter.com/VAIntermont
http://www.linkedin.com/company/
virginia-intermont-college

Virginia Intermont students in front of the College's historic bell tower.

WALSH UNIVERSITY
NORTH CANTON, OHIO

The University

Walsh University is a fully accredited, liberal arts and sciences Catholic university in North Canton, Ohio, offering fifty-five majors, seven graduate programs, and an accelerated-degree program for working adults. With 2,963 students and a 15:1 student-faculty ratio, the University offers a very friendly, supportive, and safe campus and a unique broad-based curriculum with close student-faculty interaction. Most residence halls and academic buildings on Walsh's 136-acre campus are new or have been renovated within the last several years, providing state-of-the-art facilities for students. Walsh also offers generous financial aid packages to 95 percent of full-time students.

Active and involved in campus and community life, more than 60 percent of Walsh students participate in extracurricular programs. Students also have the opportunity to participate in a variety of intramural sports. Walsh also offers seventeen intercollegiate sports including football, baseball, soccer, and volleyball. Walsh is currently Division II in the NAIA league, but has been accepted into the NCAA Division II membership process and expects to have full standing in that division by 2013.

Walsh University welcomes students from around the world of all faiths and backgrounds. The University currently has students from numerous countries and looks forward to continued growth.

Walsh University was founded in 1960 by the Brothers of Christian Instruction and is accredited by the North Central Association/Higher Learning Commission, National League for Nursing Accrediting Commission, Ohio Department of Education, Ohio Board of Counseling and Social Work, American Physical Therapy Association, the Commission on Accreditation in Physical Therapy Education, Council for Accreditation of Counseling and Related Educational Programs, and the National Council for Accreditation of Teacher Education. Walsh is a member of the Ohio College Association, the National Association of Independent Colleges and Universities, and the Association of Catholic Colleges and Universities.

In addition to its undergraduate degree programs, Walsh offers seven graduate degree programs that include an accelerated M.B.A., a Master of Science in Nursing, Master of Arts in Counseling and Human Development, Master of Arts in Education (M.A.Ed.), Master of Arts in Theology, Doctor of Nursing Practice (D.N.P.), and a Doctor of Physical Therapy.

Location

Walsh University has a beautiful, tree-lined campus located just 3 miles east of I-77 in North Canton, a safe, pleasant residential suburban community. Canton, which is about 5 miles south of the Walsh campus, is a city of 84,000 that offers a wide array of cultural, recreational, and athletic activities. Home of the Professional Football Hall of Fame, the President McKinley National Memorial, and the National First Ladies Library, the city also hosts a symphony orchestra, an art museum, and a civic opera, theater guild, and ballet. A number of major companies are headquartered in Stark County, including the Hoover Company, the Timken Company, and Diebold, Inc.

Majors and Degrees

Bachelor of Arts and Bachelor of Science degrees are offered in the following majors: accounting (general and specialized CPA tracks), bioinformatics, biology, chemistry, clinical laboratory science, communication, comprehensive science, computer science, corporate communication, criminal justice–sociology, education (early childhood, middle childhood, adolescence to young adulthood, integrated language arts, integrated mathematics teacher licensure, integrated science teacher licensure, integrated social studies teacher, intervention specialist, life science/biology teacher licensure, life science/biology and chemistry teacher licensure, multiage physical education, and physical education), English, family studies–sociology, finance, French, general business, general studies, global business, history, international relations, Latin American business, management, management information systems, marketing, mathematics, museum studies, nursing, philosophy/theology, physical education, political science, psychology, psychology–community/clinical, research methods and data analysis–sociology, and Spanish.

Walsh offers preprofessional programs in dentistry, law, medicine, natural resources, optometry, physical therapy, podiatry, and veterinary science. Each is developed within the context of a regular academic major. Walsh's physical therapy graduates have the option to continue their studies by entering Walsh's newly accredited Doctor of Physical Therapy degree program. Students enrolled in the University's B.A./M.A. program can earn a bachelor's degree in behavioral science and a master's degree in counseling and human development in 5½ years. An affiliation with Case Western Reserve University's (CWRU) program in dentistry leads to a B.S. from Walsh and ultimately a D.D.S. from CWRU.

In addition, Walsh offers the Associate of Arts degree in accounting, finance, human services, liberal arts, management, and marketing.

Academic Programs

The student's academic program comprises courses within the liberal arts, a major field of study, and elective courses. Major course work, constituting one fourth or more of a student's program of studies, is designed to help students prepare for their careers. Forty percent of a student's program of studies is within the liberal arts. Elective courses, which constitute the remaining portion of a student's program of studies, enable students to develop personal interests, take more courses within their major field, or enroll in additional core courses. The University encourages students to give careful thought to selecting a program of study and a major. While many students select double majors as a way to improve their career opportunities, the design of individual programs requires consultation with a faculty adviser and a division chair. To earn a bachelor's degree, students must successfully complete 130 semester hours.

Designed for the academically gifted, the honors program offers challenges that lead students to achieve academic excellence. Honors students take advantage of such offerings

as special seminars, independent studies, internships, and research projects.

The University's School for Professional Studies Program is for working adults who have earned college credits and who wish to earn their bachelor's degree in an accelerated format. Classes are scheduled on nights and weekends to accommodate busy schedules.

Academic Facilities

The Walsh Library contains 141,000 volumes, 270 current periodical subscriptions on paper, and 41,071 electronically. Databases bring many full-text articles immediately for download or print, and information technology systems enable online requests for physical delivery of material, often via rapid courier. Library staff members give introductory lectures on research techniques. The library has a quiet study room, a snack lounge, and a mini-theater. All library resources are available via the Internet.

Faculty

Walsh University fosters close working relationships between faculty members and students. Beyond classroom teaching, faculty members serve as student counselors and tutors and take on roles as advisers for student organizations. The Walsh faculty is composed of full-time, part-time, and adjunct members. The student-faculty ratio is 15:1. The majority of full-time faculty members hold Ph.D.'s or terminal degrees in their respective fields.

Student Government

Walsh University Student Government provides capable, responsible student governance. Through its executive, legislative, and judicial branches, it fosters student involvement in the governance of the University, serves as a forum for student opinion, and functions as a liaison between students, faculty and staff members, and the administration. Along with the Student Affairs staff, it plans student activities and community projects.

Costs

Tuition for the 2011–12 academic year was $22,500. Tuition, fees, and room and board charges total approximately $32,190 per year and vary by residence hall. Books and personal expenses cost an estimated $700–$900 for the year. The University reserves the right to change the cost structure without notice.

Financial Aid

Walsh is dedicated to providing outstanding liberal arts education at an affordable price. The primary purpose of Walsh University's financial aid program is to assist deserving students who cannot otherwise meet the costs of a college education. Financial aid takes the form of scholarships, work-study awards, grants, or loans, depending upon the resources available. The University offers a number of scholarships in amounts from $1500 to full tuition, in addition to institutional need-based grants. The Alumni Association offers scholarships as well. State and federal grants and loans are available to students along with the University's work-study program that provides work compatible with a student's academic schedule. Financial aid is awarded for one year and is renewable in subsequent years if the student shows a continuing need and maintains an appropriate academic record.

Applicants for admission may apply for financial aid by submitting the Free Application for Federal Student Aid (FAFSA) and the University's financial aid form. To allow for timely notification of financial awards, the University recommends that the FAFSA be mailed by March 15 in order to receive full analysis by May 1. Prospective students may obtain a FAFSA from their high school guidance counselor or from the University's financial aid office. The Walsh financial aid form is available from the financial aid and admissions offices of the University.

Admission Requirements

Every student seeking admission to Walsh University is reviewed individually to assess the student's ability to meet the rigors of the University's curriculum. The composition of high school classes, grades achieved, class rank, and standardized test scores are all taken into consideration before an admission decision is rendered. Essays and interviews are highly recommended but not required.

Walsh grants credit for college-level work completed in high school and for credits earned through the College Level Examination Program. Qualified high school juniors and seniors may enroll for college credit under the University's postsecondary enrollment program. The University seeks a diverse student body.

Application and Information

Early application is recommended. Walsh University operates under a rolling admissions policy. The completed admission application, $25 application fee, ACT or SAT scores, and a high school transcript are required for a student's application to be considered for admission. Transfer students must also submit transcripts from all colleges and universities attended.

Interested students are encouraged to contact:

Brett Freshour
Dean of Enrollment Management
Walsh University
2020 East Maple Street NW
North Canton, Ohio 44720-3336
Phone: 330-492-7172
      800-362-9846 (toll-free)
Fax: 330-490-7165
E-mail: admissions@walsh.edu
Web site: http://www.walsh.edu
     http://www.facebook.com/walshu
     http://www.twitter.com/walshuniversity
     http://www.youtube.com/ohiowalshuniversity

On the campus of Walsh University.

WARREN WILSON COLLEGE
ASHEVILLE, NORTH CAROLINA

The College

Warren Wilson College is distinctive among American colleges and universities. Strong environmental and international emphases enhance a learning triad of academics, work, and service. The College also is recognized as a campus leader in sustainable practices and facilities. As Samuel Schuman described Warren Wilson in his book Old Main: "Rather like Orwell's barnyard menagerie, all small colleges are unique, but some are more unique than others. [Warren Wilson's] program, emphases, population, and atmosphere are unmistakably its own."

Since its founding in 1894, Warren Wilson College has educated students with its unique blending of a strong liberal arts program, work for the College, and service to those in need—a triad that makes Warren Wilson unlike any other college. Its 900 undergraduate students come from forty-five states and twenty countries, creating a diverse and vibrant academic community.

The academic program features a first-rate faculty that does all of the teaching and frequently participates in research with students. About 85 percent of classes have fewer than 20 students, and discussion is an important part of teaching. Twenty-one majors are offered, with a commitment to quality in each program. Art, English, creative writing, biology, outdoor leadership, and the nationally recognized environmental studies program are the most popular majors.

Students at Warren Wilson are integral to the day-to-day operation of the College. Each student works 15 hours a week at a job that is essential to running the school. This experience helps build student confidence (students learn that there is no job they cannot learn to do) and a strong sense of community at the College. Many juniors and seniors have work assignments that coincide with their majors. Students receive a work stipend in the amount of $3480 each year for the work they do.

Service is also integral to the College's way of thinking. Warren Wilson is one of only a few colleges in the country that require student participation in community service for graduation. Service is offered to a wide range of nonprofit organizations and agencies in the Asheville area and beyond. Students must engage in an average of at least 25 hours of service to community each year as a graduation requirement.

The College's 1,100-acre campus includes a 300-acre working farm, 600 acres of managed forest, a 6-acre fruit and vegetable garden and 20 miles of hiking trails. The campus and surrounding area are havens for outdoor activities such as white-water sports, hiking, camping, mountain biking, and rock climbing.

About 90 percent of students and 30 percent of the faculty and staff members live on campus. The College offers men's and women's intercollegiate basketball, cross-country, soccer, and swimming, and its mountain bike team has finished in the top three nationally (Division II) for the past seven years. The College also offers intramural sports, a wellness program, and a wide range of outdoor programs among other activities.

Location

Warren Wilson, on the edge of the city of Asheville, North Carolina, is in the heart of the Blue Ridge Mountains. Asheville, a city of about 80,000 people, is considered one of the most livable cities in the United States and was selected by the National League of Cities as the All-America City for 1998.

Surrounded by more than 1 million acres of national forest, Asheville is located in an ideal setting, presenting views of outstanding beauty throughout all four seasons. In the spring and summer, variations in altitude together with warm southern sun favor native vegetation; dogwood, wildflowers, rhododendron, mountain laurel, and azaleas cover the mountains. The arresting beauty of the autumn colors attracts photographers, artists, and sports enthusiasts from the world over. During the winter, natural snow is enhanced by machine-made snow, producing excellent downhill skiing.

A short drive from the Warren Wilson campus are Great Smoky Mountains National Park, Pisgah National Forest, and the Blue Ridge Parkway, offering panoramic views, excellent camping facilities, and a perfect setting for class field trips.

Majors and Degrees

The bachelor's degree is awarded in art, biology, chemistry, creative writing, English, environmental studies, gender and women's studies, history and political science, global studies, integrative studies, mathematics, modern language, outdoor leadership, philosophy, psychology, religious studies, social work, and sociology/anthropology.

Academic Programs

The goal of the degree program at Warren Wilson College is the completion of three well-designed areas of study. First, students are expected to complete a core of required courses based on the theme "ways of knowing." A student earns 4 credits in each of the ten core areas. Second, students must develop a strength in one or more disciplines. A minimum of 128 semester hours is required for the baccalaureate degree, including the core plus major hours. Finally, a student must demonstrate the ability to work effectively with others by participation in the work and service programs.

There is a required freshman seminar designed to provide new students the opportunity to explore various fields. A senior seminar, designed as a capstone experience, is required, as is a senior letter to evaluate the student's college experiences.

All Warren Wilson students must demonstrate competence in writing and mathematics either through testing or by completing core courses.

Each semester in the academic calendar is broken into two 8-week terms. A student typically takes four courses per semester (3 or 4 credit hours per course).

Off-Campus Programs

In addition to academics, work, and service, all qualified students are afforded the opportunity to study abroad. The College heavily subsidizes the cost for a cross-cultural international experience taken during the junior year or summer.

Academic Facilities

The Martha Ellison Library houses a collection of 120,000 books and 450 periodicals. It provides written records in all areas of the College curriculum and contributes to the cultural enrichment of students. The library is open and served by librarians and student assistants 75 hours each week. The building provides

open access to books and periodicals during these hours. Individual carrels, lounge areas, and microfilm readers and printers are available, and there are Windows and Macintosh computers that students may use as word processors or for other prescribed purposes, including access to the Internet.

Computerized literature searching is available. The Martha Ellison Library is a teaching library, providing extensive and continuing bibliographic services, including courses, for the entire student body. Any resource materials not owned by the library may be acquired through interlibrary loan.

The campus arts complex includes the modern Kittredge Theater; the Kittredge Music Wing, housing classrooms, studios, and a performance area; the Holden Arts Center, with a gallery, classrooms, studios, and a lecture hall; and an outdoor amphitheater. Instruction and performance events also take place in the chapel and the Craftshop/Ceramics Studio.

Costs

Total costs for the 2011–12 school year were $34,888. From this amount, the student's work program stipend of $3480 was deducted, leaving an actual cost of $31,408 for each student before any other aid.

Financial Aid

Warren Wilson offers a comprehensive financial aid program that seeks to enroll students from all economic backgrounds. This is accomplished through a combination of work, loans, grants, entitlements, and scholarships to students who complete their file prior to May. Students and their families should file the FAFSA and the Warren Wilson Financial Aid Application to be considered for all possible funds.

Faculty

The teaching faculty consists of 70 full-time members. Of these, 93 percent hold doctoral degrees. All classes and labs are taught by faculty members, not graduate students. Faculty members—1 for every 12 students—are available after class, during regular office hours, and in their homes.

Student Government

The student body is involved in the democratic decision-making process of the College. A wide variety of leadership positions, elected and appointed, are open to students. Campuswide elections provide opportunities for student involvement in Student Caucus, Judicial Board and other College advisory committees. Student Caucus, the representative voice of the student body, is also responsible for appointing students to positions on approximately fifteen other campus committees ranging from Admission to Library to Buildings and Grounds.

Admission Requirements

Admission to Warren Wilson College is based on both the personal and the academic qualifications of the applicant.

The selection criteria are devised to choose a student body with high standards of scholarship and personal goals and a willingness to provide community service.

Each candidate for admission must present an academic transcript from a secondary school. The transcript must show at least 12 academic units (a unit is one year's study in one subject). At least 4 years of English, 2 years of algebra, 1 year of geometry, 2 years of laboratory science, and 2 years of history are recommended for admission. Performance during high school is the best predictor of success in college. Therefore, great emphasis is placed upon the high school record. Grade trends can be very important.

Applicants must submit a recommendation from their high school counselor and scores from the SAT or ACT. Students are also required to submit a personal essay.

Transfer students must present both high school and college transcripts. Transfer applicants must be in good standing with the college last attended and should also have a minimum 2.75 cumulative grade point average. At least one school year in residence at Warren Wilson is required for a transfer student to be eligible for a degree from Warren Wilson College.

There is no fee to apply for admission to Warren Wilson College.

Application and Information

An application form and further information may be obtained by contacting:

Office of Admission
Warren Wilson College
P.O. Box 9000
Asheville, North Carolina 28815-9000
Phone: 800-934-3536 (toll-free)
E-mail: admit@warren-wilson.edu
Web site: http://www.warren-wilson.edu

In the heart of the Blue Ridge Mountains, the entrance to Warren Wilson College's valley is a sight that students long remember.

WEBBER INTERNATIONAL UNIVERSITY
BABSON PARK, FLORIDA

The University

Webber International University was founded in 1927 by Roger Babson, who was an internationally known economist in the early 1900s. The four-year independent coeducational university is located on a beautiful 110-acre campus along the shoreline of Lake Caloosa, 45 minutes from Disney World, Cypress Gardens, and many other attractions. Webber is accredited by the Southern Association of Colleges and Schools and internationally by the International Assembly for Collegiate Business Education. Built on a strong tradition that sets it apart, the University exemplifies integrity, high standards, and achievement. Webber International University provides an environment that encourages success through academic excellence and hard work. About 600 students are enrolled as undergraduates at Webber; 22 percent of the students are international and represent forty-three different countries.

Webber International University offers day, evening, weekend, and online classes with the flexibility to fit any busy schedule. Webber's off-campus internship programs provide a real-world business environment for Webber students. Field trips also supplement students' business education.

Webber International University also offers a Master of Business Administration (M.B.A.) program with options in management, accounting, sport management, security management, and international business (online).

The University offers intercollegiate sports in baseball, basketball, beach volleyball, bowling, cross-country, football, golf, soccer, tennis, track and field and triathlon for men and basketball, beach volleyball, bowling, cheerleading, cross-country, golf, soccer, softball, tennis, track and field, triathlon, and volleyball for women. For the musically talented student, the University has a marching band. Intramural athletics are also available for all students. The University's physical education complex includes two gymnasiums, a fitness room, a soccer field, a junior Olympic-size swimming pool, beach volleyball court, and tennis courts. Webber students also enjoy lakeside activities such as beach volleyball, canoeing, fishing, and kayaking. Among the wide variety of social organizations and clubs are Phi Beta Lambda, a student government association, an international club, Webber ambassadors, Eta Sigma Delta and the Society of Hosteurs, a marketing club, a tourism society, FCA, a sport management club, SIFE, and athletic boosters. These groups and others help to sponsor the various social functions at Webber.

Location

The town of Babson Park, a very small rural residential community, is located in the heart of Florida's citrus country near a chain of freshwater lakes. The area has a relaxed and friendly atmosphere. Babson Park is conveniently near many major recreational facilities and national tourist attractions in central Florida.

Majors and Degrees

Webber International University offers bachelor's and associate degrees in business administration, with ten different majors: accounting, computer information systems management, corporate communications, finance, hospitality and tourism management, management, marketing, prelaw, security management, and sport management. The University also offers a Bachelor of Science degree in general business studies.

Academic Programs

The school operates on the semester system with two 15-week semesters, a six-week Summer Term A, and a six-week Summer Term B. By fall 2012, a majority of Webber's courses will be available online through its e-learning program. The University requires the completion of 60 credit hours for the Associate of Science degree and 120 credit hours for the Bachelor of Science degree with a minimum grade point average of 2.0. The average course load is 15 hours per semester. Students in the Bachelor of Science degree program are required to complete approximately 30 hours in the major, 36 hours in the business core, 36 hours in the general education core, and 18 hours of tailored electives. Students in the Associate of Science degree program are required to complete 27 hours in the business core, 18 hours in the general education core, and 15 hours in the major and tailored elective.

The Bachelor of Science degree in general business studies requires the completion of 45 hours in the general business studies core, 39 hours in the general education core, and 36 hours of tailored electives.

All students must complete 30 of the last 33 hours at Webber International University to receive a degree. Credit is awarded for successful scores on Advanced Placement (AP) and College-Level Examination Program (CLEP) general tests.

Off-Campus Programs

The hospitality and marketing departments have arrangements for internship programs with major hotels and restaurants in the Orlando area and major retail stores, both in-state and out-of-state.

The finance department places student interns in various financial institutions and financial departments of local corporations.

Other off-campus experiences include elective courses in which students observe and analyze business operations and functions of local companies and present their findings in a project format comparable to a professional business consultant's.

The departmental field trip is an opportunity for students in all ten majors to travel abroad during a summer semester and to discover business techniques in an international environment.

Academic Facilities

The Roger Babson Learning Center, located in the central part of the campus, is a modern and comprehensive business library facility. The collection currently contains about 35,500 volumes, an assortment of audiovisual materials, and a CD-ROM computer program for reference materials. The library houses computers for student use. Several research databases are available for student access.

The three computer resources centers are data processing centers and teaching facilities whose microcomputers offer the latest modern technology for developing student excellence in business, communication, and creativity.

Costs

In 2012–13, the annual fee, which includes tuition, room and board, and insurance, is $30,014. For commuting students, the annual fee is $21,940. These figures are subject to change. The University estimates that $1000 is adequate for books and supplies. Laboratory fees are additional.

Financial Aid

The Student Financial Aid Department offers students its counsel and assistance in meeting their educational expenses. Aid is awarded on the basis of an applicant's need, academic performance, and promise. Approximately 90 percent of the students at Webber International University receive financial assistance. To demonstrate need, applicants are required to file the Free Application for Federal Student Aid (FAFSA). Various types of aid, such as scholarships, grants, loans, and Federal Work-Study awards, are used to meet student needs. A limited number of no-need scholarships are available; these awards are based on academic performance, on community and college service, or on athletic ability as determined by the sport's coach. Applicants for aid must reapply each year. Webber participates in the Federal Perkins Loan, Federal Supplemental Educational Opportunity Grant, and Federal Work-Study programs. All applicants are expected to apply for any entitlement grant for which they are eligible, such as the Federal Pell Grant; Florida residents must apply for a Florida Student Assistance Grant and the Florida Resident Access Grant. Federal Student Loans are also available. Webber is nationally recognized as a military-friendly school and accepts the Post-9/11 GI Bill as well as a variety of other veteran's education benefits. Financial aid applicants should submit their requests and forms before April 1 in order to be eligible for certain financial aid programs.

Faculty

More than 70 percent of Webber's full-time faculty members hold doctoral degrees. The faculty-student ratio is 1:22, and all students are assigned a faculty adviser. All faculty members have posted office hours and are available for consultation and advising. Many of Webber's faculty members have a minimum of five years' actual professional work experience in their area of specialization in addition to their years of classroom teaching. This combination of applied and classroom work experience gives them an unusual ability to relate to the needs and concerns of their students.

Student Government

The Student Government Association, the chief governing body on Webber's campus, is composed of elected student representatives and a faculty adviser and deals with nonacademic areas of student life. The association serves as an advisory and coordinating body for student organizations and involves students in campus policy and actions. Representatives from various student organizations serve on the Student Government Association, as do members elected from the University community.

Admission Requirements

Applicants must have graduated from high school with a recommended minimum of 4 years of English and 2 to 3 years of mathematics and preparation in seven other academic subjects. Most accepted candidates rank in the top 50 percent of their high school class. Scores on the SAT or ACT are required for admission. International applicants must submit scores on the Test of English as a Foreign Language (TOEFL).

Applications from transfer students are welcome, as are those from students resuming their education or adult students who have delayed their entrance to college. Transfer students must be in good standing at their former institution.

Applicants who fail to meet regular admission requirements may be considered on an individual basis for the Fresh Start program by the Fresh Start admissions committee. An interview is required for all Fresh Start applicants.

Application and Information

An application is ready for consideration by the Admissions Committee when it has been received with a $35 application fee for domestic students and $75 for international students, the required test scores and references, and transcripts from each school attended. The University uses a system of rolling admissions. It is recommended that applications be submitted as early as possible, since on-campus housing is limited. Freshmen are required to live in the dormitory unless they reside with a parent, guardian, or spouse.

For application forms, catalogs, and additional information, students should contact:

Webber International University
1201 North Scenic Highway
P.O. Box 96
Babson Park, Florida 33827-9990
Phone: 863-638-2910
E-mail: admissions@webber.edu
Web site: http://www.webber.edu

Webber's private beach and pier.

WEBB INSTITUTE
GLEN COVE, NEW YORK

The Institute

Webb Institute was founded in 1889 to provide an opportunity for worthy young students to obtain an education in the "art and science of designing ships and their propulsion systems." The Institute has followed this basic objective to the present, and its graduates are active throughout the United States in the ship design, ship construction, yacht design, and marine operations industries and in appropriate government offices.

The 26-acre campus is the former estate of Herbert L. Pratt and is located on Long Island Sound. Because of the Institute's small size and intensive academic program, varsity sports are limited. However, Webb participates in intercollegiate basketball, cross-country, sailing, soccer, tennis, and volleyball, for which ample facilities are provided. The campus has a gymnasium, tennis courts, playing fields, and a beach. Golf and swimming facilities are available nearby.

Webb Institute maintains an enrollment that ranges from 70 to 90 students who come from all over the world and all of whom live on campus.

Location

Glen Cove is a city of more than 25,000 residents and is located on Long Island's North Shore, which is nearly an hour from New York City. Convenient train service from Glen Cove to New York brings the variety of cultural, educational, and recreational activities available in the city within easy reach of Webb students.

Majors and Degrees

Webb Institute offers an engineering program in ship design, which involves both naval architecture and marine engineering. The undergraduate degree awarded is the Bachelor of Science in naval architecture and marine engineering.

Academic Programs

The engineering program in ship design consists of fundamental foundation courses in mathematics, science, and engineering sciences, capped by extensive professional design courses. A coherent program in humanities supplements the technical program to round out undergraduate education.

In addition, students have a two-month, cooperative job experience each year in the U.S. marine and maritime industry. During this period, freshmen work as helper mechanics in shipyards, sophomores obtain seagoing experience aboard ship, and juniors and seniors work as engineering assistants in design and technical offices of various marine firms. This important part of the program provides excellent articulation of the educational and career experiences. Innovative engineering ideas are encouraged in the thesis required during the last year. The program is fully accredited. Graduates are well equipped to pursue postgraduate studies.

Semesters run from late August to mid-December and from late February to late June. January and February are winter work periods, and the period from late June to late August is designated for vacation.

Academic Facilities

Full laboratory support is provided for chemistry, physics, metallurgy, and various engineering courses. A ship-model testing tank is available for ship and boat hull studies. Computer facilities are provided on campus. The Livingston Library contains extensive holdings in naval architecture, marine engineering, and general engineering, as well as collections in literature, arts, social sciences, and music.

Costs

All U.S. citizens and green card holders admitted to Webb are accepted on a tuition-and-fee-free basis (full scholarship). For non-citizens, the tuition fee for the 2012–13 year is $39,400. Room and board costs are approximately $13,200

in 2012–13. Nearly $800 per year is required for books and supplies. A $150 room deposit fee is payable on entry and refunded, less any breakage costs, on departure. The Student Organization requires a $100 deposit on entry, also refundable on departure.

Financial Aid

As stated, a full scholarship that covers tuition and fees is awarded to all accepted candidates who are U.S. citizens or green card holders. The winter work co-op in industry provides income for students that significantly assists in covering other expenses. Supplementary aid opportunities are available through the Federal Pell Grant, Federal Stafford Student Loans, and in-house grant programs. Students requiring financial assistance must submit the Free Application for Federal Student Aid (FAFSA) after March 31 but not later than July 1 of the year of entry.

Faculty

Webb Institute has a highly qualified faculty. Many members possess engineering licenses and engage in sponsored research programs, consult for commercial firms, and research and write technical papers. Classes are limited to 25 students, and the student-faculty ratio is 8:1. Each student is assigned a faculty adviser, and consultation with individual faculty members is encouraged.

Student Government

The Student Organization is highly active in student administrative, social, and educational affairs. It is supplemented by an Honor Council and honor system. Together, these entities provide students with a high degree of responsibility for ordering and conducting student life.

Admission Requirements

Admission to Webb is highly competitive. The qualifying requirements for admission are graduation from high school with a B+ (87) or better average in 16 credits of basic high school subjects. Admission selections are based on high school standing (generally in the upper 10 percent) and scores on the College Board's SAT and Subject Tests in Mathematics (Level 1 or 2), and Physics or Chemistry. The final selection follows a personal interview conducted at Webb or at a location convenient to the applicant. The entering class is usually restricted to 25 freshmen.

All application papers must be submitted by February 15, and all required College Board tests must be taken before that date. Advanced placement is not given in any of the course offerings. Campus visits by interested students are strongly recommended; prior appointments must be made. An early decision plan is available for qualified candidates.

Webb Institute does not discriminate in admission in the areas of gender, race, or religion. Academic qualities and career motivation are the only criteria.

Application and Information

For a catalog and application forms, students may contact:

Office of Admissions
Webb Institute
Glen Cove, New York 11542
Phone: 516-671-2213, Ext. 107
E-mail: admissions@webb-institute.edu
Web site: http://www.webb-institute.edu

The academic facilities of Webb Institute are located on Long Island Sound in the former residence of Herbert L. Pratt.

WELLS COLLEGE
AURORA, NEW YORK

Wells College

The College

Wells College is ranked among the nation's top liberal arts colleges that offer high-quality education at an affordable price and has one of the most beautiful campuses in the United States. The College was established in 1868 by Henry Wells, who also founded the Wells Fargo and American Express companies.

At Wells, professors are dedicated to teaching, and because of the intimate nature of the campus community (the student body is 600), they get to know their students as individuals in and outside the classroom. Students frequently collaborate with their professors on original research and creative projects. At most other schools, these opportunities are only available to graduate students. Because faculty members at Wells know their students so well, they are especially effective advisers and mentors. Therefore, Wells students have a competitive edge entering careers and top graduate and professional schools.

Another aspect of the Wells tradition is hands-on learning. In addition to dynamic classroom teaching, Wells students have a variety of other experiential opportunities: internships, service, study abroad, and off-campus study. Professors encourage students to apply theory in practical settings and to discover what they want to do in life through involvement.

Wells currently fields intercollegiate teams at the NCAA Division III level in men's and women's cross-country, field hockey, men's and women's lacrosse, men's and women's soccer, softball, men's and women's swimming, men's and women's basketball, men's and women's golf, men's and women's volleyball, and women's tennis. There are also a number of intramural opportunities, including basketball, soccer, swimming, skiing, tennis, and volleyball. Athletic facilities include indoor and outdoor tennis courts, a gymnasium, a newly renovated fitness center, a nine-hole golf course, and a campus boathouse and dock used in teaching sailing, canoeing, and lifeguarding.

Wells has a full range of active student organizations, including a literary magazine and newspaper, music and drama groups, environmental and political organizations, and abundant opportunities for community service, among others. A busy calendar of cultural events, symposia, and lectures enhances the academic and social life of the College.

Location

Wells is located in the village of Aurora on the eastern shore of Cayuga Lake—part of New York's scenic Finger Lakes region. The area is well known for its high concentration of prestigious colleges and universities, including Cornell University, Ithaca College, Hobart and William Smith Colleges, Colgate University, Hamilton College, and Syracuse University. Aurora is 25 miles from Ithaca and 60 miles from both Rochester and Syracuse. Students have abundant opportunities for outdoor recreation and sports, including sailing, swimming, horseback riding, skiing, and hiking.

Majors and Degrees

Wells offers majors and concentrations in African American studies, American cultures, American studies, anthropology, art history, biochemistry and molecular biology, biology, chemistry, computer science, creative writing, dance, economics and management, English, environmental policies and values, environmental science, ethics and philosophy, government and politics, history, international studies, literature, management, mathematics, performing arts, physics, psychology, sociology, Spanish, studio art, theater and dance, visual arts, and women and gender studies. Students also have the option of a self-designed major. In addition, they can choose minors from a list of more than thirty programs.

Wells has also added an innovative Center for Business and Entrepreneurship, founded upon the tradition of liberal arts: learning that emphasizes critical thinking and problem solving. The role of the center is to help students build the skills and develop the discernment to know how and where they most want to serve society. As such, the center will offer students the opportunity to explore growing fields like arts administration, green businesses, not-for-profit organizations, and hospitality.

The College has pre-professional programs in dentistry, education, engineering, law, medicine, teaching, and veterinary medicine. Wells has a cross-registration agreement with nearby Ithaca College, Cayuga Community College, and Cornell University and affiliations with Cornell's engineering school.

Wells awards the Bachelor of Arts degree and has a number of programs through which students can earn their bachelor's degree at Wells and a graduate or professional degree from an affiliated university. Participating schools are Clarkson University, Columbia University, Cornell University (engineering), and the University of Rochester (business, community health, and education).

Academic Programs

All Wells students benefit from an academic environment similar to honors programs available to only a small number of students at other schools. The College has a tradition of preparing students for leadership in their chosen fields, and the breadth of knowledge they gain and the range of life experiences they encounter enable them to achieve their career goals and establish a foundation for a rich and fulfilling life.

All students entering Wells to pursue a four-year course of study leading to a bachelor's degree are required to take three themed seminars (12 semester hours) and the New Student Experience (WLLS 111). Distribution requirements are a foreign language (two courses or exemption by exam), formal reasoning (one course), arts and humanities (three courses), natural and social sciences (three courses), and physical education (four courses). Team sports and dance technique can partially satisfy requirements.

Approximately sixteen courses must be taken in the student's major, and at least six must be taken at Wells. Eighteen credit hours must be taken at the 300 level or above. A senior project or thesis and a comprehensive evaluation are required for graduation.

A student must successfully complete 120 semester hours (60 of which must be taken at Wells and through affiliated programs, such as study abroad) to be recommended by the faculty for a degree. To learn more about the academic program and requirements for transfer students, prospective students should visit the Wells College Web site.

Off-Campus Programs

Students can spend January term, a semester, or even a year in another college or university abroad or in the United States. Typically, Wells students choose to study off campus for a semester during the junior year, but many different possibilities are available depending on a student's academic program and interests.

The College offers affiliated study-abroad experiences in Belize, Denmark, France, Germany, Great Britain, Ireland, Italy, Japan, Mexico, Senegal, Spain, and Sweden. Currently, the three most popular programs are study abroad in Florence, Italy; Paris, France; and Seville, Spain. These off-campus study experiences are flexible as well as financially and academically accessible. After at least one semester at Wells, a student's financial aid applies to one semester of off-campus study.

Wells provides off-campus study options in the United States through its affiliations with American University, serving a wide range of academic and internship interests in Washington, D.C.; the Salt Center, offering documentary field studies in Portland, Maine; and the Public Leadership Education Network (PLEN), providing leadership development through seminars and internships in Washington, D.C. As part of the PLEN affiliation, students can spend a semester studying at the London School of Economics and Political Science and hold an internship in the British government. Through the School for Field Studies, Wells offers semester-long

study-abroad experiences in Africa, Australia, the Caribbean, and other locations. The College also offers credit-bearing courses during the January term that take students to a single destination in the U.S. or abroad for intensive study that requires travel in a region or country with a faculty member.

Academic Facilities

From the contemporary elegance of Weld House to the nineteenth-century Glen Park mansion, the former home of College founder Henry Wells, the residence halls encompass enough variety to satisfy every taste. Students eat their meals together in the majestic Tudor-style dining hall in Main Building.

The Louis Jefferson Long Library has received numerous awards for its architectural design. Facilities include an online computer center, individual study carrels, seminar and group-study rooms, and an art gallery. There are department libraries in art, economics, English, mathematics, music, philosophy, and the sciences located across the campus.

The Barler Hall of Music houses a recital hall with superb acoustics, vocal and instrumental practice rooms, a music library, and a listening laboratory. Facilities for printmaking, painting, ceramics, sculpture, and photography are located in the Campbell Arts Building. The Cleveland Hall of Languages contains state-of-the-art equipment for learning foreign languages. Stratton Science Hall, completed in 2007, houses state-of-the-art laboratories for chemistry, biology, environmental science, and physics as well as a computer laboratory. Morgan Hall houses the Book Arts Center and the Wells College Press. Macmillan Hall has classrooms, faculty and administrative offices, several computer laboratories, and department libraries. The east wing of Macmillan contains the Margaret Phipps Auditorium, a theater facility used for teaching, concerts, lectures, and dramatic productions.

Costs

Wells has a long-term commitment to providing talented students with access to the best education, which requires offering excellence at an affordable price. Wells is ranked among the best liberal arts colleges in the nation, yet the cost of a Wells education is considerably less than the tuition charged by comparable schools.

The cost of a Wells education for the 2012–13 academic year was $33,200 for tuition, $11,900 for room and board, and $1500 for fees.

Financial Aid

Approximately 90 percent of Wells students receive financial aid packaged in the form of grants, scholarships, loans, and work-study opportunities. The College works closely with students and their families to design a financial aid package that meets their needs and their budgets.

Award determinations are made on a rolling basis following acceptance. College financial aid is complex; however, Wells College's well-informed financial aid and admissions professionals are always pleased to answer questions and discuss methods of financing higher education with prospective students.

Applicants are considered for merit aid that is based largely on academic achievements and leadership abilities.

Faculty

At Wells, learning takes place in small, seminar-style classes where students are partners with faculty members in the learning process. Starting immediately in their first semester, students take classes with scholars who are recognized experts in their fields, not teaching assistants.

Nearly all Wells professors hold terminal degrees in their areas of expertise. They have been educated at the world's leading research universities, including Harvard, Yale, Columbia, Cornell, Brown, and Stanford. What students discover in Wells' classes is the importance of exploring ideas with others.

Wells is student centered, and academic programs focus on collaborative learning and teaching that meets the needs of students' different learning styles. As one would expect at a nationally recognized liberal arts college, professors are also engaged in research and a full range of scholarly activities. Their books are published by leading academic presses, their articles appear in top journals, and they are a presence at national and international conferences. Due to close faculty-student interaction, students have numerous opportunities to collaborate with faculty members on research, publications, and presentations.

Student Government

The student body is self-governing through the Collegiate Association. The three main governing bodies of the association are the Student-Faculty Administration Board, the Collegiate Council, and the Community Court. Students serve on faculty committees that make decisions concerning administrative and curricular matters.

Leadership development is an inherent part of the Wells experience, and students are encouraged to take an active role in student government and in the life of the campus community.

Admission Requirements

Wells admits students on the basis of the strength of their academic preparation. A student is expected to possess intellectual curiosity, motivation, and maturity to profit from the experience. In all cases, the College seeks students who have followed a solid college-preparatory program throughout high school.

Wells seeks students from varied backgrounds with diverse interests and talents in order to promote a stimulating learning community. Every admissions decision is made on an individual basis.

Wells students share an enthusiasm for academic pursuits and a serious intent to use their education in the future to enhance both their lives and the communities in which they choose to live.

Application and Information

Applications should be received early in the senior year of high school and not later than March 1 of the year in which entrance is desired. Applications from early decision and early action candidates must be received by December 15.

Transfer applications are reviewed on a rolling basis. Transfer students are eligible for merit scholarships and financial aid.

A campus visit is highly recommended for prospective students. For more information about Wells College or to schedule a campus visit, students should contact:

Admissions Office
Wells College
Aurora, New York 13026
Phone: 800-952-9355 (toll-free)
E-mail: admissions@wells.edu
Web site: http://www.wells.edu
    http://www.facebook.com/wellscollege

Main Building on the Wells College campus.

WENTWORTH INSTITUTE OF TECHNOLOGY

BOSTON, MASSACHUSETTS

The Institute

Wentworth Institute of Technology was founded in 1904 to provide education in technology. Today, Wentworth has a current undergraduate day enrollment of approximately 3,800 men and women (3,400 full-time). The education acquired at Wentworth enables graduates to assume creative and responsible careers in business and industry. Wentworth is located on a 31-acre campus on Huntington Avenue in Boston.

Wentworth provides dormitory and suite-style residence halls on campus for men and women. Students in the residence halls are on a full meal plan. Upperclass students have the option of living in on-campus apartments and students residing in the apartments may prepare their own meals. A cafeteria, snack bar, and convenience store are available for those wishing to purchase their meals.

Career counseling and placement assistance are available to all alumni and to students who have completed at least one semester of study at the Institute. While many graduates of Wentworth are employed in the Boston area, alumni have secured positions throughout the United States and abroad.

In addition to Wentworth's undergraduate programs, master's degree programs are awarded in architecture and construction management.

Location

Boston is the educational center of New England. It is a city of charm, tradition, and elegance—a major center of art, science, music, history, medicine, and education. Wentworth is situated near the heart of Boston and is surrounded by institutions that provide the cultural advantages for which the city is famous. The Museum of Fine Arts, with its store of art treasures, is diagonally across the street, and admission is free to any student with a Wentworth ID card. Symphony Hall is just a few blocks away. The Harvard Medical School, the New England Conservatory of Music, Emmanuel College, Simmons College, Massachusetts College of Pharmacy and Health Sciences, Massachusetts College of Art and Design, Roxbury Community College, and Northeastern University are among the many educational institutions within a few blocks of the campus.

Majors and Degrees

Degree programs are offered in the fields of applied mathematics, architecture, computer science, construction management, design, engineering, engineering technology, and management. Bachelor of Science (B.S.) degrees are awarded in the following majors: applied mathematics, architecture, biomedical engineering, civil engineering, civil engineering technology, computer engineering, computer engineering technology, computer networking, computer science, construction management, electromechanical engineering (optional concentration in biomedical systems engineering), electrical engineering, electronic engineering technology, engineering (interdisciplinary), facilities planning and management, industrial design, interior design, management (optional concentrations in communication, project leadership, and technology management), mechanical engineering, and mechanical engineering technology. Baccalaureate degrees in architecture and interior design are designated as first professional degrees. Completion of a Wentworth baccalaureate degree usually requires four years (five years for the electromechanical engineering degree).

Academic Programs

At Wentworth, college-level study in technological fundamentals and principles is combined with appropriate laboratory, field, and studio experience. Students apply theory to practical problems, and they acquire skills and techniques by using, operating, and controlling equipment and instruments that are particular to their area of specialization. In addition, study in the social sciences and humanities provides a balanced understanding of the world in which graduates work. Wentworth's programs of study are more practical than theoretical in approach, and the Institute's academic requirements demand extensive time and effort.

During the first two years of study in a degree program at Wentworth, students lay the foundation for more advanced study in the third and fourth (and fifth, where applicable) years. While nearly all majors allow continuous study from the freshman through the senior year, the architecture major requires a petition for acceptance to the baccalaureate program during the sophomore year.

All bachelor's degree programs are conducted as cooperative (co-op) education programs: upon entering their third year, students alternate semesters of academic study at Wentworth with semester-long periods of employment in industry. Two semesters of co-op employment are required; one additional (summer) semester of co-op is optional. Both students and the companies that hire them are enthusiastic about the co-op program and agree that it is a mutually valuable experience.

Off-Campus Programs

Students have the option to study abroad in Wentworth's established programs in Germany and Ireland. As part of various programs and classes, Wentworth students have also traveled to many destinations, such as Nicaragua, the United Kingdom, Italy, Austria, the Czech Republic, Russia, and throughout Scandinavia.

Wentworth's membership in the Colleges of the Fenway (COF) gives students the intimacy of a small college community and the resources of a major university. The COF consortium members are Emmanuel College, Massachusetts College of Art and Design, Massachusetts College of Pharmacy and Health Sciences, Simmons College, Wentworth Institute of Technology, and Wheelock College. The consortium offers the benefits of cross-registration and access to social events, intramural teams, dance and theater troupes, a chorus and orchestra, professional activities, libraries, and campus facilities at five other colleges within walking distance of one another. The COF's Global

Education Opportunities Center provides access to exchange programs and overseas institutions as well as cross-registration for faculty-led travel courses.

Academic Facilities

Wentworth's twenty-seven buildings house classrooms, laboratories, studios, administrative offices, and other facilities. Beatty Hall houses the Alumni Library, computer center, classrooms, dining areas, and office space. State-of-the-art laboratories, such as the Richard H. Lufkin Technology Center and the Davis Center for Advanced Graphics and Interactive Learning, are situated throughout the campus.

Costs

For 2012–13, tuition is $25,900, books and supplies are approximately $1000, and the average room and board are about $12,250 (this figure varies according to accommodation). Tuition includes a brand new laptop that is outfitted with the complete suite of software used in the student's academic program.

Financial Aid

Scholarships are available to students who demonstrate need and academic promise. Merit-based scholarships are also available. Wentworth also provides federal and state financial assistance, such as Federal Pell and Federal Supplemental Educational Opportunity Grants, Federal Perkins Loans, Federal Work-Study Program awards, Gilbert Matching Grants, and Massachusetts No-Interest Loans, to students with financial need in accordance with federal and state guidelines.

Wentworth participates in the Federal Direct Lending program. As a result, students are eligible to borrow under the Federal Direct Stafford Student Loan program and parents may borrow under the Federal Direct PLUS program. Individuals participating in these programs borrow money directly from the federal government rather than through lending institutions.

In addition to these need-based programs, Wentworth also participates in the MEFA loan program sponsored by the Massachusetts Educational Financing Authority. Wentworth offers several payment options through payment plans and alternative loan financing.

To apply for financial aid, new students should complete the Free Application for Federal Student Aid (FAFSA) by March 1. Applications received after that date are considered as funds allow.

Faculty

Wentworth's faculty includes 146 full-time and 123 part-time members. The primary responsibility of every faculty member is teaching. Although professors may engage in some research and related work, student development remains the central mission of Wentworth's faculty. Upon entering Wentworth, every student is assigned a faculty adviser.

Student Government

Wentworth's Student Government performs an essential function as the official representative of the student body. Its purposes are to receive and express student opinion, to advance the best interests of the student body with the administration and faculty and with other institutions and associations, to support all extracurricular activities of the student body, and to serve as a bond between the student body and the faculty to foster cooperation and understanding. The Student Government is made up of elected representatives from each class section and the officers elected by the student body at large. The Student Government sponsors social functions and student organizations and serves as an advocate for student concerns.

Admission Requirements

Applicants must be graduates of secondary schools (or have passed the GED test) and must meet specific entrance requirements. All programs require four years of English, a laboratory science, and mathematics through algebra II in a college-preparatory program. Both the electromechanical engineering and the computer science programs require a background in precalculus or trigonometry. All programs require the submission of SAT or ACT scores. International students and transfers are welcome.

Application and Information

Students are admitted to Wentworth for September and January enrollment. Notification of admission is made on a rolling basis. The preferred method for applying is online at http://www.wit.edu/apply. The online application fee is $50. An application form, the application fee, transcripts from the secondary school and any colleges previously attended, SAT or ACT scores, a personal statement, and a letter of recommendation should be sent to:

Admissions Office
Wentworth Institute of Technology
550 Huntington Avenue
Boston, Massachusetts 02115
Phone: 617-989-4000
      800-556-0610 (toll-free)
Fax: 617-989-4010
E-mail: admissions@wit.edu
Web site: http://www.wit.edu
      http://twitter.com/WITadmissions
      http://facebook.com/wentworthadmissions

Wentworth residence hall study lounge.

WEST CHESTER UNIVERSITY OF PENNSYLVANIA
WEST CHESTER, PENNSYLVANIA

The University

West Chester University of Pennsylvania (WCU) is the second largest of the fourteen institutions in the Pennsylvania State System of Higher Education and the fourth-largest university in the Philadelphia metropolitan area. Officially founded in 1871, the University traces its heritage to the West Chester Academy, which existed from 1812 to 1869. The University's 402-acre campus has well-maintained facilities, including nine residence halls and two garden-style apartment complexes, plus a new performing arts center and a student recreation center opening in Fall 2012. In keeping with West Chester's rich heritage, the University's Quadrangle buildings, part of the original campus, are on the National Register of Historic Places.

While the University attracts the majority of its students from Pennsylvania, New Jersey, and Delaware, it also enrolls many students from other areas across the United States and from more than fifty countries. The undergraduate enrollment includes approximately 12,834 women and men.

Each year, the University community schedules an impressive series of events, including programs with well-known musicians, authors, political figures, and others. More than 230 campus groups in music, theater, athletics, and other activities, as well as clubs, fraternities, sororities, service organizations, and honor societies, provide students with the opportunity to participate in a full range of programs. The University offers 24 intercollegiate sports and 24 club sports for men and women. In addition to the facilities in the health and physical education complex, the University has a field house and a gymnasium for varsity sports.

Location

The University is located in West Chester, a community in southeastern Pennsylvania that is strategically located at the center of the mid-Atlantic corridor. The seat of Chester County government for more than two centuries, West Chester retains much of its historical charm in its buildings and unspoiled countryside, yet it offers the twenty-first-century advantages of a town in the heart of a thriving suburban area. West Chester is just 25 miles west of Philadelphia and 17 miles north of Wilmington, Delaware, putting the libraries, museums, cultural resources, entertainment, and historical sites of both cities within easy reach. It is also only 2 hours from New York City and 3 hours from Washington, D.C.

Majors and Degrees

The Bachelor of Arts is offered in American studies, anthropology, art, biology, communication studies, communicative disorders, English, French, geography–geographic analysis, geography–urban/regional planning, German, history, Latin, liberal studies, literature, mathematics, philosophy, political science, political science–international relations, political science–applied public policy, psychology, Russian, sociology, Spanish, theater arts, and women's studies.

The Bachelor of Science is offered in accounting, athletic training, biochemistry, biology, biology–cell and molecular biology, biology–ecology, biology–medical technology, biology–microbiology, business management, chemistry, chemistry–biology (premed), computer science, criminal justice, economics, exercise science, finance, forensic and toxicological chemistry, geoscience–earth systems, geoscience–environmental, geosciences–geology, health and physical education, health science–general, health science–respiratory care, liberal studies–science and mathematics, liberal studies–professional studies, marketing, mathematics, nutrition and dietetics, pharmaceutical product development, physics, physics–engineering, public health–environmental, and public health–health promotion.

The Bachelor of Science in Nursing, the Bachelor of Fine Arts (studio arts), the Bachelor of Music (music education, performance, theory and composition, studies in an outside field), and the Bachelor of Social Work degrees are also offered.

The Bachelor of Science in Education degree is offered in biology, chemistry, communication–media, communication–speech, communication–theatre emphasis, early childhood education, earth-space science–astronomy, earth-space science–geology, elementary education, English, mathematics, physics, and special education.

Paraprofessional studies are available in medicine. Also available are early admission assurance programs with Drexel School of Medicine, Pennsylvania State University College of Medicine, Temple University School of Medicine, Temple University School of Dentistry, and Arcadia University Physician Assistant Program. In cooperation with Pennsylvania State University, West Chester University offers a 3-2 dual-degree program combining liberal arts, physics, and engineering. A similar, dual-degree cooperative physics/engineering program is available through affiliation with the School of Engineering and Textiles of Philadelphia University. As a member of the State System of Higher Education (PASSHE), special admission opportunities for scholarships to the Widener School of Law–Harrisburg Campus are also available.

Teacher certification programs are available in biology, chemistry, communications, early childhood education, elementary education, English, French, general science, German, health and physical education, Latin, mathematics, music education, physics, Russian, secondary education, social studies, Spanish, and special education. Certificates are also available in adapted physical education, athletic training, biology–medical technology, education for sustainability, and Russian studies.

Interdisciplinary areas of study include computer security certificate, ethnic studies, Honors College, Latin American studies, and Russian studies. Minors are available in most majors and in several interdisciplinary areas. The University also offers ROTC programs with cross-enrollment agreement with Widener University for Army ROTC and with St. Joseph's University for Air Force ROTC.

Academic Programs

West Chester University is a comprehensive institution now in its second century. The University comprises the College of Arts and Sciences, the College of Business and Public Affairs, the College of Education, the College of Health Sciences, and the College of Visual and Performing Arts. It operates on a two-semester basis; summer sessions are available.

An honors program is available to qualified students for both upper and lower division study; internships and field experiences, self-designed majors, and independent study are also offered. A variety of credit-by-examination programs are available.

Off-Campus Programs

Through the Study Abroad Program, students may spend one or more semesters in countries such as England, Italy, France, Australia, Spain, and Ireland. West Chester also sponsors a number of annual courses that include study abroad during spring, summer, and winter breaks.

West Chester University participates in the National Student Exchange Program, in which students spend up to a year at any one of more than 170 member schools across the United States, broadening their cultural and academic horizons. Automatic transfer of credit is arranged.

Academic Facilities

There are two libraries on campus: the Francis Harvey Green Library and the Presser Music Library. Library collections include more than 1,416,480 print and electronic volumes; 2,000 print journal subscriptions; 926,000 microforms; 52,500 sound recordings; 10,300 films, videos, and DVDs; 3,500 maps; Internet access to more than 130 databases (including 27,000 titles of streaming video and 67,700 albums of streaming audio); and the full-text from more

than 67,700 journals. Unique digital collections include University graduate and undergraduate catalogs from 1874 to date; title pages and autographs from the Philips Autograph Library; the letters of General Anthony Wayne; historic postcards, and other materials relating to the University and to local history. Services include free interlibrary loan, electronic and print reserves, more than one hundred public computer workstations, forty-six laptops for use in the library, and a Starbucks coffee shop.

The University's extensive computer facilities include more than 1000 PC and Macintosh workstations that are available to students in more than 72 portable/fixed computer labs. Majority of the buildings and the entire campus outdoors are wireless zones and Internet access is available in residence halls and computer labs. Students can use the computing facilities 16 hours a day during weekdays and open hours are available during the weekends.

The Merion Science Center, with modern multimedia lecture halls, extensive laboratories, and study areas where students can work together, connects to the Schmucker Science Center, which houses a fully equipped observatory and planetarium. The Center's extensive laboratories have a variety of advanced instruments such as a single-side band microscope—the world's second—as well as field inversion electrophoresis equipment for DNA analysis, and equipment for RFLP, PCR and DNA sequencing. The GIS computer lab has a first-order community base station and mobile GPS units to support coursework in geography, marketing and other subjects. Undergraduates have hands-on access to this equipment, as well as automated spectrophotometers, electron analytical equipment, atomic absorption spectrometers, and a variety of chromatographs, including gas chromatograph–mass spectrometers.

The campus includes a 100-acre natural area for environmental studies; speech and hearing and reading clinics; two theaters; music facilities with practice, rehearsal, and listening rooms; a large health and physical education complex that houses a gymnasium and a natatorium with two pool areas and a diving well; dance studios; research laboratories; physical therapy rooms; saunas; and a health resource center.

West Chester University is committed to providing barrier-free facilities for persons with impaired mobility.

Costs

West Chester University provides a high-quality education at an affordable cost. Full-time undergraduate students who are legal residents of Pennsylvania paid $6240 for annual tuition for 12 to 18 semester hours in 2011–12. For more than 18 semester hours or fewer than 12, the cost was $260 per semester hour. Out-of-state students paid $15,600 per year for 12 to 18 semester hours and $650 per semester hour for more than 18 or fewer than 12. Room and board were $7848 per year for on-campus residents in University-owned residence halls. Student fees were $1530 per year, plus a technology fee of $348 for in-state students and $526 for out-of-state students. Tuition is determined by the state.

Financial Aid

The financial aid available to students includes work-study programs, grants, loans, special awards, and scholarships. A limited number of merit scholarships are awarded based on the student's academic standing and accomplishments in high school. Students who qualify are invited to apply. About 70 percent of all full-time undergraduate students receive some form of aid.

Faculty

West Chester University has a faculty of approximately 700 members. The majority hold doctoral degrees, and many are engaged in research and serve as consultants in their field of expertise. The student-faculty ratio is 18:1.

Student Government

The Student Government Association represents all students on the West Chester campus. In addition, the Residence Hall Association represents resident students, and the Off Campus and Commuter Association represents commuting students.

Admission Requirements

Applicants to West Chester University are evaluated on the basis of scholarship, character, and potential for achievement in the programs to which they apply. The requirements for freshman admission consideration include graduation, with satisfactory scholarship, from an approved secondary school or approval by the Credentials Evaluation Division of the Pennsylvania Department of Education, or Pennsylvania Homeschoolers Accreditation Agency; satisfactory scores on either the SAT, ACT, or TOEFL (for international applicants); and completion of a personal statement. The University offers other admissions options such as early admission and special admissions programs, including the Academic Development Program. Based on the scores received on Advanced Placement (AP) tests and subject examinations administered through the College-Level Examination Program (CLEP), students may receive advanced placement or credit.

Transfer applicants must have a minimum cumulative grade point average of 2.0 for admissions consideration. Certain academic programs require specific grade point averages above a 2.0 and may require an interview or specific course prerequisites.

Application and Information

Students are admitted for the fall or spring semester. Freshman applicants for the fall semester are encouraged to apply electronically and urged to begin the application process early in their senior year of high school. Transfers should begin the process beginning in January for the fall semester. Applicants for the spring semester should apply by November 1, however certain academic programs can close early. International students must apply by March 1 for the fall semester and September 1 for the spring semester. The Office of Admissions at West Chester University completes a preliminary evaluation of applicants on a rolling basis once all information has been received and processed. The committee prioritizes applicants with the strongest academic credentials during the review process and notifies them of its decision as quickly as possible upon the completion of their file. Students are encouraged to visit WCU's campus. To arrange a visit or to attend an information session, or request additional information, students should visit www.wcupa.edu/admissions.

For additional information and required forms, students may contact:

Office of Admissions
Emil J. Messikomer Hall
West Chester University of Pennsylvania
100 West Rosedale Avenue
West Chester, Pennsylvania 19383
Phone: 610-436-3411
      877-315-2165 (toll-free)
E-mail: ugadmiss@wcupa.edu
Transfer: ugtransfer@wcupa.edu
International: uginternational@wcupa.edu
Web site: http://www.wcupa.edu/admissions
      http://www.facebook.com/WCUPA
      http://twitter.com/WCUofPA
      http://www.youtube.com/WCUofPA

Philips Memorial Building is one of the historic Quadrangle buildings on the campus of West Chester University.

WESTERN CONNECTICUT STATE UNIVERSITY
DANBURY, CONNECTICUT

The University

Founded in 1903, Western Connecticut State University (WestConn) is dedicated to providing both a high-quality university education and a memorable campus experience at an affordable cost. With programs in the arts and sciences, business, and professional studies, WestConn takes pride in providing an outstanding education to more than 4,500 full-time undergraduates and nearly 2,000 graduate or part-time students.

WestConn offers excellent educational programs through five academic units: the Ancell School of Business, the School of Arts and Sciences, the School of Professional Studies, the School of Visual and Performing Arts, and the Division of Graduate Studies and External Programs. The most popular majors include communication, theater arts, education, business, justice and law administration, music, and nursing.

In addition to the University's full menu of undergraduate degrees, the Ancell School of Business offers the Master of Business Administration, Master of Health Administration, and Master of Science in justice administration. The School of Arts and Sciences offers the Master of Arts in biological and environmental sciences, earth and planetary sciences, English, history, and mathematics; the Master of Fine Arts is offered in professional writing. The School of Professional Studies offers the Master of Science in counselor education, elementary education, nursing, and secondary education; also offered is WestConn's Doctor of Education (Ed.D.) in instructional leadership. Prelaw and pre–health professions programs also are available. WestConn's newly formed School of Visual and Performing Arts offers the Master of Fine Arts in visual arts and the Master of Music Education.

The University is also rich with a number of learning and social activities beyond the classroom. Students run academic and fraternal organizations, publish an award-winning newspaper and yearbook, and run a radio station. They stage theater and musical productions, participate in cooperative education and internship programs, and administer their own campus government association.

The University provides services for learning-disabled students, study abroad, a University Scholars program, precollegiate and access initiatives, international student services, and community service learning opportunities. A variety of NCAA Division III men's and women's sports are represented on campus, and students enjoy intramural sports and a premier recreation center that includes a swimming pool, an indoor track, and weight-lifting machines. The campus also features a child-care center, a counseling center, a health services office, a career development center, and campus ministries.

WestConn is accredited by the New England Association of Schools and Colleges; the Board of Governors for Higher Education, State of Connecticut; the Connecticut State Department of Education; the American Chemical Society; the Commission on Collegiate Nursing Education; the Council on Social Work Education (baccalaureate level); the Council for Accreditation of Counseling and Related Educational Programs; and the National Association of Schools of Music.

Location

WestConn offers two campuses in Danbury, in the heart of western Connecticut, as well as a satellite campus in Waterbury. Danbury is a major city in Fairfield County in the foothills of the Berkshire Mountains, just 65 miles north of Manhattan and 50 miles west of Hartford.

In Danbury, the Midtown campus is a 34-acre, fifteen-building campus with an interesting mix of old and new architecture, and it offers easy access to downtown entertainment, restaurants, and shopping. The 364-acre Westside campus is ideal for hikers and nature buffs who want to discover its woodland wonders while enjoying state-of-the-art facilities. The WestConn-at-Waterbury campus offers a convenient location closer to the center of the state, with the same level of excellent service.

Majors and Degrees

The Ancell School of Business offers the Bachelor of Business Administration in accounting, finance, management, management information systems, and marketing, as well as the Bachelor of Science in justice and law administration.

The School of Arts and Sciences offers the Associate in Science, Bachelor of Arts, and Bachelor of Science degrees. The Associate in Science is offered in liberal arts. The Bachelor of Arts is offered in American studies, anthropology/sociology, biology, chemistry, communication, computer science, earth and planetary sciences–astronomy, economics, English, English–professional writing, history, mathematics, political science, psychology, social sciences, and Spanish. The Bachelor of Science is offered in medical technology and meteorology.

The School of Professional Studies offers the Bachelor of Arts and Bachelor of Science degrees. The Bachelor of Arts is offered in social work. The Bachelor of Science is offered in elementary education, health education, health promotion studies, nursing, and secondary education.

The School of Visual and Performing Arts offers the Bachelor of Arts, Bachelor of Science, and Bachelor of Music degrees. The Bachelor of Arts is offered in art, music, and theater arts. The Bachelor of Science is offered in music education, and the Bachelor of Music is offered with options in classical: voice or instrument or in jazz studies. Auditions are required for entrance into any of the music degree options.

Academic Programs

The University has developed a diverse mix of programs that are designed to inspire students. From the enlightening category of the arts to specialized fields of education, the emphasis is on the individual student's learning experience.

Special offerings at WestConn include the nation's first program in computer information security management and the only licensed meteorology program in Connecticut.

Academic Facilities

A number of facilities contribute to academic life on campus. The newly renovated and expanded library holds more than 200,000 volumes and over 400,000 bound periodicals, microforms, government documents, music scores, electronic resources, and

audiovisual items. WestConn's extraordinary Science Building opened in 2005 to great acclaim for its ecology-friendly green design and cutting-edge lab and classroom equipment. Students are also encouraged to make use of WestConn's exceptional computer laboratory facilities and are invited to hone their craft in superior theater and musical facilities. Along with the rest of the greater Danbury community, they benefit from the offerings of the WestConn International Center; German Studies Center; Institute for Holistic Health Studies; Meteorological Studies and Weather Center; Jane Goodall Center for Excellence in Environmental Studies; Center for Collaboration; Center for Business Research; Center for Excellence in Learning and Teaching; Center for Excellence in the Study of Culture and Values; Center for Galactic Astronomy; Center for Graphics Research; Center for Professional Development; Center for Technology, Research, and Productivity; Westside Nature Preserve; and Westside Observatory and Planetarium.

Costs

As part of the Connecticut State System of Higher Education, WestConn provides a high-quality private university education at an exceptionally reasonable public school cost. It is estimated that a full-time, in-state undergraduate student who lives and has meals on campus will pay approximately $20,500 for 2012–13. This estimate of annual costs includes tuition, fees, and room and board. Books, laboratory fees, health insurance, and personal expenses were not included in the estimate.

WestConn participates in the New England Regional Student Program of the New England Board of Higher Education. This program offers residents of other New England states the opportunity to enroll at WestConn at Connecticut resident tuition rates, plus an additional fee, in programs that are not available in their home states. Details about the regional program can be obtained by contacting the Office of University Admissions.

Financial Aid

Any student who is matriculated at WestConn and registering for at least 6 credits per semester may apply for student aid, which includes federal, state, and institutional funding. Students must complete the Free Application for Federal Student Aid (FAFSA) and be sure to list WestConn's school code of 001380 in the college release section. If the student's file is selected for verification, appropriate signed copies of federal income tax returns must be submitted. Academic scholarships are available to students with superior academic credentials. Students with demonstrated financial need also have the opportunity to participate in work-study programs. For more information, students should contact the Financial Aid Office at 203-837-8580 or wcsufinancialaid@wcsu.edu.

Faculty

Nationally respected, WestConn's faculty members and administrators are continually cited for scholarly achievement. The faculty-student ratio is 1:15.6, and nearly 90 percent of the University's full-time faculty members have doctoral, terminal, or first professional degrees.

Admission Requirements

WestConn welcomes applications from all qualified individuals. Admission to the four undergraduate schools is competitive. University admissions criteria include grade point average, types of courses taken, extracurricular activities, and standardized test results. Applications are reviewed by admissions professionals. If an applicant feels that individual circumstances warrant special consideration, a personal letter explaining those circumstances may be submitted with the application.

Academic preparation is the most important factor in determining admission. Freshman candidates for admission must have a high school diploma from an accredited secondary school or an equivalency diploma. General Educational Development (GED) test scores must be converted into a State of Connecticut Equivalency Diploma.

WestConn applicants should present evidence of successful completion of the following academic units in high school with a cumulative grade average of B- (80) or higher: 4 years of English, including writing skills and literature; 3 years of mathematics, including algebra I, geometry, and algebra II; 2 years of social sciences, including U.S. history; 2 years of laboratory sciences; and 2 to 3 years of a single foreign language (3 years are recommended). Academic course work in computer science, visual arts, theater, music, or dance may be substituted for one of the areas above. Those applicants who do not meet these guidelines may be considered under the Educational Achievement and Access Program. For more information about the program, students should contact the Office of University Admissions.

For specific information about transfer student admission, early admission, freshman entrance with advanced standing, special transfer arrangements for associate degree recipients, guest student admission, readmit admission, fresh-start admission, and international student admission, students should contact the Office of University Admissions.

Interviews are not required, but candidates are encouraged to attend an information session before they enroll. These sessions provide information about the University and the admissions process and provide an important opportunity to assess how the University can help students meet their long-term educational goals. They also afford students the opportunity to meet with professors, other potential students, and current students. Student-guided tours are available. While on tour, students are able to visit the library, the residence halls, science and computer laboratories, the student center, and the recreation center. For information about appointments and campus visits, students should call the Office of University Admissions.

Application and Information

WestConn seeks to enroll students who will benefit from and contribute to the University. Rolling admissions for the fall semester begin December 1, with class spaces filled on a first-come basis. Rolling admissions for the spring semester begin October 1, with class spaces filled on a first-come basis. To apply, students should obtain an application from the Office of University Admissions or from a secondary school or community college guidance office. WestConn welcomes transfer and international student applications.

For application forms and more information, students should contact:

Office of University Admissions
Western Connecticut State University
181 White Street
Danbury, Connecticut 06810
Phone: 203-837-9000
        877-837-WCSU (toll-free)
E-mail: admissions@wcsu.edu
Web site: http://www.wcsu.edu
        http://www.facebook.com/WestConn
        http://twitter.com/westconn/

WESTMONT COLLEGE
SANTA BARBARA, CALIFORNIA

The College

Westmont College is a nationally ranked Christian liberal arts college in the evangelical tradition that remains focused on undergraduate education. One of the country's most dynamic interdenominational Christian colleges, Westmont combines a world-class education with an unbeatable coastal Southern California location to prepare students for fulfilling lives of leadership and service.

Residence life, athletics, off-campus programs, and opportunities for local and international outreach contribute to balanced personal and spiritual development. Alumni enter a wide variety of professions and vocations and pursue professional-, master's-, and doctoral-level programs at the world's finest research universities, including UCLA, Stanford, Harvard, Yale, Princeton, the University of Chicago, Cambridge, and many others. Westmont's 1,200 students come to Westmont from the majority of states and many countries throughout the world, the highest percentage come from California. Approximately 60 percent are women, 25 percent are students of color, and 2 percent are international students. Approximately 80 percent of the students live in the five residence halls on campus or the apartment complex off campus.

As a member of the National Association of Intercollegiate Athletics and the Golden State Athletic Conference, Westmont provides intercollegiate sports for men and women in basketball, cross-country, soccer (NAIA champions), tennis, and track and field. Men also compete in intercollegiate baseball, club polo, club rugby, club soccer, club volleyball, club Ultimate (Frisbee), and club golf. Women also compete in intercollegiate volleyball, club polo, club cheer, and club golf. The intramural program offers a wide variety of activities as well.

There are numerous clubs and organizations, including a student newspaper, literary magazine, yearbook, choral and music ensembles, multicultural club organizations, political organizations, theater productions, community service organizations, and Christian service, mission, and outreach programs. The Ruth Kerr Memorial Student Center (1983) houses the main campus dining facilities. An integral component of the Westmont experience is the Chapel Program, which students are required to attend three days a week. Chapel provides speakers and programs to inspire and challenge students to continue growing in their relationship with Christ.

Location

Westmont is located on a 111-acre campus, rich with pine, oak, and eucalyptus trees, in Montecito, an estate area of Santa Barbara between the Pacific Ocean and the Santa Ynez Mountains. Students enjoy the beach and mountain trails year-round. Santa Barbara has a wealth of history and culture, and theaters, libraries, community concerts, and other civic offerings are just minutes from the campus.

Majors and Degrees

Westmont awards Bachelor of Arts (B.A.) and Bachelor of Science (B.S.) degrees in twenty-six liberal arts majors. These include alternative major, art, biology, chemistry, communication studies, computer science, economics and business, education, engineering physics, English, English and modern languages, French, history, kinesiology, mathematics, music, philosophy, physics, political science, psychology, religious studies, social science, sociology and anthropology, Spanish, and theater arts. The College offers a teacher-preparation program, which is approved by the California Commission for Teacher Preparation and Licensing, enabling students to qualify for either the single-subject or the multiple-subject credential. Pre-professional programs include athletic training, dentistry, engineering, law, medicine, ministry and missionary studies, pharmacy, physical therapy, and veterinary studies.

Academic Programs

All majors and programs of study feature thought-provoking and inspiring ways to integrate belief, thought, and action and to come to a deeper, more accurate understanding of the world. Westmont's commitment to academic freedom is clear, not only in courses that demand students' best critical thinking, but also through a wide range of opportunities and organizations that explore the world of ideas. Students consider issues of science and religion through the Pascal Society and attend lectures in the humanities sponsored by the Erasmus Society. As an exclusively undergraduate college, Westmont has a deep understanding of the ideas and issues that absorb students. From its faculty and staff members to its alumni, Westmont is committed to helping students grow through their questions toward an ever-deeper faith.

Off-Campus Programs

Off-campus programs include the Europe Semester, which is offered each fall and provides the broadest geographical scope, with extended stays in Athens, Florence, Jerusalem, London, Paris, and Rome. The England Semester, offered every other year, combines travel and residential study in the British Isles for students of literature. Westmont in Istanbul allows students to live in Constantinople, a city that is of the past and of the future, of grace and grit, of culture and politics, of faith and skepticism. Students attending the Westmont in Mexico Semester gain skills for effective cross-cultural living, experience incarnational ministry, and improve their Spanish language abilities. Semesters in France and Spain offer French and Spanish majors the opportunity to study these languages in their home countries, as does the Latin American Studies Program, which combines the study of Spanish culture and language in Belize, Chile, Costa Rica, and Honduras. Similar programs are offered at Jerusalem University College in Israel; the Middle East Studies Program at the American University in Cairo, Egypt; and in the Russian Studies Program in Moscow, Nizhni Novgorod, and St. Petersburg (through Westmont's membership in the Council for Christian Colleges and Universities). Participants in the International Business Institute program visit the major economic and political capitals of Europe and Asia. The Westmont Economics/Business Program in Asia introduces students to the diverse economic growth in the Pacific Rim. The East Asia Program addresses contemporary world issues in China, Japan, and Taiwan. An additional summer program in Asia offers students an opportunity to study life and culture in Sri Lanka. Domestic off-campus programs include the Westmont in San Francisco Program, which studies modern American urban society and offers internships; the Washington Semester, highlighting national political processes and incorporating internships in national, international, and economic policy, justice, and journalism; the Consortium Visitor Program, enabling students to study at any of the Christian College Consortium's twelve other member colleges; and other programs sponsored by the Council for Christian Colleges and Universities.

Academic Facilities

New buildings consist of the Adams Center for the Visual Arts, which includes a museum, studios, offices and classrooms; Winter Hall for Science and Mathematics; and the newly renovated observatory. Views of these new facilities are available at http://www.westmont.edu/buildings. The tri-level Roger John Voskuyl Library, named for Westmont's third president, provides access to information resources and services to support the research and information needs of faculty, staff, students and the surrounding community. The library collections include 237,000 books, media items, music scores, and microforms; 300 print periodical titles; and 105 online databases with access to 12,000 online periodicals. The Westmont community has access to additional resources through the Gold Coast Library Network, Camino and Interlibrary Loan Services. Westmont's network consists of both wired and wireless components. Wireless coverage extends through all campus

buildings and most outdoor areas, with a total Internet bandwidth of 135 Mb/s. Students are provided Google Apps accounts through Westmont, providing e-mail, calendaring, document sharing, and 4 GB storage per student. The college provides a general access computer lab consisting of twenty-seven dual-platform iMacs located in the main floor of the library. Westmont's Learning Commons is also housed in the library. This twenty-first century space brings together library, technology, and other campus services in an environment designed to foster collaborative and creative work, and social interaction. Voskuyl Library is also home to other Westmont departments that provide student support services: the Office of Life Planning, Academic Advising and Disability Services, and Internship Programs are on the upper level; the Writer's Corner is on the main level; and the Information Technology offices are on the lower level. Porter Theatre contains state-of-the-art equipment for dramatic productions and concerts. The newly renovated George Carroll Observatory contains a 24-inch search-grade reflector telescope, the most powerful telescope between San Francisco and Los Angeles. The Mericos H. Whittier Science Building and Winter Hall for Science and Mathematics houses the College's science program and equipment, including an ultracentrifuge, a liquid scintillation counter for measuring radioactivity, physiographic units and other equipment for advanced physiological studies.

Costs

Tuition and fees for 2011–12 were $35,650, and room and board for the academic year were $11,340. The cost of books and personal expenses was estimated at $3000.

Financial Aid

Westmont has a strong financial aid program, so no student should hesitate to apply for lack of financial resources. Eighty-five percent of Westmont's students receive some form of financial assistance. Westmont offers Monroe full-tuition scholarships, which are available only to first-year applicants who apply via the early action (nonbinding) process. A select group of these applicants are invited to the campus to participate in a formal competition process. Students should contact the Office of Admission for further details. Other merit awards in the financial aid program are the Dean's, Provost's, and President's Scholarships, which ranged from $10,000 to $14,000 (2011–12). These merit scholarships are awarded to students who have demonstrated impressive academic achievement. Westmont also gives awards to students who demonstrate strength in art, music, theater arts, dance, cultural diversity, and athletics. After submitting the Free Application for Federal Student Aid (FAFSA), students may be eligible for generous state grants, aid from federal programs, institutional grants, loans, and work-study programs.

Faculty

One of the highest priorities at Westmont is the attraction and retention of outstanding Christian teachers and scholars. The College's professors are dedicated to the integration of faith and learning, while also being actively involved in the lives of students. There are 95 full-time and 52 part-time faculty members. The student-faculty ratio is 12:1; the average class size is 18. Ninety-six percent of tenure-track faculty members hold a terminal degree. Westmont's faculty members are committed to teaching at the undergraduate level, and they have additional advising responsibilities with either incoming first-year students or students in their major. A director of first-year programs is responsible for the advising and orientation of new students. Although teaching is their primary scholarly activity, many faculty members engage in research, write books, and publish articles in leading journals and periodicals.

Student Government

The Westmont College Student Association (WCSA) is an entirely self-governing body. Students elect their own WCSA representatives, who are then responsible for organizing social, cultural, and educational activities. They actively participate in and are voting members on almost all faculty committees, while also allocating the student budget to various clubs and organizations. Westmont Student Ministries, another student-managed organization, is responsible for organizing on- and off-campus ministries and mission opportunities.

Admission Requirements

Westmont selects candidates for admission from those prospective students who produce evidence that they are prepared for the academic stimulation and spiritual vitality that are central to the character of Westmont. All applicants must submit one academic letter of recommendation, official high school or college transcripts, and official SAT or ACT scores. A pastoral/character reference is optional. An interview is strongly encouraged. For transfer students from an accredited two- or four-year college or university or a Bible college or university that is accredited by the American Association of Bible Colleges, the evaluation is based on achievement in solid, transferable course work; an assessment of the personal areas covered by the application (as stated above); and the quality of the written responses. High school records must be submitted if the applicant has completed fewer than 24 college-level credits at the time of application.

Application and Information

Entrance to Westmont is possible at the beginning of either the fall or spring semester. Westmont offers an early action plan. High school seniors interested in applying for early action must submit the application by November 1; notifications are mailed on December 20. The priority deadline for regular decision is February 10 for first-year applicants and March 1 for transfers; notifications are mailed on a rolling basis. Applications should be submitted online via Common Application with an application fee of $40. The Office of Admission encourages applicants to complete the application process as early as possible. Visitors are welcome at any time. Campus visitors can stay overnight in the residence halls, attend classes and chapel, speak with professors or coaches, have a music audition, share a portfolio with the art department, and have meals with Westmont students. Several Preview Day events are planned each semester. Westmont desires to enroll a well-rounded and balanced first-year class. One of Westmont's goals is to create a dynamic as well as culturally and traditionally diverse community of learners who bring with them a variety of attributes, accomplishments, backgrounds, and interests.

For further information regarding admissions students should contact:

Office of Admission
Westmont College
955 La Paz Road
Santa Barbara, California 93108
Phone: 800-777-9011 (toll-free)
Fax: 805-565-6234
E-mail: admissions@westmont.edu
Web site: http://www.westmont.edu/
http://www.facebook.com/westmont
http://twitter.com/westmontnews

Nestled in the beautiful hills of Santa Barbara, California, Westmont is home to 1,200 undergraduate scholars, all seeking to engage the academy, church, and world.

WEST VIRGINIA WESLEYAN COLLEGE
BUCKHANNON, WEST VIRGINIA

The College

Founded in 1890, West Virginia Wesleyan College is a coeducational, residential, liberal arts college in Buckhannon, West Virginia. The College has an enrollment of 1,400 undergraduate students from thirty-five states and twenty-one countries. The average class size is 19 and the student-faculty ratio is 14:1. More than 75 percent of the faculty members hold the highest degree in their respective teaching field. Each fall, West Virginia Wesleyan enrolls approximately 400 freshmen and 50 transfers. Fifty-five percent of students originate from West Virginia, and the ratio of men to women is 1:1. Approximately 16 percent of the students are minority or international students. More than 95 percent of students live on campus, and housing is required for all four years of study. Housing options include residence halls, suites, on-campus apartments, and campus-adjacent residence units.

Wesleyan offers a modern technology infrastructure, including wireless Internet in all campus buildings and public places. The College also participates in purchase programs with the Asus and Dell computer companies, which allow students to purchase laptops directly for campus use. The College also employs a help desk staff that is authorized to service and make on-site repairs to Asus and Dell machines, including warranty work, at no cost to students.

Wesleyan students are encouraged to pursue international travel and career-related internship opportunities. The international experience is available to students during the fall and spring semesters and during the three-week optional May Term. Wesleyan students also pursue a variety of semester-long local, national, and international internship programs.

Among the many services available to students is the Academic and Career Center, which helps students with job placement, class scheduling, selection of a major program of study, internship opportunities, and international travel. The center also provides preparatory help for professional or graduate entrance exams such as the LSAT, GRE, or GMAT. The Health and Counseling Center allows students to receive personal and educational guidance, as well as health services. The Learning Center provides comprehensive learning resources for all students, as well as specific services for students with diagnosed learning differences.

In addition to challenging academic curriculum and innovative technology, Wesleyan offers a balanced and comprehensive student-life program. Cocurricular activities include nineteen NCAA Division II varsity sports, intramurals, and outdoor recreation adventures. More than seventy campus organizations include vocal and instrumental musical ensembles, theatre arts, dance, community service, clubs, special interest groups, Greek life, and spiritual and religious life programming. On-campus media opportunities include a campus radio station, student newspaper, and yearbook. The Campus Activities Board schedules cultural and social entertainment every week during the academic year.

Location

Situated in the foothills of the Allegheny Mountains, Wesleyan's picturesque 100-acre campus is located in the historic town of Buckhannon, West Virginia. Buckhannon is located two hours south of Pittsburgh, Pennsylvania, and 90 minutes north of Charleston, West Virginia. It is easily accessible by interstate highways. Buckhannon has been included in Norman Crampton's book, *The Top 100 Best Small Towns in America* and *The 120 Best College Towns in America*. Students are drawn to the attractive and friendly setting and the many restaurants, social events, and outdoor adventures available within a short distance from campus.

Majors and Degrees

The College awards Bachelor of Arts, Bachelor of Science, Bachelor of Science in Nursing, and Bachelor of Music Education degrees, in addition to a number of master's-level degrees. Majors include: accounting, art, arts administration, athletic training, biology,

business administration, five-year bachelor's + master's in business administration, chemistry, Christian formation, communication studies, computer information science, computer science, criminal justice, economics, education (combined elementary/secondary, elementary, or secondary), engineering 3-2, English (literature, education, or writing), environmental science, environmental studies, exercise science, graphic design, history, international business, international studies, management, marketing, mathematics, music (applied or theory), music education, musical theatre, nursing, painting and drawing, philosophy, photography, physics, political science, psychology, public relations, religion, sociology, and theatre arts.

Preprofessional study programs are offered in dentistry, law, medicine, optometry, pharmacy, physical therapy, and veterinary medicine. The degrees are determined by the content of the student's program.

West Virginia Wesleyan also offers the following master's degrees: Master of Science in Athletic Training, Master of Business Administration, Master of Fine Arts in Creative Writing, Master of Education, and Master of Science in Nursing.

Academic Programs

Students are required to complete 120 credit hours of course work to become eligible for graduation. Approximately one third of those hours are taken in a student's major, one third in the general studies curriculum requirement, and one third in electives. The general studies and elective courses are taken to develop and enhance a student's worldview. These classes range from contemporary issues to humanities and can be taken along with courses within the individual's major concentration throughout the four years.

Wesleyan operates on a traditional semester system. The optional May Term is a three-week intensive period of study giving students the opportunity to earn three credit hours. International travel opportunities are popular options during May Term.

The honors program is offered for superior students who meet the specific requirements and are willing to commit themselves to a rigorous and enriching curriculum that affirms the highest ideals of a liberal arts institution. Challenging classes and cultural outings are an integral part of the honors program and are offered throughout the academic year.

Advanced credit is available for students who achieve required scores on Advanced Placement exams, International Baccalaureate exams, and CLEP tests.

New students are assigned a faculty adviser who assists with course selection and student concerns. All first-year students are required to successfully complete a four-hour First Year Seminar course. In addition to helping students adapt to college life, the First Year Seminar courses are topical and apply credit toward a general studies requirement. These courses also provide students with faculty advising and student mentoring for the first semester.

Off-Campus Programs

Study abroad is highly encouraged and is an important part of the Wesleyan student's experience. In the recent past, students have studied in such countries as Australia, Austria, Bolivia, Bulgaria, England, Ireland, Italy, Kenya, Korea, Spain, and Wales, but there are a number of other countries in which students may study. Internships are required for many majors and highly encouraged for others. They are available locally, as well as in cities such as Pittsburgh, New York, Washington, D.C., and others around the globe. These off-campus opportunities can be taken for a complete semester, during the May Term, or during the summer.

Academic Facilities

Wesleyan's twenty-four buildings, including eleven modern residence hall units, house some of the most impressive facilities in the region. Residence hall facilities include Fleming Hall, which was completely

remodeled in 2008, and a brand new residence hall that opened to students in 2011. Other recent campus construction includes the Virginia Thomas Law Center for the Performing Arts, opened in 2009, and the Reemsnyder Research Center for the sciences, opened in 2011. A brand-new wellness center with Nautilus equipment, full cardio theater, separate workout rooms, and locker room facilities opened in 2012.

The Annie Merner Pfeiffer Library is a spacious facility housing more than 105,000 volumes, 700 periodicals, and 10,000 media materials. More than 220 million additional resources worldwide can be accessed through a number of online databases from students' own residence halls 24 hours a day. Located in the center of the campus is Wesley Chapel, the largest sanctuary in West Virginia, and the Martin Religious Center. The Benedum Campus and Community Center houses a convenience store, bookstore, swimming pool, the Cat's Claw restaurant, the campus radio station, the Academic and Career Center, and student services offices. The Rockefeller Health and Physical Education Center includes a main gymnasium that seats 3,700 spectators, an intramural gymnasium, weight-training rooms, and an indoor Astroturf training and recreational area. Other key campus buildings include Christopher Hall of Science and the adjacent Reemsnyder Research Center, which houses state-of-the-art laboratories and classrooms to complement the Christopher's planetarium, herbarium, and greenhouse; Loar Hall, which includes a 165-seat recital hall and state-of-the-art computer music lab; Middleton Hall, which houses the admission offices and department of nursing; Haymond Hall of Science; and the Lynch-Raine Administration Building.

Costs

The 2012–13 costs at Wesleyan are $24,780 for tuition, $7510 for room and board, and $1024 for fees. Students should allow $700 for books per year. Wesleyan offers a 10-month interest-free monthly payment plan during the academic year.

Financial Aid

Wesleyan allocates nearly $15 million each year to help supplement the financial needs of students and their families. Merit scholarships are available for students who demonstrate excellence in the classroom, as well as those who demonstrate talent in the arts and athletics. Scholarship opportunities are available for students who have a strong commitment to community service and for those who have a comprehensive cocurricular resume. A variety of need-based programs are also available, including government grants and loans, institutional grants, and student employment. All students and their families should file the Free Application for Federal Student Aid by February 15. The institutional code for West Virginia Wesleyan is 003830.

Faculty

The faculty members at Wesleyan have a primary goal of teaching and advising. More than 75 percent of the full-time faculty members hold the highest degree in their respective fields. With a 14:1 student-faculty ratio, classes are small, and personal attention is evident in all departments. Not only are faculty members teachers and advisers, but they are also mentors and friends.

Student Government

The Student Senate is structured to encourage and promote student participation. The four peer-elected officers are elected by their respective classes or representative student organizations. Student Senate meets biweekly, along with faculty members, administration, and staff members, and is recognized as the driving force behind many initiatives and decisions on campus.

Admission Requirements

Wesleyan seeks students who have proven academic credentials, combined with achievements and talents that enhance the quality of life on campus. Students are selected by the Office of Admission on the basis of their high school transcripts, college entrance exam results, letters of recommendation, campus interviews, and other supportive information. All applicants must take the SAT or ACT and submit secondary school transcripts from all schools attended, along with the application for admission. Candidates are considered on an individual basis without regard to race, color, national origin, sex, sexual orientation, age, disability, or religious affiliation.

Essays and campus interviews are strongly encouraged and may be required in some instances.

Transfer students from accredited institutions are considered for admission. All official college transcripts must be submitted, along with high school transcripts and college entrance exam results.

Applicants who complete their secondary education through an alternative program (e.g., home schooling) must present evidence that they have been adequately prepared for college work to be considered for admission. SAT or ACT results are also required.

Application and Information

Applicants must submit an application for admission, official transcripts, and ACT or SAT scores. The application review period opens each year on October 1. Applying online is free of charge at http://apply.wvwc.edu. A paper application is also available and can be submitted along with a $35 nonrefundable fee. Admission decisions are made on a rolling basis, and students are notified within three weeks of receipt of all required documents. The preferred application deadline is March 1 for the fall semester, and December 1 for the spring semester. Applicants who wish to be considered for merit scholarships must apply before March 1. Interviews, campus tours, faculty and staff appointments, and class visits are encouraged and may be arranged through the Office of Admission.

For additional information, students should contact:

Office of Admission
West Virginia Wesleyan College
59 College Avenue
Buckhannon, West Virginia 26201
Phone: 304-473-8510
      800-722-9933 (toll-free)
E-mail: admission@wvwc.edu
Web site: http://www.wvwc.edu

The Annie Merner Pfeiffer Library is a busy campus hub, and it's one of the central gathering spaces where students meet and study.

WHEATON COLLEGE
WHEATON, ILLINOIS

The College

Ranked by *U.S. News & World Report* as one of the nation's top liberal arts colleges, Wheaton College attracts exceptional students from all fifty states and more than thirty countries. An interdenominational Christian liberal arts college, Wheaton takes the pursuit of faith and learning seriously. In addition to upholding an academically rigorous curriculum, Wheaton is committed to being a community that fearlessly pursues God's truth; invests in developing whole, well-rounded students; and prepares its graduates to lead lives that make a difference in the world.

Interdenominational and international in constituency, the student body at Wheaton College consists of approximately 2,400 undergraduates (including 200 students in the Conservatory of Music). Approximately 80 percent of the undergraduate students come from outside Illinois.

Wheaton College's 150-year history demonstrates the benefits of stable leadership in private Christian higher education—it has had only 7 presidents since it was founded in 1860. Wheaton has been faithful to its original precepts, and its legacy is shown in the lives of its graduates. Many distinguished graduate schools currently enroll Wheaton graduates in the dramatic arts, education, law, medicine, music, philosophy, science, and sociology. These include Notre Dame, Princeton, SMU, Yale, and the Universities of Chicago and Missouri–Kansas City; several of the Big Ten music schools; and the A.R.T./MXAT Institute for Advanced Theater Training at Harvard. Wheaton alumni also excel in a wealth of endeavors around the world, with many holding positions in business and finance, government and foreign service, teaching, ministry, law, medicine, and the arts. Wheaton graduates actively contribute to their communities and churches, and no matter what position they hold, they strive to make a difference in the world around them.

Wheaton offers a rich, life-changing education, with graduates trained for life, not just jobs. Students are taught to think, reason, and express themselves effectively. They should be able to attain knowledge and measure it against the truth of God's word, understand the importance of service, and value faith that embraces both right belief and right action. Developing strong, life-long relationships—with classmates, professors, and Jesus Christ—is a priority. Graduates are well-positioned for whatever they want to pursue and prepared to face the challenges of life. The Wheaton experience is distinctive and living and learning at Wheaton is extraordinary.

Location

Wheaton's 80-acre campus is located in a residential suburb (population 55,000) 25 miles west of Chicago, and the educational and cultural features of the Chicago metropolitan area are easily accessible by train and regularly visited by students.

Majors and Degrees

Wheaton grants the Bachelor of Arts and Bachelor of Science degrees and, through the Wheaton Conservatory of Music, the Bachelor of Music and Bachelor of Music Education degrees.

The following majors are available in the arts and sciences: ancient languages, anthropology, applied health science, archaeology, art, biblical and theological studies, biology, business/economics, chemistry, Christian education and ministry, communication, computer science, economics, education, English, environmental studies, geology, history, interdisciplinary studies, international relations, mathematics, modern languages (French, German, and Spanish), music, philosophy, physics, political science,

psychology, and sociology. Also, 3-2 programs are offered in engineering and nursing, alongside a five-year cooperative engineering program with Illinois Institute of Technology and other engineering schools.

The Wheaton Conservatory of Music offers a full range of professional music majors, including composition, education, history/literature, performance, music with elective studies in an outside field, and music with an emphasis in a music-related field (such as media/film music, pedagogy, conducting, and collaborative piano). Students seeking these professional music degrees are accepted directly into the program by audition.

An on-campus program in military science leads to a commission in the U.S. Army at graduation. In addition to the majors offered, Wheaton has programs leading to teacher certification and to athletic training certification as well as programs preparing students for careers in business, health professions, law, and ministry.

Academic Programs

Wheaton is a distinctively Christian college where faculty members and students work together, both inside and outside the classroom, to apply Christian principles and values to the needs and problems of the individual and society. The vigorous search for knowledge and wisdom in any area of human activity is based on the belief that all truth is God's truth.

The academic curriculum combines with artistic, athletic, religious, service, and social activities to achieve a lively interaction of faith, learning, and living. Because of the College's strong commitment to developing effective servant/leaders for society worldwide and the church, there is a particularly strong integration of faith and learning in all degree programs.

A student's major is selected during the second semester of general education courses taken to meet competency and area requirements. Students must demonstrate competence (either by examination or by taking prescribed courses) in foreign language, mathematics, speech, and writing. All students must complete area requirements in applied health science, art, biblical studies, history, literature, music, natural science, philosophy, and social science. A student may be granted advanced placement or college credit on the basis of examination (SAT Subject Tests or AP). The number of credits granted and the level of placement are determined by the registrar and the chair of the department in which the course is taught.

Wheaton offers ten natural science majors—applied health science, biology, chemistry, computer science, environmental studies, geology, liberal arts engineering, liberal arts nursing, mathematics, and physics—in six academic departments. The Wheaton faculty members engage the study of science authoritatively, enthusiastically, and creatively in the classrooms and laboratories and beyond the campus. They are creative and offer more than two dozen general education courses in the natural sciences as well as the majors listed above. The programming includes the use of state-of-the-art technologies and techniques on the main Wheaton campus, cutting edge geological and biological studies in a large science station in the scientifically rich area of the Black Hills of South Dakota, and marine biology studies in Belize. In 2010, Wheaton's science departments will move into a new $80-million science and mathematics facility with expanded teaching labs and research equipment.

Off-Campus Programs

Wheaton offers a variety of off-campus opportunities to enhance students' programs of study. The Wheaton Passage program

COLLEGE CLOSE-UPS

is a popular camp experience available to new students at the College's Honey Rock Camp in northern Wisconsin. Another program, Human Needs and Global Resources (HNGR), combines classroom study with a six-month, field-based, service-learning internship in the Global South. A similar program in urban studies, Wheaton in Chicago, focuses on urban issues in U.S. cities and includes a semester living in College-owned housing in urban Chicago.

Other special summer programs for credit include field study at the Wheaton College Science Station in the Black Hills of South Dakota; working with youth at Honey Rock Camp; interdisciplinary study in East Asia; the study of English literature in England; language study in France, Germany, and Spain; the Wheaton in the Holy Lands program, involving biblical and archaeological studies; the Arts in London program, which includes course work in music, theater, and art; and an international study program based in England and the Netherlands, offering courses in economics, political science, and psychology.

Wheaton is a member of the Council of Christian Colleges and Universities, based in Washington, D.C. The council's activities increase students' learning opportunities by bringing special programs to campus and by providing off-campus study. Off-campus programs include American Studies in Washington, D.C.; the Washington Journalism Center in Washington, D.C.; the Los Angeles Film Studies Center; the Contemporary Music Center in Martha's Vineyard; Latin American Studies in Costa Rica; Middle East Studies in Cairo; the Australia Studies Center; China Studies Program; the Scholar's Semester in Oxford; Russia Studies Program; and Uganda Studies Program. Wheaton has also recently affiliated with the International Sustainable Development Studies Institute in Thailand. In addition, Wheaton's membership in the Christian College Consortium allows students a semester of study at one of the other twelve consortium colleges.

Cooperative programs in social science are available at American and Drew Universities, and students may participate in a European seminar conducted by Gordon College.

Academic Facilities

A new $80-million science and mathematics facility opened in fall 2010. The 128,000-square-feet of space includes eight teaching labs and research space designed to promote collaborative teacher-student research.

In 2009, an $11 million renovation of Adams Hall added art gallery and studio space. Edman Chapel, often the venue for concerts by world-class musicians, has undergone a $9 million renovation that added rehearsal space, including a large rehearsal room named for alum John Nelson, former conductor of Ensemble Orchestral de Paris.

In 2008, Wheaton's Memorial Student Center reopened after an extensive renovation to house the J. Dennis Hastert Center for Economics, Government, and Public Policy. The facility provides classroom, research, and public discussion space geared toward the study of economics, politics, and values in business, government, and ministry. Other recent additions to campus facilities include the Todd Beamer Student Center (2004); the Wade Center (2001), which houses the books and papers of seven British authors, including C. S. Lewis and J. R. R. Tolkien; and the Sports and Recreation Complex (2000).

Costs

Tuition for the 2012–13 year is $30,120; room and board for the year is $8560.

Financial Aid

Realizing that a private college education is a sizable investment, Wheaton is committed to providing the necessary need-based financial aid so students can attend. Last year Wheaton awarded over $20 million in grants and scholarships.

The average need-based aid package for freshmen is about $18,000 and some merit aid is also available. The Career Development Center helps students to secure part-time jobs, as well as future employment.

Faculty

Over 94 percent of Wheaton's 198 full-time faculty members hold earned doctorates, and more than one third graduated from the top twenty-five graduate schools as designated in *U.S. News & World Report*. The professors' primary commitment as educators and advisers is enriched by their considerable research, publishing, and artistic activities. In addition, the professors are active Christians who strive to show how a profound commitment to God's word structures a vision of all of life, including intellectual life. They are dedicated to honoring a Christian perspective and to modeling Christ's love to their students.

All undergraduate courses are taught by faculty members.

To ensure a rich range of perspectives and expertise, every department at Wheaton has at least 3 full-time professors, and most have 5 to 10. The student-faculty ratio is 12:1.

Student Government

Student Government ensures a student voice in institutional affairs and provides a wide range of opportunities to develop leadership abilities. Student Government's 2011–12 vision is "To further the educational, spiritual, and relational development of the Wheaton College community as elected servant leaders representing student initiative, concern, creativity, and enthusiasm."

Besides Student Government, there are over forty academic, cultural, social justice, and entertainment student groups on campus. In addition, the Office of Christian Outreach provides opportunities for student ministry through student-run mission trips and ministries in urban and suburban Chicago.

Admission Requirements

Wheaton is a selective college that seeks to enroll students who evidence a vital Christian experience, high moral character, personal integrity, social concern, strong academic ability and motivation, and the desire to pursue Christian higher education as defined in the aims and objectives of the College. These qualities are evaluated by consideration of each applicant's academic record, autobiographical essays, test scores, recommendations, optional interview, and participation in extracurricular activities. For students applying to the Conservatory of Music, strong consideration is given to the evaluation of the required audition.

Applicants must have a high school diploma or the equivalent, and at the time of graduation should have completed a college-preparatory curriculum with a minimum of 18 acceptable units.

Satisfactory scores on the SAT or on the ACT examination are required of all applicants to the freshman class. The middle 50 percent range of scores for those admitted is 26–32 (ACT) and 1230–1400 (SAT composite math and verbal scores).

Application and Information

An application packet, complete with detailed instructions and requirements, can be obtained from the Admissions Office or online. For early action (nonbinding), students seeking admission in the fall term should apply to either the College of Arts and Sciences or the Conservatory of Music by November 1. The regular action deadline is January 10; the transfer application deadline is March 1. An admissions counselor can provide more information about Wheaton in general or the application process in particular.

Further information is available from:

Admissions Office
Wheaton College
501 College Avenue
Wheaton, Illinois 60187
Phone: 630-752-5005
          800-222-2419 (toll-free)
E-mail: admissions@wheaton.edu
Web site: http://www.wheaton.edu
http://www.wheaton.edu/Admissions-and-Aid/Undergrad

WHITMAN COLLEGE
WALLA WALLA, WASHINGTON

The College

Challenging students to excel in the sciences, humanities, art, and social sciences, Whitman College is a nationally recognized liberal arts college. It combines the educational prestige of the best Eastern liberal arts colleges with the unpretentious values of the Pacific Northwest. Since 1882, students have chosen Whitman because of its commitment to undergraduate education. With 1,500 students and an average class size of 16, Whitman encourages students to be active participants in their education. In 1913, the College led the nation by requiring students to successfully complete comprehensive oral and written evaluations in their major field of study. The installation of a chapter of Phi Beta Kappa in 1919 marked the recognition of the high quality of Whitman's curriculum and the standards of teaching and learning that distinguish the College. Seventy percent of Whitman graduates enroll in graduate school within five years of earning their undergraduate degree.

Enrollment includes students from forty-five states and thirty countries. As a residential college, approximately 70 percent of Whitman students live on campus. A variety of residence hall living options are available, including coeducational housing, apartment-style living, eleven special-interest houses, four fraternity houses, and an all-women's residence hall that houses, among others, the members of four national sororities. First-year students and sophomores are required to live on campus.

Whitman has an extremely engaged student body. "Whitties" participate in more than 130 interest groups, clubs, and organizations. The debate team ranked first in the country in parliamentary debate in 2010, 2011, and 2012. The highly acclaimed theater department produces eight to ten shows each academic year, while the music department supports more than two dozen musical groups on campus. The College fields fourteen varsity teams and offers thirteen club sports and sixteen intramural activities. The Whitman club cycling team and men's and women's Ultimate (Frisbee) teams have won national championships in recent years. The varsity men's tennis and varsity women's cross-country teams have recently been nationally ranked.

Location

Whitman is located in Walla Walla, a historic community of 30,000 nestled in the foothills of the Blue Mountains of southeastern Washington. The Walla Walla Valley has four distinct seasons and enjoys 300 days of sunshine a year. With rich natural terrain at its doorstep, outdoor activities abound. These include cross-country and downhill skiing, backpacking, hiking, kayaking, rafting, and rock climbing. Whitman hosts a wide array of cultural activities on campus, including concerts, art exhibits, environmental forums, internationally renowned speakers and performers, and cinema arts films. Students also perform with the community symphony, browse in the area's seventeen art galleries, and act in the community theater. Parents appreciate the vibrant arts culture of the town as well as the wine and restaurant scene. Walla Walla is home to over 100 wineries and is a popular tourist destination.

Majors and Degrees

Whitman College confers the Bachelor of Arts (B.A.) degree, with departmental majors in anthropology; art (history, studio, and visual culture studies); Asian studies; biochemistry, biophysics, and molecular biology (BBMB); biology; chemistry; classics; economics; English; foreign languages and literatures (French, German studies, or Spanish); gender studies; geology; history; Latin American studies; mathematics; music; philosophy; physics; politics; psychology; religion; rhetoric and media studies; sociology; and theater. Combined or interdepartmental major study programs are offered in Asian studies, astronomy-geology, biology-geology, chemistry-geology, economics-mathematics, environmental studies (emphasis in biology, chemistry, economics, geology, physics, politics, or sociology), geology-physics, mathematics-physics, and physics-astronomy. Minors are available in each of the departmental

programs as well as Chinese, Japanese, Latin American and Caribbean literature, Latin American Studies, and world literature. Students with special interests may develop combined or interdepartmental major programs, subject to faculty approval. Whitman offers cooperative programs in engineering with Caltech, Columbia, Duke, the University of Washington, and Washington University in St. Louis; in environmental management or forestry with Duke; in law with Columbia School of Law; in education with the University of Puget Sound; and oceanography with the University of Washington.

Academic Programs

Whitman's goal is to provide an atmosphere in which students can learn how to learn. At the heart of Whitman's academic curriculum is the general studies program. Through this program, students develop skills in intellectual reasoning, critical analysis of major works, effective writing, solid understanding of humanity's cultural and historic roots, valid bases for judgment of values, and confident abilities to ask tough questions. The general studies program consists of a first-year Encounters course and certain distribution requirements. Encounters is a two-semester course examining contact between peoples and cultures and the formation and transformation of dominant and competing worldviews. To satisfy distribution requirements, students complete at least 6 semester credits in fine arts, humanities, science, and social sciences; take 2 courses dealing with alternative voices; and take at least 1 course in quantitative analysis. Every candidate for graduation must complete at least 124 credits in appropriate course work with acceptable grades and a senior assessment. Whitman helps fund student research and internships, and approximately 200 students present professional-level research at the Annual Whitman Undergraduate Conference. Scores of 4 and 5 on the College Board's Advanced Placement tests are accepted for credit (the economics, English, and history departments accept only a score of 5). Whitman observes a two-semester calendar with a weeklong break for Thanksgiving, a month off over the winter holiday, and two weeks for spring break.

Off-Campus Programs

Whitman has strong study-abroad and domestic off-campus study programs. Each year, nearly half of the junior class studies off campus. There are 180 different programs available, spanning six of the seven continents (excluding Antarctica). In addition to academic course work, many students pursue internships and research opportunities. The College is formally affiliated with the Institute for the International Education of Students, with programs in Australia, Austria, China, England, France, Germany, and Italy. The school for field studies has opportunities in Australia, the Caribbean, Costa Rica, Kenya, and Mexico. Students may study at the Universities of East Anglia and York in England; St. Andrews University in Scotland; Doshisha University in Kyoto, Japan; and the University of Otago in Dunedin, New Zealand, and at programs in Argentina, Botswana, China, Costa Rica, Egypt, Greece, India, Ireland, Italy, Japan, Mexico, Spain, Sri Lanka, and Taiwan. Each year, 4 Whitman graduates are selected to teach English to university students in Kunming or Xi'an in the People's Republic of China. The College offers urban-semester programs in Chicago, Philadelphia, and Washington, D.C. Students may participate in one of more than 300 science research internships available through the College. Semester in the West, a signature program, is a semester-long, interdisciplinary traveling field-study program that investigates a myriad of issues throughout the intermountain West.

Academic Facilities

To enhance Whitman's learning environment, students have access to exceptional facilities and cultural resources. Penrose Memorial Library, open 24/7, houses more than 350,000 volumes and 2,000 subscriptions. In addition, the ORBIS Cascade Alliance provides access to approximately 3.5 million volumes that can

be delivered to Whitman in less than 72 hours. Reid Campus Center, a 51,000-square-foot campus building, features a ballroom, cyber-lounge, coffeehouse performance space, and flexible dining and meeting facilities. Olin Hall of Humanities features an audiovisual center, a foreign-language learning lab, and the Donald Sheehan Art Gallery. A newer addition to Olin houses the computing equipment and is the center for the campus-wide fiber-optic network. Maxey Hall, expanded in 2011, houses the social sciences, includes a natural history and anthropology museum, a 350-seat auditorium, and animal demonstration labs. The Hall of Science houses a sophisticated physics lecture/demonstration hall and laboratory, expanded chemistry work stations, the Clise Planetarium, and support facilities for electron microscopes. It also contains laboratories for botany, ecology, vertebrate biology, physiology and developmental biology, and biochemistry and genetics; preparation and display cases for the herbarium and the preserved animal collections; a seismograph; and well-equipped student research laboratories. Some of the newest features include organic chemistry and geology labs, computer stations, and new greenhouse spaces. The 105,000-square-foot Hall of Science has more student-faculty research labs, and enhanced classroom space. Off campus, Whitman operates an observatory and the Johnston Wilderness Center—a 27-acre mountain property serving as an environmental studies field station. The Hall of Music houses an acoustically perfect performance hall and twenty-seven practice rooms that are open 24 hours a day. After a comprehensive renovation in 2011, Harper Joy Theater consists of two main stages, black box theaters, and new classrooms. Cordiner Hall is a 1,500-seat auditorium featuring a 3,000-pipe Holtkamp organ. The Fouts Center for the Arts, a 38,000-square-foot visual arts facility, opened in fall 2008.

Costs

Tuition for 2012–13 is $41,790. Room and board cost is $10,560. The estimated cost of books, supplies, and incidentals is $1400. The associated student body fee is $336.

Financial Aid

Financial aid usually combines scholarships, student employment opportunities, and low-interest loans. In 2011–12, Whitman provided more than $23 million in scholarships. Forty-seven percent of Whitman students qualified for need-based aid. Roughly 50 percent of the students are employed on campus. Whitman also has an extensive merit scholarship program that rewards students who have demonstrated excellence in academics. These scholarships range from $7000 to $12,500 and are renewable for four years. Scholarships are also available for students with exceptional talent in art, music, debate, theater, and leadership. To apply for financial aid, students must submit the Free Application for Federal Student Aid (FAFSA) and the CSS PROFILE. Early decision candidates should apply for financial aid by January 1; regular decision and transfer candidates must apply by February 1.

Faculty

Whitman College's faculty is comprised of individuals selected, retained, and promoted for demonstrated effectiveness as teachers as well as for leadership within their chosen fields. Ninety-eight percent of faculty members hold a doctoral degree or terminal degree in their field, and all serve as academic advisers. The student-faculty ratio is 10:1. Recognized nationally for faculty accessibility, Whitman offers personal attention outside the classroom, setting it apart from peer institutions. Students collaborate with professors on research projects, compete with them on athletic fields, serve with them on College committees, and dine in their homes. In the past five years, Whitman faculty members have distinguished themselves by receiving awards, honors, and fellowships from the National Institute of Mental Health, National Endowment for the Humanities, Battelle Research Institute, Washington State Arts Commission, Burlington Northern Foundation, Department of Health and Human Services, and Department of Energy.

Student Government

The College encourages students to participate and take leadership roles in self-governing campus organizations. The largest of these is the Associated Students of Whitman College (ASWC), in which every student is a member. ASWC acts through an elected student congress and executive council and is responsible for the *Whitman*

Pioneer (a weekly student newspaper), choral contest, Renaissance Faire, campus radio station KWCW (90.5 FM), and a multitude of all-campus concerts, speakers, films, and social events.

Admission Requirements

Whitman is a highly selective college that seeks academic excellence and diversity within its student body. Competition for admission is keen; about 70 percent of entering first-year students ranked in the top 10 percent of their high school class. Ninety-three percent were in the top quarter. The Admission Committee looks for evidence of intellectual achievement, motivation, creativity, responsibility, and maturity. The middle 50 percent of the class of 2015 scored in the following ranges on the SAT: 640–730 critical reading, 620–700 math, and 630–710 writing. The minimum TOEFL scores for international students are 85 on the Internet-based test and 560 on the paper test. The following pattern of high school subjects is highly recommended: 4 years of English, mathematics, science, and history or social sciences; at least 2 years of a foreign language; and 1 year of an art elective. Students who have decided early in their senior year that Whitman is their first-choice school are encouraged to apply for admission through early decision.

Application and Information

The application deadlines and notification dates for admission to Whitman are: early decision candidates apply by November 15 or January 1 and receive notification of admission by December 20 or February 1; regular decision applicants for the fall semester apply by January 15, and letters are postmarked by April 1; transfer students apply by March 1 and receive notification by April 20; and spring-semester candidates (if space is available) apply by November 15 and receive notification by December 15. First-year candidates are required to submit the following credentials: the Common Application, including the School Report Form; secondary school transcript; one teacher recommendation; and an application fee of $50. Whitman also requires test scores (SAT or ACT) and a personal supplement (a selection of writing prompts).

For more information, students should contact:

Office of Admission
Whitman College
345 Boyer Avenue
Walla Walla, Washington 99362-2046
Phone: 509-527-5176
      877-462-9448 (toll-free)
Fax: 509-527-4967
E-mail: admission@whitman.edu
Web site: http://www.whitman.edu

Students on the Whitman College campus.

WILKES UNIVERSITY
WILKES-BARRE, PENNSYLVANIA

The University

Sitting in that first class at Wilkes University, students may notice something a little unexpected: professors and instructors genuinely interested in students' thoughts and aspirations.

A crucial part of personal engagement is hands-on learning. All Wilkes students can take advantage of numerous opportunities to get real-world experience in their field of interest, from starting a business to conducting research to actually using high-tech instruments that even graduate students at other institutions rarely touch.

Located at the foothills of the Pocono Mountains, along the shore of the Susquehanna River and within walking distance of downtown Wilkes-Barre, Pennsylvania, Wilkes University is a private, comprehensive institution with about 2,200 undergraduate students.

The University is structured into the College of Arts, Humanities, and Social Sciences; the College of Science and Engineering; the Nesbitt College of Pharmacy and Nursing; the Sidhu School of Business and Leadership; the School of Education; and University College (for undecided students). Wilkes offers a broad range of bachelor's and master's degree programs in the humanities, social and natural sciences, engineering, business administration, nursing, and education as well as the Master of Fine Arts, Doctor of Pharmacy, Doctor of Education, and Doctor of Nursing Practice degrees.

The Wilkes campus features a parklike quadrangle surrounded by modern classroom buildings and historic nineteenth-century mansions that have been restored as student residences and academic buildings. Campus facilities include a sports and conference center, an outdoor athletic complex and field house, a science classroom building, a modern academic classroom/office building, a performing arts center, an indoor recreation center, and a student center with a food court, café, entertainment rooms, post office, and ballroom. A new science building is scheduled to open in fall 2013.

Programs are designed to prepare students with a well-rounded liberal arts foundation that cultivates independent thinking and gives students the credentials necessary for entrance into graduate and professional schools and professional life. Academic advising integrated with career planning is stressed, and hands-on experiences are provided in laboratory, internship, and cooperative education settings. Free tutorial services are available to all students as well.

The University is accredited by the Middle States Association of Colleges and Schools and has specialized accreditation in the sciences, engineering, nursing, education, and business. More than 97 percent of students are employed or attending graduate/professional school within one year of receiving their degrees.

First-year students enrolling prior to May 1 are guaranteed housing, and all students may have cars on campus. Campus housing is available for all four years. Architecturally, residence halls vary from modern, multifloor buildings to mansions listed on the National Register of Historic Places. Medical and dental care, department stores, specialty shops, and other services are available within three blocks of campus. A large number of nearby houses of religious worship welcome students' participation.

At Wilkes University, student activities complement academic life. Intercollegiate athletics encompass sixteen Division III sports, and an active and varied intramural program is offered. Nearly seventy clubs and organizations recognize student achievement and provide opportunities for leadership development, professional growth, and community service. The student-run Programming Board schedules movies and performances by comedians, musicians, and other entertainers, while other organizations sponsor dinner dances, block parties, and special events. The professionally run Student Development Office organizes various activities based on leadership, adventure, or cultural themes, as well as coordinates a unique e-mentor program designed to assist freshmen with the transition to college life. Wilkes students are active community volunteers, participating in numerous local and national service projects each year.

Master's degrees are awarded in bioengineering (new), business administration, creative writing, education, electrical engineering, engineering management, mechanical engineering, mathematics, and nursing. The University also offers terminal degrees in the fields of creative writing (M.F.A.), education (Ed.D.), nursing practice (D.N.P.), and pharmacy (Pharm.D.). In addition, Wilkes is the first school in Pennsylvania to offer a dual Doctor of Pharmacy and Master of Business Administration degree.

Location

The Luzerne County seat, Wilkes-Barre is a medium-sized city of 43,000 in the midst of a metropolitan area of 400,000. A wide range of recreational facilities are minutes away, including PNC Field (home of the Scranton/Wilkes-Barre Yankees Triple A baseball team); the Mohegan Sun Arena, which serves as home for the Wilkes-Barre/Scranton Penguins hockey team; the Pocono Mountain ski resorts; numerous golf courses; state parks; outdoor tennis courts; and Pocono Downs harness racing.

The University is located in the historical district, between the entertainment and residential sections of the city. The entertainment district begins at the F. M. Kirby Center of Performing Arts, featuring symphony, ballet, theatrical, and musical performances, and encompasses the Wilkes University/King's College Barnes and Noble bookstore and café, a fourteen-screen movie complex, a nightclub, and numerous shops and restaurants. Other area cultural offerings include art galleries, ethnic and community festivals, and libraries and museums. The city is also approximately 2 hours from the cultural resources of both New York City and Philadelphia.

Wilkes-Barre is in proximity to the intersection of Interstates 80, 81, and 476 and within 3 to 6 hours of other major cities, such as Washington, D.C.; Baltimore; and Boston. The Wilkes-Barre/Scranton International Airport enables travelers to arrive at most domestic destinations via one-stop or nonstop flights.

Majors and Degrees

Wilkes University offers Bachelor of Arts, Bachelor of Business Administration, and Bachelor of Science degrees. Majors include accounting; applied and engineering sciences; biochemistry; biology; chemistry; clinical laboratory sciences; communications (concentrations in journalism, organizational communications, public relations, rhetoric and public communications, and telecommunications); computer information systems; computer science; criminology; earth and environmental sciences; electrical engineering; education: elementary and early childhood, middle-level, secondary (minor with a subject-area major), and special education (all with certification); engineering management; English (concentrations in literature and creative writing); entrepreneurship; environmental engineering; finance; history; integrative media; international studies; management; marketing; mathematics (new track in computational mathematics); mechanical engineering; musical theater; nursing; philosophy; physics; political science; psychology; sociology; Spanish; and theater arts. Wilkes also offers a guaranteed-seat first-professional program leading the Doctor of Pharmacy degree.

The premedical and prelaw preparation programs are particularly strong. In addition to the University's prepharmacy program, other preprofessional programs are available in dentistry, occupational therapy, optometry, physical therapy, physician assistant, podiatry, and veterinary science. The University offers affiliated programs in medicine with the Philadelphia College of Osteopathic Medicine and The Commonwealth Medical College; in optometry with the Pennsylvania College of Optometry and the State University of New York (SUNY) College of Optometry; in podiatry with Temple University School of Podiatric Medicine; in occupational therapy with Temple University; in physical therapy with Drexel University, Temple University, and

Widener University; in medical technology/clinical laboratory sciences with Robert Packer Hospital; and in psychology with Widener University.

Academic Programs

Through a rigorous curriculum that emphasizes hands-on experience and training, Wilkes helps prepare students in all majors to adapt to a technologically and socially evolving world. To graduate, students are required to complete a core curriculum and must complete from 120 to 136 credits, depending upon their major field. Graduates demonstrate mastery of the fundamental intellectual skills as well as the essential concepts and techniques of their field. Wilkes also teaches students responsibility and independence by expecting and encouraging active participation in the classroom and laboratory.

The University operates on a dual-semester calendar, with optional summer sessions and a January intersession. Advanced Placement test credits, College Level Examination Program (CLEP) credits, and International Baccalaureate (I.B.) credits are accepted.

Off-Campus Programs

An extensive cooperative education program is available to all students, with credit applicable in most major fields. Many government offices and private businesses in northeastern Pennsylvania, as well as in New York City, Philadelphia, Harrisburg, and Washington, D.C., employ Wilkes students. The study-abroad adviser works with interested students, placing them in the situation best suited to their academic pursuits. Most recently, students have attended programs in Austria, England, the Dominican Republic, France, Germany, Italy, and Spain.

Academic Facilities

The Eugene S. Farley Library has more than 220,000 volumes of books and bound journals, 857 current print journal and newspaper subscriptions, hundreds of database searches, and 800,000 microforms. Complete laboratory facilities are available for biology, chemistry, earth and environmental sciences, engineering, nursing, pharmacy, and psychology. Student-produced programming is broadcast from WCLH-FM, the University's 2,000-watt radio station, and transmitted from a professional-quality television studio via a local cable provider. Technology-enhanced classrooms contain Intel-based Apple computers for student use. The Sordoni Art Gallery is professionally equipped and staffed and produces exhibits each year by regionally, nationally, and internationally known artists. The Dorothy Dickson Darte Center for the Performing Arts contains a fully equipped 500-seat main theater and a 45-seat black box theater presentation of plays, concerts, ballet, and other performances and lectures. Adjoining the center are studios, practice and rehearsal rooms, and faculty offices for the Division of Performing Arts. Breiseth Hall accommodates extensive computer facilities, psychology research laboratories, an integrative media lab, and modern classrooms with the latest audiovisual equipment. The University also operates a state-of-the-art distance learning facility that allows global conferencing and study using Internet and videoconferencing technology.

Costs

For the 2012–13 academic year, tuition and fees are $29,326 per year, and room and board are $11,908. Books cost approximately $900 per year.

Financial Aid

Financial aid is available to those students who demonstrate quality academic ability and/or financial need, as verified by the Free Application for Federal Student Aid (FAFSA). Merit-based and need-based aid is available from Wilkes University for qualified students. Scholarships ranging from $6000 to $13,000 per year are available to students solely on the basis of academic ability. Approximately 96 percent of the student body receive some type of financial assistance, including scholarships, grants, loans, and work-study awards.

Faculty

Wilkes University has a nationally recruited full-time faculty of 157 members, approximately 90 percent of whom have earned Ph.D.'s or terminal degrees in their chosen field. Faculty evaluation criteria emphasize teaching excellence and effective advising, while recognizing continued scholarly activities. The student-faculty ratio is 14:1.

Student Government

An active student government provides a structure for student participation in University governance and student discipline. The Inter-Residence Hall Council and Commuter Council coordinate extracurricular activities for on-campus and commuter students.

Admission Requirements

Admission to Wilkes University is traditional. SAT or ACT scores are required. In cases where a student has taken the examination more than once, scores from the highest testing in each category are used in the evaluation process. Applicants for the freshman class should either have completed or be in the process of completing a college-preparatory course of study, including 3 to 4 years of mathematics, social studies, science, and English. Additional courses should be elected in academic subjects according to individual interests. Acceptable electives include foreign language and computing, among others. Students who have not followed this pattern may still qualify for admission if there is other strong evidence of preparation for college work. Letters of recommendation are not required but may be submitted. Students intending to pursue a major in pharmacy or a major in the College of Pharmacy and Nursing should have completed algebra I and II, geometry, and trigonometry prior to enrollment. Students intending to major in nursing should have completed courses in biology and chemistry. An audition is required for all prospective musical theater and theater arts students. Transfer students must submit a transcript from every college previously attended. All students are admitted to the University and not to specific departments, with the exception of the professional Nesbitt College of Pharmacy and Nursing and the Division of Performing Arts. Students individually receive academic advisement at the time of registration and throughout their enrollment.

Wilkes University is an Equal Opportunity/Affirmative Action institution. No applicant shall be denied admission to the University because of race, color, gender, religion, national or ethnic origin, sexual orientation, or handicap.

Application and Information

Applications for admission should be completed early in the senior year of secondary school and sent to the Admissions Office. Applications are reviewed after all of the student's credentials have been received. The review of applications begins on September 15, and notification of the University's decision reaches the student two to four weeks after the application file is complete. The priority deadline for all applications is March 1; applications for the Guaranteed Seat Pharmacy Program must be received by February 1. Other health science programs may have additional deadlines; students should contact the Admissions Office for more information.

Admissions Office
Wilkes University
84 West South Street
Wilkes-Barre, Pennsylvania 18766
Phone: 570-408-4400
        800-945-5378 Ext. 4400 (toll-free)
Web site: http://www.wilkes.edu

The campus of Wilkes University.

WILLIAM PATERSON UNIVERSITY OF NEW JERSEY
WAYNE, NEW JERSEY

The University

William Paterson University offers a supportive and challenging environment that encourages students to push themselves, gain confidence, and understand that remarkable things are within their reach. A public institution located in suburban Wayne, New Jersey, it serves more than 11,500 full- and part-time students through five colleges: College of the Arts and Communication, Cotsakos College of Business, College of Education, College of Humanities and Social Sciences, and College of Science and Health.

The University is accredited by the Middle States Commission on Higher Education. Students can choose from 250 undergraduate and graduate academic programs on a beautiful campus with the facilities and equipment students need to succeed. Located on a 370-acre hilly, wooded site, William Paterson borders on High Mountain Preserve, which is nearly 1,200 acres of wetlands and woodlands; the campus is just three miles from Paterson's historic Great Falls and only 20 miles from the rich cultural, artistic, and commercial life of New York City.

William Paterson's small classes are taught by professors who are experts in their fields. Students enjoy individualized attention from faculty mentors who are committed to helping them develop strengths and uncover new ones. Financial aid is available to qualified students.

William Paterson offers students an active campus experience. Twenty-four percent of undergraduates reside on campus in ten residence halls or apartment-style facilities, which accommodate 2,600 students. Portions of the residence halls are dedicated to dynamic learning communities, as well as substance-free living.

Social, cultural, and recreational activities complement the academic programs. Cultural events take place throughout the year, featuring both William Paterson's own talent as well as renowned professional artists. Among events are concerts presenting jazz, classical, and contemporary music; theater productions; gallery exhibits; and the University's Distinguished Lecturer Series. The University Commons complex, including the John Victor Machuga Student Center, is the heart of the campus. This state-of-the-art campus center provides students with an exquisite setting for a vast array of social and extracurricular activities, dining venues, and student support services. There are more than eighty-five clubs and organizations to develop diverse activities for the entire student body. William Paterson has twenty-five social fraternities and sororities, and twenty-four honor societies. Students staff the award-winning campus radio station (WPSC) and the television station (WPC-TV), which develops a number of widely distributed television programs for local and statewide cable networks. The Recreation Center serves as the focal point for physical recreation. The 4,000-seat facility accommodates badminton, basketball, indoor tennis, volleyball, and racquetball courts, an exercise room, saunas, and Jacuzzis. "Pioneer spirit" is evident in the University's thirteen intercollegiate sports and numerous NCAA Division III post-season tournament appearances. In 2011, the Pioneers won first place in the All Girl Division college cheerleading and dance team national championship. Other club sports include the nationally ranked ice hockey, bowling, and rugby teams. Equestrian is also a club sport. The University has a competition-size indoor pool, outdoor tennis courts, and a lighted athletics field complex.

Majors and Degrees

Students can pursue B.A., B.S., B.F.A., B.M., and B.S.N. degrees through the University's five colleges.

Bachelor of Arts degrees are granted in Africana world studies, anthropology, art, art history, Asian studies, communication, communication disorders, criminology and criminal justice, early childhood education, earth science, economics, elementary education, English, French and francophone studies, geography, history, Latin American and Latino studies, legal studies, liberal studies, mathematics, music, philosophy, political science, psychology, secondary education, sociology, Spanish, sport management, and women's and gender studies.

Bachelor of Science degree programs include accounting, applied health, athletic training, biology, biotechnology, chemistry, computer science, environmental science, environmental sustainability, exercise science, global business, finance, financial planning, management, marketing, mathematics, physical education, professional sales, and public health.

The Bachelor of Fine Arts degree is awarded in fine arts. In the Bachelor of Music degree program, students can choose between performance, jazz, music education, and music management. The Bachelor of Science in Nursing is also offered.

Certification is available in bilingual education, early childhood, elementary, secondary, special education, and teacher of students with disabilities (TSD).

Academic Programs

The baccalaureate degree requires students to earn 120 credits in order to graduate. Approximately 31 to 40 of those credits are earned in University core curriculum (UCC) classes. Another 30 to 60 come from work in the student's major, and 20 to 40 can be earned in electives. UCC classes and major requirements will vary. The Career Development and Advisement Center counsels and advises students who are undecided as to their major, as well as their career choices.

Programs in the University Honors College offer students further challenges and include tracks in biopsychology, cognitive science, humanities, independent study, life science and environmental ethics, management, marketing, music, nursing, performing and literary arts, and social sciences. There are also preprofessional programs in dentistry, engineering, law, medicine (which includes dentistry, optometry, podiatry, and veterinary science), pharmacy, physical therapy, and speech-language pathology. Military experience may also be evaluated for credit.

Off-Campus Programs

William Paterson offers a special opportunity for off-campus study. Semester Abroad, a 15-credit program, is open to sophomores and juniors who wish to study for a semester at selected institutions in Australia, Denmark, Great Britain, Greece, Israel, Spain, and other countries around the world.

Academic Facilities

The newly expanded and renovated Science Complex features smart classrooms and sophisticated research laboratories designed to foster an interactive learning environment. The 1600 Valley Road facility houses the Cotsakos College of Business with its state-of-the-art Financial Learning Center, the Russ Berrie Institute, the Russ Berrie Professional Sales Lab, the College of Education, the Center for Continuing and Professional Education, and classrooms and computer laboratories. The Atrium contains computing support facilities, such as a writing center, multimedia language lab, and tutorial center. Among other academic resources are a nursing instructional facility, speech and hearing clinic, and child-care center. Hobart Hall, a state-of-the-art communication facility, houses television studios,

computer labs, a film studio, an FCC-licensed FM radio station, and an uplink and four downlink satellite dishes. The site of the Allan and Michele Gorab Alumni House contains a pond, wetlands, woods, and a living laboratory for courses in biology and the environmental sciences. The David and Lorraine Cheng Library is open seven days a week when classes are in session and contains a collection of more than 360,000 volumes and 17,000 audiovisual items, with access to more than 50,000 electronic and print periodicals and journals. Cultural activities are supported by Shea Center for Performing Arts, which houses a 922-seat theater, as well as band, choral, and orchestral practice rooms and classrooms. The Ben Shahn Center for Visual Arts features extensive galleries, as well as art studios and classrooms, while the Power Art Center includes faculty offices and studios for three-dimensional design, photography, sculpture, ceramics, printmaking, woodworking, and painting.

Costs

Annual tuition (including fees) for the 2011–12 academic year was $11,464 for full-time (12 credits or more) students who are New Jersey residents and $18,628 for full-time nonresident students. Room and board cost approximately $10,180 per year. Total annual costs for a student living on campus were $21,644 for New Jersey residents and $28,808 for out-of-state students. These amounts are subject to change by the University's Board of Trustees.

Financial Aid

William Paterson provides a first-rate education at a reasonable cost. In accordance with the University's commitment to value in education, federal and state need-based financial aid programs are offered in the forms of grants, loans, scholarships, and work-study programs. In order to apply for financial aid, students should submit the Free Application for Federal Student Aid (FAFSA) to the United States Department of Education by April 1.

Each year, more than 1,600 scholarships are awarded for academic achievement, exceptional character qualities, leadership excellence, and financial need, totalling nearly $7 million.

Faculty

William Paterson's 389 full-time and 628 part-time faculty members bring to the classroom a valuable blend of accomplished scholarship and practical, applied experience. Faculty members assist students with curriculum and career planning, which engenders open, personal communication between the students and faculty.

Through a formal reciprocal exchange relationship with various institutions worldwide, and through the Fulbright Scholarship Program, William Paterson University often receives visiting international scholars. The University's faculty members have won more than thirty-six Fulbright awards, one of the most prestigious academic distinctions in the world.

Student Government

The Student Government Association (SGA), of which all full-time and part-time students are automatically members, has become an influential voice in University decision making. Elected officers and various committees convey students' perspectives to the administration and advance their causes. The SGA is also responsible for chartering campus organizations and allocating student activity fees.

Admission Requirements

Admission is competitive. Admissions decisions for entering freshmen are based on a complete review of the students' academic record (course of study, grades, and rank) as well as the results of the SAT or ACT. Applicants are considered eligible if they have taken a minimum of 16 Carnegie units and have demonstrated strong academic ability. The students' secondary school record must show the following courses: English, 4 years (composition and literature); mathematics, 3 years (algebra I and II and geometry); laboratory science, 2 years (biology, chemistry, or physics); social science, 2 years (American history, world history, or political science); and additional college-preparatory subjects, 5 units (advanced mathematics, literature, foreign language, or social sciences). In addition, students selecting a major in art or music (except musical studies) must submit a portfolio for review by the Art Department or must audition for the Music Department.

Transfer students must present at least 12 college-level credits with a minimum 2.0 GPA; science and nursing majors must have a recommended GPA of 3.0, and teacher certification program applicants must have a minimum 2.75 GPA. Applicants with fewer than 12 college credits must submit a high school transcript. Communication disorders majors must have a GPA of 3.5 and maintain a GPA of 3.3 once admitted to the graduate portion of the program. There are some limitations on the number of credits accepted; for example, a maximum of 70 credits from a two-year institution or 90 credits from a four-year college or university. Application review is completed only upon receipt of official transcripts from high schools and especially colleges and universities. Unofficial transcripts or transcripts sent by students will not be used for admissions.

Application and Information

Application forms and transcripts from candidates for freshman status must be received by June 1 for fall admission and December 1 for spring admission. Freshmen scholarship candidates must submit completed application and supporting materials by February 15 for fall scholarship consideration; transfer students by May 1. Transfer students, readmitted students, and students seeking a second bachelor's degree must submit their materials by June 1 and December 1 for fall and spring entry, respectively. However, the University closes the application process earlier when the number of new and continuing students strains its ability to provide effective programs and services. A $50 application fee is required. Applications are reviewed on a rolling basis. Campus tours are available during the fall and spring semesters on weekdays by appointment when classes are in session. Sign up for a campus tour at www.wpunj.edu/campusvisit or take a virtual tour at www.wpunj.edu/virtualtour.

Office of Admissions
William Paterson University of New Jersey
Wayne, New Jersey 07470
Phone: 973-720-2125
E-mail: admissions@wpunj.edu
Web site: http://www.wpunj.edu
http://apps.facebook.com/williampaterson
http://twitter.com/wpunj_admission

William Paterson University's hilltop suburban campus offers an environment where students may develop both intellectually and socially.

WILLIAM PEACE UNIVERSITY
RALEIGH, NORTH CAROLINA

The University

William Peace University is a four-year private coeducational university in Raleigh, North Carolina. The University has made bold strides to meet the challenges of higher education in the twenty-first century and offers innovative academic programs rooted in the liberal arts tradition to prepare students for careers in the organizations of tomorrow. William Peace University students develop an appreciation for lifelong learning, pursue meaningful careers, and build skills for ethical citizenship. The institution was founded in 1857 and named for founding benefactor William Peace, an elder of the First Presbyterian Church of Raleigh.

On average, 90 percent of William Peace University graduates find jobs or are enrolled in graduate school within a year of graduation.

Location

William Peace University is located at 15 East Peace Street in downtown Raleigh. The State Capitol, Legislative Building, State Library, North Carolina Symphony, and several museums (art, history, and natural sciences) lie within a few blocks of the campus. Raleigh is also one of the cities that compose North Carolina's Research Triangle Park. Duke University, North Carolina State, and the University of North Carolina at Chapel Hill are all located within the Triangle. Many publications, such as *Forbes, Business Week,* and *Bloomberg,* have identified the Triangle area as business-friendly and one that creates thousands of new jobs.

Majors and Degrees

Bachelor of Arts degrees are offered in biology (allied health), communication, education (elementary, special education, or a blended program of elementary and special education), English, liberal studies, political science, pre-law, and psychology. Bachelor of Science degrees are offered in biology (pre-med, pre-dental, pre-vet, and nursing) and business administration. William Peace University also offers a Bachelor of Fine Arts degree in acting and musical theater, and several minors and concentrations in fields such as graphic design, religion, anthropology, global studies, history, leadership studies, and Spanish.

Academic Programs

The baccalaureate degree is granted upon successful completion of the appropriate curriculum presented below and upon satisfaction of the following ancillary requirements for all degrees:

- A cumulative GPA of at least 2.00 on all academic credit and a minimum of 120 earned semester hours

- A GPA of at least 2.00 on course work designated as being in the major, concentration, or minor for the baccalaureate program of study chosen; when calculating the GPA, all courses with a disciplinary designation (i.e., all English courses for English majors) and any other courses that are required for that major will be counted. All course grades

made in these courses will be calculated in the major, concentration, or minor GPA.

- Successful completion of the liberal education requirements

- Satisfactory participation in the University's Assessment Program

- Satisfaction of financial obligations to the University

The educational experience at William Peace University goes beyond the classroom. Students are taught the skills necessary to succeed in both their professional and personal lives.

A new core curriculum focuses on ethical decision making and basic knowledge needed beyond graduation. There are also mandatory courses in personal financial management, media literacy, and four years of writing courses within the English department.

Students are required to take a series of three classes focusing on career and professional development. Students are taught via a portfolio seminar how to construct a resume, build a portfolio, interview for jobs, and/or apply for graduate studies.

An academic internship related to the student's major is required in order to combine educational theory with job experience.

Students have the opportunity to expand their knowledge through living experiences in countries around the world. A signature summer program at William Peace University helps students focus on the Mexican culture and civilization while living in Yucatan, Mexico.

Students are encouraged to serve the community and embrace the concept of giving back by reaching out. On average, the student body contributes 8,000 hours of community service annually.

Academic Facilities

The Lucy Cooper Finch Library provides on-campus access to over 47,000 books, as well as journals, videos, scores, and other materials. The library's online collection includes extensive research databases for journal articles, e-books, streaming videos, and images. For materials not found in the library's collections, cooperative lending agreements with local colleges and universities as well as nationwide interlibrary loan services offer students access to the resources they need.

All academic facilities are networked and have Internet access. Computer laboratories, the library and the student publications area are equipped with state-of-the-art computer hardware and software. Other specialized computer laboratories are also available in the biology, media, theater, and visual communication departments. Student laboratories in the chemistry, general biology, and molecular and cellular biology departments are available. A recital hall in the music building, the Leggett Theater, and a dance studio are available for students in the fine arts department.

Costs

For 2012–13, tuition and fees for full-time study are $11,850 per semester.

Financial Aid

Students and/or their families are expected to pay for educational expenses to the extent that it is possible. However, it is William Peace University's goal that no student is denied the opportunity to attend because of financial need. Accordingly, the University administers a generous program of financial aid, including Federal Work-Study Program opportunities, Federal Pell Grants, Federal Supplemental Educational Opportunity Grants, and North Carolina State Contractual Scholarship Grants. The University administers loans under the Federal Family Education Loan Program and offers both scholarships and grants to all eligible students.

To apply for financial aid, students must submit a completed FAFSA, either to the processor or to the University, for electronic processing. The University's FAFSA code is 002953. Applicants must demonstrate financial need and show evidence of academic promise or academic achievement to receive assistance from federally funded programs. Students may also apply for William Peace University scholarships by completing an application form that is available from the University's Office of Financial Aid.

Faculty

Full-time faculty members teach a majority of the courses and advise students, while part-time faculty members teach courses in their areas of specialization. Because Peace is an undergraduate institution that focuses on excellent teaching, all classes, including laboratories, are taught by faculty, not teaching assistants. All are engaged in their respective academic disciplines and bring cutting-edge knowledge into their classrooms. Many faculty members involve students in their research and creative activities, and the University supports students presenting their research findings and creative pursuits at regional and national conferences. William Peace University maintains a student-faculty ratio of 11:1.

Student Government

The William Peace University Student Government Association (SGA) is comprised of student leaders, both elected and appointed, who focus on the individual and collective needs of the student body. The SGA works cooperatively with the University faculty and administration to create positive avenues of change and growth. The SGA promotes responsibility for upholding the highest standards of university life through honor and integrity. In addition to being the voice of the student body, the SGA is actively engaged in sponsoring and encouraging participation in a number of traditions and student activities throughout the year. These include Stunt Night, Honor Week, Fall Fest, and Spring Fling.

As the governing body for Peace students, the SGA has approximately 35 voting members representing various campus constituencies. Every student is a member of the SGA and its weekly meetings are open to students. All students are responsible for their self-governance at Peace under the Honor System.

Admission Requirements

William Peace University recruits and admits students who are likely to benefit from its academic programs and who are also likely to contribute to the life of the University community. The University encourages students with varied talents and interests representative of all social, economic, ethnic, and racial backgrounds to apply.

Applications are reviewed individually. Decisions are based on the following credentials: course selection, grade point average in academic courses (see minimum required courses, below), SAT or ACT scores and class rank.

Further consideration is given to an applicant's personal qualifications, potential for success, and ability to add to the social, cultural, and spiritual environment that William Peace University is known for. The major criteria for admission are the strength of the high school courses taken, the grades in the academic courses, and scores on the standardized tests.

To meet the minimum academic requirements, applicants must complete 4 units of English, 3 units of mathematics (algebra I, algebra II, and geometry), 3 units of science, 3 units of social science, and 2 units of the same foreign language. Students are encouraged to take additional courses in math and science when possible.

Application and Information

Admissions decisions are made on a rolling basis. The Admissions Committee begins reviewing applications in September for the following fall.

The University requires each freshman applicant to submit an application, a nonrefundable $25 fee, SAT or ACT scores (senior-year scores are preferred), and an official transcript of all courses taken in high school. Transfer applicants must also submit official transcripts from all colleges attended.

Inquiry cards and application forms may be completed at the University's website. Application forms and additional information may be obtained by contacting:

Office of Admissions
William Peace University
15 East Peace Street
Raleigh, North Carolina 27604
Phone: 919-508-2214
      800-PEACE-47
Fax: 919-508-2306
Web site: http://www.peace.edu

William Peace University provides a liberal arts–based higher education with innovative academic programs that prepare students for the future.

WORCESTER POLYTECHNIC INSTITUTE
WORCESTER, MASSACHUSETTS

The University

Worcester Polytechnic Institute (WPI) believes in the power of its students to make an impact. They may want to be on the first Mars mission, find alternative energy sources, or work on cancer research. To prepare them for leadership and achievement after college, students do much more than study science and technology in the classroom and lab. They complete projects on campus and around the globe where they connect what they have learned in the classroom with pressing real-life challenges, from human health and the environment to business and engineering as well as the arts and humanities. Students grow personally, professionally, and intellectually as they discover how to apply their talents and turn ideas into tangible solutions.

WPI's aim is to educate students broadly so they can achieve greatly. Though WPI has a more than 145-year history, the curriculum, like its students, is both innovative and practical. Small classes, a flexible curriculum, and one-on-one interaction with professors at the top of their field make learning at WPI an experience unlike any other.

WPI has been widely recognized for its academic program. WPI was the only technological university out of sixteen national Leadership Institutions selected by the Association of American Colleges and Universities to serve as models of outstanding practices in liberal education. WPI is consistently ranked among the top national universities by *U.S. News & World Report*. In the National Survey of Student Engagement, WPI ranked number one for student-faculty interactions, which is a measure of the quality and quantity of time faculty members spend with undergraduates.

More than thirty areas of study in engineering, science, business management, and the liberal arts allow many academic options, from molecular biology to music. Exciting new interdisciplinary programs are driven by real-world demand, such as interactive media and game development, robotics engineering, and environmental studies and engineering. The school also offers preprofessional programs and a five-year B.S./M.S. program.

With so many offerings, it is not surprising that more than 40 percent of students change their major at least once. At WPI, a comprehensive academic advising program and a wide array of academic support services help students make the right choices and reach their goals.

WPI students have received some of the nation's highest academic honors: the prestigious Marshall Scholarship, the NIH–Oxford/Cambridge Biomedical Research Scholarship, the Fulbright Scholarship, the Goldwater Scholarship, the Rotary Ambassadorial Scholarship, and the Society of Women Engineers Award. In addition, 2 students were recently named to the *USA Today* All-USA College Academic Team.

WPI is a member of the Colleges of Worcester Consortium, through which WPI students may register for courses at other colleges within the consortium and may take advantage of a wide range of cultural programming offered by consortium members. A consortium shuttle provides free transportation between campuses.

WPI has twenty varsity (NCAA Division III) athletics teams and thirty-four club and intramural sports. WPI won the Worcester Cup for four of the last six years for the highest overall winning percentage in all sports in Worcester County. There are thirteen fraternities and five sororities, more than fifteen music or theater ensembles, and dozens of academic clubs, international organizations, religious groups, and other organizations. There are more than 200 student clubs and activities.

Location

With its beautiful architecture, grassy quad, and ivy-covered walls, WPI has a traditional New England campus. Students stop and chat with their friends and professors on tree-lined paths, play pool between classes at the Campus Center, or get a coffee with friends. They study in the sun by the fountain in Reunion Plaza, go cosmic bowling, stop and smell the roses in the formal English garden behind Higgins House, or see a student play at the Little Theatre.

Home to twelve other colleges and universities and more than 35,000 college students, Worcester is a great college town. Late-night diners, clubs, museums, concert venues, and theaters are right down the hill from WPI in Worcester's vibrant downtown. Boston is less than an hour away by commuter rail, and there are great skiing and snowboarding at nearby Wachusett Mountain. Worcester is centrally located, with easy access to Providence, New York City, the Berkshires, the White Mountains, and Cape Cod.

Majors and Degrees

WPI offers the Bachelor of Science and the Bachelor of Arts degrees. Degree programs are offered in a wide variety of engineering and science: disciplines: actuarial mathematics, aerospace engineering, biochemistry, biology and biotechnology, biomedical engineering, chemical engineering, chemistry, civil engineering, computer science, electrical and computer engineering, environmental engineering, environmental science, fire protection engineering, industrial engineering, interactive media and game development, mathematical sciences, mechanical engineering, physics, and robotics engineering.

In addition, there are programs in the areas of business and liberal arts: business/management; economics; environmental and sustainability studies; history; humanities and arts; international studies; literature; management engineering; management information systems; music; philosophy and religion; professional writing; psychology/psychological science; society, technology, and policy; system dynamics; and theater.

Four new interdisciplinary majors have been added to the curriculum: interactive media and game development, environmental engineering, bioinformatics and computational biology, and robotics engineering, which is the first undergraduate program in robotics in the nation. WPI offers several preprofessional programs, including dentistry, law, medicine, and veterinary medicine. Students may also design their own majors by combining courses offered in various WPI departments. Undergraduates who wish to continue their studies toward a master's degree at WPI may enroll in a combined, continuous B.S./M.S. program.

Academic Programs

Students take the equivalent of three courses (as either traditional courses or project work) during each of four 7-week terms (two in the fall and two in the spring). At WPI, learning is about more than just theories and ideas. Students learn how to put ideas into practice through the project-enriched curriculum. WPI undergraduates complete two projects before graduation: one directly related to their major and one working with a team of students to solve a problem at the intersection of society and technology—helping to bring electricity to remote villages in Thailand or studying the bioethics of cloning, for example. Students gain valuable professional skills, a talent for teamwork, and the confidence to dive right in no matter what the challenge.

WPI's academic program encourages collaboration, not competition. Students work closely together in project-oriented classes. Learning how to work in teams prepares students to achieve results and become leaders in life after college, no matter what path they take.

Top-tier employers seek out WPI graduates for their real-world experience and ability to work collaboratively. With a placement rate of more than 90 percent, students are recruited by leading organizations such as Pfizer, General Electric, Fidelity Investments, and IBM. Each year, WPI graduates are accepted at many prestigious

graduate schools, including MIT, Yale, Princeton, Johns Hopkins, and Tufts University Medical School.

WPI graduates' starting salaries are higher than those of many other college graduates, according to the National Association of Colleges and Employers. In addition, WPI was recently recognized by the *Boston Globe* for having the third highest average starting salaries in New England and the twelfth highest of all universities in the nation.

Off-Campus Programs

WPI has sent more engineering and science students abroad than any other university as part of its hands-on, project-enriched curriculum. About half of WPI students complete projects outside the United States and two-thirds do projects off campus. With WPI's Global Perspective Program, students experience the challenge of solving real-world problems with their fellow students and immerse themselves in another culture. Students complete projects on campus or at any of the more than twenty-five project centers located on five continents around the globe, including Thailand, Australia, South Africa, Costa Rica, and the U.S. Recent project sponsors include NASA Johnson Space Center, Johnson & Johnson, Morgan Stanley, Environmental Protection Agency, and UNESCO. Through their seven-week project experience, students learn valuable professional skills, including communication, teamwork, and problem solving.

Academic Facilities

Among the many teaching, research, and project facilities available to undergraduates at WPI are a 71,000-square-foot campus center and a new Life Sciences and Bioengineering Center at Gateway Park, which is a state-of-the-art 130,000-square-foot facility at the life sciences-based campus that houses research in regenerative medicine, molecular nanotechnology, biosensors, plant systems, tissue engineering, and untethered health care. An $11-million renovation created the undergraduate Life Sciences Laboratory Center, which opened in 2009. The center has become WPI's main facility for undergraduate teaching and research in biology and biotechnology, biomedical engineering, chemistry and biochemistry, and chemical engineering. WPI's other state-of-the-art research facilities include two atomic-force microscopes, medical imaging laboratories, a fire science laboratory, a new team-based chemistry lab, a laser holography lab, a computer music lab, a satellite navigation lab, thirty multimedia classrooms and lecture halls, and a research library with thousands of electronic journals, books, databases, and nearly 300,000 volumes.

The university also has an exceptional computer and networking infrastructure. The facilities include nearly 600 computers in open-access, 24/7 labs; powerful UNIX workstations; a Web-based student information system; a high-speed data network that reaches every building and residence hall; and extensive roaming wireless access.

In addition to these existing facilities, a state-of-the-art apartment-style residence hall, with over 200 beds, opened in fall 2008. The building features recreation and fitness space, technology suites on the each floor, meeting rooms on the ground floor for group projects, and wireless access.

WPI opened a brand-new sports and recreation center in 2012. It includes a four-court gymnasium, indoor jogging track, 14,000 square feet of fitness space, racquetball and squash courts, competition pool, workout studios, and rowing tanks.

Costs

For 2012–13, full-time tuition will be $40,790. Room and board charges are $12,650.

Financial Aid

For families with established financial need, aid, including financial aid packages, on-campus jobs, and loan programs, is available. In addition, all applicants are considered for merit scholarships. More information is available from WPI's Office of Financial Aid Web site at http://www.wpi.edu/+finaid.

Faculty

Besides being passionate about teaching, WPI's 396 full- and part-time faculty members are committed researchers and scholars with world-class credentials. They are leading contributors to the fields of bioengineering, cryptography, energy, fuel cells, information technology, and more. Thirteen members of the current faculty are Fulbright Scholars, and more than 50 are fellows of top national and international societies. Since 1994, 17 WPI professors have won the National Science Foundation's CAREER Award, which is its most prestigious award for young faculty members. WPI has a 14:1 student-faculty ratio. According to *U.S. News & World Report*, faculty resources, which include salary, class size, and student-faculty ratio, rank thirtieth among national universities.

Student Government

Through the Student Government Association, the Interfraternity Council, the Panhellenic Association, and the International Student Council, students self-govern and develop their own social programs. WPI prides itself on being a caring community that respects the contributions of individuals, appreciates the diversity of the student body, and emphasizes the importance of cooperation and teamwork.

Admission Requirements

Applicants for admission must have completed 4 years of English, 4 years of mathematics (including precalculus), and 2 years of lab science. Admission requirements include a school transcript, SAT or ACT scores or alternative materials through WPI's Flex Path, recommendations from a science or math teacher and a counselor, and a personal essay. For international students whose first language is not English, a TOEFL or IELTS score is required.

The university has high standards for applicants but also looks for more than just outstanding academic performance. WPI takes care to admit students who will likely thrive at the university. They tend to be creative and curious; like to work in teams to get things done; are comfortable making their own decisions and setting their own courses; love math and science but feel just as passionate about literature, music, movies, and the arts; prefer to be leaders, not followers; and are ready to make a positive impact on the world around them.

Students are encouraged to visit the WPI campus to learn more about the university, see its facilities, and hear firsthand about the WPI experience from students and faculty members. WPI is open most school holidays and offers a wide range of options for tours, group information sessions, open houses, personal interviews, and Saturday visits. Details and schedules may be obtained from the Admissions Office Web site.

The deadline for early action round 1 is November 10, with notification by December 20. The deadline for early action round 2 is January 1, with notification by February 10. The regular decision deadline is February 1, with notification by April 1. For transfer admissions, the priority deadline is April 15; students are notified of admission decisions on a rolling basis.

Application and Information

To schedule a visit or request more information, students should contact:
Office of Admissions
Bartlett Center
Worcester Polytechnic Institute
100 Institute Road
Worcester, Massachusetts 01609-2280
Phone: 508-831-5286
Fax: 508-831-5875
E-mail: admissions@wpi.edu
Web site: http://admissions.wpi.edu
       http://www.facebook.com/WPIAdmissions
       http://twitter.com/WPIAdmissions

Indexes

Majors

INDEXES

U of Rio Grande (OH)
U of St. Francis (IL)
U of Saint Francis (IN)
U of Saint Joseph (CT)
U of Saint Mary (KS)
U of St. Thomas (MN)
U of St. Thomas (TX)
U of San Diego (CA)
The U of Scranton (PA)
U of South Alabama (AL)
U of South Carolina (SC)
The U of South Dakota (SD)
U of Southern California (CA)
U of Southern Indiana (IN)
U of Southern Maine (ME)
U of Southern Mississippi (MS)
U of South Florida (FL)
U of South Florida–St. Petersburg Campus (FL)
The U of Tampa (FL)
The U of Tennessee (TN)
The U of Tennessee at Martin (TN)
The U of Texas at Arlington (TX)
The U of Texas at Austin (TX)
The U of Texas at Dallas (TX)
The U of Texas at El Paso (TX)
The U of Texas at San Antonio (TX)
The U of Texas at Tyler (TX)
The U of Texas of the Permian Basin (TX)
The U of Texas–Pan American (TX)
U of the Cumberlands (KY)
U of the Incarnate Word (TX)
U of the Ozarks (AR)
U of the Southwest (NM)
The U of Toledo (OH)
U of Toronto (ON, Canada)
U of Tulsa (OK)
U of Utah (UT)
The U of Virginia's Coll at Wise (VA)
U of Washington (WA)
U of Washington, Bothell (WA)
The U of West Alabama (AL)
The U of Western Ontario (ON, Canada)
U of West Florida (FL)
U of West Georgia (GA)
U of Windsor (ON, Canada)
U of Wisconsin–Eau Claire (WI)
U of Wisconsin–Green Bay (WI)
U of Wisconsin–La Crosse (WI)
U of Wisconsin–Madison (WI)
U of Wisconsin–Milwaukee (WI)
U of Wisconsin–Platteville (WI)
U of Wisconsin–River Falls (WI)
U of Wisconsin–Stevens Point (WI)
U of Wisconsin–Superior (WI)
U of Wisconsin–Whitewater (WI)
U of Wyoming (WY)
Upper Iowa U (IA)
Ursuline Coll (OH)
Utah State U (UT)
Utah Valley U (UT)
Utica Coll (NY)
Valdosta State U (GA)
Valparaiso U (IN)
Vanguard U of Southern California (CA)
Villanova U (PA)
Virginia Commonwealth U (VA)
Virginia Polytechnic Inst and State U (VA)
Virginia State U (VA)
Virginia Union U (VA)
Viterbo U (WI)
Wagner Coll (NY)
Wake Forest U (NC)
Walden U (MN)
Walsh U (OH)
Wartburg Coll (IA)
Washburn U (KS)
Washington & Jefferson Coll (PA)
Washington State U (WA)
Washington U in St. Louis (MO)
Waynesburg U (PA)
Wayne State U (MI)
Webber Intl U (FL)
Weber State U (UT)
Webster U (MO)
West Chester U of Pennsylvania (PA)
Western Carolina U (NC)
Western Connecticut State U (CT)
Western Illinois U (IL)
Western Intl U (AZ)

Western Kentucky U (KY)
Western Michigan U (MI)
Western New England U (MA)
Western State Coll of Colorado (CO)
West Liberty U (WV)
Westminster Coll (MO)
Westminster Coll (UT)
West Texas A&M U (TX)
West Virginia State U (WV)
West Virginia U (WV)
West Virginia U Inst of Technology (WV)
West Virginia Wesleyan Coll (WV)
Wheeling Jesuit U (WV)
Wichita State U (KS)
Widener U (PA)
Wilkes U (PA)
William Jewell Coll (MO)
William Paterson U of New Jersey (NJ)
William Penn U (IA)
William Woods U (MO)
Wilmington Coll (OH)
Wilmington U (DE)
Wilson Coll (PA)
Wingate U (NC)
Winona State U (MN)
Wofford Coll (SC)
Woodbury U (CA)
Wright State U (OH)
Xavier U (OH)
Xavier U of Louisiana (LA)
Yeshiva U (NY)
York Coll of Pennsylvania (PA)
York Coll of the City U of New York (NY)
Youngstown State U (OH)

ACCOUNTING AND BUSINESS/MANAGEMENT

Alaska Pacific U (AK)
Babson Coll (MA)
Bethel U (TN)
Chestnut Hill Coll (PA)
East Carolina U (NC)
EDP Coll of Puerto Rico, Inc. (PR)
EDP Coll of Puerto Rico–San Sebastian (PR)
Florida Inst of Technology (FL)
Illinois State U (IL)
Keystone Coll (PA)
Maranatha Baptist Bible Coll (WI)
Mercy Coll (NY)
Mitchell Coll (CT)
Rasmussen Coll Appleton (WI)
Rasmussen Coll Fort Myers (FL)
Rasmussen Coll Green Bay (WI)
Rasmussen Coll Land O' Lakes (FL)
Rasmussen Coll New Port Richey (FL)
Rasmussen Coll Ocala (FL)
Rasmussen Coll Tampa/Brandon (FL)
Rasmussen Coll Wausau (WI)
Rocky Mountain Coll (MT)
Santa Clara U (CA)
Sierra Nevada Coll (NV)
Spalding U (KY)
Tabor Coll (KS)
U of Great Falls (MT)
U of Illinois at Urbana–Champaign (IL)
The U of Western Ontario (ON, Canada)
Washington and Lee U (VA)
Western State Coll of Colorado (CO)

ACCOUNTING AND COMPUTER SCIENCE

California State U, Chico (CA)
Fordham U (NY)
Goldey-Beacom Coll (DE)
Husson U (ME)
Southern New Hampshire U (NH)

ACCOUNTING AND FINANCE

Babson Coll (MA)
Bentley U (MA)
Bethel U (MN)
Boise State U (ID)
Bridgewater State U (MA)

Clarkson U (NY)
DEREE - The American Coll of Greece (Greece)
Drake U (IA)
Eastern U (PA)
Ferris State U (MI)
Lourdes U (OH)
Northern Michigan U (MI)
Saint Francis U (PA)
Salem State U (MA)
Simmons Coll (MA)
U of North Dakota (ND)
U of Southern Maine (ME)
The U of Western Ontario (ON, Canada)
U of Windsor (ON, Canada)
Western State Coll of Colorado (CO)

ACCOUNTING RELATED

Bentley U (MA)
Brigham Young U (UT)
Central Michigan U (MI)
Duquesne U (PA)
Franklin U (OH)
Maryville U of Saint Louis (MO)
McDaniel Coll (MD)
North Dakota State U (ND)
Northern Michigan U (MI)
Rocky Mountain Coll (MT)
Saint Mary-of-the-Woods Coll (IN)
Saint Mary's Coll of California (CA)
State U of New York at Oswego (NY)

ACCOUNTING TECHNOLOGY AND BOOKKEEPING

Canisius Coll (NY)
Ferris State U (MI)
Florida National Coll (FL)
Indiana U Southeast (IN)
Lewis-Clark State Coll (ID)
Post U (CT)
Rowan U (NJ)
St. Edward's U (TX)
U of Hawaii at Manoa (HI)

ACOUSTICS

American U (DC)

ACTING

Arcadia U (PA)
Bard Coll (NY)
Barry U (FL)
Baylor U (TX)
Bennington Coll (VT)
Boston U (MA)
Bradley U (IL)
Brigham Young U (UT)
California State U, Long Beach (CA)
Central Michigan U (MI)
Chapman U (CA)
Coe Coll (IA)
The Coll at Brockport, State U of New York (NY)
Columbia Coll Chicago (IL)
Cornish Coll of the Arts (WA)
Dalhousie U (NS, Canada)
DePaul U (IL)
Drake U (IA)
Elon U (NC)
Florida State U (FL)
Hofstra U (NY)
Illinois Wesleyan U (IL)
Ithaca Coll (NY)
Johnson State Coll (VT)
Kean U (NJ)
Keene State Coll (NH)
Lindenwood U (MO)
Long Island U–C. W. Post Campus (NY)
Marymount Manhattan Coll (NY)
New World School of the Arts (FL)
Northwest Missouri State U (MO)
Oakland U (MI)
Ohio U (OH)
Oklahoma City U (OK)
Old Dominion U (VA)
Oral Roberts U (OK)
Pace U (NY)
Penn State Abington (PA)
Penn State Altoona (PA)
Penn State Beaver (PA)

Penn State Berks (PA)
Penn State Brandywine (PA)
Penn State DuBois (PA)
Penn State Erie, The Behrend Coll (PA)
Penn State Fayette, The Eberly Campus (PA)
Penn State Greater Allegheny (PA)
Penn State Hazleton (PA)
Penn State Lehigh Valley (PA)
Penn State Mont Alto (PA)
Penn State New Kensington (PA)
Penn State Schuylkill (PA)
Penn State Shenango (PA)
Penn State U Park (PA)
Penn State Wilkes-Barre (PA)
Penn State Worthington Scranton (PA)
Penn State York (PA)
Roosevelt U (IL)
Ryerson U (ON, Canada)
Salem State U (MA)
Sarah Lawrence Coll (NY)
Seton Hill U (PA)
Shenandoah U (VA)
Slippery Rock U of Pennsylvania (PA)
Suffolk U (MA)
Tabor Coll (KS)
Temple U (PA)
Texas Christian U (TX)
Trinity U (TX)
U of Connecticut (CT)
U of Hartford (CT)
U of Maryland, Baltimore County (MD)
U of Miami (FL)
U of Northern Iowa (IA)
U of Regina (SK, Canada)
U of Southern California (CA)
The U of the Arts (PA)
U of Windsor (ON, Canada)
Virginia Intermont Coll (VA)
Webster U (MO)
Western Michigan U (MI)
Wright State U (OH)

ACTUARIAL SCIENCE

Appalachian State U (NC)
Arcadia U (PA)
Ball State U (IN)
Bellarmine U (KY)
Bernard M. Baruch Coll of the City U of New York (NY)
Bob Jones U (SC)
Bowling Green State U (OH)
Bradley U (IL)
Brigham Young U (UT)
Bryant U (RI)
Butler U (IN)
Central Coll (IA)
Central Michigan U (MI)
Concordia U (QC, Canada)
Drake U (IA)
Eastern Michigan U (MI)
Elmhurst Coll (IL)
Georgia State U (GA)
Indiana U Northwest (IN)
Indiana U South Bend (IN)
Lebanon Valley Coll (PA)
Maryville U of Saint Louis (MO)
The Master's Coll and Sem (CA)
Michigan State U (MI)
Michigan Technological U (MI)
North Central Coll (IL)
Northwestern Coll (IA)
Oakland U (MI)
The Ohio State U (OH)
Ohio U (OH)
Penn State Abington (PA)
Penn State Altoona (PA)
Penn State Beaver (PA)
Penn State Berks (PA)
Penn State Brandywine (PA)
Penn State DuBois (PA)
Penn State Erie, The Behrend Coll (PA)
Penn State Fayette, The Eberly Campus (PA)
Penn State Greater Allegheny (PA)
Penn State Hazleton (PA)
Penn State Lehigh Valley (PA)
Penn State Mont Alto (PA)
Penn State New Kensington (PA)
Penn State Schuylkill (PA)

Penn State Shenango (PA)
Penn State U Park (PA)
Penn State Wilkes-Barre (PA)
Penn State Worthington Scranton (PA)
Penn State York (PA)
Pittsburg State U (KS)
Purdue U (IN)
Queens Coll of the City U of New York (NY)
Quinnipiac U (CT)
Rider U (NJ)
Robert Morris U (PA)
Roosevelt U (IL)
St. John's U (NY)
Saint Joseph's U (PA)
Siena Coll (NY)
Simon Fraser U (BC, Canada)
Simpson Coll (IA)
Slippery Rock U of Pennsylvania (PA)
Spring Arbor U (MI)
State U of New York at Binghamton (NY)
Temple U (PA)
Texas Christian U (TX)
Thiel Coll (PA)
U at Albany, State U of New York (NY)
U of Connecticut (CT)
U of Illinois at Urbana–Champaign (IL)
The U of Iowa (IA)
U of Michigan–Flint (MI)
U of Minnesota, Duluth (MN)
U of Minnesota, Twin Cities Campus (MN)
U of Nebraska–Lincoln (NE)
U of Pennsylvania (PA)
U of Regina (SK, Canada)
U of St. Thomas (MN)
The U of Texas at Dallas (TX)
The U of Texas at San Antonio (TX)
U of Toronto (ON, Canada)
The U of Western Ontario (ON, Canada)
U of Wisconsin–Madison (WI)
U of Wisconsin–Milwaukee (WI)
Valparaiso U (IN)
Worcester Polytechnic Inst (MA)
Xavier U (OH)

ADMINISTRATIVE ASSISTANT AND SECRETARIAL SCIENCE

Baker Coll of Muskegon (MI)
Baker Coll of Owosso (MI)
Bayamón Central U (PR)
Campbellsville U (KY)
EDP Coll of Puerto Rico, Inc. (PR)
EDP Coll of Puerto Rico–San Sebastian (PR)
Faith Baptist Bible Coll and Theological Sem (IA)
Inter American U of Puerto Rico, Bayamón Campus (PR)
Lamar U (TX)
Lewis-Clark State Coll (ID)
North Carolina Ag and Tech State U (NC)
Northwest Missouri State U (MO)
Sul Ross State U (TX)
Tabor Coll (KS)
U of Puerto Rico at Humacao (PR)
Valdosta State U (GA)

ADULT AND CONTINUING EDUCATION

Auburn U (AL)
Eastern Washington U (WA)
Free Will Baptist Bible Coll (TN)
Lenoir-Rhyne U (NC)
Louisiana Coll (LA)
Louisiana State U and Ag and Mech Coll (LA)
Mars Hill Coll (NC)
San Diego Christian Coll (CA)
U of Alberta (AB, Canada)
U of Georgia (GA)
U of Minnesota, Twin Cities Campus (MN)
U of Nevada, Las Vegas (NV)
U of Regina (SK, Canada)
U of Southern Maine (ME)
The U of Toledo (OH)

ADULT AND CONTINUING EDUCATION ADMINISTRATION
Concordia Coll–New York (NY)
Marshall U (WV)
Penn State Abington (PA)
Penn State Altoona (PA)
Penn State Beaver (PA)
Penn State Berks (PA)
Penn State Brandywine (PA)
Penn State DuBois (PA)
Penn State Erie, The Behrend Coll (PA)
Penn State Fayette, The Eberly Campus (PA)
Penn State Greater Allegheny (PA)
Penn State Hazleton (PA)
Penn State Lehigh Valley (PA)
Penn State Mont Alto (PA)
Penn State New Kensington (PA)
Penn State Schuylkill (PA)
Penn State Shenango (PA)
Penn State U Park (PA)
Penn State Wilkes-Barre (PA)
Penn State Worthington Scranton (PA)
Penn State York (PA)

ADULT DEVELOPMENT AND AGING
Bowling Green State U (OH)
Madonna U (MI)
St. Thomas U (NB, Canada)
Texas State U–San Marcos (TX)
U of Guelph (ON, Canada)
York Coll of the City U of New York (NY)

ADULT HEALTH NURSING
Concordia Coll–New York (NY)
Pennsylvania Coll of Technology (PA)
Worcester State U (MA)

ADVERTISING
Acad of Art U (CA)
Adams State Coll (CO)
Appalachian State U (NC)
Art Center Coll of Design (CA)
The Art Inst of Atlanta (GA)
The Art Inst of Atlanta–Decatur (GA)
The Art Inst of Austin (TX)
The Art Inst of California, a college of Argosy U, Orange County (CA)
The Art Inst of California, a college of Argosy U, San Diego (CA)
The Art Inst of California, a college of Argosy U, San Francisco (CA)
The Art Inst of Fort Lauderdale (FL)
The Art Inst of Las Vegas (NV)
The Art Inst of Ohio–Cincinnati (OH)
The Art Inst of Philadelphia (PA)
The Art Inst of Phoenix (AZ)
The Art Inst of Pittsburgh (PA)
The Art Inst of Portland (OR)
The Art Inst of Tennessee–Nashville (TN)
The Art Inst of Tucson (AZ)
The Art Inst of Virginia Beach (VA)
The Art Inst of Washington (VA)
The Art Inst of Washington–Dulles (VA)
The Art Inst of Wisconsin (WI)
The Art Insts Intl–Kansas City (KS)
The Art Insts Intl Minnesota (MN)
Barry U (FL)
Belmont U (TN)
Bernard M. Baruch Coll of the City U of New York (NY)
Boise State U (ID)
Bowling Green State U (OH)
Bradley U (IL)
Brigham Young U (UT)
California State U, East Bay (CA)
California State U, Fullerton (CA)
Central Michigan U (MI)
Columbia Coll Chicago (IL)
Drake U (IA)
Drury U (MO)
Fashion Inst of Technology (NY)
Ferris State U (MI)
Fontbonne U (MO)

Gannon U (PA)
Grand Valley State U (MI)
Hampton U (VA)
Harding U (AR)
Hawai'i Pacific U (HI)
The Illinois Inst of Art–Chicago (IL)
The Illinois Inst of Art–Schaumburg (IL)
The Illinois Inst of Art–Tinley Park (IL)
Intl Acad of Design & Technology (FL)
Iona Coll (NY)
Iowa State U of Science and Technology (IA)
Kent State U (OH)
Lindenwood U (MO)
Louisiana Coll (LA)
Loyola U Chicago (IL)
Marquette U (WI)
Metropolitan State U (MN)
Miami Intl U of Art & Design (FL)
Michigan State U (MI)
New York Inst of Technology (NY)
Northeastern State U (OK)
Northern Arizona U (AZ)
Northwest Missouri State U (MO)
Northwood U, Florida Campus (FL)
Oklahoma Christian U (OK)
Oklahoma City U (OK)
Pace U (NY)
Penn State Abington (PA)
Penn State Altoona (PA)
Penn State Beaver (PA)
Penn State Berks (PA)
Penn State Brandywine (PA)
Penn State DuBois (PA)
Penn State Erie, The Behrend Coll (PA)
Penn State Fayette, The Eberly Campus (PA)
Penn State Greater Allegheny (PA)
Penn State Hazleton (PA)
Penn State Lehigh Valley (PA)
Penn State Mont Alto (PA)
Penn State New Kensington (PA)
Penn State Schuylkill (PA)
Penn State Shenango (PA)
Penn State U Park (PA)
Penn State Wilkes-Barre (PA)
Penn State Worthington Scranton (PA)
Penn State York (PA)
Pepperdine U, Malibu (CA)
Pittsburg State U (KS)
Point Park U (PA)
Portland State U (OR)
Purdue U Calumet (IN)
Quinnipiac U (CT)
Rider U (NJ)
Rochester Inst of Technology (NY)
Rowan U (NJ)
St. Ambrose U (IA)
St. John's U (NY)
Saint Joseph's Coll of Maine (ME)
Salem State U (MA)
San Diego State U (CA)
Simmons Coll (MA)
Southern Methodist U (TX)
Southern New Hampshire U (NH)
Spring Arbor U (MI)
Stephens Coll (MO)
Suffolk U (MA)
Syracuse U (NY)
Temple U (PA)
Texas State U–San Marcos (TX)
Texas Tech U (TX)
Texas Wesleyan U (TX)
Union U (TN)
The U of Alabama (AL)
U of Arkansas at Little Rock (AR)
U of Central Florida (FL)
U of Colorado Boulder (CO)
U of Florida (FL)
U of Georgia (GA)
U of Houston (TX)
U of Idaho (ID)
U of Illinois at Urbana–Champaign (IL)
U of Miami (FL)
U of Missouri (MO)
U of Nebraska–Lincoln (NE)
U of Oklahoma (OK)
U of Oregon (OR)
U of South Carolina (SC)

U of Southern Indiana (IN)
U of Southern Mississippi (MS)
The U of Tennessee (TN)
The U of Texas at Arlington (TX)
The U of Texas at Austin (TX)
Washington State U (WA)
Washington U in St. Louis (MO)
Waynesburg U (PA)
Webster U (MO)
Wesleyan Coll (GA)
Western Kentucky U (KY)
Western Michigan U (MI)
Western New England U (MA)
West Texas A&M U (TX)
Widener U (PA)
William Woods U (MO)
Winona State U (MN)
Xavier U (OH)
Youngstown State U (OH)

AERONAUTICAL/AEROSPACE ENGINEERING TECHNOLOGY
Bowling Green State U (OH)
New York Inst of Technology (NY)
Saint Louis U (MO)
Utah State U (UT)

AERONAUTICS/AVIATION/ AEROSPACE SCIENCE AND TECHNOLOGY
American Public U System (WV)
Arizona State U (AZ)
Bridgewater State U (MA)
Central Washington U (WA)
Delaware State U (DE)
Delta State U (MS)
Dowling Coll (NY)
Elizabeth City State U (NC)
Embry-Riddle Aeronautical U–Daytona (FL)
Embry-Riddle Aeronautical U–Prescott (AZ)
Embry-Riddle Aeronautical U–Worldwide (FL)
Florida Inst of Technology (FL)
Inter American U of Puerto Rico, Bayamón Campus (PR)
Kent State U (OH)
Liberty U (VA)
Metropolitan State Coll of Denver (CO)
Middle Tennessee State U (TN)
The Ohio State U (OH)
Ohio U (OH)
Oklahoma State U (OK)
Pacific Union Coll (CA)
Piedmont Intl U (NC)
Purdue U (IN)
South Dakota State U (SD)
Texas Southern U (TX)
U of Minnesota, Crookston (MN)
U of Oklahoma (OK)
U of the District of Columbia (DC)
Utah Valley U (UT)
Vaughn Coll of Aeronautics and Technology (NY)

AEROSPACE, AERONAUTICAL AND ASTRONAUTICAL/SPACE ENGINEERING
Arizona State U (AZ)
Auburn U (AL)
Boston U (MA)
California Polytechnic State U, San Luis Obispo (CA)
California State Polytechnic U, Pomona (CA)
California State U, Long Beach (CA)
Case Western Reserve U (OH)
Clarkson U (NY)
Daniel Webster Coll (NH)
Embry-Riddle Aeronautical U–Daytona (FL)
Embry-Riddle Aeronautical U–Prescott (AZ)
Florida Inst of Technology (FL)
Georgia Inst of Technology (GA)
Illinois Inst of Technology (IL)
Inter American U of Puerto Rico, Bayamón Campus (PR)
Iowa State U of Science and Technology (IA)

Massachusetts Inst of Technology (MA)
Mississippi State U (MS)
Missouri U of Science and Technology (MO)
New Mexico State U (NM)
North Carolina State U (NC)
The Ohio State U (OH)
Oklahoma State U (OK)
Penn State Abington (PA)
Penn State Altoona (PA)
Penn State Beaver (PA)
Penn State Berks (PA)
Penn State Brandywine (PA)
Penn State DuBois (PA)
Penn State Erie, The Behrend Coll (PA)
Penn State Fayette, The Eberly Campus (PA)
Penn State Greater Allegheny (PA)
Penn State Hazleton (PA)
Penn State Lehigh Valley (PA)
Penn State Mont Alto (PA)
Penn State New Kensington (PA)
Penn State Schuylkill (PA)
Penn State Shenango (PA)
Penn State U Park (PA)
Penn State Wilkes-Barre (PA)
Penn State Worthington Scranton (PA)
Penn State York (PA)
Purdue U (IN)
Rensselaer Polytechnic Inst (NY)
Rochester Inst of Technology (NY)
Ryerson U (ON, Canada)
Saint Louis U (MO)
San Diego State U (CA)
Stanford U (CA)
Syracuse U (NY)
Texas A&M U (TX)
Tuskegee U (AL)
United States Air Force Acad (CO)
United States Naval Acad (MD)
U at Buffalo, the State U of New York (NY)
The U of Alabama (AL)
The U of Arizona (AZ)
U of California, Davis (CA)
U of California, Irvine (CA)
U of California, Los Angeles (CA)
U of Central Florida (FL)
U of Cincinnati (OH)
U of Colorado Boulder (CO)
U of Florida (FL)
U of Illinois at Urbana–Champaign (IL)
The U of Kansas (KS)
U of Maryland, Coll Park (MD)
U of Miami (FL)
U of Michigan (MI)
U of Minnesota, Twin Cities Campus (MN)
U of Notre Dame (IN)
U of Oklahoma (OK)
U of Southern California (CA)
The U of Tennessee (TN)
The U of Texas at Arlington (TX)
The U of Texas at Austin (TX)
U of Toronto (ON, Canada)
U of Virginia (VA)
U of Washington (WA)
Utah State U (UT)
Virginia Polytechnic Inst and State U (VA)
Western Michigan U (MI)
West Virginia U (WV)
Wichita State U (KS)
Worcester Polytechnic Inst (MA)

AFRICAN AMERICAN/BLACK STUDIES
Amherst Coll (MA)
Arizona State U (AZ)
Bard Coll at Simon's Rock (MA)
Bates Coll (ME)
Berea Coll (KY)
Bowling Green State U (OH)
Brandeis U (MA)
Brown U (RI)
California State U, Dominguez Hills (CA)
California State U, East Bay (CA)
California State U, Fresno (CA)
California State U, Fullerton (CA)

California State U, Long Beach (CA)
California State U, Los Angeles (CA)
Chicago State U (IL)
City Coll of the City U of New York (NY)
Claflin U (SC)
Claremont McKenna Coll (CA)
Cleveland State U (OH)
Coe Coll (IA)
Colby Coll (ME)
Colgate U (NY)
The Coll at Brockport, State U of New York (NY)
Coll of Staten Island of the City U of New York (NY)
The Coll of William and Mary (VA)
The Coll of Wooster (OH)
Columbia U, School of General Studies (NY)
Cornell U (NY)
Dartmouth Coll (NH)
Denison U (OH)
DePaul U (IL)
DePauw U (IN)
Dillard U (LA)
Dominican U (IL)
Drew U (NJ)
Earlham Coll (IN)
East Carolina U (NC)
Eastern Illinois U (IL)
Eastern Michigan U (MI)
Emory U (GA)
Florida Ag and Mech U (FL)
Fordham U (NY)
Georgia State U (GA)
Gettysburg Coll (PA)
Guilford Coll (NC)
Hamilton Coll (NY)
Hampshire Coll (MA)
Harvard U (MA)
Hobart and William Smith Colls (NY)
Hunter Coll of the City U of New York (NY)
Indiana State U (IN)
Indiana U Bloomington (IN)
Indiana U Northwest (IN)
Indiana U–Purdue U Indianapolis (IN)
Kent State U (OH)
Knox Coll (IL)
Lehman Coll of the City U of New York (NY)
Loyola Marymount U (CA)
Loyola U Chicago (IL)
Luther Coll (IA)
Mercer U (GA)
Metropolitan State Coll of Denver (CO)
Miami U (OH)
Morehouse Coll (GA)
Mount Holyoke Coll (MA)
New York U (NY)
North Carolina State U (NC)
Northeastern U (MA)
The Ohio State U (OH)
Ohio U (OH)
Ohio Wesleyan U (OH)
Old Dominion U (VA)
Penn State Abington (PA)
Penn State Altoona (PA)
Penn State Beaver (PA)
Penn State Berks (PA)
Penn State Brandywine (PA)
Penn State DuBois (PA)
Penn State Erie, The Behrend Coll (PA)
Penn State Fayette, The Eberly Campus (PA)
Penn State Greater Allegheny (PA)
Penn State Hazleton (PA)
Penn State Lehigh Valley (PA)
Penn State Mont Alto (PA)
Penn State New Kensington (PA)
Penn State Schuylkill (PA)
Penn State Shenango (PA)
Penn State U Park (PA)
Penn State Wilkes-Barre (PA)
Penn State Worthington Scranton (PA)
Penn State York (PA)
Pitzer Coll (CA)
Pomona Coll (CA)

Portland State U (OR)
Purdue U (IN)
Ramapo Coll of New Jersey (NJ)
Rhode Island Coll (RI)
Roosevelt U (IL)
Rutgers, The State U of New Jersey, Camden (NJ)
Rutgers, The State U of New Jersey, Newark (NJ)
Saint Louis U (MO)
San Diego State U (CA)
San Francisco State U (CA)
Sarah Lawrence Coll (NY)
Scripps Coll (CA)
Smith Coll (MA)
Sonoma State U (CA)
Southern Illinois U Carbondale (IL)
Southern Methodist U (TX)
Stanford U (CA)
State U of New York at Binghamton (NY)
State U of New York at New Paltz (NY)
State U of New York Coll at Cortland (NY)
State U of New York Coll at Geneseo (NY)
Stony Brook U, State U of New York (NY)
Suffolk U (MA)
Swarthmore Coll (PA)
Syracuse U (NY)
Temple U (PA)
Tufts U (MA)
U at Albany, State U of New York (NY)
U at Buffalo, the State U of New York (NY)
The U of Alabama (AL)
The U of Alabama at Birmingham (AL)
The U of Arizona (AZ)
U of California, Berkeley (CA)
U of California, Davis (CA)
U of California, Irvine (CA)
U of California, Los Angeles (CA)
U of California, Riverside (CA)
U of California, Santa Barbara (CA)
U of Central Arkansas (AR)
U of Cincinnati (OH)
U of Delaware (DE)
U of Georgia (GA)
U of Illinois at Chicago (IL)
The U of Iowa (IA)
The U of Kansas (KS)
U of Louisville (KY)
U of Maryland, Baltimore County (MD)
U of Maryland, Coll Park (MD)
U of Massachusetts Amherst (MA)
U of Massachusetts Boston (MA)
U of Memphis (TN)
U of Miami (FL)
U of Michigan (MI)
U of Michigan–Flint (MI)
U of Minnesota, Twin Cities Campus (MN)
U of Mississippi (MS)
U of Nebraska at Omaha (NE)
U of Nevada, Las Vegas (NV)
U of New Mexico (NM)
The U of North Carolina at Chapel Hill (NC)
The U of North Carolina at Charlotte (NC)
U of Northern Colorado (CO)
U of Notre Dame (IN)
U of Oklahoma (OK)
U of Pennsylvania (PA)
U of Pittsburgh (PA)
U of Rhode Island (RI)
U of Rochester (NY)
U of South Carolina (SC)
U of Southern California (CA)
U of South Florida (FL)
The U of Texas at Austin (TX)
The U of Toledo (OH)
U of Virginia (VA)
U of Washington (WA)
U of Wisconsin–Madison (WI)
U of Wisconsin–Milwaukee (WI)
Vanderbilt U (TN)
Virginia Commonwealth U (VA)
Washington U in St. Louis (MO)
Wayne State U (MI)

Wellesley Coll (MA)
Wells Coll (NY)
Wesleyan U (CT)
Western Illinois U (IL)
Western Michigan U (MI)
Wheaton Coll (MA)
William Paterson U of New Jersey (NJ)
Wright State U (OH)
Yale U (CT)
York Coll of the City U of New York (NY)
Youngstown State U (OH)

AFRICAN LANGUAGES

Indiana U Bloomington (IN)
U of California, Los Angeles (CA)
U of Wisconsin–Madison (WI)

AFRICAN STUDIES

Agnes Scott Coll (GA)
Augustana Coll (IL)
Bard Coll (NY)
Barnard Coll (NY)
Bowdoin Coll (ME)
Bowling Green State U (OH)
Carleton Coll (MN)
Colgate U (NY)
The Coll at Brockport, State U of New York (NY)
Columbia U, School of General Studies (NY)
Connecticut Coll (CT)
Dartmouth Coll (NH)
Dickinson Coll (PA)
Drew U (NJ)
Emory U (GA)
Fordham U (NY)
Franklin & Marshall Coll (PA)
Hampshire Coll (MA)
Haverford Coll (PA)
Hobart and William Smith Colls (NY)
Hofstra U (NY)
Illinois Wesleyan U (IL)
Kennesaw State U (GA)
Kentucky State U (KY)
Lehigh U (PA)
Marlboro Coll (VT)
Oakland U (MI)
The Ohio State U (OH)
Ohio U (OH)
Portland State U (OR)
Queens Coll of the City U of New York (NY)
Rowan U (NJ)
Rutgers, The State U of New Jersey, New Brunswick (NJ)
St. Lawrence U (NY)
Sarah Lawrence Coll (NY)
Simmons Coll (MA)
Tulane U (LA)
United States Military Acad (NY)
The U of Iowa (IA)
The U of Kansas (KS)
U of Minnesota, Twin Cities Campus (MN)
U of Pennsylvania (PA)
U of Richmond (VA)
U of Toronto (ON, Canada)
Vassar Coll (NY)
Washington U in St. Louis (MO)
Wellesley Coll (MA)
Wheaton Coll (MA)
William Paterson U of New Jersey (NJ)
Yale U (CT)

AGRIBUSINESS

Abilene Christian U (TX)
Adams State Coll (CO)
American U of Beirut (Lebanon)
Andrews U (MI)
Arkansas State U (AR)
Arkansas Tech U (AR)
Brigham Young U (UT)
California Polytechnic State U, San Luis Obispo (CA)
Colorado State U (CO)
Cornell U (NY)
Delaware Valley Coll (PA)
Eastern New Mexico U (NM)
Florida Ag and Mech U (FL)
Middle Tennessee State U (TN)

Mississippi State U (MS)
Missouri State U (MO)
New Mexico State U (NM)
North Carolina Ag and Tech State U (NC)
North Carolina State U (NC)
North Dakota State U (ND)
Northwest Missouri State U (MO)
Penn State Abington (PA)
Penn State Altoona (PA)
Penn State Beaver (PA)
Penn State Berks (PA)
Penn State Brandywine (PA)
Penn State DuBois (PA)
Penn State Erie, The Behrend Coll (PA)
Penn State Fayette, The Eberly Campus (PA)
Penn State Greater Allegheny (PA)
Penn State Hazleton (PA)
Penn State Lehigh Valley (PA)
Penn State Mont Alto (PA)
Penn State New Kensington (PA)
Penn State Schuylkill (PA)
Penn State Shenango (PA)
Penn State U Park (PA)
Penn State Wilkes-Barre (PA)
Penn State Worthington Scranton (PA)
Penn State York (PA)
Purdue U (IN)
South Dakota State U (SD)
Southeast Missouri State U (MO)
Southwest Minnesota State U (MN)
Stephen F. Austin State U (TX)
Tabor Coll (KS)
Texas A&M U (TX)
Texas State U–San Marcos (TX)
U of Arkansas (AR)
U of Central Missouri (MO)
U of Delaware (DE)
U of Georgia (GA)
U of Maine (ME)
U of Minnesota, Crookston (MN)
U of Minnesota, Twin Cities Campus (MN)
U of Wisconsin–River Falls (WI)
U of Wyoming (WY)
Vermont Tech Coll (VT)
West Texas A&M U (TX)

AGRICULTURAL AND DOMESTIC ANIMAL SERVICES RELATED

Tarleton State U (TX)

AGRICULTURAL AND EXTENSION EDUCATION

North Carolina State U (NC)
Northwestern Oklahoma State U (OK)
Penn State Abington (PA)
Penn State Altoona (PA)
Penn State Beaver (PA)
Penn State Berks (PA)
Penn State Brandywine (PA)
Penn State DuBois (PA)
Penn State Erie, The Behrend Coll (PA)
Penn State Fayette, The Eberly Campus (PA)
Penn State Greater Allegheny (PA)
Penn State Hazleton (PA)
Penn State Lehigh Valley (PA)
Penn State Mont Alto (PA)
Penn State New Kensington (PA)
Penn State Schuylkill (PA)
Penn State Shenango (PA)
Penn State Wilkes-Barre (PA)
Penn State Worthington Scranton (PA)
Penn State York (PA)
Purdue U (IN)
U of Georgia (GA)
U of Illinois at Urbana–Champaign (IL)
The U of Tennessee (TN)

AGRICULTURAL AND FOOD PRODUCTS PROCESSING

Kansas State U (KS)
The Ohio State U (OH)
Texas A&M U (TX)

The U of British Columbia (BC, Canada)
U of Florida (FL)
U of Nebraska–Lincoln (NE)
Washington State U (WA)

AGRICULTURAL AND HORTICULTURAL PLANT BREEDING

Delaware State U (DE)

AGRICULTURAL ANIMAL BREEDING

U of Nevada, Reno (NV)

AGRICULTURAL BUSINESS AND MANAGEMENT

Alcorn State U (MS)
Arizona State U (AZ)
Brigham Young U (UT)
California State Polytechnic U, Pomona (CA)
California State U, Chico (CA)
California State U, Fresno (CA)
Clemson U (SC)
Cornell U (NY)
Delaware State U (DE)
Eastern Kentucky U (KY)
Florida Southern Coll (FL)
Fort Hays State U (KS)
Fort Lewis Coll (CO)
Hardin-Simmons U (TX)
Iowa State U of Science and Technology (IA)
Kansas State U (KS)
Lincoln U (MO)
Louisiana State U and Ag and Mech Coll (LA)
Michigan State U (MI)
Montana State U (MT)
Morrisville State Coll (NY)
North Carolina Ag and Tech State U (NC)
Nova Scotia Ag Coll (NS, Canada)
The Ohio State U (OH)
Oklahoma State U (OK)
Rocky Mountain Coll (MT)
South Carolina State U (SC)
Southern Arkansas U–Magnolia (AR)
Southwest Minnesota State U (MN)
Sul Ross State U (TX)
Texas A&M U (TX)
Texas A&M U–Kingsville (TX)
Texas Tech U (TX)
Tuskegee U (AL)
U of Alberta (AB, Canada)
The U of Arizona (AZ)
U of Central Missouri (MO)
U of Delaware (DE)
U of Guelph (ON, Canada)
U of Hawaii at Hilo (HI)
U of Idaho (ID)
U of Illinois at Urbana–Champaign (IL)
U of Louisiana at Monroe (LA)
U of Maryland Eastern Shore (MD)
U of Minnesota, Twin Cities Campus (MN)
U of Missouri (MO)
U of Nebraska at Kearney (NE)
U of Nebraska–Lincoln (NE)
The U of Tennessee (TN)
The U of Tennessee at Martin (TN)
U of Wisconsin–Platteville (WI)
U of Wisconsin–River Falls (WI)
Upper Iowa U (IA)
Utah State U (UT)
Washington State U (WA)
West Texas A&M U (TX)
Wilmington Coll (OH)

AGRICULTURAL BUSINESS AND MANAGEMENT RELATED

Delaware State U (DE)
Penn State New Kensington (PA)
Purdue U (IN)
U of California, Davis (CA)
U of Minnesota, Twin Cities Campus (MN)
Utah State U (UT)

AGRICULTURAL BUSINESS TECHNOLOGY

The U of Arizona (AZ)
U of Minnesota, Crookston (MN)
Washington State U (WA)

AGRICULTURAL COMMUNICATION/ JOURNALISM

Auburn U (AL)
Kansas State U (KS)
North Dakota State U (ND)
The Ohio State U (OH)
Oklahoma State U (OK)
Purdue U (IN)
South Dakota State U (SD)
Texas A&M U (TX)
Texas Tech U (TX)
U of Georgia (GA)
U of Idaho (ID)
U of Illinois at Urbana–Champaign (IL)
U of Nebraska–Lincoln (NE)
U of Wisconsin–Madison (WI)
U of Wyoming (WY)
Washington State U (WA)

AGRICULTURAL ECONOMICS

Alcorn State U (MS)
Auburn U (AL)
Brigham Young U (UT)
Clemson U (SC)
Colorado State U (CO)
Cornell U (NY)
Kansas State U (KS)
Mississippi State U (MS)
North Carolina Ag and Tech State U (NC)
North Dakota State U (ND)
Northwest Missouri State U (MO)
Nova Scotia Ag Coll (NS, Canada)
The Ohio State U (OH)
Oklahoma State U (OK)
Purdue U (IN)
South Dakota State U (SD)
Southern Illinois U Carbondale (IL)
Tarleton State U (TX)
Texas A&M U (TX)
Texas Tech U (TX)
U of Alberta (AB, Canada)
U of Central Missouri (MO)
U of Connecticut (CT)
U of Florida (FL)
U of Georgia (GA)
U of Guelph (ON, Canada)
U of Idaho (ID)
U of Illinois at Urbana–Champaign (IL)
U of Maine (ME)
U of Maryland, Coll Park (MD)
U of Massachusetts Amherst (MA)
U of Minnesota, Twin Cities Campus (MN)
U of Missouri (MO)
U of Nebraska–Lincoln (NE)
U of Nevada, Reno (NV)
U of Wisconsin–Madison (WI)
U of Wisconsin–River Falls (WI)
Utah State U (UT)
Virginia Polytechnic Inst and State U (VA)
Washington State U (WA)
West Virginia U (WV)

AGRICULTURAL ENGINEERING

Auburn U (AL)
California Lutheran U (CA)
California Polytechnic State U, San Luis Obispo (CA)
Clemson U (SC)
Cornell U (NY)
Dalhousie U (NS, Canada)
Dordt Coll (IA)
Florida Ag and Mech U (FL)
Iowa State U of Science and Technology (IA)
Kansas State U (KS)
Michigan State U (MI)
Missouri U of Science and Technology (MO)
North Carolina Ag and Tech State U (NC)

North Carolina State U (NC)
North Dakota State U (ND)
The Ohio State U (OH)
Oklahoma State U (OK)
Penn State Abington (PA)
Penn State Beaver (PA)
Penn State Brandywine (PA)
Penn State DuBois (PA)
Penn State Erie, The Behrend Coll (PA)
Penn State Fayette, The Eberly Campus (PA)
Penn State Greater Allegheny (PA)
Penn State Hazleton (PA)
Penn State Lehigh Valley (PA)
Penn State Mont Alto (PA)
Penn State New Kensington (PA)
Penn State Schuylkill (PA)
Penn State Shenango (PA)
Penn State U Park (PA)
Penn State Wilkes-Barre (PA)
Penn State Worthington Scranton (PA)
Penn State York (PA)
Purdue U (IN)
Rutgers, The State U of New Jersey, New Brunswick (NJ)
South Dakota State U (SD)
State U of New York Coll of Environmental Science and Forestry (NY)
Texas A&M U (TX)
U of Alberta (AB, Canada)
U of Arkansas (AR)
U of California, Los Angeles (CA)
U of Florida (FL)
U of Georgia (GA)
U of Hawaii at Manoa (HI)
U of Illinois at Urbana–Champaign (IL)
U of Maine (ME)
U of Maryland, Coll Park (MD)
U of Minnesota, Twin Cities Campus (MN)
U of Nebraska–Lincoln (NE)
The U of Tennessee (TN)
U of Wisconsin–Madison (WI)
U of Wisconsin–River Falls (WI)
Utah State U (UT)

AGRICULTURAL/FARM SUPPLIES RETAILING AND WHOLESALING
Texas A&M U (TX)

AGRICULTURAL MECHANIZATION
California Polytechnic State U, San Luis Obispo (CA)
Clemson U (SC)
Iowa State U of Science and Technology (IA)
Kansas State U (KS)
Montana State U (MT)
Montana State U–Northern (MT)
North Carolina Ag and Tech State U (NC)
North Carolina State U (NC)
North Dakota State U (ND)
Penn State Abington (PA)
Penn State Altoona (PA)
Penn State Beaver (PA)
Penn State Berks (PA)
Penn State Brandywine (PA)
Penn State DuBois (PA)
Penn State Erie, The Behrend Coll (PA)
Penn State Fayette, The Eberly Campus (PA)
Penn State Greater Allegheny (PA)
Penn State Hazleton (PA)
Penn State Lehigh Valley (PA)
Penn State Mont Alto (PA)
Penn State New Kensington (PA)
Penn State Schuylkill (PA)
Penn State Shenango (PA)
Penn State U Park (PA)
Penn State Wilkes-Barre (PA)
Penn State Worthington Scranton (PA)
Penn State York (PA)
Purdue U (IN)
South Dakota State U (SD)
Stephen F. Austin State U (TX)

U of Idaho (ID)
U of Illinois at Urbana–Champaign (IL)
U of Minnesota, Crookston (MN)
U of Missouri (MO)
U of Nebraska–Lincoln (NE)
U of Wisconsin–River Falls (WI)
Washington State U (WA)

AGRICULTURAL MECHANIZATION RELATED
U of Minnesota, Twin Cities Campus (MN)

AGRICULTURAL POWER MACHINERY OPERATION
U of Minnesota, Crookston (MN)

AGRICULTURAL PRODUCTION
Eastern Kentucky U (KY)
Stephen F. Austin State U (TX)
Texas A&M U (TX)

AGRICULTURAL PRODUCTION RELATED
Tarleton State U (TX)

AGRICULTURAL PUBLIC SERVICES RELATED
Oklahoma State U (OK)
U of Illinois at Urbana–Champaign (IL)

AGRICULTURAL TEACHER EDUCATION
Arkansas State U (AR)
Arkansas Tech U (AR)
Auburn U (AL)
California Polytechnic State U, San Luis Obispo (CA)
California State Polytechnic U, Pomona (CA)
California State U, Chico (CA)
California State U, Fresno (CA)
Clemson U (SC)
Coll of the Ozarks (MO)
Colorado State U (CO)
Cornell U (NY)
Delaware State U (DE)
Dordt Coll (IA)
Eastern New Mexico U (NM)
Iowa State U of Science and Technology (IA)
Kansas State U (KS)
Louisiana State U and Ag and Mech Coll (LA)
Mississippi State U (MS)
Missouri State U (MO)
Montana State U (MT)
New Mexico State U (NM)
North Carolina Ag and Tech State U (NC)
North Carolina State U (NC)
North Dakota State U (ND)
Northwest Missouri State U (MO)
The Ohio State U (OH)
Oklahoma State U (OK)
Penn State U Park (PA)
Purdue U (IN)
South Dakota State U (SD)
Southeast Missouri State U (MO)
Southern Arkansas U–Magnolia (AR)
State U of New York at Oswego (NY)
Tarleton State U (TX)
U of Arkansas (AR)
U of Connecticut (CT)
U of Delaware (DE)
U of Florida (FL)
U of Georgia (GA)
U of Idaho (ID)
U of Illinois at Urbana–Champaign (IL)
U of Maryland Eastern Shore (MD)
U of Minnesota, Twin Cities Campus (MN)
U of Missouri (MO)
U of Nebraska–Lincoln (NE)
The U of Tennessee at Martin (TN)
U of Wisconsin–Platteville (WI)

U of Wisconsin–River Falls (WI)
U of Wyoming (WY)
Utah State U (UT)
Washington State U (WA)
West Virginia U (WV)
Wilmington Coll (OH)

AGRICULTURE
Alcorn State U (MS)
American U of Beirut (Lebanon)
Auburn U (AL)
Austin Peay State U (TN)
Berea Coll (KY)
California State U, Stanislaus (CA)
Cameron U (OK)
Cornell U (NY)
Delaware State U (DE)
Dordt Coll (IA)
Eastern Kentucky U (KY)
Ferrum Coll (VA)
Florida Ag and Mech U (FL)
Fort Hays State U (KS)
Hampshire Coll (MA)
Illinois State U (IL)
Iowa State U of Science and Technology (IA)
Lincoln U (MO)
Lubbock Christian U (TX)
McNeese State U (LA)
Mississippi State U (MS)
Missouri State U (MO)
Montana State U (MT)
New Mexico State U (NM)
North Carolina Ag and Tech State U (NC)
North Carolina State U (NC)
North Dakota State U (ND)
Northwestern Oklahoma State U (OK)
Northwest Missouri State U (MO)
Nova Scotia Ag Coll (NS, Canada)
Penn State Abington (PA)
Penn State Altoona (PA)
Penn State Beaver (PA)
Penn State Berks (PA)
Penn State Brandywine (PA)
Penn State DuBois (PA)
Penn State Erie, The Behrend Coll (PA)
Penn State Fayette, The Eberly Campus (PA)
Penn State Greater Allegheny (PA)
Penn State Hazleton (PA)
Penn State Lehigh Valley (PA)
Penn State Mont Alto (PA)
Penn State New Kensington (PA)
Penn State Schuylkill (PA)
Penn State Shenango (PA)
Penn State U Park (PA)
Penn State Wilkes-Barre (PA)
Penn State Worthington Scranton (PA)
Penn State York (PA)
Prairie View A&M U (TX)
Purdue U (IN)
Rutgers, The State U of New Jersey, New Brunswick (NJ)
Sam Houston State U (TX)
South Dakota State U (SD)
Southeast Missouri State U (MO)
Southern Arkansas U–Magnolia (AR)
Southern Illinois U Carbondale (IL)
Stephen F. Austin State U (TX)
Sterling Coll (VT)
Texas A&M U (TX)
Texas A&M U–Kingsville (TX)
Texas State U–San Marcos (TX)
Texas Tech U (TX)
Truman State U (MO)
Tuskegee U (AL)
U of Alberta (AB, Canada)
U of Arkansas at Monticello (AR)
The U of British Columbia (BC, Canada)
U of Connecticut (CT)
U of Delaware (DE)
U of Georgia (GA)
U of Guam (GU)
U of Hawaii at Hilo (HI)
U of Lethbridge (AB, Canada)
U of Louisiana at Lafayette (LA)
U of Maryland, Coll Park (MD)
U of Maryland Eastern Shore (MD)

U of Minnesota, Twin Cities Campus (MN)
U of Missouri (MO)
U of Nebraska–Lincoln (NE)
The U of Tennessee at Martin (TN)
U of Vermont (VT)
U of Wisconsin–River Falls (WI)
Utah State U (UT)
Virginia State U (VA)
Washington State U (WA)
Western Illinois U (IL)
Western Kentucky U (KY)
West Texas A&M U (TX)
Wilmington Coll (OH)

AGRICULTURE AND AGRICULTURE OPERATIONS RELATED
Coll of the Atlantic (ME)
The Ohio State U (OH)
Tarleton State U (TX)
U of California, Davis (CA)
U of Minnesota, Twin Cities Campus (MN)

AGROECOLOGY AND SUSTAINABLE AGRICULTURE
Columbia U, School of General Studies (NY)
The Evergreen State Coll (WA)
Prescott Coll (AZ)
U of Minnesota, Crookston (MN)
U of New Hampshire (NH)
U of Wyoming (WY)

AGRONOMY AND CROP SCIENCE
Auburn U (AL)
California Polytechnic State U, San Luis Obispo (CA)
California State U, Chico (CA)
California State U, Fresno (CA)
Coll of the Ozarks (MO)
Colorado State U (CO)
Delaware State U (DE)
Delaware Valley Coll (PA)
Fort Hays State U (KS)
Iowa State U of Science and Technology (IA)
Kansas State U (KS)
Mississippi State U (MS)
Missouri State U (MO)
New Mexico State U (NM)
North Carolina State U (NC)
Northwest Missouri State U (MO)
The Ohio State U (OH)
Penn State Abington (PA)
Penn State Altoona (PA)
Penn State Beaver (PA)
Penn State Berks (PA)
Penn State Brandywine (PA)
Penn State DuBois (PA)
Penn State Erie, The Behrend Coll (PA)
Penn State Fayette, The Eberly Campus (PA)
Penn State Greater Allegheny (PA)
Penn State Hazleton (PA)
Penn State Mont Alto (PA)
Penn State New Kensington (PA)
Penn State Shenango (PA)
Penn State Wilkes-Barre (PA)
Penn State Worthington Scranton (PA)
Penn State York (PA)
Purdue U (IN)
South Dakota State U (SD)
Tarleton State U (TX)
Texas A&M U (TX)
Texas A&M U–Kingsville (TX)
Texas Tech U (TX)
Tuskegee U (AL)
U of Alberta (AB, Canada)
The U of Arizona (AZ)
U of Arkansas (AR)
U of Connecticut (CT)
U of Guelph (ON, Canada)
U of Illinois at Urbana–Champaign (IL)
U of Minnesota, Crookston (MN)
U of Minnesota, Twin Cities Campus (MN)
U of Nebraska–Lincoln (NE)
The U of Tennessee at Martin (TN)

U of Vermont (VT)
U of Wisconsin–Madison (WI)
U of Wisconsin–Platteville (WI)
U of Wisconsin–River Falls (WI)
Utah State U (UT)
Virginia Polytechnic Inst and State U (VA)
Washington State U (WA)
West Texas A&M U (TX)

AIRCRAFT POWERPLANT TECHNOLOGY
Embry-Riddle Aeronautical U–Daytona (FL)
Embry-Riddle Aeronautical U–Worldwide (FL)
Thomas Edison State Coll (NJ)

AIR FORCE ROTC/AIR SCIENCE
La Salle U (PA)
The U of Iowa (IA)
U of Washington (WA)
Weber State U (UT)

AIRFRAME MECHANICS AND AIRCRAFT MAINTENANCE TECHNOLOGY
Kansas State U (KS)
LeTourneau U (TX)
Purdue U (IN)
Southeastern Oklahoma State U (OK)
Thomas Edison State Coll (NJ)
Vaughn Coll of Aeronautics and Technology (NY)
Wilmington U (DE)

AIRLINE PILOT AND FLIGHT CREW
Auburn U (AL)
Averett U (VA)
Baylor U (TX)
Bridgewater State U (MA)
Delaware State U (DE)
Delta State U (MS)
Eastern Kentucky U (KY)
Eastern Michigan U (MI)
Embry-Riddle Aeronautical U–Daytona (FL)
Embry-Riddle Aeronautical U–Prescott (AZ)
Farmingdale State Coll (NY)
Indiana State U (IN)
Inter American U of Puerto Rico, Bayamón Campus (PR)
Jacksonville U (FL)
Kansas State U (KS)
LeTourneau U (TX)
Quincy U (IL)
Rocky Mountain Coll (MT)
Saint Louis U (MO)
Southeastern Oklahoma State U (OK)
U of Dubuque (IA)
U of Illinois at Urbana–Champaign (IL)
U of Louisiana at Monroe (LA)
U of Minnesota, Crookston (MN)
U of North Dakota (ND)
Utah Valley U (UT)
Western Michigan U (MI)
Westminster Coll (UT)

AIR TRAFFIC CONTROL
Arizona State U (AZ)
Daniel Webster Coll (NH)
Embry-Riddle Aeronautical U–Daytona (FL)
Embry-Riddle Aeronautical U–Prescott (AZ)
Hampton U (VA)
Inter American U of Puerto Rico, Bayamón Campus (PR)
LeTourneau U (TX)
Lewis U (IL)
Thomas Edison State Coll (NJ)
U of Maryland Eastern Shore (MD)
U of North Dakota (ND)

AIR TRANSPORTATION RELATED
Florida Inst of Technology (FL)
Thomas Edison State Coll (NJ)

U of North Dakota (ND)

ALLIED HEALTH AND MEDICAL ASSISTING SERVICES RELATED
Cedarville U (OH)
Coll of Saint Elizabeth (NJ)
Jones Coll, Jacksonville (FL)
The Ohio State U (OH)
The Ohio State U at Lima (OH)
Ramapo Coll of New Jersey (NJ)
Widener U (PA)

ALLIED HEALTH DIAGNOSTIC, INTERVENTION, AND TREATMENT PROFESSIONS RELATED
Fairleigh Dickinson U, Coll at Florham (NJ)
Fairleigh Dickinson U, Metropolitan Campus (NJ)
Georgian Court U (NJ)
Gwynedd-Mercy Coll (PA)
Hofstra U (NY)
Immaculata U (PA)
Millersville U of Pennsylvania (PA)
Northern Michigan U (MI)
Rutgers, The State U of New Jersey, Newark (NJ)
Thomas Edison State Coll (NJ)
U of Connecticut (CT)
U of Medicine and Dentistry of New Jersey (NJ)
U of Southern Maine (ME)
The U of Toledo (OH)

ALTERNATIVE AND COMPLEMENTARY MEDICINE RELATED
Johnson State Coll (VT)

AMERICAN GOVERNMENT AND POLITICS
American Jewish U (CA)
Bard Coll (NY)
Bennington Coll (VT)
Bridgewater State U (MA)
Daemen Coll (NY)
Drury U (MO)
Emory & Henry Coll (VA)
Fitchburg State U (MA)
Gallaudet U (DC)
The Master's Coll and Sem (CA)
Misericordia U (PA)
Oklahoma Christian U (OK)
Oklahoma City U (OK)
Suffolk U (MA)
United States Military Acad (NY)
The U of Akron (OH)
Wayland Baptist U (TX)
Western Michigan U (MI)

AMERICAN HISTORY
Bard Coll (NY)
Bennington Coll (VT)
The Coll of Saint Rose (NY)
Gettysburg Coll (PA)
Howard Payne U (TX)
Keene State Coll (NH)
Morningside Coll (IA)
Salem State U (MA)
Sarah Lawrence Coll (NY)
Suffolk U (MA)
Touro Coll (NY)
United States Military Acad (NY)
U of Regina (SK, Canada)
The U of Western Ontario (ON, Canada)

AMERICAN INDIAN/NATIVE AMERICAN STUDIES
Arizona State U (AZ)
Bemidji State U (MN)
Black Hills State U (SD)
California State U, East Bay (CA)
Colgate U (NY)
Concordia U (QC, Canada)
Creighton U (NE)
Dartmouth Coll (NH)
East Central U (OK)
The Evergreen State Coll (WA)
Fort Lewis Coll (CO)

Hampshire Coll (MA)
Humboldt State U (CA)
Northeastern State U (OK)
Northern Arizona U (AZ)
Northland Coll (WI)
Portland State U (OR)
St. Thomas U (NB, Canada)
San Diego State U (CA)
San Francisco State U (CA)
Sonoma State U (CA)
Stanford U (CA)
Trent U (ON, Canada)
U of Alaska Fairbanks (AK)
U of Alberta (AB, Canada)
U of California, Berkeley (CA)
U of California, Davis (CA)
U of California, Los Angeles (CA)
U of California, Riverside (CA)
U of Hawaii at Manoa (HI)
The U of Iowa (IA)
U of Lethbridge (AB, Canada)
U of Minnesota, Duluth (MN)
U of Minnesota, Twin Cities Campus (MN)
U of New Mexico (NM)
U of North Dakota (ND)
U of Oklahoma (OK)
U of Ottawa (ON, Canada)
U of Regina (SK, Canada)
U of Science and Arts of Oklahoma (OK)
The U of South Dakota (SD)
U of Toronto (ON, Canada)
U of Washington (WA)
The U of Western Ontario (ON, Canada)
U of Wisconsin–Eau Claire (WI)
U of Wisconsin–Green Bay (WI)
U of Wisconsin–Milwaukee (WI)
U of Wyoming (WY)

AMERICAN LITERATURE
Bard Coll (NY)
Bennington Coll (VT)
Castleton State Coll (VT)
The Coll at Brockport, State U of New York (NY)
Oklahoma City U (OK)
Queens U of Charlotte (NC)
Saint Joseph's Coll of Maine (ME)
St. Lawrence U (NY)
Sarah Lawrence Coll (NY)
Simmons Coll (MA)
U of California, Los Angeles (CA)
Washington U in St. Louis (MO)
Wheeling Jesuit U (WV)

AMERICAN NATIVE/NATIVE AMERICAN EDUCATION
The Coll of St. Scholastica (MN)
Northeastern State U (OK)
Queen's U at Kingston (ON, Canada)
U of Lethbridge (AB, Canada)
U of Minnesota, Duluth (MN)
U of Regina (SK, Canada)

AMERICAN NATIVE/NATIVE AMERICAN LANGUAGES
Bemidji State U (MN)
U of Alaska Fairbanks (AK)
U of Hawaii at Manoa (HI)
U of Regina (SK, Canada)

AMERICAN SIGN LANGUAGE (ASL)
Augustana Coll (SD)
Bethel Coll (IN)
California State U, Sacramento (CA)
Gardner-Webb U (NC)
Madonna U (MI)
Maryville Coll (TN)
Northeastern U (MA)
Rochester Inst of Technology (NY)
St. Catherine U (MN)
U of Houston (TX)
U of Rochester (NY)
Utah Valley U (UT)

AMERICAN STUDIES
Albright Coll (PA)
American U (DC)

Amherst Coll (MA)
Arizona State U (AZ)
Ashland U (OH)
Bard Coll (NY)
Bard Coll at Simon's Rock (MA)
Barnard Coll (NY)
Bates Coll (ME)
Baylor U (TX)
Bennington Coll (VT)
Boston U (MA)
Bowling Green State U (OH)
Brandeis U (MA)
Brown U (RI)
Cabrini Coll (PA)
California State U, Chico (CA)
California State U, Fullerton (CA)
California State U, Long Beach (CA)
California State U, San Bernardino (CA)
Carleton Coll (MN)
Case Western Reserve U (OH)
Cedarville U (OH)
Christopher Newport U (VA)
Claflin U (SC)
Claremont McKenna Coll (CA)
Clarkson U (NY)
Coe Coll (IA)
Colby Coll (ME)
Coll of Saint Elizabeth (NJ)
The Coll of Saint Rose (NY)
Coll of Staten Island of the City U of New York (NY)
The Coll of William and Mary (VA)
Columbia Coll (MO)
Columbia U, School of General Studies (NY)
Connecticut Coll (CT)
Cornell U (NY)
Creighton U (NE)
DePaul U (IL)
Dickinson Coll (PA)
Dominican Coll (NY)
Dominican U (IL)
Eckerd Coll (FL)
Elmhurst Coll (IL)
Elmira Coll (NY)
Emmanuel Coll (MA)
Emory U (GA)
Fairfield U (CT)
Fordham U (NY)
Franklin & Marshall Coll (PA)
Franklin Coll (IN)
George Fox U (OR)
Georgetown Coll (KY)
The George Washington U (DC)
Gettysburg Coll (PA)
Goucher Coll (MD)
Hamilton Coll (NY)
Hampshire Coll (MA)
Hawai`i Pacific U (HI)
Hendrix Coll (AR)
Hillsdale Coll (MI)
Hobart and William Smith Colls (NY)
Hofstra U (NY)
Idaho State U (ID)
Illinois Wesleyan U (IL)
Indiana U Bloomington (IN)
Kansas State U (KS)
Keene State Coll (NH)
Kent State U (OH)
Kenyon Coll (OH)
King Coll (TN)
Knox Coll (IL)
Lafayette Coll (PA)
Lake Forest Coll (IL)
Lehigh U (PA)
Lehman Coll of the City U of New York (NY)
Lindenwood U (MO)
Lindsey Wilson Coll (KY)
Lipscomb U (TN)
Long Island U–C. W. Post Campus (NY)
Lycoming Coll (PA)
Manhattanville Coll (NY)
Marlboro Coll (VT)
Mary Baldwin Coll (VA)
Miami U (OH)
Middlebury Coll (VT)
Mills Coll (CA)
Montana State U (MT)
Montreat Coll, Montreat (NC)
Mount Allison U (NB, Canada)

Mount Ida Coll (MA)
Mount St. Mary's Coll (CA)
Muhlenberg Coll (PA)
Nazareth Coll of Rochester (NY)
Nova Southeastern U (FL)
Occidental Coll (CA)
Oglethorpe U (GA)
Oklahoma City U (OK)
Oklahoma State U (OK)
Pace U (NY)
Penn State Abington (PA)
Penn State Berks (PA)
Penn State Brandywine (PA)
Penn State Erie, The Behrend Coll (PA)
Penn State Harrisburg (PA)
Penn State Lehigh Valley (PA)
Penn State Schuylkill (PA)
Penn State Worthington Scranton (PA)
Penn State York (PA)
Pitzer Coll (CA)
Pomona Coll (CA)
Providence Coll (RI)
Purdue U (IN)
Queens Coll of the City U of New York (NY)
Ramapo Coll of New Jersey (NJ)
Rider U (NJ)
Roger Williams U (RI)
Rutgers, The State U of New Jersey, Newark (NJ)
Rutgers, The State U of New Jersey, New Brunswick (NJ)
Saint Francis U (PA)
St. John Fisher Coll (NY)
Saint Louis U (MO)
Saint Mary's Coll of California (CA)
Saint Michael's Coll (VT)
St. Olaf Coll (MN)
Saint Peter's Coll (NJ)
Salve Regina U (RI)
San Francisco State U (CA)
Sarah Lawrence Coll (NY)
Scripps Coll (CA)
Sewanee: The U of the South (TN)
Siena Coll (NY)
Simmons Coll (MA)
Skidmore Coll (NY)
Smith Coll (MA)
Sonoma State U (CA)
Southwestern U (TX)
Stanford U (CA)
State U of New York at Fredonia (NY)
State U of New York at Oswego (NY)
State U of New York Coll at Geneseo (NY)
State U of New York Coll at Old Westbury (NY)
Stetson U (FL)
Stonehill Coll (MA)
Stony Brook U, State U of New York (NY)
Syracuse U (NY)
Temple U (PA)
Texas A&M U (TX)
Texas State U–San Marcos (TX)
Towson U (MD)
Trinity Coll (CT)
Tufts U (MA)
Tulane U (LA)
Union Coll (NY)
U at Buffalo, the State U of New York (NY)
The U of Alabama (AL)
U of Arkansas (AR)
U of California, Berkeley (CA)
U of California, Davis (CA)
U of California, Santa Cruz (CA)
U of Connecticut (CT)
U of Dayton (OH)
U of Hawaii at Manoa (HI)
U of Idaho (ID)
The U of Iowa (IA)
The U of Kansas (KS)
U of Maryland, Baltimore County (MD)
U of Maryland, Coll Park (MD)
U of Mary Washington (VA)
U of Massachusetts Boston (MA)
U of Massachusetts Lowell (MA)
U of Miami (FL)
U of Michigan (MI)

U of Michigan–Dearborn (MI)
U of Minnesota, Twin Cities Campus (MN)
U of Missouri–Kansas City (MO)
U of Mount Union (OH)
U of New England (ME)
U of New Mexico (NM)
The U of North Carolina at Chapel Hill (NC)
U of Notre Dame (IN)
U of Pennsylvania (PA)
U of Pittsburgh at Greensburg (PA)
U of Richmond (VA)
U of Rio Grande (OH)
U of Rochester (NY)
U of Southern California (CA)
U of Southern Mississippi (MS)
U of South Florida (FL)
The U of Texas at Austin (TX)
The U of Texas at Dallas (TX)
The U of Texas at San Antonio (TX)
The U of Texas–Pan American (TX)
The U of Toledo (OH)
U of Toronto (ON, Canada)
U of Washington, Bothell (WA)
The U of Western Ontario (ON, Canada)
U of Wyoming (WY)
Utah State U (UT)
Valparaiso U (IN)
Vanderbilt U (TN)
Vassar Coll (NY)
Virginia Wesleyan Coll (VA)
Washington Coll (MD)
Washington U in St. Louis (MO)
Wayne State U (MI)
Webster U (MO)
Wellesley Coll (MA)
Wells Coll (NY)
Wesleyan Coll (GA)
Wesleyan U (CT)
West Chester U of Pennsylvania (PA)
Western Connecticut State U (CT)
Western Washington U (WA)
Wheaton Coll (MA)
Wheelock Coll (MA)
Willamette U (OR)
Williams Coll (MA)
Wittenberg U (OH)
Yale U (CT)
Youngstown State U (OH)

ANALYTICAL CHEMISTRY
North Central Coll (IL)
The U of Western Ontario (ON, Canada)
West Chester U of Pennsylvania (PA)

ANATOMY
Andrews U (MI)
Minnesota State U Mankato (MN)
Tulane U (LA)
The U of Western Ontario (ON, Canada)

ANCIENT/CLASSICAL GREEK
Amherst Coll (MA)
Augustana Coll (IL)
Bard Coll (NY)
Barnard Coll (NY)
Baylor U (TX)
Boston Coll (MA)
Boston U (MA)
Brigham Young U (UT)
Bryn Mawr Coll (PA)
California State U, Long Beach (CA)
Carleton Coll (MN)
Creighton U (NE)
Dartmouth Coll (NH)
DePauw U (IN)
Duquesne U (PA)
Franklin & Marshall Coll (PA)
Gettysburg Coll (PA)
Hampden-Sydney Coll (VA)
Hobart and William Smith Colls (NY)
Howard Payne U (TX)
Hunter Coll of the City U of New York (NY)
Indiana U Bloomington (IN)
Lawrence U (WI)

Loyola U Chicago (IL)
Loyola U New Orleans (LA)
Monmouth Coll (IL)
Mount Allison U (NB, Canada)
Mount Holyoke Coll (MA)
Multnomah U (OR)
Randolph Coll (VA)
Randolph-Macon Coll (VA)
Rice U (TX)
Rockford Coll (IL)
Rutgers, The State U of New
   Jersey, New Brunswick (NJ)
St. Olaf Coll (MN)
Samford U (AL)
Santa Clara U (CA)
Smith Coll (MA)
Southwestern U (TX)
Stanford U (CA)
Swarthmore Coll (PA)
U of California, Berkeley (CA)
U of California, Los Angeles (CA)
U of Georgia (GA)
The U of Iowa (IA)
U of Miami (FL)
U of Michigan (MI)
U of Minnesota, Twin Cities
   Campus (MN)
U of Nebraska–Lincoln (NE)
U of New Hampshire (NH)
U of Notre Dame (IN)
U of Richmond (VA)
The U of Scranton (PA)
U of Vermont (VT)
U of Washington (WA)
The U of Western Ontario (ON,
   Canada)
Wake Forest U (NC)
Washington U in St. Louis (MO)
Wellesley Coll (MA)
Wheaton Coll (MA)
Yale U (CT)

ANCIENT NEAR EASTERN AND BIBLICAL LANGUAGES

Baylor U (TX)
Belmont U (TN)
Carson-Newman Coll (TN)
Concordia U (CA)
Concordia U (MI)
Concordia U Chicago (IL)
Geneva Coll (PA)
Howard Payne U (TX)
Lipscomb U (TN)
Luther Coll (IA)
The Master's Coll and Sem (CA)
Mid-Continent U (KY)
Northwest Nazarene U (ID)
Northwest U (WA)
Union U (TN)
U of Toronto (ON, Canada)

ANCIENT STUDIES

Bates Coll (ME)
Boston U (MA)
Bowdoin Coll (ME)
Colby Coll (ME)
Columbia U, School of General
   Studies (NY)
Concordia U (QC, Canada)
Lehigh U (PA)
Loyola Marymount U (CA)
Mount Holyoke Coll (MA)
Ohio Wesleyan U (OH)
Rockford Coll (IL)
St. Olaf Coll (MN)
Santa Clara U (CA)
Stanford U (CA)
The U of Iowa (IA)
The U of Kansas (KS)
U of Maryland, Baltimore County
   (MD)
U of Miami (FL)
U of Michigan (MI)
U of Minnesota, Twin Cities
   Campus (MN)
U of Nebraska–Lincoln (NE)
U of Richmond (VA)
The U of Texas at Austin (TX)
Vanderbilt U (TN)
Washington U in St. Louis (MO)
Wheaton Coll (MA)

ANIMAL-ASSISTED THERAPY

Carroll Coll (MT)

ANIMAL BEHAVIOR AND ETHOLOGY

Bucknell U (PA)
Canisius Coll (NY)
Franklin & Marshall Coll (PA)
Hampshire Coll (MA)
Southwestern U (TX)
U of Toronto (ON, Canada)

ANIMAL GENETICS

Dartmouth Coll (NH)
Jacksonville State U (AL)
Ohio Wesleyan U (OH)
Rutgers, The State U of New
   Jersey, New Brunswick (NJ)
Sarah Lawrence Coll (NY)
U of Alberta (AB, Canada)
The U of British Columbia (BC,
   Canada)
U of Toronto (ON, Canada)
Worcester Polytechnic Inst (MA)

ANIMAL HEALTH

Sul Ross State U (TX)
U of Georgia (GA)

ANIMAL/LIVESTOCK HUSBANDRY AND PRODUCTION

Angelo State U (TX)
Dordt Coll (IA)
Purdue U (IN)
Rutgers, The State U of New
   Jersey, New Brunswick (NJ)
Tarleton State U (TX)
Texas A&M U (TX)
The U of British Columbia (BC,
   Canada)
U of Illinois at Urbana–Champaign
   (IL)
U of Minnesota, Twin Cities
   Campus (MN)

ANIMAL NUTRITION

U of Georgia (GA)

ANIMAL PHYSIOLOGY

California State U, Fresno (CA)
Minnesota State U Mankato (MN)
Rutgers, The State U of New
   Jersey, New Brunswick (NJ)
Sonoma State U (CA)
Texas State U–San Marcos (TX)
The U of Akron (OH)
U of Alberta (AB, Canada)
U of Connecticut (CT)
U of Minnesota, Twin Cities
   Campus (MN)
U of Toronto (ON, Canada)
Utah State U (UT)

ANIMAL SCIENCES

Abilene Christian U (TX)
Angelo State U (TX)
Arkansas State U (AR)
Auburn U (AL)
Berry Coll (GA)
California Polytechnic State U, San
   Luis Obispo (CA)
California State Polytechnic U,
   Pomona (CA)
California State U, Chico (CA)
California State U, Fresno (CA)
Clemson U (SC)
Coll of the Ozarks (MO)
Colorado State U (CO)
Cornell U (NY)
Delaware State U (DE)
Delaware Valley Coll (PA)
Dordt Coll (IA)
Fort Hays State U (KS)
Hardin-Simmons U (TX)
Iowa State U of Science and
   Technology (IA)
Kansas State U (KS)
Louisiana State U and Ag and Mech
   Coll (LA)
Lubbock Christian U (TX)
Mercy Coll (NY)
Michigan State U (MI)
Middle Tennessee State U (TN)
Mississippi State U (MS)
Missouri State U (MO)

Montana State U (MT)
New Mexico State U (NM)
North Carolina Ag and Tech State U
   (NC)
North Carolina State U (NC)
North Dakota State U (ND)
Northwest Missouri State U (MO)
Nova Scotia Ag Coll (NS, Canada)
The Ohio State U (OH)
Oklahoma State U (OK)
Penn State Abington (PA)
Penn State Altoona (PA)
Penn State Beaver (PA)
Penn State Berks (PA)
Penn State Brandywine (PA)
Penn State DuBois (PA)
Penn State Erie, The Behrend Coll
   (PA)
Penn State Fayette, The Eberly
   Campus (PA)
Penn State Greater Allegheny (PA)
Penn State Hazleton (PA)
Penn State Lehigh Valley (PA)
Penn State Mont Alto (PA)
Penn State New Kensington (PA)
Penn State Schuylkill (PA)
Penn State Shenango (PA)
Penn State U Park (PA)
Penn State Wilkes-Barre (PA)
Penn State Worthington Scranton
   (PA)
Penn State York (PA)
Purdue U (IN)
Rutgers, The State U of New
   Jersey, New Brunswick (NJ)
South Dakota State U (SD)
Southeast Missouri State U (MO)
Southern Illinois U Carbondale (IL)
Stephen F. Austin State U (TX)
Sul Ross State U (TX)
Tarleton State U (TX)
Texas A&M U (TX)
Texas A&M U–Kingsville (TX)
Texas State U–San Marcos (TX)
Texas Tech U (TX)
Thompson Rivers U (BC, Canada)
Tuskegee U (AL)
The U of Arizona (AZ)
U of Arkansas (AR)
The U of British Columbia (BC,
   Canada)
U of California, Davis (CA)
U of Connecticut (CT)
U of Delaware (DE)
U of Denver (CO)
The U of Findlay (OH)
U of Florida (FL)
U of Guelph (ON, Canada)
U of Hawaii at Hilo (HI)
U of Hawaii at Manoa (HI)
U of Idaho (ID)
U of Illinois at Urbana–Champaign
   (IL)
U of Maine (ME)
U of Maryland, Coll Park (MD)
U of Massachusetts Amherst (MA)
U of Minnesota, Crookston (MN)
U of Minnesota, Twin Cities
   Campus (MN)
U of Missouri (MO)
U of Nebraska–Lincoln (NE)
U of Nevada, Reno (NV)
U of New Hampshire (NH)
U of Rhode Island (RI)
The U of Tennessee (TN)
The U of Tennessee at Martin (TN)
U of Vermont (VT)
U of Wisconsin–Madison (WI)
U of Wisconsin–Platteville (WI)
U of Wisconsin–River Falls (WI)
U of Wyoming (WY)
Utah State U (UT)
Virginia Polytechnic Inst and State
   U (VA)
Washington State U (WA)
West Texas A&M U (TX)
West Virginia U (WV)

ANIMAL SCIENCES RELATED

Delaware Valley Coll (PA)
North Carolina Ag and Tech State U
   (NC)
Penn State Abington (PA)
Penn State Beaver (PA)

Penn State Brandywine (PA)
Penn State DuBois (PA)
Penn State Erie, The Behrend Coll
   (PA)
Penn State Fayette, The Eberly
   Campus (PA)
Penn State Greater Allegheny (PA)
Penn State Hazleton (PA)
Penn State Lehigh Valley (PA)
Penn State Mont Alto (PA)
Penn State New Kensington (PA)
Penn State Schuylkill (PA)
Penn State Shenango (PA)
Penn State Wilkes-Barre (PA)
Penn State Worthington Scranton
   (PA)
Penn State York (PA)
Purdue U (IN)
U of California, Davis (CA)
U of Illinois at Urbana–Champaign
   (IL)

ANIMATION, INTERACTIVE TECHNOLOGY, VIDEO GRAPHICS AND SPECIAL EFFECTS

Acad of Art U (CA)
Art Center Coll of Design (CA)
The Art Inst of Atlanta (GA)
The Art Inst of Atlanta–Decatur
   (GA)
The Art Inst of Austin (TX)
The Art Inst of California, a college
   of Argosy U, Hollywood (CA)
The Art Inst of California, a college
   of Argosy U, Inland Empire (CA)
The Art Inst of California, a college
   of Argosy U, Los Angeles (CA)
The Art Inst of California, a college
   of Argosy U, Orange County (CA)
The Art Inst of California, a college
   of Argosy U, Sacramento (CA)
The Art Inst of California, a college
   of Argosy U, San Diego (CA)
The Art Inst of California, a college
   of Argosy U, San Francisco (CA)
The Art Inst of California, a college
   of Argosy U, Sunnyvale (CA)
The Art Inst of Colorado (CO)
The Art Inst of Fort Lauderdale (FL)
The Art Inst of Houston (TX)
The Art Inst of Houston - North (TX)
The Art Inst of Indianapolis (IN)
The Art Inst of Jacksonville (FL)
The Art Inst of Las Vegas (NV)
The Art Inst of Michigan–Troy (MI)
The Art Inst of Ohio–Cincinnati
   (OH)
The Art Inst of Phoenix (AZ)
The Art Inst of Pittsburgh (PA)
The Art Inst of Portland (OR)
The Art Inst of Raleigh-Durham
   (NC)
The Art Inst of Salt Lake City (UT)
The Art Inst of San Antonio (TX)
The Art Inst of Seattle (WA)
The Art Inst of Tampa (FL)
The Art Inst of Washington (VA)
Becker Coll (MA)
Bennington Coll (VT)
Bradley U (IL)
Brigham Young U (UT)
Broadview U-Salt Lake City (UT)
California Coll of the Arts (CA)
The Cleveland Inst of Art (OH)
Cogswell Polytechnical Coll (CA)
Coll for Creative Studies (MI)
Coll of the Atlantic (ME)
Concordia U (QC, Canada)
Davenport U, Grand Rapids (MI)
DePaul U (IL)
DigiPen Inst of Technology (WA)
Eastern Michigan U (MI)
East Tennessee State U (TN)
Emily Carr U of Art + Design (BC,
   Canada)
Fashion Inst of Technology (NY)
Ferris State U (MI)
George Mason U (VA)
Huntington U (IN)
The Illinois Inst of Art–Chicago (IL)
The Illinois Inst of Art–Schaumburg
   (IL)

Intl Acad of Design & Technology
   (FL)
Kansas City Art Inst (MO)
Kent State U at Tuscarawas (OH)
Loyola Marymount U (CA)
Massachusetts Coll of Art and
   Design (MA)
Miami Intl U of Art & Design (FL)
Missouri Western State U (MO)
Montclair State U (NJ)
Montserrat Coll of Art (MA)
Mount Ida Coll (MA)
Northeastern U (MA)
Northwestern Coll (MN)
Pacific Northwest Coll of Art (OR)
Purdue U Calumet (IN)
Regent U (VA)
Ringling Coll of Art and Design (FL)
Rochester Inst of Technology (NY)
Rocky Mountain Coll of Art +
   Design (CO)
Sam Houston State U (TX)
Savannah Coll of Art and Design
   (GA)
Suffolk U (MA)
U of Arkansas–Fort Smith (AR)
U of Dubuque (IA)
U of Idaho (ID)
U of Lethbridge (AB, Canada)
The U of the Arts (PA)
U of the Incarnate Word (TX)
Villa Maria Coll of Buffalo (NY)
Webster U (MO)

ANTHROPOLOGY

Adelphi U (NY)
Agnes Scott Coll (GA)
Albion Coll (MI)
Alma Coll (MI)
American U (DC)
The American U in Cairo (Egypt)
Amherst Coll (MA)
Appalachian State U (NC)
Arizona State U (AZ)
Athabasca U (AB, Canada)
Auburn U (AL)
Augustana Coll (IL)
Augustana Coll (SD)
Ball State U (IN)
Bard Coll (NY)
Barnard Coll (NY)
Bates Coll (ME)
Baylor U (TX)
Beloit Coll (WI)
Bennington Coll (VT)
Biola U (CA)
Bloomsburg U of Pennsylvania (PA)
Boise State U (ID)
Boston U (MA)
Bowdoin Coll (ME)
Brandeis U (MA)
Bridgewater State U (MA)
Brown U (RI)
Bryn Mawr Coll (PA)
Bucknell U (PA)
Buffalo State Coll, State U of New
   York (NY)
Butler U (IN)
California Baptist U (CA)
California State Polytechnic U,
   Pomona (CA)
California State U, Bakersfield (CA)
California State U, Chico (CA)
California State U, Dominguez Hills
   (CA)
California State U, East Bay (CA)
California State U, Fresno (CA)
California State U, Fullerton (CA)
California State U, Long Beach
   (CA)
California State U, Los Angeles
   (CA)
California State U, Sacramento
   (CA)
California State U, San Bernardino
   (CA)
California State U, Stanislaus (CA)
California U of Pennsylvania (PA)
Canisius Coll (NY)
Cape Breton U (NS, Canada)
Carleton Coll (MN)
Case Western Reserve U (OH)
The Catholic U of America (DC)
Central Coll (IA)
Central Connecticut State U (CT)

Central Michigan U (MI)
Central Washington U (WA)
Centre Coll (KY)
City Coll of the City U of New York (NY)
Clarion U of Pennsylvania (PA)
Cleveland State U (OH)
Colby Coll (ME)
Colgate U (NY)
Coll of Charleston (SC)
The Coll of Idaho (ID)
Coll of the Holy Cross (MA)
The Coll of William and Mary (VA)
The Colorado Coll (CO)
Colorado State U (CO)
Columbia U, School of General Studies (NY)
Concordia U (QC, Canada)
Connecticut Coll (CT)
Cornell Coll (IA)
Cornell U (NY)
Creighton U (NE)
Dalhousie U (NS, Canada)
Dartmouth Coll (NH)
Davidson Coll (NC)
Denison U (OH)
DePaul U (IL)
DePauw U (IN)
Dickinson Coll (PA)
Dowling Coll (NY)
Drake U (IA)
Drew U (NJ)
Earlham Coll (IN)
East Carolina U (NC)
Eastern Kentucky U (KY)
Eastern Michigan U (MI)
Eastern New Mexico U (NM)
Eastern Washington U (WA)
East Tennessee State U (TN)
Eckerd Coll (FL)
Edinboro U of Pennsylvania (PA)
Elmira Coll (NY)
Elon U (NC)
Emory & Henry Coll (VA)
Emory U (GA)
Florida Atlantic U (FL)
Florida Gulf Coast U (FL)
Fordham U (NY)
Fort Lewis Coll (CO)
Franciscan U of Steubenville (OH)
Franklin & Marshall Coll (PA)
George Mason U (VA)
The George Washington U (DC)
Georgia Southern U (GA)
Georgia State U (GA)
Gettysburg Coll (PA)
Goucher Coll (MD)
Grand Valley State U (MI)
Grinnell Coll (IA)
Gustavus Adolphus Coll (MN)
Hamilton Coll (NY)
Hamline U (MI)
Hampshire Coll (MA)
Hanover Coll (IN)
Hartwick Coll (NY)
Harvard U (MA)
Haverford Coll (PA)
Hawai'i Pacific U (HI)
Heidelberg U (OH)
Hendrix Coll (AR)
Hobart and William Smith Colls (NY)
Hofstra U (NY)
Humboldt State U (CA)
Hunter Coll of the City U of New York (NY)
Idaho State U (ID)
Illinois State U (IL)
Illinois Wesleyan U (IL)
Indiana State U (IN)
Indiana U Bloomington (IN)
Indiana U Northwest (IN)
Indiana U of Pennsylvania (PA)
Indiana U–Purdue U Fort Wayne (IN)
Indiana U–Purdue U Indianapolis (IN)
Indiana U South Bend (IN)
Iowa State U of Science and Technology (IA)
Ithaca Coll (NY)
Jacksonville State U (AL)
James Madison U (VA)
The Johns Hopkins U (MD)
Johnson State Coll (VT)

Juniata Coll (PA)
Kalamazoo Coll (MI)
Kansas State U (KS)
Kennesaw State U (GA)
Kent State U (OH)
Kenyon Coll (OH)
Knox Coll (IL)
Kutztown U of Pennsylvania (PA)
Lafayette Coll (PA)
Lake Forest Coll (IL)
Lakehead U (ON, Canada)
Lawrence U (WI)
Lee U (TN)
Lehigh U (PA)
Lehman Coll of the City U of New York (NY)
Lewis & Clark Coll (OR)
Lincoln U (PA)
Linfield Coll (OR)
Long Island U–C. W. Post Campus (NY)
Longwood U (VA)
Louisiana State U and Ag and Mech Coll (LA)
Loyola U Chicago (IL)
Luther Coll (IA)
Macalester Coll (MN)
Mansfield U of Pennsylvania (PA)
Marlboro Coll (VT)
Marquette U (WI)
Massachusetts Inst of Technology (MA)
Mercyhurst Coll (PA)
Metropolitan State Coll of Denver (CO)
Miami U (OH)
Michigan State U (MI)
Middle Tennessee State U (TN)
Millersville U of Pennsylvania (PA)
Mills Coll (CA)
Minnesota State U Mankato (MN)
Minnesota State U Moorhead (MN)
Mississippi State U (MS)
Missouri State U (MO)
Monmouth Coll (IL)
Monmouth U (NJ)
Montana State U (MT)
Montclair State U (NJ)
Mount Allison U (NB, Canada)
Mount Holyoke Coll (MA)
Muhlenberg Coll (PA)
Nazareth Coll of Rochester (NY)
New Coll of Florida (FL)
New Mexico State U (NM)
New York U (NY)
North Carolina State U (NC)
North Dakota State U (ND)
Northeastern Illinois U (IL)
Northern Arizona U (AZ)
Northern Illinois U (IL)
Northern Kentucky U (KY)
Oakland U (MI)
The Ohio State U (OH)
Ohio U (OH)
Ohio Wesleyan U (OH)
Pacific Lutheran U (WA)
Penn State Abington (PA)
Penn State Altoona (PA)
Penn State Beaver (PA)
Penn State Berks (PA)
Penn State Brandywine (PA)
Penn State DuBois (PA)
Penn State Erie, The Behrend Coll (PA)
Penn State Fayette, The Eberly Campus (PA)
Penn State Greater Allegheny (PA)
Penn State Hazleton (PA)
Penn State Lehigh Valley (PA)
Penn State Mont Alto (PA)
Penn State New Kensington (PA)
Penn State Schuylkill (PA)
Penn State Shenango (PA)
Penn State U Park (PA)
Penn State Wilkes-Barre (PA)
Penn State Worthington Scranton (PA)
Penn State York (PA)
Pitzer Coll (CA)
Plymouth State U (NH)
Pomona Coll (CA)
Portland State U (OR)
Princeton U (NJ)
Purchase Coll, State U of New York (NY)

Purdue U (IN)
Queens Coll of the City U of New York (NY)
Radford U (VA)
Rhode Island Coll (RI)
Rhodes Coll (TN)
Rice U (TX)
Ripon Coll (WI)
Rockford Coll (IL)
Roger Williams U (RI)
Rollins Coll (FL)
Rutgers, The State U of New Jersey, Newark (NJ)
Rutgers, The State U of New Jersey, New Brunswick (NJ)
Saint Francis U (PA)
St. John Fisher Coll (NY)
St. John's U (NY)
St. Lawrence U (NY)
Saint Louis U (MO)
Saint Martin's U (WA)
Saint Mary's Coll of California (CA)
St. Mary's Coll of Maryland (MD)
St. Thomas U (NB, Canada)
Saint Vincent Coll (PA)
San Diego State U (CA)
San Francisco State U (CA)
Santa Clara U (CA)
Sarah Lawrence Coll (NY)
Scripps Coll (CA)
Sewanee: The U of the South (TN)
Skidmore Coll (NY)
Smith Coll (MA)
Sonoma State U (CA)
Southeast Missouri State U (MO)
Southern Connecticut State U (CT)
Southern Illinois U Carbondale (IL)
Southern Illinois U Edwardsville (IL)
Southern Methodist U (TX)
Southern Oregon U (OR)
Southwestern U (TX)
Spelman Coll (GA)
Stanford U (CA)
State U of New York at Binghamton (NY)
State U of New York at New Paltz (NY)
State U of New York at Oswego (NY)
State U of New York at Plattsburgh (NY)
State U of New York Coll at Cortland (NY)
State U of New York Coll at Geneseo (NY)
State U of New York Coll at Oneonta (NY)
State U of New York Coll at Potsdam (NY)
Stony Brook U, State U of New York (NY)
Susquehanna U (PA)
Sweet Briar Coll (VA)
Syracuse U (NY)
Temple U (PA)
Texas A&M U (TX)
Texas Christian U (TX)
Texas State U–San Marcos (TX)
Texas Tech U (TX)
Thomas Edison State Coll (NJ)
Transylvania U (KY)
Trent U (ON, Canada)
Trinity Coll (CT)
Trinity U (TX)
Tufts U (MA)
Tulane U (LA)
Union Coll (NY)
U at Albany, State U of New York (NY)
U at Buffalo, the State U of New York (NY)
The U of Alabama (AL)
The U of Alabama at Birmingham (AL)
U of Alaska Anchorage (AK)
U of Alaska Fairbanks (AK)
U of Alberta (AB, Canada)
The U of Arizona (AZ)
U of Arkansas (AR)
U of Arkansas at Little Rock (AR)
The U of British Columbia (BC, Canada)
The U of British Columbia–Okanagan (BC, Canada)
U of California, Berkeley (CA)

U of California, Davis (CA)
U of California, Irvine (CA)
U of California, Los Angeles (CA)
U of California, Merced (CA)
U of California, Riverside (CA)
U of California, Santa Barbara (CA)
U of California, Santa Cruz (CA)
U of Central Florida (FL)
U of Cincinnati (OH)
U of Colorado at Colorado Springs (CO)
U of Colorado Boulder (CO)
U of Colorado Denver (CO)
U of Connecticut (CT)
U of Delaware (DE)
U of Denver (CO)
U of Florida (FL)
U of Georgia (GA)
U of Guam (GU)
U of Guelph (ON, Canada)
U of Hawaii at Hilo (HI)
U of Hawaii at Manoa (HI)
U of Hawaii–West Oahu (HI)
U of Houston (TX)
U of Houston–Clear Lake (TX)
U of Idaho (ID)
U of Illinois at Chicago (IL)
U of Illinois at Urbana–Champaign (IL)
U of Indianapolis (IN)
The U of Iowa (IA)
The U of Kansas (KS)
U of La Verne (CA)
U of Lethbridge (AB, Canada)
U of Louisiana at Lafayette (LA)
U of Louisville (KY)
U of Maine (ME)
U of Maine at Farmington (ME)
U of Maryland, Baltimore County (MD)
U of Maryland, Coll Park (MD)
U of Mary Washington (VA)
U of Massachusetts Amherst (MA)
U of Massachusetts Boston (MA)
U of Memphis (TN)
U of Miami (FL)
U of Michigan (MI)
U of Michigan–Dearborn (MI)
U of Michigan–Flint (MI)
U of Minnesota, Duluth (MN)
U of Minnesota, Twin Cities Campus (MN)
U of Mississippi (MS)
U of Missouri (MO)
U of Missouri–St. Louis (MO)
The U of Montana Western (MT)
U of Nebraska–Lincoln (NE)
U of Nevada, Las Vegas (NV)
U of Nevada, Reno (NV)
U of New Hampshire (NH)
U of New Mexico (NM)
U of New Orleans (LA)
The U of North Carolina at Chapel Hill (NC)
The U of North Carolina at Charlotte (NC)
The U of North Carolina Wilmington (NC)
U of North Dakota (ND)
U of Northern Iowa (IA)
U of North Florida (FL)
U of North Texas (TX)
U of Notre Dame (IN)
U of Oklahoma (OK)
U of Oregon (OR)
U of Ottawa (ON, Canada)
U of Pennsylvania (PA)
U of Pittsburgh (PA)
U of Pittsburgh at Greensburg (PA)
U of Redlands (CA)
U of Regina (SK, Canada)
U of Rhode Island (RI)
U of Richmond (VA)
U of Rochester (NY)
U of San Diego (CA)
U of South Alabama (AL)
U of South Carolina (SC)
The U of South Dakota (SD)
U of Southern California (CA)
U of Southern Mississippi (MS)
U of South Florida (FL)
U of South Florida–St. Petersburg Campus (FL)
The U of Tennessee (TN)
The U of Texas at Arlington (TX)

The U of Texas at Austin (TX)
The U of Texas at El Paso (TX)
The U of Texas at San Antonio (TX)
The U of Texas–Pan American (TX)
U of the District of Columbia (DC)
The U of Toledo (OH)
U of Toronto (ON, Canada)
U of Tulsa (OK)
U of Utah (UT)
U of Vermont (VT)
U of Virginia (VA)
U of Washington (WA)
The U of Western Ontario (ON, Canada)
U of West Florida (FL)
U of West Georgia (GA)
U of Windsor (ON, Canada)
U of Wisconsin–Madison (WI)
U of Wisconsin–Milwaukee (WI)
U of Wyoming (WY)
Utah State U (UT)
Vanderbilt U (TN)
Vanguard U of Southern California (CA)
Vassar Coll (NY)
Virginia Commonwealth U (VA)
Wagner Coll (NY)
Wake Forest U (NC)
Washburn U (KS)
Washington and Lee U (VA)
Washington Coll (MD)
Washington State U (WA)
Washington U in St. Louis (MO)
Wayne State U (MI)
Weber State U (UT)
Webster U (MO)
Wellesley Coll (MA)
Wells Coll (NY)
Wesleyan U (CT)
West Chester U of Pennsylvania (PA)
Western Carolina U (NC)
Western Connecticut State U (CT)
Western Kentucky U (KY)
Western Michigan U (MI)
Western Oregon U (OR)
Western State Coll of Colorado (CO)
Western Washington U (WA)
Westminster Coll (MO)
Wheaton Coll (IL)
Wheaton Coll (MA)
Whitman Coll (WA)
Wichita State U (KS)
Widener U (PA)
Willamette U (OR)
William Paterson U of New Jersey (NJ)
Williams Coll (MA)
Wright State U (OH)
Yale U (CT)
York Coll of the City U of New York (NY)
Youngstown State U (OH)

ANTHROPOLOGY RELATED

Bridgewater State U (MA)
Howard Payne U (TX)
Mary Baldwin Coll (VA)
U of Delaware (DE)
U of Michigan (MI)
U of Southern California (CA)
The U of Western Ontario (ON, Canada)
Western Washington U (WA)

APPAREL AND ACCESSORIES MARKETING

The Art Inst of Atlanta (GA)
The Art Inst of Atlanta–Decatur (GA)
The Art Inst of Austin (TX)
The Art Inst of California, a college of Argosy U, Inland Empire (CA)
The Art Inst of Charleston (SC)
The Art Inst of Dallas (TX)
The Art Inst of Houston - North (TX)
The Art Inst of Indianapolis (IN)
The Art Inst of Jacksonville (FL)
The Art Inst of Las Vegas (NV)
The Art Inst of Pittsburgh (PA)
The Art Inst of Salt Lake City (UT)
The Art Inst of San Antonio (TX)
The Art Inst of Tampa (FL)

The Art Inst of Tennessee–Nashville (TN)
The Art Inst of Virginia Beach (VA)
The Art Inst of Washington (VA)
The Art Inst of Washington–Dulles (VA)
The Art Inst of York–Pennsylvania (PA)
The Art Insts Intl Minnesota (MN)
Bluffton U (OH)
The New England Inst of Art (MA)
Philadelphia U (PA)
U of Rhode Island (RI)

APPAREL AND TEXTILE MANUFACTURING
Fashion Inst of Technology (NY)
Michigan State U (MI)
Purdue U (IN)

APPAREL AND TEXTILE MARKETING MANAGEMENT
The Art Inst of Fort Worth (TX)
The Art Inst of Philadelphia (PA)
The Art Inst of San Antonio (TX)
Auburn U (AL)
Colorado State U (CO)
Indiana Tech (IN)
Northwest Missouri State U (MO)
Purdue U (IN)
South Dakota State U (SD)
Stephens Coll (MO)
U of the Incarnate Word (TX)
Wayne State U (MI)

APPAREL AND TEXTILES
Appalachian State U (NC)
Auburn U (AL)
Bluffton U (OH)
Bob Jones U (SC)
Bowling Green State U (OH)
California State Polytechnic U, Pomona (CA)
California State U, Long Beach (CA)
Cheyney U of Pennsylvania (PA)
Delaware State U (DE)
East Carolina U (NC)
Framingham State U (MA)
Georgia Southern U (GA)
Indiana State U (IN)
Indiana U Bloomington (IN)
Iowa State U of Science and Technology (IA)
Jacksonville State U (AL)
Kansas State U (KS)
Liberty U (VA)
Lipscomb U (TN)
Michigan State U (MI)
Middle Tennessee State U (TN)
Minnesota State U Mankato (MN)
Missouri State U (MO)
New Mexico State U (NM)
North Carolina Ag and Tech State U (NC)
North Dakota State U (ND)
Northern Illinois U (IL)
The Ohio State U (OH)
Ohio U (OH)
Philadelphia U (PA)
Purdue U (IN)
Seattle Pacific U (WA)
Southern Illinois U Carbondale (IL)
Texas A&M U–Kingsville (TX)
The U of Akron (OH)
The U of Alabama (AL)
U of Alberta (AB, Canada)
U of Arkansas (AR)
U of California, Davis (CA)
U of Central Missouri (MO)
U of Delaware (DE)
U of Hawaii at Manoa (HI)
U of Idaho (ID)
U of Minnesota, Twin Cities Campus (MN)
U of Missouri (MO)
U of Nebraska–Lincoln (NE)
U of Northern Iowa (IA)
U of Rhode Island (RI)
U of Southern Mississippi (MS)
The U of Texas at Austin (TX)
U of the District of Columbia (DC)
U of Wisconsin–Madison (WI)
U of Wisconsin–Stout (WI)

Virginia Polytechnic Inst and State U (VA)
Washington State U (WA)
Western Kentucky U (KY)
Western Michigan U (MI)

APPAREL AND TEXTILES RELATED
Purdue U (IN)

APPLIED AND PROFESSIONAL ETHICS
Simpson Coll (IA)
Western Michigan U (MI)

APPLIED BEHAVIOR ANALYSIS
U of Southern Maine (ME)
Western Michigan U (MI)

APPLIED ECONOMICS
Allegheny Coll (PA)
Brigham Young U (UT)
Bryant U (RI)
The Coll of St. Scholastica (MN)
Concordia U (QC, Canada)
Farmingdale State Coll (NY)
Flagler Coll (FL)
HEC Montreal (QC, Canada)
Ithaca Coll (NY)
Penn State Abington (PA)
Penn State Beaver (PA)
Penn State Brandywine (PA)
Penn State DuBois (PA)
Penn State Erie, The Behrend Coll (PA)
Penn State Fayette, The Eberly Campus (PA)
Penn State Greater Allegheny (PA)
Penn State Hazleton (PA)
Penn State Lehigh Valley (PA)
Penn State Mont Alto (PA)
Penn State New Kensington (PA)
Penn State Schuylkill (PA)
Penn State Shenango (PA)
Penn State Wilkes-Barre (PA)
Penn State Worthington Scranton (PA)
Penn State York (PA)
Purdue U (IN)
State U of New York at Binghamton (NY)
The U of Arizona (AZ)
U of Minnesota, Twin Cities Campus (MN)
U of Northern Iowa (IA)
U of Rhode Island (RI)

APPLIED HORTICULTURE/HORTICULTURAL BUSINESS SERVICES RELATED
Delaware Valley Coll (PA)
Morrisville State Coll (NY)
U of Rhode Island (RI)

APPLIED HORTICULTURE/HORTICULTURE OPERATIONS
Colorado State U (CO)
Farmingdale State Coll (NY)
Ferrum Coll (VA)
Iowa State U of Science and Technology (IA)
Kent State U (OH)
Kent State U at Salem (OH)
Nova Scotia Ag Coll (NS, Canada)
Roger Williams U (RI)
South Dakota State U (SD)
Texas A&M U (TX)
Texas Tech U (TX)
U of Georgia (GA)
U of Illinois at Urbana–Champaign (IL)

APPLIED LINGUISTICS
Portland State U (OR)

APPLIED MATHEMATICS
American U (DC)
American U of Beirut (Lebanon)
Arizona State U (AZ)
Asbury U (KY)
Auburn U (AL)
Baylor U (TX)

Belmont U (TN)
Biola U (CA)
Bloomfield Coll (NJ)
Boise State U (ID)
Bowie State U (MD)
Brescia U (KY)
Brown U (RI)
Bryant U (RI)
California Inst of Technology (CA)
California State U, Chico (CA)
California State U, East Bay (CA)
California State U, Fullerton (CA)
California State U, Long Beach (CA)
Carnegie Mellon U (PA)
Carroll Coll (MT)
Case Western Reserve U (OH)
Clarkson U (NY)
Coastal Carolina U (SC)
The Coll of Idaho (ID)
Columbia U, School of General Studies (NY)
Creighton U (NE)
Dowling Coll (NY)
East Central U (OK)
Eastern Kentucky U (KY)
Farmingdale State Coll (NY)
Ferris State U (MI)
Fitchburg State U (MA)
Florida Inst of Technology (FL)
Geneva Coll (PA)
The George Washington U (DC)
Georgia Inst of Technology (GA)
Goshen Coll (IN)
Grand View U (IA)
Hampden-Sydney Coll (VA)
Harvard U (MA)
Hawai`i Pacific U (HI)
Hofstra U (NY)
Humboldt State U (CA)
Illinois Inst of Technology (IL)
Indiana U of Pennsylvania (PA)
Indiana U South Bend (IN)
Inter American U of Puerto Rico, Bayamón Campus (PR)
Inter American U of Puerto Rico, San Germán Campus (PR)
Iona Coll (NY)
Jamestown Coll (ND)
The Johns Hopkins U (MD)
Kent State U (OH)
Kettering U (MI)
King Coll (TN)
Lamar U (TX)
La Salle U (PA)
Lasell Coll (MA)
Long Island U–C. W. Post Campus (NY)
Longwood U (VA)
Loyola Marymount U (CA)
Loyola U Maryland (MD)
Marlboro Coll (VT)
Mary Baldwin Coll (VA)
Maryville U of Saint Louis (MO)
The Master's Coll and Sem (CA)
Metropolitan State U (MN)
Michigan Technological U (MI)
Millikin U (IL)
Millsaps Coll (MS)
Missouri U of Science and Technology (MO)
Mount Allison U (NB, Canada)
New Coll of Florida (FL)
New York City Coll of Technology of the City U of New York (NY)
North Carolina Ag and Tech State U (NC)
North Carolina State U (NC)
North Central Coll (IL)
Northern Illinois U (IL)
Oakland City U (IN)
Ohio U (OH)
Penn State Harrisburg (PA)
Purdue U (IN)
Queens U of Charlotte (NC)
Quinnipiac U (CT)
Rice U (TX)
Robert Morris U (PA)
Rutgers, The State U of New Jersey, Newark (NJ)
Saginaw Valley State U (MI)
St. Thomas Aquinas Coll (NY)
San Diego State U (CA)
San Francisco State U (CA)
Seattle U (WA)

Siena Heights U (MI)
Simon Fraser U (BC, Canada)
Sonoma State U (CA)
State U of New York at Oswego (NY)
Stony Brook U, State U of New York (NY)
Texas A&M U (TX)
Texas State U–San Marcos (TX)
Trent U (ON, Canada)
Trevecca Nazarene U (TN)
United States Naval Acad (MD)
U at Albany, State U of New York (NY)
U at Buffalo, the State U of New York (NY)
The U of Akron (OH)
U of Alberta (AB, Canada)
The U of British Columbia (BC, Canada)
U of California, Berkeley (CA)
U of California, Davis (CA)
U of California, Los Angeles (CA)
U of California, Merced (CA)
U of Colorado at Colorado Springs (CO)
U of Colorado Boulder (CO)
U of Connecticut (CT)
U of Houston–Downtown (TX)
U of Idaho (ID)
U of Massachusetts Lowell (MA)
U of Miami (FL)
U of Missouri–St. Louis (MO)
U of Nevada, Las Vegas (NV)
U of New Haven (CT)
The U of North Carolina at Chapel Hill (NC)
U of Northern Iowa (IA)
U of North Florida (FL)
U of Pittsburgh (PA)
U of Pittsburgh at Bradford (PA)
U of Pittsburgh at Greensburg (PA)
U of Rochester (NY)
U of South Carolina Aiken (SC)
U of Southern California (CA)
The U of Tennessee at Chattanooga (TN)
The U of Texas at El Paso (TX)
U of Toronto (ON, Canada)
U of Tulsa (OK)
U of Utah (UT)
U of Washington (WA)
The U of Western Ontario (ON, Canada)
U of Windsor (ON, Canada)
U of Wisconsin–Madison (WI)
U of Wisconsin–Milwaukee (WI)
U of Wisconsin–Stout (WI)
Valdosta State U (GA)
Washington State U (WA)
Washington U in St. Louis (MO)
Weber State U (UT)
Wentworth Inst of Technology (MA)
Western Michigan U (MI)
Western Washington U (WA)
West Virginia State U (WV)
William Paterson U of New Jersey (NJ)
Winona State U (MN)
Worcester Polytechnic Inst (MA)
Yale U (CT)

APPLIED MATHEMATICS RELATED
Arizona State U (AZ)
Averett U (VA)
Berea Coll (KY)
Carnegie Mellon U (PA)
DePaul U (IL)
Elizabethtown Coll (PA)
Georgia Inst of Technology (GA)
Keene State Coll (NH)
Lycoming Coll (PA)
Purdue U (IN)
Temple U (PA)
U of California, Santa Barbara (CA)
U of Dayton (OH)
U of Wisconsin–Milwaukee (WI)
Willamette U (OR)

APPLIED PSYCHOLOGY
Arizona State U (AZ)
Christian Brothers U (TN)
Florida Inst of Technology (FL)

Pace U (NY)
U of Michigan–Flint (MI)

AQUACULTURE
Auburn U (AL)
Texas A&M U (TX)
U of New England (ME)

AQUATIC BIOLOGY/LIMNOLOGY
Florida Inst of Technology (FL)
Stetson U (FL)
Texas State U–San Marcos (TX)
U of California, Santa Barbara (CA)
U of South Carolina (SC)

ARABIC
American U of Beirut (Lebanon)
Bard Coll (NY)
California State U, San Bernardino (CA)
Dartmouth Coll (NH)
DePaul U (IL)
Hope Coll (MI)
Michigan State U (MI)
Middlebury Coll (VT)
The Ohio State U (OH)
State U of New York at Binghamton (NY)
United States Military Acad (NY)
United States Naval Acad (MD)
U of Alberta (AB, Canada)
U of California, Los Angeles (CA)
U of Georgia (GA)
U of Maryland, Coll Park (MD)
U of Minnesota, Twin Cities Campus (MN)
U of Notre Dame (IN)
U of Oklahoma (OK)
U of Ottawa (ON, Canada)
U of Toronto (ON, Canada)
U of Utah (UT)
Washington U in St. Louis (MO)

ARCHEOLOGY
The American U in Cairo (Egypt)
American U of Beirut (Lebanon)
The American U of Rome (Italy)
Bard Coll (NY)
Biola U (CA)
Boston U (MA)
Bowdoin Coll (ME)
Bridgewater State U (MA)
Brown U (RI)
Bryn Mawr Coll (PA)
The Coll of Wooster (OH)
Columbia U, School of General Studies (NY)
Cornell Coll (IA)
Cornell U (NY)
Dartmouth Coll (NH)
Dickinson Coll (PA)
The George Washington U (DC)
Hamilton Coll (NY)
Haverford Coll (PA)
Hunter Coll of the City U of New York (NY)
The Johns Hopkins U (MD)
Lawrence U (WI)
Mercyhurst Coll (PA)
New York U (NY)
Penn State Abington (PA)
Penn State Altoona (PA)
Penn State Beaver (PA)
Penn State Berks (PA)
Penn State Brandywine (PA)
Penn State DuBois (PA)
Penn State Erie, The Behrend Coll (PA)
Penn State Fayette, The Eberly Campus (PA)
Penn State Greater Allegheny (PA)
Penn State Hazleton (PA)
Penn State Lehigh Valley (PA)
Penn State Mont Alto (PA)
Penn State New Kensington (PA)
Penn State Schuylkill (PA)
Penn State Shenango (PA)
Penn State York (PA)
Penn State Wilkes-Barre (PA)
Penn State Worthington Scranton (PA)
Penn State York (PA)
Saint Mary's Coll of California (CA)

Sarah Lawrence Coll (NY)
Simon Fraser U (BC, Canada)
Stanford U (CA)
State U of New York Coll at
 Potsdam (NY)
Sweet Briar Coll (VA)
Tufts U (MA)
The U of British Columbia (BC,
 Canada)
U of Cincinnati (OH)
U of Evansville (IN)
U of Indianapolis (IN)
U of Lethbridge (AB, Canada)
U of Missouri (MO)
The U of North Carolina at Chapel
 Hill (NC)
The U of Texas at Austin (TX)
U of Toronto (ON, Canada)
The U of Western Ontario (ON,
 Canada)
U of Wisconsin–La Crosse (WI)
Washington U in St. Louis (MO)
Wellesley Coll (MA)
Wesleyan U (CT)
Western Washington U (WA)
Wheaton Coll (IL)
Yale U (CT)

ARCHITECTURAL AND BUILDING SCIENCES

Pennsylvania Coll of Technology
 (PA)

ARCHITECTURAL DRAFTING AND CAD/CADD

ITT Tech Inst, Dayton (OH)

ARCHITECTURAL ENGINEERING

Andrews U (MI)
Auburn U (AL)
California Polytechnic State U, San
 Luis Obispo (CA)
Drexel U (PA)
Illinois Inst of Technology (IL)
Kansas State U (KS)
Milwaukee School of Eng (WI)
Missouri U of Science and
 Technology (MO)
North Carolina Ag and Tech State U
 (NC)
Oklahoma State U (OK)
Penn State Abington (PA)
Penn State Altoona (PA)
Penn State Beaver (PA)
Penn State Berks (PA)
Penn State Brandywine (PA)
Penn State DuBois (PA)
Penn State Erie, The Behrend Coll
 (PA)
Penn State Fayette, The Eberly
 Campus (PA)
Penn State Greater Allegheny (PA)
Penn State Hazleton (PA)
Penn State Lehigh Valley (PA)
Penn State Mont Alto (PA)
Penn State New Kensington (PA)
Penn State Schuylkill (PA)
Penn State Shenango (PA)
Penn State U Park (PA)
Penn State Wilkes-Barre (PA)
Penn State Worthington Scranton
 (PA)
Penn State York (PA)
Purdue U (IN)
Texas A&M U–Kingsville (TX)
Tufts U (MA)
U of Cincinnati (OH)
U of Colorado Boulder (CO)
The U of Kansas (KS)
U of Miami (FL)
U of Nebraska–Lincoln (NE)
U of Oklahoma (OK)
The U of Texas at Austin (TX)
U of Wyoming (WY)
Worcester Polytechnic Inst (MA)

ARCHITECTURAL ENGINEERING TECHNOLOGY

Bluefield State Coll (WV)
Delaware State U (DE)
Eastern Kentucky U (KY)
Farmingdale State Coll (NY)

Ferris State U (MI)
Fitchburg State U (MA)
Indiana State U (IN)
Indiana U–Purdue U Indianapolis
 (IN)
Keene State Coll (NH)
New England Inst of Technology
 (RI)
Northern Kentucky U (KY)
Purdue U (IN)
Purdue U North Central (IN)
Seminole State Coll of Florida (FL)
State U of New York Coll of
 Technology at Alfred (NY)
Texas Tech U (TX)
U of Hartford (CT)
U of Southern Mississippi (MS)
Vermont Tech Coll (VT)
Washington U in St. Louis (MO)

ARCHITECTURAL HISTORY AND CRITICISM

Brown U (RI)
Carnegie Mellon U (PA)
Columbia U, School of General
 Studies (NY)
Cornell U (NY)
DePaul U (IL)
Lehigh U (PA)
Sarah Lawrence Coll (NY)
Savannah Coll of Art and Design
 (GA)
Syracuse U (NY)
The U of Kansas (KS)
U of San Diego (CA)
U of Virginia (VA)

ARCHITECTURAL TECHNOLOGY

Carnegie Mellon U (PA)
New York City Coll of Technology of
 the City U of New York (NY)
U of Maine at Augusta (ME)
Washington U in St. Louis (MO)
Western Kentucky U (KY)

ARCHITECTURE

Acad of Art U (CA)
Agnes Scott Coll (GA)
American U of Beirut (Lebanon)
Andrews U (MI)
Arizona State U (AZ)
Auburn U (AL)
Ball State U (IN)
Barnard Coll (NY)
Bennington Coll (VT)
Boston Architectural Coll (MA)
California Coll of the Arts (CA)
California Polytechnic State U, San
 Luis Obispo (CA)
California State Polytechnic U,
 Pomona (CA)
Carnegie Mellon U (PA)
The Catholic U of America (DC)
City Coll of the City U of New York
 (NY)
Clemson U (SC)
Coe Coll (IA)
Columbia U, School of General
 Studies (NY)
Connecticut Coll (CT)
Cooper Union for the Advancement
 of Science and Art (NY)
Cornell Coll (IA)
Cornell U (NY)
Dalhousie U (NS, Canada)
Drexel U (PA)
Drury U (MO)
Florida Ag and Mech U (FL)
Florida Atlantic U (FL)
Georgia Inst of Technology (GA)
Hampshire Coll (MA)
Hampton U (VA)
Hobart and William Smith Colls
 (NY)
Illinois Inst of Technology (IL)
Inter American U of Puerto Rico,
 San Germán Campus (PR)
Iowa State U of Science and
 Technology (IA)
Ithaca Coll (NY)
Judson U (IL)
Keene State Coll (NH)
Kent State U (OH)

Lawrence Technological U (MI)
Lebanese American U (Lebanon)
Lehigh U (PA)
Louisiana State U and Ag and Mech
 Coll (LA)
Marywood U (PA)
Massachusetts Coll of Art and
 Design (MA)
Massachusetts Inst of Technology
 (MA)
Miami U (OH)
Mississippi State U (MS)
North Carolina State U (NC)
Northeastern U (MA)
Norwich U (VT)
The Ohio State U (OH)
Oklahoma State U (OK)
Penn State U Park (PA)
Philadelphia U (PA)
Polytechnic U of Puerto Rico (PR)
Portland State U (OR)
Prairie View A&M U (TX)
Pratt Inst (NY)
Princeton U (NJ)
Rensselaer Polytechnic Inst (NY)
Rice U (TX)
Roger Williams U (RI)
Ryerson U (ON, Canada)
Savannah Coll of Art and Design
 (GA)
Smith Coll (MA)
South Dakota State U (SD)
Southern Illinois U Carbondale (IL)
Southern Polytechnic State U (GA)
Syracuse U (NY)
Temple U (PA)
Texas A&M U (TX)
Texas Tech U (TX)
Tulane U (LA)
Tuskegee U (AL)
U at Buffalo, the State U of New
 York (NY)
The U of Arizona (AZ)
U of Arkansas (AR)
U of California, Berkeley (CA)
U of California, Los Angeles (CA)
U of Central Florida (FL)
U of Cincinnati (OH)
U of Florida (FL)
U of Houston (TX)
U of Idaho (ID)
U of Illinois at Chicago (IL)
U of Illinois at Urbana–Champaign
 (IL)
The U of Kansas (KS)
U of Louisiana at Lafayette (LA)
U of Maryland, Coll Park (MD)
U of Massachusetts Amherst (MA)
U of Memphis (TN)
U of Miami (FL)
U of Michigan (MI)
U of Minnesota, Twin Cities
 Campus (MN)
U of Missouri–Kansas City (MO)
U of Nebraska–Lincoln (NE)
U of Nevada, Las Vegas (NV)
U of New Mexico (NM)
The U of North Carolina at
 Charlotte (NC)
U of Notre Dame (IN)
U of Oklahoma (OK)
U of Oregon (OR)
U of Pennsylvania (PA)
U of Southern California (CA)
The U of Tennessee (TN)
The U of Texas at Arlington (TX)
The U of Texas at Austin (TX)
The U of Texas at San Antonio (TX)
U of the District of Columbia (DC)
U of Toronto (ON, Canada)
U of Utah (UT)
U of Virginia (VA)
U of Washington (WA)
U of Wisconsin–Milwaukee (WI)
Virginia Polytechnic Inst and State
 U (VA)
Washington State U (WA)
Washington U in St. Louis (MO)
Wellesley Coll (MA)
Wentworth Inst of Technology (MA)
Woodbury U (CA)
Yale U (CT)

ARCHITECTURE RELATED

Carnegie Mellon U (PA)

Case Western Reserve U (OH)
Coll of the Holy Cross (MA)
Georgia Inst of Technology (GA)
Lipscomb U (TN)
Mount Holyoke Coll (MA)
New York Inst of Technology (NY)
Northern Michigan U (MI)
U of Cincinnati (OH)
U of Illinois at Chicago (IL)
U of Illinois at Urbana–Champaign
 (IL)
U of Louisiana at Lafayette (LA)
U of Minnesota, Twin Cities
 Campus (MN)
U of Utah (UT)
Washington U in St. Louis (MO)

ARCHIVES/ARCHIVAL ADMINISTRATION

Emory & Henry Coll (VA)

AREA STUDIES RELATED

Appalachian State U (NC)
Boston U (MA)
Bridgewater State U (MA)
Colby Coll (ME)
Drexel U (PA)
Eastern Michigan U (MI)
Gannon U (PA)
Gettysburg Coll (PA)
Hofstra U (NY)
Illinois Wesleyan U (IL)
Lake Forest Coll (IL)
Lycoming Coll (PA)
Millersville U of Pennsylvania (PA)
Northeastern State U (OK)
Prescott Coll (AZ)
Ramapo Coll of New Jersey (NJ)
Stanford U (CA)
U of Alaska Fairbanks (AK)
U of California, Los Angeles (CA)
U of California, Santa Barbara (CA)
U of Illinois at Urbana–Champaign
 (IL)
U of Michigan–Dearborn (MI)
U of Minnesota, Twin Cities
 Campus (MN)
U of Pittsburgh (PA)
U of Virginia (VA)
Utah State U (UT)
Virginia Commonwealth U (VA)
Washington U in St. Louis (MO)
Williams Coll (MA)

ARMY ROTC/MILITARY SCIENCE

Hampton U (VA)
Jacksonville State U (AL)
La Salle U (PA)
Minnesota State U Mankato (MN)
Roger Williams U (RI)
The U of Iowa (IA)
U of Minnesota, Twin Cities
 Campus (MN)
U of Washington (WA)

ARMY ROTC, MILITARY SCIENCE AND OPERATIONS RELATED

Calvary Bible Coll and Theological
 Sem (MO)

ART

Adrian Coll (MI)
Agnes Scott Coll (GA)
Alabama State U (AL)
Albany State U (GA)
Alberta Coll of Art & Design (AB,
 Canada)
Albertus Magnus Coll (CT)
Albion Coll (MI)
Albright Coll (PA)
Alfred U (NY)
Allegheny Coll (PA)
Alma Coll (MI)
Alverno Coll (WI)
American U (DC)
The American U in Cairo (Egypt)
Amherst Coll (MA)
Anderson U (SC)
Andrews U (MI)
Angelo State U (TX)
Anna Maria Coll (MA)

Appalachian State U (NC)
Aquinas Coll (MI)
Arcadia U (PA)
Arizona State U (AZ)
Arkansas State U (AR)
Arkansas Tech U (AR)
Armstrong Atlantic State U (GA)
Art Center Coll of Design (CA)
Athens State U (AL)
Auburn U Montgomery (AL)
Augustana Coll (IL)
Augustana Coll (SD)
Austin Coll (TX)
Austin Peay State U (TN)
Averett U (VA)
Avila U (MO)
Baldwin-Wallace Coll (OH)
Ball State U (IN)
Bard Coll (NY)
Bates Coll (ME)
Baylor U (TX)
Belhaven U (MS)
Bellevue U (NE)
Belmont U (TN)
Bemidji State U (MN)
Benedictine Coll (KS)
Bennett Coll for Women (NC)
Berea Coll (KY)
Berry Coll (GA)
Bethany Coll (WV)
Bethany Lutheran Coll (MN)
Bethel Coll (IN)
Bethel U (MN)
Birmingham-Southern Coll (AL)
Bishop's U (QC, Canada)
Blackburn Coll (IL)
Black Hills State U (SD)
Bluefield Coll (VA)
Bluffton U (OH)
Bob Jones U (SC)
Boise State U (ID)
Bowie State U (MD)
Bowling Green State U (OH)
Bradley U (IL)
Brescia U (KY)
Briar Cliff U (IA)
Brown U (RI)
Bryn Mawr Coll (PA)
Bucknell U (PA)
Buena Vista U (IA)
Buffalo State Coll, State U of New
 York (NY)
Caldwell Coll (NJ)
California Baptist U (CA)
California Coll of the Arts (CA)
California Lutheran U (CA)
California State Polytechnic U,
 Pomona (CA)
California State U, Bakersfield (CA)
California State U, Chico (CA)
California State U, Dominguez Hills
 (CA)
California State U, Fresno (CA)
California State U, Fullerton (CA)
California State U, Long Beach
 (CA)
California State U, Los Angeles
 (CA)
California State U, Monterey Bay
 (CA)
California State U, Sacramento
 (CA)
California State U, San Bernardino
 (CA)
California State U, Stanislaus (CA)
California U of Pennsylvania (PA)
Calvin Coll (MI)
Cameron U (OK)
Campbellsville U (KY)
Capital U (OH)
Cardinal Stritch U (WI)
Carnegie Mellon U (PA)
Carson-Newman Coll (TN)
Castleton State Coll (VT)
The Catholic U of America (DC)
Cedar Crest Coll (PA)
Centenary Coll of Louisiana (LA)
Central Coll (IA)
Central Connecticut State U (CT)
Central Michigan U (MI)
Central State U (OH)
Central Washington U (WA)
Centre Coll (KY)
Chapman U (CA)
Cheyney U of Pennsylvania (PA)

U of Maine (ME)
U of Maine at Presque Isle (ME)
U of Mary Hardin-Baylor (TX)
U of Maryland, Coll Park (MD)
U of Maryland Eastern Shore (MD)
U of Massachusetts Dartmouth (MA)
U of Michigan–Flint (MI)
U of Minnesota, Duluth (MN)
U of Minnesota, Twin Cities Campus (MN)
U of Missouri (MO)
The U of Montana Western (MT)
U of New Mexico (NM)
The U of North Carolina at Charlotte (NC)
U of Northern Iowa (IA)
U of North Florida (FL)
U of Regina (SK, Canada)
U of Rio Grande (OH)
U of St. Francis (IL)
U of Saint Francis (IN)
U of South Carolina (SC)
U of South Carolina Upstate (SC)
The U of South Dakota (SD)
U of Southern Maine (ME)
U of South Florida (FL)
The U of Tennessee at Chattanooga (TN)
The U of Texas at El Paso (TX)
U of the Cumberlands (KY)
U of the District of Columbia (DC)
The U of Toledo (OH)
U of Vermont (VT)
U of Windsor (ON, Canada)
U of Wisconsin–La Crosse (WI)
U of Wisconsin–Madison (WI)
U of Wisconsin–Milwaukee (WI)
U of Wisconsin–River Falls (WI)
U of Wisconsin–Stout (WI)
U of Wisconsin–Superior (WI)
U of Wisconsin–Whitewater (WI)
Upper Iowa U (IA)
Ursuline Coll (OH)
Valdosta State U (GA)
Valley City State U (ND)
Valparaiso U (IN)
Virginia Commonwealth U (VA)
Virginia Intermont Coll (VA)
Virginia Wesleyan Coll (VA)
Viterbo U (WI)
Wartburg Coll (IA)
Washburn U (KS)
Washington & Jefferson Coll (PA)
Washington U in St. Louis (MO)
Wayne State U (NE)
Wayne State U (MI)
Weber State U (UT)
Western Carolina U (NC)
Western Michigan U (MI)
Western State Coll of Colorado (CO)
Western Washington U (WA)
West Liberty U (WV)
West Virginia State U (WV)
West Virginia Wesleyan Coll (WV)
William Jewell Coll (MO)
William Paterson U of New Jersey (NJ)
Williams Baptist Coll (AR)
William Woods U (MO)
Wilmington Coll (OH)
Wingate U (NC)
Winona State U (MN)
Xavier U of Louisiana (LA)
Youngstown State U (OH)

ART THERAPY
Albertus Magnus Coll (CT)
Alverno Coll (WI)
Anna Maria Coll (MA)
Arcadia U (PA)
Bethany Coll (KS)
Bowling Green State U (OH)
Capital U (OH)
Carlow U (PA)
Cedar Crest Coll (PA)
Converse Coll (SC)
DePaul U (IL)
Edgewood Coll (WI)
Emmanuel Coll (MA)
Harding U (AR)
Indiana Wesleyan U (IN)
Long Island U–C. W. Post Campus (NY)

Marywood U (PA)
Mercyhurst Coll (PA)
Millikin U (IL)
Mount Mary Coll (WI)
Nazareth Coll of Rochester (NY)
Ohio Wesleyan U (OH)
Russell Sage Coll (NY)
St. Thomas Aquinas Coll (NY)
Seton Hill U (PA)
Sierra Nevada Coll (NV)
U of Indianapolis (IN)
U of Wisconsin–Superior (WI)

ASIAN AMERICAN STUDIES
Arizona State U (AZ)
California State U, East Bay (CA)
California State U, Fullerton (CA)
California State U, Long Beach (CA)
California State U, Los Angeles (CA)
Columbia U, School of General Studies (NY)
Emory U (GA)
Pitzer Coll (CA)
Pomona Coll (CA)
San Francisco State U (CA)
Scripps Coll (CA)
Stanford U (CA)
State U of New York at Binghamton (NY)
Stony Brook U, State U of New York (NY)
U of California, Berkeley (CA)
U of California, Davis (CA)
U of California, Irvine (CA)
U of California, Los Angeles (CA)
U of California, Riverside (CA)
U of California, Santa Barbara (CA)
U of Denver (CO)
U of Southern California (CA)

ASIAN HISTORY
Bard Coll (NY)
Gettysburg Coll (PA)
Sarah Lawrence Coll (NY)
U of Regina (SK, Canada)

ASIAN STUDIES
Amherst Coll (MA)
Arizona State U (AZ)
Augustana Coll (IL)
Bard Coll (NY)
Bard Coll at Simon's Rock (MA)
Barnard Coll (NY)
Baylor U (TX)
Beloit Coll (WI)
Bennington Coll (VT)
Berea Coll (KY)
Birmingham-Southern Coll (AL)
Bowdoin Coll (ME)
Bowling Green State U (OH)
California State U, Chico (CA)
California State U, Long Beach (CA)
California State U, Los Angeles (CA)
California State U, Sacramento (CA)
Calvin Coll (MI)
Carleton Coll (MN)
Case Western Reserve U (OH)
Central Washington U (WA)
City Coll of the City U of New York (NY)
Claremont McKenna Coll (CA)
Clark U (MA)
Coe Coll (IA)
Colgate U (NY)
The Coll at Brockport, State U of New York (NY)
Coll of the Holy Cross (MA)
The Colorado Coll (CO)
Cornell U (NY)
Dartmouth Coll (NH)
Emory U (GA)
Florida Intl U (FL)
Fort Lewis Coll (CO)
Furman U (SC)
The George Washington U (DC)
Gonzaga U (WA)
Hamilton Coll (NY)
Hawai`i Pacific U (HI)

Hobart and William Smith Colls (NY)
Hofstra U (NY)
Illinois Wesleyan U (IL)
Indiana U of Pennsylvania (PA)
John Carroll U (OH)
Kean U (NJ)
Knox Coll (IL)
Lake Forest Coll (IL)
Lehigh U (PA)
Loyola Marymount U (CA)
Macalester Coll (MN)
Manhattanville Coll (NY)
Marietta Coll (OH)
Marlboro Coll (VT)
Mary Baldwin Coll (VA)
McDaniel Coll (MD)
Mount Holyoke Coll (MA)
Northeastern U (MA)
Occidental Coll (CA)
Ohio U (OH)
Old Dominion U (VA)
Penn State U Park (PA)
Pitzer Coll (CA)
Pomona Coll (CA)
Purdue U (IN)
Randolph-Macon Coll (VA)
Rice U (TX)
St. John's U (NY)
Saint Joseph's U (PA)
St. Lawrence U (NY)
St. Mary's Coll of Maryland (MD)
St. Olaf Coll (MN)
Samford U (AL)
San Diego State U (CA)
Sarah Lawrence Coll (NY)
Scripps Coll (CA)
Sewanee: The U of the South (TN)
Skidmore Coll (NY)
Stanford U (CA)
State U of New York at Binghamton (NY)
State U of New York at New Paltz (NY)
Swarthmore Coll (PA)
Temple U (PA)
Texas State U–San Marcos (TX)
Trinity U (TX)
Tufts U (MA)
Tulane U (LA)
Union Coll (NY)
U at Albany, State U of New York (NY)
U at Buffalo, the State U of New York (NY)
The U of British Columbia (BC, Canada)
U of California, Berkeley (CA)
U of California, Los Angeles (CA)
U of California, Riverside (CA)
U of California, Santa Barbara (CA)
U of Cincinnati (OH)
U of Colorado Boulder (CO)
U of Delaware (DE)
U of Florida (FL)
U of Hawaii at Manoa (HI)
The U of Iowa (IA)
U of Maryland U Coll (MD)
U of Massachusetts Boston (MA)
U of Michigan (MI)
U of Mount Union (OH)
U of New Mexico (NM)
The U of North Carolina at Chapel Hill (NC)
U of Oregon (OR)
U of Puget Sound (WA)
U of Redlands (CA)
The U of Texas at Austin (TX)
The U of Toledo (OH)
U of Toronto (ON, Canada)
U of Utah (UT)
U of Vermont (VT)
U of Washington (WA)
The U of Western Ontario (ON, Canada)
U of Wisconsin–Madison (WI)
Utah State U (UT)
Vanderbilt U (TN)
Vassar Coll (NY)
Warren Wilson Coll (NC)
Washington State U (WA)
Washington U in St. Louis (MO)
Webster U (MO)
Western Kentucky U (KY)
Wheaton Coll (MA)

Whitman Coll (WA)
Willamette U (OR)
William Paterson U of New Jersey (NJ)
Williams Coll (MA)

ASIAN STUDIES (EAST)
Bates Coll (ME)
Boston U (MA)
Brandeis U (MA)
Brown U (RI)
Bryn Mawr Coll (PA)
Bucknell U (PA)
Colby Coll (ME)
Colgate U (NY)
Columbia U, School of General Studies (NY)
Connecticut Coll (CT)
Denison U (OH)
DePaul U (IL)
DePauw U (IN)
Dickinson Coll (PA)
The George Washington U (DC)
Gettysburg Coll (PA)
Grand Valley State U (MI)
Hamline U (MN)
Hampshire Coll (MA)
Harvard U (MA)
Haverford Coll (PA)
Indiana U Bloomington (IN)
John Carroll U (OH)
The Johns Hopkins U (MD)
Lawrence U (WI)
Lewis & Clark Coll (OR)
Marlboro Coll (VT)
Miami U (OH)
Middlebury Coll (VT)
Minnesota State U Moorhead (MN)
Mount Holyoke Coll (MA)
New York U (NY)
North Central Coll (IL)
Oakland U (MI)
Ohio Wesleyan U (OH)
Penn State Abington (PA)
Penn State Altoona (PA)
Penn State Beaver (PA)
Penn State Berks (PA)
Penn State Brandywine (PA)
Penn State DuBois (PA)
Penn State Erie, The Behrend Coll (PA)
Penn State Fayette, The Eberly Campus (PA)
Penn State Greater Allegheny (PA)
Penn State Hazleton (PA)
Penn State Lehigh Valley (PA)
Penn State Mont Alto (PA)
Penn State New Kensington (PA)
Penn State Schuylkill (PA)
Penn State Shenango (PA)
Penn State Worthington Scranton (PA)
Penn State York (PA)
Pomona Coll (CA)
Portland State U (OR)
Princeton U (NJ)
Queens Coll of the City U of New York (NY)
Rutgers, The State U of New Jersey, New Brunswick (NJ)
Sarah Lawrence Coll (NY)
Seattle U (WA)
Simmons Coll (MA)
Smith Coll (MA)
Stanford U (CA)
State U of New York at Binghamton (NY)
United States Military Acad (NY)
U at Albany, State U of New York (NY)
U of Alberta (AB, Canada)
The U of Arizona (AZ)
U of Bridgeport (CT)
U of California, Davis (CA)
U of California, Irvine (CA)
U of California, Los Angeles (CA)
U of Guam (GU)
U of Illinois at Urbana–Champaign (IL)
U of Minnesota, Twin Cities Campus (MN)
U of Missouri (MO)
U of Pennsylvania (PA)
U of Southern California (CA)
U of Toronto (ON, Canada)

U of Washington (WA)
The U of Western Ontario (ON, Canada)
Valparaiso U (IN)
Washington U in St. Louis (MO)
Wayne State U (MI)
Wellesley Coll (MA)
Wesleyan U (CT)
Western Washington U (WA)
Wittenberg U (OH)
Yale U (CT)

ASIAN STUDIES (SOUTH)
Brown U (RI)
Concordia U (QC, Canada)
Gettysburg Coll (PA)
Hampshire Coll (MA)
Indiana U Bloomington (IN)
Mount Holyoke Coll (MA)
Sarah Lawrence Coll (NY)
State U of New York at Binghamton (NY)
The U of British Columbia (BC, Canada)
U of Minnesota, Twin Cities Campus (MN)
U of Missouri (MO)
U of Pennsylvania (PA)
U of Toronto (ON, Canada)
U of Washington (WA)
U of Wisconsin–Madison (WI)

ASIAN STUDIES (SOUTHEAST)
Tufts U (MA)
U of California, Berkeley (CA)
U of California, Los Angeles (CA)
U of Washington (WA)

ASIAN STUDIES (URAL-ALTAIC AND CENTRAL)
Indiana U Bloomington (IN)

ASTRONOMY
Amherst Coll (MA)
Baylor U (TX)
Benedictine Coll (KS)
Bennington Coll (VT)
Boston U (MA)
Brigham Young U (UT)
Bryn Mawr Coll (PA)
Case Western Reserve U (OH)
Central Michigan U (MI)
Colgate U (NY)
The Coll at Brockport, State U of New York (NY)
Columbia U, School of General Studies (NY)
Cornell U (NY)
Dartmouth Coll (NH)
Drake U (IA)
Eastern U (PA)
Franklin & Marshall Coll (PA)
George Mason U (VA)
Hampshire Coll (MA)
Haverford Coll (PA)
Indiana U Bloomington (IN)
Lehigh U (PA)
Lycoming Coll (PA)
Marlboro Coll (VT)
Minnesota State U Mankato (MN)
Mount Holyoke Coll (MA)
Northern Arizona U (AZ)
The Ohio State U (OH)
Ohio Wesleyan U (OH)
Penn State Abington (PA)
Penn State Altoona (PA)
Penn State Beaver (PA)
Penn State Berks (PA)
Penn State Brandywine (PA)
Penn State DuBois (PA)
Penn State Erie, The Behrend Coll (PA)
Penn State Fayette, The Eberly Campus (PA)
Penn State Greater Allegheny (PA)
Penn State Hazleton (PA)
Penn State Lehigh Valley (PA)
Penn State Mont Alto (PA)
Penn State New Kensington (PA)
Penn State Schuylkill (PA)
Penn State Shenango (PA)
Penn State U Park (PA)
Penn State Wilkes-Barre (PA)

Penn State Worthington Scranton (PA)
Penn State York (PA)
Pomona Coll (CA)
Rice U (TX)
San Diego State U (CA)
San Francisco State U (CA)
Sarah Lawrence Coll (NY)
Smith Coll (MA)
Stony Brook U, State U of New York (NY)
Swarthmore Coll (PA)
Tufts U (MA)
Union Coll (NY)
The U of Arizona (AZ)
The U of British Columbia (BC, Canada)
U of California, Santa Cruz (CA)
U of Colorado Boulder (CO)
U of Florida (FL)
U of Georgia (GA)
U of Illinois at Urbana–Champaign (IL)
The U of Iowa (IA)
The U of Kansas (KS)
U of Maryland, Coll Park (MD)
U of Massachusetts Amherst (MA)
U of Michigan (MI)
U of Minnesota, Twin Cities Campus (MN)
U of Oklahoma (OK)
U of Southern California (CA)
The U of Texas at Austin (TX)
The U of Toledo (OH)
U of Virginia (VA)
U of Washington (WA)
The U of Western Ontario (ON, Canada)
Valdosta State U (GA)
Valparaiso U (IN)
Vassar Coll (NY)
Villanova U (PA)
Wayne State U (MI)
Wellesley Coll (MA)
Wesleyan U (CT)
Whitman Coll (WA)
Williams Coll (MA)
Yale U (CT)
Youngstown State U (OH)

ASTRONOMY AND ASTROPHYSICS RELATED

Coll of Charleston (SC)
Florida Inst of Technology (FL)
Harvard U (MA)
Texas Christian U (TX)
U of Wyoming (WY)

ASTROPHYSICS

Agnes Scott Coll (GA)
Baylor U (TX)
Boston U (MA)
California Inst of Technology (CA)
Carnegie Mellon U (PA)
Colgate U (NY)
Columbia U, School of General Studies (NY)
Connecticut Coll (CT)
Franklin & Marshall Coll (PA)
Haverford Coll (PA)
Lehigh U (PA)
Marlboro Coll (VT)
Michigan State U (MI)
Ohio U (OH)
Ohio Wesleyan U (OH)
Princeton U (NJ)
Rice U (TX)
Rutgers, The State U of New Jersey, New Brunswick (NJ)
San Francisco State U (CA)
Swarthmore Coll (PA)
U of California, Berkeley (CA)
U of California, Los Angeles (CA)
U of California, Santa Cruz (CA)
U of Cincinnati (OH)
U of Minnesota, Twin Cities Campus (MN)
U of New Mexico (NM)
U of Oklahoma (OK)
The U of Western Ontario (ON, Canada)
U of Wisconsin–Madison (WI)
Villanova U (PA)
Wellesley Coll (MA)

Whitman Coll (WA)
Williams Coll (MA)
Yale U (CT)

ATHLETIC TRAINING

Albion Coll (MI)
Alfred U (NY)
Alvernia U (PA)
Anderson U (IN)
Angelo State U (TX)
Appalachian State U (NC)
Aquinas Coll (MI)
Arkansas State U (AR)
Ashland U (OH)
Augustana Coll (SD)
Averett U (VA)
Azusa Pacific U (CA)
Baldwin-Wallace Coll (OH)
Barton Coll (NC)
Baylor U (TX)
Benedictine Coll (KS)
Bethany Coll (KS)
Bethel Coll (KS)
Bethel U (MN)
Boise State U (ID)
Boston U (MA)
Bowling Green State U (OH)
Bridgewater Coll (VA)
Bridgewater State U (MA)
Brigham Young U (UT)
Buena Vista U (IA)
California Lutheran U (CA)
California State U, East Bay (CA)
California State U, Fullerton (CA)
California State U, Long Beach (CA)
California U of Pennsylvania (PA)
Campbellsville U (KY)
Canisius Coll (NY)
Capital U (OH)
Castleton State Coll (VT)
Catawba Coll (NC)
Cedarville U (OH)
Central Coll (IA)
Central Connecticut State U (CT)
Central Methodist U (MO)
Central Michigan U (MI)
Chapman U (CA)
Clarke U (IA)
Coe Coll (IA)
The Coll at Brockport, State U of New York (NY)
Coll of Charleston (SC)
Coll of Mount St. Joseph (OH)
The Coll of William and Mary (VA)
Colorado Mesa U (CO)
Colorado State U (CO)
Concordia U (CA)
Culver-Stockton Coll (MO)
Defiance Coll (OH)
Delta State U (MS)
DePauw U (IN)
Dominican Coll (NY)
Duquesne U (PA)
East Carolina U (NC)
East Central U (OK)
Eastern Illinois U (IL)
Eastern Michigan U (MI)
Eastern U (PA)
Eastern Washington U (WA)
East Stroudsburg U of Pennsylvania (PA)
East Texas Baptist U (TX)
Emory & Henry Coll (VA)
Emporia State U (KS)
Endicott Coll (MA)
Florida Gulf Coast U (FL)
Florida Southern Coll (FL)
Florida State U (FL)
Fort Lewis Coll (CO)
Franklin Coll (IN)
Free Will Baptist Bible Coll (TN)
Gardner-Webb U (NC)
George Fox U (OR)
George Mason U (VA)
Georgetown Coll (KY)
Georgia Coll & State U (GA)
Georgia Southern U (GA)
Graceland U (IA)
Grand Canyon U (AZ)
Grand Valley State U (MI)
Guilford Coll (NC)
Gustavus Adolphus Coll (MN)
Harding U (AR)
Hardin-Simmons U (TX)

Heidelberg U (OH)
Hofstra U (NY)
Hope Coll (MI)
Howard Payne U (TX)
Huntingdon Coll (AL)
Illinois State U (IL)
Indiana State U (IN)
Indiana U Bloomington (IN)
Indiana U of Pennsylvania (PA)
Indiana Wesleyan U (IN)
Ithaca Coll (NY)
James Madison U (VA)
Johnson State Coll (VT)
Kansas State U (KS)
Kean U (NJ)
Keene State Coll (NH)
Kent State U (OH)
King Coll (TN)
King's Coll (PA)
Lakehead U (ON, Canada)
Lake Superior State U (MI)
Lasell Coll (MA)
Lees-McRae Coll (NC)
Lee U (TN)
Lenoir-Rhyne U (NC)
Lewis U (IL)
Liberty U (VA)
Limestone Coll (SC)
Lincoln Memorial U (TN)
Lindenwood U (MO)
Linfield Coll (OR)
Lock Haven U of Pennsylvania (PA)
Long Island U–Brooklyn Campus (NY)
Longwood U (VA)
Loras Coll (IA)
Louisiana Coll (LA)
Louisiana State U and Ag and Mech Coll (LA)
Lubbock Christian U (TX)
Luther Coll (IA)
Lynchburg Coll (VA)
Manchester Coll (IN)
Marietta Coll (OH)
Marquette U (WI)
Marshall U (WV)
Mars Hill Coll (NC)
Marywood U (PA)
Massachusetts Coll of Liberal Arts (MA)
McKendree U (IL)
McMurry U (TX)
McNeese State U (LA)
Merrimack Coll (MA)
Messiah Coll (PA)
Miami U (OH)
Michigan State U (MI)
MidAmerica Nazarene U (KS)
Middle Tennessee State U (TN)
Midwestern State U (TX)
Millikin U (IL)
Minnesota State U Mankato (MN)
Minnesota State U Moorhead (MN)
Minot State U (ND)
Missouri State U (MO)
Montclair State U (NJ)
Nebraska Wesleyan U (NE)
Neumann U (PA)
New Mexico State U (NM)
North Carolina Central U (NC)
North Central Coll (IL)
Northern Arizona U (AZ)
Northern Illinois U (IL)
Northern Kentucky U (KY)
Northern Michigan U (MI)
North Georgia Coll & State U (GA)
Northwestern Coll (IA)
Northwest Nazarene U (ID)
Norwich U (VT)
Nova Southeastern U (FL)
Ohio Northern U (OH)
The Ohio State U (OH)
Ohio U (OH)
Oklahoma State U (OK)
Otterbein U (OH)
Pacific U (OR)
Palm Beach Atlantic U (FL)
Park U (MO)
Penn State U Park (PA)
Pepperdine U, Malibu (CA)
Plymouth State U (NH)
Point Loma Nazarene U (CA)
Presentation Coll (SD)
Purdue U (IN)
Quinnipiac U (CT)

Radford U (VA)
Roanoke Coll (VA)
Rocky Mountain Coll (MT)
Rowan U (NJ)
Sacred Heart U (CT)
Saginaw Valley State U (MI)
Saint Joseph's Coll (IN)
Saint Louis U (MO)
Salem State U (MA)
Salisbury U (MD)
Samford U (AL)
San Diego Christian Coll (CA)
Shawnee State U (OH)
Shaw U (NC)
Simpson Coll (IA)
Slippery Rock U of Pennsylvania (PA)
South Dakota State U (SD)
Southeastern Louisiana U (LA)
Southeast Missouri State U (MO)
Southern Arkansas U–Magnolia (AR)
Southern Connecticut State U (CT)
Southern Illinois U Carbondale (IL)
Southwest Baptist U (MO)
Southwestern Coll (KS)
State U of New York Coll at Cortland (NY)
Sterling Coll (KS)
Stony Brook U, State U of New York (NY)
Tabor Coll (KS)
Temple U (PA)
Texas A&M U–Corpus Christi (TX)
Texas Christian U (TX)
Texas Lutheran U (TX)
Texas State U–San Marcos (TX)
Texas Wesleyan U (TX)
Towson U (MD)
Troy U (AL)
Truman State U (MO)
Tusculum Coll (TN)
Union Coll (KY)
Union U (TN)
Université de Sherbrooke (QC, Canada)
The U of Akron (OH)
The U of Alabama (AL)
U of Alberta (AB, Canada)
U of Central Arkansas (AR)
U of Central Florida (FL)
U of Charleston (WV)
U of Cincinnati (OH)
U of Delaware (DE)
U of Evansville (IN)
U of Florida (FL)
U of Idaho (ID)
U of Illinois at Urbana–Champaign (IL)
U of Indianapolis (IN)
The U of Iowa (IA)
The U of Kansas (KS)
U of La Verne (CA)
U of Louisiana at Lafayette (LA)
U of Maine at Presque Isle (ME)
U of Mary (ND)
U of Mary Hardin-Baylor (TX)
U of Miami (FL)
U of Michigan (MI)
U of Minnesota, Duluth (MN)
U of Mobile (AL)
U of Mount Union (OH)
U of Nevada, Las Vegas (NV)
U of New England (ME)
U of New Hampshire (NH)
The U of North Carolina at Charlotte (NC)
The U of North Carolina Wilmington (NC)
U of North Dakota (ND)
U of Northern Iowa (IA)
U of North Florida (FL)
U of Pittsburgh at Bradford (PA)
U of Puerto Rico at Ponce (PR)
U of Southern Maine (ME)
U of Southern Mississippi (MS)
U of South Florida (FL)
The U of Tampa (FL)
The U of Tennessee at Martin (TN)
The U of Texas at Arlington (TX)
The U of Texas at Austin (TX)
The U of Texas of the Permian Basin (TX)
U of the Incarnate Word (TX)
U of Tulsa (OK)

U of Utah (UT)
U of Vermont (VT)
The U of West Alabama (AL)
U of Wisconsin–Eau Claire (WI)
U of Wisconsin–La Crosse (WI)
U of Wisconsin–Milwaukee (WI)
U of Wisconsin–Stevens Point (WI)
Upper Iowa U (IA)
Valdosta State U (GA)
Vanguard U of Southern California (CA)
Washburn U (KS)
Washington State U (WA)
Waynesburg U (PA)
Wayne State Coll (NE)
Weber State U (UT)
West Chester U of Pennsylvania (PA)
Western Carolina U (NC)
Western Illinois U (IL)
Western Michigan U (MI)
Westfield State U (MA)
West Virginia Wesleyan Coll (WV)
Wheeling Jesuit U (WV)
Wichita State U (KS)
William Paterson U of New Jersey (NJ)
William Woods U (MO)
Wilmington Coll (OH)
Wingate U (NC)
Winona State U (MN)
Xavier U (OH)
Youngstown State U (OH)

ATMOSPHERIC CHEMISTRY AND CLIMATOLOGY

Purdue U (IN)

ATMOSPHERIC PHYSICS AND DYNAMICS

Purdue U (IN)

ATMOSPHERIC SCIENCES AND METEOROLOGY

The Coll at Brockport, State U of New York (NY)
Cornell U (NY)
Creighton U (NE)
Dalhousie U (NS, Canada)
Embry-Riddle Aeronautical U–Daytona (FL)
Embry-Riddle Aeronautical U–Prescott (AZ)
Florida State U (FL)
Iowa State U of Science and Technology (IA)
Millersville U of Pennsylvania (PA)
North Carolina Ag and Tech State U (NC)
North Carolina State U (NC)
Northern Illinois U (IL)
Ohio U (OH)
Penn State Abington (PA)
Penn State Altoona (PA)
Penn State Beaver (PA)
Penn State Berks (PA)
Penn State Brandywine (PA)
Penn State DuBois (PA)
Penn State Erie, The Behrend Coll (PA)
Penn State Fayette, The Eberly Campus (PA)
Penn State Greater Allegheny (PA)
Penn State Hazleton (PA)
Penn State Lehigh Valley (PA)
Penn State Mont Alto (PA)
Penn State New Kensington (PA)
Penn State Schuylkill (PA)
Penn State Shenango (PA)
Penn State U Park (PA)
Penn State Wilkes-Barre (PA)
Penn State Worthington Scranton (PA)
Penn State York (PA)
Plymouth State U (NH)
Purdue U (IN)
Rutgers, The State U of New Jersey, New Brunswick (NJ)
Saint Louis U (MO)
San Francisco State U (CA)
State U of New York at Oswego (NY)
State U of New York Coll at Oneonta (NY)

State U of New York Maritime Coll (NY)
Stony Brook U, State U of New York (NY)
Texas A&M U (TX)
United States Air Force Acad (CO)
U at Albany, State U of New York (NY)
U of Alberta (AB, Canada)
The U of British Columbia (BC, Canada)
U of California, Berkeley (CA)
U of California, Davis (CA)
U of Illinois at Urbana–Champaign (IL)
The U of Kansas (KS)
U of Louisiana at Monroe (LA)
U of Louisville (KY)
U of Maryland, Coll Park (MD)
U of Miami (FL)
U of Michigan (MI)
U of Missouri (MO)
U of Nebraska–Lincoln (NE)
U of Nevada, Reno (NV)
The U of North Carolina at Asheville (NC)
U of North Dakota (ND)
U of South Alabama (AL)
U of Utah (UT)
U of Washington (WA)
U of Wisconsin–Madison (WI)
Valparaiso U (IN)
Western Connecticut State U (CT)

ATMOSPHERIC SCIENCES AND METEOROLOGY RELATED
East Carolina U (NC)
Purdue U (IN)
U of California, Los Angeles (CA)
U of the Incarnate Word (TX)

ATOMIC/MOLECULAR PHYSICS
San Diego State U (CA)

AUDIOLOGY
Biola U (CA)
California State U, Long Beach (CA)
Cleveland State U (OH)
Indiana U Bloomington (IN)
The Ohio State U (OH)
Purdue U (IN)
Stephen F. Austin State U (TX)
U of Illinois at Urbana–Champaign (IL)
U of Northern Colorado (CO)
U of Oklahoma Health Sciences Center (OK)
The U of Western Ontario (ON, Canada)

AUDIOLOGY AND SPEECH-LANGUAGE PATHOLOGY
Adelphi U (NY)
Andrews U (MI)
Arkansas State U (AR)
Auburn U (AL)
Augustana Coll (SD)
Ball State U (IN)
Bloomsburg U of Pennsylvania (PA)
Boston U (MA)
Bowling Green State U (OH)
Brescia U (KY)
Buffalo State Coll, State U of New York (NY)
California State U, East Bay (CA)
California State U, Fresno (CA)
California State U, Long Beach (CA)
California State U, Sacramento (CA)
Calvin Coll (MI)
Central Michigan U (MI)
The Coll of Idaho (ID)
The Coll of Saint Rose (NY)
Delta State U (MS)
East Carolina U (NC)
Eastern Kentucky U (KY)
Eastern New Mexico U (NM)
East Stroudsburg U of Pennsylvania (PA)
Elmhurst Coll (IL)

Elmira Coll (NY)
Fontbonne U (MO)
Fort Hays State U (KS)
The George Washington U (DC)
Governors State U (IL)
Hampton U (VA)
Hardin-Simmons U (TX)
Hofstra U (NY)
Hunter Coll of the City U of New York (NY)
Idaho State U (ID)
Illinois State U (IL)
Indiana State U (IN)
Indiana U Bloomington (IN)
Indiana U of Pennsylvania (PA)
Indiana U–Purdue U Fort Wayne (IN)
Iona Coll (NY)
Ithaca Coll (NY)
Kent State U (OH)
Lamar U (TX)
La Salle U (PA)
Lehman Coll of the City U of New York (NY)
Louisiana State U and Ag and Mech Coll (LA)
Marquette U (WI)
Marywood U (PA)
Mercy Coll (NY)
Minnesota State U Mankato (MN)
Missouri State U (MO)
Molloy Coll (NY)
Nazareth Coll of Rochester (NY)
New York U (NY)
Nicholls State U (LA)
Northeastern State U (OK)
Northeastern U (MA)
The Ohio State U (OH)
Ohio U (OH)
Old Dominion U (VA)
Otterbein U (OH)
Purdue U (IN)
The Richard Stockton Coll of New Jersey (NJ)
St. John's U (NY)
Saint Louis U (MO)
Shaw U (NC)
South Carolina State U (SC)
Southeastern Louisiana U (LA)
Southern Connecticut State U (CT)
Southern Illinois U Edwardsville (IL)
State U of New York at Fredonia (NY)
State U of New York at Plattsburgh (NY)
State U of New York Coll at Cortland (NY)
Temple U (PA)
Texas A&M U–Kingsville (TX)
Texas Woman's U (TX)
Thiel Coll (PA)
Touro Coll (NY)
U at Buffalo, the State U of New York (NY)
The U of Alabama (AL)
U of Arkansas (AR)
U of Arkansas at Little Rock (AR)
U of Central Arkansas (AR)
U of Central Florida (FL)
U of Florida (FL)
U of Hawaii at Manoa (HI)
U of Illinois at Urbana–Champaign (IL)
The U of Iowa (IA)
U of Louisiana at Lafayette (LA)
U of Louisiana at Monroe (LA)
U of Minnesota, Twin Cities Campus (MN)
U of Mississippi (MS)
U of New Mexico (NM)
U of North Texas (TX)
U of Oklahoma Health Sciences Center (OK)
U of Pittsburgh (PA)
U of Redlands (CA)
U of South Alabama (AL)
U of Southern Mississippi (MS)
U of South Florida (FL)
The U of Texas at Dallas (TX)
The U of Texas at El Paso (TX)
The U of Texas–Pan American (TX)
U of the District of Columbia (DC)
U of the Pacific (CA)
The U of Toledo (OH)
U of Tulsa (OK)

U of Utah (UT)
U of Virginia (VA)
U of Washington (WA)
The U of Western Ontario (ON, Canada)
U of Wisconsin–Madison (WI)
U of Wisconsin–Milwaukee (WI)
U of Wisconsin–Stevens Point (WI)
U of Wyoming (WY)
Utah State U (UT)
Washington State U (WA)
West Chester U of Pennsylvania (PA)
Western Michigan U (MI)
Western Washington U (WA)
West Virginia U (WV)
Yeshiva U (NY)

AUDIOVISUAL COMMUNICATIONS TECHNOLOGIES RELATED
Greenville Coll (IL)
Webster U (MO)

AUDITING
Babson Coll (MA)
Carlow U (PA)
U of Illinois at Urbana–Champaign (IL)

AUSTRALIAN/OCEANIC/PACIFIC LANGUAGES
U of Hawaii–West Oahu (HI)

AUTOBODY/COLLISION AND REPAIR TECHNOLOGY
Lewis-Clark State Coll (ID)
Pennsylvania Coll of Technology (PA)

AUTOMOBILE/AUTOMOTIVE MECHANICS TECHNOLOGY
Lewis-Clark State Coll (ID)
McPherson Coll (KS)
Montana State U–Northern (MT)
Morrisville State Coll (NY)
Pittsburg State U (KS)

AUTOMOTIVE ENGINEERING TECHNOLOGY
Central Michigan U (MI)
Ferris State U (MI)
Indiana State U (IN)
Minnesota State U Mankato (MN)
Pennsylvania Coll of Technology (PA)
Southern Illinois U Carbondale (IL)
State U of New York Coll of Technology at Alfred (NY)
Weber State U (UT)
Western Washington U (WA)

AVIATION/AIRWAY MANAGEMENT
Auburn U (AL)
Averett U (VA)
Baker Coll of Muskegon (MI)
Bridgewater State U (MA)
California State U, Los Angeles (CA)
Daniel Webster Coll (NH)
Delaware State U (DE)
Dixie State Coll of Utah (UT)
Dowling Coll (NY)
Eastern Michigan U (MI)
Eastern New Mexico U (NM)
Embry-Riddle Aeronautical U–Daytona (FL)
Embry-Riddle Aeronautical U–Worldwide (FL)
Fairmont State U (WV)
Farmingdale State Coll (NY)
Florida Inst of Technology (FL)
Hampton U (VA)
Indiana State U (IN)
Inter American U of Puerto Rico, Bayamón Campus (PR)
Jacksonville U (FL)
Lewis U (IL)
Marywood U (PA)
Metropolitan State Coll of Denver (CO)

Minnesota State U Mankato (MN)
Mountain State U (WV)
The Ohio State U (OH)
Ohio U (OH)
Purdue U (IN)
Quincy U (IL)
Rocky Mountain Coll (MT)
Saint Louis U (MO)
Salem State U (MA)
South Dakota State U (SD)
Southern Illinois U Carbondale (IL)
Tarleton State U (TX)
Texas Southern U (TX)
U of Dubuque (IA)
U of Illinois at Urbana–Champaign (IL)
U of Nebraska at Kearney (NE)
U of Nebraska at Omaha (NE)
U of North Dakota (ND)
U of North Texas (TX)
The U of Western Ontario (ON, Canada)
Vaughn Coll of Aeronautics and Technology (NY)
Western Michigan U (MI)
Westminster Coll (UT)
Wilmington U (DE)
Winona State U (MN)

AVIONICS MAINTENANCE TECHNOLOGY
Fairmont State U (WV)
LeTourneau U (TX)
Pennsylvania Coll of Technology (PA)
Purdue U (IN)
Southern Illinois U Carbondale (IL)
Vaughn Coll of Aeronautics and Technology (NY)
Western Michigan U (MI)
Wilmington U (DE)

AYURVEDIC MEDICINE
Maharishi U of Management (IA)

BAKING AND PASTRY ARTS
The Restaurant School at Walnut Hill Coll (PA)

BALLET
Brigham Young U (UT)
Friends U (KS)
Indiana U Bloomington (IN)
Texas Christian U (TX)
U of Utah (UT)

BANKING AND FINANCIAL SUPPORT SERVICES
Brescia U (KY)
Buena Vista U (IA)
Delaware State U (DE)
Emory U (GA)
Husson U (ME)
National U (CA)
Northwood U, Michigan Campus (MI)
Providence Coll (RI)
Saint Peter's Coll (NJ)
Sam Houston State U (TX)
Texas Southern U (TX)
U of Illinois at Urbana–Champaign (IL)
U of Nebraska at Omaha (NE)
U of Nebraska–Lincoln (NE)
U of North Florida (FL)
U of North Texas (TX)
The U of Texas at Arlington (TX)
U of the Incarnate Word (TX)
West Liberty U (WV)

BEHAVIORAL SCIENCES
Andrews U (MI)
Athens State U (AL)
Bemidji State U (MN)
Brown U (RI)
California Baptist U (CA)
California State U, Dominguez Hills (CA)
Carnegie Mellon U (PA)
Chaminade U of Honolulu (HI)
Coll of St. Joseph (VT)
Columbia Coll (SC)
Columbia Southern U (AL)

Concordia Coll–New York (NY)
Concordia U (CA)
Concordia U, Nebraska (NE)
Evangel U (MO)
George Fox U (OR)
Glenville State Coll (WV)
Goddard Coll (VT)
Granite State Coll (NH)
Indiana U Kokomo (IN)
Inter American U of Puerto Rico, San Germán Campus (PR)
The Johns Hopkins U (MD)
Marlboro Coll (VT)
Mars Hill Coll (NC)
Metropolitan State Coll of Denver (CO)
Minnesota State U Mankato (MN)
Missouri Baptist U (MO)
Mount Mary Coll (WI)
National U (CA)
Northeastern U (MA)
Northern Michigan U (MI)
Point Park U (PA)
Purdue U (IN)
Purdue U North Central (IN)
Saint Augustine's Coll (NC)
Sterling Coll (KS)
Tabor Coll (KS)
Trevecca Nazarene U (TN)
Tufts U (MA)
United States Air Force Acad (CO)
U of Houston–Clear Lake (TX)
The U of Kansas (KS)
U of La Verne (CA)
U of Maine at Fort Kent (ME)
U of Missouri (MO)
U of North Texas (TX)
U of Wisconsin–Green Bay (WI)
Utah Valley U (UT)
Walsh U (OH)
Western Intl U (AZ)
Widener U (PA)
William Paterson U of New Jersey (NJ)
Wilmington U (DE)
York Coll of Pennsylvania (PA)

BIBLICAL STUDIES
Abilene Christian U (TX)
Alaska Bible Coll (AK)
Amridge U (AL)
Anderson U (IN)
Andrews U (MI)
Arlington Baptist Coll (TX)
Asbury U (KY)
Azusa Pacific U (CA)
Baptist Bible Coll of Pennsylvania (PA)
The Baptist Coll of Florida (FL)
Baptist U of the Americas (TX)
Barclay Coll (KS)
Belhaven U (MS)
Belmont U (TN)
Bethel Coll (IN)
Bethel U (MN)
Beulah Heights U (GA)
Biola U (CA)
Bluefield Coll (VA)
Blue Mountain Coll (MS)
Bob Jones U (SC)
Boston Baptist Coll (MA)
Briercrest Coll (SK, Canada)
California Baptist U (CA)
Calvary Bible Coll and Theological Sem (MO)
Calvin Coll (MI)
Campbellsville U (KY)
Carolina Christian Coll (NC)
Carson-Newman Coll (TN)
Carver Bible Coll (GA)
Cedarville U (OH)
Cincinnati Christian U (OH)
Clear Creek Baptist Bible Coll (KY)
Clearwater Christian Coll (FL)
Columbia Bible Coll (BC, Canada)
Corban U (OR)
Cornerstone U (MI)
Covenant Coll (GA)
Crandall U (NB, Canada)
The Criswell Coll (TX)
Crossroads Bible Coll (IN)
Dallas Baptist U (TX)
Dallas Christian Coll (TX)
Eastern Mennonite U (VA)
Eastern U (PA)

East Texas Baptist U (TX)
Emmaus Bible Coll (IA)
Evangel U (MO)
Faith Baptist Bible Coll and
  Theological Sem (IA)
Faulkner U (AL)
Florida Coll (FL)
Free Will Baptist Bible Coll (TN)
Gardner-Webb U (NC)
Geneva Coll (PA)
George Fox U (OR)
Grace Coll (IN)
Grand Canyon U (AZ)
Great Lakes Christian Coll (MI)
Hannibal-LaGrange U (MO)
Harding U (AR)
Hardin-Simmons U (TX)
Heritage Christian U (AL)
Hope Intl U (CA)
Houghton Coll (NY)
Howard Payne U (TX)
Huntington U (IN)
Indiana Wesleyan U (IN)
John Brown U (AR)
Judson U (IL)
Kentucky Christian U (KY)
King Coll (TN)
Kingswood U (NB, Canada)
Lee U (TN)
LeTourneau U (TX)
Liberty U (VA)
Lincoln Christian U (IL)
Lipscomb U (TN)
Lubbock Christian U (TX)
Malone U (OH)
Maple Springs Baptist Bible Coll
  and Sem (MD)
Maranatha Baptist Bible Coll (WI)
Marlboro Coll (VT)
The Master's Coll and Sem (CA)
Master's Coll and Sem (ON,
  Canada)
Messiah Coll (PA)
MidAmerica Nazarene U (KS)
Mid-Atlantic Christian U (NC)
Mid-Continent U (KY)
Milligan Coll (TN)
Montreat Coll, Montreat (NC)
Moody Bible Inst (IL)
Mount Vernon Nazarene U (OH)
Multnomah U (OR)
New Hope Christian Coll (OR)
North Greenville U (SC)
Northwest Christian U (OR)
Northwestern Coll (MN)
Northwest Nazarene U (ID)
Northwest U (WA)
Nyack Coll (NY)
Oakland City U (IN)
Ohio Valley U (WV)
Oklahoma Christian U (OK)
Oklahoma City U (OK)
Oral Roberts U (OK)
Ouachita Baptist U (AR)
Palm Beach Atlantic U (FL)
Philadelphia Biblical U (PA)
Piedmont Intl U (NC)
Point Loma Nazarene U (CA)
Point U (GA)
Roberts Wesleyan Coll (NY)
Saint Louis Christian Coll (MO)
San Diego Christian Coll (CA)
Simpson U (CA)
Southeastern Bible Coll (AL)
Southwest Baptist U (MO)
Southwestern Assemblies of God U
  (TX)
Southwestern Christian U (OK)
Spring Arbor U (MI)
Tabor Coll (KS)
Taylor U (IN)
Trinity Baptist Coll (FL)
Tri-State Bible Coll (OH)
Union U (TN)
Universidad Teologica del Caribe
  (PR)
U of Evansville (IN)
U of Mary Hardin-Baylor (TX)
The U of Western Ontario (ON,
  Canada)
Valley Forge Christian Coll
  Woodbridge Campus (VA)
Vanguard Coll (AB, Canada)
Vanguard U of Southern California
  (CA)

Wheaton Coll (IL)

BILINGUAL AND MULTILINGUAL EDUCATION

Belmont U (TN)
Boise State U (ID)
Boston U (MA)
Calvin Coll (MI)
Chicago State U (IL)
Goddard Coll (VT)
Long Island U–Brooklyn Campus
  (NY)
Loyola U Chicago (IL)
Midwestern State U (TX)
Mount Mary Coll (WI)
Northeastern Illinois U (IL)
Southwestern Assemblies of God U
  (TX)
State U of New York Coll at Old
  Westbury (NY)
Texas A&M Intl U (TX)
Texas A&M U–Corpus Christi (TX)
Texas Christian U (TX)
Texas Wesleyan U (TX)
U of Alberta (AB, Canada)
U of Delaware (DE)
The U of Findlay (OH)
U of Maine at Fort Kent (ME)
U of Nebraska at Omaha (NE)
U of Regina (SK, Canada)
U of the Southwest (NM)
U of Washington (WA)
Washington State U (WA)
Western Illinois U (IL)
York Coll of the City U of New York
  (NY)

BILINGUAL, MULTILINGUAL, AND MULTICULTURAL EDUCATION RELATED

The Coll at Brockport, State U of
  New York (NY)

BIOCHEMICAL ENGINEERING

Hope Coll (MI)
U of Colorado Boulder (CO)

BIOCHEMISTRY

Abilene Christian U (TX)
Adams State Coll (CO)
Adelphi U (NY)
Agnes Scott Coll (GA)
Albright Coll (PA)
Allegheny Coll (PA)
Alma Coll (MI)
Alvernia U (PA)
American U (DC)
Anderson U (IN)
Andrews U (MI)
Angelo State U (TX)
Arizona State U (AZ)
Asbury U (KY)
Auburn U (AL)
Augustana Coll (IL)
Augustana Coll (SD)
Austin Coll (TX)
Azusa Pacific U (CA)
Barnard Coll (NY)
Bates Coll (ME)
Baylor U (TX)
Belmont U (TN)
Beloit Coll (WI)
Benedictine Coll (KS)
Berry Coll (GA)
Biola U (CA)
Bishop's U (QC, Canada)
Boston Coll (MA)
Bowdoin Coll (ME)
Bowling Green State U (OH)
Bradley U (IL)
Brandeis U (MA)
Bridgewater State U (MA)
Brown U (RI)
Bucknell U (PA)
California Lutheran U (CA)
California Polytechnic State U, San
  Luis Obispo (CA)
California State U, Chico (CA)
California State U, Dominguez Hills
  (CA)
California State U, East Bay (CA)
California State U, Fullerton (CA)

California State U, Long Beach
  (CA)
California State U, Los Angeles
  (CA)
California State U, San Bernardino
  (CA)
California State U, San Marcos
  (CA)
Calvin Coll (MI)
Canisius Coll (NY)
Capital U (OH)
Case Western Reserve U (OH)
The Catholic U of America (DC)
Cedar Crest Coll (PA)
Central Coll (IA)
Central Connecticut State U (CT)
Central Michigan U (MI)
Centre Coll (KY)
Chapman U (CA)
Chatham U (PA)
Chestnut Hill Coll (PA)
Christian Brothers U (TN)
City Coll of the City U of New York
  (NY)
Claflin U (SC)
Claremont McKenna Coll (CA)
Clarke U (IA)
Clark U (MA)
Clemson U (SC)
Coastal Carolina U (SC)
Coe Coll (IA)
Colby Coll (ME)
Colgate U (NY)
The Coll at Brockport, State U of
  New York (NY)
Coll of Mount St. Joseph (OH)
Coll of Mount Saint Vincent (NY)
Coll of Saint Benedict (MN)
Coll of Saint Elizabeth (NJ)
The Coll of Saint Rose (NY)
The Coll of St. Scholastica (MN)
Coll of Staten Island of the City U of
  New York (NY)
The Coll of Wooster (OH)
The Colorado Coll (CO)
Colorado State U (CO)
Columbia U, School of General
  Studies (NY)
Connecticut Coll (CT)
Converse Coll (SC)
Cornell Coll (IA)
Daemen Coll (NY)
Dartmouth Coll (NH)
Denison U (OH)
DePauw U (IN)
DeSales U (PA)
Dickinson Coll (PA)
Dominican U (IL)
Drake U (IA)
Drew U (NJ)
Duquesne U (PA)
Earlham Coll (IN)
East Carolina U (NC)
Eastern Connecticut State U (CT)
Eastern Mennonite U (VA)
Eastern Michigan U (MI)
Eastern New Mexico U (NM)
Eastern Oregon U (OR)
Eastern U (PA)
East Stroudsburg U of Pennsylvania
  (PA)
Eckerd Coll (FL)
Elizabethtown Coll (PA)
Elmira Coll (NY)
Emmanuel Coll (MA)
Fairfield U (CT)
Fairleigh Dickinson U, Coll at
  Florham (NJ)
Fairleigh Dickinson U, Metropolitan
  Campus (NJ)
Ferris State U (MI)
Florida Inst of Technology (FL)
Florida State U (FL)
Fort Lewis Coll (CO)
Franklin & Marshall Coll (PA)
Furman U (SC)
Geneva Coll (PA)
Georgia Inst of Technology (GA)
Georgian Court U (NJ)
Gettysburg Coll (PA)
Gonzaga U (WA)
Goucher Coll (MD)
Grinnell Coll (IA)
Grove City Coll (PA)
Gustavus Adolphus Coll (MN)

Hamilton Coll (NY)
Hamline U (MN)
Hampden-Sydney Coll (VA)
Harding U (AR)
Hartwick Coll (NY)
Harvard U (MA)
Haverford Coll (PA)
Hawai`i Pacific U (HI)
Hobart and William Smith Colls
  (NY)
Hofstra U (NY)
Holy Family U (PA)
Hood Coll (MD)
Houghton Coll (NY)
Humboldt State U (CA)
Huntingdon Coll (AL)
Idaho State U (ID)
Illinois Inst of Technology (IL)
Illinois State U (IL)
Indiana U Bloomington (IN)
Indiana U of Pennsylvania (PA)
Indiana U South Bend (IN)
Indiana Wesleyan U (IN)
Inter American U of Puerto Rico,
  Bayamón Campus (PR)
Iona Coll (NY)
Iowa State U of Science and
  Technology (IA)
Ithaca Coll (NY)
Jamestown Coll (ND)
John Brown U (AR)
Judson U (IL)
Juniata Coll (PA)
Kansas State U (KS)
Kennesaw State U (GA)
Kenyon Coll (OH)
Kettering U (MI)
Keuka Coll (NY)
King Coll (TN)
Knox Coll (IL)
Kutztown U of Pennsylvania (PA)
Lafayette Coll (PA)
LaGrange Coll (GA)
Lake Forest Coll (IL)
La Salle U (PA)
La Sierra U (CA)
Lawrence Technological U (MI)
Lawrence U (WI)
Lee U (TN)
Lehigh U (PA)
Lehman Coll of the City U of New
  York (NY)
Le Moyne Coll (NY)
Lewis U (IL)
Lipscomb U (TN)
Loras Coll (IA)
Louisiana State U and Ag and Mech
  Coll (LA)
Loyola Marymount U (CA)
Loyola U Chicago (IL)
Madonna U (MI)
Manchester Coll (IN)
Manhattan Coll (NY)
Manhattanville Coll (NY)
Mansfield U of Pennsylvania (PA)
Marietta Coll (OH)
Marlboro Coll (VT)
Maryville Coll (TN)
Maryville U of Saint Louis (MO)
McMurry U (TX)
McPherson Coll (KS)
Mercyhurst Coll (PA)
Merrimack Coll (MA)
Messiah Coll (PA)
Miami U (OH)
Michigan State U (MI)
Michigan Technological U (MI)
Middlebury Coll (VT)
Millsaps Coll (MS)
Mills Coll (CA)
Minnesota State U Mankato (MN)
Misericordia U (PA)
Mississippi Coll (MS)
Mississippi State U (MS)
Missouri Baptist U (MO)
Missouri Southern State U (MO)
Missouri Western State U (MO)
Monmouth U (IL)
Montclair State U (NJ)
Moravian Coll (PA)
Mount Allison U (NB, Canada)
Mount Holyoke Coll (MA)
Mount St. Mary's Coll (CA)
Mount St. Mary's U (MD)
Muhlenberg Coll (PA)

Nazareth Coll of Rochester (NY)
Nebraska Wesleyan U (NE)
New Coll of Florida (FL)
Newman U (KS)
New Mexico State U (NM)
New York U (NY)
Niagara U (NY)
North Carolina State U (NC)
North Central Coll (IL)
Northeastern U (MA)
Northern Michigan U (MI)
Northwestern Coll (MN)
Northwest Nazarene U (ID)
Notre Dame de Namur U (CA)
Oakland U (MI)
Occidental Coll (CA)
Ohio Northern U (OH)
The Ohio State U (OH)
Oklahoma Christian U (OK)
Oklahoma City U (OK)
Oklahoma State U (OK)
Old Dominion U (VA)
Oral Roberts U (OK)
Otterbein U (OH)
Pace U (NY)
Pacific Union Coll (CA)
Penn State Abington (PA)
Penn State Altoona (PA)
Penn State Beaver (PA)
Penn State Berks (PA)
Penn State Brandywine (PA)
Penn State DuBois (PA)
Penn State Erie, The Behrend Coll
  (PA)
Penn State Fayette, The Eberly
  Campus (PA)
Penn State Greater Allegheny (PA)
Penn State Hazleton (PA)
Penn State Lehigh Valley (PA)
Penn State Mont Alto (PA)
Penn State New Kensington (PA)
Penn State Schuylkill (PA)
Penn State Shenango (PA)
Penn State U Park (PA)
Penn State Wilkes-Barre (PA)
Penn State Worthington Scranton
  (PA)
Penn State York (PA)
Philadelphia U (PA)
Pittsburg State U (KS)
Pitzer Coll (CA)
Point Loma Nazarene U (CA)
Pomona Coll (CA)
Portland State U (OR)
Presbyterian Coll (SC)
Providence Coll (RI)
Purchase Coll, State U of New York
  (NY)
Purdue U (IN)
Queen's U at Kingston (ON,
  Canada)
Queens U of Charlotte (NC)
Quinnipiac U (CT)
Ramapo Coll of New Jersey (NJ)
Regis Coll (MA)
Regis U (CO)
Rhodes Coll (TN)
Rice U (TX)
The Richard Stockton Coll of New
  Jersey (NJ)
Rider U (NJ)
Ripon Coll (WI)
Roanoke Coll (VA)
Roberts Wesleyan Coll (NY)
Rochester Inst of Technology (NY)
Rockford Coll (IL)
Rockhurst U (MO)
Roger Williams U (RI)
Rollins Coll (FL)
Roosevelt U (IL)
Rose-Hulman Inst of Technology
  (IN)
Rosemont Coll (PA)
Rowan U (NJ)
Russell Sage Coll (NY)
Rutgers, The State U of New
  Jersey, New Brunswick (NJ)
Saginaw Valley State U (MI)
Saint Anselm Coll (NH)
St. Bonaventure U (NY)
St. Catherine U (MN)
St. Edward's U (TX)
Saint John's U (MN)
Saint Joseph's Coll (IN)
Saint Joseph's U (PA)

St. Lawrence U (NY)
Saint Louis U (MO)
Saint Mary's Coll of California (CA)
St. Mary's Coll of Maryland (MD)
St. Mary's U (TX)
Saint Mary's U of Minnesota (MN)
Saint Michael's Coll (VT)
Saint Peter's Coll (NJ)
Saint Vincent Coll (PA)
Salem State U (MA)
Samford U (AL)
San Francisco State U (CA)
Santa Clara U (CA)
Schreiner U (TX)
Scripps Coll (CA)
Seattle Pacific U (WA)
Seattle U (WA)
Seton Hill U (PA)
Siena Coll (NY)
Simmons Coll (MA)
Simon Fraser U (BC, Canada)
Simpson Coll (IA)
Slippery Rock U of Pennsylvania (PA)
Smith Coll (MA)
South Dakota State U (SD)
Southern Methodist U (TX)
Southern Oregon U (OR)
Southwestern Coll (KS)
Southwestern U (TX)
Spelman Coll (GA)
Spring Arbor U (MI)
Spring Hill Coll (AL)
State U of New York at Binghamton (NY)
State U of New York at Fredonia (NY)
State U of New York at Plattsburgh (NY)
State U of New York Coll at Geneseo (NY)
State U of New York Coll at Old Westbury (NY)
State U of New York Coll at Oneonta (NY)
State U of New York Coll at Potsdam (NY)
State U of New York Coll of Environmental Science and Forestry (NY)
Stephen F. Austin State U (TX)
Stetson U (FL)
Stevens Inst of Technology (NJ)
Stonehill Coll (MA)
Stony Brook U, State U of New York (NY)
Suffolk U (MA)
Susquehanna U (PA)
Swarthmore Coll (PA)
Syracuse U (NY)
Tabor Coll (KS)
Temple U (PA)
Texas A&M U (TX)
Texas Christian U (TX)
Texas State U–San Marcos (TX)
Texas Tech U (TX)
Texas Wesleyan U (TX)
Texas Woman's U (TX)
Thompson Rivers U (BC, Canada)
Trent U (ON, Canada)
Trinity Coll (CT)
Trinity U (TX)
Tulane U (LA)
Union Coll (NE)
Union Coll (NY)
United States Air Force Acad (CO)
Université de Sherbrooke (QC, Canada)
U at Albany, State U of New York (NY)
U at Buffalo, the State U of New York (NY)
The U of Akron (OH)
U of Alberta (AB, Canada)
The U of Arizona (AZ)
The U of British Columbia (BC, Canada)
The U of British Columbia–Okanagan (BC, Canada)
U of California, Los Angeles (CA)
U of California, Riverside (CA)
U of California, Santa Barbara (CA)
U of California, Santa Cruz (CA)
U of Cincinnati (OH)

U of Colorado at Colorado Springs (CO)
U of Colorado Boulder (CO)
U of Dallas (TX)
U of Dayton (OH)
U of Delaware (DE)
U of Denver (CO)
U of Evansville (IN)
U of Georgia (GA)
U of Guelph (ON, Canada)
U of Houston (TX)
U of Idaho (ID)
U of Illinois at Chicago (IL)
U of Illinois at Urbana–Champaign (IL)
The U of Iowa (IA)
The U of Kansas (KS)
U of Lethbridge (AB, Canada)
U of Maine (ME)
U of Maryland, Coll Park (MD)
U of Massachusetts Boston (MA)
U of Miami (FL)
U of Michigan (MI)
U of Michigan–Dearborn (MI)
U of Michigan–Flint (MI)
U of Minnesota, Duluth (MN)
U of Minnesota, Twin Cities Campus (MN)
U of Mississippi (MS)
U of Missouri (MO)
U of Missouri–St. Louis (MO)
U of Mount Union (OH)
U of Nebraska–Lincoln (NE)
U of Nevada, Las Vegas (NV)
U of Nevada, Reno (NV)
U of New England (ME)
U of New Mexico (NM)
U of Northern Iowa (IA)
U of North Texas (TX)
U of Notre Dame (IN)
U of Oklahoma (OK)
U of Oregon (OR)
U of Ottawa (ON, Canada)
U of Pennsylvania (PA)
U of Puget Sound (WA)
U of Regina (SK, Canada)
U of Rochester (NY)
U of Saint Joseph (CT)
U of St. Thomas (MN)
U of St. Thomas (TX)
U of San Diego (CA)
The U of Scranton (PA)
U of Southern California (CA)
U of Southern Indiana (IN)
The U of Tampa (FL)
The U of Texas at Arlington (TX)
The U of Texas at Austin (TX)
The U of Texas at Dallas (TX)
U of the Incarnate Word (TX)
U of the Pacific (CA)
U of the Sciences in Philadelphia (PA)
U of Toronto (ON, Canada)
U of Tulsa (OK)
U of Vermont (VT)
U of Washington (WA)
The U of Western Ontario (ON, Canada)
U of Windsor (ON, Canada)
U of Wisconsin–La Crosse (WI)
U of Wisconsin–Madison (WI)
U of Wisconsin–Milwaukee (WI)
U of Wisconsin–River Falls (WI)
U of Wisconsin–Stevens Point (WI)
Valparaiso U (IN)
Vanguard U of Southern California (CA)
Vassar Coll (NY)
Villanova U (PA)
Virginia Polytechnic Inst and State U (VA)
Viterbo U (WI)
Wabash Coll (IN)
Wartburg Coll (IA)
Washburn U (KS)
Washington Adventist U (MD)
Washington & Jefferson Coll (PA)
Washington and Lee U (VA)
Washington State U (WA)
Washington U in St. Louis (MO)
Wellesley Coll (MA)
Wells Coll (NY)
Wesleyan U (CT)
West Chester U of Pennsylvania (PA)

Western Kentucky U (KY)
Western Michigan U (MI)
Western State Coll of Colorado (CO)
Western Washington U (WA)
Westminster Coll (MO)
Wheaton Coll (MA)
Whitman Coll (WA)
Whittier Coll (CA)
Widener U (PA)
Wilkes U (PA)
William Jewell Coll (MO)
Winona State U (MN)
Worcester Polytechnic Inst (MA)
Xavier U of Louisiana (LA)
Yeshiva U (NY)

BIOCHEMISTRY AND MOLECULAR BIOLOGY

Bellarmine U (KY)
Benedictine U (IL)
Boston U (MA)
California Baptist U (CA)
California State U, Long Beach (CA)
Carroll Coll (MT)
Christopher Newport U (VA)
Culver-Stockton Coll (MO)
Dalhousie U (NS, Canada)
Florida Southern Coll (FL)
Harding U (AR)
Hardin-Simmons U (TX)
Hendrix Coll (AR)
Indiana U Bloomington (IN)
Lebanon Valley Coll (PA)
Lewis & Clark Coll (OR)
Liberty U (VA)
Marquette U (WI)
Michigan State U (MI)
Minnesota State U Moorhead (MN)
Nebraska Wesleyan U (NE)
North Dakota State U (ND)
Oklahoma City U (OK)
Purdue U (IN)
The U of British Columbia (BC, Canada)
U of California, Irvine (CA)
U of Maryland, Baltimore County (MD)
U of Massachusetts Amherst (MA)
U of New Hampshire (NH)
U of Regina (SK, Canada)
The U of Western Ontario (ON, Canada)
Whitman Coll (WA)
Wilson Coll (PA)
Wittenberg U (OH)

BIOCHEMISTRY, BIOPHYSICS AND MOLECULAR BIOLOGY RELATED

Amherst Coll (MA)
Blackburn Coll (IL)
Purdue U (IN)
Rensselaer Polytechnic Inst (NY)
Sweet Briar Coll (VA)
Towson U (MD)
U of California, Santa Barbara (CA)

BIOENGINEERING AND BIOMEDICAL ENGINEERING

Alfred U (NY)
Arizona State U (AZ)
Boston U (MA)
Brown U (RI)
Bucknell U (PA)
California Lutheran U (CA)
California Polytechnic State U, San Luis Obispo (CA)
California State U, Long Beach (CA)
Carnegie Mellon U (PA)
Case Western Reserve U (OH)
The Catholic U of America (DC)
City Coll of the City U of New York (NY)
Clemson U (SC)
The Coll of New Jersey (NJ)
Colorado School of Mines (CO)
Colorado State U (CO)
Dalhousie U (NS, Canada)
Delaware State U (DE)
Drexel U (PA)
Florida Gulf Coast U (FL)

Florida Intl U (FL)
Gannon U (PA)
George Mason U (VA)
Georgia Inst of Technology (GA)
Harding U (AR)
Hofstra U (NY)
Illinois Inst of Technology (IL)
Indiana Tech (IN)
Indiana U–Purdue U Indianapolis (IN)
The Johns Hopkins U (MD)
Lawrence Technological U (MI)
Lehigh U (PA)
LeTourneau U (TX)
Louisiana State U and Ag and Mech Coll (LA)
Marquette U (WI)
Massachusetts Inst of Technology (MA)
Michigan State U (MI)
Michigan Technological U (MI)
Milwaukee School of Eng (WI)
Mississippi State U (MS)
North Carolina Ag and Tech State U (NC)
North Carolina State U (NC)
The Ohio State U (OH)
Oral Roberts U (OK)
Penn State Abington (PA)
Penn State Altoona (PA)
Penn State Beaver (PA)
Penn State Berks (PA)
Penn State Brandywine (PA)
Penn State DuBois (PA)
Penn State Erie, The Behrend Coll (PA)
Penn State Fayette, The Eberly Campus (PA)
Penn State Greater Allegheny (PA)
Penn State Hazleton (PA)
Penn State Lehigh Valley (PA)
Penn State Mont Alto (PA)
Penn State New Kensington (PA)
Penn State Schuylkill (PA)
Penn State Shenango (PA)
Penn State U Park (PA)
Penn State Wilkes-Barre (PA)
Penn State Worthington Scranton (PA)
Penn State York (PA)
Purdue U (IN)
Rensselaer Polytechnic Inst (NY)
Rice U (TX)
Rochester Inst of Technology (NY)
Rose-Hulman Inst of Technology (IN)
Rutgers, The State U of New Jersey, New Brunswick (NJ)
Ryerson U (ON, Canada)
Saint Louis U (MO)
Santa Clara U (CA)
Stanford U (CA)
State U of New York at Binghamton (NY)
State U of New York Coll of Environmental Science and Forestry (NY)
Stevens Inst of Technology (NJ)
Stony Brook U, State U of New York (NY)
Syracuse U (NY)
Temple U (PA)
Texas A&M U (TX)
Trinity Coll (CT)
Tulane U (LA)
Union Coll (NY)
U at Buffalo, the State U of New York (NY)
The U of Akron (OH)
The U of Alabama at Birmingham (AL)
The U of Arizona (AZ)
The U of British Columbia (BC, Canada)
U of California, Berkeley (CA)
U of California, Davis (CA)
U of California, Irvine (CA)
U of California, Merced (CA)
U of California, Riverside (CA)
U of California, Santa Cruz (CA)
U of Cincinnati (OH)
U of Connecticut (CT)
U of Delaware (DE)
U of Florida (FL)
U of Guelph (ON, Canada)

U of Houston (TX)
U of Illinois at Chicago (IL)
U of Illinois at Urbana–Champaign (IL)
The U of Iowa (IA)
U of Louisville (KY)
U of Massachusetts Dartmouth (MA)
U of Memphis (TN)
U of Miami (FL)
U of Michigan (MI)
U of Ottawa (ON, Canada)
U of Pennsylvania (PA)
U of Pittsburgh (PA)
U of Rhode Island (RI)
U of Rochester (NY)
U of South Carolina (SC)
U of Southern California (CA)
The U of Texas at Austin (TX)
The U of Texas at Dallas (TX)
U of the Pacific (CA)
The U of Toledo (OH)
U of Toronto (ON, Canada)
U of Utah (UT)
U of Virginia (VA)
U of Wisconsin–Madison (WI)
Vanderbilt U (TN)
Virginia Commonwealth U (VA)
Washington State U (WA)
Washington U in St. Louis (MO)
Wayne State U (MI)
Wentworth Inst of Technology (MA)
Western New England U (MA)
Widener U (PA)
Worcester Polytechnic Inst (MA)
Wright State U (OH)
Yale U (CT)

BIOETHICS/MEDICAL ETHICS

American Jewish U (CA)
U of Rochester (NY)

BIOINFORMATICS

Baylor U (TX)
Canisius Coll (NY)
Claflin U (SC)
The Coll of Saint Rose (NY)
Dalhousie U (NS, Canada)
Davenport U, Grand Rapids (MI)
Gannon U (PA)
Indiana U Bloomington (IN)
Iowa State U of Science and Technology (IA)
Kettering U (MI)
Lakehead U (ON, Canada)
Loyola U Chicago (IL)
Michigan Technological U (MI)
Pacific Union Coll (CA)
Portland State U (OR)
Purdue U (IN)
Ramapo Coll of New Jersey (NJ)
Rensselaer Polytechnic Inst (NY)
Rochester Inst of Technology (NY)
St. Bonaventure U (NY)
St. Edward's U (TX)
Saint Vincent Coll (PA)
Stevens Inst of Technology (NJ)
U at Buffalo, the State U of New York (NY)
U of Alberta (AB, Canada)
U of California, Irvine (CA)
U of California, Santa Cruz (CA)
U of Denver (CO)
U of Maryland, Baltimore County (MD)
U of Nebraska at Omaha (NE)
U of Northern Iowa (IA)
U of Pennsylvania (PA)
U of Pittsburgh (PA)
U of St. Thomas (TX)
The U of Western Ontario (ON, Canada)
U of Windsor (ON, Canada)
Virginia Commonwealth U (VA)
Webster U (MO)
Wheaton Coll (MA)
Worcester State U (MA)

BIOLOGICAL AND BIOMEDICAL SCIENCES RELATED

Arizona State U (AZ)
Bethel U (MN)
Boston U (MA)

Cornell U (NY)
Dakota State U (SD)
Delaware State U (DE)
Eastern U (PA)
The Evergreen State Coll (WA)
Farmingdale State Coll (NY)
Grand Valley State U (MI)
Guilford Coll (NC)
Indiana U Bloomington (IN)
Indiana U–Purdue U Indianapolis (IN)
Inter American U of Puerto Rico, Bayamón Campus (PR)
Kent State U (OH)
King Coll (TN)
Logan U–Coll of Chiropractic (MO)
Louisiana State U in Shreveport (LA)
Lynchburg Coll (VA)
Messiah Coll (PA)
Mount Aloysius Coll (PA)
Oklahoma City U (OK)
Our Lady of the Lake Coll (LA)
Park U (MO)
Penn State Abington (PA)
Penn State Altoona (PA)
Penn State Beaver (PA)
Penn State Berks (PA)
Penn State Brandywine (PA)
Penn State DuBois (PA)
Penn State Erie, The Behrend Coll (PA)
Penn State Fayette, The Eberly Campus (PA)
Penn State Greater Allegheny (PA)
Penn State Hazleton (PA)
Penn State Lehigh Valley (PA)
Penn State Mont Alto (PA)
Penn State New Kensington (PA)
Penn State Schuylkill (PA)
Penn State Shenango (PA)
Penn State U Park (PA)
Penn State Wilkes-Barre (PA)
Penn State Worthington Scranton (PA)
Penn State York (PA)
Rochester Inst of Technology (NY)
Roger Williams U (RI)
Rutgers, The State U of New Jersey, Newark (NJ)
Sage Coll of Albany (NY)
Saint Mary's Coll of California (CA)
Swarthmore Coll (PA)
Texas Wesleyan U (TX)
Trevecca Nazarene U (TN)
Union Coll (NY)
U of Illinois at Urbana–Champaign (IL)
U of Louisiana at Lafayette (LA)
U of Maryland U Coll (MD)
U of Michigan (MI)
U of Minnesota, Twin Cities Campus (MN)
U of New Hampshire (NH)
U of North Alabama (AL)
U of North Dakota (ND)
U of Ottawa (ON, Canada)
U of Puerto Rico at Bayamón (PR)
U of Puerto Rico at Ponce (PR)
U of Rochester (NY)
Ursuline Coll (OH)
Utah State U (UT)
Washington U in St. Louis (MO)
Western State Coll of Colorado (CO)

BIOLOGICAL AND PHYSICAL SCIENCES
Alfred U (NY)
Allegheny Coll (PA)
Alvernia U (PA)
Angelo State U (TX)
Athabasca U (AB, Canada)
Averett U (VA)
Baldwin-Wallace Coll (OH)
Belmont U (TN)
Bemidji State U (MN)
Bennington Coll (VT)
Bishop's U (QC, Canada)
Bluefield State Coll (WV)
Brevard Coll (NC)
Buena Vista U (IA)
California State U, Fresno (CA)
Calvin Coll (MI)
Castleton State Coll (VT)

Cheyney U of Pennsylvania (PA)
Clarion U of Pennsylvania (PA)
Coe Coll (IA)
Coll of Saint Benedict (MN)
Coll of the Atlantic (ME)
Concordia U (MI)
Covenant Coll (GA)
Delta State U (MS)
DePaul U (IL)
Dominican U (IL)
Dowling Coll (NY)
Drexel U (PA)
Eastern Michigan U (MI)
East Stroudsburg U of Pennsylvania (PA)
The Evergreen State Coll (WA)
Fairleigh Dickinson U, Metropolitan Campus (NJ)
Fordham U (NY)
Fort Hays State U (KS)
Gettysburg Coll (PA)
Grand Valley State U (MI)
Houghton Coll (NY)
Huntington U (IN)
Indiana U Kokomo (IN)
Indiana U of Pennsylvania (PA)
Indiana U–Purdue U Indianapolis (IN)
Iowa Wesleyan Coll (IA)
John Brown U (AR)
John Carroll U (OH)
The Johns Hopkins U (MD)
Johnson C. Smith U (NC)
Keene State Coll (NH)
Keystone Coll (PA)
King Coll (TN)
King's Coll (PA)
Kutztown U of Pennsylvania (PA)
Lakehead U (ON, Canada)
Lee U (TN)
Le Moyne Coll (NY)
Lock Haven U of Pennsylvania (PA)
Louisiana State U in Shreveport (LA)
Mansfield U of Pennsylvania (PA)
Mars Hill Coll (NC)
Maryville U of Saint Louis (MO)
The Master's Coll and Sem (CA)
Michigan State U (MI)
Middle Tennessee State U (TN)
Minnesota State U Mankato (MN)
Mississippi State U (MS)
Mount Allison U (NB, Canada)
North Central Coll (IL)
Northwest Missouri State U (MO)
Oakland City U (IN)
Oklahoma City U (OK)
Penn State Abington (PA)
Penn State Altoona (PA)
Penn State Beaver (PA)
Penn State Berks (PA)
Penn State Brandywine (PA)
Penn State DuBois (PA)
Penn State Erie, The Behrend Coll (PA)
Penn State Fayette, The Eberly Campus (PA)
Penn State Greater Allegheny (PA)
Penn State Hazleton (PA)
Penn State Lehigh Valley (PA)
Penn State Mont Alto (PA)
Penn State New Kensington (PA)
Penn State Schuylkill (PA)
Penn State Shenango (PA)
Penn State U Park (PA)
Penn State Wilkes-Barre (PA)
Penn State Worthington Scranton (PA)
Penn State York (PA)
Peru State Coll (NE)
Philander Smith Coll (AR)
Portland State U (OR)
Purdue U (IN)
Quinnipiac U (CT)
Ramapo Coll of New Jersey (NJ)
Roberts Wesleyan Coll (NY)
Rockford Coll (IL)
Saint Anselm Coll (NH)
Saint John's U (MN)
St. Mary's Coll of Maryland (MD)
St. Norbert Coll (WI)
Saint Peter's Coll (NJ)
Saint Xavier U (IL)
Sam Houston State U (TX)
San Francisco State U (CA)

Sarah Lawrence Coll (NY)
Scripps Coll (CA)
Seattle U (WA)
Sierra Nevada Coll (NV)
Simon Fraser U (BC, Canada)
Southern Arkansas U–Magnolia (AR)
Spalding U (KY)
State U of New York at Fredonia (NY)
State U of New York Coll of Environmental Science and Forestry (NY)
State U of New York Empire State Coll (NY)
Texas Tech U (TX)
Trent U (ON, Canada)
Union Coll (NY)
Union U (TN)
United States Air Force Acad (CO)
The U of Alabama at Birmingham (AL)
U of Alaska Anchorage (AK)
U of Alaska Fairbanks (AK)
U of Alberta (AB, Canada)
U of Arkansas at Monticello (AR)
U of Central Arkansas (AR)
U of Denver (CO)
U of Dubuque (IA)
The U of Findlay (OH)
U of Georgia (GA)
U of Guam (GU)
U of Houston–Downtown (TX)
U of Massachusetts Amherst (MA)
U of Northern Iowa (IA)
U of Oregon (OR)
U of Pittsburgh (PA)
U of Puget Sound (WA)
U of Regina (SK, Canada)
U of Rochester (NY)
U of Saint Francis (IN)
U of Southern Indiana (IN)
U of Southern Mississippi (MS)
U of South Florida (FL)
The U of Texas at Austin (TX)
The U of Texas at San Antonio (TX)
The U of Toledo (OH)
The U of West Alabama (AL)
The U of Western Ontario (ON, Canada)
U of West Florida (FL)
U of Windsor (ON, Canada)
U of Wisconsin–Platteville (WI)
U of Wisconsin–River Falls (WI)
U of Wisconsin–Stevens Point (WI)
U of Wisconsin–Superior (WI)
U of Wisconsin–Whitewater (WI)
Upper Iowa U (IA)
Vanguard U of Southern California (CA)
Virginia Commonwealth U (VA)
Walsh U (OH)
Washington State U (WA)
Washington U in St. Louis (MO)
Western Washington U (WA)
Wilmington Coll (OH)
Winona State U (MN)
Xavier U (OH)

BIOLOGICAL/BIOSYSTEMS ENGINEERING
The U of Arizona (AZ)
U of Guelph (ON, Canada)
U of Idaho (ID)
U of Nebraska–Lincoln (NE)

BIOLOGY/BIOLOGICAL SCIENCES
Abilene Christian U (TX)
Acadia U (NS, Canada)
Adams State Coll (CO)
Adelphi U (NY)
Adrian Coll (MI)
Agnes Scott Coll (GA)
Alabama State U (AL)
Albany State U (GA)
Albertus Magnus Coll (CT)
Albion Coll (MI)
Albright Coll (PA)
Alcorn State U (MS)
Alfred U (NY)
Allegheny Coll (PA)
Alma Coll (MI)
Alvernia U (PA)

Alverno Coll (WI)
American U (DC)
The American U in Cairo (Egypt)
American U of Beirut (Lebanon)
Amherst Coll (MA)
Anderson U (IN)
Anderson U (SC)
Andrews U (MI)
Angelo State U (TX)
Anna Maria Coll (MA)
Appalachian State U (NC)
Aquinas Coll (MI)
Arcadia U (PA)
Arizona State U (AZ)
Arkansas State U (AR)
Arkansas Tech U (AR)
Armstrong Atlantic State U (GA)
Asbury U (KY)
Ashland U (OH)
Assumption Coll (MA)
Athens State U (AL)
Auburn U (AL)
Auburn U Montgomery (AL)
Augustana Coll (IL)
Augustana Coll (SD)
Austin Coll (TX)
Austin Peay State U (TN)
Averett U (VA)
Avila U (MO)
Azusa Pacific U (CA)
Baker U (KS)
Baldwin-Wallace Coll (OH)
Ball State U (IN)
Bard Coll (NY)
Barton Coll (NC)
Bastyr U (WA)
Bates Coll (ME)
Bayamón Central U (PR)
Baylor U (TX)
Bay Path Coll (MA)
Belhaven U (MS)
Bellarmine U (KY)
Bellevue U (NE)
Belmont Abbey Coll (NC)
Belmont U (TN)
Beloit Coll (WI)
Bemidji State U (MN)
Benedictine Coll (KS)
Benedictine U (IL)
Bennett Coll for Women (NC)
Bennington Coll (VT)
Berea Coll (KY)
Berry Coll (GA)
Bethany Coll (KS)
Bethany Coll (WV)
Bethany Lutheran Coll (MN)
Bethel Coll (IN)
Bethel Coll (KS)
Bethel U (MN)
Bethel U (TN)
Bethune-Cookman U (FL)
Biola U (CA)
Birmingham-Southern Coll (AL)
Bishop's U (QC, Canada)
Blackburn Coll (IL)
Black Hills State U (SD)
Bloomfield Coll (NJ)
Bloomsburg U of Pennsylvania (PA)
Bluefield Coll (VA)
Blue Mountain Coll (MS)
Bluffton U (OH)
Bob Jones U (SC)
Boise State U (ID)
Boston Coll (MA)
Boston U (MA)
Bowdoin Coll (ME)
Bowie State U (MD)
Bowling Green State U (OH)
Bradley U (IL)
Brandeis U (MA)
Brenau U (GA)
Brescia U (KY)
Brewton-Parker Coll (GA)
Briar Cliff U (IA)
Bridgewater Coll (VA)
Bridgewater State U (MA)
Brown U (RI)
Bryant U (RI)
Bryn Athyn Coll of the New Church (PA)
Bryn Mawr Coll (PA)
Bucknell U (PA)

Buena Vista U (IA)
Buffalo State Coll, State of New York (NY)
Butler U (IN)
Cabrini Coll (PA)
Caldwell Coll (NJ)
California Baptist U (CA)
California Inst of Technology (CA)
California Lutheran U (CA)
California Polytechnic State U, San Luis Obispo (CA)
California State Polytechnic U, Pomona (CA)
California State U, Bakersfield (CA)
California State U, Chico (CA)
California State U, Dominguez Hills (CA)
California State U, East Bay (CA)
California State U, Fresno (CA)
California State U, Fullerton (CA)
California State U, Long Beach (CA)
California State U, Los Angeles (CA)
California State U, Monterey Bay (CA)
California State U, Sacramento (CA)
California State U, San Bernardino (CA)
California State U, San Marcos (CA)
California State U, Stanislaus (CA)
California U of Pennsylvania (PA)
Calvin Coll (MI)
Cameron U (OK)
Campbellsville U (KY)
Canisius Coll (NY)
Cape Breton U (NS, Canada)
Capital U (OH)
Cardinal Stritch U (WI)
Carleton Coll (MN)
Carlow U (PA)
Carnegie Mellon U (PA)
Carroll Coll (MT)
Carson-Newman Coll (TN)
Case Western Reserve U (OH)
Castleton State Coll (VT)
Catawba Coll (NC)
The Catholic U of America (DC)
Cedar Crest Coll (PA)
Cedarville U (OH)
Centenary Coll (NJ)
Centenary Coll of Louisiana (LA)
Central Coll (IA)
Central Connecticut State U (CT)
Central Methodist U (MO)
Central State U (OH)
Central Washington U (WA)
Centre Coll (KY)
Chaminade U of Honolulu (HI)
Chapman U (CA)
Chatham U (PA)
Chestnut Hill Coll (PA)
Cheyney U of Pennsylvania (PA)
Chicago State U (IL)
Christian Brothers U (TN)
Christopher Newport U (VA)
The Citadel, The Military Coll of South Carolina (SC)
City Coll of the City U of New York (NY)
Claflin U (SC)
Claremont McKenna Coll (CA)
Clarion U of Pennsylvania (PA)
Clark Atlanta U (GA)
Clarke U (IA)
Clarkson U (NY)
Clark U (MA)
Clayton State U (GA)
Clearwater Christian Coll (FL)
Clemson U (SC)
Cleveland Chiropractic Coll–Kansas City Campus (KS)
Cleveland State U (OH)
Coastal Carolina U (SC)
Coe Coll (IA)
Colby Coll (ME)
Colgate U (NY)
The Coll at Brockport, State of New York (NY)
Coll of Charleston (SC)
Coll of Coastal Georgia (GA)
The Coll of Idaho (ID)
Coll of Mount St. Joseph (OH)

INDEXES

Coll of Mount Saint Vincent (NY)
The Coll of New Jersey (NJ)
Coll of Saint Benedict (MN)
Coll of Saint Elizabeth (NJ)
Coll of Saint Mary (NE)
The Coll of Saint Rose (NY)
The Coll of St. Scholastica (MN)
Coll of Staten Island of the City U of New York (NY)
Coll of the Atlantic (ME)
Coll of the Holy Cross (MA)
Coll of the Ozarks (MO)
The Coll of William and Mary (VA)
The Coll of Wooster (OH)
The Colorado Coll (CO)
Colorado Mesa U (CO)
Colorado State U (CO)
Columbia Coll (MO)
Columbia Coll (SC)
Columbia U, School of General Studies (NY)
Columbus State U (GA)
Concordia Coll (MN)
Concordia Coll–New York (NY)
Concordia U (CA)
Concordia U (MI)
Concordia U (QC, Canada)
Concordia U Chicago (IL)
Concordia U, Nebraska (NE)
Concordia U, St. Paul (MN)
Concordia U Texas (TX)
Connecticut Coll (CT)
Converse Coll (SC)
Cornell Coll (IA)
Cornell U (NY)
Cornerstone U (MI)
Covenant Coll (GA)
Crandall U (NB, Canada)
Creighton U (NE)
Crown Coll (MN)
Culver-Stockton Coll (MO)
Curry Coll (MA)
Daemen Coll (NY)
Dalhousie U (NS, Canada)
Dallas Baptist U (TX)
Dalton State Coll (GA)
Dartmouth Coll (NH)
Davidson Coll (NC)
Defiance Coll (OH)
Delaware State U (DE)
Delaware Valley Coll (PA)
Delta State U (MS)
Denison U (OH)
DePaul U (IL)
DePauw U (IN)
DeSales U (PA)
Dickinson Coll (PA)
Dillard U (LA)
Dixie State Coll of Utah (UT)
Doane Coll (NE)
Dominican Coll (NY)
Dominican U (IL)
Dominican U of California (CA)
Dordt Coll (IA)
Dowling Coll (NY)
Drake U (IA)
Drew U (NJ)
Drexel U (PA)
Drury U (MO)
Duquesne U (PA)
Earlham Coll (IN)
East Carolina U (NC)
East Central U (OK)
Eastern Connecticut State U (CT)
Eastern Illinois U (IL)
Eastern Kentucky U (KY)
Eastern Mennonite U (VA)
Eastern Michigan U (MI)
Eastern New Mexico U (NM)
Eastern Oregon U (OR)
Eastern U (PA)
Eastern Washington U (WA)
East Stroudsburg U of Pennsylvania (PA)
East Tennessee State U (TN)
East Texas Baptist U (TX)
Eckerd Coll (FL)
Edgewood Coll (WI)
Edinboro U of Pennsylvania (PA)
Edward Waters Coll (FL)
Elizabeth City State U (NC)
Elizabethtown Coll (PA)
Elmhurst Coll (IL)
Elmira Coll (NY)
Elon U (NC)

Emmanuel Coll (GA)
Emmanuel Coll (MA)
Emory & Henry Coll (VA)
Emory U (GA)
Emporia State U (KS)
Evangel U (MO)
Excelsior Coll (NY)
Fairfield U (CT)
Fairleigh Dickinson U, Coll at Florham (NJ)
Fairleigh Dickinson U, Metropolitan Campus (NJ)
Fairmont State U (WV)
Faulkner U (AL)
Fayetteville State U (NC)
Felician Coll (NJ)
Ferris State U (MI)
Ferrum Coll (VA)
Fitchburg State U (MA)
Florida Ag and Mech U (FL)
Florida Atlantic U (FL)
Florida Gulf Coast U (FL)
Florida Inst of Technology (FL)
Florida Intl U (FL)
Florida Southern Coll (FL)
Fontbonne U (MO)
Fordham U (NY)
Fort Hays State U (KS)
Framingham State U (MA)
Franciscan U of Steubenville (OH)
Francis Marion U (SC)
Franklin & Marshall Coll (PA)
Franklin Coll (IN)
Friends U (KS)
Furman U (SC)
Gallaudet U (DC)
Gannon U (PA)
Gardner-Webb U (NC)
Geneva Coll (PA)
George Fox U (OR)
George Mason U (VA)
Georgetown Coll (KY)
The George Washington U (DC)
Georgia Coll & State U (GA)
Georgia Gwinnett Coll (GA)
Georgia Inst of Technology (GA)
Georgian Court U (NJ)
Georgia Southern U (GA)
Georgia Southwestern State U (GA)
Georgia State U (GA)
Gettysburg Coll (PA)
Glenville State Coll (WV)
Gonzaga U (WA)
Gordon Coll (MA)
Goshen Coll (IN)
Goucher Coll (MD)
Governors State U (IL)
Grace Coll (IN)
Graceland U (IA)
Grambling State U (LA)
Grand Canyon U (AZ)
Grand Valley State U (MI)
Grand View U (IA)
Greenville Coll (IL)
Grinnell Coll (IA)
Grove City Coll (PA)
Guilford Coll (NC)
Gustavus Adolphus Coll (MN)
Gwynedd-Mercy Coll (PA)
Hamilton Coll (NY)
Hamline U (MN)
Hampden-Sydney Coll (VA)
Hampshire Coll (MA)
Hampton U (VA)
Hannibal-LaGrange U (MO)
Hanover Coll (IN)
Harding U (AR)
Hardin-Simmons U (TX)
Harrisburg U of Science and Technology (PA)
Hartwick Coll (NY)
Harvard U (MA)
Harvey Mudd Coll (CA)
Haverford Coll (PA)
Hawai`i Pacific U (HI)
Heidelberg U (OH)
Hendrix Coll (AR)
Hillsdale Coll (MI)
Hobart and William Smith Colls (NY)
Hofstra U (NY)
Hollins U (VA)
Holy Family U (PA)
Hood Coll (MD)
Hope Coll (MI)

Houghton Coll (NY)
Howard Payne U (TX)
Humboldt State U (CA)
Hunter Coll of the City U of New York (NY)
Huntingdon Coll (AL)
Huntington U (IN)
Husson U (ME)
Huston-Tillotson U (TX)
Idaho State U (ID)
Illinois Coll (IL)
Illinois Inst of Technology (IL)
Illinois State U (IL)
Illinois Wesleyan U (IL)
Immaculata U (PA)
Indiana State U (IN)
Indiana U Bloomington (IN)
Indiana U East (IN)
Indiana U Kokomo (IN)
Indiana U Northwest (IN)
Indiana U of Pennsylvania (PA)
Indiana U–Purdue U Fort Wayne (IN)
Indiana U–Purdue U Indianapolis (IN)
Indiana U South Bend (IN)
Indiana U Southeast (IN)
Indiana Wesleyan U (IN)
Inter American U of Puerto Rico, Bayamón Campus (PR)
Inter American U of Puerto Rico, Fajardo Campus (PR)
Inter American U of Puerto Rico, Ponce Campus (PR)
Inter American U of Puerto Rico, San Germán Campus (PR)
Iona Coll (NY)
Iowa State U of Science and Technology (IA)
Iowa Wesleyan Coll (IA)
Ithaca Coll (NY)
Jacksonville State U (AL)
Jacksonville U (FL)
James Madison U (VA)
Jamestown Coll (ND)
Jarvis Christian Coll (TX)
John Brown U (AR)
John Carroll U (OH)
The Johns Hopkins U (MD)
Johnson C. Smith U (NC)
Johnson State Coll (VT)
Judson Coll (AL)
Judson U (IL)
Juniata Coll (PA)
Kalamazoo Coll (MI)
Kansas State U (KS)
Kean U (NJ)
Keene State Coll (NH)
Kennesaw State U (GA)
Kent State U (OH)
Kent State U at Stark (OH)
Kentucky Christian U (KY)
Kentucky State U (KY)
Kentucky Wesleyan Coll (KY)
Kenyon Coll (OH)
Keuka Coll (NY)
Keystone Coll (PA)
King Coll (TN)
King's Coll (PA)
The King's U Coll (AB, Canada)
Knox Coll (IL)
Kutztown U of Pennsylvania (PA)
Lafayette Coll (PA)
LaGrange Coll (GA)
Lake Erie Coll (OH)
Lake Forest Coll (IL)
Lakehead U (ON, Canada)
Lamar U (TX)
Lane Coll (TN)
La Roche Coll (PA)
La Salle U (PA)
La Sierra U (CA)
Lawrence U (WI)
Lebanese American U (Lebanon)
Lebanon Valley Coll (PA)
Lees-McRae Coll (NC)
Lee U (TN)
Lehigh U (PA)
Lehman Coll of the City U of New York (NY)
Le Moyne Coll (NY)
Lenoir-Rhyne U (NC)
LeTourneau U (TX)
Lewis & Clark Coll (OR)
Lewis-Clark State Coll (ID)

Lewis U (IL)
Liberty U (VA)
Life U (GA)
Limestone Coll (SC)
Lincoln Memorial U (TN)
Lincoln U (MO)
Lincoln U (PA)
Lindenwood U (MO)
Lindsey Wilson Coll (KY)
Linfield Coll (OR)
Lipscomb U (TN)
Lock Haven U of Pennsylvania (PA)
Logan U–Coll of Chiropractic (MO)
Long Island U–Brooklyn Campus (NY)
Long Island U–C. W. Post Campus (NY)
Longwood U (VA)
Loras Coll (IA)
Louisiana Coll (LA)
Louisiana State U and Ag and Mech Coll (LA)
Louisiana State U in Shreveport (LA)
Lourdes U (OH)
Loyola Marymount U (CA)
Loyola U Chicago (IL)
Loyola U Maryland (MD)
Loyola U New Orleans (LA)
Lubbock Christian U (TX)
Luther Coll (IA)
Lycoming Coll (PA)
Lynchburg Coll (VA)
Lynn U (FL)
Lyon Coll (AR)
Macalester Coll (MN)
Macon State Coll (GA)
Madonna U (MI)
Malone U (OH)
Manchester Coll (IN)
Manhattan Coll (NY)
Manhattanville Coll (NY)
Mansfield U of Pennsylvania (PA)
Maranatha Baptist Bible Coll (WI)
Marian U (WI)
Marietta Coll (OH)
Marlboro Coll (VT)
Marquette U (WI)
Marshall U (WV)
Mars Hill Coll (NC)
Mary Baldwin Coll (VA)
Marymount Manhattan Coll (NY)
Marymount U (VA)
Maryville Coll (TN)
Maryville U of Saint Louis (MO)
Marywood U (PA)
Massachusetts Coll of Liberal Arts (MA)
Massachusetts Inst of Technology (MA)
The Master's Coll and Sem (CA)
Mayville State U (ND)
McDaniel Coll (MD)
McKendree U (IL)
McMurry U (TX)
McNeese State U (LA)
McPherson Coll (KS)
Medaille Coll (NY)
Medgar Evers Coll of the City U of New York (NY)
Mercer U (GA)
Mercy Coll (NY)
Mercyhurst Coll (PA)
Meredith Coll (NC)
Merrimack Coll (MA)
Messiah Coll (PA)
Metropolitan State Coll of Denver (CO)
Metropolitan State U (MN)
Miami Dade Coll (FL)
Michigan State U (MI)
Michigan Technological U (MI)
MidAmerica Nazarene U (KS)
Middlebury Coll (VT)
Middle Tennessee State U (TN)
Midwestern State U (TX)
Millersville U of Pennsylvania (PA)
Milligan Coll (TN)
Millikin U (IL)
Millsaps Coll (MS)
Mills Coll (CA)
Minnesota State U Mankato (MN)
Minnesota State U Moorhead (MN)
Minot State U (ND)
Misericordia U (PA)

Mississippi Coll (MS)
Mississippi State U (MS)
Mississippi U for Women (MS)
Mississippi Valley State U (MS)
Missouri Baptist U (MO)
Missouri Southern State U (MO)
Missouri State U (MO)
Missouri U of Science and Technology (MO)
Missouri Western State U (MO)
Molloy Coll (NY)
Monmouth Coll (IL)
Monmouth U (NJ)
Montana State U (MT)
Montana State U Billings (MT)
Montana State U–Northern (MT)
Montana Tech of The U of Montana (MT)
Montclair State U (NJ)
Montreat Coll, Montreat (NC)
Moravian Coll (PA)
Morehead State U (KY)
Morehouse Coll (GA)
Morningside Coll (IA)
Morris Coll (SC)
Mountain State U (WV)
Mount Allison U (NB, Canada)
Mount Aloysius Coll (PA)
Mount Holyoke Coll (MA)
Mount Ida Coll (MA)
Mount Marty Coll (SD)
Mount Mary Coll (WI)
Mount Mercy U (IA)
Mount Saint Mary Coll (NY)
Mount St. Mary's Coll (CA)
Mount St. Mary's U (MD)
Mount Vernon Nazarene U (OH)
Muhlenberg Coll (PA)
National-Louis U (IL)
National U (CA)
Nazareth Coll of Rochester (NY)
Nebraska Wesleyan U (NE)
Neumann U (PA)
Newberry Coll (SC)
New Coll of Florida (FL)
New England Coll (NH)
New Jersey City U (NJ)
Newman U (KS)
New Mexico Highlands U (NM)
New Mexico Inst of Mining and Technology (NM)
New Mexico State U (NM)
New York Inst of Technology (NY)
New York U (NY)
Niagara U (NY)
Nicholls State U (LA)
Norfolk State U (VA)
North Carolina Ag and Tech State U (NC)
North Carolina Central U (NC)
North Carolina State U (NC)
North Carolina Wesleyan Coll (NC)
North Central Coll (IL)
North Dakota State U (ND)
Northeastern Illinois U (IL)
Northeastern State U (OK)
Northeastern U (MA)
Northern Arizona U (AZ)
Northern Illinois U (IL)
Northern Kentucky U (KY)
Northern Michigan U (MI)
Northern State U (SD)
North Georgia Coll & State U (GA)
North Greenville U (SC)
Northland Coll (WI)
Northwestern Coll (IA)
Northwestern Coll (MN)
Northwestern Oklahoma State U (OK)
Northwestern State U of Louisiana (LA)
Northwest Missouri State U (MO)
Northwest Nazarene U (ID)
Norwich U (VT)
Notre Dame de Namur U (CA)
Notre Dame of Maryland U (MD)
Nova Southeastern U (FL)
Oakland City U (IN)
Oakland U (MI)
Occidental Coll (CA)
Oglethorpe U (GA)
Ohio Northern U (OH)
The Ohio State U (OH)
The Ohio State U at Lima (OH)
Ohio U (OH)

INDEXES

Ohio Wesleyan U (OH)
Oklahoma Christian U (OK)
Oklahoma City U (OK)
Oklahoma State U (OK)
Old Dominion U (VA)
Oral Roberts U (OK)
Otterbein U (OH)
Ouachita Baptist U (AR)
Our Lady of the Lake Coll (LA)
Pace U (NY)
Pacific Lutheran U (WA)
Pacific Union Coll (CA)
Pacific (OR)
Paine Coll (GA)
Palm Beach Atlantic U (FL)
Park U (MO)
Penn State Abington (PA)
Penn State Altoona (PA)
Penn State Beaver (PA)
Penn State Berks (PA)
Penn State Brandywine (PA)
Penn State DuBois (PA)
Penn State Erie, The Behrend Coll (PA)
Penn State Fayette, The Eberly Campus (PA)
Penn State Greater Allegheny (PA)
Penn State Hazleton (PA)
Penn State Lehigh Valley (PA)
Penn State Mont Alto (PA)
Penn State New Kensington (PA)
Penn State Schuylkill (PA)
Penn State Shenango (PA)
Penn State U Park (PA)
Penn State Wilkes-Barre (PA)
Penn State Worthington Scranton (PA)
Penn State York (PA)
Pepperdine U, Malibu (CA)
Peru State Coll (NE)
Philadelphia U (PA)
Philander Smith Coll (AR)
Piedmont Coll (GA)
Pine Manor Coll (MA)
Pittsburg State U (KS)
Pitzer Coll (CA)
Plymouth State U (NH)
Point Loma Nazarene U (CA)
Point Park U (PA)
Point U (GA)
Pomona Coll (CA)
Portland State U (OR)
Post U (CT)
Prairie View A&M U (TX)
Presbyterian Coll (SC)
Presentation Coll (SD)
Providence Coll (RI)
Purchase Coll, State U of New York (NY)
Purdue U (IN)
Purdue U Calumet (IN)
Purdue U North Central (IN)
Queens Coll of the City U of New York (NY)
Queen's U at Kingston (ON, Canada)
Queens U of Charlotte (NC)
Quincy U (IL)
Quinnipiac U (CT)
Radford U (VA)
Ramapo Coll of New Jersey (NJ)
Randolph Coll (VA)
Randolph-Macon Coll (VA)
Regis Coll (MA)
Regis U (CO)
Reinhardt U (GA)
Rensselaer Polytechnic Inst (NY)
Rhode Island Coll (RI)
Rhodes Coll (TN)
Rice U (TX)
The Richard Stockton Coll of New Jersey (NJ)
Rider U (NJ)
Ripon Coll (WI)
Rivier Coll (NH)
Roanoke Coll (VA)
Robert Morris U (PA)
Roberts Wesleyan Coll (NY)
Rochester Inst of Technology (NY)
Rockford Coll (IL)
Rockhurst U (MO)
Rocky Mountain Coll (MT)
Rogers State U (OK)
Roger Williams U (RI)
Rollins Coll (FL)

Roosevelt U (IL)
Rose-Hulman Inst of Technology (IN)
Rosemont Coll (PA)
Rowan U (NJ)
Russell Sage Coll (NY)
Rust Coll (MS)
Rutgers, The State U of New Jersey, Camden (NJ)
Rutgers, The State U of New Jersey, Newark (NJ)
Rutgers, The State U of New Jersey, New Brunswick (NJ)
Ryerson U (ON, Canada)
Sacred Heart U (CT)
Saginaw Valley State U (MI)
St. Ambrose U (IA)
St. Andrews U (NC)
Saint Anselm Coll (NH)
Saint Augustine's Coll (NC)
St. Bonaventure U (NY)
St. Catherine U (MN)
St. Edward's U (TX)
Saint Francis U (PA)
St. John Fisher Coll (NY)
Saint John's U (MN)
St. John's U (NY)
Saint Joseph's Coll (IN)
St. Joseph's Coll, Long Island Campus (NY)
St. Joseph's Coll, New York (NY)
Saint Joseph's Coll of Maine (ME)
Saint Joseph's U (PA)
St. Lawrence U (NY)
Saint Leo U (FL)
Saint Louis U (MO)
Saint Martin's U (WA)
Saint Mary-of-the-Woods Coll (IN)
Saint Mary's Coll (IN)
Saint Mary's Coll of California (CA)
St. Mary's Coll of Maryland (MD)
St. Mary's U (TX)
Saint Mary's U of Minnesota (MN)
Saint Michael's Coll (VT)
St. Norbert Coll (WI)
St. Olaf Coll (MN)
Saint Peter's Coll (NJ)
St. Thomas Aquinas Coll (NY)
Saint Vincent Coll (PA)
Saint Xavier U (IL)
Salem State U (MA)
Salisbury U (MD)
Salve Regina U (RI)
Samford U (AL)
Sam Houston State U (TX)
San Diego Christian Coll (CA)
San Diego State U (CA)
San Francisco State U (CA)
Santa Clara U (CA)
Sarah Lawrence Coll (NY)
Schreiner U (TX)
Scripps Coll (CA)
Seattle Pacific U (WA)
Seattle U (WA)
Seton Hill U (PA)
Sewanee: The U of the South (TN)
Shawnee State U (OH)
Shaw U (NC)
Shenandoah U (VA)
Shepherd U (WV)
Shippensburg U of Pennsylvania (PA)
Shorter U (GA)
Siena Coll (NY)
Siena Heights U (MI)
Simmons Coll (MA)
Simon Fraser U (BC, Canada)
Simpson Coll (IA)
Simpson U (CA)
Skidmore Coll (NY)
Slippery Rock U of Pennsylvania (PA)
Smith Coll (MA)
Sonoma State U (CA)
South Carolina State U (SC)
South Dakota State U (SD)
Southeastern Louisiana U (LA)
Southeastern Oklahoma State U (OK)
Southeastern U (FL)
Southeast Missouri State U (MO)
Southern Arkansas U–Magnolia (AR)
Southern Connecticut State U (CT)

Southern Illinois U Carbondale (IL)
Southern Illinois U Edwardsville (IL)
Southern Methodist U (TX)
Southern Oregon U (OR)
Southern Polytechnic State U (GA)
Southwest Baptist U (MO)
Southwestern Adventist U (TX)
Southwestern Coll (KS)
Southwestern Oklahoma State U (OK)
Southwestern U (TX)
Southwest Minnesota State U (MN)
Spelman Coll (GA)
Spring Arbor U (MI)
Spring Hill Coll (AL)
Stanford U (CA)
State U of New York at Binghamton (NY)
State U of New York at Fredonia (NY)
State U of New York at New Paltz (NY)
State U of New York at Oswego (NY)
State U of New York at Plattsburgh (NY)
State U of New York Coll at Cortland (NY)
State U of New York Coll at Geneseo (NY)
State U of New York Coll at Old Westbury (NY)
State U of New York Coll at Oneonta (NY)
State U of New York Coll at Potsdam (NY)
State U of New York Coll of Environmental Science and Forestry (NY)
Stephen F. Austin State U (TX)
Stephens Coll (MO)
Sterling Coll (KS)
Stetson U (FL)
Stevenson U (MD)
Stillman Coll (AL)
Stonehill Coll (MA)
Stony Brook U, State U of New York (NY)
Suffolk U (MA)
Sul Ross State U (TX)
Susquehanna U (PA)
Swarthmore Coll (PA)
Sweet Briar Coll (VA)
Syracuse U (NY)
Tarleton State U (TX)
Taylor U (IN)
Temple U (PA)
Texas A&M Intl U (TX)
Texas A&M U (TX)
Texas A&M U–Corpus Christi (TX)
Texas A&M U–Kingsville (TX)
Texas Christian U (TX)
Texas Coll (TX)
Texas Lutheran U (TX)
Texas Southern U (TX)
Texas State U–San Marcos (TX)
Texas Tech U (TX)
Texas Wesleyan U (TX)
Texas Woman's U (TX)
Thiel Coll (PA)
Thomas Edison State Coll (NJ)
Thomas More Coll (KY)
Thomas U (GA)
Thompson Rivers U (BC, Canada)
Touro Coll (NY)
Towson U (MD)
Transylvania U (KY)
Trent U (ON, Canada)
Trevecca Nazarene U (TN)
Trine U (IN)
Trinity Christian Coll (IL)
Trinity Coll (CT)
Trinity U (TX)
Troy U (AL)
Truett-McConnell Coll (GA)
Truman State U (MO)
Tufts U (MA)
Tulane U (LA)
Tusculum Coll (TN)
Tuskegee U (AL)
Union Coll (KY)
Union Coll (NE)
Union Coll (NY)
Union U (TN)
United States Air Force Acad (CO)

United States Military Acad (NY)
Universidad del Turabo (PR)
Université de Sherbrooke (QC, Canada)
U at Albany, State U of New York (NY)
U at Buffalo, the State U of New York (NY)
The U of Akron (OH)
The U of Alabama (AL)
The U of Alabama at Birmingham (AL)
The U of Alabama in Huntsville (AL)
U of Alaska Fairbanks (AK)
U of Alberta (AB, Canada)
The U of Arizona (AZ)
U of Arkansas (AR)
U of Arkansas at Little Rock (AR)
U of Arkansas at Monticello (AR)
U of Arkansas–Fort Smith (AR)
U of Bridgeport (CT)
The U of British Columbia (BC, Canada)
The U of British Columbia–Okanagan (BC, Canada)
U of California, Berkeley (CA)
U of California, Davis (CA)
U of California, Irvine (CA)
U of California, Los Angeles (CA)
U of California, Merced (CA)
U of California, Riverside (CA)
U of California, Santa Barbara (CA)
U of California, Santa Cruz (CA)
U of Central Arkansas (AR)
U of Central Florida (FL)
U of Central Missouri (MO)
U of Charleston (WV)
U of Cincinnati (OH)
U of Colorado at Colorado Springs (CO)
U of Colorado Denver (CO)
U of Connecticut (CT)
U of Dallas (TX)
U of Dayton (OH)
U of Delaware (DE)
U of Denver (CO)
U of Dubuque (IA)
U of Evansville (IN)
The U of Findlay (OH)
U of Florida (FL)
U of Georgia (GA)
U of Great Falls (MT)
U of Guam (GU)
U of Guelph (ON, Canada)
U of Hartford (CT)
U of Hawaii at Hilo (HI)
U of Hawaii at Manoa (HI)
U of Houston (TX)
U of Houston–Clear Lake (TX)
U of Houston–Downtown (TX)
U of Houston–Victoria (TX)
U of Idaho (ID)
U of Illinois at Chicago (IL)
U of Illinois at Springfield (IL)
U of Illinois at Urbana–Champaign (IL)
U of Indianapolis (IN)
The U of Iowa (IA)
The U of Kansas (KS)
U of La Verne (CA)
U of Lethbridge (AB, Canada)
U of Louisiana at Lafayette (LA)
U of Louisiana at Monroe (LA)
U of Louisville (KY)
U of Maine (ME)
U of Maine at Augusta (ME)
U of Maine at Farmington (ME)
U of Maine at Fort Kent (ME)
U of Maine at Presque Isle (ME)
U of Mary (ND)
U of Mary Hardin-Baylor (TX)
U of Maryland, Baltimore County (MD)
U of Maryland, Coll Park (MD)
U of Maryland Eastern Shore (MD)
U of Mary Washington (VA)
U of Massachusetts Amherst (MA)
U of Massachusetts Boston (MA)
U of Massachusetts Dartmouth (MA)
U of Massachusetts Lowell (MA)
U of Memphis (TN)
U of Miami (FL)
U of Michigan (MI)
U of Michigan–Dearborn (MI)

U of Michigan–Flint (MI)
U of Minnesota, Crookston (MN)
U of Minnesota, Duluth (MN)
U of Minnesota, Twin Cities Campus (MN)
U of Mississippi (MS)
U of Missouri (MO)
U of Missouri–Kansas City (MO)
U of Missouri–St. Louis (MO)
U of Mobile (AL)
The U of Montana Western (MT)
U of Mount Union (OH)
U of Nebraska at Kearney (NE)
U of Nebraska at Omaha (NE)
U of Nebraska–Lincoln (NE)
U of Nevada, Las Vegas (NV)
U of Nevada, Reno (NV)
U of New England (ME)
U of New Hampshire (NH)
U of New Haven (CT)
U of New Mexico (NM)
U of New Orleans (LA)
U of North Alabama (AL)
The U of North Carolina at Asheville (NC)
The U of North Carolina at Chapel Hill (NC)
The U of North Carolina at Charlotte (NC)
The U of North Carolina Wilmington (NC)
U of North Dakota (ND)
U of Northern Colorado (CO)
U of Northern Iowa (IA)
U of North Florida (FL)
U of North Texas (TX)
U of Notre Dame (IN)
U of Oregon (OR)
U of Ottawa (ON, Canada)
U of Pennsylvania (PA)
U of Pikeville (KY)
U of Pittsburgh (PA)
U of Pittsburgh at Bradford (PA)
U of Pittsburgh at Greensburg (PA)
U of Pittsburgh at Johnstown (PA)
U of Portland (OR)
U of Puerto Rico at Bayamón (PR)
U of Puerto Rico at Humacao (PR)
U of Puget Sound (WA)
U of Redlands (CA)
U of Regina (SK, Canada)
U of Rhode Island (RI)
U of Richmond (VA)
U of Rio Grande (OH)
U of Rochester (NY)
U of St. Francis (IL)
U of Saint Joseph (CT)
U of Saint Mary (KS)
U of St. Thomas (MN)
U of St. Thomas (TX)
U of San Diego (CA)
U of Science and Arts of Oklahoma (OK)
The U of Scranton (PA)
U of South Alabama (AL)
U of South Carolina (SC)
U of South Carolina Aiken (SC)
U of South Carolina Beaufort (SC)
U of South Carolina Upstate (SC)
U of Southern California (CA)
U of Southern Indiana (IN)
U of Southern Maine (ME)
U of Southern Mississippi (MS)
U of South Florida (FL)
The U of Tampa (FL)
The U of Tennessee (TN)
The U of Tennessee at Chattanooga (TN)
The U of Tennessee at Martin (TN)
The U of Texas at Arlington (TX)
The U of Texas at Austin (TX)
The U of Texas at Dallas (TX)
The U of Texas at El Paso (TX)
The U of Texas at San Antonio (TX)
The U of Texas at Tyler (TX)
The U of Texas of the Permian Basin (TX)
The U of Texas–Pan American (TX)
U of the Cumberlands (KY)
U of the District of Columbia (DC)
U of the Incarnate Word (TX)
U of the Ozarks (AR)
U of the Pacific (CA)
U of the Sciences in Philadelphia (PA)

U of the Southwest (NM)
The U of Toledo (OH)
U of Toronto (ON, Canada)
U of Tulsa (OK)
U of Utah (UT)
U of Vermont (VT)
U of Virginia (VA)
The U of Virginia's Coll at Wise (VA)
U of Washington (WA)
U of Washington, Bothell (WA)
The U of West Alabama (AL)
The U of Western Ontario (ON, Canada)
U of West Florida (FL)
U of West Georgia (GA)
U of Windsor (ON, Canada)
U of Wisconsin–Eau Claire (WI)
U of Wisconsin–Green Bay (WI)
U of Wisconsin–La Crosse (WI)
U of Wisconsin–Madison (WI)
U of Wisconsin–Milwaukee (WI)
U of Wisconsin–Platteville (WI)
U of Wisconsin–River Falls (WI)
U of Wisconsin–Stevens Point (WI)
U of Wisconsin–Superior (WI)
U of Wisconsin–Whitewater (WI)
U of Wyoming (WY)
Upper Iowa U (IA)
Ursuline Coll (OH)
Utah State U (UT)
Utah Valley U (UT)
Utica Coll (NY)
Valdosta State U (GA)
Valley City State U (ND)
Valparaiso U (IN)
Vanderbilt U (TN)
Vanguard U of Southern California (CA)
Vassar Coll (NY)
Villanova U (PA)
Virginia Commonwealth U (VA)
Virginia Intermont Coll (VA)
Virginia Polytechnic Inst and State U (VA)
Virginia State U (VA)
Virginia Union U (VA)
Virginia Wesleyan Coll (VA)
Viterbo U (WI)
Wabash Coll (IN)
Wagner Coll (NY)
Wake Forest U (NC)
Waldorf Coll (IA)
Walsh U (OH)
Warren Wilson Coll (NC)
Wartburg Coll (IA)
Washburn U (KS)
Washington Adventist U (MD)
Washington & Jefferson Coll (PA)
Washington and Lee U (VA)
Washington Coll (MD)
Washington State U (WA)
Washington U in St. Louis (MO)
Wayland Baptist U (TX)
Waynesburg U (PA)
Wayne State Coll (NE)
Wayne State U (MI)
Webster U (MO)
Wellesley Coll (MA)
Wells Coll (NY)
Wesleyan Coll (GA)
Wesleyan U (CT)
West Chester U of Pennsylvania (PA)
Western Carolina U (NC)
Western Connecticut State U (CT)
Western Illinois U (IL)
Western Kentucky U (KY)
Western Michigan U (MI)
Western New England U (MA)
Western Oregon U (OR)
Western State Coll of Colorado (CO)
Western Washington U (WA)
Westfield State U (MA)
West Liberty U (WV)
Westminster Coll (MO)
Westminster Coll (UT)
West Texas A&M U (TX)
West Virginia State U (WV)
West Virginia U (WV)
West Virginia U Inst of Technology (WV)
West Virginia Wesleyan Coll (WV)
Wheaton Coll (IL)
Wheaton Coll (MA)

Wheeling Jesuit U (WV)
Whitman Coll (WA)
Whittier Coll (CA)
Wichita State U (KS)
Widener U (PA)
Wilkes U (PA)
Willamette U (OR)
William Jewell Coll (MO)
William Paterson U of New Jersey (NJ)
William Penn U (IA)
Williams Baptist Coll (AR)
Williams Coll (MA)
William Woods U (MO)
Wilmington Coll (OH)
Wilson Coll (PA)
Wingate U (NC)
Winona State U (MN)
Winthrop U (SC)
Wittenberg U (OH)
Wofford Coll (SC)
Worcester Polytechnic Inst (MA)
Worcester State U (MA)
Wright State U (OH)
Xavier U (OH)
Xavier U of Louisiana (LA)
Yale U (CT)
Yeshiva U (NY)
York Coll of Pennsylvania (PA)
York Coll of the City U of New York (NY)
Youngstown State U (OH)

BIOLOGY/BIOTECHNOLOGY LABORATORY TECHNICIAN
Cleveland State U (OH)
The Coll at Brockport, State U of New York (NY)
Delaware State U (DE)
Gannon U (PA)
Michigan Technological U (MI)
Niagara U (NY)
Penn State Abington (PA)
Penn State Altoona (PA)
Penn State Beaver (PA)
Penn State Berks (PA)
Penn State Brandywine (PA)
Penn State DuBois (PA)
Penn State Erie, The Behrend Coll (PA)
Penn State Fayette, The Eberly Campus (PA)
Penn State Greater Allegheny (PA)
Penn State Hazleton (PA)
Penn State Lehigh Valley (PA)
Penn State Mont Alto (PA)
Penn State New Kensington (PA)
Penn State Schuylkill (PA)
Penn State Shenango (PA)
Penn State U Park (PA)
Penn State Wilkes-Barre (PA)
Penn State Worthington Scranton (PA)
Penn State York (PA)
Point Park U (PA)
Purdue U Calumet (IN)
State U of New York at Fredonia (NY)
State U of New York Coll at Oneonta (NY)
Tusculum Coll (TN)
U of Alberta (AB, Canada)
U of New Haven (CT)
Washburn U (KS)
Worcester Polytechnic Inst (MA)
York Coll of the City U of New York (NY)

BIOLOGY TEACHER EDUCATION
Abilene Christian U (TX)
Adams State Coll (CO)
Albion Coll (MI)
Alma Coll (MI)
Alvernia U (PA)
Anderson U (IN)
Appalachian State U (NC)
Arkansas State U (AR)
Arkansas Tech U (AR)
Assumption Coll (MA)
Augustana Coll (IL)
Averett U (VA)
Bethany Coll (KS)
Bethel U (MN)

Bethune-Cookman U (FL)
Biola U (CA)
Bishop's U (QC, Canada)
Blackburn Coll (IL)
Bluefield Coll (VA)
Blue Mountain Coll (MS)
Bowling Green State U (OH)
Bradley U (IL)
Brewton-Parker Coll (GA)
Bridgewater State U (MA)
Buena Vista U (IA)
Cabrini Coll (PA)
California State U, Chico (CA)
California State U, Long Beach (CA)
Calvin Coll (MI)
Campbellsville U (KY)
Carroll Coll (MT)
Cedarville U (OH)
Central Methodist U (MO)
Central Michigan U (MI)
Central Washington U (WA)
Christian Brothers U (TN)
City Coll of the City U of New York (NY)
Clearwater Christian Coll (FL)
The Coll at Brockport, State U of New York (NY)
The Coll of New Jersey (NJ)
The Coll of Saint Rose (NY)
Coll of the Ozarks (MO)
Colorado State U (CO)
Concordia Coll (MN)
Concordia U (MI)
Concordia U Chicago (IL)
Concordia U, Nebraska (NE)
Concordia U, St. Paul (MN)
Corban U (OR)
Cornerstone U (MI)
Culver-Stockton Coll (MO)
Daemen Coll (NY)
Dakota State U (SD)
Delaware State U (DE)
Dixie State Coll of Utah (UT)
Dominican Coll (NY)
Dordt Coll (IA)
Dowling Coll (NY)
East Central U (OK)
Eastern Michigan U (MI)
Eastern Washington U (WA)
East Texas Baptist U (TX)
Edgewood Coll (WI)
Elizabeth City State U (NC)
Elmhurst Coll (IL)
Elmira Coll (NY)
Evangel U (MO)
Fayetteville State U (NC)
Ferris State U (MI)
Fitchburg State U (MA)
Florida Inst of Technology (FL)
Fordham U (NY)
Fort Lewis Coll (CO)
Franklin Coll (IN)
Free Will Baptist Bible Coll (TN)
Friends U (KS)
Glenville State Coll (WV)
Grace Coll (IN)
Grambling State U (LA)
Grand Canyon U (AZ)
Grand Valley State U (MI)
Greenville Coll (IL)
Gustavus Adolphus Coll (MN)
Harding U (AR)
Hofstra U (NY)
Hope Coll (MI)
Howard Payne U (TX)
Hunter Coll of the City U of New York (NY)
Huntingdon Coll (AL)
Huntington U (IN)
Husson U (ME)
Indiana U Bloomington (IN)
Indiana U–Purdue U Fort Wayne (IN)
Indiana U South Bend (IN)
Indiana U Southeast (IN)
Indiana Wesleyan U (IN)
Indian River State Coll (FL)
Inter American U of Puerto Rico, Fajardo Campus (PR)
Inter American U of Puerto Rico, Ponce Campus (PR)
Inter American U of Puerto Rico, San Germán Campus (PR)
Iona Coll (NY)

Iowa Wesleyan Coll (IA)
Ithaca Coll (NY)
Jamestown Coll (ND)
Johnson State Coll (VT)
Juniata Coll (PA)
Keene State Coll (NH)
Kennesaw State U (GA)
Kentucky Wesleyan Coll (KY)
Keuka Coll (NY)
King Coll (TN)
Le Moyne Coll (NY)
Lenoir-Rhyne U (NC)
Liberty U (VA)
Lincoln Memorial U (TN)
Lincoln U (MO)
Lindenwood U (MO)
Lindsey Wilson Coll (KY)
Lipscomb U (TN)
Long Island U–C. W. Post Campus (NY)
Louisiana State U in Shreveport (LA)
Lubbock Christian U (TX)
Macon State Coll (GA)
Manchester Coll (IN)
Manhattanville Coll (NY)
Mansfield U of Pennsylvania (PA)
Maranatha Baptist Bible Coll (WI)
Marian U (WI)
Maryville Coll (TN)
Marywood U (PA)
Mayville State U (ND)
McKendree U (IL)
McMurry U (TX)
Mercyhurst Coll (PA)
Merrimack Coll (MA)
Messiah Coll (PA)
Metropolitan State U (MN)
Miami Dade Coll (FL)
Miami U (OH)
Michigan State U (MI)
Michigan Technological U (MI)
MidAmerica Nazarene U (KS)
Millikin U (IL)
Minnesota State U Moorhead (MN)
Minot State U (ND)
Misericordia U (PA)
Mississippi Coll (MS)
Missouri State U (MO)
Molloy Coll (NY)
Montana State U Billings (MT)
Moravian Coll (PA)
Morningside Coll (IA)
Morris Coll (SC)
Mount Mary Coll (WI)
Mount Vernon Nazarene U (OH)
Nazareth Coll of Rochester (NY)
Niagara U (NY)
North Carolina Ag and Tech State U (NC)
North Carolina Central U (NC)
North Dakota State U (ND)
Northeastern State U (OK)
Northern Michigan U (MI)
Northwestern Coll (IA)
Northwest Missouri State U (MO)
Northwest Nazarene U (ID)
Northwest U (WA)
Oakland City U (IN)
Ohio Northern U (OH)
Ohio Wesleyan U (OH)
Oklahoma City U (OK)
Pace U (NY)
Paine Coll (GA)
Palm Beach Atlantic U (FL)
Peru State Coll (NE)
Pittsburg State U (KS)
Point Park U (PA)
Rhode Island Coll (RI)
Rivier Coll (NH)
Roberts Wesleyan Coll (NY)
Rocky Mountain Coll (MT)
Rust Coll (MS)
Saginaw Valley State U (MI)
St. Ambrose U (IA)
St. Catherine U (MN)
St. Edward's U (TX)
Saint Francis U (PA)
St. John Fisher Coll (NY)
St. John's U (NY)
St. Joseph's Coll, Long Island Campus (NY)
St. Joseph's Coll, New York (NY)
Saint Joseph's Coll of Maine (ME)
Saint Mary's U of Minnesota (MN)

Saint Xavier U (IL)
Salve Regina U (RI)
Schreiner U (TX)
Seton Hill U (PA)
Southeastern U (FL)
Southern Polytechnic State U (GA)
Southwest Baptist U (MO)
Southwest Minnesota State U (MN)
Spring Arbor U (MI)
State U of New York at New Paltz (NY)
State U of New York at Plattsburgh (NY)
State U of New York Coll at Cortland (NY)
State U of New York Coll at Old Westbury (NY)
State U of New York Coll at Oneonta (NY)
State U of New York Coll of Environmental Science and Forestry (NY)
Tabor Coll (KS)
Texas A&M Intl U (TX)
Texas Wesleyan U (TX)
Trevecca Nazarene U (TN)
Trinity Christian Coll (IL)
Tusculum Coll (TN)
Union Coll (NE)
Universidad del Turabo (PR)
U of Arkansas–Fort Smith (AR)
U of California, Irvine (CA)
U of Charleston (WV)
U of Delaware (DE)
U of Dubuque (IA)
U of Evansville (IN)
U of Great Falls (MT)
U of Illinois at Chicago (IL)
The U of Iowa (IA)
U of Louisiana at Lafayette (LA)
U of Louisiana at Monroe (LA)
U of Maine (ME)
U of Maine at Farmington (ME)
U of Mary (ND)
U of Mary Hardin-Baylor (TX)
U of Minnesota, Twin Cities Campus (MN)
U of Missouri (MO)
U of Missouri–St. Louis (MO)
The U of Montana Western (MT)
U of Nebraska–Lincoln (NE)
U of New Orleans (LA)
The U of North Carolina Wilmington (NC)
U of Pittsburgh at Johnstown (PA)
U of Regina (SK, Canada)
U of Rio Grande (OH)
U of Saint Francis (IN)
U of St. Thomas (MN)
The U of South Dakota (SD)
The U of Tennessee at Martin (TN)
U of Washington (WA)
U of West Georgia (GA)
U of Windsor (ON, Canada)
U of Wisconsin–River Falls (WI)
U of Wisconsin–Superior (WI)
Utah State U (UT)
Utah Valley U (UT)
Utica Coll (NY)
Valley City State U (ND)
Valparaiso U (IN)
Virginia Intermont Coll (VA)
Viterbo U (WI)
Washburn U (KS)
Washington State U (WA)
Washington U in St. Louis (MO)
Waynesburg U (PA)
Wayne State Coll (NE)
Weber State U (UT)
Western Michigan U (MI)
Western State Coll of Colorado (CO)
Western Washington U (WA)
Wheeling Jesuit U (WV)
Widener U (PA)
William Jewell Coll (MO)
Wingate U (NC)
Winona State U (MN)
Xavier U (OH)
Xavier U of Louisiana (LA)
York Coll of Pennsylvania (PA)
Youngstown State U (OH)

BIOMATHEMATICS, BIOINFORMATICS, AND

COMPUTATIONAL BIOLOGY RELATED

Cedar Crest Coll (PA)
Florida Inst of Technology (FL)
Florida State U (FL)
U of California, Los Angeles (CA)
Walsh U (OH)
Washington U in St. Louis (MO)
Worcester Polytechnic Inst (MA)

BIOMEDICAL SCIENCES

Auburn U (AL)
Bridgewater State U (MA)
Brigham Young U (UT)
Brown U (RI)
Central Michigan U (MI)
Christian Brothers U (TN)
City Coll of the City U of New York (NY)
Colorado State U (CO)
Concordia Coll–New York (NY)
Fitchburg State U (MA)
Florida Inst of Technology (FL)
Inter American U of Puerto Rico, Ponce Campus (PR)
Inter American U of Puerto Rico, San Germán Campus (PR)
Keuka Coll (NY)
Lynchburg Coll (VA)
Marquette U (WI)
Maryville U of Saint Louis (MO)
McMurry U (TX)
Mississippi Coll (MS)
North Carolina Central U (NC)
North Carolina Wesleyan Coll (NC)
Northern Arizona U (AZ)
The Ohio State U (OH)
Oklahoma City U (OK)
Our Lady of the Lake Coll (LA)
Peru State Coll (NE)
Purdue U (IN)
Rochester Inst of Technology (NY)
Rutgers, The State U of New Jersey, New Brunswick (NJ)
Slippery Rock U of Pennsylvania (PA)
State U of New York at Fredonia (NY)
Suffolk U (MA)
Texas A&M U (TX)
Texas A&M U–Corpus Christi (TX)
Texas A&M U–Kingsville (TX)
U at Buffalo, the State U of New York (NY)
U of California, Riverside (CA)
U of Colorado Denver (CO)
U of Guelph (ON, Canada)
U of Maine (ME)
U of Michigan–Flint (MI)
U of Minnesota, Duluth (MN)
U of New England (ME)
U of New Hampshire (NH)
U of Ottawa (ON, Canada)
U of Pennsylvania (PA)
U of South Alabama (AL)
U of South Florida (FL)
Washington State U (WA)
Western Michigan U (MI)
Worcester Polytechnic Inst (MA)

BIOMEDICAL TECHNOLOGY

Andrews U (MI)
California State U, East Bay (CA)
Cleveland State U (OH)
DeVry Coll of New York (NY)
DeVry U, Phoenix (AZ)
DeVry U, Miramar (FL)
DeVry U, Orlando (FL)
DeVry U, Decatur (GA)
DeVry U, Chicago (IL)
DeVry U, North Brunswick (NJ)
DeVry U, Columbus (OH)
DeVry U, Fort Washington (PA)
DeVry U, Irving (TX)
Indiana U–Purdue U Indianapolis (IN)
Lawrence Technological U (MI)
New York Inst of Technology (NY)
Rutgers, The State U of New Jersey, Camden (NJ)
Suffolk U (MA)
Thomas Edison State Coll (NJ)
Wright State U (OH)

BIOMETRY/BIOMETRICS

Carnegie Mellon U (PA)
Cornell U (NY)
Rutgers, The State U of New Jersey, New Brunswick (NJ)
Stanford U (CA)
U of Delaware (DE)
U of Minnesota, Twin Cities Campus (MN)

BIOPHYSICS

Andrews U (MI)
Brandeis U (MA)
Brigham Young U (UT)
Brown U (RI)
Carnegie Mellon U (PA)
Centenary Coll of Louisiana (LA)
Columbia U, School of General Studies (NY)
Hampden-Sydney Coll (VA)
Haverford Coll (PA)
Illinois Inst of Technology (IL)
Iowa State U of Science and Technology (IA)
The Johns Hopkins U (MD)
King Coll (TN)
La Sierra U (CA)
Loyola U Chicago (IL)
Oakland U (MI)
Oklahoma City U (OK)
Pacific Union Coll (CA)
St. Bonaventure U (NY)
St. Lawrence U (NY)
Southwestern Oklahoma State U (OK)
State U of New York Coll at Geneseo (NY)
Suffolk U (MA)
Syracuse U (NY)
Temple U (PA)
U at Buffalo, the State U of New York (NY)
The U of British Columbia (BC, Canada)
U of California, Los Angeles (CA)
U of Connecticut (CT)
U of Illinois at Urbana–Champaign (IL)
U of Michigan (MI)
U of Pennsylvania (PA)
U of San Diego (CA)
The U of Scranton (PA)
U of Southern California (CA)
U of Southern Indiana (IN)
U of Toronto (ON, Canada)
The U of Western Ontario (ON, Canada)
Washington & Jefferson Coll (PA)
Washington U in St. Louis (MO)
Whitman Coll (WA)

BIOPSYCHOLOGY

Bucknell U (PA)
Carnegie Mellon U (PA)
Geneva Coll (PA)
Grand Valley State U (MI)
Immaculata U (PA)
Messiah Coll (PA)
Monmouth Coll (IL)
Morningside Coll (IA)
Mount Allison U (NB, Canada)
Nebraska Wesleyan U (NE)
Northwest Missouri State U (MO)
Oglethorpe U (GA)
Philadelphia U (PA)
Rider U (NJ)
Spring Hill Coll (AL)
U of California, Santa Barbara (CA)
U of Guelph (ON, Canada)
U of Pittsburgh at Johnstown (PA)
Viterbo U (WI)
Wagner Coll (NY)
Washington U in St. Louis (MO)

BIOSTATISTICS

Emmanuel Coll (MA)
Simmons Coll (MA)
Tulane U (LA)
U at Buffalo, the State U of New York (NY)
U of Minnesota, Twin Cities Campus (MN)
The U of North Carolina at Chapel Hill (NC)

U of Washington (WA)

BIOTECHNOLOGY

Bay Path Coll (MA)
California State Polytechnic U, Pomona (CA)
Calvin Coll (MI)
Claflin U (SC)
The Coll at Brockport, State U of New York (NY)
Delaware State U (DE)
East Stroudsburg U of Pennsylvania (PA)
Elizabethtown Coll (PA)
Endicott Coll (MA)
Fayetteville State U (NC)
Ferris State U (MI)
Fitchburg State U (MA)
Florida Gulf Coast U (FL)
Grand View U (IA)
Hunter Coll of the City U of New York (NY)
Indiana U Bloomington (IN)
Indiana U East (IN)
Indiana U–Purdue U Indianapolis (IN)
Inter American U of Puerto Rico, Ponce Campus (PR)
James Madison U (VA)
Kennesaw State U (GA)
Kent State U (OH)
Manhattan Coll (NY)
Marywood U (PA)
Massachusetts Coll of Liberal Arts (MA)
Missouri Baptist U (MO)
Missouri Western State U (MO)
Montana State U (MT)
North Carolina State U (NC)
North Dakota State U (ND)
Plymouth State U (NH)
Rochester Inst of Technology (NY)
Roosevelt U (IL)
Rutgers, The State U of New Jersey, New Brunswick (NJ)
Sojourner-Douglass Coll (MD)
South Dakota State U (SD)
Southeastern Oklahoma State U (OK)
State U of New York at New Paltz (NY)
State U of New York Coll of Environmental Science and Forestry (NY)
Stevenson U (MD)
U at Buffalo, the State U of New York (NY)
The U of British Columbia (BC, Canada)
U of California, Davis (CA)
U of Central Florida (FL)
U of Georgia (GA)
U of Houston (TX)
U of Illinois at Urbana–Champaign (IL)
U of Nebraska at Omaha (NE)
U of Nevada, Reno (NV)
U of Northern Iowa (IA)
U of Puerto Rico at Ponce (PR)
U of Windsor (ON, Canada)
U of Wisconsin–River Falls (WI)
Ursuline Coll (OH)
Utah Valley U (UT)
Western Kentucky U (KY)
West Texas A&M U (TX)
Worcester State U (MA)
York Coll of the City U of New York (NY)

BLOOD BANK TECHNOLOGY

Rasmussen Coll St. Cloud (MN)

BOTANY/PLANT BIOLOGY

Andrews U (MI)
Arizona State U (AZ)
Auburn U (AL)
Bennington Coll (VT)
California State U, Long Beach (CA)
Coll of the Atlantic (ME)
Colorado State U (CO)
Connecticut Coll (CT)
Goddard Coll (VT)
Humboldt State U (CA)

Idaho State U (ID)
Iowa State U of Science and Technology (IA)
Juniata Coll (PA)
Kent State U (OH)
Marlboro Coll (VT)
Miami U (OH)
Michigan State U (MI)
North Carolina State U (NC)
North Dakota State U (ND)
The Ohio State U (OH)
Ohio U (OH)
Ohio Wesleyan U (OH)
Oklahoma State U (OK)
Purdue U (IN)
Rutgers, The State U of New Jersey, Newark (NJ)
Saint Xavier U (IL)
San Francisco State U (CA)
Sonoma State U (CA)
Southern Illinois U Carbondale (IL)
State U of New York Coll of Environmental Science and Forestry (NY)
Texas State U–San Marcos (TX)
The U of Akron (OH)
U of Alberta (AB, Canada)
U of California, Berkeley (CA)
U of California, Davis (CA)
U of California, Irvine (CA)
U of California, Riverside (CA)
U of Florida (FL)
U of Georgia (GA)
U of Great Falls (MT)
U of Hawaii at Manoa (HI)
U of Illinois at Urbana–Champaign (IL)
U of Maine (ME)
U of Minnesota, Twin Cities Campus (MN)
U of Nebraska–Lincoln (NE)
U of New Hampshire (NH)
U of Oklahoma (OK)
The U of Texas at El Paso (TX)
U of Toronto (ON, Canada)
U of Vermont (VT)
U of Washington (WA)
U of Wisconsin–Madison (WI)
U of Wyoming (WY)
Utah State U (UT)
Weber State U (UT)

BOTANY/PLANT BIOLOGY RELATED

Pittsburg State U (KS)
Purdue U (IN)
U of Hawaii at Manoa (HI)
U of Minnesota, Twin Cities Campus (MN)

BRASS INSTRUMENTS

Houghton Coll (NY)
McNally Smith Coll of Music (MN)
The U of Kansas (KS)
Vanderbilt U (TN)

BROADCAST JOURNALISM

Auburn U (AL)
Barry U (FL)
Belmont U (TN)
Bemidji State U (MN)
Biola U (CA)
Bob Jones U (SC)
Bowie State U (MD)
Bowling Green State U (OH)
Brigham Young U (UT)
Buffalo State Coll, State U of New York (NY)
California State U, East Bay (CA)
California State U, Long Beach (CA)
Carson-Newman Coll (TN)
Central State U (OH)
Chapman U (CA)
Chatham U (PA)
The Coll at Brockport, State U of New York (NY)
Coll of the Ozarks (MO)
Columbia Coll Chicago (IL)
Delaware State U (DE)
Drake U (IA)
Drury U (MO)
East Carolina U (NC)
Eastern Kentucky U (KY)

Edinboro U of Pennsylvania (PA)
Elon U (NC)
Evangel U (MO)
Five Towns Coll (NY)
Fordham U (NY)
Gettysburg Coll (PA)
Gonzaga U (WA)
Hampton U (VA)
Harding U (AR)
Hardin-Simmons U (TX)
Hawai`i Pacific U (HI)
Humboldt State U (CA)
Huntington U (IN)
Ithaca Coll (NY)
John Brown U (AR)
Lamar U (TX)
La Salle U (PA)
Lindenwood U (MO)
Long Island U–C. W. Post Campus (NY)
Louisiana Coll (LA)
Manchester Coll (IN)
Massachusetts Coll of Liberal Arts (MA)
Montclair State U (NJ)
Mount Vernon Nazarene U (OH)
New England School of Communications (ME)
North Carolina Ag and Tech State U (NC)
Northern Kentucky U (KY)
North Greenville U (SC)
Ohio U (OH)
Ohio Wesleyan U (OH)
Oklahoma Christian U (OK)
Oklahoma City U (OK)
Pacific U (OR)
Point Loma Nazarene U (CA)
Point Park U (PA)
Purdue U Calumet (IN)
Quinnipiac U (CT)
Rust Coll (MS)
Southwestern Adventist U (TX)
Southwestern Assemblies of God U (TX)
State U of New York at New Paltz (NY)
State U of New York at Oswego (NY)
State U of New York at Plattsburgh (NY)
Stephens Coll (MO)
Suffolk U (MA)
Syracuse U (NY)
Troy U (AL)
Union U (TN)
U of Colorado Boulder (CO)
U of Dayton (OH)
The U of Findlay (OH)
U of Georgia (GA)
U of Illinois at Urbana–Champaign (IL)
U of La Verne (CA)
U of Miami (FL)
U of Missouri (MO)
U of Nebraska at Omaha (NE)
U of Nebraska–Lincoln (NE)
U of North Texas (TX)
U of Oklahoma (OK)
U of South Carolina (SC)
U of Southern California (CA)
The U of Texas at El Paso (TX)
U of the Ozarks (AR)
U of Wisconsin–Platteville (WI)
U of Wisconsin–River Falls (WI)
U of Wisconsin–Superior (WI)
Wartburg Coll (IA)
Washington Adventist U (MD)
Washington State U (WA)
Webster U (MO)
Western Kentucky U (KY)
West Texas A&M U (TX)
William Woods U (MO)
Winona State U (MN)

BUILDING/CONSTRUCTION FINISHING, MANAGEMENT, AND INSPECTION RELATED

California State U, Long Beach (CA)
Hampton U (VA)
John Brown U (AR)
Minnesota State U Mankato (MN)
Pratt Inst (NY)

Purdue U (IN)
U of Maryland Eastern Shore (MD)
U of the District of Columbia (DC)
U of Wisconsin–Platteville (WI)

BUILDING/CONSTRUCTION SITE MANAGEMENT

Pennsylvania Coll of Technology (PA)
Purdue U (IN)
Wentworth Inst of Technology (MA)

BUILDING CONSTRUCTION TECHNOLOGY

Purdue U (IN)
U of Massachusetts Amherst (MA)

BUILDING/HOME/ CONSTRUCTION INSPECTION

Purdue U (IN)
Tuskegee U (AL)

BUILDING/PROPERTY MAINTENANCE

Purdue U (IN)

BUSINESS ADMINISTRATION AND MANAGEMENT

Abilene Christian U (TX)
Acadia U (NS, Canada)
Adams State Coll (CO)
Adelphi U (NY)
Adrian Coll (MI)
AIB Coll of Business (IA)
Alabama State U (AL)
Alaska Pacific U (AK)
Albany State U (GA)
Albertus Magnus Coll (CT)
Albion Coll (MI)
Albright Coll (PA)
Alcorn State U (MS)
Alfred U (NY)
Alliant Intl U (CA)
Alliant Intl U–México City (Mexico)
Alma Coll (MI)
Alvernia U (PA)
Alverno Coll (WI)
Amberton U (TX)
American Public U System (WV)
American U (DC)
American U in Bulgaria (Bulgaria)
The American U in Cairo (Egypt)
American U of Beirut (Lebanon)
The American U of Rome (Italy)
Amridge U (AL)
Anderson U (IN)
Anderson U (SC)
Angelo State U (TX)
Anna Maria Coll (MA)
Antioch U Midwest (OH)
Appalachian State U (NC)
Aquinas Coll (MI)
Arcadia U (PA)
Arizona State U (AZ)
Arkansas State U (AR)
Arkansas Tech U (AR)
Ashland U (OH)
Assumption Coll (MA)
Athabasca U (AB, Canada)
Athens State U (AL)
Auburn U (AL)
Auburn U Montgomery (AL)
Augustana Coll (IL)
Augustana Coll (SD)
Austin Coll (TX)
Avila U (MO)
Azusa Pacific U (CA)
Babson Coll (MA)
Baker Coll of Auburn Hills (MI)
Baker Coll of Owosso (MI)
Baldwin-Wallace Coll (OH)
Ball State U (IN)
Baptist Bible Coll of Pennsylvania (PA)
The Baptist Coll of Florida (FL)
Baptist U of the Americas (TX)
Barclay Coll (KS)
Barry U (FL)
Barton Coll (NC)
Bauder Coll (GA)
Bayamón Central U (PR)
Baylor U (TX)
Bay Path Coll (MA)

Becker Coll (MA)
Belhaven U (MS)
Belmont Abbey Coll (NC)
Belmont U (TN)
Beloit Coll (WI)
Bemidji State U (MN)
Benedictine Coll (KS)
Bennett Coll for Women (NC)
Bentley U (MA)
Berea Coll (KY)
Bernard M. Baruch Coll of the City U of New York (NY)
Berry Coll (GA)
Bethany Coll (KS)
Bethany Lutheran Coll (MN)
Bethel Coll (IN)
Bethel U (MN)
Bethel U (TN)
Bethune-Cookman U (FL)
Biola U (CA)
Birmingham-Southern Coll (AL)
Bishop's U (QC, Canada)
Blackburn Coll (IL)
Black Hills State U (SD)
Bloomfield Coll (NJ)
Bloomsburg U of Pennsylvania (PA)
Bluefield Coll (VA)
Bluefield State Coll (WV)
Blue Mountain Coll (MS)
Bluffton U (OH)
Bob Jones U (SC)
Boise State U (ID)
Boston Coll (MA)
Boston U (MA)
Bowie State U (MD)
Bowling Green State U (OH)
Bradley U (IL)
Brevard Coll (NC)
Brewton-Parker Coll (GA)
Briar Cliff U (IA)
Bridgewater Coll (VA)
Bridgewater State U (MA)
Briercrest Coll (SK, Canada)
Broadview U (UT)
Broadview U-Boise (ID)
Broadview U-Layton (UT)
Broadview U-Orem (UT)
Bryant U (RI)
Bucknell U (PA)
Buena Vista U (IA)
Buffalo State Coll, State U of New York (NY)
Cabrini Coll (PA)
Caldwell Coll (NJ)
California Coast U (CA)
California Lutheran U (CA)
California Maritime Acad (CA)
California Polytechnic State U, San Luis Obispo (CA)
California State Polytechnic U, Pomona (CA)
California State U, Bakersfield (CA)
California State U, Chico (CA)
California State U, Dominguez Hills (CA)
California State U, East Bay (CA)
California State U, Fresno (CA)
California State U, Fullerton (CA)
California State U, Long Beach (CA)
California State U, Los Angeles (CA)
California State U, Monterey Bay (CA)
California State U, Sacramento (CA)
California State U, San Bernardino (CA)
California State U, San Marcos (CA)
California State U, Stanislaus (CA)
California U of Pennsylvania (PA)
Calumet Coll of Saint Joseph (IN)
Calvary Bible Coll and Theological Sem (MO)
Calvin Coll (MI)
Cameron U (OK)
Campbellsville U (KY)
Capella U (MN)
Capital U (OH)
Cardinal Stritch U (WI)
Caribbean U (PR)
Carlos Albizu U, Miami Campus (FL)
Carlow U (PA)

Carnegie Mellon U (PA)
Carroll Coll (MT)
Carson-Newman Coll (TN)
Case Western Reserve U (OH)
Castleton State Coll (VT)
Catawba Coll (NC)
Cedar Crest Coll (PA)
Cedarville U (OH)
Centenary Coll (NJ)
Centenary Coll of Louisiana (LA)
Central Coll (IA)
Central Connecticut State U (CT)
Central Methodist U (MO)
Central Washington U (WA)
Chaminade U of Honolulu (HI)
Chapman U (CA)
Chatham U (PA)
Chestnut Hill Coll (PA)
Cheyney U of Pennsylvania (PA)
Chicago State U (IL)
Chipola Coll (FL)
Christian Brothers U (TN)
Christopher Newport U (VA)
The Citadel, The Military Coll of South Carolina (SC)
City Coll of the City U of New York (NY)
City U of Seattle (WA)
Claflin U (SC)
Clarion U of Pennsylvania (PA)
Clark Atlanta U (GA)
Clarke U (IA)
Clarkson Coll (NE)
Clarkson U (NY)
Clark U (MA)
Clayton State U (GA)
Clearwater Christian Coll (FL)
Cleary U (MI)
Clemson U (SC)
Cleveland State U (OH)
Coastal Carolina U (SC)
Coe Coll (IA)
The Coll at Brockport, State U of New York (NY)
Coll of Charleston (SC)
Coll of Coastal Georgia (GA)
The Coll of Idaho (ID)
Coll of Mount St. Joseph (OH)
The Coll of New Jersey (NJ)
Coll of Saint Benedict (MN)
Coll of Saint Elizabeth (NJ)
Coll of St. Joseph (VT)
Coll of Saint Mary (NE)
The Coll of Saint Rose (NY)
The Coll of St. Scholastica (MN)
Coll of the Ozarks (MO)
The Coll of William and Mary (VA)
Colorado State U (CO)
Columbia Centro Universitario, Yauco (PR)
Columbia Coll (MO)
Columbia Coll (SC)
Columbia Coll Chicago (IL)
Columbia Southern U (AL)
Columbus State U (GA)
Concordia Coll (MN)
Concordia Coll–New York (NY)
Concordia U (CA)
Concordia U (MI)
Concordia U (QC, Canada)
Concordia U Chicago (IL)
Concordia U, Nebraska (NE)
Concordia U, St. Paul (MN)
Concordia U Texas (TX)
Converse Coll (SC)
Corban U (OR)
Cornerstone U (MI)
Crandall U (NB, Canada)
Crown Coll (MN)
Culver-Stockton Coll (MO)
Curry Coll (MA)
Daemen Coll (NY)
Dakota State U (SD)
Dalhousie U (NS, Canada)
Dallas Baptist U (TX)
Dallas Christian Coll (TX)
Dalton State Coll (GA)
Daniel Webster Coll (NH)
Davenport U, Grand Rapids (MI)
Delaware State U (DE)
Delaware Valley Coll (PA)
Delta State U (MS)
DePaul U (IL)
DEREE - The American Coll of Greece (Greece)

DeSales U (PA)
DeVry Coll of New York (NY)
DeVry U, Phoenix (AZ)
DeVry U, Pomona (CA)
DeVry U, Westminster (CO)
DeVry U, Miramar (FL)
DeVry U, Orlando (FL)
DeVry U, Decatur (GA)
DeVry U, Chicago (IL)
DeVry U, Kansas City (MO)
DeVry U, North Brunswick (NJ)
DeVry U, Columbus (OH)
DeVry U, Fort Washington (PA)
DeVry U, Houston (TX)
DeVry U, Irving (TX)
DeVry U, Arlington (VA)
DeVry U, Federal Way (WA)
DeVry U Online (IL)
Dillard U (LA)
Dixie State Coll of Utah (UT)
Doane Coll (NE)
Dominican Coll (NY)
Dominican U (IL)
Dominican U of California (CA)
Dordt Coll (IA)
Dowling Coll (NY)
Drake U (IA)
Drew U (NJ)
Drury U (MO)
East Carolina U (NC)
East Central U (OK)
Eastern Connecticut State U (CT)
Eastern Illinois U (IL)
Eastern Kentucky U (KY)
Eastern Mennonite U (VA)
Eastern Michigan U (MI)
Eastern New Mexico U (NM)
Eastern U (PA)
Eastern Washington U (WA)
East Stroudsburg U of Pennsylvania (PA)
East Tennessee State U (TN)
Eckerd Coll (FL)
Edgewood Coll (WI)
Edinboro U of Pennsylvania (PA)
EDP Coll of Puerto Rico, Inc. (PR)
EDP Coll of Puerto Rico–San Sebastian (PR)
Edward Waters Coll (FL)
Elizabeth City State U (NC)
Elizabethtown Coll (PA)
Elmhurst Coll (IL)
Elmira Coll (NY)
Elon U (NC)
Emmanuel Coll (MA)
Emmaus Bible Coll (IA)
Emory U (GA)
Emporia State U (KS)
Endicott Coll (MA)
Evangel U (MO)
Everest U, Lakeland (FL)
Excelsior Coll (NY)
Fairfield U (CT)
Fairleigh Dickinson U, Coll at Florham (NJ)
Fairleigh Dickinson U, Metropolitan Campus (NJ)
Fairmont State U (WV)
Farmingdale State Coll (NY)
Faulkner U (AL)
Fayetteville State U (NC)
Felician Coll (NJ)
Ferris State U (MI)
Ferrum Coll (VA)
Fitchburg State U (MA)
Five Towns Coll (NY)
Flagler Coll (FL)
Florida Ag and Mech U (FL)
Florida Atlantic U (FL)
Florida Coll (FL)
Florida Inst of Technology (FL)
Florida Intl U (FL)
Florida National Coll (FL)
Florida Southern Coll (FL)
Florida State U (FL)
Fontbonne U (MO)
Fordham U (NY)
Fort Hays State U (KS)
Fort Lewis Coll (CO)
Franciscan U of Steubenville (OH)
Francis Marion U (SC)
Franklin & Marshall Coll (PA)
Franklin U (OH)
Free Will Baptist Bible Coll (TN)
Friends U (KS)

Furman U (SC)
Gallaudet U (DC)
Gannon U (PA)
Gardner-Webb U (NC)
Geneva Coll (PA)
George Fox U (OR)
George Mason U (VA)
Georgetown Coll (KY)
The George Washington U (DC)
Georgia Coll & State U (GA)
Georgia Inst of Technology (GA)
Georgian Court U (NJ)
Georgia Southern U (GA)
Georgia Southwestern State U (GA)
Georgia State U (GA)
Gettysburg Coll (PA)
Glenville State Coll (WV)
Globe U–Appleton (WI)
Globe U–Eau Claire (WI)
Globe U–Green Bay (WI)
Globe U–La Crosse (WI)
Globe U–Madison East (WI)
Globe U–Madison West (WI)
Globe U–Minneapolis (MN)
Globe U–Sioux Falls (SD)
Globe U–Wausau (WI)
Globe U–Woodbury (MN)
Goldey-Beacom Coll (DE)
Gonzaga U (WA)
Gordon Coll (MA)
Goshen Coll (IN)
Goucher Coll (MD)
Governors State U (IL)
Grace Coll (IN)
Graceland U (IA)
Grambling State U (LA)
Grand Canyon U (AZ)
Grand View U (IA)
Greenville Coll (IL)
Guilford Coll (NC)
Gustavus Adolphus Coll (MN)
Gwynedd-Mercy Coll (PA)
Hamline U (MN)
Hampton U (VA)
Hannibal-LaGrange U (MO)
Harding U (AR)
Hardin-Simmons U (TX)
Hartwick Coll (NY)
Hawai'i Pacific U (HI)
HEC Montreal (QC, Canada)
Heidelberg U (OH)
Hellenic Coll (MA)
Hesser Coll, Concord (NH)
Hesser Coll, Manchester (NH)
Hesser Coll, Nashua (NH)
Hesser Coll, Portsmouth (NH)
Hesser Coll, Salem (NH)
Hickey Coll (MO)
Hilbert Coll (NY)
Hillsdale Coll (MI)
Hofstra U (NY)
Holy Cross Coll (IN)
Holy Family U (PA)
Hood Coll (MD)
Hope Coll (MI)
Hope Intl U (CA)
Houghton Coll (NY)
Howard Payne U (TX)
Humboldt State U (CA)
Huntingdon Coll (AL)
Huntington U (IN)
Husson U (ME)
Huston-Tillotson U (TX)
Idaho State U (ID)
Illinois Coll (IL)
Illinois Inst of Technology (IL)
Illinois State U (IL)
Illinois Wesleyan U (IL)
Immaculata U (PA)
Indiana State U (IN)
Indiana Tech (IN)
Indiana U Bloomington (IN)
Indiana U East (IN)
Indiana U of Pennsylvania (PA)
Indiana U–Purdue U Fort Wayne (IN)
Indiana Wesleyan U (IN)
Inter American U of Puerto Rico, Bayamón Campus (PR)
Inter American U of Puerto Rico, Fajardo Campus (PR)
Inter American U of Puerto Rico, Ponce Campus (PR)
Intl Business Coll, Fort Wayne (IN)
Iona Coll (NY)

Iowa State U of Science and Technology (IA)
Iowa Wesleyan Coll (IA)
Ithaca Coll (NY)
ITT Tech Inst, Bessemer (AL)
ITT Tech Inst, Madison (AL)
ITT Tech Inst, Mobile (AL)
ITT Tech Inst, Phoenix (AZ)
ITT Tech Inst, Phoenix (AZ)
ITT Tech Inst, Tempe (AZ)
ITT Tech Inst, Tucson (AZ)
ITT Tech Inst (AR)
ITT Tech Inst, Clovis (CA)
ITT Tech Inst, Concord (CA)
ITT Tech Inst, Corona (CA)
ITT Tech Inst, Culver City (CA)
ITT Tech Inst, Lathrop (CA)
ITT Tech Inst, Oakland (CA)
ITT Tech Inst, Orange (CA)
ITT Tech Inst, Oxnard (CA)
ITT Tech Inst, Rancho Cordova (CA)
ITT Tech Inst, San Bernardino (CA)
ITT Tech Inst, San Dimas (CA)
ITT Tech Inst, Sylmar (CA)
ITT Tech Inst, Torrance (CA)
ITT Tech Inst, West Covina (CA)
ITT Tech Inst, Aurora (CO)
ITT Tech Inst, Thornton (CO)
ITT Tech Inst, Bradenton (FL)
ITT Tech Inst, Fort Lauderdale (FL)
ITT Tech Inst, Fort Myers (FL)
ITT Tech Inst, Jacksonville (FL)
ITT Tech Inst, Lake Mary (FL)
ITT Tech Inst, Miami (FL)
ITT Tech Inst, Orlando (FL)
ITT Tech Inst, Pinellas Park (FL)
ITT Tech Inst, Tallahassee (FL)
ITT Tech Inst, Tampa (FL)
ITT Tech Inst (ID)
ITT Tech Inst, Fort Wayne (IN)
ITT Tech Inst, Indianapolis (IN)
ITT Tech Inst, Merrillville (IN)
ITT Tech Inst, Newburgh (IN)
ITT Tech Inst, South Bend (IN)
ITT Tech Inst, Cedar Rapids (IA)
ITT Tech Inst, Clive (IA)
ITT Tech Inst, Wichita (KS)
ITT Tech Inst, Lexington (KY)
ITT Tech Inst, Louisville (KY)
ITT Tech Inst, Baton Rouge (LA)
ITT Tech Inst, St. Rose (LA)
ITT Tech Inst, Canton (MI)
ITT Tech Inst, Dearborn (MI)
ITT Tech Inst, Swartz Creek (MI)
ITT Tech Inst, Troy (MI)
ITT Tech Inst, Wyoming (MI)
ITT Tech Inst, Brooklyn Center (MN)
ITT Tech Inst, Eden Prairie (MN)
ITT Tech Inst, Arnold (MO)
ITT Tech Inst, Earth City (MO)
ITT Tech Inst, Kansas City (MO)
ITT Tech Inst, Springfield (MO)
ITT Tech Inst (NE)
ITT Tech Inst, Henderson (NV)
ITT Tech Inst, North Las Vegas (NV)
ITT Tech Inst (NM)
ITT Tech Inst, Oklahoma City (OK)
ITT Tech Inst, Tulsa (OK)
ITT Tech Inst, Chattanooga (TN)
ITT Tech Inst, Cordova (TN)
ITT Tech Inst, Johnson City (TN)
ITT Tech Inst, Knoxville (TN)
ITT Tech Inst, Nashville (TN)
ITT Tech Inst, Arlington (TX)
ITT Tech Inst, Austin (TX)
ITT Tech Inst, DeSoto (TX)
ITT Tech Inst, Houston (TX)
ITT Tech Inst, Houston (TX)
ITT Tech Inst, Richardson (TX)
ITT Tech Inst, San Antonio (TX)
ITT Tech Inst, Waco (TX)
ITT Tech Inst, Webster (TX)
ITT Tech Inst (UT)
ITT Tech Inst, Chantilly (VA)
ITT Tech Inst, Norfolk (VA)
ITT Tech Inst, Richmond (VA)
ITT Tech Inst, Salem (VA)
ITT Tech Inst, Springfield (VA)
ITT Tech Inst, Green Bay (WI)
ITT Tech Inst, Greenfield (WI)
ITT Tech Inst, Madison (WI)
Jacksonville State U (AL)

Jacksonville U (FL)
James Madison U (VA)
Jamestown Business Coll (NY)
Jamestown Coll (ND)
Jarvis Christian Coll (TX)
John Brown U (AR)
John Carroll U (OH)
Johnson C. Smith U (NC)
Johnson State Coll (VT)
Jones Coll, Jacksonville (FL)
Jones Intl U (CO)
Judson U (IL)
Juniata Coll (PA)
Kansas State U (KS)
Kean U (NJ)
Keene State Coll (NH)
Kennesaw State U (GA)
Kent State U (OH)
Kent State U at Ashtabula (OH)
Kent State U at East Liverpool (OH)
Kent State U at Geauga (OH)
Kent State U at Salem (OH)
Kent State U at Stark (OH)
Kent State U at Trumbull (OH)
Kent State U at Tuscarawas (OH)
Kentucky Christian U (KY)
Kentucky Wesleyan Coll (KY)
Kettering U (MI)
Keuka Coll (NY)
Keystone Coll (PA)
King Coll (TN)
The King's Coll (NY)
King's Coll (PA)
The King's U Coll (AB, Canada)
Kutztown U of Pennsylvania (PA)
LaGrange Coll (GA)
Lake Erie Coll (OH)
Lakehead U (ON, Canada)
Lake Superior State U (MI)
Lamar U (TX)
Lane Coll (TN)
La Salle U (PA)
Lasell Coll (MA)
La Sierra U (CA)
Lawrence Technological U (MI)
Lebanese American U (Lebanon)
Lebanon Valley Coll (PA)
Lees-McRae Coll (NC)
Lee U (TN)
Lehman Coll of the City U of New York (NY)
Le Moyne Coll (NY)
Lenoir-Rhyne U (NC)
LeTourneau U (TX)
Lewis-Clark State Coll (ID)
Lewis U (IL)
Liberty U (VA)
Life U (GA)
Limestone Coll (SC)
Lincoln Memorial U (TN)
Lincoln U (MO)
Lincoln U (PA)
Lindenwood U (MO)
Lindsey Wilson Coll (KY)
Lipscomb U (TN)
Lock Haven U of Pennsylvania (PA)
Long Island U–Brentwood Campus (NY)
Long Island U–Brooklyn Campus (NY)
Long Island U–C. W. Post Campus (NY)
Longwood U (VA)
Loras Coll (IA)
Louisiana Coll (LA)
Louisiana State U and Ag and Mech Coll (LA)
Louisiana State U in Shreveport (LA)
Lourdes U (OH)
Loyola Marymount U (CA)
Loyola U New Orleans (LA)
Lubbock Christian U (TX)
Luther Coll (IA)
Lycoming Coll (PA)
Lynchburg Coll (VA)
Lynn U (FL)
Lyon Coll (AR)
Madonna U (MI)
Maharishi U of Management (IA)
Malone U (OH)
Manchester Coll (IN)
Manhattanville Coll (NY)
Mansfield U of Pennsylvania (PA)
Maranatha Baptist Bible Coll (WI)

Marian U (WI)
Marietta Coll (OH)
Marquette U (WI)
Marshall U (WV)
Mars Hill Coll (NC)
Mary Baldwin Coll (VA)
Marylhurst U (OR)
Marymount Coll, Palos Verdes, California (CA)
Marymount Manhattan Coll (NY)
Marymount U (VA)
Maryville Coll (TN)
Maryville U of Saint Louis (MO)
Marywood U (PA)
Massachusetts Coll of Liberal Arts (MA)
The Master's Coll and Sem (CA)
Mayville State U (ND)
McDaniel Coll (MD)
McKendree U (IL)
McMurry U (TX)
McNeese State U (LA)
McPherson Coll (KS)
Medaille Coll (NY)
Menlo Coll (CA)
Mercy Coll (NY)
Meredith Coll (NC)
Merrimack Coll (MA)
Messiah Coll (PA)
Metropolitan State Coll of Denver (CO)
Metropolitan State U (MN)
Miami U (OH)
Michigan State U (MI)
Michigan Technological U (MI)
MidAmerica Nazarene U (KS)
Mid-Continent U (KY)
Middle Tennessee State U (TN)
Millersville U of Pennsylvania (PA)
Milligan Coll (TN)
Millikin U (IL)
Millsaps Coll (MS)
Milwaukee School of Eng (WI)
Minnesota School of Business–Blaine (MN)
Minnesota School of Business–Brooklyn Center (MN)
Minnesota School of Business–Elk River (MN)
Minnesota School of Business–Lakeville (MN)
Minnesota School of Business–Plymouth (MN)
Minnesota School of Business–Richfield (MN)
Minnesota School of Business–Rochester (MN)
Minnesota School of Business–St. Cloud (MN)
Minnesota School of Business–Shakopee (MN)
Minnesota State U Mankato (MN)
Minnesota State U Moorhead (MN)
Minot State U (ND)
Misericordia U (PA)
Mississippi Coll (MS)
Mississippi State U (MS)
Mississippi U for Women (MS)
Mississippi Valley State U (MS)
Missouri Baptist U (MO)
Missouri State U (MO)
Missouri U of Science and Technology (MO)
Missouri Western State U (MO)
Mitchell Coll (CT)
Molloy Coll (NY)
Monmouth Coll (IL)
Monmouth U (NJ)
Montana State U Billings (MT)
Montana State U–Northern (MT)
Montclair State U (NJ)
Montreat Coll, Montreat (NC)
Moravian Coll (PA)
Morehead State U (KY)
Morehouse Coll (GA)
Morningside Coll (IA)
Morris Coll (SC)
Morrisville State Coll (NY)
Mount Allison U (NB, Canada)
Mount Aloysius Coll (PA)
Mount Ida Coll (MA)
Mount Marty Coll (SD)
Mount Mercy U (IA)
Mount Saint Mary Coll (NY)
Mount Vernon Nazarene U (OH)

Muhlenberg Coll (PA)
National-Louis U (IL)
National U (CA)
Nazareth Coll of Rochester (NY)
Nebraska Wesleyan U (NE)
Neumann U (PA)
Newberry Coll (SC)
Newbury Coll (MA)
New England Coll (NH)
New England Inst of Technology (RI)
New Jersey City U (NJ)
Newman U (KS)
New Mexico Highlands U (NM)
New Mexico Inst of Mining and Technology (NM)
New Mexico State U (NM)
Niagara U (NY)
Nicholls State U (LA)
Nichols Coll (MA)
North Carolina Ag and Tech State U (NC)
North Carolina Central U (NC)
North Carolina State U (NC)
North Carolina Wesleyan Coll (NC)
North Central Coll (IL)
Northcentral U (AZ)
North Dakota State U (ND)
Northeastern Illinois U (IL)
Northeastern State U (OK)
Northeastern U (MA)
Northern Arizona U (AZ)
Northern Illinois U (IL)
Northern Kentucky U (KY)
Northern Michigan U (MI)
North Georgia Coll & State U (GA)
North Greenville U (SC)
Northland Coll (WI)
Northwestern Coll (IA)
Northwestern Coll (MN)
Northwestern Oklahoma State U (OK)
Northwestern State U of Louisiana (LA)
Northwest Missouri State U (MO)
Northwest Nazarene U (ID)
Northwest U (WA)
Northwood U, Florida Campus (FL)
Northwood U, Michigan Campus (MI)
Northwood U, Texas Campus (TX)
Norwich U (VT)
Notre Dame de Namur U (CA)
Notre Dame of Maryland U (MD)
Nova Southeastern U (FL)
Nyack Coll (NY)
Oakland City U (IN)
Oglethorpe U (GA)
Ohio Northern U (OH)
The Ohio State U (OH)
The Ohio State U at Lima (OH)
The Ohio State U at Marion (OH)
The Ohio State U–Mansfield Campus (OH)
The Ohio State U–Newark Campus (OH)
Ohio U (OH)
Ohio Valley U (WV)
Ohio Wesleyan U (OH)
Okanagan Coll (BC, Canada)
Oklahoma Christian U (OK)
Oklahoma City U (OK)
Oklahoma State U (OK)
Old Dominion U (VA)
Oral Roberts U (OK)
Oregon Inst of Technology (OR)
Otterbein U (OH)
Ouachita Baptist U (AR)
Pace U (NY)
Pacific Lutheran U (WA)
Pacific States U (CA)
Pacific U (OR)
Paine Coll (GA)
Palm Beach Atlantic U (FL)
Palm Beach State Coll (FL)
Park U (MO)
Peirce Coll (PA)
Penn State Beaver (PA)
Penn State Brandywine (PA)
Penn State DuBois (PA)
Penn State Erie, The Behrend Coll (PA)
Penn State Fayette, The Eberly Campus (PA)
Penn State Greater Allegheny (PA)

Penn State Harrisburg (PA)
Penn State Hazleton (PA)
Penn State Mont Alto (PA)
Penn State New Kensington (PA)
Penn State Shenango (PA)
Penn State Wilkes-Barre (PA)
Penn State Worthington Scranton (PA)
Penn State York (PA)
Pennsylvania Coll of Technology (PA)
Pepperdine U, Malibu (CA)
Peru State Coll (NE)
Philadelphia Biblical U (PA)
Philadelphia U (PA)
Philander Smith Coll (AR)
Piedmont Coll (GA)
Pittsburg State U (KS)
Plymouth State U (NH)
Point Loma Nazarene U (CA)
Point Park U (PA)
Point U (GA)
Polytechnic U of Puerto Rico (PR)
Portland State U (OR)
Post U (CT)
Potomac Coll (DC)
Prairie View A&M U (TX)
Presbyterian Coll (SC)
Prescott Coll (AZ)
Providence Coll (RI)
Purdue U (IN)
Purdue U Calumet (IN)
Queens U of Charlotte (NC)
Quincy U (IL)
Quinnipiac U (CT)
Radford U (VA)
Ramapo Coll of New Jersey (NJ)
Rasmussen Coll Bismarck (ND)
Rasmussen Coll Bloomington (MN)
Rasmussen Coll Brooklyn Park (MN)
Rasmussen Coll Eagan (MN)
Rasmussen Coll Fargo (ND)
Rasmussen Coll Fort Myers (FL)
Rasmussen Coll Lake Elmo/Woodbury (MN)
Rasmussen Coll Land O' Lakes (FL)
Rasmussen Coll Mankato (MN)
Rasmussen Coll Moorhead (MN)
Rasmussen Coll New Port Richey (FL)
Rasmussen Coll Ocala (FL)
Rasmussen Coll Rockford (IL)
Rasmussen Coll St. Cloud (MN)
Rasmussen Coll Tampa/Brandon (FL)
Regent U (VA)
Regis U (CO)
Reinhardt U (GA)
Rensselaer Polytechnic Inst (NY)
Rhode Island Coll (RI)
Rhodes Coll (TN)
Rice U (TX)
The Richard Stockton Coll of New Jersey (NJ)
Rider U (NJ)
Ripon Coll (WI)
Rivier Coll (NH)
Roanoke Coll (VA)
Robert Morris U (PA)
Robert Morris U Illinois (IL)
Roberts Wesleyan Coll (NY)
Rochester Inst of Technology (NY)
Rockford Coll (IL)
Rockhurst U (MO)
Rocky Mountain Coll (MT)
Rogers State U (OK)
Roger Williams U (RI)
Rosemont Coll (PA)
Rowan U (NJ)
Rust Coll (MS)
Rutgers, The State U of New Jersey, Camden (NJ)
Rutgers, The State U of New Jersey, Newark (NJ)
Rutgers, The State U of New Jersey, New Brunswick (NJ)
Ryerson U (ON, Canada)
Saginaw Valley State U (MI)
St. Ambrose U (IA)
St. Andrews U (NC)
Saint Augustine's Coll (NC)
St. Bonaventure U (NY)
St. Catherine U (MN)

St. Edward's U (TX)
Saint Francis U (PA)
St. John Fisher Coll (NY)
Saint John's U (MN)
St. Joseph's Coll, Long Island Campus (NY)
St. Joseph's Coll, New York (NY)
Saint Joseph's Coll of Maine (ME)
Saint Joseph's U (PA)
Saint Leo U (FL)
Saint Louis U (MO)
Saint Martin's U (WA)
Saint Mary-of-the-Woods Coll (IN)
Saint Mary's Coll (IN)
Saint Mary's Coll of California (CA)
St. Mary's U (TX)
Saint Michael's Coll (VT)
St. Norbert Coll (WI)
Saint Peter's Coll (NJ)
St. Thomas Aquinas Coll (NY)
St. Thomas U (FL)
Saint Vincent Coll (PA)
Salem State U (MA)
Salisbury U (MD)
Salve Regina U (RI)
Samford U (AL)
Sam Houston State U (TX)
San Diego Christian Coll (CA)
San Diego State U (CA)
San Francisco State U (CA)
Schreiner U (TX)
Seattle Pacific U (WA)
Seattle U (WA)
Seminole State Coll of Florida (FL)
Seton Hill U (PA)
Shawnee State U (OH)
Shaw U (NC)
Shenandoah U (VA)
Shepherd U (WV)
Shippensburg U of Pennsylvania (PA)
Shorter U (GA)
Siena Heights U (MI)
Sierra Nevada Coll (NV)
Simmons Coll (MA)
Simon Fraser U (BC, Canada)
Simpson Coll (IA)
Simpson U (CA)
Slippery Rock U of Pennsylvania (PA)
Sojourner-Douglass Coll (MD)
Sonoma State U (CA)
South Carolina State U (SC)
Southeastern Louisiana U (LA)
Southeastern Oklahoma State U (OK)
Southeastern U (FL)
Southeast Missouri State U (MO)
Southern Arkansas U–Magnolia (AR)
Southern Connecticut State U (CT)
Southern Illinois U Carbondale (IL)
Southern Illinois U Edwardsville (IL)
Southern Methodist U (TX)
Southern New Hampshire U (NH)
Southern Oregon U (OR)
Southern Vermont Coll (VT)
South U (AL)
South U, Royal Palm Beach (FL)
South U, Tampa (FL)
South U (GA)
South U (MI)
South U, Columbia (SC)
South U (TX)
South U, Glen Allen (VA)
South U, Virginia Beach (VA)
Southwest Baptist U (MO)
Southwestern Adventist U (TX)
Southwestern Assemblies of God U (TX)
Southwestern Christian U (OK)
Southwestern Coll (KS)
Southwestern Oklahoma State U (OK)
Southwest Minnesota State U (MN)
Spring Arbor U (MI)
Spring Hill Coll (AL)
State U of New York at Binghamton (NY)
State U of New York at Fredonia (NY)
State U of New York at New Paltz (NY)
State U of New York at Oswego (NY)

State U of New York at Plattsburgh (NY)
State U of New York Coll at Geneseo (NY)
State U of New York Coll at Old Westbury (NY)
State U of New York Coll at Potsdam (NY)
State U of New York Empire State Coll (NY)
Stephen F. Austin State U (TX)
Stephens Coll (MO)
Sterling Coll (KS)
Stetson U (FL)
Stevens Inst of Business & Arts (MO)
Stevens Inst of Technology (NJ)
Stevenson U (MD)
Stillman Coll (AL)
Stonehill Coll (MA)
Stony Brook U, State U of New York (NY)
Suffolk U (MA)
Sullivan U (KY)
Sul Ross State U (TX)
Susquehanna U (PA)
Syracuse U (NY)
Tarleton State U (TX)
Taylor U (IN)
Temple U (PA)
Texas A&M Intl U (TX)
Texas A&M U (TX)
Texas A&M U–Corpus Christi (TX)
Texas A&M U–Kingsville (TX)
Texas Coll (TX)
Texas Lutheran U (TX)
Texas Southern U (TX)
Texas State U–San Marcos (TX)
Texas Tech U (TX)
Texas Wesleyan U (TX)
Texas Woman's U (TX)
Thiel Coll (PA)
Thomas Edison State Coll (NJ)
Thomas More Coll (KY)
Thomas U (GA)
Thompson Rivers U (BC, Canada)
Tiffin U (OH)
Touro Coll (NY)
Towson U (MD)
Trent U (ON, Canada)
Trevecca Nazarene U (TN)
Trident U Intl (CA)
Trine U (IN)
Trinity Christian Coll (IL)
Trinity Lutheran Coll (WA)
Trinity U (TX)
Troy U (AL)
Truett-McConnell Coll (GA)
Truman State U (MO)
Tusculum Coll (TN)
Tuskegee U (AL)
Union Coll (KY)
Union Coll (NE)
Union Inst & U (OH)
Union U (TN)
United States Air Force Acad (CO)
United States Intl U (Kenya)
United States Military Acad (NY)
Universidad del Turabo (PR)
Université de Sherbrooke (QC, Canada)
U at Albany, State U of New York (NY)
U at Buffalo, the State U of New York (NY)
The U of Akron (OH)
The U of Alabama (AL)
The U of Alabama at Birmingham (AL)
The U of Alabama in Huntsville (AL)
U of Alaska Anchorage (AK)
U of Alaska Fairbanks (AK)
U of Alberta (AB, Canada)
U of Arkansas (AR)
U of Arkansas at Little Rock (AR)
U of Arkansas at Monticello (AR)
U of Arkansas–Fort Smith (AR)
The U of British Columbia (BC, Canada)
U of California, Berkeley (CA)
U of California, Irvine (CA)
U of California, Merced (CA)
U of California, Riverside (CA)
U of Central Arkansas (AR)

U of Central Florida (FL)
U of Central Missouri (MO)
U of Charleston (WV)
U of Cincinnati (OH)
U of Colorado at Colorado Springs (CO)
U of Colorado Boulder (CO)
U of Colorado Denver (CO)
U of Dallas (TX)
U of Dayton (OH)
U of Denver (CO)
U of Dubuque (IA)
U of Evansville (IN)
The U of Findlay (OH)
U of Florida (FL)
U of Georgia (GA)
U of Great Falls (MT)
U of Guam (GU)
U of Hartford (CT)
U of Hawaii at Hilo (HI)
U of Hawaii at Manoa (HI)
U of Hawaii–West Oahu (HI)
U of Houston (TX)
U of Houston–Clear Lake (TX)
U of Houston–Downtown (TX)
U of Houston–Victoria (TX)
U of Idaho (ID)
U of Illinois at Chicago (IL)
U of Illinois at Springfield (IL)
U of Illinois at Urbana–Champaign (IL)
The U of Iowa (IA)
The U of Kansas (KS)
U of La Verne (CA)
U of Lethbridge (AB, Canada)
U of Louisiana at Lafayette (LA)
U of Maine (ME)
U of Maine at Augusta (ME)
U of Maine at Fort Kent (ME)
U of Maine at Presque Isle (ME)
U of Mary (ND)
U of Mary Hardin-Baylor (TX)
U of Maryland Eastern Shore (MD)
U of Maryland U Coll (MD)
U of Mary Washington (VA)
U of Massachusetts Amherst (MA)
U of Massachusetts Boston (MA)
U of Massachusetts Lowell (MA)
U of Memphis (TN)
U of Miami (FL)
U of Michigan (MI)
U of Michigan–Dearborn (MI)
U of Michigan–Flint (MI)
U of Minnesota, Crookston (MN)
U of Minnesota, Duluth (MN)
U of Minnesota, Twin Cities Campus (MN)
U of Mississippi (MS)
U of Missouri (MO)
U of Missouri–Kansas City (MO)
U of Missouri–St. Louis (MO)
U of Mobile (AL)
The U of Montana Western (MT)
U of Mount Union (OH)
U of Nebraska at Kearney (NE)
U of Nebraska at Omaha (NE)
U of Nebraska–Lincoln (NE)
U of Nevada, Las Vegas (NV)
U of Nevada, Reno (NV)
U of New England (ME)
U of New Hampshire (NH)
U of New Hampshire at Manchester (NH)
U of New Haven (CT)
U of New Mexico (NM)
U of New Orleans (LA)
U of North Alabama (AL)
The U of North Carolina at Asheville (NC)
The U of North Carolina at Chapel Hill (NC)
The U of North Carolina at Charlotte (NC)
The U of North Carolina Wilmington (NC)
U of North Dakota (ND)
U of Northern Colorado (CO)
U of Northern Iowa (IA)
U of North Florida (FL)
U of Oklahoma (OK)
U of Pennsylvania (PA)
U of Pikeville (KY)
U of Pittsburgh at Bradford (PA)
U of Pittsburgh at Greensburg (PA)
U of Pittsburgh at Johnstown (PA)

U of Portland (OR)
U of Puerto Rico at Humacao (PR)
U of Puget Sound (WA)
U of Redlands (CA)
U of Regina (SK, Canada)
U of Rhode Island (RI)
U of Richmond (VA)
U of Rio Grande (OH)
U of St. Francis (IL)
U of Saint Francis (IN)
U of Saint Joseph (CT)
U of Saint Mary (KS)
U of St. Thomas (MN)
U of St. Thomas (TX)
U of San Diego (CA)
The U of Scranton (PA)
U of South Alabama (AL)
U of South Carolina (SC)
U of South Carolina Aiken (SC)
U of South Carolina Beaufort (SC)
U of South Carolina Upstate (SC)
U of Southern California (CA)
U of Southern Indiana (IN)
U of Southern Maine (ME)
U of Southern Mississippi (MS)
The U of Tampa (FL)
The U of Tennessee (TN)
The U of Tennessee at Chattanooga (TN)
The U of Tennessee at Martin (TN)
The U of Texas at Arlington (TX)
The U of Texas at Austin (TX)
The U of Texas at El Paso (TX)
The U of Texas at San Antonio (TX)
The U of Texas at Tyler (TX)
The U of Texas of the Permian Basin (TX)
The U of Texas–Pan American (TX)
U of the District of Columbia (DC)
U of the Incarnate Word (TX)
U of the Ozarks (AR)
U of the Pacific (CA)
U of the Southwest (NM)
The U of Toledo (OH)
U of Toronto (ON, Canada)
U of Tulsa (OK)
U of Utah (UT)
U of Vermont (VT)
The U of Virginia's Coll at Wise (VA)
U of Washington (WA)
U of Washington, Bothell (WA)
The U of West Alabama (AL)
The U of Western Ontario (ON, Canada)
U of West Florida (FL)
U of West Georgia (GA)
U of Windsor (ON, Canada)
U of Wisconsin–Eau Claire (WI)
U of Wisconsin–Green Bay (WI)
U of Wisconsin–La Crosse (WI)
U of Wisconsin–Madison (WI)
U of Wisconsin–Platteville (WI)
U of Wisconsin–River Falls (WI)
U of Wisconsin–Stevens Point (WI)
U of Wisconsin–Stout (WI)
U of Wisconsin–Superior (WI)
U of Wisconsin–Whitewater (WI)
U of Wyoming (WY)
Upper Iowa U (IA)
Ursuline Coll (OH)
Utah State U (UT)
Utah Valley U (UT)
Utica Coll (NY)
Valdosta State U (GA)
Valley City State U (ND)
Valley Forge Christian Coll Woodbridge Campus (VA)
Vanguard U of Southern California (CA)
Vermont Tech Coll (VT)
Villanova U (PA)
Virginia Commonwealth U (VA)
Virginia Intermont Coll (VA)
Virginia Polytechnic Inst and State U (VA)
Virginia State U (VA)
Virginia Wesleyan Coll (VA)
Viterbo U (WI)
Wagner Coll (NY)
Walden U (MN)
Waldorf Coll (IA)
Walsh U (OH)
Warren Wilson Coll (NC)
Wartburg Coll (IA)
Washburn U (KS)

Washington Adventist U (MD)
Washington and Lee U (VA)
Washington Coll (MD)
Washington State U (WA)
Washington U in St. Louis (MO)
Wayland Baptist U (TX)
Waynesburg U (PA)
Wayne State Coll (NE)
Webber Intl U (FL)
Weber State U (UT)
Webster U (MO)
Wells Coll (NY)
Wesleyan Coll (GA)
West Chester U of Pennsylvania (PA)
Western Carolina U (NC)
Western Connecticut State U (CT)
Western Illinois U (IL)
Western Intl U (AZ)
Western Kentucky U (KY)
Western Michigan U (MI)
Western New England U (MA)
Western State Coll of Colorado (CO)
Western Washington U (WA)
Westfield State U (MA)
West Liberty U (WV)
Westminster Coll (MO)
West Texas A&M U (TX)
West Virginia State U (WV)
West Virginia U (WV)
West Virginia U Inst of Technology (WV)
West Virginia Wesleyan Coll (WV)
Wheeling Jesuit U (WV)
Whittier Coll (CA)
Wichita State U (KS)
Widener U (PA)
Wilkes U (PA)
William Jessup U (CA)
William Jewell Coll (MO)
William Paterson U of New Jersey (NJ)
William Penn U (IA)
Williams Baptist Coll (AR)
William Woods U (MO)
Wilmington Coll (OH)
Wilmington U (DE)
Wilson Coll (PA)
Wingate U (NC)
Winona State U (MN)
Winthrop U (SC)
Wittenberg U (OH)
Woodbury U (CA)
Worcester Polytechnic Inst (MA)
Worcester State U (MA)
Wright State U (OH)
Xavier U (OH)
Xavier U of Louisiana (LA)
Yeshiva U (NY)
York Coll of Pennsylvania (PA)
York Coll of the City U of New York (NY)
Youngstown State U (OH)

BUSINESS ADMINISTRATION, MANAGEMENT AND OPERATIONS RELATED

Adams State Coll (CO)
Albany State U (GA)
Alverno Coll (WI)
Anna Maria Coll (MA)
Babson Coll (MA)
Becker Coll (MA)
Benedictine U (IL)
Bethel U (TN)
Blackburn Coll (IL)
Bowling Green State U (OH)
Bradley U (IL)
California Polytechnic State U, San Luis Obispo (CA)
California State U, Chico (CA)
Capella U (MN)
Capital U (OH)
Carlos Albizu U, Miami Campus (FL)
Clayton State U (GA)
Colorado Mesa U (CO)
Cornerstone U (MI)
Crown Coll (MN)
Delaware State U (DE)
DePaul U (IL)
DeVry Coll of New York (NY)
DeVry U, Phoenix (AZ)

DeVry U, Pomona (CA)
DeVry U, Westminster (CO)
DeVry U, Miramar (FL)
DeVry U, Orlando (FL)
DeVry U, Decatur (GA)
DeVry U, Chicago (IL)
DeVry U, Kansas City (MO)
DeVry U, North Brunswick (NJ)
DeVry U, Columbus (OH)
DeVry U, Fort Washington (PA)
DeVry U, Houston (TX)
DeVry U, Irving (TX)
DeVry U, Arlington (VA)
DeVry U, Federal Way (WA)
DeVry U Online (IL)
Dominican U of California (CA)
Eastern New Mexico U (NM)
Eastern Oregon U (OR)
Elizabethtown Coll (PA)
Embry-Riddle Aeronautical U–
  Daytona (FL)
Embry-Riddle Aeronautical U–
  Prescott (AZ)
Embry-Riddle Aeronautical U–
  Worldwide (FL)
Florida Inst of Technology (FL)
Florida State Coll at Jacksonville
  (FL)
Franklin U (OH)
Gettysburg Coll (PA)
Grace Coll (IN)
Hodges U (FL)
Hofstra U (NY)
Howard Payne U (TX)
Huntingdon Coll (AL)
Illinois Inst of Technology (IL)
Indiana Tech (IN)
John Brown U (AR)
Judson U (IL)
Kettering U (MI)
La Roche Coll (PA)
Le Moyne Coll (NY)
Limestone Coll (SC)
Lincoln Christian U (IL)
Macon State Coll (GA)
Malone U (OH)
Marquette U (WI)
Mayville State U (ND)
Miami Dade Coll (FL)
Millikin U (IL)
Missouri Baptist U (MO)
Missouri State U (MO)
Morris Coll (SC)
Mountain State U (WV)
North Dakota State U (ND)
Northwest Christian U (OR)
Oakland City U (IN)
Ohio Northern U (OH)
Pennsylvania Coll of Technology
  (PA)
Pensacola State Coll (FL)
Polk State Coll (FL)
Prescott Coll (AZ)
Purdue U (IN)
Rider U (NJ)
Roosevelt U (IL)
Saint Mary-of-the-Woods Coll (IN)
Samford U (AL)
Stony Brook U, State U of New York
  (NY)
Texas A&M U–Kingsville (TX)
Texas Christian U (TX)
Texas Tech U (TX)
Towson U (MD)
Trinity Christian Coll (IL)
The U of Alabama at Birmingham
  (AL)
U of Charleston (WV)
U of Houston–Clear Lake (TX)
U of Illinois at Springfield (IL)
U of Louisville (KY)
U of Mary (ND)
U of Maryland, Baltimore County
  (MD)
U of Maryland U Coll (MD)
U of Michigan–Dearborn (MI)
U of Ottawa (ON, Canada)
U of Pennsylvania (PA)
U of Puerto Rico at Bayamón (PR)
U of Puerto Rico at Ponce (PR)
U of St. Thomas (MN)
The U of Scranton (PA)
U of Southern Maine (ME)
U of the Incarnate Word (TX)
The U of Toledo (OH)

The U of Western Ontario (ON,
  Canada)
U of Wisconsin–River Falls (WI)
U of Wyoming (WY)
Ursuline Coll (OH)
Valdosta State U (GA)
Viterbo U (WI)
Washington U in St. Louis (MO)
Widener U (PA)
Woodbury U (CA)

BUSINESS AND PERSONAL/ FINANCIAL SERVICES MARKETING

Oklahoma City U (OK)
Purdue U (IN)

BUSINESS AUTOMATION/ TECHNOLOGY/DATA ENTRY

East Carolina U (NC)
Inter American U of Puerto Rico,
  Bayamón Campus (PR)
Mount Vernon Nazarene U (OH)
Purdue U (IN)
Suffolk U (MA)

BUSINESS/COMMERCE

Adams State Coll (CO)
Alvernia U (PA)
American Coll of Thessaloniki
  (Greece)
American Jewish U (CA)
Anderson U (SC)
Asbury U (KY)
Auburn U Montgomery (AL)
Austin Peay State U (TN)
Avila U (MO)
Baker Coll of Jackson (MI)
Baker U (KS)
Ball State U (IN)
Bayamón Central U (PR)
Baylor U (TX)
Bellarmine U (KY)
Bellevue U (NE)
Bentley U (MA)
Bethel Coll (KS)
Bloomsburg U of Pennsylvania (PA)
Bob Jones U (SC)
Bowling Green State U (OH)
Brandeis U (MA)
Brenau U (GA)
Brescia U (KY)
California Baptist U (CA)
California State U, Dominguez Hills
  (CA)
Cambridge Coll (MA)
Canisius Coll (NY)
Caribbean U (PR)
The Catholic U of America (DC)
Central State U (OH)
Clayton State U (GA)
Coll of Staten Island of the City U of
  New York (NY)
Colorado Mesa U (CO)
Colorado Mountain Coll, Timberline
  Campus (CO)
Columbia Centro Universitario,
  Caguas (PR)
Columbia Coll (MO)
Columbus State U (GA)
Concordia U, Nebraska (NE)
Concordia U Texas (TX)
Covenant Coll (GA)
Dalhousie U (NS, Canada)
Davenport U, Grand Rapids (MI)
Delta State U (MS)
DeVry U, Phoenix (AZ)
DeVry U, Pomona (CA)
DeVry U, Westminster (CO)
DeVry U, Miramar (FL)
DeVry U, Orlando (FL)
DeVry U, Decatur (GA)
DeVry U, Chicago (IL)
DeVry U, Kansas City (MO)
DeVry U, Fort Washington (PA)
DeVry U, Houston (TX)
DeVry U, Irving (TX)
DeVry U, Arlington (VA)
DeVry U, Federal Way (WA)
DeVry U Online (IL)
Drake U (IA)
Drexel U (PA)
Earlham Coll (IN)
East Central U (OK)

Eastern Connecticut State U (CT)
Eastern Kentucky U (KY)
Eastern Michigan U (MI)
Eastern Oregon U (OR)
East Texas Baptist U (TX)
Edgewood Coll (WI)
Florida State U (FL)
Framingham State U (MA)
Franklin Coll (IN)
Franklin U (OH)
Free Will Baptist Bible Coll (TN)
Georgia Coll & State U (GA)
Georgia Gwinnett Coll (GA)
Glenville State Coll (WV)
Goshen Coll (IN)
Grace Coll (IN)
Grand Valley State U (MI)
Hawai`i Pacific U (HI)
HEC Montreal (QC, Canada)
Hillsdale Free Will Baptist Coll (OK)
Hofstra U (NY)
Hollins U (VA)
Howard Payne U (TX)
Huntingdon Coll (AL)
Idaho State U (ID)
Indiana U Bloomington (IN)
Indiana U East (IN)
Indiana U Kokomo (IN)
Indiana U Northwest (IN)
Indiana U of Pennsylvania (PA)
Indiana U–Purdue U Fort Wayne
  (IN)
Indiana U–Purdue U Indianapolis
  (IN)
Indiana U South Bend (IN)
Indiana U Southeast (IN)
Iowa Wesleyan Coll (IA)
Ithaca Coll (NY)
Jacksonville U (FL)
The Johns Hopkins U (MD)
Johnson State Coll (VT)
Judson Coll (AL)
Juniata Coll (PA)
Kansas State U (KS)
Kentucky State U (KY)
La Sierra U (CA)
Lewis U (IL)
Liberty U (VA)
Limestone Coll (SC)
Linfield Coll (OR)
Loras Coll (IA)
Lourdes U (OH)
Loyola Marymount U (CA)
Loyola U Maryland (MD)
Manchester Coll (IN)
Maryville Coll (TN)
Maryville U of Saint Louis (MO)
Massachusetts Inst of Technology
  (MA)
McMurry U (TX)
Medgar Evers Coll of the City U of
  New York (NY)
Mercer U (GA)
Midland Coll (TX)
Midwestern State U (TX)
Milwaukee School of Eng (WI)
Mississippi U for Women (MS)
Missouri Southern State U (MO)
Missouri State U (MO)
Montana State U (MT)
Montana State U Billings (MT)
Montana Tech of The U of Montana
  (MT)
Morehead State U (KY)
Mount Allison U (NB, Canada)
Mount Mercy U (IA)
Mount St. Mary's U (MD)
Mount Vernon Nazarene U (OH)
New England Inst of Technology
  (RI)
New Mexico State U (NM)
Niagara U (NY)
Nichols Coll (MA)
Norfolk State U (VA)
Northeastern Illinois U (IL)
Northeastern U (MA)
Northern Illinois U (IL)
Northern Kentucky U (KY)
Northern Michigan U (MI)
Oakland U (MI)
Ohio Northern U (OH)
The Ohio State U at Lima (OH)
The Ohio State U at Marion (OH)
The Ohio State U–Mansfield
  Campus (OH)

The Ohio State U–Newark Campus
  (OH)
Ohio Valley U (WV)
Oklahoma Christian U (OK)
Oklahoma City U (OK)
Pace U (NY)
Pacific Union Coll (CA)
Penn State Abington (PA)
Penn State Altoona (PA)
Penn State Berks (PA)
Penn State Lehigh Valley (PA)
Penn State Schuylkill (PA)
Penn State U Park (PA)
Plymouth State U (NH)
Purdue U (IN)
Queen's U at Kingston (ON,
  Canada)
Randolph Coll (VA)
Regis Coll (MA)
Reinhardt U (GA)
Rhode Island Coll (RI)
Rochester Inst of Technology (NY)
Roosevelt U (IL)
Saginaw Valley State U (MI)
St. Ambrose U (IA)
Saint Anselm Coll (NH)
Saint Joseph's Coll (IN)
Saint Leo U (FL)
Saint Mary's Coll of California (CA)
St. Thomas U (FL)
Saint Vincent Coll (PA)
Saint Xavier U (IL)
Sam Houston State U (TX)
Schreiner U (TX)
Skidmore Coll (NY)
Southern Arkansas U–Magnolia
  (AR)
Southern Methodist U (TX)
Southwestern U (TX)
Spalding U (KY)
Stephen F. Austin State U (TX)
Suffolk U (MA)
Sweet Briar Coll (VA)
Tarleton State U (TX)
Texas A&M U–Kingsville (TX)
Texas Tech U (TX)
Thompson Rivers U (BC, Canada)
Transylvania U (KY)
Trident U Intl (CA)
Trinity Coll of Florida (FL)
Troy U (AL)
The U of Arizona (AZ)
U of Arkansas (AR)
U of Arkansas at Little Rock (AR)
U of Bridgeport (CT)
The U of British Columbia (BC,
  Canada)
U of Central Arkansas (AR)
U of Central Florida (FL)
U of Connecticut (CT)
U of Delaware (DE)
U of Denver (CO)
U of Georgia (GA)
U of Hawaii at Manoa (HI)
U of Houston–Clear Lake (TX)
U of Houston–Downtown (TX)
U of Illinois at Urbana–Champaign
  (IL)
The U of Kansas (KS)
U of Maine (ME)
U of Mary Hardin-Baylor (TX)
U of Maryland, Coll Park (MD)
U of Massachusetts Dartmouth
  (MA)
U of Massachusetts Lowell (MA)
U of Minnesota, Twin Cities
  Campus (MN)
U of Missouri–St. Louis (MO)
U of Nebraska at Omaha (NE)
U of Nevada, Reno (NV)
U of North Texas (TX)
U of Notre Dame (IN)
U of Oregon (OR)
U of Pittsburgh (PA)
U of Redlands (CA)
U of Regina (SK, Canada)
U of Rhode Island (RI)
U of Science and Arts of Oklahoma
  (OK)
U of South Alabama (AL)
The U of South Dakota (SD)
U of Southern Indiana (IN)
U of South Florida (FL)
The U of Texas at Austin (TX)
The U of Texas at Dallas (TX)

The U of Texas at San Antonio (TX)
U of the Cumberlands (KY)
U of the Southwest (NM)
The U of Toledo (OH)
U of Tulsa (OK)
U of Utah (UT)
U of Virginia (VA)
U of Washington (WA)
The U of Western Ontario (ON,
  Canada)
U of West Florida (FL)
U of Windsor (ON, Canada)
U of Wisconsin–Milwaukee (WI)
U of Wisconsin–Whitewater (WI)
Utah State U (UT)
Virginia Commonwealth U (VA)
Wake Forest U (NC)
Washburn U (KS)
Washington & Jefferson Coll (PA)
Washington State U (WA)
Washington U in St. Louis (MO)
Webber Intl U (FL)
Webster U (MO)
West Chester U of Pennsylvania
  (PA)
Western Intl U (AZ)
Western Michigan U (MI)
Western New England U (MA)
Western Oregon U (OR)
Western Washington U (WA)
West Texas A&M U (TX)
Wright State U (OH)
Youngstown State U (OH)

BUSINESS/CORPORATE COMMUNICATIONS

Aquinas Coll (MI)
Augustana Coll (SD)
Babson Coll (MA)
Bentley U (MA)
Calvin Coll (MI)
Chestnut Hill Coll (PA)
Cleary U (MI)
Concordia U Chicago (IL)
Duquesne U (PA)
Elon U (NC)
Fort Hays State U (KS)
Hawai`i Pacific U (HI)
Jones Intl U (CO)
Lycoming Coll (PA)
Marietta Coll (OH)
MidAmerica Nazarene U (KS)
Morningside Coll (IA)
Mount Mary Coll (WI)
Nichols Coll (MA)
North Dakota State U (ND)
Penn State Abington (PA)
Point Loma Nazarene U (CA)
Purdue U (IN)
Rockhurst U (MO)
Roosevelt U (IL)
Saint Leo U (FL)
Stevenson U (MD)
Trinity Christian Coll (IL)
The U of Findlay (OH)
U of Houston (TX)
U of Mary (ND)
U of Rio Grande (OH)
U of St. Thomas (MN)
The U of Western Ontario (ON,
  Canada)
Walsh U (OH)
Western Intl U (AZ)

BUSINESS FAMILY AND CONSUMER SCIENCES/ HUMAN SCIENCES

Brigham Young U (UT)
The Ohio State U (OH)
Purdue U (IN)
U of Houston (TX)
Virginia Polytechnic Inst and State
  U (VA)

BUSINESS, MANAGEMENT, AND MARKETING RELATED

Adelphi U (NY)
American U (DC)
Arizona State U (AZ)
Athens State U (AL)
Baylor U (TX)
Belmont Abbey Coll (NC)
Benedictine U (IL)
Bentley U (MA)

INDEXES

Bowling Green State U (OH)
Bridgewater State U (MA)
California State U, Dominguez Hills (CA)
California State U, Stanislaus (CA)
Claflin U (SC)
Clemson U (SC)
Concordia Coll–New York (NY)
Corban U (OR)
Eastern U (PA)
The Evergreen State Coll (WA)
Farmingdale State Coll (NY)
Franklin Coll Switzerland (Switzerland)
Greenville Coll (IL)
Grove City Coll (PA)
Howard Payne U (TX)
Inter American U of Puerto Rico, Bayamón Campus (PR)
Loyola U Chicago (IL)
Mercy Coll (NY)
Mercyhurst Coll (PA)
Messiah Coll (PA)
Missouri U of Science and Technology (MO)
Nebraska Wesleyan U (NE)
New York U (NY)
Old Dominion U (VA)
Park U (MO)
Penn State U Park (PA)
Peru State Coll (NE)
Point Park U (PA)
Presentation Coll (SD)
Purdue U (IN)
Purdue U North Central (IN)
Queens U of Charlotte (NC)
Roger Williams U (RI)
Sacred Heart U (CT)
Saint Mary's U of Minnesota (MN)
Seton Hill U (PA)
Sierra Nevada Coll (NV)
Skidmore Coll (NY)
Southeastern U (FL)
Southern New Hampshire U (NH)
State U of New York at Plattsburgh (NY)
State U of New York Coll of Technology at Alfred (NY)
State U of New York Coll of Technology at Canton (NY)
State U of New York Maritime Coll (NY)
Texas Wesleyan U (TX)
Trevecca Nazarene U (TN)
Troy U (AL)
U of Louisiana at Lafayette (LA)
U of Minnesota, Crookston (MN)
U of the Southwest (NM)
The U of Toledo (OH)
The U of Western Ontario (ON, Canada)
U of Wisconsin–Stout (WI)
Utica Coll (NY)
Wentworth Inst of Technology (MA)
Western State Coll of Colorado (CO)
West Virginia U Inst of Technology (WV)

BUSINESS/MANAGERIAL ECONOMICS

Allegheny Coll (PA)
Anderson U (IN)
Andrews U (MI)
Arcadia U (PA)
Arkansas State U (AR)
Arkansas Tech U (AR)
Auburn U (AL)
Auburn U Montgomery (AL)
Ball State U (IN)
Bard Coll (NY)
Baylor U (TX)
Belmont U (TN)
Beloit Coll (WI)
Benedictine U (IL)
Bentley U (MA)
Bernard M. Baruch Coll of the City U of New York (NY)
Bethany Coll (KS)
Bethany Coll (WV)
Bishop's U (QC, Canada)
Boise State U (ID)
Boston Coll (MA)
Bradley U (IL)
Buena Vista U (IA)

California Inst of Technology (CA)
California State U, East Bay (CA)
California State U, Fullerton (CA)
California State U, Long Beach (CA)
California State U, San Bernardino (CA)
Campbellsville U (KY)
Canisius Coll (NY)
Capital U (OH)
Cardinal Stritch U (WI)
Carnegie Mellon U (PA)
Carson-Newman Coll (TN)
Catawba Coll (NC)
Chapman U (CA)
Chatham U (PA)
Clarion U of Pennsylvania (PA)
Clark Atlanta U (GA)
Cleveland State U (OH)
Coastal Carolina U (SC)
Coll of Mount Saint Vincent (NY)
Coll of the Ozarks (MO)
The Coll of Wooster (OH)
Converse Coll (SC)
Dallas Baptist U (TX)
Delaware State U (DE)
DePaul U (IL)
Drexel U (PA)
Duquesne U (PA)
Eastern Kentucky U (KY)
Eastern Michigan U (MI)
Eastern Washington U (WA)
East Tennessee State U (TN)
Elizabethtown Coll (PA)
Elmira Coll (NY)
Emory U (GA)
Fordham U (NY)
Fort Hays State U (KS)
Fort Lewis Coll (CO)
The George Washington U (DC)
Georgia Coll & State U (GA)
Georgia Inst of Technology (GA)
Georgia Southern U (GA)
Georgia State U (GA)
Gonzaga U (WA)
Grambling State U (LA)
Grand Valley State U (MI)
Grove City Coll (PA)
Gustavus Adolphus Coll (MN)
Hampden-Sydney Coll (VA)
HEC Montreal (QC, Canada)
Hofstra U (NY)
Hope Coll (MI)
Huntington U (IN)
Illinois Coll (IL)
Indiana U–Purdue U Fort Wayne (IN)
Inter American U of Puerto Rico, Bayamón Campus (PR)
Inter American U of Puerto Rico, San Germán Campus (PR)
Ithaca Coll (NY)
James Madison U (VA)
Kalamazoo Coll (MI)
Kennesaw State U (GA)
Kent State U (OH)
Lafayette Coll (PA)
Lake Forest Coll (IL)
Lake Superior State U (MI)
La Salle U (PA)
Lehigh U (PA)
Lewis U (IL)
Limestone Coll (SC)
Lincoln Memorial U (TN)
Lipscomb U (TN)
Louisiana State U and Ag and Mech Coll (LA)
Louisiana State U in Shreveport (LA)
Loyola U Chicago (IL)
Loyola U New Orleans (LA)
Marquette U (WI)
Marshall U (WV)
Mars Hill Coll (NC)
Messiah Coll (PA)
Miami U (OH)
Michigan Technological U (MI)
Middle Tennessee State U (TN)
Midwestern State U (TX)
Mills Coll (CA)
Mississippi State U (MS)
Montana State U Billings (MT)
Morehead State U (KY)
Mount Allison U (NB, Canada)
New York U (NY)

Niagara U (NY)
Nichols Coll (MA)
North Carolina State U (NC)
Northern Arizona U (AZ)
Northern Kentucky U (KY)
Northern State U (SD)
Northwest Missouri State U (MO)
Northwood U, Florida Campus (FL)
Oakland U (MI)
Oglethorpe U (GA)
The Ohio State U (OH)
The Ohio State U at Lima (OH)
The Ohio State U at Marion (OH)
The Ohio State U–Mansfield Campus (OH)
The Ohio State U–Newark Campus (OH)
Ohio U (OH)
Ohio Wesleyan U (OH)
Oklahoma City U (OK)
Oklahoma State U (OK)
Old Dominion U (VA)
Otterbein U (OH)
Park U (MO)
Penn State Abington (PA)
Penn State Altoona (PA)
Penn State Beaver (PA)
Penn State Berks (PA)
Penn State Brandywine (PA)
Penn State DuBois (PA)
Penn State Erie, The Behrend Coll (PA)
Penn State Fayette, The Eberly Campus (PA)
Penn State Greater Allegheny (PA)
Penn State Hazleton (PA)
Penn State Lehigh Valley (PA)
Penn State Mont Alto (PA)
Penn State New Kensington (PA)
Penn State Schuylkill (PA)
Penn State Shenango (PA)
Penn State Wilkes-Barre (PA)
Penn State Worthington Scranton (PA)
Penn State York (PA)
Presbyterian Coll (SC)
Purdue U (IN)
Quinnipiac U (CT)
Randolph-Macon Coll (VA)
Rhode Island Coll (RI)
Rider U (NJ)
Sacred Heart U (CT)
Saginaw Valley State U (MI)
Saint Anselm Coll (NH)
Saint Louis U (MO)
Saint Peter's Coll (NJ)
Samford U (AL)
Sam Houston State U (TX)
Seattle U (WA)
Shorter U (GA)
Sonoma State U (CA)
South Carolina State U (SC)
Southern Connecticut State U (CT)
Southern Illinois U Carbondale (IL)
Southern Illinois U Edwardsville (IL)
Spring Hill Coll (AL)
State U of New York at Plattsburgh (NY)
State U of New York Coll at Oneonta (NY)
State U of New York Coll at Potsdam (NY)
Stephen F. Austin State U (TX)
Stetson U (FL)
Texas A&M Intl U (TX)
Texas State U–San Marcos (TX)
Texas Wesleyan U (TX)
Union U (TN)
The U of Alabama (AL)
The U of Alabama at Birmingham (AL)
U of Alaska Anchorage (AK)
The U of Arizona (AZ)
U of Arkansas (AR)
U of California, Irvine (CA)
U of California, Los Angeles (CA)
U of California, Riverside (CA)
U of California, Santa Cruz (CA)
U of Central Florida (FL)
U of Dayton (OH)
U of Denver (CO)
U of Evansville (IN)
U of Georgia (GA)
U of Guelph (ON, Canada)
U of Hawaii at Manoa (HI)

U of Idaho (ID)
U of Indianapolis (IN)
The U of Iowa (IA)
U of Lethbridge (AB, Canada)
U of Louisiana at Lafayette (LA)
U of Louisville (KY)
U of Maine at Farmington (ME)
U of Mary Hardin-Baylor (TX)
U of Memphis (TN)
U of Miami (FL)
U of Mississippi (MS)
U of Missouri (MO)
U of Nebraska at Omaha (NE)
U of Nebraska–Lincoln (NE)
U of Nevada, Reno (NV)
U of New Haven (CT)
U of North Alabama (AL)
The U of North Carolina at Charlotte (NC)
The U of North Carolina Wilmington (NC)
U of North Dakota (ND)
U of North Florida (FL)
U of North Texas (TX)
U of Oklahoma (OK)
U of Pittsburgh at Johnstown (PA)
U of Rochester (NY)
U of San Diego (CA)
U of South Carolina (SC)
U of Southern Mississippi (MS)
U of South Florida (FL)
U of South Florida–St. Petersburg Campus (FL)
The U of Tennessee (TN)
The U of Tennessee at Martin (TN)
The U of Texas at Arlington (TX)
The U of Texas at San Antonio (TX)
The U of Texas of the Permian Basin (TX)
U of the Incarnate Word (TX)
The U of Toledo (OH)
The U of Western Ontario (ON, Canada)
U of West Florida (FL)
U of West Georgia (GA)
U of Windsor (ON, Canada)
U of Wisconsin–Platteville (WI)
U of Wisconsin–Superior (WI)
U of Wisconsin–Whitewater (WI)
U of Wyoming (WY)
Utica Coll (NY)
Valdosta State U (GA)
Villanova U (PA)
Virginia Commonwealth U (VA)
Virginia Polytechnic Inst and State U (VA)
Virginia State U (VA)
Washburn U (KS)
Washington U in St. Louis (MO)
Weber State U (UT)
West Chester U of Pennsylvania (PA)
Western Illinois U (IL)
Western Kentucky U (KY)
Western Michigan U (MI)
Western State Coll of Colorado (CO)
West Liberty U (WV)
Westminster Coll (UT)
West Texas A&M U (TX)
West Virginia U (WV)
West Virginia Wesleyan Coll (WV)
Wheaton Coll (IL)
Widener U (PA)
William Paterson U of New Jersey (NJ)
William Woods U (MO)
Wilmington Coll (OH)
Winona State U (MN)
Wofford Coll (SC)
Wright State U (OH)
Xavier U (OH)
Youngstown State U (OH)

BUSINESS OPERATIONS SUPPORT AND SECRETARIAL SERVICES RELATED

Delaware State U (DE)
U of Georgia (GA)

BUSINESS STATISTICS

Baylor U (TX)
Cleveland State U (OH)
Ferris State U (MI)

HEC Montreal (QC, Canada)
Purdue U (IN)
Southern Oregon U (OR)
U of Central Missouri (MO)
U of Denver (CO)
The U of Tennessee (TN)

BUSINESS TEACHER EDUCATION

Adams State Coll (CO)
Alabama State U (AL)
Alfred U (NY)
Appalachian State U (NC)
Arkansas State U (AR)
Arkansas Tech U (AR)
Armstrong Atlantic State U (GA)
Auburn U (AL)
Ball State U (IN)
Baylor U (TX)
Belmont U (TN)
Bethany Coll (KS)
Bethel Coll (IN)
Bethel U (MN)
Bethune-Cookman U (FL)
Black Hills State U (SD)
Bluefield Coll (VA)
Bowling Green State U (OH)
Buena Vista U (IA)
Buffalo State Coll, State U of New York (NY)
California State U, Dominguez Hills (CA)
Calumet Coll of Saint Joseph (IN)
Campbellsville U (KY)
Carson-Newman Coll (TN)
Central Washington U (WA)
Colorado State U (CO)
Concordia Coll (MN)
Concordia U, Nebraska (NE)
Corban U (OR)
Dakota State U (SD)
Delaware State U (DE)
Doane Coll (NE)
Dordt Coll (IA)
Dowling Coll (NY)
East Carolina U (NC)
Eastern Kentucky U (KY)
Eastern Michigan U (MI)
Eastern New Mexico U (NM)
Eastern Washington U (WA)
Edgewood Coll (WI)
Emmanuel Coll (GA)
Evangel U (MO)
Fairmont State U (WV)
Fayetteville State U (NC)
Ferris State U (MI)
Fort Hays State U (KS)
Friends U (KS)
Glenville State Coll (WV)
Grace Coll (IN)
Gwynedd-Mercy Coll (PA)
Hampton U (VA)
Hannibal-LaGrange U (MO)
Hardin-Simmons U (TX)
Hofstra U (NY)
Howard Payne U (TX)
Huntington U (IN)
Illinois State U (IL)
Immaculata U (PA)
Indiana State U (IN)
Jarvis Christian Coll (TX)
John Brown U (AR)
La Salle U (PA)
Lee U (TN)
Lehman Coll of the City U of New York (NY)
Lenoir-Rhyne U (NC)
Liberty U (VA)
Lincoln U (MO)
Lindenwood U (MO)
Louisiana Coll (LA)
Louisiana State U and Ag and Mech Coll (LA)
Maranatha Baptist Bible Coll (WI)
McKendree U (IL)
Mercyhurst Coll (PA)
Michigan Technological U (MI)
MidAmerica Nazarene U (KS)
Middle Tennessee State U (TN)
Minot State U (ND)
Mississippi Coll (MS)
Mississippi State U (MS)
Missouri Baptist U (MO)
Missouri State U (MO)
Montana State U–Northern (MT)

Morehead State U (KY)
Mount Mary Coll (WI)
Mount Vernon Nazarene U (OH)
Nazareth Coll of Rochester (NY)
Niagara U (NY)
Nicholls State U (LA)
Norfolk State U (VA)
North Carolina Ag and Tech State U (NC)
Northern Kentucky U (KY)
Northwestern Coll (IA)
Northwest Missouri State U (MO)
Oakland City U (IN)
Ohio Wesleyan U (OH)
Oklahoma City U (OK)
Oral Roberts U (OK)
Peru State Coll (NE)
Purdue U (IN)
Rider U (NJ)
Robert Morris U (PA)
Rust Coll (MS)
St. Ambrose U (IA)
Saint Mary's Coll (IN)
Saint Vincent Coll (PA)
Schreiner U (TX)
South Carolina State U (SC)
Southeast Missouri State U (MO)
Southern Arkansas U–Magnolia (AR)
Southern New Hampshire U (NH)
Tabor Coll (KS)
Temple U (PA)
Texas Wesleyan U (TX)
Thomas More Coll (KY)
Trevecca Nazarene U (TN)
Trinity Christian Coll (IL)
Tusculum Coll (TN)
Union Coll (NE)
Union U (TN)
U of Alberta (AB, Canada)
The U of British Columbia (BC, Canada)
U of Central Arkansas (AR)
U of Central Missouri (MO)
The U of Findlay (OH)
U of Illinois at Urbana–Champaign (IL)
U of Indianapolis (IN)
U of Lethbridge (AB, Canada)
U of Maine at Fort Kent (ME)
U of Mary (ND)
U of Mary Hardin-Baylor (TX)
U of Maryland Eastern Shore (MD)
U of Minnesota, Twin Cities Campus (MN)
U of Missouri (MO)
U of Missouri–St. Louis (MO)
The U of Montana Western (MT)
U of Nebraska at Kearney (NE)
U of Nebraska–Lincoln (NE)
U of North Dakota (ND)
U of Northern Iowa (IA)
U of Regina (SK, Canada)
U of Rio Grande (OH)
U of Saint Francis (IN)
U of Southern Indiana (IN)
U of Southern Mississippi (MS)
U of South Florida (FL)
The U of Tennessee at Martin (TN)
The U of Toledo (OH)
U of West Georgia (GA)
U of Wisconsin–Superior (WI)
U of Wisconsin–Whitewater (WI)
Upper Iowa U (IA)
Utah State U (UT)
Utah Valley U (UT)
Utica Coll (NY)
Valley City State U (ND)
Virginia Intermont Coll (VA)
Virginia State U (VA)
Virginia Union U (VA)
Viterbo U (WI)
Wayland Baptist U (TX)
Wayne State Coll (NE)
Weber State U (UT)
Western Kentucky U (KY)
Western Michigan U (MI)
West Virginia State U (WV)
William Penn U (IA)
Wilmington Coll (OH)
Winona State U (MN)
Wright State U (OH)
Youngstown State U (OH)

CAD/CADD DRAFTING/DESIGN TECHNOLOGY
Cameron U (OK)
Eastern Michigan U (MI)

CANADIAN GOVERNMENT AND POLITICS
The U of British Columbia (BC, Canada)

CANADIAN HISTORY
U of Regina (SK, Canada)

CANADIAN STUDIES
Acadia U (NS, Canada)
Athabasca U (AB, Canada)
Bishop's U (QC, Canada)
Dalhousie U (NS, Canada)
Franklin Coll (IN)
Mount Allison U (NB, Canada)
Queen's U at Kingston (ON, Canada)
St. Lawrence U (NY)
Simon Fraser U (BC, Canada)
Thompson Rivers U (BC, Canada)
Trent U (ON, Canada)
U of Alberta (AB, Canada)
The U of British Columbia (BC, Canada)
U of Lethbridge (AB, Canada)
U of Ottawa (ON, Canada)
U of Regina (SK, Canada)
U of Toronto (ON, Canada)
U of Vermont (VT)
U of Washington (WA)
The U of Western Ontario (ON, Canada)
Western Washington U (WA)

CARDIOVASCULAR TECHNOLOGY
Gwynedd-Mercy Coll (PA)
Medical U of South Carolina (SC)
Pennsylvania Coll of Technology (PA)
U of Medicine and Dentistry of New Jersey (NJ)

CARIBBEAN STUDIES
Columbia U, School of General Studies (NY)
Hofstra U (NY)

CASINO MANAGEMENT
Central Michigan U (MI)

CELL AND MOLECULAR BIOLOGY
Adams State Coll (CO)
Bennington Coll (VT)
Bradley U (IL)
Bridgewater State U (MA)
Bucknell U (PA)
Cedarville U (OH)
Christopher Newport U (VA)
The Coll at Brockport, State U of New York (NY)
Concordia U (QC, Canada)
Connecticut Coll (CT)
Florida State U (FL)
Fort Lewis Coll (CO)
Grand Valley State U (MI)
Harvard U (MA)
Missouri State U (MO)
Northwest Nazarene U (ID)
Ohio U (OH)
Oklahoma City U (OK)
Pittsburg State U (KS)
Purdue U (IN)
Salem State U (MA)
State U of New York at Binghamton (NY)
Texas A&M U (TX)
Texas Tech U (TX)
Thompson Rivers U (BC, Canada)
The U of Arizona (AZ)
U of California, Berkeley (CA)
U of California, Los Angeles (CA)
U of Colorado Boulder (CO)
U of Illinois at Urbana–Champaign (IL)
U of Michigan (MI)

The U of Tennessee at Martin (TN)
Western Washington U (WA)

CELL BIOLOGY AND ANATOMICAL SCIENCES RELATED
Purdue U (IN)
Rutgers, The State U of New Jersey, New Brunswick (NJ)
Tulane U (LA)
U of Connecticut (CT)
Washington & Jefferson Coll (PA)
Yale U (CT)

CELL BIOLOGY AND ANATOMY
Huntingdon Coll (AL)
Purdue U (IN)
The U of Western Ontario (ON, Canada)
Western State Coll of Colorado (CO)

CELL BIOLOGY AND HISTOLOGY
Beloit Coll (WI)
California State U, Dominguez Hills (CA)
California State U, Fresno (CA)
California State U, Long Beach (CA)
California State U, San Marcos (CA)
Colby Coll (ME)
The Coll at Brockport, State U of New York (NY)
The Coll of Saint Rose (NY)
Humboldt State U (CA)
Juniata Coll (PA)
Mansfield U of Pennsylvania (PA)
Marlboro Coll (VT)
Montana State U (MT)
Northeastern State U (OK)
Purdue U (IN)
Rutgers, The State U of New Jersey, New Brunswick (NJ)
San Francisco State U (CA)
Sonoma State U (CA)
Thompson Rivers U (BC, Canada)
Tulane U (LA)
U of Alberta (AB, Canada)
The U of British Columbia (BC, Canada)
U of California, Davis (CA)
U of California, Irvine (CA)
U of California, Santa Barbara (CA)
U of California, Santa Cruz (CA)
U of Georgia (GA)
U of Illinois at Urbana–Champaign (IL)
U of Maine (ME)
U of Minnesota, Duluth (MN)
U of Minnesota, Twin Cities Campus (MN)
U of Utah (UT)
U of Washington (WA)
Western Washington U (WA)
Worcester Polytechnic Inst (MA)

CELL PHYSIOLOGY
Purdue U (IN)

CELTIC LANGUAGES
U of California, Berkeley (CA)

CERAMIC ARTS AND CERAMICS
Adams State Coll (CO)
Alberta Coll of Art & Design (AB, Canada)
Alfred U (NY)
Aquinas Coll (MI)
Arcadia U (PA)
Bard Coll at Simon's Rock (MA)
Bennington Coll (VT)
Bethany Coll (KS)
Bowling Green State U (OH)
Bradley U (IL)
Brigham Young U (UT)
California Coll of the Arts (CA)
California State U, East Bay (CA)
California State U, Long Beach (CA)

The Cleveland Inst of Art (OH)
Coe Coll (IA)
The Coll at Brockport, State U of New York (NY)
Coll of the Atlantic (ME)
Columbia Coll (MO)
Concordia U (QC, Canada)
Emily Carr U of Art + Design (BC, Canada)
Hampton U (VA)
Hofstra U (NY)
Indiana Wesleyan U (IN)
Inter American U of Puerto Rico, San Germán Campus (PR)
Kansas City Art Inst (MO)
Marlboro Coll (VT)
Maryland Inst Coll of Art (MD)
Marywood U (PA)
Massachusetts Coll of Art and Design (MA)
Minnesota State U Mankato (MN)
Northern Michigan U (MI)
Northwest Nazarene U (ID)
Ohio Northern U (OH)
Ohio U (OH)
Pittsburg State U (KS)
Pratt Inst (NY)
Providence Coll (RI)
Rochester Inst of Technology (NY)
Rutgers, The State U of New Jersey, New Brunswick (NJ)
Salve Regina U (RI)
School of the Museum of Fine Arts, Boston (MA)
Seton Hill U (PA)
State U of New York at New Paltz (NY)
Syracuse U (NY)
Temple U (PA)
Texas Christian U (TX)
U of Dallas (TX)
U of Hartford (CT)
The U of Iowa (IA)
The U of Kansas (KS)
U of Massachusetts Dartmouth (MA)
U of Miami (FL)
U of Michigan (MI)
U of Oregon (OR)
U of Regina (SK, Canada)
The U of Texas at El Paso (TX)
U of the District of Columbia (DC)
U of Washington (WA)
Virginia Intermont Coll (VA)
Washington U in St. Louis (MO)
Western State Coll of Colorado (CO)
Western Washington U (WA)
West Virginia Wesleyan Coll (WV)

CERAMIC SCIENCES AND ENGINEERING
Alfred U (NY)
Clemson U (SC)
Missouri U of Science and Technology (MO)
Rutgers, The State U of New Jersey, New Brunswick (NJ)
U of Illinois at Urbana–Champaign (IL)
U of Washington (WA)

CHEMICAL AND BIOMOLECULAR ENGINEERING
Massachusetts Inst of Technology (MA)
Milwaukee School of Eng (WI)
Purdue U (IN)

CHEMICAL ENGINEERING
American U of Beirut (Lebanon)
Arizona State U (AZ)
Auburn U (AL)
Brown U (RI)
Bucknell U (PA)
California Inst of Technology (CA)
California State Polytechnic U, Pomona (CA)
California State U, Long Beach (CA)
Calvin Coll (MI)
Carnegie Mellon U (PA)
Case Western Reserve U (OH)

Christian Brothers U (TN)
City Coll of the City U of New York (NY)
Clarkson U (NY)
Clemson U (SC)
Cleveland State U (OH)
Colorado School of Mines (CO)
Colorado State U (CO)
Cooper Union for the Advancement of Science and Art (NY)
Cornell U (NY)
Dalhousie U (NS, Canada)
Drexel U (PA)
Elon U (NC)
Florida Ag and Mech U (FL)
Florida Inst of Technology (FL)
Gannon U (PA)
Georgia Inst of Technology (GA)
Hampton U (VA)
Hope Coll (MI)
Illinois Inst of Technology (IL)
Iowa State U of Science and Technology (IA)
The Johns Hopkins U (MD)
Kansas State U (KS)
Kettering U (MI)
Lafayette Coll (PA)
Lakehead U (ON, Canada)
Lamar U (TX)
Lehigh U (PA)
Louisiana State U and Ag and Mech Coll (LA)
Manhattan Coll (NY)
Massachusetts Inst of Technology (MA)
Miami U (OH)
Michigan State U (MI)
Michigan Technological U (MI)
Mississippi State U (MS)
Missouri U of Science and Technology (MO)
Montana State U (MT)
New Mexico Inst of Mining and Technology (NM)
New Mexico State U (NM)
North Carolina Ag and Tech State U (NC)
North Carolina State U (NC)
Northeastern U (MA)
The Ohio State U (OH)
Ohio U (OH)
Oklahoma State U (OK)
Penn State Abington (PA)
Penn State Altoona (PA)
Penn State Beaver (PA)
Penn State Berks (PA)
Penn State Brandywine (PA)
Penn State DuBois (PA)
Penn State Erie, The Behrend Coll (PA)
Penn State Fayette, The Eberly Campus (PA)
Penn State Greater Allegheny (PA)
Penn State Hazleton (PA)
Penn State Lehigh Valley (PA)
Penn State Mont Alto (PA)
Penn State New Kensington (PA)
Penn State Schuylkill (PA)
Penn State Shenango (PA)
Penn State U Park (PA)
Penn State Wilkes-Barre (PA)
Penn State Worthington Scranton (PA)
Penn State York (PA)
Polytechnic U of Puerto Rico (PR)
Prairie View A&M U (TX)
Princeton U (NJ)
Purdue U (IN)
Queen's U at Kingston (ON, Canada)
Rensselaer Polytechnic Inst (NY)
Rice U (TX)
Rochester Inst of Technology (NY)
Rose-Hulman Inst of Technology (IN)
Rowan U (NJ)
Rutgers, The State U of New Jersey, New Brunswick (NJ)
Ryerson U (ON, Canada)
South Dakota School of Mines and Technology (SD)
Stanford U (CA)
State U of New York Coll of Environmental Science and Forestry (NY)

Stevens Inst of Technology (NJ)
Stony Brook U, State U of New York (NY)
Syracuse U (NY)
Texas A&M U (TX)
Texas Tech U (TX)
Thiel Coll (PA)
Trine U (IN)
Tufts U (MA)
Tulane U (LA)
Tuskegee U (AL)
United States Military Acad (NY)
Université de Sherbrooke (QC, Canada)
U at Buffalo, the State U of New York (NY)
The U of Akron (OH)
The U of Alabama (AL)
The U of Alabama in Huntsville (AL)
U of Alberta (AB, Canada)
The U of Arizona (AZ)
U of Arkansas (AR)
The U of British Columbia (BC, Canada)
U of California, Berkeley (CA)
U of California, Davis (CA)
U of California, Irvine (CA)
U of California, Los Angeles (CA)
U of California, Riverside (CA)
U of California, Santa Barbara (CA)
U of Cincinnati (OH)
U of Colorado Boulder (CO)
U of Connecticut (CT)
U of Dayton (OH)
U of Delaware (DE)
U of Florida (FL)
U of Georgia (GA)
U of Houston (TX)
U of Idaho (ID)
U of Illinois at Chicago (IL)
U of Illinois at Urbana–Champaign (IL)
The U of Iowa (IA)
The U of Kansas (KS)
U of Louisiana at Lafayette (LA)
U of Louisville (KY)
U of Maine (ME)
U of Maryland, Baltimore County (MD)
U of Maryland, Coll Park (MD)
U of Massachusetts Amherst (MA)
U of Massachusetts Lowell (MA)
U of Michigan (MI)
U of Minnesota, Duluth (MN)
U of Minnesota, Twin Cities Campus (MN)
U of Mississippi (MS)
U of Missouri (MO)
U of Nebraska–Lincoln (NE)
U of Nevada, Reno (NV)
U of New Hampshire (NH)
U of New Haven (CT)
U of New Mexico (NM)
U of North Dakota (ND)
U of Notre Dame (IN)
U of Oklahoma (OK)
U of Ottawa (ON, Canada)
U of Pennsylvania (PA)
U of Pittsburgh (PA)
U of Rhode Island (RI)
U of Rochester (NY)
U of South Alabama (AL)
U of South Carolina (SC)
U of Southern California (CA)
U of South Florida (FL)
The U of Tennessee (TN)
The U of Tennessee at Chattanooga (TN)
The U of Texas at Austin (TX)
The U of Toledo (OH)
U of Toronto (ON, Canada)
U of Tulsa (OK)
U of Utah (UT)
U of Virginia (VA)
U of Washington (WA)
The U of Western Ontario (ON, Canada)
U of Wisconsin–Madison (WI)
U of Wyoming (WY)
Vanderbilt U (TN)
Villanova U (PA)
Virginia Commonwealth U (VA)
Virginia Polytechnic Inst and State U (VA)
Washington State U (WA)

Washington U in St. Louis (MO)
Wayne State U (MI)
Western Michigan U (MI)
West Virginia U (WV)
West Virginia U Inst of Technology (WV)
Widener U (PA)
Winona State U (MN)
Worcester Polytechnic Inst (MA)
Xavier U (OH)
Yale U (CT)
Youngstown State U (OH)

CHEMICAL ENGINEERING RELATED
Purdue U (IN)

CHEMICAL ENGINEERING TECHNOLOGY
Purdue U (IN)

CHEMICAL PHYSICS
Adams State Coll (CO)
Augustana Coll (SD)
Bowdoin Coll (ME)
Carnegie Mellon U (PA)
Columbia U, School of General Studies (NY)
Hamilton Coll (NY)
Hendrix Coll (AR)
Lewis U (IL)
Maryville Coll (TN)
Michigan State U (MI)
Michigan Technological U (MI)
Mississippi Coll (MS)
Saginaw Valley State U (MI)
Simon Fraser U (BC, Canada)
Swarthmore Coll (PA)
U of Guelph (ON, Canada)

CHEMICAL TECHNOLOGY
Inter American U of Puerto Rico, Bayamón Campus (PR)
Lenoir-Rhyne U (NC)
Norwich U (VT)
U of Regina (SK, Canada)

CHEMISTRY
Abilene Christian U (TX)
Acadia U (NS, Canada)
Adams State Coll (CO)
Adelphi U (NY)
Adrian Coll (MI)
Agnes Scott Coll (GA)
Alabama State U (AL)
Albany Coll of Pharmacy and Health Sciences (NY)
Albany State U (GA)
Albertus Magnus Coll (CT)
Albion Coll (MI)
Albright Coll (PA)
Alcorn State U (MS)
Alfred U (NY)
Allegheny Coll (PA)
Alma Coll (MI)
Alvernia U (PA)
Alverno Coll (WI)
American U (DC)
The American U in Cairo (Egypt)
American U of Beirut (Lebanon)
Amherst Coll (MA)
Anderson U (IN)
Andrews U (MI)
Angelo State U (TX)
Appalachian State U (NC)
Aquinas Coll (MI)
Arcadia U (PA)
Arizona State U (AZ)
Arkansas State U (AR)
Arkansas Tech U (AR)
Armstrong Atlantic State U (GA)
Asbury U (KY)
Ashland U (OH)
Assumption Coll (MA)
Athens State U (AL)
Auburn U (AL)
Augustana Coll (IL)
Augustana Coll (SD)
Austin Coll (TX)
Austin Peay State U (TN)
Azusa Pacific U (CA)
Baker U (KS)
Baldwin-Wallace Coll (OH)

Ball State U (IN)
Bard Coll (NY)
Bard Coll at Simon's Rock (MA)
Barnard Coll (NY)
Barry U (FL)
Barton Coll (NC)
Bates Coll (ME)
Bayamón Central U (PR)
Baylor U (TX)
Belhaven U (MS)
Bellarmine U (KY)
Belmont U (TN)
Beloit Coll (WI)
Bemidji State U (MN)
Benedictine Coll (KS)
Benedictine U (IL)
Bennett Coll for Women (NC)
Bennington Coll (VT)
Berea Coll (KY)
Berry Coll (GA)
Bethany Coll (KS)
Bethany Coll (WV)
Bethany Lutheran Coll (MN)
Bethel Coll (IN)
Bethel Coll (KS)
Bethel U (MN)
Bethel U (TN)
Bethune-Cookman U (FL)
Biola U (CA)
Birmingham-Southern Coll (AL)
Bishop's U (QC, Canada)
Blackburn Coll (IL)
Black Hills State U (SD)
Bloomfield Coll (NJ)
Bloomsburg U of Pennsylvania (PA)
Bluefield Coll (VA)
Bluffton U (OH)
Bob Jones U (SC)
Boise State U (ID)
Boston Coll (MA)
Boston U (MA)
Bowdoin Coll (ME)
Bowling Green State U (OH)
Bradley U (IL)
Brandeis U (MA)
Brescia U (KY)
Briar Cliff U (IA)
Bridgewater Coll (VA)
Bridgewater State U (MA)
Brown U (RI)
Bryn Mawr Coll (PA)
Bucknell U (PA)
Buena Vista U (IA)
Buffalo State Coll, State U of New York (NY)
Butler U (IN)
Cabrini Coll (PA)
Caldwell Coll (NJ)
California Baptist U (CA)
California Inst of Technology (CA)
California Lutheran U (CA)
California Polytechnic State U, San Luis Obispo (CA)
California State Polytechnic U, Pomona (CA)
California State U, Bakersfield (CA)
California State U, Chico (CA)
California State U, Dominguez Hills (CA)
California State U, East Bay (CA)
California State U, Fresno (CA)
California State U, Fullerton (CA)
California State U, Long Beach (CA)
California State U, Los Angeles (CA)
California State U, Sacramento (CA)
California State U, San Bernardino (CA)
California State U, San Marcos (CA)
California State U, Stanislaus (CA)
California U of Pennsylvania (PA)
Calvin Coll (MI)
Cameron U (OK)
Campbellsville U (KY)
Canisius Coll (NY)
Cape Breton U (NS, Canada)
Capital U (OH)
Cardinal Stritch U (WI)
Carleton Coll (MN)
Carlow U (PA)
Carnegie Mellon U (PA)
Carroll Coll (MT)

Carson-Newman Coll (TN)
Case Western Reserve U (OH)
Catawba Coll (NC)
The Catholic U of America (DC)
Cedar Crest Coll (PA)
Cedarville U (OH)
Centenary Coll of Louisiana (LA)
Central Coll (IA)
Central Connecticut State U (CT)
Central Methodist U (MO)
Central Michigan U (MI)
Central State U (OH)
Central Washington U (WA)
Centre Coll (KY)
Chapman U (CA)
Chatham U (PA)
Chestnut Hill Coll (PA)
Cheyney U of Pennsylvania (PA)
Chicago State U (IL)
Christian Brothers U (TN)
Christopher Newport U (VA)
The Citadel, The Military Coll of South Carolina (SC)
City Coll of the City U of New York (NY)
Claflin U (SC)
Claremont McKenna Coll (CA)
Clarion U of Pennsylvania (PA)
Clark Atlanta U (GA)
Clarke U (IA)
Clarkson U (NY)
Clark U (MA)
Clayton State U (GA)
Clemson U (SC)
Cleveland State U (OH)
Coastal Carolina U (SC)
Coe Coll (IA)
Colby Coll (ME)
Colgate U (NY)
The Coll at Brockport, State U of New York (NY)
Coll of Charleston (SC)
The Coll of Idaho (ID)
Coll of Mount St. Joseph (OH)
Coll of Mount Saint Vincent (NY)
The Coll of New Jersey (NJ)
Coll of Saint Benedict (MN)
Coll of Saint Elizabeth (NJ)
Coll of Saint Mary (NE)
The Coll of Saint Rose (NY)
The Coll of St. Scholastica (MN)
Coll of Staten Island of the City U of New York (NY)
Coll of the Holy Cross (MA)
Coll of the Ozarks (MO)
The Coll of William and Mary (VA)
The Coll of Wooster (OH)
The Colorado Coll (CO)
Colorado School of Mines (CO)
Colorado State U (CO)
Columbia Coll (MO)
Columbia Coll (SC)
Columbia U, School of General Studies (NY)
Columbus State U (GA)
Concordia Coll (MN)
Concordia U (CA)
Concordia U (QC, Canada)
Concordia U Chicago (IL)
Concordia U, Nebraska (NE)
Connecticut Coll (CT)
Converse Coll (SC)
Cornell Coll (IA)
Cornell U (NY)
Covenant Coll (GA)
Creighton U (NE)
Dalhousie U (NS, Canada)
Dalton State Coll (GA)
Dartmouth Coll (NH)
Davidson Coll (NC)
Delaware State U (DE)
Delaware Valley Coll (PA)
Delta State U (MS)
Denison U (OH)
DePaul U (IL)
DePauw U (IN)
DeSales U (PA)
Dickinson Coll (PA)
Dillard U (LA)
Doane Coll (NE)
Dominican U (IL)
Dominican U of California (CA)
Dordt Coll (IA)
Dowling Coll (NY)
Drake U (IA)

Drew U (NJ)
Drexel U (PA)
Drury U (MO)
Duquesne U (PA)
Earlham Coll (IN)
East Carolina U (NC)
East Central U (OK)
Eastern Illinois U (IL)
Eastern Kentucky U (KY)
Eastern Mennonite U (VA)
Eastern Michigan U (MI)
Eastern New Mexico U (NM)
Eastern Oregon U (OR)
Eastern U (PA)
Eastern Washington U (WA)
East Stroudsburg U of Pennsylvania (PA)
East Tennessee State U (TN)
East Texas Baptist U (TX)
Eckerd Coll (FL)
Edgewood Coll (WI)
Edinboro U of Pennsylvania (PA)
Edward Waters Coll (FL)
Elizabeth City State U (NC)
Elizabethtown Coll (PA)
Elmhurst Coll (IL)
Elmira Coll (NY)
Elon U (NC)
Emmanuel Coll (MA)
Emory & Henry Coll (VA)
Emory U (GA)
Emporia State U (KS)
Evangel U (MO)
Excelsior Coll (NY)
Fairfield U (CT)
Fairleigh Dickinson U, Coll at Florham (NJ)
Fairleigh Dickinson U, Metropolitan Campus (NJ)
Fairmont State U (WV)
Fayetteville State U (NC)
Ferris State U (MI)
Ferrum Coll (VA)
Florida Ag and Mech U (FL)
Florida Atlantic U (FL)
Florida Gulf Coast U (FL)
Florida Inst of Technology (FL)
Florida Intl U (FL)
Florida Southern Coll (FL)
Florida State U (FL)
Fordham U (NY)
Fort Hays State U (KS)
Fort Lewis Coll (CO)
Framingham State U (MA)
Franciscan U of Steubenville (OH)
Francis Marion U (SC)
Franklin & Marshall Coll (PA)
Franklin Coll (IN)
Friends U (KS)
Furman U (SC)
Gallaudet U (DC)
Gannon U (PA)
Gardner-Webb U (NC)
Geneva Coll (PA)
George Fox U (OR)
George Mason U (VA)
Georgetown Coll (KY)
The George Washington U (DC)
Georgia Coll & State U (GA)
Georgia Inst of Technology (GA)
Georgian Court U (NJ)
Georgia Southern U (GA)
Georgia Southwestern State U (GA)
Georgia State U (GA)
Gettysburg Coll (PA)
Glenville State Coll (WV)
Gonzaga U (WA)
Gordon Coll (MA)
Goshen Coll (IN)
Goucher Coll (MD)
Governors State U (IL)
Graceland U (IA)
Grambling State U (LA)
Grand Valley State U (MI)
Greenville Coll (IL)
Grinnell Coll (IA)
Grove City Coll (PA)
Guilford Coll (NC)
Gustavus Adolphus Coll (MN)
Hamilton Coll (NY)
Hamline U (MN)
Hampden-Sydney Coll (VA)
Hampshire Coll (MA)
Hampton U (VA)
Hanover Coll (IN)

Stevens Inst of Technology (NJ)
Stevenson U (MD)
Stonehill Coll (MA)
Stony Brook U, State U of New York (NY)
Suffolk U (MA)
Sul Ross State U (TX)
Susquehanna U (PA)
Swarthmore Coll (PA)
Sweet Briar Coll (VA)
Syracuse U (NY)
Tabor Coll (KS)
Tarleton State U (TX)
Taylor U (IN)
Temple U (PA)
Texas A&M Intl U (TX)
Texas A&M U (TX)
Texas A&M U–Corpus Christi (TX)
Texas A&M U–Kingsville (TX)
Texas Christian U (TX)
Texas Lutheran U (TX)
Texas Southern U (TX)
Texas State U–San Marcos (TX)
Texas Tech U (TX)
Texas Wesleyan U (TX)
Texas Woman's U (TX)
Thiel Coll (PA)
Thomas More Coll (KY)
Thompson Rivers U (BC, Canada)
Towson U (MD)
Transylvania U (KY)
Trent U (ON, Canada)
Trevecca Nazarene U (TN)
Trine U (IN)
Trinity Christian Coll (IL)
Trinity Coll (CT)
Trinity U (TX)
Troy U (AL)
Truman State U (MO)
Tufts U (MA)
Tulane U (LA)
Tuskegee U (AL)
Union Coll (KY)
Union Coll (NE)
Union Coll (NY)
Union U (TN)
United States Air Force Acad (CO)
United States Military Acad (NY)
United States Naval Acad (MD)
Universidad del Turabo (PR)
Université de Sherbrooke (QC, Canada)
U at Albany, State U of New York (NY)
U at Buffalo, the State U of New York (NY)
The U of Akron (OH)
The U of Alabama (AL)
The U of Alabama at Birmingham (AL)
The U of Alabama in Huntsville (AL)
U of Alaska Anchorage (AK)
U of Alaska Fairbanks (AK)
U of Alberta (AB, Canada)
The U of Arizona (AZ)
U of Arkansas (AR)
U of Arkansas at Little Rock (AR)
U of Arkansas at Monticello (AR)
U of Arkansas–Fort Smith (AR)
The U of British Columbia (BC, Canada)
The U of British Columbia–Okanagan (BC, Canada)
U of California, Berkeley (CA)
U of California, Davis (CA)
U of California, Irvine (CA)
U of California, Los Angeles (CA)
U of California, Merced (CA)
U of California, Riverside (CA)
U of California, Santa Barbara (CA)
U of California, Santa Cruz (CA)
U of Central Arkansas (AR)
U of Central Florida (FL)
U of Central Missouri (MO)
U of Charleston (WV)
U of Cincinnati (OH)
U of Colorado at Colorado Springs (CO)
U of Colorado Boulder (CO)
U of Colorado Denver (CO)
U of Connecticut (CT)
U of Dallas (TX)
U of Dayton (OH)
U of Delaware (DE)
U of Denver (CO)

U of Evansville (IN)
The U of Findlay (OH)
U of Florida (FL)
U of Georgia (GA)
U of Great Falls (MT)
U of Guam (GU)
U of Guelph (ON, Canada)
U of Hartford (CT)
U of Hawaii at Hilo (HI)
U of Hawaii at Manoa (HI)
U of Houston (TX)
U of Houston–Clear Lake (TX)
U of Houston–Downtown (TX)
U of Idaho (ID)
U of Illinois at Chicago (IL)
U of Illinois at Springfield (IL)
U of Illinois at Urbana–Champaign (IL)
The U of Iowa (IA)
The U of Kansas (KS)
U of La Verne (CA)
U of Lethbridge (AB, Canada)
U of Louisiana at Lafayette (LA)
U of Louisville (KY)
U of Maine (ME)
U of Mary Hardin-Baylor (TX)
U of Maryland, Baltimore County (MD)
U of Maryland, Coll Park (MD)
U of Maryland Eastern Shore (MD)
U of Mary Washington (VA)
U of Massachusetts Amherst (MA)
U of Massachusetts Boston (MA)
U of Massachusetts Dartmouth (MA)
U of Massachusetts Lowell (MA)
U of Memphis (TN)
U of Miami (FL)
U of Michigan (MI)
U of Michigan–Dearborn (MI)
U of Michigan–Flint (MI)
U of Minnesota, Duluth (MN)
U of Minnesota, Twin Cities Campus (MN)
U of Mississippi (MS)
U of Missouri (MO)
U of Missouri–Kansas City (MO)
U of Missouri–St. Louis (MO)
U of Mount Union (OH)
U of Nebraska at Kearney (NE)
U of Nebraska at Omaha (NE)
U of Nebraska–Lincoln (NE)
U of Nevada, Las Vegas (NV)
U of Nevada, Reno (NV)
U of New England (ME)
U of New Hampshire (NH)
U of New Haven (CT)
U of New Mexico (NM)
U of New Orleans (LA)
U of North Alabama (AL)
The U of North Carolina at Asheville (NC)
The U of North Carolina at Chapel Hill (NC)
The U of North Carolina at Charlotte (NC)
The U of North Carolina Wilmington (NC)
U of North Dakota (ND)
U of Northern Colorado (CO)
U of Northern Iowa (IA)
U of North Florida (FL)
U of North Texas (TX)
U of Notre Dame (IN)
U of Oklahoma (OK)
U of Oregon (OR)
U of Ottawa (ON, Canada)
U of Pennsylvania (PA)
U of Pikeville (KY)
U of Pittsburgh (PA)
U of Pittsburgh at Bradford (PA)
U of Pittsburgh at Greensburg (PA)
U of Pittsburgh at Johnstown (PA)
U of Portland (OR)
U of Puerto Rico at Humacao (PR)
U of Puget Sound (WA)
U of Redlands (CA)
U of Regina (SK, Canada)
U of Rhode Island (RI)
U of Richmond (VA)
U of Rio Grande (OH)
U of Rochester (NY)
U of Saint Francis (IN)
U of Saint Joseph (CT)
U of Saint Mary (KS)

U of St. Thomas (MN)
U of St. Thomas (TX)
U of San Diego (CA)
U of Science and Arts of Oklahoma (OK)
The U of Scranton (PA)
U of South Alabama (AL)
U of South Carolina (SC)
U of South Carolina Aiken (SC)
U of South Carolina Upstate (SC)
The U of South Dakota (SD)
U of Southern California (CA)
U of Southern Indiana (IN)
U of Southern Maine (ME)
U of Southern Mississippi (MS)
U of South Florida (FL)
The U of Tampa (FL)
The U of Tennessee (TN)
The U of Tennessee at Chattanooga (TN)
The U of Tennessee at Martin (TN)
The U of Texas at Arlington (TX)
The U of Texas at Austin (TX)
The U of Texas at Dallas (TX)
The U of Texas at El Paso (TX)
The U of Texas at San Antonio (TX)
The U of Texas at Tyler (TX)
The U of Texas of the Permian Basin (TX)
The U of Texas–Pan American (TX)
U of the Cumberlands (KY)
U of the District of Columbia (DC)
U of the Incarnate Word (TX)
U of the Ozarks (AR)
U of the Pacific (CA)
U of the Sciences in Philadelphia (PA)
The U of Toledo (OH)
U of Tulsa (OK)
U of Utah (UT)
U of Vermont (VT)
U of Virginia (VA)
The U of Virginia's Coll at Wise (VA)
U of Washington (WA)
The U of West Alabama (AL)
The U of Western Ontario (ON, Canada)
U of West Florida (FL)
U of West Georgia (GA)
U of Windsor (ON, Canada)
U of Wisconsin–Eau Claire (WI)
U of Wisconsin–Green Bay (WI)
U of Wisconsin–La Crosse (WI)
U of Wisconsin–Madison (WI)
U of Wisconsin–Milwaukee (WI)
U of Wisconsin–River Falls (WI)
U of Wisconsin–Stevens Point (WI)
U of Wisconsin–Superior (WI)
U of Wisconsin–Whitewater (WI)
U of Wyoming (WY)
Upper Iowa U (IA)
Utah State U (UT)
Utah Valley U (UT)
Utica Coll (NY)
Valdosta State U (GA)
Valley City State U (ND)
Valparaiso U (IN)
Vanderbilt U (TN)
Vanguard U of Southern California (CA)
Vassar Coll (NY)
Villanova U (PA)
Virginia Commonwealth U (VA)
Virginia Polytechnic Inst and State U (VA)
Virginia State U (VA)
Virginia Union U (VA)
Virginia Wesleyan Coll (VA)
Viterbo U (WI)
Wabash Coll (IN)
Wagner Coll (NY)
Wake Forest U (NC)
Walsh U (OH)
Warren Wilson Coll (NC)
Wartburg Coll (IA)
Washburn U (KS)
Washington Adventist U (MD)
Washington & Jefferson Coll (PA)
Washington and Lee U (VA)
Washington Coll (MD)
Washington State U (WA)
Washington U in St. Louis (MO)
Wayland Baptist U (TX)
Waynesburg U (PA)
Wayne State Coll (NE)

Wayne State U (MI)
Weber State U (UT)
Wellesley Coll (MA)
Wells Coll (NY)
Wesleyan Coll (GA)
Wesleyan U (CT)
West Chester U of Pennsylvania (PA)
Western Carolina U (NC)
Western Connecticut State U (CT)
Western Illinois U (IL)
Western Kentucky U (KY)
Western Michigan U (MI)
Western New England U (MA)
Western Oregon U (OR)
Western State Coll of Colorado (CO)
Western Washington U (WA)
Westfield State U (MA)
West Liberty U (WV)
Westminster Coll (MO)
Westminster Coll (UT)
West Texas A&M U (TX)
West Virginia State U (WV)
West Virginia U (WV)
West Virginia U Inst of Technology (WV)
West Virginia Wesleyan Coll (WV)
Wheaton Coll (IL)
Wheaton Coll (MA)
Wheeling Jesuit U (WV)
Whitman Coll (WA)
Whittier Coll (CA)
Wichita State U (KS)
Widener U (PA)
Wilkes U (PA)
Willamette U (OR)
William Jewell Coll (MO)
William Paterson U of New Jersey (NJ)
Williams Coll (MA)
Wilmington Coll (OH)
Wilson Coll (PA)
Wingate U (NC)
Winona State U (MN)
Winthrop U (SC)
Wittenberg U (OH)
Wofford Coll (SC)
Worcester Polytechnic Inst (MA)
Worcester State U (MA)
Wright State U (OH)
Xavier U (OH)
Xavier U of Louisiana (LA)
Yale U (CT)
Yeshiva U (NY)
York Coll of Pennsylvania (PA)
York Coll of the City U of New York (NY)
Youngstown State U (OH)

CHEMISTRY RELATED

Boston U (MA)
Bridgewater State U (MA)
California State U, Chico (CA)
Carnegie Mellon U (PA)
Coll of Charleston (SC)
Connecticut Coll (CT)
Dartmouth Coll (NH)
Delaware State U (DE)
Duquesne U (PA)
Eastern U (PA)
Edinboro U of Pennsylvania (PA)
Florida Inst of Technology (FL)
Florida State U (FL)
Keene State Coll (NH)
Loyola U New Orleans (LA)
Northern Michigan U (MI)
Northland Coll (WI)
Ohio Northern U (OH)
Purdue U (IN)
Roger Williams U (RI)
Saginaw Valley State U (MI)
Saint Anselm Coll (NH)
Saint Mary's Coll of California (CA)
Saint Vincent Coll (PA)
Sam Houston State U (TX)
Stony Brook U, State U of New York (NY)
Taylor U (IN)
Towson U (MD)
U at Buffalo, the State U of New York (NY)
U of California, Berkeley (CA)
U of California, Santa Barbara (CA)
U of Denver (CO)

U of Georgia (GA)
U of Houston–Downtown (TX)
U of Northern Iowa (IA)
U of Notre Dame (IN)
The U of Scranton (PA)
U of Southern Mississippi (MS)
U of the Pacific (CA)
U of Wisconsin–Eau Claire (WI)
U of Wisconsin–Madison (WI)
U of Wisconsin–Milwaukee (WI)
U of Wisconsin–Whitewater (WI)
Washington U in St. Louis (MO)
Wayne State U (MI)
Western Illinois U (IL)
Western Michigan U (MI)
Western State Coll of Colorado (CO)
Whitman Coll (WA)

CHEMISTRY TEACHER EDUCATION

Adams State Coll (CO)
Alma Coll (MI)
Alvernia U (PA)
Anderson U (IN)
Appalachian State U (NC)
Arkansas State U (AR)
Assumption Coll (MA)
Augustana Coll (IL)
Bethany Coll (KS)
Bethel U (MN)
Bethune-Cookman U (FL)
Bishop's U (QC, Canada)
Bluefield Coll (VA)
Boston U (MA)
Bowling Green State U (OH)
Bradley U (IL)
Buena Vista U (IA)
Cabrini Coll (PA)
California State U, Chico (CA)
Calvin Coll (MI)
Cameron U (OK)
Campbellsville U (KY)
Carroll Coll (MT)
Cedarville U (OH)
Central Methodist U (MO)
Central Washington U (WA)
Christian Brothers U (TN)
City Coll of the City U of New York (NY)
The Coll at Brockport, State U of New York (NY)
The Coll of New Jersey (NJ)
The Coll of Saint Rose (NY)
Coll of the Ozarks (MO)
Colorado State U (CO)
Concordia Coll (MN)
Concordia U Chicago (IL)
Concordia U, Nebraska (NE)
Concordia U, St. Paul (MN)
Delaware State U (DE)
Dordt Coll (IA)
Dowling Coll (NY)
East Central U (OK)
Eastern Michigan U (MI)
Eastern Washington U (WA)
East Texas Baptist U (TX)
Edgewood Coll (WI)
Elizabeth City State U (NC)
Elmhurst Coll (IL)
Elmira Coll (NY)
Evangel U (MO)
Ferris State U (MI)
Florida Inst of Technology (FL)
Fordham U (NY)
Fort Lewis Coll (CO)
Franklin Coll (IN)
Glenville State Coll (WV)
Grand Canyon U (AZ)
Grand Valley State U (MI)
Greenville Coll (IL)
Grove City Coll (PA)
Gustavus Adolphus Coll (MN)
Hofstra U (NY)
Hope Coll (MI)
Huntingdon Coll (AL)
Huntington U (IN)
Husson U (ME)
Indiana U Bloomington (IN)
Indiana U–Purdue U Fort Wayne (IN)
Indiana U South Bend (IN)
Indiana U Southeast (IN)
Indiana Wesleyan U (IN)

Inter American U of Puerto Rico, San Germán Campus (PR)
Iowa Wesleyan Coll (IA)
Ithaca Coll (NY)
Jamestown Coll (ND)
Juniata Coll (PA)
Keene State Coll (NH)
Kent State U (OH)
Kentucky Wesleyan Coll (KY)
King Coll (TN)
Le Moyne Coll (NY)
Lenoir-Rhyne U (NC)
Lincoln Memorial U (TN)
Lincoln U (MO)
Lindenwood U (MO)
Lipscomb U (TN)
Long Island U–Brooklyn Campus (NY)
Long Island U–C. W. Post Campus (NY)
Louisiana State U in Shreveport (LA)
Lubbock Christian U (TX)
Manchester Coll (IN)
Manhattanville Coll (NY)
Mansfield U of Pennsylvania (PA)
Maryville Coll (TN)
Mayville State U (ND)
McMurry U (TX)
Mercyhurst Coll (PA)
Merrimack Coll (MA)
Messiah Coll (PA)
Miami Dade Coll (FL)
Miami U (OH)
Michigan State U (MI)
Millikin U (IL)
Minnesota State U Moorhead (MN)
Minot State U (ND)
Misericordia U (PA)
Mississippi Coll (MS)
Missouri State U (MO)
Montana State U Billings (MT)
Moravian Coll (PA)
Morningside Coll (IA)
Mount Marty Coll (SD)
Mount Mary Coll (WI)
Mount Vernon Nazarene U (OH)
Nazareth Coll of Rochester (NY)
Niagara U (NY)
North Carolina Ag and Tech State U (NC)
North Carolina Central U (NC)
North Dakota State U (ND)
Northeastern State U (OK)
Northern Michigan U (MI)
Northwest Missouri State U (MO)
Northwest Nazarene U (ID)
Ohio Northern U (OH)
Ohio Wesleyan U (OH)
Pace U (NY)
Peru State Coll (NE)
Pittsburg State U (KS)
Purdue U (IN)
Rhode Island Coll (RI)
Roberts Wesleyan Coll (NY)
Saginaw Valley State U (MI)
St. Ambrose U (IA)
St. Catherine U (MN)
St. Edward's U (TX)
Saint Francis U (PA)
St. John Fisher Coll (NY)
St. Joseph's Coll, Long Island Campus (NY)
St. Joseph's Coll, New York (NY)
Saint Joseph's Coll of Maine (ME)
Saint Mary's U of Minnesota (MN)
Schreiner U (TX)
Seton Hill U (PA)
Southern Polytechnic State U (GA)
Southwest Baptist U (MO)
Southwest Minnesota State U (MN)
Spring Arbor U (MI)
State U of New York at New Paltz (NY)
State U of New York at Plattsburgh (NY)
State U of New York Coll at Cortland (NY)
State U of New York Coll at Old Westbury (NY)
State U of New York Coll at Oneonta (NY)
State U of New York Coll of Environmental Science and Forestry (NY)

Syracuse U (NY)
Tabor Coll (KS)
Transylvania U (KY)
Trevecca Nazarene U (TN)
Trinity Christian Coll (IL)
Union Coll (NE)
Universidad del Turabo (PR)
U of Arkansas–Fort Smith (AR)
U of Delaware (DE)
U of Evansville (IN)
U of Great Falls (MT)
U of Illinois at Chicago (IL)
U of Illinois at Urbana–Champaign (IL)
The U of Iowa (IA)
U of Louisiana at Lafayette (LA)
U of Louisiana at Monroe (LA)
U of Maine (ME)
U of Mary Hardin-Baylor (TX)
U of Michigan–Dearborn (MI)
U of Missouri (MO)
U of Missouri–St. Louis (MO)
U of Nebraska–Lincoln (NE)
U of New Orleans (LA)
The U of North Carolina at Charlotte (NC)
The U of North Carolina Wilmington (NC)
U of Pittsburgh at Johnstown (PA)
U of Regina (SK, Canada)
U of Saint Francis (IN)
U of St. Thomas (MN)
The U of Tennessee at Martin (TN)
U of West Georgia (GA)
U of Windsor (ON, Canada)
U of Wisconsin–River Falls (WI)
U of Wisconsin–Superior (WI)
Utah State U (UT)
Utah Valley U (UT)
Utica Coll (NY)
Valley City State U (ND)
Valparaiso U (IN)
Viterbo U (WI)
Washburn U (KS)
Washington State U (WA)
Washington U in St. Louis (MO)
Waynesburg U (PA)
Wayne State Coll (NE)
Weber State U (UT)
Western Michigan U (MI)
Western State Coll of Colorado (CO)
Western Washington U (WA)
Wheeling Jesuit U (WV)
Widener U (PA)
William Jewell Coll (MO)
Winona State U (MN)
Xavier U (OH)
Xavier U of Louisiana (LA)

CHILD-CARE AND SUPPORT SERVICES MANAGEMENT
American Public U System (WV)
Brigham Young U (UT)
Chestnut Hill Coll (PA)
Ferris State U (MI)
Messiah Coll (PA)
National-Louis U (IL)
Rust Coll (MS)
Ryerson U (ON, Canada)
Saint Mary-of-the-Woods Coll (IN)
Seton Hill U (PA)
Siena Heights U (MI)
Thomas Edison State Coll (NJ)
U of Minnesota, Twin Cities Campus (MN)
Wheelock Coll (MA)

CHILD-CARE PROVISION
Brigham Young U (UT)
Wayne State Coll (NE)

CHILD DEVELOPMENT
Albertus Magnus Coll (CT)
Alcorn State U (MS)
Appalachian State U (NC)
Ashland U (OH)
Auburn U (AL)
Bennington Coll (VT)
Bowling Green State U (OH)
Brigham Young U (UT)
California State U, East Bay (CA)
California State U, Fresno (CA)

California State U, Long Beach (CA)
California State U, Los Angeles (CA)
California State U, Sacramento (CA)
Carson-Newman Coll (TN)
Central Michigan U (MI)
Coll of the Ozarks (MO)
Concordia U, St. Paul (MN)
Delaware State U (DE)
East Carolina U (NC)
Eastern Washington U (WA)
East Tennessee State U (TN)
Gallaudet U (DC)
Goddard Coll (VT)
Goodwin Coll (CT)
Hampton U (VA)
Hannibal-LaGrange U (MO)
Harding U (AR)
Humboldt State U (CA)
Kansas State U (KS)
Lenoir-Rhyne U (NC)
Lewis-Clark State Coll (ID)
Madonna U (MI)
Meredith Coll (NC)
Michigan State U (MI)
Milligan Coll (TN)
Minnesota State U Mankato (MN)
Missouri Baptist U (MO)
Mount Ida Coll (MA)
National U (CA)
North Carolina Ag and Tech State U (NC)
Nova Southeastern U (FL)
Oklahoma Christian U (OK)
Pittsburg State U (KS)
Point Loma Nazarene U (CA)
Point U (GA)
Portland State U (OR)
Post U (CT)
Quinnipiac U (CT)
St. Joseph's Coll, Long Island Campus (NY)
St. Joseph's Coll, New York (NY)
San Diego State U (CA)
Seton Hill U (PA)
Southern New Hampshire U (NH)
State U of New York Coll at Oneonta (NY)
Texas Southern U (TX)
Texas Tech U (TX)
Texas Woman's U (TX)
Towson U (MD)
Tufts U (MA)
Union Inst & U (OH)
The U of Akron (OH)
U of Alaska Fairbanks (AK)
U of Alberta (AB, Canada)
U of Georgia (GA)
U of Guelph (ON, Canada)
U of Illinois at Urbana–Champaign (IL)
U of La Verne (CA)
U of Maine (ME)
U of Maryland Eastern Shore (MD)
U of Nevada, Reno (NV)
The U of North Carolina at Charlotte (NC)
U of Saint Joseph (CT)
U of Saint Mary (KS)
The U of Tennessee at Martin (TN)
The U of Texas at Arlington (TX)
U of the Incarnate Word (TX)
The U of Western Ontario (ON, Canada)
Vanderbilt U (TN)
Weber State U (UT)
Western Michigan U (MI)
West Virginia U (WV)
Wheelock Coll (MA)
Youngstown State U (OH)

CHINESE
Bard Coll (NY)
Bates Coll (ME)
Bennington Coll (VT)
Boston U (MA)
California State U, Long Beach (CA)
California State U, Los Angeles (CA)
Calvin Coll (MI)
Carnegie Mellon U (PA)
Colgate U (NY)

Coll of the Holy Cross (MA)
Concordia Coll (MN)
Connecticut Coll (CT)
Dartmouth Coll (NH)
DePaul U (IL)
Emory U (GA)
The George Washington U (DC)
Grinnell Coll (IA)
Hamilton Coll (NY)
Hobart and William Smith Colls (NY)
Hofstra U (NY)
Hope Coll (MI)
Hunter Coll of the City U of New York (NY)
Lawrence U (WI)
Lehigh U (PA)
Lincoln U (PA)
Macalester Coll (MN)
Michigan State U (MI)
Middlebury Coll (VT)
New Coll of Florida (FL)
North Georgia Coll & State U (GA)
The Ohio State U (OH)
Oklahoma City U (OK)
Pacific Lutheran U (WA)
Pacific U (OR)
Penn State U Park (PA)
Pomona Coll (CA)
Portland State U (OR)
Queens Coll of the City U of New York (NY)
Rutgers, The State U of New Jersey, New Brunswick (NJ)
San Francisco State U (CA)
Scripps Coll (CA)
Southwestern U (TX)
Stanford U (CA)
Swarthmore Coll (PA)
Trinity Coll (CT)
Trinity U (TX)
Tufts U (MA)
United States Military Acad (NY)
U of Alberta (AB, Canada)
The U of British Columbia (BC, Canada)
U of California, Berkeley (CA)
U of California, Davis (CA)
U of California, Irvine (CA)
U of California, Los Angeles (CA)
U of California, Santa Barbara (CA)
U of Colorado Boulder (CO)
U of Georgia (GA)
U of Hawaii at Manoa (HI)
U of Houston (TX)
The U of Iowa (IA)
U of Maryland, Coll Park (MD)
U of Massachusetts Amherst (MA)
U of Minnesota, Twin Cities Campus (MN)
U of Mississippi (MS)
U of Notre Dame (IN)
U of Oklahoma (OK)
U of Oregon (OR)
U of Pittsburgh (PA)
U of Puget Sound (WA)
U of Regina (SK, Canada)
U of Richmond (VA)
U of Utah (UT)
U of Vermont (VT)
U of Washington (WA)
U of Wisconsin–Madison (WI)
Vassar Coll (NY)
Wake Forest U (NC)
Washington U in St. Louis (MO)
Wellesley Coll (MA)
Williams Coll (MA)
Wofford Coll (SC)
Yale U (CT)

CHINESE STUDIES
The Coll of William and Mary (VA)
Drew U (NJ)
Gettysburg Coll (PA)
Occidental Coll (CA)
Pacific Lutheran U (WA)
Sarah Lawrence Coll (NY)
U at Albany, State U of New York (NY)
U of California, Irvine (CA)
U of North Dakota (ND)

CHIROPRACTIC ASSISTANT
Hawai'i Pacific U (HI)

CHRISTIAN STUDIES
Anderson U (SC)
Bethany Coll (KS)
Bethany Lutheran Coll (MN)
Bethel Coll (IN)
Bethel U (TN)
Bluefield Coll (VA)
California Baptist U (CA)
The Coll of St. Scholastica (MN)
Crossroads Bible Coll (IN)
Crown Coll (MN)
Dallas Baptist U (TX)
Friends U (KS)
Gordon Coll (MA)
Grand Canyon U (AZ)
Hardin-Simmons U (TX)
Hillsdale Coll (MI)
Howard Payne U (TX)
Iowa Wesleyan Coll (IA)
Lindenwood U (MO)
Loyola U New Orleans (LA)
McMurry U (TX)
Mississippi Coll (MS)
Missouri Baptist U (MO)
Ouachita Baptist U (AR)
Roanoke Coll (VA)
Saint Mary's U of Minnesota (MN)
Simpson U (CA)
Stonehill Coll (MA)
Truett-McConnell Coll (GA)
U of Mary Hardin-Baylor (TX)
Ursuline Coll (OH)
Wayland Baptist U (TX)

CINEMATOGRAPHY AND FILM/ VIDEO PRODUCTION
Acad of Art U (CA)
American U (DC)
Art Center Coll of Design (CA)
The Art Inst of Atlanta (GA)
The Art Inst of Austin (TX)
The Art Inst of California, a college of Argosy U, Hollywood (CA)
The Art Inst of California, a college of Argosy U, Los Angeles (CA)
The Art Inst of California, a college of Argosy U, Orange County (CA)
The Art Inst of California, a college of Argosy U, Sacramento (CA)
The Art Inst of California, a college of Argosy U, San Francisco (CA)
The Art Inst of California, a college of Argosy U, Sunnyvale (CA)
The Art Inst of Charleston (SC)
The Art Inst of Charlotte (NC)
The Art Inst of Colorado (CO)
The Art Inst of Dallas (TX)
The Art Inst of Fort Lauderdale (FL)
The Art Inst of Houston (TX)
The Art Inst of Houston - North (TX)
The Art Inst of Jacksonville (FL)
The Art Inst of Las Vegas (NV)
The Art Inst of Ohio–Cincinnati (OH)
The Art Inst of Philadelphia (PA)
The Art Inst of Phoenix (AZ)
The Art Inst of Pittsburgh (PA)
The Art Inst of Portland (OR)
The Art Inst of Salt Lake City (UT)
The Art Inst of Seattle (WA)
The Art Inst of Tampa (FL)
The Art Inst of Tennessee– Nashville (TN)
The Art Inst of Tucson (AZ)
The Art Inst of Washington (VA)
The Art Inst of Wisconsin (WI)
The Art Insts Intl–Kansas City (KS)
The Art Insts Intl Minnesota (MN)
Bard Coll (NY)
Bennington Coll (VT)
Biola U (CA)
Bob Jones U (SC)
Brigham Young U (UT)
California State U, Long Beach (CA)
Calvin Coll (MI)
Chapman U (CA)
City Coll of the City U of New York (NY)
Cleveland State U (OH)
Columbia Coll Chicago (IL)
Concordia U (QC, Canada)
DePaul U (IL)
Drexel U (PA)

Eastern New Mexico U (NM)
Eastern Washington U (WA)
Emily Carr U of Art + Design (BC, Canada)
The Evergreen State Coll (WA)
Fairleigh Dickinson U, Coll at Florham (NJ)
Fitchburg State U (MA)
Five Towns Coll (NY)
George Fox U (OR)
George Mason U (VA)
Grand Canyon U (AZ)
Hawai`i Pacific U (HI)
Hunter Coll of the City U of New York (NY)
The Illinois Inst of Art–Chicago (IL)
The Illinois Inst of Art–Schaumburg (IL)
Ithaca Coll (NY)
John Brown U (AR)
Keene State Coll (NH)
Long Island U–C. W. Post Campus (NY)
Loyola Marymount U (CA)
Maharishi U of Management (IA)
Massachusetts Coll of Art and Design (MA)
Mercy Coll (NY)
Miami Dade Coll (FL)
Miami Intl U of Art & Design (FL)
Middlebury Coll (VT)
Missouri Western State U (MO)
Montana State U (MT)
Montclair State U (NJ)
The New England Inst of Art (MA)
New England School of Communications (ME)
New Mexico Highlands U (NM)
New Mexico State U (NM)
New York U (NY)
Northern Michigan U (MI)
Ohio U (OH)
Oklahoma City U (OK)
Pacific Union Coll (CA)
Palm Beach Atlantic U (FL)
Point Park U (PA)
Pratt Inst (NY)
Purchase Coll, State U of New York (NY)
Quinnipiac U (CT)
Regent U (VA)
Rochester Inst of Technology (NY)
Ryerson U (ON, Canada)
Sarah Lawrence Coll (NY)
Savannah Coll of Art and Design (GA)
School of the Museum of Fine Arts, Boston (MA)
Southern Illinois U Carbondale (IL)
Stanford U (CA)
State U of New York at Binghamton (NY)
Syracuse U (NY)
Taylor U (IN)
The U of Arizona (AZ)
U of Central Arkansas (AR)
U of Central Florida (FL)
U of Illinois at Chicago (IL)
The U of Iowa (IA)
U of Miami (FL)
U of New Mexico (NM)
U of North Carolina School of the Arts (NC)
The U of North Carolina Wilmington (NC)
U of Oregon (OR)
U of Regina (SK, Canada)
U of Rhode Island (RI)
U of Southern California (CA)
The U of the Arts (PA)
Vanguard U of Southern California (CA)
Virginia Commonwealth U (VA)
Wayne State U (MI)
Webster U (MO)
Wheeling Jesuit U (WV)

CITY/URBAN, COMMUNITY AND REGIONAL PLANNING

Appalachian State U (NC)
Arizona State U (AZ)
Ball State U (IN)
Bridgewater State U (MA)
Buffalo State Coll, State U of New York (NY)

California Polytechnic State U, San Luis Obispo (CA)
California State Polytechnic U, Pomona (CA)
California State U, Chico (CA)
Concordia U (QC, Canada)
Cornell U (NY)
Dalhousie U (NS, Canada)
East Carolina U (NC)
Eastern Washington U (WA)
Florida Atlantic U (FL)
Indiana U of Pennsylvania (PA)
Iowa State U of Science and Technology (IA)
Mansfield U of Pennsylvania (PA)
Massachusetts Inst of Technology (MA)
Miami U (OH)
Michigan State U (MI)
Minnesota State U Mankato (MN)
Missouri State U (MO)
The Ohio State U (OH)
Plymouth State U (NH)
Portland State U (OR)
Rowan U (NJ)
Ryerson U (ON, Canada)
Savannah Coll of Art and Design (GA)
Sojourner-Douglass Coll (MD)
State U of New York Coll of Environmental Science and Forestry (NY)
Stony Brook U, State U of New York (NY)
Temple U (PA)
Texas A&M U (TX)
Texas State U–San Marcos (TX)
The U of Akron (OH)
The U of Arizona (AZ)
U of California, Davis (CA)
U of Cincinnati (OH)
U of Illinois at Urbana–Champaign (IL)
U of Missouri–Kansas City (MO)
U of Nevada, Las Vegas (NV)
U of New Hampshire (NH)
U of Virginia (VA)
U of Washington (WA)
The U of Western Ontario (ON, Canada)
Western Michigan U (MI)
Westfield State U (MA)

CIVIL ENGINEERING

American U of Beirut (Lebanon)
Arizona State U (AZ)
Arkansas State U (AR)
Auburn U (AL)
Boise State U (ID)
Bradley U (IL)
Brown U (RI)
Bucknell U (PA)
California Baptist U (CA)
California Polytechnic State U, San Luis Obispo (CA)
California State Polytechnic U, Pomona (CA)
California State U, Chico (CA)
California State U, Fresno (CA)
California State U, Fullerton (CA)
California State U, Long Beach (CA)
California State U, Los Angeles (CA)
California State U, Sacramento (CA)
Calvin Coll (MI)
Caribbean U (PR)
Carnegie Mellon U (PA)
Carroll Coll (MT)
Case Western Reserve U (OH)
The Catholic U of America (DC)
Central Connecticut State U (CT)
Christian Brothers U (TN)
The Citadel, The Military Coll of South Carolina (SC)
City Coll of the City U of New York (NY)
Clarkson U (NY)
Clemson U (SC)
Cleveland State U (OH)
The Coll of New Jersey (NJ)
Colorado State U (CO)
Concordia U (QC, Canada)

Cooper Union for the Advancement of Science and Art (NY)
Cornell U (NY)
Delaware State U (DE)
Dordt Coll (IA)
Drexel U (PA)
Florida Ag and Mech U (FL)
Florida Atlantic U (FL)
Florida Gulf Coast U (FL)
Florida Inst of Technology (FL)
Florida Intl U (FL)
George Fox U (OR)
George Mason U (VA)
The George Washington U (DC)
Georgia Inst of Technology (GA)
Georgia Southern U (GA)
Gonzaga U (WA)
Hofstra U (NY)
Hope Coll (MI)
Idaho State U (ID)
Illinois Inst of Technology (IL)
Indiana U–Purdue U Fort Wayne (IN)
Iowa State U of Science and Technology (IA)
The Johns Hopkins U (MD)
Kansas State U (KS)
Lafayette Coll (PA)
Lakehead U (ON, Canada)
Lamar U (TX)
Lawrence Technological U (MI)
Lebanese American U (Lebanon)
Lehigh U (PA)
Louisiana State U and Ag and Mech Coll (LA)
Loyola Marymount U (CA)
Manhattan Coll (NY)
Marquette U (WI)
Massachusetts Inst of Technology (MA)
Merrimack Coll (MA)
Michigan State U (MI)
Michigan Technological U (MI)
Milwaukee School of Eng (WI)
Minnesota State U Mankato (MN)
Mississippi State U (MS)
Missouri U of Science and Technology (MO)
Montana State U (MT)
New Mexico Inst of Mining and Technology (NM)
New Mexico State U (NM)
North Carolina Ag and Tech State U (NC)
North Carolina State U (NC)
North Dakota State U (ND)
Northeastern U (MA)
Northern Arizona U (AZ)
Norwich U (VT)
Ohio Northern U (OH)
The Ohio State U (OH)
Ohio U (OH)
Oklahoma State U (OK)
Old Dominion U (VA)
Oregon Inst of Technology (OR)
Penn State Abington (PA)
Penn State Altoona (PA)
Penn State Beaver (PA)
Penn State Berks (PA)
Penn State Brandywine (PA)
Penn State DuBois (PA)
Penn State Erie, The Behrend Coll (PA)
Penn State Fayette, The Eberly Campus (PA)
Penn State Greater Allegheny (PA)
Penn State Harrisburg (PA)
Penn State Hazleton (PA)
Penn State Lehigh Valley (PA)
Penn State Mont Alto (PA)
Penn State New Kensington (PA)
Penn State Schuylkill (PA)
Penn State Shenango (PA)
Penn State U Park (PA)
Penn State Wilkes-Barre (PA)
Penn State Worthington Scranton (PA)
Penn State York (PA)
Polytechnic Inst of NYU (NY)
Polytechnic U of Puerto Rico (PR)
Portland State U (OR)
Prairie View A&M U (TX)
Princeton U (NJ)
Purdue U (IN)
Purdue U Calumet (IN)

Queen's U at Kingston (ON, Canada)
Rensselaer Polytechnic Inst (NY)
Rice U (TX)
Rose-Hulman Inst of Technology (IN)
Rowan U (NJ)
Rutgers, The State U of New Jersey, New Brunswick (NJ)
Ryerson U (ON, Canada)
Saint Louis U (MO)
Saint Martin's U (WA)
San Diego State U (CA)
San Francisco State U (CA)
Santa Clara U (CA)
Seattle U (WA)
South Dakota School of Mines and Technology (SD)
South Dakota State U (SD)
Southern Illinois U Carbondale (IL)
Southern Illinois U Edwardsville (IL)
Southern Methodist U (TX)
Southern Polytechnic State U (GA)
Stanford U (CA)
Stevens Inst of Technology (NJ)
Stony Brook U, State U of New York (NY)
Syracuse U (NY)
Temple U (PA)
Texas A&M U (TX)
Texas A&M U–Kingsville (TX)
Texas Tech U (TX)
Trine U (IN)
Tufts U (MA)
United States Air Force Acad (CO)
United States Coast Guard Acad (CT)
United States Military Acad (NY)
Université de Sherbrooke (QC, Canada)
U at Buffalo, the State U of New York (NY)
The U of Akron (OH)
The U of Alabama (AL)
The U of Alabama at Birmingham (AL)
The U of Alabama in Huntsville (AL)
U of Alaska Anchorage (AK)
U of Alaska Fairbanks (AK)
U of Alberta (AB, Canada)
The U of Arizona (AZ)
U of Arkansas (AR)
The U of British Columbia (BC, Canada)
The U of British Columbia–Okanagan (BC, Canada)
U of California, Berkeley (CA)
U of California, Davis (CA)
U of California, Irvine (CA)
U of California, Los Angeles (CA)
U of Central Florida (FL)
U of Cincinnati (OH)
U of Colorado Boulder (CO)
U of Colorado Denver (CO)
U of Connecticut (CT)
U of Dayton (OH)
U of Delaware (DE)
U of Evansville (IN)
U of Florida (FL)
U of Hartford (CT)
U of Hawaii at Manoa (HI)
U of Houston (TX)
U of Idaho (ID)
U of Illinois at Chicago (IL)
U of Illinois at Urbana–Champaign (IL)
The U of Iowa (IA)
The U of Kansas (KS)
U of Louisiana at Lafayette (LA)
U of Louisville (KY)
U of Maine (ME)
U of Maryland, Coll Park (MD)
U of Massachusetts Amherst (MA)
U of Massachusetts Dartmouth (MA)
U of Massachusetts Lowell (MA)
U of Memphis (TN)
U of Miami (FL)
U of Michigan (MI)
U of Minnesota, Duluth (MN)
U of Minnesota, Twin Cities Campus (MN)
U of Mississippi (MS)
U of Missouri (MO)
U of Missouri–Kansas City (MO)

U of Missouri–St. Louis (MO)
U of Mount Union (OH)
U of Nebraska–Lincoln (NE)
U of Nevada, Las Vegas (NV)
U of Nevada, Reno (NV)
U of New Hampshire (NH)
U of New Haven (CT)
U of New Mexico (NM)
U of New Orleans (LA)
The U of North Carolina at Charlotte (NC)
U of North Dakota (ND)
U of North Florida (FL)
U of Notre Dame (IN)
U of Oklahoma (OK)
U of Ottawa (ON, Canada)
U of Pittsburgh (PA)
U of Portland (OR)
U of Rhode Island (RI)
U of South Alabama (AL)
U of South Carolina (SC)
U of Southern California (CA)
U of South Florida (FL)
The U of Tennessee (TN)
The U of Tennessee at Chattanooga (TN)
The U of Texas at Arlington (TX)
The U of Texas at Austin (TX)
The U of Texas at El Paso (TX)
The U of Texas at San Antonio (TX)
The U of Texas at Tyler (TX)
U of the District of Columbia (DC)
U of the Pacific (CA)
The U of Toledo (OH)
U of Toronto (ON, Canada)
U of Utah (UT)
U of Vermont (VT)
U of Virginia (VA)
U of Washington (WA)
The U of Western Ontario (ON, Canada)
U of Windsor (ON, Canada)
U of Wisconsin–Madison (WI)
U of Wisconsin–Milwaukee (WI)
U of Wisconsin–Platteville (WI)
U of Wyoming (WY)
Utah State U (UT)
Valparaiso U (IN)
Vanderbilt U (TN)
Villanova U (PA)
Virginia Polytechnic Inst and State U (VA)
Washington State U (WA)
Wayne State U (MI)
Wentworth Inst of Technology (MA)
Western Kentucky U (KY)
Western Michigan U (MI)
West Virginia U (WV)
West Virginia U Inst of Technology (WV)
Widener U (PA)
Worcester Polytechnic Inst (MA)
Youngstown State U (OH)

CIVIL ENGINEERING RELATED

Bradley U (IL)
California Polytechnic State U, San Luis Obispo (CA)
Carnegie Mellon U (PA)
Drexel U (PA)
Embry-Riddle Aeronautical U–Daytona (FL)
Ohio Northern U (OH)
Purdue U (IN)

CIVIL ENGINEERING TECHNOLOGY

Bluefield State Coll (WV)
Central Connecticut State U (CT)
Delaware State U (DE)
Fairleigh Dickinson U, Metropolitan Campus (NJ)
Fairmont State U (WV)
Georgia Southern U (GA)
Lakehead U (ON, Canada)
Lincoln U (PA)
Metropolitan State Coll of Denver (CO)
Montana State U–Northern (MT)
Pennsylvania Coll of Technology (PA)
Point Park U (PA)
Purdue U (IN)
Rochester Inst of Technology (NY)

Long Island U–C. W. Post Campus (NY)
Loras Coll (IA)
Louisiana Coll (LA)
Loyola U Chicago (IL)
Madonna U (MI)
Malone U (OH)
Manchester Coll (IN)
Mansfield U of Pennsylvania (PA)
Marquette U (WI)
Marshall U (WV)
Mary Baldwin Coll (VA)
Maryville U of Saint Louis (MO)
Marywood U (PA)
Mayville State U (ND)
McKendree U (IL)
McNeese State U (LA)
Mercy Coll (NY)
Miami U (OH)
Michigan State U (MI)
Michigan Technological U (MI)
Midwestern State U (TX)
Minnesota State U Mankato (MN)
Minnesota State U Moorhead (MN)
Minot State U (ND)
Misericordia U (PA)
Mississippi State U (MS)
Missouri Southern State U (MO)
Missouri State U (MO)
Missouri Western State U (MO)
Monmouth U (NJ)
Moravian Coll (PA)
Morningside Coll (IA)
Mount Marty Coll (SD)
Mount Mercy U (IA)
Mount Saint Mary Coll (NY)
Mount Vernon Nazarene U (OH)
Norfolk State U (VA)
North Dakota State U (ND)
Northeastern State U (OK)
Northern Illinois U (IL)
Northern Michigan U (MI)
Northern State U (SD)
Northwestern Coll (IA)
Northwest Missouri State U (MO)
Oakland U (MI)
Ohio Northern U (OH)
The Ohio State U (OH)
Oklahoma Christian U (OK)
Old Dominion U (VA)
Oral Roberts U (OK)
Our Lady of the Lake Coll (LA)
Peru State Coll (NE)
Prairie View A&M U (TX)
Purdue U (IN)
Purdue U Calumet (IN)
Quincy U (IL)
Ramapo Coll of New Jersey (NJ)
Rhode Island Coll (RI)
Rochester Inst of Technology (NY)
Rockhurst U (MO)
Roosevelt U (IL)
Rutgers, The State U of New Jersey, Camden (NJ)
Rutgers, The State U of New Jersey, Newark (NJ)
Rutgers, The State U of New Jersey, New Brunswick (NJ)
Sage Coll of Albany (NY)
Saginaw Valley State U (MI)
St. Catherine U (MN)
St. Edward's U (TX)
Saint Francis U (PA)
St. John's U (NY)
Saint Joseph's Coll (IN)
St. Joseph's Coll, Long Island Campus (NY)
St. Joseph's Coll, New York (NY)
Saint Leo U (FL)
Saint Louis U (MO)
Saint Mary-of-the-Woods Coll (IN)
Saint Mary's U of Minnesota (MN)
St. Thomas Aquinas Coll (NY)
Salem State U (MA)
Salisbury U (MD)
Salve Regina U (RI)
Seattle U (WA)
Seton Hill U (PA)
South Dakota State U (SD)
Southeast Missouri State U (MO)
Southern Arkansas U–Magnolia (AR)
Southwest Baptist U (MO)
Southwestern Adventist U (TX)

Southwestern Oklahoma State U (OK)
State U of New York at Fredonia (NY)
State U of New York at Plattsburgh (NY)
State U of New York Upstate Medical U (NY)
Stony Brook U, State of New York (NY)
Tabor Coll (KS)
Tarleton State U (TX)
Texas A&M U–Corpus Christi (TX)
Texas Southern U (TX)
Texas State U–San Marcos (TX)
Texas Woman's U (TX)
Thiel Coll (PA)
Thomas Edison State Coll (NJ)
Thomas More Coll (KY)
Trevecca Nazarene U (TN)
Tuskegee U (AL)
Union Coll (NE)
Union U (TN)
U at Buffalo, the State U of New York (NY)
The U of Alabama at Birmingham (AL)
U of Bridgeport (CT)
U of Central Arkansas (AR)
U of Central Florida (FL)
U of Central Missouri (MO)
U of Cincinnati (OH)
U of Connecticut (CT)
U of Delaware (DE)
U of Evansville (IN)
The U of Findlay (OH)
U of Hartford (CT)
U of Hawaii at Manoa (HI)
U of Idaho (ID)
U of Illinois at Springfield (IL)
U of Indianapolis (IN)
The U of Iowa (IA)
The U of Kansas (KS)
U of Louisiana at Monroe (LA)
U of Maine (ME)
U of Mary (ND)
U of Mary Hardin-Baylor (TX)
U of Maryland Eastern Shore (MD)
U of Massachusetts Dartmouth (MA)
U of Medicine and Dentistry of New Jersey (NJ)
U of Michigan–Flint (MI)
U of Minnesota, Twin Cities Campus (MN)
U of Mississippi (MS)
U of Missouri–Kansas City (MO)
U of Mount Union (OH)
U of Nebraska Medical Center (NE)
U of Nevada, Las Vegas (NV)
U of New England (ME)
U of New Hampshire (NH)
The U of North Carolina at Chapel Hill (NC)
The U of North Carolina at Charlotte (NC)
U of North Dakota (ND)
U of North Texas (TX)
U of Oklahoma (OK)
U of Rhode Island (RI)
U of Rio Grande (OH)
U of St. Francis (IL)
U of Saint Francis (IN)
The U of Scranton (PA)
U of Southern Mississippi (MS)
U of South Florida (FL)
The U of Tennessee (TN)
The U of Texas at Arlington (TX)
The U of Texas at Austin (TX)
The U of Texas at El Paso (TX)
The U of Texas at San Antonio (TX)
The U of Texas at Tyler (TX)
The U of Texas–Pan American (TX)
U of the District of Columbia (DC)
U of the Sciences in Philadelphia (PA)
The U of Toledo (OH)
U of Utah (UT)
U of Vermont (VT)
The U of Virginia's Coll at Wise (VA)
U of Washington (WA)
U of West Florida (FL)
U of Wisconsin–La Crosse (WI)
U of Wisconsin–Milwaukee (WI)
U of Wisconsin–Stevens Point (WI)

Utah State U (UT)
Virginia Commonwealth U (VA)
Wake Forest U (NC)
Walsh U (OH)
Wartburg Coll (IA)
Washburn U (KS)
Wayne State U (MI)
Weber State U (UT)
Western Carolina U (NC)
Western Connecticut State U (CT)
Western Illinois U (IL)
Western Kentucky U (KY)
West Liberty U (WV)
West Texas A&M U (TX)
West Virginia U (WV)
Wichita State U (KS)
Wilkes U (PA)
Winona State U (MN)
Wright State U (OH)
Xavier U (OH)
York Coll of Pennsylvania (PA)
York Coll of the City U of New York (NY)
Youngstown State U (OH)

CLINICAL/MEDICAL LABORATORY SCIENCE AND ALLIED PROFESSIONS RELATED

Allen Coll (IA)
Auburn U (AL)
Bloomfield Coll (NJ)
The Coll of Idaho (ID)
Hunter Coll of the City U of New York (NY)
Roosevelt U (IL)
Saint Louis U (MO)
U of Massachusetts Lowell (MA)

CLINICAL/MEDICAL LABORATORY TECHNOLOGY

Auburn U (AL)
Barry U (FL)
California State U, East Bay (CA)
Clarion U of Pennsylvania (PA)
Delaware State U (DE)
Farmingdale State Coll (NY)
Indiana U–Purdue U Fort Wayne (IN)
Long Island U–C. W. Post Campus (NY)
Northern State U (SD)
Our Lady of the Lake Coll (LA)
Penn State DuBois (PA)
St. Thomas Aquinas Coll (NY)
Sonoma State U (CA)
U of Alberta (AB, Canada)
The U of British Columbia (BC, Canada)
U of Maryland Eastern Shore (MD)
U of Missouri–Kansas City (MO)
U of New Mexico (NM)
U of Science and Arts of Oklahoma (OK)
Viterbo U (WI)
Washburn U (KS)
Winona State U (MN)
York Coll of the City U of New York (NY)

CLINICAL/MEDICAL SOCIAL WORK

New Mexico Highlands U (NM)

CLINICAL NUTRITION

Kent State U (OH)
Loyola U Chicago (IL)
Messiah Coll (PA)
U of North Dakota (ND)

CLINICAL PSYCHOLOGY

Biola U (CA)
Husson U (ME)
Keene State Coll (NH)
Lakehead U (ON, Canada)
Lamar U (TX)
Mansfield U of Pennsylvania (PA)
Moravian Coll (PA)
Simon Fraser U (BC, Canada)
U of Alberta (AB, Canada)
The U of British Columbia (BC, Canada)
U of Windsor (ON, Canada)

Western State Coll of Colorado (CO)

COGNITIVE PSYCHOLOGY AND PSYCHOLINGUISTICS

Averett U (VA)
Brown U (RI)
California State U, Stanislaus (CA)
Dartmouth Coll (NH)
Fitchburg State U (MA)
Free Will Baptist Bible Coll (TN)
The Johns Hopkins U (MD)
Lawrence U (WI)
Scripps Coll (CA)
State U of New York at Oswego (NY)
Tulane U (LA)
U of California, Santa Cruz (CA)
Vassar Coll (NY)
Washington U in St. Louis (MO)
Wellesley Coll (MA)
Yale U (CT)

COGNITIVE SCIENCE

California State U, Fresno (CA)
Carnegie Mellon U (PA)
Case Western Reserve U (OH)
Central Michigan U (MI)
George Fox U (OR)
Hampshire Coll (MA)
Indiana U Bloomington (IN)
Lawrence U (WI)
Lehigh U (PA)
Massachusetts Inst of Technology (MA)
Millsaps Coll (MS)
Occidental Coll (CA)
Pomona Coll (CA)
Queen's U at Kingston (ON, Canada)
Rensselaer Polytechnic Inst (NY)
Simon Fraser U (BC, Canada)
State U of New York at Oswego (NY)
United States Military Acad (NY)
The U of British Columbia (BC, Canada)
U of California, Berkeley (CA)
U of California, Los Angeles (CA)
U of California, Merced (CA)
U of Connecticut (CT)
U of Delaware (DE)
U of Evansville (IN)
U of Georgia (GA)
U of Pennsylvania (PA)
U of Richmond (VA)
U of Rochester (NY)
The U of Texas at Dallas (TX)
U of Wisconsin–Stout (WI)
Vanderbilt U (TN)

COLLEGE STUDENT COUNSELING AND PERSONNEL SERVICES

Bob Jones U (SC)
Bowling Green State U (OH)

COMMERCIAL AND ADVERTISING ART

Acad of Art U (CA)
Alberta Coll of Art & Design (AB, Canada)
Arcadia U (PA)
Arkansas State U (AR)
Art Center Coll of Design (CA)
The Art Inst of Dallas (TX)
The Art Inst of Fort Worth (TX)
The Art Inst of Houston (TX)
The Art Inst of Houston - North (TX)
The Art Inst of San Antonio (TX)
Ashland U (OH)
Baker Coll of Owosso (MI)
Bemidji State U (MN)
Biola U (CA)
Black Hills State U (SD)
Bob Jones U (SC)
Boise State U (ID)
Bowling Green State U (OH)
Buena Vista U (IA)
Buffalo State Coll, State U of New York (NY)
California Coll of the Arts (CA)
California State U, East Bay (CA)

California State U, Fresno (CA)
California State U, Long Beach (CA)
California U of Pennsylvania (PA)
Cardinal Stritch U (WI)
Carson-Newman Coll (TN)
Centenary Coll (NJ)
Clark U (MA)
Coll for Creative Studies (MI)
The Coll of New Jersey (NJ)
The Coll of Saint Rose (NY)
Columbia Coll Chicago (IL)
Columbus Coll of Art & Design (OH)
Concordia U (PA)
Concordia U, Nebraska (NE)
Curry Coll (MA)
Dominican U (IL)
Dordt Coll (IA)
Drake U (IA)
Drexel U (PA)
Eastern Kentucky U (KY)
Emmanuel Coll (MA)
Fairmont State U (WV)
Fashion Inst of Technology (NY)
Fontbonne U (MO)
Fordham U (NY)
Graceland U (IA)
Hampton U (VA)
Indiana U Bloomington (IN)
Indiana U–Purdue U Fort Wayne (IN)
Iowa State U of Science and Technology (IA)
Keene State Coll (NH)
Kent State U (OH)
Kutztown U of Pennsylvania (PA)
Lamar U (TX)
Lewis U (IL)
Lipscomb U (TN)
Louisiana Coll (LA)
Loyola U New Orleans (LA)
Lycoming Coll (PA)
Marietta Coll (OH)
Marymount Manhattan Coll (NY)
Massachusetts Coll of Art and Design (MA)
Mercy Coll (NY)
Miami U (OH)
Millikin U (IL)
Minnesota State U Mankato (MN)
Mitchell Coll (CT)
Montana State U–Northern (MT)
New York City Coll of Technology of the City U of New York (NY)
New York Inst of Technology (NY)
Northeastern State U (OK)
Northern Kentucky U (KY)
North Georgia Coll & State U (GA)
Northwest Nazarene U (ID)
Ohio Northern U (OH)
Oklahoma Christian U (OK)
Oklahoma City U (OK)
O'More Coll of Design (TN)
Oral Roberts U (OK)
Otis Coll of Art and Design (CA)
Pennsylvania Coll of Technology (PA)
Peru State Coll (NE)
Philadelphia U (PA)
Pittsburg State U (KS)
Portland State U (OR)
Pratt Inst (NY)
Purchase Coll, State U of New York (NY)
Ringling Coll of Art and Design (FL)
Rochester Inst of Technology (NY)
Rutgers, The State U of New Jersey, New Brunswick (NJ)
St. Norbert Coll (WI)
St. Thomas Aquinas Coll (NY)
Salem State U (MA)
Savannah Coll of Art and Design (GA)
Seton Hill U (PA)
Simmons Coll (MA)
Southwest Baptist U (MO)
Southwestern Oklahoma State U (OK)
State U of New York at Fredonia (NY)
State U of New York at New Paltz (NY)
State U of New York at Oswego (NY)
Suffolk U (MA)

Syracuse U (NY)
U of Central Missouri (MO)
U of Cincinnati (OH)
U of Dayton (OH)
U of Denver (CO)
U of Indianapolis (IN)
U of Massachusetts Dartmouth (MA)
U of Minnesota, Duluth (MN)
U of New Haven (CT)
U of North Texas (TX)
The U of Tennessee (TN)
The U of Texas at El Paso (TX)
U of the Pacific (CA)
U of Washington (WA)
U of Wisconsin–Platteville (WI)
U of Wisconsin–Stevens Point (WI)
Upper Iowa U (IA)
Villa Maria Coll of Buffalo (NY)
Wartburg Coll (IA)
Washington U in St. Louis (MO)
Waynesburg U (PA)
Weber State U (UT)
West Liberty U (WV)
West Texas A&M U (TX)
West Virginia Wesleyan Coll (WV)
William Paterson U of New Jersey (NJ)
William Woods U (MO)
Winona State U (MN)
Woodbury U (CA)
York Coll of Pennsylvania (PA)

COMMERCIAL PHOTOGRAPHY
Acad of Art U (CA)
Appalachian State U (NC)
The Art Inst of Atlanta (GA)
The Art Inst of Atlanta–Decatur (GA)
The Art Inst of Charleston (SC)
The Art Inst of Tennessee–Nashville (TN)
The Art Inst of Washington (VA)
Fashion Inst of Technology (NY)
Harrington Coll of Design (IL)
Rochester Inst of Technology (NY)
Savannah Coll of Art and Design (GA)

COMMUNICATION
Arkansas State U (AR)
Asbury U (KY)
Bellevue U (NE)
Bethany Lutheran Coll (MN)
Boston U (MA)
Cleveland State U (OH)
The Coll of New Jersey (NJ)
Concordia Coll (MN)
Concordia U (CA)
DEREE - The American Coll of Greece (Greece)
DeSales U (PA)
DeVry U, Pomona (CA)
DeVry U, Westminster (CO)
DeVry U, Miramar (FL)
DeVry U, Orlando (FL)
DeVry U, Decatur (GA)
DeVry U, Chicago (IL)
DeVry U, Kansas City (MO)
DeVry U, Fort Washington (PA)
DeVry U, Houston (TX)
DeVry U, Irving (TX)
DeVry U Online (IL)
Eastern Illinois U (IL)
Edgewood Coll (WI)
Fairfield U (CT)
Florida Coll (FL)
Florida Inst of Technology (FL)
Fordham U (NY)
Geneva Coll (PA)
Hamilton Coll (NY)
Holy Cross Coll (IN)
Huntingdon Coll (AL)
Huntington U (IN)
Indiana Wesleyan U (IN)
Kentucky Mountain Bible Coll (KY)
Lake Forest Coll (IL)
Lebanese American U (Lebanon)
Le Moyne Coll (NY)
Marymount U (VA)
Massachusetts Coll of Liberal Arts (MA)
Merrimack Coll (MA)
Misericordia U (PA)

Neumann U (PA)
Nyack Coll (NY)
Oakland U (MI)
Oklahoma City U (OK)
Pacific Union Coll (CA)
Paine Coll (GA)
Portland State U (OR)
Purdue U (IN)
Randolph-Macon Coll (VA)
Roanoke Coll (VA)
Rowan U (NJ)
Saint Anselm Coll (NH)
St. John Fisher Coll (NY)
Saint Joseph's U (PA)
Simpson Coll (IA)
Southwestern Coll (KS)
Spalding U (KY)
Stetson U (FL)
Thomas More Coll (KY)
U of Arkansas–Fort Smith (AR)
U of Delaware (DE)
U of Evansville (IN)
U of Houston–Clear Lake (TX)
U of Houston–Downtown (TX)
U of Illinois at Chicago (IL)
U of Illinois at Springfield (IL)
U of Michigan–Flint (MI)
U of Minnesota, Crookston (MN)
U of Mount Union (OH)
U of North Dakota (ND)
U of San Diego (CA)
The U of Tampa (FL)
The U of Texas of the Permian Basin (TX)
U of Wisconsin–Eau Claire (WI)
U of Wisconsin–Green Bay (WI)
U of Wisconsin–Stevens Point (WI)
Walden U (MN)
Wheeling Jesuit U (WV)
Xavier U (OH)

COMMUNICATION AND JOURNALISM RELATED
The American U of Paris (France)
Arizona State U (AZ)
Arkansas State U (AR)
Auburn U (AL)
Benedictine U (IL)
Berry Coll (GA)
Bowling Green State U (OH)
Brigham Young U (UT)
California Lutheran U (CA)
California State U, Chico (CA)
Carlow U (PA)
Cedarville U (OH)
Centenary Coll of Louisiana (LA)
Chestnut Hill Coll (PA)
Clarke U (IA)
Clemson U (SC)
The Coll at Brockport, State U of New York (NY)
Columbia Coll (SC)
Concordia U (QC, Canada)
Dalhousie U (NS, Canada)
Dominican U of California (CA)
Drexel U (PA)
The Evergreen State Coll (WA)
Farmingdale State Coll (NY)
Flagler Coll (FL)
Florida Inst of Technology (FL)
Friends U (KS)
Hannibal-LaGrange U (MO)
Hawai'i Pacific U (HI)
Hope Coll (MI)
Immaculata U (PA)
Indiana U Bloomington (IN)
Indiana U Kokomo (IN)
Judson U (IL)
Lake Erie Coll (OH)
Lehman Coll of the City U of New York (NY)
Madonna U (MI)
Malone U (OH)
Marquette U (WI)
Mary Baldwin Coll (VA)
Mercer U (GA)
Mercy Coll (NY)
Milwaukee School of Eng (WI)
Minot State U (ND)
Newbury Coll (MA)
New England School of Communications (ME)
New York U (NY)
Norfolk State U (VA)
Northwest Christian U (OR)

Notre Dame de Namur U (CA)
Ohio Northern U (OH)
The Ohio State U (OH)
Oklahoma Christian U (OK)
Oklahoma City U (OK)
Penn State Abington (PA)
Penn State Altoona (PA)
Penn State Beaver (PA)
Penn State Berks (PA)
Penn State Brandywine (PA)
Penn State DuBois (PA)
Penn State Erie, The Behrend Coll (PA)
Penn State Fayette, The Eberly Campus (PA)
Penn State Greater Allegheny (PA)
Penn State Hazleton (PA)
Penn State Lehigh Valley (PA)
Penn State Mont Alto (PA)
Penn State New Kensington (PA)
Penn State Schuylkill (PA)
Penn State Shenango (PA)
Penn State U Park (PA)
Penn State Wilkes-Barre (PA)
Penn State Worthington Scranton (PA)
Penn State York (PA)
Point Park U (PA)
Quincy U (IL)
Quinnipiac U (CT)
Reinhardt U (GA)
Saint Mary's Coll of California (CA)
Siena Heights U (MI)
Southeastern Oklahoma State U (OK)
Sterling Coll (KS)
Tabor Coll (KS)
Tiffin U (OH)
Trevecca Nazarene U (TN)
Trinity Lutheran Coll (WA)
U of Illinois at Urbana–Champaign (IL)
U of Minnesota, Duluth (MN)
U of Minnesota, Twin Cities Campus (MN)
U of Wisconsin–Green Bay (WI)
Washington U in St. Louis (MO)
Webster U (MO)
West Virginia U (WV)
Wheeling Jesuit U (WV)

COMMUNICATION AND MEDIA RELATED
Adelphi U (NY)
Alma Coll (MI)
Athabasca U (AB, Canada)
Bennington Coll (VT)
Burlington Coll (VT)
Calumet Coll of Saint Joseph (IN)
Cameron U (OK)
Carnegie Mellon U (PA)
The Coll at Brockport, State U of New York (NY)
Concordia U (QC, Canada)
Crown Coll (MN)
DePaul U (IL)
Dowling Coll (NY)
Eastern Mennonite U (VA)
Elizabethtown Coll (PA)
Elon U (NC)
Fairleigh Dickinson U, Metropolitan Campus (NJ)
Florida State U (FL)
Franklin Coll Switzerland (Switzerland)
Gardner-Webb U (NC)
Georgetown Coll (KY)
Georgian Court U (NJ)
Greenville Coll (IL)
Hood Coll (MD)
Houghton Coll (NY)
Judson U (IL)
King's Coll (PA)
Lane Coll (TN)
La Roche Coll (PA)
Lasell Coll (MA)
Loyola U Chicago (IL)
Lycoming Coll (PA)
Lynn U (FL)
Macon State Coll (GA)
Marquette U (WI)
Milligan Coll (TN)
Missouri Baptist U (MO)
Montreat Coll, Montreat (NC)
New York U (NY)

Oklahoma City U (OK)
Penn State Erie, The Behrend Coll (PA)
Purdue U Calumet (IN)
Reinhardt U (GA)
Rochester Inst of Technology (NY)
Roger Williams U (RI)
Rollins Coll (FL)
St. Edward's U (TX)
St. Thomas U (FL)
Southern New Hampshire U (NH)
Southern Polytechnic State U (GA)
Southwestern Coll (KS)
Spring Arbor U (MI)
Stanford U (CA)
Taylor U (IN)
Université de Sherbrooke (QC, Canada)
U of Central Missouri (MO)
U of Colorado Boulder (CO)
U of Mobile (AL)
U of the Incarnate Word (TX)
The U of Western Ontario (ON, Canada)
Virginia Wesleyan Coll (VA)
Walsh U (OH)
Wheelock Coll (MA)
Wilmington U (DE)

COMMUNICATION DISORDERS SCIENCES AND SERVICES RELATED
Long Island U–Brooklyn Campus (NY)
Ouachita Baptist U (AR)
U of Minnesota, Duluth (MN)
U of Missouri (MO)
U of New Hampshire (NH)
U of Oklahoma Health Sciences Center (OK)
The U of Western Ontario (ON, Canada)

COMMUNICATION SCIENCES AND DISORDERS
Appalachian State U (NC)
Arizona State U (AZ)
Auburn U (AL)
Augustana Coll (IL)
Baldwin-Wallace Coll (OH)
Baylor U (TX)
Biola U (CA)
Bob Jones U (SC)
Boston U (MA)
Bowling Green State U (OH)
Bridgewater State U (MA)
Butler U (IN)
California Baptist U (CA)
California State U, Chico (CA)
California State U, Fresno (CA)
California State U, Fullerton (CA)
California State U, Long Beach (CA)
California State U, Los Angeles (CA)
California U of Pennsylvania (PA)
Carlos Albizu U (PR)
Case Western Reserve U (OH)
Central Michigan U (MI)
Eastern Illinois U (IL)
Eastern Kentucky U (KY)
Edinboro U of Pennsylvania (PA)
Fontbonne U (MO)
Hampton U (VA)
Harding U (AR)
Kansas State U (KS)
Lamar U (TX)
Longwood U (VA)
Minnesota State U Mankato (MN)
Minot State U (ND)
Northern Illinois U (IL)
Pace U (NY)
Penn State Abington (PA)
Penn State Altoona (PA)
Penn State Beaver (PA)
Penn State Berks (PA)
Penn State Brandywine (PA)
Penn State DuBois (PA)
Penn State Erie, The Behrend Coll (PA)
Penn State Fayette, The Eberly Campus (PA)
Penn State Greater Allegheny (PA)
Penn State Hazleton (PA)

Penn State Lehigh Valley (PA)
Penn State Mont Alto (PA)
Penn State New Kensington (PA)
Penn State Schuylkill (PA)
Penn State Shenango (PA)
Penn State U Park (PA)
Penn State Wilkes-Barre (PA)
Penn State Worthington Scranton (PA)
Penn State York (PA)
Portland State U (OR)
Queens Coll of the City U of New York (NY)
Radford U (VA)
Saint Mary's Coll (IN)
San Diego State U (CA)
San Francisco State U (CA)
Southeast Missouri State U (MO)
Southern Illinois U Carbondale (IL)
State U of New York at Fredonia (NY)
State U of New York at New Paltz (NY)
Syracuse U (NY)
Texas State U–San Marcos (TX)
Truman State U (MO)
The U of Arizona (AZ)
The U of British Columbia (BC, Canada)
U of Cincinnati (OH)
U of Colorado Boulder (CO)
U of Georgia (GA)
U of Houston (TX)
The U of Kansas (KS)
U of Maine (ME)
U of Maryland, Coll Park (MD)
U of Massachusetts Amherst (MA)
U of Minnesota, Duluth (MN)
U of Minnesota, Twin Cities Campus (MN)
U of Mississippi (MS)
U of Nebraska at Kearney (NE)
U of North Dakota (ND)
U of Oklahoma Health Sciences Center (OK)
U of Oregon (OR)
U of Redlands (CA)
U of Rhode Island (RI)
U of South Alabama (AL)
The U of South Dakota (SD)
The U of Texas at Austin (TX)
The U of Toledo (OH)
U of Vermont (VT)
The U of Western Ontario (ON, Canada)
U of Wisconsin–Eau Claire (WI)
U of Wisconsin–River Falls (WI)
U of Wisconsin–Stevens Point (WI)
Wayne State U (MI)
Western Carolina U (NC)
Western Illinois U (IL)
Western Kentucky U (KY)
West Texas A&M U (TX)
Wichita State U (KS)
William Paterson U of New Jersey (NJ)
Winthrop U (SC)
Worcester State U (MA)
Xavier U of Louisiana (LA)

COMMUNICATIONS TECHNOLOGIES AND SUPPORT SERVICES RELATED
Alverno Coll (WI)
Chestnut Hill Coll (PA)
Framingham State U (MA)
Indiana U Bloomington (IN)
Lewis U (IL)
Minot State U (ND)
Saint Mary-of-the-Woods Coll (IN)
Salve Regina U (RI)
U of Windsor (ON, Canada)

COMMUNICATIONS TECHNOLOGY
Cedarville U (OH)
Eastern Michigan U (MI)
East Stroudsburg U of Pennsylvania (PA)
Inter American U of Puerto Rico, Bayamón Campus (PR)
Lawrence Technological U (MI)
Sacred Heart U (CT)
Saint Mary-of-the-Woods Coll (IN)

INDEXES

Salve Regina U (RI)
Suffolk U (MA)
York Coll of the City U of New York (NY)

COMMUNITY HEALTH AND PREVENTIVE MEDICINE
Carroll Coll (MT)
Florida Gulf Coast U (FL)
George Mason U (VA)
Governors State U (IL)
Hofstra U (NY)
Indiana U Bloomington (IN)
Minnesota State U Moorhead (MN)
Pine Manor Coll (MA)
Portland State U (OR)
Texas A&M U–Kingsville (TX)
Tufts U (MA)
U of Florida (FL)
U of Illinois at Urbana–Champaign (IL)
U of Wisconsin–Eau Claire (WI)
U of Wisconsin–La Crosse (WI)
Western Kentucky U (KY)

COMMUNITY HEALTH SERVICES COUNSELING
Carroll Coll (MT)
Central Washington U (WA)
Delaware State U (DE)
Eastern Kentucky U (KY)
Eastern Washington U (WA)
Indiana State U (IN)
Indiana U–Purdue U Fort Wayne (IN)
James Madison U (VA)
Johnson C. Smith U (NC)
Marian U (WI)
Morris Coll (SC)
Northeastern Illinois U (IL)
Northern Illinois U (IL)
Northern Michigan U (MI)
Ohio U (OH)
Prairie View A&M U (TX)
Texas A&M U (TX)
U of Central Arkansas (AR)
The U of Kansas (KS)
U of Massachusetts Lowell (MA)
U of Nebraska at Omaha (NE)
U of Northern Iowa (IA)
U of Pennsylvania (PA)
U of the Cumberlands (KY)
U of West Florida (FL)
Western Connecticut State U (CT)
Western Washington U (WA)
Worcester State U (MA)
Youngstown State U (OH)

COMMUNITY ORGANIZATION AND ADVOCACY
Alverno Coll (WI)
Bemidji State U (MN)
Bryant U (RI)
Cape Breton U (NS, Canada)
Central Michigan U (MI)
Cleveland State U (OH)
DePaul U (IL)
Emory & Henry Coll (VA)
Goddard Coll (VT)
Indiana Wesleyan U (IN)
Lewis U (IL)
Mercer U (GA)
Missouri Baptist U (MO)
Montana State U–Northern (MT)
New Mexico State U (NM)
New York U (NY)
Northern State U (SD)
Northland Coll (WI)
Notre Dame of Maryland U (MD)
Providence Coll (RI)
Saint Martin's U (WA)
Siena Heights U (MI)
Southern Arkansas U–Magnolia (AR)
State U of New York Empire State Coll (NY)
Thomas Edison State Coll (NJ)
Touro Coll (NY)
U of Alaska Fairbanks (AK)
U of Hartford (CT)
U of Massachusetts Boston (MA)
U of Saint Mary (KS)
The U of Texas at El Paso (TX)
The U of Toledo (OH)

COMMUNITY PSYCHOLOGY
Clayton State U (GA)
Goddard Coll (VT)
Montana State U Billings (MT)
New York Inst of Technology (NY)
Rogers State U (OK)
U of Miami (FL)
U of Saint Mary (KS)
U of Washington, Bothell (WA)

COMPARATIVE LITERATURE
Agnes Scott Coll (GA)
The American U in Cairo (Egypt)
The American U of Paris (France)
Arcadia U (PA)
Bard Coll (NY)
Barnard Coll (NY)
Barry U (FL)
Beloit Coll (WI)
Bernard M. Baruch Coll of the City U of New York (NY)
Bishop's U (QC, Canada)
Blackburn Coll (IL)
Boston U (MA)
Brandeis U (MA)
Brown U (RI)
Bryn Mawr Coll (PA)
California State U, Long Beach (CA)
Carson-Newman Coll (TN)
Case Western Reserve U (OH)
Castleton State Coll (VT)
Christendom Coll (VA)
City Coll of the City U of New York (NY)
Clark U (MA)
Coe Coll (IA)
The Coll at Brockport, State U of New York (NY)
Coll of the Atlantic (ME)
Coll of the Holy Cross (MA)
Coll of the Humanities and Sciences, Harrison Middleton U (AZ)
The Coll of Wooster (OH)
The Colorado Coll (CO)
Columbia U, School of General Studies (NY)
Cornell U (NY)
Dalhousie U (NS, Canada)
Dartmouth Coll (NH)
Earlham Coll (IN)
Eckerd Coll (FL)
Emory U (GA)
Fordham U (NY)
Franklin Coll Switzerland (Switzerland)
Gettysburg Coll (PA)
Gonzaga U (WA)
Graceland U (IA)
Hamilton Coll (NY)
Harvard U (MA)
Haverford Coll (PA)
Hillsdale Coll (MI)
Hobart and William Smith Colls (NY)
Hofstra U (NY)
Houghton Coll (NY)
Hunter Coll of the City U of New York (NY)
Indiana U Bloomington (IN)
Inter American U of Puerto Rico, San Germán Campus (PR)
John Carroll U (OH)
The Johns Hopkins U (MD)
Johnson State Coll (VT)
Lake Superior State U (MI)
Lycoming Coll (PA)
Manchester Coll (IN)
Marlboro Coll (VT)
Mills Coll (CA)
Minnesota State U Mankato (MN)
Mount Allison U (NB, Canada)
New Coll of Florida (FL)
New England Coll (NH)
New York U (NY)
Northwest U (WA)
The Ohio State U (OH)
Ohio Wesleyan U (OH)
Otterbein U (OH)
Pacific U (OR)
Penn State Abington (PA)
Penn State Altoona (PA)
Penn State Beaver (PA)
Penn State Berks (PA)

Penn State Brandywine (PA)
Penn State DuBois (PA)
Penn State Erie, The Behrend Coll (PA)
Penn State Fayette, The Eberly Campus (PA)
Penn State Greater Allegheny (PA)
Penn State Hazleton (PA)
Penn State Lehigh Valley (PA)
Penn State Mont Alto (PA)
Penn State New Kensington (PA)
Penn State Schuylkill (PA)
Penn State Shenango (PA)
Penn State U Park (PA)
Penn State Wilkes-Barre (PA)
Penn State Worthington Scranton (PA)
Penn State York (PA)
Princeton U (NJ)
Purchase Coll, State U of New York (NY)
Purdue U (IN)
Queens Coll of the City U of New York (NY)
Quinnipiac U (CT)
Ramapo Coll of New Jersey (NJ)
Rockford Coll (IL)
Rutgers, The State U of New Jersey, New Brunswick (NJ)
St. Catherine U (MN)
Saint Francis U (PA)
Saint Mary's Coll of California (CA)
San Diego State U (CA)
San Francisco State U (CA)
Sarah Lawrence Coll (NY)
Sewanee: The U of the South (TN)
Shimer Coll (IL)
Smith Coll (MA)
Sonoma State U (CA)
Stanford U (CA)
State U of New York at Binghamton (NY)
State U of New York Coll at Geneseo (NY)
State U of New York Coll at Old Westbury (NY)
Stony Brook U, State U of New York (NY)
Swarthmore Coll (PA)
Syracuse U (NY)
Touro Coll (NY)
Trent U (ON, Canada)
Trinity Coll (CT)
United States Military Acad (NY)
U of Alberta (AB, Canada)
U of California, Berkeley (CA)
U of California, Davis (CA)
U of California, Irvine (CA)
U of California, Los Angeles (CA)
U of California, Merced (CA)
U of California, Santa Barbara (CA)
U of California, Santa Cruz (CA)
U of Delaware (DE)
U of Georgia (GA)
U of Illinois at Urbana–Champaign (IL)
The U of Iowa (IA)
U of La Verne (CA)
U of Massachusetts Amherst (MA)
U of Michigan (MI)
U of Minnesota, Twin Cities Campus (MN)
U of Nevada, Las Vegas (NV)
U of New Mexico (NM)
The U of North Carolina at Chapel Hill (NC)
U of Oregon (OR)
U of Pennsylvania (PA)
U of Pittsburgh at Greensburg (PA)
U of Pittsburgh at Johnstown (PA)
U of Redlands (CA)
U of Rochester (NY)
U of South Carolina (SC)
U of Southern California (CA)
The U of Texas at Dallas (TX)
The U of Toledo (OH)
U of Toronto (ON, Canada)
U of Utah (UT)
U of Virginia (VA)
U of Washington (WA)
The U of Western Ontario (ON, Canada)
U of Wisconsin–Madison (WI)
U of Wisconsin–Milwaukee (WI)
Washington U in St. Louis (MO)

Wellesley Coll (MA)
West Virginia Wesleyan Coll (WV)
Willamette U (OR)
William Paterson U of New Jersey (NJ)
Williams Coll (MA)
William Woods U (MO)
Yale U (CT)

COMPARATIVE PSYCHOLOGY
Prescott Coll (AZ)

COMPUTATIONAL AND APPLIED MATHEMATICS
Mary Baldwin Coll (VA)
U of Notre Dame (IN)

COMPUTATIONAL BIOLOGY
Case Western Reserve U (OH)
Purdue U (IN)

COMPUTATIONAL MATHEMATICS
Arizona State U (AZ)
Asbury U (KY)
California Inst of Technology (CA)
Carnegie Mellon U (PA)
Coll of Saint Benedict (MN)
Embry-Riddle Aeronautical U–Daytona (FL)
Indiana U–Purdue U Fort Wayne (IN)
Marquette U (WI)
Michigan State U (MI)
Michigan Technological U (MI)
Rochester Inst of Technology (NY)
Saint John's U (MN)
Siena Coll (NY)
Southwestern U (TX)
Stevens Inst of Technology (NJ)
U of California, Davis (CA)
U of California, Los Angeles (CA)
U of Illinois at Urbana–Champaign (IL)
U of Puerto Rico at Humacao (PR)
U of Southern California (CA)

COMPUTATIONAL SCIENCE
Purdue U (IN)
The Richard Stockton Coll of New Jersey (NJ)

COMPUTER AND INFORMATION SCIENCES
Adelphi U (NY)
Albany State U (GA)
Alcorn State U (MS)
Alverno Coll (WI)
Amberton U (TX)
American U (DC)
American U in Bulgaria (Bulgaria)
The American U of Paris (France)
Andrews U (MI)
Angelo State U (TX)
Anna Maria Coll (MA)
Aquinas Coll (MI)
Arcadia U (PA)
Arizona State U (AZ)
Arkansas State U (AR)
Arkansas Tech U (AR)
Assumption Coll (MA)
Athabasca U (AB, Canada)
Auburn U (AL)
Austin Peay State U (TN)
Avila U (MO)
Baker Coll of Muskegon (MI)
Ball State U (IN)
Barnard Coll (NY)
Barton Coll (NC)
Bellarmine U (KY)
Bellevue U (NE)
Bennington Coll (VT)
Bentley U (MA)
Berea Coll (KY)
Bernard M. Baruch Coll of the City U of New York (NY)
Bethel U (MN)
Bishop's U (QC, Canada)
Bloomfield Coll (NJ)
Bluefield State Coll (WV)
Bob Jones U (SC)
Boise State U (ID)
Boston Coll (MA)

Bowie State U (MD)
Bowling Green State U (OH)
Brewton-Parker Coll (GA)
Bryant U (RI)
Bucknell U (PA)
Butler U (IN)
Caldwell Coll (NJ)
California Lutheran U (CA)
California State U, Fresno (CA)
California State U, Los Angeles (CA)
California State U, San Bernardino (CA)
California State U, Stanislaus (CA)
California U of Pennsylvania (PA)
Cameron U (OK)
Cape Breton U (NS, Canada)
Carroll Coll (MT)
Castleton State Coll (VT)
The Catholic U of America (DC)
Cedar Crest Coll (PA)
Central Connecticut State U (CT)
Central State U (OH)
Central Washington U (WA)
Chaminade U of Honolulu (HI)
Chapman U (CA)
Chestnut Hill Coll (PA)
Christopher Newport U (VA)
The Citadel, The Military Coll of South Carolina (SC)
Clarion U of Pennsylvania (PA)
Clark Atlanta U (GA)
Clarke U (IA)
Clemson U (SC)
Cleveland State U (OH)
Coastal Carolina U (SC)
Coll of Charleston (SC)
Coll of Mount St. Joseph (OH)
The Coll of New Jersey (NJ)
Coll of Saint Elizabeth (NJ)
The Coll of Saint Rose (NY)
The Coll of St. Scholastica (MN)
Coll of the Holy Cross (MA)
The Coll of William and Mary (VA)
Colorado Mesa U (CO)
Colorado State U (CO)
Columbia Coll (MO)
Columbus State U (GA)
Concordia U Chicago (IL)
Concordia U, Nebraska (NE)
Cornell U (NY)
Covenant Coll (GA)
Dakota State U (SD)
Dallas Baptist U (TX)
Delaware State U (DE)
DEREE - The American Coll of Greece (Greece)
Dickinson Coll (PA)
Dixie State Coll of Utah (UT)
Doane Coll (NE)
Dominican Coll (NY)
Dowling Coll (NY)
Earlham Coll (IN)
East Central U (OK)
Eastern Connecticut State U (CT)
Eastern Kentucky U (KY)
Eastern Michigan U (MI)
Eastern New Mexico U (NM)
Eastern Oregon U (OR)
Eastern Washington U (WA)
East Stroudsburg U of Pennsylvania (PA)
East Tennessee State U (TN)
Edgewood Coll (WI)
Edinboro U of Pennsylvania (PA)
Elizabethtown Coll (PA)
Elon U (NC)
Emmanuel Coll (GA)
Emmaus Bible Coll (IA)
Emporia State U (KS)
Excelsior Coll (NY)
Fairfield U (CT)
Fairleigh Dickinson U, Coll at Florham (NJ)
Felician Coll (NJ)
Fitchburg State U (MA)
Florida Ag and Mech U (FL)
Florida Atlantic U (FL)
Florida Gulf Coast U (FL)
Florida Intl U (FL)
Fordham U (NY)
Fort Lewis Coll (CO)
Framingham State U (MA)
Franciscan U of Steubenville (OH)
Francis Marion U (SC)

Franklin Coll (IN)
Franklin U (OH)
Friends U (KS)
Gallaudet U (DC)
Gannon U (PA)
Gardner-Webb U (NC)
Geneva Coll (PA)
George Fox U (OR)
George Mason U (VA)
Georgetown Coll (KY)
The George Washington U (DC)
Georgia Coll & State U (GA)
Georgia Inst of Technology (GA)
Georgia Southern U (GA)
Georgia State U (GA)
Goshen Coll (IN)
Grand Valley State U (MI)
Greenville Coll (IL)
Grove City Coll (PA)
Guilford Coll (NC)
Gwynedd-Mercy Coll (PA)
Hamilton Coll (NY)
Hannibal-LaGrange U (MO)
Harrisburg U of Science and
  Technology (PA)
Hartwick Coll (NY)
Hawai`i Pacific U (HI)
Herzing U, Madison (WI)
Holy Family U (PA)
Hope Coll (MI)
Howard Payne U (TX)
Huston-Tillotson U (TX)
Idaho State U (ID)
Illinois Inst of Technology (IL)
Indiana State U (IN)
Indiana U Bloomington (IN)
Indiana U Kokomo (IN)
Indiana U Northwest (IN)
Indiana U of Pennsylvania (PA)
Indiana U–Purdue U Fort Wayne
  (IN)
Indiana U–Purdue U Indianapolis
  (IN)
Indiana U South Bend (IN)
Indiana U Southeast (IN)
Indiana Wesleyan U (IN)
Inter American U of Puerto Rico,
  Fajardo Campus (PR)
Iowa Wesleyan Coll (IA)
Ithaca Coll (NY)
Jacksonville State U (AL)
Jacksonville U (FL)
James Madison U (VA)
John Jay Coll of Criminal Justice of
  the City U of New York (NY)
The Johns Hopkins U (MD)
Johnson C. Smith U (NC)
Jones Coll, Jacksonville (FL)
Juniata Coll (PA)
Kansas State U (KS)
Kean U (NJ)
Keene State Coll (NH)
Kennesaw State U (GA)
Kent State U (OH)
Kentucky State U (KY)
Kentucky Wesleyan Coll (KY)
King's Coll (PA)
Knox Coll (IL)
LaGrange Coll (GA)
Lane Coll (TN)
La Roche Coll (PA)
La Salle U (PA)
Lehman Coll of the City U of New
  York (NY)
Le Moyne Coll (NY)
Lenoir-Rhyne U (NC)
Lewis-Clark State Coll (ID)
Liberty U (VA)
Lincoln Memorial U (TN)
Lincoln U (PA)
Lindenwood U (MO)
Lock Haven U of Pennsylvania (PA)
Long Island U–Brooklyn Campus
  (NY)
Long Island U–C. W. Post Campus
  (NY)
Loyola Marymount U (CA)
Loyola U Chicago (IL)
Loyola U Maryland (MD)
Lubbock Christian U (TX)
Mansfield U of Pennsylvania (PA)
Marquette U (WI)
Marshall U (WV)
Mars Hill Coll (NC)
Maryville Coll (TN)

Massachusetts Coll of Liberal Arts
  (MA)
The Master's Coll and Sem (CA)
Mayville State U (ND)
McDaniel Coll (MD)
McMurry U (TX)
Mercy Coll (NY)
Mercyhurst Coll (PA)
Meredith Coll (NC)
Merrimack Coll (MA)
Metropolitan State Coll of Denver
  (CO)
Miami U (OH)
Michigan State U (MI)
Midwestern State U (TX)
Millersville U of Pennsylvania (PA)
Milligan Coll (TN)
Millsaps Coll (MS)
Minot State U (ND)
Misericordia U (PA)
Mississippi Coll (MS)
Mississippi State U (MS)
Missouri Southern State U (MO)
Missouri Western State U (MO)
Monmouth U (NJ)
Montana State U–Northern (MT)
Montreat Coll, Montreat (NC)
Morehead State U (KY)
Morehouse Coll (GA)
Morrisville State Coll (NY)
Mount St. Mary's U (MD)
Mount Vernon Nazarene U (OH)
Neumann U (PA)
Neumont U (UT)
New England Coll (NH)
New England Inst of Technology
  (RI)
New Jersey City U (NJ)
New Mexico Highlands U (NM)
New Mexico State U (NM)
New York Inst of Technology (NY)
New York U (NY)
Norfolk State U (VA)
North Carolina Wesleyan Coll (NC)
Northeastern Illinois U (IL)
Northeastern U (MA)
Northern Kentucky U (KY)
Northern Michigan U (MI)
North Georgia Coll & State U (GA)
Northwest Missouri State U (MO)
Northwood U, Florida Campus (FL)
Northwood U, Michigan Campus
  (MI)
Notre Dame de Namur U (CA)
Nova Southeastern U (FL)
Oakland U (MI)
The Ohio State U (OH)
Ohio U (OH)
Okanagan Coll (BC, Canada)
Oklahoma City U (OK)
Oklahoma State U (OK)
Old Dominion U (VA)
Oral Roberts U (OK)
Oregon Inst of Technology (OR)
Park U (MO)
Penn State Abington (PA)
Penn State Altoona (PA)
Penn State Beaver (PA)
Penn State Berks (PA)
Penn State Brandywine (PA)
Penn State DuBois (PA)
Penn State Erie, The Behrend Coll
  (PA)
Penn State Fayette, The Eberly
  Campus (PA)
Penn State Greater Allegheny (PA)
Penn State Harrisburg (PA)
Penn State Hazleton (PA)
Penn State Lehigh Valley (PA)
Penn State Mont Alto (PA)
Penn State New Kensington (PA)
Penn State Schuylkill (PA)
Penn State Shenango (PA)
Penn State U Park (PA)
Penn State Wilkes-Barre (PA)
Penn State Worthington Scranton
  (PA)
Penn State York (PA)
Philadelphia U (PA)
Portland State U (OR)
Prairie View A&M U (TX)
Purdue U (IN)
Purdue U Calumet (IN)
Ramapo Coll of New Jersey (NJ)
Rhode Island Coll (RI)

Rice U (TX)
Rider U (NJ)
Roanoke Coll (VA)
Rochester Inst of Technology (NY)
Rollins Coll (FL)
Rowan U (NJ)
Rutgers, The State U of New
  Jersey, Camden (NJ)
Rutgers, The State U of New
  Jersey, Newark (NJ)
Sacred Heart U (CT)
Saginaw Valley State U (MI)
Saint Augustine's Coll (NC)
St. Bonaventure U (NY)
St. Catherine U (MN)
St. Edward's U (TX)
St. John Fisher Coll (NY)
St. John's U (NY)
Saint Joseph's Coll (IN)
St. Joseph's Coll, Long Island
  Campus (NY)
St. Joseph's Coll, New York (NY)
Saint Joseph's U (PA)
Saint Leo U (FL)
Saint Louis U (MO)
Saint Mary-of-the-Woods Coll (IN)
St. Mary's Coll of Maryland (MD)
St. Norbert Coll (WI)
Saint Peter's Coll (NJ)
Saint Vincent Coll (PA)
Saint Xavier U (IL)
Salem State U (MA)
Salisbury U (MD)
Sam Houston State U (TX)
Shaw U (NC)
Shepherd U (WV)
Shippensburg U of Pennsylvania
  (PA)
Shorter U (GA)
Siena Coll (NY)
Siena Heights U (MI)
Sierra Nevada Coll (NV)
Simmons Coll (MA)
Simpson Coll (IA)
Skidmore Coll (NY)
South Carolina State U (SC)
South Dakota State U (SD)
Southeastern Oklahoma State U
  (OK)
Southeast Missouri State U (MO)
Southern Arkansas U–Magnolia
  (AR)
Southern New Hampshire U (NH)
Southwest Baptist U (MO)
Southwestern Oklahoma State U
  (OK)
Southwestern U (TX)
Spring Hill Coll (AL)
State U of New York at Binghamton
  (NY)
State U of New York at New Paltz
  (NY)
State U of New York at Plattsburgh
  (NY)
State U of New York Coll at Old
  Westbury (NY)
State U of New York Coll at
  Potsdam (NY)
Stephen F. Austin State U (TX)
Sterling Coll (KS)
Stetson U (FL)
Stevenson U (MD)
Suffolk U (MA)
Swarthmore Coll (PA)
Syracuse U (NY)
Tarleton State U (TX)
Taylor U (IN)
Temple U (PA)
Texas A&M U–Kingsville (TX)
Texas Christian U (TX)
Texas Southern U (TX)
Texas State U–San Marcos (TX)
Texas Tech U (TX)
Texas Wesleyan U (TX)
Texas Woman's U (TX)
Thompson Rivers U (BC, Canada)
Tiffin U (OH)
Towson U (MD)
Transylvania U (KY)
Trinity U (TX)
Troy U (AL)
Truman State U (MO)
Tulane U (LA)
Union Coll (NY)
United States Military Acad (NY)

United States Naval Acad (MD)
U at Albany, State U of New York
  (NY)
The U of Alabama (AL)
The U of Alabama at Birmingham
  (AL)
The U of Alabama in Huntsville (AL)
U of Alaska Fairbanks (AK)
The U of Arizona (AZ)
U of Arkansas (AR)
U of Arkansas–Fort Smith (AR)
U of California, Irvine (CA)
U of California, Los Angeles (CA)
U of Central Arkansas (AR)
U of Central Florida (FL)
U of Central Missouri (MO)
U of Cincinnati (OH)
U of Colorado at Colorado Springs
  (CO)
U of Colorado Denver (CO)
U of Delaware (DE)
U of Dubuque (IA)
U of Florida (FL)
U of Great Falls (MT)
U of Hartford (CT)
U of Hawaii at Manoa (HI)
U of Houston (TX)
U of Houston–Clear Lake (TX)
U of Houston–Downtown (TX)
U of Illinois at Urbana–Champaign
  (IL)
The U of Kansas (KS)
U of Louisiana at Lafayette (LA)
U of Maine at Augusta (ME)
U of Mary (ND)
U of Mary Hardin-Baylor (TX)
U of Maryland, Coll Park (MD)
U of Maryland U Coll (MD)
U of Mary Washington (VA)
U of Massachusetts Boston (MA)
U of Massachusetts Dartmouth
  (MA)
U of Michigan (MI)
U of Michigan–Dearborn (MI)
U of Michigan–Flint (MI)
U of Minnesota, Duluth (MN)
U of Mississippi (MS)
U of Missouri (MO)
U of Mobile (AL)
U of Nebraska at Kearney (NE)
U of Nebraska–Lincoln (NE)
U of Nevada, Reno (NV)
U of New Hampshire (NH)
U of New Haven (CT)
U of New Mexico (NM)
U of North Alabama (AL)
U of North Dakota (ND)
U of North Florida (FL)
U of North Texas (TX)
U of Notre Dame (IN)
U of Oregon (OR)
U of Ottawa (ON, Canada)
U of Pikeville (KY)
U of Pittsburgh at Greensburg (PA)
U of Puerto Rico at Bayamón (PR)
U of Puerto Rico at Ponce (PR)
U of Rhode Island (RI)
U of Saint Mary (KS)
U of St. Thomas (MN)
U of Science and Arts of Oklahoma
  (OK)
U of South Alabama (AL)
U of South Carolina (SC)
U of South Carolina Beaufort (SC)
U of South Carolina Upstate (SC)
The U of South Dakota (SD)
U of Southern California (CA)
U of Southern Indiana (IN)
U of Southern Mississippi (MS)
U of South Florida (FL)
The U of Tampa (FL)
The U of Texas at Austin (TX)
The U of Texas at Dallas (TX)
The U of Texas at Tyler (TX)
The U of Texas of the Permian
  Basin (TX)
The U of Texas–Pan American (TX)
U of the Incarnate Word (TX)
U of Vermont (VT)
U of Virginia (VA)
The U of Virginia's Coll at Wise (VA)
U of Washington (WA)
U of Washington, Bothell (WA)
The U of Western Ontario (ON,
  Canada)

U of West Florida (FL)
U of West Georgia (GA)
U of Windsor (ON, Canada)
U of Wisconsin–Eau Claire (WI)
U of Wisconsin–La Crosse (WI)
U of Wisconsin–Madison (WI)
U of Wisconsin–Milwaukee (WI)
U of Wisconsin–River Falls (WI)
U of Wisconsin–Stevens Point (WI)
U of Wisconsin–Superior (WI)
U of Wisconsin–Whitewater (WI)
Utah State U (UT)
Utica Coll (NY)
Valdosta State U (GA)
Valley City State U (ND)
Vassar Coll (NY)
Virginia Commonwealth U (VA)
Virginia Polytechnic Inst and State
  U (VA)
Viterbo U (WI)
Wake Forest U (NC)
Walden U (MN)
Wartburg Coll (IA)
Washburn U (KS)
Washington State U (WA)
Washington U in St. Louis (MO)
Waynesburg U (PA)
Wayne State Coll (NE)
Wayne State U (MI)
Webber Intl U (FL)
Weber State U (UT)
Webster U (MO)
Wentworth Inst of Technology (MA)
West Chester U of Pennsylvania
  (PA)
Western Illinois U (IL)
Western Kentucky U (KY)
Western Michigan U (MI)
Western Washington U (WA)
Westminster Coll (UT)
West Texas A&M U (TX)
West Virginia Wesleyan Coll (WV)
Wheeling Jesuit U (WV)
Wichita State U (KS)
Widener U (PA)
Wilkes U (PA)
Williams Baptist Coll (AR)
William Woods U (MO)
Winona State U (MN)
Worcester Polytechnic Inst (MA)
Worcester State U (MA)
Wright State U (OH)
Xavier U of Louisiana (LA)
Yale U (CT)
Yeshiva U (NY)

**COMPUTER AND
INFORMATION SCIENCES AND
SUPPORT SERVICES RELATED**
Amridge U (AL)
Arizona State U (AZ)
Bloomsburg U of Pennsylvania (PA)
Cabrini Coll (PA)
California State U, Chico (CA)
California State U, Los Angeles
  (CA)
Capella U (MN)
City U of Seattle (WA)
Cleary U (MI)
Coll of Staten Island of the City U of
  New York (NY)
Columbia Coll (SC)
Columbia Coll Chicago (IL)
Delaware Valley Coll (PA)
DePaul U (IL)
The Evergreen State Coll (WA)
Ferris State U (MI)
Hofstra U (NY)
Husson U (ME)
Indiana Tech (IN)
Indiana U East (IN)
Indiana U–Purdue U Indianapolis
  (IN)
Inter American U of Puerto Rico,
  Bayamón Campus (PR)
John Jay Coll of Criminal Justice of
  the City U of New York (NY)
Keene State Coll (NH)
Lehigh U (PA)
Limestone Coll (SC)
Long Island U–C. W. Post Campus
  (NY)
Mayville State U (ND)

Missouri U of Science and Technology (MO)
Morrisville State Coll (NY)
Mountain State U (WV)
New York U (NY)
Park U (MO)
Potomac Coll (DC)
Purdue U (IN)
Purdue U Calumet (IN)
Purdue U North Central (IN)
Roberts Wesleyan Coll (NY)
State U of New York Coll of Technology at Alfred (NY)
Taylor U (IN)
Tiffin U (OH)
U of Evansville (IN)
U of Great Falls (MT)
U of Michigan–Flint (MI)
U of Mount Union (OH)
U of Northern Iowa (IA)
U of Notre Dame (IN)
U of Pittsburgh (PA)
U of Washington, Bothell (WA)
Utah State U (UT)
Valley City State U (ND)
Washington U in St. Louis (MO)

COMPUTER AND INFORMATION SCIENCES RELATED

California State U, Dominguez Hills (CA)
California State U, Monterey Bay (CA)
Carnegie Mellon U (PA)
Coll of Charleston (SC)
The Colorado Coll (CO)
Columbia U, School of General Studies (NY)
DigiPen Inst of Technology (WA)
Eastern Illinois U (IL)
Kent State U at East Liverpool (OH)
Limestone Coll (SC)
Maryville Coll (TN)
Missouri State U (MO)
Neumont U (UT)
Taylor U (IN)
Université de Sherbrooke (QC, Canada)
U of Great Falls (MT)
U of Windsor (ON, Canada)
U of Wisconsin–Stout (WI)
Wagner Coll (NY)
West Virginia U (WV)

COMPUTER AND INFORMATION SYSTEMS SECURITY

American Public U System (WV)
Auburn U Montgomery (AL)
Capella U (MN)
Dakota State U (SD)
Davenport U, Grand Rapids (MI)
DePaul U (IL)
East Stroudsburg U of Pennsylvania (PA)
Fountainhead Coll of Technology (TN)
Franklin U (OH)
Hilbert Coll (NY)
Indiana Tech (IN)
ITT Tech Inst, Bessemer (AL)
ITT Tech Inst, Madison (AL)
ITT Tech Inst, Mobile (AL)
ITT Tech Inst, Phoenix (AZ)
ITT Tech Inst, Phoenix (AZ)
ITT Tech Inst, Tempe (AZ)
ITT Tech Inst, Tucson (AZ)
ITT Tech Inst (AR)
ITT Tech Inst, Clovis (CA)
ITT Tech Inst, Concord (CA)
ITT Tech Inst, Corona (CA)
ITT Tech Inst, Culver City (CA)
ITT Tech Inst, Lathrop (CA)
ITT Tech Inst, Oakland (CA)
ITT Tech Inst, Orange (CA)
ITT Tech Inst, Oxnard (CA)
ITT Tech Inst, Rancho Cordova (CA)
ITT Tech Inst, San Bernardino (CA)
ITT Tech Inst, San Diego (CA)
ITT Tech Inst, San Dimas (CA)
ITT Tech Inst, Sylmar (CA)
ITT Tech Inst, Torrance (CA)

ITT Tech Inst, West Covina (CA)
ITT Tech Inst, Aurora (CO)
ITT Tech Inst, Thornton (CO)
ITT Tech Inst, Bradenton (FL)
ITT Tech Inst, Deerfield Beach (FL)
ITT Tech Inst, Fort Lauderdale (FL)
ITT Tech Inst, Fort Myers (FL)
ITT Tech Inst, Jacksonville (FL)
ITT Tech Inst, Lake Mary (FL)
ITT Tech Inst, Miami (FL)
ITT Tech Inst, Orlando (FL)
ITT Tech Inst, Pinellas Park (FL)
ITT Tech Inst, Tallahassee (FL)
ITT Tech Inst, Tampa (FL)
ITT Tech Inst, West Palm Beach (FL)
ITT Tech Inst, Atlanta (GA)
ITT Tech Inst, Duluth (GA)
ITT Tech Inst, Kennesaw (GA)
ITT Tech Inst (ID)
ITT Tech Inst, Mount Prospect (IL)
ITT Tech Inst, Oak Brook (IL)
ITT Tech Inst, Orland Park (IL)
ITT Tech Inst, Fort Wayne (IN)
ITT Tech Inst, Indianapolis (IN)
ITT Tech Inst, Indianapolis (IN)
ITT Tech Inst, Merrillville (IN)
ITT Tech Inst, Newburgh (IN)
ITT Tech Inst, South Bend (IN)
ITT Tech Inst, Cedar Rapids (IA)
ITT Tech Inst, Clive (IA)
ITT Tech Inst, Overland Park (KS)
ITT Tech Inst, Wichita (KS)
ITT Tech Inst, Lexington (KY)
ITT Tech Inst, Louisville (KY)
ITT Tech Inst, Baton Rouge (LA)
ITT Tech Inst, St. Rose (LA)
ITT Tech Inst, Hanover (MD)
ITT Tech Inst, Owings Mills (MD)
ITT Tech Inst, Norwood (MA)
ITT Tech Inst, Wilmington (MA)
ITT Tech Inst, Canton (MI)
ITT Tech Inst, Dearborn (MI)
ITT Tech Inst, Grand Rapids (MI)
ITT Tech Inst, Southfield (MI)
ITT Tech Inst, Swartz Creek (MI)
ITT Tech Inst, Troy (MI)
ITT Tech Inst, Wyoming (MI)
ITT Tech Inst, Brooklyn Center (MN)
ITT Tech Inst, Eden Prairie (MN)
ITT Tech Inst, Arnold (MO)
ITT Tech Inst, Earth City (MO)
ITT Tech Inst, Kansas City (MO)
ITT Tech Inst, Springfield (MO)
ITT Tech Inst (NE)
ITT Tech Inst, Henderson (NV)
ITT Tech Inst, North Las Vegas (NV)
ITT Tech Inst (NM)
ITT Tech Inst, Cary (NC)
ITT Tech Inst, Charlotte (NC)
ITT Tech Inst, Charlotte (NC)
ITT Tech Inst, Durham (NC)
ITT Tech Inst, High Point (NC)
ITT Tech Inst, Akron (OH)
ITT Tech Inst, Columbus (OH)
ITT Tech Inst, Dayton (OH)
ITT Tech Inst, Hilliard (OH)
ITT Tech Inst, Maumee (OH)
ITT Tech Inst, Norwood (OH)
ITT Tech Inst, Strongsville (OH)
ITT Tech Inst, Warrensville Heights (OH)
ITT Tech Inst, Youngstown (OH)
ITT Tech Inst, Oklahoma City (OK)
ITT Tech Inst, Tulsa (OK)
ITT Tech Inst, Portland (OR)
ITT Tech Inst, Salem (OR)
ITT Tech Inst, Columbia (SC)
ITT Tech Inst, Greenville (SC)
ITT Tech Inst, Myrtle Beach (SC)
ITT Tech Inst, North Charleston (SC)
ITT Tech Inst, Chattanooga (TN)
ITT Tech Inst, Cordova (TN)
ITT Tech Inst, Johnson City (TN)
ITT Tech Inst, Knoxville (TN)
ITT Tech Inst, Nashville (TN)
ITT Tech Inst, Arlington (TX)
ITT Tech Inst, Austin (TX)
ITT Tech Inst, DeSoto (TX)
ITT Tech Inst, Houston (TX)
ITT Tech Inst, Houston (TX)
ITT Tech Inst, Richardson (TX)

ITT Tech Inst, San Antonio (TX)
ITT Tech Inst, Waco (TX)
ITT Tech Inst, Webster (TX)
ITT Tech Inst (UT)
ITT Tech Inst, Chantilly (VA)
ITT Tech Inst, Norfolk (VA)
ITT Tech Inst, Richmond (VA)
ITT Tech Inst, Salem (VA)
ITT Tech Inst, Springfield (VA)
ITT Tech Inst, Everett (WA)
ITT Tech Inst, Seattle (WA)
ITT Tech Inst, Spokane Valley (WA)
ITT Tech Inst, Germantown (WI)
ITT Tech Inst, Green Bay (WI)
ITT Tech Inst, Greenfield (WI)
ITT Tech Inst, Madison (WI)
Kennesaw State U (GA)
Lewis U (IL)
Limestone Coll (SC)
Loyola U Chicago (IL)
Mercy Coll (NY)
Metropolitan State U (MN)
Pennsylvania Coll of Technology (PA)
Pittsburg State U (KS)
Potomac Coll (DC)
Rasmussen Coll Appleton (WI)
Rasmussen Coll Bismarck (ND)
Rasmussen Coll Blaine (MN)
Rasmussen Coll Bloomington (MN)
Rasmussen Coll Brooklyn Park (MN)
Rasmussen Coll Eagan (MN)
Rasmussen Coll Fargo (ND)
Rasmussen Coll Fort Myers (FL)
Rasmussen Coll Green Bay (WI)
Rasmussen Coll Lake Elmo/Woodbury (MN)
Rasmussen Coll Land O' Lakes (FL)
Rasmussen Coll Mankato (MN)
Rasmussen Coll Moorhead (MN)
Rasmussen Coll New Port Richey (FL)
Rasmussen Coll Ocala (FL)
Rasmussen Coll St. Cloud (MN)
Rasmussen Coll Tampa/Brandon (FL)
Rasmussen Coll Wausau (WI)
Rochester Inst of Technology (NY)
St. John's U (NY)
Southeast Missouri State U (MO)
State U of New York Coll of Technology at Alfred (NY)
U of Colorado at Colorado Springs (CO)
U of Great Falls (MT)
U of Illinois at Urbana–Champaign (IL)
U of Maryland U Coll (MD)
U of Miami (FL)
Weber State U (UT)

COMPUTER ENGINEERING

American U of Beirut (Lebanon)
Arizona State U (AZ)
Auburn U (AL)
Bellarmine U (KY)
Bethune-Cookman U (FL)
Bob Jones U (SC)
Boston U (MA)
Bradley U (IL)
Brown U (RI)
Bucknell U (PA)
California Baptist U (CA)
California Inst of Technology (CA)
California Polytechnic State U, San Luis Obispo (CA)
California State Polytechnic U, Pomona (CA)
California State U, Chico (CA)
California State U, Fresno (CA)
California State U, Fullerton (CA)
California State U, Long Beach (CA)
California State U, Sacramento (CA)
Capital U (OH)
Carnegie Mellon U (PA)
Case Western Reserve U (OH)
Cedarville U (OH)
Christopher Newport U (VA)
Claflin U (SC)
Clarkson U (NY)
Clemson U (SC)

Cleveland State U (OH)
The Coll of New Jersey (NJ)
Colorado State U (CO)
Concordia U (QC, Canada)
DigiPen Inst of Technology (WA)
Dordt Coll (IA)
Drexel U (PA)
Elizabethtown Coll (PA)
Embry-Riddle Aeronautical U–Daytona (FL)
Embry-Riddle Aeronautical U–Prescott (AZ)
Fairfield U (CT)
Florida Ag and Mech U (FL)
Florida Atlantic U (FL)
Florida Inst of Technology (FL)
Florida Intl U (FL)
George Fox U (OR)
George Mason U (VA)
The George Washington U (DC)
Georgia Inst of Technology (GA)
Gonzaga U (WA)
Harding U (AR)
Hofstra U (NY)
Hope Coll (MI)
Illinois Inst of Technology (IL)
Indiana Tech (IN)
Indiana U East (IN)
Indiana U–Purdue U Fort Wayne (IN)
Indiana U–Purdue U Indianapolis (IN)
Iowa State U of Science and Technology (IA)
The Johns Hopkins U (MD)
Johnson C. Smith U (NC)
Kansas State U (KS)
Kettering U (MI)
Lakehead U (ON, Canada)
Lawrence Technological U (MI)
Lebanese American U (Lebanon)
Lehigh U (PA)
LeTourneau U (TX)
Liberty U (VA)
Lipscomb U (TN)
Louisiana State U and Ag and Mech Coll (LA)
Manhattan Coll (NY)
Marquette U (WI)
Miami U (OH)
Michigan State U (MI)
Michigan Technological U (MI)
Midwestern State U (TX)
Milwaukee School of Eng (WI)
Minnesota State U Mankato (MN)
Mississippi State U (MS)
Missouri U of Science and Technology (MO)
Montana State U (MT)
North Carolina Ag and Tech State U (NC)
North Carolina State U (NC)
North Dakota State U (ND)
Northeastern U (MA)
Norwich U (VT)
Oakland U (MI)
Ohio Northern U (OH)
The Ohio State U (OH)
Oklahoma Christian U (OK)
Oklahoma State U (OK)
Old Dominion U (VA)
Oral Roberts U (OK)
Penn State Abington (PA)
Penn State Altoona (PA)
Penn State Beaver (PA)
Penn State Berks (PA)
Penn State Brandywine (PA)
Penn State DuBois (PA)
Penn State Erie, The Behrend Coll (PA)
Penn State Fayette, The Eberly Campus (PA)
Penn State Greater Allegheny (PA)
Penn State Hazleton (PA)
Penn State Lehigh Valley (PA)
Penn State Mont Alto (PA)
Penn State New Kensington (PA)
Penn State Schuylkill (PA)
Penn State Shenango (PA)
Penn State U Park (PA)
Penn State Wilkes-Barre (PA)
Penn State Worthington Scranton (PA)
Penn State York (PA)
Polytechnic Inst of NYU (NY)

Polytechnic U of Puerto Rico (PR)
Portland State U (OR)
Princeton U (NJ)
Purdue U (IN)
Purdue U Calumet (IN)
Queen's U at Kingston (ON, Canada)
Rice U (TX)
Rochester Inst of Technology (NY)
Roger Williams U (RI)
Rose-Hulman Inst of Technology (IN)
Rutgers, The State U of New Jersey, New Brunswick (NJ)
Ryerson U (ON, Canada)
Saint Louis U (MO)
St. Mary's U (TX)
San Diego State U (CA)
San Francisco State U (CA)
Santa Clara U (CA)
Seattle Pacific U (WA)
Shepherd U (WV)
South Dakota School of Mines and Technology (SD)
Southern Illinois U Carbondale (IL)
Southern Illinois U Edwardsville (IL)
Southern Methodist U (TX)
Stanford U (CA)
State U of New York at Binghamton (NY)
State U of New York at New Paltz (NY)
Stevens Inst of Technology (NJ)
Suffolk U (MA)
Syracuse U (NY)
Taylor U (IN)
Texas A&M U (TX)
Texas Tech U (TX)
Trine U (IN)
Trinity Coll (CT)
Tufts U (MA)
Universidad del Turabo (PR)
Université de Sherbrooke (QC, Canada)
U at Buffalo, the State U of New York (NY)
The U of Akron (OH)
The U of Alabama in Huntsville (AL)
U of Alaska Fairbanks (AK)
U of Alberta (AB, Canada)
U of Arkansas (AR)
U of Bridgeport (CT)
The U of British Columbia (BC, Canada)
U of California, Irvine (CA)
U of California, Los Angeles (CA)
U of California, Merced (CA)
U of California, Riverside (CA)
U of California, Santa Barbara (CA)
U of California, Santa Cruz (CA)
U of Central Florida (FL)
U of Cincinnati (OH)
U of Colorado at Colorado Springs (CO)
U of Colorado Boulder (CO)
U of Connecticut (CT)
U of Dayton (OH)
U of Delaware (DE)
U of Denver (CO)
U of Evansville (IN)
U of Florida (FL)
U of Georgia (GA)
U of Guelph (ON, Canada)
U of Hartford (CT)
U of Houston (TX)
U of Houston–Clear Lake (TX)
U of Idaho (ID)
U of Illinois at Chicago (IL)
U of Illinois at Urbana–Champaign (IL)
U of Indianapolis (IN)
The U of Kansas (KS)
U of La Verne (CA)
U of Louisiana at Lafayette (LA)
U of Louisville (KY)
U of Maine (ME)
U of Maryland, Baltimore County (MD)
U of Maryland, Coll Park (MD)
U of Massachusetts Amherst (MA)
U of Massachusetts Dartmouth (MA)
U of Massachusetts Lowell (MA)
U of Memphis (TN)
U of Miami (FL)

INDEXES

INDEXES

Seminole State Coll of Florida (FL)
South Dakota State U (SD)
Southern Illinois U Edwardsville (IL)
Texas A&M U (TX)
Texas State U–San Marcos (TX)
Thomas Edison State Coll (NJ)
Tuskegee U (AL)
The U of Akron (OH)
U of Arkansas at Little Rock (AR)
U of Florida (FL)
U of Houston (TX)
U of Louisiana at Monroe (LA)
U of Maine (ME)
U of Maryland Eastern Shore (MD)
U of Nebraska–Lincoln (NE)
U of Nevada, Reno (NV)
U of North Florida (FL)
U of North Texas (TX)
The U of Toledo (OH)
Wayne State U (MI)
Western Carolina U (NC)
Western Kentucky U (KY)

CONSTRUCTION MANAGEMENT

Appalachian State U (NC)
Arizona State U (AZ)
California Baptist U (CA)
California State U, Fresno (CA)
Central Connecticut State U (CT)
Clemson U (SC)
Colorado State U (CO)
Eastern Michigan U (MI)
Ferris State U (MI)
Illinois State U (IL)
ITT Tech Inst, Bessemer (AL)
ITT Tech Inst, Mobile (AL)
ITT Tech Inst, Tempe (AZ)
ITT Tech Inst, Tucson (AZ)
ITT Tech Inst (AR)
ITT Tech Inst, Clovis (CA)
ITT Tech Inst, Lathrop (CA)
ITT Tech Inst, Orange (CA)
ITT Tech Inst, Rancho Cordova (CA)
ITT Tech Inst, San Bernardino (CA)
ITT Tech Inst, San Diego (CA)
ITT Tech Inst, San Dimas (CA)
ITT Tech Inst, Sylmar (CA)
ITT Tech Inst, Torrance (CA)
ITT Tech Inst, Thornton (CO)
ITT Tech Inst, Fort Lauderdale (FL)
ITT Tech Inst, Lake Mary (FL)
ITT Tech Inst, Miami (FL)
ITT Tech Inst, Tampa (FL)
ITT Tech Inst, Atlanta (GA)
ITT Tech Inst, Duluth (GA)
ITT Tech Inst, Kennesaw (GA)
ITT Tech Inst (ID)
ITT Tech Inst, Mount Prospect (IL)
ITT Tech Inst, Oak Brook (IL)
ITT Tech Inst, Orland Park (IL)
ITT Tech Inst, Fort Wayne (IN)
ITT Tech Inst, Indianapolis (IN)
ITT Tech Inst, Lexington (KY)
ITT Tech Inst, Louisville (KY)
ITT Tech Inst, St. Rose (LA)
ITT Tech Inst, Owings Mills (MD)
ITT Tech Inst, Canton (MI)
ITT Tech Inst, Swartz Creek (MI)
ITT Tech Inst, Troy (MI)
ITT Tech Inst, Wyoming (MI)
ITT Tech Inst, Arnold (MO)
ITT Tech Inst, Earth City (MO)
ITT Tech Inst, Kansas City (MO)
ITT Tech Inst (NE)
ITT Tech Inst, Henderson (NV)
ITT Tech Inst (NM)
ITT Tech Inst, Cary (NC)
ITT Tech Inst, Charlotte (NC)
ITT Tech Inst, Charlotte (NC)
ITT Tech Inst, Durham (NC)
ITT Tech Inst, High Point (NC)
ITT Tech Inst, Akron (OH)
ITT Tech Inst, Columbus (OH)
ITT Tech Inst, Dayton (OH)
ITT Tech Inst, Hilliard (OH)
ITT Tech Inst, Maumee (OH)
ITT Tech Inst, Norwood (OH)
ITT Tech Inst, Strongsville (OH)
ITT Tech Inst, Warrensville Heights (OH)
ITT Tech Inst, Youngstown (OH)
ITT Tech Inst, Oklahoma City (OK)
ITT Tech Inst, Tulsa (OK)

ITT Tech Inst, Portland (OR)
ITT Tech Inst, Greenville (SC)
ITT Tech Inst, Cordova (TN)
ITT Tech Inst, Knoxville (TN)
ITT Tech Inst, Nashville (TN)
ITT Tech Inst, Arlington (TX)
ITT Tech Inst, Houston (TX)
ITT Tech Inst, Houston (TX)
ITT Tech Inst, Richardson (TX)
ITT Tech Inst, San Antonio (TX)
ITT Tech Inst (UT)
ITT Tech Inst, Chantilly (VA)
ITT Tech Inst, Norfolk (VA)
ITT Tech Inst, Richmond (VA)
ITT Tech Inst, Springfield (VA)
ITT Tech Inst, Everett (WA)
ITT Tech Inst, Seattle (WA)
ITT Tech Inst, Spokane Valley (WA)
ITT Tech Inst, Green Bay (WI)
ITT Tech Inst, Greenfield (WI)
John Brown U (AR)
Lawrence Technological U (MI)
Louisiana State U and Ag and Mech Coll (LA)
Michigan State U (MI)
Milwaukee School of Eng (WI)
Minnesota State U Moorhead (MN)
Mississippi State U (MS)
Missouri State U (MO)
North Dakota State U (ND)
Northern Arizona U (AZ)
Northern Kentucky U (KY)
Ohio Northern U (OH)
The Ohio State U (OH)
Pittsburg State U (KS)
Purdue U (IN)
Purdue U Calumet (IN)
Southern Polytechnic State U (GA)
State U of New York Coll of Environmental Science and Forestry (NY)
U of Denver (CO)
U of Northern Iowa (IA)
U of Oklahoma (OK)
The U of Texas at Tyler (TX)
U of Washington (WA)
U of Wisconsin–Stout (WI)
Vermont Tech Coll (VT)
Virginia Polytechnic Inst and State U (VA)
Washington State U (WA)
Wentworth Inst of Technology (MA)
Western Carolina U (NC)
Western Illinois U (IL)

CONSTRUCTION TRADES

Purdue U (IN)

CONSTRUCTION TRADES RELATED

John Brown U (AR)
Purdue U (IN)
State U of New York Coll of Technology at Alfred (NY)

CONSUMER ECONOMICS

Delaware State U (DE)
South Dakota State U (SD)
U of Georgia (GA)
U of Illinois at Urbana–Champaign (IL)
The U of Tennessee (TN)
U of Utah (UT)

CONSUMER MERCHANDISING/ RETAILING MANAGEMENT

Belmont U (TN)
Bradley U (IL)
Eastern Kentucky U (KY)
Fontbonne U (MO)
Governors State U (IL)
HEC Montreal (QC, Canada)
Madonna U (MI)
Newbury Coll (MA)
Purdue U (IN)
San Francisco State U (CA)
Simmons Coll (MA)
U of Memphis (TN)
U of Nebraska–Lincoln (NE)
Winona State U (MN)

CONSUMER SERVICES AND ADVOCACY

Carson-Newman Coll (TN)
Purdue U (IN)
State U of New York Coll at Oneonta (NY)
U of Wisconsin–Madison (WI)

CORRECTIONS

Adams State Coll (CO)
Asbury U (KY)
Bowling Green State U (OH)
California State U, East Bay (CA)
California U of Pennsylvania (PA)
The Coll at Brockport, State U of New York (NY)
Coll of the Ozarks (MO)
Excelsior Coll (NY)
Jacksonville State U (AL)
Lake Superior State U (MI)
Lamar U (TX)
Lewis-Clark State Coll (ID)
Mercyhurst Coll (PA)
Minnesota State U Mankato (MN)
Oklahoma City U (OK)
Saint Louis U (MO)
Southeast Missouri State U (MO)
Spring Arbor U (MI)
Stephen F. Austin State U (TX)
Texas State U–San Marcos (TX)
Tiffin U (OH)
Tulane U (LA)
U of Great Falls (MT)
U of Minnesota, Crookston (MN)
U of New Mexico (NM)
U of Pittsburgh (PA)
Washburn U (KS)
Weber State U (UT)
Western Oregon U (OR)
Winona State U (MN)

CORRECTIONS ADMINISTRATION

Inter American U of Puerto Rico, Fajardo Campus (PR)
Inter American U of Puerto Rico, Ponce Campus (PR)
U of Great Falls (MT)
U of Mary (ND)

CORRECTIONS AND CRIMINAL JUSTICE RELATED

Albany State U (GA)
Averett U (VA)
Bethune-Cookman U (FL)
Bob Jones U (SC)
Cameron U (OK)
Caribbean U (PR)
The Coll at Brockport, State U of New York (NY)
Corban U (OR)
Delaware State U (DE)
DeVry U, Phoenix (AZ)
DeVry U, Pomona (CA)
DeVry U, Miramar (CA)
DeVry U, Orlando (FL)
DeVry U, Decatur (GA)
DeVry U, Chicago (IL)
DeVry U, Kansas City (MO)
DeVry U, Houston (TX)
DeVry U, Arlington (VA)
DeVry U, Federal Way (WA)
DeVry U Online (IL)
Emporia State U (KS)
Florida Inst of Technology (FL)
Goldey-Beacom Coll (DE)
Indiana Tech (IN)
La Roche Coll (PA)
Limestone Coll (SC)
Rasmussen Coll Bloomington (MN)
Rasmussen Coll Brooklyn Park (MN)
Rasmussen Coll Eagan (MN)
Rasmussen Coll Fargo (ND)
Rasmussen Coll Fort Myers (FL)
Rasmussen Coll Lake Elmo/ Woodbury (MN)
Rasmussen Coll Land O' Lakes (FL)
Rasmussen Coll Mankato (MN)
Rasmussen Coll Moorhead (MN)
Rasmussen Coll New Port Richey (FL)
Rasmussen Coll Ocala (FL)

Rasmussen Coll St. Cloud (MN)
Rasmussen Coll Tampa/Brandon (FL)
Roger Williams U (RI)
Russell Sage Coll (NY)
Sam Houston State U (TX)
Southern New Hampshire U (NH)
The U of Alabama at Birmingham (AL)
U of Alaska Fairbanks (AK)
U of Great Falls (MT)
U of Michigan–Flint (MI)
Vincennes U (IN)
Weber State U (UT)

COSTUME DESIGN

Shenandoah U (VA)

COUNSELING PSYCHOLOGY

Bob Jones U (SC)
Crown Coll (MN)
Delaware Valley Coll (PA)
Eastern Washington U (WA)
Emmanuel Coll (MA)
Emmaus Bible Coll (IA)
Fort Lewis Coll (CO)
Grace Coll (IN)
Great Lakes Christian Coll (MI)
Hope Intl U (CA)
Jamestown Coll (ND)
Mid-Atlantic Christian U (NC)
Mid-Continent U (KY)
Midwestern State U (TX)
Morningside Coll (IA)
Newman U (KS)
Oregon Inst of Technology (OR)
Pittsburg State U (KS)
Point U (GA)
Prescott Coll (AZ)
Saint Xavier U (IL)
San Diego Christian Coll (CA)
Southwestern Assemblies of God U (TX)
Universidad del Turabo (PR)
U of North Alabama (AL)
Washington Adventist U (MD)
Wayne State U (NE)

COUNSELOR EDUCATION/ SCHOOL COUNSELING AND GUIDANCE

Amberton U (TX)
Auburn U Montgomery (AL)
Belmont U (TN)
Bowling Green State U (OH)
Buena Vista U (IA)
Clemson U (SC)
East Central U (OK)
Eastern New Mexico U (NM)
Florida Gulf Coast U (FL)
Goddard Coll (VT)
John Brown U (AR)
Lamar U (TX)
Lenoir-Rhyne U (NC)
Marshall U (WV)
Midwestern State U (TX)
Tarleton State U (TX)
Texas A&M U–Corpus Christi (TX)
Université de Sherbrooke (QC, Canada)
U of Hawaii at Manoa (HI)
The U of South Dakota (SD)
U of Southern Maine (ME)
U of Windsor (ON, Canada)
U of Wisconsin–River Falls (WI)
Wright State U (OH)

COURT REPORTING

AIB Coll of Business (IA)

CRAFTS, FOLK ART AND ARTISANRY

Bowling Green State U (OH)
Bridgewater State U (MA)
Brigham Young U (UT)
The Cleveland Inst of Art (OH)
Coll for Creative Studies (MI)
Indiana U–Purdue U Fort Wayne (IN)
Kent State U (OH)
Kutztown U of Pennsylvania (PA)
Montserrat Coll of Art (MA)
Oregon Coll of Art & Craft (OR)

Rochester Inst of Technology (NY)
U of Illinois at Urbana–Champaign (IL)
The U of the Arts (PA)
Virginia Commonwealth U (VA)

CREATIVE WRITING

Adams State Coll (CO)
Agnes Scott Coll (GA)
Albion Coll (MI)
Allegheny Coll (PA)
Arcadia U (PA)
Arkansas Tech U (AR)
Asbury U (KY)
Ashland U (OH)
Augustana Coll (IL)
Baldwin-Wallace Coll (OH)
Bard Coll (NY)
Bard Coll at Simon's Rock (MA)
Belhaven U (MS)
Beloit Coll (WI)
Bennington Coll (VT)
Bernard M. Baruch Coll of the City U of New York (NY)
Biola U (CA)
Bluffton U (OH)
Bob Jones U (SC)
Bowie State U (MD)
Bowling Green State U (OH)
Brandeis U (MA)
Briar Cliff U (IA)
Bridgewater State U (MA)
Brown U (RI)
Bucknell U (PA)
Butler U (IN)
California Coll of the Arts (CA)
California State U, East Bay (CA)
California State U, Long Beach (CA)
California State U, San Bernardino (CA)
Calvary Bible Coll and Theological Sem (MO)
Canisius Coll (NY)
Capital U (OH)
Cardinal Stritch U (WI)
Carlow U (PA)
Carnegie Mellon U (PA)
Carson-Newman Coll (TN)
Chapman U (CA)
Chatham U (PA)
Chester Coll of New England (NH)
City Coll of the City U of New York (NY)
Coe Coll (IA)
Colby Coll (ME)
The Coll at Brockport, State U of New York (NY)
The Coll of Idaho (ID)
Coll of the Atlantic (ME)
The Colorado Coll (CO)
Colorado State U (CO)
Columbia Coll Chicago (IL)
Columbia U, School of General Studies (NY)
Concordia U (QC, Canada)
Converse Coll (SC)
Corban U (OR)
Cornell Coll (IA)
Dartmouth Coll (NH)
Denison U (OH)
Dominican U of California (CA)
Eastern Michigan U (MI)
Eckerd Coll (FL)
Emily Carr U of Art + Design (BC, Canada)
Emory U (GA)
Fairleigh Dickinson U, Coll at Florham (NJ)
Florida State U (FL)
Fordham U (NY)
Franklin & Marshall Coll (PA)
Franklin Coll Switzerland (Switzerland)
Gettysburg Coll (PA)
Goddard Coll (VT)
Hamilton Coll (NY)
Hamline U (MN)
Hampshire Coll (MA)
Hofstra U (NY)
Hope Coll (MI)
Houghton Coll (NY)
Indiana Wesleyan U (IN)
Ithaca Coll (NY)
The Johns Hopkins U (MD)

Johnson State Coll (VT)
Kansas City Art Inst (MO)
Knox Coll (IL)
Lehman Coll of the City U of New York (NY)
Lewis-Clark State Coll (ID)
Linfield Coll (OR)
Loras Coll (IA)
Loyola U Maryland (MD)
Lycoming Coll (PA)
Marlboro Coll (VT)
Massachusetts Coll of Liberal Arts (MA)
Massachusetts Inst of Technology (MA)
McMurry U (TX)
Mills Coll (CA)
Minnesota State U Mankato (MN)
Moravian Coll (PA)
Morehead State U (KY)
New England Coll (NH)
North Central Coll (IL)
Northern Michigan U (MI)
Northland Coll (WI)
Oakland U (MI)
Ohio Northern U (OH)
Ohio U (OH)
Ohio Wesleyan U (OH)
Oklahoma Christian U (OK)
Pacific U (OR)
Pittsburg State U (KS)
Point Loma Nazarene U (CA)
Pratt Inst (NY)
Prescott Coll (AZ)
Purchase Coll, State U of New York (NY)
Purdue U (IN)
Randolph Coll (VA)
Rhode Island Coll (RI)
Roanoke Coll (VA)
Rocky Mountain Coll (MT)
St. Catherine U (MN)
Saint Joseph's Coll (IN)
St. Lawrence U (NY)
Saint Mary's Coll (IN)
San Francisco State U (CA)
Sarah Lawrence Coll (NY)
Savannah Coll of Art and Design (GA)
Seattle U (WA)
Seton Hill U (PA)
Siena Heights U (MI)
Sierra Nevada Coll (NV)
Slippery Rock U of Pennsylvania (PA)
Southern Methodist U (TX)
Southern New Hampshire U (NH)
Southern Vermont Coll (VT)
Southwestern Coll (KS)
Southwest Minnesota State U (MN)
Spalding U (KY)
State U of New York at Binghamton (NY)
State U of New York at Oswego (NY)
Stephen F. Austin State U (TX)
Stephens Coll (MO)
Suffolk U (MA)
Susquehanna U (PA)
Sweet Briar Coll (VA)
Texas Christian U (TX)
Trinity Coll (CT)
Truman State U (MO)
The U of Arizona (AZ)
The U of British Columbia (BC, Canada)
The U of British Columbia–Okanagan (BC, Canada)
U of California, Riverside (CA)
U of Cincinnati (OH)
U of Denver (CO)
U of Evansville (IN)
The U of Findlay (OH)
U of Great Falls (MT)
U of Houston (TX)
U of Idaho (ID)
U of Maine at Farmington (ME)
U of Maine at Presque Isle (ME)
U of Miami (FL)
U of Michigan (MI)
U of Mount Union (OH)
U of Nebraska at Omaha (NE)
U of New Mexico (NM)
The U of North Carolina Wilmington (NC)

U of Pittsburgh (PA)
U of Pittsburgh at Bradford (PA)
U of Pittsburgh at Greensburg (PA)
U of Pittsburgh at Johnstown (PA)
U of Redlands (CA)
U of St. Thomas (MN)
U of Southern California (CA)
U of Southern Maine (ME)
The U of Texas at El Paso (TX)
U of Windsor (ON, Canada)
Valparaiso U (IN)
Virginia Intermont Coll (VA)
Waldorf Coll (IA)
Warren Wilson Coll (NC)
Washington U in St. Louis (MO)
Waynesburg U (PA)
Wells Coll (NY)
Western Michigan U (MI)
Western New England U (MA)
Western State Coll of Colorado (CO)
Western Washington U (WA)
West Virginia Wesleyan Coll (WV)
Wheeling Jesuit U (WV)
Wichita State U (KS)
Wofford Coll (SC)
Yeshiva U (NY)

CRIMINALISTICS AND CRIMINAL SCIENCE

Florida Gulf Coast U (FL)
Indiana Tech (IN)
Inter American U of Puerto Rico, Ponce Campus (PR)
Saint Leo U (FL)
West Virginia U Inst of Technology (WV)

CRIMINAL JUSTICE/LAW ENFORCEMENT ADMINISTRATION

Abilene Christian U (TX)
Adams State Coll (CO)
Adelphi U (NY)
Adrian Coll (MI)
Albertus Magnus Coll (CT)
Alfred U (NY)
Alvernia U (PA)
American Public U System (WV)
American U (DC)
Anderson U (IN)
Anderson U (SC)
Anna Maria Coll (MA)
Arcadia U (PA)
Arizona State U (AZ)
Athens State U (AL)
Austin Peay State U (TN)
Averett U (VA)
Barton Coll (NC)
Bay Path Coll (MA)
Becker Coll (MA)
Bemidji State U (MN)
Bethel U (TN)
Blackburn Coll (IL)
Bluefield Coll (VA)
Bob Jones U (SC)
Boise State U (ID)
Bowie State U (MD)
Bowling Green State U (OH)
Bradley U (IL)
Brevard Coll (NC)
Briar Cliff U (IA)
Broadview U (UT)
Broadview U-Boise (ID)
Broadview U-Layton (UT)
Broadview U-Orem (UT)
Buffalo State Coll, State U of New York (NY)
California Baptist U (CA)
California Coast U (CA)
California Lutheran U (CA)
California State U, Bakersfield (CA)
California State U, East Bay (CA)
California State U, Long Beach (CA)
California State U, Sacramento (CA)
California State U, San Bernardino (CA)
California State U, Stanislaus (CA)
Calumet Coll of Saint Joseph (IN)
Calvary Bible Coll and Theological Sem (MO)
Campbellsville U (KY)

Canisius Coll (NY)
Castleton State Coll (VT)
Cedarville U (OH)
Central Washington U (WA)
Chestnut Hill Coll (PA)
The Citadel, The Military Coll of South Carolina (SC)
Claflin U (SC)
The Coll at Brockport, State U of New York (NY)
The Coll of New Jersey (NJ)
Coll of St. Joseph (VT)
The Coll of Saint Rose (NY)
Columbia Coll (MO)
Concordia U (MI)
Concordia U Texas (TX)
Culver-Stockton Coll (MO)
Curry Coll (MA)
Dallas Baptist U (TX)
Dalton State Coll (GA)
Delaware State U (DE)
Delaware Valley Coll (PA)
Dordt Coll (IA)
East Central U (OK)
East Tennessee State U (TN)
East Texas Baptist U (TX)
Edward Waters Coll (FL)
Elmira Coll (NY)
Evangel U (MO)
Excelsior Coll (NY)
Fairleigh Dickinson U, Metropolitan Campus (NJ)
Farmingdale State Coll (NY)
Faulkner U (AL)
Fayetteville State U (NC)
Felician Coll (NJ)
Ferris State U (MI)
Florida National Coll (FL)
Franklin U (OH)
The George Washington U (DC)
Georgia Coll & State U (GA)
Globe U–Appleton (WI)
Globe U–Eau Claire (WI)
Globe U–Green Bay (WI)
Globe U–La Crosse (WI)
Globe U–Madison East (WI)
Globe U–Madison West (WI)
Globe U–Minneapolis (MN)
Globe U–Sioux Falls (SD)
Globe U–Wausau (WI)
Globe U–Woodbury (MN)
Gonzaga U (WA)
Governors State U (IL)
Graceland U (IA)
Grand Valley State U (MI)
Grand View U (IA)
Granite State Coll (NH)
Greenville Coll (IL)
Gustavus Adolphus Coll (MN)
Hampton U (VA)
Hannibal-LaGrange U (MO)
Hawai`i Pacific U (HI)
Hesser Coll, Concord (NH)
Hesser Coll, Manchester (NH)
Hesser Coll, Nashua (NH)
Hesser Coll, Portsmouth (NH)
Hesser Coll, Salem (NH)
Holy Family U (PA)
Indiana Tech (IN)
Iona Coll (NY)
ITT Tech Inst, Bessemer (AL)
ITT Tech Inst, Madison (AL)
ITT Tech Inst, Mobile (AL)
ITT Tech Inst, Phoenix (AZ)
ITT Tech Inst, Tempe (AZ)
ITT Tech Inst, Tucson (AZ)
ITT Tech Inst (AR)
ITT Tech Inst, Clovis (CA)
ITT Tech Inst, Culver City (CA)
ITT Tech Inst, Lathrop (CA)
ITT Tech Inst, Orange (CA)
ITT Tech Inst, Oxnard (CA)
ITT Tech Inst, Rancho Cordova (CA)
ITT Tech Inst, San Bernardino (CA)
ITT Tech Inst, San Diego (CA)
ITT Tech Inst, San Dimas (CA)
ITT Tech Inst, Sylmar (CA)
ITT Tech Inst, Torrance (CA)
ITT Tech Inst, West Covina (CA)
ITT Tech Inst, Thornton (CO)
ITT Tech Inst, Bradenton (FL)
ITT Tech Inst, Fort Lauderdale (FL)
ITT Tech Inst, Jacksonville (FL)
ITT Tech Inst, Lake Mary (FL)

ITT Tech Inst, Miami (FL)
ITT Tech Inst, Orlando (FL)
ITT Tech Inst, Tampa (FL)
ITT Tech Inst, Atlanta (GA)
ITT Tech Inst, Duluth (GA)
ITT Tech Inst, Kennesaw (GA)
ITT Tech Inst (ID)
ITT Tech Inst, Mount Prospect (IL)
ITT Tech Inst, Oak Brook (IL)
ITT Tech Inst, Orland Park (IL)
ITT Tech Inst, Springfield (IL)
ITT Tech Inst, Fort Wayne (IN)
ITT Tech Inst, Indianapolis (IN)
ITT Tech Inst, Newburgh (IN)
ITT Tech Inst, South Bend (IN)
ITT Tech Inst, Clive (IA)
ITT Tech Inst, Lexington (KY)
ITT Tech Inst, Louisville (KY)
ITT Tech Inst, Baton Rouge (LA)
ITT Tech Inst, St. Rose (LA)
ITT Tech Inst, Canton (MI)
ITT Tech Inst, Swartz Creek (MI)
ITT Tech Inst, Troy (MI)
ITT Tech Inst, Wyoming (MI)
ITT Tech Inst, Arnold (MO)
ITT Tech Inst, Earth City (MO)
ITT Tech Inst, Kansas City (MO)
ITT Tech Inst, Springfield (MO)
ITT Tech Inst, Henderson (NV)
ITT Tech Inst, North Las Vegas (NV)
ITT Tech Inst (NM)
ITT Tech Inst, Cary (NC)
ITT Tech Inst, Charlotte (NC)
ITT Tech Inst, Charlotte (NC)
ITT Tech Inst, Durham (NC)
ITT Tech Inst, High Point (NC)
ITT Tech Inst, Akron (OH)
ITT Tech Inst, Columbus (OH)
ITT Tech Inst, Dayton (OH)
ITT Tech Inst, Hilliard (OH)
ITT Tech Inst, Maumee (OH)
ITT Tech Inst, Norwood (OH)
ITT Tech Inst, Strongsville (OH)
ITT Tech Inst, Warrensville Heights (OH)
ITT Tech Inst, Youngstown (OH)
ITT Tech Inst, Oklahoma City (OK)
ITT Tech Inst, Tulsa (OK)
ITT Tech Inst, Portland (OR)
ITT Tech Inst, Columbia (SC)
ITT Tech Inst, Greenville (SC)
ITT Tech Inst, Cordova (TN)
ITT Tech Inst, Knoxville (TN)
ITT Tech Inst, Nashville (TN)
ITT Tech Inst (UT)
ITT Tech Inst, Chantilly (VA)
ITT Tech Inst, Norfolk (VA)
ITT Tech Inst, Richmond (VA)
ITT Tech Inst, Springfield (VA)
ITT Tech Inst, Everett (WA)
ITT Tech Inst, Seattle (WA)
ITT Tech Inst, Spokane Valley (WA)
ITT Tech Inst, Green Bay (WI)
Jacksonville State U (AL)
John Jay Coll of Criminal Justice of the City U of New York (NY)
Judson Coll (AL)
Kean U (NJ)
Kent State U at East Liverpool (OH)
Keuka Coll (NY)
Keystone Coll (PA)
Lake Erie Coll (OH)
Lake Superior State U (MI)
Lamar U (TX)
Lees-McRae Coll (NC)
Limestone Coll (SC)
Lincoln Memorial U (TN)
Lincoln U (MO)
Lindsey Wilson Coll (KY)
Lock Haven U of Pennsylvania (PA)
Longwood U (VA)
Lubbock Christian U (TX)
Mansfield U of Pennsylvania (PA)
Mars Hill Coll (NC)
McKendree U (IL)
Mercy Coll (NY)
Merrimack Coll (MA)
Michigan State U (MI)
MidAmerica Nazarene U (KS)
Middle Tennessee State U (TN)
Midwestern State U (TX)
Minnesota School of Business–Blaine (MN)

Minnesota School of Business–Brooklyn Center (MN)
Minnesota School of Business–Elk River (MN)
Minnesota School of Business–Lakeville (MN)
Minnesota School of Business–Richfield (MN)
Minnesota School of Business–Rochester (MN)
Minnesota School of Business–St. Cloud (MN)
Minnesota School of Business–Shakopee (MN)
Mississippi Coll (MS)
Mississippi Valley State U (MS)
Missouri Southern State U (MO)
Mitchell Coll (CT)
Moravian Coll (PA)
Morris Coll (SC)
Morrisville State Coll (NY)
Mount Aloysius Coll (PA)
Mount Ida Coll (MA)
Mount Mary Coll (WI)
Mount Mercy U (IA)
Mount Vernon Nazarene U (OH)
National U (CA)
New England Coll (NH)
New England Inst of Technology (RI)
Newman U (KS)
New York Inst of Technology (NY)
Niagara U (NY)
North Carolina Wesleyan Coll (NC)
Northeastern State U (OK)
Northwest Nazarene U (ID)
Norwich U (VT)
Oakland City U (IN)
Ohio Northern U (OH)
Ohio U–Zanesville (OH)
Oklahoma City U (OK)
Pace U (NY)
Penn State Abington (PA)
Penn State Altoona (PA)
Penn State Beaver (PA)
Penn State Berks (PA)
Penn State Brandywine (PA)
Penn State DuBois (PA)
Penn State Erie, The Behrend Coll (PA)
Penn State Fayette, The Eberly Campus (PA)
Penn State Greater Allegheny (PA)
Penn State Hazleton (PA)
Penn State Lehigh Valley (PA)
Penn State Mont Alto (PA)
Penn State New Kensington (PA)
Penn State Schuylkill (PA)
Penn State Shenango (PA)
Penn State U Park (PA)
Penn State Wilkes-Barre (PA)
Penn State Worthington Scranton (PA)
Penn State York (PA)
Peru State Coll (NE)
Piedmont Coll (GA)
Point Park U (PA)
Portland State U (OR)
Post U (CT)
Radford U (VA)
Regent U (VA)
Regis U (CO)
Roberts Wesleyan Coll (NY)
Rochester Inst of Technology (NY)
Rogers State U (OK)
Roger Williams U (RI)
Rutgers, The State U of New Jersey, New Brunswick (NJ)
Sacred Heart U (CT)
Saint Augustine's Coll (NC)
Saint Francis U (PA)
St. John's U (NY)
St. Joseph's Coll, Long Island Campus (NY)
St. Joseph's Coll, New York (NY)
Saint Louis U (MO)
Saint Martin's U (WA)
St. Mary's U (TX)
St. Thomas Aquinas Coll (NY)
St. Thomas U (FL)
Salem State U (MA)
Salve Regina U (RI)
San Diego State U (CA)
San Francisco State U (CA)
Seattle U (WA)

Shenandoah U (VA)
Simpson Coll (IA)
Sojourner-Douglass Coll (MD)
Sonoma State U (CA)
South Carolina State U (SC)
Southeastern U (FL)
Southern Illinois U Carbondale (IL)
Southern Vermont Coll (VT)
South U (AL)
South U, Royal Palm Beach (FL)
South U (GA)
South U (MI)
South U, Columbia (SC)
South U, Glen Allen (VA)
South U, Virginia Beach (VA)
Southwest Baptist U (MO)
Southwestern Oklahoma State U (OK)
Southwest Minnesota State U (MN)
State U of New York at Fredonia (NY)
State U of New York at Oswego (NY)
State U of New York Coll of Technology at Canton (NY)
Suffolk U (MA)
Sul Ross State U (TX)
Texas A&M U–Corpus Christi (TX)
Texas Southern U (TX)
Thomas Edison State Coll (NJ)
Thomas U (GA)
Tiffin U (OH)
Trevecca Nazarene U (TN)
Trine U (IN)
Trinity Christian Coll (IL)
Union Coll (KY)
Union Inst & U (OH)
U at Albany, State U of New York (NY)
U of Alaska Anchorage (AK)
U of Alberta (AB, Canada)
U of Arkansas at Little Rock (AR)
U of Arkansas–Fort Smith (AR)
U of Central Missouri (MO)
U of Colorado at Colorado Springs (CO)
U of Colorado Denver (CO)
U of Dayton (OH)
U of Dubuque (IA)
The U of Findlay (OH)
U of Great Falls (MT)
U of Guam (GU)
U of Guelph (ON, Canada)
U of Hawaii–West Oahu (HI)
U of Louisville (KY)
U of Maine at Augusta (ME)
U of Maine at Presque Isle (ME)
U of Mary Hardin-Baylor (TX)
U of Maryland Eastern Shore (MD)
U of Massachusetts Lowell (MA)
U of Memphis (TN)
U of Minnesota, Crookston (MN)
U of Mississippi (MS)
U of Missouri–Kansas City (MO)
U of Nevada, Las Vegas (NV)
U of New Haven (CT)
U of North Alabama (AL)
U of Oklahoma (OK)
U of Pittsburgh at Bradford (PA)
U of Pittsburgh at Greensburg (PA)
U of Regina (SK, Canada)
U of St. Francis (IL)
U of South Alabama (AL)
U of South Carolina (SC)
U of South Carolina Upstate (SC)
The U of South Dakota (SD)
The U of Tennessee at Chattanooga (TN)
The U of Tennessee at Martin (TN)
The U of Texas at El Paso (TX)
The U of Texas–Pan American (TX)
U of the Incarnate Word (TX)
U of the Southwest (NM)
U of Washington (WA)
U of Wisconsin–Platteville (WI)
Utah Valley U (UT)
Utica Coll (NY)
Villanova U (PA)
Virginia Commonwealth U (VA)
Walden U (MN)
Waldorf Coll (IA)
Washburn U (KS)
Washington State U (WA)
Wayland Baptist U (TX)
Waynesburg U (PA)

Western Illinois U (IL)
Western Intl U (AZ)
Western Oregon U (OR)
West Liberty U (WV)
West Texas A&M U (TX)
West Virginia State U (WV)
West Virginia Wesleyan Coll (WV)
Widener U (PA)
Wilmington Coll (OH)
Wilmington U (DE)
Winona State U (MN)
York Coll of Pennsylvania (PA)

CRIMINAL JUSTICE/POLICE SCIENCE

American U (DC)
Athabasca U (AB, Canada)
Bemidji State U (MN)
Bowling Green State U (OH)
California State U, East Bay (CA)
Caribbean U (PR)
Coll of the Ozarks (MO)
Columbia Southern U (AL)
East Central U (OK)
Fairmont State U (WV)
Ferris State U (MI)
George Mason U (VA)
Grambling State U (LA)
Heidelberg U (OH)
Hilbert Coll (NY)
Husson U (ME)
Jacksonville State U (AL)
Kent State U at Tuscarawas (OH)
Lake Superior State U (MI)
Lamar U (TX)
Louisiana Coll (LA)
Marian U (WI)
Metropolitan State U (MN)
Middle Tennessee State U (TN)
Minnesota State U Mankato (MN)
Newbury Coll (MA)
Northern State U (SD)
Northwestern Oklahoma State U (OK)
Ohio Northern U (OH)
Oklahoma City U (OK)
Rowan U (NJ)
Stephen F. Austin State U (TX)
Texas State U–San Marcos (TX)
U of Great Falls (MT)
U of Guam (GU)
U of Hartford (CT)
U of Pittsburgh at Greensburg (PA)
U of Regina (SK, Canada)
U of Toronto (ON, Canada)
U of Wisconsin–Superior (WI)
Weber State U (UT)
Western Connecticut State U (CT)
Western Oregon U (OR)
Winona State U (MN)

CRIMINAL JUSTICE/SAFETY

Alabama State U (AL)
Albany State U (GA)
Alcorn State U (MS)
American U (DC)
Angelo State U (TX)
Anna Maria Coll (MA)
Appalachian State U (NC)
Auburn U Montgomery (AL)
Baldwin-Wallace Coll (OH)
Ball State U (IN)
Bauder Coll (GA)
Becker Coll (MA)
Bellarmine U (KY)
Benedictine U (IL)
Bethany Coll (KS)
Bethel Coll (IN)
Bloomsburg U of Pennsylvania (PA)
Bluefield State Coll (WV)
Bluffton U (OH)
Bowling Green State U (OH)
Bridgewater State U (MA)
Buena Vista U (IA)
Caldwell Coll (NJ)
California State U, Chico (CA)
California State U, Dominguez Hills (CA)
California State U, Fresno (CA)
California State U, Fullerton (CA)
California State U, Los Angeles (CA)
Capella U (MN)
Central Methodist U (MO)

Central Penn Coll (PA)
Central State U (OH)
Chicago State U (IL)
Clark Atlanta U (GA)
Clayton State U (GA)
Colorado Mesa U (CO)
Columbus State U (GA)
Concordia U, St. Paul (MN)
Delta State U (MS)
DeSales U (PA)
Dominican Coll (NY)
East Carolina U (NC)
Eastern New Mexico U (NM)
Edgewood Coll (WI)
Edinboro U of Pennsylvania (PA)
Elizabeth City State U (NC)
Endicott Coll (MA)
Everest U, Lakeland (FL)
Excelsior Coll (NY)
Ferrum Coll (VA)
Fitchburg State U (MA)
Florida Ag and Mech U (FL)
Florida Atlantic U (FL)
Florida Gulf Coast U (FL)
Florida Intl U (FL)
Florida National Coll (FL)
Fort Hays State U (KS)
Friends U (KS)
Gannon U (PA)
Georgia Gwinnett Coll (GA)
Georgian Court U (NJ)
Georgia Southern U (GA)
Georgia State U (GA)
Grace Coll (IN)
Grand Canyon U (AZ)
Granite State Coll (NH)
Guilford Coll (NC)
Hamline U (MN)
Harding U (AR)
Hardin-Simmons U (TX)
Holy Family U (PA)
Howard Payne U (TX)
Husson U (ME)
Huston-Tillotson U (TX)
Illinois State U (IL)
Immaculata U (PA)
Indiana U Bloomington (IN)
Indiana U East (IN)
Indiana U Kokomo (IN)
Indiana U Northwest (IN)
Indiana U–Purdue U Indianapolis (IN)
Indiana U South Bend (IN)
Indiana U Southeast (IN)
Indiana Wesleyan U (IN)
Indian River State Coll (FL)
Inter American U of Puerto Rico, Fajardo Campus (PR)
Inter American U of Puerto Rico, Ponce Campus (PR)
Iowa Wesleyan Coll (IA)
Jamestown Coll (ND)
Judson U (IL)
Kennesaw State U (GA)
Kent State U (OH)
Kent State U at Ashtabula (OH)
Kent State U at Salem (OH)
Kent State U at Stark (OH)
Kent State U at Trumbull (OH)
Kentucky State U (KY)
Kentucky Wesleyan Coll (KY)
King's Coll (PA)
Kutztown U of Pennsylvania (PA)
Lane Coll (TN)
La Roche Coll (PA)
La Salle U (PA)
Lasell Coll (MA)
La Sierra U (CA)
Lewis U (IL)
Liberty U (VA)
Limestone Coll (SC)
Lincoln U (PA)
Lindenwood U (MO)
Long Island U–Brentwood Campus (NY)
Long Island U–C. W. Post Campus (NY)
Longwood U (VA)
Loras Coll (IA)
Louisiana State U in Shreveport (LA)
Lourdes U (OH)
Loyola U Chicago (IL)
Lubbock Christian U (TX)
Lynn U (FL)

Madonna U (MI)
Marshall U (WV)
Marymount U (VA)
Marywood U (PA)
McNeese State U (LA)
Medaille Coll (NY)
Mercer U (GA)
Mercyhurst Coll (PA)
Messiah Coll (PA)
Metropolitan State Coll of Denver (CO)
Metropolitan State U (MN)
Michigan State U (MI)
Minnesota State U Moorhead (MN)
Minot State U (ND)
Missouri Baptist U (MO)
Missouri Western State U (MO)
Mitchell Coll (CT)
Molloy Coll (NY)
Monmouth U (NJ)
Montana State U Billings (MT)
Mountain State U (WV)
Mount Marty Coll (SD)
Mount Vernon Nazarene U (OH)
Neumann U (PA)
New Jersey City U (NJ)
New Mexico Highlands U (NM)
New Mexico State U (NM)
Nichols Coll (MA)
North Carolina Ag and Tech State U (NC)
North Carolina Central U (NC)
North Dakota State U (ND)
Northeastern Illinois U (IL)
Northeastern U (MA)
Northern Kentucky U (KY)
Northern Michigan U (MI)
North Georgia Coll & State U (GA)
Northwestern Coll (MN)
Northwestern State U of Louisiana (LA)
Nova Southeastern U (FL)
Nyack Coll (NY)
Ohio Northern U (OH)
Penn State Abington (PA)
Penn State Altoona (PA)
Penn State Erie, The Behrend Coll (PA)
Penn State Fayette, The Eberly Campus (PA)
Penn State Harrisburg (PA)
Penn State Schuylkill (PA)
Penn State U Park (PA)
Penn State Wilkes-Barre (PA)
Plymouth State U (NH)
Point Park U (PA)
Post U (CT)
Prairie View A&M U (TX)
Quincy U (IL)
Quinnipiac U (CT)
Rhode Island Coll (RI)
Roanoke Coll (VA)
Rochester Inst of Technology (NY)
Roosevelt U (IL)
Rosemont Coll (PA)
Rowan U (NJ)
Rutgers, The State U of New Jersey, Camden (NJ)
Rutgers, The State U of New Jersey, Newark (NJ)
Ryerson U (ON, Canada)
Saginaw Valley State U (MI)
St. Ambrose U (IA)
Saint Anselm Coll (NH)
St. Edward's U (TX)
Saint Joseph's Coll (IN)
Saint Joseph's Coll of Maine (ME)
Saint Leo U (FL)
Saint Martin's U (WA)
Saint Peter's Coll (NJ)
Saint Xavier U (IL)
Sam Houston State U (TX)
San Diego State U (CA)
Seton Hill U (PA)
Shaw U (NC)
Shippensburg U of Pennsylvania (PA)
Siena Heights U (MI)
Southeastern Louisiana U (LA)
Southeastern Oklahoma State U (OK)
Southern Arkansas U–Magnolia (AR)
Southern Illinois U Edwardsville (IL)

Southwestern Assemblies of God U (TX)
Southwest Minnesota State U (MN)
State U of New York at Plattsburgh (NY)
State U of New York Coll at Oneonta (NY)
State U of New York Coll at Potsdam (NY)
Sullivan U (KY)
Tarleton State U (TX)
Temple U (PA)
Texas A&M Intl U (TX)
Texas Christian U (TX)
Texas Coll (TX)
Texas State U–San Marcos (TX)
Texas Woman's U (TX)
Thiel Coll (PA)
Thomas Edison State Coll (NJ)
Thomas More Coll (KY)
Troy U (AL)
Truman State U (MO)
The U of Akron (OH)
The U of Alabama (AL)
U of Arkansas (AR)
U of Arkansas at Monticello (AR)
U of Bridgeport (CT)
U of Central Florida (FL)
U of Cincinnati (OH)
U of Evansville (IN)
U of Georgia (GA)
U of Great Falls (MT)
U of Houston–Downtown (TX)
U of Houston–Victoria (TX)
U of Illinois at Chicago (IL)
U of Illinois at Springfield (IL)
U of Louisiana at Lafayette (LA)
U of Louisiana at Monroe (LA)
U of Mary (ND)
U of Maryland U Coll (MD)
U of Massachusetts Boston (MA)
U of Michigan–Dearborn (MI)
U of Mount Union (OH)
U of Nebraska at Kearney (NE)
U of Nebraska at Omaha (NE)
The U of North Carolina at Charlotte (NC)
The U of North Carolina Wilmington (NC)
U of North Dakota (ND)
U of Northern Colorado (CO)
U of North Florida (FL)
U of North Texas (TX)
U of Pikeville (KY)
U of Portland (OR)
U of Regina (SK, Canada)
U of Richmond (VA)
The U of Scranton (PA)
U of Southern Indiana (IN)
U of Southern Mississippi (MS)
The U of Texas at Arlington (TX)
The U of Texas at San Antonio (TX)
The U of Texas at Tyler (TX)
The U of Texas of the Permian Basin (TX)
U of the Cumberlands (KY)
U of the Incarnate Word (TX)
The U of Toledo (OH)
The U of Virginia's Coll at Wise (VA)
U of West Florida (FL)
U of Wisconsin–Eau Claire (WI)
U of Wisconsin–Milwaukee (WI)
U of Wisconsin–Superior (WI)
U of Wyoming (WY)
Valdosta State U (GA)
Virginia State U (VA)
Virginia Wesleyan Coll (VA)
Viterbo U (WI)
Wayne State Coll (NE)
Wayne State U (MI)
Weber State U (UT)
West Chester U of Pennsylvania (PA)
Western Carolina U (NC)
Western Michigan U (MI)
Western New England U (MA)
Westfield State U (MA)
Westminster Coll (UT)
Wichita State U (KS)
Wilkes U (PA)
Worcester State U (MA)
Xavier U (OH)
Youngstown State U (OH)

CRIMINOLOGY

Adams State Coll (CO)
Albright Coll (PA)
Arcadia U (PA)
Arkansas State U (AR)
Auburn U (AL)
Barry U (FL)
Biola U (CA)
Butler U (IN)
Cabrini Coll (PA)
California State U, Fresno (CA)
Capital U (OH)
Castleton State Coll (VT)
Cedar Crest Coll (PA)
Centenary Coll (NJ)
Central Connecticut State U (CT)
Chaminade U of Honolulu (HI)
Chatham U (PA)
Cleveland State U (OH)
Coll of Mount St. Joseph (OH)
Delaware State U (DE)
Dominican U (IL)
Drury U (MO)
Eastern Michigan U (MI)
Eastern Washington U (WA)
Elizabethtown Coll (PA)
Elmhurst Coll (IL)
Emmanuel Coll (MA)
Fairleigh Dickinson U, Coll at Florham (NJ)
Florida Southern Coll (FL)
Florida State U (FL)
Framingham State U (MA)
Hofstra U (NY)
Howard Payne U (TX)
Husson U (ME)
Indiana State U (IN)
Indiana U of Pennsylvania (PA)
John Jay Coll of Criminal Justice of the City U of New York (NY)
Johnson C. Smith U (NC)
Lakehead U (ON, Canada)
Lebanon Valley Coll (PA)
Le Moyne Coll (NY)
Lindenwood U (MO)
Loyola U New Orleans (LA)
Lycoming Coll (PA)
Lynchburg Coll (VA)
Marquette U (WI)
Mary Baldwin Coll (VA)
Marymount U (VA)
Maryville U of Saint Louis (MO)
Mississippi State U (MS)
Missouri State U (MO)
Mount St. Mary's U (MD)
Niagara U (NY)
North Carolina State U (NC)
Northern Arizona U (AZ)
Notre Dame of Maryland U (MD)
The Ohio State U (OH)
Ohio U (OH)
Ohio U–Chillicothe (OH)
Old Dominion U (VA)
Regis U (CO)
The Richard Stockton Coll of New Jersey (NJ)
Rivier Coll (NH)
Sage Coll of Albany (NY)
St. Edward's U (TX)
Saint Francis U (PA)
Saint Joseph's U (PA)
St. Mary's U (TX)
St. Thomas U (NB, Canada)
Simon Fraser U (BC, Canada)
Slippery Rock U of Pennsylvania (PA)
Southern Oregon U (OR)
State U of New York Coll at Cortland (NY)
State U of New York Coll at Old Westbury (NY)
Stonehill Coll (MA)
Suffolk U (MA)
Texas A&M U–Kingsville (TX)
Thomas U (GA)
Universidad del Turabo (PR)
U of Alberta (AB, Canada)
U of California, Irvine (CA)
U of Delaware (DE)
U of Denver (CO)
U of Florida (FL)
U of Houston–Clear Lake (TX)
U of La Verne (CA)
U of Maryland, Coll Park (MD)
U of Massachusetts Dartmouth (MA)
U of Memphis (TN)
U of Miami (FL)
U of Minnesota, Duluth (MN)
U of Minnesota, Twin Cities Campus (MN)
U of Missouri–Kansas City (MO)
U of Missouri–St. Louis (MO)
U of Mount Union (OH)
U of Nevada, Reno (NV)
U of New Hampshire (NH)
U of Northern Iowa (IA)
U of Ottawa (ON, Canada)
U of Saint Mary (KS)
U of St. Thomas (MN)
U of Southern Maine (ME)
U of South Florida (FL)
U of South Florida–St. Petersburg Campus (FL)
The U of Tampa (FL)
The U of Texas at Dallas (TX)
The U of Texas of the Permian Basin (TX)
U of Toronto (ON, Canada)
The U of Western Ontario (ON, Canada)
U of West Georgia (GA)
U of Windsor (ON, Canada)
Upper Iowa U (IA)
Valparaiso U (IN)
Virginia Union U (VA)
Virginia Wesleyan Coll (VA)
Western State Coll of Colorado (CO)
Wheeling Jesuit U (WV)
William Penn U (IA)
Wright State U (OH)

CRISIS/EMERGENCY/DISASTER MANAGEMENT

American Public U System (WV)
Arkansas Tech U (AR)
Union Inst & U (OH)
Walden U (MN)

CROP PRODUCTION

Delaware Valley Coll (PA)
North Dakota State U (ND)
U of Minnesota, Crookston (MN)
U of Minnesota, Twin Cities Campus (MN)
Washington State U (WA)

CULINARY ARTS

The Art Inst of Tucson (AZ)
The Art Insts Intl–Kansas City (KS)
Coll of the Ozarks (MO)
Drexel U (PA)
Mountain State U (WV)
Newbury Coll (MA)
Nicholls State U (LA)
The Restaurant School at Walnut Hill Coll (PA)
Southern New Hampshire U (NH)
U of Nevada, Las Vegas (NV)

CULINARY ARTS RELATED

Mississippi U for Women (MS)
Newbury Coll (MA)
U of Nevada, Las Vegas (NV)

CULINARY SCIENCE

Mississippi State U (MS)

CULTURAL ANTHROPOLOGY

Prescott Coll (AZ)

CULTURAL RESOURCE MANAGEMENT AND POLICY ANALYSIS

California State U, Dominguez Hills (CA)

CULTURAL STUDIES/CRITICAL THEORY AND ANALYSIS

American Public U System (WV)
Goddard Coll (VT)
Howard Payne U (TX)
Northern Arizona U (AZ)
Occidental Coll (CA)
The U of Tampa (FL)

Western Kentucky U (KY)

CURRICULUM AND INSTRUCTION

Albertus Magnus Coll (CT)
Eastern Washington U (WA)
Free Will Baptist Bible Coll (TN)
Midwestern State U (TX)
Northwest Missouri State U (MO)
Pittsburg State U (KS)
Randolph Coll (VA)
Tarleton State U (TX)
U of Minnesota, Twin Cities Campus (MN)
U of Regina (SK, Canada)
The U of South Dakota (SD)
U of Southern Maine (ME)
Utah State U (UT)
Walden U (MN)
Wright State U (OH)

CUSTOMER SERVICE MANAGEMENT

Bellevue U (NE)
Southwest Baptist U (MO)

CYBER/COMPUTER FORENSICS AND COUNTERTERRORISM

ITT Tech Inst, Indianapolis (IN)

CYTOGENETICS/GENETICS/ CLINICAL GENETICS TECHNOLOGY

Northern Michigan U (MI)
Saint Mary's U of Minnesota (MN)

CYTOTECHNOLOGY

Albany Coll of Pharmacy and Health Sciences (NY)
Barry U (FL)
Edgewood Coll (WI)
Elmhurst Coll (IL)
Illinois Coll (IL)
Indiana U Bloomington (IN)
Indiana U–Purdue U Indianapolis (IN)
Indiana U South Bend (IN)
Indiana U Southeast (IN)
Long Island U–Brooklyn Campus (NY)
Long Island U–C. W. Post Campus (NY)
Marian U (WI)
Marshall U (WV)
Massachusetts Coll of Liberal Arts (MA)
Michigan Technological U (MI)
Oakland U (MI)
Saint Louis U (MO)
Saint Mary's U of Minnesota (MN)
Slippery Rock U of Pennsylvania (PA)
State U of New York at Plattsburgh (NY)
Stony Brook U, State U of New York (NY)
Thiel Coll (PA)
U of Connecticut (CT)
The U of Kansas (KS)
U of North Dakota (ND)
U of North Texas (TX)
Winona State U (MN)

DAIRY HUSBANDRY AND PRODUCTION

U of Vermont (VT)

DAIRY SCIENCE

California Polytechnic State U, San Luis Obispo (CA)
Delaware Valley Coll (PA)
Eastern New Mexico U (NM)
Iowa State U of Science and Technology (IA)
Morrisville State Coll (NY)
South Dakota State U (SD)
Texas A&M U (TX)
U of Alberta (AB, Canada)
U of Georgia (GA)
U of Minnesota, Twin Cities Campus (MN)
U of New Hampshire (NH)

U of Wisconsin–Madison (WI)
U of Wisconsin–River Falls (WI)
Utah State U (UT)
Virginia Polytechnic Inst and State U (VA)

DANCE

Adelphi U (NY)
Agnes Scott Coll (GA)
Alma Coll (MI)
Amherst Coll (MA)
Anderson U (IN)
Appalachian State U (NC)
Arizona State U (AZ)
Ball State U (IN)
Bard Coll (NY)
Bard Coll at Simon's Rock (MA)
Barnard Coll (NY)
Bates Coll (ME)
Belhaven U (MS)
Bennington Coll (VT)
Brenau U (GA)
Butler U (IN)
California State U, East Bay (CA)
California State U, Fresno (CA)
California State U, Fullerton (CA)
California State U, Long Beach (CA)
California State U, Los Angeles (CA)
California State U, Sacramento (CA)
Cedar Crest Coll (PA)
Chapman U (CA)
The Coll at Brockport, State U of New York (NY)
The Colorado Coll (CO)
Colorado State U (CO)
Columbia Coll (SC)
Columbia Coll Chicago (IL)
Columbia U, School of General Studies (NY)
Concordia U (QC, Canada)
Connecticut Coll (CT)
Cornell U (NY)
Cornish Coll of the Arts (WA)
Denison U (OH)
DeSales U (PA)
Dickinson Coll (PA)
Dominican U of California (CA)
Drexel U (PA)
East Carolina U (NC)
Eastern Michigan U (MI)
Eastern U (PA)
Elon U (NC)
Emory U (GA)
Florida State U (FL)
Fordham U (NY)
Franklin & Marshall Coll (PA)
George Mason U (VA)
The George Washington U (DC)
Georgian Court U (NJ)
Goucher Coll (MD)
Grand Canyon U (AZ)
Grand Valley State U (MI)
Gustavus Adolphus Coll (MN)
Hamilton Coll (NY)
Hampshire Coll (MA)
Hobart and William Smith Colls (NY)
Hofstra U (NY)
Hollins U (VA)
Hope Coll (MI)
Hunter Coll of the City U of New York (NY)
Indiana U Bloomington (IN)
Ithaca Coll (NY)
Jacksonville U (FL)
Johnson State Coll (VT)
The Juilliard School (NY)
Keene State Coll (NH)
Kennesaw State U (GA)
Kent State U (OH)
Kenyon Coll (OH)
Lamar U (TX)
La Roche Coll (PA)
Lehman Coll of the City U of New York (NY)
Lindenwood U (MO)
Long Island U–Brooklyn Campus (NY)
Long Island U–C. W. Post Campus (NY)
Loyola Marymount U (CA)
Manhattanville Coll (NY)

Marlboro Coll (VT)
Marymount Manhattan Coll (NY)
Mercyhurst Coll (PA)
Meredith Coll (NC)
Middlebury Coll (VT)
Mills Coll (CA)
Montclair State U (NJ)
Mount Holyoke Coll (MA)
Muhlenberg Coll (PA)
New Mexico State U (NM)
New World School of the Arts (FL)
New York U (NY)
Nova Southeastern U (FL)
Oakland U (MI)
The Ohio State U (OH)
Ohio U (OH)
Oklahoma City U (OK)
Oral Roberts U (OK)
Palm Beach Atlantic U (FL)
Pitzer Coll (CA)
Point Park U (PA)
Pomona Coll (CA)
Purchase Coll, State of New York (NY)
Radford U (VA)
Randolph Coll (VA)
Rhode Island Coll (RI)
Rider U (NJ)
Roger Williams U (RI)
Rutgers, The State U of New Jersey, New Brunswick (NJ)
Ryerson U (ON, Canada)
Saint Mary's Coll of California (CA)
St. Olaf Coll (MN)
Sam Houston State U (TX)
San Diego State U (CA)
San Francisco State U (CA)
Sarah Lawrence Coll (NY)
Scripps Coll (CA)
Seton Hill U (PA)
Shenandoah U (VA)
Simon Fraser U (BC, Canada)
Skidmore Coll (NY)
Slippery Rock U of Pennsylvania (PA)
Smith Coll (MA)
Southern Methodist U (TX)
State U of New York at Fredonia (NY)
Stephen F. Austin State U (TX)
Stephens Coll (MO)
Swarthmore Coll (PA)
Sweet Briar Coll (VA)
Temple U (PA)
Texas Christian U (TX)
Texas State U–San Marcos (TX)
Texas Tech U (TX)
Texas Woman's U (TX)
Towson U (MD)
Trinity Coll (CT)
Tulane U (LA)
U at Buffalo, the State U of New York (NY)
The U of Akron (OH)
The U of Alabama (AL)
U of Alberta (AB, Canada)
The U of Arizona (AZ)
U of Arkansas at Little Rock (AR)
U of California, Berkeley (CA)
U of California, Irvine (CA)
U of California, Santa Barbara (CA)
U of Cincinnati (OH)
U of Colorado Boulder (CO)
U of Florida (FL)
U of Georgia (GA)
U of Hartford (CT)
U of Hawaii at Manoa (HI)
U of Houston (TX)
U of Idaho (ID)
U of Illinois at Urbana–Champaign (IL)
The U of Iowa (IA)
The U of Kansas (KS)
U of Maryland, Baltimore County (MD)
U of Maryland, Coll Park (MD)
U of Massachusetts Amherst (MA)
U of Michigan (MI)
U of Minnesota, Twin Cities Campus (MN)
U of Missouri–Kansas City (MO)
U of Nebraska–Lincoln (NE)
U of Nevada, Las Vegas (NV)
U of New Mexico (NM)

INDEXES

INDEXES

California State Polytechnic U, Pomona (CA)
California State U, Chico (CA)
California State U, Fresno (CA)
California State U, Long Beach (CA)
California State U, Los Angeles (CA)
California State U, San Bernardino (CA)
Carson-Newman Coll (TN)
Case Western Reserve U (OH)
Central Michigan U (MI)
Coll of Saint Elizabeth (NJ)
Coll of the Ozarks (MO)
Delaware State U (DE)
Dominican U (IL)
East Carolina U (NC)
Eastern Kentucky U (KY)
Eastern Michigan U (MI)
Florida Intl U (FL)
Fontbonne U (MO)
Georgia State U (GA)
Harding U (AR)
Idaho State U (ID)
Immaculata U (PA)
Iowa State U of Science and Technology (IA)
Jacksonville State U (AL)
Kansas State U (KS)
Keene State Coll (NH)
Lamar U (TX)
Lehman Coll of the City U of New York (NY)
Life U (GA)
Lipscomb U (TN)
Mansfield U of Pennsylvania (PA)
Marshall U (WV)
Marywood U (PA)
Meredith Coll (NC)
Miami U (OH)
Michigan State U (MI)
Minnesota State U Mankato (MN)
Missouri State U (MO)
Mount Mary Coll (WI)
Nicholls State U (LA)
North Dakota State U (ND)
Northern Illinois U (IL)
Northwest Missouri State U (MO)
The Ohio State U (OH)
Ohio U (OH)
Ouachita Baptist U (AR)
Point Loma Nazarene U (CA)
Purdue U (IN)
St. Catherine U (MN)
San Diego State U (CA)
San Francisco State U (CA)
Seton Hill U (PA)
Simmons Coll (MA)
State U of New York Coll at Oneonta (NY)
Texas Christian U (TX)
Texas Southern U (TX)
Texas Tech U (TX)
Tuskegee U (AL)
Universidad del Turabo (PR)
The U of Alabama (AL)
The U of British Columbia (BC, Canada)
U of Central Missouri (MO)
U of Cincinnati (OH)
U of Connecticut (CT)
U of Dayton (OH)
U of Delaware (DE)
U of Georgia (GA)
U of Illinois at Chicago (IL)
U of Illinois at Urbana–Champaign (IL)
U of Louisiana at Lafayette (LA)
U of Maryland Eastern Shore (MD)
U of Medicine and Dentistry of New Jersey (NJ)
U of Minnesota, Twin Cities Campus (MN)
U of Missouri (MO)
U of Nebraska at Kearney (NE)
U of New Haven (CT)
U of North Dakota (ND)
U of Northern Colorado (CO)
U of Oklahoma Health Sciences Center (OK)
U of Pittsburgh (PA)
U of Rhode Island (RI)
U of Southern Mississippi (MS)
The U of Tennessee at Martin (TN)

The U of Texas–Pan American (TX)
U of Vermont (VT)
The U of Western Ontario (ON, Canada)
U of Wisconsin–Stevens Point (WI)
U of Wisconsin–Stout (WI)
Viterbo U (WI)
Wayne State U (MI)
West Chester U of Pennsylvania (PA)
Western Carolina U (NC)
Youngstown State U (OH)

DIETETICS AND CLINICAL NUTRITION SERVICES RELATED

Coll of Saint Benedict (MN)
Madonna U (MI)
Purdue U (IN)
Saint John's U (MN)
Texas Christian U (TX)
Universidad del Turabo (PR)
Western Michigan U (MI)

DIETETIC TECHNOLOGY

Purdue U (IN)

DIGITAL ARTS

Bethany Lutheran Coll (MN)
Concordia U (QC, Canada)
DeSales U (PA)
Kansas City Art Inst (MO)
Lake Erie Coll (OH)
Marymount Coll, Palos Verdes, California (CA)
Memphis Coll of Art (TN)
Point Park U (PA)
Prescott Coll (AZ)
Southwestern Coll (KS)
State U of New York Coll of Technology at Alfred (NY)
Stetson U (FL)
Syracuse U (NY)
U of Central Florida (FL)
U of Florida (FL)
U of Massachusetts Dartmouth (MA)
U of Oregon (OR)
The U of Tampa (FL)

DIGITAL COMMUNICATION AND MEDIA/MULTIMEDIA

Abilene Christian U (TX)
The Art Inst of Atlanta (GA)
The Art Inst of Atlanta–Decatur (GA)
The Art Inst of Austin (TX)
The Art Inst of California, a college of Argosy U, Hollywood (CA)
The Art Inst of California, a college of Argosy U, Inland Empire (CA)
The Art Inst of California, a college of Argosy U, Los Angeles (CA)
The Art Inst of California, a college of Argosy U, Orange County (CA)
The Art Inst of California, a college of Argosy U, Sacramento (CA)
The Art Inst of California, a college of Argosy U, San Diego (CA)
The Art Inst of California, a college of Argosy U, San Francisco (CA)
The Art Inst of California, a college of Argosy U, Sunnyvale (CA)
The Art Inst of Colorado (CO)
The Art Inst of Dallas (TX)
The Art Inst of Fort Lauderdale (FL)
The Art Inst of Fort Worth (TX)
The Art Inst of Michigan (MI)
The Art Inst of Philadelphia (PA)
The Art Inst of Phoenix (AZ)
The Art Inst of Pittsburgh (PA)
The Art Inst of Portland (OR)
The Art Inst of Salt Lake City (UT)
The Art Inst of San Antonio (TX)
The Art Inst of Seattle (WA)
The Art Inst of Tampa (FL)
The Art Inst of Tennessee–Nashville (TN)
The Art Inst of Tucson (AZ)
The Art Inst of Virginia Beach (VA)
The Art Inst of Washington (VA)
The Art Inst of Washington–Dulles (VA)

The Art Inst of Wisconsin (WI)
The Art Inst of York–Pennsylvania (PA)
The Art Insts Intl Minnesota (MN)
Baldwin-Wallace Coll (OH)
Baylor U (TX)
Bradley U (IL)
Butler U (IN)
California Baptist U (CA)
California Coll of the Arts (CA)
California Lutheran U (CA)
California State U, Dominguez Hills (CA)
Calvin Coll (MI)
Canisius Coll (NY)
Cedar Crest Coll (PA)
Clarkson U (NY)
Cogswell Polytechnical Coll (CA)
Concordia Coll–New York (NY)
Corcoran Coll of Art and Design (DC)
Dordt Coll (IA)
Eastern Mennonite U (VA)
Fitchburg State U (MA)
Florida Atlantic U (FL)
Georgia Inst of Technology (GA)
Georgia Southern U (GA)
Harding U (AR)
Hilbert Coll (NY)
Howard Payne U (TX)
Huntington U (IN)
The Illinois Inst of Art–Chicago (IL)
The Illinois Inst of Art–Schaumburg (IL)
The Illinois Inst of Art–Tinley Park (IL)
Indiana U Bloomington (IN)
Indiana U–Purdue U Indianapolis (IN)
John Brown U (AR)
Juniata Coll (PA)
Kutztown U of Pennsylvania (PA)
Lebanon Valley Coll (PA)
Lee U (TN)
Lewis U (IL)
Limestone Coll (SC)
Lindenwood U (MO)
Lycoming Coll (PA)
Marywood U (PA)
Miami U (OH)
Michigan Technological U (MI)
Mount Marty Coll (SD)
Mount Mercy U (IA)
The New England Inst of Art (MA)
Northern Michigan U (MI)
Notre Dame of Maryland U (MD)
Ohio U (OH)
Point Park U (PA)
Rensselaer Polytechnic Inst (NY)
Rochester Inst of Technology (NY)
St. Edward's U (TX)
Saint Joseph's Coll of Maine (ME)
San Diego State U (CA)
Savannah Coll of Art and Design (GA)
Simpson Coll (IA)
Slippery Rock U of Pennsylvania (PA)
Southern New Hampshire U (NH)
Southwestern Coll (KS)
State U of New York Coll of Technology at Alfred (NY)
Texas A&M U (TX)
Tiffin U (OH)
Trevecca Nazarene U (TN)
Trinity Lutheran Coll (WA)
U of Denver (CO)
U of Idaho (ID)
U of Miami (FL)
U of Mississippi (MS)
U of Northern Iowa (IA)
U of Rochester (NY)
The U of Scranton (PA)
The U of Tampa (FL)
The U of Texas at Arlington (TX)
The U of Texas at Dallas (TX)
The U of the Arts (PA)
U of the Incarnate Word (TX)
U of Toronto (ON, Canada)
The U of Western Ontario (ON, Canada)
Valparaiso U (IN)
Washington State U (WA)
Webster U (MO)
Wellesley Coll (MA)

Wheeling Jesuit U (WV)
Wilkes U (PA)

DIRECTING AND THEATRICAL PRODUCTION

Bard Coll (NY)
Bennington Coll (VT)
Boston U (MA)
Bradley U (IL)
Brigham Young U (UT)
California State U, Long Beach (CA)
Coe Coll (IA)
Cornish Coll of the Arts (WA)
Drake U (IA)
Hofstra U (NY)
Juniata Coll (PA)
Keene State Coll (NH)
Lindenwood U (MO)
Lubbock Christian U (TX)
Purdue U (IN)
Rider U (NJ)
Saint Joseph's Coll (IN)
Sarah Lawrence Coll (NY)
State U of New York at Binghamton (NY)
Temple U (PA)
Texas Christian U (TX)
U of Illinois at Urbana–Champaign (IL)
The U of the Arts (PA)
Webster U (MO)

DIVINITY/MINISTRY

Azusa Pacific U (CA)
Baptist Bible Coll of Pennsylvania (PA)
Barclay Coll (KS)
Belmont U (TN)
Bethel Coll (IN)
Bluefield Coll (VA)
Briercrest Coll (SK, Canada)
Campbellsville U (KY)
Cardinal Stritch U (WI)
Cincinnati Christian U (OH)
Clear Creek Baptist Bible Coll (KY)
Corban U (OR)
Dallas Baptist U (TX)
Faith Baptist Bible Coll and Theological Sem (IA)
Faulkner U (AL)
Great Lakes Christian Coll (MI)
Hope Coll (MI)
Huntington U (IN)
Indiana Wesleyan U (IN)
John Brown U (AR)
Kingswood U (NB, Canada)
The Master's Coll and Sem (CA)
Master's Coll and Sem (ON, Canada)
Moody Bible Inst (IL)
New Hope Christian Coll (OR)
Northwest Nazarene U (ID)
Northwest U (WA)
Oakland City U (IN)
Providence Coll (RI)
Regent U (VA)
Roberts Wesleyan Coll (NY)
San Diego Christian Coll (CA)
Shorter U (GA)
Southwestern Assemblies of God U (TX)
Trevecca Nazarene U (TN)
Tri-State Bible Coll (OH)
The U of Western Ontario (ON, Canada)
Valley Forge Christian Coll Woodbridge Campus (VA)
Viterbo U (WI)
Williams Baptist Coll (AR)

DOCUMENTARY PRODUCTION

Burlington Coll (VT)
Ithaca Coll (NY)
Prescott Coll (AZ)
U at Albany, State U of New York (NY)

DRAFTING AND DESIGN TECHNOLOGY

Baker Coll of Owosso (MI)
East Carolina U (NC)

East Central U (OK)
Grambling State U (LA)
Herzing U, Madison (WI)
Lewis-Clark State Coll (ID)
Montana State U–Northern (MT)
Northern Michigan U (MI)
Prairie View A&M U (TX)
Purdue U (IN)
Texas Southern U (TX)
Trine U (IN)
U of Maine (ME)
U of Rio Grande (OH)
Western Michigan U (MI)

DRAFTING/DESIGN ENGINEERING TECHNOLOGIES RELATED

National U (CA)
Purdue U (IN)
Thomas Edison State Coll (NJ)

DRAMA AND DANCE TEACHER EDUCATION

Adams State Coll (CO)
Appalachian State U (NC)
Bishop's U (QC, Canada)
Boston U (MA)
Bowling Green State U (OH)
Bradley U (IL)
Brenau U (GA)
Bridgewater State U (MA)
Central Washington U (WA)
Columbia Coll (SC)
Columbus State U (GA)
Concordia U, Nebraska (NE)
Dordt Coll (IA)
East Carolina U (NC)
East Central U (OK)
East Texas Baptist U (TX)
Edgewood Coll (WI)
Hardin-Simmons U (TX)
Hope Coll (MI)
Howard Payne U (TX)
Jacksonville U (FL)
Johnson State Coll (VT)
Keene State Coll (NH)
Lees-McRae Coll (NC)
Lee U (TN)
Lipscomb U (TN)
Marquette U (WI)
Maryville Coll (TN)
Meredith Coll (NC)
Missouri Baptist U (MO)
Montclair State U (NJ)
North Carolina Central U (NC)
Ohio Wesleyan U (OH)
Oklahoma City U (OK)
Point Park U (PA)
St. Catherine U (MN)
St. Edward's U (TX)
Shenandoah U (VA)
Trevecca Nazarene U (TN)
The U of Akron (OH)
U of Evansville (IN)
The U of Iowa (IA)
U of Lethbridge (AB, Canada)
The U of Montana Western (MT)
The U of North Carolina at Charlotte (NC)
U of Regina (SK, Canada)
The U of South Dakota (SD)
U of South Florida (FL)
The U of the Arts (PA)
U of Windsor (ON, Canada)
Utah Valley U (UT)
Valparaiso U (IN)
Virginia Intermont Coll (VA)
Viterbo U (WI)
Washington U in St. Louis (MO)
Wayne State Coll (NE)
Weber State U (UT)
Western Washington U (WA)
William Jewell Coll (MO)

DRAMA THERAPY

Virginia Union U (VA)

DRAMATIC/THEATER ARTS

Abilene Christian U (TX)
Acadia U (NS, Canada)
Adelphi U (NY)
Adrian Coll (MI)
Agnes Scott Coll (GA)

INDEXES

Alabama State U (AL)
Albertus Magnus Coll (CT)
Albion Coll (MI)
Albright Coll (PA)
Alfred U (NY)
Allegheny Coll (PA)
Alma Coll (MI)
Alvernia U (PA)
American U (DC)
The American U in Cairo (Egypt)
Amherst Coll (MA)
Anderson U (IN)
Anderson U (SC)
Angelo State U (TX)
Appalachian State U (NC)
Aquinas Coll (MI)
Arcadia U (PA)
Arizona State U (AZ)
Arkansas State U (AR)
Armstrong Atlantic State U (GA)
Asbury U (KY)
Ashland U (OH)
Auburn U (AL)
Augustana Coll (IL)
Augustana Coll (SD)
Averett U (VA)
Avila U (MO)
Baker U (KS)
Ball State U (IN)
Bard Coll (NY)
Bard Coll at Simon's Rock (MA)
Barnard Coll (NY)
Barry U (FL)
Barton Coll (NC)
Bates Coll (ME)
Baylor U (TX)
Belhaven U (MS)
Belmont U (TN)
Beloit Coll (WI)
Bemidji State U (MN)
Benedictine Coll (KS)
Bennington Coll (VT)
Berea Coll (KY)
Bethany Coll (WV)
Bethany Lutheran Coll (MN)
Bethel Coll (IN)
Bethel U (MN)
Bethel U (TN)
Birmingham-Southern Coll (AL)
Bishop's U (QC, Canada)
Bloomsburg U of Pennsylvania (PA)
Bluefield Coll (VA)
Bob Jones U (SC)
Boise State U (ID)
Boston Coll (MA)
Boston U (MA)
Bowling Green State U (OH)
Bradley U (IL)
Brandeis U (MA)
Brenau U (GA)
Brevard Coll (NC)
Briar Cliff U (IA)
Bridgewater State U (MA)
Brown U (RI)
Bucknell U (PA)
Buffalo State Coll, State U of New York (NY)
Butler U (IN)
California Baptist U (CA)
California Lutheran U (CA)
California Polytechnic State U, San Luis Obispo (CA)
California State Polytechnic U, Pomona (CA)
California State U, Bakersfield (CA)
California State U, Chico (CA)
California State U, Dominguez Hills (CA)
California State U, East Bay (CA)
California State U, Fresno (CA)
California State U, Fullerton (CA)
California State U, Long Beach (CA)
California State U, Los Angeles (CA)
California State U, Sacramento (CA)
California State U, San Bernardino (CA)
California State U, Stanislaus (CA)
California U of Pennsylvania (PA)
Calvary Bible Coll and Theological Sem (MO)
Calvin Coll (MI)
Capital U (OH)

Cardinal Stritch U (WI)
Carleton Coll (MN)
Carnegie Mellon U (PA)
Carroll Coll (MT)
Carson-Newman Coll (TN)
Case Western Reserve U (OH)
Castleton State Coll (VT)
Catawba Coll (NC)
The Catholic U of America (DC)
Cedar Crest Coll (PA)
Cedarville U (OH)
Centenary Coll of Louisiana (LA)
Central Coll (IA)
Central Methodist U (MO)
Central Washington U (WA)
Centre Coll (KY)
Chapman U (CA)
Cheyney U of Pennsylvania (PA)
Christopher Newport U (VA)
City Coll of the City U of New York (NY)
Claremont McKenna Coll (CA)
Clarion U of Pennsylvania (PA)
Clarke U (IA)
Clark U (MA)
Clayton State U (GA)
Cleveland State U (OH)
Coastal Carolina U (SC)
Coe Coll (IA)
Colby Coll (ME)
Colgate U (NY)
The Coll at Brockport, State U of New York (NY)
Coll of Charleston (SC)
The Coll of Idaho (ID)
Coll of Saint Benedict (MN)
Coll of Staten Island of the City U of New York (NY)
Coll of the Holy Cross (MA)
Coll of the Ozarks (MO)
The Coll of William and Mary (VA)
The Coll of Wooster (OH)
The Colorado Coll (CO)
Colorado Mesa U (CO)
Colorado State U (CO)
Columbia Coll Chicago (IL)
Columbia U, School of General Studies (NY)
Columbus State U (GA)
Concordia Coll (MN)
Concordia U (CA)
Concordia U (QC, Canada)
Concordia U Chicago (IL)
Concordia U, Nebraska (NE)
Concordia U, St. Paul (MN)
Connecticut Coll (CT)
Converse Coll (SC)
Cornell Coll (IA)
Cornell U (NY)
Cornish Coll of the Arts (WA)
Covenant Coll (GA)
Creighton U (NE)
Culver-Stockton Coll (MO)
Dalhousie U (NS, Canada)
Dartmouth Coll (NH)
Davidson Coll (NC)
Denison U (OH)
DePaul U (IL)
DePauw U (IN)
DeSales U (PA)
Dickinson Coll (PA)
Dillard U (LA)
Doane Coll (NE)
Dominican U (IL)
Dordt Coll (IA)
Drake U (IA)
Drew U (NJ)
Drury U (MO)
Duquesne U (PA)
Earlham Coll (IN)
East Carolina U (NC)
East Central U (OK)
Eastern Illinois U (IL)
Eastern Kentucky U (KY)
Eastern Mennonite U (VA)
Eastern Michigan U (MI)
Eastern New Mexico U (NM)
Eastern Oregon U (OR)
Eastern Washington U (WA)
East Stroudsburg U of Pennsylvania (PA)
East Tennessee State U (TN)
East Texas Baptist U (TX)
Eckerd Coll (FL)
Edgewood Coll (WI)

Elizabethtown Coll (PA)
Elmhurst Coll (IL)
Elmira Coll (NY)
Elon U (NC)
Emory U (GA)
Emporia State U (KS)
The Evergreen State Coll (WA)
Fairfield U (CT)
Fairleigh Dickinson U, Coll at Florham (NJ)
Fairmont State U (WV)
Faulkner U (AL)
Ferrum Coll (VA)
Fitchburg State U (MA)
Five Towns Coll (NY)
Flagler Coll (FL)
Florida Ag and Mech U (FL)
Florida Atlantic U (FL)
Florida Gulf Coast U (FL)
Florida Intl U (FL)
Florida Southern Coll (FL)
Florida State U (FL)
Fontbonne U (MO)
Fordham U (NY)
Fort Hays State U (KS)
Fort Lewis Coll (CO)
Franciscan U of Steubenville (OH)
Francis Marion U (SC)
Franklin & Marshall Coll (PA)
Franklin Coll (IN)
Friends U (KS)
Furman U (SC)
Gannon U (PA)
Gardner-Webb U (NC)
George Fox U (OR)
George Mason U (VA)
Georgetown Coll (KY)
The George Washington U (DC)
Georgia Coll & State U (GA)
Georgia Southern U (GA)
Georgia Southwestern State U (GA)
Gettysburg Coll (PA)
Gonzaga U (WA)
Goshen Coll (IN)
Goucher Coll (MD)
Grace Coll (IN)
Graceland U (IA)
Grambling State U (LA)
Grand Canyon U (AZ)
Grand Valley State U (MI)
Grand View U (IA)
Greenville Coll (IL)
Grinnell Coll (IA)
Guilford Coll (NC)
Gustavus Adolphus Coll (MN)
Hamilton Coll (NY)
Hamline U (MN)
Hampshire Coll (MA)
Hampton U (VA)
Hannibal-LaGrange U (MO)
Hanover Coll (IN)
Harding U (AR)
Hardin-Simmons U (TX)
Hartwick Coll (NY)
Heidelberg U (OH)
Hendrix Coll (AR)
Hillsdale Coll (MI)
Hofstra U (NY)
Hollins U (VA)
Hope Coll (MI)
Howard Payne U (TX)
Humboldt State U (CA)
Hunter Coll of the City U of New York (NY)
Huntington U (IN)
Idaho State U (ID)
Illinois Coll (IL)
Illinois State U (IL)
Illinois Wesleyan U (IL)
Indiana State U (IN)
Indiana U Bloomington (IN)
Indiana U Northwest (IN)
Indiana U of Pennsylvania (PA)
Indiana U–Purdue U Fort Wayne (IN)
Indiana U South Bend (IN)
Iowa State U of Science and Technology (IA)
Ithaca Coll (NY)
Jacksonville State U (AL)
Jacksonville U (FL)
James Madison U (VA)
Jamestown Coll (ND)
Johnson State Coll (VT)
The Juilliard School (NY)

Juniata Coll (PA)
Kalamazoo Coll (MI)
Kansas State U (KS)
Kean U (NJ)
Kennesaw State U (GA)
Kent State U (OH)
Kenyon Coll (OH)
King's Coll (PA)
Knox Coll (IL)
Kutztown U of Pennsylvania (PA)
Lafayette Coll (PA)
LaGrange Coll (GA)
Lake Forest Coll (IL)
Lamar U (TX)
Lawrence U (WI)
Lees-McRae Coll (NC)
Lee U (TN)
Lehigh U (PA)
Lehman Coll of the City U of New York (NY)
Le Moyne Coll (NY)
Lenoir-Rhyne U (NC)
Lewis & Clark Coll (OR)
Lewis U (IL)
Liberty U (VA)
Limestone Coll (SC)
Lindenwood U (MO)
Linfield Coll (OR)
Lipscomb U (TN)
Lock Haven U of Pennsylvania (PA)
Long Island U–C. W. Post Campus (NY)
Longwood U (VA)
Louisiana Coll (LA)
Louisiana State U and Ag and Mech Coll (LA)
Loyola Marymount U (CA)
Loyola U Chicago (IL)
Loyola U New Orleans (LA)
Lubbock Christian U (TX)
Luther Coll (IA)
Lycoming Coll (PA)
Lynchburg Coll (VA)
Lyon Coll (AR)
Macalester Coll (MN)
Manchester Coll (IN)
Marietta Coll (OH)
Marlboro Coll (VT)
Marquette U (WI)
Mars Hill Coll (NC)
Mary Baldwin Coll (VA)
Marymount Manhattan Coll (NY)
Maryville Coll (TN)
Marywood U (PA)
McDaniel Coll (MD)
McMurry U (TX)
McPherson Coll (KS)
Meredith Coll (NC)
Messiah Coll (PA)
Metropolitan State Coll of Denver (CO)
Metropolitan State U (MN)
Miami U (OH)
Michigan State U (MI)
MidAmerica Nazarene U (KS)
Middlebury Coll (VT)
Middle Tennessee State U (TN)
Millikin U (IL)
Minnesota State U Mankato (MN)
Minnesota State U Moorhead (MN)
Missouri Southern State U (MO)
Missouri State U (MO)
Monmouth Coll (IL)
Monmouth U (NJ)
Montana State U Billings (MT)
Montclair State U (NJ)
Moravian Coll (PA)
Morehead State U (KY)
Morehouse Coll (GA)
Morningside Coll (IA)
Mount Allison U (NB, Canada)
Mount Holyoke Coll (MA)
Mount Marty Coll (SD)
Mount Vernon Nazarene U (OH)
Muhlenberg Coll (PA)
Naropa U (CO)
Nazareth Coll of Rochester (NY)
Nebraska Wesleyan U (NE)
Neumann U (PA)
Newberry Coll (SC)
New England Coll (NH)
New Mexico State U (NM)
New World School of the Arts (FL)
New York U (NY)
Niagara U (NY)

North Carolina Ag and Tech State U (NC)
North Carolina Central U (NC)
North Carolina Wesleyan Coll (NC)
North Central Coll (IL)
North Dakota State U (ND)
Northeastern State U (OK)
Northeastern U (MA)
Northern Arizona U (AZ)
Northern Illinois U (IL)
Northern Kentucky U (KY)
Northern Michigan U (MI)
Northern State U (SD)
North Greenville U (SC)
Northwestern Coll (IA)
Northwestern Coll (MN)
Northwestern State U of Louisiana (LA)
Northwest Missouri State U (MO)
Northwest U (WA)
Notre Dame de Namur U (CA)
Notre Dame of Maryland U (MD)
Nova Southeastern U (FL)
Oakland U (MI)
Occidental Coll (CA)
Ohio Northern U (OH)
The Ohio State U (OH)
Ohio U (OH)
Ohio Wesleyan U (OH)
Oklahoma Christian U (OK)
Oklahoma City U (OK)
Oklahoma State U (OK)
Old Dominion U (VA)
Oral Roberts U (OK)
Otterbein U (OH)
Ouachita Baptist U (AR)
Pacific U (OR)
Palm Beach Atlantic U (FL)
Park U (MO)
Pepperdine U, Malibu (CA)
Piedmont Coll (GA)
Pitzer Coll (CA)
Plymouth State U (NH)
Point Loma Nazarene U (CA)
Point Park U (PA)
Pomona Coll (CA)
Portland State U (OR)
Prairie View A&M U (TX)
Presbyterian Coll (SC)
Purchase Coll, State U of New York (NY)
Purdue U (IN)
Queens Coll of the City U of New York (NY)
Queen's U at Kingston (ON, Canada)
Queens U of Charlotte (NC)
Quinnipiac U (CT)
Radford U (VA)
Ramapo Coll of New Jersey (NJ)
Randolph Coll (VA)
Randolph-Macon Coll (VA)
Rhode Island Coll (RI)
Rhodes Coll (TN)
Ripon Coll (WI)
Roanoke Coll (VA)
Rockford Coll (IL)
Rocky Mountain Coll (MT)
Roger Williams U (RI)
Rollins Coll (FL)
Roosevelt U (IL)
Rowan U (NJ)
Russell Sage Coll (NY)
Rutgers, The State U of New Jersey, Camden (NJ)
Rutgers, The State U of New Jersey, Newark (NJ)
Rutgers, The State U of New Jersey, New Brunswick (NJ)
Saginaw Valley State U (MI)
St. Ambrose U (IA)
St. Bonaventure U (NY)
St. Catherine U (MN)
St. Edward's U (TX)
Saint John's U (MN)
St. John's U (NY)
St. Lawrence U (NY)
Saint Louis U (MO)
Saint Martin's U (WA)
Saint Mary-of-the-Woods Coll (IN)
Saint Mary's Coll (IN)
Saint Mary's Coll of California (CA)
St. Mary's Coll of Maryland (MD)
Saint Mary's U of Minnesota (MN)
Saint Michael's Coll (VT)

St. Norbert Coll (WI)
St. Olaf Coll (MN)
Saint Vincent Coll (PA)
Salem State U (MA)
Salisbury U (MD)
Salve Regina U (RI)
Samford U (AL)
Sam Houston State U (TX)
San Diego State U (CA)
San Francisco State U (CA)
Santa Clara U (CA)
Sarah Lawrence Coll (NY)
Savannah Coll of Art and Design (GA)
Schreiner U (TX)
Scripps Coll (CA)
Seattle Pacific U (WA)
Seattle U (WA)
Seton Hill U (PA)
Sewanee: The U of the South (TN)
Shaw U (NC)
Shenandoah U (VA)
Shorter U (GA)
Siena Heights U (MI)
Simon Fraser U (BC, Canada)
Simpson Coll (IA)
Skidmore Coll (NY)
Slippery Rock U of Pennsylvania (PA)
Smith Coll (MA)
Sonoma State U (CA)
South Carolina State U (SC)
Southeastern Oklahoma State U (OK)
Southeastern U (FL)
Southeast Missouri State U (MO)
Southern Arkansas U–Magnolia (AR)
Southern Connecticut State U (CT)
Southern Illinois U Carbondale (IL)
Southern Illinois U Edwardsville (IL)
Southern Methodist U (TX)
Southern Oregon U (OR)
Southwest Baptist U (MO)
Southwestern Assemblies of God U (TX)
Southwestern Coll (KS)
Southwestern U (TX)
Southwest Minnesota State U (MN)
Spelman Coll (GA)
Spring Arbor U (MI)
Spring Hill Coll (AL)
Stanford U (CA)
State U of New York at Binghamton (NY)
State U of New York at Fredonia (NY)
State U of New York at New Paltz (NY)
State U of New York at Oswego (NY)
State U of New York at Plattsburgh (NY)
State U of New York Coll at Geneseo (NY)
State U of New York Coll at Oneonta (NY)
Stephen F. Austin State U (TX)
Stephens Coll (MO)
Sterling Coll (KS)
Stetson U (FL)
Stevenson U (MD)
Stony Brook U, State U of New York (NY)
Suffolk U (MA)
Sul Ross State U (TX)
Susquehanna U (PA)
Swarthmore Coll (PA)
Sweet Briar Coll (VA)
Syracuse U (NY)
Tarleton State U (TX)
Taylor U (IN)
Temple U (PA)
Texas A&M U (TX)
Texas A&M U–Corpus Christi (TX)
Texas A&M U–Kingsville (TX)
Texas Christian U (TX)
Texas Lutheran U (TX)
Texas Southern U (TX)
Texas State U–San Marcos (TX)
Texas Tech U (TX)
Texas Wesleyan U (TX)
Texas Woman's U (TX)
Thomas Edison State Coll (NJ)
Thomas More Coll (KY)

Thompson Rivers U (BC, Canada)
Towson U (MD)
Transylvania U (KY)
Trevecca Nazarene U (TN)
Trinity Coll (CT)
Trinity U (TX)
Truman State U (MO)
Tufts U (MA)
Tulane U (LA)
Union Coll (KY)
Union U (TN)
U at Buffalo, the State U of New York (NY)
The U of Akron (OH)
The U of Alabama (AL)
The U of Alabama at Birmingham (AL)
U of Alaska Anchorage (AK)
U of Alberta (AB, Canada)
The U of Arizona (AZ)
U of Arkansas (AR)
U of Arkansas at Little Rock (AR)
U of Arkansas–Fort Smith (AR)
The U of British Columbia (BC, Canada)
The U of British Columbia–Okanagan (BC, Canada)
U of California, Berkeley (CA)
U of California, Irvine (CA)
U of California, Los Angeles (CA)
U of California, Riverside (CA)
U of California, Santa Barbara (CA)
U of California, Santa Cruz (CA)
U of Central Arkansas (AR)
U of Central Florida (FL)
U of Central Missouri (MO)
U of Cincinnati (OH)
U of Colorado Boulder (CO)
U of Colorado Denver (CO)
U of Connecticut (CT)
U of Dallas (TX)
U of Dayton (OH)
U of Denver (CO)
U of Evansville (IN)
The U of Findlay (OH)
U of Florida (FL)
U of Georgia (GA)
U of Guelph (ON, Canada)
U of Hawaii at Manoa (HI)
U of Houston (TX)
U of Idaho (ID)
U of Illinois at Chicago (IL)
U of Illinois at Urbana–Champaign (IL)
U of Indianapolis (IN)
The U of Iowa (IA)
The U of Kansas (KS)
U of La Verne (CA)
U of Lethbridge (AB, Canada)
U of Louisville (KY)
U of Maine at Farmington (ME)
U of Mary Hardin-Baylor (TX)
U of Maryland, Baltimore County (MD)
U of Maryland, Coll Park (MD)
U of Massachusetts Amherst (MA)
U of Massachusetts Boston (MA)
U of Memphis (TN)
U of Miami (FL)
U of Michigan (MI)
U of Michigan–Flint (MI)
U of Minnesota, Duluth (MN)
U of Minnesota, Twin Cities Campus (MN)
U of Mississippi (MS)
U of Missouri (MO)
U of Missouri–Kansas City (MO)
U of Missouri–St. Louis (MO)
U of Mobile (AL)
U of Mount Union (OH)
U of Nebraska at Kearney (NE)
U of Nebraska at Omaha (NE)
U of Nebraska–Lincoln (NE)
U of Nevada, Las Vegas (NV)
U of Nevada, Reno (NV)
U of New Hampshire (NH)
U of New Mexico (NM)
The U of North Carolina at Asheville (NC)
The U of North Carolina at Chapel Hill (NC)
The U of North Carolina at Charlotte (NC)
U of North Carolina School of the Arts (NC)

The U of North Carolina Wilmington (NC)
U of North Dakota (ND)
U of Northern Colorado (CO)
U of Northern Iowa (IA)
U of North Texas (TX)
U of Notre Dame (IN)
U of Oklahoma (OK)
U of Oregon (OR)
U of Ottawa (ON, Canada)
U of Pennsylvania (PA)
U of Pittsburgh (PA)
U of Pittsburgh at Johnstown (PA)
U of Portland (OR)
U of Puget Sound (WA)
U of Regina (SK, Canada)
U of Rhode Island (RI)
U of Richmond (VA)
U of Saint Mary (KS)
U of St. Thomas (TX)
U of San Diego (CA)
U of Science and Arts of Oklahoma (OK)
The U of Scranton (PA)
U of South Alabama (AL)
U of South Carolina (SC)
The U of South Dakota (SD)
U of Southern California (CA)
U of Southern Indiana (IN)
U of Southern Maine (ME)
U of Southern Mississippi (MS)
U of South Florida (FL)
The U of Tampa (FL)
The U of Tennessee (TN)
The U of Tennessee at Chattanooga (TN)
The U of Tennessee at Martin (TN)
The U of Texas at Arlington (TX)
The U of Texas at Austin (TX)
The U of Texas at El Paso (TX)
The U of Texas–Pan American (TX)
U of the Cumberlands (KY)
U of the District of Columbia (DC)
U of the Incarnate Word (TX)
U of the Ozarks (AR)
U of the Pacific (CA)
U of the Toledo (OH)
U of Tulsa (OK)
U of Utah (UT)
U of Vermont (VT)
U of Virginia (VA)
The U of Virginia's Coll at Wise (VA)
U of Washington (WA)
U of West Florida (FL)
U of West Georgia (GA)
U of Windsor (ON, Canada)
U of Wisconsin–Eau Claire (WI)
U of Wisconsin–Green Bay (WI)
U of Wisconsin–La Crosse (WI)
U of Wisconsin–Madison (WI)
U of Wisconsin–Milwaukee (WI)
U of Wisconsin–River Falls (WI)
U of Wisconsin–Stevens Point (WI)
U of Wisconsin–Superior (WI)
U of Wisconsin–Whitewater (WI)
U of Wyoming (WY)
Utah State U (UT)
Utah Valley U (UT)
Valdosta State U (GA)
Valparaiso U (IN)
Vanderbilt U (TN)
Vanguard U of Southern California (CA)
Vassar Coll (NY)
Virginia Commonwealth U (VA)
Virginia Intermont Coll (VA)
Virginia Polytechnic Inst and State U (VA)
Virginia Wesleyan Coll (VA)
Viterbo U (WI)
Wabash Coll (IN)
Wagner Coll (NY)
Wake Forest U (NC)
Waldorf Coll (IA)
Wartburg Coll (IA)
Washburn U (KS)
Washington and Lee U (VA)
Washington Coll (MD)
Washington U in St. Louis (MO)
Wayland Baptist U (TX)
Wayne State Coll (NE)
Wayne State U (MI)
Weber State U (UT)
Webster U (MO)
Wellesley Coll (MA)

Wells Coll (NY)
Wesleyan U (CT)
West Chester U of Pennsylvania (PA)
Western Carolina U (NC)
Western Connecticut State U (CT)
Western Illinois U (IL)
Western Kentucky U (KY)
Western Oregon U (OR)
Western State Coll of Colorado (CO)
Western Washington U (WA)
Westfield State U (MA)
Westminster Coll (UT)
West Texas A&M U (TX)
West Virginia U (WV)
West Virginia Wesleyan Coll (WV)
Wheaton Coll (MA)
Wheeling Jesuit U (WV)
Whitman Coll (WA)
Whittier Coll (CA)
Wichita State U (KS)
Wilkes U (PA)
Willamette U (OR)
William Jewell Coll (MO)
William Paterson U of New Jersey (NJ)
Williams Coll (MA)
William Woods U (MO)
Wilmington Coll (OH)
Winona State U (MN)
Winthrop U (SC)
Wittenberg U (OH)
Wofford Coll (SC)
Wright State U (OH)
Yale U (CT)
York Coll of Pennsylvania (PA)
York Coll of the City U of New York (NY)
Youngstown State U (OH)

DRAMATIC/THEATER ARTS AND STAGECRAFT RELATED

Adams State Coll (CO)
Baldwin-Wallace Coll (OH)
Brigham Young U (UT)
California State U, Chico (CA)
Clarke U (IA)
Coastal Carolina U (SC)
Dalhousie U (NS, Canada)
DePaul U (IL)
Drake U (IA)
Fayetteville State U (NC)
Grand Canyon U (AZ)
Indiana U South Bend (IN)
Lindenwood U (MO)
Meredith Coll (NC)
Nebraska Wesleyan U (NE)
North Central Coll (IL)
North Greenville U (SC)
Palm Beach Atlantic U (FL)
Pepperdine U, Malibu (CA)
Purdue U (IN)
Saint Augustine's Coll (NC)
Seton Hill U (PA)
Southern Illinois U Carbondale (IL)
Southwestern Coll (KS)
Southwest Minnesota State U (MN)
Thompson Rivers U (BC, Canada)
U at Buffalo, the State U of New York (NY)
U of Connecticut (CT)
U of Lethbridge (AB, Canada)
U of Miami (FL)
U of Michigan–Flint (MI)
U of Nevada, Las Vegas (NV)
U of Northern Colorado (CO)
U of Regina (SK, Canada)
Webster U (MO)
Western Kentucky U (KY)
Western Michigan U (MI)

DRAWING

Acad of Art U (CA)
Adams State Coll (CO)
Albany State U (GA)
Alberta Coll of Art & Design (AB, Canada)
Aquinas Coll (MI)
Arcadia U (PA)
Bard Coll at Simon's Rock (MA)
Bennington Coll (VT)
Bethany Coll (KS)
Biola U (CA)

Birmingham-Southern Coll (AL)
Boise State U (ID)
Bowling Green State U (OH)
Bradley U (IL)
Brigham Young U (UT)
Buffalo State Coll, State U of New York (NY)
California Coll of the Arts (CA)
California State U, East Bay (CA)
California State U, Long Beach (CA)
Carson-Newman Coll (TN)
The Cleveland Inst of Art (OH)
The Coll at Brockport, State U of New York (NY)
Coll of the Atlantic (ME)
Colorado State U (CO)
Columbus State U (GA)
Drake U (IA)
Emily Carr U of Art + Design (BC, Canada)
Ferris State U (MI)
Georgia State U (GA)
Governors State U (IL)
Grace Coll (IN)
Hampton U (VA)
Indiana U–Purdue U Fort Wayne (IN)
Inter American U of Puerto Rico, San Germán Campus (PR)
Lewis U (IL)
Lindenwood U (MO)
Longwood U (VA)
Lyme Acad Coll of Fine Arts (CT)
Marlboro Coll (VT)
Maryland Inst Coll of Art (MD)
Minnesota State U Mankato (MN)
Montserrat Coll of Art (MA)
Mount Allison U (NB, Canada)
New England Coll (NH)
Northern Michigan U (MI)
Oakland U (MI)
Otis Coll of Art and Design (CA)
Portland State U (OR)
Pratt Inst (NY)
Providence Coll (RI)
Rutgers, The State U of New Jersey, New Brunswick (NJ)
Sarah Lawrence Coll (NY)
Savannah Coll of Art and Design (GA)
School of the Museum of Fine Arts, Boston (MA)
Seton Hill U (PA)
Sewanee: The U of the South (TN)
Sonoma State U (CA)
State U of New York at Fredonia (NY)
U of Alberta (AB, Canada)
U of Hartford (CT)
The U of Iowa (IA)
U of Michigan (MI)
U of Missouri–St. Louis (MO)
U of Regina (SK, Canada)
The U of Texas at El Paso (TX)
The U of Toledo (OH)
U of Windsor (ON, Canada)
Virginia Intermont Coll (VA)
Washington U in St. Louis (MO)
Western Washington U (WA)
West Virginia Wesleyan Coll (WV)
Winona State U (MN)

DRIVER AND SAFETY TEACHER EDUCATION

William Penn U (IA)

DUTCH/FLEMISH

U of California, Berkeley (CA)

EARLY CHILDHOOD EDUCATION

Adams State Coll (CO)
Alabama State U (AL)
Albany State U (GA)
Alma Coll (MI)
Alvernia U (PA)
Anderson U (SC)
Anna Maria Coll (MA)
Antioch U Midwest (OH)
Arcadia U (PA)
Arizona State U (AZ)
Arkansas State U (AR)
Arkansas Tech U (AR)

Arlington Baptist Coll (TX)
Auburn U (AL)
Baldwin-Wallace Coll (OH)
Bayamón Central U (PR)
Baylor U (TX)
Bay Path Coll (MA)
Becker Coll (MA)
Bennington Coll (VT)
Berry Coll (GA)
Bethel Coll (IN)
Bloomsburg U of Pennsylvania (PA)
Bob Jones U (SC)
Boston U (MA)
Bradley U (IL)
Brewton-Parker Coll (GA)
Bridgewater State U (MA)
Brigham Young U (UT)
Bucknell U (PA)
Butler U (IN)
California Baptist U (CA)
California State U, Chico (CA)
California State U, Dominguez Hills (CA)
California State U, Fullerton (CA)
California State U, Los Angeles (CA)
California State U, Stanislaus (CA)
Calvin Coll (MI)
Cameron U (OK)
Canisius Coll (NY)
Capital U (OH)
Carlow U (PA)
The Catholic U of America (DC)
Cedar Crest Coll (PA)
Cedarville U (OH)
Central Methodist U (MO)
Central State U (OH)
Central Washington U (WA)
Chaminade U of Honolulu (HI)
Chatham U (PA)
Chestnut Hill Coll (PA)
Chicago State U (IL)
Christian Brothers U (TN)
City Coll of the City U of New York (NY)
Claflin U (SC)
Clarion U of Pennsylvania (PA)
Clark Atlanta U (GA)
Clemson U (SC)
Cleveland State U (OH)
Coastal Carolina U (SC)
The Coll at Brockport, State U of New York (NY)
Coll of Central Florida (FL)
Coll of Charleston (SC)
Coll of Mount St. Joseph (OH)
The Coll of New Jersey (NJ)
Coll of Saint Mary (NE)
Coll of the Ozarks (MO)
Colorado State U (CO)
Columbia Coll (SC)
Columbia Coll Chicago (IL)
Columbus State U (GA)
Concordia Coll–New York (NY)
Concordia U Chicago (IL)
Concordia U, Nebraska (NE)
Concordia U, St. Paul (MN)
Daemen Coll (NY)
Delaware State U (DE)
DePaul U (IL)
Dominican U (IL)
Dowling Coll (NY)
Duquesne U (PA)
East Central U (OK)
Eastern Connecticut State U (CT)
Eastern New Mexico U (NM)
Eastern Washington U (WA)
East Stroudsburg U of Pennsylvania (PA)
Edgewood Coll (WI)
Elizabethtown Coll (PA)
Endicott Coll (MA)
Evangel U (MO)
Fayetteville State U (NC)
Fitchburg State U (MA)
Felician Coll (NJ)
Florida Ag and Mech U (FL)
Florida Atlantic U (FL)
Florida Gulf Coast U (FL)
Florida Intl U (FL)
Florida State Coll at Jacksonville (FL)
Florida State U (FL)
Fort Lewis Coll (CO)
Francis Marion U (SC)

Free Will Baptist Bible Coll (TN)
Gannon U (PA)
Georgia Coll & State U (GA)
Georgia Gwinnett Coll (GA)
Governors State U (IL)
Granite State Coll (NH)
Greenville Coll (IL)
Grove City Coll (PA)
Hannibal-LaGrange U (MO)
Harding U (AR)
Hardin-Simmons U (TX)
Hillsdale Coll (MI)
Hofstra U (NY)
Holy Family U (PA)
Hood Coll (MD)
Idaho State U (ID)
Illinois Coll (IL)
Illinois State U (IL)
Indiana U Bloomington (IN)
Indiana U Kokomo (IN)
Indiana U of Pennsylvania (PA)
Indiana U–Purdue U Indianapolis (IN)
Inter American U of Puerto Rico, San Germán Campus (PR)
Iona Coll (NY)
Iowa Wesleyan Coll (IA)
John Brown U (AR)
Judson U (IL)
Juniata Coll (PA)
Keene State Coll (NH)
Kennesaw State U (GA)
Kent State U (OH)
Kent State U at Salem (OH)
Kent State U at Tuscarawas (OH)
Keystone Coll (PA)
King's Coll (PA)
Kutztown U of Pennsylvania (PA)
LaGrange Coll (GA)
Lake Erie Coll (OH)
Lake Superior State U (MI)
La Roche Coll (PA)
Lasell Coll (MA)
Lebanon Valley Coll (PA)
Lindenwood U (MO)
Louisiana State U and Ag and Mech Coll (LA)
Lourdes U (OH)
Loyola U Chicago (IL)
Lubbock Christian U (TX)
Lyon Coll (AR)
Macon State Coll (GA)
Malone U (OH)
Maranatha Baptist Bible Coll (WI)
Marian U (WI)
Marywood U (PA)
Mayville State U (ND)
McMurry U (TX)
McNeese State U (LA)
Merrimack Coll (MA)
Messiah Coll (PA)
Miami U (OH)
Michigan State U (MI)
Midwestern State U (TX)
Millersville U of Pennsylvania (PA)
Milligan Coll (TN)
Millikin U (IL)
Minnesota State U Moorhead (MN)
Misericordia U (PA)
Missouri Baptist U (MO)
Missouri State U (MO)
Missouri Western State U (MO)
Mitchell Coll (CT)
Morehead State U (KY)
Morehouse Coll (GA)
Morris Coll (SC)
Mount Aloysius Coll (PA)
Mount Ida Coll (MA)
Mount Saint Mary Coll (NY)
Mount Vernon Nazarene U (OH)
Naropa U (CO)
National-Louis U (IL)
Neumann U (PA)
Newman U (KS)
New Mexico State U (NM)
New York U (NY)
Nicholls State U (LA)
Northeastern Illinois U (IL)
Northeastern State U (OK)
Northern Arizona U (AZ)
Northern Illinois U (IL)
North Georgia Coll & State U (GA)
North Greenville U (SC)
Northwestern Coll (MN)

Northwestern Oklahoma State U (OK)
Northwestern State U of Louisiana (LA)
Nyack Coll (NY)
Ohio Northern U (OH)
Ohio U (OH)
Ohio U–Chillicothe (OH)
Ohio Wesleyan U (OH)
Oklahoma Christian U (OK)
Oklahoma City U (OK)
Oral Roberts U (OK)
Ouachita Baptist U (AR)
Pacific Union Coll (CA)
Park U (MO)
Peru State Coll (NE)
Pine Manor Coll (MA)
Pittsburg State U (KS)
Plymouth State U (NH)
Point Park U (PA)
Point U (GA)
Presbyterian Coll (SC)
Prescott Coll (AZ)
Purdue U (IN)
Purdue U North Central (IN)
Reinhardt U (GA)
Rhode Island Coll (RI)
Ripon Coll (WI)
Rivier Coll (NH)
Roberts Wesleyan Coll (NY)
Roosevelt U (IL)
Rowan U (NJ)
Ryerson U (ON, Canada)
St. Ambrose U (IA)
Salem State U (MA)
Salisbury U (MD)
Salve Regina U (RI)
San Francisco State U (CA)
Sarah Lawrence Coll (NY)
Schreiner U (TX)
Shawnee State U (OH)
Shippensburg U of Pennsylvania (PA)
Simmons Coll (MA)
Sojourner-Douglass Coll (MD)
South Carolina State U (SC)
South Dakota State U (SD)
Southeastern Louisiana U (LA)
Southeast Missouri State U (MO)
Southern Arkansas U–Magnolia (AR)
Southern Connecticut State U (CT)
Southern Illinois U Carbondale (IL)
Southern Illinois U Edwardsville (IL)
Southern New Hampshire U (NH)
Southwest Baptist U (MO)
Southwestern Coll (KS)
Spring Hill Coll (AL)
State U of New York Coll at Geneseo (NY)
State U of New York Coll at Old Westbury (NY)
Stephens Coll (MO)
Stonehill Coll (MA)
Texas Christian U (TX)
Thomas U (GA)
Towson U (MD)
Trevecca Nazarene U (TN)
Trinity Lutheran Coll (WA)
Troy U (AL)
Truett-McConnell Coll (GA)
Tusculum Coll (TN)
Universidad del Turabo (PR)
The U of Alabama (AL)
The U of Alabama at Birmingham (AL)
U of Arkansas (AR)
U of Arkansas–Fort Smith (AR)
U of Central Florida (FL)
U of Delaware (DE)
U of Hartford (CT)
U of Hawaii–West Oahu (HI)
U of Illinois at Urbana–Champaign (IL)
The U of Kansas (KS)
U of Maine at Farmington (ME)
U of Mary (ND)
U of Mary Hardin-Baylor (TX)
U of Michigan–Dearborn (MI)
U of Michigan–Flint (MI)
U of Minnesota, Crookston (MN)
U of Missouri (MO)
U of Missouri–Kansas City (MO)
U of Missouri–St. Louis (MO)
U of Mobile (AL)

The U of Montana Western (MT)
U of Mount Union (OH)
U of New Mexico (NM)
U of New Orleans (LA)
The U of North Carolina at Chapel Hill (NC)
U of North Dakota (ND)
U of North Florida (FL)
U of Oklahoma (OK)
U of Regina (SK, Canada)
U of Science and Arts of Oklahoma (OK)
The U of Scranton (PA)
U of South Carolina Aiken (SC)
U of South Carolina Beaufort (SC)
U of Southern Indiana (IN)
U of South Florida (FL)
The U of Tennessee at Chattanooga (TN)
U of Tulsa (OK)
U of Vermont (VT)
The U of West Alabama (AL)
U of West Florida (FL)
U of Wisconsin–Stevens Point (WI)
U of Wisconsin–Stout (WI)
U of Wisconsin–Whitewater (WI)
Ursuline Coll (OH)
Valdosta State U (GA)
Valley Forge Christian Coll Woodbridge Campus (VA)
Vanderbilt U (TN)
Virginia Intermont Coll (VA)
Walsh U (OH)
Washington State U (WA)
Wayland Baptist U (TX)
Wayne State Coll (NE)
Weber State U (UT)
Wesleyan Coll (GA)
West Chester U of Pennsylvania (PA)
Western Kentucky U (KY)
Western Michigan U (MI)
Western Washington U (WA)
Wheeling Jesuit U (WV)
Wheelock Coll (MA)
Widener U (PA)
Wilmington U (DE)
Worcester State U (MA)
Wright State U (OH)
Xavier U (OH)
Xavier U of Louisiana (LA)
Yeshiva U (NY)
York Coll of Pennsylvania (PA)
Youngstown State U (OH)

EARTH SCIENCE EDUCATION
Calvin Coll (MI)
Central Michigan U (MI)
Florida Inst of Technology (FL)
Purdue U (IN)
Syracuse U (NY)
The U of Montana Western (MT)
U of Wisconsin–Madison (WI)
Western Michigan U (MI)

EAST ASIAN LANGUAGES
Arizona State U (AZ)
Eckerd Coll (FL)
Grinnell Coll (IA)
Indiana U Bloomington (IN)
Michigan State U (MI)
Smith Coll (MA)
U of Illinois at Urbana–Champaign (IL)
The U of Kansas (KS)
U of Pennsylvania (PA)
U of Puget Sound (WA)
U of Southern California (CA)
The U of Texas at Austin (TX)
Washington and Lee U (VA)

EAST ASIAN LANGUAGES RELATED
Columbia U, School of General Studies (NY)
Dartmouth Coll (NH)
Indiana U Bloomington (IN)
Michigan State U (MI)
U of Florida (FL)
U of Minnesota, Twin Cities Campus (MN)
U of Southern California (CA)
Washington U in St. Louis (MO)

ECOLOGY
Appalachian State U (NC)
Bard Coll at Simon's Rock (MA)
Barry U (FL)
Bemidji State U (MN)
Bennington Coll (VT)
California State U, Chico (CA)
California State U, Dominguez Hills (CA)
California State U, East Bay (CA)
California State U, Fresno (CA)
California State U, Long Beach (CA)
California State U, San Marcos (CA)
Clark U (MA)
Columbia U, School of General Studies (NY)
Concordia Coll–New York (NY)
Concordia U (QC, Canada)
Cornell U (NY)
Dartmouth Coll (NH)
Defiance Coll (OH)
Eastern Kentucky U (KY)
Fort Lewis Coll (CO)
Georgetown Coll (KY)
Idaho State U (ID)
Iowa State U of Science and Technology (IA)
Jacksonville State U (AL)
Juniata Coll (PA)
Lawrence U (WI)
Le Moyne Coll (NY)
Manchester Coll (IN)
Marlboro Coll (VT)
Mars Hill Coll (NC)
Medgar Evers Coll of the City U of New York (NY)
Michigan Technological U (MI)
Minnesota State U Mankato (MN)
New Mexico State U (NM)
New York U (NY)
Northern Michigan U (MI)
Oklahoma City U (OK)
Pomona Coll (CA)
Princeton U (NJ)
Rice U (TX)
Rocky Mountain Coll (MT)
Rutgers, The State U of New Jersey, New Brunswick (NJ)
San Francisco State U (CA)
Sarah Lawrence Coll (NY)
Sierra Nevada Coll (NV)
Sonoma State U (CA)
State U of New York at Plattsburgh (NY)
State U of New York Coll of Environmental Science and Forestry (NY)
Sterling Coll (VT)
Stony Brook U, State U of New York (NY)
Susquehanna U (PA)
Thompson Rivers U (BC, Canada)
Towson U (MD)
Tufts U (MA)
Tulane U (LA)
Université de Sherbrooke (QC, Canada)
U at Buffalo, the State U of New York (NY)
The U of Akron (OH)
U of California, Los Angeles (CA)
U of California, Santa Cruz (CA)
U of Connecticut (CT)
U of Delaware (DE)
U of Denver (CO)
U of Georgia (GA)
U of Guelph (ON, Canada)
U of Illinois at Urbana–Champaign (IL)
U of Maine (ME)
U of Maryland, Coll Park (MD)
U of Maryland Eastern Shore (MD)
U of Michigan–Flint (MI)
U of Minnesota, Twin Cities Campus (MN)
U of New Haven (CT)
U of Northern Iowa (IA)
U of Pittsburgh (PA)
U of Pittsburgh at Johnstown (PA)
U of Rio Grande (OH)
The U of Western Ontario (ON, Canada)
Utah State U (UT)

Washington Coll (MD)
Washington U in St. Louis (MO)
William Paterson U of New Jersey (NJ)
Winona State U (MN)
Yale U (CT)

ECOLOGY AND EVOLUTIONARY BIOLOGY
Bradley U (IL)
Purdue U (IN)
The U of Arizona (AZ)
U of California, Irvine (CA)
U of Michigan (MI)
U of Pittsburgh (PA)
Vanderbilt U (TN)

ECOLOGY, EVOLUTION, SYSTEMATICS AND POPULATION BIOLOGY RELATED
Angelo State U (TX)
Hofstra U (NY)
The Ohio State U (OH)
Prescott Coll (AZ)
The U of British Columbia–Okanagan (BC, Canada)
U of California, Davis (CA)
U of California, Santa Barbara (CA)
U of Colorado Boulder (CO)
U of Guelph (ON, Canada)

E-COMMERCE
Bloomfield Coll (NJ)
Delaware State U (DE)
DePaul U (IL)
Friends U (KS)
Harrisburg U of Science and Technology (PA)
King Coll (TN)
Maryville U of Saint Louis (MO)
National U (CA)
Philadelphia U (PA)
Thiel Coll (PA)
Tiffin U (OH)
Trevecca Nazarene U (TN)
U of La Verne (CA)
U of North Texas (TX)
U of Ottawa (ON, Canada)
U of Pennsylvania (PA)
The U of Scranton (PA)
U of Toronto (ON, Canada)
Western Michigan U (MI)
Winthrop U (SC)

ECONOMETRICS AND QUANTITATIVE ECONOMICS
Baldwin-Wallace Coll (OH)
Bowdoin Coll (ME)
Bucknell U (PA)
The Colorado Coll (CO)
Hampden-Sydney Coll (VA)
Haverford Coll (PA)
Hofstra U (NY)
Scripps Coll (CA)
State U of New York at Oswego (NY)
United States Naval Acad (MD)
U of California, Irvine (CA)
U of California, Santa Barbara (CA)
U of Guelph (ON, Canada)
U of Minnesota, Twin Cities Campus (MN)
U of Rhode Island (RI)
Wake Forest U (NC)
Weber State U (UT)
Western Kentucky U (KY)

ECONOMICS
Acadia U (NS, Canada)
Adams State Coll (CO)
Adelphi U (NY)
Adrian Coll (MI)
Agnes Scott Coll (GA)
Albion Coll (MI)
Albright Coll (PA)
Alfred U (NY)
Allegheny Coll (PA)
Alma Coll (MI)
American U (DC)
American U in Bulgaria (Bulgaria)
The American U in Cairo (Egypt)
American U of Beirut (Lebanon)

The American U of Paris (France)
Amherst Coll (MA)
Andrews U (MI)
Appalachian State U (NC)
Aquinas Coll (MI)
Arizona State U (AZ)
Arkansas State U (AR)
Armstrong Atlantic State U (GA)
Ashland U (OH)
Assumption Coll (MA)
Auburn U (AL)
Augustana Coll (IL)
Augustana Coll (SD)
Austin Coll (TX)
Babson Coll (MA)
Baker U (KS)
Baldwin-Wallace Coll (OH)
Ball State U (IN)
Bard Coll (NY)
Barnard Coll (NY)
Barry U (FL)
Barton Coll (NC)
Bates Coll (ME)
Baylor U (TX)
Bellarmine U (KY)
Belmont U (TN)
Beloit Coll (WI)
Bemidji State U (MN)
Benedictine Coll (KS)
Benedictine U (IL)
Berea Coll (KY)
Bernard M. Baruch Coll of the City U of New York (NY)
Berry Coll (GA)
Bethany Coll (WV)
Bethel U (MN)
Birmingham-Southern Coll (AL)
Bishop's U (QC, Canada)
Bloomsburg U of Pennsylvania (PA)
Bluffton U (OH)
Boise State U (ID)
Boston Coll (MA)
Boston U (MA)
Bowdoin Coll (ME)
Bowie State U (MD)
Bowling Green State U (OH)
Bradley U (IL)
Brandeis U (MA)
Bridgewater Coll (VA)
Bridgewater State U (MA)
Brown U (RI)
Bryant U (RI)
Bryn Mawr Coll (PA)
Bucknell U (PA)
Buffalo State Coll, State U of New York (NY)
Butler U (IN)
Caldwell Coll (NJ)
California Inst of Technology (CA)
California Lutheran U (CA)
California Polytechnic State U, San Luis Obispo (CA)
California State Polytechnic U, Pomona (CA)
California State U, Bakersfield (CA)
California State U, Chico (CA)
California State U, East Bay (CA)
California State U, Fresno (CA)
California State U, Fullerton (CA)
California State U, Long Beach (CA)
California State U, Los Angeles (CA)
California State U, Sacramento (CA)
California State U, San Bernardino (CA)
California State U, San Marcos (CA)
California State U, Stanislaus (CA)
Calvin Coll (MI)
Campbellsville U (KY)
Canisius Coll (NY)
Cape Breton U (NS, Canada)
Capital U (OH)
Carleton Coll (MN)
Carnegie Mellon U (PA)
Carson-Newman Coll (TN)
Case Western Reserve U (OH)
The Catholic U of America (DC)
Centenary Coll of Louisiana (LA)
Central Coll (IA)
Central Connecticut State U (CT)
Central Methodist U (MO)
Central Michigan U (MI)

Central State U (OH)
Central Washington U (WA)
Centre Coll (KY)
Cheyney U of Pennsylvania (PA)
Chicago State U (IL)
Christopher Newport U (VA)
City Coll of the City U of New York (NY)
Claremont McKenna Coll (CA)
Clarion U of Pennsylvania (PA)
Clark U (MA)
Clemson U (SC)
Cleveland State U (OH)
Coastal Carolina U (SC)
Coe Coll (IA)
Colby Coll (ME)
Colgate U (NY)
The Coll at Brockport, State U of New York (NY)
Coll of Charleston (SC)
Coll of Mount Saint Vincent (NY)
The Coll of New Jersey (NJ)
Coll of Saint Benedict (MN)
Coll of Saint Elizabeth (NJ)
Coll of Staten Island of the City U of New York (NY)
Coll of the Atlantic (ME)
Coll of the Holy Cross (MA)
The Coll of William and Mary (VA)
The Coll of Wooster (OH)
The Colorado Coll (CO)
Colorado School of Mines (CO)
Colorado State U (CO)
Columbia U, School of General Studies (NY)
Concordia U (CA)
Concordia U (QC, Canada)
Connecticut Coll (CT)
Converse Coll (SC)
Cornell Coll (IA)
Cornell U (NY)
Creighton U (NE)
Dalhousie U (NS, Canada)
Dartmouth Coll (NH)
Davidson Coll (NC)
Denison U (OH)
DePaul U (IL)
DePauw U (IN)
DEREE - The American Coll of Greece (Greece)
Dickinson Coll (PA)
Dillard U (LA)
Doane Coll (NE)
Dominican Coll (NY)
Dominican U (IL)
Dowling Coll (NY)
Drew U (NJ)
Drury U (MO)
Duquesne U (PA)
Earlham Coll (IN)
East Carolina U (NC)
Eastern Connecticut State U (CT)
Eastern Illinois U (IL)
Eastern Kentucky U (KY)
Eastern Mennonite U (VA)
Eastern Michigan U (MI)
Eastern U (PA)
Eastern Washington U (WA)
East Stroudsburg U of Pennsylvania (PA)
East Tennessee State U (TN)
Eckerd Coll (FL)
Edgewood Coll (WI)
Edinboro U of Pennsylvania (PA)
Elizabethtown Coll (PA)
Elmhurst Coll (IL)
Elmira Coll (NY)
Elon U (NC)
Emmanuel Coll (MA)
Emory & Henry Coll (VA)
Emory U (GA)
Emporia State U (KS)
Excelsior Coll (NY)
Fairfield U (CT)
Fairleigh Dickinson U, Coll at Florham (NJ)
Fairleigh Dickinson U, Metropolitan Campus (NJ)
Fairmont State U (WV)
Fitchburg State U (MA)
Florida Ag and Mech U (FL)
Florida Atlantic U (FL)
Florida Gulf Coast U (FL)
Florida Intl U (FL)
Florida Southern Coll (FL)

Florida State U (FL)
Fordham U (NY)
Fort Hays State U (KS)
Fort Lewis Coll (CO)
Framingham State U (MA)
Franciscan U of Steubenville (OH)
Francis Marion U (SC)
Franklin & Marshall Coll (PA)
Franklin Coll (IN)
Franklin U (OH)
Furman U (SC)
Gardner-Webb U (NC)
George Fox U (OR)
George Mason U (VA)
Georgetown Coll (KY)
The George Washington U (DC)
Georgia Southern U (GA)
Georgia State U (GA)
Gettysburg Coll (PA)
Goldey-Beacom Coll (DE)
Gonzaga U (WA)
Gordon Coll (MA)
Goucher Coll (MD)
Graceland U (IA)
Grand Valley State U (MI)
Grinnell Coll (IA)
Grove City Coll (PA)
Guilford Coll (NC)
Gustavus Adolphus Coll (MN)
Hamilton Coll (NY)
Hamline U (MN)
Hampden-Sydney Coll (VA)
Hampshire Coll (MA)
Hampton U (VA)
Hanover Coll (IN)
Harding U (AR)
Hardin-Simmons U (TX)
Hartwick Coll (NY)
Harvard U (MA)
Haverford Coll (PA)
Hawai`i Pacific U (HI)
Heidelberg U (OH)
Hendrix Coll (AR)
Hillsdale Coll (MI)
Hobart and William Smith Colls (NY)
Hofstra U (NY)
Hollins U (VA)
Holy Family U (PA)
Hood Coll (MD)
Hope Coll (MI)
Humboldt State U (CA)
Hunter Coll of the City U of New York (NY)
Huntington U (IN)
Idaho State U (ID)
Illinois Coll (IL)
Illinois State U (IL)
Illinois Wesleyan U (IL)
Immaculata U (PA)
Indiana State U (IN)
Indiana U Bloomington (IN)
Indiana U Northwest (IN)
Indiana U of Pennsylvania (PA)
Indiana U–Purdue U Fort Wayne (IN)
Indiana U–Purdue U Indianapolis (IN)
Indiana U South Bend (IN)
Indiana U Southeast (IN)
Indiana Wesleyan U (IN)
Inter American U of Puerto Rico, San Germán Campus (PR)
Iona Coll (NY)
Iowa State U of Science and Technology (IA)
Ithaca Coll (NY)
Jacksonville State U (AL)
Jacksonville U (FL)
James Madison U (VA)
John Brown U (AR)
John Carroll U (OH)
John Jay Coll of Criminal Justice of the City U of New York (NY)
The Johns Hopkins U (MD)
Johnson C. Smith U (NC)
Juniata Coll (PA)
Kansas State U (KS)
Kean U (NJ)
Keene State Coll (NH)
Kenyon Coll (OH)
King Coll (TN)
King's Coll (PA)
Knox Coll (IL)
Lafayette Coll (PA)

Lake Forest Coll (IL)
Lakehead U (ON, Canada)
Lamar U (TX)
La Salle U (PA)
La Sierra U (CA)
Lawrence U (WI)
Lebanese American U (Lebanon)
Lebanon Valley Coll (PA)
Lehman Coll of the City U of New York (NY)
Le Moyne Coll (NY)
Lenoir-Rhyne U (NC)
Lewis & Clark Coll (OR)
Liberty U (VA)
Lincoln Memorial U (TN)
Lincoln U (PA)
Lindenwood U (MO)
Linfield Coll (OR)
Long Island U–Brooklyn Campus (NY)
Long Island U–C. W. Post Campus (NY)
Longwood U (VA)
Loras Coll (IA)
Louisiana Coll (LA)
Louisiana State U and Ag and Mech Coll (LA)
Loyola Marymount U (CA)
Loyola U Maryland (MD)
Loyola U New Orleans (LA)
Lubbock Christian U (TX)
Luther Coll (IA)
Lycoming Coll (PA)
Lynchburg Coll (VA)
Lyon Coll (AR)
Macalester Coll (MN)
Manchester Coll (IN)
Manhattan Coll (NY)
Manhattanville Coll (NY)
Mansfield U of Pennsylvania (PA)
Marietta Coll (OH)
Marlboro Coll (VT)
Marquette U (WI)
Marshall U (WV)
Mars Hill Coll (NC)
Mary Baldwin Coll (VA)
Marymount U (VA)
Maryville Coll (TN)
Massachusetts Inst of Technology (MA)
McDaniel Coll (MD)
McKendree U (IL)
Mercer U (GA)
Meredith Coll (NC)
Merrimack Coll (MA)
Messiah Coll (PA)
Metropolitan State Coll of Denver (CO)
Metropolitan State U (MN)
Miami U (OH)
Michigan State U (MI)
Michigan Technological U (MI)
Middlebury Coll (VT)
Middle Tennessee State U (TN)
Midwestern State U (TX)
Millersville U of Pennsylvania (PA)
Millsaps Coll (MS)
Mills Coll (CA)
Minnesota State U Mankato (MN)
Minnesota State U Moorhead (MN)
Mississippi State U (MS)
Missouri State U (MO)
Missouri U of Science and Technology (MO)
Missouri Western State U (MO)
Monmouth Coll (IL)
Montana State U (MT)
Montclair State U (NJ)
Moravian Coll (PA)
Morehouse Coll (GA)
Mount Allison U (NB, Canada)
Mount Holyoke Coll (MA)
Mount St. Mary's U (MD)
Muhlenberg Coll (PA)
National U (CA)
Nazareth Coll of Rochester (NY)
Nebraska Wesleyan U (NE)
New Coll of Florida (FL)
New Jersey City U (NJ)
New Mexico State U (NM)
New York Inst of Technology (NY)
New York U (NY)
Niagara U (NY)
Nichols Coll (MA)

INDEXES

Alverno Coll (WI)
Anderson U (IN)
Andrews U (MI)
Anna Maria Coll (MA)
Arcadia U (PA)
Arlington Baptist Coll (TX)
Ashland U (OH)
Auburn U (AL)
Baldwin-Wallace Coll (OH)
Ball State U (IN)
Baptist Bible Coll of Pennsylvania (PA)
The Baptist Coll of Florida (FL)
Barnard Coll (NY)
Barry U (FL)
Baylor U (TX)
Becker Coll (MA)
Bellevue U (NE)
Belmont Abbey Coll (NC)
Belmont U (TN)
Beloit Coll (WI)
Bemidji State U (MN)
Bennington Coll (VT)
Berea Coll (KY)
Bernard M. Baruch Coll of the City U of New York (NY)
Bethany Coll (KS)
Bethany Coll (WV)
Bethel Coll (IN)
Bethune-Cookman U (FL)
Biola U (CA)
Birmingham-Southern Coll (AL)
Bishop's U (QC, Canada)
Bloomfield Coll (NJ)
Bluefield Coll (VA)
Boise State U (ID)
Boston U (MA)
Bowie State U (MD)
Bowling Green State U (OH)
Brandeis U (MA)
Brewton-Parker Coll (GA)
Briar Cliff U (IA)
Brown U (RI)
Bucknell U (PA)
Cabrini Coll (PA)
California Baptist U (CA)
Cape Breton U (NS, Canada)
Cardinal Stritch U (WI)
Carson-Newman Coll (TN)
Catawba Coll (NC)
The Catholic U of America (DC)
Cedar Crest Coll (PA)
Centenary Coll (NJ)
Central Methodist U (MO)
Chapman U (CA)
Cheyney U of Pennsylvania (PA)
Christian Brothers U (TN)
Cincinnati Christian U (OH)
City Coll of the City U of New York (NY)
Clark Atlanta U (GA)
Clarke U (IA)
Clark U (MA)
Coe Coll (IA)
Colgate U (NY)
The Coll at Brockport, State U of New York (NY)
Coll of Mount Saint Vincent (NY)
Coll of Saint Mary (NE)
Coll of the Atlantic (ME)
Coll of the Humanities and Sciences, Harrison Middleton U (AZ)
Colorado State U (CO)
Concordia Coll–New York (NY)
Concordia U (QC, Canada)
Concordia U Chicago (IL)
Concordia U, Nebraska (NE)
Concordia U, St. Paul (MN)
Converse Coll (SC)
Corban U (OR)
Cornerstone U (MI)
Crandall U (NB, Canada)
Crown Coll (MN)
Curry Coll (MA)
Dallas Baptist U (TX)
Dallas Christian Coll (TX)
Defiance Coll (OH)
Dominican Coll (NY)
Dordt Coll (IA)
Duquesne U (PA)
Eastern Kentucky U (KY)
Eastern New Mexico U (NM)
Eastern Washington U (WA)
East Texas Baptist U (TX)

Edward Waters Coll (FL)
Elmhurst Coll (IL)
Elmira Coll (NY)
Elon U (NC)
Emmanuel Coll (MA)
Emory U (GA)
Fairmont State U (WV)
Faulkner U (AL)
Felician Coll (NJ)
Ferrum Coll (VA)
Fitchburg State U (MA)
Florida Gulf Coast U (FL)
Fontbonne U (MO)
Fordham U (NY)
Framingham State U (MA)
Free Will Baptist Bible Coll (TN)
Furman U (SC)
Gallaudet U (DC)
Gardner-Webb U (NC)
Georgia Southern U (GA)
Gettysburg Coll (PA)
Glenville State Coll (WV)
Goddard Coll (VT)
Goshen Coll (IN)
Goucher Coll (MD)
Graceland U (IA)
Gustavus Adolphus Coll (MN)
Hamline U (MN)
Hampshire Coll (MA)
Hampton U (VA)
Hannibal-LaGrange U (MO)
Hardin-Simmons U (TX)
Haverford Coll (PA)
Hebrew Coll (MA)
Heidelberg U (OH)
Hillsdale Coll (MI)
Holy Family U (PA)
Humboldt State U (CA)
Huntington U (IN)
Huston-Tillotson U (TX)
Illinois Coll (IL)
Illinois Wesleyan U (IL)
Indiana U–Purdue U Fort Wayne (IN)
Indiana U Southeast (IN)
Indiana Wesleyan U (IN)
Inter American U of Puerto Rico, San Germán Campus (PR)
Iowa State U of Science and Technology (IA)
Iowa Wesleyan Coll (IA)
Jacksonville State U (AL)
John Brown U (AR)
John Carroll U (OH)
Johnson State Coll (VT)
Juniata Coll (PA)
Kent State U (OH)
King Coll (TN)
Knox Coll (IL)
Lake Forest Coll (IL)
Lakehead U (ON, Canada)
Lake Superior State U (MI)
Lamar U (TX)
La Salle U (PA)
Lasell Coll (MA)
Lebanese American U (Lebanon)
Lee U (TN)
Lenoir-Rhyne U (NC)
Limestone Coll (SC)
Lincoln Memorial U (TN)
Lincoln U (PA)
Lindenwood U (MO)
Lindsey Wilson Coll (KY)
Lipscomb U (TN)
Long Island U–Brooklyn Campus (NY)
Long Island U–C. W. Post Campus (NY)
Longwood U (VA)
Loras Coll (IA)
Loyola U Maryland (MD)
Macalester Coll (MN)
Manchester Coll (IN)
Manhattan Coll (NY)
Manhattanville Coll (NY)
Mansfield U of Pennsylvania (PA)
Marietta Coll (OH)
Mars Hill Coll (NC)
Maryville Coll (TN)
Massachusetts Coll of Liberal Arts (MA)
The Master's Coll and Sem (CA)
Mayville State U (ND)
Mercyhurst Coll (PA)
Merrimack Coll (MA)

Miami Dade Coll (FL)
Michigan State U (MI)
Milligan Coll (TN)
Millsaps Coll (MS)
Minnesota State U Mankato (MN)
Mississippi Valley State U (MS)
Missouri Baptist U (MO)
Missouri Southern State U (MO)
Molloy Coll (NY)
Monmouth U (NJ)
Montana State U Billings (MT)
Moravian Coll (PA)
Morehouse Coll (GA)
Mount Marty Coll (SD)
Mount Mary Coll (WI)
Mount St. Mary's Coll (CA)
Mount Vernon Nazarene U (OH)
Nazareth Coll of Rochester (NY)
Newberry Coll (SC)
New England Coll (NH)
Newman U (KS)
New Mexico State U (NM)
Niagara U (NY)
North Carolina Ag and Tech State U (NC)
North Carolina State U (NC)
North Carolina Wesleyan Coll (NC)
North Central Coll (IL)
Northern Illinois U (IL)
Northern State U (SD)
Northwest U (WA)
Notre Dame of Maryland U (MD)
Nova Southeastern U (FL)
Oakland City U (IN)
Ohio Northern U (OH)
Ohio Wesleyan U (OH)
Oklahoma City U (OK)
Oklahoma State U (OK)
Otterbein U (OH)
Ouachita Baptist U (AR)
Pacific Lutheran U (WA)
Pacific U (OR)
Pepperdine U, Malibu (CA)
Peru State Coll (NE)
Purdue U (IN)
Purdue U Calumet (IN)
Queen's U at Kingston (ON, Canada)
Queens U of Charlotte (NC)
Quinnipiac U (CT)
Regent U (VA)
Regis U (CO)
Reinhardt U (GA)
Ripon Coll (WI)
Rivier Coll (NH)
Rockford Coll (IL)
Roger Williams U (RI)
Rowan U (NJ)
Sacred Heart U (CT)
St. Ambrose U (IA)
St. Catherine U (MN)
Saint Francis U (PA)
St. Joseph's Coll, Long Island Campus (NY)
St. Joseph's Coll, New York (NY)
Saint Joseph's Coll of Maine (ME)
Saint Louis U (MO)
Saint Martin's U (WA)
Saint Mary-of-the-Woods Coll (IN)
Saint Mary's Coll (IN)
St. Mary's U (TX)
Saint Michael's Coll (VT)
St. Thomas Aquinas Coll (NY)
St. Thomas U (NB, Canada)
Salem State U (MA)
San Diego Christian Coll (CA)
Sarah Lawrence Coll (NY)
Schreiner U (TX)
Shawnee State U (OH)
Simmons Coll (MA)
Simon Fraser U (BC, Canada)
Simpson Coll (IA)
Skidmore Coll (NY)
Smith Coll (MA)
Southern New Hampshire U (NH)
Southwestern Assemblies of God U (TX)
Southwestern Christian U (OK)
Southwestern Oklahoma State U (OK)
Southwestern U (TX)
Southwest Minnesota State U (MN)
Spalding U (KY)
State U of New York at Fredonia (NY)

State U of New York at New Paltz (NY)
State U of New York at Oswego (NY)
State U of New York at Plattsburgh (NY)
State U of New York Coll at Geneseo (NY)
State U of New York Coll at Oneonta (NY)
State U of New York Empire State Coll (NY)
Stetson U (FL)
Suffolk U (MA)
Tabor Coll (KS)
Tarleton State U (TX)
Texas Lutheran U (TX)
Texas Wesleyan U (TX)
Trent U (ON, Canada)
Trine U (IN)
Trinity Coll (CT)
Union Coll (KY)
Union U (TN)
Université de Sherbrooke (QC, Canada)
U of Alaska Anchorage (AK)
U of Alberta (AB, Canada)
U of Arkansas at Little Rock (AR)
The U of British Columbia (BC, Canada)
The U of British Columbia–Okanagan (BC, Canada)
U of California, Santa Cruz (CA)
U of Central Missouri (MO)
U of Charleston (WV)
U of Cincinnati (OH)
U of Dallas (TX)
U of Dayton (OH)
The U of Findlay (OH)
U of Guam (GU)
U of Hawaii at Manoa (HI)
U of Houston–Victoria (TX)
U of Indianapolis (IN)
U of Lethbridge (AB, Canada)
U of Maine (ME)
U of Maine at Fort Kent (ME)
U of Maine at Presque Isle (ME)
U of Mary Hardin-Baylor (TX)
U of Maryland Eastern Shore (MD)
U of Mary Washington (VA)
U of Massachusetts Amherst (MA)
U of Massachusetts Boston (MA)
U of Michigan–Dearborn (MI)
U of Minnesota, Duluth (MN)
U of Minnesota, Twin Cities Campus (MN)
U of Missouri (MO)
U of Missouri–St. Louis (MO)
The U of Montana Western (MT)
U of Nevada, Las Vegas (NV)
U of Oregon (OR)
U of Pittsburgh at Greensburg (PA)
U of Pittsburgh at Johnstown (PA)
U of Portland (OR)
U of Redlands (CA)
U of Regina (SK, Canada)
U of Rio Grande (OH)
U of Saint Francis (IN)
U of Saint Mary (KS)
U of St. Thomas (TX)
The U of South Dakota (SD)
U of the Pacific (CA)
The U of Toledo (OH)
U of Toronto (ON, Canada)
U of Tulsa (OK)
U of Utah (UT)
U of Vermont (VT)
U of Washington (WA)
U of Washington, Bothell (WA)
The U of Western Ontario (ON, Canada)
U of Windsor (ON, Canada)
U of Wisconsin–Green Bay (WI)
U of Wisconsin–Milwaukee (WI)
U of Wisconsin–Platteville (WI)
U of Wisconsin–River Falls (WI)
U of Wisconsin–Stevens Point (WI)
U of Wisconsin–Superior (WI)
U of Wisconsin–Whitewater (WI)
Upper Iowa U (IA)
Valley City State U (ND)
Vanderbilt U (TN)
Vanguard U of Southern California (CA)
Villanova U (PA)

Virginia Intermont Coll (VA)
Viterbo U (WI)
Wagner Coll (NY)
Walsh U (OH)
Washburn U (KS)
Washington & Jefferson Coll (PA)
Washington State U (WA)
Washington U in St. Louis (MO)
Webster U (MO)
Wells Coll (NY)
Westfield State U (MA)
West Liberty U (WV)
West Virginia State U (WV)
West Virginia Wesleyan Coll (WV)
Wheeling Jesuit U (WV)
Wilkes U (PA)
William Jessup U (CA)
William Paterson U of New Jersey (NJ)
William Penn U (IA)
Williams Baptist Coll (AR)
William Woods U (MO)
Wilmington Coll (OH)
Winona State U (MN)
Wittenberg U (OH)
Xavier U (OH)
Xavier U of Louisiana (LA)
Youngstown State U (OH)

EDUCATIONAL ADMINISTRATION AND SUPERVISION RELATED
Philander Smith Coll (AR)
Purdue U (IN)

EDUCATIONAL ASSESSMENT, EVALUATION, AND RESEARCH RELATED
Penn State Altoona (PA)
Penn State Berks (PA)
Penn State U Park (PA)
Purdue U (IN)

EDUCATIONAL ASSESSMENT, TESTING, AND MEASUREMENT
Purdue U (IN)

EDUCATIONAL EVALUATION AND RESEARCH
Purdue U (IN)

EDUCATIONAL, INSTRUCTIONAL, AND CURRICULUM SUPERVISION
Purdue U (IN)
St. John's U (NY)
U of Wisconsin–River Falls (WI)
Wright State U (OH)

EDUCATIONAL/ INSTRUCTIONAL TECHNOLOGY
Bayamón Central U (PR)
Bowling Green State U (OH)
Bridgewater State U (MA)
California State U, Chico (CA)
Cameron U (OK)
Eastern Washington U (WA)
Jacksonville State U (AL)
Midwestern State U (TX)
Minnesota State U Moorhead (MN)
Purdue U (IN)
State U of New York Coll at Potsdam (NY)
U of Maine (ME)
The U of Toledo (OH)
Western Illinois U (IL)
Western Oregon U (OR)
Widener U (PA)

EDUCATIONAL LEADERSHIP AND ADMINISTRATION
Auburn U Montgomery (AL)
Cleveland State U (OH)
DePaul U (IL)
Eastern Washington U (WA)
Free Will Baptist Bible Coll (TN)
Lamar U (TX)
Midwestern State U (TX)
Purdue U (IN)
Tarleton State U (TX)

INDEXES

U of Minnesota, Crookston (MN)
U of Regina (SK, Canada)
U of Southern Maine (ME)
U of the Incarnate Word (TX)
U of Wisconsin–Superior (WI)
Wright State U (OH)

EDUCATIONAL PSYCHOLOGY
DePaul U (IL)
Jacksonville State U (AL)
Mississippi State U (MS)
Purdue U (IN)
Saint Vincent Coll (PA)
U of Georgia (GA)
U of Pittsburgh (PA)
U of Regina (SK, Canada)
U of Southern Maine (ME)

EDUCATIONAL STATISTICS AND RESEARCH METHODS
Bucknell U (PA)
Purdue U (IN)

EDUCATIONAL SYSTEM ADMINISTRATION AND SUPERINTENDENCY
Dordt Coll (IA)
Purdue U (IN)

EDUCATION (MULTIPLE LEVELS)
Adams State Coll (CO)
Adrian Coll (MI)
Augustana Coll (SD)
Austin Peay State U (TN)
Averett U (VA)
Baptist Bible Coll of Pennsylvania (PA)
Biola U (CA)
Birmingham-Southern Coll (AL)
Bowling Green State U (OH)
Canisius Coll (NY)
Central State U (OH)
Coll of Coastal Georgia (GA)
Coll of Saint Elizabeth (NJ)
Coll of Saint Mary (NE)
The Coll of St. Scholastica (MN)
Concordia U Chicago (IL)
Crandall U (NB, Canada)
Crossroads Bible Coll (IN)
DePaul U (IL)
Dordt Coll (IA)
Dowling Coll (NY)
Eastern Oregon U (OR)
Eastern Washington U (WA)
Edinboro U of Pennsylvania (PA)
Felician Coll (NJ)
Gannon U (PA)
Gardner-Webb U (NC)
Geneva Coll (PA)
Goddard Coll (VT)
Hamline U (MN)
Harding U (AR)
Hillsdale Coll (MI)
Hofstra U (NY)
Illinois Coll (IL)
Indiana U Bloomington (IN)
Indiana Wesleyan U (IN)
Ithaca Coll (NY)
John Carroll U (OH)
Juniata Coll (PA)
Keystone Coll (PA)
Lake Superior State U (MI)
Liberty U (VA)
Lindenwood U (MO)
Lubbock Christian U (TX)
Manchester Coll (IN)
Manhattan Coll (NY)
Martin Luther Coll (MN)
McKendree U (IL)
Merrimack Coll (MA)
Mount Mary Coll (WI)
Mount Saint Mary Coll (NY)
New England Coll (NH)
Northland Coll (WI)
Northwest Christian U (OR)
Northwestern Coll (IA)
Nyack Coll (NY)
Ohio Northern U (OH)
Ohio Wesleyan U (OH)
Purdue U (IN)
Queen's U at Kingston (ON, Canada)

Quincy U (IL)
Rhode Island Coll (RI)
The Richard Stockton Coll of New Jersey (NJ)
Roger Williams U (RI)
St. Ambrose U (IA)
Saint Augustine's Coll (NC)
Saint Mary-of-the-Woods Coll (IN)
Samford U (AL)
San Diego Christian Coll (CA)
Shawnee State U (OH)
Tarleton State U (TX)
Texas Lutheran U (TX)
Troy U (AL)
U of Great Falls (MT)
U of Illinois at Urbana–Champaign (IL)
U of Louisville (KY)
U of Maine (ME)
U of Maine at Fort Kent (ME)
U of Memphis (TN)
U of Minnesota, Duluth (MN)
The U of Montana Western (MT)
U of Nebraska–Lincoln (NE)
U of North Alabama (AL)
U of Puerto Rico at Bayamón (PR)
U of Rio Grande (OH)
U of St. Thomas (MN)
U of Southern Maine (ME)
U of South Florida (FL)
U of South Florida–St. Petersburg Campus (FL)
The U of Tennessee at Martin (TN)
U of the Southwest (NM)
U of Washington (WA)
The U of West Alabama (AL)
U of Windsor (ON, Canada)
Utah State U (UT)
Virginia Wesleyan Coll (VA)
Wake Forest U (NC)
Washington State U (WA)
Washington U in St. Louis (MO)
Wayland Baptist U (TX)
Western Kentucky U (KY)
West Virginia Wesleyan Coll (WV)
William Jewell Coll (MO)
Wright State U (OH)

EDUCATION POLICY ANALYSIS
Purdue U (IN)

EDUCATION RELATED
Albany State U (GA)
Arizona State U (AZ)
Bowling Green State U (OH)
Brigham Young U (UT)
Cedarville U (OH)
Central State U (OH)
Concordia U, St. Paul (MN)
Delaware State U (DE)
DePaul U (IL)
Eastern Oregon U (OR)
Edgewood Coll (WI)
The Evergreen State Coll (WA)
Grace Coll (IN)
Grambling State U (LA)
Indiana U Bloomington (IN)
Lindsey Wilson Coll (KY)
Mercer U (GA)
Midwestern State U (TX)
Mitchell Coll (CT)
Mount Holyoke Coll (MA)
Northwest Missouri State U (MO)
Northwest Nazarene U (ID)
Ohio Northern U (OH)
Park U (MO)
Point Park U (PA)
Prescott Coll (AZ)
Purdue U (IN)
Quincy U (IL)
Saginaw Valley State U (MI)
State U of New York Coll at Potsdam (NY)
Sterling Coll (VT)
Swarthmore Coll (PA)
Thomas More Coll (KY)
Towson U (MD)
Trinity Christian Coll (IL)
U of Arkansas at Monticello (AR)
U of Lethbridge (AB, Canada)
U of Minnesota, Duluth (MN)
U of Minnesota, Twin Cities Campus (MN)

U of Nevada, Reno (NV)
Vanderbilt U (TN)
Waldorf Coll (IA)
Wayne State U (MI)
Wright State U (OH)

EDUCATION (SPECIFIC LEVELS AND METHODS) RELATED
Anderson (SC)
Bayamón Central U (PR)
Boston U (MA)
Brigham Young U (UT)
Colorado State U (CO)
Columbia Coll Chicago (IL)
Concordia Coll–New York (NY)
Delaware State U (DE)
Immaculata U (PA)
Inter American U of Puerto Rico, San Germán Campus (PR)
John Brown U (AR)
Lynchburg Coll (VA)
Northern Arizona U (AZ)
Purdue U (IN)
Roger Williams U (RI)
Rowan U (NJ)
U of Southern Maine (ME)
The U of Toledo (OH)
Washington U in St. Louis (MO)
Weber State U (UT)
Western Washington U (WA)
Wright State U (OH)
Xavier U (OH)

EDUCATION (SPECIFIC SUBJECT AREAS) RELATED
Appalachian State U (NC)
Averett U (VA)
Avila U (MO)
Bayamón Central U (PR)
Baylor U (TX)
Bowling Green State U (OH)
Brigham Young U (UT)
Central Michigan U (MI)
The Coll of Saint Rose (NY)
Columbia Coll Chicago (IL)
Drexel U (PA)
Eastern Kentucky U (KY)
Eastern Michigan U (MI)
Gardner-Webb U (NC)
Graceland U (IA)
Hope Coll (MI)
Indiana U Bloomington (IN)
Juniata Coll (PA)
Madonna U (MI)
Marquette U (WI)
Marywood U (PA)
Minot State U (ND)
Mississippi State U (MS)
Missouri State U (MO)
Missouri Western State U (MO)
Northern Michigan U (MI)
Old Dominion U (VA)
Plymouth State U (NH)
Point Park U (PA)
Purdue U (IN)
Regent U (VA)
St. Edward's U (TX)
Southwestern Coll (KS)
Taylor U (IN)
Tusculum Coll (TN)
The U of Akron (OH)
U of Lethbridge (AB, Canada)
U of Louisiana at Lafayette (LA)
U of Louisiana at Monroe (LA)
U of Michigan–Flint (MI)
U of Minnesota, Duluth (MN)
U of Nebraska–Lincoln (NE)
U of New Hampshire (NH)
U of New Orleans (LA)
The U of North Carolina Wilmington (NC)
U of Ottawa (ON, Canada)
U of Regina (SK, Canada)
U of St. Thomas (MN)
The U of Toledo (OH)
U of Wisconsin–Eau Claire (WI)
U of Wisconsin–Stout (WI)
Utah State U (UT)
Wayne State Coll (NE)
Weber State U (UT)
Western Washington U (WA)
Wright State U (OH)

ELECTRICAL AND ELECTRONIC ENGINEERING TECHNOLOGIES RELATED
Inter American U of Puerto Rico, San Germán Campus (PR)
North Carolina Ag and Tech State U (NC)
Penn State Berks (PA)
Pennsylvania Coll of Technology (PA)
Point Park U (PA)
Purdue U (IN)
Rochester Inst of Technology (NY)
Southern Illinois U Carbondale (IL)
Vaughn Coll of Aeronautics and Technology (NY)
Virginia State U (VA)
Wayne State U (MI)

ELECTRICAL AND ELECTRONICS ENGINEERING
Alfred U (NY)
The American U in Cairo (Egypt)
American U of Beirut (Lebanon)
Arizona State U (AZ)
Arkansas State U (AR)
Arkansas Tech U (AR)
Auburn U (AL)
Baylor U (TX)
Bloomsburg U of Pennsylvania (PA)
Bob Jones U (SC)
Boise State U (ID)
Boston U (MA)
Bradley U (IL)
Brown U (RI)
Bucknell U (PA)
California Inst of Technology (CA)
California Polytechnic State U, San Luis Obispo (CA)
California State Polytechnic U, Pomona (CA)
California State U, Chico (CA)
California State U, Fresno (CA)
California State U, Fullerton (CA)
California State U, Long Beach (CA)
California State U, Los Angeles (CA)
California State U, Sacramento (CA)
Calvin Coll (MI)
Carnegie Mellon U (PA)
Case Western Reserve U (OH)
The Catholic U of America (DC)
Cedarville U (OH)
Central Connecticut State U (CT)
Central Michigan U (MI)
Christian Brothers U (TN)
The Citadel, The Military Coll of South Carolina (SC)
City Coll of the City U of New York (NY)
Clarkson U (NY)
Clemson U (SC)
Cleveland State U (OH)
The Coll of New Jersey (NJ)
Colorado State U (CO)
Concordia U (QC, Canada)
Cooper Union for the Advancement of Science and Art (NY)
Cornell U (NY)
Dalhousie U (NS, Canada)
Delaware State U (DE)
Dominican U (IL)
Dordt Coll (IA)
Drexel U (PA)
Eastern Washington U (WA)
Embry-Riddle Aeronautical U–Daytona (FL)
Embry-Riddle Aeronautical U–Prescott (AZ)
Fairfield U (CT)
Fairleigh Dickinson U, Metropolitan Campus (NJ)
Florida Ag and Mech U (FL)
Florida Atlantic U (FL)
Florida Inst of Technology (FL)
Florida Intl U (FL)
Franklin W. Olin Coll of Eng (MA)
Gannon U (PA)
George Fox U (OR)
George Mason U (VA)
The George Washington U (DC)
Georgia Inst of Technology (GA)

Georgia Southern U (GA)
Gonzaga U (WA)
Grove City Coll (PA)
Hampton U (VA)
Harding U (AR)
Hofstra U (NY)
Hope Coll (MI)
Idaho State U (ID)
Illinois Inst of Technology (IL)
Indiana Tech (IN)
Indiana U–Purdue U Fort Wayne (IN)
Indiana U–Purdue U Indianapolis (IN)
Inter American U of Puerto Rico, Bayamón Campus (PR)
Inter American U of Puerto Rico, Ponce Campus (PR)
Iowa State U of Science and Technology (IA)
Jacksonville U (FL)
John Brown U (AR)
The Johns Hopkins U (MD)
Kansas State U (KS)
Kettering U (MI)
Lafayette Coll (PA)
Lakehead U (ON, Canada)
Lake Superior State U (MI)
Lamar U (TX)
Lawrence Technological U (MI)
Lebanese American U (Lebanon)
Lehigh U (PA)
LeTourneau U (TX)
Louisiana State U and Ag and Mech Coll (LA)
Loyola Marymount U (CA)
Loyola U Maryland (MD)
Manhattan Coll (NY)
Marquette U (WI)
Massachusetts Inst of Technology (MA)
Merrimack Coll (MA)
Miami U (OH)
Michigan State U (MI)
Michigan Technological U (MI)
Milwaukee School of Eng (WI)
Minnesota State U Mankato (MN)
Mississippi State U (MS)
Missouri U of Science and Technology (MO)
Montana State U (MT)
Montana Tech of The U of Montana (MT)
New England Inst of Technology (RI)
New Mexico Highlands U (NM)
New Mexico Inst of Mining and Technology (NM)
New Mexico State U (NM)
New York Inst of Technology (NY)
Norfolk State U (VA)
North Carolina Ag and Tech State U (NC)
North Carolina State U (NC)
North Dakota State U (ND)
Northeastern U (MA)
Northern Arizona U (AZ)
Northern Illinois U (IL)
Norwich U (VT)
Oakland U (MI)
Ohio Northern U (OH)
The Ohio State U (OH)
Ohio U (OH)
Oklahoma Christian U (OK)
Oklahoma State U (OK)
Old Dominion U (VA)
Oral Roberts U (OK)
Penn State Abington (PA)
Penn State Altoona (PA)
Penn State Beaver (PA)
Penn State Berks (PA)
Penn State Brandywine (PA)
Penn State DuBois (PA)
Penn State Erie, The Behrend Coll (PA)
Penn State Fayette, The Eberly Campus (PA)
Penn State Greater Allegheny (PA)
Penn State Harrisburg (PA)
Penn State Hazleton (PA)
Penn State Lehigh Valley (PA)
Penn State Mont Alto (PA)
Penn State New Kensington (PA)
Penn State Schuylkill (PA)
Penn State Shenango (PA)

Penn State U Park (PA)
Penn State Wilkes-Barre (PA)
Penn State Worthington Scranton (PA)
Penn State York (PA)
Polytechnic Inst of NYU (NY)
Polytechnic U of Puerto Rico (PR)
Portland State U (OR)
Prairie View A&M U (TX)
Princeton U (NJ)
Purdue U (IN)
Purdue U Calumet (IN)
Purdue U North Central (IN)
Queen's U at Kingston (ON, Canada)
Rensselaer Polytechnic Inst (NY)
Rice U (TX)
Rochester Inst of Technology (NY)
Rose-Hulman Inst of Technology (IN)
Rowan U (NJ)
Rutgers, The State U of New Jersey, New Brunswick (NJ)
Ryerson U (ON, Canada)
Saginaw Valley State U (MI)
Saint Louis U (MO)
St. Mary's U (TX)
San Diego State U (CA)
San Francisco State U (CA)
Santa Clara U (CA)
Seattle Pacific U (WA)
Seattle U (WA)
South Dakota School of Mines and Technology (SD)
South Dakota State U (SD)
Southern Illinois U Carbondale (IL)
Southern Illinois U Edwardsville (IL)
Southern Methodist U (TX)
Southern Polytechnic State U (GA)
Stanford U (CA)
State U of New York at Binghamton (NY)
State U of New York at New Paltz (NY)
State U of New York Maritime Coll (NY)
Stevens Inst of Technology (NJ)
Stony Brook U, State U of New York (NY)
Suffolk U (MA)
Syracuse U (NY)
Temple U (PA)
Texas A&M U (TX)
Texas A&M U–Kingsville (TX)
Texas State U–San Marcos (TX)
Texas Tech U (TX)
Trine U (IN)
Trinity Coll (CT)
Tufts U (MA)
Tulane U (LA)
Tuskegee U (AL)
Union Coll (NY)
United States Air Force Acad (CO)
United States Coast Guard Acad (CT)
United States Military Acad (NY)
United States Naval Acad (MD)
Universidad del Turabo (PR)
Université de Sherbrooke (QC, Canada)
U at Buffalo, the State U of New York (NY)
The U of Akron (OH)
The U of Alabama (AL)
The U of Alabama at Birmingham (AL)
The U of Alabama in Huntsville (AL)
U of Alaska Fairbanks (AK)
U of Alberta (AB, Canada)
U of Arkansas (AR)
The U of British Columbia (BC, Canada)
The U of British Columbia–Okanagan (BC, Canada)
U of California, Berkeley (CA)
U of California, Davis (CA)
U of California, Irvine (CA)
U of California, Los Angeles (CA)
U of California, Riverside (CA)
U of California, Santa Barbara (CA)
U of California, Santa Cruz (CA)
U of Central Florida (FL)
U of Cincinnati (OH)
U of Colorado at Colorado Springs (CO)

U of Colorado Boulder (CO)
U of Colorado Denver (CO)
U of Connecticut (CT)
U of Dayton (OH)
U of Delaware (DE)
U of Denver (CO)
U of Evansville (IN)
U of Florida (FL)
U of Hartford (CT)
U of Hawaii at Manoa (HI)
U of Houston (TX)
U of Idaho (ID)
U of Illinois at Chicago (IL)
U of Illinois at Urbana–Champaign (IL)
The U of Iowa (IA)
The U of Kansas (KS)
U of Louisiana at Lafayette (LA)
U of Louisville (KY)
U of Maine (ME)
U of Maryland, Coll Park (MD)
U of Massachusetts Amherst (MA)
U of Massachusetts Dartmouth (MA)
U of Massachusetts Lowell (MA)
U of Memphis (TN)
U of Miami (FL)
U of Michigan (MI)
U of Michigan–Dearborn (MI)
U of Minnesota, Duluth (MN)
U of Minnesota, Twin Cities Campus (MN)
U of Mississippi (MS)
U of Missouri (MO)
U of Missouri–Kansas City (MO)
U of Missouri–St. Louis (MO)
U of Nebraska–Lincoln (NE)
U of Nevada, Las Vegas (NV)
U of Nevada, Reno (NV)
U of New Hampshire (NH)
U of New Haven (CT)
U of New Mexico (NM)
U of New Orleans (LA)
The U of North Carolina at Charlotte (NC)
U of North Dakota (ND)
U of North Florida (FL)
U of North Texas (TX)
U of Notre Dame (IN)
U of Oklahoma (OK)
U of Ottawa (ON, Canada)
U of Pennsylvania (PA)
U of Pittsburgh (PA)
U of Portland (OR)
U of Regina (SK, Canada)
U of Rhode Island (RI)
U of Rochester (NY)
U of St. Thomas (MN)
U of San Diego (CA)
The U of Scranton (PA)
U of South Alabama (AL)
U of South Carolina (SC)
U of Southern California (CA)
U of Southern Maine (ME)
U of South Florida (FL)
The U of Tennessee (TN)
The U of Tennessee at Chattanooga (TN)
The U of Texas at Arlington (TX)
The U of Texas at Austin (TX)
The U of Texas at Dallas (TX)
The U of Texas at El Paso (TX)
The U of Texas at San Antonio (TX)
The U of Texas at Tyler (TX)
The U of Texas–Pan American (TX)
U of the District of Columbia (DC)
U of the Pacific (CA)
The U of Toledo (OH)
U of Toronto (ON, Canada)
U of Tulsa (OK)
U of Utah (UT)
U of Vermont (VT)
U of Virginia (VA)
U of Washington (WA)
U of Washington, Bothell (WA)
The U of Western Ontario (ON, Canada)
U of West Florida (FL)
U of Windsor (ON, Canada)
U of Wisconsin–Madison (WI)
U of Wisconsin–Milwaukee (WI)
U of Wisconsin–Platteville (WI)
U of Wyoming (WY)
Utah State U (UT)
Valparaiso U (IN)

Vanderbilt U (TN)
Villanova U (PA)
Virginia Commonwealth U (VA)
Virginia Polytechnic Inst and State U (VA)
Washington State U (WA)
Washington U in St. Louis (MO)
Wayne State U (MI)
Wentworth Inst of Technology (MA)
Western Carolina U (NC)
Western Kentucky U (KY)
Western Michigan U (MI)
Western New England U (MA)
West Virginia U (WV)
West Virginia U Inst of Technology (WV)
Wichita State U (KS)
Widener U (PA)
Wilkes U (PA)
Worcester Polytechnic Inst (MA)
Wright State U (OH)
Yale U (CT)
York Coll of Pennsylvania (PA)
Youngstown State U (OH)

ELECTRICAL, ELECTRONIC AND COMMUNICATIONS ENGINEERING TECHNOLOGY

Arizona State U (AZ)
Baker Coll of Owosso (MI)
Bluefield State Coll (WV)
Bowling Green State U (OH)
Buffalo State Coll, State U of New York (NY)
California State Polytechnic U, Pomona (CA)
California State U, Long Beach (CA)
California U of Pennsylvania (PA)
Cameron U (OK)
Caribbean U (PR)
Central Washington U (WA)
Cleveland State U (OH)
Delaware State U (DE)
DeVry Coll of New York (NY)
DeVry U, Phoenix (AZ)
DeVry U, Pomona (CA)
DeVry U, Westminster (CO)
DeVry U, Miramar (FL)
DeVry U, Orlando (FL)
DeVry U, Decatur (GA)
DeVry U, Chicago (IL)
DeVry U, Kansas City (MO)
DeVry U, North Brunswick (NJ)
DeVry U, Columbus (OH)
DeVry U, Fort Washington (PA)
DeVry U, Houston (TX)
DeVry U, Irving (TX)
DeVry U, Arlington (VA)
DeVry U, Federal Way (WA)
DeVry U Online (IL)
Eastern Michigan U (MI)
Fairleigh Dickinson U, Metropolitan Campus (NJ)
Fairmont State U (WV)
Farmingdale State Coll (NY)
Ferris State U (MI)
Fitchburg State U (MA)
Florida Ag and Mech U (FL)
Georgia Southern U (GA)
Grambling State U (LA)
Hampton U (VA)
Herzing U, Madison (WI)
Indiana State U (IN)
Indiana U–Purdue U Fort Wayne (IN)
Indiana U–Purdue U Indianapolis (IN)
Inter American U of Puerto Rico, Bayamón Campus (PR)
Inter American U of Puerto Rico, San Germán Campus (PR)
ITT Tech Inst, Bessemer (AL)
ITT Tech Inst, Madison (AL)
ITT Tech Inst, Mobile (AL)
ITT Tech Inst, Phoenix (AZ)
ITT Tech Inst, Phoenix (AZ)
ITT Tech Inst, Tempe (AZ)
ITT Tech Inst, Tucson (AZ)
ITT Tech Inst (AR)
ITT Tech Inst, Clovis (CA)
ITT Tech Inst, Concord (CA)
ITT Tech Inst, Corona (CA)
ITT Tech Inst, Culver City (CA)

ITT Tech Inst, Lathrop (CA)
ITT Tech Inst, Oakland (CA)
ITT Tech Inst, Orange (CA)
ITT Tech Inst, Oxnard (CA)
ITT Tech Inst, Rancho Cordova (CA)
ITT Tech Inst, San Bernardino (CA)
ITT Tech Inst, San Diego (CA)
ITT Tech Inst, San Dimas (CA)
ITT Tech Inst, Sylmar (CA)
ITT Tech Inst, Torrance (CA)
ITT Tech Inst, West Covina (CA)
ITT Tech Inst, Aurora (CO)
ITT Tech Inst, Thornton (CO)
ITT Tech Inst, Bradenton (FL)
ITT Tech Inst, Deerfield Beach (FL)
ITT Tech Inst, Fort Lauderdale (FL)
ITT Tech Inst, Fort Myers (FL)
ITT Tech Inst, Jacksonville (FL)
ITT Tech Inst, Lake Mary (FL)
ITT Tech Inst, Miami (FL)
ITT Tech Inst, Orlando (FL)
ITT Tech Inst, Pinellas Park (FL)
ITT Tech Inst, Tallahassee (FL)
ITT Tech Inst, Tampa (FL)
ITT Tech Inst, West Palm Beach (FL)
ITT Tech Inst, Atlanta (GA)
ITT Tech Inst, Duluth (GA)
ITT Tech Inst, Kennesaw (GA)
ITT Tech Inst (ID)
ITT Tech Inst, Mount Prospect (IL)
ITT Tech Inst, Oak Brook (IL)
ITT Tech Inst, Orland Park (IL)
ITT Tech Inst, Fort Wayne (IN)
ITT Tech Inst, Indianapolis (IN)
ITT Tech Inst, Indianapolis (IN)
ITT Tech Inst, Merrillville (IN)
ITT Tech Inst, Newburgh (IN)
ITT Tech Inst, South Bend (IN)
ITT Tech Inst, Cedar Rapids (IA)
ITT Tech Inst, Clive (IA)
ITT Tech Inst, Overland Park (KS)
ITT Tech Inst, Wichita (KS)
ITT Tech Inst, Lexington (KY)
ITT Tech Inst, Louisville (KY)
ITT Tech Inst, Baton Rouge (LA)
ITT Tech Inst, St. Rose (LA)
ITT Tech Inst, Hanover (MD)
ITT Tech Inst, Owings Mills (MD)
ITT Tech Inst, Norwood (MA)
ITT Tech Inst, Wilmington (MA)
ITT Tech Inst, Canton (MI)
ITT Tech Inst, Dearborn (MI)
ITT Tech Inst, Grand Rapids (MI)
ITT Tech Inst, Southfield (MI)
ITT Tech Inst, Swartz Creek (MI)
ITT Tech Inst, Troy (MI)
ITT Tech Inst, Wyoming (MI)
ITT Tech Inst, Brooklyn Center (MN)
ITT Tech Inst, Eden Prairie (MN)
ITT Tech Inst, Arnold (MO)
ITT Tech Inst, Earth City (MO)
ITT Tech Inst, Kansas City (MO)
ITT Tech Inst, Springfield (MO)
ITT Tech Inst (NE)
ITT Tech Inst, Henderson (NV)
ITT Tech Inst, North Las Vegas (NV)
ITT Tech Inst (NM)
ITT Tech Inst, Cary (NC)
ITT Tech Inst, Charlotte (NC)
ITT Tech Inst, Charlotte (NC)
ITT Tech Inst, Durham (NC)
ITT Tech Inst, High Point (NC)
ITT Tech Inst, Akron (OH)
ITT Tech Inst, Columbus (OH)
ITT Tech Inst, Hilliard (OH)
ITT Tech Inst, Maumee (OH)
ITT Tech Inst, Norwood (OH)
ITT Tech Inst, Strongsville (OH)
ITT Tech Inst, Warrensville Heights (OH)
ITT Tech Inst, Youngstown (OH)
ITT Tech Inst, Oklahoma City (OK)
ITT Tech Inst, Tulsa (OK)
ITT Tech Inst, Portland (OR)
ITT Tech Inst, Salem (OR)
ITT Tech Inst, Columbia (SC)
ITT Tech Inst, Greenville (SC)
ITT Tech Inst, Myrtle Beach (SC)
ITT Tech Inst, North Charleston (SC)
ITT Tech Inst, Chattanooga (TN)

ITT Tech Inst, Cordova (TN)
ITT Tech Inst, Johnson City (TN)
ITT Tech Inst, Knoxville (TN)
ITT Tech Inst, Nashville (TN)
ITT Tech Inst, Arlington (TX)
ITT Tech Inst, Austin (TX)
ITT Tech Inst, DeSoto (TX)
ITT Tech Inst, Houston (TX)
ITT Tech Inst, Houston (TX)
ITT Tech Inst, Richardson (TX)
ITT Tech Inst, San Antonio (TX)
ITT Tech Inst, Waco (TX)
ITT Tech Inst, Webster (TX)
ITT Tech Inst (UT)
ITT Tech Inst, Chantilly (VA)
ITT Tech Inst, Norfolk (VA)
ITT Tech Inst, Richmond (VA)
ITT Tech Inst, Salem (VA)
ITT Tech Inst, Springfield (VA)
ITT Tech Inst, Everett (WA)
ITT Tech Inst, Seattle (WA)
ITT Tech Inst, Spokane Valley (WA)
ITT Tech Inst, Germantown (WI)
ITT Tech Inst, Green Bay (WI)
ITT Tech Inst, Greenfield (WI)
ITT Tech Inst, Madison (WI)
Jacksonville State U (AL)
Kansas State U (KS)
Kent State U at Tuscarawas (OH)
Lakehead U (ON, Canada)
Lake Superior State U (MI)
LeTourneau U (TX)
Metropolitan State Coll of Denver (CO)
Miami Dade Coll (FL)
Michigan Technological U (MI)
Milwaukee School of Eng (WI)
Minnesota State U Mankato (MN)
Missouri Western State U (MO)
Morehead State U (KY)
New England Inst of Technology (RI)
New York Inst of Technology (NY)
Norfolk State U (VA)
North Carolina Ag and Tech State U (NC)
Northern Kentucky U (KY)
Northwestern State U of Louisiana (LA)
Oklahoma State U (OK)
Oregon Inst of Technology (OR)
Penn State Erie, The Behrend Coll (PA)
Pittsburg State U (KS)
Prairie View A&M U (TX)
Purdue U (IN)
Purdue U Calumet (IN)
Roger Williams U (RI)
South Carolina State U (SC)
South Dakota State U (SD)
Southern Polytechnic State U (GA)
State U of New York Coll of Technology at Alfred (NY)
Texas A&M U (TX)
Texas A&M U–Corpus Christi (TX)
Texas Southern U (TX)
Thomas Edison State Coll (NJ)
Troy U (AL)
The U of Akron (OH)
U of Arkansas at Little Rock (AR)
U of Central Missouri (MO)
U of Dayton (OH)
U of Hartford (CT)
U of Houston (TX)
U of Maine (ME)
U of Maryland Eastern Shore (MD)
U of Massachusetts Lowell (MA)
U of Memphis (TN)
U of New Hampshire (NH)
U of New Hampshire at Manchester (NH)
The U of North Carolina at Charlotte (NC)
U of North Texas (TX)
U of Pittsburgh at Johnstown (PA)
U of Puerto Rico at Bayamón (PR)
U of Regina (SK, Canada)
U of Southern Mississippi (MS)
The U of Toledo (OH)
Vaughn Coll of Aeronautics and Technology (NY)
Vermont Tech Coll (VT)
Wayne State U (MI)
Wentworth Inst of Technology (MA)
Western Carolina U (NC)

Western Washington U (WA)
Youngstown State U (OH)

ELECTRICAL, ELECTRONICS AND COMMUNICATIONS ENGINEERING RELATED

Marquette U (WI)
The U of Arizona (AZ)

ELECTRICAL/ELECTRONICS EQUIPMENT INSTALLATION AND REPAIR

Cape Breton U (NS, Canada)
Lewis-Clark State Coll (ID)

ELECTROMECHANICAL ENGINEERING

Wentworth Inst of Technology (MA)

ELECTROMECHANICAL TECHNOLOGY

Bowling Green State U (OH)
Buffalo State Coll, State U of New York (NY)
Excelsior Coll (NY)
John Brown U (AR)
Rochester Inst of Technology (NY)
State U of New York Coll of Technology at Alfred (NY)
Temple U (PA)
U of Northern Iowa (IA)
The U of Toledo (OH)
Vermont Tech Coll (VT)
Wayne State U (MI)

ELEMENTARY AND MIDDLE SCHOOL ADMINISTRATION/PRINCIPALSHIP

Berea Coll (KY)
Philander Smith Coll (AR)
Piedmont Coll (GA)
Purdue U (IN)

ELEMENTARY EDUCATION

Abilene Christian U (TX)
Acadia U (NS, Canada)
Adrian Coll (MI)
Alabama State U (AL)
Alaska Pacific U (AK)
Albright Coll (PA)
Alcorn State U (MS)
Alfred U (NY)
Alma Coll (MI)
Alvernia U (PA)
Alverno Coll (WI)
American U (DC)
American U of Beirut (Lebanon)
Anderson U (IN)
Anderson U (SC)
Andrews U (MI)
Anna Maria Coll (MA)
Appalachian State U (NC)
Arcadia U (PA)
Arizona State U (AZ)
Arlington Baptist Coll (TX)
Asbury U (KY)
Ashland U (OH)
Assumption Coll (MA)
Athens State U (AL)
Auburn U (AL)
Auburn U Montgomery (AL)
Augustana Coll (IL)
Augustana Coll (SD)
Avila U (MO)
Baker U (KS)
Ball State U (IN)
Baptist Bible Coll of Pennsylvania (PA)
The Baptist Coll of Florida (FL)
Barclay Coll (KS)
Barry U (FL)
Barton Coll (NC)
Bayamón Central U (PR)
Baylor U (TX)
Bay Path Coll (MA)
Becker Coll (MA)
Belhaven U (MS)
Bellarmine U (KY)
Belmont Abbey Coll (NC)
Belmont U (TN)
Beloit Coll (WI)
Bemidji State U (MN)

Benedictine Coll (KS)
Benedictine U (IL)
Bennett Coll for Women (NC)
Bennington Coll (VT)
Bethany Coll (KS)
Bethany Lutheran Coll (MN)
Bethel Coll (IN)
Bethel Coll (KS)
Bethel U (MN)
Bethel U (TN)
Bethune-Cookman U (FL)
Biola U (CA)
Birmingham-Southern Coll (AL)
Bishop's U (QC, Canada)
Blackburn Coll (IL)
Black Hills State U (SD)
Bluefield Coll (VA)
Bluefield State Coll (WV)
Blue Mountain Coll (MS)
Bluffton U (OH)
Bob Jones U (SC)
Boise State U (ID)
Boston Coll (MA)
Boston U (MA)
Bowie State U (MD)
Bowling Green State U (OH)
Bradley U (IL)
Brenau U (GA)
Brescia U (KY)
Briar Cliff U (IA)
Bridgewater State U (MA)
Bryn Athyn Coll of the New Church (PA)
Bucknell U (PA)
Buena Vista U (IA)
Buffalo State Coll, State U of New York (NY)
Butler U (IN)
Cabrini Coll (PA)
Caldwell Coll (NJ)
California U of Pennsylvania (PA)
Calumet Coll of Saint Joseph (IN)
Calvary Bible Coll and Theological Sem (MO)
Calvin Coll (MI)
Cameron U (OK)
Campbellsville U (KY)
Canisius Coll (NY)
Cardinal Stritch U (WI)
Caribbean U (PR)
Carlos Albizu U, Miami Campus (FL)
Carroll Coll (MT)
Carson-Newman Coll (TN)
Catawba Coll (NC)
The Catholic U of America (DC)
Cedar Crest Coll (PA)
Centenary Coll (NJ)
Central Coll (IA)
Central Connecticut State U (CT)
Central Methodist U (MO)
Central Washington U (WA)
Centre Coll (KY)
Chaminade U of Honolulu (HI)
Chatham U (PA)
Chestnut Hill Coll (PA)
Cheyney U of Pennsylvania (PA)
Chicago State U (IL)
Christian Brothers U (TN)
City Coll of the City U of New York (NY)
City U of Seattle (WA)
Claflin U (SC)
Clarion U of Pennsylvania (PA)
Clark U (MA)
Clearwater Christian Coll (FL)
Clemson U (SC)
Coastal Carolina U (SC)
Coe Coll (IA)
The Coll at Brockport, State U of New York (NY)
Coll of Charleston (SC)
Coll of Mount Saint Vincent (NY)
The Coll of New Jersey (NJ)
Coll of Saint Benedict (MN)
Coll of St. Joseph (VT)
Coll of Saint Mary (NE)
The Coll of Saint Rose (NY)
The Coll of St. Scholastica (MN)
Coll of the Atlantic (ME)
Coll of the Ozarks (MO)
Columbia Coll (SC)
Concordia Coll (MN)
Concordia Coll–New York (NY)
Concordia U (MI)

Concordia U (QC, Canada)
Concordia U Chicago (IL)
Concordia U, Nebraska (NE)
Concordia U, St. Paul (MN)
Concordia U Texas (TX)
Converse Coll (SC)
Corban U (OR)
Cornell Coll (IA)
Cornerstone U (MI)
Covenant Coll (GA)
Creighton U (NE)
Crown Coll (MN)
Culver-Stockton Coll (MO)
Curry Coll (MA)
Daemen Coll (NY)
Dakota State U (SD)
Dallas Baptist U (TX)
Dalton State Coll (GA)
Defiance Coll (OH)
Delaware State U (DE)
Delta State U (MS)
DePaul U (IL)
DePauw U (IN)
DeSales U (PA)
Dixie State Coll of Utah (UT)
Doane Coll (NE)
Dominican Coll (NY)
Dominican U (IL)
Dordt Coll (IA)
Dowling Coll (NY)
Drake U (IA)
Drury U (MO)
East Carolina U (NC)
East Central U (OK)
Eastern Connecticut State U (CT)
Eastern Illinois U (IL)
Eastern Kentucky U (KY)
Eastern Michigan U (MI)
Eastern New Mexico U (NM)
Eastern U (PA)
East Stroudsburg U of Pennsylvania (PA)
East Texas Baptist U (TX)
Edgewood Coll (WI)
Edinboro U of Pennsylvania (PA)
Edward Waters Coll (FL)
Elizabeth City State U (NC)
Elmhurst Coll (IL)
Elmira Coll (NY)
Elon U (NC)
Emmanuel Coll (GA)
Emmanuel Coll (MA)
Emmaus Bible Coll (IA)
Emporia State U (KS)
Endicott Coll (MA)
Evangel U (MO)
Fairmont State U (WV)
Faith Baptist Bible Coll and Theological Sem (IA)
Faulkner U (AL)
Fayetteville State U (NC)
Felician Coll (NJ)
Ferris State U (MI)
Fitchburg State U (MA)
Five Towns Coll (NY)
Flagler Coll (FL)
Florida Ag and Mech U (FL)
Florida Atlantic U (FL)
Florida Coll (FL)
Florida Gulf Coast U (FL)
Florida Intl U (FL)
Florida Southern Coll (FL)
Fontbonne U (MO)
Fordham U (NY)
Fort Hays State U (KS)
Fort Lewis Coll (CO)
Franciscan U of Steubenville (OH)
Francis Marion U (SC)
Franklin Coll (IN)
Free Will Baptist Bible Coll (TN)
Friends U (KS)
Furman U (SC)
Gannon U (PA)
Gardner-Webb U (NC)
Geneva Coll (PA)
George Fox U (OR)
Georgetown Coll (KY)
Georgian Court U (NJ)
Georgia Southern U (GA)
Georgia Southwestern State U (GA)
Gettysburg Coll (PA)
Glenville State Coll (WV)
Goddard Coll (VT)
Gonzaga U (WA)
Gordon Coll (MA)

Goshen Coll (IN)
Governors State U (IL)
Grace Coll (IN)
Graceland U (IA)
Grambling State U (LA)
Grand Canyon U (AZ)
Grand Valley State U (MI)
Grand View U (IA)
Granite State Coll (NH)
Greenville Coll (IL)
Grove City Coll (PA)
Guilford Coll (NC)
Gustavus Adolphus Coll (MN)
Gwynedd-Mercy Coll (PA)
Hamline U (MN)
Hampton U (VA)
Hannibal-LaGrange U (MO)
Hanover Coll (IN)
Harding U (AR)
Hawai`i Pacific U (HI)
Heidelberg U (OH)
Hellenic Coll (MA)
Hillsdale Coll (MI)
Hofstra U (NY)
Holy Cross Coll (IN)
Holy Family U (PA)
Hope Intl U (CA)
Houghton Coll (NY)
Howard Payne U (TX)
Humboldt State U (CA)
Hunter Coll of the City U of New York (NY)
Huntingdon Coll (AL)
Huntington U (IN)
Husson U (ME)
Huston-Tillotson U (TX)
Idaho State U (ID)
Illinois Coll (IL)
Illinois State U (IL)
Illinois Wesleyan U (IL)
Immaculata U (PA)
Indiana State U (IN)
Indiana Tech (IN)
Indiana U Bloomington (IN)
Indiana U East (IN)
Indiana U Kokomo (IN)
Indiana U Northwest (IN)
Indiana U of Pennsylvania (PA)
Indiana U–Purdue U Fort Wayne (IN)
Indiana U–Purdue U Indianapolis (IN)
Indiana U South Bend (IN)
Indiana U Southeast (IN)
Indiana Wesleyan U (IN)
Inter American U of Puerto Rico, Fajardo Campus (PR)
Inter American U of Puerto Rico, Ponce Campus (PR)
Inter American U of Puerto Rico, San Germán Campus (PR)
Iona Coll (NY)
Iowa State U of Science and Technology (IA)
Iowa Wesleyan Coll (IA)
Jacksonville State U (AL)
Jacksonville U (FL)
Jamestown Coll (ND)
Jarvis Christian Coll (TX)
John Brown U (AR)
John Carroll U (OH)
Johnson C. Smith U (NC)
Johnson State Coll (VT)
Jones Coll, Jacksonville (FL)
Judson Coll (AL)
Judson U (IL)
Juniata Coll (PA)
Kansas State U (KS)
Kean U (NJ)
Keene State Coll (NH)
Kennesaw State U (GA)
Kentucky Christian U (KY)
Kentucky Mountain Bible Coll (KY)
Kentucky State U (KY)
Kentucky Wesleyan Coll (KY)
Keuka Coll (NY)
King's Coll (PA)
The King's U Coll (AB, Canada)
Kingswood U (NB, Canada)
Knox Coll (IL)
Kutztown U of Pennsylvania (PA)
Lakehead U (ON, Canada)
Lake Superior State U (MI)
Lamar U (TX)
La Roche Coll (PA)

La Salle U (PA)
Lasell Coll (MA)
Lees-McRae Coll (NC)
Lee U (TN)
Le Moyne Coll (NY)
Lenoir-Rhyne U (NC)
LeTourneau U (TX)
Lewis-Clark State Coll (ID)
Lewis U (IL)
Liberty U (VA)
Limestone Coll (SC)
Lincoln Memorial U (TN)
Lincoln U (MO)
Lincoln U (PA)
Lindenwood U (MO)
Lindsey Wilson Coll (KY)
Linfield Coll (OR)
Lipscomb U (TN)
Lock Haven U of Pennsylvania (PA)
Long Island U–Brooklyn Campus (NY)
Long Island U–C. W. Post Campus (NY)
Longwood U (VA)
Loras Coll (IA)
Louisiana Coll (LA)
Louisiana State U and Ag and Mech Coll (LA)
Louisiana State U in Shreveport (LA)
Loyola U Chicago (IL)
Loyola U Maryland (MD)
Lubbock Christian U (TX)
Luther Coll (IA)
Lynchburg Coll (VA)
Lynn U (FL)
Maharishi U of Management (IA)
Manchester Coll (IN)
Manhattan Coll (NY)
Manhattanville Coll (NY)
Mansfield U of Pennsylvania (PA)
Maranatha Baptist Bible Coll (WI)
Marian U (WI)
Marietta Coll (OH)
Marquette U (WI)
Marshall U (WV)
Mars Hill Coll (NC)
Martin Luther Coll (MN)
Maryville U of Saint Louis (MO)
Marywood U (PA)
The Master's Coll and Sem (CA)
Mayville State U (ND)
McKendree U (IL)
McMurry U (TX)
McNeese State U (LA)
Medaille Coll (NY)
Medgar Evers Coll of the City U of New York (NY)
Mercer U (GA)
Mercyhurst Coll (PA)
Merrimack Coll (MA)
Messiah Coll (PA)
Metropolitan State U (MN)
Michigan State U (MI)
MidAmerica Nazarene U (KS)
Mid-Atlantic Christian U (NC)
Mid-Continent U (KY)
Millersville U of Pennsylvania (PA)
Millikin U (IL)
Minnesota State U Mankato (MN)
Minnesota State U Moorhead (MN)
Minot State U (ND)
Misericordia U (PA)
Mississippi Coll (MS)
Mississippi State U (MS)
Mississippi U for Women (MS)
Mississippi Valley State U (MS)
Missouri Baptist U (MO)
Missouri Southern State U (MO)
Missouri State U (MO)
Missouri Western State U (MO)
Molloy Coll (NY)
Monmouth Coll (IL)
Montana State U (MT)
Montana State U Billings (MT)
Montana State U–Northern (MT)
Montreat Coll, Montreat (NC)
Moravian Coll (PA)
Morehead State U (KY)
Morningside Coll (IA)
Morris Coll (SC)
Mount Marty Coll (SD)
Mount Mercy U (IA)
Mount St. Mary's Coll (CA)
Mount St. Mary's U (MD)

Multnomah U (OR)
National-Louis U (IL)
Nazareth Coll of Rochester (NY)
Nebraska Wesleyan U (NE)
Neumann U (PA)
Newberry Coll (SC)
New England Coll (NH)
New Jersey City U (NJ)
Newman U (KS)
New Mexico Highlands U (NM)
New Mexico State U (NM)
New York U (NY)
Niagara U (NY)
Nicholls State U (LA)
North Carolina Ag and Tech State U (NC)
North Carolina Central U (NC)
North Carolina State U (NC)
North Carolina Wesleyan Coll (NC)
North Central Coll (IL)
Northeastern Illinois U (IL)
Northeastern State U (OK)
Northern Arizona U (AZ)
Northern Illinois U (IL)
Northern Kentucky U (KY)
Northern Michigan U (MI)
Northern State U (SD)
North Greenville U (SC)
Northwestern Coll (IA)
Northwestern Coll (MN)
Northwestern Oklahoma State U (OK)
Northwestern State U of Louisiana (LA)
Northwest Florida State Coll (FL)
Northwest Missouri State U (MO)
Northwest Nazarene U (ID)
Northwest U (WA)
Notre Dame of Maryland U (MD)
Nova Southeastern U (FL)
Nyack Coll (NY)
Oakland City U (IN)
Oakland U (MI)
The Ohio State U at Lima (OH)
The Ohio State U at Marion (OH)
The Ohio State U–Mansfield Campus (OH)
The Ohio State U–Newark Campus (OH)
Ohio U–Zanesville (OH)
Ohio Valley U (WV)
Ohio Wesleyan U (OH)
Oklahoma Christian U (OK)
Oklahoma City U (OK)
Oklahoma State U (OK)
Oral Roberts U (OK)
Otterbein U (OH)
Pace U (NY)
Pacific Union Coll (CA)
Pacific U (OR)
Paine Coll (GA)
Palm Beach Atlantic U (FL)
Park U (MO)
Penn State Abington (PA)
Penn State Altoona (PA)
Penn State Beaver (PA)
Penn State Berks (PA)
Penn State Brandywine (PA)
Penn State DuBois (PA)
Penn State Erie, The Behrend Coll (PA)
Penn State Fayette, The Eberly Campus (PA)
Penn State Greater Allegheny (PA)
Penn State Harrisburg (PA)
Penn State Hazleton (PA)
Penn State Lehigh Valley (PA)
Penn State Mont Alto (PA)
Penn State New Kensington (PA)
Penn State Schuylkill (PA)
Penn State Shenango (PA)
Penn State U Park (PA)
Penn State Wilkes-Barre (PA)
Penn State Worthington Scranton (PA)
Penn State York (PA)
Pepperdine U, Malibu (CA)
Peru State Coll (NE)
Philadelphia Biblical U (PA)
Piedmont Intl U (NC)
Pittsburg State U (KS)
Plymouth State U (NH)
Point Park U (PA)
Presbyterian Coll (SC)
Prescott Coll (AZ)

Purdue U (IN)
Purdue U Calumet (IN)
Purdue U North Central (IN)
Queens Coll of the City U of New York (NY)
Queen's U at Kingston (ON, Canada)
Queens U of Charlotte (NC)
Quincy U (IL)
Regis U (CO)
Rhode Island Coll (RI)
Rider U (NJ)
Ripon Coll (WI)
Rivier Coll (NH)
Robert Morris U (PA)
Roberts Wesleyan Coll (NY)
Rockford Coll (IL)
Rockhurst U (MO)
Rocky Mountain Coll (MT)
Roger Williams U (RI)
Rollins Coll (FL)
Roosevelt U (IL)
Rosemont Coll (PA)
Rowan U (NJ)
Russell Sage Coll (NY)
Rust Coll (MS)
Sacred Heart U (CT)
Saginaw Valley State U (MI)
St. Ambrose U (IA)
St. Andrews U (NC)
Saint Anselm Coll (NH)
St. Bonaventure U (NY)
St. Catherine U (MN)
Saint Francis U (PA)
St. John Fisher Coll (NY)
Saint John's U (MN)
St. John's U (NY)
Saint Joseph's Coll (IN)
St. Joseph's Coll, Long Island Campus (NY)
St. Joseph's Coll, New York (NY)
Saint Joseph's Coll of Maine (ME)
Saint Joseph's U (PA)
Saint Leo U (FL)
Saint Louis U (MO)
Saint Martin's U (WA)
Saint Mary-of-the-Woods Coll (IN)
Saint Mary's Coll (IN)
Saint Mary's U of Minnesota (MN)
Saint Michael's Coll (VT)
St. Norbert Coll (WI)
Saint Peter's Coll (NJ)
St. Thomas Aquinas Coll (NY)
St. Thomas U (FL)
Saint Vincent Coll (PA)
Saint Xavier U (IL)
Salem State U (MA)
Salisbury U (MD)
Salve Regina U (RI)
San Diego Christian Coll (CA)
Sarah Lawrence Coll (NY)
Schreiner U (TX)
Seattle Pacific U (WA)
Seton Hill U (PA)
Shaw U (NC)
Shepherd U (WV)
Shorter U (GA)
Siena Heights U (MI)
Simmons Coll (MA)
Simpson Coll (IA)
Skidmore Coll (NY)
Slippery Rock U of Pennsylvania (PA)
South Carolina State U (SC)
Southeastern Louisiana U (LA)
Southeastern Oklahoma State U (OK)
Southeastern U (FL)
Southeast Missouri State U (MO)
Southern Connecticut State U (CT)
Southern Illinois U Carbondale (IL)
Southern Illinois U Edwardsville (IL)
Southern New Hampshire U (NH)
Southwest Baptist U (MO)
Southwestern Adventist U (TX)
Southwestern Assemblies of God U (TX)
Southwestern Coll (KS)
Southwestern Oklahoma State U (OK)
Southwestern U (TX)
Southwest Minnesota State U (MN)
Spalding U (KY)
Spring Arbor U (MI)
Spring Hill Coll (AL)

State U of New York at Fredonia (NY)
State U of New York at New Paltz (NY)
State U of New York at Oswego (NY)
State U of New York at Plattsburgh (NY)
State U of New York Coll at Cortland (NY)
State U of New York Coll at Geneseo (NY)
State U of New York Coll at Old Westbury (NY)
State U of New York Coll at Oneonta (NY)
State U of New York Coll at Potsdam (NY)
Stephens Coll (MO)
Sterling Coll (KS)
Stetson U (FL)
Stevenson U (MD)
Stillman Coll (AL)
Stonehill Coll (MA)
Sul Ross State U (TX)
Susquehanna U (PA)
Tabor Coll (KS)
Tarleton State U (TX)
Taylor U (IN)
Temple U (PA)
Texas Christian U (TX)
Texas Coll (TX)
Texas Lutheran U (TX)
Texas Wesleyan U (TX)
Thiel Coll (PA)
Thomas More Coll (KY)
Thompson Rivers U (BC, Canada)
Towson U (MD)
Transylvania U (KY)
Trent U (ON, Canada)
Trevecca Nazarene U (TN)
Trine U (IN)
Trinity Baptist Coll (FL)
Trinity Christian Coll (IL)
Trinity Coll of Florida (FL)
Trinity Lutheran Coll (WA)
Troy U (AL)
Tufts U (MA)
Tusculum Coll (TN)
Tuskegee U (AL)
Union Coll (KY)
Union Coll (NE)
Union Inst & U (OH)
Union U (TN)
Universidad del Turabo (PR)
Université de Sherbrooke (QC, Canada)
The U of Alabama (AL)
The U of Alabama at Birmingham (AL)
The U of Alabama in Huntsville (AL)
U of Alaska Anchorage (AK)
U of Alaska Fairbanks (AK)
U of Alberta (AB, Canada)
The U of Arizona (AZ)
U of Arkansas at Little Rock (AR)
The U of British Columbia (BC, Canada)
U of Central Florida (FL)
U of Central Missouri (MO)
U of Charleston (WV)
U of Cincinnati (OH)
U of Connecticut (CT)
U of Dallas (TX)
U of Dayton (OH)
U of Delaware (DE)
U of Dubuque (IA)
U of Evansville (IN)
The U of Findlay (OH)
U of Florida (FL)
U of Great Falls (MT)
U of Guam (GU)
U of Hartford (CT)
U of Hawaii at Hilo (HI)
U of Hawaii at Manoa (HI)
U of Hawaii–West Oahu (HI)
U of Idaho (ID)
U of Illinois at Chicago (IL)
U of Illinois at Urbana–Champaign (IL)
U of Indianapolis (IN)
The U of Iowa (IA)
The U of Kansas (KS)
U of Louisiana at Lafayette (LA)
U of Louisiana at Monroe (LA)

U of Louisville (KY)
U of Maine (ME)
U of Maine at Farmington (ME)
U of Maine at Fort Kent (ME)
U of Maine at Presque Isle (ME)
U of Mary (ND)
U of Mary Hardin-Baylor (TX)
U of Maryland, Coll Park (MD)
U of Maryland Eastern Shore (MD)
U of Mary Washington (VA)
U of Miami (FL)
U of Michigan (MI)
U of Michigan–Dearborn (MI)
U of Michigan–Flint (MI)
U of Minnesota, Duluth (MN)
U of Minnesota, Twin Cities Campus (MN)
U of Mississippi (MS)
U of Missouri (MO)
U of Missouri–Kansas City (MO)
U of Missouri–St. Louis (MO)
U of Mobile (AL)
The U of Montana Western (MT)
U of Nebraska at Kearney (NE)
U of Nebraska–Lincoln (NE)
U of Nevada, Las Vegas (NV)
U of Nevada, Reno (NV)
U of New England (ME)
U of New Mexico (NM)
U of New Orleans (LA)
U of North Alabama (AL)
The U of North Carolina at Chapel Hill (NC)
The U of North Carolina at Charlotte (NC)
The U of North Carolina Wilmington (NC)
U of North Dakota (ND)
U of Northern Iowa (IA)
U of North Florida (FL)
U of Oklahoma (OK)
U of Pennsylvania (PA)
U of Pikeville (KY)
U of Pittsburgh at Bradford (PA)
U of Pittsburgh at Johnstown (PA)
U of Portland (OR)
U of Puerto Rico at Humacao (PR)
U of Puerto Rico at Ponce (PR)
U of Redlands (CA)
U of Regina (SK, Canada)
U of Rhode Island (RI)
U of Rio Grande (OH)
U of St. Francis (IL)
U of Saint Francis (IN)
U of Saint Mary (KS)
U of St. Thomas (MN)
U of St. Thomas (TX)
U of Science and Arts of Oklahoma (OK)
The U of Scranton (PA)
U of South Alabama (AL)
U of South Carolina (SC)
U of South Carolina Aiken (SC)
U of South Carolina Upstate (SC)
The U of South Dakota (SD)
U of Southern Indiana (IN)
U of Southern Mississippi (MS)
U of South Florida (FL)
The U of Tampa (FL)
The U of Tennessee at Martin (TN)
U of the Cumberlands (KY)
U of the District of Columbia (DC)
U of the Incarnate Word (TX)
U of the Ozarks (AR)
U of the Southwest (NM)
The U of Toledo (OH)
U of Tulsa (OK)
U of Utah (UT)
U of Vermont (VT)
U of Washington (WA)
The U of West Alabama (AL)
The U of Western Ontario (ON, Canada)
U of West Florida (FL)
U of West Georgia (GA)
U of Windsor (ON, Canada)
U of Wisconsin–Eau Claire (WI)
U of Wisconsin–La Crosse (WI)
U of Wisconsin–Madison (WI)
U of Wisconsin–Platteville (WI)
U of Wisconsin–River Falls (WI)
U of Wisconsin–Stevens Point (WI)
U of Wisconsin–Superior (WI)
U of Wisconsin–Whitewater (WI)
U of Wyoming (WY)

Upper Iowa U (IA)
Utah State U (UT)
Utah Valley U (UT)
Utica Coll (NY)
Valley City State U (ND)
Valley Forge Christian Coll Woodbridge Campus (VA)
Valparaiso U (IN)
Vanderbilt U (TN)
Vanguard U of Southern California (CA)
Virginia Commonwealth U (VA)
Virginia Intermont Coll (VA)
Virginia Union U (VA)
Virginia Wesleyan Coll (VA)
Viterbo U (WI)
Wagner Coll (NY)
Waldorf Coll (IA)
Wartburg Coll (IA)
Washburn U (KS)
Washington Adventist U (MD)
Washington State U (WA)
Washington U in St. Louis (MO)
Wayland Baptist U (TX)
Waynesburg U (PA)
Wayne State Coll (NE)
Wayne State U (MI)
Weber State U (UT)
Webster U (MO)
Wells Coll (NY)
West Chester U of Pennsylvania (PA)
Western Carolina U (NC)
Western Connecticut State U (CT)
Western Illinois U (IL)
Western Kentucky U (KY)
Western Michigan U (MI)
Western New England U (MA)
Western Washington U (WA)
Westfield State U (MA)
West Liberty U (WV)
Westminster Coll (MO)
Westminster Coll (UT)
West Virginia State U (WV)
West Virginia U (WV)
West Virginia Wesleyan Coll (WV)
Wheaton Coll (IL)
Wheeling Jesuit U (WV)
Wheelock Coll (MA)
Wichita State U (KS)
Widener U (PA)
Wilkes U (PA)
William Jewell Coll (MO)
William Paterson U of New Jersey (NJ)
William Penn U (IA)
Williams Baptist Coll (AR)
William Woods U (MO)
Wilmington Coll (OH)
Wilson Coll (PA)
Wingate U (NC)
Winona State U (MN)
Winthrop U (SC)
Worcester State U (MA)
Wright State U (OH)
Xavier U (OH)
Xavier U of Louisiana (LA)
Yeshiva U (NY)
York Coll of Pennsylvania (PA)
York Coll of the City U of New York (NY)
Youngstown State U (OH)

ELEMENTARY PARTICLE PHYSICS
Purdue U (IN)

EMERGENCY CARE ATTENDANT (EMT AMBULANCE)
Loyola U Chicago (IL)

EMERGENCY MEDICAL TECHNOLOGY (EMT PARAMEDIC)
Central Washington U (WA)
Concordia U Chicago (IL)
Creighton U (NE)
The George Washington U (DC)
Indiana U Bloomington (IN)
U of Maryland, Baltimore County (MD)
U of New Mexico (NM)

Western Carolina U (NC)

ENERGY MANAGEMENT AND SYSTEMS TECHNOLOGY
Ferris State U (MI)
Fitchburg State U (MA)
Illinois State U (IL)
Lamar U (TX)
State U of New York Coll of Technology at Canton (NY)
Vermont Tech Coll (VT)

ENGINEERING
Albion Coll (MI)
Arizona State U (AZ)
Arkansas State U (AR)
Auburn U (AL)
Ball State U (IN)
Barry U (FL)
Bates Coll (ME)
Baylor U (TX)
Beloit Coll (WI)
Bethany Lutheran Coll (MN)
Bethel Coll (IN)
Biola U (CA)
Boston U (MA)
Brown U (RI)
Buffalo State Coll, State U of New York (NY)
California Baptist U (CA)
California State Polytechnic U, Pomona (CA)
California State U, Long Beach (CA)
California State U, Los Angeles (CA)
Calvin Coll (MI)
Cape Breton U (NS, Canada)
Case Western Reserve U (OH)
The Catholic U of America (DC)
Clarkson U (NY)
Clark U (MA)
Coll of Staten Island of the City U of New York (NY)
Colorado School of Mines (CO)
Cooper Union for the Advancement of Science and Art (NY)
Cornell U (NY)
Dalhousie U (NS, Canada)
Dartmouth Coll (NH)
Dordt Coll (IA)
Drexel U (PA)
East Carolina U (NC)
Elizabethtown Coll (PA)
Elon U (NC)
Florida Inst of Technology (FL)
Franklin W. Olin Coll of Eng (MA)
Geneva Coll (PA)
George Fox U (OR)
George Mason U (VA)
The George Washington U (DC)
Gonzaga U (WA)
Grand Valley State U (MI)
Harvard U (MA)
Harvey Mudd Coll (CA)
Hope Coll (MI)
Indiana U–Purdue U Indianapolis (IN)
Inter American U of Puerto Rico, Bayamón Campus (PR)
Inter American U of Puerto Rico, San Germán Campus (PR)
Iowa State U of Science and Technology (IA)
James Madison U (VA)
John Brown U (AR)
The Johns Hopkins U (MD)
Juniata Coll (PA)
Kent State U (OH)
King Coll (TN)
Lafayette Coll (PA)
LaGrange Coll (GA)
Lakehead U (ON, Canada)
LeTourneau U (TX)
Liberty U (VA)
Loyola U Maryland (MD)
Lubbock Christian U (TX)
Manchester Coll (IN)
Manhattan Coll (NY)
Marshall U (WV)
Maryville Coll (TN)
Massachusetts Maritime Acad (MA)
McNeese State U (LA)
Mercer U (GA)

Messiah Coll (PA)
Miami U (OH)
Michigan State U (MI)
Michigan Technological U (MI)
Mills Coll (CA)
Milwaukee School of Eng (WI)
Missouri U of Science and Technology (MO)
Montana State U (MT)
Montana Tech of The U of Montana (MT)
New Mexico Highlands U (NM)
North Carolina Ag and Tech State U (NC)
North Carolina State U (NC)
Northeastern U (MA)
Northland Coll (WI)
Northwestern Coll (MN)
Nova Scotia Ag Coll (NS, Canada)
Oglethorpe U (GA)
Ohio Northern U (OH)
The Ohio State U (OH)
Oklahoma Christian U (OK)
Old Dominion U (VA)
Oral Roberts U (OK)
Pacific Lutheran U (WA)
Purdue U (IN)
Purdue U Calumet (IN)
Queen's U at Kingston (ON, Canada)
Rensselaer Polytechnic Inst (NY)
Robert Morris U (PA)
Rochester Inst of Technology (NY)
Roger Williams U (RI)
Rutgers, The State U of New Jersey, Camden (NJ)
Rutgers, The State U of New Jersey, Newark (NJ)
Saint Anselm Coll (NH)
Saint Augustine's Coll (NC)
Saint Francis U (PA)
Saint Louis U (MO)
Saint Mary's Coll of California (CA)
Saint Vincent Coll (PA)
Schreiner U (TX)
Seattle Pacific U (WA)
Spelman Coll (GA)
Stanford U (CA)
State U of New York at Binghamton (NY)
Stony Brook U, State U of New York (NY)
Swarthmore Coll (PA)
Syracuse U (NY)
Texas Christian U (TX)
Trinity Coll (CT)
Tufts U (MA)
United States Air Force Acad (CO)
United States Naval Acad (MD)
U at Buffalo, the State U of New York (NY)
The U of Akron (OH)
U of Alberta (AB, Canada)
U of California, Irvine (CA)
U of Cincinnati (OH)
U of Delaware (DE)
U of Denver (CO)
U of Georgia (GA)
U of Hartford (CT)
U of Illinois at Urbana–Champaign (IL)
The U of Iowa (IA)
U of Louisiana at Lafayette (LA)
U of Louisville (KY)
U of Mary (ND)
U of Maryland, Baltimore County (MD)
U of Michigan (MI)
U of Minnesota, Twin Cities Campus (MN)
U of Mississippi (MS)
U of Missouri–Kansas City (MO)
U of Nebraska–Lincoln (NE)
U of New Haven (CT)
The U of North Carolina at Asheville (NC)
U of Oklahoma (OK)
U of Portland (OR)
U of Regina (SK, Canada)
U of Southern Indiana (IN)
U of South Florida (FL)
The U of Tennessee at Chattanooga (TN)
The U of Tennessee at Martin (TN)
The U of Toledo (OH)

U of Toronto (ON, Canada)
U of Utah (UT)
U of Virginia (VA)
U of Washington (WA)
U of Windsor (ON, Canada)
Vaughn Coll of Aeronautics and Technology (NY)
Wake Forest U (NC)
Wartburg Coll (IA)
Washington U in St. Louis (MO)
Weber State U (UT)
Wells Coll (NY)
Wentworth Inst of Technology (MA)
Western Illinois U (IL)
West Virginia U Inst of Technology (WV)
Widener U (PA)
Wilkes U (PA)
Winona State U (MN)
Youngstown State U (OH)

ENGINEERING ACOUSTICS
Purdue U (IN)

ENGINEERING CHEMISTRY
Oakland U (MI)
Purdue U (IN)

ENGINEERING DESIGN
Purdue U (IN)

ENGINEERING FIELDS RELATED
California State U, Chico (CA)
Purdue U (IN)

ENGINEERING/INDUSTRIAL MANAGEMENT
Arizona State U (AZ)
California State U, Chico (CA)
California State U, Long Beach (CA)
Claremont McKenna Coll (CA)
Clarkson U (NY)
Clemson U (SC)
Eastern Michigan U (MI)
Farmingdale State Coll (NY)
Fort Lewis Coll (CO)
Grove City Coll (PA)
Illinois Inst of Technology (IL)
John Brown U (AR)
Lake Superior State U (MI)
Lawrence Technological U (MI)
Massachusetts Maritime Acad (MA)
Miami U (OH)
Middle Tennessee State U (TN)
Missouri State U (MO)
Missouri U of Science and Technology (MO)
Morehead State U (KY)
Purdue U (IN)
Saginaw Valley State U (MI)
South Dakota State U (SD)
Stanford U (CA)
State U of New York Coll of Technology at Canton (NY)
Stevens Inst of Technology (NJ)
Sweet Briar Coll (VA)
United States Merchant Marine Acad (NY)
United States Military Acad (NY)
Universidad del Turabo (PR)
The U of Arizona (AZ)
U of Illinois at Chicago (IL)
U of Michigan–Flint (MI)
U of Portland (OR)
The U of Scranton (PA)
The U of Tennessee at Chattanooga (TN)
U of the Incarnate Word (TX)
U of the Pacific (CA)
U of Vermont (VT)
Washburn U (KS)
Western Michigan U (MI)
Widener U (PA)
Wilkes U (PA)
Worcester Polytechnic Inst (MA)

ENGINEERING MECHANICS
Carroll Coll (MT)
Clemson U (SC)
Dordt Coll (IA)
Fairfield U (CT)

The Johns Hopkins U (MD)
Lehigh U (PA)
Lipscomb U (TN)
Michigan Technological U (MI)
Purdue U (IN)
United States Air Force Acad (CO)
U of Illinois at Urbana–Champaign (IL)
U of Windsor (ON, Canada)
U of Wisconsin–Madison (WI)
Virginia Polytechnic Inst and State U (VA)
Worcester Polytechnic Inst (MA)

ENGINEERING PHYSICS/ APPLIED PHYSICS
Adams State Coll (CO)
Arkansas Tech U (AR)
Augustana Coll (IL)
Augustana Coll (SD)
Bemidji State U (MN)
Bradley U (IL)
Brown U (RI)
Case Western Reserve U (OH)
Christian Brothers U (TN)
Colorado School of Mines (CO)
Colorado State U (CO)
Cornell U (NY)
Dartmouth Coll (NH)
Delaware State U (DE)
Eastern Michigan U (MI)
Embry-Riddle Aeronautical U–Daytona (FL)
Fairfield U (CT)
Fordham U (NY)
Fort Lewis Coll (CO)
Illinois Inst of Technology (IL)
Jacksonville U (FL)
John Carroll U (OH)
Juniata Coll (PA)
Kettering U (MI)
Lehigh U (PA)
Loras Coll (IA)
Loyola Marymount U (CA)
Miami U (OH)
Michigan Technological U (MI)
Mississippi Coll (MS)
Morehouse Coll (GA)
Morningside Coll (IA)
New Mexico State U (NM)
North Carolina Ag and Tech State U (NC)
Northwest Nazarene U (ID)
Oakland U (MI)
The Ohio State U (OH)
Oral Roberts U (OK)
Point Loma Nazarene U (CA)
Providence Coll (RI)
Purdue U (IN)
Queen's U at Kingston (ON, Canada)
Randolph Coll (VA)
Rensselaer Polytechnic Inst (NY)
Rose-Hulman Inst of Technology (IN)
St. Ambrose U (IA)
Saint Louis U (MO)
Saint Mary's U of Minnesota (MN)
Samford U (AL)
Santa Clara U (CA)
South Dakota State U (SD)
Southeast Missouri State U (MO)
Southwestern Oklahoma State U (OK)
Stevens Inst of Technology (NJ)
Tarleton State U (TX)
Taylor U (IN)
Thiel Coll (PA)
Tufts U (MA)
U at Buffalo, the State U of New York (NY)
U of Alberta (AB, Canada)
The U of British Columbia (BC, Canada)
U of California, Berkeley (CA)
U of Colorado Boulder (CO)
U of Connecticut (CT)
U of Illinois at Chicago (IL)
U of Illinois at Urbana–Champaign (IL)
The U of Kansas (KS)
U of Maine (ME)
U of Massachusetts Boston (MA)
U of Michigan (MI)
U of Nebraska at Omaha (NE)

U of Nevada, Reno (NV)
U of Northern Iowa (IA)
U of Oklahoma (OK)
U of Pittsburgh (PA)
U of the Pacific (CA)
The U of Toledo (OH)
U of Tulsa (OK)
U of Wisconsin–Madison (WI)
Washington and Lee U (VA)
West Virginia Wesleyan Coll (WV)
Worcester Polytechnic Inst (MA)
Wright State U (OH)
Yale U (CT)

ENGINEERING RELATED
Agnes Scott Coll (GA)
Alfred U (NY)
Anderson U (SC)
Arizona State U (AZ)
Auburn U (AL)
Boston U (MA)
California State U, Chico (CA)
California State U, Long Beach (CA)
Carnegie Mellon U (PA)
The Coll of Idaho (ID)
Eastern Illinois U (IL)
Gettysburg Coll (PA)
Hawai'i Pacific U (HI)
Indiana Tech (IN)
Indiana U–Purdue U Indianapolis (IN)
Iowa State U of Science and Technology (IA)
Kentucky Wesleyan Coll (KY)
Lehigh U (PA)
Loras Coll (IA)
Maryville U of Saint Louis (MO)
McNally Smith Coll of Music (MN)
Milwaukee School of Eng (WI)
Mississippi State U (MS)
Norfolk State U (VA)
Northern Michigan U (MI)
Oakland U (MI)
Ohio Northern U (OH)
The Ohio State U (OH)
Ohio Wesleyan U (OH)
Park U (MO)
Penn State Altoona (PA)
Penn State Berks (PA)
Penn State U Park (PA)
Purdue U (IN)
Queen's U at Kingston (ON, Canada)
Rochester Inst of Technology (NY)
Rose-Hulman Inst of Technology (IN)
State U of New York at Oswego (NY)
Transylvania U (KY)
Tufts U (MA)
The U of Alabama in Huntsville (AL)
U of California, Davis (CA)
U of Connecticut (CT)
U of Delaware (DE)
U of Maryland, Coll Park (MD)
U of Massachusetts Lowell (MA)
U of Michigan–Dearborn (MI)
U of Pennsylvania (PA)
U of the Cumberlands (KY)
The U of Virginia's Coll at Wise (VA)
Waynesburg U (PA)
Wentworth Inst of Technology (MA)
Western Michigan U (MI)
Wheaton Coll (IL)
Worcester Polytechnic Inst (MA)
Wright State U (OH)
York Coll of Pennsylvania (PA)

ENGINEERING-RELATED TECHNOLOGIES
Purdue U (IN)
Rochester Inst of Technology (NY)
United States Merchant Marine Acad (NY)

ENGINEERING SCIENCE
Abilene Christian U (TX)
Belmont U (TN)
Benedictine U (IL)
Bethel U (MN)
Bob Jones U (SC)
California Polytechnic State U, San Luis Obispo (CA)

INDEXES

Felician Coll (NJ)
Ferrum Coll (VA)
Fitchburg State U (MA)
Flagler Coll (FL)
Florida Ag and Mech U (FL)
Florida Atlantic U (FL)
Florida Gulf Coast U (FL)
Florida Intl U (FL)
Florida Southern Coll (FL)
Florida State U (FL)
Fontbonne U (MO)
Fordham U (NY)
Fort Hays State U (KS)
Fort Lewis Coll (CO)
Framingham State U (MA)
Franciscan U of Steubenville (OH)
Francis Marion U (SC)
Franklin & Marshall Coll (PA)
Franklin Coll (IN)
Free Will Baptist Bible Coll (TN)
Friends U (KS)
Furman U (SC)
Gallaudet U (DC)
Gardner-Webb U (NC)
Geneva Coll (PA)
George Fox U (OR)
George Mason U (VA)
Georgetown Coll (KY)
The George Washington U (DC)
Georgia Coll & State U (GA)
Georgia Gwinnett Coll (GA)
Georgian Court U (NJ)
Georgia Southern U (GA)
Georgia Southwestern State U (GA)
Georgia State U (GA)
Gettysburg Coll (PA)
Glenville State Coll (WV)
Goldey-Beacom Coll (DE)
Gonzaga U (WA)
Gordon Coll (MA)
Goshen Coll (IN)
Goucher Coll (MD)
Governors State U (IL)
Grace Coll (IN)
Graceland U (IA)
Grambling State U (LA)
Grand Valley State U (MI)
Grand View U (IA)
Greenville Coll (IL)
Grinnell Coll (IA)
Grove City Coll (PA)
Guilford Coll (NC)
Gustavus Adolphus Coll (MN)
Gwynedd-Mercy Coll (PA)
Hamilton Coll (NY)
Hamline U (MN)
Hampden-Sydney Coll (VA)
Hampshire Coll (MA)
Hampton U (VA)
Hannibal-LaGrange U (MO)
Hanover Coll (IN)
Harding U (AR)
Hardin-Simmons U (TX)
Hartwick Coll (NY)
Harvard U (MA)
Haverford Coll (PA)
Hawai'i Pacific U (HI)
Heidelberg U (OH)
Hendrix Coll (AR)
Hilbert Coll (NY)
Hillsdale Coll (MI)
Hobart and William Smith Colls (NY)
Hofstra U (NY)
Hollins U (VA)
Holy Cross Coll (IN)
Holy Family U (PA)
Hood Coll (MD)
Hope Coll (MI)
Hope Intl U (CA)
Houghton Coll (NY)
Howard Payne U (TX)
Humboldt State U (CA)
Hunter Coll of the City U of New York (NY)
Huntingdon Coll (AL)
Huntington U (IN)
Husson U (ME)
Huston-Tillotson U (TX)
Idaho State U (ID)
Illinois Coll (IL)
Illinois State U (IL)
Immaculata U (PA)
Indiana State U (IN)
Indiana U Bloomington (IN)

Indiana U East (IN)
Indiana U Kokomo (IN)
Indiana U Northwest (IN)
Indiana U of Pennsylvania (PA)
Indiana U–Purdue U Fort Wayne (IN)
Indiana U–Purdue U Indianapolis (IN)
Indiana U South Bend (IN)
Indiana U Southeast (IN)
Indiana Wesleyan U (IN)
Inter American U of Puerto Rico, San Germán Campus (PR)
Iona Coll (NY)
Iowa State U of Science and Technology (IA)
Iowa Wesleyan Coll (IA)
Ithaca Coll (NY)
Jacksonville State U (AL)
Jacksonville U (FL)
James Madison U (VA)
Jamestown Coll (ND)
Jarvis Christian Coll (TX)
John Brown U (AR)
John Carroll U (OH)
John Jay Coll of Criminal Justice of the City U of New York (NY)
The Johns Hopkins U (MD)
Johnson C. Smith U (NC)
Johnson State Coll (VT)
Judson Coll (AL)
Judson U (IL)
Juniata Coll (PA)
Kalamazoo Coll (MI)
Kansas State U (KS)
Kean U (NJ)
Keene State Coll (NH)
Kennesaw State U (GA)
Kent State U (OH)
Kent State U at Ashtabula (OH)
Kent State U at East Liverpool (OH)
Kent State U at Salem (OH)
Kent State U at Stark (OH)
Kent State U at Trumbull (OH)
Kentucky State U (KY)
Kentucky Wesleyan Coll (KY)
Kenyon Coll (OH)
Keuka Coll (NY)
King Coll (TN)
King's Coll (PA)
The King's U Coll (AB, Canada)
Knox Coll (IL)
Kutztown U of Pennsylvania (PA)
Lafayette Coll (PA)
LaGrange Coll (GA)
Lake Erie Coll (OH)
Lake Forest Coll (IL)
Lakehead U (ON, Canada)
Lake Superior State U (MI)
Lamar U (TX)
Lane Coll (TN)
La Roche Coll (PA)
La Salle U (PA)
Lasell Coll (MA)
La Sierra U (CA)
Lawrence Technological U (MI)
Lawrence U (WI)
Lebanese American U (Lebanon)
Lebanon Valley Coll (PA)
Lees-McRae Coll (NC)
Lee U (TN)
Lehigh U (PA)
Lehman Coll of the City U of New York (NY)
Le Moyne Coll (NY)
Lenoir-Rhyne U (NC)
LeTourneau U (TX)
Lewis & Clark Coll (OR)
Lewis-Clark State Coll (ID)
Lewis U (IL)
Liberty U (VA)
Limestone Coll (SC)
Lincoln Memorial U (TN)
Lincoln U (MO)
Lincoln U (PA)
Lindenwood U (MO)
Lindsey Wilson Coll (KY)
Linfield Coll (OR)
Lipscomb U (TN)
Lock Haven U of Pennsylvania (PA)
Long Island U–Brooklyn Campus (NY)
Long Island U–C. W. Post Campus (NY)
Longwood U (VA)

Loras Coll (IA)
Louisiana Coll (LA)
Louisiana State U and Ag and Mech Coll (LA)
Louisiana State U in Shreveport (LA)
Lourdes U (OH)
Loyola Marymount U (CA)
Loyola U Chicago (IL)
Loyola U Maryland (MD)
Loyola U New Orleans (LA)
Lubbock Christian U (TX)
Luther Coll (IA)
Lycoming Coll (PA)
Lynchburg Coll (VA)
Lynn U (FL)
Lyon Coll (AR)
Macalester Coll (MN)
Macon State Coll (GA)
Madonna U (MI)
Maharishi U of Management (IA)
Malone U (OH)
Manchester Coll (IN)
Manhattan Coll (NY)
Manhattanville Coll (NY)
Mansfield U of Pennsylvania (PA)
Maranatha Baptist Bible Coll (WI)
Marian U (WI)
Marietta Coll (OH)
Marlboro Coll (VT)
Marquette U (WI)
Marshall U (WV)
Mars Hill Coll (NC)
Mary Baldwin Coll (VA)
Marylhurst U (OR)
Marymount Manhattan Coll (NY)
Marymount U (VA)
Maryville Coll (TN)
Maryville U of Saint Louis (MO)
Marywood U (PA)
Massachusetts Coll of Liberal Arts (MA)
Massachusetts Inst of Technology (MA)
The Master's Coll and Sem (CA)
Mayville State U (ND)
McDaniel Coll (MD)
McKendree U (IL)
McMurry U (TX)
McNeese State U (LA)
McPherson Coll (KS)
Medaille Coll (NY)
Mercer U (GA)
Mercy Coll (NY)
Mercyhurst Coll (PA)
Meredith Coll (NC)
Merrimack Coll (MA)
Messiah Coll (PA)
Metropolitan State Coll of Denver (CO)
Metropolitan State U (MN)
Miami U (OH)
Michigan State U (MI)
Michigan Technological U (MI)
MidAmerica Nazarene U (KS)
Mid-Continent U (KY)
Middlebury Coll (VT)
Middle Tennessee State U (TN)
Midwestern State U (TX)
Millersville U of Pennsylvania (PA)
Milligan Coll (TN)
Millikin U (IL)
Millsaps Coll (MS)
Mills Coll (CA)
Minnesota State U Mankato (MN)
Minot State U (ND)
Misericordia U (PA)
Mississippi Coll (MS)
Mississippi State U (MS)
Mississippi U for Women (MS)
Mississippi Valley State U (MS)
Missouri Baptist U (MO)
Missouri Southern State U (MO)
Missouri State U (MO)
Missouri U of Science and Technology (MO)
Missouri Western State U (MO)
Molloy Coll (NY)
Monmouth Coll (IL)
Monmouth U (NJ)
Montana State U (MT)
Montana State U Billings (MT)
Montclair State U (NJ)
Montreat Coll, Montreal (NC)
Moravian Coll (PA)

Morehead State U (KY)
Morehouse Coll (GA)
Morningside Coll (IA)
Morris Coll (SC)
Mount Allison U (NB, Canada)
Mount Aloysius Coll (PA)
Mount Holyoke Coll (MA)
Mount Ida Coll (MA)
Mount Marty Coll (SD)
Mount Mercy U (IA)
Mount Saint Mary Coll (NY)
Mount St. Mary's Coll (CA)
Mount St. Mary's U (MD)
Mount Vernon Nazarene U (OH)
Muhlenberg Coll (PA)
Multnomah U (OR)
Naropa U (CO)
National-Louis U (IL)
National U (CA)
Nazareth Coll of Rochester (NY)
Nebraska Wesleyan U (NE)
Neumann U (PA)
Newberry Coll (SC)
New Coll of Florida (FL)
New England Coll (NH)
New Jersey City U (NJ)
Newman U (KS)
New Mexico Highlands U (NM)
New Mexico State U (NM)
New York U (NY)
Niagara U (NY)
Nicholls State U (LA)
Nichols Coll (MA)
Norfolk State U (VA)
North Carolina Ag and Tech State U (NC)
North Carolina Central U (NC)
North Carolina State U (NC)
North Carolina Wesleyan Coll (NC)
North Central Coll (IL)
North Dakota State U (ND)
Northeastern Illinois U (IL)
Northeastern State U (OK)
Northeastern U (MA)
Northern Arizona U (AZ)
Northern Illinois U (IL)
Northern Kentucky U (KY)
Northern Michigan U (MI)
Northern State U (SD)
North Georgia Coll & State U (GA)
North Greenville U (SC)
Northwest Christian U (OR)
Northwestern Coll (IA)
Northwestern Coll (MN)
Northwestern Oklahoma State U (OK)
Northwestern State U of Louisiana (LA)
Northwest Missouri State U (MO)
Northwest Nazarene U (ID)
Northwest U (WA)
Norwich U (VT)
Notre Dame de Namur U (CA)
Notre Dame of Maryland U (MD)
Nova Southeastern U (FL)
Nyack Coll (NY)
Oakland U (MI)
Occidental Coll (CA)
Oglethorpe U (GA)
The Ohio State U (OH)
The Ohio State U at Lima (OH)
The Ohio State U at Marion (OH)
The Ohio State U–Mansfield Campus (OH)
The Ohio State U–Newark Campus (OH)
Ohio U (OH)
Ohio Wesleyan U (OH)
Oklahoma Christian U (OK)
Oklahoma City U (OK)
Oklahoma State U (OK)
Old Dominion U (VA)
Oral Roberts U (OK)
Otterbein U (OH)
Ouachita Baptist U (AR)
Pace U (NY)
Pacific Lutheran U (WA)
Pacific Union Coll (CA)
Pacific U (OR)
Paine Coll (GA)
Palm Beach Atlantic U (FL)
Park U (MO)
Penn State Abington (PA)
Penn State Altoona (PA)
Penn State Beaver (PA)

Penn State Berks (PA)
Penn State Brandywine (PA)
Penn State DuBois (PA)
Penn State Erie, The Behrend Coll (PA)
Penn State Fayette, The Eberly Campus (PA)
Penn State Greater Allegheny (PA)
Penn State Harrisburg (PA)
Penn State Hazleton (PA)
Penn State Lehigh Valley (PA)
Penn State Mont Alto (PA)
Penn State New Kensington (PA)
Penn State Schuylkill (PA)
Penn State Shenango (PA)
Penn State U Park (PA)
Penn State Wilkes-Barre (PA)
Penn State Worthington Scranton (PA)
Penn State York (PA)
Pepperdine U, Malibu (CA)
Peru State Coll (NE)
Philander Smith Coll (AR)
Piedmont Coll (GA)
Pine Manor Coll (MA)
Pittsburg State U (KS)
Pitzer Coll (CA)
Plymouth State U (NH)
Point Loma Nazarene U (CA)
Point Park U (PA)
Point U (GA)
Pomona Coll (CA)
Portland State U (OR)
Prairie View A&M U (TX)
Presbyterian Coll (SC)
Princeton U (NJ)
Providence Coll (RI)
Purdue U (IN)
Purdue U Calumet (IN)
Purdue U North Central (IN)
Queens Coll of the City U of New York (NY)
Queen's U at Kingston (ON, Canada)
Queens U of Charlotte (NC)
Quincy U (IL)
Quinnipiac U (CT)
Radford U (VA)
Randolph Coll (VA)
Randolph-Macon Coll (VA)
Regent U (VA)
Regis Coll (MA)
Regis U (CO)
Reinhardt U (GA)
Rhode Island Coll (RI)
Rhodes Coll (TN)
Rice U (TX)
The Richard Stockton Coll of New Jersey (NJ)
Rider U (NJ)
Ripon Coll (WI)
Rivier Coll (NH)
Roanoke Coll (VA)
Robert Morris U (PA)
Roberts Wesleyan Coll (NY)
Rockford Coll (IL)
Rockhurst U (MO)
Rocky Mountain Coll (MT)
Roger Williams U (RI)
Rollins Coll (FL)
Roosevelt U (IL)
Rosemont Coll (PA)
Rowan U (NJ)
Russell Sage Coll (NY)
Rust Coll (MS)
Rutgers, The State U of New Jersey, Camden (NJ)
Rutgers, The State U of New Jersey, Newark (NJ)
Rutgers, The State U of New Jersey, New Brunswick (NJ)
Sacred Heart U (CT)
Saginaw Valley State U (MI)
St. Ambrose U (IA)
St. Andrews U (NC)
Saint Anselm Coll (NH)
Saint Augustine's Coll (NC)
St. Bonaventure U (NY)
St. Catherine U (MN)
St. Edward's U (TX)
Saint Francis U (PA)
St. John Fisher Coll (NY)
Saint John's U (MN)
St. John's U (NY)
Saint Joseph's Coll (IN)

St. Joseph's Coll, Long Island
Campus (NY)
St. Joseph's Coll, New York (NY)
Saint Joseph's Coll of Maine (ME)
Saint Joseph's U (PA)
St. Lawrence U (NY)
Saint Leo U (FL)
Saint Louis U (MO)
Saint Martin's U (WA)
Saint Mary-of-the-Woods Coll (IN)
Saint Mary's U (IN)
Saint Mary's Coll of California (CA)
St. Mary's Coll of Maryland (MD)
St. Mary's U (TX)
Saint Michael's Coll (VT)
St. Norbert Coll (WI)
St. Olaf Coll (MN)
Saint Peter's Coll (NJ)
St. Thomas Aquinas Coll (NY)
St. Thomas U (FL)
St. Thomas U (NB, Canada)
Saint Vincent Coll (PA)
Saint Xavier U (IL)
Salem State U (MA)
Salisbury U (MD)
Salve Regina U (RI)
Samford U (AL)
Sam Houston State U (TX)
San Diego Christian Coll (CA)
San Diego State U (CA)
San Francisco State U (CA)
Santa Clara U (CA)
Sarah Lawrence Coll (NY)
Schreiner U (TX)
Scripps Coll (CA)
Seattle Pacific U (WA)
Seattle U (WA)
Seton Hill U (PA)
Sewanee: The U of the South (TN)
Shawnee State U (OH)
Shaw U (NC)
Shenandoah U (VA)
Shepherd U (WV)
Shippensburg U of Pennsylvania
(PA)
Shorter U (GA)
Siena Coll (NY)
Siena Heights U (MI)
Sierra Nevada Coll (NV)
Simmons Coll (MA)
Simon Fraser U (BC, Canada)
Simpson Coll (IA)
Simpson U (CA)
Skidmore Coll (NY)
Slippery Rock U of Pennsylvania
(PA)
Smith Coll (MA)
Sonoma State U (CA)
South Carolina State U (SC)
South Dakota State U (SD)
Southeastern Baptist Theological
Sem (NC)
Southeastern Louisiana U (LA)
Southeastern Oklahoma State U
(OK)
Southeastern U (FL)
Southeast Missouri State U (MO)
Southern Arkansas U–Magnolia
(AR)
Southern Connecticut State U (CT)
Southern Illinois U Carbondale (IL)
Southern Illinois U Edwardsville (IL)
Southern Methodist U (TX)
Southern New Hampshire U (NH)
Southern Oregon U (OR)
Southern Vermont Coll (VT)
Southwest Baptist U (MO)
Southwestern Adventist U (TX)
Southwestern Assemblies of God U
(TX)
Southwestern Christian U (OK)
Southwestern Coll (KS)
Southwestern Oklahoma State U
(OK)
Southwestern U (TX)
Southwest Minnesota State U (MN)
Spelman Coll (GA)
Spring Arbor U (MI)
Spring Hill Coll (AL)
Stanford U (CA)
State U of New York at Binghamton
(NY)
State U of New York at Fredonia
(NY)

State U of New York at New Paltz
(NY)
State U of New York at Oswego
(NY)
State U of New York at Plattsburgh
(NY)
State U of New York Coll at
Cortland (NY)
State U of New York Coll at
Geneseo (NY)
State U of New York Coll at
Oneonta (NY)
State U of New York Coll at
Potsdam (NY)
Stephen F. Austin State U (TX)
Stephens Coll (MO)
Sterling Coll (KS)
Stetson U (FL)
Stevens Inst of Technology (NJ)
Stevenson U (MD)
Stillman Coll (AL)
Stonehill Coll (MA)
Stony Brook U, State U of New York
(NY)
Suffolk U (MA)
Sul Ross State U (TX)
Susquehanna U (PA)
Swarthmore Coll (PA)
Sweet Briar Coll (VA)
Syracuse U (NY)
Tabor Coll (KS)
Tarleton State U (TX)
Taylor U (IN)
Temple U (PA)
Texas A&M Intl U (TX)
Texas A&M U (TX)
Texas A&M U–Corpus Christi (TX)
Texas A&M U–Kingsville (TX)
Texas Christian U (TX)
Texas Coll (TX)
Texas Lutheran U (TX)
Texas Southern U (TX)
Texas State U–San Marcos (TX)
Texas Tech U (TX)
Texas Wesleyan U (TX)
Texas Woman's U (TX)
Thiel Coll (PA)
Thomas Edison State Coll (NJ)
Thomas More Coll (KY)
Thomas U (GA)
Thompson Rivers U (BC, Canada)
Tiffin U (OH)
Touro Coll (NY)
Towson U (MD)
Transylvania U (KY)
Trent U (ON, Canada)
Trevecca Nazarene U (TN)
Trinity Christian Coll (IL)
Trinity Coll (CT)
Trinity U (TX)
Troy U (AL)
Truett-McConnell Coll (GA)
Truman State U (MO)
Tufts U (MA)
Tulane U (LA)
Tusculum Coll (TN)
Tuskegee U (AL)
Union Coll (KY)
Union Coll (NE)
Union Coll (NY)
Union U (TN)
United States Air Force Acad (CO)
United States Naval Acad (MD)
Université de Sherbrooke (QC,
Canada)
U at Albany, State U of New York
(NY)
U at Buffalo, the State U of New
York (NY)
The U of Akron (OH)
The U of Alabama (AL)
The U of Alabama at Birmingham
(AL)
The U of Alabama in Huntsville (AL)
U of Alaska Anchorage (AK)
U of Alaska Fairbanks (AK)
U of Alberta (AB, Canada)
The U of Arizona (AZ)
U of Arkansas (AR)
U of Arkansas at Little Rock (AR)
U of Arkansas at Monticello (AR)
U of Arkansas–Fort Smith (AR)
U of Bridgeport (CT)
The U of British Columbia (BC,
Canada)

The U of British Columbia–
Okanagan (BC, Canada)
U of California, Berkeley (CA)
U of California, Davis (CA)
U of California, Irvine (CA)
U of California, Los Angeles (CA)
U of California, Riverside (CA)
U of California, Santa Barbara (CA)
U of Central Arkansas (AR)
U of Central Florida (FL)
U of Central Missouri (MO)
U of Charleston (WV)
U of Cincinnati (OH)
U of Colorado at Colorado Springs
(CO)
U of Colorado Boulder (CO)
U of Colorado Denver (CO)
U of Connecticut (CT)
U of Dallas (TX)
U of Dayton (OH)
U of Delaware (DE)
U of Denver (CO)
U of Dubuque (IA)
U of Evansville (IN)
The U of Findlay (OH)
U of Florida (FL)
U of Georgia (GA)
U of Great Falls (MT)
U of Guam (GU)
U of Guelph (ON, Canada)
U of Hartford (CT)
U of Hawaii at Hilo (HI)
U of Hawaii at Manoa (HI)
U of Hawaii–West Oahu (HI)
U of Houston (TX)
U of Houston–Clear Lake (TX)
U of Houston–Downtown (TX)
U of Houston–Victoria (TX)
U of Idaho (ID)
U of Illinois at Chicago (IL)
U of Illinois at Springfield (IL)
U of Illinois at Urbana–Champaign
(IL)
U of Indianapolis (IN)
The U of Iowa (IA)
The U of Kansas (KS)
U of La Verne (CA)
U of Lethbridge (AB, Canada)
U of Louisiana at Lafayette (LA)
U of Louisiana at Monroe (LA)
U of Louisville (KY)
U of Maine (ME)
U of Maine at Farmington (ME)
U of Maine at Fort Kent (ME)
U of Maine at Presque Isle (ME)
U of Mary (ND)
U of Mary Hardin-Baylor (TX)
U of Maryland, Baltimore County
(MD)
U of Maryland, Coll Park (MD)
U of Maryland Eastern Shore (MD)
U of Maryland U Coll (MD)
U of Mary Washington (VA)
U of Massachusetts Amherst (MA)
U of Massachusetts Boston (MA)
U of Massachusetts Dartmouth
(MA)
U of Massachusetts Lowell (MA)
U of Memphis (TN)
U of Miami (FL)
U of Michigan (MI)
U of Michigan–Dearborn (MI)
U of Michigan–Flint (MI)
U of Minnesota, Duluth (MN)
U of Minnesota, Twin Cities
Campus (MN)
U of Mississippi (MS)
U of Missouri (MO)
U of Missouri–Kansas City (MO)
U of Missouri–St. Louis (MO)
U of Mobile (AL)
The U of Montana Western (MT)
U of Mount Union (OH)
U of Nebraska at Kearney (NE)
U of Nebraska at Omaha (NE)
U of Nebraska–Lincoln (NE)
U of Nevada, Las Vegas (NV)
U of Nevada, Reno (NV)
U of New England (ME)
U of New Hampshire (NH)
U of New Hampshire at Manchester
(NH)
U of New Haven (CT)
U of New Mexico (NM)
U of New Orleans (LA)

U of North Alabama (AL)
The U of North Carolina at Asheville
(NC)
The U of North Carolina at Chapel
Hill (NC)
The U of North Carolina at
Charlotte (NC)
The U of North Carolina Wilmington
(NC)
U of North Dakota (ND)
U of Northern Colorado (CO)
U of Northern Iowa (IA)
U of North Florida (FL)
U of North Texas (TX)
U of Notre Dame (IN)
U of Oklahoma (OK)
U of Oregon (OR)
U of Ottawa (ON, Canada)
U of Pennsylvania (PA)
U of Pikeville (KY)
U of Pittsburgh at Bradford (PA)
U of Pittsburgh at Greensburg (PA)
U of Pittsburgh at Johnstown (PA)
U of Portland (OR)
U of Puget Sound (WA)
U of Redlands (CA)
U of Regina (SK, Canada)
U of Rhode Island (RI)
U of Richmond (VA)
U of Rio Grande (OH)
U of Rochester (NY)
U of St. Francis (IL)
U of Saint Francis (IN)
U of Saint Joseph (CT)
U of Saint Mary (KS)
U of St. Thomas (MN)
U of St. Thomas (TX)
U of San Diego (CA)
U of Science and Arts of Oklahoma
(OK)
The U of Scranton (PA)
U of South Alabama (AL)
U of South Carolina (SC)
U of South Carolina Aiken (SC)
U of South Carolina Beaufort (SC)
U of South Carolina Upstate (SC)
The U of South Dakota (SD)
U of Southern California (CA)
U of Southern Indiana (IN)
U of Southern Maine (ME)
U of Southern Mississippi (MS)
U of South Florida (FL)
U of South Florida–St. Petersburg
Campus (FL)
The U of Tampa (FL)
The U of Tennessee (TN)
The U of Tennessee at
Chattanooga (TN)
The U of Tennessee at Martin (TN)
The U of Texas at Arlington (TX)
The U of Texas at Austin (TX)
The U of Texas at El Paso (TX)
The U of Texas at San Antonio (TX)
The U of Texas at Tyler (TX)
The U of Texas of the Permian
Basin (TX)
The U of Texas–Pan American (TX)
U of the Cumberlands (KY)
U of the Incarnate Word (TX)
U of the Ozarks (AR)
U of the Pacific (CA)
U of the Southwest (NM)
The U of Toledo (OH)
U of Toronto (ON, Canada)
U of Tulsa (OK)
U of Utah (UT)
U of Vermont (VT)
U of Virginia (VA)
The U of Virginia's Coll at Wise (VA)
U of Washington (WA)
The U of West Alabama (AL)
The U of Western Ontario (ON,
Canada)
U of West Florida (FL)
U of West Georgia (GA)
U of Windsor (ON, Canada)
U of Wisconsin–Eau Claire (WI)
U of Wisconsin–Green Bay (WI)
U of Wisconsin–La Crosse (WI)
U of Wisconsin–Madison (WI)
U of Wisconsin–Milwaukee (WI)
U of Wisconsin–Platteville (WI)
U of Wisconsin–River Falls (WI)
U of Wisconsin–Stevens Point (WI)
U of Wisconsin–Superior (WI)

U of Wisconsin–Whitewater (WI)
U of Wyoming (WY)
Upper Iowa U (IA)
Ursuline Coll (OH)
Utah State U (UT)
Utah Valley U (UT)
Utica Coll (NY)
Valdosta State U (GA)
Valley City State U (ND)
Valparaiso U (IN)
Vanderbilt U (TN)
Vanguard U of Southern California
(CA)
Vassar Coll (NY)
Villanova U (PA)
Virginia Commonwealth U (VA)
Virginia Intermont Coll (VA)
Virginia Polytechnic Inst and State
U (VA)
Virginia State U (VA)
Virginia Union U (VA)
Virginia Wesleyan Coll (VA)
Viterbo U (WI)
Wabash Coll (IN)
Wagner Coll (NY)
Wake Forest U (NC)
Waldorf Coll (IA)
Walsh U (OH)
Warren Wilson Coll (NC)
Wartburg Coll (IA)
Washburn U (KS)
Washington Adventist U (MD)
Washington & Jefferson Coll (PA)
Washington and Lee U (VA)
Washington Coll (MD)
Washington State U (WA)
Washington U in St. Louis (MO)
Wayland Baptist U (TX)
Waynesburg U (PA)
Wayne State Coll (NE)
Wayne State U (MI)
Weber State U (UT)
Webster U (MO)
Wellesley Coll (MA)
Wells Coll (NY)
Wesleyan Coll (GA)
Wesleyan U (CT)
West Chester U of Pennsylvania
(PA)
Western Carolina U (NC)
Western Connecticut State U (CT)
Western Illinois U (IL)
Western Kentucky U (KY)
Western Michigan U (MI)
Western New England U (MA)
Western Oregon U (OR)
Western State Coll of Colorado
(CO)
Western Washington U (WA)
Westfield State U (MA)
West Liberty U (WV)
Westminster Coll (MO)
Westminster Coll (UT)
West Texas A&M U (TX)
West Virginia State U (WV)
West Virginia U (WV)
West Virginia Wesleyan Coll (WV)
Wheaton Coll (IL)
Wheaton Coll (MA)
Wheeling Jesuit U (WV)
Whitman Coll (WA)
Whittier Coll (CA)
Wichita State U (KS)
Widener U (PA)
Wilkes U (PA)
Willamette U (OR)
William Jessup U (CA)
William Jewell Coll (MO)
William Paterson U of New Jersey
(NJ)
Williams Baptist Coll (AR)
Williams Coll (MA)
William Woods U (MO)
Wilmington Coll (OH)
Wilson Coll (PA)
Wingate U (NC)
Winona State U (MN)
Winthrop U (SC)
Wittenberg U (OH)
Wofford Coll (SC)
Worcester State U (MA)
Wright State U (OH)
Xavier U (OH)
Xavier U of Louisiana (LA)
Yale U (CT)

Yeshiva U (NY)
York Coll of Pennsylvania (PA)
York Coll of the City U of New York (NY)
Youngstown State U (OH)

ENGLISH AS A SECOND/FOREIGN LANGUAGE (TEACHING)

American U (DC)
Bayamón Central U (PR)
Bethel U (MN)
Briercrest Coll (SK, Canada)
Brigham Young U (UT)
Calvin Coll (MI)
Carroll Coll (MT)
The Catholic U of America (DC)
Concordia U (QC, Canada)
Concordia U, Nebraska (NE)
Concordia U, St. Paul (MN)
Crown Coll (MN)
Doane Coll (NE)
Eastern Washington U (WA)
Gardner-Webb U (NC)
Goshen Coll (IN)
Grand Canyon U (AZ)
Granite State Coll (NH)
Hawai`i Pacific U (HI)
Houghton Coll (NY)
Howard Payne U (TX)
Huntington U (IN)
Indiana Wesleyan U (IN)
Inter American U of Puerto Rico, Fajardo Campus (PR)
Inter American U of Puerto Rico, Ponce Campus (PR)
Inter American U of Puerto Rico, San Germán Campus (PR)
Kent State U (OH)
Lebanese American U (Lebanon)
Le Moyne Coll (NY)
Lenoir-Rhyne U (NC)
Liberty U (VA)
Lipscomb U (TN)
Maryville Coll (TN)
Multnomah U (OR)
Niagara U (NY)
Northwestern Coll (MN)
Northwest U (WA)
Nyack Coll (NY)
Oklahoma Christian U (OK)
Oklahoma City U (OK)
Queens Coll of the City U of New York (NY)
Salisbury U (MD)
Simmons Coll (MA)
Stony Brook U, State U of New York (NY)
Tarleton State U (TX)
Union U (TN)
U of Alberta (AB, Canada)
The U of British Columbia (BC, Canada)
The U of Findlay (OH)
U of Minnesota, Twin Cities Campus (MN)
U of Northern Iowa (IA)
U of Puerto Rico at Humacao (PR)
U of Southern Maine (ME)
U of Washington (WA)
U of Wisconsin–River Falls (WI)
Washington State U (WA)
Wichita State U (KS)
William Penn U (IA)
Winona State U (MN)
Wright State U (OH)

ENGLISH/FRENCH AS A SECOND/FOREIGN LANGUAGE (TEACHING) RELATED

U of Ottawa (ON, Canada)

ENGLISH LANGUAGE AND LITERATURE RELATED

Burlington Coll (VT)
Columbia Coll (SC)
Columbia U, School of General Studies (NY)
Concordia Coll–New York (NY)
Dakota State U (SD)
Doane Coll (NE)
Drexel U (PA)
Eastern U (PA)

Emmanuel Coll (MA)
Fort Lewis Coll (CO)
Harvard U (MA)
Hofstra U (NY)
Middlebury Coll (VT)
Milligan Coll (TN)
Moravian Coll (PA)
Mount Mary Coll (WI)
Oklahoma City U (OK)
Patrick Henry Coll (VA)
Point Loma Nazarene U (CA)
Purdue U (IN)
Rowan U (NJ)
Saint Leo U (FL)
Saint Mary-of-the-Woods Coll (IN)
Saint Mary's Coll of California (CA)
Saint Mary's U of Minnesota (MN)
Sarah Lawrence Coll (NY)
State U of New York at Binghamton (NY)
Tabor Coll (KS)
Thiel Coll (PA)
U of Great Falls (MT)
U of Maine at Augusta (ME)
U of Michigan (MI)
U of Pennsylvania (PA)
The U of Western Ontario (ON, Canada)
Viterbo U (WI)
Washington U in St. Louis (MO)
Webster U (MO)
Western Kentucky U (KY)

ENGLISH/LANGUAGE ARTS TEACHER EDUCATION

Abilene Christian U (TX)
Adams State Coll (CO)
Albion Coll (MI)
Alma Coll (MI)
Alvernia U (PA)
Alverno Coll (WI)
Anderson U (IN)
Anderson U (SC)
Anna Maria Coll (MA)
Appalachian State U (NC)
Aquinas Coll (MI)
Arkansas State U (AR)
Arkansas Tech U (AR)
Arlington Baptist Coll (TX)
Assumption Coll (MA)
Auburn U (AL)
Augustana Coll (IL)
The Baptist Coll of Florida (FL)
Barry U (FL)
Bayamón Central U (PR)
Baylor U (TX)
Bethany Coll (KS)
Bethel Coll (IN)
Bethel U (MN)
Bethune-Cookman U (FL)
Bishop's U (QC, Canada)
Blackburn Coll (IL)
Bluefield Coll (VA)
Blue Mountain Coll (MS)
Bob Jones U (SC)
Boston U (MA)
Bowling Green State U (OH)
Bradley U (IL)
Brewton-Parker Coll (GA)
Bridgewater State U (MA)
Buena Vista U (IA)
Buffalo State Coll, State U of New York (NY)
Cabrini Coll (PA)
California State U, Chico (CA)
California State U, Long Beach (CA)
Calumet Coll of Saint Joseph (IN)
Cameron U (OK)
Campbellsville U (KY)
Capital U (OH)
Carroll Coll (MT)
The Catholic U of America (DC)
Cedarville U (OH)
Central Washington U (WA)
Christian Brothers U (TN)
Claflin U (SC)
Clearwater Christian Coll (FL)
The Coll at Brockport, State U of New York (NY)
The Coll of New Jersey (NJ)
The Coll of Saint Rose (NY)
Coll of the Ozarks (MO)
Colorado State U (CO)
Columbus State U (GA)

Concordia U (MI)
Concordia U Chicago (IL)
Concordia U, Nebraska (NE)
Corban U (OR)
Cornerstone U (MI)
Covenant Coll (GA)
Crown Coll (MN)
Culver-Stockton Coll (MO)
Daemen Coll (NY)
Dakota State U (SD)
Delaware State U (DE)
Delta State U (MS)
Dixie State Coll of Utah (UT)
Dominican Coll (NY)
Dowling Coll (NY)
Duquesne U (PA)
East Carolina U (NC)
East Central U (OK)
Eastern Michigan U (MI)
Eastern Washington U (WA)
East Texas Baptist U (TX)
Edgewood Coll (WI)
Elizabeth City State U (NC)
Elmhurst Coll (IL)
Elmira Coll (NY)
Emmanuel Coll (GA)
Faith Baptist Bible Coll and Theological Sem (IA)
Fayetteville State U (NC)
Ferris State U (MI)
Fitchburg State U (MA)
Florida Ag and Mech U (FL)
Florida Atlantic U (FL)
Fordham U (NY)
Fort Lewis Coll (CO)
Franklin Coll (IN)
Free Will Baptist Bible Coll (TN)
Friends U (KS)
Gardner-Webb U (NC)
Glenville State Coll (WV)
Goddard Coll (VT)
Grace Coll (IN)
Grambling State U (LA)
Grand Canyon U (AZ)
Grand Valley State U (MI)
Greenville Coll (IL)
Hannibal-LaGrange U (MO)
Harding U (AR)
Hardin-Simmons U (TX)
Hofstra U (NY)
Hope Coll (MI)
Howard Payne U (TX)
Huntingdon Coll (AL)
Huntington U (IN)
Indiana U Bloomington (IN)
Indiana U Northwest (IN)
Indiana U–Purdue U Fort Wayne (IN)
Indiana U–Purdue U Indianapolis (IN)
Indiana U South Bend (IN)
Indiana U Southeast (IN)
Indiana Wesleyan U (IN)
Inter American U of Puerto Rico, San Germán Campus (PR)
Iona Coll (NY)
Iowa Wesleyan Coll (IA)
Ithaca Coll (NY)
Jamestown Coll (ND)
Johnson C. Smith U (NC)
Johnson State Coll (VT)
Judson Coll (AL)
Juniata Coll (PA)
Keene State Coll (NH)
Kennesaw State U (GA)
Kentucky Christian U (KY)
Kentucky Wesleyan Coll (KY)
Keuka Coll (NY)
King Coll (TN)
La Roche Coll (PA)
Le Moyne Coll (NY)
Lenoir-Rhyne U (NC)
Lewis-Clark State Coll (ID)
Liberty U (VA)
Limestone Coll (SC)
Lincoln U (MO)
Lincoln U (PA)
Lipscomb U (TN)
Long Island U–Brooklyn Campus (NY)
Long Island U–C. W. Post Campus (NY)
Louisiana State U in Shreveport (LA)
Malone U (OH)

Manchester Coll (IN)
Manhattanville Coll (NY)
Mansfield U of Pennsylvania (PA)
Maranatha Baptist Bible Coll (WI)
Marian U (WI)
Maryville Coll (TN)
Marywood U (PA)
Mayville State U (ND)
McKendree U (IL)
McMurry U (TX)
Medaille Coll (NY)
Mercyhurst Coll (PA)
Merrimack Coll (MA)
Messiah Coll (PA)
Metropolitan State U (MN)
Miami U (OH)
Michigan Technological U (MI)
MidAmerica Nazarene U (KS)
Midwestern State U (TX)
Millikin U (IL)
Minnesota State U Moorhead (MN)
Minot State U (ND)
Misericordia U (PA)
Mississippi Coll (MS)
Mississippi Valley State U (MS)
Missouri State U (MO)
Missouri Western State U (MO)
Molloy Coll (NY)
Montana State U Billings (MT)
Montana State U–Northern (MT)
Morningside Coll (IA)
Morris Coll (SC)
Mount Marty Coll (SD)
Mount Mary Coll (WI)
Mount Vernon Nazarene U (OH)
Nazareth Coll of Rochester (NY)
Nebraska Wesleyan U (NE)
Nicholls State U (LA)
North Carolina Ag and Tech State U (NC)
North Carolina Central U (NC)
North Carolina State U (NC)
North Dakota State U (ND)
Northeastern State U (OK)
Northern Michigan U (MI)
North Greenville U (SC)
Northwestern Coll (MN)
Northwestern Oklahoma State U (OK)
Northwestern State U of Louisiana (LA)
Northwest Missouri State U (MO)
Northwest Nazarene U (ID)
Northwest U (WA)
Nyack Coll (NY)
Ohio Northern U (OH)
The Ohio State U at Lima (OH)
The Ohio State U at Marion (OH)
The Ohio State U–Mansfield Campus (OH)
The Ohio State U–Newark Campus (OH)
Oklahoma Christian U (OK)
Oklahoma City U (OK)
Oral Roberts U (OK)
Pace U (NY)
Paine Coll (GA)
Palm Beach Atlantic U (FL)
Peru State Coll (NE)
Philadelphia Biblical U (PA)
Piedmont Intl U (NC)
Pittsburg State U (KS)
Point Park U (PA)
Queens U of Charlotte (NC)
Reinhardt U (GA)
Rhode Island Coll (RI)
Rivier Coll (NH)
Roberts Wesleyan Coll (NY)
Rocky Mountain Coll (MT)
Rust Coll (MS)
Saginaw Valley State U (MI)
St. Ambrose U (IA)
St. Catherine U (MN)
Saint Francis U (PA)
St. John Fisher Coll (NY)
St. John's U (NY)
St. Joseph's Coll, Long Island Campus (NY)
St. Joseph's Coll, New York (NY)
Saint Joseph's Coll of Maine (ME)
Saint Joseph's U (PA)
Saint Mary's U of Minnesota (MN)
Saint Xavier U (IL)
Salve Regina U (RI)
Samford U (AL)

Schreiner U (TX)
Seattle Pacific U (WA)
Seton Hill U (PA)
Shaw U (NC)
Simpson U (CA)
Southeastern Louisiana U (LA)
Southeastern Oklahoma State U (OK)
Southeastern U (FL)
Southeast Missouri State U (MO)
Southern New Hampshire U (NH)
Southwest Baptist U (MO)
Southwestern Assemblies of God U (TX)
Southwestern Christian U (OK)
Southwestern Coll (KS)
Southwestern Oklahoma State U (OK)
Southwest Minnesota State U (MN)
Spring Arbor U (MI)
State U of New York at New Paltz (NY)
State U of New York at Plattsburgh (NY)
State U of New York Coll at Oneonta (NY)
Syracuse U (NY)
Tabor Coll (KS)
Taylor U (IN)
Temple U (PA)
Texas A&M Intl U (TX)
Texas Christian U (TX)
Texas Wesleyan U (TX)
Tiffin U (OH)
Trevecca Nazarene U (TN)
Trinity Christian Coll (IL)
Tusculum Coll (TN)
Union Coll (NE)
Universidad del Turabo (PR)
The U of Akron (OH)
U of Arkansas–Fort Smith (AR)
U of Central Florida (FL)
U of Delaware (DE)
U of Dubuque (IA)
U of Evansville (IN)
U of Georgia (GA)
U of Great Falls (MT)
U of Idaho (ID)
U of Illinois at Chicago (IL)
U of Illinois at Urbana–Champaign (IL)
U of Indianapolis (IN)
U of Lethbridge (AB, Canada)
U of Louisiana at Monroe (LA)
U of Maine (ME)
U of Maine at Farmington (ME)
U of Maine at Fort Kent (ME)
U of Mary (ND)
U of Mary Hardin-Baylor (TX)
U of Michigan–Flint (MI)
U of Minnesota, Twin Cities Campus (MN)
U of Mississippi (MS)
U of Missouri–St. Louis (MO)
The U of Montana Western (MT)
U of Nebraska–Lincoln (NE)
U of New Orleans (LA)
The U of North Carolina at Charlotte (NC)
The U of North Carolina Wilmington (NC)
U of Oklahoma (OK)
U of Pittsburgh at Johnstown (PA)
U of Regina (SK, Canada)
U of Rio Grande (OH)
U of St. Francis (IL)
U of Saint Francis (IN)
U of St. Thomas (MN)
The U of South Dakota (SD)
U of South Florida (FL)
The U of Tennessee at Chattanooga (TN)
The U of Tennessee at Martin (TN)
The U of Toledo (OH)
U of Vermont (VT)
U of Windsor (ON, Canada)
U of Wisconsin–River Falls (WI)
U of Wisconsin–Superior (WI)
Ursuline Coll (OH)
Utah Valley U (UT)
Utica Coll (NY)
Valley City State U (ND)
Valparaiso U (IN)
Virginia Intermont Coll (VA)
Viterbo U (WI)

Penn State Schuylkill (PA)
Penn State Shenango (PA)
Penn State U Park (PA)
Penn State Wilkes-Barre (PA)
Penn State Worthington Scranton (PA)
Penn State York (PA)
Polytechnic U of Puerto Rico (PR)
Rensselaer Polytechnic Inst (NY)
Rice U (TX)
Roger Williams U (RI)
San Diego State U (CA)
Seattle U (WA)
South Dakota School of Mines and Technology (SD)
Southern Methodist U (TX)
Stanford U (CA)
State U of New York Coll of Environmental Science and Forestry (NY)
Stevens Inst of Technology (NJ)
Suffolk U (MA)
Syracuse U (NY)
Taylor U (IN)
Texas Tech U (TX)
Tufts U (MA)
Tulane U (LA)
United States Air Force Acad (CO)
United States Military Acad (NY)
U at Buffalo, the State U of New York (NY)
U of Alberta (AB, Canada)
U of California, Berkeley (CA)
U of California, Irvine (CA)
U of California, Merced (CA)
U of California, Riverside (CA)
U of Central Florida (FL)
U of Cincinnati (OH)
U of Colorado Boulder (CO)
U of Connecticut (CT)
U of Delaware (DE)
U of Florida (FL)
U of Georgia (GA)
U of Illinois at Urbana–Champaign (IL)
U of Miami (FL)
U of Nevada, Reno (NV)
U of New Hampshire (NH)
U of North Dakota (ND)
U of Notre Dame (IN)
U of Oklahoma (OK)
U of Pennsylvania (PA)
U of Regina (SK, Canada)
U of Southern California (CA)
U of Vermont (VT)
The U of Western Ontario (ON, Canada)
U of Windsor (ON, Canada)
U of Wisconsin–Platteville (WI)
Utah State U (UT)
Wilkes U (PA)
Worcester Polytechnic Inst (MA)
Yale U (CT)

ENVIRONMENTAL HEALTH

American U of Beirut (Lebanon)
Baylor U (TX)
Boise State U (ID)
Bowling Green State U (OH)
Colorado State U (CO)
Drury U (MO)
East Carolina U (NC)
East Central U (OK)
Eastern Kentucky U (KY)
East Tennessee State U (TN)
Illinois State U (IL)
Indiana U of Pennsylvania (PA)
Iowa Wesleyan Coll (IA)
Mississippi Valley State U (MS)
New Mexico State U (NM)
Oakland U (MI)
Ohio U (OH)
Purdue U (IN)
Roger Williams U (RI)
Texas Southern U (TX)
U of Arkansas at Little Rock (AR)
U of Georgia (GA)
U of Illinois at Urbana–Champaign (IL)
U of Massachusetts Lowell (MA)
The U of North Carolina at Chapel Hill (NC)
U of Regina (SK, Canada)
U of Southern Maine (ME)
U of Washington (WA)

Western Carolina U (NC)
Western Kentucky U (KY)
Wright State U (OH)
York Coll of the City U of New York (NY)

ENVIRONMENTAL PSYCHOLOGY

Embry-Riddle Aeronautical U–Daytona (FL)
Prescott Coll (AZ)
Purdue U (IN)

ENVIRONMENTAL SCIENCE

Abilene Christian U (TX)
Adrian Coll (MI)
Alaska Pacific U (AK)
Albright Coll (PA)
Allegheny Coll (PA)
Alverno Coll (WI)
American Public U System (WV)
Anna Maria Coll (MA)
Appalachian State U (NC)
Assumption Coll (MA)
Auburn U (AL)
Barnard Coll (NY)
Bayamón Central U (PR)
Baylor U (TX)
Bellarmine U (KY)
Benedictine U (IL)
Bennington Coll (VT)
Berry Coll (GA)
Bethel U (MN)
Bethune-Cookman U (FL)
Blackburn Coll (IL)
Bradley U (IL)
Briar Cliff U (IA)
Bridgewater Coll (VA)
Brigham Young U (UT)
Brown U (RI)
Bryant U (RI)
Buena Vista U (IA)
California Lutheran U (CA)
California State U, Fresno (CA)
California State U, Long Beach (CA)
California State U, Monterey Bay (CA)
California U of Pennsylvania (PA)
Calvin Coll (MI)
Canisius Coll (NY)
Capital U (OH)
Cedarville U (OH)
Central Methodist U (MO)
Central Michigan U (MI)
Chatham U (PA)
Chestnut Hill Coll (PA)
Claflin U (SC)
Clarion U of Pennsylvania (PA)
Clarkson U (NY)
Cleveland State U (OH)
Coe Coll (IA)
Colby Coll (ME)
The Colorado Coll (CO)
Colorado Mesa U (CO)
Columbia Coll (MO)
Columbia U, School of General Studies (NY)
Concordia U (QC, Canada)
Concordia U Chicago (IL)
Concordia U Texas (TX)
Dalhousie U (NS, Canada)
Delaware State U (DE)
DePaul U (IL)
DEREE - The American Coll of Greece (Greece)
Dickinson Coll (PA)
Dominican U (IL)
Drake U (IA)
Drury U (MO)
Duquesne U (PA)
Earlham Coll (IN)
Eastern Connecticut State U (CT)
Eastern New Mexico U (NM)
Eastern Washington U (WA)
Edinboro U of Pennsylvania (PA)
Elon U (NC)
Endicott Coll (MA)
The Evergreen State Coll (WA)
Fairleigh Dickinson U, Metropolitan Campus (NJ)
Florida Ag and Mech U (FL)
Florida Inst of Technology (FL)
Fordham U (NY)

Franklin & Marshall Coll (PA)
Gannon U (PA)
Gardner-Webb U (NC)
Geneva Coll (PA)
George Mason U (VA)
Georgia Coll & State U (GA)
Gettysburg Coll (PA)
Gonzaga U (WA)
Goshen Coll (IN)
Hardin-Simmons U (TX)
Hartwick Coll (NY)
Hawai'i Pacific U (HI)
Heidelberg U (OH)
Hood Coll (MD)
Humboldt State U (CA)
Hunter Coll of the City U of New York (NY)
Idaho State U (ID)
Indiana U Bloomington (IN)
Indiana U–Purdue U Indianapolis (IN)
Inter American U of Puerto Rico, Ponce Campus (PR)
Inter American U of Puerto Rico, San Germán Campus (PR)
John Brown U (AR)
The Johns Hopkins U (MD)
Juniata Coll (PA)
Kean U (NJ)
Keuka Coll (NY)
King's Coll (PA)
Kutztown U of Pennsylvania (PA)
Lewis U (IL)
Lincoln U (MO)
Lindenwood U (MO)
Lipscomb U (TN)
Long Island U–C. W. Post Campus (NY)
Louisiana State U and Ag and Mech Coll (LA)
Lourdes U (OH)
Loyola Marymount U (CA)
Loyola U Chicago (IL)
Lynchburg Coll (VA)
Madonna U (MI)
Marietta Coll (OH)
Marshall U (WV)
Marylhurst U (OR)
Maryville U of Saint Louis (MO)
Marywood U (PA)
Massachusetts Coll of Liberal Arts (MA)
Massachusetts Maritime Acad (MA)
McDaniel Coll (MD)
Mercer U (GA)
Messiah Coll (PA)
Metropolitan State Coll of Denver (CO)
Miami U (OH)
Michigan State U (MI)
Michigan Technological U (MI)
Midwestern State U (TX)
Mills Coll (CA)
Monmouth Coll (IL)
Montana State U (MT)
Muhlenberg Coll (PA)
National U (CA)
Nazareth Coll of Rochester (NY)
New England Coll (NH)
New Mexico State U (NM)
North Carolina Central U (NC)
North Carolina State U (NC)
Northeastern State U (OK)
Northern Arizona U (AZ)
Northern Kentucky U (KY)
Northern Michigan U (MI)
Northwest U (WA)
Oakland U (MI)
The Ohio State U (OH)
Oklahoma State U (OK)
Otterbein U (OH)
Pace U (NY)
Piedmont Coll (GA)
Pitzer Coll (CA)
Point Loma Nazarene U (CA)
Point Park U (PA)
Post U (CT)
Queens Coll of the City U of New York (NY)
Queen's U at Kingston (ON, Canada)
Queens U of Charlotte (NC)
Ramapo Coll of New Jersey (NJ)
Randolph Coll (VA)
Rensselaer Polytechnic Inst (NY)

Rochester Inst of Technology (NY)
Rocky Mountain Coll (MT)
Roger Williams U (RI)
St. Bonaventure U (NY)
Saint Francis U (PA)
Saint Joseph's Coll of Maine (ME)
Saint Louis U (MO)
St. Norbert Coll (WI)
Saint Vincent Coll (PA)
Salisbury U (MD)
Samford U (AL)
Sam Houston State U (TX)
Santa Clara U (CA)
Scripps Coll (CA)
Siena Heights U (MI)
Sierra Nevada Coll (NV)
Simmons Coll (MA)
Simon Fraser U (BC, Canada)
Simpson Coll (IA)
Skidmore Coll (NY)
Southeast Missouri State U (MO)
Southern Methodist U (TX)
Southwest Minnesota State U (MN)
State U of New York Coll at Cortland (NY)
Stephen F. Austin State U (TX)
Stetson U (FL)
Suffolk U (MA)
Sweet Briar Coll (VA)
Taylor U (IN)
Temple U (PA)
Texas A&M U (TX)
Texas A&M U–Corpus Christi (TX)
Texas Christian U (TX)
Texas State U–San Marcos (TX)
Thomas Edison State Coll (NJ)
Thomas More Coll (KY)
Trinity Coll (CT)
Troy U (AL)
United States Military Acad (NY)
U at Albany, State U of New York (NY)
The U of Alabama (AL)
U of Alberta (AB, Canada)
The U of Arizona (AZ)
U of Arkansas (AR)
U of California, Los Angeles (CA)
U of California, Riverside (CA)
U of Charleston (WV)
U of Delaware (DE)
U of Denver (CO)
U of Dubuque (IA)
U of Evansville (IN)
U of Florida (FL)
U of Guelph (ON, Canada)
U of Hawaii at Manoa (HI)
U of Houston (TX)
U of Houston–Clear Lake (TX)
U of Idaho (ID)
U of Illinois at Chicago (IL)
U of Illinois at Urbana–Champaign (IL)
U of Lethbridge (AB, Canada)
U of Maine (ME)
U of Maryland, Baltimore County (MD)
U of Maryland, Coll Park (MD)
U of Massachusetts Amherst (MA)
U of Michigan–Dearborn (MI)
U of Michigan–Flint (MI)
U of Minnesota, Duluth (MN)
U of Mobile (AL)
The U of Montana Western (MT)
U of Mount Union (OH)
U of Nebraska at Omaha (NE)
U of New England (ME)
U of New Hampshire (NH)
U of New Mexico (NM)
The U of North Carolina at Chapel Hill (NC)
The U of North Carolina Wilmington (NC)
U of Northern Iowa (IA)
U of Notre Dame (IN)
U of Oklahoma (OK)
U of Oregon (OR)
U of Ottawa (ON, Canada)
U of Rochester (NY)
U of St. Francis (IL)
U of St. Thomas (TX)
The U of Scranton (PA)
U of South Carolina (SC)
U of Southern Maine (ME)
U of South Florida (FL)

U of South Florida–St. Petersburg Campus (FL)
The U of Tennessee at Chattanooga (TN)
The U of Texas at Arlington (TX)
The U of Texas at San Antonio (TX)
U of the Incarnate Word (TX)
U of the Sciences in Philadelphia (PA)
U of Utah (UT)
U of Vermont (VT)
U of Virginia (VA)
U of Washington, Bothell (WA)
The U of Western Ontario (ON, Canada)
U of West Florida (FL)
U of West Georgia (GA)
U of Windsor (ON, Canada)
U of Wisconsin–Green Bay (WI)
U of Wisconsin–Madison (WI)
U of Wisconsin–River Falls (WI)
Upper Iowa U (IA)
Valdosta State U (GA)
Valparaiso U (IN)
Vassar Coll (NY)
Villanova U (PA)
Virginia Intermont Coll (VA)
Washington State U (WA)
Wayland Baptist U (TX)
Wayne State U (MI)
Wesleyan Coll (GA)
Western Carolina U (NC)
Western Washington U (WA)
Westminster Coll (MO)
West Texas A&M U (TX)
West Virginia Wesleyan Coll (WV)
Wheaton Coll (MA)
Wheeling Jesuit U (WV)
Willamette U (OR)
Williams Coll (MA)
Wilson Coll (PA)
Youngstown State U (OH)

ENVIRONMENTAL STUDIES

Acadia U (NS, Canada)
Adelphi U (NY)
Adrian Coll (MI)
Alaska Pacific U (AK)
Albion Coll (MI)
Alfred U (NY)
Allegheny Coll (PA)
American U (DC)
Amherst Coll (MA)
Appalachian State U (NC)
Ashland U (OH)
Augustana Coll (IL)
Bard Coll (NY)
Bard Coll at Simon's Rock (MA)
Barton Coll (NC)
Bates Coll (ME)
Baylor U (TX)
Bellarmine U (KY)
Beloit Coll (WI)
Bemidji State U (MN)
Bennington Coll (VT)
Bethany Coll (WV)
Bethel U (MN)
Birmingham-Southern Coll (AL)
Bishop's U (QC, Canada)
Black Hills State U (SD)
Boise State U (ID)
Boston Coll (MA)
Bowdoin Coll (ME)
Bowling Green State U (OH)
Brandeis U (MA)
Brevard Coll (NC)
Brown U (RI)
Bucknell U (PA)
California State U, East Bay (CA)
California State U, Monterey Bay (CA)
California State U, Sacramento (CA)
California State U, San Bernardino (CA)
Calvin Coll (MI)
Canisius Coll (NY)
Cape Breton U (NS, Canada)
Carleton Coll (MN)
Carroll Coll (MT)
Case Western Reserve U (OH)
Castleton State Coll (VT)
Catawba Coll (NC)
Central Coll (IA)
Chaminade U of Honolulu (HI)

Chatham U (PA)
Christopher Newport U (VA)
City Coll of the City U of New York (NY)
Claremont McKenna Coll (CA)
Cleveland State U (OH)
Coe Coll (IA)
Colby Coll (ME)
Colgate U (NY)
The Coll at Brockport, State U of New York (NY)
The Coll of Idaho (ID)
Coll of Saint Benedict (MN)
Coll of the Atlantic (ME)
Coll of the Holy Cross (MA)
The Coll of William and Mary (VA)
The Colorado Coll (CO)
Colorado Mountain Coll, Timberline Campus (CO)
Columbia Southern U (AL)
Concordia Coll (MN)
Concordia U Texas (TX)
Connecticut Coll (CT)
Cornell Coll (IA)
Creighton U (NE)
Curry Coll (MA)
Dalhousie U (NS, Canada)
Dartmouth Coll (NH)
Davidson Coll (NC)
Denison U (OH)
DePaul U (IL)
DePauw U (IN)
Dickinson Coll (PA)
Doane Coll (NE)
Dordt Coll (IA)
Drake U (IA)
Drew U (NJ)
Drexel U (PA)
Drury U (MO)
Earlham Coll (IN)
Eastern Kentucky U (KY)
Eastern Mennonite U (VA)
Eastern U (PA)
Eckerd Coll (FL)
Edinboro U of Pennsylvania (PA)
Elmhurst Coll (IL)
Elmira Coll (NY)
Elon U (NC)
Emory & Henry Coll (VA)
Emory U (GA)
The Evergreen State Coll (WA)
Ferrum Coll (VA)
Florida Intl U (FL)
Fort Lewis Coll (CO)
Framingham State U (MA)
Franklin & Marshall Coll (PA)
Franklin Coll Switzerland (Switzerland)
Furman U (SC)
The George Washington U (DC)
Georgia Coll & State U (GA)
Gettysburg Coll (PA)
Goddard Coll (VT)
Goodwin Coll (CT)
Goucher Coll (MD)
Guilford Coll (NC)
Gustavus Adolphus Coll (MN)
Hamilton Coll (NY)
Hamline U (MN)
Hampshire Coll (MA)
Hampton U (VA)
Harvard U (MA)
Hawai`i Pacific U (HI)
Heidelberg U (OH)
Hendrix Coll (AR)
Hobart and William Smith Colls (NY)
Hofstra U (NY)
Hollins U (VA)
Humboldt State U (CA)
Illinois Coll (IL)
Illinois Wesleyan U (IL)
Immaculata U (PA)
Indiana U Bloomington (IN)
Inter American U of Puerto Rico, San Germán Campus (PR)
Iowa State U of Science and Technology (IA)
Ithaca Coll (NY)
Jacksonville U (FL)
John Brown U (AR)
John Carroll U (OH)
The Johns Hopkins U (MD)
Johnson State Coll (VT)
Judson U (IL)

Juniata Coll (PA)
Keene State Coll (NH)
Keystone Coll (PA)
King's Coll (PA)
The King's U Coll (AB, Canada)
Knox Coll (IL)
Lake Forest Coll (IL)
Lakehead U (ON, Canada)
Lake Superior State U (MI)
Lamar U (TX)
La Salle U (PA)
Lasell Coll (MA)
Lawrence U (WI)
Lehigh U (PA)
Le Moyne Coll (NY)
Lenoir-Rhyne U (NC)
Lewis & Clark Coll (OR)
Lincoln Memorial U (TN)
Lincoln U (PA)
Linfield Coll (OR)
Lipscomb U (TN)
Long Island U–C. W. Post Campus (NY)
Luther Coll (IA)
Lynchburg Coll (VA)
Macalester Coll (MN)
Maharishi U of Management (IA)
Manchester Coll (IN)
Mansfield U of Pennsylvania (PA)
Marietta Coll (OH)
Marlboro Coll (VT)
Maryville Coll (TN)
Maryville U of Saint Louis (MO)
Massachusetts Coll of Liberal Arts (MA)
Massachusetts Maritime Acad (MA)
McDaniel Coll (MD)
McKendree U (IL)
Merrimack Coll (MA)
Messiah Coll (PA)
Miami U (OH)
Michigan State U (MI)
Middlebury Coll (VT)
Mills Coll (CA)
Minnesota State U Mankato (MN)
Minnesota State U Moorhead (MN)
Mitchell Coll (CT)
Molloy Coll (NY)
Montana State U Billings (MT)
Montreat Coll, Montreat (NC)
Moravian Coll (PA)
Mount Allison U (NB, Canada)
Mount Holyoke Coll (MA)
Mount St. Mary's U (MD)
Naropa U (CO)
Neumann U (PA)
New Coll of Florida (FL)
New England Coll (NH)
New Mexico Highlands U (NM)
New Mexico Inst of Mining and Technology (NM)
North Carolina Wesleyan Coll (NC)
Northeastern Illinois U (IL)
Northeastern U (MA)
Northern Arizona U (AZ)
Northern Illinois U (IL)
Northern State U (SD)
Northland Coll (WI)
Norwich U (VT)
Nova Scotia Ag Coll (NS, Canada)
Nova Southeastern U (FL)
Ohio Northern U (OH)
The Ohio State U (OH)
Ohio Wesleyan U (OH)
Oklahoma City U (OK)
Oregon Inst of Technology (OR)
Pace U (NY)
Pacific Lutheran U (WA)
Pacific Union Coll (CA)
Pacific U (OR)
Penn State U Altoona (PA)
Penn State U Park (PA)
Piedmont Coll (GA)
Plymouth State U (NH)
Pomona Coll (CA)
Portland State U (OR)
Post U (CT)
Prescott Coll (AZ)
Purchase Coll, State U of New York (NY)
Queens Coll of the City U of New York (NY)
Queens U of Charlotte (NC)
Ramapo Coll of New Jersey (NJ)
Randolph Coll (VA)

Randolph-Macon Coll (VA)
Regis U (CO)
The Richard Stockton Coll of New Jersey (NJ)
Rider U (NJ)
Ripon Coll (WI)
Roanoke Coll (VA)
Robert Morris U (PA)
Rocky Mountain Coll (MT)
Rollins Coll (FL)
Rosemont Coll (PA)
Rowan U (NJ)
Rutgers, The State U of New Jersey, Newark (NJ)
Rutgers, The State U of New Jersey, New Brunswick (NJ)
Saint Anselm Coll (NH)
St. Edward's U (TX)
Saint Francis U (PA)
Saint John's U (MN)
St. John's U (NY)
Saint Joseph's Coll of Maine (ME)
Saint Joseph's U (PA)
St. Lawrence U (NY)
Saint Leo U (FL)
Saint Michael's Coll (VT)
St. Olaf Coll (MN)
St. Thomas U (FL)
St. Thomas U (NB, Canada)
Saint Vincent Coll (PA)
San Diego State U (CA)
San Francisco State U (CA)
Santa Clara U (CA)
Sarah Lawrence Coll (NY)
Seattle U (WA)
Sewanee: The U of the South (TN)
Shaw U (NC)
Shenandoah U (VA)
Shepherd U (WV)
Shippensburg U of Pennsylvania (PA)
Shorter U (GA)
Siena Coll (NY)
Skidmore Coll (NY)
Smith Coll (MA)
Sonoma State U (CA)
South Dakota State U (SD)
Southern Methodist U (TX)
Southern New Hampshire U (NH)
Southern Oregon U (OR)
Southwestern U (TX)
Spelman Coll (GA)
Stanford U (CA)
State U of New York at Binghamton (NY)
State U of New York at Fredonia (NY)
State U of New York at Plattsburgh (NY)
State U of New York Coll at Cortland (NY)
State U of New York Coll at Oneonta (NY)
State U of New York Coll of Environmental Science and Forestry (NY)
Sterling Coll (VT)
Stonehill Coll (MA)
Stony Brook U, State U of New York (NY)
Sul Ross State U (TX)
Sweet Briar Coll (VA)
Tarleton State U (TX)
Temple U (PA)
Texas A&M U (TX)
Texas A&M U–Corpus Christi (TX)
Texas Southern U (TX)
Thiel Coll (PA)
Thomas Edison State Coll (NJ)
Trent U (ON, Canada)
Trine U (IN)
Tufts U (MA)
Tulane U (LA)
Tusculum Coll (TN)
Tuskegee U (AL)
United States Military Acad (NY)
Université de Sherbrooke (QC, Canada)
U of Alberta (AB, Canada)
The U of Arizona (AZ)
The U of British Columbia (BC, Canada)
The U of British Columbia–Okanagan (BC, Canada)
U of California, Davis (CA)

U of California, Irvine (CA)
U of California, Santa Barbara (CA)
U of California, Santa Cruz (CA)
U of Central Arkansas (AR)
U of Cincinnati (OH)
U of Colorado Boulder (CO)
U of Connecticut (CT)
U of Dayton (OH)
U of Delaware (DE)
U of Dubuque (IA)
U of Evansville (IN)
The U of Findlay (OH)
U of Georgia (GA)
U of Guelph (ON, Canada)
U of Indianapolis (IN)
The U of Iowa (IA)
The U of Kansas (KS)
U of Maine at Farmington (ME)
U of Maine at Fort Kent (ME)
U of Maine at Presque Isle (ME)
U of Maryland, Baltimore County (MD)
U of Maryland Eastern Shore (MD)
U of Michigan (MI)
U of Michigan–Dearborn (MI)
U of Minnesota, Duluth (MN)
U of Minnesota, Twin Cities Campus (MN)
U of Missouri (MO)
U of Missouri–Kansas City (MO)
The U of Montana Western (MT)
U of Nebraska–Lincoln (NE)
U of Nevada, Las Vegas (NV)
U of New England (ME)
U of New Orleans (LA)
The U of North Carolina at Asheville (NC)
The U of North Carolina at Chapel Hill (NC)
The U of North Carolina Wilmington (NC)
U of North Dakota (ND)
U of Oklahoma (OK)
U of Oregon (OR)
U of Ottawa (ON, Canada)
U of Pennsylvania (PA)
U of Pittsburgh at Bradford (PA)
U of Pittsburgh at Johnstown (PA)
U of Portland (OR)
U of Redlands (CA)
U of Rhode Island (RI)
U of Richmond (VA)
U of Rochester (NY)
U of Saint Francis (IN)
U of St. Thomas (TX)
U of San Diego (CA)
U of Southern California (CA)
U of Southern Maine (ME)
The U of Tampa (FL)
The U of Tennessee at Martin (TN)
U of the District of Columbia (DC)
U of the Ozarks (AR)
U of the Pacific (CA)
The U of Toledo (OH)
U of Toronto (ON, Canada)
U of Tulsa (OK)
U of Utah (UT)
U of Vermont (VT)
The U of Virginia's Coll at Wise (VA)
U of Washington (WA)
U of Washington, Bothell (WA)
The U of Western Ontario (ON, Canada)
U of West Georgia (GA)
U of Windsor (ON, Canada)
U of Wisconsin–Green Bay (WI)
U of Wisconsin–Madison (WI)
U of Wisconsin–River Falls (WI)
U of Wyoming (WY)
Vassar Coll (NY)
Villanova U (PA)
Virginia Commonwealth U (VA)
Virginia Polytechnic Inst and State U (VA)
Virginia Wesleyan Coll (VA)
Warren Wilson Coll (NC)
Washington & Jefferson Coll (PA)
Washington and Lee U (VA)
Washington Coll (MD)
Washington U in St. Louis (MO)
Waynesburg U (PA)
Wellesley Coll (MA)
Wells Coll (NY)
Wesleyan U (CT)
Western Michigan U (MI)

Western State Coll of Colorado (CO)
Western Washington U (WA)
Westminster Coll (MO)
Westminster Coll (UT)
Wheaton Coll (IL)
Wheeling Jesuit U (WV)
Widener U (PA)
William Paterson U of New Jersey (NJ)
Williams Coll (MA)
Wofford Coll (SC)
Worcester Polytechnic Inst (MA)
Yale U (CT)

ENVIRONMENTAL TOXICOLOGY
Clarkson U (NY)
U of California, Davis (CA)

EPIDEMIOLOGY
U of Rochester (NY)

EQUESTRIAN STUDIES
Asbury U (KY)
Averett U (VA)
Becker Coll (MA)
Centenary Coll (NJ)
Colorado State U (CO)
Houghton Coll (NY)
Judson Coll (AL)
Lake Erie Coll (OH)
Mount Ida Coll (MA)
North Dakota State U (ND)
Otterbein U (OH)
Post U (CT)
Rocky Mountain Coll (MT)
Rutgers, The State U of New Jersey, New Brunswick (NJ)
Saint Mary-of-the-Woods Coll (IN)
Stephens Coll (MO)
Sul Ross State U (TX)
The U of Findlay (OH)
The U of Montana Western (MT)
U of Wisconsin–River Falls (WI)
Virginia Intermont Coll (VA)
West Texas A&M U (TX)
William Woods U (MO)
Wilson Coll (PA)

ETHICS
Bridgewater State U (MA)
Carnegie Mellon U (PA)
Carroll Coll (MT)
Drake U (IA)
Syracuse U (NY)
U of Michigan–Flint (MI)
U of Ottawa (ON, Canada)
U of Southern California (CA)
U of Washington, Bothell (WA)
The U of Western Ontario (ON, Canada)

ETHNIC, CULTURAL MINORITY, GENDER, AND GROUP STUDIES RELATED
Albion Coll (MI)
American U (DC)
Arizona State U (AZ)
Bard Coll at Simon's Rock (MA)
Boston U (MA)
Bowling Green State U (OH)
Burlington Coll (VT)
California Polytechnic State U, San Luis Obispo (CA)
California State Polytechnic U, Pomona (CA)
California State U, Chico (CA)
California State U, Stanislaus (CA)
Carnegie Mellon U (PA)
Chatham U (PA)
The Colorado Coll (CO)
Columbia U, School of General Studies (NY)
Connecticut Coll (CT)
Cornell Coll (IA)
The Evergreen State Coll (WA)
Grinnell Coll (IA)
Hampshire Coll (MA)
Hawai`i Pacific U (HI)
Indiana U Bloomington (IN)
Lawrence U (WI)
Marlboro Coll (VT)

Metropolitan State U (MN)
Mills Coll (CA)
Mount Holyoke Coll (MA)
Saint Michael's Coll (VT)
Santa Clara U (CA)
Skidmore Coll (NY)
Stanford U (CA)
Stonehill Coll (MA)
U at Buffalo, the State U of New York (NY)
U of Alberta (AB, Canada)
U of California, Berkeley (CA)
U of Colorado at Colorado Springs (CO)
U of Colorado Boulder (CO)
U of Denver (CO)
U of Hawaii at Manoa (HI)
U of Illinois at Chicago (IL)
U of Nebraska–Lincoln (NE)
U of Pittsburgh (PA)
U of Regina (SK, Canada)
U of Southern California (CA)
U of Utah (UT)
The U of Western Ontario (ON, Canada)
Washington State U (WA)
Washington U in St. Louis (MO)
Wellesley Coll (MA)
Westfield State U (MA)
Whitman Coll (WA)
Wichita State U (KS)
Williams Coll (MA)
Yale U (CT)

ETHNIC STUDIES
Arizona State U (AZ)
Colorado State U (CO)
Goddard Coll (VT)
Minnesota State U Moorhead (MN)
St. Olaf Coll (MN)
U of San Diego (CA)
The U of Texas at Austin (TX)

EUROPEAN HISTORY
Bard Coll (NY)
Bennington Coll (VT)
Gettysburg Coll (PA)
Howard Payne U (TX)
Keene State Coll (NH)
Salem State U (MA)
Sarah Lawrence Coll (NY)
Suffolk U (MA)
U of Regina (SK, Canada)

EUROPEAN STUDIES
American U in Bulgaria (Bulgaria)
The American U of Paris (France)
Amherst Coll (MA)
Bard Coll (NY)
Bard Coll at Simon's Rock (MA)
Belmont U (TN)
Beloit Coll (WI)
Bennington Coll (VT)
Bowling Green State U (OH)
Brandeis U (MA)
California State U, Fullerton (CA)
Canisius Coll (NY)
Carnegie Mellon U (PA)
Central Michigan U (MI)
The Coll at Brockport, State U of New York (NY)
Dalhousie U (NS, Canada)
Fort Lewis Coll (CO)
Georgetown Coll (KY)
The George Washington U (DC)
Gettysburg Coll (PA)
Hampshire Coll (MA)
Hillsdale Coll (MI)
Hobart and William Smith Colls (NY)
Loyola Marymount U (CA)
Marlboro Coll (VT)
Middlebury Coll (VT)
Millsaps Coll (MS)
Mount Holyoke Coll (MA)
New Coll of Florida (FL)
New York U (NY)
Ohio U (OH)
Portland State U (OR)
Sacred Heart U (CT)
Saint Joseph's U (PA)
Saint Mary's Coll of California (CA)
San Diego State U (CA)
Sarah Lawrence Coll (NY)

Scripps Coll (CA)
Seattle Pacific U (WA)
Sewanee: The U of the South (TN)
Stony Brook U, State U of New York (NY)
Texas State U–San Marcos (TX)
Trinity U (TX)
United States Military Acad (NY)
The U of British Columbia (BC, Canada)
U of California, Irvine (CA)
U of California, Los Angeles (CA)
U of Delaware (DE)
U of Guelph (ON, Canada)
The U of Kansas (KS)
U of Minnesota, Twin Cities Campus (MN)
U of Missouri (MO)
U of New Hampshire (NH)
U of New Mexico (NM)
The U of North Carolina at Chapel Hill (NC)
U of Richmond (VA)
U of South Carolina (SC)
The U of Texas at Austin (TX)
The U of Toledo (OH)
U of Toronto (ON, Canada)
U of Vermont (VT)
U of Washington (WA)
Vanderbilt U (TN)
Washington U in St. Louis (MO)

EUROPEAN STUDIES (WESTERN)
Illinois Wesleyan U (IL)
Seattle U (WA)
U of Nebraska–Lincoln (NE)

EVOLUTIONARY BIOLOGY
Bennington Coll (VT)
Case Western Reserve U (OH)
Coll of the Atlantic (ME)
Columbia U, School of General Studies (NY)
Dartmouth Coll (NH)
Harvard U (MA)
Rice U (TX)
Rutgers, The State U of New Jersey, New Brunswick (NJ)
Tulane U (LA)
Yale U (CT)

EXECUTIVE ASSISTANT/ EXECUTIVE SECRETARY
Bowling Green State U (OH)
Caribbean U (PR)
Inter American U of Puerto Rico, Bayamón Campus (PR)
U of Puerto Rico at Bayamón (PR)
U of Puerto Rico at Ponce (PR)

EXERCISE PHYSIOLOGY
Baldwin-Wallace Coll (OH)
Baylor U (TX)
Bethany Lutheran Coll (MN)
Biola U (CA)
The Coll at Brockport, State U of New York (NY)
The Coll of St. Scholastica (MN)
East Carolina U (NC)
Fitchburg State U (MA)
Grand Canyon U (AZ)
Lynchburg Coll (VA)
Merrimack Coll (MA)
Ohio Northern U (OH)
Saint Francis U (PA)
U at Buffalo, the State U of New York (NY)
U of California, Davis (CA)
U of Delaware (DE)
U of Florida (FL)
U of Massachusetts Amherst (MA)
U of Southern Maine (ME)
West Virginia U (WV)

EXPERIMENTAL PSYCHOLOGY
Keene State Coll (NH)
Marlboro Coll (VT)
Moravian Coll (PA)
Northern Michigan U (MI)
Tiffin U (OH)
Tufts U (MA)
U of Alberta (AB, Canada)

The U of British Columbia (BC, Canada)
U of South Carolina (SC)
The U of Toledo (OH)

FACILITIES PLANNING AND MANAGEMENT
Eastern Michigan U (MI)
Missouri State U (MO)
New York City Coll of Technology of the City U of New York (NY)

FAMILY AND COMMUNITY SERVICES
Andrews U (MI)
Bowling Green State U (OH)
Curry Coll (MA)
East Carolina U (NC)
Eastern Kentucky U (KY)
Harding U (AR)
Iowa State U of Science and Technology (IA)
John Brown U (AR)
Keystone Coll (PA)
La Roche Coll (PA)
Lubbock Christian U (TX)
Messiah Coll (PA)
Michigan State U (MI)
Oklahoma Christian U (OK)
Prairie View A&M U (TX)
Stevenson U (MD)
Texas Tech U (TX)
Union U (TN)
U of California, Santa Cruz (CA)
U of Florida (FL)
U of Maryland, Coll Park (MD)
U of Miami (FL)
U of Minnesota, Twin Cities Campus (MN)
U of Northern Iowa (IA)
U of Wisconsin–Madison (WI)
Youngstown State U (OH)

FAMILY AND CONSUMER ECONOMICS RELATED
Andrews U (MI)
Ashland U (OH)
Bob Jones U (SC)
Bowling Green State U (OH)
Brigham Young U (UT)
California State U, Fresno (CA)
California State U, Sacramento (CA)
Carson-Newman Coll (TN)
Fairmont State U (WV)
Iowa State U of Science and Technology (IA)
Louisiana Coll (LA)
Minnesota State U Mankato (MN)
The U of Akron (OH)
U of Alberta (AB, Canada)
U of Hawaii at Manoa (HI)
U of Maryland Eastern Shore (MD)
U of Minnesota, Twin Cities Campus (MN)
U of Missouri (MO)
U of Nebraska at Kearney (NE)
U of Nebraska–Lincoln (NE)
U of Northern Iowa (IA)
U of Wisconsin–Stevens Point (WI)
Utah State U (UT)
Virginia State U (VA)

FAMILY AND CONSUMER SCIENCES/HOME ECONOMICS TEACHER EDUCATION
Appalachian State U (NC)
Ashland U (OH)
Baylor U (TX)
Bluffton U (OH)
Bowling Green State U (OH)
Bradley U (IL)
Bridgewater Coll (VA)
Carson-Newman Coll (TN)
Cheyney U of Pennsylvania (PA)
Colorado State U (CO)
Concordia U, Nebraska (NE)
East Carolina U (NC)
Eastern Kentucky U (KY)
Fairmont State U (WV)
Fontbonne U (MO)
Georgia Southern U (GA)
Hampton U (VA)

Harding U (AR)
Immaculata U (PA)
Iowa State U of Science and Technology (IA)
Jacksonville State U (AL)
Lamar U (TX)
Liberty U (VA)
Marywood U (PA)
Mercyhurst Coll (PA)
Messiah Coll (PA)
Michigan State U (MI)
Minnesota State U Mankato (MN)
Missouri State U (MO)
Mount Vernon Nazarene U (OH)
New Mexico State U (NM)
North Carolina Ag and Tech State U (NC)
North Dakota State U (ND)
Northern Illinois U (IL)
Northwest Missouri State U (MO)
The Ohio State U (OH)
The Ohio State U at Lima (OH)
Ohio U (OH)
Pittsburg State U (KS)
Queens Coll of the City U of New York (NY)
St. Catherine U (MN)
Seton Hill U (PA)
South Carolina State U (SC)
Southeast Missouri State U (MO)
State U of New York Coll at Oneonta (NY)
The U of Akron (OH)
U of Alberta (AB, Canada)
U of Central Arkansas (AR)
U of Georgia (GA)
U of Guam (GU)
U of Louisiana at Monroe (LA)
U of Maryland Eastern Shore (MD)
U of Minnesota, Twin Cities Campus (MN)
The U of Tennessee at Martin (TN)
U of the District of Columbia (DC)
U of Wisconsin–Stevens Point (WI)
U of Wisconsin–Stout (WI)
Utah State U (UT)
Virginia Polytechnic Inst and State U (VA)
Washington State U (WA)
Wayne State Coll (NE)
Western Kentucky U (KY)
Western Michigan U (MI)
Winthrop U (SC)
Youngstown State U (OH)

FAMILY AND CONSUMER SCIENCES/HUMAN SCIENCES
Ashland U (OH)
Auburn U (AL)
Ball State U (IN)
Baylor U (TX)
Berea Coll (KY)
Bluffton U (OH)
Bowling Green State U (OH)
Bradley U (IL)
Bridgewater Coll (VA)
Brigham Young U (UT)
California State U, East Bay (CA)
California State U, Long Beach (CA)
Carson-Newman Coll (TN)
Central Washington U (WA)
Coll of the Atlantic (ME)
Coll of the Ozarks (MO)
Colorado State U (CO)
Delaware State U (DE)
Delta State U (MS)
East Central U (OK)
Eastern Illinois U (IL)
Eastern Kentucky U (KY)
Eastern New Mexico U (NM)
East Tennessee State U (TN)
Fairmont State U (WV)
Fontbonne U (MO)
Framingham State U (MA)
George Fox U (OR)
Great Lakes Christian Coll (MI)
Harding U (AR)
Idaho State U (ID)
Illinois State U (IL)
Indiana State U (IN)
Indiana U of Pennsylvania (PA)
Iowa State U of Science and Technology (IA)
Jacksonville State U (AL)

Lamar U (TX)
Liberty U (VA)
Lipscomb U (TN)
Louisiana State U and Ag and Mech Coll (LA)
Madonna U (MI)
Marshall U (WV)
The Master's Coll and Sem (CA)
Meredith Coll (NC)
Michigan State U (MI)
Minnesota State U Mankato (MN)
Mississippi State U (MS)
Montana State U (MT)
Montclair State U (NJ)
Mount Vernon Nazarene U (OH)
New Mexico Highlands U (NM)
Nicholls State U (LA)
North Carolina Ag and Tech State U (NC)
North Carolina Central U (NC)
Northeastern State U (OK)
Northwestern State U of Louisiana (LA)
Pittsburg State U (KS)
Point Loma Nazarene U (CA)
Prairie View A&M U (TX)
Purdue U (IN)
Queens Coll of the City U of New York (NY)
Regis U (CO)
Rutgers, The State U of New Jersey, New Brunswick (NJ)
St. Catherine U (MN)
Sam Houston State U (TX)
San Francisco State U (CA)
Seattle Pacific U (WA)
Seton Hill U (PA)
Shepherd U (WV)
South Carolina State U (SC)
Southeastern Louisiana U (LA)
Southeast Missouri State U (MO)
State U of New York Coll at Oneonta (NY)
Stephen F. Austin State U (TX)
Tarleton State U (TX)
Texas A&M U–Kingsville (TX)
Texas Southern U (TX)
Texas State U–San Marcos (TX)
Texas Tech U (TX)
Texas Woman's U (TX)
The U of Alabama (AL)
U of Alberta (AB, Canada)
U of Arkansas (AR)
The U of British Columbia (BC, Canada)
U of Central Arkansas (AR)
U of Central Missouri (MO)
U of Maryland Eastern Shore (MD)
U of Minnesota, Twin Cities Campus (MN)
U of New Mexico (NM)
U of North Alabama (AL)
U of Saint Joseph (CT)
The U of Tennessee at Martin (TN)
The U of Texas at Austin (TX)
The U of Western Ontario (ON, Canada)
U of Wyoming (WY)
Washington State U (WA)
Wayne State Coll (NE)
Western Illinois U (IL)
Youngstown State U (OH)

FAMILY AND CONSUMER SCIENCES/HUMAN SCIENCES BUSINESS SERVICES RELATED
Brigham Young U (UT)
U of Illinois at Urbana–Champaign (IL)

FAMILY AND CONSUMER SCIENCES/HUMAN SCIENCES COMMUNICATION
U of Georgia (GA)

FAMILY AND CONSUMER SCIENCES/HUMAN SCIENCES RELATED
California State U, Long Beach (CA)
Norfolk State U (VA)
U of Minnesota, Twin Cities Campus (MN)

The U of Western Ontario (ON, Canada)

FAMILY PRACTICE NURSING
Grand Valley State U (MI)
Michigan State U (MI)
Ryerson U (ON, Canada)
The U of Virginia's Coll at Wise (VA)
The U of Western Ontario (ON, Canada)
U of Windsor (ON, Canada)

FAMILY PSYCHOLOGY
Corban U (OR)

FAMILY RESOURCE MANAGEMENT
Arizona State U (AZ)
Brigham Young U (UT)
Iowa State U of Science and Technology (IA)
Middle Tennessee State U (TN)
The Ohio State U (OH)
The Ohio State U at Lima (OH)
Ohio U (OH)
Pittsburg State U (KS)
South Dakota State U (SD)
Texas Tech U (TX)
The U of Alabama (AL)
U of Georgia (GA)

FAMILY SYSTEMS
Anderson U (IN)
Bowling Green State U (OH)
Central Michigan U (MI)
John Brown U (AR)
Lipscomb U (TN)
Lubbock Christian U (TX)
Mid-Atlantic Christian U (NC)
Mississippi U for Women (MS)
Spring Arbor U (MI)
Towson U (MD)
The U of Akron (OH)
U of Minnesota, Twin Cities Campus (MN)
U of Southern Mississippi (MS)
Weber State U (UT)
Western Michigan U (MI)

FARM AND RANCH MANAGEMENT
Colorado State U (CO)
Eastern Kentucky U (KY)
Iowa State U of Science and Technology (IA)
Lake Erie Coll (OH)
Tarleton State U (TX)
Texas A&M U (TX)
Texas Christian U (TX)
U of Alberta (AB, Canada)
The U of Findlay (OH)
U of Illinois at Urbana–Champaign (IL)
U of Minnesota, Crookston (MN)

FASHION/APPAREL DESIGN
Acad of Art U (CA)
The Art Inst of California, a college of Argosy U, Hollywood (CA)
The Art Inst of California, a college of Argosy U, Inland Empire (CA)
The Art Inst of California, a college of Argosy U, Los Angeles (CA)
The Art Inst of California, a college of Argosy U, Orange County (CA)
The Art Inst of California, a college of Argosy U, San Diego (CA)
The Art Inst of California, a college of Argosy U, San Francisco (CA)
The Art Inst of Colorado (CO)
The Art Inst of Dallas (TX)
The Art Inst of Fort Lauderdale (FL)
The Art Inst of Houston (TX)
The Art Inst of Indianapolis (IN)
The Art Inst of Philadelphia (PA)
The Art Inst of Pittsburgh (PA)
The Art Inst of Portland (OR)
The Art Inst of Seattle (WA)
The Art Inst of Tucson (AZ)
Baylor U (TX)
Bennington Coll (VT)
Bowling Green State U (OH)
Brenau U (GA)

Buffalo State Coll, State U of New York (NY)
California Coll of the Arts (CA)
Centenary Coll (NJ)
Clark Atlanta U (GA)
Columbia Coll Chicago (IL)
Columbus Coll of Art & Design (OH)
Dalhousie U (NS, Canada)
Dominican U (IL)
Drexel U (PA)
Escuela de Artes Plasticas de Puerto Rico (PR)
Fashion Inst of Technology (NY)
Ferris State U (MI)
Hampton U (VA)
The Illinois Inst of Art–Chicago (IL)
The Illinois Inst of Art–Schaumburg (IL)
Intl Acad of Design & Technology (FL)
Iowa State U of Science and Technology (IA)
Kent State U (OH)
Lamar U (TX)
Lasell Coll (MA)
Lindenwood U (MO)
Marymount U (VA)
Massachusetts Coll of Art and Design (MA)
Meredith Coll (NC)
Miami Intl U of Art & Design (FL)
Michigan State U (MI)
Montclair State U (NJ)
Moore Coll of Art & Design (PA)
Mount Ida Coll (MA)
Mount Mary Coll (WI)
O'More Coll of Design (TN)
Otis Coll of Art and Design (CA)
Philadelphia U (PA)
Point Loma Nazarene U (CA)
Pratt Inst (NY)
Ryerson U (ON, Canada)
Sacred Heart U (CT)
St. Catherine U (MN)
Savannah Coll of Art and Design (GA)
Stephens Coll (MO)
Syracuse U (NY)
Texas Tech U (TX)
Texas Woman's U (TX)
U of Cincinnati (OH)
U of Delaware (DE)
U of Maryland Eastern Shore (MD)
U of Minnesota, Twin Cities Campus (MN)
U of North Texas (TX)
U of the Incarnate Word (TX)
Ursuline Coll (OH)
Villa Maria Coll of Buffalo (NY)
Virginia Commonwealth U (VA)
Washington U in St. Louis (MO)
Woodbury U (CA)

FASHION MERCHANDISING
The Art Inst of California, a college of Argosy U, Hollywood (CA)
The Art Inst of California, a college of Argosy U, Los Angeles (CA)
The Art Inst of California, a college of Argosy U, Orange County (CA)
The Art Inst of California, a college of Escuela of Argosy U, San Diego (CA)
The Art Inst of California, a college of Argosy U, San Francisco (CA)
The Art Inst of California, a college of Argosy U, Sunnyvale (CA)
The Art Inst of Charlotte (NC)
The Art Inst of Colorado (CO)
The Art Inst of Fort Lauderdale (FL)
The Art Inst of Houston (TX)
The Art Inst of Michigan (MI)
The Art Inst of Michigan–Troy (MI)
The Art Inst of Ohio–Cincinnati (OH)
The Art Inst of Phoenix (AZ)
The Art Inst of Portland (OR)
The Art Inst of Raleigh-Durham (NC)
The Art Inst of Seattle (WA)
The Art Inst of Tucson (AZ)
The Art Inst of Wisconsin (WI)
The Art Insts Intl–Kansas City (KS)
Ashland U (OH)
Baylor U (TX)
Bowling Green State U (OH)

Bradley U (IL)
Brenau U (GA)
Buffalo State Coll, State U of New York (NY)
California State U, Long Beach (CA)
Carson-Newman Coll (TN)
Central Washington U (WA)
Delaware State U (DE)
Dominican U (IL)
East Central U (OK)
Eastern Kentucky U (KY)
Eastern Michigan U (MI)
Fashion Inst of Technology (NY)
Fontbonne U (MO)
Hampton U (VA)
Harding U (AR)
The Illinois Inst of Art–Chicago (IL)
The Illinois Inst of Art–Schaumburg (IL)
The Illinois Inst of Art–Tinley Park (IL)
Immaculata U (PA)
Indiana U of Pennsylvania (PA)
Intl Acad of Design & Technology (FL)
Kent State U (OH)
Lamar U (TX)
Lasell Coll (MA)
Liberty U (VA)
Lindenwood U (MO)
Lipscomb U (TN)
Louisiana State U and Ag and Mech Coll (LA)
Mars Hill Coll (NC)
Marymount U (VA)
Mercyhurst Coll (PA)
Meredith Coll (NC)
Miami Intl U of Art & Design (FL)
Mount Ida Coll (MA)
Mount Mary Coll (WI)
Newbury Coll (MA)
Northern Arizona U (AZ)
Northwood U, Michigan Campus (MI)
Philadelphia U (PA)
Pittsburg State U (KS)
Sacred Heart U (CT)
St. Catherine U (MN)
State U of New York Coll at Oneonta (NY)
Stephen F. Austin State U (TX)
Stephens Coll (MO)
Stevens Inst of Business & Arts (MO)
Texas Christian U (TX)
Texas State U–San Marcos (TX)
Texas Tech U (TX)
Texas Woman's U (TX)
U of Bridgeport (CT)
U of Georgia (GA)
U of Illinois at Urbana–Champaign (IL)
U of Louisiana at Lafayette (LA)
U of Maryland Eastern Shore (MD)
U of Minnesota, Twin Cities Campus (MN)
U of North Texas (TX)
The U of Tennessee at Martin (TN)
Ursuline Coll (OH)
Utah State U (UT)
Woodbury U (CA)
Youngstown State U (OH)

FIBER, TEXTILE AND WEAVING ARTS
Acad of Art U (CA)
Adams State Coll (CO)
Alberta Coll of Art & Design (AB, Canada)
Bowling Green State U (OH)
California Coll of the Arts (CA)
California State U, Long Beach (CA)
The Cleveland Inst of Art (OH)
Cornell U (NY)
Kansas City Art Inst (MO)
Maryland Inst Coll of Art (MD)
Massachusetts Coll of Art and Design (MA)
Mercyhurst Coll (PA)
Philadelphia U (PA)
Savannah Coll of Art and Design (GA)
Temple U (PA)

The U of Kansas (KS)
U of Massachusetts Dartmouth (MA)
U of Michigan (MI)
U of Oregon (OR)
U of Washington (WA)
Western Washington U (WA)

FILIPINO/TAGALOG
U of Hawaii at Manoa (HI)

FILM/CINEMA/VIDEO STUDIES
American U (DC)
The American U of Paris (France)
The American U of Rome (Italy)
Baldwin-Wallace Coll (OH)
Bard Coll (NY)
Barnard Coll (NY)
Bennington Coll (VT)
Bishop's U (QC, Canada)
Boston Coll (MA)
Bowling Green State U (OH)
Brandeis U (MA)
Brigham Young U (UT)
Brown U (RI)
Burlington Coll (VT)
California Baptist U (CA)
California Coll of the Arts (CA)
California State U, Long Beach (CA)
California State U, Sacramento (CA)
Calvin Coll (MI)
Carleton Coll (MN)
Carson-Newman Coll (TN)
Centenary Coll of Louisiana (LA)
Chapman U (CA)
Claremont McKenna Coll (CA)
Clark U (MA)
The Cleveland Inst of Art (OH)
Coll of Staten Island of the City U of New York (NY)
The Colorado Coll (CO)
Columbia Coll Chicago (IL)
Columbia U, School of General Studies (NY)
Concordia U (QC, Canada)
Connecticut Coll (CT)
Cornell U (NY)
Curry Coll (MA)
Dartmouth Coll (NH)
Denison U (OH)
DeSales U (PA)
Eastern Michigan U (MI)
Eastern Washington U (WA)
Emory U (GA)
The Evergreen State Coll (WA)
Florida State U (FL)
Fordham U (NY)
Georgia State U (GA)
Grace Coll (IN)
Grand Valley State U (MI)
Hunter Coll of the City U of New York (NY)
Huntington U (IN)
Ithaca Coll (NY)
John Brown U (AR)
The Johns Hopkins U (MD)
Kean U (NJ)
Keene State Coll (NH)
Lafayette Coll (PA)
La Salle U (PA)
Long Island U–C. W. Post Campus (NY)
Marlboro Coll (VT)
McDaniel Coll (MD)
Memphis Coll of Art (TN)
Minnesota State U Moorhead (MN)
Mount Holyoke Coll (MA)
Northeastern U (MA)
Northwest U (WA)
Oakland U (MI)
The Ohio State U (OH)
Pace U (NY)
Penn State Abington (PA)
Penn State Altoona (PA)
Penn State Beaver (PA)
Penn State Berks (PA)
Penn State Brandywine (PA)
Penn State DuBois (PA)
Penn State Erie, The Behrend Coll (PA)
Penn State Fayette, The Eberly Campus (PA)

Penn State Greater Allegheny (PA)
Penn State Hazleton (PA)
Penn State Lehigh Valley (PA)
Penn State Mont Alto (PA)
Penn State New Kensington (PA)
Penn State Schuylkill (PA)
Penn State Shenango (PA)
Penn State U Park (PA)
Penn State Wilkes-Barre (PA)
Penn State Worthington Scranton (PA)
Penn State York (PA)
Pitzer Coll (CA)
Pomona Coll (CA)
Purchase Coll, State U of New York (NY)
Queens Coll of the City U of New York (NY)
Queen's U at Kingston (ON, Canada)
Quinnipiac U (CT)
Rhode Island Coll (RI)
Roger Williams U (RI)
Rowan U (NJ)
Rutgers, The State U of New Jersey, New Brunswick (NJ)
Saint Augustine's Coll (NC)
San Francisco State U (CA)
Sarah Lawrence Coll (NY)
Savannah Coll of Art and Design (GA)
School of the Museum of Fine Arts, Boston (MA)
Simon Fraser U (BC, Canada)
Smith Coll (MA)
Southeastern U (FL)
Southern Methodist U (TX)
Southwestern Coll (KS)
Stanford U (CA)
State U of New York at Fredonia (NY)
Stephens Coll (MO)
Stevenson U (MD)
Suffolk U (MA)
Temple U (PA)
U at Buffalo, the State U of New York (NY)
U of Alaska Fairbanks (AK)
U of Alberta (AB, Canada)
The U of British Columbia (BC, Canada)
U of California, Berkeley (CA)
U of California, Davis (CA)
U of California, Irvine (CA)
U of California, Los Angeles (CA)
U of California, Santa Barbara (CA)
U of California, Santa Cruz (CA)
U of Colorado Boulder (CO)
U of Georgia (GA)
U of Hartford (CT)
U of Illinois at Urbana–Champaign (IL)
The U of Iowa (IA)
The U of Kansas (KS)
U of Michigan (MI)
U of Minnesota, Twin Cities Campus (MN)
U of Nebraska–Lincoln (NE)
U of Nevada, Las Vegas (NV)
U of New Mexico (NM)
U of North Carolina School of the Arts (NC)
U of Oklahoma (OK)
U of Pennsylvania (PA)
U of Pittsburgh (PA)
U of Regina (SK, Canada)
U of Richmond (VA)
U of Rochester (NY)
U of Southern California (CA)
The U of Tampa (FL)
The U of Toledo (OH)
U of Tulsa (OK)
U of Utah (UT)
U of Vermont (VT)
The U of Western Ontario (ON, Canada)
U of Windsor (ON, Canada)
U of Wisconsin–Milwaukee (WI)
Vanderbilt U (TN)
Vassar Coll (NY)
Washington U in St. Louis (MO)
Watkins Coll of Art, Design, & Film (TN)
Wayne State U (MI)
Webster U (MO)

Wellesley Coll (MA)
Wesleyan U (CT)
Wheaton Coll (MA)
Whitman Coll (WA)
Wright State U (OH)
Yale U (CT)

FILM/VIDEO AND PHOTOGRAPHIC ARTS RELATED

Arizona State U (AZ)
Art Center Coll of Design (CA)
Birmingham-Southern Coll (AL)
Brigham Young U (UT)
Calvary Bible Coll and Theological Sem (MO)
Chatham U (PA)
Cleveland State U (OH)
Coe Coll (IA)
Coll of the Atlantic (ME)
Columbus Coll of Art & Design (OH)
Fairfield U (CT)
Five Towns Coll (NY)
Hampshire Coll (MA)
Hollins U (VA)
Kansas City Art Inst (MO)
La Roche Coll (PA)
Maryland Inst Coll of Art (MD)
New England School of Communications (ME)
Northern Michigan U (MI)
Oklahoma City U (OK)
Pratt Inst (NY)
Ringling Coll of Art and Design (FL)
Ryerson U (ON, Canada)
Saint Joseph's U (PA)
School of the Museum of Fine Arts, Boston (MA)
Scripps Coll (CA)
Spring Arbor U (MI)
Swarthmore Coll (PA)
U of Illinois at Chicago (IL)
U of Minnesota, Twin Cities Campus (MN)
U of Regina (SK, Canada)
U of Southern California (CA)
The U of the Arts (PA)
Wellesley Coll (MA)
Western Michigan U (MI)
Woodbury U (CA)

FINANCE

Abilene Christian U (TX)
Adams State Coll (CO)
Adelphi U (NY)
Alabama State U (AL)
Albertus Magnus Coll (CT)
Albright Coll (PA)
Alfred U (NY)
American U (DC)
The American U of Paris (France)
Anderson U (IN)
Angelo State U (TX)
Appalachian State U (NC)
Arcadia U (PA)
Arizona State U (AZ)
Arkansas State U (AR)
Ashland U (OH)
Auburn U (AL)
Auburn U Montgomery (AL)
Averett U (VA)
Avila U (MO)
Babson Coll (MA)
Baldwin-Wallace Coll (OH)
Ball State U (IN)
Barry U (FL)
Bayamón Central U (PR)
Baylor U (TX)
Bellarmine U (KY)
Belmont U (TN)
Benedictine U (IL)
Bentley U (MA)
Bernard M. Baruch Coll of the City U of New York (NY)
Berry Coll (GA)
Bethany Coll (KS)
Bishop's U (QC, Canada)
Bob Jones U (SC)
Boise State U (ID)
Boston Coll (MA)
Boston U (MA)
Bowling Green State U (OH)
Bradley U (IL)
Brescia U (KY)

Bridgewater State U (MA)
Bryant U (RI)
Butler U (IN)
Cabrini Coll (PA)
California State U, Bakersfield (CA)
California State U, Chico (CA)
California State U, Dominguez Hills (CA)
California State U, East Bay (CA)
California State U, Fresno (CA)
California State U, Fullerton (CA)
California State U, Long Beach (CA)
California State U, San Bernardino (CA)
Canisius Coll (NY)
Cape Breton U (NS, Canada)
Capella U (MN)
Carroll Coll (MT)
Castleton State Coll (VT)
The Catholic U of America (DC)
Cedarville U (OH)
Centenary Coll (NJ)
Central Connecticut State U (CT)
Central Michigan U (MI)
Christopher Newport U (VA)
Clarion U of Pennsylvania (PA)
Cleary U (MI)
Clemson U (SC)
Cleveland State U (OH)
Coastal Carolina U (SC)
The Coll at Brockport, State U of New York (NY)
The Coll of St. Scholastica (MN)
The Coll of William and Mary (VA)
Colorado State U (CO)
Columbia Coll (MO)
Columbus State U (GA)
Concordia U (QC, Canada)
Concordia U, St. Paul (MN)
Converse Coll (SC)
Corban U (OR)
Cornerstone U (MI)
Creighton U (NE)
Culver-Stockton Coll (MO)
Dakota State U (SD)
Dalhousie U (NS, Canada)
Dallas Baptist U (TX)
Davenport U, Grand Rapids (MI)
Delaware State U (DE)
Delta State U (MS)
DePaul U (IL)
DeSales U (PA)
Dominican Coll (NY)
Dowling Coll (NY)
Drake U (IA)
Drury U (MO)
Duquesne U (PA)
East Carolina U (NC)
East Central U (OK)
Eastern Illinois U (IL)
Eastern Kentucky U (KY)
Eastern Michigan U (MI)
Eastern Washington U (WA)
East Tennessee State U (TN)
Elmhurst Coll (IL)
Elon U (NC)
Emory U (GA)
Emporia State U (KS)
Excelsior Coll (NY)
Fairfield U (CT)
Fairleigh Dickinson U, Coll at Florham (NJ)
Fairleigh Dickinson U, Metropolitan Campus (NJ)
Fairmont State U (WV)
Fayetteville State U (NC)
Ferris State U (MI)
Fitchburg State U (MA)
Florida Atlantic U (FL)
Florida Gulf Coast U (FL)
Florida Intl U (FL)
Florida State U (FL)
Fordham U (NY)
Fort Hays State U (KS)
Fort Lewis Coll (CO)
Francis Marion U (SC)
Franklin U (OH)
Friends U (KS)
Gannon U (PA)
Gardner-Webb U (NC)
George Fox U (OR)
George Mason U (VA)
The George Washington U (DC)
Georgia Southern U (GA)

Georgia State U (GA)
Goldey-Beacom Coll (DE)
Gonzaga U (WA)
Governors State U (IL)
Grace Coll (IN)
Grand Valley State U (MI)
Hamline U (MN)
Hampton U (VA)
Harding U (AR)
Hardin-Simmons U (TX)
Hawai`i Pacific U (HI)
HEC Montreal (QC, Canada)
Hillsdale Coll (MI)
Hofstra U (NY)
Howard Payne U (TX)
Husson U (ME)
Idaho State U (ID)
Illinois Coll (IL)
Illinois State U (IL)
Immaculata U (PA)
Indiana State U (IN)
Indiana U Bloomington (IN)
Indiana U of Pennsylvania (PA)
Indiana U–Purdue U Fort Wayne (IN)
Indiana Wesleyan U (IN)
Inter American U of Puerto Rico, Bayamón Campus (PR)
Inter American U of Puerto Rico, Ponce Campus (PR)
Inter American U of Puerto Rico, San Germán Campus (PR)
Iona Coll (NY)
Iowa State U of Science and Technology (IA)
Ithaca Coll (NY)
Jacksonville State U (AL)
Jacksonville U (FL)
James Madison U (VA)
John Carroll U (OH)
Juniata Coll (PA)
Kansas State U (KS)
Kean U (NJ)
Kennesaw State U (GA)
Kent State U (OH)
King Coll (TN)
King's Coll (PA)
Kutztown U of Pennsylvania (PA)
Lake Erie Coll (OH)
Lake Forest Coll (IL)
Lakehead U (ON, Canada)
Lake Superior State U (MI)
Lamar U (TX)
La Roche Coll (PA)
La Salle U (PA)
Lasell Coll (MA)
La Sierra U (CA)
Lehigh U (PA)
Le Moyne Coll (NY)
Lenoir-Rhyne U (NC)
LeTourneau U (TX)
Lewis U (IL)
Lincoln Memorial U (TN)
Lincoln U (PA)
Lindenwood U (MO)
Linfield Coll (OR)
Long Island U–Brooklyn Campus (NY)
Long Island U–C. W. Post Campus (NY)
Longwood U (VA)
Loras Coll (IA)
Louisiana Coll (LA)
Louisiana State U and Ag and Mech Coll (LA)
Louisiana State U in Shreveport (LA)
Loyola U Chicago (IL)
Loyola U Maryland (MD)
Loyola U New Orleans (LA)
Lubbock Christian U (TX)
Lycoming Coll (PA)
Manchester Coll (IN)
Manhattan Coll (NY)
Manhattanville Coll (NY)
Marian U (WI)
Marietta Coll (OH)
Marquette U (WI)
Marshall U (WV)
Mars Hill Coll (NC)
The Master's Coll and Sem (CA)
McKendree U (IL)
McMurry U (TX)
McNeese State U (LA)
McPherson Coll (KS)

Menlo Coll (CA)
Merrimack Coll (MA)
Metropolitan State Coll of Denver (CO)
Metropolitan State U (MN)
Miami U (OH)
Michigan State U (MI)
Michigan Technological U (MI)
Middle Tennessee State U (TN)
Midwestern State U (TX)
Millikin U (IL)
Minnesota State U Mankato (MN)
Minnesota State U Moorhead (MN)
Minot State U (ND)
Mississippi Coll (MS)
Mississippi State U (MS)
Missouri State U (MO)
Missouri Western State U (MO)
Montana State U Billings (MT)
Morehead State U (KY)
Mount Mercy U (IA)
Mount Vernon Nazarene U (OH)
National U (CA)
New England Coll (NH)
New Mexico Highlands U (NM)
New Mexico State U (NM)
New York Inst of Technology (NY)
New York U (NY)
Nicholls State U (LA)
Nichols Coll (MA)
North Carolina Ag and Tech State U (NC)
North Central Coll (IL)
North Dakota State U (ND)
Northeastern Illinois U (IL)
Northeastern State U (OK)
Northeastern U (MA)
Northern Arizona U (AZ)
Northern Illinois U (IL)
Northern Kentucky U (KY)
Northern Michigan U (MI)
Northern State U (SD)
North Georgia Coll & State U (GA)
Northwestern Coll (MN)
Northwest Missouri State U (MO)
Northwest Nazarene U (ID)
Northwood U, Florida Campus (FL)
Northwood U, Michigan Campus (MI)
Nova Southeastern U (FL)
Oakland U (MI)
Ohio Northern U (OH)
The Ohio State U (OH)
Ohio U (OH)
Oklahoma Christian U (OK)
Oklahoma City U (OK)
Oklahoma State U (OK)
Old Dominion U (VA)
Oral Roberts U (OK)
Otterbein U (OH)
Pace U (NY)
Pacific U (OR)
Palm Beach Atlantic U (FL)
Penn State Abington (PA)
Penn State Altoona (PA)
Penn State Beaver (PA)
Penn State Berks (PA)
Penn State Brandywine (PA)
Penn State DuBois (PA)
Penn State Erie, The Behrend Coll (PA)
Penn State Fayette, The Eberly Campus (PA)
Penn State Greater Allegheny (PA)
Penn State Harrisburg (PA)
Penn State Hazleton (PA)
Penn State Lehigh Valley (PA)
Penn State Mont Alto (PA)
Penn State New Kensington (PA)
Penn State Schuylkill (PA)
Penn State Shenango (PA)
Penn State U Park (PA)
Penn State Wilkes-Barre (PA)
Penn State Worthington Scranton (PA)
Penn State York (PA)
Philadelphia U (PA)
Pittsburg State U (KS)
Plymouth State U (NH)
Polytechnic U of Puerto Rico (PR)
Portland State U (OR)
Post U (CT)
Prairie View A&M U (TX)
Providence Coll (RI)
Purdue U Calumet (IN)

Queens Coll of the City U of New York (NY)
Quincy U (IL)
Quinnipiac U (CT)
Radford U (VA)
Regis U (CO)
Rhode Island Coll (RI)
Rider U (NJ)
Rivier Coll (NH)
Robert Morris U (PA)
Rochester Inst of Technology (NY)
Rockford Coll (IL)
Roger Williams U (RI)
Roosevelt U (IL)
Rowan U (NJ)
Rutgers, The State U of New Jersey, Camden (NJ)
Rutgers, The State U of New Jersey, Newark (NJ)
Rutgers, The State U of New Jersey, New Brunswick (NJ)
Ryerson U (ON, Canada)
Sacred Heart U (CT)
Saginaw Valley State U (MI)
St. Ambrose U (IA)
Saint Anselm Coll (NH)
St. Bonaventure U (NY)
St. Edward's U (TX)
Saint Francis U (PA)
St. John Fisher Coll (NY)
St. John's U (NY)
Saint Joseph's Coll of Maine (ME)
Saint Joseph's U (PA)
Saint Louis U (MO)
St. Mary's U (TX)
St. Thomas Aquinas Coll (NY)
St. Thomas U (FL)
Saint Vincent Coll (PA)
Salem State U (MA)
Salisbury U (MD)
Salve Regina U (RI)
Samford U (AL)
Sam Houston State U (TX)
San Diego State U (CA)
San Francisco State U (CA)
Santa Clara U (CA)
Schreiner U (TX)
Seattle U (WA)
Shippensburg U of Pennsylvania (PA)
Siena Coll (NY)
Sierra Nevada Coll (NV)
Simmons Coll (MA)
Slippery Rock U of Pennsylvania (PA)
Southeastern Louisiana U (LA)
Southeastern Oklahoma State U (OK)
Southeastern U (FL)
Southeast Missouri State U (MO)
Southern Connecticut State U (CT)
Southern Illinois U Carbondale (IL)
Southern Methodist U (TX)
Southwest Baptist U (MO)
Southwestern Christian U (OK)
Southwestern Coll (KS)
Southwestern Oklahoma State U (OK)
Southwest Minnesota State U (MN)
Spring Arbor U (MI)
State U of New York at Binghamton (NY)
State U of New York at Fredonia (NY)
State U of New York at New Paltz (NY)
State U of New York at Oswego (NY)
State U of New York at Plattsburgh (NY)
State U of New York Coll at Old Westbury (NY)
State U of New York Coll of Technology at Canton (NY)
Stephen F. Austin State U (TX)
Stetson U (FL)
Stonehill Coll (MA)
Suffolk U (MA)
Sullivan U (KY)
Syracuse U (NY)
Tarleton State U (TX)
Taylor U (IN)
Temple U (PA)
Texas A&M Intl U (TX)
Texas A&M U (TX)

FINANCE AND FINANCIAL MANAGEMENT SERVICES RELATED

FINANCIAL FORENSICS AND FRAUD INVESTIGATION

FINANCIAL MATHEMATICS

FINANCIAL PLANNING AND SERVICES

FINE AND STUDIO ARTS MANAGEMENT

FINE ARTS RELATED

FINE/STUDIO ARTS

Carleton Coll (MN)
Carlow U (PA)
Centenary Coll of Louisiana (LA)
Central Michigan U (MI)
Chapman U (CA)
Chatham U (PA)
Chester Coll of New England (NH)
Christian Brothers U (TN)
Christopher Newport U (VA)
Claflin U (SC)
Clark U (MA)
Coastal Carolina U (SC)
Coe Coll (IA)
Colby Coll (ME)
The Coll at Brockport, State U of New York (NY)
Coll for Creative Studies (MI)
Coll of Charleston (SC)
The Coll of Idaho (ID)
Coll of Mount St. Joseph (OH)
The Coll of New Jersey (NJ)
Coll of Saint Benedict (MN)
Coll of the Holy Cross (MA)
Coll of the Ozarks (MO)
The Coll of Wooster (OH)
The Colorado Coll (CO)
Colorado State U (CO)
Columbia Coll (SC)
Columbia Coll Chicago (IL)
Concordia U (QC, Canada)
Concordia U, Nebraska (NE)
Concordia U, St. Paul (MN)
Converse Coll (SC)
Cooper Union for the Advancement of Science and Art (NY)
Corcoran Coll of Art and Design (DC)
Cornell U (NY)
Cornish Coll of the Arts (WA)
Culver-Stockton Coll (MO)
Daemen Coll (NY)
Dartmouth Coll (NH)
Denison U (OH)
DePauw U (IN)
Dickinson Coll (PA)
Dominican U (IL)
Drake U (IA)
Drury U (MO)
East Carolina U (NC)
Eastern Kentucky U (KY)
Eastern Washington U (WA)
Edinboro U of Pennsylvania (PA)
Elizabeth City State U (NC)
Elizabethtown Coll (PA)
Elmira Coll (NY)
Emily Carr U of Art + Design (BC, Canada)
Emmanuel Coll (MA)
Emory U (GA)
Endicott Coll (MA)
The Evergreen State Coll (WA)
Fairfield U (CT)
Fashion Inst of Technology (NY)
Ferris State U (MI)
Flagler Coll (FL)
Florida Ag and Mech U (FL)
Florida Intl U (FL)
Florida Southern Coll (FL)
Florida State U (FL)
Fontbonne U (MO)
Fordham U (NY)
Fort Hays State U (KS)
Franklin & Marshall Coll (PA)
Furman U (SC)
Gallaudet U (DC)
Gardner-Webb U (NC)
Georgetown Coll (KY)
The George Washington U (DC)
Gettysburg Coll (PA)
Governors State U (IL)
Graceland U (IA)
Grand View U (IA)
Hamilton Coll (NY)
Hamline U (MN)
Hampden-Sydney Coll (VA)
Harding U (AR)
Hardin-Simmons U (TX)
Hobart and William Smith Colls (NY)
Hofstra U (NY)
Hope Coll (MI)
Howard Payne U (TX)
Humboldt State U (CA)
Hunter Coll of the City U of New York (NY)

Huntingdon Coll (AL)
Huntington U (IN)
Illinois State U (IL)
Indiana State U (IL)
Indiana U Bloomington (IN)
Indiana U of Pennsylvania (PA)
Indiana U–Purdue U Fort Wayne (IN)
Indiana U–Purdue U Indianapolis (IN)
Indiana U South Bend (IN)
Indiana U Southeast (IN)
Iowa Wesleyan Coll (IA)
Ithaca Coll (NY)
Jacksonville U (FL)
Jamestown Coll (ND)
Johnson State Coll (VT)
Judson U (IL)
Juniata Coll (PA)
Kean U (NJ)
Keene State Coll (NH)
Kentucky State U (KY)
Keystone Coll (PA)
Knox Coll (IL)
Kutztown U of Pennsylvania (PA)
Lafayette Coll (PA)
Lamar U (TX)
La Sierra U (CA)
Lawrence U (WI)
Lebanese American U (Lebanon)
Limestone Coll (SC)
Lincoln U (MO)
Lindenwood U (MO)
Lindsey Wilson Coll (KY)
Linfield Coll (OR)
Lipscomb U (TN)
Lock Haven U of Pennsylvania (PA)
Long Island U–C. W. Post Campus (NY)
Longwood U (VA)
Loras Coll (IA)
Louisiana Coll (LA)
Louisiana State U and Ag and Mech Coll (LA)
Loyola Marymount U (CA)
Loyola U Chicago (IL)
Lycoming Coll (PA)
Madonna U (MI)
Maharishi U of Management (IA)
Malone U (OH)
Manchester Coll (IN)
Manhattanville Coll (NY)
Marian U (WI)
Marietta Coll (OH)
Marlboro Coll (VT)
Mars Hill Coll (NC)
Maryland Inst Coll of Art (MD)
Marylhurst U (OR)
Marymount Manhattan Coll (NY)
Marymount U (VA)
Maryville Coll (TN)
Maryville U of Saint Louis (MO)
Massachusetts Coll of Art and Design (MA)
McMurry U (TX)
Memphis Coll of Art (TN)
Mercyhurst Coll (PA)
Meredith Coll (NC)
Merrimack Coll (MA)
Messiah Coll (PA)
Middlebury Coll (VT)
Milligan Coll (TN)
Millikin U (IL)
Millsaps Coll (MS)
Mills Coll (CA)
Minnesota State U Mankato (MN)
Minnesota State U Moorhead (MN)
Mississippi Coll (MS)
Missouri Western State U (MO)
Montana State U (MT)
Montclair State U (NJ)
Montserrat Coll of Art (MA)
Moore Coll of Art & Design (PA)
Moravian Coll (PA)
Morehead State U (KY)
Morningside Coll (IA)
Mount Allison U (NB, Canada)
Mount Holyoke Coll (MA)
Mount Vernon Nazarene U (OH)
Naropa U (CO)
Nazareth Coll of Rochester (NY)
New Coll of Florida (FL)
New England Coll (NH)
New Mexico State U (NM)
New York Inst of Technology (NY)

New York U (NY)
Northeastern State U (OK)
Northeastern U (MA)
Northern Illinois U (IL)
Northern Kentucky U (KY)
North Georgia Coll & State U (GA)
North Greenville U (SC)
Northwestern Coll (MN)
Northwestern State U of Louisiana (LA)
Northwest Missouri State U (MO)
Notre Dame de Namur U (CA)
Nova Southeastern U (FL)
Oakland U (MI)
Ohio Northern U (OH)
The Ohio State U (OH)
Ohio U (OH)
Ohio Wesleyan U (OH)
Oklahoma City U (OK)
Oral Roberts U (OK)
Otis Coll of Art and Design (CA)
Ouachita Baptist U (AR)
Pace U (NY)
Pacific Lutheran U (WA)
Pacific Northwest Coll of Art (OR)
Pacific Union Coll (CA)
Paier Coll of Art, Inc. (CT)
Palm Beach Atlantic U (FL)
Park U (MO)
Pennsylvania Coll of Art & Design (PA)
Piedmont Coll (GA)
Pitzer Coll (CA)
Plymouth State U (NH)
Point Loma Nazarene U (CA)
Pomona Coll (CA)
Pratt Inst (NY)
Presbyterian Coll (SC)
Providence Coll (RI)
Queens Coll of the City U of New York (NY)
Queens U of Charlotte (NC)
Randolph Coll (VA)
Randolph-Macon Coll (VA)
Rhode Island Coll (RI)
Rhodes Coll (TN)
Rice U (TX)
The Richard Stockton Coll of New Jersey (NJ)
Ringling Coll of Art and Design (FL)
Rivier Coll (NH)
Rochester Inst of Technology (NY)
Rosemont Coll (PA)
Sage Coll of Albany (NY)
Saginaw Valley State U (MI)
St. Ambrose U (IA)
St. Catherine U (MN)
Saint John's U (MN)
Saint Joseph's Coll (IN)
St. Lawrence U (NY)
Saint Louis U (MO)
Saint Mary-of-the-Woods Coll (IN)
Saint Mary's U of Minnesota (MN)
Saint Peter's Coll (NJ)
St. Thomas Aquinas Coll (NY)
Saint Vincent Coll (PA)
Salisbury U (MD)
Salve Regina U (RI)
Santa Clara U (CA)
Sarah Lawrence Coll (NY)
School of the Museum of Fine Arts, Boston (MA)
Scripps Coll (CA)
Seattle U (WA)
Seton Hill U (PA)
Sewanee: The U of the South (TN)
Shawnee State U (OH)
Shorter U (GA)
Siena Coll (NY)
Sierra Nevada Coll (NV)
Simpson Coll (IA)
Slippery Rock U of Pennsylvania (PA)
Smith Coll (MA)
Sonoma State U (CA)
South Carolina State U (SC)
Southern Arkansas U–Magnolia (AR)
Southern Connecticut State U (CT)
Southern Illinois U Carbondale (IL)
Southern Illinois U Edwardsville (IL)
Southern Methodist U (TX)
Spring Hill Coll (AL)
Stanford U (CA)

State U of New York at Fredonia (NY)
State U of New York at New Paltz (NY)
State U of New York at Plattsburgh (NY)
State U of New York Coll at Cortland (NY)
State U of New York Coll at Oneonta (NY)
Stonehill Coll (MA)
Stony Brook U, State U of New York (NY)
Suffolk U (MA)
Susquehanna U (PA)
Swarthmore Coll (PA)
Sweet Briar Coll (VA)
Syracuse U (NY)
Tarleton State U (TX)
Texas A&M U–Corpus Christi (TX)
Texas A&M U–Kingsville (TX)
Texas Christian U (TX)
Texas Southern U (TX)
Texas State U–San Marcos (TX)
Thomas More Coll (KY)
Thompson Rivers U (BC, Canada)
Trinity Christian Coll (IL)
Trinity Coll (CT)
Truman State U (MO)
Tulane U (LA)
Union Coll (NE)
Union Coll (NY)
U at Buffalo, the State U of New York (NY)
The U of Alabama (AL)
U of Alberta (AB, Canada)
The U of Arizona (AZ)
The U of British Columbia (BC, Canada)
U of California, Davis (CA)
U of California, Irvine (CA)
U of California, Riverside (CA)
U of California, Santa Barbara (CA)
U of Central Florida (FL)
U of Central Missouri (MO)
U of Cincinnati (OH)
U of Colorado Boulder (CO)
U of Colorado Denver (CO)
U of Connecticut (CT)
U of Dallas (TX)
U of Dayton (OH)
U of Delaware (DE)
U of Florida (FL)
U of Georgia (GA)
U of Great Falls (MT)
U of Guelph (ON, Canada)
U of Houston–Clear Lake (TX)
U of Idaho (ID)
U of Illinois at Chicago (IL)
U of Illinois at Springfield (IL)
U of Indianapolis (IN)
The U of Kansas (KS)
U of Lethbridge (AB, Canada)
U of Louisiana at Monroe (LA)
U of Louisville (KY)
U of Maine (ME)
U of Maine at Augusta (ME)
U of Maine at Presque Isle (ME)
U of Mary Hardin-Baylor (TX)
U of Maryland, Coll Park (MD)
U of Massachusetts Amherst (MA)
U of Miami (FL)
U of Michigan–Flint (MI)
U of Minnesota, Duluth (MN)
U of Minnesota, Twin Cities Campus (MN)
U of Mississippi (MS)
U of Missouri–Kansas City (MO)
U of Missouri–St. Louis (MO)
U of Mount Union (OH)
U of Nebraska–Lincoln (NE)
U of Nevada, Las Vegas (NV)
U of New Hampshire (NH)
U of New Haven (CT)
U of New Orleans (LA)
U of North Alabama (AL)
The U of North Carolina at Asheville (NC)
The U of North Carolina at Chapel Hill (NC)
The U of North Carolina at Charlotte (NC)
The U of North Carolina Wilmington (NC)
U of Northern Colorado (CO)

U of Northern Iowa (IA)
U of North Florida (FL)
U of North Texas (TX)
U of Notre Dame (IN)
U of Oklahoma (OK)
U of Oregon (OR)
U of Ottawa (ON, Canada)
U of Pennsylvania (PA)
U of Pittsburgh (PA)
U of Redlands (CA)
U of Rhode Island (RI)
U of Richmond (VA)
U of Rochester (NY)
U of St. Thomas (TX)
U of Science and Arts of Oklahoma (OK)
U of South Carolina (SC)
U of South Carolina Aiken (SC)
U of South Carolina Beaufort (SC)
U of South Carolina Upstate (SC)
U of Southern California (CA)
U of Southern Maine (ME)
U of South Florida (FL)
The U of Tennessee (TN)
The U of Texas at Arlington (TX)
The U of Texas at Austin (TX)
The U of Texas at El Paso (TX)
The U of Texas–Pan American (TX)
The U of the Arts (PA)
U of the Cumberlands (KY)
U of the District of Columbia (DC)
U of the Incarnate Word (TX)
U of the Ozarks (AR)
U of the Pacific (CA)
The U of Toledo (OH)
U of Tulsa (OK)
U of Vermont (VT)
The U of Western Ontario (ON, Canada)
U of West Florida (FL)
U of Windsor (ON, Canada)
U of Wisconsin–Stevens Point (WI)
U of Wisconsin–Superior (WI)
Ursuline Coll (OH)
Vanderbilt U (TN)
Vassar Coll (NY)
Virginia Intermont Coll (VA)
Virginia Union U (VA)
Viterbo U (WI)
Wake Forest U (NC)
Washington and Lee U (VA)
Washington State U (WA)
Washington U in St. Louis (MO)
Watkins Coll of Art, Design, & Film (TN)
Webster U (MO)
Wellesley Coll (MA)
Wells Coll (NY)
Wesleyan Coll (GA)
Wesleyan U (CT)
West Chester U of Pennsylvania (PA)
Western Carolina U (NC)
Western Illinois U (IL)
Western Kentucky U (KY)
Western Michigan U (MI)
Western State Coll of Colorado (CO)
Westminster Coll (UT)
West Texas A&M U (TX)
West Virginia Wesleyan Coll (WV)
Wheaton Coll (MA)
Wheeling Jesuit U (WV)
Willamette U (OR)
William Paterson U of New Jersey (NJ)
Williams Baptist Coll (AR)
Williams Coll (MA)
William Woods U (MO)
Wingate U (NC)
Winona State U (MN)
Xavier U (OH)
York Coll of Pennsylvania (PA)
Youngstown State U (OH)

FIRE PREVENTION AND SAFETY TECHNOLOGY

Cogswell Polytechnical Coll (CA)
Delaware State U (DE)
Oklahoma State U (OK)
Thomas Edison State Coll (NJ)
U of New Haven (CT)

FIRE PROTECTION RELATED
The U of Akron (OH)
U of New Haven (CT)

FIRE SCIENCE/FIREFIGHTING
Anna Maria Coll (MA)
Columbia Southern U (AL)
Hampton U (VA)
Holy Family U (PA)
Idaho State U (ID)
John Jay Coll of Criminal Justice of the City U of New York (NY)
Lake Superior State U (MI)
Lewis-Clark State Coll (ID)
Madonna U (MI)
Providence Coll (RI)
U of Florida (FL)
Utah Valley U (UT)

FIRE SERVICES ADMINISTRATION
American Public U System (WV)
Bowling Green State U (OH)
California State U, Los Angeles (CA)
Cogswell Polytechnical Coll (CA)
Colorado State U (CO)
Eastern Oregon U (OR)
Fayetteville State U (NC)
Florida State Coll at Jacksonville (FL)
Holy Family U (PA)
John Jay Coll of Criminal Justice of the City U of New York (NY)
Lewis U (IL)
Lindenwood U (MO)
Salem State U (MA)
Southern Illinois U Carbondale (IL)
U of Cincinnati (OH)
U of Maryland U Coll (MD)
The U of North Carolina at Charlotte (NC)
Utah Valley U (UT)
Waldorf Coll (IA)
Western Oregon U (OR)

FISHING AND FISHERIES SCIENCES AND MANAGEMENT
Albion Coll (MI)
Clemson U (SC)
Colorado State U (CO)
Delaware State U (DE)
Humboldt State U (CA)
Iowa State U of Science and Technology (IA)
Lake Superior State U (MI)
Mansfield U of Pennsylvania (PA)
Michigan State U (MI)
The Ohio State U (OH)
State U of New York Coll of Environmental Science and Forestry (NY)
U of Alaska Fairbanks (AK)
The U of British Columbia (BC, Canada)
U of Georgia (GA)
U of Idaho (ID)
U of Minnesota, Twin Cities Campus (MN)
U of Missouri (MO)
U of Rhode Island (RI)
The U of Tennessee at Martin (TN)
U of Washington (WA)

FLIGHT INSTRUCTION
South Dakota State U (SD)
U of North Dakota (ND)

FOODS AND NUTRITION RELATED
California State U, Long Beach (CA)
Samford U (AL)
The U of British Columbia (BC, Canada)
Utah State U (UT)

FOOD SCIENCE
Acadia U (NS, Canada)
American U of Beirut (Lebanon)
Auburn U (AL)
California Polytechnic State U, San Luis Obispo (CA)

California State Polytechnic U, Pomona (CA)
Clemson U (SC)
Cornell U (NY)
Dalhousie U (NS, Canada)
Delaware Valley Coll (PA)
Dominican U (IL)
Framingham State U (MA)
Kansas State U (KS)
Lamar U (TX)
Michigan State U (MI)
Mississippi State U (MS)
North Carolina Ag and Tech State U (NC)
North Carolina State U (NC)
North Dakota State U (ND)
The Ohio State U (OH)
Oklahoma State U (OK)
Penn State Abington (PA)
Penn State Altoona (PA)
Penn State Beaver (PA)
Penn State Berks (PA)
Penn State Brandywine (PA)
Penn State DuBois (PA)
Penn State Erie, The Behrend Coll (PA)
Penn State Fayette, The Eberly Campus (PA)
Penn State Greater Allegheny (PA)
Penn State Hazleton (PA)
Penn State Lehigh Valley (PA)
Penn State Mont Alto (PA)
Penn State New Kensington (PA)
Penn State Schuylkill (PA)
Penn State Shenango (PA)
Penn State U Park (PA)
Penn State Wilkes-Barre (PA)
Penn State Worthington Scranton (PA)
Penn State York (PA)
Purdue U (IN)
Rutgers, The State U of New Jersey, New Brunswick (NJ)
Simmons Coll (MA)
Texas A&M U (TX)
Texas Tech U (TX)
Tuskegee U (AL)
U of Alberta (AB, Canada)
U of Arkansas (AR)
The U of British Columbia (BC, Canada)
U of California, Davis (CA)
U of Delaware (DE)
U of Florida (FL)
U of Georgia (GA)
U of Guelph (ON, Canada)
U of Idaho (ID)
U of Illinois at Urbana–Champaign (IL)
U of Maine (ME)
U of Maryland, Coll Park (MD)
U of Massachusetts Amherst (MA)
U of Minnesota, Twin Cities Campus (MN)
U of Missouri (MO)
U of Nebraska–Lincoln (NE)
The U of Tennessee (TN)
U of the District of Columbia (DC)
U of Wisconsin–Madison (WI)
U of Wisconsin–River Falls (WI)
Virginia Polytechnic Inst and State U (VA)
Washington State U (WA)

FOOD SCIENCE AND TECHNOLOGY RELATED
North Dakota State U (ND)
The U of British Columbia (BC, Canada)
U of Illinois at Urbana–Champaign (IL)

FOOD SERVICE SYSTEMS ADMINISTRATION
Dominican U (IL)
Iowa State U of Science and Technology (IA)
Lipscomb U (TN)
Northwest Missouri State U (MO)
Ohio U (OH)
Rochester Inst of Technology (NY)
Simmons Coll (MA)
State U of New York Coll at Oneonta (NY)

U of Wisconsin–Stout (WI)
Western Michigan U (MI)

FOODS, NUTRITION, AND WELLNESS
Acadia U (NS, Canada)
Alcorn State U (MS)
Andrews U (MI)
Arizona State U (AZ)
Ashland U (OH)
Auburn U (AL)
Bastyr U (WA)
Benedictine U (IL)
Bluffton U (OH)
Bob Jones U (SC)
Bowling Green State U (OH)
Bradley U (IL)
Bridgewater Coll (VA)
California State U, Fresno (CA)
California State U, Los Angeles (CA)
California State U, San Bernardino (CA)
Carson-Newman Coll (TN)
Cedar Crest Coll (PA)
Central Washington U (WA)
Coll of the Ozarks (MO)
Delaware State U (DE)
Dominican U (IL)
Georgia Southern U (GA)
Goddard Coll (VT)
Hunter Coll of the City U of New York (NY)
Indiana State U (IN)
Indiana U of Pennsylvania (PA)
Iowa State U of Science and Technology (IA)
Ithaca Coll (NY)
Jacksonville State U (AL)
James Madison U (VA)
Lehman Coll of the City U of New York (NY)
Lincoln U (MO)
Madonna U (MI)
The Master's Coll and Sem (CA)
Middle Tennessee State U (TN)
Minnesota State U Mankato (MN)
Montclair State U (NJ)
Morrisville State Coll (NY)
New Mexico State U (NM)
New York U (NY)
North Carolina Ag and Tech State U (NC)
Northeastern State U (OK)
Northern Illinois U (IL)
The Ohio State U (OH)
Ohio U (OH)
Oklahoma State U (OK)
Pepperdine U, Malibu (CA)
Point Loma Nazarene U (CA)
Prairie View A&M U (TX)
Purdue U (IN)
Radford U (VA)
St. Catherine U (MN)
Saint Louis U (MO)
Samford U (AL)
Seattle Pacific U (WA)
South Carolina State U (SC)
South Dakota State U (SD)
Southern Illinois U Carbondale (IL)
State U of New York at Plattsburgh (NY)
Stephen F. Austin State U (TX)
Texas A&M U (TX)
Texas Southern U (TX)
Texas State U–San Marcos (TX)
Texas Tech U (TX)
Texas Woman's U (TX)
Trevecca Nazarene U (TN)
Tuskegee U (AL)
U of Alberta (AB, Canada)
U of Arkansas (AR)
The U of British Columbia (BC, Canada)
U of Central Arkansas (AR)
U of Dayton (OH)
U of Delaware (DE)
U of Georgia (GA)
U of Idaho (ID)
U of Maine (ME)
U of Minnesota, Twin Cities Campus (MN)
U of Missouri (MO)
U of Nebraska–Lincoln (NE)
U of Nevada, Reno (NV)

U of New Mexico (NM)
The U of North Carolina at Chapel Hill (NC)
U of Northern Iowa (IA)
U of Ottawa (ON, Canada)
U of Rhode Island (RI)
The U of Tennessee (TN)
The U of Texas at Austin (TX)
U of Toronto (ON, Canada)
The U of Western Ontario (ON, Canada)
Virginia Polytechnic Inst and State U (VA)
Waldorf Coll (IA)
Washington State U (WA)
Wayne State U (MI)
Youngstown State U (OH)

FOOD TECHNOLOGY AND PROCESSING
Brigham Young U (UT)
Iowa State U of Science and Technology (IA)
U of Illinois at Urbana–Champaign (IL)

FOREIGN LANGUAGES AND LITERATURES
Arkansas State U (AR)
Arkansas Tech U (AR)
Assumption Coll (MA)
Auburn U (AL)
Auburn U Montgomery (AL)
Augustana Coll (SD)
Austin Peay State U (TN)
Bennington Coll (VT)
Boston U (MA)
California Polytechnic State U, San Luis Obispo (CA)
Cameron U (OK)
Carnegie Mellon U (PA)
Central Methodist U (MO)
Central Washington U (WA)
The Citadel, The Military Coll of South Carolina (SC)
Colorado State U (CO)
Covenant Coll (GA)
Delta State U (MS)
Duquesne U (PA)
Eastern Illinois U (IL)
East Tennessee State U (TN)
Elmira Coll (NY)
Elon U (NC)
Emporia State U (KS)
Excelsior Coll (NY)
Framingham State U (MA)
Francis Marion U (SC)
Gannon U (PA)
George Mason U (VA)
Georgia Inst of Technology (GA)
Gordon Coll (MA)
Grace Coll (IN)
Hamilton Coll (NY)
Indiana U Bloomington (IN)
James Madison U (VA)
Juniata Coll (PA)
Kansas State U (KS)
Kenyon Coll (OH)
Knox Coll (IL)
Lake Erie Coll (OH)
Lewis & Clark Coll (OR)
Long Island U–Brooklyn Campus (NY)
Long Island U–C. W. Post Campus (NY)
Loyola U New Orleans (LA)
Lycoming Coll (PA)
Manchester Coll (IN)
Marshall U (WV)
Massachusetts Inst of Technology (MA)
McNeese State U (LA)
Mercyhurst Coll (PA)
Middle Tennessee State U (TN)
Mississippi State U (MS)
Monmouth U (NJ)
Montana State U (MT)
New Mexico State U (NM)
New York U (NY)
Northern Arizona U (AZ)
Notre Dame of Maryland U (MD)
Oakland U (MI)
Occidental Coll (CA)
Old Dominion U (VA)

Pace U (NY)
Penn State Berks (PA)
Penn State Lehigh Valley (PA)
Pitzer Coll (CA)
Presbyterian Coll (SC)
Purdue U (IN)
Purdue U Calumet (IN)
Queens U of Charlotte (NC)
Radford U (VA)
The Richard Stockton Coll of New Jersey (NJ)
Roger Williams U (RI)
Rutgers, The State U of New Jersey, New Brunswick (NJ)
St. Joseph's Coll, New York (NY)
St. Lawrence U (NY)
St. Mary's Coll of Maryland (MD)
Saint Peter's Coll (NJ)
Samford U (AL)
Sarah Lawrence Coll (NY)
Scripps Coll (CA)
South Carolina State U (SC)
Southern Illinois U Edwardsville (IL)
Stanford U (CA)
State U of New York Coll at Old Westbury (NY)
Stonehill Coll (MA)
Suffolk U (MA)
Sweet Briar Coll (VA)
Syracuse U (NY)
Texas A&M U (TX)
Thomas Edison State Coll (NJ)
Tulane U (LA)
Union Coll (NY)
Union U (TN)
The U of Alabama (AL)
The U of Alabama at Birmingham (AL)
The U of Alabama in Huntsville (AL)
U of Alaska Anchorage (AK)
U of Alaska Fairbanks (AK)
U of Arkansas at Monticello (AR)
U of California, Riverside (CA)
U of California, Santa Cruz (CA)
U of Central Florida (FL)
U of Delaware (DE)
U of Hartford (CT)
U of Idaho (ID)
U of Louisiana at Lafayette (LA)
U of Maine (ME)
U of Maryland, Baltimore County (MD)
U of Mary Washington (VA)
U of Memphis (TN)
U of Minnesota, Twin Cities Campus (MN)
U of Nebraska at Omaha (NE)
U of New Mexico (NM)
U of North Alabama (AL)
U of North Dakota (ND)
U of Northern Colorado (CO)
U of Northern Iowa (IA)
U of Ottawa (ON, Canada)
U of Puget Sound (WA)
U of Rochester (NY)
The U of Scranton (PA)
U of South Alabama (AL)
U of South Carolina Beaufort (SC)
U of Southern Mississippi (MS)
The U of Tennessee at Chattanooga (TN)
The U of Texas at Arlington (TX)
The U of Texas at Tyler (TX)
The U of Virginia's Coll at Wise (VA)
U of Wisconsin–River Falls (WI)
Utica Coll (NY)
Virginia Commonwealth U (VA)
Washington Coll (MD)
Washington State U (WA)
Wayne State Coll (NE)
Wayne State U (MI)
Western Washington U (WA)
West Virginia U (WV)
Wichita State U (KS)
Widener U (PA)
Wright State U (OH)
Youngstown State U (OH)

FOREIGN LANGUAGES RELATED
Arizona State U (AZ)
Augustana Coll (SD)
Bennington Coll (VT)
The Evergreen State Coll (WA)
Excelsior Coll (NY)

INDEXES

Georgia Southern U (GA)
Hood Coll (MD)
Indiana State U (IN)
Indiana U of Pennsylvania (PA)
Kennesaw State U (GA)
Mississippi Coll (MS)
New York U (NY)
Purchase Coll, State U of New York (NY)
Saint Mary's Coll of California (CA)
Southern Illinois U Carbondale (IL)
State U of New York at Binghamton (NY)
U of Alaska Fairbanks (AK)
U of California, Berkeley (CA)
U of California, Los Angeles (CA)
U of Lethbridge (AB, Canada)
U of Michigan–Flint (MI)
U of Northern Iowa (IA)
U of St. Thomas (MN)
U of West Georgia (GA)
Western Washington U (WA)
Winona State U (MN)
Yale U (CT)

FOREIGN LANGUAGE TEACHER EDUCATION

Arkansas State U (AR)
Arkansas Tech U (AR)
Auburn U (AL)
Baylor U (TX)
Boston U (MA)
Bowling Green State U (OH)
Buffalo State Coll, State U of New York (NY)
Cameron U (OK)
Central Methodist U (MO)
The Coll at Brockport, State U of New York (NY)
Concordia Coll (MN)
Dowling Coll (NY)
Eastern Michigan U (MI)
Elmira Coll (NY)
Gannon U (PA)
Gardner-Webb U (NC)
Grand Valley State U (MI)
Hofstra U (NY)
Indiana U Bloomington (IN)
Lincoln U (PA)
Long Island U–C. W. Post Campus (NY)
Manchester Coll (IN)
Mercyhurst Coll (PA)
Miami U (OH)
Moravian Coll (PA)
Nazareth Coll of Rochester (NY)
New York U (NY)
Ohio Northern U (OH)
Ohio Wesleyan U (OH)
Oral Roberts U (OK)
Penn State Abington (PA)
Penn State Altoona (PA)
Penn State Beaver (PA)
Penn State Berks (PA)
Penn State Brandywine (PA)
Penn State DuBois (PA)
Penn State Erie, The Behrend Coll (PA)
Penn State Fayette, The Eberly Campus (PA)
Penn State Greater Allegheny (PA)
Penn State Mont Alto (PA)
Penn State Shenango (PA)
Penn State U Park (PA)
Penn State Worthington Scranton (PA)
Penn State York (PA)
Rhode Island Coll (RI)
Saint Francis U (PA)
Saint Joseph's U (PA)
Seton Hill U (PA)
Southeast Missouri State U (MO)
State U of New York at New Paltz (NY)
State U of New York Coll at Old Westbury (NY)
Temple U (PA)
U of Central Florida (FL)
U of Georgia (GA)
U of Illinois at Urbana–Champaign (IL)
U of Maine (ME)
U of Minnesota, Duluth (MN)
U of Nebraska–Lincoln (NE)
U of Nevada, Reno (NV)

U of Northern Iowa (IA)
U of Oklahoma (OK)
U of St. Thomas (MN)
The U of South Dakota (SD)
U of South Florida (FL)
The U of Tennessee at Chattanooga (TN)
U of Vermont (VT)
U of Windsor (ON, Canada)
Valparaiso U (IN)
Virginia Wesleyan Coll (VA)
Washington State U (WA)
Wayne State Coll (NE)
Wheeling Jesuit U (WV)
William Jewell Coll (MO)
Youngstown State U (OH)

FORENSIC CHEMISTRY

Chestnut Hill Coll (PA)
Delaware State U (DE)
Emmanuel Coll (MA)
Maryville U of Saint Louis (MO)
St. Edward's U (TX)
Slippery Rock U of Pennsylvania (PA)
U of Rhode Island (RI)

FORENSIC PSYCHOLOGY

Bay Path Coll (MA)
The Coll of Saint Rose (NY)
Florida Inst of Technology (FL)
Gwynedd-Mercy Coll (PA)
John Jay Coll of Criminal Justice of the City U of New York (NY)
St. Ambrose U (IA)
Tiffin U (OH)
Walden U (MN)
Western State Coll of Colorado (CO)

FORENSIC SCIENCE AND TECHNOLOGY

Alvernia U (PA)
American Public U System (WV)
Anna Maria Coll (MA)
Arkansas State U (AR)
Bay Path Coll (MA)
Becker Coll (MA)
Bethany Coll (KS)
Bluefield Coll (VA)
Buffalo State Coll, State U of New York (NY)
Cedar Crest Coll (PA)
Cedarville U (OH)
Chaminade U of Honolulu (HI)
Chestnut Hill Coll (PA)
The Coll of Saint Rose (NY)
Columbia Coll (MO)
Defiance Coll (OH)
Delaware State U (DE)
Eastern Kentucky U (KY)
Eastern New Mexico U (NM)
Fayetteville State U (NC)
Friends U (KS)
George Mason U (VA)
Heidelberg U (OH)
Hilbert Coll (NY)
Hofstra U (NY)
Indiana U–Purdue U Indianapolis (IN)
Inter American U of Puerto Rico, Bayamón Campus (PR)
ITT Tech Inst, Indianapolis (IN)
Jacksonville State U (AL)
John Jay Coll of Criminal Justice of the City U of New York (NY)
Keystone Coll (PA)
King Coll (TN)
Lewis U (IL)
Long Island U–C. W. Post Campus (NY)
Loyola U Chicago (IL)
Madonna U (MI)
Marian U (WI)
Marymount U (VA)
Mercyhurst Coll (PA)
Mountain State U (WV)
Mount Ida Coll (MA)
Mount Marty Coll (SD)
Newman U (KS)
New Mexico Highlands U (NM)
Northwest Nazarene U (ID)
Pace U (NY)
Penn State Altoona (PA)

Penn State Berks (PA)
Penn State U Park (PA)
Point Park U (PA)
Roberts Wesleyan Coll (NY)
Russell Sage Coll (NY)
St. Andrews U (NC)
Saint Augustine's Coll (NC)
St. Edward's U (TX)
Saint Francis U (PA)
Seattle U (WA)
Seton Hill U (PA)
Simpson Coll (IA)
State U of New York Coll of Technology at Alfred (NY)
Syracuse U (NY)
Texas A&M U (TX)
Thomas More Coll (KY)
Tiffin U (OH)
Towson U (MD)
Trine U (IN)
U of Central Florida (FL)
The U of Findlay (OH)
U of Great Falls (MT)
U of Maryland U Coll (MD)
U of Nebraska–Lincoln (NE)
U of New Haven (CT)
U of North Dakota (ND)
The U of Scranton (PA)
The U of Tampa (FL)
U of Toronto (ON, Canada)
U of Windsor (ON, Canada)
Utah Valley U (UT)
Virginia Commonwealth U (VA)
Washburn U (KS)
Waynesburg U (PA)
Weber State U (UT)
Western Carolina U (NC)
West Virginia U (WV)
Wichita State U (KS)
York Coll of Pennsylvania (PA)
Youngstown State U (OH)

FOREST ENGINEERING

State U of New York Coll of Environmental Science and Forestry (NY)
U of Maine (ME)
U of Washington (WA)

FOREST/FOREST RESOURCES MANAGEMENT

Clemson U (SC)
Elizabethtown Coll (PA)
Lakehead U (ON, Canada)
Louisiana State U and Ag and Mech Coll (LA)
North Carolina State U (NC)
State U of New York Coll of Environmental Science and Forestry (NY)
Stephen F. Austin State U (TX)
Texas A&M U (TX)
U of Alberta (AB, Canada)
The U of British Columbia (BC, Canada)
U of California, Berkeley (CA)
U of Idaho (ID)
U of Toronto (ON, Canada)
U of Washington (WA)
West Virginia U (WV)

FORESTRY

Albion Coll (MI)
Albright Coll (PA)
Baylor U (TX)
California Polytechnic State U, San Luis Obispo (CA)
Coll of Saint Benedict (MN)
Delaware State U (DE)
Georgia Southern U (GA)
Humboldt State U (CA)
Iowa State U of Science and Technology (IA)
Iowa Wesleyan Coll (IA)
Lakehead U (ON, Canada)
Lenoir-Rhyne U (NC)
Michigan State U (MI)
Michigan Technological U (MI)
Mississippi State U (MS)
New Mexico Highlands U (NM)
The Ohio State U (OH)
Oklahoma State U (OK)
Purdue U (IN)
Saint John's U (MN)

Sewanee: The U of the South (TN)
Southern Illinois U Carbondale (IL)
State U of New York Coll of Environmental Science and Forestry (NY)
Stephen F. Austin State U (TX)
Texas A&M U (TX)
U of Alberta (AB, Canada)
U of Arkansas at Monticello (AR)
The U of British Columbia (BC, Canada)
U of California, Berkeley (CA)
U of Florida (FL)
U of Georgia (GA)
U of Illinois at Urbana–Champaign (IL)
U of Maine (ME)
U of Massachusetts Amherst (MA)
U of Minnesota, Twin Cities Campus (MN)
U of Missouri (MO)
U of Nevada, Reno (NV)
U of New Hampshire (NH)
The U of Tennessee (TN)
U of the District of Columbia (DC)
U of Toronto (ON, Canada)
U of Vermont (VT)
U of Washington (WA)
U of Wisconsin–Stevens Point (WI)
Utah State U (UT)
Virginia Polytechnic Inst and State U (VA)

FORESTRY RELATED

Roger Williams U (RI)
Sterling Coll (VT)
U of Minnesota, Twin Cities Campus (MN)
Utah State U (UT)

FOREST SCIENCES AND BIOLOGY

Auburn U (AL)
Colorado State U (CO)
Northern Arizona U (AZ)
Ohio Northern U (OH)
Penn State Abington (PA)
Penn State Altoona (PA)
Penn State Beaver (PA)
Penn State Berks (PA)
Penn State Brandywine (PA)
Penn State DuBois (PA)
Penn State Erie, The Behrend Coll (PA)
Penn State Fayette, The Eberly Campus (PA)
Penn State Greater Allegheny (PA)
Penn State Hazleton (PA)
Penn State Lehigh Valley (PA)
Penn State Mont Alto (PA)
Penn State New Kensington (PA)
Penn State Schuylkill (PA)
Penn State Shenango (PA)
Penn State U Park (PA)
Penn State Wilkes-Barre (PA)
Penn State Worthington Scranton (PA)
Penn State York (PA)
State U of New York Coll of Environmental Science and Forestry (NY)
U of Idaho (ID)
U of Illinois at Urbana–Champaign (IL)
U of Washington (WA)
U of Wisconsin–Madison (WI)

FOREST TECHNOLOGY

Penn State Abington (PA)
Penn State Altoona (PA)
Penn State Beaver (PA)
Penn State Berks (PA)
Penn State Brandywine (PA)
Penn State DuBois (PA)
Penn State Erie, The Behrend Coll (PA)
Penn State Fayette, The Eberly Campus (PA)
Penn State Greater Allegheny (PA)
Penn State Hazleton (PA)
Penn State Lehigh Valley (PA)
Penn State Mont Alto (PA)
Penn State New Kensington (PA)
Penn State Schuylkill (PA)

Penn State Shenango (PA)
Penn State U Park (PA)
Penn State Wilkes-Barre (PA)
Penn State Worthington Scranton (PA)
Penn State York (PA)

FRANCHISING

St. Catherine U (MN)

FRENCH

Acadia U (NS, Canada)
Adelphi U (NY)
Adrian Coll (MI)
Agnes Scott Coll (GA)
Albion Coll (MI)
Albright Coll (PA)
Alfred U (NY)
Allegheny Coll (PA)
Alma Coll (MI)
American U (DC)
The American U of Paris (France)
Amherst Coll (MA)
Anderson U (IN)
Andrews U (MI)
Angelo State U (TX)
Appalachian State U (NC)
Aquinas Coll (MI)
Arcadia U (PA)
Arizona State U (AZ)
Asbury U (KY)
Ashland U (OH)
Assumption Coll (MA)
Athabasca U (AB, Canada)
Auburn U (AL)
Augustana Coll (IL)
Augustana Coll (SD)
Austin Coll (TX)
Baker U (KS)
Baldwin-Wallace Coll (OH)
Ball State U (IN)
Bard Coll (NY)
Bard Coll at Simon's Rock (MA)
Barnard Coll (NY)
Barry U (FL)
Bates Coll (ME)
Baylor U (TX)
Beloit Coll (WI)
Benedictine Coll (KS)
Bennington Coll (VT)
Berea Coll (KY)
Berry Coll (GA)
Birmingham-Southern Coll (AL)
Bishop's U (QC, Canada)
Boise State U (ID)
Boston Coll (MA)
Boston U (MA)
Bowdoin Coll (ME)
Bowling Green State U (OH)
Bradley U (IL)
Brandeis U (MA)
Bridgewater Coll (VA)
Brown U (RI)
Bryn Mawr Coll (PA)
Bucknell U (PA)
Buffalo State Coll, State U of New York (NY)
Butler U (IN)
Cabrini Coll (PA)
Caldwell Coll (NJ)
California Lutheran U (CA)
California State U, Chico (CA)
California State U, East Bay (CA)
California State U, Fresno (CA)
California State U, Fullerton (CA)
California State U, Long Beach (CA)
California State U, Los Angeles (CA)
California State U, Sacramento (CA)
California State U, San Bernardino (CA)
California State U, Stanislaus (CA)
California U of Pennsylvania (PA)
Calvin Coll (MI)
Canisius Coll (NY)
Cape Breton U (NS, Canada)
Capital U (OH)
Cardinal Stritch U (WI)
Carleton Coll (MN)
Carnegie Mellon U (PA)
Carroll Coll (MT)
Case Western Reserve U (OH)

The Catholic U of America (DC)
Centenary Coll of Louisiana (LA)
Central Coll (IA)
Central Connecticut State U (CT)
Central Methodist U (MO)
Central Michigan U (MI)
Centre Coll (KY)
Chapman U (CA)
Chestnut Hill Coll (PA)
Cheyney U of Pennsylvania (PA)
Christopher Newport U (VA)
City Coll of the City U of New York (NY)
Claremont McKenna Coll (CA)
Clarion U of Pennsylvania (PA)
Clark Atlanta U (GA)
Clark U (MA)
Cleveland State U (OH)
Coe Coll (IA)
Colby Coll (ME)
Colgate U (NY)
The Coll at Brockport, State U of New York (NY)
Coll of Charleston (SC)
Coll of Mount Saint Vincent (NY)
Coll of Saint Benedict (MN)
Coll of the Holy Cross (MA)
The Coll of William and Mary (VA)
The Coll of Wooster (OH)
The Colorado Coll (CO)
Colorado State U (CO)
Columbia U, School of General Studies (NY)
Columbus State U (GA)
Concordia Coll (MN)
Concordia U (QC, Canada)
Connecticut Coll (CT)
Cornell Coll (IA)
Cornell U (NY)
Creighton U (NE)
Daemen Coll (NY)
Dalhousie U (NS, Canada)
Dartmouth Coll (NH)
Davidson Coll (NC)
Delaware State U (DE)
Denison U (OH)
DePaul U (IL)
DePauw U (IN)
Dickinson Coll (PA)
Doane Coll (NE)
Dominican U (IL)
Drew U (NJ)
Drury U (MO)
Earlham Coll (IN)
East Carolina U (NC)
Eastern Kentucky U (KY)
Eastern Michigan U (MI)
Eastern U (PA)
Eastern Washington U (WA)
East Stroudsburg U of Pennsylvania (PA)
Eckerd Coll (FL)
Edgewood Coll (WI)
Elizabethtown Coll (PA)
Elmhurst Coll (IL)
Elmira Coll (NY)
Elon U (NC)
Emory U (GA)
Fairfield U (CT)
Fairleigh Dickinson U, Coll at Florham (NJ)
Fairleigh Dickinson U, Metropolitan Campus (NJ)
Fairmont State U (WV)
Florida Atlantic U (FL)
Florida Intl U (FL)
Fordham U (NY)
Fort Hays State U (KS)
Franciscan U of Steubenville (OH)
Francis Marion U (SC)
Franklin & Marshall Coll (PA)
Franklin Coll (IN)
Furman U (SC)
Gardner-Webb U (NC)
Georgetown Coll (KY)
The George Washington U (DC)
Georgia Coll & State U (GA)
Georgia Southern U (GA)
Georgia State U (GA)
Gettysburg Coll (PA)
Gonzaga U (WA)
Gordon Coll (MA)
Goucher Coll (MD)
Grace Coll (IN)
Grambling State U (LA)

Grand Valley State U (MI)
Grinnell Coll (IA)
Grove City Coll (PA)
Guilford Coll (NC)
Gustavus Adolphus Coll (MN)
Hamilton Coll (NY)
Hampden-Sydney Coll (VA)
Hanover Coll (IN)
Harding U (AR)
Hartwick Coll (NY)
Haverford Coll (PA)
Hendrix Coll (AR)
Hillsdale Coll (MI)
Hobart and William Smith Colls (NY)
Hofstra U (NY)
Hollins U (VA)
Hood Coll (MD)
Hope Coll (MI)
Humboldt State U (CA)
Hunter Coll of the City U of New York (NY)
Idaho State U (ID)
Illinois Coll (IL)
Illinois State U (IL)
Illinois Wesleyan U (IL)
Immaculata U (PA)
Indiana U Bloomington (IN)
Indiana U Northwest (IN)
Indiana U of Pennsylvania (PA)
Indiana U–Purdue U Fort Wayne (IN)
Indiana U–Purdue U Indianapolis (IN)
Indiana U South Bend (IN)
Indiana U Southeast (IN)
Iona Coll (NY)
Iowa State U of Science and Technology (IA)
Ithaca Coll (NY)
Jacksonville State U (AL)
Jacksonville U (FL)
Jamestown Coll (ND)
John Carroll U (OH)
The Johns Hopkins U (MD)
Johnson C. Smith U (NC)
Juniata Coll (PA)
Kalamazoo Coll (MI)
Keene State Coll (NH)
Kent State U (OH)
Kenyon Coll (OH)
King Coll (TN)
King's Coll (PA)
Knox Coll (IL)
Kutztown U of Pennsylvania (PA)
Lafayette Coll (PA)
Lake Erie Coll (OH)
Lake Forest Coll (IL)
Lakehead U (ON, Canada)
Lamar U (TX)
Lane Coll (TN)
La Salle U (PA)
Lawrence U (WI)
Lebanon Valley Coll (PA)
Lee U (TN)
Lehigh U (PA)
Lehman Coll of the City U of New York (NY)
Le Moyne Coll (NY)
Lenoir-Rhyne U (NC)
Lewis & Clark Coll (OR)
Lincoln U (PA)
Lindenwood U (MO)
Linfield Coll (OR)
Lipscomb U (TN)
Lock Haven U of Pennsylvania (PA)
Long Island U–C. W. Post Campus (NY)
Longwood U (VA)
Loras Coll (IA)
Louisiana Coll (LA)
Louisiana State U and Ag and Mech Coll (LA)
Loyola Marymount U (CA)
Loyola U Chicago (IL)
Loyola U Maryland (MD)
Loyola U New Orleans (LA)
Luther Coll (IA)
Lycoming Coll (PA)
Lynchburg Coll (VA)
Macalester Coll (MN)
Manchester Coll (IN)
Manhattan Coll (NY)
Manhattanville Coll (NY)
Marlboro Coll (VT)

Marquette U (WI)
Mary Baldwin Coll (VA)
Marywood U (PA)
McDaniel Coll (MD)
Mercer U (GA)
Merrimack Coll (MA)
Messiah Coll (PA)
Miami U (OH)
Michigan State U (MI)
Middlebury Coll (VT)
Millersville U of Pennsylvania (PA)
Millsaps Coll (MS)
Mills Coll (CA)
Minnesota State U Mankato (MN)
Mississippi Coll (MS)
Missouri Southern State U (MO)
Missouri State U (MO)
Missouri Western State U (MO)
Molloy Coll (NY)
Monmouth Coll (IL)
Montclair State U (NJ)
Moravian Coll (PA)
Morehead State U (KY)
Morehouse Coll (GA)
Mount Allison U (NB, Canada)
Mount Holyoke Coll (MA)
Mount St. Mary's Coll (CA)
Mount St. Mary's U (MD)
Muhlenberg Coll (PA)
Nazareth Coll of Rochester (NY)
Nebraska Wesleyan U (NE)
New Coll of Florida (FL)
New York U (NY)
Niagara U (NY)
North Carolina Ag and Tech State U (NC)
North Carolina Central U (NC)
North Carolina State U (NC)
North Central Coll (IL)
North Dakota State U (ND)
Northeastern Illinois U (IL)
Northern Illinois U (IL)
Northern Kentucky U (KY)
Northern Michigan U (MI)
Northern State U (SD)
North Georgia Coll & State U (GA)
Notre Dame of Maryland U (MD)
Oakland U (MI)
Occidental Coll (CA)
Oglethorpe U (GA)
Ohio Northern U (OH)
The Ohio State U (OH)
Ohio U (OH)
Ohio Wesleyan U (OH)
Oklahoma City U (OK)
Oklahoma State U (OK)
Oral Roberts U (OK)
Otterbein U (OH)
Ouachita Baptist U (AR)
Pacific Lutheran U (WA)
Pacific U (OR)
Penn State Abington (PA)
Penn State Altoona (PA)
Penn State Beaver (PA)
Penn State Berks (PA)
Penn State Brandywine (PA)
Penn State DuBois (PA)
Penn State Erie, The Behrend Coll (PA)
Penn State Fayette, The Eberly Campus (PA)
Penn State Greater Allegheny (PA)
Penn State Hazleton (PA)
Penn State Lehigh Valley (PA)
Penn State Mont Alto (PA)
Penn State New Kensington (PA)
Penn State Schuylkill (PA)
Penn State Shenango (PA)
Penn State U Park (PA)
Penn State Wilkes-Barre (PA)
Penn State Worthington Scranton (PA)
Penn State York (PA)
Pepperdine U, Malibu (CA)
Pittsburg State U (KS)
Plymouth State U (NH)
Pomona Coll (CA)
Portland State U (OR)
Presbyterian Coll (SC)
Princeton U (NJ)
Providence Coll (RI)
Purchase Coll, State U of New York (NY)
Purdue U Calumet (IN)

Queens Coll of the City U of New York (NY)
Queen's U at Kingston (ON, Canada)
Randolph Coll (VA)
Randolph-Macon Coll (VA)
Regis U (CO)
Rhode Island Coll (RI)
Rhodes Coll (TN)
Rice U (TX)
Rider U (NJ)
Ripon Coll (WI)
Roanoke Coll (VA)
Rockford Coll (IL)
Rockhurst U (MO)
Rollins Coll (FL)
Rosemont Coll (PA)
Rutgers, The State U of New Jersey, Camden (NJ)
Rutgers, The State U of New Jersey, Newark (NJ)
Rutgers, The State U of New Jersey, New Brunswick (NJ)
Sacred Heart U (CT)
Saginaw Valley State U (MI)
St. Ambrose U (IA)
Saint Anselm Coll (NH)
St. Bonaventure U (NY)
St. Catherine U (MN)
St. Edward's U (TX)
Saint Francis U (PA)
St. John Fisher Coll (NY)
Saint John's U (MN)
St. John's U (NY)
Saint Joseph's U (PA)
St. Lawrence U (NY)
Saint Louis U (MO)
Saint Mary's Coll (IN)
Saint Mary's Coll of California (CA)
St. Mary's U (TX)
Saint Michael's Coll (VT)
St. Norbert Coll (WI)
St. Olaf Coll (MN)
St. Thomas U (NB, Canada)
Saint Vincent Coll (PA)
Salisbury U (MD)
Salve Regina U (RI)
Samford U (AL)
San Diego State U (CA)
San Francisco State U (CA)
Santa Clara U (CA)
Sarah Lawrence Coll (NY)
Scripps Coll (CA)
Seattle U (WA)
Sewanee: The U of the South (TN)
Shippensburg U of Pennsylvania (PA)
Siena Coll (NY)
Simmons Coll (MA)
Simon Fraser U (BC, Canada)
Simpson Coll (IA)
Skidmore Coll (NY)
Slippery Rock U of Pennsylvania (PA)
Smith Coll (MA)
Sonoma State U (CA)
South Dakota State U (SD)
Southeast Missouri State U (MO)
Southern Connecticut State U (CT)
Southern Illinois U Carbondale (IL)
Southern Methodist U (TX)
Southern Oregon U (OR)
Southwestern U (TX)
Spelman Coll (GA)
Stanford U (CA)
State U of New York at Binghamton (NY)
State U of New York at Fredonia (NY)
State U of New York at New Paltz (NY)
State U of New York at Oswego (NY)
State U of New York at Plattsburgh (NY)
State U of New York Coll at Cortland (NY)
State U of New York Coll at Geneseo (NY)
State U of New York Coll at Oneonta (NY)
State U of New York Coll at Potsdam (NY)
Stephen F. Austin State U (TX)
Stetson U (FL)

Stonehill Coll (MA)
Stony Brook U, State U of New York (NY)
Suffolk U (MA)
Susquehanna U (PA)
Swarthmore Coll (PA)
Sweet Briar Coll (VA)
Syracuse U (NY)
Taylor U (IN)
Temple U (PA)
Texas A&M U (TX)
Texas Christian U (TX)
Texas Southern U (TX)
Texas State U–San Marcos (TX)
Texas Tech U (TX)
Transylvania U (KY)
Trent U (ON, Canada)
Trinity Coll (CT)
Trinity U (TX)
Truman State U (MO)
Tufts U (MA)
Tulane U (LA)
Union Coll (NE)
Union Coll (NY)
Union U (TN)
United States Military Acad (NY)
Université de Sherbrooke (QC, Canada)
U at Buffalo, the State U of New York (NY)
The U of Akron (OH)
U of Alberta (AB, Canada)
The U of Arizona (AZ)
U of Arkansas (AR)
U of Arkansas at Little Rock (AR)
The U of British Columbia (BC, Canada)
The U of British Columbia–Okanagan (BC, Canada)
U of California, Berkeley (CA)
U of California, Davis (CA)
U of California, Irvine (CA)
U of California, Los Angeles (CA)
U of California, Riverside (CA)
U of California, Santa Barbara (CA)
U of Central Arkansas (AR)
U of Central Florida (FL)
U of Central Missouri (MO)
U of Cincinnati (OH)
U of Colorado Boulder (CO)
U of Colorado Denver (CO)
U of Connecticut (CT)
U of Dallas (TX)
U of Dayton (OH)
U of Denver (CO)
U of Evansville (IN)
U of Florida (FL)
U of Georgia (GA)
U of Hawaii at Manoa (HI)
U of Houston (TX)
U of Idaho (ID)
U of Illinois at Chicago (IL)
U of Illinois at Urbana–Champaign (IL)
U of Indianapolis (IN)
The U of Iowa (IA)
The U of Kansas (KS)
U of La Verne (CA)
U of Lethbridge (AB, Canada)
U of Louisiana at Lafayette (LA)
U of Louisiana at Monroe (LA)
U of Louisville (KY)
U of Maine (ME)
U of Maine at Fort Kent (ME)
U of Maryland, Coll Park (MD)
U of Massachusetts Amherst (MA)
U of Massachusetts Boston (MA)
U of Massachusetts Dartmouth (MA)
U of Miami (FL)
U of Michigan (MI)
U of Michigan–Dearborn (MI)
U of Michigan–Flint (MI)
U of Minnesota, Twin Cities Campus (MN)
U of Mississippi (MS)
U of Missouri (MO)
U of Missouri–Kansas City (MO)
U of Missouri–St. Louis (MO)
U of Mount Union (OH)
U of Nebraska at Kearney (NE)
U of Nebraska at Omaha (NE)
U of Nebraska–Lincoln (NE)
U of Nevada, Las Vegas (NV)
U of Nevada, Reno (NV)

INDEXES

GENETICS

GENETICS RELATED

GEOCHEMISTRY

GEOGRAPHIC INFORMATION SCIENCE AND CARTOGRAPHY

GEOGRAPHY

The U of North Carolina at Chapel Hill (NC)
The U of North Carolina at Charlotte (NC)
The U of North Carolina Wilmington (NC)
U of North Dakota (ND)
U of Northern Colorado (CO)
U of Northern Iowa (IA)
U of North Texas (TX)
U of Oklahoma (OK)
U of Oregon (OR)
U of Ottawa (ON, Canada)
U of Pittsburgh at Johnstown (PA)
U of Regina (SK, Canada)
U of Richmond (VA)
U of St. Thomas (MN)
U of South Alabama (AL)
U of South Carolina (SC)
U of Southern California (CA)
U of Southern Mississippi (MS)
U of South Florida (FL)
The U of Tennessee (TN)
The U of Tennessee at Martin (TN)
The U of Texas at Austin (TX)
The U of Texas at El Paso (TX)
The U of Texas at San Antonio (TX)
U of the District of Columbia (DC)
The U of Toledo (OH)
U of Toronto (ON, Canada)
U of Utah (UT)
U of Vermont (VT)
U of Washington (WA)
The U of Western Ontario (ON, Canada)
U of West Georgia (GA)
U of Wisconsin–Eau Claire (WI)
U of Wisconsin–La Crosse (WI)
U of Wisconsin–Madison (WI)
U of Wisconsin–Milwaukee (WI)
U of Wisconsin–River Falls (WI)
U of Wisconsin–Stevens Point (WI)
U of Wisconsin–Whitewater (WI)
U of Wyoming (WY)
Utah State U (UT)
Valparaiso U (IN)
Vassar Coll (NY)
Villanova U (PA)
Virginia Polytechnic Inst and State U (VA)
Wayne State Coll (NE)
Weber State U (UT)
West Chester U of Pennsylvania (PA)
Western Carolina U (NC)
Western Illinois U (IL)
Western Kentucky U (KY)
Western Michigan U (MI)
Western Oregon U (OR)
Western Washington U (WA)
West Texas A&M U (TX)
West Virginia U (WV)
William Paterson U of New Jersey (NJ)
Wittenberg U (OH)
Worcester State U (MA)
Wright State U (OH)
Youngstown State U (OH)

GEOGRAPHY RELATED

Bridgewater State U (MA)
Brigham Young U (UT)
Northern Michigan U (MI)
Ohio U (OH)
Prescott Coll (AZ)
South Dakota State U (SD)
Temple U (PA)
U of California, Los Angeles (CA)

GEOGRAPHY TEACHER EDUCATION

Bishop's U (QC, Canada)
Central Michigan U (MI)
Concordia U, Nebraska (NE)
Grand Valley State U (MI)
Mayville State U (ND)
Michigan State U (MI)
Northern Michigan U (MI)
Rhode Island Coll (RI)
U of Delaware (DE)
The U of Tennessee at Martin (TN)
U of Windsor (ON, Canada)
Valparaiso U (IN)
Wayne State Coll (NE)

Western Michigan U (MI)

GEOLOGICAL AND EARTH SCIENCES/GEOSCIENCES RELATED

Allegheny Coll (PA)
Baylor U (TX)
Boston U (MA)
Bridgewater State U (MA)
Brigham Young U (UT)
California State U, Chico (CA)
Cedarville U (OH)
The Coll at Brockport, State U of New York (NY)
Cornell U (NY)
Earlham Coll (IN)
Eckerd Coll (FL)
Georgia Inst of Technology (GA)
Hamilton Coll (NY)
Lehigh U (PA)
Montclair State U (NJ)
Northeastern U (MA)
Northland Coll (WI)
Old Dominion U (VA)
Pacific Lutheran U (WA)
Penn State Abington (PA)
Penn State Altoona (PA)
Penn State Beaver (PA)
Penn State Berks (PA)
Penn State Brandywine (PA)
Penn State DuBois (PA)
Penn State Erie, The Behrend Coll (PA)
Penn State Fayette, The Eberly Campus (PA)
Penn State Greater Allegheny (PA)
Penn State Hazleton (PA)
Penn State Lehigh Valley (PA)
Penn State Mont Alto (PA)
Penn State New Kensington (PA)
Penn State Schuylkill (PA)
Penn State Shenango (PA)
Penn State U Park (PA)
Penn State Wilkes-Barre (PA)
Penn State Worthington Scranton (PA)
Penn State York (PA)
Princeton U (NJ)
Salisbury U (MD)
Stanford U (CA)
Texas A&M U (TX)
Towson U (MD)
Union Coll (NY)
The U of Akron (OH)
U of Arkansas (AR)
U of California, Los Angeles (CA)
U of Guelph (ON, Canada)
U of Illinois at Urbana–Champaign (IL)
U of Miami (FL)
U of Nevada, Las Vegas (NV)
The U of North Carolina at Charlotte (NC)
U of Northern Iowa (IA)
U of Oklahoma (OK)
U of Pittsburgh (PA)
The U of Texas at Arlington (TX)
U of Utah (UT)
U of West Georgia (GA)
U of Wyoming (WY)
Utah Valley U (UT)
Utica Coll (NY)
Western State Coll of Colorado (CO)
Western Washington U (WA)
Whitman Coll (WA)
Wittenberg U (OH)
Yale U (CT)

GEOLOGICAL/GEOPHYSICAL ENGINEERING

Colorado School of Mines (CO)
Michigan Technological U (MI)
Missouri U of Science and Technology (MO)
Montana Tech of The U of Montana (MT)
Queen's U at Kingston (ON, Canada)
Rutgers, The State U of New Jersey, Newark (NJ)
South Dakota School of Mines and Technology (SD)
Tufts U (MA)

U of Alaska Fairbanks (AK)
The U of British Columbia (BC, Canada)
U of California, Berkeley (CA)
U of California, Los Angeles (CA)
U of Michigan (MI)
U of Minnesota, Twin Cities Campus (MN)
U of Mississippi (MS)
U of Nevada, Reno (NV)
U of North Dakota (ND)
U of Rochester (NY)
U of Toronto (ON, Canada)
U of Utah (UT)
U of Wisconsin–Madison (WI)

GEOLOGY/EARTH SCIENCE

Acadia U (NS, Canada)
Adams State Coll (CO)
Adrian Coll (MI)
Alaska Pacific U (AK)
Albion Coll (MI)
Alfred U (NY)
Allegheny Coll (PA)
American U of Beirut (Lebanon)
Amherst Coll (MA)
Appalachian State U (NC)
Arizona State U (AZ)
Arkansas Tech U (AR)
Ashland U (OH)
Auburn U (AL)
Augustana Coll (IL)
Austin Peay State U (TN)
Ball State U (IN)
Bates Coll (ME)
Baylor U (TX)
Beloit Coll (WI)
Bemidji State U (MN)
Bloomsburg U of Pennsylvania (PA)
Boise State U (ID)
Boston Coll (MA)
Boston U (MA)
Bowdoin Coll (ME)
Bowling Green State U (OH)
Bridgewater State U (MA)
Brown U (RI)
Bryn Mawr Coll (PA)
Bucknell U (PA)
Buffalo State Coll, State U of New York (NY)
California Inst of Technology (CA)
California Lutheran U (CA)
California Polytechnic State U, San Luis Obispo (CA)
California State Polytechnic U, Pomona (CA)
California State U, Bakersfield (CA)
California State U, Chico (CA)
California State U, Dominguez Hills (CA)
California State U, East Bay (CA)
California State U, Fresno (CA)
California State U, Fullerton (CA)
California State U, Long Beach (CA)
California State U, Los Angeles (CA)
California State U, Sacramento (CA)
California State U, San Bernardino (CA)
California State U, Stanislaus (CA)
California U of Pennsylvania (PA)
Calvin Coll (MI)
Carleton Coll (MN)
Case Western Reserve U (OH)
Castleton State Coll (VT)
Cedarville U (OH)
Centenary Coll of Louisiana (LA)
Central Connecticut State U (CT)
Central Michigan U (MI)
Central State U (OH)
Central Washington U (WA)
City Coll of the City U of New York (NY)
Clarion U of Pennsylvania (PA)
Clark U (MA)
Clemson U (SC)
Cleveland State U (OH)
Colby Coll (ME)
Colgate U (NY)
The Coll at Brockport, State U of New York (NY)
Coll of Charleston (SC)
The Coll of William and Mary (VA)

The Coll of Wooster (OH)
The Colorado Coll (CO)
Colorado State U (CO)
Columbia U, School of General Studies (NY)
Columbus State U (GA)
Concordia U Chicago (IL)
Cornell Coll (IA)
Cornell U (NY)
Dalhousie U (NS, Canada)
Dartmouth Coll (NH)
Denison U (OH)
DePauw U (IN)
Dickinson Coll (PA)
Dowling Coll (NY)
East Carolina U (NC)
Eastern Illinois U (IL)
Eastern Kentucky U (KY)
Eastern Michigan U (MI)
Eastern New Mexico U (NM)
Eastern Washington U (WA)
East Stroudsburg U of Pennsylvania (PA)
East Tennessee State U (TN)
Edinboro U of Pennsylvania (PA)
Elizabeth City State U (NC)
Emporia State U (KS)
Excelsior Coll (NY)
Florida Atlantic U (FL)
Florida Intl U (FL)
Florida State U (FL)
Fort Hays State U (KS)
Fort Lewis Coll (CO)
Franklin & Marshall Coll (PA)
Furman U (SC)
George Mason U (VA)
The George Washington U (DC)
Georgia Southern U (GA)
Georgia Southwestern State U (GA)
Georgia State U (GA)
Grand Valley State U (MI)
Guilford Coll (NC)
Gustavus Adolphus Coll (MN)
Hamilton Coll (NY)
Hanover Coll (IN)
Hardin-Simmons U (TX)
Hartwick Coll (NY)
Harvard U (MA)
Haverford Coll (PA)
Hobart and William Smith Colls (NY)
Hofstra U (NY)
Hope Coll (MI)
Humboldt State U (CA)
Idaho State U (ID)
Illinois State U (IL)
Indiana State U (IN)
Indiana U Bloomington (IN)
Indiana U Northwest (IN)
Indiana U of Pennsylvania (PA)
Indiana U–Purdue U Fort Wayne (IN)
Indiana U–Purdue U Indianapolis (IN)
Iowa State U of Science and Technology (IA)
Jacksonville State U (AL)
James Madison U (VA)
The Johns Hopkins U (MD)
Juniata Coll (PA)
Kansas State U (KS)
Kean U (NJ)
Keene State Coll (NH)
Kent State U (OH)
Kutztown U of Pennsylvania (PA)
Lafayette Coll (PA)
Lakehead U (ON, Canada)
Lake Superior State U (MI)
Lamar U (TX)
La Salle U (PA)
Lawrence U (WI)
Lehman Coll of the City U of New York (NY)
Lock Haven U of Pennsylvania (PA)
Long Island U–C. W. Post Campus (NY)
Louisiana State U and Ag and Mech Coll (LA)
Macalester Coll (MN)
Mansfield U of Pennsylvania (PA)
Marietta Coll (OH)
Marshall U (WV)
Massachusetts Inst of Technology (MA)
Mercyhurst Coll (PA)

Miami U (OH)
Michigan State U (MI)
Michigan Technological U (MI)
Middlebury Coll (VT)
Middle Tennessee State U (TN)
Midwestern State U (TX)
Millersville U of Pennsylvania (PA)
Millsaps Coll (MS)
Minnesota State U Mankato (MN)
Minnesota State U Moorhead (MN)
Minot State U (ND)
Mississippi State U (MS)
Missouri State U (MO)
Missouri U of Science and Technology (MO)
Montana State U (MT)
Montclair State U (NJ)
Moravian Coll (PA)
Morehead State U (KY)
Mount Allison U (NB, Canada)
Mount Holyoke Coll (MA)
National U (CA)
New Jersey City U (NJ)
New Mexico Highlands U (NM)
New Mexico Inst of Mining and Technology (NM)
New Mexico State U (NM)
North Carolina State U (NC)
North Dakota State U (ND)
Northeastern Illinois U (IL)
Northeastern U (MA)
Northern Arizona U (AZ)
Northern Illinois U (IL)
Northern Kentucky U (KY)
Northern Michigan U (MI)
Northwest Missouri State U (MO)
Norwich U (VT)
Occidental Coll (CA)
The Ohio State U (OH)
Ohio U (OH)
Ohio Wesleyan U (OH)
Oklahoma State U (OK)
Pace U (NY)
Pacific Lutheran U (WA)
Penn State Abington (PA)
Penn State Altoona (PA)
Penn State Beaver (PA)
Penn State Berks (PA)
Penn State Brandywine (PA)
Penn State DuBois (PA)
Penn State Erie, The Behrend Coll (PA)
Penn State Fayette, The Eberly Campus (PA)
Penn State Greater Allegheny (PA)
Penn State Hazleton (PA)
Penn State Lehigh Valley (PA)
Penn State Mont Alto (PA)
Penn State New Kensington (PA)
Penn State Schuylkill (PA)
Penn State Shenango (PA)
Penn State U Park (PA)
Penn State Wilkes-Barre (PA)
Penn State Worthington Scranton (PA)
Penn State York (PA)
Piedmont Coll (GA)
Pomona Coll (CA)
Portland State U (OR)
Prescott Coll (AZ)
Purdue U (IN)
Queens Coll of the City U of New York (NY)
Queen's U at Kingston (ON, Canada)
Radford U (VA)
Rensselaer Polytechnic Inst (NY)
Rice U (TX)
The Richard Stockton Coll of New Jersey (NJ)
Rider U (NJ)
Rocky Mountain Coll (MT)
Rutgers, The State U of New Jersey, Newark (NJ)
Rutgers, The State U of New Jersey, New Brunswick (NJ)
St. Lawrence U (NY)
Saint Louis U (MO)
St. Mary's U (TX)
St. Norbert Coll (WI)
Salem State U (MA)
Sam Houston State U (TX)
San Diego State U (CA)
San Francisco State U (CA)
Sarah Lawrence Coll (NY)

Scripps Coll (CA)
Sewanee: The U of the South (TN)
Shawnee State U (OH)
Shippensburg U of Pennsylvania (PA)
Simon Fraser U (BC, Canada)
Skidmore Coll (NY)
Slippery Rock U of Pennsylvania (PA)
Smith Coll (MA)
Sonoma State U (CA)
South Dakota School of Mines and Technology (SD)
Southern Connecticut State U (CT)
Southern Illinois U Carbondale (IL)
Southern Methodist U (TX)
Southern Oregon U (OR)
Stanford U (CA)
State U of New York at Binghamton (NY)
State U of New York at Fredonia (NY)
State U of New York at New Paltz (NY)
State U of New York at Oswego (NY)
State U of New York at Plattsburgh (NY)
State U of New York Coll at Cortland (NY)
State U of New York Coll at Geneseo (NY)
State U of New York Coll at Oneonta (NY)
State U of New York Coll at Potsdam (NY)
Stephen F. Austin State U (TX)
Stony Brook U, State U of New York (NY)
Sul Ross State U (TX)
Susquehanna U (PA)
Syracuse U (NY)
Tarleton State U (TX)
Taylor U (IN)
Temple U (PA)
Texas A&M U (TX)
Texas A&M U–Corpus Christi (TX)
Texas A&M U–Kingsville (TX)
Texas Christian U (TX)
Texas Tech U (TX)
Towson U (MD)
Trinity U (TX)
Tufts U (MA)
Tulane U (LA)
Union Coll (NY)
U at Buffalo, the State U of New York (NY)
The U of Akron (OH)
The U of Alabama (AL)
U of Alaska Fairbanks (AK)
U of Alberta (AB, Canada)
The U of Arizona (AZ)
U of Arkansas (AR)
U of Arkansas at Little Rock (AR)
The U of British Columbia (BC, Canada)
U of California, Berkeley (CA)
U of California, Davis (CA)
U of California, Irvine (CA)
U of California, Los Angeles (CA)
U of California, Merced (CA)
U of California, Riverside (CA)
U of California, Santa Barbara (CA)
U of California, Santa Cruz (CA)
U of Central Missouri (MO)
U of Cincinnati (OH)
U of Colorado Boulder (CO)
U of Connecticut (CT)
U of Dayton (OH)
U of Delaware (DE)
U of Florida (FL)
U of Georgia (GA)
U of Hawaii at Hilo (HI)
U of Hawaii at Manoa (HI)
U of Houston (TX)
U of Idaho (ID)
U of Illinois at Chicago (IL)
U of Illinois at Urbana–Champaign (IL)
U of Indianapolis (IN)
The U of Iowa (IA)
The U of Kansas (KS)
U of Louisiana at Lafayette (LA)
U of Maine (ME)
U of Maine at Farmington (ME)

U of Maine at Presque Isle (ME)
U of Maryland, Coll Park (MD)
U of Massachusetts Amherst (MA)
U of Massachusetts Boston (MA)
U of Memphis (TN)
U of Miami (FL)
U of Michigan (MI)
U of Michigan–Dearborn (MI)
U of Minnesota, Duluth (MN)
U of Minnesota, Twin Cities Campus (MN)
U of Mississippi (MS)
U of Missouri (MO)
U of Missouri–Kansas City (MO)
U of Mount Union (OH)
U of Nebraska at Omaha (NE)
U of Nebraska–Lincoln (NE)
U of Nevada, Las Vegas (NV)
U of Nevada, Reno (NV)
U of New Hampshire (NH)
U of New Mexico (NM)
U of New Orleans (LA)
U of North Alabama (AL)
The U of North Carolina at Chapel Hill (NC)
The U of North Carolina at Charlotte (NC)
The U of North Carolina Wilmington (NC)
U of North Dakota (ND)
U of Northern Colorado (CO)
U of Northern Iowa (IA)
U of Oklahoma (OK)
U of Oregon (OR)
U of Ottawa (ON, Canada)
U of Pennsylvania (PA)
U of Pittsburgh (PA)
U of Pittsburgh at Johnstown (PA)
U of Puget Sound (WA)
U of Regina (SK, Canada)
U of Rhode Island (RI)
U of Rochester (NY)
U of St. Thomas (MN)
U of South Alabama (AL)
U of South Carolina (SC)
The U of South Dakota (SD)
U of Southern California (CA)
U of Southern Indiana (IN)
U of Southern Maine (ME)
U of Southern Mississippi (MS)
U of South Florida (FL)
The U of Tennessee (TN)
The U of Tennessee at Chattanooga (TN)
The U of Tennessee at Martin (TN)
The U of Texas at Arlington (TX)
The U of Texas at Austin (TX)
The U of Texas at Dallas (TX)
The U of Texas at El Paso (TX)
The U of Texas at San Antonio (TX)
The U of Texas of the Permian Basin (TX)
U of the Pacific (CA)
The U of Toledo (OH)
U of Tulsa (OK)
U of Utah (UT)
U of Vermont (VT)
U of Washington (WA)
The U of Western Ontario (ON, Canada)
U of West Georgia (GA)
U of Windsor (ON, Canada)
U of Wisconsin–Eau Claire (WI)
U of Wisconsin–Green Bay (WI)
U of Wisconsin–Madison (WI)
U of Wisconsin–Milwaukee (WI)
U of Wisconsin–Platteville (WI)
U of Wisconsin–River Falls (WI)
U of Wisconsin–Stevens Point (WI)
U of Wyoming (WY)
Utah State U (UT)
Utah Valley U (UT)
Valparaiso U (IN)
Vanderbilt U (TN)
Vassar Coll (NY)
Virginia Polytechnic Inst and State U (VA)
Virginia Wesleyan Coll (VA)
Washington and Lee U (VA)
Washington State U (WA)
Washington U in St. Louis (MO)
Wayland Baptist U (TX)
Wayne State U (MI)
Weber State U (UT)
Wellesley Coll (MA)

Wesleyan U (CT)
West Chester U of Pennsylvania (PA)
Western Carolina U (NC)
Western Connecticut State U (CT)
Western Illinois U (IL)
Western Kentucky U (KY)
Western Michigan U (MI)
Western State Coll of Colorado (CO)
Western Washington U (WA)
West Texas A&M U (TX)
West Virginia U (WV)
Wheaton Coll (IL)
Whitman Coll (WA)
Wichita State U (KS)
Wilkes U (PA)
William Paterson U of New Jersey (NJ)
Williams Coll (MA)
Winona State U (MN)
Wittenberg U (OH)
Wright State U (OH)
York Coll of the City U of New York (NY)
Youngstown State U (OH)

GEOPHYSICS AND SEISMOLOGY

Baylor U (TX)
Boise State U (ID)
Boston Coll (MA)
Boston U (MA)
Bowdoin Coll (ME)
Bowling Green State U (OH)
Brown U (RI)
California Inst of Technology (CA)
Eastern Michigan U (MI)
Michigan State U (MI)
Michigan Technological U (MI)
Missouri U of Science and Technology (MO)
New Mexico Inst of Mining and Technology (NM)
Occidental Coll (CA)
Rice U (TX)
St. Lawrence U (NY)
Saint Louis U (MO)
Southern Methodist U (TX)
Stanford U (CA)
State U of New York at Fredonia (NY)
State U of New York Coll at Geneseo (NY)
Texas A&M U (TX)
The U of Akron (OH)
U of Alberta (AB, Canada)
The U of British Columbia (BC, Canada)
U of California, Los Angeles (CA)
U of California, Riverside (CA)
U of California, Santa Barbara (CA)
U of Houston (TX)
U of Minnesota, Twin Cities Campus (MN)
U of Nevada, Reno (NV)
U of Oklahoma (OK)
U of Ottawa (ON, Canada)
U of South Carolina (SC)
The U of Texas at Austin (TX)
The U of Texas at El Paso (TX)
U of Tulsa (OK)
U of Utah (UT)
U of Washington (WA)
Western Michigan U (MI)
Western Washington U (WA)

GEOTECHNICAL AND GEOENVIRONMENTAL ENGINEERING

U of Illinois at Urbana–Champaign (IL)

GERMAN

Adrian Coll (MI)
Agnes Scott Coll (GA)
Albion Coll (MI)
Alfred U (NY)
Allegheny Coll (PA)
Alma Coll (MI)
American U (DC)
Amherst Coll (MA)
Angelo State U (TX)
Aquinas Coll (MI)

Arizona State U (AZ)
Auburn U (AL)
Augustana Coll (IL)
Augustana Coll (SD)
Austin Coll (TX)
Baker U (KS)
Baldwin-Wallace Coll (OH)
Ball State U (IN)
Bard Coll (NY)
Bard Coll at Simon's Rock (MA)
Barnard Coll (NY)
Bates Coll (ME)
Baylor U (TX)
Beloit Coll (WI)
Bemidji State U (MN)
Berea Coll (KY)
Berry Coll (GA)
Birmingham-Southern Coll (AL)
Bishop's U (QC, Canada)
Boise State U (ID)
Boston Coll (MA)
Boston U (MA)
Bowdoin Coll (ME)
Bowling Green State U (OH)
Brandeis U (MA)
Brown U (RI)
Bryn Mawr Coll (PA)
Bucknell U (PA)
Butler U (IN)
California Lutheran U (CA)
California State U, Chico (CA)
California State U, Long Beach (CA)
Calvin Coll (MI)
Canisius Coll (NY)
Carleton Coll (MN)
Carnegie Mellon U (PA)
Case Western Reserve U (OH)
The Catholic U of America (DC)
Central Connecticut State U (CT)
Central Michigan U (MI)
Centre Coll (KY)
Christopher Newport U (VA)
Coe Coll (IA)
Colby Coll (ME)
Colgate U (NY)
Coll of Charleston (SC)
Coll of Saint Benedict (MN)
Coll of the Holy Cross (MA)
The Coll of William and Mary (VA)
The Coll of Wooster (OH)
The Colorado Coll (CO)
Colorado State U (CO)
Columbia U, School of General Studies (NY)
Concordia Coll (MN)
Converse Coll (SC)
Cornell Coll (IA)
Cornell U (NY)
Creighton U (NE)
Dalhousie U (NS, Canada)
Dartmouth Coll (NH)
Davidson Coll (NC)
Delaware State U (DE)
Denison U (OH)
DePaul U (IL)
DePauw U (IN)
Dickinson Coll (PA)
Doane Coll (NE)
Drew U (NJ)
Drury U (MO)
Earlham Coll (IN)
East Carolina U (NC)
Eastern Michigan U (MI)
Edinboro U of Pennsylvania (PA)
Elizabethtown Coll (PA)
Elmhurst Coll (IL)
Emory U (GA)
Fairfield U (CT)
Fordham U (NY)
Fort Hays State U (KS)
Franciscan U of Steubenville (OH)
Franklin & Marshall Coll (PA)
Furman U (SC)
Georgetown Coll (KY)
The George Washington U (DC)
Georgia Southern U (GA)
Georgia State U (GA)
Gettysburg Coll (PA)
Gonzaga U (WA)
Gordon Coll (MA)
Grinnell Coll (IA)
Guilford Coll (NC)
Gustavus Adolphus Coll (MN)
Hamline U (MN)

Hampden-Sydney Coll (VA)
Hanover Coll (IN)
Hartwick Coll (NY)
Harvard U (MA)
Haverford Coll (PA)
Heidelberg U (OH)
Hendrix Coll (AR)
Hillsdale Coll (MI)
Hofstra U (NY)
Hood Coll (MD)
Hope Coll (MI)
Hunter Coll of the City U of New York (NY)
Idaho State U (ID)
Illinois Coll (IL)
Illinois State U (IL)
Illinois Wesleyan U (IL)
Immaculata U (PA)
Indiana U Bloomington (IN)
Indiana U–Purdue U Fort Wayne (IN)
Indiana U–Purdue U Indianapolis (IN)
Indiana U South Bend (IN)
Indiana U Southeast (IN)
Iowa State U of Science and Technology (IA)
Ithaca Coll (NY)
Jacksonville State U (AL)
Jamestown Coll (ND)
John Carroll U (OH)
The Johns Hopkins U (MD)
Juniata Coll (PA)
Kalamazoo Coll (MI)
Kent State U (OH)
Kenyon Coll (OH)
Knox Coll (IL)
Kutztown U of Pennsylvania (PA)
Lafayette Coll (PA)
Lake Erie Coll (OH)
La Salle U (PA)
Lawrence U (WI)
Lebanon Valley Coll (PA)
Lehigh U (PA)
Lenoir-Rhyne U (NC)
Lewis & Clark Coll (OR)
Linfield Coll (OR)
Lipscomb U (TN)
Lock Haven U of Pennsylvania (PA)
Longwood U (VA)
Loyola U Maryland (MD)
Luther Coll (IA)
Lycoming Coll (PA)
Macalester Coll (MN)
Marlboro Coll (VT)
Marquette U (WI)
McDaniel Coll (MD)
Mercer U (GA)
Messiah Coll (PA)
Miami U (OH)
Michigan State U (MI)
Middlebury Coll (VT)
Millersville U of Pennsylvania (PA)
Minnesota State U Mankato (MN)
Minot State U (ND)
Missouri Southern State U (MO)
Missouri State U (MO)
Moravian Coll (PA)
Mount Allison U (NB, Canada)
Mount St. Mary's U (MD)
Muhlenberg Coll (PA)
Nazareth Coll of Rochester (NY)
Nebraska Wesleyan U (NE)
New Coll of Florida (FL)
New York U (NY)
North Central Coll (IL)
Northern Illinois U (IL)
Northern Kentucky U (KY)
Northern State U (SD)
Oakland U (MI)
The Ohio State U (OH)
Ohio U (OH)
Ohio Wesleyan U (OH)
Oklahoma City U (OK)
Oklahoma State U (OK)
Pacific Lutheran U (WA)
Pacific U (OR)
Penn State Abington (PA)
Penn State Altoona (PA)
Penn State Beaver (PA)
Penn State Berks (PA)
Penn State Brandywine (PA)
Penn State DuBois (PA)
Penn State Erie, The Behrend Coll (PA)

Penn State Fayette, The Eberly Campus (PA)
Penn State Greater Allegheny (PA)
Penn State Hazleton (PA)
Penn State Lehigh Valley (PA)
Penn State Mont Alto (PA)
Penn State New Kensington (PA)
Penn State Schuylkill (PA)
Penn State Shenango (PA)
Penn State U Park (PA)
Penn State Wilkes-Barre (PA)
Penn State Worthington Scranton (PA)
Penn State York (PA)
Pepperdine U, Malibu (CA)
Pomona Coll (CA)
Portland State U (OR)
Presbyterian Coll (SC)
Princeton U (NJ)
Queens Coll of the City U of New York (NY)
Queen's U at Kingston (ON, Canada)
Randolph-Macon Coll (VA)
Rhodes Coll (TN)
Rice U (TX)
Rider U (NJ)
Ripon Coll (WI)
Rosemont Coll (PA)
Rutgers, The State U of New Jersey, Camden (NJ)
Rutgers, The State U of New Jersey, Newark (NJ)
Rutgers, The State U of New Jersey, New Brunswick (NJ)
St. Ambrose U (IA)
Saint John's U (MN)
Saint Joseph's U (PA)
St. Lawrence U (NY)
Saint Louis U (MO)
Saint Mary's Coll of California (CA)
St. Norbert Coll (WI)
St. Olaf Coll (MN)
Samford U (AL)
San Diego State U (CA)
San Francisco State U (CA)
Santa Clara U (CA)
Sarah Lawrence Coll (NY)
Scripps Coll (CA)
Seattle U (WA)
Sewanee: The U of the South (TN)
Simpson Coll (IA)
Skidmore Coll (NY)
Smith Coll (MA)
South Dakota State U (SD)
Southeast Missouri State U (MO)
Southern Connecticut State U (CT)
Southern Illinois U Carbondale (IL)
Southern Methodist U (TX)
Southern Oregon U (OR)
Southwestern U (TX)
Stanford U (CA)
State U of New York at Binghamton (NY)
State U of New York at New Paltz (NY)
State U of New York at Oswego (NY)
State U of New York Coll at Cortland (NY)
Stetson U (FL)
Stony Brook U, State U of New York (NY)
Suffolk U (MA)
Susquehanna U (PA)
Swarthmore Coll (PA)
Sweet Briar Coll (VA)
Syracuse U (NY)
Temple U (PA)
Texas A&M U (TX)
Texas Christian U (TX)
Texas State U–San Marcos (TX)
Texas Tech U (TX)
Transylvania U (KY)
Trent U (ON, Canada)
Trinity Coll (CT)
Trinity U (TX)
Truman State U (MO)
Tufts U (MA)
Tulane U (LA)
Union Coll (NE)
Union Coll (NY)
United States Military Acad (NY)
U at Buffalo, the State U of New York (NY)

U of Alberta (AB, Canada)
The U of Arizona (AZ)
U of Arkansas (AR)
The U of British Columbia (BC, Canada)
U of California, Berkeley (CA)
U of California, Davis (CA)
U of California, Los Angeles (CA)
U of California, Santa Barbara (CA)
U of California, Santa Cruz (CA)
U of Central Missouri (MO)
U of Cincinnati (OH)
U of Connecticut (CT)
U of Dallas (TX)
U of Dayton (OH)
U of Denver (CO)
U of Evansville (IN)
U of Florida (FL)
U of Georgia (GA)
U of Hawaii at Manoa (HI)
U of Houston (TX)
U of Illinois at Urbana–Champaign (IL)
U of Indianapolis (IN)
The U of Iowa (IA)
U of Lethbridge (AB, Canada)
U of Maine (ME)
U of Maryland, Coll Park (MD)
U of Miami (FL)
U of Michigan (MI)
U of Minnesota, Duluth (MN)
U of Minnesota, Twin Cities Campus (MN)
U of Mississippi (MS)
U of Missouri (MO)
U of Missouri–Kansas City (MO)
U of Missouri–St. Louis (MO)
U of Mount Union (OH)
U of Nebraska at Kearney (NE)
U of Nebraska at Omaha (NE)
U of Nebraska–Lincoln (NE)
U of Nevada, Las Vegas (NV)
U of Nevada, Reno (NV)
U of New Hampshire (NH)
U of New Mexico (NM)
The U of North Carolina at Asheville (NC)
The U of North Carolina at Chapel Hill (NC)
The U of North Carolina at Charlotte (NC)
The U of North Carolina Wilmington (NC)
U of North Dakota (ND)
U of Northern Colorado (CO)
U of Northern Iowa (IA)
U of North Texas (TX)
U of Notre Dame (IN)
U of Oregon (OR)
U of Ottawa (ON, Canada)
U of Pennsylvania (PA)
U of Pittsburgh (PA)
U of Puget Sound (WA)
U of Redlands (CA)
U of Regina (SK, Canada)
U of Rhode Island (RI)
U of Rochester (NY)
U of St. Thomas (MN)
The U of Scranton (PA)
U of South Carolina (SC)
The U of South Dakota (SD)
U of Southern Indiana (IN)
U of South Florida (FL)
The U of Tennessee (TN)
The U of Texas at Arlington (TX)
The U of Texas at Austin (TX)
The U of Texas at El Paso (TX)
U of the Pacific (CA)
The U of Toledo (OH)
U of Toronto (ON, Canada)
U of Tulsa (OK)
U of Utah (UT)
U of Virginia (VA)
U of Washington (WA)
The U of Western Ontario (ON, Canada)
U of Windsor (ON, Canada)
U of Wisconsin–La Crosse (WI)
U of Wisconsin–Milwaukee (WI)
U of Wisconsin–Platteville (WI)
U of Wisconsin–River Falls (WI)
U of Wisconsin–Stevens Point (WI)
U of Wisconsin–Whitewater (WI)
U of Wyoming (WY)
Utah State U (UT)

Valparaiso U (IN)
Vanderbilt U (TN)
Vassar Coll (NY)
Virginia Polytechnic Inst and State U (VA)
Virginia Wesleyan Coll (VA)
Wabash Coll (IN)
Wake Forest U (NC)
Wartburg Coll (IA)
Washburn U (KS)
Washington & Jefferson Coll (PA)
Washington and Lee U (VA)
Washington Coll (MD)
Washington U in St. Louis (MO)
Wayne State U (MI)
Weber State U (UT)
Webster U (MO)
Wellesley Coll (MA)
Wesleyan U (CT)
West Chester U of Pennsylvania (PA)
Western Carolina U (NC)
Western Kentucky U (KY)
Western Michigan U (MI)
Western Oregon U (OR)
Western Washington U (WA)
Wheaton Coll (IL)
Wheaton Coll (MA)
Whitman Coll (WA)
Willamette U (OR)
Williams Coll (MA)
Wittenberg U (OH)
Wofford Coll (SC)
Wright State U (OH)
Xavier U (OH)
Yale U (CT)
Youngstown State U (OH)

GERMANIC LANGUAGES

Bennington Coll (VT)
Eastern Michigan U (MI)
Grand Valley State U (MI)
Indiana U Bloomington (IN)
New Coll of Florida (FL)
U of Colorado Boulder (CO)
The U of Kansas (KS)
U of Oklahoma (OK)
The U of Texas at San Antonio (TX)
U of Wisconsin–Eau Claire (WI)
U of Wisconsin–Green Bay (WI)
U of Wisconsin–Madison (WI)
Washington U in St. Louis (MO)

GERMANIC LANGUAGES RELATED

Calvin Coll (MI)
Columbia U, School of General Studies (NY)
Ohio Northern U (OH)

GERMAN LANGUAGE TEACHER EDUCATION

Albion Coll (MI)
Alma Coll (MI)
Auburn U (AL)
Augustana Coll (IL)
California Lutheran U (CA)
California State U, Chico (CA)
Calvin Coll (MI)
The Catholic U of America (DC)
Central Michigan U (MI)
Central Washington U (WA)
Colorado State U (CO)
Concordia Coll (MN)
Delaware State U (DE)
East Carolina U (NC)
Eastern Michigan U (MI)
Elmhurst Coll (IL)
Grand Valley State U (MI)
Hofstra U (NY)
Hope Coll (MI)
Hunter Coll of the City U of New York (NY)
Indiana U Bloomington (IN)
Indiana U–Purdue U Fort Wayne (IN)
Indiana U–Purdue U Indianapolis (IN)
Ithaca Coll (NY)
Juniata Coll (PA)
Messiah Coll (PA)
Miami U (OH)
Michigan State U (MI)
Minot State U (ND)

Missouri State U (MO)
Moravian Coll (PA)
Ohio Northern U (OH)
Ohio U (OH)
Ohio Wesleyan U (OH)
St. Ambrose U (IA)
State U of New York at New Paltz (NY)
U of Delaware (DE)
U of Evansville (IN)
U of Illinois at Chicago (IL)
U of Illinois at Urbana–Champaign (IL)
The U of Iowa (IA)
U of Lethbridge (AB, Canada)
U of Louisiana at Lafayette (LA)
U of Minnesota, Duluth (MN)
U of Missouri–St. Louis (MO)
U of Nebraska–Lincoln (NE)
The U of North Carolina at Charlotte (NC)
The U of South Dakota (SD)
The U of Tennessee at Martin (TN)
The U of Toledo (OH)
U of Windsor (ON, Canada)
U of Wisconsin–River Falls (WI)
Valparaiso U (IN)
Washburn U (KS)
Washington U in St. Louis (MO)
Weber State U (UT)
Western Michigan U (MI)
Western Washington U (WA)

GERMAN STUDIES

American U (DC)
Bard Coll (NY)
Bard Coll at Simon's Rock (MA)
Barnard Coll (NY)
Brown U (RI)
Case Western Reserve U (OH)
Central Coll (IA)
Coe Coll (IA)
Coll of the Holy Cross (MA)
The Coll of Wooster (OH)
Connecticut Coll (CT)
Cornell U (NY)
Fordham U (NY)
Franklin & Marshall Coll (PA)
Georgetown Coll (KY)
Hamilton Coll (NY)
Ithaca Coll (NY)
Kutztown U of Pennsylvania (PA)
Manhattanville Coll (NY)
Moravian Coll (PA)
Mount Holyoke Coll (MA)
North Carolina State U (NC)
Northern Michigan U (MI)
Queen's U at Kingston (ON, Canada)
Smith Coll (MA)
Stanford U (CA)
Suffolk U (MA)
Sweet Briar Coll (VA)
U of California, Irvine (CA)
U of California, Riverside (CA)
U of Illinois at Chicago (IL)
U of Massachusetts Amherst (MA)
U of Minnesota, Duluth (MN)
U of Nevada, Reno (NV)
U of Richmond (VA)
The U of Scranton (PA)
The U of Western Ontario (ON, Canada)
U of Windsor (ON, Canada)
Wellesley Coll (MA)

GERONTOLOGY

Alfred U (NY)
Barton Coll (NC)
Bethune-Cookman U (FL)
Bishop's U (QC, Canada)
Bowling Green State U (OH)
California State U, Chico (CA)
California State U, East Bay (CA)
California State U, Sacramento (CA)
California U of Pennsylvania (PA)
Case Western Reserve U (OH)
Central Washington U (WA)
Dowling Coll (NY)
Gwynedd-Mercy Coll (PA)
Indiana U Kokomo (IN)
Ithaca Coll (NY)
John Carroll U (OH)

Lakehead U (ON, Canada)
Lindenwood U (MO)
Madonna U (MI)
Miami U (OH)
Minnesota State U Moorhead (MN)
Missouri State U (MO)
Mount St. Mary's Coll (CA)
Quinnipiac U (CT)
St. Bonaventure U (NY)
St. Thomas U (NB, Canada)
San Diego State U (CA)
Sojourner-Douglass Coll (MD)
State U of New York at Fredonia (NY)
State U of New York Coll at Oneonta (NY)
Thomas Edison State Coll (NJ)
Towson U (MD)
U of Maryland U Coll (MD)
U of Nebraska at Omaha (NE)
U of Nevada, Las Vegas (NV)
U of Northern Iowa (IA)
U of North Texas (TX)
U of Regina (SK, Canada)
U of Southern California (CA)
U of South Florida (FL)
Weber State U (UT)
Wichita State U (KS)
York Coll of the City U of New York (NY)
Youngstown State U (OH)

GRAPHIC AND PRINTING EQUIPMENT OPERATION/ PRODUCTION

Fairmont State U (WV)
Ferris State U (MI)
Georgia Southern U (GA)
Lewis-Clark State Coll (ID)
Western Illinois U (IL)

GRAPHIC COMMUNICATIONS

Arizona State U (AZ)
California Polytechnic State U, San Luis Obispo (CA)
Clemson U (SC)
Eastern Washington U (WA)
Grand View U (IA)
Illinois State U (IL)
Lynn U (FL)
Point Loma Nazarene U (CA)
Rochester Inst of Technology (NY)
Roger Williams U (RI)
Ryerson U (ON, Canada)
State U of New York Coll of Technology at Canton (NY)
U of Maryland U Coll (MD)
U of North Dakota (ND)
U of Northern Iowa (IA)

GRAPHIC COMMUNICATIONS RELATED

Rasmussen Coll Appleton (WI)
Rasmussen Coll Aurora (IL)
Rasmussen Coll Bismarck (ND)
Rasmussen Coll Blaine (MN)
Rasmussen Coll Bloomington (MN)
Rasmussen Coll Brooklyn Park (MN)
Rasmussen Coll Eagan (MN)
Rasmussen Coll Fargo (ND)
Rasmussen Coll Fort Myers (FL)
Rasmussen Coll Green Bay (WI)
Rasmussen Coll Lake Elmo/ Woodbury (MN)
Rasmussen Coll Land O' Lakes (FL)
Rasmussen Coll Mankato (MN)
Rasmussen Coll Mokena/Tinley Park (IL)
Rasmussen Coll New Port Richey (FL)
Rasmussen Coll Ocala (FL)
Rasmussen Coll Rockford (IL)
Rasmussen Coll Romeoville/Joliet (IL)
Rasmussen Coll St. Cloud (MN)
Rasmussen Coll Tampa/Brandon (FL)
Rasmussen Coll Wausau (WI)
U of the District of Columbia (DC)
U of Wisconsin–Stout (WI)

GRAPHIC DESIGN

Abilene Christian U (TX)
Acad of Art U (CA)
Adams State Coll (CO)
Alberta Coll of Art & Design (AB, Canada)
Albertus Magnus Coll (CT)
Alma Coll (MI)
American U (DC)
American U of Beirut (Lebanon)
Anna Maria Coll (MA)
Appalachian State U (NC)
Arizona State U (AZ)
Art Center Coll of Design (CA)
The Art Inst of Atlanta (GA)
The Art Inst of Atlanta–Decatur (GA)
The Art Inst of Austin (TX)
The Art Inst of California, a college of Argosy U, Hollywood (CA)
The Art Inst of California, a college of Argosy U, Inland Empire (CA)
The Art Inst of California, a college of Argosy U, Los Angeles (CA)
The Art Inst of California, a college of Argosy U, Orange County (CA)
The Art Inst of California, a college of Argosy U, Sacramento (CA)
The Art Inst of California, a college of Argosy U, San Diego (CA)
The Art Inst of California, a college of Argosy U, San Francisco (CA)
The Art Inst of California, a college of Argosy U, Sunnyvale (CA)
The Art Inst of Charleston (SC)
The Art Inst of Charlotte (NC)
The Art Inst of Colorado (CO)
The Art Inst of Dallas (TX)
The Art Inst of Fort Lauderdale (FL)
The Art Inst of Fort Worth (TX)
The Art Inst of Houston (TX)
The Art Inst of Houston - North (TX)
The Art Inst of Indianapolis (IN)
The Art Inst of Jacksonville (FL)
The Art Inst of Las Vegas (NV)
The Art Inst of Michigan (MI)
The Art Inst of Michigan–Troy (MI)
The Art Inst of Ohio–Cincinnati (OH)
The Art Inst of Philadelphia (PA)
The Art Inst of Phoenix (AZ)
The Art Inst of Pittsburgh (PA)
The Art Inst of Portland (OR)
The Art Inst of Raleigh-Durham (NC)
The Art Inst of Salt Lake City (UT)
The Art Inst of San Antonio (TX)
The Art Inst of Seattle (WA)
The Art Inst of Tampa (FL)
The Art Inst of Tennessee–Nashville (TN)
The Art Inst of Tucson (AZ)
The Art Inst of Virginia Beach (VA)
The Art Inst of Washington (VA)
The Art Inst of Washington–Dulles (VA)
The Art Inst of Wisconsin (WI)
The Art Inst of York–Pennsylvania (PA)
The Art Insts Intl–Kansas City (KS)
The Art Insts Intl Minnesota (MN)
Assumption Coll (MA)
Auburn U (AL)
Augustana Coll (IL)
Becker Coll (MA)
Belhaven U (MS)
Bellevue U (NE)
Benedictine U (IL)
Bluffton U (OH)
Boston U (MA)
Bradley U (IL)
Brescia U (KY)
Briar Cliff U (IA)
Bridgewater State U (MA)
Brigham Young U (UT)
Broadview U-Salt Lake City (UT)
Burlington Coll (VT)
Cabrini Coll (PA)
Caldwell Coll (NJ)
California State Polytechnic U, Pomona (CA)
California State U, Chico (CA)
California State U, Dominguez Hills (CA)
California State U, Fresno (CA)

California State U, Long Beach (CA)
California State U, Sacramento (CA)
California U of Pennsylvania (PA)
Calvary Bible Coll and Theological Sem (MO)
Cedarville U (OH)
Centenary Coll (NJ)
Chapman U (CA)
Chatham U (PA)
Chester Coll of New England (NH)
City Coll of the City U of New York (NY)
The Cleveland Inst of Art (OH)
Coastal Carolina U (SC)
Coll for Creative Studies (MI)
Coll of Mount St. Joseph (OH)
Colorado Mesa U (CO)
Colorado State U (CO)
Columbia Coll (MO)
Concordia U (CA)
Corcoran Coll of Art and Design (DC)
Cornish Coll of the Arts (WA)
Creighton U (NE)
Culver-Stockton Coll (MO)
Curry Coll (MA)
Daemen Coll (NY)
Dominican U of California (CA)
Dordt Coll (IA)
Dowling Coll (NY)
Drake U (IA)
East Central U (OK)
Eastern U (PA)
Eastern Washington U (WA)
East Stroudsburg U of Pennsylvania (PA)
Edgewood Coll (WI)
Elizabeth City State U (NC)
Emmanuel Coll (MA)
Fashion Inst of Technology (NY)
Ferris State U (MI)
Fitchburg State U (MA)
Flagler Coll (FL)
Florida Ag and Mech U (FL)
Florida Southern Coll (FL)
Florida State U (FL)
Fort Hays State U (KS)
Georgia Southern U (GA)
Grace Coll (IN)
Grand View U (IA)
Harding U (AR)
Hardin-Simmons U (TX)
Huntington U (IN)
The Illinois Inst of Art–Schaumburg (IL)
The Illinois Inst of Art–Tinley Park (IL)
Indiana U–Purdue U Fort Wayne (IN)
Intl Acad of Design & Technology (FL)
Iowa State U of Science and Technology (IA)
ITT Tech Inst (UT)
John Brown U (AR)
Judson U (IL)
Kansas City Art Inst (MO)
Lasell Coll (MA)
Lebanese American U (Lebanon)
Lenoir-Rhyne U (NC)
Limestone Coll (SC)
Madonna U (MI)
Mansfield U of Pennsylvania (PA)
Marietta Coll (OH)
Mars Hill Coll (NC)
Maryland Inst Coll of Art (MD)
Marymount U (VA)
Maryville U of Saint Louis (MO)
Marywood U (PA)
Meredith Coll (NC)
Miami Intl U of Art & Design (FL)
MidAmerica Nazarene U (KS)
Mississippi Coll (MS)
Missouri Western State U (MO)
Montana State U–Northern (MT)
Montclair State U (NJ)
Montserrat Coll of Art (MA)
Moore Coll of Art & Design (PA)
Moravian Coll (PA)
Morningside Coll (IA)
Mountain State U (WV)
Mount Ida Coll (MA)
Mount Mary Coll (WI)

Mount Mercy U (IA)
Mount Vernon Nazarene U (OH)
Newbury Coll (MA)
The New England Inst of Art (MA)
North Carolina Ag and Tech State U (NC)
North Carolina State U (NC)
North Central Coll (IL)
Northeastern U (MA)
Northern Michigan U (MI)
Northwestern Coll (IA)
Northwestern Coll (MN)
Northwest Nazarene U (ID)
Ohio Northern U (OH)
Ohio U (OH)
Oklahoma City U (OK)
Oral Roberts U (OK)
Ouachita Baptist U (AR)
Pacific Northwest Coll of Art (OR)
Pacific Union Coll (CA)
Paier Coll of Art, Inc. (CT)
Palm Beach Atlantic U (FL)
Park U (MO)
Penn State Abington (PA)
Penn State Altoona (PA)
Penn State Beaver (PA)
Penn State Berks (PA)
Penn State Brandywine (PA)
Penn State DuBois (PA)
Penn State Erie, The Behrend Coll (PA)
Penn State Fayette, The Eberly Campus (PA)
Penn State Greater Allegheny (PA)
Penn State Hazleton (PA)
Penn State Lehigh Valley (PA)
Penn State Mont Alto (PA)
Penn State New Kensington (PA)
Penn State Schuylkill (PA)
Penn State Shenango (PA)
Penn State U Park (PA)
Penn State Wilkes-Barre (PA)
Penn State Worthington Scranton (PA)
Penn State York (PA)
Pennsylvania Coll of Art & Design (PA)
Pensacola State Coll (FL)
Peru State Coll (NE)
Philadelphia U (PA)
Plymouth State U (NH)
Point Loma Nazarene U (CA)
Portland State U (OR)
Pratt Inst (NY)
Queens Coll of the City U of New York (NY)
Queens U of Charlotte (NC)
Quincy U (IL)
Rider U (NJ)
Ringling Coll of Art and Design (FL)
Rivier Coll (NH)
Robert Morris U Illinois (IL)
Rochester Inst of Technology (NY)
Rocky Mountain Coll of Art + Design (CO)
Sacred Heart U (CT)
Sage Coll of Albany (NY)
St. Ambrose U (IA)
St. Edward's U (TX)
St. John's U (NY)
Saint Mary's U of Minnesota (MN)
Saint Vincent Coll (PA)
Salve Regina U (RI)
Samford U (AL)
San Diego State U (CA)
Savannah Coll of Art and Design (GA)
School of the Museum of Fine Arts, Boston (MA)
Schreiner U (TX)
Simpson Coll (IA)
South Dakota State U (SD)
Southern New Hampshire U (NH)
South U, Columbia (SC)
Spring Arbor U (MI)
Spring Hill Coll (AL)
Stephens Coll (MO)
Stonehill Coll (MA)
Susquehanna U (PA)
Tabor Coll (KS)
Temple U (PA)
Texas Christian U (TX)
Union Coll (NE)
Universidad del Turabo (PR)
The U of Akron (OH)

U of Arkansas–Fort Smith (AR)
U of Bridgeport (CT)
U of Denver (CO)
U of Florida (FL)
U of Hartford (CT)
U of Houston (TX)
U of Illinois at Chicago (IL)
U of Illinois at Urbana–Champaign (IL)
The U of Kansas (KS)
U of Miami (FL)
U of Michigan (MI)
U of Minnesota, Duluth (MN)
U of Missouri–St. Louis (MO)
U of North Dakota (ND)
U of Rio Grande (OH)
U of South Florida (FL)
The U of Tampa (FL)
The U of Tennessee at Martin (TN)
The U of the Arts (PA)
U of the Incarnate Word (TX)
Ursuline Coll (OH)
Villa Maria Coll of Buffalo (NY)
Virginia Commonwealth U (VA)
Viterbo U (WI)
Washington U in St. Louis (MO)
Waynesburg U (PA)
Wayne State Coll (NE)
Western Michigan U (MI)
Western State Coll of Colorado (CO)
West Virginia U Inst of Technology (WV)
Wichita State U (KS)
York Coll of Pennsylvania (PA)
Youngstown State U (OH)

GREENHOUSE MANAGEMENT

U of Minnesota, Crookston (MN)

HAZARDOUS MATERIALS MANAGEMENT AND WASTE TECHNOLOGY

Rochester Inst of Technology (NY)

HEALTH AND MEDICAL ADMINISTRATIVE SERVICES RELATED

Bellevue U (NE)
Clayton State U (GA)
Concordia Coll–New York (NY)
Missouri Southern State U (MO)
Mount Mercy U (IA)
National-Louis U (IL)
Pennsylvania Coll of Technology (PA)
U of Minnesota, Duluth (MN)
Ursuline Coll (OH)
Washburn U (KS)
Weber State U (UT)
Western Michigan U (MI)

HEALTH AND PHYSICAL EDUCATION/FITNESS

Abilene Christian U (TX)
Adrian Coll (MI)
American U (DC)
Angelo State U (TX)
Arkansas State U (AR)
Asbury U (KY)
Austin Peay State U (TN)
Averett U (VA)
Baker U (KS)
Baldwin-Wallace Coll (OH)
Baylor U (TX)
Belmont U (TN)
Berea Coll (KY)
Bethel Coll (IN)
Bethel Coll (KS)
Bethel U (MN)
Bethel U (TN)
Biola U (CA)
Blackburn Coll (IL)
Black Hills State U (SD)
Blue Mountain Coll (MS)
Bluffton U (OH)
Bob Jones U (SC)
Bridgewater Coll (VA)
California Polytechnic State U, San Luis Obispo (CA)
California State Polytechnic U, Pomona (CA)
California State U, Chico (CA)

California State U, Dominguez Hills (CA)
California State U, Fullerton (CA)
California State U, Monterey Bay (CA)
Cameron U (OK)
Canisius Coll (NY)
Capital U (OH)
Carroll Coll (MT)
Castleton State Coll (VT)
Cedarville U (OH)
Central Michigan U (MI)
Claflin U (SC)
Cleveland State U (OH)
The Coll at Brockport, State U of New York (NY)
Coll of the Ozarks (MO)
Concordia Coll (MN)
Concordia U (CA)
Concordia U (MI)
Concordia U, Nebraska (NE)
Concordia U Texas (TX)
Delaware State U (DE)
DePaul U (IL)
Doane Coll (NE)
Dordt Coll (IA)
East Central U (OK)
Eastern Michigan U (MI)
Eastern Washington U (WA)
East Tennessee State U (TN)
East Texas Baptist U (TX)
Elmhurst Coll (IL)
Emory & Henry Coll (VA)
Evangel U (MO)
Ferrum Coll (VA)
Free Will Baptist Bible Coll (TN)
Friends U (KS)
Gardner-Webb U (NC)
George Fox U (OR)
Georgia Southern U (GA)
Guilford Coll (NC)
Hanover Coll (IN)
Hardin-Simmons U (TX)
Houghton Coll (NY)
Howard Payne U (TX)
Indiana U of Pennsylvania (PA)
Iowa State U of Science and Technology (IA)
Iowa Wesleyan Coll (IA)
Ithaca Coll (NY)
Jacksonville State U (AL)
James Madison U (VA)
Jarvis Christian Coll (TX)
John Brown U (AR)
Johnson State Coll (VT)
Keene State Coll (NH)
La Sierra U (CA)
Liberty U (VA)
Lincoln Memorial U (TN)
Lincoln U (PA)
Linfield Coll (OR)
Loras Coll (IA)
Lubbock Christian U (TX)
Luther Coll (IA)
Lynchburg Coll (VA)
Maryville Coll (TN)
Marywood U (PA)
The Master's Coll and Sem (CA)
Mayville State U (ND)
McDaniel Coll (MD)
Miami U (OH)
Middle Tennessee State U (TN)
Milligan Coll (TN)
Mississippi U for Women (MS)
Missouri Western State U (MO)
Monmouth Coll (IL)
Monmouth U (NJ)
Montana State U Billings (MT)
Morehead State U (KY)
Morehouse Coll (GA)
Mount Vernon Nazarene U (OH)
New England Coll (NH)
North Carolina Central U (NC)
Northern Illinois U (IL)
Northern Michigan U (MI)
Northwestern Coll (MN)
Northwestern State U of Louisiana (LA)
Northwest Nazarene U (ID)
Ohio Northern U (OH)
The Ohio State U (OH)
Ohio U (OH)
Oral Roberts U (OK)
Pacific Union Coll (CA)
Philander Smith Coll (AR)

Plymouth State U (NH)
Point Loma Nazarene U (CA)
Prairie View A&M U (TX)
Queen's U at Kingston (ON, Canada)
Quincy U (IL)
Randolph Coll (VA)
Rocky Mountain Coll (MT)
Rowan U (NJ)
St. Ambrose U (IA)
St. Catherine U (MN)
Saint Joseph's Coll (IN)
Saint Mary's Coll of California (CA)
St. Mary's U (TX)
Salem State U (MA)
Samford U (AL)
San Diego State U (CA)
Shawnee State U (OH)
Slippery Rock U of Pennsylvania (PA)
South Carolina State U (SC)
South Dakota State U (SD)
Southeast Missouri State U (MO)
Southwest Baptist U (MO)
Southwestern Adventist U (TX)
Southwestern Christian U (OK)
Southwest Minnesota State U (MN)
Spring Arbor U (MI)
Stephen F. Austin State U (TX)
Sterling Coll (KS)
Syracuse U (NY)
Texas A&M Intl U (TX)
Texas A&M U (TX)
Texas A&M U–Kingsville (TX)
Texas Christian U (TX)
Texas Coll (TX)
Texas Southern U (TX)
Texas Wesleyan U (TX)
Tusculum Coll (TN)
U of Arkansas (AR)
U of Arkansas at Monticello (AR)
U of Delaware (DE)
U of Great Falls (MT)
U of Guam (GU)
The U of Kansas (KS)
U of Louisville (KY)
U of Mary (ND)
U of Massachusetts Boston (MA)
U of Mobile (AL)
The U of Montana Western (MT)
U of Nebraska at Omaha (NE)
U of Nebraska–Lincoln (NE)
The U of North Carolina at Chapel Hill (NC)
The U of North Carolina at Charlotte (NC)
The U of North Carolina Wilmington (NC)
U of Northern Iowa (IA)
U of North Texas (TX)
U of Ottawa (ON, Canada)
U of Regina (SK, Canada)
U of Rio Grande (OH)
U of St. Thomas (MN)
U of Science and Arts of Oklahoma (OK)
U of Southern Maine (ME)
U of Southern Mississippi (MS)
The U of Tampa (FL)
The U of Tennessee at Martin (TN)
The U of Texas at Austin (TX)
The U of Texas at San Antonio (TX)
The U of Texas at Tyler (TX)
The U of Texas–Pan American (TX)
U of the Cumberlands (KY)
U of Toronto (ON, Canada)
U of Utah (UT)
U of West Florida (FL)
U of Windsor (ON, Canada)
U of Wisconsin–La Crosse (WI)
U of Wisconsin–Stevens Point (WI)
U of Wisconsin–Superior (WI)
Utah Valley U (UT)
Valley City State U (ND)
Valparaiso U (IN)
Vanguard U of Southern California (CA)
Virginia Intermont Coll (VA)
Walsh U (OH)
Washington Adventist U (MD)
Weber State U (UT)
Wesleyan U (CT)
West Chester U of Pennsylvania (PA)
Western Washington U (WA)

West Texas A&M U (TX)
West Virginia U (WV)
West Virginia Wesleyan Coll (WV)
William Penn U (IA)
Wingate U (NC)
Wright State U (OH)
Youngstown State U (OH)

HEALTH AND PHYSICAL EDUCATION RELATED

Adelphi U (NY)
Arizona State U (AZ)
Averett U (VA)
Avila U (MO)
Bethany Coll (KS)
Bloomsburg U of Pennsylvania (PA)
Bowling Green State U (OH)
Brewton-Parker Coll (GA)
Bridgewater State U (MA)
California State U, Long Beach (CA)
Coe Coll (IA)
The Coll at Brockport, State U of New York (NY)
Concordia Coll (MN)
Cornell Coll (IA)
East Carolina U (NC)
East Stroudsburg U of Pennsylvania (PA)
Edinboro U of Pennsylvania (PA)
Gustavus Adolphus Coll (MN)
Ithaca Coll (NY)
John Brown U (AR)
Limestone Coll (SC)
Lincoln U (PA)
Lock Haven U of Pennsylvania (PA)
Mayville State U (ND)
Midwestern State U (TX)
Missouri Southern State U (MO)
Naropa U (CO)
North Greenville U (SC)
Ohio Northern U (OH)
Pittsburg State U (KS)
Regis Coll (MA)
Reinhardt U (GA)
Rocky Mountain Coll (MT)
Saint Mary's Coll of California (CA)
South Dakota State U (SD)
Tabor Coll (KS)
Texas Lutheran U (TX)
Towson U (MD)
Tusculum Coll (TN)
The U of Iowa (IA)
U of New England (ME)
U of Utah (UT)
U of Wisconsin–Superior (WI)
Valdosta State U (GA)
Virginia Intermont Coll (VA)
Wayne State Coll (NE)

HEALTH AND WELLNESS

Antioch U Midwest (OH)
Daemen Coll (NY)
Indiana U Kokomo (IN)
Indiana Wesleyan U (IN)
Johnson C. Smith U (NC)
Keene State Coll (NH)
Oklahoma City U (OK)
Prescott Coll (AZ)
Texas Tech U (TX)
Texas Woman's U (TX)
Trevecca Nazarene U (TN)
U of Houston (TX)
U of Wisconsin–La Crosse (WI)
U of Wisconsin–Stout (WI)

HEALTH COMMUNICATION

Grand Valley State U (MI)
Juniata Coll (PA)
North Dakota State U (ND)
U of Houston (TX)

HEALTH/HEALTH-CARE ADMINISTRATION

Adams State Coll (CO)
Alaska Pacific U (AK)
Appalachian State U (NC)
Arcadia U (PA)
Auburn U (AL)
Augustana Coll (SD)
Baker Coll of Auburn Hills (MI)
Baker Coll of Owosso (MI)
Baker Coll of Port Huron (MI)
Baldwin-Wallace Coll (OH)

Baptist Coll of Health Sciences (TN)
Belhaven U (MS)
Belmont U (TN)
Benedictine U (IL)
Black Hills State U (SD)
Bowling Green State U (OH)
Brandeis U (MA)
Broadview U (UT)
Broadview U-Boise (ID)
Broadview U-Layton (UT)
Broadview U-Orem (UT)
California Baptist U (CA)
California Coast U (CA)
California State U, Dominguez Hills (CA)
California State U, Long Beach (CA)
California State U, San Bernardino (CA)
Calumet Coll of Saint Joseph (IN)
Capella U (MN)
Carlow U (PA)
Chestnut Hill Coll (PA)
Clayton State U (GA)
Cleary U (MI)
Coastal Carolina U (SC)
The Coll at Brockport, State U of New York (NY)
Columbia Southern U (AL)
Concordia U (CA)
Concordia U, St. Paul (MN)
Corban U (OR)
Creighton U (NE)
Dallas Baptist U (TX)
Davenport U, Grand Rapids (MI)
DeVry U, Pomona (CA)
DeVry U, Westminster (CO)
DeVry U, Miramar (FL)
DeVry U, Orlando (FL)
DeVry U, Decatur (GA)
DeVry U, Houston (TX)
DeVry U Online (IL)
Dillard U (LA)
Dominican Coll (NY)
Drexel U (PA)
East Carolina U (NC)
Eastern Kentucky U (KY)
Eastern Michigan U (MI)
Eastern Washington U (WA)
Ferris State U (MI)
Florida Ag and Mech U (FL)
Florida Atlantic U (FL)
Florida Inst of Technology (FL)
Florida Intl U (FL)
Franklin U (OH)
Globe U–Appleton (WI)
Globe U–Eau Claire (WI)
Globe U–La Crosse (WI)
Globe U–Madison East (WI)
Globe U–Madison West (WI)
Globe U–Minneapolis (MN)
Globe U–Sioux Falls (SD)
Globe U–Wausau (WI)
Globe U–Woodbury (MN)
Goldey-Beacom Coll (DE)
Governors State U (IL)
Grand Canyon U (AZ)
Granite State Coll (NH)
Harding U (AR)
Heidelberg U (OH)
Hodges U (FL)
Howard Payne U (TX)
Husson U (ME)
Idaho State U (ID)
Immaculata U (PA)
Indiana U Bloomington (IN)
Indiana U–Purdue U Fort Wayne (IN)
Indiana U–Purdue U Indianapolis (IN)
Indian River State Coll (FL)
Iona Coll (NY)
Ithaca Coll (NY)
James Madison U (VA)
Lebanon Valley Coll (PA)
Lee U (TN)
Lehman Coll of the City U of New York (NY)
Lewis U (IL)
Limestone Coll (SC)
Lindenwood U (MO)
Lourdes U (OH)
Loyola U Chicago (IL)
Madonna U (MI)
Marian U (WI)

Mary Baldwin Coll (VA)
Marywood U (PA)
Mercy Coll of Health Sciences (IA)
Mercy Coll of Ohio (OH)
Metropolitan State Coll of Denver (CO)
Minnesota School of Business–Blaine (MN)
Minnesota School of Business–Brooklyn Center (MN)
Minnesota School of Business–Elk River (MN)
Minnesota School of Business–Lakeville (MN)
Minnesota School of Business–Richfield (MN)
Minnesota School of Business–Rochester (MN)
Minnesota School of Business–St. Cloud (MN)
Minnesota School of Business–Shakopee (MN)
Misericordia U (PA)
Missouri Baptist U (MO)
Montana State U Billings (MT)
Mount Mercy U (IA)
Mount St. Mary's Coll (CA)
Newbury Coll (MA)
New England Coll (NH)
Norfolk State U (VA)
Northeastern State U (OK)
Ohio U (OH)
Our Lady of the Lake Coll (LA)
Peirce Coll (PA)
Penn State Abington (PA)
Penn State Altoona (PA)
Penn State Beaver (PA)
Penn State Berks (PA)
Penn State Brandywine (PA)
Penn State DuBois (PA)
Penn State Erie, The Behrend Coll (PA)
Penn State Fayette, The Eberly Campus (PA)
Penn State Greater Allegheny (PA)
Penn State Hazleton (PA)
Penn State Lehigh Valley (PA)
Penn State Mont Alto (PA)
Penn State New Kensington (PA)
Penn State Schuylkill (PA)
Penn State Shenango (PA)
Penn State U Park (PA)
Penn State Wilkes-Barre (PA)
Penn State Worthington Scranton (PA)
Penn State York (PA)
Potomac Coll (DC)
Providence Coll (RI)
Rasmussen Coll Appleton (WI)
Rasmussen Coll Aurora (IL)
Rasmussen Coll Bismarck (ND)
Rasmussen Coll Blaine (MN)
Rasmussen Coll Bloomington (MN)
Rasmussen Coll Brooklyn Park (MN)
Rasmussen Coll Eagan (MN)
Rasmussen Coll Fargo (ND)
Rasmussen Coll Fort Myers (FL)
Rasmussen Coll Green Bay (WI)
Rasmussen Coll Lake Elmo/Woodbury (MN)
Rasmussen Coll Land O' Lakes (FL)
Rasmussen Coll Mankato (MN)
Rasmussen Coll Mokena/Tinley Park (IL)
Rasmussen Coll Moorhead (MN)
Rasmussen Coll New Port Richey (FL)
Rasmussen Coll Ocala (FL)
Rasmussen Coll Rockford (IL)
Rasmussen Coll Romeoville/Joliet (IL)
Rasmussen Coll St. Cloud (MN)
Rasmussen Coll Tampa/Brandon (FL)
Rasmussen Coll Wausau (WI)
Rhode Island Coll (RI)
Roberts Wesleyan Coll (NY)
Roger Williams U (RI)
St. John's U (NY)
St. Joseph's Coll, Long Island Campus (NY)
St. Joseph's Coll, New York (NY)
Saint Leo U (FL)

Saint Peter's Coll (NJ)
St. Thomas U (FL)
Shippensburg U of Pennsylvania (PA)
Simpson U (CA)
Sojourner-Douglass Coll (MD)
Southern Illinois U Carbondale (IL)
Southern Vermont Coll (VT)
South U (AL)
South U, Royal Palm Beach (FL)
South U, Tampa (FL)
South U (GA)
South U (MI)
South U, Columbia (SC)
South U (TX)
South U, Glen Allen (VA)
South U, Virginia Beach (VA)
Southwestern Adventist U (TX)
Southwestern Oklahoma State U (OK)
Spring Arbor U (MI)
State U of New York at Fredonia (NY)
State U of New York Coll of Technology at Canton (NY)
Stonehill Coll (MA)
Texas Southern U (TX)
Texas State U–San Marcos (TX)
Thomas More Coll (KY)
Towson U (MD)
Trident U Intl (CA)
U of Central Florida (FL)
U of Connecticut (CT)
U of Evansville (IN)
U of Great Falls (MT)
U of Hawaii–West Oahu (HI)
U of Houston–Clear Lake (TX)
U of La Verne (CA)
U of Medicine and Dentistry of New Jersey (NJ)
U of Michigan–Dearborn (MI)
U of Michigan–Flint (MI)
U of Minnesota, Crookston (MN)
U of Minnesota, Duluth (MN)
U of Nevada, Las Vegas (NV)
U of New England (ME)
U of New Hampshire (NH)
The U of North Carolina at Chapel Hill (NC)
U of North Florida (FL)
U of Pennsylvania (PA)
U of Rhode Island (RI)
U of St. Francis (IL)
U of Saint Francis (IN)
The U of Scranton (PA)
U of Southern Indiana (IN)
U of Southern Maine (ME)
U of South Florida (FL)
The U of Texas at El Paso (TX)
U of Wisconsin–Eau Claire (WI)
Upper Iowa U (IA)
Ursuline Coll (OH)
Valparaiso U (IN)
Vincennes U (IN)
Walden U (MN)
Washington Adventist U (MD)
Washington U in St. Louis (MO)
Waynesburg U (PA)
Webster U (MO)
West Chester U of Pennsylvania (PA)
Western Carolina U (NC)
Western Illinois U (IL)
Western Kentucky U (KY)
West Virginia U Inst of Technology (WV)
Wichita State U (KS)

HEALTH INFORMATION/ MEDICAL RECORDS ADMINISTRATION

Alabama State U (AL)
Arkansas Tech U (AR)
Baker Coll of Auburn Hills (MI)
Bowling Green State U (OH)
Chicago State U (IL)
Coll of Coastal Georgia (GA)
The Coll of St. Scholastica (MN)
Dakota State U (SD)
Dalhousie U (NS, Canada)
Davenport U, Grand Rapids (MI)
Duquesne U (PA)
East Carolina U (NC)
Eastern Washington U (WA)

Fairleigh Dickinson U, Metropolitan Campus (NJ)
Ferris State U (MI)
Florida Ag and Mech U (FL)
Georgian Court U (NJ)
Gwynedd-Mercy Coll (PA)
Illinois State U (IL)
Indiana U Bloomington (IN)
Indiana U East (IN)
Indiana U Kokomo (IN)
Indiana U Northwest (IN)
Indiana U–Purdue U Indianapolis (IN)
Indiana U South Bend (IN)
Indiana U Southeast (IN)
Kean U (NJ)
Long Island U–C. W. Post Campus (NY)
Macon State Coll (GA)
Missouri Western State U (MO)
The Ohio State U (OH)
The Ohio State U at Lima (OH)
Pennsylvania Coll of Technology (PA)
Rasmussen Coll Appleton (WI)
Rasmussen Coll Aurora (IL)
Rasmussen Coll Bismarck (ND)
Rasmussen Coll Blaine (MN)
Rasmussen Coll Bloomington (MN)
Rasmussen Coll Brooklyn Park (MN)
Rasmussen Coll Eagan (MN)
Rasmussen Coll Fargo (ND)
Rasmussen Coll Fort Myers (FL)
Rasmussen Coll Green Bay (WI)
Rasmussen Coll Lake Elmo/Woodbury (MN)
Rasmussen Coll Land O' Lakes (FL)
Rasmussen Coll Mankato (MN)
Rasmussen Coll Mokena/Tinley Park (IL)
Rasmussen Coll Moorhead (MN)
Rasmussen Coll New Port Richey (FL)
Rasmussen Coll Ocala (FL)
Rasmussen Coll Rockford (IL)
Rasmussen Coll Romeoville/Joliet (IL)
Rasmussen Coll St. Cloud (MN)
Rasmussen Coll Tampa/Brandon (FL)
Rasmussen Coll Wausau (WI)
Regis U (CO)
Ryerson U (ON, Canada)
Saint Louis U (MO)
Southwestern Oklahoma State U (OK)
Stephens Coll (MO)
Temple U (PA)
Texas Southern U (TX)
Texas State U–San Marcos (TX)
The U of Alabama at Birmingham (AL)
U of Central Florida (FL)
U of Cincinnati (OH)
U of Illinois at Chicago (IL)
The U of Kansas (KS)
U of Louisiana at Lafayette (LA)
U of Medicine and Dentistry of New Jersey (NJ)
U of Pittsburgh (PA)
The U of Toledo (OH)
Weber State U (UT)
Western Carolina U (NC)

HEALTH INFORMATION/MEDICAL RECORDS TECHNOLOGY
Franklin U (OH)
Gwynedd-Mercy Coll (PA)
Indiana U Bloomington (IN)
St. John's U (NY)

HEALTH/MEDICAL PHYSICS
Bloomsburg U of Pennsylvania (PA)
California State U, Dominguez Hills (CA)
Ryerson U (ON, Canada)
U of Guelph (ON, Canada)
U of Nevada, Las Vegas (NV)

HEALTH/MEDICAL PREPARATORY PROGRAMS RELATED
Abilene Christian U (TX)
Allegheny Coll (PA)
Arizona State U (AZ)
Asbury U (KY)
Austin Peay State U (TN)
Avila U (MO)
Baylor U (TX)
Benedictine U (IL)
Bloomsburg U of Pennsylvania (PA)
Bob Jones U (SC)
Cedarville U (OH)
Cleveland State U (OH)
Concordia U, Nebraska (NE)
Duquesne U (PA)
Emory & Henry Coll (VA)
Gannon U (PA)
Guilford Coll (NC)
Hodges U (FL)
Hofstra U (NY)
Ithaca Coll (NY)
Juniata Coll (PA)
Kent State U (OH)
Kent State U at Ashtabula (OH)
Lee U (TN)
Le Moyne Coll (NY)
Lipscomb U (TN)
Lock Haven U of Pennsylvania (PA)
Lubbock Christian U (TX)
Madonna U (MI)
Maryville U of Saint Louis (MO)
Mercer U (GA)
Mercyhurst Coll (PA)
Meredith Coll (NC)
Northern Illinois U (IL)
Northern Michigan U (MI)
Pittsburg State U (KS)
Point Park U (PA)
State U of New York at Binghamton (NY)
Tusculum Coll (TN)
The U of Akron (OH)
U of Minnesota, Twin Cities Campus (MN)
U of Missouri (MO)
U of Regina (SK, Canada)
U of South Alabama (AL)
Utica Coll (NY)
Valley City State U (ND)
Virginia Intermont Coll (VA)
Western Washington U (WA)

HEALTH/MEDICAL PSYCHOLOGY
Bridgewater State U (MA)
Massachusetts Coll of Pharmacy and Health Sciences (MA)
Prescott Coll (AZ)

HEALTH OCCUPATIONS TEACHER EDUCATION
Baylor U (TX)
Midwestern State U (TX)
Northwest U (WA)
U of Maine at Farmington (ME)

HEALTH PROFESSIONS RELATED
Alma Coll (MI)
Arizona State U (AZ)
Armstrong Atlantic State U (GA)
Athens State U (AL)
Azusa Pacific U (CA)
Baldwin-Wallace Coll (OH)
Bastyr U (WA)
Boise State U (ID)
Boston U (MA)
Bowling Green State U (OH)
Bradley U (IL)
California State U, East Bay (CA)
California State U, Fresno (CA)
California State U, Long Beach (CA)
California State U, Los Angeles (CA)
California State U, Sacramento (CA)
California State U, San Bernardino (CA)
Castleton State Coll (VT)
Clemson U (SC)

Cleveland State U (OH)
The Coll at Brockport, State U of New York (NY)
Concordia Coll–New York (NY)
Corban U (OR)
Dalhousie U (NS, Canada)
East Tennessee State U (TN)
Elizabethtown Coll (PA)
The Evergreen State Coll (WA)
Excelsior Coll (NY)
Fairmont State U (WV)
Florida Atlantic U (FL)
Furman U (SC)
George Mason U (VA)
Gettysburg Coll (PA)
Grand Canyon U (AZ)
Gwynedd-Mercy Coll (PA)
Inter American U of Puerto Rico, Ponce Campus (PR)
Inter American U of Puerto Rico, San Germán Campus (PR)
Johnson State Coll (VT)
King Coll (TN)
King's Coll (PA)
Lamar U (TX)
Lock Haven U of Pennsylvania (PA)
Long Island U–Brooklyn Campus (NY)
Long Island U–C. W. Post Campus (NY)
Manchester Coll (IN)
Marquette U (WI)
Maryville U of Saint Louis (MO)
Massachusetts Coll of Pharmacy and Health Sciences (MA)
Mercy Coll (NY)
Milligan Coll (TN)
Minnesota State U Mankato (MN)
Missouri Southern State U (MO)
Morrisville State Coll (NY)
New Jersey City U (NJ)
Newman U (KS)
Northeastern State U (OK)
Northeastern U (MA)
Northern Illinois U (IL)
Norwich U (VT)
Oakland U (MI)
The Ohio State U (OH)
Old Dominion U (VA)
Pacific U (OR)
Point Park U (PA)
Purdue U (IN)
Randolph Coll (VA)
Saint Augustine's Coll (NC)
St. Joseph's Coll, Long Island Campus (NY)
St. Joseph's Coll, New York (NY)
Saint Joseph's U (PA)
Saint Louis U (MO)
San Francisco State U (CA)
Sonoma State U (CA)
South U (AL)
South U, Royal Palm Beach (FL)
South U, Tampa (FL)
South U, Columbia (SC)
South U, Glen Allen (VA)
South U, Virginia Beach (VA)
State U of New York Coll at Cortland (NY)
Stony Brook U, State U of New York (NY)
Syracuse U (NY)
Texas A&M U–Corpus Christi (TX)
Texas Christian U (TX)
Thomas Edison State Coll (NJ)
Touro Coll (NY)
Towson U (MD)
The U of Alabama (AL)
U of Alaska Anchorage (AK)
U of Arkansas (AR)
U of Arkansas at Little Rock (AR)
U of Bridgeport (CT)
The U of British Columbia–Okanagan (BC, Canada)
U of California, Santa Cruz (CA)
U of Central Arkansas (AR)
U of Charleston (WV)
U of Cincinnati (OH)
U of Colorado at Colorado Springs (CO)
U of Delaware (DE)
U of Hartford (CT)
U of Louisiana at Monroe (LA)
U of Maryland, Baltimore County (MD)

U of Massachusetts Lowell (MA)
U of Nevada, Reno (NV)
U of New England (ME)
The U of North Carolina Wilmington (NC)
U of Northern Iowa (IA)
U of Pennsylvania (PA)
U of Pittsburgh (PA)
U of Saint Francis (IN)
U of St. Thomas (MN)
The U of Tennessee at Martin (TN)
The U of Texas at El Paso (TX)
The U of Texas at Tyler (TX)
The U of Western Ontario (ON, Canada)
U of Wisconsin–Stevens Point (WI)
Washington U in St. Louis (MO)
Wayne State U (MI)
West Liberty U (WV)
William Paterson U of New Jersey (NJ)
Winona State U (MN)
Worcester State U (MA)
Youngstown State U (OH)

HEALTH SERVICES ADMINISTRATION
Chapman U (CA)
East Stroudsburg U of Pennsylvania (PA)
Florida National Coll (FL)
Indiana U Northwest (IN)
Indiana U–Purdue U Fort Wayne (IN)
Indiana U–Purdue U Indianapolis (IN)
Indiana U South Bend (IN)
Inter American U of Puerto Rico, Ponce Campus (PR)
Macon State Coll (GA)
Minnesota State U Moorhead (MN)
Robert Morris U (PA)
Saint Louis U (MO)
Slippery Rock U of Pennsylvania (PA)
Sullivan U (KY)
U of Illinois at Urbana–Champaign (IL)
Ursuline Coll (OH)

HEALTH SERVICES/ALLIED HEALTH/HEALTH SCIENCES
Albany Coll of Pharmacy and Health Sciences (NY)
Anna Maria Coll (MA)
Boston U (MA)
Brenau U (GA)
Brevard Coll (NC)
California Baptist U (CA)
California State U, Chico (CA)
California State U, Dominguez Hills (CA)
California State U, Fullerton (CA)
Carroll Coll (MT)
Chicago State U (IL)
The Coll of Idaho (ID)
The Coll of St. Scholastica (MN)
Coll of the Ozarks (MO)
Columbus State U (GA)
Corban U (OR)
Dalhousie U (NS, Canada)
Fairleigh Dickinson U, Coll at Florham (NJ)
Ferrum Coll (VA)
Florida Ag and Mech U (FL)
Florida Atlantic U (FL)
Florida Gulf Coast U (FL)
Friends U (KS)
Goodwin Coll (CT)
Graceland U (IA)
Gwynedd-Mercy Coll (PA)
Heidelberg U (OH)
Hendrix Coll (AR)
Hofstra U (NY)
Idaho State U (ID)
Lebanon Valley Coll (PA)
Liberty U (VA)
Marywood U (PA)
Mercy Coll (NY)
Mercy Coll of Health Sciences (IA)
Mercy Coll of Ohio (OH)
Merrimack Coll (MA)
Miami Dade Coll (FL)
Misericordia U (PA)

Monmouth U (NJ)
Montclair State U (NJ)
Mountain State U (WV)
National U (CA)
Nicholls State U (LA)
Northern Kentucky U (KY)
Northwestern State U of Louisiana (LA)
Nova Southeastern U (FL)
The Richard Stockton Coll of New Jersey (NJ)
Sacred Heart U (CT)
Saginaw Valley State U (MI)
Saint Joseph's U (PA)
San Diego State U (CA)
Spalding U (KY)
Stephen F. Austin State U (TX)
Stetson U (FL)
Texas A&M U (TX)
Texas A&M U–Kingsville (TX)
Texas Southern U (TX)
Texas Woman's U (TX)
Thompson Rivers U (BC, Canada)
Trident U Intl (CA)
U of Central Florida (FL)
U of Florida (FL)
U of Hartford (CT)
U of Medicine and Dentistry of New Jersey (NJ)
U of Miami (FL)
U of Michigan–Flint (MI)
U of Minnesota, Crookston (MN)
U of Missouri–Kansas City (MO)
U of North Florida (FL)
U of North Texas (TX)
U of Ottawa (ON, Canada)
U of Southern Mississippi (MS)
U of South Florida–St. Petersburg Campus (FL)
The U of Texas at San Antonio (TX)
The U of Texas–Pan American (TX)
U of the Sciences in Philadelphia (PA)
U of Utah (UT)
The U of Western Ontario (ON, Canada)
U of West Florida (FL)
Ursuline Coll (OH)
Walden U (MN)
Washington U in St. Louis (MO)
Western Kentucky U (KY)
Westminster Coll (UT)
Wheaton Coll (IL)
Wheeling Jesuit U (WV)
Widener U (PA)

HEALTH TEACHER EDUCATION
Alma Coll (MI)
Appalachian State U (NC)
Armstrong Atlantic State U (GA)
Ashland U (OH)
Auburn U (AL)
Austin Peay State U (TN)
Averett U (VA)
Ball State U (IN)
Baylor U (TX)
Belmont U (TN)
Bemidji State U (MN)
Bethel U (MN)
Bluefield Coll (VA)
Bowling Green State U (OH)
Bridgewater State U (MA)
California State U, Chico (CA)
California State U, San Bernardino (CA)
Campbellsville U (KY)
Capital U (OH)
Cedarville U (OH)
Central Michigan U (MI)
Central Washington U (WA)
The Coll at Brockport, State U of New York (NY)
Concordia Coll (MN)
Concordia U (MI)
Concordia U, Nebraska (NE)
Concordia U, St. Paul (MN)
Curry Coll (MA)
Defiance Coll (OH)
Delaware State U (DE)
DePaul U (IL)
East Carolina U (NC)
Eastern Illinois U (IL)
Eastern Kentucky U (KY)
Eastern Oregon U (OR)

Eastern Washington U (WA)
East Stroudsburg U of Pennsylvania (PA)
Elon U (NC)
Fayetteville State U (NC)
Gardner-Webb U (NC)
George Mason U (VA)
Georgia Coll & State U (GA)
Graceland U (IA)
Grand Valley State U (MI)
Gustavus Adolphus Coll (MN)
Hampton U (VA)
Harding U (AR)
Heidelberg U (OH)
Hofstra U (NY)
Houghton Coll (NY)
Hunter Coll of the City U of New York (NY)
Idaho State U (ID)
Illinois State U (IL)
Indiana U Bloomington (IN)
Indiana U Southeast (IN)
Inter American U of Puerto Rico, San Germán Campus (PR)
Iowa State U of Science and Technology (IA)
Iowa Wesleyan Coll (IA)
Ithaca Coll (NY)
Jacksonville State U (AL)
John Brown U (AR)
Kent State U (OH)
Lamar U (TX)
Lee U (TN)
Lehman Coll of the City U of New York (NY)
Liberty U (VA)
Lincoln Memorial U (TN)
Long Island U–C. W. Post Campus (NY)
Longwood U (VA)
Louisiana Coll (LA)
Malone U (OH)
Maryville Coll (TN)
Mayville State U (ND)
Miami U (OH)
Michigan State U (MI)
Middle Tennessee State U (TN)
Minnesota State U Mankato (MN)
Minnesota State U Moorhead (MN)
Missouri Baptist U (MO)
Montana State U Billings (MT)
Montana State U–Northern (MT)
Montclair State U (NJ)
Morehead State U (KY)
Mount Vernon Nazarene U (OH)
New Mexico Highlands U (NM)
North Carolina Central U (NC)
North Dakota State U (ND)
Northeastern State U (OK)
Northern Illinois U (IL)
Northern Michigan U (MI)
Northern State U (SD)
Northwestern Oklahoma State U (OK)
Ohio Northern U (OH)
Ohio Wesleyan U (OH)
Oral Roberts U (OK)
Otterbein U (OH)
Peru State Coll (NE)
Portland State U (OR)
Rhode Island Coll (RI)
Rocky Mountain Coll (MT)
Roger Williams U (RI)
St. Ambrose U (IA)
Salisbury U (MD)
Southern Illinois U Carbondale (IL)
Southern Illinois U Edwardsville (IL)
Southern Oregon U (OR)
Southwest Baptist U (MO)
Southwest Minnesota State U (MN)
State U of New York at Oswego (NY)
State U of New York Coll at Cortland (NY)
Texas A&M U–Corpus Christi (TX)
Trident U Intl (CA)
Union Coll (KY)
The U of Alabama at Birmingham (AL)
U of Arkansas at Little Rock (AR)
U of Charleston (WV)
U of Cincinnati (OH)
U of Dayton (OH)
U of Georgia (GA)
U of Great Falls (MT)

U of Maine (ME)
U of Maine at Farmington (ME)
U of Maryland, Coll Park (MD)
U of Massachusetts Lowell (MA)
U of Minnesota, Duluth (MN)
U of Minnesota, Twin Cities Campus (MN)
The U of Montana Western (MT)
U of Mount Union (OH)
U of Nevada, Las Vegas (NV)
U of New Mexico (NM)
U of Northern Iowa (IA)
U of Regina (SK, Canada)
U of Rio Grande (OH)
U of Saint Francis (IN)
U of St. Thomas (MN)
The U of South Dakota (SD)
U of the Cumberlands (KY)
U of the District of Columbia (DC)
The U of Toledo (OH)
U of Toronto (ON, Canada)
U of Windsor (ON, Canada)
U of Wisconsin–La Crosse (WI)
Utah State U (UT)
Utah Valley U (UT)
Valley City State U (ND)
Virginia Commonwealth U (VA)
Washington State U (WA)
Wayne State U (IL)
Western Connecticut State U (CT)
Western Illinois U (IL)
Western Michigan U (MI)
West Liberty U (WV)
West Virginia State U (WV)
West Virginia Wesleyan Coll (WV)
William Paterson U of New Jersey (NJ)
William Penn U (IA)
Wilmington Coll (OH)
Winona State U (MN)
York Coll of the City U of New York (NY)
Youngstown State U (OH)

HEALTH UNIT MANAGEMENT/ WARD SUPERVISION
Ryerson U (ON, Canada)
U of Mary (ND)

HEATING, AIR CONDITIONING, VENTILATION AND REFRIGERATION MAINTENANCE TECHNOLOGY
Lewis-Clark State Coll (ID)

HEAVY EQUIPMENT MAINTENANCE TECHNOLOGY
Ferris State U (MI)
Pittsburg State U (KS)

HEBREW
Bard Coll (NY)
Bernard M. Baruch Coll of the City U of New York (NY)
Brandeis U (MA)
Brigham Young U (UT)
Columbia U, School of General Studies (NY)
Dartmouth Coll (NH)
Hofstra U (NY)
Hunter Coll of the City U of New York (NY)
Lehman Coll of the City U of New York (NY)
Multnomah U (OR)
New York U (NY)
The Ohio State U (OH)
Queens Coll of the City U of New York (NY)
State U of New York at Binghamton (NY)
Temple U (PA)
U of Alberta (AB, Canada)
U of California, Los Angeles (CA)
U of Cincinnati (OH)
U of Illinois at Urbana–Champaign (IL)
U of Michigan (MI)
U of Minnesota, Twin Cities Campus (MN)
U of Utah (UT)
U of Wisconsin–Madison (WI)

Washington U in St. Louis (MO)
Yeshiva U (NY)

HERBALISM
Bastyr U (WA)

HISPANIC-AMERICAN, PUERTO RICAN, AND MEXICAN-AMERICAN/ CHICANO STUDIES
Arizona State U (AZ)
Boston Coll (MA)
Bowling Green State U (OH)
Brown U (RI)
California State U, Dominguez Hills (CA)
California State U, East Bay (CA)
California State U, Fresno (CA)
California State U, Fullerton (CA)
California State U, Long Beach (CA)
California State U, Los Angeles (CA)
Cedar Crest Coll (PA)
Claremont McKenna Coll (CA)
The Colorado Coll (CO)
Columbia U, School of General Studies (NY)
Connecticut Coll (CT)
Dartmouth Coll (NH)
Fordham U (NY)
Fort Lewis Coll (CO)
Gettysburg Coll (PA)
Hofstra U (NY)
Hunter Coll of the City U of New York (NY)
Lewis & Clark Coll (OR)
Loyola Marymount U (CA)
Metropolitan State Coll of Denver (CO)
Mills Coll (CA)
Pitzer Coll (CA)
Pomona Coll (CA)
Rutgers, The State U of New Jersey, Newark (NJ)
Rutgers, The State U of New Jersey, New Brunswick (NJ)
San Diego State U (CA)
San Francisco State U (CA)
Scripps Coll (CA)
Sonoma State U (CA)
Southern Methodist U (TX)
Stanford U (CA)
State U of New York Coll at Oneonta (NY)
Sul Ross State U (TX)
Trent U (ON, Canada)
Tulane U (LA)
U at Albany, State U of New York (NY)
U of California, Berkeley (CA)
U of California, Davis (CA)
U of California, Irvine (CA)
U of California, Los Angeles (CA)
U of California, Riverside (CA)
U of California, Santa Barbara (CA)
U of California, Santa Cruz (CA)
U of Michigan (MI)
U of Minnesota, Twin Cities Campus (MN)
U of Northern Colorado (CO)
The U of Scranton (PA)
U of Southern California (CA)
The U of Texas at El Paso (TX)
The U of Texas at San Antonio (TX)
The U of Texas–Pan American (TX)
U of Washington (WA)
Wheaton Coll (MA)

HISPANIC AND LATIN AMERICAN LANGUAGES
Hamilton Coll (NY)

HISTOLOGIC TECHNOLOGY/ HISTOTECHNOLOGIST
Michigan Technological U (MI)
Oakland U (MI)

HISTORIC PRESERVATION AND CONSERVATION
Coll of Charleston (SC)
Delaware State U (DE)
Roger Williams U (RI)

Saint Mary's Coll of California (CA)
Salve Regina U (RI)
Savannah Coll of Art and Design (GA)
Southeast Missouri State U (MO)
U of Delaware (DE)
U of Mary Washington (VA)
Ursuline Coll (OH)

HISTORY
Abilene Christian U (TX)
Acadia U (NS, Canada)
Adams State Coll (CO)
Adelphi U (NY)
Adrian Coll (MI)
Agnes Scott Coll (GA)
Alabama State U (AL)
Albany State U (GA)
Albertus Magnus Coll (CT)
Albion Coll (MI)
Albright Coll (PA)
Alcorn State U (MS)
Alfred U (NY)
Allegheny Coll (PA)
Alma Coll (MI)
Alvernia U (PA)
Alverno Coll (WI)
American Public U System (WV)
American U (DC)
American U in Bulgaria (Bulgaria)
The American U in Cairo (Egypt)
American U of Beirut (Lebanon)
The American U of Paris (France)
Amherst Coll (MA)
Anderson U (IN)
Anderson U (SC)
Andrews U (MI)
Angelo State U (TX)
Anna Maria Coll (MA)
Appalachian State U (NC)
Aquinas Coll (MI)
Arcadia U (PA)
Arizona State U (AZ)
Arkansas State U (AR)
Arkansas Tech U (AR)
Armstrong Atlantic State U (GA)
Asbury U (KY)
Ashland U (OH)
Assumption Coll (MA)
Athabasca U (AB, Canada)
Athens State U (AL)
Auburn U (AL)
Auburn U Montgomery (AL)
Augustana Coll (IL)
Augustana Coll (SD)
Austin Coll (TX)
Austin Peay State U (TN)
Averett U (VA)
Avila U (MO)
Azusa Pacific U (CA)
Baker U (KS)
Baldwin-Wallace Coll (OH)
Ball State U (IN)
Bard Coll (NY)
Barnard Coll (NY)
Barry U (FL)
Barton Coll (NC)
Bates Coll (ME)
Baylor U (TX)
Belhaven U (MS)
Bellarmine U (KY)
Bellevue U (NE)
Belmont Abbey Coll (NC)
Belmont U (TN)
Beloit Coll (WI)
Bemidji State U (MN)
Benedictine Coll (KS)
Benedictine U (IL)
Bennington Coll (VT)
Bentley U (MA)
Berea Coll (KY)
Bernard M. Baruch Coll of the City U of New York (NY)
Berry Coll (GA)
Bethany Coll (KS)
Bethany Coll (WV)
Bethany Lutheran Coll (MN)
Bethel Coll (IN)
Bethel Coll (KS)
Bethel U (MN)
Bethel U (TN)
Biola U (CA)
Birmingham-Southern Coll (AL)
Bishop's U (QC, Canada)
Blackburn Coll (IL)

Black Hills State U (SD)
Bloomfield Coll (NJ)
Bloomsburg U of Pennsylvania (PA)
Bluefield Coll (VA)
Blue Mountain Coll (MS)
Bluffton U (OH)
Bob Jones U (SC)
Boise State U (ID)
Boston Coll (MA)
Boston U (MA)
Bowdoin Coll (ME)
Bowie State U (MD)
Bowling Green State U (OH)
Bradley U (IL)
Brandeis U (MA)
Brenau U (GA)
Brescia U (KY)
Brevard Coll (NC)
Brewton-Parker Coll (GA)
Briar Cliff U (IA)
Bridgewater Coll (VA)
Bridgewater State U (MA)
Brown U (RI)
Bryant U (RI)
Bryn Athyn Coll of the New Church (PA)
Bryn Mawr Coll (PA)
Bucknell U (PA)
Buena Vista U (IA)
Buffalo State Coll, State U of New York (NY)
Butler U (IN)
Cabrini Coll (PA)
Caldwell Coll (NJ)
California Baptist U (CA)
California Inst of Technology (CA)
California Lutheran U (CA)
California Polytechnic State U, San Luis Obispo (CA)
California State Polytechnic U, Pomona (CA)
California State U, Bakersfield (CA)
California State U, Chico (CA)
California State U, Dominguez Hills (CA)
California State U, East Bay (CA)
California State U, Fresno (CA)
California State U, Fullerton (CA)
California State U, Long Beach (CA)
California State U, Los Angeles (CA)
California State U, Sacramento (CA)
California State U, San Bernardino (CA)
California State U, San Marcos (CA)
California State U, Stanislaus (CA)
California U of Pennsylvania (PA)
Calvary Bible Coll and Theological Sem (MO)
Calvin Coll (MI)
Cameron U (OK)
Campbellsville U (KY)
Canisius Coll (NY)
Cape Breton U (NS, Canada)
Capital U (OH)
Cardinal Stritch U (WI)
Carleton Coll (MN)
Carlow U (PA)
Carroll Coll (MT)
Carson-Newman Coll (TN)
Case Western Reserve U (OH)
Castleton State Coll (VT)
Catawba Coll (NC)
The Catholic U of America (DC)
Cedar Crest Coll (PA)
Cedarville U (OH)
Centenary Coll (NJ)
Centenary Coll of Louisiana (LA)
Central Coll (IA)
Central Connecticut State U (CT)
Central Methodist U (MO)
Central State U (OH)
Central Washington U (WA)
Centre Coll (KY)
Chaminade U of Honolulu (HI)
Chapman U (CA)
Chatham U (PA)
Chestnut Hill Coll (PA)
Chicago State U (IL)
Christendom Coll (VA)
Christian Brothers U (TN)
Christopher Newport U (VA)

The Citadel, The Military Coll of South Carolina (SC)
City Coll of the City U of New York (NY)
Claflin U (SC)
Claremont McKenna Coll (CA)
Clarion U of Pennsylvania (PA)
Clark Atlanta U (GA)
Clarke U (IA)
Clarkson U (NY)
Clark U (MA)
Clayton State U (GA)
Clearwater Christian Coll (FL)
Clemson U (SC)
Cleveland State U (OH)
Coastal Carolina U (SC)
Coe Coll (IA)
Colby Coll (ME)
Colgate U (NY)
The Coll at Brockport, State U of New York (NY)
Coll of Charleston (SC)
The Coll of Idaho (ID)
Coll of Mount St. Joseph (OH)
Coll of Mount Saint Vincent (NY)
The Coll of New Jersey (NJ)
Coll of Saint Benedict (MN)
Coll of Saint Elizabeth (NJ)
Coll of St. Joseph (VT)
The Coll of St. Scholastica (MN)
Coll of Staten Island of the City U of New York (NY)
Coll of the Holy Cross (MA)
Coll of the Ozarks (MO)
The Coll of William and Mary (VA)
The Coll of Wooster (OH)
The Colorado Coll (CO)
Colorado Mesa U (CO)
Colorado State U (CO)
Columbia Coll (MO)
Columbia Coll (SC)
Columbia U, School of General Studies (NY)
Columbus State U (GA)
Concordia Coll (MN)
Concordia Coll–New York (NY)
Concordia U (CA)
Concordia U (MI)
Concordia U (QC, Canada)
Concordia U Chicago (IL)
Concordia U, Nebraska (NE)
Concordia U, St. Paul (MN)
Concordia U Texas (TX)
Connecticut Coll (CT)
Converse Coll (SC)
Corban U (OR)
Cornell Coll (IA)
Cornell U (NY)
Cornerstone U (MI)
Covenant Coll (GA)
Crandall U (NB, Canada)
Creighton U (NE)
Crown Coll (MN)
Culver-Stockton Coll (MO)
Curry Coll (MA)
Daemen Coll (NY)
Dalhousie U (NS, Canada)
Dallas Baptist U (TX)
Dalton State Coll (GA)
Dartmouth Coll (NH)
Davidson Coll (NC)
Defiance Coll (OH)
Delaware State U (DE)
Delta State U (MS)
Denison U (OH)
DePaul U (IL)
DePauw U (IN)
DEREE - The American Coll of Greece (Greece)
DeSales U (PA)
Dickinson Coll (PA)
Dillard U (LA)
Doane Coll (NE)
Dominican Coll (NY)
Dominican U (IL)
Dominican U of California (CA)
Dordt Coll (IA)
Dowling Coll (NY)
Drake U (IA)
Drew U (NJ)
Drexel U (PA)
Drury U (MO)
Duquesne U (PA)
Earlham Coll (IN)
East Carolina U (NC)

East Central U (OK)
Eastern Connecticut State U (CT)
Eastern Illinois U (IL)
Eastern Kentucky U (KY)
Eastern Mennonite U (VA)
Eastern Michigan U (MI)
Eastern New Mexico U (NM)
Eastern Oregon U (OR)
Eastern U (PA)
Eastern Washington U (WA)
East Stroudsburg U of Pennsylvania (PA)
East Tennessee State U (TN)
East Texas Baptist U (TX)
Eckerd Coll (FL)
Edgewood Coll (WI)
Edinboro U of Pennsylvania (PA)
Edward Waters Coll (FL)
Elizabeth City State U (NC)
Elizabethtown Coll (PA)
Elmhurst Coll (IL)
Elmira Coll (NY)
Elon U (NC)
Emmanuel Coll (MA)
Emory & Henry Coll (VA)
Emory U (GA)
Emporia State U (KS)
Endicott Coll (MA)
Evangel U (MO)
Excelsior Coll (NY)
Fairfield U (CT)
Fairleigh Dickinson U, Coll at Florham (NJ)
Fairleigh Dickinson U, Metropolitan Campus (NJ)
Fairmont State U (WV)
Faulkner U (AL)
Fayetteville State U (NC)
Felician Coll (NJ)
Ferris State U (MI)
Ferrum Coll (VA)
Fitchburg State U (MA)
Flagler Coll (FL)
Florida Ag and Mech U (FL)
Florida Atlantic U (FL)
Florida Gulf Coast U (FL)
Florida Intl U (FL)
Florida Southern Coll (FL)
Florida State U (FL)
Fontbonne U (MO)
Fordham U (NY)
Fort Hays State U (KS)
Fort Lewis Coll (CO)
Framingham State U (MA)
Franciscan U of Steubenville (OH)
Francis Marion U (SC)
Franklin & Marshall Coll (PA)
Franklin Coll (IN)
Franklin Coll Switzerland (Switzerland)
Free Will Baptist Bible Coll (TN)
Friends U (KS)
Furman U (SC)
Gannon U (PA)
Gardner-Webb U (NC)
Geneva Coll (PA)
George Fox U (OR)
George Mason U (VA)
Georgetown Coll (KY)
The George Washington U (DC)
Georgia Coll & State U (GA)
Georgia Gwinnett Coll (GA)
Georgian Court U (NJ)
Georgia Southern U (GA)
Georgia Southwestern State U (GA)
Georgia State U (GA)
Gettysburg Coll (PA)
Glenville State Coll (WV)
Gonzaga U (WA)
Gordon Coll (MA)
Goshen Coll (IN)
Goucher Coll (MD)
Grace Coll (IN)
Graceland U (IA)
Grambling State U (LA)
Grand Canyon U (AZ)
Grand Valley State U (MI)
Grand View U (IA)
Great Lakes Christian Coll (MI)
Greenville Coll (IL)
Grinnell Coll (IA)
Grove City Coll (PA)
Guilford Coll (NC)
Gustavus Adolphus Coll (MN)
Gwynedd-Mercy Coll (PA)

Hamilton Coll (NY)
Hamline U (MN)
Hampden-Sydney Coll (VA)
Hampshire Coll (MA)
Hampton U (VA)
Hannibal-LaGrange U (MO)
Hanover Coll (IN)
Harding U (AR)
Hardin-Simmons U (TX)
Hartwick Coll (NY)
Harvard U (MA)
Haverford Coll (PA)
Hawai`i Pacific U (HI)
Heidelberg U (OH)
Hendrix Coll (AR)
Hillsdale Coll (MI)
Hobart and William Smith Colls (NY)
Hofstra U (NY)
Hollins U (VA)
Holy Cross Coll (IN)
Holy Family U (PA)
Hood Coll (MD)
Hope Coll (MI)
Houghton Coll (NY)
Howard Payne U (TX)
Humboldt State U (CA)
Hunter Coll of the City U of New York (NY)
Huntingdon Coll (AL)
Huntington U (IN)
Huston-Tillotson U (TX)
Idaho State U (ID)
Illinois Coll (IL)
Illinois State U (IL)
Illinois Wesleyan U (IL)
Immaculata U (PA)
Indiana State U (IN)
Indiana U Bloomington (IN)
Indiana U East (IN)
Indiana U Northwest (IN)
Indiana U of Pennsylvania (PA)
Indiana U–Purdue U Fort Wayne (IN)
Indiana U–Purdue U Indianapolis (IN)
Indiana U South Bend (IN)
Indiana U Southeast (IN)
Indiana Wesleyan U (IN)
Iona Coll (NY)
Iowa State U of Science and Technology (IA)
Iowa Wesleyan Coll (IA)
Ithaca Coll (NY)
Jacksonville State U (AL)
Jacksonville U (FL)
James Madison U (VA)
Jamestown Coll (ND)
Jarvis Christian Coll (TX)
John Brown U (AR)
John Carroll U (OH)
The Johns Hopkins U (MD)
Johnson C. Smith U (NC)
Johnson State Coll (VT)
Judson Coll (AL)
Judson U (IL)
Juniata Coll (PA)
Kalamazoo Coll (MI)
Kansas State U (KS)
Kean U (NJ)
Keene State Coll (NH)
Kennesaw State U (GA)
Kent State U (OH)
Kent State U at Stark (OH)
Kentucky Christian U (KY)
Kentucky Wesleyan Coll (KY)
Kenyon Coll (OH)
Keuka Coll (NY)
King Coll (TN)
King's Coll (PA)
The King's U Coll (AB, Canada)
Knox Coll (IL)
Kutztown U of Pennsylvania (PA)
Lafayette Coll (PA)
LaGrange Coll (GA)
Lake Erie Coll (OH)
Lake Forest Coll (IL)
Lakehead U (ON, Canada)
Lake Superior State U (MI)
Lamar U (TX)
Lane Coll (TN)
La Roche Coll (PA)
La Salle U (PA)
Lasell Coll (MA)
La Sierra U (CA)

Lawrence U (WI)
Lebanese American U (Lebanon)
Lebanon Valley Coll (PA)
Lee U (TN)
Lehigh U (PA)
Lehman Coll of the City U of New York (NY)
Le Moyne Coll (NY)
Lenoir-Rhyne U (NC)
LeTourneau U (TX)
Lewis & Clark Coll (OR)
Lewis U (IL)
Liberty U (VA)
Limestone Coll (SC)
Lincoln Memorial U (TN)
Lincoln U (MO)
Lincoln U (PA)
Lindenwood U (MO)
Lindsey Wilson Coll (KY)
Linfield Coll (OR)
Lipscomb U (TN)
Lock Haven U of Pennsylvania (PA)
Long Island U–Brooklyn Campus (NY)
Long Island U–C. W. Post Campus (NY)
Longwood U (VA)
Loras Coll (IA)
Louisiana Coll (LA)
Louisiana State U and Ag and Mech Coll (LA)
Louisiana State U in Shreveport (LA)
Lourdes U (OH)
Loyola Marymount U (CA)
Loyola U Chicago (IL)
Loyola U Maryland (MD)
Loyola U New Orleans (LA)
Lubbock Christian U (TX)
Luther Coll (IA)
Lycoming Coll (PA)
Lynchburg Coll (VA)
Lyon Coll (AR)
Macalester Coll (MN)
Macon State Coll (GA)
Madonna U (MI)
Malone U (OH)
Manchester Coll (IN)
Manhattan Coll (NY)
Manhattanville Coll (NY)
Mansfield U of Pennsylvania (PA)
Marian U (WI)
Marietta Coll (OH)
Marlboro Coll (VT)
Marquette U (WI)
Marshall U (WV)
Mars Hill Coll (NC)
Mary Baldwin Coll (VA)
Marymount Manhattan Coll (NY)
Marymount U (VA)
Maryville Coll (TN)
Maryville U of Saint Louis (MO)
Marywood U (PA)
Massachusetts Coll of Liberal Arts (MA)
Massachusetts Inst of Technology (MA)
The Master's Coll and Sem (CA)
McDaniel Coll (MD)
McKendree U (IL)
McMurry U (TX)
McNeese State U (LA)
McPherson Coll (KS)
Mercer U (GA)
Mercy Coll (NY)
Mercyhurst Coll (PA)
Meredith Coll (NC)
Merrimack Coll (MA)
Messiah Coll (PA)
Metropolitan State Coll of Denver (CO)
Metropolitan State U (MN)
Miami U (OH)
Michigan State U (MI)
Michigan Technological U (MI)
MidAmerica Nazarene U (KS)
Middlebury Coll (VT)
Middle Tennessee State U (TN)
Midwestern State U (TX)
Millersville U of Pennsylvania (PA)
Milligan Coll (TN)
Millikin U (IL)
Millsaps Coll (MS)
Mills Coll (CA)
Minnesota State U Mankato (MN)

Minnesota State U Moorhead (MN)
Minot State U (ND)
Misericordia U (PA)
Mississippi Coll (MS)
Mississippi State U (MS)
Mississippi U for Women (MS)
Mississippi Valley State U (MS)
Missouri Baptist U (MO)
Missouri Southern State U (MO)
Missouri State U (MO)
Missouri U of Science and Technology (MO)
Missouri Western State U (MO)
Molloy Coll (NY)
Monmouth Coll (IL)
Monmouth U (NJ)
Montana State U (MT)
Montana State U Billings (MT)
Montclair State U (NJ)
Montreat Coll, Montreat (NC)
Moravian Coll (PA)
Morehead State U (KY)
Morehouse Coll (GA)
Morningside Coll (IA)
Morris Coll (SC)
Mount Allison U (NB, Canada)
Mount Holyoke Coll (MA)
Mount Marty Coll (SD)
Mount Mary Coll (WI)
Mount Mercy U (IA)
Mount Saint Mary Coll (NY)
Mount St. Mary's Coll (CA)
Mount St. Mary's U (MD)
Mount Vernon Nazarene U (OH)
Muhlenberg Coll (PA)
Multnomah U (OR)
National U (CA)
Nazareth Coll of Rochester (NY)
Nebraska Wesleyan U (NE)
Newberry Coll (SC)
New Coll of Florida (FL)
New England Coll (NH)
New Jersey City U (NJ)
Newman U (KS)
New Mexico Highlands U (NM)
New Mexico State U (NM)
New York U (NY)
Niagara U (NY)
Nicholls State U (LA)
Norfolk State U (VA)
North Carolina Ag and Tech State U (NC)
North Carolina Central U (NC)
North Carolina State U (NC)
North Carolina Wesleyan Coll (NC)
North Central Coll (IL)
North Dakota State U (ND)
Northeastern Illinois U (IL)
Northeastern State U (OK)
Northeastern U (MA)
Northern Arizona U (AZ)
Northern Illinois U (IL)
Northern Kentucky U (KY)
Northern Michigan U (MI)
Northern State U (SD)
North Georgia Coll & State U (GA)
North Greenville U (SC)
Northwest Christian U (OR)
Northwestern Coll (IA)
Northwestern Coll (MN)
Northwestern Oklahoma State U (OK)
Northwestern State U of Louisiana (LA)
Northwest Missouri State U (MO)
Northwest Nazarene U (ID)
Northwest U (WA)
Norwich U (VT)
Notre Dame de Namur U (CA)
Notre Dame of Maryland U (MD)
Nova Southeastern U (FL)
Nyack Coll (NY)
Oakland U (MI)
Oglethorpe U (GA)
Ohio Northern U (OH)
The Ohio State U (OH)
The Ohio State U at Lima (OH)
The Ohio State U at Marion (OH)
The Ohio State U–Mansfield Campus (OH)
The Ohio State U–Newark Campus (OH)
Ohio U (OH)
Ohio U–Chillicothe (OH)
Ohio Valley U (WV)

Ohio Wesleyan U (OH)
Oklahoma Christian U (OK)
Oklahoma City U (OK)
Oklahoma State U (OK)
Old Dominion U (VA)
Oral Roberts U (OK)
Otterbein U (OH)
Ouachita Baptist U (AR)
Pace U (NY)
Pacific Lutheran U (WA)
Pacific Union Coll (CA)
Pacific U (OR)
Paine Coll (GA)
Palm Beach Atlantic U (FL)
Park U (MO)
Patrick Henry Coll (VA)
Penn State Abington (PA)
Penn State Altoona (PA)
Penn State Beaver (PA)
Penn State Berks (PA)
Penn State Brandywine (PA)
Penn State DuBois (PA)
Penn State Erie, The Behrend Coll (PA)
Penn State Fayette, The Eberly Campus (PA)
Penn State Greater Allegheny (PA)
Penn State Hazleton (PA)
Penn State Lehigh Valley (PA)
Penn State Mont Alto (PA)
Penn State New Kensington (PA)
Penn State Schuylkill (PA)
Penn State Shenango (PA)
Penn State U Park (PA)
Penn State Wilkes-Barre (PA)
Penn State Worthington Scranton (PA)
Penn State York (PA)
Pepperdine U, Malibu (CA)
Peru State Coll (NE)
Piedmont Coll (GA)
Pine Manor Coll (MA)
Pittsburg State U (KS)
Pitzer Coll (CA)
Plymouth State U (NH)
Point Loma Nazarene U (CA)
Point Park U (PA)
Pomona Coll (CA)
Portland State U (OR)
Post U (CT)
Prairie View A&M U (TX)
Presbyterian Coll (SC)
Princeton U (NJ)
Providence Coll (RI)
Purchase Coll, State U of New York (NY)
Purdue U (IN)
Purdue U Calumet (IN)
Queens Coll of the City U of New York (NY)
Queen's U at Kingston (ON, Canada)
Queens U of Charlotte (NC)
Quincy U (IL)
Quinnipiac U (CT)
Radford U (VA)
Ramapo Coll of New Jersey (NJ)
Randolph Coll (VA)
Randolph-Macon Coll (VA)
Regent U (VA)
Regis Coll (MA)
Regis U (CO)
Reinhardt U (GA)
Rhode Island Coll (RI)
Rhodes Coll (TN)
Rice U (TX)
The Richard Stockton Coll of New Jersey (NJ)
Rider U (NJ)
Ripon Coll (WI)
Rivier Coll (NH)
Roanoke Coll (VA)
Roberts Wesleyan Coll (NY)
Rockford Coll (IL)
Rockhurst U (MO)
Rocky Mountain Coll (MT)
Roger Williams U (RI)
Rollins Coll (FL)
Roosevelt U (IL)
Rosemont Coll (PA)
Rowan U (NJ)
Russell Sage Coll (NY)
Rutgers, The State U of New Jersey, Camden (NJ)

Rutgers, The State U of New Jersey, Newark (NJ)
Rutgers, The State U of New Jersey, New Brunswick (NJ)
Sacred Heart U (CT)
Saginaw Valley State U (MI)
St. Ambrose U (IA)
Saint Anselm Coll (NH)
Saint Augustine's Coll (NC)
St. Bonaventure U (NY)
St. Catherine U (MN)
St. Edward's U (TX)
St. John Fisher Coll (NY)
Saint John's U (MN)
St. John's U (NY)
Saint Joseph's Coll (IN)
St. Joseph's Coll, Long Island Campus (NY)
St. Joseph's Coll, New York (NY)
Saint Joseph's Coll of Maine (ME)
Saint Joseph's U (PA)
St. Lawrence U (NY)
Saint Leo U (FL)
Saint Louis U (MO)
Saint Mary's Coll (IN)
Saint Mary's Coll of California (CA)
St. Mary's Coll of Maryland (MD)
St. Mary's U (TX)
Saint Mary's U of Minnesota (MN)
Saint Michael's Coll (VT)
St. Norbert Coll (WI)
St. Olaf Coll (MN)
Saint Peter's Coll (NJ)
St. Thomas Aquinas Coll (NY)
St. Thomas U (FL)
St. Thomas U (NB, Canada)
Saint Vincent Coll (PA)
Saint Xavier U (IL)
Salem State U (MA)
Salisbury U (MD)
Salve Regina U (RI)
Samford U (AL)
Sam Houston State U (TX)
San Diego Christian Coll (CA)
San Diego State U (CA)
San Francisco State U (CA)
Santa Clara U (CA)
Sarah Lawrence Coll (NY)
Schreiner U (TX)
Scripps Coll (CA)
Seattle Pacific U (WA)
Seattle U (WA)
Seton Hill U (PA)
Sewanee: The U of the South (TN)
Shawnee State U (OH)
Shenandoah U (VA)
Shepherd U (WV)
Shippensburg U of Pennsylvania (PA)
Shorter U (GA)
Siena Coll (NY)
Siena Heights U (MI)
Simmons Coll (MA)
Simon Fraser U (BC, Canada)
Simpson Coll (IA)
Simpson U (CA)
Skidmore Coll (NY)
Slippery Rock U of Pennsylvania (PA)
Smith Coll (MA)
Sonoma State U (CA)
South Carolina State U (SC)
South Dakota State U (SD)
Southeastern Baptist Theological Sem (NC)
Southeastern Louisiana U (LA)
Southeastern Oklahoma State U (OK)
Southeastern U (FL)
Southeast Missouri State U (MO)
Southern Arkansas U–Magnolia (AR)
Southern Connecticut State U (CT)
Southern Illinois U Carbondale (IL)
Southern Illinois U Edwardsville (IL)
Southern Methodist U (TX)
Southern New Hampshire U (NH)
Southern Oregon U (OR)
Southern Vermont Coll (VT)
Southwest Baptist U (MO)
Southwestern Adventist U (TX)
Southwestern Assemblies of God U (TX)
Southwestern Coll (KS)

Southwestern Oklahoma State U (OK)
Southwestern U (TX)
Southwest Minnesota State U (MN)
Spelman Coll (GA)
Spring Arbor U (MI)
Spring Hill Coll (AL)
Stanford U (CA)
State U of New York at Binghamton (NY)
State U of New York at Fredonia (NY)
State U of New York at New Paltz (NY)
State U of New York at Oswego (NY)
State U of New York at Plattsburgh (NY)
State U of New York Coll at Cortland (NY)
State U of New York Coll at Geneseo (NY)
State U of New York Coll at Old Westbury (NY)
State U of New York Coll at Oneonta (NY)
State U of New York Coll at Potsdam (NY)
State U of New York Empire State Coll (NY)
Stephen F. Austin State U (TX)
Sterling Coll (KS)
Stetson U (FL)
Stevens Inst of Technology (NJ)
Stevenson U (MD)
Stillman Coll (AL)
Stonehill Coll (MA)
Stony Brook U, State U of New York (NY)
Suffolk U (MA)
Sul Ross State U (TX)
Susquehanna U (PA)
Swarthmore Coll (PA)
Sweet Briar Coll (VA)
Syracuse U (NY)
Tabor Coll (KS)
Tarleton State U (TX)
Taylor U (IN)
Temple U (PA)
Texas A&M Intl U (TX)
Texas A&M U (TX)
Texas A&M U–Corpus Christi (TX)
Texas A&M U–Kingsville (TX)
Texas Christian U (TX)
Texas Coll (TX)
Texas Lutheran U (TX)
Texas Southern U (TX)
Texas State U–San Marcos (TX)
Texas Tech U (TX)
Texas Wesleyan U (TX)
Texas Woman's U (TX)
Thiel Coll (PA)
Thomas Edison State Coll (NJ)
Thomas More Coll (KY)
Thompson Rivers U (BC, Canada)
Tiffin U (OH)
Touro Coll (NY)
Towson U (MD)
Transylvania U (KY)
Trent U (ON, Canada)
Trevecca Nazarene U (TN)
Trinity Christian Coll (IL)
Trinity Coll (CT)
Trinity U (TX)
Troy U (AL)
Truett-McConnell Coll (GA)
Truman State U (MO)
Tufts U (MA)
Tulane U (LA)
Tusculum Coll (TN)
Tuskegee U (AL)
Union Coll (KY)
Union Coll (NE)
Union Coll (NY)
Union U (TN)
United States Air Force Acad (CO)
United States Naval Acad (MD)
Université de Sherbrooke (QC, Canada)
U at Albany, State U of New York (NY)
U at Buffalo, the State U of New York (NY)
The U of Alabama (AL)

The U of Alabama at Birmingham (AL)
The U of Alabama in Huntsville (AL)
U of Alaska Anchorage (AK)
U of Alaska Fairbanks (AK)
U of Alberta (AB, Canada)
The U of Arizona (AZ)
U of Arkansas (AR)
U of Arkansas at Little Rock (AR)
U of Arkansas at Monticello (AR)
U of Arkansas–Fort Smith (AR)
The U of British Columbia (BC, Canada)
The U of British Columbia–Okanagan (BC, Canada)
U of California, Berkeley (CA)
U of California, Davis (CA)
U of California, Irvine (CA)
U of California, Los Angeles (CA)
U of California, Merced (CA)
U of California, Riverside (CA)
U of California, Santa Barbara (CA)
U of California, Santa Cruz (CA)
U of Central Arkansas (AR)
U of Central Florida (FL)
U of Central Missouri (MO)
U of Charleston (WV)
U of Cincinnati (OH)
U of Colorado at Colorado Springs (CO)
U of Colorado Boulder (CO)
U of Colorado Denver (CO)
U of Connecticut (CT)
U of Dallas (TX)
U of Dayton (OH)
U of Delaware (DE)
U of Denver (CO)
U of Evansville (IN)
The U of Findlay (OH)
U of Florida (FL)
U of Georgia (GA)
U of Great Falls (MT)
U of Guam (GU)
U of Guelph (ON, Canada)
U of Hartford (CT)
U of Hawaii at Hilo (HI)
U of Hawaii at Manoa (HI)
U of Hawaii–West Oahu (HI)
U of Houston (TX)
U of Houston–Clear Lake (TX)
U of Houston–Downtown (TX)
U of Houston–Victoria (TX)
U of Idaho (ID)
U of Illinois at Chicago (IL)
U of Illinois at Springfield (IL)
U of Illinois at Urbana–Champaign (IL)
U of Indianapolis (IN)
The U of Iowa (IA)
The U of Kansas (KS)
U of La Verne (CA)
U of Lethbridge (AB, Canada)
U of Louisiana at Lafayette (LA)
U of Louisiana at Monroe (LA)
U of Louisville (KY)
U of Maine (ME)
U of Maine at Farmington (ME)
U of Maine at Presque Isle (ME)
U of Mary Hardin-Baylor (TX)
U of Maryland, Baltimore County (MD)
U of Maryland, Coll Park (MD)
U of Maryland Eastern Shore (MD)
U of Maryland U Coll (MD)
U of Mary Washington (VA)
U of Massachusetts Amherst (MA)
U of Massachusetts Boston (MA)
U of Massachusetts Dartmouth (MA)
U of Massachusetts Lowell (MA)
U of Memphis (TN)
U of Miami (FL)
U of Michigan (MI)
U of Michigan–Dearborn (MI)
U of Michigan–Flint (MI)
U of Minnesota, Duluth (MN)
U of Minnesota, Twin Cities Campus (MN)
U of Mississippi (MS)
U of Missouri (MO)
U of Missouri–Kansas City (MO)
U of Missouri–St. Louis (MO)
U of Mobile (AL)
The U of Montana Western (MT)
U of Mount Union (OH)

The U of Nebraska at Kearney (NE)
U of Nebraska at Omaha (NE)
U of Nebraska–Lincoln (NE)
U of Nevada, Las Vegas (NV)
U of Nevada, Reno (NV)
U of New England (ME)
U of New Hampshire (NH)
U of New Hampshire at Manchester (NH)
U of New Haven (CT)
U of New Mexico (NM)
U of New Orleans (LA)
U of North Alabama (AL)
The U of North Carolina at Asheville (NC)
The U of North Carolina at Chapel Hill (NC)
The U of North Carolina at Charlotte (NC)
The U of North Carolina Wilmington (NC)
U of North Dakota (ND)
U of Northern Colorado (CO)
U of Northern Iowa (IA)
U of North Florida (FL)
U of North Texas (TX)
U of Notre Dame (IN)
U of Oklahoma (OK)
U of Oregon (OR)
U of Ottawa (ON, Canada)
U of Pennsylvania (PA)
U of Pikeville (KY)
U of Pittsburgh (PA)
U of Pittsburgh at Bradford (PA)
U of Pittsburgh at Johnstown (PA)
U of Portland (OR)
U of Puget Sound (WA)
U of Redlands (CA)
U of Regina (SK, Canada)
U of Rhode Island (RI)
U of Richmond (VA)
U of Rio Grande (OH)
U of Rochester (NY)
U of St. Francis (IL)
U of Saint Francis (IN)
U of Saint Joseph (CT)
U of Saint Mary (KS)
U of St. Thomas (MN)
U of St. Thomas (TX)
U of San Diego (CA)
U of Science and Arts of Oklahoma (OK)
The U of Scranton (PA)
U of South Alabama (AL)
U of South Carolina (SC)
U of South Carolina Aiken (SC)
U of South Carolina Beaufort (SC)
U of South Carolina Upstate (SC)
The U of South Dakota (SD)
U of Southern California (CA)
U of Southern Indiana (IN)
U of Southern Maine (ME)
U of Southern Mississippi (MS)
U of South Florida (FL)
U of South Florida–St. Petersburg Campus (FL)
The U of Tampa (FL)
The U of Tennessee (TN)
The U of Tennessee at Chattanooga (TN)
The U of Tennessee at Martin (TN)
The U of Texas at Arlington (TX)
The U of Texas at Austin (TX)
The U of Texas at Dallas (TX)
The U of Texas at El Paso (TX)
The U of Texas at San Antonio (TX)
The U of Texas at Tyler (TX)
The U of Texas of the Permian Basin (TX)
The U of Texas–Pan American (TX)
U of the Cumberlands (KY)
U of the Incarnate Word (TX)
U of the Ozarks (AR)
U of the Pacific (CA)
U of the Southwest (NM)
The U of Toledo (OH)
U of Toronto (ON, Canada)
U of Tulsa (OK)
U of Utah (UT)
U of Vermont (VT)
U of Virginia (VA)
The U of Virginia's Coll at Wise (VA)
U of Washington (WA)
The U of West Alabama (AL)

HISTORY AND PHILOSOPHY OF SCIENCE AND TECHNOLOGY

HISTORY RELATED

HISTORY TEACHER EDUCATION

HOLOCAUST AND RELATED STUDIES

HOME FURNISHINGS AND EQUIPMENT INSTALLATION

HOMELAND SECURITY

HOMELAND SECURITY, LAW ENFORCEMENT, FIREFIGHTING AND PROTECTIVE SERVICES RELATED

HORSE HUSBANDRY/EQUINE SCIENCE AND MANAGEMENT

HORTICULTURAL SCIENCE

Washington State U (WA)

HOSPITAL AND HEALTH-CARE FACILITIES ADMINISTRATION
Avila U (MO)
Black Hills State U (SD)
Carlow U (PA)
Carson-Newman Coll (TN)
Clayton State U (GA)
Gwynedd-Mercy Coll (PA)
Indiana Tech (IN)
Ithaca Coll (NY)
Long Island U–C. W. Post Campus (NY)
Newman U (KS)
New York City Coll of Technology of the City U of New York (NY)
St. Joseph's Coll, Long Island Campus (NY)
St. Joseph's Coll, New York (NY)
Saint Joseph's U (PA)
State U of New York Coll of Technology at Canton (NY)
Thomas Edison State Coll (NJ)
The U of Alabama (AL)
The U of South Dakota (SD)
The U of Toledo (OH)
U of Wisconsin–Milwaukee (WI)
Ursuline Coll (OH)
Youngstown State U (OH)

HOSPITALITY ADMINISTRATION
American Public U System (WV)
Appalachian State U (NC)
Arkansas Tech U (AR)
The Art Inst of Austin (TX)
The Art Insts Intl Minnesota (MN)
Becker Coll (MA)
Boston U (MA)
Bowling Green State U (OH)
Bradley U (IL)
Buffalo State Coll, State U of New York (NY)
Burlington Coll (VT)
California State Polytechnic U, Pomona (CA)
Cape Breton U (NS, Canada)
Central Michigan U (MI)
Coll of Charleston (SC)
Coll of the Ozarks (MO)
Colorado Mesa U (CO)
Columbia Southern U (AL)
Delaware State U (DE)
Delta State U (MS)
DePaul U (IL)
East Carolina U (NC)
Eastern Michigan U (MI)
East Stroudsburg U of Pennsylvania (PA)
Endicott Coll (MA)
Fairleigh Dickinson U, Coll at Florham (NJ)
Fairleigh Dickinson U, Metropolitan Campus (NJ)
Ferris State U (MI)
Florida Atlantic U (FL)
Florida Intl U (FL)
Florida State U (FL)
Georgia State U (GA)
Grand Valley State U (MI)
Husson U (ME)
The Illinois Inst of Art–Chicago (IL)
The Illinois Inst of Art–Schaumburg (IL)
Indiana U of Pennsylvania (PA)
Indiana U–Purdue U Fort Wayne (IN)
James Madison U (VA)
Johnson State Coll (VT)
Kent State U (OH)
Kent State U at Ashtabula (OH)
Lasell Coll (MA)
Lebanese American U (Lebanon)
Lewis-Clark State Coll (ID)
Madonna U (MI)
Marywood U (PA)
Mercyhurst Coll (PA)
Metropolitan State Coll of Denver (CO)
Metropolitan State U (MN)
Michigan State U (MI)
Missouri State U (MO)
Morrisville State Coll (NY)

National U (CA)
New Mexico State U (NM)
New York City Coll of Technology of the City U of New York (NY)
North Carolina Central U (NC)
North Dakota State U (ND)
Northern Arizona U (AZ)
Northern Michigan U (MI)
Northwestern State U of Louisiana (LA)
The Ohio State U (OH)
Oklahoma State U (OK)
Philander Smith Coll (AR)
The Richard Stockton Coll of New Jersey (NJ)
Robert Morris U (PA)
Rochester Inst of Technology (NY)
Roosevelt U (IL)
Rutgers, The State U of New Jersey, Camden (NJ)
Ryerson U (ON, Canada)
St. John's U (NY)
Saint Leo U (FL)
Saint Louis U (MO)
Salem State U (MA)
San Diego State U (CA)
San Francisco State U (CA)
Seton Hill U (PA)
Sojourner-Douglass Coll (MD)
Southeast Missouri State U (MO)
Southern New Hampshire U (NH)
Stephen F. Austin State U (TX)
Sullivan U (KY)
Temple U (PA)
Thomas Edison State Coll (NJ)
Thompson Rivers U (BC, Canada)
Tiffin U (OH)
Trident U Intl (CA)
Tuskegee U (AL)
U of Central Florida (FL)
U of Cincinnati (OH)
U of Delaware (DE)
U of Denver (CO)
U of Illinois at Urbana–Champaign (IL)
U of Louisiana at Lafayette (LA)
U of Massachusetts Amherst (MA)
U of Memphis (TN)
U of Mississippi (MS)
U of Nebraska–Lincoln (NE)
U of Nevada, Las Vegas (NV)
U of New Hampshire (NH)
U of New Haven (CT)
U of New Orleans (LA)
U of North Texas (TX)
U of Pittsburgh at Bradford (PA)
U of South Carolina (SC)
U of South Carolina Beaufort (SC)
U of South Florida (FL)
U of West Florida (FL)
U of Wisconsin–Stout (WI)
Utah Valley U (UT)
Virginia State U (VA)
Washington State U (WA)
Webber Intl U (FL)
Western Carolina U (NC)
Western Kentucky U (KY)
Youngstown State U (OH)

HOSPITALITY ADMINISTRATION RELATED
Auburn U (AL)
California State U, Dominguez Hills (CA)
California State U, Fullerton (CA)
Delaware State U (DE)
DEREE - The American Coll of Greece (Greece)
Drexel U (PA)
Lynn U (FL)
Mitchell Coll (CT)
Morrisville State Coll (NY)
Niagara U (NY)
Penn State Abington (PA)
Penn State Altoona (PA)
Penn State Beaver (PA)
Penn State Berks (PA)
Penn State Brandywine (PA)
Penn State DuBois (PA)
Penn State Erie, The Behrend Coll (PA)
Penn State Fayette, The Eberly Campus (PA)
Penn State Greater Allegheny (PA)
Penn State Hazleton (PA)

Penn State Lehigh Valley (PA)
Penn State Mont Alto (PA)
Penn State New Kensington (PA)
Penn State Schuylkill (PA)
Penn State Shenango (PA)
Penn State U Park (PA)
Penn State Wilkes-Barre (PA)
Penn State Worthington Scranton (PA)
Penn State York (PA)
Southern Illinois U Carbondale (IL)
Thompson Rivers U (BC, Canada)
U of Central Florida (FL)
U of Louisiana at Lafayette (LA)
U of Nevada, Las Vegas (NV)
U of Southern Mississippi (MS)
Widener U (PA)

HOSPITALITY AND RECREATION MARKETING
Cape Breton U (NS, Canada)
Ferris State U (MI)
Rochester Inst of Technology (NY)
Tuskegee U (AL)
U of Minnesota, Twin Cities Campus (MN)

HOTEL/MOTEL ADMINISTRATION
The Art Inst of Pittsburgh (PA)
Ashland U (OH)
Auburn U (AL)
Becker Coll (MA)
Bethune-Cookman U (FL)
Buffalo State Coll, State U of New York (NY)
California State U, Long Beach (CA)
Central Michigan U (MI)
Cheyney U of Pennsylvania (PA)
Cornell U (NY)
Ferris State U (MI)
Georgia Southern U (GA)
Grambling State U (LA)
Grand Valley State U (MI)
Hampton U (VA)
Indiana U–Purdue U Fort Wayne (IN)
Inter American U of Puerto Rico, Fajardo Campus (PR)
Inter American U of Puerto Rico, Ponce Campus (PR)
Iowa State U of Science and Technology (IA)
Kansas State U (KS)
Keuka Coll (NY)
Mount Ida Coll (MA)
Newbury Coll (MA)
New York Inst of Technology (NY)
New York U (NY)
Niagara U (NY)
Northwood U, Florida Campus (FL)
Northwood U, Michigan Campus (MI)
The Ohio State U (OH)
Pace U (NY)
Purdue U Calumet (IN)
The Restaurant School at Walnut Hill Coll (PA)
Rochester Inst of Technology (NY)
Ryerson U (ON, Canada)
St. Thomas U (FL)
South Dakota State U (SD)
Southern Oregon U (OR)
Southwest Minnesota State U (MN)
State U of New York at Plattsburgh (NY)
State U of New York Coll of Technology at Delhi (NY)
Texas Tech U (TX)
United States Intl U (Kenya)
The U of Akron (OH)
U of Central Missouri (MO)
U of Delaware (DE)
U of Denver (CO)
The U of Findlay (OH)
U of Guelph (ON, Canada)
U of Houston (TX)
U of Maryland Eastern Shore (MD)
U of Memphis (TN)
U of Missouri (MO)
U of Nevada, Las Vegas (NV)
U of New Haven (CT)
U of Southern Mississippi (MS)

The U of Tennessee (TN)
Virginia Polytechnic Inst and State U (VA)
Widener U (PA)

HOUSING AND HUMAN ENVIRONMENTS
Eastern Kentucky U (KY)
Harding U (AR)
Missouri State U (MO)
Ohio U (OH)
Oklahoma State U (OK)
The U of Akron (OH)
U of Arkansas (AR)
U of Georgia (GA)
U of Minnesota, Twin Cities Campus (MN)
U of Missouri (MO)
U of Northern Iowa (IA)
Utah State U (UT)

HOUSING AND HUMAN ENVIRONMENTS RELATED
Bob Jones U (SC)
U of Nevada, Reno (NV)

HUMAN BIOLOGY
Daemen Coll (NY)
Scripps Coll (CA)
The U of Kansas (KS)
U of Wisconsin–Green Bay (WI)

HUMAN COMPUTER INTERACTION
U of Guelph (ON, Canada)

HUMAN DEVELOPMENT AND FAMILY STUDIES
Abilene Christian U (TX)
Amberton U (TX)
Antioch U Midwest (OH)
Ashland U (OH)
Auburn U (AL)
Baylor U (TX)
Boston Coll (MA)
Bowling Green State U (OH)
Brigham Young U (UT)
California State U, East Bay (CA)
California State U, Long Beach (CA)
California State U, San Bernardino (CA)
Colorado State U (CO)
Concordia U (MI)
Concordia U, St. Paul (MN)
Connecticut Coll (CT)
Cornell U (NY)
Eastern Kentucky U (KY)
Eckerd Coll (FL)
Florida State U (FL)
Georgia Southern U (GA)
Hellenic Coll (MA)
Hope Intl U (CA)
Howard Payne U (TX)
Indiana State U (IN)
Indiana U of Pennsylvania (PA)
Kansas State U (KS)
Kent State U (OH)
Kent State U at Stark (OH)
Kentucky State U (KY)
Lee U (TN)
Liberty U (VA)
Lubbock Christian U (TX)
Miami U (OH)
Missouri State U (MO)
Mitchell Coll (CT)
New Mexico State U (NM)
North Dakota State U (ND)
Northern Illinois U (IL)
Northwest Missouri State U (MO)
The Ohio State U (OH)
Ohio U (OH)
Oklahoma State U (OK)
Penn State Abington (PA)
Penn State Altoona (PA)
Penn State Beaver (PA)
Penn State Berks (PA)
Penn State Brandywine (PA)
Penn State DuBois (PA)
Penn State Erie, The Behrend Coll (PA)
Penn State Fayette, The Eberly Campus (PA)

Penn State Greater Allegheny (PA)
Penn State Harrisburg (PA)
Penn State Hazleton (PA)
Penn State Lehigh Valley (PA)
Penn State Mont Alto (PA)
Penn State New Kensington (PA)
Penn State Schuylkill (PA)
Penn State Shenango (PA)
Penn State U Park (PA)
Penn State Wilkes-Barre (PA)
Penn State Worthington Scranton (PA)
Penn State York (PA)
Purdue U (IN)
Purdue U Calumet (IN)
Rockford Coll (IL)
St. Joseph's Coll, Long Island Campus (NY)
St. Joseph's Coll, New York (NY)
Samford U (AL)
San Diego Christian Coll (CA)
Sarah Lawrence Coll (NY)
Seattle Pacific U (WA)
Sojourner-Douglass Coll (MD)
South Dakota State U (SD)
Southwestern Christian U (OK)
State U of New York at Oswego (NY)
State U of New York at Plattsburgh (NY)
State U of New York Empire State Coll (NY)
Stephen F. Austin State U (TX)
Stephens Coll (MO)
Syracuse U (NY)
Texas Tech U (TX)
Texas Woman's U (TX)
The U of Alabama (AL)
U of Arkansas (AR)
U of California, Davis (CA)
U of Connecticut (CT)
U of Guelph (ON, Canada)
U of Houston (TX)
U of Idaho (ID)
U of Illinois at Urbana–Champaign (IL)
U of Louisiana at Lafayette (LA)
U of Maine (ME)
U of Memphis (TN)
U of Missouri (MO)
U of Nevada, Reno (NV)
U of New Hampshire (NH)
U of New Mexico (NM)
The U of North Carolina at Charlotte (NC)
U of North Texas (TX)
U of Rhode Island (RI)
The U of Tennessee (TN)
The U of Texas at Austin (TX)
The U of Texas of the Permian Basin (TX)
U of Utah (UT)
U of Vermont (VT)
U of Wisconsin–Madison (WI)
U of Wisconsin–Stout (WI)
Utah State U (UT)
Vanguard U of Southern California (CA)
Virginia Polytechnic Inst and State U (VA)
Walden U (MN)
Washington State U (WA)
Wheelock Coll (MA)
Youngstown State U (OH)

HUMAN DEVELOPMENT AND FAMILY STUDIES RELATED
Auburn U (AL)
Ball State U (IN)
Bowling Green State U (OH)
Columbia Coll (SC)
Harding U (AR)
Hope Intl U (CA)
LaGrange Coll (GA)
State U of New York at Binghamton (NY)
The U of Alabama (AL)
U of Louisiana at Lafayette (LA)

HUMANITIES
Adelphi U (NY)
Albertus Magnus Coll (CT)
Anna Maria Coll (MA)
Antioch U Midwest (OH)

Athens State U (AL)
Baylor U (TX)
Belhaven U (MS)
Bemidji State U (MN)
Benedictine U (IL)
Bennington Coll (VT)
Biola U (CA)
Bishop's U (QC, Canada)
Bluefield State Coll (WV)
Bob Jones U (SC)
Bradley U (IL)
Briercrest Coll (SK, Canada)
Bucknell U (PA)
Buffalo State Coll, State U of New
    York (NY)
California State U, Chico (CA)
California State U, Monterey Bay
    (CA)
California State U, Sacramento
    (CA)
California State U, San Bernardino
    (CA)
Catawba Coll (NC)
Chaminade U of Honolulu (HI)
Clarkson U (NY)
Clearwater Christian Coll (FL)
Colgate U (NY)
Coll of Saint Benedict (MN)
Coll of Saint Mary (NE)
The Coll of St. Scholastica (MN)
Coll of the Humanities and
    Sciences, Harrison Middleton U
    (AZ)
Concordia Coll (MN)
Concordia U (CA)
Concordia U (QC, Canada)
Corban U (OR)
DePaul U (IL)
Dominican Coll (NY)
Dominican U of California (CA)
Dowling Coll (NY)
Eastern Oregon U (OR)
Eastern Washington U (WA)
East Stroudsburg U of Pennsylvania
    (PA)
Eckerd Coll (FL)
Edinboro U of Pennsylvania (PA)
Elmira Coll (NY)
The Evergreen State Coll (WA)
Fairleigh Dickinson U, Coll at
    Florham (NJ)
Fairleigh Dickinson U, Metropolitan
    Campus (NJ)
Faulkner U (AL)
Felician Coll (NJ)
Florida Inst of Technology (FL)
Florida Southern Coll (FL)
Florida State U (FL)
Fort Lewis Coll (CO)
Franciscan U of Steubenville (OH)
Free Will Baptist Bible Coll (TN)
The George Washington U (DC)
Georgian Court U (NJ)
Hampden-Sydney Coll (VA)
Harding U (AR)
Hawai`i Pacific U (HI)
Hillsdale Free Will Baptist Coll (OK)
Holy Family U (PA)
Houghton Coll (NY)
Howard Payne U (TX)
Hunter Coll of the City U of New
    York (NY)
Indiana U East (IN)
Indiana U Kokomo (IN)
Jacksonville U (FL)
John Carroll U (OH)
Johnson State Coll (VT)
Juniata Coll (PA)
Kansas State U (KS)
Kent State U (OH)
Kentucky Christian U (KY)
The King's Coll (NY)
Lasell Coll (MA)
Lawrence Technological U (MI)
Lee U (TN)
Lincoln Memorial U (TN)
Long Island U–Brooklyn Campus
    (NY)
Loyola Marymount U (CA)
Lubbock Christian U (TX)
Maranatha Baptist Bible Coll (WI)
Marlboro Coll (VT)
Marshall U (WV)
Marylhurst U (OR)
Messiah Coll (PA)

Michigan State U (MI)
Midwestern State U (TX)
Milligan Coll (TN)
Minnesota State U Mankato (MN)
Montclair State U (NJ)
Mount Allison U (NB, Canada)
New Coll of Florida (FL)
New York U (NY)
North Central Coll (IL)
Northland Coll (WI)
Northwestern Coll (IA)
Northwest Missouri State U (MO)
Northwest Nazarene U (ID)
Nova Southeastern U (FL)
Oakland City U (IN)
The Ohio State U (OH)
Ohio Wesleyan U (OH)
Oklahoma City U (OK)
Our Lady of the Lake Coll (LA)
Pacific U (OR)
Penn State Harrisburg (PA)
Pepperdine U, Malibu (CA)
Plymouth State U (NH)
Point U (GA)
Pomona Coll (CA)
Portland State U (OR)
Prescott Coll (AZ)
Providence Coll (RI)
Purchase Coll, State U of New York
    (NY)
Purdue U (IN)
Quincy U (IL)
Regis U (CO)
Roberts Wesleyan Coll (NY)
Rockford Coll (IL)
Rollins Coll (FL)
Rosemont Coll (PA)
Ryerson U (ON, Canada)
Sage Coll of Albany (NY)
St. Andrews U (NC)
Saint John's U (MN)
Saint Louis U (MO)
Saint Mary-of-the-Woods Coll (IN)
Saint Mary's Coll (IN)
St. Norbert Coll (WI)
Saint Peter's Coll (NJ)
St. Thomas Aquinas Coll (NY)
San Diego State U (CA)
San Francisco State U (CA)
Sarah Lawrence Coll (NY)
Schreiner U (TX)
Scripps Coll (CA)
Seattle U (WA)
Shimer Coll (IL)
Siena Heights U (MI)
Sierra Nevada Coll (NV)
Simon Fraser U (BC, Canada)
Southeastern Baptist Theological
    Sem (NC)
Spring Hill Coll (AL)
State U of New York Coll at Old
    Westbury (NY)
State U of New York Empire State
    Coll (NY)
Stetson U (FL)
Stevens Inst of Technology (NJ)
Stonehill Coll (MA)
Stony Brook U, State U of New York
    (NY)
Suffolk U (MA)
Texas Wesleyan U (TX)
Thomas Edison State Coll (NJ)
Thomas More Coll (KY)
Thomas U (GA)
Touro Coll (NY)
Trent U (ON, Canada)
Trinity U (TX)
Truett-McConnell Coll (GA)
Union Coll (NY)
United States Air Force Acad (CO)
United States Military Acad (NY)
Universidad del Turabo (PR)
The U of Akron (OH)
U of Alberta (AB, Canada)
U of Bridgeport (CT)
U of California, Irvine (CA)
U of California, Riverside (CA)
U of Central Florida (FL)
U of Colorado Boulder (CO)
U of Hawaii–West Oahu (HI)
U of Houston–Clear Lake (TX)
U of Houston–Downtown (TX)
U of Houston–Victoria (TX)
U of Illinois at Urbana–Champaign
    (IL)

The U of Kansas (KS)
U of Lethbridge (AB, Canada)
U of Louisville (KY)
U of Massachusetts Amherst (MA)
U of Michigan (MI)
U of Michigan–Dearborn (MI)
U of Minnesota, Twin Cities
    Campus (MN)
U of Mobile (AL)
U of New Hampshire (NH)
U of New Hampshire at Manchester
    (NH)
U of New Mexico (NM)
U of Northern Iowa (IA)
U of Oklahoma (OK)
U of Oregon (OR)
U of Ottawa (ON, Canada)
U of Pennsylvania (PA)
U of Pittsburgh (PA)
U of Pittsburgh at Bradford (PA)
U of Pittsburgh at Greensburg (PA)
U of Pittsburgh at Johnstown (PA)
U of Regina (SK, Canada)
U of Rio Grande (OH)
U of San Diego (CA)
U of Southern Maine (ME)
U of South Florida (FL)
The U of Tennessee at
    Chattanooga (TN)
The U of Texas at Austin (TX)
The U of Texas at San Antonio (TX)
The U of Texas of the Permian
    Basin (TX)
U of the Ozarks (AR)
U of the Southwest (NM)
The U of Toledo (OH)
U of Toronto (ON, Canada)
U of Utah (UT)
U of Washington (WA)
U of Washington, Bothell (WA)
U of West Florida (FL)
U of Wisconsin–Green Bay (WI)
U of Wyoming (WY)
Ursuline Coll (OH)
Valparaiso U (IN)
Villanova U (PA)
Virginia Wesleyan Coll (VA)
Waldorf Coll (IA)
Washington Coll (MD)
Washington State U (WA)
Washington U in St. Louis (MO)
Webster U (MO)
Wesleyan Coll (GA)
Wesleyan U (CT)
Western Oregon U (OR)
Western Washington U (WA)
Wheelock Coll (MA)
Widener U (PA)
Willamette U (OR)
William Paterson U of New Jersey
    (NJ)
Wofford Coll (SC)
Worcester Polytechnic Inst (MA)
Yale U (CT)

HUMAN/MEDICAL GENETICS
Sarah Lawrence Coll (NY)

HUMAN NUTRITION
Baylor U (TX)
Cape Breton U (NS, Canada)
Case Western Reserve U (OH)
Colorado State U (CO)
Kansas State U (KS)
Life U (GA)
Metropolitan State Coll of Denver
    (CO)
The Ohio State U (OH)
Penn State Abington (PA)
Penn State Altoona (PA)
Penn State Beaver (PA)
Penn State Berks (PA)
Penn State Brandywine (PA)
Penn State DuBois (PA)
Penn State Erie, The Behrend Coll
    (PA)
Penn State Fayette, The Eberly
    Campus (PA)
Penn State Greater Allegheny (PA)
Penn State Hazleton (PA)
Penn State Lehigh Valley (PA)
Penn State Mont Alto (PA)
Penn State New Kensington (PA)
Penn State Schuylkill (PA)

Penn State Shenango (PA)
Penn State U Park (PA)
Penn State Wilkes-Barre (PA)
Penn State Worthington Scranton
    (PA)
Penn State York (PA)
Rochester Inst of Technology (NY)
Ryerson U (ON, Canada)
Syracuse U (NY)
Tarleton State U (TX)
The U of British Columbia (BC,
    Canada)
U of Guelph (ON, Canada)
U of Houston (TX)
U of Illinois at Urbana–Champaign
    (IL)
Washington State U (WA)

HUMAN RESOURCES DEVELOPMENT
Clemson U (SC)
Concordia U Texas (TX)
Hawai`i Pacific U (HI)
Limestone Coll (SC)
Midwestern State U (TX)
Nichols Coll (MA)
Oakland U (MI)
The Ohio State U (OH)
Park U (MO)
Pittsburg State U (KS)
Texas A&M U (TX)
U of Arkansas (AR)
U of Houston (TX)
U of Regina (SK, Canada)
The U of Texas at Tyler (TX)
U of Wisconsin–Milwaukee (WI)

HUMAN RESOURCES MANAGEMENT
Alvernia U (PA)
Amberton U (TX)
Anderson U (SC)
Antioch U Midwest (OH)
Arcadia U (PA)
Athabasca U (AB, Canada)
Athens State U (AL)
Auburn U (AL)
Auburn U Montgomery (AL)
Avila U (MO)
Baker Coll of Owosso (MI)
Baldwin-Wallace Coll (OH)
Ball State U (IN)
Barton Coll (NC)
Bayamón Central U (PR)
Baylor U (TX)
Bellevue U (NE)
Bernard M. Baruch Coll of the City
    U of New York (NY)
Bishop's U (QC, Canada)
Black Hills State U (SD)
Bob Jones U (SC)
Boise State U (ID)
Boston Coll (MA)
Bowling Green State U (OH)
Bradley U (IL)
Brescia U (KY)
Briar Cliff U (IA)
Brigham Young U (UT)
Buena Vista U (IA)
Cabrini Coll (PA)
California Coast U (CA)
California State U, Chico (CA)
California State U, East Bay (CA)
California State U, Fresno (CA)
California State U, Long Beach
    (CA)
Cape Breton U (NS, Canada)
Capella U (MN)
The Catholic U of America (DC)
Central Michigan U (MI)
Chestnut Hill Coll (PA)
Cleary U (MI)
Coll of Saint Elizabeth (NJ)
Columbia Coll (MO)
Columbia Southern U (AL)
Concordia U (QC, Canada)
Concordia U, St. Paul (MN)
Concordia U Texas (TX)
Converse Coll (SC)
Davenport U, Grand Rapids (MI)
Delaware State U (DE)
DePaul U (IL)
Dominican Coll (NY)
East Central U (OK)

Eastern Washington U (WA)
Excelsior Coll (NY)
Faulkner U (AL)
Ferris State U (MI)
Florida Atlantic U (FL)
Florida Intl U (FL)
Fordham U (NY)
Fort Hays State U (KS)
Franklin U (OH)
Friends U (KS)
The George Washington U (DC)
Georgia Southwestern State U (GA)
Goldey-Beacom Coll (DE)
Governors State U (IL)
Hawai`i Pacific U (HI)
HEC Montreal (QC, Canada)
Huntington U (IN)
Idaho State U (ID)
Indiana State U (IN)
Indiana U of Pennsylvania (PA)
Inter American U of Puerto Rico,
    Bayamón Campus (PR)
Inter American U of Puerto Rico,
    Fajardo Campus (PR)
Inter American U of Puerto Rico,
    Ponce Campus (PR)
Inter American U of Puerto Rico,
    San Germán Campus (PR)
John Carroll U (OH)
Judson U (IL)
Juniata Coll (PA)
King's Coll (PA)
Kutztown U of Pennsylvania (PA)
Lake Erie Coll (OH)
Lakehead U (ON, Canada)
La Salle U (PA)
La Sierra U (CA)
Lewis U (IL)
Lindenwood U (MO)
Lipscomb U (TN)
Loras Coll (IA)
Lourdes U (OH)
Loyola U Chicago (IL)
Lynchburg Coll (VA)
Madonna U (MI)
Mansfield U of Pennsylvania (PA)
Marian U (IN)
Marietta Coll (OH)
Marquette U (WI)
Mercyhurst Coll (PA)
Messiah Coll (PA)
Metropolitan State U (MN)
Michigan State U (MI)
MidAmerica Nazarene U (KS)
Mount Mercy U (IA)
National U (CA)
Nazareth Coll of Rochester (NY)
Neumann U (PA)
New York Inst of Technology (NY)
Niagara U (NY)
Nichols Coll (MA)
North Central Coll (IL)
Northeastern Illinois U (IL)
Northeastern U (MA)
Oakland City U (IN)
Oakland U (MI)
The Ohio State U (OH)
Ohio U (OH)
Ohio U–Chillicothe (OH)
Ohio Valley U (WV)
Pace U (NY)
Peirce Coll (PA)
Point Park U (PA)
Portland State U (OR)
Purdue U North Central (IN)
Quinnipiac U (CT)
Rasmussen Coll Bismarck (ND)
Rasmussen Coll Bloomington (MN)
Rasmussen Coll Brooklyn Park
    (MN)
Rasmussen Coll Eagan (MN)
Rasmussen Coll Fort Myers (FL)
Rasmussen Coll Lake Elmo/
    Woodbury (MN)
Rasmussen Coll Land O' Lakes
    (FL)
Rasmussen Coll Mankato (MN)
Rasmussen Coll Moorhead (MN)
Rasmussen Coll New Port Richey
    (FL)
Rasmussen Coll Ocala (FL)
Rasmussen Coll Tampa/Brandon
    (FL)
Regis U (CO)
Roberts Wesleyan Coll (NY)

INDEXES

Salisbury U (MD)
San Francisco State U (CA)
Slippery Rock U of Pennsylvania (PA)
Southeastern Oklahoma State U (OK)
Southern Illinois U Carbondale (IL)
Southwestern Adventist U (TX)
State U of New York at Fredonia (NY)
State U of New York at Oswego (NY)
State U of New York Coll at Old Westbury (NY)
Stevenson U (MD)
Stony Brook U, State U of New York (NY)
Suffolk U (MA)
Susquehanna U (PA)
Syracuse U (NY)
Taylor U (IN)
Texas A&M Intl U (TX)
Texas A&M U–Corpus Christi (TX)
Texas Lutheran U (TX)
Texas Tech U (TX)
Thiel Coll (PA)
Touro Coll (NY)
Towson U (MD)
Tulane U (LA)
Union U (TN)
United States Military Acad (NY)
Université de Sherbrooke (QC, Canada)
U at Albany, State U of New York (NY)
U at Buffalo, the State U of New York (NY)
U of Alberta (AB, Canada)
U of Arkansas at Little Rock (AR)
U of Bridgeport (CT)
U of California, Santa Cruz (CA)
U of Cincinnati (OH)
U of Dayton (OH)
U of Great Falls (MT)
U of Hartford (CT)
U of Houston (TX)
U of Illinois at Chicago (IL)
The U of Iowa (IA)
U of Mary (ND)
U of Mary Hardin-Baylor (TX)
U of Maryland, Baltimore County (MD)
U of Maryland, Coll Park (MD)
U of Maryland U Coll (MD)
U of Massachusetts Lowell (MA)
U of Miami (FL)
U of Michigan–Flint (MI)
U of Nebraska at Omaha (NE)
U of New Haven (CT)
The U of North Carolina at Chapel Hill (NC)
U of North Texas (TX)
U of Oklahoma (OK)
U of Pittsburgh (PA)
The U of Scranton (PA)
U of South Alabama (AL)
U of South Carolina (SC)
U of South Carolina Upstate (SC)
U of South Florida (FL)
The U of Texas at El Paso (TX)
The U of Texas of the Permian Basin (TX)
U of the District of Columbia (DC)
U of the Pacific (CA)
The U of Toledo (OH)
U of Tulsa (OK)
U of Vermont (VT)
U of Washington (WA)
U of Washington, Bothell (WA)
The U of Western Ontario (ON, Canada)
U of Wisconsin–Green Bay (WI)
U of Wisconsin–Milwaukee (WI)
U of Wisconsin–River Falls (WI)
U of Wisconsin–Superior (WI)
Utah State U (UT)
Utah Valley U (UT)
Valdosta State U (GA)
Virginia Commonwealth U (VA)
Virginia Polytechnic Inst and State U (VA)
Walden U (MN)
Washington Adventist U (MD)
Washington U in St. Louis (MO)
Wayne State Coll (NE)

Wayne State U (MI)
Weber State U (UT)
Westfield State U (MA)
West Liberty U (WV)
West Virginia Wesleyan Coll (WV)
Wheeling Jesuit U (WV)
Widener U (PA)
Wilkes U (PA)
Winona State U (MN)
Woodbury U (CA)
Worcester Polytechnic Inst (MA)
York Coll of the City U of New York (NY)

INFORMATION TECHNOLOGY

Abilene Christian U (TX)
American Public U System (WV)
Arkansas Tech U (AR)
Armstrong Atlantic State U (GA)
Baylor U (TX)
Bellevue U (NE)
Bluefield Coll (VA)
Bluffton U (OH)
Bob Jones U (SC)
Brigham Young U (UT)
Broadview U (UT)
Broadview U-Boise (ID)
Broadview U-Layton (UT)
Broadview U-Orem (UT)
Bryant U (RI)
Cabrini Coll (PA)
Caldwell Coll (NJ)
California State U, Chico (CA)
California State U, Dominguez Hills (CA)
California State U, Fullerton (CA)
California State U, Los Angeles (CA)
Calvary Bible Coll and Theological Sem (MO)
Cameron U (OK)
Capella U (MN)
Carnegie Mellon U (PA)
Central Michigan U (MI)
Clayton State U (GA)
Coll of the Ozarks (MO)
Columbia Southern U (AL)
Columbus State U (GA)
Cornell U (NY)
Curry Coll (MA)
DePaul U (IL)
DEREE - The American Coll of Greece (Greece)
East Carolina U (NC)
Fairleigh Dickinson U, Metropolitan Campus (NJ)
Ferris State U (MI)
Florida Ag and Mech U (FL)
Florida Intl U (FL)
Franklin U (OH)
Furman U (SC)
George Mason U (VA)
Georgia Gwinnett Coll (GA)
Georgia Southwestern State U (GA)
Globe U–Eau Claire (WI)
Globe U–Green Bay (WI)
Globe U–La Crosse (WI)
Globe U–Madison East (WI)
Globe U–Madison West (WI)
Globe U–Minneapolis (MN)
Globe U–Wausau (WI)
Globe U–Woodbury (MN)
Harding U (AR)
Houghton Coll (NY)
Humboldt State U (CA)
Illinois Inst of Technology (IL)
Illinois State U (IL)
Indiana State U (IN)
Indiana U Bloomington (IN)
Indiana U East (IN)
Indiana U Kokomo (IN)
Indiana U Northwest (IN)
Indiana U–Purdue U Fort Wayne (IN)
Indiana U–Purdue U Indianapolis (IN)
Indiana U South Bend (IN)
Indiana U Southeast (IN)
Jamestown Coll (ND)
Johnson C. Smith U (NC)
Juniata Coll (PA)
Kentucky State U (KY)
Keystone Coll (PA)
Kutztown U of Pennsylvania (PA)
La Roche Coll (PA)

Lawrence Technological U (MI)
Liberty U (VA)
Lindenwood U (MO)
Lipscomb U (TN)
Long Island U–C. W. Post Campus (NY)
Loyola U Chicago (IL)
Macon State Coll (GA)
Marian U (WI)
Marquette U (WI)
Marymount U (VA)
McMurry U (TX)
Merrimack Coll (MA)
Minnesota School of Business–Blaine (MN)
Minnesota School of Business–Brooklyn Center (MN)
Minnesota School of Business–Elk River (MN)
Minnesota School of Business–Lakeville (MN)
Minnesota School of Business–Moorhead (MN)
Minnesota School of Business–Plymouth (MN)
Minnesota School of Business–Richfield (MN)
Minnesota School of Business–Rochester (MN)
Minnesota School of Business–St. Cloud (MN)
Minnesota School of Business–Shakopee (MN)
Missouri Baptist U (MO)
Montclair State U (NJ)
Morrisville State Coll (NY)
Mount Aloysius Coll (PA)
Mount Marty Coll (SD)
Mount Saint Mary Coll (NY)
National U (CA)
Nazareth Coll of Rochester (NY)
Neumont U (UT)
Newbury Coll (MA)
New England Inst of Technology (RI)
New Mexico Inst of Mining and Technology (NM)
New Mexico State U (NM)
Northern Kentucky U (KY)
Oakland U (MI)
Ohio U (OH)
Ohio U–Chillicothe (OH)
Oklahoma City U (OK)
Peirce Coll (PA)
Plymouth State U (NH)
Point Park U (PA)
Regent U (VA)
Rensselaer Polytechnic Inst (NY)
Rivier Coll (NH)
Robert Morris U Illinois (IL)
Rochester Inst of Technology (NY)
Ryerson U (ON, Canada)
Sacred Heart U (CT)
San Diego State U (CA)
Seminole State Coll of Florida (FL)
Simmons Coll (MA)
Slippery Rock U of Pennsylvania (PA)
Sojourner-Douglass Coll (MD)
Southern New Hampshire U (NH)
Southern Polytechnic State U (GA)
South U (AL)
South U, Royal Palm Beach (FL)
South U, Tampa (FL)
South U (GA)
South U (MI)
South U, Columbia (SC)
South U (TX)
South U, Glen Allen (VA)
South U, Virginia Beach (VA)
Southwest Minnesota State U (MN)
State U of New York Coll of Technology at Alfred (NY)
State U of New York Coll of Technology at Canton (NY)
Stephen F. Austin State U (TX)
Temple U (PA)
Texas Christian U (TX)
Thomas More Coll (KY)
Tiffin U (OH)
Trevecca Nazarene U (TN)
Trident U Intl (CA)
United States Intl U (Kenya)
United States Military Acad (NY)

Université de Sherbrooke (QC, Canada)
The U of British Columbia–Okanagan (BC, Canada)
U of Central Florida (FL)
U of Cincinnati (OH)
U of Denver (CO)
U of Great Falls (MT)
U of Houston–Clear Lake (TX)
U of Massachusetts Boston (MA)
U of Missouri–Kansas City (MO)
U of New Hampshire (NH)
U of Rio Grande (OH)
U of St. Francis (IL)
U of Saint Mary (KS)
U of South Alabama (AL)
U of South Florida (FL)
U of Tulsa (OK)
The U of Western Ontario (ON, Canada)
U of West Florida (FL)
U of Wisconsin–Stevens Point (WI)
U of Wisconsin–Whitewater (WI)
Vanguard U of Southern California (CA)
Vermont Tech Coll (VT)
Virginia State U (VA)
Washington & Jefferson Coll (PA)
Webster U (MO)
Western Illinois U (IL)
Western Intl U (AZ)
Western Kentucky U (KY)
Wilmington U (DE)
Youngstown State U (OH)

INFORMATION TECHNOLOGY PROJECT MANAGEMENT

Bauder Coll (GA)
ITT Tech Inst, Oxnard (CA)
ITT Tech Inst, Orland Park (IL)
ITT Tech Inst, Owings Mills (MD)
ITT Tech Inst, Swartz Creek (MI)
ITT Tech Inst, Wyoming (MI)
ITT Tech Inst, Arnold (MO)
ITT Tech Inst, Green Bay (WI)
Pace U (NY)

INORGANIC CHEMISTRY

The U of Western Ontario (ON, Canada)

INSTITUTIONAL FOOD WORKERS

Immaculata U (PA)

INSTRUMENTATION TECHNOLOGY

Northern Michigan U (MI)

INSURANCE

Appalachian State U (NC)
Baylor U (TX)
Bowling Green State U (OH)
Bradley U (IL)
Delta State U (MS)
Eastern Kentucky U (KY)
Excelsior Coll (NY)
Gannon U (PA)
Georgia State U (GA)
Idaho State U (ID)
Illinois State U (IL)
Illinois Wesleyan U (IL)
Indiana State U (IN)
Mississippi State U (MS)
Missouri State U (MO)
Northern Michigan U (MI)
The Ohio State U (OH)
St. John's U (NY)
Saint Joseph's U (PA)
Seattle U (WA)
Southern Methodist U (TX)
Temple U (PA)
U of Central Arkansas (AR)
U of Connecticut (CT)
U of Florida (FL)
U of Georgia (GA)
U of Hartford (CT)
U of Houston–Downtown (TX)
U of Illinois at Urbana–Champaign (IL)
U of Louisiana at Lafayette (LA)
U of Louisiana at Monroe (LA)

U of Minnesota, Twin Cities Campus (MN)
U of Mississippi (MS)
U of Nebraska–Lincoln (NE)
U of North Texas (TX)
U of Pennsylvania (PA)
U of South Carolina (SC)
U of Wisconsin–La Crosse (WI)
U of Wisconsin–Madison (WI)

INTELLIGENCE

Henley-Putnam U (CA)

INTERCULTURAL/ MULTICULTURAL AND DIVERSITY STUDIES

Biola U (CA)
Calvary Bible Coll and Theological Sem (MO)
Columbia Bible Coll (BC, Canada)
Concordia U (QC, Canada)
Evangel U (MO)
The Evergreen State Coll (WA)
Goddard Coll (VT)
Indiana Wesleyan U (IN)
Judson U (IL)
Macalester Coll (MN)
Northwest U (WA)
St. Catherine U (MN)
Trinity Lutheran Coll (WA)
U of the Incarnate Word (TX)
Vanguard U of Southern California (CA)
Villanova U (PA)
Western Oregon U (OR)

INTERDISCIPLINARY STUDIES

Agnes Scott Coll (GA)
Albright Coll (PA)
Alfred U (NY)
Amberton U (TX)
The American U of Rome (Italy)
Amherst Coll (MA)
Angelo State U (TX)
Austin Peay State U (TN)
Bard Coll (NY)
Bard Coll at Simon's Rock (MA)
Barnard Coll (NY)
Bay Path Coll (MA)
Beloit Coll (WI)
Bennett Coll for Women (NC)
Bernard M. Baruch Coll of the City U of New York (NY)
Bethany Coll (WV)
Birmingham-Southern Coll (AL)
Blackburn Coll (IL)
Bloomfield Coll (NJ)
Bluefield Coll (VA)
Boise State U (ID)
Boston Coll (MA)
Boston U (MA)
Bryn Athyn Coll of the New Church (PA)
Bucknell U (PA)
Burlington Coll (VT)
California Baptist U (CA)
California Lutheran U (CA)
California State U, Bakersfield (CA)
California State U, East Bay (CA)
California State U, Long Beach (CA)
California State U, Los Angeles (CA)
California State U, San Bernardino (CA)
Calvin Coll (MI)
Carleton Coll (MN)
Carson-Newman Coll (TN)
Catawba Coll (NC)
Cedarville U (OH)
Centenary Coll of Louisiana (LA)
Central Coll (IA)
Central Methodist U (MO)
Christopher Newport U (VA)
Clark U (MA)
Coe Coll (IA)
The Coll at Brockport, State U of New York (NY)
Coll of the Atlantic (ME)
The Coll of William and Mary (VA)
The Coll of Wooster (OH)
Columbia Coll Chicago (IL)
Connecticut Coll (CT)
Corban U (OR)

Cornell Coll (IA)
Cornerstone U (MI)
Crandall U (NB, Canada)
Dallas Baptist U (TX)
DePauw U (IN)
Earlham Coll (IN)
Eckerd Coll (FL)
Elmhurst Coll (IL)
Elmira Coll (NY)
Emory U (GA)
Fairleigh Dickinson U, Metropolitan Campus (NJ)
Florida Inst of Technology (FL)
Fordham U (NY)
Franklin U (OH)
Geneva Coll (PA)
George Fox U (OR)
The George Washington U (DC)
Gettysburg Coll (PA)
Goddard Coll (VT)
Grinnell Coll (IA)
Guilford Coll (NC)
Gustavus Adolphus Coll (MN)
Hamilton Coll (NY)
Harrisburg U of Science and Technology (PA)
Hendrix Coll (AR)
Hillsdale Coll (MI)
Hillsdale Free Will Baptist Coll (OK)
Hollins U (VA)
Huston-Tillotson U (TX)
Illinois Coll (IL)
Iowa State U of Science and Technology (IA)
Ithaca Coll (NY)
Jacksonville U (FL)
John Brown U (AR)
John Carroll U (OH)
The Johns Hopkins U (MD)
Jones Coll, Jacksonville (FL)
Judson Coll (AL)
Kalamazoo Coll (MI)
Kentucky Wesleyan Coll (KY)
Keuka Coll (NY)
King Coll (TN)
Lake Superior State U (MI)
Lamar U (TX)
Lasell Coll (MA)
Lees-McRae Coll (NC)
Lee U (TN)
Lehman Coll of the City U of New York (NY)
LeTourneau U (TX)
Lewis-Clark State Coll (ID)
Long Island U–Brooklyn Campus (NY)
Long Island U–C. W. Post Campus (NY)
Louisiana Coll (LA)
Loyola U Maryland (MD)
Macon State Coll (GA)
Maranatha Baptist Bible Coll (WI)
Marlboro Coll (VT)
Mars Hill Coll (NC)
Martin Luther Coll (MN)
Massachusetts Coll of Liberal Arts (MA)
McPherson Coll (KS)
Middle Tennessee State U (TN)
Midwestern State U (TX)
Mills Coll (CA)
Minnesota State U Moorhead (MN)
Molloy Coll (NY)
Mount Allison U (NB, Canada)
Mount Saint Mary Coll (NY)
National U (CA)
Nebraska Wesleyan U (NE)
Newbury Coll (MA)
North Dakota State U (ND)
North Greenville U (SC)
Northwest U (WA)
Notre Dame of Maryland U (MD)
Nyack Coll (NY)
Oakland City U (IN)
Oglethorpe U (GA)
Pepperdine U, Malibu (CA)
Piedmont Coll (GA)
Pittsburg State U (KS)
Pomona Coll (CA)
Prairie View A&M U (TX)
Rhodes Coll (TN)
Ripon Coll (WI)
Rochester Inst of Technology (NY)
Rocky Mountain Coll (MT)
Russell Sage Coll (NY)

Rutgers, The State U of New Jersey, New Brunswick (NJ)
St. Andrews U (NC)
Saint Joseph's Coll of Maine (ME)
Saint Mary's Coll (IN)
Saint Mary's Coll of California (CA)
St. Thomas U (NB, Canada)
San Diego Christian Coll (CA)
Sarah Lawrence Coll (NY)
Seattle Pacific U (WA)
Sierra Nevada Coll (NV)
Simpson Coll (IA)
Smith Coll (MA)
Sonoma State U (CA)
South Dakota School of Mines and Technology (SD)
Southern Oregon U (OR)
Southwestern Coll (KS)
Stanford U (CA)
State U of New York at Fredonia (NY)
State U of New York Coll at Oneonta (NY)
State U of New York Empire State Coll (NY)
Stephens Coll (MO)
Sterling Coll (KS)
Stevenson U (MD)
Suffolk U (MA)
Sweet Briar Coll (VA)
Syracuse U (NY)
Tarleton State U (TX)
Texas A&M U–Corpus Christi (TX)
Texas Southern U (TX)
Towson U (MD)
Trent U (ON, Canada)
Trinity Baptist Coll (FL)
Trinity Coll (CT)
United States Air Force Acad (CO)
Université de Sherbrooke (QC, Canada)
U at Albany, State U of New York (NY)
The U of Alabama (AL)
U of Alaska Anchorage (AK)
U of Alberta (AB, Canada)
The U of Arizona (AZ)
U of Bridgeport (CT)
The U of British Columbia (BC, Canada)
U of California, Santa Barbara (CA)
U of Central Florida (FL)
U of Evansville (IN)
U of Hartford (CT)
U of Hawaii at Hilo (HI)
The U of Iowa (IA)
U of Maine at Farmington (ME)
U of Massachusetts Dartmouth (MA)
U of Memphis (TN)
U of Michigan–Flint (MI)
U of Minnesota, Duluth (MN)
U of Missouri (MO)
U of Nevada, Las Vegas (NV)
U of North Alabama (AL)
U of North Dakota (ND)
U of Northern Colorado (CO)
U of North Florida (FL)
U of North Texas (TX)
U of Oklahoma (OK)
U of Portland (OR)
U of Puget Sound (WA)
U of Redlands (CA)
U of Saint Mary (KS)
U of St. Thomas (MN)
The U of Tennessee at Martin (TN)
The U of Texas at Dallas (TX)
The U of Texas at El Paso (TX)
The U of Texas at Tyler (TX)
The U of Texas–Pan American (TX)
U of the Pacific (CA)
U of Vermont (VT)
The U of Virginia's Coll at Wise (VA)
The U of Western Ontario (ON, Canada)
Vanguard U of Southern California (CA)
Vassar Coll (NY)
Virginia Polytechnic Inst and State U (VA)
Virginia State U (VA)
Virginia Wesleyan Coll (VA)
Walden U (MN)
Warren Wilson Coll (NC)

Wayne State Coll (NE)
Webster U (MO)
Wesleyan Coll (GA)
Wesleyan U (CT)
Western Oregon U (OR)
Western State Coll of Colorado (CO)
West Liberty U (WV)
West Texas A&M U (TX)
William Woods U (MO)
Woodbury U (CA)
Worcester Polytechnic Inst (MA)
Yeshiva U (NY)

INTERIOR ARCHITECTURE

Arizona State U (AZ)
Auburn U (AL)
Boston Architectural Coll (MA)
Bowling Green State U (OH)
California Coll of the Arts (CA)
Central Michigan U (MI)
Chatham U (PA)
Indiana State U (IN)
La Roche Coll (PA)
Lawrence Technological U (MI)
Lebanese American U (Lebanon)
Louisiana State U and Ag and Mech Coll (LA)
Miami U (OH)
Mississippi State U (MS)
Philadelphia U (PA)
Stephen F. Austin State U (TX)
Texas Tech U (TX)
U of Houston (TX)
U of Louisiana at Lafayette (LA)
U of Missouri (MO)
U of Nebraska–Lincoln (NE)
U of Nevada, Las Vegas (NV)
U of New Haven (CT)
U of Oregon (OR)
U of Southern Mississippi (MS)
The U of Texas at Arlington (TX)
The U of Texas at San Antonio (TX)
U of Washington (WA)
Villa Maria Coll of Buffalo (NY)
Woodbury U (CA)

INTERIOR DESIGN

Abilene Christian U (TX)
Acad of Art U (CA)
Adrian Coll (MI)
Anderson U (SC)
Appalachian State U (NC)
Arcadia U (PA)
Art Center Coll of Design (CA)
The Art Inst of Atlanta (GA)
The Art Inst of Atlanta–Decatur (GA)
The Art Inst of Austin (TX)
The Art Inst of California, a college of Argosy U, Hollywood (CA)
The Art Inst of California, a college of Argosy U, Inland Empire (CA)
The Art Inst of California, a college of Argosy U, Los Angeles (CA)
The Art Inst of California, a college of Argosy U, Orange County (CA)
The Art Inst of California, a college of Argosy U, Sacramento (CA)
The Art Inst of California, a college of Argosy U, San Diego (CA)
The Art Inst of California, a college of Argosy U, San Francisco (CA)
The Art Inst of California, a college of Argosy U, Sunnyvale (CA)
The Art Inst of Charleston (SC)
The Art Inst of Charlotte (NC)
The Art Inst of Colorado (CO)
The Art Inst of Dallas (TX)
The Art Inst of Fort Lauderdale (FL)
The Art Inst of Fort Worth (TX)
The Art Inst of Houston (TX)
The Art Inst of Houston - North (TX)
The Art Inst of Indianapolis (IN)
The Art Inst of Jacksonville (FL)
The Art Inst of Las Vegas (NV)
The Art Inst of Michigan (MI)
The Art Inst of Michigan–Troy (MI)
The Art Inst of Ohio–Cincinnati (OH)
The Art Inst of Philadelphia (PA)
The Art Inst of Phoenix (AZ)
The Art Inst of Pittsburgh (PA)
The Art Inst of Portland (OR)

The Art Inst of Raleigh-Durham (NC)
The Art Inst of Salt Lake City (UT)
The Art Inst of San Antonio (TX)
The Art Inst of Seattle (WA)
The Art Inst of Tampa (FL)
The Art Inst of Tennessee–Nashville (TN)
The Art Inst of Tucson (AZ)
The Art Inst of Virginia Beach (VA)
The Art Inst of Washington (WA)
The Art Inst of Washington–Dulles (VA)
The Art Inst of Wisconsin (WI)
The Art Inst of York–Pennsylvania (PA)
The Art Insts Intl–Kansas City (KS)
The Art Insts Intl Minnesota (MN)
Auburn U (AL)
Baylor U (TX)
Bay Path Coll (MA)
Becker Coll (MA)
Brenau U (GA)
California State U, Chico (CA)
California State U, Fresno (CA)
California State U, Long Beach (CA)
California State U, Sacramento (CA)
Carson-Newman Coll (TN)
Chaminade U of Honolulu (HI)
The Cleveland Inst of Art (OH)
Coll for Creative Studies (MI)
Coll of Mount St. Joseph (OH)
Colorado State U (CO)
Columbia Coll Chicago (IL)
Columbus Coll of Art & Design (OH)
Converse Coll (SC)
Corcoran Coll of Art and Design (DC)
Cornish Coll of the Arts (WA)
Drexel U (PA)
East Carolina U (NC)
Eastern Michigan U (MI)
East Tennessee State U (TN)
EDP Coll of Puerto Rico, Inc. (PR)
Endicott Coll (MA)
Fashion Inst of Technology (NY)
Ferris State U (MI)
Florida Intl U (FL)
Florida State U (FL)
Fort Hays State U (KS)
Georgia Southern U (GA)
Hampton U (VA)
Harding U (AR)
Harrington Coll of Design (IL)
The Illinois Inst of Art–Chicago (IL)
The Illinois Inst of Art–Schaumburg (IL)
The Illinois Inst of Art–Tinley Park (IL)
Indiana U Bloomington (IN)
Indiana U of Pennsylvania (PA)
Indiana U–Purdue U Fort Wayne (IN)
Indiana U–Purdue U Indianapolis (IN)
Indiana Wesleyan U (IN)
Intl Acad of Design & Technology (FL)
Iowa State U of Science and Technology (IA)
Kansas State U (KS)
Kean U (NJ)
Kent State U (OH)
Lamar U (TX)
Lebanese American U (Lebanon)
Maryland Inst Coll of Art (MD)
Marylhurst U (OR)
Marymount U (VA)
Maryville U of Saint Louis (MO)
Marywood U (PA)
McPherson Coll (KS)
Mercyhurst Coll (PA)
Meredith Coll (NC)
Miami Intl U of Art & Design (FL)
Michigan State U (MI)
Middle Tennessee State U (TN)
Mississippi Coll (MS)
Moore Coll of Art & Design (PA)
Mount Ida Coll (MA)
Mount Mary Coll (WI)
Newbury Coll (MA)
The New England Inst of Art (MA)

New England Inst of Technology (RI)
New York Inst of Technology (NY)
New York School of Interior Design (NY)
North Dakota State U (ND)
Northern Arizona U (AZ)
The Ohio State U (OH)
Oklahoma Christian U (OK)
O'More Coll of Design (TN)
Otis Coll of Art and Design (CA)
Paier Coll of Art, Inc. (CT)
Park U (MO)
Philadelphia U (PA)
Pittsburg State U (KS)
Point Loma Nazarene U (CA)
Pratt Inst (NY)
Queens U of Charlotte (NC)
Ringling Coll of Art and Design (FL)
Rochester Inst of Technology (NY)
Rocky Mountain Coll of Art + Design (CO)
Ryerson U (ON, Canada)
Samford U (AL)
San Diego State U (CA)
San Francisco State U (CA)
Savannah Coll of Art and Design (GA)
Seattle Pacific U (WA)
Seminole State Coll of Florida (FL)
South Dakota State U (SD)
Southern Illinois U Carbondale (IL)
Stephens Coll (MO)
Stevens Inst of Business & Arts (MO)
Suffolk U (MA)
Sullivan Coll of Technology and Design (KY)
Syracuse U (NY)
Texas Christian U (TX)
Texas State U–San Marcos (TX)
Universidad del Turabo (PR)
The U of Alabama (AL)
U of Bridgeport (CT)
U of Central Arkansas (AR)
U of Central Missouri (MO)
U of Cincinnati (OH)
U of Florida (FL)
U of Idaho (ID)
The U of Kansas (KS)
U of Minnesota, Twin Cities Campus (MN)
U of Northern Iowa (IA)
U of North Texas (TX)
U of Oklahoma (OK)
The U of Tennessee (TN)
The U of Tennessee at Chattanooga (TN)
The U of Tennessee at Martin (TN)
The U of Texas at Austin (TX)
The U of Texas at San Antonio (TX)
U of the Incarnate Word (TX)
U of Wisconsin–Madison (WI)
U of Wisconsin–Stevens Point (WI)
Utah State U (UT)
Valdosta State U (GA)
Virginia Commonwealth U (VA)
Virginia Polytechnic Inst and State U (VA)
Washington State U (WA)
Watkins Coll of Art, Design, & Film (TN)
Wentworth Inst of Technology (MA)
Western Carolina U (NC)
Western Michigan U (MI)
William Woods U (MO)

INTERMEDIA/MULTIMEDIA

Acad of Art U (CA)
Alberta Coll of Art & Design (AB, Canada)
American U (DC)
Art Center Coll of Design (CA)
The Art Inst of Atlanta (GA)
The Art Inst of California, a college of Argosy U, Hollywood (CA)
The Art Inst of California, a college of Argosy U, Orange County (CA)
The Art Inst of California, a college of Argosy U, San Diego (CA)
The Art Inst of California, a college of Argosy U, San Francisco (CA)
Bard Coll at Simon's Rock (MA)
Bennington Coll (VT)
Biola U (CA)

INDEXES

Calumet Coll of Saint Joseph (IN)
City Coll of the City U of New York (NY)
The Cleveland Inst of Art (OH)
The Coll of New Jersey (NJ)
Columbia Coll Chicago (IL)
Concordia U (QC, Canada)
The Evergreen State Coll (WA)
Hawai'i Pacific U (HI)
Indiana U of Pennsylvania (PA)
Long Island U–C. W. Post Campus (NY)
Maryland Inst Coll of Art (MD)
Massachusetts Coll of Art and Design (MA)
Mills Coll (CA)
Missouri State U (MO)
Montserrat Coll of Art (MA)
National U (CA)
Northeastern U (MA)
Pacific Northwest Coll of Art (OR)
Purchase Coll, State U of New York (NY)
Ramapo Coll of New Jersey (NJ)
Rochester Inst of Technology (NY)
School of the Museum of Fine Arts, Boston (MA)
State U of New York at Fredonia (NY)
U of Hartford (CT)
U of Regina (SK, Canada)
The U of the Arts (PA)
Weber State U (UT)
Western Washington U (WA)
Worcester Polytechnic Inst (MA)

INTERNATIONAL AGRICULTURE
Cornell U (NY)
Iowa State U of Science and Technology (IA)
Tarleton State U (TX)
U of California, Davis (CA)
U of Illinois at Urbana–Champaign (IL)
U of Missouri (MO)
Utah State U (UT)

INTERNATIONAL AND INTERCULTURAL COMMUNICATION
Pacific Union Coll (CA)

INTERNATIONAL BUSINESS/ TRADE/COMMERCE
Adams State Coll (CO)
Adrian Coll (MI)
Albertus Magnus Coll (CT)
Albright Coll (PA)
Alliant Intl U (CA)
Alliant Intl U–México City (Mexico)
Alverno Coll (WI)
The American U of Paris (France)
The American U of Rome (Italy)
Anderson U (IN)
Angelo State U (TX)
Appalachian State U (NC)
Aquinas Coll (MI)
Arcadia U (PA)
Arkansas State U (AR)
Assumption Coll (MA)
Auburn U (AL)
Augustana Coll (IL)
Avila U (MO)
Babson Coll (MA)
Baker U (KS)
Baldwin-Wallace Coll (OH)
Barry U (FL)
Baylor U (TX)
Belmont U (TN)
Benedictine U (IL)
Bentley U (MA)
Bernard M. Baruch Coll of the City U of New York (NY)
Bethany Coll (KS)
Bethel Coll (IN)
Bethune-Cookman U (FL)
Biola U (CA)
Birmingham-Southern Coll (AL)
Bishop's U (QC, Canada)
Bob Jones U (SC)
Boise State U (ID)
Boston U (MA)
Bowling Green State U (OH)

Bradley U (IL)
Bridgewater State U (MA)
Bryant U (RI)
Buena Vista U (IA)
Butler U (IN)
Caldwell Coll (NJ)
California State U, Dominguez Hills (CA)
California State U, Fresno (CA)
California State U, Fullerton (CA)
California State U, Long Beach (CA)
Canisius Coll (NY)
Cardinal Stritch U (WI)
The Catholic U of America (DC)
Cedarville U (OH)
Central Coll (IA)
Central Michigan U (MI)
Chatham U (PA)
Chestnut Hill Coll (PA)
City U of Seattle (WA)
Clarion U of Pennsylvania (PA)
Clemson U (SC)
Cleveland State U (OH)
The Coll at Brockport, State U of New York (NY)
The Coll of Idaho (ID)
The Coll of St. Scholastica (MN)
Coll of the Ozarks (MO)
Columbia Coll (MO)
Concordia Coll (MN)
Concordia Coll–New York (NY)
Concordia U (QC, Canada)
Converse Coll (SC)
Cornell Coll (IA)
Creighton U (NE)
Dalhousie U (NS, Canada)
Davenport U, Grand Rapids (MI)
DEREE - The American Coll of Greece (Greece)
DeSales U (PA)
Dickinson Coll (PA)
Dillard U (LA)
Dominican Coll (NY)
Dominican U (IL)
Drake U (IA)
Duquesne U (PA)
Eastern Mennonite U (VA)
Eastern Michigan U (MI)
Eckerd Coll (FL)
Elizabethtown Coll (PA)
Elmhurst Coll (IL)
Elmira Coll (NY)
Elon U (NC)
Excelsior Coll (NY)
Fairfield U (CT)
Felician Coll (NJ)
Florida Atlantic U (FL)
Florida Inst of Technology (FL)
Florida Intl U (FL)
Fordham U (NY)
Fort Lewis Coll (CO)
Franklin Coll Switzerland (Switzerland)
Friends U (KS)
Gannon U (PA)
Gardner-Webb U (NC)
George Fox U (OR)
The George Washington U (DC)
Georgia Southern U (GA)
Gettysburg Coll (PA)
Goldey-Beacom Coll (DE)
Gonzaga U (WA)
Grace Coll (IN)
Graceland U (IA)
Grand Valley State U (MI)
Grove City Coll (PA)
Gustavus Adolphus Coll (MN)
Hamline U (MN)
Harding U (AR)
Hawai'i Pacific U (HI)
HEC Montreal (QC, Canada)
Hofstra U (NY)
Holy Family U (PA)
Husson U (ME)
Illinois State U (IL)
Illinois Wesleyan U (IL)
Indiana U of Pennsylvania (PA)
Inter American U of Puerto Rico, Ponce Campus (PR)
Iona Coll (NY)
Iowa State U of Science and Technology (IA)
Ithaca Coll (NY)

Jacksonville U (FL)
James Madison U (VA)
Jamestown Coll (ND)
John Brown U (AR)
John Carroll U (OH)
Juniata Coll (PA)
Kennesaw State U (GA)
King Coll (TN)
King's Coll (PA)
Kutztown U of Pennsylvania (PA)
Lake Erie Coll (OH)
La Roche Coll (PA)
La Salle U (PA)
Lasell Coll (MA)
Lawrence Technological U (MI)
Lenoir-Rhyne U (NC)
LeTourneau U (TX)
Lewis U (IL)
Lindenwood U (MO)
Linfield Coll (OR)
Lipscomb U (TN)
Loras Coll (IA)
Louisiana State U and Ag and Mech Coll (LA)
Loyola U Chicago (IL)
Loyola U Maryland (MD)
Loyola U New Orleans (LA)
Madonna U (MI)
Mansfield U of Pennsylvania (PA)
Marietta Coll (OH)
Marshall U (WV)
Mars Hill Coll (NC)
Maryville Coll (TN)
Maryville U of Saint Louis (MO)
Marywood U (PA)
Massachusetts Coll of Liberal Arts (MA)
Massachusetts Maritime Acad (MA)
McPherson Coll (KS)
Menlo Coll (CA)
Merrimack Coll (MA)
Messiah Coll (PA)
Metropolitan State U (MN)
Midwestern State U (TX)
Millikin U (IL)
Milwaukee School of Eng (WI)
Minnesota State U Mankato (MN)
Minot State U (ND)
Monmouth Coll (IL)
Monmouth U (NJ)
Moravian Coll (PA)
Mount Allison U (NB, Canada)
Mount St. Mary's Coll (CA)
Mount Vernon Nazarene U (OH)
Nazareth Coll of Rochester (NY)
Nebraska Wesleyan U (NE)
Neumann U (PA)
Newbury Coll (MA)
New Mexico State U (NM)
New York Inst of Technology (NY)
New York U (NY)
Niagara U (NY)
Nichols Coll (MA)
North Central Coll (IL)
Northeastern State U (OK)
Northeastern U (MA)
Northern State U (SD)
North Greenville U (SC)
Northwestern Coll (MN)
Northwest Missouri State U (MO)
Northwest Nazarene U (ID)
Northwood U, Florida Campus (FL)
Northwood U, Michigan Campus (MI)
Ohio Northern U (OH)
The Ohio State U (OH)
Ohio U (OH)
Ohio Wesleyan U (OH)
Oklahoma City U (OK)
Oklahoma State U (OK)
Oral Roberts U (OK)
Otterbein U (OH)
Pace U (NY)
Palm Beach Atlantic U (FL)
Penn State DuBois (PA)
Penn State Erie, The Behrend Coll (PA)
Penn State Harrisburg (PA)
Penn State Lehigh Valley (PA)
Penn State Schuylkill (PA)
Pepperdine U, Malibu (CA)
Philadelphia U (PA)
Pittsburg State U (KS)
Potomac Coll (DC)

Queens Coll of the City U of New York (NY)
Quinnipiac U (CT)
Ramapo Coll of New Jersey (NJ)
Rhodes Coll (TN)
Rider U (NJ)
Rochester Inst of Technology (NY)
Roger Williams U (RI)
Rollins Coll (FL)
Saginaw Valley State U (MI)
St. Ambrose U (IA)
Saint Anselm Coll (NH)
St. Catherine U (MN)
St. Edward's U (TX)
Saint Francis U (PA)
Saint Joseph's Coll of Maine (ME)
Saint Joseph's U (PA)
Saint Louis U (MO)
Saint Mary's Coll of California (CA)
St. Mary's U (TX)
Saint Mary's U of Minnesota (MN)
St. Norbert Coll (WI)
Saint Peter's Coll (NJ)
St. Thomas U (FL)
Saint Vincent Coll (PA)
Saint Xavier U (IL)
Salem State U (MA)
Samford U (AL)
Sam Houston State U (TX)
San Diego State U (CA)
San Francisco State U (CA)
Schreiner U (TX)
Seattle U (WA)
Seton Hill U (PA)
Sierra Nevada Coll (NV)
Simmons Coll (MA)
Simpson Coll (IA)
Southeastern U (FL)
Southeast Missouri State U (MO)
Southern New Hampshire U (NH)
Southwestern Adventist U (TX)
Spring Hill Coll (AL)
State U of New York at Binghamton (NY)
State U of New York at New Paltz (NY)
State U of New York at Plattsburgh (NY)
Stephen F. Austin State U (TX)
Stetson U (FL)
Stonehill Coll (MA)
Suffolk U (MA)
Tarleton State U (TX)
Taylor U (IN)
Temple U (PA)
Texas A&M U–Kingsville (TX)
Texas Christian U (TX)
Texas Tech U (TX)
Thiel Coll (PA)
Thomas Edison State Coll (NJ)
Tiffin U (OH)
Trinity U (TX)
Union Coll (KY)
United States Intl U (Kenya)
U of Alberta (AB, Canada)
U of Arkansas (AR)
U of Arkansas at Little Rock (AR)
U of Bridgeport (CT)
The U of British Columbia (BC, Canada)
U of Cincinnati (OH)
U of Dayton (OH)
U of Delaware (DE)
U of Denver (CO)
U of Evansville (IN)
The U of Findlay (OH)
U of Georgia (GA)
U of Guam (GU)
U of Hawaii at Manoa (HI)
U of Houston–Downtown (TX)
U of Indianapolis (IN)
U of La Verne (CA)
U of Lethbridge (AB, Canada)
U of Mary Hardin-Baylor (TX)
U of Maryland, Coll Park (MD)
U of Maryland U Coll (MD)
U of Memphis (TN)
U of Miami (FL)
U of Michigan–Flint (MI)
U of Minnesota, Twin Cities Campus (MN)
U of Missouri (MO)
U of Missouri–St. Louis (MO)
U of Mount Union (OH)
U of Nebraska–Lincoln (NE)

U of Nevada, Las Vegas (NV)
U of Nevada, Reno (NV)
U of New Haven (CT)
The U of North Carolina at Charlotte (NC)
U of North Florida (FL)
U of Ottawa (ON, Canada)
U of Pennsylvania (PA)
U of Pittsburgh (PA)
U of Portland (OR)
U of Puerto Rico at Humacao (PR)
U of Rhode Island (RI)
U of Rio Grande (OH)
U of St. Thomas (MN)
U of San Diego (CA)
The U of Scranton (PA)
U of South Carolina (SC)
U of Southern Mississippi (MS)
U of South Florida (FL)
The U of Tampa (FL)
The U of Tennessee at Martin (TN)
The U of Texas at Arlington (TX)
The U of Texas at Dallas (TX)
The U of Texas at San Antonio (TX)
The U of Texas–Pan American (TX)
U of the Incarnate Word (TX)
U of the Southwest (NM)
The U of Toledo (OH)
U of Tulsa (OK)
U of Washington (WA)
The U of Western Ontario (ON, Canada)
U of Wisconsin–Eau Claire (WI)
U of Wisconsin–La Crosse (WI)
U of Wisconsin–Madison (WI)
Utica Coll (NY)
Valdosta State U (GA)
Valparaiso U (IN)
Vanguard U of Southern California (CA)
Villanova U (PA)
Waldorf Coll (IA)
Warren Wilson Coll (NC)
Wartburg Coll (IA)
Washington & Jefferson Coll (PA)
Washington State U (WA)
Washington U in St. Louis (MO)
Waynesburg U (PA)
Wayne State U (MI)
Webster U (MO)
Wesleyan Coll (GA)
Western Kentucky U (KY)
Western Washington U (WA)
Westminster Coll (MO)
Westminster Coll (UT)
Wichita State U (KS)
Widener U (PA)
William Jewell Coll (MO)
William Paterson U of New Jersey (NJ)
William Woods U (MO)
Wright State U (OH)
Xavier U (OH)
Yeshiva U (NY)

INTERNATIONAL ECONOMICS
The American U of Paris (France)
Austin Coll (TX)
California State U, Chico (CA)
Carson-Newman Coll (TN)
The Coll of Idaho (ID)
The Colorado Coll (CO)
Elon U (NC)
Fitchburg State U (MA)
Fordham U (NY)
Franklin Coll Switzerland (Switzerland)
Georgia State U (GA)
Gettysburg Coll (PA)
HEC Montreal (QC, Canada)
John Carroll U (OH)
Lawrence U (WI)
Marlboro Coll (VT)
Mary Baldwin Coll (VA)
Rhodes Coll (TN)
Rockford Coll (IL)
Ryerson U (ON, Canada)
St. Catherine U (MN)
St. Lawrence U (NY)
Salve Regina U (RI)
Seattle U (WA)
State U of New York at Oswego (NY)
Suffolk U (MA)
Texas Christian U (TX)

INDEXES

Texas Tech U (TX)
U of California, Los Angeles (CA)
U of California, Santa Cruz (CA)
U of Puget Sound (WA)
U of Richmond (VA)
U of St. Thomas (MN)
U of West Georgia (GA)
Valparaiso U (IN)
Washington U in St. Louis (MO)
Weber State U (UT)

INTERNATIONAL FINANCE

Babson Coll (MA)
Boston U (MA)
Brigham Young U (UT)
The Catholic U of America (DC)
Franklin Coll Switzerland
(Switzerland)
HEC Montreal (QC, Canada)
Lycoming Coll (PA)
Texas Christian U (TX)
The U of Western Ontario (ON,
Canada)
Washington U in St. Louis (MO)

INTERNATIONAL/GLOBAL STUDIES

Abilene Christian U (TX)
Adelphi U (NY)
Adrian Coll (MI)
Albertus Magnus Coll (CT)
Albion Coll (MI)
Alfred U (NY)
Alverno Coll (WI)
American Public U System (WV)
American U (DC)
The American U of Rome (Italy)
Appalachian State U (NC)
Arcadia U (PA)
Arizona State U (AZ)
Arkansas Tech U (AR)
Assumption Coll (MA)
Baker U (KS)
Baldwin-Wallace Coll (OH)
Belhaven U (MS)
Benedictine U (IL)
Bennington Coll (VT)
Bentley U (MA)
Brandeis U (MA)
Briercrest Coll (SK, Canada)
Bryant U (RI)
California Baptist U (CA)
Carnegie Mellon U (PA)
Case Western Reserve U (OH)
Cedar Crest Coll (PA)
Cedarville U (OH)
Central Coll (IA)
Central Connecticut State U (CT)
Chatham U (PA)
Chicago State U (IL)
City Coll of the City U of New York
(NY)
Colby Coll (ME)
Coll of Charleston (SC)
Coll of Saint Elizabeth (NJ)
Colorado State U (CO)
Concordia Coll (MN)
Concordia Coll–New York (NY)
Concordia U (CA)
Doane Coll (NE)
Dominican U of California (CA)
East Texas Baptist U (TX)
Emmanuel Coll (MA)
Endicott Coll (MA)
The Evergreen State Coll (WA)
Gannon U (PA)
George Fox U (OR)
Georgia Inst of Technology (GA)
Greenville Coll (IL)
Hamline U (MN)
Hampshire Coll (MA)
Hanover Coll (IN)
Harding U (AR)
Hawai`i Pacific U (HI)
Hope Coll (MI)
Illinois Wesleyan U (IL)
Iona Coll (NY)
John Brown U (AR)
Juniata Coll (PA)
Kenyon Coll (OH)
Knox Coll (IL)
La Sierra U (CA)
Lebanon Valley Coll (PA)
Le Moyne Coll (NY)

Louisiana State U and Ag and Mech
Coll (LA)
Macalester Coll (MN)
Manchester Coll (IN)
Maryville U of Saint Louis (MO)
McKendree U (IL)
Mercyhurst Coll (PA)
Meredith Coll (NC)
Michigan State U (MI)
Midwestern State U (TX)
Minnesota State U Moorhead (MN)
Mississippi Coll (MS)
Missouri State U (MO)
Monmouth Coll (IL)
Morningside Coll (IA)
Mount Mary Coll (WI)
National U (CA)
Nebraska Wesleyan U (NE)
New Coll of Florida (FL)
North Carolina State U (NC)
North Dakota State U (ND)
The Ohio State U (OH)
Pacific Lutheran U (WA)
Pittsburg State U (KS)
Pitzer Coll (CA)
Point Loma Nazarene U (CA)
Point Park U (PA)
Presbyterian Coll (SC)
Prescott Coll (AZ)
Providence Coll (RI)
Randolph Coll (VA)
Randolph-Macon Coll (VA)
Reinhardt U (GA)
Rockford Coll (IL)
Roger Williams U (RI)
Russell Sage Coll (NY)
Sacred Heart U (CT)
St. Bonaventure U (NY)
St. Edward's U (TX)
St. Lawrence U (NY)
Saint Mary's U of Minnesota (MN)
Salisbury U (MD)
Salve Regina U (RI)
Samford U (AL)
Scripps Coll (CA)
Sierra Nevada Coll (NV)
South Dakota State U (SD)
Southeast Missouri State U (MO)
Southern Illinois U Carbondale (IL)
Southern Methodist U (TX)
Spring Arbor U (MI)
State U of New York Coll at
Cortland (NY)
Tabor Coll (KS)
Texas A&M U (TX)
Texas State U–San Marcos (TX)
Thomas More Coll (KY)
U at Albany, State U of New York
(NY)
The U of Arizona (AZ)
U of California, Irvine (CA)
U of California, Los Angeles (CA)
U of California, Riverside (CA)
U of California, Santa Barbara (CA)
U of Central Arkansas (AR)
U of Central Florida (FL)
U of Colorado Boulder (CO)
U of Colorado Denver (CO)
U of Florida (FL)
U of Hartford (CT)
U of Illinois at Springfield (IL)
U of Illinois at Urbana–Champaign
(IL)
The U of Iowa (IA)
The U of Kansas (KS)
U of La Verne (CA)
U of Maine at Farmington (ME)
U of Michigan (MI)
U of Nebraska at Omaha (NE)
U of New Mexico (NM)
U of New Orleans (LA)
The U of North Carolina at Chapel
Hill (NC)
The U of North Carolina at
Charlotte (NC)
U of North Dakota (ND)
U of North Florida (FL)
U of North Texas (TX)
U of Oklahoma (OK)
U of Oregon (OR)
U of Ottawa (ON, Canada)
U of Pennsylvania (PA)
U of Regina (SK, Canada)
U of Saint Joseph (CT)
The U of South Dakota (SD)

The U of Texas at Austin (TX)
U of Utah (UT)
U of Washington, Bothell (WA)
The U of Western Ontario (ON,
Canada)
U of Wisconsin–Madison (WI)
U of Wisconsin–Milwaukee (WI)
U of Wisconsin–River Falls (WI)
U of Wisconsin–Stevens Point (WI)
U of Wisconsin–Whitewater (WI)
U of Wyoming (WY)
Villanova U (PA)
Warren Wilson Coll (NC)
Washington & Jefferson Coll (PA)
Western Michigan U (MI)
Western New England U (MA)
Westminster Coll (MO)
Wheeling Jesuit U (WV)
Willamette U (OR)
Winona State U (MN)

INTERNATIONAL MARKETING

Fashion Inst of Technology (NY)
Oral Roberts U (OK)
Pace U (NY)
Southwestern Christian U (OK)
Texas Christian U (TX)

INTERNATIONAL POLICY ANALYSIS

Southern Methodist U (TX)

INTERNATIONAL PUBLIC HEALTH

Clemson U (SC)
The U of Iowa (IA)

INTERNATIONAL RELATIONS AND AFFAIRS

Adrian Coll (MI)
Agnes Scott Coll (GA)
Allegheny Coll (PA)
Alliant Intl U (CA)
Alliant Intl U–México City (Mexico)
Alverno Coll (WI)
American Coll of Thessaloniki
(Greece)
American Public U System (WV)
American U (DC)
American U in Bulgaria (Bulgaria)
The American U of Rome (Italy)
Aquinas Coll (MI)
Augustana Coll (SD)
Austin Coll (TX)
Azusa Pacific U (CA)
Bard Coll (NY)
Barry U (FL)
Baylor U (TX)
Bellevue U (NE)
Beloit Coll (WI)
Benedictine U (IL)
Bennington Coll (VT)
Berry Coll (GA)
Bethany Coll (WV)
Bethel U (MN)
Bethune-Cookman U (FL)
Bishop's U (QC, Canada)
Bob Jones U (SC)
Boston U (MA)
Bowling Green State U (OH)
Bradley U (IL)
Bridgewater Coll (VA)
Bridgewater State U (MA)
Brown U (RI)
Bryant U (RI)
Bucknell U (PA)
Butler U (IN)
California Baptist U (CA)
California Lutheran U (CA)
California State U, Chico (CA)
California State U, East Bay (CA)
California State U, Long Beach
(CA)
California State U, Monterey Bay
(CA)
Calvin Coll (MI)
Canisius Coll (NY)
Capital U (OH)
Carleton Coll (MN)
Carroll Coll (MT)
Case Western Reserve U (OH)
Catawba Coll (NC)
Cedarville U (OH)

Centenary Coll (NJ)
Central Michigan U (MI)
Centre Coll (KY)
Chaminade U of Honolulu (HI)
Chatham U (PA)
City Coll of the City U of New York
(NY)
Claremont McKenna Coll (CA)
Clark U (MA)
Cleveland State U (OH)
Colgate U (NY)
The Coll at Brockport, State U of
New York (NY)
The Coll of Idaho (ID)
The Coll of New Jersey (NJ)
Coll of Staten Island of the City U of
New York (NY)
The Coll of William and Mary (VA)
The Coll of Wooster (OH)
Concordia Coll–New York (NY)
Connecticut Coll (CT)
Cornell Coll (IA)
Creighton U (NE)
Dalhousie U (NS, Canada)
Denison U (OH)
DePaul U (IL)
Dickinson Coll (PA)
Dominican U (IL)
Drake U (IA)
Drury U (MO)
Duquesne U (PA)
Eastern Michigan U (MI)
Eastern Washington U (WA)
East Tennessee State U (TN)
Eckerd Coll (FL)
Edgewood Coll (WI)
Elmira Coll (NY)
Elon U (NC)
Embry-Riddle Aeronautical U–
Prescott (AZ)
Emory U (GA)
Fairfield U (CT)
Fairleigh Dickinson U, Metropolitan
Campus (NJ)
Ferrum Coll (VA)
Fitchburg State U (MA)
Florida Intl U (FL)
Florida State U (FL)
Fordham U (NY)
Francis Marion U (SC)
Franklin Coll Switzerland
(Switzerland)
George Mason U (VA)
The George Washington U (DC)
Georgia Inst of Technology (GA)
Georgia Southern U (GA)
Gettysburg Coll (PA)
Gonzaga U (WA)
Gordon Coll (MA)
Goucher Coll (MD)
Graceland U (IA)
Grand Valley State U (MI)
Guilford Coll (NC)
Hamilton Coll (NY)
Hampden-Sydney Coll (VA)
Hampshire Coll (MA)
Hawai`i Pacific U (HI)
Heidelberg U (OH)
Hendrix Coll (AR)
Hillsdale Coll (MI)
Hobart and William Smith Colls
(NY)
Hollins U (VA)
Howard Payne U (TX)
Idaho State U (ID)
Illinois Coll (IL)
Illinois Wesleyan U (IL)
Immaculata U (PA)
Indiana U Bloomington (IN)
Indiana U of Pennsylvania (PA)
Indiana U–Purdue U Indianapolis
(IN)
Indiana U Southeast (IN)
Indiana Wesleyan U (IN)
Iowa State U of Science and
Technology (IA)
Jacksonville U (FL)
James Madison U (VA)
John Brown U (AR)
John Carroll U (OH)
The Johns Hopkins U (MD)
Juniata Coll (PA)
Kennesaw State U (GA)
Kent State U (OH)
Kenyon Coll (OH)

Knox Coll (IL)
Lafayette Coll (PA)
Lake Forest Coll (IL)
La Roche Coll (PA)
Lawrence U (WI)
Lebanese American U (Lebanon)
Lee U (TN)
Lehigh U (PA)
Lenoir-Rhyne U (NC)
Lewis & Clark Coll (OR)
Liberty U (VA)
Lincoln U (PA)
Lindenwood U (MO)
Lock Haven U of Pennsylvania (PA)
Long Island U–C. W. Post Campus
(NY)
Loras Coll (IA)
Loyola U Chicago (IL)
Lynchburg Coll (VA)
Lynn U (FL)
Manhattan Coll (NY)
Manhattanville Coll (NY)
Mansfield U of Pennsylvania (PA)
Marlboro Coll (VT)
Marshall U (WV)
Mars Hill Coll (NC)
Mary Baldwin Coll (VA)
Marymount Manhattan Coll (NY)
Maryville Coll (TN)
McKendree U (IL)
Mercer U (GA)
Meredith Coll (NC)
Miami U (OH)
Michigan State U (MI)
Middlebury Coll (VT)
Middle Tennessee State U (TN)
Mills Coll (CA)
Minnesota State U Mankato (MN)
Missouri Southern State U (MO)
Morehouse Coll (GA)
Morningside Coll (IA)
Mount Allison U (NB, Canada)
Mount Holyoke Coll (MA)
Mount Mercy U (IA)
Mount St. Mary's U (MD)
Muhlenberg Coll (PA)
Nazareth Coll of Rochester (NY)
New York U (NY)
Niagara U (NY)
Northeastern U (MA)
Northern Arizona U (AZ)
Northern Kentucky U (KY)
Northern Michigan U (MI)
North Georgia Coll & State U (GA)
Northwest Nazarene U (ID)
Norwich U (VT)
Notre Dame of Maryland U (MD)
Nova Southeastern U (FL)
Oakland U (MI)
Occidental Coll (CA)
Oglethorpe U (GA)
Ohio Northern U (OH)
The Ohio State U (OH)
Ohio U (OH)
Ohio Wesleyan U (OH)
Old Dominion U (VA)
Oral Roberts U (OK)
Otterbein U (OH)
Pacific U (OR)
Penn State Abington (PA)
Penn State Altoona (PA)
Penn State Beaver (PA)
Penn State Berks (PA)
Penn State Brandywine (PA)
Penn State DuBois (PA)
Penn State Erie, The Behrend Coll
(PA)
Penn State Fayette, The Eberly
Campus (PA)
Penn State Greater Allegheny (PA)
Penn State Hazleton (PA)
Penn State Lehigh Valley (PA)
Penn State Mont Alto (PA)
Penn State New Kensington (PA)
Penn State Schuylkill (PA)
Penn State Shenango (PA)
Penn State U Park (PA)
Penn State Wilkes-Barre (PA)
Penn State Worthington Scranton
(PA)
Penn State York (PA)
Pepperdine U, Malibu (CA)
Point Park U (PA)
Pomona Coll (CA)
Portland State U (OR)

Queens U of Charlotte (NC)
Quinnipiac U (CT)
Regis Coll (MA)
Rhodes Coll (TN)
Rider U (NJ)
Roanoke Coll (VA)
Rochester Inst of Technology (NY)
Rockhurst U (MO)
Rollins Coll (FL)
Roosevelt U (IL)
Saginaw Valley State U (MI)
Saint Anselm Coll (NH)
St. Catherine U (MN)
Saint Francis U (PA)
St. John Fisher Coll (NY)
Saint Joseph's Coll (IN)
Saint Joseph's U (PA)
Saint Leo U (FL)
Saint Louis U (MO)
Saint Mary's Coll of California (CA)
St. Mary's U (TX)
St. Norbert Coll (WI)
Saint Xavier U (IL)
Samford U (AL)
San Diego State U (CA)
San Francisco State U (CA)
Sarah Lawrence Coll (NY)
Seattle U (WA)
Seton Hill U (PA)
Sewanee: The U of the South (TN)
Shawnee State U (OH)
Shaw U (NC)
Simmons Coll (MA)
Simpson Coll (IA)
Skidmore Coll (NY)
Sonoma State U (CA)
Southern Oregon U (OR)
Southern Polytechnic State U (GA)
Southwestern Adventist U (TX)
Southwestern U (TX)
Spring Hill Coll (AL)
Stanford U (CA)
State U of New York at Binghamton (NY)
State U of New York at New Paltz (NY)
State U of New York at Oswego (NY)
State U of New York Coll at Cortland (NY)
State U of New York Coll at Geneseo (NY)
State U of New York Coll at Oneonta (NY)
Stetson U (FL)
Stonehill Coll (MA)
Suffolk U (MA)
Susquehanna U (PA)
Sweet Briar Coll (VA)
Syracuse U (NY)
Taylor U (IN)
Temple U (PA)
Texas Christian U (TX)
Texas State U–San Marcos (TX)
Texas Wesleyan U (TX)
Tiffin U (OH)
Towson U (MD)
Trent U (ON, Canada)
Trinity Coll (CT)
Tufts U (MA)
Tulane U (LA)
United States Intl U (Kenya)
United States Military Acad (NY)
The U of Akron (OH)
The U of Alabama (AL)
U of Alberta (AB, Canada)
U of Arkansas (AR)
U of Arkansas at Little Rock (AR)
U of Bridgeport (CT)
The U of British Columbia (BC, Canada)
The U of British Columbia–Okanagan (BC, Canada)
U of California, Davis (CA)
U of Cincinnati (OH)
U of Dayton (OH)
U of Delaware (DE)
U of Denver (CO)
U of Evansville (IN)
U of Georgia (GA)
U of Hartford (CT)
U of Idaho (ID)
U of Indianapolis (IN)
U of La Verne (CA)
U of Maine (ME)

U of Mary Washington (VA)
U of Memphis (TN)
U of Miami (FL)
U of Minnesota, Duluth (MN)
U of Minnesota, Twin Cities Campus (MN)
U of Mississippi (MS)
U of Mount Union (OH)
U of Nebraska at Kearney (NE)
U of Nebraska–Lincoln (NE)
U of Nevada, Reno (NV)
U of Ottawa (ON, Canada)
U of Pennsylvania (PA)
U of Redlands (CA)
U of Richmond (VA)
U of Rochester (NY)
U of St. Thomas (TX)
U of San Diego (CA)
The U of Scranton (PA)
U of South Carolina (SC)
U of Southern California (CA)
U of Southern Indiana (IN)
U of Southern Mississippi (MS)
U of South Florida (FL)
The U of Tennessee at Martin (TN)
U of the Incarnate Word (TX)
U of the Pacific (CA)
The U of Toledo (OH)
U of Toronto (ON, Canada)
U of Virginia (VA)
U of Washington (WA)
The U of Western Ontario (ON, Canada)
U of West Florida (FL)
U of West Georgia (GA)
U of Windsor (ON, Canada)
U of Wisconsin–Platteville (WI)
U of Wisconsin–Stevens Point (WI)
U of Wisconsin–Superior (WI)
U of Wisconsin–Whitewater (WI)
Utica Coll (NY)
Valparaiso U (IN)
Vassar Coll (NY)
Virginia Polytechnic Inst and State U (VA)
Virginia Wesleyan Coll (VA)
Wagner Coll (NY)
Walsh U (OH)
Wartburg Coll (IA)
Washington Coll (MD)
Washington U in St. Louis (MO)
Webster U (MO)
Wellesley Coll (MA)
Wells Coll (NY)
Wesleyan Coll (GA)
Western Kentucky U (KY)
Western Oregon U (OR)
Westminster Coll (MO)
West Virginia Wesleyan Coll (WV)
Wheaton Coll (IL)
Wheaton Coll (MA)
Whittier Coll (CA)
Widener U (PA)
Wilkes U (PA)
William Jewell Coll (MO)
William Woods U (MO)
Wilson Coll (PA)
Wittenberg U (OH)
Wofford Coll (SC)
Wright State U (OH)
Xavier U (OH)
York Coll of Pennsylvania (PA)

INVESTMENTS AND SECURITIES
Babson Coll (MA)
Bernard M. Baruch Coll of the City U of New York (NY)
Central Michigan U (MI)
U of Nebraska at Omaha (NE)
U of Nebraska–Lincoln (NE)
U of North Dakota (ND)

IRANIAN LANGUAGES
U of Maryland, Coll Park (MD)
U of Utah (UT)
Washington U in St. Louis (MO)

IRISH STUDIES
Sacred Heart U (CT)

ISLAMIC STUDIES
Boston Coll (MA)
DePaul U (IL)

The Ohio State U (OH)
Swarthmore Coll (PA)
U of Minnesota, Twin Cities Campus (MN)
The U of Texas at Austin (TX)
The U of Western Ontario (ON, Canada)
Villanova U (PA)
Washington U in St. Louis (MO)
Wellesley Coll (MA)

ITALIAN
The American U of Rome (Italy)
Arizona State U (AZ)
Bard Coll (NY)
Barnard Coll (NY)
Bennington Coll (VT)
Bishop's U (QC, Canada)
Boston Coll (MA)
Boston U (MA)
Brown U (RI)
Bryn Mawr Coll (PA)
California State U, Long Beach (CA)
Central Connecticut State U (CT)
Coll of the Holy Cross (MA)
The Colorado Coll (CO)
Columbia U, School of General Studies (NY)
Concordia U (QC, Canada)
Connecticut Coll (CT)
Cornell U (NY)
Dartmouth Coll (NH)
DePaul U (IL)
Dominican U (IL)
Emory U (GA)
Fairfield U (CT)
Florida Intl U (FL)
Fordham U (NY)
Gettysburg Coll (PA)
Gonzaga U (WA)
Haverford Coll (PA)
Hofstra U (NY)
Hunter Coll of the City U of New York (NY)
Indiana U Bloomington (IN)
Iona Coll (NY)
Ithaca Coll (NY)
The Johns Hopkins U (MD)
Lake Erie Coll (OH)
La Salle U (PA)
Lehman Coll of the City U of New York (NY)
Long Island U–C. W. Post Campus (NY)
Loyola U Chicago (IL)
Marlboro Coll (VT)
Middlebury Coll (VT)
Montclair State U (NJ)
Mount Holyoke Coll (MA)
Nazareth Coll of Rochester (NY)
New York U (NY)
The Ohio State U (OH)
Penn State Abington (PA)
Penn State Altoona (PA)
Penn State Beaver (PA)
Penn State Berks (PA)
Penn State Brandywine (PA)
Penn State DuBois (PA)
Penn State Erie, The Behrend Coll (PA)
Penn State Fayette, The Eberly Campus (PA)
Penn State Greater Allegheny (PA)
Penn State Hazleton (PA)
Penn State Lehigh Valley (PA)
Penn State Mont Alto (PA)
Penn State New Kensington (PA)
Penn State Schuylkill (PA)
Penn State Shenango (PA)
Penn State U Park (PA)
Penn State Wilkes-Barre (PA)
Penn State Worthington Scranton (PA)
Penn State York (PA)
Providence Coll (RI)
Queens Coll of the City U of New York (NY)
Rosemont Coll (PA)
Rutgers, The State U of New Jersey, Newark (NJ)
Rutgers, The State U of New Jersey, New Brunswick (NJ)
St. John's U (NY)
Saint Joseph's U (PA)

Saint Louis U (MO)
Saint Mary's Coll (IN)
Saint Mary's Coll of California (CA)
San Francisco State U (CA)
Santa Clara U (CA)
Sarah Lawrence Coll (NY)
Scripps Coll (CA)
Smith Coll (MA)
Southern Connecticut State U (CT)
Southern Methodist U (TX)
Stanford U (CA)
State U of New York at Binghamton (NY)
Stony Brook U, State U of New York (NY)
Susquehanna U (PA)
Syracuse U (NY)
Temple U (PA)
Trinity Coll (CT)
Tulane U (LA)
U at Buffalo, the State U of New York (NY)
U of Alberta (AB, Canada)
The U of Arizona (AZ)
The U of British Columbia (BC, Canada)
U of California, Berkeley (CA)
U of California, Davis (CA)
U of California, Los Angeles (CA)
U of California, Santa Barbara (CA)
U of Colorado Boulder (CO)
U of Connecticut (CT)
U of Delaware (DE)
U of Denver (CO)
U of Georgia (GA)
U of Houston (TX)
U of Illinois at Chicago (IL)
U of Illinois at Urbana–Champaign (IL)
The U of Iowa (IA)
U of Maryland, Coll Park (MD)
U of Massachusetts Amherst (MA)
U of Massachusetts Boston (MA)
U of Michigan (MI)
U of Minnesota, Twin Cities Campus (MN)
U of Notre Dame (IN)
U of Oklahoma (OK)
U of Oregon (OR)
U of Ottawa (ON, Canada)
U of Pennsylvania (PA)
U of Pittsburgh (PA)
U of Rhode Island (RI)
The U of Scranton (PA)
U of Southern California (CA)
U of South Florida (FL)
The U of Tennessee (TN)
The U of Texas at Austin (TX)
U of Toronto (ON, Canada)
U of Virginia (VA)
U of Washington (WA)
U of Windsor (ON, Canada)
U of Wisconsin–Madison (WI)
U of Wisconsin–Milwaukee (WI)
Vassar Coll (NY)
Villanova U (PA)
Washington U in St. Louis (MO)
Wellesley Coll (MA)
Wesleyan U (CT)
Yale U (CT)
York Coll of the City U of New York (NY)
Youngstown State U (OH)

ITALIAN STUDIES
Arcadia U (PA)
Assumption Coll (MA)
Boston U (MA)
Brown U (RI)
Coll of the Holy Cross (MA)
The Colorado Coll (CO)
Columbia U, School of General Studies (NY)
Dalhousie U (NS, Canada)
Dickinson Coll (PA)
Fordham U (NY)
Franklin Coll Switzerland (Switzerland)
Merrimack Coll (MA)
Miami U (OH)
Scripps Coll (CA)
Southern Methodist U (TX)
Tulane U (LA)
U of California, Santa Cruz (CA)
U of Richmond (VA)

The U of Scranton (PA)
U of Vermont (VT)
U of Windsor (ON, Canada)
Wellesley Coll (MA)
Wheaton Coll (MA)

JAPANESE
Aquinas Coll (MI)
Ball State U (IN)
Bates Coll (ME)
Bennington Coll (VT)
Boston U (MA)
California State U, Fullerton (CA)
California State U, Long Beach (CA)
California State U, Los Angeles (CA)
California State U, Monterey Bay (CA)
Calvin Coll (MI)
Carnegie Mellon U (PA)
Colgate U (NY)
Connecticut Coll (CT)
Dartmouth Coll (NH)
Eastern Michigan U (MI)
Elizabethtown Coll (PA)
Emory U (GA)
Gettysburg Coll (PA)
Gustavus Adolphus Coll (MN)
Hobart and William Smith Colls (NY)
Lawrence U (WI)
Lincoln U (PA)
Linfield Coll (OR)
Macalester Coll (MN)
Michigan State U (MI)
Middlebury Coll (VT)
North Central Coll (IL)
Oakland U (MI)
The Ohio State U (OH)
Pacific U (OR)
Penn State Abington (PA)
Penn State Altoona (PA)
Penn State Beaver (PA)
Penn State Berks (PA)
Penn State Brandywine (PA)
Penn State DuBois (PA)
Penn State Erie, The Behrend Coll (PA)
Penn State Fayette, The Eberly Campus (PA)
Penn State Greater Allegheny (PA)
Penn State Hazleton (PA)
Penn State Lehigh Valley (PA)
Penn State Mont Alto (PA)
Penn State New Kensington (PA)
Penn State Schuylkill (PA)
Penn State Shenango (PA)
Penn State U Park (PA)
Penn State Wilkes-Barre (PA)
Penn State Worthington Scranton (PA)
Penn State York (PA)
Pomona Coll (CA)
Portland State U (OR)
San Diego State U (CA)
San Francisco State U (CA)
Sarah Lawrence Coll (NY)
Scripps Coll (CA)
Stanford U (CA)
Swarthmore Coll (PA)
Trinity Coll (CT)
U of Alaska Fairbanks (AK)
U of Alberta (AB, Canada)
U of California, Berkeley (CA)
U of California, Davis (CA)
U of California, Irvine (CA)
U of California, Los Angeles (CA)
U of California, Santa Barbara (CA)
U of Colorado Boulder (CO)
The U of Findlay (OH)
U of Georgia (GA)
U of Hawaii at Hilo (HI)
U of Hawaii at Manoa (HI)
The U of Iowa (IA)
U of Maryland, Coll Park (MD)
U of Massachusetts Amherst (MA)
U of Minnesota, Twin Cities Campus (MN)
U of Mount Union (OH)
The U of North Carolina at Charlotte (NC)
U of Notre Dame (IN)
U of Oregon (OR)
U of Pittsburgh (PA)

INDEXES

Albion Coll (MI)
Alma Coll (MI)
American Public U System (WV)
Anderson U (SC)
Appalachian State U (NC)
Arizona State U (AZ)
Arkansas State U (AR)
Augustana Coll (SD)
Baker U (KS)
Barry U (FL)
Bastyr U (WA)
Becker Coll (MA)
Belhaven U (MS)
Bellarmine U (KY)
Berea Coll (KY)
Berry Coll (GA)
Bethany Lutheran Coll (MN)
Bethel Coll (IN)
Bethel U (MN)
Biola U (CA)
Bluefield Coll (VA)
Boise State U (ID)
Boston U (MA)
Brevard Coll (NC)
Bridgewater State U (MA)
Brigham Young U (UT)
Buffalo State Coll, State U of New York (NY)
Cabrini Coll (PA)
California Baptist U (CA)
California Lutheran U (CA)
California State U, Chico (CA)
California State U, East Bay (CA)
California State U, Long Beach (CA)
California State U, Los Angeles (CA)
California State U, Sacramento (CA)
Calvin Coll (MI)
Capital U (OH)
Carson-Newman Coll (TN)
Castleton State Coll (VT)
Cedarville U (OH)
Central Coll (IA)
Central Washington U (WA)
Chatham U (PA)
Clearwater Christian Coll (FL)
Coastal Carolina U (SC)
The Coll at Brockport, State U of New York (NY)
The Coll of Idaho (ID)
Colorado Mesa U (CO)
Colorado State U (CO)
Columbus State U (GA)
Concordia U (QC, Canada)
Concordia U Chicago (IL)
Concordia U, Nebraska (NE)
Concordia U, St. Paul (MN)
Concordia U Texas (TX)
Corban U (OR)
Cornell Coll (IA)
Cornerstone U (MI)
Creighton U (NE)
Dakota State U (SD)
Dalhousie U (NS, Canada)
Defiance Coll (OH)
DePauw U (IN)
DeSales U (PA)
Dordt Coll (IA)
Drury U (MO)
East Central U (OK)
Eastern Illinois U (IL)
Eastern Michigan U (MI)
Eastern U (PA)
Eastern Washington U (WA)
East Stroudsburg U of Pennsylvania (PA)
Elmhurst Coll (IL)
Elon U (NC)
Emmanuel Coll (GA)
Fitchburg State U (MA)
Florida Atlantic U (FL)
Florida Gulf Coast U (FL)
Florida Southern Coll (FL)
Florida State U (FL)
Gannon U (PA)
Georgetown Coll (KY)
The George Washington U (DC)
Georgia Gwinnett Coll (GA)
Georgian Court U (NJ)
Georgia Southern U (GA)
Gonzaga U (WA)
Gordon Coll (MA)
Greenville Coll (IL)

Grove City Coll (PA)
Hanover Coll (IN)
Harding U (AR)
Hardin-Simmons U (TX)
Hendrix Coll (AR)
Hillsdale Free Will Baptist Coll (OK)
Hope Coll (MI)
Humboldt State U (CA)
Huntingdon Coll (AL)
Huntington U (IN)
Huston-Tillotson U (TX)
Illinois State U (IL)
Immaculata U (PA)
Indiana U Bloomington (IN)
Indiana Wesleyan U (IN)
Iowa Wesleyan Coll (IA)
Ithaca Coll (NY)
Jacksonville State U (AL)
Jacksonville U (FL)
John Brown U (AR)
Johnson State Coll (VT)
Kansas State U (KS)
Keene State Coll (NH)
Kennesaw State U (GA)
Kent State U (OH)
Kentucky Wesleyan Coll (KY)
Lakehead U (ON, Canada)
Lake Superior State U (MI)
Lasell Coll (MA)
La Sierra U (CA)
Lenoir-Rhyne U (NC)
Lewis-Clark State Coll (ID)
Liberty U (VA)
Lincoln Memorial U (TN)
Lindenwood U (MO)
Linfield Coll (OR)
Lipscomb U (TN)
Longwood U (VA)
Loras Coll (IA)
Louisiana Coll (LA)
Lubbock Christian U (TX)
Malone U (OH)
Manchester Coll (IN)
Marshall U (WV)
Mars Hill Coll (NC)
Marymount U (VA)
The Master's Coll and Sem (CA)
McDaniel Coll (MD)
McMurry U (TX)
Meredith Coll (NC)
Messiah Coll (PA)
Miami U (OH)
Michigan State U (MI)
MidAmerica Nazarene U (KS)
Minnesota State U Moorhead (MN)
Mississippi Coll (MS)
Missouri Baptist U (MO)
Missouri State U (MO)
Morehead State U (KY)
Morehouse Coll (GA)
Mount Vernon Nazarene U (OH)
Nebraska Wesleyan U (NE)
Norfolk State U (VA)
North Carolina Wesleyan Coll (NC)
North Central Coll (IL)
Northeastern State U (OK)
Northern Arizona U (AZ)
Northern Michigan U (MI)
Northwestern Coll (IA)
Northwestern Coll (MN)
Northwest Nazarene U (ID)
Notre Dame de Namur U (CA)
Nova Southeastern U (FL)
Occidental Coll (CA)
Ohio Northern U (OH)
The Ohio State U (OH)
Ohio U (OH)
Oklahoma City U (OK)
Oral Roberts U (OK)
Ouachita Baptist U (AR)
Pacific Union Coll (CA)
Pacific U (OR)
Penn State Abington (PA)
Penn State Altoona (PA)
Penn State Beaver (PA)
Penn State Berks (PA)
Penn State Brandywine (PA)
Penn State DuBois (PA)
Penn State Erie, The Behrend Coll (PA)
Penn State Fayette, The Eberly Campus (PA)
Penn State Greater Allegheny (PA)
Penn State Hazleton (PA)
Penn State Lehigh Valley (PA)

Penn State Mont Alto (PA)
Penn State New Kensington (PA)
Penn State Schuylkill (PA)
Penn State Shenango (PA)
Penn State U Park (PA)
Penn State Wilkes-Barre (PA)
Penn State Worthington Scranton (PA)
Penn State York (PA)
Pepperdine U, Malibu (CA)
Point Loma Nazarene U (CA)
Queens Coll of the City U of New York (NY)
Rice U (TX)
Roanoke Coll (VA)
Rocky Mountain Coll (MT)
Rutgers, The State U of New Jersey, New Brunswick (NJ)
Sacred Heart U (CT)
Saginaw Valley State U (MI)
St. Edward's U (TX)
Saint Joseph's Coll of Maine (ME)
Saint Louis U (MO)
Saint Mary's Coll of California (CA)
St. Mary's U (TX)
St. Olaf Coll (MN)
Salem State U (MA)
Salisbury U (MD)
Samford U (AL)
Sam Houston State U (TX)
San Diego Christian Coll (CA)
San Francisco State U (CA)
Schreiner U (TX)
Seattle Pacific U (WA)
Shaw U (NC)
Shippensburg U of Pennsylvania (PA)
Simmons Coll (MA)
Simon Fraser U (BC, Canada)
Simpson Coll (IA)
Skidmore Coll (NY)
Slippery Rock U of Pennsylvania (PA)
Sonoma State U (CA)
Southern Arkansas U–Magnolia (AR)
Southern Illinois U Carbondale (IL)
Southern Illinois U Edwardsville (IL)
Southwestern Adventist U (TX)
Southwestern Christian U (OK)
Southwestern U (TX)
Southwest Minnesota State U (MN)
Spring Arbor U (MI)
State U of New York Coll at Cortland (NY)
Stephen F. Austin State U (TX)
Syracuse U (NY)
Tarleton State U (TX)
Taylor U (IN)
Temple U (PA)
Texas A&M U–Corpus Christi (TX)
Texas Lutheran U (TX)
Texas Southern U (TX)
Texas Tech U (TX)
Texas Wesleyan U (TX)
Texas Woman's U (TX)
Towson U (MD)
Transylvania U (KY)
Trinity Christian Coll (IL)
Truman State U (MO)
Tusculum Coll (TN)
Union Coll (NE)
Union U (TN)
United States Military Acad (NY)
Université de Sherbrooke (QC, Canada)
The U of Akron (OH)
U of Alberta (AB, Canada)
The U of British Columbia (BC, Canada)
The U of British Columbia–Okanagan (BC, Canada)
U of Central Arkansas (AR)
U of Dayton (OH)
U of Delaware (DE)
U of Evansville (IN)
U of Guelph (ON, Canada)
U of Hawaii at Manoa (HI)
U of Houston (TX)
U of Houston–Clear Lake (TX)
U of Idaho (ID)
U of Illinois at Chicago (IL)
U of Illinois at Urbana–Champaign (IL)
U of Indianapolis (IN)

The U of Iowa (IA)
U of La Verne (CA)
U of Lethbridge (AB, Canada)
U of Louisiana at Monroe (LA)
U of Mary (ND)
U of Maryland, Coll Park (MD)
U of Memphis (TN)
U of Miami (FL)
U of Michigan (MI)
U of Minnesota, Duluth (MN)
U of Minnesota, Twin Cities Campus (MN)
U of Mississippi (MS)
U of Mount Union (OH)
U of Nebraska at Omaha (NE)
U of Nevada, Las Vegas (NV)
U of New England (ME)
U of New Hampshire (NH)
U of Northern Colorado (CO)
U of Oklahoma (OK)
U of Ottawa (ON, Canada)
U of Puget Sound (WA)
U of Regina (SK, Canada)
U of Rhode Island (RI)
The U of Scranton (PA)
U of South Carolina (SC)
U of South Carolina Aiken (SC)
U of Southern California (CA)
U of Southern Indiana (IN)
The U of Tennessee (TN)
The U of Tennessee at Chattanooga (TN)
The U of Texas at Arlington (TX)
The U of Texas at Austin (TX)
The U of Texas at Tyler (TX)
The U of Texas of the Permian Basin (TX)
U of the Incarnate Word (TX)
U of the Pacific (CA)
U of the Sciences in Philadelphia (PA)
The U of Toledo (OH)
U of Tulsa (OK)
U of Utah (UT)
U of Vermont (VT)
U of Virginia (VA)
The U of Western Ontario (ON, Canada)
U of Windsor (ON, Canada)
U of Wisconsin–Eau Claire (WI)
U of Wisconsin–La Crosse (WI)
U of Wisconsin–Madison (WI)
U of Wisconsin–Milwaukee (WI)
U of Wisconsin–Superior (WI)
U of Wyoming (WY)
Upper Iowa U (IA)
Valdosta State U (GA)
Valparaiso U (IN)
Vanguard U of Southern California (CA)
Viterbo U (WI)
Wake Forest U (NC)
Washington State U (WA)
Waynesburg U (PA)
Western Illinois U (IL)
Western Kentucky U (KY)
Western Michigan U (MI)
Western Oregon U (OR)
Western State Coll of Colorado (CO)
West Liberty U (WV)
West Virginia Wesleyan Coll (WV)
Wichita State U (KS)
Willamette U (OR)
William Paterson U of New Jersey (NJ)
Wilson Coll (PA)
Winona State U (MN)
Youngstown State U (OH)

KINESIOTHERAPY

Boston U (MA)
Bridgewater State U (MA)
California State U, Long Beach (CA)
Loyola Marymount U (CA)
U of Regina (SK, Canada)

KNOWLEDGE MANAGEMENT

Framingham State U (MA)
Saint Joseph's U (PA)
Saint Louis U (MO)

KOREAN

Brigham Young U (UT)
The Ohio State U (OH)
U of California, Irvine (CA)
U of California, Los Angeles (CA)
U of Hawaii at Manoa (HI)

LABOR AND INDUSTRIAL RELATIONS

Athabasca U (AB, Canada)
Bowling Green State U (OH)
Clarion U of Pennsylvania (PA)
Cleveland State U (OH)
Cornell U (NY)
Governors State U (IL)
Indiana U Bloomington (IN)
Indiana U–Purdue U Fort Wayne (IN)
Indiana U Southeast (IN)
Ithaca Coll (NY)
Lakehead U (ON, Canada)
New York U (NY)
Penn State Abington (PA)
Penn State Altoona (PA)
Penn State Beaver (PA)
Penn State Berks (PA)
Penn State Brandywine (PA)
Penn State DuBois (PA)
Penn State Erie, The Behrend Coll (PA)
Penn State Fayette, The Eberly Campus (PA)
Penn State Greater Allegheny (PA)
Penn State Hazleton (PA)
Penn State Lehigh Valley (PA)
Penn State Mont Alto (PA)
Penn State New Kensington (PA)
Penn State Schuylkill (PA)
Penn State Shenango (PA)
Penn State U Park (PA)
Penn State Wilkes-Barre (PA)
Penn State Worthington Scranton (PA)
Penn State York (PA)
Rider U (NJ)
Rutgers, The State U of New Jersey, New Brunswick (NJ)
Saint Francis U (PA)
San Francisco State U (CA)
State U of New York at Fredonia (NY)
State U of New York Coll at Old Westbury (NY)
State U of New York Coll at Potsdam (NY)
State U of New York Empire State Coll (NY)
Temple U (PA)
U of Alberta (AB, Canada)
U of Bridgeport (CT)
The U of Iowa (IA)
U of Maine (ME)
U of Minnesota, Twin Cities Campus (MN)
U of Toronto (ON, Canada)
West Virginia U Inst of Technology (WV)

LABOR STUDIES

California State U, Dominguez Hills (CA)
Eastern Michigan U (MI)
Hofstra U (NY)
Indiana U Bloomington (IN)
Indiana U Kokomo (IN)
Indiana U Northwest (IN)
Indiana U–Purdue U Indianapolis (IN)
Indiana U South Bend (IN)
Queens Coll of the City U of New York (NY)
U of Windsor (ON, Canada)
Wayne State U (MI)

LANDSCAPE ARCHITECTURE

Acad of Art U (CA)
American U of Beirut (Lebanon)
Arizona State U (AZ)
Ball State U (IN)
Boston Architectural Coll (MA)
California Polytechnic State U, San Luis Obispo (CA)
California State Polytechnic U, Pomona (CA)

INDEXES

Clemson U (SC)
Coll of the Atlantic (ME)
Colorado State U (CO)
Cornell U (NY)
Iowa State U of Science and Technology (IA)
Louisiana State U and Ag and Mech Coll (LA)
Michigan State U (MI)
Mississippi State U (MS)
North Carolina Ag and Tech State U (NC)
North Carolina State U (NC)
North Dakota State U (ND)
The Ohio State U (OH)
Oklahoma State U (OK)
Penn State Brandywine (PA)
Penn State Lehigh Valley (PA)
Penn State Schuylkill (PA)
Penn State U Park (PA)
Penn State Wilkes-Barre (PA)
Philadelphia U (PA)
Purdue U (IN)
State U of New York Coll of Environmental Science and Forestry (NY)
Temple U (PA)
Texas A&M U (TX)
Texas Tech U (TX)
U of Arkansas (AR)
The U of British Columbia (BC, Canada)
U of California, Berkeley (CA)
U of California, Davis (CA)
U of Connecticut (CT)
U of Delaware (DE)
U of Florida (FL)
U of Georgia (GA)
U of Idaho (ID)
U of Illinois at Urbana–Champaign (IL)
U of Maryland, Coll Park (MD)
U of Massachusetts Amherst (MA)
U of Minnesota, Twin Cities Campus (MN)
U of Nebraska–Lincoln (NE)
U of Nevada, Las Vegas (NV)
U of Oregon (OR)
U of Rhode Island (RI)
U of Washington (WA)
U of Wisconsin–Madison (WI)
Utah State U (UT)
Virginia Polytechnic Inst and State U (VA)
Washington State U (WA)
West Virginia U (WV)

LANDSCAPING AND GROUNDSKEEPING
Andrews U (MI)
Florida Southern Coll (FL)
Mississippi State U (MS)
Oklahoma State U (OK)
Penn State Abington (PA)
Penn State Altoona (PA)
Penn State Beaver (PA)
Penn State Berks (PA)
Penn State Brandywine (PA)
Penn State DuBois (PA)
Penn State Erie, The Behrend Coll (PA)
Penn State Fayette, The Eberly Campus (PA)
Penn State Greater Allegheny (PA)
Penn State Hazleton (PA)
Penn State Lehigh Valley (PA)
Penn State Mont Alto (PA)
Penn State New Kensington (PA)
Penn State Schuylkill (PA)
Penn State Shenango (PA)
Penn State U Park (PA)
Penn State Wilkes-Barre (PA)
Penn State Worthington Scranton (PA)
Penn State York (PA)
South Dakota State U (SD)
U of Maine (ME)
U of Minnesota, Crookston (MN)
U of Nebraska–Lincoln (NE)

LAND USE PLANNING AND MANAGEMENT
California State U, Bakersfield (CA)
Central Michigan U (MI)

Metropolitan State Coll of Denver (CO)
Montana State U (MT)
State U of New York Coll of Environmental Science and Forestry (NY)
U of Alberta (AB, Canada)
The U of Western Ontario (ON, Canada)
U of Wisconsin–Platteville (WI)
U of Wisconsin–River Falls (WI)

LANGUAGE INTERPRETATION AND TRANSLATION
Bard Coll (NY)
Brigham Young U (UT)
Concordia U (QC, Canada)
Mississippi Coll (MS)
Northwestern Coll (IA)
U of Ottawa (ON, Canada)

LASER AND OPTICAL ENGINEERING
Delaware State U (DE)
U of Rochester (NY)

LASER AND OPTICAL TECHNOLOGY
Oregon Inst of Technology (OR)

LATIN
Acadia U (NS, Canada)
Amherst Coll (MA)
Augustana Coll (IL)
Austin Coll (TX)
Ball State U (IN)
Bard Coll (NY)
Barnard Coll (NY)
Baylor U (TX)
Boston Coll (MA)
Boston U (MA)
Bowling Green State U (OH)
Bryn Mawr Coll (PA)
Butler U (IN)
Calvin Coll (MI)
Carleton Coll (MN)
The Catholic U of America (DC)
Colgate U (NY)
The Coll of Wooster (OH)
Concordia Coll (MN)
Creighton U (NE)
Dartmouth Coll (NH)
DePauw U (IN)
Duquesne U (PA)
Emory U (GA)
Fordham U (NY)
Franklin & Marshall Coll (PA)
Furman U (SC)
Gettysburg Coll (PA)
Hampden-Sydney Coll (VA)
Haverford Coll (PA)
Hobart and William Smith Colls (NY)
Hofstra U (NY)
Hunter Coll of the City U of New York (NY)
Indiana U Bloomington (IN)
John Carroll U (OH)
Kent State U (OH)
Lawrence U (WI)
Lehman Coll of the City U of New York (NY)
Lenoir-Rhyne U (NC)
Loyola U Chicago (IL)
Marlboro Coll (VT)
Mercer U (GA)
Missouri State U (MO)
Monmouth Coll (IL)
Montclair State U (NJ)
Mount Allison U (NB, Canada)
Mount Holyoke Coll (MA)
Notre Dame of Maryland U (MD)
Queens Coll of the City U of New York (NY)
Randolph Coll (VA)
Randolph-Macon Coll (VA)
Rhodes Coll (TN)
Rice U (TX)
Rockford Coll (IL)
Rutgers, The State U of New Jersey, New Brunswick (NJ)
Saint Joseph's U (PA)
Saint Mary's Coll of California (CA)

St. Olaf Coll (MN)
Samford U (AL)
Santa Clara U (CA)
Sarah Lawrence Coll (NY)
Sewanee: The U of the South (TN)
Smith Coll (MA)
Southwestern U (TX)
Stanford U (CA)
State U of New York at Binghamton (NY)
Swarthmore Coll (PA)
Tufts U (MA)
Tulane U (LA)
U of Alberta (AB, Canada)
The U of British Columbia (BC, Canada)
U of California, Berkeley (CA)
U of California, Irvine (CA)
U of Georgia (GA)
The U of Iowa (IA)
U of Maine (ME)
U of Miami (FL)
U of Michigan (MI)
U of Minnesota, Twin Cities Campus (MN)
U of Missouri (MO)
U of Nebraska–Lincoln (NE)
U of New Hampshire (NH)
U of Ottawa (ON, Canada)
U of Richmond (VA)
U of St. Thomas (MN)
The U of Scranton (PA)
The U of Texas at Austin (TX)
U of Toronto (ON, Canada)
U of Vermont (VT)
U of Washington (WA)
The U of Western Ontario (ON, Canada)
U of Windsor (ON, Canada)
U of Wisconsin–Madison (WI)
Virginia Wesleyan Coll (VA)
Wabash Coll (IN)
Wake Forest U (NC)
Washington U in St. Louis (MO)
Wellesley Coll (MA)
West Chester U of Pennsylvania (PA)
Western Michigan U (MI)
Wheaton Coll (MA)
Wright State U (OH)
Yale U (CT)

LATIN AMERICAN AND CARIBBEAN STUDIES
Burlington Coll (VT)
Coll of Charleston (SC)
Mount Holyoke Coll (MA)
Rollins Coll (FL)
Union Coll (NY)
U of Michigan (MI)
U of Wisconsin–Madison (WI)

LATIN AMERICAN STUDIES
Adelphi U (NY)
Albion Coll (MI)
Albright Coll (PA)
American U (DC)
Assumption Coll (MA)
Bard Coll (NY)
Bard Coll at Simon's Rock (MA)
Barnard Coll (NY)
Baylor U (TX)
Beloit Coll (WI)
Bennington Coll (VT)
Blackburn Coll (IL)
Boston U (MA)
Bowdoin Coll (ME)
Bowling Green State U (OH)
Brandeis U (MA)
Brown U (RI)
Bucknell U (PA)
California State U, Chico (CA)
California State U, East Bay (CA)
California State U, Fullerton (CA)
California State U, Los Angeles (CA)
Carleton Coll (MN)
Carnegie Mellon U (PA)
City Coll of the City U of New York (NY)
Colby Coll (ME)
Colgate U (NY)
The Coll at Brockport, State U of New York (NY)

The Coll of William and Mary (VA)
Columbia U, School of General Studies (NY)
Connecticut Coll (CT)
Cornell Coll (IA)
Dartmouth Coll (NH)
Davidson Coll (NC)
Denison U (OH)
DePaul U (IL)
Dickinson Coll (PA)
Earlham Coll (IN)
Emory U (GA)
Flagler Coll (FL)
Fordham U (NY)
Fort Lewis Coll (CO)
George Mason U (VA)
The George Washington U (DC)
Gettysburg Coll (PA)
Gustavus Adolphus Coll (MN)
Hamline U (MN)
Hampshire Coll (MA)
Haverford Coll (PA)
Hobart and William Smith Colls (NY)
Hofstra U (NY)
Hood Coll (MD)
Hunter Coll of the City U of New York (NY)
Illinois Wesleyan U (IL)
The Johns Hopkins U (MD)
Kent State U (OH)
Lake Forest Coll (IL)
Lehman Coll of the City U of New York (NY)
Macalester Coll (MN)
Marlboro Coll (VT)
Miami U (OH)
Middlebury Coll (VT)
Millsaps Coll (MS)
New Coll of Florida (FL)
New York U (NY)
Oakland U (MI)
Occidental Coll (CA)
Ohio U (OH)
Ohio Wesleyan U (OH)
Pace U (NY)
Penn State Abington (PA)
Penn State Altoona (PA)
Penn State Beaver (PA)
Penn State Berks (PA)
Penn State Brandywine (PA)
Penn State DuBois (PA)
Penn State Erie, The Behrend Coll (PA)
Penn State Fayette, The Eberly Campus (PA)
Penn State Greater Allegheny (PA)
Penn State Hazleton (PA)
Penn State Lehigh Valley (PA)
Penn State Mont Alto (PA)
Penn State New Kensington (PA)
Penn State Schuylkill (PA)
Penn State Shenango (PA)
Penn State U Park (PA)
Penn State Wilkes-Barre (PA)
Penn State Worthington Scranton (PA)
Penn State York (PA)
Pomona Coll (CA)
Portland State U (OR)
Queens Coll of the City U of New York (NY)
Rhode Island Coll (RI)
Rice U (TX)
Ripon Coll (WI)
Rutgers, The State U of New Jersey, New Brunswick (NJ)
St. Edward's U (TX)
Saint Louis U (MO)
Saint Mary's Coll of California (CA)
St. Olaf Coll (MN)
Samford U (AL)
San Diego State U (CA)
Sarah Lawrence Coll (NY)
Scripps Coll (CA)
Seattle Pacific U (WA)
Skidmore Coll (NY)
Smith Coll (MA)
Southern Methodist U (TX)
Southwestern U (TX)
Stanford U (CA)
State U of New York at Binghamton (NY)
State U of New York at New Paltz (NY)

State U of New York at Plattsburgh (NY)
Swarthmore Coll (PA)
Syracuse U (NY)
Temple U (PA)
Texas Tech U (TX)
Trinity U (TX)
Tulane U (LA)
United States Military Acad (NY)
U at Albany, State U of New York (NY)
The U of Alabama (AL)
U of Alberta (AB, Canada)
The U of Arizona (AZ)
The U of British Columbia (BC, Canada)
U of California, Berkeley (CA)
U of California, Los Angeles (CA)
U of California, Riverside (CA)
U of California, Santa Cruz (CA)
U of Connecticut (CT)
U of Delaware (DE)
U of Denver (CO)
U of Georgia (GA)
U of Idaho (ID)
U of Illinois at Chicago (IL)
U of Illinois at Urbana–Champaign (IL)
The U of Iowa (IA)
The U of Kansas (KS)
U of Miami (FL)
U of Minnesota, Twin Cities Campus (MN)
U of Missouri (MO)
U of Nebraska at Omaha (NE)
U of Nebraska–Lincoln (NE)
U of New Mexico (NM)
The U of North Carolina at Chapel Hill (NC)
The U of North Carolina at Charlotte (NC)
U of Oregon (OR)
U of Pennsylvania (PA)
U of Richmond (VA)
U of South Carolina (SC)
The U of Texas at Austin (TX)
The U of Texas at El Paso (TX)
The U of Toledo (OH)
U of Toronto (ON, Canada)
U of Utah (UT)
U of Vermont (VT)
U of Washington (WA)
The U of Western Ontario (ON, Canada)
U of Wisconsin–Eau Claire (WI)
Vanderbilt U (TN)
Vassar Coll (NY)
Villanova U (PA)
Warren Wilson Coll (NC)
Washington Coll (MD)
Washington U in St. Louis (MO)
Wellesley Coll (MA)
Wesleyan U (CT)
Westminster Coll (UT)
Willamette U (OR)
William Paterson U of New Jersey (NJ)
Yale U (CT)

LATIN TEACHER EDUCATION
Assumption Coll (MA)
Boston U (MA)
Brigham Young U (UT)
Concordia Coll (MN)
Duquesne U (PA)
Indiana U Bloomington (IN)
Miami U (OH)
Missouri State U (MO)
Ohio Wesleyan U (OH)
U of Delaware (DE)
U of Illinois at Urbana–Champaign (IL)
Western Michigan U (MI)

LAW ENFORCEMENT INTELLIGENCE ANALYSIS
Bellevue U (NE)

LAY MINISTRY
Kentucky Mountain Bible Coll (KY)
Saint Mary's U of Minnesota (MN)
Southeastern Bible Coll (AL)
Trevecca Nazarene U (TN)

LEGAL ADMINISTRATIVE ASSISTANT/SECRETARY
Clayton State U (GA)
Lewis-Clark State Coll (ID)

LEGAL ASSISTANT/ PARALEGAL
Anna Maria Coll (MA)
Bauder Coll (GA)
Boston U (MA)
Broadview U (UT)
Broadview U-Boise (ID)
Broadview U-Layton (UT)
Broadview U-Orem (UT)
California State U, Chico (CA)
Calumet Coll of Saint Joseph (IN)
Clayton State U (GA)
Coll of Mount St. Joseph (OH)
Coll of Saint Mary (NE)
Daemen Coll (NY)
Davenport U, Grand Rapids (MI)
East Central U (OK)
Eastern Michigan U (MI)
Faulkner U (AL)
Florida Gulf Coast U (FL)
Gannon U (PA)
Globe U–Appleton (WI)
Globe U–Eau Claire (WI)
Globe U–Green Bay (WI)
Globe U–La Crosse (WI)
Globe U–Madison East (WI)
Globe U–Madison West (WI)
Globe U–Minneapolis (MN)
Globe U–Sioux Falls (SD)
Globe U–Wausau (WI)
Globe U–Woodbury (WI)
Grambling State U (LA)
Grand Valley State U (MI)
Hampton U (VA)
Hilbert Coll (NY)
Husson U (ME)
Indiana Tech (IN)
Jones Coll, Jacksonville (FL)
Kent State U (OH)
Lake Erie Coll (OH)
Lewis-Clark State Coll (ID)
Lewis U (IL)
Madonna U (MI)
Marymount U (VA)
Maryville U of Saint Louis (MO)
Minnesota School of Business–Blaine (MN)
Minnesota School of Business–Brooklyn Center (MN)
Minnesota School of Business–Elk River (MN)
Minnesota School of Business–Lakeville (MN)
Minnesota School of Business–Moorhead (MN)
Minnesota School of Business–Richfield (MN)
Minnesota School of Business–Rochester (MN)
Minnesota School of Business–St. Cloud (MN)
Minnesota School of Business–Shakopee (MN)
Minnesota State U Moorhead (MN)
Mississippi Coll (MS)
Mississippi U for Women (MS)
Morehead State U (KY)
New York City Coll of Technology of the City U of New York (NY)
Nova Southeastern U (FL)
Peirce Coll (PA)
Pennsylvania Coll of Technology (PA)
Post U (CT)
Quinnipiac U (CT)
Roger Williams U (RI)
Roosevelt U (IL)
Saint Mary-of-the-Woods Coll (IN)
Southern Illinois U Carbondale (IL)
State U of New York Coll of Technology at Canton (NY)
Stephen F. Austin State U (TX)
Stevens Inst of Business & Arts (MO)
Stevenson U (MD)
Suffolk U (MA)
Sullivan U (KY)
Texas Woman's U (TX)
Thomas Edison State Coll (NJ)

U of Central Florida (FL)
U of Cincinnati (OH)
U of Evansville (IN)
U of Great Falls (MT)
U of Hartford (CT)
U of Houston–Clear Lake (TX)
U of La Verne (CA)
U of Mississippi (MS)
U of Southern Mississippi (MS)
The U of Tennessee at Chattanooga (TN)
U of West Florida (FL)
Ursuline Coll (OH)
Valdosta State U (GA)
Washburn U (KS)
Winona State U (MN)

LEGAL PROFESSIONS AND STUDIES RELATED
Armstrong Atlantic State U (GA)
Ball State U (IN)
California U of Pennsylvania (PA)
Central Penn Coll (PA)
Hamline U (MN)
Hodges U (FL)
Maryville U of Saint Louis (MO)
Missouri Southern State U (MO)
Montclair State U (NJ)
Ramapo Coll of New Jersey (NJ)
Roger Williams U (RI)
St. John's U (NY)
Temple U (PA)
Texas Wesleyan U (TX)
Tulane U (LA)
U of Illinois at Springfield (IL)
U of Nebraska–Lincoln (NE)
U of Pennsylvania (PA)
U of Tulsa (OK)

LEGAL STUDIES
Adams State Coll (CO)
American Public U System (WV)
American U (DC)
Amherst Coll (MA)
Anna Maria Coll (MA)
Arizona State U (AZ)
Bay Path Coll (MA)
Becker Coll (MA)
Bellevue U (NE)
Brenau U (GA)
Bridgewater State U (MA)
Burlington Coll (VT)
California State U, Chico (CA)
Cape Breton U (NS, Canada)
Central Michigan U (MI)
Claremont McKenna Coll (CA)
Coll of the Atlantic (ME)
DeSales U (PA)
Dickinson Coll (PA)
Dominican U (IL)
Emory & Henry Coll (VA)
Florida National Coll (FL)
Franciscan U of Steubenville (OH)
Goldey-Beacom Coll (DE)
Hampshire Coll (MA)
Harding U (AR)
Hood Coll (MD)
James Madison U (VA)
John Jay Coll of Criminal Justice of the City U of New York (NY)
Lasell Coll (MA)
Lipscomb U (TN)
Manhattanville Coll (NY)
Minnesota State U Moorhead (MN)
Montclair State U (NJ)
Mountain State U (WV)
National U (CA)
Newbury Coll (MA)
North Carolina Wesleyan Coll (NC)
Northwest U (WA)
Park U (MO)
Point Park U (PA)
Quinnipiac U (CT)
Sage Coll of Albany (NY)
St. John's U (NY)
Saint Joseph's U (PA)
Saint Louis U (MO)
Scripps Coll (CA)
South U (AL)
South U, Royal Palm Beach (FL)
South U (GA)
South U (MI)
South U, Columbia (SC)
South U, Glen Allen (VA)

South U, Virginia Beach (VA)
State U of New York at Fredonia (NY)
Stevenson U (MD)
Suffolk U (MA)
Tiffin U (OH)
United States Air Force Acad (CO)
Université de Sherbrooke (QC, Canada)
U of Alberta (AB, Canada)
U of California, Berkeley (CA)
U of California, Santa Barbara (CA)
U of California, Santa Cruz (CA)
U of Hartford (CT)
U of Maryland U Coll (MD)
U of Massachusetts Amherst (MA)
U of Miami (FL)
U of New Haven (CT)
U of Pittsburgh (PA)
The U of Western Ontario (ON, Canada)
U of Windsor (ON, Canada)
U of Wisconsin–Madison (WI)
U of Wisconsin–Superior (WI)
Virginia Intermont Coll (VA)
Webster U (MO)
Western Intl U (AZ)
Western New England U (MA)
Wilmington U (DE)
Winona State U (MN)

LIBERAL ARTS AND SCIENCES AND HUMANITIES RELATED
Anna Maria Coll (MA)
Auburn U (AL)
Barton Coll (NC)
Belhaven U (MS)
Bennington Coll (VT)
Bishop's U (QC, Canada)
Brigham Young U (UT)
California Polytechnic State U, San Luis Obispo (CA)
California State U, Dominguez Hills (CA)
Carnegie Mellon U (PA)
Chester Coll of New England (NH)
The Colorado Coll (CO)
Concordia Coll (MN)
Crown Coll (MN)
Fairfield U (CT)
Florida Atlantic U (FL)
George Mason U (VA)
Georgia Coll & State U (GA)
Goddard Coll (VT)
Hampshire Coll (MA)
Howard Payne U (TX)
The Johns Hopkins U (MD)
Kent State U at Stark (OH)
Kent State U at Tuscarawas (OH)
Loyola U New Orleans (LA)
Malone U (OH)
Marshall U (WV)
Marymount Coll, Palos Verdes, California (CA)
Missouri Baptist U (MO)
Mitchell Coll (CT)
Mount Aloysius Coll (PA)
North Carolina State U (NC)
Oakland U (MI)
Ohio U (OH)
Ohio U–Chillicothe (OH)
Prescott Coll (AZ)
Purdue U (IN)
Roger Williams U (RI)
Sacred Heart U (CT)
Saint Anselm Coll (NH)
St. John's Coll (NM)
Saint Louis U (MO)
Saint Mary's Coll of California (CA)
Salem State U (MA)
Sarah Lawrence Coll (NY)
Shimer Coll (IL)
Southern Methodist U (TX)
Southwestern U (TX)
State U of New York Maritime Coll (NY)
Tulane U (LA)
The U of Akron (OH)
U of California, Los Angeles (CA)
U of California, Santa Barbara (CA)
U of Illinois at Urbana–Champaign (IL)
U of Maryland U Coll (MD)
U of Mary Washington (VA)
U of Massachusetts Amherst (MA)

U of Minnesota, Twin Cities Campus (MN)
U of Oklahoma (OK)
U of Rhode Island (RI)
U of Wisconsin–Milwaukee (WI)
U of Wisconsin–River Falls (WI)
U of Wisconsin–Whitewater (WI)
Valdosta State U (GA)
Vassar Coll (NY)
Walsh U (OH)
Wayland Baptist U (TX)
Western Illinois U (IL)

LIBERAL ARTS AND SCIENCES/ LIBERAL STUDIES
Abilene Christian U (TX)
Adams State Coll (CO)
Alaska Pacific U (AK)
Albion Coll (MI)
Alcorn State U (MS)
Alliant Intl U (CA)
Alliant Intl U–México City (Mexico)
Alvernia U (PA)
Alverno Coll (WI)
American Jewish U (CA)
American U (DC)
Amridge U (AL)
Angelo State U (TX)
Anna Maria Coll (MA)
Antioch U Midwest (OH)
Appalachian State U (NC)
Aquinas Coll (MI)
Arcadia U (PA)
Arizona State U (AZ)
Armstrong Atlantic State U (GA)
Ashland U (OH)
Athabasca U (AB, Canada)
Auburn U Montgomery (AL)
Augustana Coll (IL)
Augustana Coll (SD)
Austin Peay State U (TN)
Averett U (VA)
Azusa Pacific U (CA)
Ball State U (IN)
Barry U (FL)
Bay Path Coll (MA)
Beacon Coll (FL)
Becker Coll (MA)
Bellarmine U (KY)
Bemidji State U (MN)
Benedictine Coll (KS)
Bennington Coll (VT)
Bentley U (MA)
Bernard M. Baruch Coll of the City U of New York (NY)
Bethany Lutheran Coll (MN)
Bethel Coll (IN)
Bethune-Cookman U (FL)
Biola U (CA)
Bishop's U (QC, Canada)
Bluefield Coll (VA)
Boise State U (ID)
Bowling Green State U (OH)
Bradley U (IL)
Brenau U (GA)
Brescia U (KY)
Bridgewater Coll (VA)
Brigham Young U (UT)
Buffalo State Coll, State U of New York (NY)
Butler U (IN)
Cabrini Coll (PA)
California Baptist U (CA)
California Lutheran U (CA)
California Polytechnic State U, San Luis Obispo (CA)
California State Polytechnic U, Pomona (CA)
California State U, Bakersfield (CA)
California State U, Chico (CA)
California State U, Dominguez Hills (CA)
California State U, East Bay (CA)
California State U, Fresno (CA)
California State U, Fullerton (CA)
California State U, Long Beach (CA)
California State U, Los Angeles (CA)
California State U, Monterey Bay (CA)
California State U, Sacramento (CA)
California State U, San Bernardino (CA)

California State U, San Marcos (CA)
California State U, Stanislaus (CA)
California U of Pennsylvania (PA)
Calumet Coll of Saint Joseph (IN)
Cambridge Coll (MA)
Canisius Coll (NY)
Cardinal Stritch U (WI)
Carlow U (PA)
Carnegie Mellon U (PA)
Carson-Newman Coll (TN)
The Catholic U of America (DC)
Cedar Crest Coll (PA)
Central Michigan U (MI)
Chapman U (CA)
Charter Oak State Coll (CT)
Chatham U (PA)
Chestnut Hill Coll (PA)
Chicago State U (IL)
Christian Brothers U (TN)
Clarkson U (NY)
Clayton State U (GA)
Cleveland State U (OH)
Coastal Carolina U (SC)
Coe Coll (IA)
Coll of Mount St. Joseph (OH)
Coll of Mount Saint Vincent (NY)
Coll of Saint Benedict (MN)
Coll of St. Joseph (VT)
The Coll of Saint Rose (NY)
Coll of Staten Island of the City U of New York (NY)
Coll of the Atlantic (ME)
Colorado Mesa U (CO)
Colorado State U (CO)
Columbia Coll (SC)
Columbia Coll Chicago (IL)
Columbus State U (GA)
Concordia Coll–New York (NY)
Concordia U (CA)
Concordia U Texas (TX)
Corban U (OR)
Cornell Coll (IA)
Cornell U (NY)
Culver-Stockton Coll (MO)
Dakota State U (SD)
Dallas Baptist U (TX)
Defiance Coll (OH)
DEREE - The American Coll of Greece (Greece)
DeSales U (PA)
Dominican U of California (CA)
Dowling Coll (NY)
Duquesne U (PA)
East Carolina U (NC)
Eastern Illinois U (IL)
Eastern Mennonite U (VA)
Eastern New Mexico U (NM)
Eastern Oregon U (OR)
East Stroudsburg U of Pennsylvania (PA)
East Tennessee State U (TN)
Elmira Coll (NY)
Emmanuel Coll (MA)
Emory U (GA)
Emory U, Oxford Coll (GA)
Endicott Coll (MA)
The Evergreen State Coll (WA)
Excelsior Coll (NY)
Faulkner U (AL)
Felician Coll (NJ)
Ferrum Coll (VA)
Fitchburg State U (MA)
Flagler Coll (FL)
Florida Atlantic U (FL)
Florida Coll (FL)
Florida Gulf Coast U (FL)
Florida Intl U (FL)
Fontbonne U (MO)
Fordham U (NY)
Fort Hays State U (KS)
Fort Lewis Coll (CO)
Framingham State U (MA)
Francis Marion U (SC)
Friends U (KS)
Gannon U (PA)
George Mason U (VA)
Georgetown Coll (KY)
The George Washington U (DC)
Gettysburg Coll (PA)
Gonzaga U (WA)
Governors State U (IL)
Graceland U (IA)
Grand Valley State U (MI)
Grand View U (IA)

INDEXES

Granite State Coll (NH)
Greenville Coll (IL)
Hannibal-LaGrange U (MO)
Harvard U (MA)
Hillsdale Free Will Baptist Coll (OK)
Hofstra U (NY)
Holy Cross Coll (IN)
Hope Intl U (CA)
Houghton Coll (NY)
Howard Payne U (TX)
Humboldt State U (CA)
Husson U (ME)
Illinois Coll (IL)
Illinois Inst of Technology (IL)
Illinois Wesleyan U (IL)
Immaculata U (PA)
Indiana State U (IN)
Indiana U Bloomington (IN)
Iona Coll (NY)
Iowa State U of Science and
 Technology (IA)
Iowa Wesleyan Coll (IA)
Ithaca Coll (NY)
Jacksonville U (FL)
James Madison U (VA)
The Johns Hopkins U (MD)
Johnson C. Smith U (NC)
Johnson State Coll (VT)
Juniata Coll (PA)
Kent State U (OH)
Kent State U at Ashtabula (OH)
Kent State U at Tuscarawas (OH)
Kentucky State U (KY)
Keuka Coll (NY)
Lakehead U (ON, Canada)
Lake Superior State U (MI)
Lamar U (TX)
La Roche Coll (PA)
Lasell Coll (MA)
La Sierra U (CA)
Lenoir-Rhyne U (NC)
Lewis U (IL)
Liberty U (VA)
Limestone Coll (SC)
Lincoln Memorial U (TN)
Lincoln U (MO)
Lindenwood U (MO)
Lock Haven U of Pennsylvania (PA)
Long Island U–Brooklyn Campus
 (NY)
Long Island U–C. W. Post Campus
 (NY)
Longwood U (VA)
Louisiana Coll (LA)
Louisiana State U and Ag and Mech
 Coll (LA)
Loyola Marymount U (CA)
Lubbock Christian U (TX)
Lynn U (FL)
Manchester Coll (IN)
Manhattan Coll (NY)
Mansfield U of Pennsylvania (PA)
Marian U (WI)
Marietta Coll (OH)
Mars Hill Coll (NC)
Marymount Coll, Palos Verdes,
 California (CA)
Marymount Manhattan Coll (NY)
Marymount U (VA)
Maryville U of Saint Louis (MO)
Massachusetts Coll of Liberal Arts
 (MA)
Massachusetts Inst of Technology
 (MA)
The Master's Coll and Sem (CA)
McNeese State U (LA)
Medaille Coll (NY)
Mercy Coll (NY)
Merrimack Coll (MA)
Metropolitan State U (MN)
Miami U (OH)
Michigan Technological U (MI)
Middlebury Coll (VT)
Middle Tennessee State U (TN)
Midwestern State U (TX)
Misericordia U (PA)
Mississippi State U (MS)
Mississippi U for Women (MS)
Mitchell Coll (CT)
Monmouth Coll (IL)
Montana State U (MT)
Montana State U Billings (MT)
Montana State U–Northern (MT)
Montana Tech of The U of Montana
 (MT)

Morris Coll (SC)
Mount Allison U (NB, Canada)
Mount Aloysius Coll (PA)
Mount Ida Coll (MA)
Mount Marty Coll (SD)
Mount Mary Coll (WI)
Mount St. Mary's Coll (CA)
National-Louis U (IL)
Neumann U (PA)
New Coll of Florida (FL)
Newman U (KS)
New Mexico Highlands U (NM)
New Saint Andrews Coll (ID)
New York City Coll of Technology of
 the City U of New York (NY)
New York U (NY)
Niagara U (NY)
North Carolina Ag and Tech State U
 (NC)
North Carolina State U (NC)
North Central Coll (IL)
Northeastern Illinois U (IL)
Northern Arizona U (AZ)
Northern Illinois U (IL)
Northern Kentucky U (KY)
Northern Michigan U (MI)
North Greenville U (SC)
Northwestern U (IA)
Northwestern State U of Louisiana
 (LA)
Northwest Nazarene U (ID)
Notre Dame de Namur U (CA)
Notre Dame of Maryland U (MD)
Oakland U (MI)
Occidental Coll (CA)
Ohio Valley U (WV)
Oklahoma Christian U (OK)
Oklahoma City U (OK)
Oklahoma State U (OK)
Oral Roberts U (OK)
Pacific U (OR)
Park U (MO)
Patrick Henry Coll (VA)
Penn State Abington (PA)
Penn State Altoona (PA)
Penn State Beaver (PA)
Penn State Berks (PA)
Penn State Brandywine (PA)
Penn State DuBois (PA)
Penn State Erie, The Behrend Coll
 (PA)
Penn State Fayette, The Eberly
 Campus (PA)
Penn State Greater Allegheny (PA)
Penn State Lehigh Valley (PA)
Penn State Mont Alto (PA)
Penn State New Kensington (PA)
Penn State Schuylkill (PA)
Penn State Shenango (PA)
Penn State U Park (PA)
Penn State Wilkes-Barre (PA)
Penn State Worthington Scranton
 (PA)
Penn State York (PA)
Pepperdine U, Malibu (CA)
Peru State Coll (NE)
Point Loma Nazarene U (CA)
Point Park U (PA)
Pomona Coll (CA)
Portland State U (OR)
Post U (CT)
Providence Coll (RI)
Purchase Coll, State U of New York
 (NY)
Purdue U North Central (IN)
Quincy U (IL)
Quinnipiac U (CT)
Ramapo Coll of New Jersey (NJ)
Randolph Coll (VA)
Regis Coll (MA)
Regis U (CO)
Reinhardt U (GA)
Rhode Island Coll (RI)
The Richard Stockton Coll of New
 Jersey (NJ)
Rider U (NJ)
Rivier Coll (NH)
Roberts Wesleyan Coll (NY)
Rogers State U (OK)
Roger Williams U (RI)
Roosevelt U (IL)
Rowan U (NJ)
Rutgers, The State U of New
 Jersey, Camden (NJ)

Rutgers, The State U of New
 Jersey, New Brunswick (NJ)
Sacred Heart Major Sem (MI)
St. Edward's U (TX)
St. John Fisher Coll (NY)
St. John's Coll (MD)
St. John's Coll (NM)
Saint John's U (MN)
St. John's U (NY)
St. Joseph's Coll, Long Island
 Campus (NY)
St. Joseph's Coll, New York (NY)
Saint Joseph's Coll of Maine (ME)
Saint Joseph Sem Coll (LA)
Saint Joseph's U (PA)
Saint Leo U (FL)
Saint Mary-of-the-Woods Coll (IN)
Saint Mary's Coll of California (CA)
St. Olaf Coll (MN)
Saint Peter's Coll (NJ)
St. Thomas U (FL)
Saint Vincent Coll (PA)
Saint Xavier U (IL)
Salisbury U (MD)
Salve Regina U (RI)
San Diego Christian Coll (CA)
San Diego State U (CA)
San Francisco State U (CA)
Santa Clara U (CA)
Sarah Lawrence Coll (NY)
Schreiner U (TX)
Seattle Pacific U (WA)
Seattle U (WA)
Shaw U (NC)
Shenandoah U (VA)
Shimer Coll (IL)
Shorter U (GA)
Simmons Coll (MA)
Simon Fraser U (BC, Canada)
Simpson U (CA)
Skidmore Coll (NY)
Soka U of America (CA)
Sonoma State U (CA)
South Dakota State U (SD)
Southern Connecticut State U (CT)
Southern Illinois U Carbondale (IL)
Southern Illinois U Edwardsville (IL)
Southern Oregon U (OR)
Southern Vermont Coll (VT)
Southwestern Christian U (OK)
Southwestern Coll (KS)
Spalding U (KY)
State U of New York at Fredonia
 (NY)
State U of New York at New Paltz
 (NY)
State U of New York at Plattsburgh
 (NY)
State U of New York Coll at
 Oneonta (NY)
Stephen F. Austin State U (TX)
Stephens Coll (MO)
Suffolk U (MA)
Susquehanna U (PA)
Sweet Briar Coll (VA)
Syracuse U (NY)
Tabor Coll (KS)
Tarleton State U (TX)
Texas Christian U (TX)
Texas Coll (TX)
Texas Tech U (TX)
Thomas Aquinas Coll (CA)
Thomas Edison State Coll (NJ)
Thomas More Coll (KY)
Thomas More Coll of Liberal Arts
 (NH)
Thomas U (GA)
Thompson Rivers U (BC, Canada)
Touro Coll (NY)
Transylvania U (KY)
Trent U (ON, Canada)
Trine U (IN)
Troy U (AL)
Tulane U (LA)
Union Coll (NY)
Union Inst & U (OH)
U at Buffalo, the State U of New
 York (NY)
The U of Akron (OH)
U of Alaska Fairbanks (AK)
U of Alberta (AB, Canada)
U of Arkansas at Little Rock (AR)
The U of British Columbia (BC,
 Canada)
U of California, Riverside (CA)

U of California, Santa Barbara (CA)
U of Cincinnati (OH)
U of Delaware (DE)
U of Evansville (IN)
U of Georgia (GA)
U of Hawaii at Manoa (HI)
U of Houston (TX)
U of Houston–Downtown (TX)
U of Houston–Victoria (TX)
U of Illinois at Springfield (IL)
U of Illinois at Urbana–Champaign
 (IL)
The U of Iowa (IA)
The U of Kansas (KS)
U of La Verne (CA)
U of Lethbridge (AB, Canada)
U of Louisville (KY)
U of Maine (ME)
U of Maine at Augusta (ME)
U of Maine at Farmington (ME)
U of Maine at Fort Kent (ME)
U of Maine at Presque Isle (ME)
U of Maryland Eastern Shore (MD)
U of Mary Washington (VA)
U of Massachusetts Dartmouth
 (MA)
U of Massachusetts Lowell (MA)
U of Memphis (TN)
U of Michigan–Dearborn (MI)
U of Michigan–Flint (MI)
U of Minnesota, Twin Cities
 Campus (MN)
U of Mississippi (MS)
U of Missouri–St. Louis (MO)
U of Nebraska–Lincoln (NE)
U of New England (ME)
U of New Haven (CT)
U of New Mexico (NM)
The U of North Carolina at Asheville
 (NC)
The U of North Carolina at Chapel
 Hill (NC)
U of Northern Iowa (IA)
U of North Florida (FL)
U of Notre Dame (IN)
U of Oklahoma (OK)
U of Pennsylvania (PA)
U of Pittsburgh (PA)
U of Redlands (CA)
U of Regina (SK, Canada)
U of St. Francis (IL)
U of Saint Francis (IN)
U of Saint Mary (KS)
U of St. Thomas (TX)
U of San Diego (CA)
The U of Scranton (PA)
U of South Carolina (SC)
U of South Carolina Aiken (SC)
U of South Carolina Beaufort (SC)
The U of South Dakota (SD)
U of Southern Indiana (IN)
U of Southern Maine (ME)
U of South Florida (FL)
The U of Tampa (FL)
The U of Texas at Austin (TX)
The U of Texas at Tyler (TX)
U of the Incarnate Word (TX)
The U of Toledo (OH)
U of Tulsa (OK)
U of Vermont (VT)
U of Virginia (VA)
The U of Virginia's Coll at Wise (VA)
U of Washington (WA)
The U of Western Ontario (ON,
 Canada)
U of Wisconsin–Eau Claire (WI)
U of Wisconsin–Green Bay (WI)
U of Wisconsin–Platteville (WI)
U of Wisconsin–River Falls (WI)
U of Wisconsin–Whitewater (WI)
Utah State U (UT)
Utica Coll (NY)
Valdosta State U (GA)
Villanova U (PA)
Virginia State U (VA)
Viterbo U (WI)
Walsh U (OH)
Washburn U (KS)
Washington Adventist U (MD)
Washington Coll (MD)
Washington State U (WA)
Washington U in St. Louis (MO)
Weber State U (UT)
Webster U (MO)

West Chester U of Pennsylvania
 (PA)
Western Carolina U (NC)
Western Connecticut State U (CT)
Western Illinois U (IL)
Western New England U (MA)
Western Washington U (WA)
Westfield State U (MA)
West Virginia U (WV)
Wheeling Jesuit U (WV)
Wheelock Coll (MA)
Whittier Coll (CA)
Wilkes U (PA)
William Jewell Coll (MO)
William Paterson U of New Jersey
 (NJ)
Williams Baptist Coll (AR)
Wilmington Coll (OH)
Wingate U (NC)
Wittenberg U (OH)
Wright State U (OH)
Xavier U (OH)
York Coll of the City U of New York
 (NY)
Youngstown State U (OH)

**LIBRARY AND INFORMATION
SCIENCE**

Ball State U (IN)
Clarion U of Pennsylvania (PA)
Kutztown U of Pennsylvania (PA)
Southern Connecticut State U (CT)
U of Maine at Augusta (ME)
U of Minnesota, Twin Cities
 Campus (MN)
U of Nebraska at Omaha (NE)
U of Southern Mississippi (MS)

LIBRARY SCIENCE RELATED

Delaware State U (DE)
U of Great Falls (MT)

**LICENSED PRACTICAL/
VOCATIONAL NURSE
TRAINING**

Crown Coll (MN)
The U of Western Ontario (ON,
 Canada)
York Coll of Pennsylvania (PA)

**LINGUISTIC AND
COMPARATIVE LANGUAGE
STUDIES RELATED**

Brigham Young U (UT)
Iowa State U of Science and
 Technology (IA)
U of California, Los Angeles (CA)
U of California, Santa Barbara (CA)

LINGUISTICS

Baylor U (TX)
Bethel U (MN)
Biola U (CA)
Boston U (MA)
Brandeis U (MA)
Brown U (RI)
California State U, Chico (CA)
California State U, Dominguez Hills
 (CA)
California State U, Fresno (CA)
California State U, Fullerton (CA)
California State U, Monterey Bay
 (CA)
Calvin Coll (MI)
Carleton Coll (MN)
Carnegie Mellon U (PA)
Central Coll (IA)
City Coll of the City U of New York
 (NY)
Cleveland State U (OH)
The Coll of William and Mary (VA)
Concordia U (QC, Canada)
Cornell U (NY)
Crown Coll (MN)
Dartmouth Coll (NH)
Eastern Michigan U (MI)
Emory U (GA)
Florida Atlantic U (FL)
Georgia State U (GA)
Gordon Coll (MA)
Hampshire Coll (MA)
Harvard U (MA)
Hofstra U (NY)

Indiana U Bloomington (IN)
Inter American U of Puerto Rico, San Germán Campus (PR)
Iowa State U of Science and Technology (IA)
Lawrence U (WI)
Lehman Coll of the City U of New York (NY)
Liberty U (VA)
Macalester Coll (MN)
Marlboro Coll (VT)
Massachusetts Inst of Technology (MA)
Miami U (OH)
Michigan State U (MI)
Mid-Atlantic Christian U (NC)
Montclair State U (NJ)
New York U (NY)
Northeastern Illinois U (IL)
Northeastern U (MA)
Oakland U (MI)
The Ohio State U (OH)
Ohio U (OH)
Pitzer Coll (CA)
Pomona Coll (CA)
Portland State U (OR)
Purdue U (IN)
Queens Coll of the City U of New York (NY)
Queen's U at Kingston (ON, Canada)
Rice U (TX)
Rutgers, The State U of New Jersey, New Brunswick (NJ)
San Diego State U (CA)
Scripps Coll (CA)
Seattle Pacific U (WA)
Simon Fraser U (BC, Canada)
Southern Illinois U Carbondale (IL)
Stanford U (CA)
State U of New York at Binghamton (NY)
State U of New York at Oswego (NY)
Stony Brook U, State U of New York (NY)
Swarthmore Coll (PA)
Syracuse U (NY)
Temple U (PA)
Truman State U (MO)
Tulane U (LA)
U at Albany, State U of New York (NY)
U at Buffalo, the State U of New York (NY)
U of Alaska Fairbanks (AK)
U of Alberta (AB, Canada)
The U of Arizona (AZ)
The U of British Columbia (BC, Canada)
U of California, Berkeley (CA)
U of California, Davis (CA)
U of California, Los Angeles (CA)
U of California, Riverside (CA)
U of California, Santa Barbara (CA)
U of California, Santa Cruz (CA)
U of Cincinnati (OH)
U of Colorado Boulder (CO)
U of Connecticut (CT)
U of Delaware (DE)
U of Florida (FL)
U of Georgia (GA)
U of Hawaii at Hilo (HI)
U of Houston (TX)
U of Illinois at Urbana–Champaign (IL)
The U of Iowa (IA)
The U of Kansas (KS)
U of Maryland, Coll Park (MD)
U of Massachusetts Amherst (MA)
U of Michigan (MI)
U of Minnesota, Twin Cities Campus (MN)
U of Mississippi (MS)
U of Missouri (MO)
U of New Hampshire (NH)
U of New Mexico (NM)
The U of North Carolina at Chapel Hill (NC)
U of Oklahoma (OK)
U of Oregon (OR)
U of Ottawa (ON, Canada)
U of Pennsylvania (PA)
U of Pittsburgh (PA)
U of Regina (SK, Canada)

U of Rochester (NY)
U of Southern California (CA)
U of Southern Maine (ME)
The U of Texas at Arlington (TX)
The U of Texas at Austin (TX)
The U of Texas at El Paso (TX)
The U of Toledo (OH)
U of Toronto (ON, Canada)
U of Utah (UT)
U of Washington (WA)
The U of Western Ontario (ON, Canada)
U of Wisconsin–Madison (WI)
U of Wisconsin–Milwaukee (WI)
Washington State U (WA)
Washington U in St. Louis (MO)
Wayne State U (MI)
Wellesley Coll (MA)
Western Washington U (WA)
Yale U (CT)

LITERATURE

American U (DC)
Calvin Coll (MI)
Concordia U, St. Paul (MN)
Duquesne U (PA)
Franklin Coll Switzerland (Switzerland)
Huntington U (IN)
Massachusetts Coll of Liberal Arts (MA)
Mississippi Coll (MS)
Saint Mary's U of Minnesota (MN)
Southwestern Coll (KS)
Washington U in St. Louis (MO)
Williams Coll (MA)
Yeshiva U (NY)

LITERATURE RELATED

The American U of Paris (France)

LIVESTOCK MANAGEMENT

Fort Hays State U (KS)

LOGIC

Carnegie Mellon U (PA)
U of Pennsylvania (PA)

LOGISTICS, MATERIALS, AND SUPPLY CHAIN MANAGEMENT

Albany State U (GA)
American Public U System (WV)
Auburn U (AL)
Baylor U (TX)
Bowling Green State U (OH)
Brigham Young U (UT)
California State U, Dominguez Hills (CA)
Central Michigan U (MI)
Clarkson U (NY)
Clayton State U (GA)
Concordia U (QC, Canada)
Duquesne U (PA)
Eastern Michigan U (MI)
Elmhurst Coll (IL)
Florida Inst of Technology (FL)
Georgia Southern U (GA)
Hofstra U (NY)
Iowa State U of Science and Technology (IA)
Lehigh U (PA)
Michigan State U (MI)
Missouri State U (MO)
Niagara U (NY)
Northeastern State U (OK)
Northeastern U (MA)
The Ohio State U (OH)
Park U (MO)
Penn State Beaver (PA)
Penn State Brandywine (PA)
Penn State Fayette, The Eberly Campus (PA)
Penn State Greater Allegheny (PA)
Penn State Hazleton (PA)
Penn State Lehigh Valley (PA)
Penn State New Kensington (PA)
Penn State Schuylkill (PA)
Penn State Shenango (PA)
Penn State York (PA)
Portland State U (OR)
Shippensburg U of Pennsylvania (PA)
Southeastern Louisiana U (LA)

State U of New York at Binghamton (NY)
State U of New York at New Paltz (NY)
Sullivan U (KY)
Syracuse U (NY)
U of Arkansas (AR)
The U of Findlay (OH)
U of Illinois at Urbana–Champaign (IL)
The U of Kansas (KS)
U of Maryland, Coll Park (MD)
U of Memphis (TN)
U of North Texas (TX)
U of Puerto Rico at Bayamón (PR)
The U of Tennessee (TN)
The U of Texas at Austin (TX)
The U of Toledo (OH)
U of Wisconsin–Stout (WI)
Weber State U (UT)
Western Illinois U (IL)
Western Michigan U (MI)
Wright State U (OH)
York Coll of Pennsylvania (PA)

MAGNETIC RESONANCE IMAGING (MRI) TECHNOLOGY

Saint Louis U (MO)

MANAGEMENT INFORMATION SYSTEMS

Adams State Coll (CO)
Albany State U (GA)
Amberton U (TX)
American U (DC)
Angelo State U (TX)
Anna Maria Coll (MA)
Appalachian State U (NC)
Arcadia U (PA)
Auburn U (AL)
Auburn U Montgomery (AL)
Augustana Coll (SD)
Avila U (MO)
Azusa Pacific U (CA)
Babson Coll (MA)
Baker Coll of Flint (MI)
Ball State U (IN)
Barry U (FL)
Bayamón Central U (PR)
Baylor U (TX)
Bellevue U (NE)
Bernard M. Baruch Coll of the City U of New York (NY)
Bethel U (TN)
Biola U (CA)
Bishop's U (QC, Canada)
Boston Coll (MA)
Boston U (MA)
Bowling Green State U (OH)
Bradley U (IL)
Briar Cliff U (IA)
Bridgewater Coll (VA)
Bridgewater State U (MA)
Buena Vista U (IA)
California State U, Chico (CA)
California State U, East Bay (CA)
California State U, Fresno (CA)
California State U, Long Beach (CA)
California State U, San Bernardino (CA)
Calvin Coll (MI)
Canisius Coll (NY)
Carson-Newman Coll (TN)
Cedarville U (OH)
Central Connecticut State U (CT)
Central Michigan U (MI)
Claflin U (SC)
Clarkson U (NY)
Cleary U (MI)
Clemson U (SC)
Cleveland State U (OH)
Colorado Mesa U (CO)
Colorado State U (CO)
Columbia Coll (MO)
Columbus State U (GA)
Concordia U (QC, Canada)
Concordia U, Nebraska (NE)
Concordia U, St. Paul (MN)
Corban U (OR)
Cornerstone U (MI)
Creighton U (NE)
Dallas Baptist U (TX)
Dalton State Coll (GA)

Daniel Webster Coll (NH)
Delaware Valley Coll (PA)
Delta State U (MS)
DePaul U (IL)
DeSales U (PA)
Dominican Coll (NY)
Dordt Coll (IA)
Drexel U (PA)
Drury U (MO)
Duquesne U (PA)
East Carolina U (NC)
Eastern Connecticut State U (CT)
Eastern Kentucky U (KY)
Eastern Michigan U (MI)
Eastern New Mexico U (NM)
Eastern U (PA)
Eastern Washington U (WA)
Edgewood Coll (WI)
Elizabethtown Coll (PA)
Elmhurst Coll (IL)
Excelsior Coll (NY)
Fairfield U (CT)
Fayetteville State U (NC)
Felician Coll (NJ)
Ferrum Coll (VA)
Florida Atlantic U (FL)
Florida Inst of Technology (FL)
Florida Intl U (FL)
Fordham U (NY)
Fort Hays State U (KS)
Francis Marion U (SC)
Franklin U (OH)
Gannon U (PA)
Gardner-Webb U (NC)
George Fox U (OR)
Georgia Southern U (GA)
Goldey-Beacom Coll (DE)
Governors State U (IL)
Grace Coll (IN)
Graceland U (IA)
Grand View U (IA)
Greenville Coll (IL)
Hardin-Simmons U (TX)
HEC Montreal (QC, Canada)
Hofstra U (NY)
Holy Family U (PA)
Howard Payne U (TX)
Husson U (ME)
Illinois Coll (IL)
Immaculata U (PA)
Indiana State U (IN)
Indiana U East (IN)
Indiana U of Pennsylvania (PA)
Inter American U of Puerto Rico, Bayamón Campus (PR)
Inter American U of Puerto Rico, Fajardo Campus (PR)
Inter American U of Puerto Rico, Ponce Campus (PR)
Inter American U of Puerto Rico, San Germán Campus (PR)
Iona Coll (NY)
Iowa State U of Science and Technology (IA)
Jacksonville U (FL)
Jamestown Coll (ND)
John Brown U (AR)
Johnson State Coll (VT)
Judson U (IL)
King Coll (TN)
Lakehead U (ON, Canada)
La Salle U (PA)
Lehigh U (PA)
Le Moyne Coll (NY)
Lenoir-Rhyne U (NC)
LeTourneau U (TX)
Lewis U (IL)
Liberty U (VA)
Lindenwood U (MO)
Lipscomb U (TN)
Longwood U (VA)
Loras Coll (IA)
Loyola U Chicago (IL)
Lubbock Christian U (TX)
Luther Coll (IA)
Madonna U (MI)
Marshall U (WV)
Maryville U of Saint Louis (MO)
Massachusetts Coll of Liberal Arts (MA)
The Master's Coll and Sem (CA)
McMurry U (TX)
Menlo Coll (CA)
Metropolitan State U (MN)
Miami U (OH)

Michigan Technological U (MI)
Middle Tennessee State U (TN)
Millikin U (IL)
Milwaukee School of Eng (WI)
Minot State U (ND)
Misericordia U (PA)
Mississippi State U (MS)
Missouri State U (MO)
Morehead State U (KY)
Mount Mercy U (IA)
Mount Vernon Nazarene U (OH)
National-Louis U (IL)
National U (CA)
Newman U (KS)
New Mexico Highlands U (NM)
New York Inst of Technology (NY)
Nicholls State U (LA)
Nichols Coll (MA)
North Central Coll (IL)
North Dakota State U (ND)
Northeastern State U (OK)
Northeastern U (MA)
Northern Arizona U (AZ)
Northern Illinois U (IL)
Northern Kentucky U (KY)
Northern Michigan U (MI)
Northern State U (SD)
Northwestern Coll (MN)
Northwest Missouri State U (MO)
Northwood U, Michigan Campus (MI)
Oakland U (MI)
Ohio Northern U (OH)
The Ohio State U (OH)
Ohio U (OH)
Oklahoma City U (OK)
Oklahoma State U (OK)
Old Dominion U (VA)
Oral Roberts U (OK)
Oregon Inst of Technology (OR)
Park U (MO)
Penn State Abington (PA)
Penn State Altoona (PA)
Penn State Beaver (PA)
Penn State Berks (PA)
Penn State Brandywine (PA)
Penn State DuBois (PA)
Penn State Erie, The Behrend Coll (PA)
Penn State Fayette, The Eberly Campus (PA)
Penn State Greater Allegheny (PA)
Penn State Harrisburg (PA)
Penn State Hazleton (PA)
Penn State Lehigh Valley (PA)
Penn State Mont Alto (PA)
Penn State New Kensington (PA)
Penn State Schuylkill (PA)
Penn State Shenango (PA)
Penn State U Park (PA)
Penn State Wilkes-Barre (PA)
Penn State Worthington Scranton (PA)
Penn State York (PA)
Peru State Coll (NE)
Philadelphia U (PA)
Pittsburg State U (KS)
Point Loma Nazarene U (CA)
Post U (CT)
Prairie View A&M U (TX)
Regis U (CO)
Rhode Island Coll (RI)
Robert Morris U (PA)
Rochester Inst of Technology (NY)
Rockford Coll (IL)
Rocky Mountain Coll (MT)
Roger Williams U (RI)
Rowan U (NJ)
St. Catherine U (MN)
Saint Francis U (PA)
St. John's U (NY)
Saint Joseph's U (PA)
Saint Louis U (MO)
Saint Mary's Coll (IN)
Salem State U (MA)
Santa Clara U (CA)
Schreiner U (TX)
Seattle U (WA)
Seton Hill U (PA)
Shawnee State U (OH)
Simmons Coll (MA)
Simon Fraser U (BC, Canada)
Sojourner-Douglass Coll (MD)
Southeastern U (FL)
Southern Illinois U Edwardsville (IL)

Southwestern Coll (KS)
Spring Arbor U (MI)
State U of New York at Binghamton (NY)
State U of New York at Plattsburgh (NY)
State U of New York Coll at Old Westbury (NY)
State U of New York Coll of Technology at Canton (NY)
Stetson U (FL)
Suffolk U (MA)
Tarleton State U (TX)
Temple U (PA)
Texas A&M U–Corpus Christi (TX)
Texas A&M U–Kingsville (TX)
Texas Southern U (TX)
Texas State U–San Marcos (TX)
Texas Wesleyan U (TX)
Thiel Coll (PA)
Trident U Intl (CA)
Troy U (AL)
Universidad del Turabo (PR)
The U of Alabama (AL)
The U of Alabama at Birmingham (AL)
The U of Alabama in Huntsville (AL)
U of Alaska Anchorage (AK)
U of Alberta (AB, Canada)
The U of Arizona (AZ)
U of Arkansas at Monticello (AR)
U of Bridgeport (CT)
The U of British Columbia (BC, Canada)
U of Central Arkansas (AR)
U of Central Missouri (MO)
U of Colorado Boulder (CO)
U of Connecticut (CT)
U of Dayton (OH)
U of Delaware (DE)
U of Denver (CO)
U of Evansville (IN)
U of Georgia (GA)
U of Hawaii at Manoa (HI)
U of Houston (TX)
U of Houston–Downtown (TX)
U of Idaho (ID)
U of Illinois at Springfield (IL)
U of Illinois at Urbana–Champaign (IL)
The U of Iowa (IA)
The U of Kansas (KS)
U of Lethbridge (AB, Canada)
U of Louisiana at Lafayette (LA)
U of Louisiana at Monroe (LA)
U of Louisville (KY)
U of Maine (ME)
U of Mary (ND)
U of Mary Hardin-Baylor (TX)
U of Massachusetts Dartmouth (MA)
U of Memphis (TN)
U of Michigan–Dearborn (MI)
U of Minnesota, Twin Cities Campus (MN)
U of Mississippi (MS)
U of Missouri (MO)
U of Missouri–St. Louis (MO)
U of Nevada, Las Vegas (NV)
U of New Orleans (LA)
U of North Alabama (AL)
The U of North Carolina at Charlotte (NC)
The U of North Carolina Wilmington (NC)
U of Northern Iowa (IA)
U of North Texas (TX)
U of Notre Dame (IN)
U of Oklahoma (OK)
U of Ottawa (ON, Canada)
U of Pennsylvania (PA)
U of Puget Sound (WA)
U of Redlands (CA)
U of Southern Mississippi (MS)
U of South Florida (FL)
U of South Florida–St. Petersburg Campus (FL)
The U of Tennessee at Martin (TN)
The U of Texas at Arlington (TX)
The U of Texas at Austin (TX)
The U of Texas at Dallas (TX)
The U of Texas at San Antonio (TX)
The U of Texas–Pan American (TX)
U of the Cumberlands (KY)
U of the Incarnate Word (TX)

The U of Toledo (OH)
U of Tulsa (OK)
U of Utah (UT)
U of Washington (WA)
The U of West Alabama (AL)
The U of Western Ontario (ON, Canada)
U of West Florida (FL)
U of West Georgia (GA)
U of Wisconsin–Green Bay (WI)
U of Wisconsin–La Crosse (WI)
U of Wisconsin–Madison (WI)
U of Wisconsin–Milwaukee (WI)
U of Wisconsin–River Falls (WI)
U of Wisconsin–Whitewater (WI)
Upper Iowa U (IA)
Ursuline Coll (OH)
Villanova U (PA)
Virginia Union U (VA)
Viterbo U (WI)
Wake Forest U (NC)
Washington State U (WA)
Wayne State U (MI)
Weber State U (UT)
Webster U (MO)
Western Carolina U (NC)
Western Connecticut State U (CT)
Western Kentucky U (KY)
Western New England U (MA)
Western State Coll of Colorado (CO)
Western Washington U (WA)
Westminster Coll (MO)
West Texas A&M U (TX)
West Virginia U (WV)
West Virginia U Inst of Technology (WV)
Wichita State U (KS)
William Woods U (MO)
Winona State U (MN)
Worcester Polytechnic Inst (MA)
Wright State U (OH)
Xavier U (OH)
Yeshiva U (NY)
York Coll of Pennsylvania (PA)
York Coll of the City U of New York (NY)
Youngstown State U (OH)

MANAGEMENT INFORMATION SYSTEMS AND SERVICES RELATED

Buena Vista U (IA)
California State U, Chico (CA)
Fordham U (NY)
Midwestern State U (TX)
Montana Tech of The U of Montana (MT)
Northern Michigan U (MI)
Rogers State U (OK)
St. Bonaventure U (NY)
Thomas Edison State Coll (NJ)
Westminster Coll (UT)
Widener U (PA)

MANAGEMENT SCIENCE

Bridgewater State U (MA)
California Coast U (CA)
Cambridge Coll (MA)
Canisius Coll (NY)
The Catholic U of America (DC)
Centenary Coll (NJ)
Central Methodist U (MO)
Dalhousie U (NS, Canada)
DePaul U (IL)
DEREE - The American Coll of Greece (Greece)
Duquesne U (PA)
Eastern Illinois U (IL)
Elon U (NC)
Fitchburg State U (MA)
Georgia Inst of Technology (GA)
Grand Valley State U (MI)
Granite State Coll (NH)
Hardin-Simmons U (TX)
Hawai`i Pacific U (HI)
HEC Montreal (QC, Canada)
Inter American U of Puerto Rico, Bayamón Campus (PR)
Inter American U of Puerto Rico, San Germán Campus (PR)
John Brown U (AR)
La Roche Coll (PA)
Lehigh U (PA)

Lenoir-Rhyne U (NC)
Louisiana State U and Ag and Mech Coll (LA)
Lourdes U (OH)
Manhattan Coll (NY)
Minnesota State U Mankato (MN)
National-Louis U (IL)
Northeastern U (MA)
Northern Illinois U (IL)
Oakland City U (IN)
Ohio Northern U (OH)
Oklahoma City U (OK)
Oral Roberts U (OK)
Peninsula Coll (WA)
Pine Manor Coll (MA)
Portland State U (OR)
Quincy U (IL)
Rider U (NJ)
Rocky Mountain Coll (MT)
Roosevelt U (IL)
Rowan U (NJ)
Rutgers, The State U of New Jersey, New Brunswick (NJ)
St. Ambrose U (IA)
Saint Joseph's Coll of Maine (ME)
Saint Leo U (FL)
Salve Regina U (RI)
Shippensburg U of Pennsylvania (PA)
Siena Coll (NY)
Simon Fraser U (BC, Canada)
Southeastern Oklahoma State U (OK)
Southern Illinois U Carbondale (IL)
Southwestern Assemblies of God U (TX)
State U of New York at Oswego (NY)
Texas A&M U (TX)
Texas Christian U (TX)
Trinity U (TX)
Tuskegee U (AL)
United States Coast Guard Acad (CT)
The U of Alabama (AL)
U of California, Merced (CA)
U of Connecticut (CT)
U of Delaware (DE)
U of Florida (FL)
U of Great Falls (MT)
U of Illinois at Chicago (IL)
U of Illinois at Urbana–Champaign (IL)
The U of Iowa (IA)
U of Mary (ND)
U of Maryland, Coll Park (MD)
U of Memphis (TN)
U of Miami (FL)
U of Minnesota, Duluth (MN)
U of Missouri–St. Louis (MO)
U of Nebraska–Lincoln (NE)
U of St. Francis (IL)
U of South Carolina (SC)
The U of Tennessee at Martin (TN)
The U of Texas at San Antonio (TX)
U of the Southwest (NM)
U of Washington (WA)
The U of Western Ontario (ON, Canada)
U of Wyoming (WY)
Valparaiso U (IN)
Vaughn Coll of Aeronautics and Technology (NY)
Virginia Polytechnic Inst and State U (VA)
Wake Forest U (NC)
Western Kentucky U (KY)
Wheeling Jesuit U (WV)

MANAGEMENT SCIENCES AND QUANTITATIVE METHODS RELATED

George Mason U (VA)
Georgia Coll & State U (GA)
Indiana State U (IN)
Inter American U of Puerto Rico, Fajardo Campus (PR)
Inter American U of Puerto Rico, Ponce Campus (PR)
Pace U (NY)
Penn State Lehigh Valley (PA)
Penn State Schuylkill (PA)
Rutgers, The State U of New Jersey, New Brunswick (NJ)

Southwest Minnesota State U (MN)
The U of Iowa (IA)
U of Pennsylvania (PA)
The U of Toledo (OH)

MANUFACTURING ENGINEERING

Boston U (MA)
Bradley U (IL)
Brigham Young U (UT)
California Polytechnic State U, San Luis Obispo (CA)
California State Polytechnic U, Pomona (CA)
Cape Breton U (NS, Canada)
Central Michigan U (MI)
Central State U (OH)
Fairfield U (CT)
Hofstra U (NY)
Miami U (OH)
New England Inst of Technology (RI)
North Dakota State U (ND)
Robert Morris U (PA)
Southern Illinois U Edwardsville (IL)
Texas State U–San Marcos (TX)
U of California, Berkeley (CA)
U of Connecticut (CT)
U of Illinois at Urbana–Champaign (IL)
U of Michigan–Dearborn (MI)
The U of Texas–Pan American (TX)
U of Toronto (ON, Canada)
U of Wisconsin–Milwaukee (WI)
U of Wisconsin–Stout (WI)
Virginia State U (VA)
Washington State U (WA)
Western Michigan U (MI)
Wichita State U (KS)

MANUFACTURING ENGINEERING TECHNOLOGY

Arizona State U (AZ)
Berea Coll (KY)
Bradley U (IL)
California State U, Long Beach (CA)
Central Connecticut State U (CT)
Central Michigan U (MI)
East Carolina U (NC)
Eastern Michigan U (MI)
Farmingdale State Coll (NY)
Ferris State U (MI)
Fitchburg State U (MA)
Indiana State U (IN)
Lewis-Clark State Coll (ID)
Midwestern State U (TX)
Missouri Western State U (MO)
Morehead State U (KY)
New England Inst of Technology (RI)
North Carolina Ag and Tech State U (NC)
Ohio Northern U (OH)
Pennsylvania Coll of Technology (PA)
Pittsburg State U (KS)
Rochester Inst of Technology (NY)
Roger Williams U (RI)
South Dakota State U (SD)
State U of New York Coll of Technology at Alfred (NY)
Tarleton State U (TX)
Temple U (PA)
Texas A&M U (TX)
Texas State U–San Marcos (TX)
Thomas Edison State Coll (NJ)
The U of Akron (OH)
U of Memphis (TN)
U of Northern Iowa (IA)
U of North Texas (TX)
U of Regina (SK, Canada)
U of Southern Indiana (IN)
Wayne State U (MI)
Western Carolina U (NC)
Western Kentucky U (KY)
Western Washington U (WA)

MARINE BIOLOGY AND BIOLOGICAL OCEANOGRAPHY

Alabama State U (AL)
Alaska Pacific U (AK)
Auburn U (AL)

Barry U (FL)
Bemidji State U (MN)
Boston U (MA)
Brown U (RI)
California State U, Long Beach (CA)
Coastal Carolina U (SC)
Coll of Charleston (SC)
Coll of the Atlantic (ME)
Dalhousie U (NS, Canada)
East Stroudsburg U of Pennsylvania (PA)
Eckerd Coll (FL)
Fairleigh Dickinson U, Coll at Florham (NJ)
Fairleigh Dickinson U, Metropolitan Campus (NJ)
Florida Inst of Technology (FL)
Florida Intl U (FL)
Gettysburg Coll (PA)
Hampton U (VA)
Hawai`i Pacific U (HI)
Humboldt State U (CA)
Jacksonville State U (AL)
Juniata Coll (PA)
Michigan Technological U (MI)
Monmouth U (NJ)
New Coll of Florida (FL)
Northeastern U (MA)
Northwest Missouri State U (MO)
Nova Southeastern U (FL)
Prescott Coll (AZ)
The Richard Stockton Coll of New Jersey (NJ)
Roger Williams U (RI)
Rollins Coll (FL)
Rutgers, The State U of New Jersey, New Brunswick (NJ)
Saint Francis U (PA)
Saint Joseph's Coll of Maine (ME)
Salem State U (MA)
Samford U (AL)
San Francisco State U (CA)
Sarah Lawrence Coll (NY)
Sonoma State U (CA)
Southwestern Coll (KS)
Spring Hill Coll (AL)
Stony Brook U, State U of New York (NY)
Suffolk U (MA)
Troy U (AL)
The U of Alabama (AL)
The U of British Columbia (BC, Canada)
U of California, Los Angeles (CA)
U of California, Santa Barbara (CA)
U of California, Santa Cruz (CA)
U of Connecticut (CT)
U of Guelph (ON, Canada)
U of Hawaii at Hilo (HI)
U of Hawaii at Manoa (HI)
U of Maine (ME)
U of Maryland Eastern Shore (MD)
U of Miami (FL)
U of Mobile (AL)
U of New England (ME)
U of New Haven (CT)
U of North Alabama (AL)
The U of North Carolina Wilmington (NC)
U of Oregon (OR)
U of Puerto Rico at Humacao (PR)
U of Puerto Rico at Ponce (PR)
U of Rhode Island (RI)
U of San Diego (CA)
U of South Carolina (SC)
U of Southern Mississippi (MS)
The U of Tampa (FL)
The U of West Alabama (AL)
U of West Florida (FL)
Waynesburg U (PA)
Western Washington U (WA)

MARINE MAINTENANCE AND SHIP REPAIR TECHNOLOGY

California Maritime Acad (CA)
Lamar U (TX)

MARINE SCIENCE/MERCHANT MARINE OFFICER

Hampton U (VA)
Jacksonville U (FL)
Massachusetts Maritime Acad (MA)

United States Merchant Marine Acad (NY)
U of Delaware (DE)
U of South Carolina (SC)

MARINE SCIENCES
California State U, Monterey Bay (CA)

MARINE TRANSPORTATION RELATED
United States Merchant Marine Acad (NY)

MARITIME STUDIES
Coll of the Atlantic (ME)
United States Merchant Marine Acad (NY)

MARKETING/MARKETING MANAGEMENT
Abilene Christian U (TX)
Adams State Coll (CO)
Alabama State U (AL)
Albany State U (GA)
Albertus Magnus Coll (CT)
Albright Coll (PA)
Alfred U (NY)
Alvernia U (PA)
Alverno Coll (WI)
Amberton U (TX)
American Public U System (WV)
Anderson U (IN)
Andrews U (MI)
Angelo State U (TX)
Appalachian State U (NC)
Arcadia U (PA)
Arizona State U (AZ)
Arkansas State U (AR)
Ashland U (OH)
Assumption Coll (MA)
Athabasca U (AB, Canada)
Auburn U (AL)
Auburn U Montgomery (AL)
Averett U (VA)
Avila U (MO)
Azusa Pacific U (CA)
Babson Coll (MA)
Baker Coll of Auburn Hills (MI)
Baker Coll of Owosso (MI)
Baldwin-Wallace Coll (OH)
Ball State U (IN)
Barry U (FL)
Barton Coll (NC)
Bayamón Central U (PR)
Baylor U (TX)
Bay Path Coll (MA)
Becker Coll (MA)
Belmont U (TN)
Benedictine U (IL)
Bentley U (MA)
Bernard M. Baruch Coll of the City U of New York (NY)
Berry Coll (GA)
Bethany Coll (KS)
Biola U (CA)
Bishop's U (QC, Canada)
Blackburn Coll (IL)
Black Hills State U (SD)
Bob Jones U (SC)
Boston Coll (MA)
Boston U (MA)
Bowie State U (MD)
Bradley U (IL)
Brenau U (GA)
Bridgewater State U (MA)
Bryant U (RI)
Buena Vista U (IA)
Butler U (IN)
Cabrini Coll (PA)
Caldwell Coll (NJ)
California Baptist U (CA)
California Coast U (CA)
California Lutheran U (CA)
California State U, Chico (CA)
California State U, Dominguez Hills (CA)
California State U, East Bay (CA)
California State U, Fresno (CA)
California State U, Fullerton (CA)
California State U, Long Beach (CA)
California State U, Sacramento (CA)

California State U, San Bernardino (CA)
Calvary Bible Coll and Theological Sem (MO)
Campbellsville U (KY)
Canisius Coll (NY)
Cape Breton U (NS, Canada)
Capella U (MN)
Capital U (OH)
Caribbean U (PR)
Carson-Newman Coll (TN)
Castleton State Coll (VT)
Catawba Coll (NC)
Cedarville U (OH)
Centenary Coll (NJ)
Central Connecticut State U (CT)
Central Michigan U (MI)
Chaminade U of Honolulu (HI)
Chatham U (PA)
Chestnut Hill Coll (PA)
Christopher Newport U (VA)
Claflin U (SC)
Clarion U of Pennsylvania (PA)
Clayton State U (GA)
Cleary U (MI)
Clemson U (SC)
Cleveland State U (OH)
Coastal Carolina U (SC)
The Coll at Brockport, State U of New York (NY)
The Coll of St. Scholastica (MN)
Coll of the Ozarks (MO)
The Coll of William and Mary (VA)
Colorado State U (CO)
Columbia Coll (MO)
Columbia Coll Chicago (IL)
Columbia Southern U (AL)
Columbus State U (GA)
Concordia U (QC, Canada)
Concordia U Chicago (IL)
Concordia U, St. Paul (MN)
Converse Coll (SC)
Cornerstone U (MI)
Creighton U (NE)
Dakota State U (SD)
Dalhousie U (NS, Canada)
Dallas Baptist U (TX)
Dalton State Coll (GA)
Daniel Webster Coll (NH)
Davenport U, Grand Rapids (MI)
Delaware State U (DE)
Delaware Valley Coll (PA)
Delta State U (MS)
DePaul U (IL)
DEREE - The American Coll of Greece (Greece)
DeSales U (PA)
Dominican Coll (NY)
Dowling Coll (NY)
Drake U (IA)
Drexel U (PA)
Drury U (MO)
Duquesne U (PA)
East Carolina U (NC)
Eastern Illinois U (IL)
Eastern Kentucky U (KY)
Eastern Michigan U (MI)
Eastern Washington U (WA)
East Tennessee State U (TN)
Elizabethtown Coll (PA)
Elmhurst Coll (IL)
Elmira Coll (NY)
Elon U (NC)
Emory U (GA)
Emporia State U (KS)
Evangel U (MO)
Excelsior Coll (NY)
Fairfield U (CT)
Fairleigh Dickinson U, Coll at Florham (NJ)
Fairleigh Dickinson U, Metropolitan Campus (NJ)
Faulkner U (AL)
Fayetteville State U (NC)
Felician Coll (NJ)
Ferris State U (MI)
Fitchburg State U (MA)
Florida Atlantic U (FL)
Florida Gulf Coast U (FL)
Florida Inst of Technology (FL)
Florida Intl U (FL)
Fontbonne U (MO)
Fordham U (NY)
Fort Hays State U (KS)
Fort Lewis Coll (CO)

Francis Marion U (SC)
Franklin U (OH)
Friends U (KS)
Gannon U (PA)
Gardner-Webb U (NC)
George Fox U (OR)
George Mason U (VA)
The George Washington U (DC)
Georgia Coll & State U (GA)
Georgia Southern U (GA)
Georgia Southwestern State U (GA)
Georgia State U (GA)
Goldey-Beacom Coll (DE)
Gonzaga U (WA)
Governors State U (IL)
Grace Coll (IN)
Grambling State U (LA)
Grand Canyon U (AZ)
Grand Valley State U (MI)
Greenville Coll (IL)
Grove City Coll (PA)
Hamline U (MN)
Hampton U (VA)
Hannibal-LaGrange U (MO)
Harding U (AR)
Hardin-Simmons U (TX)
Hawai`i Pacific U (HI)
HEC Montreal (QC, Canada)
Hillsdale Coll (MI)
Hofstra U (NY)
Holy Family U (PA)
Howard Payne U (TX)
Huntington U (IN)
Husson U (ME)
Idaho State U (ID)
Illinois State U (IL)
Immaculata U (PA)
Indiana State U (IN)
Indiana U of Pennsylvania (PA)
Indiana U–Purdue U Fort Wayne (IN)
Indiana Wesleyan U (IN)
Inter American U of Puerto Rico, Bayamón Campus (PR)
Inter American U of Puerto Rico, Fajardo Campus (PR)
Inter American U of Puerto Rico, Ponce Campus (PR)
Inter American U of Puerto Rico, San Germán Campus (PR)
Iona Coll (NY)
Iowa State U of Science and Technology (IA)
Ithaca Coll (NY)
Jacksonville State U (AL)
Jacksonville U (FL)
James Madison U (VA)
Jamestown Coll (ND)
John Brown U (AR)
John Carroll U (OH)
Johnson State Coll (VT)
Juniata Coll (PA)
Kansas State U (KS)
Kean U (NJ)
Kennesaw State U (GA)
Kent State U (OH)
Keuka Coll (NY)
King's Coll (PA)
Kutztown U of Pennsylvania (PA)
Lake Erie Coll (OH)
Lakehead U (ON, Canada)
Lamar U (TX)
La Roche Coll (PA)
La Salle U (PA)
Lasell Coll (MA)
La Sierra U (CA)
Lehigh U (PA)
Le Moyne Coll (NY)
Lenoir-Rhyne U (NC)
LeTourneau U (TX)
Lewis U (IL)
Limestone Coll (SC)
Lincoln Memorial U (TN)
Lindenwood U (MO)
Lipscomb U (TN)
Long Island U–Brooklyn Campus (NY)
Long Island U–C. W. Post Campus (NY)
Longwood U (VA)
Loras Coll (IA)
Louisiana Coll (LA)
Louisiana State U and Ag and Mech Coll (LA)

Louisiana State U in Shreveport (LA)
Loyola U Chicago (IL)
Loyola U New Orleans (LA)
Lubbock Christian U (TX)
Lynchburg Coll (VA)
Madonna U (MI)
Manchester Coll (IN)
Manhattan Coll (NY)
Mansfield U of Pennsylvania (PA)
Maranatha Baptist Bible Coll (WI)
Marian U (WI)
Marietta Coll (OH)
Marquette U (WI)
Marshall U (WV)
Mars Hill Coll (NC)
Maryville U of Saint Louis (MO)
Marywood U (PA)
Massachusetts Coll of Liberal Arts (MA)
McKendree U (IL)
McMurry U (TX)
McNeese State U (LA)
Menlo Coll (CA)
Merrimack Coll (MA)
Messiah Coll (PA)
Metropolitan State Coll of Denver (CO)
Metropolitan State U (MN)
Miami U (OH)
Michigan State U (MI)
Michigan Technological U (MI)
MidAmerica Nazarene U (KS)
Middle Tennessee State U (TN)
Midwestern State U (TX)
Millikin U (IL)
Minnesota State U Mankato (MN)
Minot State U (ND)
Misericordia U (PA)
Mississippi Coll (MS)
Mississippi State U (MS)
Missouri Baptist U (MO)
Missouri State U (MO)
Missouri Western State U (MO)
Mitchell Coll (CT)
Montana State U (MT)
Montana State U Billings (MT)
Morehead State U (KY)
Mount Mary Coll (WI)
Mount Mercy U (IA)
Mount St. Mary's Coll (CA)
Mount Vernon Nazarene U (OH)
National U (CA)
Nazareth Coll of Rochester (NY)
Neumann U (PA)
New England Coll (NH)
New England School of Communications (ME)
New Mexico Highlands U (NM)
New Mexico State U (NM)
New York Inst of Technology (NY)
Niagara U (NY)
Nicholls State U (LA)
Nichols Coll (MA)
North Carolina Ag and Tech State U (NC)
North Central Coll (IL)
North Dakota State U (ND)
Northeastern Illinois U (IL)
Northeastern State U (OK)
Northeastern U (MA)
Northern Arizona U (AZ)
Northern Illinois U (IL)
Northern Kentucky U (KY)
Northern Michigan U (MI)
Northern State U (SD)
North Georgia Coll & State U (GA)
North Greenville U (SC)
Northwestern Coll (MN)
Northwest Missouri State U (MO)
Northwest Nazarene U (ID)
Northwest U (WA)
Northwood U, Florida Campus (FL)
Northwood U, Michigan Campus (MI)
Northwood U, Texas Campus (TX)
Nova Southeastern U (FL)
Oakland U (MI)
The Ohio State U (OH)
Ohio U (OH)
Ohio Valley U (WV)
Oklahoma Christian U (OK)
Oklahoma City U (OK)
Oklahoma State U (OK)
Old Dominion U (VA)

Oral Roberts U (OK)
Otterbein U (OH)
Pace U (NY)
Pacific U (OR)
Palm Beach Atlantic U (FL)
Park U (MO)
Penn State Abington (PA)
Penn State Altoona (PA)
Penn State Beaver (PA)
Penn State Berks (PA)
Penn State Brandywine (PA)
Penn State DuBois (PA)
Penn State Erie, The Behrend Coll (PA)
Penn State Fayette, The Eberly Campus (PA)
Penn State Greater Allegheny (PA)
Penn State Harrisburg (PA)
Penn State Hazleton (PA)
Penn State Lehigh Valley (PA)
Penn State Mont Alto (PA)
Penn State New Kensington (PA)
Penn State Schuylkill (PA)
Penn State Shenango (PA)
Penn State U Park (PA)
Penn State Wilkes-Barre (PA)
Penn State Worthington Scranton (PA)
Penn State York (PA)
Peru State Coll (NE)
Philadelphia U (PA)
Pittsburg State U (KS)
Plymouth State U (NH)
Polytechnic U of Puerto Rico (PR)
Portland State U (OR)
Post U (CT)
Prairie View A&M U (TX)
Providence Coll (RI)
Purdue U Calumet (IN)
Quincy U (IL)
Quinnipiac U (CT)
Radford U (VA)
Rasmussen Coll Bloomington (MN)
Rasmussen Coll Brooklyn Park (MN)
Rasmussen Coll Eagan (MN)
Rasmussen Coll Fort Myers (FL)
Rasmussen Coll Lake Elmo/Woodbury (MN)
Rasmussen Coll Land O' Lakes (FL)
Rasmussen Coll Mankato (MN)
Rasmussen Coll Moorhead (MN)
Rasmussen Coll New Port Richey (FL)
Rasmussen Coll Ocala (FL)
Rasmussen Coll St. Cloud (MN)
Rasmussen Coll Tampa/Brandon (FL)
Regis U (CO)
Rhode Island Coll (RI)
Rider U (NJ)
Rivier Coll (NH)
Robert Morris U (PA)
Roberts Wesleyan Coll (NY)
Rochester Inst of Technology (NY)
Rockford Coll (IL)
Roger Williams U (RI)
Roosevelt U (IL)
Rowan U (NJ)
Rutgers, The State U of New Jersey, Camden (NJ)
Rutgers, The State U of New Jersey, Newark (NJ)
Rutgers, The State U of New Jersey, New Brunswick (NJ)
Ryerson U (ON, Canada)
Sacred Heart U (CT)
Sage Coll of Albany (NY)
Saginaw Valley State U (MI)
St. Ambrose U (IA)
St. Bonaventure U (NY)
St. Catherine U (MN)
St. Edward's U (TX)
Saint Francis U (PA)
St. John's U (NY)
St. Joseph's Coll, Long Island Campus (NY)
St. Joseph's Coll, New York (NY)
Saint Joseph's Coll of Maine (ME)
Saint Joseph's U (PA)
Saint Leo U (FL)
Saint Louis U (MO)
Saint Mary-of-the-Woods Coll (IN)
Saint Mary's Coll (IN)

INDEXES

St. Mary's U (TX)
Saint Mary's U of Minnesota (MN)
Saint Peter's Coll (NJ)
St. Thomas Aquinas Coll (NY)
St. Thomas U (FL)
Saint Vincent Coll (PA)
Salem State U (MA)
Salisbury U (MD)
Salve Regina U (RI)
Samford U (AL)
Sam Houston State U (TX)
San Diego State U (CA)
San Francisco State U (CA)
Santa Clara U (CA)
Schreiner U (TX)
Seattle U (WA)
Seton Hill U (PA)
Shippensburg U of Pennsylvania (PA)
Siena Coll (NY)
Simmons Coll (MA)
Simpson Coll (IA)
Slippery Rock U of Pennsylvania (PA)
South Carolina State U (SC)
Southeastern Louisiana U (LA)
Southeastern Oklahoma State U (OK)
Southeastern U (FL)
Southeast Missouri State U (MO)
Southern Connecticut State U (CT)
Southern Illinois U Carbondale (IL)
Southern Methodist U (TX)
Southern New Hampshire U (NH)
Southern Oregon U (OR)
Southwest Baptist U (MO)
Southwestern Assemblies of God U (TX)
Southwestern Christian U (OK)
Southwestern Coll (KS)
Southwestern Oklahoma State U (OK)
Southwest Minnesota State U (MN)
Spring Hill Coll (AL)
State U of New York at Binghamton (NY)
State U of New York at Fredonia (NY)
State U of New York at Oswego (NY)
State U of New York at Plattsburgh (NY)
State U of New York Coll at Old Westbury (NY)
Stephen F. Austin State U (TX)
Stephens Coll (MO)
Stetson U (FL)
Stonehill Coll (MA)
Suffolk U (MA)
Syracuse U (NY)
Tabor Coll (KS)
Taylor U (IN)
Temple U (PA)
Texas A&M Intl U (TX)
Texas A&M U (TX)
Texas A&M U–Corpus Christi (TX)
Texas A&M U–Kingsville (TX)
Texas Christian U (TX)
Texas Southern U (TX)
Texas State U–San Marcos (TX)
Texas Tech U (TX)
Texas Wesleyan U (TX)
Texas Woman's U (TX)
Thomas Edison State Coll (NJ)
Thompson Rivers U (BC, Canada)
Tiffin U (OH)
Trevecca Nazarene U (TN)
Trine U (IN)
Trinity U (TX)
Tulane U (LA)
Tuskegee U (AL)
Union Coll (KY)
Union U (TN)
Universidad del Turabo (PR)
Université de Sherbrooke (QC, Canada)
The U of Akron (OH)
The U of Alabama (AL)
The U of Alabama at Birmingham (AL)
The U of Alabama in Huntsville (AL)
U of Alaska Anchorage (AK)
U of Alberta (AB, Canada)
The U of Arizona (AZ)
U of Arkansas (AR)

U of Arkansas at Little Rock (AR)
U of Bridgeport (CT)
The U of British Columbia (BC, Canada)
The U of British Columbia–Okanagan (BC, Canada)
U of Central Arkansas (AR)
U of Central Florida (FL)
U of Central Missouri (MO)
U of Charleston (WV)
U of Cincinnati (OH)
U of Colorado Boulder (CO)
U of Connecticut (CT)
U of Dayton (OH)
U of Delaware (DE)
U of Denver (CO)
U of Evansville (IN)
The U of Findlay (OH)
U of Florida (FL)
U of Georgia (GA)
U of Great Falls (MT)
U of Guam (GU)
U of Guelph (ON, Canada)
U of Hartford (CT)
U of Hawaii at Manoa (HI)
U of Houston (TX)
U of Houston–Clear Lake (TX)
U of Houston–Downtown (TX)
U of Houston–Victoria (TX)
U of Idaho (ID)
U of Illinois at Chicago (IL)
U of Illinois at Urbana–Champaign (IL)
U of Indianapolis (IN)
The U of Iowa (IA)
The U of Kansas (KS)
U of La Verne (CA)
U of Lethbridge (AB, Canada)
U of Louisiana at Lafayette (LA)
U of Louisiana at Monroe (LA)
U of Louisville (KY)
U of Mary (ND)
U of Mary Hardin-Baylor (TX)
U of Maryland, Coll Park (MD)
U of Maryland U Coll (MD)
U of Massachusetts Amherst (MA)
U of Massachusetts Dartmouth (MA)
U of Memphis (TN)
U of Miami (FL)
U of Michigan–Dearborn (MI)
U of Michigan–Flint (MI)
U of Minnesota, Crookston (MN)
U of Minnesota, Duluth (MN)
U of Minnesota, Twin Cities Campus (MN)
U of Mississippi (MS)
U of Missouri (MO)
U of Missouri–St. Louis (MO)
U of Mount Union (OH)
U of Nebraska at Omaha (NE)
U of Nebraska–Lincoln (NE)
U of Nevada, Las Vegas (NV)
U of Nevada, Reno (NV)
U of New Haven (CT)
U of New Orleans (LA)
U of North Alabama (AL)
The U of North Carolina at Charlotte (NC)
The U of North Carolina Wilmington (NC)
U of North Dakota (ND)
U of Northern Iowa (IA)
U of North Florida (FL)
U of North Texas (TX)
U of Notre Dame (IN)
U of Oklahoma (OK)
U of Ottawa (ON, Canada)
U of Pennsylvania (PA)
U of Pittsburgh (PA)
U of Portland (OR)
U of Puerto Rico at Bayamón (PR)
U of Puerto Rico at Ponce (PR)
U of Regina (SK, Canada)
U of Rhode Island (RI)
U of Rio Grande (OH)
U of St. Francis (IL)
U of St. Thomas (MN)
U of St. Thomas (TX)
U of San Diego (CA)
The U of Scranton (PA)
U of South Alabama (AL)
U of South Carolina (SC)
The U of South Dakota (SD)
U of Southern Indiana (IN)

U of Southern Maine (ME)
U of Southern Mississippi (MS)
U of South Florida (FL)
U of South Florida–St. Petersburg Campus (FL)
The U of Tampa (FL)
The U of Tennessee (TN)
The U of Tennessee at Martin (TN)
The U of Texas at Arlington (TX)
The U of Texas at Austin (TX)
The U of Texas at Dallas (TX)
The U of Texas at El Paso (TX)
The U of Texas at San Antonio (TX)
The U of Texas at Tyler (TX)
The U of Texas of the Permian Basin (TX)
The U of Texas–Pan American (TX)
U of the Incarnate Word (TX)
U of the Ozarks (AR)
The U of Toledo (OH)
U of Tulsa (OK)
U of Utah (UT)
The U of Western Ontario (ON, Canada)
U of West Florida (FL)
U of West Georgia (GA)
U of Windsor (ON, Canada)
U of Wisconsin–Eau Claire (WI)
U of Wisconsin–La Crosse (WI)
U of Wisconsin–Madison (WI)
U of Wisconsin–Milwaukee (WI)
U of Wisconsin–River Falls (WI)
U of Wisconsin–Superior (WI)
U of Wisconsin–Whitewater (WI)
U of Wyoming (WY)
Upper Iowa U (IA)
Ursuline Coll (OH)
Utah State U (UT)
Valdosta State U (GA)
Valparaiso U (IN)
Vanguard U of Southern California (CA)
Villanova U (PA)
Virginia Commonwealth U (VA)
Virginia Intermont Coll (VA)
Virginia Polytechnic Inst and State U (VA)
Virginia State U (VA)
Virginia Union U (VA)
Viterbo U (WI)
Walsh U (OH)
Wartburg Coll (IA)
Washburn U (KS)
Washington State U (WA)
Washington U in St. Louis (MO)
Waynesburg U (PA)
Wayne State U (MI)
Webber Intl U (FL)
Weber State U (UT)
Webster U (MO)
Western Carolina U (NC)
Western Connecticut State U (CT)
Western Illinois U (IL)
Western Intl U (AZ)
Western Kentucky U (KY)
Western Michigan U (MI)
Western New England U (MA)
Western State Coll of Colorado (CO)
Western Washington U (WA)
West Liberty U (WV)
Westminster Coll (UT)
West Texas A&M U (TX)
West Virginia U (WV)
West Virginia Wesleyan Coll (WV)
Wheeling Jesuit U (WV)
Wichita State U (KS)
Widener U (PA)
Wilmington Coll (OH)
Wilmington U (DE)
Wingate U (NC)
Winona State U (MN)
Woodbury U (CA)
Wright State U (OH)
Xavier U (OH)
Xavier U of Louisiana (LA)
Yeshiva U (NY)
York Coll of Pennsylvania (PA)
York Coll of the City U of New York (NY)
Youngstown State U (OH)

MARKETING RELATED
Babson Coll (MA)
Bowling Green State U (OH)

Delaware State U (DE)
Duquesne U (PA)
Eastern U (PA)
Franklin U (OH)
Lourdes U (OH)
Mary Baldwin Coll (VA)
Newbury Coll (MA)
Oklahoma City U (OK)
Pace U (NY)
Siena Coll (NY)
Sullivan U (KY)
Tabor Coll (KS)
Troy U (AL)
The U of Akron (OH)
The U of Iowa (IA)
U of Minnesota, Duluth (MN)
U of Mississippi (MS)
U of St. Thomas (TX)
U of South Florida (FL)
Washington U in St. Louis (MO)
Western Carolina U (NC)
Western Michigan U (MI)
Western New England U (MA)
Wheeling Jesuit U (WV)
Yeshiva U (NY)

MARKETING RESEARCH
Ashland U (OH)
Baker Coll of Jackson (MI)
Boston U (MA)
Bowling Green State U (OH)
Fashion Inst of Technology (NY)
Inter American U of Puerto Rico, Bayamón Campus (PR)
Ithaca Coll (NY)
Newbury Coll (MA)
Ohio Northern U (OH)
Salve Regina U (RI)
U of Illinois at Urbana–Champaign (IL)
The U of Toledo (OH)

MARRIAGE AND FAMILY THERAPY/COUNSELING
DeSales U (PA)
John Brown U (AR)
Michigan State U (MI)
Piedmont Intl U (NC)
U of Nevada, Las Vegas (NV)

MASS COMMUNICATION/ MEDIA
Acad of Art U (CA)
Adams State Coll (CO)
Albany State U (GA)
Albion Coll (MI)
Alcorn State U (MS)
Allegheny Coll (PA)
American Jewish U (CA)
American U (DC)
American U in Bulgaria (Bulgaria)
The American U in Cairo (Egypt)
The American U of Paris (France)
Anderson U (IN)
Andrews U (MI)
Anna Maria Coll (MA)
Arcadia U (PA)
Ashland U (OH)
Auburn U (AL)
Augustana Coll (IL)
Austin Peay State U (TN)
Baker U (KS)
Baldwin-Wallace Coll (OH)
Barry U (FL)
Barton Coll (NC)
Belmont U (TN)
Beloit Coll (WI)
Bemidji State U (MN)
Benedictine Coll (KS)
Bennett Coll for Women (NC)
Bentley U (MA)
Berea Coll (KY)
Bethel Coll (KS)
Bethel U (MN)
Bethune-Cookman U (FL)
Black Hills State U (SD)
Bloomsburg U of Pennsylvania (PA)
Bluefield Coll (VA)
Boise State U (ID)
Bowie State U (MD)
Brenau U (GA)
Briar Cliff U (IA)
Bridgewater Coll (VA)
Buena Vista U (IA)

Buffalo State Coll, State U of New York (NY)
California Lutheran U (CA)
California State U, Bakersfield (CA)
California State U, Chico (CA)
California State U, East Bay (CA)
California State U, Fresno (CA)
California State U, Long Beach (CA)
California State U, Sacramento (CA)
Calvary Bible Coll and Theological Sem (MO)
Calvin Coll (MI)
Campbellsville U (KY)
Carlow U (PA)
Carson-Newman Coll (TN)
Catawba Coll (NC)
Cedar Crest Coll (PA)
Cedarville U (OH)
Centenary Coll (NJ)
Central Penn Coll (PA)
Central Washington U (WA)
Chaminade U of Honolulu (HI)
Chestnut Hill Coll (PA)
Cheyney U of Pennsylvania (PA)
City Coll of the City U of New York (NY)
City U of Seattle (WA)
Claflin U (SC)
Clark U (MA)
Clemson U (SC)
The Coll at Brockport, State U of New York (NY)
Coll of Mount Saint Vincent (NY)
The Coll of Wooster (OH)
Colorado Mesa U (CO)
Concordia U (QC, Canada)
Concordia U, Nebraska (NE)
Concordia U, St. Paul (MN)
Concordia U Texas (TX)
Cornerstone U (MI)
Crandall U (NB, Canada)
Culver-Stockton Coll (MO)
Curry Coll (MA)
Defiance Coll (OH)
Denison U (OH)
DePaul U (IL)
DePauw U (IN)
Dillard U (LA)
Dordt Coll (IA)
Drake U (IA)
East Central U (OK)
Eastern Kentucky U (KY)
Eastern Oregon U (OR)
East Tennessee State U (TN)
East Texas Baptist U (TX)
Edinboro U of Pennsylvania (PA)
Emmanuel Coll (GA)
Endicott Coll (MA)
Excelsior Coll (NY)
Felician Coll (NJ)
Five Towns Coll (NY)
Florida Gulf Coast U (FL)
Florida Intl U (FL)
Fordham U (NY)
Francis Marion U (SC)
Gardner-Webb U (NC)
The George Washington U (DC)
Gonzaga U (WA)
Goucher Coll (MD)
Governors State U (IL)
Grambling State U (LA)
Grand View U (IA)
Greenville Coll (IL)
Gustavus Adolphus Coll (MN)
Hampton U (VA)
Hanover Coll (IN)
Hardin-Simmons U (TX)
Hawai`i Pacific U (HI)
Heidelberg U (OH)
Hobart and William Smith Colls (NY)
Hofstra U (NY)
Hollins U (VA)
Howard Payne U (TX)
Hunter Coll of the City U of New York (NY)
Huntington U (IN)
Huston-Tillotson U (TX)
Idaho State U (ID)
Illinois Coll (IL)
Illinois State U (IL)
Indiana U–Purdue U Fort Wayne (IN)

Indiana U South Bend (IN)
Indiana Wesleyan U (IN)
Inter American U of Puerto Rico, Bayamón Campus (PR)
Iona Coll (NY)
Iowa State U of Science and Technology (IA)
Ithaca Coll (NY)
Jamestown Coll (ND)
John Brown U (AR)
John Carroll U (OH)
Johnson C. Smith U (NC)
Lamar U (TX)
La Salle U (PA)
Lees-McRae Coll (NC)
Lee U (TN)
Lehman Coll of the City U of New York (NY)
Lewis U (IL)
Lincoln Memorial U (TN)
Lindenwood U (MO)
Lindsey Wilson Coll (KY)
Linfield Coll (OR)
Lipscomb U (TN)
Loras Coll (IA)
Louisiana Coll (LA)
Louisiana State U and Ag and Mech Coll (LA)
Louisiana State U in Shreveport (LA)
Lubbock Christian U (TX)
Lynn U (FL)
Macalester Coll (MN)
Manchester Coll (IN)
Mansfield U of Pennsylvania (PA)
Mars Hill Coll (NC)
Marylhurst U (OR)
Marymount Coll, Palos Verdes, California (CA)
Maryville U of Saint Louis (MO)
Massachusetts Inst of Technology (MA)
The Master's Coll and Sem (CA)
McNeese State U (LA)
Medaille Coll (NY)
Mercer U (GA)
Mercy Coll (NY)
Meredith Coll (NC)
Miami U (OH)
Michigan State U (MI)
MidAmerica Nazarene U (KS)
Middle Tennessee State U (TN)
Midwestern State U (TX)
Minnesota State U Mankato (MN)
Minnesota State U Moorhead (MN)
Mississippi Coll (MS)
Mississippi Valley State U (MS)
Missouri State U (MO)
Mitchell Coll (CT)
Morris Coll (SC)
Mount Saint Mary Coll (NY)
Newberry Coll (SC)
New England Coll (NH)
Newman U (KS)
Niagara U (NY)
Nicholls State U (LA)
North Carolina Ag and Tech State U (NC)
North Carolina Central U (NC)
Northeastern U (MA)
North Greenville U (SC)
Northwestern Oklahoma State U (OK)
Northwest Nazarene U (ID)
Oklahoma Christian U (OK)
Oklahoma City U (OK)
Ouachita Baptist U (AR)
Pace U (NY)
Pacific U (OR)
Piedmont Coll (GA)
Point Loma Nazarene U (CA)
Point Park U (PA)
Queens Coll of the City U of New York (NY)
Queens U of Charlotte (NC)
Quinnipiac U (CT)
Robert Morris U (PA)
Rutgers, The State U of New Jersey, New Brunswick (NJ)
Sacred Heart U (CT)
St. Ambrose U (IA)
St. Catherine U (MN)
Saint Francis U (PA)
Saint Joseph's Coll (IN)
Saint Joseph's Coll of Maine (ME)

Saint Mary-of-the-Woods Coll (IN)
St. Mary's U (TX)
St. Thomas Aquinas Coll (NY)
St. Thomas U (FL)
St. Thomas U (NB, Canada)
Sam Houston State U (TX)
Scripps Coll (CA)
Seattle U (WA)
Shaw U (NC)
Sonoma State U (CA)
South Carolina State U (SC)
Southern Illinois U Edwardsville (IL)
Southern Vermont Coll (VT)
Southwestern Adventist U (TX)
Southwestern Oklahoma State U (OK)
Spalding U (KY)
State U of New York at Fredonia (NY)
State U of New York at Oswego (NY)
State U of New York at Plattsburgh (NY)
State U of New York Coll at Oneonta (NY)
Stephens Coll (MO)
Suffolk U (MA)
Sul Ross State U (TX)
Taylor U (IN)
Texas State U–San Marcos (TX)
Thiel Coll (PA)
Tiffin U (OH)
Towson U (MD)
Tulane U (LA)
Tusculum Coll (TN)
Union Coll (KY)
Union U (TN)
U at Albany, State U of New York (NY)
U at Buffalo, the State U of New York (NY)
U of Alaska Anchorage (AK)
U of Bridgeport (CT)
U of California, Berkeley (CA)
U of Charleston (WV)
U of Dayton (OH)
U of Denver (CO)
U of Dubuque (IA)
U of Guam (GU)
U of Hawaii at Manoa (HI)
U of Houston (TX)
U of Illinois at Urbana–Champaign (IL)
The U of Iowa (IA)
U of Louisiana at Lafayette (LA)
U of Louisiana at Monroe (LA)
U of Maine (ME)
U of Mary (ND)
U of Mary Hardin-Baylor (TX)
U of Maryland, Baltimore County (MD)
U of Maryland Eastern Shore (MD)
U of Memphis (TN)
U of Miami (FL)
U of Minnesota, Twin Cities Campus (MN)
U of Missouri (MO)
U of Missouri–Kansas City (MO)
U of Missouri–St. Louis (MO)
U of Nebraska at Kearney (NE)
U of Nevada, Las Vegas (NV)
U of New Hampshire at Manchester (NH)
U of New Mexico (NM)
The U of North Carolina at Asheville (NC)
The U of North Carolina at Chapel Hill (NC)
U of North Florida (FL)
U of Oregon (OR)
U of Pittsburgh (PA)
U of Pittsburgh at Greensburg (PA)
U of Pittsburgh at Johnstown (PA)
U of Portland (OR)
U of Rio Grande (OH)
U of St. Francis (IL)
U of Southern Indiana (IN)
U of Southern Maine (ME)
U of South Florida (FL)
U of South Florida–St. Petersburg Campus (FL)
The U of Tennessee at Chattanooga (TN)
The U of Texas at El Paso (TX)
The U of Texas at San Antonio (TX)

The U of Texas of the Permian Basin (TX)
U of the District of Columbia (DC)
U of the Incarnate Word (TX)
U of the Ozarks (AR)
The U of Toledo (OH)
U of Toronto (ON, Canada)
U of Utah (UT)
U of Washington, Bothell (WA)
The U of Western Ontario (ON, Canada)
U of West Florida (FL)
U of Wisconsin–Eau Claire (WI)
U of Wisconsin–Platteville (WI)
U of Wisconsin–Superior (WI)
Upper Iowa U (IA)
Valdosta State U (GA)
Valley City State U (ND)
Vassar Coll (NY)
Villanova U (PA)
Virginia Commonwealth U (VA)
Virginia State U (VA)
Virginia Wesleyan Coll (VA)
Wartburg Coll (IA)
Washburn U (KS)
Washington Adventist U (MD)
Washington State U (WA)
Wayland Baptist U (TX)
Wayne State Coll (NE)
Western Kentucky U (KY)
Western New England U (MA)
West Liberty U (WV)
West Texas A&M U (TX)
Wheeling Jesuit U (WV)
Widener U (PA)
William Paterson U of New Jersey (NJ)
William Penn U (IA)
Wilmington Coll (OH)
Wilson Coll (PA)
Winona State U (MN)
Winthrop U (SC)
Worcester State U (MA)
Wright State U (OH)
Xavier U of Louisiana (LA)
York Coll of Pennsylvania (PA)

MATERIALS ENGINEERING

Alfred U (NY)
Arizona State U (AZ)
Auburn U (AL)
Boise State U (ID)
Brown U (RI)
California Polytechnic State U, San Luis Obispo (CA)
California State U, Long Beach (CA)
Case Western Reserve U (OH)
Clemson U (SC)
Cornell U (NY)
Drexel U (PA)
Georgia Inst of Technology (GA)
Iowa State U of Science and Technology (IA)
The Johns Hopkins U (MD)
Lehigh U (PA)
Massachusetts Inst of Technology (MA)
Michigan State U (MI)
Michigan Technological U (MI)
New Mexico Inst of Mining and Technology (NM)
North Carolina State U (NC)
The Ohio State U (OH)
Purdue U (IN)
Rensselaer Polytechnic Inst (NY)
Rice U (TX)
U at Albany, State U of New York (NY)
The U of Alabama at Birmingham (AL)
The U of British Columbia (BC, Canada)
U of California, Davis (CA)
U of California, Irvine (CA)
U of California, Los Angeles (CA)
U of California, Merced (CA)
U of Cincinnati (OH)
U of Connecticut (CT)
U of Florida (FL)
U of Idaho (ID)
U of Illinois at Urbana–Champaign (IL)
U of Maryland, Coll Park (MD)
U of Michigan (MI)

U of Minnesota, Twin Cities Campus (MN)
U of Pennsylvania (PA)
U of Pittsburgh (PA)
The U of Tennessee (TN)
U of Toronto (ON, Canada)
U of Utah (UT)
U of Washington (WA)
The U of Western Ontario (ON, Canada)
U of Windsor (ON, Canada)
U of Wisconsin–Madison (WI)
U of Wisconsin–Milwaukee (WI)
Virginia Polytechnic Inst and State U (VA)
Washington State U (WA)
Winona State U (MN)
Worcester Polytechnic Inst (MA)
Wright State U (OH)

MATERIALS SCIENCE

California Inst of Technology (CA)
Carnegie Mellon U (PA)
Case Western Reserve U (OH)
The Johns Hopkins U (MD)
Michigan State U (MI)
The Ohio State U (OH)
Penn State Abington (PA)
Penn State Altoona (PA)
Penn State Beaver (PA)
Penn State Berks (PA)
Penn State Brandywine (PA)
Penn State DuBois (PA)
Penn State Erie, The Behrend Coll (PA)
Penn State Fayette, The Eberly Campus (PA)
Penn State Greater Allegheny (PA)
Penn State Hazleton (PA)
Penn State Lehigh Valley (PA)
Penn State Mont Alto (PA)
Penn State New Kensington (PA)
Penn State Schuylkill (PA)
Penn State Shenango (PA)
Penn State U Park (PA)
Penn State Wilkes-Barre (PA)
Penn State Worthington Scranton (PA)
Penn State York (PA)
Rice U (TX)
Stanford U (CA)
United States Air Force Acad (CO)
The U of Arizona (AZ)
U of California, Berkeley (CA)
U of California, Los Angeles (CA)
U of California, Riverside (CA)
U of Illinois at Urbana–Champaign (IL)
U of North Texas (TX)
U of Pennsylvania (PA)
U of Toronto (ON, Canada)
U of Wisconsin–Eau Claire (WI)
Worcester Polytechnic Inst (MA)

MATERNAL AND CHILD HEALTH

Union Inst & U (OH)

MATHEMATICAL BIOLOGY

Tabor Coll (KS)
Trevecca Nazarene U (TN)
U of Houston (TX)

MATHEMATICAL STATISTICS AND PROBABILITY

Carnegie Mellon U (PA)
Concordia Coll–New York (NY)
Concordia U (QC, Canada)
U of Alaska Fairbanks (AK)
U of Miami (FL)
The U of Western Ontario (ON, Canada)

MATHEMATICS

Abilene Christian U (TX)
Acadia U (NS, Canada)
Adams State Coll (CO)
Adelphi U (NY)
Adrian Coll (MI)
Agnes Scott Coll (GA)
Alabama State U (AL)
Albany State U (GA)
Albertus Magnus Coll (CT)

Albion Coll (MI)
Albright Coll (PA)
Alcorn State U (MS)
Alfred U (NY)
Allegheny Coll (PA)
Alma Coll (MI)
Alvernia U (PA)
Alverno Coll (WI)
American U (DC)
American U in Bulgaria (Bulgaria)
The American U in Cairo (Egypt)
American U of Beirut (Lebanon)
Amherst Coll (MA)
Anderson U (IN)
Anderson U (SC)
Andrews U (MI)
Angelo State U (TX)
Antioch U Midwest (OH)
Appalachian State U (NC)
Aquinas Coll (MI)
Arcadia U (PA)
Arizona State U (AZ)
Arkansas State U (AR)
Arkansas Tech U (AR)
Armstrong Atlantic State U (GA)
Asbury U (KY)
Ashland U (OH)
Assumption Coll (MA)
Athens State U (AL)
Auburn U (AL)
Auburn U Montgomery (AL)
Augustana Coll (IL)
Augustana Coll (SD)
Austin Coll (TX)
Austin Peay State U (TN)
Averett U (VA)
Avila U (MO)
Azusa Pacific U (CA)
Baker U (KS)
Baldwin-Wallace Coll (OH)
Ball State U (IN)
Bard Coll (NY)
Bard Coll at Simon's Rock (MA)
Barnard Coll (NY)
Barry U (FL)
Barton Coll (NC)
Bates Coll (ME)
Baylor U (TX)
Belhaven U (MS)
Bellarmine U (KY)
Belmont Abbey Coll (NC)
Belmont U (TN)
Beloit Coll (WI)
Bemidji State U (MN)
Benedictine Coll (KS)
Benedictine U (IL)
Bennett Coll for Women (NC)
Bennington Coll (VT)
Bentley U (MA)
Berea Coll (KY)
Bernard M. Baruch Coll of the City U of New York (NY)
Berry Coll (GA)
Bethany Coll (KS)
Bethany Coll (WV)
Bethany Lutheran Coll (MN)
Bethel Coll (IN)
Bethel Coll (KS)
Bethel U (MN)
Bethel U (TN)
Bethune-Cookman U (FL)
Biola U (CA)
Birmingham-Southern Coll (AL)
Bishop's U (QC, Canada)
Blackburn Coll (IL)
Black Hills State U (SD)
Bloomfield Coll (NJ)
Bloomsburg U of Pennsylvania (PA)
Bluefield Coll (VA)
Blue Mountain Coll (MS)
Bluffton U (OH)
Bob Jones U (SC)
Boise State U (ID)
Boston Coll (MA)
Boston U (MA)
Bowdoin Coll (ME)
Bowie State U (MD)
Bowling Green State U (OH)
Bradley U (IL)
Brandeis U (MA)
Brevard Coll (NC)
Briar Cliff U (IA)
Bridgewater Coll (VA)
Bridgewater State U (MA)
Brown U (RI)

INDEXES

Bryn Mawr Coll (PA)
Bucknell U (PA)
Buena Vista U (IA)
Buffalo State Coll, State U of New York (NY)
Butler U (IN)
Cabrini Coll (PA)
Caldwell Coll (NJ)
California Baptist U (CA)
California Inst of Technology (CA)
California Lutheran U (CA)
California Polytechnic State U, San Luis Obispo (CA)
California State Polytechnic U, Pomona (CA)
California State U, Bakersfield (CA)
California State U, Chico (CA)
California State U, Dominguez Hills (CA)
California State U, East Bay (CA)
California State U, Fresno (CA)
California State U, Fullerton (CA)
California State U, Long Beach (CA)
California State U, Los Angeles (CA)
California State U, Monterey Bay (CA)
California State U, Sacramento (CA)
California State U, San Bernardino (CA)
California State U, San Marcos (CA)
California State U, Stanislaus (CA)
California U of Pennsylvania (PA)
Calvary Bible Coll and Theological Sem (MO)
Calvin Coll (MI)
Cameron U (OK)
Campbellsville U (KY)
Canisius Coll (NY)
Cape Breton U (NS, Canada)
Capital U (OH)
Cardinal Stritch U (WI)
Carleton Coll (MN)
Carlow U (PA)
Carnegie Mellon U (PA)
Carroll Coll (MT)
Carson-Newman Coll (TN)
Case Western Reserve U (OH)
Castleton State Coll (VT)
Catawba Coll (NC)
The Catholic U of America (DC)
Cedar Crest Coll (PA)
Cedarville U (OH)
Centenary Coll (NJ)
Centenary Coll of Louisiana (LA)
Central Coll (IA)
Central Connecticut State U (CT)
Central Methodist U (MO)
Central State U (OH)
Central Washington U (WA)
Centre Coll (KY)
Chapman U (CA)
Chatham U (PA)
Chestnut Hill Coll (PA)
Cheyney U of Pennsylvania (PA)
Chicago State U (IL)
Christian Brothers U (TN)
Christopher Newport U (VA)
The Citadel, The Military Coll of South Carolina (SC)
City Coll of the City U of New York (NY)
Claflin U (SC)
Claremont McKenna Coll (CA)
Clarion U of Pennsylvania (PA)
Clark Atlanta U (GA)
Clarke U (IA)
Clarkson U (NY)
Clark U (MA)
Clayton State U (GA)
Clearwater Christian Coll (FL)
Clemson U (SC)
Cleveland State U (OH)
Coe Coll (IA)
Colby Coll (ME)
Colgate U (NY)
The Coll at Brockport, State U of New York (NY)
Coll of Charleston (SC)
Coll of Coastal Georgia (GA)
The Coll of Idaho (ID)
Coll of Mount St. Joseph (OH)

Coll of Mount Saint Vincent (NY)
The Coll of New Jersey (NJ)
Coll of Saint Benedict (MN)
Coll of Saint Elizabeth (NJ)
Coll of Saint Mary (NE)
The Coll of Saint Rose (NY)
The Coll of St. Scholastica (MN)
Coll of Staten Island of the City U of New York (NY)
Coll of the Holy Cross (MA)
Coll of the Ozarks (MO)
The Coll of William and Mary (VA)
The Coll of Wooster (OH)
The Colorado Coll (CO)
Colorado Mesa U (CO)
Colorado School of Mines (CO)
Colorado State U (CO)
Columbia Coll (MO)
Columbia Coll (SC)
Columbia U, School of General Studies (NY)
Columbus State U (GA)
Concordia Coll (MN)
Concordia Coll–New York (NY)
Concordia U (CA)
Concordia U (MI)
Concordia U (QC, Canada)
Concordia U Chicago (IL)
Concordia U, Nebraska (NE)
Concordia U, St. Paul (MN)
Concordia U Texas (TX)
Connecticut Coll (CT)
Converse Coll (SC)
Corban U (OR)
Cornell Coll (IA)
Cornell U (NY)
Covenant Coll (GA)
Creighton U (NE)
Culver-Stockton Coll (MO)
Daemen Coll (NY)
Dalhousie U (NS, Canada)
Dallas Baptist U (TX)
Dalton State Coll (GA)
Dartmouth Coll (NH)
Davidson Coll (NC)
Defiance Coll (OH)
Delaware State U (DE)
Delaware Valley Coll (PA)
Delta State U (MS)
Denison U (OH)
DePaul U (IL)
DePauw U (IN)
DeSales U (PA)
Dickinson Coll (PA)
Dillard U (LA)
Dixie State Coll of Utah (UT)
Doane Coll (NE)
Dominican Coll (NY)
Dominican U (IL)
Dordt Coll (IA)
Dowling Coll (NY)
Drake U (IA)
Drew U (NJ)
Drexel U (PA)
Drury U (MO)
Duquesne U (PA)
Earlham Coll (IN)
East Carolina U (NC)
East Central U (OK)
Eastern Connecticut State U (CT)
Eastern Illinois U (IL)
Eastern Kentucky U (KY)
Eastern Mennonite U (VA)
Eastern Michigan U (MI)
Eastern New Mexico U (NM)
Eastern Oregon U (OR)
Eastern U (PA)
Eastern Washington U (WA)
East Stroudsburg U of Pennsylvania (PA)
East Tennessee State U (TN)
East Texas Baptist U (TX)
Eckerd Coll (FL)
Edgewood Coll (WI)
Edinboro U of Pennsylvania (PA)
Edward Waters Coll (FL)
Elizabeth City State U (NC)
Elizabethtown Coll (PA)
Elmhurst Coll (IL)
Elmira Coll (NY)
Elon U (NC)
Emmanuel Coll (GA)
Emmanuel Coll (MA)
Emory & Henry Coll (VA)
Emory U (GA)

Emporia State U (KS)
Evangel U (MO)
Excelsior Coll (NY)
Fairfield U (CT)
Fairleigh Dickinson U, Coll at Florham (NJ)
Fairleigh Dickinson U, Metropolitan Campus (NJ)
Fairmont State U (WV)
Fayetteville State U (NC)
Felician Coll (NJ)
Ferris State U (MI)
Ferrum Coll (VA)
Fitchburg State U (MA)
Florida Ag and Mech U (FL)
Florida Atlantic U (FL)
Florida Gulf Coast U (FL)
Florida Inst of Technology (FL)
Florida Intl U (FL)
Florida Southern Coll (FL)
Florida State U (FL)
Fontbonne U (MO)
Fordham U (NY)
Fort Hays State U (KS)
Fort Lewis Coll (CO)
Framingham State U (MA)
Franciscan U of Steubenville (OH)
Francis Marion U (SC)
Franklin & Marshall Coll (PA)
Franklin Coll (IN)
Friends U (KS)
Furman U (SC)
Gallaudet U (DC)
Gannon U (PA)
Gardner-Webb U (NC)
George Fox U (OR)
George Mason U (VA)
Georgetown Coll (KY)
The George Washington U (DC)
Georgia Coll & State U (GA)
Georgia Gwinnett Coll (GA)
Georgian Court U (NJ)
Georgia Southern U (GA)
Georgia Southwestern State U (GA)
Georgia State U (GA)
Gettysburg Coll (PA)
Gonzaga U (WA)
Gordon Coll (MA)
Goshen Coll (IN)
Goucher Coll (MD)
Governors State U (IL)
Grace Coll (IN)
Graceland U (IA)
Grambling State U (LA)
Grand Valley State U (MI)
Greenville Coll (IL)
Grinnell Coll (IA)
Grove City Coll (PA)
Guilford Coll (NC)
Gustavus Adolphus Coll (MN)
Gwynedd-Mercy Coll (PA)
Hamilton Coll (NY)
Hamline U (MN)
Hampden-Sydney Coll (VA)
Hampshire Coll (MA)
Hampton U (VA)
Hannibal-LaGrange U (MO)
Hanover Coll (IN)
Harding U (AR)
Hardin-Simmons U (TX)
Hartwick Coll (NY)
Harvard U (MA)
Harvey Mudd Coll (CA)
Haverford Coll (PA)
Heidelberg U (OH)
Hendrix Coll (AR)
Hillsdale Coll (MI)
Hobart and William Smith Colls (NY)
Hofstra U (NY)
Hollins U (VA)
Holy Family U (PA)
Hood Coll (MD)
Hope Coll (MI)
Houghton Coll (NY)
Howard Payne U (TX)
Humboldt State U (CA)
Hunter Coll of the City U of New York (NY)
Huntingdon Coll (AL)
Huntington U (IN)
Huston-Tillotson U (TX)
Idaho State U (ID)
Illinois Coll (IL)
Illinois State U (IL)

Illinois Wesleyan U (IL)
Immaculata U (PA)
Indiana State U (IN)
Indiana U Bloomington (IN)
Indiana U Kokomo (IN)
Indiana U Northwest (IN)
Indiana U of Pennsylvania (PA)
Indiana U–Purdue U Fort Wayne (IN)
Indiana U–Purdue U Indianapolis (IN)
Indiana U South Bend (IN)
Indiana U Southeast (IN)
Indiana Wesleyan U (IN)
Inter American U of Puerto Rico, Bayamón Campus (PR)
Inter American U of Puerto Rico, San Germán Campus (PR)
Iona Coll (NY)
Iowa State U of Science and Technology (IA)
Ithaca Coll (NY)
Jacksonville State U (AL)
Jacksonville U (FL)
James Madison U (VA)
Jamestown Coll (ND)
Jarvis Christian Coll (TX)
John Brown U (AR)
John Carroll U (OH)
The Johns Hopkins U (MD)
Johnson C. Smith U (NC)
Johnson State Coll (VT)
Judson Coll (AL)
Judson U (IL)
Juniata Coll (PA)
Kalamazoo Coll (MI)
Kansas State U (KS)
Kean U (NJ)
Keene State Coll (NH)
Kennesaw State U (GA)
Kent State U (OH)
Kentucky State U (KY)
Kentucky Wesleyan Coll (KY)
Kenyon Coll (OH)
Keuka Coll (NY)
King Coll (TN)
King's Coll (PA)
Knox Coll (IL)
Kutztown U of Pennsylvania (PA)
Lafayette Coll (PA)
LaGrange Coll (GA)
Lake Erie Coll (OH)
Lake Forest Coll (IL)
Lakehead U (ON, Canada)
Lake Superior State U (MI)
Lamar U (TX)
Lane Coll (TN)
La Roche Coll (PA)
La Salle U (PA)
La Sierra U (CA)
Lawrence Technological U (MI)
Lawrence U (WI)
Lebanese American U (Lebanon)
Lebanon Valley Coll (PA)
Lee U (TN)
Lehigh U (PA)
Lehman Coll of the City U of New York (NY)
Le Moyne Coll (NY)
Lenoir-Rhyne U (NC)
LeTourneau U (TX)
Lewis & Clark Coll (OR)
Lewis-Clark State Coll (ID)
Lewis U (IL)
Liberty U (VA)
Limestone Coll (SC)
Lincoln Memorial U (TN)
Lincoln U (MO)
Lincoln U (PA)
Lindenwood U (MO)
Linfield Coll (OR)
Lipscomb U (TN)
Lock Haven U of Pennsylvania (PA)
Long Island U–Brooklyn Campus (NY)
Long Island U–C. W. Post Campus (NY)
Loras Coll (IA)
Louisiana Coll (LA)
Louisiana State U and Ag and Mech Coll (LA)
Louisiana State U in Shreveport (LA)
Loyola Marymount U (CA)
Loyola U Chicago (IL)

Loyola U Maryland (MD)
Loyola U New Orleans (LA)
Lubbock Christian U (TX)
Luther Coll (IA)
Lycoming Coll (PA)
Lynchburg Coll (VA)
Lyon Coll (AR)
Macalester Coll (MN)
Macon State Coll (GA)
Madonna U (MI)
Maharishi U of Management (IA)
Malone U (OH)
Manchester Coll (IN)
Manhattan Coll (NY)
Manhattanville Coll (NY)
Mansfield U of Pennsylvania (PA)
Marian U (WI)
Marietta Coll (OH)
Marlboro Coll (VT)
Marquette U (WI)
Marshall U (WV)
Mars Hill Coll (NC)
Mary Baldwin Coll (VA)
Marymount U (VA)
Maryville Coll (TN)
Maryville U of Saint Louis (MO)
Marywood U (PA)
Massachusetts Coll of Liberal Arts (MA)
Massachusetts Inst of Technology (MA)
The Master's Coll and Sem (CA)
Mayville State U (ND)
McDaniel Coll (MD)
McKendree U (IL)
McMurry U (TX)
McNeese State U (LA)
McPherson Coll (KS)
Medaille Coll (NY)
Mercer U (GA)
Mercy Coll (NY)
Mercyhurst Coll (PA)
Meredith Coll (NC)
Merrimack Coll (MA)
Messiah Coll (PA)
Metropolitan State Coll of Denver (CO)
Miami U (OH)
Michigan State U (MI)
Michigan Technological U (MI)
MidAmerica Nazarene U (KS)
Mid-Continent U (KY)
Middlebury Coll (VT)
Middle Tennessee State U (TN)
Midwestern State U (TX)
Millersville U of Pennsylvania (PA)
Milligan Coll (TN)
Millsaps Coll (MS)
Mills Coll (CA)
Minnesota State U Mankato (MN)
Minnesota State U Moorhead (MN)
Minot State U (ND)
Misericordia U (PA)
Mississippi Coll (MS)
Mississippi State U (MS)
Mississippi U for Women (MS)
Mississippi Valley State U (MS)
Missouri Baptist U (MO)
Missouri Southern State U (MO)
Missouri State U (MO)
Missouri Western State U (MO)
Molloy Coll (NY)
Monmouth Coll (IL)
Monmouth U (NJ)
Montana State U (MT)
Montana State U Billings (MT)
Montana State U–Northern (MT)
Montana Tech of The U of Montana (MT)
Montclair State U (NJ)
Moravian Coll (PA)
Morehead State U (KY)
Morehouse Coll (GA)
Morningside Coll (IA)
Morris Coll (SC)
Mount Allison U (NB, Canada)
Mount Holyoke Coll (MA)
Mount Marty Coll (SD)
Mount Mary Coll (WI)
Mount Mercy U (IA)
Mount Saint Mary Coll (NY)
Mount St. Mary's Coll (CA)
Mount St. Mary's U (MD)
Mount Vernon Nazarene U (OH)
Muhlenberg Coll (PA)

INDEXES

U of Saint Joseph (CT)
U of Saint Mary (KS)
U of St. Thomas (MN)
U of St. Thomas (TX)
U of San Diego (CA)
U of Science and Arts of Oklahoma (OK)
The U of Scranton (PA)
U of South Alabama (AL)
U of South Carolina (SC)
U of South Carolina Upstate (SC)
The U of South Dakota (SD)
U of Southern California (CA)
U of Southern Indiana (IN)
U of Southern Maine (ME)
U of Southern Mississippi (MS)
U of South Florida (FL)
The U of Tampa (FL)
The U of Tennessee (TN)
The U of Tennessee at Chattanooga (TN)
The U of Tennessee at Martin (TN)
The U of Texas at Arlington (TX)
The U of Texas at Austin (TX)
The U of Texas at Dallas (TX)
The U of Texas at El Paso (TX)
The U of Texas at San Antonio (TX)
The U of Texas at Tyler (TX)
The U of Texas of the Permian Basin (TX)
The U of Texas–Pan American (TX)
U of the Cumberlands (KY)
U of the District of Columbia (DC)
U of the Incarnate Word (TX)
U of the Ozarks (AR)
U of the Pacific (CA)
The U of Toledo (OH)
U of Tulsa (OK)
U of Utah (UT)
U of Vermont (VT)
U of Virginia (VA)
The U of Virginia's Coll at Wise (VA)
U of Washington (WA)
The U of West Alabama (AL)
The U of Western Ontario (ON, Canada)
U of West Florida (FL)
U of West Georgia (GA)
U of Windsor (ON, Canada)
U of Wisconsin–Eau Claire (WI)
U of Wisconsin–Green Bay (WI)
U of Wisconsin–La Crosse (WI)
U of Wisconsin–Madison (WI)
U of Wisconsin–Milwaukee (WI)
U of Wisconsin–Platteville (WI)
U of Wisconsin–River Falls (WI)
U of Wisconsin–Stevens Point (WI)
U of Wisconsin–Superior (WI)
U of Wisconsin–Whitewater (WI)
U of Wyoming (WY)
Upper Iowa U (IA)
Ursuline Coll (OH)
Utah State U (UT)
Utah Valley U (UT)
Utica Coll (NY)
Valdosta State U (GA)
Valley City State U (ND)
Valparaiso U (IN)
Vanderbilt U (TN)
Vanguard U of Southern California (CA)
Vassar Coll (NY)
Villanova U (PA)
Virginia Commonwealth U (VA)
Virginia Polytechnic Inst and State U (VA)
Virginia State U (VA)
Virginia Union U (VA)
Virginia Wesleyan Coll (VA)
Viterbo U (WI)
Wabash Coll (IN)
Wagner Coll (NY)
Wake Forest U (NC)
Walsh U (OH)
Warren Wilson Coll (NC)
Wartburg Coll (IA)
Washburn U (KS)
Washington Adventist U (MD)
Washington & Jefferson Coll (PA)
Washington and Lee U (VA)
Washington Coll (MD)
Washington State U (WA)
Washington U in St. Louis (MO)
Wayland Baptist U (TX)
Waynesburg U (PA)

Wayne State Coll (NE)
Wayne State U (MI)
Weber State U (UT)
Webster U (MO)
Wellesley Coll (MA)
Wells Coll (NY)
Wesleyan Coll (GA)
Wesleyan U (CT)
West Chester U of Pennsylvania (PA)
Western Carolina U (NC)
Western Connecticut State U (CT)
Western Illinois U (IL)
Western Kentucky U (KY)
Western Michigan U (MI)
Western New England U (MA)
Western Oregon U (OR)
Western State Coll of Colorado (CO)
Western Washington U (WA)
Westfield State U (MA)
West Liberty U (WV)
Westminster Coll (MO)
Westminster Coll (UT)
West Texas A&M U (TX)
West Virginia State U (WV)
West Virginia U (WV)
West Virginia U Inst of Technology (WV)
West Virginia Wesleyan Coll (WV)
Wheaton Coll (IL)
Wheaton Coll (MA)
Wheeling Jesuit U (WV)
Whitman Coll (WA)
Whittier Coll (CA)
Wichita State U (KS)
Widener U (PA)
Wilkes U (PA)
Willamette U (OR)
William Jessup U (CA)
William Jewell Coll (MO)
William Paterson U of New Jersey (NJ)
Williams Coll (MA)
William Woods U (MO)
Wilmington Coll (OH)
Wilson Coll (PA)
Wingate U (NC)
Winona State U (MN)
Winthrop U (SC)
Wittenberg U (OH)
Wofford Coll (SC)
Worcester Polytechnic Inst (MA)
Worcester State U (MA)
Wright State U (OH)
Xavier U (OH)
Xavier U of Louisiana (LA)
Yale U (CT)
Yeshiva U (NY)
York Coll of Pennsylvania (PA)
York Coll of the City U of New York (NY)
Youngstown State U (OH)

MATHEMATICS AND COMPUTER SCIENCE

Anderson U (IN)
Bennington Coll (VT)
Boston U (MA)
Bowdoin Coll (ME)
Brescia U (KY)
Brown U (RI)
Cardinal Stritch U (WI)
Central Coll (IA)
Chestnut Hill Coll (PA)
The Colorado Coll (CO)
Delaware State U (DE)
DePaul U (IL)
Dominican U (IL)
Dowling Coll (NY)
Drew U (NJ)
Eastern Illinois U (IL)
Florida Southern Coll (FL)
George Mason U (VA)
Hampden-Sydney Coll (VA)
Hofstra U (NY)
Immaculata U (PA)
Indiana U–Purdue U Fort Wayne (IN)
Ithaca Coll (NY)
Lake Superior State U (MI)
Lawrence Technological U (MI)
Lawrence U (WI)
Long Island U–C. W. Post Campus (NY)

Loyola U Chicago (IL)
Manchester Coll (IN)
Massachusetts Inst of Technology (MA)
Mount Allison U (NB, Canada)
Piedmont Coll (GA)
Rochester Inst of Technology (NY)
Saint Francis U (PA)
St. Joseph's Coll, Long Island Campus (NY)
St. Joseph's Coll, New York (NY)
St. Lawrence U (NY)
Saint Mary's Coll (IN)
Saint Mary's Coll of California (CA)
Saint Mary's U of Minnesota (MN)
Salem State U (MA)
Santa Clara U (CA)
Southern Oregon U (OR)
Stanford U (CA)
Temple U (PA)
Tusculum Coll (TN)
U at Albany, State U of New York (NY)
U of Illinois at Chicago (IL)
U of Illinois at Urbana–Champaign (IL)
U of Oregon (OR)
U of Regina (SK, Canada)
U of St. Francis (IL)
The U of Tampa (FL)
The U of Texas at Austin (TX)
U of Windsor (ON, Canada)
Washington U in St. Louis (MO)
Western Washington U (WA)
Whitman Coll (WA)
Yale U (CT)

MATHEMATICS AND STATISTICS

Colby Coll (ME)
Dakota State U (SD)
Luther Coll (IA)
U of South Alabama (AL)

MATHEMATICS AND STATISTICS RELATED

The American U of Paris (France)
Anderson U (IN)
Bernard M. Baruch Coll of the City U of New York (NY)
Carnegie Mellon U (PA)
Columbia U, School of General Studies (NY)
Delaware State U (DE)
The Evergreen State Coll (WA)
Hofstra U (NY)
Indiana U of Pennsylvania (PA)
Lycoming Coll (PA)
New York U (NY)
Ohio U (OH)
Purchase Coll, State U of New York (NY)
St. Joseph's Coll, Long Island Campus (NY)
St. Joseph's Coll, New York (NY)
Saint Mary's Coll of California (CA)
Seattle Pacific U (WA)
Taylor U (IN)
Tulane U (LA)
The U of British Columbia–Okanagan (BC, Canada)
U of Minnesota, Duluth (MN)
U of Missouri–Kansas City (MO)
U of New Hampshire (NH)
The U of North Carolina at Charlotte (NC)
U of Pittsburgh (PA)
U of Regina (SK, Canada)
U of Rochester (NY)
Western State Coll of Colorado (CO)

MATHEMATICS RELATED

California Baptist U (CA)
Hillsdale Coll (MI)
Ohio Northern U (OH)
Reinhardt U (GA)
Seton Hill U (PA)
Sweet Briar Coll (VA)
United States Military Acad (NY)
U of California, Los Angeles (CA)
U of Miami (FL)
U of Pittsburgh (PA)
Wheelock Coll (MA)

MATHEMATICS TEACHER EDUCATION

Abilene Christian U (TX)
Adams State Coll (CO)
Albion Coll (MI)
Alma Coll (MI)
Alvernia U (PA)
Anderson U (IN)
Anderson U (SC)
Appalachian State U (NC)
Arkansas State U (AR)
Arkansas Tech U (AR)
Assumption Coll (MA)
Auburn U (AL)
Augustana Coll (IL)
Averett U (VA)
Baptist Bible Coll of Pennsylvania (PA)
Bayamón Central U (PR)
Baylor U (TX)
Berry Coll (GA)
Bethany Coll (KS)
Bethel Coll (IN)
Bethel U (MN)
Biola U (CA)
Bishop's U (QC, Canada)
Blackburn Coll (IL)
Black Hills State U (SD)
Bluefield Coll (VA)
Blue Mountain Coll (MS)
Bob Jones U (SC)
Boston U (MA)
Bowdoin Coll (ME)
Bowie State U (MD)
Bowling Green State U (OH)
Bradley U (IL)
Buena Vista U (IA)
Buffalo State Coll, State U of New York (NY)
Cabrini Coll (PA)
California Baptist U (CA)
California Lutheran U (CA)
California State U, Chico (CA)
California State U, Long Beach (CA)
Calvin Coll (MI)
Cameron U (OK)
Campbellsville U (KY)
Capital U (OH)
Carroll Coll (MT)
Castleton State Coll (VT)
Cedarville U (OH)
Central Michigan U (MI)
Central Washington U (WA)
Chipola Coll (FL)
Christian Brothers U (TN)
City Coll of the City U of New York (NY)
Claflin U (SC)
Clearwater Christian Coll (FL)
Clemson U (SC)
The Coll at Brockport, State U of New York (NY)
The Coll of New Jersey (NJ)
The Coll of Saint Rose (NY)
Coll of the Ozarks (MO)
Colorado State U (CO)
Columbus State U (GA)
Concordia Coll (MN)
Concordia U (MI)
Concordia U Chicago (IL)
Concordia U, Nebraska (NE)
Concordia U, St. Paul (MN)
Corban U (OR)
Cornerstone U (MI)
Covenant Coll (GA)
Culver-Stockton Coll (MO)
Daemen Coll (NY)
Dakota State U (SD)
Delaware State U (DE)
Delta State U (MS)
Dixie State Coll of Utah (UT)
Dominican Coll (NY)
Dowling Coll (NY)
Duquesne U (PA)
East Carolina U (NC)
East Central U (OK)
Eastern Michigan U (MI)
Eastern Washington U (WA)
East Texas Baptist U (TX)
Edgewood Coll (WI)
Elizabeth City State U (NC)
Elmhurst Coll (IL)
Elmira Coll (NY)
Emmanuel Coll (GA)

Fayetteville State U (NC)
Felician Coll (NJ)
Ferris State U (MI)
Fitchburg State U (MA)
Florida Ag and Mech U (FL)
Florida Atlantic U (FL)
Florida Inst of Technology (FL)
Fordham U (NY)
Franklin Coll (IN)
Friends U (KS)
Gardner-Webb U (NC)
Geneva Coll (PA)
Glenville State Coll (WV)
Grace Coll (IN)
Grambling State U (LA)
Grand Canyon U (AZ)
Grand Valley State U (MI)
Greenville Coll (IL)
Gustavus Adolphus Coll (MN)
Gwynedd-Mercy Coll (PA)
Hannibal-LaGrange U (MO)
Harding U (AR)
Hardin-Simmons U (TX)
Hawai'i Pacific U (HI)
Hofstra U (NY)
Hope Coll (MI)
Howard Payne U (TX)
Hunter Coll of the City U of New York (NY)
Huntingdon Coll (AL)
Huntington U (IN)
Indiana U Bloomington (IN)
Indiana U Northwest (IN)
Indiana U–Purdue U Fort Wayne (IN)
Indiana U South Bend (IN)
Indiana U Southeast (IN)
Indiana Wesleyan U (IN)
Indian River State Coll (FL)
Inter American U of Puerto Rico, San Germán Campus (PR)
Iona Coll (NY)
Iowa Wesleyan Coll (IA)
Ithaca Coll (NY)
Jamestown Coll (ND)
John Brown U (AR)
Johnson C. Smith U (NC)
Johnson State Coll (VT)
Judson Coll (AL)
Juniata Coll (PA)
Keene State Coll (NH)
Kennesaw State U (GA)
Kent State U (OH)
Kentucky Christian U (KY)
Kentucky Wesleyan Coll (KY)
Keuka Coll (NY)
Keystone Coll (PA)
King Coll (TN)
Le Moyne Coll (NY)
Lenoir-Rhyne U (NC)
Lewis-Clark State Coll (ID)
Liberty U (VA)
Limestone Coll (SC)
Lincoln Memorial U (TN)
Lincoln U (MO)
Lincoln U (PA)
Lindenwood U (MO)
Lindsey Wilson Coll (KY)
Lipscomb U (TN)
Long Island U–Brooklyn Campus (NY)
Long Island U–C. W. Post Campus (NY)
Louisiana State U in Shreveport (LA)
Loyola U Chicago (IL)
Macon State Coll (GA)
Madonna U (MI)
Manchester Coll (IN)
Manhattanville Coll (NY)
Mansfield U of Pennsylvania (PA)
Maranatha Baptist Bible Coll (WI)
Marquette U (WI)
Maryville Coll (TN)
Marywood U (PA)
Mayville State U (ND)
McKendree U (IL)
McMurry U (TX)
Medaille Coll (NY)
Mercyhurst Coll (PA)
Merrimack Coll (MA)
Messiah Coll (PA)
Metropolitan State U (MN)
Miami Dade Coll (FL)
Miami U (OH)

Michigan State U (MI)
Michigan Technological U (MI)
MidAmerica Nazarene U (KS)
Midwestern State U (TX)
Millikin U (IL)
Minnesota State U Moorhead (MN)
Minot State U (ND)
Misericordia U (PA)
Mississippi Coll (MS)
Mississippi Valley State U (MS)
Missouri State U (MO)
Molloy Coll (NY)
Montana State U Billings (MT)
Moravian Coll (PA)
Morningside Coll (IA)
Morris Coll (SC)
Mount Marty Coll (SD)
Mount Mary Coll (WI)
Mount Vernon Nazarene U (OH)
Nazareth Coll of Rochester (NY)
New York U (NY)
Niagara U (NY)
Nicholls State U (LA)
North Carolina Ag and Tech State U (NC)
North Carolina Central U (NC)
North Carolina State U (NC)
North Dakota State U (ND)
Northeastern State U (OK)
Northern Michigan U (MI)
North Greenville U (SC)
Northwestern Coll (MN)
Northwestern Oklahoma State U (OK)
Northwest Florida State Coll (FL)
Northwest Missouri State U (MO)
Northwest Nazarene U (ID)
Northwest U (WA)
Notre Dame of Maryland U (MD)
Nyack Coll (NY)
Oakland City U (IN)
Ohio Northern U (OH)
Ohio Valley U (WV)
Ohio Wesleyan U (OH)
Oklahoma Christian U (OK)
Oklahoma City U (OK)
Oral Roberts U (OK)
Pace U (NY)
Paine Coll (GA)
Palm Beach Atlantic U (FL)
Pepperdine U, Malibu (CA)
Peru State Coll (NE)
Philadelphia Biblical U (PA)
Pittsburg State U (KS)
Point Park U (PA)
Queens U of Charlotte (NC)
Regis Coll (MA)
Rhode Island Coll (RI)
Rivier Coll (NH)
Roberts Wesleyan Coll (NY)
Rocky Mountain Coll (MT)
Rust Coll (MS)
Saginaw Valley State U (MI)
St. Ambrose U (IA)
St. Catherine U (MN)
St. Edward's U (TX)
Saint Francis U (PA)
St. John Fisher Coll (NY)
St. John's U (NY)
St. Joseph's Coll, Long Island Campus (NY)
St. Joseph's Coll, New York (NY)
Saint Joseph's Coll of Maine (ME)
Saint Joseph's U (PA)
Saint Mary's U of Minnesota (MN)
Saint Xavier U (IL)
Salve Regina U (RI)
Schreiner U (TX)
Seattle Pacific U (WA)
Seton Hill U (PA)
Shawnee State U (OH)
Shaw U (NC)
Shorter U (GA)
Simpson U (CA)
Southeastern Oklahoma State U (OK)
Southeastern U (FL)
Southeast Missouri State U (MO)
Southern New Hampshire U (NH)
Southern Polytechnic State U (GA)
Southwest Baptist U (MO)
Southwestern Coll (KS)
Southwest Minnesota State U (MN)
Spring Arbor U (MI)

State U of New York at New Paltz (NY)
State U of New York Coll at Cortland (NY)
State U of New York Coll at Old Westbury (NY)
State U of New York Coll at Oneonta (NY)
State U of New York Coll at Potsdam (NY)
Syracuse U (NY)
Tabor Coll (KS)
Taylor U (IN)
Temple U (PA)
Texas A&M Intl U (TX)
Texas A&M U–Corpus Christi (TX)
Texas Christian U (TX)
Texas Lutheran U (TX)
Texas Wesleyan U (TX)
Trevecca Nazarene U (TN)
Trine U (IN)
Trinity Christian Coll (IL)
Tusculum Coll (TN)
Union Coll (NE)
Universidad del Turabo (PR)
The U of Akron (OH)
U of Arkansas–Fort Smith (AR)
U of Central Arkansas (AR)
U of Central Florida (FL)
U of Cincinnati (OH)
U of Delaware (DE)
U of Evansville (IN)
U of Georgia (GA)
U of Great Falls (MT)
U of Illinois at Chicago (IL)
U of Illinois at Urbana–Champaign (IL)
U of Indianapolis (IN)
The U of Iowa (IA)
U of Lethbridge (AB, Canada)
U of Louisiana at Monroe (LA)
U of Maine (ME)
U of Maine at Farmington (ME)
U of Maine at Fort Kent (ME)
U of Mary (ND)
U of Mary Hardin-Baylor (TX)
U of Michigan–Dearborn (MI)
U of Michigan–Flint (MI)
U of Minnesota, Duluth (MN)
U of Mississippi (MS)
U of Missouri (MO)
U of Missouri–St. Louis (MO)
The U of Montana Western (MT)
U of Nebraska–Lincoln (NE)
U of New Hampshire (NH)
U of New Orleans (LA)
The U of North Carolina at Charlotte (NC)
The U of North Carolina Wilmington (NC)
U of North Dakota (ND)
U of Northern Iowa (IA)
U of North Florida (FL)
U of Oklahoma (OK)
U of Pittsburgh at Johnstown (PA)
U of Regina (SK, Canada)
U of Rio Grande (OH)
U of St. Francis (IL)
U of Saint Francis (IN)
U of St. Thomas (MN)
The U of South Dakota (SD)
U of South Florida (FL)
The U of Tennessee at Chattanooga (TN)
The U of Tennessee at Martin (TN)
The U of Toledo (OH)
U of Tulsa (OK)
U of Vermont (VT)
U of Windsor (ON, Canada)
U of Wisconsin–River Falls (WI)
U of Wisconsin–Superior (WI)
Ursuline Coll (OH)
Utah State U (UT)
Utah Valley U (UT)
Utica Coll (NY)
Valley City State U (ND)
Valparaiso U (IN)
Vincennes U (IN)
Viterbo U (WI)
Walsh U (OH)
Wartburg Coll (IA)
Washburn U (KS)
Washington Adventist U (MD)
Washington State U (WA)
Washington U in St. Louis (MO)

Waynesburg U (PA)
Wayne State Coll (NE)
Wayne State U (MI)
Weber State U (UT)
Western Carolina U (NC)
Western Michigan U (MI)
Western State Coll of Colorado (CO)
Western Washington U (WA)
West Virginia Wesleyan Coll (WV)
Wheeling Jesuit U (WV)
Widener U (PA)
William Penn U (IA)
William Woods U (MO)
Wingate U (NC)
Winona State U (MN)
York Coll of Pennsylvania (PA)
Youngstown State U (OH)

MECHANICAL DRAFTING AND CAD/CADD

Eastern Michigan U (MI)
Indiana U–Purdue U Indianapolis (IN)
Purdue U (IN)

MECHANICAL ENGINEERING

Alfred U (NY)
The American U in Cairo (Egypt)
American U of Beirut (Lebanon)
Andrews U (MI)
Arizona State U (AZ)
Arkansas State U (AR)
Arkansas Tech U (AR)
Auburn U (AL)
Baker Coll of Flint (MI)
Baylor U (TX)
Boston U (MA)
Bradley U (IL)
Brown U (RI)
Bucknell U (PA)
California Baptist U (CA)
California Inst of Technology (CA)
California Maritime Acad (CA)
California Polytechnic State U, San Luis Obispo (CA)
California State Polytechnic U, Pomona (CA)
California State U, Chico (CA)
California State U, Fresno (CA)
California State U, Fullerton (CA)
California State U, Long Beach (CA)
California State U, Los Angeles (CA)
California State U, Sacramento (CA)
Calvin Coll (MI)
Carnegie Mellon U (PA)
Case Western Reserve U (OH)
The Catholic U of America (DC)
Cedarville U (OH)
Central Michigan U (MI)
Christian Brothers U (TN)
City Coll of the City U of New York (NY)
Clarkson U (NY)
Clemson U (SC)
Cleveland State U (OH)
The Coll of New Jersey (NJ)
Colorado State U (CO)
Concordia U (QC, Canada)
Cooper Union for the Advancement of Science and Art (NY)
Cornell U (NY)
Daniel Webster Coll (NH)
Delaware State U (DE)
Dordt Coll (IA)
Drexel U (PA)
Eastern Washington U (WA)
Embry-Riddle Aeronautical U–Daytona (FL)
Embry-Riddle Aeronautical U–Prescott (AZ)
Fairfield U (CT)
Florida Ag and Mech U (FL)
Florida Atlantic U (FL)
Florida Inst of Technology (FL)
Florida Intl U (FL)
Franklin W. Olin Coll of Eng (MA)
Gannon U (PA)
George Fox U (OR)
The George Washington U (DC)
Georgia Inst of Technology (GA)

Georgia Southern U (GA)
Gonzaga U (WA)
Grove City Coll (PA)
Harding U (AR)
Hofstra U (NY)
Hope Coll (MI)
Idaho State U (ID)
Illinois Inst of Technology (IL)
Indiana Tech (IN)
Indiana U East (IN)
Indiana U–Purdue U Fort Wayne (IN)
Indiana U–Purdue U Indianapolis (IN)
Inter American U of Puerto Rico, Bayamón Campus (PR)
Iowa State U of Science and Technology (IA)
Jacksonville U (FL)
John Brown U (AR)
The Johns Hopkins U (MD)
Kansas State U (KS)
Kettering U (MI)
Lafayette Coll (PA)
Lakehead U (ON, Canada)
Lake Superior State U (MI)
Lamar U (TX)
Lawrence Technological U (MI)
Lebanese American U (Lebanon)
Lehigh U (PA)
LeTourneau U (TX)
Lipscomb U (TN)
Louisiana State U and Ag and Mech Coll (LA)
Loyola Marymount U (CA)
Manhattan Coll (NY)
Marquette U (WI)
Massachusetts Inst of Technology (MA)
Merrimack Coll (MA)
Miami U (OH)
Michigan State U (MI)
Michigan Technological U (MI)
Milwaukee School of Eng (WI)
Minnesota State U Mankato (MN)
Mississippi State U (MS)
Missouri U of Science and Technology (MO)
Montana State U (MT)
New England Inst of Technology (RI)
New Mexico Inst of Mining and Technology (NM)
New Mexico State U (NM)
New York Inst of Technology (NY)
North Carolina Ag and Tech State U (NC)
North Carolina State U (NC)
North Dakota State U (ND)
Northeastern U (MA)
Northern Arizona U (AZ)
Northern Illinois U (IL)
Norwich U (VT)
Oakland U (MI)
Ohio Northern U (OH)
The Ohio State U (OH)
Ohio U (OH)
Oklahoma Christian U (OK)
Oklahoma State U (OK)
Old Dominion U (VA)
Oral Roberts U (OK)
Penn State Abington (PA)
Penn State Altoona (PA)
Penn State Beaver (PA)
Penn State Berks (PA)
Penn State Brandywine (PA)
Penn State DuBois (PA)
Penn State Erie, The Behrend Coll (PA)
Penn State Fayette, The Eberly Campus (PA)
Penn State Greater Allegheny (PA)
Penn State Harrisburg (PA)
Penn State Hazleton (PA)
Penn State Lehigh Valley (PA)
Penn State Mont Alto (PA)
Penn State New Kensington (PA)
Penn State Schuylkill (PA)
Penn State Shenango (PA)
Penn State U Park (PA)
Penn State Wilkes-Barre (PA)
Penn State Worthington Scranton (PA)
Penn State York (PA)
Polytechnic Inst of NYU (NY)

Polytechnic U of Puerto Rico (PR)
Portland State U (OR)
Prairie View A&M U (TX)
Princeton U (NJ)
Purdue U (IN)
Purdue U Calumet (IN)
Purdue U North Central (IN)
Queen's U at Kingston (ON, Canada)
Rensselaer Polytechnic Inst (NY)
Rice U (TX)
Rochester Inst of Technology (NY)
Rose-Hulman Inst of Technology (IN)
Rowan U (NJ)
Rutgers, The State U of New Jersey, New Brunswick (NJ)
Ryerson U (ON, Canada)
Saginaw Valley State U (MI)
Saint Louis U (MO)
Saint Martin's U (WA)
San Diego State U (CA)
San Francisco State U (CA)
Santa Clara U (CA)
Seattle U (WA)
South Dakota School of Mines and Technology (SD)
South Dakota State U (SD)
Southern Illinois U Carbondale (IL)
Southern Illinois U Edwardsville (IL)
Southern Methodist U (TX)
Southern Polytechnic State U (GA)
Stanford U (CA)
State U of New York at Binghamton (NY)
State U of New York Maritime Coll (NY)
Stevens Inst of Technology (NJ)
Stony Brook U, State U of New York (NY)
Syracuse U (NY)
Temple U (PA)
Texas A&M U (TX)
Texas A&M U–Corpus Christi (TX)
Texas A&M U–Kingsville (TX)
Texas Christian U (TX)
Texas Tech U (TX)
Trine U (IN)
Trinity Coll (CT)
Tufts U (MA)
Tuskegee U (AL)
Union Coll (NY)
United States Air Force Acad (CO)
United States Coast Guard Acad (CT)
United States Military Acad (NY)
United States Naval Acad (MD)
Universidad del Turabo (PR)
Université de Sherbrooke (QC, Canada)
U at Buffalo, the State U of New York (NY)
The U of Akron (OH)
The U of Alabama (AL)
The U of Alabama at Birmingham (AL)
The U of Alabama in Huntsville (AL)
U of Alaska Fairbanks (AK)
U of Alberta (AB, Canada)
The U of Arizona (AZ)
U of Arkansas (AR)
The U of British Columbia (BC, Canada)
The U of British Columbia–Okanagan (BC, Canada)
U of California, Berkeley (CA)
U of California, Davis (CA)
U of California, Irvine (CA)
U of California, Los Angeles (CA)
U of California, Merced (CA)
U of California, Riverside (CA)
U of California, Santa Barbara (CA)
U of Central Florida (FL)
U of Cincinnati (OH)
U of Colorado at Colorado Springs (CO)
U of Colorado Boulder (CO)
U of Colorado Denver (CO)
U of Connecticut (CT)
U of Dayton (OH)
U of Delaware (DE)
U of Denver (CO)
U of Evansville (IN)
U of Florida (FL)
U of Guelph (ON, Canada)

U of Hartford (CT)
U of Hawaii at Manoa (HI)
U of Houston (TX)
U of Idaho (ID)
U of Illinois at Chicago (IL)
U of Illinois at Urbana–Champaign (IL)
U of Indianapolis (IN)
The U of Iowa (IA)
The U of Kansas (KS)
U of Louisiana at Lafayette (LA)
U of Louisville (KY)
U of Maine (ME)
U of Maryland, Baltimore County (MD)
U of Maryland, Coll Park (MD)
U of Massachusetts Amherst (MA)
U of Massachusetts Dartmouth (MA)
U of Massachusetts Lowell (MA)
U of Memphis (TN)
U of Miami (FL)
U of Michigan (MI)
U of Michigan–Dearborn (MI)
U of Michigan–Flint (MI)
U of Minnesota, Duluth (MN)
U of Minnesota, Twin Cities Campus (MN)
U of Mississippi (MS)
U of Missouri (MO)
U of Missouri–Kansas City (MO)
U of Missouri–St. Louis (MO)
U of Mount Union (OH)
U of Nebraska–Lincoln (NE)
U of Nevada, Las Vegas (NV)
U of Nevada, Reno (NV)
U of New Hampshire (NH)
U of New Haven (CT)
U of New Mexico (NM)
U of New Orleans (LA)
The U of North Carolina at Charlotte (NC)
U of North Dakota (ND)
U of North Florida (FL)
U of North Texas (TX)
U of Notre Dame (IN)
U of Oklahoma (OK)
U of Ottawa (ON, Canada)
U of Pennsylvania (PA)
U of Pittsburgh (PA)
U of Portland (OR)
U of Rhode Island (RI)
U of Rochester (NY)
U of St. Thomas (MN)
U of San Diego (CA)
U of South Alabama (AL)
U of South Carolina (SC)
U of Southern California (CA)
U of Southern Maine (ME)
U of South Florida (FL)
The U of Tennessee (TN)
The U of Tennessee at Chattanooga (TN)
The U of Texas at Arlington (TX)
The U of Texas at Austin (TX)
The U of Texas at Dallas (TX)
The U of Texas at El Paso (TX)
The U of Texas at San Antonio (TX)
The U of Texas at Tyler (TX)
The U of Texas of the Permian Basin (TX)
The U of Texas–Pan American (TX)
U of the District of Columbia (DC)
U of the Pacific (CA)
The U of Toledo (OH)
U of Toronto (ON, Canada)
U of Tulsa (OK)
U of Utah (UT)
U of Vermont (VT)
U of Virginia (VA)
U of Washington (WA)
The U of Western Ontario (ON, Canada)
U of Windsor (ON, Canada)
U of Wisconsin–Madison (WI)
U of Wisconsin–Milwaukee (WI)
U of Wisconsin–Platteville (WI)
U of Wyoming (WY)
Utah State U (UT)
Valparaiso U (IN)
Vanderbilt U (TN)
Villanova U (PA)
Virginia Commonwealth U (VA)
Virginia Polytechnic Inst and State U (VA)

Washington State U (WA)
Washington U in St. Louis (MO)
Wayne State U (MI)
Wentworth Inst of Technology (MA)
Western Kentucky U (KY)
Western Michigan U (MI)
Western New England U (MA)
West Texas A&M U (TX)
West Virginia U (WV)
West Virginia U Inst of Technology (WV)
Wichita State U (KS)
Widener U (PA)
Wilkes U (PA)
William Penn U (IA)
Winona State U (MN)
Worcester Polytechnic Inst (MA)
Wright State U (OH)
Yale U (CT)
York Coll of Pennsylvania (PA)
Youngstown State U (OH)

MECHANICAL ENGINEERING/ MECHANICAL TECHNOLOGY

Arizona State U (AZ)
Bluefield State Coll (WV)
Boise State U (ID)
Bowling Green State U (OH)
Buffalo State Coll, State U of New York (NY)
California State U, Long Beach (CA)
California State U, Sacramento (CA)
Central Connecticut State U (CT)
Central Michigan U (MI)
Central Washington U (WA)
Colorado Mesa U (CO)
Delaware State U (DE)
Eastern Michigan U (MI)
Eastern Washington U (WA)
Fairleigh Dickinson U, Metropolitan Campus (NJ)
Fairmont State U (WV)
Farmingdale State Coll (NY)
Ferris State U (MI)
Georgia Southern U (GA)
Indiana U–Purdue U Fort Wayne (IN)
Kent State U at Tuscarawas (OH)
Lakehead U (ON, Canada)
Lake Superior State U (MI)
LeTourneau U (TX)
Metropolitan State Coll of Denver (CO)
Michigan Technological U (MI)
Midwestern State U (TX)
Milwaukee School of Eng (WI)
Montana State U (MT)
Nicholls State U (LA)
Northern Michigan U (MI)
Oklahoma State U (OK)
Oregon Inst of Technology (OR)
Penn State Erie, The Behrend Coll (PA)
Pennsylvania Coll of Technology (PA)
Pittsburg State U (KS)
Point Park U (PA)
Purdue U Calumet (IN)
Roger Williams U (RI)
South Carolina State U (SC)
Southern Polytechnic State U (GA)
State U of New York Coll of Technology at Alfred (NY)
Texas A&M U–Corpus Christi (TX)
Texas Tech U (TX)
Thomas Edison State Coll (NJ)
United States Military Acad (NY)
The U of Akron (OH)
U of Arkansas at Little Rock (AR)
The U of British Columbia (BC, Canada)
U of Dayton (OH)
U of Hartford (CT)
U of Houston (TX)
U of Maine (ME)
U of New Hampshire (NH)
U of New Hampshire at Manchester (NH)
The U of North Carolina at Charlotte (NC)
U of North Texas (TX)
U of Pittsburgh at Johnstown (PA)
U of Rio Grande (OH)

U of the District of Columbia (DC)
The U of Toledo (OH)
Virginia State U (VA)
Wayne State U (MI)
Wentworth Inst of Technology (MA)
Youngstown State U (OH)

MECHANICAL ENGINEERING TECHNOLOGIES RELATED

Cleveland State U (OH)
Delaware State U (DE)
Indiana State U (IN)
Indiana U–Purdue U Indianapolis (IN)
New York Inst of Technology (NY)
Pennsylvania Coll of Technology (PA)
Purdue U (IN)
Purdue U North Central (IN)
U of Hartford (CT)
U of Massachusetts Lowell (MA)
Vaughn Coll of Aeronautics and Technology (NY)

MECHANICS AND REPAIR

Lewis-Clark State Coll (ID)

MECHATRONICS, ROBOTICS, AND AUTOMATION ENGINEERING

Lawrence Technological U (MI)

MEDICAL ADMINISTRATIVE ASSISTANT AND MEDICAL SECRETARY

Baker Coll of Auburn Hills (MI)
Mercyhurst Coll (PA)
Minnesota School of Business–Shakopee (MN)

MEDICAL ANTHROPOLOGY

Creighton U (NE)

MEDICAL/HEALTH MANAGEMENT AND CLINICAL ASSISTANT

Davenport U, Grand Rapids (MI)
Lewis-Clark State Coll (ID)

MEDICAL ILLUSTRATION

Arcadia U (PA)
The Cleveland Inst of Art (OH)
Iowa State U of Science and Technology (IA)
Rochester Inst of Technology (NY)

MEDICAL INFORMATICS

Capella U (MN)
Misericordia U (PA)
Montana Tech of The U of Montana (MT)
Montclair State U (NJ)
Simmons Coll (MA)

MEDICAL MICROBIOLOGY AND BACTERIOLOGY

Adams State Coll (CO)
Auburn U (AL)
Bowling Green State U (OH)
California Polytechnic State U, San Luis Obispo (CA)
Dalhousie U (NS, Canada)
Eastern Kentucky U (KY)
Humboldt State U (CA)
Indiana U Bloomington (IN)
Inter American U of Puerto Rico, Bayamón Campus (PR)
Inter American U of Puerto Rico, San Germán Campus (PR)
Michigan Technological U (MI)
Minnesota State U Mankato (MN)
Mississippi State U (MS)
Montana State U (MT)
New Mexico State U (NM)
Ohio Wesleyan U (OH)
Penn State Abington (PA)
Penn State Altoona (PA)
Penn State Beaver (PA)
Penn State Berks (PA)
Penn State Brandywine (PA)
Penn State DuBois (PA)

Penn State Erie, The Behrend Coll (PA)
Penn State Fayette, The Eberly Campus (PA)
Penn State Greater Allegheny (PA)
Penn State Hazleton (PA)
Penn State Lehigh Valley (PA)
Penn State Mont Alto (PA)
Penn State New Kensington (PA)
Penn State Schuylkill (PA)
Penn State Shenango (PA)
Penn State U Park (PA)
Penn State Wilkes-Barre (PA)
Penn State Worthington Scranton (PA)
Penn State York (PA)
Pomona Coll (CA)
Quinnipiac U (CT)
Rutgers, The State U of New Jersey, New Brunswick (NJ)
San Francisco State U (CA)
Sonoma State U (CA)
Université de Sherbrooke (QC, Canada)
U of Alberta (AB, Canada)
The U of British Columbia (BC, Canada)
U of California, Los Angeles (CA)
U of California, Santa Barbara (CA)
U of Central Florida (FL)
U of Delaware (DE)
U of Florida (FL)
U of Louisiana at Lafayette (LA)
U of Maine (ME)
U of Miami (FL)
U of Minnesota, Twin Cities Campus (MN)
U of Rhode Island (RI)
U of Rochester (NY)
U of South Florida (FL)
The U of Texas at El Paso (TX)
U of Toronto (ON, Canada)
U of Vermont (VT)
U of Washington (WA)
U of Wisconsin–La Crosse (WI)
Utah State U (UT)
Wagner Coll (NY)
Worcester Polytechnic Inst (MA)
Xavier U of Louisiana (LA)

MEDICAL OFFICE ASSISTANT

Lewis-Clark State Coll (ID)

MEDICAL OFFICE MANAGEMENT

Eastern Kentucky U (KY)

MEDICAL RADIOLOGIC TECHNOLOGY

Arkansas State U (AR)
Avila U (MO)
Ball State U (IN)
Baptist Coll of Health Sciences (TN)
Bloomsburg U of Pennsylvania (PA)
Boise State U (ID)
California State U, Long Beach (CA)
Clarion U of Pennsylvania (PA)
Fairleigh Dickinson U, Coll at Florham (NJ)
Grand Valley State U (MI)
Idaho State U (ID)
Indiana U Bloomington (IN)
Indiana U Kokomo (IN)
Indiana U–Purdue U Indianapolis (IN)
Indiana U South Bend (IN)
Indiana U Southeast (IN)
Kent State U at Salem (OH)
La Roche Coll (PA)
Long Island U–C. W. Post Campus (NY)
Massachusetts Coll of Pharmacy and Health Sciences (MA)
Minot State U (ND)
Misericordia U (PA)
Missouri Southern State U (MO)
Morehead State U (KY)
Mount Aloysius Coll (PA)
Mount Marty Coll (SD)
New York City Coll of Technology of the City U of New York (NY)
North Central Coll (IL)
Notre Dame of Maryland U (MD)

Oakland U (MI)
The Ohio State U (OH)
Oregon Health & Science U (OR)
Rhode Island Coll (RI)
Roosevelt U (IL)
Saint Louis U (MO)
Southern Illinois U Carbondale (IL)
Southern Vermont Coll (VT)
State U of New York Upstate Medical U (NY)
Texas State U–San Marcos (TX)
Thomas Edison State Coll (NJ)
U of Central Arkansas (AR)
U of Cincinnati (OH)
The U of Findlay (OH)
U of Hartford (CT)
U of Michigan–Flint (MI)
U of Missouri (MO)
U of Nebraska Medical Center (NE)
U of Nevada, Las Vegas (NV)
U of New Mexico (NM)
The U of North Carolina at Chapel Hill (NC)
U of St. Francis (IL)
U of Southern Indiana (IN)
U of Vermont (VT)
U of Wisconsin–La Crosse (WI)
Wayne State U (MI)
Weber State U (UT)

MEDICAL STAFF SERVICES TECHNOLOGY

Converse Coll (SC)
Mount Vernon Nazarene U (OH)
St. Joseph's Coll, Long Island Campus (NY)
St. Joseph's Coll, New York (NY)

MEDICINAL AND PHARMACEUTICAL CHEMISTRY

King Coll (TN)
Michigan Technological U (MI)
Pittsburg State U (KS)
U of Guelph (ON, Canada)
U of Michigan (MI)
U of the Sciences in Philadelphia (PA)
Worcester Polytechnic Inst (MA)

MEDIEVAL AND RENAISSANCE STUDIES

Bard Coll (NY)
Barnard Coll (NY)
Brown U (RI)
The Catholic U of America (DC)
Cleveland State U (OH)
Coll of the Holy Cross (MA)
The Coll of William and Mary (VA)
Cornell Coll (IA)
Dickinson Coll (PA)
Emory U (GA)
Fordham U (NY)
Hanover Coll (IN)
Marlboro Coll (VT)
Mount Allison U (NB, Canada)
Mount Holyoke Coll (MA)
New Coll of Florida (FL)
The Ohio State U (OH)
Ohio Wesleyan U (OH)
Penn State Abington (PA)
Penn State Altoona (PA)
Penn State Beaver (PA)
Penn State Berks (PA)
Penn State Brandywine (PA)
Penn State DuBois (PA)
Penn State Erie, The Behrend Coll (PA)
Penn State Fayette, The Eberly Campus (PA)
Penn State Greater Allegheny (PA)
Penn State Hazleton (PA)
Penn State Lehigh Valley (PA)
Penn State Mont Alto (PA)
Penn State New Kensington (PA)
Penn State Schuylkill (PA)
Penn State Shenango (PA)
Penn State U Park (PA)
Penn State Wilkes-Barre (PA)
Penn State Worthington Scranton (PA)
Penn State York (PA)
Rutgers, The State U of New Jersey, New Brunswick (NJ)

St. Olaf Coll (MN)
Sewanee: The U of the South (TN)
Smith Coll (MA)
Southern Methodist U (TX)
State U of New York at Binghamton (NY)
Swarthmore Coll (PA)
Tulane U (LA)
U at Albany, State U of New York (NY)
U of California, Santa Barbara (CA)
The U of Iowa (IA)
U of Michigan (MI)
U of Nebraska–Lincoln (NE)
U of Notre Dame (IN)
U of Oregon (OR)
U of Ottawa (ON, Canada)
U of Regina (SK, Canada)
The U of Toledo (OH)
Vassar Coll (NY)
Washington and Lee U (VA)
Wellesley Coll (MA)
Wesleyan U (CT)

MEETING AND EVENT PLANNING
Lasell Coll (MA)
U of Central Florida (FL)

MENTAL AND SOCIAL HEALTH SERVICES AND ALLIED PROFESSIONS RELATED
Clarion U of Pennsylvania (PA)
Old Dominion U (VA)
Pennsylvania Coll of Technology (PA)
Roger Williams U (RI)
U of Maine at Augusta (ME)
U of Puerto Rico at Ponce (PR)
The U of Toledo (OH)
Washburn U (KS)

MENTAL HEALTH COUNSELING
Governors State U (IL)
U of Maine at Farmington (ME)

MERCHANDISING, SALES, AND MARKETING OPERATIONS RELATED (GENERAL)
Dalhousie U (NS, Canada)
Eastern Michigan U (MI)
Georgia State U (GA)
Lincoln U (MO)
Post U (CT)
U of Hartford (CT)
Washington U in St. Louis (MO)

MERCHANDISING, SALES, AND MARKETING OPERATIONS RELATED (SPECIALIZED)
Baylor U (TX)
Carlow U (PA)
Fashion Inst of Technology (NY)
Gannon U (PA)
Saint Joseph's U (PA)

METAL AND JEWELRY ARTS
Acad of Art U (CA)
Adams State Coll (CO)
Alberta Coll of Art & Design (AB, Canada)
Arcadia U (PA)
Bowling Green State U (OH)
California Coll of the Arts (CA)
California State U, Long Beach (CA)
The Cleveland Inst of Art (OH)
The Coll at Brockport, State U of New York (NY)
Colorado State U (CO)
Ferris State U (MI)
Hofstra U (NY)
Massachusetts Coll of Art and Design (MA)
Northern Michigan U (MI)
Pittsburg State U (KS)
Pratt Inst (NY)
Rochester Inst of Technology (NY)
Savannah Coll of Art and Design (GA)

School of the Museum of Fine Arts, Boston (MA)
Seton Hill U (PA)
State U of New York at New Paltz (NY)
Syracuse U (NY)
Temple U (PA)
The U of Iowa (IA)
The U of Kansas (KS)
U of Massachusetts Dartmouth (MA)
U of Michigan (MI)
U of Oregon (OR)
U of Washington (WA)
Western State Coll of Colorado (CO)

METALLURGICAL ENGINEERING
Cleveland State U (OH)
Colorado School of Mines (CO)
Michigan Technological U (MI)
Missouri U of Science and Technology (MO)
Montana Tech of The U of Montana (MT)
South Dakota School of Mines and Technology (SD)
The U of Alabama (AL)
U of Alberta (AB, Canada)
The U of British Columbia (BC, Canada)
U of Illinois at Urbana–Champaign (IL)
U of Minnesota, Twin Cities Campus (MN)
U of Nevada, Reno (NV)
The U of Texas at El Paso (TX)
U of Toronto (ON, Canada)
U of Utah (UT)
U of Washington (WA)

METEOROLOGY
Central Michigan U (MI)
The Coll at Brockport, State U of New York (NY)
Dalhousie U (NS, Canada)
Florida Inst of Technology (FL)
Florida State U (FL)
Metropolitan State Coll of Denver (CO)
U of Hawaii at Manoa (HI)
U of Miami (FL)
The U of North Carolina at Charlotte (NC)
U of Oklahoma (OK)
U of the Incarnate Word (TX)
U of Utah (UT)
U of Wisconsin–Milwaukee (WI)
Virginia Polytechnic Inst and State U (VA)
Western Illinois U (IL)
Western Kentucky U (KY)

MICROBIOLOGICAL SCIENCES AND IMMUNOLOGY RELATED
Dalhousie U (NS, Canada)
The U of Western Ontario (ON, Canada)

MICROBIOLOGY
Arizona State U (AZ)
Auburn U (AL)
Brigham Young U (UT)
California State U, Chico (CA)
California State U, Dominguez Hills (CA)
California State U, Long Beach (CA)
California State U, Los Angeles (CA)
Clemson U (SC)
Colorado State U (CO)
Idaho State U (ID)
Indiana U Bloomington (IN)
Inter American U of Puerto Rico, Ponce Campus (PR)
Inter American U of Puerto Rico, San Germán Campus (PR)
Iowa State U of Science and Technology (IA)
Juniata Coll (PA)
Kansas State U (KS)

Louisiana State U and Ag and Mech Coll (LA)
Miami U (OH)
Michigan State U (MI)
Michigan Technological U (MI)
North Carolina State U (NC)
North Dakota State U (ND)
Northern Arizona U (AZ)
Northern Michigan U (MI)
The Ohio State U (OH)
Ohio U (OH)
Oklahoma State U (OK)
San Diego State U (CA)
South Dakota State U (SD)
Southern Illinois U Carbondale (IL)
Texas A&M U (TX)
Texas State U–San Marcos (TX)
Texas Tech U (TX)
The U of Akron (OH)
The U of Alabama (AL)
The U of Arizona (AZ)
The U of British Columbia–Okanagan (BC, Canada)
U of California, Berkeley (CA)
U of California, Davis (CA)
U of California, Santa Barbara (CA)
U of Georgia (GA)
U of Guelph (ON, Canada)
U of Hawaii at Manoa (HI)
U of Houston–Downtown (TX)
U of Idaho (ID)
U of Illinois at Urbana–Champaign (IL)
The U of Iowa (IA)
The U of Kansas (KS)
U of Louisiana at Lafayette (LA)
U of Maryland, Coll Park (MD)
U of Massachusetts Amherst (MA)
U of Michigan (MI)
U of Michigan–Dearborn (MI)
U of Northern Iowa (IA)
U of Oklahoma (OK)
U of Pittsburgh (PA)
U of Puerto Rico at Humacao (PR)
U of Rhode Island (RI)
The U of Texas at Arlington (TX)
U of the Sciences in Philadelphia (PA)
U of Toronto (ON, Canada)
U of Vermont (VT)
The U of Western Ontario (ON, Canada)
U of Wisconsin–La Crosse (WI)
U of Wisconsin–Madison (WI)
U of Wisconsin–Milwaukee (WI)
U of Wyoming (WY)
Washington State U (WA)
Weber State U (UT)

MICROBIOLOGY AND IMMUNOLOGY
U of California, Irvine (CA)

MIDDLE/NEAR EASTERN AND SEMITIC LANGUAGES
U of Pennsylvania (PA)
The U of Texas at Austin (TX)

MIDDLE/NEAR EASTERN AND SEMITIC LANGUAGES RELATED
Bryn Mawr Coll (PA)
Columbia U, School of General Studies (NY)
Indiana U Bloomington (IN)
Sarah Lawrence Coll (NY)
U of Michigan (MI)
Wayne State U (MI)

MIDDLE SCHOOL EDUCATION
Abilene Christian U (TX)
Alaska Pacific U (AK)
Albany State U (GA)
Albertus Magnus Coll (CT)
Alverno Coll (WI)
Anna Maria Coll (MA)
Appalachian State U (NC)
Arkansas State U (AR)
Arkansas Tech U (AR)
Arlington Baptist Coll (TX)
Armstrong Atlantic State U (GA)
Asbury U (KY)
Ashland U (OH)

Assumption Coll (MA)
Avila U (MO)
Baker U (KS)
Baldwin-Wallace Coll (OH)
Barton Coll (NC)
Bayamón Central U (PR)
Bellarmine U (KY)
Bennington Coll (VT)
Berea Coll (KY)
Berry Coll (GA)
Bethel Coll (IN)
Black Hills State U (SD)
Bloomsburg U of Pennsylvania (PA)
Bluefield Coll (VA)
Bluffton U (OH)
Bob Jones U (SC)
Bowling Green State U (OH)
Brenau U (GA)
Brescia U (KY)
Brewton-Parker Coll (GA)
Butler U (IN)
Capital U (OH)
Carlow U (PA)
Catawba Coll (NC)
Cedarville U (OH)
Central Methodist U (MO)
Central State U (OH)
Claflin U (SC)
Clarion U of Pennsylvania (PA)
Clark U (MA)
Clayton State U (GA)
Cleveland State U (OH)
Coastal Carolina U (SC)
The Coll at Brockport, State U of New York (NY)
Coll of Charleston (SC)
Coll of Mount St. Joseph (OH)
Coll of the Atlantic (ME)
Coll of the Ozarks (MO)
Columbia Coll (SC)
Columbus State U (GA)
Concordia Coll–New York (NY)
Concordia U, Nebraska (NE)
Concordia U, St. Paul (MN)
Concordia U Texas (TX)
Delaware State U (DE)
Dowling Coll (NY)
Duquesne U (PA)
East Carolina U (NC)
Eastern Kentucky U (KY)
Edinboro U of Pennsylvania (PA)
Elizabeth City State U (NC)
Elizabethtown Coll (PA)
Elmira Coll (NY)
Elon U (NC)
Emmanuel Coll (GA)
Evangel U (MO)
Fayetteville State U (NC)
Fitchburg State U (MA)
Florida Inst of Technology (FL)
Fontbonne U (MO)
Gardner-Webb U (NC)
Geneva Coll (PA)
Georgetown Coll (KY)
Georgia Coll & State U (GA)
Georgia Southern U (GA)
Georgia Southwestern State U (GA)
Gettysburg Coll (PA)
Gordon Coll (MA)
Governors State U (IL)
Grambling State U (LA)
Grand Valley State U (MI)
Granite State Coll (NH)
Grove City Coll (PA)
Hampton U (VA)
Harding U (AR)
Howard Payne U (TX)
Huntington U (IN)
Indiana Wesleyan U (IN)
Iowa Wesleyan Coll (IA)
Ithaca Coll (NY)
Jacksonville State U (AL)
Johnson State Coll (VT)
Kennesaw State U (GA)
Kent State U (OH)
Kent State U at Geauga (OH)
Kent State U at Stark (OH)
Kentucky Christian U (KY)
Kentucky Wesleyan Coll (KY)
Keystone Coll (PA)
King Coll (TN)
Kutztown U of Pennsylvania (PA)
Lake Erie Coll (OH)
Lake Superior State U (MI)
Lee U (TN)

Lenoir-Rhyne U (NC)
Lincoln U (MO)
Lindenwood U (MO)
Lindsey Wilson Coll (KY)
Lourdes U (OH)
Lubbock Christian U (TX)
Macon State Coll (GA)
Malone U (OH)
Manchester Coll (IN)
Manhattan Coll (NY)
Marian U (WI)
Mars Hill Coll (NC)
Maryville U of Saint Louis (MO)
The Master's Coll and Sem (CA)
McKendree U (IL)
McMurry U (TX)
Medaille Coll (NY)
Mercer U (GA)
Merrimack Coll (MA)
Miami U (OH)
Michigan State U (MI)
MidAmerica Nazarene U (KS)
Millersville U of Pennsylvania (PA)
Misericordia U (PA)
Missouri Baptist U (MO)
Missouri State U (MO)
Morehead State U (KY)
Mount Aloysius Coll (PA)
Mount Mary Coll (WI)
Mount Mercy U (IA)
Mount Vernon Nazarene U (OH)
Nebraska Wesleyan U (NE)
Newberry Coll (SC)
Nicholls State U (LA)
North Carolina Central U (NC)
North Carolina State U (NC)
North Carolina Wesleyan Coll (NC)
Northern Kentucky U (KY)
North Georgia Coll & State U (GA)
Northwest Missouri State U (MO)
Nova Southeastern U (FL)
Oakland City U (IN)
Ohio Northern U (OH)
The Ohio State U (OH)
The Ohio State U at Lima (OH)
The Ohio State U at Marion (OH)
The Ohio State U–Mansfield Campus (OH)
The Ohio State U–Newark Campus (OH)
Ohio Wesleyan U (OH)
Otterbein U (OH)
Ouachita Baptist U (AR)
Paine Coll (GA)
Peru State Coll (NE)
Piedmont Coll (GA)
Point U (GA)
Presbyterian Coll (SC)
Reinhardt U (GA)
Roger Williams U (RI)
Saint Leo U (FL)
Saint Louis U (MO)
Salem State U (MA)
Schreiner U (TX)
Shippensburg U of Pennsylvania (PA)
Shorter U (GA)
South Carolina State U (SC)
Southeastern Louisiana U (LA)
Southeast Missouri State U (MO)
Southern Arkansas U–Magnolia (AR)
Southwest Baptist U (MO)
State U of New York Coll at Cortland (NY)
State U of New York Coll at Old Westbury (NY)
State U of New York Coll at Oneonta (NY)
Stevenson U (MD)
Tarleton State U (TX)
Texas Lutheran U (TX)
Thomas More Coll (KY)
Thomas U (GA)
Transylvania U (KY)
Tusculum Coll (TN)
Union Coll (KY)
The U of Akron (OH)
U of Arkansas at Monticello (AR)
U of Arkansas–Fort Smith (AR)
U of Central Arkansas (AR)
U of Central Missouri (MO)
U of Cincinnati (OH)
U of Georgia (GA)
U of Great Falls (MT)

The U of Kansas (KS)
U of Mary Hardin-Baylor (TX)
U of Maryland, Coll Park (MD)
U of Minnesota, Duluth (MN)
U of Missouri (MO)
U of Missouri–Kansas City (MO)
U of Mount Union (OH)
The U of North Carolina at Chapel Hill (NC)
The U of North Carolina at Charlotte (NC)
The U of North Carolina Wilmington (NC)
U of North Dakota (ND)
U of Northern Iowa (IA)
U of North Florida (FL)
U of Pikeville (KY)
U of Regina (SK, Canada)
U of St. Thomas (MN)
The U of Scranton (PA)
U of South Carolina (SC)
U of South Carolina Aiken (SC)
U of South Carolina Upstate (SC)
The U of Tennessee at Chattanooga (TN)
U of the Cumberlands (KY)
U of the Ozarks (AR)
U of Vermont (VT)
The U of Western Ontario (ON, Canada)
U of West Florida (FL)
U of West Georgia (GA)
U of Wisconsin–Platteville (WI)
Ursuline Coll (OH)
Valdosta State U (GA)
Virginia Wesleyan Coll (VA)
Walsh U (OH)
Washington U in St. Louis (MO)
Wayland Baptist U (TX)
Wayne State Coll (NE)
West Chester U of Pennsylvania (PA)
Western Carolina U (NC)
Western Kentucky U (KY)
Westminster Coll (MO)
West Virginia Wesleyan Coll (WV)
Wheeling Jesuit U (WV)
William Jewell Coll (MO)
William Woods U (MO)
Wilmington U (DE)
Wingate U (NC)
Winona State U (MN)
Wright State U (OH)
Xavier U (OH)
Xavier U of Louisiana (LA)
Youngstown State U (OH)

MILITARY APPLIED SCIENCES RELATED
United States Military Acad (NY)

MILITARY HISTORY
American Public U System (WV)
Rogers State U (OK)

MILITARY STUDIES
American Public U System (WV)
Hawai`i Pacific U (HI)
Pacific Lutheran U (WA)
United States Air Force Acad (CO)

MILITARY TECHNOLOGIES AND APPLIED SCIENCES RELATED
Alcorn State U (MS)

MINING AND MINERAL ENGINEERING
Colorado School of Mines (CO)
Missouri U of Science and Technology (MO)
Montana Tech of The U of Montana (MT)
New Mexico Inst of Mining and Technology (NM)
Penn State Abington (PA)
Penn State Altoona (PA)
Penn State Beaver (PA)
Penn State Berks (PA)
Penn State Brandywine (PA)
Penn State DuBois (PA)
Penn State Erie, The Behrend Coll (PA)

Penn State Fayette, The Eberly Campus (PA)
Penn State Greater Allegheny (PA)
Penn State Hazleton (PA)
Penn State Lehigh Valley (PA)
Penn State Mont Alto (PA)
Penn State New Kensington (PA)
Penn State Schuylkill (PA)
Penn State Shenango (PA)
Penn State U Park (PA)
Penn State Wilkes-Barre (PA)
Penn State Worthington Scranton (PA)
Penn State York (PA)
Queen's U at Kingston (ON, Canada)
South Dakota School of Mines and Technology (SD)
Southern Illinois U Carbondale (IL)
U of Alaska Fairbanks (AK)
U of Alberta (AB, Canada)
The U of Arizona (AZ)
The U of British Columbia (BC, Canada)
U of Minnesota, Twin Cities Campus (MN)
U of Nevada, Reno (NV)
U of Toronto (ON, Canada)
U of Utah (UT)
Virginia Polytechnic Inst and State U (VA)
West Virginia U (WV)

MINING TECHNOLOGY
Bluefield State Coll (WV)

MISSIONARY STUDIES AND MISSIOLOGY
Abilene Christian U (TX)
Asbury U (KY)
Baptist Bible Coll of Pennsylvania (PA)
Bethel Coll (IN)
Biola U (CA)
Bob Jones U (SC)
Briercrest Coll (SK, Canada)
Calvary Bible Coll and Theological Sem (MO)
Cedarville U (OH)
City Vision Coll (MO)
Columbia Bible Coll (BC, Canada)
Concordia U, St. Paul (MN)
Corban U (OR)
Crown Coll (MN)
Dordt Coll (IA)
Eastern U (PA)
East Texas Baptist U (TX)
Emmaus Bible Coll (IA)
Faith Baptist Bible Coll and Theological Sem (IA)
Free Will Baptist Bible Coll (TN)
Gardner-Webb U (NC)
Harding U (AR)
Hardin-Simmons U (TX)
Hillsdale Free Will Baptist Coll (OK)
Hope Intl U (CA)
Howard Payne U (TX)
Huntington U (IN)
Indiana Wesleyan U (IN)
Judson U (IL)
Kentucky Mountain Bible Coll (KY)
LeTourneau U (TX)
Liberty U (VA)
Lincoln Christian U (IL)
Lipscomb U (TN)
Lubbock Christian U (TX)
Maranatha Baptist Bible Coll (WI)
MidAmerica Nazarene U (KS)
Mid-Atlantic Christian U (NC)
Mid-Continent U (KY)
Moody Bible Inst (IL)
Mount Vernon Nazarene U (OH)
Multnomah U (OR)
New Hope Christian Coll (OR)
North Greenville U (SC)
Northwestern Coll (MN)
Northwest Nazarene U (ID)
Northwest U (WA)
Nyack Coll (NY)
Oklahoma Christian U (OK)
Oral Roberts U (OK)
Ouachita Baptist U (AR)
Palm Beach Atlantic U (FL)
Piedmont Intl U (NC)

Simpson U (CA)
Southeastern Baptist Theological Sem (NC)
Southeastern U (FL)
Southwest Baptist U (MO)
Southwestern Christian U (OK)
Tabor Coll (KS)
Trevecca Nazarene U (TN)
Trinity Baptist Coll (FL)
Trinity Coll of Florida (FL)
Vanguard U of Southern California (CA)
William Jessup U (CA)

MODELING, VIRTUAL ENVIRONMENTS AND SIMULATION
Daniel Webster Coll (NH)
DigiPen Inst of Technology (WA)
U of Colorado at Colorado Springs (CO)

MODERN GREEK
Belmont U (TN)
Boston U (MA)
Butler U (IN)
Calvin Coll (MI)
Colgate U (NY)
Emory U (GA)
Fordham U (NY)
Furman U (SC)
Haverford Coll (PA)
John Carroll U (OH)
Lehman Coll of the City U of New York (NY)
Marlboro Coll (VT)
The Ohio State U (OH)
Rhodes Coll (TN)
Saint Mary's Coll of California (CA)
Sewanee: The U of the South (TN)
Trent U (ON, Canada)
Tufts U (MA)
Tulane U (LA)
U of Alberta (AB, Canada)
U of Michigan (MI)
U of Toronto (ON, Canada)
Wabash Coll (IN)
Wright State U (OH)

MODERN LANGUAGES
Alma Coll (MI)
Beloit Coll (WI)
Bemidji State U (MN)
Bishop's U (QC, Canada)
Clark U (MA)
Clemson U (SC)
Coll of Mount Saint Vincent (NY)
The Coll of William and Mary (VA)
Cornell Coll (IA)
Fordham U (NY)
Franklin Coll Switzerland (Switzerland)
Gettysburg Coll (PA)
Hampton U (VA)
King Coll (TN)
La Salle U (PA)
Lee U (TN)
Long Island U–Brooklyn Campus (NY)
Louisiana Coll (LA)
Marlboro Coll (VT)
Metropolitan State Coll of Denver (CO)
Middlebury Coll (VT)
Minnesota State U Mankato (MN)
Mount Allison U (NB, Canada)
Nazareth Coll of Rochester (NY)
Pacific U (OR)
Pomona Coll (CA)
Presbyterian Coll (SC)
Purchase Coll, State U of New York (NY)
Rivier Coll (NH)
St. Bonaventure U (NY)
Saint Francis U (PA)
St. Lawrence U (NY)
Saint Mary's Coll of California (CA)
Saint Michael's Coll (VT)
Saint Peter's Coll (NJ)
St. Thomas Aquinas Coll (NY)
Sarah Lawrence Coll (NY)
Suffolk U (MA)
Trent U (ON, Canada)
Trinity Coll (CT)

U of Alberta (AB, Canada)
U of Louisiana at Lafayette (LA)
U of Maine (ME)
U of Ottawa (ON, Canada)
U of Toronto (ON, Canada)
The U of Western Ontario (ON, Canada)
U of Windsor (ON, Canada)
Walsh U (OH)
Washington U in St. Louis (MO)
Widener U (PA)
Wilmington Coll (OH)
Wright State U (OH)

MOLECULAR BIOCHEMISTRY
Clarkson U (NY)
Michigan Technological U (MI)
Simon Fraser U (BC, Canada)
U of California, Davis (CA)
U of Richmond (VA)

MOLECULAR BIOLOGY
Alverno Coll (WI)
Arizona State U (AZ)
Assumption Coll (MA)
Auburn U (AL)
Beloit Coll (WI)
Blackburn Coll (IL)
Boston U (MA)
Brown U (RI)
California Lutheran U (CA)
California State U, Fresno (CA)
California State U, San Marcos (CA)
Central Connecticut State U (CT)
Centre Coll (KY)
Chestnut Hill Coll (PA)
Claremont McKenna Coll (CA)
Clarion U of Pennsylvania (PA)
Clark U (MA)
Coe Coll (IA)
Colby Coll (ME)
Colgate U (NY)
The Coll at Brockport, State U of New York (NY)
The Coll of Wooster (OH)
Connecticut Coll (CT)
Dartmouth Coll (NH)
Florida Inst of Technology (FL)
Gettysburg Coll (PA)
Goshen Coll (IN)
Grove City Coll (PA)
Hampton U (VA)
Humboldt State U (CA)
Juniata Coll (PA)
Kenyon Coll (OH)
Lakehead U (ON, Canada)
Lawrence Technological U (MI)
Lehigh U (PA)
Marlboro Coll (VT)
Messiah Coll (PA)
Middlebury Coll (VT)
Millikin U (IL)
Montclair State U (NJ)
Ohio Northern U (OH)
Otterbein U (OH)
Pitzer Coll (CA)
Pomona Coll (CA)
Princeton U (NJ)
Rollins Coll (FL)
Rutgers, The State U of New Jersey, New Brunswick (NJ)
San Francisco State U (CA)
Sarah Lawrence Coll (NY)
Scripps Coll (CA)
Simon Fraser U (BC, Canada)
Stetson U (FL)
Thompson Rivers U (BC, Canada)
Tulane U (LA)
U at Albany, State U of New York (NY)
U of Alberta (AB, Canada)
The U of British Columbia–Okanagan (BC, Canada)
U of California, Santa Barbara (CA)
U of California, Santa Cruz (CA)
U of Denver (CO)
U of Guelph (ON, Canada)
U of Idaho (ID)
The U of Kansas (KS)
U of Maine (ME)
U of Michigan–Flint (MI)
U of Minnesota, Duluth (MN)
U of Pittsburgh (PA)

U of Puget Sound (WA)
The U of Scranton (PA)
The U of Texas at Dallas (TX)
U of Toronto (ON, Canada)
U of Vermont (VT)
U of Washington (WA)
U of Wisconsin–Eau Claire (WI)
U of Wisconsin–Madison (WI)
U of Wyoming (WY)
Vanderbilt U (TN)
Wayland Baptist U (TX)
Wells Coll (NY)
Wesleyan U (CT)
Western New England U (MA)
Whitman Coll (WA)
William Jewell Coll (MO)
Worcester Polytechnic Inst (MA)
Yale U (CT)
Yeshiva U (NY)

MOLECULAR GENETICS
Michigan State U (MI)
The Ohio State U (OH)
Texas A&M U (TX)
U of Guelph (ON, Canada)
U of Rochester (NY)
U of Vermont (VT)
Washington State U (WA)

MOLECULAR PHARMACOLOGY
The U of Scranton (PA)

MONTESSORI TEACHER EDUCATION
Oklahoma City U (OK)
Siena Heights U (MI)
Xavier U (OH)

MOVEMENT THERAPY AND MOVEMENT EDUCATION
Pacific Lutheran U (WA)
Texas Christian U (TX)
U of Vermont (VT)

MULTICULTURAL EDUCATION
Carnegie Mellon U (PA)
Fort Lewis Coll (CO)
Goddard Coll (VT)
Indiana Wesleyan U (IN)

MULTI/INTERDISCIPLINARY STUDIES RELATED
Abilene Christian U (TX)
Adams State Coll (CO)
Adelphi U (NY)
Agnes Scott Coll (GA)
Albright Coll (PA)
Allegheny Coll (PA)
American U (DC)
Anderson U (IN)
Angelo State U (TX)
Anna Maria Coll (MA)
Arcadia U (PA)
Arizona State U (AZ)
Arkansas State U (AR)
Arkansas Tech U (AR)
Austin Coll (TX)
Baldwin-Wallace Coll (OH)
Bates Coll (ME)
Baylor U (TX)
Bellarmine U (KY)
Bennington Coll (VT)
Bentley U (MA)
Berea Coll (KY)
Berry Coll (GA)
Bethel U (MN)
Bethel U (TN)
Bluffton U (OH)
Boston U (MA)
Bowdoin Coll (ME)
Bowling Green State U (OH)
Brandeis U (MA)
Brevard Coll (NC)
Bryn Athyn Coll of the New Church (PA)
Bucknell U (PA)
Buena Vista U (IA)
Buffalo State Coll, State U of New York (NY)
Caldwell Coll (NJ)
California Baptist U (CA)

INDEXES

California Lutheran U (CA)
California Polytechnic State U, San Luis Obispo (CA)
California State U, Chico (CA)
California State U, Dominguez Hills (CA)
California State U, Long Beach (CA)
California State U, Los Angeles (CA)
California State U, Monterey Bay (CA)
California State U, Stanislaus (CA)
Cameron U (OK)
Capital U (OH)
Carroll Coll (MT)
Central Connecticut State U (CT)
Chester Coll of New England (NH)
Chestnut Hill Coll (PA)
Christopher Newport U (VA)
Claremont McKenna Coll (CA)
Clarkson U (NY)
Cleveland State U (OH)
Colby Coll (ME)
The Coll of Idaho (ID)
The Coll of New Jersey (NJ)
Coll of Saint Benedict (MN)
Coll of Saint Elizabeth (NJ)
The Coll of Saint Rose (NY)
The Coll of William and Mary (VA)
The Coll of Wooster (OH)
The Colorado Coll (CO)
Columbia Coll Chicago (IL)
Cornell Coll (IA)
Cornell U (NY)
Cornerstone U (MI)
Covenant Coll (GA)
Dalhousie U (NS, Canada)
Dallas Baptist U (TX)
Dallas Christian Coll (TX)
Dartmouth Coll (NH)
Davidson Coll (NC)
Delta State U (MS)
DePauw U (IN)
Dixie State Coll of Utah (UT)
Earlham Coll (IN)
East Central U (OK)
Eastern Illinois U (IL)
Eastern Mennonite U (VA)
Eastern Michigan U (MI)
Eastern New Mexico U (NM)
Eastern Oregon U (OR)
Eastern Washington U (WA)
East Tennessee State U (TN)
East Texas Baptist U (TX)
Edgewood Coll (WI)
Embry-Riddle Aeronautical U–Daytona (FL)
Embry-Riddle Aeronautical U–Prescott (AZ)
Emmanuel Coll (MA)
Emporia State U (KS)
The Evergreen State Coll (WA)
Florida Inst of Technology (FL)
Florida Southern Coll (FL)
Franklin & Marshall Coll (PA)
Franklin U (OH)
Gannon U (PA)
Georgetown Coll (KY)
Georgia Inst of Technology (GA)
Georgian Court U (NJ)
Georgia State U (GA)
Glenville State Coll (WV)
Goshen Coll (IN)
Goucher Coll (MD)
Grand Canyon U (AZ)
Granite State Coll (NH)
Greenville Coll (IL)
Hamline U (MN)
Hampshire Coll (MA)
Hood Coll (MD)
Hope Coll (MI)
Howard Payne U (TX)
Humboldt State U (CA)
Illinois Wesleyan U (IL)
Immaculata U (PA)
Indiana U Bloomington (IN)
Indiana U–Purdue U Indianapolis (IN)
Indiana U Southeast (IN)
Iowa State U of Science and Technology (IA)
Ithaca Coll (NY)
John Brown U (AR)
Judson U (IL)

Juniata Coll (PA)
Keene State Coll (NH)
Kennesaw State U (GA)
Kentucky Christian U (KY)
Kentucky Wesleyan Coll (KY)
Kenyon Coll (OH)
Knox Coll (IL)
Lake Erie Coll (OH)
Lane Coll (TN)
Lasell Coll (MA)
Lebanon Valley Coll (PA)
Lewis-Clark State Coll (ID)
Lewis U (IL)
Liberty U (VA)
Long Island U–Brooklyn Campus (NY)
Louisiana State U and Ag and Mech Coll (LA)
Lourdes U (OH)
Loyola Marymount U (CA)
Luther Coll (IA)
Lycoming Coll (PA)
Manchester Coll (IN)
Marian U (WI)
Marquette U (WI)
Marylhurst U (OR)
Maryville Coll (TN)
McDaniel Coll (MD)
McMurry U (TX)
Mercer U (GA)
Mercyhurst Coll (PA)
Meredith Coll (NC)
Messiah Coll (PA)
Metropolitan State U (MN)
Michigan State U (MI)
Mid-Continent U (KY)
Middle Tennessee State U (TN)
Millikin U (IL)
Millsaps Coll (MS)
Minnesota State U Moorhead (MN)
Mississippi State U (MS)
Mississippi U for Women (MS)
Missouri Baptist U (MO)
Missouri Western State U (MO)
Monmouth U (NJ)
Montana State U Billings (MT)
Montclair State U (NJ)
Mountain State U (WV)
Mount Holyoke Coll (MA)
Mount Mary Coll (WI)
Mount Mercy U (IA)
Mount St. Mary's U (MD)
Naropa U (CO)
National-Louis U (IL)
Newman U (KS)
New York Inst of Technology (NY)
Norfolk State U (VA)
North Central Coll (IL)
Northeastern State U (OK)
Northern Illinois U (IL)
Northland Coll (WI)
Northwest Christian U (OR)
Northwestern Coll (MN)
Northwestern Oklahoma State U (OK)
Northwest Missouri State U (MO)
The Ohio State U (OH)
Ohio Wesleyan U (OH)
Old Dominion U (VA)
Otterbein U (OH)
Pace U (NY)
Park U (MO)
Penn State Erie, The Behrend Coll (PA)
Penn State Harrisburg (PA)
Plymouth State U (NH)
Point Park U (PA)
Prairie View A&M U (TX)
Princeton U (NJ)
Queens Coll of the City U of New York (NY)
Radford U (VA)
Regis Coll (MA)
Rice U (TX)
The Richard Stockton Coll of New Jersey (NJ)
Robert Morris U (PA)
Robert Morris U Illinois (IL)
Rocky Mountain Coll (MT)
Rogers State U (OK)
Roger Williams U (RI)
Rollins Coll (FL)
Rowan U (NJ)
Rutgers, The State U of New Jersey, Camden (NJ)

Rutgers, The State U of New Jersey, Newark (NJ)
Ryerson U (ON, Canada)
Sage Coll of Albany (NY)
St. Ambrose U (IA)
Saint Anselm Coll (NH)
Saint John's U (MN)
Saint Martin's U (WA)
Saint Mary's Coll of California (CA)
St. Mary's Coll of Maryland (MD)
Sam Houston State U (TX)
San Diego Christian Coll (CA)
San Diego State U (CA)
San Francisco State U (CA)
Scripps Coll (CA)
Shippensburg U of Pennsylvania (PA)
Simmons Coll (MA)
Sonoma State U (CA)
South Dakota State U (SD)
Southeastern Oklahoma State U (OK)
Southeast Missouri State U (MO)
Southern Arkansas U–Magnolia (AR)
Southern Illinois U Carbondale (IL)
Southern Methodist U (TX)
State U of New York at Binghamton (NY)
State U of New York Coll at Potsdam (NY)
Stephen F. Austin State U (TX)
Stonehill Coll (MA)
Stony Brook U, State U of New York (NY)
Tarleton State U (TX)
Temple U (PA)
Texas A&M U (TX)
Texas A&M U–Kingsville (TX)
Texas State U–San Marcos (TX)
Texas Tech U (TX)
Texas Wesleyan U (TX)
Texas Woman's U (TX)
Thomas Edison State Coll (NJ)
Thomas More Coll (KY)
Truett-McConnell Coll (GA)
Truman State U (MO)
Tulane U (LA)
Tusculum Coll (TN)
U at Albany, State U of New York (NY)
U at Buffalo, the State U of New York (NY)
The U of Akron (OH)
The U of Alabama in Huntsville (AL)
U of Alaska Fairbanks (AK)
The U of Arizona (AZ)
U of Arkansas at Monticello (AR)
U of Arkansas–Fort Smith (AR)
U of California, Berkeley (CA)
U of California, Davis (CA)
U of California, Irvine (CA)
U of California, Los Angeles (CA)
U of California, Santa Barbara (CA)
U of Central Arkansas (AR)
U of Cincinnati (OH)
U of Colorado at Colorado Springs (CO)
U of Colorado Denver (CO)
U of Connecticut (CT)
U of Denver (CO)
U of Evansville (IN)
U of Florida (FL)
U of Houston (TX)
U of Houston–Clear Lake (TX)
U of Houston–Downtown (TX)
U of Houston–Victoria (TX)
U of Idaho (ID)
U of Lethbridge (AB, Canada)
U of Maryland, Baltimore County (MD)
U of Maryland, Coll Park (MD)
U of Maryland U Coll (MD)
U of Mary Washington (VA)
U of Massachusetts Amherst (MA)
U of Massachusetts Boston (MA)
U of Massachusetts Dartmouth (MA)
U of Memphis (TN)
U of Michigan (MI)
U of Michigan–Dearborn (MI)
U of Michigan–Flint (MI)
U of Minnesota, Crookston (MN)
U of Minnesota, Duluth (MN)

U of Minnesota, Twin Cities Campus (MN)
U of Missouri–St. Louis (MO)
U of Mobile (AL)
U of Nebraska at Omaha (NE)
U of New Hampshire (NH)
U of New Orleans (LA)
U of North Dakota (ND)
U of Northern Colorado (CO)
U of North Texas (TX)
U of Oregon (OR)
U of Pikeville (KY)
U of Pittsburgh (PA)
U of Richmond (VA)
U of St. Francis (IL)
U of Saint Mary (KS)
U of St. Thomas (MN)
The U of South Dakota (SD)
U of Southern California (CA)
U of South Florida (FL)
The U of Tennessee (TN)
The U of Texas at Arlington (TX)
The U of Texas at Austin (TX)
The U of Texas at Tyler (TX)
The U of Texas of the Permian Basin (TX)
The U of Texas–Pan American (TX)
The U of Toledo (OH)
U of Virginia (VA)
U of Washington, Bothell (WA)
The U of Western Ontario (ON, Canada)
U of Wisconsin–Green Bay (WI)
U of Wisconsin–Milwaukee (WI)
U of Wisconsin–River Falls (WI)
U of Wisconsin–Stevens Point (WI)
U of Wisconsin–Superior (WI)
U of Wyoming (WY)
Utah State U (UT)
Utah Valley U (UT)
Valparaiso U (IN)
Vanderbilt U (TN)
Vassar Coll (NY)
Villanova U (PA)
Virginia Commonwealth U (VA)
Virginia Intermont Coll (VA)
Virginia Wesleyan Coll (VA)
Viterbo U (WI)
Waldorf Coll (IA)
Washburn U (KS)
Washington & Jefferson Coll (PA)
Washington and Lee U (VA)
Washington Coll (MD)
Washington State U (WA)
Washington U in St. Louis (MO)
Western Kentucky U (KY)
Western Michigan U (MI)
Western Washington U (WA)
West Texas A&M U (TX)
Wheaton Coll (IL)
Wichita State U (KS)
Wilkes U (PA)
Wilson Coll (PA)
Xavier U (OH)
Yale U (CT)
Yeshiva U (NY)

MUSEUM STUDIES

Beloit Coll (WI)
Centenary Coll of Louisiana (LA)
Coll of the Atlantic (ME)
Juniata Coll (PA)
Moore Coll of Art & Design (PA)
Randolph Coll (VA)
Tusculum Coll (TN)
The U of Iowa (IA)
Walsh U (OH)

MUSIC

Abilene Christian U (TX)
Acadia U (NS, Canada)
Adams State Coll (CO)
Adelphi U (NY)
Adrian Coll (MI)
Agnes Scott Coll (GA)
Alabama State U (AL)
Albany State U (GA)
Albion Coll (MI)
Albright Coll (PA)
Allegheny Coll (PA)
Alma Coll (MI)
Alverno Coll (WI)
American U (DC)
Amherst Coll (MA)

Anderson U (SC)
Andrews U (MI)
Angelo State U (TX)
Anna Maria Coll (MA)
Aquinas Coll (MI)
Arizona State U (AZ)
Arkansas State U (AR)
Arkansas Tech U (AR)
Arlington Baptist Coll (TX)
Armstrong Atlantic State U (GA)
Asbury U (KY)
Ashland U (OH)
Assumption Coll (MA)
Auburn U (AL)
Augustana Coll (IL)
Augustana Coll (SD)
Austin Coll (TX)
Austin Peay State U (TN)
Averett U (VA)
Avila U (MO)
Azusa Pacific U (CA)
Baker U (KS)
Baldwin-Wallace Coll (OH)
Ball State U (IN)
Baptist Bible Coll of Pennsylvania (PA)
Bard Coll (NY)
Bard Coll at Simon's Rock (MA)
Barnard Coll (NY)
Bates Coll (ME)
Baylor U (TX)
Belhaven U (MS)
Bellarmine U (KY)
Belmont U (TN)
Beloit Coll (WI)
Bemidji State U (MN)
Benedictine Coll (KS)
Benedictine U (IL)
Bennett Coll for Women (NC)
Bennington Coll (VT)
Berea Coll (KY)
Berklee Coll of Music (MA)
Bernard M. Baruch Coll of the City U of New York (NY)
Berry Coll (GA)
Bethany Coll (KS)
Bethany Coll (WV)
Bethany Lutheran Coll (MN)
Bethel Coll (IN)
Bethel U (MN)
Bethel U (TN)
Biola U (CA)
Birmingham-Southern Coll (AL)
Bishop's U (QC, Canada)
Blackburn Coll (IL)
Black Hills State U (SD)
Bloomsburg U of Pennsylvania (PA)
Bluefield Coll (VA)
Blue Mountain Coll (MS)
Bluffton U (OH)
Boise State U (ID)
Boston Coll (MA)
Boston U (MA)
Bowdoin Coll (ME)
Bowling Green State U (OH)
Bradley U (IL)
Brandeis U (MA)
Brenau U (GA)
Brevard Coll (NC)
Briar Cliff U (IA)
Bridgewater State U (MA)
Brown U (RI)
Bryn Mawr Coll (PA)
Bucknell U (PA)
Buffalo State Coll, State U of New York (NY)
Butler U (IN)
Caldwell Coll (NJ)
California Baptist U (CA)
California Lutheran U (CA)
California Polytechnic State U, San Luis Obispo (CA)
California State Polytechnic U, Pomona (CA)
California State U, Bakersfield (CA)
California State U, Chico (CA)
California State U, Dominguez Hills (CA)
California State U, East Bay (CA)
California State U, Fresno (CA)
California State U, Fullerton (CA)
California State U, Long Beach (CA)
California State U, Los Angeles (CA)

California State U, Monterey Bay (CA)
California State U, Sacramento (CA)
California State U, San Bernardino (CA)
California State U, Stanislaus (CA)
Calvin Coll (MI)
Cameron U (OK)
Campbellsville U (KY)
Canisius Coll (NY)
Capital U (OH)
Cardinal Stritch U (WI)
Carleton Coll (MN)
Carson-Newman U (TN)
Case Western Reserve U (OH)
Castleton State Coll (VT)
Catawba Coll (NC)
The Catholic U of America (DC)
Cedar Crest Coll (PA)
Cedarville U (OH)
Centenary Coll of Louisiana (LA)
Central Coll (IA)
Central Connecticut State U (CT)
Central Methodist U (MO)
Central Michigan U (MI)
Central Washington U (WA)
Centre Coll (KY)
Chapman U (CA)
Chatham U (PA)
Chestnut Hill Coll (PA)
Cheyney U of Pennsylvania (PA)
Chicago State U (IL)
Christopher Newport U (VA)
City Coll of the City U of New York (NY)
Claflin U (SC)
Clark Atlanta U (GA)
Clarke U (IA)
Clark U (MA)
Clayton State U (GA)
Clearwater Christian Coll (FL)
Cleveland State U (OH)
Coastal Carolina U (SC)
Coe Coll (IA)
Colby Coll (ME)
Colgate U (NY)
Coll of Charleston (SC)
The Coll of Idaho (ID)
Coll of Mount St. Joseph (OH)
The Coll of New Jersey (NJ)
Coll of Saint Benedict (MN)
Coll of Saint Elizabeth (NJ)
The Coll of Saint Rose (NY)
Coll of Staten Island of the City U of New York (NY)
Coll of the Atlantic (ME)
Coll of the Holy Cross (MA)
Coll of the Ozarks (MO)
The Coll of William and Mary (VA)
The Coll of Wooster (OH)
The Colorado Coll (CO)
Colorado Mesa U (CO)
Colorado State U (CO)
Columbia Coll (SC)
Columbia Coll Chicago (IL)
Columbia U, School of General Studies (NY)
Columbus State U (GA)
Concordia Coll (MN)
Concordia Coll–New York (NY)
Concordia U (MI)
Concordia U (QC, Canada)
Concordia U Chicago (IL)
Concordia U, Nebraska (NE)
Concordia U, St. Paul (MN)
Connecticut Coll (CT)
Converse Coll (SC)
Corban U (OR)
Cornell Coll (IA)
Cornell U (NY)
Cornerstone U (MI)
Cornish Coll of the Arts (WA)
Covenant Coll (GA)
Creighton U (NE)
Crown Coll (MN)
Culver-Stockton Coll (MO)
Dalhousie U (NS, Canada)
Dallas Baptist U (TX)
Dartmouth Coll (NH)
Davidson Coll (NC)
Delaware State U (DE)
Delta State U (MS)
Denison U (OH)
DePaul U (IL)

DePauw U (IN)
DEREE - The American Coll of Greece (Greece)
Dickinson Coll (PA)
Dillard U (LA)
Dixie State Coll of Utah (UT)
Doane Coll (NE)
Dominican U (IL)
Dominican U of California (CA)
Dordt Coll (IA)
Dowling Coll (NY)
Drake U (IA)
Drew U (NJ)
Drexel U (PA)
Drury U (MO)
Earlham Coll (IN)
East Central U (OK)
Eastern Illinois U (IL)
Eastern Kentucky U (KY)
Eastern Mennonite U (VA)
Eastern Michigan U (MI)
Eastern New Mexico U (NM)
Eastern Oregon U (OR)
Eastern U (PA)
Eastern Washington U (WA)
East Tennessee State U (TN)
East Texas Baptist U (TX)
Eckerd Coll (FL)
Edgewood Coll (WI)
Edinboro U of Pennsylvania (PA)
Elizabeth City State U (NC)
Elizabethtown Coll (PA)
Elmhurst Coll (IL)
Elmira Coll (NY)
Elon U (NC)
Emmanuel Coll (GA)
Emory U (GA)
Emporia State U (KS)
Evangel U (MO)
Excelsior Coll (NY)
Fairfield U (CT)
Fayetteville State U (NC)
Felician Coll (NJ)
Five Towns Coll (NY)
Florida Ag and Mech U (FL)
Florida Atlantic U (FL)
Florida Coll (FL)
Florida Intl U (FL)
Florida Southern Coll (FL)
Florida State U (FL)
Fordham U (NY)
Fort Hays State U (KS)
Fort Lewis Coll (CO)
Francis Marion U (SC)
Franklin & Marshall Coll (PA)
Free Will Baptist Bible Coll (TN)
Friends U (KS)
Furman U (SC)
Gardner-Webb U (NC)
Geneva Coll (PA)
George Fox U (OR)
Georgetown Coll (KY)
The George Washington U (DC)
Georgia Coll & State U (GA)
Georgian Court U (NJ)
Georgia Southern U (GA)
Georgia Southwestern State U (GA)
Gettysburg Coll (PA)
Gonzaga U (WA)
Gordon Coll (MA)
Goshen Coll (IN)
Goucher Coll (MD)
Graceland U (IA)
Grand Valley State U (MI)
Grand View U (IA)
Greenville Coll (IL)
Grinnell Coll (IA)
Grove City Coll (PA)
Guilford Coll (NC)
Gustavus Adolphus Coll (MN)
Hamilton Coll (NY)
Hamline U (MN)
Hampshire Coll (MA)
Hampton U (VA)
Hannibal-LaGrange U (MO)
Hanover Coll (IN)
Harding U (AR)
Hardin-Simmons U (TX)
Hartwick Coll (NY)
Harvard U (MA)
Haverford Coll (PA)
Hebrew Coll (MA)
Heidelberg U (OH)
Hendrix Coll (AR)
Hillsdale Coll (MI)

Hobart and William Smith Colls (NY)
Hofstra U (NY)
Hollins U (VA)
Hood Coll (MD)
Hope Coll (MI)
Houghton Coll (NY)
Humboldt State U (CA)
Hunter Coll of the City U of New York (NY)
Huntington U (IN)
Huston-Tillotson U (TX)
Idaho State U (ID)
Illinois Coll (IL)
Illinois State U (IL)
Illinois Wesleyan U (IL)
Immaculata U (PA)
Indiana State U (IN)
Indiana U Bloomington (IN)
Indiana U of Pennsylvania (PA)
Indiana U–Purdue U Fort Wayne (IN)
Indiana U South Bend (IN)
Indiana U Southeast (IN)
Inter American U of Puerto Rico, San Germán Campus (PR)
Iowa State U of Science and Technology (IA)
Iowa Wesleyan Coll (IA)
Ithaca Coll (NY)
Jacksonville State U (AL)
Jacksonville U (FL)
Jamestown Coll (ND)
John Brown U (AR)
The Johns Hopkins U (MD)
Johnson C. Smith U (NC)
Johnson State Coll (VT)
Judson Coll (AL)
The Juilliard School (NY)
Kalamazoo Coll (MI)
Kansas State U (KS)
Kean U (NJ)
Kennesaw State U (GA)
Kent State U (OH)
Kentucky State U (KY)
Kenyon Coll (OH)
King Coll (TN)
The King's U Coll (AB, Canada)
Kingswood U (NB, Canada)
Knox Coll (IL)
Kutztown U of Pennsylvania (PA)
Lafayette Coll (PA)
LaGrange Coll (GA)
Lake Forest Coll (IL)
Lakehead U (ON, Canada)
Lamar U (TX)
Lane Coll (TN)
La Sierra U (CA)
Lawrence U (WI)
Lee U (TN)
Lehigh U (PA)
Lehman Coll of the City U of New York (NY)
Lenoir-Rhyne U (NC)
Lewis & Clark Coll (OR)
Lewis U (IL)
Liberty U (VA)
Limestone Coll (SC)
Lincoln U (PA)
Lindenwood U (MO)
Linfield Coll (OR)
Lock Haven U of Pennsylvania (PA)
Long Island U–C. W. Post Campus (NY)
Longwood U (VA)
Loras Coll (IA)
Louisiana Coll (LA)
Louisiana State U and Ag and Mech Coll (LA)
Loyola Marymount U (CA)
Loyola U Chicago (IL)
Loyola U New Orleans (LA)
Lubbock Christian U (TX)
Luther Coll (IA)
Lycoming Coll (PA)
Lynchburg Coll (VA)
Lynn U (FL)
Lyon Coll (AR)
Macalester Coll (MN)
Madonna U (MI)
Malone U (OH)
Manchester Coll (IN)
Manhattanville Coll (NY)
Mansfield U of Pennsylvania (PA)
Marian U (WI)

Marietta Coll (OH)
Marlboro Coll (VT)
Mars Hill Coll (NC)
Mary Baldwin Coll (VA)
Marylhurst U (OR)
Maryville Coll (TN)
Massachusetts Coll of Liberal Arts (MA)
Massachusetts Inst of Technology (MA)
The Master's Coll and Sem (CA)
McDaniel Coll (MD)
McKendree U (IL)
McMurry U (TX)
McPherson Coll (KS)
Mercer U (GA)
Mercyhurst Coll (PA)
Meredith Coll (NC)
Messiah Coll (PA)
Metropolitan State Coll of Denver (CO)
Miami U (OH)
Michigan State U (MI)
Middlebury Coll (VT)
Middle Tennessee State U (TN)
Midwestern State U (TX)
Millersville U of Pennsylvania (PA)
Milligan Coll (TN)
Millikin U (IL)
Millsaps Coll (MS)
Mills Coll (CA)
Minnesota State U Mankato (MN)
Minnesota State U Moorhead (MN)
Minot State U (ND)
Mississippi Coll (MS)
Mississippi State U (MS)
Mississippi U for Women (MS)
Mississippi Valley State U (MS)
Missouri Baptist U (MO)
Missouri State U (MO)
Missouri Western State U (MO)
Molloy Coll (NY)
Monmouth Coll (IL)
Monmouth U (NJ)
Montana State U (MT)
Montana State U Billings (MT)
Montclair State U (NJ)
Moravian Coll (PA)
Morehead State U (KY)
Morehouse Coll (GA)
Morningside Coll (IA)
Mount Allison U (NB, Canada)
Mount Holyoke Coll (MA)
Mount Marty Coll (SD)
Mount Mercy U (IA)
Mount St. Mary's Coll (CA)
Mount Vernon Nazarene U (OH)
Muhlenberg Coll (PA)
Musicians Inst (CA)
Nazareth Coll of Rochester (NY)
Nebraska Wesleyan U (NE)
Newberry Coll (SC)
New Coll of Florida (FL)
New Jersey City U (NJ)
New Mexico Highlands U (NM)
Nicholls State U (LA)
Norfolk State U (VA)
North Carolina Ag and Tech State U (NC)
North Carolina Central U (NC)
North Central Coll (IL)
North Dakota State U (ND)
Northeastern Illinois U (IL)
Northeastern State U (OK)
Northeastern U (MA)
Northern Arizona U (AZ)
Northern Illinois U (IL)
Northern Kentucky U (KY)
Northern Michigan U (MI)
Northern State U (SD)
North Georgia Coll & State U (GA)
Northwest Christian U (OR)
Northwestern Coll (IA)
Northwestern Coll (MN)
Northwestern Oklahoma State U (OK)
Northwest Missouri State U (MO)
Northwest Nazarene U (ID)
Northwest U (WA)
Notre Dame de Namur U (CA)
Notre Dame of Maryland U (MD)
Nova Southeastern U (FL)
Nyack Coll (NY)
Oakland City U (IN)
Oakland U (MI)

Occidental Coll (CA)
Ohio Northern U (OH)
The Ohio State U (OH)
Ohio Wesleyan U (OH)
Oklahoma Christian U (OK)
Oklahoma City U (OK)
Oklahoma State U (OK)
Oral Roberts U (OK)
Otterbein U (OH)
Ouachita Baptist U (AR)
Pacific Lutheran U (WA)
Pacific Union Coll (CA)
Pacific U (OR)
Palm Beach Atlantic U (FL)
Park U (MO)
Peabody Conservatory of The Johns Hopkins U (MD)
Penn State Altoona (PA)
Penn State Beaver (PA)
Penn State Berks (PA)
Penn State Brandywine (PA)
Penn State DuBois (PA)
Penn State Greater Allegheny (PA)
Penn State Hazleton (PA)
Penn State Mont Alto (PA)
Penn State New Kensington (PA)
Penn State Shenango (PA)
Penn State U Park (PA)
Penn State Wilkes-Barre (PA)
Penn State Worthington Scranton (PA)
Penn State York (PA)
Pepperdine U, Malibu (CA)
Peru State Coll (NE)
Philadelphia Biblical U (PA)
Philander Smith Coll (AR)
Piedmont Coll (GA)
Pittsburg State U (KS)
Pitzer Coll (CA)
Plymouth State U (NH)
Point Loma Nazarene U (CA)
Point U (GA)
Pomona Coll (CA)
Portland State U (OR)
Prairie View A&M U (TX)
Presbyterian Coll (SC)
Princeton U (NJ)
Providence Coll (RI)
Queen's U at Kingston (ON, Canada)
Queens U of Charlotte (NC)
Quincy U (IL)
Radford U (VA)
Ramapo Coll of New Jersey (NJ)
Randolph-Macon Coll (VA)
Reinhardt U (GA)
Rhode Island Coll (RI)
Rhodes Coll (TN)
Rice U (TX)
Rider U (NJ)
Ripon Coll (WI)
Roanoke Coll (VA)
Roberts Wesleyan Coll (NY)
Rockford Coll (IL)
Roger Williams U (RI)
Rollins Coll (FL)
Rowan U (NJ)
Rust Coll (MS)
Rutgers, The State U of New Jersey, Camden (NJ)
Rutgers, The State U of New Jersey, Newark (NJ)
Rutgers, The State U of New Jersey, New Brunswick (NJ)
Saginaw Valley State U (MI)
St. Ambrose U (IA)
Saint Augustine's Coll (NC)
St. Catherine U (MN)
Saint John's U (MN)
Saint Joseph's U (PA)
St. Lawrence U (NY)
Saint Louis U (MO)
Saint Martin's U (WA)
Saint Mary-of-the-Woods Coll (IN)
Saint Mary's Coll (IN)
Saint Mary's Coll of California (CA)
St. Mary's Coll of Maryland (MD)
St. Mary's U (TX)
Saint Mary's U of Minnesota (MN)
Saint Michael's Coll (VT)
St. Norbert Coll (WI)
St. Olaf Coll (MN)
Saint Vincent Coll (PA)
Saint Xavier U (IL)
Salem State U (MA)

Salisbury U (MD)
Salve Regina U (RI)
Sam Houston State U (TX)
San Diego Christian Coll (CA)
San Francisco Conservatory of Music (CA)
San Francisco State U (CA)
Santa Clara U (CA)
Sarah Lawrence Coll (NY)
Schreiner U (TX)
Scripps Coll (CA)
Seattle Pacific U (WA)
Seton Hill U (PA)
Sewanee: The U of the South (TN)
Shaw U (NC)
Shenandoah U (VA)
Shepherd U (WV)
Shorter U (GA)
Simmons Coll (MA)
Simon Fraser U (BC, Canada)
Simpson Coll (IA)
Simpson U (CA)
Slippery Rock U of Pennsylvania (PA)
Smith Coll (MA)
Sonoma State U (CA)
South Dakota State U (SD)
Southeastern Baptist Theological Sem (NC)
Southeastern Oklahoma State U (OK)
Southeastern U (FL)
Southeast Missouri State U (MO)
Southern Arkansas U–Magnolia (AR)
Southern Connecticut State U (CT)
Southern Illinois U Carbondale (IL)
Southern Illinois U Edwardsville (IL)
Southern Methodist U (TX)
Southern Oregon U (OR)
Southwest Baptist U (MO)
Southwestern Adventist U (TX)
Southwestern Christian U (OK)
Southwestern Coll (KS)
Southwestern Oklahoma State U (OK)
Southwestern U (TX)
Southwest Minnesota State U (MN)
Spelman Coll (GA)
Spring Arbor U (MI)
Stanford U (CA)
State U of New York at Binghamton (NY)
State U of New York at Fredonia (NY)
State U of New York at New Paltz (NY)
State U of New York at Oswego (NY)
State U of New York at Plattsburgh (NY)
State U of New York Coll at Geneseo (NY)
State U of New York Coll at Oneonta (NY)
State U of New York Coll at Potsdam (NY)
Stephen F. Austin State U (TX)
Sterling Coll (KS)
Stetson U (FL)
Stillman Coll (AL)
Stony Brook U, State U of New York (NY)
Sul Ross State U (TX)
Susquehanna U (PA)
Swarthmore Coll (PA)
Sweet Briar Coll (VA)
Syracuse U (NY)
Tabor Coll (KS)
Tarleton State U (TX)
Taylor U (IN)
Temple U (PA)
Texas A&M U (TX)
Texas A&M U–Corpus Christi (TX)
Texas A&M U–Kingsville (TX)
Texas Christian U (TX)
Texas Coll (TX)
Texas Lutheran U (TX)
Texas Southern U (TX)
Texas State U–San Marcos (TX)
Texas Tech U (TX)
Texas Wesleyan U (TX)
Texas Woman's U (TX)
Thomas Edison State Coll (NJ)
Tiffin U (OH)

Towson U (MD)
Trinity Baptist Coll (FL)
Trinity Christian Coll (IL)
Trinity Coll (CT)
Trinity U (TX)
Troy U (AL)
Truett-McConnell Coll (GA)
Truman State U (MO)
Tufts U (MA)
Tulane U (LA)
Union Coll (NE)
Union U (TN)
U at Albany, State U of New York (NY)
U at Buffalo, the State U of New York (NY)
The U of Akron (OH)
The U of Alabama (AL)
The U of Alabama at Birmingham (AL)
The U of Alabama in Huntsville (AL)
U of Alaska Anchorage (AK)
U of Alaska Fairbanks (AK)
U of Alberta (AB, Canada)
The U of Arizona (AZ)
U of Arkansas at Little Rock (AR)
U of Arkansas at Monticello (AR)
U of Arkansas–Fort Smith (AR)
U of Bridgeport (CT)
The U of British Columbia (BC, Canada)
U of California, Berkeley (CA)
U of California, Davis (CA)
U of California, Irvine (CA)
U of California, Los Angeles (CA)
U of California, Riverside (CA)
U of California, Santa Barbara (CA)
U of California, Santa Cruz (CA)
U of Central Arkansas (AR)
U of Central Missouri (MO)
U of Cincinnati (OH)
U of Colorado Boulder (CO)
U of Colorado Denver (CO)
U of Connecticut (CT)
U of Dayton (OH)
U of Delaware (DE)
U of Denver (CO)
U of Evansville (IN)
U of Florida (FL)
U of Georgia (GA)
U of Guelph (ON, Canada)
U of Hartford (CT)
U of Hawaii at Hilo (HI)
U of Hawaii at Manoa (HI)
U of Houston (TX)
U of Idaho (ID)
U of Illinois at Chicago (IL)
U of Illinois at Urbana–Champaign (IL)
U of Indianapolis (IN)
The U of Iowa (IA)
The U of Kansas (KS)
U of La Verne (CA)
U of Lethbridge (AB, Canada)
U of Louisiana at Lafayette (LA)
U of Louisville (KY)
U of Maine (ME)
U of Maine at Augusta (ME)
U of Maine at Farmington (ME)
U of Mary Hardin-Baylor (TX)
U of Maryland, Baltimore County (MD)
U of Maryland, Coll Park (MD)
U of Mary Washington (VA)
U of Massachusetts Amherst (MA)
U of Massachusetts Boston (MA)
U of Massachusetts Dartmouth (MA)
U of Massachusetts Lowell (MA)
U of Memphis (TN)
U of Miami (FL)
U of Michigan (MI)
U of Michigan–Flint (MI)
U of Minnesota, Duluth (MN)
U of Minnesota, Twin Cities Campus (MN)
U of Mississippi (MS)
U of Missouri (MO)
U of Missouri–Kansas City (MO)
U of Missouri–St. Louis (MO)
U of Mobile (AL)
U of Mount Union (OH)
U of Nebraska at Kearney (NE)
U of Nebraska at Omaha (NE)
U of Nebraska–Lincoln (NE)

U of Nevada, Las Vegas (NV)
U of Nevada, Reno (NV)
U of New Hampshire (NH)
U of New Haven (CT)
U of New Orleans (LA)
U of North Alabama (AL)
The U of North Carolina at Asheville (NC)
The U of North Carolina at Chapel Hill (NC)
The U of North Carolina at Charlotte (NC)
The U of North Carolina Wilmington (NC)
U of North Dakota (ND)
U of Northern Colorado (CO)
U of Northern Iowa (IA)
U of North Florida (FL)
U of North Texas (TX)
U of Notre Dame (IN)
U of Oklahoma (OK)
U of Oregon (OR)
U of Ottawa (ON, Canada)
U of Pennsylvania (PA)
U of Pittsburgh (PA)
U of Portland (OR)
U of Puget Sound (WA)
U of Redlands (CA)
U of Regina (SK, Canada)
U of Rhode Island (RI)
U of Richmond (VA)
U of Rio Grande (OH)
U of Rochester (NY)
U of St. Francis (IL)
U of St. Thomas (MN)
U of St. Thomas (TX)
U of San Diego (CA)
U of Science and Arts of Oklahoma (OK)
U of South Alabama (AL)
U of South Carolina (SC)
U of Southern California (CA)
U of Southern Maine (ME)
U of Southern Mississippi (MS)
The U of Tampa (FL)
The U of Tennessee (TN)
The U of Tennessee at Chattanooga (TN)
The U of Tennessee at Martin (TN)
The U of Texas at Arlington (TX)
The U of Texas at Austin (TX)
The U of Texas at El Paso (TX)
The U of Texas at San Antonio (TX)
The U of Texas at Tyler (TX)
The U of Texas–Pan American (TX)
U of the Cumberlands (KY)
U of the Incarnate Word (TX)
U of the Ozarks (AR)
U of the Pacific (CA)
The U of Toledo (OH)
U of Tulsa (OK)
U of Utah (UT)
U of Vermont (VT)
U of Virginia (VA)
U of Washington (WA)
The U of Western Ontario (ON, Canada)
U of Windsor (ON, Canada)
U of Wisconsin–Eau Claire (WI)
U of Wisconsin–Green Bay (WI)
U of Wisconsin–La Crosse (WI)
U of Wisconsin–Madison (WI)
U of Wisconsin–Milwaukee (WI)
U of Wisconsin–Platteville (WI)
U of Wisconsin–River Falls (WI)
U of Wisconsin–Stevens Point (WI)
U of Wisconsin–Superior (WI)
U of Wisconsin–Whitewater (WI)
U of Wyoming (WY)
Utah State U (UT)
Utah Valley U (UT)
Valdosta State U (GA)
Valley City State U (ND)
Valparaiso U (IN)
Vanguard U of Southern California (CA)
Vassar Coll (NY)
Villa Maria Coll of Buffalo (NY)
Virginia Polytechnic Inst and State U (VA)
Virginia State U (VA)
Virginia Union U (VA)
Virginia Wesleyan Coll (VA)
Viterbo U (WI)
Wabash Coll (IN)

Wagner Coll (NY)
Wake Forest U (NC)
Waldorf Coll (IA)
Wartburg Coll (IA)
Washburn U (KS)
Washington Adventist U (MD)
Washington & Jefferson Coll (PA)
Washington and Lee U (VA)
Washington Coll (MD)
Washington State U (WA)
Washington U in St. Louis (MO)
Wayland Baptist U (TX)
Wayne State Coll (NE)
Wayne State U (MI)
Weber State U (UT)
Webster U (MO)
Wellesley Coll (MA)
Wesleyan Coll (GA)
Wesleyan U (CT)
West Chester U of Pennsylvania (PA)
Western Carolina U (NC)
Western Connecticut State U (CT)
Western Illinois U (IL)
Western Michigan U (MI)
Western Oregon U (OR)
Western State Coll of Colorado (CO)
Western Washington U (WA)
Westfield State U (MA)
Westminster Coll (UT)
West Texas A&M U (TX)
West Virginia U (WV)
West Virginia Wesleyan Coll (WV)
Wheaton Coll (IL)
Wheaton Coll (MA)
Wheeling Jesuit U (WV)
Whitman Coll (WA)
Whittier Coll (CA)
Wichita State U (KS)
Willamette U (OR)
William Jessup U (CA)
William Jewell Coll (MO)
William Paterson U of New Jersey (NJ)
William Penn U (IA)
Williams Baptist Coll (AR)
Williams Coll (MA)
Wingate U (NC)
Winona State U (MN)
Winthrop U (SC)
Wittenberg U (OH)
Worcester Polytechnic Inst (MA)
Wright State U (OH)
Xavier U (OH)
Xavier U of Louisiana (LA)
Yale U (CT)
York Coll of Pennsylvania (PA)
York Coll of the City U of New York (NY)
Youngstown State U (OH)

MUSICAL INSTRUMENT FABRICATION AND REPAIR
Barton Coll (NC)
Delaware State U (DE)
U of Washington (WA)

MUSICAL THEATER
Brenau U (GA)
Central Michigan U (MI)
Creighton U (NE)
Culver-Stockton Coll (MO)
Elon U (NC)
Lees-McRae Coll (NC)
Lindenwood U (MO)
Millikin U (IL)
Missouri Baptist U (MO)
Oakland U (MI)
Pace U (NY)
Roosevelt U (IL)
Shenandoah U (VA)
Southwestern Coll (KS)
Texas Christian U (TX)
The U of Arizona (AZ)
U of California, Irvine (CA)
U of Idaho (ID)
U of Michigan (MI)
U of North Dakota (ND)
U of Oklahoma (OK)
The U of Tampa (FL)
The U of the Arts (PA)
Virginia Intermont Coll (VA)
Western Michigan U (MI)

MUSIC HISTORY, LITERATURE, AND THEORY
American U (DC)
Baldwin-Wallace Coll (OH)
Bard Coll (NY)
Baylor U (TX)
Belmont U (TN)
Bennington Coll (VT)
Birmingham-Southern Coll (AL)
Boston U (MA)
Bowling Green State U (OH)
Bridgewater Coll (VA)
Brigham Young U (UT)
Bucknell U (PA)
California State U, Long Beach (CA)
Calvin Coll (MI)
The Catholic U of America (DC)
The Coll of Wooster (OH)
Concordia Coll–New York (NY)
Converse Coll (SC)
Dalhousie U (NS, Canada)
Florida State U (FL)
Fordham U (NY)
Hardin-Simmons U (TX)
Hofstra U (NY)
Keene State Coll (NH)
Lafayette Coll (PA)
Lehigh U (PA)
Loyola Marymount U (CA)
Marlboro Coll (VT)
Mount Allison U (NB, Canada)
Nazareth Coll of Rochester (NY)
New Coll of Florida (FL)
New England Conservatory of Music (MA)
The Ohio State U (OH)
Ohio U (OH)
Otterbein U (OH)
Ouachita Baptist U (AR)
Randolph Coll (VA)
Rice U (TX)
St. Bonaventure U (NY)
Saint Joseph's Coll (IN)
Sarah Lawrence Coll (NY)
Sewanee: The U of the South (TN)
Skidmore Coll (NY)
Southwestern U (TX)
State U of New York at Fredonia (NY)
Syracuse U (NY)
Temple U (PA)
U of Alberta (AB, Canada)
The U of British Columbia (BC, Canada)
U of California, Los Angeles (CA)
U of Cincinnati (OH)
U of Delaware (DE)
U of Hartford (CT)
U of Idaho (ID)
U of Illinois at Urbana–Champaign (IL)
U of Mary Hardin-Baylor (TX)
U of Michigan (MI)
U of Minnesota, Twin Cities Campus (MN)
U of North Texas (TX)
U of Redlands (CA)
U of Regina (SK, Canada)
U of the Pacific (CA)
U of Toronto (ON, Canada)
U of Vermont (VT)
U of Washington (WA)
The U of Western Ontario (ON, Canada)
U of Windsor (ON, Canada)
Washington U in St. Louis (MO)
Western Washington U (WA)
Wheaton Coll (IL)
Whitman Coll (WA)
Wright State U (OH)
Youngstown State U (OH)

MUSIC MANAGEMENT
Anderson U (IN)
Appalachian State U (NC)
Belmont U (TN)
Berklee Coll of Music (MA)
Berry Coll (GA)
Bethel U (TN)
Boise State U (ID)
Bradley U (IL)
Butler U (IN)
Capital U (OH)

Whitman Coll (WA)
Willamette U (OR)
William Jewell Coll (MO)
Wright State U (OH)
Xavier U of Louisiana (LA)
Youngstown State U (OH)

MUSIC RELATED
Acad of Art U (CA)
Alverno Coll (WI)
Ball State U (IN)
Bellarmine U (KY)
Bethel Coll (KS)
Bob Jones U (SC)
Brigham Young U (UT)
Brown U (RI)
California State U, Chico (CA)
Calvary Bible Coll and Theological Sem (MO)
Capital U (OH)
Concordia U (CA)
Connecticut Coll (CT)
DePaul U (IL)
Duquesne U (PA)
Friends U (KS)
Greenville Coll (IL)
Hampton U (VA)
Huntingdon Coll (AL)
Illinois Wesleyan U (IL)
Indiana U Bloomington (IN)
Indiana U–Purdue U Indianapolis (IN)
Indiana U South Bend (IN)
Keene State Coll (NH)
Kent State U (OH)
Kent State U at Stark (OH)
Lee U (TN)
Long Island U–Brooklyn Campus (NY)
Loyola U New Orleans (LA)
Mercer U (GA)
Messiah Coll (PA)
Milligan Coll (TN)
Mississippi Coll (MS)
Ohio Northern U (OH)
Palm Beach Atlantic U (FL)
Peru State Coll (NE)
Roosevelt U (IL)
Saint Mary's U of Minnesota (MN)
Southwestern Christian U (OK)
Tabor Coll (KS)
Texas Wesleyan U (TX)
The U of Akron (OH)
U of Delaware (DE)
U of Denver (CO)
U of Hartford (CT)
U of Lethbridge (AB, Canada)
U of Massachusetts Lowell (MA)
U of Memphis (TN)
U of Miami (FL)
U of Michigan (MI)
U of Minnesota, Duluth (MN)
The U of North Carolina at Asheville (NC)
U of Saint Francis (IN)
U of Tulsa (OK)
The U of Western Ontario (ON, Canada)
Valparaiso U (IN)
Vanderbilt U (TN)
Western Illinois U (IL)
Western Kentucky U (KY)
West Virginia U (WV)
Wheaton Coll (IL)
Wichita State U (KS)

MUSIC TEACHER EDUCATION
Abilene Christian U (TX)
Acadia U (NS, Canada)
Adams State Coll (CO)
Adrian Coll (MI)
Alabama State U (AL)
Albany State U (GA)
Albion Coll (MI)
Alma Coll (MI)
Alverno Coll (WI)
Anderson U (IN)
Anderson U (SC)
Andrews U (MI)
Anna Maria Coll (MA)
Appalachian State U (NC)
Aquinas Coll (MI)
Arizona State U (AZ)
Arkansas State U (AR)

Arkansas Tech U (AR)
Arlington Baptist Coll (TX)
Armstrong Atlantic State U (GA)
Asbury U (KY)
Ashland U (OH)
Auburn U (AL)
Augustana Coll (IL)
Augustana Coll (SD)
Baker U (KS)
Baldwin-Wallace Coll (OH)
Baptist Bible Coll of Pennsylvania (PA)
The Baptist Coll of Florida (FL)
Baylor U (TX)
Belmont U (TN)
Beloit Coll (WI)
Bemidji State U (MN)
Benedictine Coll (KS)
Benedictine U (IL)
Bennett Coll for Women (NC)
Berea Coll (KY)
Berklee Coll of Music (MA)
Berry Coll (GA)
Bethany Coll (KS)
Bethel Coll (IN)
Bethel U (MN)
Bethel U (TN)
Bethune-Cookman U (FL)
Biola U (CA)
Birmingham-Southern Coll (AL)
Bishop's U (QC, Canada)
Bluefield Coll (VA)
Blue Mountain Coll (MS)
Bluffton U (OH)
Bob Jones U (SC)
Boise State U (ID)
Boston U (MA)
Bowling Green State U (OH)
Bradley U (IL)
Brenau U (GA)
Brevard Coll (NC)
Bridgewater State U (MA)
Bucknell U (PA)
Buena Vista U (IA)
Buffalo State Coll, State U of New York (NY)
Butler U (IN)
California Baptist U (CA)
California Lutheran U (CA)
California State U, Chico (CA)
California State U, Fresno (CA)
California State U, Fullerton (CA)
Calvary Bible Coll and Theological Sem (MO)
Calvin Coll (MI)
Cameron U (OK)
Campbellsville U (KY)
Capital U (OH)
Carson-Newman Coll (TN)
Case Western Reserve U (OH)
Castleton State Coll (VT)
Catawba Coll (NC)
Cedarville U (OH)
Central Coll (IA)
Central Connecticut State U (CT)
Central Methodist U (MO)
Central State U (OH)
Central Washington U (WA)
Chapman U (CA)
Chestnut Hill Coll (PA)
Chicago State U (IL)
City Coll of the City U of New York (NY)
Claflin U (SC)
Clarion U of Pennsylvania (PA)
Clarke U (IA)
Clearwater Christian Coll (FL)
Coe Coll (IA)
The Coll of New Jersey (NJ)
The Coll of Saint Rose (NY)
Coll of the Ozarks (MO)
The Coll of Wooster (OH)
Colorado State U (CO)
Columbia Coll (SC)
Columbus State U (GA)
Concordia Coll (MN)
Concordia U (MI)
Concordia U Chicago (IL)
Concordia U, Nebraska (NE)
Concordia U, St. Paul (MN)
Conservatorio de Musica (PR)
Converse Coll (SC)
Corban U (OR)
Cornell Coll (IA)
Cornerstone U (MI)

Crown Coll (MN)
Culver-Stockton Coll (MO)
Dallas Baptist U (TX)
Delaware State U (DE)
Delta State U (MS)
DePaul U (IL)
DePauw U (IN)
Dixie State Coll of Utah (UT)
Dordt Coll (IA)
Dowling Coll (NY)
Drake U (IA)
Drury U (MO)
Duquesne U (PA)
East Carolina U (NC)
East Central U (OK)
Eastern Kentucky U (KY)
Eastern Michigan U (MI)
Eastern Washington U (WA)
East Texas Baptist U (TX)
Edgewood Coll (WI)
Elmhurst Coll (IL)
Elon U (NC)
Emmanuel Coll (GA)
Emmaus Bible Coll (IA)
Emporia State U (KS)
Evangel U (MO)
Fairfield U (CT)
Fairmont State U (WV)
Faith Baptist Bible Coll and Theological Sem (IA)
Fayetteville State U (NC)
Five Towns Coll (NY)
Florida Ag and Mech U (FL)
Florida Atlantic U (FL)
Florida Southern Coll (FL)
Fort Hays State U (KS)
Fort Lewis Coll (CO)
Free Will Baptist Bible Coll (TN)
Friends U (KS)
Furman U (SC)
Gardner-Webb U (NC)
Geneva Coll (PA)
George Fox U (OR)
Georgetown Coll (KY)
Georgia Coll & State U (GA)
Georgia Southern U (GA)
Gettysburg Coll (PA)
Glenville State Coll (WV)
Gonzaga U (WA)
Gordon Coll (MA)
Graceland U (IA)
Grambling State U (LA)
Grand Valley State U (MI)
Greenville Coll (IL)
Grove City Coll (PA)
Gustavus Adolphus Coll (MN)
Hampton U (VA)
Hannibal-LaGrange U (MO)
Harding U (AR)
Hardin-Simmons U (TX)
Hartwick Coll (NY)
Heidelberg U (OH)
Hofstra U (NY)
Hope Coll (MI)
Houghton Coll (NY)
Howard Payne U (TX)
Humboldt State U (CA)
Huntingdon Coll (AL)
Huntington U (IN)
Idaho State U (ID)
Illinois State U (IL)
Illinois Wesleyan U (IL)
Immaculata U (PA)
Indiana U Bloomington (IN)
Indiana U–Purdue U Fort Wayne (IN)
Indiana U South Bend (IN)
Indiana Wesleyan U (IN)
Inter American U of Puerto Rico, San Germán Campus (PR)
Iowa State U of Science and Technology (IA)
Iowa Wesleyan Coll (IA)
Ithaca Coll (NY)
Jacksonville State U (AL)
Jacksonville U (FL)
Jamestown Coll (ND)
Jarvis Christian Coll (TX)
John Brown U (AR)
Johnson State Coll (VT)
Judson Coll (AL)
Judson U (IL)
Kansas State U (KS)
Kean U (NJ)
Keene State Coll (NH)

Kennesaw State U (GA)
Kent State U (OH)
Lamar U (TX)
La Sierra U (CA)
Lawrence U (WI)
Lebanon Valley Coll (PA)
Lee U (TN)
Lenoir-Rhyne U (NC)
Liberty U (VA)
Limestone Coll (SC)
Lincoln U (MO)
Lincoln U (PA)
Lindenwood U (MO)
Lipscomb U (TN)
Long Island U–Brooklyn Campus (NY)
Long Island U–C. W. Post Campus (NY)
Longwood U (VA)
Louisiana Coll (LA)
Louisiana State U and Ag and Mech Coll (LA)
Loyola U New Orleans (LA)
Lubbock Christian U (TX)
Malone U (OH)
Manchester Coll (IN)
Manhattanville Coll (NY)
Mansfield U of Pennsylvania (PA)
Maranatha Baptist Bible Coll (WI)
Marian U (WI)
Marietta Coll (OH)
Mars Hill Coll (NC)
Maryville Coll (TN)
Marywood U (PA)
The Master's Coll and Sem (CA)
McKendree U (IL)
Mercer U (GA)
Mercyhurst Coll (PA)
Meredith Coll (NC)
Messiah Coll (PA)
Metropolitan State Coll of Denver (CO)
Miami U (OH)
Michigan State U (MI)
MidAmerica Nazarene U (KS)
Midwestern State U (TX)
Milligan Coll (TN)
Millikin U (IL)
Minnesota State U Mankato (MN)
Minnesota State U Moorhead (MN)
Minot State U (ND)
Mississippi Coll (MS)
Mississippi State U (MS)
Mississippi Valley State U (MS)
Missouri Baptist U (MO)
Missouri State U (MO)
Missouri Western State U (MO)
Montana State U (MT)
Montana State U Billings (MT)
Moravian Coll (PA)
Morningside Coll (IA)
Mount Marty Coll (SD)
Mount Mercy U (IA)
Mount Vernon Nazarene U (OH)
Nazareth Coll of Rochester (NY)
Nebraska Wesleyan U (NE)
Newberry Coll (SC)
New Jersey City U (NJ)
New Mexico State U (NM)
New York U (NY)
Nicholls State U (LA)
North Carolina Ag and Tech State U (NC)
North Carolina Central U (NC)
North Central Coll (IL)
North Dakota State U (ND)
Northeastern State U (OK)
Northern Arizona U (AZ)
Northern Illinois U (IL)
Northern Michigan U (MI)
Northern State U (SD)
North Georgia Coll & State U (GA)
North Greenville U (SC)
Northwestern Coll (IA)
Northwestern Coll (MN)
Northwestern Oklahoma State U (OK)
Northwestern State U of Louisiana (LA)
Northwest Missouri State U (MO)
Northwest Nazarene U (ID)
Northwest U (WA)
Notre Dame of Maryland U (MD)
Nyack Coll (NY)
Oakland City U (IN)

Oakland U (MI)
Ohio Northern U (OH)
The Ohio State U (OH)
Ohio Wesleyan U (OH)
Oklahoma Christian U (OK)
Oklahoma City U (OK)
Oklahoma State U (OK)
Oral Roberts U (OK)
Otterbein U (OH)
Ouachita Baptist U (AR)
Pacific Lutheran U (WA)
Pacific Union Coll (CA)
Pacific U (OR)
Palm Beach Atlantic U (FL)
Peabody Conservatory of The Johns Hopkins U (MD)
Penn State U Park (PA)
Pepperdine U, Malibu (CA)
Peru State Coll (NE)
Piedmont Intl U (NC)
Pittsburg State U (KS)
Plymouth State U (NH)
Point Loma Nazarene U (CA)
Presbyterian Coll (SC)
Providence Coll (RI)
Queens Coll of the City U of New York (NY)
Quincy U (IL)
Rhode Island Coll (RI)
Rider U (NJ)
Ripon Coll (WI)
Roberts Wesleyan Coll (NY)
Rocky Mountain Coll (MT)
Roosevelt U (IL)
Rowan U (NJ)
Rutgers, The State U of New Jersey, New Brunswick (NJ)
Saginaw Valley State U (MI)
St. Ambrose U (IA)
St. Catherine U (MN)
Saint Mary-of-the-Woods Coll (IN)
Saint Mary's Coll (IN)
Saint Mary's U of Minnesota (MN)
St. Norbert Coll (WI)
St. Olaf Coll (MN)
Saint Xavier U (IL)
Salve Regina U (RI)
Samford U (AL)
San Diego Christian Coll (CA)
San Diego State U (CA)
Schreiner U (TX)
Seton Hill U (PA)
Shenandoah U (VA)
Shorter U (GA)
Simpson Coll (IA)
Simpson U (CA)
Sonoma State U (CA)
South Carolina State U (SC)
South Dakota State U (SD)
Southeastern Oklahoma State U (OK)
Southeastern U (FL)
Southeast Missouri State U (MO)
Southern Arkansas U–Magnolia (AR)
Southern Methodist U (TX)
Southern New Hampshire U (NH)
Southwest Baptist U (MO)
Southwestern Assemblies of God U (TX)
Southwestern Coll (KS)
Southwestern Oklahoma State U (OK)
Southwestern U (TX)
Southwest Minnesota State U (MN)
Spring Arbor U (MI)
State U of New York at Fredonia (NY)
State U of New York Coll at Potsdam (NY)
Sterling Coll (KS)
Stetson U (FL)
Susquehanna U (PA)
Syracuse U (NY)
Tabor Coll (KS)
Tarleton State U (TX)
Taylor U (IN)
Temple U (PA)
Texas A&M U–Corpus Christi (TX)
Texas Christian U (TX)
Texas Lutheran U (TX)
Texas Wesleyan U (TX)
Towson U (MD)
Transylvania U (KY)
Trevecca Nazarene U (TN)

Trinity Christian Coll (IL)
Union Coll (NE)
Union U (TN)
The U of Akron (OH)
The U of Alabama (AL)
U of Alaska Anchorage (AK)
U of Alberta (AB, Canada)
U of Arizona (AZ)
U of Arkansas at Monticello (AR)
U of Arkansas–Fort Smith (AR)
The U of British Columbia (BC, Canada)
U of Central Florida (FL)
U of Central Missouri (MO)
U of Cincinnati (OH)
U of Colorado Boulder (CO)
U of Connecticut (CT)
U of Dayton (OH)
U of Delaware (DE)
U of Evansville (IN)
U of Florida (FL)
U of Georgia (GA)
U of Guam (GU)
U of Hartford (CT)
U of Idaho (ID)
U of Illinois at Urbana–Champaign (IL)
U of Indianapolis (IN)
The U of Iowa (IA)
The U of Kansas (KS)
U of Lethbridge (AB, Canada)
U of Louisiana at Lafayette (LA)
U of Louisiana at Monroe (LA)
U of Louisville (KY)
U of Maine (ME)
U of Mary (ND)
U of Mary Hardin-Baylor (TX)
U of Maryland, Coll Park (MD)
U of Maryland Eastern Shore (MD)
U of Miami (FL)
U of Michigan (MI)
U of Michigan–Flint (MI)
U of Minnesota, Duluth (MN)
U of Minnesota, Twin Cities Campus (MN)
U of Missouri (MO)
U of Missouri–Kansas City (MO)
U of Missouri–St. Louis (MO)
The U of Montana Western (MT)
U of Mount Union (OH)
U of Nebraska at Omaha (NE)
U of Nebraska–Lincoln (NE)
U of Nevada, Reno (NV)
U of New Mexico (NM)
U of New Orleans (LA)
The U of North Carolina at Charlotte (NC)
The U of North Carolina Wilmington (NC)
U of North Dakota (ND)
U of Northern Colorado (CO)
U of Northern Iowa (IA)
U of North Florida (FL)
U of Oklahoma (OK)
U of Oregon (OR)
U of Portland (OR)
U of Puget Sound (WA)
U of Redlands (CA)
U of Regina (SK, Canada)
U of Rhode Island (RI)
U of Rio Grande (OH)
U of Rochester (NY)
U of St. Francis (IL)
U of St. Thomas (MN)
U of St. Thomas (TX)
U of South Carolina (SC)
U of South Carolina Aiken (SC)
The U of South Dakota (SD)
U of Southern California (CA)
U of Southern Maine (ME)
U of Southern Mississippi (MS)
U of South Florida (FL)
The U of Tampa (FL)
The U of Tennessee at Chattanooga (TN)
The U of Tennessee at Martin (TN)
U of the Cumberlands (KY)
U of the District of Columbia (DC)
U of the Incarnate Word (TX)
U of the Pacific (CA)
The U of Toledo (OH)
U of Toronto (ON, Canada)
U of Tulsa (OK)
U of Vermont (VT)
U of Washington (WA)

U of West Florida (FL)
U of West Georgia (GA)
U of Windsor (ON, Canada)
U of Wisconsin–Green Bay (WI)
U of Wisconsin–Madison (WI)
U of Wisconsin–Milwaukee (WI)
U of Wisconsin–River Falls (WI)
U of Wisconsin–Stevens Point (WI)
U of Wisconsin–Superior (WI)
U of Wisconsin–Whitewater (WI)
U of Wyoming (WY)
Utah State U (UT)
Utah Valley U (UT)
Valdosta State U (GA)
Valley City State U (ND)
Valparaiso U (IN)
Vanderbilt U (TN)
VanderCook Coll of Music (IL)
Vanguard U of Southern California (CA)
Viterbo U (WI)
Wartburg Coll (IA)
Washburn U (KS)
Washington Adventist U (MD)
Washington State U (WA)
Wayland Baptist U (TX)
Wayne State Coll (NE)
Weber State U (UT)
Webster U (MO)
Western Carolina U (NC)
Western Connecticut State U (CT)
Western Michigan U (MI)
Western State Coll of Colorado (CO)
Western Washington U (WA)
West Liberty U (WV)
West Virginia State U (WV)
West Virginia Wesleyan Coll (WV)
Wheaton Coll (IL)
Wichita State U (KS)
William Jewell Coll (MO)
William Paterson U of New Jersey (NJ)
Williams Baptist Coll (AR)
Wilmington Coll (OH)
Wingate U (NC)
Winona State U (MN)
Winthrop U (SC)
Wright State U (OH)
Xavier U (OH)
Xavier U of Louisiana (LA)
York Coll of Pennsylvania (PA)
Youngstown State U (OH)

MUSIC TECHNOLOGY

Bethune-Cookman U (FL)
Cogswell Polytechnical Coll (CA)
McNally Smith Coll of Music (MN)
Shenandoah U (VA)
Stetson U (FL)
Transylvania U (KY)
U of Michigan (MI)

MUSIC THEORY AND COMPOSITION

Adams State Coll (CO)
American U (DC)
Arizona State U (AZ)
Augustana Coll (IL)
Baldwin-Wallace Coll (OH)
Bard Coll (NY)
Bard Coll at Simon's Rock (MA)
Baylor U (TX)
Bennington Coll (VT)
Berklee Coll of Music (MA)
Biola U (CA)
Birmingham-Southern Coll (AL)
Boston U (MA)
Bowling Green State U (OH)
Bradley U (IL)
Bucknell U (PA)
Butler U (IN)
California Baptist U (CA)
California State U, Chico (CA)
California State U, Long Beach (CA)
Calvin Coll (MI)
Capital U (OH)
Carnegie Mellon U (PA)
Carson-Newman Coll (TN)
The Catholic U of America (DC)
Cedarville U (OH)
Central Michigan U (MI)
Central Washington U (WA)

Chapman U (CA)
Christopher Newport U (VA)
City Coll of the City U of New York (NY)
Coe Coll (IA)
The Coll of Wooster (OH)
Colorado State U (CO)
Concordia Coll (MN)
Concordia U (QC, Canada)
Concordia U Chicago (IL)
Dalhousie U (NS, Canada)
Dallas Baptist U (TX)
DePaul U (IL)
DePauw U (IN)
Drury U (MO)
East Carolina U (NC)
Florida Southern Coll (FL)
Florida State U (FL)
Gardner-Webb U (NC)
Georgia Southern U (GA)
Hardin-Simmons U (TX)
Hofstra U (NY)
Hope Coll (MI)
Houghton Coll (NY)
Illinois Wesleyan U (IL)
Indiana U Bloomington (IN)
Indiana Wesleyan U (IN)
Ithaca Coll (NY)
Jacksonville U (FL)
Keene State Coll (NH)
Lawrence U (WI)
Linfield Coll (OR)
Lipscomb U (TN)
Long Island U–Brooklyn Campus (NY)
Loyola U New Orleans (LA)
Madonna U (MI)
Manchester Coll (IN)
Marylhurst U (OR)
Maryville Coll (TN)
McNally Smith Coll of Music (MN)
Meredith Coll (NC)
Michigan State U (MI)
Minnesota State U Moorhead (MN)
Mississippi Coll (MS)
Moravian Coll (PA)
New England Conservatory of Music (MA)
Northwestern Coll (MN)
Northwest Nazarene U (ID)
Nyack Coll (NY)
Ohio Northern U (OH)
The Ohio State U (OH)
Ohio U (OH)
Oklahoma City U (OK)
Oral Roberts U (OK)
Ouachita Baptist U (AR)
Palm Beach Atlantic U (FL)
Point Loma Nazarene U (CA)
Randolph Coll (VA)
Rice U (TX)
Rider U (NJ)
Roosevelt U (IL)
Rowan U (NJ)
St. Olaf Coll (MN)
Samford U (AL)
San Francisco Conservatory of Music (CA)
Sarah Lawrence Coll (NY)
Shenandoah U (VA)
Southern Methodist U (TX)
Southwestern U (TX)
State U of New York Coll at Potsdam (NY)
Stetson U (FL)
Susquehanna U (PA)
Syracuse U (NY)
Temple U (PA)
Texas Christian U (TX)
Trinity U (TX)
Tulane U (LA)
The U of British Columbia (BC, Canada)
U of Central Missouri (MO)
U of Cincinnati (OH)
U of Delaware (DE)
U of Georgia (GA)
U of Idaho (ID)
U of Illinois at Urbana–Champaign (IL)
The U of Kansas (KS)
U of Mary Hardin-Baylor (TX)
U of Miami (FL)
U of Michigan (MI)
U of Minnesota, Duluth (MN)

U of Missouri–Kansas City (MO)
U of Nebraska at Omaha (NE)
U of Nevada, Las Vegas (NV)
U of Northern Iowa (IA)
U of North Texas (TX)
U of Oregon (OR)
U of Redlands (CA)
U of Regina (SK, Canada)
U of Rhode Island (RI)
U of Rochester (NY)
U of Southern California (CA)
U of Southern Maine (ME)
The U of Texas at Austin (TX)
The U of Texas at San Antonio (TX)
The U of the Arts (PA)
U of the Pacific (CA)
U of Tulsa (OK)
U of Washington (WA)
The U of Western Ontario (ON, Canada)
U of West Georgia (GA)
U of Windsor (ON, Canada)
Valparaiso U (IN)
Vanderbilt U (TN)
Wartburg Coll (IA)
Washington State U (WA)
Washington U in St. Louis (MO)
Webster U (MO)
Western Connecticut State U (CT)
Western Michigan U (MI)
Western Washington U (WA)
West Texas A&M U (TX)
Wheaton Coll (IL)
Whitman Coll (WA)
Willamette U (OR)
William Jewell Coll (MO)
Youngstown State U (OH)

MUSIC THERAPY

Alverno Coll (WI)
Anna Maria Coll (MA)
Appalachian State U (NC)
Arizona State U (AZ)
Baldwin-Wallace Coll (OH)
Berklee Coll of Music (MA)
The Coll of Wooster (OH)
Colorado State U (CO)
Converse Coll (SC)
Drury U (MO)
Duquesne U (PA)
East Carolina U (NC)
Eastern Michigan U (MI)
Elizabethtown Coll (PA)
Florida State U (FL)
Georgia Coll & State U (GA)
Immaculata U (PA)
Indiana U–Purdue U Fort Wayne (IN)
Loyola U New Orleans (LA)
Lubbock Christian U (TX)
Marylhurst U (OR)
Maryville U of Saint Louis (MO)
Marywood U (PA)
Molloy Coll (NY)
Montclair State U (NJ)
Nazareth Coll of Rochester (NY)
Queens U of Charlotte (NC)
Saint Mary-of-the-Woods Coll (IN)
Sam Houston State U (TX)
Seattle Pacific U (WA)
Seton Hill U (PA)
Shenandoah U (VA)
Slippery Rock U of Pennsylvania (PA)
Southern Methodist U (TX)
Southwestern Oklahoma State U (OK)
State U of New York at Fredonia (NY)
State U of New York at New Paltz (NY)
Temple U (PA)
U of Dayton (OH)
U of Evansville (IN)
U of Georgia (GA)
The U of Iowa (IA)
The U of Kansas (KS)
U of Louisville (KY)
U of Miami (FL)
U of Minnesota, Twin Cities Campus (MN)
U of Missouri–Kansas City (MO)
U of North Dakota (ND)
U of the Incarnate Word (TX)
U of the Pacific (CA)

Utah State U (UT)
Wartburg Coll (IA)
Western Michigan U (MI)
West Texas A&M U (TX)

NANOTECHNOLOGY

U at Albany, State U of New York (NY)
U of Guelph (ON, Canada)

NATURAL RESOURCE ECONOMICS

Baldwin-Wallace Coll (OH)
Colorado State U (CO)
Juniata Coll (PA)
Michigan State U (MI)
U of Guelph (ON, Canada)
U of New Hampshire (NH)
The U of Tennessee (TN)

NATURAL RESOURCE RECREATION AND TOURISM

U of Idaho (ID)

NATURAL RESOURCES AND CONSERVATION RELATED

Bowling Green State U (OH)
California Polytechnic State U, San Luis Obispo (CA)
Lakehead U (ON, Canada)
Mount Mercy U (IA)
Northwest Missouri State U (MO)
Penn State Abington (PA)
Penn State Altoona (PA)
Penn State Beaver (PA)
Penn State Berks (PA)
Penn State Brandywine (PA)
Penn State DuBois (PA)
Penn State Erie, The Behrend Coll (PA)
Penn State Fayette, The Eberly Campus (PA)
Penn State Greater Allegheny (PA)
Penn State Hazleton (PA)
Penn State Lehigh Valley (PA)
Penn State Mont Alto (PA)
Penn State New Kensington (PA)
Penn State Schuylkill (PA)
Penn State Shenango (PA)
Penn State U Park (PA)
Penn State Wilkes-Barre (PA)
Penn State Worthington Scranton (PA)
Penn State York (PA)
Sterling Coll (VT)
Texas A&M U–Kingsville (TX)
U of Alaska Fairbanks (AK)
The U of British Columbia (BC, Canada)
U of California, Davis (CA)
U of Louisiana at Lafayette (LA)
U of New Hampshire (NH)
U of Wisconsin–Stevens Point (WI)
Utah State U (UT)

NATURAL RESOURCES/ CONSERVATION

Ball State U (IN)
Clemson U (SC)
Colorado State U (CO)
Cornell U (NY)
The Evergreen State Coll (WA)
Grand Valley State U (MI)
Gustavus Adolphus Coll (MN)
Humboldt State U (CA)
Indiana U Bloomington (IN)
Kent State U (OH)
Manchester Coll (IN)
Marlboro Coll (VT)
Montana State U (MT)
Morrisville State Coll (NY)
North Carolina State U (NC)
Northern Michigan U (MI)
Northland Coll (WI)
The Ohio State U (OH)
Penn State Abington (PA)
Penn State Altoona (PA)
Penn State Beaver (PA)
Penn State Berks (PA)
Penn State Brandywine (PA)
Penn State DuBois (PA)
Penn State Erie, The Behrend Coll (PA)

Penn State Fayette, The Eberly Campus (PA)
Penn State Greater Allegheny (PA)
Penn State Hazleton (PA)
Penn State Lehigh Valley (PA)
Penn State Mont Alto (PA)
Penn State New Kensington (PA)
Penn State Schuylkill (PA)
Penn State Shenango (PA)
Penn State U Park (PA)
Penn State Wilkes-Barre (PA)
Penn State Worthington Scranton (PA)
Penn State York (PA)
Peru State Coll (NE)
Purdue U (IN)
Rutgers, The State U of New Jersey, New Brunswick (NJ)
Southeastern Oklahoma State U (OK)
State U of New York at Plattsburgh (NY)
State U of New York Coll of Environmental Science and Forestry (NY)
Stony Brook U, State U of New York (NY)
Suffolk U (MA)
Texas A&M U (TX)
Texas Tech U (TX)
Thompson Rivers U (BC, Canada)
Tusculum Coll (TN)
U of Alberta (AB, Canada)
The U of Arizona (AZ)
The U of British Columbia (BC, Canada)
U of California, Berkeley (CA)
U of California, Davis (CA)
U of Connecticut (CT)
U of Georgia (GA)
U of Illinois at Urbana–Champaign (IL)
U of Louisiana at Lafayette (LA)
U of Maryland, Coll Park (MD)
U of Maryland U Coll (MD)
U of Massachusetts Amherst (MA)
U of Michigan–Flint (MI)
U of Minnesota, Crookston (MN)
U of Minnesota, Twin Cities Campus (MN)
U of Missouri (MO)
U of Nebraska–Lincoln (NE)
U of Nevada, Reno (NV)
U of New Hampshire (NH)
U of Vermont (VT)
U of Wisconsin–River Falls (WI)
U of Wisconsin–Stevens Point (WI)
Upper Iowa U (IA)
Washington State U (WA)
Washington U in St. Louis (MO)
Winona State U (MN)

NATURAL RESOURCES/ CONSERVATION RELATED
Sierra Nevada Coll (NV)
Stanford U (CA)
U of Illinois at Urbana–Champaign (IL)

NATURAL RESOURCES LAW ENFORCEMENT AND PROTECTIVE SERVICES
Texas Tech U (TX)
U of Minnesota, Crookston (MN)

NATURAL RESOURCES MANAGEMENT AND POLICY
Alaska Pacific U (AK)
Angelo State U (TX)
Bowling Green State U (OH)
California State U, Chico (CA)
Carnegie Mellon U (PA)
Clark U (MA)
Colorado State U (CO)
Delaware State U (DE)
Dominican U of California (CA)
Fort Hays State U (KS)
Humboldt State U (CA)
Iowa State U of Science and Technology (IA)
Johnson State Coll (VT)
Louisiana State U and Ag and Mech Coll (LA)
New Mexico Highlands U (NM)

North Carolina State U (NC)
North Dakota State U (ND)
Roanoke Coll (VA)
Rochester Inst of Technology (NY)
Sewanee: The U of the South (TN)
South Dakota State U (SD)
State U of New York Coll of Environmental Science and Forestry (NY)
Texas A&M U (TX)
Tuskegee U (AL)
U of Alberta (AB, Canada)
The U of British Columbia (BC, Canada)
U of California, Berkeley (CA)
U of Delaware (DE)
U of Guelph (ON, Canada)
U of Hawaii at Manoa (HI)
U of Idaho (ID)
U of Illinois at Urbana–Champaign (IL)
U of La Verne (CA)
U of Maine (ME)
U of Miami (FL)
U of Minnesota, Crookston (MN)
U of Minnesota, Twin Cities Campus (MN)
U of Nebraska–Lincoln (NE)
U of Nevada, Reno (NV)
U of Rhode Island (RI)
The U of Tennessee at Martin (TN)
U of Washington (WA)
U of Wisconsin–Stevens Point (WI)
Western Carolina U (NC)
Xavier U (OH)

NATURAL RESOURCES MANAGEMENT AND POLICY RELATED
Central Washington U (WA)
Delaware State U (DE)
Glenville State Coll (WV)
Humboldt State U (CA)
Keystone Coll (PA)
Massachusetts Maritime Acad (MA)
Moravian Coll (PA)
Morrisville State Coll (NY)
The Ohio State U (OH)
Rutgers, The State U of New Jersey, New Brunswick (NJ)
Sterling Coll (VT)
The U of British Columbia (BC, Canada)
U of Illinois at Urbana–Champaign (IL)
U of Minnesota, Twin Cities Campus (MN)
The U of Tennessee at Martin (TN)

NATURAL SCIENCES
Arcadia U (PA)
Azusa Pacific U (CA)
Bayamón Central U (PR)
Bemidji State U (MN)
Benedictine Coll (KS)
Bernard M. Baruch Coll of the City U of New York (NY)
Bethel Coll (KS)
Bishop's U (QC, Canada)
Blue Mountain Coll (MS)
California State U, Dominguez Hills (CA)
California State U, Fresno (CA)
California State U, Los Angeles (CA)
California State U, San Bernardino (CA)
Calvin Coll (MI)
Case Western Reserve U (OH)
Castleton State Coll (VT)
Central Coll (IA)
Christian Brothers U (TN)
Colgate U (NY)
Coll of Mount St. Joseph (OH)
Coll of Saint Benedict (MN)
Coll of Saint Mary (NE)
The Coll of St. Scholastica (MN)
Coll of the Atlantic (ME)
Coll of the Humanities and Sciences, Harrison Middleton U (AZ)
Colorado State U (CO)
Concordia Coll (MN)
Concordia U Chicago (IL)

Concordia U, Nebraska (NE)
Daemen Coll (NY)
Defiance Coll (OH)
Doane Coll (NE)
Dominican U (IL)
Dordt Coll (IA)
Eastern Kentucky U (KY)
Edgewood Coll (WI)
The Evergreen State Coll (WA)
Felician Coll (NJ)
Fordham U (NY)
Georgian Court U (NJ)
Houghton Coll (NY)
Humboldt State U (CA)
Indiana U East (IN)
Inter American U of Puerto Rico, San Germán Campus (PR)
Iowa Wesleyan Coll (IA)
The Johns Hopkins U (MD)
Johnson C. Smith U (NC)
Juniata Coll (PA)
Kansas State U (KS)
Lakehead U (ON, Canada)
Lee U (TN)
LeTourneau U (TX)
Lewis-Clark State Coll (ID)
Longwood U (VA)
Loyola Marymount U (CA)
Madonna U (MI)
Marlboro Coll (VT)
The Master's Coll and Sem (CA)
McPherson Coll (KS)
Minnesota State U Mankato (MN)
Mount Allison U (NB, Canada)
Mount Saint Mary Coll (NY)
Muhlenberg Coll (PA)
New Coll of Florida (FL)
Pacific Union Coll (CA)
Park U (MO)
Pepperdine U, Malibu (CA)
Peru State Coll (NE)
Saint John's U (MN)
Saint Peter's Coll (NJ)
St. Thomas Aquinas Coll (NY)
Sarah Lawrence Coll (NY)
Shimer Coll (IL)
Shorter U (GA)
Siena Heights U (MI)
Spelman Coll (GA)
State U of New York Coll at Geneseo (NY)
Tabor Coll (KS)
Taylor U (IN)
Thomas Edison State Coll (NJ)
Trent U (ON, Canada)
Universidad del Turabo (PR)
U of Alaska Anchorage (AK)
The U of Arizona (AZ)
U of Hawaii at Hilo (HI)
U of La Verne (CA)
U of Maine (ME)
U of Nebraska at Omaha (NE)
U of Pennsylvania (PA)
U of Pittsburgh at Greensburg (PA)
U of Pittsburgh at Johnstown (PA)
U of Puget Sound (WA)
U of Science and Arts of Oklahoma (OK)
The U of Toledo (OH)
U of Wisconsin–River Falls (WI)
U of Wisconsin–Stevens Point (WI)
Virginia Wesleyan Coll (VA)
Viterbo U (WI)
Washington U in St. Louis (MO)
Western Oregon U (OR)
Winona State U (MN)
Xavier U (OH)

NAVAL ARCHITECTURE AND MARINE ENGINEERING
Massachusetts Maritime Acad (MA)
State U of New York Maritime Coll (NY)
Stevens Inst of Technology (NJ)
United States Coast Guard Acad (CT)
United States Merchant Marine Acad (NY)
United States Naval Acad (MD)
U of Michigan (MI)
U of Minnesota, Twin Cities Campus (MN)
U of New Orleans (LA)
Webb Inst (NY)

NAVAL SCIENCE AND OPERATIONAL STUDIES
U of Wisconsin–Madison (WI)

NAVY/MARINE CORPS ROTC/ NAVAL SCIENCE
Hampton U (VA)
State U of New York Maritime Coll (NY)
U of Washington (WA)

NEAR AND MIDDLE EASTERN STUDIES
The American U in Cairo (Egypt)
Bard Coll (NY)
Brandeis U (MA)
Brown U (RI)
Claremont McKenna Coll (CA)
Columbia U, School of General Studies (NY)
Cornell U (NY)
Dartmouth Coll (NH)
Dickinson Coll (PA)
Emory U (GA)
Fordham U (NY)
The George Washington U (DC)
Hampshire Coll (MA)
Harvard U (MA)
Hood Coll (MD)
The Johns Hopkins U (MD)
Mount Holyoke Coll (MA)
New York U (NY)
Portland State U (OR)
Princeton U (NJ)
Rutgers, The State U of New Jersey, New Brunswick (NJ)
Sarah Lawrence Coll (NY)
Scripps Coll (CA)
Smith Coll (MA)
Swarthmore Coll (PA)
Syracuse U (NY)
Texas State U–San Marcos (TX)
United States Military Acad (NY)
The U of Arizona (AZ)
U of California, Berkeley (CA)
U of California, Santa Barbara (CA)
U of Massachusetts Amherst (MA)
U of Michigan (MI)
U of Minnesota, Twin Cities Campus (MN)
U of Richmond (VA)
The U of Texas at Austin (TX)
The U of Toledo (OH)
U of Toronto (ON, Canada)
U of Utah (UT)
U of Washington (WA)
Washington U in St. Louis (MO)
Wellesley Coll (MA)

NETWORK AND SYSTEM ADMINISTRATION
Bellevue U (NE)
Dordt Coll (IA)
Michigan Technological U (MI)
Rochester Inst of Technology (NY)
Simmons Coll (MA)
State U of New York Coll of Technology at Alfred (NY)
U of Great Falls (MT)

NEUROBIOLOGY AND ANATOMY
Andrews U (MI)
Harvard U (MA)
New Coll of Florida (FL)
St. Lawrence U (NY)
U of California, Davis (CA)
U of California, Irvine (CA)

NEUROBIOLOGY AND BEHAVIOR
Fitchburg State U (MA)

NEUROSCIENCE
Agnes Scott Coll (GA)
Allegheny Coll (PA)
Amherst Coll (MA)
Augustana Coll (IL)
Baldwin-Wallace Coll (OH)
Bard Coll (NY)
Barnard Coll (NY)
Bates Coll (ME)

Baylor U (TX)
Bishop's U (QC, Canada)
Boston U (MA)
Bowdoin Coll (ME)
Bowling Green State U (OH)
Brandeis U (MA)
Brown U (RI)
Bucknell U (PA)
Carnegie Mellon U (PA)
Cedar Crest Coll (PA)
Centenary Coll of Louisiana (LA)
Central Michigan U (MI)
Christopher Newport U (VA)
Claremont McKenna Coll (CA)
Clark U (MA)
Colby Coll (ME)
Colgate U (NY)
Coll of Mount St. Joseph (OH)
The Coll of William and Mary (VA)
The Coll of Wooster (OH)
The Colorado Coll (CO)
Columbia U, School of General Studies (NY)
Concordia U (QC, Canada)
Connecticut Coll (CT)
Dalhousie U (NS, Canada)
Dickinson Coll (PA)
Dominican U (IL)
Drake U (IA)
Drew U (NJ)
Earlham Coll (IN)
Eastern U (PA)
Emmanuel Coll (MA)
Emory U (GA)
Franklin & Marshall Coll (PA)
Furman U (SC)
George Mason U (VA)
Georgia State U (GA)
Hamilton Coll (NY)
Hampshire Coll (MA)
Haverford Coll (PA)
Hope Coll (MI)
Indiana U Bloomington (IN)
John Carroll U (OH)
The Johns Hopkins U (MD)
Kenyon Coll (OH)
King Coll (TN)
King's Coll (PA)
Knox Coll (IL)
Lake Forest Coll (IL)
Lawrence U (WI)
Lehigh U (PA)
Macalester Coll (MN)
Massachusetts Inst of Technology (MA)
Middlebury Coll (VT)
Mount Holyoke Coll (MA)
Muhlenberg Coll (PA)
New York U (NY)
Northeastern U (MA)
Northwest Nazarene U (ID)
Ohio U (OH)
Ohio Wesleyan U (OH)
Pitzer Coll (CA)
Pomona Coll (CA)
Regis U (CO)
Rice U (TX)
St. Lawrence U (NY)
Scripps Coll (CA)
Skidmore Coll (NY)
Smith Coll (MA)
Stonehill Coll (MA)
Syracuse U (NY)
Temple U (PA)
Texas Christian U (TX)
Thiel Coll (PA)
Trinity Coll (CT)
Trinity U (TX)
Tulane U (LA)
Union Coll (NY)
The U of Alabama at Birmingham (AL)
The U of Arizona (AZ)
U of California, Los Angeles (CA)
U of California, Riverside (CA)
U of California, Santa Cruz (CA)
U of Cincinnati (OH)
U of Delaware (DE)
U of Evansville (IN)
U of Illinois at Chicago (IL)
U of Lethbridge (AB, Canada)
U of Miami (FL)
U of Michigan (MI)
U of Minnesota, Twin Cities Campus (MN)

INDEXES

U of Mount Union (OH)
U of New Hampshire (NH)
U of Pennsylvania (PA)
U of Pittsburgh (PA)
U of Rochester (NY)
The U of Scranton (PA)
U of Southern California (CA)
The U of Texas at Dallas (TX)
The U of Western Ontario (ON, Canada)
U of Windsor (ON, Canada)
Vanderbilt U (TN)
Washington and Lee U (VA)
Washington State U (WA)
Washington U in St. Louis (MO)
Wellesley Coll (MA)
Western Washington U (WA)
Westminster Coll (UT)
Wheaton Coll (MA)

NONPROFIT MANAGEMENT

Alaska Pacific U (AK)
Arizona State U (AZ)
Austin Peay State U (TN)
City Vision Coll (MO)
Cleveland State U (OH)
Concordia U Chicago (IL)
Dalhousie U (NS, Canada)
Fairleigh Dickinson U, Metropolitan Campus (NJ)
Franklin U (OH)
Friends U (KS)
Gettysburg Coll (PA)
Grace Coll (IN)
Hardin-Simmons U (TX)
Hawai'i Pacific U (HI)
Hope Intl U (CA)
Huntington U (IN)
Pace U (NY)
Rogers State U (OK)
Southwestern Christian U (OK)
Southwest Minnesota State U (MN)
Tiffin U (OH)
Trevecca Nazarene U (TN)
U of Minnesota, Twin Cities Campus (MN)
U of South Carolina Upstate (SC)
U of Southern Maine (ME)
Warren Wilson Coll (NC)
William Jewell Coll (MO)

NORWEGIAN

Brigham Young U (UT)
Pacific Lutheran U (WA)
St. Olaf Coll (MN)
U of North Dakota (ND)

NUCLEAR AND INDUSTRIAL RADIOLOGIC TECHNOLOGIES RELATED

Mount Mary Coll (WI)

NUCLEAR ENGINEERING

Georgia Inst of Technology (GA)
Idaho State U (ID)
Kansas State U (KS)
Massachusetts Inst of Technology (MA)
Missouri U of Science and Technology (MO)
North Carolina State U (NC)
Penn State Abington (PA)
Penn State Altoona (PA)
Penn State Beaver (PA)
Penn State Berks (PA)
Penn State Brandywine (PA)
Penn State DuBois (PA)
Penn State Erie, The Behrend Coll (PA)
Penn State Fayette, The Eberly Campus (PA)
Penn State Greater Allegheny (PA)
Penn State Hazleton (PA)
Penn State Lehigh Valley (PA)
Penn State Mont Alto (PA)
Penn State New Kensington (PA)
Penn State Schuylkill (PA)
Penn State Shenango (PA)
Penn State U Park (PA)
Penn State Wilkes-Barre (PA)
Penn State Worthington Scranton (PA)
Penn State York (PA)
Purdue U (IN)

Rensselaer Polytechnic Inst (NY)
South Carolina State U (SC)
Texas A&M U (TX)
United States Military Acad (NY)
U of California, Berkeley (CA)
U of Florida (FL)
U of Illinois at Urbana–Champaign (IL)
U of Michigan (MI)
U of New Mexico (NM)
The U of Tennessee (TN)
U of Wisconsin–Madison (WI)
Worcester Polytechnic Inst (MA)

NUCLEAR ENGINEERING TECHNOLOGY

Thomas Edison State Coll (NJ)
United States Merchant Marine Acad (NY)
United States Military Acad (NY)

NUCLEAR MEDICAL TECHNOLOGY

Allen Coll (IA)
Baptist Coll of Health Sciences (TN)
Barry U (FL)
Benedictine U (IL)
Cedar Crest Coll (PA)
Dalhousie U (NS, Canada)
Ferris State U (MI)
Indiana U Bloomington (IN)
Indiana U East (IN)
Indiana U of Pennsylvania (PA)
Indiana U–Purdue U Indianapolis (IN)
Indiana U South Bend (IN)
Indiana U Southeast (IN)
Lewis U (IL)
Long Island U–Brooklyn Campus (NY)
Long Island U–C. W. Post Campus (NY)
Loras Coll (IA)
Manhattan Coll (NY)
Massachusetts Coll of Pharmacy and Health Sciences (MA)
North Central Coll (IL)
Oakland U (MI)
Old Dominion U (VA)
Peru State Coll (NE)
Robert Morris U (PA)
Roosevelt U (IL)
Saint Louis U (MO)
Saint Mary's U of Minnesota (MN)
Salem State U (MA)
Thomas Edison State Coll (NJ)
U at Buffalo, the State U of New York (NY)
The U of Alabama at Birmingham (AL)
U of Central Arkansas (AR)
U of Cincinnati (OH)
The U of Findlay (OH)
The U of Iowa (IA)
U of Medicine and Dentistry of New Jersey (NJ)
U of Missouri (MO)
U of Nebraska Medical Center (NE)
U of Nevada, Las Vegas (NV)
U of Oklahoma Health Sciences Center (OK)
U of St. Francis (IL)
U of the Incarnate Word (TX)
U of Vermont (VT)
U of Wisconsin–La Crosse (WI)
Weber State U (UT)
Wheeling Jesuit U (WV)
York Coll of Pennsylvania (PA)

NUCLEAR/NUCLEAR POWER TECHNOLOGY

U of North Texas (TX)

NUCLEAR PHYSICS

Arkansas Tech U (AR)

NURSE MIDWIFE/NURSING MIDWIFERY

Ryerson U (ON, Canada)
U of Toronto (ON, Canada)

NURSING ADMINISTRATION

Central Methodist U (MO)

Clarkson Coll (NE)
Clayton State U (GA)
Huntington U (IN)
Midwestern State U (TX)
Nebraska Wesleyan U (NE)
Nova Southeastern U (FL)
Ohio Northern U (OH)
Ryerson U (ON, Canada)
Seattle Pacific U (WA)
The U of Western Ontario (ON, Canada)
Wheeling Jesuit U (WV)

NURSING EDUCATION

Macon State Coll (GA)

NURSING PRACTICE

Benedictine Coll (KS)
Bluefield Coll (VA)
Brenau U (GA)
Christian Brothers U (TN)
Concordia Coll–New York (NY)
Florida National Coll (FL)
Lebanese American U (Lebanon)
Misericordia U (PA)
Siena Heights U (MI)

NURSING SCIENCE

Cedar Crest Coll (PA)
Clarkson Coll (NE)
Coll of Saint Elizabeth (NJ)
Columbia Centro Universitario, Caguas (PR)
EDP Coll of Puerto Rico–San Sebastian (PR)
Holy Family U (PA)
Kean U (NJ)
Kent State U at Geauga (OH)
Kent State U at Trumbull (OH)
Millersville U of Pennsylvania (PA)
Monmouth U (NJ)
National U (CA)
New Jersey City U (NJ)
North Carolina Ag and Tech State U (NC)
The Ohio State U (OH)
Oklahoma City U (OK)
Pensacola State Coll (FL)
Queens U of Charlotte (NC)
Saint Peter's Coll (NJ)
Siena Heights U (MI)
Simmons Coll (MA)
South U (AL)
South U, Royal Palm Beach (FL)
South U, Tampa (FL)
South U, Columbia (SC)
South U, Glen Allen (VA)
State U of New York Upstate Medical U (NY)
Thompson Rivers U (BC, Canada)
Trinity Coll of Nursing and Health Sciences (IL)
U of California, Irvine (CA)
U of Illinois at Chicago (IL)
U of New Hampshire at Manchester (NH)
U of Pittsburgh at Johnstown (PA)
Wayne State U (MI)
Xavier U (OH)

NUTRITION SCIENCES

Auburn U (AL)
Boston U (MA)
California State U, Los Angeles (CA)
Case Western Reserve U (OH)
Coll of Saint Benedict (MN)
Concordia Coll (MN)
Cornell U (NY)
Drexel U (PA)
Elmhurst Coll (IL)
Goddard Coll (VT)
La Salle U (PA)
Lebanese American U (Lebanon)
Louisiana State U and Ag and Mech Coll (LA)
McNeese State U (LA)
Messiah Coll (PA)
Michigan State U (MI)
New York Inst of Technology (NY)
North Carolina State U (NC)
The Ohio State U (OH)
Russell Sage Coll (NY)

Rutgers, The State U of New Jersey, New Brunswick (NJ)
Saint John's U (MN)
Southern Illinois U Carbondale (IL)
Syracuse U (NY)
Texas Woman's U (TX)
The U of Arizona (AZ)
U of California, Berkeley (CA)
U of California, Davis (CA)
U of Connecticut (CT)
U of Delaware (DE)
U of Guelph (ON, Canada)
U of Hawaii at Manoa (HI)
U of Illinois at Chicago (IL)
U of Massachusetts Amherst (MA)
U of Massachusetts Lowell (MA)
U of Minnesota, Twin Cities Campus (MN)
U of Nevada, Las Vegas (NV)
U of Nevada, Reno (NV)
U of New Hampshire (NH)
U of Northern Colorado (CO)
U of Saint Joseph (CT)
U of Southern Indiana (IN)
U of the District of Columbia (DC)
U of the Incarnate Word (TX)
U of Vermont (VT)
U of Wisconsin–Madison (WI)

OCCUPATIONAL HEALTH AND INDUSTRIAL HYGIENE

California State U, Fresno (CA)
Grand Valley State U (MI)
Indiana U Bloomington (IN)
Montana Tech of The U of Montana (MT)
North Carolina Ag and Tech State U (NC)
Oakland U (MI)
Ohio U (OH)
Roger Williams U (RI)
Ryerson U (ON, Canada)

OCCUPATIONAL SAFETY AND HEALTH TECHNOLOGY

Bayamón Central U (PR)
California State U, Fresno (CA)
Central Washington U (WA)
Columbia Southern U (AL)
Embry-Riddle Aeronautical U–Daytona (FL)
Fairmont State U (WV)
Grand Valley State U (MI)
Indiana State U (IN)
Indiana U of Pennsylvania (PA)
Indiana U Southeast (IN)
Jacksonville State U (AL)
Keene State Coll (NH)
Marshall U (WV)
Millersville U of Pennsylvania (PA)
National U (CA)
Rochester Inst of Technology (NY)
Slippery Rock U of Pennsylvania (PA)
Southeastern Louisiana U (LA)
Southeastern Oklahoma State U (OK)
Southwest Baptist U (MO)
U of Central Missouri (MO)
U of Houston–Downtown (TX)
U of North Dakota (ND)
U of Regina (SK, Canada)
U of Wisconsin–Whitewater (WI)

OCCUPATIONAL THERAPY

Alabama State U (AL)
Baker Coll of Flint (MI)
Bay Path Coll (MA)
Boston U (MA)
Calvin Coll (MI)
Coll of Saint Benedict (MN)
Dalhousie U (NS, Canada)
Dominican Coll (NY)
Dominican U (IL)
Dominican U of California (CA)
Duquesne U (PA)
Eastern Kentucky U (KY)
Eastern Michigan U (MI)
Eastern Washington U (WA)
Elizabethtown Coll (PA)
Elmhurst Coll (IL)
Grand Valley State U (MI)
Hawai'i Pacific U (HI)
Husson U (ME)

Illinois Coll (IL)
Ithaca Coll (NY)
Keuka Coll (NY)
Lenoir-Rhyne U (NC)
Long Island U–Brooklyn Campus (NY)
McKendree U (IL)
Mount Mary Coll (WI)
Nazareth Coll of Rochester (NY)
New York Inst of Technology (NY)
Penn State Mont Alto (PA)
Queen's U at Kingston (ON, Canada)
Quinnipiac U (CT)
Sacred Heart U (CT)
St. Catherine U (MN)
Saint Francis U (PA)
Saint John's U (MN)
Saint Louis U (MO)
Saint Vincent Coll (PA)
Spalding U (KY)
Stephens Coll (MO)
Stony Brook U, State U of New York (NY)
Towson U (MD)
Tuskegee U (AL)
U at Buffalo, the State U of New York (NY)
U of Alberta (AB, Canada)
The U of Findlay (OH)
The U of Kansas (KS)
U of Minnesota, Twin Cities Campus (MN)
U of Missouri (MO)
U of New England (ME)
U of New Hampshire (NH)
U of Ottawa (ON, Canada)
U of Pittsburgh (PA)
The U of Scranton (PA)
U of Southern California (CA)
U of Southern Indiana (IN)
U of Southern Maine (ME)
U of the Sciences in Philadelphia (PA)
U of Utah (UT)
U of Washington (WA)
The U of Western Ontario (ON, Canada)
U of Wisconsin–Milwaukee (WI)
Wartburg Coll (IA)
Western Michigan U (MI)
Worcester State U (MA)
Xavier U (OH)
York Coll of the City U of New York (NY)

OCEAN ENGINEERING

California State U, Long Beach (CA)
Florida Atlantic U (FL)
Florida Inst of Technology (FL)
Texas A&M U (TX)
United States Naval Acad (MD)
U of Rhode Island (RI)
Virginia Polytechnic Inst and State U (VA)

OCEANOGRAPHY (CHEMICAL AND PHYSICAL)

Central Michigan U (MI)
Coll of the Atlantic (ME)
Dalhousie U (NS, Canada)
Elizabeth City State U (NC)
Florida Inst of Technology (FL)
Hawai'i Pacific U (HI)
Humboldt State U (CA)
Kutztown U of Pennsylvania (PA)
Lamar U (TX)
Louisiana State U and Ag and Mech Coll (LA)
Millersville U of Pennsylvania (PA)
North Carolina State U (NC)
Rider U (NJ)
United States Coast Guard Acad (CT)
United States Naval Acad (MD)
The U of British Columbia (BC, Canada)
U of Miami (FL)
U of Michigan (MI)
U of South Carolina (SC)
U of Washington (WA)
U of West Florida (FL)

OFFICE MANAGEMENT

Adams State Coll (CO)
Babson Coll (MA)
Ball State U (IN)
Bob Jones U (SC)
Bowling Green State U (OH)
Central Washington U (WA)
Clayton State U (GA)
East Central U (OK)
Eastern Kentucky U (KY)
Eastern Michigan U (MI)
Indiana State U (IN)
Indiana U of Pennsylvania (PA)
Inter American U of Puerto Rico, Fajardo Campus (PR)
Inter American U of Puerto Rico, Ponce Campus (PR)
Inter American U of Puerto Rico, San Germán Campus (PR)
Loyola U Chicago (IL)
Maranatha Baptist Bible Coll (WI)
Middle Tennessee State U (TN)
Mississippi Valley State U (MS)
Mount Vernon Nazarene U (OH)
Rider U (NJ)
Roosevelt U (IL)
Southeast Missouri State U (MO)
Southwest Baptist U (MO)
Tabor Coll (KS)
Tarleton State U (TX)
Universidad del Turabo (PR)
U of Central Missouri (MO)
U of South Carolina (SC)
U of Southern Indiana (IN)
Valley City State U (ND)

OPERATIONS MANAGEMENT

Arizona State U (AZ)
Auburn U (AL)
Babson Coll (MA)
Ball State U (IN)
Bethany Coll (KS)
Boise State U (ID)
Boston Coll (MA)
Boston U (MA)
Bowling Green State U (OH)
California State U, Chico (CA)
California State U, Dominguez Hills (CA)
California State U, Long Beach (CA)
Central Michigan U (MI)
Central Washington U (WA)
Cleveland State U (OH)
Concordia U (QC, Canada)
Dalton State Coll (GA)
Eastern Washington U (WA)
Excelsior Coll (NY)
Farmingdale State Coll (NY)
Ferris State U (MI)
Fort Lewis Coll (CO)
Franklin U (OH)
Georgia Inst of Technology (GA)
Indiana U–Purdue U Fort Wayne (IN)
Indiana U–Purdue U Indianapolis (IN)
Inter American U of Puerto Rico, Ponce Campus (PR)
Iowa State U of Science and Technology (IA)
Le Moyne Coll (NY)
Loyola U Chicago (IL)
Marian U (WI)
Metropolitan State U (MN)
Miami U (OH)
Michigan Technological U (MI)
Minnesota State U Moorhead (MN)
Missouri Baptist U (MO)
National U (CA)
Northeastern State U (OK)
Northern Illinois U (IL)
Oakland U (MI)
The Ohio State U (OH)
Purdue U (IN)
Purdue U North Central (IN)
Roger Williams U (RI)
Saginaw Valley State U (MI)
Seattle U (WA)
Southern New Hampshire U (NH)
State U of New York Coll of Technology at Canton (NY)
Tabor Coll (KS)
Texas Southern U (TX)
Thomas Edison State Coll (NJ)

Trine U (IN)
The U of Akron (OH)
The U of Arizona (AZ)
U of Cincinnati (OH)
U of Delaware (DE)
U of Houston (TX)
U of Idaho (ID)
U of Illinois at Urbana–Champaign (IL)
U of Indianapolis (IN)
U of Massachusetts Amherst (MA)
U of Massachusetts Dartmouth (MA)
U of Michigan–Flint (MI)
U of Minnesota, Crookston (MN)
U of Minnesota, Twin Cities Campus (MN)
U of Nebraska at Kearney (NE)
The U of North Carolina at Asheville (NC)
The U of North Carolina at Charlotte (NC)
U of North Dakota (ND)
U of North Texas (TX)
U of Pennsylvania (PA)
U of St. Thomas (MN)
The U of Scranton (PA)
U of Southern Indiana (IN)
The U of Texas at San Antonio (TX)
The U of Toledo (OH)
U of Utah (UT)
U of Wisconsin–Madison (WI)
U of Wisconsin–Milwaukee (WI)
U of Wisconsin–Stout (WI)
U of Wisconsin–Whitewater (WI)
Utah State U (UT)
Utah Valley U (UT)
Washington State U (WA)
Washington U in St. Louis (MO)
Wentworth Inst of Technology (MA)
Western Washington U (WA)
Widener U (PA)

OPERATIONS RESEARCH

Babson Coll (MA)
Bernard M. Baruch Coll of the City U of New York (NY)
Bowling Green State U (OH)
California State U, Fullerton (CA)
Carnegie Mellon U (PA)
Cornell U (NY)
Long Island U–Brooklyn Campus (NY)
New York U (NY)
Princeton U (NJ)
Southern Methodist U (TX)
United States Air Force Acad (CO)
United States Coast Guard Acad (CT)
United States Military Acad (NY)
United States Naval Acad (MD)
U of California, Berkeley (CA)
U of Illinois at Urbana–Champaign (IL)
U of Toronto (ON, Canada)

OPHTHALMIC AND OPTOMETRIC SUPPORT SERVICES AND ALLIED PROFESSIONS RELATED

Indiana U Bloomington (IN)
Saint Joseph's Coll of Maine (ME)

OPHTHALMIC LABORATORY TECHNOLOGY

Abilene Christian U (TX)
U of Ottawa (ON, Canada)

OPTICAL SCIENCES

The Ohio State U (OH)
Saginaw Valley State U (MI)
U of Rochester (NY)
Western Washington U (WA)

OPTOMETRIC TECHNICIAN

Indiana U Bloomington (IN)
Texas A&M U–Corpus Christi (TX)

ORGANIC CHEMISTRY

Concordia U (QC, Canada)
Sarah Lawrence Coll (NY)
The U of Western Ontario (ON, Canada)

ORGANIZATIONAL BEHAVIOR

Anderson U (IN)
Anderson U (SC)
Athabasca U (AB, Canada)
Benedictine U (IL)
Bluffton U (OH)
Boston U (MA)
Bowling Green State U (OH)
Brown U (RI)
Calvary Bible Coll and Theological Sem (MO)
Central Michigan U (MI)
Claflin U (SC)
Coll of Mount St. Joseph (OH)
The Coll of St. Scholastica (MN)
Denison U (OH)
DePaul U (IL)
Eastern Mennonite U (VA)
Edgewood Coll (WI)
Goodwin Coll (CT)
Greenville Coll (IL)
Indian River State Coll (FL)
John Brown U (AR)
Lewis U (IL)
Loyola U Chicago (IL)
Manhattan Coll (NY)
Miami U (OH)
Mid-Continent U (KY)
National U (CA)
Neumann U (PA)
Northern Kentucky U (KY)
Oakland City U (IN)
Oral Roberts U (OK)
Palm Beach Atlantic U (FL)
Penn State Abington (PA)
Penn State Altoona (PA)
Penn State Beaver (PA)
Penn State Berks (PA)
Penn State Brandywine (PA)
Penn State DuBois (PA)
Penn State Erie, The Behrend Coll (PA)
Penn State Fayette, The Eberly Campus (PA)
Penn State Greater Allegheny (PA)
Penn State Harrisburg (PA)
Penn State Hazleton (PA)
Penn State Lehigh Valley (PA)
Penn State Mont Alto (PA)
Penn State New Kensington (PA)
Penn State Schuylkill (PA)
Penn State Shenango (PA)
Penn State U Park (PA)
Penn State Wilkes-Barre (PA)
Penn State Worthington Scranton (PA)
Penn State York (PA)
Philander Smith Coll (AR)
Pitzer Coll (CA)
Regent U (VA)
Rider U (NJ)
Robert Morris U (PA)
Roosevelt U (IL)
St. Ambrose U (IA)
Saint Joseph's U (PA)
Saint Louis U (MO)
Santa Clara U (CA)
Scripps Coll (CA)
Simpson U (CA)
Temple U (PA)
United States Military Acad (NY)
U of Cincinnati (OH)
U of Illinois at Urbana–Champaign (IL)
U of Michigan (MI)
U of Mobile (AL)
U of North Texas (TX)
U of Oklahoma (OK)
U of Richmond (VA)
U of St. Francis (IL)
U of the Incarnate Word (TX)
The U of Toledo (OH)
U of Tulsa (OK)
The U of Western Ontario (ON, Canada)
Waldorf Coll (IA)
Wayne State U (MI)
Woodbury U (CA)

ORGANIZATIONAL COMMUNICATION

Aquinas Coll (MI)
Assumption Coll (MA)
Bloomsburg U of Pennsylvania (PA)

Bradley U (IL)
Brigham Young U (UT)
Buena Vista U (IA)
California State U, Chico (CA)
Calvin Coll (MI)
Capital U (OH)
Cedarville U (OH)
Cleveland State U (OH)
The Coll at Brockport, State U of New York (NY)
Emmanuel Coll (GA)
Fairleigh Dickinson U, Metropolitan Campus (NJ)
Franklin U (OH)
George Fox U (OR)
Howard Payne U (TX)
Indiana U–Purdue U Fort Wayne (IN)
Lindenwood U (MO)
Lipscomb U (TN)
Lubbock Christian U (TX)
Marian U (WI)
Marylhurst U (OR)
McKendree U (IL)
Missouri State U (MO)
Montana State U Billings (MT)
North Central Coll (IL)
Northwest Missouri State U (MO)
Northwest U (WA)
Ohio Northern U (OH)
Pace U (NY)
Palm Beach Atlantic U (FL)
Roosevelt U (IL)
Shorter U (GA)
Southeastern U (FL)
Southeast Missouri State U (MO)
Suffolk U (MA)
Temple U (PA)
Trevecca Nazarene U (TN)
The U of Akron (OH)
U of Idaho (ID)
U of Illinois at Urbana–Champaign (IL)
U of Mount Union (OH)
U of Northern Iowa (IA)
Viterbo U (WI)
Washington State U (WA)
Western Kentucky U (KY)
Western Michigan U (MI)
William Jewell Coll (MO)
Xavier U (OH)

ORGANIZATIONAL LEADERSHIP

Auburn U Montgomery (AL)
Beulah Heights U (GA)
Brenau U (GA)
California Baptist U (CA)
Calvary Bible Coll and Theological Sem (MO)
Cleveland State U (OH)
Columbia Southern U (AL)
Gannon U (PA)
Indiana Tech (IN)
Indiana Wesleyan U (IN)
LaGrange Coll (GA)
Lincoln Christian U (IL)
Marquette U (WI)
Mid-Atlantic Christian U (NC)
Oral Roberts U (OK)
Point U (GA)
St. Thomas U (FL)
Spring Hill Coll (AL)
Union Inst & U (OH)
U of Evansville (IN)
U of Houston (TX)
U of Wisconsin–Eau Claire (WI)
Western Kentucky U (KY)
Wheeling Jesuit U (WV)

ORNAMENTAL HORTICULTURE

California Polytechnic State U, San Luis Obispo (CA)
California State U, Fresno (CA)
Delaware Valley Coll (PA)
Iowa State U of Science and Technology (IA)
The Ohio State U (OH)
Tarleton State U (TX)
Texas A&M U (TX)
U of Florida (FL)
U of Illinois at Urbana–Champaign (IL)

U of the District of Columbia (DC)
U of Wisconsin–Platteville (WI)

ORTHOPTICS

St. Catherine U (MN)

ORTHOTICS/PROSTHETICS

U of Washington (WA)

OUTDOOR EDUCATION

Huntington U (IN)
Northland Coll (WI)
Prescott Coll (AZ)
Sierra Nevada Coll (NV)

PACIFIC AREA/PACIFIC RIM STUDIES

Hawai`i Pacific U (HI)
U of Hawaii–West Oahu (HI)

PACKAGING SCIENCE

Michigan State U (MI)
U of Wisconsin–Stout (WI)

PAINTING

Acad of Art U (CA)
Adams State Coll (CO)
Alberta Coll of Art & Design (AB, Canada)
Aquinas Coll (MI)
Arcadia U (PA)
Art Center Coll of Design (CA)
Bennington Coll (VT)
Bethany Coll (KS)
Biola U (CA)
Birmingham-Southern Coll (AL)
Boston U (MA)
Bowling Green State U (OH)
Bradley U (IL)
Brigham Young U (UT)
Buffalo State Coll, State U of New York (NY)
California Coll of the Arts (CA)
California State U, East Bay (CA)
California State U, Long Beach (CA)
The Cleveland Inst of Art (OH)
Coe Coll (IA)
The Coll at Brockport, State U of New York (NY)
Colorado State U (CO)
Columbia Coll (MO)
Concordia U (QC, Canada)
Drake U (IA)
Emily Carr U of Art + Design (BC, Canada)
Escuela de Artes Plasticas de Puerto Rico (PR)
Ferris State U (MI)
Harding U (AR)
Hofstra U (NY)
Indiana U–Purdue U Fort Wayne (IN)
Indiana Wesleyan U (IN)
Inter American U of Puerto Rico, San Germán Campus (PR)
Kansas City Art Inst (MO)
Kent State U (OH)
Lewis U (IL)
Lyme Acad Coll of Fine Arts (CT)
Maryland Inst Coll of Art (MD)
Marywood U (PA)
Massachusetts Coll of Art and Design (MA)
Montserrat Coll of Art (MA)
Northern Michigan U (MI)
Northwest Nazarene U (ID)
Oakland U (MI)
Ohio Northern U (OH)
Ohio U (OH)
Pacific Northwest Coll of Art (OR)
Pittsburg State U (KS)
Pratt Inst (NY)
Providence Coll (RI)
Ringling Coll of Art and Design (FL)
Rochester Inst of Technology (NY)
Rutgers, The State U of New Jersey, New Brunswick (NJ)
Salem State U (MA)
Salve Regina U (RI)
Sarah Lawrence Coll (NY)
Savannah Coll of Art and Design (GA)

School of the Museum of Fine Arts, Boston (MA)
Seton Hill U (PA)
State U of New York at New Paltz (NY)
Syracuse U (NY)
Temple U (PA)
Texas Christian U (TX)
U of Dallas (TX)
U of Hartford (CT)
U of Houston (TX)
U of Illinois at Chicago (IL)
U of Illinois at Urbana–Champaign (IL)
The U of Iowa (IA)
The U of Kansas (KS)
U of Massachusetts Dartmouth (MA)
U of Miami (FL)
U of Missouri–St. Louis (MO)
U of Oregon (OR)
U of Regina (SK, Canada)
The U of the Arts (PA)
U of Washington (WA)
U of Windsor (ON, Canada)
Virginia Commonwealth U (VA)
Virginia Intermont Coll (VA)
Washington U in St. Louis (MO)
Western State Coll of Colorado (CO)
Western Washington U (WA)
West Virginia Wesleyan Coll (WV)

PALEONTOLOGY
Bowling Green State U (OH)
Mercyhurst Coll (PA)
U of Alberta (AB, Canada)

PALLIATIVE CARE NURSING
Madonna U (MI)

PAPER SCIENCE AND ENGINEERING
U of Wisconsin–Stevens Point (WI)
Western Michigan U (MI)

PARASITOLOGY
Bowling Green State U (OH)

PARKS, RECREATION AND LEISURE
Alabama State U (AL)
Alaska Pacific U (AK)
Alcorn State U (MS)
Arizona State U (AZ)
Ashland U (OH)
Belmont U (TN)
Bemidji State U (MN)
Bethune-Cookman U (FL)
Biola U (CA)
Black Hills State U (SD)
Bluffton U (OH)
Boston U (MA)
Bowling Green State U (OH)
Brevard Coll (NC)
Bridgewater State U (MA)
California Polytechnic State U, San Luis Obispo (CA)
California State U, Chico (CA)
California State U, East Bay (CA)
California State U, Fresno (CA)
California State U, Long Beach (CA)
California State U, Sacramento (CA)
Calvin Coll (MI)
Campbellsville U (KY)
Carson-Newman Coll (TN)
Catawba Coll (NC)
Central State U (OH)
Central Washington U (WA)
Cheyney U of Pennsylvania (PA)
The Coll at Brockport, State U of New York (NY)
Concordia U (QC, Canada)
Dalhousie U (NS, Canada)
Dordt Coll (IA)
East Central U (OK)
Eastern Washington U (WA)
Elon U (NC)
Emporia State U (KS)
Evangel U (MO)
Ferrum Coll (VA)

Fort Lewis Coll (CO)
Georgia Coll & State U (GA)
Georgia Southern U (GA)
Gordon Coll (MA)
Graceland U (IA)
Grambling State U (LA)
Grand Canyon U (AZ)
Greenville Coll (IL)
Houghton Coll (NY)
Humboldt State U (CA)
Huntington U (IN)
Indiana U Bloomington (IN)
Ithaca Coll (NY)
Jacksonville State U (AL)
Johnson State Coll (VT)
Kutztown U of Pennsylvania (PA)
Lakehead U (ON, Canada)
Lake Superior State U (MI)
Limestone Coll (SC)
Lindenwood U (MO)
Lindsey Wilson Coll (KY)
Lock Haven U of Pennsylvania (PA)
Manchester Coll (IN)
Mars Hill Coll (NC)
Maryville Coll (TN)
Messiah Coll (PA)
Metropolitan State Coll of Denver (CO)
Michigan State U (MI)
Minnesota State U Mankato (MN)
Missouri State U (MO)
Montclair State U (NJ)
Montreat Coll, Montreat (NC)
Morris Coll (SC)
New England Coll (NH)
New Mexico Highlands U (NM)
North Dakota State U (ND)
Northern Arizona U (AZ)
Northern Michigan U (MI)
North Greenville U (SC)
Northwest Nazarene U (ID)
The Ohio State U (OH)
Ohio U (OH)
Oklahoma State U (OK)
Presentation Coll (SD)
Radford U (VA)
St. Andrews U (NC)
St. Thomas Aquinas Coll (NY)
Salem State U (MA)
San Diego State U (CA)
San Francisco State U (CA)
Shaw U (NC)
Shepherd U (WV)
Shorter U (GA)
Simpson U (CA)
Southeastern Oklahoma State U (OK)
Southeast Missouri State U (MO)
Southern Connecticut State U (CT)
Southern Illinois U Carbondale (IL)
Southwest Baptist U (MO)
Southwestern Oklahoma State U (OK)
Spring Arbor U (MI)
State U of New York at Plattsburgh (NY)
State U of New York Coll at Cortland (NY)
State U of New York Coll of Environmental Science and Forestry (NY)
Sterling Coll (VT)
Temple U (PA)
Texas A&M U (TX)
U of Alberta (AB, Canada)
U of Arkansas (AR)
U of Central Missouri (MO)
U of Dubuque (IA)
U of Illinois at Urbana–Champaign (IL)
The U of Iowa (IA)
U of Maine at Presque Isle (ME)
U of Mary Hardin-Baylor (TX)
U of Minnesota, Duluth (MN)
U of Minnesota, Twin Cities Campus (MN)
U of Missouri (MO)
U of Nebraska at Kearney (NE)
U of Nebraska at Omaha (NE)
U of Nevada, Las Vegas (NV)
U of Northern Iowa (IA)
U of Ottawa (ON, Canada)
U of South Alabama (AL)
The U of South Dakota (SD)
U of Southern Mississippi (MS)

The U of Toledo (OH)
U of Utah (UT)
Upper Iowa U (IA)
Utah State U (UT)
Virginia Commonwealth U (VA)
Virginia Wesleyan Coll (VA)
Western Michigan U (MI)
Western State Coll of Colorado (CO)
Western Washington U (WA)
Westfield State U (MA)
West Virginia State U (WV)
William Jewell Coll (MO)
William Paterson U of New Jersey (NJ)
William Penn U (IA)
Wingate U (NC)
Winona State U (MN)
York Coll of Pennsylvania (PA)

PARKS, RECREATION AND LEISURE FACILITIES MANAGEMENT
Appalachian State U (NC)
Arkansas Tech U (AR)
Asbury U (KY)
California State U, Chico (CA)
California State U, Fresno (CA)
California State U, Sacramento (CA)
California U of Pennsylvania (PA)
Chicago State U (IL)
Clemson U (SC)
Coll of the Ozarks (MO)
Colorado State U (CO)
Delaware State U (DE)
East Carolina U (NC)
Eastern Illinois U (IL)
Eastern Michigan U (MI)
Eastern Washington U (WA)
East Stroudsburg U of Pennsylvania (PA)
Ferris State U (MI)
Florida Intl U (FL)
Georgia Southwestern State U (GA)
Hannibal-LaGrange U (MO)
Humboldt State U (CA)
Illinois State U (IL)
Indiana State U (IN)
Indiana Tech (IN)
Indiana U Bloomington (IN)
Indiana Wesleyan U (IN)
John Brown U (AR)
Kansas State U (KS)
Kean U (NJ)
Kent State U (OH)
Keystone Coll (PA)
Lake Superior State U (MI)
Marshall U (WV)
Middle Tennessee State U (TN)
Minnesota State U Mankato (MN)
Missouri Western State U (MO)
Mount Marty Coll (SD)
New England Coll (NH)
New Mexico Highlands U (NM)
New Mexico State U (NM)
New York U (NY)
North Carolina Ag and Tech State U (NC)
North Carolina Central U (NC)
North Carolina State U (NC)
Northwest Missouri State U (MO)
Old Dominion U (VA)
Oral Roberts U (OK)
Penn State Abington (PA)
Penn State Altoona (PA)
Penn State Beaver (PA)
Penn State Berks (PA)
Penn State Brandywine (PA)
Penn State DuBois (PA)
Penn State Erie, The Behrend Coll (PA)
Penn State Fayette, The Eberly Campus (PA)
Penn State Greater Allegheny (PA)
Penn State Hazleton (PA)
Penn State Lehigh Valley (PA)
Penn State Mont Alto (PA)
Penn State New Kensington (PA)
Penn State Schuylkill (PA)
Penn State Shenango (PA)
Penn State U Park (PA)
Penn State Wilkes-Barre (PA)

Penn State Worthington Scranton (PA)
Penn State York (PA)
Pittsburg State U (KS)
St. Joseph's Coll, Long Island Campus (NY)
St. Joseph's Coll, New York (NY)
Slippery Rock U of Pennsylvania (PA)
South Dakota State U (SD)
State U of New York Coll at Cortland (NY)
State U of New York Coll of Technology at Delhi (NY)
Texas A&M U (TX)
Texas State U–San Marcos (TX)
Thomas U (GA)
Trine U (IN)
Union Coll (KY)
Union U (TN)
U of Alberta (AB, Canada)
The U of British Columbia (BC, Canada)
U of Connecticut (CT)
U of Delaware (DE)
U of Florida (FL)
U of Idaho (ID)
U of Maine (ME)
U of Minnesota, Crookston (MN)
U of Minnesota, Twin Cities Campus (MN)
U of Mississippi (MS)
U of New Hampshire (NH)
The U of North Carolina at Chapel Hill (NC)
The U of North Carolina Wilmington (NC)
U of North Dakota (ND)
U of Northern Colorado (CO)
U of North Texas (TX)
U of St. Francis (IL)
U of Vermont (VT)
U of West Georgia (GA)
U of Wisconsin–La Crosse (WI)
Wayland Baptist U (TX)
Webber Intl U (FL)
Western Carolina U (NC)
Western Illinois U (IL)
Western Kentucky U (KY)
Western State Coll of Colorado (CO)
West Virginia U (WV)
Winona State U (MN)

PARKS, RECREATION, LEISURE, AND FITNESS STUDIES RELATED
Belhaven U (MS)
Brigham Young U (UT)
The Coll at Brockport, State U of New York (NY)
Franklin Coll (IN)
New England Coll (NH)
Plymouth State U (NH)
St. Edward's U (TX)
U of North Alabama (AL)
The U of Toledo (OH)
Utah State U (UT)
Western State Coll of Colorado (CO)

PASTORAL COUNSELING AND SPECIALIZED MINISTRIES RELATED
Abilene Christian U (TX)
Brescia U (KY)
Calvary Bible Coll and Theological Sem (MO)
Crossroads Bible Coll (IN)
Greenville Coll (IL)
John Brown U (AR)
Lipscomb U (TN)
Madonna U (MI)
Malone U (OH)
Maranatha Baptist Bible Coll (WI)
Multnomah U (OR)
Northwestern Coll (MN)
Ouachita Baptist U (AR)

PASTORAL STUDIES/COUNSELING
Baptist Bible Coll of Pennsylvania (PA)

The Baptist Coll of Florida (FL)
Barclay Coll (KS)
Belmont U (TN)
Bethel Coll (IN)
Biola U (CA)
California Baptist U (CA)
Calvary Bible Coll and Theological Sem (MO)
Campbellsville U (KY)
Cedarville U (OH)
Clearwater Christian Coll (FL)
Coll of Mount St. Joseph (OH)
Columbia Bible Coll (BC, Canada)
Concordia U, Nebraska (NE)
Corban U (OR)
Cornerstone U (MI)
Crossroads Bible Coll (IN)
Crown Coll (MN)
Dallas Baptist U (TX)
Dominican U (IL)
East Texas Baptist U (TX)
Emmanuel Coll (GA)
Faith Baptist Bible Coll and Theological Sem (IA)
Faulkner U (AL)
Free Will Baptist Bible Coll (TN)
Gardner-Webb U (NC)
George Fox U (OR)
Greenville Coll (IL)
Hillsdale Free Will Baptist Coll (OK)
Houghton Coll (NY)
Indiana Wesleyan U (IN)
John Brown U (AR)
Kentucky Christian U (KY)
Kentucky Mountain Bible Coll (KY)
Lee U (TN)
Lindenwood U (MO)
Loyola U Chicago (IL)
Maple Springs Baptist Bible Coll and Sem (MD)
Maranatha Baptist Bible Coll (WI)
The Master's Coll and Sem (CA)
Milligan Coll (TN)
Moody Bible Inst (IL)
Mount Vernon Nazarene U (OH)
Multnomah U (OR)
New Hope Christian Coll (OR)
Newman U (KS)
Northwest Nazarene U (ID)
Northwest U (WA)
Oral Roberts U (OK)
Ouachita Baptist U (AR)
Saint Francis U (PA)
Saint Joseph's Coll (IN)
St. Thomas U (FL)
San Diego Christian Coll (CA)
Simpson U (CA)
Southeastern Baptist Theological Sem (NC)
Southwest Baptist U (MO)
Southwestern Assemblies of God U (TX)
Southwestern Christian U (OK)
Spring Arbor U (MI)
Trinity Baptist Coll (FL)
Trinity Coll of Florida (FL)
Union Coll (NE)
Universidad Teolgica del Caribe (PR)
U of Mary Hardin-Baylor (TX)
U of Saint Mary (KS)
U of St. Thomas (TX)
Valley Forge Christian Coll Woodbridge Campus (VA)
Vanguard U of Southern California (CA)
Walsh U (OH)
William Jessup U (CA)
Williams Baptist Coll (AR)

PATHOLOGIST ASSISTANT
St. John's U (NY)
Wayne State U (MI)

PATHOLOGY/EXPERIMENTAL PATHOLOGY
Penn State Berks (PA)
U of Connecticut (CT)
The U of North Carolina at Chapel Hill (NC)

PEACE STUDIES AND CONFLICT RESOLUTION
Bennington Coll (VT)

Dordt Coll (IA)
Dowling Coll (NY)
Drake U (IA)
Drew U (NJ)
Drury U (MO)
Duquesne U (PA)
Earlham Coll (IN)
East Carolina U (NC)
Eastern Illinois U (IL)
Eastern Kentucky U (KY)
Eastern Michigan U (MI)
Eastern U (PA)
Eastern Washington U (WA)
East Stroudsburg U of Pennsylvania (PA)
East Tennessee State U (TN)
Eckerd Coll (FL)
Edinboro U of Pennsylvania (PA)
Elizabethtown Coll (PA)
Elmhurst Coll (IL)
Elmira Coll (NY)
Elon U (NC)
Emory & Henry Coll (VA)
Emory U (GA)
Excelsior Coll (NY)
Fairfield U (CT)
Fairleigh Dickinson U, Coll at Florham (NJ)
Fairleigh Dickinson U, Metropolitan Campus (NJ)
Felician Coll (NJ)
Ferrum Coll (VA)
Flagler Coll (FL)
Florida Atlantic U (FL)
Florida Gulf Coast U (FL)
Florida Intl U (FL)
Florida Southern Coll (FL)
Florida State U (FL)
Fordham U (NY)
Fort Hays State U (KS)
Fort Lewis Coll (CO)
Franciscan U of Steubenville (OH)
Franklin & Marshall Coll (PA)
Franklin Coll (IN)
Furman U (SC)
Gallaudet U (DC)
Gannon U (PA)
Geneva Coll (PA)
George Fox U (OR)
George Mason U (VA)
Georgetown Coll (KY)
The George Washington U (DC)
Georgia Coll & State U (GA)
Georgia Southern U (GA)
Georgia State U (GA)
Gettysburg Coll (PA)
Gonzaga U (WA)
Gordon Coll (MA)
Goucher Coll (MD)
Grand Valley State U (MI)
Greenville Coll (IL)
Grinnell Coll (IA)
Grove City Coll (PA)
Guilford Coll (NC)
Gustavus Adolphus Coll (MN)
Hamilton Coll (NY)
Hamline U (MN)
Hampden-Sydney Coll (VA)
Hampshire Coll (MA)
Hanover Coll (IN)
Hardin-Simmons U (TX)
Hartwick Coll (NY)
Harvard U (MA)
Haverford Coll (PA)
Heidelberg U (OH)
Hendrix Coll (AR)
Hillsdale Coll (MI)
Hobart and William Smith Colls (NY)
Hofstra U (NY)
Hollins U (VA)
Hood Coll (MD)
Hope Coll (MI)
Houghton Coll (NY)
Howard Payne U (TX)
Humboldt State U (CA)
Hunter Coll of the City U of New York (NY)
Huntington U (IN)
Idaho State U (ID)
Illinois Coll (IL)
Illinois State U (IL)
Illinois Wesleyan U (IL)
Indiana State U (IN)
Indiana U Bloomington (IN)

Indiana U Northwest (IN)
Indiana U of Pennsylvania (PA)
Indiana U–Purdue U Fort Wayne (IN)
Indiana U–Purdue U Indianapolis (IN)
Indiana U South Bend (IN)
Indiana U Southeast (IN)
Indiana Wesleyan U (IN)
Iona Coll (NY)
Iowa State U of Science and Technology (IA)
Ithaca Coll (NY)
Jacksonville U (FL)
John Carroll U (OH)
The Johns Hopkins U (MD)
Juniata Coll (PA)
Kalamazoo Coll (MI)
Kansas State U (KS)
Kennesaw State U (GA)
Kent State U (OH)
Kenyon Coll (OH)
King Coll (TN)
King's Coll (PA)
The King's U Coll (AB, Canada)
Knox Coll (IL)
Kutztown U of Pennsylvania (PA)
Lafayette Coll (PA)
Lake Forest Coll (IL)
Lakehead U (ON, Canada)
La Salle U (PA)
Lawrence U (WI)
Lebanese American U (Lebanon)
Lebanon Valley Coll (PA)
Lehigh U (PA)
Lehman Coll of the City U of New York (NY)
Le Moyne Coll (NY)
Lenoir-Rhyne U (NC)
Lewis & Clark Coll (OR)
Lewis U (IL)
Liberty U (VA)
Lincoln Christian U (IL)
Northern Illinois U (IL)
Lincoln U (PA)
Lindenwood U (MO)
Linfield Coll (OR)
Lipscomb U (TN)
Lock Haven U of Pennsylvania (PA)
Long Island U–Brooklyn Campus (NY)
Long Island U–C. W. Post Campus (NY)
Loras Coll (IA)
Louisiana Coll (LA)
Louisiana State U and Ag and Mech Coll (LA)
Loyola Marymount U (CA)
Loyola U Chicago (IL)
Loyola U Maryland (MD)
Loyola U New Orleans (LA)
Luther Coll (IA)
Lycoming Coll (PA)
Lynchburg Coll (VA)
Macalester Coll (MN)
Malone U (OH)
Manchester Coll (IN)
Manhattan Coll (NY)
Manhattanville Coll (NY)
Mansfield U of Pennsylvania (PA)
Marietta Coll (OH)
Marlboro Coll (VT)
Marquette U (WI)
Mary Baldwin Coll (VA)
Marymount U (VA)
Maryville Coll (TN)
Massachusetts Coll of Liberal Arts (MA)
Massachusetts Inst of Technology (MA)
McDaniel Coll (MD)
McKendree U (IL)
McPherson Coll (KS)
Mercer U (GA)
Mercyhurst Coll (PA)
Merrimack Coll (MA)
Messiah Coll (PA)
Metropolitan State Coll of Denver (CO)
Metropolitan State U (MN)
Miami U (OH)
Michigan State U (MI)
Middlebury Coll (VT)
Middle Tennessee State U (TN)
Millersville U of Pennsylvania (PA)
Millikin U (IL)

Millsaps Coll (MS)
Mills Coll (CA)
Minnesota State U Mankato (MN)
Minnesota State U Moorhead (MN)
Misericordia U (PA)
Mississippi State U (MS)
Missouri State U (MO)
Missouri U of Science and Technology (MO)
Missouri Western State U (MO)
Molloy Coll (NY)
Monmouth Coll (IL)
Montana State U (MT)
Montclair State U (NJ)
Moravian Coll (PA)
Morehead State U (KY)
Morehouse Coll (GA)
Morningside Coll (IA)
Mount Allison U (NB, Canada)
Mount Holyoke Coll (MA)
Mount Mary Coll (WI)
Mount Mercy U (IA)
Mount St. Mary's Coll (CA)
Mount St. Mary's U (MD)
Mount Vernon Nazarene U (OH)
Muhlenberg Coll (PA)
Nazareth Coll of Rochester (NY)
Nebraska Wesleyan U (NE)
Newberry Coll (SC)
New Coll of Florida (FL)
New England Coll (NH)
New Jersey City U (NJ)
Newman U (KS)
New Mexico State U (NM)
New York U (NY)
Niagara U (NY)
North Carolina State U (NC)
North Central Coll (IL)
North Dakota State U (ND)
Northeastern Illinois U (IL)
Northeastern U (MA)
Northern Arizona U (AZ)
Northern Illinois U (IL)
Northern Kentucky U (KY)
Northern Michigan U (MI)
Northwestern Coll (IA)
Northwest Missouri State U (MO)
Northwest Nazarene U (ID)
Northwest U (WA)
Notre Dame de Namur U (CA)
Notre Dame of Maryland U (MD)
Nova Southeastern U (FL)
Nyack Coll (NY)
Oakland U (MI)
Occidental Coll (CA)
Oglethorpe U (GA)
Ohio Northern U (OH)
The Ohio State U (OH)
Ohio U (OH)
Ohio Wesleyan U (OH)
Oklahoma City U (OK)
Oklahoma State U (OK)
Old Dominion U (VA)
Otterbein U (OH)
Ouachita Baptist U (AR)
Pacific Lutheran U (WA)
Pacific U (OR)
Palm Beach Atlantic U (FL)
Penn State Abington (PA)
Penn State Altoona (PA)
Penn State Beaver (PA)
Penn State Berks (PA)
Penn State Brandywine (PA)
Penn State DuBois (PA)
Penn State Erie, The Behrend Coll (PA)
Penn State Fayette, The Eberly Campus (PA)
Penn State Greater Allegheny (PA)
Penn State Hazleton (PA)
Penn State Lehigh Valley (PA)
Penn State Mont Alto (PA)
Penn State New Kensington (PA)
Penn State Schuylkill (PA)
Penn State Shenango (PA)
Penn State U Park (PA)
Penn State Wilkes-Barre (PA)
Penn State Worthington Scranton (PA)
Penn State York (PA)
Pepperdine U, Malibu (CA)
Piedmont Coll (GA)
Pitzer Coll (CA)
Plymouth State U (NH)
Point Loma Nazarene U (CA)

Pomona Coll (CA)
Portland State U (OR)
Presbyterian Coll (SC)
Princeton U (NJ)
Providence Coll (RI)
Purchase Coll, State U of New York (NY)
Purdue U (IN)
Purdue U Calumet (IN)
Queens Coll of the City U of New York (NY)
Queen's U at Kingston (ON, Canada)
Queens U of Charlotte (NC)
Randolph Coll (VA)
Randolph-Macon Coll (VA)
Regis U (CO)
Rensselaer Polytechnic Inst (NY)
Rhode Island Coll (RI)
Rhodes Coll (TN)
Rice U (TX)
Rider U (NJ)
Ripon Coll (WI)
Roanoke Coll (VA)
Rochester Inst of Technology (NY)
Rockford Coll (IL)
Rockhurst U (MO)
Rocky Mountain Coll (MT)
Roger Williams U (RI)
Rollins Coll (FL)
Roosevelt U (IL)
Rosemont Coll (PA)
Rutgers, The State U of New Jersey, Camden (NJ)
Rutgers, The State U of New Jersey, Newark (NJ)
Rutgers, The State U of New Jersey, New Brunswick (NJ)
Sacred Heart Major Sem (MI)
Sacred Heart U (CT)
St. Ambrose U (IA)
Saint Anselm Coll (NH)
St. Bonaventure U (NY)
St. Catherine U (MN)
Saint Charles Borromeo Sem, Overbrook (PA)
St. Edward's U (TX)
Saint Francis U (PA)
St. John Fisher Coll (NY)
Saint John's U (MN)
St. John's U (NY)
Saint Joseph's Coll (IN)
Saint Joseph's Coll of Maine (ME)
Saint Joseph's U (PA)
St. Lawrence U (NY)
Saint Louis U (MO)
Saint Mary's Coll (IN)
Saint Mary's Coll of California (CA)
St. Mary's Coll of Maryland (MD)
St. Mary's Coll (TX)
Saint Mary's U of Minnesota (MN)
Saint Michael's Coll (VT)
St. Norbert Coll (WI)
St. Olaf Coll (MN)
Saint Peter's Coll (NJ)
St. Thomas Aquinas Coll (NY)
St. Thomas U (NB, Canada)
Saint Vincent Coll (PA)
Saint Xavier U (IL)
Salisbury U (MD)
Salve Regina U (RI)
Samford U (AL)
Sam Houston State U (TX)
San Diego State U (CA)
San Francisco State U (CA)
Santa Clara U (CA)
Sarah Lawrence Coll (NY)
Scripps Coll (CA)
Seattle Pacific U (WA)
Seattle U (WA)
Sewanee: The U of the South (TN)
Shaw U (NC)
Siena Coll (NY)
Siena Heights U (MI)
Simmons Coll (MA)
Simon Fraser U (BC, Canada)
Simpson Coll (IA)
Skidmore Coll (NY)
Slippery Rock U of Pennsylvania (PA)
Smith Coll (MA)
Sonoma State U (CA)
Southeast Missouri State U (MO)
Southern Connecticut State U (CT)
Southern Illinois U Carbondale (IL)

Southern Illinois U Edwardsville (IL)
Southern Methodist U (TX)
Southwestern U (TX)
Southwest Minnesota State U (MN)
Spelman Coll (GA)
Spring Arbor U (MI)
Spring Hill Coll (AL)
Stanford U (CA)
State U of New York at Binghamton (NY)
State U of New York at Fredonia (NY)
State U of New York at New Paltz (NY)
State U of New York at Oswego (NY)
State U of New York at Plattsburgh (NY)
State U of New York Coll at Cortland (NY)
State U of New York Coll at Geneseo (NY)
State U of New York Coll at Old Westbury (NY)
State U of New York Coll at Oneonta (NY)
State U of New York Coll at Potsdam (NY)
Stephen F. Austin State U (TX)
Stetson U (FL)
Stevens Inst of Technology (NJ)
Stonehill Coll (MA)
Stony Brook U, State U of New York (NY)
Suffolk U (MA)
Susquehanna U (PA)
Swarthmore Coll (PA)
Sweet Briar Coll (VA)
Syracuse U (NY)
Tabor Coll (KS)
Taylor U (IN)
Temple U (PA)
Texas A&M U (TX)
Texas Christian U (TX)
Texas Lutheran U (TX)
Texas State U–San Marcos (TX)
Texas Tech U (TX)
Thiel Coll (PA)
Thomas Edison State Coll (NJ)
Thomas More Coll (KY)
Towson U (MD)
Transylvania U (KY)
Trent U (ON, Canada)
Trinity Christian Coll (IL)
Trinity Coll (CT)
Trinity U (TX)
Tufts U (MA)
Tulane U (LA)
Union Coll (NY)
Union U (TN)
Université de Sherbrooke (QC, Canada)
U at Albany, State U of New York (NY)
U at Buffalo, the State U of New York (NY)
The U of Akron (OH)
The U of Alabama (AL)
The U of Alabama at Birmingham (AL)
The U of Alabama in Huntsville (AL)
U of Alaska Fairbanks (AK)
U of Alberta (AB, Canada)
The U of Arizona (AZ)
U of Arkansas (AR)
U of Arkansas at Little Rock (AR)
The U of British Columbia (BC, Canada)
The U of British Columbia–Okanagan (BC, Canada)
U of California, Berkeley (CA)
U of California, Davis (CA)
U of California, Irvine (CA)
U of California, Los Angeles (CA)
U of California, Riverside (CA)
U of California, Santa Barbara (CA)
U of California, Santa Cruz (CA)
U of Central Arkansas (AR)
U of Central Florida (FL)
U of Cincinnati (OH)
U of Colorado at Colorado Springs (CO)
U of Colorado Boulder (CO)
U of Colorado Denver (CO)
U of Connecticut (CT)

U of Dallas (TX)
U of Dayton (OH)
U of Delaware (DE)
U of Denver (CO)
U of Dubuque (IA)
U of Evansville (IN)
The U of Findlay (OH)
U of Florida (FL)
U of Georgia (GA)
U of Guelph (ON, Canada)
U of Hartford (CT)
U of Hawaii at Hilo (HI)
U of Hawaii at Manoa (HI)
U of Hawaii–West Oahu (HI)
U of Houston (TX)
U of Houston–Downtown (TX)
U of Idaho (ID)
U of Illinois at Chicago (IL)
U of Illinois at Springfield (IL)
U of Illinois at Urbana–Champaign (IL)
U of Indianapolis (IN)
The U of Iowa (IA)
The U of Kansas (KS)
U of La Verne (CA)
U of Lethbridge (AB, Canada)
U of Louisiana at Lafayette (LA)
U of Louisville (KY)
U of Maine (ME)
U of Maryland, Baltimore County (MD)
U of Maryland, Coll Park (MD)
U of Mary Washington (VA)
U of Massachusetts Amherst (MA)
U of Massachusetts Boston (MA)
U of Massachusetts Dartmouth (MA)
U of Massachusetts Lowell (MA)
U of Memphis (TN)
U of Miami (FL)
U of Michigan (MI)
U of Michigan–Dearborn (MI)
U of Michigan–Flint (MI)
U of Minnesota, Duluth (MN)
U of Minnesota, Twin Cities Campus (MN)
U of Mississippi (MS)
U of Missouri (MO)
U of Missouri–Kansas City (MO)
U of Missouri–St. Louis (MO)
U of Mount Union (OH)
U of Nebraska at Omaha (NE)
U of Nebraska–Lincoln (NE)
U of Nevada, Las Vegas (NV)
U of Nevada, Reno (NV)
U of New Hampshire (NH)
U of New Mexico (NM)
U of New Orleans (LA)
The U of North Carolina at Asheville (NC)
The U of North Carolina at Chapel Hill (NC)
The U of North Carolina at Charlotte (NC)
U of North Dakota (ND)
U of Northern Colorado (CO)
U of Northern Iowa (IA)
U of North Florida (FL)
U of North Texas (TX)
U of Notre Dame (IN)
U of Oklahoma (OK)
U of Oregon (OR)
U of Ottawa (ON, Canada)
U of Pennsylvania (PA)
U of Pittsburgh (PA)
U of Portland (OR)
U of Puget Sound (WA)
U of Redlands (CA)
U of Regina (SK, Canada)
U of Rhode Island (RI)
U of Richmond (VA)
U of Rochester (NY)
U of Saint Francis (IN)
U of Saint Joseph (CT)
U of St. Thomas (MN)
U of St. Thomas (TX)
U of San Diego (CA)
The U of Scranton (PA)
U of South Alabama (AL)
U of South Carolina (SC)
The U of South Dakota (SD)
U of Southern California (CA)
U of Southern Indiana (IN)
U of Southern Maine (ME)
U of Southern Mississippi (MS)

U of South Florida (FL)
The U of Tampa (FL)
The U of Tennessee (TN)
The U of Tennessee at Martin (TN)
The U of Texas at Arlington (TX)
The U of Texas at Austin (TX)
The U of Texas at El Paso (TX)
The U of Texas at San Antonio (TX)
The U of Texas–Pan American (TX)
U of the Incarnate Word (TX)
U of the Ozarks (AR)
U of the Pacific (CA)
The U of Toledo (OH)
U of Tulsa (OK)
U of Utah (UT)
U of Vermont (VT)
U of Virginia (VA)
U of Washington (WA)
The U of Western Ontario (ON, Canada)
U of West Florida (FL)
U of West Georgia (GA)
U of Windsor (ON, Canada)
U of Wisconsin–Eau Claire (WI)
U of Wisconsin–Green Bay (WI)
U of Wisconsin–La Crosse (WI)
U of Wisconsin–Madison (WI)
U of Wisconsin–Milwaukee (WI)
U of Wisconsin–Platteville (WI)
U of Wisconsin–Stevens Point (WI)
U of Wyoming (WY)
Ursuline Coll (OH)
Utah State U (UT)
Utah Valley U (UT)
Utica Coll (NY)
Valdosta State U (GA)
Valparaiso U (IN)
Vanderbilt U (TN)
Vassar Coll (NY)
Villanova U (PA)
Virginia Commonwealth U (VA)
Virginia Polytechnic Inst and State U (VA)
Virginia Wesleyan Coll (VA)
Wabash Coll (IN)
Wagner Coll (NY)
Wake Forest U (NC)
Walsh U (OH)
Warren Wilson Coll (NC)
Wartburg Coll (IA)
Washburn U (KS)
Washington & Jefferson Coll (PA)
Washington and Lee U (VA)
Washington Coll (MD)
Washington State U (WA)
Washington U in St. Louis (MO)
Wayne State U (MI)
Weber State U (UT)
Webster U (MO)
Wellesley Coll (MA)
Wells Coll (NY)
Wesleyan Coll (GA)
Wesleyan U (CT)
West Chester U of Pennsylvania (PA)
Western Carolina U (NC)
Western Illinois U (IL)
Western Michigan U (MI)
Western New England U (MA)
Western Oregon U (OR)
Western Washington U (WA)
Westminster Coll (MO)
Westminster Coll (UT)
West Virginia U (WV)
West Virginia Wesleyan Coll (WV)
Wheaton Coll (IL)
Wheaton Coll (MA)
Wheeling Jesuit U (WV)
Whitman Coll (WA)
Whittier Coll (CA)
Wichita State U (KS)
Wilkes U (PA)
Willamette U (OR)
William Jewell Coll (MO)
William Paterson U of New Jersey (NJ)
Williams Coll (MA)
Wilmington Coll (OH)
Wilson Coll (PA)
Wingate U (NC)
Wittenberg U (OH)
Wofford Coll (SC)
Worcester Polytechnic Inst (MA)
Wright State U (OH)
Xavier U (OH)

Xavier U of Louisiana (LA)
Yale U (CT)
Yeshiva U (NY)
York Coll of Pennsylvania (PA)
York Coll of the City U of New York (NY)
Youngstown State U (OH)

PHILOSOPHY AND RELIGIOUS STUDIES

Arizona State U (AZ)
Bethune-Cookman U (FL)
Concordia Coll–New York (NY)
Emmanuel Coll (MA)
LaGrange Coll (GA)
Montreat Coll, Montreat (NC)
Oklahoma City U (OK)
Pace U (NY)
Paine Coll (GA)
The Richard Stockton Coll of New Jersey (NJ)
St. Andrews U (NC)
St. Joseph's Coll, Long Island Campus (NY)
St. Joseph's Coll, New York (NY)
Southwestern Coll (KS)

PHILOSOPHY AND RELIGIOUS STUDIES RELATED

Barton Coll (NC)
Berry Coll (GA)
Bethune-Cookman U (FL)
Bridgewater Coll (VA)
Buena Vista U (IA)
Claflin U (SC)
Coll of the Humanities and Sciences, Harrison Middleton U (AZ)
Covenant Coll (GA)
Eastern Mennonite U (VA)
The Evergreen State Coll (WA)
Florida Ag and Mech U (FL)
Friends U (KS)
Graceland U (IA)
Hendrix Coll (AR)
Iowa Wesleyan Coll (IA)
James Madison U (VA)
John Brown U (AR)
Juniata Coll (PA)
Lyon Coll (AR)
Mary Baldwin Coll (VA)
Marymount Manhattan Coll (NY)
Millsaps Coll (MS)
Ouachita Baptist U (AR)
Point Loma Nazarene U (CA)
Quincy U (IL)
Radford U (VA)
The Richard Stockton Coll of New Jersey (NJ)
Roberts Wesleyan Coll (NY)
Rocky Mountain Coll (MT)
Rowan U (NJ)
Saint Joseph's Coll (IN)
Samford U (AL)
San Francisco State U (CA)
Sarah Lawrence Coll (NY)
State U of New York at Oswego (NY)
Sterling Coll (KS)
Stillman Coll (AL)
Syracuse U (NY)
Union U (TN)
U of Maine at Farmington (ME)
U of Mary Washington (VA)
The U of North Carolina Wilmington (NC)
U of Notre Dame (IN)
The U of Tennessee at Chattanooga (TN)
U of the Ozarks (AR)
Viterbo U (WI)
Washington U in St. Louis (MO)
West Virginia Wesleyan Coll (WV)

PHILOSOPHY RELATED

Lewis U (IL)
Marlboro Coll (VT)
Ohio Northern U (OH)
The U of Arizona (AZ)
U of Massachusetts Boston (MA)
U of Pennsylvania (PA)
U of Regina (SK, Canada)
Washington U in St. Louis (MO)
Wheeling Jesuit U (WV)

PHOTOGRAPHIC AND FILM/VIDEO TECHNOLOGY

New England School of Communications (ME)
Rochester Inst of Technology (NY)
St. John's U (NY)
Towson U (MD)
Villa Maria Coll of Buffalo (NY)

PHOTOGRAPHY

Acad of Art U (CA)
Adams State Coll (CO)
Alberta Coll of Art & Design (AB, Canada)
Albertus Magnus Coll (CT)
Aquinas Coll (MI)
Arcadia U (PA)
Art Center Coll of Design (CA)
The Art Inst of Austin (TX)
The Art Inst of California, a college of Argosy U, Hollywood (CA)
The Art Inst of Charlotte (NC)
The Art Inst of Colorado (CO)
The Art Inst of Dallas (TX)
The Art Inst of Fort Lauderdale (FL)
The Art Inst of Fort Worth (TX)
The Art Inst of Houston (TX)
The Art Inst of Houston - North (TX)
The Art Inst of Indianapolis (IN)
The Art Inst of Jacksonville (FL)
The Art Inst of Las Vegas (NV)
The Art Inst of Michigan (MI)
The Art Inst of Michigan–Troy (MI)
The Art Inst of Philadelphia (PA)
The Art Inst of Phoenix (AZ)
The Art Inst of Pittsburgh (PA)
The Art Inst of Portland (OR)
The Art Inst of Raleigh-Durham (NC)
The Art Inst of Salt Lake City (UT)
The Art Inst of San Antonio (TX)
The Art Inst of Seattle (WA)
The Art Inst of Tampa (FL)
The Art Inst of Tucson (AZ)
The Art Inst of Virginia Beach (VA)
The Art Inst of Washington–Dulles (VA)
The Art Insts Intl–Kansas City (KS)
The Art Insts Intl Minnesota (MN)
Bard Coll (NY)
Bard Coll at Simon's Rock (MA)
Barry U (FL)
Bennington Coll (VT)
Bowling Green State U (OH)
Bradley U (IL)
Bridgewater State U (MA)
Buffalo State Coll, State U of New York (NY)
Burlington Coll (VT)
California Coll of the Arts (CA)
California State U, East Bay (CA)
California State U, Long Beach (CA)
California State U, Sacramento (CA)
Calvary Bible Coll and Theological Sem (MO)
Carson-Newman Coll (TN)
Chatham U (PA)
Chester Coll of New England (NH)
The Cleveland Inst of Art (OH)
Coe Coll (IA)
Coll for Creative Studies (MI)
Colorado State U (CO)
Columbia Coll (MO)
Columbia Coll Chicago (IL)
Concordia U (QC, Canada)
Corcoran Coll of Art and Design (DC)
Dominican U (IL)
Drexel U (PA)
Eastern Mennonite U (VA)
Emily Carr U of Art + Design (BC, Canada)
Ferris State U (MI)
Fitchburg State U (MA)
Fordham U (NY)
Gallaudet U (DC)
Governors State U (IL)
Grand Valley State U (MI)
Hampton U (VA)
Hofstra U (NY)
The Illinois Inst of Art–Chicago (IL)

The Illinois Inst of Art–Schaumburg (IL)
The Illinois Inst of Art–Tinley Park (IL)
Indiana U–Purdue U Fort Wayne (IN)
Indiana Wesleyan U (IN)
Inter American U of Puerto Rico, San Germán Campus (PR)
Intl Acad of Design & Technology (FL)
Ithaca Coll (NY)
John Brown U (AR)
Kansas City Art Inst (MO)
King Coll (TN)
Long Island U–C. W. Post Campus (NY)
Marlboro Coll (VT)
Maryland Inst Coll of Art (MD)
Marymount Manhattan Coll (NY)
Marywood U (PA)
Massachusetts Coll of Art and Design (MA)
Memphis Coll of Art (TN)
Miami Intl U of Art & Design (FL)
Montserrat Coll of Art (MA)
Moore Coll of Art & Design (PA)
Morningside Coll (IA)
Mount Allison U (NB, Canada)
New England Coll (NH)
The New England Inst of Art (MA)
New York U (NY)
Northeastern State U (OK)
Northern Arizona U (AZ)
Northern Michigan U (MI)
Oakland U (MI)
Ohio U (OH)
Otis Coll of Art and Design (CA)
Pacific Northwest Coll of Art (OR)
Pacific Union Coll (CA)
Paier Coll of Art, Inc. (CT)
Pennsylvania Coll of Art & Design (PA)
Point Park U (PA)
Pratt Inst (NY)
Purchase Coll, State U of New York (NY)
Ringling Coll of Art and Design (FL)
Rivier Coll (NH)
Rutgers, The State U of New Jersey, New Brunswick (NJ)
Ryerson U (ON, Canada)
Sage Coll of Albany (NY)
St. Edward's U (TX)
St. John's U (NY)
Salem State U (MA)
Salve Regina U (RI)
Sam Houston State U (TX)
Sarah Lawrence Coll (NY)
Savannah Coll of Art and Design (GA)
School of the Museum of Fine Arts, Boston (MA)
Seattle U (WA)
State U of New York at New Paltz (NY)
Syracuse U (NY)
Temple U (PA)
Texas Christian U (TX)
Texas State U–San Marcos (TX)
Thomas Edison State Coll (NJ)
The U of Akron (OH)
U of Central Florida (FL)
U of Central Missouri (MO)
U of Dayton (OH)
U of Hartford (CT)
U of Houston (TX)
U of Illinois at Chicago (IL)
U of Illinois at Urbana–Champaign (IL)
The U of Iowa (IA)
U of La Verne (CA)
U of Massachusetts Dartmouth (MA)
U of Miami (FL)
U of Missouri–St. Louis (MO)
U of Oregon (OR)
The U of the Arts (PA)
U of Washington (WA)
Virginia Commonwealth U (VA)
Virginia Intermont Coll (VA)
Washington U in St. Louis (MO)
Watkins Coll of Art, Design, & Film (TN)
Weber State U (UT)

INDEXES

Webster U (MO)
Western State Coll of Colorado (CO)
Western Washington U (WA)
Youngstown State U (OH)

PHOTOJOURNALISM

Bradley U (IL)
Central Michigan U (MI)
Corcoran Coll of Art and Design (DC)
Hawai'i Pacific U (HI)
Kent State U (OH)
Ohio U (OH)
Pittsburg State U (KS)
Point Park U (PA)
Prescott Coll (AZ)
Rochester Inst of Technology (NY)
St. John's U (NY)
Sierra Nevada Coll (NV)
U of Miami (FL)
U of Missouri (MO)
Western Kentucky U (KY)

PHYSICAL AND BIOLOGICAL ANTHROPOLOGY

The U of Western Ontario (ON, Canada)

PHYSICAL CHEMISTRY

Rice U (TX)
The U of Western Ontario (ON, Canada)

PHYSICAL EDUCATION TEACHING AND COACHING

Abilene Christian U (TX)
Adams State Coll (CO)
Adelphi U (NY)
Alabama State U (AL)
Albany State U (GA)
Alma Coll (MI)
Anderson U (IN)
Anderson U (SC)
Appalachian State U (NC)
Aquinas Coll (MI)
Arkansas State U (AR)
Arkansas Tech U (AR)
Armstrong Atlantic State U (GA)
Asbury U (KY)
Athens State U (AL)
Auburn U (AL)
Augustana Coll (SD)
Averett U (VA)
Azusa Pacific U (CA)
Ball State U (IN)
Baptist Bible Coll of Pennsylvania (PA)
Barry U (FL)
Barton Coll (NC)
Bayamón Central U (PR)
Baylor U (TX)
Bellevue U (NE)
Belmont U (TN)
Bemidji State U (MN)
Benedictine Coll (KS)
Benedictine U (IL)
Berry Coll (GA)
Bethany Coll (KS)
Bethany Coll (WV)
Bethel Coll (IN)
Bethel U (MN)
Bethune-Cookman U (FL)
Biola U (CA)
Blackburn Coll (IL)
Bluefield Coll (VA)
Blue Mountain Coll (MS)
Boise State U (ID)
Boston U (MA)
Bowling Green State U (OH)
Brewton-Parker Coll (GA)
Briar Cliff U (IA)
Bridgewater Coll (VA)
Bridgewater State U (MA)
Buena Vista U (IA)
California Lutheran U (CA)
California State U, Bakersfield (CA)
California State U, Chico (CA)
California State U, East Bay (CA)
California State U, Fresno (CA)
California State U, Long Beach (CA)
California State U, San Bernardino (CA)

California State U, Stanislaus (CA)
Calvin Coll (MI)
Cameron U (OK)
Campbellsville U (KY)
Canisius Coll (NY)
Capital U (OH)
Carroll Coll (MT)
Carson-Newman Coll (TN)
Castleton State Coll (VT)
Catawba Coll (NC)
Cedarville U (OH)
Central Connecticut State U (CT)
Central Methodist U (MO)
Central Washington U (WA)
Chicago State U (IL)
The Citadel, The Military Coll of South Carolina (SC)
Clarke U (IA)
Clearwater Christian Coll (FL)
Cleveland State U (OH)
Coastal Carolina U (SC)
Coe Coll (IA)
The Coll at Brockport, State U of New York (NY)
Coll of Charleston (SC)
The Coll of Idaho (ID)
The Coll of New Jersey (NJ)
Coll of the Ozarks (MO)
Columbus State U (GA)
Concordia Coll (MN)
Concordia U (MI)
Concordia U Chicago (IL)
Concordia U, Nebraska (NE)
Concordia U, St. Paul (MN)
Corban U (OR)
Cornell Coll (IA)
Cornerstone U (MI)
Crown Coll (MN)
Culver-Stockton Coll (MO)
Dakota State U (SD)
Defiance Coll (OH)
Delaware State U (DE)
Delta State U (MS)
Denison U (OH)
DePaul U (IL)
DePauw U (IN)
Doane Coll (NE)
Dordt Coll (IA)
Dowling Coll (NY)
Drury U (MO)
East Carolina U (NC)
East Central U (OK)
Eastern Connecticut State U (CT)
Eastern Kentucky U (KY)
Eastern Mennonite U (VA)
Eastern Michigan U (MI)
Eastern New Mexico U (NM)
East Stroudsburg U of Pennsylvania (PA)
East Texas Baptist U (TX)
Edward Waters Coll (FL)
Elizabeth City State U (NC)
Elmhurst Coll (IL)
Elon U (NC)
Endicott Coll (MA)
Evangel U (MO)
Fairmont State U (WV)
Faulkner U (AL)
Fayetteville State U (NC)
Florida Ag and Mech U (FL)
Florida Intl U (FL)
Florida Southern Coll (FL)
Fort Hays State U (KS)
Fort Lewis Coll (CO)
Franklin Coll (IN)
Free Will Baptist Bible Coll (TN)
Friends U (KS)
Gallaudet U (DC)
Gardner-Webb U (NC)
George Mason U (VA)
Georgia Coll & State U (GA)
Georgia Southern U (GA)
Georgia Southwestern State U (GA)
Georgia State U (GA)
Gettysburg Coll (PA)
Glenville State Coll (WV)
Gonzaga U (WA)
Goshen Coll (IN)
Graceland U (IA)
Grambling State U (LA)
Grand Canyon U (AZ)
Grand Valley State U (MI)
Grand View U (IA)
Greenville Coll (IL)
Gustavus Adolphus Coll (MN)

Hampton U (VA)
Hannibal-LaGrange U (MO)
Hardin-Simmons U (TX)
Heidelberg U (OH)
Hillsdale Coll (MI)
Hofstra U (NY)
Hope Coll (MI)
Houghton Coll (NY)
Howard Payne U (TX)
Humboldt State U (CA)
Hunter Coll of the City U of New York (NY)
Huntingdon Coll (AL)
Huntington U (IN)
Husson U (ME)
Huston-Tillotson U (TX)
Idaho State U (ID)
Illinois Coll (IL)
Illinois State U (IL)
Indiana State U (IN)
Indiana Tech (IN)
Indiana U Bloomington (IN)
Indiana U–Purdue U Indianapolis (IN)
Indiana Wesleyan U (IN)
Inter American U of Puerto Rico, San Germán Campus (PR)
Iowa Wesleyan Coll (IA)
Ithaca Coll (NY)
Jacksonville State U (AL)
Jacksonville U (FL)
Jamestown Coll (ND)
Jarvis Christian Coll (TX)
John Carroll U (OH)
Johnson C. Smith U (NC)
Johnson State Coll (VT)
Judson U (IL)
Kean U (NJ)
Keene State Coll (NH)
Kennesaw State U (GA)
Kent State U (OH)
Kentucky State U (KY)
Kentucky Wesleyan Coll (KY)
King Coll (TN)
Lakehead U (ON, Canada)
Lamar U (TX)
Lane Coll (TN)
Lees-McRae Coll (NC)
Lee U (TN)
Lenoir-Rhyne U (NC)
LeTourneau U (TX)
Lewis-Clark State Coll (ID)
Liberty U (VA)
Limestone Coll (SC)
Lincoln Memorial U (TN)
Lincoln U (MO)
Lindenwood U (MO)
Lindsey Wilson Coll (KY)
Lipscomb U (TN)
Lock Haven U of Pennsylvania (PA)
Long Island U–Brooklyn Campus (NY)
Long Island U–C. W. Post Campus (NY)
Longwood U (VA)
Loras Coll (IA)
Louisiana Coll (LA)
Louisiana State U and Ag and Mech Coll (LA)
Lubbock Christian U (TX)
Madonna U (MI)
Malone U (OH)
Manchester Coll (IN)
Manhattan Coll (NY)
Maranatha Baptist Bible Coll (WI)
Marshall U (WV)
Mars Hill Coll (NC)
Maryville Coll (TN)
The Master's Coll and Sem (CA)
Mayville State U (ND)
McKendree U (IL)
McMurry U (TX)
McNeese State U (LA)
McPherson Coll (KS)
Meredith Coll (NC)
Messiah Coll (PA)
Miami U (OH)
Michigan State U (MI)
MidAmerica Nazarene U (KS)
Millikin U (IL)
Minnesota State U Mankato (MN)
Minnesota State U Moorhead (MN)
Minot State U (ND)
Mississippi Coll (MS)
Mississippi State U (MS)

Mississippi Valley State U (MS)
Missouri Baptist U (MO)
Missouri State U (MO)
Monmouth Coll (IL)
Montana State U Billings (MT)
Montclair State U (NJ)
Morehead State U (KY)
Mount Vernon Nazarene U (OH)
Nebraska Wesleyan U (NE)
Newberry Coll (SC)
New England Coll (NH)
New Mexico Highlands U (NM)
New Mexico State U (NM)
Nicholls State U (LA)
North Carolina Central U (NC)
North Central Coll (IL)
North Dakota State U (ND)
Northeastern Illinois U (IL)
Northeastern State U (OK)
Northern Illinois U (IL)
Northern Kentucky U (KY)
Northern Michigan U (MI)
Northern State U (SD)
North Georgia Coll & State U (GA)
Northwestern Coll (IA)
Northwestern Coll (MN)
Northwestern Oklahoma State U (OK)
Northwestern State U of Louisiana (LA)
Northwest Missouri State U (MO)
Northwest Nazarene U (ID)
Norwich U (VT)
Oakland City U (IN)
Ohio Northern U (OH)
The Ohio State U (OH)
Ohio U (OH)
Ohio Valley U (WV)
Ohio Wesleyan U (OH)
Oklahoma Christian U (OK)
Oklahoma City U (OK)
Oklahoma State U (OK)
Old Dominion U (VA)
Oral Roberts U (OK)
Otterbein U (OH)
Ouachita Baptist U (AR)
Pacific Union Coll (CA)
Palm Beach Atlantic U (FL)
Pepperdine U, Malibu (CA)
Peru State Coll (NE)
Philadelphia Biblical U (PA)
Piedmont Intl U (NC)
Pittsburg State U (KS)
Prescott Coll (AZ)
Purdue U (IN)
Queens Coll of the City U of New York (NY)
Queen's U at Kingston (ON, Canada)
Quincy U (IL)
Radford U (VA)
Reinhardt U (GA)
Rhode Island Coll (RI)
Ripon Coll (WI)
Roanoke Coll (VA)
Roberts Wesleyan Coll (NY)
Rockford Coll (IL)
Rocky Mountain Coll (MT)
Rowan U (NJ)
Sage Coll of Albany (NY)
Saginaw Valley State U (MI)
St. Ambrose U (IA)
St. Andrews U (NC)
St. Bonaventure U (NY)
St. Catherine U (MN)
St. Edward's U (TX)
Saint Joseph's Coll of Maine (ME)
Salem State U (MA)
Salisbury U (MD)
Samford U (AL)
San Diego Christian Coll (CA)
San Francisco State U (CA)
Schreiner U (TX)
Shenandoah U (VA)
Simpson Coll (IA)
Slippery Rock U of Pennsylvania (PA)
Sonoma State U (CA)
South Carolina State U (SC)
Southeastern Louisiana U (LA)
Southeastern Oklahoma State U (OK)
Southeast Missouri State U (MO)
Southern Arkansas U–Magnolia (AR)

Southern Illinois U Carbondale (IL)
Southern Illinois U Edwardsville (IL)
Southern Oregon U (OR)
Southwest Baptist U (MO)
Southwestern Christian U (OK)
Southwestern Coll (KS)
Southwestern Oklahoma State U (OK)
Southwestern U (TX)
Southwest Minnesota State U (MN)
Spring Arbor U (MI)
State U of New York Coll at Cortland (NY)
State U of New York Coll at Potsdam (NY)
Sterling Coll (KS)
Stillman Coll (AL)
Sul Ross State U (TX)
Syracuse U (NY)
Tabor Coll (KS)
Tarleton State U (TX)
Taylor U (IN)
Texas A&M Intl U (TX)
Texas A&M U–Corpus Christi (TX)
Texas Christian U (TX)
Texas Lutheran U (TX)
Texas Wesleyan U (TX)
Towson U (MD)
Transylvania U (KY)
Trevecca Nazarene U (TN)
Trine U (IN)
Trinity Christian Coll (IL)
Tusculum Coll (TN)
Union Coll (KY)
Union Coll (NE)
Union U (TN)
Universidad del Turabo (PR)
Université de Sherbrooke (QC, Canada)
The U of Akron (OH)
The U of Alabama (AL)
The U of Alabama at Birmingham (AL)
U of Alaska Anchorage (AK)
U of Alberta (AB, Canada)
U of Arkansas at Monticello (AR)
U of Central Arkansas (AR)
U of Central Florida (FL)
U of Central Missouri (MO)
U of Connecticut (CT)
U of Dubuque (IA)
The U of Findlay (OH)
U of Georgia (GA)
U of Great Falls (MT)
U of Guam (GU)
U of Idaho (ID)
U of Illinois at Urbana–Champaign (IL)
U of Indianapolis (IN)
The U of Kansas (KS)
U of Lethbridge (AB, Canada)
U of Louisiana at Lafayette (LA)
U of Louisiana at Monroe (LA)
U of Maine (ME)
U of Maine at Presque Isle (ME)
U of Mary (ND)
U of Mary Hardin-Baylor (TX)
U of Maryland, Coll Park (MD)
U of Maryland Eastern Shore (MD)
U of Memphis (TN)
U of Michigan (MI)
U of Minnesota, Duluth (MN)
U of Minnesota, Twin Cities Campus (MN)
U of Missouri–St. Louis (MO)
The U of Montana Western (MT)
U of Mount Union (OH)
U of Nebraska at Kearney (NE)
U of Nebraska–Lincoln (NE)
U of Nevada, Las Vegas (NV)
U of New Mexico (NM)
The U of North Carolina Wilmington (NC)
U of North Dakota (ND)
U of Northern Iowa (IA)
U of North Florida (FL)
U of Pittsburgh (PA)
U of Pittsburgh at Bradford (PA)
U of Regina (SK, Canada)
U of Rio Grande (OH)
U of St. Thomas (MN)
U of South Alabama (AL)
U of South Carolina (SC)
U of South Carolina Upstate (SC)
The U of South Dakota (SD)

The U of Alabama at Birmingham (AL)
The U of Alabama in Huntsville (AL)
U of Alaska Fairbanks (AK)
U of Alberta (AB, Canada)
The U of Arizona (AZ)
U of Arkansas (AR)
U of Arkansas at Little Rock (AR)
The U of British Columbia (BC, Canada)
The U of British Columbia–Okanagan (BC, Canada)
U of California, Berkeley (CA)
U of California, Davis (CA)
U of California, Irvine (CA)
U of California, Los Angeles (CA)
U of California, Merced (CA)
U of California, Riverside (CA)
U of California, Santa Barbara (CA)
U of California, Santa Cruz (CA)
U of Central Arkansas (AR)
U of Central Florida (FL)
U of Central Missouri (MO)
U of Cincinnati (OH)
U of Colorado at Colorado Springs (CO)
U of Colorado Boulder (CO)
U of Colorado Denver (CO)
U of Connecticut (CT)
U of Dallas (TX)
U of Dayton (OH)
U of Delaware (DE)
U of Denver (CO)
U of Evansville (IN)
U of Florida (FL)
U of Georgia (GA)
U of Guelph (ON, Canada)
U of Hartford (CT)
U of Hawaii at Hilo (HI)
U of Hawaii at Manoa (HI)
U of Houston (TX)
U of Houston–Clear Lake (TX)
U of Idaho (ID)
U of Illinois at Chicago (IL)
U of Illinois at Urbana–Champaign (IL)
U of Indianapolis (IN)
The U of Iowa (IA)
The U of Kansas (KS)
U of La Verne (CA)
U of Lethbridge (AB, Canada)
U of Louisiana at Lafayette (LA)
U of Louisville (KY)
U of Maine (ME)
U of Maryland, Baltimore County (MD)
U of Maryland, Coll Park (MD)
U of Mary Washington (VA)
U of Massachusetts Amherst (MA)
U of Massachusetts Boston (MA)
U of Massachusetts Dartmouth (MA)
U of Massachusetts Lowell (MA)
U of Memphis (TN)
U of Miami (FL)
U of Michigan (MI)
U of Michigan–Dearborn (MI)
U of Michigan–Flint (MI)
U of Minnesota, Duluth (MN)
U of Minnesota, Twin Cities Campus (MN)
U of Mississippi (MS)
U of Missouri (MO)
U of Missouri–Kansas City (MO)
U of Missouri–St. Louis (MO)
U of Mount Union (OH)
U of Nebraska at Kearney (NE)
U of Nebraska at Omaha (NE)
U of Nebraska–Lincoln (NE)
U of Nevada, Las Vegas (NV)
U of Nevada, Reno (NV)
U of New Hampshire (NH)
U of New Mexico (NM)
U of New Orleans (LA)
U of North Alabama (AL)
The U of North Carolina at Asheville (NC)
The U of North Carolina at Chapel Hill (NC)
The U of North Carolina at Charlotte (NC)
The U of North Carolina Wilmington (NC)
U of North Dakota (ND)
U of Northern Colorado (CO)

U of North Florida (FL)
U of North Texas (TX)
U of Notre Dame (IN)
U of Oklahoma (OK)
U of Oregon (OR)
U of Ottawa (ON, Canada)
U of Pennsylvania (PA)
U of Pittsburgh (PA)
U of Portland (OR)
U of Puerto Rico at Humacao (PR)
U of Puget Sound (WA)
U of Redlands (CA)
U of Regina (SK, Canada)
U of Rhode Island (RI)
U of Richmond (VA)
U of Rochester (NY)
U of St. Thomas (MN)
U of San Diego (CA)
U of Science and Arts of Oklahoma (OK)
The U of Scranton (PA)
U of South Alabama (AL)
U of South Carolina (SC)
The U of South Dakota (SD)
U of Southern California (CA)
U of Southern Maine (ME)
U of Southern Mississippi (MS)
U of South Florida (FL)
The U of Tennessee (TN)
The U of Tennessee at Chattanooga (TN)
The U of Texas at Arlington (TX)
The U of Texas at Austin (TX)
The U of Texas at Dallas (TX)
The U of Texas at El Paso (TX)
The U of Texas at San Antonio (TX)
The U of Texas–Pan American (TX)
U of the Cumberlands (KY)
U of the District of Columbia (DC)
U of the Pacific (CA)
U of the Sciences in Philadelphia (PA)
The U of Toledo (OH)
U of Tulsa (OK)
U of Utah (UT)
U of Vermont (VT)
U of Virginia (VA)
U of Washington (WA)
The U of Western Ontario (ON, Canada)
U of West Florida (FL)
U of West Georgia (GA)
U of Windsor (ON, Canada)
U of Wisconsin–Eau Claire (WI)
U of Wisconsin–La Crosse (WI)
U of Wisconsin–Madison (WI)
U of Wisconsin–Milwaukee (WI)
U of Wisconsin–River Falls (WI)
U of Wisconsin–Stevens Point (WI)
U of Wisconsin–Whitewater (WI)
U of Wyoming (WY)
Utah State U (UT)
Utah Valley U (UT)
Utica Coll (NY)
Valdosta State U (GA)
Valparaiso U (IN)
Vanderbilt U (TN)
Vassar Coll (NY)
Villanova U (PA)
Virginia Commonwealth U (VA)
Virginia Polytechnic Inst and State U (VA)
Virginia State U (VA)
Wabash Coll (IN)
Wagner Coll (NY)
Wake Forest U (NC)
Wartburg Coll (IA)
Washburn U (KS)
Washington & Jefferson Coll (PA)
Washington and Lee U (VA)
Washington Coll (MD)
Washington State U (WA)
Washington U in St. Louis (MO)
Wayne State U (MI)
Weber State U (UT)
Wellesley Coll (MA)
Wells Coll (NY)
Wesleyan U (CT)
West Chester U of Pennsylvania (PA)
Western Illinois U (IL)
Western Kentucky U (KY)
Western Michigan U (MI)
Western State Coll of Colorado (CO)

Western Washington U (WA)
Westminster Coll (MO)
Westminster Coll (UT)
West Texas A&M U (TX)
West Virginia U (WV)
West Virginia Wesleyan Coll (WV)
Wheaton Coll (IL)
Wheaton Coll (MA)
Wheeling Jesuit U (WV)
Whitman Coll (WA)
Whittier Coll (CA)
Wichita State U (KS)
Widener U (PA)
Willamette U (OR)
William Jewell Coll (MO)
Williams Coll (MA)
Winona State U (MN)
Wittenberg U (OH)
Wofford Coll (SC)
Worcester Polytechnic Inst (MA)
Wright State U (OH)
Xavier U (OH)
Xavier U of Louisiana (LA)
Yale U (CT)
Yeshiva U (NY)
York Coll of the City U of New York (NY)
Youngstown State U (OH)

PHYSICS RELATED

Angelo State U (TX)
Arcadia U (PA)
Bridgewater Coll (VA)
Bridgewater State U (MA)
Brigham Young U (UT)
California State U, Chico (CA)
Carson-Newman Coll (TN)
The Coll at Brockport, State U of New York (NY)
Coll of Saint Benedict (MN)
The Coll of Wooster (OH)
Delaware State U (DE)
Drexel U (PA)
Embry-Riddle Aeronautical U–Daytona (FL)
Embry-Riddle Aeronautical U–Prescott (AZ)
Florida Inst of Technology (FL)
Fort Lewis Coll (CO)
Hampden-Sydney Coll (VA)
Illinois Inst of Technology (IL)
Indiana U of Pennsylvania (PA)
Lawrence Technological U (MI)
Linfield Coll (OR)
Morehouse Coll (GA)
Ohio Northern U (OH)
Presbyterian Coll (SC)
Rensselaer Polytechnic Inst (NY)
Rutgers, The State U of New Jersey, Newark (NJ)
Saint John's U (MN)
Saint Mary's U of Minnesota (MN)
Southern Arkansas U–Magnolia (AR)
Spring Arbor U (MI)
U of Alaska Fairbanks (AK)
U of California, Davis (CA)
U of Minnesota, Duluth (MN)
U of Nevada, Las Vegas (NV)
U of Northern Iowa (IA)
U of North Texas (TX)
U of Notre Dame (IN)
U of Regina (SK, Canada)
U of Rhode Island (RI)
U of Rochester (NY)
The U of Western Ontario (ON, Canada)
Whitman Coll (WA)

PHYSICS TEACHER EDUCATION

Alma Coll (MI)
Anderson U (IN)
Appalachian State U (NC)
Arkansas State U (AR)
Auburn U (AL)
Bethel U (MN)
Bishop's U (QC, Canada)
Bowling Green State U (OH)
Bradley U (IL)
Buena Vista U (IA)
Cedarville U (OH)
Central Methodist U (MO)
Central Michigan U (MI)

Christian Brothers U (TN)
City Coll of the City U of New York (NY)
The Coll at Brockport, State U of New York (NY)
The Coll of New Jersey (NJ)
Colorado State U (CO)
Concordia Coll (MN)
Concordia U, Nebraska (NE)
Delaware State U (DE)
East Central U (OK)
Eastern Michigan U (MI)
Eastern Washington U (WA)
Elmhurst Coll (IL)
Florida Inst of Technology (FL)
Fordham U (NY)
Grambling State U (LA)
Grand Valley State U (MI)
Greenville Coll (IL)
Grove City Coll (PA)
Gustavus Adolphus Coll (MN)
Hofstra U (NY)
Hope Coll (MI)
Husson U (ME)
Indiana U Bloomington (IN)
Indiana–Purdue U Fort Wayne (IN)
Indiana U South Bend (IN)
Iowa Wesleyan Coll (IA)
Ithaca Coll (NY)
Juniata Coll (PA)
King Coll (TN)
Le Moyne Coll (NY)
Lincoln U (MO)
Lipscomb U (TN)
Louisiana State U in Shreveport (LA)
Manchester Coll (IN)
Mansfield U of Pennsylvania (PA)
Messiah Coll (PA)
Miami Dade Coll (FL)
Miami U (OH)
Michigan State U (MI)
Minnesota State U Moorhead (MN)
Minot State U (ND)
Missouri State U (MO)
Moravian Coll (PA)
Morningside Coll (IA)
Mount Vernon Nazarene U (OH)
North Carolina Ag and Tech State U (NC)
North Carolina Central U (NC)
North Dakota State U (ND)
Northeastern State U (OK)
Northern Michigan U (MI)
Northwest Missouri State U (MO)
Ohio Northern U (OH)
Ohio Wesleyan U (OH)
Pittsburg State U (KS)
Queens Coll of the City U of New York (NY)
Rhode Island Coll (RI)
Roberts Wesleyan Coll (NY)
Saginaw Valley State U (MI)
St. Ambrose U (IA)
St. John Fisher Coll (NY)
St. John's U (NY)
Saint Mary's U of Minnesota (MN)
Saint Vincent Coll (PA)
Southern Polytechnic State U (GA)
State U of New York at New Paltz (NY)
State U of New York Coll at Cortland (NY)
State U of New York Coll at Oneonta (NY)
State U of New York Coll at Potsdam (NY)
Syracuse U (NY)
Trevecca Nazarene U (TN)
Union Coll (NE)
U of Central Missouri (MO)
U of Delaware (DE)
U of Evansville (IN)
U of Illinois at Chicago (IL)
U of Illinois at Urbana–Champaign (IL)
U of Louisiana at Lafayette (LA)
U of Maryland, Baltimore County (MD)
U of Missouri (MO)
U of Missouri–St. Louis (MO)
U of Nebraska–Lincoln (NE)
U of Regina (SK, Canada)
U of Rio Grande (OH)

U of St. Thomas (MN)
The U of South Dakota (SD)
U of West Georgia (GA)
U of Windsor (ON, Canada)
U of Wisconsin–River Falls (WI)
Utah State U (UT)
Utica Coll (NY)
Valparaiso U (IN)
Washington State U (WA)
Washington U in St. Louis (MO)
Weber State U (UT)
Western Michigan U (MI)
Wheeling Jesuit U (WV)
William Jewell Coll (MO)
Winona State U (MN)
Xavier U (OH)

PHYSIOLOGICAL PSYCHOLOGY/ PSYCHOBIOLOGY

Albright Coll (PA)
Arcadia U (PA)
Carnegie Mellon U (PA)
Centre Coll (KY)
Florida Atlantic U (FL)
Holy Family U (PA)
Houghton Coll (NY)
The Johns Hopkins U (MD)
La Sierra U (CA)
Lebanon Valley Coll (PA)
Lincoln U (PA)
Mills Coll (CA)
Mount Allison U (NB, Canada)
Northwest Missouri State U (MO)
Occidental Coll (CA)
Pace U (NY)
Quinnipiac U (CT)
Ripon Coll (WI)
Saint Mary's Coll of California (CA)
Simmons Coll (MA)
State U of New York at Binghamton (NY)
Swarthmore Coll (PA)
U of California, Los Angeles (CA)
U of Colorado Denver (CO)
U of Michigan (MI)
U of New England (ME)
U of St. Thomas (TX)
The U of Western Ontario (ON, Canada)
Vassar Coll (NY)
Washington Coll (MD)
Wilson Coll (PA)

PHYSIOLOGY

Brigham Young U (UT)
California State U, Long Beach (CA)
Marquette U (WI)
Michigan State U (MI)
Northern Michigan U (MI)
Oklahoma State U (OK)
Southern Illinois U Carbondale (IL)
U of Alberta (AB, Canada)
The U of Arizona (AZ)
The U of British Columbia (BC, Canada)
U of California, Los Angeles (CA)
U of California, Santa Barbara (CA)
U of Colorado Boulder (CO)
U of Illinois at Urbana–Champaign (IL)
U of Oregon (OR)
U of Ottawa (ON, Canada)
The U of Western Ontario (ON, Canada)
U of Wyoming (WY)

PLANETARY ASTRONOMY AND SCIENCE

California Inst of Technology (CA)
Florida Inst of Technology (FL)
The U of Western Ontario (ON, Canada)

PLANT MOLECULAR BIOLOGY

Pittsburg State U (KS)
U of Illinois at Urbana–Champaign (IL)

PLANT NURSERY MANAGEMENT

Colorado State U (CO)

INDEXES

Hollins U (VA)
Hood Coll (MD)
Hope Coll (MI)
Houghton Coll (NY)
Howard Payne U (TX)
Humboldt State U (CA)
Hunter Coll of the City U of New York (NY)
Huntingdon Coll (AL)
Huntington U (IN)
Huston-Tillotson U (TX)
Idaho State U (ID)
Illinois Coll (IL)
Illinois Inst of Technology (IL)
Illinois State U (IL)
Illinois Wesleyan U (IL)
Immaculata U (PA)
Indiana State U (IN)
Indiana U Bloomington (IN)
Indiana U East (IN)
Indiana U Northwest (IN)
Indiana U of Pennsylvania (PA)
Indiana U–Purdue U Fort Wayne (IN)
Indiana U–Purdue U Indianapolis (IN)
Indiana U South Bend (IN)
Indiana U Southeast (IN)
Indiana Wesleyan U (IN)
Inter American U of Puerto Rico, San Germán Campus (PR)
Iona Coll (NY)
Iowa State U of Science and Technology (IA)
Ithaca Coll (NY)
Jacksonville State U (AL)
Jacksonville U (FL)
James Madison U (VA)
John Brown U (AR)
John Carroll U (OH)
John Jay Coll of Criminal Justice of the City U of New York (NY)
The Johns Hopkins U (MD)
Johnson C. Smith U (NC)
Johnson State Coll (VT)
Juniata Coll (PA)
Kalamazoo Coll (MI)
Kansas State U (KS)
Kean U (NJ)
Keene State Coll (NH)
Kennesaw State U (GA)
Kent State U (OH)
Kentucky State U (KY)
Kentucky Wesleyan Coll (KY)
Kenyon Coll (OH)
King Coll (TN)
King's Coll (PA)
Knox Coll (IL)
Kutztown U of Pennsylvania (PA)
Lafayette Coll (PA)
LaGrange Coll (GA)
Lake Erie Coll (OH)
Lake Forest Coll (IL)
Lakehead U (ON, Canada)
Lake Superior State U (MI)
Lamar U (TX)
La Roche Coll (PA)
La Salle U (PA)
Lawrence U (WI)
Lebanese American U (Lebanon)
Lebanon Valley Coll (PA)
Lee U (TN)
Lehigh U (PA)
Lehman Coll of the City U of New York (NY)
Le Moyne Coll (NY)
Lenoir-Rhyne U (NC)
Lewis & Clark Coll (OR)
Lewis U (IL)
Liberty U (VA)
Lincoln U (MO)
Lincoln U (PA)
Lindenwood U (MO)
Linfield Coll (OR)
Lipscomb U (TN)
Lock Haven U of Pennsylvania (PA)
Long Island U–Brooklyn Campus (NY)
Long Island U–C. W. Post Campus (NY)
Longwood U (VA)
Loras Coll (IA)
Louisiana State U and Ag and Mech Coll (LA)

Louisiana State U in Shreveport (LA)
Loyola Marymount U (CA)
Loyola U Chicago (IL)
Loyola U Maryland (MD)
Loyola U New Orleans (LA)
Luther Coll (IA)
Lycoming Coll (PA)
Lynchburg Coll (VA)
Lyon Coll (AR)
Macalester Coll (MN)
Malone U (OH)
Manchester Coll (IN)
Manhattan Coll (NY)
Manhattanville Coll (NY)
Mansfield U of Pennsylvania (PA)
Marian U (WI)
Marietta Coll (OH)
Marlboro Coll (VT)
Marquette U (WI)
Marshall U (WV)
Mars Hill Coll (NC)
Mary Baldwin Coll (VA)
Marymount Manhattan Coll (NY)
Marymount U (VA)
Maryville Coll (TN)
Massachusetts Coll of Liberal Arts (MA)
Massachusetts Inst of Technology (MA)
The Master's Coll and Sem (CA)
McDaniel Coll (MD)
McKendree U (IL)
McMurry U (TX)
McNeese State U (LA)
Mercer U (GA)
Mercy Coll (NY)
Mercyhurst Coll (PA)
Meredith Coll (NC)
Merrimack Coll (MA)
Messiah Coll (PA)
Metropolitan State Coll of Denver (CO)
Miami U (OH)
Michigan State U (MI)
Middlebury Coll (VT)
Middle Tennessee State U (TN)
Midwestern State U (TX)
Millersville U of Pennsylvania (PA)
Millikin U (IL)
Millsaps Coll (MS)
Mills Coll (CA)
Minnesota State U Mankato (MN)
Minnesota State U Moorhead (MN)
Mississippi Coll (MS)
Mississippi State U (MS)
Mississippi U for Women (MS)
Mississippi Valley State U (MS)
Missouri Southern State U (MO)
Missouri State U (MO)
Missouri Western State U (MO)
Molloy Coll (NY)
Monmouth Coll (IL)
Monmouth U (NJ)
Montana State U (MT)
Montclair State U (NJ)
Moravian Coll (PA)
Morehead State U (KY)
Morehouse Coll (GA)
Morningside Coll (IA)
Morris Coll (SC)
Mount Allison U (NB, Canada)
Mount Holyoke Coll (MA)
Mount Mercy U (IA)
Mount Saint Mary Coll (NY)
Mount St. Mary's Coll (CA)
Mount St. Mary's U (MD)
Muhlenberg Coll (PA)
National-Louis U (IL)
Nazareth Coll of Rochester (NY)
Nebraska Wesleyan U (NE)
Neumann U (PA)
Newberry Coll (SC)
New Coll of Florida (FL)
New England Coll (NH)
New Jersey City U (NJ)
New Mexico Highlands U (NM)
New Mexico State U (NM)
New York Inst of Technology (NY)
New York U (NY)
Niagara U (NY)
Nicholls State U (LA)
Norfolk State U (VA)
North Carolina Ag and Tech State U (NC)

North Carolina Central U (NC)
North Carolina State U (NC)
North Carolina Wesleyan Coll (NC)
North Central Coll (IL)
North Dakota State U (ND)
Northeastern Illinois U (IL)
Northeastern State U (OK)
Northeastern U (MA)
Northern Arizona U (AZ)
Northern Illinois U (IL)
Northern Kentucky U (KY)
Northern Michigan U (MI)
Northern State U (SD)
North Georgia Coll & State U (GA)
Northwestern Coll (IA)
Northwestern Oklahoma State U (OK)
Northwest Missouri State U (MO)
Northwest Nazarene U (ID)
Northwest U (WA)
Norwich U (VT)
Notre Dame de Namur U (CA)
Notre Dame of Maryland U (MD)
Oakland U (MI)
Occidental Coll (CA)
Oglethorpe U (GA)
Ohio Northern U (OH)
The Ohio State U (OH)
Ohio U (OH)
Ohio Wesleyan U (OH)
Oklahoma City U (OK)
Oklahoma State U (OK)
Old Dominion U (VA)
Oral Roberts U (OK)
Otterbein U (OH)
Ouachita Baptist U (AR)
Pace U (NY)
Pacific Lutheran U (WA)
Pacific U (OR)
Palm Beach Atlantic U (FL)
Park U (MO)
Patrick Henry Coll (VA)
Penn State Abington (PA)
Penn State Altoona (PA)
Penn State Beaver (PA)
Penn State Berks (PA)
Penn State Brandywine (PA)
Penn State DuBois (PA)
Penn State Erie, The Behrend Coll (PA)
Penn State Fayette, The Eberly Campus (PA)
Penn State Greater Allegheny (PA)
Penn State Hazleton (PA)
Penn State Lehigh Valley (PA)
Penn State Mont Alto (PA)
Penn State New Kensington (PA)
Penn State Schuylkill (PA)
Penn State Shenango (PA)
Penn State U Park (PA)
Penn State Wilkes-Barre (PA)
Penn State Worthington Scranton (PA)
Penn State York (PA)
Pepperdine U, Malibu (CA)
Philander Smith Coll (AR)
Piedmont Coll (GA)
Pine Manor Coll (MA)
Pittsburg State U (KS)
Pitzer Coll (CA)
Plymouth State U (NH)
Point Loma Nazarene U (CA)
Point Park U (PA)
Pomona Coll (CA)
Portland State U (OR)
Prairie View A&M U (TX)
Presbyterian Coll (SC)
Princeton U (NJ)
Providence Coll (RI)
Purchase Coll, State U of New York (NY)
Purdue U (IN)
Purdue U Calumet (IN)
Queens Coll of the City U of New York (NY)
Queen's U at Kingston (ON, Canada)
Queens U of Charlotte (NC)
Quincy U (IL)
Quinnipiac U (CT)
Radford U (VA)
Ramapo Coll of New Jersey (NJ)
Randolph Coll (VA)
Randolph-Macon Coll (VA)
Regis Coll (MA)

Regis U (CO)
Reinhardt U (GA)
Rhode Island Coll (RI)
Rhodes Coll (TN)
Rice U (TX)
The Richard Stockton Coll of New Jersey (NJ)
Rider U (NJ)
Ripon Coll (WI)
Rivier Coll (NH)
Roanoke Coll (VA)
Rochester Inst of Technology (NY)
Rockford Coll (IL)
Rockhurst U (MO)
Rocky Mountain Coll (MT)
Roger Williams U (RI)
Rollins Coll (FL)
Roosevelt U (IL)
Rosemont Coll (PA)
Rowan U (NJ)
Russell Sage Coll (NY)
Rust Coll (MS)
Rutgers, The State U of New Jersey, Camden (NJ)
Rutgers, The State U of New Jersey, Newark (NJ)
Rutgers, The State U of New Jersey, New Brunswick (NJ)
Saginaw Valley State U (MI)
St. Ambrose U (IA)
Saint Anselm Coll (NH)
Saint Augustine's Coll (NC)
St. Bonaventure U (NY)
St. Catherine U (MN)
St. Edward's U (TX)
Saint Francis U (PA)
St. John Fisher Coll (NY)
Saint John's U (MN)
St. John's U (NY)
Saint Joseph's Coll (IN)
Saint Joseph's Coll of Maine (ME)
Saint Joseph's U (PA)
St. Lawrence U (NY)
Saint Leo U (FL)
Saint Louis U (MO)
Saint Martin's U (WA)
Saint Mary's Coll (IN)
Saint Mary's Coll of California (CA)
St. Mary's Coll of Maryland (MD)
St. Mary's U (TX)
Saint Michael's Coll (VT)
St. Norbert Coll (WI)
St. Olaf Coll (MN)
Saint Peter's Coll (NJ)
St. Thomas U (FL)
St. Thomas U (NB, Canada)
Saint Vincent Coll (PA)
Saint Xavier U (IL)
Salem State U (MA)
Salisbury U (MD)
Salve Regina U (RI)
Samford U (AL)
Sam Houston State U (TX)
San Diego State U (CA)
San Francisco State U (CA)
Santa Clara U (CA)
Sarah Lawrence Coll (NY)
Schreiner U (TX)
Scripps Coll (CA)
Seattle Pacific U (WA)
Seattle U (WA)
Seton Hill U (PA)
Sewanee: The U of the South (TN)
Shaw U (NC)
Shenandoah U (VA)
Shepherd U (WV)
Shippensburg U of Pennsylvania (PA)
Siena Coll (NY)
Simmons Coll (MA)
Simon Fraser U (BC, Canada)
Simpson Coll (IA)
Skidmore Coll (NY)
Slippery Rock U of Pennsylvania (PA)
Smith Coll (MA)
Sojourner-Douglass Coll (MD)
Sonoma State U (CA)
South Carolina State U (SC)
South Dakota State U (SD)
Southeastern Louisiana U (LA)
Southeastern Oklahoma State U (OK)
Southeast Missouri State U (MO)

Southern Arkansas U–Magnolia (AR)
Southern Connecticut State U (CT)
Southern Illinois U Carbondale (IL)
Southern Illinois U Edwardsville (IL)
Southern Methodist U (TX)
Southern New Hampshire U (NH)
Southern Oregon U (OR)
Southern Polytechnic State U (GA)
Southwest Baptist U (MO)
Southwestern Oklahoma State U (OK)
Southwestern U (TX)
Southwest Minnesota State U (MN)
Spelman Coll (GA)
Spring Arbor U (MI)
Spring Hill Coll (AL)
Stanford U (CA)
State U of New York at Binghamton (NY)
State U of New York at Fredonia (NY)
State U of New York at New Paltz (NY)
State U of New York at Oswego (NY)
State U of New York at Plattsburgh (NY)
State U of New York Coll at Cortland (NY)
State U of New York Coll at Geneseo (NY)
State U of New York Coll at Oneonta (NY)
State U of New York Coll at Potsdam (NY)
Stephen F. Austin State U (TX)
Stetson U (FL)
Stonehill Coll (MA)
Stony Brook U, State U of New York (NY)
Suffolk U (MA)
Sul Ross State U (TX)
Susquehanna U (PA)
Swarthmore Coll (PA)
Sweet Briar Coll (VA)
Syracuse U (NY)
Tarleton State U (TX)
Taylor U (IN)
Temple U (PA)
Texas A&M Intl U (TX)
Texas A&M U (TX)
Texas A&M U–Corpus Christi (TX)
Texas A&M U–Kingsville (TX)
Texas Christian U (TX)
Texas Coll (TX)
Texas Lutheran U (TX)
Texas Southern U (TX)
Texas State U–San Marcos (TX)
Texas Tech U (TX)
Texas Wesleyan U (TX)
Texas Woman's U (TX)
Thiel Coll (PA)
Thomas Edison State Coll (NJ)
Thomas More Coll (KY)
Thomas U (GA)
Thompson Rivers U (BC, Canada)
Touro Coll (NY)
Towson U (MD)
Transylvania U (KY)
Trent U (ON, Canada)
Trinity Christian Coll (IL)
Trinity Coll (CT)
Trinity U (TX)
Troy U (AL)
Truman State U (MO)
Tufts U (MA)
Tulane U (LA)
Tuskegee U (AL)
Union Coll (NY)
Union U (TN)
United States Air Force Acad (CO)
United States Coast Guard Acad (CT)
United States Military Acad (NY)
United States Naval Acad (MD)
U at Albany, State U of New York (NY)
U at Buffalo, the State U of New York (NY)
The U of Alabama (AL)
The U of Alabama at Birmingham (AL)
The U of Alabama in Huntsville (AL)
U of Alaska Anchorage (AK)

U of Alaska Fairbanks (AK)
U of Alberta (AB, Canada)
The U of Arizona (AZ)
U of Arkansas (AR)
U of Arkansas at Little Rock (AR)
U of Arkansas at Monticello (AR)
The U of British Columbia (BC, Canada)
The U of British Columbia–Okanagan (BC, Canada)
U of California, Berkeley (CA)
U of California, Davis (CA)
U of California, Irvine (CA)
U of California, Los Angeles (CA)
U of California, Merced (CA)
U of California, Riverside (CA)
U of California, Santa Barbara (CA)
U of California, Santa Cruz (CA)
U of Central Arkansas (AR)
U of Central Florida (FL)
U of Central Missouri (MO)
U of Charleston (WV)
U of Cincinnati (OH)
U of Colorado at Colorado Springs (CO)
U of Colorado Boulder (CO)
U of Colorado Denver (CO)
U of Connecticut (CT)
U of Dallas (TX)
U of Dayton (OH)
U of Delaware (DE)
U of Denver (CO)
U of Evansville (IN)
The U of Findlay (OH)
U of Florida (FL)
U of Georgia (GA)
U of Great Falls (MT)
U of Guam (GU)
U of Hartford (CT)
U of Hawaii at Hilo (HI)
U of Hawaii at Manoa (HI)
U of Hawaii–West Oahu (HI)
U of Houston (TX)
U of Houston–Downtown (TX)
U of Idaho (ID)
U of Illinois at Chicago (IL)
U of Illinois at Springfield (IL)
U of Illinois at Urbana–Champaign (IL)
U of Indianapolis (IN)
The U of Iowa (IA)
The U of Kansas (KS)
U of La Verne (CA)
U of Lethbridge (AB, Canada)
U of Louisiana at Lafayette (LA)
U of Louisiana at Monroe (LA)
U of Louisville (KY)
U of Maine (ME)
U of Maine at Farmington (ME)
U of Mary Hardin-Baylor (TX)
U of Maryland, Baltimore County (MD)
U of Maryland, Coll Park (MD)
U of Maryland U Coll (MD)
U of Mary Washington (VA)
U of Massachusetts Amherst (MA)
U of Massachusetts Boston (MA)
U of Massachusetts Dartmouth (MA)
U of Massachusetts Lowell (MA)
U of Memphis (TN)
U of Miami (FL)
U of Michigan (MI)
U of Michigan–Dearborn (MI)
U of Michigan–Flint (MI)
U of Minnesota, Duluth (MN)
U of Minnesota, Twin Cities Campus (MN)
U of Mississippi (MS)
U of Missouri (MO)
U of Missouri–Kansas City (MO)
U of Missouri–St. Louis (MO)
U of Mobile (AL)
The U of Montana Western (MT)
U of Mount Union (OH)
U of Nebraska at Kearney (NE)
U of Nebraska at Omaha (NE)
U of Nebraska–Lincoln (NE)
U of Nevada, Las Vegas (NV)
U of Nevada, Reno (NV)
U of New England (ME)
U of New Hampshire (NH)
U of New Haven (CT)
U of New Mexico (NM)
U of New Orleans (LA)

U of North Alabama (AL)
The U of North Carolina at Asheville (NC)
The U of North Carolina at Chapel Hill (NC)
The U of North Carolina at Charlotte (NC)
The U of North Carolina Wilmington (NC)
U of North Dakota (ND)
U of Northern Colorado (CO)
U of Northern Iowa (IA)
U of North Florida (FL)
U of North Texas (TX)
U of Notre Dame (IN)
U of Oklahoma (OK)
U of Oregon (OR)
U of Ottawa (ON, Canada)
U of Pennsylvania (PA)
U of Pittsburgh (PA)
U of Pittsburgh at Bradford (PA)
U of Pittsburgh at Greensburg (PA)
U of Pittsburgh at Johnstown (PA)
U of Portland (OR)
U of Puget Sound (WA)
U of Redlands (CA)
U of Regina (SK, Canada)
U of Rhode Island (RI)
U of Richmond (VA)
U of Rio Grande (OH)
U of Rochester (NY)
U of St. Francis (IL)
U of Saint Mary (KS)
U of St. Thomas (MN)
U of St. Thomas (TX)
U of San Diego (CA)
U of Science and Arts of Oklahoma (OK)
The U of Scranton (PA)
U of South Alabama (AL)
U of South Carolina (SC)
U of South Carolina Aiken (SC)
U of South Carolina Upstate (SC)
The U of South Dakota (SD)
U of Southern California (CA)
U of Southern Indiana (IN)
U of Southern Maine (ME)
U of Southern Mississippi (MS)
U of South Florida (FL)
U of South Florida–St. Petersburg Campus (FL)
The U of Tampa (FL)
The U of Tennessee (TN)
The U of Tennessee at Chattanooga (TN)
The U of Tennessee at Martin (TN)
The U of Texas at Arlington (TX)
The U of Texas at Austin (TX)
The U of Texas at Dallas (TX)
The U of Texas at El Paso (TX)
The U of Texas at San Antonio (TX)
The U of Texas at Tyler (TX)
The U of Texas of the Permian Basin (TX)
The U of Texas–Pan American (TX)
U of the Cumberlands (KY)
U of the District of Columbia (DC)
U of the Incarnate Word (TX)
U of the Ozarks (AR)
U of the Pacific (CA)
The U of Toledo (OH)
U of Toronto (ON, Canada)
U of Tulsa (OK)
U of Utah (UT)
U of Vermont (VT)
U of Virginia (VA)
The U of Virginia's Coll at Wise (VA)
U of Washington (WA)
The U of Western Ontario (ON, Canada)
U of West Florida (FL)
U of West Georgia (GA)
U of Windsor (ON, Canada)
U of Wisconsin–Eau Claire (WI)
U of Wisconsin–Green Bay (WI)
U of Wisconsin–La Crosse (WI)
U of Wisconsin–Madison (WI)
U of Wisconsin–Milwaukee (WI)
U of Wisconsin–Platteville (WI)
U of Wisconsin–River Falls (WI)
U of Wisconsin–Stevens Point (WI)
U of Wisconsin–Superior (WI)
U of Wisconsin–Whitewater (WI)
U of Wyoming (WY)
Utah State U (UT)

Utah Valley U (UT)
Utica Coll (NY)
Valdosta State U (GA)
Valparaiso U (IN)
Vanderbilt U (TN)
Vanguard U of Southern California (CA)
Vassar Coll (NY)
Villanova U (PA)
Virginia Commonwealth U (VA)
Virginia Polytechnic Inst and State U (VA)
Virginia State U (VA)
Virginia Union U (VA)
Virginia Wesleyan Coll (VA)
Wabash Coll (IN)
Wagner Coll (NY)
Wake Forest U (NC)
Walsh U (OH)
Wartburg Coll (IA)
Washburn U (KS)
Washington Adventist U (MD)
Washington & Jefferson Coll (PA)
Washington and Lee U (VA)
Washington Coll (MD)
Washington State U (WA)
Washington U in St. Louis (MO)
Wayne State Coll (NE)
Wayne State U (MI)
Weber State U (UT)
Webster U (MO)
Wellesley Coll (MA)
Wells Coll (NY)
Wesleyan Coll (GA)
Wesleyan U (CT)
West Chester U of Pennsylvania (PA)
Western Carolina U (NC)
Western Connecticut State U (CT)
Western Illinois U (IL)
Western Kentucky U (KY)
Western Michigan U (MI)
Western New England U (MA)
Western Oregon U (OR)
Western State Coll of Colorado (CO)
Western Washington U (WA)
Westfield State U (MA)
West Liberty U (WV)
Westminster Coll (MO)
Westminster Coll (UT)
West Texas A&M U (TX)
West Virginia State U (WV)
West Virginia U (WV)
West Virginia Wesleyan Coll (WV)
Wheaton Coll (IL)
Wheaton Coll (MA)
Wheeling Jesuit U (WV)
Whitman Coll (WA)
Whittier Coll (CA)
Wichita State U (KS)
Widener U (PA)
Wilkes U (PA)
Willamette U (OR)
William Jessup U (CA)
William Jewell Coll (MO)
William Paterson U of New Jersey (NJ)
William Penn U (IA)
Williams Coll (MA)
William Woods U (MO)
Wilmington Coll (OH)
Winona State U (MN)
Winthrop U (SC)
Wittenberg U (OH)
Wofford Coll (SC)
Woodbury U (CA)
Wright State U (OH)
Xavier U (OH)
Xavier U of Louisiana (LA)
Yale U (CT)
Yeshiva U (NY)
York Coll of Pennsylvania (PA)
York Coll of the City U of New York (NY)
Youngstown State U (OH)

POLITICAL SCIENCE AND GOVERNMENT RELATED

American Jewish U (CA)
American U in Bulgaria (Bulgaria)
Bennington Coll (VT)
Brandeis U (MA)
Buena Vista U (IA)
Capital U (OH)

Claflin U (SC)
Clarion U of Pennsylvania (PA)
Columbia U, School of General Studies (NY)
Delaware State U (DE)
George Mason U (VA)
Georgetown Coll (KY)
Lebanese American U (Lebanon)
McDaniel Coll (MD)
Muhlenberg Coll (PA)
Regis U (CO)
Ryerson U (ON, Canada)
Sacred Heart U (CT)
Saint Mary's Coll of California (CA)
Saint Mary's U of Minnesota (MN)
Southern Vermont Coll (VT)
Trevecca Nazarene U (TN)
U of California, Davis (CA)
U of Guelph (ON, Canada)
U of Hartford (CT)
U of Northern Iowa (IA)
U of Saint Francis (IN)
Virginia Intermont Coll (VA)
Western Michigan U (MI)
Whitman Coll (WA)

POLYMER CHEMISTRY

Clemson U (SC)
Georgia Inst of Technology (GA)
Pittsburg State U (KS)
State U of New York Coll of Environmental Science and Forestry (NY)
The U of Akron (OH)
U of Wisconsin–Stevens Point (WI)
Winona State U (MN)

POLYMER/PLASTICS ENGINEERING

Case Western Reserve U (OH)
Penn State Erie, The Behrend Coll (PA)
The U of Akron (OH)
U of Illinois at Urbana–Champaign (IL)
U of Massachusetts Lowell (MA)
U of Southern California (CA)
U of Wisconsin–Stout (WI)
Winona State U (MN)

PORTUGUESE

Florida Intl U (FL)
Indiana U Bloomington (IN)
Marlboro Coll (VT)
The Ohio State U (OH)
Rhode Island Coll (RI)
Rutgers, The State U of New Jersey, New Brunswick (NJ)
Smith Coll (MA)
Tulane U (LA)
United States Military Acad (NY)
U of California, Los Angeles (CA)
U of California, Santa Barbara (CA)
U of Florida (FL)
U of Illinois at Urbana–Champaign (IL)
The U of Iowa (IA)
U of Massachusetts Amherst (MA)
U of Massachusetts Dartmouth (MA)
U of New Mexico (NM)
The U of Texas at Austin (TX)
U of Toronto (ON, Canada)
U of Wisconsin–Madison (WI)
Yale U (CT)

POULTRY SCIENCE

Auburn U (AL)
Delaware State U (DE)
Mississippi State U (MS)
North Carolina State U (NC)
Stephen F. Austin State U (TX)
Texas A&M U (TX)
Tuskegee U (AL)
U of Arkansas (AR)
U of Georgia (GA)
U of Maryland Eastern Shore (MD)
U of Wisconsin–Madison (WI)
Virginia Polytechnic Inst and State U (VA)

PRACTICAL NURSING, VOCATIONAL NURSING AND

NURSING ASSISTANTS RELATED

St. Joseph's Coll, Long Island Campus (NY)
St. Joseph's Coll, New York (NY)

PRE-CHIROPRACTIC

Augustana Coll (SD)
Millikin U (IL)
Oklahoma City U (OK)

PRE-DENTISTRY STUDIES

Abilene Christian U (TX)
Acadia U (NS, Canada)
Albertus Magnus Coll (CT)
Allegheny Coll (PA)
Alma Coll (MI)
American U (DC)
Anderson U (IN)
Arcadia U (PA)
Ashland U (OH)
Auburn U (AL)
Augustana Coll (SD)
Baldwin-Wallace Coll (OH)
Ball State U (IN)
Barry U (FL)
Belmont Abbey Coll (NC)
Beloit Coll (WI)
Bethany Coll (WV)
Birmingham-Southern Coll (AL)
Blackburn Coll (IL)
Boise State U (ID)
Boston U (MA)
Bowling Green State U (OH)
Buffalo State Coll, State U of New York (NY)
California State U, Chico (CA)
California State U, East Bay (CA)
Calvin Coll (MI)
Campbellsville U (KY)
Cardinal Stritch U (WI)
Cedar Crest Coll (PA)
Cedarville U (OH)
Centenary Coll of Louisiana (LA)
Chapman U (CA)
City Coll of the City U of New York (NY)
Clark U (MA)
Coe Coll (IA)
The Coll at Brockport, State U of New York (NY)
Coll of Mount Saint Vincent (NY)
Coll of Saint Benedict (MN)
Concordia U Chicago (IL)
Concordia U, Nebraska (NE)
Cornerstone U (MI)
Dalhousie U (NS, Canada)
Defiance Coll (OH)
Dordt Coll (IA)
Drake U (IA)
Elmhurst Coll (IL)
Elmira Coll (NY)
Evangel U (MO)
Florida Southern Coll (FL)
Fordham U (NY)
Furman U (SC)
Gardner-Webb U (NC)
The George Washington U (DC)
Georgia Southern U (GA)
Gettysburg Coll (PA)
Graceland U (IA)
Grand Valley State U (MI)
Gustavus Adolphus Coll (MN)
Hamline U (MN)
Hampton U (VA)
Heidelberg U (OH)
Hillsdale Coll (MI)
Hobart and William Smith Colls (NY)
Hofstra U (NY)
Houghton Coll (NY)
Illinois Coll (IL)
Indiana U–Purdue U Fort Wayne (IN)
Indiana Wesleyan U (IN)
Iowa State U of Science and Technology (IA)
Iowa Wesleyan Coll (IA)
Jacksonville U (FL)
John Carroll U (OH)
Juniata Coll (PA)
Kentucky Wesleyan Coll (KY)

Keuka Coll (NY)
King's Coll (PA)
Lake Superior State U (MI)
Lamar U (TX)
La Salle U (PA)
Lawrence U (WI)
Lehigh U (PA)
Le Moyne Coll (NY)
LeTourneau U (TX)
Limestone Coll (SC)
Lindenwood U (MO)
Lindsey Wilson Coll (KY)
Lipscomb U (TN)
Lock Haven U of Pennsylvania (PA)
Longwood U (VA)
Loyola U New Orleans (LA)
Madonna U (MI)
Manchester Coll (IN)
Maryville U of Saint Louis (MO)
Mayville State U (ND)
McKendree U (IL)
Mercer U (GA)
Mercyhurst Coll (PA)
Michigan Technological U (MI)
Midwestern State U (TX)
Millikin U (IL)
Minnesota State U Mankato (MN)
Molloy Coll (NY)
Mount Allison U (NB, Canada)
Mount Mercy U (IA)
Mount Vernon Nazarene U (OH)
Nazareth Coll of Rochester (NY)
Newman U (KS)
Niagara U (NY)
North Central Coll (IL)
Northern Michigan U (MI)
Northern State U (SD)
Northwestern Oklahoma State U (OK)
Northwest Nazarene U (ID)
Oglethorpe U (GA)
Ohio Northern U (OH)
The Ohio State U (OH)
Ohio Wesleyan U (OH)
Oklahoma City U (OK)
Otterbein U (OH)
Ouachita Baptist U (AR)
Pacific U (OR)
Pepperdine U, Malibu (CA)
Peru State Coll (NE)
Pittsburg State U (KS)
Purdue U Calumet (IN)
Queens U of Charlotte (NC)
Quinnipiac U (CT)
Regis U (CO)
Rhode Island Coll (RI)
Ripon Coll (WI)
Rivier Coll (NH)
Roberts Wesleyan Coll (NY)
Rochester Inst of Technology (NY)
Rockford Coll (IL)
Rutgers, The State U of New Jersey, New Brunswick (NJ)
Sacred Heart U (CT)
Saint Anselm Coll (NH)
St. Catherine U (MN)
Saint Francis U (PA)
Saint John's U (MN)
Saint Mary-of-the-Woods Coll (IN)
Saint Michael's Coll (VT)
St. Thomas U (FL)
Sarah Lawrence Coll (NY)
Simpson Coll (IA)
Sonoma State U (CA)
Southwestern Oklahoma State U (OK)
Southwest Minnesota State U (MN)
Spring Hill Coll (AL)
State U of New York at Oswego (NY)
State U of New York Coll at Cortland (NY)
State U of New York Coll at Geneseo (NY)
State U of New York Coll at Oneonta (NY)
State U of New York Coll of Environmental Science and Forestry (NY)
Stetson U (FL)
Stevens Inst of Technology (NJ)
Sul Ross State U (TX)
Susquehanna U (PA)
Syracuse U (NY)
Tarleton State U (TX)

Texas A&M U–Corpus Christi (TX)
Texas Wesleyan U (TX)
Thiel Coll (PA)
Thompson Rivers U (BC, Canada)
Trinity U (TX)
Union U (TN)
U of Alberta (AB, Canada)
U of Bridgeport (CT)
U of Central Missouri (MO)
U of Dallas (TX)
U of Dayton (OH)
U of Evansville (IN)
U of Hartford (CT)
U of Illinois at Chicago (IL)
U of Indianapolis (IN)
The U of Iowa (IA)
U of Maryland, Coll Park (MD)
U of Maryland Eastern Shore (MD)
U of Massachusetts Amherst (MA)
U of Minnesota, Duluth (MN)
U of Minnesota, Twin Cities Campus (MN)
U of Nebraska–Lincoln (NE)
U of New England (ME)
U of Pittsburgh at Johnstown (PA)
U of Portland (OR)
U of Regina (SK, Canada)
U of Rio Grande (OH)
U of St. Francis (IL)
The U of Tennessee at Martin (TN)
The U of Toledo (OH)
U of Windsor (ON, Canada)
U of Wisconsin–River Falls (WI)
Upper Iowa U (IA)
Utah State U (UT)
Utica Coll (NY)
Valley City State U (ND)
Virginia Wesleyan Coll (VA)
Wagner Coll (NY)
Walsh U (OH)
Washburn U (KS)
Washington Adventist U (MD)
Washington Coll (MD)
Washington U in St. Louis (MO)
Waynesburg U (PA)
Wells Coll (NY)
West Liberty U (WV)
West Virginia State U (WV)
West Virginia Wesleyan Coll (WV)
Widener U (PA)
William Paterson U of New Jersey (NJ)
William Penn U (IA)
Williams Baptist Coll (AR)
Wilmington Coll (OH)
Winona State U (MN)
Wofford Coll (SC)
Youngstown State U (OH)

PRE-ENGINEERING

Asbury U (KY)
Augustana Coll (SD)
Azusa Pacific U (CA)
Baldwin-Wallace Coll (OH)
Bethel U (TN)
Delaware State U (DE)
Drake U (IA)
Faulkner U (AL)
Houghton Coll (NY)
Le Moyne Coll (NY)
Midwestern State U (TX)
Northwest Nazarene U (ID)
Ouachita Baptist U (AR)
Peru State Coll (NE)
Pittsburg State U (KS)
Roberts Wesleyan Coll (NY)
Saint Joseph's Coll of Maine (ME)
Scripps Coll (CA)
Simpson Coll (IA)
Slippery Rock U of Pennsylvania (PA)
Spring Hill Coll (AL)
U of Mary Hardin-Baylor (TX)
The U of Scranton (PA)
Valley City State U (ND)
Wagner Coll (NY)
Waynesburg U (PA)
Wheeling Jesuit U (WV)
Yeshiva U (NY)

PRE-LAW STUDIES

Abilene Christian U (TX)
Acadia U (NS, Canada)
Adrian Coll (MI)

Albertus Magnus Coll (CT)
Albright Coll (PA)
Allegheny Coll (PA)
Alma Coll (MI)
Alvernia U (PA)
American U (DC)
Anderson U (IN)
Andrews U (MI)
Aquinas Coll (MI)
Arcadia U (PA)
Ashland U (OH)
Auburn U (AL)
Augustana Coll (SD)
Azusa Pacific U (CA)
Babson Coll (MA)
Bard Coll (NY)
Barry U (FL)
Baylor U (TX)
Belmont Abbey Coll (NC)
Beloit Coll (WI)
Bemidji State U (MN)
Bennington Coll (VT)
Bethany Coll (WV)
Bethel Coll (IN)
Biola U (CA)
Birmingham-Southern Coll (AL)
Blackburn Coll (IL)
Bowling Green State U (OH)
Buffalo State Coll, State U of New York (NY)
California State U, Dominguez Hills (CA)
California State U, Fresno (CA)
Calumet Coll of Saint Joseph (IN)
Calvin Coll (MI)
Campbellsville U (KY)
Cardinal Stritch U (WI)
Cedar Crest Coll (PA)
Cedarville U (OH)
Centenary Coll of Louisiana (LA)
City Coll of the City U of New York (NY)
Clark U (MA)
Clearwater Christian Coll (FL)
Coe Coll (IA)
The Coll at Brockport, State U of New York (NY)
Coll of Mount Saint Vincent (NY)
Coll of Saint Benedict (MN)
The Coll of Saint Rose (NY)
Concordia Coll–New York (NY)
Concordia U Chicago (IL)
Concordia U, Nebraska (NE)
Corban U (OR)
Creighton U (NE)
Crown Coll (MN)
Curry Coll (MA)
Dalhousie U (NS, Canada)
Defiance Coll (OH)
Dominican Coll (NY)
Dominican U (IL)
Dordt Coll (IA)
Drake U (IA)
Elmhurst Coll (IL)
Elmira Coll (NY)
Emmanuel Coll (GA)
Emory & Henry Coll (VA)
Evangel U (MO)
Faulkner U (AL)
Florida Inst of Technology (FL)
Fontbonne U (MO)
Fordham U (NY)
Fort Hays State U (KS)
Francis Marion U (SC)
Furman U (SC)
Gannon U (PA)
Gardner-Webb U (NC)
The George Washington U (DC)
Gettysburg Coll (PA)
Grambling State U (LA)
Grand View U (IA)
Gustavus Adolphus Coll (MN)
Hamline U (MN)
Hampton U (VA)
Hartwick Coll (NY)
Haverford Coll (PA)
Hawai'i Pacific U (HI)
Heidelberg U (OH)
Hobart and William Smith Colls (NY)
Hofstra U (NY)
Houghton Coll (NY)
Howard Payne U (TX)
Huntington U (IN)
Illinois Coll (IL)

Indiana Tech (IN)
Indiana Wesleyan U (IN)
Iowa State U of Science and Technology (IA)
Iowa Wesleyan Coll (IA)
Ithaca Coll (NY)
Jacksonville U (FL)
John Carroll U (OH)
Juniata Coll (PA)
Kentucky Wesleyan Coll (KY)
Keuka Coll (NY)
Keystone Coll (PA)
King Coll (TN)
King's Coll (PA)
Lakehead U (ON, Canada)
Lake Superior State U (MI)
Lawrence U (WI)
Le Moyne Coll (NY)
Lenoir-Rhyne U (NC)
LeTourneau U (TX)
Limestone Coll (SC)
Lincoln Memorial U (TN)
Lindenwood U (MO)
Lindsey Wilson Coll (KY)
Lipscomb U (TN)
Longwood U (VA)
Louisiana Coll (LA)
Lubbock Christian U (TX)
Madonna U (MI)
Manchester Coll (IN)
Mansfield U of Pennsylvania (PA)
Marlboro Coll (VT)
Mars Hill Coll (NC)
Massachusetts Coll of Liberal Arts (MA)
The Master's Coll and Sem (CA)
Mayville State U (ND)
McKendree U (IL)
Michigan State U (MI)
Michigan Technological U (MI)
Midwestern State U (TX)
Millikin U (IL)
Minnesota State U Mankato (MN)
Molloy Coll (NY)
Mount Allison U (NB, Canada)
Mount Mercy U (IA)
Mount Vernon Nazarene U (OH)
National U (CA)
Nazareth Coll of Rochester (NY)
New England Coll (NH)
Newman U (KS)
Niagara U (NY)
North Central Coll (IL)
Northern Arizona U (AZ)
Northern Michigan U (MI)
Northern State U (SD)
Northwestern Oklahoma State U (OK)
Northwest Nazarene U (ID)
Notre Dame de Namur U (CA)
Nova Southeastern U (FL)
Oakland City U (IN)
Oglethorpe U (GA)
Ohio Northern U (OH)
Ohio Wesleyan U (OH)
Oklahoma Christian U (OK)
Oklahoma City U (OK)
Otterbein U (OH)
Ouachita Baptist U (AR)
Pacific Lutheran U (WA)
Pacific Union Coll (CA)
Palm Beach Atlantic U (FL)
Pepperdine U, Malibu (CA)
Peru State Coll (NE)
Pittsburg State U (KS)
Purdue U Calumet (IN)
Queens U of Charlotte (NC)
Quinnipiac U (CT)
Regis U (CO)
Rensselaer Polytechnic Inst (NY)
Rhode Island Coll (RI)
Ripon Coll (WI)
Rivier Coll (NH)
Roberts Wesleyan Coll (NY)
Rochester Inst of Technology (NY)
Rockford Coll (IL)
Rutgers, The State U of New Jersey, New Brunswick (NJ)
Saint Anselm Coll (NH)
St. Catherine U (MN)
Saint Francis U (PA)
Saint John's U (MN)
St. Joseph's Coll, Long Island Campus (NY)
St. Joseph's Coll, New York (NY)

Saint Mary-of-the-Woods Coll (IN)
Saint Michael's Coll (VT)
St. Thomas U (FL)
Sarah Lawrence Coll (NY)
Seattle Pacific U (WA)
Seton Hill U (PA)
Siena Heights U (MI)
Simpson Coll (IA)
Smith Coll (MA)
Sonoma State U (CA)
Southern Oregon U (OR)
Southwestern Oklahoma State U (OK)
Southwest Minnesota State U (MN)
State U of New York at Binghamton (NY)
State U of New York at Fredonia (NY)
State U of New York at New Paltz (NY)
State U of New York at Oswego (NY)
State U of New York Coll at Cortland (NY)
State U of New York Coll at Geneseo (NY)
State U of New York Coll at Oneonta (NY)
State U of New York Coll of Environmental Science and Forestry (NY)
Stephens Coll (MO)
Stetson U (FL)
Stevens Inst of Technology (NJ)
Suffolk U (MA)
Sul Ross State U (TX)
Susquehanna U (PA)
Syracuse U (NY)
Texas A&M U–Corpus Christi (TX)
Texas Wesleyan U (TX)
Thiel Coll (PA)
Trine U (IN)
Trinity U (TX)
Tusculum Coll (TN)
Union U (TN)
United States Military Acad (NY)
U of Alberta (AB, Canada)
U of Bridgeport (CT)
U of California, Santa Barbara (CA)
U of California, Santa Cruz (CA)
U of Dallas (TX)
U of Dayton (OH)
The U of Findlay (OH)
U of Illinois at Urbana–Champaign (IL)
U of Indianapolis (IN)
The U of Iowa (IA)
U of Louisiana at Lafayette (LA)
U of Maryland, Coll Park (MD)
U of Maryland Eastern Shore (MD)
U of Minnesota, Twin Cities Campus (MN)
U of Pittsburgh at Greensburg (PA)
U of Pittsburgh at Johnstown (PA)
U of Portland (OR)
U of Regina (SK, Canada)
U of Rio Grande (OH)
U of St. Francis (IL)
The U of Toledo (OH)
U of Windsor (ON, Canada)
U of Wisconsin–River Falls (WI)
U of Wisconsin–Superior (WI)
Utah State U (UT)
Utica Coll (NY)
Valley City State U (ND)
Vanguard U of Southern California (CA)
Wabash Coll (IN)
Wagner Coll (NY)
Washburn U (KS)
Washington Adventist U (MD)
Washington Coll (MD)
Wayland Baptist U (TX)
Waynesburg U (PA)
Webber Intl U (FL)
Wells Coll (NY)
Western State Coll of Colorado (CO)
West Liberty U (WV)
Westminster Coll (MO)
West Texas A&M U (TX)
West Virginia Wesleyan Coll (WV)
William Paterson U of New Jersey (NJ)
William Penn U (IA)

INDEXES

Williams Baptist Coll (AR)
Wilmington Coll (OH)
Wingate U (NC)
Winona State U (MN)
Wofford Coll (SC)
Xavier U of Louisiana (LA)
Youngstown State U (OH)

PREMEDICAL STUDIES

Abilene Christian U (TX)
Acadia U (NS, Canada)
Adrian Coll (MI)
Albertus Magnus Coll (CT)
Allegheny Coll (PA)
Alma Coll (MI)
Alvernia U (PA)
American U (DC)
Anderson U (IN)
Andrews U (MI)
Arcadia U (PA)
Ashland U (OH)
Auburn U (AL)
Augustana Coll (IL)
Augustana Coll (SD)
Baldwin-Wallace Coll (OH)
Ball State U (IN)
Bard Coll (NY)
Bard Coll at Simon's Rock (MA)
Barry U (FL)
Belmont Abbey Coll (NC)
Beloit Coll (WI)
Bemidji State U (MN)
Bennington Coll (VT)
Bethany Coll (WV)
Bethel Coll (IN)
Birmingham-Southern Coll (AL)
Blackburn Coll (IL)
Bluffton U (OH)
Bob Jones U (SC)
Boise State U (ID)
Bowling Green State U (OH)
Buffalo State Coll, State U of New
   York (NY)
California State U, Chico (CA)
California State U, East Bay (CA)
Calvin Coll (MI)
Campbellsville U (KY)
Cardinal Stritch U (WI)
Cedar Crest Coll (PA)
Cedarville U (OH)
Centenary Coll of Louisiana (LA)
Chapman U (CA)
City Coll of the City U of New York
   (NY)
Clark U (MA)
Clearwater Christian Coll (FL)
Coe Coll (IA)
The Coll at Brockport, State U of
   New York (NY)
Coll of Mount Saint Vincent (NY)
Coll of Saint Benedict (MN)
Concordia U (MI)
Concordia U Chicago (IL)
Concordia U, Nebraska (NE)
Cornerstone U (MI)
Dalhousie U (NS, Canada)
Defiance Coll (OH)
Dominican U (IL)
Dordt Coll (IA)
Drake U (IA)
Earlham Coll (IN)
Elmhurst Coll (IL)
Elmira Coll (NY)
Evangel U (MO)
Florida Southern Coll (FL)
Fordham U (NY)
Furman U (SC)
Gannon U (PA)
Gardner-Webb U (NC)
The George Washington U (DC)
Georgia Southern U (GA)
Gettysburg Coll (PA)
Graceland U (IA)
Grand Valley State U (MI)
Gustavus Adolphus Coll (MN)
Hamline U (MN)
Hampton U (VA)
Hartwick Coll (NY)
Haverford Coll (PA)
Hawai`i Pacific U (HI)
Heidelberg U (OH)
Hillsdale Coll (MI)
Hobart and William Smith Colls
   (NY)
Hofstra U (NY)

Houghton Coll (NY)
Huntington U (IN)
Illinois Coll (IL)
Immaculata U (PA)
Indiana U–Purdue U Fort Wayne
   (IN)
Indiana Wesleyan U (IN)
Inter American U of Puerto Rico,
   Bayamón Campus (PR)
Iowa State U of Science and
   Technology (IA)
Iowa Wesleyan Coll (IA)
Ithaca Coll (NY)
Jacksonville U (FL)
John Carroll U (OH)
Johnson State Coll (VT)
Juniata Coll (PA)
Kentucky Wesleyan Coll (KY)
Keuka Coll (NY)
Keystone Coll (PA)
King Coll (TN)
King's Coll (PA)
La Salle U (PA)
Lawrence U (WI)
Lees-McRae Coll (NC)
Lehigh U (PA)
Le Moyne Coll (NY)
Lenoir-Rhyne U (NC)
LeTourneau U (TX)
Limestone Coll (SC)
Lincoln Memorial U (TN)
Lindenwood U (MO)
Lindsey Wilson Coll (KY)
Lipscomb U (TN)
Lock Haven U of Pennsylvania (PA)
Longwood U (VA)
Loyola U New Orleans (LA)
Madonna U (MI)
Manchester Coll (IN)
Marlboro Coll (VT)
Mars Hill Coll (NC)
Maryville U of Saint Louis (MO)
Massachusetts Coll of Liberal Arts
   (MA)
Massachusetts Coll of Pharmacy
   and Health Sciences (MA)
The Master's Coll and Sem (CA)
Mayville State U (ND)
McKendree U (IL)
Mercy Coll of Health Sciences (IA)
Michigan State U (MI)
Michigan Technological U (MI)
Midwestern State U (TX)
Millikin U (IL)
Minnesota State U Mankato (MN)
Molloy Coll (NY)
Mount Allison U (NB, Canada)
Mount Mercy U (IA)
Mount Vernon Nazarene U (OH)
Nazareth Coll of Rochester (NY)
Newman U (KS)
New York Inst of Technology (NY)
Niagara U (NY)
North Carolina Wesleyan Coll (NC)
North Central Coll (IL)
Northern Michigan U (MI)
Northern State U (SD)
Northwestern Oklahoma State U
   (OK)
Northwest Nazarene U (ID)
Notre Dame de Namur U (CA)
Nova Southeastern U (FL)
Oakland City U (IN)
Oglethorpe U (GA)
Ohio Northern U (OH)
Ohio Wesleyan U (OH)
Oklahoma City U (OK)
Oregon Inst of Technology (OR)
Otterbein U (OH)
Ouachita Baptist U (AR)
Pacific Lutheran U (WA)
Pacific U (OR)
Penn State Abington (PA)
Penn State Altoona (PA)
Penn State Beaver (PA)
Penn State Berks (PA)
Penn State Brandywine (PA)
Penn State DuBois (PA)
Penn State Erie, The Behrend Coll
   (PA)
Penn State Fayette, The Eberly
   Campus (PA)
Penn State Greater Allegheny (PA)
Penn State Hazleton (PA)
Penn State Lehigh Valley (PA)

Penn State Mont Alto (PA)
Penn State New Kensington (PA)
Penn State Schuylkill (PA)
Penn State Shenango (PA)
Penn State Park (PA)
Penn State Wilkes-Barre (PA)
Penn State Worthington Scranton
   (PA)
Penn State York (PA)
Pepperdine U, Malibu (CA)
Peru State Coll (NE)
Philadelphia U (PA)
Pittsburg State U (KS)
Pomona Coll (CA)
Purdue U Calumet (IN)
Queens U of Charlotte (NC)
Quinnipiac U (CT)
Regis U (CO)
Rensselaer Polytechnic Inst (NY)
Rhode Island Coll (RI)
Ripon Coll (WI)
Rivier Coll (NH)
Roberts Wesleyan Coll (NY)
Rochester Inst of Technology (NY)
Rockford Coll (IL)
Rutgers, The State U of New
   Jersey, New Brunswick (NJ)
Sacred Heart U (CT)
St. Andrews U (NC)
Saint Anselm Coll (NH)
St. Catherine U (MN)
Saint Francis U (PA)
Saint John's U (MN)
Saint Mary-of-the-Woods Coll (IN)
Saint Michael's Coll (VT)
St. Thomas Aquinas Coll (NY)
St. Thomas U (FL)
Samford U (AL)
Sarah Lawrence Coll (NY)
Simpson Coll (IA)
Slippery Rock U of Pennsylvania
   (PA)
Smith Coll (MA)
Sonoma State U (CA)
Southeastern U (FL)
Southern Oregon U (OR)
Southwestern Oklahoma State U
   (OK)
Southwest Minnesota State U (MN)
Spring Hill Coll (AL)
State U of New York at Binghamton
   (NY)
State U of New York at Fredonia
   (NY)
State U of New York at Oswego
   (NY)
State U of New York Coll at
   Cortland (NY)
State U of New York Coll at
   Geneseo (NY)
State U of New York Coll at
   Oneonta (NY)
State U of New York Coll of
   Environmental Science and
   Forestry (NY)
Stetson U (FL)
Stevens Inst of Technology (NJ)
Sul Ross State U (TX)
Susquehanna U (PA)
Syracuse U (NY)
Tarleton State U (TX)
Texas A&M U–Corpus Christi (TX)
Texas Lutheran U (TX)
Thiel Coll (PA)
Thompson Rivers U (BC, Canada)
Trine U (IN)
Trinity U (TX)
Tusculum Coll (TN)
Union U (TN)
Université de Sherbrooke (QC,
   Canada)
U of Alberta (AB, Canada)
U of Arkansas (AR)
U of Bridgeport (CT)
U of California, Santa Cruz (CA)
U of Central Missouri (MO)
U of Dallas (TX)
U of Dayton (OH)
U of Evansville (IN)
The U of Findlay (OH)
U of Hartford (CT)
U of Indianapolis (IN)
The U of Iowa (IA)
U of Maine (ME)
U of Maryland Eastern Shore (MD)

U of Massachusetts Amherst (MA)
U of Minnesota, Duluth (MN)
U of Minnesota, Twin Cities
   Campus (MN)
U of Nebraska–Lincoln (NE)
U of New England (ME)
U of Notre Dame (IN)
U of Pittsburgh at Johnstown (PA)
U of Portland (OR)
U of Regina (SK, Canada)
U of Rio Grande (OH)
U of St. Francis (IL)
The U of Tennessee at Martin (TN)
The U of Toledo (OH)
U of Windsor (ON, Canada)
U of Wisconsin–Madison (WI)
U of Wisconsin–Milwaukee (WI)
U of Wisconsin–River Falls (WI)
Upper Iowa U (IA)
Utah State U (UT)
Utica Coll (NY)
Valley City State U (ND)
Vanguard U of Southern California
   (CA)
Virginia Intermont Coll (VA)
Virginia Wesleyan Coll (VA)
Wabash Coll (IN)
Wagner Coll (NY)
Walsh U (OH)
Washburn U (KS)
Washington Adventist U (MD)
Washington Coll (MD)
Washington State U (WA)
Washington U in St. Louis (MO)
Waynesburg U (PA)
Wells Coll (NY)
West Chester U of Pennsylvania
   (PA)
West Liberty U (WV)
West Virginia State U (WV)
West Virginia Wesleyan Coll (WV)
Wheeling Jesuit U (WV)
Widener U (PA)
William Paterson U of New Jersey
   (NJ)
William Penn U (IA)
Williams Baptist Coll (AR)
Wilmington Coll (OH)
Wingate U (NC)
Winona State U (MN)
Wofford Coll (SC)
Xavier U of Louisiana (LA)
Youngstown State U (OH)

PRENURSING STUDIES

Allegheny Coll (PA)
American U (DC)
Baylor U (TX)
Brigham Young U (UT)
California State U, Fullerton (CA)
Cleveland State U (OH)
The Coll of Idaho (ID)
Concordia U, Nebraska (NE)
Delaware State U (DE)
Gettysburg Coll (PA)
Juniata Coll (PA)
Limestone Coll (SC)
Lindenwood U (MO)
Lipscomb U (TN)
Madonna U (MI)
McMurry U (TX)
Missouri Baptist U (MO)
Oklahoma City U (OK)
Ouachita Baptist U (AR)
Peru State Coll (NE)
San Diego State U (CA)
Simpson Coll (IA)
State U of New York Coll at
   Geneseo (NY)
Wright State U (OH)

PRE-OCCUPATIONAL
THERAPY

Augustana Coll (SD)
Millikin U (IL)

PRE-OPTOMETRY

Augustana Coll (SD)
Lehigh U (PA)
Le Moyne Coll (NY)
Millikin U (IL)
Oklahoma City U (OK)
Peru State Coll (NE)
Simpson Coll (IA)

U of Evansville (IN)

PRE-PHARMACY STUDIES

Abilene Christian U (TX)
Allegheny Coll (PA)
American U (DC)
Ashland U (OH)
Auburn U (AL)
Augustana Coll (SD)
Baldwin-Wallace Coll (OH)
Barry U (FL)
Belmont Abbey Coll (NC)
Benedictine U (IL)
Bethel U (TN)
Coll of Saint Benedict (MN)
Concordia U, Nebraska (NE)
Dalhousie U (NS, Canada)
Dordt Coll (IA)
Elmhurst Coll (IL)
Emory & Henry Coll (VA)
Fordham U (NY)
Gardner-Webb U (NC)
Georgia Southern U (GA)
Gettysburg Coll (PA)
Hamline U (MN)
Houghton Coll (NY)
Iowa Wesleyan Coll (IA)
Juniata Coll (PA)
King Coll (TN)
King's Coll (PA)
Le Moyne Coll (NY)
Limestone Coll (SC)
Lindsey Wilson Coll (KY)
Lipscomb U (TN)
Long Island U–C. W. Post Campus
   (NY)
Longwood U (VA)
Mayville State U (ND)
Michigan Technological U (MI)
Midwestern State U (TX)
Millikin U (IL)
Mount Allison U (NB, Canada)
Mount Vernon Nazarene U (OH)
Northern Michigan U (MI)
Northwest Nazarene U (ID)
Oklahoma City U (OK)
Ouachita Baptist U (AR)
Peru State Coll (NE)
Pittsburg State U (KS)
Roberts Wesleyan Coll (NY)
Saint John's U (MN)
Saint Joseph's Coll of Maine (ME)
Saint Mary-of-the-Woods Coll (IN)
Simpson Coll (IA)
Slippery Rock U of Pennsylvania
   (PA)
Tarleton State U (TX)
Texas Southern U (TX)
Tusculum Coll (TN)
Union U (TN)
U of Central Missouri (MO)
U of Charleston (WV)
U of Connecticut (CT)
U of Evansville (IN)
The U of Iowa (IA)
U of Minnesota, Duluth (MN)
U of Minnesota, Twin Cities
   Campus (MN)
U of Nebraska–Lincoln (NE)
U of Regina (SK, Canada)
U of St. Francis (IL)
U of Saint Francis (IN)
The U of Tennessee at Martin (TN)
U of Windsor (ON, Canada)
U of Wisconsin–River Falls (WI)
Valley City State U (ND)
Walsh U (OH)
Washburn U (KS)
Washington U in St. Louis (MO)
Western New England U (MA)
West Virginia Wesleyan Coll (WV)
Wheeling Jesuit U (WV)
Wingate U (NC)
Youngstown State U (OH)

PRE-PHYSICAL THERAPY

Asbury U (KY)
Augustana Coll (SD)
Iowa Wesleyan Coll (IA)
Massachusetts Coll of Liberal Arts
   (MA)
Midwestern State U (TX)
Millikin U (IL)
Oklahoma City U (OK)

Saint Mary's U of Minnesota (MN)
Simpson Coll (IA)
Virginia Intermont Coll (VA)
Walsh U (OH)

PRE-THEOLOGY/PRE-MINISTERIAL STUDIES
Adrian Coll (MI)
Alma Coll (MI)
Ashland U (OH)
Augustana Coll (SD)
Baptist Bible Coll of Pennsylvania (PA)
California Baptist U (CA)
Coll of Saint Benedict (MN)
Columbia Bible Coll (BC, Canada)
Concordia Coll–New York (NY)
Concordia U (MI)
Concordia U Chicago (IL)
Concordia U, Nebraska (NE)
Corban U (OR)
Cornerstone U (MI)
Emmaus Bible Coll (IA)
John Brown U (AR)
Loras Coll (IA)
Manchester Coll (IN)
Martin Luther Coll (MN)
Mid-Atlantic Christian U (NC)
Mount Allison U (NB, Canada)
Northwestern Coll (MN)
Nyack Coll (NY)
Ohio Northern U (OH)
Ohio Wesleyan U (OH)
Oral Roberts U (OK)
Point Loma Nazarene U (CA)
Point U (GA)
Saint John's U (MN)
Shorter U (GA)
Simpson Coll (IA)
Southeastern U (FL)
Trinity Christian Coll (IL)
Trinity Coll of Florida (FL)
U of Dallas (TX)
U of Indianapolis (IN)
U of Rio Grande (OH)
Washburn U (KS)
Waynesburg U (PA)

PRE-VETERINARY STUDIES
Abilene Christian U (TX)
Acadia U (NS, Canada)
Adrian Coll (MI)
Albertus Magnus Coll (CT)
Allegheny Coll (PA)
Alma Coll (MI)
American U (DC)
American U of Beirut (Lebanon)
Anderson U (IN)
Andrews U (MI)
Arcadia U (PA)
Ashland U (OH)
Auburn U (AL)
Augustana Coll (SD)
Baldwin-Wallace Coll (OH)
Barry U (FL)
Becker Coll (MA)
Belmont Abbey Coll (NC)
Bemidji State U (MN)
Bethany Coll (WV)
Blackburn Coll (IL)
Boise State U (ID)
Buffalo State Coll, State U of New York (NY)
California State U, Chico (CA)
California State U, East Bay (CA)
Calvin Coll (MI)
Campbellsville U (KY)
Cardinal Stritch U (WI)
Cedar Crest Coll (PA)
Cedarville U (OH)
Centenary Coll of Louisiana (LA)
Chapman U (CA)
City Coll of the City U of New York (NY)
Clark U (MA)
Coe Coll (IA)
The Coll at Brockport, State U of New York (NY)
Coll of Saint Benedict (MN)
Coll of the Atlantic (ME)
Concordia Coll–New York (NY)
Concordia U, Nebraska (NE)
Cornerstone U (MI)
Dalhousie U (NS, Canada)

Defiance Coll (OH)
Delaware State U (DE)
Dordt Coll (IA)
Drake U (IA)
Elmhurst Coll (IL)
Elmira Coll (NY)
Emory & Henry Coll (VA)
Evangel U (MO)
Florida Southern Coll (FL)
Fordham U (NY)
Furman U (SC)
Gardner-Webb U (NC)
Georgia Southern U (GA)
Gettysburg Coll (PA)
Grand Valley State U (MI)
Gustavus Adolphus Coll (MN)
Hamline U (MN)
Hampton U (VA)
Hartwick Coll (NY)
Heidelberg U (OH)
Hillsdale Coll (MI)
Hobart and William Smith Colls (NY)
Hofstra U (NY)
Houghton Coll (NY)
Illinois Coll (IL)
Indiana U–Purdue U Fort Wayne (IN)
Indiana Wesleyan U (IN)
Iowa State U of Science and Technology (IA)
Iowa Wesleyan Coll (IA)
Jacksonville U (FL)
John Carroll U (OH)
Juniata Coll (PA)
Kentucky Wesleyan Coll (KY)
Keuka Coll (NY)
King Coll (TN)
King's Coll (PA)
La Salle U (PA)
Lawrence U (WI)
Lees-McRae Coll (NC)
Le Moyne Coll (NY)
LeTourneau U (TX)
Limestone Coll (SC)
Lincoln Memorial U (TN)
Lindenwood U (MO)
Lindsey Wilson Coll (KY)
Lipscomb U (TN)
Lock Haven U of Pennsylvania (PA)
Longwood U (VA)
Loyola U New Orleans (LA)
Manchester Coll (IN)
Marlboro Coll (VT)
Mars Hill Coll (NC)
Mayville State U (ND)
McKendree U (IL)
Mercyhurst Coll (PA)
Michigan Technological U (MI)
Midwestern State U (TX)
Millikin U (IL)
Minnesota State U Mankato (MN)
Molloy Coll (NY)
Montana State U (MT)
Mount Allison U (NB, Canada)
Mount Mercy U (IA)
Mount Vernon Nazarene U (OH)
Nazareth Coll of Rochester (NY)
Newman U (KS)
Niagara U (NY)
North Central Coll (IL)
Northern Michigan U (MI)
Northwest Missouri State U (MO)
Northwest Nazarene U (ID)
Nova Scotia Ag Coll (NS, Canada)
Oakland City U (IN)
Oglethorpe U (GA)
Ohio Northern U (OH)
Ohio Wesleyan U (OH)
Oklahoma City U (OK)
Otterbein U (OH)
Ouachita Baptist U (AR)
Pacific U (OR)
Penn State U Park (PA)
Peru State Coll (NE)
Pittsburg State U (KS)
Purdue U (IN)
Purdue U Calumet (IN)
Queens U of Charlotte (NC)
Quinnipiac U (CT)
Regis U (CO)
Rhode Island Coll (RI)
Ripon Coll (WI)
Rivier Coll (NH)

Roberts Wesleyan Coll (NY)
Rochester Inst of Technology (NY)
Rockford Coll (IL)
Sacred Heart U (CT)
St. Andrews U (NC)
St. Catherine U (MN)
Saint Francis U (PA)
Saint John's U (MN)
Saint Mary-of-the-Woods Coll (IN)
Saint Michael's Coll (VT)
Sarah Lawrence Coll (NY)
Simpson Coll (IA)
Sonoma State U (CA)
Southwestern Oklahoma State U (OK)
Southwest Minnesota State U (MN)
Spring Hill Coll (AL)
State U of New York at Binghamton (NY)
State U of New York at Fredonia (NY)
State U of New York at Oswego (NY)
State U of New York Coll at Geneseo (NY)
State U of New York Coll at Oneonta (NY)
State U of New York Coll of Environmental Science and Forestry (NY)
Stetson U (FL)
Sul Ross State U (TX)
Susquehanna U (PA)
Syracuse U (NY)
Tarleton State U (TX)
Texas A&M U (TX)
Texas A&M U–Corpus Christi (TX)
Thiel Coll (PA)
Thompson Rivers U (BC, Canada)
Trinity U (TX)
Tusculum Coll (TN)
U of Alberta (AB, Canada)
U of Bridgeport (CT)
The U of British Columbia (BC, Canada)
U of Central Missouri (MO)
U of Delaware (DE)
U of Evansville (IN)
The U of Findlay (OH)
U of Illinois at Chicago (IL)
U of Illinois at Urbana–Champaign (IL)
U of Indianapolis (IN)
The U of Iowa (IA)
U of Maine (ME)
U of Maryland, Coll Park (MD)
U of Massachusetts Amherst (MA)
U of Minnesota, Crookston (MN)
U of Minnesota, Duluth (MN)
U of Minnesota, Twin Cities Campus (MN)
U of Nebraska–Lincoln (NE)
U of Nevada, Reno (NV)
U of Pittsburgh at Johnstown (PA)
U of Regina (SK, Canada)
U of Rio Grande (OH)
U of St. Francis (IL)
The U of Tennessee at Martin (TN)
The U of Toledo (OH)
U of Wisconsin–River Falls (WI)
Upper Iowa U (IA)
Utah State U (UT)
Utica Coll (NY)
Valley City State U (ND)
Virginia Intermont Coll (VA)
Virginia Wesleyan Coll (VA)
Wabash Coll (IN)
Walsh U (OH)
Washburn U (KS)
Washington Adventist U (MD)
Washington Coll (MD)
Washington U in St. Louis (MO)
Waynesburg U (PA)
Wells Coll (NY)
West Virginia State U (WV)
West Virginia Wesleyan Coll (WV)
Widener U (PA)
Wilmington Coll (OH)
Wingate U (NC)
Winona State U (MN)
Wofford Coll (SC)
Youngstown State U (OH)

PRINTING MANAGEMENT
Coll of the Ozarks (MO)

Ferris State U (MI)
Kean U (NJ)
Pittsburg State U (KS)
Rochester Inst of Technology (NY)
West Virginia U Inst of Technology (WV)

PRINTMAKING
Acad of Art U (CA)
Adams State Coll (CO)
Alberta Coll of Art & Design (AB, Canada)
Aquinas Coll (MI)
Bennington Coll (VT)
Birmingham-Southern Coll (AL)
Bowling Green State U (OH)
Bradley U (IL)
Brigham Young U (UT)
Buffalo State Coll, State U of New York (NY)
California Coll of the Arts (CA)
California State U, East Bay (CA)
California State U, Long Beach (CA)
Central Michigan U (MI)
The Cleveland Inst of Art (OH)
Columbia Coll (MO)
Concordia U (QC, Canada)
Daemen Coll (NY)
Drake U (IA)
Emily Carr U of Art + Design (BC, Canada)
Indiana U–Purdue U Fort Wayne (IN)
Indiana Wesleyan U (IN)
Inter American U of Puerto Rico, San Germán Campus (PR)
Kansas City Art Inst (MO)
Longwood U (VA)
Maryland Inst Coll of Art (MD)
Massachusetts Coll of Art and Design (MA)
Montserrat Coll of Art (MA)
Mount Allison U (NB, Canada)
Northern Michigan U (MI)
Northwest Nazarene U (ID)
Ohio Northern U (OH)
Ohio U (OH)
Pacific Northwest Coll of Art (OR)
Pratt Inst (NY)
Purchase Coll, State U of New York (NY)
Ringling Coll of Art and Design (FL)
Rutgers, The State U of New Jersey, New Brunswick (NJ)
Salem State U (MA)
Sarah Lawrence Coll (NY)
Savannah Coll of Art and Design (GA)
School of the Museum of Fine Arts, Boston (MA)
Seton Hill U (PA)
Sonoma State U (CA)
State U of New York at New Paltz (NY)
Syracuse U (NY)
Temple U (PA)
Texas Christian U (TX)
U of Alberta (AB, Canada)
U of Dallas (TX)
U of Hartford (CT)
The U of Iowa (IA)
The U of Kansas (KS)
U of Miami (FL)
U of Michigan (MI)
U of Missouri–St. Louis (MO)
U of Oregon (OR)
U of Regina (SK, Canada)
The U of Texas at El Paso (TX)
The U of the Arts (PA)
U of Washington (WA)
U of Windsor (ON, Canada)
Virginia Intermont Coll (VA)
Washington U in St. Louis (MO)
Western State Coll of Colorado (CO)
Western Washington U (WA)

PROFESSIONAL, TECHNICAL, BUSINESS, AND SCIENTIFIC WRITING
Arizona State U (AZ)
Bob Jones U (SC)
Boise State U (ID)

Bowling Green State U (OH)
Brescia U (KY)
Carlow U (PA)
Carnegie Mellon U (PA)
Cedarville U (OH)
Chatham U (PA)
Concordia U, St. Paul (MN)
Dakota State U (SD)
Drexel U (PA)
Eastern Michigan U (MI)
Eastern Washington U (WA)
Elizabethtown Coll (PA)
Farmingdale State Coll (NY)
Ferris State U (MI)
Fitchburg State U (MA)
Indiana U–Purdue U Fort Wayne (IN)
Iowa State U of Science and Technology (IA)
James Madison U (VA)
Juniata Coll (PA)
King Coll (TN)
Lubbock Christian U (TX)
Madonna U (MI)
Maryville Coll (TN)
Massachusetts Coll of Liberal Arts (MA)
Michigan State U (MI)
Michigan Technological U (MI)
Missouri State U (MO)
Montana Tech of The U of Montana (MT)
New Mexico Inst of Mining and Technology (NM)
New York Inst of Technology (NY)
Ohio Northern U (OH)
Penn State Berks (PA)
Penn State Lehigh Valley (PA)
Pittsburg State U (KS)
Saint Leo U (FL)
Salem State U (MA)
San Francisco State U (CA)
Slippery Rock U of Pennsylvania (PA)
Spring Arbor U (MI)
Tarleton State U (TX)
Taylor U (IN)
Texas Tech U (TX)
U of Arkansas at Little Rock (AR)
U of Arkansas–Fort Smith (AR)
U of Hartford (CT)
U of Houston–Downtown (TX)
U of Idaho (ID)
U of Rhode Island (RI)
U of Wisconsin–Stout (WI)
Valparaiso U (IN)
Webster U (MO)
Winthrop U (SC)
Worcester Polytechnic Inst (MA)
Yeshiva U (NY)
York Coll of Pennsylvania (PA)
Youngstown State U (OH)

PROJECT MANAGEMENT
Bellevue U (NE)
Huntington U (IN)
ITT Tech Inst, Bessemer (AL)
ITT Tech Inst, Madison (AL)
ITT Tech Inst, Mobile (AL)
ITT Tech Inst, Phoenix (AZ)
ITT Tech Inst, Phoenix (AZ)
ITT Tech Inst, Tempe (AZ)
ITT Tech Inst, Tucson (AZ)
ITT Tech Inst (AR)
ITT Tech Inst, Clovis (CA)
ITT Tech Inst, Concord (CA)
ITT Tech Inst, Corona (CA)
ITT Tech Inst, Culver City (CA)
ITT Tech Inst, Lathrop (CA)
ITT Tech Inst, Oakland (CA)
ITT Tech Inst, Orange (CA)
ITT Tech Inst, Oxnard (CA)
ITT Tech Inst, Rancho Cordova (CA)
ITT Tech Inst, San Bernardino (CA)
ITT Tech Inst, San Diego (CA)
ITT Tech Inst, San Dimas (CA)
ITT Tech Inst, Sylmar (CA)
ITT Tech Inst, Torrance (CA)
ITT Tech Inst, West Covina (CA)
ITT Tech Inst, Aurora (CO)
ITT Tech Inst, Thornton (CO)
ITT Tech Inst, Bradenton (FL)
ITT Tech Inst, Deerfield Beach (FL)
ITT Tech Inst, Fort Lauderdale (FL)

ITT Tech Inst, Fort Myers (FL)
ITT Tech Inst, Jacksonville (FL)
ITT Tech Inst, Lake Mary (FL)
ITT Tech Inst, Miami (FL)
ITT Tech Inst, Orlando (FL)
ITT Tech Inst, Pinellas Park (FL)
ITT Tech Inst, Tallahassee (FL)
ITT Tech Inst, Tampa (FL)
ITT Tech Inst, West Palm Beach (FL)
ITT Tech Inst, Duluth (GA)
ITT Tech Inst, Kennesaw (GA)
ITT Tech Inst (ID)
ITT Tech Inst, Mount Prospect (IL)
ITT Tech Inst, Oak Brook (IL)
ITT Tech Inst, Orland Park (IL)
ITT Tech Inst, Fort Wayne (IN)
ITT Tech Inst, Indianapolis (IN)
ITT Tech Inst, Indianapolis (IN)
ITT Tech Inst, Merrillville (IN)
ITT Tech Inst, Newburgh (IN)
ITT Tech Inst, South Bend (IN)
ITT Tech Inst, Cedar Rapids (IA)
ITT Tech Inst, Clive (IA)
ITT Tech Inst, Overland Park (KS)
ITT Tech Inst, Wichita (KS)
ITT Tech Inst, Lexington (KY)
ITT Tech Inst, Louisville (KY)
ITT Tech Inst, Baton Rouge (LA)
ITT Tech Inst, St. Rose (LA)
ITT Tech Inst, Canton (MI)
ITT Tech Inst, Dearborn (MI)
ITT Tech Inst, Grand Rapids (MI)
ITT Tech Inst, Southfield (MI)
ITT Tech Inst, Swartz Creek (MI)
ITT Tech Inst, Troy (MI)
ITT Tech Inst, Wyoming (MI)
ITT Tech Inst, Brooklyn Center (MN)
ITT Tech Inst, Eden Prairie (MN)
ITT Tech Inst, Arnold (MO)
ITT Tech Inst, Earth City (MO)
ITT Tech Inst, Kansas City (MO)
ITT Tech Inst, Springfield (MO)
ITT Tech Inst (NE)
ITT Tech Inst, Henderson (NV)
ITT Tech Inst, North Las Vegas (NV)
ITT Tech Inst (NM)
ITT Tech Inst, Cary (NC)
ITT Tech Inst, Charlotte (NC)
ITT Tech Inst, Charlotte (NC)
ITT Tech Inst, Durham (NC)
ITT Tech Inst, High Point (NC)
ITT Tech Inst, Oklahoma City (OK)
ITT Tech Inst, Tulsa (OK)
ITT Tech Inst, Portland (OR)
ITT Tech Inst, Salem (OR)
ITT Tech Inst, Columbia (SC)
ITT Tech Inst, Greenville (SC)
ITT Tech Inst, Myrtle Beach (SC)
ITT Tech Inst, North Charleston (SC)
ITT Tech Inst, Chattanooga (TN)
ITT Tech Inst, Cordova (TN)
ITT Tech Inst, Johnson City (TN)
ITT Tech Inst, Knoxville (TN)
ITT Tech Inst, Nashville (TN)
ITT Tech Inst, Arlington (TX)
ITT Tech Inst, Austin (TX)
ITT Tech Inst, DeSoto (TX)
ITT Tech Inst, Houston (TX)
ITT Tech Inst, Houston (TX)
ITT Tech Inst, Richardson (TX)
ITT Tech Inst, San Antonio (TX)
ITT Tech Inst, Waco (TX)
ITT Tech Inst, Webster (TX)
ITT Tech Inst (UT)
ITT Tech Inst, Chantilly (VA)
ITT Tech Inst, Norfolk (VA)
ITT Tech Inst, Richmond (VA)
ITT Tech Inst, Salem (VA)
ITT Tech Inst, Springfield (VA)
ITT Tech Inst, Everett (WA)
ITT Tech Inst, Seattle (WA)
ITT Tech Inst, Spokane Valley (WA)
ITT Tech Inst, Germantown (WI)
ITT Tech Inst, Green Bay (WI)
ITT Tech Inst, Greenfield (WI)
ITT Tech Inst, Madison (WI)

PSYCHIATRIC/MENTAL HEALTH SERVICES TECHNOLOGY

Franciscan U of Steubenville (OH)
Indiana U–Purdue U Fort Wayne (IN)
Northern Kentucky U (KY)

PSYCHOLOGY

Abilene Christian U (TX)
Acadia U (NS, Canada)
Adams State Coll (CO)
Adelphi U (NY)
Adrian Coll (MI)
Agnes Scott Coll (GA)
Alabama State U (AL)
Alaska Pacific U (AK)
Albany State U (GA)
Albertus Magnus Coll (CT)
Albion Coll (MI)
Albright Coll (PA)
Alcorn State U (MS)
Alfred U (NY)
Allegheny Coll (PA)
Alliant Intl U (CA)
Alliant Intl U–México City (Mexico)
Alma Coll (MI)
Alvernia U (PA)
Alverno Coll (WI)
American Jewish U (CA)
American Public U System (WV)
American U (DC)
The American U in Cairo (Egypt)
American U of Beirut (Lebanon)
The American U of Paris (France)
Amherst Coll (MA)
Anderson U (IN)
Anderson U (SC)
Andrews U (MI)
Angelo State U (TX)
Anna Maria Coll (MA)
Appalachian State U (NC)
Aquinas Coll (MI)
Arcadia U (PA)
Arizona State U (AZ)
Arkansas State U (AR)
Arkansas Tech U (AR)
Armstrong Atlantic State U (GA)
Asbury U (KY)
Ashland U (OH)
Assumption Coll (MA)
Athabasca U (AB, Canada)
Athens State U (AL)
Auburn U (AL)
Auburn U Montgomery (AL)
Augustana Coll (IL)
Augustana Coll (SD)
Austin Coll (TX)
Austin Peay State U (TN)
Averett U (VA)
Avila U (MO)
Azusa Pacific U (CA)
Baker U (KS)
Baldwin-Wallace Coll (OH)
Ball State U (IN)
Baptist Bible Coll of Pennsylvania (PA)
Barclay Coll (KS)
Bard Coll (NY)
Bard Coll at Simon's Rock (MA)
Barnard Coll (NY)
Barry U (FL)
Barton Coll (NC)
Bastyr U (WA)
Bates Coll (ME)
Bayamón Central U (PR)
Baylor U (TX)
Bay Path Coll (MA)
Becker Coll (MA)
Belhaven U (MS)
Bellarmine U (KY)
Bellevue U (NE)
Belmont Abbey Coll (NC)
Belmont U (TN)
Beloit Coll (WI)
Bemidji State U (MN)
Benedictine Coll (KS)
Benedictine U (IL)
Bennett Coll for Women (NC)
Bennington Coll (VT)
Berea Coll (KY)
Bernard M. Baruch Coll of the City U of New York (NY)
Berry Coll (GA)

Bethany Coll (KS)
Bethany Coll (WV)
Bethany Lutheran Coll (MN)
Bethel Coll (IN)
Bethel Coll (KS)
Bethel U (MN)
Bethel U (TN)
Bethune-Cookman U (FL)
Biola U (CA)
Birmingham-Southern Coll (AL)
Bishop's U (QC, Canada)
Blackburn Coll (IL)
Black Hills State U (SD)
Bloomfield Coll (NJ)
Bloomsburg U of Pennsylvania (PA)
Bluefield Coll (VA)
Blue Mountain Coll (MS)
Bluffton U (OH)
Boise State U (ID)
Boston Coll (MA)
Boston U (MA)
Bowdoin Coll (ME)
Bowie State U (MD)
Bowling Green State U (OH)
Brandeis U (MA)
Brenau U (GA)
Brescia U (KY)
Brevard Coll (NC)
Brewton-Parker Coll (GA)
Briar Cliff U (IA)
Bridgewater Coll (VA)
Bridgewater State U (MA)
Brown U (RI)
Bryant U (RI)
Bryn Athyn Coll of the New Church (PA)
Bryn Mawr Coll (PA)
Bucknell U (PA)
Buena Vista U (IA)
Buffalo State Coll, State U of New York (NY)
Burlington Coll (VT)
Butler U (IN)
Cabrini Coll (PA)
Caldwell Coll (NJ)
California Baptist U (CA)
California Coast U (CA)
California Lutheran U (CA)
California Polytechnic State U, San Luis Obispo (CA)
California State Polytechnic U, Pomona (CA)
California State U, Bakersfield (CA)
California State U, Chico (CA)
California State U, Dominguez Hills (CA)
California State U, East Bay (CA)
California State U, Fresno (CA)
California State U, Fullerton (CA)
California State U, Long Beach (CA)
California State U, Los Angeles (CA)
California State U, Monterey Bay (CA)
California State U, Sacramento (CA)
California State U, San Bernardino (CA)
California State U, San Marcos (CA)
California State U, Stanislaus (CA)
California U of Pennsylvania (PA)
Calumet Coll of Saint Joseph (IN)
Calvin Coll (MI)
Cambridge Coll (MA)
Cameron U (OK)
Campbellsville U (KY)
Canisius Coll (NY)
Cape Breton U (NS, Canada)
Capella U (MN)
Capital U (OH)
Cardinal Stritch U (WI)
Carleton Coll (MN)
Carlos Albizu U (PR)
Carlos Albizu U, Miami Campus (FL)
Carlow U (PA)
Carnegie Mellon U (PA)
Carroll Coll (MT)
Carson-Newman Coll (TN)
Case Western Reserve U (OH)
Castleton State Coll (VT)
Catawba Coll (NC)
The Catholic U of America (DC)

Cedar Crest Coll (PA)
Cedarville U (OH)
Centenary Coll (NJ)
Centenary Coll of Louisiana (LA)
Central Coll (IA)
Central Connecticut State U (CT)
Central Methodist U (MO)
Central Michigan U (MI)
Central State U (OH)
Central Washington U (WA)
Centre Coll (KY)
Chaminade U of Honolulu (HI)
Chapman U (CA)
Chatham U (PA)
Chestnut Hill Coll (PA)
Cheyney U of Pennsylvania (PA)
Chicago State U (IL)
Christian Brothers U (TN)
Christopher Newport U (VA)
Cincinnati Christian U (OH)
The Citadel, The Military Coll of South Carolina (SC)
City Coll of the City U of New York (NY)
City U of Seattle (WA)
Claremont McKenna Coll (CA)
Clarion U of Pennsylvania (PA)
Clarke U (IA)
Clarkson U (NY)
Clark U (MA)
Clearwater Christian Coll (FL)
Clemson U (SC)
Cleveland State U (OH)
Coastal Carolina U (SC)
Coe Coll (IA)
Colby Coll (ME)
Colgate U (NY)
Coll of Charleston (SC)
Coll of Coastal Georgia (GA)
The Coll of Idaho (ID)
Coll of Mount St. Joseph (OH)
Coll of Mount Saint Vincent (NY)
The Coll of New Jersey (NJ)
Coll of Saint Benedict (MN)
Coll of Saint Elizabeth (NJ)
Coll of St. Joseph (VT)
Coll of Saint Mary (NE)
The Coll of Saint Rose (NY)
The Coll of St. Scholastica (MN)
Coll of Staten Island of the City U of New York (NY)
Coll of the Atlantic (ME)
Coll of the Holy Cross (MA)
Coll of the Ozarks (MO)
The Coll of William and Mary (VA)
The Coll of Wooster (OH)
The Colorado Coll (CO)
Colorado Mesa U (CO)
Colorado State U (CO)
Columbia Coll (MO)
Columbia Coll (SC)
Columbia U, School of General Studies (NY)
Columbus State U (GA)
Concordia Coll (MN)
Concordia Coll–New York (NY)
Concordia U (CA)
Concordia U (MI)
Concordia U (QC, Canada)
Concordia U Chicago (IL)
Concordia U, Nebraska (NE)
Concordia U, St. Paul (MN)
Connecticut Coll (CT)
Converse Coll (SC)
Corban U (OR)
Cornell Coll (IA)
Cornell U (NY)
Cornerstone U (MI)
Covenant Coll (GA)
Crandall U (NB, Canada)
Creighton U (NE)
Crown Coll (MN)
Culver-Stockton Coll (MO)
Curry Coll (MA)
Daemen Coll (NY)
Dalhousie U (NS, Canada)
Dallas Baptist U (TX)
Dallas Christian Coll (TX)
Daniel Webster Coll (NH)
Dartmouth Coll (NH)
Davidson Coll (NC)
Defiance Coll (OH)
Delaware State U (DE)
Delta State U (MS)

Denison U (OH)
DePaul U (IL)
DePauw U (IN)
DEREE - The American Coll of Greece (Greece)
DeSales U (PA)
Dickinson Coll (PA)
Dillard U (LA)
Dixie State Coll of Utah (UT)
Doane Coll (NE)
Dominican Coll (NY)
Dominican U (IL)
Dominican U of California (CA)
Dordt Coll (IA)
Dowling Coll (NY)
Drake U (IA)
Drew U (NJ)
Drexel U (PA)
Drury U (MO)
Duquesne U (PA)
Earlham Coll (IN)
East Carolina U (NC)
East Central U (OK)
Eastern Connecticut State U (CT)
Eastern Illinois U (IL)
Eastern Kentucky U (KY)
Eastern Mennonite U (VA)
Eastern Michigan U (MI)
Eastern New Mexico U (NM)
Eastern Oregon U (OR)
Eastern U (PA)
Eastern Washington U (WA)
East Stroudsburg U of Pennsylvania (PA)
East Tennessee State U (TN)
East Texas Baptist U (TX)
Eckerd Coll (FL)
Edgewood Coll (WI)
Edinboro U of Pennsylvania (PA)
Edward Waters Coll (FL)
Elizabeth City State U (NC)
Elizabethtown Coll (PA)
Elmhurst Coll (IL)
Elmira Coll (NY)
Elon U (NC)
Emmanuel Coll (GA)
Emmanuel Coll (MA)
Emory & Henry Coll (VA)
Emory U (GA)
Emporia State U (KS)
Endicott Coll (MA)
Evangel U (MO)
Excelsior Coll (NY)
Fairfield U (CT)
Fairleigh Dickinson U, Coll at Florham (NJ)
Fairleigh Dickinson U, Metropolitan Campus (NJ)
Fairmont State U (WV)
Faulkner U (AL)
Fayetteville State U (NC)
Felician Coll (NJ)
Ferris State U (MI)
Ferrum Coll (VA)
Fitchburg State U (MA)
Flagler Coll (FL)
Florida Ag and Mech U (FL)
Florida Atlantic U (FL)
Florida Gulf Coast U (FL)
Florida Inst of Technology (FL)
Florida Intl U (FL)
Florida Southern Coll (FL)
Florida State U (FL)
Fontbonne U (MO)
Fordham U (NY)
Fort Hays State U (KS)
Fort Lewis Coll (CO)
Framingham State U (MA)
Franciscan U of Steubenville (OH)
Francis Marion U (SC)
Franklin & Marshall Coll (PA)
Franklin Coll (IN)
Friends U (KS)
Furman U (SC)
Gallaudet U (DC)
Gannon U (PA)
Gardner-Webb U (NC)
Geneva Coll (PA)
George Fox U (OR)
George Mason U (VA)
Georgetown Coll (KY)
The George Washington U (DC)
Georgia Coll & State U (GA)
Georgia Gwinnett Coll (GA)
Georgian Court U (NJ)

INDEXES

Saint Martin's U (WA)
Saint Mary-of-the-Woods Coll (IN)
Saint Mary's Coll (IN)
Saint Mary's Coll of California (CA)
St. Mary's Coll of Maryland (MD)
St. Mary's U (TX)
Saint Mary's U of Minnesota (MN)
Saint Michael's Coll (VT)
St. Norbert Coll (WI)
St. Olaf Coll (MN)
Saint Peter's Coll (NJ)
St. Thomas Aquinas Coll (NY)
St. Thomas U (FL)
St. Thomas U (NB, Canada)
Saint Vincent Coll (PA)
Salem State U (MA)
Salisbury U (MD)
Salve Regina U (RI)
Samford U (AL)
Sam Houston State U (TX)
San Diego Christian Coll (CA)
San Diego State U (CA)
San Francisco State U (CA)
Santa Clara U (CA)
Sarah Lawrence Coll (NY)
Schreiner U (TX)
Scripps Coll (CA)
Seattle Pacific U (WA)
Seattle U (WA)
Seton Hill U (PA)
Sewanee: The U of the South (TN)
Shawnee State U (OH)
Shaw U (NC)
Shenandoah U (VA)
Shepherd U (WV)
Shippensburg U of Pennsylvania (PA)
Shorter U (GA)
Siena Coll (NY)
Siena Heights U (MI)
Sierra Nevada Coll (NV)
Simmons Coll (MA)
Simon Fraser U (BC, Canada)
Simpson Coll (IA)
Simpson U (CA)
Skidmore Coll (NY)
Slippery Rock U of Pennsylvania (PA)
Smith Coll (MA)
Sojourner-Douglass Coll (MD)
Sonoma State U (CA)
South Carolina State U (SC)
South Dakota State U (SD)
Southeastern Louisiana U (LA)
Southeastern Oklahoma State U (OK)
Southeastern U (FL)
Southeast Missouri State U (MO)
Southern Arkansas U–Magnolia (AR)
Southern Connecticut State U (CT)
Southern Illinois U Carbondale (IL)
Southern Illinois U Edwardsville (IL)
Southern Methodist U (TX)
Southern New Hampshire U (NH)
Southern Oregon U (OR)
Southern Polytechnic State U (GA)
Southern Vermont Coll (VT)
South U (AL)
South U, Royal Palm Beach (FL)
South U, Tampa (FL)
South U (GA)
South U (MI)
South U, Columbia (SC)
South U (TX)
South U, Glen Allen (VA)
South U, Virginia Beach (VA)
Southwest Baptist U (MO)
Southwestern Adventist U (TX)
Southwestern Coll (KS)
Southwestern Oklahoma State U (OK)
Southwestern U (TX)
Southwest Minnesota State U (MN)
Spalding U (KY)
Spelman Coll (GA)
Spring Arbor U (MI)
Spring Hill Coll (AL)
Stanford U (CA)
State U of New York at Binghamton (NY)
State U of New York at Fredonia (NY)

State U of New York at New Paltz (NY)
State U of New York at Oswego (NY)
State U of New York at Plattsburgh (NY)
State U of New York Coll at Cortland (NY)
State U of New York Coll at Geneseo (NY)
State U of New York Coll at Old Westbury (NY)
State U of New York Coll at Oneonta (NY)
State U of New York Coll at Potsdam (NY)
Stephen F. Austin State U (TX)
Stephens Coll (MO)
Stetson U (FL)
Stevenson U (MD)
Stillman Coll (AL)
Stonehill Coll (MA)
Stony Brook U, State U of New York (NY)
Suffolk U (MA)
Sul Ross State U (TX)
Susquehanna U (PA)
Swarthmore Coll (PA)
Sweet Briar Coll (VA)
Syracuse U (NY)
Tabor Coll (KS)
Tarleton State U (TX)
Taylor U (IN)
Temple U (PA)
Texas A&M Intl U (TX)
Texas A&M U (TX)
Texas A&M U–Corpus Christi (TX)
Texas A&M U–Kingsville (TX)
Texas Christian U (TX)
Texas Lutheran U (TX)
Texas Southern U (TX)
Texas State U–San Marcos (TX)
Texas Tech U (TX)
Texas Wesleyan U (TX)
Texas Woman's U (TX)
Thiel Coll (PA)
Thomas Edison State Coll (NJ)
Thomas More Coll (KY)
Thomas U (GA)
Thompson Rivers U (BC, Canada)
Tiffin U (OH)
Touro Coll (NY)
Towson U (MD)
Transylvania U (KY)
Trent U (ON, Canada)
Trevecca Nazarene U (TN)
Trine U (IN)
Trinity Christian Coll (IL)
Trinity Coll (CT)
Trinity Coll of Florida (FL)
Trinity Lutheran Coll (WA)
Trinity U (TX)
Troy U (AL)
Truett-McConnell Coll (GA)
Truman State U (MO)
Tufts U (MA)
Tulane U (LA)
Tusculum Coll (TN)
Tuskegee U (AL)
Union Coll (KY)
Union Coll (NE)
Union Coll (NY)
Union U (TN)
United States Intl U (Kenya)
United States Military Acad (NY)
Universidad del Turabo (PR)
Université de Sherbrooke (QC, Canada)
U at Albany, State U of New York (NY)
U at Buffalo, the State U of New York (NY)
The U of Akron (OH)
The U of Alabama (AL)
The U of Alabama at Birmingham (AL)
The U of Alabama in Huntsville (AL)
U of Alaska Anchorage (AK)
U of Alaska Fairbanks (AK)
U of Alberta (AB, Canada)
The U of Arizona (AZ)
U of Arkansas (AR)
U of Arkansas at Little Rock (AR)
U of Arkansas at Monticello (AR)
U of Arkansas–Fort Smith (AR)

U of Bridgeport (CT)
The U of British Columbia (BC, Canada)
The U of British Columbia–Okanagan (BC, Canada)
U of California, Berkeley (CA)
U of California, Davis (CA)
U of California, Irvine (CA)
U of California, Los Angeles (CA)
U of California, Merced (CA)
U of California, Riverside (CA)
U of California, Santa Barbara (CA)
U of California, Santa Cruz (CA)
U of Central Arkansas (AR)
U of Central Florida (FL)
U of Central Missouri (MO)
U of Charleston (WV)
U of Cincinnati (OH)
U of Colorado at Colorado Springs (CO)
U of Colorado Boulder (CO)
U of Colorado Denver (CO)
U of Connecticut (CT)
U of Dallas (TX)
U of Dayton (OH)
U of Delaware (DE)
U of Denver (CO)
U of Dubuque (IA)
U of Evansville (IN)
The U of Findlay (OH)
U of Florida (FL)
U of Georgia (GA)
U of Great Falls (MT)
U of Guam (GU)
U of Guelph (ON, Canada)
U of Hartford (CT)
U of Hawaii at Hilo (HI)
U of Hawaii at Manoa (HI)
U of Hawaii–West Oahu (HI)
U of Houston (TX)
U of Houston–Clear Lake (TX)
U of Houston–Downtown (TX)
U of Houston–Victoria (TX)
U of Idaho (ID)
U of Illinois at Chicago (IL)
U of Illinois at Springfield (IL)
U of Illinois at Urbana–Champaign (IL)
U of Indianapolis (IN)
The U of Iowa (IA)
The U of Kansas (KS)
U of La Verne (CA)
U of Lethbridge (AB, Canada)
U of Louisiana at Lafayette (LA)
U of Louisiana at Monroe (LA)
U of Louisville (KY)
U of Maine (ME)
U of Maine at Farmington (ME)
U of Maine at Presque Isle (ME)
U of Mary (ND)
U of Mary Hardin-Baylor (TX)
U of Maryland, Baltimore County (MD)
U of Maryland, Coll Park (MD)
U of Maryland U Coll (MD)
U of Mary Washington (VA)
U of Massachusetts Amherst (MA)
U of Massachusetts Boston (MA)
U of Massachusetts Dartmouth (MA)
U of Massachusetts Lowell (MA)
U of Memphis (TN)
U of Miami (FL)
U of Michigan (MI)
U of Michigan–Dearborn (MI)
U of Michigan–Flint (MI)
U of Minnesota, Duluth (MN)
U of Minnesota, Twin Cities Campus (MN)
U of Mississippi (MS)
U of Missouri (MO)
U of Missouri–Kansas City (MO)
U of Missouri–St. Louis (MO)
U of Mobile (AL)
The U of Montana Western (MT)
U of Mount Union (OH)
U of Nebraska at Kearney (NE)
U of Nebraska at Omaha (NE)
U of Nebraska–Lincoln (NE)
U of Nevada, Las Vegas (NV)
U of Nevada, Reno (NV)
U of New England (ME)
U of New Hampshire (NH)
U of New Hampshire at Manchester (NH)

U of New Haven (CT)
U of New Mexico (NM)
U of New Orleans (LA)
U of North Alabama (AL)
The U of North Carolina at Asheville (NC)
The U of North Carolina at Chapel Hill (NC)
The U of North Carolina at Charlotte (NC)
The U of North Carolina Wilmington (NC)
U of North Dakota (ND)
U of Northern Colorado (CO)
U of Northern Iowa (IA)
U of North Florida (FL)
U of North Texas (TX)
U of Notre Dame (IN)
U of Oklahoma (OK)
U of Oregon (OR)
U of Ottawa (ON, Canada)
U of Pennsylvania (PA)
U of Pikeville (KY)
U of Pittsburgh (PA)
U of Pittsburgh at Bradford (PA)
U of Pittsburgh at Greensburg (PA)
U of Pittsburgh at Johnstown (PA)
U of Portland (OR)
U of Puerto Rico at Ponce (PR)
U of Puget Sound (WA)
U of Redlands (CA)
U of Regina (SK, Canada)
U of Rhode Island (RI)
U of Richmond (VA)
U of Rochester (NY)
U of St. Francis (IL)
U of Saint Francis (IN)
U of Saint Joseph (CT)
U of Saint Mary (KS)
U of St. Thomas (MN)
U of St. Thomas (TX)
U of San Diego (CA)
U of Science and Arts of Oklahoma (OK)
The U of Scranton (PA)
U of South Alabama (AL)
U of South Carolina Aiken (SC)
U of South Carolina Beaufort (SC)
U of South Carolina Upstate (SC)
The U of South Dakota (SD)
U of Southern California (CA)
U of Southern Indiana (IN)
U of Southern Maine (ME)
U of Southern Mississippi (MS)
U of South Florida (FL)
U of South Florida–St. Petersburg Campus (FL)
The U of Tampa (FL)
The U of Tennessee (TN)
The U of Tennessee at Chattanooga (TN)
The U of Tennessee at Martin (TN)
The U of Texas at Arlington (TX)
The U of Texas at Austin (TX)
The U of Texas at Dallas (TX)
The U of Texas at El Paso (TX)
The U of Texas at San Antonio (TX)
The U of Texas at Tyler (TX)
The U of Texas of the Permian Basin (TX)
The U of Texas–Pan American (TX)
U of the Cumberlands (KY)
U of the District of Columbia (DC)
U of the Incarnate Word (TX)
U of the Ozarks (AR)
U of the Pacific (CA)
U of the Sciences in Philadelphia (PA)
U of the Southwest (NM)
The U of Toledo (OH)
U of Tulsa (OK)
U of Utah (UT)
U of Vermont (VT)
U of Virginia (VA)
The U of Virginia's Coll at Wise (VA)
U of Washington (WA)
The U of West Alabama (AL)
The U of Western Ontario (ON, Canada)
U of West Florida (FL)
U of West Georgia (GA)
U of Windsor (ON, Canada)
U of Wisconsin–Eau Claire (WI)
U of Wisconsin–Green Bay (WI)
U of Wisconsin–La Crosse (WI)

U of Wisconsin–Madison (WI)
U of Wisconsin–Milwaukee (WI)
U of Wisconsin–Platteville (WI)
U of Wisconsin–River Falls (WI)
U of Wisconsin–Stevens Point (WI)
U of Wisconsin–Stout (WI)
U of Wisconsin–Superior (WI)
U of Wisconsin–Whitewater (WI)
U of Wyoming (WY)
Upper Iowa U (IA)
Ursuline Coll (OH)
Utah State U (UT)
Utah Valley U (UT)
Utica Coll (NY)
Valdosta State U (GA)
Valley City State U (ND)
Valparaiso U (IN)
Vanderbilt U (TN)
Vanguard U of Southern California (CA)
Vassar Coll (NY)
Villanova U (PA)
Virginia Commonwealth U (VA)
Virginia Intermont Coll (VA)
Virginia Polytechnic Inst and State U (VA)
Virginia State U (VA)
Virginia Union U (VA)
Virginia Wesleyan Coll (VA)
Viterbo U (WI)
Wabash Coll (IN)
Wagner Coll (NY)
Wake Forest U (NC)
Walden U (MN)
Waldorf Coll (IA)
Walsh U (OH)
Warren Wilson Coll (NC)
Wartburg Coll (IA)
Washburn U (KS)
Washington Adventist U (MD)
Washington & Jefferson Coll (PA)
Washington and Lee U (VA)
Washington Coll (MD)
Washington State U (WA)
Washington U in St. Louis (MO)
Wayland Baptist U (TX)
Waynesburg U (PA)
Wayne State Coll (NE)
Wayne State U (MI)
Weber State U (UT)
Webster U (MO)
Wellesley Coll (MA)
Wells Coll (NY)
Wesleyan Coll (GA)
Wesleyan U (CT)
West Chester U of Pennsylvania (PA)
Western Carolina U (NC)
Western Connecticut State U (CT)
Western Illinois U (IL)
Western Kentucky U (KY)
Western Michigan U (MI)
Western New England U (MA)
Western Oregon U (OR)
Western State Coll of Colorado (CO)
Western Washington U (WA)
Westfield State U (MA)
West Liberty U (WV)
Westminster Coll (MO)
Westminster Coll (UT)
West Texas A&M U (TX)
West Virginia State U (WV)
West Virginia U (WV)
West Virginia U Inst of Technology (WV)
West Virginia Wesleyan Coll (WV)
Wheaton Coll (IL)
Wheaton Coll (MA)
Wheeling Jesuit U (WV)
Whitman Coll (WA)
Whittier Coll (CA)
Wichita State U (KS)
Widener U (PA)
Wilkes U (PA)
Willamette U (OR)
William Jessup U (CA)
William Jewell Coll (MO)
William Paterson U of New Jersey (NJ)
William Penn U (IA)
Williams Baptist Coll (AR)
Williams Coll (MA)
William Woods U (MO)
Wilmington Coll (OH)

Wilmington U (DE)
Wilson Coll (PA)
Wingate U (NC)
Winona State U (MN)
Winthrop U (SC)
Wittenberg U (OH)
Wofford Coll (SC)
Woodbury U (CA)
Worcester State U (MA)
Wright State U (OH)
Xavier U (OH)
Xavier U of Louisiana (LA)
Yale U (CT)
Yeshiva U (NY)
York Coll of Pennsylvania (PA)
York Coll of the City U of New York (NY)
Youngstown State U (OH)

PSYCHOLOGY RELATED

Adams State Coll (CO)
Alvernia U (PA)
American Jewish U (CA)
Buena Vista U (IA)
Burlington Coll (VT)
California Baptist U (CA)
East Central U (OK)
The Evergreen State Coll (WA)
Kean U (NJ)
Loyola U New Orleans (LA)
Madonna U (MI)
Mary Baldwin Coll (VA)
Mayville State U (ND)
Northwest Christian U (OR)
Ohio Northern U (OH)
Prescott Coll (AZ)
Saint Mary's Coll of California (CA)
St. Mary's Coll of Maryland (MD)
State U of New York at Oswego (NY)
Swarthmore Coll (PA)
Towson U (MD)
U of Michigan–Flint (MI)
U of New England (ME)
U of St. Thomas (MN)
The U of Toledo (OH)
The U of Western Ontario (ON, Canada)
Valley Forge Christian Coll Woodbridge Campus (VA)
Western State Coll of Colorado (CO)

PSYCHOLOGY TEACHER EDUCATION

Albion Coll (MI)
Alma Coll (MI)
Bradley U (IL)
Brigham Young U (UT)
California Lutheran U (CA)
Campbellsville U (KY)
Concordia U (MI)
Lee U (TN)
Lenoir-Rhyne U (NC)
Ohio Wesleyan U (OH)
Pittsburg State U (KS)
Rocky Mountain Coll (MT)
St. Ambrose U (IA)
Tusculum Coll (TN)
U of Delaware (DE)
U of Missouri–St. Louis (MO)
Valparaiso U (IN)
Wayne State Coll (NE)
Widener U (PA)

PUBLIC ADMINISTRATION

Alfred U (NY)
American U of Beirut (Lebanon)
Athabasca U (AB, Canada)
Auburn U (AL)
Auburn U Montgomery (AL)
Augustana Coll (IL)
Bayamón Central U (PR)
Baylor U (TX)
Bernard M. Baruch Coll of the City U of New York (NY)
Biola U (CA)
Blackburn Coll (IL)
Bowling Green State U (OH)
Buena Vista U (IA)
California Lutheran U (CA)
California State U, Bakersfield (CA)
California State U, Chico (CA)

California State U, Dominguez Hills (CA)
California State U, East Bay (CA)
California State U, Fresno (CA)
California State U, Fullerton (CA)
California State U, San Bernardino (CA)
Calvin Coll (MI)
Capital U (OH)
Cedarville U (OH)
Central Methodist U (MO)
Cleveland State U (OH)
Colorado Mesa U (CO)
Concordia U (QC, Canada)
Doane Coll (NE)
Eastern Michigan U (MI)
Eastern Washington U (WA)
Edward Waters Coll (FL)
Elizabethtown Coll (PA)
Elon U (NC)
Evangel U (MO)
The Evergreen State Coll (WA)
Ferris State U (MI)
Flagler Coll (FL)
Florida Atlantic U (FL)
Florida Intl U (FL)
George Mason U (VA)
Governors State U (IL)
Grand Valley State U (MI)
Harding U (AR)
Hawai`i Pacific U (HI)
Heidelberg U (OH)
Indiana U Bloomington (IN)
Indiana U East (IN)
Indiana U Kokomo (IN)
Indiana U Northwest (IN)
Indiana U–Purdue U Fort Wayne (IN)
Indiana U–Purdue U Indianapolis (IN)
Indiana U South Bend (IN)
Inter American U of Puerto Rico, San Germán Campus (PR)
Iowa State U of Science and Technology (IA)
James Madison U (VA)
John Carroll U (OH)
John Jay Coll of Criminal Justice of the City U of New York (NY)
Juniata Coll (PA)
Kean U (NJ)
Kentucky State U (KY)
Kutztown U of Pennsylvania (PA)
La Salle U (PA)
Lewis U (IL)
Lincoln U (MO)
Lincoln U (PA)
Lipscomb U (TN)
Long Island U–C. W. Post Campus (NY)
Louisiana Coll (LA)
Metropolitan State U (MN)
Miami U (OH)
MidAmerica Nazarene U (KS)
Midwestern State U (TX)
Millsaps Coll (MS)
Minnesota State U Mankato (MN)
Mississippi U for Women (MS)
Mississippi Valley State U (MS)
Missouri State U (MO)
New York U (NY)
Northern Michigan U (MI)
Northern State U (SD)
Northwest Missouri State U (MO)
Oakland U (MI)
Ohio Wesleyan U (OH)
Park U (MO)
Plymouth State U (NH)
Point Park U (PA)
Regent U (VA)
Regis U (CO)
Rhode Island Coll (RI)
Rogers State U (OK)
Roger Williams U (RI)
Roosevelt U (IL)
Ryerson U (ON, Canada)
Saginaw Valley State U (MI)
St. Ambrose U (IA)
Saint Francis U (PA)
St. John's U (NY)
Saint Joseph's U (PA)
St. Thomas U (FL)
Samford U (AL)
San Diego State U (CA)
Seattle U (WA)

Shaw U (NC)
Shenandoah U (VA)
Shippensburg U of Pennsylvania (PA)
Siena Heights U (MI)
Sojourner-Douglass Coll (MD)
Southern New Hampshire U (NH)
Southwest Minnesota State U (MN)
Stephen F. Austin State U (TX)
Stonehill Coll (MA)
Suffolk U (MA)
Syracuse U (NY)
Texas Southern U (TX)
Texas State U–San Marcos (TX)
Thomas Edison State Coll (NJ)
Union Inst & U (OH)
Universidad del Turabo (PR)
U at Albany, State U of New York (NY)
U of Central Arkansas (AR)
U of Central Florida (FL)
U of Guam (GU)
U of Guelph (ON, Canada)
U of Hawaii–West Oahu (HI)
U of Houston–Clear Lake (TX)
The U of Kansas (KS)
U of La Verne (CA)
U of Maine at Augusta (ME)
U of Maine at Fort Kent (ME)
U of Michigan–Flint (MI)
U of Missouri–St. Louis (MO)
U of New Haven (CT)
U of North Dakota (ND)
U of Northern Iowa (IA)
U of North Texas (TX)
U of Oklahoma (OK)
U of Oregon (OR)
U of Ottawa (ON, Canada)
U of Pittsburgh (PA)
U of Regina (SK, Canada)
U of St. Thomas (MN)
The U of Tennessee (TN)
The U of Tennessee at Martin (TN)
The U of Texas at Dallas (TX)
U of Toronto (ON, Canada)
U of Washington (WA)
The U of Western Ontario (ON, Canada)
U of Wisconsin–Green Bay (WI)
U of Wisconsin–La Crosse (WI)
U of Wisconsin–Stevens Point (WI)
U of Wisconsin–Whitewater (WI)
Upper Iowa U (IA)
Virginia State U (VA)
Wagner Coll (NY)
Walden U (MN)
Washburn U (KS)
Waynesburg U (PA)
Wayne State U (MI)
Western Carolina U (NC)
Western Oregon U (OR)
West Texas A&M U (TX)
West Virginia U Inst of Technology (WV)
Winona State U (MN)

PUBLIC ADMINISTRATION AND SOCIAL SERVICE PROFESSIONS RELATED

Columbia Coll (SC)
Delaware State U (DE)
Emory & Henry Coll (VA)
The Evergreen State Coll (WA)
Kentucky Wesleyan Coll (KY)
Lasell Coll (MA)
Milligan Coll (TN)
National-Louis U (IL)
New York U (NY)
Northeastern Illinois U (IL)
Prescott Coll (AZ)
State U of New York Empire State Coll (NY)
Trevecca Nazarene U (TN)
Troy U (AL)
U of Maryland U Coll (MD)
U of Massachusetts Boston (MA)
U of Minnesota, Twin Cities Campus (MN)
U of Southern Maine (ME)

PUBLIC/APPLIED HISTORY

Arkansas Tech U (AR)
Concordia U (QC, Canada)
East Carolina U (NC)

McMurry U (TX)
North Dakota State U (ND)
Salem State U (MA)
U of California, Santa Barbara (CA)
Western Michigan U (MI)

PUBLIC HEALTH

Agnes Scott Coll (GA)
Alma Coll (MI)
American Public U System (WV)
Bluffton U (OH)
Boise State U (ID)
Bowling Green State U (OH)
California State U, Long Beach (CA)
Cape Breton U (NS, Canada)
Delaware State U (DE)
Dillard U (LA)
East Tennessee State U (TN)
Elon U (NC)
Fort Lewis Coll (CO)
Hunter Coll of the City U of New York (NY)
Indiana U Bloomington (IN)
The Johns Hopkins U (MD)
Marshall U (WV)
Minnesota State U Mankato (MN)
Northern Arizona U (AZ)
Purdue U (IN)
Rutgers, The State U of New Jersey, New Brunswick (NJ)
Ryerson U (ON, Canada)
Saint Francis U (PA)
St. Joseph's Coll, Long Island Campus (NY)
St. Joseph's Coll, New York (NY)
Saint Louis U (MO)
Santa Clara U (CA)
Slippery Rock U of Pennsylvania (PA)
Southern Connecticut State U (CT)
State U of New York Coll at Old Westbury (NY)
Trident U Intl (CA)
Tufts U (MA)
U at Albany, State U of New York (NY)
The U of Arizona (AZ)
U of Colorado Denver (CO)
U of Lethbridge (AB, Canada)
U of Massachusetts Amherst (MA)
U of Rochester (NY)
U of Southern Mississippi (MS)
The U of Tampa (FL)
The U of Texas at Austin (TX)
U of Washington (WA)
Walden U (MN)
West Chester U of Pennsylvania (PA)
Westminster Coll (UT)
William Paterson U of New Jersey (NJ)
Winona State U (MN)

PUBLIC HEALTH/COMMUNITY NURSING

Capital U (OH)
Hawai`i Pacific U (HI)
Northern Illinois U (IL)
The U of Western Ontario (ON, Canada)
Wright State U (OH)

PUBLIC HEALTH EDUCATION AND PROMOTION

Appalachian State U (NC)
Baldwin-Wallace Coll (OH)
California State U, Long Beach (CA)
Central Michigan U (MI)
Chicago State U (IL)
Coastal Carolina U (SC)
Dalhousie U (NS, Canada)
East Carolina U (NC)
Eastern Washington U (WA)
Georgia Southern U (GA)
Inter American U of Puerto Rico, Ponce Campus (PR)
Ithaca Coll (NY)
Liberty U (VA)
Louisiana State U in Shreveport (LA)
Lynchburg Coll (VA)

Malone U (OH)
Marymount U (VA)
Mississippi U for Women (MS)
Montana State U–Northern (MT)
New Mexico State U (NM)
North Carolina Central U (NC)
Oklahoma State U (OK)
Plymouth State U (NH)
Simmons Coll (MA)
Southeastern Louisiana U (LA)
Temple U (PA)
Texas State U–San Marcos (TX)
Thomas Edison State Coll (NJ)
U of Georgia (GA)
The U of Iowa (IA)
U of Michigan–Flint (MI)
The U of North Carolina at Charlotte (NC)
The U of North Carolina Wilmington (NC)
U of St. Thomas (MN)
The U of Scranton (PA)
U of Southern California (CA)
The U of Toledo (OH)
U of Utah (UT)
U of Wisconsin–La Crosse (WI)

PUBLIC HEALTH RELATED

Franklin & Marshall Coll (PA)
Hampshire Coll (MA)
Indiana U Bloomington (IN)
Indiana U–Purdue U Indianapolis (IN)
The Richard Stockton Coll of New Jersey (NJ)
U of California, Berkeley (CA)
U of California, Irvine (CA)
U of Illinois at Urbana–Champaign (IL)
U of Maryland, Coll Park (MD)
U of South Carolina (SC)
Utah State U (UT)

PUBLIC POLICY ANALYSIS

Albion Coll (MI)
Anna Maria Coll (MA)
Arizona State U (AZ)
Bentley U (MA)
Bernard M. Baruch Coll of the City U of New York (NY)
Brigham Young U (UT)
Carnegie Mellon U (PA)
Central Washington U (WA)
Chatham U (PA)
Coll of the Atlantic (ME)
The Coll of William and Mary (VA)
Cornell U (NY)
DePaul U (IL)
Dickinson Coll (PA)
The George Washington U (DC)
Georgia Inst of Technology (GA)
Georgia State U (GA)
Hamilton Coll (NY)
Hampshire Coll (MA)
Hobart and William Smith Colls (NY)
Howard Payne U (TX)
Indiana U–Purdue U Fort Wayne (IN)
Indiana Wesleyan U (IN)
Massachusetts Coll of Liberal Arts (MA)
Michigan State U (MI)
Mills Coll (CA)
New Coll of Florida (FL)
Penn State Harrisburg (PA)
Pomona Coll (CA)
Princeton U (NJ)
Regent U (VA)
Rice U (TX)
Rochester Inst of Technology (NY)
Sage Coll of Albany (NY)
St. Mary's Coll of Maryland (MD)
Saint Peter's Coll (NJ)
Saint Vincent Coll (PA)
Sarah Lawrence Coll (NY)
Scripps Coll (CA)
Simmons Coll (MA)
Southeastern U (FL)
Southern Methodist U (TX)
Stanford U (CA)
Suffolk U (MA)
Trevecca Nazarene U (TN)
Trinity Coll (CT)

U at Albany, State U of New York (NY)
U of California, Riverside (CA)
U of Charleston (WV)
U of Delaware (DE)
U of Denver (CO)
U of Michigan (MI)
U of Mississippi (MS)
The U of North Carolina at Chapel Hill (NC)
U of Pennsylvania (PA)
U of Regina (SK, Canada)
U of Rhode Island (RI)
U of Southern California (CA)
U of Southern Maine (ME)
The U of Texas at Dallas (TX)
The U of Toledo (OH)
U of Wisconsin–Whitewater (WI)
Vanderbilt U (TN)
Virginia Polytechnic Inst and State U (VA)
Wagner Coll (NY)
Washington State U (WA)
Wells Coll (NY)

PUBLIC POLICY ANALYSIS RELATED

Carlow U (PA)

PUBLIC RELATIONS, ADVERTISING, AND APPLIED COMMUNICATION

Butler U (IN)
California State U, Dominguez Hills (CA)
Goshen Coll (IN)
Houghton Coll (NY)
Howard Payne U (TX)
Lake Erie Coll (OH)
Lasell Coll (MA)
Massachusetts Coll of Liberal Arts (MA)
Oklahoma City U (OK)
Simpson Coll (IA)
Syracuse U (NY)
Taylor U (IN)
Texas Christian U (TX)

PUBLIC RELATIONS, ADVERTISING, AND APPLIED COMMUNICATION RELATED

Abilene Christian U (TX)
Belmont U (TN)
Bradley U (IL)
Brigham Young U (UT)
Buena Vista U (IA)
California Lutheran U (CA)
The Coll at Brockport, State U of New York (NY)
The Coll of St. Scholastica (MN)
Columbia Coll (MO)
DePaul U (IL)
Duquesne U (PA)
Eastern Kentucky U (KY)
Grace Coll (IN)
Hardin-Simmons U (TX)
Howard Payne U (TX)
John Brown U (AR)
Marietta Coll (OH)
Marywood U (PA)
Metropolitan State Coll of Denver (CO)
Missouri Western State U (MO)
Northern Michigan U (MI)
Ohio Northern U (OH)
Oklahoma City U (OK)
Oklahoma State U (OK)
Rochester Inst of Technology (NY)
St. John's U (NY)
Saint Mary's U of Minnesota (MN)
Southern New Hampshire U (NH)
Spring Arbor U (MI)
Spring Hill Coll (AL)
State U of New York at Plattsburgh (NY)
Temple U (PA)
Thompson Rivers U (BC, Canada)
U of Central Arkansas (AR)
The U of Tampa (FL)
U of Vermont (VT)
U of Wisconsin–River Falls (WI)
Virginia State U (VA)
Washington State U (WA)

Weber State U (UT)
Western Michigan U (MI)

PUBLIC RELATIONS/IMAGE MANAGEMENT

American U (DC)
Andrews U (MI)
Appalachian State U (NC)
Auburn U (AL)
Avila U (MO)
Baldwin-Wallace Coll (OH)
Barry U (FL)
Biola U (CA)
Bob Jones U (SC)
Boston U (MA)
Bowie State U (MD)
Bowling Green State U (OH)
Bradley U (IL)
Buffalo State Coll, State U of New York (NY)
California Baptist U (CA)
California Lutheran U (CA)
California State U, Chico (CA)
California State U, Dominguez Hills (CA)
California State U, East Bay (CA)
California State U, Fresno (CA)
California State U, Fullerton (CA)
California State U, Long Beach (CA)
Capital U (OH)
Cardinal Stritch U (WI)
Carroll Coll (MT)
Castleton State Coll (VT)
Central Washington U (WA)
Chapman U (CA)
Chatham U (PA)
Cleveland State U (OH)
Coe Coll (IA)
The Coll at Brockport, State U of New York (NY)
Coll of the Ozarks (MO)
Colorado State U (CO)
Columbia Coll Chicago (IL)
Curry Coll (MA)
Delaware State U (DE)
Dominican U (IL)
Drake U (IA)
Drury U (MO)
Duquesne U (PA)
Eastern Kentucky U (KY)
Eastern Michigan U (MI)
Ferris State U (MI)
Florida Ag and Mech U (FL)
Florida Southern Coll (FL)
Fort Hays State U (KS)
Franklin U (OH)
Georgia Southern U (GA)
Gonzaga U (WA)
Goshen Coll (IN)
Greenville Coll (IL)
Hampton U (VA)
Harding U (AR)
Hawai`i Pacific U (HI)
Heidelberg U (OH)
Hofstra U (NY)
Huntington U (IN)
Illinois State U (IL)
Indiana Wesleyan U (IN)
Inter American U of Puerto Rico, Ponce Campus (PR)
Iona Coll (NY)
Ithaca Coll (NY)
John Brown U (AR)
Kent State U (OH)
La Salle U (PA)
Lasell Coll (MA)
Lee U (TN)
Lewis U (IL)
Lipscomb U (TN)
Long Island U–C. W. Post Campus (NY)
Loras Coll (IA)
Mansfield U of Pennsylvania (PA)
Marquette U (WI)
The Master's Coll and Sem (CA)
McKendree U (IL)
McPherson Coll (KS)
Miami U (OH)
MidAmerica Nazarene U (KS)
Middle Tennessee State U (TN)
Minnesota State U Mankato (MN)
Mississippi Coll (MS)
Missouri Baptist U (MO)
Monmouth Coll (IL)

Montana State U Billings (MT)
Mount Mary Coll (WI)
Mount Mercy U (IA)
Mount Saint Mary Coll (NY)
Mount Vernon Nazarene U (OH)
New England Coll (NH)
New England School of Communications (ME)
North Carolina Ag and Tech State U (NC)
North Dakota State U (ND)
Northeastern State U (OK)
Northern Arizona U (AZ)
Northern Kentucky U (KY)
Northern Michigan U (MI)
Northwestern Coll (IA)
Northwestern Coll (MN)
Northwest Missouri State U (MO)
Ohio U–Zanesville (OH)
Oklahoma Christian U (OK)
Oklahoma City U (OK)
Otterbein U (OH)
Pepperdine U, Malibu (CA)
Point Park U (PA)
Quinnipiac U (CT)
Rider U (NJ)
Rochester Inst of Technology (NY)
Roosevelt U (IL)
Rowan U (NJ)
St. Ambrose U (IA)
Saint Francis U (PA)
Saint Joseph's Coll of Maine (ME)
Salem State U (MA)
San Diego State U (CA)
Seattle U (WA)
Simmons Coll (MA)
Slippery Rock U of Pennsylvania (PA)
Southern Methodist U (TX)
State U of New York at New Paltz (NY)
State U of New York at Oswego (NY)
Stephens Coll (MO)
Suffolk U (MA)
Syracuse U (NY)
Taylor U (IN)
Temple U (PA)
Texas State U–San Marcos (TX)
Texas Tech U (TX)
Tiffin U (OH)
Union Coll (NE)
Union U (TN)
The U of Akron (OH)
The U of Alabama (AL)
U of Central Missouri (MO)
U of Dayton (OH)
The U of Findlay (OH)
U of Florida (FL)
U of Georgia (GA)
U of Houston (TX)
U of Idaho (ID)
U of Louisiana at Lafayette (LA)
U of Northern Iowa (IA)
U of Oregon (OR)
U of Ottawa (ON, Canada)
U of Pittsburgh at Bradford (PA)
U of Rhode Island (RI)
U of Rio Grande (OH)
U of South Carolina (SC)
U of Southern California (CA)
The U of Tennessee (TN)
The U of Texas at Arlington (TX)
The U of Texas at Austin (TX)
U of Toronto (ON, Canada)
U of Wisconsin–River Falls (WI)
Ursuline Coll (OH)
Utica Coll (NY)
Wartburg Coll (IA)
Washington State U (WA)
Wayne State U (MI)
Weber State U (UT)
Webster U (MO)
Western Kentucky U (KY)
Western New England U (MA)
West Virginia Wesleyan Coll (WV)
William Penn U (IA)
William Woods U (MO)
Winona State U (MN)
Xavier U (OH)
York Coll of Pennsylvania (PA)

PUBLISHING

California State U, Chico (CA)

Graceland U (IA)
Rochester Inst of Technology (NY)
U of Missouri (MO)

PURCHASING, PROCUREMENT/ ACQUISITIONS AND CONTRACTS MANAGEMENT

Arizona State U (AZ)
California State U, East Bay (CA)
Central Michigan U (MI)
Northwest Florida State Coll (FL)
Potomac Coll (DC)
Saint Joseph's U (PA)
U of Houston–Downtown (TX)
U of Illinois at Urbana–Champaign (IL)
U of the District of Columbia (DC)

QUALITY CONTROL AND SAFETY TECHNOLOGIES RELATED

Madonna U (MI)
Rochester Inst of Technology (NY)

QUALITY CONTROL TECHNOLOGY

Bowling Green State U (OH)
California State U, Dominguez Hills (CA)
California State U, Long Beach (CA)
Ferris State U (MI)
Winona State U (MN)

RABBINICAL STUDIES

Ohr Somayach/Joseph Tanenbaum Educational Center (NY)

RADIATION BIOLOGY

Suffolk U (MA)

RADIATION PROTECTION/ HEALTH PHYSICS TECHNOLOGY

Indiana U Bloomington (IN)
Indiana U East (IN)
Indiana U Kokomo (IN)
Indiana U–Purdue U Indianapolis (IN)
Indiana U South Bend (IN)
Indiana U Southeast (IN)
Lewis U (IL)
Thomas Edison State Coll (NJ)

RADIO AND TELEVISION

American U (DC)
Appalachian State U (NC)
Arkansas State U (AR)
Auburn U (AL)
Ball State U (IN)
Barry U (FL)
Belmont U (TN)
Bemidji State U (MN)
Biola U (CA)
Bob Jones U (SC)
Boston U (MA)
Bowling Green State U (OH)
Bradley U (IL)
Buffalo State Coll, State U of New York (NY)
Butler U (IN)
California State U, Fresno (CA)
California State U, Fullerton (CA)
California State U, Long Beach (CA)
California State U, Los Angeles (CA)
California State U, Monterey Bay (CA)
Castleton State Coll (VT)
Cedarville U (OH)
Central Washington U (WA)
Chicago State U (IL)
The Coll at Brockport, State U of New York (NY)
Colorado State U (CO)
Columbia Coll Chicago (IL)
Curry Coll (MA)
Delaware State U (DE)
Drake U (IA)
Eastern Kentucky U (KY)

Evangel U (MO)
Fordham U (NY)
The George Washington U (DC)
Georgia Southern U (GA)
Grand Valley State U (MI)
Grand View U (IA)
Hardin-Simmons U (TX)
Hofstra U (NY)
Iona Coll (NY)
Ithaca Coll (NY)
John Brown U (AR)
Kent State U (OH)
Lamar U (TX)
La Salle U (PA)
Lasell Coll (MA)
Lebanese American U (Lebanon)
Lewis U (IL)
Loyola Marymount U (CA)
Marietta Coll (OH)
The Master's Coll and Sem (CA)
Messiah Coll (PA)
Minot State U (ND)
Missouri Baptist U (MO)
New York Inst of Technology (NY)
North Carolina Ag and Tech State U (NC)
North Central Coll (IL)
Northern Arizona U (AZ)
North Greenville U (SC)
Northwestern Coll (MN)
Northwest Missouri State U (MO)
Ohio Northern U (OH)
Ohio U (OH)
Oklahoma Christian U (OK)
Oklahoma City U (OK)
Otterbein U (OH)
Pacific U (OR)
Pittsburg State U (KS)
Point Park U (PA)
Rider U (NJ)
Ryerson U (ON, Canada)
St. Ambrose U (IA)
San Diego State U (CA)
San Francisco State U (CA)
Southeastern U (FL)
Southern Illinois U Carbondale (IL)
Southwestern Coll (KS)
Southwest Minnesota State U (MN)
State U of New York at Fredonia (NY)
State U of New York at Plattsburgh (NY)
Stephen F. Austin State U (TX)
Stephens Coll (MO)
Syracuse U (NY)
Temple U (PA)
Texas Christian U (TX)
Texas Southern U (TX)
Texas State U–San Marcos (TX)
Texas Tech U (TX)
Texas Wesleyan U (TX)
Troy U (AL)
Union U (TN)
The U of Akron (OH)
The U of Alabama (AL)
U of Arkansas at Little Rock (AR)
U of Central Florida (FL)
U of Central Missouri (MO)
U of Dayton (OH)
U of Florida (FL)
U of Houston (TX)
U of Miami (FL)
U of Missouri (MO)
U of North Texas (TX)
U of Pittsburgh at Bradford (PA)
U of Southern California (CA)
U of Southern Indiana (IN)
The U of Texas at Arlington (TX)
The U of Texas at Austin (TX)
U of the Incarnate Word (TX)
The U of Western Ontario (ON, Canada)
U of Wisconsin–River Falls (WI)
U of Wisconsin–Superior (WI)
Vanguard U of Southern California (CA)
Wartburg Coll (IA)
Waynesburg U (PA)
Wayne State U (MI)
Webster U (MO)
Western Illinois U (IL)
Western Kentucky U (KY)
William Woods U (MO)
Winona State U (MN)
Xavier U (OH)

Youngstown State U (OH)

RADIO AND TELEVISION BROADCASTING TECHNOLOGY

Asbury U (KY)
The Coll of Saint Rose (NY)
Coll of the Ozarks (MO)
Ferris State U (MI)
Gannon U (PA)
Gardner-Webb U (NC)
Goshen Coll (IN)
New England Inst of Technology (RI)
New England School of Communications (ME)
New York U (NY)
Northwest Nazarene U (ID)
Point Park U (PA)
Rowan U (NJ)
Suffolk U (MA)
Trevecca Nazarene U (TN)
U of Georgia (GA)

RADIOLOGIC TECHNOLOGY/ SCIENCE

Austin Peay State U (TN)
Baptist Coll of Health Sciences (TN)
Bluefield State Coll (WV)
Coll of St. Joseph (VT)
Colorado Mesa U (CO)
Dalhousie U (NS, Canada)
Fort Hays State U (KS)
Friends U (KS)
The George Washington U (DC)
Holy Family U (PA)
Indiana U Bloomington (IN)
Indiana U Kokomo (IN)
Indiana U Northwest (IN)
Indiana U South Bend (IN)
Indiana U Southeast (IN)
Inter American U of Puerto Rico, Ponce Campus (PR)
Inter American U of Puerto Rico, San Germán Campus (PR)
Jamestown Coll (ND)
Manhattan Coll (NY)
Marian U (WI)
Marshall U (WV)
Massachusetts Coll of Pharmacy and Health Sciences (MA)
McNeese State U (LA)
Missouri State U (MO)
North Dakota State U (ND)
Northern Michigan U (MI)
Northwestern State U of Louisiana (LA)
Oakland U (MI)
The Ohio State U (OH)
Oregon Inst of Technology (OR)
Presentation Coll (SD)
Quinnipiac U (CT)
St. John's U (NY)
Southeastern Louisiana U (LA)
State U of New York Upstate Medical U (NY)
U of Arkansas–Fort Smith (AR)
U of Charleston (WV)
U of Louisiana at Monroe (LA)
U of Mary (ND)
U of Missouri (MO)
U of Nebraska Medical Center (NE)
U of Oklahoma Health Sciences Center (OK)
U of Pittsburgh at Bradford (PA)
U of St. Francis (IL)
U of South Alabama (AL)
U of Toronto (ON, Canada)
Virginia Commonwealth U (VA)
Widener U (PA)
York Coll of Pennsylvania (PA)

RADIO, TELEVISION, AND DIGITAL COMMUNICATION RELATED

Brigham Young U (UT)
Clark Atlanta U (GA)
The Coll at Brockport, State U of New York (NY)
Drake U (IA)
Drury U (MO)
Hofstra U (NY)
Howard Payne U (TX)

John Brown U (AR)
Keystone Coll (PA)
Madonna U (MI)
Marquette U (WI)
Mitchell Coll (CT)
Neumann U (PA)
North Dakota State U (ND)
Rogers State U (OK)
Sacred Heart U (CT)
San Francisco State U (CA)
Spring Hill Coll (AL)
Texas Christian U (TX)
The U of Akron (OH)
Washington State U (WA)
Western Carolina U (NC)

RANGE SCIENCE AND MANAGEMENT

Colorado State U (CO)
Fort Hays State U (KS)
Humboldt State U (CA)
Montana State U (MT)
New Mexico State U (NM)
North Dakota State U (ND)
South Dakota State U (SD)
Sul Ross State U (TX)
Tarleton State U (TX)
Texas A&M U (TX)
Texas Tech U (TX)
U of Alberta (AB, Canada)
U of Idaho (ID)
U of Nebraska–Lincoln (NE)
U of Wyoming (WY)
Utah State U (UT)

READING TEACHER EDUCATION

Aquinas Coll (MI)
Baylor U (TX)
Boise State U (ID)
Catawba Coll (NC)
Clarion U of Pennsylvania (PA)
Concordia U Chicago (IL)
Dordt Coll (IA)
East Central U (OK)
Eastern Michigan U (MI)
Eastern Washington U (WA)
Grand Valley State U (MI)
Harding U (AR)
Hardin-Simmons U (TX)
Iowa Wesleyan Coll (IA)
Longwood U (VA)
Michigan State U (MI)
Midwestern State U (TX)
Roger Williams U (RI)
St. Joseph's Coll, Long Island Campus (NY)
St. Joseph's Coll, New York (NY)
Southeastern Louisiana U (LA)
State U of New York Coll at Cortland (NY)
State U of New York Coll at Oneonta (NY)
Texas A&M Intl U (TX)
Texas A&M U–Corpus Christi (TX)
Texas Wesleyan U (TX)
U of Alberta (AB, Canada)
U of Central Missouri (MO)
U of Great Falls (MT)
U of Northern Iowa (IA)
U of Southern Maine (ME)
U of Wisconsin–River Falls (WI)
U of Wisconsin–Superior (WI)
Upper Iowa U (IA)
Washington State U (WA)
Wheelock Coll (MA)
William Penn U (IA)
Wingate U (NC)
Winona State U (MN)
Wright State U (OH)

REAL ESTATE

Angelo State U (TX)
Arizona State U (AZ)
Baylor U (TX)
Bernard M. Baruch Coll of the City U of New York (NY)
Bowling Green State U (OH)
California State U, Dominguez Hills (CA)
California State U, East Bay (CA)
California State U, Fresno (CA)
Central Michigan U (MI)
Clarion U of Pennsylvania (PA)

Colorado State U (CO)
DePaul U (IL)
Eastern Kentucky U (KY)
Florida Atlantic U (FL)
Florida Intl U (FL)
Georgia State U (GA)
La Roche Coll (PA)
Marquette U (WI)
Marylhurst U (OR)
Menlo Coll (CA)
Minnesota State U Mankato (MN)
Mississippi State U (MS)
New Mexico State U (NM)
New York U (NY)
The Ohio State U (OH)
Portland State U (OR)
San Diego State U (CA)
Southern Methodist U (TX)
Syracuse U (NY)
Temple U (PA)
Texas Christian U (TX)
Thomas Edison State Coll (NJ)
The U of British Columbia (BC, Canada)
U of Central Florida (FL)
U of Cincinnati (OH)
U of Connecticut (CT)
U of Denver (CO)
U of Florida (FL)
U of Georgia (GA)
U of Guelph (ON, Canada)
U of Illinois at Urbana–Champaign (IL)
U of Miami (FL)
U of Mississippi (MS)
U of Missouri (MO)
U of Nebraska at Omaha (NE)
U of Nevada, Las Vegas (NV)
U of Northern Iowa (IA)
U of North Texas (TX)
U of Pennsylvania (PA)
U of St. Thomas (MN)
U of San Diego (CA)
U of South Carolina (SC)
The U of Texas at Arlington (TX)
The U of Texas at El Paso (TX)
U of West Georgia (GA)
U of Wisconsin–Madison (WI)
U of Wisconsin–Milwaukee (WI)
U of Wisconsin–Stout (WI)
Villanova U (PA)
Virginia Commonwealth U (VA)
Washington State U (WA)

RECORDING ARTS TECHNOLOGY

American U (DC)
The Art Inst of Atlanta (GA)
The Art Inst of Austin (TX)
The Art Inst of California, a college of Argosy U, Inland Empire (CA)
The Art Inst of California, a college of Argosy U, Los Angeles (CA)
The Art Inst of California, a college of Argosy U, San Diego (CA)
The Art Inst of California, a college of Argosy U, San Francisco (CA)
The Art Inst of Houston (TX)
The Art Inst of Las Vegas (NV)
The Art Inst of Philadelphia (PA)
The Art Inst of Seattle (WA)
The Art Inst of Tennessee–Nashville (TN)
The Art Inst of Washington (VA)
The Art Insts Intl Minnesota (MN)
Berklee Coll of Music (MA)
Butler U (IN)
Columbia Coll Chicago (IL)
Five Towns Coll (NY)
Greenville Coll (IL)
The Illinois Inst of Art–Chicago (IL)
The Illinois Inst of Art–Schaumburg (IL)
Indiana U Bloomington (IN)
Intl Acad of Design & Technology (FL)
Ithaca Coll (NY)
Lebanon Valley Coll (PA)
Loyola Marymount U (CA)
Malone U (OH)
Miami Intl U of Art & Design (FL)
Michigan Technological U (MI)
New England Inst of Technology (RI)

New England School of Communications (ME)
Peabody Conservatory of The Johns Hopkins U (MD)
Savannah Coll of Art and Design (GA)
State U of New York at Fredonia (NY)
Texas Southern U (TX)
Texas State U–San Marcos (TX)
U of Hartford (CT)
York Coll of Pennsylvania (PA)

REGIONAL STUDIES

The Colorado Coll (CO)
Columbia U, School of General Studies (NY)
Houghton Coll (NY)
Mercer U (GA)
Prescott Coll (AZ)
United States Military Acad (NY)
U of Mississippi (MS)
U of Southern Maine (ME)
Washington U in St. Louis (MO)

REGISTERED NURSING, NURSING ADMINISTRATION, NURSING RESEARCH AND CLINICAL NURSING RELATED

Anna Maria Coll (MA)
Cleveland State U (OH)
Rowan U (NJ)
St. Joseph's Coll, Long Island Campus (NY)
St. Joseph's Coll, New York (NY)
Union Coll (KY)

REGISTERED NURSING/ REGISTERED NURSE

Abilene Christian U (TX)
Adams State Coll (CO)
Adelphi U (NY)
Albany State U (GA)
Alcorn State U (MS)
Allen Coll (IA)
Alvernia U (PA)
Alverno Coll (WI)
American Public U System (WV)
American U of Beirut (Lebanon)
Anderson U (IN)
Andrews U (MI)
Angelo State U (TX)
Anna Maria Coll (MA)
Appalachian State U (NC)
Arizona State U (AZ)
Arkansas State U (AR)
Arkansas Tech U (AR)
Armstrong Atlantic State U (GA)
Athabasca U (AB, Canada)
Auburn U (AL)
Auburn U Montgomery (AL)
Augustana Coll (SD)
Austin Peay State U (TN)
Azusa Pacific U (CA)
Baker U (KS)
Ball State U (IN)
Baptist Coll of Health Sciences (TN)
Barry U (FL)
Barton Coll (NC)
Bayamón Central U (PR)
Baylor U (TX)
Becker Coll (MA)
Bellarmine U (KY)
Belmont U (TN)
Bemidji State U (MN)
Benedictine U (IL)
Berea Coll (KY)
Berry Coll (GA)
Bethel Coll (IN)
Bethel Coll (KS)
Bethel U (MN)
Bethel U (TN)
Bethune-Cookman U (FL)
Biola U (CA)
Blessing-Rieman Coll of Nursing (IL)
Bloomfield Coll (NJ)
Bloomsburg U of Pennsylvania (PA)
Bob Jones U (SC)
Boise State U (ID)
Boston Coll (MA)
Bowie State U (MD)
Bowling Green State U (OH)
Bradley U (IL)

Briar Cliff U (IA)
Caldwell Coll (NJ)
California Baptist U (CA)
California State U, Bakersfield (CA)
California State U, Chico (CA)
California State U, Dominguez Hills (CA)
California State U, East Bay (CA)
California State U, Fresno (CA)
California State U, Fullerton (CA)
California State U, Long Beach (CA)
California State U, Los Angeles (CA)
California State U, Sacramento (CA)
California State U, San Bernardino (CA)
California State U, Stanislaus (CA)
California U of Pennsylvania (PA)
Calvin Coll (MI)
Cape Breton U (NS, Canada)
Capella U (MN)
Capital U (OH)
Cardinal Stritch U (WI)
Carlow U (PA)
Carroll Coll (MT)
Carson-Newman Coll (TN)
Case Western Reserve U (OH)
Castleton State Coll (VT)
The Catholic U of America (DC)
Cedarville U (OH)
Central Connecticut State U (CT)
Central Methodist U (MO)
Chamberlain Coll of Nursing (AZ)
Chamberlain Coll of Nursing, Jacksonville (FL)
Chamberlain Coll of Nursing, Miramar (FL)
Chamberlain Coll of Nursing, Addison (IL)
Chamberlain Coll of Nursing, Chicago (IL)
Chamberlain Coll of Nursing (MO)
Chamberlain Coll of Nursing (OH)
Chamberlain Coll of Nursing (TX)
Chamberlain Coll of Nursing (VA)
Chaminade U of Honolulu (HI)
Chatham U (PA)
Chicago State U (IL)
Chipola Coll (FL)
Clarion U of Pennsylvania (PA)
Clarke U (IA)
Clarkson Coll (NE)
Clayton State U (GA)
Clemson U (SC)
Cleveland State U (OH)
Coastal Carolina U (SC)
Coe Coll (IA)
The Coll at Brockport, State U of New York (NY)
Coll of Coastal Georgia (GA)
Coll of Mount St. Joseph (OH)
Coll of Mount Saint Vincent (NY)
The Coll of New Jersey (NJ)
Coll of Saint Benedict (MN)
Coll of Saint Mary (NE)
The Coll of St. Scholastica (MN)
Coll of Staten Island of the City U of New York (NY)
Coll of the Ozarks (MO)
Colorado Mesa U (CO)
Columbia Centro Universitario, Yauco (PR)
Columbus State U (GA)
Concordia Coll (MN)
Concordia U (CA)
Concordia U Texas (TX)
Creighton U (NE)
Crown Coll (MN)
Culver-Stockton Coll (MO)
Curry Coll (MA)
Daemen Coll (NY)
Dalhousie U (NS, Canada)
Dalton State Coll (GA)
Davenport U, Grand Rapids (MI)
Defiance Coll (OH)
Delaware State U (DE)
Delta State U (MS)
DePaul U (IL)
DeSales U (PA)
Dillard U (LA)
Dixie State Coll of Utah (UT)
Dominican Coll (NY)
Dominican U (IL)

Dominican U of California (CA)
Dordt Coll (IA)
Drexel U (PA)
Duquesne U (PA)
East Carolina U (NC)
East Central U (OK)
Eastern Illinois U (IL)
Eastern Mennonite U (VA)
Eastern Michigan U (MI)
Eastern New Mexico U (NM)
Eastern U (PA)
Eastern Washington U (WA)
East Stroudsburg U of Pennsylvania (PA)
East Tennessee State U (TN)
East Texas Baptist U (TX)
Edgewood Coll (WI)
Edinboro U of Pennsylvania (PA)
Elmhurst Coll (IL)
Elmira Coll (NY)
Emory U (GA)
Emporia State U (KS)
Endicott Coll (MA)
Fairfield U (CT)
Fairleigh Dickinson U, Metropolitan Campus (NJ)
Fairmont State U (WV)
Farmingdale State Coll (NY)
Fayetteville State U (NC)
Felician Coll (NJ)
Ferris State U (MI)
Fitchburg State U (MA)
Florida Ag and Mech U (FL)
Florida Atlantic U (FL)
Florida Intl U (FL)
Florida National Coll (FL)
Florida Southern Coll (FL)
Florida State Coll at Jacksonville (FL)
Fort Hays State U (KS)
Framingham State U (MA)
Franciscan U of Steubenville (OH)
Francis Marion U (SC)
Gannon U (PA)
Gardner-Webb U (NC)
George Fox U (OR)
George Mason U (VA)
Georgia Coll & State U (GA)
Georgian Court U (NJ)
Georgia Southern U (GA)
Georgia Southwestern State U (GA)
Georgia State U (GA)
Glenville State Coll (WV)
Goldfarb School of Nursing at Barnes-Jewish Coll (MO)
Gonzaga U (WA)
Goodwin Coll (CT)
Goshen Coll (IN)
Governors State U (IL)
Graceland U (IA)
Grambling State U (LA)
Grand Valley State U (MI)
Grand View U (IA)
Gustavus Adolphus Coll (MN)
Gwynedd-Mercy Coll (PA)
Hampton U (VA)
Hannibal-LaGrange U (MO)
Harding U (AR)
Hardin-Simmons U (TX)
Hartwick Coll (NY)
Hawai'i Pacific U (HI)
Hope Coll (MI)
Humboldt State U (CA)
Hunter Coll of the City U of New York (NY)
Husson U (ME)
Idaho State U (ID)
Illinois State U (IL)
Illinois Wesleyan U (IL)
Immaculata U (PA)
Indiana State U (IN)
Indiana U Bloomington (IN)
Indiana U East (IN)
Indiana U Kokomo (IN)
Indiana U Northwest (IN)
Indiana U of Pennsylvania (PA)
Indiana U–Purdue U Fort Wayne (IN)
Indiana U–Purdue U Indianapolis (IN)
Indiana U South Bend (IN)
Indiana U Southeast (IN)
Indiana Wesleyan U (IN)
Indian River State Coll (FL)

Inter American U of Puerto Rico, San Germán Campus (PR)
Iowa Wesleyan Coll (IA)
Jacksonville State U (AL)
Jacksonville U (FL)
James Madison U (VA)
Jamestown Coll (ND)
The Johns Hopkins U (MD)
Keene State Coll (NH)
Kennesaw State U (GA)
Kent State U (OH)
Kent State U at Salem (OH)
Kent State U at Stark (OH)
Kent State U at Tuscarawas (OH)
Kentucky Christian U (KY)
Kentucky Mountain Bible Coll (KY)
Kentucky State U (KY)
Keuka Coll (NY)
King Coll (TN)
LaGrange Coll (GA)
Lakehead U (ON, Canada)
Lake Superior State U (MI)
Lamar U (TX)
La Roche Coll (PA)
La Salle U (PA)
Lehman Coll of the City U of New York (NY)
Le Moyne Coll (NY)
Lenoir-Rhyne U (NC)
Lewis-Clark State Coll (ID)
Lewis U (IL)
Lincoln Memorial U (TN)
Lincoln U (MO)
Lindsey Wilson Coll (KY)
Linfield Coll (OR)
Lipscomb U (TN)
Lock Haven U of Pennsylvania (PA)
Long Island U–Brooklyn Campus (NY)
Long Island U–C. W. Post Campus (NY)
Longwood U (VA)
Lourdes U (OH)
Loyola U Chicago (IL)
Lubbock Christian U (TX)
Luther Coll (IA)
Lynchburg Coll (VA)
Madonna U (MI)
Malone U (OH)
Mansfield U of Pennsylvania (PA)
Maranatha Baptist Bible Coll (WI)
Maria Coll (NY)
Marian U (WI)
Marquette U (WI)
Marshall U (WV)
Marymount U (VA)
Maryville Coll (TN)
Maryville U of Saint Louis (MO)
Massachusetts Coll of Pharmacy and Health Sciences (MA)
McKendree U (IL)
McMurry U (TX)
McNeese State U (LA)
Medcenter One Coll of Nursing (ND)
Medgar Evers Coll of the City U of New York (NY)
Medical U of South Carolina (SC)
Mercy Coll (NY)
Mercy Coll of Health Sciences (IA)
Mercy Coll of Ohio (OH)
Messiah Coll (PA)
Metropolitan State Coll of Denver (CO)
Metropolitan State U (MN)
Miami Dade Coll (FL)
Miami U (OH)
Michigan State U (MI)
MidAmerica Nazarene U (KS)
Middle Tennessee State U (TN)
Midwestern State U (TX)
Milligan Coll (TN)
Millikin U (IL)
Milwaukee School of Eng (WI)
Minnesota School of Business–Richfield (MN)
Minnesota State U Mankato (MN)
Minnesota State U Moorhead (MN)
Minot State U (ND)
Misericordia U (PA)
Mississippi Coll (MS)
Mississippi U for Women (MS)
Missouri Southern State U (MO)
Missouri State U (MO)

Missouri Western State U (MO)
Molloy Coll (NY)
Montana State U (MT)
Montana State U–Northern (MT)
Montana Tech of The U of Montana (MT)
Montreat Coll, Montreat (NC)
Moravian Coll (PA)
Morehead State U (KY)
Morningside Coll (IA)
Morrisville State Coll (NY)
Mountain State U (WV)
Mount Aloysius Coll (PA)
Mount Carmel Coll of Nursing (OH)
Mount Marty Coll (SD)
Mount Mercy U (IA)
Mount Saint Mary Coll (NY)
Mount St. Mary's Coll (CA)
Mount Vernon Nazarene U (OH)
Nazareth Coll of Rochester (NY)
Neumann U (PA)
Newberry Coll (SC)
Newman U (KS)
New Mexico Highlands U (NM)
New Mexico State U (NM)
New York City Coll of Technology of the City U of New York (NY)
New York Inst of Technology (NY)
New York U (NY)
Niagara U (NY)
Nicholls State U (LA)
Norfolk State U (VA)
North Carolina Ag and Tech State U (NC)
North Carolina Central U (NC)
North Dakota State U (ND)
Northeastern State U (OK)
Northeastern U (MA)
Northern Arizona U (AZ)
Northern Illinois U (IL)
Northern Kentucky U (KY)
Northern Michigan U (MI)
North Georgia Coll & State U (GA)
Northwestern Coll (IA)
Northwestern Oklahoma State U (OK)
Northwestern State U of Louisiana (LA)
Northwest Florida State Coll (FL)
Northwest Missouri State U (MO)
Northwest Nazarene U (ID)
Northwest U (WA)
Norwich U (VT)
Notre Dame of Maryland U (MD)
Nova Southeastern U (FL)
Nyack Coll (NY)
Oakland U (MI)
The Ohio State U (OH)
The Ohio State U at Lima (OH)
The Ohio State U at Marion (OH)
The Ohio State U–Mansfield Campus (OH)
Ohio U (OH)
Ohio U–Chillicothe (OH)
Oklahoma Christian U (OK)
Oklahoma City U (OK)
Old Dominion U (VA)
Olympic Coll (WA)
Oral Roberts U (OK)
Oregon Health & Science U (OR)
Otterbein U (OH)
Our Lady of the Lake Coll (LA)
Pace U (NY)
Pacific Lutheran U (WA)
Pacific Union Coll (CA)
Palm Beach Atlantic U (FL)
Penn State Abington (PA)
Penn State Altoona (PA)
Penn State Beaver (PA)
Penn State Berks (PA)
Penn State Brandywine (PA)
Penn State DuBois (PA)
Penn State Erie, The Behrend Coll (PA)
Penn State Fayette, The Eberly Campus (PA)
Penn State Greater Allegheny (PA)
Penn State Harrisburg (PA)
Penn State Hazleton (PA)
Penn State Lehigh Valley (PA)
Penn State Mont Alto (PA)
Penn State New Kensington (PA)
Penn State Schuylkill (PA)
Penn State Shenango (PA)
Penn State U Park (PA)

Penn State Wilkes-Barre (PA)
Penn State Worthington Scranton (PA)
Penn State York (PA)
Piedmont Coll (GA)
Pittsburg State U (KS)
Plymouth State U (NH)
Point Loma Nazarene U (CA)
Polk State Coll (FL)
Prairie View A&M U (TX)
Presentation Coll (SD)
Purdue U (IN)
Purdue U North Central (IN)
Queen's U at Kingston (ON, Canada)
Quincy U (IL)
Quinnipiac U (CT)
Radford U (VA)
Ramapo Coll of New Jersey (NJ)
Rasmussen Coll Fort Myers (FL)
Rasmussen Coll Land O' Lakes (FL)
Rasmussen Coll New Port Richey (FL)
Rasmussen Coll Tampa/Brandon (FL)
Regis Coll (MA)
Regis U (CO)
Research Coll of Nursing (MO)
Rhode Island Coll (RI)
The Richard Stockton Coll of New Jersey (NJ)
Rivier Coll (NH)
Robert Morris U (PA)
Roberts Wesleyan Coll (NY)
Rockford Coll (IL)
Rockhurst U (MO)
Rogers State U (OK)
Rowan U (NJ)
Russell Sage Coll (NY)
Rutgers, The State U of New Jersey, Camden (NJ)
Rutgers, The State U of New Jersey, Newark (NJ)
Rutgers, The State U of New Jersey, New Brunswick (NJ)
Ryerson U (ON, Canada)
Sacred Heart U (CT)
Sage Coll of Albany (NY)
Saginaw Valley State U (MI)
St. Ambrose U (IA)
St. Catherine U (MN)
Saint Francis Medical Center Coll of Nursing (IL)
Saint Francis U (PA)
St. John Fisher Coll (NY)
Saint John's U (MN)
Saint Joseph's Coll (IN)
St. Joseph's Coll, Long Island Campus (NY)
St. Joseph's Coll, New York (NY)
Saint Joseph's Coll of Maine (ME)
Saint Louis U (MO)
Saint Mary's Coll (IN)
Saint Mary's Coll of California (CA)
St. Olaf Coll (MN)
Saint Xavier U (IL)
Salem State U (MA)
Salisbury U (MD)
Salve Regina U (RI)
Samford U (AL)
Samuel Merritt U (CA)
San Diego State U (CA)
San Francisco State U (CA)
Seattle Pacific U (WA)
Seattle U (WA)
Shawnee State U (OH)
Shenandoah U (VA)
Shepherd U (WV)
Shorter U (GA)
Siena Heights U (MI)
Simmons Coll (MA)
Simpson U (CA)
Slippery Rock U of Pennsylvania (PA)
Sonoma State U (CA)
South Carolina State U (SC)
South Dakota State U (SD)
Southeastern Louisiana U (LA)
Southeast Missouri State U (MO)
Southern Arkansas U–Magnolia (AR)
Southern Connecticut State U (CT)
Southern Illinois U Edwardsville (IL)
Southern Oregon U (OR)

Southern Vermont Coll (VT)
South U (AL)
South U, Royal Palm Beach (FL)
South U, Tampa (FL)
South U (GA)
South U, Columbia (SC)
South U, Glen Allen (VA)
South U, Virginia Beach (VA)
Southwest Baptist U (MO)
Southwestern Adventist U (TX)
Southwestern Assemblies of God U (TX)
Southwestern Oklahoma State U (OK)
Spalding U (KY)
Spring Hill Coll (AL)
State Coll of Florida Manatee-Sarasota (FL)
State U of New York at Binghamton (NY)
State U of New York at New Paltz (NY)
State U of New York at Plattsburgh (NY)
State U of New York Coll of Technology at Canton (NY)
State U of New York Empire State Coll (NY)
Stephen F. Austin State U (TX)
Stevenson U (MD)
Stillman Coll (AL)
Stony Brook U, State of New York (NY)
Sullivan U (KY)
Tarleton State U (TX)
Temple U (PA)
Texas A&M Intl U (TX)
Texas A&M U–Corpus Christi (TX)
Texas Christian U (TX)
Texas State U–San Marcos (TX)
Texas Woman's U (TX)
Thomas Edison State Coll (NJ)
Thomas More Coll (KY)
Thomas U (GA)
Thompson Rivers U (BC, Canada)
Towson U (MD)
Trent U (ON, Canada)
Trevecca Nazarene U (TN)
Trinity Christian Coll (IL)
Trinity Coll of Nursing and Health Sciences (IL)
Troy U (AL)
Truman State U (MO)
Tuskegee U (AL)
Union Coll (NE)
Union U (TN)
Universidad del Turabo (PR)
Université de Sherbrooke (QC, Canada)
U at Buffalo, the State U of New York (NY)
The U of Alabama (AL)
The U of Alabama at Birmingham (AL)
The U of Alabama in Huntsville (AL)
U of Alaska Anchorage (AK)
U of Alberta (AB, Canada)
The U of Arizona (AZ)
U of Arkansas (AR)
U of Arkansas at Little Rock (AR)
U of Arkansas at Monticello (AR)
U of Arkansas–Fort Smith (AR)
The U of British Columbia (BC, Canada)
The U of British Columbia–Okanagan (BC, Canada)
U of Central Arkansas (AR)
U of Central Florida (FL)
U of Central Missouri (MO)
U of Charleston (WV)
U of Cincinnati (OH)
U of Colorado at Colorado Springs (CO)
U of Colorado Denver (CO)
U of Connecticut (CT)
U of Delaware (DE)
U of Dubuque (IA)
U of Evansville (IN)
U of Florida (FL)
U of Guam (GU)
U of Hartford (CT)
U of Hawaii at Hilo (HI)
U of Hawaii at Manoa (HI)
U of Houston–Victoria (TX)
U of Illinois at Chicago (IL)

INDEXES

The U of Iowa (IA)
The U of Kansas (KS)
U of Lethbridge (AB, Canada)
U of Louisiana at Lafayette (LA)
U of Louisiana at Monroe (LA)
U of Louisville (KY)
U of Maine (ME)
U of Maine at Augusta (ME)
U of Maine at Fort Kent (ME)
U of Mary (ND)
U of Mary Hardin-Baylor (TX)
U of Massachusetts Amherst (MA)
U of Massachusetts Boston (MA)
U of Massachusetts Dartmouth (MA)
U of Massachusetts Lowell (MA)
U of Memphis (TN)
U of Miami (FL)
U of Michigan (MI)
U of Michigan–Flint (MI)
U of Missouri (MO)
U of Missouri–Kansas City (MO)
U of Missouri–St. Louis (MO)
U of Mobile (AL)
U of Nebraska Medical Center (NE)
U of Nevada, Las Vegas (NV)
U of Nevada, Reno (NV)
U of New England (ME)
U of New Hampshire (NH)
U of New Mexico (NM)
U of North Alabama (AL)
The U of North Carolina at Chapel Hill (NC)
The U of North Carolina at Charlotte (NC)
The U of North Carolina Wilmington (NC)
U of North Dakota (ND)
U of Northern Colorado (CO)
U of North Florida (FL)
U of Oklahoma Health Sciences Center (OK)
U of Ottawa (ON, Canada)
U of Pennsylvania (PA)
U of Pikeville (KY)
U of Pittsburgh (PA)
U of Pittsburgh at Bradford (PA)
U of Portland (OR)
U of Puerto Rico at Humacao (PR)
U of Regina (SK, Canada)
U of Rhode Island (RI)
U of Rochester (NY)
U of St. Francis (IL)
U of Saint Francis (IN)
U of Saint Joseph (CT)
U of Saint Mary (KS)
The U of Scranton (PA)
U of South Alabama (AL)
U of South Carolina (SC)
U of South Carolina Aiken (SC)
U of South Carolina Beaufort (SC)
U of South Carolina Upstate (SC)
The U of South Dakota (SD)
U of Southern Indiana (IN)
U of Southern Maine (ME)
U of Southern Mississippi (MS)
U of South Florida (FL)
The U of Tampa (FL)
The U of Tennessee (TN)
The U of Tennessee at Chattanooga (TN)
The U of Tennessee at Martin (TN)
The U of Texas at Arlington (TX)
The U of Texas at Austin (TX)
The U of Texas at El Paso (TX)
The U of Texas at Tyler (TX)
The U of Texas Health Science Center at Houston (TX)
The U of Texas–Pan American (TX)
U of the Incarnate Word (TX)
The U of Toledo (OH)
U of Toronto (ON, Canada)
U of Tulsa (OK)
U of Utah (UT)
U of Vermont (VT)
U of Virginia (VA)
U of Washington, Bothell (WA)
The U of Western Ontario (ON, Canada)
U of West Florida (FL)
U of West Georgia (GA)
U of Windsor (ON, Canada)
U of Wisconsin–Eau Claire (WI)
U of Wisconsin–Green Bay (WI)
U of Wisconsin–Madison (WI)

U of Wisconsin–Milwaukee (WI)
U of Wyoming (WY)
Ursuline Coll (OH)
Utah Valley U (UT)
Utica Coll (NY)
Valdosta State U (GA)
Valparaiso U (IN)
Vanguard U of Southern California (CA)
Villanova U (PA)
Virginia Commonwealth U (VA)
Viterbo U (WI)
Wagner Coll (NY)
Walden U (MN)
Walsh U (OH)
Washburn U (KS)
Washington Adventist U (MD)
Washington State U (WA)
Wayland Baptist U (TX)
Waynesburg U (PA)
Webster U (MO)
West Chester U of Pennsylvania (PA)
Western Carolina U (NC)
Western Connecticut State U (CT)
Western Illinois U (IL)
Western Kentucky U (KY)
Western Michigan U (MI)
Westfield State U (MA)
West Liberty U (WV)
Westminster Coll (UT)
West Texas A&M U (TX)
West Virginia U (WV)
West Virginia U Inst of Technology (WV)
West Virginia Wesleyan Coll (WV)
Wheeling Jesuit U (WV)
Wichita State U (KS)
Widener U (PA)
Wilkes U (PA)
William Jewell Coll (MO)
William Paterson U of New Jersey (NJ)
Wilmington U (DE)
Winona State U (MN)
Worcester State U (MA)
Wright State U (OH)
York Coll of Pennsylvania (PA)
York Coll of the City U of New York (NY)
Youngstown State U (OH)

REHABILITATION AND THERAPEUTIC PROFESSIONS RELATED

Assumption Coll (MA)
Baker Coll of Muskegon (MI)
Boston U (MA)
California State U, Los Angeles (CA)
Coll of Saint Mary (NE)
East Stroudsburg U of Pennsylvania (PA)
Georgian Court U (NJ)
Hilbert Coll (NY)
Indiana U of Pennsylvania (PA)
Ithaca Coll (NY)
Montana State U Billings (MT)
Penn State Abington (PA)
Penn State Altoona (PA)
Penn State Beaver (PA)
Penn State Berks (PA)
Penn State Brandywine (PA)
Penn State DuBois (PA)
Penn State Erie, The Behrend Coll (PA)
Penn State Fayette, The Eberly Campus (PA)
Penn State Greater Allegheny (PA)
Penn State Hazleton (PA)
Penn State Lehigh Valley (PA)
Penn State Mont Alto (PA)
Penn State New Kensington (PA)
Penn State Schuylkill (PA)
Penn State Shenango (PA)
Penn State U Park (PA)
Penn State Wilkes-Barre (PA)
Penn State Worthington Scranton (PA)
Penn State York (PA)
Prescott Coll (AZ)
Southern Illinois U Carbondale (IL)
Stephen F. Austin State U (TX)
Thomas U (GA)

Troy U (AL)
U of Maine at Farmington (ME)
U of Maryland Eastern Shore (MD)
U of Massachusetts Lowell (MA)
U of Medicine and Dentistry of New Jersey (NJ)
U of North Texas (TX)
The U of Texas–Pan American (TX)
The U of Western Ontario (ON, Canada)
Wilson Coll (PA)

REHABILITATION SCIENCE

Arkansas Tech U (AR)
Stephen F. Austin State U (TX)
U of North Dakota (ND)
U of Pittsburgh (PA)
U of the Incarnate Word (TX)

RELIGIOUS EDUCATION

Andrews U (MI)
Asbury U (KY)
Ashland U (OH)
Baptist Bible Coll of Pennsylvania (PA)
Barclay Coll (KS)
Biola U (CA)
Bob Jones U (SC)
Campbellsville U (KY)
Cardinal Stritch U (WI)
Cedarville U (OH)
Cincinnati Christian U (OH)
Coll of Mount St. Joseph (OH)
Coll of Saint Benedict (MN)
Columbia Coll (SC)
Concordia Coll–New York (NY)
Concordia U (CA)
Concordia U (MI)
Concordia U Chicago (IL)
Concordia U, Nebraska (NE)
Concordia U, St. Paul (MN)
Concordia U Texas (TX)
Corban U (OR)
Crossroads Bible Coll (IN)
Crown Coll (MN)
Dallas Baptist U (TX)
Defiance Coll (OH)
Edgewood Coll (WI)
Faith Baptist Bible Coll and Theological Sem (IA)
Florida Southern Coll (FL)
Franciscan U of Steubenville (OH)
Free Will Baptist Bible Coll (TN)
Gardner-Webb U (NC)
Great Lakes Christian Coll (MI)
Hannibal-LaGrange U (MO)
Harding U (AR)
Hebrew Coll (MA)
Hillsdale Free Will Baptist Coll (OK)
Holy Family U (PA)
Houghton Coll (NY)
Howard Payne U (TX)
Huntingdon Coll (AL)
Indiana Wesleyan U (IN)
Inter American U of Puerto Rico, Fajardo Campus (PR)
John Carroll U (OH)
Kingswood U (NB, Canada)
La Salle U (PA)
Lee U (TN)
Lenoir-Rhyne U (NC)
Lincoln Christian U (IL)
Lindsey Wilson Coll (KY)
Louisiana Coll (LA)
Loyola U Chicago (IL)
Loyola U New Orleans (LA)
Malone U (OH)
The Master's Coll and Sem (CA)
Master's Coll and Sem (ON, Canada)
Messiah Coll (PA)
Mid-Continent U (KY)
Moody Bible Inst (IL)
Morris Coll (SC)
Mount Vernon Nazarene U (OH)
Multnomah U (OR)
New Hope Christian Coll (OR)
Northwestern Coll (IA)
Northwest Nazarene U (ID)
Northwest U (WA)
Nyack Coll (NY)
Oakland City U (IN)
Oklahoma Christian U (OK)
Oklahoma City U (OK)

Oral Roberts U (OK)
Pepperdine U, Malibu (CA)
Piedmont Intl U (NC)
Presbyterian Coll (SC)
Saint John's U (MN)
Saint Louis Christian Coll (MO)
Saint Mary's U of Minnesota (MN)
Saint Vincent Coll (PA)
Seattle Pacific U (WA)
Simpson U (CA)
Southwest Baptist U (MO)
Southwestern Christian U (OK)
Sterling Coll (KS)
Texas Wesleyan U (TX)
Thiel Coll (PA)
Tri-State Bible Coll (OH)
Union Coll (KY)
Universidad Teologica del Caribe (PR)
U of Dayton (OH)
U of the Cumberlands (KY)
Valley Forge Christian Coll Woodbridge Campus (VA)
Vanguard U of Southern California (CA)
Washington Adventist U (MD)
Wayland Baptist U (TX)
West Virginia Wesleyan Coll (WV)
Wheaton Coll (IL)
William Jessup U (CA)
Williams Baptist Coll (AR)

RELIGIOUS/SACRED MUSIC

Anderson U (IN)
Anderson U (SC)
Aquinas Coll (MI)
Asbury U (KY)
Baptist Bible Coll of Pennsylvania (PA)
Barclay Coll (KS)
Baylor U (TX)
Belmont U (TN)
Bethany Lutheran Coll (MN)
Bethel U (MN)
Bethel U (TN)
Bluefield Coll (VA)
Blue Mountain Coll (MS)
Bowling Green State U (OH)
Briercrest Coll (SK, Canada)
Calvary Bible Coll and Theological Sem (MO)
Calvin Coll (MI)
Campbellsville U (KY)
Cedarville U (OH)
Cincinnati Christian U (OH)
Clarke U (IA)
Clearwater Christian Coll (FL)
Coll of the Ozarks (MO)
Concordia Coll–New York (NY)
Concordia U (MI)
Concordia U Chicago (IL)
Concordia U, Nebraska (NE)
Concordia U, St. Paul (MN)
Concordia U Texas (TX)
Corban U (OR)
Crown Coll (MN)
Dallas Baptist U (TX)
Drake U (IA)
East Central U (OK)
East Texas Baptist U (TX)
Emmanuel Coll (GA)
Evangel U (MO)
Faith Baptist Bible Coll and Theological Sem (IA)
Franciscan U of Steubenville (OH)
Free Will Baptist Bible Coll (TN)
Furman U (SC)
Gardner-Webb U (NC)
Great Lakes Christian Coll (MI)
Gustavus Adolphus Coll (MN)
Hannibal-LaGrange U (MO)
Hardin-Simmons U (TX)
Hebrew Coll (MA)
Hillsdale Free Will Baptist Coll (OK)
Hope Intl U (CA)
Howard Payne U (TX)
Huntington U (IN)
Indiana Wesleyan U (IN)
John Brown U (AR)
Judson U (IL)
Kentucky Christian U (KY)
Kentucky Mountain Bible Coll (KY)
Lee U (TN)
Lenoir-Rhyne U (NC)
Liberty U (VA)

Lincoln Christian U (IL)
Lincoln U (MO)
Louisiana Coll (LA)
Madonna U (MI)
Malone U (OH)
Maranatha Baptist Bible Coll (WI)
The Master's Coll and Sem (CA)
Mississippi Coll (MS)
Missouri Baptist U (MO)
Moody Bible Inst (IL)
Moravian Coll (PA)
Mount Vernon Nazarene U (OH)
Multnomah U (OR)
Newberry Coll (SC)
New Hope Christian Coll (OR)
North Carolina Central U (NC)
North Greenville U (SC)
Northwest Nazarene U (ID)
Northwest U (WA)
Nyack Coll (NY)
Oklahoma City U (OK)
Oral Roberts U (OK)
Ouachita Baptist U (AR)
Piedmont Intl U (NC)
Point Loma Nazarene U (CA)
Presbyterian Coll (SC)
Rider U (NJ)
Saint Louis Christian Coll (MO)
Saint Mary's U of Minnesota (MN)
St. Olaf Coll (MN)
Samford U (AL)
San Diego Christian Coll (CA)
Seton Hill U (PA)
Shenandoah U (VA)
Shorter U (GA)
Southeastern U (FL)
Southwestern Assemblies of God U (TX)
Southwestern Christian U (OK)
Southwestern Oklahoma State U (OK)
Texas Christian U (TX)
Trevecca Nazarene U (TN)
Trinity Lutheran Coll (WA)
Union U (TN)
U of Hartford (CT)
U of Mary (ND)
U of Mary Hardin-Baylor (TX)
U of Mobile (AL)
Vanguard Coll (AB, Canada)
Wartburg Coll (IA)
Wayland Baptist U (TX)
William Jewell Coll (MO)
Williams Baptist Coll (AR)

RELIGIOUS STUDIES

Adrian Coll (MI)
Agnes Scott Coll (GA)
Albertus Magnus Coll (CT)
Albion Coll (MI)
Albright Coll (PA)
Allegheny Coll (PA)
Alma Coll (MI)
Alvernia U (PA)
Alverno Coll (WI)
American Public U System (WV)
American U (DC)
Amherst Coll (MA)
Anderson U (IN)
Anderson U (SC)
Andrews U (MI)
Appalachian State U (NC)
Aquinas Coll (MI)
Arizona State U (AZ)
Arlington Baptist Coll (TX)
Ashland U (OH)
Athens State U (AL)
Augustana Coll (IL)
Augustana Coll (SD)
Austin Coll (TX)
Averett U (VA)
Avila U (MO)
Azusa Pacific U (CA)
Baker U (KS)
Baldwin-Wallace Coll (OH)
Ball State U (IN)
Bard Coll (NY)
Barnard Coll (NY)
Bates Coll (ME)
Bayamón Central U (PR)
Baylor U (TX)
Beloit Coll (WI)
Bemidji State U (MN)
Benedictine Coll (KS)
Berea Coll (KY)

INDEXES

Bernard M. Baruch Coll of the City U of New York (NY)
Bethany Coll (KS)
Bethany Coll (WV)
Bethany Lutheran Coll (MN)
Bethel Coll (KS)
Biola U (CA)
Birmingham-Southern Coll (AL)
Bishop's U (QC, Canada)
Bloomfield Coll (NJ)
Bluefield Coll (VA)
Bluffton U (OH)
Boston U (MA)
Bowdoin Coll (ME)
Bradley U (IL)
Brevard Coll (NC)
Brewton-Parker Coll (GA)
Briercrest Coll (SK, Canada)
Brown U (RI)
Bryn Mawr Coll (PA)
Bucknell U (PA)
Butler U (IN)
Cabrini Coll (PA)
California Lutheran U (CA)
California State U, Bakersfield (CA)
California State U, East Bay (CA)
California State U, Fresno (CA)
California State U, Fullerton (CA)
California State U, Long Beach (CA)
California State U, Sacramento (CA)
Calumet Coll of Saint Joseph (IN)
Calvin Coll (MI)
Campbellsville U (KY)
Canisius Coll (NY)
Cape Breton U (NS, Canada)
Capital U (OH)
Cardinal Stritch U (WI)
Carleton Coll (MN)
Carson-Newman Coll (TN)
Case Western Reserve U (OH)
Catawba Coll (NC)
The Catholic U of America (DC)
Centenary Coll of Louisiana (LA)
Central Coll (IA)
Central Methodist U (MO)
Central Michigan U (MI)
Central Washington U (WA)
Centre Coll (KY)
Chaminade U of Honolulu (HI)
Chapman U (CA)
Christian Brothers U (TN)
Claremont McKenna Coll (CA)
Clark Atlanta U (GA)
Clarke U (IA)
Cleveland State U (OH)
Coe Coll (IA)
Colby Coll (ME)
Colgate U (NY)
Coll of Charleston (SC)
The Coll of Idaho (ID)
Coll of Mount St. Joseph (OH)
Coll of Mount Saint Vincent (NY)
The Coll of Saint Rose (NY)
The Coll of St. Scholastica (MN)
Coll of the Holy Cross (MA)
The Coll of William and Mary (VA)
The Coll of Wooster (OH)
The Colorado Coll (CO)
Columbia Bible Coll (BC, Canada)
Columbia Coll (SC)
Columbia U, School of General Studies (NY)
Concordia Coll (MN)
Concordia Coll–New York (NY)
Concordia U (CA)
Concordia U (MI)
Concordia U (QC, Canada)
Concordia U Chicago (IL)
Connecticut Coll (CT)
Converse Coll (SC)
Corban U (OR)
Cornell Coll (IA)
Cornell U (NY)
Crandall U (NB, Canada)
The Criswell Coll (TX)
Culver-Stockton Coll (MO)
Daemen Coll (NY)
Dalhousie U (NS, Canada)
Dartmouth Coll (NH)
Davidson Coll (NC)
Defiance Coll (OH)
Denison U (OH)
DePaul U (IL)

DePauw U (IN)
Dickinson Coll (PA)
Doane Coll (NE)
Dominican U of California (CA)
Dordt Coll (IA)
Drake U (IA)
Drew U (NJ)
Drury U (MO)
Earlham Coll (IN)
Eastern New Mexico U (NM)
East Texas Baptist U (TX)
Eckerd Coll (FL)
Edgewood Coll (WI)
Elizabethtown Coll (PA)
Elmira Coll (NY)
Elon U (NC)
Emory & Henry Coll (VA)
Emory U (GA)
Fairfield U (CT)
Faulkner U (AL)
Felician Coll (NJ)
Ferrum Coll (VA)
Florida Intl U (FL)
Florida Southern Coll (FL)
Fontbonne U (MO)
Fordham U (NY)
Franklin & Marshall Coll (PA)
Franklin Coll (IN)
Furman U (SC)
Gardner-Webb U (NC)
George Mason U (VA)
Georgetown Coll (KY)
The George Washington U (DC)
Georgian Court U (NJ)
Georgia State U (GA)
Gettysburg Coll (PA)
Gonzaga U (WA)
Goshen Coll (IN)
Goucher Coll (MD)
Graceland U (IA)
Grand Canyon U (AZ)
Grand View U (IA)
Greenville Coll (IL)
Grinnell Coll (IA)
Grove City Coll (PA)
Guilford Coll (NC)
Gustavus Adolphus Coll (MN)
Hamilton Coll (NY)
Hamline U (MN)
Hampden-Sydney Coll (VA)
Hampshire Coll (MA)
Hampton U (VA)
Hartwick Coll (NY)
Harvard U (MA)
Haverford Coll (PA)
Heidelberg U (OH)
Hellenic Coll (MA)
Hendrix Coll (AR)
Hillsdale Coll (MI)
Hobart and William Smith Colls (NY)
Hofstra U (NY)
Hollins U (VA)
Holy Family U (PA)
Hood Coll (MD)
Hope Coll (MI)
Hope Intl U (CA)
Houghton Coll (NY)
Humboldt State U (CA)
Hunter Coll of the City U of New York (NY)
Huntingdon Coll (AL)
Huntington U (IN)
Illinois Coll (IL)
Illinois Wesleyan U (IL)
Indiana U Bloomington (IN)
Indiana U of Pennsylvania (PA)
Indiana U–Purdue U Indianapolis (IN)
Iona Coll (NY)
Iowa State U of Science and Technology (IA)
Jamestown Coll (ND)
Jarvis Christian Coll (TX)
John Brown U (AR)
John Carroll U (OH)
Judson Coll (AL)
Juniata Coll (PA)
Kalamazoo Coll (MI)
Kentucky Mountain Bible Coll (KY)
Kenyon Coll (OH)
King Coll (TN)
Kingswood U (NB, Canada)
Lafayette Coll (PA)
LaGrange Coll (GA)

Lake Forest Coll (IL)
Lane Coll (TN)
La Roche Coll (PA)
La Salle U (PA)
La Sierra U (CA)
Lawrence U (WI)
Lebanon Valley Coll (PA)
Lees-McRae Coll (NC)
Lehigh U (PA)
Le Moyne Coll (NY)
Lenoir-Rhyne U (NC)
LeTourneau U (TX)
Lewis & Clark Coll (OR)
Lewis U (IL)
Liberty U (VA)
Lincoln U (PA)
Lindenwood U (MO)
Linfield Coll (OR)
Loras Coll (IA)
Louisiana Coll (LA)
Lourdes U (OH)
Loyola U Maryland (MD)
Loyola U New Orleans (LA)
Luther Coll (IA)
Lycoming Coll (PA)
Lynchburg Coll (VA)
Macalester Coll (MN)
Madonna U (MI)
Manchester Coll (IN)
Manhattan Coll (NY)
Manhattanville Coll (NY)
Marian U (WI)
Marlboro Coll (VT)
Mars Hill Coll (NC)
Mary Baldwin Coll (VA)
Marylhurst U (OR)
Marymount U (VA)
Maryville Coll (TN)
Marywood U (PA)
The Master's Coll and Sem (CA)
McDaniel Coll (MD)
McKendree U (IL)
Medgar Evers Coll of the City U of New York (NY)
Mercyhurst Coll (PA)
Meredith Coll (NC)
Merrimack Coll (MA)
Miami U (OH)
Michigan State U (MI)
MidAmerica Nazarene U (KS)
Middlebury Coll (VT)
Millsaps Coll (MS)
Missouri State U (MO)
Molloy Coll (NY)
Monmouth Coll (IL)
Montclair State U (NJ)
Moravian Coll (PA)
Morehouse Coll (GA)
Morningside Coll (IA)
Mountain State U (WV)
Mount Allison U (NB, Canada)
Mount Holyoke Coll (MA)
Mount Marty Coll (SD)
Mount Mary Coll (WI)
Mount Mercy U (IA)
Mount St. Mary's Coll (CA)
Mount Vernon Nazarene U (OH)
Muhlenberg Coll (PA)
Naropa U (CO)
Nazareth Coll of Rochester (NY)
Nebraska Wesleyan U (NE)
Newberry Coll (SC)
New Coll of Florida (FL)
New York U (NY)
Niagara U (NY)
North Carolina State U (NC)
North Carolina Wesleyan Coll (NC)
North Central Coll (IL)
Northeastern U (MA)
Northwestern Coll (IA)
Northwest Nazarene U (ID)
Northwest U (WA)
Notre Dame de Namur U (CA)
Notre Dame of Maryland U (MD)
Nyack Coll (NY)
Oakland City U (IN)
Occidental Coll (CA)
Ohio Northern U (OH)
Ohio U (OH)
Ohio Valley U (WV)
Ohio Wesleyan U (OH)
Oklahoma Christian U (OK)
Oklahoma City U (OK)
Otterbein U (OH)
Pacific Lutheran U (WA)

Pacific Union Coll (CA)
Penn State Abington (PA)
Penn State Altoona (PA)
Penn State Beaver (PA)
Penn State Berks (PA)
Penn State Brandywine (PA)
Penn State DuBois (PA)
Penn State Erie, The Behrend Coll (PA)
Penn State Fayette, The Eberly Campus (PA)
Penn State Greater Allegheny (PA)
Penn State Hazleton (PA)
Penn State Lehigh Valley (PA)
Penn State Mont Alto (PA)
Penn State New Kensington (PA)
Penn State Schuylkill (PA)
Penn State Shenango (PA)
Penn State U Park (PA)
Penn State Wilkes-Barre (PA)
Penn State Worthington Scranton (PA)
Penn State York (PA)
Pepperdine U, Malibu (CA)
Philadelphia Biblical U (PA)
Philander Smith Coll (AR)
Piedmont Coll (GA)
Pitzer Coll (CA)
Pomona Coll (CA)
Portland State U (OR)
Presbyterian Coll (SC)
Princeton U (NJ)
Queens Coll of the City U of New York (NY)
Queen's U at Kingston (ON, Canada)
Queens U of Charlotte (NC)
Randolph Coll (VA)
Randolph-Macon Coll (VA)
Regis U (CO)
Reinhardt U (GA)
Rhodes Coll (TN)
Rice U (TX)
Ripon Coll (WI)
Roanoke Coll (VA)
Roberts Wesleyan Coll (NY)
Rocky Mountain Coll (MT)
Rollins Coll (FL)
Rosemont Coll (PA)
Rutgers, The State U of New Jersey, New Brunswick (NJ)
Sacred Heart U (CT)
Saint Francis U (PA)
St. John Fisher Coll (NY)
Saint Joseph's Coll of Maine (ME)
Saint Joseph's U (PA)
St. Lawrence U (NY)
Saint Leo U (FL)
Saint Martin's U (WA)
Saint Mary-of-the-Woods Coll (IN)
Saint Mary's Coll (IN)
Saint Mary's Coll of California (CA)
St. Mary's Coll of Maryland (MD)
Saint Michael's Coll (VT)
St. Norbert Coll (WI)
St. Olaf Coll (MN)
Saint Peter's Coll (NJ)
St. Thomas Aquinas Coll (NY)
St. Thomas U (FL)
St. Thomas U (NB, Canada)
Saint Xavier U (IL)
Salve Regina U (RI)
Samford U (AL)
San Diego State U (CA)
Santa Clara U (CA)
Sarah Lawrence Coll (NY)
Schreiner U (TX)
Scripps Coll (CA)
Seattle U (WA)
Seton Hill U (PA)
Sewanee: The U of the South (TN)
Shaw U (NC)
Shenandoah U (VA)
Shorter U (GA)
Siena Coll (NY)
Siena Heights U (MI)
Simpson Coll (IA)
Skidmore Coll (NY)
Smith Coll (MA)
Southern Methodist U (TX)
Southwest Baptist U (MO)
Southwestern Adventist U (TX)
Southwestern Christian U (OK)
Southwestern U (TX)
Spelman Coll (GA)

Spring Arbor U (MI)
Spring Hill Coll (AL)
Stanford U (CA)
State U of New York Coll at Old Westbury (NY)
Stetson U (FL)
Stonehill Coll (MA)
Stony Brook U, State U of New York (NY)
Susquehanna U (PA)
Swarthmore Coll (PA)
Sweet Briar Coll (VA)
Syracuse U (NY)
Temple U (PA)
Texas Christian U (TX)
Texas Coll (TX)
Texas Wesleyan U (TX)
Thiel Coll (PA)
Thomas Edison State Coll (NJ)
Thomas More Coll (KY)
Towson U (MD)
Transylvania U (KY)
Trinity Christian Coll (IL)
Trinity Coll (CT)
Trinity U (TX)
Tulane U (LA)
Union Coll (KY)
Union Coll (NY)
Union U (TN)
U at Albany, State U of New York (NY)
The U of Alabama (AL)
U of Alberta (AB, Canada)
The U of Arizona (AZ)
U of Bridgeport (CT)
The U of British Columbia (BC, Canada)
U of California, Berkeley (CA)
U of California, Davis (CA)
U of California, Irvine (CA)
U of California, Los Angeles (CA)
U of California, Riverside (CA)
U of California, Santa Barbara (CA)
U of Central Arkansas (AR)
U of Central Florida (FL)
U of Colorado Boulder (CO)
U of Dayton (OH)
U of Denver (CO)
U of Dubuque (IA)
The U of Findlay (OH)
U of Florida (FL)
U of Georgia (GA)
U of Great Falls (MT)
U of Hawaii at Manoa (HI)
U of Illinois at Urbana–Champaign (IL)
U of Indianapolis (IN)
The U of Iowa (IA)
The U of Kansas (KS)
U of La Verne (CA)
U of Lethbridge (AB, Canada)
U of Mary (ND)
U of Mary Hardin-Baylor (TX)
U of Mary Washington (VA)
U of Miami (FL)
U of Michigan (MI)
U of Minnesota, Twin Cities Campus (MN)
U of Mississippi (MS)
U of Missouri (MO)
U of Mobile (AL)
U of Mount Union (OH)
U of Nebraska at Omaha (NE)
U of New Mexico (NM)
The U of North Carolina at Asheville (NC)
The U of North Carolina at Chapel Hill (NC)
The U of North Carolina at Charlotte (NC)
U of North Dakota (ND)
U of Northern Iowa (IA)
U of Oklahoma (OK)
U of Oregon (OR)
U of Ottawa (ON, Canada)
U of Pennsylvania (PA)
U of Pikeville (KY)
U of Pittsburgh (PA)
U of Puget Sound (WA)
U of Redlands (CA)
U of Regina (SK, Canada)
U of Richmond (VA)
U of Rochester (NY)
U of Saint Francis (IN)
U of Saint Joseph (CT)

U of St. Thomas (MN)
U of San Diego (CA)
The U of Scranton (PA)
U of South Carolina (SC)
U of Southern California (CA)
U of Southern Mississippi (MS)
U of South Florida (FL)
The U of Tennessee (TN)
The U of Texas at Austin (TX)
U of the Incarnate Word (TX)
U of the Ozarks (AR)
U of the Pacific (CA)
The U of Toledo (OH)
U of Tulsa (OK)
U of Vermont (VT)
U of Virginia (VA)
U of Washington (WA)
The U of Western Ontario (ON, Canada)
U of Wisconsin–Eau Claire (WI)
U of Wisconsin–Madison (WI)
U of Wisconsin–Milwaukee (WI)
U of Wyoming (WY)
Vanderbilt U (TN)
Vanguard U of Southern California (CA)
Vassar Coll (NY)
Villanova U (PA)
Virginia Commonwealth U (VA)
Virginia Intermont Coll (VA)
Virginia Wesleyan Coll (VA)
Viterbo U (WI)
Wabash Coll (IN)
Wake Forest U (NC)
Warren Wilson Coll (NC)
Wartburg Coll (IA)
Washburn U (KS)
Washington and Lee U (VA)
Washington State U (WA)
Washington U in St. Louis (MO)
Webster U (MO)
Wellesley Coll (MA)
Wesleyan Coll (GA)
Wesleyan U (CT)
Western Illinois U (IL)
Western Kentucky U (KY)
Western Michigan U (MI)
Westminster Coll (MO)
West Virginia Wesleyan Coll (WV)
Wheeling Jesuit U (WV)
Whitman Coll (WA)
Whittier Coll (CA)
Willamette U (OR)
William Jewell Coll (MO)
Williams Baptist Coll (AR)
Williams Coll (MA)
Wilmington Coll (OH)
Wilson Coll (PA)
Wingate U (NC)
Wittenberg U (OH)
Wofford Coll (SC)
Wright State U (OH)
Xavier U (OH)
Yale U (CT)
Youngstown State U (OH)

RELIGIOUS STUDIES RELATED
Bryn Athyn Coll of the New Church (PA)
Colby Coll (ME)
Ohio Northern U (OH)
St. Edward's U (TX)
Sarah Lawrence Coll (NY)
U of Regina (SK, Canada)
The U of Western Ontario (ON, Canada)
Ursuline Coll (OH)

REPRODUCTIVE BIOLOGY
Bradley U (IL)

RESEARCH AND EXPERIMENTAL PSYCHOLOGY RELATED
U of Michigan–Flint (MI)

RESORT MANAGEMENT
California State U, Chico (CA)
Coastal Carolina U (SC)
Florida Gulf Coast U (FL)
Mitchell Coll (CT)
Rochester Inst of Technology (NY)
Sierra Nevada Coll (NV)

RESPIRATORY CARE THERAPY
Armstrong Atlantic State U (GA)
Ball State U (IN)
Baptist Coll of Health Sciences (TN)
Bellarmine U (KY)
Boise State U (ID)
Dakota State U (SD)
Dalhousie U (NS, Canada)
Fairleigh Dickinson U, Coll at Florham (NJ)
Florida Ag and Mech U (FL)
Gannon U (PA)
Georgia State U (GA)
Gwynedd-Mercy Coll (PA)
Indiana U Bloomington (IN)
Indiana U East (IN)
Indiana U Kokomo (IN)
Indiana U of Pennsylvania (PA)
Indiana U–Purdue U Indianapolis (IN)
Indiana U South Bend (IN)
Indiana U Southeast (IN)
Long Island U–Brooklyn Campus (NY)
Macon State Coll (GA)
Marshall U (WV)
Midwestern State U (TX)
Missouri State U (MO)
North Dakota State U (ND)
Northern Michigan U (MI)
The Ohio State U (OH)
St. Catherine U (MN)
Salisbury U (MD)
Shenandoah U (VA)
State U of New York Upstate Medical U (NY)
Stony Brook U, State U of New York (NY)
Texas Southern U (TX)
Texas State U–San Marcos (TX)
Thomas Edison State Coll (NJ)
Thompson Rivers U (BC, Canada)
The U of Akron (OH)
The U of Alabama at Birmingham (AL)
U of Hartford (CT)
U of Indianapolis (IN)
The U of Kansas (KS)
U of Mary (ND)
U of Medicine and Dentistry of New Jersey (NJ)
U of Missouri (MO)
The U of North Carolina at Charlotte (NC)
U of South Alabama (AL)
Weber State U (UT)
Wheeling Jesuit U (WV)
York Coll of Pennsylvania (PA)
Youngstown State U (OH)

RESPIRATORY THERAPY TECHNICIAN
Dalhousie U (NS, Canada)

RESTAURANT, CULINARY, AND CATERING MANAGEMENT
The Art Inst of Atlanta (GA)
The Art Inst of Austin (TX)
The Art Inst of California, a college of Argosy U, Hollywood (CA)
The Art Inst of California, a college of Argosy U, Inland Empire (CA)
The Art Inst of California, a college of Argosy U, Los Angeles (CA)
The Art Inst of California, a college of Argosy U, Orange County (CA)
The Art Inst of California, a college of Argosy U, Sacramento (CA)
The Art Inst of California, a college of Argosy U, San Diego (CA)
The Art Inst of California, a college of Argosy U, San Francisco (CA)
The Art Inst of California, a college of Argosy U, Sunnyvale (CA)
The Art Inst of Charleston (SC)
The Art Inst of Charlotte (NC)
The Art Inst of Colorado (CO)
The Art Inst of Dallas (TX)
The Art Inst of Fort Lauderdale (FL)
The Art Inst of Houston (TX)
The Art Inst of Indianapolis (IN)
The Art Inst of Jacksonville (FL)
The Art Inst of Las Vegas (NV)

The Art Inst of Michigan (MI)
The Art Inst of Ohio–Cincinnati (OH)
The Art Inst of Philadelphia (PA)
The Art Inst of Phoenix (AZ)
The Art Inst of Pittsburgh (PA)
The Art Inst of Portland (OR)
The Art Inst of Raleigh-Durham (NC)
The Art Inst of Salt Lake City (UT)
The Art Inst of San Antonio (TX)
The Art Inst of Seattle (WA)
The Art Inst of Tampa (FL)
The Art Inst of Tennessee–Nashville (TN)
The Art Inst of Virginia Beach (VA)
The Art Inst of Washington (VA)
The Art Insts Intl Minnesota (MN)
Bowling Green State U (OH)
Coll of the Ozarks (MO)
The Illinois Inst of Art–Chicago (IL)
Pennsylvania Coll of Technology (PA)
State U of New York Coll of Technology at Delhi (NY)
U of Hawaii–West Oahu (HI)
U of Illinois at Urbana–Champaign (IL)

RESTAURANT/FOOD SERVICES MANAGEMENT
Coll of the Ozarks (MO)
Colorado State U (CO)
The Culinary Inst of America (NY)
Lindenwood U (MO)
Messiah Coll (PA)
Morrisville State Coll (NY)
Niagara U (NY)
The Ohio State U (OH)
The Restaurant School at Walnut Hill Coll (PA)
Rochester Inst of Technology (NY)
Southwest Minnesota State U (MN)
The U of Alabama (AL)
U of Central Florida (FL)
U of Missouri (MO)

RETAILING
American Public U System (WV)
Bowling Green State U (OH)
Capella U (MN)
Central Michigan U (MI)
Purdue U Calumet (IN)
Ryerson U (ON, Canada)
Southern New Hampshire U (NH)
Stevens Inst of Business & Arts (MO)
U of Minnesota, Twin Cities Campus (MN)
U of South Carolina (SC)
U of Wisconsin–Madison (WI)

RETAIL MANAGEMENT
The U of Arizona (AZ)

RHETORIC AND COMPOSITION
Albany State U (GA)
Ashland U (OH)
Auburn U (AL)
Bates Coll (ME)
Belmont U (TN)
Bemidji State U (MN)
Black Hills State U (SD)
Bob Jones U (SC)
Bowling Green State U (OH)
Brigham Young U (UT)
California Polytechnic State U, San Luis Obispo (CA)
California State U, East Bay (CA)
California State U, Fresno (CA)
California State U, Fullerton (CA)
California State U, Long Beach (CA)
California State U, Los Angeles (CA)
Calvin Coll (MI)
Cape Breton U (NS, Canada)
Carson-Newman Coll (TN)
Clark Atlanta U (GA)
Clemson U (SC)
Coe Coll (IA)
The Coll at Brockport, State U of New York (NY)

Coll of Saint Benedict (MN)
Columbus State U (GA)
Concordia U, Nebraska (NE)
Cornell Coll (IA)
Cornerstone U (MI)
Creighton U (NE)
Denison U (OH)
Drake U (IA)
Duquesne U (PA)
East Central U (OK)
Eastern Kentucky U (KY)
East Tennessee State U (TN)
East Texas Baptist U (TX)
Evangel U (MO)
Fairmont State U (WV)
Ferris State U (MI)
George Mason U (VA)
The George Washington U (DC)
Georgia Coll & State U (GA)
Georgia Southern U (GA)
Gonzaga U (WA)
Governors State U (IL)
Graceland U (IA)
Greenville Coll (IL)
Gustavus Adolphus Coll (MN)
Hardin-Simmons U (TX)
Humboldt State U (CA)
Illinois Coll (IL)
Indiana U South Bend (IN)
Iowa State U of Science and Technology (IA)
Ithaca Coll (NY)
Lehman Coll of the City U of New York (NY)
Lipscomb U (TN)
Lock Haven U of Pennsylvania (PA)
Long Island U–Brooklyn Campus (NY)
Louisiana Coll (LA)
Louisiana State U in Shreveport (LA)
Manchester Coll (IN)
Marietta Coll (OH)
Marshall U (WV)
The Master's Coll and Sem (CA)
McKendree U (IL)
Metropolitan State Coll of Denver (CO)
Miami U (OH)
Minnesota State U Mankato (MN)
Mississippi Valley State U (MS)
Newberry Coll (SC)
North Carolina Ag and Tech State U (NC)
North Central Coll (IL)
Northeastern Illinois U (IL)
Northern Arizona U (AZ)
Northern State U (SD)
Northwestern Coll (IA)
Northwestern Oklahoma State U (OK)
Northwest Missouri State U (MO)
Oglethorpe U (GA)
Ohio U (OH)
Oklahoma Christian U (OK)
Oklahoma City U (OK)
Old Dominion U (VA)
Ouachita Baptist U (AR)
Pace U (NY)
Pepperdine U, Malibu (CA)
Portland State U (OR)
Rider U (NJ)
St. Catherine U (MN)
Saint John's U (MN)
St. John's U (NY)
St. Joseph's Coll, Long Island Campus (NY)
St. Joseph's Coll, New York (NY)
Shippensburg U of Pennsylvania (PA)
South Dakota State U (SD)
Southern Illinois U Carbondale (IL)
Southern Illinois U Edwardsville (IL)
State U of New York at New Paltz (NY)
State U of New York Coll at Cortland (NY)
State U of New York Coll at Oneonta (NY)
Stephen F. Austin State U (TX)
Tarleton State U (TX)
Temple U (PA)
Texas A&M U (TX)
Texas Southern U (TX)
Texas State U–San Marcos (TX)

Texas Tech U (TX)
Texas Wesleyan U (TX)
Trinity U (TX)
Troy U (AL)
Union U (TN)
U at Albany, State U of New York (NY)
U of Arkansas at Little Rock (AR)
U of California, Berkeley (CA)
U of Central Arkansas (AR)
U of Central Missouri (MO)
U of Cincinnati (OH)
U of Dubuque (IA)
U of Georgia (GA)
U of Illinois at Urbana–Champaign (IL)
The U of Iowa (IA)
U of Minnesota, Twin Cities Campus (MN)
U of Nebraska at Kearney (NE)
U of Nebraska at Omaha (NE)
U of New Mexico (NM)
U of North Alabama (AL)
U of North Texas (TX)
U of Pittsburgh (PA)
U of Rhode Island (RI)
U of Richmond (VA)
The U of South Dakota (SD)
U of South Florida (FL)
The U of Texas at Arlington (TX)
The U of Texas at El Paso (TX)
The U of Texas at Tyler (TX)
U of Wisconsin–Platteville (WI)
U of Wisconsin–River Falls (WI)
U of Wisconsin–Superior (WI)
U of Wisconsin–Whitewater (WI)
Utah State U (UT)
Wabash Coll (IN)
West Chester U of Pennsylvania (PA)
West Texas A&M U (TX)
West Virginia Wesleyan Coll (WV)
Willamette U (OR)
William Jewell Coll (MO)
Winona State U (MN)
Yeshiva U (NY)
York Coll of the City U of New York (NY)
Youngstown State U (OH)

RHETORIC AND COMPOSITION/WRITING RELATED
Syracuse U (NY)

ROBOTICS TECHNOLOGY
Alcorn State U (MS)
Indiana State U (IN)
Indiana U–Purdue U Indianapolis (IN)
Lake Superior State U (MI)
Purdue U (IN)
U of Rio Grande (OH)

ROMANCE LANGUAGES
Bard Coll (NY)
Beloit Coll (WI)
Bernard M. Baruch Coll of the City U of New York (NY)
Bowdoin Coll (ME)
Bryn Mawr Coll (PA)
Carleton Coll (MN)
City Coll of the City U of New York (NY)
Colgate U (NY)
Dartmouth Coll (NH)
DePauw U (IN)
Elmira Coll (NY)
Fordham U (NY)
Franklin Coll Switzerland (Switzerland)
Gettysburg Coll (PA)
Harvard U (MA)
Haverford Coll (PA)
Hunter Coll of the City U of New York (NY)
Marlboro Coll (VT)
Merrimack Coll (MA)
Mount Allison U (NB, Canada)
Mount Holyoke Coll (MA)
Point Loma Nazarene U (CA)
Pomona Coll (CA)
Ripon Coll (WI)
Rockford Coll (IL)

INDEXES

St. Thomas Aquinas Coll (NY)
Sarah Lawrence Coll (NY)
Stanford U (CA)
Truman State U (MO)
Tufts U (MA)
U of Alberta (AB, Canada)
The U of British Columbia (BC, Canada)
U of Georgia (GA)
U of Hawaii at Manoa (HI)
U of Illinois at Chicago (IL)
U of Maine (ME)
U of Maryland, Coll Park (MD)
U of Michigan (MI)
U of Nevada, Las Vegas (NV)
U of Notre Dame (IN)
U of Oregon (OR)
U of Toronto (ON, Canada)
U of Washington (WA)
Vanderbilt U (TN)
Washington and Lee U (VA)
Washington U in St. Louis (MO)
Wesleyan U (CT)
Wheeling Jesuit U (WV)

ROMANCE LANGUAGES RELATED

Dowling Coll (NY)
Hood Coll (MD)
North Carolina Ag and Tech State U (NC)
U of Lethbridge (AB, Canada)
U of Michigan–Flint (MI)
The U of North Carolina at Chapel Hill (NC)
U of Pennsylvania (PA)

RURAL SOCIOLOGY

U of Wisconsin–Madison (WI)

RUSSIAN

American U (DC)
Amherst Coll (MA)
Arizona State U (AZ)
Bard Coll (NY)
Barnard Coll (NY)
Bates Coll (ME)
Baylor U (TX)
Beloit Coll (WI)
Boston Coll (MA)
Boston U (MA)
Bowdoin Coll (ME)
Bowling Green State U (OH)
Brandeis U (MA)
Bryn Mawr Coll (PA)
Bucknell U (PA)
Carleton Coll (MN)
Colgate U (NY)
Coll of the Holy Cross (MA)
Columbia U, School of General Studies (NY)
Cornell Coll (IA)
Dalhousie U (NS, Canada)
Dartmouth Coll (NH)
Dickinson Coll (PA)
Emory U (GA)
Fordham U (NY)
The George Washington U (DC)
Goucher Coll (MD)
Grinnell Coll (IA)
Gustavus Adolphus Coll (MN)
Haverford Coll (PA)
Hofstra U (NY)
Hope Coll (MI)
Hunter Coll of the City U of New York (NY)
Juniata Coll (PA)
Kent State U (OH)
La Salle U (PA)
Lawrence U (WI)
Lehman Coll of the City U of New York (NY)
Luther Coll (IA)
Macalester Coll (MN)
Michigan State U (MI)
Middlebury Coll (VT)
New Coll of Florida (FL)
New York U (NY)
Northern Illinois U (IL)
The Ohio State U (OH)
Ohio U (OH)
Oklahoma State U (OK)
Penn State Abington (PA)
Penn State Altoona (PA)

Penn State Beaver (PA)
Penn State Berks (PA)
Penn State Brandywine (PA)
Penn State DuBois (PA)
Penn State Erie, The Behrend Coll (PA)
Penn State Fayette, The Eberly Campus (PA)
Penn State Greater Allegheny (PA)
Penn State Hazleton (PA)
Penn State Lehigh Valley (PA)
Penn State Mont Alto (PA)
Penn State New Kensington (PA)
Penn State Schuylkill (PA)
Penn State Shenango (PA)
Penn State U Park (PA)
Penn State Wilkes-Barre (PA)
Penn State Worthington Scranton (PA)
Penn State York (PA)
Pomona Coll (CA)
Portland State U (OR)
Queens Coll of the City U of New York (NY)
Rider U (NJ)
Rutgers, The State U of New Jersey, New Brunswick (NJ)
Saint Louis U (MO)
St. Olaf Coll (MN)
San Diego State U (CA)
Sarah Lawrence Coll (NY)
Scripps Coll (CA)
Seattle Pacific U (WA)
Sewanee: The U of the South (TN)
Smith Coll (MA)
Swarthmore Coll (PA)
Syracuse U (NY)
Temple U (PA)
Texas A&M U (TX)
Trinity Coll (CT)
Trinity U (TX)
Truman State U (MO)
Tufts U (MA)
Tulane U (LA)
United States Military Acad (NY)
U of Alberta (AB, Canada)
The U of Arizona (AZ)
The U of British Columbia (BC, Canada)
U of California, Davis (CA)
U of California, Los Angeles (CA)
U of Denver (CO)
U of Florida (FL)
U of Georgia (GA)
U of Hawaii at Manoa (HI)
U of Illinois at Chicago (IL)
U of Illinois at Urbana–Champaign (IL)
The U of Iowa (IA)
U of Maryland, Coll Park (MD)
U of Michigan (MI)
U of Minnesota, Twin Cities Campus (MN)
U of Missouri (MO)
U of Nebraska–Lincoln (NE)
U of New Hampshire (NH)
U of Northern Iowa (IA)
U of Notre Dame (IN)
U of Oklahoma (OK)
U of Ottawa (ON, Canada)
U of Pennsylvania (PA)
U of Pittsburgh (PA)
U of Rochester (NY)
U of South Carolina (SC)
U of Southern California (CA)
U of South Florida (FL)
The U of Tennessee (TN)
The U of Texas at Arlington (TX)
The U of Texas at Austin (TX)
U of Toronto (ON, Canada)
U of Utah (UT)
U of Vermont (VT)
U of Washington (WA)
U of Wisconsin–Madison (WI)
U of Wisconsin–Milwaukee (WI)
U of Wyoming (WY)
Vanderbilt U (TN)
Vassar Coll (NY)
Wake Forest U (NC)
Wellesley Coll (MA)
Wesleyan U (CT)
West Chester U of Pennsylvania (PA)
Wheaton Coll (MA)
Williams Coll (MA)

Yale U (CT)

RUSSIAN, CENTRAL EUROPEAN, EAST EUROPEAN AND EURASIAN STUDIES

Bowdoin Coll (ME)
Columbia U, School of General Studies (NY)
Fordham U (NY)
Hawai'i Pacific U (HI)
Marlboro Coll (VT)
Michigan State U (MI)
Middlebury Coll (VT)
Portland State U (OR)
Rutgers, The State U of New Jersey, New Brunswick (NJ)
Sarah Lawrence Coll (NY)
U of Alberta (AB, Canada)
The U of British Columbia (BC, Canada)
U of Missouri (MO)
U of Toronto (ON, Canada)
Wayne State U (MI)
Wesleyan U (CT)

RUSSIAN STUDIES

American U (DC)
Bard Coll (NY)
Beloit Coll (WI)
Boston Coll (MA)
Boston U (MA)
Bowling Green State U (OH)
Brown U (RI)
Carleton Coll (MN)
Carnegie Mellon U (PA)
Colby Coll (ME)
Colgate U (NY)
Coll of the Holy Cross (MA)
The Coll of Wooster (OH)
The Colorado Coll (CO)
Columbia U, School of General Studies (NY)
Cornell Coll (IA)
Dalhousie U (NS, Canada)
Dartmouth Coll (NH)
DePauw U (IN)
Fordham U (NY)
George Mason U (VA)
The George Washington U (DC)
Grand Valley State U (MI)
Gustavus Adolphus Coll (MN)
Hamilton Coll (NY)
Hobart and William Smith Colls (NY)
Kent State U (OH)
Lafayette Coll (PA)
La Salle U (PA)
Lawrence U (WI)
Marlboro Coll (VT)
Middlebury Coll (VT)
Mount Holyoke Coll (MA)
Muhlenberg Coll (PA)
Rhodes Coll (TN)
Rutgers, The State U of New Jersey, New Brunswick (NJ)
St. Olaf Coll (MN)
San Diego State U (CA)
Scripps Coll (CA)
Sewanee: The U of the South (TN)
Smith Coll (MA)
Stetson U (FL)
Syracuse U (NY)
Texas Tech U (TX)
Tufts U (MA)
Tulane U (LA)
United States Military Acad (NY)
U of Alaska Fairbanks (AK)
U of Alberta (AB, Canada)
The U of British Columbia (BC, Canada)
U of California, Los Angeles (CA)
U of California, Riverside (CA)
U of California, Santa Cruz (CA)
U of Colorado Boulder (CO)
U of Delaware (DE)
U of Illinois at Urbana–Champaign (IL)
The U of Kansas (KS)
U of Maryland, Coll Park (MD)
U of Massachusetts Amherst (MA)
U of Michigan (MI)
U of Minnesota, Twin Cities Campus (MN)
U of Missouri (MO)

U of Northern Iowa (IA)
U of Oregon (OR)
U of Richmond (VA)
U of Rochester (NY)
The U of Texas at Austin (TX)
U of Toronto (ON, Canada)
U of Tulsa (OK)
U of Vermont (VT)
U of Washington (WA)
Vanderbilt U (TN)
Washington and Lee U (VA)
Washington U in St. Louis (MO)
Wellesley Coll (MA)
Wesleyan U (CT)
Wheaton Coll (MA)
Wittenberg U (OH)
Yale U (CT)

SALES AND MARKETING/ MARKETING AND DISTRIBUTION TEACHER EDUCATION

Bowling Green State U (OH)
Colorado State U (CO)
East Carolina U (NC)
Eastern Michigan U (MI)
Eastern New Mexico U (NM)
Fayetteville State U (NC)
Middle Tennessee State U (TN)
North Carolina State U (NC)
Rider U (NJ)
State U of New York at Oswego (NY)
U of Minnesota, Twin Cities Campus (MN)
U of Wisconsin–Stout (WI)
Utah State U (UT)
Western Michigan U (MI)
Wright State U (OH)

SALES, DISTRIBUTION, AND MARKETING OPERATIONS

Babson Coll (MA)
Baylor U (TX)
Black Hills State U (SD)
Bowling Green State U (OH)
Cleary U (MI)
Concordia U, St. Paul (MN)
Dalton State Coll (GA)
Hampton U (VA)
Harding U (AR)
HEC Montreal (QC, Canada)
Husson U (ME)
Kennesaw State U (GA)
McKendree U (IL)
Metropolitan State U (MN)
Middle Tennessee State U (TN)
New York U (NY)
Quinnipiac U (CT)
Ryerson U (ON, Canada)
St. Catherine U (MN)
Seton Hill U (PA)
Simmons Coll (MA)
Texas A&M U (TX)
Tuskegee U (AL)
The U of Akron (OH)
The U of Findlay (OH)
U of Houston (TX)
U of Illinois at Urbana–Champaign (IL)
U of Memphis (TN)
U of Minnesota, Twin Cities Campus (MN)
U of North Texas (TX)
U of Pennsylvania (PA)
U of the Incarnate Word (TX)
U of Wisconsin–Stout (WI)
U of Wisconsin–Superior (WI)
West Chester U of Pennsylvania (PA)

SANSKRIT AND CLASSICAL INDIAN LANGUAGES

Bard Coll (NY)
Harvard U (MA)

SCANDINAVIAN LANGUAGES

Augustana Coll (IL)
Gustavus Adolphus Coll (MN)
Luther Coll (IA)
U of Alberta (AB, Canada)
U of California, Berkeley (CA)
U of California, Los Angeles (CA)

U of Minnesota, Twin Cities Campus (MN)
The U of Texas at Austin (TX)
U of Washington (WA)

SCANDINAVIAN STUDIES

Concordia Coll (MN)
Gustavus Adolphus Coll (MN)
Pacific Lutheran U (WA)
U of Washington (WA)
U of Wisconsin–Madison (WI)

SCHOOL LIBRARIAN/SCHOOL LIBRARY MEDIA

The Coll of St. Scholastica (MN)
East Central U (OK)
U of Great Falls (MT)

SCHOOL PSYCHOLOGY

Eastern Washington U (WA)
Fort Hays State U (KS)
U of Southern Maine (ME)
U of Wisconsin–River Falls (WI)

SCIENCE TEACHER EDUCATION

Abilene Christian U (TX)
Adams State Coll (CO)
Adrian Coll (MI)
Albany State U (GA)
Albion Coll (MI)
Alfred U (NY)
Alma Coll (MI)
Alvernia U (PA)
Alverno Coll (WI)
Andrews U (MI)
Aquinas Coll (MI)
Arcadia U (PA)
Arkansas Tech U (AR)
Ashland U (OH)
Assumption Coll (MA)
Athens State U (AL)
Auburn U (AL)
Ball State U (IN)
Baptist Bible Coll of Pennsylvania (PA)
Bayamón Central U (PR)
Baylor U (TX)
Beloit Coll (WI)
Bemidji State U (MN)
Bethel Coll (IN)
Biola U (CA)
Bishop's U (QC, Canada)
Black Hills State U (SD)
Bluefield Coll (VA)
Bob Jones U (SC)
Boise State U (ID)
Boston U (MA)
Bowie State U (MD)
Bowling Green State U (OH)
Bradley U (IL)
Brewton-Parker Coll (GA)
Brigham Young U (UT)
Buena Vista U (IA)
Buffalo State Coll, State U of New York (NY)
California Lutheran U (CA)
California State U, San Marcos (CA)
Calumet Coll of Saint Joseph (IN)
Calvin Coll (MI)
Cameron U (OK)
Campbellsville U (KY)
Capital U (OH)
Cardinal Stritch U (WI)
Castleton State Coll (VT)
Cedarville U (OH)
Central Methodist U (MO)
Central Michigan U (MI)
Central Washington U (WA)
Chipola Coll (FL)
City Coll of the City U of New York (NY)
Clemson U (SC)
Coe Coll (IA)
The Coll at Brockport, State U of New York (NY)
Coll of Saint Mary (NE)
The Coll of Saint Rose (NY)
Coll of the Atlantic (ME)
Coll of the Ozarks (MO)
Colorado State U (CO)
Columbus State U (GA)
Concordia Coll–New York (NY)

Concordia U (MI)
Concordia U Chicago (IL)
Concordia U, Nebraska (NE)
Cornerstone U (MI)
Covenant Coll (GA)
Crown Coll (MN)
Dallas Baptist U (TX)
Defiance Coll (OH)
Delaware State U (DE)
Dixie State Coll of Utah (UT)
Doane Coll (NE)
Dordt Coll (IA)
Dowling Coll (NY)
East Carolina U (NC)
East Central U (OK)
Eastern Illinois U (IL)
Eastern Kentucky U (KY)
Eastern Michigan U (MI)
Eastern Washington U (WA)
Edgewood Coll (WI)
Elizabethtown Coll (PA)
Elmira Coll (NY)
Elon U (NC)
Evangel U (MO)
Fairmont State U (WV)
Florida Ag and Mech U (FL)
Florida Atlantic U (FL)
Florida Inst of Technology (FL)
Fort Hays State U (KS)
Gettysburg Coll (PA)
Glenville State Coll (WV)
Governors State U (IL)
Graceland U (IA)
Grand Valley State U (MI)
Grove City Coll (PA)
Hannibal-LaGrange U (MO)
Harding U (AR)
Hardin-Simmons U (TX)
Heidelberg U (OH)
Hofstra U (NY)
Hope Coll (MI)
Hunter Coll of the City U of New York (NY)
Huntington U (IN)
Indiana State U (IN)
Indiana U Bloomington (IN)
Indiana U–Purdue U Fort Wayne (IN)
Indiana U South Bend (IN)
Indiana U Southeast (IN)
Indiana Wesleyan U (IN)
Indian River State Coll (FL)
Inter American U of Puerto Rico, San Germán Campus (PR)
Ithaca Coll (NY)
Judson Coll (AL)
Juniata Coll (PA)
Keene State Coll (NH)
Kent State U (OH)
Lakehead U (ON, Canada)
La Salle U (PA)
Le Moyne Coll (NY)
Lenoir-Rhyne U (NC)
Lewis-Clark State Coll (ID)
Lincoln Memorial U (TN)
Lindenwood U (MO)
Longwood U (VA)
Louisiana Coll (LA)
Loyola U Chicago (IL)
Lubbock Christian U (TX)
Madonna U (MI)
Malone U (OH)
Manchester Coll (IN)
Mansfield U of Pennsylvania (PA)
Maranatha Baptist Bible Coll (WI)
Marian U (WI)
Mars Hill Coll (NC)
Marywood U (PA)
The Master's Coll and Sem (CA)
Mercyhurst Coll (PA)
Merrimack Coll (MA)
Miami Dade Coll (FL)
Miami U (OH)
Michigan State U (MI)
Michigan Technological U (MI)
Midwestern State U (TX)
Minnesota State U Mankato (MN)
Minot State U (ND)
Mississippi Valley State U (MS)
Missouri Baptist U (MO)
Missouri State U (MO)
Montana State U (MT)
Montana State U Billings (MT)
Montana State U–Northern (MT)
Moravian Coll (PA)

Morningside Coll (IA)
Mount Mary Coll (WI)
Mount Mercy U (IA)
Mount Vernon Nazarene U (OH)
Nebraska Wesleyan U (NE)
New Mexico Highlands U (NM)
New York U (NY)
Niagara U (NY)
Nicholls State U (LA)
North Carolina Ag and Tech State U (NC)
North Carolina State U (NC)
North Dakota State U (ND)
Northeastern State U (OK)
Northern Michigan U (MI)
Northland Coll (WI)
Northwestern Oklahoma State U (OK)
Northwest Florida State Coll (FL)
Northwest Missouri State U (MO)
Notre Dame of Maryland U (MD)
Oakland City U (IN)
Ohio Northern U (OH)
Oklahoma Christian U (OK)
Oklahoma City U (OK)
Oral Roberts U (OK)
Otterbein U (OH)
Ouachita Baptist U (AR)
Pace U (NY)
Peru State Coll (NE)
Queen's U at Kingston (ON, Canada)
Rhode Island Coll (RI)
St. Ambrose U (IA)
Saint Francis U (PA)
Saint Joseph's U (PA)
Seattle Pacific U (WA)
Shawnee State U (OH)
Southeastern Oklahoma State U (OK)
Southeastern U (FL)
Southeast Missouri State U (MO)
Southern Illinois U Edwardsville (IL)
Southern New Hampshire U (NH)
Southwest Baptist U (MO)
Southwestern Oklahoma State U (OK)
State U of New York at Fredonia (NY)
State U of New York at New Paltz (NY)
State U of New York at Oswego (NY)
State U of New York Coll at Cortland (NY)
State U of New York Coll at Old Westbury (NY)
State U of New York Coll at Oneonta (NY)
State U of New York Coll of Environmental Science and Forestry (NY)
Tarleton State U (TX)
Temple U (PA)
Texas A&M Intl U (TX)
Texas A&M U–Corpus Christi (TX)
Texas Christian U (TX)
Texas Wesleyan U (TX)
Trine U (IN)
Union U (TN)
Universidad del Turabo (PR)
The U of Akron (OH)
U of Alberta (AB, Canada)
The U of British Columbia (BC, Canada)
U of Central Arkansas (AR)
U of Central Florida (FL)
U of Charleston (WV)
U of Dayton (OH)
The U of Findlay (OH)
U of Georgia (GA)
U of Great Falls (MT)
U of Illinois at Urbana–Champaign (IL)
U of Indianapolis (IN)
The U of Iowa (IA)
U of Lethbridge (AB, Canada)
U of Louisiana at Lafayette (LA)
U of Maine (ME)
U of Maine at Farmington (ME)
U of Maine at Presque Isle (ME)
U of Mary Hardin-Baylor (TX)
U of Michigan–Dearborn (MI)
U of Minnesota, Duluth (MN)

U of Minnesota, Twin Cities Campus (MN)
U of Mississippi (MS)
U of Missouri (MO)
The U of Montana Western (MT)
U of Nebraska–Lincoln (NE)
U of North Dakota (ND)
U of Northern Iowa (IA)
U of North Florida (FL)
U of Notre Dame (IN)
U of Oklahoma (OK)
U of Pittsburgh at Johnstown (PA)
U of Regina (SK, Canada)
U of Rio Grande (OH)
U of St. Francis (IL)
U of Saint Francis (IN)
U of St. Thomas (MN)
The U of South Dakota (SD)
U of South Florida (FL)
The U of Tennessee at Chattanooga (TN)
The U of Tennessee at Martin (TN)
The U of Toledo (OH)
U of Toronto (ON, Canada)
U of Vermont (VT)
U of Washington (WA)
U of Windsor (ON, Canada)
U of Wisconsin–Eau Claire (WI)
U of Wisconsin–La Crosse (WI)
U of Wisconsin–Madison (WI)
U of Wisconsin–Platteville (WI)
U of Wisconsin–River Falls (WI)
U of Wisconsin–Stout (WI)
U of Wisconsin–Superior (WI)
U of Wisconsin–Whitewater (WI)
Upper Iowa U (IA)
Ursuline Coll (OH)
Utah State U (UT)
Utah Valley U (UT)
Valley City State U (ND)
Valparaiso U (IN)
Vincennes U (IN)
Viterbo U (WI)
Walsh U (OH)
Washington State U (WA)
Washington U in St. Louis (MO)
Wayland Baptist U (TX)
Waynesburg U (PA)
Wayne State Coll (NE)
Wayne State U (MI)
Weber State U (UT)
Western Carolina U (NC)
Western State Coll of Colorado (CO)
Western Washington U (WA)
West Virginia State U (WV)
Widener U (PA)
William Penn U (IA)
William Woods U (MO)
Wilmington Coll (OH)
Wilmington U (DE)
Winona State U (MN)
Wright State U (OH)
Xavier U (OH)
Xavier U of Louisiana (LA)
York Coll of Pennsylvania (PA)
Youngstown State U (OH)

SCIENCE TECHNOLOGIES
Marylhurst U (OR)

SCIENCE TECHNOLOGIES RELATED
Arizona State U (AZ)
Athens State U (AL)
Bridgewater State U (MA)
Clemson U (SC)
Kean U (NJ)
Kent State U at Geauga (OH)
Madonna U (MI)
North Carolina State U (NC)
Northern Arizona U (AZ)
The U of Arizona (AZ)
U of Wisconsin–Stout (WI)
Willamette U (OR)

SCIENCE, TECHNOLOGY AND SOCIETY
Arizona State U (AZ)
Butler U (IN)
California State Polytechnic U, Pomona (CA)
Claremont McKenna Coll (CA)
Colby Coll (ME)

Cornell U (NY)
Dalhousie U (NS, Canada)
Eastern Michigan U (MI)
Georgia Inst of Technology (GA)
James Madison U (VA)
Lehigh U (PA)
Massachusetts Inst of Technology (MA)
Morrisville State Coll (NY)
North Carolina State U (NC)
Pitzer Coll (CA)
Rensselaer Polytechnic Inst (NY)
Rutgers, The State U of New Jersey, Newark (NJ)
Scripps Coll (CA)
Slippery Rock U of Pennsylvania (PA)
Stanford U (CA)
Texas Tech U (TX)
U of Alaska Anchorage (AK)
U of Puget Sound (WA)
U of Washington, Bothell (WA)
U of Windsor (ON, Canada)
Vanderbilt U (TN)
Vassar Coll (NY)
Washington U in St. Louis (MO)
Wesleyan U (CT)
Worcester Polytechnic Inst (MA)

SCULPTURE
Acad of Art U (CA)
Alberta Coll of Art & Design (AB, Canada)
Aquinas Coll (MI)
Bard Coll at Simon's Rock (MA)
Bennington Coll (VT)
Bethany Coll (KS)
Biola U (CA)
Birmingham-Southern Coll (AL)
Boston U (MA)
Bowling Green State U (OH)
Bradley U (IL)
Brigham Young U (UT)
Buffalo State Coll, State U of New York (NY)
California Coll of the Arts (CA)
California State U, East Bay (CA)
California State U, Long Beach (CA)
The Cleveland Inst of Art (OH)
The Coll at Brockport, State U of New York (NY)
Colorado State U (CO)
Concordia U (QC, Canada)
Dominican U (IL)
Drake U (IA)
Emily Carr U of Art + Design (BC, Canada)
Escuela de Artes Plasticas de Puerto Rico (PR)
Ferris State U (MI)
Indiana U–Purdue U Fort Wayne (IN)
Inter American U of Puerto Rico, San Germán Campus (PR)
Kansas City Art Inst (MO)
Lyme Acad Coll of Fine Arts (CT)
Marlboro Coll (VT)
Maryland Inst Coll of Art (MD)
Marywood U (PA)
Massachusetts Coll of Art and Design (MA)
Minnesota State U Mankato (MN)
Montserrat Coll of Art (MA)
Mount Allison U (NB, Canada)
Northern Michigan U (MI)
Northwest Nazarene U (ID)
Ohio Northern U (OH)
Ohio U (OH)
Otis Coll of Art and Design (CA)
Pacific Northwest Coll of Art (OR)
Portland State U (OR)
Pratt Inst (NY)
Ringling Coll of Art and Design (FL)
Rochester Inst of Technology (NY)
Rutgers, The State U of New Jersey, New Brunswick (NJ)
Salem State U (MA)
Sarah Lawrence Coll (NY)
Savannah Coll of Art and Design (GA)
School of the Museum of Fine Arts, Boston (MA)
Seton Hill U (PA)
Sonoma State U (CA)

State U of New York at New Paltz (NY)
Syracuse U (NY)
Temple U (PA)
Texas Christian U (TX)
U of Alberta (AB, Canada)
U of Dallas (TX)
U of Hartford (CT)
U of Houston (TX)
U of Illinois at Urbana–Champaign (IL)
The U of Iowa (IA)
The U of Kansas (KS)
U of Massachusetts Dartmouth (MA)
U of Miami (FL)
U of Michigan (MI)
U of Oregon (OR)
U of Regina (SK, Canada)
The U of Texas at El Paso (TX)
The U of the Arts (PA)
U of Washington (WA)
U of Windsor (ON, Canada)
Virginia Commonwealth U (VA)
Virginia Intermont Coll (VA)
Washington U in St. Louis (MO)
Western State Coll of Colorado (CO)
Western Washington U (WA)

SECONDARY EDUCATION
Abilene Christian U (TX)
Acadia U (NS, Canada)
Adrian Coll (MI)
Alabama State U (AL)
Albertus Magnus Coll (CT)
Albright Coll (PA)
Alfred U (NY)
Alma Coll (MI)
American U (DC)
Andrews U (MI)
Anna Maria Coll (MA)
Arcadia U (PA)
Arizona State U (AZ)
Ashland U (OH)
Assumption Coll (MA)
Athens State U (AL)
Auburn U (AL)
Auburn U Montgomery (AL)
Augustana Coll (SD)
Baker U (KS)
Baptist Bible Coll of Pennsylvania (PA)
Baylor U (TX)
Beloit Coll (WI)
Bemidji State U (MN)
Benedictine Coll (KS)
Bennington Coll (VT)
Bethel Coll (IN)
Biola U (CA)
Birmingham-Southern Coll (AL)
Bishop's U (QC, Canada)
Blackburn Coll (IL)
Black Hills State U (SD)
Bluefield Coll (VA)
Boise State U (ID)
Boston Coll (MA)
Bowie State U (MD)
Brewton-Parker Coll (GA)
Briar Cliff U (IA)
Bucknell U (PA)
Buffalo State Coll, State U of New York (NY)
Butler U (IN)
Caldwell Coll (NJ)
Calumet Coll of Saint Joseph (IN)
Calvary Bible Coll and Theological Sem (MO)
Calvin Coll (MI)
Campbellsville U (KY)
Canisius Coll (NY)
Cardinal Stritch U (WI)
Caribbean U (PR)
Carroll Coll (MT)
Carson-Newman Coll (TN)
Catawba Coll (NC)
The Catholic U of America (DC)
Cedar Crest Coll (PA)
Centenary Coll (NJ)
Central Methodist U (MO)
Central State U (OH)
Cheyney U of Pennsylvania (PA)
Chipola Coll (FL)
The Citadel, The Military Coll of South Carolina (SC)

INDEXES

City Coll of the City U of New York (NY)
Clarke U (IA)
Clark U (MA)
Clemson U (SC)
Coe Coll (IA)
The Coll at Brockport, State U of New York (NY)
Coll of Charleston (SC)
The Coll of New Jersey (NJ)
Coll of Saint Benedict (MN)
Coll of St. Joseph (VT)
Coll of Saint Mary (NE)
Coll of the Atlantic (ME)
Coll of the Ozarks (MO)
Concordia U (MI)
Concordia U Chicago (IL)
Concordia U, Nebraska (NE)
Concordia U, St. Paul (MN)
Concordia U Texas (TX)
Converse Coll (SC)
Corban U (OR)
Cornell Coll (IA)
Cornerstone U (MI)
Dallas Baptist U (TX)
Defiance Coll (OH)
Delaware State U (DE)
Delaware Valley Coll (PA)
DePaul U (IL)
Dixie State Coll of Utah (UT)
Dominican Coll (NY)
Dordt Coll (IA)
Drake U (IA)
Duquesne U (PA)
East Central U (OK)
Eastern Connecticut State U (CT)
Eastern Kentucky U (KY)
East Stroudsburg U of Pennsylvania (PA)
Edward Waters Coll (FL)
Elmhurst Coll (IL)
Elmira Coll (NY)
Elon U (NC)
Emmanuel Coll (MA)
Emporia State U (KS)
Evangel U (MO)
Fairmont State U (WV)
Faulkner U (AL)
Felician Coll (NJ)
Fitchburg State U (MA)
Flagler Coll (FL)
Florida Gulf Coast U (FL)
Florida Southern Coll (FL)
Fontbonne U (MO)
Fordham U (NY)
Fort Lewis Coll (CO)
Free Will Baptist Bible Coll (TN)
Furman U (SC)
Gannon U (PA)
Gardner-Webb U (NC)
Gettysburg Coll (PA)
Glenville State Coll (WV)
Gonzaga U (WA)
Graceland U (IA)
Grand Canyon U (AZ)
Grand Valley State U (MI)
Granite State Coll (NH)
Grove City Coll (PA)
Guilford Coll (NC)
Gustavus Adolphus Coll (MN)
Gwynedd-Mercy Coll (PA)
Hamline U (MN)
Hampton U (VA)
Hannibal-LaGrange U (MO)
Harding U (AR)
Heidelberg U (OH)
Hillsdale Coll (MI)
Hillsdale Free Will Baptist Coll (OK)
Hofstra U (NY)
Holy Family U (PA)
Houghton Coll (NY)
Howard Payne U (TX)
Humboldt State U (CA)
Hunter Coll of the City U of New York (NY)
Huntington U (IN)
Huston-Tillotson U (TX)
Idaho State U (ID)
Illinois Coll (IL)
Indiana U Bloomington (IN)
Indiana U East (IN)
Indiana U Kokomo (IN)
Indiana U Northwest (IN)
Indiana U–Purdue U Fort Wayne (IN)

Indiana U South Bend (IN)
Indiana U Southeast (IN)
Indiana Wesleyan U (IN)
Inter American U of Puerto Rico, San Germán Campus (PR)
Iona Coll (NY)
Iowa State U of Science and Technology (IA)
Iowa Wesleyan Coll (IA)
Ithaca Coll (NY)
Jacksonville State U (AL)
Jacksonville U (FL)
Jarvis Christian Coll (TX)
John Brown U (AR)
John Carroll U (OH)
Johnson State Coll (VT)
Judson U (IL)
Juniata Coll (PA)
Kansas State U (KS)
Keene State Coll (NH)
Kentucky Wesleyan Coll (KY)
Keuka Coll (NY)
The King's U Coll (AB, Canada)
Knox Coll (IL)
Lake Erie Coll (OH)
Lakehead U (ON, Canada)
Lake Superior State U (MI)
Lamar U (TX)
La Salle U (PA)
Lasell Coll (MA)
Lawrence U (WI)
Lee U (TN)
Le Moyne Coll (NY)
Lenoir-Rhyne U (NC)
LeTourneau U (TX)
Lewis U (IL)
Lincoln Memorial U (TN)
Lincoln U (MO)
Lindenwood U (MO)
Lindsey Wilson Coll (KY)
Lock Haven U of Pennsylvania (PA)
Long Island U–Brooklyn Campus (NY)
Long Island U–C. W. Post Campus (NY)
Longwood U (VA)
Loras Coll (IA)
Louisiana Coll (LA)
Lourdes U (OH)
Loyola U Chicago (IL)
Lubbock Christian U (TX)
Maharishi U of Management (IA)
Manchester Coll (IN)
Manhattanville Coll (NY)
Mansfield U of Pennsylvania (PA)
Marian U (WI)
Marietta Coll (OH)
Marquette U (WI)
Marshall U (WV)
Mars Hill Coll (NC)
The Master's Coll and Sem (CA)
McKendree U (IL)
McMurry U (TX)
McNeese State U (LA)
Medaille Coll (NY)
Mercyhurst Coll (PA)
Merrimack Coll (MA)
Miami U (OH)
Michigan State U (MI)
Michigan Technological U (MI)
MidAmerica Nazarene U (KS)
Midwestern State U (TX)
Minnesota State U Mankato (MN)
Mississippi State U (MS)
Missouri Southern State U (MO)
Missouri State U (MO)
Missouri U of Science and Technology (MO)
Molloy Coll (NY)
Monmouth U (NJ)
Montana State U Billings (MT)
Moravian Coll (PA)
Mount Aloysius Coll (PA)
Mount Marty Coll (SD)
Mount Mercy U (IA)
Mount Saint Mary Coll (NY)
Mount Vernon Nazarene U (OH)
Nazareth Coll of Rochester (NY)
Newberry Coll (SC)
New England Coll (NH)
Newman U (KS)
New Mexico State U (NM)
Niagara U (NY)
Nichols Coll (MA)

North Carolina Ag and Tech State U (NC)
North Carolina Wesleyan Coll (NC)
North Central Coll (IL)
Northern Michigan U (MI)
Northern State U (SD)
Northland Coll (WI)
Northwestern Coll (IA)
Northwestern Oklahoma State U (OK)
Northwestern State U of Louisiana (LA)
Northwest Nazarene U (ID)
Northwest U (WA)
Notre Dame of Maryland U (MD)
Nova Southeastern U (FL)
Oakland City U (IN)
Ohio U (OH)
Ohio U–Chillicothe (OH)
Ohio Valley U (WV)
Ohio Wesleyan U (OH)
Oklahoma Christian U (OK)
Oklahoma City U (OK)
Oklahoma State U (OK)
Otterbein U (OH)
Ouachita Baptist U (AR)
Pacific U (OR)
Penn State Abington (PA)
Penn State Altoona (PA)
Penn State Beaver (PA)
Penn State Berks (PA)
Penn State Brandywine (PA)
Penn State DuBois (PA)
Penn State Erie, The Behrend Coll (PA)
Penn State Fayette, The Eberly Campus (PA)
Penn State Greater Allegheny (PA)
Penn State Hazleton (PA)
Penn State Lehigh Valley (PA)
Penn State Mont Alto (PA)
Penn State New Kensington (PA)
Penn State Schuylkill (PA)
Penn State Shenango (PA)
Penn State U Park (PA)
Penn State Wilkes-Barre (PA)
Penn State Worthington Scranton (PA)
Penn State York (PA)
Pepperdine U, Malibu (CA)
Peru State Coll (NE)
Prescott Coll (AZ)
Presentation Coll (SD)
Providence Coll (RI)
Purdue U Calumet (IN)
Purdue U North Central (IN)
Queens U of Charlotte (NC)
Rhode Island Coll (RI)
Rider U (NJ)
Ripon Coll (WI)
Rivier Coll (NH)
Rockford Coll (IL)
Rockhurst U (MO)
Rocky Mountain Coll (MT)
Roger Williams U (RI)
Sacred Heart U (CT)
St. Ambrose U (IA)
Saint Anselm Coll (NH)
St. Catherine U (MN)
Saint Francis U (PA)
Saint John's U (MN)
Saint Joseph's U (PA)
Saint Mary-of-the-Woods Coll (IN)
Saint Michael's Coll (VT)
St. Thomas Aquinas Coll (NY)
St. Thomas U (FL)
Salem State U (MA)
Salve Regina U (RI)
San Diego Christian Coll (CA)
Seattle Pacific U (WA)
Shepherd U (WV)
Siena Coll (NY)
Siena Heights U (MI)
Simmons Coll (MA)
Simpson Coll (IA)
Slippery Rock U of Pennsylvania (PA)
Southern Connecticut State U (CT)
Southwestern Assemblies of God U (TX)
Southwestern Oklahoma State U (OK)
Spring Arbor U (MI)
Spring Hill Coll (AL)

State U of New York at Fredonia (NY)
State U of New York at New Paltz (NY)
State U of New York at Oswego (NY)
State U of New York Coll at Cortland (NY)
State U of New York Coll at Old Westbury (NY)
State U of New York Coll at Oneonta (NY)
Stetson U (FL)
Susquehanna U (PA)
Tabor Coll (KS)
Tarleton State U (TX)
Texas Christian U (TX)
Thiel Coll (PA)
Thomas More Coll (KY)
Thomas U (GA)
Trent U (ON, Canada)
Trine U (IN)
Trinity Baptist Coll (FL)
Troy U (AL)
Tusculum Coll (TN)
Union Coll (KY)
Union Inst & U (OH)
Union U (TN)
Université de Sherbrooke (QC, Canada)
The U of Alabama (AL)
The U of Alabama at Birmingham (AL)
U of Alaska Anchorage (AK)
U of Alberta (AB, Canada)
The U of British Columbia (BC, Canada)
U of Central Missouri (MO)
U of Cincinnati (OH)
U of Dallas (TX)
U of Dayton (OH)
U of Dubuque (IA)
The U of Findlay (OH)
U of Great Falls (MT)
U of Guam (GU)
U of Hartford (CT)
U of Hawaii at Hilo (HI)
U of Hawaii at Manoa (HI)
U of Idaho (ID)
U of Illinois at Urbana–Champaign (IL)
U of Indianapolis (IN)
The U of Iowa (IA)
The U of Kansas (KS)
U of Louisiana at Lafayette (LA)
U of Maine (ME)
U of Maine at Farmington (ME)
U of Maine at Presque Isle (ME)
U of Maryland, Coll Park (MD)
U of Michigan (MI)
U of Michigan–Dearborn (MI)
U of Minnesota, Twin Cities Campus (MN)
U of Missouri (MO)
U of Missouri–Kansas City (MO)
U of Missouri–St. Louis (MO)
The U of Montana Western (MT)
U of Nebraska at Omaha (NE)
U of Nevada, Las Vegas (NV)
U of New Mexico (NM)
U of New Orleans (LA)
U of North Alabama (AL)
U of North Florida (FL)
U of Pittsburgh at Bradford (PA)
U of Pittsburgh at Johnstown (PA)
U of Portland (OR)
U of Redlands (CA)
U of Regina (SK, Canada)
U of Rhode Island (RI)
U of Rio Grande (OH)
U of St. Thomas (TX)
The U of Scranton (PA)
U of South Alabama (AL)
U of South Carolina Aiken (SC)
U of South Carolina Upstate (SC)
The U of South Dakota (SD)
The U of Tampa (FL)
The U of Tennessee at Chattanooga (TN)
U of the Cumberlands (KY)
U of the Ozarks (AR)
U of the Southwest (NM)
The U of Toledo (OH)
U of Vermont (VT)
U of Washington (WA)

The U of Western Ontario (ON, Canada)
U of West Georgia (GA)
U of Windsor (ON, Canada)
U of Wisconsin–Platteville (WI)
U of Wisconsin–River Falls (WI)
U of Wisconsin–Stevens Point (WI)
U of Wisconsin–Whitewater (WI)
U of Wyoming (WY)
Utah State U (UT)
Utica Coll (NY)
Valley City State U (ND)
Valparaiso U (IN)
Vanderbilt U (TN)
Vanguard U of Southern California (CA)
Villanova U (PA)
Virginia Intermont Coll (VA)
Virginia Polytechnic Inst and State U (VA)
Virginia Wesleyan Coll (VA)
Wagner Coll (NY)
Waldorf Coll (IA)
Walsh U (OH)
Wartburg Coll (IA)
Washington State U (WA)
Washington U in St. Louis (MO)
Waynesburg U (PA)
Wells Coll (NY)
Western Connecticut State U (CT)
Western New England U (MA)
Western Oregon U (OR)
West Liberty U (WV)
Westminster Coll (MO)
West Virginia State U (WV)
West Virginia Wesleyan Coll (WV)
Wheaton Coll (IL)
Wheeling Jesuit U (WV)
Wichita State U (KS)
William Jewell Coll (MO)
William Paterson U of New Jersey (NJ)
William Penn U (IA)
William Woods U (MO)
Wilmington Coll (OH)
Winona State U (MN)
Wright State U (OH)
Xavier U of Louisiana (LA)
York Coll of the City U of New York (NY)
Youngstown State U (OH)

SECURITIES SERVICES ADMINISTRATION

American Public U System (WV)
Central Penn Coll (PA)
The Coll at Brockport, State U of New York (NY)
Davenport U, Grand Rapids (MI)
St. John's U (NY)
Vincennes U (IN)
Washburn U (KS)
Webber Intl U (FL)

SECURITY AND LOSS PREVENTION

Eastern Kentucky U (KY)
Farmingdale State Coll (NY)
Lewis U (IL)
Northern Michigan U (MI)
Saint Louis U (MO)

SELLING SKILLS AND SALES

Bellevue U (NE)
Bradley U (IL)
St. Catherine U (MN)
U of Memphis (TN)
Weber State U (UT)

SIGN LANGUAGE INTERPRETATION AND TRANSLATION

Augustana Coll (SD)
Bethel Coll (IN)
Bloomsburg U of Pennsylvania (PA)
Columbia Coll Chicago (IL)
Eastern Kentucky U (KY)
Gallaudet U (DC)
Goshen Coll (IN)
Idaho State U (ID)
Indiana U–Purdue U Indianapolis (IN)
Kent State U (OH)

Maryville Coll (TN)
Mount Aloysius Coll (PA)
Quincy U (IL)
Rochester Inst of Technology (NY)
Troy U (AL)
Universidad del Turabo (PR)
U of Arkansas at Little Rock (AR)
U of Louisville (KY)
U of New Hampshire at Manchester (NH)
U of New Mexico (NM)
U of Northern Colorado (CO)
U of North Florida (FL)
Valdosta State U (GA)
Western Oregon U (OR)
William Woods U (MO)
Wright State U (OH)

SLAVIC, BALTIC, AND ALBANIAN LANGUAGES RELATED

Rutgers, The State U of New Jersey, Newark (NJ)

SLAVIC LANGUAGES

Boston Coll (MA)
Columbia U, School of General Studies (NY)
Harvard U (MA)
Indiana U Bloomington (IN)
Princeton U (NJ)
Stanford U (CA)
U of Alberta (AB, Canada)
The U of British Columbia (BC, Canada)
U of California, Berkeley (CA)
U of California, Los Angeles (CA)
U of California, Santa Barbara (CA)
U of Illinois at Chicago (IL)
U of Illinois at Urbana–Champaign (IL)
The U of Kansas (KS)
U of Minnesota, Twin Cities Campus (MN)
The U of North Carolina at Chapel Hill (NC)
U of Pittsburgh (PA)
U of Toronto (ON, Canada)
U of Virginia (VA)
U of Washington (WA)
Wayne State U (MI)

SLAVIC STUDIES

Barnard Coll (NY)
Baylor U (TX)
Columbia U, School of General Studies (NY)
Connecticut Coll (CT)
Lawrence U (WI)
U of Ottawa (ON, Canada)

SMALL BUSINESS ADMINISTRATION

Adams State Coll (CO)
Arcadia U (PA)
Avila U (MO)
Babson Coll (MA)
Bradley U (IL)
Carson-Newman Coll (TN)
Dalhousie U (NS, Canada)
Huntington U (IN)
Husson U (ME)
Lewis-Clark State Coll (ID)
North Central Coll (IL)
Northern Michigan U (MI)
Saint Joseph's U (PA)
U of Nebraska at Omaha (NE)

SOCIAL AND PHILOSOPHICAL FOUNDATIONS OF EDUCATION

Eastern Washington U (WA)
Hope Intl U (CA)
Transylvania U (KY)
Washington U in St. Louis (MO)

SOCIAL PSYCHOLOGY

Bennington Coll (VT)
Brigham Young U (UT)
Clarion U of Pennsylvania (PA)
Florida Atlantic U (FL)
Grand Valley State U (MI)
Keene State Coll (NH)

Lawrence U (WI)
Maryville U of Saint Louis (MO)
Moravian Coll (PA)
Northwest Missouri State U (MO)
Penn State Abington (PA)
U of California, Irvine (CA)
U of New England (ME)
U of Wisconsin–Superior (WI)
Western Michigan U (MI)

SOCIAL SCIENCES

Adelphi U (NY)
Adrian Coll (MI)
Albertus Magnus Coll (CT)
Albion Coll (MI)
Alvernia U (PA)
Alverno Coll (WI)
American U (DC)
Andrews U (MI)
Aquinas Coll (MI)
Arizona State U (AZ)
Asbury U (KY)
Ashland U (OH)
Azusa Pacific U (CA)
Ball State U (IN)
Belhaven U (MS)
Bellevue U (NE)
Bemidji State U (MN)
Benedictine Coll (KS)
Benedictine U (IL)
Bennington Coll (VT)
Berry Coll (GA)
Bethany Lutheran Coll (MN)
Bethel Coll (IN)
Bethel U (MN)
Biola U (CA)
Bishop's U (QC, Canada)
Black Hills State U (SD)
Bluefield Coll (VA)
Bluefield State Coll (WV)
Blue Mountain Coll (MS)
Bluffton U (OH)
Boise State U (ID)
Bowling Green State U (OH)
Brescia U (KY)
Brewton-Parker Coll (GA)
Buena Vista U (IA)
Caldwell Coll (NJ)
California Lutheran U (CA)
California Polytechnic State U, San Luis Obispo (CA)
California State Polytechnic U, Pomona (CA)
California State U, Los Angeles (CA)
California State U, Monterey Bay (CA)
California State U, Sacramento (CA)
California State U, San Bernardino (CA)
California State U, San Marcos (CA)
California State U, Stanislaus (CA)
California U of Pennsylvania (PA)
Calvin Coll (MI)
Campbellsville U (KY)
Cardinal Stritch U (WI)
Castleton State Coll (VT)
Central Coll (IA)
Central Connecticut State U (CT)
Central Michigan U (MI)
Chaminade U of Honolulu (HI)
Cheyney U of Pennsylvania (PA)
Clarkson U (NY)
Cleveland State U (OH)
Colgate U (NY)
Coll of Mount Saint Vincent (NY)
Coll of Saint Benedict (MN)
Coll of Saint Mary (NE)
The Coll of St. Scholastica (MN)
Coll of the Humanities and Sciences, Harrison Middleton U (AZ)
Colorado Mesa U (CO)
Colorado State U (CO)
Concordia Coll (MN)
Concordia Coll–New York (NY)
Concordia U (MI)
Concordia U, Nebraska (NE)
Corban U (OR)
Defiance Coll (OH)
Delta State U (MS)
DePaul U (IL)
Doane Coll (NE)

Dominican Coll (NY)
Dordt Coll (IA)
Dowling Coll (NY)
Drexel U (PA)
Eastern Mennonite U (VA)
Eastern Michigan U (MI)
Eastern New Mexico U (NM)
East Stroudsburg U of Pennsylvania (PA)
Edgewood Coll (WI)
Edinboro U of Pennsylvania (PA)
Edward Waters Coll (FL)
Elizabethtown Coll (PA)
Elmira Coll (NY)
Emporia State U (KS)
Faulkner U (AL)
Ferrum Coll (VA)
Florida Atlantic U (FL)
Florida Southern Coll (FL)
Florida State U (FL)
Fontbonne U (MO)
Fordham U (NY)
Gardner-Webb U (NC)
Gettysburg Coll (PA)
Governors State U (IL)
Grand Valley State U (MI)
Gustavus Adolphus Coll (MN)
Hampton U (VA)
Harding U (AR)
Harvard U (MA)
Hawai'i Pacific U (HI)
Holy Family U (PA)
Hope Intl U (CA)
Howard Payne U (TX)
Humboldt State U (CA)
Illinois Inst of Technology (IL)
Indiana U Bloomington (IN)
Inter American U of Puerto Rico, San Germán Campus (PR)
Ithaca Coll (NY)
James Madison U (VA)
The Johns Hopkins U (MD)
Johnson C. Smith U (NC)
Juniata Coll (PA)
Kansas State U (KS)
Keene State Coll (NH)
Kentucky State U (KY)
Keuka Coll (NY)
Keystone Coll (PA)
The King's U Coll (AB, Canada)
Kutztown U of Pennsylvania (PA)
Lake Erie Coll (OH)
Lake Superior State U (MI)
La Salle U (PA)
Lewis-Clark State Coll (ID)
Liberty U (VA)
Lock Haven U of Pennsylvania (PA)
Long Island U–Brooklyn Campus (NY)
Loyola U New Orleans (LA)
Manchester Coll (IN)
Mansfield U of Pennsylvania (PA)
Marlboro Coll (VT)
Mars Hill Coll (NC)
Marylhurst U (OR)
Marywood U (PA)
Mayville State U (ND)
McKendree U (IL)
Mercy Coll (NY)
Mercyhurst Coll (PA)
Metropolitan State U (MN)
Michigan State U (MI)
Michigan Technological U (MI)
Mid-Continent U (KY)
Minnesota State U Mankato (MN)
Minot State U (ND)
Misericordia U (PA)
Mississippi U for Women (MS)
Missouri Baptist U (MO)
Montreat Coll, Montreat (NC)
Moravian Coll (PA)
Morehead State U (KY)
Mount Saint Mary Coll (NY)
Mount St. Mary's Coll (CA)
Muhlenberg Coll (PA)
National-Louis U (IL)
Nazareth Coll of Rochester (NY)
New Coll of Florida (FL)
New York Inst of Technology (NY)
New York U (NY)
Niagara U (NY)
North Carolina Ag and Tech State U (NC)
North Central Coll (IL)
North Dakota State U (ND)

Northern Kentucky U (KY)
North Georgia Coll & State U (GA)
Northwestern Oklahoma State U (OK)
Northwest Nazarene U (ID)
Notre Dame de Namur U (CA)
Oakland City U (IN)
Pace U (NY)
Peru State Coll (NE)
Piedmont Coll (GA)
Plymouth State U (NH)
Point Loma Nazarene U (CA)
Point Park U (PA)
Point U (GA)
Portland State U (OR)
Providence Coll (RI)
Purdue U (IN)
Quinnipiac U (CT)
Radford U (VA)
Ramapo Coll of New Jersey (NJ)
Regis U (CO)
Rhode Island Coll (RI)
Robert Morris U (PA)
Rockford Coll (IL)
Rogers State U (OK)
Roger Williams U (RI)
Roosevelt U (IL)
Rosemont Coll (PA)
Rust Coll (MS)
Sage Coll of Albany (NY)
St. Andrews U (NC)
St. Catherine U (MN)
Saint John's U (MN)
St. John's U (NY)
St. Joseph's Coll, Long Island Campus (NY)
St. Joseph's Coll, New York (NY)
Saint Mary-of-the-Woods Coll (IN)
Saint Mary's Coll of California (CA)
Saint Mary's U of Minnesota (MN)
Saint Peter's Coll (NJ)
St. Thomas Aquinas Coll (NY)
Saint Xavier U (IL)
San Diego Christian Coll (CA)
San Diego State U (CA)
Sarah Lawrence Coll (NY)
Sewanee: The U of the South (TN)
Shawnee State U (OH)
Shimer Coll (IL)
Shorter U (GA)
Siena Heights U (MI)
South Carolina State U (SC)
Southern Arkansas U–Magnolia (AR)
Southern Illinois U Carbondale (IL)
Southern New Hampshire U (NH)
Southern Oregon U (OR)
Southwestern Adventist U (TX)
Spalding U (KY)
Spring Arbor U (MI)
Spring Hill Coll (AL)
State U of New York at Binghamton (NY)
State U of New York at New Paltz (NY)
State U of New York Coll at Old Westbury (NY)
State U of New York Empire State Coll (NY)
Stetson U (FL)
Suffolk U (MA)
Sul Ross State U (TX)
Tabor Coll (KS)
Texas A&M Intl U (TX)
Texas Wesleyan U (TX)
Thomas Edison State Coll (NJ)
Thomas U (GA)
Thompson Rivers U (BC, Canada)
Touro Coll (NY)
Towson U (MD)
Trent U (ON, Canada)
Trine U (IN)
Troy U (AL)
Union Coll (KY)
Union Coll (NY)
United States Air Force Acad (CO)
Universidad del Turabo (PR)
U at Buffalo, the State U of New York (NY)
The U of Akron (OH)
U of Arkansas at Monticello (AR)
U of Bridgeport (CT)
The U of British Columbia (BC, Canada)
U of California, Irvine (CA)

U of Central Florida (FL)
U of Cincinnati (OH)
U of Dallas (TX)
U of Denver (CO)
The U of Findlay (OH)
U of Great Falls (MT)
U of Hawaii–West Oahu (HI)
U of Houston–Downtown (TX)
U of Houston–Victoria (TX)
U of La Verne (CA)
U of Lethbridge (AB, Canada)
U of Maine at Augusta (ME)
U of Maine at Fort Kent (ME)
U of Mary (ND)
U of Maryland Eastern Shore (MD)
U of Maryland U Coll (MD)
U of Massachusetts Boston (MA)
U of Michigan (MI)
U of Michigan–Dearborn (MI)
U of Mobile (AL)
The U of Montana Western (MT)
U of Nevada, Las Vegas (NV)
U of North Dakota (ND)
U of Northern Colorado (CO)
U of North Texas (TX)
U of Oregon (OR)
U of Ottawa (ON, Canada)
U of Pennsylvania (PA)
U of Pittsburgh (PA)
U of Pittsburgh at Bradford (PA)
U of Pittsburgh at Greensburg (PA)
U of Pittsburgh at Johnstown (PA)
U of Puerto Rico at Humacao (PR)
U of Regina (SK, Canada)
U of Rio Grande (OH)
U of St. Thomas (MN)
U of South Carolina Beaufort (SC)
U of Southern Indiana (IN)
U of South Florida (FL)
U of South Florida–St. Petersburg Campus (FL)
The U of Texas–Pan American (TX)
U of the Pacific (CA)
U of the Southwest (NM)
U of Utah (UT)
U of Washington (WA)
U of West Florida (FL)
U of Windsor (ON, Canada)
U of Wisconsin–Platteville (WI)
U of Wisconsin–River Falls (WI)
U of Wisconsin–Stevens Point (WI)
U of Wisconsin–Stout (WI)
U of Wisconsin–Superior (WI)
U of Wisconsin–Whitewater (WI)
U of Wyoming (WY)
Upper Iowa U (IA)
Utica Coll (NY)
Valley City State U (ND)
Valparaiso U (IN)
Vanderbilt U (TN)
Virginia Wesleyan Coll (VA)
Viterbo U (WI)
Washington State U (WA)
Washington U in St. Louis (MO)
Wayland Baptist U (TX)
Waynesburg U (PA)
Wayne State Coll (NE)
Webster U (MO)
Wesleyan Coll (GA)
Wesleyan U (CT)
Western Connecticut State U (CT)
Western Kentucky U (KY)
Western Oregon U (OR)
West Liberty U (WV)
Westminster Coll (UT)
West Texas A&M U (TX)
Widener U (PA)
William Paterson U of New Jersey (NJ)
Wilmington Coll (OH)
Wilson Coll (PA)
Winona State U (MN)
Worcester Polytechnic Inst (MA)
Wright State U (OH)
Youngstown State U (OH)

SOCIAL SCIENCES RELATED

Abilene Christian U (TX)
Adelphi U (NY)
Anna Maria Coll (MA)
Bard Coll at Simon's Rock (MA)
Bennington Coll (VT)
Bloomsburg U of Pennsylvania (PA)
Boston U (MA)
Bowling Green State U (OH)

INDEXES

California Polytechnic State U, San Luis Obispo (CA)
California U of Pennsylvania (PA)
Caribbean U (PR)
Cleveland State U (OH)
The Coll of Idaho (ID)
Coll of Staten Island of the City U of New York (NY)
Concordia U (QC, Canada)
Concordia U Texas (TX)
Covenant Coll (GA)
Eastern Oregon U (OR)
Elizabethtown Coll (PA)
The Evergreen State Coll (WA)
Gettysburg Coll (PA)
Hamline U (MN)
Indiana U Bloomington (IN)
Indiana U Kokomo (IN)
Indiana U of Pennsylvania (PA)
John Jay Coll of Criminal Justice of the City U of New York (NY)
Mary Baldwin Coll (VA)
Marywood U (PA)
Midwestern State U (TX)
Millersville U of Pennsylvania (PA)
Monmouth U (NJ)
Mount Aloysius Coll (PA)
Mount Holyoke Coll (MA)
Mount Mary Coll (WI)
New Mexico Highlands U (NM)
New York U (NY)
Northern Arizona U (AZ)
Northwest Missouri State U (MO)
Plymouth State U (NH)
Purchase Coll, State U of New York (NY)
Roger Williams U (RI)
Rutgers, The State U of New Jersey, New Brunswick (NJ)
Saint Mary's Coll of California (CA)
Sarah Lawrence Coll (NY)
Simon Fraser U (BC, Canada)
Skidmore Coll (NY)
Southwestern Christian U (OK)
Tabor Coll (KS)
Towson U (MD)
United States Military Acad (NY)
The U of Akron (OH)
The U of Alabama at Birmingham (AL)
U of California, Berkeley (CA)
U of Denver (CO)
U of Massachusetts Amherst (MA)
U of New England (ME)
U of Pittsburgh (PA)
U of Regina (SK, Canada)
U of Rhode Island (RI)
U of Rochester (NY)
U of Southern Maine (ME)
The U of Tennessee at Chattanooga (TN)
The U of Western Ontario (ON, Canada)
U of West Florida (FL)
U of Wisconsin–Green Bay (WI)
Washington U in St. Louis (MO)
Whitman Coll (WA)

SOCIAL SCIENCE TEACHER EDUCATION

Arkansas State U (AR)
Auburn U (AL)
Averett U (VA)
Baylor U (TX)
Biola U (CA)
Blackburn Coll (IL)
Blue Mountain Coll (MS)
Bowling Green State U (OH)
Bradley U (IL)
Brigham Young U (UT)
Buena Vista U (IA)
California Lutheran U (CA)
Campbellsville U (KY)
Carroll Coll (MT)
Central Methodist U (MO)
Central Michigan U (MI)
Central Washington U (WA)
Concordia U Chicago (IL)
Concordia U, Nebraska (NE)
Corban U (OR)
Cornerstone U (MI)
Delta State U (MS)
Dominican Coll (NY)
Dordt Coll (IA)
Dowling Coll (NY)

Eastern Illinois U (IL)
Eastern Michigan U (MI)
Eastern Washington U (WA)
East Stroudsburg U of Pennsylvania (PA)
Elmira Coll (NY)
Emmanuel Coll (GA)
Emporia State U (KS)
Fayetteville State U (NC)
Ferris State U (MI)
Florida Ag and Mech U (FL)
Florida Atlantic U (FL)
Fordham U (NY)
Gardner-Webb U (NC)
Johnson State Coll (VT)
Judson Coll (AL)
Knox Coll (IL)
Lenoir-Rhyne U (NC)
Lewis-Clark State Coll (ID)
Liberty U (VA)
Lincoln U (MO)
Lindenwood U (MO)
Lindsey Wilson Coll (KY)
Manchester Coll (IN)
Mansfield U of Pennsylvania (PA)
Marywood U (PA)
Mayville State U (ND)
McKendree U (IL)
Medaille Coll (NY)
Mercyhurst Coll (PA)
Michigan State U (MI)
Millikin U (IL)
Minot State U (ND)
Mississippi Valley State U (MS)
Montana State U (MT)
Montana State U Billings (MT)
Montana State U–Northern (MT)
Mount St. Mary's U (MD)
Nebraska Wesleyan U (NE)
Northern Michigan U (MI)
Northwest Missouri State U (MO)
Northwest Nazarene U (ID)
Oakland City U (IN)
Pacific Union Coll (CA)
Peru State Coll (NE)
Rhode Island Coll (RI)
Rust Coll (MS)
St. Ambrose U (IA)
Saint Mary's U of Minnesota (MN)
Seattle Pacific U (WA)
Shawnee State U (OH)
Simpson U (CA)
Southeastern U (FL)
Southwest Baptist U (MO)
Southwestern Oklahoma State U (OK)
State U of New York at New Paltz (NY)
State U of New York Coll at Oneonta (NY)
Tabor Coll (KS)
Union Coll (NE)
Universidad del Turabo (PR)
U of Central Florida (FL)
U of Evansville (IN)
U of Great Falls (MT)
U of Illinois at Urbana–Champaign (IL)
U of Maine at Farmington (ME)
U of Maine at Fort Kent (ME)
U of Mary (ND)
The U of Montana Western (MT)
U of Nebraska–Lincoln (NE)
U of North Dakota (ND)
U of Northern Iowa (IA)
U of Rio Grande (OH)
The U of South Dakota (SD)
U of South Florida (FL)
U of Utah (UT)
U of Wisconsin–River Falls (WI)
U of Wisconsin–Superior (WI)
Upper Iowa U (IA)
Utica Coll (NY)
Valley City State U (ND)
Valparaiso U (IN)
Wartburg Coll (IA)
Washington U in St. Louis (MO)
Wayne State Coll (NE)
Weber State U (UT)
Western Michigan U (MI)
Western State Coll of Colorado (CO)
Western Washington U (WA)
William Penn U (IA)
Winona State U (MN)

Youngstown State U (OH)

SOCIAL STUDIES TEACHER EDUCATION

Abilene Christian U (TX)
Adams State Coll (CO)
Alma Coll (MI)
Alvernia U (PA)
Alverno Coll (WI)
Anderson U (IN)
Aquinas Coll (MI)
Arkansas Tech U (AR)
Augustana Coll (SD)
Averett U (VA)
Baptist Bible Coll of Pennsylvania (PA)
The Baptist Coll of Florida (FL)
Baylor U (TX)
Bethany Coll (KS)
Bethel Coll (IN)
Bethel U (MN)
Bethune-Cookman U (FL)
Bluefield Coll (VA)
Bob Jones U (SC)
Boston U (MA)
Bowling Green State U (OH)
Bradley U (IL)
Buffalo State Coll, State U of New York (NY)
Cabrini Coll (PA)
Calumet Coll of Saint Joseph (IN)
Calvin Coll (MI)
Cameron U (OK)
Campbellsville U (KY)
Capital U (OH)
Carroll Coll (MT)
Castleton State Coll (VT)
Cedarville U (OH)
Central Michigan U (MI)
City Coll of the City U of New York (NY)
Clearwater Christian Coll (FL)
Cleveland State U (OH)
The Coll at Brockport, State U of New York (NY)
The Coll of Saint Rose (NY)
Coll of the Ozarks (MO)
Colorado State U (CO)
Columbus State U (GA)
Concordia Coll (MN)
Concordia U (MI)
Concordia U, St. Paul (MN)
Corban U (OR)
Cornerstone U (MI)
Crown Coll (MN)
Daemen Coll (NY)
Dordt Coll (IA)
Dowling Coll (NY)
Duquesne U (PA)
East Carolina U (NC)
East Central U (OK)
Eastern Michigan U (MI)
Eastern Washington U (WA)
East Texas Baptist U (TX)
Elmira Coll (NY)
Ferris State U (MI)
Franklin Coll (IN)
Gannon U (PA)
Glenville State Coll (WV)
Grace Coll (IN)
Grambling State U (LA)
Grand Valley State U (MI)
Gustavus Adolphus Coll (MN)
Harding U (AR)
Hardin-Simmons U (TX)
Hofstra U (NY)
Hope Coll (MI)
Howard Payne U (TX)
Huntington U (IN)
Huston-Tillotson U (TX)
Illinois State U (IL)
Indiana State U (IN)
Indiana U Bloomington (IN)
Indiana U Northwest (IN)
Indiana U–Purdue U Fort Wayne (IN)
Indiana U–Purdue U Indianapolis (IN)
Indiana U South Bend (IN)
Indiana U Southeast (IN)
Indiana Wesleyan U (IN)
Inter American U of Puerto Rico, Fajardo Campus (PR)
Inter American U of Puerto Rico, San Germán Campus (PR)

Iona Coll (NY)
Iowa Wesleyan Coll (IA)
Ithaca Coll (NY)
John Brown U (AR)
Johnson C. Smith U (NC)
Johnson State Coll (VT)
Juniata Coll (PA)
Keene State Coll (NH)
Kennesaw State U (GA)
Kent State U (OH)
Kentucky Christian U (KY)
Kentucky Wesleyan Coll (KY)
Keuka Coll (NY)
Keystone Coll (PA)
Le Moyne Coll (NY)
Lenoir-Rhyne U (NC)
Long Island U–Brooklyn Campus (NY)
Long Island U–C. W. Post Campus (NY)
Louisiana State U in Shreveport (LA)
Lubbock Christian U (TX)
Madonna U (MI)
Malone U (OH)
Manchester Coll (IN)
Manhattanville Coll (NY)
Mansfield U of Pennsylvania (PA)
Maranatha Baptist Bible Coll (WI)
Marian U (WI)
Maryville Coll (TN)
Merrimack Coll (MA)
Messiah Coll (PA)
Metropolitan State U (MN)
Miami U (OH)
Michigan State U (MI)
MidAmerica Nazarene U (KS)
Midwestern State U (TX)
Minnesota State U Mankato (MN)
Minnesota State U Moorhead (MN)
Mississippi Coll (MS)
Molloy Coll (NY)
Moravian Coll (PA)
Morris Coll (SC)
Mount Mary Coll (WI)
Mount Vernon Nazarene U (OH)
Nazareth Coll of Rochester (NY)
New York U (NY)
Niagara U (NY)
Nicholls State U (LA)
North Carolina State U (NC)
North Dakota State U (ND)
Northeastern State U (OK)
Northern Michigan U (MI)
North Greenville U (SC)
Northland Coll (WI)
Northwestern Coll (MN)
Northwest U (WA)
Nyack Coll (NY)
Oakland City U (IN)
Ohio Northern U (OH)
Ohio Wesleyan U (OH)
Oklahoma Christian U (OK)
Oral Roberts U (OK)
Ouachita Baptist U (AR)
Pace U (NY)
Penn State Harrisburg (PA)
Philadelphia Biblical U (PA)
Pittsburg State U (KS)
Queens Coll of the City U of New York (NY)
Rhode Island Coll (RI)
Rivier Coll (NH)
Roberts Wesleyan Coll (NY)
Rocky Mountain Coll (MT)
St. Catherine U (MN)
St. Edward's U (TX)
Saint Francis U (PA)
St. John Fisher Coll (NY)
St. John's U (NY)
St. Joseph's Coll, Long Island Campus (NY)
St. Joseph's Coll, New York (NY)
St. Mary's U (TX)
St. Olaf Coll (MN)
St. Thomas U (FL)
Siena Heights U (MI)
Southeastern Louisiana U (LA)
Southeastern Oklahoma State U (OK)
Southeast Missouri State U (MO)
Southern New Hampshire U (NH)
Southwestern Assemblies of God U (TX)
Spring Arbor U (MI)

State U of New York at New Paltz (NY)
State U of New York Coll at Cortland (NY)
State U of New York Coll at Old Westbury (NY)
State U of New York Coll at Potsdam (NY)
Syracuse U (NY)
Taylor U (IN)
Temple U (PA)
Texas A&M Intl U (TX)
Texas A&M U–Corpus Christi (TX)
Texas Christian U (TX)
Texas Lutheran U (TX)
Texas Wesleyan U (TX)
Trine U (IN)
The U of Akron (OH)
U of Central Arkansas (AR)
U of Charleston (WV)
U of Evansville (IN)
U of Georgia (GA)
U of Great Falls (MT)
U of Illinois at Urbana–Champaign (IL)
U of Indianapolis (IN)
The U of Iowa (IA)
U of Lethbridge (AB, Canada)
U of Louisiana at Lafayette (LA)
U of Louisiana at Monroe (LA)
U of Maine (ME)
U of Mary Hardin-Baylor (TX)
U of Michigan–Dearborn (MI)
U of Michigan–Flint (MI)
U of Minnesota, Duluth (MN)
U of Minnesota, Twin Cities Campus (MN)
U of Mississippi (MS)
U of Missouri (MO)
U of Missouri–St. Louis (MO)
U of New Orleans (LA)
U of Oklahoma (OK)
U of Pittsburgh at Johnstown (PA)
U of Regina (SK, Canada)
U of St. Francis (IL)
U of Saint Francis (IN)
U of St. Thomas (MN)
The U of Tennessee at Chattanooga (TN)
U of the Cumberlands (KY)
The U of Toledo (OH)
U of Vermont (VT)
U of Wisconsin–Eau Claire (WI)
U of Wisconsin–La Crosse (WI)
U of Wisconsin–Madison (WI)
U of Wisconsin–River Falls (WI)
U of Wisconsin–Superior (WI)
Ursuline Coll (OH)
Utah State U (UT)
Utica Coll (NY)
Virginia Intermont Coll (VA)
Virginia Wesleyan Coll (VA)
Viterbo U (WI)
Washington State U (WA)
Washington U in St. Louis (MO)
Wayland Baptist U (TX)
Waynesburg U (PA)
Wayne State U (MI)
Weber State U (UT)
Western Carolina U (NC)
Western Michigan U (MI)
Western Washington U (WA)
Wheaton Coll (IL)
Wheeling Jesuit U (WV)
Widener U (PA)
William Jewell Coll (MO)
Wingate U (NC)
Xavier U of Louisiana (LA)
York Coll of Pennsylvania (PA)
Youngstown State U (OH)

SOCIAL WORK

Abilene Christian U (TX)
Adams State Coll (CO)
Adelphi U (NY)
Adrian Coll (MI)
Alabama State U (AL)
Albany State U (GA)
Albertus Magnus Coll (CT)
Alvernia U (PA)
Anderson U (IN)
Andrews U (MI)
Anna Maria Coll (MA)
Appalachian State U (NC)
Arizona State U (AZ)

Arkansas State U (AR)
Asbury U (KY)
Ashland U (OH)
Auburn U (AL)
Austin Peay State U (TN)
Avila U (MO)
Azusa Pacific U (CA)
Ball State U (IN)
Barton Coll (NC)
Bayamón Central U (PR)
Baylor U (TX)
Belmont U (TN)
Bemidji State U (MN)
Bennett Coll for Women (NC)
Bethany Coll (WV)
Bethel Coll (KS)
Bethel U (MN)
Biola U (CA)
Bloomsburg U of Pennsylvania (PA)
Bluffton U (OH)
Boise State U (ID)
Bowie State U (MD)
Bowling Green State U (OH)
Bradley U (IL)
Brescia U (KY)
Briar Cliff U (IA)
Bridgewater State U (MA)
Buena Vista U (IA)
Buffalo State Coll, State U of New York (NY)
Cabrini Coll (PA)
California State U, East Bay (CA)
California State U, Fresno (CA)
California State U, Long Beach (CA)
California State U, Los Angeles (CA)
California State U, Sacramento (CA)
California State U, San Bernardino (CA)
California U of Pennsylvania (PA)
Calvin Coll (MI)
Campbellsville U (KY)
Capital U (OH)
Caribbean U (PR)
Carlow U (PA)
Castleton State Coll (VT)
The Catholic U of America (DC)
Cedar Crest Coll (PA)
Cedarville U (OH)
Centenary Coll (NJ)
Central Connecticut State U (CT)
Central Michigan U (MI)
Central State U (OH)
Chapman U (CA)
Chatham U (PA)
Christopher Newport U (VA)
Clark Atlanta U (GA)
Clarke U (IA)
Cleveland State U (OH)
Coll of Mount St. Joseph (OH)
The Coll of Saint Rose (NY)
The Coll of St. Scholastica (MN)
Coll of Staten Island of the City U of New York (NY)
Coll of the Ozarks (MO)
Colorado State U (CO)
Columbia Coll (SC)
Concordia Coll (MN)
Concordia Coll–New York (NY)
Concordia U Chicago (IL)
Cornerstone U (MI)
Creighton U (NE)
Daemen Coll (NY)
Dalhousie U (NS, Canada)
Dalton State Coll (GA)
Defiance Coll (OH)
Delaware State U (DE)
Delta State U (MS)
Dominican Coll (NY)
Dordt Coll (IA)
East Carolina U (NC)
East Central U (OK)
Eastern Connecticut State U (CT)
Eastern Kentucky U (KY)
Eastern Mennonite U (VA)
Eastern Michigan U (MI)
Eastern New Mexico U (NM)
Eastern U (PA)
Eastern Washington U (WA)
East Tennessee State U (TN)
Edinboro U of Pennsylvania (PA)
Edward Waters Coll (FL)
Elizabeth City State U (NC)

Elizabethtown Coll (PA)
Elmira Coll (NY)
Evangel U (MO)
Ferris State U (MI)
Ferrum Coll (VA)
Florida Ag and Mech U (FL)
Florida Atlantic U (FL)
Florida Gulf Coast U (FL)
Florida Intl U (FL)
Florida State U (FL)
Fontbonne U (MO)
Fordham U (NY)
Fort Hays State U (KS)
Franciscan U of Steubenville (OH)
Gannon U (PA)
George Fox U (OR)
George Mason U (VA)
Georgian Court U (NJ)
Georgia State U (GA)
Gordon Coll (MA)
Goshen Coll (IN)
Governors State U (IL)
Graceland U (IA)
Grambling State U (LA)
Grand Valley State U (MI)
Greenville Coll (IL)
Gwynedd-Mercy Coll (PA)
Hampton U (VA)
Harding U (AR)
Hardin-Simmons U (TX)
Hawai'i Pacific U (HI)
Hood Coll (MD)
Hope Coll (MI)
Howard Payne U (TX)
Humboldt State U (CA)
Huntington U (IN)
Idaho State U (ID)
Illinois State U (IL)
Indiana State U (IN)
Indiana U Bloomington (IN)
Indiana U East (IN)
Indiana U Northwest (IN)
Indiana U–Purdue U Indianapolis (IN)
Indiana Wesleyan U (IN)
Inter American U of Puerto Rico, Fajardo Campus (PR)
Iona Coll (NY)
Jacksonville State U (AL)
James Madison U (VA)
Johnson C. Smith U (NC)
Judson Coll (AL)
Juniata Coll (PA)
Kansas State U (KS)
Kentucky Christian U (KY)
Kentucky State U (KY)
Keuka Coll (NY)
Kutztown U of Pennsylvania (PA)
Lakehead U (ON, Canada)
Lamar U (TX)
La Salle U (PA)
La Sierra U (CA)
Lebanese American U (Lebanon)
Lehman Coll of the City U of New York (NY)
Lewis-Clark State Coll (ID)
Lewis U (IL)
Limestone Coll (SC)
Lincoln Memorial U (TN)
Lincoln U (MO)
Lindenwood U (MO)
Lipscomb U (TN)
Lock Haven U of Pennsylvania (PA)
Long Island U–Brooklyn Campus (NY)
Long Island U–C. W. Post Campus (NY)
Longwood U (VA)
Loras Coll (IA)
Louisiana Coll (LA)
Lourdes U (OH)
Loyola U Chicago (IL)
Lubbock Christian U (TX)
Luther Coll (IA)
Madonna U (MI)
Malone U (OH)
Manchester Coll (IN)
Mansfield U of Pennsylvania (PA)
Marian U (WI)
Marshall U (WV)
Mars Hill Coll (NC)
Mary Baldwin Coll (VA)
Marywood U (PA)
McDaniel Coll (MD)
McKendree U (IL)

Medgar Evers Coll of the City U of New York (NY)
Mercy Coll (NY)
Mercyhurst Coll (PA)
Meredith Coll (NC)
Messiah Coll (PA)
Metropolitan State Coll of Denver (CO)
Metropolitan State U (MN)
Miami U (OH)
Michigan State U (MI)
Middle Tennessee State U (TN)
Midwestern State U (TX)
Millersville U of Pennsylvania (PA)
Millikin U (IL)
Minnesota State U Mankato (MN)
Minnesota State U Moorhead (MN)
Minot State U (ND)
Misericordia U (PA)
Mississippi Coll (MS)
Mississippi State U (MS)
Mississippi Valley State U (MS)
Missouri State U (MO)
Missouri Western State U (MO)
Molloy Coll (NY)
Monmouth U (NJ)
Montclair State U (NJ)
Morehead State U (KY)
Mountain State U (WV)
Mount Mary Coll (WI)
Mount Mercy U (IA)
Mount Saint Mary Coll (NY)
Mount St. Mary's Coll (CA)
Mount Vernon Nazarene U (OH)
Nazareth Coll of Rochester (NY)
Nebraska Wesleyan U (NE)
New Mexico State U (NM)
New York U (NY)
Niagara U (NY)
Norfolk State U (VA)
North Carolina Ag and Tech State U (NC)
North Carolina Central U (NC)
North Carolina State U (NC)
Northeastern Illinois U (IL)
Northeastern State U (OK)
Northern Arizona U (AZ)
Northern Kentucky U (KY)
Northern Michigan U (MI)
Northwestern Coll (IA)
Northwestern Oklahoma State U (OK)
Northwestern State U of Louisiana (LA)
Northwest Nazarene U (ID)
Nyack Coll (NY)
Oakland U (MI)
Oglethorpe U (GA)
The Ohio State U (OH)
Ohio U (OH)
Oral Roberts U (OK)
Pacific Lutheran U (WA)
Pacific Union Coll (CA)
Pacific U (OR)
Park U (MO)
Philadelphia Biblical U (PA)
Philander Smith Coll (AR)
Pittsburg State U (KS)
Plymouth State U (NH)
Point Loma Nazarene U (CA)
Portland State U (OR)
Post U (CT)
Prairie View A&M U (TX)
Presentation Coll (SD)
Providence Coll (RI)
Purdue U North Central (IN)
Radford U (VA)
Ramapo Coll of New Jersey (NJ)
Regis Coll (MA)
Rhode Island Coll (RI)
The Richard Stockton Coll of New Jersey (NJ)
Roberts Wesleyan Coll (NY)
Rockford Coll (IL)
Rust Coll (MS)
Rutgers, The State U of New Jersey, Camden (NJ)
Rutgers, The State U of New Jersey, Newark (NJ)
Rutgers, The State U of New Jersey, New Brunswick (NJ)
Ryerson U (ON, Canada)
Sacred Heart U (CT)
Saginaw Valley State U (MI)
St. Catherine U (MN)

St. Edward's U (TX)
Saint Francis U (PA)
Saint Joseph's Coll of Maine (ME)
Saint Leo U (FL)
Saint Louis U (MO)
Saint Mary's Coll (IN)
St. Olaf Coll (MN)
St. Thomas U (NB, Canada)
Salem State U (MA)
Salisbury U (MD)
Salve Regina U (RI)
San Diego State U (CA)
San Francisco State U (CA)
Seattle U (WA)
Seton Hill U (PA)
Shaw U (NC)
Shepherd U (WV)
Shippensburg U of Pennsylvania (PA)
Siena Coll (NY)
Siena Heights U (MI)
Skidmore Coll (NY)
Slippery Rock U of Pennsylvania (PA)
Sojourner-Douglass Coll (MD)
South Carolina State U (SC)
Southeastern Louisiana U (LA)
Southeastern U (FL)
Southeast Missouri State U (MO)
Southern Arkansas U–Magnolia (AR)
Southern Connecticut State U (CT)
Southern Illinois U Carbondale (IL)
Southern Illinois U Edwardsville (IL)
Southwestern Adventist U (TX)
Southwestern Assemblies of God U (TX)
Southwestern Oklahoma State U (OK)
Southwest Minnesota State U (MN)
Spalding U (KY)
Spring Arbor U (MI)
State U of New York at Fredonia (NY)
State U of New York at New Paltz (NY)
State U of New York at Plattsburgh (NY)
State U of New York Coll at Cortland (NY)
Stephen F. Austin State U (TX)
Stony Brook U, State U of New York (NY)
Suffolk U (MA)
Syracuse U (NY)
Tabor Coll (KS)
Tarleton State U (TX)
Taylor U (IN)
Temple U (PA)
Texas A&M U–Kingsville (TX)
Texas Christian U (TX)
Texas Coll (TX)
Texas Southern U (TX)
Texas State U–San Marcos (TX)
Texas Tech U (TX)
Texas Woman's U (TX)
Thomas U (GA)
Thompson Rivers U (BC, Canada)
Trevecca Nazarene U (TN)
Trinity Christian Coll (IL)
Troy U (AL)
Tuskegee U (AL)
Union Coll (KY)
Union Coll (NE)
Union Inst & U (OH)
Union U (TN)
Universidad del Turabo (PR)
Université de Sherbrooke (QC, Canada)
U at Albany, State U of New York (NY)
The U of Akron (OH)
The U of Alabama (AL)
The U of Alabama at Birmingham (AL)
U of Alaska Anchorage (AK)
U of Alaska Fairbanks (AK)
U of Arkansas (AR)
U of Arkansas at Little Rock (AR)
U of Arkansas at Monticello (AR)
The U of British Columbia (BC, Canada)
The U of British Columbia–Okanagan (BC, Canada)
U of California, Berkeley (CA)

U of Central Florida (FL)
U of Central Missouri (MO)
U of Cincinnati (OH)
The U of Findlay (OH)
U of Georgia (GA)
U of Guam (GU)
U of Hawaii at Manoa (HI)
U of Houston–Clear Lake (TX)
U of Houston–Downtown (TX)
U of Illinois at Chicago (IL)
U of Illinois at Springfield (IL)
U of Indianapolis (IN)
The U of Iowa (IA)
The U of Kansas (KS)
U of Louisiana at Monroe (LA)
U of Louisville (KY)
U of Maine (ME)
U of Maine at Presque Isle (ME)
U of Mary (ND)
U of Mary Hardin-Baylor (TX)
U of Maryland, Baltimore County (MD)
U of Maryland Eastern Shore (MD)
U of Memphis (TN)
U of Michigan–Flint (MI)
U of Minnesota, Twin Cities Campus (MN)
U of Mississippi (MS)
U of Missouri (MO)
U of Missouri–St. Louis (MO)
U of Nebraska at Kearney (NE)
U of Nevada, Las Vegas (NV)
U of Nevada, Reno (NV)
U of New Hampshire (NH)
U of North Alabama (AL)
The U of North Carolina at Charlotte (NC)
The U of North Carolina Wilmington (NC)
U of North Dakota (ND)
U of Northern Iowa (IA)
U of North Texas (TX)
U of Oklahoma (OK)
U of Ottawa (ON, Canada)
U of Pikeville (KY)
U of Pittsburgh (PA)
U of Portland (OR)
U of Puerto Rico at Humacao (PR)
U of Regina (SK, Canada)
U of Rio Grande (OH)
U of St. Francis (IL)
U of Saint Francis (IN)
U of Saint Joseph (CT)
U of St. Thomas (MN)
U of South Alabama (AL)
U of South Carolina (SC)
The U of South Dakota (SD)
U of Southern Indiana (IN)
U of Southern Maine (ME)
U of Southern Mississippi (MS)
U of South Florida (FL)
The U of Tennessee (TN)
The U of Tennessee at Chattanooga (TN)
The U of Tennessee at Martin (TN)
The U of Texas at Arlington (TX)
The U of Texas at Austin (TX)
The U of Texas at El Paso (TX)
The U of Texas of the Permian Basin (TX)
The U of Texas–Pan American (TX)
U of the Cumberlands (KY)
U of the District of Columbia (DC)
The U of Toledo (OH)
U of Utah (UT)
U of Vermont (VT)
U of Washington (WA)
The U of Western Ontario (ON, Canada)
U of West Florida (FL)
U of Windsor (ON, Canada)
U of Wisconsin–Eau Claire (WI)
U of Wisconsin–Green Bay (WI)
U of Wisconsin–Madison (WI)
U of Wisconsin–Milwaukee (WI)
U of Wisconsin–River Falls (WI)
U of Wisconsin–Superior (WI)
U of Wisconsin–Whitewater (WI)
U of Wyoming (WY)
Ursuline Coll (OH)
Utah State U (UT)
Valparaiso U (IN)
Virginia Commonwealth U (VA)
Virginia Intermont Coll (VA)
Virginia State U (VA)

Marymount U (VA)
Maryville Coll (TN)
Maryville U of Saint Louis (MO)
Massachusetts Coll of Liberal Arts (MA)
McDaniel Coll (MD)
McKendree U (IL)
McMurry U (TX)
McNeese State U (LA)
McPherson Coll (KS)
Mercer U (GA)
Mercy Coll (NY)
Mercyhurst Coll (PA)
Meredith Coll (NC)
Merrimack Coll (MA)
Messiah Coll (PA)
Metropolitan State Coll of Denver (CO)
Miami U (OH)
Michigan State U (MI)
MidAmerica Nazarene U (KS)
Middlebury Coll (VT)
Middle Tennessee State U (TN)
Midwestern State U (TX)
Millersville U of Pennsylvania (PA)
Milligan Coll (TN)
Millikin U (IL)
Mills Coll (CA)
Minnesota State U Mankato (MN)
Minnesota State U Moorhead (MN)
Minot State U (ND)
Mississippi Coll (MS)
Mississippi State U (MS)
Mississippi Valley State U (MS)
Missouri Southern State U (MO)
Missouri State U (MO)
Missouri Western State U (MO)
Molloy Coll (NY)
Monmouth Coll (IL)
Monmouth U (NJ)
Montana State U (MT)
Montana State U Billings (MT)
Montclair State U (NJ)
Moravian Coll (PA)
Morehead State U (KY)
Morehouse Coll (GA)
Morris Coll (SC)
Mount Allison U (NB, Canada)
Mount Holyoke Coll (MA)
Mount Mercy U (IA)
Mount Saint Mary Coll (NY)
Mount St. Mary's Coll (CA)
Mount St. Mary's U (MD)
Mount Vernon Nazarene U (OH)
Muhlenberg Coll (PA)
National U (CA)
Nazareth Coll of Rochester (NY)
Nebraska Wesleyan U (NE)
Newberry Coll (SC)
New Coll of Florida (FL)
New England Coll (NH)
New Jersey City U (NJ)
Newman U (KS)
New Mexico State U (NM)
New York Inst of Technology (NY)
New York U (NY)
Niagara U (NY)
Nicholls State U (LA)
Norfolk State U (VA)
North Carolina Ag and Tech State U (NC)
North Carolina Central U (NC)
North Carolina State U (NC)
North Carolina Wesleyan Coll (NC)
North Central Coll (IL)
North Dakota State U (ND)
Northeastern Illinois U (IL)
Northeastern State U (OK)
Northeastern U (MA)
Northern Arizona U (AZ)
Northern Illinois U (IL)
Northern Kentucky U (KY)
Northern Michigan U (MI)
Northern State U (SD)
North Georgia Coll & State U (GA)
Northland Coll (WI)
Northwestern Coll (IA)
Northwestern Oklahoma State U (OK)
Northwest Missouri State U (MO)
Notre Dame de Namur U (CA)
Nova Southeastern U (FL)
Nyack Coll (NY)
Oakland U (MI)
Occidental Coll (CA)

Oglethorpe U (GA)
Ohio Northern U (OH)
The Ohio State U (OH)
Ohio U (OH)
Ohio Wesleyan U (OH)
Oklahoma City U (OK)
Oklahoma State U (OK)
Old Dominion U (VA)
Otterbein U (OH)
Ouachita Baptist U (AR)
Pacific Lutheran U (WA)
Pacific U (OR)
Paine Coll (GA)
Park U (MO)
Penn State Abington (PA)
Penn State Altoona (PA)
Penn State Beaver (PA)
Penn State Berks (PA)
Penn State Brandywine (PA)
Penn State DuBois (PA)
Penn State Erie, The Behrend Coll (PA)
Penn State Fayette, The Eberly Campus (PA)
Penn State Greater Allegheny (PA)
Penn State Harrisburg (PA)
Penn State Hazleton (PA)
Penn State Lehigh Valley (PA)
Penn State Mont Alto (PA)
Penn State New Kensington (PA)
Penn State Schuylkill (PA)
Penn State Shenango (PA)
Penn State U Park (PA)
Penn State Wilkes-Barre (PA)
Penn State Worthington Scranton (PA)
Penn State York (PA)
Pepperdine U, Malibu (CA)
Philander Smith Coll (AR)
Piedmont Coll (GA)
Pittsburg State U (KS)
Pitzer Coll (CA)
Plymouth State U (NH)
Point Loma Nazarene U (CA)
Pomona Coll (CA)
Portland State U (OR)
Post U (CT)
Prairie View A&M U (TX)
Presbyterian Coll (SC)
Princeton U (NJ)
Providence Coll (RI)
Purchase Coll, State U of New York (NY)
Purdue U (IN)
Purdue U Calumet (IN)
Queens Coll of the City U of New York (NY)
Queen's U at Kingston (ON, Canada)
Queens U of Charlotte (NC)
Quinnipiac U (CT)
Radford U (VA)
Ramapo Coll of New Jersey (NJ)
Randolph Coll (VA)
Randolph-Macon Coll (VA)
Regis Coll (MA)
Regis U (CO)
Reinhardt U (GA)
Rhode Island Coll (RI)
Rhodes Coll (TN)
Rice U (TX)
The Richard Stockton Coll of New Jersey (NJ)
Rider U (NJ)
Ripon Coll (WI)
Rivier Coll (NH)
Roanoke Coll (VA)
Rockford Coll (IL)
Rocky Mountain Coll (MT)
Roger Williams U (RI)
Rollins Coll (FL)
Roosevelt U (IL)
Rosemont Coll (PA)
Rowan U (NJ)
Russell Sage Coll (NY)
Rust Coll (MS)
Rutgers, The State U of New Jersey, Camden (NJ)
Rutgers, The State U of New Jersey, Newark (NJ)
Rutgers, The State U of New Jersey, New Brunswick (NJ)
Ryerson U (ON, Canada)
Sacred Heart U (CT)
Saginaw Valley State U (MI)

St. Ambrose U (IA)
Saint Anselm Coll (NH)
Saint Augustine's Coll (NC)
St. Bonaventure U (NY)
St. Catherine U (MN)
St. Edward's U (TX)
Saint Francis U (PA)
St. John Fisher Coll (NY)
Saint John's U (MN)
St. John's U (NY)
Saint Joseph's Coll (IN)
Saint Joseph's Coll of Maine (ME)
Saint Joseph's U (PA)
St. Lawrence U (NY)
Saint Leo U (FL)
Saint Louis U (MO)
Saint Mary's Coll (IN)
Saint Mary's Coll of California (CA)
St. Mary's Coll of Maryland (MD)
St. Mary's U (TX)
Saint Mary's U of Minnesota (MN)
Saint Michael's Coll (VT)
St. Norbert Coll (WI)
St. Olaf Coll (MN)
Saint Peter's Coll (NJ)
St. Thomas U (NB, Canada)
Saint Vincent Coll (PA)
Saint Xavier U (IL)
Salem State U (MA)
Salisbury U (MD)
Salve Regina U (RI)
Samford U (AL)
Sam Houston State U (TX)
San Diego State U (CA)
San Francisco State U (CA)
Santa Clara U (CA)
Sarah Lawrence Coll (NY)
Scripps Coll (CA)
Seattle Pacific U (WA)
Seattle U (WA)
Seton Hill U (PA)
Shawnee State U (OH)
Shaw U (NC)
Shenandoah U (VA)
Shepherd U (WV)
Shippensburg U of Pennsylvania (PA)
Shorter U (GA)
Siena Coll (NY)
Simmons Coll (MA)
Simon Fraser U (BC, Canada)
Simpson Coll (IA)
Skidmore Coll (NY)
Smith Coll (MA)
Sojourner-Douglass Coll (MD)
Sonoma State U (CA)
South Carolina State U (SC)
South Dakota State U (SD)
Southeastern Louisiana U (LA)
Southeastern Oklahoma State U (OK)
Southern Connecticut State U (CT)
Southern Illinois U Carbondale (IL)
Southern Illinois U Edwardsville (IL)
Southern Methodist U (TX)
Southern Oregon U (OR)
Southwest Baptist U (MO)
Southwestern U (TX)
Southwest Minnesota State U (MN)
Spelman Coll (GA)
Spring Arbor U (MI)
Stanford U (CA)
State U of New York at Binghamton (NY)
State U of New York at Fredonia (NY)
State U of New York at New Paltz (NY)
State U of New York at Oswego (NY)
State U of New York at Plattsburgh (NY)
State U of New York Coll at Cortland (NY)
State U of New York Coll at Geneseo (NY)
State U of New York Coll at Old Westbury (NY)
State U of New York Coll at Oneonta (NY)
State U of New York Coll at Potsdam (NY)
Stephen F. Austin State U (TX)
Stetson U (FL)
Stonehill Coll (MA)

Stony Brook U, State U of New York (NY)
Suffolk U (MA)
Susquehanna U (PA)
Sweet Briar Coll (VA)
Syracuse U (NY)
Tabor Coll (KS)
Tarleton State U (TX)
Taylor U (IN)
Temple U (PA)
Texas A&M Intl U (TX)
Texas A&M U (TX)
Texas A&M U–Corpus Christi (TX)
Texas A&M U–Kingsville (TX)
Texas Christian U (TX)
Texas Coll (TX)
Texas Lutheran U (TX)
Texas Southern U (TX)
Texas State U–San Marcos (TX)
Texas Tech U (TX)
Texas Woman's U (TX)
Thiel Coll (PA)
Thomas Edison State Coll (NJ)
Thomas More Coll (KY)
Thomas U (GA)
Thompson Rivers U (BC, Canada)
Touro Coll (NY)
Transylvania U (KY)
Trent U (ON, Canada)
Trevecca Nazarene U (TN)
Trinity Christian Coll (IL)
Trinity Coll (CT)
Trinity U (TX)
Troy U (AL)
Truman State U (MO)
Tufts U (MA)
Tulane U (LA)
Tuskegee U (AL)
Union Coll (NY)
Union U (TN)
United States Military Acad (NY)
Universidad del Turabo (PR)
U at Albany, State U of New York (NY)
U at Buffalo, the State U of New York (NY)
The U of Akron (OH)
The U of Alabama (AL)
The U of Alabama at Birmingham (AL)
The U of Alabama in Huntsville (AL)
U of Alaska Anchorage (AK)
U of Alaska Fairbanks (AK)
U of Alberta (AB, Canada)
The U of Arizona (AZ)
U of Arkansas (AR)
U of Arkansas at Little Rock (AR)
The U of British Columbia (BC, Canada)
The U of British Columbia–Okanagan (BC, Canada)
U of California, Berkeley (CA)
U of California, Davis (CA)
U of California, Irvine (CA)
U of California, Los Angeles (CA)
U of California, Merced (CA)
U of California, Riverside (CA)
U of California, Santa Barbara (CA)
U of California, Santa Cruz (CA)
U of Central Arkansas (AR)
U of Central Florida (FL)
U of Central Missouri (MO)
U of Cincinnati (OH)
U of Colorado at Colorado Springs (CO)
U of Colorado Boulder (CO)
U of Colorado Denver (CO)
U of Connecticut (CT)
U of Dayton (OH)
U of Delaware (DE)
U of Denver (CO)
U of Dubuque (IA)
U of Evansville (IN)
The U of Findlay (OH)
U of Florida (FL)
U of Georgia (GA)
U of Great Falls (MT)
U of Guam (GU)
U of Guelph (ON, Canada)
U of Hartford (CT)
U of Hawaii at Hilo (HI)
U of Hawaii at Manoa (HI)
U of Hawaii–West Oahu (HI)
U of Houston (TX)
U of Houston–Clear Lake (TX)

U of Houston–Downtown (TX)
U of Idaho (ID)
U of Illinois at Chicago (IL)
U of Illinois at Urbana–Champaign (IL)
U of Indianapolis (IN)
The U of Iowa (IA)
The U of Kansas (KS)
U of La Verne (CA)
U of Lethbridge (AB, Canada)
U of Louisiana at Lafayette (LA)
U of Louisiana at Monroe (LA)
U of Louisville (KY)
U of Maine (ME)
U of Maine at Farmington (ME)
U of Mary Hardin-Baylor (TX)
U of Maryland, Baltimore County (MD)
U of Maryland, Coll Park (MD)
U of Maryland Eastern Shore (MD)
U of Mary Washington (VA)
U of Massachusetts Amherst (MA)
U of Massachusetts Boston (MA)
U of Massachusetts Dartmouth (MA)
U of Massachusetts Lowell (MA)
U of Memphis (TN)
U of Miami (FL)
U of Michigan (MI)
U of Michigan–Dearborn (MI)
U of Michigan–Flint (MI)
U of Minnesota, Duluth (MN)
U of Minnesota, Twin Cities Campus (MN)
U of Mississippi (MS)
U of Missouri (MO)
U of Missouri–Kansas City (MO)
U of Missouri–St. Louis (MO)
U of Mobile (AL)
The U of Montana Western (MT)
U of Mount Union (OH)
U of Nebraska at Kearney (NE)
U of Nebraska at Omaha (NE)
U of Nebraska–Lincoln (NE)
U of Nevada, Las Vegas (NV)
U of Nevada, Reno (NV)
U of New England (ME)
U of New Hampshire (NH)
U of New Mexico (NM)
U of New Orleans (LA)
U of North Alabama (AL)
The U of North Carolina at Asheville (NC)
The U of North Carolina at Chapel Hill (NC)
The U of North Carolina Wilmington (NC)
U of North Dakota (ND)
U of Northern Colorado (CO)
U of Northern Iowa (IA)
U of North Florida (FL)
U of North Texas (TX)
U of Notre Dame (IN)
U of Oklahoma (OK)
U of Oregon (OR)
U of Ottawa (ON, Canada)
U of Pennsylvania (PA)
U of Pikeville (KY)
U of Pittsburgh (PA)
U of Pittsburgh at Bradford (PA)
U of Pittsburgh at Johnstown (PA)
U of Portland (OR)
U of Puget Sound (WA)
U of Redlands (CA)
U of Regina (SK, Canada)
U of Rhode Island (RI)
U of Richmond (VA)
U of Rio Grande (OH)
U of Saint Francis (IN)
U of St. Thomas (MN)
U of San Diego (CA)
U of Science and Arts of Oklahoma (OK)
The U of Scranton (PA)
U of South Alabama (AL)
U of South Carolina (SC)
U of South Carolina Aiken (SC)
U of South Carolina Beaufort (SC)
U of South Carolina Upstate (SC)
The U of South Dakota (SD)
U of Southern California (CA)
U of Southern Indiana (IN)
U of Southern Maine (ME)
U of Southern Mississippi (MS)
U of South Florida (FL)

INDEXES

The U of Tampa (FL)
The U of Tennessee (TN)
The U of Tennessee at Martin (TN)
The U of Texas at Arlington (TX)
The U of Texas at Austin (TX)
The U of Texas at Dallas (TX)
The U of Texas at El Paso (TX)
The U of Texas at San Antonio (TX)
The U of Texas at Tyler (TX)
The U of Texas of the Permian Basin (TX)
The U of Texas–Pan American (TX)
U of the District of Columbia (DC)
U of the Incarnate Word (TX)
U of the Ozarks (AR)
U of the Pacific (CA)
The U of Toledo (OH)
U of Toronto (ON, Canada)
U of Tulsa (OK)
U of Utah (UT)
U of Vermont (VT)
U of Virginia (VA)
The U of Virginia's Coll at Wise (VA)
U of Washington (WA)
The U of West Alabama (AL)
The U of Western Ontario (ON, Canada)
U of West Florida (FL)
U of West Georgia (GA)
U of Windsor (ON, Canada)
U of Wisconsin–Eau Claire (WI)
U of Wisconsin–La Crosse (WI)
U of Wisconsin–Madison (WI)
U of Wisconsin–Milwaukee (WI)
U of Wisconsin–River Falls (WI)
U of Wisconsin–Stevens Point (WI)
U of Wisconsin–Superior (WI)
U of Wisconsin–Whitewater (WI)
U of Wyoming (WY)
Upper Iowa U (IA)
Ursuline Coll (OH)
Utah State U (UT)
Utica Coll (NY)
Valdosta State U (GA)
Valparaiso U (IN)
Vanderbilt U (TN)
Vanguard U of Southern California (CA)
Vassar Coll (NY)
Villanova U (PA)
Virginia Commonwealth U (VA)
Virginia Polytechnic Inst and State U (VA)
Virginia State U (VA)
Virginia Wesleyan Coll (VA)
Viterbo U (WI)
Wagner Coll (NY)
Wake Forest U (NC)
Walsh U (OH)
Warren Wilson Coll (NC)
Wartburg Coll (IA)
Washburn U (KS)
Washington & Jefferson Coll (PA)
Washington and Lee U (VA)
Washington Coll (MD)
Washington State U (WA)
Wayland Baptist U (TX)
Waynesburg U (PA)
Wayne State Coll (NE)
Wayne State U (MI)
Weber State U (UT)
Webster U (MO)
Wellesley Coll (MA)
Wells Coll (NY)
Wesleyan U (CT)
West Chester U of Pennsylvania (PA)
Western Carolina U (NC)
Western Connecticut State U (CT)
Western Illinois U (IL)
Western Kentucky U (KY)
Western Michigan U (MI)
Western New England U (MA)
Western Oregon U (OR)
Western State Coll of Colorado (CO)
Western Washington U (WA)
Westfield State U (MA)
West Liberty U (WV)
Westminster Coll (MO)
Westminster Coll (UT)
West Texas A&M U (TX)
West Virginia State U (WV)
West Virginia U (WV)
West Virginia Wesleyan Coll (WV)

Wheaton Coll (IL)
Wheaton Coll (MA)
Whitman Coll (WA)
Whittier Coll (CA)
Wichita State U (KS)
Widener U (PA)
Wilkes U (PA)
Willamette U (OR)
William Paterson U of New Jersey (NJ)
William Penn U (IA)
Williams Coll (MA)
Wilson Coll (PA)
Wingate U (NC)
Winona State U (MN)
Winthrop U (SC)
Wittenberg U (OH)
Wofford Coll (SC)
Worcester State U (MA)
Wright State U (OH)
Xavier U (OH)
Xavier U of Louisiana (LA)
Yale U (CT)
Yeshiva U (NY)
York Coll of Pennsylvania (PA)
York Coll of the City U of New York (NY)
Youngstown State U (OH)

SOCIOLOGY AND ANTHROPOLOGY
Alma Coll (MI)
American U of Beirut (Lebanon)
Goucher Coll (MD)
Millsaps Coll (MS)
Oakland U (MI)
Pace U (NY)
Rochester Inst of Technology (NY)
Swarthmore Coll (PA)
Transylvania U (KY)
U of Illinois at Springfield (IL)

SOIL CHEMISTRY AND PHYSICS
The U of Tennessee (TN)

SOIL SCIENCE AND AGRONOMY
California Polytechnic State U, San Luis Obispo (CA)
Colorado State U (CO)
Michigan State U (MI)
New Mexico State U (NM)
North Dakota State U (ND)
Oklahoma State U (OK)
Penn State Abington (PA)
Penn State Altoona (PA)
Penn State Beaver (PA)
Penn State Berks (PA)
Penn State Brandywine (PA)
Penn State DuBois (PA)
Penn State Erie, The Behrend Coll (PA)
Penn State Fayette, The Eberly Campus (PA)
Penn State Greater Allegheny (PA)
Penn State Hazleton (PA)
Penn State Lehigh Valley (PA)
Penn State Mont Alto (PA)
Penn State New Kensington (PA)
Penn State Schuylkill (PA)
Penn State Shenango (PA)
Penn State Wilkes-Barre (PA)
Penn State Worthington Scranton (PA)
Penn State York (PA)
The U of British Columbia (BC, Canada)
U of California, Davis (CA)
U of Florida (FL)
U of Maine (ME)
U of Minnesota, Twin Cities Campus (MN)
U of Nebraska–Lincoln (NE)
U of New Hampshire (NH)
The U of Tennessee at Martin (TN)
U of Wisconsin–Madison (WI)
U of Wisconsin–River Falls (WI)
U of Wisconsin–Stevens Point (WI)
Utah State U (UT)
Washington State U (WA)

SOIL SCIENCES RELATED
Brigham Young U (UT)
North Carolina State U (NC)
U of Hawaii at Manoa (HI)

SOLAR ENERGY TECHNOLOGY
Appalachian State U (NC)

SOUTH ASIAN LANGUAGES
The U of British Columbia (BC, Canada)
U of Minnesota, Twin Cities Campus (MN)
Yale U (CT)

SPANISH
Abilene Christian U (TX)
Adams State Coll (CO)
Adelphi U (NY)
Adrian Coll (MI)
Agnes Scott Coll (GA)
Albany State U (GA)
Albertus Magnus Coll (CT)
Albion Coll (MI)
Albright Coll (PA)
Alfred U (NY)
Allegheny Coll (PA)
Alma Coll (MI)
American U (DC)
Amherst Coll (MA)
Anderson U (IN)
Anderson U (SC)
Andrews U (MI)
Angelo State U (TX)
Anna Maria Coll (MA)
Appalachian State U (NC)
Aquinas Coll (MI)
Arcadia U (PA)
Arizona State U (AZ)
Armstrong Atlantic State U (GA)
Asbury U (KY)
Ashland U (OH)
Assumption Coll (MA)
Auburn U (AL)
Auburn U Montgomery (AL)
Augustana Coll (IL)
Augustana Coll (SD)
Austin Coll (TX)
Austin Peay State U (TN)
Azusa Pacific U (CA)
Baker U (KS)
Baldwin-Wallace Coll (OH)
Ball State U (IN)
Baptist U of the Americas (TX)
Bard Coll (NY)
Bard Coll at Simon's Rock (MA)
Barnard Coll (NY)
Barry U (FL)
Barton Coll (NC)
Bates Coll (ME)
Baylor U (TX)
Bellarmine U (KY)
Belmont U (TN)
Beloit Coll (WI)
Bemidji State U (MN)
Benedictine Coll (KS)
Benedictine U (IL)
Bennington Coll (VT)
Berea Coll (KY)
Bernard M. Baruch Coll of the City U of New York (NY)
Berry Coll (GA)
Bethany Coll (WV)
Bethel Coll (IN)
Bethel U (MN)
Biola U (CA)
Birmingham-Southern Coll (AL)
Bishop's U (QC, Canada)
Blackburn Coll (IL)
Black Hills State U (SD)
Bloomsburg U of Pennsylvania (PA)
Blue Mountain Coll (MS)
Bluffton U (OH)
Bob Jones U (SC)
Boise State U (ID)
Boston Coll (MA)
Boston U (MA)
Bowdoin Coll (ME)
Bowling Green State U (OH)
Bradley U (IL)
Brandeis U (MA)
Brescia U (KY)
Briar Cliff U (IA)
Bridgewater Coll (VA)

Bridgewater State U (MA)
Brown U (RI)
Bryn Mawr Coll (PA)
Bucknell U (PA)
Buena Vista U (IA)
Buffalo State Coll, State U of New York (NY)
Butler U (IN)
Cabrini Coll (PA)
Caldwell Coll (NJ)
California Baptist U (CA)
California Lutheran U (CA)
California State Polytechnic U, Pomona (CA)
California State U, Bakersfield (CA)
California State U, Dominguez Hills (CA)
California State U, East Bay (CA)
California State U, Fresno (CA)
California State U, Fullerton (CA)
California State U, Long Beach (CA)
California State U, Los Angeles (CA)
California State U, Monterey Bay (CA)
California State U, Sacramento (CA)
California State U, San Bernardino (CA)
California State U, San Marcos (CA)
California State U, Stanislaus (CA)
California U of Pennsylvania (PA)
Calvin Coll (MI)
Canisius Coll (NY)
Capital U (OH)
Cardinal Stritch U (WI)
Carleton Coll (MN)
Carnegie Mellon U (PA)
Carroll Coll (MT)
Carson-Newman Coll (TN)
Case Western Reserve U (OH)
Castleton State Coll (VT)
Catawba Coll (NC)
The Catholic U of America (DC)
Cedarville U (OH)
Central Coll (IA)
Central Connecticut State U (CT)
Central Methodist U (MO)
Central Michigan U (MI)
Centre Coll (KY)
Chapman U (CA)
Chestnut Hill Coll (PA)
Cheyney U of Pennsylvania (PA)
Chicago State U (IL)
Christopher Newport U (VA)
City Coll of the City U of New York (NY)
Claremont McKenna Coll (CA)
Clarion U of Pennsylvania (PA)
Clark Atlanta U (GA)
Clarke U (IA)
Clark U (MA)
Cleveland State U (OH)
Coastal Carolina U (SC)
Coe Coll (IA)
Colby Coll (ME)
Colgate U (NY)
The Coll at Brockport, State U of New York (NY)
Coll of Charleston (SC)
The Coll of Idaho (ID)
Coll of Mount Saint Vincent (NY)
The Coll of New Jersey (NJ)
Coll of Saint Benedict (MN)
Coll of Saint Elizabeth (NJ)
The Coll of Saint Rose (NY)
The Coll of St. Scholastica (MN)
Coll of Staten Island of the City U of New York (NY)
Coll of the Holy Cross (MA)
Coll of the Ozarks (MO)
The Coll of Wooster (OH)
The Colorado Coll (CO)
Colorado Mesa U (CO)
Colorado State U (CO)
Columbia Coll (SC)
Columbus State U (GA)
Concordia Coll (MN)
Concordia U (QC, Canada)
Concordia U Chicago (IL)
Concordia U, Nebraska (NE)
Connecticut Coll (CT)
Converse Coll (SC)

Cornell Coll (IA)
Cornell U (NY)
Cornerstone U (MI)
Creighton U (NE)
Daemen Coll (NY)
Dalhousie U (NS, Canada)
Dartmouth Coll (NH)
Davidson Coll (NC)
Delaware State U (DE)
Denison U (OH)
DePaul U (IL)
DePauw U (IN)
DeSales U (PA)
Dickinson Coll (PA)
Doane Coll (NE)
Dominican Coll (NY)
Dominican U (IL)
Dordt Coll (IA)
Drew U (NJ)
Drury U (MO)
Duquesne U (PA)
Earlham Coll (IN)
East Carolina U (NC)
East Central U (OK)
Eastern Connecticut State U (CT)
Eastern Kentucky U (KY)
Eastern Mennonite U (VA)
Eastern Michigan U (MI)
Eastern New Mexico U (NM)
Eastern Washington U (WA)
East Stroudsburg U of Pennsylvania (PA)
East Texas Baptist U (TX)
Eckerd Coll (FL)
Edgewood Coll (WI)
Edinboro U of Pennsylvania (PA)
Elizabethtown Coll (PA)
Elmhurst Coll (IL)
Elmira Coll (NY)
Elon U (NC)
Emmanuel Coll (MA)
Emory U (GA)
Evangel U (MO)
Fairfield U (CT)
Fairleigh Dickinson U, Coll at Florham (NJ)
Fairleigh Dickinson U, Metropolitan Campus (NJ)
Fayetteville State U (NC)
Ferrum Coll (VA)
Flagler Coll (FL)
Florida Atlantic U (FL)
Florida Gulf Coast U (FL)
Florida Intl U (FL)
Florida Southern Coll (FL)
Fordham U (NY)
Fort Hays State U (KS)
Fort Lewis Coll (CO)
Franciscan U of Steubenville (OH)
Francis Marion U (SC)
Franklin & Marshall Coll (PA)
Franklin Coll (IN)
Friends U (KS)
Furman U (SC)
Gallaudet U (DC)
Gardner-Webb U (NC)
George Fox U (OR)
Georgetown Coll (KY)
The George Washington U (DC)
Georgia Coll & State U (GA)
Georgian Court U (NJ)
Georgia State U (GA)
Gettysburg Coll (PA)
Gonzaga U (WA)
Gordon Coll (MA)
Goshen Coll (IN)
Goucher Coll (MD)
Grace Coll (IN)
Grambling State U (LA)
Grand Valley State U (MI)
Greenville Coll (IL)
Grinnell Coll (IA)
Grove City Coll (PA)
Guilford Coll (NC)
Gustavus Adolphus Coll (MN)
Hamline U (MN)
Hampden-Sydney Coll (VA)
Hanover Coll (IN)
Harding U (AR)
Hardin-Simmons U (TX)
Hartwick Coll (NY)
Haverford Coll (PA)
Heidelberg U (OH)
Hendrix Coll (AR)

INDEXES

The U of North Carolina Wilmington (NC)
U of North Dakota (ND)
U of Northern Colorado (CO)
U of Northern Iowa (IA)
U of North Florida (FL)
U of North Texas (TX)
U of Notre Dame (IN)
U of Oklahoma (OK)
U of Oregon (OR)
U of Ottawa (ON, Canada)
U of Pennsylvania (PA)
U of Pittsburgh (PA)
U of Pittsburgh at Greensburg (PA)
U of Portland (OR)
U of Puget Sound (WA)
U of Redlands (CA)
U of Regina (SK, Canada)
U of Rhode Island (RI)
U of Richmond (VA)
U of Rochester (NY)
U of Saint Joseph (CT)
U of St. Thomas (MN)
U of St. Thomas (TX)
U of San Diego (CA)
The U of Scranton (PA)
U of South Carolina (SC)
U of South Carolina Beaufort (SC)
U of South Carolina Upstate (SC)
The U of South Dakota (SD)
U of Southern California (CA)
U of Southern Indiana (IN)
U of South Florida (FL)
The U of Tampa (FL)
The U of Tennessee (TN)
The U of Tennessee at Martin (TN)
The U of Texas at Arlington (TX)
The U of Texas at Austin (TX)
The U of Texas at El Paso (TX)
The U of Texas at San Antonio (TX)
The U of Texas at Tyler (TX)
The U of Texas of the Permian Basin (TX)
The U of Texas–Pan American (TX)
U of the Cumberlands (KY)
U of the District of Columbia (DC)
U of the Incarnate Word (TX)
U of the Ozarks (AR)
U of the Pacific (CA)
The U of Toledo (OH)
U of Toronto (ON, Canada)
U of Tulsa (OK)
U of Utah (UT)
U of Vermont (VT)
U of Virginia (VA)
The U of Virginia's Coll at Wise (VA)
U of Washington (WA)
The U of Western Ontario (ON, Canada)
U of West Florida (FL)
U of Windsor (ON, Canada)
U of Wisconsin–Eau Claire (WI)
U of Wisconsin–Green Bay (WI)
U of Wisconsin–La Crosse (WI)
U of Wisconsin–Madison (WI)
U of Wisconsin–Milwaukee (WI)
U of Wisconsin–Platteville (WI)
U of Wisconsin–River Falls (WI)
U of Wisconsin–Stevens Point (WI)
U of Wisconsin–Whitewater (WI)
U of Wyoming (WY)
Utah State U (UT)
Utah Valley U (UT)
Valdosta State U (GA)
Valley City State U (ND)
Valparaiso U (IN)
Vanderbilt U (TN)
Vassar Coll (NY)
Villanova U (PA)
Virginia Polytechnic Inst and State U (VA)
Virginia Wesleyan Coll (VA)
Viterbo U (WI)
Wabash Coll (IN)
Wagner Coll (NY)
Wake Forest U (NC)
Walsh U (OH)
Warren Wilson Coll (NC)
Wartburg Coll (IA)
Washburn U (KS)
Washington & Jefferson Coll (PA)
Washington and Lee U (VA)
Washington Coll (MD)
Washington State U (WA)
Washington U in St. Louis (MO)

Wayland Baptist U (TX)
Wayne State Coll (NE)
Weber State U (UT)
Webster U (MO)
Wellesley Coll (MA)
Wells Coll (NY)
Wesleyan Coll (GA)
Wesleyan U (CT)
West Chester U of Pennsylvania (PA)
Western Carolina U (NC)
Western Connecticut State U (CT)
Western Illinois U (IL)
Western Kentucky U (KY)
Western Michigan U (MI)
Western Oregon U (OR)
Western State Coll of Colorado (CO)
Western Washington U (WA)
Westfield State U (MA)
Westminster Coll (MO)
West Texas A&M U (TX)
Wheaton Coll (IL)
Wheeling Jesuit U (WV)
Whitman Coll (WA)
Whittier Coll (CA)
Widener U (PA)
Wilkes U (PA)
Willamette U (OR)
William Jewell Coll (MO)
William Paterson U of New Jersey (NJ)
Williams Coll (MA)
William Woods U (MO)
Wilmington Coll (OH)
Wilson Coll (PA)
Winona State U (MN)
Wittenberg U (OH)
Wofford Coll (SC)
Worcester State U (MA)
Wright State U (OH)
Xavier U (OH)
Xavier U of Louisiana (LA)
Yale U (CT)
York Coll of Pennsylvania (PA)
York Coll of the City U of New York (NY)
Youngstown State U (OH)

SPANISH AND IBERIAN STUDIES
Bard Coll (NY)
Bard Coll at Simon's Rock (MA)
Coe Coll (IA)
Fordham U (NY)
The U of Western Ontario (ON, Canada)

SPANISH LANGUAGE TEACHER EDUCATION
Abilene Christian U (TX)
Adams State Coll (CO)
Albion Coll (MI)
Alma Coll (MI)
Anderson U (IN)
Appalachian State U (NC)
Assumption Coll (MA)
Auburn U (AL)
Augustana Coll (IL)
Bayamón Central U (PR)
Baylor U (TX)
Bethel Coll (IN)
Bethel U (MN)
Bishop's U (QC, Canada)
Blue Mountain Coll (MS)
Bob Jones U (SC)
Buena Vista U (IA)
California Lutheran U (CA)
Calvin Coll (MI)
Carroll Coll (MT)
The Catholic U of America (DC)
Cedarville U (OH)
Central Michigan U (MI)
Central Washington U (WA)
The Coll at Brockport, State U of New York (NY)
Coll of Saint Mary (NE)
The Coll of Saint Rose (NY)
Colorado State U (CO)
Concordia Coll (MN)
Concordia U, Nebraska (NE)
Daemen Coll (NY)
Delaware State U (DE)
Dordt Coll (IA)

Dowling Coll (NY)
Duquesne U (PA)
East Carolina U (NC)
Eastern Michigan U (MI)
Eastern Washington U (WA)
East Texas Baptist U (TX)
Edgewood Coll (WI)
Elmhurst Coll (IL)
Elmira Coll (NY)
Evangel U (MO)
Fayetteville State U (NC)
Franklin Coll (IN)
Friends U (KS)
Gardner-Webb U (NC)
Georgia Southern U (GA)
Grace Coll (IN)
Grand Valley State U (MI)
Greenville Coll (IL)
Harding U (AR)
Hardin-Simmons U (TX)
Hofstra U (NY)
Hope Coll (MI)
Howard Payne U (TX)
Indiana U Bloomington (IN)
Indiana U Northwest (IN)
Indiana U–Purdue U Fort Wayne (IN)
Indiana U–Purdue U Indianapolis (IN)
Indiana U South Bend (IN)
Indiana Wesleyan U (IN)
Inter American U of Puerto Rico, Fajardo Campus (PR)
Inter American U of Puerto Rico, San Germán Campus (PR)
Iona Coll (NY)
Ithaca Coll (NY)
Juniata Coll (PA)
Keene State Coll (NH)
Kentucky Wesleyan Coll (KY)
King Coll (TN)
Lee U (TN)
Le Moyne Coll (NY)
Liberty U (VA)
Lindenwood U (MO)
Lipscomb U (TN)
Long Island U–Brooklyn Campus (NY)
Long Island U–C. W. Post Campus (NY)
Lubbock Christian U (TX)
Malone U (OH)
Manchester Coll (IN)
Manhattanville Coll (NY)
Mansfield U of Pennsylvania (PA)
Marian U (WI)
Maryville Coll (TN)
Marywood U (PA)
McMurry U (TX)
Messiah Coll (PA)
Miami U (OH)
Michigan State U (MI)
MidAmerica Nazarene U (KS)
Minnesota State U Moorhead (MN)
Minot State U (ND)
Missouri Western State U (MO)
Molloy Coll (NY)
Montana State U Billings (MT)
Moravian Coll (PA)
Morningside Coll (IA)
Mount Mary Coll (WI)
Mount Vernon Nazarene U (OH)
Niagara U (NY)
North Carolina Ag and Tech State U (NC)
North Carolina Central U (NC)
North Carolina State U (NC)
North Dakota State U (ND)
Northeastern State U (OK)
Northern Michigan U (MI)
Northwest Missouri State U (MO)
Northwest Nazarene U (ID)
Ohio Northern U (OH)
Ohio U (OH)
Ohio Wesleyan U (OH)
Oral Roberts U (OK)
Pace U (NY)
Pittsburg State U (KS)
Rhode Island Coll (RI)
Roberts Wesleyan Coll (NY)
Saginaw Valley State U (MI)
St. Ambrose U (IA)
St. Catherine U (MN)
St. Edward's U (TX)
St. John Fisher Coll (NY)

St. John's U (NY)
St. Joseph's Coll, Long Island Campus (NY)
St. Joseph's Coll, New York (NY)
Saint Mary's U of Minnesota (MN)
Saint Xavier U (IL)
Salem State U (MA)
Salve Regina U (RI)
Southeastern Oklahoma State U (OK)
Southwest Minnesota State U (MN)
State U of New York at New Paltz (NY)
State U of New York at Plattsburgh (NY)
State U of New York Coll at Cortland (NY)
State U of New York Coll at Old Westbury (NY)
State U of New York Coll at Oneonta (NY)
Taylor U (IN)
Texas A&M Intl U (TX)
Texas A&M U–Corpus Christi (TX)
Universidad del Turabo (PR)
The U of Akron (OH)
U of Arkansas–Fort Smith (AR)
U of Delaware (DE)
U of Evansville (IN)
U of Illinois at Chicago (IL)
U of Illinois at Urbana–Champaign (IL)
U of Indianapolis (IN)
The U of Iowa (IA)
U of Louisiana at Lafayette (LA)
U of Maine (ME)
U of Mary Hardin-Baylor (TX)
U of Michigan–Flint (MI)
U of Minnesota, Duluth (MN)
U of Missouri–St. Louis (MO)
U of Nebraska–Lincoln (NE)
The U of North Carolina at Charlotte (NC)
The U of North Carolina Wilmington (NC)
The U of South Dakota (SD)
The U of Tennessee at Martin (TN)
The U of Toledo (OH)
U of Wisconsin–River Falls (WI)
Utah Valley U (UT)
Valdosta State U (GA)
Valley City State U (ND)
Valparaiso U (IN)
Viterbo U (WI)
Washburn U (KS)
Washington State U (WA)
Washington U in St. Louis (MO)
Weber State U (UT)
Western Carolina U (NC)
Western Michigan U (MI)
Western State Coll of Colorado (CO)
Western Washington U (WA)
Wheeling Jesuit U (WV)
Widener U (PA)
William Jewell Coll (MO)
Winona State U (MN)
Xavier U of Louisiana (LA)
York Coll of Pennsylvania (PA)
Youngstown State U (OH)

SPECIAL EDUCATION
Abilene Christian U (TX)
Adams State Coll (CO)
Alabama State U (AL)
Albany State U (GA)
Alvernia U (PA)
Anderson U (SC)
Arizona State U (AZ)
Armstrong Atlantic State U (GA)
Asbury U (KY)
Ashland U (OH)
Athens State U (AL)
Auburn U (AL)
Augustana Coll (SD)
Austin Peay State U (TN)
Avila U (MO)
Barry U (FL)
Barton Coll (NC)
Bayamón Central U (PR)
Baylor U (TX)
Bellarmine U (KY)
Belmont U (TN)
Benedictine Coll (KS)
Benedictine U (IL)

Bennett Coll for Women (NC)
Bethel U (TN)
Black Hills State U (SD)
Bloomsburg U of Pennsylvania (PA)
Boise State U (ID)
Boston U (MA)
Bowie State U (MD)
Bowling Green State U (OH)
Brescia U (KY)
Bridgewater State U (MA)
Brigham Young U (UT)
Buena Vista U (IA)
Buffalo State Coll, State U of New York (NY)
Cabrini Coll (PA)
California U of Pennsylvania (PA)
Calvin Coll (MI)
Canisius Coll (NY)
Capital U (OH)
Cardinal Stritch U (WI)
Caribbean U (PR)
Carson-Newman Coll (TN)
Cedarville U (OH)
Centenary Coll (NJ)
Central State U (OH)
Central Washington U (WA)
Cheyney U of Pennsylvania (PA)
Christian Brothers U (TN)
City U of Seattle (WA)
Clarion U of Pennsylvania (PA)
Clemson U (SC)
Cleveland State U (OH)
Coastal Carolina U (SC)
Coll of Charleston (SC)
Coll of Mount St. Joseph (OH)
The Coll of New Jersey (NJ)
The Coll of Saint Rose (NY)
Columbia Coll (SC)
Columbus State U (GA)
Concordia U Chicago (IL)
Concordia U, Nebraska (NE)
Converse Coll (SC)
Curry Coll (MA)
Daemen Coll (NY)
Delaware State U (DE)
DePaul U (IL)
Doane Coll (NE)
Dominican Coll (NY)
Dowling Coll (NY)
East Carolina U (NC)
East Central U (OK)
Eastern Illinois U (IL)
Eastern Kentucky U (KY)
Eastern New Mexico U (NM)
Eastern Washington U (WA)
East Stroudsburg U of Pennsylvania (PA)
East Tennessee State U (TN)
Edinboro U of Pennsylvania (PA)
Elizabeth City State U (NC)
Elmhurst Coll (IL)
Elon U (NC)
Evangel U (MO)
Fairmont State U (WV)
Felician Coll (NJ)
Fitchburg State U (MA)
Florida Atlantic U (FL)
Florida Gulf Coast U (FL)
Florida Intl U (FL)
Fontbonne U (MO)
Furman U (SC)
Gannon U (PA)
Geneva Coll (PA)
Georgia Coll & State U (GA)
Georgia Gwinnett Coll (GA)
Georgia Southern U (GA)
Georgia Southwestern State U (GA)
Glenville State Coll (WV)
Gonzaga U (WA)
Gordon Coll (MA)
Goshen Coll (IN)
Goucher Coll (MD)
Grace Coll (IN)
Grambling State U (LA)
Grand Canyon U (AZ)
Grand Valley State U (MI)
Greenville Coll (IL)
Grove City Coll (PA)
Gwynedd-Mercy Coll (PA)
Hampton U (VA)
Heidelberg U (OH)
Holy Family U (PA)
Houghton Coll (NY)
Huntington U (IN)
Idaho State U (ID)

INDEXES

Pace U (NY)
State U of New York Coll at
  Cortland (NY)
U of Nebraska at Omaha (NE)
The U of Toledo (OH)
Wayne State U (MI)

**SPECIAL EDUCATION–
INDIVIDUALS WITH VISION
IMPAIRMENTS**

Eastern Michigan U (MI)
Kutztown U of Pennsylvania (PA)
The U of Toledo (OH)

**SPECIAL EDUCATION–JUNIOR
HIGH/MIDDLE SCHOOL**

Clarion U of Pennsylvania (PA)
Virginia Intermont Coll (VA)

**SPECIAL EDUCATION
RELATED**

Auburn U (AL)
Bowling Green State U (OH)
Dakota State U (SD)
Delaware State U (DE)
East Carolina U (NC)
Hood Coll (MD)
Inter American U of Puerto Rico,
  San Germán Campus (PR)
Juniata Coll (PA)
Kean U (NJ)
Keene State Coll (NH)
Lincoln U (MO)
Lock Haven U of Pennsylvania (PA)
Minot State U (ND)
Southeastern Oklahoma State U
  (OK)
Southern New Hampshire U (NH)
U of Hartford (CT)
U of Missouri (MO)
U of Nebraska–Lincoln (NE)
The U of North Carolina at
  Charlotte (NC)
U of Southern Indiana (IN)
The U of Toledo (OH)
Wright State U (OH)
York Coll of Pennsylvania (PA)

**SPECIAL EDUCATION–
SECONDARY SCHOOL**

Oklahoma City U (OK)
Virginia Intermont Coll (VA)

**SPECIAL PRODUCTS
MARKETING**

Buffalo State Coll, State U of New
  York (NY)
Central Washington U (WA)
Dominican U (IL)
Fashion Inst of Technology (NY)
Iowa State U of Science and
  Technology (IA)
Rochester Inst of Technology (NY)
Saint Joseph's U (PA)
Stephen F. Austin State U (TX)
U of Alberta (AB, Canada)
U of Maryland Eastern Shore (MD)
U of North Texas (TX)

**SPEECH COMMUNICATION
AND RHETORIC**

Abilene Christian U (TX)
Adrian Coll (MI)
Alabama State U (AL)
Albertus Magnus Coll (CT)
Albion Coll (MI)
Albright Coll (PA)
Alfred U (NY)
Allegheny Coll (PA)
Alliant Intl U (CA)
Alvernia U (PA)
Alverno Coll (WI)
American U (DC)
The American U of Rome (Italy)
Anderson U (SC)
Angelo State U (TX)
Appalachian State U (NC)
Aquinas Coll (MI)
Arcadia U (PA)
Arizona State U (AZ)
Arkansas Tech U (AR)
Auburn U Montgomery (AL)

Augustana Coll (SD)
Austin Coll (TX)
Avila U (MO)
Azusa Pacific U (CA)
Baldwin-Wallace Coll (OH)
Ball State U (IN)
Baptist Bible Coll of Pennsylvania
  (PA)
Barry U (FL)
Baylor U (TX)
Belhaven U (MS)
Bellarmine U (KY)
Benedictine U (IL)
Bethany Coll (KS)
Bethany Coll (WV)
Bethany Lutheran Coll (MN)
Bethel Coll (IN)
Bethel U (MN)
Bethune-Cookman U (FL)
Biola U (CA)
Blackburn Coll (IL)
Bluffton U (OH)
Bob Jones U (SC)
Boston Coll (MA)
Boston U (MA)
Bowling Green State U (OH)
Brewton-Parker Coll (GA)
Bridgewater State U (MA)
Bryant U (RI)
Buena Vista U (IA)
Buffalo State Coll, State U of New
  York (NY)
Butler U (IN)
Cabrini Coll (PA)
Caldwell Coll (NJ)
California Baptist U (CA)
California State Polytechnic U,
  Pomona (CA)
California State U, Chico (CA)
California State U, Dominguez Hills
  (CA)
California State U, Fresno (CA)
California State U, Fullerton (CA)
California State U, Los Angeles
  (CA)
California State U, Sacramento
  (CA)
California State U, San Marcos
  (CA)
California State U, Stanislaus (CA)
California U of Pennsylvania (PA)
Calumet Coll of Saint Joseph (IN)
Calvin Coll (MI)
Canisius Coll (NY)
Cape Breton U (NS, Canada)
Capital U (OH)
Cardinal Stritch U (WI)
Carlos Albizu U (PR)
Carroll Coll (MT)
The Catholic U of America (DC)
Cedar Crest Coll (PA)
Cedarville U (OH)
Central Coll (IA)
Central Connecticut State U (CT)
Central Methodist U (MO)
Chapman U (CA)
Christopher Newport U (VA)
Clarkson U (NY)
Clayton State U (GA)
Clearwater Christian Coll (FL)
Cleveland State U (OH)
Coastal Carolina U (SC)
The Coll at Brockport, State U of
  New York (NY)
Coll of Charleston (SC)
Coll of Mount St. Joseph (OH)
Coll of Saint Elizabeth (NJ)
The Coll of Saint Rose (NY)
The Coll of St. Scholastica (MN)
Coll of Staten Island of the City U of
  New York (NY)
Coll of the Ozarks (MO)
The Coll of Wooster (OH)
Colorado State U (CO)
Columbia Coll (MO)
Columbia Coll (SC)
Concordia Coll (MN)
Concordia U Chicago (IL)
Concordia U, Nebraska (NE)
Corban U (OR)
Cornell U (NY)
Creighton U (NE)
Culver-Stockton Coll (MO)
Dallas Baptist U (TX)
DePaul U (IL)

Dixie State Coll of Utah (UT)
Dominican U (IL)
Drury U (MO)
Duquesne U (PA)
East Carolina U (NC)
East Central U (OK)
Eastern Connecticut State U (CT)
Eastern Michigan U (MI)
Eastern New Mexico U (NM)
Eastern U (PA)
Eastern Washington U (WA)
East Stroudsburg U of Pennsylvania
  (PA)
Eckerd Coll (FL)
Edinboro U of Pennsylvania (PA)
Elizabeth City State U (NC)
Elmhurst Coll (IL)
Embry-Riddle Aeronautical U–
  Daytona (FL)
Emmanuel Coll (MA)
Emporia State U (KS)
The Evergreen State Coll (WA)
Fairleigh Dickinson U, Coll at
  Florham (NJ)
Fayetteville State U (NC)
Felician Coll (NJ)
Ferris State U (MI)
Fitchburg State U (MA)
Florida Atlantic U (FL)
Florida Intl U (FL)
Florida Southern Coll (FL)
Fontbonne U (MO)
Franciscan U of Steubenville (OH)
Furman U (SC)
Gallaudet U (DC)
George Fox U (OR)
George Mason U (VA)
Georgian Court U (NJ)
Georgia Southern U (GA)
Georgia State U (GA)
Gordon Coll (MA)
Goshen Coll (IN)
Governors State U (IL)
Grace Coll (IN)
Grand Valley State U (MI)
Great Lakes Christian Coll (MI)
Grove City Coll (PA)
Hamline U (MN)
Hampshire Coll (MA)
Hannibal-LaGrange U (MO)
Harding U (AR)
Hardin-Simmons U (TX)
Hawai'i Pacific U (HI)
Hillsdale Coll (MI)
Hillsdale Free Will Baptist Coll (OK)
Hofstra U (NY)
Hope Coll (MI)
Houghton Coll (NY)
Howard Payne U (TX)
Huntington U (IN)
Idaho State U (ID)
Illinois State U (IL)
Indiana State U (IN)
Indiana Tech (IN)
Indiana U Bloomington (IN)
Indiana U East (IN)
Indiana U Kokomo (IN)
Indiana U Northwest (IN)
Indiana U of Pennsylvania (PA)
Indiana U–Purdue U Fort Wayne
  (IN)
Indiana U–Purdue U Indianapolis
  (IN)
Indiana U Southeast (IN)
Indiana Wesleyan U (IN)
Inter American U of Puerto Rico,
  Bayamón Campus (PR)
Iona Coll (NY)
Iowa Wesleyan Coll (IA)
Jacksonville State U (AL)
Jacksonville U (FL)
James Madison U (VA)
Jamestown Coll (ND)
John Brown U (AR)
Judson U (IL)
Juniata Coll (PA)
Kansas State U (KS)
Kean U (NJ)
Keene State Coll (NH)
Kennesaw State U (GA)
Kent State U (OH)
Kent State U at Ashtabula (OH)
Kent State U at East Liverpool (OH)
Kent State U at Salem (OH)
Kent State U at Stark (OH)

Kent State U at Trumbull (OH)
Kent State U at Tuscarawas (OH)
Kentucky Wesleyan Coll (KY)
Keuka Coll (NY)
La Sierra U (CA)
Lawrence Technological U (MI)
Lenoir-Rhyne U (NC)
Lewis & Clark Coll (OR)
Lewis-Clark State Coll (ID)
Lewis U (IL)
Liberty U (VA)
Lincoln U (MO)
Lindenwood U (MO)
Linfield Coll (OR)
Long Island U–Brooklyn Campus
  (NY)
Long Island U–C. W. Post Campus
  (NY)
Longwood U (VA)
Louisiana State U and Ag and Mech
  Coll (LA)
Loyola Marymount U (CA)
Loyola U Chicago (IL)
Loyola U Maryland (MD)
Loyola U New Orleans (LA)
Lubbock Christian U (TX)
Luther Coll (IA)
Lynchburg Coll (VA)
Manchester Coll (IN)
Marian U (WI)
Marietta Coll (OH)
Marylhurst U (OR)
Marymount Manhattan Coll (NY)
Mayville State U (ND)
McDaniel Coll (MD)
McKendree U (IL)
McPherson Coll (KS)
Mercyhurst Coll (PA)
Meredith Coll (NC)
Merrimack Coll (MA)
Messiah Coll (PA)
Metropolitan State U (MN)
Michigan State U (MI)
Michigan Technological U (MI)
Millersville U of Pennsylvania (PA)
Millikin U (IL)
Millsaps Coll (MS)
Minnesota State U Moorhead (MN)
Mississippi Coll (MS)
Mississippi State U (MS)
Mississippi U for Women (MS)
Missouri Southern State U (MO)
Missouri State U (MO)
Missouri Western State U (MO)
Molloy Coll (NY)
Monmouth Coll (IL)
Monmouth U (NJ)
Montclair State U (NJ)
Moody Bible Inst (IL)
Morehead State U (KY)
Mount Mary Coll (WI)
Mount Mercy U (IA)
Mount St. Mary's U (MD)
Mount Vernon Nazarene U (OH)
Nazareth Coll of Rochester (NY)
Nebraska Wesleyan U (NE)
Neumann U (PA)
New Jersey City U (NJ)
New Mexico Highlands U (NM)
New York U (NY)
North Carolina Ag and Tech State U
  (NC)
North Carolina State U (NC)
Northeastern State U (OK)
Northern Illinois U (IL)
Northern Michigan U (MI)
Northwest Christian U (OR)
Northwestern Coll (MN)
Northwest Nazarene U (ID)
Norwich U (VT)
Notre Dame de Namur U (CA)
Notre Dame of Maryland U (MD)
Nova Southeastern U (FL)
Oglethorpe U (GA)
Ohio Northern U (OH)
The Ohio State U (OH)
Ohio U (OH)
Oral Roberts U (OK)
Oregon Inst of Technology (OR)
Ouachita Baptist U (AR)
Pace U (NY)
Park U (MO)
Penn State Abington (PA)
Penn State Altoona (PA)
Penn State Beaver (PA)

Penn State Berks (PA)
Penn State Brandywine (PA)
Penn State DuBois (PA)
Penn State Erie, The Behrend Coll
  (PA)
Penn State Fayette, The Eberly
  Campus (PA)
Penn State Greater Allegheny (PA)
Penn State Harrisburg (PA)
Penn State Hazleton (PA)
Penn State Lehigh Valley (PA)
Penn State Mont Alto (PA)
Penn State New Kensington (PA)
Penn State Schuylkill (PA)
Penn State Shenango (PA)
Penn State U Park (PA)
Penn State Wilkes-Barre (PA)
Penn State Worthington Scranton
  (PA)
Penn State York (PA)
Pepperdine U, Malibu (CA)
Pine Manor Coll (MA)
Plymouth State U (NH)
Point Loma Nazarene U (CA)
Prairie View A&M U (TX)
Purchase Coll, State U of New York
  (NY)
Purdue U (IN)
Purdue U Calumet (IN)
Purdue U North Central (IN)
Radford U (VA)
Ramapo Coll of New Jersey (NJ)
Randolph Coll (VA)
Regent U (VA)
Regis Coll (MA)
Regis U (CO)
Rensselaer Polytechnic Inst (NY)
Rhode Island Coll (RI)
The Richard Stockton Coll of New
  Jersey (NJ)
Rider U (NJ)
Ripon Coll (WI)
Robert Morris U (PA)
Roberts Wesleyan Coll (NY)
Rochester Inst of Technology (NY)
Rockhurst U (MO)
Rocky Mountain Coll (MT)
Roger Williams U (RI)
Roosevelt U (IL)
Rosemont Coll (PA)
Rutgers, The State U of New
  Jersey, New Brunswick (NJ)
Saginaw Valley State U (MI)
Saint Anselm Coll (NH)
St. John's U (NY)
Saint Joseph's U (PA)
Saint Louis U (MO)
Saint Mary's Coll (IN)
Saint Mary's Coll of California (CA)
St. Mary's U (TX)
St. Norbert Coll (WI)
Saint Peter's Coll (NJ)
Saint Vincent Coll (PA)
Saint Xavier U (IL)
Salem State U (MA)
Salisbury U (MD)
Samford U (AL)
Sam Houston State U (TX)
San Diego Christian Coll (CA)
San Francisco State U (CA)
Santa Clara U (CA)
Schreiner U (TX)
Seattle Pacific U (WA)
Seton Hill U (PA)
Shenandoah U (VA)
Shepherd U (WV)
Simmons Coll (MA)
Simon Fraser U (BC, Canada)
Simpson U (CA)
Slippery Rock U of Pennsylvania
  (PA)
Sonoma State U (CA)
Southeastern Louisiana U (LA)
Southeastern Oklahoma State U
  (OK)
Southeast Missouri State U (MO)
Southern Connecticut State U (CT)
Southern Oregon U (OR)
Southwest Baptist U (MO)
Southwestern Assemblies of God U
  (TX)
Southwestern Coll (KS)
Southwestern U (TX)
Southwest Minnesota State U (MN)
Spalding U (KY)

Spring Arbor U (MI)
State U of New York at New Paltz (NY)
State U of New York Coll at Cortland (NY)
State U of New York Coll at Old Westbury (NY)
Stonehill Coll (MA)
Suffolk U (MA)
Susquehanna U (PA)
Syracuse U (NY)
Tabor Coll (KS)
Texas A&M Intl U (TX)
Texas A&M U–Corpus Christi (TX)
Texas A&M U–Kingsville (TX)
Texas Christian U (TX)
Texas Lutheran U (TX)
Texas Southern U (TX)
Thiel Coll (PA)
Thomas Edison State Coll (NJ)
Thomas U (GA)
Tiffin U (OH)
Towson U (MD)
Trevecca Nazarene U (TN)
Trine U (IN)
Trinity U (TX)
Truman State U (MO)
Universidad del Turabo (PR)
U at Albany, State U of New York (NY)
U at Buffalo, the State U of New York (NY)
The U of Akron (OH)
The U of Alabama (AL)
The U of Alabama at Birmingham (AL)
The U of Alabama in Huntsville (AL)
U of Alaska Fairbanks (AK)
The U of Arizona (AZ)
U of Arkansas (AR)
U of Arkansas at Monticello (AR)
U of California, Davis (CA)
U of California, Santa Barbara (CA)
U of Central Florida (FL)
U of Cincinnati (OH)
U of Colorado at Colorado Springs (CO)
U of Colorado Boulder (CO)
U of Colorado Denver (CO)
U of Connecticut (CT)
U of Delaware (DE)
U of Denver (CO)
U of Hartford (CT)
U of Hawaii at Manoa (HI)
U of Houston (TX)
U of Illinois at Chicago (IL)
U of Illinois at Urbana–Champaign (IL)
U of Indianapolis (IN)
The U of Iowa (IA)
The U of Kansas (KS)
U of La Verne (CA)
U of Louisiana at Lafayette (LA)
U of Louisville (KY)
U of Maine (ME)
U of Mary Hardin-Baylor (TX)
U of Maryland, Coll Park (MD)
U of Maryland U Coll (MD)
U of Massachusetts Amherst (MA)
U of Memphis (TN)
U of Miami (FL)
U of Michigan (MI)
U of Michigan–Dearborn (MI)
U of Minnesota, Duluth (MN)
U of Minnesota, Twin Cities Campus (MN)
U of Missouri (MO)
U of Missouri–St. Louis (MO)
U of Mobile (AL)
U of Nebraska–Lincoln (NE)
U of Nevada, Las Vegas (NV)
U of Nevada, Reno (NV)
U of New Hampshire (NH)
U of New Haven (CT)
U of New Mexico (NM)
U of New Orleans (LA)
The U of North Carolina at Chapel Hill (NC)
The U of North Carolina at Charlotte (NC)
The U of North Carolina Wilmington (NC)
U of Northern Colorado (CO)
U of Northern Iowa (IA)
U of Oklahoma (OK)

U of Ottawa (ON, Canada)
U of Pennsylvania (PA)
U of Pikeville (KY)
U of Puget Sound (WA)
U of Rhode Island (RI)
U of Rio Grande (OH)
U of Saint Francis (IN)
U of St. Thomas (TX)
U of Science and Arts of Oklahoma (OK)
The U of Scranton (PA)
U of South Alabama (AL)
U of South Carolina Aiken (SC)
U of South Carolina Upstate (SC)
U of Southern California (CA)
U of Southern Maine (ME)
U of Southern Mississippi (MS)
The U of Tennessee (TN)
The U of Tennessee at Chattanooga (TN)
The U of Texas at Austin (TX)
The U of Texas at San Antonio (TX)
The U of Texas–Pan American (TX)
U of the Cumberlands (KY)
U of the Incarnate Word (TX)
U of the Pacific (CA)
The U of Toledo (OH)
U of Tulsa (OK)
U of Utah (UT)
The U of Virginia's Coll at Wise (VA)
U of Washington (WA)
U of Wisconsin–La Crosse (WI)
U of Wisconsin–Madison (WI)
U of Wisconsin–River Falls (WI)
U of Wisconsin–Stevens Point (WI)
U of Wisconsin–Whitewater (WI)
U of Wyoming (WY)
Utica Coll (NY)
Valdosta State U (GA)
Valparaiso U (IN)
Vanderbilt U (TN)
Vanguard U of Southern California (CA)
Virginia Polytechnic Inst and State U (VA)
Wake Forest U (NC)
Waldorf Coll (IA)
Wartburg Coll (IA)
Washburn U (KS)
Washington U in St. Louis (MO)
Wayland Baptist U (TX)
Waynesburg U (PA)
Wayne State Coll (NE)
Wayne State U (MI)
Webber Intl U (FL)
Weber State U (UT)
Webster U (MO)
Wesleyan Coll (GA)
Western Carolina U (NC)
Western Connecticut State U (CT)
Western Illinois U (IL)
Western Kentucky U (KY)
Western Michigan U (MI)
Western New England U (MA)
Western Washington U (WA)
Westfield State U (MA)
Westminster Coll (UT)
West Virginia U (WV)
West Virginia Wesleyan Coll (WV)
Wheaton Coll (IL)
Whitman Coll (WA)
Wichita State U (KS)
Wilkes U (PA)
William Jewell Coll (MO)
William Penn U (IA)
William Woods U (MO)
Wingate U (NC)
Wittenberg U (OH)
Woodbury U (CA)
Worcester State U (MA)
Wright State U (OH)
York Coll of Pennsylvania (PA)

SPEECH-LANGUAGE PATHOLOGY

Abilene Christian U (TX)
Biola U (CA)
Bob Jones U (SC)
Caribbean U (PR)
Cleveland State U (OH)
Columbia Coll (SC)
Duquesne U (PA)
Eastern Michigan U (MI)
Eastern Washington U (WA)
Edinboro U of Pennsylvania (PA)

Geneva Coll (PA)
Grambling State U (LA)
Harding U (AR)
Inter American U of Puerto Rico, Fajardo Campus (PR)
Inter American U of Puerto Rico, Ponce Campus (PR)
James Madison U (VA)
Lehman Coll of the City U of New York (NY)
Loyola U Maryland (MD)
Marshall U (WV)
Marymount Manhattan Coll (NY)
Miami U (OH)
Minnesota State U Moorhead (MN)
Mississippi U for Women (MS)
Nazareth Coll of Rochester (NY)
Northern Michigan U (MI)
Oklahoma State U (OK)
Rockhurst U (MO)
Saint Xavier U (IL)
Texas Christian U (TX)
Towson U (MD)
Universidad del Turabo (PR)
U of Central Missouri (MO)
U of Nebraska–Lincoln (NE)
U of Northern Colorado (CO)
U of Northern Iowa (IA)
U of Oklahoma Health Sciences Center (OK)
U of Science and Arts of Oklahoma (OK)
The U of Toledo (OH)
The U of Western Ontario (ON, Canada)
U of West Georgia (GA)
U of Wisconsin–Whitewater (WI)
Valdosta State U (GA)
Xavier U of Louisiana (LA)

SPEECH TEACHER EDUCATION

Albion Coll (MI)
Anderson U (IN)
Arkansas Tech U (AR)
Augustana Coll (SD)
Baptist Bible Coll of Pennsylvania (PA)
Bemidji State U (MN)
Boston U (MA)
Bowling Green State U (OH)
Brigham Young U (UT)
Buena Vista U (IA)
Capital U (OH)
Carroll Coll (MT)
Colorado State U (CO)
Concordia U, Nebraska (NE)
Culver-Stockton Coll (MO)
Dordt Coll (IA)
East Central U (OK)
East Texas Baptist U (TX)
Elmira Coll (NY)
Evangel U (MO)
Harding U (AR)
Hardin-Simmons U (TX)
Howard Payne U (TX)
Indiana U Bloomington (IN)
Indiana U–Purdue U Fort Wayne (IN)
Indiana U–Purdue U Indianapolis (IN)
King Coll (TN)
Lubbock Christian U (TX)
McKendree U (IL)
Northwestern Coll (IA)
Northwest U (WA)
Oklahoma City U (OK)
Saginaw Valley State U (MI)
St. Ambrose U (IA)
St. Catherine U (MN)
Southeast Missouri State U (MO)
Southwest Baptist U (MO)
Southwestern Coll (KS)
Southwest Minnesota State U (MN)
State U of New York at New Paltz (NY)
Texas A&M U–Corpus Christi (TX)
Texas Wesleyan U (TX)
Trevecca Nazarene U (TN)
U of Indianapolis (IN)
The U of Iowa (IA)
U of Louisiana at Lafayette (LA)
U of Maine (ME)
U of Mary Hardin-Baylor (TX)

U of Michigan–Flint (MI)
U of Northern Iowa (IA)
U of Rio Grande (OH)
U of St. Thomas (MN)
The U of South Dakota (SD)
U of Windsor (ON, Canada)
Wartburg Coll (IA)
Wayne State Coll (NE)
Western Washington U (WA)
William Jewell Coll (MO)
William Woods U (MO)

SPORT AND FITNESS ADMINISTRATION/ MANAGEMENT

Abilene Christian U (TX)
Adelphi U (NY)
Albertus Magnus Coll (CT)
Alvernia U (PA)
American U (DC)
Anna Maria Coll (MA)
Arkansas State U (AR)
Asbury U (KY)
Augustana Coll (SD)
Averett U (VA)
Baker U (KS)
Baldwin-Wallace Coll (OH)
Barry U (FL)
Barton Coll (NC)
Becker Coll (MA)
Belhaven U (MS)
Belmont Abbey Coll (NC)
Bemidji State U (MN)
Bethany Coll (KS)
Bethany Coll (WV)
Bethel Coll (IN)
Blackburn Coll (IL)
Black Hills State U (SD)
Bluffton U (OH)
Bowling Green State U (OH)
Bridgewater State U (MA)
Buena Vista U (IA)
California U of Pennsylvania (PA)
Calvin Coll (MI)
Canisius Coll (NY)
Cape Breton U (NS, Canada)
Cedarville U (OH)
Centenary Coll (NJ)
Central Methodist U (MO)
Central Washington U (WA)
Claflin U (SC)
Clarke U (IA)
Clayton State U (GA)
Cleveland State U (OH)
Coastal Carolina U (SC)
The Coll at Brockport, State U of New York (NY)
The Coll of Idaho (ID)
Coll of Mount St. Joseph (OH)
Colorado Mesa U (CO)
Columbia Coll (MO)
Concordia Coll–New York (NY)
Concordia U Chicago (IL)
Concordia U, Nebraska (NE)
Concordia U, St. Paul (MN)
Corban U (OR)
Cornerstone U (MI)
Crown Coll (MN)
Culver-Stockton Coll (MO)
Daniel Webster Coll (NH)
Davenport U, Grand Rapids (MI)
Defiance Coll (OH)
Delaware State U (DE)
DeSales U (PA)
Eastern Connecticut State U (CT)
Eastern Mennonite U (VA)
Eastern Michigan U (MI)
East Tennessee State U (TN)
Elmhurst Coll (IL)
Elon U (NC)
Emmanuel Coll (GA)
Emory & Henry Coll (VA)
Endicott Coll (MA)
Faulkner U (AL)
Ferrum Coll (VA)
Fitchburg State U (MA)
Flagler Coll (FL)
Florida Inst of Technology (FL)
Fontbonne U (MO)
Fort Lewis Coll (CO)
Friends U (KS)
Gannon U (PA)
Gardner-Webb U (NC)
Geneva Coll (PA)

Georgia Southern U (GA)
Glenville State Coll (WV)
Goldey-Beacom Coll (DE)
Gonzaga U (WA)
Grace Coll (IN)
Grand Canyon U (AZ)
Greenville Coll (IL)
Guilford Coll (NC)
Hamline U (MN)
Hampton U (VA)
Harding U (AR)
Holy Family U (PA)
Howard Payne U (TX)
Huntingdon Coll (AL)
Husson U (ME)
Indiana Tech (IN)
Indiana Wesleyan U (IN)
Inter American U of Puerto Rico, San Germán Campus (PR)
Ithaca Coll (NY)
Jamestown Coll (ND)
John Brown U (AR)
Johnson C. Smith U (NC)
Johnson State Coll (VT)
Judson U (IL)
Kennesaw State U (GA)
Kent State U (OH)
Kentucky Wesleyan Coll (KY)
Keystone Coll (PA)
King Coll (TN)
Lake Erie Coll (OH)
Lasell Coll (MA)
Lees-McRae Coll (NC)
Lenoir-Rhyne U (NC)
LeTourneau U (TX)
Lewis U (IL)
Liberty U (VA)
Limestone Coll (SC)
Lindenwood U (MO)
Lock Haven U of Pennsylvania (PA)
Loras Coll (IA)
Louisiana State U and Ag and Mech Coll (LA)
Lubbock Christian U (TX)
Lynchburg Coll (VA)
Madonna U (MI)
Malone U (OH)
Manchester Coll (IN)
Maranatha Baptist Bible Coll (WI)
Marian U (WI)
Marietta Coll (OH)
Mars Hill Coll (NC)
Marymount U (VA)
Maryville U of Saint Louis (MO)
McKendree U (IL)
Medaille Coll (NY)
Menlo Coll (CA)
Messiah Coll (PA)
Miami U (OH)
MidAmerica Nazarene U (KS)
Midwestern State U (TX)
Millikin U (IL)
Minnesota State U Mankato (MN)
Minot State U (ND)
Misericordia U (PA)
Mississippi Coll (MS)
Missouri Baptist U (MO)
Mitchell Coll (CT)
Montana State U (MT)
Montana State U Billings (MT)
Morehead State U (KY)
Mount Ida Coll (MA)
Mount St. Mary's U (MD)
Mount Vernon Nazarene U (OH)
National U (CA)
Nebraska Wesleyan U (NE)
Neumann U (PA)
Newbury Coll (MA)
New England Coll (NH)
Niagara U (NY)
Nichols Coll (MA)
North Carolina Ag and Tech State U (NC)
North Carolina State U (NC)
North Central Coll (IL)
North Dakota State U (ND)
Northern Kentucky U (KY)
Northern Michigan U (MI)
Northern State U (SD)
North Greenville U (SC)
Northwestern Coll (IA)
Northwood U, Florida Campus (FL)
Northwood U, Michigan Campus (MI)
Nova Southeastern U (FL)

Ohio Northern U (OH)
The Ohio State U (OH)
Oklahoma Christian U (OK)
Oklahoma City U (OK)
Otterbein U (OH)
Plymouth State U (NH)
Post U (CT)
Quincy U (IL)
Reinhardt U (GA)
Rice U (TX)
Roanoke Coll (VA)
Robert Morris U (PA)
Rockhurst U (MO)
Rocky Mountain Coll (MT)
Rogers State U (OK)
Sacred Heart U (CT)
St. Ambrose U (IA)
St. Bonaventure U (NY)
St. John Fisher Coll (NY)
St. John's U (NY)
Saint Joseph's Coll (IN)
Saint Joseph's Coll of Maine (ME)
Saint Leo U (FL)
Saint Mary's Coll of California (CA)
St. Thomas Aquinas Coll (NY)
St. Thomas U (FL)
Salem State U (MA)
Samford U (AL)
Schreiner U (TX)
Seattle Pacific U (WA)
Seton Hill U (PA)
Shawnee State U (OH)
Siena Heights U (MI)
Simpson Coll (IA)
Slippery Rock U of Pennsylvania (PA)
Southeastern Louisiana U (LA)
Southeastern U (FL)
Southeast Missouri State U (MO)
Southern Illinois U Carbondale (IL)
Southern New Hampshire U (NH)
Southern Vermont Coll (VT)
Southwest Baptist U (MO)
Southwestern Assemblies of God U (TX)
Southwestern Christian U (OK)
Southwestern Coll (KS)
Spring Arbor U (MI)
State U of New York at Oswego (NY)
Stetson U (FL)
Syracuse U (NY)
Tabor Coll (KS)
Taylor U (IN)
Texas A&M U (TX)
Texas Lutheran U (TX)
Texas Southern U (TX)
Texas State U–San Marcos (TX)
Texas Wesleyan U (TX)
Thomas More Coll (KY)
Tiffin U (OH)
Towson U (MD)
Trevecca Nazarene U (TN)
Trine U (IN)
Troy U (AL)
Tusculum Coll (TN)
Union Coll (KY)
Union Coll (NE)
Union U (TN)
The U of Akron (OH)
U of Alberta (AB, Canada)
U of Cincinnati (OH)
U of Dayton (OH)
U of Delaware (DE)
U of Evansville (IN)
U of Florida (FL)
U of Georgia (GA)
U of Houston (TX)
U of Illinois at Urbana–Champaign (IL)
U of Indianapolis (IN)
The U of Iowa (IA)
U of Louisville (KY)
U of Mary (ND)
U of Mary Hardin-Baylor (TX)
U of Massachusetts Amherst (MA)
U of Memphis (TN)
U of Miami (FL)
U of Michigan (MI)
U of Minnesota, Crookston (MN)
U of Minnesota, Twin Cities Campus (MN)
U of Mount Union (OH)
U of Nebraska at Kearney (NE)
U of Nevada, Las Vegas (NV)

U of New England (ME)
U of North Florida (FL)
U of Pittsburgh at Bradford (PA)
U of Regina (SK, Canada)
U of Saint Mary (KS)
U of South Carolina (SC)
U of Southern Indiana (IN)
The U of Tampa (FL)
The U of Tennessee (TN)
The U of Texas at Austin (TX)
U of the Cumberlands (KY)
U of the Incarnate Word (TX)
U of Tulsa (OK)
U of Windsor (ON, Canada)
Valparaiso U (IN)
Virginia Intermont Coll (VA)
Viterbo U (WI)
Waldorf Coll (IA)
Wartburg Coll (IA)
Washington State U (WA)
Wayland Baptist U (TX)
Wayne State Coll (NE)
Western Carolina U (NC)
Western New England U (MA)
Western State Coll of Colorado (CO)
West Virginia U (WV)
Widener U (PA)
William Paterson U of New Jersey (NJ)
William Penn U (IA)
Wilmington Coll (OH)
Wilmington U (DE)
Wilson Coll (PA)
Wingate U (NC)
Winona State U (MN)
Winthrop U (SC)
Xavier U (OH)
York Coll of Pennsylvania (PA)

SPORTS COMMUNICATION

Bradley U (IL)
Lasell Coll (MA)
Oklahoma State U (OK)
Queens U of Charlotte (NC)
U of Evansville (IN)

SPORTS STUDIES

Bethel Coll (IN)
Central Michigan U (MI)
Huntington U (IN)
Lees-McRae Coll (NC)
Southwestern Coll (KS)
Texas Christian U (TX)
Trevecca Nazarene U (TN)
Western Kentucky U (KY)

STATISTICS

American U (DC)
American U of Beirut (Lebanon)
Appalachian State U (NC)
Arizona State U (AZ)
Barnard Coll (NY)
Baylor U (TX)
Bernard M. Baruch Coll of the City U of New York (NY)
Bowling Green State U (OH)
California Polytechnic State U, San Luis Obispo (CA)
California State U, East Bay (CA)
California State U, Fullerton (CA)
California State U, Long Beach (CA)
Carnegie Mellon U (PA)
Case Western Reserve U (OH)
Central Michigan U (MI)
Colorado State U (CO)
Columbia U, School of General Studies (NY)
Concordia U (QC, Canada)
Cornell U (NY)
Dalhousie U (NS, Canada)
Eastern Kentucky U (KY)
Eastern Michigan U (MI)
Elon U (NC)
Ferris State U (MI)
Florida Intl U (FL)
Florida State U (FL)
The George Washington U (DC)
Grand Valley State U (MI)
Harvard U (MA)
Hunter Coll of the City U of New York (NY)
Idaho State U (ID)

Indiana U Bloomington (IN)
Indiana U–Purdue U Fort Wayne (IN)
Iowa State U of Science and Technology (IA)
Kansas State U (KS)
Lehigh U (PA)
Loyola U Chicago (IL)
Mercyhurst Coll (PA)
Miami U (OH)
Michigan State U (MI)
Michigan Technological U (MI)
Montana State U (MT)
Mount Holyoke Coll (MA)
North Carolina State U (NC)
North Dakota State U (ND)
Northwest Missouri State U (MO)
Oakland U (MI)
Ohio Northern U (OH)
Ohio Wesleyan U (OH)
Oklahoma State U (OK)
Penn State Abington (PA)
Penn State Altoona (PA)
Penn State Beaver (PA)
Penn State Berks (PA)
Penn State Brandywine (PA)
Penn State DuBois (PA)
Penn State Erie, The Behrend Coll (PA)
Penn State Fayette, The Eberly Campus (PA)
Penn State Greater Allegheny (PA)
Penn State Hazleton (PA)
Penn State Lehigh Valley (PA)
Penn State Mont Alto (PA)
Penn State New Kensington (PA)
Penn State Schuylkill (PA)
Penn State Shenango (PA)
Penn State U Park (PA)
Penn State Wilkes-Barre (PA)
Penn State Worthington Scranton (PA)
Penn State York (PA)
Purdue U (IN)
Queen's U at Kingston (ON, Canada)
Rice U (TX)
Rochester Inst of Technology (NY)
Rutgers, The State U of New Jersey, New Brunswick (NJ)
St. John Fisher Coll (NY)
San Diego State U (CA)
San Francisco State U (CA)
Simon Fraser U (BC, Canada)
Slippery Rock U of Pennsylvania (PA)
Sonoma State U (CA)
Southern Methodist U (TX)
Stanford U (CA)
State U of New York Coll at Oneonta (NY)
The U of Akron (OH)
U of Alberta (AB, Canada)
The U of British Columbia (BC, Canada)
U of California, Berkeley (CA)
U of California, Davis (CA)
U of California, Los Angeles (CA)
U of California, Riverside (CA)
U of California, Santa Barbara (CA)
U of Central Florida (FL)
U of Connecticut (CT)
U of Delaware (DE)
U of Florida (FL)
U of Georgia (GA)
U of Guelph (ON, Canada)
U of Illinois at Chicago (IL)
U of Illinois at Urbana–Champaign (IL)
The U of Iowa (IA)
U of Maryland, Baltimore County (MD)
U of Michigan (MI)
U of Minnesota, Duluth (MN)
U of Minnesota, Twin Cities Campus (MN)
U of Missouri (MO)
U of Nebraska at Kearney (NE)
U of Nevada, Las Vegas (NV)
U of New Mexico (NM)
The U of North Carolina Wilmington (NC)
U of North Florida (FL)
U of Ottawa (ON, Canada)
U of Pennsylvania (PA)

U of Pittsburgh (PA)
U of Regina (SK, Canada)
U of Rochester (NY)
U of South Carolina (SC)
U of Southern Maine (ME)
U of South Florida (FL)
The U of Tennessee (TN)
The U of Tennessee at Martin (TN)
The U of Texas at El Paso (TX)
The U of Texas at San Antonio (TX)
U of Vermont (VT)
U of Washington (WA)
The U of Western Ontario (ON, Canada)
U of Wisconsin–Madison (WI)
U of Wyoming (WY)
Utah State U (UT)
Virginia Polytechnic Inst and State U (VA)
Washington U in St. Louis (MO)
Western Michigan U (MI)
Winona State U (MN)
Wright State U (OH)
Xavier U of Louisiana (LA)

STATISTICS RELATED

Carnegie Mellon U (PA)
Ohio Northern U (OH)
Saint Mary's Coll (IN)
United States Military Acad (NY)

STRINGED INSTRUMENTS

Acadia U (NS, Canada)
Bard Coll (NY)
Bennington Coll (VT)
Berklee Coll of Music (MA)
Brigham Young U (UT)
Butler U (IN)
Carnegie Mellon U (PA)
Conservatorio de Musica (PR)
Converse Coll (SC)
Cornish Coll of the Arts (WA)
Five Towns Coll (NY)
Hardin-Simmons U (TX)
Heidelberg U (OH)
Hope Coll (MI)
Houghton Coll (NY)
Inter American U of Puerto Rico, San Germán Campus (PR)
Lamar U (TX)
Lawrence U (WI)
McNally Smith Coll of Music (MN)
Mount Allison U (NB, Canada)
New England Conservatory of Music (MA)
Northwestern Coll (MN)
Oklahoma City U (OK)
Otterbein U (OH)
Peabody Conservatory of The Johns Hopkins U (MD)
Roosevelt U (IL)
San Francisco Conservatory of Music (CA)
Sarah Lawrence Coll (NY)
State U of New York at Fredonia (NY)
Stetson U (FL)
Syracuse U (NY)
Texas Christian U (TX)
U of Alberta (AB, Canada)
The U of British Columbia (BC, Canada)
The U of Iowa (IA)
The U of Kansas (KS)
U of Nebraska at Omaha (NE)
U of Southern California (CA)
U of Washington (WA)
The U of Western Ontario (ON, Canada)
Vanderbilt U (TN)
Willamette U (OR)
Xavier U of Louisiana (LA)

STRUCTURAL BIOLOGY

U of Connecticut (CT)

STRUCTURAL ENGINEERING

Penn State Harrisburg (PA)
U at Buffalo, the State U of New York (NY)
U of Central Florida (FL)
U of Illinois at Urbana–Champaign (IL)
U of Southern California (CA)

The U of Toledo (OH)
Western Michigan U (MI)

STUDENT COUNSELING AND PERSONNEL SERVICES RELATED

Samford U (AL)

SUBSTANCE ABUSE/ ADDICTION COUNSELING

Alvernia U (PA)
City Vision Coll (MO)
The Coll at Brockport, State U of New York (NY)
Coll of St. Joseph (VT)
Indiana U–Purdue U Fort Wayne (IN)
Indiana Wesleyan U (IN)
Keene State Coll (NH)
Metropolitan State U (MN)
Minot State U (ND)
Newman U (KS)
Northwestern State U of Louisiana (LA)
Rhode Island Coll (RI)
Roger Williams U (RI)
Sojourner-Douglass Coll (MD)
Tiffin U (OH)
U of Central Arkansas (AR)
U of Cincinnati (OH)
U of Great Falls (MT)
U of Lethbridge (AB, Canada)
U of Mary (ND)
The U of South Dakota (SD)
The U of Texas–Pan American (TX)
Viterbo U (WI)
Washburn U (KS)

SURVEYING ENGINEERING

Ferris State U (MI)
Florida Atlantic U (FL)
North Carolina Ag and Tech State U (NC)
U of Maine (ME)

SURVEYING TECHNOLOGY

East Tennessee State U (TN)
Ferris State U (MI)
Idaho State U (ID)
Metropolitan State Coll of Denver (CO)
Michigan Technological U (MI)
New Mexico State U (NM)
Nicholls State U (LA)
The Ohio State U (OH)
Oregon Inst of Technology (OR)
Penn State Wilkes-Barre (PA)
Polytechnic U of Puerto Rico (PR)
Roger Williams U (RI)
South Carolina State U (SC)
Southern Polytechnic State U (GA)
State U of New York Coll of Technology at Alfred (NY)
Texas A&M U–Corpus Christi (TX)
Troy U (AL)
The U of Akron (OH)
U of Alaska Anchorage (AK)
U of Arkansas at Little Rock (AR)
U of Arkansas at Monticello (AR)
U of Florida (FL)
U of Maine (ME)

SUSTAINABILITY STUDIES

Aquinas Coll (MI)
Arizona State U (AZ)
Cleary U (MI)
Creighton U (NE)
The Evergreen State Coll (WA)
Furman U (SC)
George Mason U (VA)
Goddard Coll (VT)
Kean U (NJ)
Messiah Coll (PA)
Prescott Coll (AZ)
Rensselaer Polytechnic Inst (NY)
The Richard Stockton Coll of New Jersey (NJ)
Roosevelt U (IL)
Sierra Nevada Coll (NV)
Stephen F. Austin State U (TX)
Stony Brook U, State U of New York (NY)
U of Florida (FL)

INDEXES

The U of Western Ontario (ON, Canada)
U of Wisconsin–Stout (WI)
Western New England U (MA)
Wheeling Jesuit U (WV)

SWEDISH
Brigham Young U (UT)

SYSTEM, NETWORKING, AND LAN/WAN MANAGEMENT
Alcorn State U (MS)
Capella U (MN)
Dakota State U (SD)
Northern Michigan U (MI)
Rochester Inst of Technology (NY)
State U of New York Coll of Technology at Alfred (NY)
Texas A&M U (TX)
U of Great Falls (MT)
U of Hawaii–West Oahu (HI)

SYSTEMS ENGINEERING
Case Western Reserve U (OH)
Delaware State U (DE)
Ferris State U (MI)
George Mason U (VA)
The George Washington U (DC)
Providence Coll (RI)
Rochester Inst of Technology (NY)
Southern Polytechnic State U (GA)
Stanford U (CA)
Stevens Inst of Technology (NJ)
United States Military Acad (NY)
United States Naval Acad (MD)
The U of Arizona (AZ)
U of Florida (FL)
U of Maine (ME)
The U of North Carolina at Charlotte (NC)
U of Pennsylvania (PA)
U of Southern California (CA)
U of Virginia (VA)
U of Wyoming (WY)
Washington U in St. Louis (MO)

SYSTEMS SCIENCE AND THEORY
Boston U (MA)
Carnegie Mellon U (PA)
Indiana U Bloomington (IN)
James Madison U (VA)
Marshall U (WV)
Stanford U (CA)
United States Military Acad (NY)
U of Wyoming (WY)
Washington U in St. Louis (MO)
Yale U (CT)

TAXATION
Fontbonne U (MO)
Grand Valley State U (MI)

TECHNICAL AND SCIENTIFIC COMMUNICATION
Illinois Inst of Technology (IL)
Lehigh U (PA)

TECHNICAL TEACHER EDUCATION
Auburn U (AL)
Bowling Green State U (OH)
Eastern Illinois U (IL)
Eastern Kentucky U (KY)
Ferris State U (MI)
Montana State U (MT)
The Ohio State U (OH)
Oklahoma State U (OK)
Pittsburg State U (KS)
Queen's U at Kingston (ON, Canada)
Rhode Island Coll (RI)
South Dakota State U (SD)
The U of Akron (OH)
U of Arkansas (AR)
U of Georgia (GA)
U of Idaho (ID)
U of Illinois at Urbana–Champaign (IL)
U of Minnesota, Twin Cities Campus (MN)
U of Missouri (MO)

U of Nebraska at Kearney (NE)
U of Wisconsin–Stout (WI)
Utah State U (UT)
Valley City State U (ND)
Wayne State U (MI)
Western Michigan U (MI)
Wright State U (OH)

TECHNOLOGY/INDUSTRIAL ARTS TEACHER EDUCATION
Appalachian State U (NC)
Ball State U (IN)
Bemidji State U (MN)
Berea Coll (KY)
Bowling Green State U (OH)
Buffalo State Coll, State U of New York (NY)
Central Connecticut State U (CT)
Central Michigan U (MI)
Central Washington U (WA)
Chicago State U (IL)
The Coll of New Jersey (NJ)
Colorado State U (CO)
Concordia U, Nebraska (NE)
Eastern Kentucky U (KY)
Eastern Michigan U (MI)
Fitchburg State U (MA)
Georgia Southern U (GA)
Illinois State U (IL)
Keene State Coll (NH)
Lindenwood U (MO)
Michigan Technological U (MI)
Middle Tennessee State U (TN)
Montana State U–Northern (MT)
New Mexico Highlands U (NM)
New York City Coll of Technology of the City U of New York (NY)
North Carolina Ag and Tech State U (NC)
North Carolina State U (NC)
Ohio Northern U (OH)
The Ohio State U (OH)
Pittsburg State U (KS)
Purdue U (IN)
Rhode Island Coll (RI)
South Carolina State U (SC)
Southeast Missouri State U (MO)
Southwestern Oklahoma State U (OK)
State U of New York at Oswego (NY)
State U of New York Coll at Potsdam (NY)
Texas A&M U–Corpus Christi (TX)
U of Minnesota, Twin Cities Campus (MN)
The U of Montana Western (MT)
U of New Mexico (NM)
U of Northern Iowa (IA)
U of Southern Maine (ME)
U of the Ozarks (AR)
U of Wisconsin–Stout (WI)
U of Wyoming (WY)
Utah State U (UT)
Valley City State U (ND)
Viterbo U (WI)
Wayland Baptist U (TX)
Wayne State Coll (NE)
Western Michigan U (MI)
Western Washington U (WA)
Westfield State U (MA)

TELECOMMUNICATIONS TECHNOLOGY
California State U, East Bay (CA)
Ferris State U (MI)
Inter American U of Puerto Rico, Bayamón Campus (PR)
Lawrence Technological U (MI)
National U (CA)
New York City Coll of Technology of the City U of New York (NY)
New York Inst of Technology (NY)
Pace U (NY)
Pacific U (OR)
Pepperdine U, Malibu (CA)
Rochester Inst of Technology (NY)
St. John's U (NY)
Southern Polytechnic State U (GA)
U of Wisconsin–Platteville (WI)

TERRORISM AND COUNTERTERRORISM OPERATIONS
Henley-Putnam U (CA)

TEXTILE SCIENCE
Michigan State U (MI)

TEXTILE SCIENCES AND ENGINEERING
Auburn U (AL)
Clemson U (SC)
Georgia Inst of Technology (GA)
North Carolina State U (NC)
Philadelphia U (PA)
U of Massachusetts Dartmouth (MA)

THEATER DESIGN AND TECHNOLOGY
The Art Inst of California, a college of Argosy U, Hollywood (CA)
Bard Coll at Simon's Rock (MA)
Baylor U (TX)
Bennington Coll (VT)
Biola U (CA)
Boston U (MA)
Brenau U (GA)
Brigham Young U (UT)
Broadview U-Salt Lake City (UT)
Centenary Coll (NJ)
Central Michigan U (MI)
Coe Coll (IA)
Coll of the Ozarks (MO)
Columbia Coll Chicago (IL)
Concordia U (QC, Canada)
Cornish Coll of the Arts (WA)
DePaul U (IL)
Dixie State Coll of Utah (UT)
Doane Coll (NE)
Elon U (NC)
Fitchburg State U (MA)
Florida Southern Coll (FL)
Huntington U (IN)
Illinois Wesleyan U (IL)
Ithaca Coll (NY)
Kean U (NJ)
Keene State Coll (NH)
Lindenwood U (MO)
Michigan Technological U (MI)
Millikin U (IL)
New York City Coll of Technology of the City U of New York (NY)
Northwest Missouri State U (MO)
Oakland U (MI)
Oklahoma City U (OK)
Oral Roberts U (OK)
Penn State Abington (PA)
Penn State Altoona (PA)
Penn State Beaver (PA)
Penn State Berks (PA)
Penn State Brandywine (PA)
Penn State DuBois (PA)
Penn State Erie, The Behrend Coll (PA)
Penn State Fayette, The Eberly Campus (PA)
Penn State Greater Allegheny (PA)
Penn State Hazleton (PA)
Penn State Lehigh Valley (PA)
Penn State Mont Alto (PA)
Penn State New Kensington (PA)
Penn State Schuylkill (PA)
Penn State Shenango (PA)
Penn State U Park (PA)
Penn State Wilkes-Barre (PA)
Penn State Worthington Scranton (PA)
Penn State York (PA)
Purchase Coll, State U of New York (NY)
Rocky Mountain Coll (MT)
Ryerson U (ON, Canada)
Salem State U (MA)
Seton Hill U (PA)
Shenandoah U (VA)
Slippery Rock U of Pennsylvania (PA)
Southwestern Coll (KS)
State U of New York at Binghamton (NY)
State U of New York at New Paltz (NY)

Stephens Coll (MO)
Texas Christian U (TX)
Trinity U (TX)
U of Alaska Fairbanks (AK)
U of Alberta (AB, Canada)
The U of Arizona (AZ)
U of Cincinnati (OH)
U of Connecticut (CT)
The U of Kansas (KS)
U of Lethbridge (AB, Canada)
U of Miami (FL)
U of Michigan (MI)
U of Michigan–Flint (MI)
U of New Mexico (NM)
U of North Carolina School of the Arts (NC)
U of Regina (SK, Canada)
U of Southern California (CA)
The U of the Arts (PA)
Vanguard U of Southern California (CA)
Virginia Intermont Coll (VA)
Webster U (MO)
Western Michigan U (MI)
Western State Coll of Colorado (CO)
William Woods U (MO)
Wright State U (OH)

THEATER LITERATURE, HISTORY AND CRITICISM
Albertus Magnus Coll (CT)
Averett U (VA)
Bard Coll (NY)
Bard Coll at Simon's Rock (MA)
Bennington Coll (VT)
Bowdoin Coll (ME)
Buena Vista U (IA)
Clark Atlanta U (GA)
Dalhousie U (NS, Canada)
DePaul U (IL)
Keene State Coll (NH)
Marymount Manhattan Coll (NY)
Moravian Coll (PA)
Saint Mary's Coll of California (CA)
Salem State U (MA)
State U of New York at New Paltz (NY)
Suffolk U (MA)
U of Connecticut (CT)
U of Illinois at Urbana–Champaign (IL)
Washington & Jefferson Coll (PA)
Washington U in St. Louis (MO)
Western Michigan U (MI)
West Virginia U (WV)

THEATER/THEATER ARTS MANAGEMENT
Berry Coll (GA)
Bethany Coll (KS)
Biola U (CA)
Cedarville U (OH)
DEREE - The American Coll of Greece (Greece)
Juniata Coll (PA)
Massachusetts Coll of Liberal Arts (MA)
Nazareth Coll of Rochester (NY)
Oglethorpe U (GA)
Ohio Northern U (OH)
Oklahoma City U (OK)
Pace U (NY)
Pittsburg State U (KS)
Regent U (VA)
Reinhardt U (GA)
Seton Hill U (PA)
Slippery Rock U of Pennsylvania (PA)
Stephens Coll (MO)
The U of British Columbia (BC, Canada)
U of Evansville (IN)
U of Miami (FL)
U of Minnesota, Duluth (MN)
U of Regina (SK, Canada)
U of Richmond (VA)
U of Southern California (CA)

THEOLOGICAL AND MINISTERIAL STUDIES RELATED
Baptist Bible Coll of Pennsylvania (PA)

California Christian Coll (CA)
Concordia U (QC, Canada)
Concordia U, St. Paul (MN)
Faith Theological Sem (MD)
Hardin-Simmons U (TX)
Hope Intl U (CA)
Howard Payne U (TX)
Huntington U (IN)
John Brown U (AR)
Judson U (IL)
Lincoln Christian U (IL)
Marquette U (WI)
Northwest Christian U (OR)
Northwestern Coll (MN)
Point Loma Nazarene U (CA)
Trinity Coll of Florida (FL)
U of Saint Francis (IN)
Viterbo U (WI)

THEOLOGY
Alvernia U (PA)
Anderson U (IN)
Andrews U (MI)
Anna Maria Coll (MA)
Apex School of Theology (NC)
Assumption Coll (MA)
Azusa Pacific U (CA)
Barry U (FL)
Bellarmine U (KY)
Belmont Abbey Coll (NC)
Benedictine U (IL)
Biola U (CA)
Bluefield Coll (VA)
Bob Jones U (SC)
Boston Coll (MA)
Brescia U (KY)
Brewton-Parker Coll (GA)
Briar Cliff U (IA)
Briercrest Coll (SK, Canada)
Caldwell Coll (NJ)
Calumet Coll of Saint Joseph (IN)
Calvin Coll (MI)
Carlow U (PA)
Carroll Coll (MT)
Cedarville U (OH)
Christendom Coll (VA)
Coll of Saint Benedict (MN)
Coll of Saint Elizabeth (NJ)
Coll of Saint Mary (NE)
Concordia U (CA)
Concordia U (QC, Canada)
Concordia U Chicago (IL)
Concordia U, Nebraska (NE)
Concordia U, St. Paul (MN)
Creighton U (NE)
Crown Coll (MN)
DeSales U (PA)
Dominican U (IL)
Dordt Coll (IA)
Duquesne U (PA)
Eastern Mennonite U (VA)
Eastern U (PA)
Elmhurst Coll (IL)
Faulkner U (AL)
Fordham U (NY)
Franciscan U of Steubenville (OH)
Gannon U (PA)
Hanover Coll (IN)
Hardin-Simmons U (TX)
Hellenic Coll (MA)
Hillsdale Free Will Baptist Coll (OK)
Holy Cross Coll (IN)
Holy Trinity Orthodox Sem (NY)
Houghton Coll (NY)
Howard Payne U (TX)
Huntington U (IN)
Immaculata U (PA)
Indiana Wesleyan U (IN)
John Brown U (AR)
King's Coll (PA)
The King's U Coll (AB, Canada)
Lee U (TN)
Lincoln Christian U (IL)
Louisiana Coll (LA)
Loyola Marymount U (CA)
Loyola U Chicago (IL)
Lubbock Christian U (TX)
Marquette U (WI)
Martin Luther Coll (MN)
The Master's Coll and Sem (CA)
Master's Coll and Sem (ON, Canada)
MidAmerica Nazarene U (KS)
Moody Bible Inst (IL)
Morris Coll (SC)

INDEXES

Mount Mary Coll (WI)
Mount St. Mary's U (MD)
Mount Vernon Nazarene U (OH)
Multnomah U (OR)
Newman U (KS)
Northwest Nazarene U (ID)
Oakland City U (IN)
Oral Roberts U (OK)
Ouachita Baptist U (AR)
Pacific Lutheran U (WA)
Pacific Union Coll (CA)
Palm Beach Atlantic U (FL)
Piedmont Intl U (NC)
Point U (GA)
Providence Coll (RI)
Queen's U at Kingston (ON, Canada)
Rockhurst U (MO)
St. Ambrose U (IA)
Saint Anselm Coll (NH)
St. Bonaventure U (NY)
St. Catherine U (MN)
Saint John's U (MN)
St. John's U (NY)
Saint Joseph's Coll of Maine (ME)
Saint Louis Christian Coll (MO)
Saint Louis U (MO)
Saint Mary-of-the-Woods Coll (IN)
Saint Mary's Coll of California (CA)
St. Mary's U (TX)
Saint Mary's U of Minnesota (MN)
Saint Peter's Coll (NJ)
Saint Vincent Coll (PA)
San Diego Christian Coll (CA)
Seattle Pacific U (WA)
Southeastern Baptist Theological Sem (NC)
Southwest Baptist U (MO)
Southwestern Adventist U (TX)
Southwestern Assemblies of God U (TX)
Southwestern Christian U (OK)
Spring Arbor U (MI)
Texas Lutheran U (TX)
Trinity Christian Coll (IL)
Trinity Lutheran Coll (WA)
Union Coll (NE)
Union U (TN)
U of Dallas (TX)
U of Dubuque (IA)
U of Evansville (IN)
U of Great Falls (MT)
U of Mary (ND)
U of Mary Hardin-Baylor (TX)
U of Minnesota, Twin Cities Campus (MN)
U of Notre Dame (IN)
U of Portland (OR)
U of St. Francis (IL)
U of Saint Francis (IN)
U of Saint Mary (KS)
U of St. Thomas (TX)
U of the Southwest (NM)
The U of Western Ontario (ON, Canada)
Valparaiso U (IN)
Vanguard Coll (AB, Canada)
Vanguard U of Southern California (CA)
Walsh U (OH)
Washington Adventist U (MD)
Wheeling Jesuit U (WV)
William Jessup U (CA)
Williams Baptist Coll (AR)
Xavier U of Louisiana (LA)

THEOLOGY AND RELIGIOUS VOCATIONS RELATED
Abilene Christian U (TX)
Arlington Baptist Coll (TX)
Baptist Bible Coll of Pennsylvania (PA)
Cedarville U (OH)
Concordia Coll–New York (NY)
Kentucky Mountain Bible Coll (KY)
Master's Coll and Sem (ON, Canada)
Missouri Baptist U (MO)
Newman U (KS)
Ouachita Baptist U (AR)
St. Edward's U (TX)
Simpson U (CA)
Southeastern U (FL)
Thiel Coll (PA)
Trinity Christian Coll (IL)

Union U (TN)
U of St. Thomas (TX)

THEORETICAL AND MATHEMATICAL PHYSICS
Chapman U (CA)
Sweet Briar Coll (VA)
U at Buffalo, the State U of New York (NY)
U of Guelph (ON, Canada)
U of Ottawa (ON, Canada)
The U of Western Ontario (ON, Canada)

THERAPEUTIC RECREATION
Brigham Young U (UT)
California State U, Chico (CA)
California State U, East Bay (CA)
Calvin Coll (MI)
Catawba Coll (NC)
The Coll at Brockport, State U of New York (NY)
Concordia U (QC, Canada)
Dalhousie U (NS, Canada)
East Carolina U (NC)
Eastern Michigan U (MI)
Eastern Washington U (WA)
Grand Valley State U (MI)
Hampton U (VA)
Indiana Tech (IN)
Ithaca Coll (NY)
Lincoln U (PA)
Longwood U (VA)
Minnesota State U Mankato (MN)
Pittsburg State U (KS)
St. Andrews U (NC)
Shaw U (NC)
Slippery Rock U of Pennsylvania (PA)
Southwestern Oklahoma State U (OK)
State U of New York Coll at Cortland (NY)
Temple U (PA)
The U of Akron (OH)
The U of Iowa (IA)
U of Nebraska at Kearney (NE)
The U of North Carolina Wilmington (NC)
U of Southern Maine (ME)
U of Wisconsin–La Crosse (WI)
U of Wisconsin–Milwaukee (WI)
Utica Coll (NY)
Western Carolina U (NC)
West Virginia State U (WV)
Winona State U (MN)

TOOL AND DIE TECHNOLOGY
Utah State U (UT)

TOURISM AND TRAVEL SERVICES MANAGEMENT
Arizona State U (AZ)
Becker Coll (MA)
Black Hills State U (SD)
Bowling Green State U (OH)
California State U, Chico (CA)
Cape Breton U (NS, Canada)
Delaware State U (DE)
Fort Hays State U (KS)
Fort Lewis Coll (CO)
George Mason U (VA)
Hawai`i Pacific U (HI)
Indiana U East (IN)
Indiana U–Purdue U Indianapolis (IN)
Johnson State Coll (VT)
Mansfield U of Pennsylvania (PA)
Niagara U (NY)
Northeastern State U (OK)
Plymouth State U (NH)
St. Thomas U (FL)
Salem State U (MA)
Southern New Hampshire U (NH)
State U of New York Coll of Technology at Delhi (NY)
State U of New York Maritime Coll (NY)
Texas A&M U (TX)
United States Intl U (Kenya)
U of Central Florida (FL)
U of Guelph (ON, Canada)
U of Hawaii at Manoa (HI)
U of Nevada, Las Vegas (NV)

U of South Carolina (SC)
The U of Texas at San Antonio (TX)

TOURISM AND TRAVEL SERVICES MARKETING
Mitchell Coll (CT)
Rochester Inst of Technology (NY)
Thompson Rivers U (BC, Canada)
U of Central Missouri (MO)
Western Michigan U (MI)

TOURISM PROMOTION
Bowling Green State U (OH)
Cape Breton U (NS, Canada)

TOXICOLOGY
Ashland U (OH)
Eastern Michigan U (MI)
Penn State Beaver (PA)
Penn State Berks (PA)
Penn State DuBois (PA)
Penn State Fayette, The Eberly Campus (PA)
Penn State Greater Allegheny (PA)
Penn State Hazleton (PA)
Penn State Mont Alto (PA)
Penn State New Kensington (PA)
Penn State Shenango (PA)
Penn State U Park (PA)
Penn State Wilkes-Barre (PA)
Penn State York (PA)
St. John's U (NY)
U of California, Berkeley (CA)
U of Guelph (ON, Canada)
U of Louisiana at Monroe (LA)
U of Toronto (ON, Canada)
The U of Western Ontario (ON, Canada)

TRADE AND INDUSTRIAL TEACHER EDUCATION
Athens State U (AL)
Auburn U (AL)
Bemidji State U (MN)
Bowling Green State U (OH)
Buffalo State Coll, State U of New York (NY)
California State U, Long Beach (CA)
California State U, San Bernardino (CA)
Central Washington U (WA)
The Coll of Saint Rose (NY)
Colorado State U (CO)
Concordia U, Nebraska (NE)
Delaware State U (DE)
Eastern Kentucky U (KY)
Eastern New Mexico U (NM)
Fitchburg State U (MA)
Florida Ag and Mech U (FL)
Indiana State U (IN)
Indiana U of Pennsylvania (PA)
Iowa State U of Science and Technology (IA)
Kent State U (OH)
Lindenwood U (MO)
Norfolk State U (VA)
North Carolina Ag and Tech State U (NC)
Northern Kentucky U (KY)
Prairie View A&M U (TX)
San Diego State U (CA)
Southern Illinois U Carbondale (IL)
State U of New York at Oswego (NY)
Temple U (PA)
Texas A&M U–Corpus Christi (TX)
Universidad del Turabo (PR)
U of Alberta (AB, Canada)
U of Central Florida (FL)
U of Louisville (KY)
U of Minnesota, Twin Cities Campus (MN)
U of North Florida (FL)
U of Southern Maine (ME)
U of South Florida (FL)
U of the District of Columbia (DC)
The U of Toledo (OH)
U of West Florida (FL)
U of Wyoming (WY)
Upper Iowa U (IA)
Valdosta State U (GA)
Virginia State U (VA)
Wayland Baptist U (TX)

Western Kentucky U (KY)
Western Michigan U (MI)

TRANSPORTATION AND HIGHWAY ENGINEERING
U of Toronto (ON, Canada)

TRANSPORTATION AND MATERIALS MOVING RELATED
Eastern Kentucky U (KY)
Lewis U (IL)
Niagara U (NY)
United States Merchant Marine Acad (NY)
The U of British Columbia (BC, Canada)

TRANSPORTATION/MOBILITY MANAGEMENT
Bridgewater State U (MA)
North Carolina Ag and Tech State U (NC)
U of North Florida (FL)
U of Pennsylvania (PA)
U of Wisconsin–Superior (WI)

TURF AND TURFGRASS MANAGEMENT
Clemson U (SC)
Delaware Valley Coll (PA)
Florida Southern Coll (FL)
New Mexico State U (NM)
North Carolina State U (NC)
North Dakota State U (ND)
The Ohio State U (OH)
Penn State Abington (PA)
Penn State Altoona (PA)
Penn State Beaver (PA)
Penn State Berks (PA)
Penn State Brandywine (PA)
Penn State DuBois (PA)
Penn State Erie, The Behrend Coll (PA)
Penn State Fayette, The Eberly Campus (PA)
Penn State Greater Allegheny (PA)
Penn State Hazleton (PA)
Penn State Lehigh Valley (PA)
Penn State Mont Alto (PA)
Penn State New Kensington (PA)
Penn State Schuylkill (PA)
Penn State Shenango (PA)
Penn State U Park (PA)
Penn State Wilkes-Barre (PA)
Penn State Worthington Scranton (PA)
Penn State York (PA)
Rutgers, The State U of New Jersey, New Brunswick (NJ)
Texas A&M U (TX)
U of Georgia (GA)
U of Minnesota, Crookston (MN)
U of Nebraska–Lincoln (NE)
U of Rhode Island (RI)

TURKISH
U of Utah (UT)

URBAN EDUCATION AND LEADERSHIP
The Coll of New Jersey (NJ)
U of Delaware (DE)
U of Wisconsin–Milwaukee (WI)

URBAN FORESTRY
Texas A&M U (TX)
U of California, Davis (CA)
U of Illinois at Urbana–Champaign (IL)
U of Minnesota, Crookston (MN)

URBAN MINISTRY
Crossroads Bible Coll (IN)
Crown Coll (MN)
Trinity Baptist Coll (FL)

URBAN STUDIES/AFFAIRS
Albertus Magnus Coll (CT)
The American U of Paris (France)
Aquinas Coll (MI)
Arizona State U (AZ)
Ball State U (IN)

Barnard Coll (NY)
Boston U (MA)
Brown U (RI)
Bryn Mawr Coll (PA)
Buffalo State Coll, State U of New York (NY)
Butler U (IN)
California State U, Dominguez Hills (CA)
Calvary Bible Coll and Theological Sem (MO)
Canisius Coll (NY)
Cleveland State U (OH)
Coll of Charleston (SC)
Coll of Mount Saint Vincent (NY)
The Coll of Wooster (OH)
Columbia U, School of General Studies (NY)
Concordia U (QC, Canada)
Connecticut Coll (CT)
Delaware State U (DE)
DePaul U (IL)
Dillard U (LA)
Eastern U (PA)
Elmhurst Coll (IL)
Fordham U (NY)
Furman U (SC)
Hampshire Coll (MA)
Haverford Coll (PA)
Hobart and William Smith Colls (NY)
Hunter Coll of the City U of New York (NY)
Lipscomb U (TN)
Loyola Marymount U (CA)
Manhattan Coll (NY)
Minnesota State U Mankato (MN)
Morehouse Coll (GA)
New Coll of Florida (FL)
New Jersey City U (NJ)
New York U (NY)
Northeastern Illinois U (IL)
Occidental Coll (CA)
Oglethorpe U (GA)
Ohio U (OH)
Ohio Wesleyan U (OH)
Portland State U (OR)
Purchase Coll, State U of New York (NY)
Queens Coll of the City U of New York (NY)
Rhodes Coll (TN)
Rutgers, The State U of New Jersey, Camden (NJ)
Rutgers, The State U of New Jersey, New Brunswick (NJ)
Ryerson U (ON, Canada)
Saint Louis U (MO)
Saint Peter's Coll (NJ)
San Diego State U (CA)
San Francisco State U (CA)
Sarah Lawrence Coll (NY)
Sojourner-Douglass Coll (MD)
Stanford U (CA)
Temple U (PA)
Towson U (MD)
Trinity U (TX)
Tufts U (MA)
U at Albany, State U of New York (NY)
U of Alberta (AB, Canada)
The U of British Columbia (BC, Canada)
U of California, Berkeley (CA)
U of California, Irvine (CA)
U of Cincinnati (OH)
U of Connecticut (CT)
U of Illinois at Chicago (IL)
U of Lethbridge (AB, Canada)
U of Minnesota, Duluth (MN)
U of Minnesota, Twin Cities Campus (MN)
U of Missouri–Kansas City (MO)
U of New Orleans (LA)
U of Pennsylvania (PA)
U of Pittsburgh (PA)
The U of Texas at Austin (TX)
The U of Toledo (OH)
U of Utah (UT)
The U of Western Ontario (ON, Canada)
U of Wisconsin–Green Bay (WI)
Vassar Coll (NY)
Virginia Commonwealth U (VA)
Washington U in St. Louis (MO)

INDEXES

Wayne State U (MI)
Worcester State U (MA)
Wright State U (OH)

VEHICLE AND VEHICLE PARTS AND ACCESSORIES MARKETING
Northwood U, Florida Campus (FL)
Northwood U, Michigan Campus (MI)

VEHICLE MAINTENANCE AND REPAIR TECHNOLOGIES RELATED
McPherson Coll (KS)

VETERINARY/ANIMAL HEALTH TECHNOLOGY
Brigham Young U (UT)
Globe U–Madison East (WI)
Globe U–Woodbury (MN)
Medaille Coll (NY)
Michigan State U (MI)
Minnesota School of Business–Plymouth (MN)
Mississippi State U (MS)
Mount Ida Coll (MA)
North Dakota State U (ND)
Purdue U (IN)
State U of New York Coll of Technology at Canton (NY)
State U of New York Coll of Technology at Delhi (NY)
Thomas Edison State Coll (NJ)
U of Nebraska–Lincoln (NE)
Wilson Coll (PA)

VISION SCIENCE/ PHYSIOLOGICAL OPTICS
U of the Incarnate Word (TX)

VISUAL AND PERFORMING ARTS
American U (DC)
Angelo State U (TX)
Arizona State U (AZ)
Armstrong Atlantic State U (GA)
Art Center Coll of Design (CA)
Assumption Coll (MA)
Bard Coll at Simon's Rock (MA)
Barnard Coll (NY)
Bennington Coll (VT)
Blackburn Coll (IL)
Bloomfield Coll (NJ)
Blue Mountain Coll (MS)
Brown U (RI)
Bucknell U (PA)
California Baptist U (CA)
California State U, San Marcos (CA)
Centenary Coll of Louisiana (LA)
Clemson U (SC)
Columbia U, School of General Studies (NY)
Concordia U (QC, Canada)
Cooper Union for the Advancement of Science and Art (NY)
Delta State U (MS)
DEREE - The American Coll of Greece (Greece)
Dowling Coll (NY)
Eastern Connecticut State U (CT)
East Stroudsburg U of Pennsylvania (PA)
Eckerd Coll (FL)
The Evergreen State Coll (WA)
Fairleigh Dickinson U, Coll at Florham (NJ)
Fairleigh Dickinson U, Metropolitan Campus (NJ)
Fayetteville State U (NC)
Ferrum Coll (VA)
Gannon U (PA)
George Mason U (VA)
Gettysburg Coll (PA)
Harvard U (MA)
Indiana U of Pennsylvania (PA)
Inter American U of Puerto Rico, San Germán Campus (PR)
Iowa State U of Science and Technology (IA)
Ithaca Coll (NY)
Jacksonville U (FL)

Johnson C. Smith U (NC)
Johnson State Coll (VT)
Kent State U (OH)
King Coll (TN)
LaGrange Coll (GA)
Lindenwood U (MO)
Long Island U–C. W. Post Campus (NY)
Loras Coll (IA)
Maryland Inst Coll of Art (MD)
Massachusetts Coll of Liberal Arts (MA)
Miami Intl U of Art & Design (FL)
Mississippi State U (MS)
Mississippi U for Women (MS)
Missouri State U (MO)
Naropa U (CO)
New Mexico Highlands U (NM)
New Mexico State U (NM)
Occidental Coll (CA)
Ohio Northern U (OH)
Oklahoma City U (OK)
Penn State Abington (PA)
Penn State Altoona (PA)
Penn State Beaver (PA)
Penn State Berks (PA)
Penn State Brandywine (PA)
Penn State DuBois (PA)
Penn State Erie, The Behrend Coll (PA)
Penn State Fayette, The Eberly Campus (PA)
Penn State Greater Allegheny (PA)
Penn State Hazleton (PA)
Penn State Lehigh Valley (PA)
Penn State Mont Alto (PA)
Penn State New Kensington (PA)
Penn State Schuylkill (PA)
Penn State Shenango (PA)
Penn State U Park (PA)
Penn State Wilkes-Barre (PA)
Penn State Worthington Scranton (PA)
Penn State York (PA)
Pine Manor Coll (MA)
Prescott Coll (AZ)
Providence Coll (RI)
Purchase Coll, State U of New York (NY)
Ramapo Coll of New Jersey (NJ)
Regis U (CO)
Rensselaer Polytechnic Inst (NY)
The Richard Stockton Coll of New Jersey (NJ)
Rogers State U (OK)
Roger Williams U (RI)
Rutgers, The State U of New Jersey, New Brunswick (NJ)
Saint Augustine's Coll (NC)
St. Bonaventure U (NY)
Saint Joseph's U (PA)
Saint Peter's Coll (NJ)
Sarah Lawrence Coll (NY)
Savannah Coll of Art and Design (GA)
Shenandoah U (VA)
South Dakota State U (SD)
Southeast Missouri State U (MO)
Southern Polytechnic State U (GA)
State U of New York at New Paltz (NY)
State U of New York Coll at Old Westbury (NY)
State U of New York Coll at Potsdam (NY)
Stonehill Coll (MA)
Suffolk U (MA)
Texas Southern U (TX)
Thompson Rivers U (BC, Canada)
Tusculum Coll (TN)
The U of Arizona (AZ)
The U of British Columbia (BC, Canada)
The U of British Columbia–Okanagan (BC, Canada)
U of Colorado at Colorado Springs (CO)
U of Houston–Downtown (TX)
U of Louisiana at Lafayette (LA)
U of Maryland, Baltimore County (MD)
U of Mary Washington (VA)
The U of Montana Western (MT)
U of Mount Union (OH)

U of North Carolina School of the Arts (NC)
U of Pennsylvania (PA)
U of Regina (SK, Canada)
U of Rio Grande (OH)
U of St. Francis (IL)
U of Saint Mary (KS)
The U of South Dakota (SD)
U of Southern California (CA)
U of Southern Mississippi (MS)
The U of Tennessee at Martin (TN)
The U of Texas at Austin (TX)
The U of Texas at Dallas (TX)
U of Toronto (ON, Canada)
U of Utah (UT)
U of Windsor (ON, Canada)
U of Wisconsin–Superior (WI)
Valdosta State U (GA)
Vassar Coll (NY)
Virginia State U (VA)
Viterbo U (WI)
Western Washington U (WA)
Wheelock Coll (MA)
Wichita State U (KS)
Worcester State U (MA)

VISUAL AND PERFORMING ARTS RELATED
Adelphi U (NY)
Baldwin-Wallace Coll (OH)
The Baptist Coll of Florida (FL)
Bard Coll at Simon's Rock (MA)
Brigham Young U (UT)
Cameron U (OK)
Clemson U (SC)
Columbia U, School of General Studies (NY)
Illinois State U (IL)
Illinois Wesleyan U (IL)
Indiana U Bloomington (IN)
Marywood U (PA)
Millikin U (IL)
New York U (NY)
Ohio Northern U (OH)
Oklahoma City U (OK)
Penn State Altoona (PA)
Prescott Coll (AZ)
Providence Coll (RI)
Purchase Coll, State U of New York (NY)
Rice U (TX)
Sacred Heart U (CT)
Saint Mary's Coll of California (CA)
Samford U (AL)
Sarah Lawrence Coll (NY)
School of the Museum of Fine Arts, Boston (MA)
Seton Hill U (PA)
Simon Fraser U (BC, Canada)
Spring Arbor U (MI)
State U of New York Coll at Geneseo (NY)
Thompson Rivers U (BC, Canada)
U of California, Davis (CA)
U of Lethbridge (AB, Canada)
U of Michigan (MI)
U of New Haven (CT)
U of South Florida (FL)
U of Washington, Bothell (WA)
U of Wisconsin–Green Bay (WI)
Webster U (MO)
Western State Coll of Colorado (CO)

VITICULTURE AND ENOLOGY
Cornell U (NY)

VOCATIONAL REHABILITATION COUNSELING
Bowling Green State U (OH)
East Carolina U (NC)
East Central U (OK)
Emporia State U (KS)
Maryville U of Saint Louis (MO)
U of Illinois at Urbana–Champaign (IL)
U of Wisconsin–Madison (WI)
U of Wisconsin–Stout (WI)
Wright State U (OH)

VOICE AND OPERA
Abilene Christian U (TX)

Acadia U (NS, Canada)
Andrews U (MI)
Anna Maria Coll (MA)
Baldwin-Wallace Coll (OH)
Bard Coll (NY)
Barry U (FL)
Belmont U (TN)
Bennington Coll (VT)
Berklee Coll of Music (MA)
Biola U (CA)
Birmingham-Southern Coll (AL)
Black Hills State U (SD)
Boston U (MA)
Bowling Green State U (OH)
Brigham Young U (UT)
Butler U (IN)
California Baptist U (CA)
California State U, Long Beach (CA)
Calvary Bible Coll and Theological Sem (MO)
Calvin Coll (MI)
Campbellsville U (KY)
Capital U (OH)
Carnegie Mellon U (PA)
Carson-Newman Coll (TN)
Catawba Coll (NC)
The Catholic U of America (DC)
Central Washington U (WA)
Chapman U (CA)
Cincinnati Christian U (OH)
Concordia U, Nebraska (NE)
Conservatorio de Musica (PR)
Converse Coll (SC)
Cornish Coll of the Arts (WA)
Delaware State U (DE)
Dordt Coll (IA)
Drake U (IA)
Drury U (MO)
East Central U (OK)
East Texas Baptist U (TX)
Five Towns Coll (NY)
Furman U (SC)
Hannibal-LaGrange U (MO)
Hardin-Simmons U (TX)
Heidelberg U (OH)
Hope Coll (MI)
Houghton Coll (NY)
Howard Payne U (TX)
Illinois Wesleyan U (IL)
Indiana U Bloomington (IN)
Indiana U–Purdue U Fort Wayne (IN)
Ithaca Coll (NY)
Jacksonville U (FL)
Lamar U (TX)
Lawrence U (WI)
Lee U (TN)
Lipscomb U (TN)
Long Island U–C. W. Post Campus (NY)
Louisiana Coll (LA)
Maryville Coll (TN)
The Master's Coll and Sem (CA)
McNally Smith Coll of Music (MN)
MidAmerica Nazarene U (KS)
Millikin U (IL)
Minnesota State U Mankato (MN)
Mississippi Coll (MS)
Mount Allison U (NB, Canada)
Newberry Coll (SC)
New England Conservatory of Music (MA)
Northern State U (SD)
Northwestern Coll (MN)
Notre Dame de Namur U (CA)
Nyack Coll (NY)
Oakland U (MI)
The Ohio State U (OH)
Ohio U (OH)
Oklahoma Christian U (OK)
Oklahoma City U (OK)
Oral Roberts U (OK)
Otterbein U (OH)
Ouachita Baptist U (AR)
Palm Beach Atlantic U (FL)
Peabody Conservatory of The Johns Hopkins U (MD)
Peru State Coll (NE)
Point Loma Nazarene U (CA)
Queens U of Charlotte (NC)
Rider U (NJ)
Roberts Wesleyan Coll (NY)
Roosevelt U (IL)
Samford U (AL)

San Diego Christian Coll (CA)
San Francisco Conservatory of Music (CA)
Sarah Lawrence Coll (NY)
Shorter U (GA)
Southeastern U (FL)
Southern Methodist U (TX)
Southwestern Oklahoma State U (OK)
State U of New York at Fredonia (NY)
State U of New York at New Paltz (NY)
Stetson U (FL)
Syracuse U (NY)
Temple U (PA)
Texas Christian U (TX)
Trinity U (TX)
Union U (TN)
U of Alberta (AB, Canada)
The U of British Columbia (BC, Canada)
U of Cincinnati (OH)
U of Delaware (DE)
U of Idaho (ID)
U of Illinois at Urbana–Champaign (IL)
The U of Iowa (IA)
The U of Kansas (KS)
U of Miami (FL)
U of Mobile (AL)
U of Nebraska at Omaha (NE)
U of North Carolina School of the Arts (NC)
U of Redlands (CA)
U of Southern California (CA)
The U of Tennessee at Martin (TN)
U of the Pacific (CA)
U of Tulsa (OK)
U of Washington (WA)
The U of Western Ontario (ON, Canada)
Valparaiso U (IN)
Vanderbilt U (TN)
Washington U in St. Louis (MO)
Weber State U (UT)
Western Michigan U (MI)
Willamette U (OR)
William Paterson U of New Jersey (NJ)

WATER RESOURCES ENGINEERING
Central State U (OH)
State U of New York Coll of Environmental Science and Forestry (NY)
U of Guelph (ON, Canada)
U of Illinois at Urbana–Champaign (IL)
U of Nevada, Reno (NV)

WATER, WETLANDS, AND MARINE RESOURCES MANAGEMENT
Colorado State U (CO)
Florida Gulf Coast U (FL)
Stony Brook U, State U of New York (NY)
Texas State U–San Marcos (TX)
U of Georgia (GA)
U of Minnesota, Crookston (MN)
U of New Hampshire (NH)
Western State Coll of Colorado (CO)

WEB/MULTIMEDIA MANAGEMENT AND WEBMASTER
American Public U System (WV)
Bellevue U (NE)
Hawai`i Pacific U (HI)
Indiana Tech (IN)
Lewis-Clark State Coll (ID)
Limestone Coll (SC)
Mars Hill Coll (NC)
Morrisville State Coll (NY)
Neumont U (UT)
New England School of Communications (ME)
Northern Michigan U (MI)
Rochester Inst of Technology (NY)

State U of New York Coll of Technology at Alfred (NY)
Trevecca Nazarene U (TN)
U of Dubuque (IA)
U of Great Falls (MT)
U of St. Francis (IL)

WEB PAGE, DIGITAL/ MULTIMEDIA AND INFORMATION RESOURCES DESIGN

Acad of Art U (CA)
The Art Inst of Atlanta (GA)
The Art Inst of Atlanta–Decatur (GA)
The Art Inst of Austin (TX)
The Art Inst of California, a college of Argosy U, Hollywood (CA)
The Art Inst of California, a college of Argosy U, Inland Empire (CA)
The Art Inst of California, a college of Argosy U, Los Angeles (CA)
The Art Inst of California, a college of Argosy U, Orange County (CA)
The Art Inst of California, a college of Argosy U, Sacramento (CA)
The Art Inst of California, a college of Argosy U, San Diego (CA)
The Art Inst of California, a college of Argosy U, San Francisco (CA)
The Art Inst of California, a college of Argosy U, Sunnyvale (CA)
The Art Inst of Charleston (SC)
The Art Inst of Charlotte (NC)
The Art Inst of Colorado (CO)
The Art Inst of Dallas (TX)
The Art Inst of Fort Lauderdale (FL)
The Art Inst of Fort Worth (TX)
The Art Inst of Houston (TX)
The Art Inst of Houston - North (TX)
The Art Inst of Indianapolis (IN)
The Art Inst of Jacksonville (FL)
The Art Inst of Las Vegas (NV)
The Art Inst of Michigan (MI)
The Art Inst of Michigan–Troy (MI)
The Art Inst of Ohio–Cincinnati (OH)
The Art Inst of Philadelphia (PA)
The Art Inst of Phoenix (AZ)
The Art Inst of Pittsburgh (PA)
The Art Inst of Portland (OR)
The Art Inst of Raleigh-Durham (NC)
The Art Inst of Salt Lake City (UT)
The Art Inst of San Antonio (TX)
The Art Inst of Seattle (WA)
The Art Inst of Tampa (FL)
The Art Inst of Tennessee–Nashville (TN)
The Art Inst of Tucson (AZ)
The Art Inst of Virginia Beach (VA)
The Art Inst of Washington (VA)
The Art Inst of Washington–Dulles (VA)
The Art Inst of Wisconsin (WI)
The Art Inst of York–Pennsylvania (PA)
The Art Insts Intl–Kansas City (KS)
The Art Insts Intl Minnesota (MN)
Azusa Pacific U (CA)
Bishop's U (QC, Canada)
Bradley U (IL)
Columbia Coll Chicago (IL)
Concordia U (QC, Canada)
DeVry U, Phoenix (AZ)
DeVry U, Pomona (CA)
DeVry U, Westminster (CO)
DeVry U, Miramar (FL)
DeVry U, Orlando (FL)
DeVry U, Decatur (GA)
DeVry U, Chicago (IL)
DeVry U, Kansas City (MO)
DeVry U, North Brunswick (NJ)
DeVry U, Columbus (OH)
DeVry U, Fort Washington (PA)
DeVry U, Houston (TX)
DeVry U, Irving (TX)
DeVry U, Arlington (VA)
DeVry U, Federal Way (WA)
DeVry U Online (IL)
Drexel U (PA)
Duquesne U (PA)
Emily Carr U of Art + Design (BC, Canada)

Franklin U (OH)
Grace Coll (IN)
Hampshire Coll (MA)
Harding U (AR)
The Illinois Inst of Art–Schaumburg (IL)
Indiana Wesleyan U (IN)
Intl Acad of Design & Technology (FL)
Iona Coll (NY)
Iowa Wesleyan Coll (IA)
Lasell Coll (MA)
Miami Intl U of Art & Design (FL)
Neumont U (UT)
The New England Inst of Art (MA)
New York City Coll of Technology of the City U of New York (NY)
Northwest Missouri State U (MO)
Pennsylvania Coll of Technology (PA)
Quinnipiac U (CT)
Rasmussen Coll Bloomington (MN)
Rasmussen Coll Brooklyn Park (MN)
Rasmussen Coll Eagan (MN)
Rasmussen Coll Fort Myers (FL)
Rasmussen Coll Lake Elmo/ Woodbury (MN)
Rasmussen Coll Land O' Lakes (FL)
Rasmussen Coll Mankato (MN)
Rasmussen Coll Moorhead (MN)
Rasmussen Coll New Port Richey (FL)
Rasmussen Coll Ocala (FL)
Rasmussen Coll Rockford (IL)
Rasmussen Coll St. Cloud (MN)
Rasmussen Coll Tampa/Brandon (FL)
Rider U (NJ)
Rochester Inst of Technology (NY)
Santa Clara U (CA)
Thiel Coll (PA)
Trevecca Nazarene U (TN)
U of Dubuque (IA)
U of Great Falls (MT)
U of Mount Union (OH)
The U of North Carolina at Asheville (NC)
U of Wisconsin–Stevens Point (WI)
Utah Valley U (UT)

WELDING TECHNOLOGY

LeTourneau U (TX)
Lewis-Clark State Coll (ID)
The Ohio State U (OH)

WILDLIFE BIOLOGY

Adams State Coll (CO)
Clemson U (SC)
Coll of the Atlantic (ME)
Colorado State U (CO)
Friends U (KS)
Kansas State U (KS)
Keystone Coll (PA)
Lees-McRae Coll (NC)
Northeastern State U (OK)
Ohio U (OH)
State U of New York Coll of Environmental Science and Forestry (NY)
Texas State U–San Marcos (TX)
U of Alaska Fairbanks (AK)
U of Guelph (ON, Canada)
U of Michigan–Flint (MI)
U of Vermont (VT)
U of Wyoming (WY)
Winona State U (MN)

WILDLIFE, FISH AND WILDLANDS SCIENCE AND MANAGEMENT

Albion Coll (MI)
Arkansas State U (AR)
Arkansas Tech U (AR)
Auburn U (AL)
Delaware State U (DE)
Delaware Valley Coll (PA)
Eastern Kentucky U (KY)
Eastern New Mexico U (NM)
Fort Hays State U (KS)
Humboldt State U (CA)
Juniata Coll (PA)
Lake Superior State U (MI)

Lincoln Memorial U (TN)
McNeese State U (LA)
Michigan State U (MI)
Michigan Technological U (MI)
Mississippi State U (MS)
Missouri State U (MO)
Missouri Western State U (MO)
Montana State U (MT)
New Mexico State U (NM)
Northwest Missouri State U (MO)
The Ohio State U (OH)
Peru State Coll (NE)
Purdue U (IN)
South Dakota State U (SD)
State U of New York Coll of Environmental Science and Forestry (NY)
Stephen F. Austin State U (TX)
Sterling Coll (VT)
Sul Ross State U (TX)
Tarleton State U (TX)
Texas A&M U (TX)
Texas A&M U–Kingsville (TX)
Texas Tech U (TX)
U of Alaska Fairbanks (AK)
U of Alberta (AB, Canada)
U of Arkansas at Monticello (AR)
The U of British Columbia (BC, Canada)
U of Delaware (DE)
U of Florida (FL)
U of Georgia (GA)
U of Idaho (ID)
U of Illinois at Urbana–Champaign (IL)
U of Maine (ME)
U of Minnesota, Twin Cities Campus (MN)
U of Missouri (MO)
U of Nevada, Reno (NV)
U of New Hampshire (NH)
U of Puerto Rico at Humacao (PR)
U of Rhode Island (RI)
The U of Tennessee (TN)
The U of Tennessee at Martin (TN)
U of Washington (WA)
U of Wisconsin–Madison (WI)
U of Wisconsin–Stevens Point (WI)
Utah State U (UT)
Valley City State U (ND)
Washington State U (WA)
West Texas A&M U (TX)
West Virginia U (WV)

WOMEN'S MINISTRY

Corban U (OR)

WOMEN'S STUDIES

Agnes Scott Coll (GA)
Albion Coll (MI)
Albright Coll (PA)
Allegheny Coll (PA)
Alverno Coll (WI)
American U (DC)
Amherst Coll (MA)
Appalachian State U (NC)
Arizona State U (AZ)
Armstrong Atlantic State U (GA)
Athabasca U (AB, Canada)
Augustana Coll (IL)
Ball State U (IN)
Bard Coll at Simon's Rock (MA)
Barnard Coll (NY)
Bates Coll (ME)
Beloit Coll (WI)
Bennington Coll (VT)
Berea Coll (KY)
Bishop's U (QC, Canada)
Bowdoin Coll (ME)
Bowling Green State U (OH)
Brandeis U (MA)
Brown U (RI)
Bucknell U (PA)
California State U, Fresno (CA)
California State U, Fullerton (CA)
California State U, Long Beach (CA)
California State U, San Marcos (CA)
Carleton Coll (MN)
Case Western Reserve U (OH)
Central Michigan U (MI)
Chatham U (PA)

City Coll of the City U of New York (NY)
Clark U (MA)
Cleveland State U (OH)
Colby Coll (ME)
Colgate U (NY)
The Coll at Brockport, State U of New York (NY)
Coll of Charleston (SC)
The Coll of New Jersey (NJ)
Coll of Saint Benedict (MN)
Coll of Saint Elizabeth (NJ)
The Coll of Saint Rose (NY)
Coll of Staten Island of the City U of New York (NY)
The Coll of William and Mary (VA)
The Coll of Wooster (OH)
The Colorado Coll (CO)
Columbia U, School of General Studies (NY)
Concordia U (QC, Canada)
Concordia U Chicago (IL)
Connecticut Coll (CT)
Cornell Coll (IA)
Curry Coll (MA)
Dalhousie U (NS, Canada)
Dartmouth Coll (NH)
Denison U (OH)
DePaul U (IL)
DePauw U (IN)
Dickinson Coll (PA)
Dominican U of California (CA)
Drew U (NJ)
Duquesne U (PA)
Earlham Coll (IN)
East Carolina U (NC)
Eastern Michigan U (MI)
Eastern Washington U (WA)
East Tennessee State U (TN)
Eckerd Coll (FL)
Edinboro U of Pennsylvania (PA)
Emory U (GA)
Florida Intl U (FL)
Fordham U (NY)
Fort Lewis Coll (CO)
Georgia State U (GA)
Gettysburg Coll (PA)
Goucher Coll (MD)
Grand Valley State U (MI)
Guilford Coll (NC)
Gustavus Adolphus Coll (MN)
Hamilton Coll (NY)
Hamline U (MN)
Hampshire Coll (MA)
Harvard U (MA)
Haverford Coll (PA)
Hobart and William Smith Colls (NY)
Hofstra U (NY)
Hollins U (VA)
Hope Coll (MI)
Hunter Coll of the City U of New York (NY)
Illinois Wesleyan U (IL)
Indiana U Bloomington (IN)
Indiana U–Purdue U Fort Wayne (IN)
Indiana U South Bend (IN)
Iowa State U of Science and Technology (IA)
Kansas State U (KS)
Keene State Coll (NH)
Kenyon Coll (OH)
Knox Coll (IL)
Lafayette Coll (PA)
Lakehead U (ON, Canada)
Lehigh U (PA)
Loyola Marymount U (CA)
Loyola U Chicago (IL)
Luther Coll (IA)
Macalester Coll (MN)
Manchester Coll (IN)
Marlboro Coll (VT)
Mars Hill Coll (NC)
Metropolitan State U (MN)
Miami U (OH)
Michigan State U (MI)
Middlebury Coll (VT)
Mills Coll (CA)
Minnesota State U Mankato (MN)
Minnesota State U Moorhead (MN)
Montclair State U (NJ)
Nazareth Coll of Rochester (NY)
Nebraska Wesleyan U (NE)
New Jersey City U (NJ)

New Mexico State U (NM)
North Carolina State U (NC)
North Dakota State U (ND)
Northeastern Illinois U (IL)
Northern Arizona U (AZ)
Oakland U (MI)
The Ohio State U (OH)
Ohio U (OH)
Ohio Wesleyan U (OH)
Old Dominion U (VA)
Pace U (NY)
Pacific Lutheran U (WA)
Penn State Abington (PA)
Penn State Altoona (PA)
Penn State Beaver (PA)
Penn State Berks (PA)
Penn State Brandywine (PA)
Penn State DuBois (PA)
Penn State Erie, The Behrend Coll (PA)
Penn State Fayette, The Eberly Campus (PA)
Penn State Greater Allegheny (PA)
Penn State Hazleton (PA)
Penn State Lehigh Valley (PA)
Penn State Mont Alto (PA)
Penn State New Kensington (PA)
Penn State Schuylkill (PA)
Penn State Shenango (PA)
Penn State U Park (PA)
Penn State Wilkes-Barre (PA)
Penn State Worthington Scranton (PA)
Penn State York (PA)
Pitzer Coll (CA)
Pomona Coll (CA)
Portland State U (OR)
Prescott Coll (AZ)
Providence Coll (RI)
Purchase Coll, State U of New York (NY)
Queens Coll of the City U of New York (NY)
Queen's U at Kingston (ON, Canada)
Randolph-Macon Coll (VA)
Rhode Island Coll (RI)
Rice U (TX)
Rosemont Coll (PA)
Rutgers, The State U of New Jersey, Newark (NJ)
Rutgers, The State U of New Jersey, New Brunswick (NJ)
Sacred Heart U (CT)
St. Bonaventure U (NY)
St. Catherine U (MN)
Saint John's U (MN)
Saint Louis U (MO)
Saint Mary's Coll of California (CA)
St. Olaf Coll (MN)
St. Thomas U (NB, Canada)
San Diego State U (CA)
San Francisco State U (CA)
Santa Clara U (CA)
Sarah Lawrence Coll (NY)
Scripps Coll (CA)
Simmons Coll (MA)
Simon Fraser U (BC, Canada)
Smith Coll (MA)
Sonoma State U (CA)
Southwestern U (TX)
Spelman Coll (GA)
Stanford U (CA)
State U of New York at Fredonia (NY)
State U of New York at New Paltz (NY)
State U of New York at Oswego (NY)
State U of New York at Plattsburgh (NY)
State U of New York Coll at Potsdam (NY)
Stony Brook U, State U of New York (NY)
Suffolk U (MA)
Swarthmore Coll (PA)
Syracuse U (NY)
Temple U (PA)
Texas A&M U (TX)
Towson U (MD)
Trent U (ON, Canada)
Trinity Coll (CT)
Tufts U (MA)
Tulane U (LA)

U at Albany, State U of New York (NY)
U of Alberta (AB, Canada)
The U of Arizona (AZ)
The U of British Columbia (BC, Canada)
U of California, Berkeley (CA)
U of California, Davis (CA)
U of California, Irvine (CA)
U of California, Los Angeles (CA)
U of California, Riverside (CA)
U of California, Santa Barbara (CA)
U of California, Santa Cruz (CA)
U of Cincinnati (OH)
U of Colorado Boulder (CO)
U of Connecticut (CT)
U of Delaware (DE)
U of Florida (FL)
U of Georgia (GA)
U of Hartford (CT)
U of Hawaii at Manoa (HI)
U of Houston–Clear Lake (TX)
U of Illinois at Chicago (IL)
U of Illinois at Urbana–Champaign (IL)
The U of Iowa (IA)
The U of Kansas (KS)
U of Lethbridge (AB, Canada)
U of Louisville (KY)
U of Maryland, Baltimore County (MD)
U of Maryland, Coll Park (MD)
U of Mary Washington (VA)
U of Massachusetts Amherst (MA)
U of Massachusetts Boston (MA)
U of Massachusetts Dartmouth (MA)
U of Miami (FL)
U of Michigan (MI)
U of Michigan–Dearborn (MI)
U of Minnesota, Duluth (MN)
U of Minnesota, Twin Cities Campus (MN)
U of Nebraska at Omaha (NE)
U of Nebraska–Lincoln (NE)
U of Nevada, Las Vegas (NV)
U of Nevada, Reno (NV)
U of New Hampshire (NH)
U of New Mexico (NM)
U of New Orleans (LA)
The U of North Carolina at Asheville (NC)
The U of North Carolina at Chapel Hill (NC)
U of Oklahoma (OK)
U of Oregon (OR)
U of Ottawa (ON, Canada)
U of Pennsylvania (PA)
U of Regina (SK, Canada)
U of Rhode Island (RI)
U of Richmond (VA)
U of Rochester (NY)
U of Saint Joseph (CT)
U of St. Thomas (MN)
The U of Scranton (PA)
U of South Carolina (SC)
U of Southern Maine (ME)
U of South Florida (FL)
The U of Texas at Austin (TX)
The U of Toledo (OH)
U of Toronto (ON, Canada)
U of Utah (UT)
U of Vermont (VT)
U of Washington (WA)
The U of Western Ontario (ON, Canada)
U of Windsor (ON, Canada)

U of Wisconsin–Eau Claire (WI)
U of Wisconsin–La Crosse (WI)
U of Wisconsin–Madison (WI)
U of Wisconsin–Milwaukee (WI)
U of Wisconsin–Whitewater (WI)
U of Wyoming (WY)
Vanderbilt U (TN)
Vassar Coll (NY)
Villanova U (PA)
Virginia Commonwealth U (VA)
Virginia Wesleyan Coll (VA)
Warren Wilson Coll (NC)
Washington State U (WA)
Washington U in St. Louis (MO)
Wellesley Coll (MA)
Wells Coll (NY)
Wesleyan Coll (GA)
Wesleyan U (CT)
West Chester U of Pennsylvania (PA)
Western Illinois U (IL)
Western Michigan U (MI)
Wheaton Coll (MA)
Wichita State U (KS)
Willamette U (OR)
William Paterson U of New Jersey (NJ)
Wright State U (OH)
Yale U (CT)

WOOD SCIENCE AND WOOD PRODUCTS/PULP AND PAPER TECHNOLOGY

North Carolina State U (NC)
State U of New York Coll of Environmental Science and Forestry (NY)
The U of British Columbia (BC, Canada)
U of Idaho (ID)
U of Maine (ME)
U of Minnesota, Twin Cities Campus (MN)
U of Toronto (ON, Canada)
U of Washington (WA)
U of Wisconsin–Stevens Point (WI)
West Virginia U (WV)

WOODWIND INSTRUMENTS

Acadia U (NS, Canada)
Berklee Coll of Music (MA)
Five Towns Coll (NY)
Houghton Coll (NY)
Lawrence U (WI)
Maryville Coll (TN)
Minnesota State U Mankato (MN)
Mount Allison U (NB, Canada)
New England Conservatory of Music (MA)
Oklahoma Christian U (OK)
Oklahoma City U (OK)
Otterbein U (OH)
Peabody Conservatory of The Johns Hopkins U (MD)
Peru State Coll (NE)
San Francisco Conservatory of Music (CA)
Sarah Lawrence Coll (NY)
Southwestern Oklahoma State U (OK)
State U of New York at Fredonia (NY)
U of Alberta (AB, Canada)
The U of Iowa (IA)
The U of Kansas (KS)
U of Michigan (MI)

Vanderbilt U (TN)
Xavier U of Louisiana (LA)

WOODWORKING

Burlington Coll (VT)
Rochester Inst of Technology (NY)

WOODWORKING RELATED

Pittsburg State U (KS)

WORK AND FAMILY STUDIES

Brigham Young U (UT)
The U of North Carolina at Charlotte (NC)

WRITING

Augustana Coll (IL)
Baylor U (TX)
Bennington Coll (VT)
Brigham Young U (UT)
Calvin Coll (MI)
Carroll Coll (MT)
Columbia U, School of General Studies (NY)
DePauw U (IN)
Drury U (MO)
Eastern Michigan U (MI)
Ferris State U (MI)
Florida Southern Coll (FL)
Geneva Coll (PA)
Georgia Southern U (GA)
Gettysburg Coll (PA)
Graceland U (IA)
Grand Valley State U (MI)
Huntington U (IN)
Indiana U–Purdue U Fort Wayne (IN)
Indiana U South Bend (IN)
Indiana Wesleyan U (IN)
Jamestown Coll (ND)
La Roche Coll (PA)
Lee U (TN)
Marian U (WI)
Marquette U (WI)
Massachusetts Coll of Liberal Arts (MA)
Metropolitan State U (MN)
Mississippi Coll (MS)
Northwest U (WA)
Oakland U (MI)
Oral Roberts U (OK)
Perelandra Coll (CA)
St. Edward's U (TX)
Salem State U (MA)
Spring Hill Coll (AL)
Thiel Coll (PA)
U of Central Arkansas (AR)
U of Colorado Denver (CO)
U of Evansville (IN)
U of Great Falls (MT)
U of Illinois at Urbana–Champaign (IL)
U of Michigan–Flint (MI)
U of Minnesota, Twin Cities Campus (MN)
U of Mount Union (OH)
The U of Tampa (FL)
The U of Texas at Austin (TX)
Wartburg Coll (IA)
Western Michigan U (MI)
William Woods U (MO)

YOUTH MINISTRY

Abilene Christian U (TX)
Anderson U (IN)

Andrews U (MI)
Asbury U (KY)
Baptist Bible Coll of Pennsylvania (PA)
Benedictine Coll (KS)
Bethel Coll (IN)
Bethel U (MN)
Bluffton U (OH)
Briercrest Coll (SK, Canada)
Calvary Bible Coll and Theological Sem (MO)
Cedarville U (OH)
Corban U (OR)
Crossroads Bible Coll (IN)
Crown Coll (MN)
Dordt Coll (IA)
Eastern U (PA)
East Texas Baptist U (TX)
Emmaus Bible Coll (IA)
Florida Southern Coll (FL)
Geneva Coll (PA)
Gordon Coll (MA)
Grace Coll (IN)
Great Lakes Christian Coll (MI)
Greenville Coll (IL)
Harding U (AR)
Hardin-Simmons U (TX)
Hillsdale Free Will Baptist Coll (OK)
Hope Intl U (CA)
Howard Payne U (TX)
Huntingdon Coll (AL)
Huntington U (IN)
Indiana Wesleyan U (IN)
John Brown U (AR)
Judson U (IL)
Kentucky Mountain Bible Coll (KY)
King Coll (TN)
Lee U (TN)
Lincoln Christian U (IL)
Lipscomb U (TN)
Lubbock Christian U (TX)
Malone U (OH)
Maranatha Baptist Bible Coll (WI)
Master's Coll and Sem (ON, Canada)
MidAmerica Nazarene U (KS)
Mid-Atlantic Christian U (NC)
Mount Vernon Nazarene U (OH)
Multnomah U (OR)
New Hope Christian Coll (OR)
North Greenville U (SC)
Northwestern Coll (MN)
Northwest U (WA)
Nyack Coll (NY)
Ohio Northern U (OH)
Piedmont Intl U (NC)
Simpson U (CA)
Southwestern Assemblies of God U (TX)
Southwestern Christian U (OK)
Spring Arbor U (MI)
Tabor Coll (KS)
Trevecca Nazarene U (TN)
Trinity Coll of Florida (FL)
U of Indianapolis (IN)
Valley Forge Christian Coll Woodbridge Campus (VA)
Vanguard U of Southern California (CA)
William Jessup U (CA)

YOUTH SERVICES

Roger Williams U (RI)
Southwestern Christian U (OK)
U of Hawaii at Manoa (HI)

The U of Western Ontario (ON, Canada)
Wheelock Coll (MA)

ZOOLOGY/ANIMAL BIOLOGY

Andrews U (MI)
Auburn U (AL)
Bennington Coll (VT)
California State U, Long Beach (CA)
Coll of the Atlantic (ME)
Colorado State U (CO)
Delaware Valley Coll (PA)
Humboldt State U (CA)
Idaho State U (ID)
Juniata Coll (PA)
Kent State U (OH)
Malone U (OH)
Mars Hill Coll (NC)
Miami U (OH)
Michigan State U (MI)
North Carolina State U (NC)
North Dakota State U (ND)
Northern Michigan U (MI)
The Ohio State U (OH)
Ohio U (OH)
Ohio Wesleyan U (OH)
Oklahoma State U (OK)
Rutgers, The State U of New Jersey, Newark (NJ)
San Francisco State U (CA)
Sonoma State U (CA)
Southern Illinois U Carbondale (IL)
State U of New York at Oswego (NY)
State U of New York Coll of Environmental Science and Forestry (NY)
Tarleton State U (TX)
Texas A&M U (TX)
Texas State U–San Marcos (TX)
Texas Tech U (TX)
The U of Akron (OH)
U of Alberta (AB, Canada)
The U of British Columbia (BC, Canada)
The U of British Columbia–Okanagan (BC, Canada)
U of California, Davis (CA)
U of California, Santa Barbara (CA)
U of Florida (FL)
U of Guelph (ON, Canada)
U of Hawaii at Manoa (HI)
U of Maine (ME)
U of Minnesota, Twin Cities Campus (MN)
U of New Hampshire (NH)
U of Oklahoma (OK)
U of Rhode Island (RI)
The U of Texas at El Paso (TX)
U of Toronto (ON, Canada)
U of Vermont (VT)
U of Washington (WA)
U of Wisconsin–Madison (WI)
U of Wyoming (WY)
Utah State U (UT)
Washington State U (WA)
Weber State U (UT)
Winona State U (MN)

ZOOLOGY/ANIMAL BIOLOGY RELATED

Canisius Coll (NY)
Thompson Rivers U (BC, Canada)

INDEXES

Entrance Difficulty

This index groups colleges by their own assessment of their entrance difficulty level. The colleges were asked to select the level that most closely corresponds to their entrance difficulty, according to the guidelines below. Institutions for which high school class rank and/or standardized test scores do not apply as admission criteria were asked to select the level that best indicates their entrance difficulty as compared to other institutions.

MOST DIFFICULT

More than 75 percent of the freshmen were in the top 10 percent of their high school class and scored over 1310 on the SAT (critical reading and mathematical combined) or over 29 on the ACT (composite); about 30 percent or fewer of the applicants were accepted.

Amherst Coll (MA)
Barnard Coll (NY)
Bates Coll (ME)
Bowdoin Coll (ME)
Brandeis U (MA)
Brown U (RI)
Bryn Mawr Coll (PA)
Bucknell U (PA)
California Inst of Technology (CA)
Carnegie Mellon U (PA)
Claremont McKenna Coll (CA)
Colby Coll (ME)
Colgate U (NY)
The Coll of William and Mary (VA)
Columbia U, School of General Studies (NY)
Cooper Union for the Advancement of Science and Art (NY)
Cornell U (NY)
Dartmouth Coll (NH)
Emory U (GA)
Franklin W. Olin Coll of Eng (MA)
Gettysburg Coll (PA)
Harvard U (MA)
Harvey Mudd Coll (CA)
Haverford Coll (PA)
The Johns Hopkins U (MD)
The Juilliard School (NY)
Lafayette Coll (PA)
Lehigh U (PA)
Massachusetts Inst of Technology (MA)
Middlebury Coll (VT)
New York U (NY)
Pomona Coll (CA)
Princeton U (NJ)
Queen's U at Kingston (ON, Canada)
Rice U (TX)
Stanford U (CA)
Swarthmore Coll (PA)
Trinity Coll (CT)
Tufts U (MA)
United States Air Force Acad (CO)
United States Military Acad (NY)
U of Chicago (IL)
U of Notre Dame (IN)
U of Pennsylvania (PA)
U of Southern California (CA)
Vanderbilt U (TN)
Washington and Lee U (VA)
Washington U in St. Louis (MO)
Webb Inst (NY)
Wellesley Coll (MA)
Wesleyan U (CT)
Williams Coll (MA)
Yale U (CT)

VERY DIFFICULT

More than 50 percent of the freshmen were in the top 10 percent of their high school class and scored over 1230 on the SAT or over 26 on the ACT; about 60 percent or fewer applicants were accepted.

Agnes Scott Coll (GA)
Albany Coll of Pharmacy and Health Sciences (NY)
Allegheny Coll (PA)
American U (DC)
American U in Bulgaria (Bulgaria)
The American U in Cairo (Egypt)
Art Center Coll of Design (CA)
Austin Coll (TX)
Babson Coll (MA)
Bard Coll (NY)
Beloit Coll (WI)
Bennington Coll (VT)
Bentley U (MA)
Bernard M. Baruch Coll of the City U of New York (NY)
Boston Coll (MA)
Boston U (MA)
Butler U (IN)
Carleton Coll (MN)
Case Western Reserve U (OH)
Centre Coll (KY)
Chapman U (CA)
Clarkson U (NY)
The Coll of New Jersey (NJ)
Coll of the Atlantic (ME)
Coll of the Holy Cross (MA)
The Colorado Coll (CO)
Colorado School of Mines (CO)
Connecticut Coll (CT)
Davidson Coll (NC)
Denison U (OH)
Dickinson Coll (PA)
Earlham Coll (IN)
Emory U, Oxford Coll (GA)
Florida State U (FL)
Fordham U (NY)
Franklin & Marshall Coll (PA)
Furman U (SC)
The George Washington U (DC)
Georgia Inst of Technology (GA)
Grinnell Coll (IA)
Grove City Coll (PA)
Gustavus Adolphus Coll (MN)
Hamilton Coll (NY)
Hendrix Coll (AR)
Hillsdale Coll (MI)
Hobart and William Smith Colls (NY)
Illinois Wesleyan U (IL)
James Madison U (VA)
Kalamazoo Coll (MI)
Kenyon Coll (OH)
Kettering U (MI)
Knox Coll (IL)
Lawrence U (WI)
Lewis & Clark Coll (OR)
Loyola Marymount U (CA)
Macalester Coll (MN)
Maryland Inst Coll of Art (MD)
Massachusetts Coll of Art and Design (MA)
Medical U of South Carolina (SC)
Missouri U of Science and Technology (MO)
Mount Holyoke Coll (MA)
Muhlenberg Coll (PA)
New Coll of Florida (FL)
New England Conservatory of Music (MA)
North Carolina State U (NC)
Northeastern U (MA)
Occidental Coll (CA)
Oglethorpe U (GA)
The Ohio State U (OH)
Ohio Wesleyan U (OH)
Patrick Henry Coll (VA)
Peabody Conservatory of The Johns Hopkins U (MD)
Penn State Abington (PA)
Penn State Altoona (PA)
Penn State Berks (PA)
Penn State Erie, The Behrend Coll (PA)
Penn State Harrisburg (PA)
Penn State U Park (PA)
Pepperdine U, Malibu (CA)
Polytechnic Inst of NYU (NY)
Pratt Inst (NY)
Presbyterian Coll (SC)
Providence Coll (RI)
Queens Coll of the City U of New York (NY)
Rensselaer Polytechnic Inst (NY)
Rhodes Coll (TN)
The Richard Stockton Coll of New Jersey (NJ)
Rollins Coll (FL)
Rose-Hulman Inst of Technology (IN)
St. John's Coll (NM)
St. Lawrence U (NY)
St. Mary's Coll of Maryland (MD)
St. Olaf Coll (MN)
Sarah Lawrence Coll (NY)
Scripps Coll (CA)
Sewanee: The U of the South (TN)
Skidmore Coll (NY)
Smith Coll (MA)
Soka U of America (CA)
Southwestern U (TX)
Spelman Coll (GA)
State U of New York at Binghamton (NY)
State U of New York at New Paltz (NY)
State U of New York Coll at Geneseo (NY)
State U of New York Coll at Oneonta (NY)
State U of New York Coll of Environmental Science and Forestry (NY)
State U of New York Maritime Coll (NY)
Stevens Inst of Technology (NJ)
Stonehill Coll (MA)
Stony Brook U, State U of New York (NY)
Texas Christian U (TX)
Thomas Aquinas Coll (CA)
Transylvania U (KY)
Trinity U (TX)
Tulane U (LA)
Union Coll (NY)
United States Coast Guard Acad (CT)
United States Merchant Marine Acad (NY)
United States Naval Acad (MD)
U at Albany, State U of New York (NY)
The U of British Columbia (BC, Canada)
U of California, Davis (CA)
U of California, Irvine (CA)
U of California, Los Angeles (CA)
U of California, Riverside (CA)
U of California, Santa Barbara (CA)
U of California, Santa Cruz (CA)
U of Florida (FL)
U of Illinois at Urbana–Champaign (IL)
U of Mary Washington (VA)
U of Miami (FL)
U of Michigan (MI)
The U of North Carolina at Chapel Hill (NC)
U of North Carolina School of the Arts (NC)
U of North Florida (FL)
U of Puerto Rico at Bayamón (PR)
U of Puget Sound (WA)
U of Richmond (VA)
U of Rochester (NY)
U of San Diego (CA)
The U of Texas at Austin (TX)
The U of Texas at Dallas (TX)
U of Toronto (ON, Canada)
U of Tulsa (OK)
U of Virginia (VA)
The U of Western Ontario (ON, Canada)
U of Wisconsin–Madison (WI)
Vassar Coll (NY)
Villanova U (PA)
Wake Forest U (NC)

Washington & Jefferson Coll (PA)
Wheaton Coll (IL)
Wheaton Coll (MA)
Whitman Coll (WA)
Willamette U (OR)
Wofford Coll (SC)
Worcester Polytechnic Inst (MA)

MODERATELY DIFFICULT

*More than 75 percent of the freshmen were in the top half
of their high school class and scored over 1010 on the SAT
or over 18 on the ACT; about 85 percent or fewer of the
applicants were accepted.*

Abilene Christian U (TX)
Acadia U (NS, Canada)
Adams State Coll (CO)
Adelphi U (NY)
Adrian Coll (MI)
Alaska Pacific U (AK)
Alberta Coll of Art & Design (AB, Canada)
Albertus Magnus Coll (CT)
Albion Coll (MI)
Albright Coll (PA)
Alcorn State U (MS)
Alfred U (NY)
Allen Coll (IA)
Alliant Intl U–México City (Mexico)
Alma Coll (MI)
Alvernia U (PA)
Alverno Coll (WI)
American Jewish U (CA)
The American U of Paris (France)
The American U of Rome (Italy)
Anderson U (IN)
Andrews U (MI)
Angelo State U (TX)
Antioch U Santa Barbara (CA)
Apex School of Theology (NC)
Appalachian State U (NC)
Aquinas Coll (MI)
Arcadia U (PA)
Arizona State U (AZ)
Arkansas State U (AR)
Arkansas Tech U (AR)
Asbury U (KY)
Ashland U (OH)
Assumption Coll (MA)
Auburn U (AL)
Auburn U Montgomery (AL)
Augustana Coll (IL)
Augustana Coll (SD)
Austin Peay State U (TN)
Averett U (VA)
Azusa Pacific U (CA)
Baker U (KS)
Baldwin-Wallace Coll (OH)
Ball State U (IN)
Baptist Coll of Health Sciences (TN)
Bard Coll at Simon's Rock (MA)
Barry U (FL)
Bayamón Central U (PR)
Baylor U (TX)
Bay Path Coll (MA)
Beacon Coll (FL)
Becker Coll (MA)
Belhaven U (MS)
Bellarmine U (KY)
Belmont Abbey Coll (NC)
Belmont U (TN)
Bemidji State U (MN)
Benedictine Coll (KS)
Benedictine U (IL)
Bennett Coll for Women (NC)
Berea Coll (KY)
Berklee Coll of Music (MA)
Berry Coll (GA)
Bethany Coll (KS)
Bethany Coll (WV)
Bethany Lutheran Coll (MN)
Bethel Coll (KS)
Bethel U (MN)

Biola U (CA)
Birmingham-Southern Coll (AL)
Bishop's U (QC, Canada)
Blackburn Coll (IL)
Blessing-Rieman Coll of Nursing (IL)
Bloomfield Coll (NJ)
Bloomsburg U of Pennsylvania (PA)
Blue Mountain Coll (MS)
Bluffton U (OH)
Boise State U (ID)
Boston Baptist Coll (MA)
Bowling Green State U (OH)
Bradley U (IL)
Brenau U (GA)
Brescia U (KY)
Briar Cliff U (IA)
Bridgewater Coll (VA)
Bridgewater State U (MA)
Brigham Young U (UT)
Bryant U (RI)
Buena Vista U (IA)
Buffalo State Coll, State U of New York (NY)
Burlington Coll (VT)
Cabrini Coll (PA)
Caldwell Coll (NJ)
California Coll of the Arts (CA)
California Lutheran U (CA)
California Maritime Acad (CA)
California Polytechnic State U, San Luis Obispo (CA)
California State Polytechnic U, Pomona (CA)
California State U, Bakersfield (CA)
California State U, Chico (CA)
California State U, Dominguez Hills (CA)
California State U, East Bay (CA)
California State U, Fullerton (CA)
California State U, Long Beach (CA)
California State U, Los Angeles (CA)
California State U, Monterey Bay (CA)
California State U, Sacramento (CA)
California State U, San Bernardino (CA)
California State U, San Marcos (CA)
California State U, Stanislaus (CA)
California U of Pennsylvania (PA)
Calvin Coll (MI)
Campbellsville U (KY)
Canisius Coll (NY)
Cape Breton U (NS, Canada)
Capital U (OH)
Cardinal Stritch U (WI)
Carlow U (PA)
Carroll Coll (MT)
Carson-Newman Coll (TN)
Castleton State Coll (VT)
Catawba Coll (NC)
The Catholic U of America (DC)
Cedar Crest Coll (PA)
Cedarville U (OH)
Centenary Coll (NJ)
Centenary Coll of Louisiana (LA)
Central Coll (IA)
Central Connecticut State U (CT)
Central Methodist U (MO)
Central Michigan U (MI)
Central Washington U (WA)
Chamberlain Coll of Nursing, Miramar (FL)
Chamberlain Coll of Nursing (MO)
Chamberlain Coll of Nursing (TX)
Chaminade U of Honolulu (HI)
Chatham U (PA)
Chester Coll of New England (NH)
Chestnut Hill Coll (PA)
Christendom Coll (VA)
Christian Brothers U (TN)
The Citadel, The Military Coll of South Carolina (SC)
City Coll of the City U of New York (NY)
Clark Atlanta U (GA)
Clarke U (IA)
Clarkson Coll (NE)
Clark U (MA)
Cleary U (MI)
Clemson U (SC)
The Cleveland Inst of Art (OH)
Cleveland State U (OH)

Coastal Carolina U (SC)
Coe Coll (IA)
Cogswell Polytechnical Coll (CA)
The Coll at Brockport, State U of New York (NY)
Coll for Creative Studies (MI)
Coll of Charleston (SC)
The Coll of Idaho (ID)
Coll of Mount St. Joseph (OH)
Coll of Mount Saint Vincent (NY)
Coll of Saint Benedict (MN)
Coll of Saint Elizabeth (NJ)
The Coll of Saint Rose (NY)
The Coll of St. Scholastica (MN)
Coll of Staten Island of the City U of New York (NY)
Coll of the Ozarks (MO)
The Coll of Wooster (OH)
Colorado State U (CO)
Columbia Coll (MO)
Columbia Coll (SC)
Columbia Coll Chicago (IL)
Columbus Coll of Art & Design (OH)
Concordia Coll (MN)
Concordia Coll–New York (NY)
Concordia U (CA)
Concordia U (MI)
Concordia U (QC, Canada)
Concordia U Chicago (IL)
Concordia U, Nebraska (NE)
Concordia U Texas (TX)
Conservatorio de Musica (PR)
Converse Coll (SC)
Corban U (OR)
Corcoran Coll of Art and Design (DC)
Cornell Coll (IA)
Cornish Coll of the Arts (WA)
Covenant Coll (GA)
Creighton U (NE)
The Culinary Inst of America (NY)
Culver-Stockton Coll (MO)
Curry Coll (MA)
Daemen Coll (NY)
Dalhousie U (NS, Canada)
Dallas Baptist U (TX)
Daniel Webster Coll (NH)
Defiance Coll (OH)
Delaware State U (DE)
Delaware Valley Coll (PA)
DePaul U (IL)
DePauw U (IN)
DEREE - The American Coll of Greece (Greece)
DeSales U (PA)
Dillard U (LA)
Doane Coll (NE)
Dominican U (IL)
Dominican U of California (CA)
Dordt Coll (IA)
Dowling Coll (NY)
Drake U (IA)
Drew U (NJ)
Drexel U (PA)
Drury U (MO)
Duquesne U (PA)
East Carolina U (NC)
Eastern Connecticut State U (CT)
Eastern Illinois U (IL)
Eastern Mennonite U (VA)
Eastern Michigan U (MI)
Eastern Oregon U (OR)
Eastern U (PA)
Eastern Washington U (WA)
East Stroudsburg U of Pennsylvania (PA)
East Tennessee State U (TN)
East Texas Baptist U (TX)
Eckerd Coll (FL)
Edgewood Coll (WI)
Edinboro U of Pennsylvania (PA)
Elizabeth City State U (NC)
Elizabethtown Coll (PA)
Elmhurst Coll (IL)
Elmira Coll (NY)
Elon U (NC)
Embry-Riddle Aeronautical U–Daytona (FL)
Embry-Riddle Aeronautical U–Prescott (AZ)

Emily Carr U of Art + Design (BC, Canada)
Emmanuel Coll (GA)
Emmanuel Coll (MA)
Endicott Coll (MA)
Escuela de Artes Plasticas de Puerto Rico (PR)
Evangel U (MO)
The Evergreen State Coll (WA)
Fairfield U (CT)
Fairleigh Dickinson U, Coll at Florham (NJ)
Fairleigh Dickinson U, Metropolitan Campus (NJ)
Farmingdale State Coll (NY)
Fashion Inst of Technology (NY)
Felician Coll (NJ)
Fitchburg State U (MA)
Five Towns Coll (NY)
Flagler Coll (FL)
Florida Ag and Mech U (FL)
Florida Atlantic U (FL)
Florida Coll (FL)
Florida Gulf Coast U (FL)
Florida Inst of Technology (FL)
Florida Intl U (FL)
Florida National Coll (FL)
Florida Southern Coll (FL)
Fontbonne U (MO)
Fort Lewis Coll (CO)
Framingham State U (MA)
Franciscan U of Steubenville (OH)
Francis Marion U (SC)
Franklin Coll (IN)
Franklin Coll Switzerland (Switzerland)
Friends U (KS)
Gallaudet U (DC)
Gannon U (PA)
Gardner-Webb U (NC)
Geneva Coll (PA)
George Fox U (OR)
George Mason U (VA)
Georgetown Coll (KY)
Georgia Coll & State U (GA)
Georgian Court U (NJ)
Georgia Southern U (GA)
Georgia Southwestern State U (GA)
Georgia State U (GA)
Goddard Coll (VT)
Goldey-Beacom Coll (DE)
Gonzaga U (WA)
Gordon Coll (MA)
Goshen Coll (IN)
Goucher Coll (MD)
Grace Coll (IN)
Graceland U (IA)
Grand Canyon U (AZ)
Grand Valley State U (MI)
Great Lakes Christian Coll (MI)
Greenville Coll (IL)
Guilford Coll (NC)
Gwynedd-Mercy Coll (PA)
Hamline U (MN)
Hampden-Sydney Coll (VA)
Hampshire Coll (MA)
Hampton U (VA)
Hanover Coll (IN)
Harding U (AR)
Hardin-Simmons U (TX)
Hartwick Coll (NY)
Hawai`i Pacific U (HI)
HEC Montreal (QC, Canada)
Heidelberg U (OH)
Hofstra U (NY)
Hollins U (VA)
Holy Cross Coll (IN)
Holy Family U (PA)
Hood Coll (MD)
Hope Coll (MI)
Hope Intl U (CA)
Houghton Coll (NY)
Howard Payne U (TX)
Humboldt State U (CA)
Hunter Coll of the City U of New York (NY)
Huntingdon Coll (AL)
Huntington U (IN)
Husson U (ME)

Huston-Tillotson U (TX)
Illinois Coll (IL)
Illinois Inst of Technology (IL)
Illinois State U (IL)
Immaculata U (PA)
Indiana State U (IN)
Indiana Tech (IN)
Indiana U Bloomington (IN)
Indiana U East (IN)
Indiana U of Pennsylvania (PA)
Indiana U–Purdue U Indianapolis (IN)
Indiana U South Bend (IN)
Indiana Wesleyan U (IN)
Inter American U of Puerto Rico, Fajardo Campus (PR)
Inter American U of Puerto Rico, Ponce Campus (PR)
Inter American U of Puerto Rico, San Germán Campus (PR)
Iona Coll (NY)
Iowa State U of Science and Technology (IA)
Iowa Wesleyan Coll (IA)
Ithaca Coll (NY)
Jacksonville U (FL)
John Brown U (AR)
John Carroll U (OH)
John Jay Coll of Criminal Justice of the City U of New York (NY)
Johnson C. Smith U (NC)
Johnson State Coll (VT)
Judson Coll (AL)
Judson U (IL)
Juniata Coll (PA)
Kansas City Art Inst (MO)
Kean U (NJ)
Kennesaw State U (GA)
Kent State U (OH)
Kentucky Christian U (KY)
Kentucky Wesleyan Coll (KY)
Keuka Coll (NY)
King Coll (TN)
The King's Coll (NY)
King's Coll (PA)
The King's U Coll (AB, Canada)
Kingswood U (NB, Canada)
Kutztown U of Pennsylvania (PA)
LaGrange Coll (GA)
Lake Erie Coll (OH)
Lake Forest Coll (IL)
Lakehead U (ON, Canada)
Lake Superior State U (MI)
La Salle U (PA)
Lasell Coll (MA)
Lawrence Technological U (MI)
Lebanese American U (Lebanon)
Lebanon Valley Coll (PA)
Lehman Coll of the City U of New York (NY)
Le Moyne Coll (NY)
Lenoir-Rhyne U (NC)
LeTourneau U (TX)
Lewis U (IL)
Lincoln Christian U (IL)
Lincoln Memorial U (TN)
Lincoln U (PA)
Lindenwood U (MO)
Linfield Coll (OR)
Lipscomb U (TN)
Lock Haven U of Pennsylvania (PA)
Logan U–Coll of Chiropractic (MO)
Long Island U–Brooklyn Campus (NY)
Long Island U–C. W. Post Campus (NY)
Longwood U (VA)
Loras Coll (IA)
Louisiana Coll (LA)
Louisiana State U and Ag and Mech Coll (LA)
Louisiana State U in Shreveport (LA)
Loyola U Chicago (IL)
Loyola U Maryland (MD)
Loyola U New Orleans (LA)
Lubbock Christian U (TX)
Luther Coll (IA)
Lycoming Coll (PA)
Lyme Acad Coll of Fine Arts (CT)
Lynchburg Coll (VA)
Lynn U (FL)
Lyon Coll (AR)

Madonna U (MI)
Maharishi U of Management (IA)
Malone U (OH)
Manchester Coll (IN)
Manhattan Coll (NY)
Manhattanville Coll (NY)
Mansfield U of Pennsylvania (PA)
Marian U (WI)
Marietta Coll (OH)
Marlboro Coll (VT)
Marquette U (WI)
Marshall U (WV)
Mars Hill Coll (NC)
Martin Luther Coll (MN)
Mary Baldwin Coll (VA)
Marymount Manhattan Coll (NY)
Marymount U (VA)
Maryville Coll (TN)
Maryville U of Saint Louis (MO)
Marywood U (PA)
Massachusetts Coll of Liberal Arts (MA)
Massachusetts Maritime Acad (MA)
The Master's Coll and Sem (CA)
McDaniel Coll (MD)
McKendree U (IL)
McMurry U (TX)
McNally Smith Coll of Music (MN)
McNeese State U (LA)
McPherson Coll (KS)
Medaille Coll (NY)
Medcenter One Coll of Nursing (ND)
Memphis Coll of Art (TN)
Menlo Coll (CA)
Mercer U (GA)
Mercy Coll (NY)
Mercy Coll of Ohio (OH)
Mercyhurst Coll (PA)
Meredith Coll (NC)
Merrimack Coll (MA)
Messiah Coll (PA)
Miami U (OH)
Michigan State U (MI)
Michigan Technological U (MI)
MidAmerica Nazarene U (KS)
Middle Tennessee State U (TN)
Midwestern State U (TX)
Millersville U of Pennsylvania (PA)
Milligan Coll (TN)
Millikin U (IL)
Millsaps Coll (MS)
Mills Coll (CA)
Milwaukee School of Eng (WI)
Minnesota State U Mankato (MN)
Minnesota State U Moorhead (MN)
Minot State U (ND)
Misericordia U (PA)
Mississippi Coll (MS)
Mississippi State U (MS)
Mississippi U for Women (MS)
Missouri Baptist U (MO)
Missouri Southern State U (MO)
Missouri State U (MO)
Mitchell Coll (CT)
Molloy Coll (NY)
Monmouth Coll (IL)
Monmouth U (NJ)
Montana State U (MT)
Montana State U Billings (MT)
Montana State U–Northern (MT)
Montana Tech of The U of Montana (MT)
Montclair State U (NJ)
Montreat Coll, Montreat (NC)
Montserrat Coll of Art (MA)
Moody Bible Inst (IL)
Moore Coll of Art & Design (PA)
Moravian Coll (PA)
Morehouse Coll (GA)
Morningside Coll (IA)
Morrisville State Coll (NY)
Mount Allison U (NB, Canada)
Mount Carmel Coll of Nursing (OH)
Mount Ida Coll (MA)
Mount Mary Coll (WI)

Mount Mercy U (IA)
Mount Saint Mary Coll (NY)
Mount St. Mary's Coll (CA)
Mount St. Mary's U (MD)
Mount Vernon Nazarene U (OH)
Multnomah U (OR)
Naropa U (CO)
Nazareth Coll of Rochester (NY)
Nebraska Wesleyan U (NE)
Neumont U (UT)
Newberry Coll (SC)
New Jersey City U (NJ)
New Mexico Inst of Mining and Technology (NM)
New Mexico State U (NM)
New Saint Andrews Coll (ID)
New York Inst of Technology (NY)
New York School of Interior Design (NY)
Niagara U (NY)
Nichols Coll (MA)
Norfolk State U (VA)
North Carolina Ag and Tech State U (NC)
North Carolina Wesleyan Coll (NC)
North Central Coll (IL)
North Dakota State U (ND)
Northeastern State U (OK)
Northern Arizona U (AZ)
Northern Illinois U (IL)
Northern Kentucky U (KY)
North Georgia Coll & State U (GA)
Northland Coll (WI)
Northwest Christian U (OR)
Northwestern Coll (IA)
Northwestern Coll (MN)
Northwestern Oklahoma State U (OK)
Northwestern State U of Louisiana (LA)
Northwest Missouri State U (MO)
Northwest Nazarene U (ID)
Northwest U (WA)
Northwood U, Florida Campus (FL)
Northwood U, Michigan Campus (MI)
Northwood U, Texas Campus (TX)
Norwich U (VT)
Notre Dame de Namur U (CA)
Notre Dame of Maryland U (MD)
Nova Southeastern U (FL)
Oakland U (MI)
Ohio Northern U (OH)
Ohio U (OH)
Ohr Somayach/Joseph Tanenbaum Educational Center (NY)
Oklahoma City U (OK)
Oklahoma State U (OK)
Old Dominion U (VA)
O'More Coll of Design (TN)
Oral Roberts U (OK)
Oregon Coll of Art & Craft (OR)
Oregon Inst of Technology (OR)
Otis Coll of Art and Design (CA)
Otterbein U (OH)
Ouachita Baptist U (AR)
Pace U (NY)
Pacific Lutheran U (WA)
Pacific Union Coll (CA)
Pacific U (OR)
Palm Beach Atlantic U (FL)
Park U (MO)
Penn State Beaver (PA)
Penn State Brandywine (PA)
Penn State DuBois (PA)
Penn State Fayette, The Eberly Campus (PA)
Penn State Greater Allegheny (PA)
Penn State Hazleton (PA)
Penn State Lehigh Valley (PA)
Penn State Mont Alto (PA)
Penn State New Kensington (PA)
Penn State Schuylkill (PA)
Penn State Shenango (PA)
Penn State Wilkes-Barre (PA)
Penn State Worthington Scranton (PA)
Penn State York (PA)
Pennsylvania Coll of Art & Design (PA)
Philadelphia Biblical U (PA)
Philadelphia U (PA)
Piedmont Coll (GA)

Pine Manor Coll (MA)
Pitzer Coll (CA)
Plymouth State U (NH)
Point Loma Nazarene U (CA)
Point Park U (PA)
Point U (GA)
Portland State U (OR)
Post U (CT)
Prairie View A&M U (TX)
Prescott Coll (AZ)
Purchase Coll, State U of New York (NY)
Purdue U (IN)
Purdue U Calumet (IN)
Queens U of Charlotte (NC)
Quincy U (IL)
Quinnipiac U (CT)
Radford U (VA)
Ramapo Coll of New Jersey (NJ)
Randolph Coll (VA)
Randolph-Macon Coll (VA)
Regis Coll (MA)
Regis U (CO)
Reinhardt U (GA)
Research Coll of Nursing (MO)
Rhode Island Coll (RI)
Rider U (NJ)
Ringling Coll of Art and Design (FL)
Ripon Coll (WI)
Rivier Coll (NH)
Roanoke Coll (VA)
Roberts Wesleyan Coll (NY)
Rochester Inst of Technology (NY)
Rockford Coll (IL)
Rockhurst U (MO)
Rocky Mountain Coll (MT)
Rocky Mountain Coll of Art + Design (CO)
Roger Williams U (RI)
Roosevelt U (IL)
Rosemont Coll (PA)
Rowan U (NJ)
Russell Sage Coll (NY)
Rutgers, The State U of New Jersey, Camden (NJ)
Rutgers, The State U of New Jersey, Newark (NJ)
Rutgers, The State U of New Jersey, New Brunswick (NJ)
Ryerson U (ON, Canada)
Sacred Heart Major Sem (MI)
Sacred Heart U (CT)
Saginaw Valley State U (MI)
St. Ambrose U (IA)
St. Andrews U (NC)
Saint Anselm Coll (NH)
Saint Augustine's Coll (NC)
St. Bonaventure U (NY)
St. Catherine U (MN)
Saint Charles Borromeo Sem, Overbrook (PA)
St. Edward's U (TX)
Saint Francis U (PA)
St. John Fisher Coll (NY)
St. John's Coll (MD)
Saint John's U (MN)
St. John's U (NY)
Saint Joseph's Coll (IN)
St. Joseph's Coll, Long Island Campus (NY)
St. Joseph's Coll, New York (NY)
Saint Joseph's Coll of Maine (ME)
Saint Joseph's U (PA)
St. Louis Coll of Pharmacy (MO)
Saint Louis U (MO)
Saint Martin's U (WA)
Saint Mary-of-the-Woods Coll (IN)
Saint Mary's Coll (IN)
Saint Mary's Coll of California (CA)
St. Mary's U (TX)
Saint Mary's U of Minnesota (MN)
Saint Michael's Coll (VT)
St. Norbert Coll (WI)
Saint Peter's Coll (NJ)
St. Thomas Aquinas Coll (NY)
St. Thomas U (NB, Canada)
Saint Vincent Coll (PA)
Saint Xavier U (IL)
Salisbury U (MD)
Salve Regina U (RI)

Samford U (AL)
Sam Houston State U (TX)
Samuel Merritt U (CA)
San Diego Christian Coll (CA)
San Diego State U (CA)
San Francisco Conservatory of Music (CA)
San Francisco State U (CA)
Santa Clara U (CA)
Savannah Coll of Art and Design (GA)
School of the Museum of Fine Arts, Boston (MA)
Schreiner U (TX)
Seattle Pacific U (WA)
Seattle U (WA)
Seton Hill U (PA)
Shenandoah U (VA)
Shepherd U (WV)
Shimer Coll (IL)
Shippensburg U of Pennsylvania (PA)
Shorter U (GA)
Siena Coll (NY)
Siena Heights U (MI)
Sierra Nevada Coll (NV)
Simmons Coll (MA)
Simon Fraser U (BC, Canada)
Simpson Coll (IA)
Simpson U (CA)
Slippery Rock U of Pennsylvania (PA)
Sonoma State U (CA)
South Dakota School of Mines and Technology (SD)
Southeastern Louisiana U (LA)
Southeastern Oklahoma State U (OK)
Southeast Missouri State U (MO)
Southern Arkansas U–Magnolia (AR)
Southern Connecticut State U (CT)
Southern Illinois U Carbondale (IL)
Southern Illinois U Edwardsville (IL)
Southern Methodist U (TX)
Southern New Hampshire U (NH)
Southern Oregon U (OR)
Southern Polytechnic State U (GA)
Southern Utah U (UT)
Southwest Baptist U (MO)
Spalding U (KY)
Spring Arbor U (MI)
Spring Hill Coll (AL)
State U of New York at Fredonia (NY)
State U of New York at Oswego (NY)
State U of New York at Plattsburgh (NY)
State U of New York Coll at Cortland (NY)
State U of New York Coll at Old Westbury (NY)
State U of New York Coll at Potsdam (NY)
State U of New York Coll of Technology at Alfred (NY)
State U of New York Coll of Technology at Delhi (NY)
State U of New York Upstate Medical U (NY)
Stephen F. Austin State U (TX)
Stephens Coll (MO)
Sterling Coll (VT)
Stetson U (FL)
Stevens Inst of Business & Arts (MO)
Stevenson U (MD)
Suffolk U (MA)
Sullivan Coll of Technology and Design (KY)
Susquehanna U (PA)
Sweet Briar Coll (VA)
Syracuse U (NY)
Tabor Coll (KS)
Tarleton State U (TX)
Taylor U (IN)
Temple U (PA)
Texas A&M Intl U (TX)
Texas A&M U (TX)
Texas A&M U–Corpus Christi (TX)
Texas A&M U–Kingsville (TX)
Texas Lutheran U (TX)
Texas State U–San Marcos (TX)
Texas Tech U (TX)
Texas Wesleyan U (TX)
Thiel Coll (PA)
Thomas More Coll (KY)
Thomas More Coll of Liberal Arts (NH)
Tiffin U (OH)
Touro Coll (NY)
Towson U (MD)

Trent U (ON, Canada)
Trevecca Nazarene U (TN)
Trine U (IN)
Trinity Baptist Coll (FL)
Trinity Christian Coll (IL)
Trinity Coll of Nursing and Health Sciences (IL)
Troy U (AL)
Truman State U (MO)
Tusculum Coll (TN)
Tuskegee U (AL)
Union Coll (KY)
Union Coll (NE)
Union U (TN)
United States Intl U (Kenya)
Université de Sherbrooke (QC, Canada)
U at Buffalo, the State U of New York (NY)
The U of Akron (OH)
The U of Alabama (AL)
The U of Alabama at Birmingham (AL)
The U of Alabama in Huntsville (AL)
U of Alberta (AB, Canada)
The U of Arizona (AZ)
U of Arkansas (AR)
U of Bridgeport (CT)
The U of British Columbia–Okanagan (BC, Canada)
U of California, Merced (CA)
U of Central Arkansas (AR)
U of Central Florida (FL)
U of Central Missouri (MO)
U of Charleston (WV)
U of Cincinnati (OH)
U of Colorado at Colorado Springs (CO)
U of Colorado Boulder (CO)
U of Colorado Denver (CO)
U of Connecticut (CT)
U of Dallas (TX)
U of Dayton (OH)
U of Delaware (DE)
U of Denver (CO)
U of Dubuque (IA)
U of Evansville (IN)
The U of Findlay (OH)
U of Georgia (GA)
U of Guelph (ON, Canada)
U of Hartford (CT)
U of Hawaii at Hilo (HI)
U of Hawaii at Manoa (HI)
U of Hawaii–West Oahu (HI)
U of Houston (TX)
U of Idaho (ID)
U of Illinois at Chicago (IL)
U of Illinois at Springfield (IL)
U of Indianapolis (IN)
The U of Iowa (IA)
The U of Kansas (KS)
U of La Verne (CA)
U of Lethbridge (AB, Canada)
U of Louisiana at Lafayette (LA)
U of Louisiana at Monroe (LA)
U of Louisville (KY)
U of Maine (ME)
U of Maine at Farmington (ME)
U of Mary Hardin-Baylor (TX)
U of Maryland, Baltimore County (MD)
U of Maryland, Coll Park (MD)
U of Maryland Eastern Shore (MD)
U of Massachusetts Amherst (MA)
U of Massachusetts Boston (MA)
U of Massachusetts Dartmouth (MA)
U of Massachusetts Lowell (MA)
U of Memphis (TN)
U of Michigan–Dearborn (MI)
U of Michigan–Flint (MI)
U of Minnesota, Crookston (MN)
U of Minnesota, Duluth (MN)
U of Minnesota, Twin Cities Campus (MN)
U of Mississippi (MS)
U of Missouri (MO)
U of Missouri–Kansas City (MO)
U of Missouri–St. Louis (MO)
U of Mobile (AL)
U of Mount Union (OH)
U of Nebraska at Kearney (NE)

U of Nebraska–Lincoln (NE)
U of Nevada, Las Vegas (NV)
U of Nevada, Reno (NV)
U of New England (ME)
U of New Hampshire (NH)
U of New Hampshire at Manchester (NH)
U of New Haven (CT)
U of New Mexico (NM)
U of New Orleans (LA)
The U of North Carolina at Asheville (NC)
The U of North Carolina at Charlotte (NC)
The U of North Carolina Wilmington (NC)
U of Northern Colorado (CO)
U of Northern Iowa (IA)
U of Oklahoma (OK)
U of Oregon (OR)
U of Ottawa (ON, Canada)
U of Pittsburgh (PA)
U of Pittsburgh at Greensburg (PA)
U of Pittsburgh at Johnstown (PA)
U of Portland (OR)
U of Puerto Rico at Humacao (PR)
U of Puerto Rico at Ponce (PR)
U of Redlands (CA)
U of Rhode Island (RI)
U of St. Francis (IL)
U of Saint Francis (IN)
U of Saint Joseph (CT)
U of Saint Mary (KS)
U of St. Thomas (MN)
U of St. Thomas (TX)
U of Science and Arts of Oklahoma (OK)
The U of Scranton (PA)
U of South Alabama (AL)
U of South Carolina (SC)
U of South Carolina Aiken (SC)
U of South Carolina Upstate (SC)
The U of South Dakota (SD)
U of Southern Indiana (IN)
U of Southern Maine (ME)
U of Southern Mississippi (MS)
U of South Florida (FL)
The U of Tampa (FL)
The U of Tennessee (TN)
The U of Tennessee at Chattanooga (TN)
The U of Tennessee at Martin (TN)
The U of Texas at Arlington (TX)
The U of Texas at Tyler (TX)
The U of Texas Health Science Center at Houston (TX)
The U of Texas of the Permian Basin (TX)
The U of the Arts (PA)
U of the Cumberlands (KY)
U of the Incarnate Word (TX)
U of the Ozarks (AR)
U of the Pacific (CA)
U of the Sciences in Philadelphia (PA)
U of the Southwest (NM)
U of Utah (UT)
U of Vermont (VT)
The U of Virginia's Coll at Wise (VA)
U of Washington (WA)
U of Washington, Bothell (WA)
U of West Florida (FL)
U of Windsor (ON, Canada)
U of Wisconsin–Eau Claire (WI)
U of Wisconsin–Green Bay (WI)
U of Wisconsin–La Crosse (WI)
U of Wisconsin–Milwaukee (WI)
U of Wisconsin–River Falls (WI)
U of Wisconsin–Stevens Point (WI)
U of Wisconsin–Stout (WI)
U of Wisconsin–Superior (WI)
U of Wisconsin–Whitewater (WI)
U of Wyoming (WY)
Upper Iowa U (IA)
Utah State U (UT)
Utica Coll (NY)
Valdosta State U (GA)
Valparaiso U (IN)
VanderCook Coll of Music (IL)
Vanguard U of Southern California (CA)
Vaughn Coll of Aeronautics and Technology (NY)
Vermont Tech Coll (VT)

Virginia Intermont Coll (VA)
Virginia Polytechnic Inst and State U (VA)
Virginia Union U (VA)
Virginia Wesleyan Coll (VA)
Viterbo U (WI)
Wabash Coll (IN)
Wagner Coll (NY)
Waldorf Coll (IA)
Walsh U (OH)
Warren Wilson Coll (NC)
Wartburg Coll (IA)
Washington Adventist U (MD)
Washington Coll (MD)
Washington State U (WA)
Watkins Coll of Art, Design, & Film (TN)
Waynesburg U (PA)
Webber Intl U (FL)
Webster U (MO)
Wells Coll (NY)
Wentworth Inst of Technology (MA)
Wesleyan Coll (GA)
West Chester U of Pennsylvania (PA)
Western Carolina U (NC)
Western Connecticut State U (CT)
Western Illinois U (IL)
Western Intl U (AZ)
Western Michigan U (MI)
Western New England U (MA)
Western Oregon U (OR)
Western State Coll of Colorado (CO)
Western Washington U (WA)
Westfield State U (MA)
Westminster Coll (MO)
Westminster Coll (UT)
West Texas A&M U (TX)
West Virginia U (WV)
West Virginia Wesleyan Coll (WV)
Wheeling Jesuit U (WV)
Whittier Coll (CA)
Widener U (PA)
Wilkes U (PA)
William Jessup U (CA)
William Jewell Coll (MO)
William Paterson U of New Jersey (NJ)
William Penn U (IA)
William Woods U (MO)
Wilmington Coll (OH)
Wilson Coll (PA)
Wingate U (NC)
Winona State U (MN)
Winthrop U (SC)
Wittenberg U (OH)
Woodbury U (CA)
Worcester State U (MA)
Xavier U (OH)
Xavier U of Louisiana (LA)
Yeshiva U (NY)
York Coll of Pennsylvania (PA)
York Coll of the City U of New York (NY)

MINIMALLY DIFFICULT

Most freshmen were not in the top half of their high school class and scored somewhat below 1010 on the SAT or below 19 on the ACT; up to 95 percent of the applicants were accepted.

AIB Coll of Business (IA)
Alabama State U (AL)
Alaska Bible Coll (AK)
Albany State U (GA)
Amberton U (TX)
American Coll of Thessaloniki (Greece)
Amridge U (AL)
Anderson U (SC)
Anna Maria Coll (MA)
Armstrong Atlantic State U (GA)
Avila U (MO)
Baker Coll of Allen Park (MI)
Baker Coll of Auburn Hills (MI)
Baker Coll of Cadillac (MI)
Baker Coll of Clinton Township (MI)
Baker Coll of Flint (MI)

Baker Coll of Jackson (MI)
Baker Coll of Muskegon (MI)
Baker Coll of Owosso (MI)
Baker Coll of Port Huron (MI)
Baptist Bible Coll of Pennsylvania (PA)
Barclay Coll (KS)
Barton Coll (NC)
Bethel Coll (IN)
Bethel U (TN)
Bethune-Cookman U (FL)
Black Hills State U (SD)
Bluefield Coll (VA)
Bob Jones U (SC)
Bowie State U (MD)
Brevard Coll (NC)
Brewton-Parker Coll (GA)
Bryn Athyn Coll of the New Church (PA)
California Baptist U (CA)
California State U, Fresno (CA)
Calvary Bible Coll and Theological Sem (MO)
Capella U (MN)
Caribbean U (PR)
Central Penn Coll (PA)
Central State U (OH)
Cheyney U of Pennsylvania (PA)
Chicago State U (IL)
Cincinnati Christian U (OH)
Claflin U (SC)
Clarion U of Pennsylvania (PA)
Clayton State U (GA)
Clearwater Christian Coll (FL)
Coll of Business and Technology (FL)
Coll of Coastal Georgia (GA)
Coll of St. Joseph (VT)
Coll of Saint Mary (NE)
Colorado Mesa U (CO)
Columbus State U (GA)
Concordia U, St. Paul (MN)
Cornerstone U (MI)
Crandall U (NB, Canada)
The Criswell Coll (TX)
Crown Coll (MN)
Dakota State U (SD)
Dallas Christian Coll (TX)
Davenport U, Grand Rapids (MI)
DeVry Coll of New York (NY)
DeVry U, Phoenix (AZ)
DeVry U, Pomona (CA)
DeVry U, Miramar (FL)
DeVry U, Orlando (FL)
DeVry U, Decatur (GA)
DeVry U, Chicago (IL)
DeVry U, Kansas City (MO)
DeVry U, North Brunswick (NJ)
DeVry U, Columbus (OH)
DeVry U, Fort Washington (PA)
DeVry U, Houston (TX)
DeVry U, Irving (TX)
DeVry U, Arlington (VA)
DeVry U, Federal Way (WA)
DeVry U Online (IL)
DigiPen Inst of Technology (WA)
East Central U (OK)
EDP Coll of Puerto Rico, Inc. (PR)
EDP Coll of Puerto Rico–San Sebastian (PR)
Embry-Riddle Aeronautical U–Worldwide (FL)
Everest U, Lakeland (FL)
Fairmont State U (WV)
Faith Baptist Bible Coll and Theological Sem (IA)
Faulkner U (AL)
Fayetteville State U (NC)
Ferris State U (MI)
Ferrum Coll (VA)
Goodwin Coll (CT)
Grand View U (IA)
Hannibal-LaGrange U (MO)
Harrisburg U of Science and Technology (PA)
Hebrew Coll (MA)
Hellenic Coll (MA)
Hilbert Coll (NY)
Hodges U (FL)
Idaho State U (ID)
Indiana U Kokomo (IN)

Indiana U Northwest (IN)
Indiana U–Purdue U Fort Wayne (IN)
Indiana U Southeast (IN)
ITT Tech Inst, Bessemer (AL)
ITT Tech Inst, Madison (AL)
ITT Tech Inst, Mobile (AL)
ITT Tech Inst, Phoenix (AZ)
ITT Tech Inst, Tempe (AZ)
ITT Tech Inst, Tucson (AZ)
ITT Tech Inst (AR)
ITT Tech Inst, Clovis (CA)
ITT Tech Inst, Concord (CA)
ITT Tech Inst, Corona (CA)
ITT Tech Inst, Lathrop (CA)
ITT Tech Inst, Orange (CA)
ITT Tech Inst, Oxnard (CA)
ITT Tech Inst, Rancho Cordova (CA)
ITT Tech Inst, San Bernardino (CA)
ITT Tech Inst, San Diego (CA)
ITT Tech Inst, San Dimas (CA)
ITT Tech Inst, Sylmar (CA)
ITT Tech Inst, Torrance (CA)
ITT Tech Inst, Aurora (CO)
ITT Tech Inst, Thornton (CO)
ITT Tech Inst, Deerfield Beach (FL)
ITT Tech Inst, Fort Lauderdale (FL)
ITT Tech Inst, Fort Myers (FL)
ITT Tech Inst, Jacksonville (FL)
ITT Tech Inst, Lake Mary (FL)
ITT Tech Inst, Miami (FL)
ITT Tech Inst, Pinellas Park (FL)
ITT Tech Inst, Tallahassee (FL)
ITT Tech Inst, Tampa (FL)
ITT Tech Inst, West Palm Beach (FL)
ITT Tech Inst, Atlanta (GA)
ITT Tech Inst, Duluth (GA)
ITT Tech Inst, Kennesaw (GA)
ITT Tech Inst (ID)
ITT Tech Inst, Mount Prospect (IL)
ITT Tech Inst, Oak Brook (IL)
ITT Tech Inst, Orland Park (IL)
ITT Tech Inst, Springfield (IL)
ITT Tech Inst, Fort Wayne (IN)
ITT Tech Inst, Indianapolis (IN)
ITT Tech Inst, Indianapolis (IN)
ITT Tech Inst, Merrillville (IN)
ITT Tech Inst, Newburgh (IN)
ITT Tech Inst, South Bend (IN)
ITT Tech Inst, Cedar Rapids (IA)
ITT Tech Inst, Clive (IA)
ITT Tech Inst, Overland Park (KS)
ITT Tech Inst, Wichita (KS)
ITT Tech Inst, Lexington (KY)
ITT Tech Inst, Louisville (KY)
ITT Tech Inst, St. Rose (LA)
ITT Tech Inst, Hanover (MD)
ITT Tech Inst, Owings Mills (MD)
ITT Tech Inst, Norwood (MA)
ITT Tech Inst, Wilmington (MA)
ITT Tech Inst, Canton (MI)
ITT Tech Inst, Grand Rapids (MI)
ITT Tech Inst, Southfield (MI)
ITT Tech Inst, Swartz Creek (MI)
ITT Tech Inst, Troy (MI)
ITT Tech Inst, Wyoming (MI)
ITT Tech Inst, Eden Prairie (MN)
ITT Tech Inst (MS)
ITT Tech Inst, Arnold (MO)
ITT Tech Inst, Earth City (MO)
ITT Tech Inst, Kansas City (MO)
ITT Tech Inst, Springfield (MO)
ITT Tech Inst (NE)
ITT Tech Inst, Henderson (NV)
ITT Tech Inst (NM)
ITT Tech Inst, Cary (NC)
ITT Tech Inst, Charlotte (NC)
ITT Tech Inst, Charlotte (NC)
ITT Tech Inst, Durham (NC)
ITT Tech Inst, High Point (NC)
ITT Tech Inst, Akron (OH)
ITT Tech Inst, Columbus (OH)
ITT Tech Inst, Dayton (OH)
ITT Tech Inst, Hilliard (OH)

ITT Tech Inst, Norwood (OH)
ITT Tech Inst, Strongsville (OH)
ITT Tech Inst, Warrensville Heights (OH)
ITT Tech Inst, Youngstown (OH)
ITT Tech Inst, Oklahoma City (OK)
ITT Tech Inst, Tulsa (OK)
ITT Tech Inst, Portland (OR)
ITT Tech Inst, Salem (OR)
ITT Tech Inst, Greenville (SC)
ITT Tech Inst, Chattanooga (TN)
ITT Tech Inst, Cordova (TN)
ITT Tech Inst, Johnson City (TN)
ITT Tech Inst, Knoxville (TN)
ITT Tech Inst, Nashville (TN)
ITT Tech Inst, Arlington (TX)
ITT Tech Inst, Austin (TX)
ITT Tech Inst, DeSoto (TX)
ITT Tech Inst, Houston (TX)
ITT Tech Inst, Houston (TX)
ITT Tech Inst, Richardson (TX)
ITT Tech Inst, San Antonio (TX)
ITT Tech Inst, Webster (TX)
ITT Tech Inst (UT)
ITT Tech Inst, Chantilly (VA)
ITT Tech Inst, Norfolk (VA)
ITT Tech Inst, Richmond (VA)
ITT Tech Inst, Salem (VA)
ITT Tech Inst, Springfield (VA)
ITT Tech Inst, Everett (WA)
ITT Tech Inst, Seattle (WA)
ITT Tech Inst, Spokane Valley (WA)
ITT Tech Inst, Germantown (WI)
ITT Tech Inst, Green Bay (WI)
ITT Tech Inst, Greenfield (WI)
ITT Tech Inst, Madison (WI)
Jacksonville State U (AL)
Jamestown Business Coll (NY)
Jamestown Coll (ND)
Jarvis Christian Coll (TX)
Kentucky Mountain Bible Coll (KY)
Kentucky State U (KY)
Keystone Coll (PA)
Lamar U (TX)
Lane Coll (TN)
La Roche Coll (PA)
La Sierra U (CA)
Lees-McRae Coll (NC)
Lee U (TN)
Lewis-Clark State Coll (ID)
Liberty U (VA)
Life U (GA)
Limestone Coll (SC)
Lindsey Wilson Coll (KY)
Lourdes U (OH)
Macon State Coll (GA)
Maple Springs Baptist Bible Coll and Sem (MD)
Maria Coll (NY)
Marymount Coll, Palos Verdes, California (CA)
Metropolitan State Coll of Denver (CO)
Metropolitan State U (MN)
Mid-Atlantic Christian U (NC)
Mid-Continent U (KY)
Mississippi Valley State U (MS)
Morehead State U (KY)
Mount Aloysius Coll (PA)
Mount Marty Coll (SD)
Musicians Inst (CA)
National-Louis U (IL)
National U (CA)
Neumann U (PA)
Newbury Coll (MA)
New England Coll (NH)
New England School of Communications (ME)
New Hope Christian Coll (OR)
Newman U (KS)
New Mexico Highlands U (NM)
North Carolina Central U (NC)
Northcentral U (AZ)
Northeastern Illinois U (IL)
Northern Michigan U (MI)
Northern State U (SD)
North Greenville U (SC)
Nova Scotia Ag Coll (NS, Canada)

INDEXES

Oakland City U (IN)
Ohio Valley U (WV)
Our Lady of the Lake Coll (LA)
Pacific Northwest Coll of Art (OR)
Paier Coll of Art, Inc. (CT)
Paine Coll (GA)
Perelandra Coll (CA)
Philander Smith Coll (AR)
Pittsburg State U (KS)
Polytechnic U of Puerto Rico (PR)
Purdue U North Central (IN)
Rasmussen Coll Appleton (WI)
Rasmussen Coll Aurora (IL)
Rasmussen Coll Bismarck (ND)
Rasmussen Coll Blaine (MN)
Rasmussen Coll Bloomington (MN)
Rasmussen Coll Brooklyn Park (MN)
Rasmussen Coll Eagan (MN)
Rasmussen Coll Fargo (ND)
Rasmussen Coll Fort Myers (FL)
Rasmussen Coll Green Bay (WI)
Rasmussen Coll Lake Elmo/Woodbury (MN)
Rasmussen Coll Land O' Lakes (FL)
Rasmussen Coll Mankato (MN)
Rasmussen Coll Mokena/Tinley Park (IL)
Rasmussen Coll Moorhead (MN)
Rasmussen Coll New Port Richey (FL)
Rasmussen Coll Ocala (FL)
Rasmussen Coll Ocala School of Nursing (FL)
Rasmussen Coll Rockford (IL)
Rasmussen Coll Romeoville/Joliet (IL)
Rasmussen Coll St. Cloud (MN)
Rasmussen Coll Tampa/Brandon (FL)
Rasmussen Coll Wausau (WI)
Regent U (VA)
Robert Morris U (PA)
Robert Morris U Illinois (IL)
Rust Coll (MS)
Sage Coll of Albany (NY)
Saint Joseph Sem Coll (LA)
Saint Leo U (FL)
Saint Louis Christian Coll (MO)
St. Thomas U (FL)
Salem State U (MA)
Shaw U (NC)
South Carolina State U (SC)
South Dakota State U (SD)
Southeastern Baptist Theological Sem (NC)
Southeastern U (FL)
Southern Vermont Coll (VT)
Southwestern Adventist U (TX)
Southwestern Christian U (OK)
Southwestern Coll (KS)
Southwestern Oklahoma State U (OK)
Southwest Minnesota State U (MN)
State U of New York Coll of Technology at Canton (NY)
State U of New York Empire State Coll (NY)
Sterling Coll (KS)
Stillman Coll (AL)
Sullivan U (KY)
Texas Woman's U (TX)
Trident U Intl (CA)
Trinity Coll of Florida (FL)
Trinity Lutheran Coll (WA)
Truett-McConnell Coll (GA)
Universidad del Turabo (PR)
U of Alaska Fairbanks (AK)
U of Arkansas at Little Rock (AR)
U of Arkansas–Fort Smith (AR)
U of Houston–Clear Lake (TX)
U of Houston–Victoria (TX)
U of Maine at Fort Kent (ME)
U of Maine at Presque Isle (ME)
U of Mary (ND)
The U of Montana Western (MT)
U of Nebraska at Omaha (NE)
U of North Alabama (AL)
U of North Dakota (ND)
U of Pittsburgh at Bradford (PA)
U of Regina (SK, Canada)
U of South Carolina Beaufort (SC)
The U of Texas at El Paso (TX)

The U of West Alabama (AL)
U of West Georgia (GA)
U of Wisconsin–Platteville (WI)
Ursuline Coll (OH)
Valley Forge Christian Coll Woodbridge Campus (VA)
Villa Maria Coll of Buffalo (NY)
Virginia State U (VA)
Wayland Baptist U (TX)
Wayne State U (MI)
Western Kentucky U (KY)
West Liberty U (WV)
West Virginia State U (WV)
West Virginia U Inst of Technology (WV)
Wheelock Coll (MA)
Williams Baptist Coll (AR)
Wright State U (OH)

NONCOMPETITIVE

Virtually all applicants were accepted regardless of high school rank or test scores.

Acad of Art U (CA)
American Baptist Coll of American Baptist Theological Sem (TN)
American Public U System (WV)
Antioch U Midwest (OH)
Arlington Baptist Coll (TX)
Athabasca U (AB, Canada)
Athens State U (AL)
The Baptist Coll of Florida (FL)
Bellevue U (NE)
Beulah Heights U (GA)
Bluefield State Coll (WV)
Boston Architectural Coll (MA)
Briercrest Coll (SK, Canada)
California Christian Coll (CA)
Calumet Coll of Saint Joseph (IN)
Cambridge Coll (MA)
Cameron U (OK)
Carlos Albizu U (PR)
Carolina Christian Coll (NC)
Carver Bible Coll (GA)
Charter Oak State Coll (CT)
Chipola Coll (FL)
City U of Seattle (WA)
Clear Creek Baptist Bible Coll (KY)
Cleveland Chiropractic Coll–Kansas City Campus (KS)
Coll of Central Florida (FL)
Colorado Mountain Coll (CO)
Colorado Mountain Coll, Alpine Campus (CO)
Colorado Mountain Coll, Timberline Campus (CO)
Columbia Bible Coll (BC, Canada)
Columbia Centro Universitario, Caguas (PR)
Columbia Southern U (AL)
Crossroads Bible Coll (IN)
Dalton State Coll (GA)
Delta State U (MS)
DeVry U, Westminster (CO)
Dixie State Coll of Utah (UT)
Dominican Coll (NY)
Eastern Kentucky U (KY)
Eastern New Mexico U (NM)
Edward Waters Coll (FL)
Emmaus Bible Coll (IA)
Emporia State U (KS)
Florida State Coll at Jacksonville (FL)
Fort Hays State U (KS)
Fountainhead Coll of Technology (TN)
Franklin U (OH)
Free Will Baptist Bible Coll (TN)
Glenville State Coll (WV)
Grambling State U (LA)
Granite State Coll (NH)
Gulf Coast State Coll (FL)
Harrington Coll of Design (IL)
Heritage Christian U (AL)
Hillsdale Free Will Baptist Coll (OK)
Holy Trinity Orthodox Sem (NY)
Indian River State Coll (FL)
Intl Acad of Design & Technology (FL)
Jones Coll, Jacksonville (FL)

Jones Intl U (CO)
Kansas State U (KS)
Kent State U at Ashtabula (OH)
Kent State U at East Liverpool (OH)
Kent State U at Geauga (OH)
Kent State U at Salem (OH)
Kent State U at Stark (OH)
Kent State U at Trumbull (OH)
Kent State U at Tuscarawas (OH)
Lincoln U (MO)
Maranatha Baptist Bible Coll (WI)
Marylhurst U (OR)
Master's Coll and Sem (ON, Canada)
Mayville State U (ND)
Medgar Evers Coll of the City U of New York (NY)
Miami Dade Coll (FL)
Midland Coll (TX)
Missouri Western State U (MO)
Morris Coll (SC)
Mountain State U (WV)
New England Inst of Technology (RI)
New World School of the Arts (FL)
New York City Coll of Technology of the City U of New York (NY)
Nicholls State U (LA)
Northwest Florida State Coll (FL)
The Ohio State U at Lima (OH)
The Ohio State U at Marion (OH)
The Ohio State U–Mansfield Campus (OH)
The Ohio State U–Newark Campus (OH)
Ohio U–Chillicothe (OH)
Ohio U–Zanesville (OH)
Oklahoma Christian U (OK)
Oklahoma State U, Oklahoma City (OK)
Olympic Coll (WA)
Pacific States U (CA)
Palm Beach State Coll (FL)
Peirce Coll (PA)
Peninsula Coll (WA)
Pennsylvania Coll of Technology (PA)
Pensacola State Coll (FL)
Peru State Coll (NE)
Piedmont Intl U (NC)
Polk State Coll (FL)
Potomac Coll (DC)
Presentation Coll (SD)
Rogers State U (OK)
Seminole State Coll of Florida (FL)
Shawnee State U (OH)
Sojourner-Douglass Coll (MD)
Southeastern Bible Coll (AL)
Southwestern Assemblies of God U (TX)
State Coll of Florida Manatee-Sarasota (FL)
Sul Ross State U (TX)
Texas Coll (TX)
Texas Southern U (TX)
Thomas Edison State Coll (NJ)
Thomas U (GA)
Union Inst & U (OH)
The U of Akron–Wayne Coll (OH)
U of Alaska Anchorage (AK)
U of Arkansas at Monticello (AR)
U of Great Falls (MT)
U of Guam (GU)
U of Houston–Downtown (TX)
U of Maine at Augusta (ME)
U of Maryland U Coll (MD)
U of Pikeville (KY)
U of Rio Grande (OH)
The U of Texas–Pan American (TX)
U of the District of Columbia (DC)
The U of Toledo (OH)
Utah Valley U (UT)
Valley City State U (ND)
Vincennes U (IN)
Washburn U (KS)
Wayne State Coll (NE)
Weber State U (UT)
Wichita State U (KS)
Wilmington U (DE)
Youngstown State U (OH)

INDEXES

Cost Ranges

LESS THAN $2000

Colleges with Room and Board
United States Coast Guard Acad (CT)
United States Military Acad (NY)
United States Naval Acad (MD)

$2000–$3999

Colleges with No Room and Board or with Room Only
Chipola Coll (FL)
Coll of Central Florida (FL)
Coll of the Humanities and Sciences, Harrison Middleton U (AZ)
Emily Carr U of Art + Design (BC, Canada)
Florida State Coll at Jacksonville (FL)
Miami Dade Coll (FL)
Oklahoma State U, Oklahoma City (OK)
Olympic Coll (WA)
Palm Beach State Coll (FL)
Pensacola State Coll (FL)
Polk State Coll (FL)
U of Puerto Rico at Bayamón (PR)

$4000–$5999

Colleges with No Room and Board or with Room Only
Amberton U (TX)
Athens State U (AL)
Bayamón Central U (PR)
Bluefield State Coll (WV)
City Coll of the City U of New York (NY)
Coll of Staten Island of the City U of New York (NY)
Columbia Southern U (AL)
Escuela de Artes Plasticas de Puerto Rico (PR)
Inter American U of Puerto Rico, Bayamón Campus (PR)
Inter American U of Puerto Rico, Fajardo Campus (PR)
Inter American U of Puerto Rico, Ponce Campus (PR)
John Jay Coll of Criminal Justice of the City U of New York (NY)
Kent State U at Ashtabula (OH)
Kent State U at East Liverpool (OH)
Kent State U at Geauga (OH)
Kent State U at Salem (OH)
Kent State U at Stark (OH)
Kent State U at Trumbull (OH)
Kent State U at Tuscarawas (OH)
Lewis-Clark State Coll (ID)
Logan U–Coll of Chiropractic (MO)
Maple Springs Baptist Bible Coll and Sem (MD)
Medgar Evers Coll of the City U of New York (NY)
Metropolitan State Coll of Denver (CO)
New York City Coll of Technology of the City U of New York (NY)
Ohio U–Zanesville (OH)
State U of New York Empire State Coll (NY)
Thomas Edison State Coll (NJ)
Université de Sherbrooke (QC, Canada) **(room only)**
The U of Akron–Wayne Coll (OH)
U of Hawaii–West Oahu (HI)
U of Houston–Downtown (TX)
U of Oklahoma Health Sciences Center (OK)
Utah Valley U (UT)
York Coll of the City U of New York (NY)

$6000–$7999

Colleges with No Room and Board or with Room Only
American Public U System (WV)
Baker Coll of Allen Park (MI)
Baker Coll of Auburn Hills (MI)
Baker Coll of Cadillac (MI)
Baker Coll of Clinton Township (MI)
Baker Coll of Jackson (MI)
Baker Coll of Port Huron (MI)
California State U, San Marcos (CA)
Carlos Albizu U (PR)
Carolina Christian Coll (NC)
Cleveland Chiropractic Coll–Kansas City Campus (KS)
EDP Coll of Puerto Rico–San Sebastian (PR)
Embry-Riddle Aeronautical U–Worldwide (FL)
Granite State Coll (NH)
Indiana U East (IN)
Indiana U Kokomo (IN)
Indiana U Northwest (IN)
Jones Coll, Jacksonville (FL)
Metropolitan State U (MN)
The Ohio State U at Lima (OH)
The Ohio State U at Marion (OH)
Purdue U North Central (IN)
Southern Utah U (UT) **(room only)**
U of Maine at Augusta (ME)
U of Maryland U Coll (MD)
Vanguard Coll (AB, Canada)
Wilmington U (DE)

Colleges with Room and Board
Berea Coll (KY)
Coll of the Ozarks (MO)
Midland Coll (TX)
Universidad Teolgica del Caribe (PR)

$8000–$9999

Colleges with No Room and Board or with Room Only
Amridge U (AL)
Bellevue U (NE)
Columbia Centro Universitario, Caguas (PR)
Columbia Centro Universitario, Yauco (PR)
Governors State U (IL)
Northcentral U (AZ)
Northeastern Illinois U (IL)
Rogers State U (OK) **(room only)**
Southeastern Baptist Theological Sem (NC) **(room only)**
Trident U Intl (CA)
U of Arkansas–Fort Smith (AR) **(room only)**
U of Guam (GU) **(room only)**
U of Nebraska Medical Center (NE)

Colleges with Room and Board
Cameron U (OK)
Dalton State Coll (GA)
Dixie State Coll of Utah (UT)
East Central U (OK)
Eastern New Mexico U (NM)
Elizabeth City State U (NC)
Inter American U of Puerto Rico, San Germán Campus (PR)
Northeastern State U (OK)
Northwestern Oklahoma State U (OK)
Southeastern Oklahoma State U (OK)
Southwestern Oklahoma State U (OK)
The U of Montana Western (MT)

$10,000–$11,999

Colleges with No Room and Board or with Room Only
Baker Coll of Flint (MI) **(room only)**
Baker Coll of Muskegon (MI) **(room only)**
Baker Coll of Owosso (MI) **(room only)**
Baptist Coll of Health Sciences (TN) **(room only)**
Hodges U (FL)
Hunter Coll of the City U of New York (NY) **(room only)**
Jamestown Business Coll (NY)
Louisiana State U in Shreveport (LA) **(room only)**
Medcenter One Coll of Nursing (ND)
National U (CA)
New Saint Andrews Coll (ID)
Potomac Coll (DC)
Union Inst & U (OH)
U of Massachusetts Boston (MA)
U of Michigan–Dearborn (MI)
U of South Florida (FL) **(room only)**
The U of Texas at El Paso (TX) **(room only)**

Colleges with Room and Board
Albany State U (GA)
American U in Bulgaria (Bulgaria)
Arkansas Tech U (AR)
Arlington Baptist Coll (TX)
Auburn U Montgomery (AL)
Boise State U (ID)
Brigham Young U (UT)
California Christian Coll (CA)
Coll of Coastal Georgia (GA)
Conservatorio de Musica (PR)
Delta State U (MS)
Emporia State U (KS)
Fayetteville State U (NC)
Grambling State U (LA)
Idaho State U (ID)
Macon State Coll (GA)
Mayville State U (ND)
McNeese State U (LA)
Minot State U (ND)
Mississippi U for Women (MS)
Mississippi Valley State U (MS)
Missouri Southern State U (MO)
Montana State U Billings (MT)
Montana State U–Northern (MT)
New Mexico Highlands U (NM)
New Mexico Inst of Mining and Technology (NM)
North Carolina Ag and Tech State U (NC)
Peru State Coll (NE)
Pittsburg State U (KS)
Rust Coll (MS)
Southeastern Louisiana U (LA)
Southern Arkansas U–Magnolia (AR)
U of Arkansas at Monticello (AR)
U of Louisiana at Lafayette (LA)
U of Louisiana at Monroe (LA)
U of Puerto Rico at Humacao (PR)
U of Science and Arts of Oklahoma (OK)
The U of Texas–Pan American (TX)
Utah State U (UT)
Valley City State U (ND)
Wayne State Coll (NE)
Weber State U (UT)
West Texas A&M U (TX)
West Virginia State U (WV)

$12,000–$13,999

Colleges with No Room and Board or with Room Only
Cambridge Coll (MA)
Carlos Albizu U, Miami Campus (FL)
Crossroads Bible Coll (IN) **(room only)**

Florida National Coll (FL)
Franklin U (OH)
Indiana U–Purdue U Fort Wayne (IN) **(room only)**
Indiana U South Bend (IN) **(room only)**
Indiana U Southeast (IN) **(room only)**
Jones Intl U (CO)
Lehman Coll of the City U of New York (NY) **(room only)**
Paier Coll of Art, Inc. (CT)
Penn State Abington (PA)
Penn State Brandywine (PA)
Penn State DuBois (PA)
Penn State Fayette, The Eberly Campus (PA)
Penn State Lehigh Valley (PA)
Penn State New Kensington (PA)
Penn State Schuylkill (PA)
Penn State Shenango (PA)
Penn State Wilkes-Barre (PA)
Penn State Worthington Scranton (PA)
Penn State York (PA)
Stevens Inst of Business & Arts (MO)
U of New Hampshire at Manchester (NH)
Walden U (MN)
Western Intl U (AZ)

Colleges with Room and Board
Adams State Coll (CO)
Alabama State U (AL)
Alcorn State U (MS)
Appalachian State U (NC)
Arkansas State U (AR)
Austin Peay State U (TN)
Blue Mountain Coll (MS)
Cape Breton U (NS, Canada)
Clayton State U (GA)
Columbus State U (GA)
Dakota State U (SD)
East Carolina U (NC)
Eastern Kentucky U (KY)
East Tennessee State U (TN)
Fairmont State U (WV)
Florida Ag and Mech U (FL)
Fort Lewis Coll (CO)
Georgia Gwinnett Coll (GA)
Georgia Southwestern State U (GA)
Glenville State Coll (WV)
Jacksonville State U (AL)
Kentucky State U (KY)
Midwestern State U (TX)
Minnesota State U Mankato (MN)
Mississippi State U (MS)
Missouri State U (MO)
Missouri Western State U (MO)
Montana Tech of The U of Montana (MT)
Morehead State U (KY)
New Mexico State U (NM)
North Dakota State U (ND)
Northern State U (SD)
North Georgia Coll & State U (GA)
Northwestern State U of Louisiana (LA)
Oklahoma State U (OK)
Shepherd U (WV)
South Dakota State U (SD)
Southern Polytechnic State U (GA)
Sul Ross State U (TX)
Tarleton State U (TX)
Texas A&M Intl U (TX)
Texas A&M U–Kingsville (TX)
Texas Woman's U (TX)
Trinity Baptist Coll (FL)
U of Alaska Fairbanks (AK)
U of Arkansas at Little Rock (AR)
U of Central Arkansas (AR)
U of Hawaii at Hilo (HI)
U of Houston–Victoria (TX)
U of Idaho (ID)
U of Memphis (TN)
U of Nebraska at Kearney (NE)
U of New Mexico (NM)
U of New Orleans (LA)
U of North Alabama (AL)
The U of North Carolina at Asheville (NC)
The U of North Carolina at Charlotte (NC)
The U of North Carolina Wilmington (NC)

U of North Dakota (ND)
U of North Florida (FL)
U of Ottawa (ON, Canada)
U of Regina (SK, Canada)
U of South Alabama (AL)
The U of South Dakota (SD)
U of Southern Indiana (IN)
U of Southern Mississippi (MS)
The U of Tennessee at Martin (TN)
The U of Texas of the Permian Basin (TX)
U of the District of Columbia (DC)
U of Utah (UT)
The U of West Alabama (AL)
U of West Georgia (GA)
U of Wisconsin–Eau Claire (WI)
U of Wisconsin–Platteville (WI)
U of Wisconsin–River Falls (WI)
U of Wisconsin–Stevens Point (WI)
U of Wisconsin–Superior (WI)
U of Wisconsin–Whitewater (WI)
U of Wyoming (WY)
Valdosta State U (GA)
Washburn U (KS)
Webb Inst (NY)
Western Carolina U (NC)
Western State Coll of Colorado (CO)
West Liberty U (WV)
West Virginia U Inst of Technology (WV)
Wichita State U (KS)

$14,000–$15,999

Colleges with No Room and Board or with Room Only
Calumet Coll of Saint Joseph (IN)
Chamberlain Coll of Nursing (MO)
DeVry Coll of New York (NY)
DeVry U, Phoenix (AZ)
DeVry U, Pomona (CA)
DeVry U, Westminster (CO)
DeVry U, Miramar (FL)
DeVry U, Orlando (FL)
DeVry U, Decatur (GA)
DeVry U, Chicago (IL)
DeVry U, Kansas City (MO)
DeVry U, North Brunswick (NJ)
DeVry U, Columbus (OH)
DeVry U, Fort Washington (PA)
DeVry U, Houston (TX)
DeVry U, Irving (TX)
DeVry U, Arlington (VA)
DeVry U, Federal Way (WA)
DeVry U Online (IL)
Medical U of South Carolina (SC)
Mount Carmel Coll of Nursing (OH) **(room only)**
Peirce Coll (PA)
Salem State U (MA) **(room only)**
Southeastern Bible Coll (AL) **(room only)**
Trinity Coll of Nursing and Health Sciences (IL)
U of Colorado at Colorado Springs (CO) **(room only)**
U of Houston–Clear Lake (TX) **(room only)**

Colleges with Room and Board
Acadia U (NS, Canada)
Angelo State U (TX)
Armstrong Atlantic State U (GA)
Bemidji State U (MN)
Bloomsburg U of Pennsylvania (PA)
Bowie State U (MD)
California State U, Bakersfield (CA)
California State U, Los Angeles (CA)
California State U, Monterey Bay (CA)
California State U, San Bernardino (CA)
California State U, Stanislaus (CA)
Calvary Bible Coll and Theological Sem (MO)
Central State U (OH)
Clarion U of Pennsylvania (PA)
Colorado Mesa U (CO)
Eastern Oregon U (OR)
Eastern Washington U (WA)
East Stroudsburg U of Pennsylvania (PA)

Florida Gulf Coast U (FL)
Florida State U (FL)
Francis Marion U (SC)
Georgia Southern U (GA)
Goddard Coll (VT)
Indiana State U (IN)
Iowa State U of Science and Technology (IA)
Kansas State U (KS)
Kennesaw State U (GA)
The King's U Coll (AB, Canada)
Lakehead U (ON, Canada)
Lamar U (TX)
Lane Coll (TN)
Lincoln U (MO)
Lock Haven U of Pennsylvania (PA)
Louisiana State U and Ag and Mech Coll (LA)
Marshall U (WV)
Martin Luther Coll (MN)
Middle Tennessee State U (TN)
Minnesota State U Moorhead (MN)
Montana State U (MT)
Morris Coll (SC)
Mount Allison U (NB, Canada)
New Coll of Florida (FL)
Nicholls State U (LA)
Norfolk State U (VA)
North Carolina Central U (NC)
North Carolina State U (NC)
Northern Kentucky U (KY)
Northwest Missouri State U (MO)
The Ohio State U–Mansfield Campus (OH)
The Ohio State U–Newark Campus (OH)
Park U (MO)
Prairie View A&M U (TX)
Purdue U Calumet (IN)
Radford U (VA)
Saginaw Valley State U (MI)
Salisbury U (MD)
Sam Houston State U (TX)
Shawnee State U (OH)
South Dakota School of Mines and Technology (SD)
Southeast Missouri State U (MO)
Southwest Minnesota State U (MN)
Stephen F. Austin State U (TX)
Texas State U–San Marcos (TX)
Troy U (AL)
Truman State U (MO)
U of Alaska Anchorage (AK)
U of Arkansas (AR)
U of Central Florida (FL)
U of Central Missouri (MO)
U of Florida (FL)
U of Maine at Fort Kent (ME)
U of Maine at Presque Isle (ME)
U of Maryland Eastern Shore (MD)
U of Mississippi (MS)
U of Nebraska at Omaha (NE)
U of Nevada, Reno (NV)
U of North Carolina School of the Arts (NC)
U of Northern Iowa (IA)
U of North Texas (TX)
U of Oklahoma (OK)
U of South Carolina Aiken (SC)
U of South Carolina Beaufort (SC)
The U of Tennessee at Chattanooga (TN)
The U of Texas at Tyler (TX)
U of West Florida (FL)
U of Wisconsin–Green Bay (WI)
U of Wisconsin–La Crosse (WI)
U of Wisconsin–Stout (WI)
Virginia State U (VA)
Western Kentucky U (KY)
West Virginia U (WV)
Youngstown State U (OH)

$16,000–$17,999

Colleges with No Room and Board or with Room Only
AIB Coll of Business (IA) **(room only)**

Bernard M. Baruch Coll of the City U of New York (NY) **(room only)**
City U of Seattle (WA)
Herzing U, Madison (WI)
Thomas U (GA) **(room only)**
Villa Maria Coll of Buffalo (NY)

Colleges with Room and Board

Ball State U (IN)
Bob Jones U (SC)
Bowling Green State U (OH)
Bridgewater State U (MA)
Buffalo State Coll, State U of New York (NY)
California State Polytechnic U, Pomona (CA)
California State U, Dominguez Hills (CA)
California State U, East Bay (CA)
California State U, Fresno (CA)
California State U, Fullerton (CA)
California State U, Long Beach (CA)
California State U, Sacramento (CA)
Castleton State Coll (VT)
Central Connecticut State U (CT)
Central Washington U (WA)
Cheyney U of Pennsylvania (PA)
Chicago State U (IL)
The Citadel, The Military Coll of South Carolina (SC)
Coastal Carolina U (SC)
The Coll at Brockport, State U of New York (NY)
Colorado State U (CO)
Eastern Michigan U (MI)
Edinboro U of Pennsylvania (PA)
Edward Waters Coll (FL)
The Evergreen State Coll (WA)
Farmingdale State Coll (NY)
Fashion Inst of Technology (NY)
Fitchburg State U (MA)
Florida Atlantic U (FL)
Florida Intl U (FL)
Framingham State U (MA)
Georgia Coll & State U (GA)
Grand Valley State U (MI)
Hillsdale Free Will Baptist Coll (OK)
Humboldt State U (CA)
Indiana U Bloomington (IN)
Indiana U–Purdue U Indianapolis (IN)
James Madison U (VA)
Kutztown U of Pennsylvania (PA)
Lake Superior State U (MI)
Lincoln U (PA)
Louisiana Coll (LA)
Mansfield U of Pennsylvania (PA)
Massachusetts Coll of Liberal Arts (MA)
Massachusetts Maritime Acad (MA)
Millersville U of Pennsylvania (PA)
Missouri U of Science and Technology (MO)
Morrisville State Coll (NY)
Mountain State U (WV)
Northern Arizona U (AZ)
Northern Michigan U (MI)
Oakland U (MI)
Old Dominion U (VA)
Piedmont Intl U (NC)
Purchase Coll, State U of New York (NY)
Queens Coll of the City U of New York (NY)
Queen's U at Kingston (ON, Canada)
Rhode Island Coll (RI)
San Francisco State U (CA)
Shippensburg U of Pennsylvania (PA)
Slippery Rock U of Pennsylvania (PA)
Sonoma State U (CA)
Southern Illinois U Edwardsville (IL)
Southern Oregon U (OR)
State U of New York at Fredonia (NY)
State U of New York at New Paltz (NY)
State U of New York at Plattsburgh (NY)
State U of New York Coll at Cortland (NY)
State U of New York Coll at Geneseo (NY)
State U of New York Coll at Old Westbury (NY)
State U of New York Coll at Oneonta (NY)
State U of New York Coll at Potsdam (NY)
State U of New York Coll of Technology at Alfred (NY)
State U of New York Coll of Technology at Canton (NY)
State U of New York Maritime Coll (NY)

State U of New York Upstate Medical U (NY)
Stony Brook U, State U of New York (NY)
Texas A&M U (TX)
Texas A&M U–Corpus Christi (TX)
Texas Coll (TX)
Texas Tech U (TX)
Towson U (MD)
The U of Alabama (AL)
The U of Alabama at Birmingham (AL)
The U of Alabama in Huntsville (AL)
U of Colorado Denver (CO)
U of Guelph (ON, Canada)
U of Houston (TX)
The U of Iowa (IA)
The U of Kansas (KS)
U of Louisville (KY)
U of Maine at Farmington (ME)
U of Mary Washington (VA)
U of Michigan–Flint (MI)
U of Minnesota, Crookston (MN)
U of Missouri (MO)
U of Missouri–Kansas City (MO)
U of Missouri–St. Louis (MO)
U of Nebraska–Lincoln (NE)
U of Nevada, Las Vegas (NV)
The U of North Carolina at Chapel Hill (NC)
U of Northern Colorado (CO)
U of South Carolina Upstate (SC)
The U of Tennessee (TN)
The U of Texas at Arlington (TX)
The U of Texas at San Antonio (TX)
The U of Virginia's Coll at Wise (VA)
U of Washington (WA)
U of Wisconsin–Madison (WI)
Virginia Polytechnic Inst and State U (VA)
West Chester U of Pennsylvania (PA)
Western Michigan U (MI)
Western Oregon U (OR)
Western Washington U (WA)
Westfield State U (MA)
Winona State U (MN)
Wright State U (OH)

$18,000–$19,999

Colleges with No Room and Board or with Room Only

Goldfarb School of Nursing at Barnes-Jewish Coll (MO)
Goodwin Coll (CT)
Harrington Coll of Design (IL)
Marylhurst U (OR)
National-Louis U (IL)
New England Inst of Technology (RI)
Pennsylvania Coll of Art & Design (PA)
St. Joseph's Coll, Long Island Campus (NY)
St. Joseph's Coll, New York (NY)
U of Washington, Bothell (WA) **(room only)**

Colleges with Room and Board

Auburn U (AL)
Boston Baptist Coll (MA)
Brewton-Parker Coll (GA)
California Polytechnic State U, San Luis Obispo (CA)
California State U, Chico (CA)
California U of Pennsylvania (PA)
Central Michigan U (MI)
Christopher Newport U (VA)
Clemson U (SC)
Coll of Charleston (SC)
Delaware State U (DE)
Eastern Connecticut State U (CT)
Eastern Illinois U (IL)
Emmaus Bible Coll (IA)
Ferris State U (MI)
George Mason U (VA)
Georgia Inst of Technology (GA)
Heritage Christian U (AL)
Huston-Tillotson U (TX)
Indiana U of Pennsylvania (PA)
Johnson State Coll (VT)
Kent State U (OH)

Lee U (TN)
Longwood U (VA)
Maranatha Baptist Bible Coll (WI)
Mid-Atlantic Christian U (NC)
New Hope Christian Coll (OR)
New Jersey City U (NJ)
The Ohio State U (OH)
Ohio U (OH)
Paine Coll (GA)
Philander Smith Coll (AR)
Polytechnic U of Puerto Rico (PR)
Portland State U (OR)
Purdue U (IN)
San Diego State U (CA)
South Carolina State U (SC)
Southern Connecticut State U (CT)
Southern Illinois U Carbondale (IL)
State U of New York at Binghamton (NY)
State U of New York at Oswego (NY)
State U of New York Coll of Environmental Science and Forestry (NY)
Trinity Coll of Florida (FL)
U at Albany, State U of New York (NY)
U at Buffalo, the State U of New York (NY)
The U of Arizona (AZ)
U of Colorado Boulder (CO)
U of Georgia (GA)
U of Hawaii at Manoa (HI)
U of Maine (ME)
U of Mary (ND)
U of Maryland, Baltimore County (MD)
U of Maryland, Coll Park (MD)
U of Minnesota, Duluth (MN)
U of Oregon (OR)
U of South Carolina (SC)
U of Southern Maine (ME)
The U of Texas at Dallas (TX)
U of the Southwest (NM)
The U of Toledo (OH)
U of Toronto (ON, Canada)
U of Wisconsin–Milwaukee (WI)
Virginia Commonwealth U (VA)
Wayland Baptist U (TX)
Wayne State U (MI)
Western Connecticut State U (CT)
Western Illinois U (IL)
Williams Baptist Coll (AR)
Winthrop U (SC)
Worcester State U (MA)

$20,000–$24,999

Colleges with No Room and Board or with Room Only

American U of Beirut (Lebanon) **(room only)**
Antioch U Midwest (OH)
Creative Center (NE)
Hebrew Coll (MA)
O'More Coll of Design (TN)
Pacific States U (CA) **(room only)**
Regent U (VA) **(room only)**

Colleges with Room and Board

Allen Coll (IA)
Alliant Intl U (CA)
Arizona State U (AZ)
Baptist Bible Coll of Pennsylvania (PA)
Barclay Coll (KS)
Bennett Coll for Women (NC)
Bethel U (TN)
Bethune-Cookman U (FL)
Blackburn Coll (IL)
Central Penn Coll (PA)
Cincinnati Christian U (OH)
Claflin U (SC)
Clearwater Christian Coll (FL)
Cleveland State U (OH)
The Coll of New Jersey (NJ)
The Coll of William and Mary (VA)
Colorado School of Mines (CO)
Columbia Coll (MO)

Davenport U, Grand Rapids (MI)
Dillard U (LA)
Emmanuel Coll (GA)
Evangel U (MO)
Faith Baptist Bible Coll and Theological Sem (IA)
Faulkner U (AL)
Flagler Coll (FL)
Florida Coll (FL)
Free Will Baptist Bible Coll (TN)
Gallaudet U (DC)
Georgia State U (GA)
Great Lakes Christian Coll (MI)
Grove City Coll (PA)
Hannibal-LaGrange U (MO)
Harding U (AR)
Husson U (ME)
Illinois State U (IL)
Intl Acad of Design & Technology (FL)
Jamestown Coll (ND)
Jarvis Christian Coll (TX)
Johnson C. Smith U (NC)
Judson Coll (AL)
Kean U (NJ)
Keene State Coll (NH)
Kentucky Christian U (KY)
Life U (GA)
Lincoln Christian U (IL)
Lincoln Memorial U (TN)
Lindenwood U (MO)
Lourdes U (OH)
Lubbock Christian U (TX)
Madonna U (MI)
Massachusetts Coll of Art and Design (MA)
Miami U (OH)
Michigan State U (MI)
Michigan Technological U (MI)
Mid-Continent U (KY)
Mississippi Coll (MS)
Montclair State U (NJ)
New England School of Communications (ME)
Northern Illinois U (IL)
North Greenville U (SC)
Oakland City U (IN)
Ohio Valley U (WV)
Penn State Altoona (PA)
Penn State Beaver (PA)
Penn State Berks (PA)
Penn State Erie, The Behrend Coll (PA)
Penn State Greater Allegheny (PA)
Penn State Harrisburg (PA)
Penn State Hazleton (PA)
Penn State Mont Alto (PA)
Pennsylvania Coll of Technology (PA)
Plymouth State U (NH)
Point U (GA)
Presentation Coll (SD)
Ramapo Coll of New Jersey (NJ)
Reinhardt U (GA)
The Richard Stockton Coll of New Jersey (NJ)
Rowan U (NJ)
Rutgers, The State U of New Jersey, Camden (NJ)
Rutgers, The State U of New Jersey, Newark (NJ)
Rutgers, The State U of New Jersey, New Brunswick (NJ)
Sacred Heart Major Sem (MI)
Saint Augustine's Coll (NC)
Shaw U (NC)
Southwest Baptist U (MO)
Southwestern Adventist U (TX)
Southwestern Assemblies of God U (TX)
Stillman Coll (AL)
Temple U (PA)
Texas Southern U (TX)
Truett-McConnell Coll (GA)
Union Coll (NE)
U of California, Merced (CA)
U of Cincinnati (OH)
U of Connecticut (CT)
U of Delaware (DE)
U of Illinois at Chicago (IL)
U of Illinois at Springfield (IL)
U of Illinois at Urbana–Champaign (IL)
U of Massachusetts Amherst (MA)
U of Massachusetts Dartmouth (MA)

U of Massachusetts Lowell (MA)
U of Michigan (MI)
U of Minnesota, Twin Cities Campus (MN)
U of New Hampshire (NH)
U of Pikeville (KY)
U of Pittsburgh at Bradford (PA)
U of Pittsburgh at Greensburg (PA)
U of Pittsburgh at Johnstown (PA)
U of Rhode Island (RI)
The U of Texas at Austin (TX)
U of the Cumberlands (KY)
U of Vermont (VT)
U of Virginia (VA)
Vermont Tech Coll (VT)
Virginia Union U (VA)
Washington State U (WA)
William Paterson U of New Jersey (NJ)
York Coll of Pennsylvania (PA)

$25,000–$29,999

Colleges with No Room and Board or with Room Only

Bastyr U (WA) **(room only)**
Burlington Coll (VT) **(room only)**
DigiPen Inst of Technology (WA)
Goldey-Beacom Coll (DE) **(room only)**
Harrisburg U of Science and Technology (PA) **(room only)**
Neumont U (UT) **(room only)**
The Restaurant School at Walnut Hill Coll (PA) **(room only)**
Rocky Mountain Coll of Art + Design (CO)
Shimer Coll (IL)
Watkins Coll of Art, Design, & Film (TN) **(room only)**

Colleges with Room and Board

Alverno Coll (WI)
Anderson U (SC)
Asbury U (KY)
Avila U (MO)
Belhaven U (MS)
Benedictine Coll (KS)
Bethany Coll (KS)
Bethany Lutheran Coll (MN)
Bethel Coll (KS)
Bluefield Coll (VA)
Brescia U (KY)
Bryn Athyn Coll of the New Church (PA)
Campbellsville U (KY)
Carson-Newman Coll (TN)
Cedarville U (OH)
Central Methodist U (MO)
Chaminade U of Honolulu (HI)
Christendom Coll (VA)
Clark Atlanta U (GA)
Coll of St. Joseph (VT)
Concordia U (MI)
Concordia U, Nebraska (NE)
Cornerstone U (MI)
Crown Coll (MN)
Dallas Baptist U (TX)
Daniel Webster Coll (NH)
Drury U (MO)
East Texas Baptist U (TX)
Fontbonne U (MO)
Franciscan U of Steubenville (OH)
Friends U (KS)
Grace Coll (IN)
Graceland U (IA)
Grand Canyon U (AZ)
Grand View U (IA)
Greenville Coll (IL)
Hampton U (VA)
Hardin-Simmons U (TX)
Hawai'i Pacific U (HI)
Hilbert Coll (NY)
Hillsdale Coll (MI)
Howard Payne U (TX)
Huntingdon Coll (AL)
Indiana Wesleyan U (IN)
John Brown U (AR)
Kentucky Wesleyan Coll (KY)

Keystone Coll (PA)
Liberty U (VA)
Limestone Coll (SC)
Lindsey Wilson Coll (KY)
Marian U (WI)
McMurry U (TX)
McNally Smith Coll of Music (MN)
McPherson Coll (KS)
Mercy Coll (NY)
MidAmerica Nazarene U (KS)
Missouri Baptist U (MO)
Mount Aloysius Coll (PA)
Mount Marty Coll (SD)
Mount Vernon Nazarene U (OH)
Multnomah U (OR)
Newman U (KS)
Nyack Coll (NY)
Oklahoma Christian U (OK)
Oral Roberts U (OK)
Ouachita Baptist U (AR)
Penn State U Park (PA)
Philadelphia Biblical U (PA)
Piedmont Coll (GA)
Rocky Mountain Coll (MT)
Saint Joseph Sem Coll (LA)
Saint Leo U (FL)
Saint Louis Christian Coll (MO)
St. Mary's Coll of Maryland (MD)
Shorter U (GA)
Siena Heights U (MI)
Simpson U (CA)
Southeastern U (FL)
Southwestern Coll (KS)
Spalding U (KY)
Spring Arbor U (MI)
Sterling Coll (KS)
Sullivan Coll of Technology and Design (KY)
Tabor Coll (KS)
Texas Wesleyan U (TX)
Tiffin U (OH)
Touro Coll (NY)
Trevecca Nazarene U (TN)
Trinity Lutheran Coll (WA)
Tusculum Coll (TN)
Tuskegee U (AL)
Union Coll (KY)
U of California, Berkeley (CA)
U of California, Davis (CA)
U of California, Irvine (CA)
U of California, Los Angeles (CA)
U of California, Riverside (CA)
U of California, Santa Barbara (CA)
U of California, Santa Cruz (CA)
U of Dubuque (IA)
U of Great Falls (MT)
U of Mary Hardin-Baylor (TX)
U of Mobile (AL)
U of Pittsburgh (PA)
U of Rio Grande (OH)
U of Saint Mary (KS)
U of the Ozarks (AR)
Vaughn Coll of Aeronautics and Technology (NY)
Viterbo U (WI)
Waldorf Coll (IA)
Washington Adventist U (MD)
Waynesburg U (PA)
Webber Intl U (FL)
Wesleyan Coll (GA)
Westminster Coll (MO)
William Woods U (MO)
Xavier U of Louisiana (LA)

$30,000 AND OVER

Colleges with No Room and Board or with Room Only

Art Center Coll of Design (CA)
California Coll of the Arts (CA) **(room only)**
Chatham U (PA) **(room only)**
The King's Coll (NY) **(room only)**
Long Island U–Brentwood Campus (NY)

Musicians Inst (CA)
New York School of Interior Design (NY) **(room only)**
Otis Coll of Art and Design (CA)
Prescott Coll (AZ) **(room only)**
Samuel Merritt U (CA)
San Francisco Conservatory of Music (CA)
School of the Museum of Fine Arts, Boston (MA) **(room only)**

Colleges with Room and Board

Abilene Christian U (TX)
Acad of Art U (CA)
Adelphi U (NY)
Adrian Coll (MI)
Agnes Scott Coll (GA)
Alaska Pacific U (AK)
Albany Coll of Pharmacy and Health Sciences (NY)
Albertus Magnus Coll (CT)
Albion Coll (MI)
Albright Coll (PA)
Alfred U (NY)
Allegheny Coll (PA)
Alma Coll (MI)
Alvernia U (PA)
American Jewish U (CA)
American U (DC)
Amherst Coll (MA)
Anderson U (IN)
Andrews U (MI)
Anna Maria Coll (MA)
Aquinas Coll (MI)
Arcadia U (PA)
Ashland U (OH)
Assumption Coll (MA)
Augustana Coll (IL)
Augustana Coll (SD)
Austin Coll (TX)
Averett U (VA)
Azusa Pacific U (CA)
Babson Coll (MA)
Baker U (KS)
Baldwin-Wallace Coll (OH)
Bard Coll (NY)
Bard Coll at Simon's Rock (MA)
Barnard Coll (NY)
Barry U (FL)
Barton Coll (NC)
Bates Coll (ME)
Baylor U (TX)
Bay Path Coll (MA)
Beacon Coll (FL)
Becker Coll (MA)
Bellarmine U (KY)
Belmont Abbey Coll (NC)
Belmont U (TN)
Beloit Coll (WI)
Benedictine U (IL)
Bennington Coll (VT)
Bentley U (MA)
Berry Coll (GA)
Bethany Coll (WV)
Bethel Coll (IN)
Bethel U (MN)
Biola U (CA)
Birmingham-Southern Coll (AL)
Bloomfield Coll (NJ)
Bluffton U (OH)
Boston Coll (MA)
Boston U (MA)
Bowdoin Coll (ME)
Bradley U (IL)
Brandeis U (MA)
Brenau U (GA)
Brevard Coll (NC)
Briar Cliff U (IA)
Bridgewater Coll (VA)
Brown U (RI)
Bryant U (RI)
Bryn Mawr Coll (PA)
Bucknell U (PA)
Buena Vista U (IA)
Butler U (IN)
Cabrini Coll (PA)

Caldwell Coll (NJ)
California Baptist U (CA)
California Inst of Technology (CA)
California Lutheran U (CA)
Calvin Coll (MI)
Canisius Coll (NY)
Capital U (OH)
Cardinal Stritch U (WI)
Carleton Coll (MN)
Carlow U (PA)
Carnegie Mellon U (PA)
Carroll Coll (MT)
Case Western Reserve U (OH)
Catawba Coll (NC)
The Catholic U of America (DC)
Cedar Crest Coll (PA)
Centenary Coll (NJ)
Centenary Coll of Louisiana (LA)
Central Coll (IA)
Centre Coll (KY)
Chapman U (CA)
Chestnut Hill Coll (PA)
Christian Brothers U (TN)
Claremont McKenna Coll (CA)
Clarke U (IA)
Clarkson U (NY)
Clark U (MA)
The Cleveland Inst of Art (OH)
Coe Coll (IA)
Cogswell Polytechnical Coll (CA)
Colby Coll (ME)
Colgate U (NY)
Coll for Creative Studies (MI)
The Coll of Idaho (ID)
Coll of Mount St. Joseph (OH)
Coll of Mount Saint Vincent (NY)
Coll of Saint Benedict (MN)
Coll of Saint Elizabeth (NJ)
Coll of Saint Mary (NE)
The Coll of Saint Rose (NY)
The Coll of St. Scholastica (MN)
Coll of the Atlantic (ME)
Coll of the Holy Cross (MA)
The Coll of Wooster (OH)
The Colorado Coll (CO)
Columbia Coll (SC)
Columbia Coll Chicago (IL)
Columbia U, School of General Studies (NY)
Columbus Coll of Art & Design (OH)
Concordia Coll (MN)
Concordia Coll–New York (NY)
Concordia U (CA)
Concordia U Chicago (IL)
Concordia U, St. Paul (MN)
Concordia U Texas (TX)
Connecticut Coll (CT)
Converse Coll (SC)
Cooper Union for the Advancement of Science and Art (NY)
Corban U (OR)
Corcoran Coll of Art and Design (DC)
Cornell Coll (IA)
Cornell U (NY)
Covenant Coll (GA)
Creighton U (NE)
Culver-Stockton Coll (MO)
Curry Coll (MA)
Daemen Coll (NY)
Dartmouth Coll (NH)
Davidson Coll (NC)
Defiance Coll (OH)
Delaware Valley Coll (PA)
Denison U (OH)
DePaul U (IL)
DePauw U (IN)
DeSales U (PA)
Dickinson Coll (PA)
Doane Coll (NE)
Dominican Coll (NY)
Dominican U (IL)
Dominican U of California (CA)
Dordt Coll (IA)
Dowling Coll (NY)
Drake U (IA)

Drew U (NJ)
Drexel U (PA)
Duquesne U (PA)
Earlham Coll (IN)
Eastern Mennonite U (VA)
Eastern U (PA)
Eckerd Coll (FL)
Edgewood Coll (WI)
Elizabethtown Coll (PA)
Elmhurst Coll (IL)
Elmira Coll (NY)
Elon U (NC)
Embry-Riddle Aeronautical U–Daytona (FL)
Embry-Riddle Aeronautical U–Prescott (AZ)
Emmanuel Coll (MA)
Emory & Henry Coll (VA)
Emory U (GA)
Endicott Coll (MA)
Fairfield U (CT)
Fairleigh Dickinson U, Coll at Florham (NJ)
Fairleigh Dickinson U, Metropolitan Campus (NJ)
Felician Coll (NJ)
Five Towns Coll (NY)
Florida Inst of Technology (FL)
Florida Southern Coll (FL)
Fordham U (NY)
Franklin & Marshall Coll (PA)
Franklin Coll (IN)
Franklin Coll Switzerland (Switzerland)
Franklin W. Olin Coll of Eng (MA)
Furman U (SC)
Gannon U (PA)
Gardner-Webb U (NC)
Geneva Coll (PA)
George Fox U (OR)
Georgetown Coll (KY)
The George Washington U (DC)
Georgian Court U (NJ)
Gettysburg Coll (PA)
Gonzaga U (WA)
Gordon Coll (MA)
Goshen Coll (IN)
Goucher Coll (MD)
Grinnell Coll (IA)
Guilford Coll (NC)
Gustavus Adolphus Coll (MN)
Gwynedd-Mercy Coll (PA)
Hamilton Coll (NY)
Hamline U (MN)
Hampden-Sydney Coll (VA)
Hampshire Coll (MA)
Hanover Coll (IN)
Hartwick Coll (NY)
Harvard U (MA)
Harvey Mudd Coll (CA)
Haverford Coll (PA)
Heidelberg U (OH)
Hellenic Coll (MA)
Hendrix Coll (AR)
Hobart and William Smith Colls (NY)
Hofstra U (NY)
Hollins U (VA)
Holy Cross Coll (IN)
Holy Family U (PA)
Hood Coll (MD)
Hope Coll (MI)
Hope Intl U (CA)
Houghton Coll (NY)
Huntington U (IN)
Illinois Coll (IL)
Illinois Inst of Technology (IL)
Illinois Wesleyan U (IL)
Immaculata U (PA)
Indiana Tech (IN)
Iona Coll (NY)
Iowa Wesleyan Coll (IA)
Ithaca Coll (NY)
Jacksonville U (FL)
John Carroll U (OH)
The Johns Hopkins U (MD)
Judson U (IL)
Juniata Coll (PA)
Kalamazoo Coll (MI)

INDEXES

Kenyon Coll (OH)
Kettering U (MI)
Keuka Coll (NY)
King Coll (TN)
King's Coll (PA)
Knox Coll (IL)
Lafayette Coll (PA)
LaGrange Coll (GA)
Lake Erie Coll (OH)
Lake Forest Coll (IL)
La Roche Coll (PA)
La Salle U (PA)
Lasell Coll (MA)
La Sierra U (CA)
Lawrence Technological U (MI)
Lawrence U (WI)
Lebanon Valley Coll (PA)
Lees-McRae Coll (NC)
Lehigh U (PA)
Le Moyne Coll (NY)
Lenoir-Rhyne U (NC)
LeTourneau U (TX)
Lewis & Clark Coll (OR)
Lewis U (IL)
Linfield Coll (OR)
Lipscomb U (TN)
Long Island U–Brooklyn Campus (NY)
Long Island U–C. W. Post Campus (NY)
Loras Coll (IA)
Loyola Marymount U (CA)
Loyola U Chicago (IL)
Loyola U Maryland (MD)
Loyola U New Orleans (LA)
Luther Coll (IA)
Lycoming Coll (PA)
Lyme Acad Coll of Fine Arts (CT)
Lynchburg Coll (VA)
Lynn U (FL)
Lyon Coll (AR)
Macalester Coll (MN)
Maharishi U of Management (IA)
Malone U (OH)
Manchester Coll (IN)
Manhattan Coll (NY)
Manhattanville Coll (NY)
Marietta Coll (OH)
Marlboro Coll (VT)
Marquette U (WI)
Mars Hill Coll (NC)
Mary Baldwin Coll (VA)
Maryland Inst Coll of Art (MD)
Marymount Coll, Palos Verdes, California (CA)
Marymount Manhattan Coll (NY)
Marymount U (VA)
Maryville Coll (TN)
Maryville U of Saint Louis (MO)
Marywood U (PA)
Massachusetts Coll of Pharmacy and Health Sciences (MA)
Massachusetts Inst of Technology (MA)
The Master's Coll and Sem (CA)
McDaniel Coll (MD)
McKendree U (IL)
Medaille Coll (NY)
Memphis Coll of Art (TN)
Menlo Coll (CA)
Mercer U (GA)
Mercyhurst Coll (PA)
Meredith Coll (NC)
Merrimack Coll (MA)
Messiah Coll (PA)
Middlebury Coll (VT)
Milligan Coll (TN)
Millikin U (IL)
Millsaps Coll (MS)
Mills Coll (CA)
Milwaukee School of Eng (WI)
Misericordia U (PA)
Molloy Coll (NY)
Monmouth Coll (IL)
Monmouth U (NJ)
Montreat Coll, Montreat (NC)
Moravian Coll (PA)
Morehouse Coll (GA)

Morningside Coll (IA)
Mount Holyoke Coll (MA)
Mount Ida Coll (MA)
Mount Mary Coll (WI)
Mount Mercy U (IA)
Mount Saint Mary Coll (NY)
Mount St. Mary's Coll (CA)
Mount St. Mary's U (MD)
Muhlenberg Coll (PA)
Naropa U (CO)
Nazareth Coll of Rochester (NY)
Nebraska Wesleyan U (NE)
Neumann U (PA)
Newberry Coll (SC)
Newbury Coll (MA)
New England Coll (NH)
New England Conservatory of Music (MA)
New York Inst of Technology (NY)
New York U (NY)
Niagara U (NY)
North Carolina Wesleyan Coll (NC)
North Central Coll (IL)
Northeastern U (MA)
Northland Coll (WI)
Northwest Christian U (OR)
Northwestern Coll (IA)
Northwestern Coll (MN)
Northwest Nazarene U (ID)
Northwest U (WA)
Norwich U (VT)
Notre Dame de Namur U (CA)
Notre Dame of Maryland U (MD)
Nova Southeastern U (FL)
Occidental Coll (CA)
Oglethorpe U (GA)
Ohio Northern U (OH)
Ohio Wesleyan U (OH)
Oklahoma City U (OK)
Otterbein U (OH)
Pace U (NY)
Pacific Lutheran U (WA)
Pacific Northwest Coll of Art (OR)
Pacific Union Coll (CA)
Pacific U (OR)
Palm Beach Atlantic U (FL)
Patrick Henry Coll (VA)
Peabody Conservatory of The Johns Hopkins U (MD)
Pepperdine U, Malibu (CA)
Philadelphia U (PA)
Pine Manor Coll (MA)
Pitzer Coll (CA)
Point Loma Nazarene U (CA)
Point Park U (PA)
Polytechnic Inst of NYU (NY)
Pomona Coll (CA)
Post U (CT)
Pratt Inst (NY)
Presbyterian Coll (SC)
Princeton U (NJ)
Providence Coll (RI)
Queens U of Charlotte (NC)
Quincy U (IL)
Quinnipiac U (CT)
Randolph Coll (VA)
Randolph-Macon Coll (VA)
Regis Coll (MA)
Regis U (CO)
Rensselaer Polytechnic Inst (NY)
Research Coll of Nursing (MO)
Rhodes Coll (TN)
Rice U (TX)
Rider U (NJ)
Ringling Coll of Art and Design (FL)
Ripon Coll (WI)
Rivier Coll (NH)
Roanoke Coll (VA)
Robert Morris U (PA)
Robert Morris U Illinois (IL)
Roberts Wesleyan Coll (NY)
Rochester Inst of Technology (NY)
Rockford Coll (IL)
Rockhurst U (MO)
Roger Williams U (RI)

Rollins Coll (FL)
Roosevelt U (IL)
Rose-Hulman Inst of Technology (IN)
Rosemont Coll (PA)
Russell Sage Coll (NY)
Sacred Heart U (CT)
Sage Coll of Albany (NY)
St. Ambrose U (IA)
St. Andrews U (NC)
Saint Anselm Coll (NH)
St. Bonaventure U (NY)
St. Catherine U (MN)
St. Edward's U (TX)
Saint Francis U (PA)
St. John Fisher Coll (NY)
St. John's Coll (MD)
St. John's Coll (NM)
Saint John's U (MN)
St. John's U (NY)
Saint Joseph's Coll (IN)
Saint Joseph's Coll of Maine (ME)
Saint Joseph's U (PA)
St. Lawrence U (NY)
St. Louis Coll of Pharmacy (MO)
Saint Louis U (MO)
Saint Martin's U (WA)
Saint Mary-of-the-Woods Coll (IN)
Saint Mary's Coll (IN)
Saint Mary's Coll of California (CA)
St. Mary's U (TX)
Saint Mary's U of Minnesota (MN)
Saint Michael's Coll (VT)
St. Norbert Coll (WI)
St. Olaf Coll (MN)
Saint Peter's Coll (NJ)
St. Thomas Aquinas Coll (NY)
St. Thomas U (FL)
Saint Vincent Coll (PA)
Saint Xavier U (IL)
Salve Regina U (RI)
Samford U (AL)
San Diego Christian Coll (CA)
Santa Clara U (CA)
Sarah Lawrence Coll (NY)
Savannah Coll of Art and Design (GA)
Schreiner U (TX)
Scripps Coll (CA)
Seattle Pacific U (WA)
Seattle U (WA)
Seton Hill U (PA)
Sewanee: The U of the South (TN)
Shenandoah U (VA)
Siena Coll (NY)
Sierra Nevada Coll (NV)
Simmons Coll (MA)
Simpson Coll (IA)
Skidmore Coll (NY)
Smith Coll (MA)
Soka U of America (CA)
Southern Methodist U (TX)
Southern New Hampshire U (NH)
Southern Vermont Coll (VT)
Southwestern U (TX)
Spelman Coll (GA)
Spring Hill Coll (AL)
Stanford U (CA)
Stephens Coll (MO)
Sterling Coll (VT)
Stetson U (FL)
Stevens Inst of Technology (NJ)
Stevenson U (MD)
Stonehill Coll (MA)
Suffolk U (MA)
Susquehanna U (PA)
Swarthmore Coll (PA)
Sweet Briar Coll (VA)
Syracuse U (NY)
Taylor U (IN)
Texas Christian U (TX)
Texas Lutheran U (TX)
Thiel Coll (PA)
Thomas Aquinas Coll (CA)
Thomas More Coll (KY)

Transylvania U (KY)
Trine U (IN)
Trinity Christian Coll (IL)
Trinity Coll (CT)
Trinity U (TX)
Tufts U (MA)
Tulane U (LA)
Union Coll (NY)
Union U (TN)
United States Intl U (Kenya)
U of Bridgeport (CT)
U of Charleston (WV)
U of Chicago (IL)
U of Dallas (TX)
U of Dayton (OH)
U of Denver (CO)
U of Evansville (IN)
The U of Findlay (OH)
U of Hartford (CT)
U of Indianapolis (IN)
U of La Verne (CA)
U of Miami (FL)
U of Mount Union (OH)
U of New England (ME)
U of New Haven (CT)
U of Notre Dame (IN)
U of Pennsylvania (PA)
U of Portland (OR)
U of Puget Sound (WA)
U of Redlands (CA)
U of Richmond (VA)
U of Rochester (NY)
U of St. Francis (IL)

U of Saint Francis (IN)
U of Saint Joseph (CT)
U of St. Thomas (MN)
U of St. Thomas (TX)
U of San Diego (CA)
The U of Scranton (PA)
U of Southern California (CA)
The U of Tampa (FL)
The U of the Arts (PA)
U of the Incarnate Word (TX)
U of the Pacific (CA)
U of the Sciences in Philadelphia (PA)
U of Tulsa (OK)
Upper Iowa U (IA)
Ursuline Coll (OH)
Utica Coll (NY)
Valparaiso U (IN)
Vanderbilt U (TN)
VanderCook Coll of Music (IL)
Vanguard U of Southern California (CA)
Vassar Coll (NY)
Villanova U (PA)
Virginia Intermont Coll (VA)
Virginia Wesleyan Coll (VA)
Wabash Coll (IN)
Wagner Coll (NY)
Wake Forest U (NC)
Walsh U (OH)
Warren Wilson Coll (NC)
Wartburg Coll (IA)
Washington & Jefferson Coll (PA)
Washington and Lee U (VA)
Washington Coll (MD)

Washington U in St. Louis (MO)
Webster U (MO)
Wellesley Coll (MA)
Wells Coll (NY)
Wentworth Inst of Technology (MA)
Wesleyan U (CT)
Western New England U (MA)
Westminster Coll (UT)
West Virginia Wesleyan Coll (WV)
Wheaton Coll (IL)
Wheaton Coll (MA)
Wheeling Jesuit U (WV)
Wheelock Coll (MA)
Whitman Coll (WA)
Whittier Coll (CA)
Widener U (PA)
Wilkes U (PA)
Willamette U (OR)
William Jessup U (CA)
William Jewell Coll (MO)
Williams Coll (MA)
Wilmington Coll (OH)
Wilson Coll (PA)
Wingate U (NC)
Wittenberg U (OH)
Wofford Coll (SC)
Woodbury U (CA)
Worcester Polytechnic Inst (MA)
Xavier U (OH)
Yale U (CT)
Yeshiva U (NY)

INDEXES

Advertisers Index

The following schools have provided and paid for a half-page or full-page display ad, which appears in the **Profiles** section on the page noted in this index.

INDEXES

Alphabetical Listing of Colleges and Universities

INDEXES

INDEXES

INDEXES

INDEXES

INDEXES

INDEXES

INDEXES

Geographical Listing of Close-Ups

INDEXES

NOTES

NOTES

NOTES

NOTES

NOTES